COMPLETE
BOOK OF COLLEGES

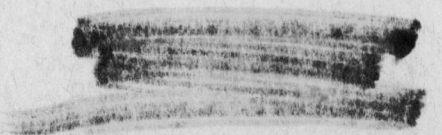

The
Princeton
Review

PrincetonReview.com

COMPLETE
BOOK OF COLLEGES

Random House, Inc., New York
2009 Edition

The Princeton Review, Inc.
2315 Broadway
New York, NY 10024
Email: bookeditor@review.com

ISBN 978-0-375-42874-6

VP: Publisher: Robert Franek
Editor: Adam O. Davis
Senior Production Editor: M. Tighe Wall
Executive Director, Print Production: Scott Harris

Printed in the United States of America.

9 8 7 6 5 4 3 2 1

2009 Edition

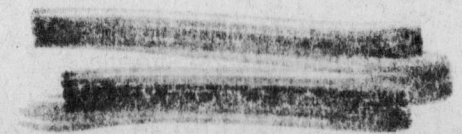

ACKNOWLEDGMENTS

The *Complete Book of Colleges* is the largest undergraduate guide produced by The Princeton Review. Our publication contains information on 1,821 colleges. There are many people both to thank and praise for their creativity, dedication, and attentiveness to detail: To each, a well-deserved *thank you*.

My thanks go to the entire undergrad data collection staff, under the direction of Ben Zelevansky and David Soto. Both gave their best to ensure that we had quality data from each school and to build a positive relationship with our administrative contact at each school. I confidently state that our entire staff are pros at explaining the collection process, how to use our tools, how each school's data should be used, and at allaying the fears of everyone in the process. Thanks also go to our account management team, especially Russ Arthur. Under the direction of the always fair Jung Shin, our representatives invite schools to supply individual profiles to our guide; each year hundreds do. Without their efforts this book would not be the greatest resource for prospective college students available.

Scott Harris and M. Tighe Wall and their team members earn my most sincere thanks. Their savvy editing and design skills make this book a success each year; coupled with their professional manner, they make this project a pleasure to work on as well. My special thanks go to Ben Zelevansky. Over the past years Ben quickly assumed and successfully delivered all book pouring for this and other similar publications. Thanks also go to David Soto for his quick and unflinching ability to balance even the most minute requests from our partner schools. Lastly, I extend a special thank you to Adam Davis for his always stylish management of this book's front matter.

Again, to all who worked so hard on this publication, thank you. Your efforts do not go unnoticed.

Robert Franek
VP—Publisher

CONTENTS

...So Much More Online!

More Guidance...

- Find school matches with Counselor-O-Matic
- Explore majors with the click of the mouse
- Advice on everything from raising test scores to career planning
- Help with selecting a summer program, a study abroad program, or finding an internship
- Get the inside scoop of scholarships and financial aid

More Information...

- Articles on college life for students and parents alike
- Our College Hopes & Worries Survey
- Detailed profiles for hundreds of colleges help you find the school that is right for you
- Dozens of Top 10 ranking lists including Quality of Professors, Worst Campus Food, Most Beautiful Campus, Party Schools, Diverse Student Population, and tons more

More Good Stuff...

- Discover other Princeton Review titles that will help you ace the big test or find your best fit college
- Discuss issues with your peers on our discussion board
- Info on grad, med, business, and law schools
- And much, much more!

princetonreview.com

FOREWORD

Welcome. You have found the best place to begin, fine-tune, and execute the search for your perfect college. With the understanding that choosing a school wisely is a top priority for each prospective student, we have provided a significant breadth of information in this text to help you navigate the exciting, amazing, and sometimes confusing process of choosing the right college.

The design of this guidebook will allow you to narrow your search of colleges from 1,821 to a few dozen. Here you'll find all the individual college statistics you'll need to make informed choices about the competitiveness, size, location, and academic offerings of the schools available to you. In addition, you can find even more information about individual schools at The Princeton Review's website, PrincetonReview.com. The site includes college search features, college profiles, college discussion boards, a college majors search engine, and much more.

By using this book, you can search for, choose, and apply to colleges with the confidence of a pro—or at the very least a well-informed undergraduate hopeful! We supply the information and guidance, and you ultimately make your own decision.

The college selection, application, and interview processes can be overwhelming at times. They can also be rewarding experiences. For most, choosing a college is the first major life decision. I know it was mine. Remember that your college decision is yours alone, so arm yourself with the best available information. Badger teachers, friends, high school and college admissions counselors, brothers, sisters, and parents; ask them how they chose their colleges and why. The more you know when beginning the process, the more in control of the situation you'll feel.

Whatever it is that you choose as your path in life, your college selection will forever be your first step in that direction. The friends you make, the professors you meet, and the classes you take are all springboards to the next phase of your life.

I wish you much luck and success at whichever college you decide to attend. My sincere hope is that this publication and other Princeton Review tools will be helpful in the process.

Robert Franek
VP—Publisher

INTRODUCTION

Before you dive into the *Complete Book of Colleges*, we want to give you some tips for your college search—especially on how to get the most out of this book and what to do once you've made your choices and are ready to apply. Since the most important thing for you to do now is to start your search, we want to start right off by revealing the secret to getting admitted to the college of your choice.

It's almost never the focus of talk about college admissions in the media, and parents and students discuss the subject all the time without even realizing that it's the crucial element to getting admitted. We're talking about matchmaking: That is, finding colleges that have the educational and social environments you're looking for, where you are well-suited academically and have something the college is looking for in return. You have a lot more control over where you end up going to college than you might think.

Matchmaking is a two-step process. You should begin with a thorough self-examination or personal inventory. Your personal inventory is best structured in the form of a spreadsheet or chart, so that when you begin to consider your options, you can check off those colleges that satisfy the various needs or wants you've identified. In this way, your best college choices will gradually begin to identify themselves.

Divide your inventory into two sections. One section should be biographical, including your high school course selection, GPA, SAT or ACT scores, class rank, and personal information like extracurricular activities—especially those you plan to continue in college. This will help you to assess how you stack up against each college's admissions standards and student body. The second section is a listing of the characteristics you need or want in the college you'll choose to attend. This list should include anything and everything you consider important, such as location, size of the student body, availability of scholarships, dormitory options, clubs and activities, even school colors if you want. This part of your inventory should grow continuously as you become more and more aware of what is important to you in your choice of colleges.

Armed with your personal inventory, you can begin to take advantage of the numerous resources available to help you narrow your choices of where to apply. There are five sources for information and advice that have become standard for most college-bound students:

1. College admissions viewbooks, videos, brochures, and catalogs

If you are a junior or senior in high school, you probably know more about the kinds of information these materials should include than the people who are responsible for designing and writing them. No college that spends half a million dollars on glossy literature is going to be objective about its content. In the best of this material, you can probably get a decent idea of the academic offerings and the basic admissions requirements. In all of it, you will never see anything but the most appealing architecture and the best-looking students on campus, nor will you hear about the recent tuition increases that were greater than the rate of inflation. Look these materials over, but don't make any decisions based solely on what you read or see.

2. Your friends

No one knows colleges and universities better than the students who currently attend them. Seek out any and all of your friends, sons and daughters of family friends, and recent graduates of your high school who attend colleges that you are considering. Talk to them when they come home. Arrange to stay with them when you visit their colleges. Pick their brains for everything they know. It doesn't get any more direct and honest than this.

3. Books and college guides

There are two types of books that can be helpful to you in your search: those that discuss specific aspects of going to college and college guides. A great narrative guide that stresses students' own opinions of colleges is our own *The Best 368 Colleges*. In addition, look at *The Fiske Guide to Colleges* or the *Yale Daily News' Insiders Guide to Colleges* for good second opinions. As for comprehensive guides—those that emphasize data over narrative content—you're holding the most up-to-date and useful one in your hands.

4. Computers

There's a lot of help out there. Using our site, PrincetonReview.com, is the best way to find the right school for you and prepare for college. For more information about our *free* online tools and features see page 10.

5. Your counselor

Since it's *critically* important, we'll say it again: Once you've developed some ideas about your personal inventory and college options, schedule a meeting with your guidance counselor. The more research you've done before you get together, the more help you're likely to get. Good advice comes out of thoughtful discussion, not from the expectation that your counselor will do your work. When it comes time to file applications, look over the materials and requirements together, and allow plenty of time to put forth your best.

USING COLLEGE INFORMATION IN THE *COMPLETE BOOK OF COLLEGES* AND ELSEWHERE

Throughout the course of your college search, you'll confront an amazing array of statistics and other data related to every college you consider. In order for all of this information to be helpful, you need to have some sense of how to interpret it. We've included a detailed key to the college entries in this book a few pages deeper into this introduction. Almost all the statistics we've compiled are self-explanatory, but there are a few that will be more useful with some elaboration.

Let's start with student/teacher ratio. Don't use it to assess average class size; they are not interchangeable terms. At almost every college, the average class size is larger than its student/teacher ratio. At many big universities, it is considerably larger. What is useful about the ratio is that it can give you an idea of how accessible your professors will be outside of the classroom. Once you are in college, you'll grow to realize just how important this is.

In the same way, the percentage of faculty who hold PhDs is useful information. When you're paying thousands of dollars in tuition each year, there's something comforting about knowing that your professors have a considerably broader and deeper grasp of what you're studying than you do. In contrast, teaching assistants (TAs) may often be just one or two steps ahead of you.

Another interesting group of statistics deals with the percentage of students who go on to graduate or professional school. Never allow yourself to be swayed by such statistics, unless you've taken the time to ponder their meaning and visited the college in question. High percentages almost always mean one of two things: that the college is an intellectual enclave that inspires students onward to further their education, or that it is a pre-professional bastion of aggressive careerists. There isn't anything inherently wrong with either scenario, but neither has universal appeal to prospective students. Colleges that are exceptions to this rule are rare and precious. The most misleading figures provided to prospective students are those for medical school acceptance rates. Virtually every college in the country can boast of high acceptance rates to medical school for its graduates; premed programs are designed to weed out those who will not be strong candidates before they even get to apply! If you're thinking about medical school, ask colleges how many of their students apply to medical school each year. Also, try to get a sense of the attrition rate within the premed program.

One final piece of advice about statistics relates to the college's acceptance rate. Simply knowing the percentage of applicants who are admitted each year is helpful, but it is even more helpful if you know how many applied, as well. When you compare these figures to the freshman profile, you have the most accurate picture of just how tough it is to get in. An 80 percent acceptance rate doesn't mean there's an open door if you don't match up well to the academic achievements of the college's typical freshman. Beyond this, keep an eye out for colleges that have relatively self-selecting applicant pools. In these cases, high acceptance rates may be misleading. When evaluating highly selective public colleges as an out-of-state applicant, remember that you will likely face a more selective evaluation than state residents.

New! Online Degree Programs

Offerings in online degree programs are multiplying at an impressive rate and as always, The Princeton Review will keep you fully up-to-date about the most current and innovative curricula. Traditional degree programs aren't the best matches for everyone. With scores of offerings in the online realm, students can now take classes, communicate with professors, and interact with classmates—all without ever leaving their apartments, favorite coffeehouses, or the library.

A Few Final Thoughts

Once you've narrowed down your options and decided where to apply, find the applications on PrincetonReview.com and get to work filling them out. The admissions process is stressful enough without putting extra pressure on yourself by waiting until the last minute. The first thing you should do when you receive the necessary forms is go over them with your guidance counselor. Immediately remove the recommendation forms (if they are required) and give them to the teachers and counselor(s) who will be completing them for you. They'll have a better opportunity to write a thorough and supportive recommendation if you give them enough time to complete them. This is also the time to make your request for official transcripts. Again, it takes time to do these things. Plan ahead.

As for completing the applications, organize yourself and all the materials. Keep everything in folders and accessible in case you need to speak with an admissions officer over the telephone. When essays and information on your extracurricular activities are required, do some outlining and rough draft-writing before you commit yourself to the actual forms or online tools.

Paying for college requires some of your attention too. Though we don't have nearly enough space to go into such a complicated and stressful subject now, it's very important that you get to work on your financial circumstances right away. Keep in mind that while college is costly, few people pay the "sticker price." Regardless, you have to have your finances in order before you can get the most financial aid possible. We've developed a financial center on PrincetonReview.com to help demystify the sometimes bewildering task of financing your education. You can also find the most exhaustive strategies for financing your education in our book *Paying for College Without Going Broke*.

Last but not least, **don't take it easy during your senior year!** Colleges routinely request mid-year grades, and they expect you to continue taking challenging academic courses and keep your grades up throughout your high school career. Doing so takes you one step closer to getting good news. On behalf of The Princeton Review, have a good time, and good luck. See you on campus!

Nota Bene

The data reported in this book, unless otherwise noted, was collected from the profiled colleges from the fall of 2007 through the summer of 2008. In some cases, we were unable to publish the most recent data because schools did not report the necessary statistics to us in time, despite our repeated outreach efforts. Because enrollment and financial statistics as well as application and financial aid deadlines fluctuate from one year to another, we recommend that you check to make sure you have the most current information before applying. Best of luck!

HOW THE *COMPLETE BOOK* OF COLLEGES IS ORGANIZED

There are two types of profiles in this book. Not every school listed will have both. All of the 1,821 colleges and universities included in this book have their own informational profiles, and each entry follows the same basic format. More than 225 of the institutions also have special two-page portraits located at the back of the book. These are written by the colleges and universities that wanted to present detailed descriptions of their campuses and programs.

Unless noted in the descriptions below, the Admissions Services Division of The Princeton Review collected all of the data presented in the informational profiles. As is customary with college guides, all data reflect figures for the academic year prior to publication, unless otherwise indicated. Since college offerings and demographics vary significantly from one institution to another and some colleges report data more thoroughly than others, few entries will include all of the individual data points described below.

The Heading

This section includes school name, address, telephone number, fax number, e-mail address, Internet site, financial aid telephone number, and college code numbers for both the College Board (CEEB) and the American College Testing Program (ACT) when applicable. All Internet site addresses were accurate and functioning at the time of publication. Check PrincetonReview.com for the most up-to-date links to colleges.

The Icons

The icons are a feature we hope will make using the *Complete Book of Colleges* easier. Icons appear under the school name for schools that are profiled in *The Best 368 Colleges*.

The Blurb

Describes the college or university. Includes all available data that relate to the date of founding of the school, religious affiliation, whether the school is public or private, and campus size.

Ratings

This section includes the school's Fire Safety Rating, it's Admissions Selectivity Rating, and it's Green Rating.

Selectivity Rating

The number listed for each college is The Princeton Review's exclusive rating of admissions competitiveness. It is a very general assessment determined by several factors, among which are the school's acceptance rate, and the class rank and average test scores of entering first-year students. By incorporating all these factors, the rating adjusts for "self-selecting" applicant pools. *Note:* The Selectivity Rating for visual and performing arts schools are approximations only. Estimated Selectivity Ratings are included to give you a general idea of where they fit in the selectivity scale, but auditions and portfolios carry the greatest weight in admissions decisions.

Schools that received an Admissions Selectivity rating of 60* did not supply sufficient data for proper calculation of this rating. By default, these schools are given this rating, although their rating may have been significantly higher had they supplied sufficient data.

Fire Safety

We asked all the schools from which we collect data annually to answer several questions about their efforts to ensure fire safety for campus residents. Each school's responses to nine of those questions were considered when calculating its Fire Safety Rating. The questions were developed in consultation with the Center for Campus Fire Safety (www.Campusfire.org), and they cover: 1) The percentage of student housing sleeping rooms protected by an automatic fire sprinkler system with a fire sprinkler head located in the individual sleeping rooms; 2) The percentage of student housing sleeping rooms equipped with a smoke detector connected to a supervised fire alarm system; 3) The number of malicious fire alarms that occur in student housing per year; 4) The number of unwanted fire alarms that occur in student housing per year; 5) The banning of certain hazardous items and activities in residence halls, like candles, smoking, halogen lamps, etc.; 6) The percentage of student housing building fire alarm systems that, if activated, result in a local alarm only; 7) The percentage of student housing building fire alarm systems that, if activated, result in a signal being transmitted to a monitored location, where security investigates before notifying the fire department; 8) The percentage of student housing building fire alarm systems that, if activated, result in a signal being transmitted immediately to a continuously monitored location which can then immediately notify the fire department to initiate a response; 9) How often fire safety rules-compliance inspections are conducted each year.

Schools that did not report answers to any of the above questions receive a Fire Safety Rating of 60*. The schools have an opportunity to update their fire safety data every year and will have their fire safety ratings re-calculated and published annually.

Each individual rating places a college on a continuum for purposes of comparing all colleges within this academic year only. Though similar, these ratings are not intended to be compared directly to those that appeared on PrincetonReview.com in any prior academic year or within any Princeton Review print publication, except for *The Best 368 Colleges, 2009 Edition* and *The Best Northeastern Colleges, 2009 Edition*. Our ratings computations are refined and change annually.

Green Rating

We asked all the schools we collect data from annually to answer a number of questions that evaluate the comprehensive measure of their performance as an environmentally aware and responsible institution. The questions were developed in consultation with ecoAmerica, a research and partnership-based environmental nonprofit that convened an expert committee to design this comprehensive rating system, and cover: 1) whether students have a campus quality of life that is both healthy and sustainable; 2) how well a school is preparing students not only for employment in the clean energy economy of the 21st century, but also for citizenship in a world now defined by environmental challenges; and 3) how environmentally responsible a school's policies are.

Colleges that did not supply answers to a sufficient number of the green campus questions for us to fairly compare them to other colleges receive a Green Rating of 60*. The schools have an opportunity to update their green data every year and will have their green ratings re-calculated and published annually.

Each individual rating places a college on a continuum for purposes of comparing all colleges within this academic year only. Though similar, these ratings are not intended to be compared directly to those that appeared on PrincetonReview.com in any prior academic year or within any Princeton Review print publication, except for the those editions published in the same year, as our ratings computations are refined and change annually.

Students & Faculty
Enrollment
The total number of full-time undergraduates.

Student Body
The percentage of male, female, out-of-state, and international students, and the number of foreign countries represented.

Ethnic Representation
By percentage according to ethnic group. Figures may not add up to 100 percent, as student reporting of ethnicity is voluntary by law.

Retention and Graduation
The percentage of freshmen who return for sophomore year. The percentage of last year's seniors who entered as freshmen and graduated in four years. The percentage of graduates who pursue further study within one year. The percentage of graduates who pursue further study at law school. The percentage of graduates who pursue further study at business school. The percentage of graduates who pursue further study at medical school.

Faculty
The ratio of undergraduates to full-time faculty. The number of full-time instructional faculty. The percentage of faculty who hold PhDs. The percentage of faculty members who teach undergraduates.

Academics
Degrees
The types of degrees awarded to students.

Academic Requirements

Areas in which all or most students are required to complete some course work prior to graduation. Can include general education (nonspecific), arts/fine arts, computer literacy, philosophy, foreign languages, history, humanities, mathematics, English (including composition), sciences (biological or physical), social sciences, and other requirements as specified by each school.

Classes

Number of students in an average regular class and an average lab/discussion section.

Majors with Highest Enrollment

The most popular majors.

Disciplines with Highest Percent of Degrees Awarded

These include arts and humanities, business, math and sciences, social sciences, education, and pre-professional enrollments. May add up to more or less than 100 percent, since not all majors fall into these broad categories, and pre-professional students must also have a true major.

Special Study Options

May include accelerated programs, cross registration, cooperative (work-study) program, distance learning, double majors, dual enrollment, English as a Second Language, student exchange programs (domestic), external degree programs, honors programs, independent study, internships, liberal arts/career combinations, student-designed majors, study abroad, teacher certification programs, weekend college, and other options as specified by each school.

Facilities

Housing

Types of school-owned or affiliated housing available. May include coed dorms, women's dorms, men's dorms, apartments for married students, apartments for single students, special housing for disabled students, special housing for international students, fraternity/sorority housing, cooperative housing, and other options as specified by the school. The availability of assistance in finding off-campus housing. Any housing requirements that may exist, such as required on-campus residence for freshmen.

Library Holdings

The number of bound volumes, periodical subscriptions, microform items, and audiovisual titles held by the school's library.

Special Academic Facilities/Equipment

Other facilities and equipment of note (e.g., nuclear reactor, on-campus elementary school for student teachers, scanning electron microscopes, and so forth).

Campus Life

Activities

Standard activities available. May include choral groups, concert band, dance, drama/theater, jazz band, literary magazine, musical ensembles, musical theater, opera, pep band, radio station, student film society, student government, student newspaper, symphony orchestra, television station, and yearbook.

Organizations
Total number of registered organizations, honor societies, religious organizations, fraternities (with percentage of males who are members), sororities (with percentage of females who are members).

Athletics
Intercollegiate athletics available, listed by sex.

Admissions

Freshman Academic Profile
Average high school GPA. Class rank distribution. The percentage from public high schools. Average SAT (Math, Critical Reading, and Writing sections) and/or ACT composite scores. Median range of SAT (Math, Critical Reading, and Writing sections) and/or ACT composite scores. Test of English as a Foreign Language (TOEFL) requirements for international studies.

Basis for Candidate Selection
The criteria considered by the admissions committee in evaluating candidates. May include secondary school record, class rank, recommendations, standardized test scores, essay, interview, extracurricular activities, talent/ability, character/personal qualities, alumni/-ae relations, geographic residence, state residency, religious affiliation/commitment, minority status, volunteer work, work experience.

Freshman Admission Requirements
High school diploma/GED requirements. The number of academic units required or recommended in total and by academic subject. (Individual subject totals may not equal the complete sum of academic units required; in most cases, the difference is made up with electives. Check with the admissions office for any additional requirements.)

Freshman Admissions Statistics
The number of students who applied, the percentage of applicants who were accepted, and the percentage of those accepted who ultimately enrolled.

Transfer Admissions Requirements
Application requirements (may include high school transcript, college transcript, essay, interview, standardized tests, statement of good standing from prior school). Minimum high school GPA required. Minimum college GPA required. Lowest course grade transferable.

General Admissions Information
Application fee. Application deadlines. Admission notification date. "Rolling" indicates that decisions are sent to candidates as they are made, rather than held for a common notification date. Registration policy for terms other than the fall term. Common Application participation. Credit policies for College Entrance Examination Board Advanced Placement tests. Deferred admission policy.

Costs and Financial Aid

Tuition, room & board, fees, and books.

Required Forms and Deadlines

Forms that applicants for financial aid must file and their respective deadlines. May include FAFSA, institution's own financial aid form, CSS/Financial Aid PROFILE, business/farm supplement, state aid form, noncustodial (divorced/separated) parent statement, and other forms specified by the school. Deadlines for filing financial aid forms.

Notification of Awards

The date that notification of financial aid awards occurs. "Rolling" indicates that notification is ongoing—the sooner you complete all of your required financial aid paperwork, the sooner you'll hear about your package.

Types of Aid

Need-based scholarships and grants may include Federal Pell, SEOG, state scholarships/grants, private scholarships, college/university gift aid from institutional funds, United Negro College Fund, Federal Nursing Scholarship, and other resources as specified by the school. Loans may include Direct Subsidized Stafford Loans, Direct Unsubsidized Stafford Loans, Direct PLUS Loans, Direct Consolidation Loan, FFEL Subsidized Stafford Loans, FFEL Unsubsidized Stafford Loans, FFEL PLUS Loans, FFEL Consolidation Loans, Federal Perkins Loans, Federal Nursing Loans, state loans, college/university loans from institutional funds, and other resources as specified by the school.

Student Employment

Availability of Federal Work-Study, a federal program that is need-based and part of most financial aid packages. Availability of part-time jobs direct from the college that are not based on need. The college's own assessment of part-time employment opportunities off campus.

Financial Aid Statistics

The percentage of freshmen who received some form of need-based financial aid. The percentage of undergraduates who received some form of need-based financial aid. The number of freshmen and undergrads who received an athletic scholarship or grant. The average amount of freshman scholarships and grants. The average amount of freshman loans. The average income from an on-campus job.

ONLINE DEGREE PROGRAMS

Distance learning programs are hardly anything new. However, increasingly sophisticated technologies that make the global sharing of information infinitely easier and faster have led to an explosion of revolutionary new programs that lend new credibility to the option of off-campus learning. The Princeton Review is here to give you the scoop on the world of online learning, and we'll tell you everything you need to know to stay fully up-to-date on all your college options. We're here to tell you what kind of programs they are, how they work, and why they just might be the best option for you.

Why Online Learning?

It's a fact: The traditional path to gaining a degree doesn't work for everyone. There's work. There's family. There's life! But you shouldn't let a little thing like scheduling conflicts stand between you and your degree. By taking the classroom out of the equation, online degree programs introduce a level of freedom and flexibility never afforded to students of more traditional programs. Gone are any worries about showing up on time—or showing up at all. While there are probably going to be requirements for how often or how long you log in for class discussions and lessons, when and where you fulfill those components of the course are largely at your discretion. Students log on at any hour of any day, from home, work, or anywhere they can find access to the Internet. This level of flexibility makes online classes an increasingly popular option for working professionals who are interested in strengthening their professional marketability without sacrificing the size or frequency of their paychecks.

Speaking of paychecks, it is important to remember that education beyond high school is not without its financial rewards. Individuals with college training can expect to earn higher salaries than those without post-secondary education. A 2003 study conducted by the National Center for Education Statistics (NCES) compared wages of working adults at different levels of education. It found that Caucasians with a Bachelor's degree, on average, out-earned those with only a high school diploma by 49 percent. For Latinos and African Americans, that number increases to 57 and 60 percent respectively. Another NCES study conducted in 2002 tracked the salary gap by gender; the results showed that men and women with Bachelor's degrees out-earned their high school graduate counterparts by 65 and 71 percent respectively. This is, of course, a long way of saying what you already know: College graduates make more money, so if you're looking to make more money too, it's a good idea to consider all your options.

How do I go about selecting an Online Program?

Regardless of whether you're thinking about pursuing a degree online or on campus, the need to choose a program that will best fit your needs is a critical one. The Princeton Review provides educational services to help you navigate the selection process, but neither we, nor anyone else, can make that decision for you. What we can do—what this guide aims to do—is help you to more fully understand the breadth of your choices.

Online degree programs provide some of the same offerings you would expect from conventional campus-based programs. Both online and traditional college catalogs are usually organized by department, division, or school, and reflect the distribution of faculty within the college or university. A subject index may also indicate whether a particular curriculum is offered. However, relying on these "text" methods for information on a particular program is not enough. Many colleges and universities will allow students to shape, at least in part, their own programs. It is a rare program indeed that is entirely prescribed. Before you design your course of study, however, you have to go through the process of selecting an institution that's going to best suit your needs. When choosing a distance learning program, you need to look at many of the traditional college criteria, including the nature and type of program, its quality, cost, and fit with your personal and professional goals. You should also investigate important personal criteria, such as its convenience, the ability it affords you to control your own study schedule, and the time it takes to degree completion. When you have narrowed your choices, you can review the important issues specific to distance learning programs.

What are Online Classes like?

Just like you'd expect from a traditional class, an online course is going to have an instructor, a group of students, and a specific curriculum with reading and writing components you must complete according to a specific schedule. Unlike a traditional class, which may meet once or twice a week, students in online courses may drop in and participate in class discussions several times a week. Instructors may require that students in the course log on for a minimum of one hour three times a week. The instructor will do the same, contributing his or her thoughts and observations to the discussion, helping to move it along, and ensuring that important curricular issues are covered. Bear in mind that all parties log on at times convenient for them, which vary by participant. In a one-week period, a class of 20 students may contribute upwards of 60 messages for each discussion theme. This makes for a lot of interaction, maybe even more than in the conventional classroom, where for various reasons fewer students can be relied upon to participate.

After a week, the class may move on to the next item on the syllabus, following the same format. The instructor can also modify this format by introducing volunteer student discussion leaders who take responsibility for moving the discussion along. Each week a different discussion leader puts his or her spin on the material. The most commonly used software programs permit instructors to create syllabi with many sub-units, develop and distribute exams, and facilitate group projects. As both software and hardware technology continue to improve, electronic courses will become more sophisticated, integrating video, voice, and graphics in imaginative and highly productive ways.

In addition to the online discussions, students complete the full complement of written assignments, including reports and term papers they can submit electronically, by fax, or by mail. These written assignments can also be posted electronically to other students in the class so each can see what the others have written, a feature not usually offered in traditional classes. Students may also e-mail privately with the instructor or with each other one-to-one; phone conversations and office meetings are also available.

What are my financial aid options? Do I have any?

Until recently, your options for federal aid to help pay for online courses would have been fairly limited. If your school offered fewer than half its classes on campus, you were automatically disqualified for federal student aid. In early 2006 however, the U.S. Congress expanded the federal aid budget, dropping the 50 percent stipulation and opening the door to schools whose only campuses were virtual ones. This legislation has allowed an increasing number of students to take classe and obtain degrees online. It has also benefited the growing for-profit education industry whose bread and butter is the online classroom—more than anyone.

But is it legitimate?

It's a fair question. Although online and asynchronous education have made distance learning available at many respected schools, any decision that can so dramatically affect your personal and financial future should be accompanied by a healthy level of skepticism. After all, how can a lesson taught by a teacher in a classroom full of students be compared to one without any of that face-to-face interaction? Even with all of the new technologies available, is it really possible to trade the campus for the computer and not necessarily be the worse off for it? While the proprietors of many online programs will argue that their programs are statistically as effective as a conventional classroom education, if not more so, many traditional programs consider this a dubious claim. They point to the notorious diploma mills of distance learning's past and say that very little has changed, and the truth is distance learning does have an occasionally shady history. With a majority of conventional universities providing some kind of online education, the question today seems to be less about the educational effectiveness of the technology, and more about the nature of the institutions (rather, corporations) that provide so many of the services.

Traditional universities and colleges argue that as for-profit entities, many online programs are, by default, more concerned with the bottom line than they are with the quality of education they provide to their students. This is clearly a concern for those who view the public's growing interest in taking classes from these institutions, not to mention the extraordinary boosts in enrollment expected with the abolition of the 50 percent rule, as a dangerous path toward the privatization of an educational system whose proprietors will seek to profit from what has long been considered a public service.

Don't go into this blindly. Do a fair amount of research. Pay specific attention to the institution's track record. How effectively do they serve students away from campus? Assess the strength of both the academic and student support systems by asking questions about academic advising, consultations with faculty, and whether the help desk is available 24 hours a day, 7 days a week. In short, make sure you know what you're getting into. There are a lot of great opportunities for an online education, and you shouldn't let fear of being hoodwinked quash your quest for a degree before it's begun. You should, however, be smart about how you proceed and make sure that you find the program that's going to suit you best.

The Best 368 Colleges Icon

 Indicates whether the school can be found in our book, *The Best 368 Colleges*. In that book, each school has a detailed profile that includes the results of our surveys regarding students' opinion, about many aspects of their schools and their educations.

PRINCETONREVIEW.COM

PrincetonReview.com has a ton of FREE information to help you through the entire college admissions process. This book is one step in the right direction, but we can also help you **RESEARCH** more schools, **PREPARE** for the SAT/ACT, **APPLY** to college directly through our website, and learn how to **PAY** for college!

Try out **Counselor-O-Matic**, our dynamic college search engine that asks you a little bit about yourself and what you're looking for in a college, and SHAZAM—it generates schools that are Good Matches, Safeties, and Reach Schools. And it doesn't stop there. We also have relationships with thousands of colleges looking to fill their lecture halls with our PrincetonReview.com users. That's right—once you fill out Counselor-O-Matic, we can get your name in front of colleges who want YOU!

We've also got the most powerful **Scholarship Search** on the Web! And no, we won't sell your name as other popular scholarship sites do. For all this and much, much more, visit **PrincetonReview.com**.

Paying For College 101

It's not a long shot to bet that you're reading this book because you're thinking of going to college. We're near psychic, right?! The odds are also good that you understand if you want to get into the college of your choice, you need the grades and the scores, and you need to demonstrate the things you dig outside the four walls of your classroom.

Positioning yourself for college admissions is not gambling; it's an investment. You've been investing your time and effort to be the best candidate for your prospective colleges and now, you've invested a little bit of money—right now by buying and reading this book! We applaud you for it!

But what else do you need to know to go to college?

If you answered, How am I going to pay for it? Then you're not alone and you're solidly on the right track to figuring it out. We think we can help.

Your college education is an investment in your future, and paying for college is a big part of that investment. In the next pages you'll find lots of basic information on that big scary subject -- financial aid. While we tried to stick to "need to know" nuggets, the information you'll read about here is powerful because it diffuses frenzy around the aid process and equips you with the knowledge to navigate the process as an educated consumer. We ask that you take a little bit of time right now to learn about what it takes to afford yourself an excellent education.

More Great Titles from The Princeton Review
Paying for College Without Going Broke

WHAT ARE THE COSTS INVOLVED?

The first thing that comes to mind when you think about how much it costs to go to school is tuition, right? Well, tuition may be the first thing, but don't make the mistake of thinking that's it. The total cost of a year at college involves more than just the tuition amount that the school lists.

Let's break it down:

- Tuition and fees
- Room and board
- Books and supplies
- Personal expenses
- Travel expenses

All of these things together make up the total cost of attendance (COA) for a year at a particular college. So your tuition might be $20,000, but add on room and board, the cost of books, lab fees, not to mention the cost of travel back and forth for breaks, and miscellaneous personal expenses (you will need to buy toothpaste occasionally), and your COA could be as much as $30,000—that's a big difference.

According to a study by The College Board, during the 2006-2007 school year, the cost of attending a four-year private college for that year averaged approximately $30,367. The same study found that the total cost of attending a public university for that year was, on average, $12,796.

Check out the Tuition Cost Calculator
PrincetonReview.com/college/finance/tcc

Paying for college is hard, yes; just about everyone needs some kind of financial assistance. More than 17 million students attend college each year—and only 20 percent manage to pay for it without some kind of financial aid package. That means almost 14 million students receive help.

WHAT'S IN A FINANCIAL AID PACKAGE?

A typical financial aid package contains money, from the school, federal government, or state, in various forms: grants, scholarships, work-study programs, and loans.

Check out the Aid Comparison Calculator
PrincetonReview.com/college/finance/acc/calc.asp

Grants

Grants are essentially gifts—free money given to you by the federal government, state agencies, and an individual college. They are usually need-based, and you are not required to pay them back.

Some states have grant programs established specifically to help financially needy students, usually to attend schools within that state. Different states have different standards and application requirements.

Scholarships

Scholarships are also free money, but unlike grants, they are merit-based. Some are also based on your financial need; others are based on different qualifications, and are often need-blind.

Scholarships can be based on anything: academic achievement or test scores (the National Merit Scholarship is a well-known one), athletic achievements, musical or artistic talent, religious affiliations or ethnicity, and so on.

They don't have to come from colleges, either. Corporations, churches, volunteer organizations, unions, advocacy groups, and many other organizations offer merit-based, need-based, or simply existence-based scholarships.

Check out the Scholarship Search page
PrincetonReview.com/college/finance

When considering outside scholarships, make sure you know how the college(s) you're applying to treat them. Some schools (but not all!) will count any money you receive from outside sources as income, and reduce the amount of any aid package accordingly.

Work-Study Programs

The federal government subsidizes a nationwide program that provides part-time, on-campus jobs to students who need financial aid to attend school. Work-study participants can work in academic departments, deans' offices, libraries, and so on. You get a paycheck, like you would at any job, and you can spend the money however you like—but it's meant for tuition, books, and food.

My Family Doesn't Have $30,000 Lying Around!

You and your family are not alone. In many cases, a school's financial aid package doesn't cover all of your costs, and you might not have the resources to make up the difference. When a school doesn't offer enough in the way of aid to cover the cost of attendance, many families turn to loans.

Let's start with the biggest source of student loans—the federal government.

Federal student aid is intended to bridge the gap between what college costs and what you and your family can actually afford to pay. The government does this in two ways: It makes money available to colleges, which then, through their financial aid offices, make the money available to students in the form of aid packages; and it helps students get affordable loans themselves, through guarantees to loan lenders and other ways (which we'll discuss in a minute).

Last year the federal government gave more than $86 billion in student aid.

How Does the Government Decide How Much to Give Me?

When you're applying for financial aid, you'll be filling out a lot of forms. The most important of those forms will be the Free Application for Federal Student Aid (FAFSA). Basically, the FAFSA will want to know the following information:

- Your parents' available income
- Your parents' available assets
- Your available income
- Your available assets

The federal government will take all this information and apply a complex formula to determine what your family's expected contribution should be.

For help filling out the FAFSA, check out MyRichUncle's easy-to-use FAFSA-Assistant tool at MyRichUncle.com/TPR

What Is This "Expected Contribution"?

This is how much of your and your family's income and assets the government thinks you can afford to put toward the cost of attending college. This amount is called the Expected Family Contribution, or EFC.

Your financial need (i.e., the money you need in order to attend college) is defined as the difference between the school's total cost of attendance (tuition, room and board, books, etc.) and your expected family contribution. Or, to put it another way:

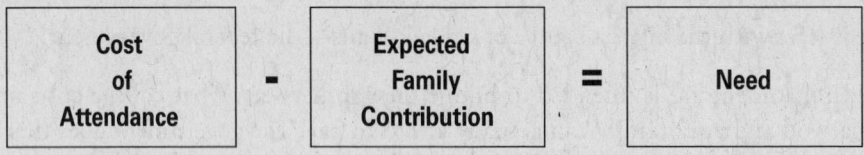

| Cost of Attendance | **-** | Expected Family Contribution | **=** | Need |

When you are accepted to a college, the school's financial aid office will then put together an aid package that, hopefully, will make up this difference and cover the cost of your need.

What Do You Mean, "Hopefully"?

The idea is that your EFC will be the same for every school, regardless of the cost of the school. This means that if your EFC is determined to be $9,500, that is the amount you would be expected to pay if you go to State U., where the COA is $14,000, or if you go to Private U., where the COA is $37,000. Ideally, the school will then provide you with a financial aid package that makes up the difference—$4,500 in the case of State U., $27,500 for Private U.

Ideally?

Yes, in a perfect world, where a school offers to meet 100% of your need, you and your family would pay no more than your EFC, and your EFC would always be exactly what you and your family believe you can afford.

In reality, this doesn't happen nearly as often as we'd like. Some schools have larger endowments for financial aid and can meet your need 100%. Other schools may not.

When that happens, you and your family may want to investigate student loans.

LOANS

The federal government and private commercial lenders offer educational loans to students. Federally-guaranteed loans are usually the "first resort" for borrowers because many are subsidized by the federal government and offer capped interest rates. Private loans, on the other hand, have fewer restrictions or borrowing limits, but may have higher interest rates and more stringent credit-based qualification process—but not always, as we'll see later on.

Federal Loans

For many students seeking financial aid, the Stafford loan is the typical place to start. The federal Stafford loan program features a low capped interest rate and yearly caps on the maximum amount a student can borrow. Stafford loans can either be subsidized (the government pays the interest while you're in school) or unsubsidized (you are responsible for the interest that accrues while in school). Most students who get Stafford loans will end up with a combination of the two. Stafford loans do not have to be repaid until you've graduated or dropped below part-time status.

Here's the thing you might not know about Stafford loans:

Many people assumed that the government sets the rate on student loans, and that that rate is locked in stone. That's not true. The government merely sets the maximum rate lenders can charge (which is 6.8% as of 2007). Lenders are free to charge less than that if they want to.

Historically, however, most lenders have charged the maximum rate because Stafford loans are distributed via colleges' financial aid offices, which maintain preferred lender lists of a limited number of lenders to choose from. Reduced numbers of lenders meant little competition for borrowers, which meant the lenders had very little incentive to offer more competitive rates.

In the last few years, though, a lot has changed. More students now know that they are not required to take a loan from a lender on a preferred lender list. And there are more lenders now willing to compete on price. It's vital that you, as the person making this important and, frankly, expensive investment in your future, educate yourself fully as to all your options when it comes to student loans.

Know Your Rights

You have the right to shop for and secure the best rates possible for your student loans. You have the right to choose the lending institution you prefer. You do not have to use the lenders recommended by your college. All your college must do— and all it is legally allowed to do—is to certify for the lending institution of your choice that you are indeed enrolled and the amount you are eligible to receive.

Let's say you have no credit history or a credit-worthy co-borrower. You might consider Preprime™: an underwriting methodology pioneered by MyRichUncle. Instead of focusing solely on credit history, MyRichUncle with its Preprime™ option, also takes into account academic performance, student behavior, and other factors that can indicate that a student will be a responsible borrower. www.myrichuncle.com/ PreprimeLoans.aspx

Here's a tip: *don't default.* If you ever feel that you are going to be unable to pay off your loans, contact your lender immediately. They will be happy to help you figure out a way to repay your loans, as long as you are upfront and honest with them about the difficulties you may be having.

Private Loans

Student loans from private lenders can make it possible to cover the costs of higher education when other sources of funding have been exhausted.

When you apply for a private loan, the lending institution will check your credit score and determine your capacity to pay back the money you borrow. For individuals whose credit history is less than positive, or if you have no credit history, lenders may require a co-borrower: a credit-worthy individual—often a parent—who also agrees to be accountable to the terms of the loan. While private loans do have annual borrowing limits, they are usually higher than government loans, around $40,000; they also have higher interest rates and have floating rate caps, not fixed as in federal loans.

Do Your Research

All student loan lenders are not created equal, so investigate all your options, and look for lenders that are offering loans at rates less than the federally mandated maximum (remember, that's 6.1% for subsidized Staffords, and 6.8% for unsubsidized as of July 2008).

One lending institution that's been in the news lately is MyRichUncle. MyRichUncle offers federal loans, including subsidized and unsubsidized Stafford loans and private loans. However, MyRichUncle has remembered that the government sets the maximum interest rate for Stafford loans, and has chosen to discount the rate upon repayment. Those discounts will not disappear, like they may with other lenders, unless you default on the loan.

So, Why MyRichUncle?

Well, we here at The Princeton Review think it's important that you have all the information when you're figuring out how to pay for college, and we think MyRichUncle is doing something different—and helpful—with their approach to student loans.

They know that getting a student loan can be a complicated and intimidating process. They believe, as does The Princeton Review, that students should have access to the best education even if they don't yet have a credit history, or at least an opportunity to prove they can be credit-worthy borrowers. They also believe student loan debt can be a serious problem so your loans should be about getting the tools necessary for the best education possible that will position you for the most opportunities when you graduate.

Something else to remember: Your student loan will, ultimately, be your responsibility. When you enter into a loan agreement, you're entering into a long-term relationship with your lender—10 to 15 years, on average. The right student loan, from the right lender, can help you avoid years of unnecessary fees and payments.

THE BOTTOM LINE

College is expensive, period. But if you're reading this book, you're already invested in getting the best education that you can. You owe it to yourself and your future to invest just as much in learning about all your financial options—and opportunities—as well.

IS THIS BOOK JUST LIKE YOUR COURSE?

Since the book came out, many students and teachers have asked us, "Is this book just like your course?" The short answer is no.

It isn't easy to raise SAT scores. Our course is more than 50 hours long and requires class participation, quizzes, homework, four practice examinations, and possibly additional tutoring.

We like to think that this book is fun, informative, and well written, but no book can capture the magic of our instructors and course structure. Each Princeton Review instructor has attended a top college and has excelled on the SAT. Moreover, each of our instructors undergoes rigorous training.

While this book contains many of the techniques we teach in our course, some of our techniques are too difficult to include in a book without a trained and experienced Princeton Review teacher to explain and demonstrate them. Moreover, this book is written for the average student. Each class in our course is tailored so that we can gear our techniques to each student's level.

We're Flattered, But...

Some tutors and schools use this book to run their own "Princeton Review course." While we are flattered, we are also concerned.

It has taken us many years of teaching tens of thousands of students across the country to develop our SAT program, and we're still learning. Many teachers think that our course is simply a collection of techniques that can be taught by anyone. It isn't that easy.

We train each Princeton Review instructor for many hours for every hour he or she will teach class. Each of the instructors is monitored, evaluated, and supervised throughout the course.

Another concern is that many of our techniques conflict with traditional math and English techniques as taught in high school. For example, in the Math section, we tell our students to avoid setting up algebraic equations. Can you imagine your math teacher telling you that? And in the Critical Reading section, we tell our students not to read the passage too carefully. Can you imagine your English teacher telling you that?

While we also teach traditional math and English in our course, some teachers may not completely agree with some of our approaches.

Beware of Princeton Review Clones

We have nothing against people who use our techniques, but we do object to tutors or high schools who claim to "teach The Princeton Review method." If you want to find out whether your teacher has been trained by The Princeton Review or whether you're taking an official Princeton Review course, call us toll-free at 1-800-2REVIEW.

If You'd Like More Information

Princeton Review sites are in hundreds of cities around the country. For the office nearest you, call 1-800-2REVIEW.

COLLEGE DIRECTORY

ABILENE CHRISTIAN UNIVERSITY

ACU Box 29000, Abilene, TX 79699
Phone: 325-674-2650 **E-mail:** info@admissions.acu.edu **CEEB Code:** 6001
Fax: 325-674-2130 **Website:** www.acu.edu **ACT Code:** 4050
Financial Aid Phone: 325-674-2643

This private school, affiliated with the Church of Christ, was founded in 1906. It has a 208-acre campus.

RATINGS
Admissions Selectivity Rating: 85   **Fire Safety Rating:** 67   **Green Rating:** 82

STUDENTS AND FACULTY
Enrollment: 4,099. **Student Body:** 55% female, 45% male, 19% out-of-state, 4% international (57 countries represented). African American 7%, Caucasian 75%, Hispanic 6%. **Retention and Graduation:** 75% freshmen return for sophomore year. 34% freshmen graduate within 4 years. 35% grads go on to further study within 1 year. 16% grads pursue arts and sciences degrees. 8% grads pursue business degrees. 3% grads pursue law degrees. 4% grads pursue medical degrees. **Faculty:** Student/faculty ratio 16:1. 223 full-time faculty, 78% hold PhDs. 98% faculty teach undergrads.

ACADEMICS
Degrees: Associate, bachelor's, doctoral, first professional, master's, post-bachelor's certificate, post-master's certificate. **Academic Requirements:** Arts/fine arts, English (including composition), foreign languages, history, humanities, mathematics, sciences (biological or physical), social science, Bible. **Classes:** Most classes have 20–29 students. Most lab/discussion sections have 10–19 students. **Majors with Highest Enrollment:** Business administration/management, elementary education and teaching, psychology. **Disciplines with Highest Percentage of Degrees Awarded:** Business/marketing 20%, education 13%, interdisciplinary studies 10%, visual and performing arts 8%, health professions and related sciences 7%. **Special Study Options:** Cross-registration, distance learning, double major, dual enrollment, English as a Second Language (ESL), honors program, independent study, internships, student-designed major, study abroad, teacher certification program.

FACILITIES
Housing: Men's dorms, women's dorms, apartments for married students, apartments for single students, special housing for disabled students. **Special Academic Facilities/Equipment:** Museum of university's history, biblical restoration studies center, voice institute, demonstration farm and ranch, observatory. **Computers:** 5% of classrooms are wireless, 69% of public computers are PCs, 31% of public computers are Macs, network access in dorm rooms, network access in dorm lounges, online registration, online administrative functions (other than registration), remote student-access to Web through college's connection.

CAMPUS LIFE
Activities: Choral groups, concert band, drama/theater, jazz band, literary magazine, marching band, music ensembles, musical theater, opera, radio station, student government, student newspaper, symphony orchestra, television station, yearbook. **Organizations:** 108 registered organizations, 14 honor societies, 16 religious organizations. 6 fraternities (16% men join), 6 sororities (20% women join). **Athletics (Intercollegiate):** *Men:* Baseball, basketball, cross-country, football, tennis, track/field (indoor), track/field (outdoor). *Women:* Basketball, cross-country, softball, tennis, track/field (indoor), track/field (outdoor), volleyball.

ADMISSIONS
Freshman Academic Profile: 18% in top 10% of high school class, 47% in top 25% of high school class, 80% in top 50% of high school class. 79% from public high schools. SAT Math middle 50% range 490-620. SAT Critical Reading middle 50% range 480-610. ACT middle 50% range 20-26. TOEFL required of all international applicants, minimum paper TOEFL 525, minimum computer TOEFL 197. **Basis for Candidate Selection:** *Very important factors considered include:* Character/personal qualities, rigor of secondary school record, standardized test scores. *Important factors considered include:* Academic GPA, class rank, interview, recommendation(s), religious affiliation/commitment, talent/ability. *Other factors considered include:* Alumni/ae relation, extracurricular activities, first generation, level of applicant's interest, racial/ethnic status, volunteer work, work experience. **Freshman Admission Requirements:** High school diploma is required, and GED is accepted. *Academic units recommended:* 4 English, 3 math, 3 science (2 science labs), 2 foreign language. **Freshman Admission Statistics:** 3,661 applied, 52% admitted, 50% enrolled. **Transfer Admission Requirements:** High school transcript, college transcript(s), interview. Minimum college GPA of 2.0 required. Lowest grade transferable C. **General Admission Information:** Application fee $25. Regular application deadline 8/1. Regular notification is rolling. Nonfall registration accepted. Credit offered for CEEB Advanced Placement tests.

COSTS AND FINANCIAL AID
Annual tuition $16,710. Room and board $6,350. Required fees $700. Average book expense $1,100. **Required Forms and Deadlines:** FAFSA, institution's own financial aid form. Financial aid filing deadline 3/1. **Notification of Awards:** Applicants will be notified of awards on a rolling basis beginning on or about 4/1. **Types of Aid:** *Need-based scholarships/grants:* Pell, SEOG, state scholarships/grants, private scholarships, the school's own gift aid, United Negro College Fund. *Loans:* FFEL Subsidized Stafford, FFEL Unsubsidized Stafford, FFEL PLUS, Federal Perkins, state loans, college/university loans from institutional funds. **Student Employment:** Federal Work-Study Program available. Institutional employment available. Off-campus job opportunities are good. **Financial Aid Statistics:** 63% freshmen, 58% undergrads receive need-based scholarship or grant aid. 48% freshmen, 48% undergrads receive need-based self-help aid. 40 freshmen, 206 undergrads receive athletic scholarships. 94% freshmen, 89% undergrads receive any aid. Highest amount earned per year from on-campus jobs $1,850.

ACADEMY OF ART UNIVERSITY

79 New Montgomery Street, San Francisco, CA 94105
Phone: 415-274-2222 **E-mail:** info@academyart.edu
Fax: 415-263-4130 **Website:** www.academyart.edu **ACT Code:** 0155
Financial Aid Phone: 800-544-2787

This private school was founded in 1929. It has a 20-acre campus.

RATINGS
Admissions Selectivity Rating: 60*   **Fire Safety Rating:** 60*   **Green Rating:** 60*

STUDENTS AND FACULTY
Enrollment: 6,596. **Student Body:** 50% female, 50% male, 23% out-of-state, 15% international. African American 4%, Asian 12%, Caucasian 42%, Hispanic 7%. **Retention and Graduation:** 58% freshmen return for sophomore year. 2% freshmen graduate within 4 years. **Faculty:** Student/faculty ratio 18:1. 135 full-time faculty, 11% hold PhDs. 80% faculty teach undergrads.

ACADEMICS
Degrees: Associate, bachelor's, certificate, master's. **Academic Requirements:** Arts/fine arts, computer literacy, English (including composition), history, humanities, arts/performing. **Classes:** Most classes have 10–19 students. **Majors with Highest Enrollment:** Cinematography and film/video production, computer graphics, fashion/apparel design. **Disciplines with Highest Percentage of Degrees Awarded:** Visual and performing arts 62%, communication technologies 21%, computer and information sciences 10%, business/marketing 7%. **Special Study Options:** Accelerated program, cooperative education program, distance learning, English as a Second Language (ESL), independent study, internships, weekend college, portfolio developement, personal enrichment program.

FACILITIES
Housing: Coed dorms, men's dorms, women's dorms, apartments for married students, apartments for single students. **Special Academic Facilities/Equipment:** 4 art galleries (public) for display of student work. **Computers:** Network access in dorm rooms, online registration, online administrative functions (other than registration), remote student-access to Web through college's connection.

CAMPUS LIFE
Activities: Concert band, dance, drama/theater, musical theater, student newspaper, student-run film society. **Organizations:** 13 registered organizations. **Athletics (Intercollegiate):** *Men:* Soccer. *Women:* Soccer, volleyball.

ADMISSIONS
Basis for Candidate Selection: *Important factors considered include:* Interview. *Factors considered include:* Rigor of secondary school record. **Freshman Admission Requirements:** High school diploma is required, and GED is accepted. **Freshman Admission Statistics:** 1,407 applied, 100% admitted, 72% enrolled. **Transfer Admission Requirements:** High school transcript, college transcript(s), interview. Minimum college GPA of 2.0 required. Lowest grade transferable C. **General Admission Information:** Application fee $100. Regular notification is rolling. Nonfall registration accepted. Admission may be deferred for a maximum of 24 months.

COSTS AND FINANCIAL AID
Annual tuition $16,800. Room and board $13,500. Required fees $280. Average

book expense $1,566. **Required Forms and Deadlines:** FAFSA, institution's own financial aid form. Financial aid filing deadline 7/10. **Types of Aid:** *Need-based scholarships/grants:* Pell, SEOG, state scholarships/grants. *Loans:* Direct Subsidized Stafford, Direct Unsubsidized Stafford, Direct PLUS, FFEL Subsidized Stafford, FFEL Unsubsidized Stafford, FFEL PLUS. **Financial Aid Statistics:** 14% freshmen, 19% undergrads receive need-based scholarship or grant aid. 29% freshmen, 35% undergrads receive need-based self-help aid. 60% undergrads receive any aid. **Financial Aid Phone:** 800-544-2787.

ACADIA UNIVERSITY

Admissions Office, Wolfville, NS B4P 2R6, Canada
Phone: 902-585-1222 **E-mail:** admissions@acadiau.ca
Fax: 902-585-1092 **Website:** www.acadiau.ca
Financial Aid Phone: 902-585-1543

This public school was founded in 1838. It has a 200-acre campus.

RATINGS
Admissions Selectivity Rating: 60* **Fire Safety Rating:** 60* **Green Rating:** 60*

STUDENTS AND FACULTY
Enrollment: 3,326. **Student Body:** 55% female, 45% male, 35% out-of-state. **Retention and Graduation:** 82% freshmen return for sophomore year. **Faculty:** Student/faculty ratio 12:1. 254 full-time faculty. 100% faculty teach undergrads.

ACADEMICS
Degrees: Bachelor's, certificate, diploma, master's. **Academic Requirements:** Arts/fine arts, English (including composition), humanities, sciences (biological or physical), social science. **Majors with Highest Enrollment:** Business administration/management, computer and information sciences. **Disciplines with Highest Percentage of Degrees Awarded:** Social sciences 17%, education 15%, business/marketing 15%, parks and recreation 11%, biological/life sciences 8%, psychology 7%. **Special Study Options:** Cooperative education program, distance learning, double major, English as a Second Language (ESL), exchange student program (domestic), honors program, independent study, internships, study abroad.

FACILITIES
Housing: Coed dorms, men's dorms, women's dorms, apartments for single students, special housing for disabled students. **Computers:** 100% of public computers are PCs, network access in dorm rooms, network access in dorm lounges, online registration, online administrative functions (other than registration), remote student-access to Web through college's connection.

CAMPUS LIFE
Activities: Choral groups, concert band, dance, drama/theater, jazz band, literary magazine, music ensembles, pep band, radio station, student government, student newspaper, symphony orchestra, yearbook. **Organizations:** 60 registered organizations, 3 religious organizations. **Athletics (Intercollegiate):** *Men:* Basketball, cheerleading, football, ice hockey, rugby, soccer, swimming, volleyball. *Women:* Basketball, cheerleading, ice hockey, rugby, soccer, swimming, volleyball.

ADMISSIONS
Freshman Academic Profile: 80% from public high schools. TOEFL required of all international applicants, minimum paper TOEFL 550. **Basis for Candidate Selection:** *Very important factors considered include:* Academic GPA, rigor of secondary school record. *Important factors considered include:* Recommendation(s), talent/ability. *Factors considered include:* Character/personal qualities, class rank, extracurricular activities, geographical residence, standardized test scores, volunteer work, work experience. **Freshman Admission Requirements:** High school diploma is required, and GED is not accepted. *Academic units required:* 1 English, 1 math. *Academic units recommended:* 1 English, 2 math, 1 science, 1 foreign language, 1 social studies, 1 history, 2 academic electives. **Freshman Admission Statistics:** 3,200 applied, 26% admitted, 72% enrolled. **Transfer Admission Requirements:** College transcript(s). **Admission Information:** Application fee $25. Regular notification is rolling. Nonfall registration accepted. Admission may be deferred for a maximum of 1 year. Common Application not accepted. Credit and/or placement offered for CEEB Advanced Placement tests.

COSTS AND FINANCIAL AID
In-province tuition $7,760. Out-of-province tuition $7,760. International tuition $13,810. Room & board $6,223. Required fees $345. Average book expense $1,000. **Student Employment:** Off-campus job opportunities are excellent..

ADAMS STATE COLLEGE

Office of Admissions, Alamosa, CO 81102
Phone: 719-587-7712 **E-mail:** ascadmit@adams.edu **CEEB Code:** 4001
Fax: 719-587-7522 **Website:** www2.adams.edu **ACT Code:** 0496
Financial Aid Phone: 800-824-6494

This public school was founded in 1921. It has a 90-acre campus.

RATINGS
Admissions Selectivity Rating: 74 **Fire Safety Rating:** 69 **Green Rating:** 72

STUDENTS AND FACULTY
Enrollment: 2,108. **Student Body:** 57% female, 43% male, 11% out-of-state. African American 6%, Caucasian 59%, Hispanic 29%, Native American 2%. **Retention and Graduation:** 56% freshmen return for sophomore year. 14% freshmen graduate within 4 years. **Faculty:** Student/faculty ratio 14:1. 106 full-time faculty, 75% hold PhDs. 100% faculty teach undergrads.

ACADEMICS
Degrees: Associate, bachelor's, master's. **Academic Requirements:** Arts/fine arts, computer literacy, English (including composition), history, humanities, mathematics, sciences (biological or physical), social science, wellness. Computer literacy is a proficiency requirement; may be met by passing a class or an examination. **Classes:** Most classes have fewer than 10 students. Most lab/discussion sections have 10–19 students. **Majors with Highest Enrollment:** Business administration/management, kinesiology and exercise science, liberal arts and sciences studies and humanities. **Disciplines with Highest Percentage of Degrees Awarded:** Liberal arts/general studies 25%, business/marketing 24%, social sciences 11%, psychology 8%, parks and recreation 7%, visual and performing arts 7%. **Special Study Options:** Accelerated program, distance learning, double major, independent study, internships, study abroad, teacher certification program, weekend college, high school dual enrollment.

FACILITIES
Housing: Coed dorms, men's dorms, women's dorms, apartments for married students, apartments for single students, Learning Community. **Special Academic Facilities/Equipment:** Luther Bean Museum, Hatfield Gallery, Gallery 114, Leon Memorial Music Hall, Zacheis Planetarium. **Computers:** 87% of public computers are PCs, 13% of public computers are Macs, network access in dorm rooms, network access in dorm lounges, online registration, online administrative functions (other than registration), remote student-access to Web through college's connection.

CAMPUS LIFE
Activities: Choral groups, concert band, dance, drama/theater, jazz band, literary magazine, marching band, music ensembles, musical theater, pep band, radio station, student government, student newspaper. **Organizations:** 42 registered organizations, 3 religious organizations. 3 fraternities. **Athletics (Intercollegiate):** *Men:* Basketball, cross-country, football, golf, track/field (indoor), track/field (outdoor), wrestling. *Women:* Basketball, cross-country, golf, soccer, softball, track/field (indoor), track/field (outdoor), volleyball. **Environmental Initiatives:** Hosting Focus of the Nation Event 1/30-31/08. Establishment of EARTH (Environmental Action for Resources, Transportation, & Health) group on campus. Water Project Phase 1-convert supply to non-potable water Phase 2-update inefficient system with one with a weather station.

ADMISSIONS
Freshman Academic Profile: 11% in top 10% of high school class, 25% in top 25% of high school class, 49% in top 50% of high school class. SAT Math middle 50% range 420-510. SAT Critical Reading middle 50% range 420-553. SAT Writing middle 50% range 390-480. ACT middle 50% range 17-22. TOEFL required of all international applicants, minimum paper TOEFL 550, minimum computer TOEFL 213. **Basis for Candidate Selection:** *Very important factors considered include:* Rigor of secondary school record, standardized test scores. *Important factors considered include:* Academic GPA. *Factors considered include:* Character/personal qualities, class rank, extracurricular activities, geographical residence, interview, recommendation(s), state residency. **Freshman Admission Requirements:** High school diploma is required, and GED is accepted. *Academic units recommended:* 4 English, 2 math, 2 science, 2 foreign language, 3 social studies, 1 history. **Freshman Admission Statistics:** 1,875 applied, 62% admitted, 44% enrolled. **Transfer Admission Requirements:** College transcript(s), minimum college GPA of 2.0 required. Lowest grade transferable D. **General Admission Information:** Application fee $20. Regular notification continuous. Nonfall registration accepted. Admission may be deferred for a maximum of 2 years. Credit offered for CEEB Advanced Placement tests.

COSTS AND FINANCIAL AID

Annual in-state tuition $8,062. Annual out-of-state tuition $8,062. Room and board $8,284. Required fees $180. Average book expense $1,200. **Required Forms and Deadlines:** FAFSA. **Notification of Awards:** Applicants will be notified of awards on a rolling basis beginning on or about 3/1. **Types of Aid:** *Need-based scholarships/grants:* Pell, SEOG, state scholarships/grants, private scholarships, the school's own gift aid. *Loans:* FFEL Subsidized Stafford, FFEL Unsubsidized Stafford, FFEL PLUS, Federal Perkins, alternative loans. **Student Employment:** Federal Work-Study Program available. Institutional employment available. Off-campus job opportunities are good. **Financial Aid Statistics:** 49% freshmen, 57% undergrads receive need-based scholarship or grant aid. 42% freshmen, 55% undergrads receive need-based self-help aid. 54 freshmen, 177 undergrads receive athletic scholarships. 89% freshmen, 87% undergrads receive any aid. Highest amount earned per year from on-campus jobs $922.

ADELPHI UNIVERSITY

Levermore Hall 114, 1 South Avenue, Garden City, NY 11530
Phone: 516-877-3050 **E-mail:** admissions@adelphi.edu **CEEB Code:** 2003
Fax: 516-877-3039 **Website:** www.adelphi.edu **ACT Code:** 2664
Financial Aid Phone: 516-877-2240

This private school was founded in 1896. It has a 75-acre campus.

RATINGS

Admissions Selectivity Rating: 79   **Fire Safety Rating:** 99   **Green Rating:** 73

STUDENTS AND FACULTY

Enrollment: 4,916. **Student Body:** 73% female, 27% male, 8% out-of-state, 4% international (40 countries represented). African American 14%, Asian 6%, Caucasian 47%, Hispanic 8%. **Retention and Graduation:** 78% freshmen return for sophomore year. 51% freshmen graduate within 4 years. 38% grads go on to further study within 1 year. **Faculty:** Student/faculty ratio 11:1. 280 full-time faculty, 90% hold PhDs. 100% faculty teach undergrads.

ACADEMICS

Degrees: Associate, bachelor's, doctoral, master's, post-bachelor's certificate, post-master's certificate. **Academic Requirements:** Arts/fine arts, English (including composition), humanities, mathematics, sciences (biological or physical), social science. **Classes:** Most classes have 20–29 students. Most lab/discussion sections have 10–19 students. **Majors with Highest Enrollment:** Business administration/management, education, nursing. **Disciplines with Highest Percentage of Degrees Awarded:** Health professions and related sciences 20%, business/marketing 19%, social sciences 12%, psychology 8%, visual and performing arts 7%. **Special Study Options:** Accelerated program, distance learning, double major, dual enrollment, English as a Second Language (ESL), honors program, independent study, internships, liberal arts/career combination, student-designed major, study abroad, teacher certification program, weekend college, joint degrees, learning disabilities program, distance learning program is being restructured.

FACILITIES

Housing: Coed dorms, special housing for disabled students. **Special Academic Facilities/Equipment:** Art gallery, sculpture and ceramics studios, bronze-casting foundry, theater, language labs. **Computers:** 100% of classrooms are wired, 46% of classrooms are wireless, 94% of public computers are PCs, 6% of public computers are Macs, network access in dorm rooms, network access in dorm lounges, online registration, online administrative functions (other than registration), support for handheld computing, remote student-access to Web through college's connection.

CAMPUS LIFE

Activities: Choral groups, concert band, dance, drama/theater, jazz band, literary magazine, music ensembles, musical theater, radio station, student government, student newspaper, student-run film society, symphony orchestra, yearbook. **Organizations:** 79 registered organizations, 21 honor society, 5 religious organizations. 2 fraternities (5% men join), 5 sororities (4% women join). **Athletics (Intercollegiate):** *Men:* Baseball, basketball, cross-country, golf, lacrosse, soccer, swimming, tennis, track/field (indoor), track/field (outdoor). *Women:* Basketball, bowling, cross-country, lacrosse, soccer, softball, swimming, tennis, track/field (indoor), track/field (outdoor), volleyball. **Environmental Initiatives:** LEED silver rating fro the CSPA project. Pending installation of a 30 KW Solar PV system on the Fine Arts Building. Use of Geo-thermal heating and cooling systems in the newly constructed residence halls.

ADMISSIONS

Freshman Academic Profile: 17% in top 10% of high school class, 48% in top

25% of high school class, 85% in top 50% of high school class. 75% from public high schools. SAT Math middle 50% range 490–590. SAT Math middle 50% range 490-590. SAT Critical Reading middle 50% range 480-580. SAT Writing middle 50% range 480-580. ACT middle 50% range 20-24. TOEFL required of all international applicants, minimum paper TOEFL 550, minimum computer TOEFL 213. **Basis for Candidate Selection:** *Very important factors considered include:* Rigor of secondary school record. *Important factors considered include:* Academic GPA, application essay, character/personal qualities, class rank, extracurricular activities, standardized test scores, talent/ability, volunteer work. *Factors considered include:* Alumni/ae relation, first generation, interview, level of applicant's interest, recommendation(s), work experience. **Freshman Admission Requirements:** High school diploma is required, and GED is accepted. *Academic units recommended:* 4 English, 3 math, 3 science, 2 foreign language, 4 social studies. **Freshman Admission Statistics:** 5,496 applied, 68% admitted, 23% enrolled. **Transfer Admission Requirements:** College transcript(s), essay or personal statement. Minimum college GPA of 2.3 required. Lowest grade transferable C-. **General Admission Information:** Application fee $35. Regular notification is rolling. Nonfall registration accepted. Admission may be deferred for a maximum of 1 year. Credit and/or placement offered for CEEB Advanced Placement tests.

COSTS AND FINANCIAL AID

Annual tuition $21,000. Room and board $9,900. Required fees $1,200. Average book expense $1,000. **Required Forms and Deadlines:** FAFSA, state aid form. Financial aid filing deadline 3/1. **Notification of Awards:** Applicants will be notified of awards on a rolling basis beginning on or about 3/1. **Types of Aid:** *Need-based scholarships/grants:* Pell, SEOG, state scholarships/grants, private scholarships, the school's own gift aid, United Negro College Fund, Donor (endowed and restricted) funds. *Loans:* FFEL Subsidized Stafford, FFEL Unsubsidized Stafford, FFEL PLUS, Federal Perkins, Federal Nursing, non-federal alternative loans. **Financial Aid Statistics:** 58% freshmen, 59% undergrads receive need-based scholarship or grant aid. 58% freshmen, 58% undergrads receive need-based self-help aid. 18 freshmen, 78 undergrads receive athletic scholarships. 93% freshmen, 90% undergrads receive any aid.

See page 1048.

ADRIAN COLLEGE

110 South Madison Street, Adrian, MI 49221
Phone: 517-265-5161 **E-mail:** admissions@adrian.edu **CEEB Code:** 1001
Fax: 517-264-3331 **Website:** www.adrian.edu **ACT Code:** 1954
Financial Aid Phone: 517-265-5161

This private school, affiliated with the Methodist Church, was founded in 1859. It has a 100-acre campus.

RATINGS

Admissions Selectivity Rating: 71   **Fire Safety Rating:** 60*   **Green Rating:** 60*

STUDENTS AND FACULTY

Enrollment: 1,010. **Student Body:** 54% female, 46% male, 20% out-of-state, 1% international (8 countries represented). African American 6%, Caucasian 75%, Hispanic 1%. **Retention and Graduation:** 63% freshmen return for sophomore year. 32% freshmen graduate within 4 years. 25% grads go on to further study within 1 year. **Faculty:** Student/faculty ratio 13:1. 66 full-time faculty, 71% hold PhDs. 100% faculty teach undergrads.

ACADEMICS

Degrees: Associate, bachelor's. **Academic Requirements:** Arts/fine arts, English (including composition), foreign languages, history, humanities, mathematics, philosophy, sciences (biological or physical), social science, 1 non-Western perspectives; 1 religion or philosopy. **Classes:** Most classes have 10–19 students. Most lab/discussion sections have fewer than 10 students. **Majors with Highest Enrollment:** Art/art studies, business administration/management, English language and literature. **Disciplines with Highest Percentage of Degrees Awarded:** Business/marketing 20%, social sciences 14%, English 12%, visual and performing arts 11%, education 8%. **Special Study Options:** Cooperative education program, double major, dual enrollment, English as a Second Language (ESL), exchange student program (domestic), honors program, independent study, internships, liberal arts/career combination, student-designed major, study abroad, teacher certification program.

FACILITIES

Housing: Coed dorms, special housing for disabled students, fraternity/sorority housing. **Special Academic Facilities/Equipment:** Art gallery, studio theater, arboretum, education resource center, language lab, observatory, planetarium, solar greenhouse, nuclear magnetic resonance spectrometer, differential scanning calorimeter. **Computers:** 95% of public computers are PCs, 5% of public computers are Macs, network access in dorm rooms, online registration, remote student-access to Web through college's connection.

CAMPUS LIFE

Activities: Choral groups, concert band, dance, drama/theater, jazz band, literary magazine, music ensembles, musical theater, opera, radio station, student government, student newspaper, symphony orchestra. **Organizations:** 65 registered organizations, 13 honor societies, 8 religious organizations. 4 fraternities (30% men join), 3 sororities (30% women join). **Athletics (Intercollegiate):** *Men:* Baseball, basketball, cross-country, football, golf, soccer, tennis, track/field (indoor), track/field (outdoor). *Women:* Basketball, cross-country, golf, soccer, softball, tennis, track/field (indoor), track/field (outdoor), volleyball.

ADMISSIONS

Freshman Academic Profile: 13% in top 10% of high school class, 32% in top 25% of high school class, 61% in top 50% of high school class. ACT middle 50% range 18–23. TOEFL required of all international applicants; minimum paper TOEFL 500, minimum computer TOEFL 173. **Basis for Candidate Selection:** *Very important factors considered include:* Rigor of secondary school record. *Important factors considered include:* Standardized test scores. *Factors considered include:* Character/personal qualities, class rank, extracurricular activities, interview, racial/ethnic status, talent/ability, volunteer work, work experience. **Freshman Admission Requirements:** High school diploma is required, and GED is accepted. *Academic units recommended:* 4 English, 2 math, 2 science (1 science lab), 2 foreign language, 1 social studies, 1 history, 3 academic electives. **Freshman Admission Statistics:** 1,209 applied, 84% admitted, 29% enrolled. **Transfer Admission Requirements:** High school transcript, college transcript(s). Lowest grade transferable C. **General Admission Information:** Application fee $20. Regular application deadline 8/15. Regular notification is rolling. Nonfall registration not accepted. Admission may be deferred for a maximum of 1 year. Common Application accepted. Credit and/or placement offered for CEEB Advanced Placement tests.

COSTS AND FINANCIAL AID

Annual tuition $16,470. Room and board $5,380. Average book expense $400. **Required Forms and Deadlines:** FAFSA. Financial aid filing deadline 3/1. **Notification of Awards:** Applicants will be notified of awards on a rolling basis beginning on or about 3/15. **Types of Aid:** *Need-based scholarships/grants:* Pell, SEOG, state scholarships/grants, private scholarships, the school's own gift aid. *Loans:* FFEL Subsidized Stafford, FFEL Unsubsidized Stafford, FFEL PLUS, Federal Perkins. **Student Employment:** Federal Work-Study Program available. Institutional employment available. Off-campus job opportunities are good. **Financial Aid Statistics:** 82% freshmen, 74% undergrads receive need-based scholarship or grant aid. 76% freshmen, 68% undergrads receive need-based self-help aid. 98% freshmen, 92% undergrads receive any aid. Highest amount earned per year from on-campus jobs $1,700.

AGNES SCOTT COLLEGE

141 East College Avenue, Atlanta/Decatur, GA 30030-3797
Phone: 404-471-6285 **E-mail:** admission@agnesscott.edu **CEEB Code:** 5002
Fax: 404-471-6414 **Website:** www.agnesscott.edu **ACT Code:** 0780
Financial Aid Phone: 404-471-6396

This private school, affiliated with the Presbyterian Church, was founded in 1889. It has a 100-acre campus.

RATINGS

Admissions Selectivity Rating: 92   **Fire Safety Rating:** 96   **Green Rating:** 79

STUDENTS AND FACULTY

Enrollment: 815. **Student Body:** 100% female, 45% out-of-state, 5% international (26 countries represented). African American 20%, Asian 5%, Caucasian 55%, Hispanic 4%. **Retention and Graduation:** 78% freshmen return for sophomore year. 63% freshmen graduate within 4 years. 35% grads go on to further study within 1 year. 25% grads pursue arts and sciences degrees. 1% grads pursue business degrees. 4% grads pursue law degrees. 2% grads pursue medical degrees. **Faculty:** Student/faculty ratio 10:1. 82 full-time faculty, 98% hold PhDs. 98% faculty teach undergrads.

ACADEMICS

Degrees: Bachelor's, master's, post-bachelor's certificate. **Academic Requirements:** Arts/fine arts, English (including composition), foreign languages, history, humanities, mathematics, philosophy, sciences (biological or physical), social science. **Classes:** Most classes have 10–19 students. Most lab/discussion sections have 10–19 students. **Majors with Highest Enrollment:** Biology/biological sciences, English language and literature, psychology. **Disciplines with Highest Percentage of Degrees Awarded:** Social sciences 26%, psychology 14%, biological/life sciences 10%, foreign languages and literature 10%, English 10%, history 8%. **Special Study Options:** Accelerated program, cross-registration, double major, dual enrollment, exchange student program (domestic), independent study, internships, student-designed major, study abroad, teacher certification program.

FACILITIES

Housing: Women's dorms, apartments for single students, theme houses, limited number of college-owned housing available for nontraditional age students. CHOICE Housing (Choosing Healthy Options in a Community Environment). **Special Academic Facilities/Equipment:** Art galleries, state-of-the-art science building, collaborative learning centers, language lab, electron microscope, observatory, 30-inch Beck telescope, planetarium, interactive learning center, multimedia presentation classrooms, instructional technology center, multimedia production facility. **Computers:** 98% of public computers are PCs, 1% of public computers are Macs, 1% of public computers are UNIX, network access in dorm rooms, network access in dorm lounges, online administrative functions (other than registration), remote student-access to Web through college's connection.

CAMPUS LIFE

Activities: Choral groups, dance, drama/theater, jazz band, literary magazine, music ensembles, musical theater, pep band, student government, student newspaper, symphony orchestra, television station, yearbook. **Organizations:** 75 registered organizations, 12 honor societies, 12 religious organizations. **Athletics (Intercollegiate):** Basketball, cross-country, soccer, softball, swimming, tennis, volleyball. **Environmental Initiatives:** Spring into Green event for campus with sign-ups for taking action on sustainability, recycling, and climate change. Formation of an inclusive sustainability steering committee with active Board and alumnae representatives as well as students, faculty, staff and all management. Charrette planned for March 14th, 2008 to engage not only the campus community but also local and national advisors and technical experts.

ADMISSIONS

Freshman Academic Profile: 36% in top 10% of high school class, 70% in top 25% of high school class, 97% in top 50% of high school class. 77% from public high schools. SAT Math middle 50% range 500-610. SAT Critical Reading middle 50% range 550-680. SAT Writing middle 50% range 550-660. ACT middle 50% range 22-29. TOEFL required of all international applicants, minimum paper TOEFL 577, minimum computer TOEFL 250. **Basis for Candidate Selection:** *Very important factors considered include:* Academic GPA, application essay, character/personal qualities, class rank, recommendation(s), rigor of secondary school record, standardized test scores, talent/ability. *Important factors considered include:* Extracurricular activities, volunteer work, work experience. *Factors considered include:* Alumni/ae relation, first generation, geographical residence, interview, level of applicant's interest, racial/ethnic status, state residency. **Freshman Admission Requirements:** High school diploma is required, and GED is accepted. *Academic units recommended:* 4 English, 3 math, 2 science (2 science labs), 2 foreign language, 2 social studies, 2 history. **Freshman Admission Statistics:** 1,541 applied, 47% admitted, 30% enrolled. **Transfer Admission Requirements:** High school transcript, college transcript(s), essay or personal statement, standardized test score, statement of good standing from prior institution(s). Minimum college GPA of 3.0 required. Lowest grade transferable C. **General Admission Information:** Application fee $35. Early decision application deadline 11/15. Regular notification within 3 weeks of completion of file. Nonfall registration accepted. Admission may be deferred for a maximum of 1 year. Credit and/or placement offered for CEEB Advanced Placement tests.

COSTS AND FINANCIAL AID

Annual tuition $26,600. Room and board $9,350. Required fees $787. Average book expense $1,000. **Required Forms and Deadlines:** FAFSA, federal tax return. Financial aid filing deadline 5/1. Financial aid filing deadline 2/15. **Notification of Awards:** Applicants will be notified of awards on a rolling basis beginning on or about 3/1. **Types of Aid:** *Need-based scholarships/grants:* Pell, SEOG, state scholarships/grants, private scholarships, the school's own gift aid. *Loans:* FFEL Subsidized Stafford, FFEL Unsubsidized Stafford, FFEL PLUS, college/university loans from institutional funds. **Student Employment:** Federal Work-Study Program available. Institutional employment available. Off-campus job opportunities are excellent. **Financial Aid Statistics:** 74% freshmen, 66% undergrads receive need-based scholarship or grant aid. 57% freshmen, 57% undergrads receive need-based self-help aid. 99% freshmen, 88% undergrads receive any aid. Highest amount earned per year from on-campus jobs $2,000.

ALABAMA A&M UNIVERSITY

PO Box 908, Normal, AL 35762
Phone: 256-851-5245 **E-mail:** juan.alexander@aamu.edu **CEEB Code:** 1003
Fax: 256-851-5249 **Website:** www.aamu.edu **ACT Code:** 0002
Financial Aid Phone: 256-851-4862

This public school was founded in 1875. It has an 880-acre campus.

RATINGS
Admissions Selectivity Rating: 60*   **Fire Safety Rating:** 60*   **Green Rating:** 62

STUDENTS AND FACULTY
Enrollment: 4,958. **Student Body:** 53% female, 47% male, 35% out-of-state, 3% international (42 countries represented). African American 95%, Caucasian 2%. **Retention and Graduation:** 69% freshmen return for sophomore year. 11% freshmen graduate within 4 years. 77% grads go on to further study within 1 year. 40% grads pursue arts and sciences degrees. 45% grads pursue business degrees. 2% grads pursue law degrees. 11% grads pursue medical degrees. **Faculty:** Student/faculty ratio 14:1. 319 full-time faculty, 69% hold PhDs. 95% faculty teach undergrads.

ACADEMICS
Degrees: Bachelor's, doctoral, master's, post-master's certificate. **Academic Requirements:** Arts/fine arts, computer literacy, English (including composition), history, humanities, mathematics, philosophy, sciences (biological or physical), social science. **Classes:** Most classes have fewer than 10 students. Most lab/discussion sections have 20–29 students. **Disciplines with Highest Percentage of Degrees Awarded:** Business/marketing 22%, education 18%, engineering 8%, biological/life sciences 8%, public administration and social services 6%, psychology 6%, computer and information sciences 6%. **Special Study Options:** Accelerated program, cooperative education program, distance learning, double major, dual enrollment, exchange student program (domestic), honors program, independent study, internships, study abroad, teacher certification program, weekend college.

FACILITIES
Housing: Men's dorms, women's dorms. **Special Academic Facilities/Equipment:** State Black Archives. **Computers:** 99% of public computers are PCs, 1% of public computers are UNIX, network access in dorm rooms, network access in dorm lounges, online registration, remote student-access to Web through college's connection.

CAMPUS LIFE
Activities: Choral groups, concert band, dance, drama/theater, jazz band, literary magazine, marching band, music ensembles, pep band, radio station, student government, student newspaper, television station, yearbook. **Organizations:** 76 registered organizations, 14 honor societies, 3 religious organizations. 4 fraternities, 4 sororities. **Athletics (Intercollegiate):** *Men:* Baseball, basketball, cross-country, football, golf, soccer, track/field (outdoor). *Women:* Basketball, cross-country, soccer, softball, track/field (outdoor), volleyball.

ADMISSIONS
Freshman Academic Profile: 90% from public high schools. ACT middle 50% range 16–20. TOEFL required of all international applicants, minimum paper TOEFL 550, minimum computer TOEFL 213. **Basis for Candidate Selection:** *Very important factors considered include:* Alumni/ae relation, geographical residence, standardized test scores, state residency. *Important factors considered include:* Racial/ethnic status. *Factors considered include:* Class rank, recommendation(s). **Freshman Admission Requirements:** High school diploma is required, and GED is accepted. *Academic units required:* 4 English, 4 math, 4 science (2 science labs), 4 social studies, 4 history. **Freshman Admission Statistics:** 7,457 applied, 43% admitted, 34% enrolled. **Transfer Admission Requirements:** High school transcript, college transcript(s), standardized test score. Minimum college GPA of 2.5 required. Lowest grade transferable C. **General Admission Information:** Application fee $10. Regular application deadline 7/1. Regular notification is rolling. Nonfall registration accepted. Admission may be deferred for a maximum of 1 year. Neither credit nor placement offered for CEEB Advanced Placement tests.

COSTS AND FINANCIAL AID
Annual in-state tuition $4,290. Annual out-of-state tuition $8,580. Room and board $3,592. Required fees $640. Average book expense $850. **Required Forms and Deadlines:** FAFSA, institution's own financial aid form. Financial aid filing deadline 4/15. **Types of Aid:** *Need-based scholarships/grants:* Pell, SEOG, state scholarships/grants, private scholarships, the school's own gift aid, United Negro College Fund. *Loans:* Direct Subsidized Stafford, Direct Unsubsidized Stafford, Direct PLUS, Federal Perkins, state loans, college/

university loans from institutional funds. **Financial Aid Statistics:** Highest amount earned per year from on-campus jobs $5,400.

ALABAMA STATE UNIVERSITY

915 South Jackson Street, Montgomery, AL 36104
Phone: 334-229-4291 **E-mail:** dlamar@asunet.alasu.edu
Fax: 334-229-4984 **Website:** www.alasu.edu **ACT Code:** 0008
Financial Aid Phone: 334-229-4862

This public school was founded in 1867.

RATINGS
Admissions Selectivity Rating: 60*   **Fire Safety Rating:** 60*   **Green Rating:** 60*

STUDENTS AND FACULTY
Enrollment: 5,125. **Student Body:** 59% female, 41% male, 35% out-of-state. African American 95%, Caucasian 4%. **Retention and Graduation:** 68% freshmen return for sophomore year. 50% grads go on to further study within 1 year. **Faculty:** Student/faculty ratio 19:1. 229 full-time faculty, 59% hold PhDs.

ACADEMICS
Degrees: Bachelor's, doctoral, master's. **Academic Requirements:** Arts/fine arts, computer literacy, English (including composition), history, humanities, mathematics, sciences (biological or physical), social science. **Majors with Highest Enrollment:** Computer and information sciences, criminal justice/safety studies, elementary education and teaching. **Disciplines with Highest Percentage of Degrees Awarded:** Education 27%, business/marketing 14%, computer and information sciences 11%, biological/life sciences 10%. **Special Study Options:** Cooperative education program, cross-registration, double major, honors program, internships, teacher certification program.

FACILITIES
Housing: Men's dorms, women's dorms, apartments for single students, honor dorms. **Special Academic Facilities/Equipment:** Levi Watkins Learning Center Special Collections. **Computers:** 85% of public computers are PCs, 14% of public computers are Macs, 1% of public computers are UNIX, network access in dorm rooms, network access in dorm lounges, online registration, online administrative functions (other than registration), remote student-access to Web through college's connection.

CAMPUS LIFE
Activities: Choral groups, concert band, dance, drama/theater, jazz band, marching band, music ensembles, musical theater, pep band, radio station, student government, student newspaper, symphony orchestra, yearbook. **Organizations:** 64 registered organizations, 17 honor societies. 5 fraternities (8% men join), 4 sororities (6% women join). **Athletics (Intercollegiate):** *Men:* Baseball, basketball, cheerleading, cross-country, football, golf, tennis, track/field (indoor), track/field (outdoor). *Women:* Basketball, cheerleading, cross-country, golf, softball, tennis, track/field (indoor), track/field (outdoor), volleyball.

ADMISSIONS
Freshman Academic Profile: SAT Math middle 50% range 340–444. SAT Critical Reading middle 50% range 350–457. ACT middle 50% range 14–18. TOEFL required of all international applicants, minimum paper TOEFL 500. **Basis for Candidate Selection:** *Very important factors considered include:* Rigor of secondary school record. *Important factors considered include:* Class rank, standardized test scores. *Factors considered include:* Recommendation(s). **Freshman Admission Requirements:** High school diploma is required, and GED is accepted. *Academic units recommended:* 3 English, 2 math, 2 science, 2 foreign language, 2 social studies. **Freshman Admission Statistics:** 11,462 applied, 50% admitted, 22% enrolled. **Transfer Admission Requirements:** College transcript(s). Minimum college GPA of 2.0 required. Lowest grade transferable C. **General Admission Information:** Regular application deadline 7/30. Regular notification is rolling. Nonfall registration accepted. Common Application accepted. Credit and/or placement offered for CEEB Advanced Placement tests.

COSTS AND FINANCIAL AID
Annual in-state tuition $2,904. Annual out-of-state tuition $5,808. Room and board $3,700. Average book expense $800. **Required Forms and Deadlines:** FAFSA, state aid form. Financial aid filing deadline 5/1. **Notification of Awards:** Applicants will be notified of awards on a rolling basis beginning on or about 5/15. **Types of Aid:** *Need-based scholarships/grants:* Pell, SEOG, state scholarships/grants, private scholarships, the school's own gift aid. *Loans:* FFEL Subsidized Stafford, FFEL Unsubsidized Stafford, FFEL PLUS, Federal Perkins. **Student Employment:** Federal Work-Study Program available.

Institutional employment available. Off-campus job opportunities are good. **Financial Aid Statistics:** 70% freshmen, 68% undergrads receive need-based scholarship or grant aid. 73% freshmen, 72% undergrads receive need-based self-help aid. 40 freshmen, 211 undergrads receive athletic scholarships. Highest amount earned per year from on-campus jobs $2,400.

ALASKA BIBLE COLLEGE

PO Box 289, Glennallen, AK 99588
Phone: 907-822-3201 **E-mail:** info@akbible.edu
Fax: 907-822-5027 **Website:** www.akbible.edu

This private school, affiliated with the Christian (Nondenominational) Church, was founded in 1966. It has a 90-acre campus.

RATINGS
Admissions Selectivity Rating: 60*   **Fire Safety Rating:** 60*   **Green Rating:** 60*

STUDENTS AND FACULTY
Enrollment: 35. **Student Body:** 60% out-of-state. Caucasian 97%, Native American 3%. **Retention and Graduation:** 67% freshmen return for sophomore year. **Faculty:** Student/faculty ratio 7:1. 4 full-time faculty, 25% hold PhDs.

ACADEMICS
Degrees: Associate, bachelor's, certificate, terminal. **Academic Requirements:** English (including composition), history, humanities, mathematics, philosophy, sciences (biological or physical), social science. **Majors with Highest Enrollment:** Bible/biblical studies. **Special Study Options:** Cooperative education program, double major, independent study, internships.

FACILITIES
Housing: Men's dorms, women's dorms, apartments for married students, apartments for single students. **Computers:** 100% of public computers are PCs.

ADMISSIONS
Freshman Academic Profile: TOEFL required of all international applicants, minimum paper TOEFL 500, minimum computer TOEFL 173. **Basis for Candidate Selection:** *Very important factors considered include:* Application essay, character/personal qualities, interview, recommendation(s), religious affiliation/commitment, rigor of secondary school record, standardized test scores. *Important factors considered include:* Volunteer work, work experience. *Factors considered include:* Extracurricular activities, racial/ethnic status, talent/ability. **Freshman Admission Requirements:** High school diploma is required, and GED is accepted. **Freshman Admission Statistics:** 11 applied, 100% admitted, 100% enrolled. **Transfer Admission Requirements:** High school transcript, college transcript(s), essay or personal statement, interview, standardized test score, statement of good standing from prior institution(s). Minimum college GPA of 2.0 required. Lowest grade transferable C. **General Admission Information:** Application fee $35. Regular application deadline 7/1. Nonfall registration accepted. Admission may be deferred for a maximum of 1 year. Common Application not accepted.

COSTS AND FINANCIAL AID
Annual tuition $5,720. Room and board $4,570. Average book expense $400.

ALASKA PACIFIC UNIVERSITY

4101 University Drive, Anchorage, AK 99508
Phone: 907-564-8248 **E-mail:** admissions@alaskapacific.edu **CEEB Code:** 4201
Fax: 907-562-4276 **Website:** www.alaskapacific.edu **ACT Code:** 0062
Financial Aid Phone: 907-564-8341

This private school was founded in 1957. It has a 170-acre campus.

RATINGS
Admissions Selectivity Rating: 70   **Fire Safety Rating:** 84   **Green Rating:** 90

STUDENTS AND FACULTY
Enrollment: 428. **Student Body:** 64% female, 36% male, 32% out-of-state. African American 7%, Asian 3%, Caucasian 71%, Hispanic 5%, Native American 14%. **Retention and Graduation:** 59% freshmen return for sophomore year. 20% freshmen graduate within 4 years. **Faculty:** Student/faculty ratio 9:1. 45 full-time faculty, 67% hold PhDs. 95% faculty teach undergrads.

ACADEMICS
Degrees: Associate, bachelor's, certificate, master's, post-bachelor's certificate, terminal. **Academic Requirements:** English (including composition), foreign languages, humanities, mathematics, sciences (biological or physical), social science, ethics and/or religion. 12 credit senior project in major. **Classes:** Most classes have fewer than 10 students. Most lab/discussion sections have fewer than 10 students. **Majors with Highest Enrollment:** Elementary education and teaching; environmental science; parks, recreation, and leisure facilities management. **Disciplines with Highest Percentage of Degrees Awarded:** Business/marketing 24%, parks and recreation 21%, education 18%, psychology 14%, liberal arts/general studies 9%. **Special Study Options:** Distance learning, double major, independent study, internships, student-designed major, study abroad, teacher certification program. Degree Completion program for adult students and a distance education program for Rural Alaskan Native Adults.

FACILITIES
Housing: Coed dorms, cooperative housing, several theme houses—example "Nordic Skiers House" for ski team members. **Special Academic Facilities/Equipment:** Alaskana collection GIS lab; gym with pool; student center with weight room and indoor climbing wall; outdoor recreation center with classes and rental equipment; lake for canoeing and kayaking; trails for running, skiing, hiking, biking, etc.; connected to city's trail system. **Computers:** 90% of classrooms are wired, 70% of public computers are PCs, 20% of public computers are Macs, network access in dorm rooms, network access in dorm lounges, online registration, online administrative functions (other than registration), remote student-access to Web through college's connection.

CAMPUS LIFE
Activities: Drama/theater, literary magazine, music ensembles, student government, student newspaper, yearbook. **Organizations:** 15 registered organizations, 1 religious organization. **Environmental Initiatives:** Kellogg Farm dedicated to organic and sustainable enterprises. APU does not use paper plates, plastic silverware, etc. Also paperless initiative. Committed to building a LEEDs level student center.

ADMISSIONS
Freshman Academic Profile: 11% in top 10% of high school class, 50% in top 25% of high school class, 68% in top 50% of high school class. AT Math middle 50% range 450–580. SAT Critical Reading middle 50% range 460–620. ACT middle 50% range 18–26. TOEFL required of all international applicants, minimum paper TOEFL 550, minimum computer TOEFL 79. **Basis for Candidate Selection:** *Very important factors considered include:* Academic GPA, application essay, rigor of secondary school record. *Important factors considered include:* Recommendation(s), standardized test scores. *Factors considered include:* Character/personal qualities, class rank, extracurricular activities, talent/ability, volunteer work, work experience. **Freshman Admission Requirements:** High school diploma is required, and GED is accepted. *Academic units recommended:* 4 English, 3 math, 2 science (1 science lab), 2 foreign language, 1 social studies, 1 history. **Freshman Admission Statistics:** 128 applied, 93% admitted, 49% enrolled. **Transfer Admission Requirements:** College transcript(s), essay or personal statement, statement of good standing from prior institution(s). Minimum college GPA of 2.0 required. Lowest grade transferable C. **General Admission Information:** Application fee $25. Regular application deadline 8/15. Regular notification is rolling. Nonfall registration accepted. Admission may be deferred for a maximum of 1 year. Credit offered for CEEB Advanced Placement tests.

COSTS AND FINANCIAL AID
Annual tuition $20,900. Room and board $7,600. Required fees $110. Average book expense $1,000. **Required Forms and Deadlines:** FAFSA. Financial aid filing deadline 4/15. **Notification of Awards:** Applicants will be notified of awards on a rolling basis beginning on or about 2/1. **Types of Aid:** *Need-based scholarships/grants:* Pell, SEOG, state scholarships/grants, private scholarships, the school's own gift aid. *Loans:* FFEL Subsidized Stafford, FFEL Unsubsidized Stafford, FFEL PLUS, state loans, college/university loans from institutional funds. **Financial Aid Statistics:** 81% freshmen, 64% undergrads receive need-based scholarship or grant aid. 71% freshmen, 59% undergrads receive need-based self-help aid. 1 undergrad receives athletic scholarships. 85% freshmen, 59% undergrads receive any aid.

ALBANY COLLEGE OF PHARMACY

106 New Scotland Avenue, Albany, NY 12208
Phone: 518-694-7221 **E-mail:** admissions@acp.edu **CEEB Code:** 2013
Fax: 518-694-7202 **Website:** www.acp.edu **ACT Code:** 2672
Financial Aid Phone: 518-445-7221

This private school was founded in 1881. It has a 1-acre campus.

RATINGS
Admissions Selectivity Rating: 91   **Fire Safety Rating:** 60*   **Green Rating:** 60*

STUDENTS AND FACULTY
Enrollment: 892. **Student Body:** 57% female, 43% male, 10% international (6 countries represented). African American 2%, Asian 16%, Caucasian 71%, Hispanic 1%. **Retention and Graduation:** 81% freshmen return for sophomore year. 1% grads pursue medical degrees. **Faculty:** 100% faculty teach undergrads.

ACADEMICS
Degrees: Bachelor's, certificate, first professional. **Academic Requirements:** Arts/fine arts, English (including composition), humanities, mathematics, sciences (biological or physical). **Classes:** Most classes have 20–29 students. Most lab/discussion sections have 20–29 students. **Majors with Highest Enrollment:** Pharmacy (PharMD, BS/BPharm). **Disciplines with Highest Percentage of Degrees Awarded:** Health professions and related sciences 100%. **Special Study Options:** Accelerated program, cross-registration, dual enrollment, internships, liberal arts/career combination.

FACILITIES
Housing: Coed dorms, apartments for single students, special housing for disabled students. **Special Academic Facilities/Equipment:** Pharmaceutical museum. **Computers:** 100% of classrooms are wired, 100% of classrooms are wireless, network access in dorm rooms, network access in dorm lounges, online administrative functions (other than registration), remote student-access to Web through college's connection, tuition includes personal computer. undergraduates are required to own a computer.

CAMPUS LIFE
Activities: Choral groups, concert band, dance, literary magazine, student government, student newspaper, yearbook. **Organizations:** 5 honor societies, 1 religious organization. **Athletics (Intercollegiate):** *Men:* Basketball, soccer. *Women:* Basketball, soccer.

ADMISSIONS
Freshman Academic Profile: 42% in top 10% of high school class, 83% in top 25% of high school class, 98% in top 50% of high school class. SAT Math middle 50% range 570–650. SAT Critical Reading middle 50% range 530–620. SAT Writing middle 50% range 510–600. ACT middle 50% range 23–28. TOEFL required of all international applicants, minimum paper TOEFL 600, minimum computer TOEFL 250. **Basis for Candidate Selection:** *Very important factors considered include:* Academic GPA, standardized test scores. *Important factors considered include:* Class rank, rigor of secondary school record. *Factors considered include:* Alumni/ae relation, application essay, character/personal qualities, extracurricular activities, geographical residence, level of applicant's interest, recommendation(s), talent/ability, volunteer work, work experience. **Freshman Admission Requirements:** High school diploma is required, and GED is accepted. *Academic units required:* 4 English, 4 math, 3 science (3 science labs), 4 social studies. *Academic units recommended:* 4 English, 4 math, 4 science (4 science labs), 4 foreign language, 4 social studies. **Freshman Admission Statistics:** 1,049 applied, 61% admitted, 41% enrolled. **Transfer Admission Requirements:** College transcript(s), minimum college GPA of 3.2 required. Lowest grade transferable C. **General Admission Information:** Application fee $75. Early decision application deadline 11/1. Regular application deadline 3/1. Nonfall registration not accepted. Admission may be deferred for a maximum of 1 year. Credit offered for CEEB Advanced Placement tests.

COSTS AND FINANCIAL AID
Annual tuition $18,300. Room & board $6,200. Required fees $357. Average book expense $700. **Required Forms and Deadlines:** FAFSA. Financial aid filing deadline 3/1. **Notification of Awards:** Applicants will be notified of awards on or about 3/25. **Types of Aid:** *Need-based scholarships/grants:* Pell, SEOG, state scholarships/grants, private scholarships, the school's own gift aid. *Loans:* FFEL Subsidized Stafford, FFEL Unsubsidized Stafford, FFEL PLUS, Federal Perkins. **Financial Aid Statistics:** 66% freshmen, 58% undergrads receive need-based scholarship or grant aid. 64% freshmen, 67% undergrads receive need-based self-help aid. 97% undergrads receive any aid.

ALBANY STATE UNIVERSITY

504 College Drive, Albany, GA 31705
Phone: 229-430-4646 **E-mail:** fsuttles@asurams.edu **CEEB Code:** 5004
Fax: 229-430-3936 **Website:** www.asurams.edu **ACT Code:** 0782
Financial Aid Phone: 229-430-4650

This public school was founded in 1903. It has a 206-acre campus.

RATINGS
Admissions Selectivity Rating: 60*   **Fire Safety Rating:** 60*   **Green Rating:** 60*

STUDENTS AND FACULTY
Enrollment: 2,936. **Student Body:** 67% female, 33% male, 4% international. African American 84%, Caucasian 4%. **Retention and Graduation:** 84% freshmen return for sophomore year. 7% freshmen graduate within 4 years. **Faculty:** Student/faculty ratio 20:1. 40% faculty teach undergrads.

ACADEMICS
Degrees: Bachelor's, master's, post-master's certificate. **Academic Requirements:** Arts/fine arts, computer literacy, sciences (biological or physical), social science, education, health professions, engineering. **Majors with Highest Enrollment:** Business administration/management, criminal justice/safety studies, nursing–registered nurse training (ASN, BSN, MSN, RN). **Disciplines with Highest Percentage of Degrees Awarded:** Education 20%, business/marketing 17%, health professions and related sciences 14%, social sciences 12%, psychology 8%. **Special Study Options:** Distance learning, dual enrollment, honors program, internships, weekend college.

FACILITIES
Housing: Men's dorms, women's dorms, special housing for disabled students. **Computers:** 11% of public computers are PCs, network access in dorm rooms, network access in dorm lounges, online administrative functions (other than registration).

CAMPUS LIFE
Activities: Choral groups, concert band, dance, drama/theater, jazz band, marching band, music ensembles, pep band, student government, student newspaper, student-run film society, yearbook. **Organizations:** 47 registered organizations, 5 honor societies, 4 religious organizations. 3 fraternities, 3 sororities. **Athletics (Intercollegiate):** *Men:* Baseball, basketball, cross-country, football, track/field (outdoor). *Women:* Basketball, cross-country, softball, tennis, track/field (outdoor), volleyball.

ADMISSIONS
Freshman Academic Profile: 4% in top 10% of high school class, 11% in top 25% of high school class, 27% in top 50% of high school class. TOEFL required of all international applicants, minimum paper TOEFL 523, minimum computer TOEFL 193. **Basis for Candidate Selection:** *Very important factors considered include:* Rigor of secondary school record, standardized test scores. **Freshman Admission Requirements:** High school diploma is required, and GED is accepted. *Academic units required:* 4 English, 4 math, 2 foreign language, 1 social studies, 2 history. **Freshman Admission Statistics:** 2,233 applied, 57% admitted, 50% enrolled. **Transfer Admission Requirements:** College transcript(s), statement of good standing from prior institution(s). Minimum college GPA of 2.0 required. Lowest grade transferable C. **General Admission Information:** Application fee $20. Regular application deadline 7/1. Nonfall registration accepted. Admission may be deferred for a maximum of 1 year. Common Application not accepted. Credit and/or placement offered for CEEB Advanced Placement tests.

COSTS AND FINANCIAL AID
Required Forms and Deadlines: FAFSA, institution's own financial aid form. **Types of Aid:** *Need-based scholarships/grants:* Pell, SEOG, state scholarships/grants, private scholarships, the school's own gift aid, Federal Nursing Scholarships, Thurgood Marshall Scholarship. **Student Employment:** Federal Work-Study Program available. Off-campus job opportunities are good.

ALBERTA COLLEGE OF ART & DESIGN

1407 14 Avenue Northwest, Calgary, AB T2N 4R3, Canada
Phone: 403-284-7617 **E-mail:** admissions@acad.ca
Fax: 403-284-7644 **Website:** www.acad.ca
Financial Aid Phone: 403-284-7685

This public school was founded in 1926.

RATINGS
Admissions Selectivity Rating: 60*   **Fire Safety Rating:** 60*   **Green Rating:** 60*

STUDENTS AND FACULTY
Enrollment: 2,244. **Student Body:** 50% female, 50% male, 15% out-of-state. **Faculty:** Student/faculty ratio 9:1. 42 full-time faculty. 100% faculty teach undergrads.

ACADEMICS
Degrees: Bachelor's. **Academic Requirements:** Arts/fine arts, English (including composition), humanities, social science. **Majors with Highest Enrollment:** Drawing, painting, sculpture. **Disciplines with Highest Percentage of Degrees Awarded:** Visual and performing arts 100%. **Special Study Options:** Cross-registration, study abroad, mobility and exchange.

FACILITIES
Housing: Assisted off-campus housing search. **Special Academic Facilities/Equipment:** 2 art galleries. **Computers:** 16% of public computers are PCs, 16% of public computers are Macs, network access in dorm rooms, online registration, online administrative functions (other than registration).

CAMPUS LIFE
Activities: Student government. **Athletics (Intercollegiate):** *Men:* Basketball, ice hockey, volleyball. *Women:* Basketball, volleyball.

ADMISSIONS
Freshman Academic Profile: TOEFL required of all international applicants, minimum paper TOEFL 560, minimum computer TOEFL 220. **Basis for Candidate Selection:** *Very important factors considered include:* Talent/ability. *Important factors considered include:* Application essay, rigor of secondary school record *Factors considered include:* Character/personal qualities, class rank, extracurricular activities, recommendation(s), standardized test scores, work experience. **Freshman Admission Requirements:** High school diploma is required, and GED is not accepted. *Academic units required:* 4 English, 4 social studies. **Freshman Admission Statistics:** 710 applied, 48% admitted, 100% enrolled. **Transfer Admission Requirements:** College transcript(s), essay or personal statement. **Admission Information:** Application fee $50. Early decision application deadline 3/1. Regular application deadline 4/1. Regular notification 6/15. Nonfall registration not accepted. Common Application not accepted.

COSTS AND FINANCIAL AID
Room & board $10,200. Required fees $577. Average book expense $2,500. **Student Employment:** Off-campus job opportunities are good.

ALBERTSON COLLEGE OF IDAHO

2112 Cleveland Boulevard, Caldwell, ID 83605
Phone: 208-459-5305 **E-mail:** admission@albertson.edu **CEEB Code:** 4060
Fax: 208-459-5757 **Website:** www.albertson.edu **ACT Code:** 0916
Financial Aid Phone: 208-459-5308

This private school was founded in 1891. It has a 50-acre campus.

RATINGS
Admissions Selectivity Rating: 86   **Fire Safety Rating:** 66   **Green Rating:** 81

STUDENTS AND FACULTY
Enrollment: 778. **Student Body:** 59% female, 41% male, 27% out-of-state, 1% international (8 countries represented). African American 1%, Asian 3%, Caucasian 68%, Hispanic 6%. **Retention and Graduation:** 82% freshmen return for sophomore year. **Faculty:** Student/faculty ratio 9:1. 75 full-time faculty, 65% hold PhDs. 100% faculty teach undergrads.

ACADEMICS
Degrees: Bachelor's, master's. **Academic Requirements:** Arts/fine arts, English (including composition), history, humanities, mathematics, sciences (biological or physical), social science. **Classes:** Most classes have fewer than 10 students. **Majors with Highest Enrollment:** Biology/biological sciences, business administration/management, psychology. **Disciplines with Highest Percentage of Degrees Awarded:** Business/marketing 18%, psychology 13%, biological/life sciences 11%, visual and performing arts 11%, history 8%, parks and recreation 6%. **Special Study Options:** Cross-registration, double major, exchange student program (domestic), honor's program, independent study, internships, liberal arts/career combination, student-designed major, study abroad, teacher certification program.

FACILITIES
Housing: Coed dorms, apartments for single students, special housing for disabled students, fraternity/sorority housing, college-owned houses. **Special Academic Facilities/Equipment:** Art and natural history museums, gem and mineral collections, observatory, planetarium, nuclear magnetic resonance spectrometer, gas chromatograph, gamma camera, graphic computer, art gallery, Robert E. Smylie Archives. **Computers:** 75% of classrooms are wired, 100% of classrooms are wireless, 99% of public computers are PCs, 1% of public computers are Macs, network access in dorm rooms, network access in dorm lounges, online registration, online administrative functions (other than registration), remote student-access to Web through college's connection. Undergraduates are required to own a computer.

CAMPUS LIFE
Activities: Choral groups, concert band, dance, drama/theater, jazz band, literary magazine, music ensembles, musical theater, opera, pep band, radio station, student government, student newspaper, student-run film society, symphony orchestra, yearbook. **Organizations:** 43 registered organizations, 4 honor societies, 3 religious organizations, 3 fraternities (46% men join), 4 sororities (87% women join). **Athletics (Intercollegiate):** *Men:* Baseball, basketball, cross-country, golf, skiing (downhill/alpine), skiing (nordic/cross-country), snowboarding, soccer, swimming. *Women:* Basketball, cross-country, golf, skiing (downhill/alpine), skiing (nordic/cross-country), snowboarding, soccer, softball, swimming, tennis, volleyball. **Environmental Initiatives:** Caldwell, ID's downtown revitalization project. Environmental Studies major. Students from The College of Idaho's The Environmental Resource and Recreation Association (TERRA) participated in the national Step It Up event on Saturday, Nov. 3.

ADMISSIONS
Freshman Academic Profile: 40% in top 10% of high school class, 67% in top 25% of high school class, 87% in top 50% of high school class. SAT Math middle 50% range 498-633. SAT Critical Reading middle 50% range 188-640. SAT Writing middle 50% range 470-618. ACT middle 50% range 21-27. TOEFL required of all international applicants, minimum paper TOEFL 550, minimum computer TOEFL 213. **Basis for Candidate Selection:** *Very important factors considered include:* Academic GPA, application essay, character/personal qualities, extracurricular activities, level of applicant's interest, recommendation(s), rigor of secondary school record, standardized test scores. *Important factors considered include:* Class rank, interview, volunteer work. *Other factors considered include:* Alumni/ae relation, first generation, geographical residence, racial/ethnic status, talent/ability, work experience. **Freshman Admission Requirements:** High school diploma is required, and GED is accepted. *Academic units required:* 4 English, 3 math, 2 science, 3 history, 3 academic electives. *Academic units recommended:* 4 English, 4 math, 4 science, 4 foreign language, 2 social studies, 3 history, 3 academic electives. **Freshman Admission Statistics:** 838 applied, 74% admitted, 34% enrolled. **Transfer Admission Requirements:** College transcript(s), essay or personal statement, statement of good standing from prior institution(s). Minimum college GPA of 2.2 required. Lowest grade transferable D-. **General Admission Information:** Application fee $50. Early decision application deadline 3/1. Regular application deadline 8/1. Regular notification is rolling. Nonfall registration accepted. Admission may be deferred for a maximum of 1 year. Credit and/or placement offered for CEEB Advanced Placement tests.

COSTS AND FINANCIAL AID
Annual tuition $18,300. Room and board $6,631. Required fees $690. Average book expense $900. **Required Forms and Deadlines:** FAFSA, institution's own financial aid form. Financial aid filing deadline 2/15. **Notification of Awards:** Applicants will be notified of awards on a rolling basis beginning on or about 3/1. **Types of Aid:** *Need-based scholarships/grants:* Pell, SEOG, state scholarships/grants, private scholarships, the school's own gift aid. *Loans:* FFEL Subsidized Stafford, FFEL Unsubsidized Stafford, FFEL PLUS, Federal Perkins, alternative loans. **Student Employment:** Federal Work-Study Program available. Institutional employment available. Off-campus job

opportunities are good. **Financial Aid Statistics:** 35% freshmen, 54% undergrads receive need-based scholarship or grant aid. 41% freshmen, 70% undergrads receive need-based self-help aid. 52 freshmen, 183 undergrads receive athletic scholarships. 95% freshmen, 66% undergrads receive any aid.

ALBERTUS MAGNUS COLLEGE

700 Prospect Street, New Haven, CT 06511
Phone: 203-773-8501 **E-mail:** admissions@albertus.edu **CEEB Code:** 3001
Fax: 203-773-5248 **Website:** www.albertus.edu **ACT Code:** 0549
Financial Aid Phone: 203-773-8508

This private school, affiliated with the Roman Catholic Church, was founded in 1925. It has a 50-acre campus.

RATINGS
Admissions Selectivity Rating: 60*   **Fire Safety Rating:** 60*   **Green Rating:** 60*

STUDENTS AND FACULTY
Enrollment: 1,769. **Student Body:** 69% female, 31% male, 15% out-of-state. African American 27%, Asian 1%, Caucasian 57%, Hispanic 9%. **Retention and Graduation:** 74% freshmen return for sophomore year. 40% grads go on to further study within 1 year. 10% grads pursue arts and sciences degrees. 20% grads pursue business degrees. 5% grads pursue law degrees. 5% grads pursue medical degrees. **Faculty:** Student/faculty ratio 13:1. 37 full-time faculty. 100% faculty teach undergrads.

ACADEMICS
Degrees: Associate, bachelor's, certificate, master's. **Academic Requirements:** Arts/fine arts, English (including composition), foreign languages, history, humanities, mathematics, philosophy, sciences (biological or physical), social science. **Classes:** Most classes have 10–19 students. **Majors with Highest Enrollment:** Business administration/management, communications and media studies; psychology. **Disciplines with Highest Percentage of Degrees Awarded:** Biological/life sciences 41%, business/marketing 25%, psychology 20%, social sciences 15%, area and ethnic studies 15%, English 7%. **Special Study Options:** Accelerated program, double major, honors program, independent study, internships, student-designed major, study abroad, teacher certification program.

FACILITIES
Housing: Coed dorms, women's dorms, Mansion-style residence halls. **Special Academic Facilities/Equipment:** Margart McDonough Art Gallery. **Computers:** 100% of classrooms are wired, 99% of classrooms are wireless, 100% of public computers are PCs, network access in dorm rooms, network access in dorm lounges, remote student-access to Web through college's connection.

CAMPUS LIFE
Activities: Choral groups, dance, drama/theater, literary magazine, musical theater, student government, yearbook. **Organizations:** 1 honor society, 1 religious organization. **Athletics (Intercollegiate):** *Men:* Baseball, basketball, cross-country, lacrosse, soccer, tennis. *Women:* Basketball, cross-country, lacrosse, soccer, softball, tennis, volleyball.

ADMISSIONS
Freshman Academic Profile: 70% from public high schools. SAT Math middle 50% range 470-500. SAT Critical Reading middle 50% range 490-560. SAT Writing middle 50% range 430-560. TOEFL required of all international applicants, minimum paper TOEFL 550, minimum computer TOEFL 213. **Basis for Candidate Selection:** *Very important factors considered include:* Academic GPA, recommendation(s), rigor of secondary school record, talent/ability. *Important factors considered include:* Application essay, class rank, interview, standardized test scores. *Factors considered include:* Alumni/ae relation, character/personal qualities, extracurricular activities, first generation, level of applicant's interest, volunteer work, work experience. **Freshman Admission Requirements:** High school diploma is required, and GED is accepted. *Academic units required:* 4 English. *Academic units recommended:* 3 math, 2 science (1 science lab), 2 foreign language, 1 social studies, 2 history. **Freshman Admission Statistics:** 556 applied, 84% admitted, 26% enrolled. **Transfer Admission Requirements:** College transcript(s). Minimum college GPA of 2.0 required. Lowest grade transferable C. **General Admission Information:** Application fee $35. Regular notification is rolling. Nonfall registration accepted. Admission may be deferred for a maximum of 1 year. Credit offered for CEEB Advanced Placement tests.

COSTS AND FINANCIAL AID
Annual tuition $20,166. Room and board $8,907. Required fees $908. Average

book expense $920. **Required Forms and Deadlines:** FAFSA, institution's own financial aid form. Financial aid filing deadline 2/28. **Notification of Awards:** Applicants will be notified of awards on or about 3/1. **Types of Aid:** *Need-based scholarships/grants:* Pell, SEOG, state scholarships/grants, the school's own gift aid. *Loans:* Direct Subsidized Stafford, Direct Unsubsidized Stafford, Direct PLUS, FFEL Subsidized Stafford, FFEL Unsubsidized Stafford, FFEL PLUS, Federal Perkins. **Student Employment:** Federal Work-Study Program available. **Financial Aid Statistics:** 87% freshmen, 75% undergrads receive any aid.

See page 1050.

ALBION COLLEGE

Best 368

611 East Porter, Albion, MI 49224
Phone: 517-629-0321 **E-mail:** admissions@albion.edu **CEEB Code:** 1007
Fax: 517-629-0569 **Website:** www.albion.edu **ACT Code:** 1956
Financial Aid Phone: 517-629-0440

This private school, affiliated with the Methodist Church, was founded in 1835. It has a 585-acre campus.

RATINGS
Admissions Selectivity Rating: 84   **Fire Safety Rating:** 68   **Green Rating:** 87

STUDENTS AND FACULTY
Enrollment: 1,953. **Student Body:** 56% female, 44% male, 10% out-of-state. African American 4%, Asian 2%, Caucasian 89%. **Retention and Graduation:** 86% freshmen return for sophomore year. 67% freshmen graduate within 4 years. 38% grads go on to further study within 1 year. 16% grads pursue arts and sciences degrees. 1% grads pursue business degrees. 6% grads pursue law degrees. 15% grads pursue medical degrees. **Faculty:** Student/faculty ratio 13:1. 139 full-time faculty, 91% hold PhDs. 100% faculty teach undergrads.

ACADEMICS
Degrees: Bachelor's. **Academic Requirements:** Arts/fine arts, humanities, sciences (biological or physical), social science, Students complete courses in 5 modes of inquiry and 4 categories of learning. (See catalog.) **Classes:** Most classes have 10–19 students. Most lab/discussion sections have 10–19 students. **Majors with Highest Enrollment:** Biology/biological sciences, economics, psychology. **Disciplines with Highest Percentage of Degrees Awarded:** Social sciences 20%, psychology 11%, biological/life sciences 9%, physical sciences 9%, visual and performing arts 9%, English 8%. **Special Study Options:** Double major, dual enrollment, honors program, independent study, internships, liberal arts/career combination, student-designed major, study abroad, teacher certification program.

FACILITIES
Housing: Coed dorms, men's dorms, women's dorms, apartments for married students, apartments for single students, special housing for disabled students, special housing for international students, fraternity/sorority housing, cooperative housing. **Special Academic Facilities/Equipment:** Visual arts museum, nature center, science complex museum, shark aquarium, greenhouse, geographic information systems/computer-aided mapping lab, observatory. **Computers:** 100% of classrooms are wired, 99% of classrooms are wireless, 97% of public computers are PCs, 1% of public computers are Macs, 2% of public computers are UNIX, network access in dorm rooms, network access in dorm lounges, online registration, online administrative functions (other than registration), support for handheld computing, remote student-access to Web through college's connection.

CAMPUS LIFE
Activities: Choral groups, concert band, dance, drama/theater, jazz band, literary magazine, marching band, music ensembles, musical theater, pep band, radio station, student government, student newspaper, symphony orchestra, television station, yearbook. **Organizations:** 122 registered organizations, 16 honor societies, 11 religious organization. 6 fraternities (32% men join), 7 sororities (32% women join). **Athletics (Intercollegiate):** *Men:* Baseball, basketball, cross-country, diving, football, golf, soccer, swimming, tennis, track/field (indoor), track/field (outdoor). *Women:* Basketball, cross-country, diving, equestrian sports, golf, soccer, softball, swimming, tennis, track/field (indoor), track/field (outdoor), volleyball.

ADMISSIONS

Freshman Academic Profile: 30% in top 10% of high school class, 64% in top 25% of high school class, 90% in top 50% of high school class. 75% from public high schools. SAT Math middle 50% range 530-650. SAT Critical Reading middle 50% range 520-660. ACT middle 50% range 23-28. TOEFL required of all international applicants, minimum paper TOEFL 550, minimum computer TOEFL 270. **Basis for Candidate Selection:** *Very important factors considered include:* Academic GPA, character/personal qualities, interview, level of applicant's interest, recommendation(s), rigor of secondary school record. *Important factors considered include:* Application essay, extracurricular activities, standardized test scores, talent/ability, volunteer work. *Factors considered include:* Alumni/ae relation, class rank, geographical residence, racial/ethnic status, work experience. **Freshman Admission Requirements:** High school diploma is required, and GED is accepted. *Academic units required:* 4 English, 3 math, 3 science (1 science lab), 3 social studies, 1 history. *Academic units recommended:* 4 English, 3 math, 3 science, 3 foreign language, 3 social studies, 3 history. **Freshman Admission Statistics:** 1,946 applied, 82% admitted, 36% enrolled. **Transfer Admission Requirements:** High school transcript, college transcript(s), statement of good standing from prior institution(s). Minimum college GPA of 2.5 required. Lowest grade transferable C. **General Admission Information:** Application fee $20. Regular application deadline 3/1. Regular notification is rolling. Nonfall registration accepted. Admission may be deferred for a maximum of 1 year. Credit and/or placement offered for CEEB Advanced Placement tests.

COSTS AND FINANCIAL AID

Annual tuition $27,054. Room and board $7,806. Required fees $476. Average book expense $700. **Required Forms and Deadlines:** FAFSA. Financial aid filing deadline 3/1. **Notification of Awards:** Applicants will be notified of awards on a rolling basis beginning on or about 3/15. **Types of Aid:** *Need-based scholarships/grants:* Pell, SEOG, state scholarships/grants, private scholarships, the school's own gift aid. *Loans:* FFEL Subsidized Stafford, FFEL Unsubsidized Stafford, FFEL PLUS, Federal Perkins, state loans. **Financial Aid Statistics:** 60% freshmen, 60% undergrads receive need-based scholarship or grant aid. 43% freshmen, 46% undergrads receive need-based self-help aid. 95% freshmen, 94% undergrads receive any aid. Highest amount earned per year from on-campus jobs $3,500.

ALBRIGHT COLLEGE

PO Box 15234, 13th and Bern Streets, Reading, PA 19612-5234
Phone: 610-921-7799 **E-mail:** admission@albright.edu **CEEB Code:** 2004
Fax: 610-921-7294 **Website:** www.albright.edu **ACT Code:** 2004
Financial Aid Phone: 610-921-7515

This private school, affiliated with the Methodist Church, was founded in 1856. It has a 118-acre campus.

RATINGS

Admissions Selectivity Rating: 80 **Fire Safety Rating:** 60* **Green Rating:** 60*

STUDENTS AND FACULTY

Enrollment: 2,074. **Student Body:** 58% female, 42% male, 33% out-of-state, 3% international (26 countries represented). African American 9%, Asian 2%, Caucasian 78%, Hispanic 4%. **Retention and Graduation:** 76% freshmen return for sophomore year. 52% freshmen graduate within 4 years. 23% grads go on to further study within 1 year. 15% grads pursue arts and sciences degrees. 5% grads pursue business degrees. 9% grads pursue law degrees. 7% grads pursue medical degrees. **Faculty:** Student/faculty ratio 14:1. 103 full-time faculty, 83% hold PhDs. 100% faculty teach undergrads.

ACADEMICS

Degrees: Bachelor's, certificate, master's. **Academic Requirements:** Arts/fine arts, computer literacy, English (including composition), foreign languages, history, humanities, mathematics, philosophy, sciences (biological or physical), social science, interdisciplinary. **Classes:** Most classes have 10–19 students. Most lab/discussion sections have 10–19 students. **Majors with Highest Enrollment:** Business administration/management, sociology. **Disciplines with Highest Percentage of Degrees Awarded:** Business/marketing 28%, social sciences 15%, psychology 14%, visual and performing arts 11%, computer and information sciences 7%. **Special Study Options:** Accelerated program, cross-registration, dual enrollment, English as a Second Language (ESL), exchange student program (domestic), honors program, independent study, internships, liberal arts/career combination, student-designed major, study abroad, teacher certification program, interdisciplinary.

FACILITIES

Housing: Coed dorms, men's dorms, women's dorms, apartments for single students, honors-special interest-freshmen floors vs. dorms. **Special Academic Facilities/Equipment:** Freedman Art Gallery. **Computers:** 95% of classrooms are wireless, 5% of public computers are PCs, network access in dorm rooms, network access in dorm lounges, remote student-access to Web through college's connection.

CAMPUS LIFE

Activities: Choral groups, concert band, dance, drama/theater, jazz band, literary magazine, music ensembles, musical theater, pep band, radio station, student government, student newspaper, television station, yearbook. **Organizations:** 84 registered organizations, 10 honor societies, 3 religious organizations. 4 fraternities (25% men join), 3 sororities (30% women join). **Athletics (Intercollegiate):** *Men:* Baseball, basketball, cheerleading, cross-country, football, golf, soccer, swimming, tennis, track/field (indoor), track/field (outdoor), wrestling. *Women:* Badminton, basketball, cheerleading, cross-country, field hockey, soccer, softball, swimming, tennis, track/field (indoor), track/field (outdoor), volleyball.

ADMISSIONS

Freshman Academic Profile: 23% in top 10% of high school class, 48% in top 25% of high school class, 79% in top 50% of high school class. 77% from public high schools. SAT Math middle 50% range 460-570. SAT Critical Reading middle 50% range 470-580. **Basis for Candidate Selection:** *Very important factors considered include:* Rigor of secondary school record. *Important factors considered include:* Academic GPA, application essay, character/personal qualities, class rank, recommendation(s), standardized test scores. *Factors considered include:* Alumni/ae relation, extracurricular activities, talent/ability, volunteer work, work experience. **Freshman Admission Requirements:** High school diploma is required, and GED is accepted. *Academic units required:* 4 English, 2 math, 3 science (1 science lab), 2 foreign language, 2 social studies, 1 history, 2 academic electives. *Academic units recommended:* 4 English, 3 math, 4 science (2 science labs), 3 foreign language, 2 social studies, 2 history, 2 academic electives. **Freshman Admission Statistics:** 3,013 applied, 71% admitted, 21% enrolled. **Transfer Admission Requirements:** College transcript(s), essay or personal statement, statement of good standing from prior institution(s). Minimum college GPA of 2.0 required. Lowest grade transferable C-. **General Admission Information:** Application fee $25. Regular notification is rolling. Nonfall registration accepted. Admission may be deferred for a maximum of 1 year. Common Application accepted. Credit and/or placement offered for CEEB Advanced Placement tests.

COSTS AND FINANCIAL AID

Annual tuition $25,232. Room and board $7,888. Required fees $800. Average book expense $800. **Required Forms and Deadlines:** FAFSA. Financial aid filing deadline 3/1. **Notification of Awards:** Applicants will be notified of awards on or about 2/14. **Types of Aid:** *Need-based scholarships/grants:* Pell, SEOG, state scholarships/grants, private scholarships, the school's own gift aid. *Loans:* FFEL Subsidized Stafford, FFEL Unsubsidized Stafford, FFEL PLUS, Federal Perkins, private educational loans. **Student Employment:** Federal Work-Study Program available. Institutional employment available. Off-campus job opportunities are good. **Financial Aid Statistics:** 81% freshmen, 68% undergrads receive need-based scholarship or grant aid. 67% freshmen, 59% undergrads receive need-based self-help aid. 95% freshmen, 94% undergrads receive any aid. Highest amount earned per year from on-campus jobs $1,100.

ALCORN STATE UNIVERSITY

1000 ASU Drive #300, Alcorn State, MS 39096
Phone: 601-877-6147 **E-mail:** ebarnes@alcorn.edu **CEEB Code:** 1008
Fax: 601-877-6347 **Website:** www.alcorn.edu **ACT Code:** 2176
Financial Aid Phone: 601-877-6190

This public school was founded in 1871. It has a 1,756-acre campus.

RATINGS

Admissions Selectivity Rating: 60* **Fire Safety Rating:** 60* **Green Rating:** 60*

STUDENTS AND FACULTY

Enrollment: 2,962. **Student Body:** 63% female, 37% male, 16% out-of-state, 2% international (14 countries represented). African American 92%, Caucasian 6%. **Retention and Graduation:** 74% freshmen return for sophomore year. 24% freshmen graduate within 4 years. 38% grads go on to further study within 1 year. **Faculty:** Student/faculty ratio 16:1. 175 full-time faculty, 64% hold PhDs.

ACADEMICS

Degrees: Associate, bachelor's, master's, post-master's certificate. **Academic Requirements:** Arts/fine arts, computer literacy, English (including composition), history, humanities, mathematics, sciences (biological or physical), social science, oral communication, physical education, student adjustment. **Classes:** Most classes have fewer than 10 students. Most lab/discussion sections have fewer than 10 students. **Majors with Highest Enrollment:** Elementary education and teaching, liberal arts and sciences/liberal studies. **Disciplines with Highest Percentage of Degrees Awarded:** Liberal arts/general studies 21%, health professions and related sciences 11%, education 10%, business/marketing 10%, biological/life sciences 8%, social sciences 8%, engineering technologies 5%. **Special Study Options:** Accelerated program, cooperative education program, distance learning, double major, honors program, independent study, internships, liberal arts/career combination, teacher certification program, undergrads may take grad level classes (restrictions apply).

FACILITIES

Housing: Men's dorms, women's dorms. **Special Academic Facilities/Equipment:** Honors resident hall. **Computers:** Network access in dorm rooms, network access in dorm lounges, online registration, online administrative functions (other than registration), remote student-access to Web through college's connection.

CAMPUS LIFE

Activities: Choral groups, concert band, dance, drama/theater, jazz band, marching band, music ensembles, radio station, student government, student newspaper, television station, yearbook. **Organizations:** 6 honor societies, 13 religious organizations. 4 fraternities (7% men join), 4 sororities (12% women join). **Athletics (Intercollegiate):** *Men:* Baseball, basketball, cross-country, football, golf, tennis, track/field (outdoor). *Women:* Basketball, cross-country, golf, soccer, softball, tennis, track/field (outdoor), volleyball.

ADMISSIONS

Freshman Academic Profile: 75% in top 50% of high school class. 99% from public high schools. ACT middle 50% range 16–19. TOEFL required of all international applicants, minimum paper TOEFL 525. **Basis for Candidate Selection:** *Very important factors considered include:* Class rank, rigor of secondary school record. *Important factors considered include:* Standardized test scores. *Factors considered include:* Interview, racial/ethnic status, recommendation(s). **Freshman Admission Requirements:** High school diploma is required, and GED is accepted. *Academic units required:* 4 English, 3 math, 3 science (2 science labs), 3 social studies, 2 academic electives. *Academic units recommended:* 1 foreign language. **Freshman Admission Statistics:** 2,335 applied, 68% admitted, 31% enrolled. **Transfer Admission Requirements:** College transcript(s), statement of good standing from prior institution(s). Minimum college GPA of 2.0 required. Lowest grade transferable C. **General Admission Information:** Regular notification is rolling. Nonfall registration accepted. Common Application not accepted. Credit and/or placement offered for CEEB Advanced Placement tests.

COSTS AND FINANCIAL AID

Annual in-state tuition $3,919. Annual out-of-state tuition $8,887. Room and board $4,272. Average book expense $1,320. **Required Forms and Deadlines:** FAFSA, institution's own financial aid form. Financial aid filing deadline 4/1. **Notification of Awards:** Applicants will be notified of awards on a rolling basis beginning on or about 4/1. *Types of Aid: Need-based scholarships/grants:* Pell, SEOG, state scholarships/grants, private scholarships, the school's own gift aid. *Loans:* Direct Subsidized Stafford, Direct Unsubsidized Stafford, Direct PLUS. **Student Employment:** Federal Work-Study Program available. Institutional employment available. Off-campus job opportunities are poor. **Financial Aid Statistics:** 58% freshmen, 66% undergrads receive need-based scholarship or grant aid. 48% freshmen, 60% undergrads receive need-based self-help aid. 55 freshmen, 253 undergrads receive athletic scholarships. Highest amount earned per year from on-campus jobs $500.

ALDERSON-BROADDUS COLLEGE

PO Box 2003, Philippi, WV 26416
Phone: 800-263-1549 **E-mail:** admissions@ab.edu **CEEB Code:** 5005
Fax: 304-457-6239 **Website:** www.ab.edu **ACT Code:** 4508
Financial Aid Phone: 304-457-6354

This private school, affiliated with the American Baptist Church, was founded in 1871. It has a 170-acre campus.

RATINGS

Admissions Selectivity Rating: 76   **Fire Safety Rating:** 71   **Green Rating:** 60*

STUDENTS AND FACULTY

Enrollment: 623. **Student Body:** 68% female, 32% male, 19% out-of-state, 2% international (7 countries represented). African American 2%, Asian 1%, Caucasian 81%, Hispanic 1%. **Retention and Graduation:** 69% freshmen return for sophomore year. 15% grads go on to further study within 1 year. 6% grads pursue arts and sciences degrees. 3% grads pursue business degrees. 2% grads pursue law degrees. 4% grads pursue medical degrees. **Faculty:** Student/faculty ratio 11:1. 58 full-time faculty, 34% hold PhDs. 100% faculty teach undergrads.

ACADEMICS

Degrees: Associate, bachelor's, certificate, master's. **Academic Requirements:** Arts/fine arts, computer literacy, English (including composition), history, humanities, mathematics, philosophy, sciences (biological or physical), social science, religion, personal health. **Classes:** Most classes have fewer than 10 students. **Majors with Highest Enrollment:** Biology/biological sciences, nursing–registered nurse training (ASN, BSN, MSN, RN), physician assistant. **Disciplines with Highest Percentage of Degrees Awarded:** Health professions and related sciences 51%, education 20%, business/marketing 10%, visual and performing arts 9%, biological/life sciences 7%. **Special Study Options:** Double major, dual enrollment, honors program, independent study, internships, liberal arts/career combination, student-designed major, study abroad, teacher certification program.

FACILITIES

Housing: Coed dorms, women's dorms, apartments for married students, apartments for single students, special housing for disabled students. **Special Academic Facilities/Equipment:** Art gallery in New Main Hall, Campbell School House. **Computers:** 95% of public computers are PCs, 5% of public computers are Macs, network access in dorm rooms, online administrative functions (other than registration), remote student-access to Web through college's connection.

CAMPUS LIFE

Activities: Choral groups, concert band, dance, drama/theater, jazz band, literary magazine, music ensembles, musical theater, opera, radio station, student government, student newspaper, television station, yearbook. **Organizations:** 36 registered organizations, 3 honor societies, 2 religious organizations. 1 fraternity (2% men join), 3 sororities (3% women join). **Athletics (Intercollegiate):** *Men:* Baseball, basketball, cross-country, golf, soccer. *Women:* Basketball, cross-country, golf, softball, volleyball.

ADMISSIONS

Freshman Academic Profile: 20% in top 10% of high school class, 45% in top 25% of high school class, 78% in top 50% of high school class. 95% from public high schools. SAT Math middle 50% range 390–530. SAT Critical Reading middle 50% range 420–560. ACT middle 50% range 19–24. TOEFL required of all international applicants, minimum paper TOEFL 500, minimum computer TOEFL 173. **Basis for Candidate Selection:** *Very important factors considered include:* Academic GPA, standardized test scores. *Important factors considered include:* Application essay, interview, level of applicant's interest. *Other factors considered include:* Alumni/ae relation, first generation, recommendation(s), religious affiliation/commitment, rigor of secondary school record, talent/ability, work experience. **Freshman Admission Requirements:** High school diploma is required, and GED is accepted. *Academic units required:* 4 English, 3 math, (3 science labs), 1 foreign language, 2 social studies. *Academic units recommended:* 4 English, 3 math, 3 science, 1 foreign language, 2 social studies, 2 history. **Freshman Admission Statistics:** 480 applied, 75% admitted, 35% enrolled. **Transfer Admission Requirements:** College transcript(s), statement of good standing from prior institution(s). Minimum college GPA of 2.0 required. Lowest grade transferable C. **General Admission Information:** Application fee $10. Regular application deadline 8/25. Regular notification is rolling. Nonfall registration accepted. Common Application not accepted. Credit and/or placement offered for CEEB Advanced Placement tests.

COSTS AND FINANCIAL AID

Annual tuition $18,890. Room and board $6,150. Required fees $200. Average book expense $800. **Required Forms and Deadlines:** FAFSA, state aid form. Financial aid filing deadline 3/1. **Notification of Awards:** Applicants will be notified of awards on a rolling basis beginning on or about 2/15. **Types of Aid:** *Need-based scholarships/grants:* Pell, SEOG, state scholarships/grants, private scholarships, the school's own gift aid, Federal Nursing Scholarships, National Health Service Corp, scholarship for disadvantaged students. *Loans:* FFEL Subsidized Stafford, FFEL Unsubsidized Stafford, FFEL PLUS, Federal Perkins, Federal Nursing, college/university loans from institutional funds. **Student Employment:** Federal Work-Study Program available. Institutional employment available. Off-campus job opportunities are fair. **Financial Aid Statistics:** 92% freshmen, 91% undergrads receive need-based scholarship or grant aid. 73% freshmen, 85% undergrads receive need-based self-help aid. 1 freshmen, 6 undergrads receive athletic scholarships. 92% freshmen, 95% undergrads receive any aid. Highest amount earned per year from on-campus jobs $1,400.

ALFRED UNIVERSITY

Best 368

Alumni Hall, 1 Saxon Drive, Alfred, NY 14802-1205
Phone: 607-871-2115 **E-mail:** admissions@alfred.edu **CEEB Code:** 2005
Fax: 607-871-2198 **Website:** www.alfred.edu **ACT Code:** 2666
Financial Aid Phone: 607-871-2159

This private school was founded in 1836. It has a 600-acre campus.

RATINGS
Admissions Selectivity Rating: 78   **Fire Safety Rating:** 60*   **Green Rating:** 60*

STUDENTS AND FACULTY
Enrollment: 1,971. **Student Body:** 49% female, 51% male, 35% out-of-state, 2% international. African American 6%, Asian 2%, Caucasian 76%, Hispanic 4%. **Retention and Graduation:** 82% freshmen return for sophomore year. 49% freshmen graduate within 4 years. 29% grads go on to further study within 1 year. **Faculty:** Student/faculty ratio 12:1. 172 full-time faculty, 87% hold PhDs. 100% faculty teach undergrads.

ACADEMICS
Degrees: Bachelor's, doctoral, master's, post-master's certificate. **Academic Requirements:** Arts/fine arts, English (including composition), foreign languages, history, mathematics, philosophy, sciences (biological or physical), social science. Please note that general education requirements vary by college. Those checked above are representative of the College of Liberal Arts and Sciences, the largest college at Alfred University. In addition, there is a physical education requirement for all students. **Classes:** Most classes have 10–19 students. Most lab/discussion sections have 10–19 students. **Majors with Highest Enrollment:** Business administration/management; ceramic sciences and engineering, fine/studio arts. **Disciplines with Highest Percentage of Degrees Awarded:** Visual and performing arts 31%, engineering 17%, business/marketing 15%, psychology 9%, communication technologies 5%. **Special Study Options:** Cooperative education program, cross-registration, double major, English as a Second Language (ESL), exchange student program (domestic), honors program, independent study, internships, liberal arts/career combination, student-designed major, study abroad, teacher certification program.

FACILITIES
Housing: Coed dorms, apartments for single students, theme housing (i.e. Environmental Studies House, Language House, etc.). **Special Academic Facilities/Equipment:** Art museums, carillon, language labs, electron microscope, observatory, extensive engineering equipment, performing arts center. **Computers:** 40% of classrooms are wireless, 75% of public computers are PCs, 25% of public computers are Macs, network access in dorm rooms, network access in dorm lounges, online registration, online administrative functions (other than registration), remote student-access to Web through college's connection.

CAMPUS LIFE
Activities: Choral groups, concert band, dance, drama/theater, literary magazine, music ensembles, musical theater, pep band, radio station, student government, student newspaper, student-run film society, television station, yearbook. **Organizations:** 90 registered organizations, 13 honor societies, 3 religious organizations. **Athletics (Intercollegiate): Men:** Basketball, cross-country, diving, equestrian sports, football, lacrosse, skiing (downhill/alpine), soccer, swimming, tennis, track/field (indoor), track/field (outdoor). **Women:** Basketball, cross-country, diving, equestrian sports, lacrosse, skiing (downhill/alpine), soccer, softball, swimming, tennis, track/field (indoor), track/field (outdoor), volleyball.

ADMISSIONS
Freshman Academic Profile: 15% in top 10% of high school class, 47% in top 25% of high school class, 84% in top 50% of high school class. SAT Math middle 50% range 500–610. SAT Critical Reading middle 50% range 500–610. ACT middle 50% range 21–27. TOEFL required of all international applicants, minimum paper TOEFL 550, minimum computer TOEFL 213. **Basis for Candidate Selection:** *Very important factors considered:* Character/personal qualities, class rank, extracurricular activities, recommendation(s), rigor of secondary school record. *Important factors considered:* Application essay, standardized test scores, volunteer work, work experience.

Other factors considered include: Interview, racial/ethnic status, talent/ability. **Freshman Admission Requirements:** High school diploma is required, and GED is accepted. *Academic units required:* 4 English, 2 math, 2 science (2 science labs), 2 social studies. *Academic units recommended:* 4 math, 3 science (3 science labs), 3 social studies. **Freshman Admission Statistics:** 2,243 applied, 73% admitted, 31% enrolled. **Transfer Admission Requirements:** College transcript(s), statement of good standing from prior institution(s). Minimum college GPA of 2.5 required. Lowest grade transferable C. **General Admission Information:** Application fee $40. Early decision application deadline 12/1. Regular notification is rolling. Nonfall registration accepted. Admission may be deferred for a maximum of 2 years. Common Application accepted.

COSTS AND FINANCIAL AID
Annual tuition $22,312. Room and board $10,384. Required fees $850. Average book expense $900. **Required Forms and Deadlines:** FAFSA, institution's own financial aid form, state aid form, Noncustodial PROFILE, Business/Farm Supplement. Financial aid filing deadline 3/15. **Notification of Awards:** Applicants will be notified of awards on a rolling basis beginning on or about 2/15. **Types of Aid:** *Need-based scholarships/grants:* Pell, SEOG, state scholarships/grants, private scholarships, the school's own gift aid. *Loans:* FFEL Subsidized Stafford, FFEL Unsubsidized Stafford, FFEL PLUS, Federal Perkins, college/university loans from institutional funds, private alternative loans. **Student Employment:** Federal Work-Study Program available. Institutional employment available. Off-campus job opportunities are poor. **Financial Aid Statistics:** 80% freshmen, 80% undergrads receive need-based scholarship or grant aid. 72% freshmen, 74% undergrads receive need-based self-help aid. 92% freshmen, 90% undergrads receive any aid.

ALICE LLOYD COLLEGE

100 Purpose Road, Pippa Passes, KY 41844
Phone: 606-368-6036 **E-mail:** admissions@alc.edu **CEEB Code:** 1098
Fax: 606-368-6215 **Website:** www.alc.edu **ACT Code:** 1502
Financial Aid Phone: 606-368-6059

This private school was founded in 1923. It has a 225-acre campus.

RATINGS
Admissions Selectivity Rating: 84   **Fire Safety Rating:** 89   **Green Rating:** 60*

STUDENTS AND FACULTY
Enrollment: 607. **Student Body:** 52% female, 48% male, 16% out-of-state. African American 1%, Caucasian 98%. **Retention and Graduation:** 68% freshmen return for sophomore year. 28% freshmen graduate within 4 years. 55% grads go on to further study within 1 year. 35% grads pursue arts and sciences degrees. 10% grads pursue business degrees. 5% grads pursue law degrees. 5% grads pursue medical degrees. **Faculty:** Student/faculty ratio 18:1. 29 full-time faculty, 62% hold PhDs. 100% faculty teach undergrads.

ACADEMICS
Degrees: Bachelor's. **Academic Requirements:** Arts/fine arts, computer literacy, English (including composition), foreign languages, history, humanities, mathematics, philosophy, sciences (biological or physical), social science. **Classes:** Most classes have 20–29 students. **Disciplines with Highest Percentage of Degrees Awarded:** Education 30%, biological/life sciences 29%, social sciences 15%, business/marketing 13%, parks and recreation 8%. **Special Study Options:** Cooperative education program, double major, honors program, independent study, internships, liberal arts/career combination, study abroad, teacher certification program.

FACILITIES
Housing: Men's dorms, women's dorms. **Special Academic Facilities/Equipment:** Photographic archives; oral history museum; Appalachian collection; on-campus day care center; kindergarten, elementary, and secondary school. **Computers:** 35% of public computers are PCs, network access in dorm rooms, online administrative functions (other than registration), remote student-access to Web through college's connection.

CAMPUS LIFE
Activities: Choral groups, drama/theater, music ensembles, musical theater, pep band, radio station, student government, student newspaper, yearbook. **Organizations:** 19 registered organizations, 2 honor societies, 1 religious organization. **Athletics (Intercollegiate): Men:** Baseball, basketball, cheerleading, cross-country, golf, tennis. **Women:** Basketball, cheerleading, cross-country, golf, softball, tennis.

ADMISSIONS

Freshman Academic Profile: 30% in top 10% of high school class, 61% in top 25% of high school class, 87% in top 50% of high school class. 90% from public high schools. SAT Math middle 50% range 480–570. SAT Critical Reading middle 50% range 440–590. SAT Writing middle 50% range 430–520. ACT middle 50% range 17–23. TOEFL required of all international applicants, minimum paper TOEFL 550, minimum computer TOEFL 213. **Basis for Candidate Selection:** *Very important factors considered include:* Character/ personal qualities, geographical residence, rigor of secondary school record, standardized test scores. *Important factors considered include:* Alumni/ae relation, class rank, recommendation(s), state residency. *Other factors considered include:* Application essay, extracurricular activities, interview, talent/ ability, volunteer work, work experience. **Freshman Admission Requirements:** High school diploma is required, and GED is accepted. *Academic units required:* 4 English, 3 math, 2 science, 2 social studies, 1 history. *Academic units recommended:* 4 English, 3 math, 2 science, 2 foreign language, 2 social studies. **Freshman Admission Statistics:** 994 applied, 56% admitted, 35% enrolled. **Transfer Admission Requirements:** High school transcript, college transcript(s), standardized test score, statement of good standing from prior institution(s). Minimum college GPA of 2.0 required. Lowest grade transferable C. **General Admission Information:** Regular application deadline 5/1. Regular notification is rolling. Nonfall registration accepted. Credit and/or placement offered for CEEB Advanced Placement tests.

COSTS AND FINANCIAL AID

Room and board $4,250. Required fees $1,300. Average book expense $850. **Required Forms and Deadlines:** FAFSA. Financial aid filing deadline 3/15. **Notification of Awards:** Applicants will be notified of awards on a rolling basis beginning on or about 4/1. **Types of Aid:** *Need-based scholarships/grants:* Pell, SEOG, state scholarships/grants, private scholarships, the school's own gift aid. *Loans:* FFEL Subsidized Stafford, FFEL Unsubsidized Stafford, FFEL PLUS, Federal Perkins, state loans, college/university loans from institutional funds. **Financial Aid Statistics:** 69% freshmen, 69% undergrads receive need-based scholarship or grant aid. 69% freshmen, 69% undergrads receive need-based self-help aid. 32 undergrads receive athletic scholarships. 100% freshmen, 100% undergrads receive any aid.

ALLEGHENY COLLEGE

Best 368

Allegheny College, Admissions Office, Box 5, 520 North Main Street, Meadville, PA 16335
Phone: 814-332-4351 **E-mail:** admissions@allegheny.edu **CEEB Code:** 2006
Fax: 814-337-0431 **Website:** www.allegheny.edu **ACT Code:** 3520
Financial Aid Phone: 800-835-7780

This private school, affiliated with the United Methodist Church, was founded in 1815. It has a 542-acre campus.

RATINGS

Admissions Selectivity Rating: 91   **Fire Safety Rating:** 79   **Green Rating:** 93

STUDENTS AND FACULTY

Enrollment: 2,057. **Student Body:** 54% female, 46% male, 36% out-of-state. African American 2%, Asian 3%, Caucasian 93%, Hispanic 1%. **Retention and Graduation:** 88% freshmen return for sophomore year. 70% freshmen graduate within 4 years. 48% grads go on to further study within 1 year. 21% grads pursue arts and sciences degrees. 3% grads pursue business degrees. 3% grads pursue law degrees. 14% grads pursue medical degrees. **Faculty:** Student/faculty ratio 14:1. 137 full-time faculty, 93% hold PhDs. 100% faculty teach undergrads.

ACADEMICS

Degrees: Bachelor's. **Academic Requirements:** Humanities, sciences (biological or physical), social science. Students must major in 1 academic division, minor in another, and complete 8 credits from the third academic division. **Classes:** Most classes have 10–19 students. **Majors with Highest Enrollment:** Biology/biological sciences, English language and literature, psychology. **Disciplines with Highest Percentage of Degrees Awarded:** Psychology 14%, biological/life sciences 11%, English 10%, interdisciplinary studies 7%, physical sciences 6%, communications/journalism 6%. **Special Study Options:** Combined degree programs, cooperative program in teacher education, double major, dual enrollment, English as a second language (ESL),

experiential learning terms, independent study, internships, marine biology study program, medical school partnerships, pre-professional programs, student-designed major, study abroad, Washington Semester.

FACILITIES

Housing: Coed dorms, men's dorms, women's dorms, apartments for single students, special housing for disabled students, fraternity/sorority housing, special interest housing, wellness floors, quiet study floors, townhouses. **Special Academic Facilities/Equipment:** Newly expanded and renovated campus center with bookstore, coffee house, cultural center, attractive gathering spaces, and areas for student organizations and activities, radio and television stations. **Computers:** 90% of public computers are PCs, 10% of public computers are Macs, network access in dorm rooms, network access in dorm lounges, online registration, online administrative functions (other than registration), remote student-access to Web through college's connection.

CAMPUS LIFE

Activities: Choral groups, concert band, dance, drama/theater, jazz band, literary magazine, music ensembles, musical theater, pep band, radio station, student government, student newspaper, symphony orchestra, television station, yearbook. **Organizations:** 83 registered organizations, 13 honor societies, 7 religious organizations. 5 fraternities (21% men join), 4 sororities (28% women join). **Athletics (Intercollegiate):** *Men:* Baseball, basketball, cross-country, diving, football, golf, soccer, swimming, tennis, track/field (indoor), track/field (outdoor). *Women:* Basketball, cross-country, diving, golf, lacrosse, soccer, softball, swimming, tennis, track/field (indoor), track/field (outdoor), volleyball. **Environmental Initiatives:** Wind energy. Composting. Commitment to LEED Silver on new construction.

ADMISSIONS

Freshman Academic Profile: 41% in top 10% of high school class, 75% in top 25% of high school class, 98% in top 50% of high school class. 84% from public high schools. SAT Math middle 50% range 555–650. SAT Critical Reading middle 50% range 560–660. ACT middle 50% range 24–28. TOEFL required of all international applicants, minimum paper TOEFL 550, minimum computer TOEFL 213. **Basis for Candidate Selection:** *Very important factors considered include:* Academic GPA, class rank, rigor of secondary school record. *Important factors considered include:* Character/personal qualities, extracurricular activities, interview, recommendation(s), standardized test scores. *Other factors considered include:* Alumni/ae relation, application essay, first generation, geographical residence, level of applicant's interest, racial/ ethnic status, talent/ability, volunteer work, work experience. **Freshman Admission Requirements:** High school diploma is required, and GED is accepted. *Academic units required:* 4 English, 3 math, 3 science, 2 foreign language, 3 social studies, 1 academic elective. **Freshman Admission Statistics:** 3,668 applied, 63% admitted, 25% enrolled. **Transfer Admission Requirements:** High school transcript, college transcript(s), essay or personal statement, standardized test score, statement of good standing from prior institution(s). Minimum college GPA of 2.5 required. Lowest grade transferable C. **General Admission Information:** Application fee $35. Early decision application deadline 11/15. Regular application deadline 2/15. Regular notification 4/1. Nonfall registration accepted. Admission may be deferred for a maximum of 1 year. Credit and/or placement offered for CEEB Advanced Placement tests.

COSTS AND FINANCIAL AID

Annual tuition $31,680. Room and board $8,000. Required fees $320. Average book expense $900. **Required Forms and Deadlines:** FAFSA. Financial aid filing deadline 2/15. **Notification of Awards:** Applicants will be notified of awards on a rolling basis beginning on or about 3/1. **Types of Aid:** *Need-based scholarships/grants:* Pell, SEOG, state scholarships/grants, private scholarships, the school's own gift aid, Federal Academic Competitiveness Grant, National SMART Grant, Veterans Educational Benefits. *Loans:* FFEL Subsidized Stafford, FFEL Unsubsidized Stafford, FFEL PLUS, Federal Perkins, Private loans from commercial lenders. **Financial Aid Statistics:** 70% freshmen, 67% undergrads receive need-based scholarship or grant aid. 61% freshmen, 57% undergrads receive need-based self-help aid. 98% freshmen, 98% undergrads receive any aid. Highest amount earned per year from on-campus jobs $2,304.

ALLEN COLLEGE

1825 Logan Avenue, Waterloo, IA 50703
Phone: 319-226-2000 **E-mail:** allencollegeadmissions@ihs.org
Fax: 319-226-2051 **Website:** www.allencollege.edu
Financial Aid Phone: 319-226-2003

This private school was founded in 1989.

RATINGS
Admissions Selectivity Rating: 80   **Fire Safety Rating:** 94   **Green Rating:** 60*

STUDENTS AND FACULTY
Enrollment: 359. **Student Body:** 94% female, 6% male, 5% out-of-state. Caucasian 97%. **Retention and Graduation:** 72% freshmen return for sophomore year. 52% freshmen graduate within 4 years. 10% grads go on to further study within 1 year. **Faculty:** Student/faculty ratio 13:1. 19 full-time faculty, 16% hold PhDs. 100% faculty teach undergrads.

ACADEMICS
Degrees: Associate, bachelor's, master's, post-master's certificate. **Academic Requirements:** English (including composition), humanities, sciences (biological or physical), social science. **Classes:** Most classes have 10–19 students. Most lab/discussion sections have fewer than 10 students. **Majors with Highest Enrollment:** Family practice nurse nurse practitioner, health services/allied health, nursing–registered nurse training (ASN, BSN, MSN, RN). **Disciplines with Highest Percentage of Degrees Awarded:** Health professions and related sciences 100%. **Special Study Options:** Cooperative education program, distance learning, independent study, internships.

FACILITIES
Housing: Housing also available at a cooperating institution. **Computers:** 1% of classrooms are wired, 1% of classrooms are wireless, 100% of public computers are PCs, network access in dorm rooms, network access in dorm lounges, online administrative functions (other than registration), remote student-access to Web through college's connection.

CAMPUS LIFE
Activities: Student government, student newspaper, yearbook. **Organizations:** 4 registered organizations, 1 honor society, 1 religious organization.

ADMISSIONS
Freshman Academic Profile: 19% in top 10% of high school class, 58% in top 25% of high school class, 100% in top 50% of high school class. ACT middle 50% range 20–24. TOEFL required of all international applicants, minimum paper TOEFL 550, minimum computer TOEFL 213. **Basis for Candidate Selection:** *Very important factors considered include:* Class rank, rigor of secondary school record, standardized test scores. *Important factors considered include:* Application essay, recommendation(s). *Other factors considered include:* Character/personal qualities, extracurricular activities, first generation, interview, talent/ability. **Freshman Admission Requirements:** High school diploma is required, and GED is accepted. *Academic units required:* 8 English, 6 math, 6 science, 6 social studies. **Freshman Admission Statistics:** 61 applied, 66% admitted, 78% enrolled. **Transfer Admission Requirements:** High school transcript, college transcript(s), essay or personal statement, standardized test score, minimum college GPA of 2.7 required. Lowest grade transferable C. **General Admission Information:** Application fee $50. Regular application deadline 3/1. Regular notification is rolling. Nonfall registration accepted. Credit offered for CEEB Advanced Placement tests.

COSTS AND FINANCIAL AID
Annual tuition $13,359. Room and board $6,178. Required fees $536. Average book expense $964. **Required Forms and Deadlines:** FAFSA, institution's own financial aid form. Financial aid filing deadline 6/30. **Notification of Awards:** Applicants will be notified of awards on a rolling basis beginning on or about 3/15. **Types of Aid:** *Need-based scholarships/grants:* Pell, SEOG, state scholarships/grants, private scholarships, the school's own gift aid, Federal Nursing Scholarships. *Loans:* Direct Subsidized Stafford, Direct Unsubsidized Stafford, Direct PLUS, Federal Perkins, Federal Nursing, college/university loans from institutional funds, alternative loans. **Student Employment:** Federal Work-Study Program available. Off-campus job opportunities are excellent. **Financial Aid Statistics:** 51% freshmen, 54% undergrads receive need-based scholarship or grant aid. 64% freshmen, 69% undergrads receive need-based self-help aid. 91% freshmen, 92% undergrads receive any aid.

ALLIANT INTERNATIONAL UNIVERSITY

Admissions Processing Center, 10455 Pomerado Road, San Diego, CA 94131-1799
Phone: 866-825-5426 **E-mail:** admissions@alliant.edu **CEEB Code:** 4039
Fax: 858-635-4355 **Website:** www.alliant.edu **ACT Code:** 0443
Financial Aid Phone: 858-635-4559

This private school was founded in 1952. It has a 60-acre campus.

RATINGS
Admissions Selectivity Rating: 60*   **Fire Safety Rating:** 60*   **Green Rating:** 60*

STUDENTS AND FACULTY
Enrollment: 344. **Student Body:** 50% female, 50% male, 16% out-of-state, 32% international (59 countries represented). African American 6%, Asian 6%, Caucasian 26%, Hispanic 22%. **Retention and Graduation:** 38% freshmen return for sophomore year. 29% freshmen graduate within 4 years. 14% grads go on to further study within 1 year. 50% grads pursue arts and sciences degrees. 50% grads pursue business degrees. **Faculty:** Student/faculty ratio 15:1. 161 full-time faculty, 100% hold PhDs. 7% faculty teach undergrads.

ACADEMICS
Degrees: Bachelor's, certificate, doctoral, master's, post-bachelor's certificate. **Academic Requirements:** Computer literacy, English (including composition), foreign languages, humanities, mathematics, sciences (biological or physical), social science, community service. **Classes:** Most classes have fewer than 10 students. **Majors with Highest Enrollment:** Business administration/management, international business, psychology. **Disciplines with Highest Percentage of Degrees Awarded:** Business/marketing 66%, psychology 10%, social sciences 10%, liberal arts/general studies 9%, education 3%, communication technologies 1%. **Special Study Options:** English as a Second Language (ESL), honors program, independent study, internships, study abroad.

FACILITIES
Housing: Coed dorms. **Special Academic Facilities/Equipment:** Legler Benbough Theater, AIU SportCenter. **Computers:** 90% of public computers are PCs, 10% of public computers are Macs, network access in dorm rooms, network access in dorm lounges, online registration, online administrative functions (other than registration), remote student-access to Web through college's connection.

CAMPUS LIFE
Activities: Student government, student newspaper, yearbook. **Organizations:** 12 registered organizations. **Athletics (Intercollegiate):** *Men:* Cross-country, soccer, tennis, track/field (outdoor). *Women:* Cross-country, soccer, tennis, track/field (outdoor), volleyball.

ADMISSIONS
Freshman Academic Profile: TOEFL required of all international applicants, minimum paper TOEFL 550, minimum computer TOEFL 213. **Basis for Candidate Selection:** *Very important factors considered include:* Rigor of secondary school record. *Other factors considered include:* Character/personal qualities, class rank, extracurricular activities, recommendation(s), talent/ability, volunteer work, work experience. **Freshman Admission Requirements:** High school diploma is required, and GED is accepted. **Freshman Admission Statistics:** 222 applied, 88% admitted, 39% enrolled. **Transfer Admission Requirements:** High school transcript, college transcript(s), minimum college GPA of 2.7 required. Lowest grade transferable C. **General Admission Information:** Application fee $40. Regular notification is rolling. Nonfall registration accepted. Admission may be deferred for a maximum of 1 year. Common Application accepted. Credit and/or placement offered for CEEB Advanced Placement tests.

COSTS AND FINANCIAL AID
Annual tuition $18,990. Room & board $7,430. Required fees $250. Average book expense $1,224. **Required Forms and Deadlines:** FAFSA, institution's own financial aid form. Financial aid filing deadline 3/2. **Notification of Awards:** Applicants will be notified of awards on a rolling basis beginning on or about 10/1. **Types of Aid:** *Need-based scholarships/grants:* Pell, SEOG, state scholarships/grants, private scholarships, the school's own gift aid. *Loans:* FFEL Subsidized Stafford, FFEL Unsubsidized Stafford, FFEL PLUS, Federal Perkins. **Student Employment:** Federal Work-Study Program available. Institutional employment available. Off-campus job opportunities are good. **Financial Aid Statistics:** 55% freshmen, 60% undergrads receive need-based scholarship or grant aid. 55% freshmen, 63% undergrads receive need-based self-help aid. 8 freshmen, 55 undergrads receive athletic scholarships. 91% freshmen, 89% undergrads receive any aid.

ALMA COLLEGE

614 West Superior Street, Alma, MI 48801-1599
Phone: 989-463-7139 **E-mail:** admissions@alma.edu **CEEB Code:** 1010
Fax: 989-463-7057 **Website:** www.alma.edu **ACT Code:** 1958
Financial Aid Phone: 989-463-7347

This private school, affiliated with the Presbyterian Church, was founded in 1886. It has a 125-acre campus.

RATINGS
Admissions Selectivity Rating: 84   **Fire Safety Rating:** 60*   **Green Rating:** 70

STUDENTS AND FACULTY
Enrollment: 1,175. **Student Body:** 59% female, 41% male, 5% out-of-state. African American 2%, Asian 1%, Caucasian 94%, Hispanic 2%. **Retention and Graduation:** 80% freshmen return for sophomore year. 60% freshmen graduate within 4 years. **Faculty:** Student/faculty ratio 12:1. 87 full-time faculty, 87% hold PhDs. 100% faculty teach undergrads.

ACADEMICS
Degrees: Bachelor's. **Academic Requirements:** Arts/fine arts, English (including composition), foreign languages, history, humanities, mathematics, philosophy, sciences (biological or physical), social science. **Classes:** Most classes have 10–19 students. Most lab/discussion sections have 10–19 students. **Majors with Highest Enrollment:** Business administration/management, education, kinesiology and exercise science. **Disciplines with Highest Percentage of Degrees Awarded:** Business/marketing 13%, education 11%, social sciences 11%, biological/life sciences 10%, visual and performing arts 10%, psychology 9%. **Special Study Options:** Double major, dual enrollment, honors program, independent study, internships, student-designed major, study abroad, teacher certification program.

FACILITIES
Housing: Coed dorms, women's dorms, apartments for single students, fraternity/sorority housing, academic theme houses. **Special Academic Facilities/Equipment:** Music and arts centers, science lab, planetarium, a DNA synthesizer and sequencer, and a multinuclear magnetic resonance spectrometer. **Computers:** 28% of public computers are PCs, 69% of public computers are Macs, 3% of public computers are UNIX, network access in dorm rooms, network access in dorm lounges, online registration, remote student-access to Web through college's connection.

CAMPUS LIFE
Activities: Choral groups, concert band, dance, drama/theater, jazz band, marching band, music ensembles, musical theater, radio station, student government, student newspaper, symphony orchestra, yearbook. **Organizations:** 93 registered organizations, 22 honor societies, 4 religious organizations. 5 fraternities (17% men join), 5 sororities (30% women join). **Athletics (Intercollegiate):** *Men:* Baseball, basketball, cross-country, diving, football, golf, soccer, swimming, tennis, track/field (outdoor). *Women:* Basketball, cross-country, diving, golf, soccer, softball, swimming, tennis, track/field (outdoor), volleyball. **Environmental Initiatives:** Alma's "green" residence hall, Wright Hall, was completed in January 2005. The modern, 60-bed apartment-style hall features a number of environmentally friendly features, including geothermal heating and cooling, recycled-content ceiling tiles and carpeting, energy-efficient windows, rooftop solar heating panels, energy-efficient showers and washing machines, and a computerized energy monitoring system. Alma College's partnership with the Pine River Superfund Citizen Task Force was selected as a finalist for Michigan's 2007 Carter Partnership Award. Organized by Michigan Campus Compact, the Jimmy and Rosalynn Carter Partnership Award for Campus-Community Collaboration recognizes colleges and community groups that work together in exceptional ways to improve peoples' lives and help college students learn the value of community service. The Task Force works to clean the Pine River. Alma College and the Pine River Superfund Task Force are organizing an international conference that examines the impact of DDT on human health and the environment. The Eugene Kenaga International DDT Conference on Environment and Health will take place March 14, 2008 at Alma College. It will bring together international experts to frame and lead discussions of current knowledge of DDT and other persistent organic pollutants (POPs).

ADMISSIONS
Freshman Academic Profile: 31% in top 10% of high school class, 60% in top 25% of high school class, 90% in top 50% of high school class. 90% from public high schools. SAT Math middle 50% range 520–668. SAT Critical Reading middle 50% range 498–665. SAT Writing middle 50% range 503–623. ACT middle 50% range 21–27. TOEFL required of all international applicants, minimum paper TOEFL 525, minimum computer TOEFL 195. **Basis for**

Candidate Selection: *Very important factors considered include:* Academic GPA, standardized test scores. *Important factors considered include:* Rigor of secondary school record. *Other factors considered include:* Alumni/ae relation, application essay, character/personal qualities, class rank, extracurricular activities, interview, level of applicant's interest, recommendation(s), talent/ability, volunteer work, work experience. **Freshman Admission Requirements:** High school diploma is required, and GED is accepted. *Academic units required:* 4 English, 3 math, 3 science, 3 social studies. *Academic units recommended:* 2 foreign language. **Freshman Admission Statistics:** 1,878 applied, 70% admitted, 24% enrolled. **Transfer Admission Requirements:** High school transcript, college transcript(s), standardized test score, statement of good standing from prior institution(s). Minimum college GPA of 3.0 required. Lowest grade transferable C. **General Admission Information:** Application fee $25. Regular notification is rolling. Nonfall registration accepted. Admission may be deferred for a maximum of 1 year. Credit and/or placement offered for CEEB Advanced Placement tests.

COSTS AND FINANCIAL AID
Annual tuition $24,630. Room and board $8,120. Required fees $220. Average book expense $722. **Required Forms and Deadlines:** FAFSA. **Notification of Awards:** Applicants will be notified of awards on a rolling basis beginning on or about 3/1. **Types of Aid:** *Need-based scholarships/grants:* Pell, SEOG, state scholarships/grants, private scholarships, the school's own gift aid. *Loans:* Direct Subsidized Stafford, Direct Unsubsidized Stafford, Direct PLUS, Federal Perkins, college/university loans from institutional funds, alternative loans. **Student Employment:** Federal Work-Study Program available. Institutional employment available. **Financial Aid Statistics:** 78% freshmen, 77% undergrads receive need-based scholarship or grant aid. 60% freshmen, 64% undergrads receive need-based self-help aid. 99% freshmen, 99% undergrads receive any aid. Highest amount earned per year from on-campus jobs $1,000.

ALVERNIA COLLEGE

400 St. Bernardine Street, Reading, PA 19607
Phone: 610-796-8220 **E-mail:** admissions@alvernia.edu
Fax: 610-796-8336 **Website:** www.alvernia.edu
Financial Aid Phone: 610-796-8356

This private school, affiliated with the Roman Catholic Church, was founded in 1958. It has an 80-acre campus.

RATINGS
Admissions Selectivity Rating: 71   **Fire Safety Rating:** 60*   **Green Rating:** 60*

STUDENTS AND FACULTY
Enrollment: 2,019. **Student Body:** 71% female, 29% male, 14% out-of-state. African American 11%, Caucasian 74%, Hispanic 6%. **Retention and Graduation:** 77% freshmen return for sophomore year. 40% freshmen graduate within 4 years. **Faculty:** Student/faculty ratio 13:1. 74 full-time faculty, 68% hold PhDs. 100% faculty teach undergrads.

ACADEMICS
Degrees: Associate, bachelor's, certificate, doctoral, master's, post-bachelor's certificate, post-master's certificate. **Academic Requirements:** Arts/fine arts; English (including composition); foreign languages; history; humanities; mathematics; philosophy; sciences (biological or physical); social science; theology; human diversity; nutrition, health, and wellness. **Classes:** Most classes have 10–19 students. Most lab/discussion sections have 10–19 students. **Majors with Highest Enrollment:** Criminal justice/law enforcement administration, elementary education and teaching, substance abuse/addiction counseling. **Disciplines with Highest Percentage of Degrees Awarded:** Education 26%, health professions and related sciences 21%, business/marketing 18%, security and protective services 15%, computer and information sciences 3% 3%. **Special Study Options:** Accelerated program, cross-registration, double major, dual enrollment, English as a Second Language (ESL), honors program, independent study, internships, student-designed major, study abroad, teacher certification program.

FACILITIES
Housing: Coed dorms, women's dorms, special housing for disabled students, single-sex suites in townhouses, single-sex floors in dorms. **Computers:** 15% of classrooms are wired, 10% of classrooms are wireless, 100% of public computers are PCs, network access in dorm rooms, network access in dorm lounges, online registration, online administrative functions (other than registration), remote student-access to Web through college's connection.

CAMPUS LIFE
Activities: Choral groups, dance, drama/theater, literary magazine, music

ensembles, student government, student newspaper, yearbook. **Organizations:** 35 registered organizations, 5 honor societies, 5 religious organizations. **Athletics (Intercollegiate):** *Men:* Baseball, basketball, cross-country, golf, lacrosse, soccer, tennis. *Women:* Basketball, cheerleading, cross-country, field hockey, lacrosse, soccer, softball, tennis, volleyball.

ADMISSIONS

Freshman Academic Profile: 8% in top 10% of high school class, 27% in top 25% of high school class, 53% in top 50% of high school class. 74% from public high schools. SAT Math middle 50% range 420–530. SAT Critical Reading middle 50% range 420–520. TOEFL required of all international applicants, minimum paper TOEFL 550, minimum computer TOEFL 213. **Basis for Candidate Selection:** *Very important factors considered include:* Academic GPA, standardized test scores. *Important factors considered include:* Application essay, character/personal qualities, class rank, extracurricular activities, interview, level of applicant's interest, recommendation(s), rigor of secondary school record, talent/ability, volunteer work, work experience. *Other factors considered include:* Religious affiliation/commitment. **Freshman Admission Requirements:** High school diploma is required, and GED is accepted. **Freshman Admission Statistics:** 922 applied, 76% admitted, 41% enrolled. **Transfer Admission Requirements:** High school transcript, college transcript(s), essay or personal statement, minimum college GPA of 2.0 required. Lowest grade transferable C. **General Admission Information:** Application fee $25. Regular notification immediately. Nonfall registration accepted. Admission may be deferred for a maximum of 1 year. Common Application accepted. Credit and/or placement offered for CEEB Advanced Placement tests.

COSTS AND FINANCIAL AID

Annual tuition $20,220. Room and board $8,220. Required fees $202. Average book expense $1,200. **Required Forms and Deadlines:** FAFSA. Financial aid filing deadline 5/1. **Notification of Awards:** Applicants will be notified of awards on a rolling basis beginning on or about 2/10. **Types of Aid:** *Need-based scholarships/grants:* Pell, SEOG, state scholarships/grants, private scholarships. *Loans:* FFEL Subsidized Stafford, FFEL Unsubsidized Stafford, FFEL PLUS. **Financial Aid Statistics:** 84% freshmen, 94% undergrads receive need-based scholarship or grant aid. 80% freshmen, 90% undergrads receive need-based self-help aid. 94% freshmen, 98% undergrads receive any aid. Highest amount earned per year from on-campus jobs $3,886.

See page 1052.

ALVERNO COLLEGE

3400 South 43rd Street, PO Box 343922, Milwaukee, WI 53234-3922
Phone: 414-382-6100 **E-mail:** admissions@alverno.edu **CEEB Code:** 1012
Fax: 414-382-6354 **Website:** www.alverno.edu **ACT Code:** 4558
Financial Aid Phone: 414-382-6046

This private school, affiliated with the Roman Catholic Church, was founded in 1887. It has a 47-acre campus.

RATINGS
Admissions Selectivity Rating: 60*   **Fire Safety Rating:** 62   **Green Rating:** 71

STUDENTS AND FACULTY

Enrollment: 2,123. **Student Body:** 100% female, 2% out-of-state. African American 19%, Asian 5%, Caucasian 64%, Hispanic 11%, Native American 1%. **Retention and Graduation:** 71% freshmen return for sophomore year. 17% freshmen graduate within 4 years. **Faculty:** Student/faculty ratio 12:1. 107 full-time faculty, 90% hold PhDs. 100% faculty teach undergrads.

ACADEMICS

Degrees: Associate, bachelor's, master's, post-bachelor's certificate, post-master's certificate. **Academic Requirements:** Arts/fine arts, computer literacy, English (including composition), humanities, mathematics, sciences (biological or physical), social science, communication and global studies. **Classes:** Most classes have 10–19 students. Most lab/discussion sections have 10–19 students. **Majors with Highest Enrollment:** Education, nursing–registered nurse training (ASN, BSN, MSN, RN), psychology. **Disciplines with Highest Percentage of Degrees Awarded:** Health professions and related sciences 31%, business/marketing 20%, education 11%, communications/journalism 9%, psychology 6%. **Special Study Options:** Double major, independent study, internships, student-designed major, study abroad, teacher certification program, weekend college.

FACILITIES

Housing: Women's dorms. **Special Academic Facilities/Equipment:** Art gallery, career center, fitness center, Reiman Gymnasium, nursing skills lab,

student centered multi-media production facility, diagnostic digital portfolio. **Computers:** 100% of classrooms are wired, 3% of classrooms are wireless, 92% of public computers are PCs, 8% of public computers are Macs, network access in dorm rooms, network access in dorm lounges, online registration, online administrative functions (other than registration), remote student-access to Web through college's connection.

CAMPUS LIFE

Activities: Choral groups, dance, drama/theater, literary magazine, music ensembles, student newspaper. **Organizations:** 23 registered organizations, 3 honor societies, 2 religious organizations. 4 sororities (2% women join). **Athletics (Intercollegiate):** *Women:* Basketball, cross-country, soccer, softball, volleyball. **Environmental Initiatives:** Recycle paper, plastic, cans. When remodeling, Alverno uses energy efficient lighting. In areas changed over from steam to hot water heat.

ADMISSIONS

Freshman Academic Profile: 85% from public high schools. ACT middle 50% range 17–22. TOEFL required of all international applicants, minimum paper TOEFL 520, minimum computer TOEFL 190. **Basis for Candidate Selection:** *Very important factors considered include:* Academic GPA, standardized test scores. *Important factors considered include:* Application essay, class rank, rigor of secondary school record. *Other factors considered include:* Interview, recommendation(s). **Freshman Admission Requirements:** High school diploma is required, and GED is accepted. *Academic units required:* 4 English, 3 math, 3 science, 3 social studies. *Academic units recommended:* 2 foreign language. **Freshman Admission Statistics:** 911 applied, 59% admitted, 53% enrolled. **Transfer Admission Requirements:** High school transcript, college transcript(s), minimum college GPA of 2.0 required. Lowest grade transferable C. **General Admission Information:** Application fee $20. Regular notification is rolling. Nonfall registration accepted. Admission may be deferred for a maximum of 1 year. Credit and/or placement offered for CEEB Advanced Placement tests.

COSTS AND FINANCIAL AID

Average book expense $1,050. **Required Forms and Deadlines:** FAFSA, institution's own financial aid form, Business/Farm Supplement, tax forms if chosen for verification. Financial aid filing deadline 4/15. **Notification of Awards:** Applicants will be notified of awards on a rolling basis beginning on or about 4/15. **Types of Aid:** *Need-based scholarships/grants:* Pell, SEOG, state scholarships/grants, private scholarships, the school's own gift aid, Federal Nursing Scholarships, transfer scholarships/referral scholarships. *Loans:* FFEL Subsidized Stafford, FFEL Unsubsidized Stafford, FFEL PLUS, Federal Perkins. **Student Employment:** Federal Work-Study Program available. Institutional employment available. Off-campus job opportunities are good. **Financial Aid Statistics:** 96% freshmen, 87% undergrads receive any aid. Highest amount earned per year from on-campus jobs $2,500.

AMERICAN ACADEMY FOR DRAMATIC ARTS—EAST

120 Madison Avenue, New York, NY 10016
Phone: 212-686-0620 **E-mail:** admissions-ny@aada.org
Fax: 212-696-1284 **Website:** www.aada.org **Financial Aid Phone:** 212-686-0250

This private school was founded in 1884.

RATINGS
Admissions Selectivity Rating: 60*   **Fire Safety Rating:** 60*   **Green Rating:** 60*

STUDENTS AND FACULTY
Faculty: Student/faculty ratio 15:1. 12 full-time faculty.

ACADEMICS
Degrees: Associate, terminal. **Classes:** Most classes have 10–19 students.

FACILITIES
Housing: All Academy students are responsible for securing own housing arrangements. Students are provided with information pertaining to living accommodations. Suggested residences are not owned or maintained by the Academy. **Computers:** Online administrative functions (other than registration).

ADMISSIONS
Freshman Academic Profile: 26% from public high schools. **Basis for Candidate Selection:** *Very important factors considered include:* Interview, talent/ability. *Important factors considered include:* Recommendation(s). *Other factors considered include:* Alumni/ae relation, application essay, character/

personal qualities, rigor of secondary school record, work experience. **Freshman Admission Requirements:** High school diploma is required, and GED is accepted. **Freshman Admission Statistics:** 458 applied. **General Admission Information:** Application fee $50. Nonfall registration accepted. Admission may be deferred for a maximum of 1 year. Common Application not accepted.

COSTS AND FINANCIAL AID

Annual tuition $12,200. Required fees $400. Average book expense $400. **Required Forms and Deadlines:** FAFSA. **Types of Aid:** *Need-based scholarships/grants:* Pell, SEOG, state scholarships/grants, private scholarships. *Loans:* FFEL Subsidized Stafford, FFEL Unsubsidized Stafford, FFEL PLUS. **Student Employment:** Federal Work-Study Program available. Institutional employment available. Off-campus job opportunities are good. **Financial Aid Statistics:** 28% freshmen, 41% undergrads receive need-based scholarship or grant aid. 44% freshmen, 41% undergrads receive need-based self-help aid. Highest amount earned per year from on-campus jobs $2,340.

AMERICAN ACADEMY FOR DRAMATIC ARTS— WEST

1336 North LaBrea Avenue, Hollywood, CA 90028
Phone: 800-222-2867 **E-mail:** admissions-ca@aada.org
Fax: 626-229-9977 **Website:** www.aada.org
Financial Aid Phone: 800-222-2867

This private school was founded in 1884. It has a 2-acre campus.

RATINGS
Admissions Selectivity Rating: 60*   **Fire Safety Rating:** 60*   **Green Rating:** 60*

STUDENTS AND FACULTY
Enrollment: 104. **Student Body:** 53% female, 47% male, 4% international. African American 4%, Caucasian 24%, Hispanic 6%. **Faculty:** Student/faculty ratio 12:1.

ACADEMICS
Degrees: Associate, terminal. **Classes:** Most classes have 10–19 students. Most lab/discussion sections have 10–19 students.

ADMISSIONS
Basis for Candidate Selection: *Very important factors considered include:* Interview, talent/ability. *Important factors considered include:* Recommendation(s). *Other factors considered include:* Alumni/ae relation, application essay, character/personal qualities, extracurricular activities, rigor of secondary school record, work experience. **Freshman Admission Requirements:** High school diploma is required, and GED is accepted. **Freshman Admission Statistics:** 230 applied, 79% admitted, 57% enrolled. **Transfer Admission Requirements:** High school transcript, college transcript(s), essay or personal statement, interview. **Admission Information:** Application fee $50. Regular notification 4 weeks after audition. Nonfall registration accepted. Admission may be deferred for a maximum of 1 year. Common Application not accepted.

COSTS AND FINANCIAL AID
Annual tuition $11,700. **Required Forms and Deadlines:** FAFSA. **Student Employment:** Federal Work-Study Program available. Institutional employment available. Off-campus job opportunities are good. **Financial Aid Statistics:** 9% freshmen, 45% undergrads receive need-based scholarship or grant aid. 62% freshmen, 52% undergrads receive need-based self-help aid. Highest amount earned per year from on-campus jobs $1,510.

AMERICAN CONSERVATORY OF MUSIC

252 Wildwood Road, Hammond, IN 46324
Phone: 219-931-6000 **E-mail:** registrar@americanconservatory.edu
Fax: 219-931-6089 **Website:** www.americanconservatory.edu

This private school, affiliated with the Greek Orthodox Church, was founded in 1886.

RATINGS
Admissions Selectivity Rating: 60*   **Fire Safety Rating:** 60*   **Green Rating:** 60*

STUDENTS AND FACULTY
Faculty: Student/faculty ratio 1:1.

ACADEMICS
Degrees: Associate, bachelor's, certificate, diploma, doctoral, first professional certificate, master's. **Academic Requirements:** Arts/fine arts, computer literacy, English (including composition), history, philosophy, acoustics, music literature. Use of Finale and similar software. **Majors with Highest Enrollment:** Conducting, music performance, music theory and composition. **Disciplines with Highest Percentage of Degrees Awarded:** Visual and performing arts 100%. **Special Study Options:** Accelerated program, distance learning, double major, English as a Second Language (ESL).

FACILITIES
Computers: 20% of public computers are PCs, 50% of public computers are Macs, 30% of public computers are UNIX. undergraduates are required to own a computer.

CAMPUS LIFE
Activities: Choral groups, jazz band, music ensembles, opera, symphony orchestra.

ADMISSIONS
Transfer Admission Requirements: High school transcript, college transcript(s), essay or personal statement, interview, statement of good standing from prior institution(s). Minimum college GPA of 2.0 required. Lowest grade transferable C.

COSTS AND FINANCIAL AID
Average book expense $2,400.

AMERICAN INDIAN COLLEGE OF THE ASSEMBLIES OF GOD, INC.

10020 North 15th Avenue, Phoenix, AZ 85021
Phone: 602-944-3335 **E-mail:** aicadm@aicag.edu
Fax: 602-943-8299 **Website:** www.aicag.edu **ACT Code:** 6005
Financial Aid Phone: 602-944-3335

This private school, affiliated with the Assemblies of God Church, was founded in 1957. It has a 10-acre campus.

RATINGS
Admissions Selectivity Rating: 60*   **Fire Safety Rating:** 60*   **Green Rating:** 60*

STUDENTS AND FACULTY
Enrollment: 70. **Student Body:** 44% female, 56% male, 2% out-of-state, 1% international (2 countries represented). African American 4%, Asian 6%, Caucasian 14%, Hispanic 6%, Native American 69%. **Faculty:** Student/faculty ratio 5:1. 8 full-time faculty, 88% hold PhDs. 100% faculty teach undergrads.

ACADEMICS
Degrees: Associate, bachelor's. **Academic Requirements:** Arts/fine arts, computer literacy, English (including composition), history, mathematics, sciences (biological or physical), social science, theology, Bible, behavioral science, religion. **Classes:** Most classes have fewer than 10 students. Most lab/discussion sections have fewer than 10 students. **Majors with Highest Enrollment:** Bible/biblical studies, pastoral studies/counseling, religion/religious studies. **Disciplines with Highest Percentage of Degrees Awarded:** Education 33%. **Special Study Options:** Double major.

FACILITIES
Housing: Men's dorms, women's dorms, special housing for disabled students.

CAMPUS LIFE
Activities: Student government, yearbook.

ADMISSIONS
Freshman Academic Profile: TOEFL required of all international applicants, minimum paper TOEFL 500, minimum computer TOEFL 150. **Basis for Candidate Selection:** *Very important factors considered include:* Character/personal qualities, class rank, recommendation(s), religious affiliation/commitment, rigor of secondary school record, standardized test scores. *Important factors considered include:* Application essay. *Other factors considered include:* Extracurricular activities, interview, talent/ability, volunteer work, work experience. **Freshman Admission Requirements:** High school diploma is required, and GED is accepted. **Freshman Admission Statistics:** 18 applied, 44% admitted. **Transfer Admission Requirements:** High school transcript, college transcript(s), standardized test score, minimum college GPA

of 2.0 required. Lowest grade transferable C. **General Admission Information:** Nonfall registration accepted. Common Application not accepted.

COSTS AND FINANCIAL AID
Annual tuition $4,950. Room & board $3,850. Required fees $605. Average book expense $500. **Required Forms and Deadlines:** FAFSA, institution's own financial aid form, CSS/Financial Aid PROFILE, state aid form, Noncustodial PROFILE, Business/Farm Supplement. **Types of Aid:** *Need-based scholarships/grants:* Pell, SEOG, state scholarships/grants, private scholarships, the school's own gift aid. *Loans:* FFEL Subsidized Stafford, FFEL Unsubsidized Stafford, FFEL PLUS. **Student Employment:** Off-campus job opportunities are fair. **Financial Aid Statistics:** 46% undergrads receive any aid.

AMERICAN INTERCONTINENTAL UNIVERSITY

5550 Prarie Stone Parkway, Suite 400, Hoffman Estates, IL 60192
Phone: 877-701-3800 **E-mail:** info@aiuonline.edu
Fax: 877-701-3800 **Website:** www.aiuonline.edu

This proprietary school was founded in 1973.

RATINGS
Admissions Selectivity Rating: 60*   Fire Safety Rating: 60*   Green Rating: 60*

STUDENTS AND FACULTY
Enrollment: 981. **Student Body:** 35% out-of-state, 27% international (120 countries represented). African American 27%, Asian 1%, Caucasian 33%, Hispanic 2%. **Faculty:** 100% faculty teach undergrads.

ACADEMICS
Degrees: Associate, bachelor's, master's. **Academic Requirements:** Arts/fine arts, computer literacy, English (including composition), history, humanities, mathematics, sciences (biological or physical). **Special Study Options:** Accelerated program, distance learning, double major, English as a Second Language (ESL), independent study, internships, study abroad.

FACILITIES
Housing: Coed dorms. **Computers:** Undergraduates are required to own a computer.

CAMPUS LIFE
Activities: Student government.

ADMISSIONS
Freshman Academic Profile: TOEFL required of all international applicants, minimum paper TOEFL 500. **Basis for Candidate Selection:** *Very important factors considered include:* Alumni/ae relation, application essay, character/personal qualities, extracurricular activities, interview, recommendation(s), rigor of secondary school record, talent/ability, volunteer work, work experience. *Important factors considered include:* Racial/ethnic status. *Other factors considered include:* Standardized test scores. **Freshman Admission Requirements:** High school diploma is required, and GED is accepted. **Transfer Admission Requirements:** High school transcript, college transcript(s), essay or personal statement, interview, minimum college GPA of 2.0 required. Lowest grade transferable 2. **General Admission Information:** Application fee $35. Regular application deadline is rolling. Regular notification is rolling. Nonfall registration accepted. Admission may be deferred for a maximum of 1 year.

COSTS AND FINANCIAL AID
Annual tuition $10,868. Room $4,253. Average book expense $1,000. **Financial Aid Statistics:** 54% freshmen, 48% undergrads receive need-based scholarship or grant aid. 54% freshmen, 48% undergrads receive need-based self-help aid.

AMERICAN INTERNATIONAL COLLEGE

1000 State Street, Springfield, MA 01109-3184
Phone: 413-205-3201 **E-mail:** inquiry@aic.edu **CEEB Code:** 3002
Fax: 413-205-3051 **Website:** www.aic.edu **ACT Code:** 1772
Financial Aid Phone: 413-205-3259

This private school was founded in 1885. It has a 58-acre campus.

RATINGS
Admissions Selectivity Rating: 60*   Fire Safety Rating: 60*   Green Rating: 60*

STUDENTS AND FACULTY
Enrollment: 1,227. **Student Body:** 53% female, 47% male, 53% out-of-state, 4% international. African American 26%, Asian 3%, Caucasian 55%, Hispanic 8%. **Retention and Graduation:** 55% freshmen return for sophomore year. 20% grads go on to further study within 1 year. 9% grads pursue arts and sciences degrees. 15% grads pursue business degrees. 5% grads pursue law degrees. 2% grads pursue medical degrees. **Faculty:** Student/faculty ratio 12:1. 70 full-time faculty. 100% faculty teach undergrads.

ACADEMICS
Degrees: Associate, bachelor's, certificate, doctoral, master's, post-master's certificate, terminal. **Academic Requirements:** Arts/fine arts, computer literacy, English (including composition), humanities, mathematics, sciences (biological or physical), social science. All majors have a general education requirement comprised of a liberal arts core. **Classes:** Most classes have fewer than 10 students. Most lab/discussion sections have fewer than 10 students. **Disciplines with Highest Percentage of Degrees Awarded:** Business/marketing 22%, health professions and related sciences 20%, social sciences 12%, computer and information sciences 8%, communication technologies 7%. **Special Study Options:** Cross-registration, double major, English as a Second Language (ESL), independent study, internships, liberal arts/career combination, study abroad, teacher certification program, off-campus study in Washington, DC, undergrads may take grad level courses.

FACILITIES
Housing: Coed dorms, women's dorms. **Special Academic Facilities/Equipment:** Centers for child development, cultural arts, and human technology.

CAMPUS LIFE
Activities: Choral groups, dance, drama/theater, literary magazine, music ensembles, radio station, student government, student newspaper, yearbook. **Organizations:** 45 registered organizations, 5 honor societies, 3 religious organizations. **Athletics (Intercollegiate):** *Men:* Baseball, basketball, football, golf, ice hockey, lacrosse, soccer, tennis, wrestling. *Women:* Basketball, softball, tennis, volleyball.

ADMISSIONS
Freshman Academic Profile: 15% in top 10% of high school class, 25% in top 25% of high school class, 70% in top 50% of high school class. 79% from public high schools. SAT Math middle 50% range 420–570. SAT Critical Reading middle 50% range 410–560. ACT middle 50% range 17–23. TOEFL required of all international applicants, minimum paper TOEFL 500, minimum computer TOEFL 173. **Basis for Candidate Selection:** *Very important factors considered include:* Rigor of secondary school record. *Important factors considered include:* Alumni/ae relation, character/personal qualities, class rank, interview, standardized test scores. *Other factors considered include:* Application essay, extracurricular activities, recommendation(s), talent/ability, volunteer work, work experience. **Freshman Admission Requirements:** High school diploma is required, and GED is accepted. *Academic units required:* 4 English, 2 math, 2 science (1 science lab), 1 social studies, 1 history, 5 academic electives. *Academic units recommended:* 4 English, 3 math, 2 science (1 science lab), 2 foreign language, 1 social studies, 1 history, 3 academic electives. **Freshman Admission Statistics:** 1,274 applied, 85% admitted, 27% enrolled. **Transfer Admission Requirements:** High school transcript, college transcript(s), minimum college GPA of 2.0 required. Lowest grade transferable C. **General Admission Information:** Application fee $20. Regular notification is rolling. Nonfall registration accepted. Admission may be deferred for a maximum of 1 year. Common Application accepted. Credit and/or placement offered for CEEB Advanced Placement tests.

COSTS AND FINANCIAL AID
Annual tuition $18,000. Room & board $8,390. Average book expense $800. **Required Forms and Deadlines:** FAFSA. Financial aid filing deadline 5/1. **Notification of Awards:** Applicants will be notified of awards on a rolling basis beginning on or about 3/15. **Types of Aid:** *Need-based scholarships/grants:*

Pell, SEOG, state scholarships/grants, private scholarships, the school's own gift aid, Federal Nursing Scholarships. *Loans:* Direct Subsidized Stafford, Direct Unsubsidized Stafford, Direct PLUS, FFEL Subsidized Stafford, FFEL Unsubsidized Stafford, FFEL PLUS, Federal Perkins, Federal Nursing, college/university loans from institutional funds. **Student Employment:** Federal Work-Study Program available. Institutional employment available. Off-campus job opportunities are good. **Financial Aid Statistics:** 84% freshmen, 90% undergrads receive need-based scholarship or grant aid. 84% freshmen, 90% undergrads receive need-based self-help aid. 39 freshmen, 140 undergrads receive athletic scholarships. 85% freshmen, 85% undergrads receive any aid. Highest amount earned per year from on-campus jobs $2,200.

See page 1054.

AMERICAN PUBLIC UNIVERSITY SYSTEM

111 West Congress Street, Charles Town, WV 25414
Phone: 877-468-6268 **E-mail:** Info@apus.edu
Fax: 304-724-3788 **Website:** www.apus.edu
Financial Aid Phone: 866-487-3692/3690

This private school was founded in 1991.

RATINGS
Admissions Selectivity Rating: 60*   **Fire Safety Rating:** 60*   **Green Rating:** 60*

STUDENTS AND FACULTY
Enrollment: 421. **Student Body:** 32% female, 68% male. **Retention and Graduation:** 84% freshmen return for sophomore year. **Faculty:** 79 full-time faculty.

ACADEMICS
Degrees: Associate, bachelor's, certificate, master's, post-bachelor's certificate, post-master's certificate. **Academic Requirements:** Computer literacy, English (including composition), history, humanities, mathematics, sciences (biological or physical), social science. **Majors with Highest Enrollment:** Business administration/management, general studies, military technologies. **Special Study Options:** Distance learning, independent study.

FACILITIES
Computers: Online registration, online administrative functions (other than registration).

ADMISSIONS
Freshman Admission Requirements: High school diploma is required, and GED is accepted. **Freshman Admission Statistics:** 7,204 applied, 89% admitted. **Transfer Admission Requirements:** High school transcript, college transcript(s). Lowest grade transferable C. **General Admission Information:** Regular notification accepted immediately. Nonfall registration accepted. Admission may be deferred for a maximum of 1 year.

COSTS AND FINANCIAL AID
Annual tuition $3,000. **Types of Aid:** *Need-based scholarships/grants:* Undergraduate students using military tuition dollars are eligible to receive their textbooks free through a university grant.

AMERICAN UNIVERSITY

4400 Massachusetts Avenue, Northwest, Washington, DC 20016-8001
Phone: 202-885-6000 **E-mail:** admissions@american.edu **CEEB Code:** 5007
Fax: 202-885-1025 **Website:** www.american.edu **ACT Code:** 0648
Financial Aid Phone: 202-885-6100

This private school, affiliated with the Methodist Church, was founded in 1893. It has an 84-acre campus.

RATINGS
Admissions Selectivity Rating: 93   **Fire Safety Rating:** 94   **Green Rating:** 75

STUDENTS AND FACULTY
Enrollment: 5,788. **Student Body:** 62% female, 38% male, 75% out-of-state, 6% international (102 countries represented). African American 6%, Asian 5%, Caucasian 63%, Hispanic 5%. **Retention and Graduation:** 89% freshmen return for sophomore year. 63% freshmen graduate within 4 years. 73% grads go on to further study within 1 year. **Faculty:** Student/faculty ratio 14:1. 513 full-time faculty, 96% hold PhDs. 81% faculty teach undergrads.

ACADEMICS
Degrees: Associate, bachelor's, certificate, doctoral, first professional, master's, post-bachelor's certificate. **Academic Requirements:** Arts/fine arts, English (including composition), humanities, mathematics, sciences (biological or physical), social science. AU's general education program core curriculum requires course work in 5 curricular areas: The creative arts, traditions that shape the Western world, global and multicultural perspectives, social institutions and behavior, and the natural sciences. **Classes:** Most classes have 10–19 students. **Majors with Highest Enrollment:** Business administration/management, international relations and affairs, mass communications/media studies. **Disciplines with Highest Percentage of Degrees Awarded:** Social sciences 35%, business/marketing 18%, communication technologies 13%, visual and performing arts 7%, psychology 5%. **Special Study Options:** Accelerated program, cooperative education program, cross-registration, double major, exchange student program (domestic), honors program, independent study, internships, student-designed major, study abroad, teacher certification program, weekend college. Summer programs include pre-college programs in leadership, college writing skills and the media (script writing, photography, video production, news writing), and a swim school. Online courses offered in communication and international relations research, contemporary journalism, special education, global justice and human rights, justice and terrorism, and human rights and foreign policy. College-level options include institutes in art and craft of lobbying; campaign management; Civil War; discovering North America; human rights in the 21st century; nuclear studies; peace, conflict resolution, and development; Washington semester summer internship program, film and video institute; TESOL institute; and summer study abroad programs in Cuba (politics), Europe (international trade, security, and human rights); Southeast Asia (globalization, and Japan (nuclear studies) and summer internship opportunities in Brussels, London, Madrid, Monterrey (Mexico), Santiago, South Africa, Berlin/Prague, Prague (photography); Washington Internships for Native Students (WINS).

FACILITIES
Housing: Coed dorms, apartments for married students, apartments for single students, special housing for international students, honors floors, community service floor, intercultural/international hall available. Housing for disabled students handled individually. **Special Academic Facilities/Equipment:** Student-run radio and TV facilities, Watkins Art Gallery, Katzen Arts Center, experimental theater, Greenberg Theatre, Friedheim Journalism Center, William I. Jacobs Fitness Center, language resource center, multimedia center, audiotechnology lab, UNIX and Oracle labs, Kay Spiritual Life Center (interdenominational). **Computers:** 100% of classrooms are wired, 100% of classrooms are wireless, 75% of public computers are PCs, 25% of public computers are Macs, network access in dorm rooms, network access in dorm lounges, online registration, online administrative functions (other than registration), support for handheld computing, remote student-access to Web through college's connection.

CAMPUS LIFE
Activities: Choral groups, dance, drama/theater, jazz band, literary magazine, music ensembles, musical theater, opera, pep band, radio station, student government, student newspaper, student-run film society, symphony orchestra, television station, yearbook. **Organizations:** 128 registered organizations, 15 honor societies, 17 religious organizations. 11 fraternities (14% men join), 11 sororities (16% women join). **Athletics (Intercollegiate):** *Men:* Basketball, cross-country, diving, soccer, swimming, track/field (indoor), track/field (outdoor), wrestling. *Women:* Basketball, cross-country, diving, field hockey, lacrosse, soccer, swimming, track/field (indoor), track/field (outdoor), volleyball.

ADMISSIONS
Freshman Academic Profile: 47% in top 10% of high school class, 82% in top 25% of high school class, 98% in top 50% of high school class. SAT Math middle 50% range 580–670. SAT Critical Reading middle 50% range 590–690. SAT Writing middle 50% range 580–690. ACT middle 50% range 25–30. TOEFL required of all international applicants, minimum paper TOEFL 590, minimum computer TOEFL 213. **Basis for Candidate Selection:** *Very important factors considered include:* Rigor of secondary school record, standardized test scores. *Important factors considered include:* Academic GPA, application essay, class rank, extracurricular activities, recommendation(s), volunteer work. *Other factors considered include:* Alumni/ae relation, character/personal qualities, first generation, geographical residence, interview, level of applicant's interest, racial/ethnic status, talent/ability, work experience. **Freshman Admission Requirements:** High school diploma is required, and GED is accepted. *Academic units*

required: 4 English, 3 math, 2 science (2 science labs), 2 foreign language, 2 social studies, 3 academic electives. *Academic units recommended:* 4 English, 4 math, 4 science, 3 foreign language, 4 social studies, 4 academic electives. **Freshman Admission Statistics:** 13,583 applied, 51% admitted, 18% enrolled. **Transfer Admission Requirements:** College transcript(s), essay or personal statement, minimum college GPA of 2.0 required. Lowest grade transferable C. **General Admission Information:** Application fee $45. Early decision application deadline 11/15. Regular application deadline 1/15. Regular notification 4/1. Nonfall registration accepted. Admission may be deferred for a maximum of 1 year. Credit and/or placement offered for CEEB Advanced Placement tests.

COSTS AND FINANCIAL AID

Annual tuition $32,816. Room and board $12,418. Required fees $467. Average book expense $600. **Required Forms and Deadlines:** FAFSA, institution's own financial aid form. Financial aid filing deadline 2/15. **Notification of Awards:** Applicants will be notified of awards on or about 4/1. **Types of Aid:** *Need-based scholarships/grants:* Pell, SEOG, state scholarships/grants, private scholarships, the school's own gift aid, academic merit scholarships: presidential scholarships, dean's scholarships, leadership scholarships, Phi Theta Kappa scholarships (transfers only), tuition exchange. *Loans:* Direct Subsidized Stafford, Direct Unsubsidized Stafford, Direct PLUS, FFEL PLUS, Federal Perkins, college/university loans from institutional funds. **Financial Aid Statistics:** 39% freshmen, 5% undergrads receive need-based scholarship or grant aid. 45% freshmen, 6% undergrads receive need-based self-help aid. 44 freshmen, 173 undergrads receive athletic scholarships. 82% freshmen, 69% undergrads receive any aid.

See page 1056.

AMERICAN UNIVERSITY IN DUBAI

Sheikh Zayed Road, PO Box 28282, Dubai, United Arab Emirates
Phone: 00971-4-3999000 ext. 170/171/172/173 **E-mail:** admissions@aud.edu
Fax: 00971-4-3998899 **Website:** www.aud.edu

This is a proprietary school.

RATINGS
Admissions Selectivity Rating: 60*   **Fire Safety Rating:** 60*   **Green Rating:** 60*

STUDENTS AND FACULTY
Enrollment: 1,967. **Student Body:** 47% female, 53% male. **Retention and Graduation:** 74% freshmen return for sophomore year. 7% freshmen graduate within 4 years. **Faculty:** Student/faculty ratio 18:1. 76 full-time faculty.

ACADEMICS
Degrees: Bachelor's, master's. **Academic Requirements:** Computer literacy, English (including composition), humanities, mathematics, sciences (biological or physical), social science. **Classes:** Most classes have 20–29 students. Most lab/discussion sections have fewer than 10 students. **Disciplines with Highest Percentage of Degrees Awarded:** Business/marketing 71%, computer and information sciences 47%, visual and performing arts 31%, engineering 17%. **Special Study Options:** Double major, English as a Second Language (ESL), internships, study abroad.

FACILITIES
Housing: Men's dorms, women's dorms, special housing for disabled students.

CAMPUS LIFE
Activities: Dance, drama/theater, student government, student newspaper, yearbook.

ADMISSIONS
Basis for Candidate Selection: *Very important factors considered include:* Academic GPA, character/personal qualities, recommendation(s), rigor of secondary school record, standardized test scores. *Important factors considered include:* Alumni/ae relation, application essay, class rank, interview, level of applicant's interest. *Other factors considered include:* Extracurricular activities, first generation, talent/ability. **Freshman Admission Requirements:** High school diploma is required, and GED is not accepted. **Freshman Admission Statistics:** 976 applied, 31% admitted, 100% enrolled. **Transfer Admission Requirements:** High school transcript, college transcript(s), essay or personal statement, standardized test score, statement of good standing from prior institution(s). Minimum college GPA of 2.0 required. Lowest grade transferable C. **General Admission Information:** Application fee $50. Regular application deadline 8/20. Regular notification is rolling. Nonfall registration accepted.

COSTS AND FINANCIAL AID
Room $3,870. Required fees $55. Average book expense $600.

THE AMERICAN UNIVERSITY OF PARIS

6, rue du Colonel Combes, Paris, 75007 France
Phone: 33-1-40-62-07-20 **E-mail:** admissions@aup.edu
Fax: 33-1-47-05-34-32 **Website:** www.aup.edu

This private school was founded in 1962.

RATINGS
Admissions Selectivity Rating: 60*   **Fire Safety Rating:** 60*   **Green Rating:** 60*

STUDENTS AND FACULTY
Faculty: Student/faculty ratio 13:1. 51 full-time faculty, 73% hold PhDs. 100% faculty teach undergrads.

ACADEMICS
Degrees: Bachelor's, master's. **Academic Requirements:** English (including composition), foreign languages, humanities, sciences (biological or physical). **Majors with Highest Enrollment:** Business administration/management, English language and literature/letters, international relations and affairs. **Special Study Options:** Double major, exchange student program (domestic), independent study, internships, study abroad.

FACILITIES
Computers: 80% of public computers are PCs, 20% of public computers are Macs, online administrative functions (other than registration), remote student-access to Web through college's connection.

CAMPUS LIFE
Activities: Drama/theater, literary magazine, musical theater, student government, student newspaper, yearbook. **Organizations:** 20 registered organizations, 4 honor societies. **Athletics (Intercollegiate):** *Men:* Basketball, football, rugby, soccer, swimming, volleyball. *Women:* Basketball, football, soccer, swimming, volleyball.

ADMISSIONS
Freshman Academic Profile: SAT Math middle 50% range 520–640. SAT Critical Reading middle 50% range 550–660. TOEFL required of all international applicants, minimum computer TOEFL 600, minimum computer TOEFL 250. **Basis for Candidate Selection:** *Very important factors considered include:* Class rank, rigor of secondary school record. *Important factors considered include:* Application essay, character/personal qualities, extracurricular activities, recommendation(s), standardized test scores. *Other factors considered include:* Alumni/ae relation, interview, talent/ability, volunteer work, work experience. **Freshman Admission Requirements:** High school diploma is required, and GED is accepted. *Academic units recommended:* 4 English, 2 math, 2 science (1 science lab), 2 foreign language, 2 social studies, 2 history. **Freshman Admission Statistics:** 482 applied, 62% admitted, 55% enrolled. **Transfer Admission Requirements:** College transcript(s), essay or personal statement, statement of good standing from prior institution(s). Minimum college GPA of 3.0 required. Lowest grade transferable C. **General Admission Information:** Application fee $50. Regular notification 2–3 weeks after application is completed. Non-fall registration accepted. Admission may be deferred for a maximum of 1 year. Common Application not accepted. Credit and/or placement offered for CEEB Advanced Placement tests.

COSTS AND FINANCIAL AID
Room & board $10,000. Required fees $1,516. Average book expense $1,200. **Required Forms and Deadlines:** FAFSA, institution's own financial aid form **Types of Aid:** *Need-based scholarships/grants:* the school's own gift aid. *Loans:* FFEL Subsidized Stafford, FFEL Unsubsidized Stafford, FFEL PLUS. **Student Employment:** Off-campus job opportunities are fair. **Financial Aid Statistics:** Highest amount earned per year from on-campus jobs $1,600.

THE AMERICAN UNIVERSITY OF PARIS (CO)

US Admissions Office, 950 South Cherry Street Suite 210, Denver, CO 80246
Phone: 303-757-6333 **E-mail:** usoffice@aup.edu **CEEB Code:** 0866
Fax: 303-757-6444 **Website:** www.aup.edu **ACT Code:** 5295
Financial Aid Phone: 001-40620720

This private school was founded in 1962.

RATINGS
Admissions Selectivity Rating: 60*   **Fire Safety Rating:** 60*   **Green Rating:** 60*

STUDENTS AND FACULTY

Enrollment: 925. **Student Body:** 67% female, 33% male. **Retention and Graduation:** 64% freshmen return for sophomore year. 32% freshmen graduate within 4 years. **Faculty:** Student/faculty ratio 12:1. 56 full-time faculty, 80% hold PhDs. 100% faculty teach undergrads.

ACADEMICS

Degrees: Bachelor's, master's. **Academic Requirements:** English (including composition), foreign languages, humanities, mathematics, sciences (biological or physical), social science. **Classes:** Most classes have 10–19 students. Most lab/discussion sections have 10–19 students. **Majors with Highest Enrollment:** Business administration/management, international relations and affairs. **Disciplines with Highest Percentage of Degrees Awarded:** Business/marketing 36%, social sciences 25%, communications/journalism 24%, history 4%, English 3%. **Special Study Options:** Double major, exchange student program (domestic), independent study, internships, study abroad.

FACILITIES

Housing: Students are housed in independent rooms or with French families. **Computers:** 100% of classrooms are wireless, 66% of public computers are PCs, 33% of public computers are Macs, online administrative functions (other than registration), remote student-access to Web through college's connection.

CAMPUS LIFE

Activities: Drama/theater, literary magazine, musical theater, student government, student newspaper, yearbook. **Organizations:** 20 registered organizations. **Athletics (Intercollegiate):** *Men:* Basketball, football, rugby, soccer, swimming, volleyball. *Women:* Basketball, football, soccer, swimming, volleyball.

ADMISSIONS

Freshman Academic Profile: SAT Math middle 50% range 520–640. SAT Critical Reading middle 50% range 550–660. TOEFL required of all international applicants, minimum paper TOEFL 600, minimum computer TOEFL 250. **Basis for Candidate Selection:** *Very important factors considered include:* Application essay, class rank, recommendation(s), rigor of secondary school record. *Important factors considered include:* Academic GPA, character/personal qualities, extracurricular activities, level of applicant's interest, standardized test scores. *Other factors considered include:* Alumni/ae relation, interview, talent/ability, volunteer work, work experience. **Freshman Admission Requirements:** High school diploma is required, and GED is accepted. *Academic units recommended:* 4 English, 3 math, 2 science (1 science lab), 3 foreign language, 3 social studies, 2 history. **Freshman Admission Statistics:** 541 applied, 71% admitted, 41% enrolled. **Transfer Admission Requirements:** College transcript(s), essay or personal statement, statement of good standing from prior institution(s). Minimum college GPA of 3.0 required. Lowest grade transferable C. **General Admission Information:** Application fee $50. Regular notification approximately 3 weeks after application is completed. Non-fall registration accepted. Admission may be deferred for a maximum of 1 year. Common Application not accepted. Credit and/or placement offered for CEEB Advanced Placement tests.

COSTS AND FINANCIAL AID

Average book expense $1,200. **Required Forms and Deadlines:** FAFSA, institution's own financial aid form. **Types of Aid:** *Need-based scholarships/grants:* the school's own gift aid. *Loans:* FFEL Subsidized Stafford, FFEL Unsubsidized Stafford, FFEL PLUS. **Financial Aid Statistics:** 37% freshmen, 33% undergrads receive need-based scholarship or grant aid. 12% freshmen, 10% undergrads receive need-based self-help aid. Highest amount earned per year from on-campus jobs $2,500.

AMERICAN UNIVERSITY OF PUERTO RICO

PO Box 2037, Bayamon, PR 00960-2037
Phone: 787-740-6410 **E-mail:** mcruz@aupr.edu
Fax: 787-785-7377 **Website:** www.aupr.edu
Financial Aid Phone: 787-620-2040

This private school was founded in 1963.

RATINGS

Admissions Selectivity Rating: 60*   **Fire Safety Rating:** 60*   **Green Rating:** 60*

STUDENTS AND FACULTY

Enrollment: 4,060. **Student Body:** 59% female, 41% male. Hispanic 100%.

ACADEMICS

Degrees: Associate, bachelor's, master's. **Academic Requirements:** English (including composition), history, humanities, mathematics, sciences (biological

---

or physical), social science. **Special Study Options:** Cooperative education program, distance learning, English as a Second Language (ESL), honors program, independent study, liberal arts/career combination, student-designed major.

CAMPUS LIFE

Activities: Dance, drama/theater, literary magazine. **Athletics (Intercollegiate):** *Men:* Baseball, basketball, soccer, tennis, volleyball. *Women:* Baseball, basketball, soccer, tennis, volleyball.

ADMISSIONS

Freshman Academic Profile: 66% from public high schools. **Basis for Candidate Selection:** *Very important factors considered include:* Rigor of secondary school record, standardized test scores. *Other factors considered include:* Character/personal qualities, interview, talent/ability. **Freshman Admission Requirements:** High school diploma is required, and GED is accepted. **Freshman Admission Statistics:** 1,131 applied, 100% admitted, 71% enrolled. **General Admission Information:** Application fee $15. Nonfall registration accepted. Common Application not accepted.

COSTS AND FINANCIAL AID

Annual tuition $1,740. Required fees $160. Average book expense $160. **Types of Aid:** *Need-based scholarships/grants:* Pell, SEOG, state scholarships/grants. *Loans:* Direct Subsidized Stafford, state loans. **Student Employment:** Federal Work-Study Program available. Off-campus job opportunities are good. **Financial Aid Statistics:** 87% freshmen, 85% undergrads receive need-based scholarship or grant aid. 80% freshmen, 46% undergrads receive need-based self-help aid. 12 freshmen, 108 undergrads receive athletic scholarships.

AMHERST COLLEGE

Campus Box 2231, PO Box 5000, Amherst, MA 01002
Phone: 413-542-2328 **E-mail:** admission@amherst.edu **CEEB Code:** 3003
Fax: 413-542-2040 **Website:** www.amherst.edu **ACT Code:** 1774
Financial Aid Phone: 413-542-2296

This private school was founded in 1821. It has a 1,000-acre campus.

RATINGS

Admissions Selectivity Rating: 98   **Fire Safety Rating:** 60*   **Green Rating:** 60*

STUDENTS AND FACULTY

Enrollment: 1,648. **Student Body:** 50% female, 50% male, 88% out-of-state, 7% international (39 countries represented). African American 9%, Asian 13%, Caucasian 45%, Hispanic 7%. **Retention and Graduation:** 98% freshmen return for sophomore year. 88% freshmen graduate within 4 years. 33% grads go on to further study within 1 year. 14% grads pursue arts and sciences degrees. 9% grads pursue law degrees. 10% grads pursue medical degrees. **Faculty:** Student/faculty ratio 8:1. 195 full-time faculty, 93% hold PhDs. 100% faculty teach undergrads.

ACADEMICS

Degrees: Bachelor's. **Academic Requirements:** Amherst offers an open curriculum with no core or distribution requirements. **Classes:** Most classes have 10–19 students. Most lab/discussion sections have 10–19 students. **Majors with Highest Enrollment:** Economics, English language and literature, political science and government. **Disciplines with Highest Percentage of Degrees Awarded:** Social sciences 22%, foreign languages and literature 11%, English 9%, psychology 9%, biological/life sciences 8%. **Special Study Options:** Cross-registration, double major, exchange student program (domestic), honors program, independent study, student-designed major, study abroad, teacher certification program.

FACILITIES

Housing: Coed dorms, cooperative housing, French/Spanish language house, German/Russian language house, Latino culture house, African American culture house, health and wellness house, arts house, food cooperative house, and single sex floors for men and women within specific dorms. **Special Academic Facilities/Equipment:** Art, natural history, geology museums, language labs, observatory, planetarium, the Amherst Center for Russian Culture, the Dickinson Homestead. **Computers:** 3% of classrooms are wired, 10% of classrooms are wireless, 70% of public computers are PCs, 30% of public computers are Macs, network access in dorm rooms, network access in dorm lounges, online administrative functions (other than registration), remote student-access to Web through college's connection.

CAMPUS LIFE

Activities: Choral groups, concert band, dance, drama/theater, jazz band, literary magazine, music ensembles, musical theater, opera, radio station, student government, student newspaper, symphony orchestra, yearbook. **Organizations:** 100 registered organizations, 2 honor societies, 7 religious organizations. **Athletics (Intercollegiate):** *Men:* Baseball, basketball, cross-country, diving, football, golf, ice hockey, lacrosse, soccer, squash, swimming, tennis, track/field (indoor), track/field (outdoor). *Women:* Basketball, cross-country, diving, field hockey, golf, ice hockey, lacrosse, soccer, softball, squash, swimming, tennis, track/field (indoor), track/field (outdoor), volleyball.

ADMISSIONS

Freshman Academic Profile: 86% in top 10% of high school class, 97% in top 25% of high school class, 100% in top 50% of high school class. 59% from public high schools. SAT Math middle 50% range 660–760. SAT Critical Reading middle 50% range 670–770. SAT Writing middle 50% range 670–760. ACT middle 50% range 29–34. TOEFL required of all international applicants, minimum paper TOEFL 600, minimum computer TOEFL 250. **Basis for Candidate Selection:** *Very important factors considered include:* Academic GPA, application essay, character/personal qualities, extracurricular activities, first generation, recommendation(s), rigor of secondary school record, standardized test scores, talent/ability. *Important factors considered include:* Alumni/ae relation, class rank, volunteer work. *Other factors considered include:* Geographical residence, state residency, work experience. **Freshman Admission Requirements:** High school diploma or equivalent is not required. *Academic units recommended:* 4 English, 4 math, 3 science (1 science lab), 4 foreign language, 2 social studies, 2 history. **Freshman Admission Statistics:** 6,142 applied, 19% admitted, 38% enrolled. **Transfer Admission Requirements:** High school transcript, college transcript(s), essay or personal statement, statement of good standing from prior institution(s). Minimum college GPA of 3.5 required. Lowest grade transferable C. **General Admission Information:** Application fee $55. Early decision application deadline 11/15. Regular application deadline 1/1. Regular notification 4/5. Nonfall registration not accepted. Admission may be deferred for a maximum of 2 years. Neither credit nor placement offered for CEEB Advanced Placement tests.

COSTS AND FINANCIAL AID

Annual tuition $35,580. Room and board $9,420. Required fees $652. Average book expense $1,000. **Required Forms and Deadlines:** FAFSA, CSS/Financial Aid PROFILE, Noncustodial PROFILE, Business/Farm Supplement, income documentation submitted through college. Financial aid filing deadline 2/15. **Notification of Awards:** Applicants will be notified of awards on or about 4/5. **Types of Aid:** *Need-based scholarships/grants:* Pell, SEOG, state scholarships/grants, private scholarships, the school's own gift aid. *Loans:* Direct Subsidized Stafford, Direct Unsubsidized Stafford, Direct PLUS, Federal Perkins, college/university loans from institutional funds. **Student Employment:** Federal Work-Study Program available. Institutional employment available. Off-campus job opportunities are good. **Financial Aid Statistics:** 52% freshmen, 46% undergrads receive need-based scholarship or grant aid. 52% freshmen, 47% undergrads receive need-based self-help aid. 47% freshmen, 48% undergrads receive any aid. Highest amount earned per year from on-campus jobs $1,450.

ANDERSON UNIVERSITY

316 Boulevard, Anderson, SC 29621
Phone: 864-231-5607 **E-mail:** admissions@ac.edu **CEEB Code:** 5008
Fax: 864-231-2033 **Website:** www.ac.edu **ACT Code:** 3832
Financial Aid Phone: 864-231-2070

This private school, affiliated with the South Carolina Baptist Convention Church, was founded in 1911. It has a 56-acre campus.

RATINGS

Admissions Selectivity Rating: 76   **Fire Safety Rating:** 79   **Green Rating:** 60*

STUDENTS AND FACULTY

Enrollment: 1,418. **Student Body:** 63% female, 37% male, 11% out-of-state, 2% international. African American 17%, Caucasian 85%, Hispanic 1%. **Retention and Graduation:** 62% freshmen return for sophomore year. 15% grads go on to further study within 1 year. **Faculty:** Student/faculty ratio 15:1. 68 full-time faculty, 60% hold PhDs. 100% faculty teach undergrads.

ACADEMICS

Degrees: Bachelor's, master's. **Academic Requirements:** Arts/fine arts, computer literacy, English (including composition), foreign languages, history, humanities, mathematics, sciences (biological or physical), social science, religion, fine arts, lifetime wellness, liberal arts laboratory. **Classes:** Most classes have 20–29 students. **Majors with Highest Enrollment:** Business administration/management, elementary education and teaching, graphic design. **Disciplines with Highest Percentage of Degrees Awarded:** Business/marketing 34%, education 25%, visual and performing arts 11%, psychology 8%, parks and recreation 7%. **Special Study Options:** Accelerated program, cooperative education program, distance learning, double major, dual enrollment, honors program, independent study, internships, liberal arts/career combination, study abroad, teacher certification program.

FACILITIES

Housing: Coed dorms, men's dorms, women's dorms. **Special Academic Facilities/Equipment:** Electronic classrooms, art gallery, recording studio. **Computers:** 20% of classrooms are wireless, 95% of public computers are PCs, 5% of public computers are Macs, network access in dorm rooms, network access in dorm lounges, online administrative functions (other than registration), remote student-access to Web through college's connection.

CAMPUS LIFE

Activities: Choral groups, concert band, dance, drama/theater, jazz band, literary magazine, music ensembles, musical theater, student government, student newspaper, symphony orchestra, yearbook. **Organizations:** 27 registered organizations, 1 honor society, 6 religious organizations. **Athletics (Intercollegiate):** *Men:* Baseball, basketball, cross-country, equestrian sports, golf, soccer, tennis, track/field (outdoor), wrestling. *Women:* Basketball, cheerleading, cross-country, equestrian sports, golf, soccer, softball, tennis, track/field (outdoor), volleyball.

ADMISSIONS

Freshman Academic Profile: 17% in top 10% of high school class, 44% in top 25% of high school class, 81% in top 50% of high school class. 94% from public high schools. SAT Math middle 50% range 450–560. SAT Critical Reading middle 50% range 44–550. SAT Writing middle 50% range 430–550. ACT middle 50% range 18–23. TOEFL required of all international applicants, minimum paper TOEFL 550, minimum computer TOEFL 220. **Basis for Candidate Selection:** *Very important factors considered include:* Rigor of secondary school record, standardized test scores. *Important factors considered include:* Character/personal qualities, class rank. *Other factors considered include:* Alumni/ae relation, application essay, interview, racial/ethnic status, recommendation(s), religious affiliation/commitment, talent/ability, volunteer work. **Freshman Admission Requirements:** High school diploma is required, and GED is accepted. *Academic units required:* 4 English, 3 math, 3 science (2 science labs), 2 foreign language, 2 social studies, 2 history, 4 academic electives. *Academic units recommended:* 4 English, 4 math, 4 science (2 science labs), 2 foreign language, 2 social studies, 2 history, 4 academic electives. **Freshman Admission Statistics:** 1,079 applied, 78% admitted, 44% enrolled. **Transfer Admission Requirements:** College transcript(s), minimum college GPA of 2.0 required. Lowest grade transferable C. **General Admission Information:** Application fee $25. Regular application deadline 7/1. Regular notification is rolling. Nonfall registration accepted. Admission may be deferred for a maximum of 1 year. Common Application not accepted. Credit and/or placement offered for CEEB Advanced Placement tests.

COSTS AND FINANCIAL AID

Annual tuition $16,600. Room and board $6,750. Required fees $1,250. Average book expense $1,650. **Required Forms and Deadlines:** FAFSA. Financial aid filing deadline 6/30. **Notification of Awards:** Applicants will be notified of awards on a rolling basis beginning on or about 3/15. **Types of Aid:** *Need-based scholarships/grants:* Pell, SEOG, state scholarships/grants, the school's own gift aid. *Loans:* FFEL Subsidized Stafford, FFEL Unsubsidized Stafford, FFEL PLUS, Federal Perkins. **Financial Aid Statistics:** 87% freshmen, 82% undergrads receive need-based scholarship or grant aid. 45% freshmen, 50% undergrads receive need-based self-help aid. 59 freshmen, 163 undergrads receive athletic scholarships.

ANDERSON UNIVERSITY (IN)

1100 East Fifth Street, Anderson, IN 46012
Phone: 765-641-4080 **E-mail:** info@anderson.edu **CEEB Code:** 1016
Fax: 765-641-4091 **Website:** www.anderson.edu **ACT Code:** 1174
Financial Aid Phone: 765-641-4180

This private school, affiliated with the Church of God, was founded in 1917. It has a 100-acre campus.

RATINGS
Admissions Selectivity Rating: 76   **Fire Safety Rating:** 63   **Green Rating:** 60*

STUDENTS AND FACULTY
Enrollment: 2,194. **Student Body:** 58% female, 42% male, 34% out-of-state, 2% international (31 countries represented). African American 5%, Caucasian 89%, Hispanic 1%. **Retention and Graduation:** 77% freshmen return for sophomore year. 39% freshmen graduate within 4 years. 20% grads go on to further study within 1 year. **Faculty:** Student/faculty ratio 151:1. 141 full-time faculty, 65% hold PhDs. 95% faculty teach undergrads.

ACADEMICS
Degrees: Associate, bachelor's, doctoral, first professional, master's. **Academic Requirements:** Arts/fine arts, English (including composition), foreign languages, history, humanities, mathematics, philosophy, sciences (biological or physical), social science. **Classes:** Most classes have 10–19 students. Most lab/discussion sections have 10–19 students. **Majors with Highest Enrollment:** Business administration and management, elementary education and teaching, nursing–registered nurse training (ASN, BSN, MSN, RN). **Disciplines with Highest Percentage of Degrees Awarded:** Business/marketing 21%, education 18%, health professions and related sciences 8%, communications/journalism 6%, visual and performing arts 6%, family and consumer sciences 5%, psychology 5%. **Special Study Options:** Accelerated program, cross-registration, double major, honors program, independent study, internships, student-designed major, study abroad, teacher certification program, Summer overseas service program.

FACILITIES
Housing: Coed dorms, men's dorms, women's dorms, apartments for married students, apartments for single students, 1 house. **Special Academic Facilities/Equipment:** Gustav Jeeninga Museum of Bible and Near Eastern Studies, Wilson Galleries, Archives of the Church of God. **Computers:** 90% of classrooms are wireless, 90% of public computers are PCs, 10% of public computers are Macs, network access in dorm rooms, online registration, online administrative functions (other than registration), support for handheld computing, remote student-access to Web through college's connection.

CAMPUS LIFE
Activities: Choral groups, concert band, dance, drama/theater, jazz band, literary magazine, music ensembles, musical theater, opera, pep band, radio station, student government, student newspaper, symphony orchestra, yearbook. **Organizations:** 33 registered organizations, 12 honor societies, 15 religious organizations. **Athletics (Intercollegiate):** *Men:* Baseball, basketball, cheerleading, cross-country, football, golf, soccer, tennis, track/field (outdoor). *Women:* Basketball, cheerleading, cross-country, golf, soccer, softball, tennis, track/field (outdoor), volleyball.

ADMISSIONS
Freshman Academic Profile: 22% in top 10% of high school class, 46% in top 25% of high school class, 78% in top 50% of high school class. 95% from public high schools. SAT Math middle 50% range 460–580. SAT Critical Reading middle 50% range 460–580. ACT middle 50% range 20–26. TOEFL required of all international applicants, minimum paper TOEFL 515, minimum computer TOEFL 187. **Basis for Candidate Selection:** *Very important factors considered include:* Recommendation(s), religious affiliation/commitment, rigor of secondary school record. *Important factors considered include:* Character/personal qualities, class rank, extracurricular activities, interview, standardized test scores, volunteer work. *Other factors considered include:* Alumni/ae relation, application essay, first generation, level of applicant's interest, racial/ethnic status, talent/ability. **Freshman Admission Requirements:** High school diploma is required, and GED is not accepted. *Academic units required:* 4 English, 3 math, 3 science (3 science labs), 2 foreign language, 1 social studies, 1 history. *Academic units recommended:* 4 English, 4 math, 4 science (4 science labs), 3 foreign language, 2 social studies, 2 history, 5 academic electives. **Freshman Admission Statistics:** 1,986 applied, 91% admitted, 25% enrolled. **Transfer Admission Requirements:** High school transcript, college transcript(s), standardized test score, statement of good standing from prior institution(s). Minimum college GPA of 2.0 required. Lowest grade transferable C-. **General Admission Information:** Application fee $25. Regular application deadline 7/1. Regular notification is rolling. Nonfall registration accepted. Admission may be deferred for a maximum of 1 year. Credit and/or placement offered for CEEB Advanced Placement tests.

COSTS AND FINANCIAL AID
Annual tuition $19,990. Room & board $6,460. Average book expense $850. **Required Forms and Deadlines:** FAFSA. Financial aid filing deadline 3/1. **Notification of Awards:** Applicants will be notified of awards on a rolling basis beginning on or about 2/15. **Types of Aid:** *Need-based scholarships/grants:* Pell, SEOG, state scholarships/grants, private scholarships, the school's own gift aid. *Loans:* FFEL Subsidized Stafford, FFEL Unsubsidized Stafford, FFEL PLUS, Federal Perkins, college/university loans from institutional funds. **Student Employment:** Federal Work-Study Program available. **Financial Aid Statistics:** 79% freshmen, 76% undergrads receive need-based scholarship or grant aid. 78% freshmen, 75% undergrads receive need-based self-help aid.

ANDREWS UNIVERSITY

Office of Admissions, Andrews University, Berrien Springs, MI 49104
Phone: 269-471-6343 **E-mail:** enroll@andrews.edu **CEEB Code:** 1030
Fax: 269-471-2670 **Website:** www.andrews.edu **ACT Code:** 1992
Financial Aid Phone: 800-253-2874

This private school, affiliated with the Seventh Day Adventist Church, was founded in 1874. It has a 1,600-acre campus.

RATINGS
Admissions Selectivity Rating: 80   **Fire Safety Rating:** 60*   **Green Rating:** 60*

STUDENTS AND FACULTY
Enrollment: 1,746. **Student Body:** 56% female, 44% male, 42% out-of-state, 15% international. African American 21%, Asian 10%, Caucasian 52%, Hispanic 8%. **Retention and Graduation:** 69% freshmen return for sophomore year. 24% grads go on to further study within 1 year. 24% grads pursue arts and sciences degrees.

ACADEMICS
Degrees: Associate, bachelor's, diploma, doctoral, first professional, master's. **Special Study Options:** Study abroad, undergrads may take grad level classes.

FACILITIES
Housing: Men's dorms, women's dorms, apartments for married students, apartments for single students. **Special Academic Facilities/Equipment:** Audio-visual center, lab school, natural history and archaeological museums, observatory, physical therapy facilities.

CAMPUS LIFE
Activities: Choral groups, concert band, radio station, student government, student newspaper, yearbook. **Organizations:** 2 religious organizations.

ADMISSIONS
Freshman Academic Profile: 14% in top 10% of high school class, 35% in top 25% of high school class, 69% in top 50% of high school class. 23% from public high schools. SAT Math middle 50% range 420–600. SAT Critical Reading middle 50% range 440–610. ACT middle 50% range 19–27. **Freshman Admission Requirements:** High school diploma is required, and GED is accepted. *Academic units recommended:* 4 English, 2 math, 2 science, 2 history. **Transfer Admission Requirements:** Minimum college GPA of 2.0 required. Lowest grade transferable C. **General Admission Information:** Application fee $30. Early decision application deadline 1/1. Regular application deadline is rolling. Regular notification is rolling. Nonfall registration accepted. Common Application not accepted. Credit offered for CEEB Advanced Placement tests.

COSTS AND FINANCIAL AID
Annual tuition $11,685. Room & board $3,630. Required fees $285. Average book expense $1,128. **Required Forms and Deadlines:** FAFSA, institution's own financial aid form, state aid form. **Types of Aid:** *Need-based scholarships/grants:* state scholarships/grants. *Loans:* FFEL Subsidized Stafford, FFEL PLUS. **Student Employment:** Federal Work-Study Program available. Institutional employment available. Off-campus job opportunities are good. Highest amount earned per year from on-campus jobs $1,200.

ANGELO STATE UNIVERSITY

2601 West Avenue N, San Angelo, TX 76909
Phone: 325-942-2041 **E-mail:** admissions@angelo.edu **CEEB Code:** 6644
Fax: 325-942-2078 **Website:** www.angelo.edu **ACT Code:** 4164
Financial Aid Phone: 800-253-2874

This public school was founded in 1928. It has a 268-acre campus.

RATINGS
Admissions Selectivity Rating: 65   **Fire Safety Rating:** 60*   **Green Rating:** 60*

STUDENTS AND FACULTY
Enrollment: 5,712. **Student Body:** 54% female, 46% male, 4% out-of-state. African American 6%, Asian 1%, Caucasian 67%, Hispanic 24%. **Retention and Graduation:** 59% freshmen return for sophomore year. 17% freshmen graduate within 4 years. **Faculty:** Student/faculty ratio 20:1. 235 full-time faculty, 73% hold PhDs. 95% faculty teach undergrads.

ACADEMICS
Degrees: Associate, bachelor's, master's. **Academic Requirements:** Arts/fine arts, computer literacy, English (including composition), history, humanities, mathematics, sciences (biological or physical), social science, physical activity. **Classes:** Most classes have 20–29 students. Most lab/discussion sections have 20–29 students. **Majors with Highest Enrollment:** Business administration and management, health and physical education, multi/interdisciplinary studies. **Disciplines with Highest Percentage of Degrees Awarded:** Business/marketing 22%, parks and recreation 14%, education 13%, psychology 10%, communications/journalism 8%. **Special Study Options:** Accelerated program, distance learning, double major, dual enrollment, honors program, independent study, internships, study abroad, teacher certification program, 3–2 engineering-physics and 3–2 agriculture-education programs with Texas A&M and University of Texas El Paso.

FACILITIES
Housing: Coed dorms, women's dorms, apartments for single students, rooms for disabled students. **Special Academic Facilities/Equipment:** Planetarium; West Texas collection; Management, Instruction, and Research (MIR, agriculture) center. **Computers:** 95% of public computers are PCs, 5% of public computers are UNIX, network access in dorm rooms, network access in dorm lounges, online registration, online administrative functions (other than registration), remote student-access to Web through college's connection.

CAMPUS LIFE
Activities: Choral groups, concert band, dance, drama/theater, jazz band, literary magazine, marching band, music ensembles, musical theater, pep band, radio station, student government, student newspaper, student-run film society, television station. **Organizations:** 76 registered organizations, 11 honor societies, 9 religious organizations. 4 fraternities (3% men join), 2 sororities (4% women join). **Athletics (Intercollegiate):** *Men:* Baseball, basketball, cross-country, football, track/field (outdoor). *Women:* Basketball, cross-country, soccer, softball, track/field (outdoor), volleyball.

ADMISSIONS
Freshman Academic Profile: 12% in top 10% of high school class, 35% in top 25% of high school class, 70% in top 50% of high school class. 96% from public high schools. SAT Math middle 50% range 430–540. SAT Critical Reading middle 50% range 420–525. SAT Writing middle 50% range 410–520. ACT middle 50% range 17–23. TOEFL required of all international applicants, minimum paper TOEFL 550, minimum computer TOEFL 213. **Basis for Candidate Selection:** *Very important factors considered include:* Class rank, rigor of secondary school record, standardized test scores. *Other factors considered include:* Academic GPA, first generation. **Freshman Admission Requirements:** High school diploma is required, and GED is accepted. *Academic units recommended:* 4 English, 3 math, 3 science, 2 foreign language, 3 social studies, 1 academic elective. **Freshman Admission Statistics:** 2,747 applied, 84% admitted, 63% enrolled. **Transfer Admission Requirements:** College transcript(s), statement of good standing from prior institution(s). Minimum college GPA of 2.0 required. Lowest grade transferable D. **General Admission Information:** Application fee $25. Regular application deadline 8/15. Regular notification is rolling. Nonfall registration accepted. Admission may be deferred for a maximum of 1 year. Credit offered for CEEB Advanced Placement tests.

COSTS AND FINANCIAL AID
Annual in-state tuition $3,180. Out-of-state tuition $11,460. Room & board $5,314. Required fees $1,110. Average book expense $1,000. **Required Forms and Deadlines:** FAFSA, institution's own financial aid form. Financial aid

filing deadline 5/1. **Notification of Awards:** Applicants will be notified of awards on a rolling basis beginning on or about 4/1. **Types of Aid:** *Need-based scholarships/grants:* Pell, SEOG, state scholarships/grants, private scholarships, the school's own gift aid. *Loans:* FFEL Subsidized Stafford, FFEL Unsubsidized Stafford, FFEL PLUS, Federal Perkins, state loans, college/university loans from institutional funds. **Student Employment:** Institutional employment available. Off-campus job opportunities are good. **Financial Aid Statistics:** 45% freshmen, 49% undergrads receive need-based scholarship or grant aid. 43% freshmen, 44% undergrads receive need-based self-help aid. 4 freshmen, 23 undergrads receive athletic scholarships. 76% freshmen, 72% undergrads receive any aid.

ANNA MARIA COLLEGE

50 Sunset Lane, Box O, Paxton, MA 01612-1198
Phone: 508-849-3360 **E-mail:** admission@annamaria.edu **CEEB Code:** 3005
Fax: 508-849-3362 **Website:** www.annamaria.edu **ACT Code:** 3232
Financial Aid Phone: 508-849-3367

This private school, affiliated with the Roman Catholic Church, was founded in 1946. It has a 180-acre campus.

RATINGS
Admissions Selectivity Rating: 63   **Fire Safety Rating:** 73   **Green Rating:** 78

STUDENTS AND FACULTY
Enrollment: 784. **Student Body:** 59% female, 41% male, 12% out-of-state. African American 3%, Asian 1%, Caucasian 70%, Hispanic 3%. **Retention and Graduation:** 59% freshmen return for sophomore year. 43% freshmen graduate within 4 years. **Faculty:** Student/faculty ratio 10:1. 40 full-time faculty, 45% hold PhDs.

ACADEMICS
Degrees: Associate, bachelor's, master's, post-bachelor's certificate, post-master's certificate. **Academic Requirements:** Arts/fine arts, computer literacy, English (including composition), foreign languages, history, humanities, mathematics, philosophy, sciences (biological or physical), social science. **Classes:** Most classes have 10–19 students. Most lab/discussion sections have 10–19 students. **Majors with Highest Enrollment:** Business administration/management, criminal justice/law enforcement administration, human development and family studies. **Disciplines with Highest Percentage of Degrees Awarded:** Security and protective services 20%, English 14%, public administration and social services 13%, health professions and related sciences 12%, education 10%. **Special Study Options:** Accelerated program, cooperative education program, cross-registration, double major, dual enrollment, independent study, internships, liberal arts/career combination, student-designed major, study abroad, teacher certification program.

FACILITIES
Housing: Coed dorms, special housing for disabled students. **Computers:** 1% of classrooms are wireless, 86% of public computers are PCs, 14% of public computers are Macs, network access in dorm rooms, network access in dorm lounges, online administrative functions (other than registration), remote student-access to Web through college's connection.

CAMPUS LIFE
Activities: Choral groups, drama/theater, jazz band, music ensembles, student government, yearbook. **Athletics (Intercollegiate):** *Men:* Baseball, basketball, cross-country, golf, soccer. *Women:* Basketball, cheerleading, cross-country, field hockey, golf, soccer, softball, volleyball. **Environmental Initiatives:** Performed a comprehensive audit. Anna Maria moving to a paperless environment and have recently digitized many administrative forms which are currently utilized by staff and faculty.

ADMISSIONS
Freshman Academic Profile: 39% in top 50% of high school class. SAT Math middle 50% range 380–470. SAT Math middle 50% range 370–480. SAT Critical Reading middle 50% range 380–480. ACT middle 50% range 16–19. TOEFL required of all international applicants, minimum paper TOEFL 470, minimum computer TOEFL 150. **Basis for Candidate Selection:** *Important factors considered include:* Academic GPA, application essay, extracurricular activities, level of applicant's interest, recommendation(s), rigor of secondary school record, standardized test scores. *Other factors considered include:* Alumni/ae relation, character/personal qualities, class rank, first generation, interview, talent/ability, volunteer work, work experience. **Freshman Admission Requirements:** High school diploma is required, and GED is

accepted. *Academic units required:* 4 English, 3 math, 3 science (1 science lab), 2 foreign language, 2 social studies, 2 history, 4 academic electives. **Freshman Admission Statistics:** 712 applied, 87% admitted, 29% enrolled. **Transfer Admission Requirements:** High school transcript, college transcript(s), statement of good standing from prior institution(s). Minimum college GPA of 2.0 required. Lowest grade transferable C. **General Admission Information:** Application fee $40. Regular notification is rolling. Nonfall registration accepted. Admission may be deferred for a maximum of 1 year. Neither credit nor placement offered for CEEB Advanced Placement tests.

COSTS AND FINANCIAL AID

Annual tuition $22,360. Room and board $8,915. Required fees $2,257. Average book expense $800. **Required Forms and Deadlines:** FAFSA, state aid form. Financial aid filing deadline 3/1. **Notification of Awards:** Applicants will be notified of awards on a rolling basis beginning on or about 4/1. **Types of Aid:** *Need–based scholarships/grants:* Pell, SEOG, state scholarships/grants, private scholarships, the school's own gift aid, United Negro College Fund, Federal Nursing Scholarships. *Loans:* FFEL Subsidized Stafford, FFEL Unsubsidized Stafford, FFEL PLUS, Federal Perkins, state loans, college/university loans from institutional funds. **Financial Aid Statistics:** 81% freshmen, 81% undergrads receive need-based scholarship or grant aid. 81% freshmen, 81% undergrads receive need-based self-help aid.

See page 1058.

ANTIOCH COLLEGE

795 Livermore Street, Yellow Springs, OH 45387
Phone: 937-769-1100 **E-mail:** admissions@antioch-college.edu **CEEB Code:** 1017
Fax: 937-769-1111 **Website:** www.antioch-college.edu **ACT Code:** 3232
Financial Aid Phone: 800-543-9436

This private school was founded in 1852. It has a 100-acre campus.

RATINGS
Admissions Selectivity Rating: 84   **Fire Safety Rating:** 60*   **Green Rating:** 60*

STUDENTS AND FACULTY
Enrollment: 120. **Student Body:** 68% female, 32% male, 66% out-of-state. **Retention and Graduation:** 60% freshmen return for sophomore year. 28% freshmen graduate within 4 years. **Faculty:** Student/faculty ratio 8:1. 45 full-time faculty, 78% hold PhDs. 100% faculty teach undergrads.

ACADEMICS
Degrees: Bachelor's. **Academic Requirements:** Arts/fine arts, English (including composition), humanities, mathematics, sciences (biological or physical), social science. **Classes:** Most classes have fewer than 10 students. **Disciplines with Highest Percentage of Degrees Awarded:** Area and ethnic studies 29%, interdisciplinary studies 25%, liberal arts/general studies 14%, visual and performing arts 11%, agriculture 9%. **Special Study Options:** Cooperative education program, cross-registration, dual enrollment, independent study, internships, liberal arts/career combination, student-designed major, study abroad.

FACILITIES
Housing: Coed dorms, special housing for disabled students, special housing for international students, gender-specific floors. **Special Academic Facilities/ Equipment:** 1,000-acre nature preserve.

CAMPUS LIFE
Activities: Choral groups, dance, drama/theater, literary magazine, music ensembles, musical theater, radio station, student government, student newspaper. **Organizations:** 16 registered organizations.

ADMISSIONS
Freshman Academic Profile: 14% in top 10% of high school class, 42% in top 25% of high school class, 70% in top 50% of high school class. SAT Math middle 50% range 500–620. SAT Critical Reading middle 50% range 550–690. ACT middle 50% range 22–27. TOEFL required of all international applicants, minimum paper TOEFL 525. **Basis for Candidate Selection:** *Very important factors considered include:* Academic GPA, application essay, character/personal qualities, interview, level of applicant's interest, recommendation(s), rigor of secondary school record. *Important factors considered include:* Class rank, volunteer work, work experience. *Other factors considered include:* Alumni/ae relation, extracurricular activities, first generation, standardized test scores, talent/ability. **Freshman Admission Requirements:** High school diploma is required, and GED is accepted. *Academic units required:* 4 English. *Academic units recommended:* 4 math, 4 science (3 science labs), 4 foreign language, 4 social studies, 4 history, 2 academic electives. **Freshman Admission Statistics:**

1,204 applied, 60% admitted, 15% enrolled. **Transfer Admission Requirements:** High school transcript, college transcript(s), essay or personal statement, statement of good standing from prior institution(s). **General Admission Information:** Regular notification is rolling. Nonfall registration not accepted. Admission may be deferred for a maximum of 1 year. Credit and/ or placement offered for CEEB Advanced Placement tests.

COSTS AND FINANCIAL AID
Annual tuition $27,800. Room and board $7,354. Required fees $750. Average book expense $2,000. **Required Forms and Deadlines:** FAFSA, institution's own financial aid form. Financial aid filing deadline 3/1. **Notification of Awards:** Applicants will be notified of awards on a rolling basis beginning on or about 3/15. **Types of Aid:** *Need-based scholarships/grants:* Pell, SEOG, state scholarships/grants, private scholarships, the school's own gift aid. *Loans:* Direct Subsidized Stafford, Direct Unsubsidized Stafford, Direct PLUS, FFEL Subsidized Stafford, FFEL Unsubsidized Stafford, FFEL PLUS, Federal Perkins. **Student Employment:** Federal Work-Study Program available. Institutional employment available. Off-campus job opportunities are fair. **Financial Aid Statistics:** 61% freshmen, 72% undergrads receive need-based scholarship or grant aid. 63% freshmen, 69% undergrads receive need-based self-help aid.

ANTIOCH UNIVERSITY—LOS ANGELES

Office of Admissions, Culver City, CA 90230
Phone: 310-578-1090 **E-mail:** admissions@atiochla.edu **CEEB Code:** 1862
Fax: 310-822-4824 **Website:** www.antiochla.edu
Financial Aid Phone: 310-578-1080

This private school was founded in 1852. It has an 800-acre campus.

RATINGS
Admissions Selectivity Rating: 60*   **Fire Safety Rating:** 60*   **Green Rating:** 60*

STUDENTS AND FACULTY
Enrollment: 188. **Student Body:** 100% female. African American 24%, Asian 5%, Caucasian 80%, Hispanic 11%, Native American 2%. **Retention and Graduation:** 73% grads go on to further study within 1 year. 82% grads pursue arts and sciences degrees. 12% grads pursue business degrees. 4% grads pursue law degrees. **Faculty:** Student/faculty ratio 14:1. 21 full-time faculty, 81% hold PhDs. 35% faculty teach undergrads.

ACADEMICS
Degrees: Bachelor's, certificate, diploma, master's, post-bachelor's certificate, post-master's certificate. **Academic Requirements:** Arts/fine arts, computer literacy, English (including composition), humanities, mathematics, sciences (biological or physical), social science, educational foundations course, non-classroom learning experience. **Classes:** Most classes have 10–19 students. **Majors with Highest Enrollment:** Creative writing, liberal arts and sciences/ liberal studies, psychology. **Disciplines with Highest Percentage of Degrees Awarded:** Liberal arts/general studies 88%. **Special Study Options:** Cross-registration, double major, independent study, internships, teacher certification program, weekend college.

FACILITIES
Computers: 50% of public computers are PCs, 50% of public computers are Macs, remote student-access to Web through college's connection.

CAMPUS LIFE
Organizations: 1 registered organization.

ADMISSIONS
Freshman Academic Profile: TOEFL required of all international applicants, minimum paper TOEFL 600, minimum computer TOEFL 250. **Transfer Admission Requirements:** College transcript(s), essay or personal statement. Lowest grade transferable C. **General Admission Information:** Application fee $60. Regular application deadline 8/1. Regular notification is rolling. Nonfall registration not accepted. Admission may be deferred for a maximum of 1 year. Common Application not accepted. Credit and/or placement offered for CEEB Advanced Placement tests.

COSTS AND FINANCIAL AID
Annual tuition $15,380. Required fees $260. **Required Forms and Deadlines:** FAFSA, institution's own financial aid form. Financial aid filing deadline 3/24. **Notification of Awards:** Applicants will be notified of awards on a rolling basis beginning on or about 4/15. **Types of Aid:** *Need-based scholarships/grants:* Pell, SEOG, state scholarships/grants, private scholarships, the school's own gift aid. *Loans:* FFEL Subsidized Stafford, FFEL Unsubsidized Stafford, FFEL PLUS, Federal Perkins. **Student Employment:** Federal Work-Study Program available.

Institutional employment available. Off-campus job opportunities are excellent. **Financial Aid Statistics:** 67% undergrads receive need-based scholarship or grant aid. 74% undergrads receive need-based self-help aid.

ANTIOCH UNIVERSITY—SANTA BARBARA

801 Garden Street, Santa Barbara, CA 93101
Phone: 805-962-8179 **E-mail:** admissions@antiochsb.edu
Fax: 805-962-4786 **Website:** www.antiochsb.edu
Financial Aid Phone: 805-962-8179

This private school was founded in 1852.

RATINGS
Admissions Selectivity Rating: 60*　　　Fire Safety Rating: 60*　　　Green Rating: 60*

STUDENTS AND FACULTY
Enrollment: 94. **Student Body:** 69% female, 31% male. **Faculty:** 16 full-time faculty.

ACADEMICS
Degrees: Bachelor's, doctoral, master's. **Disciplines with Highest Percentage of Degrees Awarded:** Liberal arts/general studies 100%. **Special Study Options:** Cross-registration, double major, independent study, internships, liberal arts/career combination, study abroad, teacher certification program, weekend college.

ADMISSIONS
Freshman Academic Profile: TOEFL required of all international applicants, minimum paper TOEFL 550, minimum computer TOEFL 213. **Transfer Admission Requirements:** High school transcript, college transcript(s), essay or personal statement, interview, statement of good standing from prior institution(s). Minimum college GPA of 2.0 required. Lowest grade transferable C. **General Admission Information:** Application fee $60. Nonfall registration accepted.

COSTS AND FINANCIAL AID
Annual tuition $13,935. Required fees $48. **Required Forms and Deadlines:** FAFSA, institution's own financial aid form. Financial aid filing deadline 4/15.

ANTIOCH UNIVERSITY—SEATTLE

Admissions Office, 2326 Sixth Avenue, Seattle, WA 98121
Phone: 206-268-4202 **E-mail:** admissions@antiochsea.edu
Fax: 206-268-4242 **Website:** www.antiochsea.edu

This is a private school.

RATINGS
Admissions Selectivity Rating: 60*　　　Fire Safety Rating: 60*　　　Green Rating: 60*

STUDENTS AND FACULTY
Student Body: 2% out-of-state.

ACADEMICS
Degrees: Bachelor's, doctoral, master's, post-bachelor's certificate, post-master's certificate. **Academic Requirements:** Arts/fine arts, English (including composition), history, humanities, social science. **Disciplines with Highest Percentage of Degrees Awarded:** Liberal arts/general studies 94%. **Special Study Options:** Accelerated program, cross-registration, double major, independent study, liberal arts/career combination, student-designed major, teacher certification program.

FACILITIES
Housing: Off-campus housing.

CAMPUS LIFE
Activities: Literary magazine.

ADMISSIONS
Transfer Admission Requirements: High school transcript, college transcript(s), essay or personal statement, interview. Lowest grade transferable C-.

COSTS AND FINANCIAL AID
Required fees $180.

APPALACHIAN STATE UNIVERSITY

Office of Admissions, ASU Box 32004, Boone, NC 28608-2004
Phone: 828-262-2120 **E-mail:** admissions@appstate.edu **CEEB Code:** 5010
Fax: 828-262-3296 **Website:** www.appstate.edu **ACT Code:** 3062
Financial Aid Phone: 828-262-2190

This public school was founded in 1899. It has a 1,100-acre campus.

RATINGS
Admissions Selectivity Rating: 82　　　Fire Safety Rating: 71　　　Green Rating: 73

STUDENTS AND FACULTY
Enrollment: 13,114. **Student Body:** 50% female, 50% male, 9% out-of-state. African American 3%, Asian 1%, Caucasian 90%, Hispanic 2%. **Retention and Graduation:** 84% freshmen return for sophomore year. 34% freshmen graduate within 4 years. **Faculty:** Student/faculty ratio 17:1. 703 full-time faculty, 98% hold PhDs. 100% faculty teach undergrads.

ACADEMICS
Degrees: Bachelor's, certificate, doctoral, master's, post-bachelor's certificate, post-master's certificate. **Academic Requirements:** Arts/fine arts, computer literacy, English (including composition), history, humanities, mathematics, sciences (biological or physical), social science, physical activity/wellness. **Classes:** Most classes have 20–29 students. Most lab/discussion sections have 20–29 students. **Majors with Highest Enrollment:** Business administration/management, elementary education and teaching, psychology. **Disciplines with Highest Percentage of Degrees Awarded:** Business/marketing 20%, education 19%, communications/journalism 9%, social sciences 8%, visual and performing arts 6%. **Special Study Options:** Distance learning, double major, dual enrollment, English as a Second Language (ESL), exchange student program (domestic), honors program, independent study, internships, liberal arts/career combination, student-designed major, study abroad, teacher certification program.

FACILITIES
Housing: Coed dorms, men's dorms, women's dorms, apartments for married students, apartments for single students, special housing for disabled students, special housing for international students, sorority housing. **Special Academic Facilities/Equipment:** Museum of Appalachian history, language lab, observatory, meteorological reporting station, Catherine Smith Gallery. **Computers:** 70% of public computers are PCs, 30% of public computers are Macs, network access in dorm rooms, network access in dorm lounges, online registration, online administrative functions (other than registration), remote student-access to Web through college's connection.

CAMPUS LIFE
Activities: Choral groups, concert band, dance, drama/theater, jazz band, literary magazine, marching band, music ensembles, musical theater, opera, pep band, radio station, student government, student newspaper, student-run film society, symphony orchestra, television studio. **Organizations:** 213 registered organizations, 30 honor societies, 40 religious organizations. 11 fraternities (8% men join), 8 sororities (9% women join). **Athletics (Intercollegiate):** *Men:* Baseball, basketball, cheerleading, cross-country, football, golf, soccer, tennis, track/field (indoor), track/field (outdoor), wrestling. *Women:* Basketball, cheerleading, cross-country, field hockey, golf, soccer, tennis, track/field (indoor), track/field (outdoor), volleyball.

ADMISSIONS
Freshman Academic Profile: 16% in top 10% of high school class, 50% in top 25% of high school class, 87% in top 50% of high school class. SAT Math middle 50% range 530–610. SAT Critical Reading middle 50% range 510–600. SAT Writing middle 50% range 490–590. ACT middle 50% range 21–26. TOEFL required of all international applicants, minimum paper TOEFL 500. **Basis for Candidate Selection:** *Very important factors considered include:* Academic GPA, class rank, rigor of secondary school record, standardized test scores. *Other factors considered include:* Application essay, character/personal qualities, extracurricular activities, first generation, interview, recommendation(s), talent/ability, volunteer work, work experience. **Freshman Admission Requirements:** High school diploma is required, and GED is not accepted. *Academic units required:* 4 English, 4 math, 3 science (1 science lab), 2 foreign language, 1 social studies, 1 history. **Freshman Admission Statistics:** 10,419 applied, 69% admitted, 38% enrolled. **Transfer Admission Requirements:** High school transcript, college transcript(s), minimum college GPA of 2.0 required. Lowest grade transferable D. **General Admission Information:** Application fee $45. Regular notification 10/15. Nonfall registration accepted. Credit and/or placement offered for CEEB Advanced Placement tests.

COSTS AND FINANCIAL AID

Annual in-state tuition $2,221. Annual out-of-state tuition $11,963. Room and board $5,990. Required fees $2,020. Average book expense $600. **Required Forms and Deadlines:** FAFSA. Financial aid filing deadline 3/15. **Notification of Awards:** Applicants will be notified of awards on or about 4/1. **Types of Aid:** *Need-based scholarships/grants:* Pell, SEOG, state scholarships/grants, private scholarships, the school's own gift aid. *Loans:* FFEL Subsidized Stafford, FFEL Unsubsidized Stafford, FFEL PLUS, Federal Perkins. **Financial Aid Statistics:** 27% freshmen, 30% undergrads receive need-based scholarship or grant aid. 22% freshmen, 28% undergrads receive need-based self-help aid. 46 freshmen, 197 undergrads receive athletic scholarships.

AQUINAS COLLEGE

1607 Robinson Road SE, Grand Rapids, MI 49506-1799
Phone: 616-632-2900 **E-mail:** admissions@aquinas.edu **CEEB Code:** 1018
Fax: 616-732-4469 **Website:** www.aquinas.edu **ACT Code:** 1962
Financial Aid Phone: 616-632-2893

This private school, affiliated with the Roman Catholic Church, was founded in 1886. It has a 107-acre campus.

RATINGS
Admissions Selectivity Rating: 79   **Fire Safety Rating:** 64   **Green Rating:** 84

STUDENTS AND FACULTY
Enrollment: 1,726. **Student Body:** 64% female, 36% male, 4% out-of-state. African American 3%, Asian 1%, Caucasian 68%, Hispanic 3%. **Retention and Graduation:** 69% freshmen return for sophomore year. 25% freshmen graduate within 4 years. 13% grads go on to further study within 1 year. 11% grads pursue arts and sciences degrees. 1% grads pursue business degrees. 1% grads pursue law degrees. 2% grads pursue medical degrees. **Faculty:** Student/faculty ratio 14:1. 94 full-time faculty, 65% hold PhDs. 100% faculty teach undergrads.

ACADEMICS
Degrees: Associate, bachelor's, master's. **Academic Requirements:** Arts/fine arts, computer literacy, English (including composition), foreign languages, history, humanities, mathematics, philosophy, sciences (biological or physical), social science. **Classes:** Most classes have 10–19 students. **Majors with Highest Enrollment:** Communications studies/speech communication and rhetoric, English/language arts teacher education, history. **Disciplines with Highest Percentage of Degrees Awarded:** Education 21%, business/marketing 19%, social sciences 8%, liberal arts/general studies 6%, visual and performing arts 6%, biological/life sciences 5%, communications/journalism 5%, English 5%. **Special Study Options:** Accelerated program, cooperative education program, cross-registration, distance learning, double major, dual enrollment, exchange student program (domestic), honors program, independent study, internships, liberal arts/career combination, student-designed major, study abroad, teacher certification program. Service learning experiences in Peru, Haiti, and Mexico. Semester abroad in Costa Rica, France, Germany, Spain, Japan, and Ireland. Domestic exchange in California, Florida, and Chicago.

FACILITIES
Housing: Coed dorms, apartments for single students, project/theme houses. **Special Academic Facilities/Equipment:** Observatory and Jarecki Center for Advanced Learning featuring high-speed, 2-way interactive video conferencing for courses and a virtual connection for external experts to interact with classes (sound, video, graphics) using a laptop computer equipped with a camera that is housed in a self-contained briefcase. The package includes all the technology needed to accomplish the connection through a standard phone jack. This "virtual faculty briefcase" can be shipped to a guest lecturer at another location anywhere in the world and they are able to conduct an interactive lecture or discussion with an Aquinas classroom. **Computers:** 100% of classrooms are wired, 10% of classrooms are wireless, 95% of public computers are PCs, 5% of public computers are Macs, network access in dorm rooms, network access in dorm lounges, online administrative functions (other than registration), remote student-access to Web through college's connection.

CAMPUS LIFE
Activities: Choral groups, dance, drama/theater, jazz band, literary magazine, music ensembles, radio station, student government, student newspaper. **Organizations:** 42 registered organizations, 4 honor societies, 2 religious organizations. **Athletics (Intercollegiate):** *Men:* Baseball, basketball, cheerleading, cross-country, golf, soccer, tennis, track/field (indoor), track/field

(outdoor). *Women:* Basketball, cheerleading, cross-country, golf, soccer, softball, tennis, track/field (indoor), track/field (outdoor), volleyball. **Environmental Initiatives:** Sustainable Business practices restore environmental quality, promote stable and healthy communities, and increase long-term profitability. The Aquinas Sustainable Business Degree program fosters ecological and social intelligence in all business decisions and is the only undergraduate program of its kind in Michigan and possibly the United States. The West Michigan Sustainable Business Forum is an association of over 90 businesses, including Aquinas College, that have come together to research and promote "best sustainable business practices" in West Michigan. Aquinas is offering employees of any member business a 20% tuition discount for SB program classes. The Aquinas Campus Sustainability Initiative process has begun. There are currently 14 proposals in progress, 6 more that are of preliminary status (in need of further development) and 3 which have been accepted and implemented. Proposals focus on a variety of campus processes including native plant landscaping, healthy cleaning products, an intelligent campus-wide recycling system, food waste composting with a campus vegetable garden, a smokeless campus, and a number of energy related proposals. Ideas are submitted to the student senate sustainability committee who help to further develop the proposals.

ADMISSIONS
Freshman Academic Profile: 19% in top 10% of high school class, 44% in top 25% of high school class, 71% in top 50% of high school class. 79% from public high schools. ACT middle 50% range 20–25. TOEFL required of all international applicants, minimum paper TOEFL 550, minimum computer TOEFL 213. **Basis for Candidate Selection:** *Very important factors considered include:* Academic GPA, rigor of secondary school record, standardized test scores. *Other factors considered include:* Character/personal qualities, extracurricular activities, recommendation(s), talent/ability, volunteer work, work experience. **Freshman Admission Requirements:** High school diploma is required, and GED is not accepted. *Academic units required:* 4 English, 4 math, 3 science, 4 social studies. **Freshman Admission Statistics:** 1,896 applied, 81% admitted, 25% enrolled. **Transfer Admission Requirements:** High school transcript, college transcript(s), minimum college GPA of 2.0 required. Lowest grade transferable D. **General Admission Information:** Regular notification is rolling. Nonfall registration accepted. Admission may be deferred for a maximum of 1 year. Credit offered for CEEB Advanced Placement tests.

COSTS AND FINANCIAL AID
Annual tuition $20,048. Room & board $6,422. Average book expense $737. **Required Forms and Deadlines:** FAFSA. Financial aid filing deadline 3/1. **Notification of Awards:** Applicants will be notified of awards on a rolling basis beginning on or about 3/1. **Types of Aid:** *Need-based scholarships/grants:* Pell, SEOG, state scholarships/grants, private scholarships, the school's own gift aid. *Loans:* FFEL Subsidized Stafford, FFEL Unsubsidized Stafford, FFEL PLUS, Federal Perkins. **Student Employment:** Off-campus job opportunities are excellent. **Financial Aid Statistics:** 73% undergrads receive need-based scholarship or grant aid. 76% freshmen, 73% undergrads receive need-based self-help aid. 18 freshmen, 58 undergrads receive athletic scholarships. 97% freshmen, 94% undergrads receive any aid. Highest amount earned per year from on-campus jobs $12,500.

See page 1060.

AQUINAS COLLEGE (TN)

4210 Harding Road, Nashville, TN 37205
Phone: 615-297-7545 **E-mail:** admissions@aquinas-tn.edu
Fax: 615-297-7970 **Website:** www.aquinas-tn.edu **ACT Code:** 3942
Financial Aid Phone: 615-297-7545

This private school, affiliated with the Roman Catholic Church, was founded in 1961. It has an 80-acre campus.

RATINGS
Admissions Selectivity Rating: 60*   **Fire Safety Rating:** 60*   **Green Rating:** 60*

STUDENTS AND FACULTY
Enrollment: 329. **Student Body:** 77% female, 23% male. **Faculty:** Student/faculty ratio 12:1. 21 full-time faculty, 43% hold PhDs. 100% faculty teach undergrads.

ACADEMICS
Degrees: Associate, bachelor's, post-bachelor's certificate, terminal. **Academic Requirements:** English (including composition), history, humanities,

mathematics, sciences (biological or physical), social science, religion. **Special Study Options:** Liberal arts/career combination, teacher certification program, weekend college.

FACILITIES
Computers: 100% of public computers are PCs, remote student-access to Web through college's connection.

CAMPUS LIFE
Activities: Student government, student newspaper. **Organizations:** 5 registered organizations. **Athletics (Intercollegiate):** *Men:* Baseball, basketball. *Women:* Cheerleading.

ADMISSIONS
Freshman Academic Profile: 7% in top 10% of high school class, 20% in top 25% of high school class, 65% in top 50% of high school class. 80% from public high schools. TOEFL required of all international applicants, minimum paper TOEFL 525. **Basis for Candidate Selection:** *Very important factors considered include:* Rigor of secondary school record, standardized test scores. *Other factors considered include:* Alumni/ae relation, character/personal qualities, extracurricular activities, interview, recommendation(s), work experience. **Freshman Admission Requirements:** High school diploma is required, and GED is accepted. *Academic units recommended:* 4 English, 3 math, 3 science, 1 foreign language, 1 social studies, 1 history. **Freshman Admission Statistics:** 329 applied, 73% admitted, 28% enrolled. **Transfer Admission Requirements:** College transcript(s), minimum college GPA of 2.0 required. Lowest grade transferable C. **General Admission Information:** Application fee $10. Regular notification is rolling. Nonfall registration accepted. Admission may be deferred for a maximum of 1 year. Common Application not accepted. Credit offered for CEEB Advanced Placement tests.

COSTS AND FINANCIAL AID
Annual tuition $9,000. Required fees $400. Average book expense $600. **Required Forms and Deadlines:** FAFSA, institution's own financial aid form. Financial aid filing deadline 2/15. **Notification of Awards:** Applicants will be notified of awards on a rolling basis beginning on or about 3/1. **Types of Aid:** *Need-based scholarships/grants:* Pell, SEOG, state scholarships/grants, private scholarships, the school's own gift aid. *Loans:* FFEL Subsidized Stafford, FFEL Unsubsidized Stafford, FFEL PLUS. **Student Employment:** Federal Work-Study Program available. Off-campus job opportunities are excellent. **Financial Aid Statistics:** 33% undergrads receive need-based scholarship or grant aid. 51% undergrads receive need-based self-help aid. 2 freshmen, 3 undergrads receive athletic scholarships.

ARCADIA UNIVERSITY

450 South Easton Road, Glenside, PA 19038
Phone: 215-572-2910 **E-mail:** admiss@arcadia.edu **CEEB Code:** 2039
Fax: 215-572-4049 **Website:** www.arcadia.edu
Financial Aid Phone: 215-572-2980

This private school, affiliated with the Presbyterian Church, was founded in 1853. It has a 60-acre campus.

RATINGS
Admissions Selectivity Rating: 79   **Fire Safety Rating:** 60*   **Green Rating:** 60*

STUDENTS AND FACULTY
Enrollment: 2,063. **Student Body:** 73% female, 27% male, 36% out-of-state. 1% international (13 countries represented). African American 8%, Asian 2%, Caucasian 81%, Hispanic 3%. **Retention and Graduation:** 80% freshmen return for sophomore year. 54% freshmen graduate within 4 years. 25% grads go on to further study within 1 year. 18% grads pursue arts and sciences degrees. 3% grads pursue business degrees. 2% grads pursue law degrees. 2% grads pursue medical degrees. **Faculty:** Student/faculty ratio 13:1. 102 full-time faculty. 92% faculty teach undergrads.

ACADEMICS
Degrees: Bachelor's, doctoral, master's, post-bachelor's certificate, post-master's certificate. **Academic Requirements:** Arts/fine arts, English (including composition), foreign languages, history, humanities, mathematics, sciences (biological or physical), social science. Common core courses include justice, multicultural interpretations and pluralism in the United States. **Classes:** Most classes have 10–19 students. Most lab/discussion sections have 10–19 students. **Majors with Highest Enrollment:** Business administration/management, education, psychology. **Disciplines with Highest Percentage of Degrees Awarded:** Business/marketing 16%, education 15%, psychology

15%, visual and performing arts 12%, social sciences 9%. **Special Study Options:** Cooperative education program, cross-registration, double major, exchange student program (domestic), honors program, independent study, internships, liberal arts/career combination, student-designed major, study abroad, teacher certification program, Arcadia also offers programs in Washington, DC. and a Philadelphia Urban Semester. Undergraduate students may also take gradutate courses. The university also offers evening and some weekend classes.

FACILITIES
Housing: Coed dorms, women's dorms, apartments for single students, special housing for disabled students, Living Learning Communities. **Special Academic Facilities/Equipment:** Art gallery, language lab, observatory. **Computers:** Network access in dorm rooms, network access in dorm lounges, online registration, online administrative functions (other than registration), remote student-access to Web through college's connection.

CAMPUS LIFE
Activities: Choral groups, dance, drama/theater, literary magazine, music ensembles, musical theater, radio station, student government, student newspaper, television station, yearbook. **Organizations:** 40 registered organizations, 8 honor societies, 3 religious organizations. **Athletics (Intercollegiate):** *Men:* Baseball, basketball, cheerleading, golf, soccer, swimming, tennis. *Women:* Basketball, cheerleading, field hockey, lacrosse, soccer, softball, swimming, tennis, volleyball.

ADMISSIONS
Freshman Academic Profile: 30% in top 10% of high school class, 67% in top 25% of high school class, 91% in top 50% of high school class. 72% from public high schools. SAT Math middle 50% range 480–590. SAT Critical Reading middle 50% range 500–620. SAT Writing middle 50% range 490–600. ACT middle 50% range 21–26. TOEFL required of all international applicants, minimum paper TOEFL 550, minimum computer TOEFL 213. **Basis for Candidate Selection:** *Very important factors considered include:* Academic GPA, rigor of secondary school record. *Important factors considered include:* Application essay, class rank, extracurricular activities, recommendation(s), standardized test scores. *Other factors considered include:* Alumni/ae relation, character/personal qualities, interview, talent/ability, volunteer work, work experience. **Freshman Admission Requirements:** High school diploma is required, and GED is accepted. *Academic units recommended:* 4 English, 3 math, 3 science (3 science labs), 2 foreign language, 2 social studies, 2 history. **Freshman Admission Statistics:** 3,226 applied, 79% admitted, 22% enrolled. **Transfer Admission Requirements:** College transcript(s), essay or personal statement, minimum college GPA of 2.5 required. Lowest grade transferable C-. **General Admission Information:** Application fee $30. Early decision application deadline 10/15. Regular application deadline 8/1. Regular notification is rolling. Nonfall registration accepted. Admission may be deferred for a maximum of 1 year. Credit and/or placement offered for CEEB Advanced Placement tests.

COSTS AND FINANCIAL AID
Annual tuition $25,650. Room & board $9,660. Required fees $340. Average book expense $800. **Required Forms and Deadlines:** FAFSA, institution's own financial aid form. Financial aid filing deadline 3/1. **Notification of Awards:** Applicants will be notified of awards on a rolling basis beginning on or about 2/15. **Types of Aid:** *Need-based scholarships/grants:* Pell, SEOG, state scholarships/grants, private scholarships, the school's own gift aid. *Loans:* FFEL Subsidized Stafford, FFEL Unsubsidized Stafford, FFEL PLUS, Federal Perkins, college/university loans from institutional funds. **Student Employment:** Off-campus job opportunities are good. **Financial Aid Statistics:** 77% freshmen, 75% undergrads receive need-based scholarship or grant aid. 66% freshmen, 69% undergrads receive need-based self-help aid. 97% freshmen, receive any aid.

See page 1062.

ARIZONA STATE UNIVERSITY— POLYTECHNIC CAMPUS

AZ State University, PO Box 870112, Tempe, AZ 85287-0112
Phone: 480-965-7788 **E-mail:** poly@asu.edu **CEEB Code:** 4007
Fax: 480-727-1008 **Website:** www.asu.edu **ACT Code:** 0088
Financial Aid Phone: 480-727-1041

This public school was founded in 1994. It has a 605-acre campus.

RATINGS
Admissions Selectivity Rating: 76   **Fire Safety Rating:** 60*   **Green Rating:** 60*

STUDENTS AND FACULTY
Enrollment: 2,590. **Student Body:** 44% female, 56% male, 12% out-of-state, 2% international (44 countries represented). African American 3%, Asian 4%, Caucasian 72%, Hispanic 12%, Native American 3%. **Retention and Graduation:** 70% freshmen return for sophomore year. **Faculty:** Student/faculty ratio 16:1. 158 full-time faculty, 77% hold PhDs.

ACADEMICS
Degrees: Bachelor's, master's, post-bachelor's certificate, doctoral. **Academic Requirements:** Arts/fine arts, computer literacy, English (including composition), history, humanities, mathematics, philosophy, sciences (biological or physical), social science. **Classes:** Most classes have 10–19 students. Most lab/discussion sections have 10–19 students. **Disciplines with Highest Percentage of Degrees Awarded:** Business/marketing 34%, education 21%, agriculture 7%, science technologies 7%, engineering technologies 7%, family and consumer sciences 7%. **Special Study Options:** Distance learning, double major, English as a second language (ESL), honor program, independent study, internships, liberal arts/career combination, student-designed major, study abroad, teacher certification program.

FACILITIES
Housing: Coed dorms, apartments for married students, apartments for single students, special housing for disabled students, theme housing based on academic interest, housing for students with families and single students, special freshman dorm. **Computers:** 3% of classrooms are wired, 100% of classrooms are wireless, 74% of public computers are PCs, 8% of public computers are Macs, 18% of public computers are UNIX, network access in dorm rooms, network access in dorm lounges, online registration, online administrative functions (other than registration), support for handheld computing, remote student-access to Web through college's connection.

CAMPUS LIFE
Activities: Choral groups, student government. **Organizations:** 31 registered organizations, 3 honor societies.

ADMISSIONS
Freshman Academic Profile: 23% in top 10% of high school class, 51% in top 25% of high school class, 79% in top 50% of high school class. SAT Math middle 50% range 480–610. SAT Critical Reading middle 50% range 460–570. ACT middle 50% range 19–25. TOEFL required of all international applicants, minimum paper TOEFL 500, minimum computer TOEFL 173. **Basis for Candidate Selection:** *Very important factors considered include:* Academic GPA, rigor of secondary school record, standardized test scores, state residency. **Freshman Admission Requirements:** High school diploma is required, and GED is accepted. *Academic units required:* 4 English, 4 math, 3 science (3 science labs), 2 foreign language, 1 social studies, 1 history, 1 fine arts. **Freshman Admission Statistics:** 1,151 applied, 87% admitted, 25% enrolled. **Transfer Admission Requirements:** College transcript(s), statement of good standing from prior institution(s). Lowest grade transferable C. **General Admission Information:** Application fee $50. Regular notification is rolling. Nonfall registration accepted. Credit offered for CEEB Advanced Placement tests.

COSTS AND FINANCIAL AID
Annual in-state tuition $4,400. Annual out-of-state tuition $15,750. Room and board $6,150. Average book expense $950. **Required Forms and Deadlines:** FAFSA. Financial aid filing deadline 3/1. **Notification of Awards:** Applicants will be notified of awards on a rolling basis beginning on or about 4/15. **Types of Aid:** *Need-based scholarships/grants:* Pell, SEOG, state scholarships/grants, private scholarships, the school's own gift aid. *Loans:* Direct Subsidized Stafford, Direct Unsubsidized Stafford, Direct PLUS, FFEL PLUS, Federal Perkins. **Financial Aid Statistics:** 45% freshmen, 41% undergrads receive need-based scholarship or grant aid. 26% freshmen, 40% undergrads receive need-based self-help aid.

ARIZONA STATE UNIVERSITY AT THE TEMPE CAMPUS

Box 870112, Tempe, AZ 85287-0112
Phone: 480-965-7788 **E-mail:** ugradinq@asu.edu **CEEB Code:** 4007
Fax: 480-965-3610 **Website:** www.asu.edu **ACT Code:** 0088
Financial Aid Phone: 480-965-3355 **Financial Aid Phone:** 480-965-3355

This public school was founded in 1885. It has a 716-acre campus.

RATINGS
Admissions Selectivity Rating: 78   **Fire Safety Rating:** 87   **Green Rating:** 99

STUDENTS AND FACULTY
Enrollment: 38,984. **Student Body:** 49% female, 51% male, 25% out-of-state, 3% international (114 countries represented). African American 4%, Asian 5%, Caucasian 69%, Hispanic 13%, Native American 2%. **Retention and Graduation:** 79% freshmen return for sophomore year. 28% freshmen graduate within 4 years. **Faculty:** Student/faculty ratio 23:1. 1,769 full-time faculty, 90% hold PhDs. 70% faculty teach undergrads.

ACADEMICS
Degrees: Bachelor's, doctoral, first professional, master's, post-bachelor's certificate, post-master's certificate. **Academic Requirements:** Arts/fine arts, computer literacy, English (including composition), foreign languages, history, humanities, mathematics, sciences (biological or physical), social science. **Classes:** Most classes have 10–19 students. Most lab/discussion sections have 20–29 students. **Majors with Highest Enrollment:** Business administration and management, journalism, psychology. **Disciplines with Highest Percentage of Degrees Awarded:** Business/marketing 17%, interdisciplinary studies 10%, communications/journalism 9%, education 9%, engineering 8%. **Special Study Options:** Accelerated program, cooperative education program, distance learning, double major, dual enrollment, exchange student program (domestic), honors program, independent study, internships, study abroad, teacher certification program, weekend college.

FACILITIES
Housing: Coed dorms, apartments for single students, special housing for disabled students, fraternity/sorority housing, freshmen. **Special Academic Facilities/Equipment:** Art, anthropology, geology, history, and sports museums; early childhood development lab; herbarium; robotics lab; semiconductor clean room; high-resolution electron microscope facility; gamma cell irradiation chamber; solar research facilities; nuclear reactor. **Computers:** 100% of classrooms are wired, 50% of classrooms are wireless, 80% of public computers are PCs, 15% of public computers are Macs, 5% of public computers are UNIX, network access in dorm rooms, network access in dorm lounges, online registration, online administrative functions (other than registration), support for handheld computing, remote student-access to Web through college's connection.

CAMPUS LIFE
Activities: Choral groups, concert band, dance, drama/theater, jazz band, literary magazine, marching band, music ensembles, musical theater, opera, pep band, radio station, student government, student newspaper, symphony orchestra, television station. **Organizations:** 521 registered organizations, 13 honor societies, 47 religious organizations. 31 fraternities (7% men join), 20 sororities (8% women join). **Athletics (Intercollegiate):** *Men:* Baseball, basketball, cross-country, diving, football, golf, swimming, tennis, track/field (outdoor), wrestling. *Women:* Basketball, cross-country, diving, golf, gymnastics, soccer, softball, swimming, tennis, track/field (outdoor), volleyball, water polo. **Environmental Initiatives:** Active Community Engagement. Zero Waste. Carbon Neutrality.

ADMISSIONS
Freshman Academic Profile: 28% in top 10% of high school class, 55% in top 25% of high school class, 83% in top 50% of high school class. SAT Math middle 50% range 490–620. SAT Critical Reading middle 50% range 470–600. ACT middle 50% range 20–26. TOEFL required of all international applicants, minimum paper TOEFL 500, minimum computer TOEFL 173. **Basis for Candidate Selection:** *Very important factors considered include:* Academic GPA, class rank, standardized test scores. *Important factors considered include:*

State residency. **Freshman Admission Requirements:** High school diploma is required, and GED is accepted. *Academic units required:* 4 English, 4 math, 3 science (3 science labs), 2 foreign language, 1 social studies, 1 history, 1 fine arts. **Freshman Admission Statistics:** 20,702 applied, 92% admitted, 41% enrolled. **Transfer Admission Requirements:** College transcript(s), standardized test score, minimum college GPA of 2.0 required. Lowest grade transferable C. **General Admission Information:** Application fee $50. Nonfall registration accepted. Credit offered for CEEB Advanced Placement tests.

COSTS AND FINANCIAL AID
Annual in-state tuition $5,063. Annual out-of-state tuition $17,697. Room and board $8,797. Required fees $252. Average book expense $1,130. **Required Forms and Deadlines:** FAFSA. Financial aid filing deadline 3/1. **Types of Aid:** *Need-based scholarships/grants:* Pell, SEOG, state scholarships/grants, private scholarships, the school's own gift aid, Federal Nursing Scholarships. *Loans:* Direct Subsidized Stafford, Direct Unsubsidized Stafford, Direct PLUS, FFEL PLUS, Federal Perkins. **Student Employment:** Federal Work-Study Program available. Institutional employment available. Off-campus job opportunities are good. **Financial Aid Statistics:** 35% freshmen, 34% undergrads receive need-based scholarship or grant aid. 20% freshmen, 29% undergrads receive need-based self-help aid. 52 freshmen, 295 undergrads receive athletic scholarships. 73% freshmen, 65% undergrads receive any aid.

ARIZONA STATE UNIVERSITY—WEST

PO Box 37100, Phoenix, AZ 85069-7100
Phone: 602-543-8203 **E-mail:** west-admissions@asu.edu **CEEB Code:** 4007
Fax: 602-543-8312 **Website:** www.west.asu.edu **ACT Code:** 0088
Financial Aid Phone: 602-543-8178

This public school was founded in 1984. It has a 300-acre campus.

RATINGS
Admissions Selectivity Rating: 84   **Fire Safety Rating:** 60*   **Green Rating:** 60*

STUDENTS AND FACULTY
Enrollment: 5,726. **Student Body:** 65% female, 35% male, 6% out-of-state, (74 countries represented). African American 6%, Asian 5%, Caucasian 64%, Hispanic 19%, Native American 3%. **Retention and Graduation:** 74% freshmen return for sophomore year. **Faculty:** Student/faculty ratio 21:1. 230 full-time faculty, 83% hold PhDs. 100% faculty teach undergrads.

ACADEMICS
Degrees: Bachelor's, doctoral, master's, post-bachelor's certificate. **Academic Requirements:** Arts/fine arts, computer literacy, English (including composition), foreign languages, history, humanities, mathematics, sciences (biological or physical), social science. **Classes:** Most classes have 10–19 students. Most lab/discussion sections have 20–29 students. **Majors with Highest Enrollment:** Criminal justice/law enforcement administration, elementary education and teaching, international business. **Disciplines with Highest Percentage of Degrees Awarded:** Education 27%, business/marketing 25%, security and protective services 8%, psychology 7%, communications/journalism 7%, interdisciplinary studies 5%, biological/life sciences 5%, social sciences 5%. **Special Study Options:** Distance learning, double major, honors program, independent study, internships, student-designed major, study abroad, teacher certification program.

FACILITIES
Housing: Apartments for single students, special housing for disabled students. **Computers:** 100% of classrooms are wireless, 95% of public computers are PCs, 5% of public computers are Macs, network access in dorm rooms, network access in dorm lounges, online registration, online administrative functions (other than registration), remote student-access to Web through college's connection.

CAMPUS LIFE
Activities: Drama/theater, literary magazine, student government, student newspaper. **Organizations:** 33 registered organizations, 4 honor societies, 4 religious organizations.

ADMISSIONS
Freshman Academic Profile: 32% in top 10% of high school class, 60% in top 25% of high school class, 87% in top 50% of high school class. 92% from public high schools. SAT Math middle 50% range 440–570. SAT Critical Reading middle 50% range 450–560. ACT middle 50% range 19–25. TOEFL required of all international applicants, minimum paper TOEFL 500, minimum

computer TOEFL 173. **Basis for Candidate Selection:** *Very important factors considered include:* Academic GPA, class rank, rigor of secondary school record, standardized test scores. *Important factors considered include:* State residency. *Other factors considered include:* Application essay, extracurricular activities, interview, recommendation(s), talent/ability. **Freshman Admission Requirements:** High school diploma is required, and GED is accepted. *Academic units required:* 4 English, 4 math, 3 science (3 science labs), 2 foreign language, 1 social studies, 1 history, 1 fine arts. **Freshman Admission Statistics:** 1,595 applied, 60% admitted, 56% enrolled. **Transfer Admission Requirements:** College transcript(s), minimum college GPA of 2.0 required. Lowest grade transferable C. **General Admission Information:** Application fee $25. Regular notification is continuous. Nonfall registration accepted. Credit and/or placement offered for CEEB Advanced Placement tests.

COSTS AND FINANCIAL AID
Annual in-state tuition $4,620. Annual out-of-state tuition $16,853. Required fees $146. Average book expense $950. **Required Forms and Deadlines:** FAFSA. Financial aid filing deadline 3/1. **Notification of Awards:** Applicants will be notified of awards on a rolling basis beginning on or about 3/15. **Types of Aid:** *Need-based scholarships/grants:* Pell, SEOG, state scholarships/grants, private scholarships, the school's own gift aid. *Loans:* Direct Subsidized Stafford, Direct Unsubsidized Stafford, FFEL PLUS, Federal Perkins, college/university loans from institutional funds. **Student Employment:** Federal Work-Study Program available. Institutional employment available. Off-campus job opportunities are excellent. **Financial Aid Statistics:** 44% freshmen, 45% undergrads receive need-based scholarship or grant aid. 19% freshmen, 39% undergrads receive need-based self-help aid. 68% freshmen, 57% undergrads receive any aid. Highest amount earned per year from on-campus jobs $10,970.

ARKANSAS BAPTIST COLLEGE

1600 Bishop Street, Little Rock, AR 72202
Phone: 501-374-7856 **E-mail:** ahightower@swbell.net
Fax: 501-375-9257 **Website:** www.arkansasbaptist.edu

This private school, affiliated with the Baptist Church, was founded in 1884.

RATINGS
Admissions Selectivity Rating: 61   **Fire Safety Rating:** 60*   **Green Rating:** 60*

STUDENTS AND FACULTY
Enrollment: 117. **Student Body:** 49% female, 51% male, 10% out-of-state. **Retention and Graduation:** 4% freshmen graduate within 4 years.

ACADEMICS
Degrees: Associate, bachelor's, certificate. **Academic Requirements:** Computer literacy, English (including composition), humanities, mathematics, philosophy, sciences (biological or physical), social science. **Special Study Options:** Independent study, internships, teacher certification program, weekend college.

FACILITIES
Housing: Men's dorms, women's dorms.

CAMPUS LIFE
Activities: Choral groups, student government, yearbook.

ADMISSIONS
Freshman Academic Profile: 3% in top 25% of high school class, 5% in top 50% of high school class. **Basis for Candidate Selection:** *Important factors considered include:* Rigor of secondary school record. *Other factors considered include:* Alumni/ae relation, character/personal qualities, extracurricular activities, recommendation(s), standardized test scores, volunteer work, work experience. **Freshman Admission Requirements:** High school diploma is required, and GED is accepted. *Academic units required:* 4 English, 4 math, 4 science, 3 social studies, 1 history. **Freshman Admission Statistics:** 72 applied, 100% admitted, 22% enrolled. **Transfer Admission Requirements:** High school transcript, college transcript(s), minimum college GPA of 1.7 required. Lowest grade transferable C. **General Admission Information:** Application fee $10. Regular notification is rolling. Nonfall registration accepted. Admission may be deferred for a maximum of indefinite. Common Application not accepted.

COSTS AND FINANCIAL AID
Annual tuition $2,200. Room & board $3,000. Required fees $30. Average book expense $250. **Types of Aid:** *Loans:* FFEL Subsidized Stafford, FFEL PLUS.

ARKANSAS STATE UNIVERSITY

PO Box 1630, State University, AR 72467
Phone: 870-972-3024 **E-mail:** admissions@astate.edu **CEEB Code:** 6011
Fax: 870-910-8094 **Website:** www.astate.edu **ACT Code:** 0116
Financial Aid Phone: 870-972-2310

This public school was founded in 1909. It has a 941-acre campus.

RATINGS
Admissions Selectivity Rating: 75   **Fire Safety Rating:** 60*   **Green Rating:** 60*

STUDENTS AND FACULTY
Enrollment: 9,000. **Student Body:** 59% female, 41% male, 10% out-of-state. African American 15%, Caucasian 82%. **Retention and Graduation:** 70% freshmen return for sophomore year. 15% freshmen graduate within 4 years. 3% grads go on to further study within 1 year. 1% grads pursue arts and sciences degrees. 2% grads pursue business degrees. 1% grads pursue law degrees. 1% grads pursue medical degrees. **Faculty:** Student/faculty ratio 19:1. 446 full-time faculty, 62% hold PhDs. 89% faculty teach undergrads.

ACADEMICS
Degrees: Associate, bachelor's, certificate, doctoral, master's, post-bachelor's certificate, post-master's certificate. **Academic Requirements:** Arts/fine arts, English (including composition), history, humanities, mathematics, philosophy, sciences (biological or physical), social science, physical education. **Classes:** Most classes have 20–29 students. Most lab/discussion sections have fewer than 10 students. **Majors with Highest Enrollment:** Business administration/management, data processing and data processing technology/technician. **Disciplines with Highest Percentage of Degrees Awarded:** Business/marketing 22%, education 21%, health professions and related sciences 8%, agriculture 6%, computer and information sciences 6%, social sciences 6%, communication technologies 5%, engineering 5%. **Special Study Options:** Accelerated program, cooperative education program, distance learning, double major, dual enrollment, English as a Second Language (ESL), exchange student program (domestic), honors program, independent study, internships, study abroad, teacher certification program.

FACILITIES
Housing: Men's dorms, women's dorms, apartments for married students, apartments for single students, fraternity/sorority housing, married and graduate student housing. **Special Academic Facilities/Equipment:** Art gallery, museum of Native American cultures and Arkansas artifacts, ecotoxicology research facility, electron microscope facility, geographic information system facility, equine center. **Computers:** 98% of public computers are PCs, 2% of public computers are Macs, network access in dorm rooms, online registration, online administrative functions (other than registration), remote student-access to Web through college's connection.

CAMPUS LIFE
Activities: Choral groups, concert band, dance, drama/theater, jazz band, marching band, music ensembles, musical theater, opera, pep band, radio station, student government, student newspaper, symphony orchestra, television station, yearbook. **Organizations:** 192 registered organizations, 42 honor societies, 16 religious organizations. 12 fraternities (15% men join), 9 sororities (11% women join). **Athletics (Intercollegiate):** *Men:* Baseball, basketball, cross-country, football, golf, track/field (indoor), track/field (outdoor). *Women:* Basketball, cross-country, golf, soccer, tennis, track/field (indoor), track/field (outdoor), volleyball.

ADMISSIONS
Freshman Academic Profile: 93% from public high schools. ACT middle 50% range 18–25. TOEFL required of all international applicants, minimum paper TOEFL 500, minimum computer TOEFL 173. **Basis for Candidate Selection:** *Very important factors considered include:* Rigor of secondary school record, standardized test scores. *Other factors considered include:* Class rank, recommendation(s), talent/ability. **Freshman Admission Requirements:** High school diploma is required, and GED is accepted. *Academic units recommended:* 4 English, 3 math, 3 science (3 science labs), 2 foreign language, 1 social studies, 2 history. **Freshman Admission Statistics:** 3,088 applied, 66% admitted, 75% enrolled. **Transfer Admission Requirements:** College transcript(s), minimum college GPA of 2.0 required. Lowest grade transferable C. **General Admission Information:** Application fee $15. Regular application deadline 8/23. Regular notification is rolling, upon receipt of application. Nonfall registration accepted. Common Application not accepted. Credit offered for CEEB Advanced Placement tests.

COSTS AND FINANCIAL AID
Annual in-state tuition $3,750. Out-of-state tuition $9,660. Room & board $3,640. Required fees $1,060. Average book expense $1,000. **Required Forms and Deadlines:** FAFSA, institution's own financial aid form. Financial aid filing deadline 7/1. **Notification of Awards:** Applicants will be notified of awards on a rolling basis beginning on or about 6/1. **Types of Aid:** *Need-based scholarships/grants:* Pell, SEOG, state scholarships/grants, private scholarships, the school's own gift aid. *Loans:* FFEL Subsidized Stafford, FFEL Unsubsidized Stafford, FFEL PLUS, Federal Perkins. **Student Employment:** Federal Work-Study Program available. Institutional employment available. Off-campus job opportunities are good. **Financial Aid Statistics:** 78% freshmen, 53% undergrads receive need-based scholarship or grant aid. 33% freshmen, 37% undergrads receive need-based self-help aid. 41 freshmen, 197 undergrads receive athletic scholarships. 76% freshmen, 67% undergrads receive any aid. Highest amount earned per year from on-campus jobs $3,600.

ARKANSAS TECH UNIVERSITY

ATU, Doc Bryan #141, Russellville, AR 72801
Phone: 479-968-0343 **E-mail:** tech.enroll@atu.edu **CEEB Code:** 6010
Fax: 479-964-0522 **Website:** www.atu.edu **ACT Code:** 0114
Financial Aid Phone: 479-968-0399

This public school was founded in 1909. It has a 516-acre campus.

RATINGS
Admissions Selectivity Rating: 81   **Fire Safety Rating:** 60*   **Green Rating:** 60*

STUDENTS AND FACULTY
Enrollment: 6,208. **Student Body:** 53% female, 47% male, 4% out-of-state, 3% international (32 countries represented). African American 5%, Asian 1%, Caucasian 87%, Hispanic 2%, Native American 2%. **Retention and Graduation:** 69% freshmen return for sophomore year. 21% freshmen graduate within 4 years. **Faculty:** Student/faculty ratio 18:1. 265 full-time faculty, 64% hold PhDs. 96% faculty teach undergrads.

ACADEMICS
Degrees: Associate, bachelor's, certificate, master's, post-master's certificate, terminal. **Academic Requirements:** Arts/fine arts, computer literacy, English (including composition), history, humanities, mathematics, sciences (biological or physical), social science, physical activity. **Classes:** Most classes have 20–29 students. Most lab/discussion sections have 10–19 students. **Majors with Highest Enrollment:** Business administration and management, early childhood education and teaching, nursing–registered nurse training (ASN, BSN, MSN, RN). **Disciplines with Highest Percentage of Degrees Awarded:** Education 20%, business/marketing 14%, health professions and related sciences 8%, engineering 7%, biological/life sciences 6%. **Special Study Options:** Accelerated program, cooperative education program, distance learning, double major, dual enrollment, English as a Second Language (ESL), exchange student program (domestic), external degree program, honors program, independent study, internships, student-designed major, study abroad, teacher certification program, weekend college.

FACILITIES
Housing: Coed dorms, men's dorms, women's dorms, apartments for single students, special housing for disabled students. **Special Academic Facilities/Equipment:** Arkansas Center for Energy, Natural Resources, and Environmental Studies, Crabaugh Communications Center; Museum of Prehistory and History, technology center. **Computers:** Network access in dorm rooms, network access in dorm lounges, online registration, online administrative functions (other than registration), remote student-access to Web through college's connection.

CAMPUS LIFE
Activities: Choral groups, concert band, dance, drama/theater, jazz band, literary magazine, marching band, music ensembles, musical theater, opera, pep band, radio station, student government, student newspaper, symphony orchestra, television station, yearbook. **Organizations:** 111 registered organizations, 14 honor societies, 11 religious organization. 5 fraternities (5% men join), 2 sororities (4% women join). **Athletics (Intercollegiate):** *Men:* Baseball, basketball, cheerleading, football, golf. *Women:* Basketball, cheerleading, cross-country, tennis, volleyball.

ADMISSIONS
Freshman Academic Profile: 18% in top 10% of high school class, 42% in top 25% of high school class, 70% in top 50% of high school class. SAT Math middle 50% range 430–620. SAT Critical Reading middle 50% range 350–520. ACT middle 50% range 19–26. TOEFL required of all international applicants, minimum paper TOEFL 500, minimum computer TOEFL 173. **Basis for**

Candidate Selection: *Very important factors considered include:* Academic GPA, rigor of secondary school record, standardized test scores. *Other factors considered include:* Class rank. **Freshman Admission Requirements:** High school diploma is required, and GED is accepted. *Academic units required:* 4 English, 4 math, 3 science (3 science labs), 1 social studies, 2 history, 4 academic electives, 2 various: Consult the ATU Online Catalog. *Academic units recommended:* 2 foreign language. **Freshman Admission Statistics:** 3,680 applied, 44% admitted, 94% enrolled. **Transfer Admission Requirements:** College transcript(s), minimum college GPA of 2.0 required. Lowest grade transferable C. **General Admission Information:** Regular notification is rolling, ending with requested term. Nonfall registration accepted. Admission may be deferred for a maximum of 1 year. Credit and/or placement offered for CEEB Advanced Placement tests.

COSTS AND FINANCIAL AID

Annual in-state tuition $4,590. Annual out-of-state tuition $9,180. Room and board $4,640. Required fees $530. Average book expense $1,320. **Required Forms and Deadlines:** FAFSA. Financial aid filing deadline 4/15. **Notification of Awards:** Applicants will be notified of awards on a rolling basis beginning on or about 5/1. **Types of Aid:** *Need-based scholarships/grants:* Pell, SEOG, state scholarships/grants, private scholarships, the school's own gift aid. *Loans:* FFEL Subsidized Stafford, FFEL Unsubsidized Stafford, FFEL PLUS, Federal Perkins. **Student Employment:** Federal Work-Study Program available. Institutional employment available. Off-campus job opportunities are excellent. **Financial Aid Statistics:** 48% freshmen, 47% undergrads receive need-based scholarship or grant aid. 32% freshmen, 44% undergrads receive need-based self-help aid. 68 freshmen, 194 undergrads receive athletic scholarships. 65% freshmen, 64% undergrads receive any aid.

ARLINGTON BAPTIST COLLEGE

Admissions Office, 3001 West Division, Arlington, TX 76012
Phone: 817-461-8741 **E-mail:** jhall@abconline.edu
Fax: 817-274-1138 **Website:** www.abconline.edu **ACT Code:** 4163
Financial Aid Phone: 817-461-8741

This private school, affiliated with the Baptist Church, was founded in 1939. It has a 35-acre campus.

RATINGS

Admissions Selectivity Rating: 61   **Fire Safety Rating:** 86   **Green Rating:** 60*

STUDENTS AND FACULTY

Enrollment: 152. **Student Body:** 46% female, 54% male, 17% out-of-state, 5% international (1 countries represented). African American 2%, Asian 1%, Caucasian 87%, Hispanic 4%. **Retention and Graduation:** 56% freshmen return for sophomore year. 27% freshmen graduate within 4 years. 15% grads go on to further study within 1 year. **Faculty:** Student/faculty ratio 10:1. 9 full-time faculty, 11% hold PhDs. 100% faculty teach undergrads.

ACADEMICS

Degrees: Bachelor's, certificate, diploma. **Academic Requirements:** English (including composition), history, mathematics, sciences (biological or physical). **Classes:** Most classes have fewer than 10 students. Most lab/discussion sections have fewer than 10 students. **Disciplines with Highest Percentage of Degrees Awarded:** Theology and religious vocations 54%, education 38%. **Special Study Options:** Distance learning, double major, dual enrollment, external degree program, teacher certification program.

FACILITIES

Housing: Men's dorms, women's dorms. **Special Academic Facilities/ Equipment:** Heritage Collection.

CAMPUS LIFE

Activities: Choral groups, drama/theater, student government, yearbook. **Organizations:** 5 religious organizations. **Athletics (Intercollegiate):** *Men:* Baseball, basketball. *Women:* Basketball, cheerleading, volleyball.

ADMISSIONS

Freshman Academic Profile: 31% in top 25% of high school class, 59% in top 50% of high school class. 80% from public high schools. TOEFL required of all international applicants, minimum paper TOEFL 550, minimum computer TOEFL 213. **Basis for Candidate Selection:** *Very important factors considered include:* Application essay, recommendation(s), religious affiliation/ commitment. *Important factors considered include:* Interview, level of applicant's interest. *Other factors considered include:* Character/personal qualities, extracurricular activities. **Freshman Admission Requirements:**

High school diploma is required, and GED is accepted. *Academic units required:* 3 English, 2 math, 1 science, 2 social studies. **Freshman Admission Statistics:** 38 applied, 100% admitted, 71% enrolled. **Transfer Admission Requirements:** High school transcript, college transcript(s), essay or personal statement. Lowest grade transferable C. **General Admission Information:** Application fee $15. Regular notification within a week of receiving the admissions requirements. Nonfall registration accepted. Admission may be deferred for a maximum of 3 semesters. Neither credit nor placement offered for CEEB Advanced Placement tests.

COSTS AND FINANCIAL AID

Annual tuition $5,550. Room and board $4,100. Required fees $540. Average book expense $750. **Required Forms and Deadlines:** FAFSA, institution's own financial aid form. **Notification of Awards:** Applicants will be notified of awards on a rolling basis beginning on or about 6/1. **Types of Aid:** *Need-based scholarships/grants:* Pell, SEOG, private scholarships, the school's own gift aid. *Loans:* FFEL Subsidized Stafford, FFEL Unsubsidized Stafford, FFEL PLUS. **Student Employment:** Institutional employment available. Off-campus job opportunities are excellent. **Financial Aid Statistics:** 100% freshmen, 93% undergrads receive need-based scholarship or grant aid. 100% freshmen, 93% undergrads receive need-based self-help aid. 90% freshmen, 95% undergrads receive any aid. Highest amount earned per year from on-campus jobs $5,600.

ARMSTRONG ATLANTIC STATE UNIVERSITY

11935 Abercorn Street, Savannah, GA 31419-1997
Phone: 912-927-5277 **E-mail:** adm-info@mail.armstrong.edu **CEEB Code:** 5012
Fax: 912-927-5462 **Website:** www.armstrong.edu **ACT Code:** 0786
Financial Aid Phone: 912-927-5272

This public school was founded in 1935. It has a 250-acre campus.

RATINGS

Admissions Selectivity Rating: 60*   **Fire Safety Rating:** 60*   **Green Rating:** 60*

STUDENTS AND FACULTY

Enrollment: 5,281. **Student Body:** 68% female, 32% male, 8% out-of-state, 2% international (71 countries represented). African American 22%, Asian 3%, Caucasian 65%, Hispanic 3%. **Faculty:** Student/faculty ratio 19:1. 229 full-time faculty, 70% hold PhDs. 90% faculty teach undergrads.

ACADEMICS

Degrees: Associate, bachelor's, master's, post-bachelor's certificate, post-master's certificate. **Academic Requirements:** Arts/fine arts, computer literacy, English (including composition), history, humanities, mathematics, sciences (biological or physical), social science. **Classes:** Most classes have 20–29 students. Most lab/discussion sections have fewer than 10 students. **Majors with Highest Enrollment:** Liberal arts and sciences/liberal studies, nursing–registered nurse training (ASN, BSN, MSN, RN). **Disciplines with Highest Percentage of Degrees Awarded:** Health professions and related sciences 28%, education 19%, liberal arts/general studies 12%, social sciences 11%, psychology 5%. **Special Study Options:** Cooperative education program, cross-registration, distance learning, double major, dual enrollment, honors program, independent study, internships, study abroad, teacher certification program, weekend college.

FACILITIES

Housing: Apartments for single students. **Special Academic Facilities/ Equipment:** Language lab, criminal justice training center, sports medicine clinic, speech/language pathology lab. **Computers:** Network access in dorm rooms, online registration, online administrative functions (other than registration), remote student-access to Web through college's connection.

CAMPUS LIFE

Activities: Choral groups, concert band, drama/theater, jazz band, literary magazine, music ensembles, musical theater, pep band, student government, student newspaper, symphony orchestra. **Organizations:** 55 registered organizations, 7 honor societies, 3 religious organizations. 1 fraternity, 1 sorority. **Athletics (Intercollegiate):** *Men:* Baseball, basketball, golf, tennis. *Women:* Basketball, softball, tennis, volleyball.

ADMISSIONS

Freshman Academic Profile: SAT Math middle 50% range 450–550. SAT Critical Reading middle 50% range 470–570. ACT middle 50% range 18–23. TOEFL required of all international applicants, minimum paper TOEFL 523, minimum computer TOEFL 193. **Basis for Candidate Selection:** *Important factors considered include:* Rigor of secondary school record, standardized test scores. *Other factors considered include:* Extracurricular activities, volunteer work. **Freshman Admission Requirements:** High school diploma is required, and GED is accepted. *Academic units required:* 4 English, 4 math, 3 science (2 science labs), 2 foreign language, 3 social studies. **Freshman Admission Statistics:** 1,685 applied, 65% admitted, 75% enrolled. **Transfer Admission Requirements:** College transcript(s), minimum college GPA of 2.0 required. Lowest grade transferable D. **General Admission Information:** Application fee $20. Regular application deadline 7/1. Regular notification is rolling. Nonfall registration accepted. Admission may be deferred for a maximum of 1 year. Common Application not accepted. Credit and/or placement offered for CEEB Advanced Placement tests.

COSTS AND FINANCIAL AID
Annual in-state tuition $2,212. Annual out-of-state tuition $8,842. Room and board $4,500. Required fees $390. Average book expense $800. **Required Forms and Deadlines:** FAFSA. Financial aid filing deadline 3/15. **Notification of Awards:** Applicants will be notified of awards on or about 2/1. **Types of Aid:** *Need-based scholarships/grants:* Pell, SEOG, state scholarships/grants, private scholarships, the school's own gift aid, Federal Nursing Scholarships. *Loans:* FFEL Subsidized Stafford, FFEL Unsubsidized Stafford, FFEL PLUS, state loans. **Student Employment:** Federal Work-Study Program available. Institutional employment available. Off-campus job opportunities are excellent. **Financial Aid Statistics:** 13% freshmen, 36% undergrads receive need-based scholarship or grant aid. 11% freshmen, 53% undergrads receive need-based self-help aid. 37 freshmen, 106 undergrads receive athletic scholarships. 90% freshmen, 90% undergrads receive any aid.

ART ACADEMY OF CINCINNATI

1212 Jackson Street, Cincinnati, OH 45202
Phone: 513-562-8740 **E-mail:** admissions@artacademy.edu
Fax: 513-562-8778 **Website:** www.artacademy.edu
Financial Aid Phone: 513-562-8751

This private school was founded in 1887.

RATINGS
Admissions Selectivity Rating: 60*   **Fire Safety Rating:** 60*   **Green Rating:** 63

STUDENTS AND FACULTY
Student Body: 30% out-of-state. **Faculty:** 100% faculty teach undergrads.

ACADEMICS
Degrees: Associate, bachelor's, master's. **Academic Requirements:** Arts/fine arts, computer literacy, English (including composition), humanities, social science, natural science, art history. **Disciplines with Highest Percentage of Degrees Awarded:** Visual and performing arts 100%. **Special Study Options:** Cooperative education program, cross-registration, double major, internships.

FACILITIES
Housing: Coed dorms. **Computers:** 25% of classrooms are wired, 25% of classrooms are wireless, 100% of public computers are Macs, remote student-access to Web through college's connection.

CAMPUS LIFE
Activities: Literary magazine.

ADMISSIONS
Freshman Academic Profile: SAT Math middle 50% range 420–510. SAT Critical Reading middle 50% range 480–580. ACT middle 50% range 18–23. TOEFL required of all international applicants, minimum paper TOEFL 550, minimum computer TOEFL 213. **Basis for Candidate Selection:** *Very important factors considered include:* Academic GPA, application essay, interview, recommendation(s), standardized test scores, talent/ability. *Important factors considered include:* Character/personal qualities, level of applicant's interest, rigor of secondary school record. *Other factors considered include:* Alumni/ae relation, class rank, geographical residence, state residency. **Freshman Admission Requirements:** High school diploma is required, and GED is accepted. **Freshman Admission Statistics:** 192 applied, 57% admitted, 43% enrolled. **Transfer Admission Requirements:** High school transcript, college transcript(s), essay or personal statement, interview, minimum college GPA of 2.0 required. Lowest grade transferable C. **General Admission Information:** Application fee $25. Regular application deadline 6/30. Regular notification is rolling. Nonfall registration not accepted. Admission may be deferred for a maximum of 1 year.

COSTS AND FINANCIAL AID
Annual tuition $20,950. Room and board $5,600. Required fees $350. Average book expense $1,200. **Required Forms and Deadlines:** FAFSA, state aid form. **Notification of Awards:** Applicants will be notified of awards on a rolling basis beginning on or about 2/1. **Types of Aid:** *Need-based scholarships/grants:* Pell, SEOG, state scholarships/grants, private scholarships, the school's own gift aid. *Loans:* FFEL Subsidized Stafford, FFEL Unsubsidized Stafford, FFEL PLUS, Federal Perkins. **Student Employment:** Federal Work-Study Program available. Institutional employment available.

ART CENTER COLLEGE OF DESIGN

1700 Lida Street, Pasadena, CA 91103-1999
Phone: 626-396-2373 **E-mail:** admissions@artcenter.edu **CEEB Code:** 4009
Fax: 626-795-0578 **Website:** www.artcenter.edu
Financial Aid Phone: 626-396-2215

This private school was founded in 1930. It has a 175-acre campus.

RATINGS
Admissions Selectivity Rating: 60*   **Fire Safety Rating:** 60*   **Green Rating:** 60*

STUDENTS AND FACULTY
Enrollment: 1,485. **Student Body:** 40% female, 60% male, 23% out-of-state, 16% international (32 countries represented). African American 2%, Asian 35%, Caucasian 35%, Hispanic 11%. **Retention and Graduation:** 86% freshmen return for sophomore year. 62% freshmen graduate within 4 years. **Faculty:** Student/faculty ratio 9:1. 66 full-time faculty. 98% faculty teach undergrads.

ACADEMICS
Degrees: Bachelor's, master's. **Academic Requirements:** Arts/fine arts, computer literacy, English (including composition), history, humanities, philosophy, sciences (biological or physical), social science, art history. **Classes:** Most classes have 10–19 students. **Majors with Highest Enrollment:** Graphic design, illustration, industrial design. **Disciplines with Highest Percentage of Degrees Awarded:** Visual and performing arts 100%. **Special Study Options:** Cooperative education program, independent study, internships.

FACILITIES
Special Academic Facilities/Equipment: 2 art galleries. **Computers:** 100% of public computers are Macs, online administrative functions (other than registration), remote student-access to Web through college's connection.

CAMPUS LIFE
Activities: Student government. **Organizations:** 12 registered organizations.

ADMISSIONS
Freshman Academic Profile: TOEFL required of all international applicants, minimum paper TOEFL 550, minimum computer TOEFL 213. **Basis for Candidate Selection:** *Very important factors considered include:* Academic GPA, application essay, rigor of secondary school record, talent/ability. *Important factors considered include:* Class rank, standardized test scores. *Other factors considered include:* Character/personal qualities, extracurricular activities, interview, racial/ethnic status, recommendation(s), volunteer work, work experience. **Freshman Admission Requirements:** High school diploma is required, and GED is accepted. **Freshman Admission Statistics:** 543 applied, 71% admitted, 65% enrolled. **Transfer Admission Requirements:** College transcript(s), essay or personal statement. Lowest grade transferable C. **General Admission Information:** Application fee $50. Regular notification is rolling. Nonfall registration accepted. Admission may be deferred for a maximum of 1 consecutive semester. Credit offered for CEEB Advanced Placement tests.

COSTS AND FINANCIAL AID
Annual tuition $27,710. Required fees $200. **Required Forms and Deadlines:** FAFSA. Financial aid filing deadline 1/1. **Types of Aid:** *Need-based scholarships/grants:* Pell, SEOG, state scholarships/grants, private scholarships, the school's own gift aid. *Loans:* Direct Subsidized Stafford, Direct Unsubsidized Stafford, Direct PLUS. **Student Employment:** Federal Work-Study Program available. Institutional employment available. **Financial Aid Statistics:** 43% freshmen, 55% undergrads receive need-based scholarship or grant aid. 69% freshmen, 68% undergrads receive need-based self-help aid. 78% freshmen, 79% undergrads receive any aid.

ART INSTITUTE OF ATLANTA

6600 Peachtree Dunwoody Road, 100 Embassy Row, Atlanta, GA 30328
Phone: 770-394-8300 **E-mail:** aiaadm@aii.edu
Fax: 770-394-0008 **Website:** www.aia.artinstitutes.edu **ACT Code:** 0859
Financial Aid Phone: 770-689-4824

This proprietary school was founded in 1949. It has a 7-acre campus.

RATINGS
Admissions Selectivity Rating: 60* **Fire Safety Rating:** 60* **Green Rating:** 60*

STUDENTS AND FACULTY
Enrollment: 2,646. **Student Body:** 46% female, 54% male, 38% out-of-state, 2% international (33 countries represented). African American 27%, Asian 2%, Caucasian 39%, Hispanic 3%. **Faculty:** Student/faculty ratio 21:1. 91 full-time faculty, 49% hold PhDs. 100% faculty teach undergrads.

ACADEMICS
Degrees: Associate, bachelor's, diploma. **Academic Requirements:** Arts/fine arts, computer literacy, English (including composition), history, humanities, mathematics, sciences (biological or physical), social science education courses such as math, English, and psychology. Foundation art courses for all non-culinary arts majors. **Classes:** Most classes have 20–29 students. **Majors with Highest Enrollment:** Commercial and advertising art, culinary arts/chef training, interior design. **Disciplines with Highest Percentage of Degrees Awarded:** Visual and performing arts 75%. **Special Study Options:** Accelerated program, cross-registration, distance learning, honors program, independent study, internships, study abroad, academic remediation advanced placement credit.

FACILITIES
Housing: Coed dorms, apartments for married students, apartments for single students, special housing for disabled students, apartment and roommate referral services. **Special Academic Facilities/Equipment:** Art gallery, multi-camera video studio with digital and non-linear video editing suites, and an audio studio and control room featuring Protools stations. Professional photography studios with traditional and digital darkroom facilities containing high-end professional equipment such as the Imacon scanner, Cone Piezograph B&W printers, Epson 5500 printer, and Epson 10000 printer. Photographic video editing stations consist of Dual Processor G4s with cinema displays that are color managed with Greytag MacBeth equipment. Culinary facilities with 5 teaching kitchens and a dining lab. **Computers:** 50% of public computers are PCs, 50% of public computers are Macs, network access in dorm lounges, online registration, remote student-access to Web through college's connection.

CAMPUS LIFE
Activities: Student government. **Organizations:** 16 registered organizations.

ADMISSIONS
Freshman Academic Profile: TOEFL required of all international applicants, minimum paper TOEFL 500, minimum computer TOEFL 173. **Basis for Candidate Selection:** *Very important factors considered include:* Application essay, interview, rigor of secondary school record. *Important factors considered include:* Standardized test scores, talent/ability. *Other factors considered include:* Character/personal qualities, class rank, extracurricular activities, recommendation(s), volunteer work, work experience. **Freshman Admission Requirements:** High school diploma is required, and GED is accepted. **Transfer Admission Requirements:** College transcript(s), essay or personal statement, interview, minimum college GPA of 2.0 required. Lowest grade transferable C. **General Admission Information:** Application fee $50. Regular application deadline 10/1. Regular notification continuous. Nonfall registration accepted. Admission may be deferred for a maximum of 4 quarters. Credit and/or placement offered for CEEB Advanced Placement tests.

COSTS AND FINANCIAL AID
Annual tuition $17,040. Room $7,311. Average book expense $1,440. **Required Forms and Deadlines:** FAFSA, state aid form. **Notification of Awards:** Applicants will be notified of awards on a rolling basis beginning on or about 3/15. **Types of Aid:** *Need-based scholarships/grants:* Pell, SEOG, state scholarships/grants, private scholarships, the school's own gift aid. *Loans:* Direct Subsidized Stafford, Direct Unsubsidized Stafford, Direct PLUS, FFEL Subsidized Stafford, FFEL Unsubsidized Stafford, FFEL PLUS, Federal Perkins. **Student Employment:** Federal Work-Study Program available. Institutional employment available. Off-campus job opportunities are good. **Financial Aid Statistics:** 50% freshmen, 63% undergrads receive need-based scholarship or grant aid. 97% freshmen, 87% undergrads receive need-based self-help aid. 19% freshmen, 81% undergrads receive any aid.

See page 1064.

THE ART INSTITUTE OF BOSTON
AT LESLEY UNIVERSITY

700 Beacon Street, Boston, MA 02215-2598
Phone: 617-585-6710 **E-mail:** admissions@aiboston.edu **CEEB Code:** 3777
Fax: 617-585-6720 **Website:** http://web.lesley.edu/aib/default.asp
Financial Aid Phone: 617-349-8710

This private school was founded in 1912. It has a 1-acre campus.

RATINGS
Admissions Selectivity Rating: 81 **Fire Safety Rating:** 88 **Green Rating:** 72

STUDENTS AND FACULTY
Enrollment: 1,152. **Student Body:** 76% female, 24% male, 41% out-of-state, 2% international (15 countries represented). African American 5%, Asian 4%, Caucasian 63%, Hispanic 5%. **Retention and Graduation:** 75% freshmen return for sophomore year. 36% freshmen graduate within 4 years. **Faculty:** Student/faculty ratio 10:1. 66 full-time faculty, 71% hold PhDs. 100% faculty teach undergrads.

ACADEMICS
Degrees: Associate, bachelor's, certificate, diploma, doctoral, master's, post-bachelor's certificate, post-master's certificate. **Academic Requirements:** Arts/fine arts, computer literacy, English (including composition), history, humanities, mathematics, philosophy, sciences (biological or physical), social science, multicultural perspectives. **Classes:** Most classes have 10–19 students. **Majors with Highest Enrollment:** Graphic design, illustration, photography. **Disciplines with Highest Percentage of Degrees Awarded:** Liberal arts/general studies 34%, visual and performing arts 28%, history 11%, psychology 11%, education 7%. **Special Study Options:** Accelerated program, AICAD mobility program, Bridge program, cross registration, distance learning, double major, dual enrollment, exchange student program (domestic), honors program, independent study, internships, liberal arts/career combination, NY Studio program, student-designed major, study abroad, teacher certification program.

FACILITIES
Housing: Coed dorms, women's dorms. **Special Academic Facilities/Equipment:** Art gallery with regular shows of prominant artists, art library, applied art facilities including state-of-the-art photo and computer labs, animation studio, ceramics studio, wood shop, metals studio, and printmaking studio. **Computers:** 100% of classrooms are wired, 50% of classrooms are wireless, 100% of public computers are Macs, network access in dorm lounges, network access in dorm rooms, online administrative functions (other than registration), online registration, remote student-access to Web through college's connection. Undergraduates are required to own a computer.

CAMPUS LIFE
Activities: Choral groups, dance, drama/theater, literary magazine, musical theater, student government, student newspaper, yearbook. **Organizations:** 25 registered organizations, 2 honor societies. **Athletics (Intercollegiate):** *Men:* Basketball, crew/rowing, soccer. *Women:* Basketball, crew/rowing, soccer, softball, volleyball. Environmental Initiatives: Continual enhancement of recycling, waste management, and composting programs on campus. The formation of sustainability recommendations for faculty, staff and students. Student groups on campus are involved with and sponsor sustainability events.

ADMISSIONS
Freshman Academic Profile: 15% in top 10% of high school class, 49% in top 25% of high school class, 79% in top 50% of high school class. 84% from public high schools. SAT Math middle 50% range 460–560. SAT Critical Reading middle 50% range 450–600. SAT Writing middle 50% range 480–580. ACT middle 50% range 20–26. TOEFL required of all international applicants, minimum paper TOEFL 500, minimum computer TOEFL 220. **Basis for Candidate Selection:** *Very important factors considered include:* Academic GPA, rigor of secondary school record. *Important factors considered include:* Application essay, character/personal qualities, class rank, interview, recommendation(s), standardized test scores. *Other factors considered include:* Alumni/ae relation, extracurricular activities, first generation, geographical residence, level of applicant's interest, racial/ethnic status, talent/ability, volunteer work, work experience. **Freshman Admission Requirements:** High school diploma is required, and GED is accepted. *Academic units required:* 4 English. *Academic units recommended:* 4 English, 1 math, 1 science, 1 foreign language, 2 social studies, 2 history, 2 academic electives, 2 studio art. **Freshman Admission Statistics:** 2,687 applied, 40% admitted, 28% enrolled. **Transfer Admission Requirements:** High school transcript, college transcript(s), essay or personal statement, interview, statement of good standing

from prior institution(s). Minimum college GPA of 2.0 required. Lowest grade transferable C. **General Admission Information:** Application fee $40. Regular notification is rolling. Non-fall registration accepted. Admission may be deferred for a maxiumum of 2 semesters. Credit and/or placement offered for CEEB Advanced Placement tests.

COSTS AND FINANCIAL AID
Annual tuition $24,825. Room and board $12,000. Required fees $810. Average book expense $1,575. **Required Forms and Deadlines:** FAFSA, institution's own financial aid form. Financial aid filing deadline 2/15. **Notification of Awards:** Applicants will be notified of awards on or about 3/1. **Types of Aid:** *Need-based scholarships/grants:* Pell, private scholarships, SEOG, state scholarships/grants, the school's own gift aid. *Loans:* Federal Perkins, FFEL PLUS, FFEL Subsidized Stafford, FFEL Unsubsidized Stafford, state loans. **Financial Aid Statistics:** 62% freshmen, 62% undergrads receive need-based scholarship or grant aid. 62% freshmen, 68% undergrads receive need-based self-help aid. 70% freshmen, 70% undergrads receive any aid. Highest amount earned per year from on-campus jobs: $1,200.

THE ART INSTITUTE OF CALIFORNIA— ORANGE COUNTY

3601 Sunflower Avenue, Santa Ana, CA 92704
Phone: 714-830-0200 **E-mail:** aicaocadm@aii.edu
Fax: 714-556-1923 **Website:** www.artinstitutes.edu/orangecounty/
Financial Aid Phone: 888-549-3055

This proprietary school was founded in 2000.

RATINGS
Admissions Selectivity Rating: 60*　　**Fire Safety Rating:** 60*　　**Green Rating:** 60*

ACADEMICS
Degrees: Associate, bachelor's. **Academic Requirements:** Arts/fine arts, computer literacy, English (including composition), history, humanities, mathematics, philosophy, social science. **Special Study Options:** Internships.

FACILITIES
Housing: Apartments for single students.

CAMPUS LIFE
Activities: Student newspaper.

ADMISSIONS
Basis for Candidate Selection: *Very important factors considered include:* Application essay, interview. *Important factors considered include:* Rigor of secondary school record. *Other factors considered include:* Class rank, standardized test scores, talent/ability. **Freshman Admission Requirements:** High school diploma is required, and GED is accepted. **Freshman Admission Statistics:** 1,998 applied, 100% admitted. **Transfer Admission Requirements:** College transcript(s), essay or personal statement, high school transcript. Lowest grade transferable C. **General Admission Information:** Application fee $50. Regular notification immediately upon reciept of application and review by admissions. Non-fall registration accepted. Admission may be deferred for a maxiumum of 2 semesters. Common Application not accepted.

COSTS AND FINANCIAL AID
Required fees: $150. Average book expense: $125. **Required Forms and Deadlines:** FAFSA, institution's own financial aid form, state aid form. **Notification of Awards:** Applicants will be notified of awards on a rolling basis beginning on or about 1/1. **Types of Aid:** *Need-based scholarships/grants:* Pell, SEOG, state scholarships/grants, private scholarships, the school's own gift aid. *Loans:* Direct Subsidized Stafford, Direct Unsubsidized Stafford, Direct PLUS, FFEL Subsidized Stafford, FFEL Unsubsidized Stafford, FFEL PLUS, Federal Perkins, Creative Education Loan. **Student Employment:** Federal Work-Study Program available. Institutional employment available. Off-campus job opportunities are excellent.

THE ART INSTITUTE OF CALIFORNIA— SAN DIEGO

10025 Mesa Rim Road, San Diego, CA 92121
Phone: 619-546-0602 **E-mail:** aicaadmin@aii.edu
Fax: 619-546-0274 **Website:** www.taac.edu
Financial Aid Phone: 619-546-0602

This private school was founded in 1981. It has a 2-acre campus.

RATINGS
Admissions Selectivity Rating: 60*　　**Fire Safety Rating:** 60*　　**Green Rating:** 60*

STUDENTS AND FACULTY
Enrollment: 267. **Student Body:** 37% female, 63% male. **Retention and Graduation:** 50% grads go on to further study within 1 year.

ACADEMICS
Degrees: Associate, bachelor's, certificate, diploma. **Academic Requirements:** Arts/fine arts, computer literacy, mathematics, social science. **Special Study Options:** Internships.

FACILITIES
Computers: 25% of public computers are PCs, 75% of public computers are Macs, online registration.

CAMPUS LIFE
Activities: Student newspaper.

ADMISSIONS
Basis for Candidate Selection: *Factors considered include:* Application essay, character/personal qualities, talent/ability. **Freshman Admission Requirements:** High school diploma is required, and GED is accepted. **Freshman Admission Statistics:** 164 applied, 100% admitted. **Transfer Admission Requirements:** College transcript(s), essay or personal statement, high school transcript. Lowest grade transferable C. **General Admission Information:** Application fee $30. Non-fall registration accepted. Common Application not accepted.

COSTS AND FINANCIAL AID
Annual tuition: $9,300. Average book expense: $200. **Required Forms and Deadlines:** FAFSA, institution's own financial aid form, state aid form. **Types of Aid:** *Need-based scholarships/grants:* Pell, SEOG, state scholarships/grants, private scholarships. *Loans:* Direct Subsidized Stafford, Direct Unsubsidized Stafford, Direct PLUS. **Student Employment:** Federal Work-Study Program available. Institutional employment available. Off-campus job opportunities are good. **Financial Aid Statistics:** 62% freshmen, 67% undergrads receive need-based scholarship or grant aid. 8% freshmen, 21% undergrads receive need-based self-help aid.

THE ART INSTITUTE OF CALIFORNIA— SAN FRANCISCO

1170 Market Street, San Francisco, CA 94102
Phone: 415-865-0198 **E-mail:** aisfadm@aii.edu
Fax: 415-863-6344 **Website:** www.aicasf.aii.edu
Financial Aid Phone: 415-865-0198

This proprietary school was founded in 1939. It has a 1-acre campus.

RATINGS
Admissions Selectivity Rating: 61　　**Fire Safety Rating:** 60*　　**Green Rating:** 60*

STUDENTS AND FACULTY
Enrollment: 346. **Student Body:** 44% female, 56% male, 25% out-of-state, 5% international. African American 5%, Asian 12%, Caucasian 24%, Hispanic 17%, Native American 1%. **Retention and Graduation:** 78% freshmen return for sophomore year. 5% grads go on to further study within 1 year. 5% grads pursue arts and sciences degrees. **Faculty:** Student/faculty ratio 14:1. 7 full-time faculty, 86% hold PhDs. 100% faculty teach undergrads.

ACADEMICS
Degrees: Associate, bachelor's. **Academic Requirements:** Arts/fine arts,

computer literacy, English (including composition), history, mathematics, sciences (biological or physical), social science. **Classes:** Most classes have 10–19 students. **Disciplines with Highest Percentage of Degrees Awarded:** Visual and performing arts 100%. **Special Study Options:** Accelerated program, distance learning, internships.

FACILITIES
Housing: All housing is in an apartment complex. Studio, 1, and 2 bedroom apartments are available with 2/2/4 roommates per apartment respectively. Apartments are available for married couples. **Computers:** 60% of public computers are PCs, 40% of public computers are Macs.

CAMPUS LIFE
Activities: Student government, student newspaper.

ADMISSIONS
Freshman Academic Profile: 90% from public high schools. TOEFL required of all international applicants, minimum paper TOEFL 480, minimum computer TOEFL 157. **Basis for Candidate Selection:** *Important factors considered include:* Application essay, character/personal qualities, interview, talent/ability. *Other factors considered include:* Alumni/ae relation, class rank, extracurricular activities, recommendation(s), rigor of secondary school record, standardized test scores, volunteer work, work experience. **Freshman Admission Requirements:** High school diploma is required, and GED is accepted. **Freshman Admission Statistics:** 205 applied, 100% admitted, 48% enrolled. **Transfer Admission Requirements:** College transcript(s), essay or personal statement, high school transcript, interview. Lowest grade transferable C. **General Admission Information:** Application fee $50. Regular notification 1 month after application information recieved. Non-fall registration accepted. Admission may be deferred for a maxiumum of 2 semesters. Common Application not accepted.

COSTS AND FINANCIAL AID
Annual tuition: $13,200. Average book expense: $1,125. **Required Forms and Deadlines:** FAFSA. Financial aid filing deadline 6/30. **Types of Aid:** *Need-based scholarships/grants:* Pell, private scholarships, SEOG, state scholarships/grants, the school's own gift aid, United Negro College Fund. *Loans:* FFEL Subsidized Stafford, FFEL Unsubsidized Stafford, FFEL PLUS, Federal Perkins, Federal Nursing, state loans, CELP, CEOL, independent loans from private organizations. **Student Employment:** Federal Work-Study Program available. Institutional employment available. Off-campus job opportunities are good. **Financial Aid Statistics:** 42% freshmen, 60% undergrads receive need-based scholarship or grant aid. Highest amount earned per year from on-campus jobs: $5,000.

ART INSTITUTE OF COLORADO

1200 Lincoln Street, Denver, CO 80203
Phone: 303-837-0825 **E-mail:** aicinfo@artinstitutes.edu
Fax: 303-860-8520 **Website:** www.aic.artinstitutes.edu **ACT Code:** 0495
Financial Aid Phone: 303-824-4757

This proprietary school was founded in 1952.

RATINGS
Admissions Selectivity Rating: 60*   **Fire Safety Rating:** 60*   **Green Rating:** 60*

STUDENTS AND FACULTY
Enrollment: 2,320. **Student Body:** 48% female, 52% male. African American 1%, Asian 2%, Caucasian 43%, Hispanic 6%. **Faculty:** Student/faculty ratio 20:1. 64 full-time faculty, 17% hold PhDs.

ACADEMICS
Degrees: Associate, bachelor's, certificate, diploma. **Academic Requirements:** Arts/fine arts, computer literacy, English (including composition), foreign languages, history, humanities, mathematics, philosophy, sciences (biological or physical), social science. **Special Study Options:** Independent study, internships, study abroad.

FACILITIES
Housing: Apartments for single students. **Computers:** 50% of public computers are PCs, 49% of public computers are Macs, network access in dorm rooms, online administrative functions (other than registration), remote student-access to Web through college's connection.

CAMPUS LIFE
Organizations: 3 honor societies.

ADMISSIONS
Freshman Academic Profile: TOEFL required of all international applicants, minimum paper TOEFL 480. **Basis for Candidate Selection:** *Important factors considered include:* Application essay, interview, standardized test scores. *Other factors considered include:* Rigor of secondary school record. **Freshman Admission Requirements:** High school diploma is required, and GED is accepted. **Freshman Admission Statistics:** 748 applied, 52% admitted, 96% enrolled. **Transfer Admission Requirements:** High school transcript, essay or personal statement, interview. Lowest grade transferable C. **General Admission Information:** Application fee $50. Nonfall registration accepted. Admission may be deferred for a maximum of 1 year. Common Application not accepted. Credit offered for CEEB Advanced Placement tests.

COSTS AND FINANCIAL AID
Annual tuition $14,880. Room and board $6,048. Required fees $50. Average book expense $2,250. **Required Forms and Deadlines:** FAFSA, institution's own financial aid form. Financial aid filing deadline 3/15. **Types of Aid:** *Need-based scholarships/grants:* Pell, SEOG, state scholarships/grants, private scholarships, the school's own gift aid. *Loans:* FFEL Subsidized Stafford, FFEL Unsubsidized Stafford, FFEL PLUS, Federal Perkins, state loans. **Student Employment:** Federal Work-Study Program available. Institutional employment available. Off-campus job opportunities are excellent.

THE ART INSTITUTE OF DALLAS

8080 Park Lane #100, Two Park North East, Dallas, TX 75231
Phone: 214-692-8080 **E-mail:** crispm@aii.edu **CEEB Code:** 2680
Fax: 214-750-9460 **Website:** www.artinstitutes.edu/dallas **ACT Code:** 4075
Financial Aid Phone: 800-275-4243

This private school was founded in 1964.

RATINGS
Admissions Selectivity Rating: 60*   **Fire Safety Rating:** 60*   **Green Rating:** 60*

STUDENTS AND FACULTY
Enrollment: 1,463. **Student Body:** 41% female, 59% male, 97% out-of-state. African American 5%, Asian 3%, Caucasian 35%, Hispanic 7%. **Retention and Graduation:** 8% grads go on to further study within 1 year. 8% grads pursue arts and sciences degrees. **Faculty:** Student/faculty ratio 18:1. 62 full-time faculty, 21% hold PhDs. 100% faculty teach undergrads.

ACADEMICS
Degrees: Associate, bachelor's, certificate, terminal. **Academic Requirements:** Arts/fine arts, computer literacy, English (including composition), humanities, mathematics, social science. **Classes:** Most classes have 10–19 students. **Special Study Options:** Cross registration, dual enrollment, internships, liberal arts/career combination, study abroad.

FACILITIES
Housing: Apartments for single students. **Special Academic Facilities/Equipment:** See website. **Computers:** 80% of public computers are PCs, 20% of public computers are Macs, remote student-access to Web through college's connection.

CAMPUS LIFE
Activities: Student government, student newspaper, student-run film society. **Organizations:** 5 registered organizations.

ADMISSIONS
Freshman Academic Profile: 93% from public high schools. TOEFL required of all international applicants, minimum paper TOEFL 550, minimum computer TOEFL 213. **Basis for Candidate Selection:** *Factors considered include:* Application essay, class rank, recommendation(s), rigor of secondary school record, standardized test scores. **Freshman Admission Requirements:** High school diploma is required, and GED is accepted. *Academic units required:* 4 English, 4 math, 2 science, 1 foreign language, 2 social studies, 2 history. *Academic units recommended:* 4 English, 4 math, 2 science, 1 foreign language, 2 social studies, 2 history. **Freshman Admission Statistics:** 855 applied, 53% admitted, 61% enrolled. **Transfer Admission Requirements:** Essay or personal statement, high school transcript, interview, standardized test score. Minimum college GPA of 2.0 required. Lowest grade transferable C. **General Admission Information:** Application fee $50. Non-fall registration accepted. Admission may be deferred for a maximum of 1 quarter. Common Application not accepted. Credit and/or placement offered for CEEB Advanced Placement tests.

COSTS AND FINANCIAL AID

Annual tuition: $13,770. Average book expense: $950. **Required Forms and Deadlines:** FAFSA, institution's own financial aid form. **Types of Aid:** *Need-based scholarships/grants:* Pell, SEOG, private scholarships, the school's own gift aid. *Loans:* FFEL Subsidized Stafford, FFEL Unsubsidized Stafford, FFEL PLUS. **Student Employment:** Federal Work-Study Program available. Institutional employment available. Off-campus job opportunities are excellent. **Financial Aid Statistics:** 39% freshmen, 26% undergrads receive need-based scholarship or grant aid. 4% undergrads receive need-based self-help aid. 20 freshmen, 45 undergrads receive athletic scholarships. Highest amount earned per year from on-campus jobs: $1,014.

THE ART INSTITUTE OF PITTSBURGH

420 Boulevard of the Allies, Pittsburgh, PA 15219
Phone: 412-263-6600 **E-mail:** aip_admissions@aii.edu
Fax: 412-263-6667 **Website:** www.aip.aii.edu
Financial Aid Phone: 412-291-6376

This proprietary school was founded in 1921.

RATINGS

Admissions Selectivity Rating: 60*   **Fire Safety Rating:** 60*   **Green Rating:** 60*

STUDENTS AND FACULTY

Enrollment: 4,864. **Student Body:** 55% female, 45% male. African American 2%, Caucasian 30%. **Faculty:** Student/faculty ratio 20:1. 44 full-time faculty, 50% hold PhDs. 100% faculty teach undergrads.

ACADEMICS

Degrees: Associate, bachelor's, diploma. **Academic Requirements:** Arts/fine arts, computer literacy, English (including composition), history, humanities, mathematics, natural science, philosophy, sciences (biological or physical), social science. **Highest Percentage of Degrees Awarded:** Visual and performing arts 100%. **Special Study Options:** Distance learning, English as a Second Language (ESL), internships.

FACILITIES

Housing: Single sex apartments in coed buildings. **Computers:** 50% of public computers are PCs, 50% of public computers are Macs, network access in dorm rooms, network access in dorm lounges, remote student-access to Web through college's connection.

CAMPUS LIFE

Activities: Drama/theater, student government, student newspaper, student-run film society. **Organizations:** 21 registered organizations, 2 honor societies, 1 religious organization.

ADMISSIONS

Basis for Candidate Selection: *Very important factors considered include:* Application essay, rigor of secondary school record. *Important factors considered include:* Talent/ability. *Other factors considered include:* Extracurricular activities, recommendation(s). **Freshman Admission Requirements:** High school diploma is required, and GED is accepted. *Academic units recommended:* 3 English, 3 math, 3 science. **Freshman Admission Statistics:** 2,177 applied, 46% admitted, 100% enrolled. **Transfer Admission Requirements:** Essay or personal statement, high school transcript, interview. Lowest grade transferable C. **General Admission Information:** Application fee $150. Non-fall registration accepted. Admission may be deferred for a maxiumum of 2 semesters. Common Application not accepted. Neither credit nor placement offered for CEEB Advanced Placement tests.

COSTS AND FINANCIAL AID

Annual tuition $16,740. Room and board $6,525. Average book expense $900. **Required Forms and Deadlines:** FAFSA, institution's own financial aid form, state aid form. **Types of Aid:** *Need-based scholarships/grants:* Pell, SEOG, state scholarships/grants, private scholarships, the school's own gift aid. *Loans:* FFEL Subsidized Stafford, FFEL Unsubsidized Stafford, FFEL PLUS, Federal Perkins, state loans, college/university loans from institutional funds. **Student Employment:** Federal Work-Study Program available. Institutional employment available. Off-campus job opportunities are excellent. **Financial Aid Statistics:** 88% undergrads receive any aid.

THE ART INSTITUTES INTERNATIONAL MINNESOTA

15 South 9th Street, Minneapolis, MN 55402
Phone: 612-332-3361 **E-mail:** aimadm@aii.edu
Fax: 612-332-3934 **Website:** www.artinstitutes.edu/minneapolis
Financial Aid Phone: 612-332-3361

This proprietary school was founded in 1997.

RATINGS

Admissions Selectivity Rating: 60*   **Fire Safety Rating:** 60*   **Green Rating:** 60*

STUDENTS AND FACULTY

Enrollment: 1,608. **Student Body:** 58% female, 42% male, 6% out-of-state. African American 1%, Asian 2%, Caucasian 28%. **Faculty:** Student/faculty ratio 20:1. 49 full-time faculty. 100% faculty teach undergrads.

ACADEMICS

Degrees: Associate, bachelor's, certificate. **Academic Requirements:** Arts/fine arts, computer literacy, English (including composition), foreign languages, history, humanities, mathematics, sciences (biological or physical). **Majors with Highest Enrollment:** Culinary arts/chef training, design and applied arts, design and visual communications. **Disciplines with Highest Percentage of Degrees Awarded:** Personal and culinary services 15%. **Special Study Options:** Cooperative education program, honors program, independent study, internships, study abroad, evening program, online program.

FACILITIES

Housing: Apartments for single students. **Special Academic Facilities/ Equipment:** Gallery, Gourmet Gallery (student run dining lab), learning resource center. **Computers:** 50% of public computers are PCs, 50% of public computers are Macs, network access in dorm rooms, network access in dorm lounges, remote student-access to Web through college's connection.

CAMPUS LIFE

Activities: Student government, student newspaper, student-run film society. **Organizations:** 6 registered organizations, 1 honor society.

ADMISSIONS

Freshman Academic Profile: TOEFL required of all international applicants, minimum paper TOEFL 500, minimum computer TOEFL 156. **Basis for Candidate Selection:** *Important factors considered include:* Application essay, interview. *Other factors considered include:* Recommendation(s), rigor of secondary school record, talent/ability. **Freshman Admission Requirements:** High school diploma is required, and GED is accepted. **Freshman Admission Statistics:** 715 applied, 46% admitted. **Transfer Admission Requirements:** High school transcript, college transcript(s), essay or personal statement, interview, standardized test score. Minimum college GPA of 2.0 required. Lowest grade transferable C. **General Admission Information:** Application fee $150. Non-fall registration accepted.

COSTS AND FINANCIAL AID

Annual tuition $20,688. Room and board: $6,864. Average book expense: $1,125. **Required Forms and Deadlines:** FAFSA, institution's own financial aid form, state aid form. **Types of Aid:** *Need-based scholarships/grants:* Pell, SEOG, state scholarships/grants, the school's own gift aid. *Loans:* FFEL Subsidized Stafford, FFEL Unsubsidized Stafford, FFEL PLUS, state loans. **Student Employment:** Federal Work-Study Program available. Off-campus job opportunities are good.

ART INSTITUTES INTERNATIONAL AT PORTLAND

2000 Southwest Fifth Avenue, Portland, OR 97201-4907
Phone: 503-228-6528 **E-mail:** alstonk@aii.edu **CEEB Code:** 7819
Fax: 503-228-4227 **Website:** www.aii.edu/portland
Financial Aid Phone: 503-228-6528

This proprietary school was founded in 1963. It has a 1-acre campus.

RATINGS
Admissions Selectivity Rating: 60*   **Fire Safety Rating:** 60*   **Green Rating:** 60*

STUDENTS AND FACULTY
Enrollment: 204. **Student Body:** 72% female, 28% male. **Retention and Graduation:** 57% freshmen return for sophomore year. **Faculty:** 100% faculty teach undergrads.

ACADEMICS
Degrees: Associate, bachelor's. **Academic Requirements:** Arts/fine arts, computer literacy, English (including composition), history, humanities, mathematics, philosophy, sciences (biological or physical), social science. **Special Study Options:** Independent study, internships.

FACILITIES
Computers: 60% of public computers are PCs, 40% of public computers are Macs.

CAMPUS LIFE
Organizations: 2 registered organizations.

ADMISSIONS
Freshman Academic Profile: TOEFL required of all international applicants, minimum paper TOEFL 500. **Basis for Candidate Selection:** *Very important factors considered include:* Application essay, rigor of secondary school record. *Important factors considered include:* Interview, talent/ability. *Other factors considered include:* Character/personal qualities, class rank, extracurricular activities, recommendation(s), standardized test scores, work experience. **Freshman Admission Requirements:** High school diploma is required, and GED is accepted. **Freshman Admission Statistics:** 51 applied, 96% admitted, 67% enrolled. **Transfer Admission Requirements:** High school transcript, college transcript(s), essay or personal statement, interview, minimum college GPA of 2.0 required. Lowest grade transferable C. **General Admission Information:** Application fee $50. Nonfall registration accepted. Common Application not accepted.

COSTS AND FINANCIAL AID
Annual tuition $11,250. Average book expense $1,125. **Required Forms and Deadlines:** FAFSA. **Notification of Awards:** Applicants will be notified of awards on a rolling basis beginning on or about 2/1. **Types of Aid:** *Need-based scholarships/grants:* Pell, SEOG, private scholarships, the school's own gift aid. *Loans:* FFEL Subsidized Stafford, FFEL Unsubsidized Stafford, FFEL PLUS, Federal Perkins. **Student Employment:** Off-campus job opportunities are excellent. **Financial Aid Statistics:** 37% freshmen, 21% undergrads receive need-based scholarship or grant aid. 87% freshmen, 77% undergrads receive need-based self-help aid.

ASBURY COLLEGE

1 Macklem Drive, Wilmore, KY 40390
Phone: 859-858-3511 **E-mail:** admissions@asbury.edu **CEEB Code:** 1019
Fax: 859-858-3921 **Website:** www.asbury.edu **ACT Code:** 1486
Financial Aid Phone: 859-858-3511

This private school was founded in 1890. It has a 400-acre campus.

RATINGS
Admissions Selectivity Rating: 87   **Fire Safety Rating:** 60*   **Green Rating:** 60*

STUDENTS AND FACULTY
Enrollment: 1,167. **Student Body:** 58% female, 42% male, 70% out-of-state, 1% international (10 countries represented). Caucasian 96%, Hispanic 1%. **Retention and Graduation:** 82% freshmen return for sophomore year. 49%

freshmen graduate within 4 years. **Faculty:** Student/faculty ratio 11:1. 90 full-time faculty, 78% hold PhDs. 100% faculty teach undergrads.

ACADEMICS
Degrees: Bachelor's, master's. **Academic Requirements:** Arts/fine arts, computer literacy, English (including composition), foreign languages, history, humanities, mathematics, philosophy, sciences (biological or physical), social science, Bible and theology. **Classes:** Most classes have 10–19 students. **Majors with Highest Enrollment:** Communications technologies and support services, elementary education and teaching, psychology. **Disciplines with Highest Percentage of Degrees Awarded:** Communication technologies 16%, education 14%, English 12%, psychology 7%, business/marketing 6%. **Special Study Options:** Double major, internships, teacher certification program, 3–2 programs in engineering and computer science with the University of Kentucky.

FACILITIES
Housing: Men's dorms, women's dorms, apartments for married students, apartments for single students, special housing for disabled students, Spanish House. **Special Academic Facilities/Equipment:** Art gallery, art annex, practice rooms, theater building, Luce Physical Activities Center, TV/radio studios and Mac lab. **Computers:** 65% of public computers are PCs, 35% of public computers are Macs, network access in dorm rooms, online administrative functions (other than registration), remote student-access to Web through college's connection.

CAMPUS LIFE
Activities: Choral groups, concert band, drama/theater, jazz band, literary magazine, music ensembles, opera, radio station, student government, student newspaper, symphony orchestra, television station, yearbook. **Organizations:** 41 registered organizations, 6 honor societies, 8 religious organizations. **Athletics (Intercollegiate):** *Men:* Baseball, basketball, cross-country, diving, soccer, swimming, tennis, track/field (outdoor). *Women:* Basketball, cross-country, diving, soccer, softball, swimming, tennis, track/field (outdoor), volleyball.

ADMISSIONS
Freshman Academic Profile: 32% in top 10% of high school class, 63% in top 25% of high school class, 86% in top 50% of high school class. 65% from public high schools. SAT Math middle 50% range 490–620. SAT Critical Reading middle 50% range 530–650. ACT middle 50% range 21–28. TOEFL required of all international applicants, minimum paper TOEFL 550, minimum computer TOEFL 213. **Basis for Candidate Selection:** *Very important factors considered include:* Character/personal qualities, racial/ethnic status, recommendation(s), religious affiliation/commitment, rigor of secondary school record, standardized test scores. *Important factors considered include:* Application essay, class rank, volunteer work, work experience. *Other factors considered include:* Alumni/ae relation, extracurricular activities, geographical residence, state residency, talent/ability. **Freshman Admission Requirements:** High school diploma is required, and GED is accepted. *Academic units recommended:* 4 English, 4 math, 3 science, 2 foreign language, 2 social studies. **Freshman Admission Statistics:** 820 applied, 73% admitted, 49% enrolled. **Transfer Admission Requirements:** High school transcript, college transcript(s), essay or personal statement, standardized test score, minimum college GPA of 2.5 required. Lowest grade transferable C-. **General Admission Information:** Application fee $30. Regular notification is immediately. Rolling admissions. Nonfall registration accepted. Admission may be deferred for a maximum of 1 year. Common Application not accepted. Neither credit nor placement offered for CEEB Advanced Placement tests.

COSTS AND FINANCIAL AID
Annual tuition $17,660. Room & board $4,494. Required fees $148. Average book expense $600. **Required Forms and Deadlines:** FAFSA, institution's own financial aid form. Financial aid filing deadline 6/30. **Notification of Awards:** Applicants will be notified of awards on a rolling basis beginning on or about 3/1. **Types of Aid:** *Need-based scholarships/grants:* Pell, SEOG, state scholarships/grants, the school's own gift aid. *Loans:* FFEL Subsidized Stafford, FFEL Unsubsidized Stafford, FFEL PLUS, Federal Perkins, college/university loans from institutional funds, private alternative loans. **Student Employment:** Federal Work-Study Program available. Institutional employment available. Off-campus job opportunities are good. **Financial Aid Statistics:** 72% freshmen, 69% undergrads receive need-based scholarship or grant aid. 67% freshmen, 61% undergrads receive need-based self-help aid. 2 freshmen, 2 undergrads receive athletic scholarships. Highest amount earned per year from on-campus jobs $1,200.

ASHLAND UNIVERSITY

401 College Avenue, Ashland, OH 44805
Phone: 419-289-5052 **E-mail:** enrollme@ashland.edu **CEEB Code:** 1021
Fax: 419-289-5999 **Website:** www.exploreashland.com **ACT Code:** 3234
Financial Aid Phone: 419-289-5002

This private school, affiliated with the Church of Brethren, was founded in 1878. It has a 98-acre campus.

RATINGS
Admissions Selectivity Rating: 78   **Fire Safety Rating:** 60*   **Green Rating:** 60*

STUDENTS AND FACULTY
Enrollment: 2,719. **Student Body:** 55% female, 45% male, 6% out-of-state, 2% international (28 countries represented). African American 8%, Caucasian 83%, Hispanic 3%. **Retention and Graduation:** 69% freshmen return for sophomore year. 56% freshmen graduate within 4 years. 10% grads go on to further study within 1 year. 2% grads pursue arts and sciences degrees. 1% grads pursue business degrees. 1% grads pursue law degrees. 1% grads pursue medical degrees. **Faculty:** Student/faculty ratio 13:1. 231 full-time faculty, 85% hold PhDs.

ACADEMICS
Degrees: Associate, bachelor's, certificate, diploma, doctoral, first professional, master's, terminal. **Academic Requirements:** Arts/fine arts, English (including composition), history, humanities, mathematics, sciences (biological or physical), social science, religion, wellness, international perspective. **Classes:** Most classes have 10–19 students. Most lab/discussion sections have 10–19 students. **Majors with Highest Enrollment:** Business administration/ management, education. **Disciplines with Highest Percentage of Degrees Awarded:** Education 39%, business/marketing 20%, security and protective services 7%, social sciences 7%, communication technologies 5%, health professions and related sciences 4%. **Special Study Options:** Double major, English as a Second Language (ESL), honors program, independent study, internships, student-designed major, study abroad, teacher certification program, weekend college, Ashbrook Center for Public Affairs.

FACILITIES
Housing: Coed dorms, men's dorms, women's dorms, apartments for single students, special housing for disabled students, special housing for international students, fraternity/sorority housing. **Special Academic Facilities/Equipment:** Neumismatic Center, Patterson Technology Center, Coburn Art Gallery, Hugo Young Theatre, studio theater, 33 room radio/television condex, media center, Pre-Columbian Art Exhibit, Ashbrook Center. **Computers:** 60% of public computers are PCs, 2% of public computers are Macs, 1% of public computers are UNIX, network access in dorm rooms, network access in dorm lounges, remote student-access to Web through college's connection.

CAMPUS LIFE
Activities: Choral groups, concert band, dance, drama/theater, jazz band, literary magazine, marching band, music ensembles, musical theater, pep band, radio station, student government, student newspaper, symphony orchestra, television station, yearbook. **Organizations:** 104 registered organizations, 18 honor societies, 4 religious organizations. 4 fraternities (7% men join), 5 sororities (13% women join). **Athletics (Intercollegiate):** *Men:* Baseball, basketball, cross-country, football, golf, soccer, swimming, track/field (indoor), track/field (outdoor), wrestling. *Women:* Basketball, cross-country, golf, soccer, softball, swimming, tennis, track/field (indoor), track/field (outdoor), volleyball.

ADMISSIONS
Freshman Academic Profile: 17% in top 10% of high school class, 46% in top 25% of high school class, 76% in top 50% of high school class. 89% from public high school. SAT Math middle 50% range 480–580. SAT Critical Reading middle 50% range 450–560. SAT Writing middle 50% range 450–460. ACT middle 50% range 20–25. TOEFL required of all international applicants, minimum paper TOEFL 500. **Basis for Candidate Selection:** *Very important factors considered include:* Rigor of secondary school record, standardized test scores. *Important factors considered include:* Academic GPA, alumni/ae relation, character/personal qualities, class rank, extracurricular activities, interview, level of applicant's interest. *Other factors considered include:* Geographical residence, recommendation(s), religious affiliation/commitment, work experience. **Freshman Admission Requirements:** High school diploma is required, and GED is accepted. *Academic units required:* 3 English, 2 math, 2 science, 2 social studies, 1 history. *Academic units recommended:* 4 English, 3 math, 3 science, 2 foreign language, 3 social studies, 1 history. **Freshman Admission Statistics:** 2,569 applied, 71% admitted, 31% enrolled. **Transfer Admission Requirements:** College transcript(s), essay or personal statement,

minimum college GPA of 2.5 required. Lowest grade transferable C-. **General Admission Information:** Regular application deadline 8/15. Regular notification is rolling. Nonfall registration accepted. Credit and/or placement offered for CEEB Advanced Placement tests.

COSTS AND FINANCIAL AID
Annual tuition $23,550. Room and board $8,876. Required fees $790. Average book expense $900. **Required Forms and Deadlines:** FAFSA, institution's own financial aid form. Financial aid filing deadline 3/15. **Notification of Awards:** Applicants will be notified of awards on or about 3/15. **Types of Aid:** *Need-based scholarships/grants:* Pell, SEOG, state scholarships/grants, private scholarships, the school's own gift aid. *Loans:* Direct Subsidized Stafford, Direct Unsubsidized Stafford, Direct PLUS, Federal Perkins, Federal Nursing, state loans, college/university loans from institutional funds. **Student Employment:** Federal Work-Study Program available. Off-campus job opportunities are good. **Financial Aid Statistics:** 80% freshmen, 77% undergrads receive need-based scholarship or grant aid. 71% freshmen, 69% undergrads receive need-based self-help aid. 26 freshmen, 90 undergrads receive athletic scholarships. Highest amount earned per year from on-campus jobs $1,000.

ASSUMPTION COLLEGE

500 Salisbury Street, Worcester, MA 01609-1296
Phone: 508-767-7285 **E-mail:** admiss@assumption.edu **CEEB Code:** 3009
Fax: 508-799-4412 **Website:** www.assumption.edu **ACT Code:** 1782
Financial Aid Phone: 508-767-7158

This private school, affiliated with the Roman Catholic Church, was founded in 1904. It has a 180-acre campus.

RATINGS
Admissions Selectivity Rating: 77   **Fire Safety Rating:** 82   **Green Rating:** 67

STUDENTS AND FACULTY
Enrollment: 2,125. **Student Body:** 60% female, 40% male, 69% out-of-state. African American 1%, Asian 1%, Caucasian 82%, Hispanic 2%. **Retention and Graduation:** 79% freshmen return for sophomore year. 66% freshmen graduate within 4 years. 22% grads go on to further study within 1 year. **Faculty:** Student/faculty ratio 12:1. 143 full-time faculty, 92% hold PhDs. 100% faculty teach undergrads.

ACADEMICS
Degrees: Bachelor's, master's, post master's certificate. **Academic Requirements:** Arts/fine arts, English (including composition), foreign languages, history, mathematics, philosophy, sciences (biological or physical), social science, theology. **Classes:** Most classes have 10–19 students. Most lab/ discussion sections have 10–19 students. **Majors with Highest Enrollment:** English language and literature, psychology, rehabilitation and therapeutic professions. **Disciplines with Highest Percentage of Degrees Awarded:** Business/marketing 24%, psychology 12%, communications/journalism 11%, English 9%, health professions and related sciences 8%. **Special Study Options:** Cross-registration, double major, honor program, independent study, internships, student-designed major, study abroad, teacher certification program.

FACILITIES
Housing: Coed dorms, women's dorms, special housing for disabled students, freshmen dorms, substance-free dorms, living/learning center. **Special Academic Facilities/Equipment:** French institute museum, social and rehabilitation services institute, language lab, media center, Living/Learning Center, Testa Science Center, information technology center. **Computers:** 100% of classrooms are wired, 35% of classrooms are wireless, 75% of public computers are PCs, 25% of public computers are Macs, network access in dorm rooms, network access in dorm lounges, online registration, online administrative functions (other than registration), support for handheld computing, remote student-access to Web through college's connection.

CAMPUS LIFE
Activities: Choral groups, concert band, drama/theater, literary magazine, musical theater, pep band, student government, student newspaper, student-run film society, television station, yearbook. **Organizations:** 50 registered organizations, 12 honor societies, 1 religious organization. **Athletics (Intercollegiate):** *Men:* Baseball, basketball, cross-country, football, golf, ice hockey, lacrosse, soccer, tennis, track/field (indoor), track/field (outdoor). *Women:* Basketball, crew/rowing, cross-country, field hockey, lacrosse, soccer, softball, tennis, track/field (indoor), track/field (outdoor), volleyball.

ADMISSIONS

Freshman Academic Profile: 14% in top 10% of high school class, 43% in top 25% of high school class, 84% in top 50% of high school class. 70% from public high schools. SAT Math middle 50% range 490–570. SAT Critical Reading middle 50% range 490–570. ACT middle 50% range 20–24. TOEFL required of all international applicants, minimum paper TOEFL 213, minimum computer TOEFL 40. **Basis for Candidate Selection:** *Very important factors considered include:* Academic GPA, application essay, standardized test scores. *Important factors considered include:* Interview, level of applicant's interest, recommendation(s), rigor of secondary school record, volunteer work. *Other factors considered include:* Alumni/ae relation, character/personal qualities, class rank, extracurricular activities, first generation, racial/ethnic status, talent/ability. **Freshman Admission Requirements:** High school diploma is required, and GED is accepted. *Academic units required:* 4 English, 3 math, 2 science, 2 foreign language, 2 history, 5 academic electives. **Freshman Admission Statistics:** 3,477 applied, 74% admitted, 26% enrolled. **Transfer Admission Requirements:** High school transcript, college transcript(s), essay or personal statement, standardized test score. Minimum college GPA of 2.5 required. Lowest grade transferable C. **General Admission Information:** Application fee $50. Regular application deadline 2/15. Regular notification continuous until 5/1. Nonfall registration accepted. Admission may be deferred for a maximum of 1 year. Credit and/or placement offered for CEEB Advanced Placement tests.

COSTS AND FINANCIAL AID

Annual tuition $27,320. Room and board $9,492. Required fees $165. Average book expense $850. **Required Forms and Deadlines:** FAFSA. Financial aid filing deadline 2/1. **Notification of Awards:** Applicants will be notified of awards on a rolling basis beginning on or about 2/16. **Types of Aid:** *Need-based scholarships/grants:* Pell, SEOG, state scholarships/grants, private scholarships, the school's own gift aid. *Loans:* FFEL Subsidized Stafford, FFEL Unsubsidized Stafford, FFEL PLUS, Federal Perkins, state loans, college/university loans from institutional funds. **Student Employment:** Federal Work-Study Program available. Institutional employment available. Off-campus job opportunities are good. **Financial Aid Statistics:** 71% freshmen receive need-based scholarship or grant aid. 63% freshmen, 64% undergrads receive need-based self-help aid. 5 freshmen, 23 undergrads receive athletic scholarships. 95% freshmen, 94% undergrads receive any aid. Highest amount earned per year from on-campus jobs $5,537.

See page 1066.

ATHABASCA UNIVERSITY

1 University Drive, Athabasca, AB T9S 3A3, Canada
Phone: 780-675-6100 **E-mail:** admissions@athabascau.ca
Fax: 780-675-6174 **Website:** www.athabascau.ca
Financial Aid Phone: 800-788-9041

This public school was founded in 1970.

RATINGS

Admissions Selectivity Rating: 60*   **Fire Safety Rating:** 60*   **Green Rating:** 60*

STUDENTS AND FACULTY

Student Body: 60% out-of-state. **Faculty:** 123 full-time faculty.

ACADEMICS

Degrees: Bachelor's, certificate, diploma, master's, post-bachelor's certificate, post-master's certificate. **Academic Requirements:** Arts/fine arts, English (including composition), foreign languages, history, humanities, mathematics, philosophy, sciences (biological or physical), social science, business administration, commerce, computing and information systems, counselling, distance education, French language proficiency studies, health administration, health studies, human resources and labour relations, integrated studies, managment, nursing, professional arts, public administration. **Majors with Highest Enrollment:** Business administration/management, organizational behavior studies; psychology. **Special Study Options:** Accelerated program, cross-registration, distance learning, English as a Second Language (ESL).

FACILITIES

Housing: Students can complete studies from their home or workplace. **Computers:** 100% of public computers are PCs, online registration, online administrative functions (other than registration), support for handheld computing.

CAMPUS LIFE

Activities: Student government, student newspaper.

ADMISSIONS

Freshman Admission Statistics: 14,068 applied, 100% admitted. **General Admission Information:** Application fee $56. Regular notification within 3 weeks. Nonfall registration accepted. Admission may be deferred for a maximum of 1 year. Common Application not accepted.

COSTS AND FINANCIAL AID

Annual in-state tuition $591. Annual out-of-state tuition $689. International tuition $759–$7,590.

ATHENS STATE UNIVERSITY

300 North Beaty Street, Athens, AL 35611
Phone: 205-233-8220
Fax: 205-233-6565 **Website:** www.athens.edu
Financial Aid Phone: 205-233-8122

This public school was founded in 1822.

RATINGS

Admissions Selectivity Rating: 60*   **Fire Safety Rating:** 60*   **Green Rating:** 60*

STUDENTS AND FACULTY

Student Body: 3% out-of-state. **Retention and Graduation:** 70% freshmen return for sophomore year.

ACADEMICS

Degrees: Bachelor's.

FACILITIES

Housing: Coed dorms.

CAMPUS LIFE

Activities: Literary magazine, student government, student newspaper. **Organizations:** 20 registered organizations, 5 honor societies. 1 fraternity (20% men join), 1 sorority (30% women join). **Athletics (Intercollegiate):** *Men:* Basketball, cheerleading. *Women:* Cheerleading, softball.

ADMISSIONS

Freshman Academic Profile: Minimum paper TOEFL 500. **Freshman Admission Requirements:** High school diploma is required, and GED is accepted. **General Admission Information:** Regular application deadline is rolling. Regular notification is rolling. Nonfall registration accepted. Common Application not accepted.

COSTS AND FINANCIAL AID

Annual in-state tuition $1,656. Out-of-state tuition $3,312. Room & board $4,800. Required fees $45. Average book expense $450. **Required Forms and Deadlines:** FAFSA. **Notification of Awards:** Applicants will be notified of awards on or about 6/10. **Types of Aid:** *Need-based scholarships/grants:* Pell, SEOG, state scholarships/grants, private scholarships, the school's own gift aid. *Loans:* FFEL Subsidized Stafford, FFEL Unsubsidized Stafford. **Student Employment:** Federal Work-Study Program available. Off-campus job opportunities are good.

ATLANTA CHRISTIAN COLLEGE

Office of Admissions, 2605 Ben Hill Road, East Point, GA 30344
Phone: 404-669-3202 **E-mail:** admissions@acc.edu
Fax: 404-460-2451 **Website:** www.acc.edu **ACT Code:** 0785
Financial Aid Phone: 404-669-2062

This private school, affiliated with the Christian (Nondenominational) Church, was founded in 1937. It has a 52-acre campus.

RATINGS

Admissions Selectivity Rating: 60*   **Fire Safety Rating:** 60*   **Green Rating:** 60*

STUDENTS AND FACULTY

Enrollment: 443. **Student Body:** 10% out-of-state. African American 17%, Caucasian 78%, Hispanic 2%. **Faculty:** Student/faculty ratio 16:1. 100% faculty teach undergrads.

ACADEMICS

Degrees: Associate, bachelor's. **Academic Requirements:** Computer literacy, English (including composition), history, humanities, mathematics, philosophy, sciences (biological or physical), social science. **Majors with Highest Enrollment:** Bible/biblical studies, business administration/management, elementary education and teaching. **Special Study Options:** Double major, dual enrollment, independent study, internships.

FACILITIES

Housing: Men's dorms, women's dorms, apartments for married students, apartments for single students. **Computers:** 100% of public computers are PCs, network access in dorm rooms, network access in dorm lounges, online registration, remote student-access to Web through college's connection.

CAMPUS LIFE

Activities: Choral groups, music ensembles, student government, yearbook. **Organizations:** 2 fraternities, 2 sororities. **Athletics (Intercollegiate):** *Men:* Baseball, basketball, golf, soccer. *Women:* Basketball, soccer, volleyball.

ADMISSIONS

Freshman Academic Profile: 85% from public high schools. TOEFL required of all international applicants, minimum paper TOEFL 500, minimum computer TOEFL 173. **Basis for Candidate Selection:** *Very important factors considered include:* Recommendation(s), rigor of secondary school record, standardized test scores. *Important factors considered include:* Character/personal qualities. **Freshman Admission Requirements:** High school diploma is required, and GED is accepted. **Freshman Admission Statistics:** 550 applied, 45% admitted, 42% enrolled. **Transfer Admission Requirements:** College transcript(s), statement of good standing from prior institution(s). Minimum college GPA of 2.0 required. Lowest grade transferable C. **General Admission Information:** Application fee $25. Early decision application deadline 11/15. Regular application deadline 8/1. Regular notification is rolling. Nonfall registration accepted. Admission may be deferred for a maximum of 1 semester. Common Application not accepted. Credit and/or placement offered for CEEB Advanced Placement tests.

COSTS AND FINANCIAL AID

Annual tuition $10,800. Room & board $4,400. Required fees $560. Average book expense $800. **Student Employment:** Federal Work-Study Program available. Institutional employment available. Off-campus job opportunities are excellent.

ATLANTIC UNION COLLEGE

Main Street, South Lancaster, MA 01561
Phone: 978-368-2235 **E-mail:** rlashley@atlanticuc.edu **CEEB Code:** 3010
Fax: 978-368-2517 **Website:** www.atlanticuc.edu **ACT Code:** 1784
Financial Aid Phone: 508-368-2280

This private school, affiliated with the Seventh Day Adventist Church, was founded in 1882. It has a 330-acre campus.

RATINGS

Admissions Selectivity Rating: 60*   **Fire Safety Rating:** 60*   **Green Rating:** 60*

STUDENTS AND FACULTY

Retention and Graduation: 6% grads go on to further study within 1 year. 2% grads pursue arts and sciences degrees. 1% grads pursue law degrees. 3% grads pursue medical degrees. **Faculty:** Student/faculty ratio 10:1. 48 full-time faculty.

ACADEMICS

Degrees: Associate, bachelor's, certificate, master's, post-bachelor's certificate. **Academic Requirements:** Computer literacy, English (including composition), foreign languages, history, humanities, mathematics, sciences (biological or physical), social science. **Special Study Options:** Cooperative education program, double major, English as a Second Language (ESL), honors program, study abroad.

FACILITIES

Housing: Men's dorms, women's dorms, apartments for married students, apartments for single students. **Special Academic Facilities/Equipment:** Art gallery, music conservatory, demonstration high school and elementary school near campus. **Computers:** Network access in dorm rooms, network access in dorm lounges, remote student-access to Web through college's connection.

CAMPUS LIFE

Activities: Choral groups, concert band, music ensembles, student government, yearbook. **Organizations:** 2 honor societies.

ADMISSIONS

Freshman Academic Profile: SAT Math middle 50% range 340–480. SAT Critical Reading middle 50% range 380–490. ACT middle 50% range 13–20. **Basis for Candidate Selection:** *Very important factors considered include:* Character/personal qualities, recommendation(s), religious affiliation/commitment, rigor of secondary school record, standardized test scores, state residency. *Important factors considered include:* Alumni/ae relation, racial/ethnic status, work experience. *Other factors considered include:* Application essay, class rank, geographical residence, interview, volunteer work. **Freshman Admission Requirements:** High school diploma is required, and GED is accepted. **Freshman Admission Statistics:** 713 applied, 39% admitted, 31% enrolled. **Transfer Admission Requirements:** High school transcript, college transcript(s), minimum college GPA of 2.0 required. Lowest grade transferable C-. **General Admission Information:** Application fee $25. Regular application deadline 8/1. Regular notification is rolling. Nonfall registration accepted. Admission may be deferred for a maximum of 2 semesters. Common Application accepted.

COSTS AND FINANCIAL AID

Annual tuition $13,000. Room & board $5,088. Required fees $960. Average book expense $800. **Required Forms and Deadlines:** FAFSA, institution's own financial aid form, state aid form. **Types of Aid:** *Need-based scholarships/grants:* Pell, SEOG, state scholarships/grants, private scholarships, the school's own gift aid. *Loans:* FFEL Subsidized Stafford, FFEL Unsubsidized Stafford, FFEL PLUS, Federal Perkins, college/university loans from institutional funds. **Student Employment:** Federal Work-Study Program available. Institutional employment available. Off-campus job opportunities are fair. Highest amount earned per year from on-campus jobs $2,000.

AUBURN UNIVERSITY

Best 368

108 Mary Martin Hall, Auburn, AL 36849-5149
Phone: 334-844-4080 **E-mail:** admissions@auburn.edu **CEEB Code:** 1005
Fax: 334-844-6179 **Website:** www.auburn.edu **ACT Code:** 0011
Financial Aid Phone: 334-844-4367

This public school was founded in 1856. It has a 1,875-acre campus.

RATINGS

Admissions Selectivity Rating: 60*   **Fire Safety Rating:** 60*   **Green Rating:** 60*

STUDENTS AND FACULTY

Enrollment: 19,349. **Student Body:** 49% female, 51% male, 34% out-of-state. African American 8%, Asian 2%, Caucasian 86%, Hispanic 2%. **Retention and Graduation:** 84% freshmen return for sophomore year. 33% freshmen graduate within 4 years. 35% grads go on to further study within 1 year. 5% grads pursue arts and sciences degrees. 10% grads pursue business degrees. 3% grads pursue law degrees. 8% grads pursue medical degrees. **Faculty:** Student/faculty ratio 18:1. 1,142 full-time faculty. 98% faculty teach undergrads.

ACADEMICS

Degrees: Bachelor's, doctoral, first professional, master's, post-master's certificate. **Academic Requirements:** Arts/fine arts, computer literacy, English (including composition), history, humanities, mathematics, philosophy, sciences (biological or physical), social science. **Classes:** Most classes have 20–29 students. Most lab/discussion sections have 10–19 students. **Majors with Highest Enrollment:** Business administration and management, education, engineering. **Disciplines with Highest Percentage of Degrees Awarded:** Business/marketing 26%, engineering 13%, education 9%, social sciences 8%, agriculture 5%, biological/life sciences 5%. **Special Study Options:** Accelerated program, cooperative education program, distance learning, double major, dual enrollment, English as a Second Language (ESL), honors program, independent study, internships, liberal arts/career combination, study abroad, teacher certification program.

FACILITIES

Housing: Coed dorms, men's dorms, women's dorms, apartments for married students, apartments for single students, special housing for disabled students, fraternity/sorority housing, housing for honors students. **Special Academic Facilities/Equipment:** Speech and hearing clinic, center for arts and humanities, TV studio, electron microscopes, nuclear science center, torsatron, sports museum, Jule Collins Smith Museum of Art, McWhorter Center for

60

Women's Athletics, Center for Diversity and Race Relations. **Computers:** 18% of classrooms are wired, 1% of classrooms are wireless, 84% of public computers are PCs, 13% of public computers are Macs, 3% of public computers are UNIX, network access in dorm rooms, online registration, online administrative functions (other than registration), remote student-access to Web through college's connection.

CAMPUS LIFE
Activities: Choral groups, concert band, dance, drama/theater, jazz band, literary magazine, marching band, music ensembles, musical theater, opera, pep band, radio station, student government, student newspaper, student-run film society, symphony orchestra, television station, yearbook. **Organizations:** 300 registered organizations, 56 honor societies, 15 religious organizations. 31 fraternities (23% men join), 20 sororities (34% women join). **Athletics (Intercollegiate):** *Men:* Baseball, basketball, cheerleading, cross-country, diving, football, golf, swimming, tennis, track/field (indoor), track/field (outdoor). *Women:* Basketball, cheerleading, cross-country, diving, equestrian sports, golf, gymnastics, soccer, softball, swimming, tennis, track/field (indoor), track/field (outdoor), volleyball. **Environmental Initiatives:** Incorporation of sustainability initiatives into university curricula. Campus community education and awareness of sustainability issues via Focus the Nation at AU speaker series and conference events. Hands-on student experience in administering on-campus sustainability initiatives (i.e., Haley Center Green Roof, Auburn Clean Streams projects).

ADMISSIONS
Freshman Academic Profile: 36% in top 10% of high school class, 59% in top 25% of high school class, 87% in top 50% of high school class. 86% from public high schools. SAT Math middle 50% range 520–630. SAT Critical Reading middle 50% range 500–610. ACT middle 50% range 22–27. TOEFL required of all international applicants, minimum paper TOEFL 550, minimum computer TOEFL 213. **Basis for Candidate Selection:** *Very important factors considered include:* Academic GPA, rigor of secondary school record, standardized test scores. *Important factors considered include:* State residency. *Other factors considered include:* Alumni/ae relation, application essay, class rank, extracurricular activities, first generation, geographical residence, level of applicant's interest, racial/ethnic status, recommendation(s), talent/ability, volunteer work. **Freshman Admission Requirements:** High school diploma is required, and GED is accepted. *Academic units required:* 4 English, 3 math, 2 science, 3 social studies. *Academic units recommended:* 4 English, 3 math, 3 science, 1 foreign language, 4 social studies. **Freshman Admission Statistics:** 15,919 applied, 72% admitted, 35% enrolled. **Transfer Admission Requirements:** College transcript(s), minimum college GPA of 2.5 required. Lowest grade transferable C. **General Admission Information:** Application fee $25. Regular application deadline 8/1. Regular notification is continuous. Nonfall registration accepted. Credit and/or placement offered for CEEB Advanced Placement tests.

COSTS AND FINANCIAL AID
Annual in-state tuition $5,250. Annual out-of-state tuition $15,750. Room and board $7,466. Required fees $344. Average book expense $1,100. **Required Forms and Deadlines:** FAFSA, institution's own financial aid form. Financial aid filing deadline 3/1. **Types of Aid:** *Need-based scholarships/grants:* Pell, SEOG, state scholarships/grants, private scholarships, the school's own gift aid. *Loans:* FFEL Subsidized Stafford, FFEL Unsubsidized Stafford, FFEL PLUS, Federal Perkins, college/university loans from institutional funds. **Student Employment:** Off-campus job opportunities are good. **Financial Aid Statistics:** 20% freshmen, 20% undergrads receive need-based scholarship or grant aid. 22% freshmen, 28% undergrads receive need-based self-help aid. 73 freshmen, 311 undergrads receive athletic scholarships. 55% freshmen, 56% undergrads receive any aid. Highest amount earned per year from on-campus jobs $10,920.

AUBURN UNIVERSITY MONTGOMERY

PO Box 244023, Montgomery, AL 36124-4023
Phone: 334-244-3611 **E-mail:** vsamuel@mail.aum.edu
Fax: 334-244-3795 **Website:** www.aum.edu **ACT Code:** 0057
Financial Aid Phone: 334-244-3126

This public school was founded in 1967. It has a 500-acre campus.

RATINGS
Admissions Selectivity Rating: 60*   **Fire Safety Rating:** 60*   **Green Rating:** 60*

STUDENTS AND FACULTY
Enrollment: 4,074. **Student Body:** 63% female, 37% male, 4% out-of-state.

African American 28%, Asian 2%, Caucasian 58%, Hispanic 1%. **Faculty:** 186 full-time faculty. 98% faculty teach undergrads.

ACADEMICS
Degrees: Bachelor's, doctoral, master's, post-master's certificate. **Academic Requirements:** English (including composition), history, humanities, mathematics, sciences (biological or physical), social science. **Classes:** Most classes have 20–29 students. Most lab/discussion sections have 20–29 students. **Majors with Highest Enrollment:** Business administration/management; elementary education and teaching, nursing–registered nurse training (ASN, BSN, MSN, RN). **Disciplines with Highest Percentage of Degrees Awarded:** Business/marketing 36%, education 16%, health professions and related sciences 13%, biological/life sciences 7%, security and protective services 6%. **Special Study Options:** Accelerated program, cooperative education program, cross-registration, distance learning, double major, dual enrollment, English as a Second Language (ESL), exchange student program (domestic), honors program, independent study, internships, liberal arts/career combination, study abroad, teacher certification program, weekend college, joint PhD in public administration with Auburn University, EdD in cooperation with Auburn University.

FACILITIES
Housing: Coed dorms, apartments for married students, apartments for single students, special housing for disabled students. **Computers:** Network access in dorm rooms, online registration, online administrative functions (other than registration), remote student-access to Web through college's connection.

CAMPUS LIFE
Activities: Choral groups, dance, drama/theater, literary magazine, musical theater, student government, student newspaper, student-run film society. **Organizations:** 66 registered organizations, 13 honor societies, 2 religious organizations. 6 fraternities (6% men join), 7 sororities (4% women join). **Athletics (Intercollegiate):** *Men:* Baseball, basketball, cheerleading, soccer, tennis. *Women:* Basketball, cheerleading, soccer, tennis.

ADMISSIONS
Freshman Academic Profile: ACT middle 50% range 18–23. TOEFL required of all international applicants, minimum paper TOEFL 500, minimum computer TOEFL 173. **Basis for Candidate Selection:** *Very important factors considered include:* Academic GPA, class rank, rigor of secondary school record, standardized test scores. *Other factors considered include:* Alumni/ae relation, extracurricular activities, geographical residence, recommendation(s), state residency. **Freshman Admission Requirements:** High school diploma is required, and GED is accepted. *Academic units recommended:* 4 English, 3 math, 2 science (2 science labs), 2 foreign language, 2 social studies, 2 history, 2 academic electives. **Freshman Admission Statistics:** 702 applied, 98% admitted, 95% enrolled. **Transfer Admission Requirements:** College transcript(s), minimum college GPA of 2.0 required. Lowest grade transferable D. **General Admission Information:** Application fee $25. Regular notification is a weekly basis. Nonfall registration accepted. Credit offered for CEEB Advanced Placement tests.

COSTS AND FINANCIAL AID
Average book expense $800. **Required Forms and Deadlines:** FAFSA. Financial aid filing deadline 3/15. **Notification of Awards:** Applicants will be notified of awards on or about 5/1. **Types of Aid:** *Need-based scholarships/grants:* Pell, SEOG, state scholarships/grants, private scholarships, the school's own gift aid. *Loans:* FFEL Subsidized Stafford, FFEL Unsubsidized Stafford, FFEL PLUS, Federal Perkins. **Financial Aid Statistics:** 34% freshmen, 32% undergrads receive need-based scholarship or grant aid. 39% freshmen, 39% undergrads receive need-based self-help aid.

AUGSBURG COLLEGE

2211 Riverside Avenue South, Minneapolis, MN 55454
Phone: 612-330-1001 **E-mail:** admissions@augsburg.edu **CEEB Code:** 6014
Fax: 612-330-1590 **Website:** www.augsburg.edu **ACT Code:** 2080
Financial Aid Phone: 612-330-1046

This private school, affiliated with the Lutheran Church, was founded in 1869. It has a 23-acre campus.

RATINGS
Admissions Selectivity Rating: 78   **Fire Safety Rating:** 60*   **Green Rating:** 60*

STUDENTS AND FACULTY
Enrollment: 2,783. **Student Body:** 56% female, 44% male, 14% out-of-state, 1% international (24 countries represented). African American 5%, Asian 4%,

Caucasian 72%, Hispanic 2%, Native American 1%. **Retention and Graduation:** 84% freshmen return for sophomore year. 48% freshmen graduate within 4 years. 27% grads go on to further study within 1 year. 15% grads pursue arts and sciences degrees. 4% grads pursue business degrees. 2% grads pursue law degrees. 5% grads pursue medical degrees. **Faculty:** Student/faculty ratio 15:1. 165 full-time faculty, 77% hold PhDs. 99% faculty teach undergrads.

ACADEMICS
Degrees: Bachelor's, certificate, master's. **Academic Requirements:** Arts/fine arts, English (including composition), foreign languages, history, humanities, mathematics, sciences (biological or physical), social science. **Classes:** Most classes have 10–19 students. Most lab/discussion sections have 10–19 students. **Majors with Highest Enrollment:** Business administration/management, communications studies/speech communication and rhetoric, education. **Disciplines with Highest Percentage of Degrees Awarded:** Business/marketing 26%, education 14%, social sciences 9%, health professions and related sciences 7%, visual and performing arts 7%. **Special Study Options:** Cooperative education program, cross-registration, double major, dual enrollment, honors program, independent study, internships, study abroad, teacher certification program, weekend college.

FACILITIES
Housing: Coed dorms. **Special Academic Facilities/Equipment:** Electron microscope, center for atmospheric science research, theater, pipe organ. **Computers:** 62% of public computers are PCs, 38% of public computers are Macs, network access in dorm rooms, network access in dorm lounges, online registration, online administrative functions (other than registration), remote student-access to Web through college's connection.

CAMPUS LIFE
Activities: Choral groups, concert band, dance, drama/theater, jazz band, literary magazine, music ensembles, opera, radio station, student government, student newspaper, yearbook. **Organizations:** 35 registered organizations, 1 honor society, 1 religious organization. **Athletics (Intercollegiate):** *Men:* Baseball, basketball, cross-country, football, golf, ice hockey, soccer, tennis, track/field (indoor), track/field (outdoor), wrestling. *Women:* Basketball, cheerleading, cross-country, golf, ice hockey, soccer, softball, swimming, tennis, track/field (indoor), track/field (outdoor), volleyball.

ADMISSIONS
Freshman Academic Profile: 16% in top 10% of high school class, 34% in top 25% of high school class, 66% in top 50% of high school class. SAT Math middle 50% range 500–640. SAT Critical Reading middle 50% range 510–640. SAT Writing middle 50% range 480–600. ACT middle 50% range 19–25. TOEFL required of all international applicants, minimum paper TOEFL 550, minimum computer TOEFL 213. **Basis for Candidate Selection:** *Very important factors considered include:* Academic GPA, application essay, class rank, recommendation(s), rigor of secondary school record, standardized test scores. *Important factors considered include:* Alumni/ae relation, character/personal qualities, extracurricular activities, level of applicant's interest. *Other factors considered include:* Interview, talent/ability, volunteer work, work experience. **Freshman Admission Requirements:** High school diploma is required, and GED is accepted. *Academic units required:* 4 English, 3 math, 3 science, 2 foreign language, 3 social studies. *Academic units recommended:* 4 social studies, 2 history. **Freshman Admission Statistics:** 1,320 applied, 71% admitted, 43% enrolled. **Transfer Admission Requirements:** College transcript(s), statement of good standing from prior institution(s). Minimum college GPA of 2.5 required. Lowest grade transferable B. **General Admission Information:** Application fee $25. Regular application deadline 8/15. Regular notification is rolling. Nonfall registration accepted. Admission may be deferred for a maximum of 24 months. Credit and/or placement offered for CEEB Advanced Placement tests.

COSTS AND FINANCIAL AID
Annual tuition $24,046. Room and board $6,902. Required fees $522. Average book expense $1,000. **Required Forms and Deadlines:** FAFSA. Financial aid filing deadline 8/1. **Notification of Awards:** Applicants will be notified of awards on a rolling basis beginning on or about 3/1. **Types of Aid:** *Need-based scholarships/grants:* Pell, SEOG, state scholarships/grants, private scholarships, the school's own gift aid. *Loans:* FFEL Subsidized Stafford, FFEL Unsubsidized Stafford, FFEL PLUS, Federal Perkins, Federal Nursing, state loans, supplemental loans from private lenders. **Financial Aid Statistics:** 78% freshmen, 68% undergrads receive need-based scholarship or grant aid. 32% freshmen, 29% undergrads receive need-based self-help aid. 90% freshmen, 76% undergrads receive any aid. Highest amount earned per year from on-campus jobs $3,000.

AUGUSTA STATE UNIVERSITY

2500 Walton Way, Augusta, GA 30904-2200
Phone: 706-737-1632 **E-mail:** admissio@aug.edu **CEEB Code:** 5336
Fax: 706-667-4355 **Website:** www.aug.edu **ACT Code:** 0796
Financial Aid Phone: 706-737-1431

This public school was founded in 1925. It has a 76-acre campus.

RATINGS
Admissions Selectivity Rating: 60*   **Fire Safety Rating:** 60*   **Green Rating:** 60*

STUDENTS AND FACULTY
Enrollment: 5,636. **Student Body:** 65% female, 35% male, 11% out-of-state, 1% international (58 countries represented). African American 26%, Asian 3%, Caucasian 63%, Hispanic 3%. **Retention and Graduation:** 65% freshmen return for sophomore year. 6% freshmen graduate within 4 years. **Faculty:** Student/faculty ratio 19:1. 220 full-time faculty, 66% hold PhDs. 100% faculty teach undergrads.

ACADEMICS
Degrees: Associate, bachelor's, master's, post-master's certificate, terminal. **Academic Requirements:** English (including composition), foreign languages, history, humanities, mathematics, sciences (biological or physical), social science. **Classes:** Most classes have 20–29 students. Most lab/discussion sections have 20–29 students. **Majors with Highest Enrollment:** Biology/biological sciences, elementary education and teaching, psychology. **Disciplines with Highest Percentage of Degrees Awarded:** Business/marketing 27%, education 18%, psychology 7%, communications/journalism 6%, biological/life sciences 6%. **Special Study Options:** Cooperative education program, cross-registration, distance learning, double major, dual enrollment, English as a second language (ESL), honor program, independent study, internships, study abroad, teacher certification program, Paralegal Certification.

FACILITIES
Housing: Apartments for single students. **Special Academic Facilities/Equipment:** Performing arts theater, Christenberry Field House, Forest Hill Golf Course. **Computers:** 75% of classrooms are wireless, 99% of public computers are PCs, 1% of public computers are Macs, network access in dorm rooms, network access in dorm lounges, online registration, online administrative functions (other than registration), support for handheld computing, remote student-access to Web through college's connection.

CAMPUS LIFE
Activities: Choral groups, concert band, drama/theater, jazz band, literary magazine, pep band, radio station, student government, student newspaper. **Organizations:** 60 registered organizations, 5 honor societies, 5 religious organizations. 3 fraternities (1% men join), 3 sororities (1% women join). **Athletics (Intercollegiate):** *Men:* Baseball, basketball, golf, tennis. *Women:* Basketball, golf, softball, tennis, volleyball.

ADMISSIONS
Freshman Academic Profile: 95% from public high schools. SAT Math middle 50% range 450–540. SAT Critical Reading middle 50% range 440–540. ACT middle 50% range 17–21. TOEFL required of all international applicants, minimum paper TOEFL 500, minimum computer TOEFL 250. **Basis for Candidate Selection:** *Important factors considered include:* Academic GPA, rigor of secondary school record, standardized test scores. **Freshman Admission Requirements:** High school diploma is required, and GED is accepted. *Academic units required:* 4 English, 4 math, 3 science, 2 foreign language, 3 social studies. **Freshman Admission Statistics:** 2,401 applied, 52% admitted, 76% enrolled. **Transfer Admission Requirements:** College transcript(s), Minimum college GPA of 2.0 required. Lowest grade transferable D. **General Admission Information:** Application fee $20. Regular notification whenever the application is complete. Nonfall registration accepted. Admission may be deferred for a maximum of Period is not limite. Credit and/or placement offered for CEEB Advanced Placement tests.

COSTS AND FINANCIAL AID
Average book expense $1,000. **Required Forms and Deadlines:** FAFSA, state aid form. Financial aid filing deadline 4/1. **Notification of Awards:** Applicants will be notified of awards on or about 6/1. **Types of Aid:** *Need-based scholarships/grants:* Pell, SEOG, state scholarships/grants, private scholarships, the school's own gift aid. *Loans:* FFEL Subsidized Stafford, FFEL Unsubsidized Stafford, FFEL PLUS, Federal Perkins, state loans, college/university loans from institutional funds, alternative loans. **Financial Aid Statistics:** 43% freshmen, 37% undergrads receive need-based scholarship or grant aid. 21% freshmen, 25% undergrads receive need-based self-help aid. 14

freshmen, 92 undergrads receive athletic scholarships. Highest amount earned per year from on-campus jobs $8,140.

AUGUSTANA COLLEGE (IL)

639 38th Street, Rock Island, IL 61201-2296
Phone: 309-794-7341 **E-mail:** admissions@augustana.edu **CEEB Code:** 1025
Fax: 309-794-7422 **Website:** www.augustana.edu **ACT Code:** 0946
Financial Aid Phone: 309-794-7449

This private school, affiliated with the Lutheran Church, was founded in 1860. It has a 115-acre campus.

RATINGS
Admissions Selectivity Rating: 85   **Fire Safety Rating:** 65   **Green Rating:** 77

STUDENTS AND FACULTY
Enrollment: 2,445. **Student Body:** 57% female, 43% male, 12% out-of-state, 1% international (23 countries represented). African American 2%, Asian 2%, Caucasian 90%, Hispanic 3%. **Retention and Graduation:** 85% freshmen return for sophomore year. 73% freshmen graduate within 4 years. 40% grads go on to further study within 1 year. 21% grads pursue arts and sciences degrees. 7% grads pursue business degrees. 3% grads pursue law degrees. 9% grads pursue medical degrees. **Faculty:** Student/faculty ratio 12:1. 164 full-time faculty, 94% hold PhDs. 100% faculty teach undergrads.

ACADEMICS
Degrees: Bachelor's. **Academic Requirements:** Arts/fine arts, English (including composition), foreign languages, history, humanities, mathematics, philosophy, sciences (biological or physical), social science. **Classes:** Most classes have 10–19 students. Most lab/discussion sections have fewer than 10 students. **Majors with Highest Enrollment:** Business administration/management, English language and literature, pre-medicine/pre-medical studies. **Disciplines with Highest Percentage of Degrees Awarded:** Business/marketing 18%, biological/life sciences 14%, English 11%, social sciences 10%, health professions and related sciences 9%. **Special Study Options:** Accelerated program, double major, honors program, independent study, internships, liberal arts/career combination, study abroad, teacher certification program.

FACILITIES
Housing: Coed dorms, men's dorms, women's dorms, apartments for single students. **Special Academic Facilities/Equipment:** Educational technology building, art gallery, black culture house, Hispanic culture house, geology museum, on-campus preschool, immigration research center, scanning and transmission electron microscopes, nuclear magnetic resonance, atomic absorption, and diode array mass spectrophotometers, planetarium, observatory with celestron telescope, environmental field stations. **Computers:** 92% of public computers are PCs, 7% of public computers are Macs, 1% of public computers are UNIX, network access in dorm rooms, network access in dorm lounges, online registration, online administrative functions (other than registration), remote student-access to Web through college's connection.

CAMPUS LIFE
Activities: Choral groups, concert band, dance, drama/theater, jazz band, literary magazine, music ensembles, musical theater, opera, pep band, radio station, student government, student newspaper, symphony orchestra, yearbook. **Organizations:** 110 registered organizations, 15 honor societies, 6 religious organizations. 7 fraternities (16% men join), 6 sororities (26% women join). **Athletics (Intercollegiate):** *Men:* Baseball, basketball, cross-country, diving, football, golf, soccer, swimming, tennis, track/field (indoor), track/field (outdoor), wrestling. *Women:* Basketball, cross-country, diving, golf, soccer, softball, swimming, tennis, track/field (indoor), track/field (outdoor), volleyball. **Environmental Initiatives:** Recycling Program. Geothermal heating for newest housing. LEEDS certification for new construction.

ADMISSIONS
Freshman Academic Profile: 27% in top 10% of high school class, 65% in top 25% of high school class, 92% in top 50% of high school class. 85% from public high schools. ACT middle 50% range 23.4–28.4. TOEFL required of all international applicants, minimum paper TOEFL 550, minimum computer TOEFL 213. **Basis for Candidate Selection:** *Very important factors considered include:* Academic GPA, class rank, rigor of secondary school record. *Important factors considered include:* Application essay, character/personal qualities, extracurricular activities, interview, level of applicant's interest, recommendation(s), standardized test scores, talent/ability. *Other factors considered include:* Alumni/ae relation, geographical residence, racial/ethnic status, religious affiliation/commitment, volunteer work, work experience.

Freshman Admission Requirements: High school diploma is required, and GED is accepted. *Academic units recommended:* 4 English, 3 math, 2 science, 1 foreign language, 1 social studies, 1 history, 4 academic electives. **Freshman Admission Statistics:** 3,288 applied, 75% admitted, 28% enrolled. **Transfer Admission Requirements:** High school transcript, college transcript(s), statement of good standing from prior institution(s). Minimum college GPA of 2.0 required. Lowest grade transferable D. **General Admission Information:** Application fee $35. Nonfall registration accepted. Admission may be deferred for a maximum of up to 1 year. Credit and/or placement offered for CEEB Advanced Placement tests.

COSTS AND FINANCIAL AID
Annual tuition $25,935. Room and board $7,233. Required fees $549. Average book expense $675. **Required Forms and Deadlines:** FAFSA, institution's own financial aid form. Financial aid filing deadline 4/1. **Notification of Awards:** Applicants will be notified of awards on a rolling basis beginning on or about 2/15. *Types of Aid: Need-based scholarships/grants:* Pell, SEOG, state scholarships/grants, private scholarships, the school's own gift aid. *Loans:* FFEL Subsidized Stafford, FFEL Unsubsidized Stafford, FFEL PLUS, Federal Perkins. **Student Employment:** Off-campus job opportunities are excellent. **Financial Aid Statistics:** 67% freshmen, 64% undergrads receive need-based scholarship or grant aid. 59% freshmen, 59% undergrads receive need-based self-help aid. 98% freshmen, 98% undergrads receive any aid. Highest amount earned per year from on-campus jobs $900.

AUGUSTANA COLLEGE (SD)

2001 South Summit Avenue, Sioux Falls, SD 57197
Phone: 605-274-5516 **E-mail:** admission@augie.edu **CEEB Code:** 6015
Fax: 605-274-5518 **Website:** www.augustana.edu **ACT Code:** 3902
Financial Aid Phone: 605-274-5216

This private school, affiliated with the Lutheran Church, was founded in 1860. It has a 100-acre campus.

RATINGS
Admissions Selectivity Rating: 85   **Fire Safety Rating:** 60*   **Green Rating:** 66

STUDENTS AND FACULTY
Enrollment: 1,747. **Student Body:** 63% female, 37% male, 54% out-of-state. **Retention and Graduation:** 76% freshmen return for sophomore year. 48% freshmen graduate within 4 years. 27% grads go on to further study within 1 year. **Faculty:** Student/faculty ratio 13:1. 111 full-time faculty, 74% hold PhDs. 100% faculty teach undergrads.

ACADEMICS
Degrees: Bachelor's, master's. **Academic Requirements:** Arts/fine arts, computer literacy, English (including composition), foreign languages, history, humanities, mathematics, philosophy, sciences (biological or physical), social science, new student seminar, religion, physical education, capstone course. **Classes:** Most classes have 10–19 students. **Majors with Highest Enrollment:** Business administration/management, elementary education and teaching, nursing–registered nurse training (ASN, BSN, MSN, RN). **Disciplines with Highest Percentage of Degrees Awarded:** Health professions and related sciences 18%, business/marketing 17%, education 16%, social sciences 10%, biological/life sciences 6%, foreign languages and literature 6%. **Special Study Options:** Cross-registration, distance learning, double major, honors program, independent study, internships, liberal arts/career combination, study abroad, teacher certification program. Metro-Urban Studies through HECUA. January abroad program through UMAIE. Washington, DC semesters; dual degree program in engineering; National Internship Centers in Minneapolis, Chicago, and Denver; service-learning spring breaks trips; faculty-led spring breaks abroad; honors courses in Western civilization and history.

FACILITIES
Housing: Coed dorms, apartments for married students, apartments for single students, special housing for disabled students, theme houses available for upper-class students (priority given to seniors). Senior Living Experience on-campus community housing is available. **Special Academic Facilities/Equipment:** Center for Western Studies, archeology lab, Eide/Dalrymple Gallery, Center for Liturgical Art. **Computers:** 80% of public computers are PCs, 20% of public computers are Macs, network access in dorm rooms, network access in dorm lounges, online registration, online administrative functions (other than registration), remote student-access to Web through college's connection.

CAMPUS LIFE
Activities: Choral groups, concert band, dance, drama/theater, jazz band,

literary magazine, music ensembles, musical theater, opera, pep band, radio station, student government, student newspaper, symphony orchestra, yearbook. **Organizations:** 56 registered organizations, 10 honor societies, 6 religious organizations. **Athletics (Intercollegiate):** *Men:* Baseball, basketball, cross-country, football, golf, tennis, track/field (indoor), track/field (outdoor), wrestling. *Women:* Basketball, cheerleading, cross-country, golf, soccer, softball, tennis, track/field (indoor), track/field (outdoor), volleyball. **Environmental Initiatives:** Increased recycling efforts in residential and academic buildings. Green bike program offers students the chance to use bikes for free transportation on and around campus. Student group, Augustana Green, has created multiple task forces to advance campus sustainability and create community support for broad based measures.

ADMISSIONS

Freshman Academic Profile: 28% in top 10% of high school class, 57% in top 25% of high school class, 88% in top 50% of high school class. 97% from public high schools. SAT Math middle 50% range 530–630. SAT Critical Reading middle 50% range 490–640. ACT middle 50% range 22–27. TOEFL required of all international applicants, minimum paper TOEFL 550, minimum computer TOEFL 213. **Basis for Candidate Selection:** *Very important factors considered include:* Academic GPA, rigor of secondary school record, standardized test scores. *Important factors considered include:* Class rank, extracurricular activities, recommendation(s). *Other factors considered include:* Application essay, character/personal qualities, interview, talent/ability, volunteer work. **Freshman Admission Requirements:** High school diploma is required, and GED is accepted. *Academic units recommended:* 4 English, 3 math, 3 science (3 science labs), 2 foreign language, 3 social studies, 1 computer science, 1 fine arts. **Freshman Admission Statistics:** 1,413 applied, 83% admitted, 38% enrolled. **Transfer Admission Requirements:** High school transcript, college transcript(s), statement of good standing from prior institution(s). Minimum college GPA of 2.2 required. Lowest grade transferable C-. **General Admission Information:** Regular application deadline is rolling. Regular notification is rolling. Nonfall registration accepted. Admission may be deferred for a maximum of 1 year. Credit offered for CEEB Advanced Placement tests.

COSTS AND FINANCIAL AID

Annual tuition $20,932. Room and board $5,640. Required fees $250. Average book expense $800. **Required Forms and Deadlines:** FAFSA. Financial aid filing deadline 3/1. **Notification of Awards:** Applicants will be notified of awards on a rolling basis beginning on or about 3/15. **Types of Aid:** *Need-based scholarships/grants:* Pell, SEOG, state scholarships/grants, private scholarships, the school's own aid, Federal Nursing Scholarships. *Loans:* FFEL Subsidized Stafford, FFEL Unsubsidized Stafford, FFEL PLUS, Federal Perkins, Federal Nursing, college/university loans from institutional funds. **Student Employment:** Federal Work-Study Program available. Institutional employment available. Off-campus job opportunities are excellent. **Financial Aid Statistics:** 71% freshmen, 67% undergrads receive need-based scholarship or grant aid. 54% freshmen, 54% undergrads receive need-based self-help aid. 42 freshmen, 132 undergrads receive athletic scholarships. 99% freshmen, 94% undergrads receive any aid. Highest amount earned per year from on-campus jobs $6,055.

AURORA UNIVERSITY

347 South Gladstone Avenue, Aurora, IL 60506
Phone: 630-844-5533 **E-mail:** admission@aurora.edu **CEEB Code:** 1027
Fax: 630-844-5535 **Website:** www.aurora.edu **ACT Code:** 0950
Financial Aid Phone: 630-844-5533

This private school was founded in 1893. It has a 27-acre campus.

RATINGS
Admissions Selectivity Rating: 75   **Fire Safety Rating:** 60*   **Green Rating:** 60*

STUDENTS AND FACULTY
Enrollment: 1,957. **Student Body:** 66% female, 34% male, 7% out-of-state. African American 11%, Asian 3%, Caucasian 74%, Hispanic 12%. **Retention and Graduation:** 65% freshmen return for sophomore year. 35% freshmen graduate within 4 years. **Faculty:** Student/faculty ratio 16:1. 102 full-time faculty, 82% hold PhDs. 52% faculty teach undergrads.

ACADEMICS
Degrees: Bachelor's, doctoral, master's, post-bachelor's certificate, post-master's certificate. **Academic Requirements:** Arts/fine arts, English (including composition), history, humanities, mathematics, philosophy, sciences (biological or physical), social science. **Classes:** Most classes have 10–19 students. Most lab/discussion sections have 10–19 students. **Majors with Highest Enrollment:** Elementary education and teaching; social work; teacher education and professional development, specific levels and methods.

Disciplines with Highest Percentage of Degrees Awarded: Education 21%, business/marketing 20%, health professions and related sciences 11%, public administration and social services 9%, parks and recreation 8%. **Special Study Options:** Accelerated program, cross-registration, double major, honors program, independent study, internships, liberal arts/career combination, student-designed major, study abroad, teacher certification program.

FACILITIES

Housing: Coed dorms. **Special Academic Facilities/Equipment:** Schingoethe Center for Native American Culture, Downstairs Dunham Gallery, Center For Faith And Action, Perry Theatre in the Aurora Foundation Center for Continuing Education **Computers:** 100% of classrooms are wired, 75% of classrooms are wireless, 100% of public computers are PCs, network access in dorm rooms, network access in dorm lounges, online administrative functions (other than registration), remote student-access to Web through college's connection.

CAMPUS LIFE

Activities: Choral groups, drama/theater, literary magazine, student government, student newspaper. **Organizations:** 30 registered organizations, 2 honor societies, 1 religious organization. 1 fraternity (1% men join), 5 sororities (39% women join). **Athletics (Intercollegiate):** *Men:* Baseball, basketball, cross-country, football, golf, soccer, tennis, track/field (indoor), track/field (outdoor). *Women:* Basketball, cross-country, golf, soccer, softball, tennis, track/field (indoor), track/field (outdoor), volleyball.

ADMISSIONS

Freshman Academic Profile: 12% in top 10% of high school class, 40% in top 25% of high school class, 75% in top 50% of high school class. SAT Math middle 50% range 460–560. SAT Critical Reading middle 50% range 470–570. ACT middle 50% range 20–23. TOEFL required of all international applicants, minimum paper TOEFL 550, minimum computer TOEFL 213. **Basis for Candidate Selection:** *Very important factors considered include:* Academic GPA, class rank, interview, recommendation(s), rigor of secondary school record, standardized test scores. *Other factors considered include:* Application essay, character/personal qualities, extracurricular activities, talent/ability. **Freshman Admission Requirements:** High school diploma is required, and GED is accepted. *Academic units recommended:* 4 English, 3 math, 3 science, 3 social studies, 3 academic electives. **Freshman Admission Statistics:** 1,508 applied, 71% admitted, 35% enrolled. **Transfer Admission Requirements:** College transcript(s), statement of good standing from prior institution(s). Minimum college GPA of 2.0 required. Lowest grade transferable C. **General Admission Information:** Application fee $25. Regular application deadline 5/1. Regular notification is rolling. Nonfall registration accepted. Admission may be deferred for a maximum of 2 years. Credit and/or placement offered for CEEB Advanced Placement tests.

COSTS AND FINANCIAL AID

Annual tuition $16,750. Room and board $7,034. Required fees $100. Average book expense $1,000. **Required Forms and Deadlines:** FAFSA. Financial aid filing deadline 4/15. **Notification of Awards:** Applicants will be notified of awards on a rolling basis beginning on or about 3/1. **Types of Aid:** *Need-based scholarships/grants:* Pell, SEOG, state scholarships/grants, private scholarships, the school's own gift aid. *Loans:* FFEL Subsidized Stafford, FFEL Unsubsidized Stafford, FFEL PLUS, Federal Perkins, college/university loans from institutional funds. **Student Employment:** Federal Work-Study Program available. Institutional employment available. Off-campus job opportunities are excellent. **Financial Aid Statistics:** 55% freshmen, 51% undergrads receive need-based scholarship or grant aid. 63% freshmen, 58% undergrads receive need-based self-help aid.

See page 1070.

AUSTIN COLLEGE

900 North Grand Avenue, Suite 6N, Sherman, TX 75090-4400
Phone: 903-813-3000 **E-mail:** admission@austincollege.edu **CEEB Code:** 6016
Fax: 903-813-3198 **Website:** www.austincollege.edu **ACT Code:** 4058
Financial Aid Phone: 903-813-2900

This private school, affiliated with the Presbyterian Church, was founded in 1849. It has a 70-acre campus.

RATINGS
Admissions Selectivity Rating: 83   **Fire Safety Rating:** 69   **Green Rating:** 60*

STUDENTS AND FACULTY

Enrollment: 1,313. **Student Body:** 54% female, 46% male, 7% out-of-state, 1% international (25 countries represented). African American 3%, Asian 13%, Caucasian 74%, Hispanic 8%, Native American 1%. **Retention and Graduation:** 84% freshmen return for sophomore year. 72% freshmen graduate within 4 years. 32% grads go on to further study within 1 year. 22% grads pursue arts and sciences degrees. 1% grads pursue business degrees. 2% grads pursue law degrees. 7% grads pursue medical degrees. **Faculty:** Student/faculty ratio 12:1. 92 full-time faculty, 97% hold PhDs. 100% faculty teach undergrads.

ACADEMICS

Degrees: Bachelor's, master's. **Academic Requirements:** English (including composition), foreign languages, humanities, mathematics, sciences (biological or physical), social science. **Classes:** Most classes have 10–19 students. Most lab/discussion sections have fewer than 10 students. **Majors with Highest Enrollment:** Biology/biological sciences, business administration/management; psychology. **Disciplines with Highest Percentage of Degrees Awarded:** Psychology 15%, business/marketing 14%, biological/life sciences 10%, foreign languages and literature 9%, history 7%. **Special Study Options:** Double major, exchange student program (domestic), honor program, independent study, internships, student-designed major, study abroad, teacher certification program, Phi Beta Kappa.

FACILITIES

Housing: Coed dorms, men's dorms, women's dorms, apartments for single students, special housing for disabled students, Jordan Family Language House. **Special Academic Facilities/Equipment:** Tissue culture facility, high-performance numerics and graphics computing facility. **Computers:** 50% of classrooms are wired, 30% of classrooms are wireless, 73% of public computers are PCs, 25% of public computers are Macs, 2% of public computers are UNIX, network access in dorm rooms, network access in dorm lounges, online administrative functions (other than registration), support for handheld computing, remote student-access to Web through college's connection.

CAMPUS LIFE

Activities: Choral groups, dance, drama/theater, jazz band, literary magazine, music ensembles, musical theater, pep band, student government, student newspaper, symphony orchestra, yearbook. **Organizations:** 53 registered organizations, 15 honor societies, 6 religious organizations. 7 fraternities (24% men join), 7 sororities (29% women join). **Athletics (Intercollegiate):** *Men:* Baseball, basketball, football, soccer, swimming, tennis. *Women:* Basketball, soccer, swimming, tennis, volleyball.

ADMISSIONS

Freshman Academic Profile: 48% in top 10% of high school class, 78% in top 25% of high school class, 97% in top 50% of high school class. 86% from public high schools. SAT Math middle 50% range 560–660. SAT Critical Reading middle 50% range 560–670. SAT Writing middle 50% range 530–660. ACT middle 50% range 23–28. TOEFL required of all international applicants, minimum paper TOEFL 550, minimum computer TOEFL 213. **Basis for Candidate Selection:** *Very important factors considered include:* Academic GPA, rigor of secondary school record. *Important factors considered include:* Application essay, character/personal qualities, class rank, extracurricular activities, recommendation(s), standardized test scores, talent/ability. *Other factors considered include:* Alumni/ae relation, first generation, geographical residence, interview, racial/ethnic status, religious affiliation/commitment, state residency, volunteer work, work experience. **Freshman Admission Requirements:** High school diploma is required, and GED is accepted. *Academic units required:* 4 English, 3 math, 3 science (2 science labs), 2 foreign language, 2 social studies, 1 academic elective, 1 fine art. *Academic units recommended:* 4 English, 4 math, 4 science (3 science labs), 3 foreign language, 3 social studies, 2 fine art. **Freshman Admission Statistics:** 1,385 applied, 76% admitted, 32% enrolled. **Transfer Admission Requirements:** College transcript(s), essay or personal statement, statement of good standing from prior institution(s). Minimum college GPA of 2.5 required. Lowest grade transferable C. **General Admission Information:** Application fee $35. Early Decision application deadline 12/1. Regular application deadline 5/1. Regular notification by 4/1 and rolling thereafter. Nonfall registration accepted. Admission may be deferred for a maximum of 1 year. Credit and/or placement offered for CEEB Advanced Placement tests.

COSTS AND FINANCIAL AID

Annual tuition $24,192. **Room and board** $4,030. **Required fees** $160. **Average book expense** $1,000. **Required Forms and Deadlines:** FAFSA, institution's own financial aid form. Financial aid filing deadline 4/1. **Notification of Awards:** Applicants will be notified of awards on a rolling basis beginning on or about 3/1. **Types of Aid:** *Need-based scholarships/grants:* Pell, SEOG, state scholarships/grants, private scholarships, the school's own gift aid. *Loans:* FFEL Subsidized Stafford, FFEL Unsubsidized Stafford, FFEL PLUS, Federal Perkins, state loans, college/university loans from institutional funds, Alternative loans through various sources. **Student Employment:** Federal Work-Study Program available. Institutional employment available. Off-campus job

opportunities are good. **Financial Aid Statistics:** 56% freshmen, 57% undergrads receive need-based scholarship or grant aid. 44% freshmen, 45% undergrads receive need-based self-help aid. 95% freshmen, 96% undergrads receive any aid. Highest amount earned per year from on-campus jobs $1,999.

AUSTIN PEAY STATE UNIVERSITY

PO Box 4548, Clarksville, TN 37044
Phone: 931-221-7661 **E-mail:** admissions@apsu.edu **CEEB Code:** 1028
Fax: 931-221-6168 **Website:** www.apsu.edu **ACT Code:** 3944
Financial Aid Phone: 931-221-7907

This public school was founded in 1927. It has a 210-acre campus.

RATINGS

Admissions Selectivity Rating: 76   **Fire Safety Rating:** 60*   **Green Rating:** 60*

STUDENTS AND FACULTY

Enrollment: 8,382. **Student Body:** 63% female, 37% male, 7% out-of-state. African American 17%, Asian 2%, Caucasian 64%, Hispanic 5%. **Retention and Graduation:** 64% freshmen return for sophomore year. 12% freshmen graduate within 4 years. **Faculty:** Student/faculty ratio 21:1. 279 full-time faculty. 100% faculty teach undergrads.

ACADEMICS

Degrees: Associate, bachelor's, certificate, master's, post-bachelor's certificate, post-master's certificate, terminal. **Academic Requirements:** Arts/fine arts, English (including composition), foreign languages, history, humanities, mathematics, sciences (biological or physical), social science. **Classes:** Most classes have 20–29 students. Most lab/discussion sections have 10–19 students. **Disciplines with Highest Percentage of Degrees Awarded:** Business/marketing 24%, health professions and related sciences 10%, interdisciplinary studies 7%, liberal arts/general studies 6%, communications/journalism 6%, English 4%, psychology 4%, visual and performing arts 4%. **Special Study Options:** Accelerated program, cooperative education program, distance learning, double major, dual enrollment, English as a second language (ESL), honor program, independent study, internships, study abroad, teacher certification program, Servicemembers Opportunity College (SOC) for associate and bachelor's degrees.

FACILITIES

Housing: Coed dorms, men's dorms, women's dorms, apartments for married students, apartments for single students, special housing for disabled students, fraternity/sorority housing. **Special Academic Facilities/Equipment:** Art museum, biology museum, language lab, demonstration farm, twenty-first century classroom. **Computers:** 90% of public computers are PCs, 10% of public computers are Macs, network access in dorm rooms, network access in dorm lounges, remote student-access to Web through college's connection.

CAMPUS LIFE

Activities: Choral groups, concert band, dance, drama/theater, jazz band, literary magazine, marching band, music ensembles, musical theater, opera, pep band, radio station, student government, student newspaper, student-run film society, symphony orchestra, television station. **Organizations:** 50 registered organizations, 13 honor societies, 10 religious organizations. 8 fraternities (8% men join), 6 sororities (5% women join). **Athletics (Intercollegiate):** *Men:* Baseball, basketball, cheerleading, cross-country, football, golf, tennis. *Women:* Basketball, cheerleading, cross-country, golf, riflery, soccer, softball, tennis, track/field (outdoor), volleyball.

ADMISSIONS

Freshman Academic Profile: 12% in top 10% of high school class, 31% in top 25% of high school class, 59% in top 50% of high school class. 95% from public high schools. SAT Math middle 50% range 448–515. SAT Critical Reading middle 50% range 440–550. ACT middle 50% range 20–24. TOEFL required of all international applicants, minimum paper TOEFL 500, minimum computer TOEFL 173. **Basis for Candidate Selection:** *Very important factors considered include:* Academic GPA, rigor of secondary school record, standardized test scores. **Freshman Admission Requirements:** High school diploma is required, and GED is accepted. *Academic units required:* 4 English, 3 math, 2 science (1 science lab), 2 foreign language, 1 social studies, 1 history, 1 visual/performing arts. **Freshman Admission Statistics:** 2,514 applied, 59% admitted, 92% enrolled. **Transfer Admission Requirements:** College transcript(s). Lowest grade transferable D. **General Admission Information:** Application fee $15. Regular application deadline 7/25. Regular notification with receipt of a completed application. Nonfall registration accepted. Admission may be deferred for a maximum of 1 year. Credit offered for CEEB Advanced Placement tests.

COSTS AND FINANCIAL AID

Annual in-state tuition $4,058. Annual out-of-state tuition $14,334. Room and board $5,510. Required fees $1,180. Average book expense $1,404. Average book expense $1,350. **Required Forms and Deadlines:** FAFSA. Financial aid filing deadline 3/1. **Notification of Awards:** Applicants will be notified of awards on a rolling basis beginning on or about 5/1. **Types of Aid:** *Need-based scholarships/grants:* Pell, SEOG, state scholarships/grants, private scholarships, the school's own gift aid, corporate. *Loans:* FFEL Subsidized Stafford, FFEL Unsubsidized Stafford, FFEL PLUS, Federal Perkins. **Student Employment:** Federal Work-Study Program available. Institutional employment available. Off-campus job opportunities are good. **Financial Aid Statistics:** 38% freshmen, 43% undergrads receive need-based scholarship or grant aid. 3% freshmen, 3% undergrads receive need-based self-help aid. 33 freshmen, 146 undergrads receive athletic scholarships.

AVERETT UNIVERSITY

420 West Main Street, Danville, VA 24541
Phone: 434-791-4996 **E-mail:** admit@averett.edu **CEEB Code:** 5017
Fax: 434-797-2784 **Website:** www.averett.edu **ACT Code:** 4338
Financial Aid Phone: 434-791-5890

This private school was founded in 1859. It has a 19-acre campus.

RATINGS

Admissions Selectivity Rating: 72   **Fire Safety Rating:** 75   **Green Rating:** 76

STUDENTS AND FACULTY

Enrollment: 775. **Student Body:** 49% female, 51% male, 30% out-of-state, 2% international (10 countries represented). African American 22%, Caucasian 72%, Hispanic 3%. **Retention and Graduation:** 62% freshmen return for sophomore year. 20% freshmen graduate within 4 years. **Faculty:** Student/faculty ratio 11:1. 55 full-time faculty, 76% hold PhDs. 100% faculty teach undergrads.

ACADEMICS

Degrees: Associate, bachelor's, master's. **Academic Requirements:** Arts/fine arts, computer literacy, English (including composition), history, humanities, mathematics, sciences (biological or physical), social science, religion or philosophy and general education. Foreign language required for BA only. **Classes:** Most classes have fewer than 10 students. Most lab/discussion sections have 10–19 students. **Majors with Highest Enrollment:** Management science; teacher education, multiple levels. **Disciplines with Highest Percentage of Degrees Awarded:** Business/marketing 15%, parks and recreation 12%, liberal arts/general studies 12%, education 11%, security and protective services 7%. **Special Study Options:** Accelerated program, cooperative education program, cross-registration, distance learning, double major, dual enrollment, exchange student program (domestic), honors program, independent study, internships, liberal arts/career combination, student-designed major, study abroad, teacher certification program. Also offered: interdisciplinary studies and leadership studies. Undergraduates may take grad level classes. Some online courses available.

FACILITIES

Housing: Coed dorms, men's dorms, women's dorms, apartments for single students. **Special Academic Facilities/Equipment:** Averett's Flight Center located 4 miles from the main campus at Danville Regional Airport has 2 runways (1 with ILS approach), automated weather system, and UNICOM service. Averett's facility houses aircraft, areas for ground instruction, simulator rooms, technology center. Averett's 100-acre Equestrian Center is a 15-minute drive from the main campus. It houses an indoor ring, 40 stalls with removable partitions, 3 tack rooms, wash room for horses and equipment, breeding area, offices, and a laboratory. The outdoor facilities include a round pen, riding ring, jumping area, pastures, and cross-country trails. **Computers:** 3% of classrooms are wireless, 80% of public computers are PCs, 20% of public computers are Macs, online registration, online administrative functions (other than registration), remote student-access to Web through college's connection.

CAMPUS LIFE

Activities: Choral groups, drama/theater, literary magazine, musical theater, student government, student newspaper. **Organizations:** 25 registered organizations, 4 honor societies, 4 religious organizations. 1 fraternity (3% men join), 1 sorority (2% women join). **Athletics (Intercollegiate):** *Men:* Baseball, basketball, cheerleading, cross-country, football, golf, soccer, tennis. *Women:* Basketball, cheerleading, cross-country, lacrosse, soccer, softball, tennis, volleyball.

ADMISSIONS

Freshman Academic Profile: 13% in top 10% of high school class, 27% in top 25% of high school class, 64% in top 50% of high school class. 90% from public high schools. SAT Math middle 50% range 420–460. SAT Critical Reading middle 50% range 410–450. ACT middle 50% range 16–19. TOEFL required of all international applicants, minimum paper TOEFL 500, minimum computer TOEFL 173. **Basis for Candidate Selection:** *Very important factors considered include:* Academic GPA, class rank, level of applicant's interest, rigor of secondary school record, standardized test scores. *Important factors considered include:* Extracurricular activities. *Other factors considered include:* Alumni/ae relation, application essay, character/personal qualities, interview, recommendation(s), talent/ability, volunteer work, work experience. **Freshman Admission Requirements:** High school diploma is required, and GED is accepted. *Academic units required:* 4 English, 2 math, 2 science (2 science labs), 3 social studies, 3 history, 3 academic electives. *Academic units recommended:* 4 English, 3 math, 3 science (3 science labs), 2 foreign language, 3 social studies, 3 history, 5 academic electives. **Freshman Admission Statistics:** 961 applied, 85% admitted, 20% enrolled. **Transfer Admission Requirements:** College transcript(s), statement of good standing from prior institution(s). Minimum college GPA of 2.0 required. Lowest grade transferable C. **General Admission Information:** Regular application deadline 7/15. Regular notification within 1–2 weeks of acceptance. Nonfall registration accepted. Admission may be deferred for a maximum of 2 years. Credit and/or placement offered for CEEB Advanced Placement tests.

COSTS AND FINANCIAL AID

Average book expense $900. **Required Forms and Deadlines:** FAFSA, state aid form. Financial aid filing deadline 4/1. **Notification of Awards:** Applicants will be notified of awards on a rolling basis beginning on or about 2/15. **Types of Aid:** *Need-based scholarships/grants:* Pell, SEOG, state scholarships/grants, private scholarships, the school's own gift aid. *Loans:* FFEL Subsidized Stafford, FFEL Unsubsidized Stafford, FFEL PLUS, Federal Perkins, Federal Nursing, state loans. **Financial Aid Statistics:** 78% freshmen, 80% undergrads receive need-based scholarship or grant aid. 68% freshmen, 68% undergrads receive need-based self-help aid. 96% freshmen, 97% undergrads receive any aid.

AVILA UNIVERSITY

11901 Wornall Road, Kansas City, MO 64145-1698
Phone: 816-942-8400 **E-mail:** admissions@mail.avila.edu **CEEB Code:** 6109
Fax: 816-942-3362 **Website:** www.avila.edu **ACT Code:** 2278

This private school, affiliated with the Roman Catholic Church, was founded in 1916. It has a 48-acre campus.

RATINGS

Admissions Selectivity Rating: 81   **Fire Safety Rating:** 60*   **Green Rating:** 60*

STUDENTS AND FACULTY

Enrollment: 1,096. **Student Body:** 64% female, 36% male, 34% out-of-state, 3% international. African American 18%, Asian 1%, Caucasian 70%, Hispanic 4%. **Retention and Graduation:** 69% freshmen return for sophomore year. 30% freshmen graduate within 4 years. 40% grads go on to further study within 1 year. 20% grads pursue arts and sciences degrees. 15% grads pursue business degrees. 2% grads pursue law degrees. 3% grads pursue medical degrees. **Faculty:** Student/faculty ratio 12:1. 63 full-time faculty, 71% hold PhDs. 100% faculty teach undergrads.

ACADEMICS

Degrees: Bachelor's, certificate, master's. **Academic Requirements:** Arts/fine arts, computer literacy, English (including composition), history, mathematics, philosophy, sciences (biological or physical). **Classes:** Most classes have fewer than 10 students. **Majors with Highest Enrollment:** Business administration/management, nursing, psychology. **Disciplines with Highest Percentage of Degrees Awarded:** Business/marketing 28%, health professions and related sciences 21%, psychology 10%, visual and performing arts 8%, communication technologies 7%, education 7%, social sciences 7%. **Special Study Options:** Accelerated program, double major, dual enrollment, English as a Second Language (ESL), independent study, internships, study abroad, teacher certification program.

FACILITIES

Housing: Coed dorms. **Computers:** 90% of public computers are PCs, 10% of public computers are Macs, network access in dorm rooms, network access in dorm lounges, remote student-access to Web through college's connection.

CAMPUS LIFE

Activities: Choral groups, drama/theater, literary magazine, student government, student newspaper, television station. **Organizations:** 12 religious organizations. **Athletics (Intercollegiate):** *Men:* Baseball, basketball, football, soccer, volleyball. *Women:* Basketball, cheerleading, golf, soccer, softball, volleyball.

ADMISSIONS

Freshman Academic Profile: 17% in top 10% of high school class, 39% in top 25% of high school class, 74% in top 50% of high school class. 92% from public high schools. ACT middle 50% range 18–25. TOEFL required of all international applicants, minimum paper TOEFL 550, minimum computer TOEFL 213. **Basis for Candidate Selection:** *Very important factors considered include:* Rigor of secondary school record, standardized test scores. *Other factors considered include:* Application essay, character/personal qualities, class rank, extracurricular activities, interview, recommendation(s), talent/ability. **Freshman Admission Requirements:** High school diploma is required, and GED is accepted. *Academic units recommended:* 4 English, 3 math, 2 science (1 science lab), 2 foreign language, 3 social studies, 2 history. **Freshman Admission Statistics:** 936 applied, 42% admitted, 38% enrolled. **Transfer Admission Requirements:** College transcript(s), minimum college GPA of 2.0 required. Lowest grade transferable C. **General Admission Information:** Regular notification is rolling. Nonfall registration accepted. Admission may be deferred for a maximum of 1 year. Common Application not accepted. Credit and/or placement offered for CEEB Advanced Placement tests.

COSTS AND FINANCIAL AID

Annual tuition $14,700. Room & board $5,300. Required fees $187. Average book expense $800. **Required Forms and Deadlines:** FAFSA, institution's own financial aid form. Financial aid filing deadline 4/1. **Notification of Awards:** Applicants will be notified of awards on a rolling basis beginning on or about 2/15. **Types of Aid:** *Need-based scholarships/grants:* Pell, SEOG, state scholarships/grants. *Loans:* FFEL Subsidized Stafford, FFEL Unsubsidized Stafford, FFEL PLUS, Federal Perkins. **Student Employment:** Federal Work-Study Program available. Institutional employment available. **Financial Aid Statistics:** 30% freshmen, 44% undergrads receive need-based scholarship or grant aid. 46% freshmen, 57% undergrads receive need-based self-help aid. 70 freshmen, 340 undergrads receive athletic scholarships. Highest amount earned per year from on-campus jobs $1,500.

AZUSA PACIFIC UNIVERSITY

901 East Alosta Avenue, Azusa, CA 91702-7000
Phone: 626-812-3016 **E-mail:** admissions@apu.edu **CEEB Code:** 4596
Fax: 626-812-3096 **Website:** www.apu.edu
Financial Aid Phone: 626-812-3009

This private school, affiliated with the Christian (nondenominational) Church, was founded in 1899. It has a 103-acre campus.

RATINGS

Admissions Selectivity Rating: 83   **Fire Safety Rating:** 60*   **Green Rating:** 64

STUDENTS AND FACULTY

Enrollment: 4,722. **Student Body:** 63% female, 37% male, 27% out-of-state, 2% international (68 countries represented). African American 4%, Asian 7%, Caucasian 68%, Hispanic 13%. **Retention and Graduation:** 79% freshmen return for sophomore year. 48% freshmen graduate within 4 years. **Faculty:** Student/faculty ratio 11:1. 300 full-time faculty, 76% hold PhDs. 100% faculty teach undergrads.

ACADEMICS

Degrees: Bachelor's, doctoral, first professional, master's. **Academic Requirements:** Arts/fine arts, English (including composition), foreign languages, history, humanities, mathematics, philosophy, sciences (biological or physical), social science. **Classes:** Most classes have 10–19 students. Most lab/discussion sections have 10–19 students. **Majors with Highest Enrollment:** Business, management, marketing, and related support services; liberal arts and sciences, studies, and humanities; nursing. **Disciplines with Highest Percentage of Degrees Awarded:** Liberal arts/general studies 22%, business/marketing 22%, philosophy and religious studies 8%, communications/journalism 8%, health professions and related sciences 8%, psychology 7%, visual and performing arts 7%, biological/life sciences 3%, education 2%, English 2%, public administration and social services 2%. **Special Study Options:** Accelerated program, cooperative education program, distance learning, double major, English as a second language (ESL), exchange student program (domestic), honor program, independent study, internships, study abroad, teacher certification program.

FACILITIES

Housing: Coed dorms, men's dorms, women's dorms, apartments for single students. **Special Academic Facilities/Equipment:** Electron microscope. **Computers:** 100% of classrooms are wireless, 90% of public computers are PCs, 10% of public computers are Macs, network access in dorm rooms, online registration, online administrative functions (other than registration).

CAMPUS LIFE

Activities: Choral groups, concert band, drama/theater, jazz band, marching band, music ensembles, musical theater, opera, pep band, radio station, student government, student newspaper, symphony orchestra, television station, yearbook. **Organizations:** 30 registered organizations, 7 honor societies. **Athletics (Intercollegiate):** *Men:* Baseball, basketball, cross-country, football, soccer, tennis, track/field (outdoor), volleyball. *Women:* Basketball, cheerleading, cross-country, soccer, softball, tennis, track/field (outdoor), volleyball.

ADMISSIONS

Freshman Academic Profile: 27% in top 10% of high school class, 58% in top 25% of high school class, 85% in top 50% of high school class. SAT Math middle 50% range 480–590. SAT Critical Reading middle 50% range 480–590. SAT Writing middle 50% range 960–1178. ACT middle 50% range 21–26. TOEFL required of all international applicants, minimum paper TOEFL 500, minimum computer TOEFL 173. **Basis for Candidate Selection:** *Very important factors considered include:* Academic GPA, application essay, class rank, recommendation(s), standardized test scores. *Important factors considered include:* Character/personal qualities, state residency. *Other factors considered include:* Alumni/ae relation, extracurricular activities, first generation, interview, level of applicant's interest, racial/ethnic status, rigor of secondary school record, talent/ability, volunteer work, work experience. **Freshman Admission Requirements:** High school diploma is required, and GED is accepted. *Academic units recommended:* 4 English, 3 math, 2 science, 3 foreign language, 1 social studies, 2 history. **Freshman Admission Statistics:** 3,106 applied, 74% admitted, 38% enrolled. **Transfer Admission Requirements:** College transcript(s), essay or personal statement, statement of good standing from prior institution(s). Minimum college GPA of 2.2 required. Lowest grade transferable C. **General Admission Information:** Application fee $45. Regular application deadline 6/1. Regular notification rolling basis 2 weeks after they apply. Nonfall registration accepted. Credit offered for CEEB Advanced Placement tests.

COSTS AND FINANCIAL AID

Annual tuition $24,430. Room and board $7,518. Required fees $700. Average book expense $1,386. **Required Forms and Deadlines:** FAFSA, institution's own financial aid form. Financial aid filing deadline 7/1. **Notification of Awards:** Applicants will be notified of awards on a rolling basis beginning on or about 3/1. **Types of Aid:** *Need-based scholarships/grants:* Pell, SEOG, state scholarships/grants, private scholarships, the school's own gift aid, Federal Nursing Scholarships. *Loans:* FFEL Subsidized Stafford, FFEL Unsubsidized Stafford, FFEL PLUS, Federal Perkins, Federal Nursing. **Student Employment:** Off-campus job opportunities are good. **Financial Aid Statistics:** 59% freshmen, 56% undergrads receive need-based scholarship or grant aid. 27% freshmen, 40% undergrads receive need-based self-help aid. 13 freshmen, 73 undergrads receive athletic scholarships. 82% undergrads receive any aid. Highest amount earned per year from on-campus jobs $8,000.

BABSON COLLEGE

Best 368

Lunder Hall, Babson Park, MA 02457
Phone: 781-239-5522 **E-mail:** ugradadmission@babson.edu **CEEB Code:** 3075
Fax: 781-239-4135 **Website:** www.babson.edu **ACT Code:** 1780
Financial Aid Phone: 781-239-4219

This private school was founded in 1919. It has a 370-acre campus.

RATINGS

Admissions Selectivity Rating: 93   **Fire Safety Rating:** 86   **Green Rating:** 60*

STUDENTS AND FACULTY

Enrollment: 1,776. **Student Body:** 39% female, 61% male, 70% out-of-state, 17% international (60 countries represented). African American 3%, Asian 10%, Caucasian 43%, Hispanic 7%. **Retention and Graduation:** 95% freshmen return for sophomore year. 83% freshmen graduate within 4 years. **Faculty:**

Student/faculty ratio 14:1. 152 full-time faculty, 90% hold PhDs. 100% faculty teach undergrads.

ACADEMICS

Degrees: Bachelor's, master's, post-master's certificate. **Academic Requirements:** Arts/fine arts, computer literacy, English (including composition), history, humanities, mathematics, sciences (biological or physical), social science, accounting, finance, economics, law, management, MIS, operations, organizational behavior, strategy. **Classes:** Most classes have 20–29 students. **Majors with Highest Enrollment:** Accounting, entrepreneurial and small business operations, finance. **Disciplines with Highest Percentage of Degrees Awarded:** Business/marketing 100%. **Special Study Options:** Cross-registration, exchange student program (domestic), honors program, independent study, internships, liberal arts/career combination, study abroad. We offer 24 concentrations that provide a coherent set of courses for academic and external recognition.

FACILITIES

Housing: Coed dorms, special housing for disabled students, fraternity/sorority housing, substance free, special interest housing. **Special Academic Facilities/Equipment:** The Babson World Globe, Roger Babson Museum, Isaac Newton Museum, Arthur Blank Center for Entrepreneurship. **Computers:** 70% of classrooms are wired, 1% of classrooms are wireless, 100% of public computers are PCs, network access in dorm rooms, network access in dorm lounges, online registration, online administrative functions (other than registration), support for handheld computing, remote student-access to Web through college's connection, tuition includes personal computer. Undergraduates are required to own a computer.

CAMPUS LIFE

Activities: Dance, drama/theater, jazz band, literary magazine, musical theater, radio station, student government, student newspaper, yearbook. **Organizations:** 64 registered organizations, 3 religious organizations. 4 fraternities (10% men join), 3 sororities (12% women join). **Athletics (Intercollegiate):** *Men:* Baseball, basketball, cross-country, diving, golf, ice hockey, lacrosse, skiing (downhill/alpine), soccer, swimming, tennis, track/field (indoor), track/field (outdoor). *Women:* Basketball, cross-country, diving, field hockey, lacrosse, skiing (downhill/alpine), soccer, softball, swimming, tennis, track/field (indoor), track/field (outdoor), volleyball.

ADMISSIONS

Freshman Academic Profile: 47% in top 10% of high school class, 87% in top 25% of high school class, 99% in top 50% of high school class. SAT Math middle 50% range 590–680. SAT Critical Reading middle 50% range 560–640. SAT Writing middle 50% range 570–650. ACT middle 50% range 25–29. TOEFL required of all international applicants, minimum paper TOEFL 600, minimum computer TOEFL 250. **Basis for Candidate Selection:** *Very important factors considered include:* Academic GPA, application essay, character/personal qualities, recommendation(s), rigor of secondary school record, standardized test scores. *Important factors considered include:* Class rank, extracurricular activities. *Other factors considered include:* Alumni/ae relation, first generation, geographical residence, interview, level of applicant's interest, racial/ethnic status, state residency, talent/ability, volunteer work, work experience. **Freshman Admission Requirements:** High school diploma is required, and GED is accepted. *Academic units recommended:* 4 English, 4 math, 4 science (3 science labs), 4 foreign language, 2 social studies, 2 history, 1 pre-calculus. **Freshman Admission Statistics:** 3,436 applied, 37% admitted, 35% enrolled. **Transfer Admission Requirements:** High school transcript, college transcript(s), essay or personal statement, statement of good standing from prior institution(s). Lowest grade transferable C. **General Admission Information:** Application fee $65. Early decision application deadline 11/15. Regular application deadline 1/15. Regular notification 4/1. Nonfall registration not accepted. Admission may be deferred for a maximum of 1 year. Credit and/or placement offered for CEEB Advanced Placement tests.

COSTS AND FINANCIAL AID

Required Forms and Deadlines: FAFSA, CSS/Financial Aid PROFILE, Noncustodial PROFILE, Business/Farm Supplement, federal tax returns, W-2s, and verification worksheet. Financial aid filing deadline 2/15. **Notification of Awards:** Applicants will be notified of awards on or about 4/1. **Types of Aid:** *Need-based scholarships/grants:* Pell, SEOG, state scholarships/grants, the school's own gift aid. *Loans:* FFEL Subsidized Stafford, FFEL Unsubsidized Stafford, FFEL PLUS, Federal Perkins, state loans. **Financial Aid Statistics:** 37% freshmen, 40% undergrads receive need-based scholarship or grant aid. 31% freshmen, 39% undergrads receive need-based self-help aid. 40% freshmen, 44% undergrads receive any aid. Highest amount earned per year from on-campus jobs $5,400.

See page 1072.

See page 1072.

BAKER COLLEGE OF AUBURN HILLS

1500 University Drive, Auburn Hills, MI 48326-1586
Phone: 248-340-0600 **E-mail:** bohlen_j@auburnhills.baker.edu
Fax: 248-340-0600 **Website:** www.baker.edu
Financial Aid Phone: 248-276-8214

This private school was founded in 1992. It has a 7-acre campus.

RATINGS

Admissions Selectivity Rating: 60*   **Fire Safety Rating:** 60*   **Green Rating:** 60*

STUDENTS AND FACULTY

Enrollment: 2,596. **Student Body:** African American 20%, Asian 4%, Caucasian 72%, Hispanic 4%. **Faculty:** Student/faculty ratio 19:1. 8 full-time faculty. 100% faculty teach undergrads.

ACADEMICS

Degrees: Associate, bachelor's, certificate, diploma, master's, post-bachelor's certificate, terminal. **Academic Requirements:** Computer literacy, English (including composition), mathematics. **Classes:** Most classes have 20–29 students. Most lab/discussion sections have fewer than 10 students. **Disciplines with Highest Percentage of Degrees Awarded:** Business/marketing 100%. **Special Study Options:** Accelerated program, cooperative education program, distance learning, double major, dual enrollment, external degree program, independent study, internships, weekend college.

FACILITIES

Computers: 99% of public computers are PCs, 1% of public computers are Macs, online administrative functions (other than registration), remote student-access to Web through college's connection.

CAMPUS LIFE

Activities: Literary magazine, student newspaper. **Organizations:** 3 registered organizations.

ADMISSIONS

Freshman Academic Profile: TOEFL required of all international applicants, minimum paper TOEFL 550. **Freshman Admission Requirements:** High school diploma is required, and GED is accepted. **Freshman Admission Statistics:** 748 applied, 50% admitted. **Transfer Admission Requirements:** High school transcript, college transcript(s), Lowest grade transferable C. **General Admission Information:** Application fee $20. Regular application deadline 9/19. Regular notification is rolling. Nonfall registration accepted. Admission may be deferred for a maximum of 1 quarter. Common Application not accepted.

COSTS AND FINANCIAL AID

Annual tuition $5,760. Average book expense $900. **Required Forms and Deadlines:** FAFSA, institution's own financial aid form. Financial aid filing deadline 9/1. **Types of Aid:** *Need-based scholarships/grants:* Pell, SEOG, state scholarships/grants, the school's own gift aid. *Loans:* FFEL PLUS. **Student Employment:** Federal Work-Study Program available. Off-campus job opportunities are excellent.

BAKER COLLEGE OF JACKSON

2800 Springport Road, Jackson, MI 49202
Phone: 517-788-7800 **E-mail:** kelli.stepka@baker.edu
Fax: 517-789-7331 **Website:** www.baker.edu

This is a private school. It has a 42-acre campus.

RATINGS

Admissions Selectivity Rating: 60*   **Fire Safety Rating:** 60*   **Green Rating:** 60*

STUDENTS AND FACULTY

Enrollment: 1,392. **Student Body:** African American 7%, Caucasian 90%, Hispanic 3%. **Faculty:** Student/faculty ratio 17:1.

ACADEMICS

Degrees: Associate, bachelor's, certificate, diploma, master's. **Academic Requirements:** Computer literacy, English (including composition), mathematics. **Special Study Options:** Accelerated program, cooperative education program, distance learning, double major, dual enrollment, external degree program, independent study, internships, teacher certification program.

ADMISSIONS

Freshman Admission Requirements: High school diploma is required, and GED is accepted. **General Admission Information:** Application fee $20. Regular application deadline 9/20. Nonfall registration accepted. Common Application not accepted.

COSTS AND FINANCIAL AID

Annual tuition $5,760. Required fees $20. Average book expense $900. **Types of Aid:** *Loans:* Direct Subsidized Stafford, Direct Unsubsidized Stafford, Direct PLUS.

BAKER COLLEGE OF MUSKEGON

1903 Marquette Avenue, Muskegon, MI 49442-3497
Phone: 231-777-5200 **E-mail:** kathy.jacobson@baker.edu
Fax: 231-777-5201 **Website:** www.baker.edu **ACT Code:** 1957
Financial Aid Phone: 616-777-5231

This private school was founded in 1888.

RATINGS

Admissions Selectivity Rating: 60*   **Fire Safety Rating:** 60*   **Green Rating:** 60*

STUDENTS AND FACULTY

Enrollment: 3,442. **Student Body:** African American 14%, Asian 1%, Caucasian 79%, Hispanic 4%. **Retention and Graduation:** 9% grads go on to further study within 1 year. **Faculty:** 100% faculty teach undergrads.

ACADEMICS

Degrees: Associate, bachelor's, certificate, diploma, master's. **Academic Requirements:** Computer literacy, English (including composition), mathematics, social science, oral communications. **Special Study Options:** Accelerated program, cooperative education program, distance learning, double major, dual enrollment, external degree program, independent study, internships.

FACILITIES

Housing: Coed dorms, special housing for disabled students. **Computers:** 95% of public computers are PCs, 5% of public computers are Macs, network access in dorm rooms, remote student-access to Web through college's connection.

CAMPUS LIFE

Activities: Yearbook. **Organizations:** 4 registered organizations.

ADMISSIONS

Freshman Admission Requirements: High school diploma is required, and GED is accepted. **Freshman Admission Statistics:** 2,202 applied, 100% admitted, 35% enrolled. **Transfer Admission Requirements:** High school transcript, Lowest grade transferable C. **General Admission Information:** Application fee $20. Regular application deadline 9/20. Nonfall registration not accepted. Common Application not accepted.

COSTS AND FINANCIAL AID

Annual tuition $5,760. Room $2,100. Required fees $20. Average book expense $900. **Student Employment:** Federal Work-Study Program available. Institutional employment available. Off-campus job opportunities are excellent.

BAKER COLLEGE OF OWOSSO

1020 South Washington Street, Owosso, MI 48867-4400
Phone: 989-729-3350 **E-mail:** mike.konopacke@baker.edu
Fax: 989-723-3355 **Website:** www.baker.edu

This private school was founded in 1984.

RATINGS

Admissions Selectivity Rating: 60*   **Fire Safety Rating:** 60*   **Green Rating:** 60*

STUDENTS AND FACULTY

Enrollment: 2,361. **Student Body:** African American 2%, Caucasian 96%, Hispanic 2%. **Faculty:** Student/faculty ratio 38:1.

ACADEMICS

Degrees: Associate, bachelor's, certificate, diploma, master's. **Disciplines with**

Highest Percentage of Degrees Awarded: Business/marketing 73%, health professions and related sciences 20%, computer and information sciences 7%.

FACILITIES

Housing: Coed dorms. **Computers:** Network access in dorm rooms, network access in dorm lounges, online registration, remote student-access to Web through college's connection.

ADMISSIONS

Freshman Academic Profile: TOEFL required of all international applicants, minimum paper TOEFL 500. **Freshman Admission Requirements:** High school diploma is required, and GED is accepted. **Freshman Admission Statistics:** 713 applied, 100% admitted, 99% enrolled. **Transfer Admission Requirements:** High school transcript. Lowest grade transferable C. **General Admission Information:** Application fee $20. Nonfall registration accepted. Common Application not accepted. Neither credit nor placement offered for CEEB Advanced Placement tests.

COSTS AND FINANCIAL AID

Annual tuition $5,760. Room $2,100. Required fees $20. Average book expense $900. **Types of Aid:** *Need-based scholarships/grants:* Pell, SEOG, state scholarships/grants, private scholarships. *Loans:* FFEL Subsidized Stafford, FFEL Unsubsidized Stafford, FFEL PLUS. **Student Employment:** Federal Work-Study Program available. Off-campus job opportunities are good. **Financial Aid Phone:** 517-729-3435.

BAKER COLLEGE OF PORT HURON

3403 Lapeer Road, Port Huron, MI 48060-2597
Phone: 810-985-7000 **E-mail:** kenny_d@porthuron.baker.edu
Fax: 810-985-7066 **Website:** www.baker.edu

This is a private school.

RATINGS

Admissions Selectivity Rating: 60*   **Fire Safety Rating:** 60*   **Green Rating:** 60*

STUDENTS AND FACULTY

Enrollment: 1,363. **Student Body:** African American 4%, Caucasian 93%, Hispanic 2%. **Faculty:** Student/faculty ratio 13:1. 10 full-time faculty, 10% hold PhDs.

ACADEMICS

Degrees: Associate, bachelor's, certificate, diploma, master's, terminal. **Academic Requirements:** Computer literacy, English (including composition), mathematics. **Classes:** Most classes have 20–29 students. Most lab/discussion sections have 10–19 students. **Disciplines with Highest Percentage of Degrees Awarded:** Business/marketing 25%. **Special Study Options:** Accelerated program, cooperative education program, distance learning, double major, dual enrollment, external degree program, independent study, internships.

ADMISSIONS

Freshman Admission Requirements: High school diploma is required, and GED is accepted. **Freshman Admission Statistics:** 498 applied, 84% admitted, 71% enrolled. **Transfer Admission Requirements:** High school transcript. Lowest grade transferable C. **General Admission Information:** Application fee $20. Regular application deadline 9/25. Regular notification is rolling. Nonfall registration accepted. Admission may be deferred for a maximum of 3 months. Common Application not accepted.

COSTS AND FINANCIAL AID

Annual tuition $5,760. Required fees $20. Average book expense $900. **Required Forms and Deadlines:** FAFSA, institution's own financial aid form. Financial aid filing deadline 2/21. **Notification of Awards:** Applicants will be notified of awards on a rolling basis beginning on or about 4/1. **Types of Aid:** *Need-based scholarships/grants:* Pell, SEOG, state scholarships/grants, private scholarships, the school's own gift aid. *Loans:* FFEL Subsidized Stafford, FFEL Unsubsidized Stafford, FFEL PLUS.

BAKER UNIVERSITY COLLEGE OF ARTS AND SCIENCES

PO Box 65, Baldwin City, KS 66006
Phone: 785-594-8307 **E-mail:** admissions@bakeru.edu **CEEB Code:** 6031
Fax: 785-594-8372 **Website:** www.bakeru.edu **ACT Code:** 1386
Financial Aid Phone: 785-594-4595

This private school, affiliated with the Methodist Church, was founded in 1858. It has a 36-acre campus.

RATINGS
Admissions Selectivity Rating: 83   **Fire Safety Rating:** 64   **Green Rating:** 60*

STUDENTS AND FACULTY
Enrollment: 870. **Student Body:** 52% female, 48% male, 27% out-of-state. African American 8%, Caucasian 84%, Hispanic 3%. **Retention and Graduation:** 81% freshmen return for sophomore year. 39% freshmen graduate within 4 years. 26% grads go on to further study within 1 year. 11% grads pursue arts and sciences degrees. 1% grads pursue business degrees. 6% grads pursue law degrees. 4% grads pursue medical degrees. **Faculty:** Student/faculty ratio 10:1. 73 full-time faculty, 71% hold PhDs. 100% faculty teach undergrads.

ACADEMICS
Degrees: Bachelor's. **Academic Requirements:** Arts/fine arts, English (including composition), history, humanities, mathematics, sciences (biological or physical), social science, critical thinking, non-Western studies, fitness and well-being, oral communication. **Classes:** Most classes have fewer than 10 students. Most lab/discussion sections have fewer than 10 students. **Majors with Highest Enrollment:** Biology/biological sciences, business administration/management, elementary education and teaching. **Disciplines with Highest Percentage of Degrees Awarded:** Business/marketing 24%, education 12%, biological/life sciences 11%, communications/journalism 9%, social sciences 8%. **Special Study Options:** Accelerated program, double major, honors program, independent study, internships, liberal arts/career combination, student-designed major, study abroad, teacher certification program. Students can transfer to the School of Nursing (located in a clinical setting in Topeka, KS) after completing their first 2 years of general education and pre-nursing course work. Baker also offers an Interterm program (3 1/2 weeks in January), during which students can take classes on campus, pursue travel courses, or work in internships.

FACILITIES
Housing: Coed dorms, men's dorms, women's dorms, apartments for single students, special housing for disabled students, fraternity/sorority housing. **Special Academic Facilities/Equipment:** Old Castle Museum, Quayle Bible Collection. **Computers:** 90% of public computers are PCs, 10% of public computers are Macs, network access in dorm rooms, network access in dorm lounges, online registration, online administrative functions (other than registration), remote student-access to Web through college's connection.

CAMPUS LIFE
Activities: Choral groups, concert band, drama/theater, jazz band, literary magazine, music ensembles, radio station, student government, student newspaper, television station, yearbook. **Organizations:** 60 registered organizations, 15 honor societies, 2 religious organizations. 4 fraternities (39% men join), 4 sororities (45% women join). **Athletics (Intercollegiate):** *Men:* Baseball, basketball, cheerleading, cross-country, football, golf, soccer, tennis, track/field (outdoor). *Women:* Basketball, cheerleading, cross-country, golf, soccer, softball, tennis, track/field (outdoor), volleyball.

ADMISSIONS
Freshman Academic Profile: 25% in top 10% of high school class, 52% in top 25% of high school class, 81% in top 50% of high school class. 95% from public high schools. ACT middle 50% range 21–26. TOEFL required of all international applicants, minimum paper TOEFL 525, minimum computer TOEFL 195. **Basis for Candidate Selection:** *Very important factors considered include:* Level of applicant's interest, recommendation(s), rigor of secondary school record, standardized test scores. *Important factors considered include:* Academic GPA, class rank. *Other factors considered include:* Alumni/ae relation, application essay, character/personal qualities, extracurricular activities, geographical residence, interview, talent/ability, volunteer work, work experience. **Freshman Admission Requirements:** High school diploma is required, and GED is accepted. *Academic units recommended:* 4 English, 3 math, 3 science (1 science lab), 2 foreign language, 3 social studies, 2 fine arts/computing. **Freshman Admission Statistics:** 1,051 applied, 63% admitted, 36% enrolled. **Transfer Admission Requirements:** High school transcript,

college transcript(s), standardized test score, minimum college GPA of 2.3 required. Lowest grade transferable C. **General Admission Information:** Regular notification is rolling. Nonfall registration accepted. Admission may be deferred for a maximum of 1 year. Common Application not accepted. Credit and/or placement offered for CEEB Advanced Placement tests.

COSTS AND FINANCIAL AID
Average book expense $1,000. **Required Forms and Deadlines:** FAFSA, institution's own financial aid form. Financial aid filing deadline 3/1. **Notification of Awards:** Applicants will be notified of awards on a rolling basis beginning on or about 3/1. **Types of Aid:** *Need-based scholarships/grants:* Pell, SEOG, state scholarships/grants, private scholarships, the school's own gift aid. *Loans:* FFEL Subsidized Stafford, FFEL Unsubsidized Stafford, FFEL PLUS, Federal Perkins. **Student Employment:** Federal Work-Study Program available. Institutional employment available. Off-campus job opportunities are good. **Financial Aid Statistics:** 76% freshmen, 77% undergrads receive need-based scholarship or grant aid. 76% freshmen, 78% undergrads receive need-based self-help aid. 52 freshmen, 193 undergrads receive athletic scholarships. 98% freshmen, 95% undergrads receive any aid. Highest amount earned per year from on-campus jobs $1,400.

See page 1074.

BALDWIN-WALLACE COLLEGE

275 Eastland Road, Berea, OH 44017
Phone: 440-826-2222 **E-mail:** admission@bw.edu **CEEB Code:** 1050
Fax: 440-826-3830 **Website:** www.bw.edu **ACT Code:** 3236
Financial Aid Phone: 440-826-2108

This private school, affiliated with the Methodist Church, was founded in 1845. It has a 100-acre campus.

RATINGS
Admissions Selectivity Rating: 82   **Fire Safety Rating:** 66   **Green Rating:** 80

STUDENTS AND FACULTY
Enrollment: 3,440. **Student Body:** 59% female, 41% male, 10% out-of-state, 1% international (25 countries represented). African American 6%, Asian 1%, Caucasian 82%, Hispanic 1%. **Retention and Graduation:** 81% freshmen return for sophomore year. 52% freshmen graduate within 4 years. 28% grads go on to further study within 1 year. 22% grads pursue arts and sciences degrees. 14% grads pursue business degrees. 9% grads pursue law degrees. 18% grads pursue medical degrees. **Faculty:** Student/faculty ratio 15:1. 164 full-time faculty, 82% hold PhDs. 94% faculty teach undergrads.

ACADEMICS
Degrees: Bachelor's, master's. **Academic Requirements:** Arts/fine arts, English (including composition), history, humanities, mathematics, philosophy, sciences (biological or physical), social science, international studies (including foreign language, study abroad, or selected courses with an international emphasis), HPE (traditional day students only). Please note: History is part of Cultural Heritage Core. **Classes:** Most classes have 10–19 students. Most lab/discussion sections have 10–19 students. **Majors with Highest Enrollment:** Business administration and management, early childhood education and teaching, psychology. **Disciplines with Highest Percentage of Degrees Awarded:** Business/marketing 30%, education 14%, psychology 6%, visual and performing arts 6%, English 5%. **Special Study Options:** Accelerated program, cross-registration, distance learning, double major, dual enrollment, exchange student program (domestic), honors program, independent study, internships, liberal arts/career combination, student-designed major, study abroad, teacher certification program, weekend college. BS program in Allied Health fields with 3 local community colleges; 3–2 in engineering with Case Western Reserve, Columbia University, and Washington University; 3–2 in social work with Case Western Reserve; 3–1 or 4–1 medical technology program with local hospitals; 3–2 MBA programs in accounting and human resources; 3–2 biology program with Case Western Reserve.

FACILITIES
Housing: Coed dorms, women's dorms, apartments for single students, special housing for disabled students, special housing for international students, fraternity/sorority housing, Wellness Halls, Sprout Houses (for single mothers and children). **Special Academic Facilities/Equipment:** Art gallery, electron microscope, observatory. **Computers:** 100% of classrooms are wired, 20% of classrooms are wireless, 90% of public computers are PCs, 10% of public computers are Macs, network access in dorm rooms, network access in dorm lounges, online registration, online administrative functions (other than registration), remote student-access to Web through college's connection.

CAMPUS LIFE

Activities: Choral groups, concert band, dance, drama/theater, jazz band, literary magazine, marching band, music ensembles, musical theater, opera, pep band, radio station, student government, student newspaper, symphony orchestra, television station, yearbook. **Organizations:** 112 registered organizations, 22 honor societies, 9 religious organizations. 3 fraternities (11% men join), 6 sororities (18% women join). **Athletics (Intercollegiate):** *Men:* Baseball, basketball, cross-country, football, golf, soccer, swimming, tennis, track/field (indoor), track/field (outdoor), wrestling. *Women:* Basketball, cross-country, golf, soccer, softball, swimming, tennis, track/field (indoor), track/field (outdoor), volleyball. **Environmental Initiatives:** Commitment to geo-thermal energy with all new buildings and major renovations. Creation of campus-wide sustainability committee. Considerable investments in electricity energy conservation.

ADMISSIONS

Freshman Academic Profile: 24% in top 10% of high school class, 55% in top 25% of high school class, 85% in top 50% of high school class. 84% from public high schools. SAT Math middle 50% range 490–600. SAT Critical Reading middle 50% range 500–610. SAT Writing middle 50% range 470–590. ACT middle 50% range 21–26. TOEFL required of all international applicants, minimum paper TOEFL 500, minimum computer TOEFL 173. **Basis for Candidate Selection:** *Very important factors considered include:* Rigor of secondary school record. *Important factors considered include:* Academic GPA, application essay, character/personal qualities, class rank, extracurricular activities, standardized test scores, talent/ability. *Other factors considered include:* Alumni/ae relation, first generation, geographical residence, interview, level of applicant's interest, racial/ethnic status, recommendation(s), state residency, volunteer work, work experience. **Freshman Admission Requirements:** High school diploma is required, and GED is accepted. *Academic units required:* 4 English, 3 math, 3 science (2 science labs), 2 foreign language, 2 social studies, 1 history. *Academic units recommended:* 4 English, 4 math, 1 history, 3 academic electives. **Freshman Admission Statistics:** 2,618 applied, 80% admitted, 34% enrolled. **Transfer Admission Requirements:** High school transcript, college transcript(s), minimum college GPA of 2.5 required. Lowest grade transferable C. **General Admission Information:** Application fee $25. Regular notification is rolling. Nonfall registration accepted. Admission may be deferred for a maximum of 1 year. Credit and/or placement offered for CEEB Advanced Placement tests.

COSTS AND FINANCIAL AID

Annual tuition $23,524. Room and board $7,728. Average book expense $1,000. **Required Forms and Deadlines:** FAFSA. Financial aid filing deadline 9/1. **Notification of Awards:** Applicants will be notified of awards on a rolling basis beginning on or about 2/14. **Types of Aid:** *Need-based scholarships/grants:* Pell, SEOG, state scholarships/grants, private scholarships, the school's own gift aid. *Loans:* FFEL Subsidized Stafford, FFEL Unsubsidized Stafford, FFEL PLUS, Federal Perkins. **Financial Aid Statistics:** 96% freshmen, 70% undergrads receive need-based scholarship or grant aid. 85% freshmen, 62% undergrads receive need-based self-help aid. 98% freshmen, 98% undergrads receive any aid. Highest amount earned per year from on-campus jobs $1,820.

BALL STATE UNIVERSITY

Office of Admissions, 2000 University Avenue, Muncie, IN 47306
Phone: 765-285-8300 **E-mail:** askUs@bsu.edu **CEEB Code:** 1051
Fax: 765-285-1632 **Website:** www.bsu.edu **ACT Code:** 1176
Financial Aid Phone: 765-285-5600

This public school was founded in 1918. It has a 1,035-acre campus.

RATINGS

Admissions Selectivity Rating: 71   **Fire Safety Rating:** 64   **Green Rating:** 89

STUDENTS AND FACULTY

Enrollment: 16,902. **Student Body:** 52% female, 48% male, 7% out-of-state. African American 7%, Caucasian 87%, Hispanic 2%. **Retention and Graduation:** 75% freshmen return for sophomore year. 30% grads go on to further study within 1 year. **Faculty:** Student/faculty ratio 17:1. 915 full-time faculty, 87% hold PhDs. 92% faculty teach undergrads.

ACADEMICS

Degrees: Associate, bachelor's, doctoral, master's, post-bachelor's certificate, post-master's certificate. **Academic Requirements:** Arts/fine arts, English (including composition), history, humanities, mathematics, sciences (biological or physical), social science. **Classes:** Most classes have 20–29 students. Most lab/discussion sections have fewer than 10 students. **Majors with Highest Enrollment:** Business administration/management, elementary education and teaching, radio and television. **Disciplines with Highest Percentage of Degrees Awarded:** Education 15%, business/marketing 13%, liberal arts/general studies 10%, communications/journalism 9%, architecture 7%. **Special Study Options:** Accelerated program, cooperative education program, distance learning, double major, dual enrollment, English as a Second Language (ESL), exchange student program (domestic), external degree program, honors program, independent study, internships, liberal arts/career combination, student-designed major, study abroad, teacher certification program.

FACILITIES

Housing: Coed dorms, men's dorms, women's dorms, apartments for married students, apartments for single students, special housing for disabled students, special housing for international students, fraternity/sorority housing, cooperative housing. **Special Academic Facilities/Equipment:** Art gallery, museum, on-campus school (K-12), learning center, weather station, physical therapy lab, human performance lab, planetarium/observatory, wildlife and nature preserve. **Computers:** 100% of classrooms are wired, 100% of classrooms are wireless, 85% of public computers are PCs, 10% of public computers are Macs, 5% of public computers are UNIX, network access in dorm rooms, network access in dorm lounges, online registration, online administrative functions (other than registration), support for handheld computing, remote student-access to Web through college's connection.

CAMPUS LIFE

Activities: Choral groups, concert band, dance, drama/theater, jazz band, literary magazine, marching band, music ensembles, musical theater, pep band, radio station, student government, student newspaper, student-run film society, symphony orchestra, television station. **Organizations:** 325 registered organizations, 37 honor societies, 30 religious organizations. 14 fraternities (7% men join), 14 sororities (10% women join). **Athletics (Intercollegiate):** *Men:* Baseball, basketball, cheerleading, diving, football, golf, swimming, tennis, volleyball. *Women:* Basketball, cheerleading, cross-country, diving, field hockey, golf, gymnastics, soccer, softball, swimming, tennis, track/field (indoor), track/field (outdoor), volleyball. **Environmental Initiatives:** Requirement for LEED Silver certification of all new construction. Requirement for unit-level sustainability planning. Creation of a Council on the Environment.¡

ADMISSIONS

Freshman Academic Profile: 15% in top 10% of high school class, 40% in top 25% of high school class, 79% in top 50% of high school class. 95% from public high schools. SAT Math middle 50% range 470–580. SAT Critical Reading middle 50% range 470–570. SAT Writing middle 50% range 460–560. ACT middle 50% range 19–24. TOEFL required of all international applicants, minimum paper TOEFL 500, minimum computer TOEFL 173. **Basis for Candidate Selection:** *Very important factors considered include:* Rigor of secondary school record. *Important factors considered include:* Standardized test scores, talent/ability. *Other factors considered include:* Alumni/ae relation, application essay, character/personal qualities, extracurricular activities, interview, level of applicant's interest, volunteer work, work experience. **Freshman Admission Requirements:** High school diploma is required, and GED is accepted. *Academic units required:* 4 English, 3 math, 3 science (2 science labs), 3 social studies. *Academic units recommended:* 4 math, 3 foreign language. **Freshman Admission Statistics:** 10,935 applied, 79% admitted, 46% enrolled. **Transfer Admission Requirements:** College transcript(s), minimum college GPA of 2.0 required. Lowest grade transferable C. **General Admission Information:** Regular application deadline 8/15. Application fee $25. Regular notification on a rolling basis, no specific date. Nonfall registration accepted. Admission may be deferred for a maximum of 1 year. Credit and/or placement offered for CEEB Advanced Placement tests.

COSTS AND FINANCIAL AID

Annual in-state tuition $6,736. Annual out-of-state tuition $17,804. Room and board $7,240. Required fees $476. Average book expense $930. **Required Forms and Deadlines:** FAFSA. Financial aid filing deadline 3/10. **Notification of Awards:** Applicants will be notified of awards on a rolling basis beginning on or about 4/1. **Types of Aid:** *Need-based scholarships/grants:* Pell, SEOG, state scholarships/grants, private scholarships, the school's own gift aid. *Loans:* Direct Subsidized Stafford, Direct Unsubsidized Stafford, Direct PLUS, Federal Perkins. **Financial Aid Statistics:** 42% freshmen, 37% undergrads receive need-based scholarship or grant aid. 46% freshmen, 45% undergrads receive need-based self-help aid. 73 freshmen, 318 undergrads receive athletic scholarships. 90% freshmen, 83% undergrads receive any aid.

BALTIMORE HEBREW UNIVERSITY

5800 Park Heights, Baltimore, MD 21215
Phone: 410-578-6967 **E-mail:** bhu@bhu.edu **CEEB Code:** 5035
Fax: 410-578-6940 **Website:** www.bhu.edu
Financial Aid Phone: 410-578-6913

This private school was founded in 1919.

RATINGS
Admissions Selectivity Rating: 60*   **Fire Safety Rating:** 60*   **Green Rating:** 60*

STUDENTS AND FACULTY
Enrollment: 75. **Student Body:** 63% female, 37% male. African American 3%. **Retention and Graduation:** 67% freshmen return for sophomore year. 33% freshmen graduate within 4 years. **Faculty:** Student/faculty ratio 8:1. 100% faculty teach undergrads.

ACADEMICS
Degrees: Associate, bachelor's, certificate, doctoral, master's. **Academic Requirements:** English (including composition), foreign languages, history, humanities, mathematics, philosophy, sciences (biological or physical), social science, Judaic studies. **Special Study Options:** Cross-registration, double major, dual enrollment, independent study, internships, study abroad, teacher certification program, English language skills program for non-native speakers.

FACILITIES
Facilities/Equipment: Joseph Meyerhoff Library, Cohen Auditorium. **Computers:** 100% of public computers are PCs.

CAMPUS LIFE
Organizations: 2 registered organizations.

ADMISSIONS
Freshman Academic Profile: TOEFL required of all international applicants, minimum paper TOEFL 250, minimum computer TOEFL 250. **Basis for Candidate Selection:** *Very important factors considered include:* Interview, recommendation(s). *Other factors considered include:* Character/personal qualities, class rank, rigor of secondary school record, standardized test scores. **Freshman Admission Requirements:** High school diploma is required, and GED is accepted. **Freshman Admission Statistics:** 6 applied, 100% admitted, 67% enrolled. **Transfer Admission Requirements:** College transcript(s), minimum college GPA of 2.0 required. Lowest grade transferable C. **General Admission Information:** Application fee $20. Nonfall registration accepted. Admission may be deferred for a maximum of 1 year. Common Application accepted.

COSTS AND FINANCIAL AID
Annual tuition $6,400. Required fees $30. Average book expense $600. **Required Forms and Deadlines:** FAFSA. *Types of Aid:* *Need-based scholarships/grants:* Pell, state scholarships/grants, private scholarships, the school's own gift aid. *Loans:* FFEL Subsidized Stafford, FFEL Unsubsidized Stafford, FFEL PLUS. **Student Employment:** Off-campus job opportunities are excellent. **Financial Aid Statistics:** 2% undergrads receive need-based scholarship or grant aid. 2% undergrads receive need-based self-help aid.

BAPTIST BIBLE COLLEGE AND SEMINARY OF PENNSYLVANIA

538 Venard Road, Clarks Summit, PA 18411-1297
Phone: 570-586-2400 **E-mail:** admissions@bbc.edu **CEEB Code:** 2036
Fax: 570-586-1753 **Website:** www.bbc.edu **ACT Code:** 3523
Financial Aid Phone: 570-586-2400

This private school, affiliated with the Baptist Church, was founded in 1932. It has a 121-acre campus.

RATINGS
Admissions Selectivity Rating: 73   **Fire Safety Rating:** 60*   **Green Rating:** 61

STUDENTS AND FACULTY
Enrollment: 709. **Student Body:** 56% female, 44% male, 61% out-of-state. Caucasian 92%. **Retention and Graduation:** 42% freshmen graduate within 4 years. 15% grads go on to further study within 1 year. **Faculty:** Student/faculty ratio 25:1. 32 full-time faculty, 25% hold PhDs. 100% faculty teach undergrads.

ACADEMICS
Degrees: Associate, bachelor's, certificate, doctoral, first professional, master's. **Academic Requirements:** Arts/fine arts, English (including composition), history, humanities, sciences (biological or physical). **Classes:** Most classes have fewer than 10 students. Most lab/discussion sections have 20–29 students. **Majors with Highest Enrollment:** Elementary and middle school administration/principalship, pastoral studies/counseling, youth ministry. **Disciplines with Highest Percentage of Degrees Awarded:** Education 26%, business/marketing 2%. **Special Study Options:** Distance learning, double major, dual enrollment, honors program, independent study, internships, study abroad, teacher certification program.

FACILITIES
Housing: Men's dorms, women's dorms. **Computers:** 100% of public computers are PCs, network access in dorm rooms, online registration.

CAMPUS LIFE
Activities: Choral groups, concert band, drama/theater, music ensembles, pep band, student government, yearbook. **Organizations:** 2 honor societies. **Athletics (Intercollegiate):** *Men:* Basketball, cross-country, soccer, track/field (outdoor), wrestling. *Women:* Basketball, cheerleading, cross-country, soccer, softball, track/field (outdoor), volleyball.

ADMISSIONS
Freshman Academic Profile: 10% in top 10% of high school class, 32% in top 25% of high school class, 64% in top 50% of high school class. 39% from public high schools. SAT Math middle 50% range 430–560. SAT Critical Reading middle 50% range 460–570. ACT middle 50% range 20–24. TOEFL required of all international applicants, minimum paper TOEFL 500. **Basis for Candidate Selection:** *Very important factors considered include:* Application essay, character/personal qualities, recommendation(s), religious affiliation/commitment, rigor of secondary school record, standardized test scores. *Other factors considered include:* Class rank, talent/ability. **Freshman Admission Requirements:** High school diploma is required, and GED is accepted. **Freshman Admission Statistics:** 352 applied, 87% admitted, 54% enrolled. **Transfer Admission Requirements:** High school transcript, college transcript(s), essay or personal statement. Lowest grade transferable C. **General Admission Information:** Application fee $30. Regular application deadline 8/15. Regular notification 1/25. Nonfall registration accepted. Admission may be deferred for a maximum of 1 year. Common Application not accepted. Credit offered for CEEB Advanced Placement tests.

COSTS AND FINANCIAL AID
Annual tuition $9,720. Room & board $4,892. Required fees $900. Average book expense $600. **Required Forms and Deadlines:** FAFSA. Financial aid filing deadline 5/1. **Notification of Awards:** Applicants will be notified of awards on or about 7/1. *Types of Aid:* *Need-based scholarships/grants:* Pell, state scholarships/grants, private scholarships, the school's own gift aid. *Loans:* FFEL Subsidized Stafford, FFEL Unsubsidized Stafford, FFEL PLUS. **Student Employment:** Institutional employment available. Off-campus job opportunities are excellent. **Financial Aid Statistics:** 47% undergrads receive need-based self-help aid. Highest amount earned per year from on-campus jobs $1,917.

BAPTIST COLLEGE OF FLORIDA

5400 College Drive, Graceville, FL 32440-1898
Phone: 850-263-3261 **E-mail:** admissions@baptistcollege.edu
Fax: 850-263-9026 **Website:** www.baptistcollege.edu **ACT Code:** 6870
Financial Aid Phone: 850-263-3261

This private school, affiliated with the Southern Baptist Church, was founded in 1943. It has a 217-acre campus.

RATINGS
Admissions Selectivity Rating: 64   **Fire Safety Rating:** 60*   **Green Rating:** 60*

STUDENTS AND FACULTY
Enrollment: 566. **Student Body:** 38% female, 62% male, 26% out-of-state. African American 5%, Asian 1%, Caucasian 90%, Hispanic 3%. **Retention and Graduation:** 60% grads go on to further study within 1 year. 60% grads pursue arts and sciences degrees. **Faculty:** Student/faculty ratio 12:1. 26 full-time faculty, 69% hold PhDs. 100% faculty teach undergrads.

ACADEMICS

Degrees: Associate, bachelor's, terminal. **Academic Requirements:** Arts/fine arts, computer literacy, English (including composition), history, humanities, mathematics, philosophy, sciences (biological or physical), social science, Bible. **Classes:** Most classes have 10–19 students. **Majors with Highest Enrollment:** Pastoral studies/counseling, religious education, theology/theological studies. **Disciplines with Highest Percentage of Degrees Awarded:** Theology and religious vocations 85%, education 6%. **Special Study Options:** Distance learning, double major, independent study, internships, teacher certification program, weekend college, academic remediation, advanced placement credit, learning disabilities services.

FACILITIES

Housing: Men's dorms, women's dorms, apartments for married students, special housing for disabled students. **Special Academic Facilities/Equipment:** Florida Baptist Historical Society, Heritage Village, assembly center. **Computers:** 100% of public computers are PCs, network access in dorm rooms, network access in dorm lounges, online registration, online administrative functions (other than registration), remote student-access to Web through college's connection.

CAMPUS LIFE

Activities: Choral groups, concert band, drama/theater, jazz band, music ensembles, radio station, student government. **Organizations:** 3 registered organizations, 2 religious organizations.

ADMISSIONS

Freshman Academic Profile: 10% in top 10% of high school class, 27% in top 25% of high school class, 53% in top 50% of high school class. 86% from public high schools. ACT middle 50% range 17–24. TOEFL required of all international applicants, minimum paper TOEFL 500. **Basis for Candidate Selection:** *Very important factors considered include:* Academic GPA, character/personal qualities, level of applicant's interest, recommendation(s), religious affiliation/commitment. *Important factors considered include:* Alumni/ae relation, talent/ability. *Other factors considered include:* Application essay, class rank, extracurricular activities, interview, rigor of secondary school record, standardized test scores, volunteer work. **Freshman Admission Requirements:** High school diploma is required, and GED is accepted. *Academic units recommended:* 4 English, 4 math, 3 science, 1 social studies, 2 history. **Freshman Admission Statistics:** 77 applied, 79% admitted, 77% enrolled. **Transfer Admission Requirements:** High school transcript, college transcript(s), essay or personal statement, minimum college GPA of 2.0 required. Lowest grade transferable C. **General Admission Information:** Application fee $20. Regular application deadline 8/15. Regular notification is rolling. Nonfall registration accepted. Admission may be deferred for a maximum of 1 semester. Neither credit nor placement offered for CEEB Advanced Placement tests.

COSTS AND FINANCIAL AID

Annual tuition $7,200. Room & board $3,736. Required fees $350. Average book expense $900. **Required Forms and Deadlines:** FAFSA, institution's own financial aid form, state aid form, Business/Farm Supplement. Financial aid filing deadline 5/15. **Notification of Awards:** Applicants will be notified of awards on a rolling basis beginning on or about 6/15. **Types of Aid:** *Need-based scholarships/grants:* Pell, SEOG, state scholarships/grants, private scholarships, the school's own gift aid. *Loans:* FFEL Subsidized Stafford, FFEL Unsubsidized Stafford, FFEL PLUS. **Student Employment:** Federal Work-Study Program available. Institutional employment available. Off-campus job opportunities are good. **Financial Aid Statistics:** 60% freshmen, 82% undergrads receive need-based scholarship or grant aid. 42% freshmen, 60% undergrads receive need-based self-help aid. Highest amount earned per year from on-campus jobs $7,600.

BARAT COLLEGE OF DEPAUL UNIVERSITY

700 East Westleigh Road, Lake Forest, IL 60045
Phone: 847-295-4260 **E-mail:** admissions@barat.edu **CEEB Code:** 1635
Fax: 847-604-6300 **Website:** www.barat.edu **ACT Code:** 0952
Financial Aid Phone: 847-604-6279

This private school, affiliated with the Roman Catholic Church, was founded in 1858. It has a 30-acre campus.

RATINGS

Admissions Selectivity Rating: 74   Fire Safety Rating: 60*   Green Rating: 60*

STUDENTS AND FACULTY

Enrollment: 708. **Student Body:** 72% female, 28% male, 18% out-of-state. African American 8%, Asian 3%, Caucasian 58%, Hispanic 7%. **Retention and Graduation:** 85% freshmen return for sophomore year. 15% freshmen graduate within 4 years. 35% grads go on to further study within 1 year. **Faculty:** Student/faculty ratio 12:1. 40 full-time faculty, 88% hold PhDs. 100% faculty teach undergrads.

ACADEMICS

Degrees: Bachelor's, certificate, master's, post-bachelor's certificate. **Academic Requirements:** Arts/fine arts, computer literacy, English (including composition), foreign languages, history, humanities, mathematics, philosophy, sciences (biological or physical), social science, writing experience and multi-cultural class experience. **Classes:** Most classes have 10–19 students. **Disciplines with Highest Percentage of Degrees Awarded:** Business/marketing 21%, visual and performing arts 20%, health professions and related sciences 18%, education 9%, psychology 9%, biological/life sciences 4%. **Special Study Options:** Accelerated program, cross-registration, double major, dual enrollment, exchange student program (domestic), honors program, independent study, internships, liberal arts/career combination, student-designed major, study abroad, teacher certification program.

FACILITIES

Housing: Coed dorms, women's dorms. **Special Academic Facilities/Equipment:** Drake Theater Complex, Sister Madeline Sophie Cooney Library, Cuneo Science Building. **Computers:** 75% of public computers are PCs, 25% of public computers are Macs, network access in dorm rooms, network access in dorm lounges, remote student-access to Web through college's connection.

CAMPUS LIFE

Activities: Choral groups, dance, drama/theater, literary magazine, radio station, student government, student newspaper. **Organizations:** 22 registered organizations, 2 honor societies, 1 religious organization. **Athletics (Intercollegiate):** *Men:* Basketball. *Women:* Volleyball.

ADMISSIONS

Freshman Academic Profile: 4% in top 10% of high school class, 20% in top 25% of high school class, 49% in top 50% of high school class. 60% from public high schools. SAT Math middle 50% range 470–550. SAT Critical Reading middle 50% range 520–620. ACT middle 50% range 18–24. TOEFL required of all international applicants, minimum paper TOEFL 500. **Basis for Candidate Selection:** *Very important factors considered include:* Application essay, rigor of secondary school record, standardized test scores. *Important factors considered include:* Interview, recommendation(s), talent/ability. *Other factors considered include:* Alumni/ae relation, character/personal qualities, class rank, extracurricular activities, volunteer work, work experience. **Freshman Admission Requirements:** High school diploma is required, and GED is accepted. *Academic units recommended:* 4 English, 2 math, 2 science, 2 foreign language, 2 social studies, 1 history. **Freshman Admission Statistics:** 388 applied, 62% admitted, 48% enrolled. **Transfer Admission Requirements:** College transcript(s), minimum college GPA of 2.5 required. Lowest grade transferable C. **General Admission Information:** Application fee $20. Regular notification is rolling. Nonfall registration accepted. Admission may be deferred for a maximum of 1 year. Common Application accepted. Credit and/or placement offered for CEEB Advanced Placement tests.

COSTS AND FINANCIAL AID

Annual tuition $14,630. Room & board $5,920. Average book expense $840. **Required Forms and Deadlines:** FAFSA, institution's own financial aid form. Financial aid filing deadline 5/30. **Notification of Awards:** Applicants will be notified of awards on a rolling basis beginning on or about 3/1. **Types of Aid:** *Need-based scholarships/grants:* Pell, SEOG, state scholarships/grants, private scholarships, the school's own gift aid. *Loans:* FFEL Subsidized Stafford, FFEL Unsubsidized Stafford, FFEL PLUS, Federal Perkins. **Student Employment:** Federal Work-Study Program available. Institutional employment available. Off-campus job opportunities are good. **Financial Aid Statistics:** 44% freshmen, 31% undergrads receive need-based scholarship or grant aid. 39% freshmen, 29% undergrads receive need-based self-help aid. 1 freshmen, 4 undergrads receive athletic scholarships.

BARCLAY COLLEGE

607 North Kingman, Haviland, KS 67059-0288
Phone: 620-862-5252 **E-mail:** admissions@barclaycollege.edu
Fax: 620-862-5242 **Website:** www.barclaycollege.edu **ACT Code:** 1411
Financial Aid Phone: 316-862-5252

This private school, affiliated with the Society of Friends, was founded in 1917. It has a 17-acre campus.

RATINGS
Admissions Selectivity Rating: 60*   **Fire Safety Rating:** 60*   **Green Rating:** 60*

STUDENTS AND FACULTY
Enrollment: 225. **Student Body:** 58% female, 42% male, 4% international. African American 3%. **Retention and Graduation:** 66% freshmen return for sophomore year. 19% freshmen graduate within 4 years. 4% grads go on to further study within 1 year. **Faculty:** Student/faculty ratio 8:1. 8 full-time faculty, 25% hold PhDs. 100% faculty teach undergrads.

ACADEMICS
Degrees: Associate, bachelor's. **Academic Requirements:** Arts/fine arts, computer literacy, English (including composition), history, humanities, mathematics, philosophy, sciences (biological or physical), social science. Everyone is required to take 30 hours of Bible and graduates with a degree in Bible along with their declared major. **Classes:** Most classes have fewer than 10 students. Most lab/discussion sections have fewer than 10 students. **Disciplines with Highest Percentage of Degrees Awarded:** Business/marketing 54%, psychology 12%. **Special Study Options:** Cooperative education program, distance learning, double major, dual enrollment, independent study, internships, ADVANTAGE! adult degree completion program.

FACILITIES
Housing: Men's dorms, women's dorms, special housing for disabled students. **Computers:** 100% of public computers are PCs, network access in dorm lounges, remote student-access to Web through college's connection.

CAMPUS LIFE
Activities: Choral groups, drama/theater, music ensembles, student government, yearbook. **Organizations:** 1 honor society. **Athletics (Intercollegiate):** *Men:* Baseball, basketball, cheerleading, golf, soccer, tennis. *Women:* Basketball, cheerleading, golf, softball, tennis, volleyball.

ADMISSIONS
Freshman Academic Profile: 80% from public high schools. SAT Math middle 50% range 350–540. SAT Critical Reading middle 50% range 280–490. ACT middle 50% range 18–26. **Basis for Candidate Selection:** *Very important factors considered include:* Recommendation(s). *Important factors considered include:* Character/personal qualities, interview, religious affiliation/commitment, rigor of secondary school record, standardized test scores. *Other factors considered include:* Alumni/ae relation, application essay, class rank, extracurricular activities. **Freshman Admission Requirements:** High school diploma is required, and GED is accepted. **Freshman Admission Statistics:** 66 applied, 73% admitted, 48% enrolled. **Transfer Admission Requirements:** High school transcript, college transcript(s), essay or personal statement, standardized test score. Lowest grade transferable C–. **General Admission Information:** Application fee $15. Nonfall registration accepted. Common Application not accepted. Credit and/or placement offered for CEEB Advanced Placement tests.

COSTS AND FINANCIAL AID
Annual tuition $6,240. Room & board $3,300. Required fees $955. Average book expense $500. **Required Forms and Deadlines:** FAFSA. Financial aid filing deadline 3/15. **Notification of Awards:** Applicants will be notified of awards on a rolling basis beginning on or about 4/15. **Types of Aid:** *Need-based scholarships/grants:* Pell, SEOG, state scholarships/grants, private scholarships, the school's own gift aid. *Loans:* FFEL Subsidized Stafford, FFEL Unsubsidized Stafford, FFEL PLUS. **Student Employment:** Federal Work-Study Program available. Institutional employment available. Off-campus job opportunities are fair. **Financial Aid Statistics:** 78% freshmen, 63% undergrads receive need-based scholarship or grant aid. 78% freshmen, 63% undergrads receive need-based self-help aid.

BARD COLLEGE

Office of Admissions, Annandale-on-Hudson, NY 12504
Phone: 845-758-7472 **E-mail:** admission@bard.edu **CEEB Code:** 2037
Fax: 845-758-5208 **Website:** www.bard.edu **ACT Code:** 2674
Financial Aid Phone: 845-758-7526

This private school was founded in 1860. It has a 600-acre campus.

RATINGS
Admissions Selectivity Rating: 96   **Fire Safety Rating:** 78   **Green Rating:** 90

STUDENTS AND FACULTY
Enrollment: 1,667. **Student Body:** 56% female, 44% male, 70% out-of-state, 9% international (50 countries represented). African American 2%, Asian 4%, Caucasian 74%, Hispanic 3%. **Retention and Graduation:** 87% freshmen return for sophomore year. 62% freshmen graduate within 4 years. 3% grads pursue business degrees. 5% grads pursue law degrees. 3% grads pursue medical degrees. **Faculty:** Student/faculty ratio 9:1. 136 full-time faculty, 96% hold PhDs. 100% faculty teach undergrads.

ACADEMICS
Degrees: Associate, bachelor's, doctoral, master's. **Academic Requirements:** Arts/fine arts, English (including composition), history, humanities, mathematics, sciences (biological or physical), social science, "Rethinking Diversity" (fulfills diversity requirement). **Classes:** Most classes have 10–19 students. **Majors with Highest Enrollment:** English language and literature, social sciences, visual and performing arts. **Disciplines with Highest Percentage of Degrees Awarded:** Visual and performing arts 37%, social sciences 17%, English 12%, foreign languages and literature 6%, history 6%, biological/life sciences 4%, philosophy and religious studies 4%. **Special Study Options:** Cross-registration, double major, dual enrollment, independent study, internships, student-designed major, study abroad. Intensive language studies in Italy, Germany, France, Mexico, Russia, China. Program in International Education (Central and Eastern Europe and Southern Africa).

FACILITIES
Housing: Coed dorms, women's dorms, cooperative housing. **Special Academic Facilities/Equipment:** Performing arts center, gallery, art museum, collection of contemporary art, center for curatorial studies, language lab, nursery school, ecology field station, archaeology field school, economics institute. **Computers:** 100% of classrooms are wired, 30% of classrooms are wireless, 65% of public computers are PCs, 30% of public computers are Macs, 5% of public computers are UNIX, network access in dorm rooms, network access in dorm lounges, online registration, online administrative functions (other than registration), remote student-access to Web through college's connection.

CAMPUS LIFE
Activities: Choral groups, concert band, dance, drama/theater, jazz band, literary magazine, music ensembles, opera, radio station, student government, student newspaper, student-run film society, symphony orchestra. **Organizations:** 70 registered organizations, 5 religious organizations. **Athletics (Intercollegiate):** *Men:* Basketball, cross-country, soccer, squash, tennis, volleyball. *Women:* Basketball, cross-country, soccer, tennis, volleyball. **Environmental Initiatives:** Renewable energy (geothermal) in new buildings. 100% food composting onsite. Re-use program: free store and bins throughout campus.

ADMISSIONS
Freshman Academic Profile: 59% in top 10% of high school class, 85% in top 25% of high school class, 99% in top 50% of high school class. 64% from public high schools. SAT Math middle 50% range 640–690. SAT Critical Reading middle 50% range 680–740. TOEFL required of all international applicants, minimum paper TOEFL 600, minimum computer TOEFL 250. **Basis for Candidate Selection:** *Very important factors considered include:* Academic GPA, application essay, character/personal qualities, extracurricular activities, recommendation(s), rigor of secondary school record, talent/ability. *Important factors considered include:* volunteer work, work experience. *Other factors considered include:* Alumni/ae relation, class rank, first generation, geographical residence, interview, level of applicant's interest, racial/ethnic status, religious affiliation/commitment, standardized test scores, state residency. **Freshman**

Admission Requirements: High school diploma is required, and GED is accepted. *Academic units recommended:* 4 English, 4 math, 4 science (3 science labs), 4 foreign language, 4 social studies, 4 history. **Freshman Admission Statistics:** 4,828 applied, 29% admitted, 36% enrolled. **Transfer Admission Requirements:** College transcript(s), essay or personal statement, statement of good standing from prior institution(s). Minimum college GPA of 3.0 required. Lowest grade transferable C. **General Admission Information:** Application fee $50. Regular application deadline 1/15. Regular notification 4/1. Nonfall registration not accepted. Admission may be deferred for a maximum of 1 year. Credit offered for CEEB Advanced Placement tests.

COSTS AND FINANCIAL AID

Annual tuition $34,080. Room & board $9,850. Required fees $702. Average book expense $850. **Required Forms and Deadlines:** FAFSA, CSS/Financial Aid PROFILE, state aid form, Business/Farm Supplement. Financial aid filing deadline 2/15. **Notification of Awards:** Applicants will be notified of awards on or about 4/1. **Types of Aid:** *Need-based scholarships/grants:* Pell, SEOG, state scholarships/grants, private scholarships, the school's own gift aid. *Loans:* FFEL Subsidized Stafford, FFEL Unsubsidized Stafford, FFEL PLUS, Federal Perkins, College loans from institutional funds (for international students only). **Financial Aid Statistics:** 60% freshmen, 57% undergrads receive need-based scholarship or grant aid. 54% freshmen, 52% undergrads receive need-based self-help aid. 70% freshmen, 67% undergrads receive any aid. Highest amount earned per year from on-campus jobs $1,800.

BARNARD COLLEGE

3009 Broadway, New York, NY 10027
Phone: 212-854-2014 **E-mail:** admissions@barnard.edu **CEEB Code:** 2038
Fax: 212-854-6220 **Website:** www.barnard.edu **ACT Code:** 2718
Financial Aid Phone: 212-854-2154

This private school was founded in 1889. It has a 4-acre campus.

RATINGS

Admissions Selectivity Rating: 97 **Fire Safety Rating:** 69 **Green Rating:** 86

STUDENTS AND FACULTY

Enrollment: 2,350. **Student Body:** 100% female, 64% out-of-state, 3% international (36 countries represented). African American 4%, Asian 18%, Caucasian 66%, Hispanic 8%. **Retention and Graduation:** 96% freshmen return for sophomore year. 80% freshmen graduate within 4 years. 23% grads go on to further study within 1 year. 6% grads pursue arts and sciences degrees. 7% grads pursue law degrees. 5% grads pursue medical degrees. **Faculty:** Student/faculty ratio 10:1. 201 full-time faculty, 91% hold PhDs. 100% faculty teach undergrads.

ACADEMICS

Degrees: Bachelor's. **Academic Requirements:** Arts/fine arts, English (including composition), foreign languages, history, humanities, mathematics, philosophy, physical education, sciences (biological or physical), social science. **Classes:** Most classes have 10–19 students. Most lab/discussion sections have fewer than 10 students. **Majors with Highest Enrollment:** Economics, English language and literature, psychology. **Disciplines with Highest Percentage of Degrees Awarded:** Public administration and social services 29%, psychology 13%, English 12%, visual and performing arts 11%, history 6%. **Special Study Options:** Accelerated program, cross-registration, double major, dual enrollment, exchange student program (domestic), honor program, independent study, internships, liberal arts/career combination, student-designed major, study abroad, teacher certification program.

FACILITIES

Housing: Coed dorms, women's dorms, apartments for single students, special housing for disabled students. **Special Academic Facilities/Equipment:** Professional theater, infant-toddler center, greenhouse, academic computer center. **Computers:** 5% of classrooms are wired, 1% of classrooms are wireless, 98% of public computers are PCs, 2% of public computers are Macs, network access in dorm rooms, network access in dorm lounges, online registration, online administrative functions (other than registration), remote student-access to Web through college's connection.

CAMPUS LIFE

Activities: Choral groups, concert band, dance, drama/theater, jazz band, literary magazine, marching band, music ensembles, musical theater, opera, pep band, radio station, student government, student newspaper, student-run film society, symphony orchestra, television station, yearbook. **Organizations:** 100 registered organizations, 1 honor society. **Athletics (Intercollegiate):** *Men: Women:* Archery, basketball, crew/rowing, cross-country, diving, fencing, field hockey, golf, lacrosse, soccer, softball, swimming, tennis, track/field (outdoor), volleyball. **Environmental Initiatives:** Engaged an energy consulting firm to provide energy modeling for all new building systems design and create an inventory of existing equipment to be upgraded or modified to reduce consumption, model the savings and provide a prioritized list of initiative and payback periods. Barnard is working with the USGBC, Con Edison and NYSERDA on other incentive-based or life cycle initiatives. They have set up a tripartite committee to study sustainable business practices and a website to report and track our performance.

ADMISSIONS

Freshman Academic Profile: 84% in top 10% of high school class, 96% in top 25% of high school class, 100% in top 50% of high school class. 64% from public high schools. SAT Math middle 50% range 620–700. SAT Critical Reading middle 50% range 640–740. SAT Writing middle 50% range 650–730. ACT middle 50% range 29–31. TOEFL required of all international applicants, minimum paper TOEFL 600, minimum computer TOEFL 250. **Basis for Candidate Selection:** *Very important factors considered include:* Academic GPA, application essay, character/personal qualities, extracurricular activities, recommendation(s), rigor of secondary school record. *Important factors considered include:* Class rank, standardized test scores, talent/ability, volunteer work. *Other factors considered include:* Alumni/ae relation, first generation, geographical residence, interview, level of applicant's interest, racial/ethnic status, work experience. **Freshman Admission Requirements:** High school diploma or equivalent is not required. *Academic units recommended:* 4 English, 3 math, 3 science (2 science labs), 3 foreign language, 3 history. **Freshman Admission Statistics:** 4,599 applied, 26% admitted, 47% enrolled. **Transfer Admission Requirements:** High school transcript, college transcript(s), essay or personal statement, standardized test score, statement of good standing from prior institution(s). Minimum college GPA of 3.0 required. Lowest grade transferable C-. **General Admission Information:** Application fee $55. Early Decision application deadline 11/15. Regular application deadline 1/1. Regular notification 4/1. Nonfall registration not accepted. Admission may be deferred for a maximum of 1 year. Credit and/or placement offered for CEEB Advanced Placement tests.

COSTS AND FINANCIAL AID

Annual tuition $31,714. Room & board $11,392. Required fees $1,364. Average book expense $1,080. **Required Forms and Deadlines:** FAFSA, institution's own financial aid form, CSS/Financial Aid PROFILE, state aid form, Noncustodial PROFILE, Business/Farm Supplement, parent's individual, corporate and/or partnership federal income tax returns. Financial aid filing deadline 2/1. **Notification of Awards:** Applicants will be notified of awards on or about 3/31. **Types of Aid:** *Need-based scholarships/grants:* Pell, SEOG, state scholarships/grants, private scholarships, the school's own gift aid. *Loans:* FFEL Subsidized Stafford, FFEL Unsubsidized Stafford, FFEL PLUS, Federal Perkins, state loans, college/university loans from institutional funds. **Financial Aid Statistics:** 45% freshmen, 41% undergrads receive need-based scholarship or grant aid. 47% freshmen, 43% undergrads receive need-based self-help aid. 47% freshmen, 43% undergrads receive any aid. Highest amount earned per year from on-campus jobs $3,200.

See page 1076.

BARRY UNIVERSITY

11300 North East Second Avenue, Miami Shores, FL 33161-6695
Phone: 305-899-3100 **E-mail:** des-forms@mail.barry.edu **CEEB Code:** 5053
Fax: 305-899-2971 **Website:** www.barry.edu **ACT Code:** 0718
Financial Aid Phone: 305-899-3673

This private school, affiliated with the Roman Catholic Church, was founded in 1940. It has a 122-acre campus.

RATINGS

Admissions Selectivity Rating: 60* **Fire Safety Rating:** 60* **Green Rating:** 60*

STUDENTS AND FACULTY

Enrollment: 2,800. **Student Body:** 50% female, 50% male, 16% out-of-state, 9% international (101 countries represented). African American 47%, Asian 2%,

Caucasian 58%, Hispanic 66%. **Retention and Graduation:** 64% freshmen return for sophomore year. 21% freshmen graduate within 4 years. **Faculty:** Student/faculty ratio 14:1. 353 full-time faculty, 85% hold PhDs.

ACADEMICS

Degrees: Bachelor's, doctoral, first professional, master's, post-bachelor's certificate, post-master's certificate. **Academic Requirements:** Arts/fine arts, computer literacy, English (including composition), humanities, mathematics, philosophy, sciences (biological or physical), social science, theology, orientation and Capstone Course. **Classes:** Most classes have 10–19 students. **Majors with Highest Enrollment:** Business administration/management, elementary education and teaching, information science/studies. **Disciplines with Highest Percentage of Degrees Awarded:** Education 22%, business/ marketing 19%, liberal arts/general studies 14%, health professions and related sciences 12%, computer and information sciences 8%. **Special Study Options:** Accelerated program, distance learning, double major, dual enrollment, English as a Second Language (ESL), honors program, independent study, internships, study abroad, teacher certification program.

FACILITIES

Housing: Coed dorms, men's dorms, women's dorms, special housing for disabled students. **Special Academic Facilities/Equipment:** Human performance lab; broadcasting studio, radio station; athletic training room; cell biology/biotechnology labs; Classroom of Tomorrow, biomechanics lab, photography lab, darkroom, and studio; language lab; athletic training room. **Computers:** 95% of public computers are PCs, 5% of public computers are Macs, network access in dorm rooms, network access in dorm lounges, online registration, online administrative functions (other than registration), remote student-access to Web through college's connection.

CAMPUS LIFE

Activities: Choral groups, dance, drama/theater, literary magazine, music ensembles, musical theater, radio station, student government, student newspaper, television station. **Organizations:** 67 registered organizations, 20 honor societies, 5 religious organizations. 2 fraternities, 2 sororities. **Athletics (Intercollegiate):** *Men:* Baseball, basketball, golf, soccer, tennis. *Women:* Basketball, crew/rowing, golf, soccer, softball, tennis, volleyball.

ADMISSIONS

Freshman Academic Profile: 100% in top 50% of high school class. SAT Math middle 50% range 420–520. SAT Critical Reading middle 50% range 440–520. ACT middle 50% range 18–22. TOEFL required of all international applicants, minimum paper TOEFL 550, minimum computer TOEFL 213. **Basis for Candidate Selection:** *Very important factors considered include:* Academic GPA, rigor of secondary school record, standardized test scores. *Important factors considered include:* Character/personal qualities, interview, talent/ability. *Other factors considered include:* Application essay, class rank, extracurricular activities, recommendation(s), volunteer work, work experience. **Freshman Admission Requirements:** High school diploma is required, and GED is accepted. *Academic units recommended:* 4 English, 3 math, 3 science, 3 social studies. **Freshman Admission Statistics:** 3,802 applied, 72% admitted, 21% enrolled. **Transfer Admission Requirements:** College transcript(s), Lowest grade transferable C. **General Admission Information:** Application fee $30. Regular notification is rolling. Nonfall registration accepted. Admission may be deferred for a maximum of 1 year. Common Application accepted. Credit offered for CEEB Advanced Placement tests.

COSTS AND FINANCIAL AID

Annual tuition $24,000. Room & board $7,850. **Required Forms and Deadlines:** FAFSA. **Notification of Awards:** Applicants will be notified of awards on a rolling basis beginning on or about 1/25. **Types of Aid:** *Need-based scholarships/grants:* Pell, SEOG, state scholarships/grants, private scholarships, the school's own gift aid, Federal Nursing Scholarships. *Loans:* FFEL Subsidized Stafford, FFEL Unsubsidized Stafford, FFEL PLUS, Federal Perkins, Federal Nursing, college/university loans from institutional funds, alternative loans. **Student Employment:** Federal Work-Study Program available. Institutional employment available. Off-campus job opportunities are good. **Financial Aid Statistics:** 67% freshmen, 56% undergrads receive need-based scholarship or grant aid. 70% freshmen, 68% undergrads receive need-based self-help aid. 34 freshmen, 133 undergrads receive athletic scholarships. 98% freshmen, 85% undergrads receive any aid. Highest amount earned per year from on-campus jobs $7,400.

See page 1078.

BARTON COLLEGE

Box 5000, Wilson, NC 27893-7000
Phone: 252-399-6317 **E-mail:** enroll@barton.edu **CEEB Code:** 5016
Fax: 252-399-6572 **Website:** www.barton.edu **ACT Code:** 3066
Financial Aid Phone: 252-399-6316

This private school, affiliated with the Disciples of Christ Church, was founded in 1902. It has a 76-acre campus.

RATINGS

Admissions Selectivity Rating: 74   **Fire Safety Rating:** 81   **Green Rating:** 60*

STUDENTS AND FACULTY

Enrollment: 1,113. **Student Body:** 71% female, 29% male, 18% out-of-state, 2% international (12 countries represented). African American 23%, Caucasian 65%, Hispanic 3%. **Retention and Graduation:** 68% freshmen return for sophomore year. 28% freshmen graduate within 4 years. **Faculty:** Student/ faculty ratio 12:1. 71 full-time faculty, 56% hold PhDs. 100% faculty teach undergrads.

ACADEMICS

Degrees: Bachelor's, post-bachelor's certificate. **Academic Requirements:** Computer literacy, English (including composition), humanities, mathematics, sciences (biological or physical), social science, sport science perspective, global and cross-cultural perspective. **Classes:** Most classes have 10–19 students. Most lab/discussion sections have 10–19 students. **Majors with Highest Enrollment:** Business administration and management; elementary education and teaching, nursing–registered nurse training (ASN, BSN, MSN, RN). **Disciplines with Highest Percentage of Degrees Awarded:** Business/marketing 25%, education 14%, health professions and related sciences 12%, public administration and social services 11%, communications/journalism 7%. **Special Study Options:** Cooperative education program, double major, English as a Second Language (ESL), honors program, independent study, internships, liberal arts/career combination, study abroad, teacher certification program, weekend college.

FACILITIES

Housing: Coed dorms, women's dorms, special housing for disabled students, fraternity/sorority housing. **Special Academic Facilities/Equipment:** Television station, art museum, music recording studio, greenhouse. **Computers:** 90% of public computers are PCs, 10% of public computers are Macs, network access in dorm rooms, online administrative functions (other than registration), remote student-access to Web through college's connection.

CAMPUS LIFE

Activities: Choral groups, drama/theater, literary magazine, musical theater, pep band, student government, student newspaper, symphony orchestra, television station. **Organizations:** 48 registered organizations, 7 honor societies, 4 religious organizations. 3 fraternities (3% men join), 3 sororities (10% women join). **Athletics (Intercollegiate):** *Men:* Baseball, basketball, cross-country, golf, soccer, tennis. *Women:* Basketball, cross-country, soccer, softball, tennis, volleyball.

ADMISSIONS

Freshman Academic Profile: 10% in top 10% of high school class, 36% in top 25% of high school class, 72% in top 50% of high school class. 76% from public high schools. SAT Math middle 50% range 420–530. SAT Critical Reading middle 50% range 410–510. ACT middle 50% range 17–21. TOEFL required of all international applicants, minimum paper TOEFL 525, minimum computer TOEFL 195. **Basis for Candidate Selection:** *Very important factors considered include:* Academic GPA, rigor of secondary school record, standardized test scores. *Important factors considered include:* Class rank, interview. *Other factors considered include:* Alumni/ae relation, application essay, character/personal qualities, extracurricular activities, first generation, level of applicant's interest, recommendation(s), talent/ability, volunteer work, work experience. **Freshman Admission Requirements:** High school diploma is required, and GED is accepted. *Academic units required:* 4 English, 3 math, 2 science (1 science lab), 1 academic elective, 2 social sciences. *Academic units recommended:* 2 foreign language. **Freshman Admission Statistics:** 1,303 applied, 64% admitted, 26% enrolled. **Transfer Admission Requirements:** College transcript(s), statement of good standing from prior institution(s). Minimum college GPA of 1.8 required. Lowest grade transferable C. **General Admission Information:** Application fee $25. Nonfall registration accepted. Admission may be deferred for a maximum of 1 year. Credit and/or placement offered for CEEB Advanced Placement tests.

COSTS AND FINANCIAL AID

Required Forms and Deadlines: FAFSA. Financial aid filing deadline 4/1.

Notification of Awards: Applicants will be notified of awards on a rolling basis beginning on or about 2/1. **Types of Aid:** *Need-based scholarships/grants:* Pell, SEOG, state scholarships/grants, private scholarships, the school's own gift aid. *Loans:* FFEL Subsidized Stafford, FFEL Unsubsidized Stafford, FFEL PLUS, Federal Perkins. **Student Employment:** Federal Work-Study Program available. Institutional employment available. Off-campus job opportunities are good. **Financial Aid Statistics:** 57% freshmen, 54% undergrads receive need-based scholarship or grant aid. 59% freshmen, 47% undergrads receive need-based self-help aid. 9 freshmen, 52 undergrads receive athletic scholarships. 99% freshmen, 92% undergrads receive any aid. Highest amount earned per year from on-campus jobs $1,500.

BATES COLLEGE

Best 368

23 Campus Avenue, Lindholm House, Lewiston, ME 04240
Phone: 207-786-6000 **CEEB Code:** 3076
Fax: 207-786-6025 **Website:** www.bates.edu **ACT Code:** 1634
Financial Aid Phone: 207-786-6096

This private school was founded in 1855. It has a 109-acre campus.

RATINGS
Admissions Selectivity Rating: 95   **Fire Safety Rating:** 93   **Green Rating:** 98

STUDENTS AND FACULTY
Enrollment: 1,744. **Student Body:** 52% female, 48% male, 89% out-of-state, 5% international (78 countries represented). African American 2%, Asian 5%, Caucasian 82%, Hispanic 2%. **Retention and Graduation:** 95% freshmen return for sophomore year. 86% freshmen graduate within 4 years. **Faculty:** Student/faculty ratio 10:1. 165 full-time faculty, 93% hold PhDs. 100% faculty teach undergrads.

ACADEMICS
Degrees: Bachelor's. **Academic Requirements:** Humanities, sciences (biological or physical), social science, quantitative. **Classes:** Most classes have fewer than 10 students. Most lab/discussion sections have 10–19 students. **Majors with Highest Enrollment:** Economics, English language and literature, political science and government. **Disciplines with Highest Percentage of Degrees Awarded:** Social sciences 29%, biological/life sciences 11%, English 11%, psychology 9%, foreign languages and literature 7%, history 7%, visual and performing arts 6%. **Special Study Options:** Accelerated program, cooperative education program, double major, exchange student program (domestic), honors program, independent study, internships, liberal arts/career combination, student-designed major, study abroad, teacher certification program.

FACILITIES
Housing: Coed dorms, men's dorms, women's dorms, chem-free, quiet/study and theme houses. **Special Academic Facilities/Equipment:** Art gallery, Edmund S. Muskie Archives, language labs, planetarium, 600-acre conservation area on seacoast for environmental studies, scanning electron microscope. **Computers:** 100% of classrooms are wired, 100% of classrooms are wireless, 90% of public computers are PCs, 10% of public computers are Macs, network access in dorm rooms, network access in dorm lounges, online registration, online administrative functions (other than registration), remote student-access to Web through college's connection.

CAMPUS LIFE
Activities: Choral groups, dance, drama/theater, jazz band, literary magazine, music ensembles, pep band, radio station, student government, student newspaper, student-run film society, symphony orchestra, yearbook. **Organizations:** 107 registered organizations, 3 honor societies, 7 religious organizations. **Athletics (Intercollegiate):** *Men:* Baseball, basketball, crew/rowing, cross-country, diving, football, golf, lacrosse, skiing (downhill/alpine), skiing (nordic/cross-country), soccer, squash, swimming, tennis, track/field (indoor), track/field (outdoor). *Women:* Basketball, crew/rowing, cross-country, diving, field hockey, golf, lacrosse, skiing (downhill/alpine), skiing (nordic/cross-country), soccer, softball, squash, swimming, tennis, track/field (indoor), track/field (outdoor), volleyball. **Environmental Initiatives:** In the process of developing a climate neutral action plan: Working with Master Planning Steering Committee to ensure that all new construction meets at least LEED silver equivalent environmental standards. Working with students through competitions, events, and info campaigns to improve recycling, energy conservation, waste reduction, alternative transportation options, etc.

ADMISSIONS
Freshman Academic Profile: 62% in top 10% of high school class, 92% in top 25% of high school class, 100% in top 50% of high school class. 54% from public high schools. SAT Math middle 50% range 630–700. SAT Critical Reading middle 50% range 635–710. TOEFL required of all international applicants, minimum paper TOEFL 200. **Basis for Candidate Selection:** *Very important factors considered include:* Academic GPA, application essay, character/personal qualities, class rank, extracurricular activities, interview, level of applicant's interest, recommendation(s), rigor of secondary school record, talent/ability. *Other factors considered include:* Alumni/ae relation, first generation, geographical residence, racial/ethnic status, standardized test scores, state residency, volunteer work, work experience. **Freshman Admission Requirements:** High school diploma is required, and GED is not accepted. *Academic units required:* 4 English, 3 math, 3 science (2 science labs), 2 foreign language, 3 social studies. *Academic units recommended:* 4 English, 4 math, 4 science (3 science labs), 4 foreign language, 4 social studies, 4 electives. **Freshman Admission Statistics:** 4,305 applied, 32% admitted, 36% enrolled. **Transfer Admission Requirements:** High school transcript, college transcript(s), essay or personal statement, statement of good standing from prior institution(s). Lowest grade transferable C. **General Admission Information:** Application fee $60. Early decision application deadline 11/15. Regular application deadline 1/1. Regular notification 3/31. Nonfall registration accepted. Admission may be deferred for a maximum of 1 year. Credit and/or placement offered for CEEB Advanced Placement tests.

COSTS AND FINANCIAL AID
Comprehensive fee $46,800. Average book expense $1,150. **Required Forms and Deadlines:** FAFSA, CSS/Financial Aid PROFILE, Noncustodial PROFILE, Business/Farm Supplement. Financial aid filing deadline 2/1. **Notification of Awards:** Applicants will be notified of awards on or about 4/1. **Types of Aid:** *Need-based scholarships/grants:* Pell, SEOG, state scholarships/grants, private scholarships, the school's own gift aid. *Loans:* FFEL Subsidized Stafford, FFEL Unsubsidized Stafford, FFEL PLUS, Federal Perkins, state loans. **Student Employment:** Federal Work-Study Program available. Institutional employment available. Off-campus job opportunities are good. **Financial Aid Statistics:** 33% freshmen, 37% undergrads receive need-based scholarship or grant aid. 31% freshmen, 36% undergrads receive need-based self-help aid. 33% freshmen, 38% undergrads receive any aid.

BAY PATH COLLEGE

588 Longmeadow Street, Longmeadow, MA 01106-2292
Phone: 413-565-1331 **E-mail:** admiss@baypath.edu
Fax: 413-565-1105 **Website:** www.baypath.edu
Financial Aid Phone: 413-565-1345

This private school was founded in 1897. It has a 48-acre campus.

RATINGS
Admissions Selectivity Rating: 74   **Fire Safety Rating:** 99   **Green Rating:** 60*

STUDENTS AND FACULTY
Enrollment: 1,370. **Student Body:** 100% female, 41% out-of-state. **Faculty:** Student/faculty ratio 17:1. 42 full-time faculty, 67% hold PhDs. 100% faculty teach undergrads.

ACADEMICS
Degrees: Associate, bachelor's, certificate, master's. **Academic Requirements:** Arts/fine arts, computer literacy, English (including composition), history, humanities, mathematics, sciences (biological or physical), social science, leadership. **Classes:** Most classes have 10–19 students. Most lab/discussion sections have 10–19 students. **Majors with Highest Enrollment:** Business/commerce, elementary education and teaching, psychology. **Disciplines with Highest Percentage of Degrees Awarded:** Business/marketing 52%, liberal arts/general studies 21%, psychology 12%, law/legal studies 6%, health professions and related sciences 5%. **Special Study Options:** Cooperative education program, cross-registration, double major, English as a Second Language (ESL), honors program, independent study, internships, study abroad, weekend college, directed study program.

FACILITIES
Housing: Women's dorms. **Special Academic Facilities/Equipment:** Blake Student Commons; Bashevkin Academic Development Center; Breck Fitness Center; occupational therapy laboratory; and D'Amour Hall for Business, Communications, and Technology. **Computers:** 100% of public computers are

PCs, network access in dorm rooms, network access in dorm lounges, online administrative functions (other than registration), remote student-access to Web through college's connection.

CAMPUS LIFE
Activities: Choral groups, dance, drama/theater, literary magazine, musical theater, radio station, student government, student-run film society, television station, yearbook. **Organizations:** 31 registered organizations, 2 honor societies, 1 religious organization. **Athletics (Intercollegiate):** *Women:* Basketball, cross-country, soccer, softball, tennis, volleyball.

ADMISSIONS
Freshman Academic Profile: 13% in top 10% of high school class, 34% in top 25% of high school class, 70% in top 50% of high school class. 93% from public high schools. SAT Math middle 50% range 430–520. SAT Critical Reading middle 50% range 450–550. SAT Writing middle 50% range 450–550. ACT middle 50% range 18–21. TOEFL required of all international applicants, minimum paper TOEFL 500, minimum computer TOEFL 187. **Basis for Candidate Selection:** *Very important factors considered include:* Academic GPA, rigor of secondary school record. *Important factors considered include:* Standardized test scores, talent/ability. *Other factors considered include:* Application essay, character/personal qualities, class rank, extracurricular activities, first generation, geographical residence, level of applicant's interest, recommendation(s), state residency, volunteer work, work experience. **Freshman Admission Requirements:** High school diploma is required, and GED is accepted. *Academic units required:* 4 English, 3 math, 2 science (2 science labs), 2 social studies, 1 history. *Academic units recommended:* 4 math, 3 science, 2 foreign language, 2 history. **Freshman Admission Statistics:** 497 applied, 79% admitted, 35% enrolled. **Transfer Admission Requirements:** High school transcript, college transcript(s), minimum college GPA of 2.0 required. Lowest grade transferable C. **General Admission Information:** Application fee $25. Regular notification is rolling. Nonfall registration accepted. Placement offered for CEEB Advanced Placement tests.

COSTS AND FINANCIAL AID
Average book expense $900. **Required Forms and Deadlines:** FAFSA, institution's own financial aid form. Financial aid filing deadline 3/15. **Notification of Awards:** Applicants will be notified of awards on a rolling basis beginning on or about 3/1. **Types of Aid:** *Need-based scholarships/grants:* Pell, SEOG, state scholarships/grants, private scholarships, the school's own gift aid. *Loans:* Direct Subsidized Stafford, Direct Unsubsidized Stafford, Direct PLUS, FFEL Subsidized Stafford, FFEL Unsubsidized Stafford, FFEL PLUS, Federal Perkins, state loans. **Financial Aid Statistics:** 88% freshmen, 86% undergrads receive need-based scholarship or grant aid. 77% freshmen, 78% undergrads receive need-based self-help aid. 96% freshmen, 93% undergrads receive any aid. Highest amount earned per year from on-campus jobs $2,000.

BAYLOR UNIVERSITY

Best 368

1 Bear Place #97056, Waco, TX 76798-7056
Phone: 254-710-3435 **E-mail:** admissions@baylor.edu **CEEB Code:** 6032
Fax: 254-710-3436 **Website:** www.baylor.edu **ACT Code:** 4062
Financial Aid Phone: 254-710-2611

This private school, affiliated with the Baptist Church, was founded in 1845. It has a 508-acre campus.

RATINGS
Admissions Selectivity Rating: 88　　　**Fire Safety Rating:** 79　　　**Green Rating:** 78

STUDENTS AND FACULTY
Enrollment: 11,786. **Student Body:** 59% female, 41% male, 17% out-of-state, 2% international (90 countries represented). African American 8%, Asian 7%, Caucasian 72%, Hispanic 10%. **Retention and Graduation:** 84% freshmen return for sophomore year. 49% freshmen graduate within 4 years. **Faculty:** Student/faculty ratio 16:1. 767 full-time faculty, 80% hold PhDs.

ACADEMICS
Degrees: Bachelor's, doctoral, first professional, master's, post-master's certificate. **Academic Requirements:** Arts/fine arts, English (including

composition), foreign languages, history, humanities, mathematics, sciences (biological or physical), social science, religion. **Classes:** Most classes have 20–29 students. Most lab/discussion sections have 10–19 students. **Majors with Highest Enrollment:** Biology/biological sciences, marketing/marketing management, psychology. **Disciplines with Highest Percentage of Degrees Awarded:** Business/marketing 27%, history 12%, communications/journalism 11%, health professions and related sciences 8%, biological/life sciences 8%. **Special Study Options:** Accelerated program, double major, honors program, internships, student-designed major, study abroad, teacher certification program.

FACILITIES
Housing: Men's dorms, women's dorms, apartments for married students, apartments for single students, special housing for disabled students, special housing for international students, living-learning centers. **Special Academic Facilities/Equipment:** Language and environmental studies labs, natural science museum, high definition television, Armstrong Browning library, Texas Collection Library, Strecker Museum/Bill & Vara Daniel Historical Village, television station, radio station. **Computers:** 100% of classrooms are wireless, 97% of public computers are PCs, 3% of public computers are Macs, network access in dorm rooms, network access in dorm lounges, online registration, online administrative functions (other than registration), support for handheld computing, remote student-access to Web through college's connection.

CAMPUS LIFE
Activities: Choral groups, concert band, dance, drama/theater, jazz band, literary magazine, marching band, music ensembles, musical theater, opera, pep band, radio station, student government, student newspaper, student-run film society, symphony orchestra, television station. **Organizations:** 289 registered organizations, 22 honor societies, 5 religious organizations. 18 fraternities (13% men join), 15 sororities (17% women join). **Athletics (Intercollegiate):** *Men:* Baseball, basketball, cross-country, football, golf, tennis, track/field (indoor), track/field (outdoor). *Women:* Basketball, cross-country, equestrian sports, golf, soccer, softball, tennis, track/field (indoor), track/field (outdoor), volleyball. **Environmental Initiatives:** Campus wide plan for recycling. Educational events for the community on various sustainability topics. Financing wind power generation facilities through our contract for the next 10 years to finance the construction of wind turbines.

ADMISSIONS
Freshman Academic Profile: 40% in top 10% of high school class, 70% in top 25% of high school class, 93% in top 50% of high school class. SAT Math middle 50% range 560–660. SAT Critical Reading middle 50% range 540–650. SAT Writing middle 50% range 530–640. ACT middle 50% range 23–28. TOEFL required of all international applicants, minimum paper TOEFL 540, minimum computer TOEFL 207. **Basis for Candidate Selection:** *Very important factors considered include:* Class rank, rigor of secondary school record, standardized test scores. *Important factors considered include:* Academic GPA, recommendation(s). *Other factors considered include:* Alumni/ae relation, application essay, character/personal qualities, extracurricular activities, first generation, geographical residence, interview, level of applicant's interest, religious affiliation/commitment, talent/ability, volunteer work. **Freshman Admission Requirements:** High school diploma is required, and GED is accepted. *Academic units required:* 4 English, 3 math, 2 science (2 science labs), 2 foreign language, 1 social studies, 1 history, 3 academic electives. **Freshman Admission Statistics:** 21,393 applied, 43% admitted, 31% enrolled. **Transfer Admission Requirements:** College transcript(s), minimum college GPA of 2.5 required. Lowest grade transferable C. **General Admission Information:** Application fee $50. Regular application deadline 2/1. Nonfall registration accepted. Credit and/or placement offered for CEEB Advanced Placement tests.

COSTS AND FINANCIAL AID
Annual tuition $22,220. Room & board $7,526. Required fees $2,270. Average book expense $1,548. **Required Forms and Deadlines:** FAFSA, state residency affirmation. Financial aid filing deadline 2/15. **Notification of Awards:** Applicants will be notified of awards on a rolling basis beginning on or about 3/5. **Types of Aid:** *Need-based scholarships/grants:* Pell, SEOG, state scholarships/grants, the school's own gift aid. *Loans:* FFEL Subsidized Stafford, FFEL Unsubsidized Stafford, FFEL PLUS, Federal Perkins, state loans. **Financial Aid Statistics:** 47% freshmen, 46% undergrads receive need-based scholarship or grant aid. 38% freshmen, 38% undergrads receive need-based self-help aid. 94 freshmen, 335 undergrads receive athletic scholarships.

BEACON COLLEGE

105 East Main Street, Leesburg, FL 34748
Phone: 352-787-7249 **E-mail:** admissions@beaconcollege.edu
Fax: 352-787-0721 **Website:** beaconcollege.edu **ACT Code:** 0704
Financial Aid Phone: 352-787-6306

This private school was founded in 1989.

RATINGS

Admissions Selectivity Rating: 60*　　**Fire Safety Rating:** 81　　**Green Rating:** 60*

STUDENTS AND FACULTY

Enrollment: 112. **Student Body:** 43% female, 57% male, 80% out-of-state. **Retention and Graduation:** 95% freshmen return for sophomore year. 96% freshmen graduate within 4 years. **Faculty:** Student/faculty ratio 7:1. 13 full-time faculty. 100% faculty teach undergrads.

ACADEMICS

Degrees: Associate, bachelor's. **Academic Requirements:** Arts/fine arts, computer literacy, English (including composition), history, humanities, mathematics, philosophy, sciences (biological or physical), social science. **Classes:** Most classes have fewer than 10 students. **Disciplines with Highest Percentage of Degrees Awarded:** Liberal arts/general studies 75%, public administration and social services 25%. **Special Study Options:** Cooperative education program, independent study, internships, study abroad.

FACILITIES

Housing: Students enjoy 1, 2, and 3 bedroom apartment-style living accommodations. **Computers:** 100% of public computers are PCs, remote student-access to Web through college's connection.

CAMPUS LIFE

Activities: Drama/theater, student government, student newspaper, yearbook. **Organizations:** 13 registered organizations, 1 honor society.

ADMISSIONS

Basis for Candidate Selection: *Very important factors considered include:* Interview, recommendation(s). *Important factors considered include:* Application essay, character/personal qualities, extracurricular activities, rigor of secondary school record, talent/ability. *Other factors considered include:* Standardized test scores, volunteer work, work experience. **Freshman Admission Requirements:** High school diploma is required, and GED is accepted. *Academic units required:* 4 English, 1 math, 1 science, 1 social studies, 2 history, 3 academic electives. **Freshman Admission Statistics:** 64 applied, 50% admitted, 53% enrolled. **Transfer Admission Requirements:** High school transcript, college transcript(s), essay or personal statement, interview. Lowest grade transferable C. **General Admission Information:** Application fee $50. Regular application deadline 8/20. Regular notification is rolling. Nonfall registration accepted. Credit offered for CEEB Advanced Placement tests.

COSTS AND FINANCIAL AID

Annual tuition $23,900. Room & board $7,200. Average book expense $350. **Required Forms and Deadlines:** FAFSA, institution's own financial aid form. **Student Employment:** Federal Work-Study Program available. Off-campus job opportunities are good. Highest amount earned per year from on-campus jobs $6,000.

BECKER COLLEGE

61 Sever Street, Worcester, MA 01609
Phone: 508-791-9241 **E-mail:** admissions@beckercollege.edu **CEEB Code:** 3079
Fax: 508-890-1500 **Website:** www.beckercollege.edu **ACT Code:** 1787
Financial Aid Phone: 508-791-9241

This private school was founded in 1784. It has a 100-acre campus.

RATINGS

Admissions Selectivity Rating: 66　　**Fire Safety Rating:** 60*　　**Green Rating:** 60*

STUDENTS AND FACULTY

Enrollment: 1,501. **Student Body:** 79% female, 21% male, 29% out-of-state. African American 5%, Asian 2%, Caucasian 55%, Hispanic 3%. **Retention and**

Graduation: 68% freshmen return for sophomore year. 43% grads go on to further study within 1 year. **Faculty:** Student/faculty ratio 15:1. 39 full-time faculty, 33% hold PhDs. 100% faculty teach undergrads.

ACADEMICS

Degrees: Associate, bachelor's, certificate, terminal. **Academic Requirements:** Computer literacy, English (including composition), humanities, mathematics, sciences (biological or physical), social science. **Classes:** Most classes have 10–19 students. Most lab/discussion sections have 10–19 students. **Majors with Highest Enrollment:** Business administration/management; nursing–registered nurse training (ASN, BSN, MSN, RN), veterinary/animal health technology/technician and veterinary assistant. **Disciplines with Highest Percentage of Degrees Awarded:** Business/marketing 61%, psychology 13%, health professions and related sciences 6%, visual and performing arts 6%, law/legal studies 5%, liberal arts/general studies 2%, parks and recreation 2%. **Special Study Options:** Accelerated program, cooperative education program, cross-registration, distance learning, dual enrollment, internships, liberal arts/career combination, study abroad, teacher certification program.

FACILITIES

Housing: Coed dorms, men's dorms, women's dorms. **Special Academic Facilities/Equipment:** Veterinary clinic, motion analysis lab, preschool facility. **Computers:** 100% of classrooms are wired, 17% of classrooms are wireless, 90% of public computers are PCs, 10% of public computers are Macs, network access in dorm rooms, remote student-access to Web through college's connection.

CAMPUS LIFE

Activities: Dance, drama/theater, student government, student newspaper, yearbook. **Organizations:** 25 registered organizations, 3 honor societies. **Athletics (Intercollegiate):** *Men:* Baseball, basketball, cross-country, equestrian sports, golf, lacrosse, soccer, tennis. *Women:* Basketball, cheerleading, cross-country, equestrian sports, field hockey, soccer, softball, tennis, volleyball.

ADMISSIONS

Freshman Academic Profile: SAT Math middle 50% range 370–490. SAT Critical Reading middle 50% range 390–490. ACT middle 50% range 17–19. TOEFL required of all international applicants, minimum paper TOEFL 550, minimum computer TOEFL 213. **Basis for Candidate Selection:** *Very important factors considered include:* Rigor of secondary school record. *Important factors considered include:* Recommendation(s). *Other factors considered include:* Alumni/ae relation, application essay, character/personal qualities, class rank, extracurricular activities, interview, standardized test scores, talent/ability, volunteer work, work experience. **Freshman Admission Requirements:** High school diploma is required, and GED is accepted. **Freshman Admission Statistics:** 1,790 applied, 65% admitted, 67% enrolled. **Transfer Admission Requirements:** High school transcript, college transcript(s), minimum college GPA of 2.0 required. Lowest grade transferable C-. **General Admission Information:** Application fee $30. Nonfall registration accepted. Admission may be deferred for a maximum of 1 year. Common Application accepted. Credit and/or placement offered for CEEB Advanced Placement tests.

COSTS AND FINANCIAL AID

Average book expense $1,000. **Required Forms and Deadlines:** FAFSA. Financial aid filing deadline 3/1. **Notification of Awards:** Applicants will be notified of awards on a rolling basis beginning on or about 2/1. **Types of Aid:** *Need-based scholarships/grants:* Pell, SEOG, state scholarships/grants, private scholarships, the school's own gift aid. *Loans:* FFEL Subsidized Stafford, FFEL Unsubsidized Stafford, FFEL PLUS, state loans. **Student Employment:** Federal Work-Study Program available. Institutional employment available. Off-campus job opportunities are good. **Financial Aid Statistics:** 87% freshmen, receive need-based scholarship or grant aid. 89% freshmen, receive need-based self-help aid. 49% freshmen, 89% undergrads receive any aid.

See page 1080.

BELHAVEN COLLEGE

1500 Peachtree Street, Box 153, Jackson, MS 39202
Phone: 601-968-5940 **E-mail:** admission@belhaven.edu **CEEB Code:** 1055
Fax: 601-968-8946 **Website:** www.belhaven.edu **ACT Code:** 2180
Financial Aid Phone: 601-968-5933

This private school, affiliated with the Presbyterian Church, was founded in 1883. It has a 42-acre campus.

RATINGS
Admissions Selectivity Rating: 60*   **Fire Safety Rating:** 60*   **Green Rating:** 60*

STUDENTS AND FACULTY
Enrollment: 2,195. **Student Body:** 66% female, 34% male, 41% out-of-state, 1% international. African American 41%, Caucasian 44%, Hispanic 3%. **Retention and Graduation:** 68% freshmen return for sophomore year. 31% freshmen graduate within 4 years. **Faculty:** Student/faculty ratio 18:1. 61 full-time faculty, 79% hold PhDs. 100% faculty teach undergrads.

ACADEMICS
Degrees: Associate, bachelor's, certificate, master's. **Academic Requirements:** Arts/fine arts, English (including composition), foreign languages, history, mathematics, sciences (biological or physical), biblical studies, Kingdom Life. **Classes:** Most classes have 10–19 students. Most lab/discussion sections have 10–19 students. **Disciplines with Highest Percentage of Degrees Awarded:** Business/marketing 59%, psychology 8%, visual and performing arts 7%, parks and recreation 5%, education 5%. **Special Study Options:** Accelerated program, distance learning, double major, dual enrollment, English as a Second Language (ESL), honors program, independent study, internships, student-designed major, study abroad, teacher certification program.

FACILITIES
Housing: Men's dorms, women's dorms. **Computers:** 73% of public computers are PCs, 27% of public computers are Macs, network access in dorm rooms, online administrative functions (other than registration), remote student-access to Web through college's connection.

CAMPUS LIFE
Activities: Choral groups, dance, drama/theater, literary magazine, music ensembles, student government, student newspaper, yearbook. **Organizations:** 29 registered organizations. **Athletics (Intercollegiate):** *Men:* Baseball, basketball, cheerleading, cross-country, football, golf, soccer, tennis. *Women:* Basketball, cheerleading, cross-country, golf, soccer, softball, tennis, volleyball.

ADMISSIONS
Freshman Academic Profile: SAT Math middle 50% range 470–570. SAT Critical Reading middle 50% range 490–640. ACT middle 50% range 20–26. TOEFL required of all international applicants, minimum paper TOEFL 500, minimum computer TOEFL 173. **Basis for Candidate Selection:** *Very important factors considered include:* Academic GPA, standardized test scores. *Other factors considered include:* Application essay, interview, recommendation(s). **Freshman Admission Requirements:** High school diploma is required, and GED is accepted. *Academic units required:* 4 English, 2 math, 1 science, 1 history, 8 academic electives. **Freshman Admission Statistics:** 477 applied, 64% admitted, 69% enrolled. **Transfer Admission Requirements:** College transcript(s), minimum college GPA of 2.0 required. Lowest grade transferable D. **General Admission Information:** Application fee $25. Nonfall registration accepted. Admission may be deferred for a maximum of 1 year. Credit and/or placement offered for CEEB Advanced Placement tests.

COSTS AND FINANCIAL AID
Annual tuition $16,360. Room and board $6,120. Average book expense $1,400. **Required Forms and Deadlines:** FAFSA. Financial aid filing deadline 3/1. **Notification of Awards:** Applicants will be notified of awards on a rolling basis beginning on or about 3/1. **Types of Aid:** *Need-based scholarships/grants:* Pell, SEOG, state scholarships/grants, private scholarships, the school's own gift aid. *Loans:* FFEL Subsidized Stafford, FFEL Unsubsidized Stafford, FFEL PLUS, Federal Perkins. **Financial Aid Statistics:** 49% freshmen, 66% undergrads receive need-based scholarship or grant aid. 57% freshmen, 66% undergrads receive need-based self-help aid. 108 freshmen, 326 undergrads receive athletic scholarships.

BELLARMINE UNIVERSITY

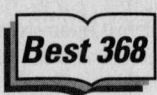

2001 Newburg Road, Louisville, KY 40205
Phone: 502-452-8131 **E-mail:** admissions@bellarmine.edu **CEEB Code:** 1056
Fax: 502-452-8002 **Website:** www.bellarmine.edu **ACT Code:** 0490
Financial Aid Phone: 502-452-8124

This private school, affiliated with the Roman Catholic Church, was founded in 1950. It has a 135-acre campus.

RATINGS
Admissions Selectivity Rating: 60*   **Fire Safety Rating:** 60*   **Green Rating:** 60*

STUDENTS AND FACULTY
Student Body: 17% out-of-state. **Retention and Graduation:** 78% freshmen return for sophomore year. 54% freshmen graduate within 4 years. 15% grads go on to further study within 1 year. 5% grads pursue arts and sciences degrees. 2% grads pursue business degrees. 2% grads pursue law degrees. 2% grads pursue medical degrees. **Faculty:** Student/faculty ratio 13:1. 101 full-time faculty, 79% hold PhDs. 100% faculty teach undergrads.

ACADEMICS
Degrees: Bachelor's, certificate, doctoral, master's, post-bachelor's certificate, post-master's certificate. **Academic Requirements:** Arts/fine arts, English (including composition), history, humanities, mathematics, philosophy, sciences (biological or physical), social science, theology, American experience, transcultural experience, senior seminar. **Classes:** Most classes have 20–29 students. **Disciplines with Highest Percentage of Degrees Awarded:** Business/marketing 25%, health professions and related sciences 18%, social sciences 12%, psychology 9%, biological/life sciences 8%. **Special Study Options:** Accelerated program, cross-registration, double major, exchange student program (domestic), honors program, independent study, internships, study abroad, teacher certification program, Washington, DC semester program.

FACILITIES
Housing: Coed dorms, men's dorms, women's dorms, special housing for disabled students, 4 bedroom or 2 bedroom suites. **Special Academic Facilities/Equipment:** Art gallery, Thomas Merton Center. **Computers:** 96% of public computers are PCs, 4% of public computers are Macs, network access in dorm rooms, network access in dorm lounges, remote student-access to Web through college's connection.

CAMPUS LIFE
Activities: Choral groups, concert band, dance, drama/theater, jazz band, literary magazine, music ensembles, musical theater, opera, pep band, student government, student newspaper, yearbook. **Organizations:** 50 registered organizations, 6 honor societies, 3 religious organizations. 1 fraternity (2% men join), 1 sorority (2% women join). **Athletics (Intercollegiate):** *Men:* Baseball, basketball, cheerleading, cross-country, golf, soccer, tennis, track/field (outdoor). *Women:* Basketball, cheerleading, cross-country, field hockey, golf, soccer, softball, tennis, track/field (outdoor), volleyball. **Environmental Initiatives:** Hire an environmental scientist in Fall 2008 (position is funded and search is under way). Develop a strategic plan for developing environmental awareness, practices and identity. Student-led recycling and educational efforts have taken place on campus the last couple of years.

ADMISSIONS
Freshman Academic Profile: 18% in top 10% of high school class, 51% in top 25% of high school class, 81% in top 50% of high school class. 50% from public high schools. SAT Math middle 50% range 510–610. SAT Critical Reading middle 50% range 500–620. ACT middle 50% range 22–27. TOEFL required of all international applicants, minimum paper TOEFL 550, minimum computer TOEFL 213. **Basis for Candidate Selection:** *Very important factors considered include:* Application essay, recommendation(s), rigor of secondary school record, standardized test scores. *Important factors considered include:* Character/personal qualities. *Other factors considered include:* Alumni/ae relation, class rank, extracurricular activities, interview, talent/ability, volunteer work, work experience. **Freshman Admission Requirements:** High school diploma is required, and GED is accepted. *Academic units required:* 4 English, 3 math, 2 science, 2 social studies. *Academic units recommended:* 4 math, 3 science, 2 foreign language. **Freshman Admission Statistics:** 1,485 applied, 82% admitted, 37% enrolled. **Transfer Admission Requirements:**

College transcript(s), minimum college GPA of 2.0 required. Lowest grade transferable D. **General Admission Information:** Application fee $25. Regular application deadline 8/15. Regular notification is rolling. Nonfall registration accepted. Admission may be deferred for a maximum of 1 year. Common Application accepted. Credit offered for CEEB Advanced Placement tests.

COSTS AND FINANCIAL AID

Annual tuition $27,000. Room and board $8,406. Required fees $1,030. Average book expense $750. **Required Forms and Deadlines:** FAFSA. Financial aid filing deadline 3/1. **Notification of Awards:** Applicants will be notified of awards on or about 4/1. **Types of Aid:** *Need-based scholarships/grants:* Pell, SEOG, state scholarships/grants, the school's own gift aid. *Loans:* FFEL Subsidized Stafford, FFEL Unsubsidized Stafford, FFEL PLUS, Federal Perkins, college/university loans from institutional funds. **Student Employment:** Federal Work-Study Program available. Institutional employment available. Off-campus job opportunities are excellent. Highest amount earned per year from on-campus jobs $1,443.

BELLEVUE UNIVERSITY

1000 Galvin Road South, Bellevue, NE 68005
Phone: 402-293-2000 **E-mail:** info@bellevue.edu
Fax: 402-293-3730 **Website:** www.bellevue.edu **ACT Code:** 2437
Financial Aid Phone: 402-293-2062

This private school was founded in 1966. It has a 38-acre campus.

RATINGS
Admissions Selectivity Rating: 60*   **Fire Safety Rating:** 60*   **Green Rating:** 60*

STUDENTS AND FACULTY
Enrollment: 3,972. **Student Body:** 49% female, 51% male, 7% international (70 countries represented). African American 10%, Asian 1%, Caucasian 71%, Hispanic 7%. **Faculty:** Student/faculty ratio 23:1. 64 full-time faculty, 47% hold PhDs. 100% faculty teach undergrads.

ACADEMICS
Degrees: Bachelor's, certificate, diploma, master's. **Academic Requirements:** English (including composition), humanities, mathematics, sciences (biological or physical), social science, Signature Series. **Majors with Highest Enrollment:** Accounting, business/commerce; computer systems networking and telecommunications. **Disciplines with Highest Percentage of Degrees Awarded:** Business/marketing 75%, health professions and related sciences 11%, computer and information sciences 8%, psychology 2%. **Special Study Options:** Accelerated program, cross-registration, distance learning, double major, dual enrollment, English as a Second Language (ESL), independent study, internships, liberal arts/career combination, weekend college.

FACILITIES
Housing: Apartments for single students. **Computers:** 100% of public computers are PCs, online registration, online administrative functions (other than registration).

CAMPUS LIFE
Activities: Literary magazine, student government, student newspaper. **Athletics (Intercollegiate):** *Men:* Baseball, basketball, soccer. *Women:* soccer, softball, volleyball.

ADMISSIONS
Freshman Academic Profile: 10% in top 10% of high school class, 39% in top 25% of high school class, 51% in top 50% of high school class. 90% from public high schools. TOEFL required of all international applicants, minimum paper TOEFL 500, minimum computer TOEFL 173. **Freshman Admission Requirements:** High school diploma is required, and GED is accepted. *Academic units recommended:* 3 English, 3 math, 3 science, 3 foreign language, 3 social studies, 3 history, 3 academic electives. **Freshman Admission Statistics:** 107 applied, 85% admitted. **Transfer Admission Requirements:** High school transcript, college transcript(s), Lowest grade transferable D. **General Admission Information:** Application fee $50. Nonfall registration accepted. Admission may be deferred for a maximum of 1 year. Common Application not accepted.

COSTS AND FINANCIAL AID
Annual tuition $4,650. Required fees $90. Average book expense $1,000. **Required Forms and Deadlines:** FAFSA, institution's own financial aid form. **Notification of Awards:** Applicants will be notified of awards on a rolling basis beginning on or about 4/1. **Types of Aid:** *Need-based scholarships/grants:* Pell,

SEOG, state scholarships/grants. *Loans:* FFEL Subsidized Stafford, FFEL Unsubsidized Stafford, FFEL PLUS. **Financial Aid Statistics:** 16 freshmen, 114 undergrads receive athletic scholarships.

BELMONT ABBEY COLLEGE

100 Belmont-Mount Holly Road, Belmont, NC 28012
Phone: 704-825-6665 **E-mail:** admissions@bac.edu **CEEB Code:** 5055
Fax: 704-825-6220 **Website:** www.belmontabbeycollege.edu **ACT Code:** 3070
Financial Aid Phone: 888-222-0110

This private school, affiliated with the Roman Catholic Church, was founded in 1876. It has a 650-acre campus.

RATINGS
Admissions Selectivity Rating: 73   **Fire Safety Rating:** 60*   **Green Rating:** 60*

STUDENTS AND FACULTY
Student Body: 60% female, 40% male, 30% out-of-state, 4% international (16 countries represented). African American 12%, Asian 1%, Caucasian 73%, Hispanic 5%. **Retention and Graduation:** 53% freshmen return for sophomore year. 41% freshmen graduate within 4 years. 35% grads go on to further study within 1 year. 20% grads pursue arts and sciences degrees. 8% grads pursue business degrees. 2% grads pursue law degrees. 5% grads pursue medical degrees. **Faculty:** Student/faculty ratio 15:1. 41 full-time faculty, 85% hold PhDs. 100% faculty teach undergrads.

ACADEMICS
Degrees: Bachelor's. **Academic Requirements:** Arts/fine arts, computer literacy, English (including composition), history, humanities, mathematics, philosophy, sciences (biological or physical), social science, theology, Great Books, international studies. **Classes:** Most classes have 10–19 students. Most lab/discussion sections have 10–19 students. **Disciplines with Highest Percentage of Degrees Awarded:** Business/marketing 43%, education 23%, social sciences 15%, computer and information sciences 6%, English 3%, liberal arts/general studies 3%. **Special Study Options:** Accelerated program, cooperative education program, distance learning, double major, dual enrollment, external degree program, honors program, independent study, internships, study abroad, teacher certification program, weekend college.

FACILITIES
Housing: Coed dorms, apartments for single students. **Special Academic Facilities/Equipment:** Museum with rare book collection. **Computers:** 95% of public computers are PCs, 5% of public computers are Macs, network access in dorm rooms, remote student-access to Web through college's connection.

CAMPUS LIFE
Activities: Choral groups, drama/theater, literary magazine, musical theater, student government, student newspaper. **Organizations:** 21 registered organizations, 5 honor societies, 3 religious organizations. 5 fraternities (20% men join), 4 sororities (20% women join). **Athletics (Intercollegiate):** *Men:* Baseball, basketball, cross-country, golf, soccer, tennis, wrestling. *Women:* Basketball, cross-country, soccer, softball, tennis, volleyball.

ADMISSIONS
Freshman Academic Profile: 6% in top 10% of high school class, 20% in top 25% of high school class, 52% in top 50% of high school class. 65% from public high schools. SAT Math middle 50% range 450–530. SAT Critical Reading middle 50% range 440–550. ACT middle 50% range 18–21. TOEFL required of all international applicants, minimum paper TOEFL 550, minimum computer TOEFL 213. **Basis for Candidate Selection:** *Very important factors considered include:* Character/personal qualities, rigor of secondary school record, standardized test scores. *Important factors considered include:* Alumni/ae relation, class rank, extracurricular activities, interview, volunteer work. *Other factors considered include:* Application essay, recommendation(s), talent/ability, work experience. **Freshman Admission Requirements:** High school diploma is required, and GED is accepted. *Academic units required:* 4 English, 3 math, 2 science, 2 foreign language, 2 social studies, 3 academic electives. *Academic units recommended:* 4 math, 3 foreign language. **Freshman Admission Statistics:** 845 applied, 69% admitted, 30% enrolled. **Transfer Admission Requirements:** College transcript(s), minimum college GPA of 2.0 required. Lowest grade transferable C. **General Admission Information:** Application fee $35. Regular application deadline 8/2. Regular notification is rolling. Nonfall registration accepted. Admission may be deferred for a maximum of 1 year. Common Application accepted. Credit offered for CEEB Advanced Placement tests.

COSTS AND FINANCIAL AID

Annual tuition $15,910. Room & board $8,588. Required fees $814. Average book expense $900. **Required Forms and Deadlines:** FAFSA. Financial aid filing deadline 4/5. **Notification of Awards:** Applicants will be notified of awards on a rolling basis beginning on or about 3/10. **Types of Aid:** *Need-based scholarships/grants:* Pell, SEOG, state scholarships/grants, private scholarships, the school's own gift aid. *Loans:* Direct Subsidized Stafford, Direct Unsubsidized Stafford, Direct PLUS, Federal Perkins, state loans. **Student Employment:** Federal Work-Study Program available. Institutional employment available. Off-campus job opportunities are excellent. **Financial Aid Statistics:** 64% freshmen, 64% undergrads receive need-based scholarship or grant aid. 55% freshmen, 59% undergrads receive need-based self-help aid. 21 freshmen, 58 undergrads receive athletic scholarships. 90% freshmen, 81% undergrads receive any aid. Highest amount earned per year from on-campus jobs $1,600.

BELMONT UNIVERSITY

1900 Belmont Boulevard, Nashville, TN 37212-3757
Phone: 615-460-6785 **E-mail:** buadmission@mail.belmont.edu **CEEB Code:** 1058
Fax: 615-460-5434 **Website:** www.belmont.edu **ACT Code:** 3946
Financial Aid Phone: 615-460-6403

This private school, affiliated with the Baptist Church, was founded in 1860. It has a 60-acre campus.

RATINGS

Admissions Selectivity Rating: 88   **Fire Safety Rating:** 90   **Green Rating:** 60*

STUDENTS AND FACULTY

Enrollment: 3,734. **Student Body:** 60% female, 40% male, 56% out-of-state. African American 4%, Asian 1%, Caucasian 89%, Hispanic 2%. **Retention and Graduation:** 76% freshmen return for sophomore year. 44% freshmen graduate within 4 years. 18% grads go on to further study within 1 year. 15% grads pursue arts and sciences degrees. 6% grads pursue business degrees. 1% grads pursue law degrees. 2% grads pursue medical degrees. **Faculty:** Student/faculty ratio 13:1. 221 full-time faculty, 79% hold PhDs. 99% faculty teach undergrads.

ACADEMICS

Degrees: Bachelor's, doctoral, master's, post-bachelor's certificate, post-master's certificate. **Academic Requirements:** Arts/fine arts, computer literacy, English (including composition), foreign languages, history, humanities, mathematics, philosophy, sciences (biological or physical), social science, religion. **Classes:** Most classes have 20–29 students. Most lab/discussion sections have 10–19 students. **Majors with Highest Enrollment:** Business administration/management, music management and merchandising; music performance. **Disciplines with Highest Percentage of Degrees Awarded:** Visual and performing arts 43%, business/marketing 15%, health professions and related sciences 11%, liberal arts/general studies 5%, social sciences 3%. **Special Study Options:** Accelerated program, cooperative education program, distance learning, double major, honors program, independent study, internships, student-designed major, study abroad, teacher certification program.

FACILITIES

Housing: Men's dorms, women's dorms, apartments for single students, special housing for international students, international house, language house, philosophy house. **Special Academic Facilities/Equipment:** Language lab, recording studio, the Belmont Mansion, Little Theater. **Computers:** 90% of classrooms are wired, 90% of classrooms are wireless, 77% of public computers are PCs, 22% of public computers are Macs, 1% of public computers are UNIX, network access in dorm rooms, network access in dorm lounges, online registration, online administrative functions (other than registration), remote student-access to Web through college's connection.

CAMPUS LIFE

Activities: Choral groups, concert band, dance, drama/theater, jazz band, literary magazine, marching band, music ensembles, musical theater, opera, pep band, radio station, student government, student newspaper, symphony orchestra, television station. **Organizations:** 74 registered organizations, 17 honor societies, 12 religious organizations. 3 fraternities (3% men join), 4 sororities (3% women join). **Athletics (Intercollegiate):** *Men:* Baseball, basketball, cross-country, golf, soccer, tennis, track/field (outdoor). *Women:* Basketball, cross-country, golf, soccer, softball, tennis, track/field (outdoor), volleyball.

ADMISSIONS

Freshman Academic Profile: 37% in top 10% of high school class, 66% in top 25% of high school class, 94% in top 50% of high school class. 59% from public high schools. SAT Math middle 50% range 530–640. SAT Critical Reading middle 50% range 540–640. ACT middle 50% range 23–28. TOEFL required of all international applicants, minimum paper TOEFL 550, minimum computer TOEFL 213. **Basis for Candidate Selection:** *Very important factors considered include:* Class rank, rigor of secondary school record, standardized test scores. *Important factors considered include:* Academic GPA, application essay, recommendation(s). *Other factors considered include:* Alumni/ae relation, character/personal qualities, extracurricular activities, first generation, level of applicant's interest, racial/ethnic status, talent/ability, volunteer work, work experience. **Freshman Admission Requirements:** High school diploma is required, and GED is accepted. *Academic units required:* 4 English, 3 math, 2 science, 2 foreign language, 2 social studies, 4 academic electives. *Academic units recommended:* 4 math, 3 science, 2 foreign language, 2 social studies, 3 academic electives. **Freshman Admission Statistics:** 2,266 applied, 69% admitted, 49% enrolled. **Transfer Admission Requirements:** High school transcript, college transcript(s), essay or personal statement, standardized test score, minimum college GPA of 2.0 required. Lowest grade transferable C. **General Admission Information:** Application fee $35. Regular application deadline 8/1. Regular notification is rolling. Nonfall registration accepted. Admission may be deferred for a maximum of 1 year. Credit and/or placement offered for CEEB Advanced Placement tests.

COSTS AND FINANCIAL AID

Comprehensive fee $20,070. Room and board $10,000. Required fees $1,040. Average book expense $1,100. **Required Forms and Deadlines:** FAFSA. Financial aid filing deadline 3/1. **Notification of Awards:** Applicants will be notified of awards on a rolling basis beginning on or about 3/15. **Types of Aid:** *Need-based scholarships/grants:* Pell, SEOG, state scholarships/grants, private scholarships, the school's own gift aid. *Loans:* FFEL Subsidized Stafford, FFEL Unsubsidized Stafford, FFEL PLUS, Federal Perkins, college/university loans from institutional funds. **Student Employment:** Federal Work-Study Program available. Off-campus job opportunities are excellent. **Financial Aid Statistics:** 37% freshmen, 35% undergrads receive need-based scholarship or grant aid. 31% freshmen, 38% undergrads receive need-based self-help aid. 51 freshmen, 217 undergrads receive athletic scholarships. 80% freshmen, 74% undergrads receive any aid. Highest amount earned per year from on-campus jobs $4,000.

See page 1082.

BELOIT COLLEGE

Best 368

700 College Street, Beloit, WI 53511
Phone: 608-363-2500 **E-mail:** admiss@beloit.edu **CEEB Code:** 1059
Fax: 608-363-2075 **Website:** www.beloit.edu **ACT Code:** 4564
Financial Aid Phone: 608-363-2663

This private school was founded in 1846. It has a 75-acre campus.

RATINGS

Admissions Selectivity Rating: 89   **Fire Safety Rating:** 70   **Green Rating:** 77

STUDENTS AND FACULTY

Enrollment: 1,329. **Student Body:** 58% female, 42% male, 81% out-of-state, 5% international (43 countries represented). African American 3%, Asian 2%, Caucasian 85%, Hispanic 3%. **Retention and Graduation:** 86% freshmen return for sophomore year. 63% freshmen graduate within 4 years. 33% grads go on to further study within 1 year. **Faculty:** Student/faculty ratio 12:1. 105 full-time faculty, 97% hold PhDs. 100% faculty teach undergrads.

ACADEMICS

Degrees: Bachelor's. **Academic Requirements:** English (including composition), humanities, sciences (biological or physical), social science. Graduates must complete 2 units each of social science, humanities, and science (1 unit must be lab science). Graduates are also expected to include international, "experiential" (hands-on), and interdisciplinary credit in their coursework. **Classes:** Most classes have 10–19 students. **Majors with Highest Enrollment:** Anthropology, political science and government, psychology. **Disciplines with Highest Percentage of Degrees Awarded:** Social sciences

27%, visual and performing arts 13%, English 12%, foreign languages and literature 12%, psychology 9%, biological/life sciences 7%. **Special Study Options:** Double major, English as a Second Language (ESL), exchange student program (domestic), independent study, internships, liberal arts/career combination, student-designed major, study abroad, teacher certification program. 3–2 programs in engineering, nursing, med tech, and forestry. Over half of our graduates earn credit off-campus for at least a semester through our comprehensive study abroad and "field term" programs.

FACILITIES

Housing: Coed dorms, women's dorms, apartments for single students, fraternity/sorority housing, cooperative housing, Wide variety of special-interest housing, particularly for languages. See Beloit College's website for a current list of special-interest housing. **Special Academic Facilities/Equipment:** Wright Museum of Ar, Logan Museum of Anthropology, center for language study, student run market research company (BELMARK), Alfred S. Thompson Observatory, Center for Entrepreneurial Leadership (CELEB). **Computers:** 100% of classrooms are wireless, 80% of public computers are PCs, 19% of public computers are Macs, 1% of public computers are UNIX, network access in dorm rooms, network access in dorm lounges, remote student-access to Web through college's connection.

CAMPUS LIFE

Activities: Choral groups, dance, drama/theater, jazz band, literary magazine, music ensembles, musical theater, pep band, radio station, student government, student newspaper, student-run film society, symphony orchestra, television station, yearbook. **Organizations:** 85 registered organizations, 6 honor societies, 3 religious organizations. 3 fraternities (8% men join), 3 sororities (6% women join). **Athletics (Intercollegiate):** *Men:* Baseball, basketball, cross-country, football, golf, soccer, swimming, tennis, track/field (indoor), track/field (outdoor), volleyball. *Women:* Basketball, cross-country, golf, soccer, softball, swimming, tennis, track/field (indoor), track/field (outdoor), volleyball. **Environmental Initiatives:** New Science Center will be silver level LEED certified (minimum). Campus-wide recycling program. Green meal plan for food service currently under discussion & development.

ADMISSIONS

Freshman Academic Profile: 35% in top 10% of high school class, 70% in top 25% of high school class, 97% in top 50% of high school class. 78% from public high schools. SAT Math middle 50% range 590–670. SAT Critical Reading middle 50% range 620–710. ACT middle 50% range 25–29. TOEFL required of all international applicants, minimum paper TOEFL 525, minimum computer TOEFL 197. **Basis for Candidate Selection:** *Very important factors considered include:* Application essay, recommendation(s), rigor of secondary school record. *Important factors considered include:* Class rank, interview, standardized test scores. *Other factors considered include:* Alumni/ae relation, character/personal qualities, extracurricular activities, talent/ability, volunteer work, work experience. **Freshman Admission Requirements:** High school diploma is required, and GED is accepted. *Academic units recommended:* 4 English, 4 math, 3 science, 2 foreign language, 4 social studies, 4 history. **Freshman Admission Statistics:** 2,048 applied, 67% admitted, 25% enrolled. **Transfer Admission Requirements:** College transcript(s), essay or personal statement, statement of good standing from prior institution(s). Minimum college GPA of 2.5 required. Lowest grade transferable C. **General Admission Information:** Application fee $35. Regular notification is rolling. Nonfall registration accepted. Admission may be deferred for a maximum of 1 year. Credit and/or placement offered for CEEB Advanced Placement tests.

COSTS AND FINANCIAL AID

Annual tuition $29,908. Room and board $6,408. Required fees $230. Average book expense $400. **Required Forms and Deadlines:** FAFSA, institution's own financial aid form, state aid form. Financial aid filing deadline 3/1. **Notification of Awards:** Applicants will be notified of awards on a rolling basis beginning on or about 4/1. **Types of Aid:** *Need-based scholarships/grants:* Pell, SEOG, state scholarships/grants, private scholarships, the school's own gift aid. *Loans:* FFEL Subsidized Stafford, FFEL Unsubsidized Stafford, FFEL PLUS, Federal Perkins, college/university loans from institutional funds. **Financial Aid Statistics:** 57% freshmen, 58% undergrads receive need-based scholarship or grant aid. 56% freshmen, 58% undergrads receive need-based self-help aid. 92% freshmen, 91% undergrads receive any aid. Highest amount earned per year from on-campus jobs $3,000.

See page 1084.

See page 1084.

BEMIDJI STATE UNIVERSITY

1500 Birchmont Drive Northeast, Deputy Hall, Bemidji, MN 56601
Phone: 218-755-2040 **E-mail:** admissions@bemidjistate.edu **CEEB Code:** 6676
Fax: 218-755-2074 **Website:** www.bemidjistate.edu **ACT Code:** 2084
Financial Aid Phone: 218-755-4143

This public school was founded in 1919. It has a 90-acre campus.

RATINGS
Admissions Selectivity Rating: 76   **Fire Safety Rating:** 61   **Green Rating:** 60*

STUDENTS AND FACULTY
Enrollment: 3,806. **Student Body:** 52% female, 48% male, 9% out-of-state. **Retention and Graduation:** 71% freshmen return for sophomore year. 41% freshmen graduate within 4 years. 34% grads go on to further study within 1 year. 27% grads pursue arts and sciences degrees. 5% grads pursue business degrees. 1% grads pursue law degrees. 1% grads pursue medical degrees. **Faculty:** Student/faculty ratio 19:1. 202 full-time faculty, 89% hold PhDs. 100% faculty teach undergrads.

ACADEMICS
Degrees: Associate, bachelor's, master's. **Academic Requirements:** English (including composition), history, mathematics, sciences (biological or physical), social science, liberal arts required. **Classes:** Most classes have fewer than 10 students. Most lab/discussion sections have 20–29 students. **Majors with Highest Enrollment:** Business administration/management, education, industrial production technologies/technicians. **Disciplines with Highest Percentage of Degrees Awarded:** Education 23%, business/marketing 12%, engineering 9%, psychology 8%, visual and performing arts 7%. **Special Study Options:** Cooperative education program, distance learning, double major, dual enrollment, English as a Second Language (ESL), exchange student program (domestic), external degree program, honors program, independent study, internships, liberal arts/career combination, study abroad, teacher certification program, Eurospring semester, Sino-summer, exchange program with other Minnesota state universities, other study-travel.

FACILITIES
Housing: Coed dorms, men's dorms, women's dorms, apartments for married students, apartments for single students, special housing for international students, cooperative housing, 2 floors for SOTA (students older than average age). Cooperative housing for international students. **Special Academic Facilities/Equipment:** Aquatics lab, waterfront C.V., Hobson forest, center for research & innovation (CRI). **Computers:** 10% of classrooms are wired, 50% of classrooms are wireless, 50% of public computers are PCs, 50% of public computers are Macs, network access in dorm rooms, network access in dorm lounges, online registration, online administrative functions (other than registration), remote student-access to Web through college's connection.

CAMPUS LIFE
Activities: Choral groups, concert band, dance, drama/theater, jazz band, literary magazine, music ensembles, musical theater, opera, pep band, radio station, student government, student newspaper, student-run film society, symphony orchestra, television station. **Organizations:** 83 registered organizations, 1 honor society, 8 religious organizations. 2 fraternities, 1 sorority. **Athletics (Intercollegiate):** *Men:* Baseball, basketball, cross-country, football, golf, ice hockey, soccer, softball, tennis, track/field (indoor), track/field (outdoor), volleyball. *Women:* Basketball, cross-country, golf, ice hockey, soccer, softball, tennis, track/field (indoor), track/field (outdoor), volleyball.

ADMISSIONS
Freshman Academic Profile: 10% in top 10% of high school class, 50% in top 25% of high school class, 90% in top 50% of high school class. 95% from public high schools. ACT middle 50% range 19–24. TOEFL required of all international applicants, minimum paper TOEFL 550, minimum computer TOEFL 200. **Basis for Candidate Selection:** *Very important factors considered include:* Rigor of secondary school record, standardized test scores. *Important factors considered include:* Class rank, recommendation(s). *Other factors considered include:* Application essay. **Freshman Admission Requirements:** High school diploma is required, and GED is accepted. *Academic units required:* 4 English, 3 math, 3 science (1 science lab), 2 foreign language, 3 social studies, 1 history, 1 art/music/world culture. *Academic units recommended:* 4 English, 3 math, 3 science (1 science lab), 2 foreign language, 3 social studies, 1 history, 1 academic elective, 1 art/music/world culture. **Freshman Admission Statistics:** 1,408 applied, 71% admitted, 65% enrolled. **Transfer Admission Requirements:** Minimum college GPA of 2.0 required. Lowest grade transferable C. **General Admission Information:** Application fee $20. Regular application deadline 8/15. Regular notification rolling. Nonfall registration accepted. Admission may be deferred for a maximum of 1 year. Placement offered for CEEB Advanced Placement tests.

COSTS AND FINANCIAL AID

Annual in-state tuition $5,900. Annual out-of-state tuition $5,900. Room and board $5,860. Required fees $790. Average book expense $800. Average book expense $800. **Required Forms and Deadlines:** Institution's own financial aid form. Financial aid filing deadline 5/15. **Notification of Awards:** Applicants will be notified of awards on a rolling basis beginning on or about 5/15. **Types of Aid:** *Need-based scholarships/grants:* Pell, SEOG, state scholarships/grants, private scholarships, the school's own gift aid. *Loans:* Direct Subsidized Stafford, Direct Unsubsidized Stafford, Direct PLUS, Federal Perkins, state loans. **Student Employment:** Federal Work-Study Program available. Institutional employment available. Off-campus job opportunities are good. **Financial Aid Statistics:** 48% freshmen, 44% undergrads receive need-based scholarship or grant aid. 55% freshmen, 51% undergrads receive need-based self-help aid. 61 freshmen, 140 undergrads receive athletic scholarships. 74% freshmen, 78% undergrads receive any aid. Highest amount earned per year from on-campus jobs $2,600.

BENEDICT COLLEGE

Harden and Blanding Streets, Columbia, SC 29204
Phone: 803-253-5143 **E-mail:** admission@benedict.edu **CEEB Code:** 5056
Fax: 803-253-5167 **Website:** www.benedict.edu **ACT Code:** 3834
Financial Aid Phone: 803-253-5143

This private school, affiliated with the Baptist Church, was founded in 1870. It has a 20-acre campus.

RATINGS
Admissions Selectivity Rating: 60*   **Fire Safety Rating:** 60*   **Green Rating:** 60*

STUDENTS AND FACULTY
Enrollment: 2,128. **Student Body:** 51% female, 49% male, 15% out-of-state. African American 53%. **Retention and Graduation:** 15% grads go on to further study within 1 year. 15% grads pursue arts and sciences degrees. **Faculty:** 100% faculty teach undergrads.

ACADEMICS
Degrees: Bachelor's. **Academic Requirements:** Arts/fine arts, English (including composition), foreign languages, history, mathematics, sciences (biological or physical), social science. **Special Study Options:** Cooperative education program, double major, dual enrollment, honors program, independent study, internships, study abroad, teacher certification program.

FACILITIES
Housing: Men's dorms, women's dorms. **Special Academic Facilities/Equipment:** Language lab.

CAMPUS LIFE
Activities: Choral groups, dance, marching band. **Organizations:** 2 honor societies, 5 religious organizations. 4 fraternities (5% men join), 4 sororities (8% women join). **Athletics (Intercollegiate):** *Men:* Baseball, basketball, football, golf, track/field (outdoor). *Women:* Basketball, cheerleading, golf, softball, track/field (outdoor), volleyball.

ADMISSIONS
Freshman Academic Profile: 98% from public high schools. SAT Math middle 50% range 320–430. SAT Critical Reading middle 50% range 320–430. ACT middle 50% range 13–17. TOEFL required of all international applicants, minimum paper TOEFL 500. **Basis for Candidate Selection:** *Very important factors considered include:* Standardized test scores. *Important factors considered include:* Class rank, rigor of secondary school record. *Other factors considered include:* Alumni/ae relation, application essay, character/personal qualities, extracurricular activities, geographical residence, racial/ethnic status, religious affiliation/commitment, state residency, volunteer work. **Freshman Admission Requirements:** High school diploma is required, and GED is accepted. *Academic units recommended:* 4 English, 3 math, 2 science, 4 social studies, 7 academic electives. **Freshman Admission Statistics:** 3,586 applied, 79% admitted. **Transfer Admission Requirements:** College transcript(s), minimum college GPA of 2.0 required. Lowest grade transferable C. **General Admission Information:** Application fee $25. Regular application deadline rolling. Regular notification is rolling. Nonfall registration accepted. Admission may be deferred for a maximum of 3 years. Common Application accepted.

COSTS AND FINANCIAL AID
Annual tuition $12,516. Room and board $6,444. Required fees $1,494. Average book expense $1,000. **Required Forms and Deadlines:** FAFSA, institution's

own financial aid form, state aid form. Financial aid filing deadline 4/15. **Types of Aid:** *Need-based scholarships/grants:* United Negro College Fund. *Loans:* FFEL Subsidized Stafford, FFEL PLUS. **Student Employment:** Federal Work-Study Program available. Institutional employment available. Off-campus job opportunities are good. Highest amount earned per year from on-campus jobs $1,600.

BENEDICTINE COLLEGE

1020 North Second Street, Atchison, KS 66002
Phone: 913-360-7476 **E-mail:** bcadmiss@benedictine.edu **CEEB Code:** 6056
Fax: 913-367-5462 **Website:** www.benedictine.edu **ACT Code:** 1444
Financial Aid Phone: 800-467-5340

This private school, affiliated with the Roman Catholic Church, was founded in 1859. It has a 225-acre campus.

RATINGS
Admissions Selectivity Rating: 72   **Fire Safety Rating:** 63   **Green Rating:** 60*

STUDENTS AND FACULTY
Enrollment: 978. **Student Body:** 49% female, 51% male, 44% out-of-state, 3% international (18 countries represented). **Retention and Graduation:** 83% freshmen return for sophomore year. 35% freshmen graduate within 4 years. 27% grads go on to further study within 1 year. 11% grads pursue arts and sciences degrees. 6% grads pursue business degrees. 8% grads pursue law degrees. **Faculty:** Student/faculty ratio 16:1. 54 full-time faculty, 81% hold PhDs. 91% faculty teach undergrads.

ACADEMICS
Degrees: Associate, bachelor's, master's. **Academic Requirements:** Arts/fine arts, English (including composition), foreign languages, history, humanities, mathematics, philosophy, sciences (biological or physical), social science, religious studies. **Classes:** Most classes have fewer than 10 students. Most lab/discussion sections have 10–19 students. **Majors with Highest Enrollment:** Business administration/management, religion/religious studies. **Disciplines with Highest Percentage of Degrees Awarded:** Education 24%, business/marketing 19%, social sciences 11%, biological/life sciences 9%, psychology 5%, communication technologies 5%. **Special Study Options:** Cooperative education program, double major, dual enrollment, English as a Second Language (ESL), independent study, internships, liberal arts/career combination, student-designed major, study abroad, teacher certification program.

FACILITIES
Housing: Coed dorms, men's dorms, women's dorms, off-campus college-owned housing. **Special Academic Facilities/Equipment:** Language and special education labs, high tech classroom, stadium, student union. **Computers:** 60% of public computers are PCs, 40% of public computers are Macs, network access in dorm rooms, network access in dorm lounges, online administrative functions (other than registration), remote student-access to Web through college's connection.

CAMPUS LIFE
Activities: Choral groups, concert band, dance, drama/theater, jazz band, literary magazine, music ensembles, musical theater, pep band, student government, student newspaper, symphony orchestra, yearbook. **Organizations:** 38 registered organizations, 14 honor societies, 4 religious organizations. **Athletics (Intercollegiate):** *Men:* Baseball, basketball, cheerleading, cross-country, football, golf, soccer, tennis, track/field (indoor), track/field (outdoor). *Women:* Basketball, cheerleading, cross-country, golf, soccer, softball, tennis, track/field (indoor), track/field (outdoor), volleyball.

ADMISSIONS
Freshman Academic Profile: 11% in top 10% of high school class, 33% in top 25% of high school class, 61% in top 50% of high school class. 44% from public high schools. SAT Math middle 50% range 480–590. SAT Critical Reading middle 50% range 460–580. ACT middle 50% range 20–26. TOEFL required of all international applicants, minimum paper TOEFL 535, minimum computer TOEFL 200. **Basis for Candidate Selection:** *Very important factors considered include:* Class rank, rigor of secondary school record, standardized test scores. *Other factors considered include:* Alumni/ae relation, application essay, character/personal qualities, extracurricular activities, interview, racial/ethnic status, recommendation(s), talent/ability, volunteer work, work experience. **Freshman Admission Requirements:** High school diploma is required, and GED is accepted. *Academic units required:* 4 English, 3 math, 2 science, 2 foreign language, 2 social studies, 2 history, 1 academic elective. *Academic units recommended:* 4 math, 4 science, 4 foreign language.

Freshman Admission Statistics: 580 applied, 96% admitted, 46% enrolled. **Transfer Admission Requirements:** College transcript(s), minimum college GPA of 2.0 required. Lowest grade transferable C. **General Admission Information:** Application fee $25. Regular notification is rolling. Nonfall registration accepted. Admission may be deferred for a maximum of 1 year. Common Application accepted. Credit and/or placement offered for CEEB Advanced Placement tests.

COSTS AND FINANCIAL AID

Annual tuition $17,700. Room and board $6,210. Average book expense $1,000. **Required Forms and Deadlines:** FAFSA. Financial aid filing deadline 3/15. **Notification of Awards:** Applicants will be notified of awards on a rolling basis beginning on or about 2/1. **Types of Aid:** *Need-based scholarships/grants:* Pell, SEOG, state scholarships/grants, private scholarships, the school's own gift aid. *Loans:* FFEL Subsidized Stafford, FFEL Unsubsidized Stafford, FFEL PLUS, Federal Perkins, alternative loans. **Student Employment:** Federal Work-Study Program available. Institutional employment available. Off-campus job opportunities are good. **Financial Aid Statistics:** 69% freshmen, 65% undergrads receive need-based scholarship or grant aid. 65% freshmen, 66% undergrads receive need-based self-help aid. 15 freshmen, 29 undergrads receive athletic scholarships. 98% freshmen, 77% undergrads receive any aid.

BENEDICTINE UNIVERSITY

5700 College Road, Lisle, IL 60532-0900
Phone: 630-829-6300 **E-mail:** admissions@ben.edu **CEEB Code:** 1707
Fax: 630-829-6301 **Website:** www.ben.edu **ACT Code:** 1132
Financial Aid Phone: 630-829-6500

This private school, affiliated with the Roman Catholic Church, was founded in 1887. It has a 108-acre campus.

RATINGS
Admissions Selectivity Rating: 74   **Fire Safety Rating:** 88   **Green Rating:** 60*

STUDENTS AND FACULTY
Enrollment: 2,582. **Student Body:** 58% female, 42% male, 3% out-of-state. African American 10%, Asian 13%, Caucasian 38%, Hispanic 6%. **Retention and Graduation:** 71% freshmen return for sophomore year. 39% freshmen graduate within 4 years. **Faculty:** Student/faculty ratio 13:1. 90 full-time faculty, 90% hold PhDs. 83% faculty teach undergrads.

ACADEMICS
Degrees: Associate, bachelor's, certificate, doctoral, master's, post-bachelor's certificate. **Academic Requirements:** Arts/fine arts, English (including composition), humanities, mathematics, philosophy, sciences (biological or physical), social science. **Classes:** Most classes have 10–19 students. Most lab/discussion sections have 40-49 students. **Majors with Highest Enrollment:** Biology/biological sciences, business/managerial operations, health/medical preparatory programs. **Disciplines with Highest Percentage of Degrees Awarded:** Business/marketing 33%, health professions and related sciences 15%, psychology 11%, biological/life sciences 9%, education 8%. **Special Study Options:** Accelerated program, cross-registration, distance learning, double major, dual enrollment, honors program, independent study, internships, study abroad, teacher certification program, weekend college.

FACILITIES
Housing: Coed dorms, men's dorms, women's dorms, apartments for married students, apartments for single students. **Special Academic Facilities/Equipment:** Natural science and history museums, exercise physiology lab. **Computers:** 1% of classrooms are wired, 1% of classrooms are wireless, 100% of public computers are PCs, network access in dorm rooms, network access in dorm lounges, online registration, online administrative functions (other than registration), remote student-access to Web through college's connection.

CAMPUS LIFE
Activities: Choral groups, concert band, jazz band, literary magazine, music ensembles, pep band, student government, student newspaper, symphony orchestra, television station. **Organizations:** 30 registered organizations, 3 religious organizations. **Athletics (Intercollegiate):** *Men:* Baseball, basketball, cross-country, football, golf, soccer, swimming, track/field (indoor), track/field (outdoor). *Women:* Basketball, cross-country, soccer, softball, swimming, tennis, track/field (indoor), track/field (outdoor), volleyball.

ADMISSIONS
Freshman Academic Profile: 19% in top 10% of high school class, 41% in top 25% of high school class, 73% in top 50% of high school class. 71% from public high schools. ACT middle 50% range 21–25. TOEFL required of all interna-

tional applicants, minimum paper TOEFL 550, minimum computer TOEFL 213. **Basis for Candidate Selection:** *Very important factors considered include:* Academic GPA, class rank, rigor of secondary school record, standardized test scores. *Other factors considered include:* Application essay, extracurricular activities, interview, recommendation(s). **Freshman Admission Requirements:** High school diploma is required, and GED is accepted. *Academic units required:* 4 English, 3 math, 2 science (1 science lab), 2 foreign language, 1 history. *Academic units recommended:* 4 math, 3 science (2 science labs). **Freshman Admission Statistics:** 1,271 applied, 85% admitted, 35% enrolled. **Transfer Admission Requirements:** College transcript(s), statement of good standing from prior institution(s). Minimum college GPA of 2.0 required. Lowest grade transferable D. **General Admission Information:** Application fee $40. Regular application deadline 8/30. Nonfall registration accepted. Credit offered for CEEB Advanced Placement tests.

COSTS AND FINANCIAL AID

Required Forms and Deadlines: FAFSA, institution's own financial aid form. **Notification of Awards:** Applicants will be notified of awards on a rolling basis beginning on or about 2/1. **Types of Aid:** *Need-based scholarships/grants:* Pell, SEOG, state scholarships/grants, private scholarships, the school's own gift aid. *Loans:* FFEL Subsidized Stafford, FFEL Unsubsidized Stafford, FFEL PLUS, Federal Perkins. **Financial Aid Statistics:** 98% freshmen, 92% undergrads receive any aid.

BENNETT COLLEGE FOR WOMEN

900 East Washinton Street, Greensboro, NC 27401
Phone: 336-370-8624 **E-mail:** admiss@bennett.edu **CEEB Code:** 5058
Fax: 336-370-8653 **Website:** www.bennett.edu **ACT Code:** 3072
Financial Aid Phone: 910-370-8677

This private school, affiliated with the Methodist Church, was founded in 1873. It has a 55-acre campus.

RATINGS
Admissions Selectivity Rating: 72   **Fire Safety Rating:** 60*   **Green Rating:** 60*

STUDENTS AND FACULTY
Enrollment: 596. **Student Body:** 100% female, 87% out-of-state, 1% international (6 countries represented). African American 97%, Caucasian 1%, Hispanic 1%. **Retention and Graduation:** 56% freshmen return for sophomore year. 17% freshmen graduate within 4 years. 30% grads go on to further study within 1 year. 20% grads pursue arts and sciences degrees. 5% grads pursue business degrees. 5% grads pursue law degrees. 15% grads pursue medical degrees. **Faculty:** Student/faculty ratio 11:1. 49 full-time faculty, 63% hold PhDs. 100% faculty teach undergrads.

ACADEMICS
Degrees: Bachelor's. **Academic Requirements:** Arts/fine arts, computer literacy, English (including composition), foreign languages, history, humanities, mathematics, philosophy, sciences (biological or physical), social science, speech. **Classes:** Most classes have 10–19 students. **Disciplines with Highest Percentage of Degrees Awarded:** Biological/life sciences 21%, communications/journalism 17%, psychology 15%, public administration and social services 11%, business/marketing 8%. **Special Study Options:** Cooperative education program, double major, honor program, internships, student-designed major, study abroad, teacher certification program.

FACILITIES
Housing: Women's dorms. **Special Academic Facilities/Equipment:** Children's House, Constance Maiteena collection, college archives, telecommunications satellite dish.

CAMPUS LIFE
Activities: Choral groups, radio station, student government, student newspaper. **Organizations:** 34 registered organizations, 5 honor societies, 1 religious organization. 4 sororities (11% women join). **Athletics (Intercollegiate):** *Women:* Basketball, cheerleading, cross-country, softball, swimming, tennis, track/field (outdoor), volleyball.

ADMISSIONS
Freshman Academic Profile: 3% in top 10% of high school class, 13% in top 25% of high school class, 34% in top 50% of high school class. 92% from public high schools. SAT Math middle 50% range 350–440. SAT Critical Reading middle 50% range 360–450. TOEFL required of all international applicants, minimum paper TOEFL 500. **Basis for Candidate Selection:** *Very important factors considered include:* Academic GPA, rigor of secondary school record, standardized test scores. *Important factors considered include:* Alumni/ae

relation, application essay, class rank, recommendation(s), talent/ability. *Other factors considered include:* extracurricular activities, interview, racial/ethnic status, religious affiliation/commitment, state residency. **Freshman Admission Requirements:** High school diploma is required, and GED is accepted. *Academic units required:* 4 English, 3 math, 2 science, 2 foreign language, 2 social studies, 5 academic electives. **Freshman Admission Statistics:** 859 applied, 54% admitted, 41% enrolled. **Transfer Admission Requirements:** College transcript(s), essay or personal statement. Minimum college GPA of 2.0 required. Lowest grade transferable C. **General Admission Information:** Application fee $30. Regular notification rolling. Nonfall registration accepted. Neither credit nor placement offered for CEEB Advanced Placement tests.

COSTS AND FINANCIAL AID

Annual tuition $6,374. Room and board $3,239. Required fees $1,900. Average book expense $1,200. **Required Forms and Deadlines:** FAFSA, institution's own financial aid form. Financial aid filing deadline 6/30. **Notification of Awards:** Applicants will be notified of awards on a rolling basis beginning on or about 1/2. **Types of Aid:** *Need-based scholarships/grants:* Pell, SEOG, state scholarships/grants, private scholarships, the school's own gift aid, United Negro College Fund, Federal Nursing Scholarships. *Loans:* FFEL Subsidized Stafford, FFEL Unsubsidized Stafford, FFEL PLUS, Federal Perkins. **Student Employment:** Federal Work-Study Program available. Institutional employment available. Off-campus job opportunities are good. **Financial Aid Statistics:** 84% freshmen, 79% undergrads receive need-based scholarship or grant aid. 81% freshmen, 80% undergrads receive need-based self-help aid. Highest amount earned per year from on-campus jobs $1,500.

BENNINGTON COLLEGE

Office of Admissions and Financial Aid, Bennington, VT 05201-6003
Phone: 802-440-4312 **E-mail:** admissions@bennington.edu **CEEB Code:** 3080
Fax: 802-440-4320 **Website:** www.bennington.edu **ACT Code:** 4296
Financial Aid Phone: 802-440-4325

This private school was founded in 1932. It has a 470-acre campus.

RATINGS

Admissions Selectivity Rating: 88   **Fire Safety Rating:** 81   **Green Rating:** 88

STUDENTS AND FACULTY

Enrollment: 523. **Student Body:** 66% female, 34% male, 96% out-of-state, 3% international (13 countries represented). African American 2%, Asian 2%, Caucasian 89%, Hispanic 2%. **Retention and Graduation:** 85% freshmen return for sophomore year. 52% freshmen graduate within 4 years. **Faculty:** Student/faculty ratio 7:1. 62 full-time faculty, 74% hold PhDs. 100% faculty teach undergrads.

ACADEMICS

Degrees: Bachelor's, master's, post-bachelor's certificate. **Academic Requirements:** Working closely with faculty advisors, each student develops an individual plan of study, including course requirements. **Classes:** Most classes have 10–19 students. Most lab/discussion sections have 10–19 students. **Majors with Highest Enrollment:** English language and literature, music, visual and performing arts. **Disciplines with Highest Percentage of Degrees Awarded:** Visual and performing arts 47%, English 18%, foreign languages and literature 6%, education 5%, social sciences 5%, liberal arts/general studies 4%. **Special Study Options:** Accelerated program, cross-registration, double major, English as a Second Language (ESL), independent study, internships, student-designed major, study abroad, teacher certification program. Post-baccalaureate program in preparation for Medical or Allied Health School grad programs.

FACILITIES

Housing: Coed dorms, special housing for disabled students, cooperative housing. **Special Academic Facilities/Equipment:** Computer center and media labs; labs for chemistry, physics, and microbiology; digital arts lab; art gallery; architecture, drawing, painting, printmaking, and sculpture studios; ceramics studio and kilns; photography darkrooms; film and video editing studio, several fully equipped theaters; dance studios and archives; scripts library; costume shop; electronic music and sound recording studios; music practice rooms and music library; radio station; student-run café and bar; fitness center; student center; observatory; greenhouse, and 470 acres of forest, ponds,

wetlands, and fields for recreation and scientific study. **Computers:** 46% of classrooms are wired, 91% of classrooms are wireless, 56% of public computers are PCs, 44% of public computers are Macs, network access in dorm rooms, network access in dorm lounges, online administrative functions (other than registration), support for handheld computing, remote student-access to Web through college's connection.

CAMPUS LIFE

Activities: Choral groups, dance, drama/theater, jazz band, literary magazine, music ensembles, musical theater, student government, student newspaper, student-run film society, symphony orchestra, yearbook. **Organizations:** 25 registered organizations. **Environmental Initiatives:** Converting to a campus-wide biomass heating system. Recycling. LEED certification on new building.

ADMISSIONS

Freshman Academic Profile: 31% in top 10% of high school class, 62% in top 25% of high school class, 91% in top 50% of high school class. SAT Math middle 50% range 540–630. SAT Critical Reading middle 50% range 580–700. SAT Writing middle 50% range 580–690. ACT middle 50% range 24–30. TOEFL required of all international applicants, minimum paper TOEFL 577, minimum computer TOEFL 233. **Basis for Candidate Selection:** *Very important factors considered include:* Academic GPA, application essay, character/personal qualities, class rank, extracurricular activities, interview, recommendation(s), rigor of secondary school record, talent/ability. *Other factors considered include:* Alumni/ae relation, first generation, geographical residence, level of applicant's interest, racial/ethnic status, standardized test scores, state residency, volunteer work, work experience. **Freshman Admission Requirements:** High school diploma is required, and GED is accepted. *Academic units recommended:* 4 English, 3 math, 3 science, 2 foreign language, 3 social studies, 3 history. **Freshman Admission Statistics:** 798 applied, 66% admitted, 24% enrolled. **Transfer Admission Requirements:** High school transcript, college transcript(s), essay or personal statement, statement of good standing from prior institution(s). Lowest grade transferable C. **General Admission Information:** Application fee $60. Early decision application deadline 11/15. Regular application deadline 1/3. Regular notification 4/1. Nonfall registration accepted. Admission may be deferred for a maximum of 1 year. Neither credit nor placement offered for CEEB Advanced Placement tests.

COSTS AND FINANCIAL AID

Required Forms and Deadlines: FAFSA, institution's own financial aid form, CSS/Financial Aid PROFILE, Noncustodial PROFILE, student and parent federal tax returns and W-2s. Financial aid filing deadline 3/1. **Notification of Awards:** Applicants will be notified of awards on or about 4/1. **Types of Aid:** *Need-based scholarships/grants:* Pell, SEOG, state scholarships/grants, private scholarships, the school's own gift aid. *Loans:* FFEL Subsidized Stafford, FFEL Unsubsidized Stafford, FFEL PLUS, college/university loans from institutional funds. Note: College/university loans from institutional funds for international students only. **Financial Aid Statistics:** 62% freshmen, 65% undergrads receive need-based scholarship or grant aid. 62% freshmen, 63% undergrads receive need-based self-help aid. 76% freshmen, 76% undergrads receive any aid. Highest amount earned per year from on-campus jobs $1,700.

BENTLEY COLLEGE

175 Forest Street, Waltham, MA 02452-4705
Phone: 781-891-2244 **E-mail:** ugadmission@bentley.edu **CEEB Code:** 3096
Fax: 781-891-3414 **Website:** www.bentley.edu **ACT Code:** 1783
Financial Aid Phone: 781-891-3441

This private school was founded in 1917. It has a 163-acre campus.

RATINGS

Admissions Selectivity Rating: 91   **Fire Safety Rating:** 99   **Green Rating:** 95

STUDENTS AND FACULTY

Enrollment: 4,195. **Student Body:** 40% female, 60% male, 49% out-of-state, 7% international (76 countries represented). African American 3%, Asian 8%, Caucasian 68%, Hispanic 4%. **Retention and Graduation:** 95% freshmen return for sophomore year. 77% freshmen graduate within 4 years. 14% grads go on to further study within 1 year. 13% grads pursue business degrees. 1% grads pursue law degrees. **Faculty:** Student/faculty ratio 12:1. 271 full-time faculty, 83% hold PhDs. 90% faculty teach undergrads.

ACADEMICS

Degrees: Associate, bachelor's, doctoral, master's, post-bachelor's certificate, post-master's certificate, terminal. **Academic Requirements:** Computer literacy, English (including composition), history, humanities, mathematics, philosophy, sciences (biological or physical), social science, business. **Classes:** Most classes have 20–29 students. **Majors with Highest Enrollment:** Business administration/management, finance, marketing/marketing management. **Disciplines with Highest Percentage of Degrees Awarded:** Business/marketing 93%, computer and information sciences 4%, mathematics 1%, public administration and social services 1%, interdisciplinary studies 1%. **Special Study Options:** Accelerated program, cross-registration, double major, honors program, independent study, internships, liberal arts/career combination, student-designed major, study abroad.

FACILITIES

Housing: Coed dorms, apartments for single students, special housing for disabled students, 2 wellness houses with an overall health and wellness theme are available to students. **Special Academic Facilities/Equipment:** Academic technology center, accounting center for electronic learning and business measurement, economic/finance/statistics learning center, center for marketing technology, center for languages and international collaboration, ESOL tutorial center, math learning center, writing center, financial trading room, design and usability center, Bentley Service Learning Center. **Computers:** 70% of classrooms are wired, 100% of classrooms are wireless, 82% of public computers are PCs, 10% of public computers are Macs, 8% of public computers are UNIX, network access in dorm rooms, network access in dorm lounges, online registration, online administrative functions (other than registration), support for handheld computing, remote student-access to Web through college's connection, tuition includes personal computer. Undergraduates are required to own a computer.

CAMPUS LIFE

Activities: Choral groups, dance, drama/theater, jazz band, pep band, radio station, student government, student newspaper, yearbook. **Organizations:** 98 registered organizations, 2 honor societies, 5 religious organizations. 7 fraternities (10% men join), 4 sororities (10% women join). **Athletics (Intercollegiate):** *Men:* Baseball, basketball, cross-country, diving, football, golf, ice hockey, lacrosse, soccer, swimming, tennis, track/field (indoor), track/field (outdoor). *Women:* Basketball, cross-country, diving, field hockey, lacrosse, soccer, softball, swimming, tennis, track/field (indoor), track/field (outdoor), volleyball. **Environmental Initiatives:** American College and University Presidents Climate Committment. LEED-EB Projects. Energy Star Partner.

ADMISSIONS

Freshman Academic Profile: 40% in top 10% of high school class, 76% in top 25% of high school class, 99% in top 50% of high school class. 72% from public high schools. SAT Math middle 50% range 600–680. SAT Critical Reading middle 50% range 550–630. SAT Writing middle 50% range 550–640. ACT middle 50% range 24–29. TOEFL required of all international applicants, minimum paper TOEFL 550, minimum computer TOEFL 213. **Basis for Candidate Selection:** *Very important factors considered include:* Rigor of secondary school record, standardized test scores. *Important factors considered include:* Academic GPA, application essay, character/personal qualities, class rank, extracurricular activities, recommendation(s), volunteer work, work experience. *Other factors considered include:* Alumni/ae relation, first generation, geographical residence, interview, level of applicant's interest, racial/ethnic status, state residency, talent/ability. **Freshman Admission Requirements:** High school diploma is required, and GED is accepted. *Academic units recommended:* 4 English; 4 math; 3 science (3 science labs); 3 foreign language; 3 history; 2 additional English, mathematics, social or lab science, foreign language, speech. **Freshman Admission Statistics:** 6,156 applied, 39% admitted, 37% enrolled. **Transfer Admission Requirements:** High school transcript, college transcript(s), essay or personal statement, statement of good standing from prior institution(s). Lowest grade transferable C. **General Admission Information:** Application fee $50. Early decision application deadline 11/15. Regular application deadline 1/15. Regular notification 4/1. Nonfall registration accepted. Admission may be deferred for a maximum of 1 year. Credit and/or placement offered for CEEB Advanced Placement tests.

COSTS AND FINANCIAL AID

Annual tuition $31,450. Room and board $10,940. Required fees $1,446. Average book expense $1,000. **Required Forms and Deadlines:** FAFSA, CSS/Financial Aid PROFILE, Noncustodial PROFILE, Business/Farm Supplement, Federal Tax Returns, including all schedules for parents and student. Financial aid filing deadline 2/1. **Notification of Awards:** Applicants will be notified of awards on a rolling basis beginning on or about 3/25. **Types of Aid:** *Need-based scholarships/grants:* Pell, SEOG, state scholarships/grants, private scholarships, the school's own gift aid. *Loans:* FFEL Subsidized Stafford, FFEL Unsubsidized Stafford, FFEL PLUS, Federal Perkins, state loans. **Student Employment:** Federal Work-Study Program available. Institutional employment available. Off-campus job opportunities are good. **Financial Aid Statistics:** 48% freshmen, 42% undergrads receive need-based

scholarship or grant aid. 50% freshmen, 46% undergrads receive need-based self-help aid. 4 freshmen, 32 undergrads receive athletic scholarships. 78% freshmen, 73% undergrads receive any aid.

See page 1086.

BEREA COLLEGE

CPO 2220, Berea, KY 40404
Phone: 859-985-3500 **E-mail:** admissions@berea.edu **CEEB Code:** 1060
Fax: 859-985-3512 **Website:** www.berea.edu **ACT Code:** 1492
Financial Aid Phone: 859-985-3310

This private school was founded in 1855. It has a 140-acre campus.

RATINGS

Admissions Selectivity Rating: 92   **Fire Safety Rating:** 85   **Green Rating:** 89

STUDENTS AND FACULTY

Enrollment: 1,520. **Student Body:** 60% female, 40% male, 59% out-of-state, 8% international (64 countries represented). African American 18%, Asian 1%, Caucasian 68%, Hispanic 2%. **Retention and Graduation:** 82% freshmen return for sophomore year. 40% freshmen graduate within 4 years. **Faculty:** Student/faculty ratio 11:1. 128 full-time faculty, 88% hold PhDs. 100% faculty teach undergrads.

ACADEMICS

Degrees: Bachelor's. **Academic Requirements:** Arts/fine arts, English (including composition), history, humanities, mathematics, sciences (biological or physical), social science, Concept of Wellness. **Classes:** Most classes have 10–19 students. **Majors with Highest Enrollment:** Biology/biological sciences, business administration/management, family and consumer sciences/human sciences. **Disciplines with Highest Percentage of Degrees Awarded:** Education 11%, social sciences 10%, family and consumer sciences 8%, biological/life sciences 8%, business/marketing 8%, psychology 6%, communications/journalism 6%, visual and performing arts 6%, physical sciences 5%, interdisciplinary studies 5%. **Special Study Options:** Double major, exchange student program (domestic), honors program, independent study, internships, student-designed major, study abroad, teacher certification program. 3–2 engineering program with Washington University, St. Louis, and University of Kentucky.

FACILITIES

Housing: Men's dorms, women's dorms, apartments for married students, apartments for single-parent students, 9 small houses which hold 9–12 upperclass students, EcoVillage. **Special Academic Facilities/Equipment:** Geology museum; nursery school lab for child psychology and development majors; language labs; 1,100-acre farm; planetarium. **Computers:** 37% of classrooms are wired, 4% of classrooms are wireless, 100% of public computers are PCs, network access in dorm rooms, network access in dorm lounges, online registration, online administrative functions (other than registration), support for handheld computing, remote student-access to Web through college's connection, tuition includes personal computer.

CAMPUS LIFE

Activities: Choral groups, dance, drama/theater, jazz band, literary magazine, music ensembles, pep band, student government, student newspaper, yearbook. **Organizations:** 77 registered organizations, 14 honor societies, 5 religious organizations. **Athletics (Intercollegiate):** *Men:* Baseball, basketball, cross-country, golf, soccer, swimming, tennis, track/field (outdoor). *Women:* Basketball, cross-country, soccer, softball, swimming, tennis, track/field (outdoor), volleyball. **Environmental Initiatives:** 1. Sustainability and Environmental Studies academic program. 2. Ecological Renovations. 3. Local Food Initiative.

ADMISSIONS

Freshman Academic Profile: 27% in top 10% of high school class, 67% in top 25% of high school class, 94% in top 50% of high school class. SAT Math middle 50% range 478–600. SAT Critical Reading middle 50% range 480–593. SAT Writing middle 50% range 470–563. ACT middle 50% range 21–25. TOEFL required of all international applicants, minimum paper TOEFL 500, minimum computer TOEFL 173. **Basis for Candidate Selection:** *Very important* *factors considered include:* Academic GPA, class rank, geographical residence, rigor of secondary school record, standardized test scores. *Important factors considered include:* Application essay, character/personal qualities, extracurricular activities, interview, racial/ethnic status, talent/ability, volunteer work. *Other factors considered include:* First generation, level of applicant's interest, recommendation(s), state residency, work experience. **Freshman Admission Requirements:** High school diploma is required, and GED is accepted. *Academic units recommended:* 4 English, 3 math, 2 science, 2 foreign language, 1 social studies, 1 history. **Freshman Admission Statistics:** 1,818 applied, 29% admitted, 73% enrolled. **Transfer Admission Requirements:** High school transcript, college transcript(s), interview. Lowest grade transferable C. **General Admission Information:** Regular application deadline 4/30. Regular notification is rolling. Nonfall registration accepted. Credit offered for CEEB Advanced Placement tests.

COSTS AND FINANCIAL AID
Required Forms and Deadlines: FAFSA. Financial aid filing deadline 4/1. **Notification of Awards:** Applicants will be notified of awards on a rolling basis beginning on or about 5/1. **Types of Aid:** *Need-based scholarships/grants:* Pell, SEOG, state scholarships/grants, private scholarships, the school's own gift aid, United Negro College Fund. *Loans:* FFEL Subsidized Stafford, FFEL Unsubsidized Stafford, FFEL PLUS, Federal Perkins, college/university loans from institutional funds. **Financial Aid Statistics:** 100% freshmen, 100% undergrads receive need-based scholarship or grant aid. 100% freshmen, 100% undergrads receive need-based self-help aid. 100% freshmen, 100% undergrads receive any aid.

BERKELEY COLLEGE

44 Rifle Camp Road, West Paterson, NJ 07424
Phone: 973-278-5400 **E-mail:** info@berkeleycollege.edu **CEEB Code:** 2061
Fax: 973-278-9141 **Website:** www.berkeleycollege.edu **ACT Code:** 2576
Financial Aid Phone: 973-278-5400

This proprietary school was founded in 1931. It has a 25-acre campus.

RATINGS
Admissions Selectivity Rating: 60*   **Fire Safety Rating:** 60*   **Green Rating:** 60*

STUDENTS AND FACULTY
Enrollment: 2,709. **Student Body:** 72% female, 28% male, 4% out-of-state, 1% international. African American 20%, Asian 5%, Caucasian 35%, Hispanic 35%. **Retention and Graduation:** 53% freshmen return for sophomore year. **Faculty:** Student/faculty ratio 24:1. 54 full-time faculty. 100% faculty teach undergrads.

ACADEMICS
Degrees: Associate, bachelor's, certificate, terminal. **Academic Requirements:** Computer literacy, English (including composition), humanities, social science. 1 class in either mathematics or sciences is required in every associate degree program. Every baccalaureate degree program requires 2 mathematics courses and an elective in the sciences. **Majors with Highest Enrollment:** Accounting, business administration/management, fashion merchandising. **Disciplines with Highest Percentage of Degrees Awarded:** Business/marketing 100%. **Special Study Options:** Accelerated program, distance learning, internships, study abroad, academic remediation. Off-campus study at Berkeley College in New York City and in White Plains.

FACILITIES
Housing: Coed dorms. **Computers:** 100% of public computers are PCs, network access in dorm rooms, online administrative functions (other than registration), remote student-access to Web through college's connection.

CAMPUS LIFE
Activities: Choral groups, literary magazine, student government, student newspaper. **Organizations:** 8 registered organizations, 1 honor society.

ADMISSIONS
Freshman Academic Profile: TOEFL required of all international applicants, minimum paper TOEFL 500, minimum computer TOEFL 173. **Basis for Candidate Selection:** *Very important factors considered include:* Interview, rigor of secondary school record. *Important factors considered include:* Standardized test scores. *Other factors considered include:* Academic GPA, character/personal qualities, class rank, extracurricular activities, recommendation(s), talent/ability, volunteer work, work experience. **Freshman Admission Requirements:** High school diploma is required, and GED is accepted. **Freshman Admission Statistics:** 1,955 applied, 84% admitted, 53% enrolled. **Transfer Admission Requirements:** High school transcript, college

transcript(s). Lowest grade transferable C. **General Admission Information:** Application fee $50. Regular notification on a continuous rolling basis. Nonfall registration accepted. Admission may be deferred for a maximum of no limit. Credit and/or placement offered for CEEB Advanced Placement tests.

COSTS AND FINANCIAL AID
Annual tuition $18,300. Room and board $9,000. Required fees $750. Average book expense $1,300. **Required Forms and Deadlines:** FAFSA. **Notification of Awards:** Applicants will be notified of awards on a rolling basis beginning on or about 3/1. **Types of Aid:** *Need-based scholarships/grants:* Pell, SEOG, state scholarships/grants, private scholarships, the school's own gift aid. *Loans:* FFEL Subsidized Stafford, FFEL Unsubsidized Stafford, FFEL PLUS, state loans. **Financial Aid Statistics:** 85% freshmen receive any aid.

BERKELEY COLLEGE—NEW YORK CITY CAMPUS

3 East 43rd Street, New York, NY 10017
Phone: 212-986-4343 **E-mail:** info@berkeleycollege.edu
Fax: 212-818-1079 **Website:** berkeleycollege.edu **ACT Code:** 2688
Financial Aid Phone: 212-986-4343

This proprietary school was founded in 1936.

RATINGS
Admissions Selectivity Rating: 60*   **Fire Safety Rating:** 60*   **Green Rating:** 60*

STUDENTS AND FACULTY
Enrollment: 2,390. **Student Body:** 70% female, 30% male, 9% out-of-state, 15% international. African American 22%, Asian 5%, Caucasian 16%, Hispanic 23%. **Retention and Graduation:** 51% freshmen return for sophomore year. **Faculty:** Student/faculty ratio 24:1. 40 full-time faculty. 100% faculty teach undergrads.

ACADEMICS
Degrees: Associate, bachelor's, certificate. **Academic Requirements:** Computer literacy, English (including composition), humanities, social science. 1 class in either mathematics or sciences is required in every associate degree program. Every baccalaureate degree program requires 2 mathematics courses and an elective in the sciences. **Majors with Highest Enrollment:** Business administration/management, fashion merchandising, marketing/marketing management. **Disciplines with Highest Percentage of Degrees Awarded:** Business/marketing 100%. **Special Study Options:** Accelerated program, distance learning, English as a Second Language (ESL), internships, study abroad. Academic remediation, off campus study at Berkeley College, White Plains, and Berkley College, New Jersey.

FACILITIES
Computers: 80% of classrooms are wireless, 100% of public computers are PCs, online administrative functions (other than registration), remote student-access to Web through college's connection.

CAMPUS LIFE
Activities: Choral groups, student government. **Organizations:** 6 registered organizations, 4 honor societies.

ADMISSIONS
Freshman Academic Profile: TOEFL required of all international applicants, minimum paper TOEFL 500, minimum computer TOEFL 173. **Basis for Candidate Selection:** *Very important factors considered include:* Interview, rigor of secondary school record. *Important factors considered include:* Standardized test scores. *Other factors considered include:* Academic GPA, character/personal qualities, class rank, extracurricular activities, recommendation(s), talent/ability, volunteer work, work experience. **Freshman Admission Requirements:** High school diploma is required, and GED is accepted. **Freshman Admission Statistics:** 2,279 applied, 73% admitted, 63% enrolled. **Transfer Admission Requirements:** College transcript(s). Lowest grade transferable C. **General Admission Information:** Application fee $50. Regular notification on a continuous rolling basis. Nonfall registration accepted. Admission may be deferred indefinitely. Credit and/or placement offered for CEEB Advanced Placement tests.

COSTS AND FINANCIAL AID
Annual tuition $18,300. Required fees $750. Average book expense $1,300. **Required Forms and Deadlines:** FAFSA, state aid form. **Notification of Awards:** Applicants will be notified of awards on or about 3/1. **Types of Aid:** *Need-based scholarships/grants:* Pell, SEOG, state scholarships/grants, private scholarships, the school's own gift aid. *Loans:* FFEL Subsidized Stafford, FFEL Unsubsidized Stafford, FFEL PLUS. **Student Employment:** Federal Work-

Study Program available. Institutional employment available. Off-campus job opportunities are excellent. **Financial Aid Statistics:** 85% freshmen receive any aid.

BERKELEY COLLEGE—WESTCHESTER CAMPUS

99 Church Street, White Plains, NY 10601
Phone: 914-694-1122 **E-mail:** info@berkeleycollege.edu
Fax: 914-328-9470 **Website:** www.berkeleycollege.edu **ACT Code:** 2695
Financial Aid Phone: 914-694-1122

This proprietary school was founded in 1945.

RATINGS
Admissions Selectivity Rating: 60*   **Fire Safety Rating:** 60*   **Green Rating:** 60*

STUDENTS AND FACULTY
Enrollment: 608. **Student Body:** 72% female, 28% male, 15% out-of-state, 6% international. African American 26%, Asian 3%, Caucasian 35%, Hispanic 21%. **Retention and Graduation:** 50% freshmen return for sophomore year. **Faculty:** Student/faculty ratio 24:1. 17 full-time faculty. 100% faculty teach undergrads.

ACADEMICS
Degrees: Associate, bachelor's, certificate. **Academic Requirements:** Computer literacy, English (including composition), humanities, social science. 1 class in either mathematics or sciences is required in every associate degree program. Every baccalaureate degree program requires 2 mathematics courses and an elective in the sciences. **Majors with Highest Enrollment:** Business administration/management, business/managerial operations, marketing/marketing management. **Disciplines with Highest Percentage of Degrees Awarded:** Business/marketing 100%. **Special Study Options:** Accelerated program, distance learning, English as a Second Language (ESL), internships, study abroad. Academic remediation, off-campus study at Berkley College, New York City and Berkeley College, New Jersey.

FACILITIES
Housing: Coed dorms. **Computers:** 100% of public computers are PCs, online administrative functions (other than registration), remote student-access to Web through college's connection.

CAMPUS LIFE
Activities: Student government. **Organizations:** 6 registered organizations, 4 honor societies. 1 fraternity, 1 sorority.

ADMISSIONS
Freshman Academic Profile: TOEFL required of all international applicants, minimum paper TOEFL 500, minimum computer TOEFL 173. **Basis for Candidate Selection:** *Very important factors considered include:* Interview, rigor of secondary school record. *Important factors considered include:* Standardized test scores. *Other factors considered include:* Academic GPA, character/personal qualities, class rank, extracurricular activities, recommendation(s), talent/ability, volunteer work, work experience. **Freshman Admission Requirements:** High school diploma is required, and GED is accepted. **Transfer Admission Requirements:** College transcript(s). Lowest grade transferable C. **General Admission Information:** Application fee $50. Regular notification notified on a continuous rolling basis. Nonfall registration accepted. Admission may be deferred indefinitely. Credit and/or placement offered for CEEB Advanced Placement tests.

COSTS AND FINANCIAL AID
Annual tuition $18,300. Room and board $9,000. Required fees $750. Average book expense $1,300. **Required Forms and Deadlines:** FAFSA, state aid form. **Notification of Awards:** Applicants will be notified of awards on a rolling basis beginning on or about 3/1. **Types of Aid:** *Need-based scholarships/grants:* Pell, SEOG, state scholarships/grants, private scholarships, the school's own gift aid. *Loans:* FFEL Subsidized Stafford, FFEL Unsubsidized Stafford, FFEL PLUS.

BERKLEE COLLEGE OF MUSIC

1140 Boylston Street, Boston, MA 02215-3693
Phone: 617-747-2222 **E-mail:** admissions@berklee.edu **CEEB Code:** 3107
Fax: 617-747-2047 **Website:** www.berklee.edu **ACT Code:** 1789
Financial Aid Phone: 800-538-3844

This private school was founded in 1945.

RATINGS
Admissions Selectivity Rating: 60*   **Fire Safety Rating:** 60*   **Green Rating:** 60*

STUDENTS AND FACULTY
Enrollment: 3,799. **Student Body:** 82% out-of-state, 25% international (75 countries represented). African American 4%, Asian 3%, Caucasian 54%, Hispanic 4%. **Faculty:** Student/faculty ratio 12:1. 193 full-time faculty.

ACADEMICS
Degrees: Bachelor's. **Academic Requirements:** Arts/fine arts, computer literacy. **Majors with Highest Enrollment:** Music performance, music. **Special Study Options:** Accelerated program, double major, internships, student-designed major, teacher certification program.

FACILITIES
Housing: Coed dorms. **Special Academic Facilities/Equipment:** Ensemble library, 10 professional recording studios, film scoring and editing studio, analog and digital music synthesis labs, 1,200-seat performance center, learning center. **Computers:** Network access in dorm rooms, network access in dorm lounges, remote student-access to Web through college's connection.

CAMPUS LIFE
Activities: Choral groups, concert band, jazz band, music ensembles, musical theater, student government, student newspaper. **Organizations:** 63 registered organizations, 2 honor societies.

ADMISSIONS
Freshman Academic Profile: TOEFL required of all international applicants, minimum paper TOEFL 500. **Basis for Candidate Selection:** *Very important factors considered include:* Extracurricular activities, interview, recommendation(s), rigor of secondary school record, talent/ability. *Important factors considered include:* Character/personal qualities, standardized test scores. *Other factors considered include:* Alumni/ae relation, application essay, class rank, geographical residence, racial/ethnic status, state residency, volunteer work, work experience. **Freshman Admission Requirements:** High school diploma is required, and GED is accepted. *Academic units required:* 4 English, 1 math, 1 science (1 science lab), 2 social studies, 6 academic electives, 2 art electives. **Freshman Admission Statistics:** 1,779 applied, 81% admitted, 42% enrolled. **Transfer Admission Requirements:** College transcript(s), essay or personal statement, minimum college GPA of 2.0 required. Lowest grade transferable C. **General Admission Information:** Application fee $75. Regular notification rolling admissions. Nonfall registration accepted. Admission may be deferred for a maximum of 6 semesters. Common Application not accepted. Credit offered for CEEB Advanced Placement tests.

COSTS AND FINANCIAL AID
Annual tuition $20,350. Room and board $10,900. Required fees $2,640. Average book expense $500. **Required Forms and Deadlines:** FAFSA, institution's own financial aid form. **Notification of Awards:** Applicants will be notified of awards on or about 4/3. **Types of Aid:** *Need-based scholarships/grants:* Pell, SEOG, state scholarships/grants, private scholarships, the school's own gift aid. *Loans:* Direct Subsidized Stafford, Direct Unsubsidized Stafford, Direct PLUS, Federal Perkins, state loans. **Student Employment:** Federal Work-Study Program available. Off-campus job opportunities are good. Highest amount earned per year from on-campus jobs $2,000.

BERRY COLLEGE

PO Box 490159, Mount Berry, GA 30149-0159
Phone: 706-236-2215 **E-mail:** admissions@berry.edu **CEEB Code:** 5059
Fax: 706-290-2178 **Website:** www.berry.edu **ACT Code:** 0798
Financial Aid Phone: 706-236-1714

This private school was founded in 1902. It has a 28,000-acre campus.

RATINGS
Admissions Selectivity Rating: 86   **Fire Safety Rating:** 78   **Green Rating:** 82

STUDENTS AND FACULTY
Enrollment: 1,708. **Student Body:** 66% female, 34% male, 15% out-of-state, 2% international (26 countries represented). African American 3%, Asian 2%, Caucasian 89%, Hispanic 2%. **Retention and Graduation:** 75% freshmen return for sophomore year. 48% freshmen graduate within 4 years. 24% grads go on to further study within 1 year. 15% grads pursue arts and sciences degrees. 4% grads pursue business degrees. 2% grads pursue law degrees. 2% grads pursue medical degrees. **Faculty:** Student/faculty ratio 12:1. 143 full-time faculty, 87% hold PhDs. 100% faculty teach undergrads.

ACADEMICS
Degrees: Bachelor's, master's, post-master's certificate. **Academic Requirements:** Arts/fine arts, computer literacy, English (including composition), history, humanities, mathematics, philosophy, sciences (biological or physical), social science. **Classes:** Most classes have 10–19 students. Most lab/discussion sections have 10–19 students. **Majors with Highest Enrollment:** Communications, journalism, and related fields; early childhood education and teaching; psychology. **Disciplines with Highest Percentage of Degrees Awarded:** Business/marketing 14%, psychology 12%, education 12%, social sciences 10%, communications/journalism 9%, communication technologies 9%, visual and performing arts 6%. **Special Study Options:** Cooperative education program, cross-registration, double major, honors program, independent study, internships, student-designed major, study abroad, teacher certification program, 3–2 nursing with Emory University, 3–2 engineering with Georgia Institute of Technology, Mercer University.

FACILITIES
Housing: Coed dorms, men's dorms, women's dorms, special housing for disabled students, traditional residence halls are single sex, apartments and townhouses are coed by site or apartment. Special-interest houses for women in math and science (primarily first-year). **Special Academic Facilities/Equipment:** Oak Hill founder's home, Martha Berry Museum, research center for animal science, nature preserve of 400 acres containing riding trails and stables, select government depository containing over 89,000 government documents, Berry Elementary School, Berry Middle School. **Computers:** 100% of public computers are PCs, network access in dorm rooms, network access in dorm lounges, online registration, online administrative functions (other than registration), remote student-access to Web through college's connection.

CAMPUS LIFE
Activities: Choral groups, concert band, dance, drama/theater, jazz band, literary magazine, music ensembles, student government, student newspaper, television station, yearbook. **Organizations:** 77 registered organizations, 15 honor societies, 11 religious organizations. **Athletics (Intercollegiate):** *Men:* Baseball, basketball, cheerleading, cross-country, golf, soccer, tennis, track/field (indoor), track/field (outdoor). *Women:* Basketball, cheerleading, cross-country, golf, soccer, tennis, track/field (indoor), track/field (outdoor), volleyball. **Environmental Initiatives:** President's Climate Commitment: Energy Star Policy, RecycleMania. Environmental Land Management: Carbon Reserve, wetland banking, and EPA Compliance-Peer Audit. Establishing an environmental science major.

ADMISSIONS
Freshman Academic Profile: 35% in top 10% of high school class, 71% in top 25% of high school class, 94% in top 50% of high school class. 84% from public high schools. SAT Math middle 50% range 510–620. SAT Writing middle 50% range 510–610. ACT middle 50% range 23–29. TOEFL required of all international applicants, minimum paper TOEFL 550, minimum computer TOEFL 213. **Basis for Candidate Selection:** *Very important factors considered include:* Rigor of secondary school record, standardized test scores. *Important factors considered include:* Extracurricular activities. *Other factors considered include:* Academic GPA, alumni/ae relation, application essay, character/personal qualities, class rank, recommendation(s), talent/ability, volunteer work, work experience. **Freshman Admission Requirements:** High school diploma is required, and GED is accepted. *Academic units required:* 4 English, 4 math, 3 science (3 science labs), 2 foreign language, 3 social studies.

Freshman Admission Statistics: 1,334 applied, 72% admitted, 45% enrolled. **Transfer Admission Requirements:** College transcript(s), statement of good standing from prior institution(s). Minimum college GPA of 2.5 required. Lowest grade transferable C. **General Admission Information:** Application fee $50. Regular application deadline 7/25. Regular notification is rolling. Nonfall registration accepted. Admission may be deferred for a maximum of up to 1 year. Credit and/or placement offered for CEEB Advanced Placement tests.

COSTS AND FINANCIAL AID
Annual tuition $20,570. Room and board $7,626. Average book expense $900. **Required Forms and Deadlines:** FAFSA, institution's own financial aid form, state aid form. Financial aid filing deadline 4/1. **Notification of Awards:** Applicants will be notified of awards on a rolling basis beginning on or about 3/1. **Types of Aid:** *Need-based scholarships/grants:* Pell, SEOG, state scholarships/grants, private scholarships, the school's own gift aid. *Loans:* FFEL Subsidized Stafford, FFEL Unsubsidized Stafford, FFEL PLUS, Federal Perkins, college/university loans from institutional funds. **Financial Aid Statistics:** 57% freshmen, 58% undergrads receive need-based scholarship or grant aid. 43% freshmen, 47% undergrads receive need-based self-help aid. 37 freshmen, 114 undergrads receive athletic scholarships.

BETHANY COLLEGE (KS)

335 East Swensson Street, Lindsborg, KS 67456-1897
Phone: 785-227-3311 **E-mail:** admissions@bethanylb.edu **CEEB Code:** 6034
Fax: 785-227-8993 **Website:** www.bethanylb.edu **ACT Code:** 1388
Financial Aid Phone: 785-227-3311

This private school, affiliated with the Lutheran Church, was founded in 1881. It has a 62-acre campus.

RATINGS
Admissions Selectivity Rating: 78   **Fire Safety Rating:** 96   **Green Rating:** 60*

STUDENTS AND FACULTY
Enrollment: 534. **Student Body:** 52% female, 48% male, 39% out-of-state, 3% international (13 countries represented). African American 9%, Caucasian 76%, Hispanic 6%. **Retention and Graduation:** 55% freshmen return for sophomore year. 27% freshmen graduate within 4 years. 20% grads go on to further study within 1 year. 3% grads pursue medical degrees. **Faculty:** Student/faculty ratio 10:1. 41 full-time faculty, 73% hold PhDs. 100% faculty teach undergrads.

ACADEMICS
Degrees: Bachelor's. **Academic Requirements:** Arts/fine arts, English (including composition), humanities, mathematics, philosophy, sciences (biological or physical), social science. **Classes:** Most classes have fewer than 10 students. Most lab/discussion sections have 10–19 students. **Majors with Highest Enrollment:** Biology/biological sciences, business administration and management, elementary education and teaching. **Disciplines with Highest Percentage of Degrees Awarded:** Education 26%, business/marketing 20%, biological/life sciences 9%, security and protective services 7%, communications/journalism 6%. **Special Study Options:** Accelerated program, cross-registration, double major, dual enrollment, exchange student program (domestic), honors program, independent study, internships, student-designed major, study abroad, teacher certification program.

FACILITIES
Housing: Coed dorms, men's dorms, women's dorms. Special interest housing—bid on by student groups, community service, and house improvements. **Special Academic Facilities/Equipment:** Mingenback Gallery, Bethany College Archives, Plym Gallery, Sandzen Gallery. **Computers:** 1% of classrooms are wired, 100% of public computers are PCs, network access in dorm rooms, remote student-access to Web through college's connection.

CAMPUS LIFE
Activities: Choral groups, concert band, dance, drama/theater, jazz band, music ensembles, musical theater, pep band, student government, student newspaper, symphony orchestra, yearbook. **Organizations:** 49 registered organizations, 8 honor societies, 9 religious organizations. 3 fraternities (15% men join), 3 sororities (18% women join). **Athletics (Intercollegiate):** *Men:* Baseball, basketball, cheerleading, cross-country, football, golf, soccer, tennis, track/field (indoor), track/field (outdoor). *Women:* Basketball, cheerleading, cross-country, soccer, softball, tennis, track/field (indoor), track/field (outdoor), volleyball.

ADMISSIONS
Freshman Academic Profile: 14% in top 10% of high school class, 40% in top

25% of high school class, 70% in top 50% of high school class. 97% from public high schools. SAT Math middle 50% range 380–520. SAT Critical Reading middle 50% range 370–480. SAT Writing middle 50% range 370–480. ACT middle 50% range 20–25. TOEFL required of all international applicants, minimum paper TOEFL 525, minimum computer TOEFL 195. **Basis for Candidate Selection:** *Very important factors considered include:* Academic GPA, class rank, standardized test scores. *Important factors considered include:* Rigor of secondary school record. *Other factors considered include:* Alumni/ae relation, application essay, character/personal qualities, extracurricular activities, interview, level of applicant's interest, recommendation(s), talent/ability. **Freshman Admission Requirements:** High school diploma is required, and GED is accepted. *Academic units recommended:* 4 English, 3 math, 3 science (2 science labs), 2 foreign language, 3 social studies. **Freshman Admission Statistics:** 1,283 applied, 60% admitted, 22% enrolled. **Transfer Admission Requirements:** College transcript(s), minimum college GPA of 2.3 required. Lowest grade transferable D. **General Admission Information:** Application fee $20. Regular application deadline 7/1. Regular notification is rolling. Nonfall registration accepted. Neither credit nor placement offered for CEEB Advanced Placement tests.

COSTS AND FINANCIAL AID

Annual tuition $17,824. Room and board $5,650. Required fees $300. Average book expense $1,000 **Required Forms and Deadlines:** FAFSA. Financial aid filing deadline 3/15. **Notification of Awards:** Applicants will be notified of awards on a rolling basis beginning on or about 2/1. **Types of Aid:** *Need-based scholarships/grants:* Pell, SEOG, state scholarships/grants, private scholarships, the school's own gift aid. *Loans:* FFEL Subsidized Stafford, FFEL Unsubsidized Stafford, FFEL PLUS, Federal Perkins. **Financial Aid Statistics:** 71% freshmen, 71% undergrads receive need-based scholarship or grant aid. 72% freshmen, 71% undergrads receive need-based self-help aid. 6 freshmen, 31 undergrads receive athletic scholarships. 98% freshmen, 98% undergrads receive any aid. Highest amount earned per year from on-campus jobs $1,500.

BETHANY COLLEGE (WV)

Office of Admission, Bethany, WV 26032
Phone: 304-829-7611 **E-mail:** admission@bethanywv.edu **CEEB Code:** 5060
Fax: 304-829-7142 **Website:** www.bethanywv.edu **ACT Code:** 4512
Financial Aid Phone: 304-829-7141

This private school, affiliated with the Disciples of Christ Church, was founded in 1840. It has a 400-acre campus.

RATINGS
Admissions Selectivity Rating: 80   **Fire Safety Rating:** 60*   **Green Rating:** 60*

STUDENTS AND FACULTY
Enrollment: 887. **Student Body:** 49% female, 51% male, 74% out-of-state, 4% international (13 countries represented). African American 2%, Caucasian 92%. **Retention and Graduation:** 79% freshmen return for sophomore year. 51% freshmen graduate within 4 years. 10% grads go on to further study within 1 year. 30% grads pursue arts and sciences degrees. 2% grads pursue business degrees. 4% grads pursue law degrees. 3% grads pursue medical degrees. **Faculty:** Student/faculty ratio 12:1. 66 full-time faculty, 65% hold PhDs. 100% faculty teach undergrads.

ACADEMICS
Degrees: Bachelor's. **Academic Requirements:** Arts/fine arts, computer literacy, English (including composition), foreign languages, history, humanities, mathematics, philosophy, sciences (biological or physical), social science, first-year seminar. **Classes:** Most classes have 10–19 students. Most lab/discussion sections have 10–19 students. **Majors with Highest Enrollment:** Education, mass communications/media studies, psychology. **Disciplines with Highest Percentage of Degrees Awarded:** Communication technologies 13%, psychology 13%, social sciences 9%, education 8%, mathematics 7%, biological/life sciences 7%, visual and performing arts 7%. **Special Study Options:** Double major, exchange student program (domestic), independent study, internships, liberal arts/career combination, student-designed major, study abroad, teacher certification program, off campus study: Washington, DC.

FACILITIES
Housing: Coed dorms, men's dorms, women's dorms, apartments for married students, apartments for single students, special housing for disabled students, fraternity/sorority housing. **Computers:** 50% of public computers are PCs, 50% of public computers are Macs, network access in dorm rooms, online administrative functions (other than registration), remote student-access to Web through college's connection.

CAMPUS LIFE
Activities: Choral groups, concert band, drama/theater, jazz band, literary magazine, music ensembles, musical theater, pep band, radio station, student government, student newspaper, student-run film society, television station, yearbook. **Organizations:** 38 registered organizations, 16 honor societies, 3 religious organizations. 6 fraternities (45% men join), 3 sororities (45% women join). **Athletics (Intercollegiate):** *Men:* Baseball, basketball, cross-country, diving, football, golf, soccer, swimming, tennis, track/field (indoor), track/field (outdoor). *Women:* Basketball, cross-country, diving, golf, soccer, softball, swimming, tennis, track/field (indoor), track/field (outdoor), volleyball.

ADMISSIONS
Freshman Academic Profile: 20% in top 10% of high school class, 47% in top 25% of high school class, 81% in top 50% of high school class. 75% from public high schools. SAT Math middle 50% range 460–560. SAT Critical Reading middle 50% range 450–540. ACT middle 50% range 19–25. TOEFL required of all international applicants, minimum paper TOEFL 500, minimum computer TOEFL 173. **Basis for Candidate Selection:** *Very important factors considered include:* Application essay, class rank, recommendation(s), rigor of secondary school record, standardized test scores. *Important factors considered include:* Interview. *Other factors considered include:* Alumni/ae relation, character/personal qualities, extracurricular activities, talent/ability, volunteer work, work experience. **Freshman Admission Requirements:** High school diploma is required, and GED is accepted. *Academic units required:* 4 English, 3 math, 3 science, 2 foreign language, 3 social studies. **Freshman Admission Statistics:** 860 applied, 75% admitted, 35% enrolled. **Transfer Admission Requirements:** College transcript(s), essay or personal statement, statement of good standing from prior institution(s). Minimum college GPA of 2.0 required. Lowest grade transferable D. **General Admission Information:** Application fee $25. Regular notification is rolling. Nonfall registration accepted. Admission may be deferred for a maximum of 1 year. Common Application accepted. Credit and/or placement offered for CEEB Advanced Placement tests.

COSTS AND FINANCIAL AID
Annual tuition $15,750. Room & board $7,770. Required fees $800. Average book expense $1,000. **Required Forms and Deadlines:** FAFSA, institution's own financial aid form. Financial aid filing deadline 4/1. **Notification of Awards:** Applicants will be notified of awards on a rolling basis beginning on or about 3/1. **Types of Aid:** *Need-based scholarships/grants:* Pell, SEOG, state scholarships/grants, private scholarships, the school's own gift aid. *Loans:* Direct Subsidized Stafford, Direct Unsubsidized Stafford, Direct PLUS, Federal Perkins. **Student Employment:** Federal Work-Study Program available. Institutional employment available. Off-campus job opportunities are fair. **Financial Aid Statistics:** 78% freshmen, 77% undergrads receive need-based scholarship or grant aid. 88% freshmen, 88% undergrads receive need-based self-help aid. 95% freshmen, 92% undergrads receive any aid. Highest amount earned per year from on-campus jobs $1,000.

BETHANY UNIVERSITY

800 Bethany Drive, Scotts Valley, CA 95066
Phone: 831-438-3800 **E-mail:** info@bethany.edu **CEEB Code:** 4021
Fax: 831-438-6104 **Website:** www.bethany.edu

This is a private school.

RATINGS
Admissions Selectivity Rating: 60*   **Fire Safety Rating:** 60*   **Green Rating:** 60*

STUDENTS AND FACULTY
Enrollment: 504. **Student Body:** 60% female, 40% male, 13% out-of-state, 2% international. African American 10%, Asian 5%, Caucasian 62%, Hispanic 18%, Native American 1%. **Retention and Graduation:** 59% freshmen return for sophomore year. 6% grads go on to further study within 1 year. 6% grads pursue arts and sciences degrees. **Faculty:** Student/faculty ratio 12:1. 25 full-time faculty, 84% hold PhDs. 90% faculty teach undergrads.

ACADEMICS
Degrees: Associate, bachelor's, certificate, master's, post-bachelor's certificate. **Academic Requirements:** English (including composition), history, humanities, mathematics, sciences (biological or physical), social science, Bible and theology. **Classes:** Most classes have 10–19 students. Most lab/discussion sections have fewer than 10 students. **Disciplines with Highest Percentage of Degrees Awarded:** Theology and religious vocations 17%, interdisciplinary studies 12%, business/marketing 11% 6%, social sciences 6%, education 4%. **Special Study Options:** Accelerated program, distance learning, double major,

external degree program, independent study, internships, teacher certification program, weekend college.

FACILITIES

Housing: Men's dorms, women's dorms, apartments for married students.

CAMPUS LIFE

Activities: Choral groups, drama/theater, jazz band, music ensembles, student government, student newspaper, yearbook. **Organizations:** 1 honor society, 1 religious organization. **Athletics (Intercollegiate):** *Men:* Basketball, cheerleading, golf. *Women:* Basketball, cheerleading, softball, volleyball.

ADMISSIONS

Freshman Academic Profile: 16% in top 10% of high school class, 59% in top 25% of high school class, 75% in top 50% of high school class. TOEFL required of all international applicants, minimum paper TOEFL 500. **Basis for Candidate Selection:** *Very important factors considered include:* Academic GPA, application essay, recommendation(s), religious affiliation/commitment, standardized test scores. *Other factors considered include:* Character/personal qualities, class rank, extracurricular activities, level of applicant's interest, rigor of secondary school record. **Freshman Admission Statistics:** 228 applied, 55% admitted, 67% enrolled. **Transfer Admission Requirements:** College transcript(s), essay or personal statement, minimum college GPA of 2.0 required. **General Admission Information:** Application fee $35. Regular application deadline 7/1. Nonfall registration accepted. Admission may be deferred for a maximum of 2 years.

COSTS AND FINANCIAL AID

Annual tuition $14,300. Room & board $6,320. Required fees $715. Average book expense $500. **Required Forms and Deadlines:** FAFSA, institution's own financial aid form. Financial aid filing deadline 3/2. **Types of Aid:** *Need-based scholarships/grants:* Pell, SEOG, state scholarships/grants, private scholarships, the school's own gift aid. *Loans:* FFEL Subsidized Stafford, FFEL Unsubsidized Stafford, FFEL PLUS, Federal Perkins, college/university loans from institutional funds. **Student Employment:** Federal Work-Study Program available.

BETHEL COLLEGE (IN)

1001 West McKinley Avenue, Mishawaka, IN 46545
Phone: 574-257-3339 **E-mail:** admissions@bethelcollege.edu **CEEB Code:** 1079
Fax: 574-257-3335 **Website:** www.bethelcollege.edu **ACT Code:** 1178
Financial Aid Phone: 574-257-3316

This private school, affiliated with the Missionary Church, was founded in 1947. It has a 75-acre campus.

RATINGS

Admissions Selectivity Rating: 73   **Fire Safety Rating:** 60*   **Green Rating:** 70

STUDENTS AND FACULTY

Enrollment: 1,974. **Student Body:** 34% female, 66% male, 27% out-of-state, 2% international (14 countries represented). African American 10%, Asian 2%, Caucasian 80%, Hispanic 3%. **Retention and Graduation:** 79% freshmen return for sophomore year. 37% freshmen graduate within 4 years. **Faculty:** Student/faculty ratio 13:1. 97 full-time faculty. 100% faculty teach undergrads.

ACADEMICS

Degrees: Associate, bachelor's, master's. **Academic Requirements:** Arts/fine arts, English (including composition), foreign languages, history, humanities, mathematics, philosophy, sciences (biological or physical), social science, Bible/religion. **Classes:** Most classes have 10–19 students. Most lab/discussion sections have fewer than 10 students. **Majors with Highest Enrollment:** Business administration/management; elementary education and teaching. nursing/registered nurse training (ASN, BSN, MSN, RN). **Disciplines with Highest Percentage of Degrees Awarded:** Business/marketing 28%, education 16%, liberal arts/general studies 14%, health professions and related sciences 6%, theology and religious vocations 6%. **Special Study Options:** Accelerated program, cross-registration, double major, independent study, internships, student-designed major, study abroad, teacher certification program.

FACILITIES

Housing: Men's dorms, women's dorms, special housing for disabled students. **Special Academic Facilities/Equipment:** Bowen Museum, Weaver Gallery. **Computers:** 90% of public computers are PCs, 10% of public computers are Macs, network access in dorm rooms, network access in dorm lounges, online administrative functions (other than registration), support for handheld computing, remote student-access to Web through college's connection.

CAMPUS LIFE

Activities: Choral groups, concert band, dance, drama/theater, jazz band, literary magazine, music ensembles, musical theater, pep band, radio station, student government, student newspaper, yearbook. **Organizations:** 18 registered organizations, 4 religious organizations. **Athletics (Intercollegiate):** *Men:* Baseball, basketball, cheerleading, cross-country, golf, soccer, tennis, track/field (indoor), track/field (outdoor), wrestling. *Women:* Basketball, cheerleading, cross-country, golf, soccer, softball, tennis, track/field (indoor), track/field (outdoor), volleyball. **Environmental Initiatives:** Recycle trash. Working with local community on MS4 program. Recycle leaves.

ADMISSIONS

Freshman Academic Profile: 15% in top 10% of high school class, 39% in top 25% of high school class, 74% in top 50% of high school class. 75% from public high schools. SAT Math middle 50% range 460–590. SAT Critical Reading middle 50% range 450–570. SAT Writing middle 50% range 435–560. ACT middle 50% range 19–25. TOEFL required of all international applicants, minimum paper TOEFL 540, minimum computer TOEFL 207. **Basis for Candidate Selection:** *Important factors considered include:* Academic GPA, application essay, character/personal qualities, class rank, extracurricular activities, recommendation(s), rigor of secondary school record, standardized test scores. *Other factors considered include:* Interview, racial/ethnic status, volunteer work. **Freshman Admission Requirements:** High school diploma is required, and GED is accepted. *Academic units recommended:* 4 English, 3 math, 1 science, (1 science lab), 2 foreign language, 1 social studies, 3 history, 3 academic electives. **Freshman Admission Statistics:** 645 applied, 91% admitted, 53% enrolled. **Transfer Admission Requirements:** High school transcript, college transcript(s), essay or personal statement, standardized test score, minimum college GPA of 2.0 required. Lowest grade transferable C-. **General Admission Information:** Application fee $25. Regular application deadline 8/15. Regular notification is rolling. Nonfall registration accepted. Admission may be deferred for a maximum of 1 year. Credit and/or placement offered for CEEB Advanced Placement tests.

COSTS AND FINANCIAL AID

Annual tuition $17,450. Room & board $5,380. Average book expense $1,600. **Required Forms and Deadlines:** FAFSA, institution's own financial aid form. Financial aid filing deadline 3/10. **Notification of Awards:** Applicants will be notified of awards on a rolling basis beginning on or about 4/15. **Types of Aid:** *Need-based scholarships/grants:* Pell, SEOG, state scholarships/grants, private scholarships, the school's own gift aid, Federal Nursing Scholarships. *Loans:* FFEL Subsidized Stafford, FFEL Unsubsidized Stafford, FFEL PLUS, Federal Perkins, college/university loans from institutional funds. **Financial Aid Statistics:** 60% freshmen, 53% undergrads receive need-based scholarship or grant aid. 73% freshmen, 67% undergrads receive need-based self-help aid. 76 freshmen, 238 undergrads receive athletic scholarships. 76% freshmen, 73% undergrads receive any aid. Highest amount earned per year from on-campus jobs $2,000.

BETHEL COLLEGE (KS)

300 East 27th Street, North Newton, KS 67117-0531
Phone: 316-284-5230 **E-mail:** admissions@bethelks.edu **CEEB Code:** 6037
Fax: 316-284-5870 **Website:** www.bethelks.edu **ACT Code:** 1390
Financial Aid Phone: 316-284-5232

This private school, affiliated with the Mennonite Church USA, was founded in 1887. It has a 60-acre campus.

RATINGS

Admissions Selectivity Rating: 84   **Fire Safety Rating:** 70   **Green Rating:** 60*

STUDENTS AND FACULTY

Enrollment: 539. **Student Body:** 48% female, 52% male, 17% out-of-state, 7% international (18 countries represented). African American 5%, Asian 2%, Caucasian 82%, Hispanic 3%. **Retention and Graduation:** 73% freshmen return for sophomore year. 45% freshmen graduate within 4 years. **Faculty:** Student/faculty ratio 10:1. 46 full-time faculty, 65% hold PhDs. 100% faculty teach undergrads.

ACADEMICS

Degrees: Bachelor's, certificate. **Academic Requirements:** Arts/fine arts, computer literacy, English (including composition), foreign languages, history, humanities, mathematics, philosophy, sciences (biological or physical), social science, cross cultural learning. Senior capstone course focusing on basic issues of faith and life, and convocation. **Classes:** Most classes have 10–19 students. Most lab/discussion sections have 10–19 students. **Majors with Highest**

Enrollment: Nursing–registered nurse training (ASN, BSN, MSN, RN), social work, visual and performing arts. **Disciplines with Highest Percentage of Degrees Awarded:** Health professions and related sciences 30%, visual and performing arts 8%, physical sciences 7%, public administration and social services 6%, interdisciplinary studies 5%, foreign languages and literature 5%, business/marketing 5%, history 5%. **Special Study Options:** Cross-registration, double major, dual enrollment, independent study, internships, liberal arts/career combination, study abroad, teacher certification program.

FACILITIES

Housing: Coed dorms, apartments for married students, apartments for single students, special housing for disabled students. **Special Academic Facilities/Equipment:** Art gallery, natural history and midwestern/Kansas history museums, 80 acre natural history field laboratory for biological studies, Mennonite Historical Library and Archives, Institute for Peace and Conflict Resolution, observatory. **Computers:** 65% of public computers are PCs, 35% of public computers are Macs, network access in dorm rooms, online administrative functions (other than registration), remote student-access to Web through college's connection.

CAMPUS LIFE

Activities: Choral groups, concert band, dance, drama/theater, jazz band, literary magazine, music ensembles, musical theater, opera, radio station, student government, student newspaper, symphony orchestra, yearbook. **Organizations:** 28 registered organizations, 2 religious organizations. **Athletics (Intercollegiate):** *Men:* Basketball, football, golf, soccer, tennis, track/field (indoor), track/field (outdoor). *Women:* Basketball, golf, soccer, tennis, track/field (indoor), track/field (outdoor), volleyball.

ADMISSIONS

Freshman Academic Profile: 27% in top 10% of high school class, 52% in top 25% of high school class, 78% in top 50% of high school class. 93% from public high schools. SAT Math middle 50% range 440–560. SAT Critical Reading middle 50% range 450–540. ACT middle 50% range 20–27. TOEFL required of all international applicants, minimum paper TOEFL 540, minimum computer TOEFL 207. **Basis for Candidate Selection:** *Very important factors considered include:* Academic GPA, standardized test scores. *Other factors considered include:* Alumni/ae relation, application essay, character/personal qualities, class rank, interview, recommendation(s), rigor of secondary school record, talent/ability. **Freshman Admission Requirements:** High school diploma is required, and GED is accepted. *Academic units recommended:* 4 English, 4 math, 3 science, 2 foreign language, 3 social studies, 1 history, 1 computer technology. **Freshman Admission Statistics:** 357 applied, 75% admitted, 39% enrolled. **Transfer Admission Requirements:** High school transcript, college transcript(s), statement of good standing from prior institution(s). Minimum college GPA of 2.0 required. Lowest grade transferable D-. **General Admission Information:** Application fee $20. Regular notification is rolling. Nonfall registration accepted. Admission may be deferred for a maximum of 1 year. Credit and/or placement offered for CEEB Advanced Placement tests.

COSTS AND FINANCIAL AID

Required Forms and Deadlines: FAFSA. **Notification of Awards:** Applicants will be notified of awards on a rolling basis beginning on or about 2/1. *Types of Aid: Need-based scholarships/grants:* Pell, SEOG, state scholarships/grants, private scholarships, the school's own gift aid. *Loans:* FFEL Subsidized Stafford, FFEL Unsubsidized Stafford, FFEL PLUS, Federal Perkins. **Financial Aid Statistics:** 71% freshmen, 66% undergrads receive need-based scholarship or grant aid. 63% freshmen, 69% undergrads receive need-based self-help aid. 55 freshmen, 179 undergrads receive athletic scholarships. 100% freshmen, 97% undergrads receive any aid. Highest amount earned per year from on-campus jobs $4,468.

BETHEL COLLEGE (TN)

325 Cherry Avenue, McKenzie, TN 38201
Phone: 731-352-4030 **E-mail:** admissions@bethel-college.edu **CEEB Code:** 1063
Fax: 731-352-4069 **Website:** www.bethel-college.edu
Financial Aid Phone: 901-352-4007

This private school, affiliated with the Cumberland Presbyterian Church, was founded in 1842. It has a 100-acre campus.

RATINGS

Admissions Selectivity Rating: 65   **Fire Safety Rating:** 60*   **Green Rating:** 60*

STUDENTS AND FACULTY

Enrollment: 924. **Student Body:** 54% female, 46% male, 12% out-of-state. **Retention and Graduation:** 60% freshmen return for sophomore year. 13% freshmen graduate within 4 years. **Faculty:** Student/faculty ratio 14:1. 35 full-time faculty, 51% hold PhDs. 100% faculty teach undergrads.

ACADEMICS

Degrees: Bachelor's, first professional, master's. **Academic Requirements:** Arts/fine arts, computer literacy, English (including composition), history, humanities, mathematics, philosophy, sciences (biological or physical), social science. **Classes:** Most classes have 10–19 students. Most lab/discussion sections have 10–19 students. **Disciplines with Highest Percentage of Degrees Awarded:** Business/marketing 63%, education 11%, biological/life sciences 6%, English 4%, health professions and related sciences 4%, social sciences 4%, liberal arts/general studies 2%, mathematics 2%, psychology 2%. **Special Study Options:** Accelerated program, double major, internships, liberal arts/career combination, student-designed major, teacher certification program, weekend college.

FACILITIES

Housing: Men's dorms, women's dorms, special housing for international students, new dorm construction in May 2003. **Computers:** 100% of public computers are PCs, network access in dorm rooms, network access in dorm lounges, remote student-access to Web through college's connection. Undergraduates are required to own a computer.

CAMPUS LIFE

Activities: Choral groups, drama/theater, musical theater, yearbook. **Organizations:** 30 registered organizations, 1 honor society, 4 religious organizations. 4 fraternities, 4 sororities. **Athletics (Intercollegiate):** *Men:* Baseball, basketball, cheerleading, football, golf, soccer, tennis, track/field (outdoor). *Women:* Basketball, cheerleading, golf, soccer, softball, tennis, track/field (outdoor), volleyball.

ADMISSIONS

Freshman Academic Profile: 12% in top 10% of high school class, 38% in top 25% of high school class, 68% in top 50% of high school class. SAT Math middle 50% range 440–580. SAT Critical Reading middle 50% range 400–540. ACT middle 50% range 17–23. **Basis for Candidate Selection:** *Very important factors considered include:* Class rank, rigor of secondary school record, standardized test scores. *Other factors considered include:* Recommendation(s). **Freshman Admission Requirements:** High school diploma is required, and GED is accepted. *Academic units required:* 4 English, 2 math, 2 science, 2 social studies. **Freshman Admission Statistics:** 452 applied, 62% admitted, 50% enrolled. **Transfer Admission Requirements:** College transcript(s), statement of good standing from prior institution(s). Minimum college GPA of 1.5 required. Lowest grade transferable D. **General Admission Information:** Application fee $30. Regular notification, rolling upon receipt of application. Nonfall registration accepted. Admission may be deferred for a maximum of 1 year. Common Application not accepted.

COSTS AND FINANCIAL AID

Annual tuition $8,180. Room & board $4,740. Required fees $850. Average book expense $1,000. **Required Forms and Deadlines:** FAFSA; institution's own financial aid form; 1040, 1040A, 1040EZ. Financial aid filing deadline 8/21. **Notification of Awards:** Applicants will be notified of awards on a rolling basis beginning on or about 3/1. **Types of Aid:** *Need-based scholarships/grants:* Pell, SEOG, state scholarships/grants, private scholarships, the school's own gift aid. *Loans:* FFEL Subsidized Stafford, FFEL Unsubsidized Stafford, FFEL PLUS, Federal Perkins. **Student Employment:** Federal Work-Study Program available. Institutional employment available. Off-campus job opportunities are fair.

BETHEL UNIVERSITY (MN)

Office of Admissions-CAS, 3900 Bethel Drive, Saint Paul, MN 55112
Phone: 651-638-6242 **E-mail:** buadmissions-cas@bethel.edu **CEEB Code:** 6038
Fax: 651-635-1490 **Website:** www.bethel.edu **ACT Code:** 2088
Financial Aid Phone: 651-638-6241

This private school, affiliated with the Baptist Church, was founded in 1871. It has a 248-acre campus.

RATINGS

Admissions Selectivity Rating: 83   **Fire Safety Rating:** 78   **Green Rating:** 84

STUDENTS AND FACULTY

Enrollment: 3,293. **Student Body:** 61% female, 39% male, 26% out-of-state. African American 3%, Asian 3%, Caucasian 90%, Hispanic 1%. **Retention and**

Graduation: 85% freshmen return for sophomore year. 62% freshmen graduate within 4 years. **Faculty:** Student/faculty ratio 13:1. 171 full-time faculty, 81% hold PhDs. 100% faculty teach undergrads.

ACADEMICS

Degrees: Associate, bachelor's, doctoral, master's, post-bachelor's certificate, post-master's certificate. **Academic Requirements:** Arts/fine arts, English (including composition), foreign languages, humanities, mathematics, sciences (biological or physical), biblical/theological studies, health. **Classes:** Most classes have 10–19 students. Most lab/discussion sections have 10–19 students. **Majors with Highest Enrollment:** Business, management, marketing, and related support services; communications studies/speech communication and rhetoric; nursing–registered nurse training (ASN, BSN, MSN, RN). **Disciplines with Highest Percentage of Degrees Awarded:** Business/marketing 24%, health professions and related sciences 19%, education 12%, psychology 7%. **Special Study Options:** Accelerated program, double major, exchange student program (domestic), honors program, independent study, internships, student-designed major, study abroad, teacher certification program. Dual degree program for engineering science with the University of Minnesota, Case Western Reserve, and Washington University; American studies program, Washington, DC; Au Sable Inst. environmental studies program, Michigan; urban studies program, Chicago; Los Angeles Film Studies Center; New York Center for Art & Media Studies (NYCAMS).

FACILITIES

Housing: Coed dorms, apartments for single students, special housing for disabled students. **Special Academic Facilities/Equipment:** Art gallery, media center, television studio, and radio station. **Computers:** 100% of classrooms are wired, 80% of classrooms are wireless, 90% of public computers are PCs, 9% of public computers are Macs, 1% of public computers are UNIX, network access in dorm rooms, network access in dorm lounges, online registration, online administrative functions (other than registration), remote student-access to Web through college's connection.

CAMPUS LIFE

Activities: Choral groups, concert band, dance, drama/theater, jazz band, literary magazine, music ensembles, musical theater, pep band, radio station, student government, student newspaper, student-run film society, symphony orchestra. **Organizations:** 61 registered organizations, 4 honor societies, 20 religious organizations. **Athletics (Intercollegiate):** *Men:* Baseball, basketball, cross-country, football, golf, ice hockey, soccer, tennis, track/field (indoor), track/field (outdoor). *Women:* Basketball, cross-country, ice hockey, soccer, softball, tennis, track/field (indoor), track/field (outdoor), volleyball.

ADMISSIONS

Freshman Academic Profile: 29% in top 10% of high school class, 54% in top 25% of high school class, 83% in top 50% of high school class. SAT Math middle 50% range 510–650. SAT Critical Reading middle 50% range 500–650. ACT middle 50% range 22–28. TOEFL required of all international applicants, minimum paper TOEFL 525, minimum computer TOEFL 195. **Basis for Candidate Selection:** *Important factors considered include:* Academic GPA, application essay, character/personal qualities, class rank, religious affiliation/commitment, rigor of secondary school record, standardized test scores. *Other factors considered include:* Alumni/ae relation, extracurricular activities, first generation, geographical residence, interview, level of applicant's interest, racial/ethnic status, recommendation(s), state residency, talent/ability, volunteer work. **Freshman Admission Requirements:** High school diploma is required, and GED is accepted. *Academic units recommended:* 4 English, 3 math, 3 science (3 science labs), 2 foreign language, 4 social studies, 2 history. **Freshman Admission Statistics:** 1,637 applied, 85% admitted, 48% enrolled. **Transfer Admission Requirements:** College transcript(s), essay or personal statement, minimum college GPA of 2.5 required. Lowest grade transferable C. **General Admission Information:** Application fee $25. Regular application deadline 8/1. Regular notification is rolling. Nonfall registration accepted. Admission may be deferred for a maximum of 1 year. Credit and/or placement offered for CEEB Advanced Placement tests.

COSTS AND FINANCIAL AID

Required Forms and Deadlines: FAFSA, institution's own financial aid form, non-need applicants do not need to submit FAFSA. Financial aid filing deadline 4/15. **Notification of Awards:** Applicants will be notified of awards on a rolling basis beginning on or about 3/1. **Types of Aid:** *Need-based scholarships/grants:* Pell, SEOG, state scholarships/grants, private scholarships, the school's own gift aid. *Loans:* FFEL Subsidized Stafford, FFEL Unsubsidized Stafford, FFEL PLUS, Federal Perkins, state loans. **Student Employment:** Federal Work-Study Program available. Institutional employment available. Off-campus job opportunities are excellent. **Financial Aid Statistics:** 66% freshmen, 65% undergrads receive need-based scholarship or grant aid. 59% freshmen, 60% undergrads receive need-based self-help aid. 95% freshmen, 94% undergrads receive any aid. Highest amount earned per year from on-campus jobs $2,200.

BETHUNE-COOKMAN COLLEGE

640 Dr. Mary McLeod Bethune Boulevard, Daytona Beach, FL 32114-3099
Phone: 386-481-2600 **E-mail:** admissions@cookman.edu **CEEB Code:** 5061
Fax: 386-481-2601 **Website:** www.bethune.cookman.edu **ACT Code:** 0720
Financial Aid Phone: 386-481-2626

This private school, affiliated with the Methodist Church, was founded in 1904. It has a 78-acre campus.

RATINGS

Admissions Selectivity Rating: 66   **Fire Safety Rating:** 60*   **Green Rating:** 60*

STUDENTS AND FACULTY

Enrollment: 3,093. **Student Body:** 58% female, 42% male, 30% out-of-state, 3% international (25 countries represented). African American 91%, Caucasian 1%, Hispanic 2%. **Retention and Graduation:** 69% freshmen return for sophomore year. 13% freshmen graduate within 4 years. 28% grads go on to further study within 1 year. 12% grads pursue arts and sciences degrees. 14% grads pursue business degrees. 1% grads pursue law degrees. 1% grads pursue medical degrees. **Faculty:** Student/faculty ratio 17:1. 161 full-time faculty, 57% hold PhDs. 100% faculty teach undergrads.

ACADEMICS

Degrees: Bachelor's, master's. **Academic Requirements:** Arts/fine arts, computer literacy, English (including composition), foreign languages, history, humanities, mathematics, philosophy, sciences (biological or physical), social science. **Classes:** Most classes have 20–29 students. Most lab/discussion sections have fewer than 10 students. **Majors with Highest Enrollment:** Business administration/management, corrections and criminal justice, elementary education and teaching. **Disciplines with Highest Percentage of Degrees Awarded:** Education 21%, business/marketing 19%, security and protective services 12%, health professions and related sciences 9%, social sciences 8%. **Special Study Options:** Accelerated program, distance learning, double major, honors program, independent study, internships, study abroad, teacher certification program, weekend college.

FACILITIES

Housing: Men's dorms, women's dorms, scholarship housing. **Special Academic Facilities/Equipment:** Historic archives, founder's home and gravesite (historic landmark), outreach center, telecommunications satellite network, art gallery/studio, audiologic recording studio, observatory. **Computers:** 80% of classrooms are wired, 80% of classrooms are wireless, 95% of public computers are PCs, 5% of public computers are Macs, 5% of public computers are UNIX, network access in dorm rooms, network access in dorm lounges, online registration, online administrative functions (other than registration), support for handheld computing, remote student-access to Web through college's connection.

CAMPUS LIFE

Activities: Choral groups, concert band, drama/theater, jazz band, marching band, music ensembles, radio station, student government, student newspaper, yearbook. **Organizations:** 40 registered organizations, 9 honor societies, 2 religious organizations. 5 fraternities (3% men join), 4 sororities (5% women join). **Athletics (Intercollegiate):** *Men:* Baseball, basketball, cross-country, football, golf, tennis, track/field (indoor), track/field (outdoor). *Women:* Basketball, cross-country, golf, softball, tennis, track/field (indoor), track/field (outdoor), volleyball.

ADMISSIONS

Freshman Academic Profile: 5% in top 10% of high school class, 15% in top 25% of high school class, 48% in top 50% of high school class. 90% from public high schools. SAT Math middle 50% range 360–460. SAT Critical Reading middle 50% range 360–460. ACT middle 50% range 14–18. TOEFL required of all international applicants, minimum paper TOEFL 550, minimum computer TOEFL 213. **Basis for Candidate Selection:** *Very important factors considered include:* Academic GPA, rigor of secondary school record, standardized test scores. *Important factors considered include:* Character/personal qualities, recommendation(s). *Other factors considered include:* Alumni/ae relation, application essay, class rank, extracurricular activities, first generation, interview, level of applicant's interest, talent/ability, volunteer work, work experience. **Freshman Admission Requirements:** High school diploma is required, and GED is accepted. *Academic units required:* 4 English, 3 math, 3 science (1 science lab), 1 social studies, 2 history, 6 academic electives. *Academic units recommended:* 2 foreign language, 1 computer literacy. **Freshman Admission Statistics:** 4,129 applied, 78% admitted, 28% enrolled. **Transfer Admission Requirements:** College transcript(s), essay or personal statement, statement of good standing from prior institution(s). Minimum college GPA of 2.2 required. Lowest grade transferable C. **General Admission Information:** Application fee $25. Regular notification immediately after evaluation. Nonfall registration accepted. Admission may be deferred for a maximum of 1 year. Credit offered for CEEB Advanced Placement tests.

COSTS AND FINANCIAL AID
Annual tuition $11,792. Room and board $7,206. Average book expense $850. **Required Forms and Deadlines:** FAFSA. Financial aid filing deadline 4/1. **Notification of Awards:** Applicants will be notified of awards on a rolling basis beginning on or about 4/1. **Types of Aid:** *Need-based scholarships/grants:* Pell, SEOG, state scholarships/grants, private scholarships, the school's own gift aid, United Negro College Fund, Federal Nursing Scholarships. *Loans:* Direct Subsidized Stafford, Direct Unsubsidized Stafford, Direct PLUS, FFEL Subsidized Stafford, FFEL Unsubsidized Stafford, FFEL PLUS. **Student Employment:** Federal Work-Study Program available. Institutional employment available. Off-campus job opportunities are good. **Financial Aid Statistics:** 76% freshmen, 71% undergrads receive need-based scholarship or grant aid. 84% freshmen, 79% undergrads receive need-based self-help aid. 72 freshmen, 253 undergrads receive athletic scholarships. 94% freshmen, 93% undergrads receive any aid. Highest amount earned per year from on-campus jobs $2,500.

BEULAH HEIGHTS BIBLE COLLEGE

892 Berne Street SE, PO Box 18145, Atlanta, GA 30316
Phone: 404-627-2681 **E-mail:** admissions@beulah.org
Fax: 404-627-0702 **Website:** www.beulah.org **ACT Code:** 0842
Financial Aid Phone: 404-627-2681

This private school, affiliated with the Pentecostal Church, was founded in 1918. It has a 5-acre campus.

RATINGS
Admissions Selectivity Rating: 60*   **Fire Safety Rating:** 60*   **Green Rating:** 60*

STUDENTS AND FACULTY
Enrollment: 557. **Student Body:** 56% female, 44% male, 13% international. African American 24%, Caucasian 2%. **Retention and Graduation:** 47% freshmen graduate within 4 years. 58% grads go on to further study within 1 year. 4% grads pursue arts and sciences degrees. 4% grads pursue business degrees. **Faculty:** Student/faculty ratio 10:1. 28 full-time faculty, 21% hold PhDs. 100% faculty teach undergrads.

ACADEMICS
Degrees: Associate, bachelor's, certificate, diploma. **Academic Requirements:** Arts/fine arts, English (including composition), history, humanities, mathematics, sciences (biological or physical), social science. **Classes:** Most classes have fewer than 10 students. **Special Study Options:** Distance learning, double major, English as a Second Language (ESL), independent study, internships.

FACILITIES
Housing: Men's dorms, women's dorms, apartments for married students, apartments for single students. **Computers:** 25% of public computers are PCs, online administrative functions (other than registration), remote student-access to Web through college's connection.

CAMPUS LIFE
Activities: Student government. **Organizations:** 2 registered organizations, 2 honor societies.

ADMISSIONS
Freshman Academic Profile: 100% from public high schools. TOEFL required of all international applicants, minimum paper TOEFL 480, minimum computer TOEFL 480. **Basis for Candidate Selection:** *Important factors considered include:* Character/personal qualities, interview. *Other factors considered include:* Application essay, extracurricular activities, recommendation(s), rigor of secondary school record, standardized test scores, talent/ability. **Freshman Admission Requirements:** High school diploma is required, and GED is accepted. **Freshman Admission Statistics:** 41 applied, 92% enrolled. **Transfer Admission Requirements:** High school transcript, college transcript(s), essay or personal statement, interview, statement of good standing from prior institution(s). Minimum college GPA of 2.0 required. Lowest grade transferable C. **General Admission Information:** Application fee $20. Regular application deadline 7/10. Regular notification on a rolling basis-no beginning date. Nonfall registration accepted. Common Application not accepted. Neither credit nor placement offered for CEEB Advanced Placement tests.

COSTS AND FINANCIAL AID
Annual tuition $3,600. Room & board $3,600. Required fees $3,600. Average book expense $200. **Required Forms and Deadlines:** FAFSA, institution's own financial aid form. Financial aid filing deadline 6/30. **Notification of Awards:** Applicants will be notified of awards on or about 7/30. **Types of Aid:** *Need-based scholarships/grants:* Pell, SEOG. *Loans:* FFEL Subsidized Stafford, FFEL Unsubsidized Stafford, FFEL PLUS. **Student Employment:** Federal Work-Study Program available. Institutional employment available. Off-campus job opportunities are good. **Financial Aid Statistics:** 2% freshmen, 42% undergrads receive need-based scholarship or grant aid. 2% freshmen, 47% undergrads receive need-based self-help aid.

BIOLA UNIVERSITY

13800 Biola Avenue, La Mirada, CA 90639
Phone: 562-903-4752 **E-mail:** admissions@biola.edu **CEEB Code:** 4017
Fax: 562-903-4709 **Website:** www.biola.edu **ACT Code:** 0172
Financial Aid Phone: 562-903-4752

This private school, affiliated with the Christian (Nondenominational) Church, was founded in 1908. It has a 95-acre campus.

RATINGS
Admissions Selectivity Rating: 60*   **Fire Safety Rating:** 84   **Green Rating:** 63

STUDENTS AND FACULTY
Enrollment: 3,922. **Student Body:** 60% female, 40% male, 25% out-of-state. **Retention and Graduation:** 86% freshmen return for sophomore year. 51% freshmen graduate within 4 years. **Faculty:** Student/faculty ratio 17:1. 201 full-time faculty, 73% hold PhDs. 100% faculty teach undergrads.

ACADEMICS
Degrees: Bachelor's, doctoral, first professional, master's, post-master's certificate. **Academic Requirements:** Arts/fine arts, English (including composition), foreign languages, history, mathematics, philosophy, sciences (biological or physical), social science, communication, physical education, biblical studies. **Classes:** Most classes have 10–19 students. Most lab/discussion sections have 10–19 students. **Majors with Highest Enrollment:** Business administration/management, elementary education and teaching, psychology. **Disciplines with Highest Percentage of Degrees Awarded:** Business/marketing 26%, theology and religious vocations 14%, communications/journalism 11%, education 9%, visual and performing arts 9%. **Special Study Options:** Double major, English as a Second Language (ESL), exchange student program (domestic), honors program, internships, study abroad.

FACILITIES
Housing: Coed dorms, men's dorms, women's dorms, apartments for married students, apartments for single students, special housing for disabled students, flex style dorms—separate floors and wings for specific genders, off campus apartments, on campus apartments. **Special Academic Facilities/Equipment:** Art gallery, electron microscope, TV production facility, film editing facility, media center, writing center, student ministry union, and tutoring services. **Computers:** 90% of classrooms are wired, 5% of classrooms are wireless, 75% of public computers are PCs, 25% of public computers are Macs, network access in dorm rooms, network access in dorm lounges, online registration, online administrative functions (other than registration), remote student-access to Web through college's connection.

CAMPUS LIFE
Activities: Choral groups, concert band, drama/theater, jazz band, music ensembles, musical theater, opera, radio station, student government, student newspaper, student-run film society, symphony orchestra, television station, yearbook. **Organizations:** 33 registered organizations, 2 honor societies. **Athletics (Intercollegiate):** *Men:* Baseball, basketball, cross-country, golf, soccer, swimming, tennis, track/field (outdoor). *Women:* Basketball, cross-country, golf, soccer, softball, swimming, tennis, track/field (outdoor), volleyball.

ADMISSIONS
Freshman Academic Profile: SAT Math middle 50% range 490–620. SAT Critical Reading middle 50% range 500–620. SAT Writing middle 50% range 500–610. ACT middle 50% range 21–26. TOEFL required of all international applicants, minimum paper TOEFL 500, minimum computer TOEFL 173. **Basis for Candidate Selection:** *Very important factors considered include:* Academic GPA, application essay, character/personal qualities, recommendation(s), religious affiliation/commitment, standardized test scores. *Important factors considered include:* Extracurricular activities, interview, rigor of secondary school record. *Other factors considered include:* Alumni/ae

relation, class rank, first generation, geographical residence, level of applicant's interest, state residency, volunteer work, work experience. **Freshman Admission Requirements:** High school diploma is required, and GED is accepted. *Academic units recommended:* 4 English, 3 math, 2 science, 4 foreign language, 2 social studies, 1 history. **Freshman Admission Statistics:** 2,287 applied, 80% admitted, 44% enrolled. **Transfer Admission Requirements:** High school transcript, college transcript(s), essay or personal statement, statement of good standing from prior institution(s). Minimum college GPA of 2.0 required. Lowest grade transferable C. **General Admission Information:** Application fee $45. Regular application deadline 3/1. Regular notification 4/1. Nonfall registration not accepted. Admission may be deferred for a maximum of 2 years. Credit offered for CEEB Advanced Placement tests.

COSTS AND FINANCIAL AID

Annual tuition $23,782. Room and board $7,410. Average book expense $1,314. **Required Forms and Deadlines:** FAFSA, state aid form. **Notification of Awards:** Applicants will be notified of awards on a rolling basis beginning on or about 3/1. **Types of Aid:** *Need-based scholarships/grants:* Pell, SEOG, state scholarships/grants, private scholarships, the school's own gift aid. *Loans:* FFEL Subsidized Stafford, FFEL Unsubsidized Stafford, FFEL PLUS, Federal Perkins, Federal Nursing, college/university loans from institutional funds. **Financial Aid Statistics:** 56% freshmen, 52% undergrads receive need-based scholarship or grant aid. 69% freshmen, 64% undergrads receive need-based self-help aid. 14 freshmen, 78 undergrads receive athletic scholarships. 89% freshmen, 96% undergrads receive any aid. Highest amount earned per year from on-campus jobs $2,000.

BIRMINGHAM-SOUTHERN COLLEGE

Box 549008, Birmingham, AL 35254
Phone: 205-226-4696 **E-mail:** admission@bsc.edu **CEEB Code:** 1064
Fax: 205-226-3074 **Website:** www.bsc.edu **ACT Code:** 0012
Financial Aid Phone: 205-226-4688

This private school, affiliated with the Methodist Church, was founded in 1856. It has a 196-acre campus.

RATINGS
Admissions Selectivity Rating: 88   **Fire Safety Rating:** 98   **Green Rating:** 84

STUDENTS AND FACULTY
Enrollment: 1,207. **Student Body:** 59% female, 41% male, 27% out-of-state. African American 8%, Asian 3%, Caucasian 86%, Hispanic 1%. **Retention and Graduation:** 86% freshmen return for sophomore year. 60% freshmen graduate within 4 years. 65% grads go on to further study within 1 year. 19% grads pursue arts and sciences degrees. 2% grads pursue business degrees. 7% grads pursue law degrees. 10% grads pursue medical degrees. **Faculty:** Student/faculty ratio 10:1. 103 full-time faculty, 96% hold PhDs. 100% faculty teach undergrads.

ACADEMICS
Degrees: Bachelor's, master's. **Academic Requirements:** Arts/fine arts, computer literacy, English (including composition), foreign languages, history, humanities, mathematics, philosophy, sciences (biological or physical), social science. **Classes:** Most classes have 10–19 students. Most lab/discussion sections have 10–19 students. **Majors with Highest Enrollment:** Business administration/management; health/medical preparatory programs. **Disciplines with Special Study Options:** Cooperative education program, cross-registration, double major, dual enrollment, exchange student program (domestic), honor program, independent study, internships, student-designed major, study abroad, teacher certification program.

FACILITIES
Housing: Men's dorms, women's dorms, apartments for married students, apartments for single students, special housing for disabled students, fraternity/sorority housing. **Special Academic Facilities/Equipment:** Theater, planetarium, environmental center (hands-on, interactive museum for ecology education), ecosite(outdoor ecology education), ropes course for leadership training. **Computers:** 1% of classrooms are wired, 1% of classrooms are wireless, 100% of public computers are PCs, network access in dorm rooms,

network access in dorm lounges, online administrative functions (other than registration), remote student-access to Web through college's connection.

CAMPUS LIFE
Activities: Choral groups, dance, drama/theater, jazz band, literary magazine, music ensembles, musical theater, opera, pep band, student government, student newspaper, yearbook. **Organizations:** 70 registered organizations, 20 honor societies, 5 religious organizations. 6 fraternities (51% men join), 7 sororities (50% women join). **Athletics (Intercollegiate):** *Men:* Baseball, basketball, cheerleading, cross-country, golf, soccer, tennis. *Women:* Basketball, cheerleading, cross-country, golf, riflery, soccer, softball, tennis, volleyball. **Environmental Initiatives:** Implemented bike share program with 100 bikes for campus use at no charge to students/faculty/staff. The Southern Environmental Center (SEC) is the largest educational facility of its kind in Alabama. In addition to its award winning interactive museum and Ecoscape Gardens, the SEC is also active in the community. Annually, 15,000 school children visit the center. Building an Urban Environmental Park that will serve as both a place of recreation for students, as well as an academic laboratory for the study of environmental issues.

ADMISSIONS
Freshman Academic Profile: 34% in top 10% of high school class, 64% in top 25% of high school class, 84% in top 50% of high school class. 65% from public high schools. SAT Math middle 50% range 520–630. SAT Critical Reading middle 50% range 530–660. SAT Writing middle 50% range 520–650. ACT middle 50% range 23–28. TOEFL required of all international applicants, minimum paper TOEFL 500, minimum computer TOEFL 173. **Basis for Candidate Selection:** *Very important factors considered include:* Academic GPA, application essay, recommendation(s), rigor of secondary school record, standardized test scores. *Important factors considered include:* Character/personal qualities, level of applicant's interest. *Other factors considered include:* Extracurricular activities, interview, talent/ability, volunteer work, work experience. **Freshman Admission Requirements:** High school diploma is required, and GED is accepted. *Academic units required:* 4 English. *Academic units recommended:* 4 math, 4 science (2 science labs), 2 foreign language, 2 social studies, 2 history, 10 academic electives. **Freshman Admission Statistics:** 2,198 applied, 57% admitted, 23% enrolled. **Transfer Admission Requirements:** High school transcript, college transcript(s), essay or personal statement, standardized test score, statement of good standing from prior institution(s). Minimum college GPA of 2.0 required. Lowest grade transferable D. **General Admission Information:** Application fee $25. Regular notification is rolling. Nonfall registration accepted. Admission may be deferred for a maximum of 1 year. Credit and/or placement offered for CEEB Advanced Placement tests.

COSTS AND FINANCIAL AID
Annual tuition $23,600. Room and board $8,273. Required fees $700. Average book expense $1,000. **Required Forms and Deadlines:** FAFSA. Financial aid filing deadline 3/1. **Notification of Awards:** Applicants will be notified of awards on or about 3/1. **Types of Aid:** *Need-based scholarships/grants:* Pell, SEOG, private scholarships, the school's own gift aid, United Negro College Fund. *Loans:* FFEL Subsidized Stafford, FFEL Unsubsidized Stafford, FFEL PLUS, Federal Perkins. **Financial Aid Statistics:** 34% freshmen, 26% undergrads receive need-based scholarship or grant aid. 34% freshmen, 28% undergrads receive need-based self-help aid. 45 freshmen, 149 undergrads receive athletic scholarships. 95% freshmen, 95% undergrads receive any aid. Highest amount earned per year from on-campus jobs $1,200.

BISHOP'S UNIVERSITY

2600 College Street, Sherbrooke, QC J1M0C8, Canada
Phone: 819-822-9600 **E-mail:** admission@ubishops.ca
Fax: 819-822-9616 **Website:** www.ubishops.ca
Financial Aid Phone: 819-822-9600

This public school was founded in 1843. It has a 550-acre campus.

RATINGS
Admissions Selectivity Rating: 60*   **Fire Safety Rating:** 60*   **Green Rating:** 60*

STUDENTS AND FACULTY
Retention and Graduation: 78% freshmen return for sophomore year. 57% freshmen graduate within 4 years. 50% grads go on to further study within 1 year. **Faculty:** Student/faculty ratio 12:1. 120 full-time faculty, 68% hold PhDs. 100% faculty teach undergrads.

ACADEMICS

Degrees: Bachelor's, certificate, master's. **Academic Requirements:** English (including composition). **Classes:** Most classes have 10–19 students. Most lab/discussion sections have 10–19 students. **Majors with Highest Enrollment:** Business administration/management, education. **Disciplines with Highest Percentage of Degrees Awarded:** Business/marketing 23%, social sciences 22%, education 13%, psychology 9%, computer and information sciences 8%. **Special Study Options:** Double major, English as a Second Language (ESL), exchange student program (domestic), honors program, independent study, liberal arts/career combination, student-designed major, study abroad, teacher certification program.

FACILITIES

Housing: Coed dorms, women's dorms, special housing for disabled students. **Special Academic Facilities/Equipment:** Eastern Townships Research Centre, Cormier Economics Centre, Dobson-Lagasse Entreprenneurship Centre, Molson Fine Arts Building, art gallery. **Computers:** 97% of public computers are PCs, 3% of public computers are Macs, network access in dorm rooms, online registration, online administrative functions (other than registration), remote student-access to Web through college's connection.

CAMPUS LIFE

Activities: Choral groups, concert band, dance, drama/theater, jazz band, literary magazine, music ensembles, musical theater, radio station, student government, student newspaper, yearbook. **Organizations:** 60 registered organizations, 2 religious organizations. **Athletics (Intercollegiate):** *Men:* Basketball, football, golf, rugby, skiing (downhill/alpine). *Women:* Basketball, rugby, skiing (downhill/alpine), soccer.

ADMISSIONS

Freshman Academic Profile: 100% in top 50% of high school class. TOEFL required of all international applicants, minimum paper TOEFL 550, minimum computer TOEFL 213. **Basis for Candidate Selection:** *Very important factors considered include:* Rigor of secondary school record. *Important factors considered include:* Standardized test scores. *Other factors considered include:* Application essay, character/personal qualities, class rank, extracurricular activities, recommendation(s), talent/ability, volunteer work. **Freshman Admission Requirements:** High school diploma is required, and GED is accepted. **Freshman Admission Statistics:** 1,569 applied, 82% admitted, 9% enrolled. **Transfer Admission Requirements:** College transcript(s). **Admission Information:** Application fee $55. Regular notification is rolling. Nonfall registration accepted. Admission may be deferred for a maximum of 1 year. Common Application accepted. Credit offered for CEEB Advanced Placement tests.

COSTS AND FINANCIAL AID

Annual in-state tuition $1,668. Annual out-of-state tuition $3,438. Room and board $4,000. Required fees $525. Average book expense $625. **Student Employment:** Off-campus job opportunities are good.

BISMARCK STATE COLLEGE

PO Box 5587, Attn: Admissions, Bismarck, ND 58506
Phone: 701-224-5429 **E-mail:** gabriel@gwmail.nodak.edu
Fax: 701-224-5643 **Website:** www.bismarckstate.com **ACT Code:** 3196
Financial Aid Phone: 701-224-5494

This public school was founded in 1939.

RATINGS

Admissions Selectivity Rating: 60*   **Fire Safety Rating:** 60*   **Green Rating:** 60*

STUDENTS AND FACULTY

Enrollment: 2,594. **Student Body:** 51% female, 49% male. Caucasian 38%.

ACADEMICS

Degrees: Associate, certificate, diploma, terminal. **Special Study Options:** Cooperative education program, distance learning, dual enrollment.

FACILITIES

Housing: Men's dorms, women's dorms, apartments for married students. **Computers:** Online registration.

CAMPUS LIFE

Activities: Choral groups, drama/theater, jazz band, music ensembles, student government, student newspaper. **Organizations:** 1 honor society, 1 religious organization. **Athletics (Intercollegiate):** *Men:* Baseball, basketball. *Women:* Basketball, volleyball.

ADMISSIONS

Freshman Academic Profile: ACT middle 50% range 17–22. TOEFL required of all international applicants, minimum paper TOEFL 525. **Freshman Admission Requirements:** High school diploma is required, and GED is accepted. **Transfer Admission Requirements:** College transcript(s), statement of good standing from prior institution(s). Lowest grade transferable D. **General Admission Information:** Application fee $25. Nonfall registration accepted.

COSTS AND FINANCIAL AID

Annual in-state tuition $1,888. Average book expense $630. **Types of Aid:** *Need-based scholarships/grants:* Pell, SEOG, state scholarships/grants, private scholarships, the school's own gift aid. *Loans:* FFEL Subsidized Stafford, FFEL Unsubsidized Stafford, FFEL PLUS, Federal Perkins, state loans.

BLACK HILLS STATE UNIVERSITY

1200 University Street Unit 9502, Spearfish, SD 57799-9502
Phone: 605-642-6343 **E-mail:** admissions@bhsu.edu **CEEB Code:** 6042
Fax: 605-642-6254 **Website:** www.bhsu.edu **ACT Code:** 3904
Financial Aid Phone: 605-642-6254

This public school was founded in 1883. It has a 123-acre campus.

RATINGS

Admissions Selectivity Rating: 67   **Fire Safety Rating:** 60*   **Green Rating:** 60*

STUDENTS AND FACULTY

Enrollment: 3,166. **Student Body:** 63% female, 37% male, 18% out-of-state. Caucasian 88%, Hispanic 1%, Native American 3%. **Retention and Graduation:** 54% freshmen return for sophomore year. 9% freshmen graduate within 4 years. 20% grads go on to further study within 1 year. 1% grads pursue arts and sciences degrees. 2% grads pursue business degrees. 2% grads pursue law degrees. 2% grads pursue medical degrees. **Faculty:** Student/faculty ratio 22:1. 115 full-time faculty, 77% hold PhDs. 100% faculty teach undergrads.

ACADEMICS

Degrees: Associate, bachelor's, master's, post-bachelor's certificate. **Academic Requirements:** Arts/fine arts, computer literacy, English (including composition), history, humanities, mathematics, sciences (biological or physical), social science. **Classes:** Most classes have 20–29 students. Most lab/discussion sections have 20–29 students. **Disciplines with Highest Percentage of Degrees Awarded:** Education 28%, business/marketing 24%, social sciences 11%, psychology 7%, communication technologies 6%. **Special Study Options:** Cooperative education program, distance learning, double major, dual enrollment, honors program, independent study, internships, teacher certification program.

FACILITIES

Housing: Coed dorms, men's dorms, women's dorms, apartments for married students, apartments for single students. **Special Academic Facilities/Equipment:** Art galleries, museum collections, Western historical studies library, center for Indian studies, center for advancement and study of tourism, small business institute, center of excellence for math and science education. **Computers:** 100% of public computers are PCs, network access in dorm rooms, network access in dorm lounges, online registration.

CAMPUS LIFE

Activities: Choral groups, concert band, drama/theater, jazz band, music ensembles, pep band, radio station, student government, student newspaper, television station. **Organizations:** 60 registered organizations, 5 honor societies, 3 religious organizations. 1 fraternity, 1 sorority. **Athletics (Intercollegiate):** *Men:* Basketball, cross-country, football, track/field (indoor), track/field (outdoor). *Women:* Basketball, cross-country, track/field (indoor), track/field (outdoor), volleyball.

ADMISSIONS

Freshman Academic Profile: 6% in top 10% of high school class, 23% in top 25% of high school class, 56% in top 50% of high school class. ACT middle 50% range 18–23. TOEFL required of all international applicants, minimum paper TOEFL 520. **Basis for Candidate Selection:** *Very important factors considered include:* Class rank, rigor of secondary school record, standardized test scores. *Other factors considered include:* Character/personal qualities, extracurricular activities, talent/ability. **Freshman Admission Requirements:** High school diploma is required, and GED is accepted. *Academic units required:* 4 English, 3 math, 3 science (3 science labs), 3 social studies, 1 fine arts. **Freshman Admission Statistics:** 1,424 applied, 49% admitted, 94% enrolled. **Transfer Admission Requirements:** High school transcript, college transcript(s), minimum college GPA of 2.0 required. Lowest grade transferable D. **General Admission Information:** Application fee $20. Nonfall registration accepted. Common Application accepted. Credit and/or placement offered for CEEB Advanced Placement tests.

COSTS AND FINANCIAL AID

Annual in-state tuition $2,382. Annual out-of-state tuition $8,074. Room and board $4,667. Required fees $2,619. Average book expense $800. **Required Forms and Deadlines:** FAFSA. Financial aid filing deadline 3/1. **Notification of Awards:** Applicants will be notified of awards on or about 5/15. **Types of Aid:** *Need-based scholarships/grants:* Pell, SEOG, state scholarships/grants, private scholarships, the school's own gift aid. *Loans:* FFEL Subsidized Stafford, FFEL Unsubsidized Stafford, FFEL PLUS, Federal Perkins. Highest amount earned per year from on-campus jobs $1,700.

BLACKBURN COLLEGE

700 College Avenue, Carlinville, IL 62626
Phone: 217-854-3231 **CEEB Code:** 1065
Fax: 217-854-3713 **Website:** www.blackburn.edu **ACT Code:** 0958
Financial Aid Phone: 217-854-3231

This private school was founded in 1837. It has an 80-acre campus.

RATINGS

Admissions Selectivity Rating: 60*   **Fire Safety Rating:** 60*   **Green Rating:** 60*

STUDENTS AND FACULTY

Student Body: 34% out-of-state. **Retention and Graduation:** 14% grads go on to further study within 1 year. 10% grads pursue arts and sciences degrees. 2% grads pursue business degrees. 1% grads pursue law degrees. 1% grads pursue medical degrees.

ACADEMICS

Degrees: Bachelor's. **Special Study Options:** Study abroad, Washington, DC, student-managed mandatory work program.

FACILITIES

Housing: Coed dorms, apartments for single students. **Special Academic Facilities/Equipment:** Electron microscope.

CAMPUS LIFE

Activities: Student government, student newspaper, yearbook. **Organizations:** 15 registered organizations, 2 honor societies, 1 religious organization. **Athletics (Intercollegiate):** *Men:* Baseball, basketball, cross-country, football, golf, soccer, volleyball. *Women:* Basketball, cross-country, softball, swimming, tennis, track/field (outdoor), volleyball.

ADMISSIONS

Freshman Academic Profile: 25% in top 10% of high school class, 55% in top 25% of high school class, 82% in top 50% of high school class. 85% from public high schools. Minimum paper TOEFL 500. **Freshman Admission Requirements:** High school diploma is required, and GED is accepted. *Academic units recommended:* 4 English, 2 math, 2 science, 2 foreign language, 2 social studies. **Transfer Admission Requirements:** Minimum college GPA of 2.0 required. Lowest grade transferable C. **General Admission Information:** Regular application deadline is rolling. Regular notification rolling. Nonfall registration accepted. Common Application not accepted. Credit and/or placement offered for CEEB Advanced Placement tests.

COSTS AND FINANCIAL AID

Annual tuition $7,795. Room & board $3,240. Average book expense $500. **Required Forms and Deadlines:** FAFSA. **Types of Aid:** *Need-based scholarships/grants:* State scholarships/grants. *Loans:* FFEL Subsidized Stafford, FFEL PLUS. **Student Employment:** Off-campus job opportunities are good.

BLESSING-RIEMAN COLLEGE OF NURSING

Broadway at 11th Street, PO Box 7005, Quincy, IL 62305-7005
Phone: 217-228-5520 **E-mail:** hmutter@blessinghospital.com
Fax: 217-223-4661 **Website:** www.brcn.edu **ACT Code:** 0956
Financial Aid Phone: 217-228-5520

This private school was founded in 1891. It has a 1-acre campus.

RATINGS

Admissions Selectivity Rating: 90   **Fire Safety Rating:** 60*   **Green Rating:** 60*

STUDENTS AND FACULTY

Enrollment: 177. **Student Body:** 97% female, 3% male, 28% out-of-state. African American 2%, Caucasian 84%, Hispanic 1%. **Retention and Graduation:** 76% freshmen return for sophomore year. 47% freshmen graduate within 4 years. **Faculty:** Student/faculty ratio 9:1. 13 full-time faculty, 31% hold PhDs. 100% faculty teach undergrads.

ACADEMICS

Degrees: Bachelor's. **Academic Requirements:** Arts/fine arts, computer literacy, English (including composition), history, humanities, mathematics, philosophy, sciences (biological or physical), social science. **Classes:** Most classes have 10–19 students. Most lab/discussion sections have fewer than 10 students. **Disciplines with Highest Percentage of Degrees Awarded:** Health professions and related sciences 100%. **Special Study Options:** Double major.

FACILITIES

Housing: Apartments for single students, men's and women's dormitories available at Culver-Stockton College and Quincy University. **Computers:** 100% of public computers are PCs, network access in dorm lounges, remote student-access to Web through college's connection.

CAMPUS LIFE

Activities: Student government. **Organizations:** 1 registered organization, 1 honor society.

ADMISSIONS

Freshman Academic Profile: 20% in top 10% of high school class, 97% in top 25% of high school class, 100% in top 50% of high school class. 89% from public high schools. ACT middle 50% range 22–27. TOEFL required of all international applicants, minimum paper TOEFL 550. **Basis for Candidate Selection:** *Very important factors considered include:* Class rank, rigor of secondary school record, standardized test scores. **Freshman Admission Requirements:** High school diploma is required, and GED is accepted. *Academic units required:* 4 English, 2 math, 3 science (2 science labs), 3 social studies. **Freshman Admission Statistics:** 153 applied, 50% admitted, 34% enrolled. **Transfer Admission Requirements:** High school transcript, college transcript(s), minimum college GPA of 2.0 required. Lowest grade transferable C. **General Admission Information:** Regular notification is rolling. Nonfall registration accepted. Common Application not accepted.

COSTS AND FINANCIAL AID

Annual tuition $11,200. Room & board $4,975. Required fees $300. Average book expense $800. **Required Forms and Deadlines:** FAFSA. **Notification of Awards:** Applicants will be notified of awards on a rolling basis beginning on or about 9/1. **Types of Aid:** *Need-based scholarships/grants:* Pell, state scholarships/grants, Federal Nursing Scholarships. *Loans:* FFEL Subsidized Stafford, FFEL Unsubsidized Stafford, FFEL PLUS, Federal Nursing, college/university loans from institutional funds. **Student Employment:** Institutional employment available. Off-campus job opportunities are excellent. **Financial Aid Statistics:** 94% undergrads receive need-based scholarship or grant aid. 40% undergrads receive need-based self-help aid.

BLOOMFIELD COLLEGE

1 Park Place, Bloomfield, NJ 07003
Phone: 973-748-9000 **E-mail:** admission@bloomfield.edu **CEEB Code:** 2044
Fax: 973-748-0916 **Website:** www.bloomfield.edu **ACT Code:** 2540
Financial Aid Phone: .973-748-9000

This private school, affiliated with the Presbyterian Church, was founded in 1868. It has a 12-acre campus.

RATINGS
Admissions Selectivity Rating: 71 **Fire Safety Rating:** 82 **Green Rating:** 67

STUDENTS AND FACULTY
Enrollment: 2,041. **Student Body:** 67% female, 33% male, 4% out-of-state, 2% international (20 countries represented). African American 51%, Asian 5%, Caucasian 16%, Hispanic 18%. **Retention and Graduation:** 63% freshmen return for sophomore year. 11% freshmen graduate within 4 years. 12% grads go on to further study within 1 year. **Faculty:** Student/faculty ratio 14:1. 69 full-time faculty, 74% hold PhDs. 100% faculty teach undergrads.

ACADEMICS
Degrees: Bachelor's, certificate, post-bachelor's certificate. **Academic Requirements:** Arts/fine arts, computer literacy, English (including composition), history, humanities, mathematics, philosophy, sciences (biological or physical), social science. **Classes:** Most classes have 10–19 students. Most lab/discussion sections have 10–19 students. **Majors with Highest Enrollment:** Business administration and management, nursing–registered nurse training (ASN, BSN, MSN, RN), sociology. **Disciplines with Highest Percentage of Degrees Awarded:** Business/marketing 23%, social sciences 18%, health professions and related sciences 13%, psychology 11%, visual and performing arts 10%. **Special Study Options:** Accelerated program, distance learning, double major, dual enrollment, English as a Second Language (ESL), honors program, independent study, internships, liberal arts/career combination, student-designed major, study abroad, teacher certification program, weekend college.

FACILITIES
Housing: Coed dorms, honors house and creative arts and technology house available. Students are also housed in a local hotel. **Special Academic Facilities/Equipment:** Westminster Theatre, art gallery, state-of-the-art library. **Computers:** 5% of classrooms are wired, 9% of classrooms are wireless, 90% of public computers are PCs, 10% of public computers are Macs, network access in dorm rooms, network access in dorm lounges, online administrative functions (other than registration), remote student-access to Web through college's connection.

CAMPUS LIFE
Activities: Choral groups, dance, drama/theater, radio station, student government, student newspaper. **Organizations:** 31 registered organizations, 4 honor societies. 5 fraternities (3% men join), 2 sororities (1% women join). **Athletics (Intercollegiate):** *Men:* Baseball, basketball, cross-country, soccer, tennis. *Women:* Basketball, cross-country, soccer, softball, volleyball. **Environmental Initiatives:** Campus-wide recycling program. EPA self-audit. Continued upgrading of newer, more efficient heating systems.

ADMISSIONS
Freshman Academic Profile: 1% in top 10% of high school class, 8% in top 25% of high school class, 33% in top 50% of high school class. 78% from public high schools. SAT Math middle 50% range 400–480. SAT Critical Reading middle 50% range 390–470. TOEFL required of all international applicants, minimum paper TOEFL 550, minimum computer TOEFL 213. **Basis for Candidate Selection:** *Very important factors considered include:* Academic GPA, application essay, recommendation(s), rigor of secondary school record, standardized test scores. *Important factors considered include:* Character/personal qualities, extracurricular activities, interview, volunteer work. *Other factors considered include:* Alumni/ae relation, class rank, talent/ability, work experience. **Freshman Admission Requirements:** High school diploma is required, and GED is accepted. **Freshman Admission Statistics:** 2,595 applied, 43% admitted, 35% enrolled. **Transfer Admission Requirements:** College transcript(s), minimum college GPA of 2.0 required. Lowest grade transferable C. **General Admission Information:** Application fee $40. Regular application deadline 7/1. Regular notification is rolling. Nonfall registration accepted. Admission may be deferred for a maximum of 24 months. Credit and/or placement offered for CEEB Advanced Placement tests.

COSTS AND FINANCIAL AID
Annual tuition $17,500. Room and board $8,650. Required fees $500. Average book expense $850. **Required Forms and Deadlines:** FAFSA. Financial aid filing deadline 6/1. **Notification of Awards:** Applicants will be notified of awards on a rolling basis beginning on or about 4/1. **Types of Aid:** *Need-based scholarships/grants:* Pell, SEOG, state scholarships/grants, private scholarships, the school's own gift aid. *Loans:* FFEL Subsidized Stafford, FFEL Unsubsidized Stafford, FFEL PLUS. **Student Employment:** Off-campus job opportunities are good. **Financial Aid Statistics:** 85% freshmen, 83% undergrads receive need-based scholarship or grant aid. 72% freshmen, 77% undergrads receive need-based self-help aid. 8 freshmen, 23 undergrads receive athletic scholarships. 94% freshmen, 84% undergrads receive any aid. Highest amount earned per year from on-campus jobs $1,600.

See page 1088.

BLOOMSBURG UNIVERSITY OF PENNSYLVANIA

104 Student Services Center, 400 East Second Street, Bloomsburg, PA 17815
Phone: 570-389-4316 **E-mail:** buadmiss@bloomu.edu **CEEB Code:** 2646
Fax: 570-389-4741 **Website:** www.bloomu.edu **ACT Code:** 3692
Financial Aid Phone: 570-389-4279

This public school was founded in 1839. It has a 282-acre campus.

RATINGS
Admissions Selectivity Rating: 77 **Fire Safety Rating:** 96 **Green Rating:** 60*

STUDENTS AND FACULTY
Enrollment: 7,634. **Student Body:** 60% female, 40% male, 10% out-of-state. African American 6%, Asian 1%, Caucasian 86%, Hispanic 2%. **Retention and Graduation:** 79% freshmen return for sophomore year. 42% freshmen graduate within 4 years. 16% grads go on to further study within 1 year. **Faculty:** Student/faculty ratio 21:1. 366 full-time faculty, 86% hold PhDs. 90% faculty teach undergrads.

ACADEMICS
Degrees: Bachelor's, doctoral, master's, post-bachelor's certificate. **Academic Requirements:** Arts/fine arts, English (including composition), foreign languages, history, humanities, mathematics, philosophy, sciences (biological or physical), social science. **Classes:** Most classes have 20–29 students. Most lab/discussion sections have 10–19 students. **Majors with Highest Enrollment:** Business administration/management; elementary education and teaching; psychology. **Disciplines with Highest Percentage of Degrees Awarded:** Business/marketing 21%, education 15%, health professions and related sciences 9%, social sciences 9%, English 8%. **Special Study Options:** Cooperative education program, distance learning, double major, dual enrollment, English as a Second Language (ESL), honors program, independent study, internships, study abroad, teacher certification program.

FACILITIES
Housing: Coed dorms, apartments for single students. **Special Academic Facilities/Equipment:** Art gallery, language lab, TV studio, radio station. **Computers:** 80% of public computers are PCs, 20% of public computers are Macs, network access in dorm rooms, network access in dorm lounges, online registration, remote student-access to Web through college's connection.

CAMPUS LIFE
Activities: Choral groups, concert band, dance, drama/theater, jazz band, literary magazine, marching band, music ensembles, pep band, radio station, student government, student newspaper, symphony orchestra, television station, yearbook. **Organizations:** 200 registered organizations, 19 honor societies, 7 religious organizations. 11 fraternities (6% men join), 13 sororities (6% women join). **Athletics (Intercollegiate):** *Men:* Baseball, basketball, cheerleading, cross-country, football, soccer, swimming, tennis, track/field (indoor), track/field (outdoor), wrestling. *Women:* Basketball, cheerleading, cross-country, field hockey, lacrosse, soccer, softball, swimming, tennis, track/field (indoor), track/field (outdoor).

ADMISSIONS
Freshman Academic Profile: 11% in top 10% of high school class, 39% in top 25% of high school class, 79% in top 50% of high school class. 90% from public high schools. SAT Math middle 50% range 470–570. SAT Critical Reading middle 50% range 460–540. SAT Writing middle 50% range 440–530. TOEFL required of all international applicants, minimum paper TOEFL 550, minimum computer TOEFL 213. **Basis for Candidate Selection:** *Very important factors considered include:* Academic GPA, class rank, rigor of secondary school record, standardized test scores. *Other factors considered include:* Application essay, character/personal qualities, extracurricular activities, interview, recommendation(s), talent/ability. **Freshman Admission Requirements:** High school diploma is required, and GED is accepted. *Academic units*

required: 4 English, 3 math, 3 science (1 science lab), 2 social studies, 2 history, 2 academic electives. *Academic units recommended:* 4 English, 4 math, 4 science (2 science labs), 2 foreign language, 2 social studies, 2 history. **Freshman Admission Statistics:** 8,943 applied, 60% admitted, 31% enrolled. **Transfer Admission Requirements:** High school transcript, college transcript(s), minimum college GPA of 2.0 required. Lowest grade transferable C. **General Admission Information:** Application fee $30. Early decision application deadline 11/15. Regular notification is rolling. Nonfall registration accepted. Admission may be deferred for a maximum of 1 year. Credit and/or placement offered for CEEB Advanced Placement tests.

COSTS AND FINANCIAL AID

Required Forms and Deadlines: FAFSA. Financial aid filing deadline 3/15. **Notification of Awards:** Applicants will be notified of awards on a rolling basis beginning on or about 4/1. **Types of Aid:** *Need-based scholarships/grants:* Pell, SEOG, state scholarships/grants, private scholarships, the school's own gift aid, Federal ACG and Federal Smart Grants. *Loans:* FFEL Subsidized Stafford, FFEL Unsubsidized Stafford, FFEL PLUS, Federal Perkins, state loans, alternative loans. **Financial Aid Statistics:** 39% freshmen, 38% undergrads receive need-based scholarship or grant aid. 44% freshmen, 48% undergrads receive need-based self-help aid. 59 freshmen, 207 undergrads receive athletic scholarships. 65% freshmen, 65% undergrads receive any aid. Highest amount earned per year from on-campus jobs $3,300.

math, 3 science (2 science labs), 2 foreign language, 1 social studies, 2 history. **Freshman Admission Statistics:** 146 applied, 47% admitted, 66% enrolled. **Transfer Admission Requirements:** College transcript(s), Lowest grade transferable C. **General Admission Information:** Application fee $10. Regular notification is rolling. Nonfall registration accepted. Admission may be deferred for a maximum of semester. Credit offered for CEEB Advanced Placement tests.

COSTS AND FINANCIAL AID

Annual tuition $6,900. Room & board $3,766. Required fees $540. Average book expense $650. **Required Forms and Deadlines:** FAFSA, institution's own financial aid form. Financial aid filing deadline 3/31. **Notification of Awards:** Applicants will be notified of awards on a rolling basis beginning on or about 4/1. **Types of Aid:** *Need-based scholarships/grants:* Pell, SEOG, state scholarships/grants, private scholarships. *Loans:* FFEL Subsidized Stafford, FFEL Unsubsidized Stafford, FFEL PLUS, Federal Perkins. **Student Employment:** Federal Work-Study Program available. Institutional employment available. Off-campus job opportunities are good. **Financial Aid Statistics:** 79% freshmen, 41% undergrads receive need-based scholarship or grant aid. 61% freshmen, 11% undergrads receive need-based self-help aid. 3 freshmen, 16 undergrads receive athletic scholarships. 95% freshmen, 96% undergrads receive any aid. Highest amount earned per year from on-campus jobs $1,400.

BLUE MOUNTAIN COLLEGE

PO Box 160, Blue Mountain, MS 38610
Phone: 662-685-4771 **E-mail:** admissions@bmc.edu
Fax: 662-685-4776 **Website:** www.bmc.edu
Financial Aid Phone: 662-685-4771

This private school, affiliated with the Baptist Church, was founded in 1873. It has a 44-acre campus.

RATINGS
Admissions Selectivity Rating: 80　　**Fire Safety Rating:** 61　　**Green Rating:** 60*

STUDENTS AND FACULTY
Enrollment: 354. **Student Body:** 70% female, 30% male, 11% out-of-state. African American 13%, Caucasian 87%. **Retention and Graduation:** 69% freshmen return for sophomore year. 42% freshmen graduate within 4 years. 14% grads go on to further study within 1 year. 14% grads pursue arts and sciences degrees. **Faculty:** Student/faculty ratio 10:1. 24 full-time faculty, 62% hold PhDs. 100% faculty teach undergrads.

ACADEMICS
Degrees: Bachelor's. **Academic Requirements:** Arts/fine arts, computer literacy, English (including composition), history, mathematics, philosophy, sciences (biological or physical), social science. **Classes:** Most classes have fewer than 10 students. Most lab/discussion sections have fewer than 10 students. **Majors with Highest Enrollment:** Bible/biblical studies; elementary education and teaching; psychology. **Disciplines with Highest Percentage of Degrees Awarded:** Education 56%, philosophy and religious studies 18%, psychology 11%, business/marketing 6%, biological/life sciences 5%. **Special Study Options:** Double major, honor program, internships, teacher certification program.

FACILITIES
Housing: Men's dorms, women's dorms. **Computers:** 25% of classrooms are wired, 100% of public computers are PCs, network access in dorm rooms, network access in dorm lounges, remote student-access to Web through college's connection.

CAMPUS LIFE
Activities: Choral groups, drama/theater, literary magazine, musical theater, student government, yearbook. **Organizations:** 28 registered organizations, 1 honor society, 1 religious organization. 2 fraternities, 3 sororities. **Athletics (Intercollegiate):** *Women:* Basketball, tennis.

ADMISSIONS
Freshman Academic Profile: 23% in top 10% of high school class, 46% in top 25% of high school class, 73% in top 50% of high school class. 83% from public high schools. ACT middle 50% range 18–22. TOEFL required of all international applicants, minimum paper TOEFL 500, minimum computer TOEFL 173. **Basis for Candidate Selection:** *Important factors considered include:* Academic GPA, standardized test scores. *Other factors considered include:* Class rank. **Freshman Admission Requirements:** High school diploma is required, and GED is accepted. *Academic units recommended:* 4 English, 3

BLUEFIELD COLLEGE

3000 College Drive, Bluefield, VA 24605
Phone: 540-326-4214 **E-mail:** thavens@mail.bluefield.edu **CEEB Code:** 5063
Fax: 540-326-4288 **Website:** www.bluefield.edu **ACT Code:** 4340
Financial Aid Phone: 800-872-0175

This private school, affiliated with the Baptist Church, was founded in 1922.

RATINGS
Admissions Selectivity Rating: 81　　**Fire Safety Rating:** 60*　　**Green Rating:** 60*

STUDENTS AND FACULTY
Enrollment: 776. **Student Body:** 60% female, 40% male, 22% out-of-state. African American 18%, Caucasian 78%. **Retention and Graduation:** 66% freshmen return for sophomore year. 36% freshmen graduate within 4 years. 23% grads go on to further study within 1 year. 10% grads pursue arts and sciences degrees. 8% grads pursue business degrees. 3% grads pursue law degrees. 2% grads pursue medical degrees. **Faculty:** Student/faculty ratio 12:1. 33 full-time faculty, 64% hold PhDs. 100% faculty teach undergrads.

ACADEMICS
Degrees: Bachelor's. **Academic Requirements:** Arts/fine arts, computer literacy, English (including composition), history, mathematics, sciences (biological or physical), social science. **Classes:** Most classes have fewer than 10 students. Most lab/discussion sections have 10–19 students. **Majors with Highest Enrollment:** Business administration/management, Christian studies, criminal justice/law enforcement administration. **Disciplines with Highest Percentage of Degrees Awarded:** Business/marketing 41%, law/legal studies 32%, psychology 6%, health professions and related sciences 5%, biological/life sciences 3%. **Special Study Options:** Accelerated program, double major, dual enrollment, honors program, internships, student-designed major, study abroad, teacher certification program, weekend college.

FACILITIES
Housing: Coed dorms, men's dorms, women's dorms. **Special Academic Facilities/Equipment:** Art center. **Computers:** 98% of public computers are PCs, 2% of public computers are Macs, network access in dorm rooms.

CAMPUS LIFE
Activities: Choral groups, drama/theater, literary magazine, music ensembles, student government, student newspaper, yearbook. **Organizations:** 18 registered organizations, 7 honor societies, 6 religious organizations. 2 fraternities (10% men join), 2 sororities (11% women join). **Athletics (Intercollegiate):** *Men:* Baseball, basketball, golf, soccer, tennis. *Women:* Basketball, soccer, softball, tennis, volleyball.

ADMISSIONS
Freshman Academic Profile: 23% in top 10% of high school class, 44% in top 25% of high school class, 83% in top 50% of high school class. 95% from public high schools. SAT Math middle 50% range 420–520. SAT Critical Reading middle 50% range 440–530. ACT middle 50% range 19–24. **Basis for Candidate Selection:** *Very important factors considered include:* Character/

personal qualities, rigor of secondary school record, standardized test scores. *Important factors considered include:* Class rank, interview. *Other factors considered include:* Alumni/ae relation, application essay, extracurricular activities, recommendation(s), talent/ability, volunteer work, work experience. **Freshman Admission Requirements:** High school diploma is required, and GED is accepted. *Academic units required:* 4 English, 3 math, 3 science (1 science lab), 3 social studies, 6 academic electives. **Freshman Admission Statistics:** 537 applied, 50% admitted, 40% enrolled. **Transfer Admission Requirements:** College transcript(s), minimum college GPA of 2.0 required. Lowest grade transferable D. **General Admission Information:** Application fee $30. Regular notification is rolling. Nonfall registration accepted. Admission may be deferred for a maximum of 1 semester. Common Application not accepted.

COSTS AND FINANCIAL AID

Annual tuition $6,900. Room & board $4,890. Average book expense $900. **Required Forms and Deadlines:** FAFSA, institution's own financial aid form, state aid form. Financial aid filing deadline 3/10. **Notification of Awards:** Applicants will be notified of awards on a rolling basis beginning on or about 3/10. **Types of Aid:** *Need-based scholarships/grants:* Pell, SEOG, state scholarships/grants, private scholarships, the school's own gift aid. *Loans:* FFEL Subsidized Stafford, FFEL Unsubsidized Stafford, FFEL PLUS, Keesee Foundation. **Student Employment:** Off-campus job opportunities are good. **Financial Aid Statistics:** 53% freshmen, 70% undergrads receive need-based scholarship or grant aid. 39% freshmen, 60% undergrads receive need-based self-help aid. Highest amount earned per year from on-campus jobs $700.

BLUEFIELD STATE COLLEGE

219 Rock Street, Bluefield, WV 24701
Phone: 304-327-4065 **E-mail:** bscadmit@bluefieldstate.edu **CEEB Code:** 5064
Fax: 304-325-7747 **Website:** www.bluefieldstate.edu **ACT Code:** 4514
Financial Aid Phone: 304-327-4020

This public school was founded in 1895. It has a 40-acre campus.

RATINGS
Admissions Selectivity Rating: 65   **Fire Safety Rating:** 60*   **Green Rating:** 60*

STUDENTS AND FACULTY
Enrollment: 3,092. **Student Body:** 65% female, 35% male, 5% out-of-state. African American 11%, Caucasian 100%. **Retention and Graduation:** 76% freshmen return for sophomore year. 26% freshmen graduate within 4 years. 9% grads go on to further study within 1 year. 4% grads pursue arts and sciences degrees. 3% grads pursue business degrees. 1% grads pursue law degrees. 1% grads pursue medical degrees. **Faculty:** Student/faculty ratio 17:1. 92 full-time faculty, 40% hold PhDs. 100% faculty teach undergrads.

ACADEMICS
Degrees: Associate, bachelor's, certificate, terminal. **Academic Requirements:** Computer literacy, English (including composition), humanities, mathematics, sciences (biological or physical), social science, PE activity. **Classes:** Most classes have 10–19 students. Most lab/discussion sections have 10–19 students. **Majors with Highest Enrollment:** Business administration/management, elementary education and teaching, nursing–registered nurse training (ASN, BSN, MSN, RN). **Disciplines with Highest Percentage of Degrees Awarded:** Engineering 22%, education 18%, business/marketing 15%, health professions and related sciences 14%, computer and information sciences 10%, liberal arts/general studies 10%. **Special Study Options:** Distance learning, dual enrollment, honors program, internships, student-designed major, teacher certification program.

FACILITIES
Housing: Off-campus housing services provided, including referrals and resources. **Computers:** 95% of public computers are PCs, 2% of public computers are Macs, online registration, online administrative functions (other than registration), remote student-access to Web through college's connection.

CAMPUS LIFE
Activities: Choral groups, student government, student newspaper, yearbook. **Organizations:** 28 registered organizations, 6 honor societies, 1 religious organization. 3 fraternities (5% men join), 4 sororities (10% women join). **Athletics (Intercollegiate):** *Men:* Baseball, basketball, cross-country, golf, tennis. *Women:* Basketball, cheerleading, cross-country, softball, tennis, volleyball.

ADMISSIONS
Freshman Academic Profile: 10% in top 10% of high school class, 27% in top

25% of high school class, 73% in top 50% of high school class. 98% from public high schools. ACT middle 50% range 21–26. TOEFL required of all international applicants, minimum paper TOEFL 550, minimum computer TOEFL 250. **Basis for Candidate Selection:** *Important factors considered include:* Rigor of secondary school record, standardized test scores. **Freshman Admission Requirements:** High school diploma is required, and GED is accepted. *Academic units required:* 4 English, 3 math, 3 science (2 science labs), 3 social studies, 1 history, 1 academic elective. *Academic units recommended:* 2 foreign language. **Freshman Admission Statistics:** 1,135 applied, 98% admitted, 53% enrolled. **Transfer Admission Requirements:** College transcript(s), lowest grade transferable D. **General Admission Information:** Regular notification continuous. Nonfall registration accepted. Admission may be deferred for a maximum of 1 semester. Common Application accepted. Credit and/or placement offered for CEEB Advanced Placement tests.

COSTS AND FINANCIAL AID
Annual in-state tuition $3,114. Out-of-state tuition $6,894. Average book expense $1,200. **Required Forms and Deadlines:** FAFSA, institution's own financial aid form, state aid form. Financial aid filing deadline 3/1. **Notification of Awards:** Applicants will be notified of awards on a rolling basis beginning on or about 6/1. **Types of Aid:** *Need-based scholarships/grants:* Pell, SEOG, state scholarships/grants, private scholarships, the school's own gift aid. *Loans:* Direct Subsidized Stafford, Direct Unsubsidized Stafford, Direct PLUS, Federal Perkins. **Financial Aid Statistics:** 66% freshmen, 38% undergrads receive need-based scholarship or grant aid. 53% freshmen, 29% undergrads receive need-based self-help aid. 30 freshmen, 110 undergrads receive athletic scholarships. Highest amount earned per year from on-campus jobs $1,500.

BLUFFTON UNIVERSITY

Office of Admissions, 1 University Drive, Bluffton, OH 45817
Phone: 419-358-3257 **E-mail:** admissions@bluffton.edu **CEEB Code:** 1067
Fax: 419-358-3232 **Website:** www.bluffton.edu **ACT Code:** 3238
Financial Aid Phone: 800-488-3257

This private school, affiliated with the Mennonite Church, was founded in 1899. It has a 65-acre campus.

RATINGS
Admissions Selectivity Rating: 75   **Fire Safety Rating:** 60*   **Green Rating:** 60*

STUDENTS AND FACULTY
Enrollment: 866. **Student Body:** 60% female, 40% male, 8% out-of-state. African American 2%, Caucasian 69%. **Retention and Graduation:** 72% freshmen return for sophomore year. 51% freshmen graduate within 4 years. 9% grads go on to further study within 1 year. 9% grads pursue arts and sciences degrees. 1% grads pursue law degrees. 1% grads pursue medical degrees. **Faculty:** Student/faculty ratio 13:1. 64 full-time faculty, 72% hold PhDs. 100% faculty teach undergrads.

ACADEMICS
Degrees: Bachelor's, master's. **Academic Requirements:** Arts/fine arts, English (including composition), foreign languages, history, humanities, mathematics, sciences (biological or physical), social science. **Classes:** Most classes have 10–19 students. Most lab/discussion sections have 10–19 students. **Disciplines with Highest Percentage of Degrees Awarded:** Business/marketing 35%, education 26%, communication technologies 4%, parks and recreation 4%, mathematics 3%, biological/life sciences 3%, social sciences 3%, English 2%, visual and performing arts 2%. **Special Study Options:** Double major, English as a Second Language (ESL), exchange student program (domestic), honors program, internships, student-designed major, study abroad, teacher certification program, American Studies program (Washington, DC). Other term-away programs available.

FACILITIES
Housing: Men's dorms, women's dorms. **Special Academic Facilities/Equipment:** Mennonite historical library, peace arts center, nature preserve. **Computers:** 90% of public computers are PCs, 10% of public computers are Macs, network access in dorm rooms, network access in dorm lounges, remote student-access to Web through college's connection.

CAMPUS LIFE
Activities: Choral groups, concert band, dance, drama/theater, jazz band, literary magazine, music ensembles, musical theater, pep band, radio station, student government, student newspaper, yearbook. **Organizations:** 50 registered organizations, 19 honor societies, 10 religious organizations. **Athletics (Intercollegiate):** *Men:* Baseball, basketball, cheerleading, cross-

country, football, golf, soccer, tennis, track/field (indoor), track/field (outdoor). *Women:* Basketball, cheerleading, cross-country, golf, soccer, softball, tennis, track/field (indoor), track/field (outdoor), volleyball.

ADMISSIONS

Freshman Academic Profile: 19% in top 10% of high school class, 46% in top 25% of high school class, 79% in top 50% of high school class. 98% from public high schools. SAT Math middle 50% range 470–580. SAT Critical Reading middle 50% range 470–600. ACT middle 50% range 20–25. TOEFL required of all international applicants, minimum paper TOEFL 500. **Basis for Candidate Selection:** *Important factors considered include:* Class rank, recommendation(s), rigor of secondary school record, standardized test scores. *Other factors considered include:* Application essay, interview. **Freshman Admission Requirements:** High school diploma is required, and GED is accepted. *Academic units recommended:* 4 English, 3 math, 3 science, 3 foreign language, 3 social studies. **Freshman Admission Statistics:** 733 applied, 86% admitted, 35% enrolled. **Transfer Admission Requirements:** College transcript(s), standardized test score, statement of good standing from prior institution(s). Minimum college GPA of 2.0 required. Lowest grade transferable C. **General Admission Information:** Application fee $20. Regular application deadline 5/31. Regular notification is rolling. Nonfall registration accepted. Admission may be deferred for a maximum of 2 years. Common Application not accepted. Credit and/or placement offered for CEEB Advanced Placement tests.

COSTS AND FINANCIAL AID

Annual tuition $15,046. Room & board $5,268. Required fees $300. Average book expense $500. **Required Forms and Deadlines:** FAFSA. Financial aid filing deadline 10/1. **Notification of Awards:** Applicants will be notified of awards on a rolling basis beginning on or about 3/1. **Types of Aid:** *Need-based scholarships/grants:* Pell, SEOG, state scholarships/grants, private scholarships, the school's own gift aid. *Loans:* FFEL Subsidized Stafford, FFEL Unsubsidized Stafford, FFEL PLUS, Federal Perkins. **Student Employment:** Federal Work-Study Program available. Institutional employment available. Off-campus job opportunities are good. **Financial Aid Statistics:** 83% freshmen, 70% undergrads receive need-based scholarship or grant aid. 72% freshmen, 64% undergrads receive need-based self-help aid. Highest amount earned per year from on-campus jobs $1,350.

BOB JONES UNIVERSITY

1700 Wade Hampton Boulevard, Greenville, SC 29614
Phone: 864-242-5100 **E-mail:** admissions@bju.edu **CEEB Code:** 5065
Fax: 800-232-9258 **Website:** www.bju.edu **ACT Code:** 3836
Financial Aid Phone: 864-242-5100

This private school was founded in 1927. It has a 225-acre campus.

RATINGS
Admissions Selectivity Rating: 60*   **Fire Safety Rating:** 60*   **Green Rating:** 60*

STUDENTS AND FACULTY

Enrollment: 3,572. **Student Body:** 54% female, 46% male, 72% out-of-state. **Retention and Graduation:** 73% freshmen return for sophomore year. 24% grads go on to further study within 1 year. 33% grads pursue arts and sciences degrees. 5% grads pursue business degrees. 1% grads pursue law degrees. **Faculty:** Student/faculty ratio 11:1. 248 full-time faculty.

ACADEMICS

Degrees: Associate, bachelor's, certificate, doctoral, first professional, master's, post-bachelor's certificate, post-master's certificate. **Academic Requirements:** Arts/fine arts, English (including composition), foreign languages, history, mathematics, philosophy, sciences (biological or physical), Bible. **Majors with Highest Enrollment:** Accounting, elementary education and teaching, nursing–registered nurse training (ASN, BSN, MSN, RN). **Disciplines with Highest Percentage of Degrees Awarded:** Theology and religious vocations 15%, education 15%, business/marketing 14%, health professions and related sciences 9%, visual and performing arts 9%. **Special Study Options:** Distance learning, English as a Second Language (ESL), internships, teacher certification program.

FACILITIES

Housing: Men's dorms, women's dorms, apartments for married students, apartments for single students, special housing for disabled students. **Special Academic Facilities/Equipment:** BJU Museum and Gallery, Davis Field House, Fremont Fitness Center, Rodeheaver Auditorium, Bob Jones Jr. Memorial Seminary & Evangelism Center, Founder's Memorial Amphitorium,

Mack Library. **Computers:** 75% of classrooms are wireless, 77% of public computers are PCs, 13% of public computers are Macs, 10% of public computers are UNIX, network access in dorm rooms, network access in dorm lounges, online registration, online administrative functions (other than registration), remote student-access to Web through college's connection.

CAMPUS LIFE

Activities: Choral groups, concert band, drama/theater, music ensembles, opera, radio station, student government, student newspaper, symphony orchestra, television station, yearbook. **Organizations:** 31 registered organizations, 18 religious organizations.

ADMISSIONS

Freshman Academic Profile: 14% from public high schools. ACT middle 50% range 19–26. TOEFL required of all international applicants, minimum paper TOEFL 500, minimum computer TOEFL 173. **Basis for Candidate Selection:** *Very important factors considered include:* Academic GPA, character/personal qualities, recommendation(s), religious affiliation/commitment, rigor of secondary school record. *Important factors considered include:* Class rank, interview, standardized test scores. *Other factors considered include:* Application essay. **Freshman Admission Requirements:** High school diploma is required, and GED is accepted. *Academic units recommended:* 3 English, 2 math, 1 science, 2 foreign language, 2 social studies. **Freshman Admission Statistics:** 1,680 applied, 82% admitted, 84% enrolled. **Transfer Admission Requirements:** High school transcript, college transcript(s), essay or personal statement, standardized test score, statement of good standing from prior institution(s). Minimum college GPA of 2.0 required. Lowest grade transferable C. **General Admission Information:** Application fee $45. Regular application deadline 8/1. Regular notification when required info is received, usually within 6 weeks. Nonfall registration accepted. Admission may be deferred for a maximum of 1 year. Credit offered for CEEB Advanced Placement tests.

COSTS AND FINANCIAL AID

Annual tuition $9,180. Room & board $4,980. Required fees $590. Average book expense $1,227. **Required Forms and Deadlines:** Institution's own financial aid form, parent's most recent federal tax return. Financial aid filing deadline 8/30. **Types of Aid:** *Need-based scholarships/grants:* State scholarships/grants, private scholarships, the school's own gift aid. *Loans:* College/university loans from institutional funds, alternative loans. **Financial Aid Statistics:** 66% freshmen, 66% undergrads receive any aid.

BOISE BIBLE COLLEGE

8695 West Marigold Street, Boise, ID 83714-1220
Phone: 208-376-7731 **E-mail:** boisebible@boisebible.edu **CEEB Code:** 0891
Fax: 208-376-7743 **Website:** www.boisebible.edu **ACT Code:** 0917
Financial Aid Phone: 208-376-7731

This private school, affiliated with the Christian (Nondenominational) Church, was founded in 1945. It has a 16-acre campus.

RATINGS
Admissions Selectivity Rating: 60*   **Fire Safety Rating:** 60*   **Green Rating:** 60*

STUDENTS AND FACULTY

Enrollment: 175. **Student Body:** 50% female, 50% male, 55% out-of-state, 2% international (3 countries represented). African American 1%, Asian 2%, Caucasian 89%, Hispanic 3%. **Retention and Graduation:** 60% freshmen return for sophomore year. **Faculty:** Student/faculty ratio 16:1. 8 full-time faculty, 12% hold PhDs.

ACADEMICS

Degrees: Associate, bachelor's, certificate. **Academic Requirements:** English (including composition), history, mathematics, philosophy. **Majors with Highest Enrollment:** Pastoral studies/counseling, religious education, theological and ministerial studies. **Disciplines with Highest Percentage of Degrees Awarded:** Theology and religious vocations 21%. **Special Study Options:** Double major, internships, teacher certification program.

FACILITIES

Housing: Men's dorms, women's dorms.

CAMPUS LIFE

Activities: Choral groups, music ensembles, student government.

ADMISSIONS

Freshman Academic Profile: SAT Math middle 50% range 410–540. SAT Critical Reading middle 50% range 460–550. ACT middle 50% range 16–21.

TOEFL required of all international applicants, minimum paper TOEFL 500, minimum computer TOEFL 173. **Basis for Candidate Selection:** *Important factors considered include:* Academic GPA, application essay, character/personal qualities, class rank, recommendation(s), religious affiliation/commitment, standardized test scores. *Other factors considered include:* Interview, level of applicant's interest. **Freshman Admission Requirements:** High school diploma is required, and GED is accepted. **Freshman Admission Statistics:** 80 applied, 99% admitted, 75% enrolled. **Transfer Admission Requirements:** College transcript(s), essay or personal statement, statement of good standing from prior institution(s). Minimum college GPA of 2.0 required. Lowest grade transferable C. **General Admission Information:** Application fee $25. Regular application deadline 8/15. Regular notification is rolling. Nonfall registration accepted. Admission may be deferred for a maximum of 1 year. Credit offered for CEEB Advanced Placement tests.

COSTS AND FINANCIAL AID

Annual tuition $6,840. Room & board $4,800. Required fees $49. Average book expense $450. **Required Forms and Deadlines:** FAFSA, institution's own financial aid form. **Types of Aid:** *Need-based scholarships/grants:* Pell, SEOG, private scholarships. *Loans:* Direct Subsidized Stafford, Direct Unsubsidized Stafford, Direct PLUS. **Student Employment:** Federal Work-Study Program available.

BOISE STATE UNIVERSITY

1910 University Drive, Boise, ID 83725
Phone: 208-426-1156 **E-mail:** bsuinfo@boisestate.edu **CEEB Code:** 4018
Fax: 208-426-3765 **Website:** www.boisestate.edu **ACT Code:** 0914
Financial Aid Phone: 208-426-1664

This public school was founded in 1932. It has a 150-acre campus.

RATINGS

Admissions Selectivity Rating: 72   **Fire Safety Rating:** 60*   **Green Rating:** 60*

STUDENTS AND FACULTY

Enrollment: 15,676. **Student Body:** 54% female, 46% male, 11% out-of-state, 1% international (42 countries represented). African American 1%, Asian 3%, Caucasian 82%, Hispanic 6%, Native American 1%. **Retention and Graduation:** 63% freshmen return for sophomore year. 15% grads go on to further study within 1 year. 4% grads pursue arts and sciences degrees. 2% grads pursue business degrees. 1% grads pursue law degrees. 1% grads pursue medical degrees. **Faculty:** Student/faculty ratio 18:1. 578 full-time faculty, 85% hold PhDs. 95% faculty teach undergrads.

ACADEMICS

Degrees: Associate, bachelor's, certificate, doctoral, master's, post-master's certificate. **Academic Requirements:** Computer literacy, English (including composition), humanities, mathematics, sciences (biological or physical), social science. **Classes:** Most classes have 10–19 students. Most lab/discussion sections have 20–29 students. **Majors with Highest Enrollment:** Communications studies/speech communication and rhetoric, computer science, information science/studies. **Disciplines with Highest Percentage of Degrees Awarded:** Business/marketing 20%, health professions and related sciences 12%, education 9%, social sciences 8%, communications/journalism 6%. **Special Study Options:** Cooperative education program, distance learning, double major, dual enrollment, honors program, independent study, internships, liberal arts/career combination, study abroad, teacher certification program, weekend college.

FACILITIES

Housing: Coed dorms, men's dorms, women's dorms, apartments for married students, apartments for single students, fraternity/sorority housing. **Computers:** 50% of classrooms are wired, 25% of classrooms are wireless, network access in dorm rooms, network access in dorm lounges, online registration, online administrative functions (other than registration), remote student-access to Web through college's connection.

CAMPUS LIFE

Activities: Choral groups, drama/theater, literary magazine, marching band, music ensembles, musical theater, pep band, radio station, student government, student newspaper, student-run film society. **Organizations:** 180 registered organizations. 4 fraternities (1% men join), 3 sororities (1% women join). **Athletics (Intercollegiate):** *Men:* Basketball, cheerleading, cross-country, football, golf, tennis, track/field (indoor), track/field (outdoor), wrestling. *Women:* Basketball, cheerleading, cross-country, golf, gymnastics, skiing (downhill/alpine), soccer, tennis, track/field (indoor), track/field (outdoor), volleyball.

ADMISSIONS

Freshman Academic Profile: 9% in top 10% of high school class, 28% in top 25% of high school class, 64% in top 50% of high school class. 94% from public high schools. SAT Math middle 50% range 460–580. SAT Critical Reading middle 50% range 460–570. ACT middle 50% range 19–24. TOEFL required of all international applicants, minimum paper TOEFL 500, minimum computer TOEFL 173. **Basis for Candidate Selection:** *Very important factors considered include:* Academic GPA, rigor of secondary school record, standardized test scores. *Other factors considered include:* Class rank, extracurricular activities, first generation, racial/ethnic status, talent/ability. **Freshman Admission Requirements:** High school diploma is required, and GED is accepted. *Academic units required:* 4 English, 3 math, 3 science, 1 foreign language, 2 social studies, 1 academic elective. **Freshman Admission Statistics:** 3,340 applied, 90% admitted, 84% enrolled. **Transfer Admission Requirements:** College transcript(s), minimum college GPA of 2.0 required. Lowest grade transferable C. **General Admission Information:** Application fee $30. Regular application deadline 7/12. Regular notification is rolling. Nonfall registration accepted. Common Application not accepted. Credit offered for CEEB Advanced Placement tests.

COSTS AND FINANCIAL AID

Annual in-state tuition $3,520. Out-of-state tuition $10,576. Room & board $5,384. Average book expense $1,014. **Required Forms and Deadlines:** FAFSA. Financial aid filing deadline 4/1. **Notification of Awards:** Applicants will be notified of awards on a rolling basis beginning on or about 4/1. **Types of Aid:** *Need-based scholarships/grants:* Pell, SEOG, state scholarships/grants, private scholarships, the school's own gift aid. *Loans:* Direct Subsidized Stafford, Direct Unsubsidized Stafford, Direct PLUS, Federal Perkins, college/university loans from institutional funds. **Student Employment:** Federal Work-Study Program available. Institutional employment available. Off-campus job opportunities are excellent. **Financial Aid Statistics:** 48% freshmen, 42% undergrads receive need-based scholarship or grant aid. 33% freshmen, 42% undergrads receive need-based self-help aid. 49 freshmen, 263 undergrads receive athletic scholarships. 70% freshmen, 80% undergrads receive any aid. Highest amount earned per year from on-campus jobs $10,000.

BOSTON ARCHITECTURAL COLLEGE

320 Newbury Street, Boston, MA 02115-2703
Phone: 617-585-0123 **E-mail:** admissions@the-bac.edu **CEEB Code:** 1168
Fax: 617-585-0121 **Website:** www.the-bac.edu
Financial Aid Phone: 617-585-0125

This private school was founded in 1889.

RATINGS

Admissions Selectivity Rating: 60*   **Fire Safety Rating:** 60*   **Green Rating:** 60*

STUDENTS AND FACULTY

Enrollment: 744. **Faculty:** Student/faculty ratio 15:1. 100% faculty teach undergrads.

ACADEMICS

Degrees: Bachelor's, certificate, first professional, master's. **Academic Requirements:** Arts/fine arts, computer literacy, English (including composition), humanities, mathematics, sciences (biological or physical), social science. **Disciplines with Highest Percentage of Degrees Awarded:** Architecture 40%. **Special Study Options:** Cross-registration, distance learning, study abroad, concurrent academic and practice-based learning.

FACILITIES

Special Academic Facilities/Equipment: McCormick Gallery. **Computers:** Remote student access to Web through college's connection.

CAMPUS LIFE

Activities: Student newspaper. **Organizations:** 2 registered organizations.

ADMISSIONS

Freshman Academic Profile: TOEFL required of all international applicants, minimum paper TOEFL 550. **Freshman Admission Requirements:** High school diploma is required, and GED is accepted. **Freshman Admission Statistics:** 368 applied, 94% admitted, 32% enrolled. **Transfer Admission Requirements:** High school transcript, college transcript(s), lowest grade transferable C. **General Admission Information:** Application fee $50. Nonfall registration accepted. Admission may be deferred for a maximum of 1 semester. Common Application not accepted. Credit and/or placement offered for CEEB Advanced Placement tests.

COSTS AND FINANCIAL AID

Annual tuition $7,438. Required fees $150. Average book expense $1,105. **Required Forms and Deadlines:** FAFSA, institution's own financial aid form. Financial aid filing deadline 3/31. **Notification of Awards:** Applicants will be notified of awards on a rolling basis beginning on or about 4/30. **Types of Aid:** *Need-based scholarships/grants:* Pell, state scholarships/grants, private scholarships. *Loans:* FFEL Subsidized Stafford, FFEL Unsubsidized Stafford, FFEL PLUS, state loans. **Student Employment:** Off-campus job opportunities are excellent.

BOSTON COLLEGE

140 Commonwealth Avenue, Devlin Hall 208, Chestnut Hill, MA 02467-3809
Phone: 617-552-3100 **CEEB Code:** 3083
Fax: 617-552-0798 **Website:** www.bc.edu **ACT Code:** 1788
Financial Aid Phone: 617-552-3300

This private school, affiliated with the Roman Catholic Church, was founded in 1863. It has a 379-acre campus.

RATINGS

Admissions Selectivity Rating: 97　　　**Fire Safety Rating:** 92　　　**Green Rating:** 88

STUDENTS AND FACULTY

Enrollment: 9,020. **Student Body:** 52% female, 48% male, 71% out-of-state, 2% international (97 countries represented). African American 6%, Asian 9%, Caucasian 72%, Hispanic 8%. **Retention and Graduation:** 96% freshmen return for sophomore year. 25% grads go on to further study within 1 year. 6% grads pursue arts and sciences degrees. 4% grads pursue business degrees. 7% grads pursue law degrees. 2% grads pursue medical degrees. **Faculty:** Student/faculty ratio 13:1. 679 full-time faculty, 98% hold PhDs. 100% faculty teach undergrads.

ACADEMICS

Degrees: Bachelor's, doctoral, first professional, master's, post-master's certificate. **Academic Requirements:** Arts/fine arts, English (including composition), history, humanities, mathematics, philosophy, sciences (biological or physical), social science, theology requirement, and students must demonstrate proficiency in a foreign language. **Classes:** Most classes have 10–19 students. **Majors with Highest Enrollment:** Communications and media studies, English language and literature, finance. **Disciplines with Highest Percentage of Degrees Awarded:** Business/marketing 21%, social sciences 17%, communications/journalism 10%, English 9%, education 8%, biological/life sciences 8%, history 8%. **Special Study Options:** Accelerated program, cross-registration, distance learning, double major, English as a Second Language (ESL), exchange student program (domestic), honors program, independent study, internships, liberal arts/career combination, student-designed major, study abroad, teacher certification program.

FACILITIES

Housing: Coed dorms, women's dorms, apartments for single students, special housing for disabled students, Greycliff Honors House, multicultural and intercultural floors, a quiet floor, social justice floor and a community living floor, and a leadership house. **Special Academic Facilities/Equipment:** Art museum, theater arts center, on-campus school for multihandicapped students, athletic facility, state-of-the-art science facilities. **Computers:** 10% of classrooms are wired, 100% of classrooms are wireless, 90% of public computers are PCs, 9% of public computers are Macs, 1% of public computers are UNIX, network access in dorm rooms, network access in dorm lounges, online registration, online administrative functions (other than registration), support for handheld computing, remote student-access to Web through college's connection.

CAMPUS LIFE

Activities: Choral groups, concert band, dance, drama/theater, jazz band, literary magazine, marching band, music ensembles, musical theater, pep band, radio station, student government, student newspaper, student-run film society, symphony orchestra, television station. **Organizations:** 214 registered organizations, 12 honor societies, 14 religious organizations. **Athletics (Intercollegiate):** *Men:* Baseball, basketball, cross-country, diving, fencing, football, golf, ice hockey, lacrosse, sailing, skiing (downhill/alpine), soccer,

swimming, tennis, track/field (indoor), track/field (outdoor). *Women:* Basketball, crew/rowing, cross-country, diving, fencing, field hockey, golf, ice hockey, lacrosse, sailing, skiing (downhill/alpine), soccer, softball, swimming, tennis, track/field (indoor), track/field (outdoor), volleyball. **Environmental Initiatives:** Master Plan-BC will have a large percentage of buildings meet or exceed LEED certified standards. Energery Conservation program and procurement. (49% of power purchased is renewable from hydropower). Comprehensive Recycling program that includes food composting, yard waste, and a goal of 85% recycled construction and demolition waste resulted in 55% of waste diverted from landfills last year.

ADMISSIONS

Freshman Academic Profile: 80% in top 10% of high school class, 95% in top 25% of high school class, 99% in top 50% of high school class. 60% from public high schools. SAT Math middle 50% range 630–720. SAT Critical Reading middle 50% range 610–710. SAT Writing middle 50% range 620–710. TOEFL required of all international applicants, minimum paper TOEFL 600, minimum computer TOEFL 250. **Basis for Candidate Selection:** *Very important factors considered include:* Academic GPA, rigor of secondary school record, standardized test scores. *Important factors considered include:* Alumni/ae relation, application essay, character/personal qualities, class rank, extracurricular activities, recommendation(s), religious affiliation/commitment, talent/ability, volunteer work. *Other factors considered include:* First generation, racial/ethnic status, work experience. **Freshman Admission Requirements:** High school diploma is required; and GED is accepted. *Academic units recommended:* 4 English, 4 math, 4 science (4 science labs), 4 foreign language, 4 social studies. **Freshman Admission Statistics:** 26,584 applied, 29% admitted, 30% enrolled. **Transfer Admission Requirements:** High school transcript, college transcript(s), essay or personal statement, standardized test score, statement of good standing from prior institution(s). Minimum college GPA of 3.0 required. Lowest grade transferable C. **General Admission Information:** Application fee $70. Regular application deadline 1/1. Regular notification 4/15. Nonfall registration accepted. Admission may be deferred for a maximum of 2 years. Placement offered for CEEB Advanced Placement tests.

COSTS AND FINANCIAL AID

Annual tuition $35,150. Room and board $11,805. Required fees $524. Average book expense $750. **Required Forms and Deadlines:** FAFSA, CSS/Financial Aid PROFILE, Noncustodial PROFILE, Business/Farm Supplement, parent and student tax returns and W-2 statements. Financial aid filing deadline 2/1. **Notification of Awards:** Applicants will be notified of awards on or about 4/15. **Types of Aid:** *Need-based scholarships/grants:* Pell, SEOG, state scholarships/grants, private scholarships, the school's own gift aid. *Loans:* FFEL Subsidized Stafford, FFEL Unsubsidized Stafford, FFEL PLUS, Federal Perkins, Federal Nursing, state loans. **Student Employment:** Federal Work-Study Program available. Institutional employment available. Off-campus job opportunities are excellent. **Financial Aid Statistics:** 38% freshmen, 36% undergrads receive need-based scholarship or grant aid. 39% freshmen, 38% undergrads receive need-based self-help aid. 60 freshmen, 282 undergrads receive athletic scholarships. 70% freshmen, 70% undergrads receive any aid. Highest amount earned per year from on-campus jobs $3,000.

BOSTON CONSERVATORY

8 the Fenway, Boston, MA 02215
Phone: 617-912-9153 **E-mail:** admissions@bostonconservatory.edu **CEEB Code:** 3084
Fax: 617-247-3159 **Website:** www.bostonconservatory.edu **ACT Code:** 1790
Financial Aid Phone: 617-912-9147

This private school was founded in 1867.

RATINGS

Admissions Selectivity Rating: 60*　　　**Fire Safety Rating:** 60*　　　**Green Rating:** 60*

STUDENTS AND FACULTY

Enrollment: 178. **Student Body:** 58% female, 42% male, 60% out-of-state. African American 1%, Asian 3%, Caucasian 11%, Hispanic 2%. **Retention and Graduation:** 68% freshmen return for sophomore year. 35% freshmen graduate within 4 years. **Faculty:** Student/faculty ratio 4:1. 44 full-time faculty. 100% faculty teach undergrads.

ACADEMICS

Degrees: Bachelor's, diploma, master's, post-bachelor's certificate, post-master's certificate. **Academic Requirements:** English (including composition), history, social science, liberal arts core 5th and 6th semester; 9 credits of electives. **Classes:** Most classes have fewer than 10 students. **Disciplines with Highest Percentage of Degrees Awarded:** Visual and performing arts 46%.

Special Study Options: Cross-registration, double major, English as a Second Language (ESL), independent study, teacher certification program.

FACILITIES

Housing: Coed dorms, women's dorms, Graduate house. **Computers:** 100% of public computers are PCs.

CAMPUS LIFE

Activities: Literary magazine, student government, student newspaper. **Organizations:** 11 registered organizations, 1 honor society, 1 religious organization.

ADMISSIONS

Freshman Academic Profile: 90% from public high schools. TOEFL required of all international applicants. **Basis for Candidate Selection:** *Very important factors considered include:* Character/personal qualities, recommendation(s), talent/ability. *Important factors considered include:* Application essay, class rank, interview, rigor of secondary school record. *Other factors considered include:* Extracurricular activities. **Freshman Admission Requirements:** High school diploma is required, and GED is accepted. *Academic units required:* 4 English, 3 math, 2 science, 2 foreign language, 2 social studies, 2 history. **Freshman Admission Statistics:** 989 applied, 43% admitted, 28% enrolled. **Transfer Admission Requirements:** High school transcript, college transcript(s), essay or personal statement, minimum college GPA of 2.5 required. Lowest grade transferable C. **General Admission Information:** Application fee $100. Regular notification 4/1. Nonfall registration accepted. Admission may be deferred for a maximum of 1 year. Common Application not accepted. Credit offered for CEEB Advanced Placement tests.

COSTS AND FINANCIAL AID

Annual tuition $21,194. Room and board $15,640. Required fees $2,690. **Required Forms and Deadlines:** FAFSA, institution's own financial aid form. Financial aid filing deadline 2/1. **Notification of Awards:** Applicants will be notified of awards on or about 4/1. **Types of Aid:** *Need-based scholarships/ grants:* Pell, SEOG, state scholarships/grants, private scholarships, the school's own gift aid. *Loans:* FFEL Subsidized Stafford, FFEL Unsubsidized Stafford, FFEL PLUS, college/university loans from institutional funds, private educational loans. **Student Employment:** Federal Work-Study Program available. Institutional employment available. Off-campus job opportunities are excellent. **Financial Aid Statistics:** 16% freshmen, 16% undergrads receive need-based scholarship or grant aid. 49% freshmen, 52% undergrads receive need-based self-help aid. Highest amount earned per year from on-campus jobs $830.

BOSTON UNIVERSITY

Best 368

121 Bay State Road, Boston, MA 02215
Phone: 617-353-2300 **E-mail:** admissions@bu.edu **CEEB Code:** 3087
Fax: 617-353-9695 **Website:** www.bu.edu **ACT Code:** 1794
Financial Aid Phone: 617-353-4176

This private school was founded in 1839. It has a 132-acre campus.

RATINGS

Admissions Selectivity Rating: 94   **Fire Safety Rating:** 60*   **Green Rating:** 60*

STUDENTS AND FACULTY

Enrollment: 16,479. **Student Body:** 60% female, 40% male, 77% out-of-state, 6% international (100 countries represented). African American 3%, Asian 13%, Caucasian 56%, Hispanic 6%. **Retention and Graduation:** 91% freshmen return for sophomore year. 70% freshmen graduate within 4 years. 29% grads go on to further study within 1 year. 23% grads pursue arts and sciences degrees. 1% grads pursue business degrees. 2% grads pursue law degrees. 2% grads pursue medical degrees. **Faculty:** Student/faculty ratio 12:1. 1,454 full-time faculty, 86% hold PhDs. 75% faculty teach undergrads.

ACADEMICS

Degrees: Bachelor's, doctoral, first professional certificate, first professional, master's, post-bachelor's certificate, post-master's certificate. **Academic Requirements:** Computer literacy, English (including composition), foreign languages, humanities, mathematics, sciences (biological or physical), social science. **Classes:**

Most classes have 10–19 students. Most lab/discussion sections have 20–29 students. **Majors with Highest Enrollment:** Business administration/management, communications and media studies, engineering. **Disciplines with Highest Percentage of Degrees Awarded:** Social sciences 19%, business/marketing 17%, communications/journalism 16%, psychology 8%, engineering 7%. **Special Study Options:** Accelerated program, cooperative education program, cross-registration, distance learning, double major, dual enrollment, English as a Second Language (ESL), honors program, independent study, internships, liberal arts/career combination, student-designed major, study abroad, teacher certification program, weekend college, field study in marine science at the Woods Hole Institute and in environmental/ecological science in Ecuador at the biodiversity station in the tropical rain forest, the Photonics Center.

FACILITIES

Housing: Coed dorms, women's dorms, apartments for married students, apartments for single students, special housing for disabled students, cooperative housing, specialty dorms/floors for groups of students with a common interest or academic major. **Special Academic Facilities/Equipment:** Center for Computational Science; Center for Advanced Biotechnology; Center for Photonics Research; art galleries; planetarium; commercial TV station; National Public Radio station; 20th century archives; professional theater and theater company; Center for Remote Sensing; Geddes Language Labratory; speech, language and hearing clinic, Culinary Center; Metcalf Center for Science and Engineering; Tsai Performance Center; and College of Communication Multimedia Lab. **Computers:** Network access in dorm rooms, network access in dorm lounges, online registration, online administrative functions (other than registration), support for handheld computing, remote student-access to Web through college's connection.

CAMPUS LIFE

Activities: Choral groups, concert band, dance, drama/theater, jazz band, literary magazine, marching band, music ensembles, musical theater, opera, radio station, student government, student newspaper, student-run film society, symphony orchestra, yearbook. **Organizations:** 400 registered organizations, 11 honor societies, 26 religious organizations. 9 fraternities (3% men join), 9 sororities (5% women join). **Athletics (Intercollegiate):** *Men:* Basketball, crew/rowing, cross-country, diving, golf, ice hockey, soccer, swimming, tennis, track/field (indoor), track/field (outdoor), wrestling. *Women:* Basketball, crew/rowing, cross-country, diving, field hockey, golf, ice hockey, lacrosse, soccer, softball, swimming, tennis, track/field (indoor), track/field (outdoor).

ADMISSIONS

Freshman Academic Profile: 53% in top 10% of high school class, 87% in top 25% of high school class, 99% in top 50% of high school class. 70% from public high schools. SAT Math middle 50% range 600–690. SAT Critical Reading middle 50% range 580–680. SAT Writing middle 50% range 590–690. ACT middle 50% range 25–29. TOEFL required of all international applicants, minimum paper TOEFL 550, minimum computer TOEFL 215. **Basis for Candidate Selection:** *Very important factors considered include:* Rigor of secondary school record. *Important factors considered include:* Academic GPA, application essay, class rank, recommendation(s), standardized test scores. *Other factors considered include:* Alumni/ae relation, character/personal qualities, extracurricular activities, first generation, geographical residence, level of applicant's interest, racial/ethnic status, state residency, volunteer work, work experience. **Freshman Admission Requirements:** High school diploma is required, and GED is accepted. *Academic units required:* 4 English, 3 math, 3 science (3 science labs), 2 foreign language, 3 social studies. *Academic units recommended:* 4 English, 4 math, 4 science (4 science labs), 4 foreign language, 4 social studies. **Freshman Admission Statistics:** 31,851 applied, 58% admitted, 22% enrolled. **Transfer Admission Requirements:** High school transcript, college transcript(s), essay or personal statement, standardized test score, statement of good standing from prior institution(s). Minimum college GPA of 3.5 required. Lowest grade transferable C. **General Admission Information:** Application fee $75. Early decision application deadline 11/1. Regular application deadline 1/1. Regular notification late-March thru mid-April. Nonfall registration accepted. Admission may be deferred for a maximum of 1 year. Credit and/or placement offered for CEEB Advanced Placement tests.

COSTS AND FINANCIAL AID

Annual tuition $34,930. Room and board $10,950. Required fees $488. Average book expense $840. **Required Forms and Deadlines:** FAFSA, CSS/Financial Aid PROFILE, state aid form, Noncustodial PROFILE, Business/Farm Supplement. Financial aid filing deadline 2/15. **Notification of Awards:** Applicants will be notified of awards on a rolling basis beginning on or about 3/15. **Types of Aid:** *Need-based scholarships/grants:* Pell, SEOG, state scholarships/grants, private scholarships, the school's own gift aid. *Loans:* Direct Subsidized Stafford, Direct Unsubsidized Stafford, Direct PLUS, Federal Perkins, state loans. **Financial Aid Statistics:** 41% freshmen, 41% undergrads receive need-based scholarship or grant aid. 39% freshmen, 39% undergrads receive need-based self-help aid. 68 freshmen, 255 undergrads receive athletic scholarships. 65% freshmen, 66% undergrads receive any aid.

See page 1090.

BOWDOIN COLLEGE

Best 368

5000 College Station, Bowdoin College, Brunswick, ME 04011-8441
Phone: 207-725-3100 **E-mail:** admissions@bowdoin.edu **CEEB Code:** 3089
Fax: 207-725-3101 **Website:** www.bowdoin.edu **ACT Code:** 1636
Financial Aid Phone: 207-725-3273

This private school was founded in 1794. It has a 205-acre campus.

RATINGS
Admissions Selectivity Rating: 99   **Fire Safety Rating:** 95   **Green Rating:** 94

STUDENTS AND FACULTY
Enrollment: 1,727. **Student Body:** 51% female, 49% male, 88% out-of-state, 3% international (31 countries represented). African American 5%, Asian 12%, Caucasian 70%, Hispanic 7%. **Retention and Graduation:** 98% freshmen return for sophomore year. 84% freshmen graduate within 4 years. 15% grads go on to further study within 1 year. 7% grads pursue arts and sciences degrees. 2% grads pursue business degrees. 3% grads pursue law degrees. 3% grads pursue medical degrees. **Faculty:** Student/faculty ratio 10:1. 161 full-time faculty, 97% hold PhDs. 100% faculty teach undergrads.

ACADEMICS
Degrees: Bachelor's. **Academic Requirements:** Arts/fine arts, humanities, mathematics, sciences (biological or physical), social science, 1 course in each of natural science and mathematics; social and behavioral sciences; and arts and humanities; and 1 course in each of the 5 distribution areas (1. mathematical, computational or statistical reasoning; 2. inquiry in the natural sciences; 3. exploring social differences; 4. international perspectives; and 5. visual and performing arts). **Classes:** Most classes have 10–19 students. Most lab/discussion sections have 10–19 students. **Majors with Highest Enrollment:** Economics, history, political science and government. **Disciplines with Highest Percentage of Degrees Awarded:** Social sciences 34%, biological/life sciences 9%, foreign languages and literature 8%, visual and performing arts 8%, English 7%, area and ethnic studies 5%, psychology 5%, history 5%. **Special Study Options:** Accelerated program, double major, exchange student program (domestic), independent study, liberal arts/career combination, student-designed major, study abroad, teacher certification program. 3–2 or 4–2 engineering degree programs with Dartmouth College, California Institute of Technology, and Columbia University; and 3–3 legal studies degree program with Columbia University Law School. Pass/fail grading options are available.

FACILITIES
Housing: Coed dorms, apartments for single students, special housing for disabled students, 6 small college houses and 6 college house system houses. **Special Academic Facilities/Equipment:** Art Museum; Arctic Museum; coastal marine biology and ornithology research facility on Orr's Island; scientific station on Kent Island; black box theater; Pickard Theater; Baldwin Center for Learning and Teaching; outdoor leadership center; visual arts center; crafts center; 10 specialized libraries, including the language media center; Coleman Farm; quantitative skills program; the Writing Project; Gibson Hall of Music; educational technology center; environmental studies center; Russwurm African-American Center; women's resource center; off-campus study office; office of health professions advising; pre-law advising office; career planning center; and a state-of-the-art science facility. **Computers:** 20% of classrooms are wired, 100% of classrooms are wireless, 45% of public computers are PCs, 45% of public computers are Macs, 10% of public computers are UNIX, network access in dorm rooms, network access in dorm lounges, online administrative functions (other than registration), support for handheld computing, remote student-access to Web through college's connection.

CAMPUS LIFE
Activities: Choral groups, concert band, dance, drama/theater, jazz band, literary magazine, music ensembles, musical theater, radio station, student government, student newspaper, student-run film society, symphony orchestra, television station, yearbook. **Organizations:** 109 registered organizations, 1 honor society, 4 religious organizations. **Athletics (Intercollegiate):** *Men:* Baseball, basketball, cross-country, diving, football, golf, ice hockey, lacrosse, sailing, skiing (nordic/cross-country), soccer, squash, swimming, tennis, track/field (indoor), track/field (outdoor). *Women:* Basketball, cross-country, diving, field hockey, golf, ice hockey, lacrosse, rugby, sailing, skiing (nordic/cross-country), soccer, softball, squash, swimming, tennis, track/field (indoor), track/field (outdoor), volleyball. **Environmental Initiatives:** On-campus heating

emissions reduction of 25% over the past 5 years due to: change in fuels from #6 heating oil to dual fuels (#2 oil and primarily Natural Gas), upgrades in steam plant, reduction in campus heating set point, renovation of 6 dormitory buildings with more efficient heating systems, plus added roof insulation and installation of 700 new energy-efficient windows.

ADMISSIONS
Freshman Academic Profile: 79% in top 10% of high school class, 96% in top 25% of high school class, 100% in top 50% of high school class. 51% from public high schools. SAT Math middle 50% range 650–730. SAT Critical Reading middle 50% range 650–740. SAT Writing middle 50% range 650–730. ACT middle 50% range 29–33. TOEFL required of all international applicants, minimum paper TOEFL 600, minimum computer TOEFL 250. **Basis for Candidate Selection:** *Very important factors considered include:* Academic GPA, application essay, character/personal qualities, class rank, extracurricular activities, recommendation(s), rigor of secondary school record, talent/ability. *Important factors considered include:* Alumni/ae relation, first generation, geographical residence, racial/ethnic status, volunteer work, work experience. *Other factors considered include:* Interview, level of applicant's interest, standardized test scores, state residency. **Freshman Admission Requirements:** High school diploma is required, and GED is not accepted. *Academic units recommended:* 4 English, 4 math, 4 science (3 science labs), 4 foreign language, 4 social studies. **Freshman Admission Statistics:** 5,401 applied, 22% admitted, 41% enrolled. **Transfer Admission Requirements:** High school transcript, college transcript(s), essay or personal statement, statement of good standing from prior institution(s). Minimum college GPA of 3.0 required. Lowest grade transferable C-. **General Admission Information:** Application fee $60. Early decision application deadline 11/15. Regular application deadline 1/1. Regular notification 4/5. Nonfall registration not accepted. Admission may be deferred for a maximum of 1 year. Credit and/or placement offered for CEEB Advanced Placement tests.

COSTS AND FINANCIAL AID
Annual tuition $35,990. Room and board $9,890. Required fees $380. Average book expense $800. **Required Forms and Deadlines:** FAFSA, institution's own financial aid form, CSS/Financial Aid PROFILE, Noncustodial PROFILE, Business/Farm Supplement. Financial aid filing deadline 2/15. **Notification of Awards:** Applicants will be notified of awards on or about 4/5. **Types of Aid:** *Need-based scholarships/grants:* Pell, SEOG, state scholarships/grants, private scholarships, the school's own gift aid. *Loans:* FFEL Subsidized Stafford, FFEL Unsubsidized Stafford, FFEL PLUS, Federal Perkins, state loans, college/university loans from institutional funds. **Student Employment:** Federal Work-Study Program available. Institutional employment available. Off-campus job opportunities are good. **Financial Aid Statistics:** 39% freshmen, 44% undergrads receive need-based scholarship or grant aid. 33% freshmen, 40% undergrads receive need-based self-help aid. 42% freshmen, 43% undergrads receive any aid. Highest amount earned per year from on-campus jobs $1,500.

BOWIE STATE UNIVERSITY

14000 Jericho Park Road, Henry Administration Building, Bowie, MD 20715
Phone: 301-860-3415 **E-mail:** schanaiwa@bowiestate.edu **CEEB Code:** 5401
Fax: 301-860-3438 **Website:** www.bowiestate.edu
Financial Aid Phone: 301-860-3543

This public school was founded in 1865. It has a 312-acre campus.

RATINGS
Admissions Selectivity Rating: 60*   **Fire Safety Rating:** 60*   **Green Rating:** 60*

STUDENTS AND FACULTY
Enrollment: 3,953. **Student Body:** 64% female, 36% male, 8% out-of-state. African American 74%, Asian 1%, Caucasian 5%, Hispanic 1%. **Retention and Graduation:** 72% freshmen return for sophomore year. 11% freshmen graduate within 4 years. 30% grads go on to further study within 1 year. **Faculty:** Student/faculty ratio 19:1. 191 full-time faculty, 68% hold PhDs. 95% faculty teach undergrads.

ACADEMICS
Degrees: Bachelor's, certificate, doctoral, master's, post-bachelor's certificate, post-master's certificate. **Academic Requirements:** Arts/fine arts, computer literacy, English (including composition), history, humanities, mathematics, philosophy, sciences (biological or physical), social science, health and wellness orientation to college. **Classes:** Most classes have 20–29 students. **Disciplines with Highest Percentage of Degrees Awarded:** Business/marketing 25%, social sciences 17%, interdisciplinary studies 13%, psychology 10%, communication technologies 9%. **Special Study Options:** Cooperative education

program, cross-registration, distance learning, double major, dual enrollment, exchange student program (domestic), honors program, independent study, internships, liberal arts/career combination, study abroad, teacher certification program, dual degree mathematics/engineering program.

FACILITIES

Housing: Coed dorms, men's dorms, women's dorms, apartments for single students, honors residence available, special interest floors. **Special Academic Facilities/Equipment:** Science and math labs, computer academy, art galleries. **Computers:** Network access in dorm rooms, online registration, online administrative functions (other than registration), remote student-access to Web through college's connection.

CAMPUS LIFE

Activities: Choral groups, concert band, dance, drama/theater, jazz band, literary magazine, marching band, music ensembles, musical theater, pep band, radio station, student government, student newspaper, television station, yearbook. **Organizations:** 71 registered organizations, 17 honor societies, 2 religious organizations. 4 fraternities (2% men join), 4 sororities (2% women join). **Athletics (Intercollegiate):** *Men:* Basketball, cross-country, football, track/field (outdoor). *Women:* Basketball, cross-country, softball, tennis, track/field (outdoor), volleyball.

ADMISSIONS

Freshman Academic Profile: 88% from public high schools. SAT Math middle 50% range 400–480. SAT Critical Reading middle 50% range 400–490. TOEFL required of all international applicants, minimum paper TOEFL 500, minimum computer TOEFL 173. **Basis for Candidate Selection:** *Very important factors considered include:* Rigor of secondary school record, standardized test scores. *Other factors considered include:* Application essay, extracurricular activities, interview, recommendation(s). **Freshman Admission Requirements:** High school diploma is required, and GED is accepted. *Academic units required:* 4 English, 3 math, 3 science, 2 foreign language, 1 social studies, 2 history. **Freshman Admission Statistics:** 2,826 applied, 52% admitted, 44% enrolled. **Transfer Admission Requirements:** College transcript(s), minimum college GPA of 2.0 required. Lowest grade transferable C. **General Admission Information:** Application fee $40. Regular notification is rolling. Nonfall registration accepted. Admission may be deferred for a maximum of 1 year. Common Application not accepted. Credit and/or placement offered for CEEB Advanced Placement tests.

COSTS AND FINANCIAL AID

Annual in-state tuition $4,286. Out-of-state tuition $13,591. Room & board $6,823. Required fees $1,195. Average book expense $1,388. **Required Forms and Deadlines:** FAFSA. **Types of Aid:** *Need-based scholarships/grants:* Pell, SEOG, state scholarships/grants, private scholarships, the school's own gift aid. *Loans:* Direct Subsidized Stafford, Direct Unsubsidized Stafford, Direct PLUS, Federal Perkins. **Student Employment:** Federal Work-Study Program available. **Financial Aid Statistics:** 46% freshmen, 44% undergrads receive need-based scholarship or grant aid. 38% freshmen, 44% undergrads receive need-based self-help aid. 55 freshmen, 258 undergrads receive athletic scholarships.

BOWLING GREEN STATE UNIVERSITY

110 McFall Center, Bowling Green, OH 43403
Phone: 419-372-2478 **E-mail:** admissions@bgsu.edu **CEEB Code:** 1069
Fax: 419-372-6955 **Website:** www.bgsu.edu **ACT Code:** 3240
Financial Aid Phone: 419-372-2651

This public school was founded in 1910. It has a 1,250-acre campus.

RATINGS

Admissions Selectivity Rating: 72   **Fire Safety Rating:** 60*   **Green Rating:** 60*

STUDENTS AND FACULTY

Enrollment: 15,875. **Student Body:** 54% female, 46% male, 9% out-of-state, 1% international. African American 9%, Caucasian 82%, Hispanic 3%. **Retention and Graduation:** 76% freshmen return for sophomore year. 34% freshmen graduate within 4 years. **Faculty:** Student/faculty ratio 19:1. 875 full-time faculty, 76% hold PhDs. 91% faculty teach undergrads.

ACADEMICS

Degrees: Bachelor's, doctoral, master's, post-master's certificate. **Academic Requirements:** English (including composition), humanities, mathematics, sciences (biological or physical), social science, multicultural perspective.

Classes: Most classes have 20–29 students. **Majors with Highest Enrollment:** Biology/biological sciences, marketing, psychology. **Disciplines with Highest Percentage of Degrees Awarded:** Education 27%, business/marketing 15%, visual and performing arts 9%, English 7%, health professions and related sciences 6%. **Special Study Options:** Accelerated program, cooperative education program, cross-registration, distance learning, double major, dual enrollment, exchange student program (domestic), honors program, independent study, internships, liberal arts/career combination, student-designed major, study abroad, teacher certification program.

FACILITIES

Housing: Coed dorms, fraternity/sorority housing, residental housing communities, no-alcohol wings. **Computers:** Network access in dorm rooms, network access in dorm lounges, online registration, online administrative functions (other than registration), remote student-access to Web through college's connection.

CAMPUS LIFE

Activities: Choral groups, concert band, dance, drama/theater, jazz band, literary magazine, marching band, music ensembles, musical theater, radio station, student government, student newspaper, student-run film society, symphony orchestra, television station, yearbook. **Organizations:** 280 registered organizations, 20 honor societies. 19 fraternities (8% men join), 17 sororities (11% women join). **Athletics (Intercollegiate):** *Men:* Baseball, basketball, cross-country, diving, football, golf, ice hockey, soccer, swimming, tennis. *Women:* Basketball, cross-country, diving, golf, gymnastics, soccer, softball, swimming, tennis, track/field (outdoor), volleyball.

ADMISSIONS

Freshman Academic Profile: 14% in top 10% of high school class, 36% in top 25% of high school class, 70% in top 50% of high school class. SAT Math middle 50% range 450–575. SAT Critical Reading middle 50% range 470–590. ACT middle 50% range 19–24. TOEFL required of all international applicants, minimum paper TOEFL 500, minimum computer TOEFL 173. **Basis for Candidate Selection:** *Very important factors considered include:* Academic GPA, rigor of secondary school record, standardized test scores. *Important factors considered include:* Class rank, talent/ability. *Other factors considered include:* Alumni/ae relation, application essay, character/personal qualities, extracurricular activities, interview, racial/ethnic status, recommendation(s), volunteer work, work experience. **Freshman Admission Requirements:** High school diploma is required, and GED is accepted. *Academic units required:* 4 English, 3 math, 3 science (2 science labs), 2 foreign language, 3 social studies, 1 visual/performing arts *Academic units recommended:* 4 English, 3 math, 3 science (2 science labs), 2 foreign language, 3 social studies, 1 visual/performing arts. **Freshman Admission Statistics:** 11,557 applied, 90% admitted, 35% enrolled. **Transfer Admission Requirements:** Minimum college GPA of 2.5 required. Lowest grade transferable C. **General Admission Information:** Application fee $40. Regular application deadline 7/15. Regular notification is rolling. Nonfall registration accepted. Admission may be deferred for a maximum of 1 year. Credit and/or placement offered for CEEB Advanced Placement tests.

COSTS AND FINANCIAL AID

Required Forms and Deadlines: FAFSA. **Notification of Awards:** Applicants will be notified of awards on a rolling basis beginning on or about 4/15. **Types of Aid:** *Need-based scholarships/grants:* Pell, SEOG, state scholarships/grants, private scholarships, the school's own gift aid. *Loans:* Direct Subsidized Stafford, Direct Unsubsidized Stafford, Direct PLUS, FFEL Subsidized Stafford, FFEL Unsubsidized Stafford, FFEL PLUS, Federal Perkins, Federal Nursing, state loans, college/university loans from institutional funds. **Student Employment:** Federal Work-Study Program available. Institutional employment available. Off-campus job opportunities are good. **Financial Aid Statistics:** 27% freshmen, 24% undergrads receive need-based scholarship or grant aid. 46% freshmen, 47% undergrads receive need-based self-help aid. 84 freshmen, 321 undergrads receive athletic scholarships. 78% freshmen, 78% undergrads receive any aid.

BRADLEY UNIVERSITY

1501 West Bradley Avenue, Peoria, IL 61625
Phone: 309-677-1000 **E-mail:** admissions@bradley.edu **CEEB Code:** 1070
Fax: 309-677-2797 **Website:** www.bradley.edu **ACT Code:** 0960
Financial Aid Phone: 309-677-3089

This private school was founded in 1897. It has an 85-acre campus.

RATINGS
Admissions Selectivity Rating: 77　　　**Fire Safety Rating:** 74　　　**Green Rating:** 60*

STUDENTS AND FACULTY
Enrollment: 5,292. **Student Body:** 55% female, 45% male, 12% out-of-state. African American 6%, Asian 3%, Caucasian 85%, Hispanic 2%. **Retention and Graduation:** 87% freshmen return for sophomore year. 17% grads go on to further study within 1 year. 16% grads pursue arts and sciences degrees. 2% grads pursue business degrees. 6% grads pursue law degrees. 1% grads pursue medical degrees. **Faculty:** Student/faculty ratio 14:1. 334 full-time faculty, 83% hold PhDs. 100% faculty teach undergrads.

ACADEMICS
Degrees: Bachelor's, doctoral, master's. **Academic Requirements:** Arts/fine arts, computer literacy, English (including composition), history, humanities, mathematics, sciences (biological or physical), social science. **Classes:** Most classes have 20–29 students. **Majors with Highest Enrollment:** Business administration and management; nursing–registered nurse training (ASN, BSN, MSN, RN); organizational communications, public relations, and advertising. **Disciplines with Highest Percentage of Degrees Awarded:** Business/marketing 22%, engineering 14%, communications/journalism 13%, education 10%, health professions and related sciences 8%. **Special Study Options:** Accelerated program, cooperative education program, distance learning, double major, honors program, independent study, liberal arts/career combination, student-designed major, study abroad, teacher certification program, limited distance learning courses available. Collaborative classes with other institutions taught through the Internet.

FACILITIES
Housing: Coed dorms, apartments for single students, fraternity/sorority housing. **Special Academic Facilities/Equipment:** Caterpillar Global Communication Center, 2 art galleries on campus. **Computers:** 12% of classrooms are wired, 68% of classrooms are wireless, 85% of public computers are PCs, 10% of public computers are Macs, 5% of public computers are UNIX, network access in dorm rooms, network access in dorm lounges, online registration, online administrative functions (other than registration).

CAMPUS LIFE
Activities: Choral groups, concert band, drama/theater, jazz band, literary magazine, music ensembles, musical theater, pep band, radio station, student government, student newspaper, student-run film society, symphony orchestra, television station, yearbook. **Organizations:** 220 registered organizations, 31 honor societies, 14 religious organizations. 16 fraternities (27% men join), 11 sororities (26% women join). **Athletics (Intercollegiate):** *Men:* Baseball, basketball, cross-country, golf, soccer, tennis. *Women:* Basketball, cross-country, golf, softball, tennis, track/field (indoor), track/field (outdoor), volleyball.

ADMISSIONS
Freshman Academic Profile: 28% in top 10% of high school class, 63% in top 25% of high school class, 92% in top 50% of high school class. SAT Math middle 50% range 530–610. SAT Critical Reading middle 50% range 510–610. ACT middle 50% range 23–27. TOEFL required of all international applicants, minimum paper TOEFL 525, minimum computer TOEFL 213. **Basis for Candidate Selection:** *Very important factors considered include:* Rigor of secondary school record. *Important factors considered include:* Academic GPA, class rank, standardized test scores. *Other factors considered include:* Alumni/ae relation, application essay, character/personal qualities, extracurricular activities, geographical residence, interview, level of applicant's interest, racial/ethnic status, recommendation(s), talent/ability, volunteer work, work experience. **Freshman Admission Requirements:** High school diploma is required, and GED is accepted. *Academic units required:* 4 English, 3 math, 2 science (2 science labs), 2 social studies. *Academic units recommended:* 5 English, 4 math, 3 science (3 science labs), 2 foreign language, 3 social studies, 2 history.

Freshman Admission Statistics: 4,321 applied, 83% admitted, 30% enrolled. **Transfer Admission Requirements:** College transcript(s), statement of good standing from prior institution(s). Minimum college GPA of 2.0 required. Lowest grade transferable C. **General Admission Information:** Application fee $35. Regular application deadline is rolling. Regular notification is rolling. Nonfall registration accepted. Admission may be deferred for a maximum of 1 year. Neither credit nor placement offered for CEEB Advanced Placement tests.

COSTS AND FINANCIAL AID
Annual tuition $21,000. Room and board $7,050. Required fees $178. Average book expense $500. **Required Forms and Deadlines:** FAFSA. Financial aid filing deadline 3/1. **Types of Aid:** *Need-based scholarships/grants:* Pell, SEOG, state scholarships/grants, private scholarships, the school's own gift aid. *Loans:* Direct Subsidized Stafford, Direct Unsubsidized Stafford, Direct PLUS, FFEL PLUS, Federal Perkins, Federal Nursing. **Financial Aid Statistics:** 64% freshmen, 69% undergrads receive need-based scholarship or grant aid. 55% freshmen, 52% undergrads receive need-based self-help aid. 17 freshmen, 102 undergrads receive athletic scholarships. 96% freshmen, 92% undergrads receive any aid.

BRANDEIS UNIVERSITY

415 South Street, MS003, Waltham, MA 02454-9110
Phone: 781-736-3500 **E-mail:** admissions@brandeis.edu **CEEB Code:** 3092
Fax: 781-736-3536 **Website:** www.brandeis.edu **ACT Code:** 1802
Financial Aid Phone: 781-736-3700

This private school was founded in 1948. It has a 235-acre campus.

RATINGS
Admissions Selectivity Rating: 97　　　**Fire Safety Rating:** 60*　　　**Green Rating:** 60*

STUDENTS AND FACULTY
Enrollment: 3,257. **Student Body:** 56% female, 44% male, 73% out-of-state, 7% international (52 countries represented). African American 3%, Asian 8%, Caucasian 61%, Hispanic 4%. **Retention and Graduation:** 96% freshmen return for sophomore year. 84% freshmen graduate within 4 years. 28% grads go on to further study within 1 year. **Faculty:** Student/faculty ratio 8:1. 352 full-time faculty, 96% hold PhDs. 99% faculty teach undergrads.

ACADEMICS
Degrees: Bachelor's, doctoral, master's, post-bachelor's certificate. **Academic Requirements:** Arts/fine arts, English (including composition), foreign languages, humanities, mathematics, social science. **Classes:** Most classes have 10–19 students. **Majors with Highest Enrollment:** Biology/biological sciences, economics, psychology. **Disciplines with Highest Percentage of Degrees Awarded:** Social sciences 31%, biological/life sciences 12%, psychology 9%, area and ethnic studies 8%, history 7%. **Special Study Options:** Cross-registration, double major, independent study, internships, student-designed major, study abroad.

FACILITIES
Housing: Coed dorms, men's dorms, women's dorms, apartments for single students, thematic learning communities. **Special Academic Facilities/Equipment:** Art museum, multicultural library, intercultural center, theater arts complex, language lab, American Jewish Historical Society headquarters, spatial orientation lab, research centers on aging, basic medical sciences, complex systems, family/children's policy, health policy, mental retardation, public policy, study of European Jewry, student leadership development room. **Computers:** 100% of classrooms are wireless, 60% of public computers are PCs, 40% of public computers are Macs, network access in dorm rooms, network access in dorm lounges, online registration, online administrative functions (other than registration), remote student-access to Web through college's connection.

CAMPUS LIFE
Activities: Choral groups, concert band, dance, drama/theater, jazz band, literary magazine, music ensembles, musical theater, radio station, student government, student newspaper, student-run film society, television station, yearbook. **Organizations:** 246 registered organizations, 4 honor societies, 19

religious organizations. **Athletics (Intercollegiate):** *Men:* Baseball, basketball, cross-country, diving, fencing, golf, sailing, soccer, swimming, tennis, track/field (indoor), track/field (outdoor), wrestling. *Women:* Basketball, cheerleading, cross-country, diving, fencing, sailing, soccer, softball, swimming, tennis, track/field (indoor), track/field (outdoor), volleyball, wrestling.

ADMISSIONS

Freshman Academic Profile: 76% in top 10% of high school class, 96% in top 25% of high school class, 99% in top 50% of high school class. 70% from public high schools. SAT Math middle 50% range 650–740. SAT Critical Reading middle 50% range 630–720. ACT middle 50% range 28–32. TOEFL required of all international applicants, minimum paper TOEFL 600, minimum computer TOEFL 250. **Basis for Candidate Selection:** *Very important factors considered include:* Academic GPA, class rank, level of applicant's interest, rigor of secondary school record, standardized test scores. *Important factors considered include:* Application essay, character/personal qualities, extracurricular activities, first generation, recommendation(s), talent/ability, volunteer work, work experience. *Other factors considered include:* Alumni/ae relation, geographical residence, interview, racial/ethnic status. **Freshman Admission Requirements:** High school diploma is required, and GED is accepted. *Academic units recommended:* 4 English, 3 math, 1 science (1 science lab), 3 foreign language, 1 history, 4 academic electives. **Freshman Admission Statistics:** 7,640 applied, 36% admitted, 28% enrolled. **Transfer Admission Requirements:** High school transcript, college transcript(s), essay or personal statement, standardized test score, statement of good standing from prior institution(s). Minimum college GPA of 3.0 required. Lowest grade transferable C-. **General Admission Information:** Application fee $55. Early decision application deadline 11/15. Regular application deadline 1/15. Regular notification 4/1. Nonfall registration accepted. Admission may be deferred for a maximum of 1 year. Credit and/or placement offered for CEEB Advanced Placement tests.

COSTS AND FINANCIAL AID

Annual tuition $34,566. Room and board $9,908. Required fees $1,136. Average book expense $700. **Required Forms and Deadlines:** FAFSA, CSS/Financial Aid PROFILE, Noncustodial PROFILE, Business/Farm Supplement. Financial aid filing deadline 1/15. **Types of Aid:** *Need-based scholarships/grants:* Pell, SEOG, state scholarships/grants, private scholarships, the school's own gift aid. *Loans:* Direct Subsidized Stafford, Direct Unsubsidized Stafford, Direct PLUS, Federal Perkins, state loans, college/university loans from institutional funds. **Student Employment:** Federal Work-Study Program available. Off-campus job opportunities are fair. **Financial Aid Statistics:** 52% freshmen, 46% undergrads receive need-based scholarship or grant aid. 39% freshmen, 41% undergrads receive need-based self-help aid. 54% freshmen, 47% undergrads receive any aid. Highest amount earned per year from on-campus jobs $1,326.

BRANDON UNIVERSITY

270-18th Street, Brandon, MB R7A 6A9, Canada
Phone: 204-727-9784 **E-mail:** admission@brandonu.ca
Fax: 204-728-3221 **Website:** www.brandonu.ca
Financial Aid Phone: 204-727-9737

This public school was founded in 1899. It has a 3-acre campus.

RATINGS

Admissions Selectivity Rating: 60*   **Fire Safety Rating:** 60*   **Green Rating:** 60*

STUDENTS AND FACULTY

Enrollment: 3,097. **Student Body:** 68% female, 32% male, 14% out-of-state. **Retention and Graduation:** 65% freshmen return for sophomore year. **Faculty:** Student/faculty ratio 11:1. 215 full-time faculty. 100% faculty teach undergrads.

ACADEMICS

Degrees: Bachelor's, certificate, master's. **Academic Requirements:** Humanities, sciences (biological or physical), social science. **Classes:** Most classes have fewer than 10 students. **Majors with Highest Enrollment:** Business administration/management; computer and information sciences; psychology. **Disciplines with Highest Percentage of Degrees Awarded:** Education 32%, liberal arts/general studies 31% health professions and related sciences 6%, business/marketing 3%. **Special Study Options:** Distance learning, double major, English as a Second Language (ESL), teacher certification program.

FACILITIES

Housing: Coed dorms, men's dorms, women's dorms, special housing for

disabled students. **Special Academic Facilities/Equipment:** B.J. Hales Museum. **Computers:** 100% of public computers are PCs, network access in dorm rooms, online administrative functions (other than registration), remote student-access to Web through college's connection.

CAMPUS LIFE

Activities: Choral groups, concert band, drama/theater, jazz band, music ensembles, musical theater, opera, radio station, student government, student newspaper, symphony orchestra. **Athletics (Intercollegiate):** *Men:* Basketball, volleyball. *Women:* Basketball, volleyball.

ADMISSIONS

Freshman Academic Profile: TOEFL required of all international applicants, minimum paper TOEFL 550, minimum computer TOEFL 213. **Basis for Candidate Selection:** *Very important factors considered include:* Academic GPA, rigor of secondary school record. **Freshman Admission Requirements:** High school diploma is required, and GED is accepted. **Freshman Admission Statistics:** 2,157 applied, 70% admitted. **Transfer Admission Requirements:** College transcript(s), statement of good standing from prior institution(s). **General Admission Information:** Application fee $125. Regular notification is rolling. Nonfall registration accepted. Admission may be deferred for a maximum of nil. Common Application not accepted.

COSTS AND FINANCIAL AID

Annual in-state tuition $3,354. Annual out-of-state tuition $3,354. Room and board $6,270. Required fees $345. Average book expense $1,000.

BRENAU UNIVERSITY THE WOMEN'S COLLEGE

500 Washington Street Southeast, Gainesville, GA 30501.
Phone: 770-534-6100 **E-mail:** wcadmissions@lib.brenau.edu **CEEB Code:** 5066
Fax: 770-538-4306 **Website:** www.brenau.edu **ACT Code:** 0800
Financial Aid Phone: 770-534-6152

This private school was founded in 1878. It has a 56-acre campus.

RATINGS

Admissions Selectivity Rating: 60*   **Fire Safety Rating:** 60*   **Green Rating:** 60*

STUDENTS AND FACULTY

Enrollment: 796. **Student Body:** 100% female, 9% out-of-state, 6% international (11 countries represented). African American 18%, Asian 2%, Caucasian 59%, Hispanic 3%. **Retention and Graduation:** 65% freshmen return for sophomore year. 28% freshmen graduate within 4 years. **Faculty:** Student/faculty ratio 10:1. 62 full-time faculty, 81% hold PhDs. 100% faculty teach undergrads.

ACADEMICS

Degrees: Bachelor's, master's. **Academic Requirements:** Arts/fine arts, computer literacy, English (including composition), foreign languages, history, humanities, mathematics, philosophy, sciences (biological or physical), social science, health. **Classes:** Most classes have 10–19 students. Most lab/discussion sections have 10–19 students. **Majors with Highest Enrollment:** Nursing–registered nurse training (ASN, BSN, MSN, RN), psychology. **Disciplines with Highest Percentage of Degrees Awarded:** Health professions and related sciences 33%, visual and performing arts 21%, education 15%, communications/journalism 6%, psychology 5%, business/marketing 5%. **Special Study Options:** Accelerated program, cross-registration, distance learning, double major, dual enrollment, exchange student program (domestic), honors program, independent study, internships, liberal arts/career combination, student-designed major, study abroad, teacher certification program, weekend college.

FACILITIES

Housing: Women's dorms, apartments for single students, special housing for disabled students, special housing for international students, fraternity/sorority housing. **Special Academic Facilities/Equipment:** Simmons Art Gallery, Wages House, Whitepath House, Natatorium Physical Fitness Center, Leo Castelli Art Gallery. **Computers:** 75% of classrooms are wireless, 100% of public computers are PCs, network access in dorm rooms, network access in dorm lounges, online registration, online administrative functions (other than registration), remote student-access to Web through college's connection.

CAMPUS LIFE

Activities: Choral groups, dance, drama/theater, literary magazine, musical theater, radio station, student government, student newspaper, yearbook. **Organizations:** 54 registered organizations, 12 honor societies, 2 religious organizations. 8 sororities (18% women join). **Athletics (Intercollegiate):** *Women:* Basketball, cross-country, soccer, softball, swimming, tennis, volleyball.

ADMISSIONS

Freshman Academic Profile: SAT Math middle 50% range 450–540. SAT Critical Reading middle 50% range 450–560. SAT Writing middle 50% range 450–560. ACT middle 50% range 19–23. TOEFL required of all international applicants, minimum paper TOEFL 550, minimum computer TOEFL 173. **Basis for Candidate Selection:** *Important factors considered include:* Academic GPA, rigor of secondary school record, standardized test scores. *Other factors considered include:* Class rank, extracurricular activities, interview, level of applicant's interest, recommendation(s), volunteer work, work experience. **Freshman Admission Requirements:** High school diploma is required, and GED is accepted. **Freshman Admission Statistics:** 2,846 applied, 43% admitted, 18% enrolled. **Transfer Admission Requirements:** College transcript(s), minimum college GPA of 2.0 required. Lowest grade transferable C. **General Admission Information:** Application fee $35. Regular notification is rolling. Nonfall registration accepted. Admission may be deferred for a maximum of 2 semesters. Credit and/or placement offered for CEEB Advanced Placement tests.

COSTS AND FINANCIAL AID

Annual tuition $15,450. Room & board $8,350. Required fees $150. Average book expense $850. **Required Forms and Deadlines:** FAFSA, state aid form. Financial aid filing deadline 4/1. **Notification of Awards:** Applicants will be notified of awards on a rolling basis beginning on or about 3/1. **Types of Aid:** *Need-based scholarships/grants:* Pell, SEOG, state scholarships/grants, private scholarships, the school's own gift aid, National Smart Grant. *Loans:* FFEL Subsidized Stafford, FFEL Unsubsidized Stafford, FFEL PLUS, Federal Perkins, state loans. **Student Employment:** Off-campus job opportunities are excellent. **Financial Aid Statistics:** 73% freshmen, 70% undergrads receive need-based scholarship or grant aid. 48% freshmen, 50% undergrads receive need-based self-help aid. 10 freshmen, 24 undergrads receive athletic scholarships. 97% freshmen, 97% undergrads receive any aid.

BRESCIA UNIVERSITY

717 Frederica Street, Owensboro, KY 42301-3023
Phone: 270-686-4241 **E-mail:** admissions@brescia.edu **CEEB Code:** 1071
Fax: 270-686-4314 **Website:** www.brescia.edu **ACT Code:** 1498
Financial Aid Phone: 270-686-4290

This private school, affiliated with the Roman Catholic Church, was founded in 1950. It has a 9-acre campus.

RATINGS

Admissions Selectivity Rating: 60*　　**Fire Safety Rating:** 60*　　**Green Rating:** 60*

STUDENTS AND FACULTY

Enrollment: 467. **Student Body:** 58% female, 42% male, 13% out-of-state, 10% international (3 countries represented). African American 4%, Caucasian 81%, Hispanic 1%. **Retention and Graduation:** 71% freshmen return for sophomore year. **Faculty:** Student/faculty ratio 9:1. 44 full-time faculty, 57% hold PhDs. 100% faculty teach undergrads.

ACADEMICS

Degrees: Associate, bachelor's, master's, post-bachelor's certificate. **Academic Requirements:** Arts/fine arts, computer literacy, English (including composition), foreign languages, history, humanities, mathematics, philosophy, sciences (biological or physical), social science. **Classes:** Most classes have fewer than 10 students. Most lab/discussion sections have fewer than 10 students. **Majors with Highest Enrollment:** Business/commerce; general studies; social sciences. **Disciplines with Highest Percentage of Degrees Awarded:** Business/marketing 25%, education 17%, public administration and social services 12%, biological/life sciences 11%, liberal arts/general studies 9%. **Special Study Options:** Cross-registration, distance learning, double major, English as a Second Language (ESL), exchange student program (domestic), honors program, independent study, internships, liberal arts/career combination, student-designed major, teacher certification program, weekend college.

FACILITIES

Housing: Coed dorms, men's dorms, women's dorms, special housing for disabled students. **Special Academic Facilities/Equipment:** Art gallery, computer labs, campus center, greenhouse, observatory, science building. **Computers:** 80% of public computers are PCs, 20% of public computers are Macs, 80% of public computers are UNIX, network access in dorm rooms, network access in dorm lounges, remote student-access to Web through college's connection.

CAMPUS LIFE

Activities: Choral groups, dance, drama/theater, literary magazine, student government, student newspaper. **Organizations:** 22 registered organizations, 2 honor societies, 2 religious organizations. **Athletics (Intercollegiate):** *Men:* Baseball, basketball, golf, soccer. *Women:* Basketball, golf, soccer, softball, tennis, volleyball.

ADMISSIONS

Freshman Academic Profile: 61% from public high schools. SAT Math middle 50% range 320–570. SAT Critical Reading middle 50% range 410–600. ACT middle 50% range 18–23. TOEFL required of all international applicants, minimum paper TOEFL 550, minimum computer TOEFL 213. **Basis for Candidate Selection:** *Very important factors considered include:* Academic GPA, standardized test scores. **Freshman Admission Requirements:** High school diploma is required, and GED is accepted. *Academic units recommended:* 4 English, 3 math, 2 science, 2 foreign language, 2 social studies, 2 history, 2 academic electives. **Freshman Admission Statistics:** 126 applied, 75% admitted, 51% enrolled. **Transfer Admission Requirements:** High school transcript, college transcript(s), minimum college GPA of 2.0 required. Lowest grade transferable C. **General Admission Information:** Application fee $25. Regular notification is rolling. Nonfall registration accepted. Admission may be deferred for a maximum of 1 year. Common Application accepted. Credit and/or placement offered for CEEB Advanced Placement tests.

COSTS AND FINANCIAL AID

Required Forms and Deadlines: FAFSA. Financial aid filing deadline 8/1. **Notification of Awards:** Applicants will be notified of awards on a rolling basis beginning on or about 3/1. **Types of Aid:** *Need-based scholarships/grants:* Pell, SEOG, state scholarships/grants, private scholarships, the school's own gift aid. *Loans:* Direct Subsidized Stafford, Direct Unsubsidized Stafford, Direct PLUS, FFEL Subsidized Stafford, FFEL Unsubsidized Stafford, FFEL PLUS, Federal Perkins, college/university loans from institutional funds. **Student Employment:** Federal Work-Study Program available. Institutional employment available. Off-campus job opportunities are excellent. Highest amount earned per year from on-campus jobs $1,236.

BREVARD COLLEGE

1 Brevard College Drive, Brevard, NC 28712
Phone: 828-884-8300 **E-mail:** admissions@brevard.edu **CEEB Code:** 5067
Fax: 828-884-3790 **Website:** www.brevard.edu **ACT Code:** 3074
Financial Aid Phone: 828-884-8287

This private school, affiliated with the Methodist Church, was founded in 1853. It has a 120-acre campus.

RATINGS

Admissions Selectivity Rating: 74　　**Fire Safety Rating:** 60*　　**Green Rating:** 83

STUDENTS AND FACULTY

Enrollment: 664. **Student Body:** 44% female, 56% male, 47% out-of-state, 2% international (12 countries represented). African American 5%, Caucasian 88%, Hispanic 2%, Native American 1%. **Retention and Graduation:** 50% freshmen return for sophomore year. 26% freshmen graduate within 4 years. 30% grads go on to further study within 1 year. 30% grads pursue arts and sciences degrees. **Faculty:** Student/faculty ratio 10:1. 57 full-time faculty, 70% hold PhDs. 100% faculty teach undergrads.

ACADEMICS

Degrees: Bachelor's. **Academic Requirements:** Arts/fine arts, computer literacy, English (including composition), environmental studies, history, humanities, mathematics, philosophy, sciences (biological or physical), social science, physical education. **Classes:** Most classes have fewer than 10 students. Most lab/discussion sections have 10–19 students. **Majors with Highest Enrollment:** Business administration and management; music/music and performing arts studies; parks, recreation, and leisure studies. **Disciplines with Highest Percentage of Degrees Awarded:** Parks and recreation 22%, visual and performing arts 19%, business/marketing 19%, interdisciplinary studies 8%, English 7%, philosophy and religious studies 6%. **Special Study Options:** Double major, dual enrollment, honors program, independent study, internships, student-designed major, study abroad, teacher certification program. Brevard College has received provisional approval from the North Carolina State Board of Education to offer licensure in the following areas: Elementary grades K–6; grades 9–12 in English, mathematics, science, and social studies; grades K–12 in art, music, physical education, and theater.

FACILITIES

Housing: Coed dorms, men's dorms, women's dorms, coed upper classperson dorm. **Special Academic Facilities/Equipment:** Porter Center for Performing Arts; Sims Art Center; Morrison Playhouse; fitness appraisal laboratory; academic enrichment center; center for career, service, and learning; medical services building; Stamey Counseling Center; 24-hour computer lab; library with wireless connection; Moore Science Annex Building. **Computers:** 25% of classrooms are wired, 1% of classrooms are wireless, 85% of public computers are PCs, 15% of public computers are Macs, network access in dorm rooms, network access in dorm lounges, remote student-access to Web through college's connection.

CAMPUS LIFE

Activities: Choral groups, concert band, dance, drama/theater, jazz band, literary magazine, music ensembles, musical theater, opera, pep band, student government, student newspaper, symphony orchestra, yearbook. **Organizations:** 27 registered organizations, 3 honor societies, 3 religious organizations. **Athletics (Intercollegiate):** *Men:* Baseball, basketball, cheerleading, cross-country, cycling, football, golf, soccer, tennis, track/field (outdoor). *Women:* Basketball, cheerleading, cross-country, cycling, soccer, softball, tennis, track/field (outdoor), volleyball.

ADMISSIONS

Freshman Academic Profile: 5% in top 10% of high school class, 22% in top 25% of high school class, 53% in top 50% of high school class. 81% from public high schools. SAT Math middle 50% range 460–560. SAT Critical Reading middle 50% range 440–540. ACT middle 50% range 18–25. TOEFL required of all international applicants, minimum paper TOEFL 537, minimum computer TOEFL 203. **Basis for Candidate Selection:** *Very important factors considered include:* Academic GPA, level of applicant's interest, rigor of secondary school record. *Important factors considered include:* Application essay, character/personal qualities, class rank, extracurricular activities, interview, standardized test scores, talent/ability, volunteer work. *Other factors considered include:* Alumni/ae relation, recommendation(s), religious affiliation/commitment, work experience. **Freshman Admission Requirements:** High school diploma is required, and GED is accepted. *Academic units recommended:* 4 English, 3 math, 3 science (1 science lab), 2 foreign language, 4 social studies, 1 history, 4 academic electives. **Freshman Admission Statistics:** 881 applied, 67% admitted, 39% enrolled. **Transfer Admission Requirements:** High school transcript, college transcript(s), essay or personal statement, standardized test score, statement of good standing from prior institution(s). Minimum college GPA of 2.0 required. Lowest grade transferable C-. **General Admission Information:** Application fee $30. Regular notification is rolling. Nonfall registration accepted. Admission may be deferred for a maximum of 1 semester. Credit and/or placement offered for CEEB Advanced Placement tests.

COSTS AND FINANCIAL AID

Annual tuition $18,700. Room and board $7,050. Required fees $50. Average book expense $1,000. **Required Forms and Deadlines:** FAFSA, state aid form. Financial aid filing deadline 4/15. **Notification of Awards:** Applicants will be notified of awards on a rolling basis beginning on or about 2/1. **Types of Aid:** *Need-based scholarships/grants:* Pell, SEOG, state scholarships/grants, private scholarships, the school's own gift aid. *Loans:* FFEL Subsidized Stafford, FFEL Unsubsidized Stafford, FFEL PLUS, Federal Perkins. **Student Employment:** Federal Work-Study Program available. Institutional employment available. Off-campus job opportunities are fair. **Financial Aid Statistics:** 71% freshmen, 69% undergrads receive need-based scholarship or grant aid. 68% freshmen, 62% undergrads receive need-based self-help aid. 35 freshmen, 60 undergrads receive athletic scholarships. 95% freshmen, 89% undergrads receive any aid. Highest amount earned per year from on-campus jobs $1,883.

See page 1092.

BREWTON-PARKER COLLEGE

PO Box 2011, Mount Vernon, GA 30445
Phone: 912-583-3265 **E-mail:** admissions@bpc.edu
Fax: 912-583-3598 **Website:** www.bpc.edu

This private school, affiliated with the Baptist Church, was founded in 1904. It has a 270-acre campus.

RATINGS

Admissions Selectivity Rating: 71   **Fire Safety Rating:** 60*   **Green Rating:** 60*

STUDENTS AND FACULTY

Enrollment: 1,124. **Student Body:** 64% female, 36% male, 5% out-of-state, 2% international (19 countries represented). African American 20%, Caucasian 65%, Hispanic 2%. **Retention and Graduation:** 59% freshmen return for sophomore year. 8% freshmen graduate within 4 years. 10% grads go on to further study within 1 year. **Faculty:** Student/faculty ratio 9:1. 52 full-time faculty, 73% hold PhDs. 100% faculty teach undergrads.

ACADEMICS

Degrees: Associate, bachelor's. **Academic Requirements:** Arts/fine arts, computer literacy, English (including composition), foreign languages, history, humanities, mathematics, philosophy, sciences (biological or physical), social science. **Classes:** Most classes have fewer than 10 students. **Majors with Highest Enrollment:** Business administration/management, education, psychology. **Disciplines with Highest Percentage of Degrees Awarded:** Education 44%, business/marketing 20%, psychology 15%, social sciences 7%, liberal arts/general studies 6%. **Special Study Options:** Double major, dual enrollment, exchange student program (domestic), honors program, independent study, internships, teacher certification program, weekend college.

FACILITIES

Housing: Men's dorms, women's dorms. **Special Academic Facilities/Equipment:** Library. **Computers:** Network access in dorm rooms, online registration, remote student-access to Web through college's connection.

CAMPUS LIFE

Activities: Choral groups, concert band, drama/theater, jazz band, literary magazine, music ensembles, musical theater, student government, student newspaper, yearbook. **Organizations:** 24 registered organizations, 1 honor society, 5 religious organizations. 3 fraternities (7% men join), 3 sororities (8% women join). **Athletics (Intercollegiate):** *Men:* Baseball, basketball, cheerleading, soccer. *Women:* Basketball, cheerleading, soccer, softball, volleyball.

ADMISSIONS

Freshman Academic Profile: 12% in top 10% of high school class, 26% in top 25% of high school class, 62% in top 50% of high school class. 80% from public high schools. SAT Math middle 50% range 400–500. SAT Critical Reading middle 50% range 390–510. ACT middle 50% range 17–21. **Basis for Candidate Selection:** *Very important factors considered include:* Standardized test scores. *Important factors considered include:* Class rank, rigor of secondary school record. **Freshman Admission Requirements:** High school diploma is required, and GED is accepted. *Academic units required:* 4 English, 3 math, 3 science, 3 social studies. **Freshman Admission Statistics:** 498 applied, 48% admitted, 49% enrolled. **Transfer Admission Requirements:** College transcript(s), statement of good standing from prior institution(s). Minimum college GPA of 2.0 required. Lowest grade transferable D. **General Admission Information:** Application fee $25. Regular notification 1/1. Nonfall registration accepted. Admission may be deferred for a maximum of 1 year. Common Application not accepted.

COSTS AND FINANCIAL AID

Annual tuition $11,500. Room & board $5,200. Required fees $1,100. Average book expense $1,000. **Required Forms and Deadlines:** FAFSA, state aid form, Certification Statement. Financial aid filing deadline 4/1. **Notification of Awards:** Applicants will be notified of awards on a rolling basis beginning on or about 2/1. **Types of Aid:** *Need-based scholarships/grants:* Pell, SEOG, state scholarships/grants, private scholarships, the school's own gift aid, Georgia Baptist Funds. *Loans:* FFEL Subsidized Stafford, FFEL Unsubsidized Stafford, FFEL PLUS, Federal Perkins, state loans, college/university loans from institutional funds. **Student Employment:** Federal Work-Study Program available. Institutional employment available. Off-campus job opportunities are fair. **Financial Aid Statistics:** 88% freshmen, 90% undergrads receive need-based scholarship or grant aid. 62% freshmen, 67% undergrads receive need-based self-help aid. 13 freshmen, 49 undergrads receive athletic scholarships. Highest amount earned per year from on-campus jobs $1,235. **Financial Aid Phone:** 912-583-3215.

BRIAR CLIFF UNIVERSITY

Admissions Office, PO Box 2100, Sioux City, IA 51104-0100
Phone: 712-279-5200 **E-mail:** admissions@briarcliff.edu **CEEB Code:** 1846
Fax: 712-279-1632 **Website:** www.briarcliff.edu **ACT Code:** 1276
Financial Aid Phone: 712-279-5239

This private school, affiliated with the Roman Catholic Church, was founded in 1930. It has a 70-acre campus.

RATINGS

Admissions Selectivity Rating: 76   **Fire Safety Rating:** 88   **Green Rating:** 71

STUDENTS AND FACULTY

Enrollment: 1,080. **Student Body:** 58% female, 42% male, 45% out-of-state. African American 4%, Asian 2%, Caucasian 89%, Hispanic 5%. **Retention and Graduation:** 67% freshmen return for sophomore year. 40% freshmen graduate within 4 years. **Faculty:** Student/faculty ratio 14:1. 56 full-time faculty, 62% hold PhDs. 100% faculty teach undergrads.

ACADEMICS

Degrees: Associate, bachelor's, master's, post-bachelor's certificate. **Academic Requirements:** Arts/fine arts, computer literacy, English (including composition), foreign languages, history, humanities, mathematics, philosophy, sciences (biological or physical), social science. **Classes:** Most classes have 10–19 students. Most lab/discussion sections have 10–19 students. **Majors with Highest Enrollment:** Business administration/management; education; nursing–registered nurse training (RN, ASN, BSN, MSN). **Disciplines with Highest Percentage of Degrees Awarded:** Business/marketing 29%, health professions and related sciences 18%, education 11%, biological/life sciences 7%, communications/journalism 6%. **Special Study Options:** Accelerated program, cross-registration, distance learning, double major, dual enrollment, honor program, independent study, internships, liberal arts/career combination, student-designed major, study abroad, teacher certification program, weekend college.

FACILITIES

Housing: Coed dorms, men's dorms, women's dorms, apartments for single students. **Special Academic Facilities/Equipment:** Nursing simulation lab, integrated multimedia center, human anatomy lab, Clausen Art Gallery. **Computers:** 100% of classrooms are wired, 100% of classrooms are wireless, 100% of public computers are PCs, network access in dorm rooms, network access in dorm lounges, online administrative functions (other than registration), support for handheld computing, remote student-access to Web through college's connection.

CAMPUS LIFE

Activities: Choral groups, drama/theater, jazz band, literary magazine, music ensembles, musical theater, opera, radio station, student government, student newspaper. **Organizations:** 36 registered organizations, 2 honor societies, 1 religious organization. **Athletics (Intercollegiate):** *Men:* Baseball, basketball, cross-country, football, golf, soccer, track/field (indoor), track/field (outdoor), wrestling. *Women:* Basketball, cross-country, golf, soccer, softball, tennis, track/field (indoor), track/field (outdoor), volleyball. **Environmental Initiatives:** Recycling. Prairie Restoration.

ADMISSIONS

Freshman Academic Profile: 13% in top 10% of high school class, 30% in top 25% of high school class, 62% in top 50% of high school class. 83% from public high schools. SAT Math middle 50% range 460–550. SAT Critical Reading middle 50% range 410–510. SAT Writing middle 50% range 350–460. ACT middle 50% range 19–23. TOEFL required of all international applicants, minimum paper TOEFL 500, minimum computer TOEFL 213. **Basis for Candidate Selection:** *Very important factors considered include:* Academic GPA, rigor of secondary school record, standardized test scores. *Other factors considered include:* Alumni/ae relation, application essay, character/personal qualities, class rank, extracurricular activities, first generation, interview, recommendation(s), talent/ability. **Freshman Admission Requirements:** High school diploma is required, and GED is accepted. *Academic units recommended:* 4 English, 3 math, 3 science, 2 foreign language, 3 social studies, 1 academic elective. **Freshman Admission Statistics:** 1,351 applied, 71% admitted, 27% enrolled. **Transfer Admission Requirements:** High school transcript, college transcript(s), statement of good standing from prior institution(s). Minimum college GPA of 2.0 required. Lowest grade transferable D. **General Admission Information:** Application fee $20. Regular notification by 5/1. Nonfall registration accepted. Admission may be deferred for a maximum of 1 year. Credit offered for CEEB Advanced Placement tests.

COSTS AND FINANCIAL AID

Annual tuition $19,446. Room and board $5,988. Required fees $549. Average book expense $825. **Required Forms and Deadlines:** FAFSA. Financial aid filing deadline 3/15. **Types of Aid:** *Need-based scholarships/grants:* Pell, SEOG, state scholarships/grants, private scholarships, the school's own gift aid. *Loans:* FFEL Subsidized Stafford, FFEL Unsubsidized Stafford, FFEL PLUS, Federal Perkins, state loans. **Financial Aid Statistics:** 77% freshmen, 80% undergrads receive need-based scholarship or grant aid. 77% freshmen, 80% undergrads receive need-based self-help aid. 38 freshmen, 90 undergrads receive athletic scholarships. 100% freshmen, 98% undergrads receive any aid. Highest amount earned per year from on-campus jobs $2,500.

BRIARWOOD COLLEGE

2279 Mount Vernon Road, Southington, CT 06489
Phone: 860-628-4751 **E-mail:** admis@briarwood.edu **CEEB Code:** 3121
Fax: 860-628-6444 **Website:** www.briarwood.edu
Financial Aid Phone: 860-628-4751

This proprietary school was founded in 1966. It has a 33-acre campus.

RATINGS

Admissions Selectivity Rating: 60*   **Fire Safety Rating:** 60*   **Green Rating:** 60*

STUDENTS AND FACULTY

Enrollment: 649. **Student Body:** 77% female, 23% male. African American 20%, Asian 1%, Caucasian 68%, Hispanic 9%.

ACADEMICS

Degrees: Associate, bachelor's, diploma. **Academic Requirements:** English (including composition), mathematics. **Special Study Options:** Accelerated program, distance learning, English as a second language (ESL), internships, weekend college.

FACILITIES

Housing: Coed dorms. **Computers:** Network access in dorm rooms, network access in dorm lounges, online registration.

CAMPUS LIFE

Activities: Choral groups, student government, yearbook.

ADMISSIONS

Basis for Candidate Selection: *Very important factors considered include:* Academic GPA, application essay, class rank, recommendation(s), rigor of secondary school record, standardized test scores. *Important factors considered include:* Alumni/ae relation, extracurricular activities, interview, level of applicant's interest. *Other factors considered include:* Character/personal qualities, first generation, geographical residence, state residency, talent/ability, volunteer work, work experience. **Freshman Admission Requirements:** High school diploma is required, and GED is accepted. **Transfer Admission Requirements:** High school transcript, college transcript(s). Lowest grade transferable C. **General Admission Information:** Application fee $25. Nonfall registration accepted. Admission may be deferred for a maximum of 1 semester. Credit and/or placement offered for CEEB Advanced Placement tests.

COSTS AND FINANCIAL AID

Annual tuition $17,100. Room $3,800. Required fees $363. Average book expense $1,000. **Student Employment:** Federal Work-Study Program available. Off-campus job opportunities are good.

BRIDGEWATER COLLEGE

402 East College Street, Bridgewater, VA 22812-1599
Phone: 540-828-5375 **E-mail:** admissions@bridgewater.edu **CEEB Code:** 5069
Fax: 540-828-5481 **Website:** www.bridgewater.edu **ACT Code:** 4342
Financial Aid Phone: 540-828-5377

This private school, affiliated with the Church of the Brethren, was founded in 1880. It has a 190-acre campus.

RATINGS

Admissions Selectivity Rating: 74   **Fire Safety Rating:** 68   **Green Rating:** 72

STUDENTS AND FACULTY

Enrollment: 1,499. **Student Body:** 57% female, 43% male, 22% out-of-state. African American 7%, Caucasian 83%, Hispanic 2%. **Retention and Graduation:** 73% freshmen return for sophomore year. 60% freshmen graduate within 4 years. **Faculty:** Student/faculty ratio 14:1. 95 full-time faculty, 79% hold PhDs. 100% faculty teach undergrads.

ACADEMICS

Degrees: Bachelor's. **Academic Requirements:** Arts/fine arts, computer literacy, English (including composition), foreign languages, history, humanities, mathematics, philosophy, sciences (biological or physical), social science, PDP 150. Personal Development and the Liberal Arts must be completed by each entering student unless the student transfers 15 or more credits to Bridgewater

College. **Classes:** Most classes have 10–19 students. Most lab/discussion sections have 10–19 students. **Majors with Highest Enrollment:** Biology/biological sciences, business administration and management, mass communications/media studies. **Disciplines with Highest Percentage of Degrees Awarded:** Business/marketing 20%, education 13%, biological/life sciences 12%, parks and recreation 11%, psychology 9%. **Special Study Options:** Double major, honors program, independent study, internships, liberal arts/career combination, study abroad, teacher certification program, dual-degree programs. Pre-professional programs in dentistry, engineering, law, medicine, ministry, nursing, occupational therapy, pharmacy, physical therapy, and veterinary science.

FACILITIES

Housing: Men's dorms, women's dorms, apartments for single students, special housing for disabled students, honor housing. **Special Academic Facilities/Equipment:** Museum of Shenandoah region and Brethren history. **Computers:** 99% of public computers are PCs, 1% of public computers are Macs, network access in dorm rooms, online administrative functions (other than registration), remote student-access to Web through college's connection.

CAMPUS LIFE

Activities: Choral groups, concert band, dance, drama/theater, jazz band, literary magazine, music ensembles, musical theater, pep band, radio station, student government, student newspaper, yearbook. **Organizations:** 80 registered organizations, 8 honor societies, 10 religious organizations. **Athletics (Intercollegiate):** *Men:* Baseball, basketball, cross-country, equestrian sports, football, golf, soccer, tennis, track/field (indoor), track/field (outdoor). *Women:* Basketball, cross-country, equestrian sports, field hockey, lacrosse, soccer, softball, tennis, track/field (indoor), track/field (outdoor), volleyball. **Environmental Initiatives:** Recycling. Environmental Committee. Dining services initiatives.

ADMISSIONS

Freshman Academic Profile: 13% in top 10% of high school class, 42% in top 25% of high school class, 78% in top 50% of high school class. 87% from public high schools. SAT Math middle 50% range 460–570. SAT Critical Reading middle 50% range 450–560. SAT Writing middle 50% range 450–550. ACT middle 50% range 18–23. TOEFL required of all international applicants, minimum paper TOEFL 500, minimum computer TOEFL 173. **Basis for Candidate Selection:** *Very important factors considered include:* Academic GPA, rigor of secondary school record, standardized test scores. *Important factors considered include:* Character/personal qualities, class rank, extracurricular activities, interview, recommendation(s), talent/ability. *Other factors considered include:* Geographical residence, level of applicant's interest, state scholarship, volunteer work, work experience. **Freshman Admission Requirements:** High school diploma is required, and GED is accepted. *Academic units required:* 4 English, 3 math, 2 science (2 science labs), 4 academic electives, 2 social studies and history. *Academic units recommended:* 4 English, 4 math, 4 science (2 science labs), 3 foreign language, 4 academic electives, 3 social studies and history. **Freshman Admission Statistics:** 1,600 applied, 85% admitted, 31% enrolled. **Transfer Admission Requirements:** High school transcript, college transcript(s), standardized test score, statement of good standing from prior institution(s). Minimum college GPA of 2.2 required. Lowest grade transferable C. **General Admission Information:** Application fee $30. Regular notification is rolling. Nonfall registration not accepted. Admission may be deferred for a maximum of 1 year. Credit and/or placement offered for CEEB Advanced Placement tests.

COSTS AND FINANCIAL AID

Annual tuition $23,090. Room and board $9,900. Average book expense $1,050. **Required Forms and Deadlines:** FAFSA, state aid form. Financial aid filing deadline 3/1. **Notification of Awards:** Applicants will be notified of awards on a rolling basis beginning on or about 3/15. **Types of Aid:** *Need-based scholarships/grants:* Pell, SEOG, state scholarships/grants, private scholarships, the school's own gift aid. *Loans:* FFEL Subsidized Stafford, FFEL Unsubsidized Stafford, FFEL PLUS, Federal Perkins. **Financial Aid Statistics:** 70% freshmen, 68% undergrads receive need-based scholarship or grant aid. 56% freshmen, 52% undergrads receive need-based self-help aid. 100% freshmen, 99% undergrads receive any aid. Highest amount earned per year from on-campus jobs $456.

BRIDGEWATER STATE COLLEGE

Gates House, Bridgewater State College, Bridgewater, MA 02325
Phone: 508-531-1237 **E-mail:** admission@bridgew.edu **CEEB Code:** 3517
Fax: 508-531-1746 **Website:** www.bridgew.edu **ACT Code:** 1900
Financial Aid Phone: 508-697-1341

This public school was founded in 1840. It has a 235-acre campus.

RATINGS

Admissions Selectivity Rating: 73   **Fire Safety Rating:** 60*   **Green Rating:** 60*

STUDENTS AND FACULTY

Enrollment: 7,573. **Student Body:** 58% female, 42% male, 4% out-of-state, 1% international (32 countries represented). African American 5%, Asian 2%, Caucasian 78%, Hispanic 2%. **Retention and Graduation:** 75% freshmen return for sophomore year. 23% freshmen graduate within 4 years. 16% grads go on to further study within 1 year. 1% grads pursue business degrees. 2% grads pursue law degrees. **Faculty:** Student/faculty ratio 20:1. 292 full-time faculty, 90% hold PhDs. 100% faculty teach undergrads.

ACADEMICS

Degrees: Bachelor's, master's, post-bachelor's certificate, post-master's certificate. **Academic Requirements:** Arts/fine arts, English (including composition), foreign languages, history, humanities, mathematics, philosophy, sciences (biological or physical), social science. **Classes:** Most classes have 20–29 students. Most lab/discussion sections have 10–19 students. **Majors with Highest Enrollment:** Business administration/management, elementary education and teaching, psychology. **Disciplines with Highest Percentage of Degrees Awarded:** Business/marketing 16%, education 14%, psychology 13%, communications/journalism 7%, security and protective services 7%. **Special Study Options:** Accelerated program, cross-registration, distance learning, double major, dual enrollment, English as a Second Language (ESL), exchange student program (domestic), honors program, independent study, internships, study abroad, teacher certification program.

FACILITIES

Housing: Coed dorms, women's dorms, apartments for single students, special housing for disabled students, break housing for athletes, student teachers, international students. **Special Academic Facilities/Equipment:** On-campus school, children's physical development clinic, human performance lab, TV studio, observatory, flight simulators, electron microscope, Moakley Technology Center. **Computers:** 89% of public computers are PCs, 10% of public computers are Macs, 1% of public computers are UNIX, network access in dorm rooms, network access in dorm lounges, online registration, online administrative functions (other than registration), remote student-access to Web through college's connection.

CAMPUS LIFE

Activities: Choral groups, concert band, dance, drama/theater, jazz band, literary magazine, marching band, music ensembles, musical theater, radio station, student government, student newspaper, yearbook. **Organizations:** 74 registered organizations, 11 honor societies, 1 religious organization. 5 fraternities, 3 sororities. **Athletics (Intercollegiate):** *Men:* Baseball, basketball, cross-country, football, soccer, swimming, tennis, track/field (outdoor), wrestling. *Women:* Basketball, cross-country, field hockey, lacrosse, soccer, softball, swimming, tennis, track/field (outdoor), volleyball.

ADMISSIONS

Freshman Academic Profile: 8% in top 10% of high school class, 32% in top 25% of high school class, 75% in top 50% of high school class. SAT Math middle 50% range 460–560. SAT Critical Reading middle 50% range 450–550. ACT middle 50% range 19–23. TOEFL required of all international applicants, minimum paper TOEFL 500. **Basis for Candidate Selection:** *Very important factors considered include:* Academic GPA, rigor of secondary school record. *Important factors considered include:* Extracurricular activities, standardized test scores. *Other factors considered include:* Alumni/ae relation, application essay, character/personal qualities, class rank, first generation, racial/ethnic status, recommendation(s), talent/ability, volunteer work, work experience. **Freshman Admission Requirements:** High school diploma is required, and GED is accepted. *Academic units required:* 4 English, 3 math, 3 science (2 science labs), 2 foreign language, 1 social studies, 1 history, 2 academic electives. **Freshman Admission Statistics:** 6,532 applied, 71% admitted, 29% enrolled. **Transfer Admission Requirements:** College transcript(s), essay or personal statement, minimum college GPA of 2.0 required. Lowest grade transferable C-. **General Admission Information:** Application fee $25. Regular notification is rolling. Nonfall registration accepted. Admission may be deferred for a maximum of 1 year. Credit and/or placement offered for CEEB Advanced Placement tests.

COSTS AND FINANCIAL AID

Annual in-state tuition $910. Annual out-of-state tuition $7,050. Room and board $6,852. Required fees $5,123. Average book expense $1,000. **Required Forms and Deadlines:** FAFSA. Financial aid filing deadline 3/1. **Notification of Awards:** Applicants will be notified of awards on a rolling basis beginning on or about 4/1. **Types of Aid:** *Need-based scholarships/grants:* Pell, SEOG, state scholarships/grants, private scholarships, the school's own gift aid. *Loans:* Direct Subsidized Stafford, Direct Unsubsidized Stafford, Direct PLUS, Federal Perkins, state loans. **Student Employment:** Federal Work-Study Program available. Institutional employment available. Off-campus job opportunities are good. **Financial Aid Statistics:** 43% freshmen, 41% undergrads receive need-based scholarship or grant aid. 48% freshmen, 45% undergrads receive need-based self-help aid. Highest amount earned per year from on-campus jobs $4,000.

See page 1094.

BRIERCREST COLLEGE

510 College Drive, Caronport, SK S0H 0S0, Canada
Phone: 800-667-5199 **E-mail:** admissions@briercrest.ca
Fax: 800-667-5500 **Website:** www.briercrest.ca

This private school, affiliated with the Nondenominational Church, was founded in 1935. It has a 160-acre campus.

RATINGS
Admissions Selectivity Rating: 60*   **Fire Safety Rating:** 60*   **Green Rating:** 60*

STUDENTS AND FACULTY
Faculty: Student/faculty ratio 16:1. 30 full-time faculty.

ACADEMICS
Degrees: Associate, bachelor's, certificate, master's, post-bachelor's certificate. **Academic Requirements:** Arts/fine arts, English (including composition), history, humanities, social science. **Special Study Options:** Distance learning, double major, English as a Second Language (ESL), independent study, internships, study abroad.

FACILITIES
Housing: Men's dorms, women's dorms, apartments for married students. **Computers:** 100% of public computers are PCs, network access in dorm rooms, online registration.

CAMPUS LIFE
Activities: Choral groups, concert band, drama/theater, music ensembles, musical theater, student government, yearbook. **Athletics (Intercollegiate):** *Men:* Basketball, ice hockey, volleyball. *Women:* Basketball, volleyball.

ADMISSIONS
Transfer Admission Requirements: High school transcript, college transcript(s), essay or personal statement. **Admission Information:** Nonfall registration accepted.

COSTS AND FINANCIAL AID
Room and board $2,000. Required fees $150. Average book expense $500.

BRIGHAM YOUNG UNIVERSITY (ID)

Admissions Office, KIM 120, Rexburg, ID 83460-1615
Phone: 208-496-1020 **E-mail:** admissions@byui.edu
Fax: 208-496-1220 **Website:** www.byui.edu **ACT Code:** 0952
Financial Aid Phone: 208-496-1015

This private school, affiliated with the Church of Jesus Christ of Latter-day Saints, was founded in 1888. It has a 255-acre campus.

RATINGS
Admissions Selectivity Rating: 60*   **Fire Safety Rating:** 60*   **Green Rating:** 60*

STUDENTS AND FACULTY
Enrollment: 11,555. **Student Body:** 54% female, 46% male, 62% out-of-state, 3% international (40 countries represented). Asian 2%, Caucasian 91%, Hispanic 3%. **Retention and Graduation:** 79% freshmen return for

sophomore year. **Faculty:** Student/faculty ratio 25:1. 441 full-time faculty. 100% faculty teach undergrads.

ACADEMICS
Degrees: Associate, bachelor's, terminal. **Academic Requirements:** Arts/fine arts, computer literacy, English (including composition), foreign languages, history, humanities, mathematics, philosophy, sciences (biological or physical), social science. **Disciplines with Highest Percentage of Degrees Awarded:** Business/marketing 40%, education 28%, health professions and related sciences 7%, parks and recreation 6%, liberal arts/general studies 5%. **Special Study Options:** Accelerated program, distance learning, double major, honors program, independent study, internships, study abroad, teacher certification program.

FACILITIES
Housing: Men's dorms, women's dorms, apartments for married students. **Special Academic Facilities/Equipment:** Outdoor learning center. **Computers:** 95% of public computers are PCs, 5% of public computers are Macs, network access in dorm rooms, network access in dorm lounges, online registration, online administrative functions (other than registration), remote student-access to Web through college's connection.

CAMPUS LIFE
Activities: Choral groups, concert band, dance, drama/theater, jazz band, literary magazine, music ensembles, musical theater, opera, pep band, radio station, student government, student newspaper, symphony orchestra, yearbook. **Organizations:** 50 registered organizations, 5 honor societies, 55 religious organizations.

ADMISSIONS
Freshman Academic Profile: 90% from public high schools. SAT Math middle 50% range 570–680. SAT Critical Reading middle 50% range 550–670. ACT middle 50% range 25–30. TOEFL required of all international applicants. **Transfer Admission Requirements:** College transcript(s), essay or personal statement, standardized test score. **Admission Information:** Regular application deadline 2/1. Credit offered for CEEB Advanced Placement tests.

COSTS AND FINANCIAL AID
Annual tuition $3,840. Room and board $6,460. Average book expense $1,170. **Types of Aid:** *Need-based scholarships/grants:* Pell, SEOG, state scholarships/grants, private scholarships, the school's own gift aid. *Loans:* Direct Subsidized Stafford, Direct Unsubsidized Stafford, Direct PLUS. **Student Employment:** Off-campus job opportunities are good. **Financial Aid Statistics:** 77% freshmen, 77% undergrads receive any aid.

BRIGHAM YOUNG UNIVERSITY (HI)

BYU—Hawaii #1973, 55-220 Kulanui Street, Laie, HI 96762
Phone: 808-293-3738 **E-mail:** admissions@byuh.edu **CEEB Code:** 4106
Fax: 808-293-3457 **Website:** www.byuh.edu **ACT Code:** 0899
Financial Aid Phone: 808-293-3530

This private school, affiliated with the Church of Jesus Christ of Latter-day Saints, was founded in 1955. It has a 60-acre campus.

RATINGS
Admissions Selectivity Rating: 60*   **Fire Safety Rating:** 60*   **Green Rating:** 60*

STUDENTS AND FACULTY
Enrollment: 430. **Student Body:** 55% female, 45% male, 63% out-of-state, 270% international (67 countries represented). African American 3%, Asian 117%, Caucasian 151%, Hispanic 12%, Native American 4%. **Retention and Graduation:** 79% freshmen return for sophomore year. 23% freshmen graduate within 4 years. **Faculty:** Student/faculty ratio 15:1. 118 full-time faculty, 58% hold PhDs. 100% faculty teach undergrads.

ACADEMICS
Degrees: Bachelor's. **Academic Requirements:** Arts/fine arts, English (including composition), history, humanities, mathematics, sciences (biological or physical), social science, religion classes. **Classes:** Most classes have 10–19 students. Most lab/discussion sections have 10–19 students. **Majors with Highest Enrollment:** Information science/studies, intercultural/multicultural and diversity studies, international business. **Disciplines with Highest Percentage of Degrees Awarded:** Business/marketing 26%, interdisciplinary studies 14%, education 12%, computer and information sciences 10%, parks and recreation 7%, psychology 7%. **Special Study Options:** Accelerated program, cooperative education program, distance learning, English as a Second Language (ESL), exchange student program (domestic), honors

program, independent study, internships, student-designed major, teacher certification program.

FACILITIES

Housing: Men's dorms, women's dorms, apartments for married students, special housing for disabled students. **Special Academic Facilities/ Equipment:** Museum of Natural History, media lab. **Computers:** 95% of public computers are PCs, 5% of public computers are Macs, network access in dorm rooms, network access in dorm lounges, online registration, online administrative functions (other than registration), remote student-access to Web through college's connection.

CAMPUS LIFE

Activities: Choral groups, concert band, dance, jazz band, literary magazine, music ensembles, pep band, student government, student newspaper, student-run film society. **Organizations:** 52 registered organizations, 3 honor societies. **Athletics (Intercollegiate):** *Men:* Basketball, cross-country, golf, soccer, tennis. *Women:* Basketball, cross-country, soccer, softball, tennis, volleyball.

ADMISSIONS

Freshman Academic Profile: SAT Math middle 50% range 480–600. SAT Critical Reading middle 50% range 460–580. ACT middle 50% range 20–27. TOEFL required of all international applicants, minimum paper TOEFL 475, minimum computer TOEFL 153. **Basis for Candidate Selection:** *Very important factors considered include:* Application essay, character/personal qualities, extracurricular activities, geographical residence, interview, recommendation(s), religious affiliation/commitment, rigor of secondary school record, standardized test scores. *Important factors considered include:* Alumni/ ae relation, class rank, talent/ability, volunteer work, work experience. *Other factors considered include:* state residency. **Freshman Admission Requirements:** High school diploma is required, and GED is not accepted. *Academic units recommended:* 4 English, 2 math, 2 science (2 science labs), 2 foreign language, 2 history. **Freshman Admission Statistics:** 2,078 applied, 19% admitted, 56% enrolled. **Transfer Admission Requirements:** College transcript(s), essay or personal statement, statement of good standing from prior institution(s). Minimum college GPA of 3.0 required. Lowest grade transferable C-. **General Admission Information:** Application fee $30. Regular application deadline 2/15. Regular notification 4/1. Nonfall registration accepted. Admission may be deferred for a maximum of 1 semester. Credit offered for CEEB Advanced Placement tests.

COSTS AND FINANCIAL AID

Annual tuition $3,600. Room and board $5,568. Average book expense $900. **Required Forms and Deadlines:** FAFSA, institution's own financial aid form. Financial aid filing deadline 3/31. **Notification of Awards:** Applicants will be notified of awards on or about 6/30. **Types of Aid:** *Need-based scholarships/ grants:* Pell, private scholarships, the school's own gift aid. *Loans:* FFEL Subsidized Stafford, FFEL Unsubsidized Stafford, FFEL PLUS, college/ university loans from institutional funds. **Student Employment:** Institutional employment available. Off-campus job opportunities are fair. **Financial Aid Statistics:** 58% freshmen, 67% undergrads receive need-based scholarship or grant aid. 44% freshmen, 54% undergrads receive need-based self-help aid. 15 freshmen, 60 undergrads receive athletic scholarships. 70% freshmen, 72% undergrads receive any aid. Highest amount earned per year from on-campus jobs $4,500.

BRIGHAM YOUNG UNIVERSITY (UT)

A-153 ASB, Provo, UT 84602-1110
Phone: 801-422-2507 **E-mail:** admissions@byu.edu **CEEB Code:** 4019
Fax: 801-422-0005 **Website:** www.byu.edu **ACT Code:** 4266
Financial Aid Phone: 801-378-4104

This private school, affiliated with the Church of Jesus Christ of Latter-day Saints, was founded in 1875. It has a 557-acre campus.

RATINGS

Admissions Selectivity Rating: 91   **Fire Safety Rating:** 63   **Green Rating:** 60*

STUDENTS AND FACULTY

Enrollment: 30,798. **Student Body:** 49% female, 51% male, 72% out-of-state, 2% international (121 countries represented). Asian 3%, Caucasian 76%,

Hispanic 3%. **Retention and Graduation:** 95% freshmen return for sophomore year. **Faculty:** Student/faculty ratio 21:1. 1,321 full-time faculty.

ACADEMICS

Degrees: Bachelor's, doctoral, first professional, master's. **Academic Requirements:** Arts/fine arts, English (including composition), foreign languages, history, mathematics, sciences (biological or physical), social science, religious education, health and wellness. **Classes:** Most classes have 20–29 students. **Majors with Highest Enrollment:** English language and literature; political science and government, psychology. **Disciplines with Highest Percentage of Degrees Awarded:** Business/marketing 16%, education 12%, visual and performing arts 7%, family and consumer sciences 6%, engineering 6%, foreign languages and literature 5%, English 5%, biological/life sciences 5%, psychology 5%, history 5%. **Special Study Options:** Accelerated program, cooperative education program, cross-registration, distance learning, double major, English as a Second Language (ESL), external degree program, honors program, independent study, internships, liberal arts/career combination, study abroad, teacher certification program.

FACILITIES

Housing: Men's dorms, women's dorms, apartments for married students, apartments for single students, special housing for disabled students, language houses are available. **Special Academic Facilities/Equipment:** Art, peoples/ cultures, life science, and earth science museums; film studio; on-campus nursery school; language research center; seismography equipment; electron microscope. **Computers:** 5% of classrooms are wireless, 90% of public computers are PCs, 5% of public computers are Macs, 5% of public computers are UNIX, network access in dorm rooms, network access in dorm lounges, online registration, online administrative functions (other than registration), support for handheld computing, remote student-access to Web through college's connection.

CAMPUS LIFE

Activities: Choral groups, concert band, dance, drama/theater, jazz band, literary magazine, marching band, music ensembles, musical theater, opera, pep band, radio station, student government, student newspaper, student-run film society, symphony orchestra, television station. **Organizations:** 390 registered organizations, 22 honor societies, 25 religious organizations. **Athletics (Intercollegiate):** *Men:* Baseball, basketball, cheerleading, cross-country, diving, football, golf, racquetball, swimming, tennis, track/field (outdoor), volleyball. *Women:* Basketball, cheerleading, cross-country, diving, golf, gymnastics, racquetball, soccer, softball, swimming, tennis, track/field (outdoor), volleyball.

ADMISSIONS

Freshman Academic Profile: 49% in top 10% of high school class, 35% in top 25% of high school class, 99% in top 50% of high school class. SAT Math middle 50% range 570–670. SAT Critical Reading middle 50% range 550–660. ACT middle 50% range 25–29. TOEFL required of all international applicants, minimum paper TOEFL 500, minimum computer TOEFL 173. **Basis for Candidate Selection:** *Very important factors considered include:* Academic GPA, character/personal qualities, interview, religious affiliation/commitment, rigor of secondary school record, standardized test scores. *Important factors considered include:* Application essay, extracurricular activities, racial/ethnic status, recommendation(s), volunteer work. *Other factors considered include:* Talent/ability, work experience. **Freshman Admission Requirements:** High school diploma is required, and GED is accepted. *Academic units required:* 4 English, 3 math, 2 science (2 science labs), 2 foreign language, 2 history, 2 literature or writing. *Academic units recommended:* 4 English, 4 math, 3 science (3 science labs), 4 foreign language. **Freshman Admission Statistics:** 8,696 applied, 78% admitted, 79% enrolled. **Transfer Admission Requirements:** College transcript(s), essay or personal statement, interview, minimum college GPA of 3.0 required. Lowest grade transferable C-. **General Admission Information:** Application fee $30. Regular application deadline 2/1. Nonfall registration accepted. Admission may be deferred for a maximum of 2 years. Credit and/or placement offered for CEEB Advanced Placement tests.

COSTS AND FINANCIAL AID

Annual tuition $3,620. Room & board $5,640. Average book expense $1,380. **Required Forms and Deadlines:** FAFSA. Financial aid filing deadline 4/15. **Notification of Awards:** Applicants will be notified of awards on or about 4/20. **Types of Aid:** *Need-based scholarships/grants:* Pell, state scholarships/grants, private scholarships, the school's own gift aid. *Loans:* FFEL Subsidized Stafford, FFEL Unsubsidized Stafford, FFEL PLUS, college/university loans from institutional funds. **Financial Aid Statistics:** 13% freshmen, 29% undergrads receive need-based scholarship or grant aid. 6% freshmen, 15% undergrads receive need-based self-help aid. 66 freshmen, 376 undergrads receive athletic scholarships. 20% freshmen, 36% undergrads receive any aid.

BROCK UNIVERSITY

500 Glenridge Avenue, St. Catharines, ON L2S 3A1, Canada
Phone: 905-688-5550 **E-mail:** admissns@brocku.ca
Fax: 905-988-5488 **Website:** www.brocku.ca
Financial Aid Phone: 905-688-5550

This public school was founded in 1964. It has a 457-acre campus.

RATINGS
Admissions Selectivity Rating: 60*   **Fire Safety Rating:** 60*   **Green Rating:** 60*

STUDENTS AND FACULTY
Student Body: 8% out-of-state. **Faculty:** Student/faculty ratio 30:1. 592 full-time faculty. 100% faculty teach undergrads.

ACADEMICS
Degrees: Bachelor's, certificate, doctoral, master's. **Academic Requirements:** Foreign languages, humanities, sciences (biological or physical), social science. **Majors with Highest Enrollment:** Business administration/management, education, health professions and related sciences. **Special Study Options:** Accelerated program, cooperative education program, double major, English as a Second Language (ESL), exchange student program (domestic), honors program, internships, liberal arts/career combination, student-designed major, study abroad, teacher certification program. Liberal arts/career combination: Students may choose from 5 concurrent education programs, combining their undergraduate degree and bachelor's of education degree.

FACILITIES
Housing: Coed dorms, women's dorms, special housing for disabled students, village residence and Quarry View Residence (townhouses). **Special Academic Facilities/Equipment:** Cool climate oenology and viticulture institute, map library, intructional resource center, Rodman Hall arts center, Cypriote Museum. **Computers:** 100% of classrooms are wireless, 93% of public computers are PCs, 7% of public computers are Macs, network access in dorm rooms, online registration, remote student access to Web through college's connection.

CAMPUS LIFE
Activities: Choral groups, concert band, dance, drama/theater, literary magazine, music ensembles, musical theater, radio station, student government, student newspaper, student-run film society, symphony orchestra, television station, yearbook. **Organizations:** 40 registered organizations, 6 religious organizations. **Athletics (Intercollegiate):** *Men:* Baseball, basketball, cheerleading, crew/rowing, cross-country, curling, fencing, golf, ice hockey, lacrosse, rugby, soccer, squash, swimming, tennis, wrestling. *Women:* Basketball, cheerleading, crew/rowing, cross-country, curling, fencing, golf, ice hockey, lacrosse, rugby, soccer, swimming, volleyball, wrestling.

ADMISSIONS
Freshman Academic Profile: TOEFL required of all international applicants, minimum paper TOEFL 580, minimum computer TOEFL 237. **Basis for Candidate Selection:** *Very important factors considered include:* Academic GPA, rigor of secondary school record. *Other factors considered include:* Standardized test scores, talent/ability. **Freshman Admission Requirements:** High school diploma is required, and GED is accepted. **Freshman Admission Statistics:** 16,870 applied. **Transfer Admission Requirements:** High school transcript, college transcript(s). **Admission Information:** Application fee $115. Regular application deadline 4/1. Regular notification is rolling. Nonfall registration accepted. Common Application not accepted. Neither credit nor placement offered for CEEB Advanced Placement tests.

COSTS AND FINANCIAL AID
Annual in-state tuition $4,852. Room and board $8,215. Average book expense $900. **Student Employment:** Federal Work-Study Program available. Institutional employment available. Off-campus job opportunities are good. **Financial Aid Statistics:** 39% undergrads receive any aid.

BROOKS INSTITUTE OF PHOTOGRAPHY

801 Alston Road, Santa Barbara, CA 93108
Phone: 805-966-3888 **E-mail:** admissions@brooks.edu
Fax: 805-564-1475 **Website:** www.brooks.edu
Financial Aid Phone: 805-966-3888

This private school was founded in 1945.

RATINGS
Admissions Selectivity Rating: 60*   **Fire Safety Rating:** 60*   **Green Rating:** 60*

STUDENTS AND FACULTY
Enrollment: 295. **Student Body:** 32% female, 68% male, 45% out-of-state, 29% international. Asian 2%, Caucasian 64%, Hispanic 4%. **Retention and Graduation:** 84% freshmen return for sophomore year.

ACADEMICS
Degrees: Associate, bachelor's, certificate, master's. **Academic Requirements:** English (including composition), humanities, mathematics, sciences (biological or physical), social science. **Special Study Options:** Double major, independent study, internships.

FACILITIES
Housing: Apartments for single students. **Special Academic Facilities/Equipment:** Photographic memorabilia—pre-1900 to present (equipment and imaging).

CAMPUS LIFE
Activities: Student government. **Organizations:** 1 honor society.

ADMISSIONS
Freshman Academic Profile: TOEFL required of all international applicants, minimum paper TOEFL 500. **Transfer Admission Requirements:** High school transcript, essay or personal statement, minimum college GPA of 2.0 required. Lowest grade transferable C. **General Admission Information:** Regular application deadline is rolling. Regular notification rolling. Nonfall registration accepted. Credit offered for CEEB Advanced Placement tests.

COSTS AND FINANCIAL AID
Annual tuition $15,000. Required fees $450. Average book expense $6,000. **Required Forms and Deadlines:** FAFSA, institution's own financial aid form. Financial aid filing deadline 3/2. **Types of Aid:** *Need-based scholarships/grants:* Pell, SEOG, state scholarships/grants, private scholarships. *Loans:* FFEL Subsidized Stafford, FFEL Unsubsidized Stafford, FFEL PLUS, alternative loans. **Student Employment:** Federal Work-Study Program available. Institutional employment available. Off-campus job opportunities are good. **Financial Aid Statistics:** 13% freshmen, 16% undergrads receive need-based scholarship or grant aid. 20% freshmen, 40% undergrads receive need-based self-help aid.

BROWN UNIVERSITY

Box 1876, 45 Prospect Street, Providence, RI 02912
Phone: 401-863-2378 **E-mail:** admission_undergraduate@brown.edu **CEEB Code:** 3094
Fax: 401-863-9300 **Website:** www.brown.edu **ACT Code:** 3800
Financial Aid Phone: 401-863-2721

This private school was founded in 1764. It has a 140-acre campus.

RATINGS
Admissions Selectivity Rating: 99   **Fire Safety Rating:** 86   **Green Rating:** 93

STUDENTS AND FACULTY
Enrollment: 5,798. **Student Body:** 51% female, 49% male, 96% out-of-state, 6% international (72 countries represented). African American 7%, Asian 14%, Caucasian 50%, Hispanic 8%. **Retention and Graduation:** 96% freshmen return for sophomore year. 35% grads go on to further study within 1 year. 10% grads pursue arts and sciences degrees. 1% grads pursue business degrees. 10%

grads pursue law degrees. 9% grads pursue medical degrees. **Faculty:** Student/faculty ratio 9:1. 702 full-time faculty, 95% hold PhDs. 100% faculty teach undergrads.

ACADEMICS

Degrees: Bachelor's, doctoral, first professional, master's. **Academic Requirements:** No requirements in specific areas; must graduate with writing competency. **Majors with Highest Enrollment:** History; international relations and affairs. **Disciplines with Highest Percentage of Degrees Awarded:** Biological/life sciences 17%, physical sciences 12%, interdisciplinary studies 1%. **Special Study Options:** Accelerated program, cross-registration, double major, exchange student program (domestic), honor program, independent study, internships, student-designed major, study abroad, teacher certification program, 8-year medical program (AB or SCB plus MD), 5-year degree program (AB and SCB).

FACILITIES

Housing: Coed dorms, women's dorms, special housing for international students, fraternity/sorority housing, cooperative housing, language houses, international house, enviromental studies house, social dormitories, cultural houses, and other special program housing. **Special Academic Facilities/Equipment:** Art gallery, anthropology museum, language lab, information technology center, NASA research center, center for modern culture/media. **Computers:** 30% of public computers are PCs, 70% of public computers are Macs, network access in dorm rooms, network access in dorm lounges, online registration, remote student-access to Web through college's connection.

CAMPUS LIFE

Activities: Choral groups, concert band, dance, drama/theater, jazz band, literary magazine, marching band, music ensembles, musical theater, radio station, student government, student newspaper, student-run film society, symphony orchestra, television station, yearbook. **Organizations:** 240 registered organizations, 10 fraternities (12% men join), 3 sororities (2% women join). **Athletics (Intercollegiate):** *Men:* Baseball, basketball, crew/rowing, cross-country, diving, fencing, football, golf, ice hockey, lacrosse, soccer, squash, swimming, tennis, track/field (indoor), track/field (outdoor), water polo, wrestling. *Women:* Basketball, crew/rowing, cross-country, diving, equestrian sports, fencing, field hockey, golf, gymnastics, ice hockey, lacrosse, skiing (downhill/alpine), soccer, softball, squash, swimming, tennis, track/field (indoor), track/field (outdoor), volleyball, water polo. **Environmental Initiatives:** Reduce GHG emissions to 42% (15% below 1990) below 2007 for existing buildings. Reduce GHG emissions for all newly constructed facilities between 25% and 50% below code requirements. Reduce GHG emissions for all newly acquired facilities by a minimum of 15% and as much as 30%.

ADMISSIONS

Freshman Academic Profile: 91% in top 10% of high school class, 99% in top 25% of high school class, 100% in top 50% of high school class. 60% from public high schools. SAT Math middle 50% range 670–770. SAT Critical Reading middle 50% range 660–760. SAT Writing middle 50% range 660–760. ACT middle 50% range 28–33. TOEFL required of all international applicants, minimum paper TOEFL 600, minimum computer TOEFL 250. **Basis for Candidate Selection:** *Very important factors considered include:* Character/personal qualities, rigor of secondary school record, talent/ability. *Important factors considered include:* Academic GPA, application essay, class rank, extracurricular activities, level of applicant's interest, recommendation(s), standardized test scores. *Other factors considered include:* Alumni/ae relation, first generation, geographical residence, interview, racial/ethnic status, state residency, volunteer work, work experience. **Freshman Admission Requirements:** High school diploma is required, and GED is not accepted. *Academic units required:* 4 English, 3 math, 3 science (2 science labs), 3 foreign language, 2 history, 1 academic elective. *Academic units recommended:* 4 English, 4 math, 4 science (3 science labs), 4 foreign language, 2 history, 1 academic elective. **Freshman Admission Statistics:** 18,316 applied, 14% admitted, 59% enrolled. **Transfer Admission Requirements:** High school transcript, college transcript(s), essay or personal statement, standardized test score, statement of good standing from prior institution(s). Lowest grade transferable C. **General Admission Information:** Application fee $70. Early Decision application deadline 11/1. Regular application deadline 1/1. Regular notification 4/1. Nonfall registration not accepted. Admission may be deferred for a maximum of 1 year. Placement offered for CEEB Advanced Placement tests.

COSTS AND FINANCIAL AID

Annual tuition $32,264. Room & board $8,796. Required fees $955. Average book expense $2,515. **Required Forms and Deadlines:** FAFSA, CSS/Financial Aid PROFILE, Noncustodial PROFILE, Business/Farm Supplement. Financial aid filing deadline 2/1. **Notification of Awards:** Applicants will be notified of awards on or about 4/1. **Types of Aid:** *Need-based scholarships/grants:* Pell, SEOG, state scholarships/grants, private scholarships, the school's own gift aid. *Loans:* Direct Subsidized Stafford, Direct Unsubsidized Stafford, Direct PLUS, Federal Perkins, state loans, college/university loans from institutional funds. **Student Employment:** Federal Work-Study Program

available. Institutional employment available. Off-campus job opportunities are excellent. **Financial Aid Statistics:** 40% freshmen, 40% undergrads receive need-based scholarship or grant aid. 32% freshmen, 39% undergrads receive need-based self-help aid. Highest amount earned per year from on-campus jobs $2,000.

BRYAN COLLEGE

PO Box 7000, Dayton, TN 37321-7000
Phone: 423-775-2041 **E-mail:** admiss@bryan.edu **CEEB Code:** 1908
Fax: 423-775-7199 **Website:** www.bryan.edu

This is a private school.

RATINGS

Admissions Selectivity Rating: 60*　　**Fire Safety Rating:** 60*　　**Green Rating:** 60*

STUDENTS AND FACULTY

Student Body: 72% out-of-state.

ACADEMICS

Degrees: Associate, bachelor's.

FACILITIES

Housing: Coed dorms, men's dorms, women's dorms.

CAMPUS LIFE

Organizations: 2 honor societies, 2 religious organizations. **Athletics (Intercollegiate):** *Men:* Basketball, cheerleading, cross-country, soccer, tennis, volleyball. *Women:* Basketball, cheerleading, cross-country, tennis, volleyball.

ADMISSIONS

Freshman Academic Profile: TOEFL required of all international applicants, minimum paper TOEFL 500. **General Admission Information:** Regular application deadline 7/31.

COSTS AND FINANCIAL AID

Annual tuition $8,450. Room and board $2,548. Required fees $60. Average book expense $1,000. **Types of Aid:** *Need-based scholarships/grants:* Pell, SEOG, state scholarships/grants, private scholarships, the school's own gift aid. *Loans:* FFEL Subsidized Stafford, FFEL Unsubsidized Stafford, FFEL PLUS, Federal Perkins, college/university loans from institutional funds. **Student Employment:** Federal Work-Study Program available. Highest amount earned per year from on-campus jobs $800.

BRYANT UNIVERSITY

1150 Douglas Pike Suite 3, Smithfield, RI 02917-1285
Phone: 401-232-6100 **E-mail:** admission@bryant.edu **CEEB Code:** 3095
Fax: 401-232-6741 **Website:** www.bryant.edu **ACT Code:** 3802
Financial Aid Phone: 401-232-6020

This private school was founded in 1863. It has a 420-acre campus.

RATINGS

Admissions Selectivity Rating: 90　　**Fire Safety Rating:** 91　　**Green Rating:** 83

STUDENTS AND FACULTY

Enrollment: 3,231. **Student Body:** 42% female, 58% male, 84% out-of-state, 2% international (31 countries represented). African American 3%, Asian 3%, Caucasian 85%, Hispanic 4%. **Retention and Graduation:** 86% freshmen return for sophomore year. 62% freshmen graduate within 4 years. 5% grads go on to further study within 1 year. 1% grads pursue arts and sciences degrees. 3% grads pursue business degrees. 1% grads pursue law degrees. **Faculty:** Student/faculty ratio 16:1. 147 full-time faculty, 86% hold PhDs. 100% faculty teach undergrads.

ACADEMICS

Degrees: Bachelor's, master's, post-master's certificate. **Academic Requirements:** Computer literacy, English (including composition), history, humanities, mathematics, sciences (biological or physical), social science, accounting, computer science, economics, finance, law, management, marketing. **Classes:** Most classes have 30–39 students. Most lab/discussion sections have 20–29 students. **Majors with Highest Enrollment:** Accounting, business administration and management, marketing/marketing management. **Disciplines with Highest Percentage of Degrees Awarded:** Business/marketing 87%, computer and information sciences 6%, communications/journalism 3%, social sciences 2%, psychology 1%, English 1%. **Special Study Options:** Double major, English as a Second Language (ESL), honors program, independent study, internships, study abroad, Beta Gamma Sigma (business honor society), Omicron Delta Epsilon (economics honor society), Lambda Pi Eta (communication honor society).

FACILITIES

Housing: Coed dorms, women's dorms, special housing for disabled students, 24 hour quiet, honors, all women for upperclass, international business. **Special Academic Facilities/Equipment:** George E. Bello Center for Information and Technology, Koffler Technology Center and Communications Complex, John H. Chafee Center for International Business, Koffler Television Studio, C.V. Starr Financial Markets Center, learning and language lab. **Computers:** 100% of classrooms are wired, 100% of classrooms are wireless, 100% of public computers are PCs, network access in dorm rooms, network access in dorm lounges, online registration, online administrative functions (other than registration), support for handheld computing, remote student-access to Web through college's connection, tuition includes personal computer. Undergraduates are required to own a computer.

CAMPUS LIFE

Activities: Choral groups, dance, drama/theater, jazz band, radio station, student government, student newspaper, yearbook. **Organizations:** 76 registered organizations, 3 honor societies, 1 religious organization. 6 fraternities, 3 sororities. **Athletics (Intercollegiate):** *Men:* Baseball, basketball, cross-country, football, golf, lacrosse, soccer, swimming, tennis, track/field (indoor), track/field (outdoor). *Women:* Basketball, cross-country, field hockey, lacrosse, soccer, softball, swimming, tennis, track/field (indoor), track/field (outdoor), volleyball. **Environmental Initiatives:** Recycling Program. Purchasing renewable energy credits. Environmental studies major.

ADMISSIONS

Freshman Academic Profile: 24% in top 10% of high school class, 63% in top 25% of high school class, 93% in top 50% of high school class. SAT Math middle 50% range 550–630. SAT Critical Reading middle 50% range 520–600. SAT Writing middle 50% range 520–600. ACT middle 50% range 22–26. TOEFL required of all international applicants, minimum paper TOEFL 550, minimum computer TOEFL 213. **Basis for Candidate Selection:** *Very important factors considered include:* Academic GPA, rigor of secondary school record. *Important factors considered include:* Application essay, class rank, recommendation(s), standardized test scores. *Other factors considered include:* Alumni/ae relation, character/personal qualities, extracurricular activities, first generation, geographical residence, interview, level of applicant's interest, racial/ethnic status, state residency, talent/ability, volunteer work, work experience. **Freshman Admission Requirements:** High school diploma is required, and GED is accepted. *Academic units required:* 4 English, 4 math, 3 science (2 science labs), 2 foreign language, 2 history/social sciences. *Academic units recommended:* 4 history/social sciences. **Freshman Admission Statistics:** 5,829 applied, 44% admitted, 32% enrolled. **Transfer Admission Requirements:** High school transcript, college transcript(s), essay or personal statement, minimum college GPA of 2.5 required. Lowest grade transferable C. **General Admission Information:** Application fee $50. Early decision application deadline 11/15. Regular application deadline 2/1. Regular notification 3/15. Nonfall registration accepted. Admission may be deferred for a maximum of 1 year. Credit and/or placement offered for CEEB Advanced Placement tests.

COSTS AND FINANCIAL AID

Annual tuition $27,639. Room and board $10,715. Average book expense $1,200. **Required Forms and Deadlines:** FAFSA. Financial aid filing deadline 2/15. **Notification of Awards:** Applicants will be notified of awards on or about 3/24. **Types of Aid:** *Need-based scholarships/grants:* Pell, SEOG, state scholarships/grants, private scholarships, the school's own gift aid. *Loans:* Direct Subsidized Stafford, Direct Unsubsidized Stafford, FFEL PLUS, Federal Perkins. **Financial Aid Statistics:** 57% freshmen, 55% undergrads receive need-based scholarship or grant aid. 60% freshmen, 60% undergrads receive need-based self-help aid. 20 freshmen, 57 undergrads receive athletic scholarships. 85% freshmen, 85% undergrads receive any aid. Highest amount earned per year from on-campus jobs $5,000.

See page 1096.

BRYN ATHYN COLLEGE OF THE NEW CHURCH

PO Box 717, Bryn Athyn, PA 19009
Phone: 215-938-2511 **E-mail:** dsjohns@newchurch.edu **CEEB Code:** 2002
Fax: 215-938-2658 **Website:** www.newchurch.edu
Financial Aid Phone: 267-502-2630

This private school, affiliated with the General Church of the New Jerusalem, was founded in 1877. It has a 130-acre campus.

RATINGS

Admissions Selectivity Rating: 60*   **Fire Safety Rating:** 71   **Green Rating:** 66

STUDENTS AND FACULTY

Enrollment: 109. **Student Body:** 57% female, 43% male, 29% out-of-state, 20% international (10 countries represented). Asian 4%, Caucasian 75%. **Retention and Graduation:** 64% freshmen return for sophomore year. 14% freshmen graduate within 4 years. **Faculty:** Student/faculty ratio 6:1. 18 full-time faculty, 78% hold PhDs. 92% faculty teach undergrads.

ACADEMICS

Degrees: Associate, bachelor's, first professional certificate, first professional, master's. **Academic Requirements:** Arts/fine arts, English (including composition), foreign languages, history, mathematics, philosophy, sciences (biological or physical), social science, religion, physical education. **Classes:** Most classes have fewer than 10 students. Most lab/discussion sections have fewer than 10 students. **Majors with Highest Enrollment:** English language and literature, history, multi/interdisciplinary studies. **Disciplines with Highest Percentage of Degrees Awarded:** Education 36%, interdisciplinary studies 29%, English 21%, biological/life sciences 7%, social sciences 7%. **Special Study Options:** Cooperative education program, distance learning, dual enrollment, English as a Second Language (ESL), independent study, internships, student-designed major, study abroad.

FACILITIES

Housing: Men's dorms, women's dorms, houses contiguous to campus. **Special Academic Facilities/Equipment:** Glencairn Museum, Swedenborg Library, Swedenborgiana Academy of the New Church Archives, John Pitcairn Archives, Raymond & Mildred Pitcairn Archives. **Computers:** 100% of public computers are PCs, network access in dorm rooms, network access in dorm lounges, remote student-access to Web through college's connection.

CAMPUS LIFE

Activities: Choral groups, dance, drama/theater, musical theater, student government, student newspaper. **Organizations:** 13 registered organizations, 1 sorority. **Environmental Initiatives:** Chemical purchase, storage and disposal plan. LEED certified construction. Recycling program for glass and paper in all buildings.

ADMISSIONS

Freshman Academic Profile: 3% from public high schools. SAT Math middle 50% range 500–580. SAT Critical Reading middle 50% range 430–570. SAT Writing middle 50% range 410–550. ACT middle 50% range 20–21. TOEFL required of all international applicants, minimum paper TOEFL 520, minimum computer TOEFL 190. **Basis for Candidate Selection:** *Very important factors considered include:* Character/personal qualities, recommendation(s), religious affiliation/commitment, rigor of secondary school record. *Important factors considered include:* Application essay, standardized test scores. *Other factors considered include:* Alumni/ae relation, class rank, extracurricular activities, interview, talent/ability, volunteer work, work experience. **Freshman Admission Requirements:** High school diploma is required, and GED is accepted. *Academic units required:* 4 English, 3 math, 3 science, 2 foreign language, 3 social studies shared with history. **Freshman Admission Statistics:** 39 applied, 97% admitted, 92% enrolled. **Transfer Admission Requirements:** College transcript(s), essay or personal statement, minimum college GPA of 2.5 required. Lowest grade transferable C-. **General Admission Information:** Application fee $30. Regular application deadline 7/1. Regular notification rolling. Nonfall registration accepted. Admission may be deferred for a maximum of 1 year. Common Application not accepted. Credit and/or placement offered for CEEB Advanced Placement tests.

COSTS AND FINANCIAL AID

Annual tuition $8,676. Room and board $5,853. Required fees $1,944. Average book expense $950. **Required Forms and Deadlines:** Institution's own financial aid form, most recent year tax return. Financial aid filing deadline 6/1. **Notification of Awards:** Applicants will be notified of awards on a rolling basis beginning on or about 6/1. **Types of Aid:** *Need-based scholarships/grants:* Private scholarships, the school's own gift aid. **Student Employment:** Institutional employment available. Off-campus job opportunities are good.

Financial Aid Statistics: 58% freshmen, 49% undergrads receive need-based scholarship or grant aid. 11% freshmen, 18% undergrads receive need-based self-help aid. 93% freshmen, 86% undergrads receive any aid.

BRYN MAWR COLLEGE

101 North Merion Avenue, Bryn Mawr, PA 19010-2859
Phone: 610-526-5152 **E-mail:** admissions@brynmawr.edu **CEEB Code:** 2049
Fax: 610-526-7471 **Website:** www.brynmawr.edu **ACT Code:** 3526
Financial Aid Phone: 610-526-5245

This private school was founded in 1885. It has a 135-acre campus.

RATINGS

Admissions Selectivity Rating: 95　　　**Fire Safety Rating:** 74　　　**Green Rating:** 85

STUDENTS AND FACULTY

Enrollment: 1,362. **Student Body:** 98% female, 2% male, 83% out-of-state, 6% international (40 countries represented). African American 6%, Asian 12%, Caucasian 49%, Hispanic 3%. **Retention and Graduation:** 96% freshmen return for sophomore year. 74% freshmen graduate within 4 years. 20% grads go on to further study within 1 year. 10% grads pursue arts and sciences degrees. 2% grads pursue business degrees. 4% grads pursue law degrees. 3% grads pursue medical degrees. **Faculty:** Student/faculty ratio 8:1. 145 full-time faculty, 97% hold PhDs. 100% faculty teach undergrads.

ACADEMICS

Degrees: Bachelor's, doctoral, master's, post-bachelor's certificate. **Academic Requirements:** English (including composition), foreign languages, humanities, mathematics, sciences (biological or physical), social science, 2 semesters of physical education, 8–10 courses in major. **Classes:** Most classes have 10–19 students. **Majors with Highest Enrollment:** English language and literature; mathematics; political science and government. **Disciplines with Highest Percentage of Degrees Awarded:** Social sciences 24%, English 13%, foreign languages and literature 13%, biological/life sciences 10%, physical sciences 8%. **Special Study Options:** Accelerated program, cross-registration, double major, dual enrollment, exchange student program (domestic), independent study, internships, liberal arts/career combination, student-designed major, study abroad, teacher certification program. AB/MA city planning 3–2 program in city and regional planning offered with the University of Pennsylvania. AB/BS 3–2 engineering programs with Cal Tech.

FACILITIES

Housing: Coed dorms, women's dorms, apartments for single students, cooperative housing, students may live at Haverford. Foreign language houses available to students studying Chinese, French, German, Hebrew, Italian, Russsian, or Spanish. Coed housing is available. **Special Academic Facilities/Equipment:** Museum of classical and Near Eastern archaeology, mineral collection, child study institute, on-campus nursery school, Newfeld Collection of African Art, language learning center. **Computers:** 80% of public computers are PCs, 20% of public computers are Macs, network access in dorm rooms, online registration, online administrative functions (other than registration), remote student-access to Web through college's connection.

CAMPUS LIFE

Activities: Choral groups, dance, drama/theater, literary magazine, music ensembles, musical theater, radio station, student government, student newspaper, student-run film society, yearbook. **Organizations:** 100 registered organizations, 11 religious organizations. **Athletics (Intercollegiate):** *Women:* Badminton, basketball, crew/rowing, cross-country, field hockey, lacrosse, soccer, swimming, tennis, track/field (outdoor), volleyball. **Environmental Initiatives:** Bryn Mawr has received two Pennsylvania Growing Greener Grants for watershed improvements under the Environmental improvement and Watershed Protection Act, and are committed to being good steward's of the waterway that pass through campus. They're currently removing all incandescent light bulbs from Campus, and are committed to reducing their consumption of electricity through the use of technology. All capital projects are required to be designed using the appropriate LEED checklist archiving a minimum of 26 points. Bryn Mawr is committed to designing sustainability into the renovations of our buildings.

ADMISSIONS

Freshman Academic Profile: 62% in top 10% of high school class, 88% in top 25% of high school class, 100% in top 50% of high school class. 64% from public high schools. SAT Math middle 50% range 580–690. SAT Critical Reading middle 50% range 620–730. SAT Writing middle 50% range 620–720. ACT middle 50% range 26–30. TOEFL required of all international applicants, minimum paper TOEFL 600, minimum computer TOEFL 250. **Basis for Candidate Selection:** *Very important factors considered include:* Recommendation(s), rigor of secondary school record. *Important factors considered include:* Academic GPA, application essay, character/personal qualities, extracurricular activities. *Other factors considered include:* Alumni/ae relation, class rank, first generation, geographical residence, interview, racial/ethnic status, standardized test scores, talent/ability, volunteer work, work experience. **Freshman Admission Requirements:** High school diploma is required, and GED is accepted. *Academic units required:* 2 academic electives. *Academic units recommended:* 4 English, 3 math, 2 science (1 science lab), 3 foreign language, 2 social studies, 2 history. **Freshman Admission Statistics:** 2,133 applied, 44% admitted, 38% enrolled. **Transfer Admission Requirements:** High school transcript, college transcript(s), essay or personal statement, standardized test score, statement of good standing from prior institution(s). Lowest grade transferable C. **General Admission Information:** Application fee $50. Early decision application deadline 11/15 Regular application deadline 1/15. Regular notification 4/15. Nonfall registration not accepted. Admission may be deferred for a maximum of 1 year. Credit and/or placement offered for CEEB Advanced Placement tests.

COSTS AND FINANCIAL AID

Annual tuition $32,230. Room & board $10,550. Required fees $780. Average book expense $1,000. **Required Forms and Deadlines:** FAFSA, CSS/Financial Aid PROFILE, Business/Farm Supplement, statement of earnings from parents' employer. Financial aid filing deadline 3/1. **Notification of Awards:** Applicants will be notified of awards on or about 3/23. **Types of Aid:** *Need-based scholarships/grants:* Pell, SEOG, state scholarships/grants, the school's own gift aid, Federal Academic Competitiveness Grant (ACG), Federal National Science and Mathematics to Retain Talent Grant (SMART). *Loans:* FFEL Subsidized Stafford, FFEL Unsubsidized Stafford, FFEL PLUS, Federal Perkins. **Financial Aid Statistics:** 55% freshmen, 56% undergrads receive need-based scholarship or grant aid. 46% freshmen, 48% undergrads receive need-based self-help aid. 73% freshmen, 68% undergrads receive any aid. Highest amount earned per year from on-campus jobs $2,000.

BUCKNELL UNIVERSITY

Freas Hall, Bucknell University, Lewisburg, PA 17837
Phone: 570-577-1101 **E-mail:** admissions@bucknell.edu **CEEB Code:** 2050
Fax: 570-577-3538 **Website:** www.bucknell.edu **ACT Code:** 3528
Financial Aid Phone: 570-577-1331

This private school was founded in 1846. It has a 446-acre campus.

RATINGS

Admissions Selectivity Rating: 96　　　**Fire Safety Rating:** 87　　　**Green Rating:** 83

STUDENTS AND FACULTY

Enrollment: 3,528. **Student Body:** 51% female, 49% male, 73% out-of-state, 3% international (41 countries represented). African American 3%, Asian 7%, Caucasian 80%, Hispanic 4%. **Retention and Graduation:** 96% freshmen return for sophomore year. 85% freshmen graduate within 4 years. 22% grads go on to further study within 1 year. 15% grads pursue arts and sciences degrees. 1% grads pursue business degrees. 4% grads pursue law degrees. 2% grads pursue medical degrees. **Faculty:** Student/faculty ratio 12:1. 301 full-time faculty, 97% hold PhDs. 100% faculty teach undergrads.

ACADEMICS

Degrees: Bachelor's, master's. **Academic Requirements:** English (including composition), humanities, mathematics, sciences (biological or physical), social science. **Classes:** Most classes have 10–19 students. Most lab/discussion sections have 10–19 students. **Majors with Highest Enrollment:** Business administration and management, economics, psychology. **Disciplines with Highest Percentage of Degrees Awarded:** Social sciences 23%, business/marketing 14%, engineering 13%, biological/life sciences 8%, psychology 7%.

Special Study Options: Double major, dual enrollment, honors program, independent study, internships, liberal arts/career combination, student-designed major, study abroad, teacher certification program.

FACILITIES

Housing: Coed dorms, women's dorms, apartments for single students, special housing for disabled students, special housing for international students, fraternity/sorority housing, substance-free, Judaic studies, Afro-American studies. **Special Academic Facilities/Equipment:** Art gallery, center for performing arts, poetry center, photography lab, observatory, 63-acre nature site, greenhouse, primate facility, gas chromatograph/mass spectrometer, electron microscope, herbarium, crafts center, engineering structural test lab, nuclear magnetic resonance spectrometer, 18-hole golf course, conference center, high ropes course. **Computers:** 100% of classrooms are wired, 100% of classrooms are wireless, 80% of public computers are PCs, 10% of public computers are Macs, 10% of public computers are UNIX, network access in dorm rooms, network access in dorm lounges, online registration, online administrative functions (other than registration), remote student-access to Web through college's connection.

CAMPUS LIFE

Activities: Choral groups, concert band, dance, drama/theater, jazz band, literary magazine, music ensembles, musical theater, opera, pep band, radio station, student government, student newspaper, student-run film society, symphony orchestra, yearbook. **Organizations:** 150 registered organizations, 23 honor societies, 15 religious organizations. 13 fraternities (39% men join), 6 sororities (40% women join). **Athletics (Intercollegiate):** *Men:* Baseball, basketball, cross-country, diving, football, golf, lacrosse, soccer, swimming, tennis, track/field (indoor), track/field (outdoor), water polo, wrestling. *Women:* Basketball, crew/rowing, cross-country, diving, field hockey, golf, lacrosse, soccer, softball, swimming, tennis, track/field (indoor), track/field (outdoor), volleyball, water polo. **Environmental Initiatives:** In September of 2007, the Bucknell University Environmental Center (BUEC) initiated a campus-wide environmental assessment of the university's operations, involving over 65 faculty, students, staff, and community members in a highly educational and collaborative project. The University will purchase Energy Star products that meet the strict efficiency guidelines of the EPA. Bucknell has also purchased 1 million kilowatt hours of electricity from renewable wind energy sources each year since 2002. Wind power now accounts for 100% of Bucknell's purchased energy.

ADMISSIONS

Freshman Academic Profile: 71% in top 10% of high school class, 94% in top 25% of high school class, 100% in top 50% of high school class. 69% from public high schools. SAT Math middle 50% range 630–710. SAT Critical Reading middle 50% range 600–690. SAT Writing middle 50% range 600–690. ACT middle 50% range 27–31. TOEFL required of all international applicants, minimum paper TOEFL 550, minimum computer TOEFL 213. **Basis for Candidate Selection:** *Very important factors considered include:* Academic GPA, character/personal qualities, class rank, rigor of secondary school record, standardized test scores, talent/ability. *Important factors considered include:* Extracurricular activities, level of applicant's interest, racial/ethnic status, recommendation(s), volunteer work. *Other factors considered include:* Alumni/ae relation, application essay, first generation, geographical residence, interview, religious affiliation/commitment, work experience. **Freshman Admission Requirements:** High school diploma is required, and GED is accepted. *Academic units required:* 4 English, 3 math, 2 science, 2 foreign language, 2 social studies, 2 history, 1 academic elective. *Academic units recommended:* 4 English, 4 math, 3 science, 4 foreign language, 2 social studies, 2 history, 1 academic elective. **Freshman Admission Statistics:** 9,021 applied, 33% admitted, 31% enrolled. **Transfer Admission Requirements:** High school transcript, college transcript(s), essay or personal statement, statement of good standing from prior institution(s). Minimum college GPA of 2.5 required. Lowest grade transferable C. **General Admission Information:** Application fee $60. Early decision application deadline 11/15. Regular application deadline 1/1. Regular notification 4/1. Nonfall registration not accepted. Admission may be deferred for a maximum of 2 years. Credit and/or placement offered for CEEB Advanced Placement tests.

COSTS AND FINANCIAL AID

Annual tuition $39,434. Room and board $8,052. Required fees $218. Average book expense $750. **Required Forms and Deadlines:** FAFSA, CSS/Financial Aid PROFILE, Noncustodial PROFILE. Financial aid filing deadline 1/1. **Notification of Awards:** Applicants will be notified of awards on or about 4/1. **Types of Aid:** *Need-based scholarships/grants:* Pell, SEOG, state scholarships/grants, private scholarships, the school's own gift aid. *Loans:* FFEL Subsidized Stafford, FFEL Unsubsidized Stafford, FFEL PLUS, Federal Perkins. **Financial Aid Statistics:** 46% freshmen, 46% undergrads receive need-based scholarship or grant aid. 46% freshmen, 48% undergrads receive need-based self-help aid. 4 freshmen, 21 undergrads receive athletic scholarships. 60% freshmen, 62% undergrads receive any aid. Highest amount earned per year from on-campus jobs $1,500.

BUENA VISTA UNIVERSITY

610 West Fourth Street, Storm Lake, IA 50588-1798
Phone: 712-749-2235 **E-mail:** admissions@bvu.edu **CEEB Code:** 6047
Fax: 712-749-1459 **Website:** www.bvu.edu **ACT Code:** 1278
Financial Aid Phone: 712-749-2164

This private school, affiliated with the Presbyterian Church, was founded in 1891. It has a 60-acre campus.

RATINGS

Admissions Selectivity Rating: 75   **Fire Safety Rating:** 71   **Green Rating:** 60*

STUDENTS AND FACULTY

Enrollment: 1,121. **Student Body:** 51% female, 49% male, 21% out-of-state. African American 4%, Asian 1%, Caucasian 91%, Hispanic 3%. **Retention and Graduation:** 71% freshmen return for sophomore year. 47% freshmen graduate within 4 years. 17% grads go on to further study within 1 year. 8% grads pursue arts and sciences degrees. 1% grads pursue business degrees. 8% grads pursue medical degrees. **Faculty:** Student/faculty ratio 12:1. 83 full-time faculty, 69% hold PhDs. 100% faculty teach undergrads.

ACADEMICS

Degrees: Bachelor's, master's. **Academic Requirements:** Arts/fine arts, computer literacy, English (including composition), humanities, mathematics, sciences (biological or physical), social science, speech. **Classes:** Most classes have 10–19 students. Most lab/discussion sections have 10–19 students. **Majors with Highest Enrollment:** Biology/biological sciences, elementary education and teaching, management science. **Disciplines with Highest Percentage of Degrees Awarded:** Business/marketing 29%, education 23%, interdisciplinary studies 10%, psychology 10%, security and protective services 8%. **Special Study Options:** Distance learning, double major, dual enrollment, English as a Second Language (ESL), exchange student program (domestic), external degree program, honors program, independent study, internships, student-designed major, study abroad, teacher certification program, off-campus study, other semester-away programs available. Academic and cultural events series brings national and world leaders and performers to campus; students earn credits for attendance.

FACILITIES

Housing: Coed dorms, men's dorms, women's dorms. **Special Academic Facilities/Equipment:** Art gallery, language lab, television station, radio station, satellite telecommunications system, computer labs/centers, electron microscope. **Computers:** 100% of classrooms are wireless, 95% of public computers are PCs, 4% of public computers are Macs, 1% of public computers are UNIX, network access in dorm rooms, network access in dorm lounges, online registration, online administrative functions (other than registration), remote student-access to Web through college's connection.

CAMPUS LIFE

Activities: Choral groups, concert band, drama/theater, jazz band, music ensembles, musical theater, pep band, radio station, student government, student newspaper, television station. **Organizations:** 70 registered organizations, 5 honor societies, 3 religious organizations. **Athletics (Intercollegiate):** *Men:* Baseball, basketball, cross-country, football, golf, soccer, tennis, track/field (indoor), track/field (outdoor), wrestling. *Women:* Basketball, cross-country, golf, soccer, softball, tennis, track/field (indoor), track/field (outdoor), volleyball.

ADMISSIONS

Freshman Academic Profile: 20% in top 10% of high school class, 42% in top 25% of high school class, 73% in top 50% of high school class. 85% from public high schools. ACT middle 50% range 19–24. TOEFL required of all international applicants, minimum paper TOEFL 550, minimum computer TOEFL 213. **Basis for Candidate Selection:** *Very important factors considered include:* Academic GPA, class rank, recommendation(s), rigor of secondary school record, standardized test scores. *Other factors considered include:* Alumni/ae relation, application essay, character/personal qualities, extracurricular activities, first generation, interview, talent/ability, volunteer work, work experience. **Freshman Admission Requirements:** High school diploma is required, and GED is accepted. *Academic units required:* 4 English, 2 science, 2 social studies. *Academic units recommended:* 4 math, 4 science, 2 foreign language, 2 history, 1 computer science. **Freshman Admission Statistics:** 1,107 applied, 79% admitted, 31% enrolled. **Transfer Admission Requirements:** College transcript(s), statement of good standing from prior institution(s). Minimum college GPA of 2.0 required. Lowest grade transferable D. **General Admission Information:** Regular notification rolling. Nonfall registration accepted. Admission may be deferred for a maximum of 1 year. Credit and/or placement offered for CEEB Advanced Placement tests.

COSTS AND FINANCIAL AID

Annual tuition $23,842. Room and board $6,712. Average book expense $1,500. **Required Forms and Deadlines:** FAFSA. Financial aid filing deadline 6/1. **Notification of Awards:** Applicants will be notified of awards on a rolling basis beginning on or about 2/20. **Types of Aid:** *Need-based scholarships/grants:* Pell, SEOG, state scholarships/grants, private scholarships, the school's own gift aid. *Loans:* FFEL Subsidized Stafford, FFEL Unsubsidized Stafford, FFEL PLUS, Federal Perkins, state loans, college/university loans from institutional funds. **Financial Aid Statistics:** 89% freshmen, 91% undergrads receive need-based scholarship or grant aid. 83% freshmen, 81% undergrads receive need-based self-help aid. 99% freshmen, 98% undergrads receive any aid. Highest amount earned per year from on-campus jobs $1,050.

BURLINGTON COLLEGE

95 North Avenue, Burlington, VT 05401
Phone: 802-862-9616 **E-mail:** admissions@burcol.edu **CEEB Code:** 3944
Fax: 802-660-4331 **Website:** www.burlingtoncollege.edu
Financial Aid Phone: 802-862-9616

This private school was founded in 1972. It has a 1-acre campus.

RATINGS

Admissions Selectivity Rating: 60*   **Fire Safety Rating:** 60*   **Green Rating:** 74

STUDENTS AND FACULTY

Enrollment: 245. **Student Body:** 64% female, 36% male, 39% out-of-state. **Retention and Graduation:** 59% freshmen return for sophomore year. 34% grads go on to further study within 1 year. 34% grads pursue arts and sciences degrees. **Faculty:** Student/faculty ratio 8:1. 100% faculty teach undergrads.

ACADEMICS

Degrees: Associate, bachelor's, certificate. **Academic Requirements:** Arts/fine arts, computer literacy, English (including composition), history, humanities, mathematics, sciences (biological or physical), social science. **Classes:** Most classes have fewer than 10 students. **Majors with Highest Enrollment:** Area, ethnic, cultural, and gender studies; film/cinema studies; social sciences. **Disciplines with Highest Percentage of Degrees Awarded:** Psychology 54%, visual and performing arts 20%, English 17%, social sciences 6%. **Special Study Options:** Cross-registration, distance learning, double major, dual enrollment, external degree program, independent study, internships, liberal arts/career combination, student-designed major, study abroad, weekend college.

FACILITIES

Housing: Apartments for married students, apartments for single students.

CAMPUS LIFE

Activities: Drama/theater, literary magazine, student government, student newspaper, student-run film society. **Environmental Initiatives:** Conducted energy audits on all buildings, completed 75% of recommendations and plan to complete the rest. Plan to build LEED-certified building. Organic Community Garden.

ADMISSIONS

Freshman Academic Profile: TOEFL required of all international applicants, minimum paper TOEFL 500. **Basis for Candidate Selection:** *Very important factors considered include:* Application essay, interview. *Important factors considered include:* Character/personal qualities, recommendation(s), rigor of secondary school record, talent/ability. *Other factors considered include:* Extracurricular activities, volunteer work, work experience. **Freshman Admission Requirements:** High school diploma is required, and GED is accepted. *Academic units recommended:* 4 English, 3 math, 3 science (1 science lab), 2 foreign language, 4 social studies, 3 history, 4 academic electives. **Freshman Admission Statistics:** 43 applied, 95% admitted, 68% enrolled. **Transfer Admission Requirements:** College transcript(s), essay or personal statement, interview, Lowest grade transferable C+. **General Admission Information:** Application fee $35. Regular application deadline 8/3. Regular notification rolling. Nonfall registration accepted. Admission may be deferred for a maximum of 1 year. Common Application accepted. Credit offered for CEEB Advanced Placement tests.

COSTS AND FINANCIAL AID

Annual tuition $18,350. Room and board $5,750. Average book expense $1,075. **Required Forms and Deadlines:** FAFSA. Financial aid filing deadline 8/1. Financial aid filing deadline 6/1. **Notification of Awards:** Applicants will be notified of awards on a rolling basis beginning on or about 4/1. **Types of Aid:** *Need-based scholarships/grants:* Pell, SEOG, state scholarships/grants, private

scholarships, the school's own gift aid, Work Study Aid. *Loans:* FFEL Subsidized Stafford, FFEL Unsubsidized Stafford, FFEL PLUS, Federal Perkins, college/university loans from institutional funds. **Student Employment:** Federal Work-Study Program available. Off-campus job opportunities are excellent. **Financial Aid Statistics:** 58% freshmen, 72% undergrads receive need-based scholarship or grant aid. 71% freshmen receive need-based self-help aid.

BUTLER UNIVERSITY

4600 Sunset Avenue, Indianapolis, IN 46208
Phone: 317-940-8100 **E-mail:** admission@butler.edu **CEEB Code:** 1073
Fax: 317-940-8150 **Website:** www.butler.edu **ACT Code:** 1180
Financial Aid Phone: 317-940-8200

This private school was founded in 1855. It has a 290-acre campus.

RATINGS

Admissions Selectivity Rating: 89   **Fire Safety Rating:** 74   **Green Rating:** 74

STUDENTS AND FACULTY

Enrollment: 3,634. **Student Body:** 62% female, 38% male, 41% out-of-state, 3% international (59 countries represented). African American 3%, Asian 2%, Caucasian 85%, Hispanic 2%. **Retention and Graduation:** 87% freshmen return for sophomore year. 53% freshmen graduate within 4 years. 20% grads go on to further study within 1 year. 13% grads pursue arts and sciences degrees. 1% grads pursue business degrees. 2% grads pursue law degrees. 4% grads pursue medical degrees. **Faculty:** Student/faculty ratio 12:1. 291 full-time faculty, 84% hold PhDs. 97% faculty teach undergrads.

ACADEMICS

Degrees: Associate, bachelor's, first professional, master's. **Academic Requirements:** Arts/fine arts, English (including composition), humanities, mathematics, sciences (biological or physical), social science, physical education, world cultures. **Classes:** Most classes have 10–19 students. Most lab/discussion sections have fewer than 10 students. **Majors with Highest Enrollment:** Biology/biological sciences, marketing/marketing management, pharmacy (PharmD, BS/BPharm). **Disciplines with Highest Percentage of Degrees Awarded:** Business/marketing 18%, health professions and related sciences 18%, communications/journalism 11%, education 10%, visual and performing arts 8%. **Special Study Options:** Cross-registration, double major, dual enrollment, exchange student program (domestic), honors program, independent study, internships, student-designed major, study abroad, teacher certification program, cooperative education program in business only.

FACILITIES

Housing: Coed dorms, women's dorms, apartments for single students, fraternity/sorority housing, service learning housing for women. **Special Academic Facilities/Equipment:** Holcomb Observatory, Clowes Memorial Hall (performing arts theater), WBTU (public TV station). **Computers:** 75% of public computers are PCs, 15% of public computers are Macs, 10% of public computers are UNIX, network access in dorm rooms, network access in dorm lounges, online registration, online administrative functions (other than registration), remote student-access to Web through college's connection.

CAMPUS LIFE

Activities: Choral groups, concert band, dance, drama/theater, jazz band, literary magazine, marching band, music ensembles, opera, pep band, student government, student newspaper, symphony orchestra, television station, yearbook. **Organizations:** 100 registered organizations, 8 honor societies, 6 religious organizations. 8 fraternities (23% men join), 8 sororities (27% women join). **Athletics (Intercollegiate):** *Men:* Baseball, basketball, cross-country, football, golf, lacrosse, soccer, swimming, tennis, track/field (indoor), track/field (outdoor). *Women:* Basketball, cross-country, golf, soccer, softball, swimming, tennis, track/field (indoor), track/field (outdoor), volleyball. **Environmental Initiatives:** College of Pharmacy and Health Sciences building will be "Leed Certified-Silver." IDEM grant for campus recycling, $25,000. Completely Green cleaning operations of custodial operation.

ADMISSIONS

Freshman Academic Profile: 49% in top 10% of high school class, 78% in top 25% of high school class, 95% in top 50% of high school class. 85% from public high schools.SAT Math middle 50% range 530–650. SAT Critical Reading middle 50% range 520–630. SAT Writing middle 50% range 520–610. ACT middle 50% range 24–29. TOEFL required of all international applicants, minimum paper TOEFL 550, minimum computer TOEFL 213. **Basis for Candidate Selection:** *Very important factors considered include:* Academic

GPA, rigor of secondary school record. *Important factors considered include:* Application essay, class rank, standardized test scores. *Other factors considered include:* Alumni/ae relation, extracurricular activities, geographical residence, level of applicant's interest, recommendation(s), state residency, volunteer work, work experience. **Freshman Admission Requirements:** High school diploma is required, and GED is accepted. *Academic units required:* 4 English, 3 math, 3 science, 2 foreign language, 2 history, 2 academic electives. **Freshman Admission Statistics:** 5,052 applied, 74% admitted, 26% enrolled. **Transfer Admission Requirements:** High school transcript, college transcript(s), essay or personal statement, standardized test score, minimum college GPA of 2.0 required. Lowest grade transferable C. **General Admission Information:** Regular application deadline 3/1. Application fee $35. Regular notification is rolling. Nonfall registration accepted. Admission may be deferred for a maximum of 1 year. Credit offered for CEEB Advanced Placement tests.

COSTS AND FINANCIAL AID

Annual tuition $26,070. Room and board $8,960. Required fees $736. Average book expense $800. **Required Forms and Deadlines:** FAFSA. Financial aid filing deadline 3/1. **Notification of Awards:** Applicants will be notified of awards on a rolling basis beginning on or about 3/15. **Types of Aid:** *Need-based scholarships/grants:* Pell, SEOG, state scholarships/grants, private scholarships, the school's own gift aid. *Loans:* FFEL Subsidized Stafford, FFEL Unsubsidized Stafford, FFEL PLUS, Federal Perkins. **Student Employment:** Federal Work-Study Program available. Institutional employment available. Off-campus job opportunities are excellent. **Financial Aid Statistics:** 90% freshmen, 88% undergrads receive any aid. Highest amount earned per year from on-campus jobs $3,000.

CABRINI COLLEGE

610 King of Prussia Road, Radnor, PA 19087-3698
Phone: 610-902-8552 **E-mail:** admit@cabrini.edu **CEEB Code:** 2071
Fax: 610-902-8508 **Website:** www.cabrini.edu **ACT Code:** 3532
Financial Aid Phone: 610-902-8420

This private school, affiliated with the Roman Catholic Church, was founded in 1957. It has a 112-acre campus.

RATINGS
Admissions Selectivity Rating: 70   **Fire Safety Rating:** 89   **Green Rating:** 60*

STUDENTS AND FACULTY
Enrollment: 1,760. **Student Body:** 67% female, 33% male, 36% out-of-state. African American 6%, Asian 2%, Caucasian 83%, Hispanic 2%. **Retention and Graduation:** 72% freshmen return for sophomore year. 45% freshmen graduate within 4 years. 21% grads go on to further study within 1 year. 16% grads pursue arts and sciences degrees. 3% grads pursue business degrees. 1% grads pursue law degrees. 1% grads pursue medical degrees. **Faculty:** Student/faculty ratio 16:1. 61 full-time faculty, 77% hold PhDs. 79% faculty teach undergrads.

ACADEMICS
Degrees: Bachelor's, certificate, master's, post-bachelor's certificate. **Academic Requirements:** Arts/fine arts, computer literacy, English (including composition), foreign languages, history, humanities, mathematics, philosophy, sciences (biological or physical), social science, 2 writing-intensive seminar courses. **Classes:** Most classes have 20–29 students. Most lab/discussion sections have 10–19 students. **Majors with Highest Enrollment:** Business, management, marketing, and related support services; communications studies/speech communication, and rhetoric; elementary education and teaching. **Disciplines with Highest Percentage of Degrees Awarded:** Business/marketing 27%, education 22%, communications/journalism 15%, visual and performing arts 6%, psychology 5%, social sciences 5%. **Special Study Options:** Accelerated program, cooperative education program, cross-registration, distance learning, double major, honors program, independent study, internships, liberal arts/career combination, student-designed major, study abroad, teacher certification program.

FACILITIES
Housing: Coed dorms, women's dorms, apartments for single students, special housing for disabled students, special interest housing is available. **Special Academic Facilities/Equipment:** Exercise science lab, communications center (includes a graphic design lab, radio station, newsroom, and television studio). Science education and technology building with state-of-the-art biology, chemistry, and physics labs, instructional technology labs, and research space. **Computers:** 25% of classrooms are wired, 100% of classrooms are wireless, 75% of public computers are PCs, 25% of public computers are Macs, network

access in dorm rooms, network access in dorm lounges, online registration, online administrative functions (other than registration), support for handheld computing, remote student-access to Web through college's connection.

CAMPUS LIFE
Activities: Choral groups, dance, drama/theater, literary magazine, music ensembles, musical theater, radio station, student government, student newspaper, student-run film society, television station, yearbook. **Organizations:** 32 registered organizations, 10 honor societies, 1 religious organization. **Athletics (Intercollegiate):** *Men:* Basketball, cross-country, golf, lacrosse, soccer, swimming, tennis, track/field (outdoor). *Women:* Basketball, cross-country, field hockey, lacrosse, soccer, softball, swimming, tennis, track/field (outdoor), volleyball.

ADMISSIONS
Freshman Academic Profile: 7% in top 10% of high school class, 22% in top 25% of high school class, 49% in top 50% of high school class. 56% from public high schools. SAT Math middle 50% range 430–520. SAT Critical Reading middle 50% range 440–530. ACT middle 50% range 16–21. TOEFL required of all international applicants, minimum paper TOEFL 500, minimum computer TOEFL 80. **Basis for Candidate Selection:** *Very important factors considered include:* Academic GPA, standardized test scores. *Important factors considered include:* Level of applicant's interest. *Other factors considered include:* Alumni/ae relation, application essay, character/personal qualities, class rank, extracurricular activities, interview, recommendation(s), rigor of secondary school record, talent/ability, volunteer work, work experience. **Freshman Admission Requirements:** High school diploma is required, and GED is accepted. *Academic units required:* 4 English, 3 math, 3 science, 2 foreign language, 3 social studies, 3 history. *Academic units recommended:* 4 English, 4 math, 3 science, 2 foreign language, 3 social studies, 3 history, 2 academic electives. **Freshman Admission Statistics:** 2,374 applied, 87% admitted, 26% enrolled. **Transfer Admission Requirements:** College transcript(s), minimum college GPA of 2.2 required. Lowest grade transferable C-. **General Admission Information:** Application fee $35. Nonfall registration accepted. Admission may be deferred for a maximum of no limit. Credit and/or placement offered for CEEB Advanced Placement tests.

COSTS AND FINANCIAL AID
Average book expense $960. **Required Forms and Deadlines:** FAFSA. Financial aid filing deadline 5/1. **Notification of Awards:** Applicants will be notified of awards on a rolling basis beginning on or about 3/1. **Types of Aid:** *Need-based scholarships/grants:* Pell, SEOG, state scholarships/grants, private scholarships, the school's own gift aid. *Loans:* FFEL Subsidized Stafford, FFEL Unsubsidized Stafford, FFEL PLUS, Federal Perkins. **Financial Aid Statistics:** 55% freshmen, 55% undergrads receive need-based scholarship or grant aid. 60% freshmen, 61% undergrads receive need-based self-help aid. 98% freshmen, 97% undergrads receive any aid. Highest amount earned per year from on-campus jobs $4,160.

See page 1098.

CALDWELL COLLEGE

9 Ryerson Avenue, Caldwell, NJ 07006-6195
Phone: 973-618-3500 **E-mail:** admissions@caldwell.edu **CEEB Code:** 2072
Fax: 973-618-3600 **Website:** www.caldwell.edu **ACT Code:** 2542
Financial Aid Phone: 973-618-3221

This private school, affiliated with the Roman Catholic Church, was founded in 1939. It has an 80-acre campus.

RATINGS
Admissions Selectivity Rating: 71   **Fire Safety Rating:** 60*   **Green Rating:** 60*

STUDENTS AND FACULTY
Enrollment: 1,563. **Student Body:** 67% female, 33% male, 14% out-of-state, 5% international (26 countries represented). African American 16%, Asian 2%, Caucasian 61%, Hispanic 12%. **Retention and Graduation:** 73% freshmen return for sophomore year. 45% freshmen graduate within 4 years. **Faculty:** Student/faculty ratio 12:1. 80 full-time faculty, 82% hold PhDs. 100% faculty teach undergrads.

ACADEMICS
Degrees: Bachelor's, certificate, master's, post-bachelor's certificate, post-master's certificate. **Academic Requirements:** Arts/fine arts, computer literacy, English (including composition), foreign languages, history, humanities, mathematics, philosophy, sciences (biological or physical), social science, religious studies. **Majors with Highest Enrollment:** Business administration/

management, elementary education and teaching, psychology. **Disciplines with Highest Percentage of Degrees Awarded:** Business/marketing 24%, psychology 15%, education 12%, communication technologies 10%, English 8%, social sciences 8%. **Special Study Options:** Accelerated program, cooperative education program, distance learning, double major, English as a Second Language (ESL), external degree program, honors program, independent study, internships, liberal arts/career combination, student-designed major, study abroad, teacher certification program, weekend college.

FACILITIES

Housing: Coed dorms. **Special Academic Facilities/Equipment:** Art gallery, theater, library with media center, TV studio, state of the art technology building with interactive television classroom, new student center. **Computers:** 94% of public computers are PCs, 6% of public computers are Macs, network access in dorm rooms, online registration, online administrative functions (other than registration).

CAMPUS LIFE

Activities: Choral groups, drama/theater, jazz band, literary magazine, music ensembles, musical theater, pep band, student government, student newspaper, yearbook. **Organizations:** 20 registered organizations, 15 honor societies, 1 religious organization. **Athletics (Intercollegiate):** *Men:* Baseball, basketball, golf, soccer, tennis. *Women:* Basketball, golf, soccer, softball, tennis.

ADMISSIONS

Freshman Academic Profile: 7% in top 10% of high school class, 14% in top 25% of high school class, 47% in top 50% of high school class. 67% from public high schools. SAT Math middle 50% range 430–530. SAT Critical Reading middle 50% range 440–520. TOEFL required of all international applicants, minimum paper TOEFL 500. **Basis for Candidate Selection:** *Very important factors considered include:* Extracurricular activities, rigor of secondary school record. *Important factors considered include:* Academic GPA, class rank, standardized test scores, talent/ability. *Other factors considered include:* Alumni/ae relation, application essay, character/personal qualities, interview, recommendation(s), volunteer work, work experience. **Freshman Admission Requirements:** High school diploma is required, and GED is accepted. *Academic units required:* 4 English, 2 math, 2 science (1 science lab), 2 foreign language, 1 history, 5 academic electives. **Freshman Admission Statistics:** 1,442 applied, 66% admitted, 30% enrolled. **Transfer Admission Requirements:** High school transcript, college transcript(s), minimum college GPA of 2.0 required. Lowest grade transferable C. **General Admission Information:** Application fee $40. Regular application deadline 4/1. Regular notification continuous. Nonfall registration accepted. Admission may be deferred for a maximum of 1 semester. Credit and/or placement offered for CEEB Advanced Placement tests.

COSTS AND FINANCIAL AID

Annual tuition $12,400. Room and board $7,000. Required fees $100. Average book expense $800. **Required Forms and Deadlines:** FAFSA, institution's own financial aid form. Financial aid filing deadline 4/15. **Notification of Awards:** Applicants will be notified of awards on a rolling basis beginning on or about 3/1. **Types of Aid:** *Need-based scholarships/grants:* Pell, SEOG, state scholarships/grants, private scholarships, the school's own gift aid. *Loans:* FFEL Subsidized Stafford, FFEL Unsubsidized Stafford, FFEL PLUS, state loans, alternative loans, such as Key, TERL, Signature. **Student Employment:** Federal Work-Study Program available. Institutional employment available. Off-campus job opportunities are excellent. **Financial Aid Statistics:** 66% freshmen, 79% undergrads receive need-based scholarship or grant aid. 58% freshmen, 60% undergrads receive need-based self-help aid. Highest amount earned per year from on-campus jobs $1,000.

See page 1100.

CALIFORNIA BAPTIST UNIVERSITY

8432 Magnolia Avenue, Riverside, CA 92504
Phone: 951-343-4212 **E-mail:** admissions@calbaptist.edu **CEEB Code:** 4094
Fax: 951-343-4525 **Website:** www.calbaptist.edu **ACT Code:** 4094
Financial Aid Phone: 951-343-4236

This private school, affiliated with the Southern Baptist Church, was founded in 1950. It has a 110-acre campus.

RATINGS

Admissions Selectivity Rating: 60*   **Fire Safety Rating:** 64   **Green Rating:** 64

STUDENTS AND FACULTY

Enrollment: 2,605. **Student Body:** 64% female, 36% male, 6% out-of-state, 3% international (27 countries represented). African American 8%, Asian 2%, Caucasian 59%, Hispanic 17%. **Retention and Graduation:** 84% freshmen return for sophomore year. 64% freshmen graduate within 4 years. **Faculty:** Student/faculty ratio 18:1. 120 full-time faculty, 62% hold PhDs. 100% faculty teach undergrads.

ACADEMICS

Degrees: Bachelor's, master's, post-bachelor's certificate. **Academic Requirements:** Arts/fine arts, computer literacy, English (including composition), humanities, mathematics, philosophy, sciences (biological or physical), social science, Christian studies. **Classes:** Most classes have 10–19 students. Most lab/discussion sections have 10–19 students. **Majors with Highest Enrollment:** Business administration/management, liberal arts and sciences/liberal studies, psychology. **Disciplines with Highest Percentage of Degrees Awarded:** Liberal arts/general studies 31%, psychology 15%, business/marketing 13%, philosophy and religious studies 8%, parks and recreation 7%. **Special Study Options:** Accelerated program, distance learning, double major, English as a Second Language (ESL), exchange student program (domestic), honors program, internships, liberal arts/career combination, study abroad, teacher certification program, weekend college.

FACILITIES

Housing: Men's dorms, women's dorms, apartments for married students, apartments for single students, cooperative housing. **Special Academic Facilities/Equipment:** Metcalf Art Gallery, Annie Gabriel Library, Wallace Theater, P. Boyd Smith Hymnology Collection, School of Music Performance and Recording Studios, Nie Wieder Collection, Lancer Sports Complex and Aquatic Center. **Computers:** 20% of classrooms are wireless, 97% of public computers are PCs, 3% of public computers are Macs, network access in dorm rooms, online registration, online administrative functions (other than registration), remote student-access to Web through college's connection.

CAMPUS LIFE

Activities: Choral groups, concert band, drama/theater, jazz band, music ensembles, musical theater, pep band, student government, student newspaper, symphony orchestra, yearbook. **Organizations:** 27 registered organizations, 2 honor societies, 6 religious organizations. **Athletics (Intercollegiate):** *Men:* Baseball, basketball, diving, golf, soccer, swimming, tennis, volleyball, water polo. *Women:* Basketball, cheerleading, diving, golf, soccer, softball, swimming, tennis, volleyball, water polo. **Environmental Initiatives:** Energy Efficient Lighting. HVAC Regulators. Strategic Landscaping Considerations.

ADMISSIONS

Freshman Academic Profile: 79% from public high schools. SAT Math middle 50% range 440–550. SAT Critical Reading middle 50% range 450–550. SAT Writing middle 50% range 440–550. ACT middle 50% range 18–23. TOEFL required of all international applicants, minimum paper TOEFL 500, minimum computer TOEFL 153. **Basis for Candidate Selection:** *Very important factors considered include:* Academic GPA, rigor of secondary school record, standardized test scores. *Important factors considered include:* Application essay, character/personal qualities, level of applicant's interest, recommendation(s). *Other factors considered include:* Class rank, extracurricular activities, interview, talent/ability. **Freshman Admission Requirements:** High school diploma is required, and GED is accepted. *Academic units required:* 4 English, 3 math, 2 science (1 science lab), 2 foreign language, 2 social studies, 2 history. *Academic units recommended:* 4 English, 4 math, 3 science (2 science labs), 3 foreign language, 3 academic electives. **Freshman Admission Statistics:** 1,325 applied, 69% admitted, 48% enrolled. **Transfer Admission Requirements:** College transcript(s), essay or personal statement, statement of good standing from prior institution(s). Minimum college GPA of 2.0 required. Lowest grade transferable C. **General Admission Information:** Application fee $45. Regular notification is rolling. Nonfall registration accepted. Admission may be deferred for a maximum of 1 year. Credit and/or placement offered for CEEB Advanced Placement tests.

COSTS AND FINANCIAL AID

Annual tuition $19,240. Room and board $7,510. Required fees $1,400. Average book expense $1,314. **Required Forms and Deadlines:** FAFSA, state aid form. Financial aid filing deadline 3/2. **Notification of Awards:** Applicants will be notified of awards on a rolling basis beginning on or about 3/2. **Types of Aid:** *Need-based scholarships/grants:* Pell, SEOG, state scholarships/grants, private scholarships, the school's own gift aid, Federal Nursing Scholarships. *Loans:* FFEL Subsidized Stafford, FFEL Unsubsidized Stafford, FFEL PLUS, Federal Perkins, Federal Nursing, alternative loans. **Student Employment:** Federal Work-Study Program available. Institutional employment available. Off-campus job opportunities are good. **Financial Aid Statistics:** 91% freshmen, 95% undergrads receive need-based scholarship or grant aid. 91% freshmen, 95% undergrads receive need-based self-help aid. 36 freshmen, 182 undergrads receive athletic scholarships. 90% freshmen, 87% undergrads receive any aid. Highest amount earned per year from on-campus jobs $1,900.

CALIFORNIA COLLEGE FOR HEALTH SCIENCES

2423 Hoover Avenue, National City, CA 91950
Phone: 619-477-4800 **E-mail:** admissns@cchs.edu
Fax: 619-477-4360 **Website:** www.cchs.edu

This proprietary school was founded in 1978. It has a 1-acre campus.

RATINGS
Admissions Selectivity Rating: 60*   **Fire Safety Rating:** 60*   **Green Rating:** 60*

STUDENTS AND FACULTY
Faculty: Student/faculty ratio 17:1. 5 full-time faculty.

ACADEMICS
Degrees: Associate, bachelor's, master's. **Academic Requirements:** English (including composition), sciences (biological or physical), social science. **Majors with Highest Enrollment:** Health services administration; health/health care administration/management; respiratory therapy/therapist. **Special Study Options:** Distance learning.

CAMPUS LIFE
Organizations: 2 honor societies.

ADMISSIONS
Freshman Admission Requirements: High school diploma is required, and GED is accepted. **Transfer Admission Requirements:** College transcript(s), lowest grade transferable C. **General Admission Information:** Application fee $35. Regular notification is rolling. Nonfall registration accepted. Admission may be deferred for a maximum of 11 months. Common Application not accepted. Neither credit nor placement offered for CEEB Advanced Placement tests.

COSTS AND FINANCIAL AID
Annual tuition $3,000. Required fees $35.

CALIFORNIA COLLEGE OF THE ARTS

1111 8th Street, San Francisco, CA 94107
Phone: 415-703-9523 **E-mail:** enroll@cca.edu **CEEB Code:** 4031
Fax: 415-703-9539 **Website:** www.cca.edu **ACT Code:** 0176
Financial Aid Phone: 415-703-9573

This private school was founded in 1907. It has a 4-acre campus.

RATINGS
Admissions Selectivity Rating: 60*   **Fire Safety Rating:** 68   **Green Rating:** 74

STUDENTS AND FACULTY
Enrollment: 1,322. **Student Body:** 59% female, 41% male, 35% out-of-state, 7% international (26 countries represented). African American 3%, Asian 12%, Caucasian 54%, Hispanic 10%. **Retention and Graduation:** 79% freshmen return for sophomore year. 21% freshmen graduate within 4 years. **Faculty:** Student/faculty ratio 14:1. 33 full-time faculty, 82% hold PhDs. 84% faculty teach undergrads.

ACADEMICS
Degrees: Bachelor's, master's. **Academic Requirements:** English (including composition), humanities, mathematics, philosophy, sciences (biological or physical), social science, art history, seminar. **Majors with Highest Enrollment:** Graphic design, illustration, painting. **Disciplines with Highest Percentage of Degrees Awarded:** Visual and performing arts 97%, architecture 3%. **Special Study Options:** Double major, exchange student program (domestic), independent study, internships, student-designed major, study abroad, academic remediation, Advanced Placement credits.

FACILITIES
Housing: Coed dorms, apartments for single students, special housing for international students, first-year student community, and transfer student housing. **Special Academic Facilities/Equipment:** Logan Gallery on the San Francisco Campus, Wattis Institute for Contemporary Art. **Computers:** 1% of public computers are PCs, 99% of public computers are Macs, network access in dorm rooms, network access in dorm lounges, remote student-access to Web through college's connection.

CAMPUS LIFE
Activities: Literary magazine, student government, student newspaper. **Organizations:** 9 registered organizations, 1 honor society. **Environmental Initiatives:** Largest solar heated facility in San Francisco, named Top Ten Green Building on Earth Day 2001. Curricular content commitment to sustainability with national experts teaching. Ongoing partnerships with Pacific Energy Center, Sustainable Cotton Project, IDSA's Okala curriculum standards, etc.

ADMISSIONS
Freshman Academic Profile: SAT Math middle 50% range 450–590. SAT Critical Reading middle 50% range 470–610. SAT Writing middle 50% range 480–590. ACT middle 50% range 18–24. TOEFL required of all international applicants, minimum paper TOEFL 550, minimum computer TOEFL 213. **Basis for Candidate Selection:** *Very important factors considered include:* Academic GPA, application essay, talent/ability. *Important factors considered include:* Interview, recommendation(s). *Other factors considered include:* Character/personal qualities, extracurricular activities, rigor of secondary school record, standardized test scores, volunteer work, work experience. **Freshman Admission Requirements:** High school diploma is required, and GED is accepted. **Freshman Admission Statistics:** 879 applied, 78% admitted, 27% enrolled. **Transfer Admission Requirements:** College transcript(s), essay or personal statement, minimum college GPA of 2.0 required. Lowest grade transferable C. **General Admission Information:** Application fee $50. Regular notification is rolling. Nonfall registration accepted. Admission may be deferred for a maximum of 1 semester. Credit and/or placement offered for CEEB Advanced Placement tests.

COSTS AND FINANCIAL AID
Annual tuition $29,280. Room and board $6,350. Required fees $290. Average book expense $1,400. **Required Forms and Deadlines:** FAFSA. Financial aid filing deadline 3/1. **Notification of Awards:** Applicants will be notified of awards on or about 4/1. *Types of Aid: Need-based scholarships/grants:* Pell, SEOG, state scholarships/grants, private scholarships, the school's own gift aid, Various. *Loans:* FFEL Subsidized Stafford, FFEL Unsubsidized Stafford, FFEL PLUS, Federal Perkins, state loans. **Financial Aid Statistics:** 52% freshmen, 63% undergrads receive need-based scholarship or grant aid. 52% freshmen, 64% undergrads receive need-based self-help aid. 75% freshmen, 75% undergrads receive any aid. Highest amount earned per year from on-campus jobs $1,500.

See page 1102.

CALIFORNIA INSTITUTE OF THE ARTS

24700 McBean Parkway, Valencia, CA 91355
Phone: 661-255-1050 **E-mail:** admiss@calarts.edu **CEEB Code:** 4049
Fax: 661-253-7710 **Website:** www.calarts.edu **ACT Code:** 0121
Financial Aid Phone: 661-253-7869

This private school was founded in 1961. It has a 60-acre campus.

RATINGS
Admissions Selectivity Rating: 60*   **Fire Safety Rating:** 60*   **Green Rating:** 60*

STUDENTS AND FACULTY
Enrollment: 821. **Student Body:** 44% female, 56% male, 53% out-of-state, 8% international. African American 7%, Asian 10%, Caucasian 61%, Hispanic 12%, Native American 1%. **Retention and Graduation:** 80% freshmen return for sophomore year. 75% freshmen graduate within 4 years. **Faculty:** Student/faculty ratio 7:1. 150 full-time faculty. 100% faculty teach undergrads.

ACADEMICS
Degrees: Bachelor's, certificate, master's, post-bachelor's certificate. **Academic Requirements:** Arts/fine arts, computer literacy, English (including composition), history, humanities, mathematics, philosophy, sciences (biological or physical), social science. **Classes:** Most classes have fewer than 10 students. **Majors with Highest Enrollment:** Acting, art/art studies, film/video and photographic arts. **Disciplines with Highest Percentage of Degrees Awarded:** Visual and performing arts 100%. **Special Study Options:** Independent study, internships, student-designed major, study abroad.

FACILITIES
Housing: Coed dorms, apartments for single students, special housing for disabled students. **Special Academic Facilities/Equipment:** 7 art galleries, TV studio, Walt Disney Theater, Roy Disney Music Hall, Sharon Disney Lund Dance Theater, Bisou Film Theater **Computers:** 100% of classrooms are wireless, 50% of public computers are PCs, 50% of public computers are Macs,

network access in dorm rooms, remote student-access to Web through college's connection.

CAMPUS LIFE

Activities: Choral groups, dance, drama/theater, jazz band, literary magazine, music ensembles, opera, radio station, student government, student newspaper, student-run film society, symphony orchestra, television station. **Organizations:** 5 registered organizations.

ADMISSIONS

Freshman Academic Profile: 25% in top 10% of high school class. TOEFL required of all international applicants, minimum paper TOEFL 550, minimum computer TOEFL 213. **Basis for Candidate Selection:** *Very important factors considered include:* Application essay, talent/ability. *Important factors considered include:* Extracurricular activities, interview, recommendation(s). *Other factors considered include:* Character/personal qualities. **Freshman Admission Requirements:** High school diploma is required, and GED is accepted. **Freshman Admission Statistics:** 2,975 applied, 12% admitted, 25% enrolled. **Transfer Admission Requirements:** High school transcript, college transcript(s), essay or personal statement. Lowest grade transferable C. **General Admission Information:** Application fee $65. Regular application deadline 1/4. Regular notification is rolling. Nonfall registration accepted. Credit offered for CEEB Advanced Placement tests.

COSTS AND FINANCIAL AID

Annual tuition $32,860. Room and board $3,663. Required fees $575. Average book expense $1,500. **Required Forms and Deadlines:** FAFSA. Financial aid filing deadline 3/1. **Notification of Awards:** Applicants will be notified of awards on a rolling basis beginning on or about 4/1. **Types of Aid:** *Need-based scholarships/grants:* Pell, SEOG, state scholarships/grants, private scholarships, the school's own gift aid. *Loans:* FFEL Subsidized Stafford, FFEL Unsubsidized Stafford, FFEL PLUS, Federal Perkins, college/university loans from institutional funds. **Financial Aid Statistics:** 54% freshmen, 66% undergrads receive need-based scholarship or grant aid. 52% freshmen, 62% undergrads receive need-based self-help aid. Highest amount earned per year from on-campus jobs $1,536.

CALIFORNIA INSTITUTE OF TECHNOLOGY

1200 East California Boulevard, Mail Code 1-94, Pasadena, CA 91125
Phone: 626-395-6341 **E-mail:** ugadmissions@caltech.edu **CEEB Code:** 4034
Fax: 626-683-3026 **Website:** www.admissions.caltech.edu **ACT Code:** 0182
Financial Aid Phone: 626-395-6280

This private school was founded in 1891. It has a 124-acre campus.

RATINGS

Admissions Selectivity Rating: 99 **Fire Safety Rating:** 60* **Green Rating:** 60*

STUDENTS AND FACULTY

Enrollment: 864. **Student Body:** 28% female, 72% male, 68% out-of-state, 8% international (30 countries represented). Asian 37%, Caucasian 46%, Hispanic 6%. **Retention and Graduation:** 97% freshmen return for sophomore year. 80% freshmen graduate within 4 years. 53% grads go on to further study within 1 year. 40% grads pursue arts and sciences degrees. 1% grads pursue law degrees. 3% grads pursue medical degrees. **Faculty:** Student/faculty ratio 3:1. 291 full-time faculty.

ACADEMICS

Degrees: Bachelor's, doctoral, master's. **Academic Requirements:** humanities, mathematics, sciences (biological or physical), social science, physical education—3 terms. **Majors with Highest Enrollment:** Mathematics, mechanical engineering, physics. **Disciplines with Highest Percentage of Degrees Awarded:** Engineering 33%, physical sciences 32%, biological/life sciences 15%, mathematics 10%, social sciences 3%. **Special Study Options:** Cross-registration, double major, English as a Second Language (ESL), exchange student program (domestic), independent study, liberal arts/career combination, student-designed major, study abroad. 3–2 engineering program with Bowdoin, Grinnell, Oberlin, Occidental, Pomona, Reed Colleges, Wesleyan University, Whitman, Ohio Wesleyan, Mt. Holyoke, and Spelman Colleges. Liberal arts and engineering Summer Undergraduate Research Opportunities (SURF) are available to all undergraduate students and are paid

10 week research opportunities during the summer at Caltech or other facilities throughout the country.

FACILITIES

Housing: Coed dorms, apartments for married students, apartments for single students, special housing for disabled students, single-unit houses. **Special Academic Facilities/Equipment:** Jet propulsion laboratory, Palomar Observatory, seismological laboratory, Beckman Institute for Fundamental Research in Biology and Chemistry, Mead Chemistry Laboratory, Moore Laboratory. **Computers:** 5% of classrooms are wired, 15% of classrooms are wireless, 100% of public computers are PCs, network access in dorm rooms, network access in dorm lounges, online registration, online administrative functions (other than registration), remote student-access to Web through college's connection.

CAMPUS LIFE

Activities: Choral groups, concert band, dance, drama/theater, jazz band, literary magazine, music ensembles, musical theater, pep band, student government, student newspaper, student-run film society, symphony orchestra, yearbook. **Organizations:** 148 registered organizations, 2 honor societies, 6 religious organizations. **Athletics (Intercollegiate):** *Men:* Baseball, basketball, cross-country, diving, fencing, soccer, swimming, tennis, track/field (outdoor), water polo. *Women:* Basketball, cross-country, diving, fencing, swimming, tennis, track/field (outdoor), volleyball, water polo.

ADMISSIONS

Freshman Academic Profile: 88% in top 10% of high school class, 97% in top 25% of high school class, 100% in top 50% of high school class. 70% from public high schools. SAT Math middle 50% range 780–800. SAT Critical Reading middle 50% range 690–770. SAT Writing middle 50% range 670–760. **Basis for Candidate Selection:** *Very important factors considered include:* Rigor of secondary school record. *Important factors considered include:* Academic GPA, application essay, character/personal qualities, class rank, extracurricular activities, recommendation(s), standardized test scores. *Other factors considered include:* Alumni/ae relation, first generation, racial/ethnic status, talent/ability, volunteer work, work experience. **Freshman Admission Requirements:** High school diploma or equivalent is not required. *Academic units required:* 3 English, 4 math, 2 science (1 science lab), 1 social studies, 1 history. *Academic units recommended:* 4 English, 4 science. **Freshman Admission Statistics:** 3,330 applied, 17% admitted, 37% enrolled. **Transfer Admission Requirements:** High school transcript, college transcript(s), essay or personal statement, statement of good standing from prior institution(s). **General Admission Information:** Application fee $60. Regular application deadline 1/1. Regular notification 4/1. Nonfall registration not accepted. Admission may be deferred for a maximum of 1 year. Neither credit nor placement offered for CEEB Advanced Placement tests.

COSTS AND FINANCIAL AID

Annual tuition $29,940. Room and board $9,540. Required fees $2,895. Average book expense $1,077. **Required Forms and Deadlines:** FAFSA, CSS/Financial Aid PROFILE, state aid form, Noncustodial PROFILE, Business/Farm Supplement, Noncustodial Parent's Statement and Business/Farm Supplement forms are required only when applicable. Financial aid filing deadline 1/15. **Notification of Awards:** Applicants will be notified of awards on or about 4/15. **Types of Aid:** *Need-based scholarships/grants:* Pell, SEOG, state scholarships/grants, private scholarships, the school's own gift aid. *Loans:* Direct Subsidized Stafford, Direct Unsubsidized Stafford, Direct PLUS, Federal Perkins, college/university loans from institutional funds. **Financial Aid Statistics:** 53% freshmen, 53% undergrads receive need-based scholarship or grant aid. 31% freshmen, 38% undergrads receive need-based self-help aid. 60% freshmen, 60% undergrads receive any aid.

CALIFORNIA LUTHERAN UNIVERSITY

60 West Olsen Road, 1350, Thousand Oaks, CA 91360
Phone: 805-493-3135 **E-mail:** cluadm@clunet.edu **CEEB Code:** 4088
Fax: 805-493-3114 **Website:** www.callutheran.edu **ACT Code:** 0183
Financial Aid Phone: 805-493-3115

This private school, affiliated with the Lutheran Church, was founded in 1959. It has a 290-acre campus.

RATINGS

Admissions Selectivity Rating: 83 **Fire Safety Rating:** 60* **Green Rating:** 60*

STUDENTS AND FACULTY

Enrollment: 1,959. **Student Body:** 56% female, 44% male, 21% out-of-state, 1% international. African American 2%, Asian 3%, Caucasian 52%, Hispanic

12%. **Retention and Graduation:** 78% freshmen return for sophomore year. 57% freshmen graduate within 4 years. 65% grads go on to further study within 1 year. **Faculty:** Student/faculty ratio 14:1. 118 full-time faculty, 86% hold PhDs. 100% faculty teach undergrads.

ACADEMICS

Degrees: Bachelor's, doctoral, master's, post-bachelor's certificate, post-master's certificate. **Academic Requirements:** Arts/fine arts, computer literacy, English (including composition), foreign languages, history, humanities, mathematics, philosophy, sciences (biological or physical), social science, religion. **Classes:** Most classes have 20–29 students. Most lab/discussion sections have 10–19 students. **Majors with Highest Enrollment:** Business administration/management, liberal arts and sciences/liberal studies. **Disciplines with Highest Percentage of Degrees Awarded:** Business/marketing 26%, social sciences 11%, computer and information sciences 10%, communication technologies 10%, liberal arts/general studies 10%, psychology 9%, biological/life sciences 5%. **Special Study Options:** Accelerated program, cooperative education program, double major, dual enrollment, exchange student program (domestic), honors program, independent study, internships, student-designed major, study abroad, teacher certification program.

FACILITIES

Housing: Coed dorms, apartments for single students, special housing for disabled students. **Special Academic Facilities/Equipment:** On-campus pre-school, hypermedia lab, multimedia center and program, film studio, Kwan Fong Art Gallery, Scandinavian Center, educational technology center. **Computers:** 80% of public computers are PCs, 20% of public computers are Macs, network access in dorm rooms, network access in dorm lounges, online registration, online administrative functions (other than registration), support for handheld computing, remote student-access to Web through college's connection.

CAMPUS LIFE

Activities: Choral groups, concert band, dance, drama/theater, jazz band, literary magazine, music ensembles, musical theater, pep band, radio station, student government, student newspaper, symphony orchestra, television station, yearbook. **Organizations:** 75 registered organizations, 11 honor societies, 3 religious organizations. **Athletics (Intercollegiate):** *Men:* Baseball, basketball, cheerleading, cross-country, diving, football, golf, soccer, swimming, tennis, track/field (outdoor), water polo. *Women:* Basketball, cheerleading, cross-country, diving, soccer, softball, swimming, tennis, track/field (outdoor), volleyball, water polo.

ADMISSIONS

Freshman Academic Profile: 29% in top 10% of high school class, 60% in top 25% of high school class, 95% in top 50% of high school class. SAT Math middle 50% range 500–600. SAT Critical Reading middle 50% range 480–590. ACT middle 50% range 21–26. TOEFL required of all international applicants, minimum paper TOEFL 550, minimum computer TOEFL 213. **Basis for Candidate Selection:** *Very important factors considered include:* Recommendation(s), rigor of secondary school record, standardized test scores. *Important factors considered include:* Application essay, extracurricular activities, talent/ability, volunteer work, work experience. *Other factors considered include:* Alumni/ae relation, character/personal qualities, class rank, geographical residence, interview, racial/ethnic status, religious affiliation/commitment, state residency. **Freshman Admission Requirements:** High school diploma is required, and GED is accepted. *Academic units required:* 4 English, 3 math, 3 science, 2 foreign language, 2 social studies, 1 history, 2 humanities. **Freshman Admission Statistics:** 1,660 applied, 73% admitted, 33% enrolled. **Transfer Admission Requirements:** College transcript(s), essay or personal statement, statement of good standing from prior institution(s). Minimum college GPA of 2.8 required. Lowest grade transferable D. **General Admission Information:** Application fee $45. Regular notification is rolling. Nonfall registration accepted. Admission may be deferred for a maximum of 1 year. Common Application accepted. Credit and/or placement offered for CEEB Advanced Placement tests.

COSTS AND FINANCIAL AID

Annual tuition $21,820. Room & board $7,570. Required fees $465. Average book expense $1,260. **Required Forms and Deadlines:** FAFSA, Student Request Form. Financial aid filing deadline 3/2. **Notification of Awards:** Applicants will be notified of awards on a rolling basis beginning on or about 4/1. **Types of Aid:** *Need-based scholarships/grants:* Pell, SEOG, state scholarships/grants, private scholarships, the school's own gift aid. *Loans:* FFEL Subsidized Stafford, FFEL Unsubsidized Stafford, FFEL PLUS, Federal Perkins, Opportunity Loans From Loan Servicer. **Student Employment:** Federal Work-Study Program available. Institutional employment available. Off-campus job opportunities are good. **Financial Aid Statistics:** 72% freshmen, 65% undergrads receive need-based scholarship or grant aid. 56% freshmen, 54% undergrads receive need-based self-help aid. 83% undergrads receive any aid. Highest amount earned per year from on-campus jobs $1,200.

CALIFORNIA MARITIME ACADEMY OF CALIFORNIA STATE UNIVERSITY

200 Maritime Academy Drive, Vallejo, CA 94590
Phone: 707-654-1330 **E-mail:** admission@csum.edu
Fax: 707-654-1336 **Website:** www.csum.edu **ACT Code:** 0184
Financial Aid Phone: 707-654-1275

This public school was founded in 1929. It has a 67-acre campus.

RATINGS

Admissions Selectivity Rating: 61   **Fire Safety Rating:** 60*   **Green Rating:** 60*

STUDENTS AND FACULTY

Enrollment: 606. **Student Body:** 17% female, 83% male, 13% out-of-state, 6% international. African American 4%, Asian 11%, Caucasian 59%, Hispanic 7%. **Retention and Graduation:** 93% freshmen return for sophomore year. 45% freshmen graduate within 4 years. **Faculty:** Student/faculty ratio 15:1. 49 full-time faculty, 53% hold PhDs. 100% faculty teach undergrads.

ACADEMICS

Degrees: Bachelor's. **Academic Requirements:** Computer literacy, English (including composition), history, humanities, mathematics, sciences (biological or physical), social science, maritime-related courses. **Disciplines with Highest Percentage of Degrees Awarded:** Engineering 38%, business/marketing 30%. **Special Study Options:** Cooperative education program, distance learning, double major, internships, all students participate in at least one 2-month training cruise around the Pacific Rim over the summer on the *Golden Bear*.

FACILITIES

Housing: Coed dorms. **Special Academic Facilities/Equipment:** Bookstore, library, gym, swimming pool. **Computers:** Network access in dorm rooms, remote student-access to Web through college's connection.

CAMPUS LIFE

Activities: Student government. **Organizations:** 16 registered organizations, **Athletics (Intercollegiate):** *Men:* Basketball, crew/rowing, golf, sailing, soccer, water polo. *Women:* Crew/rowing, sailing, volleyball.

ADMISSIONS

Freshman Academic Profile: 80% from public high schools. TOEFL required of all international applicants, minimum paper TOEFL 550, minimum computer TOEFL 213. **Basis for Candidate Selection:** *Very important factors considered include:* Rigor of secondary school record, standardized test scores. *Other factors considered include:* Alumni/ae relation, application essay, character/personal qualities, extracurricular activities, geographical residence, interview, recommendation(s), state residency, talent/ability, volunteer work, work experience. **Freshman Admission Requirements:** High school diploma is required, and GED is accepted. *Academic units required:* 4 English, 3 math, 2 science (2 science labs), 2 foreign language, 1 social studies, 1 history, 1 academic elective, 1 visual and performing arts. **Freshman Admission Statistics:** 432 applied, 83% admitted, 44% enrolled. **Transfer Admission Requirements:** College transcript(s), statement of good standing from prior institution(s). Minimum college GPA of 2.0 required. Lowest grade transferable C. **General Admission Information:** Application fee $55. Regular application deadline 5/1. Regular notification is rolling. Nonfall registration not accepted. Common Application not accepted.

COSTS AND FINANCIAL AID

Annual in-state tuition $12,106. Out-of-state tuition $8,460. Room & board $6,750. Required fees $1,050. Average book expense $846. **Required Forms and Deadlines:** FAFSA. Financial aid filing deadline 3/2. **Notification of Awards:** Applicants will be notified of awards on a rolling basis beginning on or about 4/15. **Types of Aid:** *Need-based scholarships/grants:* Pell, SEOG, state scholarships/grants, private scholarships, the school's own gift aid. *Loans:* FFEL Subsidized Stafford, FFEL Unsubsidized Stafford, FFEL PLUS, Federal Perkins. **Student Employment:** Federal Work-Study Program available. Off-campus job opportunities are fair. **Financial Aid Statistics:** 42% freshmen, 59% undergrads receive need-based scholarship or grant aid. 63% freshmen, 71% undergrads receive need-based self-help aid. Highest amount earned per year from on-campus jobs $750.

CALIFORNIA POLYTECHNIC STATE UNIVERSITY—SAN LUIS OBISPO

Admissions Office, Cal Poly, San Luis Obispo, CA 93407
Phone: 805-756-2311 **E-mail:** admissions@calpoly.edu **CEEB Code:** 4038
Fax: 805-756-5400 **Website:** www.calpoly.edu **ACT Code:** 0188
Financial Aid Phone: 805-756-2927

This public school was founded in 1901. It has a 5,000-acre campus.

RATINGS
Admissions Selectivity Rating: 90   **Fire Safety Rating:** 79   **Green Rating:** 60*

STUDENTS AND FACULTY
Enrollment: 17,671. **Student Body:** 43% female, 57% male, 6% out-of-state. African American 1%, Asian 11%, Caucasian 65%, Hispanic 10%. **Retention and Graduation:** 91% freshmen return for sophomore year. 21% freshmen graduate within 4 years. **Faculty:** Student/faculty ratio 20:1. 697 full-time faculty, 72% hold PhDs.

ACADEMICS
Degrees: Bachelor's, master's. **Academic Requirements:** Arts/fine arts, English (including composition), history, humanities, mathematics, philosophy, sciences (biological or physical), social science, technology. **Classes:** Most classes have 20–29 students. Most lab/discussion sections have 10–19 students. **Majors with Highest Enrollment:** Agricultural business and management, business administration and management, mechanical engineering. **Disciplines with Highest Percentage of Degrees Awarded:** Engineering 26%, business/marketing 15%, agriculture 14%, architecture 6%, social sciences 4%, biological/life sciences 4%, parks and recreation 4%. **Special Study Options:** Cooperative education program, cross-registration, distance learning, double major, dual enrollment, English as a Second Language (ESL), exchange student program (domestic), external degree program, honors program, independent study, internships, study abroad, teacher certification program.

FACILITIES
Housing: Coed dorms, men's dorms, women's dorms, shared, apartment-style housing. **Special Academic Facilities/Equipment:** Dairy, veterinary clinic, printing museum, art gallery. **Computers:** Network access in dorm rooms, network access in dorm lounges, online registration, online administrative functions (other than registration), remote student-access to Web through college's connection.

CAMPUS LIFE
Activities: Choral groups, concert band, dance, drama/theater, jazz band, literary magazine, marching band, music ensembles, musical theater, pep band, radio station, student government, student newspaper, television station. **Organizations:** 375 registered organizations, 13 religious organizations. 23 fraternities, 10 sororities. **Athletics (Intercollegiate):** *Men:* Baseball, basketball, cheerleading, cross-country, football, golf, soccer, swimming, tennis, track/field (outdoor), wrestling. *Women:* Basketball, cheerleading, cross-country, golf, soccer, softball, swimming, tennis, track/field (indoor), track/field (outdoor), volleyball. **Environmental Initiatives:** Completed baseline inventory. Established LEED Silver Standard or Equivalent on all new buildings. Established Energy Star Policy on Purchase of Appliances.

ADMISSIONS
Freshman Academic Profile: 39% in top 10% of high school class, 76% in top 25% of high school class, 97% in top 50% of high school class. 92% from public high schools. SAT Math middle 50% range 560–670. SAT Critical Reading middle 50% range 520–620. ACT middle 50% range 23–28. TOEFL required of all international applicants, minimum paper TOEFL 550, minimum computer TOEFL 213. **Basis for Candidate Selection:** *Very important factors considered include:* Academic GPA, rigor of secondary school record, standardized test scores. *Other factors considered include:* Extracurricular activities, first generation, geographical residence, talent/ability, volunteer work, work experience. **Freshman Admission Requirements:** High school diploma is required, and GED is accepted. *Academic units required:* 4 English, 3 math, 3 science (1 science lab), 2 foreign language, 2 social studies, 1 history, 1 academic elective, 1 visual and preforming arts. **Freshman Admission Statistics:** 26,724 applied, 47% admitted, 29% enrolled. **Transfer Admission Requirements:** College transcript(s), minimum college GPA of 2.0 required. Lowest grade transferable D. **General Admission Information:** Application fee $55. Early decision application deadline 10/31. Regular application deadline 11/30. Regular notification is rolling. Nonfall registration accepted. Credit offered for CEEB Advanced Placement tests.

COSTS AND FINANCIAL AID
Annual out-of-state tuition $10,170. Room and board $8,817. Required fees $4,689. Average book expense $1,386. **Required Forms and Deadlines:** FAFSA, institution's own financial aid form. Financial aid filing deadline 6/30. **Notification of Awards:** Applicants will be notified of awards on or about 4/15. **Types of Aid:** *Need-based scholarships/grants:* Pell, SEOG, state scholarships/grants, private scholarships, the school's own gift aid. *Loans:* FFEL Subsidized Stafford, FFEL Unsubsidized Stafford, FFEL PLUS, Federal Perkins, college/university loans from institutional funds, alternative loans. **Student Employment:** Off-campus job opportunities are fair. **Financial Aid Statistics:** 19% freshmen, 23% undergrads receive need-based scholarship or grant aid. 18% freshmen, 25% undergrads receive need-based self-help aid. 64% freshmen, 67% undergrads receive any aid.

CALIFORNIA STATE POLYTECHNIC UNIVERSITY—POMONA

3801 West Temple Avenue, Pomona, CA 91768
Phone: 909-869-3210 **E-mail:** admissions@csupomona.edu **CEEB Code:** 4082
Fax: 909-869-4529 **Website:** www.csupomona.edu **ACT Code:** 4048
Financial Aid Phone: 909-869-3700

This public school was founded in 1938. It has a 1,437-acre campus.

RATINGS
Admissions Selectivity Rating: 60*   **Fire Safety Rating:** 71   **Green Rating:** 95

STUDENTS AND FACULTY
Enrollment: 18,040. **Student Body:** 43% female, 57% male, 2% out-of-state, 5% international (112 countries represented). African American 4%, Asian 30%, Caucasian 25%, Hispanic 27%. **Retention and Graduation:** 78% freshmen return for sophomore year. 10% freshmen graduate within 4 years. **Faculty:** Student/faculty ratio 23:1. 680 full-time faculty, 75% hold PhDs. 100% faculty teach undergrads.

ACADEMICS
Degrees: Bachelor's, master's. **Academic Requirements:** Arts/fine arts, computer literacy, English (including composition), foreign languages, history, humanities, mathematics, philosophy, sciences (biological or physical), social science. **Classes:** Most classes have 20–29 students. **Majors with Highest Enrollment:** Business administration/management; computer and information sciences; electrical, electronics, and communications engineering. **Disciplines with Highest Percentage of Degrees Awarded:** Business/marketing 37%, engineering 15%, liberal arts/general studies 6%, architecture 5%, biological/life sciences 4%. **Special Study Options:** Cooperative education program, cross-registration, double major, dual enrollment, English as a Second Language (ESL), exchange student program (domestic), external degree program, honors program, internships, study abroad, teacher certification program, undergrads may take grad classes, Ocean Studies Institute, Desert Studies Consortium.

FACILITIES
Housing: Coed dorms, apartments for single students, special housing for disabled students. **Special Academic Facilities/Equipment:** Center for hospitality management; art gallery; center for regenerative studies; citrus-packing house; meat-processing building; poultry plant; feed mill; beef, sheep, swine, Arabian horse units; horse show arena; and aerospace wind tunnel. **Computers:** 90% of public computers are PCs, 10% of public computers are Macs, network access in dorm rooms, online registration, online administrative functions (other than registration), remote student-access to Web through college's connection.

CAMPUS LIFE
Activities: Choral groups, concert band, dance, drama/theater, jazz band, literary magazine, music ensembles, musical theater, opera, pep band, student government, student newspaper, symphony orchestra, yearbook. **Organizations:** 230 registered organizations, 26 honor societies, 9 religious organizations. 12 fraternities (3% men join), 8 sororities (3% women join). **Athletics (Intercollegiate):** *Men:* Baseball, basketball, cheerleading, cross-country, soccer, tennis, track/field (outdoor). *Women:* Basketball, cheerleading, cross-country, soccer, tennis, track/field (outdoor), volleyball.

ADMISSIONS
Freshman Academic Profile: 98% from public high schools. SAT Math middle 50% range 460–590. SAT Critical Reading middle 50% range 430–540. ACT middle 50% range 18–23. TOEFL required of all international applicants, minimum paper TOEFL 525, minimum computer TOEFL 195. **Basis for**

Candidate Selection: *Very important factors considered include:* Academic GPA, rigor of secondary school record, standardized test scores. **Freshman Admission Requirements:** High school diploma is required, and GED is accepted. *Academic units required:* 4 English, 3 math, 2 science (2 science labs), 2 foreign language, 1 social studies, 1 history, 1 academic elective, 1 visual/performing arts. *Academic units recommended:* 4 math. **Freshman Admission Statistics:** 19,965 applied, 72% admitted, 20% enrolled. **Transfer Admission Requirements:** College transcript(s), statement of good standing from prior institution(s). Minimum college GPA of 2.0 required. Lowest grade transferable C. **General Admission Information:** Application fee $55. Regular application deadline 11/30. Regular notification is rolling. Nonfall registration accepted. Credit and/or placement offered for CEEB Advanced Placement tests.

COSTS AND FINANCIAL AID

Annual out-of-state tuition $10,170. Room and board $8,493. Required fees $3,279. Average book expense $1,386. **Required Forms and Deadlines:** FAFSA. Financial aid filing deadline 3/2. **Notification of Awards:** Applicants will be notified of awards on a rolling basis beginning on or about 4/1. **Types of Aid:** *Need-based scholarships/grants:* Pell, SEOG, state scholarships/grants, private scholarships, the school's own gift aid. *Loans:* FFEL Subsidized Stafford, FFEL Unsubsidized Stafford, FFEL PLUS, Federal Perkins. **Financial Aid Statistics:** 35% undergrads, 37% undergrads receive need-based scholarship or grant aid. 40% freshmen, 41% undergrads receive need-based self-help aid. 27 freshmen, 125 undergrads receive athletic scholarships. 77% freshmen, 84% undergrads receive any aid. Highest amount earned per year from on-campus jobs $2,500.

CALIFORNIA STATE UNIVERSITY—BAKERSFIELD

9001 Stockdale Highway, Bakersfield, CA 93311
Phone: 661-664-3036 **E-mail:** swatkin@csub.edu **CEEB Code:** 4110
Fax: 661-664-3389 **Website:** www.csub.edu
Financial Aid Phone: 661-664-3016

This public school was founded in 1970. It has a 375-acre campus.

RATINGS
Admissions Selectivity Rating: 60*   **Fire Safety Rating:** 60*   **Green Rating:** 60*

STUDENTS AND FACULTY
Enrollment: 4,309. **Student Body:** 10% out-of-state, 2% international. African American 7%, Asian 7%, Caucasian 46%, Hispanic 27%, Native American 2%. **Retention and Graduation:** 20% grads go on to further study within 1 year. 10% grads pursue arts and sciences degrees. 10% grads pursue business degrees. **Faculty:** Student/faculty ratio 19:1.

ACADEMICS
Degrees: Bachelor's, master's. **Academic Requirements:** Arts/fine arts, computer literacy, English (including composition), foreign languages, history, humanities, mathematics, philosophy, sciences (biological or physical), social science. **Majors with Highest Enrollment:** Business, management, marketing, and related support services; liberal arts and sciences/liberal studies; psychology. **Study Options:** Accelerated program, cooperative education program, cross-registration, distance learning, double major, dual enrollment, English as a Second Language (ESL), exchange student program (domestic), external degree program, honors program, independent study, internships, liberal arts/career combination, student-designed major, study abroad, teacher certification program.

FACILITIES
Housing: Coed dorms, women's dorms. **Special Academic Facilities/ Equipment:** Todd Madigan Art Gallery, Frances Doré Theater, California Well Sample Repository, Geotechnology Training Center, Family Business Institute. **Computers:** Online registration.

CAMPUS LIFE
Activities: Choral groups, concert band, drama/theater, jazz band, literary magazine, music ensembles, musical theater, opera, pep band, student government, student newspaper. **Organizations:** 71 registered organizations, 1 honor society, 2 religious organizations. 2 fraternities (1% men join), 2 sororities (1% women join). **Athletics (Intercollegiate):** *Men:* Basketball, diving, golf, soccer, swimming, track/field (outdoor), wrestling. *Women:* Basketball, cross-country, diving, soccer, softball, swimming, tennis, track/field (outdoor), volleyball, water polo.

ADMISSIONS
Freshman Academic Profile: 100% in top 50% of high school class. 99% from public high schools. TOEFL required of all international applicants, minimum paper TOEFL 550. **Freshman Admission Requirements:** High school diploma is required, and GED is accepted. *Academic units required:* 4 English, 3 math, 1 science (2 science labs), 2 foreign language, 2 history, 1 academic elective, 1 visual/performing arts. **Transfer Admission Requirements:** College transcript(s), minimum college GPA of 2.0 required. Lowest grade transferable D. **General Admission Information:** Application fee $55. Regular notification rolling. Nonfall registration accepted. Common Application accepted. Credit and/or placement offered for CEEB Advanced Placement tests.

COSTS AND FINANCIAL AID
Annual in-state tuition $1,506. Out-of-state tuition $7,380. Room & board $5,801. Required fees $1,957. Average book expense $650. **Required Forms and Deadlines:** FAFSA, state aid form. Financial aid filing deadline 4/1. **Types of Aid:** *Need-based scholarships/grants:* Pell, SEOG, state scholarships/grants, private scholarships, the school's own gift aid, United Negro College Fund, Federal Nursing Scholarships. *Loans:* Direct Subsidized Stafford, FFEL Subsidized Stafford, Federal Perkins, Federal Nursing, state loans, college/ university loans from institutional funds. **Student Employment:** Federal Work-Study Program available. Institutional employment available. Off-campus job opportunities are good. **Financial Aid Statistics:** 55% freshmen, 53% undergrads receive need-based scholarship or grant aid. 31% freshmen, 44% undergrads receive need-based self-help aid. Highest amount earned per year from on-campus jobs $3,916.

CALIFORNIA STATE UNIVERSITY—CHICO

400 West First Street, Chico, CA 95929-0722
Phone: 530-898-4428 **E-mail:** info@csuchico.edu **CEEB Code:** 4048
Fax: 530-898-6456 **Website:** www.csuchico.edu **ACT Code:** 0212
Financial Aid Phone: 530-898-6451

This public school was founded in 1887. It has a 130-acre campus.

RATINGS
Admissions Selectivity Rating: 79   **Fire Safety Rating:** 60*   **Green Rating:** 60*

STUDENTS AND FACULTY
Enrollment: 14,927. **Student Body:** 53% female, 47% male, 1% out-of-state, 2% international. African American 2%, Asian 6%, Caucasian 66%, Hispanic 12%. **Retention and Graduation:** 82% freshmen return for sophomore year. 16% freshmen graduate within 4 years. **Faculty:** Student/faculty ratio 21:1. 533 full-time faculty, 85% hold PhDs. 100% faculty teach undergrads.

ACADEMICS
Degrees: Bachelor's, certificate, master's, post-bachelor's certificate, post-master's certificate. **Academic Requirements:** Arts/fine arts, computer literacy, English (including composition), history, humanities, mathematics, philosophy, sciences (biological or physical), social science. **Classes:** Most classes have 20–29 students. Most lab/discussion sections have 20–29 students. **Disciplines with Highest Percentage of Degrees Awarded:** Business/marketing 17%, social sciences 11%, liberal arts/general studies 10%, communications/journalism 7%, parks and recreation 6%. **Special Study Options:** Cooperative education program, cross-registration, distance learning, double major, dual enrollment, English as a Second Language (ESL), exchange student program (domestic), external degree program, honors program, independent study, internships, student-designed major, study abroad, teacher certification program.

FACILITIES
Housing: Coed dorms, apartments for single students, special housing for disabled students, special housing for international students, fraternity/sorority housing. Thematic housing for honors, engineering, minorities in engineering and science, business, and math. **Special Academic Facilities/Equipment:** Anthropology museum, center for intercultural studies, satellite communication dishes, biological field station, university farm, electron microscope.

CAMPUS LIFE
Activities: Choral groups, concert band, dance, drama/theater, jazz band, literary magazine, music ensembles, musical theater, opera, pep band, radio station, student government, student newspaper, student-run film society, symphony orchestra, yearbook. **Organizations:** 15 honor societies, 19 religious organizations. 22 fraternities (1% men join), 18 sororities (1% women join). **Athletics (Intercollegiate):** *Men:* Baseball, basketball, cross-country, soccer,

track/field (outdoor), volleyball. *Women:* Basketball, cross-country, soccer, softball, track/field (outdoor), volleyball.

ADMISSIONS

Freshman Academic Profile: 35% in top 10% of high school class, 76% in top 25% of high school class, 100% in top 50% of high school class. 39% from public high schools. SAT Math middle 50% range 460–570. SAT Critical Reading middle 50% range 440–550. ACT middle 50% range 19–24. TOEFL required of all international applicants, minimum paper TOEFL 500. **Basis for Candidate Selection:** *Very important factors considered include:* Academic GPA, standardized test scores. *Important factors considered include:* Geographical residence, state residency. **Freshman Admission Requirements:** High school diploma is required, and GED is accepted. *Academic units required:* 4 English, 3 math, 2 science (2 science labs), 2 foreign language, 2 social studies, 1 academic elective, 1 visual and performing arts. **Freshman Admission Statistics:** 12,733 applied, 90% admitted, 22% enrolled. **Transfer Admission Requirements:** College transcript(s), statement of good standing from prior institution(s). Minimum college GPA of 2.0 required. Lowest grade transferable D. **General Admission Information:** Application fee $55. Regular application deadline 11/30. Regular notification 3/1. Nonfall registration accepted. Admission may be deferred for a maximum of 1 year. Credit and/or placement offered for CEEB Advanced Placement tests.

COSTS AND FINANCIAL AID

Annual in-state tuition $3,050. Annual out-of-state tuition $13,220. Room and board $8,466. Required fees $944. Average book expense $1,351. **Required Forms and Deadlines:** FAFSA, scholarship application form. Financial aid filing deadline 3/2. **Notification of Awards:** Applicants will be notified of awards on a rolling basis beginning on or about 2/15. **Types of Aid:** *Need-based scholarships/grants:* Pell, SEOG, state scholarships/grants, private scholarships, the school's own gift aid, United Negro College Fund. *Loans:* Direct Subsidized Stafford, Direct Unsubsidized Stafford, Direct PLUS, Federal Perkins, college/university loans from institutional funds. **Student Employment:** Federal Work-Study Program available. Institutional employment available. Off-campus job opportunities are fair. **Financial Aid Statistics:** 25% freshmen, 31% undergrads receive need-based scholarship or grant aid. 27% freshmen, 31% undergrads receive need-based self-help aid. 6 freshmen, 27 undergrads receive athletic scholarships.

CALIFORNIA STATE UNIVERSITY— DOMINGUEZ HILLS

100 East Victoria Street, Carson, CA 90747
Phone: 310-243-3600 **E-mail:** lwise@csudh.edu **CEEB Code:** 4098
Fax: 310-516-3609 **Website:** www.csudh.edu
Financial Aid Phone: 310-243-3691

This public school was founded in 1960. It has a 346-acre campus.

RATINGS
Admissions Selectivity Rating: 60*   **Fire Safety Rating:** 60*   **Green Rating:** 60*

STUDENTS AND FACULTY

Enrollment: 8,698. **Student Body:** 69% female, 31% male, 1% out-of-state, 2% international. African American 27%, Asian 9%, Caucasian 13%, Hispanic 36%. **Retention and Graduation:** 67% freshmen return for sophomore year. 5% freshmen graduate within 4 years. **Faculty:** Student/faculty ratio 22:1. 252 full-time faculty, 76% hold PhDs.

ACADEMICS

Degrees: Bachelor's, certificate, master's, post-bachelor's certificate. **Academic Requirements:** English (including composition), humanities, mathematics, sciences (biological or physical), social science, cultural pluralium requirement (3 units), at least 9 units of general education classes must be completed at campus from which students graduate. **Classes:** Most classes have 20–29 students. Most lab/discussion sections have 20–29 students. **Disciplines with Highest Percentage of Degrees Awarded:** Liberal arts/general studies 20%, health professions and related sciences 17%, business/marketing 14%, social sciences 10%, interdisciplinary studies 7%. **Special Study Options:** Cooperative education program, cross-registration, distance learning, double major, dual enrollment, external degree program, honors program, independent study, internships, study abroad, teacher certification program, weekend college.

FACILITIES

Housing: Apartments for married students, apartments for single students. **Special Academic Facilities/Equipment:** University art gallery, Olympic velodrome, university theater.

College Directory

CAMPUS LIFE
Activities: Choral groups, concert band, dance, drama/theater, jazz band, music ensembles, student government, student newspaper, symphony orchestra. **Organizations:** 65 registered organizations, 6 honor societies, 3 religious organizations. 4 fraternities, 4 sororities. **Athletics (Intercollegiate):** *Men:* Baseball, basketball, golf, soccer. *Women:* Basketball, cross-country, soccer, softball, tennis, track/field (outdoor), volleyball.

ADMISSIONS
Freshman Academic Profile: 50% in top 50% of high school class. 84% from public high schools. SAT Math middle 50% range 370–480. SAT Critical Reading middle 50% range 360–470. ACT middle 50% range 13–19. TOEFL required of all international applicants, minimum paper TOEFL 550, minimum computer TOEFL 150. **Basis for Candidate Selection:** *Factors considered include:* Geographical residence, recommendation(s), state residency. **Freshman Admission Requirements:** High school diploma is required, and GED is accepted. *Academic units required:* 4 English, 3 math, 2 science (2 science labs), 2 foreign language, 2 social studies, 1 history, 1 academic elective, 1 visual/performing arts. **Freshman Admission Statistics:** 6,486 applied, 15% admitted, 75% enrolled. **Transfer Admission Requirements:** High school transcript, college transcript(s), minimum college GPA of 2.0 required. Lowest grade transferable C. **General Admission Information:** Application fee $55. Regular application deadline 6/1. Regular notification is rolling. Nonfall registration accepted. Common Application not accepted. Credit offered for CEEB Advanced Placement tests.

COSTS AND FINANCIAL AID
Annual in-state tuition $1,815. Out-of-state tuition $7,380. Room & board $5,801. Required fees $300. Average book expense $630. **Required Forms and Deadlines:** FAFSA, institution's own financial aid form, state aid form. Financial aid filing deadline 4/15. **Notification of Awards:** Applicants will be notified of awards on or about 4/19. **Types of Aid:** *Need-based scholarships/grants:* Pell, state scholarships/grants. *Loans:* Direct Subsidized Stafford, Direct Unsubsidized Stafford, FFEL PLUS, Federal Perkins. **Financial Aid Statistics:** 66% freshmen, 64% undergrads receive need-based scholarship or grant aid. 21% freshmen, 35% undergrads receive need-based self-help aid. 3 freshmen, 12 undergrads receive athletic scholarships. Highest amount earned per year from on-campus jobs $3,000.

CALIFORNIA STATE UNIVERSITY—EAST BAY

25800 Carlos Bee Boulevard, Hayward, CA 94542-3035
Phone: 510-885-2624 **E-mail:** askes@csuhayward.edu **CEEB Code:** 4011
Fax: 510-885-4059 **Website:** www.csuhayward.edu **ACT Code:** 0154
Financial Aid Phone: 510-885-2784

This public school was founded in 1957. It has a 342-acre campus.

RATINGS
Admissions Selectivity Rating: 78   **Fire Safety Rating:** 60*   **Green Rating:** 60*

STUDENTS AND FACULTY
Enrollment: 9,385. **Student Body:** 63% female, 37% male, 1% out-of-state, 3% international (86 countries represented). African American 11%, Asian 28%, Caucasian 25%, Hispanic 12%. **Retention and Graduation:** 82% freshmen return for sophomore year. 14% freshmen graduate within 4 years. **Faculty:** Student/faculty ratio 20:1. 359 full-time faculty, 82% hold PhDs. 85% faculty teach undergrads.

ACADEMICS
Degrees: Bachelor's, certificate, master's, post-bachelor's certificate, post-master's certificate. **Academic Requirements:** Arts/fine arts, computer literacy, English (including composition), history, humanities, mathematics, sciences (biological or physical), social science, critical thinking. **Classes:** Most classes have 20–29 students. Most lab/discussion sections have fewer than 10 students. **Disciplines with Highest Percentage of Degrees Awarded:** Business/marketing 30%, liberal arts/general studies 16%, social sciences 13%, psychology 5%, health professions and related sciences 5%, biological/life sciences 4%, communication technologies 4%, computer and information sciences 4%. **Special Study Options:** Cooperative education program, cross-registration, distance learning, double major, dual enrollment, English as a Second Language (ESL), exchange student program (domestic), external degree program, honors program, independent study, internships, liberal arts/career combination, student-designed major, study abroad, teacher certification program, weekend college, year round operation with state supported summer quarter. Joint master's degree in marine science offered at Moss Landing

Marine Lab. Joint MFA in creative writing in summer. Overseas MBA programs in Hong Kong, Moscow, Singapore, and Vienna.

FACILITIES

Housing: Apartments for single students, private coeducational dormitory adjacent to campus. **Special Academic Facilities/Equipment:** Anthropology museum, art gallery, scanning electron microscope facility, marine lab, ecological field station, geology summer camp. **Computers:** 75% of public computers are PCs, 20% of public computers are Macs, 5% of public computers are UNIX, network access in dorm rooms, online registration, online administrative functions (other than registration), remote student-access to Web through college's connection.

CAMPUS LIFE

Activities: Choral groups, concert band, dance, drama/theater, jazz band, literary magazine, music ensembles, musical theater, opera, pep band, radio station, student government, student newspaper, symphony orchestra, television station. **Organizations:** 89 registered organizations, 2 honor societies, 2 religious organizations. 7 fraternities, 7 sororities. **Athletics (Intercollegiate):** *Men:* Baseball, basketball, cross-country, golf, soccer. *Women:* Basketball, cross-country, golf, soccer, softball, swimming, volleyball, water polo.

ADMISSIONS

Freshman Academic Profile: 12% in top 10% of high school class, 41% in top 25% of high school class, 80% in top 50% of high school class. 80% from public high schools. SAT Math middle 50% range 420–540. SAT Critical Reading middle 50% range 380–520. ACT middle 50% range 16–21. TOEFL required of all international applicants, minimum paper TOEFL 525, minimum computer TOEFL 197. **Basis for Candidate Selection:** *Very important factors considered include:* Rigor of secondary school record, standardized test scores. *Other factors considered include:* Recommendation(s), state residency. **Freshman Admission Requirements:** High school diploma is required, and GED is accepted. *Academic units required:* 4 English, 3 math, 2 science (2 science labs), 2 foreign language, 1 social studies, 1 history, 1 academic elective, 1 visual/performing arts. **Freshman Admission Statistics:** 4,675 applied, 46% admitted, 31% enrolled. **Transfer Admission Requirements:** College transcript(s), statement of good standing from prior institution(s). Minimum college GPA of 2.0 required. Lowest grade transferable D. **General Admission Information:** Application fee $55. Early decision application deadline 3/15. Regular application deadline 6/30. Regular notification is rolling. Nonfall registration accepted. Admission may be deferred for a maximum of 2 quarters. Common Application not accepted. Credit and/or placement offered for CEEB Advanced Placement tests.

COSTS AND FINANCIAL AID

Comprehensive fee $3,264. Room and board $8,739. Required fees $2,706. Average book expense $1,224. **Required Forms and Deadlines:** FAFSA. Financial aid filing deadline ???. **Notification of Awards:** Applicants will be notified of awards on a rolling basis beginning on or about 3/15. **Types of Aid:** *Need-based scholarships/grants:* Pell, SEOG, state scholarships/grants, private scholarships, the school's own gift aid. *Loans:* FFEL Subsidized Stafford, FFEL Unsubsidized Stafford, FFEL PLUS, Federal Perkins. **Student Employment:** Federal Work-Study Program available. Institutional employment available. Off-campus job opportunities are excellent. **Financial Aid Statistics:** 40% freshmen, 35% undergrads receive need-based scholarship or grant aid. 16% freshmen, 25% undergrads receive need-based self-help aid. 43% freshmen, 42% undergrads receive any aid.

CALIFORNIA STATE UNIVERSITY—FRESNO

5150 North Maple Avenue, M/S JA 57, Fresno, CA 93740-8026
Phone: 559-278-2261 **E-mail:** vivian_franco@csufresno.edu **CEEB Code:** 4312
Fax: 559-278-4812 **Website:** www.csufresno.edu **ACT Code:** 0266
Financial Aid Phone: 559-294-2200

This public school was founded in 1911. It has a 327-acre campus.

RATINGS

Admissions Selectivity Rating: 60*   **Fire Safety Rating:** 60*   **Green Rating:** 60*

STUDENTS AND FACULTY

Enrollment: 18,951. **Student Body:** 58% female, 42% male, 2% out-of-state, 2% international (103 countries represented). African American 5%, Asian 14%, Caucasian 37%, Hispanic 31%. **Retention and Graduation:** 82% freshmen return for sophomore year. 12% freshmen graduate within 4 years. 5% grads go on to further study within 1 year. 4% grads pursue business degrees. 1% grads pursue law degrees. 1% grads pursue medical degrees. **Faculty:** 656 full-time faculty, 81% hold PhDs. 100% faculty teach undergrads.

ACADEMICS

Degrees: Bachelor's, doctoral, master's. **Academic Requirements:** Arts/fine arts, computer literacy, English (including composition), foreign languages, history, humanities, mathematics, philosophy, sciences (biological or physical), social science, speech, critical thinking, political science, behavioral/ environmental systems. **Classes:** Most classes have 20–29 students. Most lab/discussion sections have 20–29 students. **Majors with Highest Enrollment:** Business/ commerce, health services/allied health, liberal arts and sciences/liberal studies. **Disciplines with Highest Percentage of Degrees Awarded:** Liberal arts/ general studies 16%, business/marketing 16%, social sciences 10%, health professions and related sciences 9%, psychology 5%. **Special Study Options:** Accelerated program, cooperative education program, cross-registration, distance learning, double major, dual enrollment, English as a Second Language (ESL), exchange student program (domestic), honors program, independent study, internships, student-designed major, study abroad, teacher certification program.

FACILITIES

Housing: Coed dorms, men's dorms, women's dorms, apartments for married students, apartments for single students, fraternity/sorority housing. **Special Academic Facilities/Equipment:** Marine lab, Downing Planeterium. **Computers:** 75% of public computers are PCs, 25% of public computers are Macs, network access in dorm rooms, network access in dorm lounges, online registration, online administrative functions (other than registration), remote student-access to Web through college's connection. Undergraduates are required to own a computer.

CAMPUS LIFE

Activities: Choral groups, concert band, dance, drama/theater, jazz band, literary magazine, marching band, music ensembles, musical theater, radio station, student government, student newspaper, symphony orchestra, television station. **Organizations:** 250 registered organizations, 21 honor societies, 11 religious organizations. 19 fraternities (4% men join), 13 sororities (3% women join). **Athletics (Intercollegiate):** *Men:* Baseball, basketball, cheerleading, cross-country, football, golf, tennis, track/field (outdoor), wrestling. *Women:* Basketball, cheerleading, cross-country, diving, equestrian sports, golf, soccer, softball, tennis, track/field (outdoor), volleyball.

ADMISSIONS

Freshman Academic Profile: 99% from public high schools. SAT Math middle 50% range 410–540. SAT Critical Reading middle 50% range 380–510. ACT middle 50% range 16–27. TOEFL required of all international applicants, minimum paper TOEFL 500, minimum computer TOEFL 173. **Basis for Candidate Selection:** *Very important factors considered include:* Rigor of secondary school record, standardized test scores. **Freshman Admission Requirements:** High school diploma is required, and GED is accepted. *Academic units required:* 4 English, 3 math, 1 science (1 science lab), 2 foreign language, 1 history, 3 academic electives, 1 visual/performing arts. *Academic units recommended:* 1 social studies. **Freshman Admission Statistics:** 13,495 applied, 69% admitted, 28% enrolled. **Transfer Admission Requirements:** College transcript(s), minimum college GPA of 2.0 required. Lowest grade transferable D. **General Admission Information:** Application fee $55. Regular application deadline 4/1. Regular notification is rolling. Nonfall registration accepted. Credit offered for CEEB Advanced Placement tests.

COSTS AND FINANCIAL AID

Out-of-state tuition $13,209. Room & board $6,880. Required fees $3,039. Average book expense $1,240. **Required Forms and Deadlines:** FAFSA. Financial aid filing deadline 3/2. **Notification of Awards:** Applicants will be notified of awards on a rolling basis beginning on or about 4/1. **Types of Aid:** *Need-based scholarships/grants:* Pell, SEOG, state scholarships/grants, private scholarships, the school's own gift aid. *Loans:* FFEL Subsidized Stafford, FFEL Unsubsidized Stafford, FFEL PLUS, Federal Perkins, Federal Nursing, college/university loans from institutional funds. **Financial Aid Statistics:** 34% freshmen, 48% undergrads receive need-based scholarship or grant aid. 14% freshmen, 28% undergrads receive need-based self-help aid. 46 freshmen, 378 undergrads receive athletic scholarships. Highest amount earned per year from on-campus jobs $2,090.

CALIFORNIA STATE UNIVERSITY—FULLERTON

800 North State College Boulevard, Fullerton, CA 92834-6900
Phone: 714-773-2370 **E-mail:** admissions@fullerton.edu **CEEB Code:** 4589
Fax: 714-278-2356 **Website:** www.fullerton.edu
Financial Aid Phone: 714-278-3125

This public school was founded in 1957. It has a 225-acre campus.

RATINGS
Admissions Selectivity Rating: 76   **Fire Safety Rating:** 60*   **Green Rating:** 60*

STUDENTS AND FACULTY
Enrollment: 25,261. **Student Body:** 60% female, 40% male, 1% out-of-state, 4% international (78 countries represented). African American 3%, Asian 24%, Caucasian 34%, Hispanic 24%. **Retention and Graduation:** 80% freshmen return for sophomore year. 8% freshmen graduate within 4 years. **Faculty:** Student/faculty ratio 21:1. 754 full-time faculty, 84% hold PhDs.

ACADEMICS
Degrees: Bachelor's, master's. **Academic Requirements:** Arts/fine arts, English (including composition), history, humanities, mathematics, sciences (biological or physical), social science, oral and written communication. **Classes:** Most classes have 20–29 students. Most lab/discussion sections have 20–29 students. **Special Study Options:** Cooperative education program, double major, honors program, independent study, internships, student-designed major, study abroad.

FACILITIES
Housing: Apartments for single students, fraternity/sorority housing. **Computers:** 90% of public computers are PCs, 9% of public computers are Macs, 1% of public computers are UNIX, network access in dorm rooms, online registration, online administrative functions (other than registration), remote student-access to Web through college's connection.

CAMPUS LIFE
Activities: Choral groups, concert band, dance, drama/theater, jazz band, music ensembles, musical theater, radio station, student government, student newspaper. **Athletics (Intercollegiate):** *Men:* Baseball, basketball, cross-country, fencing, soccer, track/field (outdoor), wrestling. *Women:* Basketball, cross-country, fencing, gymnastics, soccer, softball, tennis, track/field (outdoor), volleyball.

ADMISSIONS
Freshman Academic Profile: 15% in top 10% of high school class, 45% in top 25% of high school class, 81% in top 50% of high school class. 82% from public high schools. SAT Math middle 50% range 440–560. SAT Critical Reading middle 50% range 420–530. ACT middle 50% range 17–23. TOEFL required of all international applicants, minimum paper TOEFL 500, minimum computer TOEFL 173. **Basis for Candidate Selection:** *Very important factors considered include:* Rigor of secondary school record, standardized test scores. *Other factors considered include:* State residency. **Freshman Admission Requirements:** High school diploma is required, and GED is accepted. *Academic units required:* 2 science (2 science labs), 2 history, 1 academic elective, 1 visual/performing arts. **Freshman Admission Statistics:** 13,721 applied, 69% admitted, 30% enrolled. **Transfer Admission Requirements:** College transcript(s), statement of good standing from prior institution(s). Minimum college GPA of 2.0 required. Lowest grade transferable C. **General Admission Information:** Application fee $55. Regular application deadline 4/15. Regular notification is rolling. Nonfall registration accepted. Common Application not accepted. Credit and/or placement offered for CEEB Advanced Placement tests.

COSTS AND FINANCIAL AID
Out-of-state tuition $5,904. Room & board $3,953. Required fees $1,881. Average book expense $1,080. **Required Forms and Deadlines:** FAFSA, state aid form. Financial aid filing deadline 3/2. **Notification of Awards:** Applicants will be notified of awards on a rolling basis beginning on or about 3/1. **Types of Aid:** *Need-based scholarships/grants:* Pell, SEOG, state scholarships/grants, private scholarships, the school's own gift aid. *Loans:* FFEL Subsidized Stafford, FFEL Unsubsidized Stafford, FFEL PLUS, Federal Perkins, college/university loans from institutional funds. **Student Employment:** Federal Work-Study Program available. Institutional employment available. Off-campus job opportunities are good. **Financial Aid Statistics:** 30% freshmen, 29% undergrads receive need-based scholarship or grant aid. 15% freshmen, 21% undergrads receive need-based self-help aid. 39 freshmen, 160 undergrads receive athletic scholarships.

CALIFORNIA STATE UNIVERSITY—LONG BEACH

1250 Bellflower Boulevard, Long Beach, CA 90840
Phone: 562-985-5471 **E-mail:** eslb@csulb.edu **CEEB Code:** 4389
Fax: 562-985-4973 **Website:** www.csulb.edu
Financial Aid Phone: 562-985-8403

This public school was founded in 1949. It has a 322-acre campus.

RATINGS
Admissions Selectivity Rating: 91   **Fire Safety Rating:** 60*   **Green Rating:** 60*

STUDENTS AND FACULTY
Enrollment: 29,540. **Student Body:** 60% female, 40% male, 1% out-of-state, 5% international. African American 6%, Asian 23%, Caucasian 32%, Hispanic 26%. **Retention and Graduation:** 85% freshmen return for sophomore year. 12% freshmen graduate within 4 years. **Faculty:** Student/faculty ratio 20:1. 1,029 full-time faculty, 83% hold PhDs. 100% faculty teach undergrads.

ACADEMICS
Degrees: Bachelor's, master's, post-bachelor's certificate. **Academic Requirements:** Arts/fine arts, English (including composition), history, humanities, mathematics, sciences (biological or physical), social science. **Classes:** Most classes have 20–29 students. Most lab/discussion sections have 20–29 students. **Majors with Highest Enrollment:** Corrections and criminal justice; management information systems, psychology. **Disciplines with Highest Percentage of Degrees Awarded:** Business/marketing 20%, English 9%, liberal arts/general studies 8%, visual and performing arts 8%, social sciences 7%, psychology 6%, health professions and related sciences 6%. **Special Study Options:** Accelerated program, cross-registration, distance learning, double major, dual enrollment, English as a Second Language (ESL), honors program, independent study, internships, student-designed major, study abroad, teacher certification program.

FACILITIES
Housing: Coed dorms, special housing for international students. **Special Academic Facilities/Equipment:** Art and science museums, Japanese garden, special events arena with meeting facilities. **Computers:** Network access in dorm rooms.

CAMPUS LIFE
Activities: Choral groups, concert band, dance, drama/theater, jazz band, literary magazine, music ensembles, musical theater, opera, radio station, student government, student newspaper, student-run film society, symphony orchestra, television station, yearbook. **Organizations:** 300 registered organizations, 25 honor societies, 20 religious organizations. 16 fraternities (4% men join), 15 sororities (4% women join). **Athletics (Intercollegiate):** *Men:* Baseball, basketball, cross-country, golf, track/field (outdoor), volleyball, water polo. *Women:* Basketball, cross-country, golf, soccer, softball, tennis, track/field (outdoor), volleyball, water polo.

ADMISSIONS
Freshman Academic Profile: 82% in top 25% of high school class, 100% in top 50% of high school class. 82% from public high schools. SAT Math middle 50% range 460–580. SAT Critical Reading middle 50% range 440–550. ACT middle 50% range 17–23. TOEFL required of all international applicants, minimum paper TOEFL 525. **Basis for Candidate Selection:** *Very important factors considered include:* Rigor of secondary school record, standardized test scores. **Freshman Admission Requirements:** High school diploma is required, and GED is accepted. *Academic units recommended:* 4 English, 3 math, 2 science (2 science labs), 2 foreign language, 1 social studies, 1 history, 1 academic elective, 1 fine arts. **Freshman Admission Statistics:** 42,815 applied, 52% admitted, 20% enrolled. **Transfer Admission Requirements:** College transcript(s), minimum college GPA of 2.0 required. Lowest grade transferable C. **General Admission Information:** Application fee $55. Regular application deadline 11/30. Regular notification is rolling. Nonfall registration accepted. Credit offered for CEEB Advanced Placement tests.

COSTS AND FINANCIAL AID
Annual out-of-state tuition $10,170. Room and board $7,940. Required fees $3,394. Average book expense $1,566. **Required Forms and Deadlines:** FAFSA. Financial aid filing deadline 3/2. **Notification of Awards:** Applicants will be notified of awards on a rolling basis beginning on or about 4/1. **Types of Aid:** *Need-based scholarships/grants:* Pell, SEOG, state scholarships/grants, private scholarships, the school's own gift aid. *Loans:* FFEL Subsidized Stafford, FFEL Unsubsidized Stafford, FFEL PLUS, Federal Perkins. **Student Employment:** Federal Work-Study Program available. Institutional employ-

ment available. Off-campus job opportunities are good. **Financial Aid Statistics:** 41% freshmen, 45% undergrads receive need-based scholarship or grant aid. 29% freshmen, 43% undergrads receive need-based self-help aid. 300 undergrads receive athletic scholarships. Highest amount earned per year from on-campus jobs $3,000.

CALIFORNIA STATE UNIVERSITY—LOS ANGELES

5151 State University Drive, Los Angeles, CA 90032
Phone: 323-343-3901 **E-mail:** admission@calstatela.edu **CEEB Code:** 4399
Fax: 323-343-6306 **ACT Code:** 0320
Financial Aid Phone: 213-343-1784

This public school was founded in 1947. It has a 175-acre campus.

RATINGS
Admissions Selectivity Rating: 60*　　**Fire Safety Rating:** 60*　　**Green Rating:** 60*

STUDENTS AND FACULTY
Enrollment: 15,352. **Student Body:** 62% female, 38% male, 3% out-of-state, 6% international. African American 9%, Asian 20%, Caucasian 11%, Hispanic 46%. **Retention and Graduation:** 75% freshmen return for sophomore year. **Faculty:** Student/faculty ratio 20:1. 569 full-time faculty.

ACADEMICS
Degrees: Bachelor's, certificate, doctoral, master's, post-bachelor's certificate. **Academic Requirements:** Arts/fine arts, computer literacy, English (including composition), history, humanities, mathematics, philosophy, sciences (biological or physical), social science. **Classes:** Most classes have 10–19 students. **Disciplines with Highest Percentage of Degrees Awarded:** Business/marketing 24%, social sciences 10%, security and protective services 10%, education 9%, liberal arts/general studies 9%. **Special Study Options:** Accelerated program, cooperative education program, cross-registration, distance learning, double major, dual enrollment, English as a Second Language (ESL), exchange student program (domestic), honors program, independent study, internships, student-designed major, study abroad, teacher certification program.

FACILITIES
Housing: Coed dorms, apartments for single students, special housing for international students, fraternity/sorority housing, (special interest housing), first-year house, quiet house, ACLP/international house, the neighborhood wellness/substance free house, the village. **Special Academic Facilities/Equipment:** Baroque pipe organ, bilingual center, entrepreneurship and small business institutes, center for study of armament and disarmament, Van de Graaff accelerator. **Computers:** 95% of public computers are PCs, 3% of public computers are Macs, 2% of public computers are UNIX, network access in dorm lounges, online administrative functions (other than registration), remote student-access to Web through college's connection.

CAMPUS LIFE
Activities: Choral groups, dance, drama/theater, jazz band, literary magazine, music ensembles, musical theater, opera, student government, student newspaper, symphony orchestra, yearbook. **Organizations:** 1 religious organization. 8 fraternities, 6 sororities. **Athletics (Intercollegiate):** *Men:* Baseball, basketball, cross-country, soccer, track/field (outdoor). *Women:* Basketball, cross-country, soccer, tennis, track/field (outdoor), volleyball.

ADMISSIONS
Freshman Academic Profile: SAT SAT Math middle 50% range 380–490. SAT Critical Reading middle 50% range 380–480. ACT middle 50% range 15–20. TOEFL required of all international applicants, minimum paper TOEFL 550, minimum computer TOEFL 213. **Basis for Candidate Selection:** *Very important factors considered include:* Academic GPA, rigor of secondary school record, standardized test scores. *Other factors considered include:* State residency. **Freshman Admission Requirements:** High school diploma is required, and GED is accepted. *Academic units required:* 4 English, 3 math, 2 science (2 science labs), 2 foreign language, 1 social studies, 1 history, 1 academic elective, 1 visual and performing arts. **Freshman Admission Statistics:** 18,725 applied, 61% admitted, 15% enrolled. **Transfer Admission Requirements:** College transcript(s), minimum college GPA of 2.0 required. Lowest grade transferable C. **General Admission Information:** Application fee $55. Regular application deadline 6/15. Regular notification is rolling. Nonfall registration accepted. Credit and/or placement offered for CEEB Advanced Placement tests.

COSTS AND FINANCIAL AID
Annual in-state tuition $2,772. Annual out-of-state tuition $12,942. Room and board $8,406. Required fees $560. Average book expense $1,386. **Required Forms and Deadlines:** FAFSA, verification/household size. Financial aid filing deadline 3/2. **Types of Aid:** *Need-based scholarships/grants:* Pell, SEOG, state scholarships/grants, private scholarships, the school's own gift aid, Federal and State Work Study. *Loans:* Direct Subsidized Stafford, Direct Unsubsidized Stafford, FFEL PLUS, Federal Perkins, Federal Nursing. **Financial Aid Statistics:** 64% freshmen, 54% undergrads receive need-based scholarship or grant aid. 10% freshmen, 23% undergrads receive need-based self-help aid.

CALIFORNIA STATE UNIVERSITY—NORTHRIDGE

The Tseng College of Extended Learning, California State University–Northridge, Northridge, CA 91330-8365
Phone: 818-677-2270 **E-mail:** lorraine.newlon@csun.edu **CEEB Code:** 4707
Fax: 818-677-5088 **Website:** www.csun.edu **ACT Code:** 0400
Financial Aid Phone: 818-677-3000

This public school was founded in 1956. It has a 350-acre campus.

RATINGS
Admissions Selectivity Rating: 60*　　**Fire Safety Rating:** 60*　　**Green Rating:** 60*

STUDENTS AND FACULTY
Enrollment: 20,955. **Student Body:** 1% out-of-state, 3% international. African American 9%, Asian 15%, Caucasian 33%, Hispanic 24%. **Retention and Graduation:** 78% freshmen return for sophomore year. 4% freshmen graduate within 4 years.

ACADEMICS
Degrees: Bachelor's, master's. **Special Study Options:** Accelerated program, English as a Second Language (ESL), honors program, student-designed major, study abroad.

FACILITIES
Housing: Coed dorms, apartments for married students, apartments for single students, special housing for international students, fraternity/sorority housing. **Special Academic Facilities/Equipment:** Anthropology museum, art galleries, deafness center, urban archives, map library, cancer research/developmental biology center, planetarium, observatory.

CAMPUS LIFE
Activities: Choral groups, concert band, drama/theater, jazz band, literary magazine, marching band, music ensembles, musical theater, radio station, student government, student newspaper, yearbook. **Organizations:** 267 registered organizations, 18 honor societies, 13 religious organizations. 24 fraternities, 12 sororities. **Athletics (Intercollegiate):** *Men:* Baseball, basketball, cross-country, diving, football, golf, soccer, swimming, track/field (indoor), track/field (outdoor), volleyball. *Women:* Basketball, cross-country, diving, football, golf, soccer, softball, swimming, tennis, track/field (indoor), track/field (outdoor), volleyball.

ADMISSIONS
Freshman Academic Profile: 33% in top 25% of high school class, 33% in top 50% of high school class. 81% from public high schools. TOEFL required of all international applicants, minimum paper TOEFL 500. **Basis for Candidate Selection:** *Very important factors considered include:* Standardized test scores. **Freshman Admission Requirements:** High school diploma is required, and GED is accepted. *Academic units required:* 4 English, 3 math, 1 science (2 science labs), 2 foreign language, 2 history, 1 academic elective, 1 visual/performing arts. **Freshman Admission Statistics:** 7,931 applied, 78% admitted, 38% enrolled. **Transfer Admission Requirements:** Lowest grade transferable D. **General Admission Information:** Application fee $55. Regular notification is rolling. Nonfall registration accepted. Common Application not accepted. Credit and/or placement offered for CEEB Advanced Placement tests.

COSTS AND FINANCIAL AID
Annual in-state tuition $1,506. Out-of-state tuition $7,874. Room & board $5,801. Average book expense $648. **Required Forms and Deadlines:** Institution's own financial aid form. **Types of Aid:** *Need-based scholarships/grants:* Pell, SEOG, state scholarships/grants, private scholarships, the school's own gift aid, Federal Nursing Scholarships. *Loans:* FFEL Subsidized Stafford, FFEL Unsubsidized Stafford, FFEL PLUS, Federal Perkins, Federal Nursing, college/university loans from institutional funds. **Student Employment:**

Federal Work-Study Program available. Institutional employment available. Off-campus job opportunities are good. Highest amount earned per year from on-campus jobs $3,000.

CALIFORNIA STATE UNIVERSITY— SACRAMENTO

6000 J Street, Lassen Hall, Sacramento, CA 95819-6048
Phone: 916-278-3901 **E-mail:** admissions@csus.edu **CEEB Code:** 4671
Fax: 916-278-5603 **Website:** www.csus.edu **ACT Code:** 0382
Financial Aid Phone: 916-278-6554

This public school was founded in 1947. It has a 300-acre campus.

RATINGS
Admissions Selectivity Rating: 60*   **Fire Safety Rating:** 61   **Green Rating:** 60*

STUDENTS AND FACULTY
Enrollment: 23,028. **Student Body:** 57% female, 43% male, 1% out-of-state, 1% international (122 countries represented). African American 7%, Asian 19%, Caucasian 43%, Hispanic 15%, Native American 1%. **Retention and Graduation:** 81% freshmen return for sophomore year. 10% freshmen graduate within 4 years. **Faculty:** Student/faculty ratio 22:1. 812 full-time faculty, 78% hold PhDs. 25% faculty teach undergrads.

ACADEMICS
Degrees: Bachelor's, doctoral, master's. **Academic Requirements:** Arts/fine arts, English (including composition), foreign languages, history, humanities, mathematics, sciences (biological or physical), social science, personal development. **Classes:** Most classes have 20–29 students. Most lab/discussion sections have 10–19 students. **Majors with Highest Enrollment:** Business administration/management, criminal justice/law enforcement administration; nursing–registered nurse training (ASN, BSN, MSN, RN). **Disciplines with Highest Percentage of Degrees Awarded:** Business/marketing 23%, social sciences 11%, security and protective services 10%, communication technologies 9%, liberal arts/general studies 9%. **Special Study Options:** Accelerated program, cooperative education program, cross-registration, distance learning, double major, dual enrollment, English as a Second Language (ESL), honors program, independent study, internships, student-designed major, study abroad, teacher certification program.

FACILITIES
Housing: Coed dorms. **Special Academic Facilities/Equipment:** CSUS Museum of Anthropology, university library gallery (art), Else Gallery (art), Witt Gallery (art). **Computers:** 1% of classrooms are wired, 50% of classrooms are wireless, 98% of public computers are PCs, 1% of public computers are Macs, 1% of public computers are UNIX, network access in dorm rooms, online registration, online administrative functions (other than registration), remote student-access to Web through college's connection.

CAMPUS LIFE
Activities: Choral groups, concert band, dance, drama/theater, jazz band, marching band, music ensembles, musical theater, opera, pep band, radio station, student government, student newspaper, symphony orchestra. **Organizations:** 222 registered organizations, 7 honor societies, 13 religious organizations. 19 fraternities (7% men join), 20 sororities (5% women join). **Athletics (Intercollegiate):** *Men:* Baseball, basketball, cheerleading, cross-country, football, golf, soccer, tennis, track/field (outdoor). *Women:* Basketball, cheerleading, crew/rowing, cross-country, golf, gymnastics, soccer, softball, tennis, track/field (outdoor), volleyball.

ADMISSIONS
Freshman Academic Profile: 100% in top 50% of high school class. 89% from public high schools. SAT Math middle 50% range 440–550. SAT Critical Reading middle 50% range 420–540. ACT middle 50% range 17–22. TOEFL required of all international applicants, minimum paper TOEFL 510, minimum computer TOEFL 180. **Basis for Candidate Selection:** *Very important factors considered include:* Rigor of secondary school record, standardized test scores. *Important factors considered include:* State residency. *Other factors considered include:* Extracurricular activities, geographical residence, interview, recommendation(s), talent/ability. **Freshman Admission Requirements:** High school diploma is required, and GED is accepted. *Academic units required:* 4 English, 3 math, 2 science (2 science labs), 2 foreign language, 1 social studies, 1 history, 1 academic elective, 1 visual/performing arts. **Freshman Admission Statistics:** 15,980 applied, 47% admitted, 34% enrolled. **Transfer Admission Requirements:** College transcript(s),

statement of good standing from prior institution(s). Minimum college GPA of 2.0 required. Lowest grade transferable D. **General Admission Information:** Application fee $55. Regular application deadline 11/30. Regular notification is rolling. Nonfall registration accepted. Admission may be deferred for a maximum of 1 semester. Common Application not accepted. Credit and/or placement offered for CEEB Advanced Placement tests.

COSTS AND FINANCIAL AID
Annual in-state tuition $3,072. Out-of-state tuition $13,242. Room & board $7,052. Required fees $276. Average book expense $1,260. **Required Forms and Deadlines:** FAFSA. Financial aid filing deadline 3/2. **Notification of Awards:** Applicants will be notified of awards on a rolling basis beginning on or about 4/1. **Types of Aid:** *Need-based scholarships/grants:* Pell, SEOG, state scholarships/grants, private scholarships, Federal Nursing Scholarships. *Loans:* Direct Subsidized Stafford, Direct Unsubsidized Stafford, Direct PLUS, Federal Perkins, Federal Nursing. **Student Employment:** Federal Work-Study Program available. Institutional employment available. Off-campus job opportunities are fair. **Financial Aid Statistics:** 43% freshmen, 39% undergrads receive need-based scholarship or grant aid. 24% freshmen, 32% undergrads receive need-based self-help aid. 50% undergrads receive any aid.

CALIFORNIA STATE UNIVERSITY— SAN BERNARDINO

5500 University Parkway, CSUSB-IR, 5500 University Parkway, San Bernardino, CA 92407-2397
Phone: 909-537-5188 **E-mail:** moreinfo@mail.csusb.edu **CEEB Code:** 4099
Fax: 909-537-7034 **Website:** www.csusb.edu **ACT Code:** 0205
Financial Aid Phone: 909-537-7800

This public school was founded in 1965. It has a 430-acre campus.

RATINGS
Admissions Selectivity Rating: 75   **Fire Safety Rating:** 60*   **Green Rating:** 60*

STUDENTS AND FACULTY
Enrollment: 12,926. **Student Body:** 65% female, 35% male, 3% international (62 countries represented). African American 12%, Asian 8%, Caucasian 31%, Hispanic 35%. **Retention and Graduation:** 84% freshmen return for sophomore year. 11% freshmen graduate within 4 years. **Faculty:** Student/faculty ratio 21:1. 450 full-time faculty.

ACADEMICS
Degrees: Bachelor's, master's. **Academic Requirements:** Arts/fine arts, computer literacy, English (including composition), foreign languages, history, humanities, mathematics, philosophy, sciences (biological or physical), social science, kinesiology or physical education. **Classes:** Most classes have 20–29 students. Most lab/discussion sections have 20–29 students. **Majors with Highest Enrollment:** Business administration/management, liberal arts and sciences/liberal studies, psychology. **Disciplines with Highest Percentage of Degrees Awarded:** Business/marketing 23%, liberal arts/general studies 17%, social sciences 9%, psychology 8%, security and protective services 7%. **Special Study Options:** Accelerated program, cooperative education program, cross-registration, distance learning, double major, dual enrollment, exchange student program (domestic), honors program, independent study, internships, study abroad, teacher certification program.

FACILITIES
Housing: Coed dorms, women's dorms, apartments for single students. **Special Academic Facilities/Equipment:** Simulation labs, electronic music studios, language lab, desert studies center, Robert V. Fullerton Art Museum, anthropology museum. **Computers:** Network access in dorm rooms, online registration, online administrative functions (other than registration), remote student-access to Web through college's connection.

CAMPUS LIFE
Activities: Choral groups, dance, drama/theater, jazz band, music ensembles, radio station, student government, student newspaper, television station. **Organizations:** 97 registered organizations, 3 religious organizations. 9 fraternities (3% men join), 6 sororities (6% women join). **Athletics (Intercollegiate):** *Men:* Baseball, basketball, golf, soccer. *Women:* Basketball, cross-country, soccer, softball, tennis, volleyball, water polo.

ADMISSIONS
Freshman Academic Profile: 18% in top 10% of high school class, 35% in top 25% of high school class, 90% in top 50% of high school class. 81% from public

high schools. SAT Math middle 50% range 410–520. SAT Critical Reading middle 50% range 400–500. SAT Writing middle 50% range 400–500. ACT middle 50% range 16–21. TOEFL required of all international applicants, minimum paper TOEFL 500, minimum computer TOEFL 173. **Basis for Candidate Selection:** *Very important factors considered include:* Academic GPA, recommendation(s), standardized test scores. *Important factors considered include:* Geographical residence. **Freshman Admission Requirements:** High school diploma is required, and GED is accepted. *Academic units required:* 4 English, 3 math, 2 science (2 science labs), 2 foreign language, 1 social studies, 1 history, 1 academic elective, 1 visual and performing arts. **Freshman Admission Statistics:** 9,555 applied, 63% admitted, 31% enrolled. **Transfer Admission Requirements:** College transcript(s), minimum college GPA of 2.0 required. Lowest grade transferable C. **General Admission Information:** Application fee $55. Nonfall registration accepted. Credit and/or placement offered for CEEB Advanced Placement tests.

COSTS AND FINANCIAL AID
Annual out-of-state tuition $8,136. Room and board $6,401. Required fees $3,440. Average book expense $1,380. **Required Forms and Deadlines:** FAFSA. Financial aid filing deadline 3/2. **Notification of Awards:** Applicants will be notified of awards on or about 4/1. **Types of Aid:** *Need-based scholarships/grants:* Pell, SEOG, state scholarships/grants, private scholarships, the school's own gift aid. *Loans:* Direct Subsidized Stafford, Direct Unsubsidized Stafford, FFEL PLUS, Federal Perkins. **Financial Aid Statistics:** 50% freshmen, 52% undergrads receive need-based scholarship or grant aid. 55% freshmen, 55% undergrads receive need-based self-help aid. 27 freshmen, 160 undergrads receive athletic scholarships.

CALIFORNIA STATE UNIVERSITY— SAN MARCOS

133 S. Twin Oaks Valley Road, San Marcos, CA 92096-0001
Phone: 760-750-4848 **E-mail:** apply@csusm.edu **CEEB Code:** 5677
Fax: 760-750-3248 **Website:** www.csusm.edu

This public school was founded in 1989. It has a 304-acre campus.

RATINGS
Admissions Selectivity Rating: 60*   **Fire Safety Rating:** 60*   **Green Rating:** 60*

STUDENTS AND FACULTY
Enrollment: 7,517. **Student Body:** 61% female, 39% male, 1% out-of-state, 2% international. African American 3%, Asian 10%, Caucasian 40%, Hispanic 17%. **Retention and Graduation:** 73% freshmen return for sophomore year. 10% freshmen graduate within 4 years. **Faculty:** Student/faculty ratio 24:1. 187 full-time faculty, 99% hold PhDs. 100% faculty teach undergrads.

ACADEMICS
Degrees: Bachelor's, master's. **Academic Requirements:** Computer literacy, English (including composition), foreign languages, history, humanities, mathematics, sciences (biological or physical), social science, U.S. history, constitution, and American ideals requirement, 2,500 word all-university writing requirement. **Classes:** Most classes have 30–39 students. Most lab/discussion sections have 20–29 students. **Disciplines with Highest Percentage of Degrees Awarded:** Business/marketing 28%, liberal arts/general studies 21%, social sciences 12% communication technologies 7%. **Special Study Options:** Cross-registration, distance learning, double major, dual enrollment, English as a Second Language (ESL), independent study, internships, student-designed major, study abroad, teacher certification program, weekend college, evening degree program, Program for Adult College Education (PACE), Saturday classes, Air Force ROTC, extended studies, open university, special sessions, including winter.

FACILITIES
Housing: Apartments for single students, special housing for disabled students, special housing for international students, our housing is privatized and operated by Allen & O'Hara. **Computers:** Online registration, remote student-access to Web through college's connection.

CAMPUS LIFE
Activities: Choral groups, dance, drama/theater, music ensembles, student newspaper. **Organizations:** 70 registered organizations, 5 honor societies, 2 religious organizations. 1 fraternity, 2 sororities. **Athletics (Intercollegiate):** *Men:* Baseball, cross-country, golf, soccer, track/field (outdoor). *Women:* Cross-country, golf, soccer, softball, track/field (outdoor).

ADMISSIONS
Freshman Academic Profile: SAT Math middle 50% range 450–550. SAT Critical Reading middle 50% range 440–530. TOEFL required of all international applicants, minimum paper TOEFL 550, minimum computer TOEFL 200. **Basis for Candidate Selection:** *Very important factors considered include:* Rigor of secondary school record, standardized test scores. **Freshman Admission Requirements:** High school diploma is required, and GED is accepted. *Academic units required:* 4 English, 3 math, 2 science (2 science labs), 2 foreign language, 2 social studies, 1 history, 1 academic elective, 1 visual performing arts. *Academic units recommended:* 4 English, 4 math, 2 science (2 science labs), 2 foreign language, 1 social studies, 1 history, 1 academic elective, 1 visual performing arts. **Freshman Admission Statistics:** 9,894 applied, 62% admitted, 22% enrolled. **Transfer Admission Requirements:** College transcript(s), minimum college GPA of 2.0 required. Lowest grade transferable C. **General Admission Information:** Application fee $55. Regular application deadline 11/30. Regular notification is rolling. Nonfall registration not accepted. Credit and/or placement offered for CEEB Advanced Placement tests.

COSTS AND FINANCIAL AID
Annual out-of-state tuition $7,510. Room and board $8,400. Required fees $3,374. Average book expense $1,386. **Required Forms and Deadlines:** FAFSA. Financial aid filing deadline 3/2. **Notification of Awards:** Applicants will be notified of awards on or about 4/15. **Types of Aid:** *Need-based scholarships/grants:* Pell, SEOG, state scholarships/grants, private scholarships, the school's own gift aid. *Loans:* Direct Subsidized Stafford, Direct Unsubsidized Stafford, Direct PLUS, FFEL PLUS, Federal Perkins, college/university loans from institutional funds. **Financial Aid Statistics:** 34% freshmen, 39% undergrads receive need-based scholarship or grant aid. 15% freshmen, 25% undergrads receive need-based self-help aid. 35 undergrads receive athletic scholarships. Highest amount earned per year from on-campus jobs $6,981. **Financial Aid Phone:** 760-750-4850.

CALIFORNIA STATE UNIVERSITY—STANISLAUS

Best 368

801 West Monte Vista Avenue, Turlock, CA 95382
Phone: 209-667-3070 **E-mail:** outreach_Help_Desk@csustan.edu **CEEB Code:** 4713
Fax: 209-667-3788 **Website:** www.csustan.edu **ACT Code:** 0435

This public school was founded in 1957. It has a 228-acre campus.

RATINGS
Admissions Selectivity Rating: 60*   **Fire Safety Rating:** 99   **Green Rating:** 94

STUDENTS AND FACULTY
Enrollment: 6,576. **Student Body:** 66% female, 34% male, 1% out-of-state, 1% international (35 countries represented). African American 4%, Asian 12%, Caucasian 40%, Hispanic 29%, Native American 1%. **Retention and Graduation:** 81% freshmen return for sophomore year. 20% freshmen graduate within 4 years. **Faculty:** Student/faculty ratio 19:1. 292 full-time faculty, 81% hold PhDs. 94% faculty teach undergrads.

ACADEMICS
Degrees: Bachelor's, master's, post-bachelor's certificate, post-master's certificate. **Academic Requirements:** Arts/fine arts, computer literacy, English (including composition), history, humanities, mathematics, philosophy, sciences (biological or physical), social science, public speaking, upper division writing. **Classes:** Most classes have 20–29 students. Most lab/discussion sections have 10–19 students. **Majors with Highest Enrollment:** Business administration/management, liberal arts and sciences/liberal studies, psychology. **Disciplines with Highest Percentage of Degrees Awarded:** Liberal arts/general studies 25%, business/marketing 18%, social sciences 13%, psychology 8%, security and protective services 6%. **Special Study Options:** Cooperative education program, distance learning, double major, dual enrollment, English as a Second Language (ESL), external degree program, honors program, independent study, internships, liberal arts/career combination, student-designed major, study abroad, teacher certification program.

FACILITIES
Housing: Coed dorms, apartments for single students. Most housing units can accomodate disabled students. Housing available in the summer months. **Special Academic Facilities/Equipment:** Marine sciences station, laser lab,

greenhouse, art gallery, mainstage theater, recital hall, observatory, science building, art complex, distance learning studios, BioAg Eco building. **Computers:** 10% of classrooms are wired, 75% of public computers are PCs, 20% of public computers are Macs, 5% of public computers are UNIX, network access in dorm rooms, online registration, online administrative functions (other than registration), remote student-access to Web through college's connection.

CAMPUS LIFE

Activities: Choral groups, concert band, dance, drama/theater, jazz band, music ensembles, musical theater, opera, radio station, student government, student newspaper, symphony orchestra. **Organizations:** 82 registered organizations, 9 honor societies, 4 religious organizations. 5 fraternities (3% men join), 7 sororities (3% women join). **Athletics (Intercollegiate):** *Men:* Baseball, basketball, cross-country, golf, soccer, track/field (indoor), track/field (outdoor). *Women:* Basketball, cross-country, soccer, softball, track/field (indoor), track/field (outdoor), volleyball.

ADMISSIONS

Freshman Academic Profile: 93% from public high schools. SAT Math middle 50% range 430–540. SAT Critical Reading middle 50% range 420–530. ACT middle 50% range 18–23. TOEFL required of all international applicants, minimum paper TOEFL 500, minimum computer TOEFL 173. **Basis for Candidate Selection:** *Very important factors considered include:* Academic GPA, rigor of secondary school record, standardized test scores. *Important factors considered include:* Class rank. **Freshman Admission Requirements:** High school diploma is required, and GED is accepted. *Academic units required:* 4 English, 3 math, 2 science (2 science labs), 2 foreign language, 1 social studies, 1 history, 1 academic elective, 1 visual and performing arts. **Freshman Admission Statistics:** 3,003 applied, 93% admitted, 34% enrolled. **Transfer Admission Requirements:** College transcript(s), statement of good standing from prior institution(s). Minimum college GPA of 2.0 required. Lowest grade transferable D. **General Admission Information:** Application fee $55. Regular application deadline 2/1. Regular notification is rolling. Nonfall registration accepted. Credit offered for CEEB Advanced Placement tests.

COSTS AND FINANCIAL AID

Annual out-of-state tuition $10,170. Room and board $7,707. Required fees $3,307. Average book expense $1,386. **Required Forms and Deadlines:** FAFSA. Financial aid filing deadline 3/2. **Notification of Awards:** Applicants will be notified of awards on a rolling basis beginning on or about 3/15. **Types of Aid:** *Need-based scholarships/grants:* Pell, SEOG, state scholarships/grants, private scholarships, the school's own gift aid, Federal Nursing Scholarships. *Loans:* FFEL Subsidized Stafford, FFEL Unsubsidized Stafford, FFEL PLUS, Federal Perkins, college/university loans from institutional funds. **Financial Aid Statistics:** 53% freshmen, 45% undergrads receive need-based scholarship or grant aid. 28% freshmen, 35% undergrads receive need-based self-help aid. 20 freshmen, 116 undergrads receive athletic scholarships. 68% freshmen, 59% undergrads receive any aid. **Financial Aid Phone:** 209-667-3336.

CALIFORNIA UNIVERSITY OF PENNSYLVANIA

250 University Avenue, California, PA 15419
Phone: 724-938-4404 **E-mail:** inquiry@cup.edu **CEEB Code:** 2647
Fax: 724-938-4564 **Website:** www.cup.edu **ACT Code:** 3694

This public school was founded in 1852. It has a 188-acre campus.

RATINGS

Admissions Selectivity Rating: 74   **Fire Safety Rating:** 95   **Green Rating:** 99

STUDENTS AND FACULTY

Enrollment: 6,199. **Student Body:** 52% female, 48% male, 6% out-of-state. African American 6%, Caucasian 67%. **Retention and Graduation:** 74% freshmen return for sophomore year. 25% freshmen graduate within 4 years. 16% grads go on to further study within 1 year. **Faculty:** Student/faculty ratio 23:1. 298 full-time faculty, 65% hold PhDs. 98% faculty teach undergrads.

ACADEMICS

Degrees: Associate, bachelor's, certificate, master's, post-bachelor's certificate, post-master's certificate, terminal. **Academic Requirements:** English (including composition), humanities, mathematics. **Classes:** Most classes have 20–29 students. Most lab/discussion sections have 20–29 students. **Majors with Highest Enrollment:** Business administration and management, criminal justice/safety studies, elementary education and teaching. **Disciplines with Highest Percentage of Degrees Awarded:** Education 21%, business/marketing 12%, engineering technologies 8%, security and protective services 8%, health professions and related sciences 8%, psychology 6%, parks and recreation 6%, liberal arts/general studies 5%. **Special Study Options:**

Accelerated program, cooperative education program, distance learning, double major, dual enrollment, exchange student program (domestic), honors program, independent study, internships, liberal arts/career combination, student-designed major, study abroad, teacher certification program, weekend college, undergrads may take grad classes.

FACILITIES

Housing: Coed dorms. **Special Academic Facilities/Equipment:** Art museum. **Computers:** 100% of public computers are PCs, network access in dorm rooms, network access in dorm lounges, online registration, online administrative functions (other than registration), remote student-access to Web through college's connection.

CAMPUS LIFE

Activities: Choral groups, concert band, dance, drama/theater, jazz band, literary magazine, marching band, music ensembles, musical theater, pep band, radio station, student government, student newspaper, television station, yearbook. **Organizations:** 25 honor societies, 1 religious organization. 6 fraternities (10% men join), 7 sororities (10% women join). **Athletics (Intercollegiate):** *Men:* Baseball, basketball, cheerleading, cross-country, football, golf, rugby, soccer, softball, track/field (indoor), track/field (outdoor), volleyball. *Women:* Basketball, cheerleading, cross-country, golf, rugby, soccer, softball, track/field (indoor), track/field (outdoor), volleyball. **Environmental Initiatives:** Multimillion Dollar Geothermal project plus replacing all residence halls in less than 5 years with Green buildings. Massive implementation of Johnson Controls systems to reduce our carbon footprint and energy usage. Campus wide sustainability awareness programs.

ADMISSIONS

Freshman Academic Profile: 7% in top 10% of high school class, 28% in top 25% of high school class, 65% in top 50% of high school class. 80% from public high schools. SAT Math middle 50% range 460–540. SAT Critical Reading middle 50% range 460–536. TOEFL required of all international applicants, minimum paper TOEFL 450, minimum computer TOEFL 133. **Basis for Candidate Selection:** *Very important factors considered include:* Class rank, rigor of secondary school record, standardized test scores. *Other factors considered include:* Application essay, extracurricular activities, interview, recommendation(s), talent/ability, work experience. **Freshman Admission Requirements:** High school diploma is required, and GED is accepted. *Academic units required:* 4 English, 3 math, 1 science (1 science lab), 2 social studies, 2 history, 6 academic electives, 1 arts & humanities. *Academic units recommended:* 4 English, 3 math, 1 science (1 science lab), 2 foreign language, 2 social studies, 2 history, 6 academic electives, 1 arts and humanities. **Freshman Admission Statistics:** 3,849 applied, 68% admitted, 51% enrolled. **Transfer Admission Requirements:** High school transcript, college transcript(s), statement of good standing from prior institution(s). Minimum college GPA of 2.3 required. Lowest grade transferable C. **General Admission Information:** Application fee $25. Regular notification with in 2 weeks. Nonfall registration accepted. Admission may be deferred for a maximum of 1 semester. Credit offered for CEEB Advanced Placement tests.

COSTS AND FINANCIAL AID

Annual in-state tuition $5,178. Annual out-of-state tuition $8,284. Room and board $8,466. Required fees $1,673. Average book expense $875. **Required Forms and Deadlines:** FAFSA. Financial aid filing deadline 5/1. **Notification of Awards:** Applicants will be notified of awards on a rolling basis beginning on or about 3/25. **Types of Aid:** *Need-based scholarships/grants:* Pell, SEOG, state scholarships/grants, private scholarships, the school's own gift aid. *Loans:* FFEL Subsidized Stafford, FFEL Unsubsidized Stafford, FFEL PLUS, Federal Perkins. **Financial Aid Statistics:** 48% freshmen, 49% undergrads receive need-based scholarship or grant aid. 58% freshmen, 62% undergrads receive need-based self-help aid. 8 freshmen, 57 undergrads receive athletic scholarships. 76% freshmen, 72% undergrads receive any aid. **Financial Aid Phone:** 724-938-4415.

See page 1104.

CALUMET COLLEGE OF SAINT JOSEPH

2400 New York Avenue, Whiting, IN 46394
Phone: 219-473-4215 **E-mail:** admissions@ccsj.edu **CEEB Code:** 1776
Fax: 219-473-4259 **Website:** www.ccsj.edu **ACT Code:** 1245

This private school, affiliated with the Roman Catholic Church, was founded in 1951. It has a 256-acre campus.

RATINGS

Admissions Selectivity Rating: 60*   **Fire Safety Rating:** 60*   **Green Rating:** 60*

STUDENTS AND FACULTY

Enrollment: 1,004. **Student Body:** 62% female, 38% male, 24% out-of-state. African American 28%, Caucasian 48%, Hispanic 17%. **Retention and Graduation:** 75% freshmen return for sophomore year. 5% freshmen graduate within 4 years. **Faculty:** Student/faculty ratio 15:1. 21 full-time faculty, 86% hold PhDs. 100% faculty teach undergrads.

ACADEMICS

Degrees: Associate, bachelor's, certificate, terminal. **Academic Requirements:** Arts/fine arts, computer literacy, English (including composition), history, humanities, mathematics, philosophy, sciences (biological or physical), social science. **Classes:** Most classes have 10–19 students. Most lab/discussion sections have 10–19 students. **Disciplines with Highest Percentage of Degrees Awarded:** Business/marketing 46%, health professions and related sciences 14%, social sciences 8%, law/legal studies 7%, psychology 5%. **Special Study Options:** Accelerated program, cooperative education program, distance learning, double major, English as a Second Language (ESL), independent study, internships, liberal arts/career combination, teacher certification program, weekend college.

FACILITIES

Academic Facilities/Equipment: Art gallery, chapel. **Computers:** Online administrative functions (other than registration).

CAMPUS LIFE

Activities: Drama/theater, literary magazine, student government, student newspaper. **Organizations:** 8 registered organizations, 19 honor societies, 6 religious organizations. 1 sorority. **Athletics (Intercollegiate):** *Men:* Basketball. *Women:* Basketball, cheerleading.

ADMISSIONS

Freshman Academic Profile: 13% in top 10% of high school class, 24% in top 25% of high school class, 59% in top 50% of high school class. 50% from public high schools. TOEFL required of all international applicants, minimum paper TOEFL 550. **Basis for Candidate Selection:** *Important factors considered include:* Interview. *Other factors considered include:* Application essay, character/personal qualities, class rank, extracurricular activities, recommendation(s), rigor of secondary school record, standardized test scores. **Freshman Admission Requirements:** High school diploma is required, and GED is accepted. *Academic units recommended:* 4 English, 3 math, 2 science, 1 foreign language, 2 social studies, 1 history, 2 academic electives. **Freshman Admission Statistics:** 412 applied, 54% admitted, 37% enrolled. **Transfer Admission Requirements:** College transcript(s), essay or personal statement, interview, statement of good standing from prior institution(s). Minimum college GPA of 2.0 required. Lowest grade transferable D. **General Admission Information:** Regular notification is rolling. Nonfall registration accepted. Common Application accepted.

COSTS AND FINANCIAL AID

Comprehensive fee $5,460. Required fees $25. Average book expense $600. **Required Forms and Deadlines:** FAFSA, institution's own financial aid form. Financial aid filing deadline 3/1. **Notification of Awards:** Applicants will be notified of awards on or about 5/1. **Types of Aid:** *Need-based scholarships/grants:* Pell, SEOG, state scholarships/grants, private scholarships, the school's own gift aid. *Loans:* FFEL Subsidized Stafford, FFEL Unsubsidized Stafford, FFEL PLUS. **Student Employment:** Federal Work-Study Program available. Institutional employment available. Off-campus job opportunities are good. Highest amount earned per year from on-campus jobs $1,500. **Financial Aid Phone:** 219-473-4296.

CALVARY BIBLE COLLEGE
AND THEOLOGICAL SEMINARY

15800 Calvary Road, Kansas City, MO 64147
Phone: 816-322-3960 **E-mail:** admissions@calvary.edu
Fax: 816-331-4474 **Website:** www.calvary.edu **ACT Code:** 2312

This private school was founded in 1932. It has a 55-acre campus.

RATINGS

Admissions Selectivity Rating: 60*   **Fire Safety Rating:** 60*   **Green Rating:** 61

STUDENTS AND FACULTY

Enrollment: 251. **Student Body:** 49% female, 51% male. African American 5%, Asian 1%, Caucasian 88%, Hispanic 3%, Native American 2%. **Retention and Graduation:** 60% freshmen return for sophomore year. **Faculty:** Student/faculty ratio 12:1. 12 full-time faculty, 33% hold PhDs.

ACADEMICS

Degrees: Associate, bachelor's, certificate, first professional, master's, terminal. **Academic Requirements:** Arts/fine arts, computer literacy, English (including composition), history, philosophy, sciences (biological or physical), social science, Bible, theology, Christian missions. **Majors with Highest Enrollment:** Bible/biblical studies, elementary education and teaching, pastoral studies/counseling. **Disciplines with Highest Percentage of Degrees Awarded:** Theology and religious vocations 67%, education 14%, business/marketing 14%, social sciences 5%. **Special Study Options:** Distance learning, double major, dual enrollment, independent study, internships, student-designed major, teacher certification program.

FACILITIES

Housing: Men's dorms, women's dorms, apartments for married students, apartments for single students, single students required to live in college housing unless living with parents or at least 23 years of age. Duplexes available for married students. **Computers:** 100% of public computers are PCs, remote student-access to Web through college's connection.

CAMPUS LIFE

Activities: Choral groups, drama/theater, music ensembles, musical theater, radio station, student government, yearbook. **Athletics (Intercollegiate):** *Men:* Basketball, soccer. *Women:* Basketball, cheerleading, volleyball.

ADMISSIONS

Freshman Academic Profile: SAT Math middle 50% range 410–600. SAT Critical Reading middle 50% range 530–620. ACT middle 50% range 20–25. **Basis for Candidate Selection:** *Very important factors considered include:* Academic GPA, character/personal qualities, recommendation(s), religious affiliation/commitment, standardized test scores. *Important factors considered include:* Alumni/ae relation. *Other factors considered include:* Application essay, class rank, rigor of secondary school record. **Freshman Admission Requirements:** High school diploma is required, and GED is accepted. **Freshman Admission Statistics:** 53 applied, 98% admitted, 85% enrolled. **Transfer Admission Requirements:** College transcript(s), essay or personal statement, minimum college GPA of 2.0 required. Lowest grade transferable C-. **General Admission Information:** Application fee $25. Regular application deadline 7/15. Nonfall registration accepted. Admission may be deferred for a maximum of 1 year.

COSTS AND FINANCIAL AID

Annual tuition $7,800. Room and board $4,000. Required fees $760. Average book expense $500. **Required Forms and Deadlines:** FAFSA, institution's own financial aid form. Financial aid filing deadline 4/1. **Notification of Awards:** Applicants will be notified of awards on a rolling basis beginning on or about 4/1. **Types of Aid:** *Need-based scholarships/grants:* Pell, SEOG, private scholarships, the school's own gift aid. *Loans:* FFEL Subsidized Stafford, FFEL Unsubsidized Stafford, FFEL PLUS, Alternative/Signature Loans. **Financial Aid Statistics:** 54% freshmen, 51% undergrads receive need-based scholarship or grant aid. 58% freshmen, 59% undergrads receive need-based self-help aid. **Financial Aid Phone:** 816-322-0110.

CALVIN COLLEGE

3201 Burton Street Southeast, Grand Rapids, MI 49546
Phone: 616-526-6106 **E-mail:** admissions@calvin.edu **CEEB Code:** 1095
Fax: 616-526-6777 **Website:** www.calvin.edu **ACT Code:** 1968

This private school, affiliated with the Christian Reformed Church, was founded in 1876. It has a 400-acre campus.

RATINGS

Admissions Selectivity Rating: 80   **Fire Safety Rating:** 67   **Green Rating:** 60*

STUDENTS AND FACULTY

Enrollment: 4,040. **Student Body:** 54% female, 46% male, 41% out-of-state. 7% international (62 countries represented). African American 1%, Asian 3%, Caucasian 85%, Hispanic 1%. **Retention and Graduation:** 88% freshmen return for sophomore year. 54% freshmen graduate within 4 years. 16% grads go on to further study within 1 year. 4% grads pursue arts and sciences degrees. 2% grads pursue business degrees. 1% grads pursue law degrees. 2% grads pursue medical degrees. **Faculty:** Student/faculty ratio 12:1. 309 full-time faculty, 82% hold PhDs. 100% faculty teach undergrads.

ACADEMICS

Degrees: Bachelor's, master's, post-bachelor's certificate. **Academic Requirements:** Arts/fine arts, computer literacy, English (including composition), foreign languages, history, humanities, mathematics, philosophy, sciences (biological or physical), social science, religion, physical education, communication, cross-cultural study. **Classes:** Most classes have 20–29 students. Most lab/discussion sections have 20–29 students. **Majors with Highest Enrollment:** Business administration/management; elementary education and teaching; engineering. **Disciplines with Highest Percentage of Degrees Awarded:** Business/marketing 11%, education 9%, health professions and related sciences 8%, social sciences 8%, English 7%. **Special Study Options:** Accelerated program, double major, dual enrollment, honors program, independent study, internships, student-designed major, study abroad, teacher certification program, academically-based service-learning.

FACILITIES

Housing: Men's dorms, women's dorms, apartments for single students, Project Neighborhood Houses. **Special Academic Facilities/Equipment:** Art gallery, observatory, ecosystem preserve, electron microscope, seismograph lab. **Computers:** 3% of classrooms are wired, 4% of classrooms are wireless, 85% of public computers are PCs, 13% of public computers are Macs, 2% of public computers are UNIX, network access in dorm rooms, network access in dorm lounges, online registration, online administrative functions (other than registration), remote student-access to Web through college's connection.

CAMPUS LIFE

Activities: Choral groups, concert band, dance, drama/theater, jazz band, literary magazine, music ensembles, musical theater, pep band, radio station, student government, student newspaper, student-run film society, symphony orchestra, yearbook. **Organizations:** 52 registered organizations, 6 honor societies, 5 religious organizations. **Athletics (Intercollegiate):** *Men:* Baseball, basketball, cross-country, golf, soccer, swimming, tennis, track/field (outdoor). *Women:* Basketball, cross-country, golf, soccer, softball, swimming, tennis, track/field (outdoor), volleyball.

ADMISSIONS

Freshman Academic Profile: 26% in top 10% of high school class, 54% in top 25% of high school class, 80% in top 50% of high school class. 42% from public high schools. SAT Math middle 50% range 540–650. SAT Critical Reading middle 50% range 530–650. ACT middle 50% range 23–28. TOEFL required of all international applicants, minimum paper TOEFL 550, minimum computer TOEFL 213. **Basis for Candidate Selection:** *Very important factors considered include:* Academic GPA, religious affiliation/commitment, rigor of secondary school record, standardized test scores. *Important factors considered include:* Application essay, character/personal qualities, extracurricular activities, recommendation(s). *Other factors considered include:* Class rank, level of applicant's interest, volunteer work, work experience. **Freshman Admission Requirements:** High school diploma is required, and GED is accepted. *Academic units required:* 3 English, 3 math, 2 science, 2 social studies, 3 academic electives. *Academic units recommended:* 4 English, 3 math, 2 science (1 science lab), 2 foreign language, 3 social studies, 3 academic electives. **Freshman Admission Statistics:** 2,156 applied, 98% admitted, 48% enrolled. **Transfer Admission Requirements:** High school transcript, college transcript(s), essay or personal statement, statement of good standing from prior institution(s). Minimum college GPA of 2.5 required. Lowest grade transferable C. **General Admission Information:** Application fee $35. Regular application deadline 8/15. Regular notification is rolling. Nonfall registration accepted. Admission may be deferred for a maximum of 1 year. Common Application accepted. Credit and/or placement offered for CEEB Advanced Placement tests.

COSTS AND FINANCIAL AID

Annual tuition $21,460. Room and board $7,460. Required fees $225. Average book expense $810. **Required Forms and Deadlines:** FAFSA, institution's own financial aid form. Financial aid filing deadline 2/15. **Notification of Awards:** Applicants will be notified of awards on a rolling basis beginning on or about 3/15. **Types of Aid:** *Need-based scholarships/grants:* Pell, SEOG, state scholarships/grants, private scholarships, the school's own gift aid. *Loans:* Direct Subsidized Stafford, Direct Unsubsidized Stafford, Direct PLUS, Federal Perkins, state loans, college/university loans from institutional funds, private alternative. **Student Employment:** Federal Work-Study Program available. Institutional employment available. Off-campus job opportunities are excellent. **Financial Aid Statistics:** 62% freshmen, 61% undergrads receive need-based scholarship or grant aid. 52% freshmen, 51% undergrads receive need-based self-help aid. 93% freshmen, 92% undergrads receive any aid. Highest amount earned per year from on-campus jobs $4,000. **Financial Aid Phone:** 800-688-0122

CAMERON UNIVERSITY

2800 West Gore Boulevard, Lawton, OK 73505
Phone: 580-581-2230 **E-mail:** admiss@cua.cameron.edu **CEEB Code:** 6080
Fax: 580-581-5514 **Website:** www.cameron.edu **ACT Code:** 3386

This public school was founded in 1908. It has a 369-acre campus.

RATINGS

Admissions Selectivity Rating: 62   **Fire Safety Rating:** 84   **Green Rating:** 60*

STUDENTS AND FACULTY

Enrollment: 5,076. **Student Body:** 60% female, 40% male, 1% out-of-state, 3% international (50 countries represented). African American 19%, Asian 3%, Caucasian 58%, Hispanic 9%, Native American 8%. **Retention and Graduation:** 56% freshmen return for sophomore year. 24% freshmen graduate within 4 years. **Faculty:** Student/faculty ratio 17:1. 180 full-time faculty, 69% hold PhDs. 100% faculty teach undergrads.

ACADEMICS

Degrees: Associate, bachelor's, master's. **Academic Requirements:** Computer literacy, English (including composition), history, humanities, mathematics, sciences (biological or physical), social science. **Classes:** Most classes have 20–29 students. Most lab/discussion sections have 10–19 students. **Majors with Highest Enrollment:** Business administration/management, criminal justice/law enforcement administration, elementary education and teaching. **Disciplines with Highest Percentage of Degrees Awarded:** Business/marketing 19%, education 13%, computer and information sciences 13%, interdisciplinary studies 10%, psychology 8%, communications/journalism 4%, social sciences 4%. **Special Study Options:** Accelerated program, distance learning, double major, dual enrollment, honors program, independent study, internships, liberal arts/career combination, teacher certification program, undergrads may take grad classes. Evening and Saturday classes offered; extension study possible.

FACILITIES

Housing: Men's dorms, women's dorms, quiet and wellness (non-smoking) areas available. **Special Academic Facilities/Equipment:** Satellite labs. **Computers:** 90% of public computers are PCs, 10% of public computers are Macs, 20% of public computers are UNIX, network access in dorm rooms, online administrative functions (other than registration), support for handheld computing.

CAMPUS LIFE

Activities: Choral groups, concert band, dance, drama/theater, jazz band, literary magazine, music ensembles, musical theater, pep band, radio station, student government, student newspaper, symphony orchestra, television station, yearbook. **Organizations:** 66 registered organizations, 19 honor societies, 4 religious organizations. 2 fraternities (2% men join), 3 sororities (2% women join). **Athletics (Intercollegiate):** *Men:* Baseball, basketball, cross-country, golf, tennis. *Women:* Basketball, golf, softball, tennis, volleyball.

ADMISSIONS

Freshman Academic Profile: 8% in top 10% of high school class, 28% in top 25% of high school class, 62% in top 50% of high school class. 99% from public high schools. ACT middle 50% range 16–22. TOEFL required of all international applicants, minimum paper TOEFL 500, minimum computer TOEFL 173. **Basis for Candidate Selection:** *Important factors considered include:* Academic GPA, class rank, geographical residence, standardized test scores, state residency. **Freshman Admission Requirements:** High school diploma is required, and GED is accepted. *Academic units required:* 4 English, 3 math, 2 science (2 science labs), 2 history, 3 academic electives. **Freshman Admission Statistics:** 1,357 applied, 100% admitted, 70% enrolled. **Transfer Admission Requirements:** College transcript(s), minimum college GPA of 2.0 required. Lowest grade transferable D. **General Admission Information:** Application fee $15. Regular notification is rolling. Nonfall registration accepted. Admission may be deferred for a maximum of 1 year. Common Application not accepted. Credit and/or placement offered for CEEB Advanced Placement tests.

COSTS AND FINANCIAL AID

Average book expense $1,050. **Required Forms and Deadlines:** FAFSA. Financial aid filing deadline 6/15. **Notification of Awards:** Applicants will be notified of awards on a rolling basis beginning on or about 4/1. **Types of Aid:** *Need-based scholarships/grants:* Pell, SEOG, state scholarships/grants, private scholarships, the school's own gift aid. *Loans:* FFEL Subsidized Stafford, FFEL Unsubsidized Stafford, FFEL PLUS. **Financial Aid Statistics:** 36% freshmen, 26% undergrads receive need-based scholarship or grant aid. 29% freshmen, 18% undergrads receive need-based self-help aid. 6 freshmen, 41 undergrads receive athletic scholarships. 36% freshmen, 26% undergrads receive any aid. **Financial Aid Phone:** 580-581-2293.

CAMPBELL UNIVERSITY

Post Office Box 546, Buies Creek, NC 27506
Phone: 910-893-1290 **E-mail:** adm@mailcenter.campbell.edu **CEEB Code:** 5100
Fax: 910-893-1288 **Website:** www.campbell.edu **ACT Code:** 3076
Financial Aid Phone: 910-893-1310

This private school, affiliated with the Southern Baptist Church, was founded in 1887. It has an 850-acre campus.

RATINGS
Admissions Selectivity Rating: 88 **Fire Safety Rating:** 60* **Green Rating:** 60*

STUDENTS AND FACULTY
Enrollment: 4,384. **Student Body:** 52% female, 48% male, 22% out-of-state, 4% international. African American 15%, Caucasian 71%, Hispanic 5%. **Retention and Graduation:** 71% freshmen return for sophomore year. 23% grads go on to further study within 1 year. 5% grads pursue arts and sciences degrees. 7% grads pursue business degrees. 4% grads pursue law degrees. **Faculty:** Student/faculty ratio 13:1. 189 full-time faculty, 93% hold PhDs. 100% faculty teach undergrads.

ACADEMICS
Degrees: Associate, bachelor's, doctoral, first professional, master's. **Academic Requirements:** Arts/fine arts, computer literacy, English (including composition), foreign languages, history, humanities, mathematics, sciences (biological or physical), social science. **Classes:** Most classes have fewer than 10 students. **Majors with Highest Enrollment:** Business administration/management, pre-pharmacy studies. **Disciplines with Highest Percentage of Degrees Awarded:** Business/marketing 36%, psychology 10%, education 9%, social sciences 7%, health professions and related sciences 5%. **Special Study Options:** Accelerated program, cooperative education program, distance learning, double major, dual enrollment, exchange student program (domestic), honors program, independent study, internships, liberal arts/career combination, study abroad, teacher certification program.

FACILITIES
Housing: Men's dorms, women's dorms, apartments for married students, apartments for single students, special housing for disabled students. Student apartments and suites for sophomores, juniors, and seniors; also graduate apartments. **Special Academic Facilities/Equipment:** Taylor Bott-Rogers fine arts building, Lundy-Fetterman School of Business museum and exhibit hall, school of pharmacy clinical research facility. **Computers:** Network access in dorm rooms, network access in dorm lounges, remote student-access to Web through college's connection.

CAMPUS LIFE
Activities: Choral groups, concert band, drama/theater, jazz band, literary magazine, music ensembles, musical theater, pep band, radio station, student government, student newspaper, yearbook. **Organizations:** 44 registered organizations, 14 honor societies, 20 religious organizations. **Athletics (Intercollegiate):** *Men:* Baseball, basketball, cross-country, golf, soccer, tennis, track/field (outdoor), wrestling. *Women:* Basketball, cheerleading, cross-country, golf, soccer, softball, swimming, tennis, track/field (outdoor), volleyball.

ADMISSIONS
Freshman Academic Profile: 38% in top 10% of high school class, 80% in top 25% of high school class, 92% in top 50% of high school class. 85% from public high schools. SAT Math middle 50% range 500–625. SAT Critical Reading middle 50% range 505–615. TOEFL required of all international applicants, minimum paper TOEFL 500, minimum computer TOEFL 173. **Basis for Candidate Selection:** *Very important factors considered include:* Academic GPA, rigor of secondary school record, standardized test scores. *Important factors considered include:* Class rank, interview, talent/ability. *Other factors considered include:* Alumni/ae relation, application essay, character/personal qualities, extracurricular activities, level of applicant's interest, recommendation(s), volunteer work, work experience. **Freshman Admission Requirements:** High school diploma is required, and GED is accepted. *Academic units required:* 4 English, 3 math, 2 science (1 science lab), 2 foreign language, 2 social science. **Freshman Admission Statistics:** 3,014 applied, 60% admitted, 46% enrolled. **Transfer Admission Requirements:** High school transcript, college transcript(s), standardized test score, statement of good standing from prior institution(s). Minimum college GPA of 2.5 required. Lowest grade transferable C. **General Admission Information:** Application fee $35. Regular notification is rolling. Nonfall registration accepted. Admission may be deferred for a maximum of 1 year. Credit and/or placement offered for CEEB Advanced Placement tests.

COSTS AND FINANCIAL AID
Annual tuition $19,600. Room and board $6,800. Required fees $700. Average book expense $1,100. **Required Forms and Deadlines:** FAFSA. Financial aid filing deadline 3/15. **Notification of Awards:** Applicants will be notified of awards on a rolling basis beginning on or about 3/1. **Types of Aid:** *Need-based scholarships/grants:* Pell, SEOG, state scholarships/grants, private scholarships, the school's own gift aid. *Loans:* FFEL Subsidized Stafford, FFEL Unsubsidized Stafford, FFEL PLUS, Federal Perkins, state loans, college/university loans from institutional funds. **Student Employment:** Federal Work-Study Program available. Institutional employment available. Off-campus job opportunities are good. **Financial Aid Statistics:** 51% freshmen, 39% undergrads receive need-based scholarship or grant aid. 60% freshmen, 47% undergrads receive need-based self-help aid. 21 freshmen, 66 undergrads receive athletic scholarships. 97% freshmen, 92% undergrads receive any aid. Highest amount earned per year from on-campus jobs $600.

CAMPBELLSVILLE UNIVERSITY

1 University Drive, Campbellsville, KY 42718-2799
Phone: 270-789-5220 **E-mail:** admissions@campbellsville.edu **CEEB Code:** 1097
Fax: 270-789-5071 **Website:** www.campbellsville.edu **ACT Code:** 1500
Financial Aid Phone: 270-789-5013

This private school, affiliated with the Baptist Church, was founded in 1906. It has an 80-acre campus.

RATINGS
Admissions Selectivity Rating: 74 **Fire Safety Rating:** 60* **Green Rating:** 60*

STUDENTS AND FACULTY
Enrollment: 1,462. **Student Body:** 54% female, 46% male, 11% out-of-state, 5% international. African American 6%, Caucasian 84%. **Retention and Graduation:** 63% freshmen return for sophomore year. 29% freshmen graduate within 4 years. 20% grads go on to further study within 1 year. 25% grads pursue arts and sciences degrees. 15% grads pursue business degrees. 1% grads pursue law degrees. 1% grads pursue medical degrees. **Faculty:** Student/faculty ratio 13:1. 91 full-time faculty, 62% hold PhDs. 100% faculty teach undergrads.

ACADEMICS
Degrees: Associate, bachelor's, master's. **Academic Requirements:** Arts/fine arts, computer literacy, English (including composition), foreign languages, history, humanities, mathematics, philosophy, sciences (biological or physical), social science. **Classes:** Most classes have fewer than 10 students. **Majors with Highest Enrollment:** Accounting; business, management, marketing, and related support services; junior high/intermediate/middle school education and teaching. **Disciplines with Highest Percentage of Degrees Awarded:** Business/marketing 24%, education 13%, theology and religious vocations 13%, psychology 9%, social sciences 8%, biological/life sciences 6%. **Special Study Options:** Cooperative education program, distance learning, double major, dual enrollment, English as a Second Language (ESL), honors program, independent study, internships, liberal arts/career combination, study abroad, teacher certification program, weekend college.

FACILITIES
Housing: Men's dorms, women's dorms, apartments for married students, apartments for single students. **Special Academic Facilities/Equipment:** Computer labs, technology lab. **Computers:** 95% of public computers are PCs, 5% of public computers are Macs, network access in dorm rooms, online registration, online administrative functions (other than registration), remote student-access to Web through college's connection.

CAMPUS LIFE
Activities: Choral groups, concert band, dance, drama/theater, jazz band, literary magazine, marching band, music ensembles, pep band, radio station, student government, student newspaper, television station, yearbook. **Organizations:** 49 registered organizations, 1 honor society, 7 religious organizations. **Athletics (Intercollegiate):** *Men:* Baseball, basketball, cheerleading, cross-country, football, soccer, tennis, track/field (outdoor), wrestling. *Women:* Basketball, cheerleading, cross-country, golf, soccer, softball, tennis, track/field (outdoor), volleyball.

ADMISSIONS
Freshman Academic Profile: 16% in top 10% of high school class, 36% in top 25% of high school class, 67% in top 50% of high school class. 90% from public high schools. SAT Math middle 50% range 470–610. SAT Critical Reading

middle 50% range 400–560. ACT middle 50% range 18–24. TOEFL required of all international applicants, minimum paper TOEFL 500, minimum computer TOEFL 173. **Basis for Candidate Selection:** *Very important factors considered include:* Rigor of secondary school record. *Important factors considered include:* Character/personal qualities, class rank, interview, recommendation(s), standardized test scores. *Other factors considered include:* Alumni/ae relation, application essay, extracurricular activities, religious affiliation/commitment, talent/ability, volunteer work, work experience. **Freshman Admission Requirements:** High school diploma is required, and GED is accepted. *Academic units recommended:* 4 English, 3 math, 3 science (1 science lab), 2 social studies, 1 history, 6 academic electives, 1 fine arts. **Freshman Admission Statistics:** 1,293 applied, 74% admitted, 37% enrolled. **Transfer Admission Requirements:** College transcript(s). Lowest grade transferable C. **General Admission Information:** Application fee $20. Regular application deadline 8/15. Regular notification is rolling. Nonfall registration accepted. Admission may be deferred for a maximum of 1 year. Credit and/or placement offered for CEEB Advanced Placement tests.

COSTS AND FINANCIAL AID

Annual tuition $17,770. Room and board $6,410. Required fees $400. Average book expense $1,000. **Required Forms and Deadlines:** FAFSA. **Notification of Awards:** Applicants will be notified of awards on a rolling basis beginning on or about 2/15. *Types of Aid: Need-based scholarships/grants:* Pell, SEOG, state scholarships/grants, private scholarships, the school's own gift aid. *Loans:* FFEL Subsidized Stafford, FFEL Unsubsidized Stafford, FFEL PLUS, Federal Perkins, college/university loans from institutional funds. **Student Employment:** Off-campus job opportunities are good. **Financial Aid Statistics:** 90% freshmen, 81% undergrads receive need-based scholarship or grant aid. 70% freshmen, 65% undergrads receive need-based self-help aid. 21 freshmen, 101 undergrads receive athletic scholarships. 97% freshmen, 95% undergrads receive any aid. Highest amount earned per year from on-campus jobs $2,000.

CANISIUS COLLEGE

2001 Main Street, Buffalo, NY 14208
Phone: 716-888-2200 **E-mail:** inquiry@canisius.edu **CEEB Code:** 2073
Fax: 716-888-3230 **Website:** www.canisius.edu **ACT Code:** 2690
Financial Aid Phone: 716-888-2300

This private school, affiliated with the Roman Catholic Church, was founded in 1870. It has a 32-acre campus.

RATINGS
Admissions Selectivity Rating: 80   **Fire Safety Rating:** 60*   **Green Rating:** 60*

STUDENTS AND FACULTY
Enrollment: 3,293. **Student Body:** 56% female, 44% male, 8% out-of-state, 3% international (32 countries represented). African American 6%, Asian 2%, Caucasian 81%, Hispanic 2%. **Retention and Graduation:** 80% freshmen return for sophomore year. 51% freshmen graduate within 4 years. 24% grads go on to further study within 1 year. **Faculty:** Student/faculty ratio 12:1. 215 full-time faculty, 93% hold PhDs. 98% faculty teach undergrads.

ACADEMICS
Degrees: Bachelor's, master's. **Academic Requirements:** Arts/fine arts, English (including composition), foreign languages, history, humanities, mathematics, philosophy, sciences (biological or physical), social science, religious studies requirement. **Classes:** Most classes have 10–19 students. Most lab/discussion sections have 20–29 students. **Majors with Highest Enrollment:** Business administration and management, organizational communication, psychology. **Disciplines with Highest Percentage of Degrees Awarded:** Business/marketing 23%, education 13%, communications/journalism 12%, social sciences 9%, psychology 9%. **Special Study Options:** Cooperative education program, cross-registration, distance learning, double major, dual enrollment, honors program, independent study, internships, study abroad, teacher certification program, 4 + 1 BS/MBA, 3 + 4 BS/DD (biology and dentistry; early assurance guaranteed for medical school admission).

FACILITIES
Housing: Coed dorms, apartments for single students, special housing for disabled students, special housing for international students, honors student housing. All college-owned housing is handicapped accessible. **Special Academic Facilities/Equipment:** TV studio, electron microscope, seismograph, language lab, digital lab, human performance lab, molecular biology and physics labs, mini-planetarium. **Computers:** 5% of classrooms are wired, 90%

of classrooms are wireless, 60% of public computers are PCs, 40% of public computers are Macs, network access in dorm rooms, network access in dorm lounges, online registration, online administrative functions (other than registration), remote student-access to Web through college's connection.

CAMPUS LIFE
Activities: Choral groups, concert band, dance, drama/theater, jazz band, literary magazine, music ensembles, musical theater, pep band, radio station, student government, student newspaper, student-run film society, television station, yearbook. **Organizations:** 102 registered organizations, 16 honor societies, 2 religious organizations. 1 fraternity (1% men join), 1 sorority (1% women join). **Athletics (Intercollegiate):** *Men:* Baseball, basketball, cross-country, diving, golf, ice hockey, lacrosse, soccer, swimming. *Women:* Basketball, cross-country, diving, lacrosse, soccer, softball, swimming, synchronized swimming, volleyball.

ADMISSIONS
Freshman Academic Profile: 25% in top 10% of high school class, 51% in top 25% of high school class, 85% in top 50% of high school class. 71% from public high schools. SAT Math middle 50% range 500–600. SAT Critical Reading middle 50% range 490–590. ACT middle 50% range 22–27. TOEFL required of all international applicants, minimum paper TOEFL 500, minimum computer TOEFL 173. **Basis for Candidate Selection:** *Very important factors considered include:* Academic GPA, rigor of secondary school record, standardized test scores. *Important factors considered include:* Application essay, character/personal qualities, interview, recommendation(s), talent/ability, volunteer work. *Other factors considered include:* Alumni/ae relation, class rank, extracurricular activities, first generation, work experience. **Freshman Admission Requirements:** High school diploma is required, and GED is accepted. *Academic units required:* 4 English, 3 math, 2 science (2 science labs), 2 foreign language, 4 social studies. *Academic units recommended:* 4 English, 3 math, 3 science (2 science labs), 3 foreign language, 4 social studies, 4 academic electives. **Freshman Admission Statistics:** 3,762 applied, 77% admitted, 26% enrolled. **Transfer Admission Requirements:** College transcript(s), statement of good standing from prior institution(s). Minimum college GPA of 2.0 required. Lowest grade transferable C. **General Admission Information:** Application fee $40. Regular application deadline 5/1. Regular notification is rolling. Nonfall registration accepted. Admission may be deferred for a maximum of 1 year. Credit and/or placement offered for CEEB Advanced Placement tests.

COSTS AND FINANCIAL AID
Average book expense $700. **Required Forms and Deadlines:** FAFSA, state aid form. Financial aid filing deadline 2/15. **Notification of Awards:** Applicants will be notified of awards on a rolling basis beginning on or about 3/1. **Types of Aid:** *Need-based scholarships/grants:* Pell, SEOG, state scholarships/grants, private scholarships. *Loans:* FFEL Subsidized Stafford, FFEL Unsubsidized Stafford, FFEL PLUS. **Student Employment:** Federal Work-Study Program available. Institutional employment available. Off-campus job opportunities are excellent. **Financial Aid Statistics:** 80% freshmen, 75% undergrads receive need-based scholarship or grant aid. 67% freshmen, 60% undergrads receive need-based self-help aid. 27 freshmen, 104 undergrads receive athletic scholarships. 96% freshmen, 94% undergrads receive any aid. Highest amount earned per year from on-campus jobs $2,200.

CAPELLA UNIVERSITY

222 South Ninth Street, Twentieth Floor, Minneapolis, MN 55402
Phone: 888-227-3552 **E-mail:** info@capella.edu
Fax: 612-339-8022 **Website:** www.capellauniversity.edu
Financial Aid Phone: 888-227-3552

This proprietary school was founded in 1993.

RATINGS
Admissions Selectivity Rating: 60*   **Fire Safety Rating:** 60*   **Green Rating:** 60*

STUDENTS AND FACULTY
Enrollment: 1,168. **Faculty:** Student/faculty ratio 20:1. 41 full-time faculty.

ACADEMICS
Degrees: Bachelor's, certificate, doctoral, master's, post-bachelor's certificate. **Majors with Highest Enrollment:** Business/commerce, computer and information sciences, information technology. **Disciplines with Highest Percentage of Degrees Awarded:** Computer and information sciences 35%. **Special Study Options:** Distance learning.

FACILITIES

Computers: Online registration, online administrative functions (other than registration).

ADMISSIONS

Freshman Academic Profile: TOEFL required of all international applicants, minimum paper TOEFL 550, minimum computer TOEFL 213. **Freshman Admission Requirements:** High school diploma is required, and GED is accepted. **Transfer Admission Requirements:** Minimum college GPA of 2.0 required. **General Admission Information:** Application fee $50. Nonfall registration not accepted. Common Application not accepted.

COSTS AND FINANCIAL AID

Required fees $50. Average book expense $300. **Types of Aid:** *Need-based scholarships/grants:* Pell, private scholarships. *Loans:* Direct Subsidized Stafford, Direct Unsubsidized Stafford.

CAPITAL UNIVERSITY

Admission Office, 1 College and Main, Columbus, OH 43209
Phone: 614-236-6101 **E-mail:** admissions@capital.edu **CEEB Code:** 1099
Fax: 614-236-6926 **Website:** www.capital.edu **ACT Code:** 3242
Financial Aid Phone: 614-236-6511

This private school, affiliated with the Lutheran Church, was founded in 1830. It has a 48-acre campus.

RATINGS

Admissions Selectivity Rating: 79   **Fire Safety Rating:** 60*   **Green Rating:** 78

STUDENTS AND FACULTY

Enrollment: 2,737. **Student Body:** 62% female, 38% male, 4% out-of-state. African American 11%, Asian 1%, Caucasian 81%, Hispanic 2%. **Retention and Graduation:** 77% freshmen return for sophomore year. 55% freshmen graduate within 4 years. **Faculty:** Student/faculty ratio 11:1. 228 full-time faculty, 70% hold PhDs. 85% faculty teach undergrads.

ACADEMICS

Degrees: Bachelor's, certificate, first professional, master's. **Academic Requirements:** Arts/fine arts, English (including composition), foreign languages, humanities, mathematics, sciences (biological or physical), social science, cultural diversity, ethical thought, speaking and listening, lifetime health, religion, global awareness. **Classes:** Most classes have fewer than 10 students. Most lab/discussion sections have 20–29 students. **Majors with Highest Enrollment:** Education, multi/interdisciplinary studies, nursing/registered nurse training (RN, ASN, BSN, MSN). **Disciplines with Highest Percentage of Degrees Awarded:** Education 15%, interdisciplinary studies 13%, social sciences 12%, health professions and related sciences 12%, public administration and social services 11%, business/marketing 10%. **Special Study Options:** Accelerated program, cooperative education program, cross-registration, double major, English as a second language (ESL), exchange student program (domestic), honors program, independent study, internships, liberal arts/career combination, student-designed major, study abroad, teacher certification program.

FACILITIES

Housing: Coed dorms, apartments for single students, special housing for disabled students, honors housing, self-governing areas, and group cluster housing. **Special Academic Facilities/Equipment:** Art gallery, conservatory of music. **Computers:** 90% of public computers are PCs, 10% of public computers are Macs, network access in dorm rooms, network access in dorm lounges, online registration, online administrative functions (other than registration), remote student-access to Web through college's connection.

CAMPUS LIFE

Activities: Choral groups, concert band, dance, drama/theater, jazz band, literary magazine, music ensembles, musical theater, radio station, student government, student newspaper, symphony orchestra, television station, yearbook. **Organizations:** 60 registered organizations, 16 honor societies, 5 religious organizations. 5 fraternities (7% men join), 5 sororities (10% women join). **Athletics (Intercollegiate):** *Men:* Baseball, basketball, cross-country, football, golf, soccer, tennis, track/field (indoor), track/field (outdoor). *Women:* Basketball, cross-country, golf, soccer, softball, tennis, track/field (indoor), track/field (outdoor), volleyball.

ADMISSIONS

Freshman Academic Profile: 26% in top 10% of high school class, 56% in top 25% of high school class, 85% in top 50% of high school class. 92% from public

high schools. SAT Math middle 50% range 470–590. SAT Critical Reading middle 50% range 470–590. ACT middle 50% range 21–26. TOEFL required of all international applicants, minimum paper TOEFL 500, minimum computer TOEFL 173. **Basis for Candidate Selection:** *Very important factors considered include:* Academic GPA, rigor of secondary school record, standardized test scores. *Important factors considered include:* Interview. *Other factors considered include:* Alumni/ae relation, character/personal qualities, class rank, extracurricular activities, racial/ethnic status, recommendation(s), religious affiliation/commitment, talent/ability. **Freshman Admission Requirements:** High school diploma is required, and GED is accepted. *Academic units required:* 4 English, 3 math, 3 science (2 science labs), 2 foreign language, 3 social studies, 1 academic elective. *Academic units recommended:* 4 English, 3 math, 3 science (2 science labs), 2 foreign language, 3 social studies, 1 academic elective. **Freshman Admission Statistics:** 3,286 applied, 77% admitted, 27% enrolled. **Transfer Admission Requirements:** College transcript(s). Minimum college GPA of 2.5 required. Lowest grade transferable C-. **General Admission Information:** Application fee $25. Regular notification is rolling. Nonfall registration accepted. Admission may be deferred for a maximum of 1 year. Credit and/or placement offered for CEEB Advanced Placement tests.

COSTS AND FINANCIAL AID

Required Forms and Deadlines: FAFSA. Financial aid filing deadline 2/28. **Notification of Awards:** Applicants will be notified of awards on a rolling basis beginning on or about 3/1. **Types of Aid:** *Need-based scholarships/grants:* Pell, SEOG, state scholarships/grants, private scholarships, the school's own gift aid. *Loans:* FFEL Subsidized Stafford, FFEL Unsubsidized Stafford, FFEL PLUS, Federal Perkins, Federal Nursing, state loans, college/university loans from institutional funds. **Student Employment:** Federal Work-Study Program available. Institutional employment available. Off-campus job opportunities are good. **Financial Aid Statistics:** 52% freshmen, 49% undergrads receive need-based scholarship or grant aid. 81% freshmen, 73% undergrads receive need-based self-help aid.

CAPITOL COLLEGE

11301 Springfield Road, Laurel, MD 20708
Phone: 800-950-1992 **E-mail:** admissions@capitol-college.edu **CEEB Code:** 5101
Fax: 301-953-1442 **Website:** www.capitol-college.edu
Financial Aid Phone: 301-369-2800

This private school was founded in 1964. It has a 52-acre campus.

RATINGS

Admissions Selectivity Rating: 60*   **Fire Safety Rating:** 60*   **Green Rating:** 60*

STUDENTS AND FACULTY

Enrollment: 452. **Student Body:** 22% female, 78% male, 14% out-of-state, 4% international. African American 36%, Asian 7%, Caucasian 48%, Hispanic 2%. **Retention and Graduation:** 60% freshmen return for sophomore year. 5% freshmen graduate within 4 years. 10% grads go on to further study within 1 year. 10% grads pursue arts and sciences degrees. **Faculty:** Student/faculty ratio 12:1. 21 full-time faculty, 33% hold PhDs. 100% faculty teach undergrads.

ACADEMICS

Degrees: Associate, bachelor's, certificate, master's, post-bachelor's certificate. **Academic Requirements:** Arts/fine arts, computer literacy, English (including composition), history, humanities, mathematics, sciences (biological or physical), social science. **Classes:** Most classes have 10–19 students. Most lab/discussion sections have fewer than 10 students. **Majors with Highest Enrollment:** Aerospace, aeronautical, and astronautical engineering; computer engineering; electrical, electronics, and communications engineering. **Disciplines with Highest Percentage of Degrees Awarded:** Engineering 69%, computer and information sciences 31%. **Special Study Options:** Cooperative education program, distance learning, double major, independent study, internships, weekend college.

FACILITIES

Housing: Men's dorms, women's dorms, apartments for single students. **Computers:** Network access in dorm rooms, remote student-access to Web through college's connection.

CAMPUS LIFE

Activities: Dance, drama/theater, literary magazine, radio station, student government, student newspaper. **Organizations:** 10 registered organizations, 3 honor societies.

ADMISSIONS

Freshman Academic Profile: 85% from public high schools. SAT Math middle 50% range 350–590. SAT Critical Reading middle 50% range 400–520. TOEFL required of all international applicants, minimum paper TOEFL 500. **Basis for Candidate Selection:** *Very important factors considered include:* Rigor of secondary school record. *Important factors considered include:* Application essay, standardized test scores. *Other factors considered include:* Alumni/ae relation, character/personal qualities, extracurricular activities, interview, recommendation(s), talent/ability, volunteer work, work experience. **Freshman Admission Requirements:** High school diploma is required, and GED is accepted. *Academic units required:* 4 English, 3 math, 3 science (2 science labs). *Academic units recommended:* 4 English, 4 math, 4 science (2 science labs), 2 social studies, 2 history. **Freshman Admission Statistics:** 190 applied, 86% admitted, 21% enrolled. **Transfer Admission Requirements:** College transcript(s), essay or personal statement. Minimum college GPA of 2.0 required. Lowest grade transferable C. **General Admission Information:** Application fee $25. Regular notification is rolling. Nonfall registration accepted. Admission may be deferred for a maximum of 1 year. Common Application accepted. Credit and/or placement offered for CEEB Advanced Placement tests.

COSTS AND FINANCIAL AID

Annual tuition $16,500. Room & board $3,710. Required fees $600. Average book expense $800. **Required Forms and Deadlines:** FAFSA, institution's own financial aid form. Financial aid filing deadline 3/1. **Notification of Awards:** Applicants will be notified of awards on a rolling basis beginning on or about 6/30. **Types of Aid:** *Need-based scholarships/grants:* Pell, SEOG, state scholarships/grants, private scholarships, the school's own gift aid. *Loans:* FFEL Subsidized Stafford, FFEL Unsubsidized Stafford, FFEL PLUS, Federal Perkins. **Student Employment:** Federal Work-Study Program available. Institutional employment available. Off-campus job opportunities are excellent. **Financial Aid Statistics:** 25% freshmen, 36% undergrads receive need-based scholarship or grant aid. 10% freshmen, 30% undergrads receive need-based self-help aid. Highest amount earned per year from on-campus jobs $2,000.

CARDINAL STRITCH COLLEGE

6801 North Yates Road, Box 237, Milwaukee, WI 53217-3985
Phone: 414-410-4040 **E-mail:** admityou@stritch.edu **CEEB Code:** 1100
Fax: 414-410-4058 **Website:** www.stritch.edu **ACT Code:** 6755
414-410-4048

This private school, affiliated with the Roman Catholic Church, was founded in 1937. It has a 40-acre campus.

RATINGS

Admissions Selectivity Rating: 74   **Fire Safety Rating:** 60*   **Green Rating:** 60*

STUDENTS AND FACULTY

Enrollment: 3,069. **Student Body:** 69% female, 31% male, 11% out-of-state, 1% international. African American 16%, Asian 2%, Caucasian 73%, Hispanic 3%. **Retention and Graduation:** 73% freshmen return for sophomore year. 19% freshmen graduate within 4 years. **Faculty:** Student/faculty ratio 18:1. 98 full-time faculty, 54% hold PhDs.

ACADEMICS

Degrees: Associate, bachelor's, certificate, doctoral, master's, post-bachelor's certificate. **Academic Requirements:** Arts/fine arts, English (including composition), foreign languages, history, humanities, mathematics, philosophy, sciences (biological or physical), social science, religious studies. **Classes:** Most classes have 10–19 students. Most lab/discussion sections have 10–19 students. **Majors with Highest Enrollment:** Business administration/management, education, management information systems. **Disciplines with Highest Percentage of Degrees Awarded:** Business/marketing 80%, education 6%, health professions and related sciences 3%, visual and performing arts 3%, communication technologies 2%, psychology 2%, computer and information sciences 1%, English 1%, social sciences 1%. **Special Study Options:** Accelerated program, cooperative education program, distance learning, double major, dual enrollment, English as a second language (ESL), external degree program, honors program, independent study, internships, student-designed major, study abroad, teacher certification program, remedial/tutoring services, academic/career counseling center, employment/placement services.

FACILITIES

Housing: Coed dorms. **Special Academic Facilities/Equipment:** Reading and learning center, children's center, art gallery. **Computers:** Network access in dorm rooms, network access in dorm lounges, remote student-access to Web through college's connection.

CAMPUS LIFE

Activities: Choral groups, concert band, dance, drama/theater, jazz band, literary magazine, music ensembles, musical theater, pep band, radio station, student government, student newspaper, yearbook. **Organizations:** 6 honor societies, 1 religious organization. **Athletics (Intercollegiate):** *Men:* Baseball, basketball, cross-country, soccer, volleyball. *Women:* Basketball, cross-country, soccer, softball, volleyball.

ADMISSIONS

Freshman Academic Profile: 14% in top 10% of high school class, 37% in top 25% of high school class, 66% in top 50% of high school class. ACT middle 50% range 19–24. TOEFL required of all international applicants, minimum paper TOEFL 550. **Basis for Candidate Selection:** *Very important factors considered include:* Rigor of secondary school record, standardized test scores. *Important factors considered include:* Application essay, character/personal qualities, recommendation(s), talent/ability. *Other factors considered include:* Class rank, extracurricular activities, interview, racial/ethnic status, volunteer work, work experience. **Freshman Admission Requirements:** High school diploma is required, and GED is accepted. *Academic units required:* 4 English, 2 math, 2 science, 2 foreign language, 1 social studies, 1 history, 4 academic electives. *Academic units recommended:* 3 math, 3 science. **Freshman Admission Statistics:** 387 applied, 71% admitted, 50% enrolled. **Transfer Admission Requirements:** College transcript(s). Minimum college GPA of 2.0 required. Lowest grade transferable C-. **General Admission Information:** Application fee $25. Regular notification is rolling. Nonfall registration accepted. Admission may be deferred for a maximum of 1 year. Common Application accepted. Credit and/or placement offered for CEEB Advanced Placement tests.

COSTS AND FINANCIAL AID

Annual tuition $12,480. Room & board $4,840. Required fees $300. Average book expense $500. **Required Forms and Deadlines:** FAFSA, institution's own financial aid form. Financial aid filing deadline 4/1. **Notification of Awards:** Applicants will be notified of awards on a rolling basis beginning on or about 4/1. **Types of Aid:** *Need-based scholarships/grants:* Pell, SEOG, state scholarships/grants, private scholarships, the school's own gift aid. *Loans:* FFEL Subsidized Stafford, FFEL Unsubsidized Stafford, FFEL PLUS, Federal Perkins, state loans. **Student Employment:** Federal Work-Study Program available. Institutional employment available. Off-campus job opportunities are excellent. **Financial Aid Statistics:** 30% freshmen, 37% undergrads receive need-based scholarship or grant aid. 42% freshmen, 69% undergrads receive need-based self-help aid. **Financial Aid Phone:** .

CARLETON COLLEGE

100 South College Street, Northfield, MN 55057
Phone: 507-646-4190 **E-mail:** admissions@acs.carleton.edu **CEEB Code:** 6081
Fax: 507-646-4526 **Website:** www.careleton.edu **ACT Code:** 2092
Financial Aid Phone: 507-646-4138

This private school was founded in 1866. It has a 955-acre campus.

RATINGS

Admissions Selectivity Rating: 97   **Fire Safety Rating:** 60*   **Green Rating:** 60*

STUDENTS AND FACULTY

Enrollment: 1,958. **Student Body:** 53% female, 47% male, 73% out-of-state, 5% international (30 countries represented). African American 6%, Asian 10%, Caucasian 74%, Hispanic 5%. **Retention and Graduation:** 96% freshmen return for sophomore year. 88% freshmen graduate within 4 years. 23% grads go on to further study within 1 year. 12% grads pursue arts and sciences degrees. 3% grads pursue law degrees. 2% grads pursue medical degrees. **Faculty:** Student/faculty ratio 9:1. 200 full-time faculty, 95% hold PhDs. 100% faculty teach undergrads.

ACADEMICS

Degrees: Bachelor's. **Academic Requirements:** Arts/fine arts, English (including composition), foreign languages, humanities, mathematics, sciences (biological or physical), social science, physical education, writing requirement, recognition and affirmation of difference requirement. **Classes:** Most classes have 10–19 students. Most lab/discussion sections have 10–19 students. **Majors**

with Highest Enrollment: Biology/biological sciences, economics, political science and government. **Disciplines with Highest Percentage of Degrees Awarded:** Social sciences 26%, physical sciences 13%, biological/life sciences 10%, English 9%, psychology 8%. **Special Study Options:** Accelerated program, cross-registration, double major, dual enrollment, independent study, internships, student-designed major, study abroad, teacher certification program.

FACILITIES

Housing: Coed dorms, apartments for single students, special housing for disabled students, 25 college-owned houses within 2 blocks of campus with varying meal plan options. Some are designated as special interest houses (green house, culinary house). **Special Academic Facilities/Equipment:** Arboretum, greenhouse, observatory, scanning and transmission electron microscopes, refractor and reflector telescopes, nuclear magnetic resonance spectrometer, art gallery. **Computers:** Network access in dorm rooms, online registration, remote student-access to Web through college's connection.

CAMPUS LIFE

Activities: Choral groups, concert band, dance, drama/theater, jazz band, literary magazine, music ensembles, musical theater, radio station, student government, student newspaper, student-run film society, symphony orchestra, yearbook. **Organizations:** 132 registered organizations, 3 honor societies, 17 religious organizations. **Athletics (Intercollegiate):** *Men:* Baseball, basketball, cross-country, diving, football, golf, soccer, swimming, tennis, track/field (indoor), track/field (outdoor). *Women:* Basketball, cross-country, diving, golf, soccer, softball, swimming, synchronized swimming, tennis, track/field (indoor), track/field (outdoor), volleyball.

ADMISSIONS

. **Freshman Academic Profile:** 78% in top 10% of high school class, 97% in top 25% of high school class, 100% in top 50% of high school class. 73% from public high schools. SAT Math middle 50% range 660–740. SAT Critical Reading middle 50% range 650–750. SAT Writing middle 50% range 650–730. ACT middle 50% range 29–33. TOEFL required of all international applicants, minimum paper TOEFL 600, minimum computer TOEFL 250. **Basis for Candidate Selection:** *Very important factors considered include:* Academic GPA, class rank, rigor of secondary school record. *Important factors considered include:* Application essay, character/personal qualities, extracurricular activities, racial/ethnic status, recommendation(s), standardized test scores, talent/ability, volunteer work, work experience. *Other factors considered include:* Alumni/ae relation, first generation, geographical residence, interview, state residency. **Freshman Admission Requirements:** High school diploma is required, and GED is accepted. *Academic units recommended:* 4 English, 3 math, 3 science (1 science lab), 3 foreign language, 3 social studies and history. **Freshman Admission Statistics:** 4,450 applied, 32% admitted, 36% enrolled. **Transfer Admission Requirements:** High school transcript, college transcript(s), essay or personal statement, standardized test score, statement of good standing from prior institution(s). Minimum college GPA of 2.0 required. Lowest grade transferable C-. **General Admission Information:** Application fee $30. Early decision application deadline 11/15. Regular application deadline 1/15. Regular notification 4/15. Nonfall registration not accepted. Admission may be deferred for a maximum of 1 year. Credit and/or placement offered for CEEB Advanced Placement tests.

COSTS AND FINANCIAL AID

Annual tuition $37,860. Room and board $9,978. Required fees $204. Average book expense $629. **Required Forms and Deadlines:** FAFSA, CSS/Financial Aid PROFILE, Noncustodial PROFILE, Business/Farm Supplement, prior year tax forms. Financial aid filing deadline 2/15. **Notification of Awards:** Applicants will be notified of awards on or about 4/1. *Types of Aid: Need-based scholarships/grants:* Pell, SEOG, state scholarships/grants, private scholarships, the school's own gift aid. *Loans:* FFEL Subsidized Stafford, FFEL Unsubsidized Stafford, FFEL PLUS, Federal Perkins, state loans, college/university loans from institutional funds, Minnesota SELF Loan program. **Financial Aid Statistics:** 50% freshmen, 56% undergrads receive need-based scholarship or grant aid. 48% freshmen, 55% undergrads receive need-based self-help aid.

CARLOS ALBIZU UNIVERSITY—CAU

2173 Northwest 99 Avenue, Miami, FL 33172
Phone: 800-672-3246 **E-mail:** admissions@albizu.edu
Fax: 305-593-1854 **Website:** www.mia.albizu.edu
Financial Aid Phone: 305-593-1223

This private school was founded in 1966. It has an 18-acre campus.

RATINGS

Admissions Selectivity Rating: 60*   **Fire Safety Rating:** 60*   **Green Rating:** 60*

STUDENTS AND FACULTY

Enrollment: 563. **Student Body:** 74% female, 26% male, 2% international. African American 17%, Caucasian 6%. **Retention and Graduation:** 60% grads go on to further study within 1 year. 85% grads pursue arts and sciences degrees. **Faculty:** Student/faculty ratio 13:1. 4 full-time faculty, 100% hold PhDs.

ACADEMICS

Degrees: Bachelor's, diploma, doctoral, master's. **Academic Requirements:** Arts/fine arts, computer literacy, English (including composition), foreign languages, history, humanities, mathematics, philosophy, social science, cross-cultral, accounting, oral communication. **Disciplines with Highest Percentage of Degrees Awarded:** Psychology 100%. **Special Study Options:** Accelerated program, cooperative education program, cross-registration, double major, dual enrollment, English as a second language (ESL), independent study, internships, teacher certification program, weekend college.

CAMPUS LIFE

Activities: Student government, student newspaper. **Organizations:** 3 registered organizations, 1 honor society.

ADMISSIONS

Basis for Candidate Selection: *Very important factors considered include:* Rigor of secondary school record. **Freshman Admission Requirements:** High school diploma is required, and GED is accepted. **Freshman Admission Statistics:** 185 applied, 64% admitted, 54% enrolled. **Transfer Admission Requirements:** Minimum college GPA of 2.0 required. Lowest grade transferable C. **General Admission Information:** Application fee $25. Nonfall registration accepted. Admission may be deferred for a maximum of 1 year. Common Application not accepted.

COSTS AND FINANCIAL AID

Annual tuition $8,250. Average book expense $690. **Required Forms and Deadlines:** FAFSA, institution's own financial aid form. Financial aid filing deadline 6/1. **Notification of Awards:** Applicants will be notified of awards on a rolling basis beginning on or about 2/1. **Student Employment:** Off-campus job opportunities are good. **Financial Aid Statistics:** 82% freshmen, 84% undergrads receive need-based scholarship or grant aid. 95% freshmen, 91% undergrads receive need-based self-help aid.

CARLOW UNIVERSITY

3333 Fifth Avenue, Pittsburgh, PA 15213-3165
Phone: 412-578-6059 **E-mail:** admissions@carlow.edu **CEEB Code:** 2421
Fax: 412-578-6668 **Website:** www.carlow.edu **ACT Code:** 3638
Financial Aid Phone: 412-578-6058

This private school, affiliated with the Roman Catholic Church, was founded in 1929. It has a 15-acre campus.

RATINGS

Admissions Selectivity Rating: 74   **Fire Safety Rating:** 60*   **Green Rating:** 60*

STUDENTS AND FACULTY

Student Body: 4% out-of-state. **Retention and Graduation:** 18% grads go on to further study within 1 year. 1% grads pursue arts and sciences degrees. 2% grads pursue business degrees. 1% grads pursue law degrees. 4% grads pursue medical degrees. **Faculty:** Student/faculty ratio 14:1. 69 full-time faculty, 77% hold PhDs. 90% faculty teach undergrads.

ACADEMICS

Degrees: Bachelor's, master's, post-master's certificate. **Academic Requirements:** Arts/fine arts, English (including composition), history, humanities, mathematics, philosophy, sciences (biological or physical), social science. **Classes:** Most classes have fewer than 10 students. Most lab/discussion sections have fewer than 10 students. **Majors with Highest Enrollment:** Business administration/management, elementary education and teaching, nursing. **Disciplines with Highest Percentage of Degrees Awarded:** Health professions and related sciences 27%, education 23%, business/marketing 13%, communication technologies 8%, computer and information sciences 6%, psychology 6%. **Special Study Options:** Accelerated program, cooperative education program, cross-registration, distance learning, double major, English as a second language (ESL), honors program, independent study, internships, liberal arts/career combination, student-designed major, study abroad, teacher certification program, weekend college. 3–2 programs with Carnegie Mellon for chemistry, engineering, environmental engineering, and mechanical engineering. Other programs with Duquesne University in athletic training (2/2), environmental science and management (3/2), occupational therapy (2/3), physical therapy (3/3), and physician assistant (2/3).

FACILITIES

Housing: Women's dorms. **Special Academic Facilities/Equipment:** The A. J. Palumbo Hall of Science and Technology features research labs, as well as a greenhouse, darkroom, biochamber, an on-site reference library and specially designed study and work zones on every floor to encourage team research. The building incorporates more than 1,000 outlets for Internet access. Also on-campus preschool and elementary school, media center, and the Bayer Children's Science Learning Lab. **Computers:** 95% of public computers are PCs, 5% of public computers are Macs, network access in dorm rooms, online registration, remote student-access to Web through college's connection.

CAMPUS LIFE

...ties: Choral groups, drama/theater, literary magazine, student government, student newspaper, yearbook. **Organizations:** 28 registered organizations, 5 honor societies, 1 religious organization. **Athletics (Intercollegiate):** ...men: Basketball, soccer, softball, tennis, volleyball.

ADMISSIONS

Freshman Academic Profile: 12% in top 10% of high school class, 32% in top 25% of high school class, 72% in top 50% of high school class. 84% from public high schools. SAT Math middle 50% range 430–550. SAT Critical Reading middle 50% range 450–570. ACT middle 50% range 18–24. TOEFL required of all international applicants, minimum paper TOEFL 500, minimum computer TOEFL 173. **Basis for Candidate Selection:** *Very important factors considered include:* Rigor of secondary school record. *Important factors considered include:* Character/personal qualities, class rank, interview, standardized test scores. *Other factors considered include:* Alumni/ae relation, application essay, extracurricular activities, racial/ethnic status, recommendation(s), talent/ability, volunteer work, work experience. **Freshman Admission Requirements:** High school diploma is required, and GED is accepted. *Academic units required:* 4 English, 3 math, 3 science, 4 academic electives, 4 arts and humanities. **Freshman Admission Statistics:** 1,356 applied, 68% admitted, 27% enrolled. **Transfer Admission Requirements:** College transcript(s). Minimum college GPA of 2.0 required. Lowest grade transferable C. **General Admission Information:** Application fee $20. Regular notification within 3 weeks of receipt of completed application. Nonfall registration accepted. Admission may be deferred for a maximum of 1 semester. Common Application accepted. Credit and/or placement offered for CEEB Advanced Placement tests.

COSTS AND FINANCIAL AID

Annual tuition $16,460. Room & board $6,538. Required fees $424. Average book expense $700. **Required Forms and Deadlines:** FAFSA. Financial aid filing deadline 4/1. **Notification of Awards:** Applicants will be notified of awards on a rolling basis beginning on or about 2/15. **Types of Aid:** *Need-based scholarships/grants:* Pell, SEOG, state scholarships/grants, private scholarships, the school's own gift aid. *Loans:* FFEL Subsidized Stafford, FFEL Unsubsidized Stafford, FFEL PLUS, Federal Perkins, Federal Nursing. **Financial Aid Statistics:** 83% freshmen, 79% undergrads receive need-based scholarship or grant aid. 79% freshmen, 78% undergrads receive need-based self-help aid. Highest amount earned per year from on-campus jobs $1,000.

CARNEGIE MELLON UNIVERSITY

5000 Forbes Avenue, Pittsburgh, PA 15213
Phone: 412-268-2082 **E-mail:** undergraduate-admissions@andrew.cmu.edu
CEEB Code: 2074 **Fax:** 412-268-7838 **Website:** www.cmu.edu **ACT Code:** 3534
Financial Aid Phone: 412-268-8186

This private school was founded in 1900. It has a 136-acre campus.

RATINGS

Admissions Selectivity Rating: 97   **Fire Safety Rating:** 77   **Green Rating:** 60*

STUDENTS AND FACULTY

Enrollment: 5,580. **Student Body:** 39% female, 61% male, 76% out-of-state, 13% international (95 countries represented). African American 5%, Asian 24%, Caucasian 40%, Hispanic 5%. **Retention and Graduation:** 94% freshmen return for sophomore year. 69% freshmen graduate within 4 years. 52% grads go on to further study within 1 year. 40% grads pursue arts and sciences degrees. 5% grads pursue business degrees. 2% grads pursue law degrees. 2% grads pursue medical degrees. **Faculty:** Student/faculty ratio 10:1. 838 full-time faculty, 98% hold PhDs.

ACADEMICS

Degrees: Bachelor's, doctoral, master's, post-master's certificate. **Academic Requirements:** Computer literacy, English (including composition), history, humanities, mathematics, social science. **Classes:** Most classes have fewer than 10 students. Most lab/discussion sections have 20–29 students. **Majors with Highest Enrollment:** Computer engineering, computer science, liberal arts and sciences/liberal studies. **Disciplines with Highest Percentage of Degrees Awarded:** Engineering 25%, business/marketing 12%, computer and information sciences 11%, visual and performing arts 11%, interdisciplinary studies 6%, physical sciences 5%. **Special Study Options:** Cooperative education program, cross-registration, distance learning, double major, dual enrollment, exchange student program (domestic), independent study, internships, liberal arts/career combination, student-designed major, study abroad, teacher certification program.

FACILITIES

Housing: Coed dorms, men's dorms, women's dorms, apartments for single students, special housing for disabled students, fraternity/sorority housing, special interest housing. **Special Academic Facilities/Equipment:** Rare books collection, entertainment technology center, art galleries, theaters, botanical institute, extensive lab facilities and equipment, recording studio, robotics institute, design studios, photo shoot studio and darkrooms, radio station, collaborative innovation center, LEED-certified green residence hall, Campo Garden, observatory, wood shops. **Computers:** 7% of classrooms are wired, 100% of classrooms are wireless, 46% of public computers are PCs, 30% of public computers are Macs, 25% of public computers are UNIX, network access in dorm rooms, network access in dorm lounges, online registration, online administrative functions (other than registration), remote student-access to Web through college's connection.

CAMPUS LIFE

Activities: Choral groups, concert band, dance, drama/theater, literary magazine, marching band, music ensembles, musical theater, pep band, radio station, student government, student newspaper, student-run film society, symphony orchestra, television station, yearbook. **Organizations:** 225 registered organizations, 19 religious organizations. 17 fraternities (8% men join), 8 sororities (9% women join). **Athletics (Intercollegiate):** *Men:* Basketball, cheerleading, cross-country, diving, football, golf, soccer, swimming, tennis, track/field (outdoor). *Women:* Basketball, cheerleading, cross-country, diving, soccer, swimming, tennis, track/field (outdoor), volleyball.

ADMISSIONS

. **Freshman Academic Profile:** 75% in top 10% of high school class, 95% in top 25% of high school class, 100% in top 50% of high school class. SAT Math middle 50% range 690–780. SAT Critical Reading middle 50% range 610–710. SAT Writing middle 50% range 610–700. ACT middle 50% range 28–32. TOEFL required of all international applicants, minimum paper TOEFL 600, minimum computer TOEFL 250. **Basis for Candidate Selection:** *Very important factors considered include:* Academic GPA, rigor of secondary school record. *Important factors considered include:* Application essay, class rank, recommendation(s), standardized test scores. *Other factors considered include:* Alumni/ae relation, character/personal qualities, extracurricular activities, first generation, geographical residence, interview, racial/ethnic status, talent/ability, volunteer work, work experience. **Freshman Admission Requirements:** High school diploma is required, and GED is accepted. *Academic units required:* 4 English, 4 math, 3 science (3 science labs), 2 foreign language, 3 academic electives. *Academic units recommended:* 4 English, 4 math, 3 science (3 science labs), 2 foreign language, 4 academic electives. **Freshman Admission Statistics:** 18,864 applied, 34% admitted, 22% enrolled. **Transfer Admission Requirements:** High school transcript, college transcript(s), essay or personal statement, standardized test score, statement of good standing from prior institution(s). **General Admission Information:** Application fee $65. Early decision application deadline 11/1. Regular application deadline 1/1. Regular notification 4/15. Nonfall registration not accepted. Admission may be deferred for a maximum of 1 year. Credit offered for CEEB Advanced Placement tests.

COSTS AND FINANCIAL AID

Annual tuition $35,580. Room and board $9,350. Required fees $404. Average book expense $966. **Required Forms and Deadlines:** FAFSA, institution's own financial aid form, parent and student federal tax returns, parent W-2 forms. Financial aid filing deadline 5/1. **Notification of Awards:** Applicants will be notified of awards on or about 3/15. **Types of Aid:** *Need-based scholarships/grants:* Pell, SEOG, state scholarships/grants, private scholarships, the school's own gift aid. *Loans:* FFEL Subsidized Stafford, FFEL Unsubsidized Stafford, FFEL PLUS, Federal Perkins, Gate Student Loan. **Student Employment:** Federal Work-Study Program available. Institutional employment available. Off-campus job opportunities are good. **Financial Aid Statistics:** 49% freshmen, 46% undergrads receive need-based scholarship or grant aid. 49% freshmen, 47% undergrads receive need-based self-help aid. 68% freshmen, 66% undergrads receive any aid.

CARROLL COLLEGE (MT)

1601 North Benton Avenue, Helena, MT 59625
Phone: 406-447-4384 **E-mail:** enroll@carroll.edu **CEEB Code:** 4041
Fax: 406-447-4533 **Website:** www.carroll.edu **ACT Code:** 2408
Financial Aid Phone: 406-447-5423

This private school, affiliated with the Roman Catholic Church, was founded in 1909. It has a 63-acre campus.

RATINGS

Admissions Selectivity Rating: 78   **Fire Safety Rating:** 60*   **Green Rating:** 60*

STUDENTS AND FACULTY

Enrollment: 1,317. **Student Body:** 57% female, 43% male, 35% out-of-state. Caucasian 70%, Hispanic 1%, Native American 1%. **Retention and Graduation:** 79% freshmen return for sophomore year. 42% freshmen graduate within 4 years. 22% grads go on to further study within 1 year. **Faculty:** Student/faculty ratio 13:1. 80 full-time faculty, 70% hold PhDs. 100% faculty teach undergrads.

ACADEMICS

Degrees: Associate, bachelor's. **Academic Requirements:** Arts/fine arts, English (including composition), history, humanities, mathematics, philosophy, sciences (biological or physical), social science, theology, communications, alpha seminar. **Classes:** Most classes have 10–19 students. Most lab/discussion sections have 20–29 students. **Majors with Highest Enrollment:** Business administration/management, nursing/registered nurse training (RN, ASN, BSN, MSN), psychology. **Disciplines with Highest Percentage of Degrees Awarded:** Business/marketing 21%, education 14%, biological/life sciences 10%, social sciences 10%, health professions and related sciences 9%, psychology 8%. **Special Study Options:** Accelerated program, cooperative education program, double major, dual enrollment, English as a second language (ESL), exchange student program (domestic), honors program, independent study, internships, liberal arts/career combination, student-designed major, study abroad, teacher certification program.

FACILITIES

Housing: Coed dorms, apartments for single students, freshman dorm. **Special Academic Facilities/Equipment:** Arts lab, observatory, seismograph station, engineering lab. **Computers:** 99% of public computers are PCs, 1% of public computers are Macs, network access in dorm rooms, network access in dorm lounges.

CAMPUS LIFE

Activities: Choral groups, dance, drama/theater, music ensembles, pep band, radio station, student government, student newspaper, yearbook. **Organizations:** 34 registered organizations, 10 honor societies, 4 religious organizations. **Athletics (Intercollegiate):** *Men:* Basketball, cheerleading, football, golf. *Women:* Basketball, cheerleading, golf, soccer, volleyball.

ADMISSIONS

Freshman Academic Profile: 22% in top 10% of high school class, 44% in top 25% of high school class, 80% in top 50% of high school class. 82% from public

---

high schools. SAT Math middle 50% range 480–600. SAT Critical Reading middle 50% range 480–590. ACT middle 50% range 21–26. **Basis for Candidate Selection:** *Very important factors considered include:* Academic GPA, rigor of secondary school record, standardized test scores. *Important factors considered include:* Application essay, character/personal qualities, class rank, recommendation(s). *Other factors considered include:* Alumni/ae relation, extracurricular activities, interview, level of applicant's interest, religious affiliation/commitment, talent/ability, volunteer work, work experience. **Freshman Admission Requirements:** High school diploma is required, and GED is accepted. *Academic units recommended:* 4 English, 3 math, 2 science (1 science lab), 2 foreign language, 1 social studies, 2 history, 2 academic electives, 1 technology. **Freshman Admission Statistics:** 1,048 applied, 79% admitted, 37% enrolled. **Transfer Admission Requirements:** College transcript(s), essay or personal statement, statement of good standing from prior institution(s). Minimum college GPA of 2.5 required. Lowest grade transferable C. **General Admission Information:** Application fee $35. Regular application deadline 6/1. Regular notification is rolling. Nonfall registration accepted. Admission may be deferred for a maximum of 1 semester. Common Application accepted. Credit and/or placement offered for CEEB Advanced Placement tests.

COSTS AND FINANCIAL AID

Annual tuition $17,986. Room & board $6,500. Required fees $300. Average book expense $700. **Required Forms and Deadlines:** FAFSA. Financial aid filing deadline 3/1. **Notification of Awards:** Applicants will be notified of awards on a rolling basis beginning on or about 3/1. **Types of Aid:** *Need-based scholarships/grants:* Pell, SEOG, state scholarships/grants, private scholarships, the school's own gift aid. *Loans:* FFEL Subsidized Stafford, FFEL Unsubsidized Stafford, FFEL PLUS, Federal Perkins, private. **Student Employment:** Federal Work-Study Program available. Institutional employment available. Off-campus job opportunities are good. **Financial Aid Statistics:** 60% freshmen, 62% undergrads receive need-based scholarship or grant aid. 43% freshmen, 41% undergrads receive need-based self-help aid. 18 freshmen, 84 undergrads receive athletic scholarships. 67% freshmen, 67% undergrads receive any aid.

CARROLL COLLEGE (WI)

100 North East Avenue, Waukesha, WI 53186
Phone: 262-524-7220 **E-mail:** ccinfo@ccadmincc.edu **CEEB Code:** 1101
Fax: 262-951-3037 **Website:** www.cc.edu **ACT Code:** 4570
Financial Aid Phone: 262-524-7297

This private school, affiliated with the Presbyterian Church, was founded in 1846. It has a 52-acre campus.

RATINGS

Admissions Selectivity Rating: 73   **Fire Safety Rating:** 60*   **Green Rating:** 60*

STUDENTS AND FACULTY

Enrollment: 2,914. **Student Body:** 67% female, 33% male, 18% out-of-state, 1% international (32 countries represented). African American 2%, Caucasian 70%, Hispanic 2%. **Retention and Graduation:** 77% freshmen return for sophomore year. 13% grads go on to further study within 1 year. **Faculty:** Student/faculty ratio 16:1. 109 full-time faculty, 63% hold PhDs. 100% faculty teach undergrads.

ACADEMICS

Degrees: Bachelor's, doctoral, master's, post-bachelor's certificate. **Academic Requirements:** Arts/fine arts, computer literacy, English (including composition), humanities, mathematics, sciences (biological or physical), social science. **Classes:** Most classes have 20–29 students. Most lab/discussion sections have 10–19 students. **Majors with Highest Enrollment:** Business administration/management, education, nursing/registered nurse training (RN, ASN, BSN, MSN). **Disciplines with Highest Percentage of Degrees Awarded:** Health professions and related sciences 16%, business/marketing 16%, psychology 11%, education 10%, communications/journalism 7%, biological/life sciences 7%. **Special Study Options:** Distance learning, double major, exchange student program (domestic), honors program, independent study, internships, student-designed major, study abroad, teacher certification program.

FACILITIES

Housing: Coed dorms, women's dorms, apartments for single students. **Computers:** 10% of classrooms are wired, 50% of classrooms are wireless, 90% of public computers are PCs, 10% of public computers are Macs, network access in dorm rooms, network access in dorm lounges, online registration, online administrative functions (other than registration), remote student-access to Web through college's connection.

The Princeton Review's **Complete Book of Colleges**

CAMPUS LIFE

Activities: Choral groups, concert band, dance, drama/theater, jazz band, literary magazine, music ensembles, radio station, student government, student newspaper, symphony orchestra, yearbook. **Organizations:** 40 registered organizations, 2 religious organizations. 2 fraternities (6% men join), 4 sororities (4% women join). **Athletics (Intercollegiate):** *Men:* Baseball, basketball, cross-country, football, golf, soccer, swimming, tennis, track/field (indoor), track/field (outdoor). *Women:* Basketball, cross-country, golf, soccer, softball, swimming, tennis, track/field (indoor), track/field (outdoor), volleyball.

ADMISSIONS

Freshman Academic Profile: 17% in top 10% of high school class, 52% in top 25% of high school class, 79% in top 50% of high school class. 87% from public high schools. ACT middle 50% range 20–25. TOEFL required of all international applicants, minimum paper TOEFL 550, minimum computer TOEFL 213. **Basis for Candidate Selection:** *Very important factors considered include:* Class rank, rigor of secondary school record, standardized test scores. *Other factors considered include:* Application essay, character/personal qualities, interview, recommendation(s). **Freshman Admission Requirements:** High school diploma is required, and GED is accepted. *Academic units recommended:* 4 English, 4 math, 3 science (1 science lab), 2 foreign language, 3 social studies, 3 history. **Freshman Admission Statistics:** 2,676 applied, 74% admitted, 35% enrolled. **Transfer Admission Requirements:** High school transcript, college transcript(s). Minimum college GPA of 2.0 required. Lowest grade transferable C. **General Admission Information:** Regular notification is rolling. Nonfall registration accepted. Admission may be deferred for a maximum of 2 years. Credit and/or placement offered for CEEB Advanced Placement tests.

COSTS AND FINANCIAL AID

Annual tuition $20,400. Room & board $6,350. Required fees $430. Average book expense $1,060. **Required Forms and Deadlines:** FAFSA. **Notification of Awards:** Applicants will be notified of awards on a rolling basis beginning on or about 3/1. **Types of Aid:** *Need-based scholarships/grants:* Pell, SEOG, state scholarships/grants, private scholarships, the school's own gift aid, Federal Nursing Scholarships. *Loans:* FFEL Subsidized Stafford, FFEL Unsubsidized Stafford, FFEL PLUS, Federal Perkins, state loans. **Financial Aid Statistics:** 70% freshmen, 73% undergrads receive need-based scholarship or grant aid. 54% freshmen, 54% undergrads receive need-based self-help aid. 98% freshmen, 98% undergrads receive any aid. Highest amount earned per year from on-campus jobs $3,000.

CARSON-NEWMAN COLLEGE

1646 Russell Avenue, Jefferson City, TN 37760
Phone: 865-471-3223 **E-mail:** admitme@.cn.edu **CEEB Code:** 1102
Fax: 865-471-3502 **Website:** www.cn.edu **ACT Code:** 3950
Financial Aid Phone: 865-471-3414

This private school, affiliated with the Baptist Church, was founded in 1851. It has a 90-acre campus.

RATINGS

Admissions Selectivity Rating: 73   **Fire Safety Rating:** 60*   **Green Rating:** 60*

STUDENTS AND FACULTY

Enrollment: 1,849. **Student Body:** 53% female, 47% male, 32% out-of-state, 3% international. African American 9%, Caucasian 85%. **Retention and Graduation:** 72% freshmen return for sophomore year. 45% freshmen graduate within 4 years. 25% grads go on to further study within 1 year. 20% grads pursue arts and sciences degrees. 1% grads pursue business degrees. 3% grads pursue law degrees. 2% grads pursue medical degrees. **Faculty:** Student/faculty ratio 13:1. 123 full-time faculty, 69% hold PhDs. 100% faculty teach undergrads.

ACADEMICS

Degrees: Associate, bachelor's, master's. **Academic Requirements:** Arts/fine arts, computer literacy, English (including composition), foreign languages, history, humanities, mathematics, sciences (biological or physical), social science. Regardless of major, all students must complete a 51-semester-hour general education core for graduation, including 2 religion classes. **Classes:** Most classes have 10–19 students. Most lab/discussion sections have 10–19 students. **Disciplines with Highest Percentage of Degrees Awarded:** Education 17%, business/marketing 12%, social sciences 8%, visual and performing arts 8%, communication technologies 7%, biological/life sciences 7%, psychology 7%, English 4%, health professions and related sciences 4%. **Special Study Options:** Cooperative education program, double major, dual

enrollment, English as a second language (ESL), honors program, independent study, internships, student-designed major, study abroad, teacher certification program.

FACILITIES

Housing: Men's dorms, women's dorms, apartments for married students, apartments for single students. **Special Academic Facilities/Equipment:** Art galleries, Appalachian History Museum, home management house, language lab. **Computers:** 90% of public computers are PCs, 10% of public computers are Macs, network access in dorm rooms, remote student-access to Web through college's connection.

CAMPUS LIFE

Activities: Choral groups, concert band, dance, drama/theater, jazz band, literary magazine, marching band, music ensembles, musical theater, opera, pep band, student government, student newspaper, television station, yearbook. **Organizations:** 45 registered organizations, 10 honor societies, 5 religious organizations. 2 fraternities, 2 sororities. **Athletics (Intercollegiate):** *Men:* Baseball, basketball, cheerleading, cross-country, football, golf, soccer, tennis, track/field (outdoor), wrestling. *Women:* Basketball, cheerleading, cross-country, soccer, softball, tennis, track/field (outdoor), volleyball.

ADMISSIONS

Freshman Academic Profile: 28% in top 10% of high school class, 49% in top 25% of high school class, 77% in top 50% of high school class. 87% from public high schools. TOEFL required of all international applicants, minimum paper TOEFL 550, minimum computer TOEFL 213. **Basis for Candidate Selection:** *Very important factors considered include:* Rigor of secondary school record, standardized test scores. *Important factors considered include:* Class rank. *Other factors considered include:* Alumni/ae relation, application essay, character/personal qualities, extracurricular activities, interview, recommendation(s), religious affiliation/commitment, talent/ability, volunteer work, work experience. **Freshman Admission Requirements:** High school diploma is required, and GED is accepted. *Academic units required:* 4 English, 2 math, 2 science (1 science lab), 1 social studies, 1 history, 4 academic electives. *Academic units recommended:* 2 foreign language. **Freshman Admission Statistics:** 1,694 applied, 82% admitted, 32% enrolled. **Transfer Admission Requirements:** College transcript(s). Minimum college GPA of 2.0 required. Lowest grade transferable D. **General Admission Information:** Application fee $25. Regular notification is rolling. Nonfall registration accepted. Admission may be deferred for a maximum of 2 years. Common Application accepted. Credit and/or placement offered for CEEB Advanced Placement tests.

COSTS AND FINANCIAL AID

Annual tuition $14,500. Room & board $5,380. Required fees $740. Average book expense $900. **Required Forms and Deadlines:** FAFSA, institution's own financial aid form. Financial aid filing deadline 3/1. **Types of Aid:** *Need-based scholarships/grants:* Pell, SEOG, state scholarships/grants, private scholarships, the school's own gift aid. *Loans:* Direct Subsidized Stafford, Direct Unsubsidized Stafford, Direct PLUS, Federal Perkins, Federal Nursing. **Student Employment:** Federal Work-Study Program available. Institutional employment available. Off-campus job opportunities are good. **Financial Aid Statistics:** 81% freshmen, 72% undergrads receive need-based scholarship or grant aid. 65% freshmen, 63% undergrads receive need-based self-help aid. 10 freshmen, 66 undergrads receive athletic scholarships. Highest amount earned per year from on-campus jobs $900.

CARTHAGE COLLEGE

2001 Alford Park Drive, Kenosha, WI 53140-1994
Phone: 262-551-6000 **E-mail:** admissions@carthage.edu **CEEB Code:** 1103
Fax: 262-551-5762 **Website:** www.carthage.edu **ACT Code:** 4571
Financial Aid Phone: 262-551-6001

This private school, affiliated with the Lutheran Church, was founded in 1847. It has a 95-acre campus.

RATINGS

Admissions Selectivity Rating: 80   **Fire Safety Rating:** 60*   **Green Rating:** 60*

STUDENTS AND FACULTY

Enrollment: 2,456. **Student Body:** 58% female, 42% male, 70% out-of-state. **Retention and Graduation:** 75% freshmen return for sophomore year. 46% freshmen graduate within 4 years. 16% grads go on to further study within 1 year. 4% grads pursue arts and sciences degrees. 1% grads pursue business degrees. 2% grads pursue law degrees. 1% grads pursue medical degrees.

Faculty: Student/faculty ratio 16:1. 126 full-time faculty, 87% hold PhDs. 100% faculty teach undergrads.

ACADEMICS

Degrees: Bachelor's, certificate, master's. **Academic Requirements:** Arts/fine arts, foreign languages, humanities, mathematics, sciences (biological or physical), social science, heritage studies, exercise and sport science, Carthage symposium, senior thesis, religion. **Classes:** Most classes have 20–29 students. Most lab/discussion sections have fewer than 10 students. **Majors with Highest Enrollment:** Biology/biological sciences, business administration/management, elementary education and teaching. **Disciplines with Highest Percentage of Degrees Awarded:** Business/marketing 24%, social sciences 10%, education 9%, biological/life sciences 5%, security and protective services 5%. **Special Study Options:** Accelerated program, cross-registration, double major, honors program, independent study, internships, student-designed major, study abroad, teacher certification program.

FACILITIES

Housing: Coed dorms, men's dorms, women's dorms, fraternity/sorority housing, Best Western Harborside through Carthage. **Special Academic Facilities/Equipment:** H.F. Johnson Art Gallery, center for children's literature, planetarium, undergraduate science research lab, graphic design lab, greenhouse, computer/math research lab, physics research lab, ScienceWorks lab, A.W. Clausen Center Boardroom. **Computers:** 11% of classrooms are wired, 100% of classrooms are wireless, 98% of public computers are PCs, 2% of public computers are Macs, network access in dorm rooms, network access in dorm lounges, online registration, online administrative functions (other than registration), remote student-access to Web through college's connection.

CAMPUS LIFE

Activities: Choral groups, concert band, dance, drama/theater, jazz band, literary magazine, music ensembles, musical theater, opera, pep band, radio station, student government, student newspaper, student-run film society, symphony orchestra, yearbook. **Organizations:** 90 registered organizations, 20 honor societies, 7 religious organizations. 8 fraternities (22% men join), 7 sororities (25% women join). **Athletics (Intercollegiate):** *Men:* Baseball, basketball, cross-country, football, golf, soccer, swimming, tennis, track/field (indoor), track/field (outdoor), volleyball. *Women:* Basketball, cross-country, golf, soccer, softball, swimming, tennis, track/field (indoor), track/field (outdoor), volleyball, water polo.

ADMISSIONS

Freshman Academic Profile: 19% in top 10% of high school class, 43% in top 25% of high school class, 75% in top 50% of high school class. 91% from public high schools. SAT Math middle 50% range 490–620. SAT Critical Reading middle 50% range 470–630. ACT middle 50% range 21–26. TOEFL required of all international applicants, minimum paper TOEFL 500, minimum computer TOEFL 173. **Basis for Candidate Selection:** *Very important factors considered include:* Academic GPA, rigor of secondary school record, standardized test scores. *Other factors considered include:* Application essay, character/personal qualities, class rank, extracurricular activities, interview, recommendation(s), talent/ability, volunteer work, work experience. **Freshman Admission Requirements:** High school diploma is required, and GED is accepted. *Academic units recommended:* 4 English, 3 math, 3 science (2 science labs), 2 foreign language, 3 social studies, 3 academic electives. **Freshman Admission Statistics:** 4,495 applied, 77% admitted, 19% enrolled. **Transfer Admission Requirements:** College transcript(s), statement of good standing from prior institution(s). Minimum college GPA of 2.0 required. Lowest grade transferable C-. **General Admission Information:** Application fee $25. Regular notification is rolling. Nonfall registration accepted. Admission may be deferred for a maximum of 1 year. Credit and/or placement offered for CEEB Advanced Placement tests.

COSTS AND FINANCIAL AID

Annual tuition $25,000. Room & board $7,000. Average book expense $1,200. **Required Forms and Deadlines:** FAFSA. Financial aid filing deadline 2/15. **Notification of Awards:** Applicants will be notified of awards on a rolling basis beginning on or about 3/1. **Types of Aid:** *Need-based scholarships/grants:* Pell, SEOG, state scholarships/grants, private scholarships, the school's own gift aid. *Loans:* FFEL Subsidized Stafford, FFEL Unsubsidized Stafford, FFEL PLUS, Federal Perkins, state loans, college/university loans from institutional funds. **Financial Aid Statistics:** 73% freshmen, 69% undergrads receive need-based scholarship or grant aid. 59% freshmen, 56% undergrads receive need-based self-help aid. 97% freshmen, 97% undergrads receive any aid. Highest amount earned per year from on-campus jobs $1,000.

CASCADE COLLEGE

9101 East Burnside Street, Portland, OR 97216-1515
Phone: 503-257-1202 **E-mail:** admissions@cascade.edu
Fax: 503-257-1222 **Website:** www.cascade.edu **ACT Code:** 3459
Financial Aid Phone: 503-257-1241

This private school, affiliated with the Church of Christ, was founded in 1993. It has a 13-acre campus. .

RATINGS

Admissions Selectivity Rating: 60*   **Fire Safety Rating:** 61   **Green Rating:** 64

STUDENTS AND FACULTY

Enrollment: 290. **Student Body:** 55% female, 45% male, 64% out-of-state, 3% international (11 countries represented). African American 6%, Asian 3%, Caucasian 78%, Hispanic 7%, Native American 1%. **Retention and Graduation:** 64% freshmen return for sophomore year. 18% freshmen graduate within 4 years. 15% grads go on to further study within 1 year. 10% grads pursue arts and sciences degrees. 1% grads pursue business degrees. 2% grads pursue law degrees. **Faculty:** Student/faculty ratio 14:1. 14 full-time faculty, 64% hold PhDs. 100% faculty teach undergrads.

ACADEMICS

Degrees: Bachelor's. **Academic Requirements:** Arts/fine arts, computer literacy, English (including composition), history, humanities, mathematics, philosophy, sciences (biological or physical), social science. All students are required to take Bible courses. **Classes:** Most classes have 10–19 students. Most lab/discussion sections have 20–29 students. **Majors with Highest Enrollment:** Business administration/management, psychology, teacher education, multiple levels. **Disciplines with Highest Percentage of Degrees Awarded:** Interdisciplinary studies 38%, theology and religious vocations 16%, education 16%, business/marketing 16%, psychology 11%, liberal arts/general studies 3%. **Special Study Options:** Double major, dual enrollment, independent study, internships, student-designed major, study abroad, teacher certification program.

FACILITIES

Housing: Men's dorms, women's dorms, apartments for married students, special housing for disabled students. **Computers:** 90% of classrooms are wired, 90% of classrooms are wireless, 100% of public computers are PCs, network access in dorm rooms, network access in dorm lounges, online administrative functions (other than registration), remote student-access to Web through college's connection.

CAMPUS LIFE

Activities: Choral groups, concert band, drama/theater, literary magazine, music ensembles, musical theater, student government, yearbook. **Organizations:** 16 registered organizations, 2 honor societies. **Athletics (Intercollegiate):** *Men:* Basketball, cross-country, soccer, track/field (indoor), track/field (outdoor). *Women:* Basketball, cross-country, soccer, track/field (indoor), track/field (outdoor), volleyball.

ADMISSIONS

Freshman Academic Profile: 85% from public high schools. TOEFL required of all international applicants, minimum paper TOEFL 500, minimum computer TOEFL 173. **Basis for Candidate Selection:** *Other factors considered include:* Academic GPA, recommendation(s), standardized test scores. **Freshman Admission Requirements:** High school diploma is required, and GED is accepted. *Academic units recommended:* 4 English, 3 math, 2 science (1 science lab), 2 foreign language, 4 social studies. **Freshman Admission Statistics:** 204 applied, 57% admitted, 57% enrolled. **Transfer Admission Requirements:** High school transcript, college transcript(s). Minimum college GPA of 2.0 required. Lowest grade transferable D. **General Admission Information:** Application fee $25. Nonfall registration accepted. Admission may be deferred for a maximum of 1 year. Credit offered for CEEB Advanced Placement tests.

COSTS AND FINANCIAL AID

Average book expense $900. **Required Forms and Deadlines:** FAFSA, institution's own financial aid form, payment plan form, FERPA release form. Financial aid filing deadline 7/31. **Notification of Awards:** Applicants will be notified of awards on a rolling basis beginning on or about 2/15. **Types of Aid:** *Need-based scholarships/grants:* Pell, SEOG, private scholarships, the school's own gift aid. *Loans:* FFEL Subsidized Stafford, FFEL Unsubsidized Stafford, FFEL PLUS, private loans. **Financial Aid Statistics:** 76% undergrads receive need-based scholarship or grant aid. 66% undergrads receive need-based self-help aid. 46 freshmen, 102 undergrads receive athletic scholarships. 100%

freshmen, 99% undergrads receive any aid. Highest amount earned per year from on-campus jobs $2,000.

CASE WESTERN RESERVE UNIVERSITY

103 Tomlinson Hall, 10900 Euclid Avenue, Cleveland, OH 44106-7055
Phone: 216-368-4450 **E-mail:** admission@case.edu **CEEB Code:** 1105
Fax: 216-368-5111 **Website:** www.case.edu **ACT Code:** 3244
Financial Aid Phone: 216-368-4530

This private school was founded in 1826. It has a 150-acre campus.

RATINGS
Admissions Selectivity Rating: 92   **Fire Safety Rating:** 68   **Green Rating:** 80

STUDENTS AND FACULTY
Enrollment: 3,998. **Student Body:** 41% female, 59% male, 45% out-of-state, 4% international (28 countries represented). African American 5%, Asian 17%, Caucasian 64%, Hispanic 2%. **Retention and Graduation:** 91% freshmen return for sophomore year. 59% freshmen graduate within 4 years. 44% grads go on to further study within 1 year. 8% grads pursue arts and sciences degrees. 2% grads pursue business degrees. 4% grads pursue law degrees. 10% grads pursue medical degrees. **Faculty:** Student/faculty ratio 9:1. 696 full-time faculty, 90% hold PhDs. 72% faculty teach undergrads.

ACADEMICS
Degrees: Bachelor's, doctoral, first professional, master's. **Academic Requirements:** English (including composition), humanities, mathematics, sciences (biological or physical), social science. **Classes:** Most classes have 10–19 students. Most lab/discussion sections have fewer than 10 students. **Majors with Highest Enrollment:** Biology/biological sciences, biomedical/medical engineering, business administration/management. **Disciplines with Highest Percentage of Degrees Awarded:** Engineering 31%, social sciences 10%, business/marketing 10%, biological/life sciences 9%, psychology 8%, health professions and related sciences 6%. **Special Study Options:** Accelerated program, cooperative education program, cross-registration, double major, dual enrollment, English as a second language (ESL), exchange student program (domestic), honors program, independent study, internships, liberal arts/career combination, student-designed major, study abroad, teacher certification program, Washington, DC semester.

FACILITIES
Housing: Coed dorms, apartments for single students, fraternity/sorority housing, secured women-only floor available, special-interest housing available, residential colleges. **Special Academic Facilities/Equipment:** Art, natural history, and auto-aviation museums; historical society; botanical garden; biology field stations; observatory. **Computers:** 100% of classrooms are wired, 100% of classrooms are wireless, 93% of public computers are PCs, 1% of public computers are Macs, 4% of public computers are UNIX, network access in dorm rooms, network access in dorm lounges, online registration, online administrative functions (other than registration), support for handheld computing, remote student-access to Web through college's connection.

CAMPUS LIFE
Activities: Choral groups, concert band, dance, drama/theater, jazz band, literary magazine, marching band, music ensembles, musical theater, pep band, radio station, student government, student newspaper, student-run film society, symphony orchestra, yearbook. **Organizations:** 120 registered organizations, 4 honor societies, 4 religious organizations. 16 fraternities (29% men join), 6 sororities (23% women join). **Athletics (Intercollegiate):** *Men:* Baseball, basketball, cross-country, football, soccer, swimming, tennis, track/field (indoor), track/field (outdoor), wrestling. *Women:* Basketball, cross-country, soccer, softball, swimming, tennis, track/field (indoor), track/field (outdoor), volleyball. Environmental Initiatives: Case Western has dedicated funding for infrastructure upgrades for increased energy efficiency and building performance, which has resulted in more than 7 million kwh saved in the last two years in academic buildings alone. Formation of the Great Lakes Advanced Energy Institute, which is partnering with Cuyahoga County and Green Energy Ohio in a wind feasibility study and implementation of a wind farm in Lake Erie. Campus food service (Bon Appetit) purchasing bulk of fresh food and supplies from local farms and food producers. Organic, seasonal, local (low carbon footprint), and delicious!

ADMISSIONS
. **Freshman Academic Profile:** 68% in top 10% of high school class, 93% in top 25% of high school class, 99% in top 50% of high school class. 70% from public high schools. SAT Math middle 50% range 620–720. SAT Critical Reading middle 50% range 580–690. SAT Writing middle 50% range 580–680. ACT middle 50% range 26–31. TOEFL required of all international applicants, minimum paper TOEFL 550, minimum computer TOEFL 213. **Basis for Candidate Selection:** *Very important factors considered include:* Extracurricular activities, rigor of secondary school record, talent/ability, volunteer work, work experience. *Important factors considered include:* Alumni/ae relation, application essay, character/personal qualities, class rank, interview, racial/ethnic status, recommendation(s), standardized test scores. *Other factors considered include:* Academic GPA, first generation, level of applicant's interest. **Freshman Admission Requirements:** High school diploma is required, and GED is accepted. *Academic units required:* 4 English, 3 math, 3 science (1 science lab), 2 foreign language, 3 social studies. *Academic units recommended:* 4 math, 3 foreign language, 4 social studies. **Freshman Admission Statistics:** 7,508 applied, 67% admitted, 20% enrolled. **Transfer Admission Requirements:** High school transcript, college transcript(s), essay or personal statement, statement of good standing from prior institution(s). Minimum college GPA of 3.0 required. Lowest grade transferable C. **General Admission Information:** Regular application deadline 1/15. Regular notification 4/1. Nonfall registration accepted. Admission may be deferred for a maximum of 1 year. Credit and/or placement offered for CEEB Advanced Placement tests.

COSTS AND FINANCIAL AID
Annual tuition $33,500. Room and board $10,590. Required fees $752. Average book expense $1,100. **Required Forms and Deadlines:** FAFSA, institution's own financial aid form, Business/Farm Supplement, parent and student income tax returns and W-2 forms. Financial aid filing deadline 2/1. **Notification of Awards:** Applicants will be notified of awards on a rolling basis beginning on or about 2/15. **Types of Aid:** *Need-based scholarships/grants:* Pell, SEOG, state scholarships/grants, private scholarships, the school's own gift aid. *Loans:* FFEL Subsidized Stafford, FFEL Unsubsidized Stafford, FFEL PLUS, Federal Perkins, Federal Nursing, state loans, college/university loans from institutional funds. **Student Employment:** Federal Work-Study Program available. Institutional employment available. Off-campus job opportunities are good. **Financial Aid Statistics:** 65% freshmen, 61% undergrads receive need-based scholarship or grant aid. 58% freshmen, 56% undergrads receive need-based self-help aid. 97% freshmen, 96% undergrads receive any aid. Highest amount earned per year from on-campus jobs $2,900.

CASTLETON STATE COLLEGE

Office of Admissions, Castleton, VT 05735
Phone: 802-468-1213 **E-mail:** info@castleton.edu **CEEB Code:** 3765
Fax: 802-468-1476 **Website:** www.castleton.edu **ACT Code:** 4314
Financial Aid Phone: 802-468-6070

This public school was founded in 1787. It has a 165-acre campus.

RATINGS
Admissions Selectivity Rating: 70   **Fire Safety Rating:** 60*   **Green Rating:** 60*

STUDENTS AND FACULTY
Enrollment: 1,907. **Student Body:** 55% female, 45% male, 33% out-of-state. Caucasian 87%. **Retention and Graduation:** 71% freshmen return for sophomore year. **Faculty:** Student/faculty ratio 14:1. 90 full-time faculty, 94% hold PhDs. 100% faculty teach undergrads.

ACADEMICS
Degrees: Associate, bachelor's, master's, post-master's certificate. **Academic Requirements:** Arts/fine arts, computer literacy, English (including composition), history, humanities, mathematics, sciences (biological or physical), social science. **Classes:** Most classes have 10–19 students. Most lab/discussion sections have 10–19 students. **Majors with Highest Enrollment:** Business administration/management, mass communications/media studies, psychology. **Disciplines with Highest Percentage of Degrees Awarded:** Business/marketing 19%, communications/journalism 15%, psychology 14%, interdisciplinary studies 9%, parks and recreation 6%, social sciences 6%, visual and performing arts 6%. **Special Study Options:** Cooperative education program, double major, dual enrollment, honors program, independent study, internships, liberal arts/career combination, student-designed major, study abroad, teacher certification program.

FACILITIES

Housing: Coed dorms. **Special Academic Facilities/Equipment:** Historical/medical museum. **Computers:** 70% of public computers are PCs, 30% of public computers are Macs, network access in dorm rooms, network access in dorm lounges, remote student-access to Web through college's connection.

CAMPUS LIFE

Activities: Choral groups, dance, drama/theater, jazz band, literary magazine, music ensembles, musical theater, radio station, student government, student newspaper, student-run film society, television station, yearbook. **Organizations:** 40 registered organizations, 7 honor societies, 2 religious organizations. **Athletics (Intercollegiate):** *Men:* Baseball, basketball, cross-country, ice hockey, lacrosse, skiing (downhill/alpine), soccer, tennis. *Women:* Basketball, cross-country, field hockey, ice hockey, lacrosse, skiing (downhill/alpine), soccer, softball, tennis. Environmental Initiatives: Student driven recycling effort. New construction is significantly green. Purchasing is significantly green.

ADMISSIONS

Freshman Academic Profile: 3% in top 10% of high school class, 15% in top 25% of high school class, 50% in top 50% of high school class. SAT Math middle 50% range 450–530. SAT Critical Reading middle 50% range 440–530. SAT Writing middle 50% range 440–520. ACT middle 50% range 18–22. TOEFL required of all international applicants, minimum paper TOEFL 500, minimum computer TOEFL 173. **Basis for Candidate Selection:** *Very important factors considered include:* Academic GPA, application essay, class rank, recommendation(s), rigor of secondary school record, standardized test scores. *Other factors considered include:* Character/personal qualities, extracurricular activities, interview, level of applicant's interest, talent/ability, volunteer work. **Freshman Admission Requirements:** High school diploma is required, and GED is accepted. *Academic units required:* 4 English, 3 math, 2 science (2 science labs), 3 social studies. *Academic units recommended:* 4 English, 3 math, 2 science (2 science labs), 2 foreign language, 4 social studies, 2 academic electives. **Freshman Admission Statistics:** 1,847 applied, 75% admitted, 34% enrolled. **Transfer Admission Requirements:** College transcript, essay or personal statement. Minimum college GPA of 2.0 required. Lowest grade transferable C-. **General Admission Information:** Application fee $35. Regular notification is rolling. Nonfall registration accepted. Admission may be deferred for a maximum of 1 year. Credit and/or placement offered for CEEB Advanced Placement tests.

COSTS AND FINANCIAL AID

Annual in-state tuition $6,648. Out-of-state tuition $14,376. Room & board $6,942. Required fees $375. Average book expense $800. **Required Forms and Deadlines:** FAFSA. Financial aid filing deadline 2/15. **Notification of Awards:** Applicants will be notified of awards on a rolling basis beginning on or about 2/15. **Types of Aid:** *Need-based scholarships/grants:* Pell, SEOG, state scholarships/grants, private scholarships, the school's own gift aid. *Loans:* FFEL Subsidized Stafford, FFEL Unsubsidized Stafford, FFEL PLUS, Federal Perkins, Federal Nursing.

See page 1106.

CATAWBA COLLEGE

2300 West Innes Street, Salisbury, NC 28144
Phone: 704-637-4402 **E-mail:** admission@catawba.edu **CEEB Code:** 5103
Fax: 704-637-4222 **Website:** www.catawba.edu **ACT Code:** 3080
Financial Aid Phone: 704-637-4416

This private school, affiliated with the United Church of Christ, was founded in 1851. It has a 276-acre campus.

RATINGS

Admissions Selectivity Rating: 79   **Fire Safety Rating:** 64   **Green Rating:** 60*

STUDENTS AND FACULTY

Enrollment: 1,235. **Student Body:** 51% female, 49% male, 30% out-of-state. **Retention and Graduation:** 72% freshmen return for sophomore year. 29% freshmen graduate within 4 years. 13% grads go on to further study within 1 year. 6% grads pursue arts and sciences degrees. 4% grads pursue business degrees. 2% grads pursue law degrees. 1% grads pursue medical degrees. **Faculty:** Student/faculty ratio 15:1. 73 full-time faculty, 79% hold PhDs. 100% faculty teach undergrads.

ACADEMICS

Degrees: Bachelor's, master's. **Academic Requirements:** Arts/fine arts, English (including composition), foreign languages, humanities, mathematics, sciences (biological or physical), social science, physical education/prescriptive fitness, non-Western perspective course. **Classes:** Most classes have 10–19 students. Most lab/discussion sections have fewer than 10 students. **Majors with Highest Enrollment:** Business administration/management, drama and dramatics/theater arts, sports and fitness administration/management. **Disciplines with Highest Percentage of Degrees Awarded:** Business/marketing 45%, education 10%, parks and recreation 7%, health professions and related sciences 6%, visual and performing arts 6%, communications/journalism 5%. **Special Study Options:** Cross-registration, double major, honors program, independent study, internships, liberal arts/career combination, student-designed major, study abroad, teacher certification program.

FACILITIES

Housing: Coed dorms, men's dorms, women's dorms, substance-free housing. **Special Academic Facilities/Equipment:** Ecology preserve (183 acres), wildlife preserve (300 acres). **Computers:** 2% of classrooms are wired, 2% of classrooms are wireless, 99% of public computers are PCs, 1% of public computers are Macs, network access in dorm rooms, online administrative functions (other than registration), remote student-access to Web through college's connection.

CAMPUS LIFE

Activities: Choral groups, concert band, dance, drama/theater, jazz band, literary magazine, music ensembles, musical theater, pep band, student government, student newspaper, symphony orchestra, yearbook. **Organizations:** 38 registered organizations, 9 honor societies, 4 religious organizations. **Athletics (Intercollegiate):** *Men:* Baseball, basketball, cross-country, football, golf, lacrosse, soccer, tennis. *Women:* Basketball, cross-country, field hockey, golf, soccer, softball, swimming, tennis, volleyball.

ADMISSIONS

Freshman Academic Profile: 9% in top 10% of high school class, 34% in top 25% of high school class, 68% in top 50% of high school class. 80% from public high schools. SAT Math middle 50% range 470–580. SAT Critical Reading middle 50% range 450–570. ACT middle 50% range 18–25. TOEFL required of all international applicants, minimum paper TOEFL 525, minimum computer TOEFL 197. **Basis for Candidate Selection:** *Very important factors considered include:* Academic GPA, application essay, class rank, recommendation(s), standardized test scores. *Important factors considered include:* Character/personal qualities, extracurricular activities, interview, level of applicant's interest, rigor of secondary school record, talent/ability. *Other factors considered include:* Volunteer work. **Freshman Admission Requirements:** High school diploma is required, and GED is accepted. *Academic units required:* 4 English, 2 math, 2 science, 2 social studies, 6 academic electives. *Academic units recommended:* 4 English, 3 math, 3 science (3 science labs), 2 foreign language, 3 social studies, 2 academic electives. **Freshman Admission Statistics:** 792 applied, 68% admitted, 45% enrolled. **Transfer Admission Requirements:** High school transcript, college transcript(s), essay or personal statement, statement of good standing from prior institution(s). Minimum college GPA of 2.0 required. Lowest grade transferable C. **General Admission Information:** Application fee $30. Regular notification is rolling. Nonfall registration accepted. Admission may be deferred for a maximum of 1 year. Credit and/or placement offered for CEEB Advanced Placement tests.

COSTS AND FINANCIAL AID

Annual tuition $20,835. Room and board $7,190. Average book expense $800. **Required Forms and Deadlines:** FAFSA, state aid form. Financial aid filing deadline 3/15. **Notification of Awards:** Applicants will be notified of awards on a rolling basis beginning on or about 2/15. **Types of Aid:** *Need-based scholarships/grants:* Pell, SEOG, state scholarships/grants, private scholarships, the school's own gift aid. *Loans:* FFEL Subsidized Stafford, FFEL Unsubsidized Stafford, FFEL PLUS, Federal Perkins, college/university loans from institutional funds, TERI Loans, Nellie Mae Loans, Advantage Loans, alternative loans. **Financial Aid Statistics:** 50% freshmen, 45% undergrads receive need-based scholarship or grant aid. 61% freshmen, 51% undergrads receive need-based self-help aid. 65 freshmen, 200 undergrads receive athletic scholarships. 96% freshmen, 96% undergrads receive any aid. Highest amount earned per year from on-campus jobs $1,210.

See page 1108.

THE CATHOLIC UNIVERSITY OF AMERICA

Office of Undergraduate Admissions, 620 Michigan Avenue, NE, Washington, DC 20064
Phone: 202-319-5305 **E-mail:** cua-admissions@cua.edu **CEEB Code:** 5104
Fax: 202-319-6533 **Website:** www.cua.edu **ACT Code:** 0654
Financial Aid Phone: 202-319-5307

This private school, affiliated with the Roman Catholic Church, was founded in 1887. It has a 193-acre campus.

RATINGS
Admissions Selectivity Rating: 84   **Fire Safety Rating:** 85   **Green Rating:** 69

STUDENTS AND FACULTY
Enrollment: 3,083. **Student Body:** 56% female, 44% male, 94% out-of-state, 2% international (76 countries represented). African American 6%, Asian 3%, Caucasian 68%, Hispanic 6%. **Retention and Graduation:** 81% freshmen return for sophomore year. 41% grads go on to further study within 1 year. 23% grads pursue arts and sciences degrees. 2% grads pursue business degrees. 13% grads pursue law degrees. 6% grads pursue medical degrees. **Faculty:** Student/faculty ratio 9:1. 344 full-time faculty, 98% hold PhDs. 69% faculty teach undergrads.

ACADEMICS
Degrees: Bachelor's, doctoral, first professional, master's, post-master's certificate. **Academic Requirements:** English (including composition), foreign languages, humanities, mathematics, philosophy, social science, religion and religious education. **Classes:** Most classes have 10–19 students. Most lab/discussion sections have 10–19 students. **Majors with Highest Enrollment:** Architecture (BArch, BA/BS, MArch, MA/MS, PhD), engineering, political science and government. **Disciplines with Highest Percentage of Degrees Awarded:** Social sciences 15%, architecture 11%, visual and performing arts 11%, health professions and related sciences 7%, business/marketing 6%, engineering 6%, psychology 6%, communications/journalism 5%, education 5%, philosophy and religious studies 5%. **Special Study Options:** Accelerated program, cross registration, distance learning, double major, dual enrollment, English as a Second Language (ESL), honors program, independent study, internships, study abroad, teacher certification program.

FACILITIES
Housing: Coed dorms, men's dorms, women's dorms, apartments for single students, special housing for disabled students, residential college, thematic housing, honors housing. **Special Academic Facilities/Equipment:** Facilities available on the university campus include: An art department museum, rare book collection, the university archives, an on-campus nuclear reactor and vitreous state laboratory. Adjacent to the campus is the Roman Catholic Basilica of the National Shrine of the Immaculate Conception, the largest church in the Western hemisphere. Directly across the street from the university is the Pope John Paul II Cultural Center, a major Catholic museum. **Computers:** 2% of classrooms are wired, 20% of classrooms are wireless, 85% of public computers are PCs, 10% of public computers are Macs, 5% of public computers are UNIX, network access in dorm rooms, network access in dorm lounges, online registration, online administrative functions (other than registration), support for handheld computing, remote student-access to Web through college's connection.

CAMPUS LIFE
Activities: Choral groups, dance, drama/theater, jazz band, literary magazine, music ensembles, musical theater, opera, radio station, student government, student newspaper, student-run film society, symphony orchestra, yearbook. **Organizations:** 117 registered organizations, 16 honor societies, 5 religious organizations. 1 fraternity (1% men join), 1 sorority (1% women join). **Athletics (Intercollegiate):** *Men:* Baseball, basketball, cross-country, football, lacrosse, soccer, swimming, tennis, track/field (indoor), track/field (outdoor). *Women:* Basketball, cross-country, field hockey, lacrosse, soccer, softball, swimming, tennis, track/field (indoor), track/field (outdoor), volleyball. **Environmental Initiatives:** LEED-NC certification pending for new dormitory. Alternative energay purchasing at 25% of consumption. comprehesvie recycling and reuse of E-waste, haz mat, universal waste and general recycling on-campus.

ADMISSIONS
Freshman Academic Profile: 25% in top 10% of high school class, 53% in top 25% of high school class, 87% in top 50% of high school class. 49% from public

high schools. SAT Math middle 50% range 510–610. SAT Critical Reading middle 50% range 520–620. SAT Writing middle 50% range 520–610. ACT middle 50% range 22–26. TOEFL required of all international applicants, minimum paper TOEFL 560, minimum computer TOEFL 220. **Basis for Candidate Selection:** *Very important factors considered include:* Academic GPA, character/personal qualities, level of applicant's interest, recommendation(s), rigor of secondary school record, standardized test scores, volunteer work. *Important factors considered include:* Application essay, extracurricular activities, first generation, interview, talent/ability. *Other factors considered include:* Alumni/ae relation, class rank, racial/ethnic status, work experience. **Freshman Admission Requirements:** High school diploma is required, and GED is accepted. *Academic units recommended:* 4 English, 3 math, 3 science (1 science lab), 2 foreign language, 4 social studies, 1 fine art or humanities. **Freshman Admission Statistics:** 3,492 applied, 81% admitted, 30% enrolled. **Transfer Admission Requirements:** High school transcript, college transcript(s), essay or personal statement, standardized test score. Minimum college GPA of 2.8 required. Lowest grade transferable C. **General Admission Information:** Application fee $55. Regular application deadline 2/15. Regular notification 3/15. Non-fall registration accepted. Admission may be deferred for a maximum of 2 semesters. Credit and/or placement offered for CEEB Advanced Placement tests.

COSTS AND FINANCIAL AID
Annual tuition $26,200. Room & board $10,322. Required fees $1,240. Average book expense $1,000. **Required Forms and Deadlines:** FAFSA, Alumni and Parish Scholarship Applications if appropriate. Financial aid filing deadline 3/1. **Notification of Awards:** Applicants will be notified of awards on a rolling basis beginning on or about 4/1. **Types of Aid:** *Need-based scholarships/grants:* Pell, SEOG, state scholarships/grants, private scholarships, the school's own gift aid, Federal Nursing Scholarships. *Loans:* FFEL Subsidized Stafford, FFEL Unsubsidized Stafford, FFEL PLUS, Federal Perkins, Federal Nursing, college/university loans from institutional funds, commercial loans. **Student Employment:** Federal Work-Study Program available. Institutional employment available. Off-campus job opportunities are good. **Financial Aid Statistics:** 55% freshmen, 51% undergrads receive need-based scholarship or grant aid. 52% freshmen, 49% undergrads receive need-based self-help aid. 99% freshmen, 92% undergrads receive any aid.

CAZENOVIA COLLEGE

3 Sullivan Street, Cazenovia, NY 13035
Phone: 315-655-7208 **E-mail:** admission@cazenovia.edu
Fax: 315-655-4860 **Website:** www.cazenovia.edu
Financial Aid Phone: 315-655-7887

This private school was founded in 1824.

RATINGS
Admissions Selectivity Rating: 71   **Fire Safety Rating:** 99   **Green Rating:** 60*

STUDENTS AND FACULTY
Enrollment: 911. **Student Body:** 78% female, 22% male, 17% out-of-state. African American 5%, Asian 1%, Caucasian 75%, Hispanic 2%, Native American 1%. **Retention and Graduation:** 62% freshmen return for sophomore year. **Faculty:** Student/faculty ratio 11:1. 52 full-time faculty, 69% hold PhDs. 100% faculty teach undergrads.

ACADEMICS
Degrees: Associate, bachelor's, certificate. **Academic Requirements:** Arts/fine arts, computer literacy, English (including composition), humanities, mathematics, science (natural, behavioral, or social), communications, research methods. **Classes:** Most classes have 10–19 students. Most lab/discussion sections have fewer than 10 students. **Majors with Highest Enrollment:** Business, management, marketing, and related support services; design and visual communications; human services. **Disciplines with Highest Percentage of Degrees Awarded:** Business/marketing 40%, visual and performing arts 31%, public administration and social services 8%, liberal arts/general studies 6%, education 5%, psychology 5%. **Special Study Options:** Accelerated program, distance learning, double major, exchange student program (domestic), honors program, independent study, internships, study abroad, teacher certification program, weekend college.

FACILITIES
Housing: Coed dorms, women's dorms, single-room suites. **Special Academic Facilities/Equipment:** State-of-the-art design and art facility and gallery, 160-acre farm and equine center, historic theater. **Computers:** 100% of classrooms are wireless, 60% of public computers are PCs, 40% of public computers are

Macs, network access in dorm rooms, network access in dorm lounges, support for handheld computing, remote student-access to Web through college's connection.

CAMPUS LIFE

Activities: Choral groups, dance, drama/theater, jazz band, music ensembles, musical theater, radio station, student government, student newspaper, student-run film society, yearbook. **Organizations:** 2 honor societies. **Athletics (Intercollegiate):** *Men:* Baseball, basketball, cheerleading, crew/rowing, cross-country, equestrian sports, golf, horseback riding, lacrosse, soccer, swimming. *Women:* Basketball, cheerleading, crew/rowing, cross-country, equestrian sports, horseback riding, lacrosse, soccer, softball, swimming, volleyball.

ADMISSIONS

Freshman Academic Profile: 6% in top 10% of high school class, 24% in top 25% of high school class, 64% in top 50% of high school class. SAT Math middle 50% range 420–530. SAT Critical Reading middle 50% range 430–540. ACT middle 50% range 18–24. TOEFL required of all international applicants, minimum paper TOEFL 550, minimum computer TOEFL 213. **Basis for Candidate Selection:** *Very important factors considered include:* Rigor of secondary school record. *Important factors considered include:* Class rank, extracurricular activities, interview, recommendation(s). *Other factors considered include:* Application essay, character/personal qualities, standardized test scores, talent/ability, volunteer work, work experience. **Freshman Admission Requirements:** High school diploma is required, and GED is accepted. *Academic units recommended:* 4 English, 2 math, 2 science, 4 social studies. **Freshman Admission Statistics:** 1,502 applied, 80% admitted, 21% enrolled. **Transfer Admission Requirements:** High school transcript, college transcript(s). Minimum college GPA of 2.0 required. Lowest grade transferable C. **General Admission Information:** Application fee $30. Regular notification is rolling. Nonfall registration accepted. Admission may be deferred for a maximum of 1 year. Credit and/or placement offered for CEEB Advanced Placement tests.

COSTS AND FINANCIAL AID

Annual tuition $21,280. Room & board $8,972. Required fees $220. Average book expense $1,000. **Required Forms and Deadlines:** FAFSA, state aid form. Financial aid filing deadline 3/15. **Notification of Awards:** Applicants will be notified of awards on a rolling basis beginning on or about 11/1. **Types of Aid:** *Need-based scholarships/grants:* Pell, SEOG, state scholarships/grants, private scholarships, the school's own gift aid. *Loans:* Direct Subsidized Stafford, Direct Unsubsidized Stafford, Direct PLUS. **Student Employment:** Federal Work-Study Program available. **Financial Aid Statistics:** 83% undergrads receive need-based scholarship or grant aid. 78% undergrads receive need-based self-help aid.

CEDAR CREST COLLEGE

100 College Drive, Allentown, PA 18104-6196
Phone: 610-740-3780 **E-mail:** cccadmis@cedarcrest.edu **CEEB Code:** 2079
Fax: 610-606-4647 **Website:** www.cedarcrest.edu **ACT Code:** 3536
Financial Aid Phone: 610-740-3785

This private school, affiliated with the United Church of Christ, was founded in 1867. It has an 84-acre campus.

RATINGS

Admissions Selectivity Rating: 79   **Fire Safety Rating:** 60*   **Green Rating:** 60*

STUDENTS AND FACULTY

Enrollment: 1,523. **Student Body:** 99% female, 1% male, 18% out-of-state, 2% international (18 countries represented). African American 5%, Asian 2%, Caucasian 83%, Hispanic 5%. **Retention and Graduation:** 83% freshmen return for sophomore year. 54% freshmen graduate within 4 years. 40% grads go on to further study within 1 year. 14% grads pursue arts and sciences degrees. 1% grads pursue business degrees. 1% grads pursue law degrees. 2% grads pursue medical degrees. **Faculty:** Student/faculty ratio 11:1. 69 full-time faculty, 75% hold PhDs. 100% faculty teach undergrads.

ACADEMICS

Degrees: Associate, bachelor's, certificate, post-bachelor's certificate. **Academic Requirements:** Arts/fine arts, English (including composition), mathematics, sciences (biological or physical), philosophy, foreign languages, history, social science. **Classes:** Most classes have 10–19 students. Most lab/discussion sections have 10–19 students. **Disciplines with Highest Percentage of Degrees Awarded:** Psychology 20%, health professions and related sciences 19%, business/marketing 15%, computer and information sciences 6%, engineering 5%, social sciences 5%, biological/life sciences 5%. **Special Study**

Options: Accelerated program, cross-registration, distance learning, double major, dual enrollment, English as a second language (ESL), honors program, independent study, internships, student-designed major, study abroad, teacher certification program, weekend college.

FACILITIES

Housing: Women's dorms, special housing for disabled students. **Special Academic Facilities/Equipment:** Art gallery, theaters, arboretum, genetic engineering labs, nutrition computer lab, radio station, sculpture garden, multimedia lecture hall, alumnae museum. **Computers:** 92% of public computers are PCs, 8% of public computers are Macs, network access in dorm rooms, network access in dorm lounges, online administrative functions (other than registration), remote student-access to Web through college's connection.

CAMPUS LIFE

Activities: Choral groups, dance, drama/theater, literary magazine, music ensembles, musical theater, radio station, student government, student newspaper, television station, yearbook. **Organizations:** 46 registered organizations, 11 honor societies, 3 religious organizations. **Women:** Basketball, cross-country, field hockey, lacrosse, soccer, softball, tennis, volleyball.

ADMISSIONS

Freshman Academic Profile: 22% in top 10% of high school class, 54% in top 25% of high school class, 88% in top 50% of high school class. 95% from public high schools. SAT Math middle 50% range 530–650. SAT Critical Reading middle 50% range 540–660. SAT Writing middle 50% range 520–640. ACT middle 50% range 23–29. TOEFL required of all international applicants, minimum paper TOEFL 500. **Basis for Candidate Selection:** *Very important factors considered include:* Class rank, rigor of secondary school record, standardized test scores. *Important factors considered include:* Application essay, character/personal qualities, extracurricular activities, interview, recommendation(s), talent/ability. *Other factors considered include:* Alumni/ae relation, volunteer work, work experience. **Freshman Admission Requirements:** High school diploma is required, and GED is accepted. *Academic units required:* 4 English, 3 math, 2 science (2 science labs), 2 foreign language, 3 social studies. *Academic units recommended:* 3 academic electives. **Freshman Admission Statistics:** 1,083 applied, 76% admitted, 21% enrolled. **Transfer Admission Requirements:** High school transcript, college transcript(s). Minimum college GPA of 2.0 required. Lowest grade transferable C. **General Admission Information:** Application fee $30. Regular notification is rolling. Nonfall registration accepted. Admission may be deferred for a maximum of 2 years. Common Application accepted. Credit and/or placement offered for CEEB Advanced Placement tests.

COSTS AND FINANCIAL AID

Annual tuition $26,668. Room and board $9,009. Average book expense $1,000. **Required Forms and Deadlines:** FAFSA, institution's own financial aid form. **Notification of Awards:** Applicants will be notified of awards on a rolling basis beginning on or about 11/1. **Types of Aid:** *Need-based scholarships/grants:* Pell, SEOG, state scholarships/grants, private scholarships, the school's own gift aid. *Loans:* FFEL Subsidized Stafford, FFEL Unsubsidized Stafford, FFEL PLUS, Federal Perkins, Federal Nursing, college/university loans from institutional funds. **Student Employment:** Federal Work-Study Program available. Institutional employment available. Off-campus job opportunities are excellent. **Financial Aid Statistics:** 89% freshmen, 84% undergrads receive need-based scholarship or grant aid. 77% freshmen, 76% undergrads receive need-based self-help aid. Highest amount earned per year from on-campus jobs $1,100.

CEDARVILLE UNIVERSITY

251 North Main Street, Cedarville, OH 45314
Phone: 937-766-7700 **E-mail:** admissions@cedarville.edu
Fax: 937-766-7575 **Website:** www.cedarville.edu **ACT Code:** 3245
Financial Aid Phone: 937-766-7866

This private school, affiliated with the Baptist Church, was founded in 1887. It has a 400-acre campus.

RATINGS

Admissions Selectivity Rating: 87   **Fire Safety Rating:** 83   **Green Rating:** 60*

STUDENTS AND FACULTY

Enrollment: 2,977. **Student Body:** 55% female, 45% male, 63% out-of-state. African American 1%, Asian 1%, Caucasian 94%, Hispanic 2%. **Retention and Graduation:** 83% freshmen return for sophomore year. 57% freshmen graduate within 4 years. 10% grads go on to further study within 1 year. 2% grads pursue arts and sciences degrees. 2% grads pursue business degrees.

Faculty: Student/faculty ratio 11:1. 208 full-time faculty, 61% hold PhDs. 96% faculty teach undergrads.

ACADEMICS

Degrees: Bachelor's, certificate, master's. **Academic Requirements:** Arts/fine arts, English (including composition), history, humanities, mathematics, sciences (biological or physical), social science, biblical, physical education. **Classes:** Most classes have 10–19 students. Most lab/discussion sections have 10–19 students. **Majors with Highest Enrollment:** Early childhood education and teaching, mechanical engineering, nursing/registered nurse training (RN, ASN, BSN, MSN). **Disciplines with Highest Percentage of Degrees Awarded:** Education 19%, business/marketing 13%, theology and religious vocations 10%, health professions and related sciences 10%, engineering 8%. **Special Study Options:** Accelerated program, distance learning, double major, dual enrollment, honors program, independent study, internships, student-designed major, study abroad, teacher certification program.

FACILITIES

Housing: Men's dorms, women's dorms, apartments for married students. **Computers:** 20% of classrooms are wired, 100% of classrooms are wireless, 99% of public computers are PCs, 1% of public computers are Macs, network access in dorm rooms, network access in dorm lounges, online registration, online administrative functions (other than registration), support for handheld computing, remote student-access to Web through college's connection.

CAMPUS LIFE

Activities: Choral groups, concert band, drama/theater, jazz band, music ensembles, musical theater, pep band, radio station, student government, student newspaper, symphony orchestra, yearbook. **Organizations:** 87 registered organizations, 4 honor societies. **Athletics (Intercollegiate):** *Men:* Baseball, basketball, cheerleading, cross-country, golf, soccer, tennis, track/field (indoor), track/field (outdoor). *Women:* Basketball, cheerleading, cross-country, soccer, softball, tennis, track/field (indoor), track/field (outdoor), volleyball.

ADMISSIONS

Freshman Academic Profile: 34% in top 10% of high school class, 67% in top 25% of high school class, 90% in top 50% of high school class. 53% from public high schools. SAT Math middle 50% range 520–640. SAT Critical Reading middle 50% range 540–650. SAT Writing middle 50% range 520–640. ACT middle 50% range 23–28. TOEFL required of all international applicants, minimum paper TOEFL 550, minimum computer TOEFL 213. **Basis for Candidate Selection:** *Very important factors considered include:* Academic GPA, application essay, character/personal qualities, religious affiliation/commitment, rigor of secondary school record, standardized test scores. *Important factors considered include:* Racial/ethnic status, recommendation(s). *Other factors considered include:* Alumni/ae relation, class rank, extracurricular activities, interview, talent/ability, volunteer work. **Freshman Admission Requirements:** High school diploma is required, and GED is accepted. *Academic units recommended:* 4 English, 4 math, 3 science (3 science labs), 3 foreign language, 3 social studies. **Freshman Admission Statistics:** 2,151 applied, 81% admitted, 41% enrolled. **Transfer Admission Requirements:** High school transcript, college transcript(s), essay or personal statement, statement of good standing from prior institution(s). Minimum college GPA of 3.0 required. Lowest grade transferable C-. **General Admission Information:** Application fee $30. Regular notification is rolling. Nonfall registration accepted. Admission may be deferred for a maximum of 1 year. Credit and/or placement offered for CEEB Advanced Placement tests.

COSTS AND FINANCIAL AID

Annual tuition $19,680. Room and board $5,010. Average book expense $900. **Required Forms and Deadlines:** FAFSA. Financial aid filing deadline 3/1. **Notification of Awards:** Applicants will be notified of awards on a rolling basis beginning on or about 3/1. *Types of Aid: Need-based scholarships/grants:* Pell, SEOG, state scholarships/grants, private scholarships, the school's own gift aid. *Loans:* FFEL Subsidized Stafford, FFEL Unsubsidized Stafford, FFEL PLUS, Federal Perkins, Federal Nursing, state loans, college/university loans from institutional funds. **Financial Aid Statistics:** 28% freshmen, 33% undergrads receive need-based scholarship or grant aid. 58% freshmen, 54% undergrads receive need-based self-help aid. 47 freshmen, 167 undergrads receive athletic scholarships. 66% freshmen, 51% undergrads receive any aid. Highest amount earned per year from on-campus jobs $2,500.

CENTENARY COLLEGE

400 Jefferson Street, Hackettstown, NJ 07840
Phone: 800-236-8679 **E-mail:** admissions@centenarycollege.edu **CEEB Code:** 2080
Fax: 908-852-3454 **Website:** www.centenarycollege.edu **ACT Code:** 2544
Financial Aid Phone: 908-852-1400

This private school, affiliated with the Methodist Church, was founded in 1867. It has a 42-acre campus.

RATINGS

Admissions Selectivity Rating: 67   **Fire Safety Rating:** 60*   **Green Rating:** 60*

STUDENTS AND FACULTY

Enrollment: 1,887. **Student Body:** 64% female, 36% male, 12% out-of-state. **Retention and Graduation:** 72% freshmen return for sophomore year. 24% grads go on to further study within 1 year. 16% grads pursue business degrees. **Faculty:** Student/faculty ratio 15:1. 63 full-time faculty, 71% hold PhDs. 100% faculty teach undergrads.

ACADEMICS

Degrees: Associate, bachelor's, master's, post-bachelor's certificate. **Academic Requirements:** Arts/fine arts, English (including composition), history, humanities, mathematics, sciences (biological or physical), social science, liberal arts core. **Classes:** Most classes have 10–19 students. Most lab/discussion sections have 10–19 students. **Majors with Highest Enrollment:** Biology/biological sciences, business administration/management, elementary education and teaching. **Disciplines with Highest Percentage of Degrees Awarded:** Business/marketing 45%, social sciences 16%, psychology 15%, English 10%, agriculture 6%. **Special Study Options:** Accelerated program, double major, English as a second language (ESL), honors program, independent study, internships, liberal arts/career combination, student-designed major, study abroad, teacher certification program.

FACILITIES

Housing: Coed dorms, women's dorms. **Special Academic Facilities/Equipment:** Art gallery, radio station (WNTI 91.9 FM), Equity-status theater, equestrian center. **Computers:** 95% of public computers are PCs, 5% of public computers are Macs, network access in dorm rooms, network access in dorm lounges, remote student-access to Web through college's connection, tuition includes personal computer. Undergraduates are required to own a computer.

CAMPUS LIFE

Activities: Choral groups, dance, drama/theater, literary magazine, radio station, student government, student newspaper, television station, yearbook. **Organizations:** 27 registered organizations, 2 honor societies, 2 fraternities (15% men join), 3 sororities (12% women join). **Athletics (Intercollegiate):** *Men:* Baseball, basketball, cross-country, golf, lacrosse, soccer, wrestling. *Women:* Basketball, cross-country, golf, lacrosse, soccer, softball, volleyball.

ADMISSIONS

Freshman Academic Profile: 3% in top 10% of high school class, 18% in top 25% of high school class, 55% in top 50% of high school class. 85% from public high schools. SAT Math middle 50% range 400–500. SAT Critical Reading middle 50% range 410–510. ACT middle 50% range 17–21. TOEFL required of all international applicants, minimum paper TOEFL 450, minimum computer TOEFL 200. **Basis for Candidate Selection:** *Very important factors considered include:* Rigor of secondary school record, standardized test scores. *Important factors considered include:* Alumni/ae relation, application essay, character/personal qualities, extracurricular activities, talent/ability, volunteer work. *Other factors considered include:* Class rank, interview, recommendation(s), work experience. **Freshman Admission Requirements:** High school diploma is required, and GED is accepted. *Academic units required:* 4 English, 3 math, 2 science (2 science labs), 2 history, 3 academic electives. *Academic units recommended:* 4 math, 4 science, 2 foreign language, 4 social studies, 3 history. **Freshman Admission Statistics:** 693 applied, 75% admitted, 52% enrolled. **Transfer Admission Requirements:** College transcript(s). Minimum college GPA of 1.8 required. Lowest grade transferable C-. **General Admission Information:** Application fee $30. Regular notification is rolling. Nonfall registration accepted. Admission may be deferred for a maximum of 1 semester. Common Application accepted. Credit offered for CEEB Advanced Placement tests.

COSTS AND FINANCIAL AID

Annual tuition $15,700. Room & board $6,850. Required fees $1,100. Average book expense $666. **Required Forms and Deadlines:** FAFSA, institution's own financial aid form. Financial aid filing deadline 6/1. **Notification of Awards:** Applicants will be notified of awards on a rolling basis beginning on or about 3/1. *Types of Aid: Need-based scholarships/grants:* Pell, SEOG, state scholarships/grants, the school's own gift aid. *Loans:* FFEL Subsidized Stafford,

FFEL Unsubsidized Stafford, FFEL PLUS, Federal Perkins. **Financial Aid Statistics:** Highest amount earned per year from on-campus jobs $645.

CENTENARY COLLEGE OF LOUISIANA

PO Box 41188, 2911 Centenary Boulevard, Shreveport, LA 71134-1188
Phone: 318-869-5131 **E-mail:** admissions@centenary.edu **CEEB Code:** 6082
Fax: 318-869-5005 **Website:** www.centenary.edu **ACT Code:** 1576
Financial Aid Phone: 318-869-5137

This private school, affiliated with the Methodist Church, was founded in 1825. It has a 68-acre campus.

RATINGS
Admissions Selectivity Rating: 83   **Fire Safety Rating:** 80   **Green Rating:** 60*

STUDENTS AND FACULTY
Enrollment: 891. **Student Body:** 59% female, 41% male, 43% out-of-state, 2% international (12 countries represented). African American 8%, Asian 2%, Caucasian 82%, Hispanic 4%. **Retention and Graduation:** 76% freshmen return for sophomore year. 43% freshmen graduate within 4 years. 50% grads go on to further study within 1 year. **Faculty:** Student/faculty ratio 10:1. 73 full-time faculty, 95% hold PhDs. 100% faculty teach undergrads.

ACADEMICS
Degrees: Bachelor's, master's. **Academic Requirements:** Arts/fine arts, English (including composition), humanities, mathematics, sciences (biological or physical), social science, foreign language for all BA students. **Classes:** Most classes have 10–19 students. **Majors with Highest Enrollment:** Biology/biological sciences; business administration/management; communications, journalism, and related fields. **Disciplines with Highest Percentage of Degrees Awarded:** Business/marketing 23%, biological/life sciences 18%, communications/journalism 12%, social sciences 10%, psychology 6%, visual and performing arts 6%. **Special Study Options:** Cross-registration, double major, dual enrollment, exchange student program (domestic), honors program, independent study, internships, liberal arts/career combination, student-designed major, study abroad, teacher certification program, weekend college. 3–2 dual degree (liberal arts/engineering) program in cooperation with Case Western Reserve University, Columbia University, Texas A&M University, University of Southern California, and Washington University in St. Louis; mathematics/computer science double degree program with Southern Methodist University; semester at Oak Ridge National Laboratory; semester in Washington, DC; British studies at Oxford summer program.

FACILITIES
Housing: Coed dorms, women's dorms, fraternity/sorority housing. **Special Academic Facilities/Equipment:** Art museum, art center, art studios, theater, performance and practice organs, piano lab, language lab, School of Music recording studio, Science Hall multimedia auditorium. **Computers:** 97% of public computers are PCs, 3% of public computers are Macs, network access in dorm rooms, network access in dorm lounges, online registration, online administrative functions (other than registration), remote student-access to Web through college's connection.

CAMPUS LIFE
Activities: Choral groups, concert band, dance, drama/theater, jazz band, literary magazine, music ensembles, musical theater, pep band, radio station, student government, student newspaper, student-run film society, yearbook. **Organizations:** 58 registered organizations, 15 honor societies, 8 religious organizations. 5 fraternities, 2 sororities. **Athletics (Intercollegiate):** *Men:* Baseball, basketball, cross-country, golf, soccer, swimming, tennis. *Women:* Basketball, cross-country, golf, gymnastics, soccer, softball, swimming, tennis, volleyball.

ADMISSIONS
Freshman Academic Profile: 37% in top 10% of high school class, 67% in top 25% of high school class, 91% in top 50% of high school class. 80% from public high schools. SAT Math middle 50% range 510–620. SAT Critical Reading middle 50% range 500–620. ACT middle 50% range 23–28. TOEFL required of all international applicants, minimum paper TOEFL 550, minimum computer TOEFL 220. **Basis for Candidate Selection:** *Very important factors considered include:* Academic GPA, rigor of secondary school record.

Important factors considered include: Alumni/ae relation, character/personal qualities, extracurricular activities, interview, level of applicant's interest, standardized test scores, talent/ability. *Other factors considered include:* Application essay, class rank, geographical residence, racial/ethnic status, recommendation(s), religious affiliation/commitment, work experience. **Freshman Admission Requirements:** High school diploma is required, and GED is accepted. *Academic units recommended:* 4 English, 3 math, 3 science (2 science labs), 2 foreign language, 3 social studies. **Freshman Admission Statistics:** 1,069 applied, 65% admitted, 34% enrolled. **Transfer Admission Requirements:** College transcript(s). Minimum college GPA of 2.0 required. Lowest grade transferable C. **General Admission Information:** Application fee $30. Early decision application deadline 12/1. Regular application deadline 8/1. Regular notification 11/15. Nonfall registration accepted. Admission may be deferred for a maximum of 1 year. Credit and/or placement offered for CEEB Advanced Placement tests.

COSTS AND FINANCIAL AID
Annual tuition $19,850. Room and board $7,050. Required fees $1,100. Average book expense $1,000. **Required Forms and Deadlines:** FAFSA, institution's own financial aid form. Financial aid filing deadline 2/15. **Notification of Awards:** Applicants will be notified of awards on or about 3/15. **Types of Aid:** *Need-based scholarships/grants:* Pell, SEOG, state scholarships/grants, private scholarships, the school's own gift aid. *Loans:* FFEL Subsidized Stafford, FFEL Unsubsidized Stafford, FFEL PLUS, Federal Perkins. **Student Employment:** Federal Work-Study Program available. Institutional employment available. Off-campus job opportunities are good. **Financial Aid Statistics:** 60% freshmen, 56% undergrads receive need-based scholarship or grant aid. 30% freshmen, 34% undergrads receive need-based self-help aid. 35 freshmen, 113 undergrads receive athletic scholarships. 98% freshmen, 95% undergrads receive any aid. Highest amount earned per year from on-campus jobs $1,500.

CENTRAL BAPTIST COLLEGE

1501 College Avenue, Conway, AR 72034
Phone: 501-329-6872 **E-mail:** ccalhoun@cbc.edu, lwatson@cbc.edu
Fax: 501-329-2941 **Website:** www.cbc.edu **ACT Code:** 0119

This private school, affiliated with the Baptist Church, was founded in 1952. It has a 13-acre campus.

RATINGS
Admissions Selectivity Rating: 67   **Fire Safety Rating:** 60*   **Green Rating:** 60*

STUDENTS AND FACULTY
Enrollment: 394. **Student Body:** 46% female, 54% male, 11% out-of-state. African American 9%, Asian 1%, Caucasian 92%, Hispanic 2%, Native American 1%. **Faculty:** Student/faculty ratio 17:1. 16 full-time faculty, 44% hold PhDs. 100% faculty teach undergrads.

ACADEMICS
Degrees: Associate, bachelor's. **Academic Requirements:** Arts/fine arts, English (including composition), history, humanities, mathematics, sciences (biological or physical), social science, religion (Bible). **Disciplines with Highest Percentage of Degrees Awarded:** Business/marketing 45%, psychology 23%.

FACILITIES
Housing: Men's dorms, women's dorms. **Computers:** Remote student-access to Web through college's connection.

CAMPUS LIFE
Activities: Choral groups, music ensembles, musical theater, student government, yearbook. **Athletics (Intercollegiate):** *Men:* Baseball, basketball. *Women:* Basketball, volleyball.

ADMISSIONS
Freshman Academic Profile: 19% in top 10% of high school class, 40% in top 25% of high school class, 70% in top 50% of high school class. TOEFL required of all international applicants, minimum paper TOEFL 500. **Basis for Candidate Selection:** *Very important factors considered include:* Character/personal qualities, class rank, recommendation(s), rigor of secondary school record, standardized test scores. *Important factors considered include:* Religious affiliation/commitment. *Other factors considered include:* Extracurricular activities, talent/ability. **Freshman Admission Requirements:** High school diploma is required, and GED is accepted. **Freshman Admission Statistics:** 164 applied, 84% admitted, 75% enrolled. **Transfer Admission Requirements:** College transcript(s), essay or personal statement, standardized test score. Minimum college GPA of 2.0 required. Lowest grade transferable C.

General Admission Information: Application fee $25. Regular application deadline 8/15. Nonfall registration accepted. Admission may be deferred for a maximum of 1 year. Common Application not accepted.

COSTS AND FINANCIAL AID
Average book expense $700. **Required Forms and Deadlines:** FAFSA. **Types of Aid:** *Need-based scholarships/grants:* Pell, SEOG, state scholarships/grants, private scholarships. *Loans:* FFEL Subsidized Stafford, FFEL Unsubsidized Stafford, FFEL PLUS. **Student Employment:** Federal Work-Study Program available. Off-campus job opportunities are good.

CENTRAL CHRISTIAN COLLEGE OF THE BIBLE

Admissions Departmen, 911 East Urbandale Drive, Moberly, MO 65270
Phone: 660-263-3900 **E-mail:** iwant2be@cccb.edu
Fax: 660-263-3936 **Website:** www.cccb.edu

This private school, affiliated with the Christian (Nondenominational) Church, was founded in 1957. It has a 40-acre campus.

RATINGS
Admissions Selectivity Rating: 60*   Fire Safety Rating: 60*   Green Rating: 60*

STUDENTS AND FACULTY
Faculty: 100% faculty teach undergrads.

ACADEMICS
Degrees: Associate, bachelor's. **Academic Requirements:** English (including composition), foreign languages, history, philosophy, sciences (biological or physical), social science, biblical studies. **Majors with Highest Enrollment:** Bible/biblical studies, pastoral studies/counseling, religion/religious studies. **Special Study Options:** Dual enrollment, internships.

FACILITIES
Housing: Men's dorms, women's dorms, apartments for single students. **Computers:** 99% of public computers are PCs, 1% of public computers are Macs, network access in dorm rooms, network access in dorm lounges.

CAMPUS LIFE
Activities: Choral groups, music ensembles, musical theater. **Organizations:** 1 religious organization. **Athletics (Intercollegiate):** *Men:* Basketball, soccer. *Women:* Basketball, volleyball.

ADMISSIONS
Freshman Academic Profile: TOEFL required of all international applicants, minimum paper TOEFL 870, minimum computer TOEFL 260. **Transfer Admission Requirements:** High school transcript, college transcript(s), standardized test score. **General Admission Information:** Nonfall registration not accepted. Common Application not accepted.

COSTS AND FINANCIAL AID
Room & board $1,930. Required fees $305. Average book expense $300. **Student Employment:** Federal Work-Study Program available. Institutional employment available. Off-campus job opportunities are excellent. **Financial Aid Phone:** 660-263-3900.

CENTRAL COLLEGE

812 University Street, Pella, IA 50219-1999
Phone: 877-462-3687 **E-mail:** admission@central.edu **CEEB Code:** 6087
Fax: 641-628-5316 **Website:** www.central.edu **ACT Code:** 1284

This private school, affiliated with the Reformed Church, was founded in 1853. It has a 133-acre campus.

RATINGS
Admissions Selectivity Rating: 79   Fire Safety Rating: 60*   Green Rating: 60*

STUDENTS AND FACULTY
Enrollment: 1,606. **Student Body:** 55% female, 45% male, 17% out-of-state. **Retention and Graduation:** 79% freshmen return for sophomore year. 63% freshmen graduate within 4 years. 15% grads go on to further study within 1 year. 9% grads pursue arts and sciences degrees. 1% grads pursue business degrees. 1% grads pursue law degrees. 4% grads pursue medical degrees.

Faculty: Student/faculty ratio 13:1. 94 full-time faculty, 97% hold PhDs. 100% faculty teach undergrads.

ACADEMICS
Degrees: Bachelor's. **Academic Requirements:** Arts/fine arts, English (including composition), foreign languages, history, humanities, mathematics, philosophy, sciences (biological or physical), social science, religion, non-Western culture. **Classes:** Most classes have 10–19 students. Most lab/discussion sections have 10–19 students. **Majors with Highest Enrollment:** Business administration/management, education, kinesiology and exercise science. **Disciplines with Highest Percentage of Degrees Awarded:** Social sciences 12%, education 11%, business/marketing 11%, foreign languages and literature 8%, communications/journalism 8%, parks and recreation 8%, biological/life sciences 6%, psychology 6%, visual and performing arts 6%. **Special Study Options:** Double major, English as a second language (ESL), honors program, independent study, internships, liberal arts/career combination, student-designed major, study abroad, teacher certification program. Off-campus study available in Washington, DC, Chicago Metro Program, study abroad in 9 countries, Exploring Student Program encourages students to go through 2 years of multidisciplinary study before selecting a major.

FACILITIES
Housing: Coed dorms, men's dorms, women's dorms, apartments for married students, apartments for single students, special housing for disabled students, special housing for international students, fraternity/sorority housing. **Special Academic Facilities/Equipment:** Art gallery, center for communication and theater, music center, language lab, glass-blowing studio. **Computers:** 25% of classrooms are wireless, 95% of public computers are PCs, 5% of public computers are Macs, network access in dorm rooms, network access in dorm lounges, online registration, online administrative functions (other than registration), remote student-access to Web through college's connection.

CAMPUS LIFE
Activities: Choral groups, concert band, drama/theater, jazz band, literary magazine, music ensembles, musical theater, radio station, student government, student newspaper, symphony orchestra, yearbook. **Organizations:** 50 registered organizations, 4 religious organizations. 4 fraternities (15% men join), 2 sororities (7% women join). **Athletics (Intercollegiate):** *Men:* Baseball, basketball, football, golf, soccer, tennis, track/field (indoor), track/field (outdoor), wrestling. *Women:* Basketball, cross-country, golf, softball, tennis, track/field (indoor), track/field (outdoor), volleyball.

ADMISSIONS
Freshman Academic Profile: 25% in top 10% of high school class, 54% in top 25% of high school class, 85% in top 50% of high school class. 98% from public high schools. SAT Math middle 50% range 410–610. SAT Critical Reading middle 50% range 440–600. ACT middle 50% range 21–25. TOEFL required of all international applicants, minimum paper TOEFL 530, minimum computer TOEFL 197. **Basis for Candidate Selection:** *Very important factors considered include:* Academic GPA, rigor of secondary school record, standardized test scores. *Important factors considered include:* Class rank. *Other factors considered include:* Alumni/ae relation, application essay, character/personal qualities, extracurricular activities, first generation, interview, recommendation(s), talent/ability, volunteer work, work experience. **Freshman Admission Requirements:** High school diploma is required, and GED is accepted. *Academic units required:* 4 English, 2 math, 2 science (2 science labs), 3 social studies, 2 history. *Academic units recommended:* 3 math, 3 science, 2 foreign language. **Freshman Admission Statistics:** 1,797 applied, 80% admitted, 29% enrolled. **Transfer Admission Requirements:** High school transcript, college transcript(s). Minimum college GPA of 2.5 required. Lowest grade transferable C-. **General Admission Information:** Application fee $25. Regular notification is rolling. Nonfall registration accepted. Admission may be deferred for a maximum of 1 year. Credit and/or placement offered for CEEB Advanced Placement tests.

COSTS AND FINANCIAL AID
Annual tuition $20,972. Room & board $7,224. Required fees $250. Average book expense $880. **Required Forms and Deadlines:** FAFSA. Financial aid filing deadline 3/15. **Notification of Awards:** Applicants will be notified of awards on a rolling basis beginning on or about 3/15. **Types of Aid:** *Need-based scholarships/grants:* Pell, SEOG, state scholarships/grants, private scholarships, the school's own gift aid. *Loans:* Direct Subsidized Stafford, Direct Unsubsidized Stafford, Direct PLUS, Federal Perkins, college/university loans from institutional funds, private alternative loans. **Financial Aid Statistics:** 83% freshmen, 78% undergrads receive need-based scholarship or grant aid. 71% freshmen, 68% undergrads receive need-based self-help aid. 100% freshmen, 99% undergrads receive any aid. Highest amount earned per year from on-campus jobs $2,600. **Financial Aid Phone:** 641-628-5336.

CENTRAL CONNECTICUT STATE UNIVERSITY

1615 Stanley Street, New Britain, CT 06050
Phone: 860-832-2278 **E-mail:** admissions@ccsu.edu **CEEB Code:** 3898
Fax: 862-832-2295 **Website:** www.ccsu.edu **ACT Code:** 0596
Financial Aid Phone: 860-832-2200

This public school was founded in 1849. It has a 294-acre campus.

RATINGS
Admissions Selectivity Rating: 70   **Fire Safety Rating:** 81   **Green Rating:** 60*

STUDENTS AND FACULTY
Enrollment: 9,114. **Student Body:** 50% female, 50% male, 5% out-of-state, 1% international (64 countries represented). African American 8%, Asian 3%, Caucasian 74%, Hispanic 6%. **Retention and Graduation:** 76% freshmen return for sophomore year. 11% freshmen graduate within 4 years. 28% grads go on to further study within 1 year. 21% grads pursue arts and sciences degrees. 6% grads pursue business degrees. 1% grads pursue law degrees. **Faculty:** Student/faculty ratio 19:1. 417 full-time faculty, 77% hold PhDs. 100% faculty teach undergrads.

ACADEMICS
Degrees: Bachelor's, certificate, doctoral, master's, post-bachelor's certificate, post-master's certificate. **Academic Requirements:** Arts/fine arts, computer literacy, English (including composition), foreign languages, history, humanities, mathematics, philosophy, sciences (biological or physical), social science. **Classes:** Most classes have 20–29 students. Most lab/discussion sections have fewer than 10 students. **Majors with Highest Enrollment:** Accounting, marketing/marketing management, psychology. **Disciplines with Highest Percentage of Degrees Awarded:** Business/marketing 26%, social sciences 12%, education 11%, psychology 9%, engineering technologies 6%. **Special Study Options:** Cooperative education program, cross-registration, distance learning, double major, dual enrollment, English as a second language (ESL), exchange student program (domestic), honors program, independent study, internships, student-designed major, study abroad, teacher certification program. Undergrads may take grad-level classes; co-op programs available in the arts, business, computer science, education, humanities, natural science, social/behavioral science, technologies.

FACILITIES
Housing: Coed dorms, women's dorms. **Special Academic Facilities/Equipment:** Art gallery, language lab, Childhood Center, Planetarium and Space Science Center, Center for Economic Education, TV studio. **Computers:** 25% of classrooms are wired, 100% of classrooms are wireless, 90% of public computers are PCs, 10% of public computers are Macs, network access in dorm rooms, network access in dorm lounges, online registration, online administrative functions (other than registration), remote student-access to Web through college's connection.

CAMPUS LIFE
Activities: Choral groups, concert band, dance, drama/theater, jazz band, literary magazine, music ensembles, musical theater, radio station, student government, student newspaper, student-run film society, television station, yearbook. **Organizations:** 101 registered organizations, 18 honor societies, 5 religious organizations. 1 sorority (1% women join). **Athletics (Intercollegiate):** *Men:* Baseball, basketball, cross-country, football, golf, soccer, track/field (outdoor). *Women:* Basketball, cross-country, diving, golf, lacrosse, soccer, softball, swimming, track/field (outdoor), volleyball.

ADMISSIONS
Freshman Academic Profile: 10% in top 10% of high school class, 26% in top 25% of high school class, 50% in top 50% of high school class. 93% from public high schools. SAT Math middle 50% range 460–560. SAT Critical Reading middle 50% range 460–540. SAT Writing middle 50% range 460–540. TOEFL required of all international applicants, minimum paper TOEFL 500. **Basis for Candidate Selection:** *Very important factors considered include:* Rigor of secondary school record. *Important factors considered include:* Class rank, standardized test scores. *Other factors considered include:* Application essay, extracurricular activities, interview, racial/ethnic status, recommendation(s), state residency, talent/ability. **Freshman Admission Requirements:** High school diploma is required, and GED is accepted. *Academic units required:* 4 English, 3 math, 2 science (1 science lab), 2 social studies, 1 history. *Academic units recommended:* 1 math, 3 foreign language. **Freshman Admission Statistics:** 5,313 applied, 60% admitted, 41% enrolled. **Transfer Admission Requirements:** High school transcript, college transcript(s), statement of good standing from prior institution(s). Minimum college GPA of 2.0 required. Lowest grade transferable C. **General Admission Information:** Application fee $50. Regular application deadline 6/1. Regular notification is rolling. Nonfall

registration accepted. Admission may be deferred. Credit offered for CEEB Advanced Placement tests.

COSTS AND FINANCIAL AID
Annual in-state tuition $3,346. Annual out-of-state tuition $10,831. Room and board $8,350. Required fees $3,388. Average book expense $1,010. **Required Forms and Deadlines:** FAFSA. Financial aid filing deadline 9/15. **Notification of Awards:** Applicants will be notified of awards on or about 3/15. **Types of Aid:** *Need-based scholarships/grants:* Pell, SEOG, state scholarships/grants, the school's own gift aid. *Loans:* Direct Subsidized Stafford, Direct Unsubsidized Stafford, Direct PLUS, FFEL PLUS, Federal Perkins. **Student Employment:** Federal Work-Study Program available. Institutional employment available. Off-campus job opportunities are good. **Financial Aid Statistics:** 34% freshmen, 36% undergrads receive need-based scholarship or grant aid. 39% freshmen, 44% undergrads receive need-based self-help aid. 32 freshmen, 166 undergrads receive athletic scholarships. 50% freshmen, 55% undergrads receive any aid. Highest amount earned per year from on-campus jobs $2,800.

See page 1110.

CENTRAL METHODIST UNIVERSITY

411 CMC Square, Fayette, MO 65248
Phone: 660-248-6251 **E-mail:** admissions@cmc.edu **CEEB Code:** 6089
Fax: 660-248-1872 **Website:** www.cmc.edu **ACT Code:** 2270
Financial Aid Phone: 660-248-6245

This private school, affiliated with the Methodist Church, was founded in 1854. It has a 90-acre campus.

RATINGS
Admissions Selectivity Rating: 72   **Fire Safety Rating:** 60*   **Green Rating:** 60*

STUDENTS AND FACULTY
Enrollment: 829. **Student Body:** 52% female, 48% male, 10% out-of-state, 2% international (15 countries represented). African American 7%, Caucasian 85%, Hispanic 1%. **Retention and Graduation:** 57% freshmen return for sophomore year. 30% freshmen graduate within 4 years. 15% grads go on to further study within 1 year. 15% grads pursue arts and sciences degrees. 5% grads pursue business degrees. 5% grads pursue law degrees. 4% grads pursue medical degrees. **Faculty:** Student/faculty ratio 14:1. 54 full-time faculty, 65% hold PhDs. 100% faculty teach undergrads.

ACADEMICS
Degrees: Associate, bachelor's, master's. **Academic Requirements:** Computer literacy, English (including composition), history, humanities, mathematics, sciences (biological or physical), social science, human character formation, development and cultural diversity. **Classes:** Most classes have fewer than 10 students. **Majors with Highest Enrollment:** Business administration/management, elementary education and teaching. **Disciplines with Highest Percentage of Degrees Awarded:** Education 25%, business/marketing 15%, biological/life sciences 10%, psychology 6%, social sciences 6%, interdisciplinary studies 5%, health professions and related sciences 5%. **Special Study Options:** Accelerated program, distance learning, double major, dual enrollment, honors program, independent study, internships, liberal arts/career combination, student-designed major, study abroad, teacher certification program.

FACILITIES
Housing: Coed dorms, men's dorms, women's dorms, apartments for married students, apartments for single students. **Special Academic Facilities/Equipment:** 2 museums, Telecommunity Technology Center, computer lab in residence halls. **Computers:** 95% of public computers are PCs, 4% of public computers are Macs, 1% of public computers are UNIX, network access in dorm rooms, network access in dorm lounges, remote student-access to Web through college's connection.

CAMPUS LIFE
Activities: Choral groups, concert band, drama/theater, jazz band, literary magazine, marching band, music ensembles, musical theater, radio station, student government, student newspaper, symphony orchestra, television station, yearbook. **Organizations:** 41 registered organizations, 13 honor societies, 2 religious organizations. 6 fraternities (12% men join), 4 sororities (14% women join). **Athletics (Intercollegiate):** *Men:* Baseball, basketball, cheerleading, cross-country, football, golf, soccer, track/field (outdoor). *Women:* Basketball, cheerleading, cross-country, golf, soccer, softball, track/field (outdoor), volleyball.

ADMISSIONS

Freshman Academic Profile: 7% in top 10% of high school class, 34% in top 25% of high school class, 70% in top 50% of high school class. ACT middle 50% range 19–23. TOEFL required of all international applicants, minimum paper TOEFL 500, minimum computer TOEFL 173. **Basis for Candidate Selection:** *Very important factors considered include:* Class rank, extracurricular activities, rigor of secondary school record, standardized test scores. *Important factors considered include:* Alumni/ae relation, character/personal qualities, racial/ethnic status, religious affiliation/commitment, talent/ability, volunteer work, work experience. *Other factors considered include:* Geographical residence, interview, recommendation(s), state residency. **Freshman Admission Requirements:** High school diploma is required, and GED is accepted. *Academic units recommended:* 4 English, 4 math, 5 science, 2 foreign language, 3 social studies. **Freshman Admission Statistics:** 1,033 applied, 73% admitted, 30% enrolled. **Transfer Admission Requirements:** High school transcript, college transcript(s), standardized test score, statement of good standing from prior institution(s). Minimum college GPA of 2.0 required. Lowest grade transferable D. **General Admission Information:** Regular application deadline 8/1. Nonfall registration accepted. Common Application accepted. Credit offered for CEEB Advanced Placement tests.

COSTS AND FINANCIAL AID

Required Forms and Deadlines: FAFSA. Financial aid filing deadline 3/15. **Notification of Awards:** Applicants will be notified of awards on a rolling basis beginning on or about 1/30. **Types of Aid:** *Need-based scholarships/grants:* Pell, SEOG, state scholarships/grants, private scholarships, the school's own gift aid. *Loans:* FFEL Subsidized Stafford, FFEL Unsubsidized Stafford, FFEL PLUS, Federal Perkins, college/university loans from institutional funds. **Student Employment:** Federal Work-Study Program available. Off-campus job opportunities are good. **Financial Aid Statistics:** 75% freshmen, 80% undergrads receive need-based scholarship or grant aid. 67% freshmen, 65% undergrads receive need-based self-help aid. 4 freshmen, 7 undergrads receive athletic scholarships.

CENTRAL MICHIGAN UNIVERSITY

105 Warriner Hall, Mount Pleasant, MI 48859
Phone: 989-774-3076 **E-mail:** cmuadmit@cmich.edu **CEEB Code:** 1106
Fax: 989-774-7267 **Website:** www.cmich.edu **ACT Code:** 1972
Financial Aid Phone: 888-392-0007

This public school was founded in 1892. It has an 854-acre campus.

RATINGS

Admissions Selectivity Rating: 78   **Fire Safety Rating:** 60*   **Green Rating:** 78

STUDENTS AND FACULTY

Enrollment: 19,814. **Student Body:** 56% female, 44% male, 2% out-of-state. African American 6%, Asian 1%, Caucasian 82%, Hispanic 2%, Native American 1%. **Retention and Graduation:** 76% freshmen return for sophomore year. 21% freshmen graduate within 4 years. **Faculty:** Student/faculty ratio 22:1. 728 full-time faculty, 81% hold PhDs. 95% faculty teach undergrads.

ACADEMICS

Degrees: Bachelor's, doctoral, master's, post-bachelor's certificate, post-master's certificate. **Academic Requirements:** Arts/fine arts, English (including composition), humanities, mathematics, philosophy, sciences (biological or physical), social science, oral English. **Classes:** Most classes have 10–19 students. Most lab/discussion sections have 20–29 students. **Majors with Highest Enrollment:** English language and literature, history, psychology. **Disciplines with Highest Percentage of Degrees Awarded:** Business/marketing 26%, education 11%, social sciences 8%, health professions and related sciences 7%, communications/journalism 7%. **Special Study Options:** Accelerated program, distance learning, double major, dual enrollment, English as a second language (ESL), exchange student program (domestic), external degree program, honors program, independent study, internships, student-designed major, study abroad, teacher certification program, Leadership Institute, pre-professional programs.

FACILITIES

Housing: Coed dorms, men's dorms, women's dorms, apartments for married students, apartments for single students, special housing for disabled students, special housing for international students, fraternity/sorority housing, residential college for health program. **Special Academic Facilities/Equipment:** Clarke Historical Library, Central Michigan University Museum of Cultural and Natural History, Gerald L. Poor School Museum, Brooks Astronomical

Observatory, university art gallery, university theater, public broadcasting, student activity center, Charles V. Park Library. **Computers:** 25% of classrooms are wired, 50% of classrooms are wireless, 75% of public computers are PCs, 20% of public computers are Macs, 5% of public computers are UNIX, network access in dorm rooms, network access in dorm lounges, online registration, online administrative functions (other than registration), remote student-access to Web through college's connection.

CAMPUS LIFE

Activities: Choral groups, concert band, dance, drama/theater, jazz band, literary magazine, marching band, music ensembles, musical theater, pep band, radio station, student government, student newspaper, student-run film society, television station, yearbook. **Organizations:** 191 registered organizations, 9 honor societies, 15 religious organizations. 12 fraternities (6% men join), 11 sororities (7% women join). **Athletics (Intercollegiate):** *Men:* Baseball, basketball, cross-country, football, track/field (indoor), track/field (outdoor), wrestling. *Women:* Basketball, cross-country, field hockey, gymnastics, soccer, softball, track/field (indoor), track/field (outdoor), volleyball. Environmental Initiatives: RecycleMania. Campus Sustainability Advisory Committee.

ADMISSIONS

Freshman Academic Profile: 15% in top 10% of high school class, 41% in top 25% of high school class, 77% in top 50% of high school class. 90% from public high schools. SAT Math middle 50% range 470–600. SAT Critical Reading middle 50% range 450–580. ACT middle 50% range 20–24. TOEFL required of all international applicants, minimum paper TOEFL 550, minimum computer TOEFL 213. **Basis for Candidate Selection:** *Very important factors considered include:* Academic GPA, rigor of secondary school record, standardized test scores. *Important factors considered include:* Class rank. *Other factors considered include:* Alumni/ae relation, application essay, character/personal qualities, extracurricular activities, first generation, interview, level of applicant's interest, racial/ethnic status, recommendation(s), talent/ability, volunteer work, work experience. **Freshman Admission Requirements:** High school diploma is required, and GED is accepted. *Academic units recommended:* 4 English, 4 math, 3 science, 2 foreign language, 2 social studies, 2 history, 2 computer literacy. **Transfer Admission Requirements:** College transcript(s). Minimum college GPA of 2.0 required. Lowest grade transferable D. **General Admission Information:** Application fee $35. Regular notification is rolling. Nonfall registration accepted. Admission may be deferred for a maximum of 1 year. Credit and/or placement offered for CEEB Advanced Placement tests.

COSTS AND FINANCIAL AID

Annual in-state tuition $7,343. Annual out-of-state tuition $17,078. Room and board $6,600. Average book expense $1,000. **Required Forms and Deadlines:** FAFSA. Financial aid filing deadline 3/1. **Notification of Awards:** Applicants will be notified of awards on a rolling basis beginning on or about 4/1. **Types of Aid:** *Need-based scholarships/grants:* Pell, SEOG, state scholarships/grants, private scholarships, the school's own gift aid. *Loans:* Direct Subsidized Stafford, Direct Unsubsidized Stafford, Direct PLUS, Federal Perkins, state loans, alternative loans. **Student Employment:** Federal Work-Study Program available. Institutional employment available. Off-campus job opportunities are good. **Financial Aid Statistics:** 46% freshmen, 39% undergrads receive need-based scholarship or grant aid. 43% freshmen, 47% undergrads receive need-based self-help aid. 41 freshmen, 198 undergrads receive athletic scholarships. 51% freshmen, 49% undergrads receive any aid. Highest amount earned per year from on-campus jobs $3,500.

CENTRAL PENNSYLVANIA COLLEGE

College Hill and Valley Roads, Summerdale, PA 17093
Phone: 717-728-2201 **E-mail:** admissions@centralpenn.edu
Fax: 717-728-2505 **Website:** www.centralpenn.edu
Financial Aid Phone: 800-759-2727

This is a proprietary school.

RATINGS

Admissions Selectivity Rating: 60*   **Fire Safety Rating:** 60*   **Green Rating:** 60*

STUDENTS AND FACULTY

Enrollment: 859. **Student Body:** 60% female, 40% male, 10% out-of-state. African American 14%, Asian 1%, Caucasian 74%, Hispanic 3%, Native American 2%. **Retention and Graduation:** 68% freshmen return for sophomore year. **Faculty:** 100% faculty teach undergrads.

ACADEMICS

Degrees: Associate, bachelor's, certificate. **Academic Requirements:** Computer literacy, English (including composition), humanities, mathematics, sciences (biological or physical), social science. **Majors with Highest Enrollment:** Business administration/management, computer and information sciences, criminal justice/safety studies. **Disciplines with Highest Percentage of Degrees Awarded:** Business/marketing 67%, computer and information sciences 7%, communication technologies 3%. **Special Study Options:** Accelerated program, distance learning, double major, honors program, independent study, internships, study abroad.

FACILITIES

Housing: All housing are either multi-person, single gender townhouses, or apartments. **Computers:** 98% of public computers are PCs, 2% of public computers are Macs, network access in dorm rooms, network access in dorm lounges, online registration, online administrative functions (other than registration).

CAMPUS LIFE

Activities: Choral groups, literary magazine, student government, student newspaper, yearbook. **Organizations:** 20 registered organizations, 1 honor society, 1 religious organization. **Athletics (Intercollegiate):** *Men:* Basketball, bowling, golf, tennis, volleyball. *Women:* Basketball, bowling, golf, tennis, volleyball.

ADMISSIONS

Freshman Academic Profile: TOEFL required of all international applicants, minimum paper TOEFL 550, minimum computer TOEFL 213. **Basis for Candidate Selection:** *Very important factors considered include:* Class rank, interview, rigor of secondary school record. *Other factors considered include:* Character/personal qualities, extracurricular activities, recommendation(s), standardized test scores, talent/ability, volunteer work, work experience. **Freshman Admission Requirements:** High school diploma is required, and GED is accepted. **Transfer Admission Requirements:** High school transcript, college transcript(s). Minimum college GPA of 2.0 required. Lowest grade transferable C. **General Admission Information:** Nonfall registration accepted. Admission may be deferred for a maximum of 1 year. Common Application not accepted. Credit and/or placement offered for CEEB Advanced Placement tests.

COSTS AND FINANCIAL AID

Annual tuition $11,520. Room & board $6,060. Required fees $645. Average book expense $990. **Required Forms and Deadlines:** FAFSA, institution's own financial aid form, Noncustodial PROFILE. Financial aid filing deadline 3/15. **Notification of Awards:** Applicants will be notified of awards on a rolling basis beginning on or about 1/1. **Types of Aid:** *Need-based scholarships/grants:* Pell, SEOG, state scholarships/grants, private scholarships, the school's own gift aid. *Loans:* FFEL Subsidized Stafford, FFEL Unsubsidized Stafford, FFEL PLUS, College Payment Plan. **Student Employment:** Federal Work-Study Program available. Institutional employment available. Off-campus job opportunities are good. **Financial Aid Statistics:** 80% freshmen, 80% undergrads receive any aid.

CENTRAL STATE UNIVERSITY

PO Box 1004, Wilberforce, OH 45384
Phone: 937-376-6348 **E-mail:** admissions@centralstate.edu **CEEB Code:** 1107
Fax: 937-376-6648 **Website:** www.centralstate.edu **ACT Code:** 3246
Financial Aid Phone: 937-376-6579

This public school was founded in 1887. It has a 60-acre campus.

RATINGS

Admissions Selectivity Rating: 72   **Fire Safety Rating:** 60*   **Green Rating:** 60*

STUDENTS AND FACULTY

Enrollment: 1,729. **Student Body:** 49% female, 51% male, 34% out-of-state. African American 90%, Caucasian 2%. **Retention and Graduation:** 50% freshmen return for sophomore year. 16% freshmen graduate within 4 years. 32% grads go on to further study within 1 year. 50% grads pursue arts and sciences degrees. 29% grads pursue business degrees. 7% grads pursue law degrees. **Faculty:** Student/faculty ratio 13:1. 102 full-time faculty.

ACADEMICS

Degrees: Bachelor's, master's. **Academic Requirements:** Arts/fine arts, computer literacy, English (including composition), history, humanities, mathematics, sciences (biological or physical), social science. **Classes:** Most classes have fewer than 10 students. Most lab/discussion sections have 10–19

students. **Majors with Highest Enrollment:** Business administration/management. **Disciplines with Highest Percentage of Degrees Awarded:** Business/marketing 41%, education 11%, psychology 7%, communication technologies 6%, social sciences 6%, computer and information sciences 4%, English 4%, engineering 4%, parks and recreation 4%, visual and performing arts 4%. **Special Study Options:** Cooperative education program, cross-registration, double major, honors program, independent study, internships, study abroad, teacher certification program.

FACILITIES

Housing: Coed dorms, men's dorms, women's dorms. **Special Academic Facilities/Equipment:** National Afro-American Museum & Cultural Center, C. J. McLin International Center for Water Resources Management, Center for Integrated Manufacturing Protocols, Architectures and Logistics Laboratory, Biology Technique Laboratory, Electrochemistry Research Laboratory, Cosby Mass Communication Center, Paul Robeson Cultural & Performing Arts Center. **Computers:** 95% of public computers are PCs, 5% of public computers are Macs, network access in dorm rooms, online administrative functions (other than registration).

CAMPUS LIFE

Activities: Choral groups, concert band, dance, drama/theater, jazz band, marching band, music ensembles, pep band, radio station, student government, student newspaper, television station. **Organizations:** 30 registered organizations, 3 honor societies, 4 religious organizations. 1 fraternity (1% men join), 3 sororities (1% women join). **Athletics (Intercollegiate):** *Men:* Basketball, cheerleading, cross-country, golf, track/field (outdoor). *Women:* Basketball, cheerleading, cross-country, golf, track/field (outdoor), volleyball.

ADMISSIONS

Freshman Academic Profile: 7% in top 10% of high school class, 20% in top 25% of high school class, 46% in top 50% of high school class. SAT Math middle 50% range 340–450. SAT Critical Reading middle 50% range 350–450. ACT middle 50% range 14–18. TOEFL required of all international applicants, minimum paper TOEFL 500. **Basis for Candidate Selection:** *Very important factors considered include:* Academic GPA, rigor of secondary school record, standardized test scores. *Important factors considered include:* Application essay, character/personal qualities, class rank, geographical residence, state residency. *Other factors considered include:* Extracurricular activities, interview, recommendation(s), talent/ability. **Freshman Admission Requirements:** High school diploma is required, and GED is accepted. *Academic units recommended:* 4 English, 3 math, 3 science, 2 foreign language, 3 social studies, 1 art. **Freshman Admission Statistics:** 5,173 applied, 41% admitted, 26% enrolled. **Transfer Admission Requirements:** College transcript(s), statement of good standing from prior institution(s). Minimum college GPA of 2.0 required. Lowest grade transferable D. **General Admission Information:** Application fee $20. Regular notification is rolling. Nonfall registration accepted. Credit and/or placement offered for CEEB Advanced Placement tests.

COSTS AND FINANCIAL AID

Average book expense $1,000. **Required Forms and Deadlines:** FAFSA, institution's own financial aid form. Financial aid filing deadline 2/15. **Notification of Awards:** Applicants will be notified of awards on a rolling basis beginning on or about 5/1. **Types of Aid:** *Need-based scholarships/grants:* Pell, SEOG, state scholarships/grants, private scholarships, the school's own gift aid, United Negro College Fund. *Loans:* Direct Subsidized Stafford, Direct Unsubsidized Stafford, Direct PLUS, college/university loans from institutional funds. **Student Employment:** Federal Work-Study Program available. Institutional employment available. Off-campus job opportunities are fair. **Financial Aid Statistics:** 75% freshmen, 73% undergrads receive need-based scholarship or grant aid. 83% freshmen, 80% undergrads receive need-based self-help aid. 13 freshmen, 89 undergrads receive athletic scholarships.

CENTRAL WASHINGTON UNIVERSITY

Admissions Office, 400 East University Way, Ellensburg, WA 98926-7463
Phone: 509-963-1211 **E-mail:** cwuadmis@cwu.edu **CEEB Code:** 4044
Fax: 509-963-3022 **Website:** www.cwu.edu **ACT Code:** 4444
Financial Aid Phone: 509-963-1611

This public school was founded in 1891. It has a 350-acre campus.

RATINGS

Admissions Selectivity Rating: 73   **Fire Safety Rating:** 63   **Green Rating:** 60*

STUDENTS AND FACULTY

Enrollment: 9,367. **Student Body:** 53% female, 47% male, 2% out-of-state, 2% international. African American 2%, Asian 6%, Caucasian 74%, Hispanic 7%, Native American 2%. **Retention and Graduation:** 78% freshmen return for sophomore year. 23% freshmen graduate within 4 years. **Faculty:** Student/faculty ratio 22:1. 372 full-time faculty, 86% hold PhDs. 99% faculty teach undergrads.

ACADEMICS

Degrees: Bachelor's, master's, post-bachelor's certificate. **Academic Requirements:** Arts/fine arts, computer literacy, English (including composition), foreign languages, history, humanities, mathematics, philosophy, sciences (biological or physical), social science. **Classes:** Most classes have 20–29 students. Most lab/discussion sections have 20–29 students. **Majors with Highest Enrollment:** Business administration/management, criminal justice/safety studies, elementary education and teaching. **Disciplines with Highest Percentage of Degrees Awarded:** Business/marketing 25%, education 25%, security and protective services 9%, social sciences 8%, visual and performing arts 4%. **Special Study Options:** Cooperative education program, distance learning, double major, dual enrollment, English as a second language (ESL), exchange student program (domestic), honors program, independent study, internships, student-designed major, study abroad, teacher certification program.

FACILITIES

Housing: Coed dorms, women's dorms, apartments for married students, apartments for single students, special housing for disabled students, special housing for international students, academic interests, upper-classmen, 21 years and older. **Special Academic Facilities/Equipment:** Chimpanzee & Human Communication Institute, Geodesy Laboratory (a data analysis facility of the Pacific Northwest Geodetic Array), Educational Technology Center, museum collection of NW Native American and Circum-Pacific artifacts for teaching and research. **Computers:** 63% of public computers are PCs, 36% of public computers are Macs, 1% of public computers are UNIX, network access in dorm rooms, online registration, online administrative functions (other than registration), remote student-access to Web through college's connection.

CAMPUS LIFE

Activities: Choral groups, concert band, dance, drama/theater, jazz band, literary magazine, marching band, music ensembles, musical theater, opera, pep band, radio station, student government, student newspaper, student-run film society, symphony orchestra. **Organizations:** 96 registered organizations, 3 honor societies, 9 religious organizations. **Athletics (Intercollegiate):** Men: Baseball, basketball, cross-country, football, track/field (indoor), track/field (outdoor). Women: Basketball, cross-country, soccer, softball, track/field (indoor), track/field (outdoor), volleyball.

ADMISSIONS

Freshman Academic Profile: 15% in top 10% of high school class, 36% in top 25% of high school class, 77% in top 50% of high school class. SAT Math middle 50% range 440–550. SAT Critical Reading middle 50% range 440–550. ACT middle 50% range 18–23. TOEFL required of all international applicants, minimum paper TOEFL 525, minimum computer TOEFL 195. **Basis for Candidate Selection:** Very important factors considered include: Academic GPA, rigor of secondary school record. Important factors considered include: Application essay, standardized test scores. Other factors considered include: Character/personal qualities, class rank, extracurricular activities, interview, level of applicant's interest, recommendation(s), talent/ability, volunteer work, work experience. **Freshman Admission Requirements:** High school diploma is required, and GED is accepted. Academic units required: 4 English, 3 math, 2 science (1 science lab), 2 foreign language, 3 social studies. Academic units recommended: 3 science, 3 social studies. **Freshman Admission Statistics:** 4,656 applied, 76% admitted, 40% enrolled. **Transfer Admission Requirements:** College transcript(s), statement of good standing from prior institution(s). Minimum college GPA of 2.5 required. Lowest grade transferable D-. **General Admission Information:** Application fee $50. Regular application deadline 4/1. Regular notification is rolling. Nonfall registration accepted. Credit and/or placement offered for CEEB Advanced Placement tests.

COSTS AND FINANCIAL AID

Annual in-state tuition $4,611. Annual out-of-state tuition $14,013. Room and board $7,842. Required fees $846. Average book expense $924. **Required Forms and Deadlines:** FAFSA. Financial aid filing deadline 3/1. **Notification of Awards:** Applicants will be notified of awards on a rolling basis beginning on or about 4/15. **Types of Aid:** Need-based scholarships/grants: Pell, SEOG, state scholarships/grants, private scholarships, the school's own gift aid. Loans: Direct Subsidized Stafford, Direct Unsubsidized Stafford, Direct PLUS, FFEL Subsidized Stafford, FFEL Unsubsidized Stafford, FFEL PLUS, Federal Perkins, state loans, college/university loans from institutional funds. **Financial Aid Statistics:** 33% freshmen, 36% undergrads receive need-based scholarship or grant aid. 36% freshmen, 44% undergrads receive need-based self-help aid.

64% freshmen, 66% undergrads receive any aid. Highest amount earned per year from on-campus jobs $10,166.

CENTRAL WYOMING COLLEGE

2660 Peck Avenue, Riverton, WY 82501
Phone: 307-855-2119 **E-mail:** admit@cwc.edu **CEEB Code:** 4115
Fax: 307-855-2093 **Website:** www.cwc.edu
Financial Aid Phone: 307-855-2150

This public school was founded in 1966. It has a 200-acre campus.

RATINGS

Admissions Selectivity Rating: 60* **Fire Safety Rating:** 60* **Green Rating:** 71

STUDENTS AND FACULTY

Enrollment: 989. **Student Body:** 69% female, 31% male, 6% out-of-state, 2% international (19 countries represented). Asian 1%, Caucasian 73%, Hispanic 4%, Native American 19%. **Retention and Graduation:** 46% freshmen return for sophomore year. **Faculty:** Student/faculty ratio 14:1. 46 full-time faculty, 20% hold PhDs. 100% faculty teach undergrads.

ACADEMICS

Degrees: Associate, certificate, diploma. **Academic Requirements:** Arts/fine arts, English (including composition), history, humanities, mathematics, sciences (biological or physical), social science, university studies (UNST), wellness, physical education activity (PEAC), oral, diversity. **Classes:** Most classes have fewer than 10 students. Most lab/discussion sections have fewer than 10 students. **Majors with Highest Enrollment:** Equestrian/equine studies, nursing/registered nurse training (RN, ASN, BSN, MSN). **Special Study Options:** Cross-registration, distance learning, double major, dual enrollment, English as a second language (ESL), honors program, independent study, student-designed major, teacher certification program.

FACILITIES

Housing: Coed dorms, apartments for married students, apartments for single students. **Special Academic Facilities/Equipment:** Fine arts center, Microsoft training lab, Cisco training lab, Wyoming Public Television station and radio station, Stewart Collection (Native American Artifacts), Sinks Canyon Center, rodeo arena, library, arts gallery. **Computers:** 75% of classrooms are wireless, 100% of public computers are PCs, network access in dorm rooms, network access in dorm lounges, online registration, online administrative functions (other than registration), remote student-access to Web through college's connection.

CAMPUS LIFE

Activities: Choral groups, concert band, dance, drama/theater, jazz band, music ensembles, musical theater, radio station, student government, student newspaper, television station. **Organizations:** 15 registered organizations, 2 honor societies, 2 religious organizations. **Athletics (Intercollegiate):** Men: Rodeo. Women: Rodeo.

ADMISSIONS

Freshman Academic Profile: 100% from public high schools. SAT Math middle 50% range 360–460. SAT Critical Reading middle 50% range 350–510. ACT middle 50% range 17–22. TOEFL required of all international applicants, minimum paper TOEFL 500, minimum computer TOEFL 175. **Freshman Admission Requirements:** High school diploma or equivalent is not required. **Freshman Admission Statistics:** 366 applied, 100% admitted, 61% enrolled. **Transfer Admission Requirements:** College transcript(s), lowest grade transferable C. **General Admission Information:** Regular notification is rolling. Nonfall registration accepted. Admission may be deferred. Credit offered for CEEB Advanced Placement tests.

COSTS AND FINANCIAL AID

Annual in-state tuition $1,560. Annual out-of-state tuition $4,680. Room and board $3,405. Required fees $504. Average book expense $900. **Required Forms and Deadlines:** FAFSA, institution's own financial aid form. Financial aid filing deadline 4/15. **Notification of Awards:** Applicants will be notified of awards on a rolling basis beginning on or about 5/1. **Types of Aid:** Need-based scholarships/grants: Pell, SEOG, state scholarships/grants, private scholarships, the school's own gift aid. Loans: FFEL Subsidized Stafford, FFEL Unsubsidized Stafford, FFEL PLUS, state loans. **Student Employment:** Federal Work-Study Program available. Institutional employment available. Off-campus job opportunities are excellent. **Financial Aid Statistics:** 40% freshmen, 47% undergrads receive need-based scholarship or grant aid. 21% freshmen, 30% undergrads receive need-based self-help aid. 42% freshmen, 50% undergrads receive any aid. Highest amount earned per year from on-campus jobs $3,000.

CENTRE COLLEGE

600 West Walnut Street, 600 West Walnut Street, Danville, KY 40422
Phone: 859-238-5350 **E-mail:** admission@centre.edu **CEEB Code:** 1109
Fax: 859-238-5373 **Website:** www.centre.edu **ACT Code:** 1506
Financial Aid Phone: 859-238-5365

This private school, affiliated with the Presbyterian Church, was founded in 1819. It has a 115-acre campus.

RATINGS

Admissions Selectivity Rating: 93   **Fire Safety Rating:** 60*   **Green Rating:** 81

STUDENTS AND FACULTY

Enrollment: 1,144. **Student Body:** 53% female, 47% male, 35% out-of-state, 2% international (12 countries represented). African American 3%, Asian 2%, Caucasian 92%, Hispanic 1%. **Retention and Graduation:** 89% freshmen return for sophomore year. 78% freshmen graduate within 4 years. 41% grads go on to further study within 1 year. 35% grads pursue arts and sciences degrees. 3% grads pursue business degrees. 21% grads pursue law degrees. 13% grads pursue medical degrees. **Faculty:** Student/faculty ratio 10:1. 101 full-time faculty, 98% hold PhDs. 100% faculty teach undergrads.

ACADEMICS

Degrees: Bachelor's. **Academic Requirements:** Foreign languages, history, humanities, mathematics, philosophy, sciences (biological or physical), social science, religion. **Classes:** Most classes have 10–19 students. Most lab/discussion sections have 10–19 students. **Majors with Highest Enrollment:** Economics, English language and literature, history. **Disciplines with Highest Percentage of Degrees Awarded:** Social sciences 21%, biological/life sciences 12%, history 12%, psychology 9%, English 9%, foreign languages and literature 8%, visual and performing arts 8%, philosophy and religious studies 6%. **Special Study Options:** Cross-registration, double major, honors program, independent study, internships, student-designed major, study abroad, teacher certification program.

FACILITIES

Housing: Coed dorms, men's dorms, women's dorms, apartments for single students, special housing for disabled students, special housing for international students, fraternity/sorority housing, theme housing. **Special Academic Facilities/Equipment:** Arts center, physical science and math facility, electron microscope, visible and infrared mass spectroscopy equipment, visual arts center. **Computers:** 10% of classrooms are wireless, 80% of public computers are PCs, 15% of public computers are Macs, 5% of public computers are UNIX, network access in dorm rooms, network access in dorm lounges, online administrative functions (other than registration), remote student-access to Web through college's connection.

CAMPUS LIFE

Activities: Choral groups, concert band, dance, drama/theater, jazz band, literary magazine, music ensembles, pep band, student government, student newspaper, student-run film society, television station, yearbook. **Organizations:** 70 registered organizations, 12 honor societies, 6 religious organizations. 5 fraternities (34% men join), 4 sororities (37% women join). **Athletics (Intercollegiate):** *Men:* Baseball, basketball, cheerleading, cross-country, diving, football, golf, soccer, swimming, tennis, track/field (outdoor). *Women:* Basketball, cheerleading, cross-country, diving, field hockey, golf, soccer, softball, swimming, tennis, track/field (outdoor), volleyball. Environmental Initiatives: All new buildings and major renovations will be designed and built to conserve energy and enhance the human environment as evaluated by LEED silver standards or equivalent. Certification through U.S.G.B.C. will be pursued as appropriate. The intention will be to purchase E.P.A. Energy Star products in all areas. Waste minimization will be promoted and pursued by policy and practice. Current efforts include participation in the Waste minimization component of the RecycleMania competition.

ADMISSIONS

. **Freshman Academic Profile:** 63% in top 10% of high school class, 88% in top 25% of high school class, 99% in top 50% of high school class. 79% from public high schools. SAT Math middle 50% range 570–650. SAT Critical Reading middle 50% range 570–690. ACT middle 50% range 26–30. TOEFL required of all international applicants, minimum paper TOEFL 580. **Basis for Candidate Selection:** *Very important factors considered include:* Academic GPA, rigor of secondary school record. *Important factors considered include:* Application essay, standardized test scores. *Other factors considered include:* Alumni/ae relation, character/personal qualities, class rank, extracurricular activities, first generation, geographical residence, interview, racial/ethnic status, recommendation(s), talent/ability. **Freshman Admission Requirements:** High school diploma or equivalent is not required. *Academic units required:* 4 English, 4 math, 2 science (2 science labs), 2 foreign language, 2 history. *Academic units recommended:* 3 science (3 science labs). **Freshman Admission Statistics:** 2,092 applied, 60% admitted, 26% enrolled. **Transfer Admission Requirements:** High school transcript, college transcript(s), essay or personal statement, standardized test score, statement of good standing from prior institution(s). Lowest grade transferable C-. **General Admission Information:** Application fee $40. Regular application deadline 2/1. Regular notification 3/15. Nonfall registration not accepted. Admission may be deferred for a maximum of 1 year. Credit and/or placement offered for CEEB Advanced Placement tests.

COSTS AND FINANCIAL AID

Annual tuition $28,000. Room and board $7,000. Average book expense $900. **Required Forms and Deadlines:** FAFSA, institution's own financial aid form. Financial aid filing deadline 3/1. **Notification of Awards:** Applicants will be notified of awards on or about 3/25. **Types of Aid:** *Need-based scholarships/grants:* Pell, SEOG, state scholarships/grants, private scholarships, the school's own gift aid, Federal ACG, Federal SMART. *Loans:* FFEL Subsidized Stafford, FFEL Unsubsidized Stafford, FFEL PLUS, Federal Perkins, college/university loans from institutional funds. **Student Employment:** Federal Work-Study Program available. Institutional employment available. Off-campus job opportunities are fair. **Financial Aid Statistics:** 64% freshmen, 58% undergrads receive need-based scholarship or grant aid. 43% freshmen, 41% undergrads receive need-based self-help aid.

CHADRON STATE COLLEGE

1000 Main Street, Chadron, NE 69337
Phone: 308-432-6263 **E-mail:** inquire@csc.edu **CEEB Code:** 6466
Fax: 308-432-6229 **Website:** www.csc.edu **ACT Code:** 2466
Financial Aid Phone: 308-432-6230

This public school was founded in 1911. It has a 281-acre campus.

RATINGS

Admissions Selectivity Rating: 75   **Fire Safety Rating:** 60*   **Green Rating:** 60*

STUDENTS AND FACULTY

Enrollment: 2,152. **Student Body:** 57% female, 43% male, 32% out-of-state. African American 1%, Caucasian 73%, Hispanic 2%, Native American 2%. **Retention and Graduation:** 70% freshmen return for sophomore year. 17% freshmen graduate within 4 years. 41% grads go on to further study within 1 year. 25% grads pursue arts and sciences degrees. 10% grads pursue business degrees. 3% grads pursue law degrees. 3% grads pursue medical degrees. **Faculty:** Student/faculty ratio 19:1. 101 full-time faculty, 57% hold PhDs. 100% faculty teach undergrads.

ACADEMICS

Degrees: Bachelor's, master's, post-master's certificate. **Academic Requirements:** Arts/fine arts, English (including composition), history, humanities, mathematics, philosophy, sciences (biological or physical), social science, ethics, communications, government, global studies, physical education. **Classes:** Most classes have fewer than 10 students. **Majors with Highest Enrollment:** Business administration/management, criminal justice/law enforcement administration, elementary education and teaching. **Special Study Options:** Accelerated program, cooperative education program, cross-registration, distance learning, double major, dual enrollment, honors program, independent study, internships, student-designed major, study abroad, teacher certification program.

FACILITIES

Housing: Coed dorms, men's dorms, women's dorms, apartments for married students, apartments for single students. **Special Academic Facilities/Equipment:** Planetarium, herbarium, geology museum, Mari Sandoz Center. **Computers:** Network access in dorm rooms, network access in dorm lounges, online registration, online administrative functions (other than registration), remote student-access to Web through college's connection.

CAMPUS LIFE

Activities: Choral groups, concert band, dance, drama/theater, jazz band, literary magazine, music ensembles, musical theater, pep band, radio station, student government, student newspaper, yearbook. **Organizations:** 65 registered organizations, 14 honor societies, 5 religious organizations. **Athletics (Intercollegiate):** *Men:* Basketball, football, track/field (indoor), track/field (outdoor), wrestling. *Women:* Basketball, golf, track/field (indoor), track/field (outdoor), volleyball.

ADMISSIONS

Freshman Academic Profile: 11% in top 10% of high school class, 33% in top 25% of high school class, 65% in top 50% of high school class. 83% from public high schools. TOEFL required of all international applicants, minimum paper TOEFL 550, minimum computer TOEFL 213. **Basis for Candidate Selection:** *Other factors considered include:* Academic GPA. **Freshman Admission Requirements:** High school diploma is required, and GED is accepted. *Academic units recommended:* 4 English, 3 math, 2 science (2 science labs), 3 social studies. **Freshman Admission Statistics:** 1,060 applied, 44% admitted, 80% enrolled. **Transfer Admission Requirements:** College transcript(s). Minimum college GPA of 2.0 required. Lowest grade transferable D. **General Admission Information:** Application fee $15. Regular notification is rolling. Nonfall registration accepted. Common Application not accepted. Credit and/or placement offered for CEEB Advanced Placement tests.

COSTS AND FINANCIAL AID

Annual in-state tuition $2,933. Annual out-of-state tuition $5,865. Room and board $4,074. Required fees $730. **Required Forms and Deadlines:** FAFSA, institution's own financial aid form. Financial aid filing deadline 6/1. **Notification of Awards:** Applicants will be notified of awards on a rolling basis beginning on or about 4/1. **Types of Aid:** *Need-based scholarships/grants:* Pell, SEOG, state scholarships/grants, private scholarships, the school's own gift aid. *Loans:* Direct Subsidized Stafford, Direct Unsubsidized Stafford, Direct PLUS, FFEL Subsidized Stafford, FFEL Unsubsidized Stafford, FFEL PLUS, Federal Perkins. **Student Employment:** Federal Work-Study Program available. Institutional employment available. **Financial Aid Statistics:** 50% freshmen, 48% undergrads receive need-based scholarship or grant aid. 36% freshmen, 41% undergrads receive need-based self-help aid.

CHAMINADE UNIVERSITY OF HONOLULU

3140 Waialae Avenue, Honolulu, HI 96816-1578
Phone: 808-735-4735 **E-mail:** admissions@chaminade.edu **CEEB Code:** 4105
Fax: 808-739-4647 **Website:** www.chaminade.edu **ACT Code:** 0898
Financial Aid Phone: 808-735-4780

This private school, affiliated with the Roman Catholic Church, was founded in 1955. It has a 67-acre campus.

RATINGS
Admissions Selectivity Rating: 72   **Fire Safety Rating:** 60*   **Green Rating:** 60*

STUDENTS AND FACULTY

Enrollment: 1,116. **Student Body:** 68% female, 32% male, 50% out-of-state, 2% international (12 countries represented). African American 3%, Asian 65%, Caucasian 23%, Hispanic 7%. **Retention and Graduation:** 65% freshmen return for sophomore year. 20% freshmen graduate within 4 years. **Faculty:** Student/faculty ratio 11:1. 85 full-time faculty, 56% hold PhDs. 100% faculty teach undergrads.

ACADEMICS

Degrees: Associate, bachelor's, master's, post-bachelor's certificate. **Academic Requirements:** Arts/fine arts, computer literacy, English (including composition), history, humanities, mathematics, philosophy, sciences (biological or physical), social science, cultural studies. **Classes:** Most classes have 10–19 students. Most lab/discussion sections have 10–19 students. **Majors with Highest Enrollment:** Business administration/management, criminal justice/safety studies, psychology. **Disciplines with Highest Percentage of Degrees Awarded:** Business/marketing 90%, security and protective services 20%, education 14%, history 12%, psychology 11%. **Special Study Options:** Accelerated program, distance learning, double major, exchange student program (domestic), independent study, internships, student-designed major, study abroad, teacher certification program.

FACILITIES

Housing: Coed dorms, women's dorms, apartments for single students, special housing for disabled students. **Special Academic Facilities/Equipment:** Montessori Lab School, observatory, black box theater. **Computers:** 1% of classrooms are wired, 100% of classrooms are wireless, 100% of public computers are PCs, network access in dorm rooms, network access in dorm lounges, online registration, online administrative functions (other than registration), remote student-access to Web through college's connection.

CAMPUS LIFE

Activities: Choral groups, drama/theater, literary magazine, musical theater, student government, student newspaper, symphony orchestra, yearbook. **Organizations:** 38 registered organizations, 7 honor societies, 1 religious organization. **Athletics (Intercollegiate):** *Men:* Basketball, cross-country, golf, tennis, water polo. *Women:* Cross-country, golf, softball, tennis, volleyball.

ADMISSIONS

Freshman Academic Profile: 16% in top 10% of high school class, 44% in top 25% of high school class, 75% in top 50% of high school class. SAT Math middle 50% range 410–530. SAT Critical Reading middle 50% range 400–510. ACT middle 50% range 18–22. TOEFL required of all international applicants, minimum paper TOEFL 450, minimum computer TOEFL 133. **Basis for Candidate Selection:** *Very important factors considered:* Academic GPA, standardized test scores. *Important factors considered include:* Application essay, character/personal qualities, extracurricular activities, interview, talent/ability, volunteer work. *Other factors considered include:* Recommendation(s), rigor of secondary school record, work experience. **Freshman Admission Requirements:** High school diploma is required, and GED is accepted. *Academic units recommended:* 4 English, 3 math, 2 science, 3 social studies, 4 academic electives. **Freshman Admission Statistics:** 984 applied, 94% admitted, 27% enrolled. **Transfer Admission Requirements:** College transcript(s), essay or personal statement, statement of good standing from prior institution(s). Minimum college GPA of 2.0 required. Lowest grade transferable C. **General Admission Information:** Application fee $50. Regular notification is rolling. Nonfall registration accepted. Admission may be deferred for a maximum of 1 year. Credit and/or placement offered for CEEB Advanced Placement tests.

COSTS AND FINANCIAL AID

Required Forms and Deadlines: FAFSA. Financial aid filing deadline 3/1. **Notification of Awards:** Applicants will be notified of awards on a rolling basis beginning on or about 2/15. **Types of Aid:** *Need-based scholarships/grants:* Pell, SEOG, private scholarships, the school's own gift aid. *Loans:* FFEL Subsidized Stafford, FFEL Unsubsidized Stafford, FFEL PLUS, Federal Perkins, CitiAssist Loans, Sallie Mae's Signature Education Loan Program, alternative loans, U.S. Bank Gap Education Loans. **Student Employment:** Federal Work-Study Program available. Institutional employment available. Off-campus job opportunities are fair. **Financial Aid Statistics:** 67% freshmen, 73% undergrads receive need-based scholarship or grant aid. 59% freshmen, 65% undergrads receive need-based self-help aid. 3 freshmen, 22 undergrads receive athletic scholarships. 99% freshmen, 96% undergrads receive any aid. Highest amount earned per year from on-campus jobs $8,056.

See page 1112.

CHAMPLAIN COLLEGE

163 South Willard Street, PO Box 670, Burlington, VT 05402-0670
Phone: 802-860-2727 **E-mail:** admission@champlain.edu **CEEB Code:** 3291
Fax: 802-860-2767 **Website:** www.champlain.edu **ACT Code:** 3291
Financial Aid Phone: 802-860-2730

This private school was founded in 1878. It has a 19-acre campus.

RATINGS
Admissions Selectivity Rating: 77   **Fire Safety Rating:** 71   **Green Rating:** 60*

STUDENTS AND FACULTY

Enrollment: 1,928. **Student Body:** 50% female, 50% male, 59% out-of-state. **Retention and Graduation:** 83% freshmen return for sophomore year. 72% freshmen graduate within 4 years. 10% grads go on to further study within 1 year. 3% grads pursue arts and sciences degrees. 6% grads pursue business degrees. 1% grads pursue law degrees. **Faculty:** Student/faculty ratio 16:1. 65 full-time faculty, 37% hold PhDs. 100% faculty teach undergrads.

ACADEMICS

Degrees: Associate, bachelor's, certificate, master's. **Academic Requirements:** Arts/fine arts, computer literacy, English (including composition), history, humanities, mathematics, philosophy, sciences (biological or physical), social science. Accounting and business coursework is included in many majors. **Classes:** Most classes have 10–19 students. Most lab/discussion sections have fewer than 10 students. **Majors with Highest Enrollment:** Business administration/management, intermedia/multimedia, liberal arts and sciences/liberal studies. **Disciplines with Highest Percentage of Degrees Awarded:** Business/marketing 42%, visual and performing arts 12%, liberal arts/general studies 11%, communications/journalism 10%, computer and information sciences 10%, education 8%. **Special Study Options:** Accelerated program, cross-registration, distance learning, double major, honors program, independent study, internships, liberal arts/career combination, study abroad, teacher certification program.

FACILITIES

Housing: Coed dorms, women's dorms, special housing for international students, wellness, performing arts, international dorm. Suites style singles with common living room and kitchenette (for selected sophomores, juniors, and seniors). **Computers:** 100% of classrooms are wireless, 80% of public computers are PCs, 20% of public computers are Macs, network access in dorm rooms, network access in dorm lounges, online registration, online administrative functions (other than registration), support for handheld computing, remote student-access to Web through college's connection.

CAMPUS LIFE

Activities: Choral groups, dance, drama/theater, literary magazine, musical theater, radio station, student government, student newspaper, television station. **Organizations:** 40 registered organizations, 2 honor societies, 1 religious organization.

ADMISSIONS

Freshman Academic Profile: 10% in top 10% of high school class, 15% in top 25% of high school class, 85% in top 50% of high school class. 85% from public high schools. SAT Math middle 50% range 500–610. SAT Critical Reading middle 50% range 500–590. ACT middle 50% range 20–25. TOEFL required of all international applicants, minimum paper TOEFL 500, minimum computer TOEFL 173. **Basis for Candidate Selection:** *Very important factors considered include:* Academic GPA, application essay, rigor of secondary school record. *Important factors considered include:* Class rank, first generation, interview, recommendation(s), standardized test scores. *Other factors considered include:* Alumni/ae relation, character/personal qualities, extracurricular activities, level of applicant's interest, talent/ability, volunteer work, work experience. **Freshman Admission Requirements:** High school diploma is required, and GED is accepted. *Academic units required:* 4 English, 3 math, 3 science (2 science labs), 4 history, 4 academic electives. *Academic units recommended:* 4 math, 4 science (3 science labs), 2 foreign language, 2 social studies. **Freshman Admission Statistics:** 2,152 applied, 58% admitted, 43% enrolled. **Transfer Admission Requirements:** High school transcript, college transcript(s), essay or personal statement. Minimum college GPA of 2.0 required. Lowest grade transferable C. **General Admission Information:** Application fee $40. Early decision application deadline 11/15. Regular application deadline 1/31. Regular notification 3/25. Nonfall registration accepted. Admission may be deferred for a maximum of 1 year with no transferred credits. Credit offered for CEEB Advanced Placement tests.

COSTS AND FINANCIAL AID

Annual tuition $22,550. Room & board $10,910. Average book expense $600. **Required Forms and Deadlines:** FAFSA, institution's own financial aid form, state aid form, Noncustodial PROFILE. Financial aid filing deadline 5/1. **Notification of Awards:** Applicants will be notified of awards on a rolling basis beginning on or about 3/1. **Types of Aid:** *Need-based scholarships/grants:* Pell, SEOG, state scholarships/grants, private scholarships, the school's own gift aid. *Loans:* FFEL Subsidized Stafford, FFEL Unsubsidized Stafford, FFEL PLUS, Federal Perkins. **Financial Aid Statistics:** 51% freshmen, 44% undergrads receive need-based scholarship or grant aid. 63% freshmen, 55% undergrads receive need-based self-help aid. 60% freshmen, 55% undergrads receive any aid. Highest amount earned per year from on-campus jobs $2,211.

CHAPMAN UNIVERSITY

Best 368

One University Drive, Orange, CA 92866
Phone: 714-997-6711 **E-mail:** admit@chapman.edu **CEEB Code:** 4047
Fax: 714-997-6713 **Website:** www.chapman.edu **ACT Code:** 0210
Financial Aid Phone: 714-997-6741

This private school, affiliated with the Disciples of Christ Church, was founded in 1861. It has a 75-acre campus.

RATINGS

Admissions Selectivity Rating: 94   **Fire Safety Rating:** 60*   **Green Rating:** 60*

STUDENTS AND FACULTY

Enrollment: 4,053. **Student Body:** 58% female, 42% male, 23% out-of-state, 2% international (51 countries represented). African American 2%, Asian 8%, Caucasian 69%, Hispanic 10%. **Retention and Graduation:** 87% freshmen return for sophomore year. 52% freshmen graduate within 4 years. **Faculty:** Student/faculty ratio 16:1. 279 full-time faculty, 90% hold PhDs. 84% faculty teach undergrads.

ACADEMICS

Degrees: Bachelor's, doctoral, first professional, master's, post-bachelor's certificate. **Academic Requirements:** Arts/fine arts, English (including composition), foreign languages, history, humanities, mathematics, philosophy, sciences (biological or physical), social science, world cultures/human diversity. Junior year writing proficiency examination (taken at completion of 60 semester credits). **Classes:** Most classes have 20–29 students. Most lab/discussion sections have 10–19 students. **Majors with Highest Enrollment:** Advertising, business administration and management, cinematography and film/video production. **Disciplines with Highest Percentage of Degrees Awarded:** Visual and performing arts 26%, business/marketing 22%, communications/journalism 15%, psychology 7%, liberal arts/general studies 5%. **Special Study Options:** Distance learning, double major, English as a second language (ESL), exchange student program (domestic), honors program, independent study, internships, liberal arts/career combination, student-designed major, study abroad, teacher certification program. In addition to our main campus in Orange, California, that enrolls approximately 5,500 students in undergraduate, graduate, doctoral, and professional programs, Chapman has 15 off-campus satellite University College campus locations in California and Washington, each offering a variety of associate and baccalaureate degree completion and graduate degree and teacher certification program formats for working adults.

FACILITIES

Housing: Coed dorms, apartments for married students, apartments for single students, special housing for disabled students. Houses for married and single students and students with dependents. **Special Academic Facilities/Equipment:** Anderson Center for Economic Research, Leatherby Center for Entrepreneurship and Business Ethics, Schmid Center for International Business, Law and Organizational Economics Center, Center for Cold War Studies, Henley Social Science Research Laboratory, Guggenhiem Art Gallery, TV studio, film/TV lab, Waltmer Theatre, Beckman Information & Technology Hall, DeMille Hall Film and TV Production and Digital Editing Studios. **Computers:** 100% of classrooms are wired, 100% of classrooms are wireless, 86% of public computers are PCs, 14% of public computers are Macs, network access in dorm rooms, network access in dorm lounges, online registration, online administrative functions (other than registration), support for handheld computing, remote student-access to Web through college's connection.

CAMPUS LIFE

Activities: Choral groups, dance, drama/theater, jazz band, literary magazine, music ensembles, musical theater, opera, pep band, radio station, student government, student newspaper, student-run film society, symphony orchestra, yearbook. **Organizations:** 65 registered organizations, 7 honor societies, 7 religious organizations. 6 fraternities (26% men join), 5 sororities (30% women join). **Athletics (Intercollegiate):** *Men:* Baseball, basketball, cross-country, football, golf, soccer, tennis, water polo. *Women:* Basketball, crew/rowing, cross-country, soccer, softball, swimming, tennis, track/field (outdoor), volleyball, water polo.

ADMISSIONS

Freshman Academic Profile: 61% in top 10% of high school class, 96% in top 25% of high school class, 99% in top 50% of high school class. 70% from public high schools. SAT Math middle 50% range 553–669. SAT Critical Reading middle 50% range 552–665. SAT Writing middle 50% range 555–667. ACT middle 50% range 25–29. TOEFL required of all international applicants, minimum paper TOEFL 550, minimum computer TOEFL 213. **Basis for Candidate Selection:** *Very important factors considered include:* Academic GPA, application essay, character/personal qualities, class rank, rigor of secondary school record, standardized test scores. *Important factors considered include:* Extracurricular activities, interview, talent/ability, volunteer work. *Other factors considered include:* Alumni/ae relation, racial/ethnic status, recommendation(s), work experience. **Freshman Admission Requirements:** High school diploma is required, and GED is accepted. *Academic units required:* 2 English, 2 math, 2 science (1 science lab), 2 foreign language, 3 social studies. **Freshman Admission Statistics:** 4,269 applied, 53% admitted, 43% enrolled. **Transfer Admission Requirements:** College transcript(s), essay or personal statement. Minimum college GPA of 2.5 required. Lowest grade transferable C-. **General Admission Information:** Application fee $55. Regular application deadline 1/15. Regular notification is rolling. Nonfall registration accepted. Credit and/or placement offered for CEEB Advanced Placement tests.

COSTS AND FINANCIAL AID

Annual tuition $33,760. Room and board $11,315. Required fees $940. Average book expense $1,100. **Required Forms and Deadlines:** FAFSA, state aid form. Financial aid filing deadline 3/2. **Notification of Awards:** Applicants will be notified of awards on a rolling basis beginning on or about 3/15. **Types of Aid:** *Need-based scholarships/grants:* Pell, SEOG, state scholarships/grants, private scholarships, the school's own gift aid. *Loans:* FFEL Subsidized Stafford, FFEL Unsubsidized Stafford, FFEL PLUS, Federal Perkins, college/university loans from institutional funds. **Student Employment:** Federal Work-Study Program available. Institutional employment available. Off-campus job opportunities are excellent. **Financial Aid Statistics:** 59% freshmen, 59% undergrads receive need-based scholarship or grant aid. 47% freshmen, 50% undergrads receive need-based self-help aid. 74% freshmen, 75% undergrads receive any aid.

See page 1114.

CHARLESTON SOUTHERN UNIVERSITY

Enrollment Services, PO Box 118087, Charleston, SC 29423
Phone: 843-863-7050 **E-mail:** enroll@csuniv.edu **CEEB Code:** 5079
Fax: 843-863-7070 **Website:** www.charlestonsouthern.edu **ACT Code:** 3833
Financial Aid Phone: 843-863-7050

This private school, affiliated with the Southern Baptist Church, was founded in 1964. It has a 300-acre campus.

RATINGS
Admissions Selectivity Rating: 78   **Fire Safety Rating:** 60*   **Green Rating:** 60*

STUDENTS AND FACULTY
Enrollment: 2,473. **Student Body:** 61% female, 39% male, 18% out-of-state, 2% international (30 countries represented). African American 27%, Asian 2%, Caucasian 55%, Hispanic 1%. **Retention and Graduation:** 60% freshmen return for sophomore year. 22% freshmen graduate within 4 years. 14% grads go on to further study within 1 year. **Faculty:** Student/faculty ratio 18:1. 107 full-time faculty, 63% hold PhDs. 100% faculty teach undergrads.

ACADEMICS
Degrees: Bachelor's, master's. **Academic Requirements:** Arts/fine arts, computer literacy, English (including composition), foreign languages, history, humanities, mathematics, sciences (biological or physical), social science. **Classes:** Most classes have 20–29 students. Most lab/discussion sections have 20–29 students. **Majors with Highest Enrollment:** Business administration/management, elementary education and teaching, psychology. **Disciplines with Highest Percentage of Degrees Awarded:** Education 20%, business/marketing 18%, social sciences 14%, psychology 11%, health professions and related sciences 10%. **Special Study Options:** Accelerated program, cooperative education program, cross-registration, distance learning, double major, dual enrollment, honors program, internships, study abroad, teacher certification program, evening division.

FACILITIES
Housing: Men's dorms, women's dorms. **Special Academic Facilities/Equipment:** Earthquake Education Center, computer labs with wireless Internet, nursing clinical lab, specialized music rehearsal modules, advanced music keyboard technology. **Computers:** 100% of classrooms are wireless, 100% of public computers are PCs, network access in dorm rooms, network access in dorm lounges, online registration, online administrative functions (other than registration), remote student-access to Web through college's connection.

CAMPUS LIFE
Activities: Choral groups, concert band, dance, drama/theater, jazz band, literary magazine, marching band, music ensembles, musical theater, pep band, student government, student newspaper, yearbook. **Organizations:** 22 registered organizations, 3 honor societies, 4 religious organizations. **Athletics (Intercollegiate):** *Men:* Baseball, basketball, cross-country, football, golf, tennis, track/field (indoor), track/field (outdoor). *Women:* Basketball, cross-country, golf, soccer, softball, tennis, track/field (indoor), track/field (outdoor), volleyball.

ADMISSIONS
Freshman Academic Profile: 18% in top 10% of high school class, 47% in top 25% of high school class, 80% in top 50% of high school class. 81% from public high schools. SAT Math middle 50% range 480–570. SAT Critical Reading middle 50% range 490–570. ACT middle 50% range 20–24. TOEFL required of all international applicants, minimum paper TOEFL 550, minimum computer TOEFL 213. **Basis for Candidate Selection:** *Very important factors considered include:* Rigor of secondary school record, standardized test scores. *Important factors considered include:* Class rank. *Other factors*

considered include: Application essay, character/personal qualities, extracurricular activities, interview, recommendation(s), religious affiliation/commitment, talent/ability, work experience. **Freshman Admission Requirements:** High school diploma is required, and GED is accepted. *Academic units required:* 4 English, 3 math, 3 science (2 science labs), 3 history, 3 academic electives. *Academic units recommended:* 4 English, 4 math, 3 science (2 science labs), 2 foreign language. **Freshman Admission Statistics:** 2,283 applied, 72% admitted, 47% enrolled. **Transfer Admission Requirements:** College transcript(s), statement of good standing from prior institution(s). Minimum college GPA of 2.0 required. Lowest grade transferable C. **General Admission Information:** Application fee $30. Regular notification is rolling. Nonfall registration accepted. Common Application not accepted. Credit and/or placement offered for CEEB Advanced Placement tests.

COSTS AND FINANCIAL AID
Average book expense $1,000. **Required Forms and Deadlines:** FAFSA. Financial aid filing deadline 4/15. **Notification of Awards:** Applicants will be notified of awards on a rolling basis beginning on or about 2/1. **Types of Aid:** *Need-based scholarships/grants:* Pell, SEOG, state scholarships/grants, private scholarships, the school's own gift aid. *Loans:* Direct Subsidized Stafford, Direct Unsubsidized Stafford, Direct PLUS, FFEL Subsidized Stafford, FFEL PLUS, Federal Perkins, state loans. **Financial Aid Statistics:** 85% freshmen, 79% undergrads receive need-based scholarship or grant aid. 69% freshmen, 63% undergrads receive need-based self-help aid. 23 freshmen, 72 undergrads receive athletic scholarships. Highest amount earned per year from on-campus jobs $2,000.

CHARTER OAK STATE COLLEGE

55 Paul J. Manafort Drive, New Britain, CT 06053-2142
Phone: 860-832-3800 **E-mail:** info@charteroak.edu
Fax: 860-832-3800 **Website:** www.cosc.edu
Financial Aid Phone: 860-832-3872

This public school was founded in 1973.

RATINGS
Admissions Selectivity Rating: 60*   **Fire Safety Rating:** 60*   **Green Rating:** 60*

STUDENTS AND FACULTY
Enrollment: 1,711. **Student Body:** 62% female, 38% male, 53% out-of-state. African American 12%, Asian 2%, Caucasian 68%, Hispanic 6%. **Retention and Graduation:** 72% freshmen return for sophomore year. **Faculty:** Student/faculty ratio 11:1. 100% faculty teach undergrads.

ACADEMICS
Degrees: Associate, bachelor's. **Academic Requirements:** Arts/fine arts, English (including composition), history, humanities, mathematics, philosophy, sciences (biological or physical), social science. **Classes:** Most classes have 10–19 students. **Disciplines with Highest Percentage of Degrees Awarded:** Liberal arts/general studies 100%. **Special Study Options:** Distance learning, external degree program, independent study, liberal arts/career combination, student-designed major.

FACILITIES
Computers: Online registration, online administrative functions (other than registration).

ADMISSIONS
Freshman Admission Requirements: High school diploma is required, and GED is accepted. **Transfer Admission Requirements:** College transcript(s), Lowest grade transferable D. **General Admission Information:** Application fee $75. Regular notification daily. Nonfall registration not accepted. Admission may be deferred for a maximum of 1 year. Credit offered for CEEB Advanced Placement tests.

COSTS AND FINANCIAL AID
Required Forms and Deadlines: FAFSA, institution's own financial aid form, Contractual Consortium Agreement form and course approval form (if applicable). **Notification of Awards:** Applicants will be notified of awards on a rolling basis beginning on or about 8/15. **Types of Aid:** *Need-based scholarships/grants:* Pell, state scholarships/grants, private scholarships, the school's own gift aid. *Loans:* FFEL Subsidized Stafford, FFEL Unsubsidized Stafford, FFEL PLUS. **Financial Aid Statistics:** 12% undergrads receive need-based scholarship or grant aid. 25% undergrads receive need-based self-help aid.

CHATHAM COLLEGE UNIVERSITY

Woodland Road, Pittsburgh, PA 15232
Phone: 412-365-1290 **E-mail:** admissions@chatham.edu **CEEB Code:** 2081
Fax: 412-365-1609 **Website:** www.chatham.edu **ACT Code:** 3538
Financial Aid Phone: 412-365-2797

This private school was founded in 1869. It has a 32-acre campus.

RATINGS
Admissions Selectivity Rating: 77   **Fire Safety Rating:** 65   **Green Rating:** 89

STUDENTS AND FACULTY
Enrollment: 568. **Student Body:** 100% female, 19% out-of-state, 6% international (17 countries represented). African American 10%, Asian 2%, Caucasian 66%, Hispanic 3%. **Retention and Graduation:** 70% freshmen return for sophomore year. 39% freshmen graduate within 4 years. 56% grads go on to further study within 1 year. 11% grads pursue arts and sciences degrees. 11% grads pursue business degrees. 1% grads pursue law degrees. 6% grads pursue medical degrees. **Faculty:** Student/faculty ratio 8:1. 78 full-time faculty, 88% hold PhDs. 80% faculty teach undergrads.

ACADEMICS
Degrees: Bachelor's, doctoral, master's, post-bachelor's certificate, post-master's certificate. **Academic Requirements:** Arts/fine arts, English (including composition), mathematics, sciences (biological or physical), first-year seminar (writing and information literacy), intercultural/international experience (can be fulfilled with foreign language or study abroad), diversity and identity in a global context, citizenship and civic engagement, wellness. **Classes:** Most classes have 10–19 students. Most lab/discussion sections have 10–19 students. **Majors with Highest Enrollment:** Biology/biological sciences, English language and literature, psychology. **Disciplines with Highest Percentage of Degrees Awarded:** Psychology 21%, English 13%, visual and performing arts 13%, social sciences 7%, biological/life sciences 7%, business/marketing 7%, public administration and social services 5%, natural resources/environmental science 5%, area and ethnic studies 4%. **Special Study Options:** Accelerated program, cooperative education program, cross-registration, distance learning, double major, dual enrollment, English as a second language (ESL), exchange student program (domestic), honors program, independent study, internships, liberal arts/career combination, student-designed major, study abroad, teacher certification program, 5-year bachelor's/master's programs in 9 fields on campus, 5-year bachelor's/master's programs also with Carnegie Mellon (e.g., engineering, public policy) and other institutions.

FACILITIES
Housing: Women's dorms, apartments for married students, apartments for single students, special housing for international students, intercultural residence hall, community service floor and environmental floor within a larger residence hall. **Special Academic Facilities/Equipment:** Athletic and fitness center, art and design center, broadcast studio, renovated art gallery, classroom space, coffee shop, campus arboretum and greenhouse, proscenium theater. **Computers:** 12% of classrooms are wired, 100% of classrooms are wireless, 95% of public computers are PCs, 5% of public computers are Macs, network access in dorm rooms, network access in dorm lounges, online registration, online administrative functions (other than registration), remote student-access to Web through college's connection, tuition includes personal computer. Undergraduates are required to own a computer.

CAMPUS LIFE
Activities: Choral groups, dance, drama/theater, literary magazine, music ensembles, musical theater, student government, student newspaper, yearbook. **Organizations:** 25 registered organizations, 10 honor societies, 6 religious organizations. **Women:** Basketball, ice hockey, soccer, softball, swimming, tennis, volleyball. Environmental Initiatives: 15% alternative energy usage. Participation in President's Climate Commitment of AC&U. Highly subsidized or free public transportation and shuttle service.

ADMISSIONS
Freshman Academic Profile: 31% in top 10% of high school class, 51% in top 25% of high school class, 88% in top 50% of high school class. SAT Math middle 50% range 440–563. SAT Critical Reading middle 50% range 480–583. ACT middle 50% range 21–26. TOEFL required of all international applicants, minimum paper TOEFL 550, minimum computer TOEFL 210. **Basis for Candidate Selection:** *Very important factors considered include:* Rigor of secondary school record. *Important factors considered include:* Academic GPA, application essay. *Other factors considered include:* Alumni/ae relation, character/personal qualities, class rank, extracurricular activities, interview, level of applicant's interest, recommendation(s), standardized test scores, talent/ability,

volunteer work, work experience. **Freshman Admission Requirements:** High school diploma is required, and GED is accepted. *Academic units required:* 4 English, 2 math, 2 science, 3 social science. *Academic units recommended:* 4 English, 3 math, 3 science, 2 foreign language, 3 social science. **Freshman Admission Statistics:** 514 applied, 76% admitted, 38% enrolled. **Transfer Admission Requirements:** College transcript(s), essay or personal statement. Minimum college GPA of 2.0 required. Lowest grade transferable C-. **General Admission Information:** Application fee $35. Regular application deadline 8/1. Regular notification is rolling. Nonfall registration accepted. Admission may be deferred for a maximum of 1 year. Credit and/or placement offered for CEEB Advanced Placement tests.

COSTS AND FINANCIAL AID
Annual tuition $25,216. Room and board $7,892. Required fees $900. Average book expense $860. **Required Forms and Deadlines:** FAFSA. Financial aid filing deadline 5/1. **Notification of Awards:** Applicants will be notified of awards on a rolling basis beginning on or about 2/15. **Types of Aid:** *Need-based scholarships/grants:* Pell, SEOG, state scholarships/grants, private scholarships, the school's own gift aid. *Loans:* FFEL Subsidized Stafford, FFEL Unsubsidized Stafford, FFEL PLUS, Federal Perkins. **Student Employment:** Federal Work-Study Program available. Institutional employment available. Off-campus job opportunities are good. **Financial Aid Statistics:** 81% freshmen, 88% undergrads receive need-based scholarship or grant aid. 81% freshmen, 90% undergrads receive need-based self-help aid. 92% freshmen, 96% undergrads receive any aid. Highest amount earned per year from on-campus jobs $2,200.

See page 1116.

CHESTNUT HILL COLLEGE

9601 Germantown Avenue, Philadelphia, PA 19118-2693
Phone: 215-248-7001 **E-mail:** chcapply@chc.edu **CEEB Code:** 2082
Fax: 215-248-7082 **Website:** www.chc.edu **ACT Code:** 3540

This private school, affiliated with the Roman Catholic Church, was founded in 1924. It has a 75-acre campus.

RATINGS
Admissions Selectivity Rating: 60*   **Fire Safety Rating:** 83   **Green Rating:** 68

STUDENTS AND FACULTY
Enrollment: 1,105. **Student Body:** 71% female, 29% male, 29% out-of-state. African American 37%, Asian 2%, Caucasian 52%, Hispanic 6%. **Retention and Graduation:** 63% freshmen return for sophomore year. 46% freshmen graduate within 4 years. 41% grads go on to further study within 1 year. 32% grads pursue arts and sciences degrees. 6% grads pursue business degrees. 3% grads pursue medical degrees. **Faculty:** Student/faculty ratio 10:1. 70 full-time faculty, 81% hold PhDs. 68% faculty teach undergrads.

ACADEMICS
Degrees: Associate, bachelor's, certificate, doctoral, master's, post-bachelor's certificate, post-master's certificate. **Academic Requirements:** Arts/fine arts, computer literacy, English (including composition), foreign languages, history, humanities, mathematics, sciences (biological or physical), social science. Core requirements also include a seminar introducing the liberal arts, a global studies seminar, religious studies, and physical education. **Classes:** Most classes have 10–19 students. Most lab/discussion sections have 10–19 students. **Majors with Highest Enrollment:** Business administration and management, elementary education and teaching, psychology. **Disciplines with Highest Percentage of Degrees Awarded:** Business/marketing 29%, public administration and social services 19%, psychology 14%, education 11%, security and protective services 9%. **Special Study Options:** Cooperative education program, cross-registration, double major, dual enrollment, English as a second language (ESL), exchange student program (domestic), honors program, independent study, internships, student-designed major, study abroad, teacher certification program. Upperclass undergraduates may take grad classes. Post-baccalaureate certificates in instructional technology, administration of human services, spirituality/spiritual direction, clinical pastoral education. Post-master's certificate programs in leadership in instructional technology, instructional technology design, education and technology, instructional technology specialist, addictions counseling, child and adolescent theorapy, marriage and family therapy, trauma studies, spiritual direction, supervision of spiritual directors, professional counseling for licensure. There is a 2–2 double bachelor's program in biology or chemistry and medical technology with Thomas Jefferson University. Bachelor's/doctoral program with College of Podiatric Medicine of Temple University. 5-year bachelor's/master's combination programs in counseling psychology, education, and computer information sciences/instructional technology.

FACILITIES

Housing: Coed dorms, on-campus housing includes singles, doubles, suites, and apartment-like units. A new on-campus residence hall opened in fall 2006. **Special Academic Facilities/Equipment:** Rare book collection, Irish literature collection, observatory, planetarium. **Computers:** 40% of classrooms are wired, 10% of classrooms are wireless, 90% of public computers are PCs, 10% of public computers are Macs, network access in dorm rooms, network access in dorm lounges, remote student-access to Web through college's connection. Undergraduates are required to own a computer.

CAMPUS LIFE

Activities: Choral groups, drama/theater, jazz band, literary magazine, music ensembles, musical theater, opera, student government, student newspaper, symphony orchestra, television station, yearbook. **Organizations:** 19 registered organizations, 9 honor societies, 1 religious organization. **Athletics (Intercollegiate):** *Men:* Baseball, basketball, cross-country, golf, softball, tennis. *Women:* Basketball, cross-country, golf, lacrosse, soccer, softball, tennis, volleyball.

ADMISSIONS

Freshman Academic Profile: 38% from public high schools. SAT Math middle 50% range 420–530. SAT Critical Reading middle 50% range 440–550. SAT Writing middle 50% range 440–540. ACT middle 50% range 17–21. TOEFL required of all international applicants, minimum paper TOEFL 500, minimum computer TOEFL 213. **Basis for Candidate Selection:** *Very important factors considered include:* Application essay, rigor of secondary school record. *Important factors considered include:* Academic GPA, character/personal qualities, extracurricular activities, interview, recommendation(s), standardized test scores. *Other factors considered include:* Alumni/ae relation, class rank, level of applicant's interest, talent/ability, volunteer work, work experience. **Freshman Admission Requirements:** High school diploma is required, and GED is accepted. *Academic units recommended:* 4 English, 3 math, 3 science, 2 foreign language, 4 social studies. **Freshman Admission Statistics:** 1,341 applied, 83% admitted, 19% enrolled. **Transfer Admission Requirements:** College transcript(s), essay or personal statement. Minimum college GPA of 2.0 required. Lowest grade transferable C. **General Admission Information:** Application fee $35. Early decision application deadline 12/10. Regular notification is rolling. Nonfall registration accepted. Admission may be deferred for a maximum of 1 year. Credit and/or placement offered for CEEB Advanced Placement tests.

COSTS AND FINANCIAL AID

Annual tuition $23,600. Room & board $7,950. Average book expense $1,160. **Required Forms and Deadlines:** FAFSA. Financial aid filing deadline 4/15. **Notification of Awards:** Applicants will be notified of awards on a rolling basis beginning on or about 1/31. **Types of Aid:** *Need-based scholarships/grants:* Pell, SEOG, state scholarships/grants, private scholarships, the school's own gift aid. *Loans:* FFEL Subsidized Stafford, FFEL Unsubsidized Stafford, FFEL PLUS, Federal Perkins. **Financial Aid Statistics:** 77% freshmen, 79% undergrads receive need-based scholarship or grant aid. 70% freshmen, 74% undergrads receive need-based self-help aid. 77% freshmen, 79% undergrads receive any aid. Highest amount earned per year from on-campus jobs $1,500.

CHEYNEY UNIVERSITY OF PENNSYLVANIA

1837 University Circle, Cheyney, PA 19319
Phone: 610-399-2275 **E-mail:** jbrown@cheyney.edu **CEEB Code:** 2648
Fax: 610-399-2099 **Website:** www.cheyney.edu
Financial Aid Phone: 610-399-2302

This public school was founded in 1837. It has a 275-acre campus.

RATINGS

Admissions Selectivity Rating: 60*   **Fire Safety Rating:** 60*   **Green Rating:** 60*

STUDENTS AND FACULTY

Enrollment: 1,351. **Student Body:** 54% female, 46% male, 19% out-of-state. African American 94%, Caucasian 1%. **Retention and Graduation:** 57% freshmen return for sophomore year. **Faculty:** Student/faculty ratio 14:1. 103 full-time faculty, 63% hold PhDs. 89% faculty teach undergrads.

ACADEMICS

Degrees: Associate, bachelor's, master's, post-bachelor's certificate. **Academic Requirements:** Arts/fine arts, computer literacy, English (including composition), foreign languages, humanities, mathematics, sciences (biological or physical), social science. **Disciplines with Highest Percentage of Degrees Awarded:** Social sciences 35%, business/marketing 28%, psychology 12%, parks and recreation 6%, communication technologies 6%, English 3%, biological/life sciences 3%. **Special Study Options:** Cooperative education

program, cross-registration, distance learning, double major, honors program, independent study, internships, study abroad, teacher certification program.

FACILITIES

Housing: Coed dorms, men's dorms, women's dorms. **Special Academic Facilities/Equipment:** Afro-American history/culture collection, planetarium, weather station, satellite communication network. **Computers:** Network access in dorm lounges, online registration, online administrative functions (other than registration), remote student-access to Web through college's connection.

CAMPUS LIFE

Activities: Choral groups, dance, drama/theater, jazz band, marching band, music ensembles, radio station, student government, student newspaper, student-run film society, television station, yearbook. **Organizations:** 41 registered organizations, 12 honor societies. 4 fraternities (5% men join), 4 sororities (8% women join). **Athletics (Intercollegiate):** *Men:* Basketball, cross-country, football, tennis, track/field (outdoor), wrestling. *Women:* Basketball, cross-country, tennis, track/field (outdoor), volleyball.

ADMISSIONS

Freshman Academic Profile: TOEFL required of all international applicants, minimum paper TOEFL 500. **Basis for Candidate Selection:** *Very important factors considered include:* Recommendation(s), rigor of secondary school record. *Important factors considered include:* Application essay, class rank, extracurricular activities, interview, standardized test scores, state residency. *Other factors considered include:* Racial/ethnic status, talent/ability. **Freshman Admission Requirements:** High school diploma is required, and GED is accepted. *Academic units required:* 4 English, 3 math, 2 science, 2 foreign language, 2 history. **Freshman Admission Statistics:** 2,751 applied, 56% admitted, 43% enrolled. **Transfer Admission Requirements:** College transcript(s), interview, statement of good standing from prior institution(s). Minimum college GPA of 2.0 required. Lowest grade transferable C. **General Admission Information:** Application fee $20. Regular application deadline 3/31. Regular notification is rolling. Nonfall registration accepted. Admission may be deferred for a maximum of 1 year. Common Application not accepted.

COSTS AND FINANCIAL AID

Annual in-state tuition $4,906. Out-of-state tuition $12,266. Room & board $5,679. Required fees $912. Average book expense $1,200. **Required Forms and Deadlines:** FAFSA. Financial aid filing deadline 5/1. **Notification of Awards:** Applicants will be notified of awards on a rolling basis beginning on or about 4/1. **Types of Aid:** *Need-based scholarships/grants:* Pell, SEOG, state scholarships/grants, private scholarships, the school's own gift aid. *Loans:* FFEL Subsidized Stafford, FFEL Unsubsidized Stafford, FFEL PLUS, Federal Perkins. **Student Employment:** Federal Work-Study Program available. Institutional employment available. Off-campus job opportunities are good. **Financial Aid Statistics:** 72% freshmen, 61% undergrads receive need-based scholarship or grant aid. 84% freshmen, 80% undergrads receive need-based self-help aid.

CHICAGO STATE UNIVERSITY

9501 South Street King Drive, ADM-200, Chicago, IL 60628
Phone: 773-995-2513 **E-mail:** ug-admissions@csu.edu
Fax: 773-995-3820 **Website:** www.csu.edu **ACT Code:** 1694
Financial Aid Phone: 773-995-2304

This public school was founded in 1867. It has a 161-acre campus.

RATINGS

Admissions Selectivity Rating: 71   **Fire Safety Rating:** 60*   **Green Rating:** 60*

STUDENTS AND FACULTY

Enrollment: 4,818. **Student Body:** 73% female, 27% male, 2% out-of-state. African American 87%, Caucasian 3%, Hispanic 6%. **Faculty:** Student/faculty ratio 13:1. 322 full-time faculty.

ACADEMICS

Degrees: Bachelor's, master's, post-bachelor's certificate. **Academic Requirements:** English (including composition), foreign languages, humanities, mathematics, sciences (biological or physical), social science. **Classes:** Most classes have 20–29 students. **Majors with Highest Enrollment:** Elementary education and teaching, liberal arts and sciences/liberal studies, nursing/registered nurse training (RN, ASN, BSN, MSN). **Disciplines with Highest Percentage of Degrees Awarded:** Liberal arts/general studies 31%, education 13%, business/marketing 12%, health professions and related sciences 9%, psychology 7%. **Special Study Options:** Cooperative education program, distance learning, double major, English as a second language (ESL), honors program, independent study, internships, student-designed major, study abroad, teacher certification program, programs for mature adults (University Without Walls, Individual Curriculum, and Board of Governors degree program).

FACILITIES

Housing: Coed dorms. **Special Academic Facilities/Equipment:** Art gallery, electron microscopes, greenhouse. **Computers:** 100% of public computers are PCs, network access in dorm rooms, online registration, remote student-access to Web through college's connection.

CAMPUS LIFE

Activities: Choral groups, concert band, dance, drama/theater, jazz band, literary magazine, music ensembles, radio station, student government, student newspaper, television station. **Organizations:** 47 registered organizations, 30 honor societies, 4 religious organizations. 4 fraternities, 4 sororities. **Athletics (Intercollegiate):** *Men:* Baseball, basketball, cross-country, golf, tennis, track/field (indoor), track/field (outdoor). *Women:* Basketball, cross-country, golf, tennis, track/field (indoor), track/field (outdoor), volleyball.

ADMISSIONS

Freshman Academic Profile: 11% in top 10% of high school class, 29% in top 25% of high school class, 58% in top 50% of high school class. 80% from public high schools. ACT middle 50% range 16–19. TOEFL required of all international applicants, minimum paper TOEFL 500. **Basis for Candidate Selection:** *Very important factors considered include:* Rigor of secondary school record, standardized test scores. **Freshman Admission Requirements:** High school diploma is required, and GED is accepted. *Academic units required:* 4 English, 3 math, 3 science, 3 social studies, 2 academic electives. **Freshman Admission Statistics:** 3,949 applied, 56% admitted, 25% enrolled. **Transfer Admission Requirements:** College transcript(s). Minimum college GPA of 2.0 required. Lowest grade transferable D. **General Admission Information:** Application fee $25. Regular application deadline 7/15. Regular notification is rolling. Nonfall registration accepted. Admission may be deferred for a maximum of 1 semester. Common Application not accepted. Credit and/or placement offered for CEEB Advanced Placement tests.

COSTS AND FINANCIAL AID

Annual in-state tuition $3,762. Out-of-state tuition $8,448. Room & board $5,700. Required fees $1,060. Average book expense $1,400. **Required Forms and Deadlines:** FAFSA, institution's own financial aid form. **Notification of Awards:** Applicants will be notified of awards on a rolling basis beginning on or about 3/1. **Types of Aid:** *Need-based scholarships/grants:* Pell, SEOG, state scholarships/grants, private scholarships, the school's own gift aid. *Loans:* FFEL Subsidized Stafford, FFEL Unsubsidized Stafford, FFEL PLUS, Federal Perkins. **Student Employment:** Federal Work-Study Program available. Institutional employment available. Off-campus job opportunities are good. **Financial Aid Statistics:** 73% freshmen, 82% undergrads receive need-based scholarship or grant aid. 26% freshmen, 45% undergrads receive need-based self-help aid. Highest amount earned per year from on-campus jobs $2,000.

CHOWAN UNIVERSITY

One University Place, Murfreesboro, NC 27855
Phone: 252-398-1236 **E-mail:** admissions@chowan.edu **CEEB Code:** 5107
Fax: 252-398-1190 **Website:** www.chowan.edu **ACT Code:** 3084
Financial Aid Phone: 252-398-6513

This private school, affiliated with the Baptist Church, was founded in 1848. It has a 300-acre campus.

RATINGS

Admissions Selectivity Rating: 73   **Fire Safety Rating:** 62   **Green Rating:** 60*

STUDENTS AND FACULTY

Enrollment: 886. **Student Body:** 46% female, 54% male, 48% out-of-state. **Retention and Graduation:** 54% freshmen return for sophomore year. 18% freshmen graduate within 4 years. 5% grads go on to further study within 1 year. 2% grads pursue arts and sciences degrees. 1% grads pursue business degrees. 1% grads pursue law degrees. 1% grads pursue medical degrees. **Faculty:** Student/faculty ratio 16:1. 47 full-time faculty, 64% hold PhDs. 100% faculty teach undergrads.

ACADEMICS

Degrees: Associate, bachelor's. **Academic Requirements:** Arts/fine arts, computer literacy, English (including composition), foreign languages, history, humanities, mathematics, philosophy, sciences (biological or physical), social science, religion, physical education. **Classes:** Most classes have fewer than 10

students. **Majors with Highest Enrollment:** Business administration/ management, graphic communications, health services/allied health. **Disciplines with Highest Percentage of Degrees Awarded:** Business/marketing 17%, parks and recreation 14%, education 14%, visual and performing arts 12%, biological/life sciences 11%, security and protective services 9%, history 9%. **Special Study Options:** Distance learning, double major, dual enrollment, honors program, independent study, internships, liberal arts/career combination, study abroad, teacher certification program.

FACILITIES

Housing: Men's dorms, women's dorms, special housing for disabled students. **Special Academic Facilities/Equipment:** Antiquities room in Whitaker Library, Ward Parlor in McDowell Columns Building, Green Hall Art Gallery, Daniel Hall Recital Hall. **Computers:** 1% of classrooms are wired, 5% of classrooms are wireless, 100% of public computers are PCs, network access in dorm rooms, online registration, online administrative functions (other than registration), remote student-access to Web through college's connection.

CAMPUS LIFE

Activities: Choral groups, concert band, drama/theater, jazz band, literary magazine, music ensembles, pep band, student government, yearbook. **Organizations:** 52 registered organizations, 5 honor societies, 2 religious organizations. 2 fraternities (5% men join), 2 sororities (5% women join). **Athletics (Intercollegiate):** *Men:* Baseball, basketball, cheerleading, football, golf, soccer, tennis. *Women:* Basketball, cheerleading, cross-country, golf, soccer, softball, tennis, volleyball.

ADMISSIONS

Freshman Academic Profile: 4% in top 10% of high school class, 35% in top 50% of high school class. 95% from public high schools. SAT Math middle 50% range 380–490. SAT Critical Reading middle 50% range 380–480. ACT middle 50% range 15–19. TOEFL required of all international applicants, minimum paper TOEFL 450, minimum computer TOEFL 133. **Basis for Candidate Selection:** *Very important factors considered include:* Academic GPA, rigor of secondary school record, standardized test scores. *Other factors considered include:* Alumni/ae relation, application essay, character/personal qualities, class rank, extracurricular activities, interview, level of applicant's interest, recommendation(s), talent/ability, volunteer work, work experience. **Freshman Admission Requirements:** High school diploma is required, and GED is accepted. *Academic units recommended:* 4 English, 3 math, 2 science (2 science labs), 3 social studies, 7 academic electives. **Freshman Admission Statistics:** 2,385 applied, 61% admitted, 24% enrolled. **Transfer Admission Requirements:** High school transcript, college transcript(s), statement of good standing from prior institution(s). Minimum college GPA of 2.0 required. Lowest grade transferable C. **General Admission Information:** Application fee $20. Regular notification is rolling. Nonfall registration accepted. Admission may be deferred for a maximum of 1 year. Credit and/or placement offered for CEEB Advanced Placement tests.

COSTS AND FINANCIAL AID

Annual tuition $15,800. Room & board $6,800. Required fees $240. Average book expense $885. **Required Forms and Deadlines:** FAFSA. Financial aid filing deadline 8/1. **Notification of Awards:** Applicants will be notified of awards on a rolling basis beginning on or about 3/1. **Types of Aid:** *Need-based scholarships/grants:* SEOG, state scholarships/grants, private scholarships, the school's own gift aid. *Loans:* FFEL Unsubsidized Stafford, FFEL PLUS, college/university loans from institutional funds, alternative loans. **Financial Aid Statistics:** 80% freshmen, 83% undergrads receive need-based scholarship or grant aid. 75% freshmen, 76% undergrads receive need-based self-help aid. 86% freshmen, 86% undergrads receive any aid. Highest amount earned per year from on-campus jobs $700.

CHRISTENDOM COLLEGE

134 Christendom Drive, Front Royal, VA 22630
Phone: 540-636-2900 **E-mail:** admissions@christendom.edu **CEEB Code:** 5691
Fax: 540-636-1655 **Website:** www.christendom.edu **ACT Code:** 4339
Financial Aid Phone: 800-877-5456

This private school, affiliated with the Roman Catholic Church, was founded in 1977. It has a 100-acre campus.

RATINGS

Admissions Selectivity Rating: 87   **Fire Safety Rating:** 60*   **Green Rating:** 60*

STUDENTS AND FACULTY

Enrollment: 379. **Student Body:** 57% female, 43% male, 78% out-of-state,

2% international (3 countries represented). Asian 2%, Caucasian 93%, Hispanic 3%. **Retention and Graduation:** 84% freshmen return for sophomore year. 53% freshmen graduate within 4 years. 25% grads go on to further study within 1 year. 15% grads pursue arts and sciences degrees. 5% grads pursue business degrees. 5% grads pursue law degrees. **Faculty:** Student/faculty ratio 12:1. 23 full-time faculty, 78% hold PhDs. 100% faculty teach undergrads.

ACADEMICS

Degrees: Associate, bachelor's, master's. **Academic Requirements:** English (including composition), foreign languages, history, humanities, mathematics, philosophy, sciences (biological or physical), social science, theology. **Classes:** Most classes have 10–19 students. **Majors with Highest Enrollment:** History, philosophy, political science and government. **Disciplines with Highest Percentage of Degrees Awarded:** Liberal arts/general studies 100%. **Special Study Options:** Double major, honors program, independent study, internships, study abroad, semester in Rome.

FACILITIES

Housing: Men's dorms, women's dorms. **Computers:** 100% of public computers are PCs.

CAMPUS LIFE

Activities: Choral groups, drama/theater, literary magazine, musical theater, student government, student newspaper, student-run film society, yearbook. **Organizations:** 5 registered organizations, 4 religious organizations. **Athletics (Intercollegiate):** *Men:* Baseball, basketball, soccer. *Women:* Basketball, soccer, softball, volleyball.

ADMISSIONS

Freshman Academic Profile: 15% in top 10% of high school class, 75% in top 25% of high school class, 100% in top 50% of high school class. 20% from public high schools. SAT Math middle 50% range 530–630. SAT Critical Reading middle 50% range 600–700. TOEFL required of all international applicants, minimum paper TOEFL 550, minimum computer TOEFL 250. **Basis for Candidate Selection:** *Very important factors considered include:* Application essay, character/personal qualities, level of applicant's interest, religious affiliation/commitment, standardized test scores. *Important factors considered include:* Interview, recommendation(s), rigor of secondary school record. *Other factors considered include:* Academic GPA, alumni/ae relation, class rank, extracurricular activities, first generation, talent/ability, volunteer work, work experience. **Freshman Admission Requirements:** High school diploma or equivalent is not required. *Academic units recommended:* 4 English, 2 math, 2 science, 2 foreign language, 1 social studies, 2 history, 1 academic elective. **Freshman Admission Statistics:** 249 applied, 76% admitted, 55% enrolled. **Transfer Admission Requirements:** College transcript(s), essay or personal statement. Minimum college GPA of 2.8 required. Lowest grade transferable C. **General Admission Information:** Application fee $25. Regular application deadline 3/1. Regular notification 4/1. Nonfall registration not accepted. Common Application accepted. Credit offered for CEEB Advanced Placement tests.

COSTS AND FINANCIAL AID

Annual tuition $16,290. Room & board $6,066. Required fees $540. Average book expense $450. **Required Forms and Deadlines:** Institution's own financial aid form. Financial aid filing deadline 3/1. **Notification of Awards:** Applicants will be notified of awards on a rolling basis beginning on or about 2/1. **Types of Aid:** *Need-based scholarships/grants:* Private scholarships, the school's own gift aid. *Loans:* College/university loans from institutional funds. **Student Employment:** Institutional employment available. Off-campus job opportunities are fair. **Financial Aid Statistics:** 43% freshmen, 47% undergrads receive need-based scholarship or grant aid. 43% freshmen, 48% undergrads receive need-based self-help aid. 80% freshmen, 65% undergrads receive any aid. Highest amount earned per year from on-campus jobs $1,850.

CHRISTIAN BROTHERS UNIVERSITY

Admissions, Box T-6, 650 East Parkway South, Memphis, TN 38104-5519
Phone: 901-321-3205 **E-mail:** admissions@cbu.edu **CEEB Code:** 1121
Fax: 901-321-3202 **Website:** www.cbu.edu **ACT Code:** 3952
Financial Aid Phone: 901-321-3306

This private school, affiliated with the Roman Catholic Church, was founded in 1871. It has a 75-acre campus.

RATINGS

Admissions Selectivity Rating: 85   **Fire Safety Rating:** 60*   **Green Rating:** 60*

STUDENTS AND FACULTY

Enrollment: 1,428. **Student Body:** 55% female, 45% male, 17% out-of-state, 2% international (21 countries represented). African American 33%, Asian 5%, Caucasian 51%, Hispanic 2%. **Retention and Graduation:** 75% freshmen return for sophomore year. 39% freshmen graduate within 4 years. **Faculty:** Student/faculty ratio 13:1. 92 full-time faculty, 88% hold PhDs. 100% faculty teach undergrads.

ACADEMICS

Degrees: Bachelor's, master's, post-bachelor's certificate. **Academic Requirements:** Computer literacy, English (including composition), mathematics, sciences (biological or physical), social science, religious studies, moral philosophy. **Classes:** Most classes have 10–19 students. Most lab/discussion sections have fewer than 10 students. **Majors with Highest Enrollment:** Biology/biological sciences, business administration/management, psychology. **Disciplines with Highest Percentage of Degrees Awarded:** Business/marketing 37%, psychology 24%, engineering 13%, physical sciences 7%, biological/life sciences 6%, education 6%. **Special Study Options:** Accelerated program, cooperative education program, cross-registration, distance learning, double major, dual enrollment, exchange student program (domestic), honors program, independent study, internships, liberal arts/career combination, study abroad, teacher certification program.

FACILITIES

Housing: Men's dorms, women's dorms, apartments for single students, juniors and seniors may live in on-campus apartments. All freshmen and sophomores whose permanent address is beyond a 30-mile radius are required to live on-campus. Some houses are available. **Special Academic Facilities/Equipment:** Art exhibits, audiovisual lab, engineering graphics lab, Gandhi Institute for Nonviolence, Facing History. **Computers:** 100% of public computers are PCs, network access in dorm rooms, network access in dorm lounges, online registration, online administrative functions (other than registration), remote student-access to Web through college's connection.

CAMPUS LIFE

Activities: Choral groups, drama/theater, literary magazine, musical theater, student government, student newspaper, yearbook. **Organizations:** 37 registered organizations, 10 honor societies, 3 religious organizations. 4 fraternities (21% men join), 5 sororities (24% women join). **Athletics (Intercollegiate):** *Men:* Baseball, basketball, cross-country, golf, soccer, tennis. *Women:* Basketball, cross-country, golf, soccer, softball, tennis, volleyball.

ADMISSIONS

Freshman Academic Profile: 30% in top 10% of high school class, 67% in top 25% of high school class, 93% in top 50% of high school class. 64% from public high schools. SAT Math middle 50% range 480–620. SAT Critical Reading middle 50% range 470–610. ACT middle 50% range 21–26. TOEFL required of all international applicants, minimum paper TOEFL 500, minimum computer TOEFL 173. **Basis for Candidate Selection:** *Very important factors considered include:* Academic GPA, rigor of secondary school record, standardized test scores. *Important factors considered include:* Application essay, character/personal qualities, class rank, extracurricular activities, interview, recommendation(s). *Other factors considered include:* Alumni/ae relation, talent/ability, volunteer work, work experience. **Freshman Admission Requirements:** High school diploma is required, and GED is accepted. *Academic units recommended:* 4 English, 4 math, 4 science. **Freshman Admission Statistics:** 1,183 applied, 64% admitted, 37% enrolled. **Transfer Admission Requirements:** College transcript(s), essay or personal statement. Minimum college GPA of 2.5 required. Lowest grade transferable C. **General Admission Information:** Application fee $25. Regular application deadline 8/1. Regular notification is rolling. Nonfall registration accepted. Admission may be deferred for a maximum of 1 year. Credit and/or placement offered for CEEB Advanced Placement tests.

COSTS AND FINANCIAL AID

Annual tuition $21,890. Room and board $5,880. Required fees $520. Average book expense $1,000. **Required Forms and Deadlines:** FAFSA. Financial aid filing deadline 2/15. **Notification of Awards:** Applicants will be notified of awards on a rolling basis beginning on or about 3/1. **Types of Aid:** *Need-based scholarships/grants:* Pell, SEOG, state scholarships/grants, private scholarships, the school's own gift aid. *Loans:* FFEL Subsidized Stafford, FFEL Unsubsidized Stafford, FFEL PLUS, Federal Perkins, state loans. **Student Employment:** Off-campus job opportunities are good. **Financial Aid Statistics:** 35% freshmen, 36% undergrads receive need-based scholarship or grant aid. 44% freshmen, 48% undergrads receive need-based self-help aid. 29 freshmen, 132 undergrads receive athletic scholarships.

CHRISTIAN HERITAGE COLLEGE

2100 Greenfield Drive, El Cajon, CA 92019-1157
Phone: 619-588-7747 **E-mail:** chcadm@adm.christianheritage.edu
Fax: 619-440-0209 **Website:** www.christianheritage.edu **ACT Code:** 0211
Financial Aid Phone: 619-590-1786

This private school was founded in 1970. It has a 32-acre campus.

RATINGS
Admissions Selectivity Rating: 60*   **Fire Safety Rating:** 60*   **Green Rating:** 60*

STUDENTS AND FACULTY
Enrollment: 503. **Student Body:** 59% female, 41% male, 13% out-of-state, 2% international (14 countries represented). African American 11%, Asian 4%, Caucasian 91%, Hispanic 14%. **Retention and Graduation:** 68% freshmen return for sophomore year. 19% freshmen graduate within 4 years. 25% grads go on to further study within 1 year. **Faculty:** 100% faculty teach undergrads.

ACADEMICS
Degrees: Bachelor's, certificate. **Academic Requirements:** Arts/fine arts, computer literacy, English (including composition), history, humanities, mathematics, philosophy, sciences (biological or physical), social science. **Special Study Options:** English as a second language (ESL), independent study, internships, student-designed major, study abroad, teacher certification program.

FACILITIES
Housing: Men's dorms, women's dorms, apartments for single students.

CAMPUS LIFE
Activities: Choral groups, music ensembles, student government, yearbook. **Organizations:** 12 registered organizations, 1 honor society. **Athletics (Intercollegiate):** *Men:* Basketball, soccer. *Women:* Basketball, cheerleading, soccer, volleyball.

ADMISSIONS
Freshman Academic Profile: 7% in top 10% of high school class, 21% in top 25% of high school class, 45% in top 50% of high school class. 70% from public high schools. TOEFL required of all international applicants, minimum paper TOEFL 500. **Basis for Candidate Selection:** *Very important factors considered include:* Application essay, recommendation(s), religious affiliation/commitment, rigor of secondary school record, standardized test scores. *Important factors considered include:* Class rank, extracurricular activities. *Other factors considered include:* Character/personal qualities, interview, volunteer work. **Freshman Admission Requirements:** High school diploma is required, and GED is accepted. *Academic units recommended:* 4 English, 3 math, 3 science (1 science lab), 2 foreign language, 3 history. **Transfer Admission Requirements:** College transcript(s), essay or personal statement, statement of good standing from prior institution(s). Minimum college GPA of 2.0 required. Lowest grade transferable C. **General Admission Information:** Application fee $25. Regular application deadline 8/1. Nonfall registration accepted. Admission may be deferred for a maximum of 1 year. Common Application not accepted. Credit and/or placement offered for CEEB Advanced Placement tests.

COSTS AND FINANCIAL AID
Annual tuition $10,240. Room & board $4,500. Average book expense $600. **Required Forms and Deadlines:** FAFSA, state aid form. Financial aid filing deadline 9/1. **Notification of Awards:** Applicants will be notified of awards on a rolling basis beginning on or about 4/1. **Types of Aid:** *Need-based scholarships/grants:* Pell, SEOG, state scholarships/grants, private scholarships, the school's own gift aid. *Loans:* Direct Subsidized Stafford, Direct Unsubsidized Stafford, Direct PLUS, Federal Perkins. **Student Employment:** Federal Work-Study Program available. Institutional employment available. Off-campus job opportunities are good. **Financial Aid Statistics:** 62% freshmen, 56% undergrads receive need-based scholarship or grant aid. 15% freshmen, 10% undergrads receive need-based self-help aid. Highest amount earned per year from on-campus jobs $1,750.

CHRISTOPHER NEWPORT UNIVERSITY

1 University Place, Newport News, VA 23606-2998
Phone: 757-594-7015 **E-mail:** admit@cnu.edu **CEEB Code:** 5128
Fax: 757-594-7333 **Website:** www.cnu.edu **ACT Code:** 4345
Financial Aid Phone: 757-594-7170

This public school was founded in 1960. It has a 175-acre campus.

RATINGS
Admissions Selectivity Rating: 85   **Fire Safety Rating:** 87   **Green Rating:** 67

STUDENTS AND FACULTY
Enrollment: 4,570. **Student Body:** 54% female, 46% male, 3% out-of-state. African American 7%, Asian 2%, Caucasian 85%, Hispanic 3%. **Retention and Graduation:** 79% freshmen return for sophomore year. 26% freshmen graduate within 4 years. **Faculty:** Student/faculty ratio 17:1. 226 full-time faculty, 88% hold PhDs. 100% faculty teach undergrads.

ACADEMICS
Degrees: Bachelor's, master's. **Academic Requirements:** Arts/fine arts, English (including composition), foreign languages, history, humanities, mathematics, philosophy, sciences (biological or physical), social science. **Classes:** Most classes have 20–29 students. Most lab/discussion sections have 20–29 students. **Majors with Highest Enrollment:** Biology/biological sciences, business administration and management, psychology. **Disciplines with Highest Percentage of Degrees Awarded:** Business/marketing 20%, social sciences 17%, psychology 12%, biological/life sciences 8%, communications/journalism 8%, English 8%. **Special Study Options:** Cross-registration, double major, dual enrollment, honors program, independent study, internships, student-designed major, study abroad.

FACILITIES
Housing: Coed dorms, apartments for single students, fraternity/sorority housing. **Special Academic Facilities/Equipment:** Falk Art Gallery, greenhouse. **Computers:** 80% of public computers are PCs, 10% of public computers are Macs, 10% of public computers are UNIX, network access in dorm rooms, network access in dorm lounges, online registration, online administrative functions (other than registration), remote student-access to Web through college's connection.

CAMPUS LIFE
Activities: Choral groups, concert band, dance, drama/theater, jazz band, literary magazine, marching band, music ensembles, musical theater, pep band, radio station, student government, student newspaper, symphony orchestra, television station. **Organizations:** 67 registered organizations, 13 honor societies, 12 religious organizations. 6 fraternities (4% men join), 5 sororities (3% women join). **Athletics (Intercollegiate):** *Men:* Baseball, basketball, cheerleading, cross-country, equestrian sports, football, golf, lacrosse, sailing, soccer, tennis, track/field (indoor), track/field (outdoor). *Women:* Basketball, cheerleading, cross-country, equestrian sports, field hockey, lacrosse, sailing, soccer, softball, tennis, track/field (indoor), track/field (outdoor), volleyball.

ADMISSIONS
Freshman Academic Profile: 17% in top 10% of high school class, 53% in top 25% of high school class, 96% in top 50% of high school class. SAT Math middle 50% range 540–620. SAT Critical Reading middle 50% range 550–630. ACT middle 50% range 22–25. TOEFL required of all international applicants, minimum paper TOEFL 530, minimum computer TOEFL 197. **Basis for Candidate Selection:** *Very important factors considered include:* Rigor of secondary school record, standardized test scores. *Important factors considered include:* Class rank. *Other factors considered include:* Application essay, character/personal qualities, extracurricular activities, interview, recommendation(s), talent/ability, volunteer work, work experience. **Freshman Admission Requirements:** High school diploma is required, and GED is accepted. *Academic units required:* 4 English, 4 math, 3 science, 2 foreign language, 3 history. *Academic units recommended:* 4 English, 4 math, 4 science, 3 foreign language, 4 history, 4 academic electives. **Freshman Admission Statistics:** 6,615 applied, 52% admitted, 34% enrolled. **Transfer Admission Requirements:** High school transcript, college transcript(s). Minimum college GPA of 3.0 required. Lowest grade transferable C. **General Admission Information:** Application fee $45. Regular application deadline 3/1. Regular notification is rolling. Nonfall registration accepted. Admission may be deferred for a maximum of 1 year. Credit and/or placement offered for CEEB Advanced Placement tests.

COSTS AND FINANCIAL AID
Average book expense $870. **Required Forms and Deadlines:** FAFSA. Financial aid filing deadline 3/1. **Notification of Awards:** Applicants will be

notified of awards on a rolling basis beginning on or about 2/21. **Types of Aid:** *Need-based scholarships/grants:* Pell, SEOG, state scholarships/grants, private scholarships, the school's own gift aid. *Loans:* FFEL Subsidized Stafford, FFEL Unsubsidized Stafford, FFEL PLUS, state loans, college/university loans from institutional funds, alternative loans. **Financial Aid Statistics:** 27% freshmen, 25% undergrads receive need-based scholarship or grant aid. 30% freshmen, 30% undergrads receive need-based self-help aid. 43% freshmen, 38% undergrads receive any aid.

CINCINNATI BIBLE COLLEGE AND SEMINARY

2700 Glenway Avenue, Cincinnati, OH 45204-1799
Phone: 513-244-8141 **E-mail:** admissions@cincybible.edu
Fax: 513-244-8140 **Website:** www.cincybible.edu **ACT Code:** 3248
Financial Aid Phone: 513-244-8132

This private school was founded in 1924. It has a 40-acre campus.

RATINGS
Admissions Selectivity Rating: 61   **Fire Safety Rating:** 60*   **Green Rating:** 60*

STUDENTS AND FACULTY
Enrollment: 625. **Student Body:** 42% female, 58% male. **Retention and Graduation:** 71% freshmen return for sophomore year. **Faculty:** Student/faculty ratio 19:1. 17 full-time faculty, 29% hold PhDs. 95% faculty teach undergrads.

ACADEMICS
Degrees: Associate, bachelor's, first professional, master's. **Academic Requirements:** Computer literacy, English (including composition), history, sciences (biological or physical), social science, Bible. **Special Study Options:** Cross-registration, double major, internships.

FACILITIES
Housing: Men's dorms, women's dorms, special housing for international students. **Computers:** 100% of public computers are PCs, network access in dorm rooms.

CAMPUS LIFE
Activities: Choral groups, concert band, drama/theater, jazz band, music ensembles, pep band, student government, yearbook. **Organizations:** 1 honor society, 2 religious organizations. **Athletics (Intercollegiate):** *Men:* Basketball, soccer. *Women:* Basketball, soccer, volleyball.

ADMISSIONS
61 (out of 100). **Freshman Academic Profile:** 90% from public high schools. TOEFL required of all international applicants, minimum paper TOEFL 550. **Basis for Candidate Selection:** *Very important factors considered include:* Recommendation(s). *Important factors considered include:* Character/personal qualities, religious affiliation/commitment, rigor of secondary school record, standardized test scores. *Other factors considered include:* Class rank, extracurricular activities, talent/ability. **Freshman Admission Requirements:** High school diploma is required, and GED is accepted. *Academic units recommended:* 4 English. **Freshman Admission Statistics:** 256 applied, 99% admitted, 79% enrolled. **Transfer Admission Requirements:** College transcript(s), statement of good standing from prior institution(s). Minimum college GPA of 2.0 required. Lowest grade transferable C. **General Admission Information:** Application fee $35. Regular application deadline 8/10. Regular notification is rolling. Nonfall registration accepted. Admission may be deferred for a maximum of 1 year. Common Application not accepted. Credit offered for CEEB Advanced Placement tests.

COSTS AND FINANCIAL AID
Annual tuition $6,560. Room & board $3,940. Required fees $300. Average book expense $600. **Required Forms and Deadlines:** FAFSA, institution's own financial aid form, state aid form. Financial aid filing deadline 5/1. **Types of Aid:** *Need-based scholarships/grants:* Pell, SEOG, state scholarships/grants, private scholarships, the school's own gift aid. *Loans:* FFEL Subsidized Stafford, FFEL Unsubsidized Stafford, FFEL PLUS. **Student Employment:** Federal Work-Study Program available. Institutional employment available. Off-campus job opportunities are excellent. **Financial Aid Statistics:** 64% freshmen, 64% undergrads receive need-based scholarship or grant aid. 71% freshmen, 70% undergrads receive need-based self-help aid. Highest amount earned per year from on-campus jobs $2,500.

CIRCLEVILLE BIBLE COLLEGE

1476 Lancaster Pike, PO Box 458, Circleville, OH 43113-9487
Phone: 740-477-7701 **E-mail:** enroll@biblecollege.edu
Fax: 740-477-7755 **Website:** www.biblecollege.edu **ACT Code:** 3030
Financial Aid Phone: 740-477-7749

This private school, affiliated with the Churches of Christ in Christian Union Church, was founded in 1948.

RATINGS
Admissions Selectivity Rating: 73   **Fire Safety Rating:** 60*   **Green Rating:** 60*

STUDENTS AND FACULTY
Enrollment: 349. **Student Body:** 51% female, 49% male, 24% out-of-state. African American 6%, Caucasian 91%, Hispanic 2%. **Retention and Graduation:** 58% freshmen return for sophomore year. **Faculty:** Student/faculty ratio 13:1. 14 full-time faculty, 64% hold PhDs.

ACADEMICS
Degrees: Associate, bachelor's. **Academic Requirements:** Arts/fine arts, computer literacy, English (including composition), history, humanities, mathematics, philosophy, sciences (biological or physical), social science. **Classes:** Most classes have 10–19 students. **Disciplines with Highest Percentage of Degrees Awarded:** Psychology 9%, education 7%. **Special Study Options:** Double major, independent study, internships, liberal arts/career combination, student-designed major.

FACILITIES
Housing: Men's dorms, women's dorms, apartments for married students, special housing for international students. **Computers:** 100% of public computers are PCs, network access in dorm rooms, network access in dorm lounges, remote student-access to Web through college's connection.

CAMPUS LIFE
Activities: Choral groups, drama/theater, music ensembles, student government, yearbook. **Athletics (Intercollegiate):** *Men:* Baseball, basketball. *Women:* Basketball, volleyball.

ADMISSIONS
Freshman Academic Profile: 21% in top 10% of high school class, 24% in top 25% of high school class, 32% in top 50% of high school class. ACT middle 50% range 17–23. **Basis for Candidate Selection:** *Very important factors considered include:* Class rank, recommendation(s), religious affiliation/commitment, rigor of secondary school record, standardized test scores. *Important factors considered include:* Application essay, character/personal qualities. *Other factors considered include:* Interview. **Freshman Admission Requirements:** High school diploma is required, and GED is accepted. *Academic units recommended:* 4 English, 3 math, 3 science, 2 foreign language, 3 social studies. **Freshman Admission Statistics:** 138 applied, 69% admitted, 75% enrolled. **Transfer Admission Requirements:** High school transcript, college transcript(s), essay or personal statement, standardized test score, statement of good standing from prior institution(s). Minimum college GPA of 2.0 required. Lowest grade transferable C. **General Admission Information:** Application fee $25. Regular notification when accepted. Nonfall registration accepted. Admission may be deferred for a maximum of 1 year. Common Application not accepted.

COSTS AND FINANCIAL AID
Annual tuition $7,950. Room & board $5,200. Required fees $850. Average book expense $500. **Required Forms and Deadlines:** FAFSA, institution's own financial aid form, CSS/Financial Aid PROFILE. Financial aid filing deadline 4/1. **Notification of Awards:** Applicants will be notified of awards on or about 6/1. **Student Employment:** Federal Work-Study Program available. Off-campus job opportunities are excellent. **Financial Aid Statistics:** 27% freshmen, 31% undergrads receive need-based scholarship or grant aid. 27% freshmen, 31% undergrads receive need-based self-help aid.

THE CITADEL—THE MILITARY COLLEGE OF SOUTH CAROLINA

171 Moultrie Street, Charleston, SC 29409
Phone: 843-953-5230 **E-mail:** admissions@citadel.edu
Fax: 843-953-7036 **Website:** www.citadel.edu **ACT Code:** 3838
Financial Aid Phone: 843-953-5187

This public school was founded in 1842. It has a 300-acre campus.

RATINGS
Admissions Selectivity Rating: 77 **Fire Safety Rating:** 60* **Green Rating:** 60*

STUDENTS AND FACULTY
Enrollment: 2,205. **Student Body:** 6% female, 94% male, 51% out-of-state, 2% international (23 countries represented). African American 7%, Asian 3%, Caucasian 84%, Hispanic 4%. **Retention and Graduation:** 82% freshmen return for sophomore year. **Faculty:** Student/faculty ratio 15:1. 163 full-time faculty, 95% hold PhDs. 100% faculty teach undergrads.

ACADEMICS
Degrees: Bachelor's, master's, post-master's certificate. **Academic Requirements:** Computer literacy, English (including composition), foreign languages, history, mathematics, physical education or ROTC, sciences (biological or physical), social science. **Classes:** Most classes have 20–29 students. Most lab/discussion sections have 10–19 students. **Majors with Highest Enrollment:** Business administration/management, criminal justice/law enforcement administration, political science and government. **Disciplines with Highest Percentage of Degrees Awarded:** Business/marketing 34%, engineering 15%, security and protective services 12%, education 9%, social sciences 9%. **Special Study Options:** Cooperative education program, double major, English as a Second Language (ESL), honors program, independent study, internships, study abroad, teacher certification program.

FACILITIES
Housing: Coed dorms. **Special Academic Facilities/Equipment:** Archives and museum. **Computers:** Network access in dorm rooms, network access in dorm lounges, online registration, online administrative functions (other than registration), remote student-access to Web through college's connection.

CAMPUS LIFE
Activities: Choral groups, concert band, drama/theater, jazz band, literary magazine, marching band, music ensembles, pep band, student government, student newspaper, yearbook. **Organizations:** 60 registered organizations, 3 honor societies. **Athletics (Intercollegiate):** *Men:* Baseball, basketball, cross-country, football, golf, tennis, track/field (indoor), track/field (outdoor), wrestling. *Women:* Cross-country, golf, soccer, track/field (indoor), track/field (outdoor), volleyball.

ADMISSIONS
Freshman Academic Profile: 12% in top 10% of high school class, 32% in top 25% of high school class, 69% in top 50% of high school class. SAT Math middle 50% range 500–600. SAT Critical Reading middle 50% range 490–580. ACT middle 50% range 20–24. TOEFL required of all international applicants, minimum paper TOEFL 550, minimum computer TOEFL 213. **Basis for Candidate Selection:** *Very important factors considered include:* Academic GPA, level of applicant's interest, standardized test scores. *Important factors considered include:* Character/personal qualities, extracurricular activities, rigor of secondary school record, state residency, talent/ability. *Other factors considered include:* Alumni/ae relation, class rank, first generation, geographical residence, interview, recommendation(s), volunteer work. **Freshman Admission Requirements:** High school diploma is required, and GED is accepted. *Academic units required:* 4 English, 3 math, 3 science (3 science labs), 2 foreign language, 2 social studies, 1 history, 4 academic electives, 1 PE or ROTC. **Freshman Admission Statistics:** 1,999 applied, 75% admitted, 36% enrolled. **Transfer Admission Requirements:** High school transcript, college transcript(s), standardized test score, statement of good standing from prior institution(s). Minimum college GPA of 2.0 required. Lowest grade transferable C. **General Admission Information:** Application fee $40. Early decision application deadline 10/26. Regular notification is rolling. Non-fall registration not accepted. Credit and/or placement offered for CEEB Advanced Placement tests.

COSTS AND FINANCIAL AID
Annual in-state tuition $7,735. Annual out-of-state tuition $19,291. Room and board $5,390. **Required Forms and Deadlines:** FAFSA. Financial aid filing deadline 3/1. **Notification of Awards:** Applicants will be notified of awards on or about 4/1. **Types of Aid:** *Need-based scholarships/grants:* Pell, SEOG, state scholarships/grants, the school's own gift aid. *Loans:* Direct Subsidized Stafford, Direct Unsubsidized Stafford, Direct PLUS, Federal Perkins. **Student Employment:** Federal Work-Study Program available. **Financial Aid Statistics:** 41% freshmen, 32% undergrads receive need-based scholarship or grant aid. 34% freshmen, 36% undergrads receive need-based self-help aid. 8 freshmen, 110 undergrads receive athletic scholarships. 63% freshmen, 67% undergrads receive any aid.

CITY UNIVERSITY

11900 Northeast First Street, Bellevue, WA 98005
Phone: 425-637-1010 **E-mail:** info@cityu.edu
Fax: 425-709-5361 **Website:** www.cityu.edu
Financial Aid Phone: 425-709-5251

This private school was founded in 1973. It has a 5-acre campus.

RATINGS
Admissions Selectivity Rating: 60* **Fire Safety Rating:** 60* **Green Rating:** 60*

STUDENTS AND FACULTY
Enrollment: 1,848. **Student Body:** 55% female, 45% male, 11% out-of-state, 5% international. African American 5%, Asian 6%, Caucasian 66%, Hispanic 3%, Native American 1%. **Faculty:** Student/faculty ratio 20:1. 36 full-time faculty, 25% hold PhDs.

ACADEMICS
Degrees: Associate, bachelor's, certificate, master's. **Academic Requirements:** English (including composition), humanities, mathematics, sciences (biological or physical), social science. **Majors with Highest Enrollment:** Business administration and management, computer and information sciences and support services, elementary education and teaching. **Disciplines with Highest Percentage of Degrees Awarded:** Business/marketing 45%, education 22%, computer and information sciences 21%, liberal arts/general studies 7%, psychology 5%. **Special Study Options:** Accelerated program, distance learning, double major, dual enrollment, English as a second language (ESL), internships, student-designed major, teacher certification program, weekend college.

FACILITIES
Housing: City University does not have housing options for students. Students must arrange their own housing. **Computers:** 15% of classrooms are wired, 100% of public computers are PCs, online administrative functions (other than registration), remote student-access to Web through college's connection.

ADMISSIONS
Freshman Academic Profile: TOEFL required of all international applicants, minimum paper TOEFL 540, minimum computer TOEFL 207. **Freshman Admission Requirements:** High school diploma is required, and GED is accepted. **Freshman Admission Statistics:** 15 applied, 100% admitted. **Transfer Admission Requirements:** High school transcript, college transcript(s). Lowest grade transferable C. **General Admission Information:** Application fee $80. Nonfall registration accepted. Admission may be deferred. Common Application not accepted.

COSTS AND FINANCIAL AID
Annual tuition $9,320. Required fees $120. Average book expense $500. **Student Employment:** Federal Work-Study Program available. **Financial Aid Statistics:** 27% freshmen, 29% undergrads receive any aid.

CITY UNIVERSITY OF NEW YORK— BARUCH COLLEGE

Best 368

Undergraduate Admissions, 1 Bernard Baruch Way Box H-0720, New York, NY 10010
Phone: 646-312-1400 **E-mail:** admissions@baruch.cuny.edu **CEEB Code:** 2034
Fax: 646-312-1361 **Website:** www.baruch.cuny.edu
Financial Aid Phone: 646-312-1360

This public school was founded in 1968.

RATINGS
Admissions Selectivity Rating: 88   **Fire Safety Rating:** 60*   **Green Rating:** 66

STUDENTS AND FACULTY
Enrollment: 12,598. **Student Body:** 53% female, 47% male, 1% out-of-state, 13% international (187 countries represented). African American 12%, Asian 29%, Caucasian 29%, Hispanic 17%. **Retention and Graduation:** 88% freshmen return for sophomore year. 27% freshmen graduate within 4 years. **Faculty:** Student/faculty ratio 18:1. 495 full-time faculty, 88% hold PhDs. 95% faculty teach undergrads.

ACADEMICS
Degrees: Bachelor's, master's, post-master's certificate. **Academic Requirements:** Arts/fine arts, computer literacy, English (including composition), foreign languages, history, humanities, mathematics, philosophy, sciences (biological or physical), social science, speech communications. **Classes:** Most classes have 20–29 students. Most lab/discussion sections have 10–19 students. **Majors with Highest Enrollment:** Accounting, computer and information sciences, finance. **Disciplines with Highest Percentage of Degrees Awarded:** Business/marketing 78%, psychology 4%, social sciences 3%, English 2%, liberal arts/general studies 2%, foreign languages and literature 1%, public administration and social services 1%, mathematics 1%, philosophy and religious studies 1%, history 1%. **Special Study Options:** Accelerated program, cross-registration, distance learning, double major, English as a Second Language (ESL), exchange student program (domestic), honors program, independent study, internships, liberal arts/career combination, student-designed major, study abroad.

FACILITIES
Special Academic Facilities/Equipment: Art gallery, Subotnik Financial Services Center & Wasserman Trading Floor. **Computers:** 94% of public computers are PCs, 5% of public computers are Macs, 1% of public computers are UNIX, online registration, online administrative functions (other than registration), remote student-access to Web through college's connection.

CAMPUS LIFE
Activities: Choral groups, dance, drama/theater, literary magazine, musical theater, radio station, student government, student newspaper, yearbook. **Organizations:** 165 registered organizations, 9 honor societies, 5 religious organizations. 4 fraternities (10% men join), 4 sororities (10% women join). **Athletics (Intercollegiate):** *Men:* Baseball, basketball, cross-country, soccer, swimming, tennis, volleyball. *Women:* Basketball, cheerleading, cross-country, softball, swimming, tennis, volleyball.

ADMISSIONS
Freshman Academic Profile: 30% in top 10% of high school class, 59% in top 25% of high school class, 86% in top 50% of high school class. 72% from public high schools. SAT Math middle 50% range 530–640. SAT Critical Reading middle 50% range 470–570. TOEFL required of all international applicants, minimum paper TOEFL 620, minimum computer TOEFL 260. **Basis for Candidate Selection:** *Very important factors considered include:* Academic GPA, rigor of secondary school record, standardized test scores. *Important factors considered include:* Application essay, recommendation(s). *Other factors considered include:* Alumni/ae relation, character/personal qualities, class rank, extracurricular activities, interview, talent/ability, work experience. **Freshman Admission Requirements:** High school diploma is required, and GED is accepted. *Academic units required:* 4 English, 3 math, 2 science (2 science labs), 2 foreign language, 4 social studies. *Academic units recommended:* 4 math, 3 foreign language, 1 academic elective. **Freshman Admission Statistics:** 15,066 applied, 31% admitted, 32% enrolled. **Transfer Admission Requirements:** High school transcript, college transcript(s), statement of good standing from prior institution(s). Minimum college GPA of 2.7 required.

Lowest grade transferable C. **General Admission Information:** Application fee $65. Early decision application deadline 12/13. Regular application deadline 2/1. Regular notification is rolling. Nonfall registration accepted. Admission may be deferred for a maximum of 6 months. Credit and/or placement offered for CEEB Advanced Placement tests.

COSTS AND FINANCIAL AID
Annual in-state tuition $4,000. Out-of-state tuition $8,640. Required fees $320. **Required Forms and Deadlines:** FAFSA, state aid form. Financial aid filing deadline 4/30. **Notification of Awards:** Applicants will be notified of awards on a rolling basis beginning on or about 4/1. **Types of Aid:** *Need-based scholarships/grants:* Pell, SEOG, state scholarships/grants, the school's own gift aid, City merit scholarships. *Loans:* Direct Subsidized Stafford, Direct Unsubsidized Stafford, Direct PLUS, Federal Perkins. **Student Employment:** Federal Work-Study Program available. Institutional employment available. Off-campus job opportunities are excellent. **Financial Aid Statistics:** 51% freshmen, 62% undergrads receive need-based scholarship or grant aid. 19% freshmen, 13% undergrads receive need-based self-help aid. 84% freshmen, 74% undergrads receive any aid.

CITY UNIVERSITY OF NEW YORK—BOROUGH OF MANHATTAN COMMUNITY COLLEGE

199 Chambers Street, New York, NY 10007-1097
Phone: 212-220-1265 **E-mail:** ebarrios@bmcc.cuny.edu
Fax: 212-346-8110 **Website:** www.bmcc.cuny.edu
Financial Aid Phone: 212-220-1430

This public school was founded in 1964. It has a 5-acre campus.

RATINGS
Admissions Selectivity Rating: 60*   **Fire Safety Rating:** 60*   **Green Rating:** 60*

STUDENTS AND FACULTY
Enrollment: 16,732. **Student Body:** 64% female, 36% male, 12% international. African American 37%, Asian 10%, Caucasian 11%, Hispanic 30%. **Retention and Graduation:** 40% grads go on to further study within 1 year. **Faculty:** Student/faculty ratio 21:1. 315 full-time faculty.

ACADEMICS
Degrees: Associate, certificate. **Academic Requirements:** English (including composition), mathematics, social science, fundamentals of speech communication. **Special Study Options:** Cooperative education program, distance learning, English as a second language (ESL), honors program, independent study, internships, study abroad, weekend college.

FACILITIES
Computers: 30% of public computers are PCs, 70% of public computers are Macs, online registration, remote student-access to Web through college's connection.

CAMPUS LIFE
Activities: Dance, drama/theater, musical theater, student government, student newspaper, yearbook.

ADMISSIONS
Freshman Admission Requirements: High school diploma is required, and GED is accepted. *Academic units recommended:* 4 English, 3 math, 2 foreign language, 4 social studies, 1 fine arts. **Freshman Admission Statistics:** 6,374 applied, 85% admitted, 60% enrolled. **Transfer Admission Requirements:** College transcript(s). **General Admission Information:** Application fee $40. Nonfall registration not accepted. Common Application not accepted.

COSTS AND FINANCIAL AID
Annual in-state tuition $2,500. Out-of-state tuition $3,076. Required fees $80. Average book expense $350. **Student Employment:** Federal Work-Study Program available. Institutional employment available. Off-campus job opportunities are good.

CITY UNIVERSITY OF NEW YORK— BROOKLYN COLLEGE

2900 Bedford Avenue, Brooklyn, NY 11210-2889
Phone: 718-951-5001 **E-mail:** adminqry@brooklyn.cuny.edu
Fax: 718-951-4506 **Website:** www.brooklyn.cuny.edu
Financial Aid Phone: 718-951-4684

This public school was founded in 1930. It has a 26-acre campus.

RATINGS
Admissions Selectivity Rating: 80 **Fire Safety Rating:** 60* **Green Rating:** 77

STUDENTS AND FACULTY
Enrollment: 11,524. **Student Body:** 60% female, 40% male, 2% out-of-state, 7% international (82 countries represented). African American 28%, Asian 13%, Caucasian 41%, Hispanic 12%. **Retention and Graduation:** 78% freshmen return for sophomore year. 18% freshmen graduate within 4 years. 40% grads go on to further study within 1 year. 6% grads pursue arts and sciences degrees. 12% grads pursue business degrees. 5% grads pursue law degrees. 2% grads pursue medical degrees. **Faculty:** Student/faculty ratio 16:1. 515 full-time faculty, 91% hold PhDs. 80% faculty teach undergrads.

ACADEMICS
Degrees: Bachelor's, certificate, master's, post-bachelor's certificate, post-master's certificate. **Academic Requirements:** Arts/fine arts, computer literacy, English (including composition), foreign languages, history, humanities, mathematics, philosophy, sciences (biological or physical), social science. **Classes:** Most classes have 20–29 students. **Majors with Highest Enrollment:** Business administration/management, education, psychology. **Disciplines with Highest Percentage of Degrees Awarded:** Business/marketing 29%, psychology 13%, education 11%, social sciences 10%, computer and information sciences 6%, health professions and related sciences 6%. **Special Study Options:** Accelerated program, cooperative education program, cross-registration, distance learning, double major, dual enrollment, English as a second language (ESL), exchange student program (domestic), honors program, independent study, internships, study abroad, teacher certification program, weekend college.

FACILITIES
Housing: No student housing available. **Special Academic Facilities/Equipment:** Art museum, language lab, TV studios, speech clinic, research centers and institutes, particle accelerator. **Computers:** 3% of classrooms are wired, 3% of classrooms are wireless, 84% of public computers are PCs, 10% of public computers are Macs, 6% of public computers are UNIX, online registration, online administrative functions (other than registration), remote student-access to Web through college's connection.

CAMPUS LIFE
Activities: Choral groups, concert band, dance, drama/theater, jazz band, literary magazine, music ensembles, radio station, student government, student newspaper, student-run film society, symphony orchestra, television station, yearbook. **Organizations:** 150 registered organizations, 5 honor societies, 6 religious organizations. 4 fraternities (2% men join), 6 sororities (2% women join). **Athletics (Intercollegiate):** *Men:* Basketball, cross-country, soccer, tennis, volleyball. *Women:* Basketball, cross-country, softball, tennis, volleyball. Environmental Initiatives: Reduce comsumption. Awareness.

ADMISSIONS
Freshman Academic Profile: 14% in top 10% of high school class, 45% in top 25% of high school class, 74% in top 50% of high school class. 60% from public high schools. SAT Math middle 50% range 490–590. SAT Critical Reading middle 50% range 450–560. TOEFL required of all international applicants, minimum paper TOEFL 500, minimum computer TOEFL 173. **Basis for Candidate Selection:** *Very important factors considered include:* Academic GPA, rigor of secondary school record, standardized test scores. *Other factors considered include:* Recommendation(s). **Freshman Admission Requirements:** High school diploma is required, and GED is accepted. *Academic units recommended:* 4 English, 3 math, 3 science, 3 foreign language, 4 social studies, 4 academic electives. **Freshman Admission Statistics:** 13,615 applied, 45% admitted, 23% enrolled. **Transfer Admission Requirements:** College transcript(s). Minimum college GPA of 2.0 required. Lowest grade transferable

C. General Admission Information: Application fee $65. Regular notification is rolling. Nonfall registration accepted. Admission may be deferred for a maximum of 1 semester. Credit and/or placement offered for CEEB Advanced Placement tests.

COSTS AND FINANCIAL AID
Annual in-state tuition $4,000. Out-of-state tuition $10,800. Required fees $381. Average book expense $850. **Required Forms and Deadlines:** FAFSA, state aid form. Financial aid filing deadline 4/1. **Notification of Awards:** Applicants will be notified of awards on or about 5/1. **Types of Aid:** *Need-based scholarships/grants:* Pell, SEOG, state scholarships/grants, private scholarships, the school's own gift aid. *Loans:* Direct Subsidized Stafford, Direct Unsubsidized Stafford, Direct PLUS, Federal Perkins. **Student Employment:** Federal Work-Study Program available. Institutional employment available. Off-campus job opportunities are excellent. **Financial Aid Statistics:** 74% freshmen, 66% undergrads receive need-based scholarship or grant aid. 69% freshmen, 68% undergrads receive need-based self-help aid. 78% freshmen, 71% undergrads receive any aid. Highest amount earned per year from on-campus jobs $12,480.

CITY UNIVERSITY OF NEW YORK— CITY COLLEGE

Convent Avenue at 138th Street, New York, NY 10031-9198
Phone: 212-650-6977 **E-mail:** admissions@ccny.cuny.edu **CEEB Code:** 2083
Fax: 212-650-6417 **Website:** www.ccny.cuny.edu
Financial Aid Phone: 212-650-5819

This public school was founded in 1847. It has a 36-acre campus.

RATINGS
Admissions Selectivity Rating: 79 **Fire Safety Rating:** 60* **Green Rating:** 60*

STUDENTS AND FACULTY
Enrollment: 9,778. **Student Body:** 49% female, 51% male, 12% out-of-state, 15% international (85 countries represented). African American 24%, Asian 19%, Caucasian 11%, Hispanic 33%. **Retention and Graduation:** 5% freshmen graduate within 4 years. 11% grads pursue arts and sciences degrees. 1% grads pursue medical degrees. **Faculty:** Student/faculty ratio 12:1. 524 full-time faculty, 90% hold PhDs. 100% faculty teach undergrads.

ACADEMICS
Degrees: Bachelor's, first professional certificate, master's, post-master's certificate. **Academic Requirements:** Arts/fine arts, computer literacy, English (including composition), foreign languages, history, humanities, mathematics, philosophy, sciences (biological or physical), social science. **Classes:** Most classes have 20–29 students. **Majors with Highest Enrollment:** Architecture (BArch, BA/BS, MArch, MA/MS, PhD); electrical, electronics, and communications engineering; psychology. **Disciplines with Highest Percentage of Degrees Awarded:** Liberal arts/general studies 13%, engineering 11%, social sciences 11%, visual and performing arts 10%, psychology 10%. **Special Study Options:** Accelerated program, cooperative education program, cross-registration, English as a second language (ESL), honors program, independent study, internships, study abroad, teacher certification program.

FACILITIES
Housing: Coed dorms, new residence hall called the Towers opened in the fall of 2006 (for information call 917-507-0070 or www.ccnytowers.com/ccny/). Service available to help students locate housing. For information, call 212-650-5370. **Special Academic Facilities/Equipment:** Art museum, electron microscope, spectroscopy lab, planetarium, aquarium, weather station. **Computers:** Network access in dorm rooms, network access in dorm lounges, online registration, online administrative functions (other than registration), remote student-access to Web through college's connection.

CAMPUS LIFE
Activities: Choral groups, dance, drama/theater, jazz band, literary magazine, radio station, student government, student newspaper, yearbook. **Organizations:** 85 registered organizations, 3 religious organizations. 3 fraternities, 1 sorority. **Athletics (Intercollegiate):** *Men:* Baseball, basketball, lacrosse, soccer, tennis, track/field (indoor), track/field (outdoor), volleyball. *Women:* Basketball, fencing, soccer, tennis, track/field (indoor), track/field (outdoor), volleyball.

ADMISSIONS

Freshman Academic Profile: 27% in top 10% of high school class, 31% in top 25% of high school class, 85% from public high schools. SAT Math middle 50% range 440–590. SAT Critical Reading middle 50% range 410–550. TOEFL required of all international applicants, minimum paper TOEFL 500, minimum computer TOEFL 173. **Basis for Candidate Selection:** *Very important factors considered include:* Academic GPA, rigor of secondary school record. *Important factors considered include:* Standardized test scores. **Freshman Admission Requirements:** High school diploma is required, and GED is accepted. *Academic units required:* 4 English, 2 math, 2 science (2 science labs), 2 foreign language, 4 social studies, 1 fine or performing arts. *Academic units recommended:* 4 English, 3 math, 2 science (2 science labs), 3 foreign language, 4 social studies, 1 fine or performing arts. **Freshman Admission Statistics:** 13,528 applied, 47% admitted, 25% enrolled. **Transfer Admission Requirements:** College transcript(s). Minimum college GPA of 2.0 required. Lowest grade transferable C. **General Admission Information:** Application fee $65. Regular notification is rolling. Nonfall registration accepted. Admission may be deferred for a maximum of 1 semester. Credit offered for CEEB Advanced Placement tests.

COSTS AND FINANCIAL AID

Annual in-state tuition $4,000. Annual out-of-state tuition $10,800. Required fees $279. **Required Forms and Deadlines:** FAFSA. **Notification of Awards:** Applicants will be notified of awards on or about 3/31. **Types of Aid:** *Need-based scholarships/grants:* Pell, SEOG, state scholarships/grants, private scholarships. *Loans:* Direct Subsidized Stafford, Direct Unsubsidized Stafford, Direct PLUS, Federal Perkins, college/university loans from institutional funds. **Student Employment:** Federal Work-Study Program available. Institutional employment available. Off-campus job opportunities are fair. **Financial Aid Statistics:** 58% freshmen, 73% undergrads receive need-based scholarship or grant aid. 36% freshmen, 42% undergrads receive need-based self-help aid. 70% freshmen, 68% undergrads receive any aid.

CITY UNIVERSITY OF NEW YORK— THE COLLEGE OF STATEN ISLAND

2800 Victory Boulevard, Building 2A, Room 102, Staten Island, NY 10314
Phone: 718-982-2010 **E-mail:** admissions@mail.csi.cuny.edu **CEEB Code:** 2778
Fax: 718-982-2500 **Website:** www.csi.cuny.edu **ACT Code:** 7002
Financial Aid Phone: 718-982-2030

This public school was founded in 1955. It has a 204-acre campus.

RATINGS
Admissions Selectivity Rating: 60* **Fire Safety Rating:** 60* **Green Rating:** 74

STUDENTS AND FACULTY

Enrollment: 10,848. **Student Body:** 59% female, 41% male, 5% international (106 countries represented). African American 11%, Asian 9%, Caucasian 63%, Hispanic 13%. **Retention and Graduation:** 79% freshmen return for sophomore year. 21% freshmen graduate within 4 years. **Faculty:** Student/faculty ratio 18:1. 328 full-time faculty, 86% hold PhDs. 86% faculty teach undergrads.

ACADEMICS

Degrees: Associate, bachelor's, master's. **Academic Requirements:** Arts/fine arts, computer literacy, English (including composition), foreign languages, history, humanities, mathematics, philosophy, sciences (biological or physical), social science. **Classes:** Most classes have 20–29 students. Most lab/discussion sections have 10–19 students. **Majors with Highest Enrollment:** Business administration/management, liberal arts and sciences/liberal studies, psychology. **Disciplines with Highest Percentage of Degrees Awarded:** Business/marketing 24%, social sciences 15%, psychology 11%, liberal arts/general studies 10%, English 9%. **Special Study Options:** Accelerated program, cooperative education program, cross-registration, distance learning, double major, dual enrollment, English as a second language (ESL), exchange student program (domestic), external degree program, honors program, independent study, internships, liberal arts/career combination, student-designed major, study abroad, teacher certification program, weekend college.

FACILITIES

Special Academic Facilities/Equipment: Astrophysical observatory, archives and special collections, Center for the Arts (CFA). **Computers:** 100% of classrooms are wireless, 100% of public computers are PCs, online registration, online administrative functions (other than registration).

CAMPUS LIFE

Activities: Choral groups, concert band, dance, drama/theater, jazz band, literary magazine, music ensembles, musical theater, radio station, student government, student newspaper, student-run film society, yearbook. **Organizations:** 47 registered organizations, 2 honor societies, 4 religious organizations. **Athletics (Intercollegiate):** *Men:* Baseball, basketball, cross-country, diving, soccer, swimming, tennis. *Women:* Basketball, cross-country, diving, soccer, softball, swimming, tennis, volleyball. **Environmental Initiatives:** Developed paper/cans, bottles, glass/waste minirecycling deposit centers on all floors of all buildings on campus. Experimenting with a biodiesel kit to convert used cooking oil from our cafeteria to biodiesel fuel for equipment. Recently registered to participate in recycle-mania. Are currently recruiting student ambassadors.

ADMISSIONS

Freshman Academic Profile: 79% from public high schools. SAT Math middle 50% range 460–550. SAT Critical Reading middle 50% range 450–540. SAT Writing middle 50% range 430–540. TOEFL required of all international applicants, minimum paper TOEFL 450, minimum computer TOEFL 133. **Basis for Candidate Selection:** *Very important factors considered include:* Rigor of secondary school record. *Important factors considered include:* Academic GPA, standardized test scores. **Freshman Admission Requirements:** High school diploma is required, and GED is accepted. *Academic units required:* 4 English, 2 math, 2 science, 2 foreign language, 4 social studies, 1 social science. *Academic units recommended:* 4 English, 3 math, 2 science, 2 foreign language, 4 social studies, 1 social science. **Freshman Admission Statistics:** 7,570 applied, 99% admitted, 30% enrolled. **Transfer Admission Requirements:** College transcript(s). Minimum college GPA of 2.0 required. **General Admission Information:** Application fee $65. Regular notification is rolling. Nonfall registration accepted. Admission may be deferred for a maximum of 1 semester. Placement offered for CEEB Advanced Placement tests.

COSTS AND FINANCIAL AID

Annual in-state tuition $4,000. Annual out-of-state tuition $8,640. Required fees $328. **Required Forms and Deadlines:** FAFSA, state aid form. Financial aid filing deadline 3/31. **Notification of Awards:** Applicants will be notified of awards on a rolling basis beginning on or about 4/30. **Types of Aid:** *Need-based scholarships/grants:* Pell, SEOG, state scholarships/grants, private scholarships, the school's own gift aid. *Loans:* Direct Subsidized Stafford, Direct Unsubsidized Stafford, Direct PLUS, Federal Perkins. **Student Employment:** Federal Work-Study Program available. Off-campus job opportunities are good. **Financial Aid Statistics:** 51% freshmen, 50% undergrads receive need-based scholarship or grant aid. 14% freshmen, 20% undergrads receive need-based self-help aid. 56% freshmen, 53% undergrads receive any aid.

CITY UNIVERSITY OF NEW YORK— HOSTOS COMMUNITY COLLEGE

120 East 149th Street, Room D210, Bronx, NY 10451
Phone: 718-518-4405 **E-mail:** admissions@hostos.cuny.edu
Fax: 718-518-6643 **Website:** www.hostos.cuny.edu

This public school was founded in 1968. It has an 8-acre campus.

RATINGS
Admissions Selectivity Rating: 60* **Fire Safety Rating:** 60* **Green Rating:** 60*

STUDENTS AND FACULTY

Enrollment: 3,577. **Student Body:** 75% female, 25% male, 9% out-of-state, 9% international. African American 26%, Asian 3%, Caucasian 3%, Hispanic 59%. **Retention and Graduation:** 56% freshmen return for sophomore year. **Faculty:** Student/faculty ratio 14:1. 155 full-time faculty, 48% hold PhDs.

ACADEMICS

Degrees: Associate, certificate. **Academic Requirements:** English (including composition), history, humanities, mathematics, social science. **Classes:** Most classes have 20–29 students. **Majors with Highest Enrollment:** Liberal arts and sciences/liberal studies, nursing/registered nurse training (RN, ASN, BSN, MSN). **Special Study Options:** Distance learning, English as a second language (ESL), honors program, internships, liberal arts/career combination, study abroad, weekend college.

FACILITIES

Special Academic Facilities/Equipment: Art gallery. **Computers:** 100% of public computers are PCs, online registration, online administrative functions (other than registration), remote student-access to Web through college's connection.

CAMPUS LIFE
Activities: Drama/theater, student government, student newspaper, television station. **Organizations:** 30 registered organizations.

ADMISSIONS
Freshman Academic Profile: 95% from public high schools. **Freshman Admission Requirements:** High school diploma is required, and GED is accepted. *Academic units required:* 4 English, 3 math, 2 science, 2 foreign language, 4 social studies, 2 art. **Freshman Admission Statistics:** 1,410 applied, 88% admitted, 51% enrolled. **Transfer Admission Requirements:** High school transcript, college transcript(s). Minimum college GPA of 2.0 required. Lowest grade transferable C. **General Admission Information:** Application fee $40. Regular application deadline 8/15. Regular notification is rolling. Nonfall registration accepted. Admission may be deferred for a maximum of 1 semester. Common Application not accepted. Neither credit nor placement offered for CEEB Advanced Placement tests.

COSTS AND FINANCIAL AID
Annual in-state tuition $2,500. Out-of-state tuition $3,076. Required fees $86. Average book expense $670. **Required Forms and Deadlines:** FAFSA, institution's own financial aid form, state aid form. Financial aid filing deadline 7/1. *Types of Aid: Need-based scholarships/grants:* Pell, state scholarships/grants. **Student Employment:** Off-campus job opportunities are good. **Financial Aid Statistics:** 31% freshmen, 29% undergrads receive need-based self-help aid.

CITY UNIVERSITY OF NEW YORK— HUNTER COLLEGE

695 Park Avenue, New York, NY 10021
Phone: 212-772-4490 **E-mail:** admissions@hunter.cuny.edu **CEEB Code:** 2301
Fax: 212-650-3336 **Website:** www.hunter.cuny.edu
Financial Aid Phone: 212-772-4820

This public school was founded in 1870.

RATINGS
Admissions Selectivity Rating: 85   **Fire Safety Rating:** 93   **Green Rating:** 76

STUDENTS AND FACULTY
Enrollment: 14,434. **Student Body:** 43% female, 57% male, 4% out-of-state, 10% international (150 countries represented). African American 14%, Asian 17%, Caucasian 39%, Hispanic 19%. **Retention and Graduation:** 82% freshmen return for sophomore year. 11% freshmen graduate within 4 years. **Faculty:** Student/faculty ratio 16:1. 635 full-time faculty, 88% hold PhDs. 96% faculty teach undergrads.

ACADEMICS
Degrees: Bachelor's, master's, post-master's certificate. **Academic Requirements:** Arts/fine arts, English (including composition), foreign languages, history, humanities, mathematics, sciences (biological or physical), social science, pluralism, diversity. **Classes:** Most classes have 20–29 students. **Majors with Highest Enrollment:** Accounting, English language and literature, psychology. **Disciplines with Highest Percentage of Degrees Awarded:** Social sciences 22%, English 14%, psychology 12%, visual and performing arts 9%, communications/journalism 8%. **Special Study Options:** Accelerated program, cross-registration, distance learning, double major, dual enrollment, exchange student program (domestic), honors program, independent study, internships, liberal arts/career combination, student-designed major, study abroad, teacher certification program.

FACILITIES
Housing: Coed dorms. **Special Academic Facilities/Equipment:** Art gallery, theater, geology lab, on-campus elementary and secondary schools. **Computers:** 40% of classrooms are wireless, 95% of public computers are PCs, 5% of public computers are Macs, network access in dorm rooms, network access in dorm lounges, online registration, online administrative functions (other than registration), support for handheld computing, remote student-access to Web through college's connection.

CAMPUS LIFE
Activities: Choral groups, concert band, dance, drama/theater, jazz band, literary magazine, music ensembles, musical theater, radio station, student government, student newspaper, student-run film society, symphony orchestra, television station, yearbook. **Organizations:** 130 registered organizations, 20 honor societies. 2 fraternities (1% men join), 2 sororities (1% women join). **Athletics (Intercollegiate):** *Men:* Basketball, cross-country, fencing, soccer, tennis, track/field (indoor), track/field (outdoor), volleyball, wrestling. *Women:* Basketball, cross-country, fencing, softball, swimming, tennis, track/field (indoor), track/field (outdoor), volleyball. Environmental Initiatives: A Hunter Sustainability Council has been established to develop an action plan for a sustainable campus by January 2009. Hunter hosts the CUNY Institute for Sustainable Cities, which conducts research and outreach on sustainability issues with both faculty and student involvement. Hunter has shown a commitment to greening its infrastructure: as examples, recent renovations of the 68th Street pool will incorporate green features, and the design of a new Science & Health Professions building will require at least LEED silver certification.

ADMISSIONS
Freshman Academic Profile: 21% in top 10% of high school class, 48% in top 25% of high school class, 78% in top 50% of high school class. 70% from public high schools. SAT Math middle 50% range 490–560. SAT Critical Reading middle 50% range 480–550. TOEFL required of all international applicants, minimum paper TOEFL 500, minimum computer TOEFL 173. **Basis for Candidate Selection:** *Very important factors considered include:* Academic GPA, rigor of secondary school record, standardized test scores. **Freshman Admission Requirements:** High school diploma is required, and GED is accepted. *Academic units required:* 2 English, 2 math, 1 science (1 science lab). *Academic units recommended:* 4 English, 3 math, 2 science (2 science labs), 2 foreign language, 4 social studies, 1 visual and performing arts. **Freshman Admission Statistics:** 21,830 applied, 34% admitted, 25% enrolled. **Transfer Admission Requirements:** College transcript(s). Minimum college GPA of 2.3 required. Lowest grade transferable C. **General Admission Information:** Application fee $65. Regular application deadline 3/15. Regular notification is rolling. Nonfall registration accepted. Admission may be deferred for a maximum of 1 semester. Credit and/or placement offered for CEEB Advanced Placement tests.

COSTS AND FINANCIAL AID
Annual in-state tuition $4,000. Room & Board $3,726. Required fees $329. Average book expense $879. **Required Forms and Deadlines:** FAFSA, state aid form, institutional direct loan request form from DL applicants. Financial aid filing deadline 5/1. **Notification of Awards:** Applicants will be notified of awards on a rolling basis beginning on or about 5/15. **Types of Aid:** *Need-based scholarships/grants:* Pell, SEOG, state scholarships/grants, private scholarships, the school's own gift aid. *Loans:* Direct Subsidized Stafford, Direct Unsubsidized Stafford, Direct PLUS, Federal Perkins, alternative loans. **Student Employment:** Federal Work-Study Program available. Institutional employment available. Off-campus job opportunities are fair. **Financial Aid Statistics:** 64% freshmen, 53% undergrads receive need-based scholarship or grant aid. 4% freshmen, 17% undergrads receive need-based self-help aid. 90% freshmen, 90% undergrads receive any aid.

CITY UNIVERSITY OF NEW YORK— JOHN JAY COLLEGE OF CRIMINAL JUSTICE

899 Tenth Avenue, New York, NY 10019
Phone: 212-237-8869 **E-mail:** admissions@jjay.cuny.edu **CEEB Code:** 2115
Fax: 212-237-8777 **Website:** www.jjay.cuny.edu
Financial Aid Phone: 212-237-8151

This public school was founded in 1964.

RATINGS
Admissions Selectivity Rating: 60*   **Fire Safety Rating:** 60*   **Green Rating:** 60*

STUDENTS AND FACULTY
Enrollment: 12,224.

ACADEMICS
Degrees: Associate, bachelor's, certificate, doctoral, master's. **Academic Requirements:** Arts/fine arts, English (including composition), foreign languages, history, mathematics, philosophy, sciences (biological or physical), social science, ethnic studies, physical education. **Special Study Options:** Cooperative education program, distance learning, English as a second

language (ESL), exchange student program (domestic), study abroad, weekend college. Undergrads may take grad level classes. Off-campus study available in Albany Internship Program, and co-op programs available in public service.

FACILITIES

Housing: List of possible housing arrangements can be obtained from Student Activities. 212-237-8698. **Special Academic Facilities/Equipment:** Criminal Justice Center, Center for Violence/Human Survival, Toxicology Research/Training Center, Fire Science Institute, Institute for Criminal Justice Ethics, Institute for the Study of Genocide, Institute on Alcohol/Substance Abuse. **Computers:** Online registration.

CAMPUS LIFE

Activities: Choral groups, dance, drama/theater, musical theater, radio station, student government, student newspaper, yearbook. **Athletics (Intercollegiate):** *Men:* Basketball, cross-country, riflery, soccer. *Women:* Cross-country, riflery, softball, tennis, volleyball.

ADMISSIONS

Freshman Academic Profile: 63% from public high schools. TOEFL required of all international applicants, minimum paper TOEFL 500, minimum computer TOEFL 173. **Freshman Admission Requirements:** High school diploma is required, and GED is accepted. *Academic units recommended:* 4 English, 3 math, 2 science, 2 social studies, 4 academic electives. **Transfer Admission Requirements:** Minimum college GPA of 2.0 required. Lowest grade transferable C. **General Admission Information:** Application fee $50. Regular application deadline 3/15. Regular notification is rolling. Nonfall registration accepted. Common Application not accepted. Credit offered for CEEB Advanced Placement tests.

COSTS AND FINANCIAL AID

Comprehensive fee $4,000. Room and board $1,802. Required fees $100. Average book expense $500. **Required Forms and Deadlines:** FAFSA. **Types of Aid:** *Need-based scholarships/grants:* Pell, SEOG, state scholarships/grants, private scholarships, the school's own gift aid. *Loans:* FFEL Subsidized Stafford, FFEL Unsubsidized Stafford, FFEL PLUS, Federal Perkins, college/university loans from institutional funds. **Student Employment:** Federal Work-Study Program available. Institutional employment available. Off-campus job opportunities are good. **Financial Aid Statistics:** Highest amount earned per year from on-campus jobs $2,500.

CITY UNIVERSITY OF NEW YORK— KINGSBOROUGH COMMUNITY COLLEGE

2001 Oriental Boulevard, Brooklyn, NY 11235
Phone: 718-368-4600 **E-mail:** info@kbcc.cuny.edu
Fax: 718-368-5356 **Website:** www.kbcc.cuny.edu
Financial Aid Phone: 718-368-4644

This public school was founded in 1963. It has a 72-acre campus.

RATINGS

Admissions Selectivity Rating: 60*   **Fire Safety Rating:** 60*   **Green Rating:** 60*

STUDENTS AND FACULTY

Enrollment: 10,751. **Student Body:** 58% female, 42% male, 1% out-of-state, 11% international (127 countries represented). African American 32%, Asian 9%, Caucasian 35%, Hispanic 13%. **Faculty:** Student/faculty ratio 26:1. 284 full-time faculty, 73% hold PhDs. 100% faculty teach undergrads.

ACADEMICS

Degrees: Associate, certificate. **Academic Requirements:** English (including composition). **Classes:** Most classes have 20–29 students. **Majors with Highest Enrollment:** Business administration/management, liberal arts and sciences/liberal studies. **Special Study Options:** Accelerated program, cross-registration, dual enrollment, English as a second language (ESL), honors program, independent study, internships, My Turn Program for senior citizens, New Start Program for students academically dismissed from 4-year institutions.

FACILITIES

Computers: 100% of public computers are PCs, online registration.

CAMPUS LIFE

Activities: Choral groups, concert band, dance, drama/theater, jazz band, literary magazine, music ensembles, musical theater, opera, radio station, student government, student newspaper, student-run film society, symphony orchestra, yearbook. **Athletics (Intercollegiate):** *Men:* Baseball, basketball,

soccer, tennis, track/field (outdoor). *Women:* Basketball, softball, tennis, track/field (outdoor), volleyball.

ADMISSIONS

Freshman Academic Profile: TOEFL required of all international applicants, minimum paper TOEFL 475, minimum computer TOEFL 150. **Freshman Admission Requirements:** High school diploma is required, and GED is accepted. *Academic units recommended:* 4 English, 3 math, 2 science, 2 foreign language, 4 social studies, 1 fine arts. **Transfer Admission Requirements:** College transcript(s). Minimum college GPA of 2 required. Lowest grade transferable C. **General Admission Information:** Application fee $65. Regular application deadline 8/15. Regular notification is rolling. Nonfall registration accepted.

COSTS AND FINANCIAL AID

Annual in-state tuition $2,800. Annual out-of-state tuition $5,700. Required fees $300. Average book expense $879.

CITY UNIVERSITY OF NEW YORK— LAGUARDIA COMMUNITY COLLEGE

31-10 Thomson Avenue, M-147, Long Island City, NY 11101
Phone: 718-482-7206 **E-mail:** admissions@lagcc.cuny.edu **CEEB Code:** 2246
Fax: 718-603-2033 **Website:** www.lagcc.cuny.edu
Financial Aid Phone: 718-482-7218

This public school was founded in 1971.

RATINGS

Admissions Selectivity Rating: 60*   **Fire Safety Rating:** 60*   **Green Rating:** 60*

STUDENTS AND FACULTY

Enrollment: 11,285. **Student Body:** 64% female, 36% male, 1% out-of-state, 18% international (156 countries represented). African American 20%, Asian 12%, Caucasian 15%, Hispanic 34%. **Retention and Graduation:** 57% grads go on to further study within 1 year. **Faculty:** Student/faculty ratio 21:1. 270 full-time faculty, 51% hold PhDs. 100% faculty teach undergrads.

ACADEMICS

Degrees: Associate, certificate. **Academic Requirements:** English (including composition), history, humanities, sciences (biological or physical), social science. **Classes:** Most classes have 20–29 students. **Majors with Highest Enrollment:** Business administration/management, liberal arts and sciences studies and humanities, nursing/registered nurse training (RN, ASN, BSN, MSN). **Special Study Options:** Cooperative education program, dual enrollment, English as a second language (ESL), honors program, independent study, internships, study abroad.

FACILITIES

Special Academic Facilities/Equipment: LaGuardia and Wagner Archives. **Computers:** 90% of public computers are PCs, 10% of public computers are Macs, online registration, remote student-access to Web through college's connection.

CAMPUS LIFE

Activities: Dance, drama/theater, literary magazine, music ensembles, radio station, student government, student newspaper, yearbook.

ADMISSIONS

Freshman Academic Profile: 55% from public high schools. TOEFL required of all international applicants, minimum paper TOEFL 450. **Freshman Admission Requirements:** High school diploma is required, and GED is accepted. *Academic units required:* 4 English, 2 math, 1 science, 2 social studies, 4 academic electives. **Freshman Admission Statistics:** 3,606 applied, 100% admitted, 58% enrolled. **Transfer Admission Requirements:** College transcript(s). **General Admission Information:** Application fee $65. Nonfall registration accepted. Admission may be deferred for a maximum of 1 year. Common Application not accepted. Credit and/or placement offered for CEEB Advanced Placement tests.

COSTS AND FINANCIAL AID

Annual in-state tuition $2,800. Out-of-state tuition $4,560. Required fees $272. **Required Forms and Deadlines:** FAFSA, state aid form. Financial aid filing deadline 4/15. **Types of Aid:** *Need-based scholarships/grants:* Pell, SEOG, state scholarships/grants, the school's own gift aid. *Loans:* Direct Subsidized Stafford, Direct Unsubsidized Stafford, Direct PLUS, Federal Perkins. **Student Employment:** Off-campus job opportunities are good.

CITY UNIVERSITY OF NEW YORK— LEHMAN COLLEGE

250 Bedford Park Boulevard West, Bronx, NY 10468
Phone: 718-960-8000 **E-mail:** wilkes@alpha.lehman.cuny.edu **CEEB Code:** 2950
Fax: 718-960-8712 **Website:** www.lehman.cuny.edu
Financial Aid Phone: 718-960-8545

This public school was founded in 1968. It has a 38-acre campus.

RATINGS
Admissions Selectivity Rating: 60*   **Fire Safety Rating:** 60*   **Green Rating:** 60*

STUDENTS AND FACULTY
Enrollment: 7,805. **Student Body:** 72% female, 28% male, 1% out-of-state, 5% international (123 countries represented). African American 34%, Asian 4%, Caucasian 10%, Hispanic 47%. **Retention and Graduation:** 74% freshmen return for sophomore year. 7% freshmen graduate within 4 years. **Faculty:** Student/faculty ratio 14:1. 337 full-time faculty, 83% hold PhDs. 76% faculty teach undergrads.

ACADEMICS
Degrees: Bachelor's, certificate, diploma, master's. **Academic Requirements:** Writing intensive courses and general education courses. **Classes:** Most classes have 20–29 students. **Majors with Highest Enrollment:** Nursing/registered nurse training (RN, ASN, BSN, MSN), social work, sociology. **Special Study Options:** Accelerated program, cooperative education program, cross-registration, distance learning, double major, dual enrollment, English as a second language (ESL), exchange student program (domestic), honors program, independent study, internships, student-designed major, study abroad, teacher certification program, weekend college, bilingual liberal arts (first 2 years may be taken in Spanish), professional writing concentration, 3–2 engineering program with City College.

FACILITIES
Special Academic Facilities/Equipment: Art gallery, concert hall, sports complex. **Computers:** 8% of classrooms are wireless, 79% of public computers are PCs, 20% of public computers are Macs, 1% of public computers are UNIX, network access in dorm rooms, network access in dorm lounges, online registration, online administrative functions (other than registration), remote student-access to Web through college's connection.

CAMPUS LIFE
Activities: Choral groups, concert band, dance, drama/theater, jazz band, literary magazine, music ensembles, musical theater, opera, radio station, student government, student newspaper, student-run film society, symphony orchestra, television station, yearbook. **Organizations:** 3 honor societies, 1 religious organization. 1 fraternity (1% men join), 1 sorority (1% women join). **Athletics (Intercollegiate):** *Men:* Baseball, basketball, cross-country, diving, softball, swimming, tennis, track/field (outdoor), volleyball. *Women:* Basketball, cross-country, diving, softball, swimming, tennis, track/field (outdoor), volleyball.

ADMISSIONS
Freshman Academic Profile: 74% from public high schools. SAT Math middle 50% range 400–500. SAT Critical Reading middle 50% range 400–490. TOEFL required of all international applicants, minimum paper TOEFL 500, minimum computer TOEFL 173. **Basis for Candidate Selection:** *Very important factors considered include:* Rigor of secondary school record, standardized test scores. *Other factors considered include:* Application essay, extracurricular activities, interview, recommendation(s), talent/ability. **Freshman Admission Requirements:** High school diploma is required, and GED is accepted. *Academic units required:* 4 English, 2 math, 2 science (1 science lab), 2 foreign language, 1 social studies, 1 history. *Academic units recommended:* 3 math, 3 science, 2 history. **Freshman Admission Statistics:** 10,193 applied, 35% admitted, 23% enrolled. **Transfer Admission Requirements:** College transcript(s). Minimum college GPA of 2 required. Lowest grade transferable C. **General Admission Information:** Application fee $50. Regular application deadline 8/15. Regular notification is monthly (December to August for fall and October to January for spring). Nonfall registration accepted. Admission may be deferred for a maximum of 1 semester. Common Application not accepted. Credit offered for CEEB Advanced Placement tests.

COSTS AND FINANCIAL AID
Annual in-state tuition $4,000. Out-of-state tuition $10,800. Required fees $290. Average book expense $938. **Required Forms and Deadlines:** FAFSA,

---

state aid form. **Notification of Awards:** Applicants will be notified of awards on a rolling basis beginning on or about 3/1. **Types of Aid:** *Need-based scholarships/grants:* Pell, SEOG, state scholarships/grants, private scholarships, the school's own gift aid, MARC, NBRS. *Loans:* Direct Subsidized Stafford, Direct Unsubsidized Stafford, Direct PLUS, Federal Perkins, state loans, college/university loans from institutional funds. **Student Employment:** Federal Work-Study Program available. Institutional employment available. Off-campus job opportunities are excellent. **Financial Aid Statistics:** 82% freshmen, 77% undergrads receive need-based scholarship or grant aid. 13% freshmen, 33% undergrads receive need-based self-help aid. 83% freshmen, 80% undergrads receive any aid.

CITY UNIVERSITY OF NEW YORK— MEDGAR EVERS COLLEGE

1655 Bedford Avenue, Brooklyn, NY 11225
Phone: 718-270-6023 **E-mail:** website@mec.cuny.edu
Fax: 718-270-6188 **Website:** www.mec.cuny.edu
Financial Aid Phone: 718-270-6139

This public school was founded in 1969.

RATINGS
Admissions Selectivity Rating: 62   **Fire Safety Rating:** 60*   **Green Rating:** 60*

STUDENTS AND FACULTY
Enrollment: 5,189. **Student Body:** 77% female, 23% male, 3% international. African American 88%, Caucasian 1%, Hispanic 4%. **Retention and Graduation:** 7% freshmen graduate within 4 years. **Faculty:** Student/faculty ratio 17:1. 162 full-time faculty, 63% hold PhDs. 100% faculty teach undergrads.

ACADEMICS
Degrees: Associate, bachelor's, certificate. **Academic Requirements:** Arts/fine arts, computer literacy, English (including composition), foreign languages, history, mathematics, philosophy, sciences (biological or physical), social science. **Classes:** Most classes have 30–39 students. Most lab/discussion sections have 10–19 students. **Majors with Highest Enrollment:** Business administration/management, psychology, special education. **Disciplines with Highest Percentage of Degrees Awarded:** Business/marketing 18%, psychology 14%, biological/life sciences 8%, health professions and related sciences 6%. **Special Study Options:** Distance learning, double major, English as a second language (ESL), honors program, independent study, internships, study abroad, weekend college.

FACILITIES
Computers: 100% of public computers are PCs, online registration, online administrative functions (other than registration), remote student-access to Web through college's connection.

CAMPUS LIFE
Activities: Choral groups, dance, drama/theater, radio station, student government, student newspaper, television station, yearbook. **Organizations:** 30 registered organizations, 3 honor societies, 3 religious organizations. **Athletics (Intercollegiate):** *Men:* Basketball, cross-country, soccer, track/field (indoor), track/field (outdoor). *Women:* Basketball, cross-country, softball, track/field (indoor), track/field (outdoor), volleyball.

ADMISSIONS
62 (out of 100). **Freshman Academic Profile:** 24% in top 25% of high school class, 45% in top 50% of high school class. SAT Math middle 50% range 380–480. SAT Critical Reading middle 50% range 380–460. **Basis for Candidate Selection:** *Important factors considered include:* Rigor of secondary school record, standardized test scores, state residency. **Freshman Admission Requirements:** High school diploma is required, and GED is accepted. *Academic units recommended:* 4 English, 3 math, 2 science, 2 history, 4 academic electives. **Freshman Admission Statistics:** 4,364 applied, 100% admitted, 22% enrolled. **Transfer Admission Requirements:** College transcript(s). Minimum college GPA of 2.0 required. Lowest grade transferable C. **General Admission Information:** Application fee $65. Regular application deadline is rolling. Regular notification is rolling. Nonfall registration accepted. Admission may be deferred for a maximum of 1 year.

COSTS AND FINANCIAL AID
Annual in-state tuition $4,000. Out-of-state tuition $8,640. Required fees $251. Average book expense $500. **Required Forms and Deadlines:** FAFSA, state aid form. Financial aid filing deadline 3/6. **Notification of Awards:** Applicants

will be notified of awards on a rolling basis beginning on or about 9/6. **Types of Aid:** *Need-based scholarships/grants:* Pell, SEOG, state scholarships/grants, private scholarships. *Loans:* Direct Subsidized Stafford, Direct Unsubsidized Stafford, Direct PLUS, FFEL Subsidized Stafford, FFEL Unsubsidized Stafford, FFEL PLUS, Federal Perkins. **Student Employment:** Federal Work-Study Program available. Institutional employment available. Off-campus job opportunities are good. **Financial Aid Statistics:** 77% freshmen, 77% undergrads receive need-based scholarship or grant aid. 14% freshmen, 26% undergrads receive need-based self-help aid. Highest amount earned per year from on-campus jobs $1,300.

CITY UNIVERSITY OF NEW YORK— NEW YORK CITY COLLEGE OF TECHNOLOGY

300 Jay Street, NG17, Brooklyn, NY 11201
Phone: 718-260-5500 **E-mail:** admissions@citytech.cuny.edu **CEEB Code:** 2550
Fax: 718-260-5504 **Website:** www.citytech.cuny.edu **ACT Code:** 2950
Financial Aid Phone: 718-260-5700

This public school was founded in 1946. It has a 3-acre campus.

RATINGS
Admissions Selectivity Rating: 60*   **Fire Safety Rating:** 60*   **Green Rating:** 60*

STUDENTS AND FACULTY
Enrollment: 12,533. **Student Body:** 49% female, 51% male, 1% out-of-state, 10% international (110 countries represented). African American 38%, Asian 13%, Caucasian 13%, Hispanic 26%. **Retention and Graduation:** 72% freshmen return for sophomore year. 9% freshmen graduate within 4 years. **Faculty:** Student/faculty ratio 17:1. 307 full-time faculty, 87% hold PhDs. 100% faculty teach undergrads.

ACADEMICS
Degrees: Associate, bachelor's, certificate. **Academic Requirements:** Computer literacy, English (including composition), humanities, mathematics, philosophy, sciences (biological or physical), social science, communication. **Classes:** Most classes have 20–29 students. Most lab/discussion sections have 20–29 students. **Majors with Highest Enrollment:** Commercial and advertising art, computer and information sciences, hotel/motel administration/management. **Disciplines with Highest Percentage of Degrees Awarded:** Computer and information sciences 29%, engineering technologies 17%, public administration and social services 16%, business/marketing 13%, visual and performing arts 12%. **Special Study Options:** Distance learning, dual enrollment, English as a second language (ESL), honors program, independent study, internships, study abroad, teacher certification program, weekend college.

FACILITIES
Housing: Some housing available at nearby university. **Computers:** 80% of public computers are PCs, 20% of public computers are Macs, online registration, online administrative functions (other than registration).

CAMPUS LIFE
Activities: Drama/theater, musical theater, student government, student newspaper. **Organizations:** 45 registered organizations, 1 honor society, 4 religious organizations. 2 fraternities, 2 sororities. **Athletics (Intercollegiate):** *Men:* Basketball, tennis, track/field (outdoor). *Women:* Basketball, tennis, track/field (outdoor).

ADMISSIONS
Freshman Academic Profile: 90% from public high schools. SAT Math middle 50% range 370–480. SAT Critical Reading middle 50% range 350–450. Minimum paper TOEFL 500. **Basis for Candidate Selection:** *Important factors considered include:* Rigor of secondary school record. *Other factors considered include:* Class rank, recommendation(s), standardized test scores. **Freshman Admission Requirements:** High school diploma is required, and GED is accepted. *Academic units required:* 4 English, 2 math, 2 science (1 science lab), 1 foreign language, 2 social studies, 1 academic elective. *Academic units recommended:* 4 English, 3 math, 2 science (2 science labs), 2 foreign language, 3 social studies, 2 academic electives. **Freshman Admission Statistics:** 11,118 applied, 87% admitted, 30% enrolled. **Transfer Admission Requirements:** High school transcript, college transcript(s), statement of good standing from prior institution(s). Minimum college GPA of 2.0 required. Lowest grade transferable C. **General Admission Information:** Application fee $65. Regular notification is rolling. Nonfall registration accepted. Admission may be deferred for a maximum of 1 semester. Credit and/or placement offered for CEEB Advanced Placement tests.

COSTS AND FINANCIAL AID
Annual in-state tuition $4,000. Annual out-of-state tuition $10,800. Required fees $289. **Required Forms and Deadlines:** FAFSA. **Types of Aid:** *Need-based scholarships/grants:* Pell, SEOG, state scholarships/grants, Federal Nursing Scholarships. *Loans:* Direct Subsidized Stafford, Direct Unsubsidized Stafford, Direct PLUS, Federal Perkins. **Financial Aid Statistics:** 80% freshmen, 75% undergrads receive need-based scholarship or grant aid. 20% freshmen, 28% undergrads receive need-based self-help aid. 81% freshmen, 81% undergrads receive any aid.

CITY UNIVERSITY OF NEW YORK— QUEENS COLLEGE

Best 368

65-30 Kissena Boulevard, Flushing, NY 11367
Phone: 718-997-5600 **E-mail:** vincent.angrisani@qc.cuny.edu **CEEB Code:** 2750
Fax: 718-997-5617 **Website:** www.qc.cuny.edu
Financial Aid Phone: 718-997-5123

This public school was founded in 1937. It has a 76-acre campus.

RATINGS
Admissions Selectivity Rating: 60*   **Fire Safety Rating:** 60*   **Green Rating:** 60*

STUDENTS AND FACULTY
Enrollment: 12,991. **Student Body:** 61% female, 39% male, 1% out-of-state, 8% international (140 countries represented). African American 9%, Asian 19%, Caucasian 47%, Hispanic 18%. **Retention and Graduation:** 82% freshmen return for sophomore year. 23% freshmen graduate within 4 years. 25% grads go on to further study within 1 year. 20% grads pursue arts and sciences degrees. 1% grads pursue business degrees. 3% grads pursue law degrees. 1% grads pursue medical degrees. **Faculty:** Student/faculty ratio 17:1. 577 full-time faculty, 87% hold PhDs. 90% faculty teach undergrads.

ACADEMICS
Degrees: Bachelor's, master's, post-bachelor's certificate, post-master's certificate. **Academic Requirements:** Arts/fine arts, English (including composition), foreign languages, humanities, sciences (biological or physical), social science, pre-industrial and/or non-Western civilizations. **Classes:** Most classes have 20–29 students. **Majors with Highest Enrollment:** Accounting, psychology, sociology. **Disciplines with Highest Percentage of Degrees Awarded:** Social sciences 20%, business/marketing 17%, psychology 13%, education 10%, English 7%. **Special Study Options:** Accelerated program, cooperative education program, cross-registration, distance learning, double major, dual enrollment, English as a second language (ESL), honors program, independent study, internships, liberal arts/career combination, student-designed major, study abroad, teacher certification program, weekend college, Albany semester, NYC internship.

FACILITIES
Special Academic Facilities/Equipment: Kupferberg Center for the Performing Arts; Louis Armstrong Archival Center; art museum; centers for Asian, Byzantine, modern Greek, Jewish studies; Italian American Institute; Art Center for the Biology of Natural Systems; art library; music library. **Computers:** 22% of classrooms are wired, 100% of classrooms are wireless, 80% of public computers are PCs, 20% of public computers are Macs, online registration, online administrative functions (other than registration), remote student-access to Web through college's connection.

CAMPUS LIFE
Activities: Choral groups, concert band, dance, drama/theater, jazz band, literary magazine, music ensembles, musical theater, radio station, student government, student newspaper, student-run film society, symphony orchestra, television station, yearbook. **Organizations:** 140 registered organizations, 22 honor societies, 8 religious organizations. 3 fraternities (1% men join), 3 sororities (1% women join). **Athletics (Intercollegiate):** *Men:* Baseball, basketball, cross-country, soccer, swimming, tennis, track/field (indoor), track/field (outdoor), water polo. *Women:* Basketball, cross-country, fencing, soccer, softball, swimming, tennis, track/field (indoor), track/field (outdoor), volleyball, water polo.

ADMISSIONS

Freshman Academic Profile: 67% from public high schools. SAT Math middle 50% range 480–580. SAT Critical Reading middle 50% range 450–550. SAT Writing middle 50% range 490–550. TOEFL required of all international applicants, minimum paper TOEFL 500, minimum computer TOEFL 173. **Basis for Candidate Selection:** *Very important factors considered include:* Academic GPA, rigor of secondary school record, standardized test scores. **Freshman Admission Requirements:** High school diploma is required, and GED is accepted. *Academic units required:* 4 English, 3 math, 2 science (2 science labs), 3 foreign language, 4 social studies. *Academic units recommended:* 4 English, 3 math, 3 science (3 science labs), 3 foreign language, 4 social studies. **Freshman Admission Statistics:** 12,911 applied, 43% admitted, 30% enrolled. **Transfer Admission Requirements:** College transcript(s), statement of good standing from prior institution(s). Minimum college GPA of 2.2 required. Lowest grade transferable C. **General Admission Information:** Application fee $65. Regular notification is rolling. Nonfall registration accepted. Admission may be deferred for a maximum of 1 semester. Credit offered for CEEB Advanced Placement tests.

COSTS AND FINANCIAL AID

Annual in-state tuition $4,000. Annual out-of-state tuition $8,640. Required fees $377. **Required Forms and Deadlines:** FAFSA, institution's own financial aid form, state aid form. Financial aid filing deadline 2/1. **Notification of Awards:** Applicants will be notified of awards on a rolling basis beginning on or about 3/1. **Types of Aid:** *Need-based scholarships/grants:* Pell, SEOG, state scholarships/grants, private scholarships, the school's own gift aid. *Loans:* Direct Subsidized Stafford, Direct Unsubsidized Stafford, Direct PLUS, Federal Perkins. **Student Employment:** Federal Work-Study Program available. Institutional employment available. Off-campus job opportunities are good. **Financial Aid Statistics:** 33% freshmen, 46% undergrads receive need-based scholarship or grant aid. 20% freshmen, 15% undergrads receive need-based self-help aid. 13 freshmen, 91 undergrads receive athletic scholarships. 76% freshmen, 44% undergrads receive any aid. Highest amount earned per year from on-campus jobs $4,125.

CITY UNIVERSITY OF NEW YORK— QUEENSBOROUGH COMMUNITY COLLEGE

222-05 56th Avenue, A-210, Queens, NY 11364
Phone: 718-631-6236 **E-mail:** wyarde@qcc.cuny.edu **CEEB Code:** 2751
Fax: 718-281-5208 **Website:** www.qcc.cuny.edu
Financial Aid Phone: 718-631-6367

This public school was founded in 1967. It has a 34-acre campus.

RATINGS
Admissions Selectivity Rating: 60*   **Fire Safety Rating:** 60*   **Green Rating:** 60*

STUDENTS AND FACULTY

Enrollment: 10,955. **Student Body:** 57% female, 43% male, 1% out-of-state, 12% international (132 countries represented). African American 25%, Asian 18%, Caucasian 24%, Hispanic 21%. **Faculty:** Student/faculty ratio 15:1. 289 full-time faculty. 100% faculty teach undergrads.

ACADEMICS

Degrees: Associate, certificate. **Academic Requirements:** Arts/fine arts, computer literacy, English (including composition), foreign languages, history, humanities, mathematics, philosophy, sciences (biological or physical), social science. **Majors with Highest Enrollment:** Accounting, business administration/management, liberal arts and sciences/liberal studies. **Special Study Options:** Cooperative education program, distance learning, double major, dual enrollment, English as a second language (ESL), honors program, independent study, internships, liberal arts/career combination, study abroad, weekend college, external education for homebound students, honors program for high school seniors.

FACILITIES

Special Academic Facilities/Equipment: Oakland Art Gallery, performing arts center, the Holocaust Center. **Computers:** Online registration, online administrative functions (other than registration), remote student-access to Web through college's connection.

CAMPUS LIFE

Activities: Choral groups, concert band, dance, drama/theater, jazz band, music ensembles, musical theater, student government, student newspaper, student-run film society, symphony orchestra, yearbook. **Organizations:** 37 registered

organizations, 3 honor societies. **Athletics (Intercollegiate):** *Men:* Baseball, basketball, cross-country, soccer, swimming, tennis, track/field (indoor), volleyball. *Women:* Basketball, cross-country, softball, swimming, tennis, volleyball.

ADMISSIONS

Freshman Academic Profile: 80% from public high schools. TOEFL required of all international applicants, minimum paper TOEFL 475, minimum computer TOEFL 163. **Basis for Candidate Selection:** *Factors considered include:* Academic GPA, standardized test scores. **Freshman Admission Requirements:** High school diploma is required, and GED is accepted. **Freshman Admission Statistics:** 7,471 applied, 99% admitted, 35% enrolled. **Transfer Admission Requirements:** High school transcript, college transcript(s). Minimum college GPA of 2.0 required. Lowest grade transferable D. **General Admission Information:** Application fee $50. Regular notification is rolling. Nonfall registration accepted. Credit offered for CEEB Advanced Placement tests.

COSTS AND FINANCIAL AID

Annual in-state tuition $2,800. Annual out-of-state tuition $4,560. Required fees $284. **Required Forms and Deadlines:** FAFSA, institution's own financial aid form. **Notification of Awards:** Applicants will be notified of awards on a rolling basis beginning on or about 7/15. **Types of Aid:** *Need-based scholarships/grants:* Pell, SEOG, state scholarships/grants, the school's own gift aid. *Loans:* Direct Subsidized Stafford, Direct Unsubsidized Stafford, Direct PLUS. **Student Employment:** Federal Work-Study Program available. Institutional employment available. Off-campus job opportunities are good.

CITY UNIVERSITY OF NEW YORK— YORK COLLEGE

94-20 Guy R. Brewer Boulevard, Jamaica, NY 11451
Phone: 718-262-2165 **E-mail:** admissions@york.cuny.edu **CEEB Code:** 2992
Fax: 718-262-2601 **Website:** www.york.cuny.edu
Financial Aid Phone: 718-262-2230

This public school was founded in 1968. It has a 50-acre campus.

RATINGS
Admissions Selectivity Rating: 60*   **Fire Safety Rating:** 60*   **Green Rating:** 60*

STUDENTS AND FACULTY

Enrollment: 5,311. **Student Body:** 71% female, 29% male, 7% international (113 countries represented). African American 44%, Asian 8%, Caucasian 4%, Hispanic 14%. **Retention and Graduation:** 77% freshmen return for sophomore year. 9% freshmen graduate within 4 years. **Faculty:** Student/faculty ratio 15:1. 166 full-time faculty, 73% hold PhDs. 100% faculty teach undergrads.

ACADEMICS

Degrees: Bachelor's. **Academic Requirements:** Arts/fine arts, English (including composition), history, mathematics, philosophy, sciences (biological or physical), social science. **Majors with Highest Enrollment:** Business administration/management, psychology, social work. **Disciplines with Highest Percentage of Degrees Awarded:** Psychology 21%, business/marketing 20%, mathematics 12%, health professions and related sciences 10%, education 9%. **Special Study Options:** Cooperative education program, double major, dual enrollment, English as a second language (ESL), honors program, independent study, internships, teacher certification program. Co-op programs available in business, computer science, health professions.

FACILITIES

Special Academic Facilities/Equipment: Center for Educational Technology, state-of-the-art cardio-pneumo-simulator. **Computers:** 100% of public computers are PCs, online registration, online administrative functions (other than registration), remote student-access to Web through college's connection.

CAMPUS LIFE

Activities: Choral groups, drama/theater, jazz band, literary magazine, student government, student newspaper, student-run film society, television station, yearbook. **Organizations:** 50 registered organizations, 1 honor society, 2 religious organizations. **Athletics (Intercollegiate):** *Men:* Basketball, cheerleading, cross-country, soccer, swimming, tennis, track/field (outdoor), volleyball. *Women:* Basketball, cheerleading, cross-country, softball, swimming, track/field (outdoor), volleyball.

ADMISSIONS

Freshman Academic Profile: 68% from public high schools. SAT Math middle 50% range 390–470. SAT Critical Reading middle 50% range 363–460. TOEFL required of all international applicants, minimum paper TOEFL 470. **Basis for Candidate Selection:** *Very important factors considered include:* Rigor of secondary school record, standardized test scores. **Freshman Admission Requirements:** High school diploma is required, and GED is accepted. *Academic units required:* 3 English, 2 math, 10 academic electives. *Academic units recommended:* 2 science (2 science labs), 1 foreign language, 1 social studies, 2 history, 2 academic electives. **Freshman Admission Statistics:** 2,389 applied, 31% admitted, 80% enrolled. **Transfer Admission Requirements:** High school transcript, college transcript(s), standardized test score. Minimum college GPA of 2.0 required. Lowest grade transferable C. **General Admission Information:** Application fee $40. Regular notification is rolling. Nonfall registration accepted. Admission may be deferred for a maximum of 1 semester. Common Application not accepted. Placement offered for CEEB Advanced Placement tests.

COSTS AND FINANCIAL AID

Annual in-state tuition $3,200. Annual out-of-state tuition $6,800. Required fees $242. Average book expense $692. **Required Forms and Deadlines:** FAFSA, state aid form. **Notification of Awards:** Applicants will be notified of awards on a rolling basis beginning on or about 3/1. **Types of Aid:** *Need-based scholarships/grants:* Pell, SEOG, state scholarships/grants, private scholarships. *Loans:* Direct Subsidized Stafford, Direct Unsubsidized Stafford, Direct PLUS, Federal Perkins, college/university loans from institutional funds. **Student Employment:** Federal Work-Study Program available.

CLAFLIN UNIVERSITY

400 Magnolia Street, Orangeburg, SC 29115
Phone: 803-535-5340 **E-mail:** mzeigler@claflin.edu **CEEB Code:** 5109
Fax: 803-535-5387 **Website:** www.claflin.edu **ACT Code:** 3840
Financial Aid Phone: 803-535-5344

This private school, affiliated with the Methodist Church, was founded in 1869. It has a 43-acre campus.

RATINGS

Admissions Selectivity Rating: 80   **Fire Safety Rating:** 92   **Green Rating:** 69

STUDENTS AND FACULTY

Enrollment: 1,625. **Student Body:** 68% female, 32% male, 10% out-of-state, 4% international (15 countries represented). African American 94%, Caucasian 1%. **Retention and Graduation:** 74% freshmen return for sophomore year. 41% freshmen graduate within 4 years. 20% grads go on to further study within 1 year. 1% grads pursue arts and sciences degrees. 5% grads pursue business degrees. 1% grads pursue law degrees. 2% grads pursue medical degrees. **Faculty:** Student/faculty ratio 12:1. 102 full-time faculty, 73% hold PhDs. 100% faculty teach undergrads.

ACADEMICS

Degrees: Bachelor's, master's. **Academic Requirements:** Arts/fine arts, computer literacy, English (including composition), foreign languages, history, humanities, mathematics, philosophy, sciences (biological or physical), social science. **Classes:** Most classes have fewer than 10 students. Most lab/discussion sections have 10–19 students. **Majors with Highest Enrollment:** Biology/biological sciences, business administration and management, sociology. **Disciplines with Highest Percentage of Degrees Awarded:** Business/marketing 29%, security and protective services 15%, social sciences 15%, biological/life sciences 10%, communications/journalism 9%, parks and recreation 5%. **Special Study Options:** Accelerated program, cooperative education program, cross-registration, double major, dual enrollment, English as a second language (ESL), honors program, independent study, internships, study abroad, teacher certification program, weekend college, (3+2) BS applied mathematics/Claflin + BS engineering/Clemson, (3+2) BS applied mathematics/Claflin + BS engineering technology/South Carolina State University, (3+2) BS biology/Claflin + doctor of chiropractic medicine/Sherman College of Straight Chiropractic.

FACILITIES

Housing: Men's dorms, women's dorms. **Special Academic Facilities/Equipment:** TV studio, NMR Wilbur R. Gregg Collection, Arthur Rose Museum. **Computers:** 90% of classrooms are wired, 10% of classrooms are wireless, 5% of public computers are PCs, network access in dorm rooms, network access in dorm lounges, online registration, remote student-access to Web through college's connection.

CAMPUS LIFE

Activities: Concert band, dance, drama/theater, jazz band, literary magazine, music ensembles, radio station, student government, student newspaper, student-run film society, television station, yearbook. **Organizations:** 3 honor societies. 4 fraternities (15% men join), 4 sororities (15% women join). **Athletics (Intercollegiate):** *Men:* Baseball, basketball, cross-country, track/field (indoor), track/field (outdoor). *Women:* Basketball, cross-country, softball, track/field (indoor), track/field (outdoor), volleyball.

ADMISSIONS

Freshman Academic Profile: 26% in top 10% of high school class, 47% in top 25% of high school class, 72% in top 50% of high school class. 100% from public high schools. SAT Math middle 50% range 400–500. SAT Critical Reading middle 50% range 420–550. TOEFL required of all international applicants, minimum paper TOEFL 500, minimum computer TOEFL 213. **Basis for Candidate Selection:** *Very important factors considered include:* Academic GPA, character/personal qualities, class rank, first generation, rigor of secondary school record, standardized test scores. *Important factors considered include:* Alumni/ae relation, application essay, extracurricular activities, level of applicant's interest, talent/ability. *Other factors considered include:* Recommendation(s), state residency, volunteer work, work experience. **Freshman Admission Requirements:** High school diploma is required, and GED is accepted. *Academic units required:* 4 English, 3 math, 2 science (1 science lab), 2 social studies, 1 history, 7 academic electives. **Freshman Admission Statistics:** 2,711 applied, 49% admitted, 30% enrolled. **Transfer Admission Requirements:** College transcript(s), statement of good standing from prior institution(s). Minimum college GPA of 2.0 required. Lowest grade transferable C. **General Admission Information:** Application fee $20. Regular application deadline 7/15. Regular notification is rolling. Nonfall registration accepted. Admission may be deferred for a maximum of 1 year. Credit offered for CEEB Advanced Placement tests.

COSTS AND FINANCIAL AID

Annual tuition $10,368. Room and board $6,640. Required fees $1,990. Average book expense $1,200. **Required Forms and Deadlines:** FAFSA, institution's own financial aid form. Financial aid filing deadline 4/15. **Notification of Awards:** Applicants will be notified of awards on a rolling basis beginning on or about 5/15. **Types of Aid:** *Need-based scholarships/grants:* Pell, SEOG, state scholarships/grants, private scholarships, the school's own gift aid, United Negro College Fund. *Loans:* FFEL Subsidized Stafford, FFEL Unsubsidized Stafford, FFEL PLUS, Federal Perkins. **Financial Aid Statistics:** 87% freshmen, 87% undergrads receive need-based scholarship or grant aid. 76% freshmen, 80% undergrads receive need-based self-help aid. 88% freshmen, 97% undergrads receive any aid.

CLAREMONT MCKENNA COLLEGE

890 Columbia Avenue, Claremont, CA 91711
Phone: 909-621-8088 **E-mail:** admission@claremontmckenna.edu **CEEB Code:** 4054
Fax: 909-621-8516 **Website:** www.cmc.edu **ACT Code:** 0224
Financial Aid Phone: 909-621-8356

This private school was founded in 1946. It has a 56-acre campus.

RATINGS

Admissions Selectivity Rating: 98   **Fire Safety Rating:** 87   **Green Rating:** 93

STUDENTS AND FACULTY

Enrollment: 1,153. **Student Body:** 46% female, 54% male, 52% out-of-state, 4% international. African American 4%, Asian 15%, Caucasian 56%, Hispanic 12%. **Retention and Graduation:** 95% freshmen return for sophomore year. 81% freshmen graduate within 4 years. 26% grads go on to further study within 1 year. 15% grads pursue arts and sciences degrees. 25% grads pursue business degrees. 25% grads pursue law degrees. 10% grads pursue medical degrees. **Faculty:** Student/faculty ratio 9:1. 112 full-time faculty, 97% hold PhDs. 100% faculty teach undergrads.

ACADEMICS

Degrees: Bachelor's. **Academic Requirements:** English (including composition), foreign languages, humanities, mathematics, philosophy, sciences (biological or physical), social science, civilization course (questions of civilization), senior thesis (major research paper), physical education. **Majors with Highest Enrollment:** Economics, international relations and affairs, political science and government. **Disciplines with Highest Percentage of Degrees Awarded:** Social sciences 44%, business/marketing 11%, psychology 9%, biological/life sciences 7%, interdisciplinary studies 6%, philosophy and religious studies 6%. **Special Study Options:** Accelerated program, cross-registration, double major, exchange student program (domestic), independent study, internships, student-designed major, study abroad.

FACILITIES

Housing: Coed dorms, apartments for single students, substance-free dormitory, living exchanges with other Claremont Colleges. **Special Academic Facilities/Equipment:** Art galleries, athenaeum complex, Centers for Black and Chicano Studies, computer lab, leadership lab, science center. **Computers:** 90% of public computers are PCs, 10% of public computers are Macs, network access in dorm rooms, network access in dorm lounges, online administrative functions (other than registration), remote student-access to Web through college's connection.

CAMPUS LIFE

Activities: Choral groups, concert band, dance, drama/theater, jazz band, literary magazine, music ensembles, musical theater, pep band, radio station, student government, student newspaper, student-run film society, symphony orchestra, yearbook. **Organizations:** 280 registered organizations, 7 honor societies, 5 religious organizations. **Athletics (Intercollegiate): Men:** Baseball, basketball, cross-country, diving, football, golf, soccer, swimming, tennis, track/field (outdoor), water polo. **Women:** Basketball, cross-country, diving, golf, lacrosse, soccer, softball, swimming, tennis, track/field (outdoor), volleyball, water polo. Environmental Initiatives: Building a LEED Silver Residence Hall. Designing a LEED certified new academic building. Signed APUPCC and joined AASHE.

ADMISSIONS

Freshman Academic Profile: 83% in top 10% of high school class, 95% in top 25% of high school class, 100% in top 50% of high school class. 73% from public high schools. SAT Math middle 50% range 630–740. SAT Critical Reading middle 50% range 620–730. TOEFL required of all international applicants, minimum paper TOEFL 600, minimum computer TOEFL 250. **Basis for Candidate Selection:** *Very important factors considered include:* Application essay, character/personal qualities, extracurricular activities, rigor of secondary school record, standardized test scores. *Important factors considered include:* Recommendation(s), talent/ability. *Other factors considered include:* Alumni/ae relation, class rank, geographical residence, interview, racial/ethnic status, state residency, volunteer work, work experience. **Freshman Admission Requirements:** High school diploma is required, and GED is accepted. *Academic units required:* 4 English, 3 math, 2 science, 3 foreign language, 2 social studies, 1 history. *Academic units recommended:* 4 English, 4 math, 3 science, 3 foreign language, 2 social studies, 2 history. **Freshman Admission Statistics:** 3,593 applied, 22% admitted, 37% enrolled. **Transfer Admission Requirements:** High school transcript, college transcript(s), essay or personal statement, statement of good standing from prior institution(s). Lowest grade transferable C. **General Admission Information:** Application fee $60. Early decision application deadline 11/15. Regular application deadline 1/2. Regular notification 4/1. Nonfall registration accepted. Admission may be deferred for a maximum of 2 semesters. Credit and/or placement offered for CEEB Advanced Placement tests.

COSTS AND FINANCIAL AID

Annual tuition $33,000. Room & board $10,740. Required fees $210. Average book expense $1,850. **Required Forms and Deadlines:** FAFSA, CSS/Financial Aid PROFILE, state aid form, Noncustodial PROFILE. Financial aid filing deadline 2/1. **Notification of Awards:** Applicants will be notified of awards on or about 4/1. **Types of Aid:** *Need-based scholarships/grants:* Pell, SEOG, state scholarships/grants, private scholarships, the school's own gift aid. *Loans:* Direct Subsidized Stafford, Direct Unsubsidized Stafford, Direct PLUS, FFEL Subsidized Stafford, FFEL Unsubsidized Stafford, Federal Perkins, Federal Nursing, college/university loans from institutional funds. **Student Employment:** Federal Work-Study Program available. Institutional employment available. Off-campus job opportunities are excellent. **Financial Aid Statistics:** 45% freshmen, 46% undergrads receive need-based scholarship or grant aid. 33% freshmen, 34% undergrads receive need-based self-help aid. 65% freshmen, 72% undergrads receive any aid.

CLARION UNIVERSITY OF PENNSYLVANIA

Admissions Office, 840 Wood Street, Clarion, PA 16214
Phone: 814-393-2306 **E-mail:** admissions@clarion.edu **CEEB Code:** 2649
Fax: 814-393-2030 **Website:** www.clarion.edu **ACT Code:** 3698
Financial Aid Phone: 814-393-2315

This public school was founded in 1867. It has a 192-acre campus.

RATINGS

Admissions Selectivity Rating: 71   **Fire Safety Rating:** 87   **Green Rating:** 77

STUDENTS AND FACULTY

Enrollment: 5,724. **Student Body:** 61% female, 39% male, 6% out-of-state. African American 5%, Caucasian 92%. **Retention and Graduation:** 73% freshmen return for sophomore year. 39% freshmen graduate within 4 years. **Faculty:** Student/faculty ratio 20:1. 247 full-time faculty, 93% hold PhDs. 100% faculty teach undergrads.

ACADEMICS

Degrees: Associate, bachelor's, certificate, master's, post-bachelor's certificate, post-master's certificate. **Academic Requirements:** Arts/fine arts, computer literacy, English (including composition), humanities, mathematics, sciences (biological or physical), social science, health and personal performance. **Classes:** Most classes have 20–29 students. **Majors with Highest Enrollment:** Business administration and management, communications studies/speech communication and rhetoric, elementary education and teaching. **Disciplines with Highest Percentage of Degrees Awarded:** Education 21%, business/marketing 18%, health professions and related sciences 8%, social sciences 6%, liberal arts/general studies 5%, English 5%. **Special Study Options:** Accelerated program, cooperative education program, distance learning, double major, dual enrollment, honors program, independent study, internships, liberal arts/career combination, study abroad, teacher certification program.

FACILITIES

Housing: Coed dorms, men's dorms, women's dorms, apartments for single students, fraternity/sorority housing. Sororities occupy floors on residence halls, and fraternities are off-campus. **Special Academic Facilities/Equipment:** Planetarium, art gallery. **Computers:** 100% of classrooms are wired, 30% of classrooms are wireless, 85% of public computers are PCs, 14% of public computers are Macs, 1% of public computers are UNIX, network access in dorm rooms, network access in dorm lounges, online registration, online administrative functions (other than registration), support for handheld computing, remote student-access to Web through college's connection.

CAMPUS LIFE

Activities: Choral groups, concert band, dance, drama/theater, jazz band, marching band, music ensembles, musical theater, pep band, radio station, student government, student newspaper, television station. **Organizations:** 150 registered organizations, 17 honor societies, 4 religious organizations. 5 fraternities (5% men join), 8 sororities (9% women join). **Athletics (Intercollegiate): Men:** Baseball, basketball, diving, football, golf, swimming, wrestling. **Women:** Basketball, cross-country, diving, soccer, softball, swimming, tennis, track/field (outdoor), volleyball.

ADMISSIONS

Freshman Academic Profile: 9% in top 10% of high school class, 27% in top 25% of high school class, 62% in top 50% of high school class. 87% from public high schools. SAT Math middle 50% range 420–530. SAT Critical Reading middle 50% range 420–520. TOEFL required of all international applicants, minimum paper TOEFL 500, minimum computer TOEFL 173. **Basis for Candidate Selection:** *Very important factors considered include:* Academic GPA, class rank, rigor of secondary school record, standardized test scores. *Important factors considered include:* Application essay, recommendation(s). *Other factors considered include:* Character/personal qualities, extracurricular activities, interview, level of applicant's interest, talent/ability, volunteer work, work experience. **Freshman Admission Requirements:** High school diploma is required, and GED is accepted. *Academic units required:* 4 English, 3 math, 3 science, 3 social studies. *Academic units recommended:* 4 English, 4 math, 4 science (1 science lab), 2 foreign language, 4 social studies. **Freshman Admission Statistics:** 3,987 applied, 73% admitted, 48% enrolled. **Transfer Admission Requirements:** High school transcript, college transcript(s), statement of good standing from prior institution(s). Minimum college GPA of 2.0 required. Lowest grade transferable C. **General Admission Information:** Application fee $30. Regular notification is rolling. Nonfall registration accepted. Credit offered for CEEB Advanced Placement tests.

COSTS AND FINANCIAL AID

Annual in-state tuition $5,177. Annual out-of-state tuition $10,345. Room and board $6,280. Required fees $1,690. Average book expense $850. **Required Forms and Deadlines:** FAFSA. Financial aid filing deadline 4/15. **Notification of Awards:** Applicants will be notified of awards on or about 3/1. **Types of Aid:** *Need-based scholarships/grants:* Pell, SEOG, state scholarships/grants, private scholarships, the school's own gift aid, United Negro College Fund, Federal Nursing Scholarships. *Loans:* FFEL Subsidized Stafford, FFEL Unsubsidized Stafford, FFEL PLUS, Federal Perkins, college/university loans from institutional funds. **Financial Aid Statistics:** 60% freshmen, 55% undergrads receive need-based scholarship or grant aid. 61% freshmen, 62% undergrads receive need-based self-help aid. 58 freshmen, 201 undergrads receive athletic scholarships. 71% freshmen, 87% undergrads receive any aid. Highest amount earned per year from on-campus jobs $11,885.

CLARK ATLANTA UNIVERSITY

223 James P. Brawley Drive at Fair Street, Atlanta, GA 30314
Phone: 404-880-8000 **E-mail:** admissions@panthernet.cau.edu **CEEB Code:** 5110
Fax: 404-880-6174 **Website:** www.cau.edu **ACT Code:** 0804
Financial Aid Phone: 404-880-8992

This private school, affiliated with the Methodist Church, was founded in 1988. It has a 123-acre campus.

RATINGS

Admissions Selectivity Rating: 60*　　**Fire Safety Rating:** 60*　　**Green Rating:** 60*

STUDENTS AND FACULTY

Enrollment: 3,667. **Student Body:** 70% female, 30% male, 56% out-of-state. African American 69%. **Retention and Graduation:** 72% freshmen return for sophomore year. 11% freshmen graduate within 4 years. **Faculty:** Student/faculty ratio 16:1. 290 full-time faculty, 84% hold PhDs.

ACADEMICS

Degrees: Bachelor's, doctoral, master's, post-bachelor's certificate, post-master's certificate. **Academic Requirements:** Arts/fine arts, computer literacy, English (including composition), foreign languages, history, humanities, mathematics, philosophy, sciences (biological or physical), social science. **Classes:** Most classes have 20–29 students. Most lab/discussion sections have 10–19 students. **Disciplines with Highest Percentage of Degrees Awarded:** Business/marketing 31%, communication technologies 18%, psychology 10%, computer and information sciences 8%. **Special Study Options:** Accelerated program, cooperative education program, cross-registration, distance learning, double major, dual enrollment, exchange student program (domestic), honors program, internships, student-designed major, study abroad, teacher certification program, weekend college. Co-op programs available in engineering.

FACILITIES

Housing: Coed dorms, men's dorms, women's dorms, special housing for disabled students, fraternity/sorority housing. **Special Academic Facilities/Equipment:** Language lab. **Computers:** Network access in dorm rooms, network access in dorm lounges, remote student-access to Web through college's connection.

CAMPUS LIFE

Activities: Choral groups, concert band, dance, drama/theater, jazz band, marching band, music ensembles, musical theater, pep band, radio station, student government, student newspaper, student-run film society, symphony orchestra, television station, yearbook. **Organizations:** 60 registered organizations, 12 honor societies. 4 fraternities, 4 sororities. **Athletics (Intercollegiate):** *Men:* Baseball, basketball, cross-country, football, tennis, track/field (outdoor), volleyball. *Women:* Basketball, cheerleading, cross-country, tennis, track/field (outdoor).

ADMISSIONS

Freshman Academic Profile: SAT Math middle 50% range 360–580. SAT Critical Reading middle 50% range 330–593. ACT middle 50% range 14–25. TOEFL required of all international applicants, minimum paper TOEFL 500. **Basis for Candidate Selection:** *Very important factors considered include:* Academic GPA, character/personal qualities, level of applicant's interest, standardized test scores, talent/ability. *Important factors considered include:* Alumni/ae relation, application essay, first generation, recommendation(s), rigor of secondary school record, state residency. *Other factors considered include:* Class rank, extracurricular activities, interview, volunteer work, work experience. **Freshman Admission Requirements:** High school diploma is required,

and GED is accepted. *Academic units required:* 4 English. *Academic units recommended:* 4 English, 3 math, 2 science (1 science lab), 2 foreign language, 3 social studies, 3 academic electives. **Freshman Admission Statistics:** 5,797 applied, 61% admitted, 30% enrolled. **Transfer Admission Requirements:** College transcript(s), essay or personal statement. Minimum college GPA of 2.0 required. Lowest grade transferable C. **General Admission Information:** Application fee $35. Early decision application deadline 3/1. Regular application deadline 6/1. Regular notification is rolling. Nonfall registration accepted. Admission may be deferred for a maximum of 1 year. Common Application not accepted. Neither credit nor placement offered for CEEB Advanced Placement tests.

COSTS AND FINANCIAL AID

Annual tuition $14,522. Room & board $10,978. Required fees $550. Average book expense $1,000. **Required Forms and Deadlines:** FAFSA, institution's own financial aid form. Financial aid filing deadline 4/1. **Notification of Awards:** Applicants will be notified of awards on or about 2/27. **Types of Aid:** *Need-based scholarships/grants:* Pell, SEOG, state scholarships/grants, private scholarships, the school's own gift aid, United Negro College Fund. *Loans:* FFEL Subsidized Stafford, FFEL Unsubsidized Stafford, FFEL PLUS, Federal Perkins, state loans. **Student Employment:** Federal Work-Study Program available. Institutional employment available. Off-campus job opportunities are fair. **Financial Aid Statistics:** 75% freshmen, 76% undergrads receive need-based scholarship or grant aid. 34% freshmen, 29% undergrads receive need-based self-help aid. 4 freshmen, 13 undergrads receive athletic scholarships. Highest amount earned per year from on-campus jobs $2,000.

CLARK UNIVERSITY

950 Main Street, Worcester, MA 01610-1477
Phone: 508-793-7431 **E-mail:** admissions@clarku.edu **CEEB Code:** 3279
Fax: 508-793-8821 **Website:** www.clarku.edu **ACT Code:** 1808
Financial Aid Phone: 508-793-7478

This private school was founded in 1887. It has a 50-acre campus.

RATINGS

Admissions Selectivity Rating: 89　　**Fire Safety Rating:** 97　　**Green Rating:** 73

STUDENTS AND FACULTY

Enrollment: 2,175. **Student Body:** 60% female, 40% male, 62% out-of-state, 8% international (58 countries represented). African American 3%, Asian 4%, Caucasian 66%, Hispanic 2%. **Retention and Graduation:** 88% freshmen return for sophomore year. 63% freshmen graduate within 4 years. 31% grads go on to further study within 1 year. 23% grads pursue arts and sciences degrees. 4% grads pursue business degrees. 3% grads pursue law degrees. 1% grads pursue medical degrees. **Faculty:** Student/faculty ratio 10:1. 172 full-time faculty, 96% hold PhDs. 100% faculty teach undergrads.

ACADEMICS

Degrees: Bachelor's, doctoral, master's, post-bachelor's certificate, post-master's certificate. **Academic Requirements:** Arts/fine arts, English (including composition), foreign languages, history, humanities, mathematics, philosophy, sciences (biological or physical), social science. **Classes:** Most classes have 10–19 students. Most lab/discussion sections have 10–19 students. **Majors with Highest Enrollment:** Biology/biological sciences, political science and government, psychology. **Disciplines with Highest Percentage of Degrees Awarded:** Social sciences 30%, psychology 12%, English 9%, visual and performing arts 9%, biological/life sciences 7%, business/marketing 6%. **Special Study Options:** Cross-registration, double major, English as a second language (ESL), independent study, internships, liberal arts/career combination, student-designed major, study abroad, teacher certification program.

FACILITIES

Housing: Coed dorms, women's dorms, apartments for single students, special housing for disabled students. **Special Academic Facilities/Equipment:** Galleries, theaters, Robert H. Goddard Historical Exhibition, rare book room, craft center, music center, map library, arboretum, herbarium, extensive darkroom facilities, satellite dish for international program reception, electron microscope, nuclear magnetic resonance spectrometer. **Computers:** 2% of classrooms are wired, 99% of classrooms are wireless, 70% of public computers are PCs, 30% of public computers are Macs, network access in dorm rooms, network access in dorm lounges, online registration, online administrative functions (other than registration), remote student-access to Web through college's connection.

CAMPUS LIFE

Activities: Choral groups, concert band, dance, drama/theater, jazz band, literary magazine, marching band, music ensembles, musical theater, pep band, radio station, student government, student newspaper, student-run film society, symphony orchestra, television station. **Organizations:** 82 registered organizations, 8 honor societies, 7 religious organizations. **Athletics (Intercollegiate):** *Men:* Baseball, basketball, crew/rowing, cross-country, diving, lacrosse, soccer, swimming, tennis. *Women:* Basketball, crew/rowing, cross-country, diving, field hockey, soccer, softball, swimming, tennis, volleyball.

ADMISSIONS

. **Freshman Academic Profile:** 31% in top 10% of high school class, 71% in top 25% of high school class, 96% in top 50% of high school class. 70% from public high schools. SAT Math middle 50% range 543–650. SAT Critical Reading middle 50% range 553–660. ACT middle 50% range 24–28.. TOEFL required of all international applicants, minimum paper TOEFL 550, minimum computer TOEFL 213. **Basis for Candidate Selection:** *Very important factors considered include:* Academic GPA, character/personal qualities, recommendation(s), rigor of secondary school record, standardized test scores. *Important factors considered include:* Application essay, extracurricular activities, talent/ability, volunteer work. *Other factors considered include:* Alumni/ae relation, class rank, first generation, geographical residence, interview, level of applicant's interest, racial/ethnic status, work experience. **Freshman Admission Requirements:** High school diploma is required, and GED is accepted. *Academic units recommended:* 4 English, 3 math, 3 science (2 science labs), 2 foreign language, 2 social studies, 2 history. **Freshman Admission Statistics:** 4,726 applied, 60% admitted, 20% enrolled. **Transfer Admission Requirements:** High school transcript, college transcript(s), essay or personal statement, standardized test score, statement of good standing from prior institution(s). Minimum college GPA of 2.8 required. **General Admission Information:** Application fee $50. Early decision application deadline 11/15. Regular application deadline 1/15. Regular notification 4/1. Nonfall registration accepted. Admission may be deferred for a maximum of 1 year. Credit and/or placement offered for CEEB Advanced Placement tests.

COSTS AND FINANCIAL AID

Annual tuition $33,900. Room and board $6,650. Required fees $320. Average book expense $800. **Required Forms and Deadlines:** FAFSA, CSS/Financial Aid PROFILE. Financial aid filing deadline 2/1. **Notification of Awards:** Applicants will be notified of awards on or about 3/31. **Types of Aid:** *Need-based scholarships/grants:* Pell, SEOG, state scholarships/grants, the school's own gift aid. *Loans:* FFEL Subsidized Stafford, FFEL Unsubsidized Stafford, FFEL PLUS, Federal Perkins, state loans. **Financial Aid Statistics:** 53% freshmen, 53% undergrads receive need-based scholarship or grant aid. 44% freshmen, 44% undergrads receive need-based self-help aid. 78% freshmen, 77% undergrads receive any aid.

CLARKE COLLEGE

1550 Clarke Drive, Dubuque, IA 52001-3198
Phone: 563-588-6316 **E-mail:** admissions@clarke.edu **CEEB Code:** 6099
Fax: 563-588-6789 **Website:** www.clarke.edu **ACT Code:** 1290
Financial Aid Phone: 563-588-6327

This private school, affiliated with the Roman Catholic Church, was founded in 1843. It has a 55-acre campus.

RATINGS

Admissions Selectivity Rating: 81   **Fire Safety Rating:** 60*   **Green Rating:** 60*

STUDENTS AND FACULTY

Enrollment: 979. **Student Body:** 71% female, 29% male, 35% out-of-state. African American 2%, Caucasian 57%, Hispanic 3%. **Retention and Graduation:** 74% freshmen return for sophomore year. 56% freshmen graduate within 4 years. 25% grads go on to further study within 1 year. 23% grads pursue arts and sciences degrees. 2% grads pursue business degrees. **Faculty:** Student/faculty ratio 11:1. 77 full-time faculty, 56% hold PhDs. 100% faculty teach undergrads.

ACADEMICS

Degrees: Associate, bachelor's, doctoral, master's. **Academic Requirements:** Arts/fine arts, computer literacy, English (including composition), foreign languages, history, humanities, mathematics, philosophy, sciences (biological or physical), social science, 2 sections of a writing/speaking/research course and capstone. **Classes:** Most classes have fewer than 10 students. Most lab/discussion sections have 10–19 students. **Majors with Highest Enrollment:** Business administration/management, nursing/registered nurse training (RN, ASN, BSN, MSN), psychology. **Disciplines with Highest Percentage of Degrees Awarded:** Education 16%, health professions and related sciences 16%, business/marketing 13%, communications/journalism 12%, visual and performing arts 12%, psychology 8%, public administration and social services 5%. **Special Study Options:** Accelerated program, cross-registration, distance learning, double major, honors program, independent study, internships, student-designed major, study abroad, teacher certification program.

FACILITIES

Housing: Coed dorms, men's dorms, women's dorms, apartments for single students. **Special Academic Facilities/Equipment:** Art gallery, computer classrooms for math, biology, and computer science, computer-interfaced chemistry lab, human gross anatomy and nursing labs, electron microscope, music performance hall, foreign language lab, distance learning classroom. **Computers:** 75% of public computers are PCs, 25% of public computers are Macs, network access in dorm rooms, network access in dorm lounges, online registration, online administrative functions (other than registration), remote student-access to Web through college's connection.

CAMPUS LIFE

Activities: Choral groups, drama/theater, jazz band, literary magazine, music ensembles, radio station, student government, student newspaper, yearbook. **Organizations:** 48 registered organizations, 5 honor societies, 1 religious organization. **Athletics (Intercollegiate):** *Men:* Baseball, basketball, cheerleading, cross-country, golf, soccer, tennis, volleyball. *Women:* Basketball, cheerleading, cross-country, golf, soccer, softball, tennis, volleyball.

ADMISSIONS

Freshman Academic Profile: 23% in top 10% of high school class, 42% in top 25% of high school class, 79% in top 50% of high school class. 81% from public high schools. SAT Math middle 50% range 460–640. SAT Critical Reading middle 50% range 480–550. SAT Writing middle 50% range 510–560. ACT middle 50% range 20–25. TOEFL required of all international applicants, minimum paper TOEFL 527, minimum computer TOEFL 197. **Basis for Candidate Selection:** *Very important factors considered include:* Academic GPA, rigor of secondary school record, standardized test scores, talent/ability. *Important factors considered include:* Class rank. *Other factors considered include:* Extracurricular activities, interview, racial/ethnic status, volunteer work. **Freshman Admission Requirements:** High school diploma is required, and GED is accepted. *Academic units required:* 4 English, 3 math, 3 science (2 science labs), 2 foreign language, 2 social studies, 4 academic electives. *Academic units recommended:* 4 math, 4 science. **Freshman Admission Statistics:** 736 applied, 66% admitted, 34% enrolled. **Transfer Admission Requirements:** High school transcript, college transcript(s), standardized test score, statement of good standing from prior institution(s). Minimum college GPA of 2.0 required. Lowest grade transferable C. **General Admission Information:** Application fee $25. Regular notification is rolling. Nonfall registration accepted. Admission may be deferred for a maximum of 1 year. Credit and/or placement offered for CEEB Advanced Placement tests.

COSTS AND FINANCIAL AID

Annual tuition $21,699. Room and board $6,574. Required fees $995. Average book expense $700. **Required Forms and Deadlines:** FAFSA. Financial aid filing deadline 4/15. **Notification of Awards:** Applicants will be notified of awards on a rolling basis beginning on or about 3/15. **Types of Aid:** *Need-based scholarships/grants:* Pell, SEOG, state scholarships/grants, private scholarships, the school's own gift aid. *Loans:* FFEL Subsidized Stafford, FFEL Unsubsidized Stafford, FFEL PLUS, Federal Perkins, Federal Nursing, state loans, college/university loans from institutional funds, alternative and private loans. **Student Employment:** Federal Work-Study Program available. Institutional employment available. Off-campus job opportunities are excellent. **Financial Aid Statistics:** 89% freshmen, 86% undergrads receive need-based scholarship or grant aid. 80% freshmen, 77% undergrads receive need-based self-help aid. Highest amount earned per year from on-campus jobs $1,422.

CLARKSON COLLEGE

101 South Forty-second Street, Omaha, NE 68131
Phone: 402-552-3041 **E-mail:** admiss@clarksoncollege.edu **CEEB Code:** 6066
Fax: 402-552-6057 **Website:** www.clarksoncollege.edu **ACT Code:** 2436
Financial Aid Phone: 402-552-2749

This private school, affiliated with the Episcopal Church, was founded in 1888. It has a 29-acre campus.

RATINGS
Admissions Selectivity Rating: 60*   **Fire Safety Rating:** 60*   **Green Rating:** 60*

STUDENTS AND FACULTY
Enrollment: 380. **Student Body:** 33% out-of-state. African American 5%, Asian 1%, Caucasian 90%, Hispanic 2%. **Retention and Graduation:** 20% grads go on to further study within 1 year. 10% grads pursue business degrees. 1% grads pursue law degrees. 1% grads pursue medical degrees. **Faculty:** Student/faculty ratio 20:1. 34 full-time faculty. 100% faculty teach undergrads.

ACADEMICS
Degrees: Associate, bachelor's, master's, post-master's certificate. **Academic Requirements:** Computer literacy, English (including composition), humanities, mathematics, sciences (biological or physical), social science. **Special Study Options:** Accelerated program, cooperative education program, distance learning, double major, independent study, internships, study abroad.

FACILITIES
Housing: Coed dorms, apartments for single students. **Special Academic Facilities/Equipment:** 2 hospitals next to campus.

CAMPUS LIFE
Activities: Student government. **Organizations:** 10 registered organizations, 4 honor societies. Environmental Initiatives: Elimination of purchase of all polystyrene product. Recommitment to divert more waste from trash to recyling wastestream. Building new and future buildings to LEED certification.

ADMISSIONS
Freshman Academic Profile: 10% in top 10% of high school class, 40% in top 25% of high school class, 90% in top 50% of high school class. TOEFL required of all international applicants, minimum paper TOEFL 600. **Basis for Candidate Selection:** *Very important factors considered include:* Rigor of secondary school record. *Important factors considered include:* Class rank. *Other factors considered include:* Application essay, recommendation(s), standardized test scores, work experience. **Freshman Admission Requirements:** High school diploma is required, and GED is accepted. *Academic units required:* 3 English, 2 math, 2 science (1 science lab), 2 social studies. *Academic units recommended:* 4 English, 4 math, 4 science (2 science labs), 4 social studies. **Transfer Admission Requirements:** High school transcript, college transcript(s), essay or personal statement. Minimum college GPA of 2.5 required. Lowest grade transferable C-. **General Admission Information:** Application fee $15. Early decision application deadline 3/1. Regular application deadline is rolling. Regular notification is rolling. Nonfall registration accepted. Admission may be deferred for a maximum of 1 year. Common Application accepted. Credit and/or placement offered for CEEB Advanced Placement tests.

COSTS AND FINANCIAL AID
Annual tuition $8,970. Room & board $2,900. Required fees $192. Average book expense $600. **Required Forms and Deadlines:** FAFSA, institution's own financial aid form. Financial aid filing deadline 4/1. **Notification of Awards:** Applicants will be notified of awards on a rolling basis beginning on or about 4/1. **Types of Aid:** *Need-based scholarships/grants:* Pell, SEOG, state scholarships/grants, private scholarships, the school's own gift aid. *Loans:* FFEL Subsidized Stafford, FFEL Unsubsidized Stafford, FFEL PLUS, Federal Nursing. **Student Employment:** Federal Work-Study Program available. Institutional employment available. Off-campus job opportunities are excellent.

CLARKSON UNIVERSITY

Box 5605, Potsdam, NY 13699
Phone: 315-268-6479 **E-mail:** admission@clarkson.edu **CEEB Code:** 2084
Fax: 315-268-7647 **Website:** www.clarkson.edu
Financial Aid Phone: 315-268-6413

This private school was founded in 1896. It has a 640-acre campus.

RATINGS
Admissions Selectivity Rating: 86   **Fire Safety Rating:** 76   **Green Rating:** 95

STUDENTS AND FACULTY
Enrollment: 2,515. **Student Body:** 26% female, 74% male, 26% out-of-state, 3% international (40 countries represented). African American 2%, Asian 2%, Caucasian 90%, Hispanic 2%. **Retention and Graduation:** 84% freshmen return for sophomore year. 58% freshmen graduate within 4 years. 29% grads go on to further study within 1 year. 23% grads pursue arts and sciences degrees. 5% grads pursue business degrees. 1% grads pursue law degrees. **Faculty:** Student/faculty ratio 16:1. 174 full-time faculty, 93% hold PhDs. 88% faculty teach undergrads.

ACADEMICS
Degrees: Bachelor's, doctoral, first professional, master's. **Academic Requirements:** Computer literacy, humanities, mathematics, sciences (biological or physical), social science, engineering, business, Clarkson Common Experience. **Classes:** Most classes have 20–29 students. Most lab/discussion sections have 10–19 students. **Majors with Highest Enrollment:** Business, management, marketing, and related support services; civil engineering; mechanical engineering. **Disciplines with Highest Percentage of Degrees Awarded:** Engineering 46%, business/marketing 32%, biological/life sciences 6%, physical sciences 4%, computer and information sciences 3%. **Special Study Options:** Accelerated program, cooperative education program, cross-registration, distance learning, double major, dual enrollment, English as a second language (ESL), honors program, independent study, internships, liberal arts/career combination, student-designed major, study abroad. Distance learning is available only in our master's program in engineering and global operations management.

FACILITIES
Housing: Coed dorms, men's dorms, women's dorms, apartments for married students, apartments for single students, special housing for disabled students, fraternity/sorority housing, theme and substance-free housing. **Special Academic Facilities/Equipment:** The Center for Advanced Materials Processing (CAMP) is dedicated to developing innovations in advanced materials processing and to transfer this technology to business and industry, and is built on Clarkson's recognized expertise in colloid and surface science and fine particle technology. The Center for the Environment facilitate the development, promotion, and operation of environmental activities within the university and among its partners. **Computers:** 4% of classrooms are wired, 25% of classrooms are wireless, 100% of public computers are PCs, network access in dorm rooms, network access in dorm lounges, online registration, online administrative functions (other than registration), remote student-access to Web through college's connection. Undergraduates are required to own a computer.

CAMPUS LIFE
Activities: Choral groups, drama/theater, jazz band, literary magazine, musical theater, pep band, radio station, student government, student newspaper, symphony orchestra, television station, yearbook. **Organizations:** 90 registered organizations, 9 honor societies, 1 religious organization. 10 fraternities (14% men join), 3 sororities (16% women join). **Athletics (Intercollegiate):** *Men:* Baseball, basketball, cross-country, diving, golf, ice hockey, lacrosse, skiing (downhill/alpine), skiing (nordic/cross-country), soccer, swimming, tennis. *Women:* Basketball, cross-country, diving, ice hockey, lacrosse, skiing (downhill/alpine), skiing (nordic/cross-country), soccer, swimming, tennis, volleyball.

ADMISSIONS
Freshman Academic Profile: 31% in top 10% of high school class, 69% in top 25% of high school class, 95% in top 50% of high school class. 85% from public high schools. SAT Math middle 50% range 560–670. SAT Critical Reading middle 50% range 510–610. SAT Writing middle 50% range 500–630. ACT middle 50% range 23–29. TOEFL required of all international applicants,

minimum paper TOEFL 550, minimum computer TOEFL 213. **Basis for Candidate Selection:** *Very important factors considered include:* Academic GPA, interview, rigor of secondary school record. *Important factors considered include:* Class rank, extracurricular activities, recommendation(s), standardized test scores, volunteer work. *Other factors considered include:* Alumni/ae relation, application essay, character/personal qualities, first generation, level of applicant's interest, talent/ability, work experience. **Freshman Admission Requirements:** High school diploma is required, and GED is accepted. *Academic units required:* 4 English, 3 math, 2 science. *Academic units recommended:* 4 math, 3 science. **Freshman Admission Statistics:** 2,428 applied, 84% admitted, 32% enrolled. **Transfer Admission Requirements:** College transcript(s). Minimum college GPA of 2.7 required. Lowest grade transferable C. **General Admission Information:** Application fee $50. Early decision application deadline 12/1. Regular application deadline 1/15. Regular notification is continuous. Nonfall registration accepted. Admission may be deferred for a maximum of 1 year. Neither credit nor placement offered for CEEB Advanced Placement tests.

COSTS AND FINANCIAL AID

Annual tuition $28,470. Room and board $10,130. Required fees $690. Average book expense $1,100. **Required Forms and Deadlines:** FAFSA, institution's own financial aid form, state aid form. Financial aid filing deadline 2/15. **Notification of Awards:** Applicants will be notified of awards on or about 3/19. **Types of Aid:** *Need-based scholarships/grants:* Pell, SEOG, state scholarships/grants, private scholarships, the school's own gift aid, HEOP. *Loans:* Direct Subsidized Stafford, Direct Unsubsidized Stafford, Direct PLUS, Federal Perkins, college/university loans from institutional funds, Nellie Mae. **Student Employment:** Federal Work-Study Program available. Institutional employment available. **Financial Aid Statistics:** 48% freshmen, 62% undergrads receive need-based scholarship or grant aid. 59% freshmen, 71% undergrads receive need-based self-help aid. 8 freshmen, 38 undergrads receive athletic scholarships. 90% freshmen, 88% undergrads receive any aid.

CLAYTON COLLEGE & STATE UNIVERSITY

5900 North Lee Street, Morrow, GA 30206-0285
Phone: 770-961-3500 **E-mail:** ccsu-info@mail.clayton.edu
Fax: 770-961-3752 **Website:** www.clayton.edu

This is a public school.

RATINGS
Admissions Selectivity Rating: 60* **Fire Safety Rating:** 60* **Green Rating:** 60*

STUDENTS AND FACULTY
Enrollment: 5,661. **Student Body:** 69% female, 31% male, 5% out-of-state, 2% international. African American 48%, Asian 4%, Caucasian 43%, Hispanic 3%. **Retention and Graduation:** 61% freshmen return for sophomore year. **Faculty:** Student/faculty ratio 28:1. 157 full-time faculty, 57% hold PhDs.

ACADEMICS
Degrees: Associate, bachelor's, certificate. **Academic Requirements:** Arts/fine arts, computer literacy, English (including composition), foreign languages, history, humanities, mathematics, philosophy, sciences (biological or physical), social science. **Classes:** Most classes have 20–29 students. Most lab/discussion sections have fewer than 10 students. **Disciplines with Highest Percentage of Degrees Awarded:** Business/marketing 31%, health professions and related sciences 30%, computer and information sciences 17%, psychology 8%, liberal arts/general studies 5%. **Special Study Options:** Cooperative education program, cross-registration, distance learning, double major, dual enrollment, exchange student program (domestic), honors program, independent study, internships, liberal arts/career combination, study abroad, teacher certification program.

FACILITIES
Housing: Apartments for single students, local private apartment living.

CAMPUS LIFE
Activities: Choral groups, drama/theater, jazz band, literary magazine, music ensembles, musical theater, opera, pep band, student government, student newspaper.

ADMISSIONS
Freshman Academic Profile: SAT Math middle 50% range 440–550. SAT Critical Reading middle 50% range 450–550. ACT middle 50% range 17–21. **Basis for Candidate Selection:** *Very important factors considered include:* Rigor of secondary school record, standardized test scores. *Other factors considered include:* Class rank, extracurricular activities, talent/ability.

Freshman Admission Requirements: High school diploma is required, and GED is accepted. *Academic units required:* 4 English, 4 math, 3 science, 2 foreign language, 3 social studies. **Freshman Admission Statistics:** 2,920 applied, 71% admitted, 63% enrolled. **Transfer Admission Requirements:** College transcript(s). Minimum college GPA of 2.0 required. Lowest grade transferable D. **General Admission Information:** Application fee $40. Regular application deadline 7/1. Regular notification is rolling. Nonfall registration accepted. Common Application not accepted.

COSTS AND FINANCIAL AID

Annual in-state tuition $2,212. Out-of-state tuition $8,848. Average book expense $1,000. **Required Forms and Deadlines:** FAFSA, state aid form. Financial aid filing deadline 7/23. **Types of Aid:** *Need-based scholarships/ grants:* Pell, SEOG, state scholarships/grants, private scholarships, the school's own gift aid, Federal Nursing Scholarships. *Loans:* FFEL Subsidized Stafford, FFEL Unsubsidized Stafford, FFEL PLUS, state loans. **Financial Aid Statistics:** 33% freshmen, 36% undergrads receive need-based scholarship or grant aid. 23% freshmen, 33% undergrads receive need-based self-help aid. 7 freshmen, 76 undergrads receive athletic scholarships.

CLEAR CREEK BAPTIST BIBLE COLLEGE

300 Clear Creek Road, Pineville, KY 40977-9754
Phone: 606-337-3196 **E-mail:** ccbbc@ccbbc.edu
Fax: 606-337-2372 **Website:** www.ccbbc.edu

This is a private school.

RATINGS
Admissions Selectivity Rating: 60* **Fire Safety Rating:** 62 **Green Rating:** 63

STUDENTS AND FACULTY
Enrollment: 182. **Student Body:** 20% female, 80% male, 48% out-of-state. African American 1%, Caucasian 99%. **Retention and Graduation:** 84% freshmen return for sophomore year. 13% freshmen graduate within 4 years. **Faculty:** Student/faculty ratio 16:1. 7 full-time faculty, 71% hold PhDs.

ACADEMICS
Degrees: Associate, bachelor's, certificate, diploma. **Academic Requirements:** Arts/fine arts, computer literacy, English (including composition), history, humanities, philosophy, sciences (biological or physical), social science. **Classes:** Most classes have fewer than 10 students. Most lab/discussion sections have 10–19 students. **Disciplines with Highest Percentage of Degrees Awarded:** Theology and religious vocations 100%. **Special Study Options:** Cooperative education program, distance learning, double major, dual enrollment, independent study, internships.

FACILITIES
Housing: Men's dorms, women's dorms, apartments for married students, apartments for single students.

CAMPUS LIFE
Activities: Choral groups, music ensembles.

ADMISSIONS
Basis for Candidate Selection: *Very important factors considered include:* Application essay, recommendation(s), religious affiliation/commitment. *Other factors considered include:* Alumni/ae relation, character/personal qualities, interview, level of applicant's interest, talent/ability. **Freshman Admission Requirements:** High school diploma is required, and GED is accepted. **Freshman Admission Statistics:** 92% enrolled. **Transfer Admission Requirements:** High school transcript, college transcript(s), essay or personal statement, interview, statement of good standing from prior institution(s). Lowest grade transferable C. **General Admission Information:** Application fee $40. Regular notification is rolling. Nonfall registration accepted. Admission may be deferred for a maximum of 2 years.

COSTS AND FINANCIAL AID
Annual tuition $4,972. Room & board $3,310. Required fees $225. Average book expense $1,000. **Required Forms and Deadlines:** FAFSA, institution's own financial aid form. Financial aid filing deadline 6/30. **Notification of Awards:** Applicants will be notified of awards on or about 7/1. **Types of Aid:** *Need-based scholarships/grants:* Pell, SEOG, private scholarships, the school's own gift aid. **Financial Aid Statistics:** 85% freshmen, 67% undergrads receive need-based scholarship or grant aid. 15% freshmen, 11% undergrads receive need-based self-help aid.

The Princeton Review's Complete Book of Colleges

CLEARWATER CHRISTIAN COLLEGE

3400 Gulf-to-Bay Boulevard, Clearwater, FL 33759-4595
Phone: 727-726-1153 **E-mail:** admissions@clearwater.edu
Fax: 727-726-8597 **Website:** www.clearwater.edu
Financial Aid Phone: 727-726-1153

This private school was founded in 1966.

RATINGS
Admissions Selectivity Rating: 60*   **Fire Safety Rating:** 96   **Green Rating:** 60*

STUDENTS AND FACULTY
Enrollment: 641. **Student Body:** 56% female, 44% male, 50% out-of-state, 2% international. African American 1%, Caucasian 91%, Hispanic 4%. **Retention and Graduation:** 34% freshmen graduate within 4 years. 19% grads go on to further study within 1 year. 15% grads pursue arts and sciences degrees. 2% grads pursue business degrees. 2% grads pursue law degrees. **Faculty:** Student/faculty ratio 18:1. 34 full-time faculty, 62% hold PhDs. 100% faculty teach undergrads.

ACADEMICS
Degrees: Associate, bachelor's. **Academic Requirements:** Arts/fine arts, computer literacy, English (including composition), history, humanities, mathematics, philosophy, sciences (biological or physical), social science, Bible. **Disciplines with Highest Percentage of Degrees Awarded:** Education 31%, business/marketing 18%, psychology 14%, biological/life sciences 9%, English 6%. **Special Study Options:** Cooperative education program, double major, dual enrollment, honors program, internships, liberal arts/career combination, study abroad, teacher certification program.

FACILITIES
Housing: Men's dorms, women's dorms. **Computers:** 100% of public computers are PCs, network access in dorm rooms, network access in dorm lounges, remote student-access to Web through college's connection.

CAMPUS LIFE
Activities: Choral groups, concert band, drama/theater, music ensembles, pep band, student government, yearbook. **Organizations:** 17 registered organizations, 1 honor society, 1 religious organization. 7 fraternities (100% men join), 7 sororities (100% women join). **Athletics (Intercollegiate):** *Men:* Baseball, basketball, golf, soccer. *Women:* Basketball, cheerleading, softball, volleyball.

ADMISSIONS
Freshman Academic Profile: 40% from public high schools.SAT Math middle 50% range 420–560. SAT Critical Reading middle 50% range 450–580. ACT middle 50% range 19–25. TOEFL required of all international applicants, minimum paper TOEFL 500. **Basis for Candidate Selection:** *Very important factors considered include:* Character/personal qualities, recommendation(s), rigor of secondary school record, standardized test scores. *Important factors considered include:* Extracurricular activities, interview, talent/ability. *Other factors considered include:* Alumni/ae relation, geographical residence, racial/ethnic status, religious affiliation/commitment, state residency, volunteer work, work experience. **Freshman Admission Requirements:** High school diploma is required, and GED is accepted. **Freshman Admission Statistics:** 306 applied, 67% admitted, 83% enrolled. **Transfer Admission Requirements:** High school transcript, college transcript(s), essay or personal statement, standardized test score, statement of good standing from prior institution(s). Minimum college GPA of 2.0 required. Lowest grade transferable C-. **General Admission Information:** Application fee $35. Regular application deadline 8/1. Nonfall registration not accepted. Common Application not accepted. Neither credit nor placement offered for CEEB Advanced Placement tests.

COSTS AND FINANCIAL AID
Annual tuition $13,390. Room and board $5,900. Required fees $650. Average book expense $1,000. **Required Forms and Deadlines:** FAFSA, institution's own financial aid form, state aid form. Financial aid filing deadline 4/5. **Types of Aid:** *Need-based scholarships/grants:* Pell, SEOG, state scholarships/grants, private scholarships, the school's own gift aid. *Loans:* FFEL Subsidized Stafford, FFEL Unsubsidized Stafford, FFEL PLUS, state loans. **Student Employment:** Federal Work-Study Program available. Off-campus job opportunities are excellent. **Financial Aid Statistics:** 77% freshmen, 49% undergrads receive need-based scholarship or grant aid. 41% freshmen, 19% undergrads receive need-based self-help aid. Highest amount earned per year from on-campus jobs $900.

CLEARY UNIVERSITY

3750 Cleary Drive, Howell, MI 48843
Phone: 517-548-3670 **E-mail:** admissions@cleary.edu **CEEB Code:** 1123
Fax: 517-552-7805 **Website:** www.cleary.edu **ACT Code:** 1974
Financial Aid Phone: 517-548-3670

This private school was founded in 1883. It has a 32-acre campus.

RATINGS
Admissions Selectivity Rating: 60*   **Fire Safety Rating:** 60*   **Green Rating:** 60*

STUDENTS AND FACULTY
Enrollment: 626. **Student Body:** 54% female, 46% male. African American 6%, Caucasian 77%, Hispanic 1%. **Retention and Graduation:** 75% freshmen return for sophomore year. **Faculty:** Student/faculty ratio 10:1. 8 full-time faculty, 25% hold PhDs. 100% faculty teach undergrads.

ACADEMICS
Degrees: Associate, bachelor's, certificate, master's. **Academic Requirements:** Computer literacy, English (including composition), humanities, mathematics, philosophy, business law, finance, accounting, marketing, management, economics, business computer systems. **Classes:** Most classes have 10–19 students. Most lab/discussion sections have 10–19 students. **Majors with Highest Enrollment:** Accounting, business administration/management, management information systems. **Disciplines with Highest Percentage of Degrees Awarded:** Business/marketing 100%. **Special Study Options:** Accelerated program, cooperative education program, distance learning, dual enrollment, independent study, internships.

FACILITIES
Special Academic Facilities/Equipment: Center for Quality, Quality Resource Collection, Center for Business Ethics and Leadership. **Computers:** 100% of public computers are PCs, online administrative functions (other than registration), remote student-access to Web through college's connection. Undergraduates are required to own a computer.

CAMPUS LIFE
Organizations: 1 registered organization.

ADMISSIONS
Freshman Academic Profile: 85% from public high schools. TOEFL required of all international applicants, minimum paper TOEFL 600, minimum computer TOEFL 250. **Basis for Candidate Selection:** *Very important factors considered include:* Rigor of secondary school record. *Important factors considered include:* Interview, standardized test scores. *Other factors considered include:* Application essay, recommendation(s). **Freshman Admission Requirements:** High school diploma is required, and GED is accepted. *Academic units recommended:* 4 English, 2 math, 2 science, 2 social studies, 2 history, 12 academic electives. **Freshman Admission Statistics:** 63 applied, 92% admitted, 69% enrolled. **Transfer Admission Requirements:** High school transcript, college transcript(s), statement of good standing from prior institution(s). Minimum college GPA of 2.5 required. Lowest grade transferable D. **General Admission Information:** Application fee $25. Regular application deadline 8/15. Regular notification is rolling. Nonfall registration not accepted. Admission may be deferred for a maximum of 1 year. Credit and/or placement offered for CEEB Advanced Placement tests.

COSTS AND FINANCIAL AID
Annual tuition $13,680. **Required Forms and Deadlines:** FAFSA, institution's own financial aid form. Financial aid filing deadline 6/15. **Types of Aid:** *Need-based scholarships/grants:* Pell, SEOG, state scholarships/grants, private scholarships, the school's own gift aid. *Loans:* FFEL Subsidized Stafford, FFEL Unsubsidized Stafford, FFEL PLUS. **Financial Aid Statistics:** 54% freshmen, 37% undergrads receive need-based scholarship or grant aid. 54% freshmen, 50% undergrads receive need-based self-help aid. 75% freshmen, 48% undergrads receive any aid.

CLEMSON UNIVERSITY

Best 368

105 Sikes Hall, Box 345124, Clemson, SC 29634-5124
Phone: 864-656-2287 **E-mail:** cuadmissions@clemson.edu **CEEB Code:** 5111
Fax: 864-656-2464 **Website:** www.clemson.edu **ACT Code:** 3842
Financial Aid Phone: 864-656-2280

This public school was founded in 1889. It has a 1,400-acre campus.

RATINGS
Admissions Selectivity Rating: 92   **Fire Safety Rating:** 60*   **Green Rating:** 60*

STUDENTS AND FACULTY
Enrollment: 13,959. **Student Body:** 46% female, 54% male, 32% out-of-state. African American 7%, Asian 2%, Caucasian 82%, Hispanic 1%. **Retention and Graduation:** 87% freshmen return for sophomore year. 28% grads go on to further study within 1 year. 25% grads pursue arts and sciences degrees. 21% grads pursue business degrees. 5% grads pursue law degrees. 8% grads pursue medical degrees. **Faculty:** Student/faculty ratio 15:1. 1,105 full-time faculty, 79% hold PhDs. 95% faculty teach undergrads.

ACADEMICS
Degrees: Bachelor's, doctoral, master's, post-master's certificate. **Academic Requirements:** Computer literacy, English (including composition), mathematics. Each major has its own specific requirements for graduation. **Classes:** Most classes have 10–19 students. Most lab/discussion sections have 10–19 students. **Majors with Highest Enrollment:** Business administration/management, engineering, secondary education and teaching. **Disciplines with Highest Percentage of Degrees Awarded:** Business/marketing 21%, engineering 15%, education 10%, health professions and related sciences 7%, social sciences 6%. **Special Study Options:** Cooperative education program, distance learning, double major, exchange student program (domestic), honors program, independent study, internships, study abroad, teacher certification program. We have an RN to BSN program located in Greenville, SC. This is an off-campus degree program for students who have a 2-year degree in nursing and an RN.

FACILITIES
Housing: Coed dorms, men's dorms, women's dorms, apartments for married students, apartments for single students, fraternity/sorority housing. **Special Academic Facilities/Equipment:** The South Carolina Botanical Gardens, Campbell Geology Museum, Brooks Center for the Performing Arts, Rudolph Lee Art Gallery, Garrison Livestock Arena, John C. Calhoun Home. **Computers:** 100% of public computers are PCs, network access in dorm rooms, network access in dorm lounges, online registration, online administrative functions (other than registration), remote student-access to Web through college's connection. Undergraduates are required to own a computer.

CAMPUS LIFE
Activities: Choral groups, concert band, dance, drama/theater, jazz band, literary magazine, marching band, music ensembles, pep band, radio station, student government, student newspaper, symphony orchestra, television station, yearbook. **Organizations:** 292 registered organizations, 23 honor societies, 24 religious organizations. 26 fraternities (11% men join), 17 sororities (14% women join). **Athletics (Intercollegiate):** *Men:* Baseball, basketball, cheerleading, cross-country, diving, football, golf, soccer, swimming, tennis, track/field (indoor), track/field (outdoor). *Women:* Basketball, cheerleading, crew/rowing, cross-country, diving, soccer, swimming, tennis, track/field (indoor), track/field (outdoor), volleyball.

ADMISSIONS
Freshman Academic Profile: 45% in top 10% of high school class, 74% in top 25% of high school class, 93% in top 50% of high school class. 89% from public high schools. SAT Math middle 50% range 590–680. SAT Critical Reading middle 50% range 540–640. ACT middle 50% range 25–29. TOEFL required of all international applicants, minimum paper TOEFL 550, minimum computer TOEFL 213. **Basis for Candidate Selection:** *Very important factors considered include:* Academic GPA, class rank, rigor of secondary school record, standardized test scores, state residency. *Important factors considered include:* Alumni/ae relation. *Other factors considered include:* Application essay, extracurricular activities, recommendation(s), talent/ability. **Freshman Admission Requirements:** High school diploma is required, and GED is accepted. *Academic units required:* 4 English, 3 math, 3 science (3 science

labs), 3 foreign language, 3 social studies, 1 history, 2 academic electives, 1 physical education or ROTC. *Academic units recommended:* 4 math, 4 science lab. **Freshman Admission Statistics:** 12,784 applied, 55% admitted, 40% enrolled. **Transfer Admission Requirements:** College transcript(s). Minimum college GPA of 2.5 required. Lowest grade transferable C. **General Admission Information:** Application fee $50. Regular application deadline 5/1. Regular notification is rolling. Nonfall registration accepted. Credit and/or placement offered for CEEB Advanced Placement tests.

COSTS AND FINANCIAL AID
Annual in-state tuition $9,868. Out-of-state tuition $20,292. Room & board $5,874. Required fees $122. Average book expense $820. **Required Forms and Deadlines:** FAFSA. Financial aid filing deadline 4/1. **Notification of Awards:** Applicants will be notified of awards on a rolling basis beginning on or about 4/1. **Types of Aid:** *Need-based scholarships/grants:* Pell, SEOG, state scholarships/grants, private scholarships, the school's own gift aid, Federal Nursing Scholarships. *Loans:* FFEL Subsidized Stafford, FFEL Unsubsidized Stafford, FFEL PLUS, Federal Perkins, state loans, college/university loans from institutional funds. **Student Employment:** Federal Work-Study Program available. Institutional employment available. Off-campus job opportunities are fair. **Financial Aid Statistics:** 15% freshmen, 18% undergrads receive need-based scholarship or grant aid. 24% freshmen, 28% undergrads receive need-based self-help aid. 99 freshmen, 389 undergrads receive athletic scholarships. 87% freshmen, 71% undergrads receive any aid. Highest amount earned per year from on-campus jobs $3,500.

See page 1118.

THE CLEVELAND INSTITUTE OF ART

11141 East Boulevard, Cleveland, OH 44106
Phone: 216-421-7418 **E-mail:** admissions@cia.edu **CEEB Code:** 1152
Fax: 216-754-3634 **Website:** www.cia.edu **ACT Code:** 3243
Financial Aid Phone: 216-421-7425

This private school was founded in 1882. It has a 488-acre campus.

RATINGS
Fire Safety: TK   **Admissions Selectivity:** TK   **Green Rating:** TK

STUDENTS AND FACULTY
Enrollment: 489. **Student Body:** 53% female, 47% male, 34% out-of-state, 1% international. African American 4%, Asian 3%, Caucasian 88%, Hispanic 3%. **Retention and Graduation:** 71% freshmen return for sophomore year. **Faculty:** Student/faculty ratio 7:1. 43 full-time faculty, 88% hold PhDs. 100% faculty teach undergrads.

ACADEMICS
Degrees: Bachelor's, master's. **Academic Requirements:** Arts/fine arts, computer literacy, English (including composition), history. There are various elective requirements for the liberal arts. **Classes:** Most classes have 10–19 students. Most lab/discussion sections have fewer than 10 students. **Majors with Highest Enrollment:** Industrial design, intermedia/multimedia, painting. **Disciplines with Highest Percentage of Degrees Awarded:** Visual and performing arts 100%. **Special Study Options:** Cooperative education program, cross registration, exchange student program (domestic), honors program, independent study, internships, study abroad, study for up to 2 semesters at an Alliance of Independent Colleges of Art and Design.

FACILITIES
Housing: Coed dorms, apartments for single students, fraternity/sorority housing. **Special Academic Facilities/Equipment:** The Reinberger Galleries. **Computers:** 50% of classrooms are wired, network access in dorm rooms, network access in dorm lounges, online registration, online administrative functions (other than registration), remote student-access to Web through college's connection.

CAMPUS LIFE
Activities: Student government, student newspaper. **Organizations:** 7 registered organizations, 2 religious organizations.

ADMISSIONS
Freshman Academic Profile: 14% in top 10% of high school class, 46% in top 25% of high school class, 81% in top 50% of high school class. SAT Math middle 50% range 500–590. SAT Critical Reading middle 50% range 480–600. ACT middle 50% range 19–24. TOEFL required of all international applicants, minimum paper TOEFL 525, minimum computer TOEFL 190. **Basis for Candidate Selection:** *Very important factors considered include:* Rigor of

secondary school record, talent/ability. *Important factors considered include:* Academic GPA, Application essay, character/personal qualities, interview, recommendation(s), standardized test scores. *Other factors considered include:* Extracurricular activities. **Freshman Admission Requirements:** High school diploma is required, and GED is accepted. *Academic units recommended:* 4 English, 3 math, 3 science, 3 social studies, 6 academic electives, 3 art. **Freshman Admission Statistics:** 446 applied, 67% admitted, 28% enrolled. **Transfer Admission Requirements:** College transcript(s), essay or personal statement. Minimum college GPA of 2.0 required. Lowest grade transferable C. **General Admission Information:** Application fee $30. Regular notification is rolling. Non-fall registration not accepted. Admission may be deferred for a maximum of 2 semesters. Credit offered for CEEB Advanced Placement tests.

COSTS AND FINANCIAL AID

Annual tuition $24,917. Room & board $9,146. Required fees $1,885. Average book expense $1,300. **Required Forms and Deadlines:** FAFSA, institution's own financial aid form. Financial aid filing deadline 3/15. **Notification of Awards:** Applicants will be notified of awards on a rolling basis beginning on or about 3/16. **Types of Aid:** *Need-based scholarships/grants:* Pell, SEOG, state scholarships/grants, private scholarships, the school's own gift aid, academic merit scholarships/grants (institutional funds). *Loans:* FFEL Subsidized Stafford, FFEL Unsubsidized Stafford, FFEL PLUS, Federal Perkins. **Student Employment:** Federal Work-Study Program available. Institutional employment available. Off-campus job opportunities are good. **Financial Aid Statistics:** 86% freshmen, 81% undergrads receive need-based scholarship or grant aid. 79% freshmen, 75% undergrads receive need-based self-help aid. 95% freshmen, 92% undergrads receive any aid.

CLEVELAND INSTITUTE OF MUSIC

Admission Office, 11021 East Boulevard, Cleveland, OH 44106-1776
Phone: 216-795-3107 **E-mail:** cimadmission@po.cwru.edu **CEEB Code:** 1124
Fax: 216-791-1530 **Website:** www.cim.edu **ACT Code:** 3250
Financial Aid Phone: 216-791-5000

This private school was founded in 1920. It has a 500-acre campus.

RATINGS

Admissions Selectivity Rating: 78   **Fire Safety Rating:** 77   **Green Rating:** 60*

STUDENTS AND FACULTY

Enrollment: 228. **Student Body:** 55% female, 45% male, 79% out-of-state, 11% international (26 countries represented). Asian 8%, Caucasian 78%, Hispanic 3%. **Retention and Graduation:** 87% freshmen return for sophomore year. 82% grads go on to further study within 1 year. 85% grads pursue arts and sciences degrees. **Faculty:** Student/faculty ratio 7:1. 31 full-time faculty, 29% hold PhDs. 100% faculty teach undergrads.

ACADEMICS

Degrees: Bachelor's, doctoral, master's. **Academic Requirements:** Arts/fine arts, English (including composition), foreign languages, 24 credit hours of liberal arts courses. **Disciplines with Highest Percentage of Degrees Awarded:** Visual and performing arts 100%. **Special Study Options:** Accelerated program, cross-registration, distance learning, double major, dual enrollment, English as a second language (ESL), independent study, internships.

FACILITIES

Housing: Coed dorms. **Computers:** Network access in dorm rooms, remote student-access to Web through college's connection.

CAMPUS LIFE

Activities: Choral groups, music ensembles, student government, symphony orchestra.

ADMISSIONS

Freshman Academic Profile: TOEFL required of all international applicants, minimum paper TOEFL 550. **Basis for Candidate Selection:** *Very important factors considered include:* Talent/ability. *Important factors considered include:* Application essay, character/personal qualities, class rank, interview, recommendation(s), rigor of secondary school record, standardized test scores. *Other factors considered include:* Extracurricular activities. **Freshman Admission Requirements:** High school diploma is required, and GED is accepted. *Academic units recommended:* 4 English, 3 math, 3 science, 3 foreign language, 3 social studies. **Freshman Admission Statistics:** 361 applied, 29% admitted, 51% enrolled. **Transfer Admission Requirements:** High school transcript, college transcript(s), essay or personal statement, standardized test score, statement of good standing from prior institution(s). Minimum college

GPA of 3.0 required. Lowest grade transferable C. **General Admission Information:** Application fee $70. Regular application deadline 12/1. Regular notification 4/1. Nonfall registration not accepted. Admission may be deferred for a maximum of 1 semester. Common Application not accepted. Credit and/or placement offered for CEEB Advanced Placement tests.

COSTS AND FINANCIAL AID

Annual tuition $17,875. Room & board $5,590. Average book expense $750. **Required Forms and Deadlines:** FAFSA, institution's own financial aid form, CSS/Financial Aid PROFILE. Financial aid filing deadline 2/15. **Notification of Awards:** Applicants will be notified of awards on or about 4/1. **Types of Aid:** *Need-based scholarships/grants:* Pell, SEOG, state scholarships/grants, private scholarships, the school's own gift aid. *Loans:* Direct Subsidized Stafford, Direct Unsubsidized Stafford, Direct PLUS, Federal Perkins. **Student Employment:** Federal Work-Study Program available. Off-campus job opportunities are good. **Financial Aid Statistics:** 60% freshmen, 65% undergrads receive need-based scholarship or grant aid. 47% freshmen, 53% undergrads receive need-based self-help aid. Highest amount earned per year from on-campus jobs $1,000.

CLEVELAND STATE UNIVERSITY

2121 Euclid Avenue, Cleveland, OH 44115
Phone: 216-687-2100 **E-mail:** admissions@csuohio.edu **CEEB Code:** 3032
Fax: 216-687-9210 **Website:** www.csuohio.edu **ACT Code:** 1221
Financial Aid Phone: 216-687-3764

This public school was founded in 1964. It has an 82-acre campus.

RATINGS

Admissions Selectivity Rating: 69   **Fire Safety Rating:** 60*   **Green Rating:** 60*

STUDENTS AND FACULTY

Enrollment: 9,087. **Student Body:** 55% female, 45% male, 2% out-of-state, 2% international (66 countries represented). African American 22%, Asian 3%, Caucasian 62%, Hispanic 3%. **Retention and Graduation:** 8% freshmen graduate within 4 years. **Faculty:** 524 full-time faculty, 91% hold PhDs. 95% faculty teach undergrads.

ACADEMICS

Degrees: Bachelor's, doctoral, first professional certificate, first professional, master's, post-bachelor's certificate, post-master's certificate. **Academic Requirements:** Arts/fine arts, computer literacy, English (including composition), foreign languages, history, humanities, mathematics, philosophy, sciences (biological or physical), social science, human diversity. **Disciplines with Highest Percentage of Degrees Awarded:** Business/marketing 19%, social sciences 14%, education 11%, communications/journalism 9%, psychology 7%. **Special Study Options:** Accelerated program, cooperative education program, cross-registration, distance learning, double major, dual enrollment, English as a second language (ESL), exchange student program (domestic), honors program, independent study, internships, liberal arts/career combination, student-designed major, study abroad, teacher certification program.

FACILITIES

Housing: Coed dorms, fraternity/sorority housing. **Computers:** 95% of public computers are PCs, 4% of public computers are Macs, 1% of public computers are UNIX, network access in dorm lounges, remote student-access to Web through college's connection.

CAMPUS LIFE

Activities: Choral groups, concert band, dance, drama/theater, jazz band, literary magazine, music ensembles, opera, pep band, radio station, student government, student newspaper, student-run film society, symphony orchestra. **Organizations:** 115 registered organizations, 8 honor societies, 9 religious organizations. 7 fraternities (5% men join), 6 sororities (5% women join). **Athletics (Intercollegiate):** *Men:* Baseball, basketball, fencing, golf, soccer, swimming, wrestling. *Women:* Basketball, cross-country, fencing, softball, swimming, tennis, track/field (indoor), track/field (outdoor), volleyball.

ADMISSIONS

69 (out of 100). **Freshman Academic Profile:** 11% in top 10% of high school class, 28% in top 25% of high school class, 64% in top 50% of high school class. SAT Math middle 50% range 400–550. SAT Critical Reading middle 50% range 400–530. ACT middle 50% range 17–22. TOEFL required of all international applicants, minimum paper TOEFL 525. **Basis for Candidate Selection:** *Very important factors considered include:* Academic GPA, rigor of secondary school record, standardized test scores. *Important factors considered include:* Class rank. **Freshman Admission Requirements:** High school diploma is required, and GED is accepted. *Academic units required:* 4 English, 4 math, 2

science, 2 foreign language, 1 social studies. *Academic units recommended:* 4 English, 3 math, 3 science (1 science lab), 2 foreign language, 3 social studies, 1 fine or performing arts. **Freshman Admission Statistics:** 3,216 applied, 74% admitted, 44% enrolled. **Transfer Admission Requirements:** College transcript(s). Minimum college GPA of 2.0 required. Lowest grade transferable D. **General Admission Information:** Application fee $30. Regular application deadline 8/15. Regular notification is rolling. Nonfall registration accepted. Admission may be deferred for a maximum of 1 year. Credit and/or placement offered for CEEB Advanced Placement tests.

COSTS AND FINANCIAL AID

Annual in-state tuition $7,920. Annual out-of-state tuition $10,664. Room and board $7,800. Average book expense $800. **Required Forms and Deadlines:** FAFSA, tax forms (for base tax year, if selected for verification by Department of Education or the institution). Financial aid filing deadline 2/15. **Notification of Awards:** Applicants will be notified of awards on a rolling basis beginning on or about 3/15. **Types of Aid:** *Need-based scholarships/grants:* Pell, SEOG, state scholarships/grants, private scholarships, the school's own gift aid. *Loans:* FFEL Subsidized Stafford, FFEL Unsubsidized Stafford, FFEL PLUS, Federal Perkins, alternative. **Student Employment:** Federal Work-Study Program available. Institutional employment available. Off-campus job opportunities are excellent. **Financial Aid Statistics:** 61% freshmen, 54% undergrads receive need-based scholarship or grant aid. 57% freshmen, 65% undergrads receive need-based self-help aid. 25 freshmen, 126 undergrads receive athletic scholarships. Highest amount earned per year from on-campus jobs $3,000.

COASTAL CAROLINA UNIVERSITY

PO Box 261954, Conway, SC 29528-6054
Phone: 843-349-2026 **E-mail:** admissions@coastal.edu **CEEB Code:** 5837
Fax: 843-349-2127 **Website:** www.coastal.edu **ACT Code:** 5837
Financial Aid Phone: 843-349-2325

This public school was founded in 1954. It has a 302-acre campus.

RATINGS

Admissions Selectivity Rating: 78   **Fire Safety Rating:** 69   **Green Rating:** 81

STUDENTS AND FACULTY

Enrollment: 6,434. **Student Body:** 52% female, 48% male, 48% out-of-state, 1% international (32 countries represented). African American 12%, Asian 1%, Caucasian 82%, Hispanic 2%. **Retention and Graduation:** 67% freshmen return for sophomore year. 20% freshmen graduate within 4 years. **Faculty:** Student/faculty ratio 19:1. 241 full-time faculty, 80% hold PhDs. 100% faculty teach undergrads.

ACADEMICS

Degrees: Bachelor's, master's, post-bachelor's certificate. **Academic Requirements:** Computer literacy, English (including composition), foreign languages, history, humanities, mathematics, sciences (biological or physical), social science, behavioral science. **Classes:** Most classes have 20–29 students. Most lab/discussion sections have 20–29 students. **Majors with Highest Enrollment:** Business administration and management, marine biology and biological oceanography, marketing/marketing management. **Disciplines with Highest Percentage of Degrees Awarded:** Business/marketing 32%, biological/life sciences 14%, education 13%, social sciences 7%, psychology 6%. **Special Study Options:** Accelerated program, cooperative education program, distance learning, double major, dual enrollment, honors program, independent study, internships, student-designed major, study abroad, teacher certification program.

FACILITIES

Housing: Coed dorms, special housing for disabled students. **Computers:** 90% of classrooms are wired, 90% of classrooms are wireless, 90% of public computers are PCs, 10% of public computers are Macs, network access in dorm rooms, network access in dorm lounges, online registration, online administrative functions (other than registration), remote student-access to Web through college's connection.

CAMPUS LIFE

Activities: Choral groups, concert band, dance, drama/theater, literary magazine, marching band, music ensembles, musical theater, pep band, student government, student newspaper. **Organizations:** 123 registered organizations, 26 honor societies, 6 religious organizations. 9 fraternities (5% men join), 8 sororities (6% women join). **Athletics (Intercollegiate):** *Men:* Baseball, basketball, cheerleading, cross-country, football, golf, soccer, tennis, track/field (outdoor). *Women:* Basketball, cheerleading, cross-country, golf, soccer, softball,

tennis, track/field (outdoor), volleyball. Environmental Initiatives: Energy Efficiency upgrades to 2 renovations. Green Power, including on-site solar. Establishment of Sustainability Initiative.

ADMISSIONS

Freshman Academic Profile: 12% in top 10% of high school class, 37% in top 25% of high school class, 76% in top 50% of high school class. 95% from public high schools. SSAT Math middle 50% range 480–570. SAT Critical Reading middle 50% range 470–550. ACT middle 50% range 20–22. TOEFL required of all international applicants, minimum paper TOEFL 500, minimum computer TOEFL 173. **Basis for Candidate Selection:** *Very important factors considered include:* Academic GPA, rigor of secondary school record, standardized test scores. *Important factors considered include:* Class rank. *Other factors considered include:* Application essay, character/personal qualities, extracurricular activities, first generation, geographical residence, interview, level of applicant's interest, recommendation(s), state residency, talent/ability, work experience. **Freshman Admission Requirements:** High school diploma is required, and GED is accepted. *Academic units required:* 4 English, 3 math, 3 science (3 science labs), 2 foreign language, 2 social studies, 1 history, 4 academic electives, 1 physical education or ROTC. **Freshman Admission Statistics:** 6,218 applied, 68% admitted, 35% enrolled. **Transfer Admission Requirements:** College transcript(s), statement of good standing from prior institution(s). Minimum college GPA of 2.0 required. Lowest grade transferable C. **General Admission Information:** Application fee $45. Regular application deadline 8/15. Regular notification is rolling. Nonfall registration accepted. Admission may be deferred for a maximum of 1 year. Credit and/or placement offered for CEEB Advanced Placement tests.

COSTS AND FINANCIAL AID

Required Forms and Deadlines: FAFSA. Financial aid filing deadline 4/1. **Notification of Awards:** Applicants will be notified of awards on a rolling basis beginning on or about 3/1. **Types of Aid:** *Need-based scholarships/grants:* Pell, SEOG, state scholarships/grants, private scholarships, the school's own gift aid. *Loans:* FFEL Subsidized Stafford, FFEL Unsubsidized Stafford, FFEL PLUS, Federal Perkins, state loans. **Financial Aid Statistics:** 21% freshmen, 25% undergrads receive need-based scholarship or grant aid. 48% freshmen, 50% undergrads receive need-based self-help aid. 68 freshmen, 304 undergrads receive athletic scholarships. 85% freshmen, 82% undergrads receive any aid. Highest amount earned per year from on-campus jobs $21,589.

COE COLLEGE

1220 First Avenue NE, Cedar Rapids, IA 52402
Phone: 319-399-8500 **E-mail:** admission@coe.edu **CEEB Code:** 6101
Fax: 319-399-8816 **Website:** www.coe.edu **ACT Code:** 1294
Financial Aid Phone: 319-399-8540

This private school, affiliated with the Presbyterian Church, was founded in 1851. It has a 53-acre campus.

RATINGS

Admissions Selectivity Rating: 88   **Fire Safety Rating:** 60*   **Green Rating:** 60*

STUDENTS AND FACULTY

Enrollment: 1,250. **Student Body:** 56% female, 44% male, 31% out-of-state, 4% international (15 countries represented). African American 2%, Caucasian 91%, Hispanic 2%. **Retention and Graduation:** 84% freshmen return for sophomore year. 55% freshmen graduate within 4 years. 28% grads go on to further study within 1 year. 18% grads pursue arts and sciences degrees. 2% grads pursue business degrees. 3% grads pursue law degrees. 3% grads pursue medical degrees. **Faculty:** Student/faculty ratio 13:1. 75 full-time faculty, 95% hold PhDs. 100% faculty teach undergrads.

ACADEMICS

Degrees: Bachelor's, master's. **Academic Requirements:** Arts/fine arts, English (including composition), humanities, sciences (biological or physical), social science, foreign culture requirement. **Classes:** Most classes have 10–19 students. Most lab/discussion sections have fewer than 10 students. **Majors with Highest Enrollment:** Biology/biological sciences, business administration and management, psychology. **Disciplines with Highest Percentage of Degrees Awarded:** Social sciences 21%, business/marketing 17%, psychology

11%, visual and performing arts 10%, biological/life sciences 8%. **Special Study Options:** Accelerated program, cross-registration, double major, dual enrollment, English as a second language (ESL), exchange student program (domestic), honors program, independent study, internships, student-designed major, study abroad, teacher certification program.

FACILITIES

Housing: Coed dorms, men's dorms, women's dorms, apartments for single students, fraternity/sorority housing. **Special Academic Facilities/Equipment:** Ornithological museum, writing lab, theater. **Computers:** 50% of classrooms are wired, 25% of classrooms are wireless, 90% of public computers are PCs, 10% of public computers are Macs, network access in dorm rooms, network access in dorm lounges, online registration, support for handheld computing, remote student-access to Web through college's connection.

CAMPUS LIFE

Activities: Choral groups, concert band, drama/theater, jazz band, literary magazine, music ensembles, pep band, radio station, student government, student newspaper, symphony orchestra, yearbook. **Organizations:** 60 registered organizations, 8 honor societies, 4 religious organizations. 5 fraternities (25% men join), 3 sororities (19% women join). **Athletics (Intercollegiate):** *Men:* Baseball, basketball, cross-country, diving, football, golf, soccer, swimming, tennis, track/field (indoor), track/field (outdoor), wrestling. *Women:* Basketball, cheerleading, cross-country, diving, golf, soccer, softball, swimming, tennis, track/field (indoor), track/field (outdoor), volleyball.

ADMISSIONS

Freshman Academic Profile: 25% in top 10% of high school class, 57% in top 25% of high school class, 93% in top 50% of high school class. 90% from public high schools. SAT Math middle 50% range 540–650. SAT Critical Reading middle 50% range 550–650. ACT middle 50% range 22–28. TOEFL required of all international applicants, minimum paper TOEFL 500, minimum computer TOEFL 173. **Basis for Candidate Selection:** *Very important factors considered include:* Rigor of secondary school record, standardized test scores. *Important factors considered include:* Application essay, class rank, recommendation(s). *Other factors considered include:* Alumni/ae relation, character/personal qualities, extracurricular activities, interview, racial/ethnic status, talent/ability, volunteer work. **Freshman Admission Requirements:** High school diploma is required, and GED is accepted. *Academic units recommended:* 4 English, 3 math, 3 science (1 science lab), 2 foreign language, 3 social studies, 2 academic electives. **Freshman Admission Statistics:** 1,177 applied, 72% admitted, 37% enrolled. **Transfer Admission Requirements:** High school transcript, college transcript(s), statement of good standing from prior institution(s). Minimum college GPA of 2.5 required. Lowest grade transferable C. **General Admission Information:** Application fee $30. Regular application deadline 3/1. Regular notification 3/15. Nonfall registration accepted. Admission may be deferred for a maximum of 2 years. Common Application accepted. Credit and/or placement offered for CEEB Advanced Placement tests.

COSTS AND FINANCIAL AID

Annual tuition $26,100. Room and board $6,600. Required fees $290. Average book expense $800. **Required Forms and Deadlines:** FAFSA. Financial aid filing deadline 3/1. **Notification of Awards:** Applicants will be notified of awards on a rolling basis beginning on or about 3/15. **Types of Aid:** *Need-based scholarships/grants:* Pell, SEOG, state scholarships/grants, private scholarships, the school's own gift aid. *Loans:* Direct Subsidized Stafford, Direct Unsubsidized Stafford, Direct PLUS, Federal Perkins, college/university loans from institutional funds. **Student Employment:** Federal Work-Study Program available. Institutional employment available. Off-campus job opportunities are excellent. **Financial Aid Statistics:** 84% freshmen, 80% undergrads receive need-based scholarship or grant aid. 69% freshmen, 71% undergrads receive need-based self-help aid. 98% freshmen, 96% undergrads receive any aid. Highest amount earned per year from on-campus jobs $500.

COGSWELL POLYTECHNICAL COLLEGE

1175 Bordeaux Drive, Sunnyvale, CA 94089-1299
Phone: 408-541-0100 **E-mail:** admissions@cogswell.edu **CEEB Code:** 1177
Fax: 408-747-0764 **Website:** www.cogswell.edu **ACT Code:** 1177
Financial Aid Phone: 408-541-0100

This private school was founded in 1887. It has a 5-acre campus.

RATINGS

Admissions Selectivity Rating: 60*   **Fire Safety Rating:** 60*   **Green Rating:** 62

STUDENTS AND FACULTY

Enrollment: 287. **Student Body:** 15% female, 85% male, 15% out-of-state. African American 1%, Asian 10%, Caucasian 60%, Hispanic 9%. **Retention and Graduation:** 70% freshmen return for sophomore year. **Faculty:** Student/faculty ratio 7:1. 9 full-time faculty, 67% hold PhDs. 100% faculty teach undergrads.

ACADEMICS

Degrees: Bachelor's. **Academic Requirements:** Arts/fine arts, computer literacy, English (including composition), history, humanities, mathematics, sciences (biological or physical), social science, digital arts, digital audio technology, digital motion picture, electrical engineering, software engineering, digital arts engineering, fire science. **Classes:** Most classes have fewer than 10 students. **Majors with Highest Enrollment:** Engineering, fire services administration, visual and performing arts. **Disciplines with Highest Percentage of Degrees Awarded:** Visual and performing arts 62%, security and protective services 32%, engineering 6%. **Special Study Options:** Cooperative education program, distance learning, double major, internships, student-designed major.

FACILITIES

Housing: Apartments for single students. **Computers:** 50% of classrooms are wireless, 75% of public computers are PCs, 20% of public computers are Macs, 5% of public computers are UNIX, remote student-access to Web through college's connection.

CAMPUS LIFE

Activities: Student government, student newspaper. **Organizations:** 5 registered organizations. Environmental Initiatives: saving energy. recycling. saving water.

ADMISSIONS

Freshman Academic Profile: TOEFL required of all international applicants, minimum paper TOEFL 550, minimum computer TOEFL 197. **Basis for Candidate Selection:** *Very important factors considered include:* Academic GPA, application essay, rigor of secondary school record. *Important factors considered include:* Recommendation(s), talent/ability. *Other factors considered include:* Interview. **Freshman Admission Requirements:** High school diploma is required, and GED is accepted. *Academic units required:* 3 English, 3 math, 1 science. **Freshman Admission Statistics:** 48 applied, 73% admitted, 91% enrolled. **Transfer Admission Requirements:** High school transcript, college transcript(s), essay or personal statement, statement of good standing from prior institution(s). Minimum college GPA of 2.5 required. Lowest grade transferable C. **General Admission Information:** Regular application deadline 3/1. Application fee $55. Regular notification within 1 month. Nonfall registration accepted. Admission may be deferred for a maximum of 1 year. Credit and/or placement offered for CEEB Advanced Placement tests.

COSTS AND FINANCIAL AID

Annual tuition $14,904. Required fees $80. **Required Forms and Deadlines:** FAFSA, institution's own financial aid form. Financial aid filing deadline 3/2. **Notification of Awards:** Applicants will be notified of awards on a rolling basis beginning on or about 4/30. **Types of Aid:** *Need-based scholarships/grants:* Pell, SEOG, state scholarships/grants, the school's own gift aid. *Loans:* FFEL Subsidized Stafford, FFEL Unsubsidized Stafford, FFEL PLUS. **Financial Aid Statistics:** 8% freshmen, 51% undergrads receive any aid.

COKER COLLEGE

300 East College Avenue, Hartsville, SC 29550
Phone: 843-383-8050 **E-mail:** admissions@coker.edu **CEEB Code:** 5112
Fax: 843-383-8056 **Website:** www.coker.edu **ACT Code:** 3844
Financial Aid Phone: 800-950-1908

This private school was founded in 1908. It has a 15-acre campus.

RATINGS

Admissions Selectivity Rating: 79   **Fire Safety Rating:** 60*   **Green Rating:** 60*

STUDENTS AND FACULTY

Enrollment: 549. **Student Body:** 59% female, 41% male, 23% out-of-state, 2% international (4 countries represented). African American 20%, Caucasian 75%, Hispanic 2%. **Retention and Graduation:** 74% freshmen return for sophomore year. 37% freshmen graduate within 4 years. **Faculty:** Student/faculty ratio 9:1. 55 full-time faculty, 85% hold PhDs. 100% faculty teach undergrads.

ACADEMICS

Degrees: Bachelor's. **Academic Requirements:** Arts/fine arts, English (including composition), foreign languages, history, humanities, mathematics, philosophy, sciences (biological or physical), social science, wellness/health class. **Classes:** Most classes have fewer than 10 students. Most lab/discussion sections have fewer than 10 students. **Majors with Highest Enrollment:** Business administration/management, graphic design, psychology. **Disciplines with Highest Percentage of Degrees Awarded:** Business/marketing 18%, visual and performing arts 14%, psychology 10%, communications/journalism 9%, social sciences 9%, education 8%, parks and recreation 8%. **Special Study Options:** Cooperative education program, double major, dual enrollment, English as a second language (ESL), honors program, independent study, internships, student-designed major, study abroad, teacher certification program, 2+2 programs with 2-year colleges, 3+1 program with regional medical facility.

FACILITIES

Housing: Coed dorms, special housing for international students, honors housing (Coker World Scholars' Program). **Special Academic Facilities/Equipment:** Art gallery, state-of-the-art performing arts center, dark rooms, botanical gardens, graduate-level science equipment. **Computers:** 80% of public computers are PCs, 20% of public computers are Macs, network access in dorm rooms, network access in dorm lounges, online administrative functions (other than registration), remote student-access to Web through college's connection.

CAMPUS LIFE

Activities: Choral groups, concert band, dance, drama/theater, literary magazine, music ensembles, musical theater, student government, student newspaper, yearbook. **Organizations:** 27 registered organizations, 4 honor societies, 2 religious organizations. **Athletics (Intercollegiate):** *Men:* Baseball, basketball, cheerleading, cross-country, golf, soccer, tennis. *Women:* Basketball, cheerleading, cross-country, soccer, softball, tennis, volleyball.

ADMISSIONS

Freshman Academic Profile: 20% in top 10% of high school class, 50% in top 25% of high school class, 82% in top 50% of high school class. SAT Math middle 50% range 440–550. SAT Critical Reading middle 50% range 430–530. ACT middle 50% range 17–22. TOEFL required of all international applicants, minimum paper TOEFL 500, minimum computer TOEFL 173. **Basis for Candidate Selection:** *Very important factors considered include:* Academic GPA, standardized test scores. *Important factors considered include:* Level of applicant's interest, rigor of secondary school record. *Other factors considered include:* Alumni/ae relation, application essay, character/personal qualities, class rank, extracurricular activities, interview, recommendation(s), talent/ability, volunteer work, work experience. **Freshman Admission Requirements:** High school diploma is required, and GED is accepted. *Academic units required:* 4 English, 3 math, 3 science, 2 foreign language, 3 social studies. **Freshman Admission Statistics:** 649 applied, 66% admitted, 35% enrolled. **Transfer Admission Requirements:** College transcript(s), statement of good standing from prior institution(s). Minimum college GPA of 2.0 required. Lowest grade transferable C. **General Admission Information:** Application fee $15. Regular notification is rolling. Nonfall registration accepted. Admission may be deferred for a maximum of 1 year. Common Application accepted. Credit and/or placement offered for CEEB Advanced Placement tests.

COSTS AND FINANCIAL AID

Annual tuition $17,472. Room & board $2,986. Required fees $480. Average book expense $1,000. **Required Forms and Deadlines:** FAFSA. Financial aid filing deadline 6/1. **Notification of Awards:** Applicants will be notified of awards on a rolling basis beginning on or about 3/1. **Types of Aid:** *Need-based scholarships/grants:* Pell, SEOG, state scholarships/grants, private scholarships, the school's own gift aid. *Loans:* FFEL Subsidized Stafford, FFEL Unsubsidized Stafford, FFEL PLUS, Federal Perkins, state loans, private source loans. **Student Employment:** Federal Work-Study Program available. Institutional employment available. Off-campus job opportunities are good. **Financial Aid Statistics:** 76% freshmen, 74% undergrads receive need-based scholarship or grant aid. 74% freshmen, 72% undergrads receive need-based self-help aid. 10 freshmen, 56 undergrads receive athletic scholarships. 100% freshmen, 100% undergrads receive any aid. Highest amount earned per year from on-campus jobs $1,072.

COLBY COLLEGE

4000 Mayflower Hill, Waterville, ME 04901-8848
Phone: 207-872-3168 **E-mail:** admissions@colby.edu **CEEB Code:** 3280
Fax: 207-859-4828 **Website:** www.colby.edu **ACT Code:** 1638
Financial Aid Phone: 207-859-4832

This private school was founded in 1813. It has a 714-acre campus.

RATINGS

Admissions Selectivity Rating: 96   **Fire Safety Rating:** 95   **Green Rating:** 95

STUDENTS AND FACULTY

Enrollment: 1,865. **Student Body:** 54% female, 46% male, 89% out-of-state, 7% international (69 countries represented). African American 2%, Asian 7%, Caucasian 81%, Hispanic 2%. **Retention and Graduation:** 94% freshmen return for sophomore year. 84% freshmen graduate within 4 years. 22% grads go on to further study within 1 year. 14% grads pursue arts and sciences degrees. 1% grads pursue business degrees. 4% grads pursue law degrees. 2% grads pursue medical degrees. **Faculty:** Student/faculty ratio 10:1. 157 full-time faculty, 94% hold PhDs. 100% faculty teach undergrads.

ACADEMICS

Degrees: Bachelor's. **Academic Requirements:** Arts/fine arts, English (including composition), foreign languages, history, humanities, mathematics, sciences (biological or physical), social science. Students must meet both diversity and wellness requirements. **Classes:** Most classes have 10–19 students. Most lab/discussion sections have 10–19 students. **Majors with Highest Enrollment:** Biology/biological sciences, economics, English language and literature. **Disciplines with Highest Percentage of Degrees Awarded:** Social sciences 23%, area and ethnic studies 13%, English 10%, biological/life sciences 9%, visual and performing arts 8%. **Special Study Options:** Cross-registration, double major, exchange student program (domestic), honors program, independent study, internships, student-designed major, study abroad, teacher certification program, summer research assistantships. Colby has coordinated 3–2 engineering programs with Dartmouth and numerous college-sponsored and approved study abroad programs (about two thirds study abroad at least once before graduating).

FACILITIES

Housing: Coed dorms, quiet halls, chem-free halls, apartments for seniors only, environmental awareness housing. **Special Academic Facilities/Equipment:** 28,000-square-foot art museum, completely renovated student center (Pulver Pavilion to be completed by fall 2007), arboretum, electronic microscopes, greenhouse, astronomical observatory, writer's center, cross-country ski trails, Goldfarb Center for Public Affairs and Civic Engagement, multicultural center, rare books and archives library, computer research classroom, language lab. **Computers:** 5% of classrooms are wired, 5% of classrooms are wireless, 47% of public computers are PCs, 47% of public computers are Macs, 6% of public computers are UNIX, network access in dorm rooms, network access in dorm lounges, online registration, online administrative functions (other than registration), remote student-access to Web through college's connection.

CAMPUS LIFE

Activities: Choral groups, concert band, dance, drama/theater, jazz band, literary magazine, music ensembles, musical theater, radio station, student government, student newspaper, student-run film society, symphony orchestra, yearbook. **Organizations:** 119 registered organizations, 9 honor societies, 6 religious organizations. **Athletics (Intercollegiate):** *Men:* Baseball, basketball, crew/rowing, cross-country, diving, football, golf, ice hockey, lacrosse, skiing (downhill/alpine), skiing (nordic/cross-country), soccer, squash, swimming, tennis, track/field (indoor), track/field (outdoor). *Women:* Basketball, crew/rowing, cross-country, diving, field hockey, golf, ice hockey, lacrosse, skiing (downhill/alpine), skiing (nordic/cross-country), soccer, softball, squash, swimming, tennis, track/field (indoor), track/field (outdoor), volleyball. Environmental Initiatives: Since October 2003 Colby has been committed to 100-percent renewal sources of electricity. A co-generation turbine in the college's steam plant produces about 13 percent of the electricity used. Colby is committed to seeking LEED certification for an new construction and has achieved it in its two newest buildings.

ADMISSIONS

Freshman Academic Profile: 63% in top 10% of high school class, 88% in top 25% of high school class, 98% in top 50% of high school class. 54% from public high schools. SAT Math middle 50% range 640–720. SAT Critical Reading middle 50% range 640–720. SAT Writing middle 50% range 630–710. ACT middle 50% range 28–31. TOEFL required of all international applicants, minimum paper TOEFL 600, minimum computer TOEFL 240. **Basis for Candidate Selection:** *Very important factors considered include:* Character/personal qualities, rigor of secondary school record. *Important factors considered include:* Academic GPA, application essay, class rank, extracurricular activities, interview, racial/ethnic status, recommendation(s), standardized test scores, talent/ability. *Other factors considered include:* Alumni/ae relation, first generation, geographical residence, level of applicant's interest, state residency, volunteer work, work experience. **Freshman Admission Requirements:** High school diploma or equivalent is not required. *Academic units recommended:* 4 English, 3 math, 2 science (2 science labs), 3 foreign language, 2 social studies, 2 academic electives. **Freshman Admission Statistics:** 4,242 applied, 33% admitted, 34% enrolled. **Transfer Admission Requirements:** High school transcript, college transcript(s), essay or personal statement, standardized test score, statement of good standing from prior institution(s). Minimum college GPA of 3.0 required. Lowest grade transferable C. **General Admission Information:** Application fee $65. Early decision application deadline 11/15. Regular application deadline 1/1. Regular notification 4/1. Nonfall registration accepted. Admission may be deferred for a maximum of 1 year. Credit and/or placement offered for CEEB Advanced Placement tests.

COSTS AND FINANCIAL AID

Comprehensive fee $46,100. Average book expense $700. **Required Forms and Deadlines:** FAFSA, either CSS/Financial Aid PROFILE or institutional application. Financial aid filing deadline 2/1. **Notification of Awards:** Applicants will be notified of awards on or about 4/1. **Types of Aid:** *Need-based scholarships/grants:* Pell, SEOG, state scholarships/grants, private scholarships, the school's own gift aid. *Loans:* Direct Subsidized Stafford, Direct Unsubsidized Stafford, Direct PLUS, FFEL Subsidized Stafford, FFEL Unsubsidized Stafford, FFEL PLUS, Federal Perkins, state loans, college/university loans from institutional funds, alternative loans. **Student Employment:** Federal Work-Study Program available. Institutional employment available. Off-campus job opportunities are fair. **Financial Aid Statistics:** 40% freshmen, 35% undergrads receive need-based scholarship or grant aid. 34% freshmen, 31% undergrads receive need-based self-help aid. 41% freshmen, 37% undergrads receive any aid.

COLBY-SAWYER COLLEGE

541 Main Street, New London, NH 03257-7835
Phone: 603-526-3700 **E-mail:** admissions@colbysawyer.edu **CEEB Code:** 3281
Fax: 603-526-3452 **Website:** www.colby-sawyer.edu **ACT Code:** 2506
Financial Aid Phone: 603-526-3717

This private school was founded in 1837. It has a 200-acre campus.

RATINGS

Admissions Selectivity Rating: 60*   **Fire Safety Rating:** 60*   **Green Rating:** 60*

STUDENTS AND FACULTY

Enrollment: 954. **Student Body:** 65% female, 35% male, 71% out-of-state, 1% international (5 countries represented). Asian 1%, Caucasian 93%. **Retention and Graduation:** 75% freshmen return for sophomore year. 50% freshmen graduate within 4 years. **Faculty:** Student/faculty ratio 12:1. 59 full-time faculty, 78% hold PhDs. 100% faculty teach undergrads.

ACADEMICS

Degrees: Associate, bachelor's. **Academic Requirements:** Arts/fine arts, computer literacy, English (including composition), history, humanities, mathematics, sciences (biological or physical), social science. 1 course (3 or 4 credit hours) from 2 of the following areas: Environmental literacy, media literacy, global perspectives, wellness. **Classes:** Most classes have 10–19 students. Most lab/discussion sections have 10–19 students. **Majors with Highest Enrollment:** Business administration and management, psychology, sports and fitness administration/management. **Disciplines with Highest Percentage of Degrees Awarded:** Psychology 21%, business/marketing 15%, parks and recreation 14%, visual and performing arts 13%, education 10%. **Special Study Options:** Accelerated program, cross-registration, double major, dual enrollment, English as a second language (ESL), exchange student program (domestic), honors program, independent study, internships, student-designed major, study abroad, teacher certification program.

FACILITIES

Housing: Coed dorms, women's dorms, special housing for disabled students, substance-free residence hall. **Special Academic Facilities/Equipment:** Sawyer Fine Arts Center, Windy Hill School (pre-school to third grade laboratory school), Ivey Science Center. **Computers:** 100% of public computers are PCs, network access in dorm rooms, remote student-access to Web through college's connection.

CAMPUS LIFE

Activities: Choral groups, dance, drama/theater, literary magazine, musical theater, radio station, student government, student newspaper, yearbook. **Organizations:** 40 registered organizations, 3 honor societies, 1 religious organization. **Athletics (Intercollegiate):** *Men:* Baseball, basketball, diving, equestrian sports, skiing (downhill/alpine), soccer, swimming, tennis, track/field (outdoor). *Women:* Basketball, diving, equestrian sports, lacrosse, skiing (downhill/alpine), soccer, swimming, tennis, track/field (outdoor), volleyball.

ADMISSIONS

Freshman Academic Profile: 79% from public high schools. SAT Math middle 50% range 450–540. SAT Critical Reading middle 50% range 430–550. ACT middle 50% range 18–21. TOEFL required of all international applicants, minimum paper TOEFL 500, minimum computer TOEFL 173. **Basis for Candidate Selection:** *Very important factors considered include:* Interview, level of applicant's interest, rigor of secondary school record. *Important factors considered include:* Academic GPA, alumni/ae relation, application essay, character/personal qualities, extracurricular activities, recommendation(s), standardized test scores, talent/ability, volunteer work, work experience. *Other factors considered include:* Geographical residence, state residency. **Freshman Admission Requirements:** High school diploma is required, and GED is accepted. *Academic units required:* 4 English, 3 math, 2 science (2 science labs), 2 foreign language, 3 social studies. **Freshman Admission Statistics:** 1,402 applied, 88% admitted, 18% enrolled. **Transfer Admission Requirements:** College transcript(s), essay or personal statement. Minimum college GPA of 2.0 required. Lowest grade transferable C. **General Admission Information:** Application fee $45. Early decision application deadline 12/1. Regular application deadline 4/1. Regular notification is rolling. Nonfall registration accepted. Admission may be deferred for a maximum of 1 year. Credit and/or placement offered for CEEB Advanced Placement tests.

COSTS AND FINANCIAL AID

Annual tuition $28,010. Room and board $9,900. Average book expense $750. **Required Forms and Deadlines:** FAFSA, institution's own financial aid form. Financial aid filing deadline 2/15. **Notification of Awards:** Applicants will be notified of awards on a rolling basis beginning on or about 3/1. **Types of Aid:** *Need-based scholarships/grants:* Pell, SEOG, state scholarships/grants, private scholarships, the school's own gift aid. *Loans:* FFEL Subsidized Stafford, FFEL Unsubsidized Stafford, FFEL PLUS, Federal Perkins, state loans, college/university loans from institutional funds. **Student Employment:** Federal Work-Study Program available. Institutional employment available. **Financial Aid Statistics:** 89% freshmen, 80% undergrads receive any aid.

COLGATE UNIVERSITY

Best 368

13 Oak Drive, Hamilton, NY 13346
Phone: 315-228-7401 **E-mail:** admission@mail.colgate.edu **CEEB Code:** 2086
Fax: 315-228-7544 **Website:** www.colgate.edu **ACT Code:** 2702
Financial Aid Phone: 315-228-7431

This private school was founded in 1819. It has a 515-acre campus.

RATINGS

Admissions Selectivity Rating: 96   **Fire Safety Rating:** 78   **Green Rating:** 86

STUDENTS AND FACULTY

Enrollment: 2,756. **Student Body:** 52% female, 48% male, 70% out-of-state, 5% international (36 countries represented). African American 5%, Asian 7%, Caucasian 75%, Hispanic 4%. **Retention and Graduation:** 94% freshmen return for sophomore year. 84% freshmen graduate within 4 years. 19% grads go on to further study within 1 year. 10% grads pursue arts and sciences degrees. 1% grads pursue business degrees. 6% grads pursue law degrees. 3% grads pursue medical degrees. **Faculty:** Student/faculty ratio 10:1. 259 full-time faculty, 96% hold PhDs. 100% faculty teach undergrads.

ACADEMICS

Degrees: Bachelor's, master's. **Academic Requirements:** Foreign languages, humanities, sciences (biological or physical), social science. Competency in foreign language must be shown by successfully completing 3 years of study of 1 language in secondary school, scoring 580 or better on an SAT Subject Test, or successfully completing at least 1 term of intermediate language at Colgate. All students must complete 4 classes in the core curriculum. **Classes:** Most classes have 10–19 students. Most lab/discussion sections have 10–19 students. **Majors with Highest Enrollment:** Economics, English language and literature, history. **Disciplines with Highest Percentage of Degrees Awarded:** Social sciences 31%, English 11%, foreign languages and literature 8%, philosophy and religious studies 7%, biological/life sciences 7%, history 7%. **Special Study Options:** Cross-registration, double major, honors program, independent study, internships, student-designed major, study abroad, teacher certification program. Extended study program allows students to further academic work with a 3–5 week off-campus experience during the winter or summer break. Trips include 13 locations around the world, including South Africa, Ireland, and China.

FACILITIES

Housing: Coed dorms, apartments for single students, special housing for disabled students, fraternity/sorority housing, cooperative housing, theme housing (peace studies, La Casa Pan Latina, Harlem Reniassance Center, French Italian House). **Special Academic Facilities/Equipment:** Art galleries, anthropology museum, language lab, cable TV station, life sciences complex, geology/fossil collection, observatory, electron microscopes, laser lab, weather lab. **Computers:** 100% of classrooms are wired, 100% of classrooms are wireless, 75% of public computers are PCs, 24% of public computers are Macs, 1% of public computers are UNIX, network access in dorm rooms, network access in dorm lounges, online registration, online administrative functions (other than registration), remote student-access to Web through college's connection.

CAMPUS LIFE

Activities: Choral groups, concert band, dance, drama/theater, jazz band, literary magazine, music ensembles, musical theater, pep band, radio station, student government, student newspaper, student-run film society, symphony orchestra, television station, yearbook. **Organizations:** 125 registered organizations, 4 honor societies, 8 religious organizations. 6 fraternities (33% men join), 4 sororities (29% women join). **Athletics (Intercollegiate):** *Men:* Basketball, crew/rowing, cross-country, diving, football, golf, ice hockey, lacrosse, soccer, swimming, tennis, track/field (outdoor). *Women:* Basketball, crew/rowing, cross-country, diving, field hockey, ice hockey, lacrosse, soccer, softball, swimming, tennis, track/field (outdoor), volleyball. Environmental Initiatives: All electricity used on campus is hydroelectric, with some supplemental nuclear power. Colgate's wood-chip-burning heating plant utilizes a renewable energy source to provide about 70 percent of our total requirement. Colgate signed an agreement with Clean Air-Cool Planet in 2004, agreeing to complete a campuswide greenhouse gas emissions inventory, raise awareness about the importance of addressing climate change within the campus community, adopt a greenhouse gas emissions reduction target, and develop and implement a strategic plan to meet established targets and monitor progress over time. Colgate routinely builds and renovates to LEED silver standards.

ADMISSIONS

. **Freshman Academic Profile:** 70% in top 10% of high school class, 92% in top 25% of high school class, 100% in top 50% of high school class. 66% from public high schools. SAT Math middle 50% range 630–710. SAT Critical Reading middle 50% range 620–720. ACT middle 50% range 29–32. Early decision application deadline 11/15. Regular application deadline 1/15. TOEFL required of all international applicants, minimum paper TOEFL 600, minimum computer TOEFL 250. **Basis for Candidate Selection:** *Very important factors considered include:* Academic GPA, class rank, rigor of secondary school record. *Important factors considered include:* Application essay, character/personal qualities, extracurricular activities, recommendation(s), standardized test scores, talent/ability. *Other factors considered include:* Alumni/ae relation, first generation, geographical residence, racial/ethnic status, volunteer work, work experience. **Freshman Admission Requirements:** High school diploma is required, and GED is accepted. *Academic units required:* 4 English, 3 math, 3 science (2 science labs), 3 foreign language, 2 social studies, 1 history. *Academic units recommended:* 4 English, 4 math, 4 science (3 science labs), 4 foreign language, 2 social studies, 3 history. **Freshman Admission Statistics:** 7,873 applied, 28% admitted, 34% enrolled. **Transfer Admission Requirements:** High school transcript, college transcript(s), essay or personal statement, standardized test score, statement of good standing from prior institution(s). Lowest grade transferable C. **General Admission Information:** Application fee $55. Early decision application deadline 11/15. Regular application deadline 1/15. Nonfall registration not accepted. Admission may be deferred for a maximum of 1 year. Credit and/or placement offered for CEEB Advanced Placement tests.

COSTS AND FINANCIAL AID

Annual tuition $37,405. Room and board $9,170. Required fees $255. Average book expense $1,880. **Required Forms and Deadlines:** FAFSA, CSS/Financial Aid PROFILE, Noncustodial PROFILE, Business/Farm Supplement. Financial aid filing deadline 1/15. **Notification of Awards:** Applicants will be notified of awards on or about 4/1. **Types of Aid:** *Need-based scholarships/grants:* Pell, SEOG, state scholarships/grants, the school's own gift aid. *Loans:* FFEL Subsidized Stafford, FFEL Unsubsidized Stafford, FFEL PLUS, Federal Perkins. **Student Employment:** Federal Work-Study Program available. Institutional employment available. Off-campus job opportunities are fair. **Financial Aid Statistics:** 34% freshmen, 36% undergrads receive need-based scholarship or grant aid. 25% freshmen, 29% undergrads receive need-based self-help aid. 48 freshmen, 124 undergrads receive athletic scholarships. 35% freshmen, 46% undergrads receive any aid. Highest amount earned per year from on-campus jobs $1,600.

COLLEGE OF THE ATLANTIC

Best 368

105 Eden Street, Admission Office, Bar Harbor, ME 04609
Phone: 207-288-5015 **E-mail:** inquiry@coa.edu **CEEB Code:** 3305
Fax: 207-288-4126 **Website:** www.coa.edu **ACT Code:** 1637
Financial Aid Phone: 207-288-5015

This private school was founded in 1969. It has a 25-acre campus.

RATINGS

Admissions Selectivity Rating: 88   **Fire Safety Rating:** 88   **Green Rating:** 99

STUDENTS AND FACULTY

Enrollment: 320. **Student Body:** 67% female, 33% male, 79% out-of-state, 16% international (40 countries represented). Caucasian 18%, Hispanic 1%. **Retention and Graduation:** 82% freshmen return for sophomore year. 55% freshmen graduate within 4 years. 25% grads go on to further study within 1 year. 20% grads pursue arts and sciences degrees. 1% grads pursue business degrees. 1% grads pursue law degrees. 1% grads pursue medical degrees. **Faculty:** Student/faculty ratio 11:1. 26 full-time faculty, 85% hold PhDs. 100% faculty teach undergrads.

ACADEMICS

Degrees: Bachelor's, master's. **Academic Requirements:** Arts/fine arts, English (including composition), history, humanities, mathematics, sciences (biological or physical). Human ecology core course required of all entering first-year students with fewer than 9 credits. **Classes:** Most classes have 10–19 students. **Majors with Highest Enrollment:** Animal behavior and ethology, wildlife biology. **Disciplines with Highest Percentage of Degrees Awarded:** Liberal arts/general studies 100%. **Special Study Options:** Cross-registration, exchange student program (domestic), independent study, internships, liberal arts/career combination, student-designed major, study abroad, teacher certification program. Winter term program in Yucatan, Mexico; EcoLeague, consortium agreement with 5 other colleges for student exchanges (Alaska Pacific University, Antioch College, Green Mountain College, Northland College, Prescott College); exchange program with Olin College of Engineering.

FACILITIES

Housing: Coed dorms, special housing for disabled students, substance-free housing. **Special Academic Facilities/Equipment:** Natural history museum, pottery studio, greenhouse, geographical information systems lab. **Computers:** 100% of classrooms are wired, 100% of classrooms are wireless, 90% of public computers are PCs, 10% of public computers are Macs, network access in dorm rooms, network access in dorm lounges, remote student-access to Web through college's connection.

CAMPUS LIFE

Activities: Choral groups, dance, drama/theater, jazz band, literary magazine, music ensembles, student government, student newspaper, yearbook. **Organizations:** 4 registered organizations, 1 religious organization. **Environmental Initiatives:** Carbon NetZero Initiative—the College is carbon net zero. Renewable Energy—the College's new student dorms, will have space heating and hot water provided by wood pellet boilers, the buildings are super-insulated, have triple pane windows, and composting toilets. Energy Conservation—Working with a energy services company, the college has recently completed an energy audit of the campus and is reviewing recommendations for making existing buildings more energy efficient. Retrofits and upgrades to buildings will begin in early 2008.

ADMISSIONS

Freshman Academic Profile: 41% in top 10% of high school class, 66% in top 25% of high school class, 90% in top 50% of high school class. 71% from public high schools. SAT Math middle 50% range 540–640. SAT Critical Reading middle 50% range 590–690. SAT Writing middle 50% range 570–670. ACT middle 50% range 24–30. TOEFL required of all international applicants, minimum paper TOEFL 567, minimum computer TOEFL 227. **Basis for Candidate Selection:** *Very important factors considered include:* Application essay, recommendation(s), rigor of secondary school record. *Important factors considered include:* Academic GPA, character/personal qualities, class rank, extracurricular activities, interview, talent/ability, volunteer work, work experience. *Other factors considered include:* Alumni/ae relation, first generation, geographical residence, level of applicant's interest, racial/ethnic status, standardized test scores, state residency. **Freshman Admission Requirements:** High school diploma is required, and GED is accepted. *Academic units required:* 4 English, 3 math, 2 science (2 science labs), 2 social studies. *Academic units recommended:* 4 math, 3 science, 2 foreign language, 2 history, 1 academic elective. **Freshman Admission Statistics:** 300 applied, 66% admitted, 37% enrolled. **Transfer Admission Requirements:** High school transcript, college transcript(s), essay or personal statement. Minimum college GPA of 3.0 required. Lowest grade transferable C. **General Admission Information:** Application fee $45. Early decision application deadline 12/1. Regular application deadline 2/15. Regular notification 4/1. Nonfall registration accepted. Admission may be deferred for a maximum of 1 year. Credit and/or placement offered for CEEB Advanced Placement tests.

COSTS AND FINANCIAL AID

Annual tuition $30,990. Room and board $8,490. Required fees $480. Average book expense $600. **Required Forms and Deadlines:** FAFSA, institution's own financial aid form, Noncustodial PROFILE, Business/Farm Supplement. Financial aid filing deadline 2/15. **Notification of Awards:** Applicants will be notified of awards on or about 4/1. **Types of Aid:** *Need-based scholarships/ grants:* Pell, SEOG, state scholarships/grants, private scholarships, the school's own gift aid. *Loans:* FFEL Subsidized Stafford, FFEL Unsubsidized Stafford, FFEL PLUS, Federal Perkins. **Financial Aid Statistics:** 85% freshmen, 83% undergrads receive need-based scholarship or grant aid. 88% freshmen, 87% undergrads receive need-based self-help aid. 92% freshmen, 92% undergrads receive any aid.

See page 1120.

COLLEGE OF CHARLESTON

Best 368

66 George Street, Charleston, SC 29424
Phone: 843-953-5670 **E-mail:** admissions@cofc.edu **CEEB Code:** 5113
Fax: 843-953-6322 **Website:** www.cofc.edu **ACT Code:** 3846
Financial Aid Phone: 843-953-5540

This public school was founded in 1770. It has a 52-acre campus.

RATINGS

Admissions Selectivity Rating: 88   **Fire Safety Rating:** 92   **Green Rating:** 73

STUDENTS AND FACULTY

Enrollment: 9,423. **Student Body:** 64% female, 36% male, 36% out-of-state, 2% international (75 countries represented). African American 6%, Asian 2%, Caucasian 83%, Hispanic 2%. **Retention and Graduation:** 81% freshmen return for sophomore year. 42% freshmen graduate within 4 years. 35% grads go on to further study within 1 year. 49% grads pursue arts and sciences degrees. 23% grads pursue business degrees. 9% grads pursue law degrees. 19% grads pursue medical degrees. **Faculty:** Student/faculty ratio 13:1. 522 full-time faculty, 85% hold PhDs. 95% faculty teach undergrads.

ACADEMICS

Degrees: Bachelor's, master's, post-bachelor's certificate. **Academic Requirements:** English (including composition), foreign languages, history,

humanities, mathematics, sciences (biological or physical), social science. **Classes:** Most classes have 20–29 students. Most lab/discussion sections have 20–29 students. **Majors with Highest Enrollment:** Biology/biological sciences, business administration/management, communications studies/speech communication and rhetoric. **Disciplines with Highest Percentage of Degrees Awarded:** Business/marketing 20%, communications/journalism 15%, social sciences 11%, education 10%, biological/life sciences 9%. **Special Study Options:** Accelerated program, cooperative education program, cross-registration, distance learning, double major, dual enrollment, English as a second language (ESL), exchange student program (domestic), honors program, independent study, internships, liberal arts/career combination, study abroad, teacher certification program, semester at sea.

FACILITIES

Housing: Coed dorms, men's dorms, women's dorms, special housing for disabled students, special housing for international students, fraternity/sorority housing, restored old Charleston houses used as residence halls, international house. **Special Academic Facilities/Equipment:** Art gallery, broadcast museum, early childhood development center, African American History and Culture Institute, observatory, marine sciences station, sculpture facility, sailing marina, sports facilities. **Computers:** 74% of classrooms are wired, 97% of classrooms are wireless, network access in dorm rooms, network access in dorm lounges, online registration, online administrative functions (other than registration), support for handheld computing, remote student-access to Web through college's connection.

CAMPUS LIFE

Activities: Choral groups, dance, drama/theater, jazz band, literary magazine, music ensembles, musical theater, pep band, radio station, student government, student newspaper, symphony orchestra, yearbook. **Organizations:** 120 registered organizations, 19 honor societies, 17 religious organizations. 14 fraternities (14% men join), 11 sororities (18% women join). **Athletics (Intercollegiate):** *Men:* Baseball, basketball, cross-country, diving, golf, sailing, soccer, swimming, tennis. *Women:* Basketball, cross-country, diving, equestrian sports, golf, sailing, soccer, softball, swimming, tennis, volleyball. Environmental Initiatives: Convened a Sustainability Committee. Signed the ACUPCC. Participate in RecycleMania.

ADMISSIONS

. **Freshman Academic Profile:** 30% in top 10% of high school class, 66% in top 25% of high school class, 95% in top 50% of high school class. 81% from public high schools. SAT Math middle 50% range 570–650. SAT Critical Reading middle 50% range 570–650. ACT middle 50% range 23–26. TOEFL required of all international applicants, minimum paper TOEFL 550, minimum computer TOEFL 213. **Basis for Candidate Selection:** *Very important factors considered include:* Academic GPA, rigor of secondary school record, standardized test scores, state residency. *Important factors considered include:* Character/personal qualities, class rank, first generation, talent/ability. *Other factors considered include:* Alumni/ae relation, application essay, extracurricular activities, geographical residence, racial/ethnic status, recommendation(s), volunteer work, work experience. **Freshman Admission Requirements:** High school diploma is required, and GED is accepted. *Academic units required:* 4 English, 3 math, 3 science (3 science labs), 3 foreign language, 3 social studies, 4 academic electives. *Academic units recommended:* 4 math, 4 science, 3 foreign language, 2 history. **Freshman Admission Statistics:** 8,673 applied, 61% admitted, 37% enrolled. **Transfer Admission Requirements:** College transcript(s). Minimum college GPA of 2.6 required. Lowest grade transferable C. **General Admission Information:** Application fee $45. Regular application deadline 4/1. Regular notification mid-December for early action. Nonfall registration accepted. Admission may be deferred for a maximum of 1 semester. Credit and/or placement offered for CEEB Advanced Placement tests.

COSTS AND FINANCIAL AID

Required Forms and Deadlines: FAFSA. Financial aid filing deadline 3/15. **Notification of Awards:** Applicants will be notified of awards on a rolling basis beginning on or about 4/10. **Types of Aid:** *Need-based scholarships/grants:* Pell, SEOG, state scholarships/grants, private scholarships, the school's own gift aid. *Loans:* Direct Subsidized Stafford, Direct Unsubsidized Stafford, Direct PLUS, Federal Perkins. **Student Employment:** Federal Work-Study Program available. Institutional employment available. Off-campus job opportunities are excellent. **Financial Aid Statistics:** 24% freshmen, 22% undergrads receive need-based scholarship or grant aid. 24% freshmen, 30% undergrads receive need-based self-help aid. 39 freshmen, 143 undergrads receive athletic scholarships. 33% freshmen, 36% undergrads receive any aid. Highest amount earned per year from on-campus jobs $9,139.

COLLEGE FOR CREATIVE STUDIES

201 East Kirby, Detroit, MI 48202-4304
Phone: 313-664-7425 **E-mail:** admissions@ccscad.edu
Fax: 313-872-2739 **Website:** www.ccscad.edu
Financial Aid Phone: 313-664-7495

This private school was founded in 1906. It has an 11-acre campus.

RATINGS
Admissions Selectivity Rating: 60*   **Fire Safety Rating:** 60*   **Green Rating:** 60*

STUDENTS AND FACULTY
Enrollment: 714. **Student Body:** 75% female, 25% male, 18% out-of-state, 8% international. African American 11%, Asian 8%, Caucasian 130%, Hispanic 7%. **Retention and Graduation:** 77% freshmen return for sophomore year. 24% freshmen graduate within 4 years. **Faculty:** Student/faculty ratio 11:1. 46 full-time faculty. 100% faculty teach undergrads.

ACADEMICS
Degrees: Bachelor's, post-bachelor's certificate. **Academic Requirements:** Arts/fine arts, computer literacy, English (including composition), history, philosophy, sciences (biological or physical), social science. **Majors with Highest Enrollment:** Commercial and advertising art, film/video and photgraphic arts, industrial design. **Special Study Options:** Cooperative education program, double major, dual enrollment, English as a second language (ESL), exchange student program (domestic), independent study, internships, study abroad, teacher certification program.

FACILITIES
Housing: Coed dorms. **Special Academic Facilities/Equipment:** Top-of-the-line technology for design, animation, and audiovisual editing; wood and metal shops; hot glass studio; gallery; private studios. **Computers:** 100% of classrooms are wired, 100% of classrooms are wireless, network access in dorm rooms, network access in dorm lounges, remote student-access to Web through college's connection.

CAMPUS LIFE
Activities: Student government. **Organizations:** 5 registered organizations.

ADMISSIONS
Freshman Academic Profile: ACT middle 50% range 18–23. TOEFL required of all international applicants, minimum paper TOEFL 525, minimum computer TOEFL 197. **Basis for Candidate Selection:** *Very important factors considered include:* Talent/ability. *Important factors considered include:* Academic GPA, standardized test scores. *Other factors considered include:* Level of applicant's interest. **Freshman Admission Requirements:** High school diploma is required, and GED is accepted. **Freshman Admission Statistics:** 1,039 applied, 36% admitted, 52% enrolled. **Transfer Admission Requirements:** High school transcript, college transcript(s). Minimum college GPA of 2.0 required. Lowest grade transferable C. **General Admission Information:** Application fee $35. Regular application deadline 8/1. Regular notification is rolling. Nonfall registration accepted. Admission may be deferred for a maximum of 4 semesters. Credit offered for CEEB Advanced Placement tests.

COSTS AND FINANCIAL AID
Annual tuition $27,090. Room and board $4,300. Required fees $1,185. Average book expense $2,500. **Required Forms and Deadlines:** FAFSA. Financial aid filing deadline 7/1. **Notification of Awards:** Applicants will be notified of awards on a rolling basis beginning on or about 3/15. **Types of Aid:** *Need-based scholarships/grants:* Pell, SEOG, state scholarships/grants, private scholarships, the school's own gift aid. *Loans:* FFEL Subsidized Stafford, FFEL Unsubsidized Stafford, FFEL PLUS, alternative loan programs. **Financial Aid Statistics:** Highest amount earned per year from on-campus jobs $1,000.

COLLEGE OF THE HOLY CROSS

Admissions Office, 1 College Street, Worcester, MA 01610-2395
Phone: 508-793-2443 **E-mail:** admissions@holycross.edu **CEEB Code:** 3282
Fax: 508-793-3888 **Website:** www.holycross.edu **ACT Code:** 1810
Financial Aid Phone: 508-793-2265

This private school, affiliated with the Roman Catholic Church, was founded in 1843. It has a 174-acre campus.

RATINGS
Admissions Selectivity Rating: 96   **Fire Safety Rating:** 95   **Green Rating:** 94

STUDENTS AND FACULTY
Enrollment: 2,790. **Student Body:** 55% female, 45% male, 62% out-of-state. African American 4%, Asian 5%, Caucasian 74%, Hispanic 5%. **Retention and Graduation:** 96% freshmen return for sophomore year. 89% freshmen graduate within 4 years. 22% grads go on to further study within 1 year. 12% grads pursue arts and sciences degrees. 1% grads pursue business degrees. 6% grads pursue law degrees. 3% grads pursue medical degrees. **Faculty:** Student/faculty ratio 11:1. 239 full-time faculty, 95% hold PhDs. 100% faculty teach undergrads.

ACADEMICS
Degrees: Bachelor's. **Academic Requirements:** Arts/fine arts, English (including composition), foreign languages, history, humanities, mathematics, philosophy, sciences (biological or physical), social science, literature, religion, cross-cultural studies. **Classes:** Most classes have 10–19 students. Most lab/discussion sections have 10–19 students. **Majors with Highest Enrollment:** Economics, political science and government, psychology. **Disciplines with Highest Percentage of Degrees Awarded:** Social sciences 33%, psychology 12%, history 11%, English 10%, foreign languages and literature 9%. **Special Study Options:** Accelerated program, cross-registration, double major, dual enrollment, honors program, independent study, internships, liberal arts/career combination, student-designed major, study abroad, teacher certification program, first-year program (integrated living and learning).

FACILITIES
Housing: Coed dorms, apartments for single students, special housing for disabled students, suites on campus available for juniors and seniors, substance-free housing also available. **Special Academic Facilities/Equipment:** Art gallery, concert hall, Taylor and Boody Tracker Organ, O'Callahan Science Library, Rehm Library, multimedia resource center, wellness center. Scientific equipment on par with the best research universities. **Computers:** 10% of classrooms are wired, 10% of classrooms are wireless, 80% of public computers are PCs, 15% of public computers are Macs, 5% of public computers are UNIX, network access in dorm rooms, network access in dorm lounges, online registration, online administrative functions (other than registration), remote student-access to Web through college's connection.

CAMPUS LIFE
Activities: Choral groups, dance, drama/theater, jazz band, literary magazine, marching band, music ensembles, musical theater, pep band, radio station, student government, student newspaper, yearbook. **Organizations:** 103 registered organizations, 20 honor societies, 4 religious organizations. **Athletics (Intercollegiate):** *Men:* Baseball, basketball, crew/rowing, cross-country, diving, football, golf, ice hockey, lacrosse, soccer, swimming, tennis, track/field (indoor), track/field (outdoor). *Women:* Basketball, crew/rowing, cross-country, diving, field hockey, golf, ice hockey, lacrosse, soccer, softball, swimming, tennis, track/field (indoor), track/field (outdoor), volleyball. **Environmental Initiatives:** College has a four-year commitment with Trans-Canada to supply electric power will reduce the school's carbon footprint by 30%. College received a grant to investigate the feasibility of wind power. College is continuously updating HVAC controls, installing windows, and replacing light fixtures to reduce overall energy consumption.

ADMISSIONS
Freshman Academic Profile: 64% in top 10% of high school class, 93% in top 25% of high school class, 100% in top 50% of high school class. 51% from public high schools. SAT Math middle 50% range 620–690. SAT Critical Reading middle 50% range 590–690. TOEFL required of all international applicants, minimum paper TOEFL 550, minimum computer TOEFL 213. **Basis for Candidate Selection:** *Very important factors considered include:*

192

Academic GPA, class rank, rigor of secondary school record. *Important factors considered include:* Alumni/ae relation, application essay, character/personal qualities, extracurricular activities, interview, recommendation(s). *Other factors considered include:* First generation, geographical residence, level of applicant's interest, racial/ethnic status, standardized test scores, talent/ability, volunteer work, work experience. **Freshman Admission Requirements:** High school diploma is required, and GED is accepted. *Academic units recommended:* 4 English, 4 math, 4 science, 3 foreign language, 2 social studies, 2 history, 1 academic elective. **Freshman Admission Statistics:** 6,706 applied, 34% admitted, 33% enrolled. **Transfer Admission Requirements:** High school transcript, college transcript(s), essay or personal statement, statement of good standing from prior institution(s). Minimum college GPA of 3.2 required. Lowest grade transferable C. **General Admission Information:** Application fee $50. Early decision application deadline 12/15. Regular application deadline 1/15. Regular notification 4/1. Nonfall registration accepted. Admission may be deferred for a maximum of 1 year. Credit offered for CEEB Advanced Placement tests.

COSTS AND FINANCIAL AID

Annual tuition $36,710. Room and board $10,260. Required fees $532. Average book expense $700. **Required Forms and Deadlines:** FAFSA, CSS/Financial Aid PROFILE, Noncustodial PROFILE, Business/Farm Supplement, parent and student federal tax returns. Financial aid filing deadline 2/1. **Notification of Awards:** Applicants will be notified of awards on or about 3/30. **Types of Aid:** *Need-based scholarships/grants:* Pell, SEOG, state scholarships/grants, private scholarships, the school's own gift aid. *Loans:* FFEL Subsidized Stafford, FFEL Unsubsidized Stafford, FFEL PLUS, Federal Perkins, MDFA. **Financial Aid Statistics:** 47% freshmen, 45% undergrads receive need-based scholarship or grant aid. 49% freshmen, 51% undergrads receive need-based self-help aid. 8 freshmen, 24 undergrads receive athletic scholarships. 64% freshmen, 59% undergrads receive any aid. Highest amount earned per year from on-campus jobs $1,401.

COLLEGE MISERICORDIA

301 Lake Street, Dallas, PA 18612
Phone: 570-674-6264 **E-mail:** admiss@misericordia.edu **CEEB Code:** 2087
Fax: 570-675-2441 **Website:** www.misericordia.edu **ACT Code:** 3539
Financial Aid Phone: 570-674-6280

This private school, affiliated with the Roman Catholic Church, was founded in 1924. It has a 120-acre campus.

RATINGS

Admissions Selectivity Rating: 77   **Fire Safety Rating:** 66   **Green Rating:** 60*

STUDENTS AND FACULTY

Enrollment: 2,001. **Student Body:** 72% female, 28% male, 16% out-of-state. African American 2%, Caucasian 96%, Hispanic 1%. **Retention and Graduation:** 80% freshmen return for sophomore year. 10% grads go on to further study within 1 year. **Faculty:** Student/faculty ratio 12:1. 94 full-time faculty, 78% hold PhDs. 92% faculty teach undergrads.

ACADEMICS

Degrees: Bachelor's, certificate, doctoral, master's, post-bachelor's certificate, post-master's certificate. **Academic Requirements:** Arts/fine arts, computer literacy, English (including composition), history, humanities, mathematics, philosophy, sciences (biological or physical), social science, religious studies. **Classes:** Most classes have 10–19 students. Most lab/discussion sections have 10–19 students. **Majors with Highest Enrollment:** Business administration/management, nursing/registered nurse training (RN, ASN, BSN, MSN), physical therapy/therapist. **Disciplines with Highest Percentage of Degrees Awarded:** Health professions and related sciences 36%, business/marketing 15%, education 14%, psychology 7%, public administration and social services 6%. **Special Study Options:** Accelerated program, cooperative education program, cross-registration, distance learning, double major, dual enrollment, English as a second language (ESL), honors program, independent study, internships, student-designed major, study abroad, teacher certification program, weekend college.

FACILITIES

Housing: Coed dorms, leadership house, service house, women with children house. **Computers:** 100% of classrooms are wired, 10% of classrooms are wireless, 100% of public computers are PCs, network access in dorm rooms, network access in dorm lounges, online registration, online administrative functions (other than registration), support for handheld computing, remote student-access to Web through college's connection.

CAMPUS LIFE

Activities: Choral groups, dance, drama/theater, jazz band, literary magazine, music ensembles, radio station, student government, student newspaper, television station, yearbook. **Organizations:** 23 registered organizations, 1 honor society, 1 religious organization. **Athletics (Intercollegiate):** *Men:* Baseball, basketball, cross-country, golf, lacrosse, soccer, swimming, track/field (outdoor). *Women:* Basketball, cheerleading, cross-country, field hockey, lacrosse, soccer, softball, swimming, tennis, track/field (outdoor), volleyball.

ADMISSIONS

Freshman Academic Profile: 17% in top 10% of high school class, 41% in top 25% of high school class, 72% in top 50% of high school class. 78% from public high schools. SAT Math middle 50% range 460–560. SAT Critical Reading middle 50% range 455–550. ACT middle 50% range 19–24. TOEFL required of all international applicants, minimum paper TOEFL 500, minimum computer TOEFL 75. **Basis for Candidate Selection:** *Very important factors considered include:* Academic GPA, rigor of secondary school record. *Important factors considered include:* Character/personal qualities, class rank, standardized test scores, volunteer work. *Other factors considered include:* Application essay, extracurricular activities, interview, racial/ethnic status, recommendation(s), work experience. **Freshman Admission Requirements:** High school diploma is required, and GED is accepted. *Academic units required:* 4 English, 4 math, 4 science, 4 social studies. **Freshman Admission Statistics:** 1,130 applied, 78% admitted, 36% enrolled. **Transfer Admission Requirements:** College transcript(s). Minimum college GPA of 2.0 required. Lowest grade transferable C. **General Admission Information:** Application fee $25. Regular notification is rolling. Nonfall registration accepted. Admission may be deferred for a maximum of 1 year. Credit and/or placement offered for CEEB Advanced Placement tests.

COSTS AND FINANCIAL AID

Annual tuition $20,830. Room and board $9,100. Required fees $1,120. Average book expense $850. **Required Forms and Deadlines:** FAFSA, institution's own financial aid form. Financial aid filing deadline 5/1. **Notification of Awards:** Applicants will be notified of awards on a rolling basis beginning on or about 3/15. **Types of Aid:** *Need-based scholarships/grants:* Pell, SEOG, state scholarships/grants, private scholarships, the school's own gift aid, Federal Nursing Scholarships. *Loans:* FFEL Subsidized Stafford, FFEL Unsubsidized Stafford, FFEL PLUS, Federal Perkins, Federal Nursing, state loans. **Student Employment:** Federal Work-Study Program available. Institutional employment available. Off-campus job opportunities are good. **Financial Aid Statistics:** 82% freshmen, 83% undergrads receive need-based scholarship or grant aid. 69% freshmen, 70% undergrads receive need-based self-help aid. 99% freshmen, 97% undergrads receive any aid. Highest amount earned per year from on-campus jobs $1,400.

COLLEGE OF MOUNT SAINT VINCENT

6301 Riverdale Avenue, Riverdale, NY 10471
Phone: 718-405-3267 **E-mail:** admissions@mountsaintvincent.edu **CEEB Code:** 2088
Fax: 718-549-7945 **Website:** www.mountsaintvincent.edu
Financial Aid Phone: 718-405-3290

This private school, affiliated with the Roman Catholic Church, was founded in 1847. It has a 70-acre campus.

RATINGS

Admissions Selectivity Rating: 73   **Fire Safety Rating:** 60*   **Green Rating:** 60*

STUDENTS AND FACULTY

Enrollment: 1,355. **Student Body:** 74% female, 26% male, 13% out-of-state. African American 10%, Asian 10%, Caucasian 45%, Hispanic 31%. **Retention and Graduation:** 75% freshmen return for sophomore year. 36% freshmen graduate within 4 years. 25% grads go on to further study within 1 year. 9% grads pursue arts and sciences degrees. 7% grads pursue business degrees. 3% grads pursue law degrees. 2% grads pursue medical degrees. **Faculty:** Student/faculty ratio 13:1. 72 full-time faculty, 86% hold PhDs. 100% faculty teach undergrads.

ACADEMICS

Degrees: Associate, bachelor's, master's, post-master's certificate. **Academic Requirements:** Arts/fine arts, computer literacy, English (including composition), foreign languages, history, humanities, mathematics, philosophy, sciences (biological or physical), social science, junior level world literature course, 2 integrated courses (1 junior level and 1 senior level). **Classes:** Most classes have 20–29 students. Most lab/discussion sections have 10–19 students. **Majors with Highest Enrollment:** Business administration/management, nursing/registered nurse training (RN, ASN, BSN, MSN), psychology. **Disciplines with**

Highest Percentage of Degrees Awarded: Health professions and related sciences 26%, communication technologies 15%, business/marketing 15%, psychology 13%, liberal arts/general studies 10%, education 5%. **Special Study Options:** Accelerated program, cross-registration, double major, honors program, independent study, internships, liberal arts/career combination, study abroad, teacher certification program.

FACILITIES

Housing: Coed dorms, women's dorms, special housing for disabled students. **Special Academic Facilities/Equipment:** Newly renovated Maryvale Hall with newly constructed wing for communications and fine arts departments, Skylight Art Gallery, nursing lab, TV studio, radio station, Elizabeth Seton Travelling Museum, new forensic laboratory equipment. **Computers:** 61% of classrooms are wired, 100% of public computers are PCs, network access in dorm rooms, network access in dorm lounges, online registration, online administrative functions (other than registration), remote student-access to Web through college's connection.

CAMPUS LIFE

Activities: Choral groups, dance, drama/theater, literary magazine, musical theater, radio station, student government, student newspaper, television station, yearbook. **Organizations:** 30 registered organizations, 15 honor societies, 1 religious organization. **Athletics (Intercollegiate):** *Men:* Baseball, basketball, cross-country, lacrosse, soccer, tennis, volleyball. *Women:* Basketball, cross-country, lacrosse, soccer, softball, swimming, tennis, track/field (outdoor), volleyball.

ADMISSIONS

Freshman Academic Profile: 17% in top 10% of high school class, 35% in top 25% of high school class, 77% in top 50% of high school class. 46% from public high schools. SAT Math middle 50% range 430–530. SAT Critical Reading middle 50% range 450–540. TOEFL required of all international applicants, minimum paper TOEFL 550, minimum computer TOEFL 213. **Basis for Candidate Selection:** *Very important factors considered include:* Academic GPA, rigor of secondary school record. *Important factors considered include:* Application essay, character/personal qualities, extracurricular activities, interview, recommendation(s), standardized test scores. *Other factors considered include:* Alumni/ae relation, class rank, first generation, geographical residence, religious affiliation/commitment, state residency, volunteer work, work experience. **Freshman Admission Requirements:** High school diploma is required, and GED is accepted. *Academic units required:* 4 English, 2 math, 2 science, 2 foreign language, 3 social studies, 3 academic electives. *Academic units recommended:* 4 English, 4 math, 3 science (3 science labs), 3 foreign language, 4 social studies, 3 academic electives. **Freshman Admission Statistics:** 2,144 applied, 68% admitted, 27% enrolled. **Transfer Admission Requirements:** College transcript(s), essay or personal statement. Minimum college GPA of 2.0 required. Lowest grade transferable C. **General Admission Information:** Application fee $35. Early decision application deadline 11/15. Regular application deadline 4/1. Regular notification is rolling. Nonfall registration accepted. Admission may be deferred for a maximum of 1 year. Credit and/or placement offered for CEEB Advanced Placement tests.

COSTS AND FINANCIAL AID

Annual tuition $21,000. Room & board $8,500. Required fees $550. Average book expense $850. **Required Forms and Deadlines:** FAFSA, state aid form. Financial aid filing deadline 2/15. **Notification of Awards:** Applicants will be notified of awards on a rolling basis beginning on or about 3/1. **Types of Aid:** *Need-based scholarships/grants:* Pell, SEOG, state scholarships/grants, private scholarships, the school's own gift aid. *Loans:* FFEL Subsidized Stafford, FFEL Unsubsidized Stafford, FFEL PLUS, Federal Perkins. **Student Employment:** Federal Work-Study Program available. Institutional employment available. Off-campus job opportunities are good. **Financial Aid Statistics:** 82% freshmen, 78% undergrads receive need-based scholarship or grant aid. 82% freshmen, 78% undergrads receive need-based self-help aid. 87% freshmen, 86% undergrads receive any aid.

COLLEGE OF MOUNT ST. JOSEPH

5701 Delhi Road, Cincinnati, OH 45233
Phone: 513-244-4531 **E-mail:** admission@mail.msj.edu **CEEB Code:** 1129
Fax: 513-244-4629 **Website:** www.msj.edu **ACT Code:** 3254
Financial Aid Phone: 513-244-4418

This private school, affiliated with the Roman Catholic Church, was founded in 1920. It has a 92-acre campus.

RATINGS

Admissions Selectivity Rating: 74   **Fire Safety Rating:** 99   **Green Rating:** 60*

STUDENTS AND FACULTY

Enrollment: 1,883. **Student Body:** 68% female, 32% male, 15% out-of-state. African American 10%, Caucasian 84%. **Retention and Graduation:** 76% freshmen return for sophomore year. 44% freshmen graduate within 4 years. 8% grads go on to further study within 1 year. 1% grads pursue arts and sciences degrees. 1% grads pursue business degrees. 1% grads pursue medical degrees. **Faculty:** Student/faculty ratio 11:1. 115 full-time faculty, 66% hold PhDs. 90% faculty teach undergrads.

ACADEMICS

Degrees: Associate, bachelor's, certificate, doctoral, master's, post-bachelor's certificate. **Academic Requirements:** Arts/fine arts, English (including composition), foreign languages, history, humanities, mathematics, philosophy, sciences (biological or physical), social science, ethics, religious studies. **Classes:** Most classes have 10–19 students. Most lab/discussion sections have 10–19 students. **Majors with Highest Enrollment:** Business administration/management, graphic design, nursing/registered nurse training (RN, ASN, BSN, MSN). **Disciplines with Highest Percentage of Degrees Awarded:** Health professions and related sciences 29%, business/marketing 14%, education 12%, visual and performing arts 11%, liberal arts/general studies 10%. **Special Study Options:** Accelerated program, cooperative education program, cross-registration, distance learning, double major, honors program, independent study, internships, liberal arts/career combination, study abroad, teacher certification program.

FACILITIES

Housing: Coed dorms. **Special Academic Facilities/Equipment:** Art studio/gallery, Student Scholar Center, computer labs, theater. **Computers:** 100% of classrooms are wireless, 90% of public computers are PCs, 10% of public computers are Macs, network access in dorm rooms, network access in dorm lounges, online registration, online administrative functions (other than registration), remote student-access to Web through college's connection. Undergraduates are required to own a computer.

CAMPUS LIFE

Activities: Choral groups, concert band, dance, drama/theater, jazz band, literary magazine, marching band, music ensembles, musical theater, pep band, student government, student newspaper. **Organizations:** 40 registered organizations, 13 honor societies, 1 religious organization. **Athletics (Intercollegiate):** *Men:* Baseball, basketball, cross-country, football, golf, lacrosse, soccer, tennis, track/field (indoor), track/field (outdoor), wrestling. *Women:* Basketball, cheerleading, cross-country, golf, soccer, softball, tennis, track/field (indoor), track/field (outdoor), volleyball. Environmental Initiatives: Recycling. Lighting retrofit campus wide with energy efficient ballasts and bulbs. Water conservation measures campus wide. This also reduces the energy used for hot water.

ADMISSIONS

Freshman Academic Profile: 9% in top 10% of high school class, 33% in top 25% of high school class, 71% in top 50% of high school class. 61% from public high schools. SAT Math middle 50% range 440–550. SAT Critical Reading middle 50% range 440–540. ACT middle 50% range 19–24. TOEFL required of all international applicants, minimum paper TOEFL 510, minimum computer TOEFL 180. **Basis for Candidate Selection:** *Very important factors considered include:* Academic GPA, rigor of secondary school record, standardized test scores. *Other factors considered include:* Alumni/ae relation, application essay, character/personal qualities, extracurricular activities, first generation, interview, level of applicant's interest, racial/ethnic status, recommendation(s), talent/ability, volunteer work, work experience. **Freshman Admission Requirements:** High school diploma is required, and GED is accepted. *Academic units required:* 4 English, 2 math, 2 science (1 science lab), 2 foreign language, 1 social studies, 1 history, 1 academic elective, 1 fine arts. *Academic units recommended:* 4 English, 4 math, 4 science (2 science labs), 2 foreign language, 2 social studies, 2 history, 1 academic elective, 2 fine arts. **Freshman Admission Statistics:** 1,144 applied, 71% admitted, 40% enrolled. **Transfer Admission Requirements:** High school transcript, college transcript(s). Minimum college GPA of 2.0 required. Lowest grade transferable C. **General Admission Information:** Application fee $25. Regular application deadline 8/15. Regular notification is rolling. Nonfall registration accepted. Admission may be deferred for a maximum of 1 year. Credit and/or placement offered for CEEB Advanced Placement tests.

COSTS AND FINANCIAL AID

Annual tuition $20,400. Room and board $6,500. Required fees $800. Average book expense $800. **Required Forms and Deadlines:** FAFSA. Financial aid filing deadline 3/1. **Notification of Awards:** Applicants will be notified of awards on a rolling basis beginning on or about 2/15. **Types of Aid:** *Need-based scholarships/grants:* Pell, SEOG, state scholarships/grants, private scholarships, the school's own gift aid. *Loans:* FFEL Subsidized Stafford, FFEL Unsubsidized Stafford, FFEL PLUS, Federal Perkins, Federal Nursing, state loans. **Student Employment:** Federal Work-Study Program available. Institutional employment available. Off-campus job opportunities are good.

Financial Aid Statistics: 80% freshmen, 80% undergrads receive need-based scholarship or grant aid. 73% freshmen, 70% undergrads receive need-based self-help aid. 99% freshmen, 90% undergrads receive any aid. Highest amount earned per year from on-campus jobs $5,000.

THE COLLEGE OF NEW JERSEY

PO Box 7718, Ewing, NJ 08628-0718
Phone: 609-771-2131 **E-mail:** tcnjinfo@tcnj.edu **CEEB Code:** 2519
Fax: 609-637-5174 **Website:** www.tcnj.com **ACT Code:** 2614
Financial Aid Phone: 609-771-2211

This public school was founded in 1855. It has a 289-acre campus.

RATINGS
Admissions Selectivity Rating: 93   **Fire Safety Rating:** 96   **Green Rating:** 91

STUDENTS AND FACULTY
Enrollment: 6,037. **Student Body:** 58% female, 42% male, 5% out-of-state. African American 6%, Asian 7%, Caucasian 75%, Hispanic 8%. **Retention and Graduation:** 95% freshmen return for sophomore year. 64% freshmen graduate within 4 years. 25% grads go on to further study within 1 year. 15% grads pursue arts and sciences degrees. 7% grads pursue business degrees. 2% grads pursue law degrees. 1% grads pursue medical degrees. **Faculty:** Student/ faculty ratio 13:1. 332 full-time faculty, 88% hold PhDs. 95% faculty teach undergrads.

ACADEMICS
Degrees: Bachelor's, master's, post-bachelor's certificate, post-master's certificate. **Academic Requirements:** Arts/fine arts, computer literacy, English (including composition), history, humanities, interdisciplinary, mathematics, philosophy, sciences (biological or physical), social science. **Classes:** Most classes have 20–29 students. Most lab/discussion sections have 10–19 students. **Majors with Highest Enrollment:** Elementary education and teaching, English language and literature. **Disciplines with Highest Percentage of Degrees Awarded:** Education 25%, business/marketing 16%, English 11%, psychology 10%, visual and performing arts 7%. **Special Study Options:** 7 year medical program with UMDNJ, double major, dual enrollment, exchange student program (domestic), honors program, independent study, internships, liberal arts/career combination, student-designed major, study abroad, summer undergraduate research program, teacher certification program.

FACILITIES
Housing: Coed dorms, men's dorms, women's dorms, apartments for single students, special housing for disabled students, housing for transfer students. **Special Academic Facilities/Equipment:** Art gallery, concert hall, observatory, scanning and transmission electron microscopes. **Computers:** 100% of classrooms are wired, 75% of public computers are PCs, 17% of public computers are Macs, 8% of public computers are UNIX, network access in dorm rooms, network access in dorm lounges, online registration, online administrative functions (other than registration), support for handheld computing, remote student-access to Web through college's connection.

CAMPUS LIFE
Activities: Choral groups, concert band, dance, drama/theater, jazz band, literary magazine, music ensembles, musical theater, opera, pep band, radio station, student government, student newspaper, symphony orchestra, yearbook. **Organizations:** 186 registered organizations, 11 honor societies, 10 religious organizations. 8 fraternities (12% men join), 7 sororities (14% women join). **Athletics (Intercollegiate):** *Men:* Baseball, basketball, cross-country, diving, football, golf, soccer, swimming, tennis, track/field (indoor), track/field (outdoor), wrestling. *Women:* Basketball, cross-country, diving, field hockey, lacrosse, soccer, softball, swimming, tennis, track/field (indoor), track/field (outdoor). Environmental Initiatives: Commitment to sustainability being incorporated into the curriculum at TCNJ. This may include Freshman seminars, liberal learning programs, research, and possible new minor or major degrees. Development of a plan to achieve climate neutrality. Strategy is being developed now. Commitment to purchase 15% of electrical energy from renewable resources.

ADMISSIONS
Admissions Selectivity Rating: 93 (out of 100). **Freshman Academic Profile:** 68% in top 10% of high school class, 93% in top 25% of high school class, 99% in top 50% of high school class. 85% from public high schools. SAT Math middle 50% range 580–680. SAT Critical Reading middle 50% range 560–650. SAT Writing middle 50% range 560–660. TOEFL required of all international applicants, minimum paper TOEFL 550, minimum computer TOEFL 215. **Basis for Candidate Selection:** *Very important factors considered include:* Application essay, character/personal qualities, class rank, extracurricular activities, rigor of secondary school record, standardized test scores, talent/ability. *Important factors considered include:* Level of applicant's interest, recommendation(s), volunteer work. *Other factors considered include:* Academic GPA, Alumni/ae relation, first generation, geographical residence, interview, racial/ethnic status, state residency, work experience. **Freshman Admission Requirements:** High school diploma is required, and GED is accepted. *Academic units required:* 4 English, 3 math, 3 science (2 science labs), 2 foreign language, 2 social studies. *Academic units recommended:* 4 English, 3 math, 3 science (3 science labs), 3 foreign language, 3 social studies. **Freshman Admission Statistics:** 8,185 applied, 44% admitted, 36% enrolled. **Transfer Admission Requirements:** High school transcript, college transcript(s), essay or personal statement, standardized test score, statement of good standing from prior institution(s). Minimum college GPA of 2.5 required. Lowest grade transferable C. **General Admission Information:** Application fee $60. Early decision application deadline 11/15. Regular application deadline 2/15. Regular notification is rolling. Non-fall registration not accepted. Credit and/or placement offered for CEEB Advanced Placement tests.

COSTS AND FINANCIAL AID
Annual in-state tuition $8,072. Annual out-of-state tuition $15,295. Room and board $9,242. Required fees $3,235. Average book expense $1,000. **Required Forms and Deadlines:** FAFSA. Financial aid filing deadline 3/1. **Notification of Awards:** Applicants will be notified of awards on a rolling basis beginning on or about 6/1. **Types of Aid:** *Need-based scholarships/grants:* Pell, SEOG, state scholarships/grants, private scholarships, the school's own gift aid. *Loans:* FFEL Subsidized Stafford, FFEL Unsubsidized Stafford, FFEL PLUS, Federal Perkins, Federal Nursing. **Financial Aid Statistics:** 16% freshmen, 16% undergrads receive need-based scholarship or grant aid. 26% freshmen, 29% undergrads receive need-based self-help aid. Highest amount earned per year from on-campus jobs $800.

See page 1122.

THE COLLEGE OF NEW ROCHELLE

29 Castle Place, New Rochelle, NY 10805-2339
Phone: 914-654-5452 **E-mail:** admission@cnr.edu **CEEB Code:** 2089
Fax: 914-654-5464 **Website:** www.cnr.edu **ACT Code:** 2712
Financial Aid Phone: 914-654-5224

This private school was founded in 1904. It has a 20-acre campus.

RATINGS
Admissions Selectivity Rating: 77   **Fire Safety Rating:** 60*   **Green Rating:** 60*

STUDENTS AND FACULTY
Enrollment: 1,041. **Student Body:** 96% female, 4% male, 12% out-of-state. African American 38%, Asian 6%, Caucasian 14%, Hispanic 13%. **Retention and Graduation:** 71% freshmen return for sophomore year. 15% grads go on to further study within 1 year. **Faculty:** Student/faculty ratio 8:1. 85 full-time faculty. 100% faculty teach undergrads.

ACADEMICS
Degrees: Bachelor's, master's, post-bachelor's certificate, post-master's certificate. **Academic Requirements:** Arts/fine arts, English (including composition), foreign languages, history, humanities, mathematics, philosophy, sciences (biological or physical), social science. **Classes:** Most classes have 10–19 students. **Majors with Highest Enrollment:** Mass communications/media studies, nursing/registered nurse training (RN, ASN, BSN, MSN), psychology. **Disciplines with Highest Percentage of Degrees Awarded:** Health professions and related sciences 56%, psychology 12%, communications/ journalism 7%, visual and performing arts 5%, English 4%. **Special Study Options:** Accelerated program, cooperative education program, cross registration, double major, exchange student program (domestic), honors program, independent study, internships, liberal arts/career combination, student-designed major, study abroad, teacher certification program.

FACILITIES

Housing: Women's dorms. **Special Academic Facilities/Equipment:** Art gallery, multimedia theater/teleconference center, language lab, centers for media, computer studies, TV studio, Learning Center for Women, Learning Center for Nursing. **Computers:** 90% of public computers are PCs, 10% of public computers are Macs, network access in dorm rooms, network access in dorm lounges, online registration, online administrative functions (other than registration), remote student-access to Web through college's connection, tuition includes personal computer.

CAMPUS LIFE

Activities: Choral groups, dance, drama/theater, literary magazine, musical theater, student government, student newspaper, yearbook. **Organizations:** 26 registered organizations, 2 honor societies, 1 religious organization. **Athletics (Intercollegiate):** *Women:* Basketball, cross-country, softball, swimming, tennis, volleyball.

ADMISSIONS

Freshman Academic Profile: 15% in top 10% of high school class, 46% in top 25% of high school class, 82% in top 50% of high school class. 76% from public high schools. SAT Math middle 50% range 440–530. SAT Critical Reading middle 50% range 440–530. ACT middle 50% range 16–22. TOEFL required of all international applicants, minimum paper TOEFL 550. **Basis for Candidate Selection:** *Very important factors considered include:* Rigor of secondary school record. *Important factors considered include:* Application essay, class rank, standardized test scores. *Other factors considered include:* Alumni/ae relation, character/personal qualities, extracurricular activities, interview, recommendation(s), talent/ability, volunteer work, work experience. **Freshman Admission Requirements:** High school diploma is required, and GED is accepted. *Academic units recommended:* 4 English, 3 math, 3 science (2 science labs), 2 foreign language, 2 social studies. **Freshman Admission Statistics:** 1,430 applied, 50% admitted, 27% enrolled. **Transfer Admission Requirements:** High school transcript, college transcript(s). Lowest grade transferable C-. **General Admission Information:** Application fee $20. Early decision application deadline 11/1. Regular notification is rolling. Non-fall registration accepted. Admission may be deferred for a maximum of 2 semesters. Common Application accepted. Credit and/or placement offered for CEEB Advanced Placement tests.

COSTS AND FINANCIAL AID

Annual tuition $23,200. Room and board $9,700. Required fees $500. Average book expense $600. **Required Forms and Deadlines:** FAFSA, institution's own financial aid form, federal income tax form(s). **Notification of Awards:** Applicants will be notified of awards on a rolling basis beginning on or about 1/1. **Types of Aid:** *Need-based scholarships/grants:* Pell, SEOG, state scholarships/grants, private scholarships, the school's own gift aid. *Loans:* Direct Subsidized Stafford, Direct Unsubsidized Stafford, FFEL PLUS, Federal Perkins, Federal Nursing. **Student Employment:** Federal Work-Study Program available. Institutional employment available. Off-campus job opportunities are excellent. **Financial Aid Statistics:** 86% freshmen, 76% undergrads receive need-based scholarship or grant aid. 88% freshmen, 89% undergrads receive need-based self-help aid. Highest amount earned per year from on-campus jobs $1,500.

COLLEGE OF NOTRE DAME OF MARYLAND

4701 North Charles Street, Baltimore, MD 21210
Phone: 410-532-5330 **E-mail:** admiss@ndm.edu **CEEB Code:** 5114
Fax: 410-532-6287 **Website:** www.ndm.edu **ACT Code:** 1727
Financial Aid Phone: 410-532-5369

This private school, affiliated with the Roman Catholic Church, was founded in 1896. It has a 58-acre campus.

RATINGS

Admissions Selectivity Rating: 81   **Fire Safety Rating:** 60*   **Green Rating:** 60*

STUDENTS AND FACULTY

Enrollment: 1,686. **Student Body:** 94% female, 6% male, 2% international. African American 26%, Asian 3%, Caucasian 66%, Hispanic 3%. **Retention and Graduation:** 87% freshmen return for sophomore year. 49% freshmen graduate within 4 years. **Faculty:** Student/faculty ratio 13:1. 83 full-time faculty, 78% hold PhDs. 100% faculty teach undergrads.

ACADEMICS

Degrees: Bachelor's, doctoral, master's, post-master's certificate. **Academic Requirements:** Arts/fine arts, English (including composition), foreign

languages, history, mathematics, philosophy, sciences (biological or physical), social science, religious studies, physical education, oral communication. **Classes:** Most classes have 20–29 students. **Majors with Highest Enrollment:** Business, management, marketing, and related support services; liberal arts and sciences/liberal studies; nursing/registered nurse training (RN, ASN, BSN, MSN). **Disciplines with Highest Percentage of Degrees Awarded:** Business/marketing 27%, liberal arts/general studies 13%, education 11%, health professions and related sciences 10%, computer and information sciences 7%, interdisciplinary studies 7%. **Special Study Options:** Accelerated program, cross-registration, double major, dual enrollment, English as a second language (ESL), exchange student program (domestic), honors program, independent study, internships, liberal arts/career combination, student-designed major, study abroad, teacher certification program, weekend college. Orientation program for all new students to college, which includes a first semester seminar course for entering freshman. Also a Career Action Plan for all students and an academic consortium with 7 local colleges and universities.

FACILITIES

Housing: Women's dorms. **Special Academic Facilities/Equipment:** Art gallery, photo labs, language labs, child care center, fitness center, television and radio studios, music practice labs, planetarium. **Computers:** Network access in dorm rooms, network access in dorm lounges, online administrative functions (other than registration), remote student-access to Web through college's connection.

CAMPUS LIFE

Activities: Choral groups, dance, drama/theater, literary magazine, music ensembles, radio station, student government, student newspaper, student-run film society, television station, yearbook. **Organizations:** 24 registered organizations, 7 honor societies. **Women:** Basketball, field hockey, lacrosse, soccer, swimming, tennis, volleyball.

ADMISSIONS

Freshman Academic Profile: 26% in top 10% of high school class, 47% in top 25% of high school class, 77% in top 50% of high school class. 71% from public high schools. SAT Math middle 50% range 450–560. SAT Critical Reading middle 50% range 490–580. **Basis for Candidate Selection:** *Very important factors considered include:* Application essay, interview, recommendation(s), rigor of secondary school record, standardized test scores. *Important factors considered include:* Extracurricular activities, volunteer work. *Other factors considered include:* Alumni/ae relation, character/personal qualities, class rank, talent/ability, work experience. **Freshman Admission Requirements:** High school diploma is required, and GED is accepted. *Academic units required:* 4 English, 3 math, 2 science (2 science labs), 3 foreign language, 2 history, 4 academic electives. **Freshman Admission Statistics:** 450 applied, 72% admitted, 46% enrolled. **Transfer Admission Requirements:** College transcript(s), essay or personal statement. Minimum college GPA of 2.5 required. Lowest grade transferable C. **General Admission Information:** Application fee $40. Regular notification is rolling. Nonfall registration accepted. Admission may be deferred for a maximum of 1 year. Common Application accepted. Credit and/or placement offered for CEEB Advanced Placement tests.

COSTS AND FINANCIAL AID

Annual tuition $19,900. Room & board $7,800. Required fees $400. Average book expense $800. **Required Forms and Deadlines:** FAFSA. Financial aid filing deadline 2/15. **Notification of Awards:** Applicants will be notified of awards on a rolling basis beginning on or about 3/1. **Types of Aid:** *Need-based scholarships/grants:* Pell, SEOG, state scholarships/grants. *Loans:* Direct Subsidized Stafford, Direct Unsubsidized Stafford, Direct PLUS, Federal Perkins. **Student Employment:** Federal Work-Study Program available. Institutional employment available. Off-campus job opportunities are good. **Financial Aid Statistics:** 85% freshmen, 65% undergrads receive need-based scholarship or grant aid. 65% freshmen, 60% undergrads receive need-based self-help aid.

COLLEGE OF THE OZARKS

Best 368

Office of Admissions, PO Box 17, Point Lookout, MO 65726
Phone: 417-334-6411 **E-mail:** admiss4@cofo.edu **CEEB Code:** 6713
Fax: 417-335-2618 **Website:** www.cofo.edu **ACT Code:** 2364
Financial Aid Phone: 417-334-6411

This private school, affiliated with the Presbyterian Church, was founded in 1906. It has a 1,000-acre campus.

RATINGS
Admissions Selectivity Rating: 89   **Fire Safety Rating:** 63   **Green Rating:** 67

STUDENTS AND FACULTY
Enrollment: 1,332. **Student Body:** 54% female, 46% male, 33% out-of-state, 1% international (13 countries represented). Caucasian 76%. **Retention and Graduation:** 81% freshmen return for sophomore year. 17% grads go on to further study within 1 year. 9% grads pursue arts and sciences degrees. 4% grads pursue business degrees. 2% grads pursue law degrees. 2% grads pursue medical degrees. **Faculty:** Student/faculty ratio 16:1. 81 full-time faculty, 54% hold PhDs. 100% faculty teach undergrads.

ACADEMICS
Degrees: Bachelor's. **Academic Requirements:** Arts/fine arts, computer literacy, English (including composition), foreign languages, history, humanities, mathematics, philosophy, sciences (biological or physical), social science. **Classes:** Most classes have 10–19 students. Most lab/discussion sections have 10–19 students. **Majors with Highest Enrollment:** Business administration/management, criminal justice/police science, elementary education and teaching. **Disciplines with Highest Percentage of Degrees Awarded:** Business/marketing 22%, education 16%, security and protective services 9%, agriculture 8%, communications/journalism 6%, psychology 6%. **Special Study Options:** Accelerated program, double major, dual enrollment, independent study, internships, student-designed major, teacher certification program.

FACILITIES
Housing: Men's dorms, women's dorms. All full-time students must live in residence halls unless they meet one of the following criteria: 21 years of age or older, married, living with parents, or veteran of the armed forces. **Special Academic Facilities/Equipment:** Ralph Foster Museum, Edwards Mill, the Keeter Center, fruitcake and jelly kitchen, greenhouses. **Computers:** 1% of classrooms are wired, 1% of classrooms are wireless, 98% of public computers are PCs, 2% of public computers are Macs, network access in dorm rooms, network access in dorm lounges, online registration, online administrative functions (other than registration), support for handheld computing, remote student-access to Web through college's connection.

CAMPUS LIFE
Activities: Choral groups, concert band, drama/theater, jazz band, literary magazine, music ensembles, musical theater, pep band, radio station, student government, student newspaper, student-run film society, yearbook. **Organizations:** 46 registered organizations, 4 honor societies, 10 religious organizations. **Athletics (Intercollegiate):** *Men:* Baseball, basketball, cheerleading. *Women:* Basketball, cheerleading, volleyball.

ADMISSIONS
. **Freshman Academic Profile:** 16% in top 10% of high school class, 48% in top 25% of high school class, 87% in top 50% of high school class. 82% from public high schools. ACT middle 50% range 21–26. TOEFL required of all international applicants, minimum paper TOEFL 550, minimum computer TOEFL 213. **Basis for Candidate Selection:** *Very important factors considered include:* Character/personal qualities, class rank, interview, rigor of secondary school record. *Important factors considered include:* Academic GPA, recommendation(s), standardized test scores, volunteer work. work experience. *Other factors considered include:* Alumni/ae relation, extracurricular activities, first generation, geographical residence, level of applicant's interest, racial/ethnic status, religious affiliation/commitment, state residency, talent/ability. **Freshman Admission Requirements:** High school diploma is required, and GED is accepted. *Academic units recommended:* 4 English, 3 math, 2 science (1 science lab), 2 foreign language, 3 social studies, 1 visual and peforming arts or public speaking. **Freshman Admission Statistics:** 2,654 applied, 12% admitted, 83% enrolled. **Transfer Admission Requirements:** College transcript(s), interview, statement of good standing from prior institution(s).

Minimum college GPA of 2.0 required. Lowest grade transferable D-. **General Admission Information:** Regular application deadline 3/15. Regular notification is rolling. Nonfall registration accepted. Credit offered for CEEB Advanced Placement tests.

COSTS AND FINANCIAL AID
Room & board $4,700. Required fees $390. Average book expense $800. **Required Forms and Deadlines:** FAFSA. Financial aid filing deadline 2/15. **Notification of Awards:** Applicants will be notified of awards on or about 2/1. **Types of Aid:** *Need-based scholarships/grants:* Pell, SEOG, state scholarships/grants, private scholarships, the school's own gift aid. **Financial Aid Statistics:** 88% freshmen, 90% undergrads receive need-based scholarship or grant aid. 76% freshmen, 70% undergrads receive need-based self-help aid. 14 freshmen, 45 undergrads receive athletic scholarships. 100% freshmen, 100% undergrads receive any aid.

COLLEGE OF SAINT BENEDICT/ SAINT JOHN'S UNIVERSITY

PO Box 7155, Collegeville, MN 56321-7155
Phone: 320-363-2196 **E-mail:** admissions@csbsju.edu **CEEB Code:** 6624
Fax: 320-363-2750 **Website:** www.csbsju.edu **ACT Code:** 2140
Financial Aid Phone: 800-544-1489

This private school, affiliated with the Roman Catholic Church, was founded in 1857. It has a 2,400-acre campus.

RATINGS
Admissions Selectivity Rating: 83   **Fire Safety Rating:** 91   **Green Rating:** 88

STUDENTS AND FACULTY
Enrollment: 3,913. **Student Body:** 52% female, 48% male, 15% out-of-state, 4% international (41 countries represented). Asian 2%, Caucasian 91%, Hispanic 1%. **Retention and Graduation:** 91% freshmen return for sophomore year. 76% freshmen graduate within 4 years. 23% grads go on to further study within 1 year. 7% grads pursue arts and sciences degrees. 3% grads pursue law degrees. 3% grads pursue medical degrees. **Faculty:** Student/faculty ratio 13:1. 288 full-time faculty, 83% hold PhDs. 100% faculty teach undergrads.

ACADEMICS
Degrees: Bachelor's, first professional, master's. **Academic Requirements:** Arts/fine arts, English (including composition), foreign languages, history, humanities, mathematics, philosophy, sciences (biological or physical), social science, first-year symposium, senior seminar, gender perspectives, global perspectives. **Classes:** Most classes have 20–29 students. Most lab/discussion sections have 10–19 students. **Majors with Highest Enrollment:** Biology/biological sciences, business administration and management, psychology. **Disciplines with Highest Percentage of Degrees Awarded:** Business/marketing 15%, social sciences 15%, English 14%, biological/life sciences 10%, psychology 8%. **Special Study Options:** Accelerated program, cross-registration, double major, dual enrollment, English as a second language (ESL), honors program, independent study, internships, liberal arts/career combination, student-designed major, study abroad, teacher certification program.

FACILITIES
Housing: Men's dorms, women's dorms, apartments for single students, special housing for disabled students, special housing for international students, health and wellness floor, WorldStar program apartments, service learning/social justice floor, global initiative. **Special Academic Facilities/Equipment:** Hill Museum and Manuscript Library, art galleries, natural science museum, arboretum, Benedicta Arts Center, Sommers Digital Lab. **Computers:** 5% of classrooms are wired, 100% of classrooms are wireless, 91% of public computers are PCs, 8% of public computers are Macs, 1% of public computers are UNIX, network access in dorm rooms, network access in dorm lounges, online registration, online administrative functions (other than registration), support for handheld computing, remote student-access to Web through college's connection.

CAMPUS LIFE
Activities: Choral groups, concert band, dance, drama/theater, jazz band, literary magazine, music ensembles, musical theater, opera, pep band, radio station, student government, student newspaper, symphony orchestra. **Organizations:** 85 registered organizations, 3 honor societies, 4 religious organizations. **Athletics (Intercollegiate):** *Men:* Baseball, basketball, cross-country, diving, football, golf, ice hockey, skiing (nordic/cross-country), soccer,

swimming, tennis, track/field (indoor), track/field (outdoor), wrestling. *Women:* Basketball, cross-country, diving, golf, ice hockey, skiing (nordic/cross-country), soccer, softball, swimming, tennis, track/field (indoor), track/field (outdoor), volleyball. Environmental Initiatives: ACUPCC signatory process. SJU arboretum. CSB Green building policy.

ADMISSIONS

Freshman Academic Profile: 31% in top 10% of high school class, 64% in top 25% of high school class, 93% in top 50% of high school class. 71% from public high schools. SAT Math middle 50% range 540–660. SAT Critical Reading middle 50% range 500–633. ACT middle 50% range 23–28. TOEFL required of all international applicants, minimum paper TOEFL 500, minimum computer TOEFL 173. **Basis for Candidate Selection:** *Very important factors considered include:* Academic GPA, application essay, rigor of secondary school record, standardized test scores. *Important factors considered include:* Class rank, extracurricular activities, geographical residence, racial/ethnic status, recommendation(s), volunteer work. *Other factors considered include:* Alumni/ae relation, character/personal qualities, first generation, interview, talent/ability, work experience. **Freshman Admission Requirements:** High school diploma is required, and GED is accepted. *Academic units required:* 4 English, 3 math, 2 science (2 science labs), 2 social studies, 4 academic electives. *Academic units recommended:* 2 foreign language. **Freshman Admission Statistics:** 2,651 applied, 86% admitted, 46% enrolled. **Transfer Admission Requirements:** High school transcript, college transcript(s), essay or personal statement, statement of good standing from prior institution(s). Minimum college GPA of 2.7 required. Lowest grade transferable C. **General Admission Information:** Regular notification is rolling. Nonfall registration accepted. Admission may be deferred for a maximum of 1 year. Credit and/or placement offered for CEEB Advanced Placement tests.

COSTS AND FINANCIAL AID

Annual tuition $24,448. Room & board $6,697. Required fees $476. Average book expense $800. **Required Forms and Deadlines:** FAFSA, institution's own financial aid form. Financial aid filing deadline 3/15. **Notification of Awards:** Applicants will be notified of awards on a rolling basis beginning on or about 3/15. **Types of Aid:** *Need-based scholarships/grants:* Pell, SEOG, state scholarships/grants, the school's own gift aid. *Loans:* FFEL Subsidized Stafford, FFEL Unsubsidized Stafford, FFEL PLUS, Federal Perkins, state loans, various private loans. **Student Employment:** Federal Work-Study Program available. Institutional employment available. Off-campus job opportunities are fair. **Financial Aid Statistics:** 59% freshmen, 59% undergrads receive need-based scholarship or grant aid. 54% freshmen, 55% undergrads receive need-based self-help aid. 97% freshmen, 94% undergrads receive any aid. Highest amount earned per year from on-campus jobs $6,400.

COLLEGE OF SAINT ELIZABETH

Admissions Office, 2 Convent Road, Morristown, NJ 07960-6989
Phone: 973-290-4700 **E-mail:** apply@cse.edu **CEEB Code:** 2090
Fax: 973-290-4710 **Website:** www.cse.edu
Financial Aid Phone: 973-290-4445

This private school, affiliated with the Roman Catholic Church, was founded in 1899. It has a 200-acre campus.

RATINGS
Admissions Selectivity Rating: 65   **Fire Safety Rating:** 96   **Green Rating:** 61

STUDENTS AND FACULTY
Enrollment: 1,204. **Student Body:** 91% female, 9% male, 6% out-of-state, 4% international (13 countries represented). African American 15%, Asian 5%, Caucasian 46%, Hispanic 15%. **Retention and Graduation:** 82% freshmen return for sophomore year. 60% freshmen graduate within 4 years. 21% grads go on to further study within 1 year. 11% grads pursue arts and sciences degrees. 6% grads pursue business degrees. 3% grads pursue medical degrees. **Faculty:** Student/faculty ratio 11:1. 63 full-time faculty, 84% hold PhDs. 76% faculty teach undergrads.

ACADEMICS
Degrees: Bachelor's, certificate, master's, post-bachelor's certificate, post-master's certificate. **Academic Requirements:** Arts/fine arts, English (including composition), foreign languages, history, humanities, mathematics, philosophy, sciences (biological or physical), social science, religious studies, fitness/wellness, perspectives on interdependent world. **Classes:** Most classes have 10–19 students. **Majors with Highest Enrollment:** Business administration/management, psychology, teacher education, multiple levels. **Disciplines with Highest Percentage of Degrees Awarded:** Business/marketing 18%,

communications/journalism 13%, education 12%, psychology 10%, health professions and related sciences 8%. **Special Study Options:** Accelerated program, cross-registration, distance learning, double major, dual enrollment, English as a second language (ESL), exchange student program (domestic), honors program, independent study, internships, student-designed major, study abroad, teacher certification program, weekend college.

FACILITIES
Housing: Women's dorms. **Computers:** 84% of public computers are PCs, 16% of public computers are Macs, network access in dorm rooms, remote student-access to Web through college's connection.

CAMPUS LIFE
Activities: Choral groups, dance, drama/theater, literary magazine, music ensembles, student government, student newspaper, yearbook. **Organizations:** 28 registered organizations, 9 honor societies, 1 religious organization. **Women:** Basketball, equestrian sports, soccer, softball, swimming, tennis.

ADMISSIONS
65 (out of 100). **Freshman Academic Profile:** 15% in top 10% of high school class, 34% in top 25% of high school class, 70% in top 50% of high school class. 75% from public high schools. SAT Math middle 50% range 370–490. SAT Critical Reading middle 50% range 390–500. SAT Writing middle 50% range 390–510. TOEFL required of all international applicants, minimum paper TOEFL 500, minimum computer TOEFL 173. **Basis for Candidate Selection:** *Very important factors considered include:* Academic GPA, class rank, recommendation(s), rigor of secondary school record, standardized test scores. *Important factors considered include:* Application essay, character/personal qualities. *Other factors considered include:* Alumni/ae relation, extracurricular activities, first generation, geographical residence, interview, level of applicant's interest, talent/ability, volunteer work, work experience. **Freshman Admission Requirements:** High school diploma is required, and GED is accepted. *Academic units required:* 3 English, 2 math, 1 science (1 science lab), 2 foreign language, 1 history, 7 academic electives. *Academic units recommended:* 4 English, 3 math, 2 science (2 science labs), 2 foreign language, 3 history, 7 academic electives. **Freshman Admission Statistics:** 469 applied, 77% admitted, 44% enrolled. **Transfer Admission Requirements:** College transcript(s), essay or personal statement. Minimum college GPA of 2.0 required. Lowest grade transferable C. **General Admission Information:** Application fee $35. Regular application deadline 8/15. Regular notification is rolling. Nonfall registration accepted. Admission may be deferred for a maximum of 1 year. Credit and/or placement offered for CEEB Advanced Placement tests.

COSTS AND FINANCIAL AID
Required Forms and Deadlines: FAFSA. Financial aid filing deadline 3/1. **Notification of Awards:** Applicants will be notified of awards on a rolling basis beginning on or about 11/15. **Types of Aid:** *Need-based scholarships/grants:* Pell, SEOG, state scholarships/grants, private scholarships, the school's own gift aid. *Loans:* FFEL Subsidized Stafford, FFEL Unsubsidized Stafford, FFEL PLUS, Federal Perkins, state loans. **Student Employment:** Federal Work-Study Program available. Institutional employment available. **Financial Aid Statistics:** 68% freshmen, 72% undergrads receive need-based scholarship or grant aid. 52% freshmen, 66% undergrads receive need-based self-help aid. Highest amount earned per year from on-campus jobs $4,290.

COLLEGE OF SAINT MARY

7000 Mercy Road, Omaha, NE 68106
Phone: 402-399-2405 **E-mail:** enroll@csm.edu **CEEB Code:** 6106
Fax: 402-399-2412 **Website:** www.csm.edu **ACT Code:** 2440
Financial Aid Phone: 402-399-2415

This private school, affiliated with the Roman Catholic Church, was founded in 1923. It has a 25-acre campus.

RATINGS
Admissions Selectivity Rating: 76   **Fire Safety Rating:** 77   **Green Rating:** 60*

STUDENTS AND FACULTY
Enrollment: 871. **Student Body:** 100% female, 10% out-of-state. African American 10%, Asian 1%, Caucasian 83%, Hispanic 4%. **Retention and Graduation:** 62% freshmen return for sophomore year..34% freshmen graduate within 4 years. **Faculty:** Student/faculty ratio 11:1. 58 full-time faculty, 48% hold PhDs. 100% faculty teach undergrads.

ACADEMICS

Degrees: Associate, bachelor's, certificate, master's, post-bachelor's certificate.
Academic Requirements: Arts/fine arts, computer literacy, English (including composition), history, mathematics, philosophy, sciences (biological or physical), social science, theology, liberal arts, physical education. **Classes:** Most classes have fewer than 10 students. Most lab/discussion sections have fewer than 10 students. **Majors with Highest Enrollment:** Business, management, marketing, and related support services; elementary education and teaching; nursing/registered nurse training (RN, ASN, BSN, MSN). **Disciplines with Highest Percentage of Degrees Awarded:** Health professions and related sciences 37%, business/marketing 16%, education 9%, law/legal studies 9%, liberal arts/general studies 9%, social sciences 7%, biological/life sciences 4%. **Special Study Options:** Accelerated program, cooperative education program, double major, independent study, internships, study abroad, teacher certification program, weekend college.

FACILITIES

Housing: Women's dorms, special housing for disabled students, women with children housing. **Special Academic Facilities/Equipment:** Hillmer Art Gallery, Saint Brigit Theatre. **Computers:** 100% of classrooms are wired, 30% of classrooms are wireless, 100% of public computers are PCs, network access in dorm rooms, online registration, online administrative functions (other than registration), support for handheld computing, remote student-access to Web through college's connection.

CAMPUS LIFE

Activities: Choral groups, drama/theater, student government. **Organizations:** 17 registered organizations, 2 honor societies, 1 religious organization. **Women:** Basketball, cheerleading, cross-country, soccer, softball, volleyball.

ADMISSIONS

Freshman Academic Profile: 19% in top 10% of high school class, 32% in top 25% of high school class, 72% in top 50% of high school class. 74% from public high schools. ACT middle 50% range 18–24. TOEFL required of all international applicants, minimum paper TOEFL 550, minimum computer TOEFL 285. **Basis for Candidate Selection:** *Very important factors considered include:* Academic GPA, class rank, standardized test scores. *Important factors considered include:* Interview. *Other factors considered include:* Alumni/ae relation, application essay, character/personal qualities, extracurricular activities, level of applicant's interest, recommendation(s), rigor of secondary school record, talent/ability. **Freshman Admission Requirements:** High school diploma is required, and GED is accepted. *Academic units required:* 4 English, 2 math, 2 science, 2 social studies. *Academic units recommended:* 3 math, 3 science, 1 history. **Freshman Admission Statistics:** 503 applied, 58% admitted, 37% enrolled. **Transfer Admission Requirements:** High school transcript, college transcript(s). Minimum college GPA of 2.0 required. Lowest grade transferable C. **General Admission Information:** Application fee $30. Regular notification is rolling. Nonfall registration accepted. Admission may be deferred for a maximum of 1 year. Credit and/or placement offered for CEEB Advanced Placement tests.

COSTS AND FINANCIAL AID

Annual tuition $19,800. Room and board $6,300. Required fees $336. Average book expense $1,000. **Required Forms and Deadlines:** FAFSA. Financial aid filing deadline 3/15. **Notification of Awards:** Applicants will be notified of awards on a rolling basis beginning on or about 3/15. **Types of Aid:** *Need-based scholarships/grants:* Pell, SEOG, state scholarships/grants, private scholarships, the school's own gift aid. *Loans:* FFEL Subsidized Stafford, FFEL Unsubsidized Stafford, FFEL PLUS, Federal Perkins, Federal Nursing. **Financial Aid Statistics:** 80% freshmen, 79% undergrads receive need-based scholarship or grant aid. 74% freshmen, 84% undergrads receive need-based self-help aid. 6 freshmen, 14 undergrads receive athletic scholarships. 83% freshmen, 55% undergrads receive any aid. Highest amount earned per year from on-campus jobs $1,500.

THE COLLEGE OF SAINT ROSE

432 Western Avenue, Albany, NY 12203
Phone: 800-637-8556 **E-mail:** admit@strose.edu **CEEB Code:** 2091
Fax: 518-454-2013 **Website:** www.strose.edu **ACT Code:** 2714
Financial Aid Phone: 518-454-2013

This private school, affiliated with the Roman Catholic Church, was founded in 1920. It has a 25-acre campus.

STUDENTS AND FACULTY

Enrollment: 3,055. **Student Body:** 72% female, 28% male, 97% out-of-state. African American 3%, Asian 1%, Caucasian 78%, Hispanic 4%. **Retention and Graduation:** 79% freshmen return for sophomore year. 45% freshmen graduate within 4 years. **Faculty:** Student/faculty ratio 15:1. 191 full-time faculty, 77% hold PhDs. 96% faculty teach undergrads.

ACADEMICS

Degrees: Bachelor's, master's, post-bachelor's certificate, post-master's certificate. **Academic Requirements:** Arts/fine arts, computer literacy, English (including composition), foreign languages, history, humanities, mathematics, philosophy, physical education, sciences (biological or physical), social science. **Classes:** Most classes have 10–19 students. Most lab/discussion sections have 10–19 students. **Disciplines with Highest Percentage of Degrees Awarded:** Education 47%, history 10%, communication technologies 8%, visual and performing arts 8%, computer and information sciences 4%, psychology 4%, security and protective services 2%, English 2%, liberal arts/general studies 2%. **Special Study Options:** Accelerated program, cross registration, double major, exchange student program (domestic), independent study, internships, liberal arts/career combination, student-designed major, study abroad, teacher certification program.

FACILITIES

Housing: Coed dorms, men's dorms, women's dorms, apartments for single students. **Special Academic Facilities/Equipment:** The Saint Rose Art Gallery, one of the largest screen printing facilities in the state of New York, full-scale television studio, a 16-track professional recording studio, music library, new fitness center, competition-size pool, weight room, regulation NCAA basketball court, private meditation rooms, and an indoor garden. **Computers:** 90% of public computers are PCs, 10% of public computers are Macs, network access in dorm rooms, remote student-access to Web through college's connection.

CAMPUS LIFE

Activities: Choral groups, concert band, dance, drama/theater, jazz band, literary magazine, music ensembles, radio station, student government, student newspaper, yearbook. **Organizations:** 38 registered organizations, 6 honor societies, 1 religious organization. **Athletics (Intercollegiate):** *Men:* Baseball, basketball, cross-country, golf, soccer, swimming, track/field (outdoor). *Women:* Basketball, cheerleading, cross-country, soccer, softball, swimming, tennis, track/field (outdoor), volleyball.

ADMISSIONS

Freshman Academic Profile: 17% in top 10% of high school class, 46% in top 25% of high school class, 83% in top 50% of high school class. 82% from public high schools. SAT Math middle 50% range 480–580. SAT Critical Reading middle 50% range 480–580. ACT middle 50% range 21–27. TOEFL required of all international applicants, minimum paper TOEFL 500, minimum computer TOEFL 175. **Basis for Candidate Selection:** *Very important factors considered include:* Academic GPA, interview, level of applicant's interest, rigor of secondary school record, talent/ability. *Important factors considered include:* Character/personal qualities, extracurricular activities, geographical residence, recommendation(s), standardized test scores, volunteer work. *Other factors considered include:* Alumni/ae relation, application essay, class rank, racial/ethnic status, state residency, work experience. **Freshman Admission Requirements:** High school diploma is required, and GED is accepted. *Academic units required:* 4 English, 3 math, 3 science (2 science labs), 3 foreign language, 4 social studies, 4 history. *Academic units recommended:* 4 English, 4 math, 4 science (3 science labs), 4 foreign language, 4 social studies, 4 history, 4 academic electives. **Freshman Admission Statistics:** 3,452 applied, 68% admitted, 27% enrolled. **Transfer Admission Requirements:** High school transcript, college transcript(s), statement of good standing from prior institution(s). Minimum college GPA of 2.5 required. Lowest grade transferable C-. **General Admission Information:** Application fee $35. Regular application deadline 2/1. Regular notification is rolling. Non-fall registration accepted. Admission may be deferred for a maximum of 2 semesters. Credit and/or placement offered for CEEB Advanced Placement tests.

COSTS AND FINANCIAL AID

Required Forms and Deadlines: FAFSA. Financial aid filing deadline 3/1. **Notification of Awards:** Applicants will be notified of awards on or about 3/15. **Types of Aid:** *Need-based scholarships/grants:* Pell, SEOG, state scholarships/grants, private scholarships, the school's own gift aid. *Loans:* FFEL Subsidized Stafford, FFEL Unsubsidized Stafford, FFEL PLUS, Federal Perkins. **Financial Aid Statistics:** 76% freshmen, 78% undergrads receive need-based scholarship or grant aid. 75% freshmen, 79% undergrads receive need-based self-help aid. 14 freshmen, 36 undergrads receive athletic scholarships.

RATINGS

Admissions Selectivity Rating: 84   **Fire Safety Rating:** 99   **Green Rating:** 60*

THE COLLEGE OF SAINT SCHOLASTICA

1200 Kenwood Avenue, Duluth, MN 55811-4199
Phone: 218-723-6046 **E-mail:** admissions@css.edu **CEEB Code:** 6107
Fax: 218-723-5991 **Website:** www.css.edu **ACT Code:** 2098
Financial Aid Phone: 218-723-6047

This private school, affiliated with the Roman Catholic Church, was founded in 1912. It has a 186-acre campus.

RATINGS
Admissions Selectivity Rating: 79 **Fire Safety Rating:** 61 **Green Rating:** 60*

STUDENTS AND FACULTY
Enrollment: 2,078. **Student Body:** 70% female, 30% male, 12% out-of-state, 5% international (19 countries represented). African American 1%, Asian 2%, Caucasian 84%, Native American 2%. **Retention and Graduation:** 81% freshmen return for sophomore year. 55% freshmen graduate within 4 years. 29% grads go on to further study within 1 year. **Faculty:** Student/faculty ratio 13:1. 142 full-time faculty, 59% hold PhDs. 100% faculty teach undergrads.

ACADEMICS
Degrees: Bachelor's, certificate, first professional, master's, post-bachelor's certificate, post-master's certificate. **Academic Requirements:** Arts/fine arts, cultural diversity, English (including composition), foreign languages, history, humanities, mathematics, philosophy, sciences (biological or physical), social science. **Classes:** Most classes have 20–29 students. Most lab/discussion sections have 10–19 students. **Majors with Highest Enrollment:** Business administration and management, computer and information sciences, nursing/registered nurse training (RN, ASN, BSN, MSN). **Disciplines with Highest Percentage of Degrees Awarded:** Business/marketing 31%, health professions and related sciences 31%, biological/life sciences 9%, computer and information sciences 6%, social sciences 6%, public administration and social services 4%, education 3%. **Special Study Options:** Accelerated program, cross registration, distance learning, double major, dual enrollment, external degree program, honors program, independent study, internships, liberal arts/career combination, student-designed major, study abroad, teacher certification program.

FACILITIES
Housing: Coed dorms, apartments for single students, special housing for disabled students, special housing for international students, apartments for students with dependent children.
Quiet or study wings available. **Computers:** 100% of classrooms are wired, 10% of classrooms are wireless, 90% of public computers are PCs, 10% of public computers are Macs, network access in dorm rooms, network access in dorm lounges, online registration, online administrative functions (other than registration), support for handheld computing, remote student-access to Web through college's connection.

CAMPUS LIFE
Activities: Choral groups, concert band, dance, drama/theater, jazz band, literary magazine, music ensembles, pep band, student government, student newspaper, television station. **Organizations:** 67 registered organizations, 2 honor societies, 7 religious organizations. **Athletics (Intercollegiate):** *Men:* Baseball, basketball, cross-country, ice hockey, soccer, tennis, track/field (indoor), track/field (outdoor). *Women:* Basketball, cross-country, soccer, softball, tennis, track/field (indoor), track/field (outdoor), volleyball.

ADMISSIONS
Freshman Academic Profile: 27% in top 10% of high school class, 58% in top 25% of high school class, 86% in top 50% of high school class. SAT Math middle 50% range 530–660. SAT Critical Reading middle 50% range 530–650. ACT middle 50% range 21–26. TOEFL required of all international applicants, minimum paper TOEFL 550, minimum computer TOEFL 213. **Basis for Candidate Selection:** *Very important factors considered include:* Academic GPA, standardized test scores. *Important factors considered include:* Application essay, interview, recommendation(s). *Other factors considered include:* Alumni/ae relation, class rank, extracurricular activities, geographical residence. **Freshman Admission Requirements:** High school diploma is required, and GED is accepted. *Academic units recommended:* 4 English, 2 math, 3 science, 3 foreign language, 3 social studies, 3 history. **Freshman Admission Statistics:** 1,521 applied, 88% admitted, 37% enrolled. **Transfer Admission Requirements:** College transcript(s), statement of good standing from prior institution(s). Minimum college GPA of 2.0 required. Lowest grade transferable C. **General Admission Information:** Application fee $25. Regular notification is rolling. Non-fall registration accepted. Admission may be deferred for a maximum of 2 semesters. Credit and/or placement offered for CEEB Advanced Placement tests.

COSTS AND FINANCIAL AID
Annual tuition $26,324. Room and board $6,720. Required fees $165. Average book expense $1,000. **Required Forms and Deadlines:** FAFSA, institution's own financial aid form. Financial aid filing deadline 3/15. **Notification of Awards:** Applicants will be notified of awards on a rolling basis beginning on or about 3/1. **Types of Aid:** *Need-based scholarships/grants:* Pell, SEOG, state scholarships/grants, private scholarships, the school's own gift aid. *Loans:* FFEL Subsidized Stafford, FFEL Unsubsidized Stafford, FFEL PLUS, Federal Perkins, Federal Nursing, state loans, private supplemental loans. **Student Employment:** Federal Work-Study Program available. Institutional employment available. Off-campus job opportunities are good. **Financial Aid Statistics:** 62% freshmen, 60% undergrads receive need-based scholarship or grant aid. 51% freshmen, 58% undergrads receive need-based self-help aid. 79% freshmen, 98% undergrads receive any aid. Highest amount earned per year from on-campus jobs $4,688.

THE COLLEGE OF SAINT THOMAS MORE

3020 Lubbock Street, Fort Worth, TX 76109-2323
Phone: 817-923-8459 **E-mail:** more-info@cstm.edu
Fax: 817-924-3206 **Website:** www.cstm.edu
Financial Aid Phone: 817-923-8459

This private school, affiliated with the Roman Catholic Church, was founded in 1981.

RATINGS
Admissions Selectivity Rating: 60* **Fire Safety Rating:** 60* **Green Rating:** 60*

STUDENTS AND FACULTY
Enrollment: 34. **Student Body:** 44% female, 56% male, 6% out-of-state, 3% international. African American 3%, Caucasian 15%, Hispanic 15%, Native American 3%. **Faculty:** Student/faculty ratio 4:1. 4 full-time faculty, 100% hold PhDs. 100% faculty teach undergrads.

ACADEMICS
Degrees: Bachelor's. **Academic Requirements:** Foreign languages, history, humanities, mathematics, philosophy, theology. **Special Study Options:** Foreign programs in Oxford, Rome, and Greece.

FACILITIES
Housing: Men's dorms, women's dorms, apartments for married students, apartments for single students. **Computers:** 100% of public computers are PCs, online registration.

CAMPUS LIFE
Activities: Dance, student government, student-run film society. **Organizations:** 1 religious organization.

ADMISSIONS
Freshman Academic Profile: 66% from public high schools. SAT Math middle 50% range 470–590. SAT Critical Reading middle 50% range 460–710. **Basis for Candidate Selection:** *Very important factors considered include:* Application essay, character/personal qualities, interview, recommendation(s), rigor of secondary school record, talent/ability. *Important factors considered include:* Class rank, extracurricular activities, standardized test scores. *Other factors considered include:* Religious affiliation/commitment, volunteer work, work experience. **Freshman Admission Requirements:** High school diploma is required, and GED is accepted. *Academic units recommended:* 2 foreign language. **Freshman Admission Statistics:** 7 applied, 43% admitted. **Transfer Admission Requirements:** College transcript(s), essay or personal statement, interview. Minimum college GPA of 2.0 required. **General Admission Information:** Application fee $25. Early decision application deadline 12/1. Regular application deadline 7/15. Regular notification 3/15. Non-fall registration accepted. Common Application not accepted.

COSTS AND FINANCIAL AID
Room $300. Required fees $400. Average book expense $200. **Required Forms and Deadlines:** FAFSA. **Notification of Awards:** Applicants will be notified of awards on a rolling basis beginning on or about 1/1. **Types of Aid:** *Need-based scholarships/grants:* State scholarships/grants, private scholarships, the school's own gift aid. *Loans:* Direct Subsidized Stafford, Direct Unsubsidized Stafford, Direct PLUS, FFEL Subsidized Stafford, FFEL Unsubsidized Stafford, FFEL PLUS. **Student Employment:** Institutional employment available. Off-campus job opportunities are excellent. Highest amount earned per year from on-campus jobs $750.

COLLEGE OF SANTA FE

1600 St. Michaels Drive, Santa Fe, NM 87505-7634
Phone: 505-473-6133 **E-mail:** admissions@csf.edu **CEEB Code:** 4676
Fax: 505-473-6129 **Website:** www.csf.edu **ACT Code:** 2648
Financial Aid Phone: 505-473-6454

This private school was founded in 1874. It has a 100-acre campus.

RATINGS
Admissions Selectivity Rating: 76   **Fire Safety Rating:** 60*   **Green Rating:** 60*

STUDENTS AND FACULTY
Enrollment: 1,225. **Student Body:** 58% female, 42% male, 73% out-of-state. African American 3%, Asian 1%, Caucasian 55%, Hispanic 26%, Native American 3%. **Retention and Graduation:** 75% freshmen return for sophomore year. 21% freshmen graduate within 4 years. **Faculty:** Student/ faculty ratio 7:1. 76 full-time faculty, 79% hold PhDs. 100% faculty teach undergrads.

ACADEMICS
Degrees: Associate, bachelor's, master's. **Academic Requirements:** Arts/fine arts, English (including composition), humanities, mathematics, philosophy, sciences (biological or physical), social science. **Classes:** Most classes have 10–19 students. Most lab/discussion sections have 10–19 students. **Majors with Highest Enrollment:** Creative writing, drama and dramatics/theater arts, film/ cinema studies. **Disciplines with Highest Percentage of Degrees Awarded:** Visual and performing arts 24%, business/marketing 22%, education 13%, computer and information sciences 11%, psychology 10%. **Special Study Options:** Accelerated program, cooperative education program, distance learning, double major, dual enrollment, exchange student program (domestic), independent study, internships, student-designed major, study abroad, teacher certification program.

FACILITIES
Housing: Coed dorms, men's dorms, women's dorms, apartments for single students, special housing for disabled students, substance-free floors, quiet floors, smoking floors. **Special Academic Facilities/Equipment:** Thaw Art History Library, Marion Center Photographic Library, Garson Studios, Visual Art Center, Greer Garson Theatre Centre. **Computers:** 80% of public computers are PCs, 20% of public computers are Macs, network access in dorm rooms, network access in dorm lounges, online administrative functions (other than registration), remote student-access to Web through college's connection.

CAMPUS LIFE
Activities: Choral groups, dance, drama/theater, literary magazine, music ensembles, musical theater, student government, student newspaper, television station. **Organizations:** 14 registered organizations, 1 honor society. **Athletics (Intercollegiate):** *Men:* Tennis. *Women:* Tennis.

ADMISSIONS
Freshman Academic Profile: 7% in top 10% of high school class, 30% in top 25% of high school class, 63% in top 50% of high school class. SAT Math middle 50% range 460–590. SAT Critical Reading middle 50% range 520–640. ACT middle 50% range 20–25. TOEFL required of all international applicants, minimum paper TOEFL 550, minimum computer TOEFL 213. **Basis for Candidate Selection:** *Very important factors considered include:* Character/ personal qualities, interview, rigor of secondary school record, talent/ability. *Important factors considered include:* Academic GPA, application essay, class rank, extracurricular activities, recommendation(s), standardized test scores, volunteer work. *Other factors considered include:* Alumni/ae relation, geographical residence, racial/ethnic status, state residency, work experience. **Freshman Admission Requirements:** High school diploma is required, and GED is accepted. *Academic units required:* 4 English, 2 math, 2 science (2 science labs), 2 social studies, 6 academic electives. *Academic units recommended:* 4 English, 3 math, 3 science (2 science labs), 2 foreign language, 2 social studies, 2 history, 4 academic electives. **Freshman Admission Statistics:** 750 applied, 78% admitted, 27% enrolled. **Transfer Admission Requirements:** High school transcript, college transcript(s), essay or personal statement. Lowest grade transferable C-. **General Admission Information:** Application fee $35. Regular notification is rolling. Nonfall registration accepted. Admission may be deferred for a maximum of 1 year. Credit and/or placement offered for CEEB Advanced Placement tests.

COSTS AND FINANCIAL AID
Annual tuition $21,530. Room & board $6,702. Required fees $746. Average book expense $840. **Required Forms and Deadlines: FAFSA. Financial aid filing deadline 3/15. **Notification of Awards:** Applicants will be notified of awards on a rolling basis beginning on or about 3/1. **Types of Aid:** *Need-based scholarships/grants:* Pell, SEOG, state scholarships/grants, private scholarships, the school's own gift aid. *Loans:* FFEL Subsidized Stafford, FFEL Unsubsidized Stafford, FFEL PLUS, Federal Perkins, state loans, college/ university loans from institutional funds. **Student Employment:** Federal Work-Study Program available. Institutional employment available. Off-campus job opportunities are excellent. **Financial Aid Statistics:** 55% freshmen, 60% undergrads receive need-based scholarship or grant aid. 58% freshmen, 62% undergrads receive need-based self-help aid. 4 undergrads receive athletic scholarships.

COLLEGE OF THE SISKIYOUS

800 College Avenue, Weed, CA 96094
Phone: 530-938-5555 **E-mail:** registration@siskiyous.edu
Fax: 530-938-5367 **Website:** www.siskiyous.edu
Financial Aid Phone: 530-938-5209

This public school was founded in 1957. It has a 260-acre campus.

RATINGS
Admissions Selectivity Rating: 60*   **Fire Safety Rating:** 60*   **Green Rating:** 60*

STUDENTS AND FACULTY
Enrollment: 1,153. **Student Body:** 57% female, 43% male, 10% out-of-state. African American 5%, Asian 4%, Caucasian 71%, Hispanic 8%, Native American 5%. **Faculty:** Student/faculty ratio 21:1. 50 full-time faculty, 16% hold PhDs.

ACADEMICS
Degrees: Associate, certificate. **Academic Requirements:** English (including composition), humanities, mathematics, sciences (biological or physical), social science, wellness requirement. **Classes:** Most classes have fewer than 10 students. Most lab/discussion sections have fewer than 10 students. **Special Study Options:** Accelerated program, cooperative education program, distance learning, English as a second language (ESL), exchange student program (domestic), independent study, liberal arts/career combination.

FACILITIES
Housing: Coed dorms, men's dorms. **Computers:** 98% of public computers are PCs, 2% of public computers are Macs, network access in dorm lounges, online registration, online administrative functions (other than registration), remote student-access to Web through college's connection.

CAMPUS LIFE
Activities: Choral groups, concert band, dance, drama/theater, jazz band, music ensembles, musical theater, student government. **Organizations:** 18 registered organizations, 1 religious organization. **Athletics (Intercollegiate):** *Men:* Baseball, basketball, football, skiing (downhill/alpine), track/field (outdoor). *Women:* Basketball, skiing (downhill/alpine), softball, track/field (outdoor), volleyball.

ADMISSIONS
Freshman Academic Profile: TOEFL required of all international applicants, minimum paper TOEFL 470, minimum computer TOEFL 150. **Freshman Admission Requirements:** High school diploma or equivalent is not required. **Transfer Admission Requirements:** Lowest grade transferable D. **General Admission Information:** Nonfall registration accepted. Common Application not accepted.

COSTS AND FINANCIAL AID
Annual in-state tuition $806. Out-of-state tuition $5,906. Room & board $6,020. Required fees $26. Average book expense $1,000. **Required Forms and Deadlines:** FAFSA, institution's own financial aid form. **Types of Aid:** *Need-based scholarships/grants:* Pell, SEOG, state scholarships/grants, private scholarships, the school's own gift aid, BOG fee waiver. *Loans:* FFEL Subsidized Stafford, FFEL Unsubsidized Stafford, FFEL PLUS, college/ university loans from institutional funds. **Financial Aid Statistics:** 66% freshmen, 45% undergrads receive need-based scholarship or grant aid. 24% freshmen, 19% undergrads receive need-based self-help aid.

COLLEGE OF THE SOUTHWEST

6610 Lovington Highway, Hobbs, NM 88240
Phone: 505-392-6563 **E-mail:** admissions@csw.edu **CEEB Code:** 4116
Fax: 505-392-6006 **Website:** www.csw.edu **ACT Code:** 2633
Financial Aid Phone: 505-392-6561

This private school was founded in 1962. It has a 162-acre campus.

RATINGS
Admissions Selectivity Rating: 79   **Fire Safety Rating:** 78   **Green Rating:** 60*

STUDENTS AND FACULTY
Enrollment: 430. **Student Body:** 64% female, 36% male, 39% out-of-state. African American 4%, Caucasian 52%, Hispanic 39%, Native American 2%. **Retention and Graduation:** 32% freshmen return for sophomore year. 10% freshmen graduate within 4 years. 30% grads go on to further study within 1 year. 30% grads pursue arts and sciences degrees. **Faculty:** Student/faculty ratio 11:1. 20 full-time faculty, 60% hold PhDs. 100% faculty teach undergrads.

ACADEMICS
Degrees: Bachelor's, master's. **Academic Requirements:** Arts/fine arts, computer literacy, English (including composition), history, humanities, mathematics, sciences (biological or physical), social science, religion. **Classes:** Most classes have fewer than 10 students. Most lab/discussion sections have fewer than 10 students. **Majors with Highest Enrollment:** Business administration/management, criminal justice/police science, elementary education and teaching. **Disciplines with Highest Percentage of Degrees Awarded:** Education 36%, business/marketing 32%, psychology 10%, biological/life sciences 4%, English 4%, natural resources/environmental science 3%. **Special Study Options:** Distance learning, double major, internships, teacher certification program.

FACILITIES
Housing: Men's dorms, women's dorms. **Computers:** 100% of public computers are PCs, network access in dorm rooms, remote student-access to Web through college's connection.

CAMPUS LIFE
Activities: Choral groups, drama/theater, literary magazine, student government, student newspaper. **Organizations:** 3 honor societies, 1 religious organization. **Athletics (Intercollegiate):** *Men:* Baseball, cross-country, golf, rodeo, soccer, track/field (outdoor). *Women:* Cross-country, golf, rodeo, soccer, softball, track/field (outdoor), volleyball.

ADMISSIONS
Freshman Academic Profile: 1% in top 10% of high school class, 16% in top 25% of high school class, 69% in top 50% of high school class. SAT Math middle 50% range 340–500. SAT Critical Reading middle 50% range 340–470. SAT Writing middle 50% range 330–460. ACT middle 50% range 14–20. TOEFL required of all international applicants, minimum paper TOEFL 550, minimum computer TOEFL 218. **Basis for Candidate Selection:** *Very important factors considered include:* Academic GPA, class rank, standardized test scores. **Freshman Admission Requirements:** High school diploma is required, and GED is accepted. **Freshman Admission Statistics:** 2,207 applied, 23% admitted, 10% enrolled. **Transfer Admission Requirements:** College transcript(s). Minimum college GPA of 2.0 required. Lowest grade transferable D. **General Admission Information:** Application fee $25. Regular notification is rolling. Nonfall registration accepted. Credit offered for CEEB Advanced Placement tests.

COSTS AND FINANCIAL AID
Annual tuition $11,700. Room & board $5,400. Average book expense $800. **Required Forms and Deadlines:** FAFSA, institution's own financial aid form. Financial aid filing deadline 6/2. **Notification of Awards:** Applicants will be notified of awards on or about 4/2. **Types of Aid:** *Need-based scholarships/grants:* Pell, SEOG, state scholarships/grants, private scholarships, the school's own gift aid. *Loans:* FFEL Subsidized Stafford, FFEL Unsubsidized Stafford, FFEL PLUS. **Financial Aid Statistics:** 61% freshmen, 60% undergrads receive need-based scholarship or grant aid. 8% freshmen, 14% undergrads receive need-based self-help aid. 6 freshmen, 98 undergrads receive athletic scholarships. 75% freshmen, 77% undergrads receive any aid. Highest amount earned per year from on-campus jobs $3,000.

THE COLLEGE OF ST. CATHERINE

2004 Randolph Avenue, Saint Paul, MN 55105
Phone: 651-690-8850 **E-mail:** admissions@stkate.edu **CEEB Code:** 6105
Fax: 651-690-8824 **Website:** www.stkate.edu **ACT Code:** 2096
Financial Aid Phone: 651-690-6540

This private school, affiliated with the Roman Catholic Church, was founded in 1905. It has a 110-acre campus.

RATINGS
Admissions Selectivity Rating: 84   **Fire Safety Rating:** 60*   **Green Rating:** 60*

STUDENTS AND FACULTY
Enrollment: 3,511. **Student Body:** 97% female, 3% male, 10% out-of-state, 2% international. African American 8%, Asian 7%, Caucasian 74%, Hispanic 3%. **Retention and Graduation:** 81% freshmen return for sophomore year. 41% freshmen graduate within 4 years. 16% grads go on to further study within 1 year. 64% grads pursue arts and sciences degrees. 10% grads pursue business degrees. 4% grads pursue law degrees. 2% grads pursue medical degrees. **Faculty:** Student/faculty ratio 11:1. 246 full-time faculty. 100% faculty teach undergrads.

ACADEMICS
Degrees: Associate, bachelor's, certificate, doctoral, master's, post-bachelor's certificate, terminal. **Academic Requirements:** 2 core classes: the Reflective Woman and Global Search for Justice, arts/fine arts, computer literacy, English (including composition), foreign languages, history, humanities, mathematics, philosophy, sciences (biological or physical), social science, theology. **Classes:** Most classes have 10–19 students. Most lab/discussion sections have 10–19 students. **Majors with Highest Enrollment:** Elementary education and teaching, nursing/registered nurse training (RN, ASN, BSN, MSN), occupational therapy/therapist. **Disciplines with Highest Percentage of Degrees Awarded:** Health professions and related sciences 25%, business/marketing 17%, education 9%, English 6%, public administration and social services 6%, communications/journalism 5%. **Special Study Options:** Cross registration, double major, exchange student program (domestic), honors program, independent study, internships, liberal arts/career combination, student-designed major, study abroad, teacher certification program, weekend college.

FACILITIES
Housing: Women's dorms, apartments for single students, apartments for single mothers. **Special Academic Facilities/Equipment:** Art gallery, theater, recital hall, experimental psychology lab, language lab, observatory. **Computers:** 90% of public computers are PCs, 10% of public computers are Macs, network access in dorm rooms, network access in dorm lounges, online administrative functions (other than registration), remote student-access to Web through college's connection.

CAMPUS LIFE
Activities: Choral groups, dance, drama/theater, literary magazine, music ensembles, musical theater, student government, student newspaper. **Organizations:** 40 registered organizations, 24 honor societies, 4 religious organizations. 1 sorority. **Athletics (Intercollegiate):** *Women:* Basketball, cross-country, diving, ice hockey, soccer, softball, swimming, tennis, track/field (indoor), track/field (outdoor), volleyball.

ADMISSIONS
Freshman Academic Profile: 34% in top 10% of high school class, 75% in top 25% of high school class, 95% in top 50% of high school class. 84% from public high schools. SAT Math middle 50% range 495–650. SAT Critical Reading middle 50% range 518–660. ACT middle 50% range 22–26. TOEFL required of all international applicants, minimum paper TOEFL 500, minimum computer TOEFL 173. **Basis for Candidate Selection:** *Very important factors considered include:* Rigor of secondary school record. *Important factors considered include:* Academic GPA, class rank, extracurricular activities, recommendation(s), standardized test scores. *Other factors considered include:* Application essay, character/personal qualities, interview, level of applicant's interest, racial/ethnic status, talent/ability, volunteer work, work experience. **Freshman Admission Requirements:** High school diploma is required, and GED is accepted. *Academic units recommended:* 4 English, 3 math, 2 science, 4 foreign language, 2 social studies. **Freshman Admission Statistics:** 1,475 applied, 78% admitted, 36% enrolled. **Transfer Admission Requirements:** High school transcript, college transcript(s), statement of good standing from prior institution(s). Minimum college GPA of 2.0 required. Lowest grade transferable C-. **General Admission Information:** Non-fall registration accepted. Admission may be deferred for a maximum of 2 semesters. Credit offered for CEEB Advanced Placement tests.

COSTS AND FINANCIAL AID

Annual tuition $22,620. Room & board $6,432. Required fees $260. Average book expense $640. **Required Forms and Deadlines:** FAFSA, institution's own financial aid form. Financial aid filing deadline 4/15. **Notification of Awards:** Applicants will be notified of awards on a rolling basis beginning on or about 3/30. **Types of Aid:** *Need-based scholarships/grants:* Pell, SEOG, state scholarships/grants, the school's own gift aid, Federal Nursing Scholarships. *Loans:* FFEL Subsidized Stafford, FFEL Unsubsidized Stafford, FFEL PLUS, Federal Perkins, Federal Nursing, state loans, alternative loans. **Student Employment:** Federal Work-Study Program available. Institutional employment available. Off-campus job opportunities are excellent. **Financial Aid Statistics:** 54% freshmen, 58% undergrads receive need-based scholarship or grant aid. 58% freshmen, 60% undergrads receive need-based self-help aid. Highest amount earned per year from on-campus jobs $2,158.

COLLEGE OF ST. JOSEPH IN VERMONT

71 Clement Road, Rutland, VT 05701
Phone: 802-773-5900 **E-mail:** admissions@csj.edu **CEEB Code:** 3297
Fax: 802-776-5258 **Website:** www.csj.edu
Financial Aid Phone: 802-776-5218

This private school, affiliated with the Roman Catholic Church, was founded in 1956. It has a 90-acre campus.

RATINGS

Admissions Selectivity Rating: 65   **Fire Safety Rating:** 62   **Green Rating:** 60*

STUDENTS AND FACULTY

Enrollment: 247. **Student Body:** 68% female, 32% male, 55% out-of-state, 2% international (1 country represented). African American 4%. **Retention and Graduation:** 59% freshmen return for sophomore year. 28% freshmen graduate within 4 years. 12% grads go on to further study within 1 year. 2% grads pursue arts and sciences degrees. 4% grads pursue business degrees. **Faculty:** Student/faculty ratio 11:1. 12 full-time faculty, 67% hold PhDs. 100% faculty teach undergrads.

ACADEMICS

Degrees: Associate, bachelor's, master's. **Academic Requirements:** Arts/fine arts, computer literacy, English (including composition), history, humanities, mathematics, sciences (biological or physical), social science, religion, philosophy. **Classes:** Most classes have fewer than 10 students. **Majors with Highest Enrollment:** Business administration/management, elementary education and teaching, psychology. **Disciplines with Highest Percentage of Degrees Awarded:** Liberal arts/general studies 13%, psychology 10%, business/marketing 10%, education 8%, communication technologies 3%, computer and information sciences 3%. **Special Study Options:** Accelerated program, double major, dual enrollment, independent study, internships, liberal arts/career combination, study abroad, teacher certification program.

FACILITIES

Housing: Men's dorms, women's dorms. **Special Academic Facilities/ Equipment:** Theater and athletic center. **Computers:** 85% of classrooms are wired, 100% of public computers are PCs, network access in dorm rooms, remote student-access to Web through college's connection.

CAMPUS LIFE

Activities: Choral groups, drama/theater, literary magazine, student government, student newspaper. **Organizations:** 20 registered organizations, 6 honor societies, 1 religious organization. **Athletics (Intercollegiate):** *Men:* Baseball, basketball, cross-country, soccer. *Women:* Basketball, cross-country, soccer, softball.

ADMISSIONS

65 (out of 100). **Freshman Academic Profile:** 6% in top 10% of high school class, 9% in top 25% of high school class, 45% in top 50% of high school class. 65% from public high schools. SAT Math middle 50% range 390–490. SAT Critical Reading middle 50% range 410–530. ACT middle 50% range 17–23. TOEFL required of all international applicants, minimum paper TOEFL 500, minimum computer TOEFL 213. **Basis for Candidate Selection:** *Very important factors considered include:* Application essay, rigor of secondary school record. *Important factors considered include:* Extracurricular activities, interview, recommendation(s), standardized test scores. *Other factors considered include:* Alumni/ae relation, character/personal qualities, class rank, talent/ability, volunteer work. **Freshman Admission Requirements:** High school diploma is required, and GED is accepted. *Academic units required:* 4 English, 3 math, 2 science, 2 social studies, 2 history, 5 academic electives.

Academic units recommended: 2 foreign language. **Freshman Admission Statistics:** 127 applied, 90% admitted, 34% enrolled. **Transfer Admission Requirements:** High school transcript, college transcript(s), essay or personal statement. Minimum college GPA of 2.0 required. Lowest grade transferable C. **General Admission Information:** Application fee $25. Regular notification is rolling. Nonfall registration accepted. Admission may be deferred for a maximum of 1 year. Common Application not accepted. Credit and/or placement offered for CEEB Advanced Placement tests.

COSTS AND FINANCIAL AID

Annual tuition $15,500. Room and board $7,600. Required fees $260. Average book expense $1,000. **Required Forms and Deadlines:** FAFSA, institution's own financial aid form. **Notification of Awards:** Applicants will be notified of awards on a rolling basis beginning on or about 3/15. **Types of Aid:** *Need-based scholarships/grants:* Pell, SEOG, state scholarships/grants, private scholarships, the school's own gift aid. *Loans:* FFEL Subsidized Stafford, FFEL Unsubsidized Stafford, FFEL PLUS, Federal Perkins. **Student Employment:** Federal Work-Study Program available. Institutional employment available. Off-campus job opportunities are good. **Financial Aid Statistics:** 87% freshmen, 68% undergrads receive need-based scholarship or grant aid. 74% undergrads receive need-based self-help aid. 1 undergrad receives athletic scholarships. 97% freshmen, 89% undergrads receive any aid. Highest amount earned per year from on-campus jobs $1,285.

THE COLLEGE OF WILLIAM & MARY

PO Box 8795, Williamsburg, VA 23187-8795
Phone: 757-221-4223 **E-mail:** admiss@wm.edu **CEEB Code:** 5115
Fax: 757-221-1242 **Website:** www.wm.edu **ACT Code:** 4344
Financial Aid Phone: 757-221-2420.

This public school was founded in 1693. It has a 1,200-acre campus.

RATINGS

Admissions Selectivity Rating: 97   **Fire Safety Rating:** 73   **Green Rating:** 84

STUDENTS AND FACULTY

Enrollment: 5,651. **Student Body:** 54% female, 46% male, 32% out-of-state, 1% international (50 countries represented). African American 7%, Asian 7%, Caucasian 67%, Hispanic 5%. **Retention and Graduation:** 95% freshmen return for sophomore year. 30% grads go on to further study within 1 year. 7% grads pursue law degrees. 4% grads pursue medical degrees. **Faculty:** Student/ faculty ratio 11:1. 594 full-time faculty, 89% hold PhDs. 99% faculty teach undergrads.

ACADEMICS

Degrees: Bachelor's, doctoral, first professional, master's, post-master's certificate. **Academic Requirements:** Arts/fine arts, computer literacy, English (including composition), foreign languages, history, humanities, mathematics, philosophy, sciences (biological or physical), social science. **Classes:** Most classes have 10—19 students. **Majors with Highest Enrollment:** Business administration/management; multi/interdisciplinary studies; psychology. **Disciplines with Highest Percentage of Degrees Awarded:** Business/marketing 10%, interdisciplinary studies 9%, psychology 9%, history 8%, English 7%. **Special Study Options:** Accelerated program, double major, dual enrollment, exchange student program (domestic), honor program, independent study, internships, student-designed major, study abroad, teacher certification program, early assurance program with Eastern Virginia Medical School.

FACILITIES

Housing: Coed dorms, men's dorms, women's dorms, apartments for married students, apartments for single students, special housing for disabled students, special housing for international students, fraternity/sorority housing. **Special Academic Facilities/Equipment:** Art museum, language lab, greenhouse, herbarium, archaeological conservation lab, electron microscope, spectrometer, chromatograph, population ecology lab, marine sciences institute, rare books collection. **Computers:** 5% of classrooms are wired, 100% of classrooms are wireless, 95% of public computers are PCs, 5% of public computers are Macs, network access in dorm rooms, network access in dorm lounges, online registration, online administrative functions (other than registration), remote student-access to Web through college's connection. Undergraduates are required to own a computer.

CAMPUS LIFE

Activities: Choral groups, concert band, dance, drama/theater, jazz band, literary magazine, music ensembles, musical theater, opera, pep band, radio station, student government, student newspaper, student-run film society, symphony orchestra, television station, yearbook. **Organizations:** 358 registered organizations, 28 honor societies, 28 religious organizations. 16 fraternities (22% men join), 11 sororities (27% women join). **Athletics (Intercollegiate):** *Men:* Baseball, basketball, cross-country, diving, football, golf, gymnastics, soccer, swimming, tennis, track/field (indoor), track/field (outdoor). *Women:* Basketball, cross-country, diving, field hockey, golf, gymnastics, lacrosse, soccer, swimming, tennis, track/field (indoor), track/field (outdoor), volleyball. Environmental Initiatives: Recycling. Retrofit of systems to improve energy consumption. Purchase of enviornmentally sustainable materials.

ADMISSIONS

. **Freshman Academic Profile:** 80% in top 10% of high school class, 16% in top 25% of high school class, 98% in top 50% of high school class. SAT Math middle 50% range 620–710. SAT Critical Reading middle 50% range 630–740. SAT Writing middle 50% range 620–710. ACT middle 50% range 27–32. TOEFL required of all international applicants, minimum paper TOEFL 600, minimum computer TOEFL 250. **Basis for Candidate Selection:** *Very important factors considered include:* Academic GPA, application essay, character/personal qualities, class rank, extracurricular activities, recommendation(s), rigor of secondary school record, standardized test scores, state residency, talent/ability. *Other factors considered include:* Alumni/ae relation, first generation, geographical residence, interview, racial/ethnic status, volunteer work, work experience. **Freshman Admission Requirements:** High school diploma is required, and GED is not accepted. *Academic units recommended:* 4 English, 4 math, 4 science (3 science labs), 4 foreign language, 4 social studies. **Freshman Admission Statistics:** 10,722 applied, 32% admitted, 39% enrolled. **Transfer Admission Requirements:** High school transcript, college transcript(s), essay or personal statement, statement of good standing from prior institution(s). Lowest grade transferable C. **General Admission Information:** Application fee $60. Early Decision application deadline 11/1. Regular application deadline 1/1. Regular notification 4/1. Nonfall registration not accepted. Admission may be deferred for a maximum of 1 year. Credit and/or placement offered for CEEB Advanced Placement tests.

COSTS AND FINANCIAL AID

Annual in-state tuition $8,490. Out-of-state tuition $25,048. Room & board $6,932. Average book expense $900. **Required Forms and Deadlines:** FAFSA, CSS/Financial Aid PROFILE. CSS/Financial Aid PROFILE required of Early Decision applicants only. Financial aid filing deadline 2/15. Financial aid filing deadline 2/15. **Notification of Awards:** Applicants will be notified of awards on a rolling basis beginning on or about 3/10. **Types of Aid:** *Need-based scholarships/grants:* Pell, SEOG, state scholarships/grants, private scholarships, the school's own gift aid. *Loans:* FFEL Subsidized Stafford, FFEL Unsubsidized Stafford, FFEL PLUS, Federal Perkins. **Student Employment:** Federal Work-Study Program available. Institutional employment available. Off-campus job opportunities are excellent. **Financial Aid Statistics:** 19% freshmen, 22% undergrads receive need-based scholarship or grant aid. 22% freshmen, 24% undergrads receive need-based self-help aid. Highest amount earned per year from on-campus jobs $1,200.

THE COLLEGE OF WOOSTER

Best 368

847 College Avenue, Wooster, OH 44691
Phone: 330-263-2322 **E-mail:** admissions@wooster.edu **CEEB Code:** 1134
Fax: 330-263-2621 **Website:** www.wooster.edu **ACT Code:** 3260
Financial Aid Phone: 800-877-3688

This private school, historically affiliated with Presbyterian Church, was founded in 1866. It has a 240-acre campus.

RATINGS

Admissions Selectivity Rating: 86   **Fire Safety Rating:** 60*   **Green Rating:** 73

STUDENTS AND FACULTY

Enrollment: 1,792. **Student Body:** 51% female, 49% male, 54% out-of-state, 5% international (30 countries represented). African American 4%, Asian 2%, Caucasian 75%, Hispanic 2%. **Retention and Graduation:** 87% freshmen return for sophomore year. 66% freshmen graduate within 4 years. 42% grads go on to further study within 1 year. 23% grads pursue arts and sciences degrees. 2% grads pursue business degrees. 5% grads pursue law degrees. 3% grads pursue medical degrees. **Faculty:** Student/faculty ratio 11:1. 137 full-time faculty, 97% hold PhDs. 100% faculty teach undergrads.

ACADEMICS

Degrees: Bachelor's. **Academic Requirements:** Arts/fine arts, English (including composition), foreign languages, history, humanities, mathematics, sciences (biological or physical), social science. **Classes:** Most classes have fewer than 10 students. Most lab/discussion sections have 10–19 students. **Majors with Highest Enrollment:** English language and literature, history, psychology. **Disciplines with Highest Percentage of Degrees Awarded:** Social sciences 24%, history 10%, psychology 9%, biological/life sciences 8%, English 8%. **Special Study Options:** Cooperative education program, double major, exchange student program (domestic), independent study, internships, student-designed major, study abroad, teacher certification program.

FACILITIES

Housing: Coed dorms, women's dorms, fraternity/sorority housing, special housing for students participating in volunteer programs. **Special Academic Facilities/Equipment:** Art museum, language lab, on-campus nursery school, science library. **Computers:** 20% of public computers are PCs, 74% of public computers are Macs, 6% of public computers are UNIX, network access in dorm rooms, network access in dorm lounges, online registration, online administrative functions (other than registration), remote student-access to Web through college's connection.

CAMPUS LIFE

Activities: Choral groups, concert band, dance, drama/theater, jazz band, literary magazine, marching band, music ensembles, musical theater, pep band, radio station, student government, student newspaper, student-run film society, symphony orchestra, yearbook. **Organizations:** 100 registered organizations, 15 honor societies. **Athletics (Intercollegiate):** *Men:* Baseball, basketball, cross-country, diving, football, golf, lacrosse, soccer, swimming, tennis, track/field (indoor), track/field (outdoor). *Women:* Basketball, cross-country, diving, field hockey, lacrosse, soccer, softball, swimming, tennis, track/field (indoor), track/field (outdoor), volleyball. Environmental Initiatives: Reusable coffee mugs. Buy locally grown, seasonal produce as well as baked goods, dairy, eggs, and other food items that are locally produced. Recently started purchasing biodegradable containers and cutlery made from sustainable crops such as sugar cane stalks and corn. Have a longstanding and comprehensive recycling policy, which includes not only the usual paper etc. but also recycling computers (through Apple) and recycling yard waste (to use as mulch). Building debris is recycled wherever possible. Parking blocks are made of recycled materials.

ADMISSIONS

Freshman Academic Profile: 27% in top 10% of high school class, 61% in top 25% of high school class, 92% in top 50% of high school class. 73% from public high schools. SAT Math middle 50% range 560–650. SAT Critical Reading middle 50% range 540–670. SAT Writing middle 50% range 550–650. ACT middle 50% range 23–29. TOEFL required of all international applicants, minimum paper TOEFL 550, minimum computer TOEFL 213. **Basis for Candidate Selection:** *Very important factors considered include:* Academic GPA, class rank, rigor of secondary school record. *Important factors considered include:* Application essay, character/personal qualities, recommendation(s), standardized test scores, talent/ability. *Other factors considered include:* Alumni/ae relation, extracurricular activities, geographical residence, interview, racial/ethnic status, state residency, volunteer work, work experience. **Freshman Admission Requirements:** High school diploma is required, and GED is accepted. *Academic units required:* 4 English, 3 math, 3 science, 2 foreign language, 3 social studies, 2 academic electives. *Academic units recommended:* 4 math, 4 science, 3 foreign language, 4 social studies. **Freshman Admission Statistics:** 2,218 applied, 91% admitted, 25% enrolled. **Transfer Admission Requirements:** High school transcript, college transcript(s), essay or personal statement, standardized test score, statement of good standing from prior institution(s). Minimum college GPA of 2.5 required. Lowest grade transferable C. **General Admission Information:** Application fee $40. Early decision application deadline 12/1. Regular application deadline 2/15. Regular notification 4/1. Non-fall registration accepted. Admission may be deferred for a maximum of 2 semesters.

COSTS AND FINANCIAL AID

Comprehensive fee $40,372. **Required Forms and Deadlines:** FAFSA, institution's own financial aid form, CSS/Financial Aid PROFILE. Financial aid filing deadline 9/1. **Notification of Awards:** Applicants will be notified of awards on or about 4/1. **Types of Aid:** *Need-based scholarships/grants:* Pell, SEOG, state scholarships/grants, private scholarships, the school's own gift aid.

Loans: Direct Subsidized Stafford, Direct Unsubsidized Stafford, Direct PLUS, Federal Perkins, college/university loans from institutional funds. **Student Employment:** Federal Work-Study Program available. Institutional employment available. **Financial Aid Statistics:** 58% freshmen, 55% undergrads receive need-based scholarship or grant aid. 59% freshmen, 55% undergrads receive need-based self-help aid. 100% freshmen, 100% undergrads receive any aid.

COLLINS COLLEGE

1140 South Priest Drive, Tempe, AZ 85281
Phone: 480-966-3000 **E-mail:** jen@alcollins.com
Fax: 480-966-2599 **Website:** www.collinscollege.edu/princeton/

This is a private school.

RATINGS
Admissions Selectivity Rating: 60*   **Fire Safety Rating:** 60*   **Green Rating:** 60*

STUDENTS AND FACULTY
Faculty: Student/faculty ratio 24:1. 57 full-time faculty.

ACADEMICS
Degrees: Associate, bachelor's, certificate. **Academic Requirements:** Arts/fine arts, computer literacy. **Special Study Options:** Honors program.

FACILITIES
Housing: Apartments for married students, apartments for single students. **Special Academic Facilities/Equipment:** Media studio, production center, library, student store, photo darkroom. **Computers:** 45% of public computers are PCs, 50% of public computers are Macs, 5% of public computers are UNIX.

ADMISSIONS
Basis for Candidate Selection: *Other factors considered include:* Application essay, rigor of secondary school record. **Freshman Admission Requirements:** High school diploma is required, and GED is accepted. **Transfer Admission Requirements:** High school transcript, college transcript(s), essay or personal statement. **General Admission Information:** Application fee $100. Nonfall registration accepted. Common Application not accepted.

COSTS AND FINANCIAL AID
Required fees $100. **Required Forms and Deadlines:** FAFSA, SEOG Federal Stafford and UNSUB CWS. **Types of Aid:** *Need-based scholarships/grants:* Pell, SEOG. *Loans:* FFEL Subsidized Stafford, FFEL Unsubsidized Stafford, FFEL PLUS, Sallie Mae.

COLORADO CHRISTIAN UNIVERSITY

8787 West Alameda Avenue, Lakewood, CO 80226
Phone: 303-963-3200 **E-mail:** ccuadmissions@ccu.edu **CEEB Code:** 4659
Fax: 303-963-3201 **Website:** www.ccu.edu **ACT Code:** 0523
Financial Aid Phone: 303-963-3230

This private school, affiliated with the Christian (Nondenominational) Church, was founded in 1914. It has a 26-acre campus.

RATINGS
Admissions Selectivity Rating: 81   **Fire Safety Rating:** 60*   **Green Rating:** 60*

STUDENTS AND FACULTY
Enrollment: 1,772. **Student Body:** 60% female, 40% male, 56% out-of-state. African American 4%, Asian 1%, Caucasian 77%, Hispanic 9%, Native American 1%. **Retention and Graduation:** 72% freshmen return for sophomore year. 34% freshmen graduate within 4 years. **Faculty:** Student/faculty ratio 21:1. 43 full-time faculty, 74% hold PhDs. 100% faculty teach undergrads.

ACADEMICS
Degrees: Associate, bachelor's, master's. **Academic Requirements:** Arts/fine arts, computer literacy, English (including composition), foreign languages, history, humanities, mathematics, philosophy, sciences (biological or physical), social science, biblical studies. **Classes:** Most classes have fewer than 10 students. Most lab/discussion sections have 10–19 students. **Majors with**

Highest Enrollment: Computer/information technology services administration and management, liberal arts and sciences/liberal studies, management information systems. **Disciplines with Highest Percentage of Degrees Awarded:** Business/marketing 37%, computer and information sciences 16%, education 14%, psychology 7%, theology and religious vocations 6%. **Special Study Options:** Accelerated program, cooperative education program, distance learning, double major, honors program, independent study, internships, student-designed major, study abroad, teacher certification program, weekend college, American Studies Program (Washington, DC), Host University for Institute for Family Studies, China Studies Program (various sites in China), Latin American Studies Program (Costa Rica), Los Angeles Film Studies Center, Middle East Studies (Cairo, Egypt), Oxford Honors Program (University of Oxford, England), Russian Studies Program (various sites in Russia), Summer Institute of Journalism (Washington, DC).

FACILITIES
Housing: Coed dorms, men's dorms, women's dorms, apartments for single students, special housing for disabled students, theme housing. **Special Academic Facilities/Equipment:** Music recording studio, electron microscope. **Computers:** 99% of public computers are PCs, 1% of public computers are Macs, network access in dorm rooms, network access in dorm lounges, online registration, online administrative functions (other than registration), remote student-access to Web through college's connection.

CAMPUS LIFE
Activities: Choral groups, concert band, drama/theater, jazz band, literary magazine, music ensembles, musical theater, student government, student newspaper, symphony orchestra. **Organizations:** 21 registered organizations, 3 honor societies, 14 religious organizations. **Athletics (Intercollegiate):** *Men:* Basketball, cross-country, golf, soccer, tennis. *Women:* Basketball, cross-country, soccer, tennis, volleyball.

ADMISSIONS
Freshman Academic Profile: 22% in top 10% of high school class, 46% in top 25% of high school class, 79% in top 50% of high school class. SAT Math middle 50% range 480–590. SAT Critical Reading middle 50% range 510–630. ACT middle 50% range 20–26. TOEFL required of all international applicants, minimum paper TOEFL 500, minimum computer TOEFL 150. **Basis for Candidate Selection:** *Very important factors considered include:* Application essay, character/personal qualities, first generation, religious affiliation/commitment, rigor of secondary school record, standardized test scores, talent/ability. *Important factors considered include:* Academic GPA, class rank, extracurricular activities, level of applicant's interest, racial/ethnic status, recommendation(s), volunteer work. *Other factors considered include:* Alumni/ae relation, interview, work experience. **Freshman Admission Requirements:** High school diploma is required, and GED is accepted. *Academic units recommended:* 4 English, 3 math, 3 science (2 science labs), 3 foreign language, 1 social studies, 2 history, 1 computer science. **Freshman Admission Statistics:** 946 applied, 77% admitted, 33% enrolled. **Transfer Admission Requirements:** College transcript(s), essay or personal statement, statement of good standing from prior institution(s). Minimum college GPA of 2.0 required. Lowest grade transferable C. **General Admission Information:** Application fee $50. Regular application deadline 8/21. Regular notification is rolling. Nonfall registration accepted. Admission may be deferred for a maximum of 1 year. Common Application accepted. Credit and/or placement offered for CEEB Advanced Placement tests.

COSTS AND FINANCIAL AID
Annual tuition $18,850. Room and board $6,682. Required fees $150. Average book expense $1,188. **Required Forms and Deadlines:** FAFSA. **Notification of Awards:** Applicants will be notified of awards on or about 4/1. **Types of Aid:** *Need-based scholarships/grants:* Pell, SEOG, private scholarships, the school's own gift aid. *Loans:* FFEL Subsidized Stafford, FFEL Unsubsidized Stafford, FFEL PLUS, Federal Perkins. **Student Employment:** Federal Work-Study Program available. Institutional employment available. Off-campus job opportunities are good. **Financial Aid Statistics:** 66% freshmen, 57% undergrads receive need-based scholarship or grant aid. 67% freshmen, 62% undergrads receive need-based self-help aid. 10 freshmen, 36 undergrads receive athletic scholarships.

COLORADO COLLEGE

14 East Cache la Poudre Street, Colorado Springs, CO 80903
Phone: 719-389-6344 **E-mail:** admission@coloradocollege.edu **CEEB Code:** 4072
Fax: 719-389-6816 **Website:** www.coloradocollege.edu **ACT Code:** 0498
Financial Aid Phone: 719-389-6651

This private school was founded in 1874. It has a 90-acre campus.

RATINGS
Admissions Selectivity Rating: 95   **Fire Safety Rating:** 60*   **Green Rating:** 97

STUDENTS AND FACULTY
Enrollment: 1,939. **Student Body:** 54% female, 46% male, 73% out-of-state, 2% international (26 countries represented). African American 2%, Asian 4%, Caucasian 79%, Hispanic 7%, Native American 1%. **Retention and Graduation:** 94% freshmen return for sophomore year. 77% freshmen graduate within 4 years. **Faculty:** Student/faculty ratio 10:1. 158 full-time faculty, 97% hold PhDs. 100% faculty teach undergrads.

ACADEMICS
Degrees: Bachelor's, master's. **Academic Requirements:** Foreign languages, humanities, sciences (biological or physical), social science. **Classes:** Most classes have 10–19 students. **Majors with Highest Enrollment:** Biology/biological sciences, economics, English language and literature. **Disciplines with Highest Percentage of Degrees Awarded:** Social sciences 32%, biological/life sciences 10%, English 10%, visual and performing arts 7%, philosophy and religious studies 6%, physical sciences 6%, psychology 6%. **Special Study Options:** Double major, English as a second language (ESL), independent study, internships, liberal arts/career combination, student-designed major, study abroad, teacher certification program.

FACILITIES
Housing: Coed dorms, men's dorms, women's dorms, apartments for single students, special housing for international students, fraternity/sorority housing, theme housing (synergy, interfaith, other choices, living and learning community). **Special Academic Facilities/Equipment:** Electronic music studio, telescope dome, multimedia computer laboratory, Balinese orchestras, Colorado electronic music studio, observatory, extensive herbarium collection, 4 greenhouses, environmental science van equipped for field research, fourier transform nuclear magnetic resonance spectrometer, Packard Hall (300-seat concert/lecture hall), photography darkrooms, Armstrong Theatre (740-seat proscenium theater), Armstrong 32 (100-seat experimental theater), 4 dance studios with Marley, variable speed CD players, drama computer lab, petrographic microscopes, X-ray diffractometer, sedimentology lab, El Pomar Sports Center, metabolic equipment (COSMED Quark PFT Ergo), hydrostatic weighing equipment, cadaver study in sports science, scanning electron microscope, transmission electron microscope. **Computers:** 50% of classrooms are wired, 98% of classrooms are wireless, 84% of public computers are PCs, 16% of public computers are Macs, network access in dorm rooms, network access in dorm lounges, online registration, online administrative functions (other than registration), remote student-access to Web through college's connection.

CAMPUS LIFE
Activities: Choral groups, concert band, dance, drama/theater, jazz band, literary magazine, music ensembles, radio station, student government, student newspaper, student-run film society, yearbook. **Organizations:** 92 registered organizations, 10 honor societies, 19 religious organizations. 3 fraternities (9% men join), 3 sororities (14% women join). **Athletics (Intercollegiate):** *Men:* Basketball, cross-country, diving, football, ice hockey, lacrosse, soccer, swimming, tennis, track/field (outdoor). *Women:* Basketball, cross-country, diving, lacrosse, soccer, softball, swimming, tennis, track/field (outdoor), volleyball. Environmental Initiatives: Brendle Group Environmental Inventory and Presidential Advisory Council on Sustainability leading to official college commitment on carbon neutrality. Joint Wind Power Generation Project with several Colorado Colleges and Universities. College radio station will become the first National Public Radio station housed in an Earthship building and completely powered by renewable energy.

ADMISSIONS
Freshman Academic Profile: 66% in top 10% of high school class, 92% in top 25% of high school class, 98% in top 50% of high school class. 58% from public high schools. SAT Math middle 50% range 620–690. SAT Critical Reading middle 50% range 610–700. SAT Writing middle 50% range 600–700. ACT middle 50% range 27–31. TOEFL required of all international applicants, minimum paper TOEFL 550, minimum computer TOEFL 213. **Basis for Candidate Selection:** *Very important factors considered include:* Rigor of secondary school record. *Important factors considered include:* Academic GPA, application essay, class rank, extracurricular activities, interview, recommendation(s), standardized test scores. *Other factors considered include:* Alumni/ae relation, character/personal qualities, first generation, level of applicant's interest, racial/ethnic status, religious affiliation/commitment, talent/ability, volunteer work, work experience. **Freshman Admission Requirements:** High school diploma or equivalent is not required. *Academic units required:* 4 English. *Academic units recommended:* 4 English. **Freshman Admission Statistics:** 4,386 applied, 34% admitted, 33% enrolled. **Transfer Admission Requirements:** High school transcript, college transcript(s), essay or personal statement, standardized test score, statement of good standing from prior institution(s). Lowest grade transferable C. **General Admission Information:** Application fee $50. Early decision application deadline 11/15. Regular application deadline 1/15. Regular notification 4/1. Nonfall registration accepted. Admission may be deferred for a maximum of 1 year. Credit and/or placement offered for CEEB Advanced Placement tests.

COSTS AND FINANCIAL AID
Annual tuition $33,972. Room and board $8,498. Average book expense $936. **Required Forms and Deadlines:** FAFSA, CSS/Financial Aid PROFILE, Noncustodial PROFILE, Federal 1040 parent and student tax returns and parent W-2 forms. Financial aid filing deadline 2/15. **Notification of Awards:** Applicants will be notified of awards on or about 3/20. **Types of Aid:** *Need-based scholarships/grants:* Pell, SEOG, state scholarships/grants, private scholarships, the school's own gift aid. *Loans:* FFEL Subsidized Stafford, FFEL Unsubsidized Stafford, FFEL PLUS, Federal Perkins. **Student Employment:** Federal Work-Study Program available. Institutional employment available. Off-campus job opportunities are good. **Financial Aid Statistics:** 33% freshmen, 38% undergrads receive need-based scholarship or grant aid. 30% freshmen, 35% undergrads receive need-based self-help aid. 12 freshmen, 36 undergrads receive athletic scholarships.

COLORADO MOUNTAIN COLLEGE— ALPINE CAMPUS

Admissions Office, 1330 Bob Adams Drive, Steamboat Springs, CO 80487
Phone: 970-870-4417 **E-mail:** joinus@coloradomtn.edu **CEEB Code:** 4140
Fax: 970-947-8324 **Website:** www.coloradomtn.edu **ACT Code:** 0499
Financial Aid Phone: 800-621-8559

This public school was founded in 1967.

RATINGS
Admissions Selectivity Rating: 60*   **Fire Safety Rating:** 60*   **Green Rating:** 60*

STUDENTS AND FACULTY
Enrollment: 1,293. **Student Body:** African American 1%, Asian 1%, Caucasian 88%, Hispanic 3%, Native American 1%. **Faculty:** Student/faculty ratio 13:1. 18 full-time faculty, 17% hold PhDs. 100% faculty teach undergrads.

ACADEMICS
Degrees: Associate, certificate. **Academic Requirements:** Arts/fine arts, computer literacy, English (including composition), humanities, mathematics, sciences (biological or physical), social science. **Special Study Options:** Distance learning, dual enrollment, honors program, independent study, internships, liberal arts/career combination, study abroad.

FACILITIES
Housing: Coed dorms. **Computers:** Network access in dorm rooms.

CAMPUS LIFE
Activities: Dance, drama/theater, student government. **Organizations:** 1 honor society. **Athletics (Intercollegiate):** *Men:* Skiing (downhill/alpine), skiing (nordic/cross-country), soccer. *Women:* Skiing (downhill/alpine), skiing (nordic/cross-country), soccer.

ADMISSIONS
Freshman Academic Profile: TOEFL required of all international applicants, minimum paper TOEFL 500, minimum computer TOEFL 173. **Basis for Candidate Selection:** *Factors considered include:* Class rank, rigor of secondary school record, standardized test scores. **Freshman Admission Requirements:** High school diploma or equivalent is not required. **Freshman**

Admission Statistics: 374 applied, 100% admitted, 57% enrolled. **Transfer Admission Requirements:** Lowest grade transferable C. **General Admission Information:** Regular notification is rolling. Nonfall registration accepted. Admission may be deferred for a maximum of 1 year. Common Application not accepted. Credit offered for CEEB Advanced Placement tests.

COSTS AND FINANCIAL AID

Annual in-state tuition $960. Out-of-state tuition $5,160. Room & board $5,000. Required fees $180. Average book expense $550. **Required Forms and Deadlines:** FAFSA. Financial aid filing deadline 3/31. **Notification of Awards:** Applicants will be notified of awards on or about 4/15. **Types of Aid:** *Need-based scholarships/grants:* Pell, SEOG, state scholarships/grants, private scholarships. *Loans:* FFEL Subsidized Stafford, FFEL Unsubsidized Stafford, FFEL PLUS. **Student Employment:** Federal Work-Study Program available. Institutional employment available. Off-campus job opportunities are excellent.

COLORADO MOUNTAIN COLLEGE— SPRING VALLEY

Admissions Office, 3000 County Road 114, Glenwood Springs, CO 81602
Phone: 970-947-8276 **E-mail:** joinus@coloradomtn.edu **CEEB Code:** 4112
Fax: 970-947-8324 **Website:** www.coloradomtn.edu **ACT Code:** 0501
Financial Aid Phone: 800-621-8559

This is a public school.

RATINGS

Admissions Selectivity Rating: 60* **Fire Safety Rating:** 60* **Green Rating:** 60*

STUDENTS AND FACULTY

Enrollment: 827. **Student Body:** 15% out-of-state. Caucasian 84%, Hispanic 4%. **Faculty:** Student/faculty ratio 13:1. 24 full-time faculty, 25% hold PhDs. 100% faculty teach undergrads.

ACADEMICS

Degrees: Associate, certificate. **Academic Requirements:** Arts/fine arts, computer literacy, humanities, mathematics, philosophy, sciences (biological or physical), social science. **Special Study Options:** Cooperative education program, distance learning, dual enrollment, internships, liberal arts/career combination, study abroad.

FACILITIES

Housing: Coed dorms. **Special Academic Facilities/Equipment:** Vet tech farm, photo studio, graphic design lab. **Computers:** Network access in dorm rooms.

CAMPUS LIFE

Activities: Dance, drama/theater, student government. **Organizations:** 10 registered organizations, 1 honor society. **Athletics (Intercollegiate):** *Men:* Skiing (downhill/alpine), skiing (nordic/cross-country), soccer. *Women:* Skiing (downhill/alpine), skiing (nordic/cross-country), soccer.

ADMISSIONS

Freshman Academic Profile: TOEFL required of all international applicants, minimum paper TOEFL 500, minimum computer TOEFL 173. **Basis for Candidate Selection:** *Factors considered include:* Class rank, rigor of secondary school record, standardized test scores. **Freshman Admission Requirements:** High school diploma or equivalent is not required. **Freshman Admission Statistics:** 557 applied, 100% admitted, 71% enrolled. **Transfer Admission Requirements:** Lowest grade transferable C. **General Admission Information:** Regular notification is rolling. Nonfall registration accepted. Admission may be deferred for a maximum of 1 year. Common Application not accepted. Credit offered for CEEB Advanced Placement tests.

COSTS AND FINANCIAL AID

Annual in-state tuition $960. Out-of-state tuition $5,160. Room & board $5,000. Required fees $130. Average book expense $550. **Required Forms and Deadlines:** FAFSA. Financial aid filing deadline 3/31. **Notification of Awards:** Applicants will be notified of awards on or about 4/15. **Types of Aid:** *Need-based scholarships/grants:* Pell, SEOG, state scholarships/grants, private scholarships. *Loans:* FFEL Subsidized Stafford, FFEL Unsubsidized Stafford, FFEL PLUS. **Student Employment:** Federal Work-Study Program available. Institutional employment available. Off-campus job opportunities are excellent.

COLORADO MOUNTAIN COLLEGE— TIMBERLINE CAMPUS

Admissions Office, 901 South Highway 24, Leadville, CO 80461
Phone: 719-486-4291 **E-mail:** joinus@coloradomtn.edu **CEEB Code:** 4113
Fax: 970-947-8324 **Website:** www.coloradomtn.edu **ACT Code:** 0503
Financial Aid Phone: 970-491-6321

This is a public school.

RATINGS

Admissions Selectivity Rating: 60* **Fire Safety Rating:** 60* **Green Rating:** 60*

STUDENTS AND FACULTY

Enrollment: 100. **Student Body:** 30% out-of-state. Asian 1%, Caucasian 77%, Hispanic 14%. **Faculty:** Student/faculty ratio 13:1. 17 full-time faculty, 18% hold PhDs. 100% faculty teach undergrads.

ACADEMICS

Degrees: Associate, certificate. **Academic Requirements:** Arts/fine arts, computer literacy, English (including composition), humanities, mathematics, sciences (biological or physical), social science. **Special Study Options:** Cooperative education program, distance learning, dual enrollment, internships, liberal arts/career combination, study abroad.

FACILITIES

Housing: Coed dorms. **Special Academic Facilities/Equipment:** Greenhouse, lab-ski trails for labs. **Computers:** Network access in dorm rooms.

CAMPUS LIFE

Athletics (Intercollegiate): *Men:* Skiing (downhill/alpine), skiing (nordic/cross-country). *Women:* Skiing (downhill/alpine), skiing (nordic/cross-country).

ADMISSIONS

Freshman Academic Profile: TOEFL required of all international applicants, minimum computer TOEFL 173. **Basis for Candidate Selection:** *Factors considered include:* Class rank, rigor of secondary school record, standardized test scores. **Freshman Admission Requirements:** High school diploma or equivalent is not required. **Freshman Admission Statistics:** 202 applied, 100% admitted, 63% enrolled. **Transfer Admission Requirements:** Lowest grade transferable C. **General Admission Information:** Regular notification is rolling. Nonfall registration accepted. Admission may be deferred for a maximum of 1 year. Common Application not accepted. Credit offered for CEEB Advanced Placement tests.

COSTS AND FINANCIAL AID

Annual in-state tuition $960. Out-of-state tuition $5,160. Room & board $5,000. Required fees $180. Average book expense $550. **Required Forms and Deadlines:** FAFSA. Financial aid filing deadline 3/31. **Notification of Awards:** Applicants will be notified of awards on or about 4/15. **Types of Aid:** *Need-based scholarships/grants:* Pell, SEOG, state scholarships/grants, private scholarships. *Loans:* FFEL Subsidized Stafford, FFEL Unsubsidized Stafford, FFEL PLUS. **Student Employment:** Federal Work-Study Program available. Institutional employment available. Off-campus job opportunities are good. **Financial Aid Phone:** 800-621-8559.

COLORADO SCHOOL OF MINES

Weaver Towers, 1811 Elm Street, Golden, CO 80401-1842
Phone: 303-273-3220 **E-mail:** admit@mines.edu **CEEB Code:** 4073
Fax: 303-273-3509 **Website:** www.mines.edu **ACT Code:** 0500
Financial Aid Phone: 303-273-3301

This public school was founded in 1874. It has a 373-acre campus.

RATINGS

Admissions Selectivity Rating: 89 **Fire Safety Rating:** 60* **Green Rating:** 60*

STUDENTS AND FACULTY

Enrollment: 3,209. **Student Body:** 22% female, 78% male, 22% out-of-state, 4% international (62 countries represented). African American 1%, Asian 5%, Caucasian 75%, Hispanic 6%, Native American 1%. **Retention and Graduation:** 84% freshmen return for sophomore year. 27% freshmen graduate within 4 years. 14% grads go on to further study within 1 year. 4% grads pursue arts and sciences degrees. 2% grads pursue business degrees. 1% grads pursue law degrees. 1% grads pursue medical degrees. **Faculty:** Student/faculty ratio 15:1. 210 full-time faculty, 98% hold PhDs. 86% faculty teach undergrads.

ACADEMICS

Degrees: Bachelor's, doctoral, master's, post-bachelor's certificate. **Academic Requirements:** Computer literacy, English (including composition), humanities, mathematics, sciences (biological or physical), social science. **Classes:** Most classes have 10–19 students. Most lab/discussion sections have 20–29 students. **Majors with Highest Enrollment:** Chemical engineering, mathematics, mechanical engineering. **Disciplines with Highest Percentage of Degrees Awarded:** Engineering 73%, physical sciences 14%, computer and information sciences 8%, business/marketing 4%, mathematics 1%. **Special Study Options:** Accelerated program, cooperative education program, double major, dual enrollment, English as a second language (ESL), honors program, independent study, internships, study abroad.

FACILITIES

Housing: Coed dorms, men's dorms, apartments for married students, apartments for single students, fraternity/sorority housing. **Special Academic Facilities/Equipment:** Geology museum, experimental mine, field camps, geophysical lab, energy research institute, other research institutes. **Computers:** 99% of public computers are PCs, 1% of public computers are Macs, network access in dorm rooms, network access in dorm lounges, online registration, online administrative functions (other than registration), remote student-access to Web through college's connection.

CAMPUS LIFE

Activities: Choral groups, concert band, drama/theater, jazz band, literary magazine, marching band, music ensembles, musical theater, student government, student newspaper, symphony orchestra, yearbook. **Organizations:** 126 registered organizations, 7 honor societies, 5 religious organizations. 7 fraternities (20% men join), 4 sororities (20% women join). **Athletics (Intercollegiate):** *Men:* Baseball, basketball, cross-country, diving, football, golf, soccer, swimming, tennis, track/field (outdoor), wrestling. *Women:* Basketball, cross-country, diving, golf, softball, swimming, track/field (outdoor), volleyball.

ADMISSIONS

. **Freshman Academic Profile:** 49% in top 10% of high school class, 82% in top 25% of high school class, 100% in top 50% of high school class. 90% from public high schools. SAT Math middle 50% range 600–690. SAT Critical Reading middle 50% range 540–640. ACT middle 50% range 25–30. TOEFL required of all international applicants, minimum paper TOEFL 550. **Basis for Candidate Selection:** *Very important factors considered include:* Class rank, rigor of secondary school record. *Important factors considered include:* Academic GPA, standardized test scores. *Other factors considered include:* Application essay, extracurricular activities, recommendation(s), talent/ability. **Freshman Admission Requirements:** High school diploma is required, and GED is accepted. *Academic units required:* 4 English, 4 math, 3 science (3 science labs), 2 social studies, 3 academic electives. *Academic units recommended:* 2 foreign language, 2 history. **Freshman Admission Statistics:** 3,142 applied, 84% admitted, 30% enrolled. **Transfer Admission Requirements:** High school transcript, college transcript(s), statement of good standing from prior institution(s). Minimum college GPA of 2.7 required. Lowest grade transferable C. **General Admission Information:** Application fee $45. Regular application deadline 6/1. Regular notification is rolling. Nonfall registration accepted. Admission may be deferred for a maximum of 1 year. Credit and/or placement offered for CEEB Advanced Placement tests.

COSTS AND FINANCIAL AID

Annual in-state tuition $8,088. Out-of-state tuition $20,624. Room & board $6,880. Required fees $922. Average book expense $1,300. **Required Forms and Deadlines:** FAFSA. Financial aid filing deadline 2/15. **Notification of Awards:** Applicants will be notified of awards on or about 3/15. **Types of Aid:** *Need-based scholarships/grants:* Pell, SEOG, state scholarships/grants, private scholarships, the school's own gift aid. *Loans:* FFEL Subsidized Stafford, FFEL Unsubsidized Stafford, FFEL PLUS, Federal Perkins. **Student Employment:** Federal Work-Study Program available. Institutional employment available. Off-campus job opportunities are good. **Financial Aid Statistics:** 59% freshmen, 59% undergrads receive need-based scholarship or grant aid. 64% freshmen, 66% undergrads receive need-based self-help aid. 97 freshmen, 430 undergrads receive athletic scholarships. Highest amount earned per year from on-campus jobs $1,000.

COLORADO STATE UNIVERSITY

Spruce Hall, Fort Collins, CO 80523-8020
Phone: 970-491-6909 **E-mail:** admissions@colostate.edu **CEEB Code:** 4075
Fax: 970-491-7799 **Website:** www.welcome.colostate.edu **ACT Code:** 0504
Financial Aid Phone: 303-273-3301

This public school was founded in 1870. It has a 579-acre campus.

RATINGS

Admissions Selectivity Rating: 78   **Fire Safety Rating:** 72   **Green Rating:** 89

STUDENTS AND FACULTY

Enrollment: 20,385. **Student Body:** 52% female, 48% male, 18% out-of-state, 1% international (86 countries represented). African American 2%, Asian 3%, Caucasian 82%, Hispanic 6%, Native American 2%. **Retention and Graduation:** 82% freshmen return for sophomore year. 35% freshmen graduate within 4 years. **Faculty:** Student/faculty ratio 18:1. 856 full-time faculty, 99% hold PhDs. 100% faculty teach undergrads.

ACADEMICS

Degrees: Bachelor's, doctoral, first professional, master's. **Academic Requirements:** Arts/fine arts, English (including composition), history, humanities, mathematics, sciences (biological or physical), social science, health/wellness, critical thinking. **Classes:** Most classes have 20–29 students. Most lab/discussion sections have 20–29 students. **Majors with Highest Enrollment:** Construction engineering technology/technician, kinesiology and exercise science, psychology. **Disciplines with Highest Percentage of Degrees Awarded:** Business/marketing 16%, social sciences 9%, family and consumer sciences 8%, English 6%, engineering 6%, agriculture 6%, psychology 6%, biological/life sciences 6%, parks and recreation 6%, liberal arts/general studies 5%, visual and performing arts 5%. **Special Study Options:** Accelerated program, cooperative education program, cross-registration, distance learning, double major, dual enrollment, English as a second language (ESL), exchange student program (domestic), honors program, independent study, internships, liberal arts/career combination, study abroad, teacher certification program.

FACILITIES

Housing: Coed dorms, apartments for married students, apartments for single students, special housing for disabled students, non-college-owned fraternity/sorority housing is available, living-learning communities, special interest floors. **Special Academic Facilities/Equipment:** International poster collection, Gustafson Gallery (historic clothing), Curfman Gallery (art), student recreation center, ropes course. **Computers:** 5% of classrooms are wired, 81% of classrooms are wireless, 85% of public computers are PCs, 8% of public computers are Macs, 7% of public computers are UNIX, network access in dorm rooms, network access in dorm lounges, online registration, online administrative functions (other than registration), support for handheld computing, remote student-access to Web through college's connection.

CAMPUS LIFE

Activities: Choral groups, concert band, dance, drama/theater, jazz band, literary magazine, marching band, music ensembles, musical theater, opera, pep band, radio station, student government, student newspaper, symphony orchestra, television station, yearbook. **Organizations:** 330 registered organizations, 29 honor societies, 27 religious organizations. 20 fraternities (5% men join), 14 sororities (5% women join). **Athletics (Intercollegiate):** *Men:* Basketball, cross-country, football, golf, track/field (indoor), track/field (outdoor). *Women:* Basketball, cross-country, diving, golf, softball, swimming, track/field (indoor), track/field (outdoor), volleyball, water polo. Environmental Initiatives: Talloires Declaration signatory, 2001. An agreement has been signed with a third-party developer to install wind turbines on the CSU-owned Maxwell Ranch near the Wyoming border. When completed it will be the largest wind development on University owned land. All university diesel vehicles operate on biodiesel.

ADMISSIONS

Freshman Academic Profile: 19% in top 10% of high school class, 48% in top 25% of high school class, 86% in top 50% of high school class. SAT Math middle 50% range 510–630. SAT Critical Reading middle 50% range 490–610. SAT Writing middle 50% range 480–590. ACT middle 50% range 22–26. TOEFL required of all international applicants, minimum paper TOEFL 525, minimum computer TOEFL 197. **Basis for Candidate Selection:** *Very important factors considered include:* Academic GPA, application essay, class rank, recommendation(s), rigor of secondary school record, standardized test scores. *Other factors considered include:* Character/personal qualities, extracurricular activities, first generation, geographical residence, interview, level of applicant's interest, racial/ethnic status, state residency, talent/ability, volunteer work, work experience. **Freshman Admission Requirements:** High school diploma is required, and GED is accepted. *Academic units required:* 4 English, 3 math, 2 science (1 science lab), 2 social studies, 3 academic electives, 1 social science, 1 natural science. Engineering majors and individual colleges have additional requirements. *Academic units recommended:* 4 English, 4 math, 3 science (1 science lab), 2 foreign language, 3 social studies, 2 academic electives, 1 social science, 1 natural science. Engineering majors and individual colleges have additional recommendations. **Freshman Admission Statistics:** 11,310 applied, 86% admitted, 42% enrolled. **Transfer Admission Requirements:** College transcript(s), statement of good standing from prior institution(s). Minimum college GPA of 2.0 required. Lowest grade transferable C. **General Admission Information:** Application fee $50. Regular application deadline 7/1. Regular notification within 3 to 4 weeks of completed application. Nonfall registration accepted. Credit and/or placement offered for CEEB Advanced Placement tests.

COSTS AND FINANCIAL AID

Annual in-state tuition $4,040. Annual out-of-state tuition $17,480. Room and board $7,382. Required fees $1,379. Average book expense $990. **Required Forms and Deadlines:** FAFSA. Financial aid filing deadline 3/1. **Notification of Awards:** Applicants will be notified of awards on a rolling basis beginning on or about 3/1. **Types of Aid:** *Need-based scholarships/grants:* Pell, SEOG, state scholarships/grants, private scholarships, the school's own gift aid. *Loans:* Direct Subsidized Stafford, Direct Unsubsidized Stafford, Direct PLUS, Federal Perkins, college/university loans from institutional funds, alternative loans. **Student Employment:** Federal Work-Study Program available. Institutional employment available. Off-campus job opportunities are excellent. **Financial Aid Statistics:** 27% freshmen, 26% undergrads receive need-based scholarship or grant aid. 25% freshmen, 32% undergrads receive need-based self-help aid. 53 freshmen, 276 undergrads receive athletic scholarships. 64% freshmen, 64% undergrads receive any aid.

See page 1124.

COLORADO STATE UNIVERSITY—PUEBLO

Admissions, 2200 Bonforte Boulevard, Pueblo, CO 81001
Phone: 719-549-2461 **E-mail:** info@colostate-pueblo.edu **CEEB Code:** 4611
Fax: 719-549-2419 **Website:** www.colostate-pueblo.edu **ACT Code:** 0524
Financial Aid Phone: 719-549-2178

This public school was founded in 1933. It has a 275-acre campus.

RATINGS
Admissions Selectivity Rating: 63   **Fire Safety Rating:** 64   **Green Rating:** 60*

STUDENTS AND FACULTY
Enrollment: 4,104. **Student Body:** 59% female, 41% male, 3% out-of-state, 3% international (27 countries represented). African American 5%, Asian 2%, Caucasian 57%, Hispanic 24%, Native American 2%. **Retention and Graduation:** 65% freshmen return for sophomore year. 8% freshmen graduate within 4 years. **Faculty:** Student/faculty ratio 18:1. 168 full-time faculty, 58% hold PhDs. 100% faculty teach undergrads.

ACADEMICS
Degrees: Bachelor's, master's. **Academic Requirements:** English (including composition), foreign languages, history, mathematics, sciences (biological or physical), social science. **Classes:** Most classes have 20–29 students. Most lab/discussion sections have 20–29 students. **Majors with Highest Enrollment:** Business, management, marketing, and related support services; social sciences; sociology. **Disciplines with Highest Percentage of Degrees Awarded:** Social sciences 21%, business/marketing 14%, health professions and related sciences 10%, communications/journalism 6%, liberal arts/general studies 6%. **Special Study Options:** Accelerated program, cooperative education program, distance learning, double major, dual enrollment, English as a Second Language (ESL), external degree program, independent study, internships, liberal arts/career combination, study abroad, teacher certification program.

FACILITIES
Housing: Coed dorms, apartments for single students, special housing for disabled students. **Special Academic Facilities/Equipment:** Recital hall,

public television and radio station. **Computers:** 50% of classrooms are wireless, 95% of public computers are PCs, 5% of public computers are Macs, network access in dorm rooms, online registration, online administrative functions (other than registration), remote student-access to Web through college's connection.

CAMPUS LIFE
Activities: Choral groups, concert band, dance, jazz band, literary magazine, music ensembles, pep band, radio station, student government, student newspaper, symphony orchestra, television station. **Organizations:** 24 registered organizations, 6 honor societies, 4 religious organizations. 2 fraternities (2% men join), 1 sorority (1% women join). **Athletics (Intercollegiate): Men:** Baseball, basketball, golf, soccer, tennis. *Women:* Basketball, cross-country, golf, soccer, softball, tennis, volleyball.

ADMISSIONS
63 (out of 100). **Freshman Academic Profile:** 7% in top 25% of high school class, 32% in top 50% of high school class. 85% from public high schools. SAT SAT Math middle 50% range 410–530. SAT Critical Reading middle 50% range 400–510. ACT middle 50% range 18–23. TOEFL required of all international applicants, minimum paper TOEFL 500, minimum computer TOEFL 173. **Basis for Candidate Selection:** *Very important factors considered include:* Academic GPA, rigor of secondary school record, standardized test scores. *Important factors considered include:* Class rank. *Other factors considered include:* Application essay, character/personal qualities, interview, level of applicant's interest, racial/ethnic status, recommendation(s), talent/ability, volunteer work, work experience. **Freshman Admission Requirements:** High school diploma is required, and GED is accepted. *Academic units recommended:* 4 English, 3 math, 3 science (2 science labs), 2 foreign language, 2 social studies, 1 history. **Freshman Admission Statistics:** 1,698 applied, 96% admitted, 41% enrolled. **Transfer Admission Requirements:** College transcript(s). Minimum college GPA of 2.3 required. Lowest grade transferable C-. **General Admission Information:** Application fee $25. Regular application deadline 8/1. Regular notification as received. Nonfall registration accepted. Admission may be deferred for a maximum of 1 semester. Credit offered for CEEB Advanced Placement tests.

COSTS AND FINANCIAL AID
Annual in-state tuition $3,866. Annual out-of-state tuition $14,506. **Required Forms and Deadlines:** FAFSA. Financial aid filing deadline 3/1. **Notification of Awards:** Applicants will be notified of awards on a rolling basis beginning on or about 3/15. **Types of Aid:** *Need-based scholarships/grants:* Pell, SEOG, state scholarships/grants, private scholarships, the school's own gift aid, academic competitiveness grant and national SMART grant. *Loans:* FFEL Subsidized Stafford, FFEL Unsubsidized Stafford, FFEL PLUS, Federal Perkins. **Financial Aid Statistics:** 61% freshmen, 62% undergrads receive need-based scholarship or grant aid. 63% freshmen, 70% undergrads receive need-based self-help aid. 25 freshmen, 92 undergrads receive athletic scholarships. 81% freshmen, 86% undergrads receive any aid. Highest amount earned per year from on-campus jobs $8,000.

COLORADO TECHNICAL UNIVERSITY

4435 North Chestnut Street, Colorado Springs, CO 80907-3896
Phone: 719-598-0200 **E-mail:** cosadmissions@coloradotech.edu **CEEB Code:** 4133
Fax: 719-598-3740 **Website:** www.colotechu.edu **ACT Code:** 0515
Financial Aid Phone: 719-598-0200

This proprietary school was founded in 1965. It has a 13-acre campus.

RATINGS
Admissions Selectivity Rating: 60*   **Fire Safety Rating:** 60*   **Green Rating:** 60*

STUDENTS AND FACULTY
Enrollment: 1,261. **Student Body:** 1% international. African American 8%, Asian 4%, Caucasian 73%, Hispanic 6%. **Retention and Graduation:** 15% grads go on to further study within 1 year. 5% grads pursue arts and sciences degrees. 10% grads pursue business degrees. **Faculty:** Student/faculty ratio 25:1. 31 full-time faculty, 52% hold PhDs. 100% faculty teach undergrads.

ACADEMICS
Degrees: Associate, bachelor's, certificate, doctoral, master's. **Academic Requirements:** Computer literacy, mathematics, sciences (biological or physical). **Classes:** Most classes have 10–19 students. **Majors with Highest Enrollment:** Computer and information sciences, information technology, management information systems. **Disciplines with Highest Percentage of Degrees Awarded:** Business/marketing 36%, computer and information sciences 34%, engineering 25%, communication technologies 5%. **Special Study Options:** Accelerated program, double major, independent study,

internships, weekend college, 16.5-month MS degree programs, 2-year doctoral programs.

FACILITIES
Computers: 100% of public computers are PCs, 100% of public computers are UNIX, online administrative functions (other than registration), remote student-access to Web through college's connection.

CAMPUS LIFE
Activities: Student government. **Organizations:** 5 registered organizations, 1 honor society.

ADMISSIONS
Freshman Academic Profile: TOEFL required of all international applicants, minimum paper TOEFL 550. **Basis for Candidate Selection:** *Factors considered include:* Alumni/ae relation, character/personal qualities, class rank, interview, recommendation(s), rigor of secondary school record, standardized test scores, work experience. **Freshman Admission Requirements:** High school diploma is required, and GED is accepted. *Academic units required:* 1 English, 1 math, 1 science (1 science lab). *Academic units recommended:* 2 English, 2 math, 2 science (1 science lab). **Transfer Admission Requirements:** High school transcript, college transcript(s), statement of good standing from prior institution(s). Lowest grade transferable C. **General Admission Information:** Application fee $50. Regular application deadline 10/2. Regular notification is rolling. Nonfall registration accepted. Common Application not accepted. Credit and/or placement offered for CEEB Advanced Placement tests.

COSTS AND FINANCIAL AID
Comprehensive fee $7,020. Required fees $171. Average book expense $1,000. **Required Forms and Deadlines:** FAFSA, institution's own financial aid form, state aid form. **Notification of Awards:** Applicants will be notified of awards on a rolling basis beginning on or about 2/1. **Types of Aid:** *Need-based scholarships/grants:* Pell, SEOG, state scholarships/grants. *Loans:* FFEL Subsidized Stafford, FFEL Unsubsidized Stafford, FFEL PLUS, Federal Perkins. **Student Employment:** Federal Work-Study Program available. Institutional employment available. Off-campus job opportunities are excellent.

See page 1126.

COLUMBIA COLLEGE (MO)

1001 Rogers Street, Columbia, MO 65216
Phone: 573-875-7352 **E-mail:** admissions@ccis.edu **CEEB Code:** 6095
Fax: 573-875-7506 **Website:** www.ccis.edu **ACT Code:** 2276
Financial Aid Phone: 573-875-7390

This private school, affiliated with the Disciples of Christ Church, was founded in 1851. It has a 27-acre campus.

RATINGS
Admissions Selectivity Rating: 76   **Fire Safety Rating:** 60*   **Green Rating:** 60*

STUDENTS AND FACULTY
Enrollment: 983. **Student Body:** 61% female, 39% male, 13% out-of-state, 6% international (27 countries represented). African American 6%, Asian 1%, Caucasian 78%, Hispanic 3%, Native American 1%. **Retention and Graduation:** 61% freshmen return for sophomore year. 30% freshmen graduate within 4 years. **Faculty:** Student/faculty ratio 13:1. 58 full-time faculty, 83% hold PhDs. 100% faculty teach undergrads.

ACADEMICS
Degrees: Associate, bachelor's, master's, terminal. **Academic Requirements:** Computer literacy, English (including composition), history, humanities, mathematics, sciences (biological or physical), social science. Students required to complete a course in ethics prior to graduation. **Classes:** Most classes have 10–19 students. Most lab/discussion sections have 10–19 students. **Majors with Highest Enrollment:** Business administration/management; criminal justice/law enforcement administration. **Disciplines with Highest Percentage of Degrees Awarded:** Business/marketing 50%, security and protective services 13%, liberal arts/general studies 13%, psychology 10%, interdisciplinary studies 4%. **Special Study Options:** Accelerated program, cooperative education program, cross-registration, distance learning, double major, dual enrollment,

English as a second language (ESL), honor program, independent study, internships, student-designed major, study abroad, teacher certification program.

FACILITIES
Housing: Coed dorms, women's dorms, apartments for single students. **Special Academic Facilities/Equipment:** Most classrooms are multimedia with SmartBoards, new student commons building, arts center, Larson Gallery, Jane Froman Archive. **Computers:** 100% of classrooms are wireless, 92% of public computers are PCs, 8% of public computers are Macs, network access in dorm rooms, network access in dorm lounges, online registration, online administrative functions (other than registration), remote student-access to Web through college's connection.

CAMPUS LIFE
Activities: Choral groups, drama/theater, literary magazine, student government, student newspaper. **Organizations:** 30 registered organizations, 11 honor societies. **Athletics (Intercollegiate):** *Men:* Basketball, soccer. *Women:* Basketball, softball, volleyball.

ADMISSIONS
Freshman Academic Profile: 7% in top 10% of high school class, 28% in top 25% of high school class, 58% in top 50% of high school class. 90% from public high schools. SAT Math middle 50% range 485–600. SAT Critical Reading middle 50% range 485–580. ACT middle 50% range 20–25. TOEFL required of all international applicants, minimum paper TOEFL 500, minimum computer TOEFL 173. **Basis for Candidate Selection:** *Very important factors considered include:* Academic GPA, class rank, rigor of secondary school record, standardized test scores. *Other factors considered include:* Alumni/ae relation, application essay, character/personal qualities, extracurricular activities, first generation, geographical residence, interview, recommendation(s), religious affiliation/commitment, talent/ability, volunteer work. **Freshman Admission Requirements:** High school diploma is required, and GED is accepted. *Academic units required:* 4 English, 3 math, 2 social studies. *Academic units recommended:* 2 science (2 science labs). **Freshman Admission Statistics:** 796 applied, 60% admitted, 40% enrolled. **Transfer Admission Requirements:** College transcript(s). Minimum college GPA of 2.0 required. Lowest grade transferable C. **General Admission Information:** Application fee $25. Regular notification is rolling. Nonfall registration accepted. Admission may be deferred for a maximum of 1 year. Credit and/or placement offered for CEEB Advanced Placement tests.

COSTS AND FINANCIAL AID
Annual tuition $13,034. Room and board $5,320. Average book expense $720. **Required Forms and Deadlines:** FAFSA, institution's own financial aid form. Financial aid filing deadline 3/1. **Notification of Awards:** Applicants will be notified of awards on a rolling basis beginning on or about 3/1. **Types of Aid:** *Need-based scholarships/grants:* Pell, SEOG, state scholarships/grants, private scholarships, the school's own gift aid. *Loans:* Direct Subsidized Stafford, Direct Unsubsidized Stafford, Direct PLUS, Federal Perkins. **Financial Aid Statistics:** 56% freshmen, 37% undergrads receive need-based scholarship or grant aid. 51% freshmen, 46% undergrads receive need-based self-help aid. 9 freshmen, 65 undergrads receive athletic scholarships. 67% freshmen, 56% undergrads receive any aid.

COLUMBIA COLLEGE (SC)

1301 Columbia College Drive, Columbia, SC 29203
Phone: 803-786-3871 **E-mail:** admissions@colacoll.edu **CEEB Code:** 5117
Fax: 803-786-3674 **Website:** www.columbiacollegesc.edu **ACT Code:** 3850
Financial Aid Phone: 803-786-3612

This private school, affiliated with the Methodist Church, was founded in 1854. It has a 33-acre campus.

RATINGS
Admissions Selectivity Rating: 77   **Fire Safety Rating:** 78   **Green Rating:** 63

STUDENTS AND FACULTY
Enrollment: 1,130. **Student Body:** 98% female, 2% male, 6% out-of-state, 2% international (16 countries represented). African American 45%, Asian 1%, Caucasian 47%, Hispanic 2%. **Retention and Graduation:** 69% freshmen return for sophomore year. 39% freshmen graduate within 4 years. **Faculty:** Student/faculty ratio 12:1. 76 full-time faculty, 80% hold PhDs. 81% faculty teach undergrads.

ACADEMICS

Degrees: Bachelor's, master's, post-bachelor's certificate. **Academic Requirements:** Arts/fine arts, English (including composition), foreign languages, history, humanities, mathematics, sciences (biological or physical), social science, physical education, health promotion. **Classes:** Most classes have 10–19 students. **Majors with Highest Enrollment:** Business administration and management, psychology, speech-language pathology/pathologist. **Disciplines with Highest Percentage of Degrees Awarded:** Education 14%, public administration and social services 12%, business/marketing 9%, psychology 8%, visual and performing arts 8%, health professions and related sciences 8%, interdisciplinary studies 6%, biological/life sciences 6%, social sciences 6%. **Special Study Options:** Distance learning, double major, dual enrollment, honors program, independent study, internships, student-designed major, study abroad, teacher certification program.

FACILITIES

Housing: Women's dorms, leadership and honors program theme housing. **Special Academic Facilities/Equipment:** Language lab, Alumnae Hall, Barbara Bush Center for Science and Technology, Breed Leadership Center for Women. **Computers:** 20% of classrooms are wired, 50% of classrooms are wireless, 95% of public computers are PCs, 5% of public computers are Macs, network access in dorm rooms, online registration, online administrative functions (other than registration), support for handheld computing, remote student-access to Web through college's connection.

CAMPUS LIFE

Activities: Choral groups, concert band, dance, drama/theater, literary magazine, music ensembles, musical theater, opera, student government, student newspaper, yearbook. **Organizations:** 53 registered organizations, 10 honor societies, 7 religious organizations. **Women:** Basketball, soccer, tennis, volleyball. Environmental Initiatives: Student-sponsored and initiated recycling program.

ADMISSIONS

Freshman Academic Profile: 24% in top 10% of high school class, 54% in top 25% of high school class, 92% in top 50% of high school class. SAT Math middle 50% range 430–530. SAT Critical Reading middle 50% range 450–540. SAT Writing middle 50% range 430–540. ACT middle 50% range 18–23. TOEFL required of all international applicants, minimum paper TOEFL 550, minimum computer TOEFL 213. **Basis for Candidate Selection:** *Very important factors considered include:* Recommendation(s), rigor of secondary school record, standardized test scores. *Important factors considered include:* Character/personal qualities, class rank. *Other factors considered include:* Alumni/ae relation, application essay, extracurricular activities, talent/ability, volunteer work. **Freshman Admission Requirements:** High school diploma is required, and GED is accepted. *Academic units recommended:* 4 English, 3 math, 2 science (2 science labs), 2 foreign language, 2 social studies, 1 history, 2 academic electives. **Freshman Admission Statistics:** 1,077 applied, 82% admitted, 29% enrolled. **Transfer Admission Requirements:** High school transcript, college transcript(s), standardized test score, statement of good standing from prior institution(s). Minimum college GPA of 2.0 required. Lowest grade transferable C. **General Admission Information:** Application fee $25. Regular application deadline 8/1. Regular notification is rolling. Nonfall registration accepted. Admission may be deferred for a maximum of 1 year. Credit offered for CEEB Advanced Placement tests.

COSTS AND FINANCIAL AID

Annual tuition $18,864. Room & board $5,818. Required fees $350. Average book expense $800. **Required Forms and Deadlines:** FAFSA. Financial aid filing deadline 4/1. **Notification of Awards:** Applicants will be notified of awards on a rolling basis beginning on or about 3/1. **Types of Aid:** *Need-based scholarships/grants:* Pell, SEOG, state scholarships/grants, private scholarships, the school's own gift aid, United Negro College Fund. *Loans:* FFEL Subsidized Stafford, FFEL Unsubsidized Stafford, FFEL PLUS, Federal Perkins, state loans, signature student loan. **Financial Aid Statistics:** 75% freshmen, 74% undergrads receive need-based scholarship or grant aid. 62% freshmen, 64% undergrads receive need-based self-help aid. 9 freshmen, 37 undergrads receive athletic scholarships. 99% freshmen, 89% undergrads receive any aid. Highest amount earned per year from on-campus jobs $1,000.

COLUMBIA COLLEGE—CHICAGO (IL)

600 South Michigan Avenue, Chicago, IL 60605-1996
Phone: 312-344-7130 **E-mail:** admissions@colum.edu **CEEB Code:** 1135
Fax: 312-344-8024 **Website:** www.colum.edu **ACT Code:** 1002
Financial Aid Phone: 312-344-7140

This private school was founded in 1890.

RATINGS

Admissions Selectivity Rating: 67   **Fire Safety Rating:** 60*   **Green Rating:** 74

STUDENTS AND FACULTY

Enrollment: 10,671. **Student Body:** 50% female, 50% male, 31% out-of-state, 1% international (61 countries represented). African American 14%, Asian 3%, Caucasian 64%, Hispanic 9%. **Retention and Graduation:** 66% freshmen return for sophomore year. 26% freshmen graduate within 4 years. 9% grads go on to further study within 1 year. 10% grads pursue arts and sciences degrees. 1% grads pursue law degrees. 1% grads pursue medical degrees. **Faculty:** Student/faculty ratio 14:1. 328 full-time faculty. 100% faculty teach undergrads.

ACADEMICS

Degrees: Bachelor's, master's, post-bachelor's certificate, post-master's certificate. **Academic Requirements:** Arts/fine arts, computer literacy, English (including composition), history, humanities, mathematics, sciences (biological or physical), social science. **Classes:** Most classes have 10–19 students. **Majors with Highest Enrollment:** Arts management, cinematography and film/video production, fine/studio arts. **Disciplines with Highest Percentage of Degrees Awarded:** Visual and performing arts 43%, business/marketing 20%, liberal arts/general studies 6%, English 4%, interdisciplinary studies 1%. **Special Study Options:** Cooperative education program, distance learning, dual enrollment, English as a second language (ESL), independent study, internships, liberal arts/career combination, student-designed major, study abroad, teacher certification program.

FACILITIES

Housing: Coed dorms, student housing available at nearby colleges and universities. **Special Academic Facilities/Equipment:** Art galleries, Center for Black Music Research, contemporary photography museum, dance center. **Computers:** Network access in dorm lounges, online registration, online administrative functions (other than registration), remote student-access to Web through college's connection.

CAMPUS LIFE

Activities: Choral groups, concert band, dance, drama/theater, jazz band, literary magazine, music ensembles, musical theater, radio station, student government, student newspaper, student-run film society, television station. **Organizations:** 64 registered organizations.

ADMISSIONS

Freshman Academic Profile: 6% in top 10% of high school class, 21% in top 25% of high school class, 51% in top 50% of high school class. ACT middle 50% range 18–25. TOEFL required of all international applicants, minimum paper TOEFL 533, minimum computer TOEFL 200. **Freshman Admission Requirements:** High school diploma is required, and GED is accepted. **Freshman Admission Statistics:** 4,043 applied, 95% admitted, 52% enrolled. **Transfer Admission Requirements:** High school transcript, college transcript(s), Lowest grade transferable C. **General Admission Information:** Application fee $35. Regular notification is rolling basis. Nonfall registration accepted. Admission may be deferred for a maximum of 1 year. Credit and/or placement offered for CEEB Advanced Placement tests.

COSTS AND FINANCIAL AID

Annual tuition $16,328. Room & board $11,326. Required fees $515. Average book expense $1,300. **Required Forms and Deadlines:** FAFSA, institution's own financial aid form. Financial aid filing deadline 5/1. **Types of Aid:** *Need-based scholarships/grants:* Pell, SEOG, state scholarships/grants, private scholarships, the school's own gift aid. *Loans:* Direct Subsidized Stafford, Direct Unsubsidized Stafford, Direct PLUS. **Student Employment:** Federal Work-Study Program available. **Financial Aid Statistics:** 63% freshmen, 62% undergrads receive any aid.

See page 1128.

COLUMBIA COLLEGE—HOLLYWOOD

18618 Oxnard Street, Tarzana, CA 91356
Phone: 818-345-8414 **E-mail:** admissions@columbiacollege.edu **CEEB Code:** 7213
Fax: 818-345-9053 **Website:** www.columbiacollege.edu
Financial Aid Phone: 818-345-8414

This private school was founded in 1952.

RATINGS
Admissions Selectivity Rating: 60*   **Fire Safety Rating:** 60*   **Green Rating:** 60*

STUDENTS AND FACULTY
Enrollment: 150. **Student Body:** 31% female, 69% male, 10% international (24 countries represented). African American 9%, Asian 5%, Caucasian 60%, Hispanic 14%. **Retention and Graduation:** 47% freshmen return for sophomore year. 36% freshmen graduate within 4 years. 5% grads go on to further study within 1 year. **Faculty:** Student/faculty ratio 6:1. 100% faculty teach undergrads.

ACADEMICS
Degrees: Associate, bachelor's. **Academic Requirements:** Arts/fine arts, English (including composition), humanities, sciences (biological or physical), social science, film/cinema, television/video. **Majors with Highest Enrollment:** Cinematography and film/video production, film/cinema studies. **Special Study Options:** Accelerated program, double major, internships, liberal arts/career combination.

FACILITIES
Housing: CCH does not offer housing, but our staff does assist students in trying to find apartments and potential roommates. **Computers:** 100% of public computers are PCs, remote student-access to Web through college's connection.

CAMPUS LIFE
Activities: Student government. **Organizations:** 1 registered organization, 3 honor societies.

ADMISSIONS
Freshman Academic Profile: 50% from public high schools. TOEFL required of all international applicants, minimum paper TOEFL 550, minimum computer TOEFL 213. **Basis for Candidate Selection:** *Very important factors considered include:* Application essay, recommendation(s), rigor of secondary school record. *Other factors considered include:* Character/personal qualities, extracurricular activities, interview, standardized test scores, talent/ability. **Freshman Admission Requirements:** High school diploma is required, and GED is accepted. **Freshman Admission Statistics:** 87 applied, 77% admitted, 90% enrolled. **Transfer Admission Requirements:** High school transcript, college transcript(s), essay or personal statement. Minimum college GPA of 2.0 required. Lowest grade transferable C. **General Admission Information:** Application fee $50. Regular notification as accepted. Nonfall registration accepted. Admission may be deferred for a maximum of 1 year. Common Application not accepted. Neither credit nor placement offered for CEEB Advanced Placement tests.

COSTS AND FINANCIAL AID
Annual tuition $11,400. Required fees $225. Average book expense $400. **Required Forms and Deadlines:** FAFSA, institution's own financial aid form. **Types of Aid:** *Need-based scholarships/grants:* Pell, SEOG, state scholarships/grants. *Loans:* FFEL Subsidized Stafford, FFEL Unsubsidized Stafford, FFEL PLUS. **Student Employment:** Federal Work-Study Program available. Off-campus job opportunities are excellent. **Financial Aid Statistics:** 48% freshmen, 50% undergrads receive need-based scholarship or grant aid. 78% freshmen, 75% undergrads receive any aid.

COLUMBIA INTERNATIONAL UNIVERSITY

PO Box 3122, Columbia, SC 29230-3122
Phone: 803-754-4100 **E-mail:** yesciu@ciu.edu
Fax: 803-786-4041 **Website:** www.ciu.edu **ACT Code:** 5016
Financial Aid Phone: 803-754-4100

This private school was founded in 1923. It has a 400-acre campus.

RATINGS
Admissions Selectivity Rating: 76   **Fire Safety Rating:** 60*   **Green Rating:** 60*

STUDENTS AND FACULTY
Enrollment: 568. **Student Body:** 54% female, 46% male, 56% out-of-state. **Retention and Graduation:** 77% freshmen return for sophomore year. 35% freshmen graduate within 4 years. **Faculty:** Student/faculty ratio 19:1. 19 full-time faculty, 58% hold PhDs. 100% faculty teach undergrads.

ACADEMICS
Degrees: Associate, bachelor's, certificate, doctoral, first professional, master's, post-bachelor's certificate. **Academic Requirements:** Arts/fine arts, computer literacy, English (including composition), history, humanities, mathematics, philosophy, sciences (biological or physical), social science. **Disciplines with Highest Percentage of Degrees Awarded:** Education 9%. **Special Study Options:** Cross-registration, distance learning, double major, dual enrollment, English as a second language (ESL), independent study, internships, liberal arts/career combination, study abroad. Cooperative studies with Midlands Technical College.

FACILITIES
Housing: Men's dorms, women's dorms, apartments for single students, mobile home park for married students. **Computers:** 60% of public computers are PCs.

CAMPUS LIFE
Activities: Choral groups, concert band, drama/theater, music ensembles, student government, symphony orchestra, yearbook. **Organizations:** 4 religious organizations.

ADMISSIONS
Freshman Academic Profile: 18% in top 10% of high school class, 40% in top 25% of high school class, 66% in top 50% of high school class. TOEFL required of all international applicants, minimum paper TOEFL 525. **Basis for Candidate Selection:** *Very important factors considered include:* Character/personal qualities, religious affiliation/commitment, rigor of secondary school record. *Important factors considered include:* Application essay, recommendation(s), standardized test scores, volunteer work. *Other factors considered include:* Class rank, extracurricular activities, interview, talent/ability. **Freshman Admission Requirements:** High school diploma is required, and GED is accepted. *Academic units recommended:* 2 math, 1 science, 2 foreign language, 2 social studies. **Freshman Admission Statistics:** 323 applied, 56% admitted, 62% enrolled. **Transfer Admission Requirements:** College transcript(s), essay or personal statement, statement of good standing from prior institution(s). Minimum college GPA of 2.0 required. Lowest grade transferable C. **General Admission Information:** Application fee $25. Regular notification is rolling. Nonfall registration accepted. Admission may be deferred. Common Application not accepted.

COSTS AND FINANCIAL AID
Annual tuition $8,980. Room & board $4,520. Required fees $160. Average book expense $800. **Required Forms and Deadlines:** FAFSA. Financial aid filing deadline 8/1. **Types of Aid:** *Need-based scholarships/grants:* Pell, SEOG, state scholarships/grants, private scholarships, the school's own gift aid. *Loans:* FFEL Subsidized Stafford, FFEL Unsubsidized Stafford, FFEL PLUS, college/university loans from institutional funds. **Student Employment:** Federal Work-Study Program available. Off-campus job opportunities are good. **Financial Aid Statistics:** 55% freshmen, 58% undergrads receive need-based scholarship or grant aid. 72% freshmen, 73% undergrads receive need-based self-help aid. Highest amount earned per year from on-campus jobs $1,200.

COLUMBIA UNION COLLEGE

7600 Flower Avenue, Takoma Park, MD 20912
Phone: 301-891-4080 **E-mail:** enroll@cuc.edu **CEEB Code:** 5890
Fax: 301-891-4230 **Website:** www.cuc.edu **ACT Code:** 1687
Financial Aid Phone: 301-891-4005

This private school, affiliated with the Seventh-Day Adventist Church, was founded in 1904. It has a 19-acre campus.

RATINGS
Admissions Selectivity Rating: 60*   **Fire Safety Rating:** 60*   **Green Rating:** 60*

STUDENTS AND FACULTY
Enrollment: 893. **Student Body:** 62% female, 38% male, 43% out-of-state, 4% international (47 countries represented). African American 54%, Asian 6%, Caucasian 15%, Hispanic 9%. **Retention and Graduation:** 59% freshmen return for sophomore year. 14% freshmen graduate within 4 years. **Faculty:** Student/faculty ratio 12:1. 50 full-time faculty, 48% hold PhDs. 100% faculty teach undergrads.

ACADEMICS

Degrees: Associate, bachelor's, master's. **Academic Requirements:** Computer literacy, English (including composition), history, humanities, mathematics, sciences (biological or physical), social science. **Classes:** Most classes have fewer than 10 students. **Majors with Highest Enrollment:** Business administration/management, communications and media studies, nursing/registered nurse training (RN, ASN, BSN, MSN). **Disciplines with Highest Percentage of Degrees Awarded:** Health professions and related sciences 24%, psychology 17%, business/marketing 16%, computer and information sciences 14%, liberal arts/general studies 6%. **Special Study Options:** Accelerated program, cooperative education program, cross-registration, distance learning, double major, dual enrollment, English as a second language (ESL), external degree program, honors program, independent study, internships, student-designed major, study abroad, teacher certification program. Co-op programs available in business, biochemistry, communication/journalism, computer science, English. Other special programs available in adult education and external degree programs.

FACILITIES

Housing: Men's dorms, women's dorms, apartments for married students, apartments for single students. **Special Academic Facilities/Equipment:** Hospital adjacent to campus for students in health fields. **Computers:** Network access in dorm rooms, network access in dorm lounges, online registration, online administrative functions (other than registration), remote student-access to Web through college's connection.

CAMPUS LIFE

Activities: Choral groups, concert band, literary magazine, music ensembles, musical theater, radio station, student government, student newspaper, symphony orchestra, yearbook. **Organizations:** 5 honor societies. **Athletics (Intercollegiate):** *Men:* Baseball, basketball, cross-country, soccer, track/field (outdoor). *Women:* Basketball, cross-country, soccer, softball, track/field (outdoor).

ADMISSIONS

Freshman Academic Profile: 53% from public high schools. SAT Math middle 50% range 340–478. SAT Critical Reading middle 50% range 386–508. ACT middle 50% range 14–22. TOEFL required of all international applicants, minimum paper TOEFL 550, minimum computer TOEFL 213. **Basis for Candidate Selection:** *Very important factors considered include:* Academic GPA, rigor of secondary school record, standardized test scores. *Important factors considered include:* Character/personal qualities, recommendation(s), religious affiliation/commitment, talent/ability. *Other factors considered include:* Application essay, extracurricular activities, volunteer work, work experience. **Freshman Admission Requirements:** High school diploma is required, and GED is accepted. *Academic units required:* 4 English, 2 math, 2 science (2 science labs), 2 history, 4 academic electives. **Freshman Admission Statistics:** 1,435 applied, 42% admitted, 24% enrolled. **Transfer Admission Requirements:** College transcript(s). Minimum college GPA of 2.0 required. Lowest grade transferable C. **General Admission Information:** Application fee $25. Regular application deadline 8/1. Regular notification is rolling. Nonfall registration accepted. Admission may be deferred for a maximum of 1 year. Credit and/or placement offered for CEEB Advanced Placement tests.

COSTS AND FINANCIAL AID

Average book expense $945. **Required Forms and Deadlines:** FAFSA, state aid form. Financial aid filing deadline 3/1. **Notification of Awards:** Applicants will be notified of awards on a rolling basis beginning on or about 5/1. **Types of Aid:** *Need-based scholarships/grants:* Pell, SEOG, state scholarships/grants, private scholarships. *Loans:* Direct Subsidized Stafford, Direct Unsubsidized Stafford, Direct PLUS, FFEL Subsidized Stafford, FFEL PLUS, Federal Perkins. **Student Employment:** Federal Work-Study Program available. Institutional employment available. Off-campus job opportunities are excellent.

COLUMBIA UNIVERSITY

212 Hamilton Hall MC 2807, 1130 Amsterdam Avenue, New York, NY 10027
Phone: 212-854-2522 **CEEB Code:** 2116 **Fax:** 212-894-1209
Website: www.studentaffairs.columbia.edu/admissions **ACT Code:** 2717
Financial Aid Phone: 212-854-3711

This private school was founded in 1754. It has a 36-acre campus.

RATINGS

Admissions Selectivity Rating: 99   **Fire Safety Rating:** 60*   **Green Rating:** 60*

STUDENTS AND FACULTY

Enrollment: 5,593. **Student Body:** 46% female, 54% male, 69% out-of-state, 8% international (87 countries represented). African American 8%, Asian 18%, Caucasian 43%, Hispanic 9%. **Retention and Graduation:** 98% freshmen return for sophomore year. 86% freshmen graduate within 4 years. **Faculty:** Student/faculty ratio 5:1. 864 full-time faculty. 100% faculty teach undergrads.

ACADEMICS

Degrees: Bachelor's. **Academic Requirements:** Computer literacy, English (including composition), foreign languages, humanities, mathematics, sciences (biological or physical), art or music, Western literature or philosophy. **Classes:** Most classes have 10–19 students. **Majors with Highest Enrollment:** Biomedical/medical engineering, economics, English language and literature. **Disciplines with Highest Percentage of Degrees Awarded:** Social sciences 23%, engineering 18%, history 9%, visual and performing arts 7%, English 7%. **Special Study Options:** Accelerated program, cooperative education program, cross-registration, double major, dual enrollment, English as a second language (ESL), exchange student program (domestic), independent study, internships, liberal arts/career combination, study abroad, teacher certification program, combined 3–2 program.

FACILITIES

Housing: Coed dorms, apartments for married students, special housing for disabled students, fraternity/sorority housing, single-gender first-year floor available. **Special Academic Facilities/Equipment:** Art and architecture galleries, theaters, cinema, observatory. **Computers:** 1% of classrooms are wired, 60% of classrooms are wireless, 70% of public computers are PCs, 10% of public computers are Macs, 20% of public computers are UNIX, network access in dorm rooms, network access in dorm lounges, online registration, online administrative functions (other than registration), remote student-access to Web through college's connection.

CAMPUS LIFE

Activities: Choral groups, concert band, dance, drama/theater, jazz band, literary magazine, marching band, music ensembles, musical theater, opera, pep band, radio station, student government, student newspaper, student-run film society, symphony orchestra, television station. **Organizations:** 300 registered organizations, 17 religious organizations. 17 fraternities (15% men join), 11 sororities (10% women join). **Athletics (Intercollegiate):** *Men:* Baseball, basketball, crew/rowing, cross-country, diving, fencing, football, golf, soccer, swimming, tennis, track/field (indoor), track/field (outdoor), wrestling. *Women:* Archery, basketball, crew/rowing, cross-country, diving, fencing, field hockey, golf, lacrosse, soccer, softball, swimming, tennis, track/field (indoor), track/field (outdoor), volleyball.

ADMISSIONS

. **Freshman Academic Profile:** 49% from public high schools. SAT Math middle 50% range 680–780. SAT Critical Reading middle 50% range 670–760. SAT Writing middle 50% range 660–760. ACT middle 50% range 28–33. TOEFL required of all international applicants, minimum paper TOEFL 600, minimum computer TOEFL 250. **Basis for Candidate Selection:** *Very important factors considered include:* Academic GPA, application essay, character/personal qualities, class rank, recommendation(s), rigor of secondary school record, standardized test scores. *Important factors considered include:* Extracurricular activities, talent/ability. *Other factors considered include:* Alumni/ae relation, geographical residence, interview, racial/ethnic status, volunteer work. **Freshman Admission Requirements:** High school diploma is required, and GED is accepted. *Academic units recommended:* 4 English, 4 math, 4 science (4 science labs), 4 foreign language, 4 history, 4 academic electives. **Freshman Admission Statistics:** 19,851 applied, 12% admitted, 58% enrolled. **Transfer Admission Requirements:** High school transcript, college transcript(s), essay or personal statement, statement of good standing from prior institution(s). Lowest grade transferable C. **General Admission Information:** Application fee $65. Early decision application deadline 11/6. Regular application deadline 1/6. Regular notification 4/6. Nonfall registration not accepted. Admission may be deferred for a maximum of 2 years. Credit and/or placement offered for CEEB Advanced Placement tests.

COSTS AND FINANCIAL AID

Required Forms and Deadlines: FAFSA, institution's own financial aid form, CSS/Financial Aid PROFILE, Noncustodial PROFILE, Business/Farm Supplement, parent and student income tax forms. Financial aid filing deadline 2/10. **Notification of Awards:** Applicants will be notified of awards on or about 4/1. **Types of Aid:** *Need-based scholarships/grants:* Pell, SEOG, state scholarships/grants, private scholarships, the school's own gift aid. *Loans:* FFEL Subsidized Stafford, FFEL Unsubsidized Stafford, FFEL PLUS, Federal Perkins, alternative loans. **Student Employment:** Federal Work-Study Program available. Institutional employment available. Off-campus job opportunities are excellent. **Financial Aid Statistics:** 48% freshmen, 46% undergrads receive need-based scholarship or grant aid. 44% freshmen, 44% undergrads receive need-based self-help aid. 61% freshmen, 56% undergrads receive any aid.

COLUMBIA UNIVERSITY—
SCHOOL OF GENERAL STUDIES

408 Lewisohn Hall, Mail Code 4101, 2970 Broadway, New York, NY 10027
Phone: 800-895-1169 **E-mail:** gs-admit@columbia.edu **CEEB Code:** 2095
Fax: 212-854-6316 **Website:** www.gs.columbia.edu **ACT Code:** 2716
Financial Aid Phone: 212-854-5410

This private school was founded in 1947. It has a 36-acre campus.

RATINGS
Admissions Selectivity Rating: 60*   **Fire Safety Rating:** 60*   **Green Rating:** 60*

STUDENTS AND FACULTY
Enrollment: 1,260. **Student Body:** 51% female, 49% male, 42% out-of-state. African American 6%, Asian 12%, Caucasian 55%, Hispanic 9%. **Faculty:** Student/faculty ratio 10:1. 784 full-time faculty, 100% hold PhDs.

ACADEMICS
Degrees: Bachelor's, post-bachelor's certificate. **Academic Requirements:** Arts/fine arts, English (including composition), foreign languages, history, humanities, mathematics, philosophy, sciences (biological or physical), social science, cultural diversity. **Majors with Highest Enrollment:** Economics, English language and literature, political science and government. **Disciplines with Highest Percentage of Degrees Awarded:** Social sciences 29%, English 18%, liberal arts/general studies 11%, history 8%, psychology 7%. **Special Study Options:** Accelerated program, cross-registration, double major, dual enrollment, English as a second language (ESL), exchange student program (domestic), independent study, internships, student-designed major, study abroad, teacher certification program.

FACILITIES
Housing: Coed dorms, apartments for married students, apartments for single students, special housing for international students, fraternity/sorority housing. **Special Academic Facilities/Equipment:** Earth Institute, Lamont-Doherty Earth Observatory. **Computers:** 100% of classrooms are wireless, 75% of public computers are PCs, 25% of public computers are Macs, network access in dorm rooms, network access in dorm lounges; online registration, online administrative functions (other than registration), remote student-access to Web through college's connection.

CAMPUS LIFE
Activities: Choral groups, concert band, dance, drama/theater, jazz band, literary magazine, music ensembles, musical theater, opera, radio station, student government, student newspaper, student-run film society, television station, yearbook. **Organizations:** 250 registered organizations, 21 religious organizations. **Athletics (Intercollegiate):** *Men:* Baseball, basketball, crew/rowing, cross-country, diving, fencing, football, golf, soccer, swimming, tennis, track/field (indoor), track/field (outdoor), wrestling. *Women:* Archery, basketball, crew/rowing, cross-country, diving, fencing, field hockey, golf, lacrosse, soccer, softball, swimming, tennis, track/field (indoor), track/field (outdoor), volleyball. Environmental Initiatives: Establishment of a Center on Climate Change. The Earth Clinic— Solutions for Sustainable Development. Extreme Poverty: A Global Emergency.

ADMISSIONS
Freshman Academic Profile: TOEFL required of all international applicants, minimum paper TOEFL 600, minimum computer TOEFL 250. **Basis for Candidate Selection:** *Very important factors considered include:* Academic GPA, application essay, character/personal qualities, first generation, interview, level of applicant's interest, rigor of secondary school record, standardized test scores, work experience. *Important factors considered include:* Class rank, extracurricular activities, racial/ethnic status, recommendation(s), talent/ability. *Other factors considered include:* Alumni/ae relation, geographical residence, state residency, volunteer work. **Freshman Admission Requirements:** High school diploma is required, and GED is accepted. **Freshman Admission Statistics:** 248 applied, 47% admitted, 59% enrolled. **Transfer Admission Requirements:** High school transcript, college transcript(s), essay or personal statement, standardized test score. Lowest grade transferable C. **General Admission Information:** Application fee $65. Regular application deadline 6/1. Regular notification is rolling. Nonfall registration accepted. Admission may be deferred for a maximum of 2 semesters. Credit and/or placement offered for CEEB Advanced Placement tests.

COSTS AND FINANCIAL AID
Annual tuition $34,380. Room and board $13,034. Required fees $1,553. Average book expense $2,000. **Required Forms and Deadlines:** FAFSA, institution's own financial aid form. Financial aid filing deadline 6/1. **Types of Aid:** *Need-based scholarships/grants:* Pell, SEOG, state scholarships/grants, private scholarships, the school's own gift aid. *Loans:* FFEL Subsidized Stafford, FFEL Unsubsidized Stafford, Federal Perkins, college/university loans from institutional funds. **Student Employment:** Federal Work-Study Program available. Institutional employment available. Off-campus job opportunities are excellent.

See page 1130.

COLUMBUS COLLEGE OF ART & DESIGN

107 North Ninth Street, Columbus, OH 43215-3875
Phone: 614-222-3261 **E-mail:** admissions@ccad.edu **CEEB Code:** 1085
Fax: 614-232-8344 **Website:** www.ccad.edu **ACT Code:** 3281
Financial Aid Phone: 614-222-3275

This private school was founded in 1879. It has a 17-acre campus.

RATINGS
Admissions Selectivity Rating: 75   **Fire Safety Rating:** 60*   **Green Rating:** 60*

STUDENTS AND FACULTY
Enrollment: 1,359. **Student Body:** 48% female, 52% male, 28% out-of-state, 5% international (29 countries represented). African American 6%, Asian 4%, Caucasian 83%, Hispanic 2%. **Retention and Graduation:** 79% freshmen return for sophomore year. 32% freshmen graduate within 4 years. 12% grads go on to further study within 1 year. 12% grads pursue arts and sciences degrees. **Faculty:** Student/faculty ratio 12:1. 72 full-time faculty, 56% hold PhDs. 100% faculty teach undergrads.

ACADEMICS
Degrees: Bachelor's. **Academic Requirements:** Arts/fine arts, computer literacy, English (including composition), sciences (biological or physical), social science. **Special Study Options:** Cooperative education program, cross-registration, internships, study abroad. Undergrads may take grad level classes. Other special programs available include evening classes for credit and Saturday school (ages 6–18).

FACILITIES
Housing: Coed dorms. **Special Academic Facilities/Equipment:** Student art exhibition hall, gallery, auditorium, recreation center. **Computers:** Remote student-access to Web through college's connection.

CAMPUS LIFE
Activities: Literary magazine, student government, student newspaper. **Organizations:** 2 registered organizations, 1 religious organization.

ADMISSIONS
Freshman Academic Profile: 10% in top 10% of high school class, 30% in top 25% of high school class, 61% in top 50% of high school class. SAT Math middle 50% range 433–550. SAT Critical Reading middle 50% range 433–580. ACT middle 50% range 18–23. TOEFL required of all international applicants, minimum paper TOEFL 500, minimum computer TOEFL 173. **Basis for Candidate Selection:** *Very important factors considered include:* Rigor of secondary school record, talent/ability. *Important factors considered include:*

Application essay, character/personal qualities, interview, recommendation(s), standardized test scores. *Other factors considered include:* Class rank, extracurricular activities. **Freshman Admission Requirements:** High school diploma is required, and GED is accepted. *Academic units recommended:* 4 English, 4 math, 4 science, 2 foreign language. **Freshman Admission Statistics:** 510 applied, 63% admitted. **Transfer Admission Requirements:** High school transcript, college transcript(s), essay or personal statement. Minimum college GPA of 2.0 required. Lowest grade transferable C. **General Admission Information:** Application fee $25. Regular notification is rolling. Nonfall registration accepted. Admission may be deferred for a maximum of 1 year. Common Application not accepted. Credit and/or placement offered for CEEB Advanced Placement tests.

COSTS AND FINANCIAL AID
Annual tuition $17,880. Room & board $6,300. Required fees $390. Average book expense $1,800. **Required Forms and Deadlines:** FAFSA. Financial aid filing deadline 6/2. **Notification of Awards:** Applicants will be notified of awards on or about 6/15. **Types of Aid:** *Need-based scholarships/grants:* Pell, SEOG, state scholarships/grants, private scholarships, the school's own gift aid. *Loans:* FFEL Subsidized Stafford, FFEL Unsubsidized Stafford, FFEL PLUS, Federal Perkins, state loans. **Student Employment:** Federal Work-Study Program available. Institutional employment available. Off-campus job opportunities are excellent. **Financial Aid Statistics:** 77% freshmen, 73% undergrads receive need-based scholarship or grant aid. 59% freshmen, 60% undergrads receive need-based self-help aid. Highest amount earned per year from on-campus jobs $2,500.

COLUMBUS STATE UNIVERSITY

4225 University Avenue, Columbus, GA 31907-5645
Phone: 706-568-2035 **E-mail:** admissions@colstate.edu
Fax: 706-568-5091 **Website:** www.colstate.edu
Financial Aid Phone: 706-568-2036

This public school was founded in 1958. It has a 132-acre campus.

RATINGS
Admissions Selectivity Rating: 60*   **Fire Safety Rating:** 60*   **Green Rating:** 60*

STUDENTS AND FACULTY
Enrollment: 6,677. **Student Body:** 62% female, 38% male, 14% out-of-state, 1% international. African American 33%, Asian 2%, Caucasian 57%, Hispanic 3%. **Retention and Graduation:** 69% freshmen return for sophomore year. 11% freshmen graduate within 4 years. **Faculty:** Student/faculty ratio 17:1. 246 full-time faculty, 74% hold PhDs.

ACADEMICS
Degrees: Associate, bachelor's, certificate, master's, post-bachelor's certificate, post-master's certificate. **Academic Requirements:** Arts/fine arts, computer literacy, English (including composition), history, humanities, mathematics, sciences (biological or physical), social science. **Classes:** Most classes have 20–29 students. Most lab/discussion sections have 20–29 students. **Majors with Highest Enrollment:** Computer and information sciences, criminal justice/law enforcement administration, curriculum and instruction. **Disciplines with Highest Percentage of Degrees Awarded:** Business/marketing 26%, education 16%, security and protective services 10%, health professions and related sciences 8%, biological/life sciences 7%. **Special Study Options:** Accelerated program, cooperative education program, distance learning, double major, dual enrollment, honors program, internships, liberal arts/career combination, study abroad, teacher certification program.

FACILITIES
Housing: Coed dorms, apartments for single students, special housing for disabled students, special housing for international students. **Special Academic Facilities/Equipment:** Fine arts and science halls. **Computers:** Network access in dorm rooms, network access in dorm lounges, online registration, online administrative functions (other than registration).

CAMPUS LIFE
Activities: Choral groups, concert band, dance, drama/theater, jazz band, literary magazine, music ensembles, musical theater, student government, student newspaper, symphony orchestra. **Organizations:** 54 registered organizations, 13 honor societies, 2 religious organizations. 5 fraternities (1% men join), 6 sororities (1% women join). **Athletics (Intercollegiate):** *Men:* Baseball, basketball, cheerleading, golf, tennis, track/field (outdoor). *Women:* Basketball, cheerleading, softball, tennis, track/field (outdoor).

ADMISSIONS
Freshman Academic Profile: SAT Math middle 50% range 40–550. SAT Critical Reading middle 50% range 450–560. ACT middle 50% range 17–22. TOEFL required of all international applicants, minimum paper TOEFL 550, minimum computer TOEFL 213. **Basis for Candidate Selection:** *Very important factors considered include:* Rigor of secondary school record. *Important factors considered include:* Academic GPA, standardized test scores. *Other factors considered include:* Extracurricular activities, geographical residence, interview, talent/ability. **Freshman Admission Requirements:** High school diploma is required, and GED is not accepted. *Academic units required:* 4 English, 4 math, 3 science (2 science labs), 2 foreign language, 3 social studies. *Academic units recommended:* 4 English, 4 math, 3 science (2 science labs), 2 foreign language, 3 social studies. **Freshman Admission Statistics:** 3,308 applied, 57% admitted, 62% enrolled. **Transfer Admission Requirements:** College transcript(s), statement of good standing from prior institution(s). Lowest grade transferable D. **General Admission Information:** Application fee $25. Regular application deadline 7/1. Regular notification is rolling. Nonfall registration accepted. Admission may be deferred for a maximum of 1 year. Credit offered for CEEB Advanced Placement tests.

COSTS AND FINANCIAL AID
Annual in-state tuition $2,706. Annual out-of-state tuition $10,823. Room and board $6,220. Required fees $646. Average book expense $814. **Required Forms and Deadlines:** FAFSA. Financial aid filing deadline 5/1. **Notification of Awards:** Applicants will be notified of awards on a rolling basis beginning on or about 2/1. **Types of Aid:** *Need-based scholarships/grants:* Pell, SEOG, state scholarships/grants, private scholarships, the school's own gift aid. *Loans:* Direct Subsidized Stafford, Direct Unsubsidized Stafford, Direct PLUS, Federal Perkins, Federal Nursing, state loans, college/university loans from institutional funds. **Student Employment:** Federal Work-Study Program available. Institutional employment available. Off-campus job opportunities are good. **Financial Aid Statistics:** 34% freshmen, 35% undergrads receive need-based scholarship or grant aid. 37% freshmen, 37% undergrads receive need-based self-help aid. 20 freshmen, 170 undergrads receive athletic scholarships.

CONCEPTION SEMINARY COLLEGE

PO Box 502, 37174 State Highway W, Conception, MO 64433
Phone: 660-944-2886 **E-mail:** vocations@conception.edu
Fax: 660-944-2829 **Website:** www.conception.edu **ACT Code:** 2280
Financial Aid Phone: 660-944-2851

This private school, affiliated with the Roman Catholic Church, was founded in 1886. It has a 30-acre campus.

RATINGS
Admissions Selectivity Rating: 60*   **Fire Safety Rating:** 60*   **Green Rating:** 60*

STUDENTS AND FACULTY
Enrollment: 96. **Student Body:** 100% male, 73% out-of-state, 5% international. Asian 10%, Caucasian 56%, Hispanic 2%. **Retention and Graduation:** 50% freshmen return for sophomore year. 60% grads go on to further study within 1 year. **Faculty:** Student/faculty ratio 4:1. 20 full-time faculty, 85% hold PhDs. 100% faculty teach undergrads.

ACADEMICS
Degrees: Bachelor's, certificate. **Academic Requirements:** Arts/fine arts, English (including composition), philosophy. **Disciplines with Highest Percentage of Degrees Awarded:** Liberal arts/general studies 14%. **Special Study Options:** Double major, English as a second language (ESL), independent study.

FACILITIES
Housing: Men's dorms. **Computers:** 100% of public computers are PCs, network access in dorm rooms, online administrative functions (other than registration), remote student-access to Web through college's connection.

CAMPUS LIFE
Activities: Drama/theater, music ensembles, student government, student newspaper, yearbook. **Organizations:** 12 registered organizations. **Athletics (Intercollegiate):** *Men:* Soccer, volleyball.

ADMISSIONS
Freshman Academic Profile: SAT Math middle 50% range 433–550. SAT Critical Reading middle 50% range 433–580. ACT middle 50% range 12–29. TOEFL required of all international applicants, minimum computer TOEFL 173. **Basis for Candidate Selection:** *Very important factors considered include:* Application essay, recommendation(s), religious affiliation/commit-

ment. *Important factors considered include:* Character/personal qualities, rigor of secondary school record, standardized test scores, talent/ability. *Other factors considered include:* Class rank, extracurricular activities, interview, volunteer work, work experience. **Freshman Admission Requirements:** High school diploma is required, and GED is accepted. *Academic units required:* 4 English, 4 science, 4 social studies. **Freshman Admission Statistics:** 17 applied, 100% admitted, 100% enrolled. **Transfer Admission Requirements:** College transcript(s), essay or personal statement. Minimum college GPA of 2.0 required. Lowest grade transferable C. **General Admission Information:** Regular application deadline 8/15. Regular notification is rolling. Nonfall registration accepted. Admission may be deferred for a maximum of 1 year. Common Application not accepted.

COSTS AND FINANCIAL AID

Annual tuition $17,880. Room and board $6,300. Required fees $390. Average book expense $1,800. **Required Forms and Deadlines:** FAFSA. Financial aid filing deadline 6/2. **Financial Aid Statistics:** 53% freshmen, 51% undergrads receive need-based scholarship or grant aid. 20% freshmen, 31% undergrads receive need-based self-help aid.

CONCORD UNIVERSITY—ATHENS

1000 Vermillion Street, PO Box 1000, Athens, WV 24712
Phone: 304-384-5248 **E-mail:** admissions@concord.edu **CEEB Code:** 5120
Fax: 304-384-9044 **Website:** www.concord.edu
Financial Aid Phone: 304-384-6069

This public school was founded in 1872. It has a 123-acre campus.

RATINGS
Admissions Selectivity Rating: 78   **Fire Safety Rating:** 60*   **Green Rating:** 60*

STUDENTS AND FACULTY

Enrollment: 3,023. **Student Body:** 57% female, 43% male, 11% out-of-state. African American 3%, Asian 1%, Caucasian 76%. **Retention and Graduation:** 64% freshmen return for sophomore year. 23% grads go on to further study within 1 year. 8% grads pursue arts and sciences degrees. 10% grads pursue business degrees. 2% grads pursue law degrees. 3% grads pursue medical degrees. **Faculty:** Student/faculty ratio 24:1. 84 full-time faculty, 69% hold PhDs.

ACADEMICS

Degrees: Associate, bachelor's. **Academic Requirements:** Arts/fine arts, English (including composition), foreign languages, mathematics, sciences (biological or physical), social science, physical education. **Classes:** Most classes have fewer than 10 students. Most lab/discussion sections have 10–19 students. **Disciplines with Highest Percentage of Degrees Awarded:** Education 26%, business/marketing 15%, liberal arts/general studies 12%, social sciences 10%, biological/life sciences 7%, psychology 7%. **Special Study Options:** Cooperative education program, double major, dual enrollment, English as a second language (ESL), honors program, student-designed major, teacher certification program.

FACILITIES

Housing: Coed dorms, men's dorms, women's dorms, apartments for married students, special housing for disabled students, special housing for international students. **Computers:** 75% of public computers are PCs, 2% of public computers are Macs, network access in dorm rooms, network access in dorm lounges, remote student-access to Web through college's connection.

CAMPUS LIFE

Activities: Choral groups, concert band, drama/theater, jazz band, pep band, radio station, student government, student newspaper, student-run film society, television station, yearbook. **Organizations:** 57 registered organizations, 1 honor society, 1 religious organization. 6 fraternities (15% men join), 4 sororities (20% women join). **Athletics (Intercollegiate):** *Men:* Baseball, basketball, cheerleading, cross-country, football, golf, soccer, tennis, track/field (outdoor). *Women:* Basketball, cheerleading, cross-country, golf, soccer, softball, tennis, track/field (outdoor), volleyball.

ADMISSIONS

Freshman Academic Profile: 17% in top 10% of high school class, 38% in top 25% of high school class, 65% in top 50% of high school class. SAT Math middle 50% range 410–560. SAT Critical Reading middle 50% range 390–560. ACT middle 50% range 23–27. TOEFL required of all international applicants, minimum paper TOEFL 500. **Basis for Candidate Selection:** *Very important factors considered include:* Rigor of secondary school record. *Important factors considered include:* Class rank, extracurricular activities, standardized test

scores. *Other factors considered include:* Alumni/ae relation, application essay, character/personal qualities, geographical residence, interview, racial/ethnic status, recommendation(s), talent/ability, volunteer work, work experience. **Freshman Admission Requirements:** High school diploma is required, and GED is accepted. *Academic units required:* 4 English, 2 math, 2 science (2 science labs), 2 social studies, 1 history, 6 academic electives. *Academic units recommended:* 3 math, 2 foreign language. **Freshman Admission Statistics:** 2,330 applied, 65% admitted, 42% enrolled. **Transfer Admission Requirements:** College transcript(s). Lowest grade transferable D. **General Admission Information:** Regular notification is rolling. Nonfall registration accepted. Admission may be deferred for a maximum of 1 year. Common Application accepted.

COSTS AND FINANCIAL AID

Annual in-state tuition $2,724. Out-of-state tuition $6,116. Room & board $4,358. Average book expense $650. **Required Forms and Deadlines:** FAFSA, institution's own financial aid form, verification worksheet. Financial aid filing deadline 3/1. **Notification of Awards:** Applicants will be notified of awards on a rolling basis beginning on or about 3/1. **Types of Aid:** *Need-based scholarships/grants:* Pell, SEOG, state scholarships/grants, the school's own gift aid. *Loans:* FFEL Subsidized Stafford, FFEL Unsubsidized Stafford, FFEL PLUS, Federal Perkins. **Student Employment:** Federal Work-Study Program available. Institutional employment available. Off-campus job opportunities are excellent. **Financial Aid Statistics:** 53% freshmen, 51% undergrads receive need-based scholarship or grant aid. 46% freshmen, 49% undergrads receive need-based self-help aid. 43 freshmen, 165 undergrads receive athletic scholarships. Highest amount earned per year from on-campus jobs $823.

CONCORDIA COLLEGE—MOORHEAD, MN

901 Eighth Street South, Moorhead, MN 56562
Phone: 218-299-3004 **E-mail:** admissions@cord.edu **CEEB Code:** 6113
Fax: 218-299-4720 **Website:** www.goconcordia.com **ACT Code:** 2104
Financial Aid Phone: 218-299-3010

This private school, affiliated with the Lutheran Church, was founded in 1891. It has a 120-acre campus.

RATINGS
Admissions Selectivity Rating: 77   **Fire Safety Rating:** 60*   **Green Rating:** 60*

STUDENTS AND FACULTY

Enrollment: 2,793. **Student Body:** 63% female, 37% male, 33% out-of-state, 6% international (42 countries represented). Asian 2%, Caucasian 92%. **Retention and Graduation:** 80% freshmen return for sophomore year. 57% freshmen graduate within 4 years. 20% grads go on to further study within 1 year. 9% grads pursue arts and sciences degrees. 3% grads pursue business degrees. 4% grads pursue law degrees. 4% grads pursue medical degrees. **Faculty:** Student/faculty ratio 14:1. 175 full-time faculty, 78% hold PhDs. 100% faculty teach undergrads.

ACADEMICS

Degrees: Bachelor's, master's. **Academic Requirements:** Arts/fine arts, English (including composition), foreign languages, history, humanities, mathematics, sciences (biological or physical), social science. **Classes:** Most classes have 20–29 students. **Disciplines with Highest Percentage of Degrees Awarded:** Education 19%, biological/life sciences 11%, business/marketing 11%, communication technologies 8%, visual and performing arts 8%, foreign languages and literature 7%, social sciences 6%, health professions and related sciences 6%. **Special Study Options:** Cooperative education program, double major, exchange student program (domestic), honors program, independent study, internships, liberal arts/career combination, study abroad, teacher certification program.

FACILITIES

Housing: Coed dorms, men's dorms, women's dorms, apartments for single students, special housing for disabled students, language houses (French, German, and Spanish). **Special Academic Facilities/Equipment:** Cyrus M. Running Gallery. **Computers:** 85% of public computers are PCs, 15% of public computers are Macs, network access in dorm rooms, network access in dorm lounges, online administrative functions (other than registration), remote student-access to Web through college's connection.

CAMPUS LIFE

Activities: Choral groups, concert band, dance, drama/theater, jazz band, literary magazine, music ensembles, musical theater, pep band, radio station, student government, student newspaper, symphony orchestra, television station, yearbook. **Organizations:** 80 registered organizations, 22 honor societies, 12 religious organizations. 2 fraternities, 2 sororities. **Athletics (Intercollegiate):** *Men:* Baseball, basketball, cross-country, football, golf, ice hockey, soccer, tennis, track/field (indoor), track/field (outdoor), wrestling. *Women:* Basketball, cross-country, diving, golf, ice hockey, soccer, softball, swimming, tennis, track/field (indoor), track/field (outdoor), volleyball.

ADMISSIONS

Freshman Academic Profile: 31% in top 10% of high school class, 62% in top 25% of high school class, 89% in top 50% of high school class. SAT Math middle 50% range 520–630. SAT Critical Reading middle 50% range 530–650. ACT middle 50% range 21–27. TOEFL required of all international applicants, minimum paper TOEFL 550, minimum computer TOEFL 200. **Basis for Candidate Selection:** *Very important factors considered include:* Rigor of secondary school record. *Important factors considered include:* Class rank, recommendation(s). *Other factors considered include:* Alumni/ae relation, character/personal qualities, extracurricular activities, racial/ethnic status, standardized test scores, talent/ability, volunteer work. **Freshman Admission Requirements:** High school diploma is required, and GED is accepted. *Academic units recommended:* 4 English, 3 math, 3 science, 2 foreign language, 3 social studies. **Freshman Admission Statistics:** 2,444 applied, 86% admitted, 37% enrolled. **Transfer Admission Requirements:** College transcript(s). Minimum college GPA of 2.0 required. Lowest grade transferable C-. **General Admission Information:** Application fee $20. Regular notification after file is complete. Nonfall registration accepted. Admission may be deferred for a maximum of 1 year. Common Application accepted. Credit and/or placement offered for CEEB Advanced Placement tests.

COSTS AND FINANCIAL AID

Annual tuition $17,620. Room & board $4,690. Required fees $150. Average book expense $700. **Required Forms and Deadlines:** FAFSA, institution's own financial aid form. **Notification of Awards:** Applicants will be notified of awards on a rolling basis beginning on or about 3/1. **Types of Aid:** *Need-based scholarships/grants:* Pell, SEOG, state scholarships/grants, private scholarships, the school's own gift aid. *Loans:* FFEL Subsidized Stafford, FFEL Unsubsidized Stafford, FFEL PLUS, Federal Perkins, state loans, college/university loans from institutional funds. **Student Employment:** Federal Work-Study Program available. Institutional employment available. Off-campus job opportunities are excellent. **Financial Aid Statistics:** 71% freshmen, 71% undergrads receive need-based scholarship or grant aid. 62% freshmen, 60% undergrads receive need-based self-help aid. 97% freshmen, 94% undergrads receive any aid.

CONCORDIA COLLEGE—NEW YORK

171 White Plains Road, Bronxville, NY 10708
Phone: 914-337-9300 **E-mail:** admission@concordia-ny.edu **CEEB Code:** 2096
Fax: 914-395-4636 **Website:** www.concordia-ny.edu **ACT Code:** 2722
Financial Aid Phone: 914-337-9300

This private school, affiliated with the Lutheran Church, was founded in 1881. It has a 33-acre campus.

RATINGS
Admissions Selectivity Rating: 70   **Fire Safety Rating:** 60*   **Green Rating:** 60*

STUDENTS AND FACULTY
Enrollment: 587. **Student Body:** 58% female, 42% male, 27% out-of-state. African American 14%, Asian 7%, Caucasian 63%, Hispanic 10%. **Retention and Graduation:** 76% freshmen return for sophomore year. 23% freshmen graduate within 4 years. 40% grads go on to further study within 1 year. 30% grads pursue arts and sciences degrees. 30% grads pursue business degrees. 2% grads pursue law degrees. 10% grads pursue medical degrees. **Faculty:** Student/faculty ratio 16:1. 33 full-time faculty, 67% hold PhDs. 100% faculty teach undergrads.

ACADEMICS
Degrees: Associate, bachelor's. **Academic Requirements:** Arts/fine arts, computer literacy, English (including composition), foreign languages, history, humanities, mathematics, philosophy, sciences (biological or physical), social science, religion. **Classes:** Most classes have 10–19 students. Most lab/discussion sections have 10–19 students. **Majors with Highest Enrollment:** Business administration/management, education, social sciences. **Disciplines with Highest Percentage of Degrees Awarded:** Business/marketing 33%, education 22%, liberal arts/general studies 15%, social sciences 12%, biological/life sciences 5%. **Special Study Options:** Accelerated program, cooperative education program, cross-registration, double major, English as a second

language (ESL), exchange student program (domestic), honors program, independent study, internships, liberal arts/career combination, student-designed major, study abroad, teacher certification program.

FACILITIES

Housing: Men's dorms, women's dorms. **Special Academic Facilities/Equipment:** Art gallery, center for worship and performing arts, English language center, distance learning classroom. **Computers:** 99% of public computers are PCs, 1% of public computers are Macs, network access in dorm rooms, network access in dorm lounges, remote student-access to Web through college's connection.

CAMPUS LIFE

Activities: Choral groups, concert band, drama/theater, jazz band, literary magazine, music ensembles, musical theater, student government, student newspaper, yearbook. **Organizations:** 35 registered organizations, 1 honor society, 3 religious organizations. **Athletics (Intercollegiate):** *Men:* Baseball, basketball, soccer, tennis, volleyball. *Women:* Basketball, soccer, softball, tennis, volleyball.

ADMISSIONS

Freshman Academic Profile: 5% in top 10% of high school class, 14% in top 25% of high school class, 44% in top 50% of high school class. 60% from public high schools. SAT Math middle 50% range 410–530. SAT Critical Reading middle 50% range 420–520. ACT middle 50% range 17–22. TOEFL required of all international applicants, minimum paper TOEFL 550, minimum computer TOEFL 213. **Basis for Candidate Selection:** *Very important factors considered include:* Rigor of secondary school record. *Important factors considered include:* Character/personal qualities, class rank, interview, standardized test scores. *Other factors considered include:* Alumni/ae relation, application essay, extracurricular activities, recommendation(s), religious affiliation/commitment, talent/ability, volunteer work, work experience. **Freshman Admission Requirements:** High school diploma is required, and GED is accepted. *Academic units required:* 4 English, 3 math, 2 science (2 science labs), 2 foreign language, 2 social studies, 2 history. **Freshman Admission Statistics:** 684 applied, 70% admitted, 37% enrolled. **Transfer Admission Requirements:** High school transcript, college transcript(s), statement of good standing from prior institution(s). Minimum college GPA of 2.0 required. Lowest grade transferable C. **General Admission Information:** Application fee $40. Regular application deadline 3/15. Regular notification is rolling. Nonfall registration accepted. Admission may be deferred for a maximum of 1 year. Credit and/or placement offered for CEEB Advanced Placement tests.

COSTS AND FINANCIAL AID

Annual tuition $20,700. Room & board $8,230. Required fees $150. Average book expense $750. **Required Forms and Deadlines:** FAFSA, state aid form. Financial aid filing deadline 5/1. **Notification of Awards:** Applicants will be notified on a rolling basis beginning on or about 3/1. **Types of Aid:** *Need-based scholarships/grants:* Pell, SEOG, state scholarships/grants, private scholarships, the school's own gift aid. *Loans:* FFEL Subsidized Stafford, FFEL Unsubsidized Stafford, FFEL PLUS, college/university loans from institutional funds. **Student Employment:** Federal Work-Study Program available. Institutional employment available. Off-campus job opportunities are excellent. **Financial Aid Statistics:** Highest amount earned per year from on-campus jobs $2,000.

CONCORDIA UNIVERSITY AT AUSTIN

3400 I-35 N, Austin, TX 78705
Phone: 512-486-1106 **E-mail:** admissions@concordia.edu **CEEB Code:** 6127
Fax: 512-486-1350 **Website:** www.concordia.edu **ACT Code:** 4124
Financial Aid Phone: 512-486-2000

This private school, affiliated with the Lutheran Church, was founded in 1926. It has a 23-acre campus.

RATINGS
Admissions Selectivity Rating: 71   **Fire Safety Rating:** 60*   **Green Rating:** 60*

STUDENTS AND FACULTY
Enrollment: 966. **Student Body:** 56% female, 44% male, 7% out-of-state. African American 9%, Asian 2%, Caucasian 67%, Hispanic 14%. **Retention and Graduation:** 56% freshmen return for sophomore year. 12% freshmen graduate within 4 years. 12% grads go on to further study within 1 year. 9% grads pursue arts and sciences degrees. 2% grads pursue business degrees. 1% grads pursue law degrees. **Faculty:** Student/faculty ratio 19:1. 33 full-time faculty, 70% hold PhDs. 100% faculty teach undergrads.

ACADEMICS

Degrees: Associate, bachelor's, certificate, diploma, master's, post-bachelor's certificate. **Academic Requirements:** Arts/fine arts, computer literacy, English (including composition), foreign languages, history, humanities, mathematics, sciences (biological or physical), social science. **Classes:** Most classes have 10–19 students. Most lab/discussion sections have 20–29 students. **Majors with Highest Enrollment:** Business/commerce, elementary education and teaching. **Disciplines with Highest Percentage of Degrees Awarded:** Business/marketing 46%, education 10%, communication technologies 8%, liberal arts/general studies 6%, biological/life sciences 5%. **Special Study Options:** Accelerated program, cooperative education program, cross-registration, distance learning, double major, dual enrollment, exchange student program (domestic), external degree program, honors program, independent study, internships, study abroad, teacher certification program.

FACILITIES

Housing: Coed dorms, men's dorms, women's dorms. **Computers:** 100% of public computers are PCs, network access in dorm rooms, remote student-access to Web through college's connection.

CAMPUS LIFE

Activities: Choral groups, drama/theater, jazz band, literary magazine, music ensembles, student government, yearbook. **Organizations:** 20 registered organizations, 4 honor societies, 5 religious organizations. **Athletics (Intercollegiate):** *Men:* Baseball, basketball, cross-country, golf, rugby, soccer, tennis. *Women:* Basketball, cross-country, golf, soccer, softball, tennis, volleyball.

ADMISSIONS

Freshman Academic Profile: 7% in top 10% of high school class, 21% in top 25% of high school class, 52% in top 50% of high school class. 86% from public high schools. SAT Math middle 50% range 450–550. SAT Critical Reading middle 50% range 430–500. ACT middle 50% range 18–24. **Basis for Candidate Selection:** *Very important factors considered include:* Rigor of secondary school record, standardized test scores. *Other factors considered include:* Application essay, class rank, recommendation(s). **Freshman Admission Requirements:** High school diploma is required, and GED is accepted. *Academic units recommended:* 4 English, 3 math, 3 science. **Freshman Admission Statistics:** 523 applied, 76% admitted, 40% enrolled. **Transfer Admission Requirements:** College transcript(s). Minimum college GPA of 2.0 required. Lowest grade transferable C. **General Admission Information:** Application fee $25. Regular notification is rolling. Nonfall registration accepted. Common Application not accepted. Credit offered for CEEB Advanced Placement tests.

COSTS AND FINANCIAL AID

Required Forms and Deadlines: FAFSA, institution's own financial aid form. Financial aid filing deadline 7/1. **Notification of Awards:** Applicants will be notified of awards on a rolling basis beginning on or about 2/1. **Types of Aid:** *Need-based scholarships/grants:* Pell, SEOG, state scholarships/grants, the school's own gift aid. *Loans:* FFEL Subsidized Stafford, FFEL Unsubsidized Stafford, FFEL PLUS, state loans. **Student Employment:** Federal Work-Study Program available. Off-campus job opportunities are excellent. **Financial Aid Statistics:** 61% freshmen, 55% undergrads receive need-based scholarship or grant aid. 55% freshmen, 50% undergrads receive need-based self-help aid. 85% undergrads receive any aid. Highest amount earned per year from on-campus jobs $1,000.

CONCORDIA UNIVERSITY—CHICAGO

7400 Augusta Street, River Forest, IL 60305-1499
Phone: 708-209-3100 **E-mail:** admission@cuchicago.edu **CEEB Code:** 1140
Fax: 708-209-3473 **Website:** www.CUChicago.edu **ACT Code:** 1004
Financial Aid Phone: 708-209-3113

This private school, affiliated with the Lutheran Church, was founded in 1864. It has a 40-acre campus.

RATINGS

Admissions Selectivity Rating: 79   **Fire Safety Rating:** 64   **Green Rating:** 60*

STUDENTS AND FACULTY

Enrollment: 1,011. **Student Body:** 62% female, 38% male. African American 13%, Asian 1%, Caucasian 70%, Hispanic 9%. **Retention and Graduation:** 79% freshmen return for sophomore year. 23% grads go on to further study within 1 year. **Faculty:** Student/faculty ratio 17:1. 99 full-time faculty. 82% faculty teach undergrads.

ACADEMICS

Degrees: Bachelor's, doctoral, master's, post-master's certificate. **Academic Requirements:** Arts/fine arts, computer literacy, English (including composition), foreign languages, history, humanities, mathematics, sciences (biological or physical), social science, ethics, theology, wellness, world studies. **Classes:** Most classes have 10–19 students. **Majors with Highest Enrollment:** Business administration/management, elementary education and teaching, kinesiology and exercise science. **Disciplines with Highest Percentage of Degrees Awarded:** Education 40%, business/marketing 21%, philosophy and religious studies 9%, social sciences 7%, psychology 6%. **Special Study Options:** Double major, exchange student program (domestic), honors program, independent study, internships, study abroad, teacher certification program.

FACILITIES

Housing: Coed dorms, men's dorms, women's dorms, special housing for disabled students. **Special Academic Facilities/Equipment:** Art museum, zoology exhibit, human performance lab, early childhood education lab school, TV studio, weather station, radio station. **Computers:** 90% of public computers are PCs, 10% of public computers are Macs, network access in dorm rooms, network access in dorm lounges, online registration, online administrative functions (other than registration), remote student-access to Web through college's connection.

CAMPUS LIFE

Activities: Choral groups, concert band, dance, drama/theater, jazz band, literary magazine, music ensembles, musical theater, pep band, radio station, student government, student newspaper, television station, yearbook. **Organizations:** 15 registered organizations, 3 honor societies, 5 religious organizations. **Athletics (Intercollegiate):** *Men:* Baseball, basketball, cheerleading, cross-country, football, soccer, tennis, track/field (outdoor). *Women:* Basketball, cheerleading, cross-country, soccer, softball, tennis, track/field (outdoor), volleyball.

ADMISSIONS

Freshman Academic Profile: 18% in top 10% of high school class, 41% in top 25% of high school class, 67% in top 50% of high school class. 80% from public high schools. ACT middle 50% range 19–26. TOEFL required of all international applicants, minimum paper TOEFL 525, minimum computer TOEFL 195. **Basis for Candidate Selection:** *Important factors considered include:* Academic GPA, class rank, rigor of secondary school record, standardized test scores. *Other factors considered include:* Application essay, character/personal qualities, extracurricular activities, interview, recommendation(s). **Freshman Admission Requirements:** High school diploma is required, and GED is accepted. *Academic units required:* 4 English, 3 math, 2 science (1 science lab), 2 social studies. *Academic units recommended:* 4 science, 2 foreign language, 1 history. **Freshman Admission Statistics:** 1,092 applied, 65% admitted, 30% enrolled. **Transfer Admission Requirements:** College transcript(s), statement of good standing from prior institution(s). Minimum college GPA of 2.0 required. Lowest grade transferable C. **General Admission Information:** Regular notification is rolling. Nonfall registration accepted. Admission may be deferred for a maximum of 1 year. Credit offered for CEEB Advanced Placement tests.

COSTS AND FINANCIAL AID

Annual tuition $20,900. Room & board $6,992. Required fees $420. Average book expense $600. **Required Forms and Deadlines:** FAFSA, institution's own financial aid form. Financial aid filing deadline 4/1. **Notification of Awards:** Applicants will be notified of awards on a rolling basis beginning on or about 2/24. **Types of Aid:** *Need-based scholarships/grants:* Pell, SEOG, state scholarships/grants, private scholarships, the school's own gift aid. *Loans:* FFEL Subsidized Stafford, FFEL Unsubsidized Stafford, FFEL PLUS, Federal Perkins. **Student Employment:** Federal Work-Study Program available. Institutional employment available. Off-campus job opportunities are good. **Financial Aid Statistics:** 72% freshmen, 69% undergrads receive need-based scholarship or grant aid. 65% freshmen, 61% undergrads receive need-based self-help aid. 81% freshmen, 77% undergrads receive any aid. Highest amount earned per year from on-campus jobs $17,000.

CONCORDIA UNIVERSITY—IRVINE

1530 Concordia West, Irvine, CA 92612-3299
Phone: 949-854-8002 **E-mail:** admission@cui.edu
Fax: 949-854-6894 **Website:** www.cui.edu **ACT Code:** 0227
Financial Aid Phone: 949-854-8002

This private school, affiliated with the Lutheran Church, was founded in 1976. It has a 70-acre campus.

RATINGS
Admissions Selectivity Rating: 80   **Fire Safety Rating:** 84   **Green Rating:** 64

STUDENTS AND FACULTY
Enrollment: 1,304. **Student Body:** 62% female, 38% male, 1% out-of-state, 2% international (14 countries represented). African American 4%, Asian 4%, Caucasian 69%, Hispanic 13%. **Retention and Graduation:** 73% freshmen return for sophomore year. 49% freshmen graduate within 4 years. **Faculty:** Student/faculty ratio 15:1. 87 full-time faculty, 61% hold PhDs. 100% faculty teach undergrads.

ACADEMICS
Degrees: Associate, bachelor's, master's, post-bachelor's certificate. **Academic Requirements:** Arts/fine arts, computer literacy, English (including composition), foreign languages, history, humanities, mathematics, philosophy, sciences (biological or physical), social science, theology. **Classes:** Most classes have 20–29 students. **Majors with Highest Enrollment:** Business administration/management, liberal arts and sciences/liberal studies, psychology. **Disciplines with Highest Percentage of Degrees Awarded:** Business/marketing 23%, liberal arts/general studies 22%, education 11%, social sciences 8%, psychology 7%. **Special Study Options:** Accelerated program, cross-registration, distance learning, double major, dual enrollment, English as a second language (ESL), exchange student program (domestic), honors program, independent study, internships, liberal arts/career combination, student-designed major, study abroad, teacher certification program.

FACILITIES
Housing: Men's dorms, women's dorms, special housing for disabled students. **Special Academic Facilities/Equipment:** An education/business/technology building on campus is nearing completion. **Computers:** 100% of classrooms are wired, 100% of public computers are PCs, network access in dorm rooms, network access in dorm lounges, online registration, remote student-access to Web through college's connection.

CAMPUS LIFE
Activities: Choral groups, concert band, dance, drama/theater, jazz band, literary magazine, music ensembles, musical theater, pep band, radio station, student government, student newspaper, student-run film society, yearbook. **Organizations:** 18 registered organizations, 5 honor societies, 8 religious organizations. **Athletics (Intercollegiate):** *Men:* Baseball, basketball, cross-country, golf, soccer, tennis, track/field (outdoor). *Women:* Basketball, cross-country, golf, soccer, softball, tennis, track/field (outdoor), volleyball.

ADMISSIONS
Freshman Academic Profile: 20% in top 10% of high school class, 54% in top 25% of high school class, 84% in top 50% of high school class. SAT Math middle 50% range 450–570. SAT Critical Reading middle 50% range 450–570. ACT middle 50% range 20–24. TOEFL required of all international applicants, minimum paper TOEFL 550, minimum computer TOEFL 213. **Basis for Candidate Selection:** *Very important factors considered include:* Academic GPA, class rank, rigor of secondary school record, standardized test scores. *Important factors considered include:* Character/personal qualities, recommendation(s), religious affiliation/commitment. *Other factors considered include:* Alumni/ae relation, application essay, extracurricular activities, interview, level of applicant's interest, racial/ethnic status, talent/ability, volunteer work, work experience. **Freshman Admission Requirements:** High school diploma is required, and GED is accepted. *Academic units required:* 4 English, 3 math, 3 science (2 science labs), 2 foreign language, 2 social studies. *Academic units recommended:* 4 social studies. **Freshman Admission Statistics:** 897 applied, 66% accepted, 42% enrolled. **Transfer Admission Requirements:** High school transcript, college transcript(s), statement of good standing from prior institution(s). Minimum college GPA of 2.3 required. Lowest grade transferable D. **General Admission Information:** Application fee $50. Regular notification 3/2. Nonfall registration accepted. Admission may be deferred for a maximum of 1 year. Credit and/or placement offered for CEEB Advanced Placement tests.

COSTS AND FINANCIAL AID
Required Forms and Deadlines: FAFSA, institution's own financial aid form, state aid form, (GPA Verification Form). Financial aid filing deadline 4/1. **Notification of Awards:** Applicants will be notified of awards on a rolling basis beginning on or about 2/1. **Types of Aid:** *Need-based scholarships/grants:* Pell, SEOG, state scholarships/grants, private scholarships, the school's own gift aid. *Loans:* FFEL Subsidized Stafford, FFEL Unsubsidized Stafford, FFEL PLUS. **Financial Aid Statistics:** 62% freshmen, 60% undergrads receive need-based scholarship or grant aid. 48% freshmen, 49% undergrads receive need-based self-help aid. 20 freshmen, 72 undergrads receive athletic scholarships. 65% freshmen, 69% undergrads receive any aid. Highest amount earned per year from on-campus jobs $2,000.

CONCORDIA UNIVERSITY—MONTREAL, QC

Office of Admissions, 1455 de Maisonneuve W., Montreal, QC H3G 1M8 Canada
Phone: 514-848-2668 **E-mail:** admreg@alcor.concordia.ca **CEEB Code:** 956
Fax: 514-848-2621 **Website:** www.concordia.ca
Financial Aid Phone: 514-848-3507

This public school was founded in 1974. It has a 135-acre campus.

RATINGS
Admissions Selectivity Rating: 77   **Fire Safety Rating:** 60*   **Green Rating:** 60*

STUDENTS AND FACULTY
Enrollment: 20,488. **Student Body:** 54% female, 46% male, 8% out-of-state, 6% international (125 countries represented). **Retention and Graduation:** 86% freshmen return for sophomore year. **Faculty:** Student/faculty ratio 20:1. 696 full-time faculty, 92% hold PhDs. 98% faculty teach undergrads.

ACADEMICS
Degrees: Bachelor's, certificate, diploma, doctoral, master's, post-bachelor's certificate, post-master's certificate. **Academic Requirements:** Arts/fine arts, computer literacy, English (including composition), humanities, social science. All students must complete a general education 12-credit core within their programs. **Classes:** Most classes have 40–49 students. **Majors with Highest Enrollment:** Accounting, computer and information sciences, marketing/marketing management. **Disciplines with Highest Percentage of Degrees Awarded:** Business/marketing 31%, liberal arts/general studies 10%, social sciences 10%, visual and performing arts 10%, computer and information sciences 6%, engineering 6%, biological/life sciences 3%, psychology 3%, mathematics 2%, education 2%. **Special Study Options:** Accelerated program, cooperative education program, cross-registration, distance learning, double major, English as a second language (ESL), exchange student program (domestic), honors program, independent study, internships, liberal arts/career combination, student-designed major, study abroad, teacher certification program.

FACILITIES
Housing: Coed dorms, off-campus housing service (the service is an extensive data bank listing that has vacant apartments and rooms and lists of people who are seeking roommates). **Computers:** 50% of public computers are PCs, 40% of public computers are Macs, 10% of public computers are UNIX, network access in dorm lounges, online registration, online administrative functions (other than registration), remote student-access to Web through college's connection.

CAMPUS LIFE
Activities: Choral groups, concert band, dance, drama/theater, jazz band, literary magazine, music ensembles, musical theater, radio station, student government, student newspaper, student-run film society, television station, yearbook. **Organizations:** 125 registered organizations, 12 honor societies, 8 religious organizations. 4 fraternities, 2 sororities. **Athletics (Intercollegiate):** *Men:* Baseball, basketball, crew/rowing, cross-country, football, ice hockey, rugby, skiing (downhill/alpine), soccer, swimming, track/field (indoor), track/field (outdoor), volleyball, wrestling. *Women:* Basketball, crew/rowing, cross-country, ice hockey, rugby, skiing (downhill/alpine), soccer, swimming, track/field (indoor), track/field (outdoor), volleyball, wrestling.

ADMISSIONS
Freshman Academic Profile: 21% in top 10% of high school class, 49% in top 25% of high school class, 85% in top 50% of high school class. 92% from public high schools. SAT Math middle 50% range 430–590. SAT Critical Reading middle 50% range 430–580. TOEFL required of all international applicants, minimum paper TOEFL 550. **Basis for Candidate Selection:** *Very important factors considered include:* Class rank, rigor of secondary school record. *Important factors considered include:* Interview, standardized test scores, talent/ability, work experience. *Other factors considered include:* Application essay,

character/personal qualities, extracurricular activities, recommendation(s). **Freshman Admission Requirements:** High school diploma is required, and GED is not accepted. *Academic units required:* 4 English. *Academic units recommended:* 4 English, 4 math, 4 science. **Freshman Admission Statistics:** 13,064 applied, 65% admitted, 59% enrolled. **Transfer Admission Requirements:** High school transcript, college transcript(s), statement of good standing from prior institution(s). Minimum college GPA of 2.5 required. Lowest grade transferable D-. **General Admission Information:** Application fee $50. Regular application deadline 3/1. Regular notification is rolling. Nonfall registration accepted. Common Application not accepted. Credit and/or placement offered for CEEB Advanced Placement tests.

COSTS AND FINANCIAL AID

In-province tuition $1,668. Out-of-province tuition $3,708. International tuition $9,168–$14,000. Room & board $4,970. Required fees $911. Average book expense $1,322. **Student Employment:** Off-campus job opportunities are excellent.

CONCORDIA UNIVERSITY—NEBRASKA

800 North Columbia Avenue, Seward, NE 68434-1556
Phone: 800-535-5494 **E-mail:** admiss@cune.edu **CEEB Code:** 6116
Fax: 402-643-4073 **Website:** www.cune.edu **ACT Code:** 2442
Financial Aid Phone: 402-643-7270

This private school, affiliated with the Lutheran Church, was founded in 1894. It has a 120-acre campus.

RATINGS

Admissions Selectivity Rating: 79   Fire Safety Rating: 68   Green Rating: 60*

STUDENTS AND FACULTY

Enrollment: 1,081. **Student Body:** 55% female, 45% male, 60% out-of-state. African American 1%, Caucasian 84%, Hispanic 1%. **Retention and Graduation:** 72% freshmen return for sophomore year. 26% freshmen graduate within 4 years. **Faculty:** Student/faculty ratio 14:1. 57 full-time faculty, 86% hold PhDs. 98% faculty teach undergrads.

ACADEMICS

Degrees: Bachelor's, master's, post-bachelor's certificate. **Academic Requirements:** Arts/fine arts, English (including composition), foreign languages, history, humanities, mathematics, sciences (biological or physical), social science, general studies, theology. **Classes:** Most classes have 10–19 students. Most lab/discussion sections have 10–19 students. **Majors with Highest Enrollment:** Biology/biological sciences, business administration/management, education. **Disciplines with Highest Percentage of Degrees Awarded:** Education 43%, theology and religious vocations 13%, business/marketing 11%, visual and performing arts 8%, biological/life sciences 6%. **Special Study Options:** Accelerated program, distance learning, double major, dual enrollment, English as a second language (ESL), exchange student program (domestic), independent study, internships, study abroad, teacher certification program. Undergradate students may take graduate level classes.

FACILITIES

Housing: Men's dorms, women's dorms, apartments for married students, apartments for single students, special housing for disabled students. **Special Academic Facilities/Equipment:** Art gallery, museum of natural history, audiovisual equipment, observatory. **Computers:** 100% of classrooms are wired, 1% of classrooms are wireless, 90% of public computers are PCs, 10% of public computers are Macs, 100% of public computers are UNIX, network access in dorm rooms, network access in dorm lounges, online registration, online administrative functions (other than registration), remote student-access to Web through college's connection.

CAMPUS LIFE

Activities: Choral groups, concert band, drama/theater, jazz band, literary magazine, music ensembles, musical theater, pep band, student government, student newspaper, symphony orchestra, yearbook. **Organizations:** 32 registered organizations, 1 honor society, 5 religious organizations. **Athletics (Intercollegiate):** *Men:* Baseball, basketball, cross-country, football, golf, soccer, tennis, track/field (indoor), track/field (outdoor). *Women:* Basketball, cross-country, golf, soccer, softball, tennis, track/field (indoor), track/field (outdoor), volleyball.

ADMISSIONS

Freshman Academic Profile: 23% in top 10% of high school class, 44% in top 25% of high school class, 74% in top 50% of high school class. SAT Math middle 50% range 460–570. SAT Critical Reading middle 50% range 470–580. ACT

middle 50% range 21–27. TOEFL required of all international applicants, minimum paper TOEFL 500, minimum computer TOEFL 173. **Basis for Candidate Selection:** *Very important factors considered include:* Academic GPA, standardized test scores. *Important factors considered include:* Character/personal qualities, class rank, rigor of secondary school record. *Other factors considered include:* Alumni/ae relation, extracurricular activities, interview, recommendation(s), religious affiliation/commitment. **Freshman Admission Requirements:** High school diploma is required, and GED is accepted. *Academic units required:* 4 English, 3 math, 2 science, 2 foreign language, 3 social studies. *Academic units recommended:* 4 English, 4 math, 4 science, 2 foreign language, 3 social studies, 1 music, 1 art, 1 physical education. **Freshman Admission Statistics:** 1,082 applied, 78% admitted, 36% enrolled. **Transfer Admission Requirements:** High school transcript, college transcript(s). Minimum college GPA of 2.0 required. Lowest grade transferable D. **General Admission Information:** Application fee $25. Regular application deadline 8/1. Regular notification is rolling. Nonfall registration accepted. Admission may be deferred for a maximum of 1 year. Credit and/or placement offered for CEEB Advanced Placement tests.

COSTS AND FINANCIAL AID

Room and board $10,800. Required fees $7,355. Average book expense $1,700. **Required Forms and Deadlines:** FAFSA. Financial aid filing deadline 3/1. **Notification of Awards:** Applicants will be notified of awards on a rolling basis beginning on or about 3/1. **Types of Aid:** *Need-based scholarships/grants:* Pell, SEOG, state scholarships/grants, private scholarships, the school's own gift aid. *Loans:* FFEL Subsidized Stafford, FFEL Unsubsidized Stafford, FFEL PLUS, Federal Perkins. **Student Employment:** Federal Work-Study Program available. Institutional employment available. Off-campus job opportunities are good. **Financial Aid Statistics:** 78% freshmen, 76% undergrads receive need-based scholarship or grant aid. 58% freshmen, 56% undergrads receive need-based self-help aid. 36 freshmen, 88 undergrads receive athletic scholarships. 98% freshmen, 98% undergrads receive any aid. Highest amount earned per year from on-campus jobs $3,500.

CONCORDIA UNIVERSITY—PORTLAND

2811 Northeast Holman Street, Portland, OR 97211-6099
Phone: 503-280-8501 **E-mail:** admissions@cu-portland.edu **CEEB Code:** 4078
Fax: 503-280-8531 **Website:** www.cu-portland.edu **ACT Code:** 3458
Financial Aid Phone: 503-288-9371

This private school, affiliated with the Lutheran Church, was founded in 1905.

RATINGS

Fire Safety: TK   Admissions Selectivity: TK   Green Rating: TK

STUDENTS AND FACULTY

Enrollment: 912. **Student Body:** 63% female, 37% male, 39% out-of-state. African American 6%, Asian 5%, Caucasian 74%, Hispanic 4%, Native American 2%. **Retention and Graduation:** 68% freshmen return for sophomore year. 30% freshmen graduate within 4 years. **Faculty:** Student/faculty ratio 17:1. 42 full-time faculty, 55% hold PhDs. 100% faculty teach undergrads.

ACADEMICS

Degrees: Bachelor's, certificate, master's, post-bachelor's certificate, post-master's certificate. **Academic Requirements:** Arts/fine arts, English (including composition), history, humanities, mathematics, sciences (biological or physical), social science, religion. **Classes:** Most classes have 10–19 students. **Disciplines with Highest Percentage of Degrees Awarded:** Education 37%, business/marketing 29%, psychology 8%, biological/life sciences 6%, theology and religious vocations 5%. **Special Study Options:** Accelerated program, cross-registration, distance learning, double major, dual enrollment, English as a second language (ESL), exchange student program (domestic), honors program, independent study, internships, study abroad, teacher certification program.

FACILITIES

Housing: Coed dorms, women's dorms, apartments for single students, university-owned rental houses. **Computers:** 100% of public computers are PCs, network access in dorm rooms, online administrative functions (other than registration), remote student-access to Web through college's connection.

CAMPUS LIFE

Activities: Choral groups, drama/theater, literary magazine, radio station, student government, student newspaper. **Organizations:** 10 registered organizations, 2 honor societies, 1 religious organization. **Athletics (Intercollegiate):** *Men:* Baseball, basketball, soccer. *Women:* Basketball, soccer, softball, volleyball.

ADMISSIONS

Freshman Academic Profile: 17% in top 10% of high school class, 49% in top 25% of high school class, 77% in top 50% of high school class. SAT Math middle 50% range 450–560. SAT Critical Reading middle 50% range 450–560. ACT middle 50% range 18–25. TOEFL required of all international applicants, minimum paper TOEFL 500. **Basis for Candidate Selection:** *Very important factors considered include:* Recommendation(s), rigor of secondary school record, standardized test scores. *Other factors considered include:* Application essay, character/personal qualities, class rank. **Freshman Admission Requirements:** High school diploma is required, and GED is accepted. *Academic units recommended:* 4 English, 3 math, 3 science, 2 foreign language, 3 social studies, 3 academic electives, 1 computer. **Freshman Admission Statistics:** 804 applied, 66% admitted, 32% enrolled. **Transfer Admission Requirements:** College transcript(s), statement of good standing from prior institution(s). Minimum college GPA of 2.0 required. Lowest grade transferable D. **General Admission Information:** Application fee $20. Regular application deadline 7/1. Regular notification is rolling. Nonfall registration accepted. Admission may be deferred for a maximum of 1 year. Common Application not accepted.

COSTS AND FINANCIAL AID

Annual tuition $20,900. Room and board $6,270. Required fees $210. Average book expense $800. **Required Forms and Deadlines:** FAFSA. **Notification of Awards:** Applicants will be notified of awards on a rolling basis beginning on or about 3/15. **Types of Aid:** *Need-based scholarships/grants:* Pell, SEOG, state scholarships/grants, the school's own gift aid. *Loans:* FFEL Subsidized Stafford, FFEL Unsubsidized Stafford, FFEL PLUS, Federal Perkins. **Student Employment:** Federal Work-Study Program available. Institutional employment available. Off-campus job opportunities are fair. **Financial Aid Statistics:** 85% freshmen, 67% undergrads receive need-based scholarship or grant aid. 85% freshmen, 81% undergrads receive need-based self-help aid. 54 freshmen, 160 undergrads receive athletic scholarships.

See page 1132.

CONCORDIA UNIVERSITY—ST. PAUL

275 Syndicate Street North, Saint Paul, MN 55104-5494
Phone: 651-641-8230 **E-mail:** admission@csp.edu **CEEB Code:** 6114
Fax: 651-603-6320 **Website:** www.csp.edu **ACT Code:** 2106
Financial Aid Phone: 651-603-6300

This private school, affiliated with the Lutheran Church, was founded in 1893. It has a 37-acre campus.

RATINGS

Admissions Selectivity Rating: 84   **Fire Safety Rating:** 60*   **Green Rating:** 60*

STUDENTS AND FACULTY

Enrollment: 1,511. **Student Body:** 60% female, 40% male, 21% out-of-state. African American 9%, Asian 6%, Caucasian 64%, Hispanic 2%. **Retention and Graduation:** 73% freshmen return for sophomore year. 27% freshmen graduate within 4 years. **Faculty:** Student/faculty ratio 12:1. 89 full-time faculty.

ACADEMICS

Degrees: Associate, bachelor's, master's, post-bachelor's certificate. **Academic Requirements:** Arts/fine arts, English (including composition), history, humanities, mathematics, sciences (biological or physical), social science. **Classes:** Most classes have 10–19 students. **Disciplines with Highest Percentage of Degrees Awarded:** Business/marketing 61%, family and consumer sciences 9%, education 8%, parks and recreation 4%, theology and religious vocations 4%, security and protective services 3%. **Special Study Options:** Accelerated program, cross-registration, distance learning, double major, dual enrollment, exchange student program (domestic), honors program, independent study, internships, study abroad, teacher certification program.

FACILITIES

Housing: Coed dorms, men's dorms, women's dorms, apartments for married students, apartments for single students. **Special Academic Facilities/Equipment:** Greenhouse, museum. **Computers:** Network access in dorm rooms, online registration, online administrative functions (other than registration), remote student-access to Web through college's connection, tuition includes personal computer.

CAMPUS LIFE

Activities: Choral groups, concert band, drama/theater, jazz band, music

---

ensembles, musical theater, student government, student newspaper, television station. **Athletics (Intercollegiate):** *Men:* Baseball, basketball, cross-country, football, golf, track/field (indoor), track/field (outdoor). *Women:* Basketball, cross-country, golf, soccer, softball, track/field (indoor), track/field (outdoor), volleyball.

ADMISSIONS

Freshman Academic Profile: 15% in top 10% of high school class, 34% in top 25% of high school class, 62% in top 50% of high school class. 80% from public high schools. ACT middle 50% range 18–24. TOEFL required of all international applicants, minimum paper TOEFL 500, minimum computer TOEFL 173. **Basis for Candidate Selection:** *Very important factors considered include:* Academic GPA, recommendation(s), rigor of secondary school record, standardized test scores. *Important factors considered include:* Character/personal qualities, class rank, interview, racial/ethnic status, religious affiliation/commitment, talent/ability. *Other factors considered include:* Application essay, extracurricular activities, level of applicant's interest. **Freshman Admission Requirements:** High school diploma is required, and GED is accepted. *Academic units required:* 4 English, 2 math, 2 science (2 science labs), 1 social studies, 1 history, 2 fine arts, 1 health. *Academic units recommended:* 1 foreign language. **Freshman Admission Statistics:** 783 applied, 65% admitted, 40% enrolled. **Transfer Admission Requirements:** College transcript(s), statement of good standing from prior institution(s). Minimum college GPA of 2.0 required. Lowest grade transferable D. **General Admission Information:** Application fee $30. Regular application deadline 8/1. Regular notification is rolling. Nonfall registration accepted. Admission may be deferred for a maximum of 1 year. Credit and/or placement offered for CEEB Advanced Placement tests.

COSTS AND FINANCIAL AID

Annual tuition $24,900. Room and board $6,900. Average book expense $700. **Required Forms and Deadlines:** FAFSA, institution's own financial aid form. Financial aid filing deadline 5/1. **Notification of Awards:** Applicants will be notified of awards on a rolling basis beginning on or about 3/1. **Types of Aid:** *Need-based scholarships/grants:* Pell, SEOG, state scholarships/grants, private scholarships, the school's own gift aid. *Loans:* FFEL Subsidized Stafford, FFEL Unsubsidized Stafford, FFEL PLUS, Federal Perkins, state loans. **Financial Aid Statistics:** 86% freshmen, 55% undergrads receive need-based scholarship or grant aid. 77% freshmen, 61% undergrads receive need-based self-help aid. 7 freshmen, 51 undergrads receive athletic scholarships. 98% freshmen receive any aid.

CONCORDIA UNIVERSITY—WISCONSIN

12800 North Lakeshore Drive, Mequon, WI 53097
Phone: 262-243-5700 **E-mail:** admission@cuw.edu **CEEB Code:** 1139
Fax: 262-243-4545 **Website:** www.cuw.edu **ACT Code:** 4574
Financial Aid Phone: 262-243-4348

This private school, affiliated with the Lutheran Church, was founded in 1881. It has a 192-acre campus.

RATINGS

Admissions Selectivity Rating: 76   **Fire Safety Rating:** 60*   **Green Rating:** 60*

STUDENTS AND FACULTY

Enrollment: 3,503. **Student Body:** 64% female, 36% male, 30% out-of-state. African American 13%, Asian 1%, Caucasian 55%, Hispanic 2%. **Retention and Graduation:** 74% freshmen return for sophomore year. **Faculty:** Student/faculty ratio 14:1. 89 full-time faculty, 69% hold PhDs.

ACADEMICS

Degrees: Associate, bachelor's, certificate, doctoral, master's, post-bachelor's certificate. **Academic Requirements:** Arts/fine arts, English (including composition), history, humanities, mathematics, sciences (biological or physical), social science. **Classes:** Most classes have 20–29 students. Most lab/discussion sections have 20–29 students. **Majors with Highest Enrollment:** Business/commerce; education; health services/allied health. **Disciplines with Highest Percentage of Degrees Awarded:** Business/marketing 35%, education 16%, health professions and related sciences 15%, security and protective services 10%, theology and religious vocations 7%. **Special Study Options:** Accelerated program, cross-registration, distance learning, double major, dual enrollment, English as a second language (ESL), exchange student program (domestic), independent study, internships, liberal arts/career combination, student-designed major, study abroad, teacher certification program, weekend college, cooperative programs with Cardinal Stritch, Marquette University, and Milwaukee Institute of Art and Design.

FACILITIES

Housing: Men's dorms, women's dorms. **Computers:** Network access in dorm rooms, remote student-access to Web through college's connection.

CAMPUS LIFE

Activities: Choral groups, concert band, dance, drama/theater, jazz band, music ensembles, musical theater, pep band, radio station, student government, student newspaper, student-run film society. **Athletics (Intercollegiate):** *Men:* Baseball, basketball, cross-country, football, soccer, tennis, track/field (outdoor), volleyball, wrestling. *Women:* Basketball, cross-country, soccer, softball, tennis, track/field (outdoor), volleyball. Environmental Initiatives: Construction of environmental education center with LEED status.

ADMISSIONS

Freshman Academic Profile: 13% in top 10% of high school class, 37% in top 25% of high school class, 70% in top 50% of high school class. ACT middle 50% range 19–25. TOEFL required of all international applicants, minimum paper TOEFL 500, minimum computer TOEFL 173. **Basis for Candidate Selection:** *Very important factors considered include:* Academic GPA, application essay, rigor of secondary school record. *Important factors considered include:* Character/personal qualities, level of applicant's interest. *Other factors considered include:* Class rank, extracurricular activities, interview, racial/ethnic status, recommendation(s), standardized test scores, talent/ability, volunteer work, work experience. **Freshman Admission Requirements:** High school diploma is required, and GED is accepted. *Academic units required:* 3 English, 2 math, 2 science, 2 social studies, 5 academic electives. *Academic units recommended:* 4 English, 3 math, 2 foreign language, 5 academic electives. **Freshman Admission Statistics:** 1,856 applied, 70% admitted, 30% enrolled. **Transfer Admission Requirements:** College transcript(s), statement of good standing from prior institution(s). Minimum college GPA of 2.0 required. Lowest grade transferable C. **General Admission Information:** Application fee $35. Regular application deadline 8/15. Regular notification is rolling. Nonfall registration accepted.

COSTS AND FINANCIAL AID

Annual tuition $18,950. Room and board $7,200. Required fees $90. Average book expense $1,100. **Required Forms and Deadlines:** FAFSA, institution's own financial aid form. Financial aid filing deadline 4/1. **Notification of Awards:** Applicants will be notified of awards on a rolling basis beginning on or about 3/1. **Types of Aid:** *Need-based scholarships/grants:* Pell, SEOG, state scholarships/grants, private scholarships, the school's own gift aid. *Loans:* Direct Subsidized Stafford, Direct Unsubsidized Stafford, Direct PLUS, state loans. **Financial Aid Statistics:** 73% freshmen, 62% undergrads receive need-based scholarship or grant aid. 70% freshmen, 73% undergrads receive need-based self-help aid. 95% freshmen receive any aid.

CONNECTICUT COLLEGE

270 Mohegan Avenue, New London, CT 06320
Phone: 860-439-2200 **E-mail:** admission@conncoll.edu **CEEB Code:** 3284
Fax: 860-439-4301 **Website:** www.conncoll.edu **ACT Code:** 0556
Financial Aid Phone: 860-439-2058

This private school was founded in 1911. It has a 750-acre campus.

RATINGS

Admissions Selectivity Rating: 95   **Fire Safety Rating:** 81   **Green Rating:** 80

STUDENTS AND FACULTY

Enrollment: 1,773. **Student Body:** 60% female, 40% male, 83% out-of-state, 6% international (41 countries represented). African American 4%, Asian 4%, Caucasian 73%, Hispanic 5%. **Retention and Graduation:** 91% freshmen return for sophomore year. 82% freshmen graduate within 4 years. **Faculty:** Student/faculty ratio 10:1. 162 full-time faculty, 91% hold PhDs. 100% faculty teach undergrads.

ACADEMICS

Degrees: Bachelor's, master's. **Academic Requirements:** Arts/fine arts, foreign languages, history, humanities, mathematics, philosophy, sciences (biological or physical), social science, writing. **Classes:** Most classes have 10–19 students. Most lab/discussion sections have 10–19 students. **Majors with Highest Enrollment:** English language and literature, political science and government, psychology. **Disciplines with Highest Percentage of Degrees Awarded:** Social sciences 32%, biological/life sciences 10%, visual and performing arts 10%, psychology 7%, foreign languages and literature 6%, English 6%. **Special Study Options:** Cross-registration, double major, dual enrollment, exchange student program (domestic), honors program, independent study, internships, student-designed major, study abroad, teacher certification program. Cross-registration with the U.S. Coast Guard Academy, Trinity College, and Wesleyan University; 3–2 Program with Washington University or Boston University for a 5-year BA/BS degree, exchange student program, 12 exchanges.

FACILITIES

Housing: Coed dorms, special housing for disabled students, cooperative housing, thematic housing (environmentalism, foreign language, substance-free housing, etc.), men's floors, women's floors. **Special Academic Facilities/Equipment:** Art museum, children's school, language lab, 750-acre arboretum, botanic garden, greenhouse, environment control labs, transmission and scanning electron microscope, ion accelerator, GIS lab, refracting telescope, observatory. **Computers:** 100% of classrooms are wireless, 82% of public computers are PCs, 18% of public computers are Macs, network access in dorm rooms, online administrative functions (other than registration), remote student-access to Web through college's connection.

CAMPUS LIFE

Activities: Choral groups, concert band, dance, drama/theater, jazz band, literary magazine, music ensembles, radio station, student government, student newspaper, student-run film society, symphony orchestra, yearbook. **Organizations:** 60 registered organizations, 5 honor societies, 6 religious organizations. **Athletics (Intercollegiate):** *Men:* Basketball, crew/rowing, cross-country, diving, ice hockey, lacrosse, sailing, soccer, squash, swimming, tennis, track/field (indoor), track/field (outdoor), water polo. *Women:* Basketball, crew/rowing, cross-country, diving, field hockey, ice hockey, lacrosse, sailing, soccer, squash, swimming, tennis, track/field (indoor), track/field (outdoor), volleyball, water polo.

ADMISSIONS

. **Freshman Academic Profile:** 52% in top 10% of high school class, 93% in top 25% of high school class, 100% in top 50% of high school class. 55% from public high schools. SAT Math middle 50% range 610–690. SAT Critical Reading middle 50% range 630–720. SAT Writing middle 50% range 630–720. ACT middle 50% range 25–29. TOEFL required of all international applicants, minimum paper TOEFL 600, minimum computer TOEFL 250. **Freshman Admission Requirements:** High school diploma is required, and GED is accepted. *Academic units recommended:* 4 English, 4 math, 4 science (3 science labs), 2 foreign language, 2 social studies, 3 history, 3 academic electives. **Freshman Admission Statistics:** 4,278 applied, 38% admitted, 30% enrolled. **Transfer Admission Requirements:** Minimum college GPA of 3.0 required. Lowest grade transferable C. **General Admission Information:** Application fee $60. Early decision application deadline 11/15. Regular application deadline 1/1. Regular notification 3/31. Nonfall registration accepted. Admission may be deferred for a maximum of 1 year. Credit and/or placement offered for CEEB Advanced Placement tests.

COSTS AND FINANCIAL AID

Average book expense $1,000. **Required Forms and Deadlines:** FAFSA, CSS/Financial Aid PROFILE, Noncustodial PROFILE, Business/Farm Supplement, federal tax returns, federal W-2 statements. Financial aid filing deadline 2/1. **Types of Aid:** *Need-based scholarships/grants:* Pell, SEOG, state scholarships/grants, the school's own gift aid. *Loans:* FFEL Subsidized Stafford, FFEL Unsubsidized Stafford, FFEL PLUS, Federal Perkins, college/university loans from institutional funds. **Student Employment:** Federal Work-Study Program available. Institutional employment available. Off-campus job opportunities are good. **Financial Aid Statistics:** 35% freshmen, 39% undergrads receive need-based scholarship or grant aid. 34% freshmen, 38% undergrads receive need-based self-help aid. 41% freshmen receive any aid. Highest amount earned per year from on-campus jobs $1,100.

See page 1134.

CONVERSE COLLEGE

580 East Main Street, Spartanburg, SC 29302
Phone: 864-596-9040 **E-mail:** admissions@converse.edu **CEEB Code:** 5121
Fax: 864-596-9225 **Website:** www.converse.edu **ACT Code:** 3852
Financial Aid Phone: 864-596-9019

This private school was founded in 1889. It has a 70-acre campus.

RATINGS
Admissions Selectivity Rating: 89   **Fire Safety Rating:** 60*   **Green Rating:** 73

STUDENTS AND FACULTY
Enrollment: 746. **Student Body:** 100% female, 28% out-of-state, 4% international. African American 12%, Caucasian 74%, Hispanic 2%. **Retention and Graduation:** 79% freshmen return for sophomore year. 53% freshmen graduate within 4 years. 20% grads go on to further study within 1 year. 12% grads pursue arts and sciences degrees. 4% grads pursue business degrees. 2% grads pursue law degrees. 2% grads pursue medical degrees. **Faculty:** Student/faculty ratio 11:1. 84 full-time faculty, 89% hold PhDs. 98% faculty teach undergrads.

ACADEMICS
Degrees: Bachelor's, master's, post-master's certificate. **Academic Requirements:** Arts/fine arts, English (including composition), foreign languages, history, humanities, mathematics, sciences (biological or physical), social science, ideas and cultures. **Classes:** Most classes have fewer than 10 students. Most lab/discussion sections have fewer than 10 students. **Majors with Highest Enrollment:** Business administration/management, education, psychology. **Disciplines with Highest Percentage of Degrees Awarded:** Education 33%, visual and performing arts 17%, business/marketing 13%, psychology 8%, English 7%. **Special Study Options:** Cross-registration, double major, English as a second language (ESL), honors program, independent study, internships, liberal arts/career combination, student-designed major, study abroad, teacher certification program. Undergrads may take grad level classes.

FACILITIES
Housing: Women's dorms. **Special Academic Facilities/Equipment:** Language lab, Phifer Science Building, Blackman Auditorium (music). **Computers:** 95% of public computers are PCs, 5% of public computers are Macs, network access in dorm rooms, online registration, online administrative functions (other than registration), remote student-access to Web through college's connection.

CAMPUS LIFE
Activities: Choral groups, concert band, dance, drama/theater, literary magazine, music ensembles, musical theater, opera, student government, student newspaper, symphony orchestra, yearbook. **Organizations:** 45 registered organizations, 16 honor societies, 7 religious organizations. **Women:** Basketball, cheerleading, cross-country, equestrian sports, soccer, tennis, volleyball. Environmental Initiatives: LEED Certified new construction. Sustainable foodstuffs bought and used by Dining Services. Student Environmental Group—WISE.

ADMISSIONS
Freshman Academic Profile: 30% in top 10% of high school class, 71% in top 25% of high school class, 95% in top 50% of high school class. 80% from public high schools. SAT Math middle 50% range 480–590. SAT Critical Reading middle 50% range 510–610. SAT Writing middle 50% range 480–580. ACT middle 50% range 20–26. **Basis for Candidate Selection:** *Very important factors considered include:* Academic GPA, rigor of secondary school record. *Important factors considered include:* Application essay, character/personal qualities, extracurricular activities, recommendation(s), standardized test scores, talent/ability. *Other factors considered include:* Alumni/ae relation, class rank, first generation, interview, volunteer work, work experience. **Freshman Admission Requirements:** High school diploma is required, and GED is accepted. *Academic units recommended:* 4 English, 2 math, 2 science (2 science labs), 2 foreign language, 1 social studies, 1 history. **Freshman Admission Statistics:** 1,361 applied, 47% admitted, 25% enrolled. **Transfer Admission Requirements:** College transcript(s), statement of good standing from prior institution(s). Minimum college GPA of 2.0 required. Lowest grade transferable C. **General Admission Information:** Application fee $40. Regular notification is rolling. Nonfall registration accepted. Admission may be deferred for a maximum of 1 year. Credit offered for CEEB Advanced Placement tests.

COSTS AND FINANCIAL AID
Annual tuition $24,500. Room and board $7,550. Average book expense $850.

Required Forms and Deadlines: FAFSA. **Notification of Awards:** Applicants will be notified of awards on a rolling basis beginning on or about 3/1. **Types of Aid:** *Need-based scholarships/grants:* Pell, SEOG, state scholarships/grants, private scholarships, the school's own gift aid. *Loans:* FFEL Subsidized Stafford, FFEL Unsubsidized Stafford, FFEL PLUS, Federal Perkins, state loans. **Student Employment:** Federal Work-Study Program available. Institutional employment available. Off-campus job opportunities are good. **Financial Aid Statistics:** 69% freshmen, 68% undergrads receive need-based scholarship or grant aid. 45% freshmen, 43% undergrads receive need-based self-help aid. 8 freshmen, 27 undergrads receive athletic scholarships. 95% freshmen, 93% undergrads receive any aid.

See page 1136.

THE COOPER UNION FOR THE ADVANCEMENT OF SCIENCE AND ART

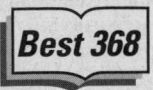

Best 368

30 Cooper Square, Office of Admissions and Records, New York, NY 10003
Phone: 212-353-4120 **E-mail:** admissions@cooper.edu **CEEB Code:** 2097
Fax: 212-353-4342 **Website:** www.cooper.edu **ACT Code:** 2724
Financial Aid Phone: 212-353-4130

This private school was founded in 1859.

RATINGS
Admissions Selectivity Rating: 98   **Fire Safety Rating:** 98   **Green Rating:** 80

STUDENTS AND FACULTY
Enrollment: 904. **Student Body:** 38% female, 62% male, 40% out-of-state, 9% international. African American 5%, Asian 22%, Caucasian 48%, Hispanic 8%. **Retention and Graduation:** 93% freshmen return for sophomore year. 77% freshmen graduate within 4 years. 60% grads go on to further study within 1 year. 15% grads pursue arts and sciences degrees. 10% grads pursue business degrees. 6% grads pursue law degrees. 3% grads pursue medical degrees. **Faculty:** Student/faculty ratio 7:1. 53 full-time faculty, 83% hold PhDs. 100% faculty teach undergrads.

ACADEMICS
Degrees: Bachelor's, certificate, master's. **Academic Requirements:** English (including composition), history, humanities, sciences (biological or physical), social science. Every enrolled student must complete a core humanities and social science program. About 1/4 to 1/3 of each professional degree program involves liberal arts coursework. **Classes:** Most classes have 10–19 students. Most lab/discussion sections have 10–19 students. **Majors with Highest Enrollment:** Architecture (BArch, BA/BS, MArch, MA/MS, PhD); electrical, electronics, and communications engineering; fine arts and art studies. **Disciplines with Highest Percentage of Degrees Awarded:** Engineering 57%, visual and performing arts 28%, architecture 16%. **Special Study Options:** Cross registration, exchange student program (domestic), honors program, independent study, internships, student-designed major, study abroad.

FACILITIES
Housing: Coed dorms. **Special Academic Facilities/Equipment:** The Great Hall, Houghton Gallery, the Brooks Lab. **Computers:** 30% of classrooms are wired, 20% of classrooms are wireless, 80% of public computers are PCs, 20% of public computers are Macs, 10% of public computers are UNIX, network access in dorm rooms, network access in dorm lounges, online administrative functions (other than registration), support for handheld computing, remote student-access to Web through college's connection.

CAMPUS LIFE
Activities: Choral groups, concert band, dance, drama/theater, jazz band, literary magazine, music ensembles, student government, student newspaper, student-run film society, symphony orchestra, yearbook. **Organizations:** 95 registered organizations, 7 honor societies, 8 religious organizations. 2 fraternities (10% men join), 1 sorority (5% women join). **Athletics (Intercollegiate):** *Men:* Baseball, basketball, golf, soccer, tennis, track/field (outdoor), volleyball. *Women:* Basketball, golf, tennis, track/field (outdoor), volleyball. Environmental Initiatives: New Academic Building.

ADMISSIONS

. **Freshman Academic Profile:** 90% in top 10% of high school class, 98% in top 25% of high school class, 98% in top 50% of high school class. 65% from public high schools. SAT Math middle 50% range 640–770. SAT Critical Reading middle 50% range 610–700. ACT middle 50% range 29–33. TOEFL required of all international applicants, minimum paper TOEFL 600, minimum computer TOEFL 250. **Basis for Candidate Selection:** *Very important factors considered include:* Academic GPA, rigor of secondary school record, standardized test scores, talent/ability. *Important factors considered include:* Application essay, character/personal qualities, extracurricular activities, level of applicant's interest. *Other factors considered include:* Class rank, first generation, interview, racial/ethnic status, recommendation(s), volunteer work, work experience. **Freshman Admission Requirements:** High school diploma is required, and GED is accepted. *Academic units required:* 4 English, 1 math, 1 science, 1 social studies, 1 history, 8 academic electives. *Academic units recommended:* 4 English, 4 math, 4 science (3 science labs), 2 foreign language, 4 social studies. **Freshman Admission Statistics:** 2,600 applied, 10% admitted, 78% enrolled. **Transfer Admission Requirements:** High school transcript, college transcript(s), essay or personal statement, statement of good standing from prior institution(s). Minimum college GPA of 3.0 required. Lowest grade transferable B. **General Admission Information:** Application fee $65. Early decision application deadline 12/1. Regular application deadline 1/1. Regular notification 4/1. Non-fall registration not accepted. Admission may be deferred for a maximum of 2 semesters. Credit and/or placement offered for CEEB Advanced Placement tests.

COSTS AND FINANCIAL AID

Annual tuition $31,500. Room and board $13,500. Required fees $1,600. Average book expense $1,800. **Required Forms and Deadlines:** FAFSA, CSS/Financial aid profile. Financial aid filing deadline 6/1. **Notification of Awards:** Applicants will be notified of awards on or about 6/1. **Types of Aid:** *Need-based scholarships/grants:* Pell, SEOG, state scholarships/grants, private scholarships, the school's own gift aid. *Loans:* FFEL Subsidized Stafford, FFEL Unsubsidized Stafford, FFEL PLUS, Federal Perkins, college/university loans from institutional funds. **Student Employment:** Federal Work-Study Program available. Institutional employment available. Off-campus job opportunities are excellent. **Financial Aid Statistics:** 34% freshmen, 31% undergrads receive need-based scholarship or grant aid. 29% freshmen, 21% undergrads receive need-based self-help aid. 222 freshmen, 928 undergrads receive athletic scholarships. 100% freshmen, 100% undergrads receive any aid.

COPPIN STATE UNIVERSITY

2500 West North Avenue, Baltimore, MD 21216
Phone: 410-951-3600 **E-mail:** admissions@coppin.edu **CEEB Code:** 5122
Fax: 410-523-7351 **Website:** www.coppin.edu **ACT Code:** 1688
Financial Aid Phone: 410-951-3636

This public school was founded in 1900. It has a 52-acre campus.

RATINGS

Admissions Selectivity Rating: 60*   **Fire Safety Rating:** 60*   **Green Rating:** 60*

STUDENTS AND FACULTY

Enrollment: 3,185. **Student Body:** 77% female, 23% male, 8% out-of-state, 3% international. African American 95%, Caucasian 2%. **Retention and Graduation:** 65% freshmen return for sophomore year. 7% freshmen graduate within 4 years. **Faculty:** Student/faculty ratio 19:1. 130 full-time faculty, 59% hold PhDs.

ACADEMICS

Degrees: Bachelor's, master's, post-master's certificate. **Academic Requirements:** Arts/fine arts, English (including composition), history, humanities, mathematics, philosophy, sciences (biological or physical), social science. **Majors with Highest Enrollment:** Criminal justice/law enforcement administration, management science, nursing/registered nurse training (RN, ASN, BSN, MSN). **Disciplines with Highest Percentage of Degrees Awarded:** Business/marketing 16%, health professions and related sciences 14%, social sciences 14%, law/legal studies 13%, psychology 13%, liberal arts/general studies 11%, computer and information sciences 7%. **Special Study Options:** Accelerated program, cooperative education program, distance learning, double major, dual enrollment, external degree program, honors program, independent study, internships, liberal arts/career combination, study abroad, teacher certification program, weekend college. 3–2 programs in engineering, pharmacy, dentistry, physical therapy.

FACILITIES

Housing: Coed dorms, special housing for disabled students. **Special Academic Facilities/Equipment:** Language lab, school of special education, TV studio. **Computers:** 100% of public computers are PCs, network access in dorm rooms, network access in dorm lounges, online registration, online administrative functions (other than registration), remote student-access to Web through college's connection.

CAMPUS LIFE

Activities: Choral groups, concert band, dance, drama/theater, music ensembles, radio station, student government, student newspaper, student-run film society, television station, yearbook. **Organizations:** 28 registered organizations, 1 honor society, 1 religious organization. 3 fraternities, 4 sororities. **Athletics (Intercollegiate):** *Men:* Baseball, basketball, cross-country, tennis, track/field (indoor), track/field (outdoor). *Women:* Basketball, bowling, cheerleading, cross-country, golf, softball, tennis, track/field (indoor), track/field (outdoor), volleyball.

ADMISSIONS

Freshman Academic Profile: SAT Math middle 50% range 370–450. SAT Critical Reading middle 50% range 380–460. TOEFL required of all international applicants, minimum paper TOEFL 500, minimum computer TOEFL 173. **Basis for Candidate Selection:** *Very important factors considered include:* Rigor of secondary school record. *Important factors considered include:* Recommendation(s), standardized test scores, talent/ability. *Other factors considered include:* Alumni/ae relation, application essay, character/personal qualities, class rank, extracurricular activities, geographical residence, interview, racial/ethnic status, state residency, volunteer work, work experience. **Freshman Admission Requirements:** High school diploma is required, and GED is accepted. *Academic units required:* 4 English, 3 math, 2 science (2 science labs), 2 foreign language, 3 social studies, 2 advanced tech prep. **Freshman Admission Statistics:** 3,075 applied, 46% admitted, 44% enrolled. **Transfer Admission Requirements:** College transcript(s). Minimum college GPA of 2.0 required. Lowest grade transferable C. **General Admission Information:** Application fee $35. Regular application deadline 7/15. Regular notification is rolling. Nonfall registration accepted. Admission may be deferred for a maximum of 1 semester. Common Application accepted. Credit and/or placement offered for CEEB Advanced Placement tests.

COSTS AND FINANCIAL AID

Required Forms and Deadlines: FAFSA. Financial aid filing deadline 3/1. **Notification of Awards:** Applicants will be notified of awards on a rolling basis beginning on or about 4/15. **Types of Aid:** *Need-based scholarships/grants:* Pell, SEOG, state scholarships/grants, private scholarships, the school's own gift aid, United Negro College Fund, Federal Nursing Scholarships. *Loans:* Direct Subsidized Stafford, Direct Unsubsidized Stafford, Direct PLUS, FFEL PLUS, Federal Perkins, college/university loans from institutional funds, Sallie Mae's Signature Loans and Key Alternative Loan. **Student Employment:** Federal Work-Study Program available. Institutional employment available. Off-campus job opportunities are excellent. **Financial Aid Statistics:** 55% freshmen, 67% undergrads receive need-based scholarship or grant aid. 61% freshmen, 66% undergrads receive need-based self-help aid. 31 freshmen, 120 undergrads receive athletic scholarships.

CORBAN COLLEGE

5000 Deer Park Drive Southeast, Salem, OR 97317
Phone: 503-375-7005 **E-mail:** admissions@corban.edu
Fax: 503-585-4316 **Website:** www.corban.edu **ACT Code:** 0477
Financial Aid Phone: 503-375-7007

This private school, affiliated with the Baptist Church, was founded in 1935. It has a 100-acre campus.

RATINGS

Admissions Selectivity Rating: 81   **Fire Safety Rating:** 60*   **Green Rating:** 60*

STUDENTS AND FACULTY

Enrollment: 805. **Student Body:** 60% female, 40% male, 35% out-of-state. Asian 2%, Caucasian 92%, Hispanic 2%, Native American 2%. **Retention and Graduation:** 72% freshmen return for sophomore year. 49% freshmen graduate within 4 years. **Faculty:** Student/faculty ratio 13:1. 36 full-time faculty, 47% hold PhDs. 100% faculty teach undergrads.

ACADEMICS

Degrees: Associate, bachelor's, master's. **Academic Requirements:** Arts/fine arts, English (including composition), history, humanities, mathematics, philosophy, sciences (biological or physical), social science, biblical/theological studies. **Classes:** Most classes have fewer than 10 students. Most lab/discussion sections have 10–19 students. **Majors with Highest Enrollment:** Business administration/management, family systems, liberal arts and sciences/liberal studies. **Disciplines with Highest Percentage of Degrees Awarded:** Business/marketing 29%, psychology 28%, education 16%, theology and religious vocations 8%, interdisciplinary studies 5%. **Special Study Options:** Accelerated program, cross-registration, distance learning, double major, exchange student program (domestic), honors program, independent study, internships, student-designed major, study abroad, teacher certification program, weekend college.

FACILITIES

Housing: Men's dorms, women's dorms, apartments for married students, apartments for single students. **Special Academic Facilities/Equipment:** Prewitt-Allen Archaeological Museum, Psalms Performing Arts Center. **Computers:** 100% of public computers are PCs, network access in dorm rooms, online registration, remote student-access to Web through college's connection.

CAMPUS LIFE

Activities: Choral groups, concert band, drama/theater, jazz band, literary magazine, music ensembles, musical theater, pep band, radio station, student government, student newspaper, symphony orchestra, yearbook. **Organizations:** 1 honor society, 10 religious organizations. **Athletics (Intercollegiate):** *Men:* Baseball, basketball, cross-country, golf, soccer. *Women:* Basketball, cross-country, golf, soccer, softball, volleyball.

ADMISSIONS

Freshman Academic Profile: 27% in top 10% of high school class, 55% in top 25% of high school class, 80% in top 50% of high school class. 40% from public high schools. SAT Math middle 50% range 475–600. SAT Critical Reading middle 50% range 490–605. SAT Writing middle 50% range 470–570. ACT middle 50% range 20–25. TOEFL required of all international applicants, minimum paper TOEFL 500, minimum computer TOEFL 250. **Basis for Candidate Selection:** *Very important factors considered include:* Academic GPA, application essay, recommendation(s), religious affiliation/commitment. *Important factors considered include:* Character/personal qualities, level of applicant's interest, rigor of secondary school record, standardized test scores. *Other factors considered include:* Alumni/ae relation, class rank, extracurricular activities, interview. **Freshman Admission Requirements:** High school diploma is required, and GED is accepted. *Academic units recommended:* 4 English, 3 math, 2 science, 2 foreign language, 3 social studies. **Freshman Admission Statistics:** 503 applied, 79% admitted, 47% enrolled. **Transfer Admission Requirements:** High school transcript, college transcript(s), essay or personal statement. Minimum college GPA of 2.0 required. Lowest grade transferable C. **General Admission Information:** Application fee $40. Regular application deadline 8/1. Regular notification is rolling. Nonfall registration accepted. Credit offered for CEEB Advanced Placement tests.

COSTS AND FINANCIAL AID

Annual tuition $19,084. Room & board $7,070. Required fees $210. Average book expense $900. **Required Forms and Deadlines:** FAFSA. Financial aid filing deadline 2/15. **Notification of Awards:** Applicants will be notified of awards on a rolling basis beginning on or about 3/1. **Types of Aid:** *Need-based scholarships/grants:* Pell, SEOG, state scholarships/grants, private scholarships, the school's own gift aid. *Loans:* Direct Subsidized Stafford, Direct Unsubsidized Stafford, Direct PLUS, Federal Perkins, state loans, alternative bank loans. **Student Employment:** Federal Work-Study Program available. Institutional employment available. Off-campus job opportunities are fair. **Financial Aid Statistics:** 85% freshmen, 85% undergrads receive need-based scholarship or grant aid. 77% freshmen, 74% undergrads receive need-based self-help aid. 9 freshmen, 38 undergrads receive athletic scholarships. 95% freshmen, 95% undergrads receive any aid. Highest amount earned per year from on-campus jobs $1,000.

STUDENTS AND FACULTY

Enrollment: 352. **Student Body:** 64% female, 36% male, 73% out-of-state, 11% international (20 countries represented). African American 7%, Asian 6%, Caucasian 51%, Hispanic 5%. **Retention and Graduation:** 64% freshmen return for sophomore year. **Faculty:** Student/faculty ratio 4:1. 31 full-time faculty, 42% hold PhDs. 100% faculty teach undergrads.

ACADEMICS

Degrees: Associate, bachelor's, certificate, master's. **Academic Requirements:** Arts/fine arts, English (including composition), humanities, philosophy. **Classes:** Most classes have fewer than 10 students. **Majors with Highest Enrollment:** Fine/studio arts; graphic design, photography. **Disciplines with Highest Percentage of Degrees Awarded:** Visual and performing arts 100%. **Special Study Options:** Cross-registration, exchange student program (domestic), internships, study abroad.

FACILITIES

Housing: Corcoran Leased Apartments and assistance in finding area housing. **Special Academic Facilities/Equipment:** Art gallery, student exhibition spaces. **Computers:** 15% of public computers are PCs, 85% of public computers are Macs, network access in dorm rooms, network access in dorm lounges, online administrative functions (other than registration), remote student-access to Web through college's connection. Undergraduates are required to own a computer.

CAMPUS LIFE

Activities: Student government, student-run film society.

ADMISSIONS

Freshman Academic Profile: 11% in top 10% of high school class, 50% in top 25% of high school class, 83% in top 50% of high school class. SAT Math middle 50% range 410–530. SAT Critical Reading middle 50% range 460–585. SAT Writing middle 50% range 430–540. ACT middle 50% range 16–28. TOEFL required of all international applicants, minimum paper TOEFL 550, minimum computer TOEFL 213. **Basis for Candidate Selection:** *Very important factors considered include:* Academic GPA, interview, rigor of secondary school record, talent/ability. *Important factors considered include:* Application essay, class rank, recommendation(s), standardized test scores. *Other factors considered include:* Alumni/ae relation, character/personal qualities, extracurricular activities, volunteer work, work experience. **Freshman Admission Requirements:** High school diploma is required, and GED is accepted. *Academic units recommended:* 4 English, 4 history, 2 art courses. **Freshman Admission Statistics:** 167 applied, 90% admitted, 26% enrolled. **Transfer Admission Requirements:** High school transcript, college transcript(s). Minimum college GPA of 2.5 required. Lowest grade transferable C. **General Admission Information:** Application fee $40. Regular notification is rolling. Nonfall registration accepted. Admission may be deferred for a maximum of 1 year. Credit and/or placement offered for CEEB Advanced Placement tests.

COSTS AND FINANCIAL AID

Annual tuition $24,289. Room & board $10,795. Required fees $200. Average book expense $2,500. **Required Forms and Deadlines:** FAFSA, institution's own financial aid form. Financial aid filing deadline 3/1. **Notification of Awards:** Applicants will be notified of awards on a rolling basis beginning on or about 4/1. **Types of Aid:** *Need-based scholarships/grants:* Pell, SEOG, state scholarships/grants, the school's own gift aid. *Loans:* Direct Subsidized Stafford, Direct Unsubsidized Stafford, Direct PLUS, FFEL Subsidized Stafford, FFEL Unsubsidized Stafford, FFEL PLUS, Federal Perkins, alternative loans, PLATO, Signature Loans. **Student Employment:** Federal Work-Study Program available. Institutional employment available. Off-campus job opportunities are excellent. **Financial Aid Statistics:** 51% freshmen, 50% undergrads receive need-based scholarship or grant aid. 58% freshmen, 61% undergrads receive need-based self-help aid.

See page 1138.

CORCORAN COLLEGE OF ART AND DESIGN

500 Seventeenth Street Northwest, Washington, DC 20006-4804
Phone: 202-639-1814 **E-mail:** admissions@corcoran.org **CEEB Code:** 5705
Fax: 202-639-1830 **Website:** www.corcoran.edu **ACT Code:** 0671
Financial Aid Phone: 202-639-1816

This private school was founded in 1890. It has a 7-acre campus.

RATINGS

Admissions Selectivity Rating: 76   **Fire Safety Rating:** 60*   **Green Rating:** 60*

CORNELL COLLEGE

600 First Street West, Mount Vernon, IA 52314-1098
Phone: 319-895-4477 **E-mail:** admissions@cornellcollege.edu **CEEB Code:** 6119
Fax: 319-895-4451 **Website:** www.cornellcollege.edu **ACT Code:** 1296
Financial Aid Phone: 319-895-4216

This private school, affiliated with the Methodist Church, was founded in 1853. It has a 129-acre campus.

RATINGS
Admissions Selectivity Rating: 87   **Fire Safety Rating:** 62   **Green Rating:** 60*

STUDENTS AND FACULTY
Enrollment: 1,115. **Student Body:** 54% female, 46% male, 69% out-of-state, 3% international (21 countries represented). African American 3%, Caucasian 84%, Hispanic 3%. **Retention and Graduation:** 85% freshmen return for sophomore year. 60% freshmen graduate within 4 years. **Faculty:** Student/faculty ratio 11:1. 86 full-time faculty, 91% hold PhDs. 100% faculty teach undergrads.

ACADEMICS
Degrees: Bachelor's. **Academic Requirements:** Arts/fine arts, English (including composition), foreign languages, humanities, mathematics, sciences (biological or physical), social science. History and philosophy are considered part of our humanities division. **Classes:** Most classes have 10–19 students. **Majors with Highest Enrollment:** Economics, English language and literature, psychology. **Disciplines with Highest Percentage of Degrees Awarded:** Social sciences 17%, psychology 11%, visual and performing arts 10%, biological/life sciences 9%, education 7%, foreign languages and literature 7%, history 7%. **Special Study Options:** Double major, English as a second language (ESL), exchange student program (domestic), independent study, internships, liberal arts/career combination, student-designed major, study abroad, teacher certification program.

FACILITIES
Housing: Coed dorms, men's dorms, women's dorms, apartments for single students. Our first-year students live on first-year only floors and/or in first-year only residence halls. **Special Academic Facilities/Equipment:** Geology center and museum, MNR machine in West Science Building. **Computers:** 99% of classrooms are wired, 60% of classrooms are wireless, 95% of public computers are PCs, 2% of public computers are Macs, 3% of public computers are UNIX, network access in dorm rooms, network access in dorm lounges, online administrative functions (other than registration), support for handheld computing, remote student-access to Web through college's connection.

CAMPUS LIFE
Activities: Choral groups, concert band, dance, drama/theater, jazz band, literary magazine, music ensembles, musical theater, opera, radio station, student government, student newspaper, symphony orchestra, yearbook. **Organizations:** 76 registered organizations, 11 honor societies, 11 religious organizations. 8 fraternities (23% men join), 7 sororities (25% women join). **Athletics (Intercollegiate):** *Men:* Baseball, basketball, cross-country, football, golf, soccer, tennis, track/field (indoor), track/field (outdoor), wrestling. *Women:* Basketball, cross-country, golf, soccer, softball, tennis, track/field (indoor), track/field (outdoor), volleyball.

ADMISSIONS
88(out of 100). **Freshman Academic Profile:** 31% in top 10% of high school class, 58% in top 25% of high school class, 85% in top 50% of high school class. 85% from public high schools. SAT Math middle 50% range 530–650. SAT Critical Reading middle 50% range 540–680. ACT middle 50% range 24–29. TOEFL required of all international applicants, minimum paper TOEFL 550, minimum computer TOEFL 213. **Basis for Candidate Selection:** *Very important factors considered include:* Academic GPA, application essay, recommendation(s), rigor of secondary school record. *Important factors considered include:* Character/personal qualities, class rank, extracurricular activities, first generation, level of applicant's interest, standardized test scores, talent/ability, volunteer work, work experience. *Other factors considered include:* Alumni/ae relation, geographical residence, interview, racial/ethnic status, state residency. **Freshman Admission Requirements:** High school diploma is required, and GED is accepted. *Academic units recommended:* 4 English, 3 math, 3 science, 2 foreign language, 3 social studies. **Freshman**

Admission Statistics: 1,718 applied, 62% admitted, 23% enrolled. **Transfer Admission Requirements:** College transcript(s), essay or personal statement, standardized test score, statement of good standing from prior institution(s). Lowest grade transferable C. **General Admission Information:** Application fee $30. Early decision application deadline 11/1. Regular application deadline 3/1. Regular notification 4/1. Nonfall registration accepted. Admission may be deferred for a maximum of 1 year. Credit and/or placement offered for CEEB Advanced Placement tests.

COSTS AND FINANCIAL AID
Annual tuition $26,100. Room and board $6,970. Required fees $180. Average book expense $720. **Required Forms and Deadlines:** FAFSA, institution's own financial aid form, Noncustodial PROFILE. Financial aid filing deadline 3/1. **Notification of Awards:** Applicants will be notified of awards on a rolling basis beginning on or about 3/1. **Types of Aid:** *Need-based scholarships/grants:* Pell, SEOG, state scholarships/grants, private scholarships, the school's own gift aid, AC and SMART Grants. *Loans:* FFEL Subsidized Stafford, FFEL Unsubsidized Stafford, FFEL PLUS, Federal Perkins, McElroy Loan, Sherman Loan, United Methodist Loan. **Financial Aid Statistics:** 73% freshmen, 72% undergrads receive need-based scholarship or grant aid. 73% freshmen, 72% undergrads receive need-based self-help aid. 84% freshmen, 82% undergrads receive any aid. Highest amount earned per year from on-campus jobs $2,600.

See page 1140.

CORNELL UNIVERSITY

Undergraduate Admissions, 410 Thurston Avenue, Ithaca, NY 14850
Phone: 607-255-5241 **E-mail:** admissions@cornell.edu **CEEB Code:** 2098
Fax: 607-255-0659 **Website:** www.cornell.edu **ACT Code:** 2726
Financial Aid Phone: 607-255-5147

This private school was founded in 1865. It has a 745-acre campus.

RATINGS
Admissions Selectivity Rating: 98   **Fire Safety Rating:** 72   **Green Rating:** 92

STUDENTS AND FACULTY
Enrollment: 13,523. **Student Body:** 49% female, 51% male, 62% out-of-state, 8% international (103 countries represented). African American 5%, Asian 16%, Caucasian 53%, Hispanic 6%. **Retention and Graduation:** 96% freshmen return for sophomore year. 84% freshmen graduate within 4 years. 33% grads go on to further study within 1 year. 3% grads pursue business degrees. 19% grads pursue law degrees. 16% grads pursue medical degrees. **Faculty:** Student/faculty ratio 9:1. 1,700 full-time faculty, 91% hold PhDs. 100% faculty teach undergrads.

ACADEMICS
Degrees: Bachelor's, doctoral, first professional, master's. **Academic Requirements:** English (including composition), social science. **Classes:** Most classes have 10–19 students. Most lab/discussion sections have 10–19 students. **Majors with Highest Enrollment:** Biology/biological sciences, business/commerce; engineering. **Disciplines with Highest Percentage of Degrees Awarded:** Engineering 18%, business/marketing 13%, agriculture 12%, biological/life sciences 12%, social sciences 10%, family and consumer sciences 4%. **Special Study Options:** Accelerated program, cooperative education program, cross-registration, distance learning, double major, English as a second language (ESL), exchange student program (domestic), honors program, independent study, internships, liberal arts/career combination, student-designed major, study abroad, teacher certification program, undergraduate research program.

FACILITIES
Housing: Coed dorms, men's dorms, women's dorms, apartments for married students, apartments for single students, special housing for disabled students, special housing for international students, fraternity/sorority housing, cooperative housing, ecology house. **Special Academic Facilities/Equipment:** Art museum, Africana Studies/Research Center, Theory Center for Supercomputing, ornithology laboratory, plantations. **Computers:** 5% of classrooms are wired, 15% of classrooms are wireless, 85% of public computers are PCs, 5% of public computers are Macs, 10% of public computers are UNIX, network access in dorm rooms, network access in dorm lounges, online

registration, online administrative functions (other than registration), support for handheld computing, remote student-access to Web through college's connection.

CAMPUS LIFE

Activities: Choral groups, concert band, dance, drama/theater, jazz band, literary magazine, marching band, music ensembles, musical theater, pep band, radio station, student government, student newspaper, student-run film society, symphony orchestra, yearbook. **Organizations:** 823 registered organizations, 11 honor societies, 64 religious organizations. 49 fraternities (28% men join), 22 sororities (22% women join). **Athletics (Intercollegiate):** *Men:* Baseball, basketball, crew/rowing, cross-country, football, golf, ice hockey, lacrosse, polo, soccer, squash, swimming, tennis, track/field (outdoor), wrestling. *Women:* Basketball, crew/rowing, cross-country, equestrian sports, fencing, field hockey, gymnastics, ice hockey, lacrosse, polo, soccer, softball, squash, swimming, tennis, track/field (outdoor), volleyball. Environmental Initiatives: Organized and Sustainable Campus Activities. Signing of President's Climate Commitment. Creation of Cornell Center for a Sustainable Future.

ADMISSIONS

. **Freshman Academic Profile:** 84% in top 10% of high school class, 97% in top 25% of high school class, 100% in top 50% of high school class. SAT Math middle 50% range 660–730. SAT Critical Reading middle 50% range 630–770. ACT middle 50% range 28–32. TOEFL required of all international applicants, minimum paper TOEFL 550, minimum computer TOEFL 250. **Basis for Candidate Selection:** *Very important factors considered include:* Academic GPA, application essay, extracurricular activities, recommendation(s), rigor of secondary school record, standardized test scores, talent/ability. *Important factors considered include:* Class rank. *Other factors considered include:* Alumni/ae relation, character/personal qualities, first generation, geographical residence, interview, racial/ethnic status, state residency, volunteer work, work experience. **Freshman Admission Requirements:** High school diploma or equivalent is not required. *Academic units required:* 4 English, 3 math. *Academic units recommended:* 3 science (3 science labs), 3 foreign language, 3 social studies, 3 history. **Freshman Admission Statistics:** 28,098 applied, 25% admitted, 47% enrolled. **Transfer Admission Requirements:** High school transcript, college transcript(s), essay or personal statement. Lowest grade transferable C. **General Admission Information:** Application fee $65. Early decision application deadline 11/1. Regular application deadline 1/1. Regular notification 4/1. Nonfall registration not accepted. Admission may be deferred. Credit and/or placement offered for CEEB Advanced Placement tests.

COSTS AND FINANCIAL AID

Annual tuition $34,600. Room and board $11,190. Required fees $181. Average book expense $720. **Required Forms and Deadlines:** FAFSA, institution's own financial aid form, CSS/Financial Aid PROFILE, Noncustodial PROFILE, Business/Farm Supplement, prior year tax returns. Financial aid filing deadline 2/11. **Notification of Awards:** Applicants will be notified of awards on or about 4/1. **Types of Aid:** *Need-based scholarships/grants:* Pell, SEOG, state scholarships/grants, private scholarships, the school's own gift aid. *Loans:* Direct Subsidized Stafford, Direct Unsubsidized Stafford, Direct PLUS, FFEL Subsidized Stafford, FFEL Unsubsidized Stafford, FFEL PLUS, Federal Perkins, college/university loans from institutional funds, Key Bank alternative loan. **Student Employment:** Federal Work-Study Program available. Institutional employment available. Off-campus job opportunities are fair. **Financial Aid Statistics:** 46% freshmen, 44% undergrads receive need-based scholarship or grant aid. 43% freshmen, 44% undergrads receive need-based self-help aid. 49% freshmen, 47% undergrads receive any aid. Highest amount earned per year from on-campus jobs $2,500.

CORNERSTONE UNIVERSITY

1001 East Beltline Avenue, NE, Grand Rapids, MI 49525-5897
Phone: 616-222-1418 **E-mail:** admissions@cornerstone.edu
Fax: 616-222-1418 **Website:** www.cornerstone.edu **ACT Code:** 2002
Financial Aid Phone: 616-949-5300

This private school, affiliated with the Christian (Nondenominational) Church, was founded in 1941. It has a 130-acre campus.

RATINGS

Admissions Selectivity Rating: 77 **Fire Safety Rating:** 96 **Green Rating:** 70

STUDENTS AND FACULTY

Enrollment: 1,953. **Student Body:** 61% female, 39% male, 19% out-of-state, 1% international (15 countries represented). African American 15%, Caucasian 80%, Hispanic 3%. **Retention and Graduation:** 65% freshmen return for

sophomore year. 15% grads go on to further study within 1 year. 10% grads pursue arts and sciences degrees. 3% grads pursue business degrees. 1% grads pursue law degrees. 1% grads pursue medical degrees. **Faculty:** Student/faculty ratio 14:1. 62 full-time faculty, 52% hold PhDs. 100% faculty teach undergrads.

ACADEMICS

Degrees: Associate, bachelor's, certificate, diploma, doctoral, first professional, master's. **Academic Requirements:** Arts/fine arts, computer literacy, English (including composition), foreign languages, history, humanities, mathematics, philosophy, sciences (biological or physical), social science, religion. **Classes:** Most classes have 10–19 students. **Majors with Highest Enrollment:** Business administration/management, education, psychology. **Disciplines with Highest Percentage of Degrees Awarded:** Business/marketing 54%, education 18%, theology and religious vocations 7%, psychology 4%, English 3%. **Special Study Options:** Accelerated program, distance learning, double major, dual enrollment, English as a second language (ESL), honors program, independent study, internships, liberal arts/career combination, study abroad, teacher certification program, weekend college.

FACILITIES

Housing: Men's dorms, women's dorms, apartments for married students, apartments for single students, special housing for disabled students. **Computers:** 100% of classrooms are wired, 85% of classrooms are wireless, 100% of public computers are PCs, network access in dorm rooms, network access in dorm lounges, online registration, online administrative functions (other than registration), remote student-access to Web through college's connection, tuition includes personal computer. Undergraduates are required to own a computer.

CAMPUS LIFE

Activities: Choral groups, concert band, drama/theater, jazz band, literary magazine, music ensembles, musical theater, pep band, radio station, student government, student newspaper, yearbook. **Organizations:** 11 registered organizations, 1 honor society, 1 religious organization. **Athletics (Intercollegiate):** *Men:* Basketball, cross-country, golf, soccer, track/field (indoor), track/field (outdoor). *Women:* Basketball, cross-country, soccer, softball, track/field (indoor), track/field (outdoor), volleyball. Environmental Initiatives: On campus dialogue and focus on sustainability issues. Joining a community organization.

ADMISSIONS

Freshman Academic Profile: 15% in top 10% of high school class, 39% in top 25% of high school class, 73% in top 50% of high school class. 60% from public high schools. SAT Math middle 50% range 490–590. SAT Critical Reading middle 50% range 460–590. ACT middle 50% range 20–26. TOEFL required of all international applicants, minimum paper TOEFL 500, minimum computer TOEFL 173. **Basis for Candidate Selection:** *Very important factors considered include:* Academic GPA, character/personal qualities, recommendation(s), religious affiliation/commitment, standardized test scores. *Important factors considered include:* Application essay, class rank, rigor of secondary school record, talent/ability. *Other factors considered include:* Extracurricular activities, level of applicant's interest. **Freshman Admission Requirements:** High school diploma is required, and GED is accepted. *Academic units recommended:* 4 English, 3 math, 2 science (1 science lab), 3 foreign language, 3 social studies, 2 history, 4 academic electives. **Freshman Admission Statistics:** 1,109 applied, 73% admitted, 45% enrolled. **Transfer Admission Requirements:** High school transcript, college transcript(s), essay or personal statement. Minimum college GPA of 2.0 required. Lowest grade transferable C-. **General Admission Information:** Application fee $25. Regular application deadline 8/15. Regular notification is rolling. Nonfall registration accepted. Credit and/or placement offered for CEEB Advanced Placement tests.

COSTS AND FINANCIAL AID

Annual tuition $19,190. Room and board $6,500. Required fees $340. Average book expense $1,000. **Required Forms and Deadlines:** FAFSA. Financial aid filing deadline 3/1. **Notification of Awards:** Applicants will be notified of awards on a rolling basis beginning on or about 3/1. **Types of Aid:** *Need-based scholarships/grants:* Pell; SEOG, state scholarships/grants, private scholarships, the school's own gift aid. *Loans:* FFEL Subsidized Stafford, FFEL Unsubsidized Stafford, FFEL PLUS, Federal Perkins, state loans. **Financial Aid Statistics:** 81% freshmen, 77% undergrads receive need-based scholarship or grant aid. 64% freshmen, 60% undergrads receive need-based self-help aid. 42 freshmen, 131 undergrads receive athletic scholarships. 98% freshmen, 92% undergrads receive any aid. Highest amount earned per year from on-campus jobs $5,500.

CORNISH COLLEGE OF THE ARTS

1000 Lenora Street, Seattle, WA 98121
Phone: 800-726-5016 **E-mail:** admissions@cornish.edu **CEEB Code:** 0058
Fax: 206-720-1011 **Website:** www.cornish.edu **ACT Code:** 4801
Financial Aid Phone: 206-726-5013

This private school was founded in 1914. It has a 4-acre campus.

RATINGS
Admissions Selectivity Rating: 60*   **Fire Safety Rating:** 60*   **Green Rating:** 60*

STUDENTS AND FACULTY
Enrollment: 649. **Student Body:** 61% female, 39% male, 35% out-of-state, 5% international (6 countries represented). African American 2%, Asian 5%, Caucasian 69%, Hispanic 4%. **Retention and Graduation:** 72% freshmen return for sophomore year. 12% grads go on to further study within 1 year. 5% grads pursue arts and sciences degrees. **Faculty:** Student/faculty ratio 9:1. 51 full-time faculty, 59% hold PhDs. 100% faculty teach undergrads.

ACADEMICS
Degrees: Bachelor's. **Academic Requirements:** Arts/fine arts, computer literacy, English (including composition), history, humanities, sciences (biological or physical), social science. All students must take 6–8 credits outside their emphasis of study in 1 of the other academic departments. These classes for non-majors are specifically listed in our schedule of classes. **Classes:** Most classes have 10–19 students. **Majors with Highest Enrollment:** Design and visual communications, drama and dramatics/theater arts, fine/studio arts. **Disciplines with Highest Percentage of Degrees Awarded:** Visual and performing arts 100%. **Special Study Options:** Cooperative education program, independent study, internships, study abroad.

FACILITIES
Special Academic Facilities/Equipment: Art galleries, extensive art studio space, theaters, electronic music studio, dance studio, concert hall. **Computers:** 50% of public computers are PCs, 50% of public computers are Macs, remote student-access to Web through college's connection.

CAMPUS LIFE
Activities: Choral groups, concert band, dance, drama/theater, jazz band, literary magazine, music ensembles, musical theater, opera, student government, student newspaper, student-run film society. **Organizations:** 18 registered organizations, 6 honor societies, 1 religious organization.

ADMISSIONS
Freshman Academic Profile: 75% from public high schools. ACT middle 50% range 122–999. TOEFL required of all international applicants, minimum paper TOEFL 525, minimum computer TOEFL 195. **Basis for Candidate Selection:** *Very important factors considered include:* Talent/ability. *Important factors considered include:* Application essay, rigor of secondary school record. *Other factors considered include:* Extracurricular activities, interview, recommendation(s), standardized test scores. **Freshman Admission Requirements:** High school diploma is required, and GED is accepted. **Freshman Admission Statistics:** 602 applied, 81% admitted, 51% enrolled. **Transfer Admission Requirements:** High school transcript, college transcript(s), essay or personal statement, interview. Minimum college GPA of 2.0 required. Lowest grade transferable C. **General Admission Information:** Application fee $35. Regular application deadline 2/15. Regular notification is rolling. Nonfall registration not accepted. Admission may be deferred for a maximum of 1 year. Common Application not accepted. Credit offered for CEEB Advanced Placement tests.

COSTS AND FINANCIAL AID
Annual tuition $14,900. Room & board $11,000. Required fees $300. Average book expense $1,600. **Required Forms and Deadlines:** FAFSA, institution's own financial aid form. Financial aid filing deadline 3/1. **Notification of Awards:** Applicants will be notified of awards on or about 5/15. **Types of Aid:** *Need-based scholarships/grants:* Pell, SEOG, state scholarships/grants, merit scholarships based on artistic merit and merit with need scholarships (both are insitutional money). *Loans:* FFEL Subsidized Stafford, FFEL Unsubsidized Stafford, FFEL PLUS, Federal Perkins. **Student Employment:** Federal Work-Study Program available. Off-campus job opportunities are excellent. **Financial Aid Statistics:** 66% undergrads receive need-based scholarship or grant aid. 66% undergrads receive need-based self-help aid. Highest amount earned per year from on-campus jobs $3,000.

COTTEY COLLEGE

1000 West Austin Boulevard, Nevada, MO 64772
Phone: 417-667-8181 **E-mail:** enrollmgt@cottey.edu
Fax: 417-667-8103 **Website:** www.cottey.edu

This is a private school.

RATINGS
Admissions Selectivity Rating: 60*   **Fire Safety Rating:** 60*   **Green Rating:** 60*

STUDENTS AND FACULTY
Enrollment: 309. **Student Body:** 100% female, 89% out-of-state. **Faculty:** Student/faculty ratio 9:1.

ACADEMICS
Degrees: Associate. **Academic Requirements:** Arts/fine arts, English (including composition), foreign languages, history, humanities, mathematics, sciences (biological or physical), social science. **Special Study Options:** Distance learning, double major, independent study, internships.

FACILITIES
Housing: All residence halls are apartment-style suites.

CAMPUS LIFE
Activities: Choral groups, concert band, dance, drama/theater, jazz band, literary magazine, music ensembles, musical theater, student government, student newspaper, yearbook.

ADMISSIONS
Basis for Candidate Selection: *Very important factors considered include:* Academic GPA, class rank, rigor of secondary school record, standardized test scores. *Other factors considered include:* Alumni/ae relation, application essay, extracurricular activities, recommendation(s), talent/ability. **Freshman Admission Requirements:** High school diploma is required, and GED is accepted. *Academic units required:* 4 English, 3 math, 2 science (2 science labs), 2 foreign language, 2 history, 1 academic elective. **Transfer Admission Requirements:** High school transcript, college transcript(s). Minimum college GPA of 2.0 required. Lowest grade transferable C. **General Admission Information:** Application fee $20. Regular notification within 2 weeks of contact. Nonfall registration accepted. Common Application accepted.

COSTS AND FINANCIAL AID
Comprehensive fee $13,200. Room and board $5,400. Required fees $760. **Required Forms and Deadlines:** FAFSA. **Notification of Awards:** Applicants will be notified of awards on a rolling basis beginning on or about 1/3. **Types of Aid:** *Need-based scholarships/grants:* Pell, SEOG, state scholarships/grants, private scholarships, the school's own gift aid. *Loans:* Direct Subsidized Stafford, Direct Unsubsidized Stafford, Direct PLUS, FFEL Subsidized Stafford, FFEL Unsubsidized Stafford, FFEL PLUS, Federal Perkins.

See page 1142.

COVENANT COLLEGE

14049 Scenic Highway, Lookout Mountain, GA 30750
Phone: 706-820-2398 **E-mail:** admissions@covenant.edu **CEEB Code:** 6124
Fax: 706-820-0893 **Website:** www.covenant.edu **ACT Code:** 3951
Financial Aid Phone: 706-419-1126

This private school, affiliated with the Presbyterian Church in America, was founded in 1955. It has a 300-acre campus.

RATINGS
Admissions Selectivity Rating: 86   **Fire Safety Rating:** 80   **Green Rating:** 60*

STUDENTS AND FACULTY
Enrollment: 918. **Student Body:** 57% female, 43% male, 75% out-of-state. African American 3%, Asian 1%, Caucasian 92%, Hispanic 2%. **Retention and Graduation:** 71% freshmen return for sophomore year. 56% freshmen graduate within 4 years. **Faculty:** Student/faculty ratio 14:1. 60 full-time faculty, 88% hold PhDs. 100% faculty teach undergrads.

ACADEMICS

Degrees: Associate, bachelor's, master's. **Academic Requirements:** Computer literacy, English (including composition), foreign languages, history, humanities, mathematics, sciences (biological or physical), social science, religion. **Classes:** Most classes have 10–19 students. Most lab/discussion sections have fewer than 10 students. **Majors with Highest Enrollment:** Business administration/management, elementary education and teaching, English language and literature. **Disciplines with Highest Percentage of Degrees Awarded:** Education 11%, social sciences 8%, philosophy and religious studies 7%, English 7%. **Special Study Options:** Double major, dual enrollment, independent study, internships, student-designed major, study abroad, teacher certification program. Dual-engineering degree with Georgia Tech, cooperative nursing program with Emory University and Chattanooga State, and bridge program for MSN with Vanderbilt University.

FACILITIES

Housing: Men's dorms, women's dorms, apartments for single students. **Computers:** 100% of classrooms are wireless, 100% of public computers are PCs, network access in dorm rooms, network access in dorm lounges, online registration, online administrative functions (other than registration), remote student-access to Web through college's connection.

CAMPUS LIFE

Activities: Choral groups, drama/theater, literary magazine, music ensembles, radio station, student government, student newspaper, student-run film society, symphony orchestra, yearbook. **Organizations:** 39 registered organizations, 2 honor societies, 1 religious organization. **Athletics (Intercollegiate):** *Men:* Baseball, basketball, cross-country, golf, soccer, tennis. *Women:* Basketball, cross-country, soccer, tennis, volleyball.

ADMISSIONS

Freshman Academic Profile: 22% in top 10% of high school class, 43% in top 25% of high school class, 77% in top 50% of high school class. 50% from public high schools. SAT Math middle 50% range 490–630. SAT Critical Reading middle 50% range 510–660. SAT Writing middle 50% range 500–640. ACT middle 50% range 21–28. TOEFL required of all international applicants, minimum paper TOEFL 540, minimum computer TOEFL 207. **Basis for Candidate Selection:** *Very important factors considered include:* Academic GPA, character/personal qualities, recommendation(s), religious affiliation/commitment, standardized test scores. *Important factors considered include:* Application essay, rigor of secondary school record. *Other factors considered include:* Class rank, extracurricular activities, level of applicant's interest, volunteer work. **Freshman Admission Requirements:** High school diploma is required, and GED is accepted. *Academic units recommended:* 4 English, 3 math, 2 science, 2 foreign language, 2 history, 3 academic electives. **Freshman Admission Statistics:** 951 applied, 65% admitted, 49% enrolled. **Transfer Admission Requirements:** High school transcript, college transcript(s), standardized test score, statement of good standing from prior institution(s). Minimum college GPA of 2.0 required. Lowest grade transferable C-. **General Admission Information:** Application fee $35. Regular notification is rolling. Nonfall registration accepted. Admission may be deferred for a maximum of 3 years. Credit offered for CEEB Advanced Placement tests.

COSTS AND FINANCIAL AID

Annual tuition $22,160. Room and board $6,490. Required fees $680. Average book expense $800. **Required Forms and Deadlines:** FAFSA, state aid form. **Notification of Awards:** Applicants will be notified of awards on a rolling basis beginning on or about 2/1. **Types of Aid:** *Need-based scholarships/grants:* Pell, SEOG, state scholarships/grants, private scholarships, the school's own gift aid. *Loans:* FFEL Subsidized Stafford, FFEL Unsubsidized Stafford, FFEL PLUS, Federal Perkins, state loans. **Student Employment:** Federal Work-Study Program available. Institutional employment available. Off-campus job opportunities are good. **Financial Aid Statistics:** 69% freshmen, 68% undergrads receive need-based scholarship or grant aid. 60% freshmen, 61% undergrads receive need-based self-help aid. 19 freshmen, 57 undergrads receive athletic scholarships. 99% freshmen, 98% undergrads receive any aid. Highest amount earned per year from on-campus jobs $4,050.

CREIGHTON UNIVERSITY

2500 California Plaza, Omaha, NE 68178
Phone: 402-280-2703 **E-mail:** admissions@creighton.edu **CEEB Code:** 6121
Fax: 402-280-2685 **Website:** www.creighton.edu **ACT Code:** 2444
Financial Aid Phone: 402-280-2731

This private school, affiliated with the Roman Catholic Church, was founded in 1878. It has a 130-acre campus.

RATINGS

Admissions Selectivity Rating: 88   **Fire Safety Rating:** 85   **Green Rating:** 89

STUDENTS AND FACULTY

Enrollment: 4,052. **Student Body:** 60% female, 40% male, 55% out-of-state, 1% international (33 countries represented). African American 3%, Asian 8%, Caucasian 79%, Hispanic 3%, Native American 1%. **Retention and Graduation:** 86% freshmen return for sophomore year. 61% freshmen graduate within 4 years. 40% grads go on to further study within 1 year. 10% grads pursue arts and sciences degrees. 8% grads pursue business degrees. 9% grads pursue law degrees. 13% grads pursue medical degrees. **Faculty:** Student/faculty ratio 12:1. 492 full-time faculty, 86% hold PhDs. 59% faculty teach undergrads.

ACADEMICS

Degrees: Associate, bachelor's, doctoral, first professional, master's. **Academic Requirements:** Arts/fine arts, English (including composition), foreign languages, history, humanities, mathematics, philosophy, sciences (biological or physical), social science, theology. **Classes:** Most classes have 20–29 students. Most lab/discussion sections have 10–19 students. **Majors with Highest Enrollment:** Business administration/management, health/medical preparatory programs, psychology. **Special Study Options:** Accelerated program, cross-registration, distance learning, double major, dual enrollment, English as a second language (ESL), exchange student program (domestic), honors program, independent study, internships, liberal arts/career combination, study abroad, teacher certification program, 3–3 engineering program with University of Detroit Mercy.

FACILITIES

Housing: Coed dorms, women's dorms, apartments for married students, apartments for single students, special housing for disabled students. **Special Academic Facilities/Equipment:** Fine arts/performing center, health science and research complex, hospital. **Computers:** 5% of classrooms are wired, 1% of classrooms are wireless, 90% of public computers are PCs, 10% of public computers are Macs, network access in dorm rooms, network access in dorm lounges, online registration, online administrative functions (other than registration), support for handheld computing, remote student-access to Web through college's connection.

CAMPUS LIFE

Activities: Choral groups, concert band, dance, drama/theater, jazz band, literary magazine, music ensembles, pep band, radio station, student government, student newspaper, symphony orchestra, television station, yearbook. **Organizations:** 182 registered organizations, 11 honor societies, 6 religious organizations. 5 fraternities (24% men join), 6 sororities (25% women join). **Athletics (Intercollegiate):** *Men:* Baseball, basketball, cross-country, golf, soccer, tennis. *Women:* Basketball, crew/rowing, cross-country, golf, soccer, softball, tennis, volleyball. Environmental Initiatives: The enhanced recycling program is directed toward a single stream of recycle commodity colection. The University is collaborating with local utilities to create a beta site for solar collection of ample size to generate electricity that can be sold on the grid. The University is undertaking initiatives to foster more use of public transportation, on campus shuttle service and carpooling.

ADMISSIONS

Freshman Academic Profile: 44% in top 10% of high school class, 70% in top 25% of high school class, 92% in top 50% of high school class. 55% from public high schools. SAT Math middle 50% range 550–660. SAT Critical Reading middle 50% range 530–640. SAT Writing middle 50% range 520–640. ACT middle 50% range 24–30. TOEFL required of all international applicants, minimum paper TOEFL 550, minimum computer TOEFL 213. **Basis for Candidate Selection:** *Very important factors considered include:* Academic GPA, rigor of secondary school record. *Important factors considered include:* Application essay, standardized test scores. *Other factors considered include:*

Character/personal qualities, class rank, extracurricular activities, first generation, level of applicant's interest, racial/ethnic status, recommendation(s), talent/ability, volunteer work. **Freshman Admission Requirements:** High school diploma is required, and GED is accepted. *Academic units recommended:* 4 English, 3 math, 2 science, 2 foreign language, 1 social studies, 1 history, 3 academic electives. **Freshman Admission Statistics:** 3,403 applied, 89% admitted, 32% enrolled. **Transfer Admission Requirements:** High school transcript, college transcript(s), statement of good standing from prior institution(s). Minimum college GPA of 2.5 required. Lowest grade transferable C. **General Admission Information:** Application fee $40. Regular application deadline 2/15. Nonfall registration accepted. Admission may be deferred for a maximum of 1 year. Credit and/or placement offered for CEEB Advanced Placement tests.

COSTS AND FINANCIAL AID
Annual tuition $25,820. Room and board $8,736. Required fees $1,260. Average book expense $1,000. **Required Forms and Deadlines:** FAFSA, institution's own financial aid form. Financial aid filing deadline 4/1. **Notification of Awards:** Applicants will be notified of awards on a rolling basis beginning on or about 3/15. *Types of Aid: Need-based scholarships/grants:* Pell, SEOG, state scholarships/grants, private scholarships, the school's own gift aid. *Loans:* FFEL Subsidized Stafford, FFEL Unsubsidized Stafford, FFEL PLUS, Federal Perkins, Federal Nursing, college/university loans from institutional funds. **Student Employment:** Federal Work-Study Program available. Institutional employment available. Off-campus job opportunities are excellent. **Financial Aid Statistics:** 60% freshmen, 49% undergrads receive need-based scholarship or grant aid. 47% freshmen, 47% undergrads receive need-based self-help aid. 46 freshmen, 142 undergrads receive athletic scholarships. 96% freshmen, 91% undergrads receive any aid. Highest amount earned per year from on-campus jobs $1,393.

CRICHTON COLLEGE

255 North Highland, Memphis, TN 38111
Phone: 901-320-9797 **E-mail:** info@crichton.edu
Fax: 901-320-9791 **Website:** www.crichton.edu

This private school was founded in 1941. It has a 55-acre campus.

RATINGS
Admissions Selectivity Rating: 60*   **Fire Safety Rating:** 60*   **Green Rating:** 60*

STUDENTS AND FACULTY
Retention and Graduation: 55% freshmen return for sophomore year. 12% freshmen graduate within 4 years.

ACADEMICS
Degrees: Bachelor's, certificate. **Special Study Options:** Accelerated program, cooperative education program, double major, independent study, internships, student-designed major, study abroad.

FACILITIES
Housing: Men's dorms, women's dorms, special housing for disabled students.

CAMPUS LIFE
Activities: Choral groups, drama/theater, student newspaper. **Athletics (Intercollegiate):** *Men:* Baseball, softball.

ADMISSIONS
Freshman Admission Requirements: High school diploma is required, and GED is accepted. *Academic units required:* 14 English, 14 math, 14 science, 14 foreign language, 14 social studies. **Freshman Admission Statistics:** 362 applied, 68% admitted, 53% enrolled. **Transfer Admission Requirements:** Lowest grade transferable C. **General Admission Information:** Application fee $25. Regular application deadline 8/31. Regular notification is rolling. Common Application not accepted.

COSTS AND FINANCIAL AID
Annual tuition $6,600. Room & Board $2,600. Average book expense $700.

CROWN COLLEGE

8700 College View Drive, St. Bonifacius, MN 55375-9001
Phone: 952-446-4142 **E-mail:** info@crown.edu
Fax: 952-446-4149 **Website:** www.crown.edu **ACT Code:** 2152
Financial Aid Phone: 952-446-4177

This private school, affiliated with the Christian and Missionary Alliance Church, was founded in 1916. It has a 215-acre campus.

RATINGS
Admissions Selectivity Rating: 76   **Fire Safety Rating:** 62   **Green Rating:** 60*

STUDENTS AND FACULTY
Enrollment: 1,054. **Student Body:** 59% female, 41% male, 23% out-of-state. African American 3%, Asian 6%, Caucasian 85%, Hispanic 2%. **Retention and Graduation:** 72% freshmen return for sophomore year. 32% freshmen graduate within 4 years. **Faculty:** Student/faculty ratio 22:1. 39 full-time faculty, 56% hold PhDs. 100% faculty teach undergrads.

ACADEMICS
Degrees: Associate, bachelor's, certificate, master's. **Academic Requirements:** Computer literacy, English (including composition), history, humanities, sciences (biological or physical), Bible classes. **Classes:** Most classes have 10–19 students. Most lab/discussion sections have fewer than 10 students. **Majors with Highest Enrollment:** Business administration/management, elementary education and teaching, psychology. **Disciplines with Highest Percentage of Degrees Awarded:** Theology and religious vocations 45%, business/marketing 18%, education 12%, psychology 8%, computer and information sciences 5%. **Special Study Options:** Accelerated program, distance learning, double major, dual enrollment, English as a second language (ESL), honors program, independent study, internships, study abroad, teacher certification program, weekend college: 2–2 with non-accredited Bible colleges.

FACILITIES
Housing: Men's dorms, women's dorms, apartments for married students, apartments for single students, special housing for disabled students, apartments for students with dependent children. **Computers:** 20% of classrooms are wired, 90% of classrooms are wireless, 86% of public computers are PCs, 14% of public computers are Macs, network access in dorm rooms, network access in dorm lounges, online administrative functions (other than registration), remote student-access to Web through college's connection.

CAMPUS LIFE
Activities: Choral groups, concert band, drama/theater, jazz band, literary magazine, music ensembles, musical theater, pep band, student government, student newspaper, yearbook. **Organizations:** 14 registered organizations. **Athletics (Intercollegiate):** *Men:* Baseball, basketball, cross-country, football, golf, soccer. *Women:* Basketball, cross-country, golf, soccer, softball, volleyball.

ADMISSIONS
Freshman Academic Profile: 13% in top 10% of high school class, 28% in top 25% of high school class, 57% in top 50% of high school class. SAT Math middle 50% range 480–600. SAT Critical Reading middle 50% range 420–610. ACT middle 50% range 19–24. TOEFL required of all international applicants, minimum paper TOEFL 450, minimum computer TOEFL 130. **Basis for Candidate Selection:** *Very important factors considered include:* Academic GPA, application essay, recommendation(s), religious affiliation/commitment, rigor of secondary school record, standardized test scores. *Important factors considered include:* Character/personal qualities, class rank. *Other factors considered include:* Extracurricular activities, interview, level of applicant's interest, talent/ability, volunteer work, work experience. **Freshman Admission Requirements:** High school diploma is required, and GED is accepted. *Academic units recommended:* 4 English, 3 math, 3 science, 2 foreign language, 3 social studies. **Freshman Admission Statistics:** 435 applied, 71% admitted, 56% enrolled. **Transfer Admission Requirements:** High school transcript, college transcript(s), essay or personal statement. Minimum college GPA of 2.0 required. Lowest grade transferable C. **General Admission Information:** Application fee $35. Regular application deadline 8/20. Regular notification within two weeks of decision. Nonfall registration accepted. Admission may be deferred for a maximum of 1 year. Common Application not accepted. Credit offered for CEEB Advanced Placement tests.

COSTS AND FINANCIAL AID
Annual tuition $19,198. Room and board $7,366. Average book expense $1,600. **Required Forms and Deadlines:** FAFSA, institution's own financial aid form. Financial aid filing deadline 8/1. **Notification of Awards:** Applicants will be notified of awards on a rolling basis beginning on or about 4/1. **Types of Aid:** *Need-based scholarships/grants:* Pell, SEOG, state scholarships/grants, private

scholarships, the school's own gift aid. *Loans:* FFEL Subsidized Stafford, FFEL Unsubsidized Stafford, FFEL PLUS, Federal Perkins, state loans, Bremer Educational loans, U.S. Bank No Fee Education loans, CitiAssist loans, Signature loans. **Student Employment:** Federal Work-Study Program available. Off-campus job opportunities are good. **Financial Aid Statistics:** 89% freshmen, 97% undergrads receive any aid. Highest amount earned per year from on-campus jobs $20,090.

THE CULINARY INSTITUTE OF AMERICA

Admissions Deptartment, 1946 Campus Drive, Hyde Park, NY 12538
Phone: 800-285-4627 **E-mail:** admissions@culinary.edu **CEEB Code:** 3301
Fax: 845-451-1068 **Website:** www.ciachef.edu
Financial Aid Phone: 845-451-1302

This private school was founded in 1946. It has a 170-acre campus.

RATINGS
Admissions Selectivity Rating: 60* **Fire Safety Rating:** 60* **Green Rating:** 60*

STUDENTS AND FACULTY
Enrollment: 2,742. **Student Body:** 39% female, 61% male, 76% out-of-state. African American 3%, Asian 4%, Caucasian 56%, Hispanic 4%. **Retention and Graduation:** 95% freshmen return for sophomore year. **Faculty:** Student/faculty ratio 18:1. 130 full-time faculty, 6% hold PhDs.

ACADEMICS
Degrees: Associate, bachelor's, certificate. **Academic Requirements:** 6-month restaurant experience needed for enrollment. **Special Study Options:** Cross-registration, internships.

FACILITIES
Housing: Coed dorms, hearing-impaired housing. **Computers:** Network access in dorm rooms, network access in dorm lounges, online administrative functions (other than registration), remote student-access to Web through college's connection.

CAMPUS LIFE
Activities: Student government, student newspaper.

ADMISSIONS
Freshman Academic Profile: TOEFL required of all international applicants, minimum paper TOEFL 550, minimum computer TOEFL 213. **Basis for Candidate Selection:** *Very important factors considered include:* Application essay, interview, rigor of secondary school record, work experience. *Important factors considered include:* Alumni/ae relation, character/personal qualities, recommendation(s), standardized test scores, talent/ability. *Other factors considered include:* Extracurricular activities, geographical residence, volunteer work. **Freshman Admission Requirements:** High school diploma is required, and GED is accepted. *Academic units recommended:* 4 English, 3 math, 2 science, 2 social studies, 2 history. **Freshman Admission Statistics:** 1,154 applied, 63% admitted, 79% enrolled. **General Admission Information:** Application fee $30. Regular notification 4 dates per year. Nonfall registration accepted. Admission may be deferred for a maximum of 16 months.

COSTS AND FINANCIAL AID
Average book expense $975. **Required Forms and Deadlines:** FAFSA, institution's own financial aid form. **Notification of Awards:** Applicants will be notified of awards on or about 2/15. **Types of Aid:** *Need-based scholarships/grants:* Pell, SEOG, state scholarships/grants, private scholarships, Veterans Administration Educational Benefits (VA). *Loans:* Direct Subsidized Stafford, Direct Unsubsidized Stafford, FFEL PLUS, Federal Perkins. **Student Employment:** Federal Work-Study Program available. Institutional employment available. **Financial Aid Statistics:** 78% undergrads receive need-based scholarship or grant aid. 82% undergrads receive need-based self-help aid.

CULVER-STOCKTON COLLEGE

One College Hill, Canton, MO 63435
Phone: 573-288-6331 **E-mail:** enrollment@culver.edu **CEEB Code:** 6123
Fax: 573-288-6618 **Website:** www.culver.edu **ACT Code:** 2290
Financial Aid Phone: 573-288-6307

This private school, affiliated with the Disciples of Christ Church, was founded in 1853. It has a 139-acre campus.

RATINGS
Admissions Selectivity Rating: 74 **Fire Safety Rating:** 62 **Green Rating:** 63

STUDENTS AND FACULTY
Enrollment: 869. **Student Body:** 58% female, 42% male, 48% out-of-state. African American 4%, Caucasian 68%, Hispanic 3%. **Retention and Graduation:** 65% freshmen return for sophomore year. 36% freshmen graduate within 4 years. 9% grads go on to further study within 1 year. 4% grads pursue arts and sciences degrees. 2% grads pursue business degrees. 1% grads pursue law degrees. 2% grads pursue medical degrees. **Faculty:** Student/faculty ratio 13:1. 46 full-time faculty, 70% hold PhDs. 100% faculty teach undergrads.

ACADEMICS
Degrees: Bachelor's. **Academic Requirements:** Arts/fine arts, computer literacy, English (including composition), humanities, lifetime physical fitness, mathematics, religion, sciences (biological or physical), service learning, social science. **Classes:** Most classes have 10–19 students. Most lab/discussion sections have 20–29 students. **Majors with Highest Enrollment:** Business administration/management, criminal justice/law enforcement administration, nursing/registered nurse training (RN, ASN, BSN, MSN). **Disciplines with Highest Percentage of Degrees Awarded:** Business/marketing 24%, education 13%, psychology 9%, security and protective services 9%, health professions and related sciences 8%, visual and performing arts 7%. **Special Study Options:** Distance learning, double major, dual enrollment, honors program, independent study, internships, liberal arts/career combination, student-designed major, study abroad, teacher certification program.

FACILITIES
Housing: Coed dorms, men's dorms, women's dorms, fraternity/sorority housing. **Special Academic Facilities/Equipment:** Art gallery, performing arts center. **Computers:** 100% of classrooms are wired, 100% of classrooms are wireless, 90% of public computers are PCs, 10% of public computers are Macs, network access in dorm rooms, network access in dorm lounges, online administrative functions (other than registration), remote student-access to Web through college's connection.

CAMPUS LIFE
Activities: Choral groups, concert band, dance, drama/theater, jazz band, literary magazine, music ensembles, musical theater, pep band, radio station, student government, student newspaper. **Organizations:** 44 registered organizations, 10 honor societies, 4 religious organizations. 4 fraternities (30% men join), 3 sororities (31% women join). **Athletics (Intercollegiate):** *Men:* Baseball, basketball, cheerleading, football, golf, soccer. *Women:* Basketball, cheerleading, golf, soccer, softball, volleyball. Environmental Initiatives: Thermostat control. Recycling focus group. Limited use of disposable containers.

ADMISSIONS
Freshman Academic Profile: 11% in top 10% of high school class, 34% in top 25% of high school class, 68% in top 50% of high school class. 90% from public high schools. ACT middle 50% range 18–24. TOEFL required of all international applicants, minimum paper TOEFL 500, minimum computer TOEFL 176. **Basis for Candidate Selection:** *Very important factors considered include:* Academic GPA, class rank, rigor of secondary school record, standardized test scores. *Other factors considered include:* Alumni/ae relation, application essay, character/personal qualities, extracurricular activities, interview, level of applicant's interest, recommendation(s), talent/ability, volunteer work, work experience. **Freshman Admission Requirements:** High school diploma is required, and GED is accepted. *Academic units recommended:* 4 English, 2 math, 2 science, 3 social studies. **Freshman Admission Statistics:** 1,295 applied, 74% admitted, 22% enrolled. **Transfer Admission Requirements:** College transcript(s). Minimum college GPA of 2.0 required. Lowest grade transferable D. **General Admission Information:** Regular notification continuous rolling. Nonfall registration accepted. Admission may be deferred for a maximum of 1 year. Credit and/or placement offered for CEEB Advanced Placement tests.

COSTS AND FINANCIAL AID
Annual tuition $16,600. Room & board $6,850. Required fees $250. Average book expense $800. Average book expense $1,000. **Required Forms and**

Deadlines: FAFSA. Financial aid filing deadline 6/1. **Notification of Awards:** Applicants will be notified of awards on a rolling basis beginning on or about 2/15. **Types of Aid:** *Need-based scholarships/grants:* Pell, SEOG, state scholarships/grants, private scholarships, the school's own gift aid. *Loans:* Direct Subsidized Stafford, Direct Unsubsidized Stafford, Direct PLUS, Federal Perkins, Federal Nursing, state loans, college/university loans from institutional funds. **Student Employment:** Federal Work-Study Program available. Institutional employment available. Off-campus job opportunities are fair. **Financial Aid Statistics:** 86% freshmen, 87% undergrads receive need-based scholarship or grant aid. 78% freshmen, 78% undergrads receive need-based self-help aid. 19 freshmen, 76 undergrads receive athletic scholarships. 100% freshmen, 96% undergrads receive any aid. Highest amount earned per year from on-campus jobs $4,409.

CUMBERLAND UNIVERSITY

Cumberland University, One Cumberland Square, Lebanon, TN 37087-3408
Phone: 615-444-2562 **E-mail:** admissions@cumberland.edu **CEEB Code:** 1146
Fax: 615-444-2569 **Website:** www.cumberland.edu **ACT Code:** 3954
Financial Aid Phone: 615-444-2562

This private school was founded in 1842. It has a 40-acre campus.

RATINGS
Admissions Selectivity Rating: 75   **Fire Safety Rating:** 60*   **Green Rating:** 60*

STUDENTS AND FACULTY
Enrollment: 921. **Student Body:** 57% female, 43% male, 15% out-of-state, 3% international (27 countries represented). African American 14%, Asian 2%, Caucasian 77%. **Retention and Graduation:** 69% freshmen return for sophomore year. 23% freshmen graduate within 4 years. 15% grads go on to further study within 1 year. 5% grads pursue arts and sciences degrees. 5% grads pursue business degrees. 3% grads pursue law degrees. 1% grads pursue medical degrees. **Faculty:** Student/faculty ratio 13:1. 79 full-time faculty, 57% hold PhDs. 98% faculty teach undergrads.

ACADEMICS
Degrees: Associate, bachelor's, master's. **Academic Requirements:** Arts/fine arts, computer literacy, English (including composition), history, humanities, mathematics, philosophy, sciences (biological or physical), social science. **Classes:** Most classes have fewer than 10 students. Most lab/discussion sections have fewer than 10 students. **Majors with Highest Enrollment:** Business/commerce, elementary education and teaching, nursing/registered nurse training (RN, ASN, BSN, MSN). **Disciplines with Highest Percentage of Degrees Awarded:** Business/marketing 26%, health professions and related sciences 19%, education 17%, biological/life sciences 7%, psychology 7%, liberal arts/general studies 5%. **Special Study Options:** Accelerated program, distance learning, double major, dual enrollment, honors program, independent study, internships, teacher certification program.

FACILITIES
Housing: Men's dorms, women's dorms, special housing for disabled students. **Special Academic Facilities/Equipment:** Cavett Wild Game Collection. **Computers:** 100% of public computers are PCs, network access in dorm rooms, remote student-access to Web through college's connection.

CAMPUS LIFE
Activities: Choral groups, dance, drama/theater, jazz band, marching band, music ensembles, musical theater, radio station, student government, student newspaper, yearbook. **Organizations:** 15 registered organizations, 13 honor societies, 2 religious organizations. 3 fraternities (6% men join), 2 sororities (3% women join). **Athletics (Intercollegiate):** *Men:* Baseball, basketball, cheerleading, cross-country, football, golf, soccer, tennis, wrestling. *Women:* Basketball, cheerleading, cross-country, golf, soccer, softball, tennis, volleyball.

ADMISSIONS
Freshman Academic Profile: 15% in top 10% of high school class, 38% in top 25% of high school class, 69% in top 50% of high school class. 89% from public high schools. SAT Math middle 50% range 380–510. SAT Critical Reading middle 50% range 410–530. ACT middle 50% range 17–22. TOEFL required of all international applicants, minimum paper TOEFL 500, minimum computer TOEFL 173. **Basis for Candidate Selection:** *Very important factors considered include:* Class rank, rigor of secondary school record, standardized test scores. *Other factors considered include:* Alumni/ae relation, application essay, recommendation(s). **Freshman Admission Requirements:** High school diploma is required, and GED is accepted. *Academic units recommended:* 4 English, 3 math, 3 science (1 science lab), 2 foreign language,

2 social studies, 1 history, 12 academic electives. **Freshman Admission Statistics:** 532 applied, 66% admitted, 59% enrolled. **Transfer Admission Requirements:** College transcript(s). Minimum college GPA of 2.0 required. Lowest grade transferable C. **General Admission Information:** Application fee $25. Regular notification is rolling. Nonfall registration accepted. Admission may be deferred for a maximum of 1 year. Common Application not accepted. Credit offered for CEEB Advanced Placement tests.

COSTS AND FINANCIAL AID
Annual tuition $12,130. Room & board $4,680. Required fees $100. Average book expense $1,040. **Required Forms and Deadlines:** FAFSA, institution's own financial aid form. Financial aid filing deadline 5/1. **Notification of Awards:** Applicants will be notified of awards on or about 5/1. **Types of Aid:** *Need-based scholarships/grants:* Pell, SEOG, state scholarships/grants, private scholarships, the school's own gift aid. *Loans:* FFEL Subsidized Stafford, FFEL Unsubsidized Stafford, FFEL PLUS, Federal Perkins, state loans. **Student Employment:** Federal Work-Study Program available. Off-campus job opportunities are excellent. **Financial Aid Statistics:** 48% freshmen, 43% undergrads receive need-based scholarship or grant aid. 58% freshmen, 52% undergrads receive need-based self-help aid. 139 freshmen, 759 undergrads receive athletic scholarships. 85% freshmen, 85% undergrads receive any aid.

CURRY COLLEGE

1071 Blue Hill Avenue, Milton, MA 02186
Phone: 617-333-2210 **E-mail:** curryadm@curry.edu **CEEB Code:** 3285
Fax: 617-333-2114 **Website:** www.curry.edu **ACT Code:** 1814
Financial Aid Phone: 617-333-2146

This private school was founded in 1879. It has a 137-acre campus.

RATINGS
Admissions Selectivity Rating: 63   **Fire Safety Rating:** 60*   **Green Rating:** 60*

STUDENTS AND FACULTY
Enrollment: 1,709. **Student Body:** 53% female, 47% male, 40% out-of-state, 1% international (20 countries represented). African American 4%, Asian 1%, Caucasian 48%, Hispanic 2%. **Retention and Graduation:** 68% freshmen return for sophomore year. 44% freshmen graduate within 4 years. 17% grads go on to further study within 1 year. 10% grads pursue arts and sciences degrees. 2% grads pursue business degrees. 1% grads pursue law degrees. **Faculty:** Student/faculty ratio 12:1. 100% faculty teach undergrads.

ACADEMICS
Degrees: Bachelor's, master's. **Academic Requirements:** Arts/fine arts, communications, computer literacy, English (including composition), humanities, mathematics, philosophy, sciences (biological or physical), social science. **Special Study Options:** Accelerated program, double major, honors program, independent study, internships, liberal arts/career combination, student-designed major, study abroad, teacher certification program, weekend college.

FACILITIES
Housing: Coed dorms, women's dorms, special housing for international students. **Special Academic Facilities/Equipment:** On-campus preschool, nursing lab, psychology lab. **Computers:** 80% of classrooms are wired, 60% of classrooms are wireless, 50% of public computers are PCs, 50% of public computers are Macs, network access in dorm rooms, network access in dorm lounges, online registration, support for handheld computing, remote student-access to Web through college's connection.

CAMPUS LIFE
Activities: Choral groups, dance, drama/theater, literary magazine, music ensembles, radio station, student government, student newspaper, television station, yearbook. **Organizations:** 1 honor society, 2 religious organizations. **Athletics (Intercollegiate):** *Men:* Baseball, basketball, cheerleading, football, ice hockey, lacrosse, soccer, tennis. *Women:* Basketball, cheerleading, cross-country, lacrosse, soccer, softball, tennis.

ADMISSIONS
63 (out of 100). **Freshman Academic Profile:** 5% in top 10% of high school class, 22% in top 25% of high school class, 65% in top 50% of high school class. 76% from public high schools. TOEFL required of all international applicants, minimum paper TOEFL 500, minimum computer TOEFL 173. **Basis for Candidate Selection:** *Important factors considered include:* Academic GPA, class rank, recommendation(s), rigor of secondary school record. *Other factors considered include:* Alumni/ae relation, application essay, character/personal qualities, extracurricular activities, interview, standardized test scores, volunteer

work, work experience. **Freshman Admission Requirements:** High school diploma is required, and GED is accepted. *Academic units required:* 4 English, 3 math, 2 science (2 science labs), 1 social studies, 1 history, 5 academic electives. **Freshman Admission Statistics:** 3,509 applied, 66% admitted, 30% enrolled. **Transfer Admission Requirements:** College transcript(s), essay or personal statement. Minimum college GPA of 2.0 required. Lowest grade transferable C-. **General Admission Information:** Application fee $40. Early decision application deadline 12/1. Regular application deadline 4/1. Regular notification is rolling. Nonfall registration accepted. Admission may be deferred for a maximum of 1 year. Common Application accepted. Credit and/or placement offered for CEEB Advanced Placement tests.

COSTS AND FINANCIAL AID
Annual tuition $17,160. Room & board $6,870. Required fees $755. Average book expense $700. **Required Forms and Deadlines:** FAFSA, institution's own financial aid form. Financial aid filing deadline 3/1. **Notification of Awards:** Applicants will be notified of awards on a rolling basis beginning on or about 3/1. **Types of Aid:** *Need-based scholarships/grants:* Pell, SEOG, state scholarships/grants, private scholarships, the school's own gift aid. *Loans:* FFEL Subsidized Stafford, FFEL Unsubsidized Stafford, FFEL PLUS, Federal Perkins, state loans. **Financial Aid Statistics:** 45% freshmen, 38% undergrads receive need-based scholarship or grant aid. 50% freshmen, 47% undergrads receive need-based self-help aid.

See page 1144.

DAEMEN COLLEGE

4380 Main Street, Amherst, NY 14226-3592
Phone: 716-839-8225 **E-mail:** admissions@daemen.edu **CEEB Code:** 2762
Fax: 716-839-8229 **Website:** www.daemen.edu **ACT Code:** 2874
Financial Aid Phone: 716-839-8254

This private school was founded in 1947. It has a 35-acre campus.

RATINGS
Admissions Selectivity Rating: 77   **Fire Safety Rating:** 81   **Green Rating:** 60*

STUDENTS AND FACULTY
Enrollment: 1,509. **Student Body:** 77% female, 23% male, 3% out-of-state. African American 12%, Asian 2%, Caucasian 83%, Hispanic 2%. **Retention and Graduation:** 72% freshmen return for sophomore year. 28% freshmen graduate within 4 years. 25% grads go on to further study within 1 year. 1% grads pursue medical degrees. **Faculty:** Student/faculty ratio 13:1. 85 full-time faculty, 76% hold PhDs. 95% faculty teach undergrads.

ACADEMICS
Degrees: Bachelor's, certificate, first professional, master's, post-master's certificate. **Academic Requirements:** Daemen's core curriculum is skill-based and requires taking course work to demonstrate competency in critical thinking, problem-solving, information literacy, communication, affective judgment, moral and ethical discernment, contextual understanding, and civic responsibility. Also required for graduation are 3 credit hours of service-learning, research and presentation, and quantitative literacy, and 9 credit hours of writing-intensive courses. **Classes:** Most classes have 10–19 students. Most lab/discussion sections have 10–19 students. **Majors with Highest Enrollment:** Health/medical preparatory programs, nursing/registered nurse training (RN, ASN, BSN, MSN), special education. **Disciplines with Highest Percentage of Degrees Awarded:** Health professions and related sciences 33%, education 25%, business/marketing 13%, psychology 7%, visual and performing arts 6%. **Special Study Options:** Accelerated program, cross-registration, distance learning, double major, dual enrollment, exchange student program (domestic), honors program, independent study, internships, student-designed major, study abroad, teacher certification program, weekend college. Washington semester through the Washington Internship Institute. Dual degree (BS/MS) awarded at the completion of the program in physician assistant studies and professional accountancy.

FACILITIES
Housing: Coed dorms, coed apartment-style residence halls, some units are handicapped accessible. **Special Academic Facilities/Equipment:** Teaching Resource Center, Franette Goldman/Carolyn Greenfield Art Gallery, Natural & Health Sciences Research Center, video conferencing center. **Computers:** 50% of classrooms are wireless, 90% of public computers are PCs, 10% of public computers are Macs, network access in dorm rooms, network access in dorm lounges, online administrative functions (other than registration), remote student-access to Web through college's connection.

CAMPUS LIFE
Activities: Choral groups, dance, drama/theater, literary magazine, student government, student newspaper, yearbook. **Organizations:** 52 registered organizations, 9 honor societies, 1 fraternity (6% men join), 4 sororities (4% women join). **Athletics (Intercollegiate):** *Men:* Basketball, cross-country, golf, soccer. *Women:* Basketball, cross-country, soccer, volleyball.

ADMISSIONS
Freshman Academic Profile: 16% in top 10% of high school class, 45% in top 25% of high school class, 77% in top 50% of high school class. SAT Math middle 50% range 460–570. SAT Critical Reading middle 50% range 450–550. ACT middle 50% range 20–25. TOEFL required of all international applicants, minimum paper TOEFL 500, minimum computer TOEFL 173. **Basis for Candidate Selection:** *Very important factors considered include:* Academic GPA, standardized test scores. *Important factors considered include:* Application essay, class rank, interview, recommendation(s), rigor of secondary school record. *Other factors considered include:* Alumni/ae relation, character/personal qualities, extracurricular activities, level of applicant's interest, talent/ability, volunteer work, work experience. **Freshman Admission Requirements:** High school diploma is required, and GED is accepted. *Academic units recommended:* 4 English, 4 math, 4 science (1 science lab), 4 social studies. **Freshman Admission Statistics:** 1,654 applied, 72% admitted, 31% enrolled. **Transfer Admission Requirements:** High school transcript, college transcript(s), statement of good standing from prior institution(s). Minimum college GPA of 2.0 required. Lowest grade transferable C. **General Admission Information:** Application fee $25. Regular notification is rolling. Nonfall registration accepted. Admission may be deferred for a maximum of 1 year. Credit offered for CEEB Advanced Placement tests.

COSTS AND FINANCIAL AID
Annual tuition $18,300. Room and board $8,610. Required fees $450. Average book expense $800. **Required Forms and Deadlines:** FAFSA, state aid form. Financial aid filing deadline 2/15. **Notification of Awards:** Applicants will be notified of awards on a rolling basis beginning on or about 2/15. **Types of Aid:** *Need-based scholarships/grants:* Pell, SEOG, state scholarships/grants, private scholarships, the school's own gift aid. *Loans:* FFEL Subsidized Stafford, FFEL Unsubsidized Stafford, FFEL PLUS, Federal Perkins, college/university loans from institutional funds, alternative loans. **Student Employment:** Federal Work-Study Program available. Institutional employment available. Off-campus job opportunities are fair. **Financial Aid Statistics:** 80% freshmen, 78% undergrads receive need-based scholarship or grant aid. 72% freshmen, 74% undergrads receive need-based self-help aid. 3 freshmen, 20 undergrads receive athletic scholarships. 87% freshmen, 84% undergrads receive any aid. Highest amount earned per year from on-campus jobs $800.

See page 1148.

DAKOTA STATE UNIVERSITY

820 North Washington Avenue, Enrollment Services, Madison, SD 57042
Phone: 605-256-5139 **E-mail:** yourfuture@dsu.edu **CEEB Code:** 6247
Fax: 605-256-5020 **Website:** www.dsu.edu **ACT Code:** 3910
Financial Aid Phone: 605-256-5152

This public school was founded in 1881. It has a 20-acre campus.

RATINGS
Admissions Selectivity Rating: 68   **Fire Safety Rating:** 66   **Green Rating:** 60*

STUDENTS AND FACULTY
Enrollment: 1,455. **Student Body:** 49% female, 51% male, 22% out-of-state. African American 1%, Caucasian 90%, Hispanic 1%, Native American 1%. **Retention and Graduation:** 66% freshmen return for sophomore year. 20% freshmen graduate within 4 years. **Faculty:** Student/faculty ratio 18:1. 80 full-time faculty, 66% hold PhDs. 100% faculty teach undergrads.

ACADEMICS
Degrees: Associate, bachelor's, certificate, doctoral, master's. **Academic Requirements:** Arts/fine arts, computer literacy, English (including composition), humanities, mathematics, sciences (biological or physical), social science. **Classes:** Most classes have 10–19 students. Most lab/discussion sections have 10–19 students. **Majors with Highest Enrollment:** Computer and information sciences, elementary education and teaching, information science/studies. **Disciplines with Highest Percentage of Degrees Awarded:** Computer and information sciences 34%, education 29%, business/marketing 24%, parks and recreation 4%, mathematics 3%. **Special Study Options:** Cooperative education program, cross-registration, distance learning, double major, dual enrollment, English as a second language (ESL), honors program, independent study, internships, teacher certification program.

FACILITIES

Housing: Coed dorms, men's dorms, women's dorms, apartments for single students. **Special Academic Facilities/Equipment:** Natural History Museum, technology classroom building. **Computers:** 100% of classrooms are wireless, 73% of public computers are PCs, 17% of public computers are Macs, 10% of public computers are UNIX, network access in dorm rooms, network access in dorm lounges, online registration, online administrative functions (other than registration), support for handheld computing, remote student-access to Web through college's connection, tuition includes personal computer. Undergraduates are required to own a computer.

CAMPUS LIFE

Activities: Choral groups, concert band, dance, drama/theater, jazz band, literary magazine, music ensembles, musical theater, radio station, student government, student newspaper. **Organizations:** 30 registered organizations, 3 honor societies, 2 religious organizations. **Athletics (Intercollegiate):** *Men:* Baseball, basketball, cheerleading, cross-country, football, track/field (indoor), track/field (outdoor). *Women:* Basketball, cheerleading, cross-country, softball, track/field (indoor), track/field (outdoor), volleyball.

ADMISSIONS

68 (out of 100). **Freshman Academic Profile:** 6% in top 10% of high school class, 25% in top 25% of high school class, 52% in top 50% of high school class. ACT middle 50% range 19–24. TOEFL required of all international applicants, minimum paper TOEFL 550, minimum computer TOEFL 213. **Basis for Candidate Selection:** *Important factors considered include:* Academic GPA, class rank, level of applicant's interest, rigor of secondary school record, standardized test scores. **Freshman Admission Requirements:** High school diploma is required, and GED is accepted. *Academic units recommended:* 4 English, 3 math, 3 science (3 science labs), 3 social studies, 1 fine arts, 1 computer studies. **Freshman Admission Statistics:** 551 applied, 96% admitted, 55% enrolled. **Transfer Admission Requirements:** College transcript(s). Minimum college GPA of 2.0 required. Lowest grade transferable D. **General Admission Information:** Application fee $20. Regular notification continuous. Nonfall registration accepted. Admission may be deferred for a maximum of 1 semester. Credit and/or placement offered for CEEB Advanced Placement tests.

COSTS AND FINANCIAL AID

Annual in-state tuition $2,478. Annual out-of-state tuition $3,716. Room and board $4,308. Required fees $3,567. Average book expense $900. **Required Forms and Deadlines:** FAFSA, Institutional Scholarship Application Form. Financial aid filing deadline 3/1. **Notification of Awards:** Applicants will be notified of awards on a rolling basis beginning on or about 4/1. **Types of Aid:** *Need-based scholarships/grants:* Pell, SEOG, state scholarships/grants, private scholarships, the school's own gift aid, Agency Assistance (Veteran Benefits/Department of Labor). *Loans:* FFEL Subsidized Stafford, FFEL Unsubsidized Stafford, FFEL PLUS, Federal Perkins, alternative commercial loans. **Financial Aid Statistics:** 28% freshmen, 31% undergrads receive need-based scholarship or grant aid. 54% freshmen, 60% undergrads receive need-based self-help aid. 44 freshmen, 144 undergrads receive athletic scholarships. 91% freshmen, 88% undergrads receive any aid. Highest amount earned per year from on-campus jobs $8,000.

DAKOTA WESLEYAN UNIVERSITY

1200 West University Avenue, Mitchell, SD 57301-4398
Phone: 605-995-2650 **E-mail:** admissions@dwu.edu **CEEB Code:** 6155
Fax: 605-995-2699 **Website:** www.dwu.edu **ACT Code:** 3906
Financial Aid Phone: 605-995-2656

This private school, affiliated with the Methodist Church, was founded in 1885. It has a 50-acre campus.

RATINGS

Admissions Selectivity Rating: 75   **Fire Safety Rating:** 60*   **Green Rating:** 60*

STUDENTS AND FACULTY

Enrollment: 654. **Student Body:** 59% female, 41% male, 24% out-of-state, 1% international (5 countries represented). African American 4%, Caucasian 90%, Hispanic 2%, Native American 2%. **Retention and Graduation:** 58% freshmen return for sophomore year. 23% freshmen graduate within 4 years. 10% grads go on to further study within 1 year. **Faculty:** Student/faculty ratio 11:1. 45 full-time faculty, 64% hold PhDs. 100% faculty teach undergrads.

ACADEMICS

Degrees: Associate, bachelor's, master's. **Academic Requirements:** Arts/fine arts, computer literacy, cultural awareness, English (including composition), history, humanities, mathematics, philosophy, sciences (biological or physical), social science. **Classes:** Most classes have 10–19 students. Most lab/discussion sections have 10–19 students. **Majors with Highest Enrollment:** Business administration/management, elementary education and teaching, human services. **Disciplines with Highest Percentage of Degrees Awarded:** Education 26%, business/marketing 20%, psychology 8%, biological/life sciences 6%, mathematics 4%, parks and recreation 4%, social sciences 4%. **Special Study Options:** Distance learning, double major, dual enrollment, honors program, independent study, internships, liberal arts/career combination, student-designed major, study abroad, teacher certification program.

FACILITIES

Housing: Coed dorms, men's dorms, women's dorms, apartments for married students, apartments for single students, Koka honor housing for upper-class women, ADA rooms, apartments available. **Special Academic Facilities/Equipment:** Friends of the Middle Border Museum and Grounds. **Computers:** 75% of classrooms are wireless, 92% of public computers are PCs, 8% of public computers are Macs, network access in dorm rooms, network access in dorm lounges, online administrative functions (other than registration), remote student-access to Web through college's connection. Undergraduates are required to own a computer.

CAMPUS LIFE

Activities: Choral groups, concert band, drama/theater, literary magazine, music ensembles, student government, student newspaper, yearbook. **Organizations:** 5 registered organizations, 6 honor societies, 3 religious organizations. **Athletics (Intercollegiate):** *Men:* Baseball, basketball, cheerleading, cross-country, football, golf, track/field (indoor), track/field (outdoor), wrestling. *Women:* Basketball, cheerleading, cross-country, golf, softball, track/field (indoor), track/field (outdoor), volleyball.

ADMISSIONS

Freshman Academic Profile: 10% in top 10% of high school class, 35% in top 25% of high school class, 75% in top 50% of high school class. 98% from public high schools. ACT middle 50% range 22–28. TOEFL required of all international applicants, minimum paper TOEFL 500, minimum computer TOEFL 200. **Basis for Candidate Selection:** *Very important factors considered include:* Class rank, rigor of secondary school record, standardized test scores. *Important factors considered include:* Application essay. *Other factors considered include:* Recommendation(s). **Freshman Admission Requirements:** High school diploma is required, and GED is accepted. *Academic units recommended:* 4 English, 4 math, 4 social studies. **Freshman Admission Statistics:** 423 applied, 79% admitted, 41% enrolled. **Transfer Admission Requirements:** College transcript(s). Minimum college GPA of 2.0 required. Lowest grade transferable D-. **General Admission Information:** Application fee $25. Regular application deadline 8/29. Regular notification is rolling. Nonfall registration accepted. Admission may be deferred. Common Application not accepted. Credit and/or placement offered for CEEB Advanced Placement tests.

COSTS AND FINANCIAL AID

Annual tuition $15,600. Room & board $4,744. Average book expense $900. **Required Forms and Deadlines:** FAFSA. Financial aid filing deadline 4/1. **Notification of Awards:** Applicants will be notified of awards on or about 3/1. **Types of Aid:** *Need-based scholarships/grants:* Pell, SEOG, private scholarships, the school's own gift aid, Federal Nursing Scholarships, South Dakota Board of Nursing Scholarships/Loans. *Loans:* FFEL Subsidized Stafford, FFEL Unsubsidized Stafford, FFEL PLUS, Federal Perkins, Methodist Loans, private alternative student loans. **Financial Aid Statistics:** 85% freshmen, 100% undergrads receive need-based scholarship or grant aid. 85% freshmen, 97% undergrads receive need-based self-help aid. 88 freshmen, 255 undergrads receive athletic scholarships. 98% freshmen, 98% undergrads receive any aid. Highest amount earned per year from on-campus jobs $3,300.

DALHOUSIE UNIVERSITY

Registrar Office, Halifax, NS B3H4H6 Canada
Phone: 902-494-2450 **E-mail:** admissions@dal.ca **CEEB Code:** 0915
Fax: 902-494-1630 **Website:** www.dal.ca
Financial Aid Phone: 902-494-2302

This public school was founded in 1818. It has an 80-acre campus.

RATINGS

Admissions Selectivity Rating: 60*   **Fire Safety Rating:** 60*   **Green Rating:** 60*

STUDENTS AND FACULTY

Retention and Graduation: 74% freshmen return for sophomore year. 44% grads pursue arts and sciences degrees. 33% grads pursue law degrees. 33% grads pursue medical degrees. **Faculty:** Student/faculty ratio 14:1. 912 full-time faculty.

ACADEMICS

Degrees: Bachelor's, diploma, doctoral, first professional, master's. **Academic Requirements:** Arts/fine arts, foreign languages, humanities, mathematics, sciences (biological or physical), social science, writing course (not necessarily English). **Majors with Highest Enrollment:** Business/commerce, computer and information sciences, engineering. **Special Study Options:** Cooperative education program, distance learning, double major, dual enrollment, English as a second language (ESL), exchange student program (domestic), honors program, internships, liberal arts/career combination, study abroad.

FACILITIES

Housing: Coed dorms, men's dorms, women's dorms, apartments for married students, apartments for single students, special housing for international students, fraternity/sorority housing. Off-campus housing office offers help to students looking for their own accommodations. **Special Academic Facilities/ Equipment:** Art gallery, Dalplex (sports complex), Rebecca Cohn Arts Center. **Computers:** Network access in dorm rooms, network access in dorm lounges, online registration, online administrative functions (other than registration), remote student-access to Web through college's connection.

CAMPUS LIFE

Activities: Choral groups, concert band, dance, drama/theater, jazz band, music ensembles, musical theater, radio station, student government, student newspaper, student-run film society, yearbook. **Organizations:** 200 registered organizations, 8 fraternities, 2 sororities. **Athletics (Intercollegiate):** *Men:* Basketball, cross-country, diving, ice hockey, soccer, swimming, track/field (outdoor), volleyball. *Women:* Basketball, cross-country, diving, soccer, swimming, track/field (outdoor), volleyball.

ADMISSIONS

Freshman Academic Profile: TOEFL required of all international applicants, minimum paper TOEFL 580, minimum computer TOEFL 237. **Basis for Candidate Selection:** *Very important factors considered include:* Rigor of secondary school record. *Important factors considered include:* Class rank, standardized test scores. *Other factors considered include:* Recommendation(s). **Freshman Admission Requirements:** High school diploma is required, and GED is not accepted. *Academic units required:* 3 English, 3 math, 1 science, 15 academic electives. *Academic units recommended:* 3 English, 3 math, 3 science, 1 foreign language, 1 social studies, 1 history, 15 academic electives. **Freshman Admission Statistics:** 8,382 applied, 67% admitted. **Transfer Admission Requirements:** College transcript(s). **General Admission Information:** Application fee $40. Regular application deadline 6/1. Regular notification is rolling. Nonfall registration accepted. Admission may be deferred for a maximum of 1 year. Common Application accepted. Credit and/or placement offered for CEEB Advanced Placement tests.

COSTS AND FINANCIAL AID

In-province tuition $5,320. Out-of-province tuition $5,320. International tuition $9,520. Room & board $6,600. Required fees $400. Average book expense $900. **Student Employment:** Off-campus job opportunities are good.

DALLAS BAPTIST UNIVERSITY

3000 Mountain Creek Parkway, Dallas, TX 75211-9299
Phone: 214-333-5360 **E-mail:** admiss@dbu.edu **CEEB Code:** 6159
Fax: 214-333-5447 **Website:** www.dbu.edu **ACT Code:** 4080
Financial Aid Phone: 214-333-5363

This private school, affiliated with the Baptist Church, was founded in 1898. It has a 293-acre campus.

RATINGS

Admissions Selectivity Rating: 82   **Fire Safety Rating:** 60*   **Green Rating:** 60*

STUDENTS AND FACULTY

Enrollment: 3,610. **Student Body:** 60% female, 40% male, 5% out-of-state, 7% international (55 countries represented). African American 19%, Asian 1%, Caucasian 62%, Hispanic 10%. **Retention and Graduation:** 68% freshmen return for sophomore year. **Faculty:** Student/faculty ratio 17:1. 111 full-time faculty, 77% hold PhDs. 100% faculty teach undergrads.

ACADEMICS

Degrees: Associate, bachelor's, certificate, doctoral, master's, post-bachelor's certificate. **Academic Requirements:** Arts/fine arts, computer literacy, English (including composition), history, mathematics, religion, sciences (biological or physical), social science. **Classes:** Most classes have 10–19 students. Most lab/discussion sections have 10–19 students. **Majors with Highest Enrollment:** Business administration/management, general studies, psychology. **Special Study Options:** Accelerated program, distance learning, double major, dual enrollment, English as a second language (ESL), honors program, independent study, internships, study abroad, teacher certification program, weekend college.

FACILITIES

Housing: Men's dorms, women's dorms, apartments for married students, apartments for single students, special housing for disabled students. **Special Academic Facilities/Equipment:** Corrie Ten Boom Collection. **Computers:** 97% of public computers are PCs, 3% of public computers are Macs, network access in dorm rooms, online registration, remote student-access to Web through college's connection.

CAMPUS LIFE

Activities: Choral groups, drama/theater, music ensembles, musical theater, opera, student government, yearbook. **Organizations:** 36 registered organizations, 4 honor societies, 3 religious organizations. **Athletics (Intercollegiate):** *Men:* Baseball, cross-country, golf, soccer, tennis, track/field (outdoor). *Women:* Cross-country, golf, soccer, tennis, track/field (outdoor), volleyball.

ADMISSIONS

Freshman Academic Profile: 18% in top 10% of high school class, 43% in top 25% of high school class, 67% in top 50% of high school class. SAT Math middle 50% range 464–575. SAT Critical Reading middle 50% range 465–590. ACT middle 50% range 19–24. TOEFL required of all international applicants, minimum paper TOEFL 525, minimum computer TOEFL 197. **Basis for Candidate Selection:** *Very important factors considered include:* Application essay, class rank, rigor of secondary school record, standardized test scores. *Important factors considered include:* Religious affiliation/commitment. *Other factors considered include:* Character/personal qualities, extracurricular activities, interview, level of applicant's interest, recommendation(s), talent/ability, volunteer work, work experience. **Freshman Admission Requirements:** High school diploma is required, and GED is accepted. *Academic units recommended:* 4 English, 3 math, 2 science, 2 foreign language, 3 social studies, 2 history. **Freshman Admission Statistics:** 1,110 applied, 55% admitted, 59% enrolled. **Transfer Admission Requirements:** College transcript(s), essay or personal statement. Minimum college GPA of 2.5 required. Lowest grade transferable C. **General Admission Information:** Application fee $25. Nonfall registration accepted. Credit offered for CEEB Advanced Placement tests.

COSTS AND FINANCIAL AID

Annual tuition $14,940. Room and board $5,148. Average book expense $1,350. **Required Forms and Deadlines:** FAFSA, institution's own financial aid form. Financial aid filing deadline 5/1. **Types of Aid:** *Need-based scholarships/grants:* Pell, SEOG, state scholarships/grants, private scholarships, the school's own gift aid. *Loans:* FFEL Subsidized Stafford, FFEL Unsubsidized Stafford, FFEL PLUS, Federal Perkins, state loans, college/university loans from institutional funds. **Student Employment:** Federal Work-Study Program available. Institutional employment available. Off-campus job opportunities are good. **Financial Aid Statistics:** 44% freshmen, 42% undergrads receive need-based scholarship or grant aid. 49% freshmen, 48% undergrads receive need-based self-help aid. 29 freshmen, 104 undergrads receive athletic scholarships. 94% freshmen, 75% undergrads receive any aid. Highest amount earned per year from on-campus jobs $2,880.

DANA COLLEGE

2848 College Drive, Blair, NE 68008-1099
Phone: 402-426-7222 **E-mail:** admissions@dana.edu
Fax: 402-426-7386 **Website:** www.dana.edu **ACT Code:** 2446
Financial Aid Phone: 402-426-7226

This private school, affiliated with the Lutheran Church, was founded in 1884. It has a 150-acre campus.

RATINGS

Admissions Selectivity Rating: 77   **Fire Safety Rating:** 83   **Green Rating:** 60*

STUDENTS AND FACULTY

Enrollment: 595. **Student Body:** 47% female, 53% male, 42% out-of-state. African American 3%, Caucasian 91%, Hispanic 4%. **Retention and Graduation:** 60% freshmen return for sophomore year. 33% freshmen graduate within 4 years. 13% grads go on to further study within 1 year. 5% grads pursue arts and sciences degrees. 1% grads pursue business degrees. 1% grads pursue law degrees. 1% grads pursue medical degrees. **Faculty:** Student/faculty ratio 13:1. 31 full-time faculty, 81% hold PhDs. 100% faculty teach undergrads.

ACADEMICS

Degrees: Bachelor's. **Academic Requirements:** Arts/fine arts, communication, English (including composition), foreign languages, history, mathematics, physical education, religion, sciences (biological or physical). **Classes:** Most classes have fewer than 10 students. Most lab/discussion sections have fewer than 10 students. **Majors with Highest Enrollment:** Business administration/management, criminal justice/law enforcement administration, education. **Disciplines with Highest Percentage of Degrees Awarded:** Education 29%, business/marketing 15%, public administration and social services 10%, psychology 8%, biological/life sciences 7%. **Special Study Options:** Accelerated program, cross-registration, double major, dual enrollment, English as a second language (ESL), honors program, independent study, internships, liberal arts/career combination, student-designed major, study abroad, teacher certification program.

FACILITIES

Housing: Coed dorms, women's dorms, apartments for married students, apartments for single students. **Special Academic Facilities/Equipment:** Danish Archives. **Computers:** 25% of classrooms are wired, 100% of classrooms are wireless, 85% of public computers are PCs, 15% of public computers are Macs, network access in dorm rooms, network access in dorm lounges, online administrative functions (other than registration), remote student-access to Web through college's connection.

CAMPUS LIFE

Activities: Choral groups, concert band, dance, drama/theater, jazz band, literary magazine, music ensembles, musical theater, radio station, student government, student newspaper, television station, yearbook. **Organizations:** 25 registered organizations, 3 honor societies, 3 religious organizations. **Athletics (Intercollegiate):** *Men:* Baseball, basketball, cross-country, football, soccer, track/field (outdoor), wrestling. *Women:* Basketball, cheerleading, cross-country, golf, soccer, softball, track/field (outdoor), volleyball.

ADMISSIONS

Freshman Academic Profile: 16% in top 10% of high school class, 37% in top 25% of high school class, 62% in top 50% of high school class. SAT Math middle 50% range 420–550. SAT Critical Reading middle 50% range 480–560. ACT middle 50% range 20–25. TOEFL required of all international applicants, minimum paper TOEFL 500, minimum computer TOEFL 173. **Basis for Candidate Selection:** *Very important factors considered include:* Academic GPA, rigor of secondary school record, standardized test scores. *Other factors considered include:* Application essay, extracurricular activities, interview, level of applicant's interest, recommendation(s), volunteer work, work experience. **Freshman Admission Requirements:** High school diploma is required, and GED is accepted. *Academic units recommended:* 4 English, 3 math, 3 science (2 science labs), 2 foreign language, 4 social studies. **Freshman Admission Statistics:** 830 applied, 72% admitted, 24% enrolled. **Transfer Admission Requirements:** College transcript(s). Minimum college GPA of 2.0 required. Lowest grade transferable C. **General Admission Information:** Regular notification is rolling. Nonfall registration accepted. Admission may be deferred for a maximum of 2 years. Credit offered for CEEB Advanced Placement tests.

COSTS AND FINANCIAL AID

Average book expense $900. **Required Forms and Deadlines:** FAFSA, institution's own financial aid form. Financial aid filing deadline 3/15. **Notification of Awards:** Applicants will be notified of awards on a rolling basis beginning on or about 3/4. **Types of Aid:** *Need-based scholarships/grants:* Pell, SEOG, state scholarships/grants, private scholarships, the school's own gift aid. *Loans:* FFEL Subsidized Stafford, FFEL Unsubsidized Stafford, FFEL PLUS, Federal Perkins. **Student Employment:** Federal Work-Study Program available. Institutional employment available. Off-campus job opportunities are good. **Financial Aid Statistics:** 39% freshmen, 48% undergrads receive need-based scholarship or grant aid. 65% freshmen, 64% undergrads receive need-based self-help aid. 99 freshmen, 345 undergrads receive athletic scholarships. Highest amount earned per year from on-campus jobs $1,500.

DANIEL WEBSTER COLLEGE

20 University Drive, Nashua, NH 03063-1300
Phone: 603-577-6600 **E-mail:** admissions@dwc.edu **CEEB Code:** 3648
Fax: 603-577-6001 **Website:** www.dwc.edu **ACT Code:** 2525
Financial Aid Phone: 603-577-6590

This private school was founded in 1965. It has a 50-acre campus.

RATINGS

Admissions Selectivity Rating: 72 **Fire Safety Rating:** 60* **Green Rating:** 60*

STUDENTS AND FACULTY

Enrollment: 785. **Student Body:** 25% female, 75% male, 72% out-of-state. African American 4%, Hispanic 3%. **Retention and Graduation:** 64% freshmen return for sophomore year. 100% freshmen graduate within 4 years. 8% grads go on to further study within 1 year. 8% grads pursue arts and sciences degrees. **Faculty:** Student/faculty ratio 14:1. 39 full-time faculty, 54% hold PhDs. 100% faculty teach undergrads.

ACADEMICS

Degrees: Associate, bachelor's, master's. **Academic Requirements:** Computer literacy, English (including composition), humanities, mathematics, sciences (biological or physical), social science. **Classes:** Most classes have 10–19 students. Most lab/discussion sections have fewer than 10 students. **Majors with Highest Enrollment:** Airline/commercial/professional pilot and flight crew, business administration/management, computer and information sciences. **Disciplines with Highest Percentage of Degrees Awarded:** Business/marketing 73%, computer and information sciences 7%. **Special Study Options:** Accelerated program, cooperative education program, cross-registration, distance learning, double major, dual enrollment, independent study, internships, study abroad.

FACILITIES

Housing: Coed dorms, men's dorms, women's dorms, men's townhouses, women's townhouses, suites. **Special Academic Facilities/Equipment:** Campus is adjacent to municipal airport; more than 35 aircraft available for flight training; 3 flight simulators; aviation center. **Computers:** Network access in dorm rooms, remote student-access to Web through college's connection.

CAMPUS LIFE

Activities: Choral groups, drama/theater, jazz band, musical theater, student government, student newspaper, student-run film society, yearbook. **Organizations:** 17 registered organizations, 2 honor societies, 1 religious organization. **Athletics (Intercollegiate):** *Men:* Baseball, basketball, cross-country, lacrosse, soccer. *Women:* Basketball, cross-country, soccer, softball, volleyball.

ADMISSIONS

Freshman Academic Profile: 7% in top 10% of high school class, 21% in top 25% of high school class, 52% in top 50% of high school class. 83% from public high schools. SAT Math middle 50% range 480–610. SAT Critical Reading middle 50% range 470–570. ACT middle 50% range 19–24. TOEFL required of all international applicants, minimum paper TOEFL 520, minimum computer TOEFL 190. **Basis for Candidate Selection:** *Very important factors considered include:* Rigor of secondary school record. *Important factors considered include:* Class rank, extracurricular activities, interview, recommendation(s), standardized test scores. *Other factors considered include:* Application essay, character/personal qualities, level of applicant's interest, talent/ability, volunteer work, work experience. **Freshman Admission Requirements:** High school diploma is required, and GED is accepted. *Academic units required:* 4 English, 3 math, 3 science (2 science labs), 2 social studies, 2 history, 2 academic electives. *Academic units recommended:* 4 math, 2 foreign language. **Freshman Admission Statistics:** 823 applied, 91% admitted, 24% enrolled. **Transfer Admission Requirements:** College transcript(s), high school transcript. Minimum college GPA of 2.5 required. Lowest grade transferable C. **General Admission Information:** Application fee $35. Regular notification is rolling. Nonfall registration accepted. Admission may be deferred for a maximum of 1 year. Credit and/or placement offered for CEEB Advanced Placement tests.

COSTS AND FINANCIAL AID

Average book expense $750. **Required Forms and Deadlines:** FAFSA, institution's own financial aid form. Financial aid filing deadline 3/1. **Notification of Awards:** Applicants will be notified of awards on a rolling basis beginning on or about 3/15. **Types of Aid:** *Need-based scholarships/grants:* Pell, SEOG, state scholarships/grants, the school's own gift aid. *Loans:* Direct Subsidized Stafford, Direct Unsubsidized Stafford, Direct PLUS, Federal Perkins. **Student Employment:** Federal Work-Study Program available. Institutional employment available. Off-campus job opportunities are excellent.

Financial Aid Statistics: 93% freshmen, 79% undergrads receive need-based scholarship or grant aid. 100% freshmen, 81% undergrads receive need-based self-help aid. Highest amount earned per year from on-campus jobs $2,000.

DARTMOUTH COLLEGE

Best 368

6016 McNutt Hall, Hanover, NH 03755
Phone: 603-646-2875 **E-mail:** admissions.office@dartmouth.edu **CEEB Code:** 3351
Fax: 603-646-1216 **Website:** www.dartmouth.edu
Financial Aid Phone: 603-646-2451

This private school was founded in 1769. It has a 265-acre campus.

RATINGS

Admissions Selectivity Rating: 98　　**Fire Safety Rating:** 60*　　**Green Rating:** 60*

STUDENTS AND FACULTY

Enrollment: 4,005. **Student Body:** 51% female, 49% male, 96% out-of-state, 5% international. African American 7%, Asian 14%, Caucasian 58%, Hispanic 6%, Native American 4%. **Retention and Graduation:** 98% freshmen return for sophomore year. 86% freshmen graduate within 4 years. **Faculty:** Student/faculty ratio 8:1. 492 full-time faculty, 93% hold PhDs. 100% faculty teach undergrads.

ACADEMICS

Degrees: Bachelor's, doctoral, first professional, master's. **Academic Requirements:** Arts/fine arts, English (including composition), foreign languages, history, humanities, mathematics, philosophy, religion, sciences (biological or physical), social science. **Classes:** Most classes have 10–19 students. Most lab/discussion sections have fewer than 10 students. **Majors with Highest Enrollment:** Economics, psychology, sociology. **Disciplines with Highest Percentage of Degrees Awarded:** Social sciences 30%, psychology 10%, history 9%, foreign languages and literature 8%, English 6%. **Special Study Options:** Double major, exchange student program (domestic), honors program, independent study, internships, student-designed major, study abroad, teacher certification program.

FACILITIES

Housing: Coed dorms, apartments for married students, apartments for single students, special housing for international students, fraternity/sorority housing, cooperative housing, academic affinity housing, faculty-in-residence programs, special interest housing. **Special Academic Facilities/Equipment:** Art museum; centers for performing arts, humanities, social science, and science; observatory; ethics; Center for Volunteer Services. **Computers:** 100% of classrooms are wireless, 60% of public computers are PCs, 40% of public computers are Macs, network access in dorm rooms, network access in dorm lounges, online registration, online administrative functions (other than registration), support for handheld computing, remote student-access to Web through college's connection. Undergraduates are required to own a computer.

CAMPUS LIFE

Activities: Choral groups, concert band, dance, drama/theater, jazz band, literary magazine, marching band, music ensembles, musical theater, opera, pep band, radio station, student government, student newspaper, student-run film society, symphony orchestra, television station. **Organizations:** 330 registered organizations, 26 religious organizations. 14 fraternities (38% men join), 6 sororities (38% women join). **Athletics (Intercollegiate):** *Men:* Baseball, basketball, crew/rowing, cross-country, diving, equestrian sports, fencing, football, golf, ice hockey, lacrosse, sailing, skiing (downhill/alpine), skiing (nordic/cross-country), soccer, squash, swimming, tennis, track/field (indoor), track/field (outdoor). *Women:* Basketball, crew/rowing, cross-country, diving, equestrian sports, fencing, field hockey, golf, ice hockey, lacrosse, sailing, skiing (downhill/alpine), skiing (nordic/cross-country), soccer, softball, squash, swimming, tennis, track/field (indoor), track/field (outdoor). Environmental Initiatives: Formed Sustainable Dining Committee. Launched Sustainable Dining Club and Sustainable Dining facilites including compostable take-out containers, increased local food items, enhanced recycling and composting. Formed Sustainable Dartmouth, a student-led roundtable. Trained and employed 50 student interns. Energy Task Force initiated. Released campus-wide energy conservation statement. Supported Dorm Energy contest. 5.5% oil reduciton in 2004-2005. Solar Thermal Project.

ADMISSIONS

Freshman Academic Profile: 90% in top 10% of high school class, 100% in top 50% of high school class. 61% from public high schools. SAT Math middle 50% range 670–780. SAT Critical Reading middle 50% range 660–770. SAT Writing middle 50% range 660–770. ACT middle 50% range 29–34. TOEFL required of all international applicants, minimum paper TOEFL 600, minimum computer TOEFL 250. **Basis for Candidate Selection:** *Very important factors considered include:* Academic GPA, application essay, character/personal qualities, class rank, extracurricular activities, recommendation(s), rigor of secondary school record, standardized test scores. *Important factors considered include:* Talent/ability, volunteer work. *Other factors considered include:* Alumni/ae relation, first generation, geographical residence, interview, racial/ethnic status, work experience. **Freshman Admission Requirements:** High school diploma or equivalent is not required. *Academic units recommended:* 4 English, 4 math, 4 science, 3 social studies, 3 history. **Freshman Admission Statistics:** 13,938 applied, 16% admitted, 49% enrolled. **Transfer Admission Requirements:** High school transcript, college transcript(s), essay or personal statement, standardized test score, statement of good standing from prior institution(s). Lowest grade transferable B. **General Admission Information:** Application fee $70. Early decision application deadline 11/1. Regular application deadline 1/1. Regular notification 4/10. Nonfall registration not accepted. Admission may be deferred for a maximum of 2 years. Credit and/or placement offered for CEEB Advanced Placement tests.

COSTS AND FINANCIAL AID

Annual tuition $34,965. Room and board $10,305. Required fees $213. Average book expense $1,412. **Required Forms and Deadlines:** FAFSA, CSS/Financial Aid PROFILE, Noncustodial PROFILE, Business/Farm Supplement, current W-2 forms or Federal Tax Returns. Financial aid filing deadline 2/1. **Notification of Awards:** Applicants will be notified of awards on or about 4/2. *Types of Aid: Need-based scholarships/grants:* Pell, SEOG, the school's own gift aid. *Loans:* FFEL Subsidized Stafford, FFEL Unsubsidized Stafford, FFEL PLUS, Federal Perkins, college/university loans from institutional funds. **Student Employment:** Federal Work-Study Program available. Institutional employment available. Off-campus job opportunities are excellent. **Financial Aid Statistics:** 48% freshmen, 50% undergrads receive need-based scholarship or grant aid. 44% freshmen, 49% undergrads receive need-based self-help aid. 48% freshmen, 50% undergrads receive any aid.

DAVENPORT UNIVERSITY

6191 Kraft Avenue Southeast, Grand Rapids, MI 49512
Phone: 616-698-7111 **E-mail:** gradmiss@davenport.edu
Fax: 616-698-0333 **Website:** www.davenport.edu
Financial Aid Phone: 313-581-4400

This private school was founded in 1866. It has a 43-acre campus.

RATINGS

Admissions Selectivity Rating: 60*　　**Fire Safety Rating:** 60*　　**Green Rating:** 60*

STUDENTS AND FACULTY

Enrollment: 11,736. **Student Body:** 76% female, 24% male, 2% out-of-state. African American 24%, Asian 1%, Caucasian 58%, Hispanic 4%. **Retention and Graduation:** 61% freshmen return for sophomore year. **Faculty:** Student/faculty ratio 14:1. 130 full-time faculty, 24% hold PhDs. 100% faculty teach undergrads.

ACADEMICS

Degrees: Associate, bachelor's, diploma, master's, post-bachelor's certificate. **Academic Requirements:** Computer literacy, English (including composition), humanities, mathematics, sciences (biological or physical), social science. **Classes:** Most classes have fewer than 10 students. Most lab/discussion sections have fewer than 10 students. **Majors with Highest Enrollment:** Accounting, business administration/management, human resources management/personnel administration. **Disciplines with Highest Percentage of Degrees Awarded:** Business/marketing 79%, computer and information sciences 15%, health professions and related sciences 5%, law/legal studies 1%. **Special Study Options:** Accelerated program, distance learning, dual enrollment, English as a second language (ESL), independent study, internships, student-designed major, study abroad.

FACILITIES

Housing: Coed dorms. **Computers:** 100% of classrooms are wired, 100% of classrooms are wireless, 100% of public computers are PCs, network access in dorm rooms, network access in dorm lounges, online registration, online administrative functions (other than registration), support for handheld computing, remote student-access to Web through college's connection.

ADMISSIONS

Freshman Academic Profile: TOEFL required of all international applicants, minimum paper TOEFL 500, minimum computer TOEFL 180. **Freshman Admission Requirements:** High school diploma is required, and GED is accepted. *Academic units required:* 6 English, 6 math, 9 social studies, 31 academic electives, 10 interdisciplinary. *Academic units recommended:* 9 math, 9 social studies, 47 academic electives, 10 interdisciplinary. **Freshman Admission Statistics:** 1,231 applied, 100% admitted, 100% enrolled. **Transfer Admission Requirements:** High school transcript, college transcript(s). Minimum college GPA of 2.0 required. Lowest grade transferable C. **General Admission Information:** Application fee $25. Regular notification is rolling. Nonfall registration accepted. Admission may be deferred. Common Application not accepted. Neither credit nor placement offered for CEEB Advanced Placement tests.

COSTS AND FINANCIAL AID

Annual tuition $8,760. Room $4,200. Required fees $120. Average book expense $1,000. **Required Forms and Deadlines:** FAFSA, scholarship application, if applicable. Financial aid filing deadline 3/15. **Notification of Awards:** Applicants will be notified of awards on a rolling basis beginning on or about 3/1. **Types of Aid:** *Need-based scholarships/grants:* Pell, SEOG, state scholarships/grants, private scholarships, the school's own gift aid, State of MI Nursing Scholarships. *Loans:* FFEL Subsidized Stafford, FFEL Unsubsidized Stafford, FFEL PLUS, state loans. **Financial Aid Statistics:** 79% freshmen, 76% undergrads receive need-based scholarship or grant aid. 72% freshmen, 78% undergrads receive need-based self-help aid. 12 freshmen, 50 undergrads receive athletic scholarships.

DAVIDSON COLLEGE

PO Box 7156, Davidson, NC 28035-5000
Phone: 704-894-2230 **E-mail:** admission@davidson.edu **CEEB Code:** 5150
Fax: 704-894-2016 **Website:** www.davidson.edu **ACT Code:** 3086
Financial Aid Phone: 704-894-2232

This private school, affiliated with the Presbyterian Church, was founded in 1837. It has a 556-acre campus.

RATINGS

Admissions Selectivity Rating: 97   **Fire Safety Rating:** 60*   **Green Rating:** 60*

STUDENTS AND FACULTY

Enrollment: 1,660. **Student Body:** 50% female, 50% male, 81% out-of-state, 3% international (29 countries represented). African American 7%, Asian 3%, Caucasian 76%, Hispanic 5%. **Retention and Graduation:** 95% freshmen return for sophomore year. 89% freshmen graduate within 4 years. 25% grads go on to further study within 1 year. **Faculty:** Student/faculty ratio 10:1. 162 full-time faculty, 98% hold PhDs. 100% faculty teach undergrads.

ACADEMICS

Degrees: Bachelor's. **Academic Requirements:** Arts/fine arts, cultural diversity, English (including composition), foreign languages, history, mathematics, philosophy, sciences (biological or physical), religion, social science. **Classes:** Most classes have 10–19 students. Most lab/discussion sections have 10–19 students. **Majors with Highest Enrollment:** Biology/biological sciences, English language and literature, history. **Disciplines with Highest Percentage of Degrees Awarded:** Social sciences 29%, English 14%, history 12%, biological/life sciences 10%, foreign languages and literature 9%. **Special Study Options:** Cross-registration, double major, exchange student program (domestic), honors program, independent study, student-designed major, study abroad, teacher certification program.

FACILITIES

Housing: Coed dorms, apartments for single students. **Special Academic Facilities/Equipment:** Art gallery, scanning electron microscopes, UV-visible spectrometer, laser systems, Baker Sports Complex, visual arts building. **Computers:** 80% of public computers are PCs, 20% of public computers are Macs, network access in dorm rooms, network access in dorm lounges, online registration, remote student-access to Web through college's connection.

CAMPUS LIFE

Activities: Choral groups, concert band, dance, drama/theater, jazz band, music ensembles, musical theater, pep band, radio station, student government, student newspaper, symphony orchestra, yearbook. **Organizations:** 151 registered organizations, 15 honor societies, 16 religious organizations. 8 fraternities (40% men join). **Athletics (Intercollegiate):** *Men:* Baseball, basketball, cross-country, diving, football, golf, soccer, swimming, tennis, track/field (outdoor), wrestling. *Women:* Basketball, cross-country, diving, field hockey, lacrosse, soccer, swimming, tennis, track/field (outdoor), volleyball.

ADMISSIONS

Freshman Academic Profile: 79% in top 10% of high school class, 97% in top 25% of high school class, 99% in top 50% of high school class. 48% from public high schools. SAT Math middle 50% range 640–710. SAT Critical Reading middle 50% range 630–730. ACT middle 50% range 28–32. TOEFL required of all international applicants, minimum paper TOEFL 600, minimum computer TOEFL 250. **Basis for Candidate Selection:** *Very important factors considered include:* Character/personal qualities, recommendation(s), rigor of secondary school record, volunteer work. *Important factors considered include:* Application essay, extracurricular activities, talent/ability. *Other factors considered include:* Class rank, racial/ethnic status, standardized test scores, work experience. **Freshman Admission Requirements:** High school diploma is required, and GED is not accepted. *Academic units required:* 4 English, 3 math, 2 science, 2 foreign language, 2 social studies and history. *Academic units recommended:* 4 math, 4 science, 4 foreign language, 4 social studies and history. **Freshman Admission Statistics:** 3,895 applied, 30% admitted, 39% enrolled. **Transfer Admission Requirements:** High school transcript, college transcript(s), essay or personal statement, standardized test score, statement of good standing from prior institution(s). Minimum college GPA of 3.0 required. Lowest grade transferable C. **General Admission Information:** Application fee $50. Early decision application deadline 11/15. Regular application deadline 1/2. Regular notification 4/1. Nonfall registration not accepted. Admission may be deferred for a maximum of 1 year. Credit and/or placement offered for CEEB Advanced Placement tests.

COSTS AND FINANCIAL AID

Annual tuition $33,148. Room and board $9,471. Required fees $331. Average book expense $1,000. **Required Forms and Deadlines:** FAFSA, CSS/Financial Aid PROFILE, Noncustodial PROFILE, Business/Farm Supplement, noncustodial (divorced/separated) parents' statement, corporate tax return and/or noncustodial parent tax return (if applicable); parent and student tax returns and W-2 forms. Financial aid filing deadline 2/15. **Notification of Awards:** Applicants will be notified of awards on or about 4/1. **Types of Aid:** *Need-based scholarships/grants:* Pell, SEOG, state scholarships/grants, private scholarships, the school's own gift aid. *Loans:* FFEL Subsidized Stafford, FFEL Unsubsidized Stafford, FFEL PLUS, Federal Perkins, alternative loans. **Student Employment:** Federal Work-Study Program available. Institutional employment available. Off-campus job opportunities are excellent. **Financial Aid Statistics:** 31% freshmen, 32% undergrads receive need-based scholarship or grant aid. 24% freshmen, 27% undergrads receive need-based self-help aid. 48 freshmen, 178 undergrads receive athletic scholarships. 35% freshmen, 35% undergrads receive any aid.

See page 1150.

DAVIS & ELKINS COLLEGE

100 Campus Drive, Elkins, WV 26241
Phone: 304-637-1230 **E-mail:** admiss@davisandelkins.edu **CEEB Code:** 5151
Fax: 304-637-1800 **Website:** www.davisandelkins.edu **ACT Code:** 4518
Financial Aid Phone: 304-637-1373

This private school, affiliated with the Presbyterian Church, was founded in 1904. It has a 170-acre campus.

RATINGS

Admissions Selectivity Rating: 76   **Fire Safety Rating:** 61   **Green Rating:** 60*

STUDENTS AND FACULTY

Enrollment: 624. **Student Body:** 63% female, 37% male, 23% out-of-state. **Retention and Graduation:** 64% freshmen return for sophomore year. 29% freshmen graduate within 4 years. 13% grads go on to further study within 1 year. 11% grads pursue business degrees. 2% grads pursue law degrees. **Faculty:** Student/faculty ratio 11:1. 44 full-time faculty, 84% hold PhDs. 100% faculty teach undergrads.

ACADEMICS

Degrees: Associate, bachelor's. **Academic Requirements:** Arts/fine arts, computer literacy, English (including composition), history, humanities, mathematics, philosophy, sciences (biological or physical), social science. **Classes:** Most classes have fewer than 10 students. Most lab/discussion sections have 20–29 students. **Majors with Highest Enrollment:** Business administration and management, marketing/marketing management, nursing/registered nurse training (RN, ASN, BSN, MSN). **Disciplines with Highest Percentage of Degrees Awarded:** Business/marketing 34%, education 14%, social sciences 8%, history 7%, psychology 6%. **Special Study Options:** Cooperative education program, cross-registration, double major, dual enrollment, external degree program, honors program, independent study, internships, student-designed major, study abroad, teacher certification program.

FACILITIES

Housing: Coed dorms, men's dorms, women's dorms. **Special Academic Facilities/Equipment:** Planetarium, Graceland Inn and Conference Center (19th-century Victorian mansion, now used as training center for the Hospitality Program), Darby Collection-Civil War collection, Comstock Collection, Pearl S. Buck collection. **Computers:** 10% of classrooms are wireless, 50% of public computers are PCs, 1% of public computers are Macs, network access in dorm rooms, online administrative functions (other than registration), remote student-access to Web through college's connection.

CAMPUS LIFE

Activities: Choral groups, concert band, drama/theater, jazz band, literary magazine, music ensembles, musical theater, radio station, student government, student newspaper, yearbook. **Organizations:** 39 registered organizations, 7 honor societies, 1 religious organization. 2 fraternities (14% men join), 2 sororities (14% women join). **Athletics (Intercollegiate):** *Men:* Baseball, basketball, cross-country, golf, skiing (downhill/alpine), soccer. *Women:* Basketball, cross-country, skiing (downhill/alpine), soccer, softball, volleyball.

ADMISSIONS

Freshman Academic Profile: 12% in top 10% of high school class, 33% in top 25% of high school class, 71% in top 50% of high school class. 91% from public high schools. SAT Math middle 50% range 420–510. SAT Critical Reading middle 50% range 420–530. ACT middle 50% range 18–22. TOEFL required of all international applicants, minimum paper TOEFL 450, minimum computer TOEFL 133. **Basis for Candidate Selection:** *Very important factors considered include:* Level of applicant's interest, rigor of secondary school record. *Important factors considered include:* Academic GPA, character/personal qualities, class rank, extracurricular activities, recommendation(s), standardized test scores, talent/ability. *Other factors considered include:* Alumni/ae relation, application essay, first generation, interview, volunteer work, work experience. **Freshman Admission Requirements:** High school diploma is required, and GED is accepted. *Academic units required:* 4 English, 1 math, 3 science (1 science lab), 1 foreign language, 3 social studies, 2 mathematics units (must include algebra I or II and geometry). *Academic units recommended:* 4 English, 1 math, 3 science (1 science lab), 1 foreign language, 3 social studies, 2 mathematics units (must include algebra I or II and geometry). **Freshman Admission Statistics:** 563 applied, 55% admitted, 34% enrolled. **Transfer Admission Requirements:** High school transcript, college transcript(s). Minimum college GPA of 2.0 required. Lowest grade transferable D. **General Admission Information:** Application fee $35. Regular notification is rolling. Nonfall registration accepted. Admission may be deferred for a maximum of 1 year. Common Application accepted. Credit and/or placement offered for CEEB Advanced Placement tests.

COSTS AND FINANCIAL AID

Average book expense $800. **Required Forms and Deadlines:** FAFSA. Financial aid filing deadline 3/1. **Notification of Awards:** Applicants will be notified of awards on or about 5/1. *Types of Aid: Need-based scholarships/grants:* Pell, SEOG, state scholarships/grants, private scholarships, the school's own gift aid. *Loans:* FFEL Subsidized Stafford, FFEL Unsubsidized Stafford, FFEL PLUS, Federal Perkins, state loans. **Student Employment:** Federal Work-Study Program available. Institutional employment available. Off-campus job opportunities are good. **Financial Aid Statistics:** 32% freshmen, 48% undergrads receive need-based scholarship or grant aid. 47% freshmen, 63% undergrads receive need-based self-help aid. 54 freshmen, 136 undergrads receive athletic scholarships. 98% freshmen, 98% undergrads receive any aid. Highest amount earned per year from on-campus jobs $1,000.

DAWSON COMMUNITY COLLEGE

300 College Drive Box 421, Glendive, MT 59330
Phone: 406-377-3396 **E-mail:** wade@dawson.cc.mt.us
Fax: 406-377-8132 **Website:** www.dawson.cc.mt.us

This is a public school.

RATINGS

Admissions Selectivity Rating: 60*   **Fire Safety Rating:** 60*   **Green Rating:** 60*

STUDENTS AND FACULTY

Enrollment: 417. **Student Body:** 48% female, 52% male, 9% out-of-state. Caucasian 87%, Native American 1%. **Retention and Graduation:** 64% freshmen return for sophomore year.

ACADEMICS

Degrees: Associate, certificate. **Academic Requirements:** Computer literacy, English (including composition), mathematics. **Special Study Options:** Independent study, internships.

FACILITIES

Housing: Coed dorms.

CAMPUS LIFE

Activities: Choral groups, drama/theater, jazz band, music ensembles, musical theater, pep band, student government.

ADMISSIONS

Freshman Admission Requirements: High school diploma is required, and GED is accepted. **Freshman Admission Statistics:** 294 applied, 100% admitted, 57% enrolled. **Transfer Admission Requirements:** High school transcript, college transcript(s), Lowest grade transferable D. **General Admission Information:** Application fee $30. Regular application deadline is rolling. Regular notification is rolling. Nonfall registration accepted. Admission may be deferred for a maximum of 1 year. Common Application not accepted.

COSTS AND FINANCIAL AID

Annual in-state tuition $840. Out-of-state tuition $4,816. Room $1,215. Required fees $560. Average book expense $550. **Required Forms and Deadlines:** FAFSA. Financial aid filing deadline 3/1. **Notification of Awards:** Applicants will be notified of awards on a rolling basis beginning on or about 4/1. **Types of Aid:** *Need-based scholarships/grants:* Pell, SEOG, state scholarships/grants, private scholarships. *Loans:* FFEL Subsidized Stafford, FFEL Unsubsidized Stafford, FFEL PLUS, Federal Perkins. **Financial Aid Statistics:** 56% freshmen, 62% undergrads receive need-based scholarship or grant aid. 46% freshmen, 51% undergrads receive need-based self-help aid. 6 freshmen, 16 undergrads receive athletic scholarships.

DEACONESS COLLEGE OF NURSING

6150 Oakland Avenue, St. Louis, MO 63139
Phone: 314-768-3044 **E-mail:** lisa.grote@tenetstl.com
Fax: 314-768-5673 **Website:** www.deaconess.edu **ACT Code:** 2293
Financial Aid Phone: 314-768-3044

This proprietary school was founded in 1889.

RATINGS

Admissions Selectivity Rating: 78   **Fire Safety Rating:** 60*   **Green Rating:** 60*

STUDENTS AND FACULTY

Enrollment: 305. **Student Body:** 93% female, 7% male, 33% out-of-state. African American 19%, Caucasian 78%, Hispanic 2%. **Retention and Graduation:** 72% freshmen return for sophomore year. 9% grads go on to further study within 1 year. 6% grads pursue arts and sciences degrees. 3% grads pursue business degrees. **Faculty:** 100% faculty teach undergrads.

ACADEMICS

Degrees: Associate, bachelor's. **Academic Requirements:** Computer literacy, English (including composition), history, humanities, mathematics, nursing, philosophy, sciences (biological or physical), social science. **Special Study Options:** Cross-registration, independent study.

FACILITIES

Housing: Men's dorms, women's dorms.

CAMPUS LIFE

Activities: Choral groups, music ensembles, student government, student newspaper, yearbook.

ADMISSIONS

Freshman Academic Profile: 10% in top 10% of high school class, 45% in top 25% of high school class, 86% in top 50% of high school class. ACT middle 50% range 20–24. TOEFL required of all international applicants, minimum paper TOEFL 500. **Basis for Candidate Selection:** *Very important factors considered include:* Class rank, rigor of secondary school record, standardized test scores. *Important factors considered include:* Application essay. *Other factors considered include:* Alumni/ae relation, character/personal qualities, extracurricular activities, recommendation(s). **Freshman Admission Requirements:** High school diploma is required, and GED is accepted. *Academic units required:* 4 English, 3 math, 3 science. **Transfer Admission Requirements:** High school transcript, college transcript(s), essay or personal statement, statement of good standing from prior institution(s). Minimum college GPA of 2.5 required. Lowest grade transferable C. **General Admission Information:** Application fee $30. Regular application deadline is rolling. Regular notification. Nonfall registration accepted. Common Application not accepted.

COSTS AND FINANCIAL AID

Annual tuition $8,100. Room & board $3,200. Average book expense $953. **Required Forms and Deadlines:** FAFSA, institution's own financial aid form. Financial aid filing deadline 4/1. **Notification of Awards:** Applicants will be notified of awards on a rolling basis beginning on or about 4/20. **Types of Aid:** *Need-based scholarships/grants:* Pell, SEOG, state scholarships/grants, private scholarships, the school's own gift aid. *Loans:* Direct Subsidized Stafford, Direct Unsubsidized Stafford, Direct PLUS, FFEL Subsidized Stafford, FFEL PLUS. **Student Employment:** Federal Work-Study Program available. Off-campus job opportunities are excellent. **Financial Aid Statistics:** Highest amount earned per year from on-campus jobs $2,535.

DEAN COLLEGE

Office of Admission, 99 Main Street, Franklin, MA 02038-1994
Phone: 508-541-1508 **E-mail:** admission@dean.edu
Fax: 508-541-8726 **Website:** www.dean.edu

This is a private school.

RATINGS
Admissions Selectivity Rating: 60*   **Fire Safety Rating:** 60*   **Green Rating:** 60*

STUDENTS AND FACULTY

Enrollment: 1,106. **Student Body:** 48% female, 52% male, 53% out-of-state, 10% international. African American 7%, Asian 1%, Caucasian 50%, Hispanic 3%. **Retention and Graduation:** 62% freshmen return for sophomore year. **Faculty:** Student/faculty ratio 19:1. 33 full-time faculty, 36% hold PhDs.

ACADEMICS

Degrees: Associate, bachelor's, certificate. **Academic Requirements:** Arts/fine arts, computer literacy, English (including composition), history, humanities, mathematics, philosophy, sciences (biological or physical), social science. **Classes:** Most classes have 10–19 students. Most lab/discussion sections have fewer than 10 students. **Disciplines with Highest Percentage of Degrees Awarded:** Visual and performing arts 100%. **Special Study Options:** Accelerated program, double major, English as a second language (ESL), honors program, independent study, internships, liberal arts/career combination, study abroad.

FACILITIES

Housing: Coed dorms, women's dorms.

CAMPUS LIFE

Activities: Dance, drama/theater, literary magazine, musical theater, radio station, student government, yearbook.

ADMISSIONS

Freshman Academic Profile: SAT Math middle 50% range 380–490. SAT Critical Reading middle 50% range 390–490. ACT middle 50% range 15–20. **Basis for Candidate Selection:** *Other factors considered include:* Academic GPA, alumni/ae relation, application essay, character/personal qualities, class rank, extracurricular activities, interview, level of applicant's interest, recommendation(s), rigor of secondary school record, standardized test scores, talent/ability. **Freshman Admission Requirements:** High school diploma is required, and GED is accepted. *Academic units required:* 3 English, 1 math, 1

science (1 science lab), 1 social studies, 1 history. *Academic units recommended:* 4 English, 2 math, 2 science (1 science lab), 1 foreign language, 2 social studies, 2 history, 1 academic elective. **Freshman Admission Statistics:** 1,910 applied, 73% admitted, 39% enrolled. **Transfer Admission Requirements:** High school transcript, college transcript(s), essay or personal statement. Lowest grade transferable C-. **General Admission Information:** Application fee $35. Regular notification is rolling. Nonfall registration accepted. Admission may be deferred for a maximum of 1 year.

COSTS AND FINANCIAL AID

Annual tuition $24,000. Room & board $10,350. Average book expense $1,000. **Required Forms and Deadlines:** FAFSA. Financial aid filing deadline 3/1. **Notification of Awards:** Applicants will be notified of awards on a rolling basis beginning on or about 3/1. **Types of Aid:** *Need-based scholarships/grants:* Pell, SEOG, state scholarships/grants, private scholarships, the school's own gift aid. *Loans:* FFEL Subsidized Stafford, FFEL Unsubsidized Stafford, FFEL PLUS, Federal Perkins. **Financial Aid Statistics:** 61% freshmen, 60% undergrads receive need-based scholarship or grant aid. 56% freshmen, 57% undergrads receive need-based self-help aid. 11 freshmen, 24 undergrads receive athletic scholarships.

DEEP SPRINGS COLLEGE

Applications Committee, HC 72 Box 45001, Dyer, NV 89010
Phone: 760-872-2000 **E-mail:** apcom@deepsprings.edu **CEEB Code:** 4281
Fax: 760-872-4466 **Website:** www.deepsprings.edu
Financial Aid Phone: 760-872-2000

This private school was founded in 1917. It has a 30,000-acre campus.

RATINGS
Admissions Selectivity Rating: 99   **Fire Safety Rating:** 82   **Green Rating:** 60*

STUDENTS AND FACULTY

Enrollment: 26. **Student Body:** 100% male, 80% out-of-state. **Retention and Graduation:** 100% freshmen return for sophomore year. 96% grads go on to further study within 1 year. 26% grads pursue arts and sciences degrees. 3% grads pursue business degrees. 11% grads pursue law degrees. 10% grads pursue medical degrees. **Faculty:** Student/faculty ratio 4:1. 3 full-time faculty, 67% hold PhDs. 100% faculty teach undergrads.

ACADEMICS

Degrees: Associate. **Academic Requirements:** English (including composition), public speaking (4 semesters). **Classes:** Most classes have fewer than 10 students. **Majors with Highest Enrollment:** Liberal arts, sciences studies, humanities. **Disciplines with Highest Percentage of Degrees Awarded:** Liberal arts/general studies 100%. **Special Study Options:** Independent study, internships.

FACILITIES

Housing: Men's dorms. **Special Academic Facilities/Equipment:** Ranch (300 cattle, 20 horses, organic farm growing hay and produce); thousands of acres of wilderness surround the college. **Computers:** 100% of classrooms are wired, 50% of public computers are PCs, 50% of public computers are Macs, remote student-access to Web through college's connection.

CAMPUS LIFE

Activities: Student government. **Organizations:** 1 registered organization.

ADMISSIONS

Freshman Academic Profile: 86% in top 10% of high school class, 93% in top 25% of high school class, 100% in top 50% of high school class. 50% from public high schools. SAT Math middle 50% range 700–800. SAT Critical Reading middle 50% range 750–800. **Basis for Candidate Selection:** *Very important factors considered include:* Application essay, character/personal qualities, interview, level of applicant's interest. *Important factors considered include:* Academic GPA, extracurricular activities, rigor of secondary school record, volunteer work. work experience. *Other factors considered include:* Class rank, racial/ethnic status, recommendation(s), standardized test scores, talent/ability. **Freshman Admission Requirements:** High school diploma or equivalent is not required. **Freshman Admission Statistics:** 170 applied, 7% admitted, 92% enrolled. **Transfer Admission Requirements:** High school

The Princeton Review's Complete Book of Colleges

transcript, college transcript(s), essay or personal statement, interview, standardized test score. **General Admission Information:** Regular application deadline 11/15. Regular notification 4/15. Nonfall registration not accepted. Neither credit nor placement offered for CEEB Advanced Placement tests.

COSTS AND FINANCIAL AID

Average book expense $1,200. **Notification of Awards:** Applicants will be notified of awards on or about 4/15. **Financial Aid Statistics:** 100% freshmen, 100% undergrads receive any aid.

DEFIANCE COLLEGE

701 North Clinton Street, Defiance, OH 43512-1695
Phone: 419-783-2359 **E-mail:** admissions@defiance.edu **CEEB Code:** 1162
Fax: 419-783-2468 **Website:** www.defiance.edu **ACT Code:** 3264
Financial Aid Phone: 419-783-2376

This private school, affiliated with the United Church of Christ, was founded in 1850. It has a 150-acre campus.

RATINGS

Admissions Selectivity Rating: 74   **Fire Safety Rating:** 60*   **Green Rating:** 60*

STUDENTS AND FACULTY

Enrollment: 888. **Student Body:** 55% female, 45% male, 21% out-of-state. African American 3%, Caucasian 69%, Hispanic 3%. **Retention and Graduation:** 73% freshmen return for sophomore year. 7% grads go on to further study within 1 year. 4% grads pursue arts and sciences degrees. 1% grads pursue business degrees. 1% grads pursue law degrees. 1% grads pursue medical degrees. **Faculty:** Student/faculty ratio 13:1. 45 full-time faculty, 47% hold PhDs. 100% faculty teach undergrads.

ACADEMICS

Degrees: Associate, bachelor's, master's. **Academic Requirements:** Arts/fine arts, computer literacy, English (including composition), history, humanities, mathematics, philosophy, sciences (biological or physical), social science. **Classes:** Most classes have fewer than 10 students. Most lab/discussion sections have 10–19 students. **Majors with Highest Enrollment:** Business administration/management, criminology. **Disciplines with Highest Percentage of Degrees Awarded:** Business/marketing 33%, education 24%, communication technologies 7%, law/legal studies 7%, social sciences 7%, health professions and related sciences 6%, computer and information sciences 5%. **Special Study Options:** Cooperative education program, distance learning, double major, dual enrollment, honors program, independent study, internships, student-designed major, study abroad, teacher certification program, weekend college.

FACILITIES

Housing: Coed dorms, apartments for single students. **Special Academic Facilities/Equipment:** Art gallery, media center, Eisenhower Archives Room, curriculum resource center, Cultural Arts Center, Indian Wars Collection. **Computers:** 10% of classrooms are wired, 5% of classrooms are wireless, network access in dorm rooms, remote student-access to Web through college's connection.

CAMPUS LIFE

Activities: Choral groups, concert band, drama/theater, literary magazine, musical theater, student government, student newspaper, yearbook. **Organizations:** 30 registered organizations, 1 honor society, 3 religious organizations. 2 fraternities (6% men join), 2 sororities (8% women join). **Athletics (Intercollegiate):** *Men:* Baseball, basketball, cheerleading, cross-country, football, soccer, tennis, track/field (indoor), track/field (outdoor). *Women:* Basketball, cheerleading, cross-country, soccer, softball, tennis, track/field (indoor), track/field (outdoor), volleyball.

ADMISSIONS

Freshman Academic Profile: 15% in top 10% of high school class, 36% in top 25% of high school class, 65% in top 50% of high school class. SAT Math middle 50% range 430–560. SAT Critical Reading middle 50% range 410–560. SAT Writing middle 50% range 380–550. ACT middle 50% range 18–23. TOEFL required of all international applicants, minimum paper TOEFL 550, minimum computer TOEFL 213. **Basis for Candidate Selection:** *Very important factors considered include:* Rigor of secondary school record, standardized test scores. *Important factors considered include:* Academic GPA, application essay, class rank. *Other factors considered include:* Alumni/ae relation, character/personal qualities, extracurricular activities, first generation, interview, volunteer work. **Freshman Admission Requirements:** High school diploma

is required, and GED is accepted. *Academic units recommended:* 4 English, 3 math, 3 science (2 science labs), 2 foreign language, 2 social studies, 1 visual and performing arts. **Freshman Admission Statistics:** 869 applied, 79% admitted, 34% enrolled. **Transfer Admission Requirements:** High school transcript, college transcript(s), essay or personal statement, statement of good standing from prior institution(s). Minimum college GPA of 2.0 required. Lowest grade transferable C. **General Admission Information:** Application fee $25. Regular application deadline 8/25. Regular notification is rolling. Nonfall registration accepted. Admission may be deferred for a maximum of 1 year. Credit and/or placement offered for CEEB Advanced Placement tests.

COSTS AND FINANCIAL AID

Required Forms and Deadlines: FAFSA. Financial aid filing deadline 3/1. **Notification of Awards:** Applicants will be notified of awards on a rolling basis beginning on or about 2/1. **Types of Aid:** *Need-based scholarships/grants:* Pell, SEOG, state scholarships/grants, private scholarships, the school's own gift aid. *Loans:* FFEL Subsidized Stafford, FFEL Unsubsidized Stafford, FFEL PLUS, Federal Perkins, alternative loans. **Student Employment:** Federal Work-Study Program available. Institutional employment available. Off-campus job opportunities are good. **Financial Aid Statistics:** Highest amount earned per year from on-campus jobs $1,650.

DELAWARE STATE UNIVERSITY

1200 North DuPont Highway, Dover, DE 19901
Phone: 302-857-6361 **E-mail:** admissions@dsc.edu **CEEB Code:** 5153
Fax: 302-857-6362 **Website:** www.dsc.edu **ACT Code:** 0630
Financial Aid Phone: 302-857-6250

This public school was founded in 1891. It has a 400-acre campus.

RATINGS

Admissions Selectivity Rating: 70   **Fire Safety Rating:** 60*   **Green Rating:** 60*

STUDENTS AND FACULTY

Enrollment: 3,149. **Student Body:** 57% female, 43% male, 44% out-of-state. African American 79%, Asian 1%, Caucasian 15%, Hispanic 2%. **Retention and Graduation:** 65% freshmen return for sophomore year. 16% freshmen graduate within 4 years. 15% grads go on to further study within 1 year. 6% grads pursue arts and sciences degrees. 8% grads pursue business degrees. 1% grads pursue law degrees. **Faculty:** Student/faculty ratio 13:1. 184 full-time faculty, 74% hold PhDs. 100% faculty teach undergrads.

ACADEMICS

Degrees: Bachelor's, master's. **Academic Requirements:** Arts/fine arts, English (including composition), fitness and health, foreign languages, history, humanities, mathematics, philosophy, sciences (biological or physical), social science, speech, university seminar. **Classes:** Most classes have fewer than 10 students. **Disciplines with Highest Percentage of Degrees Awarded:** Business/marketing 29%, education 12%, communication technologies 9%, social sciences 9%, biological/life sciences 5%, psychology 5%, computer and information sciences 4%, health professions and related sciences 4%. **Special Study Options:** Accelerated program, cooperative education program, distance learning, double major, English as a second language (ESL), exchange student program (domestic), honors program, independent study, internships, study abroad, teacher certification program, weekend college.

FACILITIES

Housing: Coed dorms, men's dorms, women's dorms, apartments for single students. **Special Academic Facilities/Equipment:** Art gallery, language lab, observatory, herbarium. **Computers:** 90% of public computers are PCs, 8% of public computers are Macs, 2% of public computers are UNIX, network access in dorm rooms, remote student-access to Web through college's connection.

CAMPUS LIFE

Activities: Choral groups, concert band, dance, jazz band, marching band, music ensembles, pep band, radio station, student government, student newspaper, television station, yearbook. **Organizations:** 63 registered organizations, 9 honor societies, 3 religious organizations. 4 fraternities, 4 sororities. **Athletics (Intercollegiate):** *Men:* Baseball, basketball, cross-country, football, tennis, track/field (outdoor), wrestling. *Women:* Basketball, cheerleading, cross-country, softball, tennis, track/field (outdoor), volleyball. Environmental Initiatives: Recycling. Wind Energy. Bio-Diesel Fuel.

ADMISSIONS

Freshman Academic Profile: 4% in top 10% of high school class, 19% in top 25% of high school class, 51% in top 50% of high school class. 80% from public high schools. SAT Math middle 50% range 340–450. SAT Critical Reading

middle 50% range 350–460. TOEFL required of all international applicants, minimum paper TOEFL 500. **Basis for Candidate Selection:** *Very important factors considered include:* Rigor of secondary school record. *Important factors considered include:* Application essay, character/personal qualities, recommendation(s), standardized test scores. *Other factors considered include:* Alumni/ae relation, class rank, extracurricular activities, interview, state residency, talent/ability, volunteer work, work experience. **Freshman Admission Requirements:** High school diploma is required, and GED is accepted. *Academic units required:* 4 English, 3 math, 3 science, 2 social studies, 4 academic electives. **Freshman Admission Statistics:** 3,177 applied, 61% admitted, 42% enrolled. **Transfer Admission Requirements:** High school transcript, college transcript(s), essay or personal statement, interview, standardized test score, statement of good standing from prior institution(s). Lowest grade transferable C. **General Admission Information:** Application fee $15. Regular application deadline 4/1. Regular notification is rolling. Nonfall registration accepted. Admission may be deferred for a maximum of 1 year. Common Application accepted. Placement offered for CEEB Advanced Placement tests.

COSTS AND FINANCIAL AID

Annual in-state tuition $3,096. Out-of-state tuition $7,088. Room & board $4,990. Required fees $600. Average book expense $1,000. **Required Forms and Deadlines:** FAFSA. Financial aid filing deadline 2/15. **Notification of Awards:** Applicants will be notified of awards on a rolling basis beginning on or about 3/30. **Types of Aid:** *Need-based scholarships/grants:* Pell, SEOG, state scholarships/grants, private scholarships, the school's own gift aid, Federal Nursing Scholarships. *Loans:* FFEL Subsidized Stafford, FFEL Unsubsidized Stafford, FFEL PLUS, Federal Perkins, Signature loans (private). **Student Employment:** Federal Work-Study Program available. Institutional employment available. Off-campus job opportunities are good. **Financial Aid Statistics:** 54% freshmen, 48% undergrads receive need-based scholarship or grant aid. 67% freshmen, 62% undergrads receive need-based self-help aid. 8 freshmen, 38 undergrads receive athletic scholarships. Highest amount earned per year from on-campus jobs $1,500.

DELAWARE VALLEY COLLEGE

700 East Butler Avenue, Doylestown, PA 18901-2697
Phone: 215-489-2211 **E-mail:** admitme@devalcol.edu **CEEB Code:** 2510
Fax: 215-230-2968 **Website:** www.devalcol.edu **ACT Code:** 3551
Financial Aid Phone: 215-489-2272

This private school was founded in 1896. It has a 600-acre campus.

RATINGS
Admissions Selectivity Rating: 78   **Fire Safety Rating:** 73   **Green Rating:** 81

STUDENTS AND FACULTY
Enrollment: 1,959. **Student Body:** 57% female, 43% male, 36% out-of-state. African American 3%, Caucasian 77%, Hispanic 2%. **Retention and Graduation:** 73% freshmen return for sophomore year. 43% freshmen graduate within 4 years. 51% grads go on to further study within 1 year. 9% grads pursue business degrees. 1% grads pursue law degrees. 10% grads pursue medical degrees. **Faculty:** Student/faculty ratio 15:1. 81 full-time faculty, 53% hold PhDs. 100% faculty teach undergrads.

ACADEMICS
Degrees: Associate, bachelor's, certificate, master's, post-bachelor's certificate, post-master's certificate. **Academic Requirements:** Arts/fine arts, computer literacy, English (including composition), history, humanities, macroeconomics, mathematics, philosophy, sciences (biological or physical), social science, speech. **Classes:** Most classes have fewer than 10 students. Most lab/discussion sections have 10–19 students. **Majors with Highest Enrollment:** Animal sciences, business administration/management, equestrian/equine studies. **Disciplines with Highest Percentage of Degrees Awarded:** Agriculture 46%, business/marketing 24%, security and protective services 8%, biological/life sciences 5%, computer and information sciences 5%, physical sciences 4%. **Special Study Options:** Cooperative education program, cross-registration, distance learning, double major, honors program, independent study, internships, liberal arts/career combination, study abroad, teacher certification program, weekend college.

FACILITIES
Housing: Coed dorms, women's dorms. **Special Academic Facilities/Equipment:** Dairy processing plant, greenhouse and nursery lab complex, small animal science labs, poultry diagnostic lab, arboretum, equine facilities, 500+ acre farm, tissue culture lab. **Computers:** 5% of classrooms are wired,

30% of classrooms are wireless, 80% of public computers are PCs, network access in dorm rooms, network access in dorm lounges, online registration, online administrative functions (other than registration), remote student-access to Web through college's connection.

CAMPUS LIFE
Activities: Choral groups, concert band, drama/theater, literary magazine, music ensembles, radio station, student government, student newspaper, yearbook. **Organizations:** 38 registered organizations, 6 honor societies, 3 religious organizations. 5 fraternities (4% men join), 3 sororities (5% women join). **Athletics (Intercollegiate):** *Men:* Baseball; basketball, cross-country, football, golf, soccer, track/field (outdoor), wrestling. *Women:* Basketball, cheerleading, cross-country, field hockey, soccer, softball, track/field (outdoor), volleyball.

ADMISSIONS
Freshman Academic Profile: 11% in top 10% of high school class, 38% in top 25% of high school class, 73% in top 50% of high school class. 85% from public high schools. SAT Math middle 50% range 460–560. SAT Critical Reading middle 50% range 460–560. SAT Writing middle 50% range 450–550. ACT middle 50% range 20–25. TOEFL required of all international applicants, minimum paper TOEFL 500, minimum computer TOEFL 173. **Basis for Candidate Selection:** *Very important factors considered include:* Academic GPA, standardized test scores. *Important factors considered include:* Class rank, interview, rigor of secondary school record. *Other factors considered include:* Alumni/ae relation, application essay, character/personal qualities, extracurricular activities, level of applicant's interest, recommendation(s), talent/ability, volunteer work, work experience. **Freshman Admission Requirements:** High school diploma is required, and GED is accepted. *Academic units required:* 3 English, 2 math, 2 science (1 science lab), 2 social studies, 6 academic electives. **Freshman Admission Statistics:** 1,579 applied, 71% admitted, 40% enrolled. **Transfer Admission Requirements:** High school transcript, college transcript(s), statement of good standing from prior institution(s). Minimum college GPA of 2.0 required. Lowest grade transferable C. **General Admission Information:** Application fee $35. Regular notification is rolling. Nonfall registration accepted. Admission may be deferred for a maximum of 1 year. Credit and/or placement offered for CEEB Advanced Placement tests.

COSTS AND FINANCIAL AID
Average book expense $1,000. **Required Forms and Deadlines:** FAFSA. Financial aid filing deadline 4/1. **Notification of Awards:** Applicants will be notified of awards on a rolling basis beginning on or about 2/1. **Types of Aid:** *Need-based scholarships/grants:* Pell, SEOG, state scholarships/grants, private scholarships, the school's own gift aid. *Loans:* FFEL Subsidized Stafford, FFEL Unsubsidized Stafford, FFEL PLUS, Federal Perkins, alternative loans. **Financial Aid Statistics:** 78% freshmen, 76% undergrads receive need-based scholarship or grant aid. 72% freshmen, 59% undergrads receive need-based self-help aid. 98% freshmen, 91% undergrads receive any aid. Highest amount earned per year from on-campus jobs $2,200.

DELTA STATE UNIVERSITY

Highway 8 West, Cleveland, MS 38733
Phone: 662-846-4018 **E-mail:** dheslep@deltastate.edu
Fax: 662-846-4683 **Website:** www.deltastate.edu **ACT Code:** 2190
Financial Aid Phone: 662-846-4670

This public school was founded in 1924. It has a 332-acre campus.

RATINGS
Admissions Selectivity Rating: 60*   **Fire Safety Rating:** 60*   **Green Rating:** 60*

STUDENTS AND FACULTY
Enrollment: 3,156. **Student Body:** 62% female, 38% male, 10% out-of-state. African American 33%, Caucasian 66%. **Retention and Graduation:** 68% freshmen return for sophomore year. 24% freshmen graduate within 4 years. **Faculty:** Student/faculty ratio 16:1. 162 full-time faculty, 60% hold PhDs.

ACADEMICS
Degrees: Bachelor's, doctoral, master's, post-master's certificate. **Academic Requirements:** Arts/fine arts, English (including composition), history, mathematics, physical education, psychology, sciences (biological or physical), social science, speech communication. **Majors with Highest Enrollment:** Business administration/management, elementary education and teaching, management information systems. **Disciplines with Highest Percentage of Degrees Awarded:** Business/marketing 31%, education 24%, health professions and related sciences 7%, biological/life sciences 5%, social sciences

5%, visual and performing arts 4%. **Special Study Options:** Cooperative education program, distance learning, double major, dual enrollment, honors program, independent study, internships, teacher certification program, weekend college.

FACILITIES

Housing: Men's dorms, women's dorms, apartments for married students, apartments for students with dependent children. **Special Academic Facilities/Equipment:** Art museum, performing arts center, natural history museum, language lab, airport facility with 12 airplanes, flight simulator, planetarium. **Computers:** Network access in dorm rooms, online registration, online administrative functions (other than registration), remote student-access to Web through college's connection.

CAMPUS LIFE

Activities: Choral groups, concert band, drama/theater, jazz band, literary magazine, marching band, music ensembles, musical theater, opera, student government, student newspaper, symphony orchestra, yearbook. **Organizations:** 46 registered organizations, 27 honor societies, 11 religious organizations. 8 fraternities (14% men join), 6 sororities (13% women join). **Athletics (Intercollegiate):** *Men:* Baseball, basketball, diving, football, golf, soccer, swimming, tennis. *Women:* Basketball, cross-country, diving, soccer, softball, swimming, tennis.

ADMISSIONS

Freshman Academic Profile: 4% in top 25% of high school class, 57% in top 50% of high school class. ACT middle 50% range 17–21. TOEFL required of all international applicants, minimum paper TOEFL 525, minimum computer TOEFL 196. **Basis for Candidate Selection:** *Very important factors considered include:* Class rank, rigor of secondary school record, standardized test scores. *Other factors considered include:* Interview, recommendation(s). **Freshman Admission Requirements:** High school diploma is required, and GED is accepted. *Academic units required:* 4 English, 3 math, 3 science (2 science labs), 1 foreign language, 3 social studies, 1 academic elective. **Freshman Admission Statistics:** 1,289 applied, 32% admitted, 79% enrolled. **Transfer Admission Requirements:** College transcript(s). Minimum college GPA of 2.0 required. Lowest grade transferable D. **General Admission Information:** Application fee $15. Regular application deadline 8/1. Regular notification is rolling. Nonfall registration accepted. Admission may be deferred. Common Application not accepted. Credit and/or placement offered for CEEB Advanced Placement tests.

COSTS AND FINANCIAL AID

Average book expense $700. **Required Forms and Deadlines:** FAFSA, institution's own financial aid form. Financial aid filing deadline 4/1. **Notification of Awards:** Applicants will be notified of awards on a rolling basis beginning on or about 5/1. **Types of Aid:** *Need-based scholarships/grants:* Pell, SEOG, private scholarships, the school's own gift aid. *Loans:* FFEL Subsidized Stafford, FFEL Unsubsidized Stafford, FFEL PLUS, Federal Perkins, college/university loans from institutional funds. **Student Employment:** Federal Work-Study Program available. Institutional employment available. Off-campus job opportunities are fair. **Financial Aid Statistics:** Highest amount earned per year from on-campus jobs $1,200.

DENISON UNIVERSITY

Box H, Granville, OH 43023
Phone: 740-587-6276 **E-mail:** admissions@denison.edu **CEEB Code:** 1164
Fax: 740-587-6306 **Website:** www.denison.edu **ACT Code:** 3266
Financial Aid Phone: 800-336-4766

This private school was founded in 1831. It has a 900-acre campus.

RATINGS

Admissions Selectivity Rating: 91   **Fire Safety Rating:** 88   **Green Rating:** 87

STUDENTS AND FACULTY

Enrollment: 2,235. **Student Body:** 57% female, 43% male, 61% out-of-state, 4% international (31 countries represented). African American 5%, Asian 3%, Caucasian 84%, Hispanic 3%. **Retention and Graduation:** 87% freshmen return for sophomore year. 73% freshmen graduate within 4 years. 22% grads go on to further study within 1 year. 15% grads pursue arts and sciences

degrees. 1% grads pursue business degrees. 2% grads pursue law degrees. 2% grads pursue medical degrees. **Faculty:** Student/faculty ratio 11:1. 192 full-time faculty, 100% hold PhDs. 100% faculty teach undergrads.

ACADEMICS

Degrees: Bachelor's. **Academic Requirements:** Arts/fine arts, English (including composition), foreign languages, humanities, sciences (biological or physical), social science. **Classes:** Most classes have 20–29 students. **Majors with Highest Enrollment:** Communications and media studies, economics, English language and literature. **Disciplines with Highest Percentage of Degrees Awarded:** Social sciences 24%, English 11%, biological/life sciences 10%, communications/journalism 10%, visual and performing arts 9%. **Special Study Options:** Double major, honors program, independent study, internships, student-designed major, study abroad, teacher certification program. 3–2 Duke U. environmental management; 3–2 U. of Michigan natural resources, 3–4 Case Western Reserve dental; 3–2 Rensselaer Poly., Washington U. (St. Louis), Case Western Reserve, Columbia U. engineering; Washington U. (St. Louis) occupational therapy.

FACILITIES

Housing: Coed dorms, men's dorms, women's dorms, apartments for single students. **Special Academic Facilities/Equipment:** Burmese art collection, language lab, research station in 350-acre biological reserve, observatory, high resolution spectrometer lab, nuclear magnetic resonance spectrometer, planetarium, economics computer laboratories. **Computers:** 10% of classrooms are wireless, 55% of public computers are PCs, 35% of public computers are Macs, 10% of public computers are UNIX, network access in dorm rooms, network access in dorm lounges, online administrative functions (other than registration), remote student-access to Web through college's connection.

CAMPUS LIFE

Activities: Choral groups, concert band, dance, drama/theater, jazz band, literary magazine, music ensembles, musical theater, pep band, radio station, student government, student newspaper, student-run film society, symphony orchestra, television station, yearbook. **Organizations:** 156 registered organizations, 15 honor societies, 7 religious organizations. 8 fraternities (25% men join), 6 sororities (30% women join). **Athletics (Intercollegiate):** *Men:* Baseball, basketball, cross-country, diving, football, golf, lacrosse, soccer, swimming, tennis, track/field (indoor), track/field (outdoor). *Women:* Basketball, cross-country, diving, field hockey, lacrosse, soccer, softball, swimming, tennis, track/field (indoor), track/field (outdoor), volleyball. **Environmental Initiatives:** Campus recycling program takes paper, cardboard, aluminum, bi-metal, paper, magazines, books, glass, year end move out materials, construction/maintenance metal, wood, debris - community has access to drop of materials too. Have begun composting operaitons for yard wastes and kitchen food scraps. Operations department collects recyclables from all construction and maintenance operations, chemicals in cleaning and grounds are 90% 'green', incandescent bulbs are no longer used (except where reuired), lamp and balasts are recycled, inventory of mercury lamps identified - replace fixture rather than relamp. Currently establishing a systematic energy conservation/retrofit program for existing buildings - anticipate going through all campus buildings in the next 3-5 years. Major renovation project currently under way and planned future projects to be LEED certified, smaller renovations and projects to follow guidelines to the extent possible, exploring LEED-EB certification for some buildings on campus.

ADMISSIONS

Freshman Academic Profile: 52% in top 10% of high school class, 34% in top 25% of high school class, 14% in top 50% of high school class. 70% from public high schools. SAT Math middle 50% range 580–670. SAT Critical Reading middle 50% range 580–690. ACT middle 50% range 31–28. TOEFL required of all international applicants, minimum paper TOEFL 550, minimum computer TOEFL 213. **Basis for Candidate Selection:** *Very important factors considered include:* Academic GPA, application essay, class rank, recommendation(s), rigor of secondary school record, standardized test scores. *Important factors considered include:* Extracurricular activities, interview, talent/ability. *Other factors considered include:* Alumni/ae relation, character/personal qualities, first generation, geographical residence, level of applicant's interest, racial/ethnic status, religious affiliation/commitment, state residency, volunteer work, work experience. **Freshman Admission Requirements:** High school diploma is required, GED is accepted. *Academic units required:* 4 English, 4 math, 4 science, 3 foreign language, 2 social studies, 1 history, 1 academic elective. **Freshman Admission Statistics:** 5,010 applied, 39% admitted, 29% enrolled. **Transfer Admission Requirements:** High school transcript, college transcript(s), essay or personal statement, standardized test score, statement of good standing from prior institution(s). Minimum college GPA of 2.7 required. Lowest grade transferable C-. **General Admission Information:** Application fee $40. Early decision application deadline 11/1. Regular application deadline 1/15. Regular notification 4/1. Nonfall registration not accepted. Admission may be deferred for a maximum of 1 year. Credit and/or placement offered for CEEB Advanced Placement tests.

COSTS AND FINANCIAL AID

Annual tuition $34,410. Room and board $8,830. Required fees $890. Average book expense $1,200. **Required Forms and Deadlines:** FAFSA, institution's own financial aid form. Financial aid filing deadline 2/15. **Notification of Awards:** Applicants will be notified of awards on or about 5/1. **Types of Aid:** *Need-based scholarships/grants:* Pell, SEOG, state scholarships/grants, private scholarships, the school's own gift aid. *Loans:* Direct Subsidized Stafford, Direct Unsubsidized Stafford, Direct PLUS, Federal Perkins, college/university loans from institutional funds. **Student Employment:** Federal Work-Study Program available. Institutional employment available. Off-campus job opportunities are fair. **Financial Aid Statistics:** 43% freshmen, 46% undergrads receive need-based scholarship or grant aid. 28% freshmen, 34% undergrads receive need-based self-help aid. 95% freshmen, 95% undergrads receive any aid. Highest amount earned per year from on-campus jobs $2,250.

See page 1152.

DEPAUL UNIVERSITY

1 East Jackson Boulevard, Chicago, IL 60604-2287
Phone: 312-362-8300 **E-mail:** admitdpu@depaul.edu **CEEB Code:** 1165
Fax: 312-362-5749 **Website:** www.depaul.edu **ACT Code:** 1012
Financial Aid Phone: 312-362-8091

This private school, affiliated with the Roman Catholic Church, was founded in 1898. It has a 36-acre campus.

RATINGS

Admissions Selectivity Rating: 82   **Fire Safety Rating:** 82   **Green Rating:** 86

STUDENTS AND FACULTY

Enrollment: 14,465. **Student Body:** 56% female, 44% male, 16% out-of-state, 1% international (85 countries represented). African American 8%, Asian 8%, Caucasian 50%, Hispanic 11%. **Retention and Graduation:** 85% freshmen return for sophomore year. 39% freshmen graduate within 4 years. **Faculty:** Student/faculty ratio 16:1. 850 full-time faculty, 87% hold PhDs. 99% faculty teach undergrads.

ACADEMICS

Degrees: Bachelor's, certificate, doctoral, first professional, master's, post-bachelor's certificate, post-master's certificate. **Academic Requirements:** Arts/fine arts, computer literacy, English (including composition), experiential service learning, foreign languages, history, humanities, mathematics, philosophy, sciences (biological or physical), senior year capstone course, social science. **Classes:** Most classes have 20–29 students. Most lab/discussion sections have fewer than 10 students. **Majors with Highest Enrollment:** Accounting, communication and rhetoric, communications studies/speech, finance. **Disciplines with Highest Percentage of Degrees Awarded:** Business/marketing 33%, liberal arts/general studies 12%, social sciences 9%, communications/journalism 8%, education 8%. **Special Study Options:** Accelerated program, cooperative education program, distance learning, double major, English as a second language (ESL), honors program, independent study, internships, student-designed major, study abroad, teacher certification program, weekend college.

FACILITIES

Housing: Coed dorms, apartments for single students, theme communities (groups of students who choose to live together in a house or apartment within residence life, to further a particular theme). **Special Academic Facilities/Equipment:** McGowan Science Center, Merle Reskin Theatre, art gallery, environmental science building, Ray Meyer Fitness and Recreational Center, three-level student center. **Computers:** 1% of classrooms are wired, 35% of classrooms are wireless, 99% of public computers are PCs, 1% of public computers are Macs, network access in dorm rooms, network access in dorm lounges, online registration, online administrative functions (other than registration), remote student-access to Web through college's connection.

CAMPUS LIFE

Activities: Choral groups, concert band, dance, drama/theater, jazz band, music ensembles, musical theater, opera, pep band, radio station, student government, student newspaper, student-run film society, symphony orchestra. **Organizations:** 170 registered organizations, 3 honor societies, 7 religious organizations.

12 fraternities, 11 sororities. **Athletics (Intercollegiate):** *Men:* Basketball, cross-country, golf, soccer, tennis, track/field (indoor), track/field (outdoor). *Women:* Basketball, cross-country, soccer, softball, tennis, track/field (indoor), track/field (outdoor), volleyball. **Environmental Initiatives:** That all new construction projects achieve a minimum LEED rating of silver. That in the next five years all existing older buildings be re-commissioned in order to operate with greater energy efficiency. To introduce new sustainable education coursework into the curriculum.

ADMISSIONS

Freshman Academic Profile: 19% in top 10% of high school class, 47% in top 25% of high school class, 79% in top 50% of high school class. 74% from public high schools. SAT Math middle 50% range 510–620. SAT Critical Reading middle 50% range 520–630. SAT Writing middle 50% range 527.5–622.5. ACT middle 50% range 22–27. TOEFL required of all international applicants, minimum paper TOEFL 550, minimum computer TOEFL 213. **Basis for Candidate Selection:** *Very important factors considered include:* Academic GPA, character/personal qualities, rigor of secondary school record. *Important factors considered include:* Application essay, class rank, extracurricular activities, recommendation(s), standardized test scores, talent/ability, volunteer work. work experience. *Other factors considered include:* Alumni/ae relation, first generation, geographical residence, interview, level of applicant's interest, racial/ethnic status, religious affiliation/commitment, state residency. **Freshman Admission Requirements:** High school diploma is required, and GED is accepted. *Academic units required:* 4 English, 2 math, 2 science (2 science labs), 2 social studies, 4 academic electives. **Freshman Admission Statistics:** 10,414 applied, 70% admitted, 35% enrolled. **Transfer Admission Requirements:** College transcript(s), essay or personal statement, statement of good standing from prior institution(s). Minimum college GPA of 2.0 required. Lowest grade transferable C-. **General Admission Information:** Application fee $40. Regular notification is rolling. Nonfall registration accepted. Admission may be deferred for a maximum of 1 year. Credit and/or placement offered for CEEB Advanced Placement tests.

COSTS AND FINANCIAL AID

Annual tuition $23,820. Room and board $9,955. Required fees $574. Average book expense $900. **Required Forms and Deadlines:** FAFSA. Financial aid filing deadline 5/1. **Notification of Awards:** Applicants will be notified of awards on a rolling basis beginning on or about 2/15. **Types of Aid:** *Need-based scholarships/grants:* Pell, SEOG, state scholarships/grants, private scholarships, the school's own gift aid. *Loans:* Direct Subsidized Stafford, Direct Unsubsidized Stafford, Direct PLUS, Federal Perkins. **Student Employment:** Off-campus job opportunities are excellent. **Financial Aid Statistics:** 47% freshmen, 47% undergrads receive need-based scholarship or grant aid. 48% freshmen, 50% undergrads receive need-based self-help aid. 38 freshmen, 183 undergrads receive athletic scholarships. 66% freshmen, 66% undergrads receive any aid. Highest amount earned per year from on-campus jobs $3,500.

DEPAUW UNIVERSITY

101 East Seminary, Greencastle, IN 46135
Phone: 765-658-4006 **E-mail:** admission@depauw.edu **CEEB Code:** 1166
Fax: 765-658-4007 **Website:** www.depauw.edu **ACT Code:** 1184
Financial Aid Phone: 765-658-4030

This private school, affiliated with the Methodist Church, was founded in 1837. It has a 1,100-acre campus.

RATINGS

Admissions Selectivity Rating: 92   **Fire Safety Rating:** 60*   **Green Rating:** 70

STUDENTS AND FACULTY

Enrollment: 2,276. **Student Body:** 56% female, 44% male, 46% out-of-state, 2% international (32 countries represented). African American 6%, Asian 3%, Caucasian 84%, Hispanic 3%. **Retention and Graduation:** 92% freshmen return for sophomore year. 79% freshmen graduate within 4 years. 23% grads go on to further study within 1 year. 15% grads pursue arts and sciences degrees. 1% grads pursue business degrees. 5% grads pursue law degrees. 2% grads pursue medical degrees. **Faculty:** Student/faculty ratio 10:1. 211 full-time faculty, 97% hold PhDs. 100% faculty teach undergrads.

ACADEMICS

Degrees: Bachelor's. **Academic Requirements:** Arts/fine arts, English (including composition), foreign languages, history, humanities, philosophy, sciences (biological or physical), social science. **Classes:** Most classes have 10–19 students. Most lab/discussion sections have 10–19 students. **Majors with Highest Enrollment:** Economics, English composition, mass communications/media studies. **Disciplines with Highest Percentage of Degrees Awarded:** Social sciences 19%, English 12%, communications/journalism 11%, foreign languages and literature 11%, biological/life sciences 10%. **Special Study Options:** Double major, dual enrollment, exchange student program (domestic), honors program, independent study, internships, student-designed major, study abroad, teacher certification program.

FACILITIES

Housing: Coed dorms, apartments for single students, special housing for international students, fraternity/sorority housing. **Special Academic Facilities/Equipment:** Recently opened Peeler Art Center housing gallery and studio space, Center for Contemporary Media, performing arts center, Anthropology Museum, Shidzuo Iikudo Museum. **Computers:** 20% of classrooms are wired, 100% of classrooms are wireless, 85% of public computers are PCs, 14% of public computers are Macs, 1% of public computers are UNIX, network access in dorm rooms, network access in dorm lounges, online registration, online administrative functions (other than registration), support for handheld computing, remote student-access to Web through college's connection. Undergraduates are required to own a computer.

CAMPUS LIFE

Activities: Choral groups, concert band, dance, drama/theater, jazz band, literary magazine, music ensembles, musical theater, opera, pep band, radio station, student government, student newspaper, student-run film society, symphony orchestra, television station, yearbook. **Organizations:** 119 registered organizations, 13 honor societies, 10 religious organizations. 13 fraternities (75% men join), 11 sororities (70% women join). **Athletics (Intercollegiate):** *Men:* Baseball, basketball, cross-country, diving, football, golf, soccer, swimming, tennis, track/field (indoor), track/field (outdoor). *Women:* Basketball, cross-country, diving, field hockey, golf, soccer, softball, swimming, tennis, track/field (indoor), track/field (outdoor), volleyball. Environmental Initiatives: LEED certified construction of the Janet Prindle Institute for Ethics. 2007–08 full year of campus programming, speakers, and colloquia on sustainability. Significant investment in/upgrades to campus utilities/infrastructure, including an HVAC audit, upgraded steam pipes, chiller planet water system replacement, lightbulb replacement, and a bike-share program, among other changes.

ADMISSIONS

Freshman Academic Profile: 46% in top 10% of high school class, 81% in top 25% of high school class, 99% in top 50% of high school class. 83% from public high schools. SAT Math middle 50% range 570–660. SAT Critical Reading middle 50% range 560–660. SAT Writing middle 50% range 550–650. ACT middle 50% range 25–29. TOEFL required of all international applicants, minimum paper TOEFL 560, minimum computer TOEFL 225. **Basis for Candidate Selection:** *Very important factors considered include:* Academic GPA, rigor of secondary school record, standardized test scores. *Important factors considered include:* Application essay, class rank, recommendation(s). *Other factors considered include:* Alumni/ae relation, character/personal qualities, extracurricular activities, first generation, geographical residence, interview, level of applicant's interest, state residency, talent/ability, volunteer work, work experience. **Freshman Admission Requirements:** High school diploma is required, and GED is accepted. *Academic units recommended:* 4 English, 4 math, 4 science (2 science labs), 4 foreign language, 4 social studies. **Freshman Admission Statistics:** 4,074 applied, 68% admitted, 22% enrolled. **Transfer Admission Requirements:** High school transcript, college transcript(s), essay or personal statement, statement of good standing from prior institution(s). Minimum college GPA of 3.0 required. Lowest grade transferable C. **General Admission Information:** Application fee $40. Early decision application deadline 11/1. Regular application deadline 2/1. Regular notification 4/1. Nonfall registration accepted. Admission may be deferred for a maximum of 1 year. Credit and/or placement offered for CEEB Advanced Placement tests.

COSTS AND FINANCIAL AID

Annual tuition $29,300. Room and board $8,100. Required fees $400. Average book expense $700. **Required Forms and Deadlines:** FAFSA, institution's own financial aid form. Financial aid filing deadline 2/15. **Notification of Awards:** Applicants will be notified of awards on or about 3/27. **Types of Aid:** *Need-based scholarships/grants:* Pell, SEOG, state scholarships/grants, private scholarships, the school's own gift aid. *Loans:* FFEL Subsidized Stafford, FFEL Unsubsidized Stafford, FFEL PLUS, Federal Perkins, college/university loans from institutional funds, alternative loans. **Student Employment:** Federal Work-Study Program available. Institutional employment available. Off-campus job opportunities are fair. **Financial Aid Statistics:** 50% freshmen, 46% undergrads receive need-based scholarship or grant aid. 37% freshmen, 35%

undergrads receive need-based self-help aid. 97% freshmen, 98% undergrads receive any aid. Highest amount earned per year from on-campus jobs $563.

DESALES UNIVERSITY

2755 Station Avenue, Center Valley, PA 18034-9568
Phone: 610-282-4443 **E-mail:** admiss@desales.edu **CEEB Code:** 2021
Fax: 610-282-0131 **Website:** www.desales.edu
Financial Aid Phone: 610-282-4443

This private school, affiliated with the Roman Catholic Church, was founded in 1964. It has a 400-acre campus.

RATINGS

Admissions Selectivity Rating: 78   **Fire Safety Rating:** 60*   **Green Rating:** 60*

STUDENTS AND FACULTY

Enrollment: 2,126. **Student Body:** 59% female, 41% male, 18% out-of-state. Caucasian 52%, Hispanic 2%. **Retention and Graduation:** 82% freshmen return for sophomore year. 59% freshmen graduate within 4 years. 27% grads go on to further study within 1 year. 19% grads pursue arts and sciences degrees. 1% grads pursue business degrees. 2% grads pursue medical degrees. **Faculty:** Student/faculty ratio 15:1. 97 full-time faculty, 74% hold PhDs. 90% faculty teach undergrads.

ACADEMICS

Degrees: Bachelor's, certificate, master's, post-bachelor's certificate, post-master's certificate. **Academic Requirements:** Arts/fine arts, computer literacy, English (including composition), foreign languages, history, humanities, mathematics, philosophy, sciences (biological or physical), social science, Catholic theology courses, foreign culture courses, foreign language. **Classes:** Most classes have 10–19 students. Most lab/discussion sections have fewer than 10 students. **Majors with Highest Enrollment:** Drama and dramatics/theater arts, elementary education and teaching, physician assistant. **Disciplines with Highest Percentage of Degrees Awarded;** Business/marketing 33%, visual and performing arts 16%, education 12%, public administration and social services 8%, computer and information sciences 6%. **Special Study Options:** Accelerated program, cross-registration, distance learning, double major, dual enrollment, honors program, independent study, internships, liberal arts/career combination, study abroad, teacher certification program, weekend college.

FACILITIES

Housing: Coed dorms, men's dorms, women's dorms, cooperative housing. Townhouses are available for upperclassmen or upperclasswomen and for common interest housing. **Computers:** 10% of classrooms are wired, 40% of classrooms are wireless, 95% of public computers are PCs, 5% of public computers are Macs, network access in dorm rooms, online registration, online administrative functions (other than registration), remote student-access to Web through college's connection. Environmental Initiatives: Computer/technology recycling program. Alternative sources of power are used or planned. An elective course on Sustainability is offered.

CAMPUS LIFE

Activities: Choral groups, dance, drama/theater, literary magazine, musical theater, pep band, radio station, student government, student newspaper, student-run film society, television station, yearbook. **Organizations:** 36 registered organizations, 7 honor societies, 1 religious organization. **Athletics (Intercollegiate):** *Men:* Baseball, basketball, cross-country, golf, lacrosse, soccer, tennis, track/field (outdoor). *Women:* Basketball, cross-country, field hockey, soccer, softball, tennis, track/field (outdoor), volleyball.

ADMISSIONS

Freshman Academic Profile: 23% in top 10% of high school class, 45% in top 25% of high school class, 80% in top 50% of high school class. 59% from public high schools. SAT Math middle 50% range 490–590. SAT Critical Reading middle 50% range 490–590. ACT middle 50% range 18–23. TOEFL required of all international applicants, minimum paper TOEFL 550, minimum computer TOEFL 213. **Basis for Candidate Selection:** *Very important factors considered include:* Academic GPA, class rank, recommendation(s), rigor of secondary school record, standardized test scores. *Important factors considered include:* Character/personal qualities, extracurricular activities, interview, talent/ability. *Other factors considered include:* Application essay, geographical residence, racial/ethnic status, state residency, volunteer work, work experience. **Freshman Admission Requirements:** High school diploma is required, and GED is accepted. *Academic units required:* 4 English, 3 math, 2 science (2 science labs), 2 foreign language, 3 social studies. *Academic units recommended:* 4 English, 4 math, 2 science (2 science labs), 2 foreign language, 4 social studies. **Freshman Admission Statistics:** 1,693 applied, 78%

admitted, 30% enrolled. **Transfer Admission Requirements:** High school transcript, college transcript(s), statement of good standing from prior institution(s). Minimum college GPA of 2.0 required. Lowest grade transferable C-. **General Admission Information:** Application fee $30. Regular application deadline 8/1. Regular notification is rolling. Nonfall registration not accepted. Admission may be deferred for a maximum of 1 year. Credit offered for CEEB Advanced Placement tests.

COSTS AND FINANCIAL AID

Annual tuition $21,200. Room & board $8,250. Required fees $900. Average book expense $900. **Required Forms and Deadlines:** FAFSA, institution's own financial aid form, non-need based on financial need according to FAFSA. Financial aid filing deadline 2/1. **Notification of Awards:** Applicants will be notified of awards on a rolling basis beginning on or about 2/15. **Types of Aid:** *Need-based scholarships/grants:* Pell, SEOG, state scholarships/grants, private scholarships, the school's own gift aid. *Loans:* FFEL Subsidized Stafford, FFEL Unsubsidized Stafford, FFEL PLUS, Federal Perkins, Federal Nursing. **Financial Aid Statistics:** 58% freshmen, 54% undergrads receive need-based scholarship or grant aid. 53% freshmen, 56% undergrads receive need-based self-help aid. Highest amount earned per year from on-campus jobs $640.

See page 1154.

DEVRY UNIVERSITY

Multiple locations nationwide
Administrative Office, One Tower Lane, Oakbrook Terrace, IL 60181
Phone: 866-338-7934 **Email:** info@devry.edu **Website:** www.devry.edu

This is a proprietary school founded in 1931.

RATINGS
Admissions Selectivity Rating: 60*   **Fire Safety Rating:** 60*   **Green Rating:** 60*

STUDENTS AND FACULTY
Enrollment: 40,932 **Student Body:** 40% female, 60% male, 1% international. African American 28%, Asian 6%, Caucasian 45%, Hispanic 15%, Native American 1%. **Faculty:** Student/faculty ratio 12:1. 720 full-time faculty.

ACADEMICS
Degrees: Associate, bachelor's, master's. **Academic Requirements:** Computer literacy, English (including composition), humanities, mathematics, sciences (biological or physical), social science. **Majors with Highest Enrollment:** Bachelor in business administration, bachelor in technical management, bachelor in computer information systems. **Disciplines with Highest Percentage of Degrees Awarded:** Business/marketing 69%, computer and information sciences 17%, engineering technologies 13%, biological/life sciences 1%, health professions and related sciences 1%. **Special Study Options:** Accelerated program, distance learning.

FACILITIES
Housing: Private apartments, student plan housing, private rooms. **Computers:** Campus-wide network, online registration.

ADMISSIONS
60 (out of 100).
Basis for Candidate Selection: *Important factors considered include:* Academic GPA, interview. *Other factors considered include:* Class rank, standardized test scores. **Freshman Admission Requirements:** High school diploma is required and GED is accepted. **Transfer Admission Requirements:** College transcript(s), interview, statement of good standing from prior institution(s). **General Admission Information:** Application fee: $50. Applications accepted on a rolling basis. Regular notification is on a rolling basis. Nonfall registration is accepted. Admission may be deferred for a maximum of 1 year. Common Application is not accepted.

COSTS AND FINANCIAL AID
Annual tuition $12,900–$14,320 (depending on location). Required fees $120–$320 (depending on location). Average book expense $650. **Required Forms and Deadlines:** FAFSA. **Types of Aid:** *Need-based scholarships/grants:* Federal Pell, SEOG, state scholarships/grants, college/university scholarship or grant aid from institutional funds. *Loans:* FFEL Subsidized Stafford Loans, FFEL Unsubsidized Stafford Loans, FFEL PLUS Loans, Federal Perkins Loans. **Student Employment:** Federal Work-Study Program available. Institutional employment available.

See page 1156.

DICKINSON COLLEGE

Best 368

PO Box 1773, Carlisle, PA 17013-2896
Phone: 717-245-1231 **E-mail:** admit@dickinson.edu **CEEB Code:** 2186
Fax: 717-245-1442 **Website:** www.dickinson.edu **ACT Code:** 3550
Financial Aid Phone: 717-245-1308

This private school was founded in 1783. It has a 120-acre campus.

RATINGS
Admissions Selectivity Rating: 93   **Fire Safety Rating:** 75   **Green Rating:** 89

STUDENTS AND FACULTY
Enrollment: 2,369. **Student Body:** 56% female, 44% male, 73% out-of-state, 6% international (37 countries represented). African American 5%, Asian 4%, Caucasian 80%, Hispanic 4%. **Retention and Graduation:** 91% freshmen return for sophomore year. 78% freshmen graduate within 4 years. 28% grads go on to further study within 1 year. 14% grads pursue arts and sciences degrees. 1% grads pursue business degrees. 5% grads pursue law degrees. 2% grads pursue medical degrees. **Faculty:** Student/faculty ratio 12:1. 177 full-time faculty, 95% hold PhDs. 100% faculty teach undergrads.

ACADEMICS
Degrees: Bachelor's. **Academic Requirements:** First-year seminar, foreign languages, humanities, physical education, quantitative reasoning, sciences (biological or physical), social science, U.S. diversity, writing intensive course. **Classes:** Most classes have 10–19 students. Most lab/discussion sections have fewer than 10 students. **Majors with Highest Enrollment:** International business, political science and government, psychology. **Disciplines with Highest Percentage of Degrees Awarded:** Social sciences 25%, biological/life sciences 9%, business/marketing 9%, psychology 9%, history 8%. **Special Study Options:** Accelerated program, cross-registration, double major, English as a second language (ESL), exchange student program (domestic), independent study, internships, liberal arts/career combination, student-designed major, study abroad, teacher certification program.

FACILITIES
Housing: Coed dorms, apartments for single students, special housing for disabled students, fraternity/sorority housing, theme houses, foreign languages, arts, environmental, multicultural. **Special Academic Facilities/Equipment:** Art gallery, center for the arts, planetarium, observatory, scanning electron microscope, archaeology. **Computers:** 53% of public computers are PCs, 47% of public computers are Macs, network access in dorm rooms, network access in dorm lounges, online registration, online administrative functions (other than registration), remote student-access to Web through college's connection.

CAMPUS LIFE
Activities: Choral groups, concert band, dance, drama/theater, jazz band, literary magazine, music ensembles, musical theater, radio station, student government, student newspaper, student-run film society, symphony orchestra, yearbook. **Organizations:** 140 registered organizations, 15 honor societies, 10 religious organizations. 6 fraternities (18% men join), 4 sororities (24% women join). **Athletics (Intercollegiate):** *Men:* Baseball, basketball, cross-country, football, golf, lacrosse, soccer, swimming, tennis, track/field (indoor), track/field (outdoor). *Women:* Basketball, cross-country, field hockey, golf, lacrosse, soccer, softball, swimming, tennis, track/field (indoor), track/field (outdoor), volleyball. Environmental Initiatives: Renewable energy sources: wind (purchasing) & solar (on campus). LEED silver certification (or comparable) for major projects. President's Climate Committee—moving toward climate neutrality.

ADMISSIONS
Freshman Academic Profile: 53% in top 10% of high school class, 84% in top 25% of high school class, 97% in top 50% of high school class. 61% from public high schools. SAT Math middle 50% range 590–680. SAT Critical Reading middle 50% range 600–690. ACT middle 50% range 27–30. TOEFL required of all international applicants, minimum paper TOEFL 600, minimum computer TOEFL 250. **Basis for Candidate Selection:** *Very important factors considered include:* Academic GPA, extracurricular activities, rigor of secondary school record, talent/ability, volunteer work. *Important factors considered include:* Alumni/ae relation, class rank, recommendation(s), standardized test scores, work experience. *Other factors considered include:* Application essay, character/personal qualities, first generation, geographical residence, interview, level of applicant's interest, racial/ethnic status, state

residency. **Freshman Admission Requirements:** High school diploma is required, and GED is accepted. *Academic units required:* 4 English, 3 math, 3 science (2 science labs), 2 foreign language, 2 social studies, 2 academic electives. *Academic units recommended:* 3 foreign language. **Freshman Admission Statistics:** 5,298 applied, 43% admitted, 27% enrolled. **Transfer Admission Requirements:** High school transcript, college transcript(s), essay or personal statement, statement of good standing from prior institution(s). Minimum college GPA of 2.0 required. Lowest grade transferable C. **General Admission Information:** Application fee $60. Early decision application deadline 11/15. Regular application deadline 2/1. Regular notification 3/31. Nonfall registration not accepted. Admission may be deferred for a maximum of 2 years. Credit and/or placement offered for CEEB Advanced Placement tests.

COSTS AND FINANCIAL AID

Annual tuition $35,450. Room and board $8,980. Required fees $334. Average book expense $1,000. **Required Forms and Deadlines:** FAFSA, CSS/Financial Aid PROFILE, state aid form, Noncustodial PROFILE, Business/Farm Supplement. Financial aid filing deadline 2/1. **Notification of Awards:** Applicants will be notified of awards on or about 3/31. **Types of Aid:** *Need-based scholarships/grants:* Pell, SEOG, state scholarships/grants, private scholarships, the school's own gift aid. *Loans:* FFEL Subsidized Stafford, FFEL Unsubsidized Stafford, FFEL PLUS, Federal Perkins, college/university loans from institutional funds. **Financial Aid Statistics:** 45% freshmen, 46% undergrads receive need-based scholarship or grant aid. 41% freshmen, 41% undergrads receive need-based self-help aid. 50% freshmen, 55% undergrads receive any aid.

DICKINSON STATE UNIVERSITY

Office of Enrollment Services, Box 173, Dickinson, ND 58601-4896
Phone: 701-483-2175 **E-mail:** dsu.hawks@dsu.nodak.edu
Fax: 701-483-2409 **Website:** www.dickinsonstate.com **ACT Code:** 3210
Financial Aid Phone: 701-483-2371

This public school was founded in 1918. It has a 137-acre campus.

RATINGS
Admissions Selectivity Rating: 69   **Fire Safety Rating:** 60*   **Green Rating:** 60*

STUDENTS AND FACULTY
Enrollment: 2,572. **Student Body:** 59% female, 41% male, 32% out-of-state, 10% international (26 countries represented). African American 2%, Caucasian 77%, Hispanic 1%, Native American 3%. **Retention and Graduation:** 59% freshmen return for sophomore year. 9% freshmen graduate within 4 years. **Faculty:** Student/faculty ratio 19:1. 86 full-time faculty, 51% hold PhDs. 100% faculty teach undergrads.

ACADEMICS
Degrees: Associate, bachelor's, certificate. **Academic Requirements:** Arts/fine arts, computer literacy, English (including composition), history, humanities, mathematics, sciences (biological or physical), social science, freshman seminar, physical education. **Classes:** Most classes have 10–19 students. **Majors with Highest Enrollment:** Business administration/management, nursing/registered nurse training (RN, ASN, BSN, MSN), teacher education. **Disciplines with Highest Percentage of Degrees Awarded:** Agriculture 4%, business/marketing 28%, education 28%, liberal arts/general studies 10%, health professions and related sciences 8%, biological/life sciences 5%, psychology 4%. **Special Study Options:** Accelerated program, distance learning, double major, dual enrollment, honors program, independent study, internships, liberal arts/career combination, student-designed major, study abroad, teacher certification program.

FACILITIES
Housing: Coed dorms, men's dorms, women's dorms, apartments for married students, apartments for single students, special housing for disabled students, apartments for upperclassmen, apartments for scholars. **Special Academic Facilities/Equipment:** Art gallery, smart classrooms. **Computers:** 90% of public computers are PCs, 10% of public computers are Macs, network access in dorm rooms, network access in dorm lounges, online registration.

CAMPUS LIFE
Activities: Choral groups, concert band, dance, drama/theater, jazz band, literary magazine, marching band, music ensembles, musical theater, pep band, student government, student newspaper, student-run film society, yearbook. **Organizations:** 47 registered organizations, 7 honor societies, 6 religious organizations. **Athletics (Intercollegiate):** *Men:* Baseball, basketball, cheerleading, cross-country, football, golf, rodeo, track/field (indoor), track/field

(outdoor), wrestling. *Women:* Basketball, cheerleading, cross-country, golf, rodeo, softball, track/field (indoor), track/field (outdoor), volleyball.

ADMISSIONS
69 (out of 100). **Freshman Academic Profile:** 5% in top 10% of high school class, 15% in top 25% of high school class, 51% in top 50% of high school class. 98% from public high schools. SAT Math middle 50% range 470–590. SAT Critical Reading middle 50% range 430–530. ACT middle 50% range 18–23. TOEFL required of all international applicants, minimum paper TOEFL 525, minimum computer TOEFL 195. **Freshman Admission Requirements:** High school diploma is required, and GED is accepted. *Academic units required:* 4 English, 3 math, 3 science, 3 history and/or social studies **Freshman Admission Statistics:** 527 applied, 96% admitted, 71% enrolled. **Transfer Admission Requirements:** College transcript(s). Minimum college GPA of 2.0 required. Lowest grade transferable D. **General Admission Information:** Application fee $35. Regular notification is rolling basis. Nonfall registration accepted. Neither credit nor placement offered for CEEB Advanced Placement tests.

COSTS AND FINANCIAL AID
Annual in-state tuition $3,828. Annual out-of-state tuition $10,222. Room and board $4,076. Required fees $945. Average book expense $900. Average book expense $800. **Required Forms and Deadlines:** FAFSA. Financial aid filing deadline 3/15. **Notification of Awards:** Applicants will be notified of awards on a rolling basis beginning on or about 4/30. **Types of Aid:** *Need-based scholarships/grants:* Pell, SEOG, state scholarships/grants, private scholarships, the school's own gift aid. *Loans:* FFEL Subsidized Stafford, FFEL Unsubsidized Stafford, FFEL PLUS, Federal Perkins, Federal Nursing. **Student Employment:** Federal Work-Study Program available. Institutional employment available. Off-campus job opportunities are good. **Financial Aid Statistics:** Highest amount earned per year from on-campus jobs $1,304.

DILLARD UNIVERSITY

2601 Gentilly Boulevard, New Orleans, LA 70122
Phone: 504-816-4670 **E-mail:** admissions@dillard.edu **CEEB Code:** 6164
Fax: 504-816-4895 **Website:** www.dillard.edu **ACT Code:** 1578
Financial Aid Phone: 504-816-4677

This private school, affiliated with the United Church of Christ, was founded in 1869. It has a 55-acre campus.

RATINGS
Admissions Selectivity Rating: 80   **Fire Safety Rating:** 60*   **Green Rating:** 60*

STUDENTS AND FACULTY
Enrollment: 2,155. **Student Body:** 78% female, 22% male, 54% out-of-state. African American 99%. **Retention and Graduation:** 78% freshmen return for sophomore year. 36% freshmen graduate within 4 years. 39% grads go on to further study within 1 year. 34% grads pursue arts and sciences degrees. 1% grads pursue business degrees. 1% grads pursue law degrees. 3% grads pursue medical degrees. **Faculty:** Student/faculty ratio 12:1. 145 full-time faculty, 68% hold PhDs. 100% faculty teach undergrads.

ACADEMICS
Degrees: Bachelor's. **Academic Requirements:** Arts/fine arts, computer literacy, English (including composition), foreign languages, history, humanities, mathematics, sciences (biological or physical), social science. **Classes:** Most classes have 10–19 students. Most lab/discussion sections have 20–29 students. **Disciplines with Highest Percentage of Degrees Awarded:** Business/marketing 19%, social sciences 17%, biological/life sciences 11%, health professions and related sciences 11%, communication technologies 10%, psychology 7%. **Special Study Options:** Double major, dual enrollment, honors program, independent study, internships, liberal arts/career combination, study abroad, teacher certification program.

FACILITIES
Housing: Coed dorms, men's dorms, women's dorms, apartments for single students. **Special Academic Facilities/Equipment:** Art gallery, language lab, communication studies facilities, electron microscope, observatory, outdoor challenge course. **Computers:** 5% of classrooms are wired, 5% of classrooms are wireless, 100% of public computers are PCs, network access in dorm rooms, network access in dorm lounges, online administrative functions (other than registration), remote student-access to Web through college's connection.

CAMPUS LIFE
Activities: Choral groups, dance, drama/theater, music ensembles, radio station, student government, student newspaper, yearbook. **Organizations:** 67

registered organizations, 6 honor societies, 3 religious organizations. 4 fraternities (4% men join), 4 sororities (11% women join). **Athletics (Intercollegiate):** *Men:* Basketball, cross-country, tennis. *Women:* Basketball, cross-country, tennis, volleyball.

ADMISSIONS

Freshman Academic Profile: 2% in top 10% of high school class, 44% in top 25% of high school class, 74% in top 50% of high school class. SAT Math middle 50% range 440–520. SAT Critical Reading middle 50% range 450–530. ACT middle 50% range 19–22. TOEFL required of all international applicants, minimum paper TOEFL 550, minimum computer TOEFL 230. **Basis for Candidate Selection:** *Very important factors considered include:* Application essay, recommendation(s), rigor of secondary school record, standardized test scores. *Other factors considered include:* Alumni/ae relation, class rank, extracurricular activities, interview. **Freshman Admission Requirements:** High school diploma is required, and GED is accepted. *Academic units required:* 4 English, 3 math, 3 science, 3 social studies, 6 academic electives. *Academic units recommended:* 2 foreign language. **Freshman Admission Statistics:** 3,106 applied, 47% admitted, 35% enrolled. **Transfer Admission Requirements:** College transcript(s), statement of good standing from prior institution(s). Minimum college GPA of 2.0 required. Lowest grade transferable C. **General Admission Information:** Application fee $20. Regular application deadline 7/1. Regular notification is rolling. Nonfall registration accepted. Common Application accepted. Credit and/or placement offered for CEEB Advanced Placement tests.

COSTS AND FINANCIAL AID

Average book expense $1,000. **Required Forms and Deadlines:** FAFSA, institution's own financial aid form. Financial aid filing deadline 5/1. **Notification of Awards:** Applicants will be notified of awards on a rolling basis beginning on or about 3/1. **Types of Aid:** *Need-based scholarships/grants:* Pell, SEOG, state scholarships/grants, private scholarships, the school's own gift aid, United Negro College Fund, Federal Nursing Scholarships. *Loans:* Direct Subsidized Stafford, Direct Unsubsidized Stafford, Direct PLUS, FFEL Subsidized Stafford, FFEL Unsubsidized Stafford, FFEL PLUS, Federal Perkins, Federal Nursing. **Student Employment:** Federal Work-Study Program available. Off-campus job opportunities are good. **Financial Aid Statistics:** 76% freshmen, 58% undergrads receive need-based scholarship or grant aid. 100% freshmen, 99% undergrads receive need-based self-help aid. 16 freshmen, 44 undergrads receive athletic scholarships. 98% freshmen, 98% undergrads receive any aid. Highest amount earned per year from on-campus jobs $2,000.

DIVINE WORD COLLEGE

Office of Admissions, PO Box 380, Epworth, IA 52045
Phone: 563-876-3332 **E-mail:** dwm@mwci.net **CEEB Code:** 6174
Fax: 563-876-5515 **Website:** www.dwci.edu
Financial Aid Phone: 563-876-3353

This private school, affiliated with the Roman Catholic Church, was founded in 1964. It has a 30-acre campus.

RATINGS

Admissions Selectivity Rating: 60*   **Fire Safety Rating:** 60*   **Green Rating:** 60*

STUDENTS AND FACULTY

Student Body: 100% out-of-state. **Faculty:** Student/faculty ratio 3:1. 22 full-time faculty, 50% hold PhDs. 100% faculty teach undergrads.

ACADEMICS

Degrees: Associate, bachelor's. **Academic Requirements:** Arts/fine arts, computer literacy, English (including composition), foreign languages, history, humanities, mathematics, philosophy, sciences (biological or physical), social science. **Special Study Options:** Double major, English as a second language (ESL), independent study, liberal arts/career combination, study abroad.

FACILITIES

Housing: Men's dorms. **Computers:** 100% of public computers are PCs, network access in dorm rooms, remote student-access to Web through college's connection.

CAMPUS LIFE

Activities: Choral groups, student government, yearbook. **Athletics (Intercollegiate):** *Men:* Soccer.

ADMISSIONS

Freshman Academic Profile: TOEFL required of all international applicants,

minimum paper TOEFL 550. **Basis for Candidate Selection:** *Very important factors considered include:* Character/personal qualities, interview, recommendation(s), religious affiliation/commitment. *Other factors considered include:* Class rank, extracurricular activities, geographical residence, rigor of secondary school record, standardized test scores, talent/ability, volunteer work, work experience. **Freshman Admission Requirements:** High school diploma is required, and GED is accepted. **Transfer Admission Requirements:** College transcript(s), essay or personal statement, interview. **General Admission Information:** Application fee $25. Regular application deadline 7/15. Nonfall registration accepted. Admission may be deferred for a maximum of 1 semester. Common Application not accepted. Credit and/or placement offered for CEEB Advanced Placement tests.

COSTS AND FINANCIAL AID

Annual tuition $10,400. Room and board $2,700. Required fees $120. Average book expense $500. **Types of Aid:** *Need-based scholarships/grants:* Pell, SEOG, state scholarships/grants, private scholarships, the school's own gift aid. *Loans:* Direct Subsidized Stafford, Direct Unsubsidized Stafford, FFEL Subsidized Stafford, FFEL PLUS, Federal Perkins, state loans. **Student Employment:** Federal Work-Study Program available.

DOANE COLLEGE

1014 Boswell Avenue, Crete, NE 68333
Phone: 402-826-8222 **E-mail:** admissions@doane.edu **CEEB Code:** 6165
Fax: 402-826-8600 **Website:** www.doane.edu **ACT Code:** 2448
Financial Aid Phone: 402-826-8260

This private school, affiliated with the United Church of Christ, was founded in 1872. It has a 300-acre campus.

RATINGS

Admissions Selectivity Rating: 75   **Fire Safety Rating:** 60*   **Green Rating:** 69

STUDENTS AND FACULTY

Enrollment: 1,555. **Student Body:** 59% female, 41% male, 17% out-of-state. African American 3%, Caucasian 76%, Hispanic 2%. **Retention and Graduation:** 78% freshmen return for sophomore year. 60% freshmen graduate within 4 years. 22% grads go on to further study within 1 year. 4% grads pursue law degrees. 7% grads pursue medical degrees. **Faculty:** Student/faculty ratio 10:1. 81 full-time faculty, 67% hold PhDs. 100% faculty teach undergrads.

ACADEMICS

Degrees: Bachelor's, master's. **Academic Requirements:** Arts/fine arts, English (including composition), history, humanities, mathematics, sciences (biological or physical), social science. **Classes:** Most classes have fewer than 10 students. **Majors with Highest Enrollment:** Biological and physical sciences, economics, elementary education and teaching. **Disciplines with Highest Percentage of Degrees Awarded:** Social sciences 32%, education 10%, English 8%, biological/life sciences 7%, business/marketing 6%. **Special Study Options:** Double major, English as a second language (ESL), honors program, independent study, internships, student-designed major, study abroad, teacher certification program.

FACILITIES

Housing: Coed dorms, men's dorms, women's dorms, special housing for Hansen Leadership students. **Special Academic Facilities/Equipment:** Art gallery, language lab, communication studies facilities, electron microscope, observatory, outdoor challenge course. **Computers:** 100% of classrooms are wired, 50% of classrooms are wireless, 75% of public computers are PCs, 25% of public computers are Macs, network access in dorm rooms, network access in dorm lounges, online registration, online administrative functions (other than registration), remote student-access to Web through college's connection.

CAMPUS LIFE

Activities: Choral groups, concert band, dance, drama/theater, jazz band, literary magazine, marching band, music ensembles, musical theater, pep band, radio station, student government, student newspaper, television station, yearbook. **Organizations:** 50 registered organizations, 8 honor societies, 2 religious organizations. 5 fraternities (31% men join), 4 sororities (28% women join). **Athletics (Intercollegiate):** *Men:* Baseball, basketball, cross-country, football, golf, soccer, tennis, track/field (indoor), track/field (outdoor). *Women:* Basketball, cross-country, golf, soccer, softball, tennis, track/field (indoor), track/field (outdoor), volleyball.

ADMISSIONS

Freshman Academic Profile: 48% in top 25% of high school class, 83% in top 50% of high school class. 89% from public high schools. SAT Math middle 50% range 460–520. SAT Critical Reading middle 50% range 440–500. ACT middle 50% range 19–25. TOEFL required of all international applicants, minimum paper TOEFL 525, minimum computer TOEFL 195. **Basis for Candidate Selection:** *Very important factors considered include:* Academic GPA, standardized test scores. *Important factors considered include:* Alumni/ae relation, application essay, character/personal qualities, level of applicant's interest, recommendation(s), rigor of secondary school record. *Other factors considered include:* Class rank, extracurricular activities, interview, racial/ethnic status, talent/ability, volunteer work, work experience. **Freshman Admission Requirements:** High school diploma is required, and GED is accepted. *Academic units recommended:* 4 English, 3 math, 3 science, 3 social studies. **Freshman Admission Statistics:** 1,150 applied, 79% admitted, 27% enrolled. **Transfer Admission Requirements:** High school transcript, college transcript(s), essay or personal statement, statement of good standing from prior institution(s). Lowest grade transferable C-. **General Admission Information:** Regular notification is rolling. Nonfall registration accepted. Admission may be deferred for a maximum of 1 semester. Credit offered for CEEB Advanced Placement tests.

COSTS AND FINANCIAL AID

Annual tuition $18,420. Room & board $5,150. Required fees $350. Average book expense $800. **Required Forms and Deadlines:** FAFSA. Financial aid filing deadline 3/1. **Notification of Awards:** Applicants will be notified of awards on a rolling basis beginning on or about 3/1. **Types of Aid:** *Need-based scholarships/grants:* Pell, SEOG, state scholarships/grants, private scholarships, the school's own gift aid, *Loans:* FFEL Subsidized Stafford, FFEL Unsubsidized Stafford, FFEL PLUS, Federal Perkins. **Financial Aid Statistics:** 84% freshmen, 75% undergrads receive need-based scholarship or grant aid. 75% freshmen, 70% undergrads receive need-based self-help aid. 97% freshmen, 93% undergrads receive any aid.

DOMINICAN COLLEGE

470 Western Highway, Orangeburg, NY 10962-1210
Phone: 845-848-7900 **E-mail:** admissions@dc.edu **CEEB Code:** 2190
Fax: 845-365-3150 **Website:** www.dc.edu **ACT Code:** 2730
Financial Aid Phone: 845-848-7818

This private school was founded in 1952. It has a 62-acre campus.

RATINGS

Admissions Selectivity Rating: 60*   **Fire Safety Rating:** 89   **Green Rating:** 66

STUDENTS AND FACULTY

Enrollment: 1,577. **Student Body:** 65% female, 35% male, 22% out-of-state. African American 16%, Asian 6%, Caucasian 45%, Hispanic 13%. **Retention and Graduation:** 75% freshmen return for sophomore year. 24% freshmen graduate within 4 years. **Faculty:** Student/faculty ratio 14:1. 62 full-time faculty, 53% hold PhDs. 88% faculty teach undergrads.

ACADEMICS

Degrees: Associate, bachelor's, doctoral, master's. **Academic Requirements:** Computer literacy, English (including composition), foreign languages, history, humanities, mathematics, philosophy, sciences (biological or physical), social science, speech. **Classes:** Most classes have 10–19 students. Most lab/discussion sections have fewer than 10 students. **Majors with Highest Enrollment:** Business administration/management, nursing/registered nurse training (RN, ASN, BSN, MSN), social sciences. **Disciplines with Highest Percentage of Degrees Awarded:** Health professions and related sciences 31%, business/marketing 20%, social sciences 17%, education 9%, English 7%. **Special Study Options:** Accelerated program, cooperative education program, distance learning, dual enrollment, honors program, independent study, internships, teacher certification program, weekend college.

FACILITIES

Housing: Coed dorms, 125 accommodations at a nearby hotel. **Special Academic Facilities/Equipment:** New Prusmack Center for Health Care Programs and Science Education. **Computers:** 100% of public computers are PCs, network access in dorm rooms, network access in dorm lounges.

CAMPUS LIFE

Activities: Choral groups, dance, drama/theater, literary magazine, musical theater, student government, student newspaper, yearbook. **Organizations:** 17 registered organizations, 6 honor societies, 1 religious organization. **Athletics (Intercollegiate):** *Men:* Baseball, basketball, cross-country, golf, lacrosse, soccer. *Women:* Basketball, cross-country, lacrosse, soccer, softball, volleyball.

ADMISSIONS

Freshman Academic Profile: 75% from public high schools. SAT Math middle 50% range 395–480. SAT Critical Reading middle 50% range 375–470. SAT Writing middle 50% range 400–480. ACT middle 50% range 18–24. TOEFL required of all international applicants, minimum paper TOEFL 550, minimum computer TOEFL 213. **Basis for Candidate Selection:** *Important factors considered include:* Academic GPA, recommendation(s), standardized test scores. *Other factors considered include:* Application essay, character/personal qualities, extracurricular activities, interview, level of applicant's interest, rigor of secondary school record, talent/ability, volunteer work, work experience. **Freshman Admission Requirements:** High school diploma is required, and GED is accepted. *Academic units required:* 4 English, 3 math, 3 science (1 science lab), 1 foreign language, 3 social studies, 3 history, 2 academic electives. *Academic units recommended:* 4 English, 3 math, 3 science (1 science lab), 2 foreign language, 4 social studies, 4 history, 2 academic electives. **Freshman Admission Statistics:** 1,160 applied, 82% admitted, 32% enrolled. **Transfer Admission Requirements:** College transcript(s). Minimum college GPA of 2.0 required. Lowest grade transferable C. **General Admission Information:** Application fee $35. Nonfall registration accepted. Admission may be deferred for a maximum of 1 year. Credit offered for CEEB Advanced Placement tests.

COSTS AND FINANCIAL AID

Annual tuition $18,830. Room and board $9,340. Required fees $680. Average book expense $1,350. **Required Forms and Deadlines:** FAFSA, state aid form. Financial aid filing deadline 2/15. **Notification of Awards:** Applicants will be notified of awards on a rolling basis beginning on or about 2/1. **Types of Aid:** *Need-based scholarships/grants:* Pell, SEOG, state scholarships/grants, private scholarships, the school's own gift aid. *Loans:* FFEL Subsidized Stafford, FFEL Unsubsidized Stafford, FFEL PLUS, Federal Perkins, Federal Nursing. **Student Employment:** Off-campus job opportunities are fair. **Financial Aid Statistics:** 81% freshmen, 75% undergrads receive need-based scholarship or grant aid. 67% freshmen, 62% undergrads receive need-based self-help aid. 19 freshmen, 58 undergrads receive athletic scholarships. 97% freshmen, 88% undergrads receive any aid. Highest amount earned per year from on-campus jobs $2,000.

DOMINICAN SCHOOL OF PHILOSOPHY AND THEOLOGY

2301 Vine Street, Berkeley, CA 94708
Phone: 510-883-2073 **E-mail:** admissions@dspt.edu
Fax: 510-849-1372 **Website:** www.dspt.edu
Financial Aid Phone: 510-649-2469

This private school, affiliated with the Roman Catholic Church, was founded in 1932.

RATINGS

Admissions Selectivity Rating: 60*   **Fire Safety Rating:** 60*   **Green Rating:** 60*

STUDENTS AND FACULTY

Enrollment: 5. **Student Body:** 40% female, 60% male. Asian 40%, Caucasian 20%, Hispanic 40%. **Retention and Graduation:** 100% freshmen return for sophomore year. 50% grads go on to further study within 1 year. **Faculty:** Student/faculty ratio 4:1. 12 full-time faculty, 100% hold PhDs. 50% faculty teach undergrads.

ACADEMICS

Degrees: Bachelor's, certificate, first professional, master's. **Academic Requirements:** Arts/fine arts, computer literacy, English (including composition), history, humanities, mathematics, philosophy, sciences (biological or physical), social science, speech. **Classes:** Most classes have 10–19 students. **Disciplines with Highest Percentage of Degrees Awarded:** Philosophy and religious studies 100%. **Special Study Options:** Cross-registration, independent study, study abroad. Select graduate level courses available to undergraduate students.

FACILITIES

Housing: Apartments for married students, apartments for single students, cooperative housing. **Computers:** 60% of public computers are PCs, 40% of public computers are Macs, online administrative functions (other than registration), remote student-access to Web through college's connection.

CAMPUS LIFE
Activities: Student government, student newspaper.

ADMISSIONS
Freshman Academic Profile: TOEFL required of all international applicants, minimum paper TOEFL 550. **Freshman Admission Requirements:** High school diploma is required, and GED is accepted. **Transfer Admission Requirements:** College transcript(s), essay or personal statement. Minimum college GPA of 2.3 required. Lowest grade transferable C. **General Admission Information:** Application fee $40. Nonfall registration not accepted. Admission may be deferred for a maximum of 1 year.

COSTS AND FINANCIAL AID
Annual tuition $11,160. Required fees $50. Average book expense $1,113. **Financial Aid Statistics:** Highest amount earned per year from on-campus jobs $3,500.

DOMINICAN UNIVERSITY

7900 West Division, River Forest, IL 60305
Phone: 708-524-6800 **E-mail:** domadmis@dom.edu **CEEB Code:** 1667
Fax: 708-524-6864 **Website:** www.dom.edu **ACT Code:** 1126
Financial Aid Phone: 708-524-6809

This private school, affiliated with the Roman Catholic Church, was founded in 1901. It has a 30-acre campus.

RATINGS
Admissions Selectivity Rating: 78   **Fire Safety Rating:** 83   **Green Rating:** 75

STUDENTS AND FACULTY
Enrollment: 1,397. **Student Body:** 70% female, 30% male, 10% out-of-state, 1% international (34 countries represented). African American 6%, Asian 3%, Caucasian 62%, Hispanic 23%. **Retention and Graduation:** 82% freshmen return for sophomore year. 56% freshmen graduate within 4 years. 30% grads go on to further study within 1 year. **Faculty:** Student/faculty ratio 12:1. 112 full-time faculty, 78% hold PhDs. 100% faculty teach undergrads.

ACADEMICS
Degrees: Bachelor's, certificate, master's, post-bachelor's certificate, post-master's certificate. **Academic Requirements:** Arts/fine arts, computer literacy, English (including composition), foreign languages, history, humanities, mathematics, philosophy, sciences (biological or physical), social science, theology. **Classes:** Most classes have 10–19 students. Most lab/discussion sections have 10–19 students. **Majors with Highest Enrollment:** Business administration/management, psychology, sociology. **Disciplines with Highest Percentage of Degrees Awarded:** Business/marketing 28%, social sciences 18%, psychology 10%, visual and performing arts 9%, communications/journalism 6%. **Special Study Options:** Accelerated program, cross-registration, distance learning, double major, dual enrollment, English as a second language (ESL), honors program, independent study, internships, liberal arts/career combination, student-designed major, study abroad, teacher certification program.

FACILITIES
Housing: Coed dorms, coed by floor. **Special Academic Facilities/Equipment:** Art gallery, technology center, language lab, recital hall. **Computers:** 20% of classrooms are wired, 80% of classrooms are wireless, 91% of public computers are PCs, 9% of public computers are Macs, network access in dorm rooms, network access in dorm lounges, online registration, online administrative functions (other than registration), remote student-access to Web through college's connection.

CAMPUS LIFE
Activities: Choral groups, dance, drama/theater, literary magazine, musical theater, student government, student newspaper. **Organizations:** 76 registered organizations, 14 honor societies, 2 religious organizations. **Athletics (Intercollegiate):** *Men:* Baseball, basketball, cross-country, soccer, tennis, volleyball. *Women:* Basketball, cross-country, soccer, softball, tennis, volleyball.

ADMISSIONS
Freshman Academic Profile: 24% in top 10% of high school class, 52% in top 25% of high school class, 85% in top 50% of high school class. 60% from public high schools. SAT Math middle 50% range 480–570. SAT Critical Reading

middle 50% range 470–580. ACT middle 50% range 20–25. TOEFL required of all international applicants, minimum paper TOEFL 550, minimum computer TOEFL 213. **Basis for Candidate Selection:** *Very important factors considered include:* Academic GPA, class rank, rigor of secondary school record. *Important factors considered include:* Interview, standardized test scores. *Other factors considered include:* Alumni/ae relation, application essay, character/personal qualities, extracurricular activities, first generation, geographical residence, recommendation(s), state residency, talent/ability, volunteer work, work experience. **Freshman Admission Requirements:** High school diploma is required, and GED is accepted. *Academic units required:* 4 English, 2 academic electives. *Academic units recommended:* 3 math, 2 science (2 science labs), 2 foreign language, 1 social studies, 2 history. **Freshman Admission Statistics:** 1,215 applied, 84% admitted, 35% enrolled. **Transfer Admission Requirements:** College transcript(s), essay or personal statement. Minimum college GPA of 2.5 required. Lowest grade transferable C-. **General Admission Information:** Application fee $25. Regular notification is rolling. Nonfall registration accepted. Admission may be deferred for a maximum of 1 year. Credit offered for CEEB Advanced Placement tests.

COSTS AND FINANCIAL AID
Required fees $100. Average book expense $1,000. **Required Forms and Deadlines:** FAFSA, parent and student tax forms. Financial aid filing deadline 6/1. **Notification of Awards:** Applicants will be notified of awards on a rolling basis beginning on or about 3/1. **Types of Aid:** *Need-based scholarships/grants:* Pell, SEOG, state scholarships/grants, private scholarships, the school's own gift aid. *Loans:* FFEL Subsidized Stafford, FFEL Unsubsidized Stafford, FFEL PLUS, Federal Perkins. **Student Employment:** Federal Work-Study Program available. Institutional employment available. Off-campus job opportunities are good. **Financial Aid Statistics:** 86% freshmen, 80% undergrads receive need-based scholarship or grant aid. 69% freshmen, 68% undergrads receive need-based self-help aid. 96% freshmen, 92% undergrads receive any aid. Highest amount earned per year from on-campus jobs $2,500.

DOMINICAN UNIVERSITY OF CALIFORNIA

Admissions, 50 Acacia Avenue, San Rafael, CA 94901-2298
Phone: 415-485-3204 **E-mail:** enroll@dominican.edu **CEEB Code:** 4284
Fax: 415-485-3214 **Website:** www.dominican.edu
Financial Aid Phone: 415-257-1350

This private school, affiliated with the Roman Catholic Church, was founded in 1890. It has a 80-acre campus.

RATINGS
Admissions Selectivity Rating: 79   **Fire Safety Rating:** 60*   **Green Rating:** 60*

STUDENTS AND FACULTY
Enrollment: 1,440. **Student Body:** 76% female, 24% male, 8% out-of-state, 2% international (22 countries represented). African American 8%, Asian 20%, Caucasian 41%, Hispanic 15%, Native American 1%. **Retention and Graduation:** 81% freshmen return for sophomore year. 42% freshmen graduate within 4 years. 1% grads pursue medical degrees. **Faculty:** Student/faculty ratio 11:1. 75 full-time faculty, 79% hold PhDs. 74% faculty teach undergrads.

ACADEMICS
Degrees: Bachelor's, master's, post-bachelor's certificate. **Academic Requirements:** Arts/fine arts, computer literacy, English (including composition), history, humanities, mathematics, philosophy, sciences (biological or physical), social science. **Classes:** Most classes have 10–19 students. Most lab/discussion sections have fewer than 10 students. **Majors with Highest Enrollment:** Business administration/management; nursing—registered nurse training (RN, ASN, BSN, MSN); teacher education, multiple levels. **Disciplines with Highest Percentage of Degrees Awarded:** Health professions and related sciences 40%, business/marketing 25%, liberal arts/general studies 24%, biological/life sciences 14%, communications/journalism 12%. **Special Study Options:** Accelerated program, cross-registration, double major, dual enrollment, English as a second language (ESL), exchange student program (domestic), honor program, independent study, internships, liberal arts/career combination, student-designed major, study abroad, teacher certification program, weekend college.

FACILITIES
Housing: Coed dorms. **Special Academic Facilities/Equipment:** Art gallery, science lab, computer labs, nursing skills lab. **Computers:** 50% of classrooms are wireless, 80% of public computers are PCs, 20% of public computers are

Macs, network access in dorm rooms, online administrative functions (other than registration), remote student-access to Web through college's connection.

CAMPUS LIFE

Activities: Choral groups, drama/theater, jazz band, literary magazine, music ensembles, radio station, student government, student newspaper, yearbook. **Organizations:** 19 registered organizations, 3 honor societies, 4 religious organizations, 1 fraternity, 1 sorority. **Athletics (Intercollegiate):** *Men:* Basketball, soccer, tennis. *Women:* Basketball, soccer, softball, tennis, volleyball.

ADMISSIONS

Freshman Academic Profile: 20% in top 10% of high school class, 32% in top 25% of high school class, 24% in top 50% of high school class. 67% from public high schools. SAT Math middle 50% range 440–550. SAT Critical Reading middle 50% range 450–550. ACT middle 50% range 18–24. TOEFL required of all international applicants, minimum paper TOEFL 550, minimum computer TOEFL 213. **Basis for Candidate Selection:** *Very important factors considered include:* Application essay, character/personal qualities, recommendation(s), rigor of secondary school record, standardized test scores. *Important factors considered include:* Class rank, extracurricular activities, interview, racial/ethnic status, talent/ability, volunteer work. *Other factors considered include:* Alumni/ae relation, work experience. **Freshman Admission Requirements:** High school diploma is required, and GED is accepted. *Academic units required:* 4 English, 2 math, 2 science (1 science lab), 2 foreign language, 1 history. **Freshman Admission Statistics:** 2,749 applied, 52% admitted, 19% enrolled. **Transfer Admission Requirements:** College transcript(s), essay or personal statement. Minimum college GPA of 2.0 required. Lowest grade transferable C. **General Admission Information:** Application fee $40. Regular notification is rolling. Nonfall registration accepted. Admission may be deferred for a maximum of one term. Placement offered for CEEB Advanced Placement tests.

COSTS AND FINANCIAL AID

Required fees $100. Average book expense $1,000. **Required Forms and Deadlines:** FAFSA, institution's own financial aid form. Financial aid filing deadline 3/2. **Notification of Awards:** Applicants will be notified of awards on a rolling basis beginning on or about 3/15. **Types of Aid:** *Need-based scholarships/grants:* Pell, SEOG, state scholarships/grants, private scholarships, the school's own gift aid. *Loans:* FFEL Subsidized Stafford, FFEL Unsubsidized Stafford, FFEL PLUS, Federal Perkins. **Student Employment:** Federal Work-Study Program available. Institutional employment available. Off-campus job opportunities are good. **Financial Aid Statistics:** 55% freshmen, 57% undergrads receive need-based scholarship or grant aid. 59% freshmen, 64% undergrads receive need-based self-help aid. 12 freshmen, 52 undergrads receive athletic scholarships. 97% freshmen, 83% undergrads receive any aid. Highest amount earned per year from on-campus jobs $3,500.

DORDT COLLEGE

498 Fourth Avenue Northeast, Sioux Center, IA 51250
Phone: 712-722-6080 **E-mail:** admissions@dordt.edu **CEEB Code:** 6171
Fax: 712-722-1967 **Website:** www.dordt.edu **ACT Code:** 1301
Financial Aid Phone: 712-722-6087

This private school, affiliated with the Christian Reformed Church, was founded in 1955. It has a 150-acre campus.

RATINGS

Admissions Selectivity Rating: 81   **Fire Safety Rating:** 60*   **Green Rating:** 60*

STUDENTS AND FACULTY

Enrollment: 1,231. **Student Body:** 54% female, 46% male, 62% out-of-state, 16% international (14 countries represented). Caucasian 78%. **Retention and Graduation:** 85% freshmen return for sophomore year. 60% freshmen graduate within 4 years. 15% grads go on to further study within 1 year. 9% grads pursue arts and sciences degrees. 3% grads pursue business degrees. 1% grads pursue law degrees. 2% grads pursue medical degrees. **Faculty:** Student/faculty ratio 14:1. 70 full-time faculty, 97% hold PhDs. 100% faculty teach undergrads.

ACADEMICS

Degrees: Associate, bachelor's, master's. **Academic Requirements:** Arts/fine arts, English (including composition), history, humanities, mathematics, philosophy, sciences (biological or physical), social science. **Classes:** Most classes have 10–19 students. Most lab/discussion sections have 10–19 students. **Majors with Highest Enrollment:** Agricultural business and management, mechanical engineering. **Disciplines with Highest Percentage of Degrees Awarded:** Education 21%, business/marketing 16%, visual and performing arts

8%, parks and recreation 7%, engineering 6%. **Special Study Options:** Double major, English as a second language (ESL), honors program, independent study, internships, liberal arts/career combination, student-designed major, study abroad, teacher certification program.

FACILITIES

Housing: Men's dorms, women's dorms, apartments for married students, apartments for single students, special housing for disabled students. **Special Academic Facilities/Equipment:** Observatories, 160-acre research farm for ag. program; modern recreation facilities that include indoor track, swimming, and ice arena. **Computers:** 7% of classrooms are wireless, 95% of public computers are PCs, 5% of public computers are Macs, network access in dorm rooms, online registration, online administrative functions (other than registration), remote student-access to Web through college's connection.

CAMPUS LIFE

Activities: Choral groups, concert band, dance, drama/theater, jazz band, literary magazine, music ensembles, musical theater, opera, pep band, radio station, student government, student newspaper, student-run film society, symphony orchestra, yearbook. **Organizations:** 40 registered organizations, 4 honor societies, 6 religious organizations. **Athletics (Intercollegiate):** *Men:* Baseball, basketball, cross-country, football, golf, ice hockey, soccer, tennis, track/field (indoor), track/field (outdoor). *Women:* Basketball, cross-country, soccer, softball, tennis, track/field (indoor), track/field (outdoor), volleyball.

ADMISSIONS

Freshman Academic Profile: 31% in top 10% of high school class, 53% in top 25% of high school class, 76% in top 50% of high school class. 25% from public high schools. SAT Math middle 50% range 500–640. SAT Critical Reading middle 50% range 480–630. SAT Writing middle 50% range 450–610. ACT middle 50% range 21–27. TOEFL required of all international applicants, minimum paper TOEFL 550, minimum computer TOEFL 213. **Basis for Candidate Selection:** *Very important factors considered include:* Religious affiliation/commitment, rigor of secondary school record, standardized test scores. *Other factors considered include:* Character/personal qualities, class rank, extracurricular activities, talent/ability. **Freshman Admission Requirements:** High school diploma is required, and GED is accepted. *Academic units required:* 3 English, 2 math, 2 science, 2 foreign language, 2 history, 6 academic electives. *Academic units recommended:* 4 English, 3 math, 4 science, 3 foreign language, 1 social studies. **Freshman Admission Statistics:** 844 applied, 89% admitted, 46% enrolled. **Transfer Admission Requirements:** High school transcript, college transcript(s), standardized test score. Minimum college GPA of 2.0 required. Lowest grade transferable C. **General Admission Information:** Application fee $25. Regular application deadline 8/1. Regular notification is rolling. Nonfall registration accepted. Credit offered for CEEB Advanced Placement tests.

COSTS AND FINANCIAL AID

Annual tuition $19,600. Room and board $5,460. Required fees $300. Average book expense $780. **Required Forms and Deadlines:** FAFSA, institution's own financial aid form. Financial aid filing deadline 4/1. **Notification of Awards:** Applicants will be notified of awards on a rolling basis beginning on or about 3/15. **Types of Aid:** *Need-based scholarships/grants:* Pell, SEOG, state scholarships/grants, private scholarships, the school's own gift aid. *Loans:* Direct Subsidized Stafford, Direct Unsubsidized Stafford, Direct PLUS, FFEL Subsidized Stafford, FFEL Unsubsidized Stafford, FFEL PLUS, Federal Perkins, college/university loans from institutional funds, alternate loans. **Student Employment:** Off-campus job opportunities are good. **Financial Aid Statistics:** 81% freshmen, 78% undergrads receive need-based scholarship or grant aid. 80% freshmen, 77% undergrads receive need-based self-help aid. 14 freshmen, 47 undergrads receive athletic scholarships. 98% freshmen, 98% undergrads receive any aid. Highest amount earned per year from on-campus jobs $1,300.

DOWLING COLLEGE

Idle Hour Boulevard, Oakdale, NY 11769-1999
Phone: 800-369-5464 **E-mail:** admissions@dowling.edu **CEEB Code:** 2011
Fax: 631-563-3827 **Website:** www.dowling.edu **ACT Code:** 2665
Financial Aid Phone: 631-244-3303

This private school was founded in 1959. It has a 157-acre campus.

RATINGS

Admissions Selectivity Rating: 66   **Fire Safety Rating:** 60*   **Green Rating:** 60*

STUDENTS AND FACULTY

Enrollment: 3,627. **Student Body:** 61% female, 39% male, 10% out-of-state, 4% international (53 countries represented). African American 9%, Asian 2%, Caucasian 59%, Hispanic 9%. **Retention and Graduation:** 66% freshmen return for sophomore year. 17% freshmen graduate within 4 years. **Faculty:** Student/faculty ratio 17:1. 124 full-time faculty, 90% hold PhDs. 55% faculty teach undergrads.

ACADEMICS

Degrees: Bachelor's, doctoral, master's, post-bachelor's certificate, post-master's certificate. **Academic Requirements:** Arts/fine arts, English (including composition), history, humanities, mathematics, philosophy, sciences (biological or physical), social science. **Classes:** Most classes have 10–19 students. **Majors with Highest Enrollment:** Business administration/management, elementary education and teaching, special education. **Disciplines with Highest Percentage of Degrees Awarded:** Business/marketing 32%, education 18%, liberal arts/general studies 10%, social sciences 8%, computer and information sciences 6%. **Special Study Options:** Accelerated program, double major, English as a second language (ESL), honors program, independent study, internships, liberal arts/career combination, student-designed major, study abroad, teacher certification program, weekend college.

FACILITIES

Housing: Coed dorms. **Special Academic Facilities/Equipment:** Art gallery, cultural study center, media center, human factors lab, meteorology lab. **Computers:** 50% of classrooms are wireless, 95% of public computers are PCs, 5% of public computers are Macs, network access in dorm rooms, online registration, online administrative functions (other than registration), remote student-access to Web through college's connection.

CAMPUS LIFE

Activities: Choral groups, drama/theater, jazz band, literary magazine, music ensembles, musical theater, student government, student newspaper, symphony orchestra, yearbook. **Organizations:** 29 registered organizations, 10 honor societies, 1 religious organization. **Athletics (Intercollegiate):** *Men:* Baseball, basketball, crew/rowing, golf, lacrosse, soccer, tennis. *Women:* Basketball, crew/rowing, cross-country, equestrian sports, soccer, softball, tennis, volleyball.

ADMISSIONS

66 (out of 100). **Freshman Academic Profile:** 6% in top 10% of high school class, 19% in top 25% of high school class, 50% in top 50% of high school class. 89% from public high schools. SAT Math middle 50% range 410–520. SAT Critical Reading middle 50% range 410–520. **Basis for Candidate Selection:** *Very important factors considered include:* Rigor of secondary school record. *Other factors considered include:* Academic GPA, alumni/ae relation, application essay, character/personal qualities, class rank, extracurricular activities, recommendation(s), standardized test scores, talent/ability. **Freshman Admission Requirements:** High school diploma is required, and GED is accepted. *Academic units recommended:* 4 English, 3 math, 2 science, 3 social studies. **Freshman Admission Statistics:** 2,399 applied, 87% admitted, 22% enrolled. **Transfer Admission Requirements:** College transcript(s). Minimum college GPA of 2.0 required. Lowest grade transferable C. **General Admission Information:** Application fee $25. Nonfall registration accepted. Admission may be deferred for a maximum of 1 year. Common Application accepted. Credit and/or placement offered for CEEB Advanced Placement tests.

COSTS AND FINANCIAL AID

Average book expense $1,000. **Required Forms and Deadlines:** FAFSA, state aid form. Financial aid filing deadline 4/30. **Notification of Awards:** Applicants will be notified of awards on a rolling basis beginning on or about 2/1. **Types of Aid:** *Need-based scholarships/grants:* Pell, SEOG, state scholarships/grants, private scholarships, the school's own gift aid. *Loans:* Direct Subsidized Stafford, Direct Unsubsidized Stafford, Direct PLUS, Federal Perkins, alternative loans. **Student Employment:** Federal Work-Study Program available. Off-campus job opportunities are good. **Financial Aid Statistics:** 69% freshmen, 65% undergrads receive need-based scholarship or grant aid. 64% freshmen, 57% undergrads receive need-based self-help aid. 10 freshmen, 80 undergrads receive athletic scholarships. 87% freshmen, 87% undergrads receive any aid.

DR. WILLIAM M. SCHOLL COLLEGE OF PODIATRIC MEDICINE

1001 North Dearborn Street, Chicago, IL 60610-2856
Phone: 312-280-2940 **E-mail:** admiss@scholl.edu
Fax: 312-280-2997 **Website:** www.scholl.edu

This is a private school.

RATINGS

Admissions Selectivity Rating: 60* **Fire Safety Rating:** 60* **Green Rating:** 60*

ACADEMICS

Degrees: Bachelor's, doctoral. **Academic Requirements:** Sciences (biological or physical). **Special Study Options:** Cooperative education program, cross-registration, external degree program, honors program, independent study, internships, study abroad, DPM/PhD program.

FACILITIES

Housing: Housing seminar held summer prior to matriculation.

CAMPUS LIFE

Activities: Student government, student newspaper.

ADMISSIONS

Freshman Admission Requirements: High school diploma is required, and GED is accepted. **Transfer Admission Requirements:** High school transcript, college transcript(s), essay or personal statement, interview, standardized test score, statement of good standing from prior institution(s). Minimum college GPA of 3.0 required. **General Admission Information:** Regular notification. Nonfall registration not accepted. Admission may be deferred for a maximum of 1 year. Common Application not accepted.

COSTS AND FINANCIAL AID

Average book expense $850. **Required Forms and Deadlines:** FAFSA, institution's own financial aid form, Noncustodial PROFILE, Financial aid filing deadline 5/1. **Notification of Awards:** Applicants will be notified of awards on or about 6/1. **Types of Aid:** *Need-based scholarships/grants:* State scholarships/grants, private scholarships, the school's own gift aid. *Loans:* FFEL Subsidized Stafford, FFEL Unsubsidized Stafford, Federal Perkins, state loans, college/university loans from institutional funds, HEAL, MEDCAP, HPSL.

DRAKE UNIVERSITY

2507 University Avenue, Des Moines, IA 50311-4505
Phone: 515-271-3181 **E-mail:** admission@drake.edu **CEEB Code:** 6168
Fax: 515-271-2831 **Website:** www.drake.edu **ACT Code:** 1302
Financial Aid Phone: 515-271-2905

This private school was founded in 1881. It has a 150-acre campus.

RATINGS

Admissions Selectivity Rating: 88 **Fire Safety Rating:** 60* **Green Rating:** 60*

STUDENTS AND FACULTY

Enrollment: 3,191. **Student Body:** 56% female, 44% male, 61% out-of-state, 6% international (56 countries represented). African American 3%, Asian 4%, Caucasian 78%, Hispanic 2%. **Retention and Graduation:** 88% freshmen return for sophomore year. 25% grads go on to further study within 1 year. 17% grads pursue arts and sciences degrees. 1% grads pursue business degrees. 5% grads pursue law degrees. 2% grads pursue medical degrees. **Faculty:** Student/faculty ratio 14:1. 246 full-time faculty, 95% hold PhDs. 100% faculty teach undergrads.

ACADEMICS

Degrees: Bachelor's, doctoral, first professional, master's, post-bachelor's certificate. **Academic Requirements:** Arts/fine arts, computer literacy, English (including composition), history, humanities, international and multicultural understanding, mathematics, philosophy, sciences (biological or physical). **Classes:** Most classes have 10–19 students. Most lab/discussion sections have 10–19 students. **Majors with Highest Enrollment:** Biology/biological sciences, journalism, marketing/marketing management. **Disciplines with Highest Percentage of Degrees Awarded:** Biological/life sciences 8%, business/marketing 32%, communications/journalism 14%, education 8%, social sciences 9%, visual and performing arts 7%. **Special Study Options:** Accelerated program, cooperative education program, cross-registration, distance learning, double major, English as a second language (ESL), exchange student program (domestic), honors program, independent study, internships, liberal arts/career combination, student-designed major, study abroad, teacher certification program.

FACILITIES

Housing: Coed dorms, apartments for single students, fraternity/sorority housing, rental houses. **Special Academic Facilities/Equipment:** Language lab, observatory, media service center, Anderson Art Gallery. **Computers:** 80% of classrooms are wireless, 50% of public computers are PCs, 45% of public computers are Macs, 5% of public computers are UNIX, network access in dorm rooms, network access in dorm lounges, online registration, online administrative functions (other than registration), remote student-access to Web through college's connection.

CAMPUS LIFE

Activities: Choral groups, concert band, dance, drama/theater, jazz band, literary magazine, marching band, music ensembles, musical theater, pep band, radio station, student government, student newspaper, student-run film society, symphony orchestra, television station. **Organizations:** 160 registered organizations, 24 honor societies, 10 religious organizations. 8 fraternities (30% men join), 6 sororities (22% women join). **Athletics (Intercollegiate):** *Men:* Basketball, cheerleading, cross-country, football, golf, soccer, tennis, track/field (indoor), track/field (outdoor). *Women:* Basketball, cheerleading, crew/rowing, cross-country, golf, soccer, softball, tennis, track/field (indoor), track/field (outdoor), volleyball.

ADMISSIONS

Freshman Academic Profile: 40% in top 10% of high school class, 68% in top 25% of high school class, 92% in top 50% of high school class. 82% from public high schools. SAT Math middle 50% range 540–660. SAT Critical Reading middle 50% range 520–650. ACT middle 50% range 23–28. TOEFL required of all international applicants, minimum paper TOEFL 545, minimum computer TOEFL 252. **Basis for Candidate Selection:** *Very important factors considered include:* Academic GPA, standardized test scores. *Important factors considered include:* Class rank, rigor of secondary school record. *Other factors considered include:* Application essay, character/personal qualities, extracurricular activities, interview, recommendation(s), talent/ability, volunteer work, work experience. **Freshman Admission Requirements:** High school diploma is required, and GED is accepted. *Academic units recommended:* 4 English, 3 math, 2 science, 2 foreign language, 4 social studies. **Freshman Admission Statistics:** 4,049 applied, 80% admitted, 24% enrolled. **Transfer Admission Requirements:** College transcript(s). Minimum college GPA of 2.0 required. Lowest grade transferable C. **General Admission Information:** Application fee $25. Regular notification is rolling. Nonfall registration accepted. Admission may be deferred for a maximum of 1 year. Credit and/or placement offered for CEEB Advanced Placement tests.

COSTS AND FINANCIAL AID

Annual tuition $22,270. Room & board $6,500. Required fees $412. Average book expense $700. **Required Forms and Deadlines:** FAFSA. Financial aid filing deadline 3/1. **Notification of Awards:** Applicants will be notified of awards on a rolling basis beginning on or about 3/1. **Types of Aid:** *Need-based scholarships/grants:* Pell, SEOG, state scholarships/grants, private scholarships, the school's own gift aid. *Loans:* FFEL Subsidized Stafford, FFEL Unsubsidized Stafford, FFEL PLUS, Federal Perkins, state loans, college/university loans from institutional funds, Federal Health Professional Loans. **Student Employment:** Off-campus job opportunities are good. **Financial Aid Statistics:** 65% freshmen, 62% undergrads receive need-based scholarship or grant aid. 54% freshmen, 54% undergrads receive need-based self-help aid. 20 freshmen, 98 undergrads receive athletic scholarships. 98% freshmen, 85% undergrads receive any aid. Highest amount earned per year from on-campus jobs $1,175.

See page 1158.

DREW UNIVERSITY

Office of College Admissions, Madison, NJ 07940-1493
Phone: 973-408-3739 **E-mail:** cadm@drew.edu **CEEB Code:** 2193
Fax: 973-408-3068 **Website:** www.drew.edu **ACT Code:** 2550
Financial Aid Phone: 973-408-3112

This private school, affiliated with the Methodist Church, was founded in 1868. It has a 186-acre campus.

RATINGS
Admissions Selectivity Rating: 87   **Fire Safety Rating:** 98   **Green Rating:** 74

STUDENTS AND FACULTY

Enrollment: 1,608. **Student Body:** 60% female, 40% male, 43% out-of-state, 1% international (11 countries represented). African American 5%, Asian 6%, Caucasian 66%, Hispanic 6%. **Retention and Graduation:** 83% freshmen return for sophomore year. 26% grads go on to further study within 1 year. 17% grads pursue arts and sciences degrees. 5% grads pursue law degrees. 2% grads pursue medical degrees. **Faculty:** Student/faculty ratio 11:1. 155 full-time faculty, 95% hold PhDs. 100% faculty teach undergrads.

ACADEMICS

Degrees: Bachelor's, doctoral, first professional, master's, post-bachelor's certificate. **Academic Requirements:** Arts/fine arts, computer literacy, English (including composition), foreign languages, history, humanities, philosophy, sciences (biological or physical), social science. **Classes:** Most classes have 10–19 students. Most lab/discussion sections have 10–19 students. **Majors with Highest Enrollment:** Economics, political science and government, psychology. **Disciplines with Highest Percentage of Degrees Awarded:** Social sciences 32%, English 11%, psychology 11%, visual and performing arts 9%, foreign languages and literature 8%. **Special Study Options:** Accelerated program, cross-registration, double major, exchange student program (domestic), independent study, internships, student-designed major, study abroad, teacher certification program. 7-year dual degree BA/MD program with UMDNJ–New Jersey Medical school; 5-year dual degree (BA/BS or BEng) programs in engineering and technologies with Columbia University, Stevens Institute of Technology, and Washington University; 5-year dual degree (BA/master of forestry or master of environmental management) program with Duke University.

FACILITIES

Housing: Coed dorms, special housing for disabled students, theme houses. **Special Academic Facilities/Equipment:** Art gallery, photography gallery, multimedia language lab, child development center, research greenhouse, arboretum, observatory, laser holography lab, nuclear magnetic resonator, electron microscope, optical and radio telescopes, computer graphics laboratory, New Jersey Shakespeare Festival (professional acting company). **Computers:** 20% of classrooms are wired, 90% of classrooms are wireless, 100% of public computers are PCs, network access in dorm rooms, network access in dorm lounges, online registration, online administrative functions (other than registration), remote student-access to Web through college's connection. Undergraduates are required to own a computer.

CAMPUS LIFE

Activities: Choral groups, dance, drama/theater, literary magazine, music ensembles, radio station, student government, student newspaper, student-run film society, symphony orchestra, television station, yearbook. **Organizations:** 80 registered organizations, 17 honor societies, 9 religious organizations. **Athletics (Intercollegiate):** *Men:* Baseball, basketball, cross-country, equestrian sports, fencing, lacrosse, soccer, swimming, tennis. *Women:* Basketball, cross-country, equestrian sports, fencing, field hockey, lacrosse, soccer, softball, swimming, tennis. Environmental Initiatives: Construction of new residence hall to meet L.E.E.D.S. silver certification. Energy efficient lighting sensors and lights. 100% composting/recycling of landscape waste.

ADMISSIONS

Freshman Academic Profile: 37% in top 10% of high school class, 68% in top 25% of high school class, 94% in top 50% of high school class. 61% from public high schools. SAT Math middle 50% range 510–630. SAT Critical Reading middle 50% range 520–650. SAT Writing middle 50% range 530–650. ACT middle 50% range 20–25. TOEFL required of all international applicants, minimum paper TOEFL 550, minimum computer TOEFL 213. **Basis for**

Candidate Selection: *Very important factors considered include:* Academic GPA, rigor of secondary school record, talent/ability. *Important factors considered include:* Application essay, extracurricular activities, interview, level of applicant's interest, recommendation(s). *Other factors considered include:* Alumni/ae relation, character/personal qualities, class rank, first generation, geographical residence, racial/ethnic status, standardized test scores, volunteer work, work experience. **Freshman Admission Requirements:** High school diploma or equivalent is not required. *Academic units recommended:* 4 English, 3 math, 2 science, 2 foreign language, 2 social studies, 2 history, 3 academic electives. **Freshman Admission Statistics:** 4,532 applied, 64% admitted, 17% enrolled. **Transfer Admission Requirements:** High school transcript, college transcript(s), essay or personal statement, statement of good standing from prior institution(s). Lowest grade transferable C. **General Admission Information:** Application fee $50. Early decision application deadline 12/1. Regular application deadline 2/15. Regular notification 3/21. Nonfall registration accepted. Admission may be deferred for a maximum of 1 year. Credit and/or placement offered for CEEB Advanced Placement tests.

COSTS AND FINANCIAL AID

Required Forms and Deadlines: FAFSA, CSS/Financial Aid PROFILE. Financial aid filing deadline 2/15. **Notification of Awards:** Applicants will be notified of awards on or about 4/1. **Types of Aid:** *Need-based scholarships/grants:* Pell, SEOG, state scholarships/grants, private scholarships, the school's own gift aid. *Loans:* FFEL Subsidized Stafford, FFEL Unsubsidized Stafford, FFEL PLUS, Federal Perkins, state loans. **Student Employment:** Federal Work-Study Program available. Institutional employment available. Off-campus job opportunities are excellent. **Financial Aid Statistics:** 51% freshmen, 48% undergrads receive need-based scholarship or grant aid. 42% freshmen, 41% undergrads receive need-based self-help aid. 90% freshmen, 82% undergrads receive any aid. Highest amount earned per year from on-campus jobs $1,200.

DREXEL UNIVERSITY

3141 Chestnut Street, Philadelphia, PA 19104
Phone: 215-895-2400 **E-mail:** enroll@drexel.edu **CEEB Code:** 2194
Fax: 215-895-5939 **Website:** www.drexel.edu **ACT Code:** 3556
Financial Aid Phone: 215-895-2537

This private school was founded in 1891. It has a 40-acre campus.

RATINGS

Admissions Selectivity Rating: 87   Fire Safety Rating: 75   Green Rating: 98

STUDENTS AND FACULTY

Enrollment: 11,936. **Student Body:** 41% female, 59% male, 44% out-of-state, 6% international (100 countries represented). African American 9%, Asian 12%, Caucasian 63%, Hispanic 3%. **Retention and Graduation:** 80% freshmen return for sophomore year. 14% freshmen graduate within 4 years. 13% grads go on to further study within 1 year. 3% grads pursue arts and sciences degrees. 3% grads pursue business degrees. 1% grads pursue law degrees. 1% grads pursue medical degrees. **Faculty:** 723 full-time faculty. 100% faculty teach undergrads.

ACADEMICS

Degrees: Associate, bachelor's, certificate, doctoral, first professional, master's, post-bachelor's certificate, post-master's certificate. **Academic Requirements:** Computer literacy, English (including composition), history, humanities, mathematics, sciences (biological or physical). **Classes:** Most classes have 10–19 students. Most lab/discussion sections have 20–29 students. **Majors with Highest Enrollment:** Biology/biological sciences, information science/studies, mechanical engineering. **Disciplines with Highest Percentage of Degrees Awarded:** Business/marketing 28%, engineering 20%, computer and information sciences 15%, health professions and related sciences 12%, visual and performing arts 8%. **Special Study Options:** Accelerated program, cooperative education program, distance learning, double major, English as a second language (ESL), honors program, independent study, internships, study abroad, teacher certification program, weekend college, 3–3 programs in engineering with Lincoln University, Indiana Univ. of Penn, Eastern Mennonite college.

FACILITIES

Housing: Coed dorms, apartments for single students, special housing for disabled students, special housing for international students, fraternity/sorority housing. Freshman required to live on campus unless living with parents. **Special Academic Facilities/Equipment:** Art museum, theater, audio-visual center, TV studio, recreational center, Center for Automation Technology, engineering center. **Computers:** 100% of classrooms are wired, 100% of classrooms are wireless, 85% of public computers are PCs, 10% of public computers are Macs, 5% of public computers are UNIX, network access in dorm rooms, network access in dorm lounges, online registration, online administrative functions (other than registration), remote student-access to Web through college's connection. Undergraduates are required to own a computer.

CAMPUS LIFE

Activities: Choral groups, concert band, dance, drama/theater, jazz band, literary magazine, music ensembles, musical theater, pep band, radio station, student government, student newspaper, student-run film society, television station, yearbook. **Organizations:** 136 registered organizations, 8 honor societies, 8 religious organizations. 12 fraternities (5% men join), 11 sororities (5% women join). **Athletics (Intercollegiate):** *Men:* Basketball, cheerleading, crew/rowing, diving, golf, lacrosse, soccer, swimming, tennis, wrestling. *Women:* Basketball, cheerleading, crew/rowing, diving, field hockey, lacrosse, soccer, softball, swimming, tennis, volleyball. Environmental Initiatives: Construction of a $69.5 million five story Integrated Sciences Building, 140,000 sq. ft. teaching facility, will be the first academic building in the U.S. to have a 30- to 40-ft., four-story biofilter wall. This feature will be part of the HVAC system—air intakes and outputs will be filtered through the living wall of vegetation that will upgrade energy efficiency and indoor air quality, along with controlled humidity in dry weather. The building will be LEED certified building. A new $41.6 million Recreation Center, 84,000 sq. ft. addition will have total storm water management. Construction of a $42 million, 140,000 sq. ft. Residence Hall with 18-stories, housing 482 students, will incorporate many environmental sustainable features including two green roofs.

ADMISSIONS

Freshman Academic Profile: 30% in top 10% of high school class, 60% in top 25% of high school class, 86% in top 50% of high school class. 70% from public high schools. SAT Math middle 50% range 560–670. SAT Critical Reading middle 50% range 530–630. ACT middle 50% range 23–28. TOEFL required of all international applicants, minimum paper TOEFL 550, minimum computer TOEFL 213. **Basis for Candidate Selection:** *Very important factors considered include:* Academic GPA, application essay, class rank, rigor of secondary school record, standardized test scores. *Important factors considered include:* Character/personal qualities, extracurricular activities, interview, recommendation(s), talent/ability. *Other factors considered include:* Alumni/ae relation, first generation, level of applicant's interest, volunteer work, work experience. **Freshman Admission Requirements:** High school diploma is required, and GED is accepted. *Academic units required:* 3 math, 1 science (1 science lab). *Academic units recommended:* 1 foreign language. **Freshman Admission Statistics:** 12,093 applied, 82% admitted, 25% enrolled. **Transfer Admission Requirements:** College transcript(s). Minimum college GPA of 2.5 required. Lowest grade transferable C. **General Admission Information:** Application fee $50. Regular application deadline 3/1. Regular notification is rolling basis. Nonfall registration accepted. Admission may be deferred for a maximum of 1 year. Common Application not accepted. Credit and/or placement offered for CEEB Advanced Placement tests.

COSTS AND FINANCIAL AID

Annual tuition $28,500. Room and board $12,135. Required fees $1,940. Average book expense $1,800. **Required Forms and Deadlines:** FAFSA. Financial aid filing deadline 3/1. **Notification of Awards:** Applicants will be notified of awards on a rolling basis beginning on or about 3/15. **Types of Aid:** *Need-based scholarships/grants:* Pell, SEOG, state scholarships/grants, private scholarships, the school's own gift aid, United Negro College Fund. *Loans:* FFEL Subsidized Stafford, FFEL Unsubsidized Stafford, FFEL PLUS, Federal Perkins, Federal Nursing, college/university loans from institutional funds. **Student Employment:** Federal Work-Study Program available. **Financial Aid Statistics:** 26% freshmen, 26% undergrads receive need-based scholarship or grant aid. 58% freshmen, 54% undergrads receive need-based self-help aid. 62 freshmen, 234 undergrads receive athletic scholarships. 90% freshmen, 83% undergrads receive any aid.

DRURY UNIVERSITY

900 North Benton Avenue, Springfield, MO 65802-3712
Phone: 417-873-7205 **E-mail:** druryad@drury.edu **CEEB Code:** 6169
Fax: 417-866-3873 **Website:** www.drury.edu **ACT Code:** 2292
Financial Aid Phone: 417-873-7312

This private school, affiliated with the UCC Church (Disciples of Christ), was founded in 1873. It has an 84-acre campus.

RATINGS
Admissions Selectivity Rating: 85   **Fire Safety Rating:** 60*   **Green Rating:** 86

STUDENTS AND FACULTY
Enrollment: 1,599. **Student Body:** 54% female, 46% male, 17% out-of-state, 4% international (21 countries represented). African American 1%, Asian 2%, Caucasian 90%, Hispanic 2%. **Retention and Graduation:** 82% freshmen return for sophomore year. 49% freshmen graduate within 4 years. 35% grads go on to further study within 1 year. 5% grads pursue arts and sciences degrees. 9% grads pursue business degrees. 5% grads pursue law degrees. 15% grads pursue medical degrees. **Faculty:** Student/faculty ratio 12:1. 121 full-time faculty, 95% hold PhDs. 100% faculty teach undergrads.

ACADEMICS
Degrees: Associate, bachelor's, master's. **Academic Requirements:** Arts/fine arts, computer literacy, English (including composition), foreign languages, health and wellness, history, humanities, mathematics, philosophy, sciences (biological or physical), social science. **Classes:** Most classes have 10–19 students. Most lab/discussion sections have 20–29 students. **Majors with Highest Enrollment:** Business administration/management, education, health/medical preparatory programs. **Disciplines with Highest Percentage of Degrees Awarded:** Communications/journalism 13%, biological/life sciences 11%, business/marketing 11%, psychology 11%, visual and performing arts 10%. **Special Study Options:** Accelerated program, cooperative education program, distance learning, double major, Drury Center in Volos (Greece), dual enrollment, English as a second language (ESL), honors program, independent study, internships, liberal arts/career combination, living-learning communities, student-designed major, study abroad, teacher certification program, Washington semester.

FACILITIES
Housing: Coed dorms, women's dorms, apartments for married students, apartments for single students, fraternity/sorority housing, living-learning communities, leadership/community service, shared interest housing. **Special Academic Facilities/Equipment:** Science center with greenhouse and astronomical observaton station, new visual art center with 2 galleries, TV studio, radio station, teleconference facility, language lab, electronic music lab, laser lab. **Computers:** 12% of classrooms are wired, 100% of classrooms are wireless, 85% of public computers are PCs, 14% of public computers are Macs, 1% of public computers are UNIX, network access in dorm rooms, network access in dorm lounges, online registration, online administrative functions (other than registration), remote student-access to Web through college's connection.

CAMPUS LIFE
Activities: Choral groups, concert band, dance, drama/theater, jazz band, literary magazine, music ensembles, musical theater, opera, pep band, radio station, student government, student newspaper, student-run film society, symphony orchestra, television station. **Organizations:** 60 registered organizations, 13 honor societies, 7 religious organizations. 4 fraternities (30% men join), 4 sororities (26% women join). **Athletics (Intercollegiate):** *Men:* Baseball, basketball, cheerleading, cross-country, diving, golf, soccer, swimming, tennis. *Women:* Basketball, cheerleading, cross-country, diving, golf, soccer, swimming, tennis, volleyball. Environmental Initiatives: Energy Management strategies on buildings (upgrading lighting, HVAC systems). Expanded recycling program and partnership with neighbor institutions. Sustainability across the curriculum developments.

ADMISSIONS
Freshman Academic Profile: 31% in top 10% of high school class, 63% in top 25% of high school class, 90% in top 50% of high school class. 85% from public high schools. SAT Math middle 50% range 485–640. SAT Critical Reading middle 50% range 480–640. SAT Writing middle 50% range 490–635. ACT

middle 50% range 22–28. TOEFL required of all international applicants, minimum paper TOEFL 530, minimum computer TOEFL 197. **Basis for Candidate Selection:** *Very important factors considered include:* Academic GPA. *Important factors considered include:* Application essay, character/personal qualities, class rank, interview, recommendation(s), standardized test scores. *Other factors considered include:* Alumni/ae relation, extracurricular activities, geographical residence, level of applicant's interest, racial/ethnic status, rigor of secondary school record, talent/ability, volunteer work, work experience. **Freshman Admission Requirements:** High school diploma is required, and GED is accepted. *Academic units required:* 4 English, 3 math, 3 science, 2 foreign language, 3 social studies. *Academic units recommended:* 4 English, 4 math, 3 science, 2 foreign language, 3 social studies. **Freshman Admission Statistics:** 1,209 applied, 77% admitted, 41% enrolled. **Transfer Admission Requirements:** High school transcript, college transcript(s), essay or personal statement. Minimum college GPA of 2.0 required. Lowest grade transferable C. **General Admission Information:** Application fee $25. Regular application deadline 8/1. Regular notification is rolling. Nonfall registration accepted. Admission may be deferred for a maximum of 1 semester. Credit and/or placement offered for CEEB Advanced Placement tests.

COSTS AND FINANCIAL AID
Annual tuition $17,900. Room and board $6,384. Required fees $364. Average book expense $1,500. **Required Forms and Deadlines:** FAFSA, institution's own financial aid form. Financial aid filing deadline 3/15. **Notification of Awards:** Applicants will be notified of awards on a rolling basis beginning on or about 3/15. **Types of Aid:** *Need-based scholarships/grants:* Pell, SEOG, state scholarships/grants, private scholarships, the school's own gift aid. *Loans:* FFEL Subsidized Stafford, FFEL Unsubsidized Stafford, FFEL PLUS, Federal Perkins. **Student Employment:** Federal Work-Study Program available. Institutional employment available. Off-campus job opportunities are excellent. **Financial Aid Statistics:** 82% freshmen, 90% undergrads receive need-based scholarship or grant aid. 81% freshmen, 85% undergrads receive need-based self-help aid. 19 freshmen, 83 undergrads receive athletic scholarships. 94% freshmen, 90% undergrads receive any aid. Highest amount earned per year from on-campus jobs $2,500.

DUKE UNIVERSITY

2138 Campus Drive, Box 90586, Durham, NC 27708-0586
Phone: 919-684-3214 **Fax:** 919-681-8941 **CEEB Code:** 5156
Website: www.admissions.duke.edu **ACT Code:** 3088
Financial Aid Phone: 919-684-6225

This private school, affiliated with the Methodist Church, was founded in 1838. It has an 8,500-acre campus.

RATINGS
Admissions Selectivity Rating: 99   **Fire Safety Rating:** 60*   **Green Rating:** 93

STUDENTS AND FACULTY
Enrollment: 6,259. **Student Body:** 48% female, 52% male, 85% out-of-state, 5% international (89 countries represented). African American 10%, Asian 14%, Caucasian 56%, Hispanic 7%. **Retention and Graduation:** 96% freshmen return for sophomore year. 86% freshmen graduate within 4 years. 38% grads go on to further study within 1 year. 14% grads pursue arts and sciences degrees. 1% grads pursue business degrees. 11% grads pursue law degrees. 12% grads pursue medical degrees. **Faculty:** Student/faculty ratio 11:1. 901 full-time faculty, 91% hold PhDs. 96% faculty teach undergrads.

ACADEMICS
Degrees: Associate, bachelor's, master's, doctoral. **Academic Requirements:** , Arts and literature, civilizations, English (including composition), foreign languages, natural sciences, mathematics, sciences (biological or physical), social science. **Classes:** Most classes have 10–19 students. Most lab/discussion sections have 10–19 students. **Majors with Highest Enrollment:** Economics, psychology, public policy analysis. **Disciplines with Highest Percentage of Degrees Awarded:** Social sciences 31%, biological/life sciences 13%, engineering 13%, psychology 9%, English 6%, computer and information sciences 3%. **Special Study Options:** Accelerated program, cross-registration, distance learning, double major, exchange student program (domestic), honors program, independent study, internships, student-designed major, study abroad,

teacher certification program. Undergrads may take grad level classes. New York Arts Program and semester and summer programs in ecology, geology, oceanography, physiology, and zoology at marine laboratory in Beaufort.

FACILITIES

Housing: Coed dorms, men's dorms, women's dorms, apartments for single students, fraternity/sorority housing, theme houses. **Special Academic Facilities/Equipment:** Art museum, language lab, university forest, primate center, phytotron, electron laser, nuclear magnetic resonance machine, nuclear lab. **Computers:** Network access in dorm rooms, network access in dorm lounges, online registration, remote student-access to Web through college's connection.

CAMPUS LIFE

Activities: Choral groups, concert band, dance, drama/theater, jazz band, literary magazine, marching band, music ensembles, musical theater, opera, pep band, radio station, student government, student newspaper, student-run film society, symphony orchestra, television station. **Organizations:** 200 registered organizations, 10 honor societies, 25 religious organizations. 21 fraternities (29% men join), 14 sororities (42% women join). **Athletics (Intercollegiate):** *Men:* Baseball, basketball, cross-country, diving, fencing, football, golf, lacrosse, soccer, swimming, tennis, track/field (indoor), track/field (outdoor), volleyball, wrestling. *Women:* Basketball, crew/rowing, cross-country, diving, fencing, field hockey, golf, lacrosse, soccer, swimming, tennis, track/field (indoor), track/field (outdoor), volleyball. Environmental Initiatives: Duke has signed the ACUPCC and signed a LEED building policy in 2003. The university now has 19 buildings that are certified or in the process of being certified. The Campus Master Plan, which guides all campus development, defines eight key principles including several that are related to the tenets of sustainability. Two of the most important of these principles are the commitment for Duke to be a "university in the forest" and a "citizen of Durham and the region."

ADMISSIONS

Freshman Academic Profile: 90% in top 10% of high school class, 98% in top 25% of high school class, 100% in top 50% of high school class. 65% from public high schools. SAT Math middle 50% range 690–800. SAT Critical Reading middle 50% range 690–770. ACT middle 50% range 29–34. **Basis for Candidate Selection:** *Very important factors considered include:* Application essay, extracurricular activities, recommendation(s), rigor of secondary school record, standardized test scores, talent/ability. *Important factors considered include:* Character/personal qualities. *Other factors considered include:* Academic GPA, alumni/ae relation, class rank, geographical residence, interview, racial/ethnic status, state residency, volunteer work, work experience. **Freshman Admission Requirements:** High school diploma is required, and GED is not accepted. *Academic units recommended:* 4 English, 4 math, 4 science, 4 foreign language, 4 social studies. **Freshman Admission Statistics:** 18,090 applied, 22% admitted, 43% enrolled. **Transfer Admission Requirements:** High school transcript, college transcript(s), essay or personal statement, standardized test score, Lowest grade transferable C. **General Admission Information:** Application fee $65. Early decision application deadline 11/1. Regular application deadline 1/2. Regular notification 4/1. Nonfall registration not accepted. Admission may be deferred for a maximum of 1 year. Common Application accepted. Credit and/or placement offered for CEEB Advanced Placement tests.

COSTS AND FINANCIAL AID

Annual tuition $31,420. Room & board $8,950. Required fees $1,180. Average book expense $970. **Required Forms and Deadlines:** FAFSA, CSS/Financial Aid PROFILE, Noncustodial PROFILE, Business/Farm Supplement, parent and student income tax returns. Financial aid filing deadline 3/1. **Notification of Awards:** Applicants will be notified of awards on or about 4/1. **Types of Aid:** *Need-based scholarships/grants:* Pell, SEOG, state scholarships/grants, private scholarships, the school's own gift aid, ROTC. *Loans:* FFEL Subsidized Stafford, FFEL Unsubsidized Stafford, FFEL PLUS, Federal Perkins, college/university loans from institutional funds, private loans. **Student Employment:** Federal Work-Study Program available. Institutional employment available. Off-campus job opportunities are good. **Financial Aid Statistics:** 38% freshmen, 37% undergrads receive need-based scholarship or grant aid. 35% freshmen, 35% undergrads receive need-based self-help aid. Highest amount earned per year from on-campus jobs $1,400.

DUQUESNE UNIVERSITY

600 Forbes Avenue, Pittsburgh, PA 15282
Phone: 412-396-6222 **E-mail:** admissions@duq.edu **CEEB Code:** 2196
Fax: 412-396-6223 **Website:** www.duq.edu **ACT Code:** 3560
Financial Aid Phone: 412-396-6607

This private school, affiliated with the Roman Catholic Church, was founded in 1878. It has a 50-acre campus.

RATINGS

Admissions Selectivity Rating: 84   Fire Safety Rating: 88   Green Rating: 84

STUDENTS AND FACULTY

Enrollment: 5,608. **Student Body:** 58% female, 42% male, 19% out-of-state, 2% international (80 countries represented). African American 3%, Asian 2%, Caucasian 80%, Hispanic 1%. **Retention and Graduation:** 87% freshmen return for sophomore year. 33% grads go on to further study within 1 year. **Faculty:** Student/faculty ratio 15:1. 442 full-time faculty, 86% hold PhDs. 94% faculty teach undergrads.

ACADEMICS

Degrees: Bachelor's, doctoral, first professional, master's, post-bachelor's certificate, post-master's certificate. **Academic Requirements:** Arts/fine arts, computer literacy, English (including composition), foreign languages, history, humanities, mathematics, philosophy, sciences (biological or physical), social science, theology. **Classes:** Most classes have 10–19 students. Most lab/discussion sections have 20–29 students. **Majors with Highest Enrollment:** Marketing/marketing management, nursing/registered nurse training (RN, ASN, BSN, MSN), pharmacy (PharMD, BS/BPharm). **Disciplines with Highest Percentage of Degrees Awarded:** Business/marketing 32%, health professions and related sciences 15%, biological/life sciences 8%, education 8%, communications/journalism 7%, social sciences 7%, liberal arts/general studies 6%. **Special Study Options:** Accelerated program, cross-registration, distance learning, double major, dual enrollment, English as a second language (ESL), exchange student program (domestic), external degree program, honors program, independent study, internships, liberal arts/career combination, student-designed major, study abroad, teacher certification program, weekend college.

FACILITIES

Housing: Coed dorms, apartments for married students, apartments for single students, special housing for disabled students, fraternity/sorority housing, single-gender wings, sorority and fraternity wings, international wings, club wings. **Special Academic Facilities/Equipment:** Student art gallery. **Computers:** 3% of classrooms are wired, 10% of classrooms are wireless, 91% of public computers are PCs, 9% of public computers are Macs, network access in dorm rooms, network access in dorm lounges, online registration, online administrative functions (other than registration), support for handheld computing, remote student-access to Web through college's connection.

CAMPUS LIFE

Activities: Choral groups, concert band, dance, drama/theater, jazz band, literary magazine, marching band, music ensembles, musical theater, opera, pep band, radio station, student government, student newspaper, student-run film society, symphony orchestra, television station. **Organizations:** 140 registered organizations, 14 honor societies, 6 religious organizations. 10 fraternities (14% men join), 9 sororities (20% women join). **Athletics (Intercollegiate):** *Men:* Baseball, basketball, cross-country, football, golf, soccer, swimming, tennis, track/field (outdoor), wrestling. *Women:* Basketball, crew/rowing, cross-country, lacrosse, soccer, swimming, tennis, track/field (indoor), track/field (outdoor), volleyball. Environmental Initiatives: Goal of LEED's certification. Climate Footprint. Campus Recycling Program Outside EHS Assessment.

ADMISSIONS

Freshman Academic Profile: 28% in top 10% of high school class, 57% in top 25% of high school class, 88% in top 50% of high school class. 77% from public high schools. SAT Math middle 50% range 510–610. SAT Critical Reading middle 50% range 510–600. SAT Writing middle 50% range 510–600. ACT middle 50% range 22–26. **Basis for Candidate Selection:** *Very important factors considered include:* Academic GPA, application essay, recommendation(s), rigor of secondary school record, standardized test scores. *Important factors considered include:* Character/personal qualities, class rank, extracurricular activities, interview, talent/ability, volunteer work. *Other factors considered include:* Alumni/ae relation, first generation, level of applicant's interest, racial/ethnic status, work experience. **Freshman Admission Requirements:** High school diploma is required, and GED is accepted. *Academic units required:* 4 English, 2 math, 2 science, 2 foreign language, 2 social studies, 4 academic electives. **Freshman Admission Statistics:** 5,252 applied, 72% admitted, 35% enrolled. **Transfer Admission Requirements:** High school transcript, college transcript(s), essay or personal statement, statement of good standing from prior institution(s). Minimum college GPA of 2.5 required. Lowest grade transferable C. **General Admission Information:** Application fee $50. Early decision application deadline 11/1. Regular application deadline 7/1. Regular notification is rolling. Nonfall registration accepted. Admission may be deferred for a maximum of 1 year. Credit and/or placement offered for CEEB Advanced Placement tests.

COSTS AND FINANCIAL AID

Annual tuition $22,054. Room and board $8,546. Required fees $1,896. Average book expense $600. **Required Forms and Deadlines:** FAFSA, institution's own financial aid form. Financial aid filing deadline 5/1. **Notification of Awards:** Applicants will be notified of awards on a rolling basis beginning on or about 3/1. **Types of Aid:** *Need-based scholarships/grants:* Pell, SEOG, state scholarships/grants, private scholarships, the school's own gift aid, United Negro College Fund. *Loans:* FFEL Subsidized Stafford, FFEL Unsubsidized Stafford, FFEL PLUS, Federal Perkins, Federal Nursing, private alternative loans. **Student Employment:** Federal Work-Study Program available. Institutional employment available. Off-campus job opportunities are good. **Financial Aid Statistics:** 73% freshmen, 64% undergrads receive need-based scholarship or grant aid. 62% freshmen, 56% undergrads receive need-based self-help aid. 63 freshmen, 294 undergrads receive athletic scholarships. 93% freshmen, 85% undergrads receive any aid. Highest amount earned per year from on-campus jobs $22,500.

D'YOUVILLE COLLEGE

One DYouville Square, 320 Porter Avenue, Buffalo, NY 14201
Phone: 716-829-7600 **E-mail:** admiss@dyc.edu **CEEB Code:** 2197
Fax: 716-829-7790 **Website:** www.dyc.edu **ACT Code:** 2732
Financial Aid Phone: 716-829-7500

This private school was founded in 1908. It has a 7-acre campus.

RATINGS
Admissions Selectivity Rating: 71   **Fire Safety Rating:** 60*   **Green Rating:** 60*

STUDENTS AND FACULTY
Enrollment: 1,136. **Student Body:** 76% female, 24% male, 26% out-of-state. **Retention and Graduation:** 72% freshmen return for sophomore year. 13% freshmen graduate within 4 years. **Faculty:** Student/faculty ratio 13:1. 105 full-time faculty, 64% hold PhDs. 75% faculty teach undergrads.

ACADEMICS
Degrees: Bachelor's, doctoral, first professional, master's, post-bachelor's certificate, post-master's certificate. **Academic Requirements:** Arts/fine arts, computer literacy, English (including composition), foreign languages, history, humanities, mathematics, philosophy, sciences (biological or physical), social science. **Classes:** Most classes have 10–19 students. Most lab/discussion sections have 10–19 students. **Majors with Highest Enrollment:** Business administration/management, education, nursing/registered nurse training (RN, ASN, BSN, MSN). **Disciplines with Highest Percentage of Degrees Awarded:** Health professions and related sciences 58%, business/marketing 16%, education 9%, liberal arts/general studies 5%, psychology 4%. **Special Study Options:** Accelerated program, cooperative education program, cross-registration, distance learning, double major, dual enrollment, exchange student program (domestic), independent study, internships, liberal arts/career combination, study abroad, teacher certification program, weekend college.

FACILITIES
Housing: Coed dorms, apartments for married students, apartments for single students, special housing for disabled students, quiet floors for third to fifth year students, separate male and female floors available, new apartment-style housing. **Special Academic Facilities/Equipment:** Kavinoky Theatre (professional theater). **Computers:** 80% of classrooms are wired, 60% of public computers are PCs, 40% of public computers are Macs, network access in dorm rooms, network access in dorm lounges, online registration, online administrative functions (other than registration), remote student-access to Web through college's connection.

CAMPUS LIFE
Activities: Choral groups, drama/theater, literary magazine, student government, student newspaper, yearbook. **Organizations:** 25 registered organizations, 3 honor societies, 1 religious organization. **Athletics (Intercollegiate):** *Men:* Baseball, basketball, golf, soccer, volleyball. *Women:* Basketball, crew/rowing, golf, soccer, softball, volleyball.

ADMISSIONS
Freshman Academic Profile: 10% in top 10% of high school class, 9% in top 25% of high school class, 81% in top 50% of high school class. 75% from public high schools. SAT Math middle 50% range 433–540. SAT Critical Reading middle 50% range 430–540. ACT middle 50% range 18–23. TOEFL required of all international applicants, minimum paper TOEFL 500, minimum computer TOEFL 173. **Basis for Candidate Selection:** *Very important factors considered include:* Rigor of secondary school record, standardized test scores. *Important factors considered include:* Class rank. *Other factors considered include:* Alumni/ae relation, character/personal qualities, extracurricular activities, interview, recommendation(s), talent/ability, volunteer work, work experience. **Freshman Admission Requirements:** High school diploma is required, and GED is accepted. *Academic units recommended:* 4 English, 3 math, 3 science, 3 foreign language, 3 social studies. **Freshman Admission Statistics:** 1,242 applied, 72% admitted, 26% enrolled. **Transfer Admission Requirements:** High school transcript, college transcript(s). Minimum college GPA of 2.0 required. Lowest grade transferable C. **General Admission Information:** Application fee $25. Regular notification is rolling. Nonfall registration accepted. Admission may be deferred for a maximum of 1 year. Common Application accepted. Credit offered for CEEB Advanced Placement tests.

COSTS AND FINANCIAL AID
Annual tuition $14,690. Room & board $7,340. Required fees $200. Average book expense $850. **Required Forms and Deadlines:** FAFSA, institution's own financial aid form, state aid form. Financial aid filing deadline 3/1. **Notification of Awards:** Applicants will be notified of awards on or about 4/15. **Types of Aid:** *Need-based scholarships/grants:* Pell, SEOG, state scholarships/grants, private scholarships, the school's own gift aid, Federal Nursing Scholarships. *Loans:* FFEL Subsidized Stafford, FFEL Unsubsidized Stafford, FFEL PLUS, Federal Perkins, Federal Nursing, college/university loans from institutional funds. **Student Employment:** Federal Work-Study Program available. Institutional employment available. Off-campus job opportunities are excellent. **Financial Aid Statistics:** 93% freshmen, 93% undergrads receive need-based scholarship or grant aid. 92% freshmen, 60% undergrads receive need-based self-help aid. Highest amount earned per year from on-campus jobs $2,000.

See page 1146.

EARLHAM COLLEGE

801 National Road West, Richmond, IN 47374-4095
Phone: 765-983-1600 **E-mail:** admissions@earlham.edu **CEEB Code:** 1195
Fax: 765-983-1560 **Website:** www.earlham.edu **ACT Code:** 1186
Financial Aid Phone: 765-983-1217

This private school, affiliated with the Society of Friends, was founded in 1847. It has an 800-acre campus.

RATINGS
Admissions Selectivity Rating: 88   **Fire Safety Rating:** 80   **Green Rating:** 60*

STUDENTS AND FACULTY
Enrollment: 1,206. **Student Body:** 57% female, 43% male, 69% out-of-state, 8% international (61 countries represented). African American 7%, Asian 2%, Caucasian 72%, Hispanic 2%. **Retention and Graduation:** 82% freshmen return for sophomore year. 62% freshmen graduate within 4 years. 21% grads go on to further study within 1 year. 17% grads pursue arts and sciences degrees. 1% grads pursue medical degrees. **Faculty:** Student/faculty ratio 12:1. 96 full-time faculty, 93% hold PhDs. 100% faculty teach undergrads.

ACADEMICS
Degrees: Bachelor's, first professional, master's. **Academic Requirements:** Arts/fine arts, computer literacy, English (including composition), foreign languages, history, humanities, mathematics, philosophy, sciences (biological or physical), social science. **Classes:** Most classes have 10–19 students. Most lab/discussion sections have 10–19 students. **Majors with Highest Enrollment:** Biology/biological sciences, history, psychology. **Disciplines with Highest Percentage of Degrees Awarded:** Social sciences 15%, foreign languages

and literature 12%, visual and performing arts 12%, psychology 11%, interdisciplinary studies 7%, biological/life sciences 6%, English 6%, area and ethnic studies 6%, physical sciences 6%. **Special Study Options:** Double major, English as a second language (ESL), independent study, internships, student-designed major, study abroad, teacher certification program, teacher certification at master's degree level only.

FACILITIES

Housing: Coed dorms, apartments for single students, special housing for disabled students, special housing for international students, cooperative housing, residence hall with quad style living, single-gender floors in some coed dorms. **Special Academic Facilities/Equipment:** Major academic building Landrum Bolling Center for Interdisciplinary and Social Studies, Natural History Museum, cultural centers, language labs, greenhouse, observatory, planetarium. **Computers:** 95% of classrooms are wireless, 71% of public computers are PCs, 20% of public computers are Macs, 9% of public computers are UNIX, network access in dorm rooms, network access in dorm lounges, online administrative functions (other than registration), remote student-access to Web through college's connection.

CAMPUS LIFE

Activities: Choral groups, concert band, dance, drama/theater, jazz band, literary magazine, music ensembles, musical theater, radio station, student government, student newspaper, student-run film society, yearbook. **Organizations:** 70 registered organizations, 1 honor society, 15 religious organizations. **Athletics (Intercollegiate):** *Men:* Baseball, basketball, cross-country, football, soccer, tennis, track/field (indoor), track/field (outdoor). *Women:* Basketball, cross-country, field hockey, soccer, tennis, track/field (indoor), track/field (outdoor), volleyball.

ADMISSIONS

Freshman Academic Profile: 31% in top 10% of high school class, 67% in top 25% of high school class, 91% in top 50% of high school class. 68% from public high schools. SAT Math middle 50% range 550–650. SAT Critical Reading middle 50% range 570–690. ACT middle 50% range 24–29. TOEFL required of all international applicants, minimum paper TOEFL 550, minimum computer TOEFL 213. **Basis for Candidate Selection:** *Very important factors considered include:* Academic GPA, application essay, character/personal qualities, recommendation(s), rigor of secondary school record. *Important factors considered include:* Class rank, extracurricular activities, interview, racial/ethnic status, standardized test scores, talent/ability, volunteer work. *Other factors considered include:* Alumni/ae relation, first generation, work experience. **Freshman Admission Requirements:** High school diploma is required, and GED is accepted. *Academic units required:* 4 English, 3 math, 3 science (2 science labs), 2 foreign language, 2 social studies, 1 history. *Academic units recommended:* 4 English, 4 math, 4 science (2 science labs), 4 foreign language, 3 social studies, 1 history. **Freshman Admission Statistics:** 1,661 applied, 68% admitted, 27% enrolled. **Transfer Admission Requirements:** High school transcript, college transcript(s), essay or personal statement, standardized test score, statement of good standing from prior institution(s). Minimum college GPA of 3.0 required. Lowest grade transferable C. **General Admission Information:** Application fee $30. Early decision application deadline 12/1. Regular application deadline 2/15. Regular notification 3/15. Nonfall registration accepted. Admission may be deferred for a maximum of 1 year. Credit offered for CEEB Advanced Placement tests.

COSTS AND FINANCIAL AID

Annual tuition $30,744. Room and board $6,504. Required fees $740. Average book expense $850. **Required Forms and Deadlines:** FAFSA, institution's own financial aid form. Financial aid filing deadline 3/1. **Notification of Awards:** Applicants will be notified of awards on a rolling basis beginning on or about 2/15. **Types of Aid:** *Need-based scholarships/grants:* Pell, SEOG, state scholarships/grants, private scholarships, the school's own gift aid. *Loans:* Direct Subsidized Stafford, Direct Unsubsidized Stafford, Direct PLUS, Federal Perkins, college/university loans from institutional funds. **Financial Aid Statistics:** 48% freshmen, 51% undergrads receive need-based scholarship or grant aid. 44% freshmen, 49% undergrads receive need-based self-help aid. 93% freshmen, 92% undergrads receive any aid. Highest amount earned per year from on-campus jobs $2,259.

EAST CAROLINA UNIVERSITY

Office of Undergraduate Admissions, 106 Whichard Building, Greenville, NC 27858-4353
Phone: 252-328-6640 **E-mail:** admis@ecu.edu **CEEB Code:** 5180
Fax: 252-328-6945 **Website:** www.ecu.edu **ACT Code:** 3094
Financial Aid Phone: 252-328-9379

This public school was founded in 1907. It has a 1,000-acre campus.

RATINGS

Admissions Selectivity Rating: 76   **Fire Safety Rating:** 60*   **Green Rating:** 60*

STUDENTS AND FACULTY

Enrollment: 18,445. **Student Body:** 60% female, 40% male, 13% out-of-state. African American 16%, Asian 2%, Caucasian 76%, Hispanic 2%. **Retention and Graduation:** 79% freshmen return for sophomore year. 27% freshmen graduate within 4 years. **Faculty:** Student/faculty ratio 18:1. 1,508 full-time faculty, 80% hold PhDs. 88% faculty teach undergrads.

ACADEMICS

Degrees: Bachelor's, doctoral, first professional, master's, post-bachelor's certificate, post-master's certificate. **Academic Requirements:** Arts/fine arts, English (including composition), health and exercise, humanities, mathematics, sciences (biological or physical), social science, sport science. **Classes:** Most classes have 20–29 students. Most lab/discussion sections have 10–19 students. **Majors with Highest Enrollment:** Elementary education and teaching, fine/studio arts, nursing/registered nurse training (RN, ASN, BSN, MSN). **Disciplines with Highest Percentage of Degrees Awarded:** Health professions and related sciences 15%, business/marketing 14%, education 14%, computer and information sciences 7%, social sciences 6%. **Special Study Options:** Accelerated program, cooperative education program, distance learning, double major, dual enrollment, exchange student program (domestic), honors program, independent study, internships, student-designed major, study abroad, teacher certification program.

FACILITIES

Housing: Coed dorms, men's dorms, women's dorms, fraternity/sorority housing, first-year students floor, leadership hall, extended quiet study hours floor, academic year residence halls. **Special Academic Facilities/Equipment:** Wellington B. Gray Gallery, Museum Without Walls, Ledonia Wright Cultural Center, A. J. Fletcher Recital Hall, Hendrix Theatre, Jenkins Fine Arts Center, McGinnis Theatre, Mendenhall Student Center. **Computers:** 76% of public computers are PCs, 21% of public computers are Macs, 3% of public computers are UNIX, network access in dorm rooms, network access in dorm lounges, online registration, online administrative functions (other than registration), support for handheld computing, remote student-access to Web through college's connection.

CAMPUS LIFE

Activities: Choral groups, concert band, dance, drama/theater, jazz band, literary magazine, marching band, music ensembles, musical theater, opera, pep band, radio station, student government, student newspaper, student-run film society, symphony orchestra, yearbook. **Organizations:** 244 registered organizations, 11 honor societies, 27 religious organizations. 22 fraternities (4% men join), 13 sororities (4% women join). **Athletics (Intercollegiate):** *Men:* Baseball, basketball, cross-country, diving, football, golf, soccer, swimming, tennis, track/field (outdoor). *Women:* Basketball, cross-country, diving, golf, soccer, softball, swimming, tennis, track/field (outdoor), volleyball.

ADMISSIONS

Freshman Academic Profile: 11% in top 10% of high school class, 37% in top 25% of high school class, 75% in top 50% of high school class. 90% from public high schools. SAT Math middle 50% range 470–560. SAT Critical Reading middle 50% range 450–540. SAT Writing middle 50% range 440–530. ACT middle 50% range 19–23. TOEFL required of all international applicants, minimum paper TOEFL 550, minimum computer TOEFL 213. **Basis for Candidate Selection:** *Very important factors considered include:* Class rank, rigor of secondary school record, standardized test scores. *Other factors considered include:* Alumni/ae relation, character/personal qualities, extracurricular activities, geographical residence, recommendation(s), state residency, talent/ability. **Freshman Admission Requirements:** High school diploma is required, and GED is accepted. *Academic units required:* 4 English, 4 math, 3 science (1 science lab), 2 foreign language, 2 social studies, 4 academic electives. *Academic units recommended:* 1 fine art, 1 U.S. history. **Freshman Admission Statistics:** 12,130 applied, 76% admitted, 37% enrolled. **Transfer Admission Requirements:** High school transcript, college transcript(s). Minimum college GPA of 2.0 required. Lowest grade transferable C. **General Admission Information:** Application fee $60. Regular application deadline 3/15. Regular notification is rolling. Nonfall registration accepted. Admission may be deferred for a maximum of 1 semester. Credit and/or placement offered for CEEB Advanced Placement tests.

COSTS AND FINANCIAL AID

Annual in-state tuition $2,335. Out-of-state tuition $12,849. Room & board $6,940. Required fees $1,668. Average book expense $900. **Required Forms and Deadlines:** FAFSA. Financial aid filing deadline 4/15. **Notification of Awards:** Applicants will be notified of awards on or about 3/15. **Types of Aid:** *Need-based scholarships/grants:* Pell, SEOG, state scholarships/grants, private scholarships, the school's own gift aid. *Loans:* FFEL Subsidized Stafford, FFEL Unsubsidized Stafford, FFEL PLUS, Federal Perkins, Federal Nursing. **Student Employment:** Federal Work-Study Program available. Institutional employment available. **Financial Aid Statistics:** 30% freshmen, 24% undergrads receive need-based scholarship or grant aid. 9% freshmen, 8% undergrads receive need-based self-help aid. 26 freshmen, 215 undergrads receive athletic scholarships.

EAST CENTRAL UNIVERSITY

Office of Admissions, Ada, OK 74820-6899
Phone: 580-332-8000 **E-mail:** tesarry@mailclerk.ecok.edu **CEEB Code:** 6186
Fax: 580-436-5495 **Website:** www.ecok.edu **ACT Code:** 3394
Financial Aid Phone: 580-332-8000

This public school was founded in 1909. It has a 130-acre campus.

RATINGS
Admissions Selectivity Rating: 60* **Fire Safety Rating:** 60* **Green Rating:** 60*

STUDENTS AND FACULTY
Student Body: 3% out-of-state. **Retention and Graduation:** 62% freshmen return for sophomore year. 12% grads go on to further study within 1 year. 10% grads pursue arts and sciences degrees. 1% grads pursue law degrees. 1% grads pursue medical degrees.

ACADEMICS
Degrees: Associate, bachelor's, master's. **Special Study Options:** Exchange student program (domestic). Undergrads may take grad level classes.

FACILITIES
Housing: Coed dorms, men's dorms, women's dorms, apartments for married students, apartments for single students, fraternity/sorority housing.

CAMPUS LIFE
Organizations: 8 religious organizations. 4 fraternities (9% men join), 3 sororities (10% women join). **Athletics (Intercollegiate):** *Men:* Baseball, basketball, cheerleading, cross-country, football, golf, softball, tennis, track/field (outdoor). *Women:* Basketball, cheerleading, cross-country, softball, tennis.

ADMISSIONS
Freshman Academic Profile: 15% in top 10% of high school class, 41% in top 25% of high school class, 77% in top 50% of high school class. 99% from public high schools. TOEFL required of all international applicants, minimum paper TOEFL 500. **Freshman Admission Requirements:** High school diploma is required, and GED is accepted. *Academic units required:* 4 English, 3 math, 2 science, 2 history. **Transfer Admission Requirements:** Minimum college GPA of 2.0 required. Lowest grade transferable D. **General Admission Information:** Early decision application deadline 5/1. Regular application deadline 8/21. Regular notification is rolling. Nonfall registration accepted. Common Application not accepted.

COSTS AND FINANCIAL AID
Annual in-state tuition $1,106. Out-of-state tuition $3,323. Room & board $2,200. Required fees $28. Average book expense $400. **Required Forms and Deadlines:** FAFSA, institution's own financial aid form. **Types of Aid:** *Need-based scholarships/grants:* Pell, SEOG, state scholarships/grants, private scholarships, the school's own gift aid. *Loans:* FFEL Subsidized Stafford, FFEL Unsubsidized Stafford, FFEL PLUS, Federal Perkins, college/university loans from institutional funds. **Student Employment:** Federal Work-Study Program available. Institutional employment available. Off-campus job opportunities are good. **Financial Aid Statistics:** Highest amount earned per year from on-campus jobs $3,200.

EAST STROUDSBURG UNIVERSITY OF PENNSYLVANIA

200 Prospect Street, East Stroudsburg, PA 18301-2999
Phone: 570-422-3542 **E-mail:** undergrads@po-box.esu.edu **CEEB Code:** 2650
Fax: 570-422-3933 **Website:** www3.esu.edu **ACT Code:** 3700
Financial Aid Phone: 570-422-3340

This public school was founded in 1893. It has a 213-acre campus.

RATINGS
Admissions Selectivity Rating: 73 **Fire Safety Rating:** 98 **Green Rating:** 65

STUDENTS AND FACULTY
Enrollment: 5,750. **Student Body:** 58% female, 42% male, 23% out-of-state. African American 4%, Asian 1%, Caucasian 87%, Hispanic 5%. **Retention and Graduation:** 78% freshmen return for sophomore year. 22% freshmen graduate within 4 years. **Faculty:** Student/faculty ratio 19:1. 259 full-time faculty, 78% hold PhDs. 89% faculty teach undergrads.

ACADEMICS
Degrees: Associate, bachelor's, master's, post-bachelor's certificate, post-master's certificate. **Academic Requirements:** Arts/fine arts, English (including composition), humanities, sciences (biological or physical), social science. **Classes:** Most classes have 20–29 students. Most lab/discussion sections have 10–19 students. **Majors with Highest Enrollment:** Business administration and management, elementary education and teaching, physical education teaching and coaching. **Disciplines with Highest Percentage of Degrees Awarded:** Education 25%, business/marketing 11%, social sciences 11%, psychology 9%, parks and recreation 8%. **Special Study Options:** Accelerated program, double major, exchange student program (domestic), honors program, independent study, internships, student-designed major, study abroad, teacher certification program.

FACILITIES
Housing: Coed dorms, apartments for single students, special housing for disabled students, special housing for international students. **Special Academic Facilities/Equipment:** Natural history museum, human performance lab, TV production studios, 52-acre student-owned/operated recreation area and wildlife sanctuary, observatory, electron microscopes. **Computers:** 88% of public computers are PCs, 12% of public computers are Macs, network access in dorm rooms, network access in dorm lounges, online registration, remote student-access to Web through college's connection.

CAMPUS LIFE
Activities: Choral groups, concert band, dance, drama/theater, literary magazine, marching band, music ensembles, musical theater, pep band, radio station, student government, student newspaper, symphony orchestra, yearbook. **Organizations:** 100 registered organizations, 14 honor societies, 3 religious organizations. 7 fraternities (4% men join), 7 sororities (3% women join). **Athletics (Intercollegiate):** *Men:* Baseball, basketball, cross-country, football, soccer, tennis, track/field (indoor), track/field (outdoor), volleyball, wrestling. *Women:* Basketball, cross-country, field hockey, lacrosse, soccer, softball, swimming, tennis, track/field (indoor), track/field (outdoor), volleyball.

ADMISSIONS
Freshman Academic Profile: 5% in top 10% of high school class, 24% in top 25% of high school class, 64% in top 50% of high school class. 90% from public high schools. SAT Math middle 50% range 450–540. SAT Critical Reading middle 50% range 440–520. SAT Writing middle 50% range 430–520. TOEFL required of all international applicants, minimum paper TOEFL 500, minimum computer TOEFL 173. **Basis for Candidate Selection:** *Very important factors considered include:* Academic GPA, rigor of secondary school record, standardized test scores. *Important factors considered include:* Racial/ethnic status. *Other factors considered include:* Alumni/ae relation, application essay, character/personal qualities, class rank, extracurricular activities, first generation, geographical residence, recommendation(s), state residency, talent/ability, volunteer work, work experience. **Freshman Admission Requirements:** High school diploma is required, and GED is accepted. *Academic units recommended:* 4 English, 4 math, 3 science (2 science labs), 2 foreign language, 3 social studies, 3 history. **Freshman Admission Statistics:** 5,562 applied, 64% admitted, 35% enrolled. **Transfer Admission Requirements:** College transcript(s). Minimum college GPA of 2.0 required. Lowest grade transferable C-. **General Admission Information:** Application fee $35. Regular application deadline 4/1. Regular notification is rolling. Nonfall registration accepted. Credit and/or placement offered for CEEB Advanced Placement tests.

COSTS AND FINANCIAL AID

Annual in-state tuition $5,178. Annual out-of-state tuition $12,944. Room and board $5,686. Required fees $1,631. Average book expense $1,000. **Required Forms and Deadlines:** FAFSA. Financial aid filing deadline 3/1. **Notification of Awards:** Applicants will be notified of awards on or about 4/1. **Types of Aid:** *Need-based scholarships/grants:* Pell, SEOG, state scholarships/grants, private scholarships, the school's own gift aid. *Loans:* FFEL Subsidized Stafford, FFEL Unsubsidized Stafford, FFEL PLUS, Federal Perkins. **Financial Aid Statistics:** 30% freshmen, 31% undergrads receive need-based scholarship or grant aid. 42% freshmen, 45% undergrads receive need-based self-help aid. 45 freshmen, 208 undergrads receive athletic scholarships.

EAST TENNESSEE STATE UNIVERSITY

ETSU Box 70731, Johnson City, TN 37614-0731
Phone: 423-439-4213 **E-mail:** go2etsu@etsu.edu **CEEB Code:** 1198
Fax: 423-439-4630 **Website:** www.etsu.edu **ACT Code:** 3958
Financial Aid Phone: 423-439-4300

This public school was founded in 1911. It has a 366-acre campus.

RATINGS
Admissions Selectivity Rating: 72   **Fire Safety Rating:** 60*   **Green Rating:** 60*

STUDENTS AND FACULTY
Enrollment: 9,895. **Student Body:** 58% female, 42% male, 9% out-of-state, 1% international (63 countries represented). African American 4%, Asian 1%, Caucasian 89%, Hispanic 1%. **Retention and Graduation:** 71% freshmen return for sophomore year. 17% freshmen graduate within 4 years. **Faculty:** Student/faculty ratio 18:1. 497 full-time faculty, 72% hold PhDs.

ACADEMICS
Degrees: Bachelor's, doctoral, first professional, master's, post-bachelor's certificate, post-master's certificate. **Academic Requirements:** Arts/fine arts, computer literacy, English (including composition), history, humanities, mathematics, philosophy, sciences (biological or physical), social science. **Classes:** Most classes have 20–29 students. Most lab/discussion sections have 20–29 students. **Majors with Highest Enrollment:** Business administration and management, multi/interdisciplinary studies, nursing/registered nurse training (RN, ASN, BSN, MSN). **Disciplines with Highest Percentage of Degrees Awarded:** Health professions and related sciences 18%, business/marketing 15%, liberal arts/general studies 8%, interdisciplinary studies 7%, family and consumer sciences 6%. **Special Study Options:** Accelerated program, cooperative education program, distance learning, double major, dual enrollment, exchange student program (domestic), honors program, independent study, internships, study abroad, teacher certification program.

FACILITIES
Housing: Coed dorms, men's dorms, women's dorms, apartments for married students, apartments for single students, special housing for disabled students, fraternity/sorority housing. **Special Academic Facilities/Equipment:** Regional history museum, art gallery, Archives of Appalachia, planetarium. **Computers:** 80% of public computers are PCs, 20% of public computers are Macs, network access in dorm rooms, online registration, online administrative functions (other than registration), support for handheld computing, remote student-access to Web through college's connection.

CAMPUS LIFE
Activities: Choral groups, concert band, drama/theater, jazz band, literary magazine, music ensembles, pep band, radio station, student government, student newspaper, television station. **Organizations:** 200 registered organizations, 19 honor societies, 13 religious organizations. 9 fraternities (6% men join), 7 sororities (5% women join). **Athletics (Intercollegiate):** *Men:* Baseball, basketball, cheerleading, cross-country, golf, soccer, tennis, track/field (indoor), track/field (outdoor). *Women:* Basketball, cheerleading, cross-country, golf, soccer, softball, tennis, track/field (indoor), track/field (outdoor), volleyball.

ADMISSIONS
Freshman Academic Profile: 14% in top 10% of high school class, 41% in top 25% of high school class, 72% in top 50% of high school class. 90% from public high schools. SAT Math middle 50% range 450–560. SAT Critical Reading middle 50% range 440–560. SAT Writing middle 50% range 430–550. ACT middle 50% range 20–25. TOEFL required of all international applicants,

minimum paper TOEFL 500, minimum computer TOEFL 173. **Basis for Candidate Selection:** *Very important factors considered include:* Academic GPA, standardized test scores. *Important factors considered include:* Rigor of secondary school record. *Other factors considered include:* Class rank, geographical residence, state residency. **Freshman Admission Requirements:** High school diploma is required, and GED is accepted. *Academic units required:* 4 English, 3 math, 2 science (1 science lab), 2 foreign language, 1 social studies, 1 history, 1 visual and performing arts. *Academic units recommended:* 4 math, 3 science. **Freshman Admission Statistics:** 2,320 applied, 97% admitted, 77% enrolled. **Transfer Admission Requirements:** College transcript(s). Minimum college GPA of 2.0 required. Lowest grade transferable D. **General Admission Information:** Application fee $15. Regular notification as application and credentials arrive. Nonfall registration accepted. Credit and/or placement offered for CEEB Advanced Placement tests.

COSTS AND FINANCIAL AID
Annual in-state tuition $4,058. Annual out-of-state tuition $14,334. Room and board $5,146. Required fees $829. Average book expense $1,008. **Required Forms and Deadlines:** FAFSA. Financial aid filing deadline 3/1. **Notification of Awards:** Applicants will be notified of awards on or about 5/15. **Types of Aid:** *Need-based scholarships/grants:* Pell, SEOG, state scholarships/grants, private scholarships, the school's own gift aid, Federal Nursing Scholarships. *Loans:* FFEL Subsidized Stafford, FFEL Unsubsidized Stafford, FFEL PLUS, Federal Perkins, state loans, college/university loans from institutional funds. **Student Employment:** Federal Work-Study Program available. Institutional employment available. Off-campus job opportunities are excellent. **Financial Aid Statistics:** 2% freshmen, 3% undergrads receive need-based scholarship or grant aid. 34% freshmen, 38% undergrads receive need-based self-help aid. 36 freshmen, 149 undergrads receive athletic scholarships.

EAST TEXAS BAPTIST UNIVERSITY

1209 North Grove, Marshall, TX 75670-1498
Phone: 903-923-2000 **E-mail:** admissions@etbu.edu **CEEB Code:** 6187
Fax: 903-923-2001 **Website:** www.etbu.edu **ACT Code:** 4086
Financial Aid Phone: 903-923-2137

This private school, affiliated with the Baptist Church, was founded in 1912. It has a 200-acre campus.

RATINGS
Admissions Selectivity Rating: 70   **Fire Safety Rating:** 61   **Green Rating:** 60*

STUDENTS AND FACULTY
Enrollment: 1,241. **Student Body:** 55% female, 45% male, 13% out-of-state. African American 15%, Caucasian 80%, Hispanic 4%. **Retention and Graduation:** 53% freshmen return for sophomore year. 26% freshmen graduate within 4 years. **Faculty:** Student/faculty ratio 15:1. 66 full-time faculty, 85% hold PhDs. 100% faculty teach undergrads.

ACADEMICS
Degrees: Associate, bachelor's. **Academic Requirements:** Arts/fine arts, English (including composition), history, humanities, mathematics, sciences (biological or physical), social science. **Classes:** Most classes have 20–29 students. Most lab/discussion sections have 10–19 students. **Majors with Highest Enrollment:** Bible/biblical studies, business administration/management, elementary education and teaching. **Disciplines with Highest Percentage of Degrees Awarded:** Education 22%, business/marketing 16%, theology and religious vocations 14%, psychology 9%, health professions and related sciences 7%. **Special Study Options:** Accelerated program, double major, dual enrollment, exchange student program (domestic), honors program, independent study, internships, liberal arts/career combination, study abroad, teacher certification program.

FACILITIES
Housing: Men's dorms, women's dorms, apartments for married students, apartments for single students. **Computers:** 100% of classrooms are wireless, 100% of public computers are PCs, network access in dorm rooms, network access in dorm lounges, online registration, online administrative functions (other than registration), remote student-access to Web through college's connection.

CAMPUS LIFE
Activities: Choral groups, concert band, drama/theater, jazz band, marching band, music ensembles, pep band, student government, student newspaper, symphony orchestra, yearbook. **Organizations:** 34 registered organizations, 6

honor societies, 2 religious organizations. 2 fraternities (2% men join), 2 sororities (3% women join). **Athletics (Intercollegiate): Men:** Baseball, basketball, cross-country, football, soccer. *Women:* Basketball, cross-country, soccer, softball, volleyball.

ADMISSIONS

Freshman Academic Profile: 16% in top 10% of high school class, 44% in top 25% of high school class, 78% in top 50% of high school class. SAT Math middle 50% range 440–560. SAT Critical Reading middle 50% range 430–540. ACT middle 50% range 18–23. TOEFL required of all international applicants, minimum paper TOEFL 500, minimum computer TOEFL 173. **Basis for Candidate Selection:** *Very important factors considered include:* Class rank, rigor of secondary school record, standardized test scores. *Important factors considered include:* Academic GPA, character/personal qualities. *Other factors considered include:* Alumni/ae relation, level of applicant's interest, religious affiliation/commitment. **Freshman Admission Requirements:** High school diploma is required, and GED is accepted. *Academic units recommended:* 4 English, 3 math, 2 science, 2 social studies, 1 academic elective, 0.5 economics, 1.5 physical education, 0.5 health education, 1 technology application. **Freshman Admission Statistics:** 851 applied, 79% admitted, 45% enrolled. **Transfer Admission Requirements:** College transcript(s), statement of good standing from prior institution(s). Minimum college GPA of 2.0 required. Lowest grade transferable D. **General Admission Information:** Application fee $25. Regular application deadline 8/14. Regular notification is rolling. Nonfall registration accepted. Admission may be deferred for a maximum of 1 year. Common Application accepted. Credit and/or placement offered for CEEB Advanced Placement tests.

COSTS AND FINANCIAL AID

Required Forms and Deadlines: FAFSA, institution's own financial aid form. Financial aid filing deadline 6/1. **Notification of Awards:** Applicants will be notified of awards on a rolling basis beginning on or about 1/15. **Types of Aid:** *Need-based scholarships/grants:* Pell, SEOG, state scholarships/grants, private scholarships, the school's own gift aid. *Loans:* FFEL Subsidized Stafford, FFEL Unsubsidized Stafford, FFEL PLUS, Federal Perkins, state loans, college/university loans from institutional funds. **Student Employment:** Federal Work-Study Program available. Institutional employment available. Off-campus job opportunities are fair. **Financial Aid Statistics:** 62% freshmen, 61% undergrads receive need-based scholarship or grant aid. 58% freshmen, 59% undergrads receive need-based self-help aid. 90% freshmen, 95% undergrads receive any aid. Highest amount earned per year from on-campus jobs $1,648.

EASTERN CONNECTICUT STATE UNIVERSITY

83 Windham Street, Willimantic, CT 06226
Phone: 860-465-5286 **E-mail:** admissions@easternct.edu **CEEB Code:** 3966
Fax: 860-465-5544 **Website:** www.easternct.edu
Financial Aid Phone: 860-365-5205

This public school was founded in 1889. It has a 182-acre campus.

RATINGS
Admissions Selectivity Rating: 69   **Fire Safety Rating:** 84   **Green Rating:** 60*

STUDENTS AND FACULTY
Enrollment: 4,742. **Student Body:** 57% female, 43% male, 6% out-of-state. African American 7%, Asian 2%, Caucasian 82%, Hispanic 5%. **Retention and Graduation:** 75% freshmen return for sophomore year. 23% freshmen graduate within 4 years. 35% grads go on to further study within 1 year. **Faculty:** Student/faculty ratio 16:1. 187 full-time faculty, 100% hold PhDs. 100% faculty teach undergrads.

ACADEMICS
Degrees: Associate, bachelor's, master's. **Academic Requirements:** Arts/fine arts, computer literacy, English (including composition), foreign languages, humanities, mathematics, sciences (biological or physical), social science. **Classes:** Most classes have 20–29 students. Most lab/discussion sections have 10–19 students. **Majors with Highest Enrollment:** Business administration/management, communications and media studies, psychology. **Disciplines with Highest Percentage of Degrees Awarded:** Business/marketing 16%, psychology 12%, communications/journalism 10%, social sciences 10%, English 9%, liberal arts/general studies 7%. **Special Study Options:** Accelerated program, cooperative education program, cross-registration, distance learning, double major, dual enrollment, exchange student program (domestic), honors program, independent study, internships, National Student Exchange (NSE), student-designed major, study abroad, teacher certification program, weekend college.

FACILITIES

Housing: Coed dorms, apartments for single students. **Special Academic Facilities/Equipment:** Art gallery, electron microscope, planetarium with teaching facilities, center for Connecticut studies, media center with TV studio. **Computers:** 25% of classrooms are wired, 100% of public computers are PCs, network access in dorm rooms, network access in dorm lounges, online registration, online administrative functions (other than registration), remote student-access to Web through college's connection.

CAMPUS LIFE
Activities: Choral groups, concert band, dance, drama/theater, literary magazine, music ensembles, musical theater, radio station, student government, student newspaper, television station, yearbook. **Organizations:** 65 registered organizations, 17 honor societies, 1 religious organization. **Athletics (Intercollegiate): Men:** Baseball, basketball, cross-country, golf, lacrosse, soccer, track/field (indoor), track/field (outdoor). *Women:* Basketball, cross-country, diving, field hockey, lacrosse, soccer, softball, swimming, track/field (indoor), track/field (outdoor), volleyball.

ADMISSIONS
Freshman Academic Profile: 5% in top 10% of high school class, 25% in top 25% of high school class, 69% in top 50% of high school class. SAT Math middle 50% range 460–550. SAT Critical Reading middle 50% range 460–550. TOEFL required of all international applicants, minimum paper TOEFL 550, minimum computer TOEFL 213. **Basis for Candidate Selection:** *Very important factors considered include:* Class rank, standardized test scores, talent/ability. *Important factors considered include:* Academic GPA, level of applicant's interest, recommendation(s), rigor of secondary school record. *Other factors considered include:* Application essay, character/personal qualities, extracurricular activities, interview, volunteer work, work experience. **Freshman Admission Requirements:** High school diploma is required, and GED is accepted. *Academic units required:* 4 English, 3 math, 2 science (1 science lab), 2 foreign language, 2 social studies, 3 history. **Freshman Admission Statistics:** 3,475 applied, 65% admitted, 42% enrolled. **Transfer Admission Requirements:** High school transcript, college transcript(s). Minimum college GPA of 2.0 required. Lowest grade transferable C-. **General Admission Information:** Application fee $50. Regular notification is rolling. Nonfall registration accepted. Admission may be deferred for a maximum of 1 year. Credit offered for CEEB Advanced Placement tests.

COSTS AND FINANCIAL AID
Comprehensive fee $3,346. Room and board $8,377. Required fees $3,615. Average book expense $1,168. Required Forms and Deadlines: FAFSA. Financial aid filing deadline 3/15. **Notification of Awards:** Applicants will be notified of awards on a rolling basis beginning on or about 2/15. **Types of Aid:** *Need-based scholarships/grants:* Pell, SEOG, state scholarships/grants, private scholarships, the school's own gift aid. *Loans:* FFEL Subsidized Stafford, FFEL Unsubsidized Stafford, FFEL PLUS, Federal Perkins. **Financial Aid Statistics:** 48% freshmen, 40% undergrads receive need-based scholarship or grant aid. 18% freshmen, 10% undergrads receive need-based self-help aid. 70% freshmen, 68% undergrads receive any aid.

EASTERN ILLINOIS UNIVERSITY

600 Lincoln Avenue, Charleston, IL 61920
Phone: 217-581-2223 **E-mail:** admissions@.eiu.edu **CEEB Code:** 1199
Fax: 217-581-7060 **Website:** www.eiu.edu **ACT Code:** 1016
Financial Aid Phone: 217-581-3714

This public school was founded in 1895. It has a 320-acre campus.

RATINGS
Admissions Selectivity Rating: 71   **Fire Safety Rating:** 69   **Green Rating:** 76

STUDENTS AND FACULTY
Enrollment: 10,477. **Student Body:** 58% female, 42% male, 1% out-of-state. African American 8%, Asian 1%, Caucasian 83%, Hispanic 2%. **Retention and Graduation:** 79% freshmen return for sophomore year. **Faculty:** Student/faculty ratio 16:1. 618 full-time faculty, 67% hold PhDs.

ACADEMICS
Degrees: Bachelor's, master's, post-bachelor's certificate, post-master's certificate. **Academic Requirements:** Arts/fine arts, computer literacy, English (including composition), foreign languages, humanities, mathematics, sciences (biological or physical), social science. **Classes:** Most classes have 20–29 students. **Majors with Highest Enrollment:** Elementary education and teaching, family and consumer sciences/human sciences, physical education

teaching and coaching. **Disciplines with Highest Percentage of Degrees Awarded:** Education 27%, business/marketing 12%, English 10%, history 10%, family and consumer sciences 8%, liberal arts/general studies 7%. **Special Study Options:** Distance learning, double major, dual enrollment, exchange student program (domestic), honors program, independent study, internships, study abroad, teacher certification program.

FACILITIES

Housing: Coed dorms, men's dorms, women's dorms, apartments for married students, apartments for single students, special housing for disabled students, special housing for international students, fraternity/sorority housing. **Special Academic Facilities/Equipment:** Arts center, electron microscope. **Computers:** 5% of classrooms are wired, 100% of classrooms are wireless, 85% of public computers are PCs, 14% of public computers are Macs, 1% of public computers are UNIX, network access in dorm rooms, network access in dorm lounges, online registration, online administrative functions (other than registration), support for handheld computing, remote student-access to Web through college's connection.

CAMPUS LIFE

Activities: Choral groups, concert band, dance, drama/theater, jazz band, literary magazine, marching band, music ensembles, musical theater, pep band, radio station, student government, student newspaper, symphony orchestra, television station, yearbook. **Organizations:** 166 registered organizations, 11 honor societies, 11 religious organizations. 12 fraternities (17% men join), 11 sororities (16% women join). **Athletics (Intercollegiate):** *Men:* Baseball, basketball, cross-country, diving, football, golf, soccer, swimming, tennis, track/field (indoor), track/field (outdoor), wrestling. *Women:* Basketball, cross-country, diving, golf, rugby, soccer, softball, swimming, tennis, track/field (indoor), track/field (outdoor), volleyball. **Environmental initiatives:** Performance contracts have cut 30% off total energy consumption. Performance contracts have cut 50% off potable water consumption. Looking to replace central thermal plant with one that will use sustainable/renewable fuel.

ADMISSIONS

Freshman Academic Profile: 9% in top 10% of high school class, 28% in top 25% of high school class, 62% in top 50% of high school class. ACT middle 50% range 19–23. TOEFL required of all international applicants, minimum paper TOEFL 500, minimum computer TOEFL 173. **Basis for Candidate Selection:** *Very important factors considered include:* Academic GPA, class rank, rigor of secondary school record, standardized test scores. *Other factors considered include:* Application essay, recommendation(s). **Freshman Admission Requirements:** High school diploma is required, and GED is accepted. *Academic units required:* 4 English, 3 math, 3 science (3 science labs), 3 social studies, 2 academic electives. *Academic units recommended:* 2 foreign language. **Freshman Admission Statistics:** 7,495 applied, 73% admitted, 33% enrolled. **Transfer Admission Requirements:** High school transcript, college transcript(s). Minimum college GPA of 2.0 required. **General Admission Information:** Application fee $30. Regular notification is rolling upon receipt of application. Nonfall registration accepted. Credit offered for CEEB Advanced Placement tests.

COSTS AND FINANCIAL AID

Annual in-state tuition $5,832. Annual out-of-state tuition $17,496. Room and board $7,124. Required fees $2,158. Average book expense $120. **Required Forms and Deadlines:** FAFSA. Financial aid filing deadline 3/1. **Notification of Awards:** Applicants will be notified of awards on or about 3/1. **Types of Aid:** *Need-based scholarships/grants:* Pell, SEOG, state scholarships/grants, private scholarships, the school's own gift aid. *Loans:* Direct Subsidized Stafford, Direct Unsubsidized Stafford, Direct PLUS, Federal Perkins, college/university loans from institutional funds. **Student Employment:** Federal Work-Study Program available. Institutional employment available. Off-campus job opportunities are fair. **Financial Aid Statistics:** 24% freshmen, 24% undergrads receive need-based scholarship or grant aid. 37% freshmen, 35% undergrads receive need-based self-help aid. 2 freshmen, 13 undergrads receive athletic scholarships. 53% freshmen, 49% undergrads receive any aid.

EASTERN KENTUCKY UNIVERSITY

SSB CPO 54, 521 Lancaster Avenue, Richmond, KY 40475
Phone: 859-622-2106 **E-mail:** admissions@eku.edu. **CEEB Code:** 1200
Fax: 859-622-8024 **Website:** www.eku.edu **ACT Code:** 1512
Financial Aid Phone: 859-622-2361

This public school was founded in 1906. It has a 675-acre campus.

STUDENTS AND FACULTY

Enrollment: 12,813. **Student Body:** 60% female, 40% male, 12% out-of-state. African American 4%, Caucasian 92%. **Retention and Graduation:** 65% freshmen return for sophomore year. **Faculty:** Student/faculty ratio 17:1. 575 full-time faculty, 72% hold PhDs.

ACADEMICS

Degrees: Associate, bachelor's, certificate, master's, post-bachelor's certificate. **Academic Requirements:** Arts/fine arts, computer literacy, English (including composition), foreign languages, history, humanities, mathematics, sciences (biological or physical), social science. **Classes:** Most classes have 10–19 students. **Majors with Highest Enrollment:** Criminal justice/law enforcement administration, elementary education and teaching, nursing/registered nurse training (RN, ASN, BSN, MSN). **Disciplines with Highest Percentage of Degrees Awarded:** Health professions and related sciences 16%, education 15%, security and protective services 12%, business/marketing 10%, communications/journalism 5%, psychology 5%. **Special Study Options:** Cooperative education program, distance learning, double major, English as a second language (ESL), honors program, independent study, internships, study abroad, teacher certification program.

FACILITIES

Housing: Coed dorms, men's dorms, women's dorms, apartments for married students, special housing for international students, fraternity/sorority housing. **Special Academic Facilities/Equipment:** Hummel Planetarium, Giles Gallery. **Computers:** 100% of classrooms are wireless, 95% of public computers are PCs, 5% of public computers are Macs, network access in dorm rooms, network access in dorm lounges, online registration, online administrative functions (other than registration), support for handheld computing, remote student-access to Web through college's connection.

CAMPUS LIFE

Activities: Choral groups, concert band, dance, drama/theater, jazz band, literary magazine, marching band, music ensembles, musical theater, pep band, radio station, student government, student newspaper, symphony orchestra. **Organizations:** 178 registered organizations, 30 honor societies, 11 religious organizations. 16 fraternities (10% men join), 13 sororities (7% women join). **Athletics (Intercollegiate):** *Men:* Baseball, basketball, cheerleading, cross-country, football, golf, tennis, track/field (indoor), track/field (outdoor). *Women:* Basketball, cheerleading, cross-country, golf, soccer, softball, tennis, track/field (indoor), track/field (outdoor), volleyball.

ADMISSIONS

Freshman Academic Profile: SAT Math middle 50% range 440–450. SAT Critical Reading middle 50% range 440–450. SAT Writing middle 50% range 420–430. ACT middle 50% range 18–19. TOEFL required of all international applicants, minimum paper TOEFL 500, minimum computer TOEFL 173. **Basis for Candidate Selection:** *Very important factors considered include:* Academic GPA, standardized test scores. *Other factors considered include:* Talent/ability. **Freshman Admission Requirements:** High school diploma is required, and GED is accepted. *Academic units required:* 4 English, 3 math, 3 science (1 science lab), 2 foreign language, 3 social studies, 7 academic electives, 3 health. **Freshman Admission Statistics:** 6,774 applied, 72% admitted, 51% enrolled. **Transfer Admission Requirements:** College transcript(s). Minimum college GPA of 2.0 required. Lowest grade transferable D. **General Admission Information:** Application fee $30. Regular application deadline 8/1. Regular notification is rolling. Nonfall registration accepted. Admission may be deferred for a maximum of 1 semester. Credit offered for CEEB Advanced Placement tests.

COSTS AND FINANCIAL AID

Annual in-state tuition $5,682. Annual out-of-state tuition $15,382. Room and board $5,288. Required fees $460. Average book expense $800. **Required Forms and Deadlines:** FAFSA. Financial aid filing deadline 3/15. **Notification of Awards:** Applicants will be notified of awards on a rolling basis beginning on or about 4/1. **Types of Aid:** *Need-based scholarships/grants:* Pell, SEOG, state scholarships/grants, private scholarships, the school's own gift aid. *Loans:* FFEL Subsidized Stafford, FFEL Unsubsidized Stafford, FFEL PLUS, Federal Perkins, college/university loans from institutional funds. **Student Employment:** Federal Work-Study Program available. Institutional employment available. Off-campus job opportunities are good. **Financial Aid Statistics:** 45% freshmen, 40% undergrads receive need-based scholarship or grant aid. 44% freshmen, 46% undergrads receive need-based self-help aid. 81 freshmen, 280 undergrads receive athletic scholarships. 94% freshmen, 86% undergrads receive any aid. Highest amount earned per year from on-campus jobs $1,800.

RATINGS

Admissions Selectivity Rating: 60*   **Fire Safety Rating:** 83   **Green Rating:** 60*

EASTERN MENNONITE UNIVERSITY

1200 Park Road, Harrisonburg, VA 22802
Phone: 540-432-4118 **E-mail:** admiss@emu.edu **CEEB Code:** 5181
Fax: 540-432-4444 **Website:** www.emu.edu **ACT Code:** 3708
Financial Aid Phone: 540-432-4137

This school, affiliated with the Mennonite Church, was founded in 1917. It has a 93-acre campus.

RATINGS
Admissions Selectivity Rating: 60*   **Fire Safety Rating:** 60*   **Green Rating:** 60*

STUDENTS AND FACULTY
Retention and Graduation: 5% grads go on to further study within 1 year. 1% grads pursue arts and sciences degrees. 2% grads pursue medical degrees. **Faculty:** 79% faculty teach undergrads.

ACADEMICS
Majors with Highest Enrollment: Business administration and management, nursing/registered nurse training (RN, ASN, BSN, MSN), psychology.

FACILITIES
Special Academic Facilities/Equipment: D. Ralph Hostetter Museum of Natural History, M. T, Brackbill Planetarium, arboretum, Menno Simons Historical Library. **Computers:** 71% of public computers are PCs, 29% of public computers are Macs, network access in dorm rooms, online administrative functions (other than registration), remote student-access to Web through college's connection.

CAMPUS LIFE
Organizations: 37 registered organizations, 2 honor societies, 4 religious organizations. **Athletics (Intercollegiate):** *Men:* Baseball, basketball, cross-country, soccer, tennis, track/field (indoor), track/field (outdoor), volleyball. *Women:* Basketball, cross-country, field hockey, soccer, softball, tennis, track/field (indoor), track/field (outdoor), volleyball.

ADMISSIONS
Freshman Academic Profile: 64% from public high schools. TOEFL required of all international applicants, minimum paper TOEFL 550, minimum computer TOEFL 213. **General Admission Information:** Credit and/or placement offered for CEEB Advanced Placement tests.

COSTS AND FINANCIAL AID
Student Employment: Federal Work-Study Program available. Institutional employment available. Off-campus job opportunities are good. **Financial Aid Statistics:** 91% freshmen, 93% undergrads receive any aid. Highest amount earned per year from on-campus jobs $3,500.

EASTERN MICHIGAN UNIVERSITY

Eastern Michigan University, 400 Pierce Hall, Ypsilanti, MI 48197
Phone: 734-487-3060 **E-mail:** admissions@emich.edu **CEEB Code:** 1201
Fax: 734-487-1484 **Website:** www.emich.edu **ACT Code:** 1990
Financial Aid Phone: 734-487-0455

This public school was founded in 1849. It has a 460-acre campus.

RATINGS
Admissions Selectivity Rating: 73   **Fire Safety Rating:** 65   **Green Rating:** 60*

STUDENTS AND FACULTY
Enrollment: 17,826. **Student Body:** 59% female, 41% male, 7% out-of-state, 1% international (75 countries represented). African American 18%, Asian 2%, Caucasian 69%, Hispanic 2%. **Retention and Graduation:** 74% freshmen return for sophomore year. 12% freshmen graduate within 4 years. 14% grads go on to further study within 1 year. 8% grads pursue arts and sciences degrees. 1% grads pursue business degrees. 1% grads pursue law degrees. 1% grads pursue medical degrees. **Faculty:** Student/faculty ratio 18:1. 764 full-time faculty, 81% hold PhDs. 100% faculty teach undergrads.

ACADEMICS
Degrees: Bachelor's, doctoral, master's, post-bachelor's certificate, post-master's certificate. **Academic Requirements:** Arts/fine arts, computer literacy, English (including composition), health education, history, humanities,

mathematics, philosophy, physical education, sciences (biological or physical), social science. **Classes:** Most classes have 20–29 students. Most lab/discussion sections have 10–19 students. **Majors with Highest Enrollment:** Business administration/management, elementary education and teaching. **Disciplines with Highest Percentage of Degrees Awarded:** Education 27%, business/marketing 21%, social sciences 8%, health professions and related sciences 7%, communications/journalism 6%, visual and performing arts 6%. **Special Study Options:** Accelerated program, cooperative education program, distance learning, double major, dual enrollment, English as a second language (ESL), honors program, independent study, internships, student-designed major, study abroad, teacher certification program, weekend college. High school students may enroll in college courses, but they are required to apply for admission to Eastern.

FACILITIES
Housing: Coed dorms, apartments for married students, apartments for single students, special housing for disabled students, special housing for international students, fraternity/sorority housing, house rental. **Special Academic Facilities/Equipment:** Intermedia art gallery, paint research center, Sherzer Observatory, Bruce T. Halle Library, Terrestial & Aquatics Ecology Research Facility, Coatings Research Institute, John W. Porter Building housing the College of Education, Marshall Building housing the College of Health and Human Services. **Computers:** 20% of classrooms are wired, 80% of classrooms are wireless, 59% of public computers are PCs, 40% of public computers are Macs, 1% of public computers are UNIX, network access in dorm rooms, network access in dorm lounges, online registration, online administrative functions (other than registration), remote student-access to Web through college's connection.

CAMPUS LIFE
Activities: Choral groups, concert band, dance, drama/theater, jazz band, literary magazine, marching band, music ensembles, musical theater, pep band, radio station, student government, student newspaper, student-run film society, symphony orchestra, television station. **Organizations:** 200 registered organizations, 9 honor societies, 26 religious organizations. 13 fraternities (4% men join), 12 sororities (4% women join). **Athletics (Intercollegiate):** *Men:* Baseball, basketball, cross-country, diving, football, golf, swimming, track/field (indoor), track/field (outdoor), wrestling. *Women:* Basketball, crew/rowing, cross-country, diving, golf, gymnastics, soccer, softball, swimming, tennis, track/field (indoor), track/field (outdoor), volleyball.

ADMISSIONS
Freshman Academic Profile: 10% in top 10% of high school class, 33% in top 25% of high school class, 66% in top 50% of high school class. 85% from public high schools. SAT Math middle 50% range 450–580. SAT Critical Reading middle 50% range 450–570. SAT Writing middle 50% range 430–540. ACT middle 50% range 18–24. TOEFL required of all international applicants, minimum paper TOEFL 500, minimum computer TOEFL 173. **Basis for Candidate Selection:** *Very important factors considered include:* Academic GPA, standardized test scores. *Important factors considered include:* Character/personal qualities. *Other factors considered include:* Extracurricular activities, interview, recommendation(s), rigor of secondary school record, talent/ability, volunteer work. **Freshman Admission Requirements:** High school diploma is required, and GED is accepted. *Academic units recommended:* 4 English, 3 math, 2 science (1 science lab), 2 foreign language, 2 social studies, 1 history, 2 traditional college preparatory classes. **Freshman Admission Statistics:** 9,915 applied, 79% admitted, 30% enrolled. **Transfer Admission Requirements:** College transcript(s). Minimum college GPA of 2.0 required. Lowest grade transferable C. **General Admission Information:** Application fee $30. Regular notification is rolling. Nonfall registration accepted. Admission may be deferred for a maximum of 1 year. Credit and/or placement offered for CEEB Advanced Placement tests.

COSTS AND FINANCIAL AID
Annual in-state tuition $6,390. Annual out-of-state tuition $18,825. Room and board $6,942. Required fees $1,200. Average book expense $900. **Required Forms and Deadlines:** FAFSA. Financial aid filing deadline 3/15. **Notification of Awards:** Applicants will be notified of awards on a rolling basis beginning on or about 3/15. **Types of Aid:** *Need-based scholarships/grants:* Pell, SEOG, state scholarships/grants, private scholarships, the school's own gift aid. *Loans:* FFEL Subsidized Stafford, FFEL Unsubsidized Stafford, FFEL PLUS, Federal Perkins, college/university loans from institutional funds, alternative (private) loans. **Student Employment:** Federal Work-Study Program available. Institutional employment available. Off-campus job opportunities are excellent. **Financial Aid Statistics:** 37% freshmen, 29% undergrads receive need-based scholarship or grant aid. 42% freshmen, 43% undergrads receive need-based self-help aid. 89 freshmen, 375 undergrads receive athletic scholarships. 49% freshmen, 67% undergrads receive any aid. Highest amount earned per year from on-campus jobs $13,375.

EASTERN NAZARENE COLLEGE

23 East Elm Avenue, Quincy, MA 02170-2999
Phone: 617-745-3711 **E-mail:** admissions@enc.edu **CEEB Code:** 3365
Fax: 617-745-3992 **Website:** www.enc.edu
Financial Aid Phone: 617-745-3869

*This private school, affiliated with the Nazarene Church, was founded in
1918. It has a 19-acre campus.*

RATINGS
Admissions Selectivity Rating: 75   **Fire Safety Rating:** 60*   **Green Rating:** 60*

STUDENTS AND FACULTY
Enrollment: 525. **Student Body:** 58% out-of-state. **Retention and
Graduation:** 22% grads go on to further study within 1 year. 17% grads pursue
arts and sciences degrees. 2% grads pursue business degrees. 1% grads pursue
law degrees. 2% grads pursue medical degrees. **Faculty:** Student/faculty ratio
15:1.

ACADEMICS
Degrees: Associate, bachelor's, diploma, first professional certificate, master's.
Academic Requirements: Arts/fine arts, English (including composition),
history, sciences (biological or physical), social science. **Majors with Highest
Enrollment:** Business administration/management, communications studies/
speech communication and rhetoric. **Special Study Options:** Accelerated
program, cooperative education program, double major, honors program,
independent study, internships, study abroad, teacher certification program.

FACILITIES
Housing: Men's dorms, women's dorms, apartments for married students,
special housing for disabled students, men's and women's suites. **Computers:**
Network access in dorm rooms.

CAMPUS LIFE
Activities: Choral groups, drama/theater, music ensembles, musical theater,
radio station, student government, student newspaper, yearbook. **Organizations:** 1 religious organization. **Athletics (Intercollegiate):** *Men:* Baseball,
basketball, cross-country, soccer, tennis. *Women:* Basketball, cross-country,
soccer, softball, tennis, volleyball.

ADMISSIONS
Freshman Academic Profile: 17% in top 10% of high school class, 40% in top
25% of high school class, 64% in top 50% of high school class. TOEFL required
of all international applicants, minimum paper TOEFL 600, minimum
computer TOEFL 250. **Basis for Candidate Selection:** *Very important
factors considered include:* Application essay, interview, recommendation(s),
rigor of secondary school record, standardized test scores. *Other factors
considered include:* Character/personal qualities, class rank, extracurricular
activities, religious affiliation/commitment, talent/ability, volunteer work, work
experience. **Freshman Admission Requirements:** High school diploma is
required, and GED is accepted. *Academic units required:* 4 English, 2 math, 1
science, 2 foreign language, 1 social studies, 1 history. *Academic units
recommended:* 4 math, 4 science, 4 foreign language, 2 social studies, 2 history.
Freshman Admission Statistics: 560 applied, 61% admitted. **Transfer
Admission Requirements:** High school transcript, college transcript(s), essay
or personal statement, interview, standardized test score. Minimum college
GPA of 2.0 required. Lowest grade transferable C. **General Admission
Information:** Application fee $25. Nonfall registration accepted. Common
Application not accepted.

COSTS AND FINANCIAL AID
Annual tuition $17,700. Room & board $6,590. Required fees $610. Average
book expense $500. **Required Forms and Deadlines:** FAFSA, institution's
own financial aid form. **Types of Aid:** *Need-based scholarships/grants:* Pell,
SEOG, state scholarships/grants, private scholarships, the school's own gift aid,
church scholarships. *Loans:* FFEL Subsidized Stafford, FFEL Unsubsidized
Stafford, FFEL PLUS, Federal Perkins, state loans. **Student Employment:**
Federal Work-Study Program available. **Financial Aid Statistics:** 30%
freshmen, 20% undergrads receive need-based scholarship or grant aid. 75%
freshmen, 68% undergrads receive need-based self-help aid. Highest amount
earned per year from on-campus jobs $3,000.

EASTERN NEW MEXICO UNIVERSITY

Station #7, ENMU, Portales, NM 88130
Phone: 505-562-2178 **E-mail:** admissions@enmu.edu **CEEB Code:** 4299
Fax: 505-562-2118 **Website:** www.enmu.edu **ACT Code:** 2636
Financial Aid Phone: 505-562-2194

This public school was founded in 1934. It has a 400-acre campus.

RATINGS
Admissions Selectivity Rating: 73   **Fire Safety Rating:** 82   **Green Rating:** 60*

STUDENTS AND FACULTY
Enrollment: 2,964. **Student Body:** 56% female, 44% male, 19% out-of-state,
1% international (16 countries represented). African American 7%, Asian 1%,
Caucasian 52%, Hispanic 31%, Native American 3%. **Retention and
Graduation:** 52% freshmen return for sophomore year. 8% freshmen graduate
within 4 years. **Faculty:** Student/faculty ratio 16:1. 148 full-time faculty, 78%
hold PhDs. 93% faculty teach undergrads.

ACADEMICS
Degrees: Associate, bachelor's, master's. **Academic Requirements:** Arts/fine
arts, English (including composition), humanities, mathematics, physical well-
being, sciences (biological or physical), social science. **Classes:** Most classes
have 10–19 students. Most lab/discussion sections have 10–19 students. **Majors
with Highest Enrollment:** Biology/biological sciences, business administration and management, elementary education and teaching. **Disciplines with
Highest Percentage of Degrees Awarded:** Education 18%, liberal arts/
general studies 16%, business/marketing 11%, visual and performing arts 6%,
communications/journalism 5%. **Special Study Options:** Accelerated program,
cooperative education program, distance learning, double major, dual
enrollment, exchange student program (domestic), honors program, independent study, internships, student-designed major, study abroad, teacher
certification program.

FACILITIES
Housing: Coed dorms, women's dorms, apartments for married students,
apartments for single students, special housing for disabled students, fraternity/
sorority housing, doubles, private housing, suites. **Special Academic
Facilities/Equipment:** Natural history and historical museums, theater, child
development center, audiovisual center, electron microscopes, laser. **Computers:** 91% of public computers are PCs, 8% of public computers are Macs, 1% of
public computers are UNIX, network access in dorm rooms, online registration,
online administrative functions (other than registration), remote student-access
to Web through college's connection.

CAMPUS LIFE
Activities: Choral groups, concert band, dance, drama/theater, jazz band,
literary magazine, marching band, music ensembles, musical theater, pep band,
radio station, student government, student newspaper, student-run film society,
symphony orchestra, television station. **Organizations:** 60 registered
organizations, 4 honor societies, 4 religious organizations. 4 fraternities, 2
sororities. **Athletics (Intercollegiate):** *Men:* Baseball, basketball, cross-
country, football, rodeo, soccer, track/field (outdoor). *Women:* Basketball, cross-
country, rodeo, soccer, softball, tennis, track/field (outdoor), volleyball.

ADMISSIONS
Freshman Academic Profile: 11% in top 10% of high school class, 29% in top
25% of high school class, 66% in top 50% of high school class. SAT Math middle
50% range 410–530. SAT Critical Reading middle 50% range 390–510. ACT
middle 50% range 16.5–22. TOEFL required of all international applicants,
minimum paper TOEFL 500. **Basis for Candidate Selection:** *Very important
factors considered include:* Academic GPA, rigor of secondary school record,
standardized test scores. *Other factors considered include:* Extracurricular
activities, interview, recommendation(s), talent/ability. **Freshman Admission
Requirements:** High school diploma is required, and GED is accepted.
Academic units recommended: 4 English, 3 math, 4 science, 1 foreign language,
2 social studies. **Freshman Admission Statistics:** 1,649 applied, 70%
admitted, 53% enrolled. **Transfer Admission Requirements:** College
transcript(s), statement of good standing from prior institution(s). Minimum
college GPA of 2.0 required. Lowest grade transferable D. **General Admission
Information:** Regular notification rolling. Nonfall registration accepted.
Admission may be deferred. Credit and/or placement offered for CEEB
Advanced Placement tests.

COSTS AND FINANCIAL AID
Required Forms and Deadlines: FAFSA. Financial aid filing deadline 3/30.
Notification of Awards: Applicants will be notified of awards on or about 4/1.
Types of Aid: *Need-based scholarships/grants:* Pell, SEOG, state scholarships/

grants, the school's own gift aid. *Loans:* FFEL Subsidized Stafford, FFEL Unsubsidized Stafford, FFEL PLUS, Federal Perkins. **Financial Aid Statistics:** 55% freshmen, 57% undergrads receive need-based scholarship or grant aid. 44% freshmen, 50% undergrads receive need-based self-help aid. 75 freshmen, 230 undergrads receive athletic scholarships. 63% freshmen, 66% undergrads receive any aid.

EASTERN OREGON UNIVERSITY

One University Boulevard, LaGrande, OR 97850
Phone: 800-452-3393 **E-mail:** admissions@eou.edu **CEEB Code:** 4300
Fax: 541-962-3418 **Website:** www.eou.edu **ACT Code:** 3460
Financial Aid Phone: 541-962-3550

This public school was founded in 1929. It has a 121-acre campus.

RATINGS
Admissions Selectivity Rating: 84   **Fire Safety Rating:** 60*   **Green Rating:** 60*

STUDENTS AND FACULTY
Enrollment: 2,855. **Student Body:** 61% female, 39% male, 30% out-of-state, 3% international (25 countries represented). African American 1%, Asian 2%, Caucasian 83%, Hispanic 4%, Native American 3%. **Retention and Graduation:** 65% freshmen return for sophomore year. **Faculty:** Student/faculty ratio 28:1. 102 full-time faculty, 62% hold PhDs. 100% faculty teach undergrads.

ACADEMICS
Degrees: Bachelor's, master's. **Academic Requirements:** Arts/fine arts, computer literacy, English (including composition), foreign languages, humanities, mathematics, sciences (biological or physical), senior project, social science. **Classes:** Most classes have 20–29 students. Most lab/discussion sections have 20–29 students. **Disciplines with Highest Percentage of Degrees Awarded:** Business/marketing 30%, liberal arts/general studies 23%, interdisciplinary studies 18%, social sciences 6%, English 4%. **Special Study Options:** Cooperative education program, cross-registration, distance learning, double major, dual enrollment, English as a second language (ESL), exchange student program (domestic), external degree program, honors program, independent study, internships, liberal arts/career combination, student-designed major, study abroad, teacher certification program, weekend college.

FACILITIES
Housing: Coed dorms, men's dorms, women's dorms, apartments for married students. **Special Academic Facilities/Equipment:** Art gallery, archaeological museum, Indian Education Institute, on-campus elementary school. **Computers:** 80% of public computers are PCs, 20% of public computers are Macs, network access in dorm rooms, network access in dorm lounges, online registration, remote student-access to Web through college's connection.

CAMPUS LIFE
Activities: Choral groups, concert band, dance, drama/theater, jazz band, literary magazine, music ensembles, musical theater, radio station, student government, student newspaper, symphony orchestra, television station. **Organizations:** 57 registered organizations, 2 honor societies, 4 religious organizations. **Athletics (Intercollegiate):** *Men:* Baseball, basketball, cheerleading, cross-country, football, rodeo, track/field (indoor), track/field (outdoor). *Women:* Basketball, cheerleading, cross-country, rodeo, soccer, softball, track/field (indoor), track/field (outdoor), volleyball.

ADMISSIONS
Freshman Academic Profile: 23% in top 10% of high school class, 46% in top 25% of high school class, 80% in top 50% of high school class. 98% from public high schools. SAT Math middle 50% range 410–530. SAT Critical Reading middle 50% range 418–530. SAT Writing middle 50% range 400–500. ACT middle 50% range 18–23. TOEFL required of all international applicants, minimum paper TOEFL 520, minimum computer TOEFL 190. **Basis for Candidate Selection:** *Very important factors considered include:* Rigor of secondary school record. *Important factors considered include:* Recommendation(s), talent/ability. *Other factors considered include:* Application essay, class rank, extracurricular activities, first generation, geographical residence, level of applicant's interest, standardized test scores, volunteer work, work experience. **Freshman Admission Requirements:** High school diploma is required, and GED is accepted. *Academic units required:* 4 English, 3 math, 2 science, 2 foreign language. *Academic units recommended:* 1 science lab. **Freshman Admission Statistics:** 941 applied, 43% admitted, 88% enrolled. **Transfer Admission Requirements:** College transcript(s). Minimum college GPA of 2.2 required. Lowest grade transferable D-. **General Admission Information:** Application fee $50. Regular application deadline 9/1. Regular notification is rolling. Nonfall registration accepted. Admission may be deferred

for a maximum of 1 year. Credit offered for CEEB Advanced Placement tests.

COSTS AND FINANCIAL AID
Annual in-state tuition $4,794. Annual out-of-state tuition $4,794. Room and board $8,635. Required fees $1,509. Average book expense $1,152. **Required Forms and Deadlines:** FAFSA. Financial aid filing deadline 3/1. **Notification of Awards:** Applicants will be notified of awards on a rolling basis beginning on or about 4/1. **Types of Aid:** *Need-based scholarships/grants:* Pell, SEOG, state scholarships/grants, private scholarships, the school's own gift aid. *Loans:* Direct Subsidized Stafford, Direct Unsubsidized Stafford, Direct PLUS, FFEL Subsidized Stafford, FFEL Unsubsidized Stafford, FFEL PLUS, Federal Perkins. **Financial Aid Statistics:** 33% freshmen, 39% undergrads receive need-based scholarship or grant aid. 62% freshmen, 63% undergrads receive need-based self-help aid. 30 freshmen, 92 undergrads receive athletic scholarships. 60% freshmen, 66% undergrads receive any aid.

EASTERN UNIVERSITY

1300 Eagle Road, St. Davids, PA 19087-3696
Phone: 610-341-5967 **E-mail:** ugadm@eastern.edu **CEEB Code:** 2220
Fax: 610-341-1723 **Website:** www.eastern.edu **ACT Code:** 3562
Financial Aid Phone: 610-341-5842

This private school, affiliated with the American Baptist Church, was founded in 1952. It has a 107-acre campus.

RATINGS
Admissions Selectivity Rating: 80   **Fire Safety Rating:** 60*   **Green Rating:** 60*

STUDENTS AND FACULTY
Enrollment: 2,054. **Student Body:** 65% female, 35% male, 52% out-of-state, 1% international. African American 12%, Asian 1%, Caucasian 77%, Hispanic 5%. **Retention and Graduation:** 77% freshmen return for sophomore year. 56% freshmen graduate within 4 years. 19% grads go on to further study within 1 year. 24% grads pursue arts and sciences degrees. 4% grads pursue business degrees. 4% grads pursue law degrees. **Faculty:** Student/faculty ratio 13:1. 79 full-time faculty, 78% hold PhDs.

ACADEMICS
Degrees: Associate, bachelor's, master's, post-bachelor's certificate, post-master's certificate. **Academic Requirements:** Biblical and theological studies, English (including composition), foreign languages, history, humanities, mathematics, philosophy, sciences (biological or physical), social science. **Classes:** Most classes have fewer than 10 students. Most lab/discussion sections have 10–19 students. **Majors with Highest Enrollment:** Business, management, marketing, and related support services; elementary education and teaching; social work. **Disciplines with Highest Percentage of Degrees Awarded:** Business/marketing 47%, health professions and related sciences 8%, education 7%, social sciences 7%, communication technologies 5%, psychology 3%. **Special Study Options:** Accelerated program, cross-registration, double major, honors program, independent study, internships, student-designed major, study abroad, teacher certification program.

FACILITIES
Housing: Coed dorms, apartments for single students. **Special Academic Facilities/Equipment:** Planetarium. **Computers:** 92% of public computers are PCs, 8% of public computers are Macs, network access in dorm rooms, network access in dorm lounges, online registration, online administrative functions (other than registration), remote student-access to Web through college's connection.

CAMPUS LIFE
Activities: Choral groups, concert band, dance, drama/theater, jazz band, literary magazine, music ensembles, musical theater, pep band, student government, student newspaper, yearbook. **Organizations:** 94 registered organizations, 10 honor societies, 20 religious organizations. **Athletics (Intercollegiate):** *Men:* Baseball, basketball, golf, soccer, tennis. *Women:* Basketball, field hockey, lacrosse, soccer, softball, tennis, volleyball.

ADMISSIONS
Freshman Academic Profile: 19% in top 10% of high school class, 47% in top 25% of high school class, 79% in top 50% of high school class. 75% from public high schools. SAT Math middle 50% range 490–590. SAT Critical Reading middle 50% range 510–610. ACT middle 50% range 19–31. TOEFL required of all international applicants, minimum paper TOEFL 213, minimum computer TOEFL 213. **Basis for Candidate Selection:** *Very important factors considered include:* Class rank, rigor of secondary school record, standardized test scores. *Important factors considered include:* Application

essay, character/personal qualities, extracurricular activities, recommendation(s), volunteer work. *Other factors considered include:* Alumni/ae relation, interview, religious affiliation/commitment, talent/ability, work experience. **Freshman Admission Requirements:** High school diploma is required, and GED is accepted. **Freshman Admission Statistics:** 1,174 applied, 77% admitted, 43% enrolled. **Transfer Admission Requirements:** High school transcript, college transcript(s), essay or personal statement. Minimum college GPA of 2.0 required. Lowest grade transferable C. **General Admission Information:** Application fee $25. Regular notification within 2–3 weeks of receiving all needed info. Nonfall registration accepted. Admission may be deferred for a maximum of 1 year. Common Application accepted. Credit and/or placement offered for CEEB Advanced Placement tests.

COSTS AND FINANCIAL AID

Annual tuition $17,700. Room & board $7,600. Required fees $40. Average book expense $830. **Required Forms and Deadlines:** FAFSA. **Types of Aid:** *Need-based scholarships/grants:* Pell, SEOG, state scholarships/grants, private scholarships, the school's own gift aid. *Loans:* FFEL Subsidized Stafford, FFEL Unsubsidized Stafford, FFEL PLUS, Federal Perkins, alternative loans. **Financial Aid Statistics:** 64% freshmen, 57% freshmen. Highest amount earned per year from on-campus jobs $1,200.

EASTERN WASHINGTON UNIVERSITY

526 Fifth Street, Cheney, WA 99004
Phone: 509-359-2397 **E-mail:** admissions@mail.ewu.edu **CEEB Code:** 4301
Fax: 509-359-6692 **Website:** www.ewu.edu **ACT Code:** 4454
Financial Aid Phone: 509-359-2314

This public school was founded in 1882. It has a 335-acre campus.

RATINGS

Admissions Selectivity Rating: 60*   **Fire Safety Rating:** 60*   **Green Rating:** 60*

STUDENTS AND FACULTY

Enrollment: 9,553. **Student Body:** 58% female, 42% male, 9% out-of-state, 1% international (35 countries represented). African American 3%, Asian 4%, Caucasian 65%, Hispanic 7%, Native American 2%. **Retention and Graduation:** 78% freshmen return for sophomore year. 21% freshmen graduate within 4 years. **Faculty:** Student/faculty ratio 20:1. 416 full-time faculty, 97% hold PhDs. 98% faculty teach undergrads.

ACADEMICS

Degrees: Bachelor's, doctoral, master's. **Academic Requirements:** Arts/fine arts, computer literacy, cultural/gender diversity, English (including composition), foreign languages, history, humanities, international studies, mathematics, philosophy, sciences (biological or physical), senior capstone, social science. Please note 1 year of college foreign language is required if student doesn't have 2 years of single foreign language in high school. **Classes:** Most classes have 20–29 students. Most lab/discussion sections have 20–29 students. **Disciplines with Highest Percentage of Degrees Awarded:** Business/marketing 23%, education 14%, health professions and related sciences 10%, social sciences 8%, psychology 6%. **Special Study Options:** Cooperative education program, distance learning, double major, dual enrollment, English as a second language (ESL), honors program, independent study, internships, nursing consortium, student-designed major, study abroad, teacher certification program, weekend college.

FACILITIES

Housing: Coed dorms, men's dorms, women's dorms, apartments for married students, special housing for disabled students, fraternity/sorority housing, apartments for students with children. **Special Academic Facilities/Equipment:** Anthropology museum, on-campus elementary school, education lab, primate research center, marine biology lab, ecological studies lab, wildlife refuge, planetarium. **Computers:** 50% of public computers are PCs, 50% of public computers are Macs, network access in dorm rooms, online registration, online administrative functions (other than registration), remote student-access to Web through college's connection.

CAMPUS LIFE

Activities: Choral groups, concert band, dance, drama/theater, jazz band, literary magazine, marching band, music ensembles, pep band, radio station, student government, student newspaper, student-run film society, symphony orchestra. **Organizations:** 100 registered organizations, 14 honor societies, 10 religious organizations. 5 fraternities, 5 sororities. **Athletics (Intercollegiate):** *Men:* Basketball, cross-country, football, golf, tennis, track/field (indoor), track/field (outdoor). *Women:* Basketball, cross-country, golf, soccer, tennis, track/field (indoor), track/field (outdoor), volleyball.

ADMISSIONS

Freshman Academic Profile: 95% from public high schools. TOEFL required of all international applicants, minimum paper TOEFL 525, minimum computer TOEFL 195. **Basis for Candidate Selection:** *Very important factors considered include:* Academic GPA, standardized test scores. *Important factors considered include:* Rigor of secondary school record. *Other factors considered include:* Application essay, interview, recommendation(s). **Freshman Admission Requirements:** High school diploma is required, and GED is accepted. *Academic units required:* 4 English, 3 math, 2 science (1 science lab), 2 foreign language, 3 social studies, 1 fine arts (or add. unit from above) *Academic units recommended:* 4 English, 4 math, 3 science, 2 foreign language, 4 social studies, 1 fine arts. **Freshman Admission Statistics:** 3,700 applied, 82% admitted, 47% enrolled. **Transfer Admission Requirements:** College transcript(s). Minimum college GPA of 2.0 required. Lowest grade transferable D-. **General Admission Information:** Application fee $50. Regular application deadline 8/15. Regular notification is rolling. Nonfall registration accepted. Admission may be deferred for a maximum of 1 year. Credit and/or placement offered for CEEB Advanced Placement tests.

COSTS AND FINANCIAL AID

Required Forms and Deadlines: FAFSA. Financial aid filing deadline 4/1. **Notification of Awards:** Applicants will be notified of awards on a rolling basis beginning on or about 4/1. **Types of Aid:** *Need-based scholarships/grants:* Pell, SEOG, state scholarships/grants, private scholarships, the school's own gift aid. *Loans:* FFEL Subsidized Stafford, FFEL Unsubsidized Stafford, FFEL PLUS, Federal Perkins, Scholarships for disadvantgaged students. **Financial Aid Statistics:** 40% freshmen, 43% undergrads receive need-based scholarship or grant aid. 47% freshmen, 48% undergrads receive need-based self-help aid. 19 freshmen, 83 undergrads receive athletic scholarships. Highest amount earned per year from on-campus jobs $2,457.

EASTMAN SCHOOL OF MUSIC—UNIVERSITY OF ROCHESTER

26 Gibbs Street, Rochester, NY 14604-2599
Phone: 716-274-1060 **E-mail:** esmadmit@mail.rochester.edu **CEEB Code:** 2224
Fax: 716-232-8601 **Website:** www.rochester.edu/eastman **ACT Code:** 2980
Financial Aid Phone: 716-274-1070

This private school was founded in 1921. It has a 5-acre campus.

RATINGS

Admissions Selectivity Rating: 60*   **Fire Safety Rating:** 60*   **Green Rating:** 60*

STUDENTS AND FACULTY

Enrollment: 495. **Student Body:** 56% female, 44% male, 83% out-of-state, 11% international (42 countries represented). African American 3%, Asian 6%, Caucasian 71%, Hispanic 2%. **Retention and Graduation:** 89% freshmen return for sophomore year. 72% freshmen graduate within 4 years. 72% grads go on to further study within 1 year. 72% grads pursue arts and sciences degrees. 3% grads pursue business degrees. 2% grads pursue law degrees. 2% grads pursue medical degrees. **Faculty:** 100% faculty teach undergrads.

ACADEMICS

Degrees: Bachelor's, certificate, diploma, doctoral, master's. **Academic Requirements:** Arts/fine arts, history, humanities. **Special Study Options:** Cooperative education program, double major, English as a second language (ESL), independent study, internships, liberal arts/career combination, study abroad, teacher certification program.

FACILITIES

Housing: Coed dorms, men's dorms, women's dorms, special housing for disabled students, fraternity/sorority housing, housing is handicapped accessible. **Computers:** 35% of public computers are PCs, 60% of public computers are Macs, 5% of public computers are UNIX, network access in dorm rooms, network access in dorm lounges, online administrative functions (other than registration), remote student-access to Web through college's connection.

CAMPUS LIFE

Activities: Choral groups, concert band, dance, jazz band, literary magazine, music ensembles, musical theater, opera, radio station, student government, student newspaper, student-run film society, symphony orchestra. **Organizations:** 8 registered organizations, 3 honor societies, 2 religious organizations. 2 fraternities (16% men join), 1 sorority (15% women join).

ADMISSIONS

Freshman Academic Profile: 80% from public high schools. SAT Math middle 50% range 510–650. SAT Critical Reading middle 50% range 500–650. ACT middle 50% range 22–28. TOEFL required of all international applicants, minimum paper TOEFL 500. **Basis for Candidate Selection:** *Very important factors considered include:* Talent/ability. *Important factors considered include:* Class rank, interview, recommendation(s), rigor of secondary school record, standardized test scores. *Other factors considered include:* Alumni/ae relation, application essay, character/personal qualities, racial/ethnic status. **Freshman Admission Requirements:** High school diploma is required, and GED is accepted. *Academic units recommended:* 4 English. **Freshman Admission Statistics:** 899 applied, 29% admitted, 47% enrolled. **Transfer Admission Requirements:** High school transcript, college transcript(s), statement of good standing from prior institution(s). Minimum college GPA of 2.0 required. Lowest grade transferable C. **General Admission Information:** Application fee $50. Regular application deadline 1/1. Regular notification is rolling. Nonfall registration accepted. Admission may be deferred for a maximum of 1 year. Common Application not accepted. Placement offered for CEEB Advanced Placement tests.

COSTS AND FINANCIAL AID

Annual tuition $20,320. Room & board $7,512. Required fees $484. Average book expense $600. **Required Forms and Deadlines:** FAFSA, institution's own financial aid form, CSS/Financial Aid PROFILE. Financial aid filing deadline 2/1. **Notification of Awards:** Applicants will be notified of awards on or about 4/15. **Types of Aid:** *Need-based scholarships/grants:* Pell, SEOG, state scholarships/grants, private scholarships, the school's own gift aid. *Loans:* Direct Subsidized Stafford, Direct Unsubsidized Stafford, Direct PLUS, Federal Perkins, college/university loans from institutional funds. **Student Employment:** Federal Work-Study Program available. Institutional employment available. Off-campus job opportunities are good. **Financial Aid Statistics:** 51% freshmen, 48% undergrads receive need-based scholarship or grant aid. 51% freshmen, 48% undergrads receive need-based self-help aid. Highest amount earned per year from on-campus jobs $300.

EAST-WEST UNIVERSITY

816 South Michigan Avenue, Chicago, IL 60605
Phone: 312-939-0111 **E-mail:** admissions@eastwest.edu
Fax: 312-939-0083 **Website:** www.eastwest.edu
Financial Aid Phone: 312-939-0111

This private school was founded in 1980.

RATINGS

Admissions Selectivity Rating: 60*   **Fire Safety Rating:** 60*   **Green Rating:** 60*

STUDENTS AND FACULTY

Enrollment: 1,113. **Student Body:** 65% female, 35% male, 14% international. African American 71%, Asian 1%, Caucasian 3%, Hispanic 11%. **Retention and Graduation:** 60% freshmen return for sophomore year. 8% freshmen graduate within 4 years. **Faculty:** Student/faculty ratio 20:1. 14 full-time faculty, 71% hold PhDs.

ACADEMICS

Degrees: Associate, bachelor's. **Academic Requirements:** Arts/fine arts, computer literacy, English (including composition), foreign languages, history, humanities, mathematics, philosophy, sciences (biological or physical), social science. **Classes:** Most classes have more than 100 students. **Majors with Highest Enrollment:** Business administration/management, computer and information sciences, liberal arts and sciences studies and humanities. **Disciplines with Highest Percentage of Degrees Awarded:** Computer and information sciences 3%, English 2%, liberal arts/general studies 2%, business/marketing 2%, engineering 1%. **Special Study Options:** Cooperative education program, double major, independent study, internships.

FACILITIES

Computers: 100% of public computers are PCs, remote student-access to Web through college's connection.

CAMPUS LIFE

Activities: Drama/theater, student government, student newspaper.

ADMISSIONS

Freshman Academic Profile: 80% from public high schools. **Basis for Candidate Selection:** *Very important factors considered include:* State residency. *Other factors considered include:* Application essay, character/personal qualities, extracurricular activities, interview, recommendation(s), rigor

of secondary school record, work experience. **Freshman Admission Requirements:** High school diploma is required, and GED is accepted. **Freshman Admission Statistics:** 947 applied, 90% admitted, 90% enrolled. **Transfer Admission Requirements:** High school transcript, college transcript(s), interview, statement of good standing from prior institution(s). Lowest grade transferable C. **General Admission Information:** Application fee $30. Nonfall registration accepted. Admission may be deferred for a maximum of 1 year. Common Application not accepted.

COSTS AND FINANCIAL AID

Comprehensive fee $9,900. Required fees $495. Average book expense $600. **Required Forms and Deadlines:** FAFSA. Financial aid filing deadline 6/1. **Types of Aid:** *Need-based scholarships/grants:* Pell, SEOG, state scholarships/grants, private scholarships, the school's own gift aid. *Loans:* Direct Subsidized Stafford, Direct Unsubsidized Stafford, FFEL Subsidized Stafford, FFEL PLUS. **Student Employment:** Federal Work-Study Program available.

ECKERD COLLEGE

4200 Fifty-Fourth Avenue South, St. Petersburg, FL 33711
Phone: 727-864-8331 **E-mail:** admissions@eckerd.edu **CEEB Code:** 5223
Fax: 727-866-2304 **Website:** www.eckerd.edu **ACT Code:** 0731
Financial Aid Phone: 727-864-8334

This private school, affiliated with the Presbyterian Church, was founded in 1958. It has a 188-acre campus.

RATINGS

Admissions Selectivity Rating: 82   **Fire Safety Rating:** 60*   **Green Rating:** 88

STUDENTS AND FACULTY

Enrollment: 1,826. **Student Body:** 56% female, 44% male, 75% out-of-state, 4% international (33 countries represented). African American 3%, Asian 2%, Caucasian 78%, Hispanic 4%. **Retention and Graduation:** 78% freshmen return for sophomore year. 53% freshmen graduate within 4 years. 36% grads go on to further study within 1 year. **Faculty:** Student/faculty ratio 13:1. 111 full-time faculty, 93% hold PhDs. 100% faculty teach undergrads.

ACADEMICS

Degrees: Bachelor's. **Academic Requirements:** Arts/fine arts, foreign languages, humanities, information technology competency, mathematics, oral competency, quantitative competency, the Quest for Meaning, sciences (biological or physical), social science, Western heritage in a global context I and II, writing competency. **Classes:** Most classes have 20–29 students. Most lab/discussion sections have 20–29 students. **Majors with Highest Enrollment:** Business administration/management, environmental studies, marine biology and biological oceanography. **Disciplines with Highest Percentage of Degrees Awarded:** Business/marketing 19%, biological/life sciences 16%, social sciences 16%, psychology 10%, visual and performing arts 10%, natural resources/environmental science 9%, communications/journalism 5%. **Special Study Options:** Accelerated program, double major, honors program, independent study, internships, liberal arts/career combination, student-designed major, study abroad.

FACILITIES

Housing: Coed dorms, men's dorms, women's dorms, apartments for single students, suite-style dorms, wellness housing, pet dorms, community service dorms. **Special Academic Facilities/Equipment:** Language lab, oral communications lab, marine science center. **Computers:** 3% of classrooms are wireless, 85% of public computers are PCs, 10% of public computers are Macs, 5% of public computers are UNIX, network access in dorm rooms, network access in dorm lounges, online registration, online administrative functions (other than registration), remote student-access to Web through college's connection.

CAMPUS LIFE

Activities: Choral groups, dance, drama/theater, literary magazine, music ensembles, musical theater, radio station, student government, student newspaper, television station, yearbook. **Organizations:** 53 registered organizations, 8 honor societies, 3 religious organizations. **Athletics (Intercollegiate):** *Men:* Baseball, basketball, golf, sailing, soccer, swimming, tennis, volleyball. *Women:* Basketball, cheerleading, cross-country, sailing, soccer, softball, swimming, tennis, volleyball. **Environmental initiatives:** All students are required to take an "Environmental Perspective" course in order to graduate. Signed the Climate Commitment in May 2007. Have a campus community "Yellow Bikes" program for free campus transportation.

ADMISSIONS

Freshman Academic Profile: SAT Math middle 50% range 500–610. SAT Critical Reading middle 50% range 510–610. SAT Writing middle 50% range 500–600. ACT middle 50% range 22–27. TOEFL required of all international applicants, minimum paper TOEFL 550, minimum computer TOEFL 213. **Basis for Candidate Selection:** *Very important factors considered include:* Academic GPA, rigor of secondary school record. *Important factors considered include:* Application essay, character/personal qualities, extracurricular activities, interview, recommendation(s), standardized test scores, talent/ability. *Other factors considered include:* Alumni/ae relation, class rank, first generation, level of applicant's interest, volunteer work, work experience. **Freshman Admission Requirements:** High school diploma is required, and GED is accepted. *Academic units required:* 4 English, 3 math, 3 science (2 science labs), 2 foreign language, 2 social studies, 1 history, 3 academic electives. *Academic units recommended:* 4 math, 4 science (3 science labs), 3 foreign language, 3 academic electives. **Freshman Admission Statistics:** 2,774 applied, 72% admitted, 27% enrolled. **Transfer Admission Requirements:** College transcript(s), essay or personal statement, statement of good standing from prior institution(s). Minimum college GPA of 2.5 required. Lowest grade transferable C. **General Admission Information:** Application fee $35. Regular notification is rolling. Nonfall registration accepted. Admission may be deferred for a maximum of 1 year. Credit and/or placement offered for CEEB Advanced Placement tests.

COSTS AND FINANCIAL AID

Annual tuition $30,304. Room and board $8,754. Required fees $286. Average book expense $1,000. **Required Forms and Deadlines:** FAFSA. Financial aid filing deadline 3/1. **Notification of Awards:** Applicants will be notified of awards on a rolling basis beginning on or about 2/1. **Types of Aid:** *Need-based scholarships/grants:* Pell, SEOG, state scholarships/grants, private scholarships, the school's own gift aid. *Loans:* FFEL Subsidized Stafford, FFEL Unsubsidized Stafford, FFEL PLUS, Federal Perkins, college/university loans from institutional funds. **Financial Aid Statistics:** 4 freshmen, 17 undergrads receive athletic scholarships. 96% freshmen, 96% undergrads receive any aid.

EDGEWOOD COLLEGE

1000 Edgewood College Drive, Madison, WI 53711-1997
Phone: 608-663-2294 **E-mail:** admissions@edgewood.edu **CEEB Code:** 1202
Fax: 608-663-3291 **Website:** www.edgewood.edu **ACT Code:** 4582
Financial Aid Phone: 608-663-2206

This private school, affiliated with the Roman Catholic Church, was founded in 1927. It has a 55-acre campus.

RATINGS
Admissions Selectivity Rating: 73　　　**Fire Safety Rating:** 60*　　　**Green Rating:** 60*

STUDENTS AND FACULTY

Enrollment: 1,790. **Student Body:** 72% female, 28% male, 5% out-of-state, 1% international (21 countries represented). African American 3%, Asian 2%, Caucasian 82%, Hispanic 2%. **Retention and Graduation:** 66% freshmen return for sophomore year. 30% freshmen graduate within 4 years. 16% grads go on to further study within 1 year. 4% grads pursue arts and sciences degrees. 4% grads pursue business degrees. 2% grads pursue law degrees. 1% grads pursue medical degrees. **Faculty:** Student/faculty ratio 13:1. 101 full-time faculty, 74% hold PhDs. 100% faculty teach undergrads.

ACADEMICS

Degrees: Associate, bachelor's, doctoral, master's. **Academic Requirements:** Arts/fine arts, computer literacy, English (including composition), foreign languages, history, humanities, mathematics, philosophy, sciences (biological or physical), social science. **Classes:** Most classes have 10–19 students. **Majors with Highest Enrollment:** Business administration/management, education, nursing/registered nurse training (RN, ASN, BSN, MSN). **Disciplines with Highest Percentage of Degrees Awarded:** Health professions and related sciences 22%, business/marketing 19%, education 17%, psychology 10%, social sciences 8%. **Special Study Options:** Accelerated program, cross-registration, distance learning, double major, dual enrollment, honors program, independent study, internships, liberal arts/career combination, student-designed major, study abroad, teacher certification program, weekend college.

FACILITIES

Housing: Coed dorms, women's dorms, apartments for single students, special housing for disabled students, student leadership house. **Special Academic Facilities/Equipment:** DeRicci Art Gallery. **Computers:** 71% of public computers are PCs, 29% of public computers are Macs, network access in dorm rooms, network access in dorm lounges, online registration, online administrative functions (other than registration), remote student-access to Web through college's connection.

CAMPUS LIFE

Activities: Choral groups, concert band, dance, drama/theater, jazz band, literary magazine, music ensembles, musical theater, student government, student newspaper, symphony orchestra. **Organizations:** 30 registered organizations, 4 honor societies, 1 religious organization. **Athletics (Intercollegiate):** *Men:* Baseball, basketball, cross-country, golf, soccer, track/field (indoor), track/field (outdoor). *Women:* Basketball, cross-country, golf, soccer, softball, tennis, track/field (indoor), track/field (outdoor), volleyball.

ADMISSIONS

Freshman Academic Profile: 11% in top 10% of high school class, 34% in top 25% of high school class, 73% in top 50% of high school class. 87% from public high schools. ACT middle 50% range 19–25. TOEFL required of all international applicants, minimum paper TOEFL 525, minimum computer TOEFL 197. **Basis for Candidate Selection:** *Very important factors considered include:* Class rank, rigor of secondary school record, standardized test scores. *Important factors considered include:* Interview, talent/ability. *Other factors considered include:* Alumni/ae relation, application essay, character/personal qualities, extracurricular activities, geographical residence, racial/ethnic status, recommendation(s), volunteer work. **Freshman Admission Requirements:** High school diploma is required, and GED is accepted. *Academic units recommended:* 4 English, 2 math, 2 science (1 science lab), 2 foreign language, 2 social studies, 1 history. **Freshman Admission Statistics:** 1,061 applied, 79% admitted, 35% enrolled. **Transfer Admission Requirements:** High school transcript, college transcript(s). Minimum college GPA of 2.0 required. **General Admission Information:** Application fee $25. Regular application deadline 8/26. Regular notification is rolling. Nonfall registration accepted. Admission may be deferred for a maximum of 1 year. Credit and/or placement offered for CEEB Advanced Placement tests.

COSTS AND FINANCIAL AID

Annual tuition $18,000. Room & board $6,056. Average book expense $800. **Required Forms and Deadlines:** FAFSA, institution's own financial aid form. Financial aid filing deadline 3/15. **Notification of Awards:** Applicants will be notified of awards on a rolling basis beginning on or about 3/15. **Types of Aid:** *Need-based scholarships/grants:* Pell, SEOG, state scholarships/grants, private scholarships, the school's own gift aid. *Loans:* FFEL Subsidized Stafford, FFEL Unsubsidized Stafford, FFEL PLUS, Federal Perkins, state loans, college/university loans from institutional funds. **Student Employment:** Off-campus job opportunities are good. **Financial Aid Statistics:** 71% freshmen, 66% undergrads receive need-based scholarship or grant aid. 67% freshmen, 64% undergrads receive need-based self-help aid. Highest amount earned per year from on-campus jobs $1,600.

EDINBORO UNIVERSITY OF PENNSYLVANIA

Edinboro, PA 16444
Phone: 814-732-2761 **E-mail:** eup_admissions@edinboro.edu **CEEB Code:** 2651
Fax: 814-732-2420 **Website:** www.edinboro.edu **ACT Code:** 3702
Financial Aid Phone: 814-732-5555

This public school was founded in 1857. It has a 585-acre campus.

RATINGS
Admissions Selectivity Rating: 70　　　**Fire Safety Rating:** 89　　　**Green Rating:** 84

STUDENTS AND FACULTY

Enrollment: 6,162. **Student Body:** 57% female, 43% male, 10% out-of-state, 1% international (36 countries represented). African American 9%, Caucasian 87%, Hispanic 1%. **Retention and Graduation:** 74% freshmen return for sophomore year. 24% freshmen graduate within 4 years. **Faculty:** Student/faculty ratio 18:1. 363 full-time faculty. 98% faculty teach undergrads.

ACADEMICS

Degrees: Associate, bachelor's, master's, post-bachelor's certificate, post-master's certificate. **Academic Requirements:** Arts/fine arts, computer literacy, English (including composition), history, mathematics, sciences (biological or physical), social science, wellness. **Classes:** Most classes have 20–

29 students. **Majors with Highest Enrollment:** Business administration/management, criminal justice/safety studies, fine/studio arts. **Disciplines with Highest Percentage of Degrees Awarded:** Visual and performing arts 17%, education 13%, security and protective services 9%, communications/journalism 9%, business/marketing 8%. **Special Study Options:** Cooperative education program, cross-registration, distance learning, double major, dual enrollment, honors program, independent study, internships, liberal arts/career combination, student-designed major, study abroad, teacher certification program, weekend college.

FACILITIES

Housing: Coed dorms, women's dorms, special housing for disabled students, special housing for international students, living and learning by major, non-smoking. **Special Academic Facilities/Equipment:** Planetarium, solar observatory, Governor George Leader Speech and Hearing Center. **Computers:** 84% of public computers are PCs, 15% of public computers are Macs, 1% of public computers are UNIX, network access in dorm rooms, network access in dorm lounges, online registration, online administrative functions (other than registration), support for handheld computing, remote student-access to Web through college's connection.

CAMPUS LIFE

Activities: Choral groups, dance, drama/theater, literary magazine, marching band, music ensembles, pep band, radio station, student government, student newspaper, student-run film society, television station. **Organizations:** 157 registered organizations, 10 honor societies, 3 religious organizations. 11 fraternities, 8 sororities. **Athletics (Intercollegiate):** *Men:* Basketball, cross-country, football, swimming, track/field (indoor), track/field (outdoor), wrestling. *Women:* Basketball, cross-country, soccer, softball, swimming, track/field (indoor), track/field (outdoor), volleyball. **Environmental initiatives:** LEED Certification for all new building projects. Use of geothermal heat pumps in new construction and HVAC renovations. Energy conservation programs include lighting retrofits, fuel switch, use of variable speed drives.

ADMISSIONS

Freshman Academic Profile: 6% in top 10% of high school class, 21% in top 25% of high school class, 51% in top 50% of high school class. SAT Math middle 50% range 400–510. SAT Critical Reading middle 50% range 410–520. ACT middle 50% range 15–20. TOEFL required of all international applicants, minimum paper TOEFL 500, minimum computer TOEFL 173. **Basis for Candidate Selection:** *Very important factors considered include:* Academic GPA, class rank, rigor of secondary school record, standardized test scores. *Important factors considered include:* Extracurricular activities, state residency. *Other factors considered include:* Alumni/ae relation, application essay, character/personal qualities, geographical residence, interview, level of applicant's interest, racial/ethnic status, recommendation(s), talent/ability, volunteer work, work experience. **Freshman Admission Requirements:** High school diploma is required, and GED is accepted. *Academic units recommended:* 4 English, 3 math, 3 science, 2 foreign language, 4 social studies, 3 academic electives, 1 keyboarding/computer. **Freshman Admission Statistics:** 3,395 applied, 84% admitted, 74% enrolled. **Transfer Admission Requirements:** High school transcript, college transcript(s), statement of good standing from prior institution(s). Minimum college GPA of 2.0 required. Lowest grade transferable C. **General Admission Information:** Application fee $30. Regular notification is rolling. Nonfall registration accepted. Admission may be deferred for a maximum of 1 year. Credit and/or placement offered for CEEB Advanced Placement tests.

COSTS AND FINANCIAL AID

Annual in-state tuition $5,177. Annual out-of-state tuition $7,766. Room and board $5,718. Required fees $1,509. Average book expense $900. **Required Forms and Deadlines:** FAFSA. Financial aid filing deadline 5/1. **Notification of Awards:** Applicants will be notified of awards on a rolling basis beginning on or about 11/1. **Types of Aid:** *Need-based scholarships/grants:* Pell, SEOG, state scholarships/grants, private scholarships, the school's own gift aid. *Loans:* FFEL Subsidized Stafford, FFEL Unsubsidized Stafford, FFEL PLUS, Federal Perkins, Federal Nursing, alternative loans. **Student Employment:** Federal Work-Study Program available. Institutional employment available. Off-campus job opportunities are good. **Financial Aid Statistics:** 78% freshmen, 72% undergrads receive need-based scholarship or grant aid. 69% freshmen, 66% undergrads receive need-based self-help aid. 128 undergrads receive athletic scholarships. 79% freshmen, 83% undergrads receive any aid. Highest amount earned per year from on-campus jobs $4,200.

ELIZABETH CITY STATE UNIVERSITY

1704 Weeksville Road, Elizabeth City, NC 27909
Phone: 252-335-3305 **E-mail:** admissions@mail.ecsu.edu **CEEB Code:** 5629
Fax: 252-335-3537 **Website:** www.ecsu.edu **ACT Code:** 3095
Financial Aid Phone: 919-335-3283

This public school was founded in 1891. It has a 114-acre campus.

RATINGS

Admissions Selectivity Rating: 66   **Fire Safety Rating:** 60*   **Green Rating:** 60*

STUDENTS AND FACULTY

Enrollment: 2,015. **Student Body:** 62% female, 38% male, 12% out-of-state. African American 77%, Caucasian 22%. **Retention and Graduation:** 39% freshmen graduate within 4 years. 20% grads go on to further study within 1 year. 20% grads pursue arts and sciences degrees. **Faculty:** Student/faculty ratio 12:1. 114 full-time faculty, 70% hold PhDs.

ACADEMICS

Degrees: Bachelor's, master's. **Academic Requirements:** Arts/fine arts, computer literacy, English (including composition), history, mathematics, sciences (biological or physical). **Classes:** Most classes have fewer than 10 students. **Disciplines with Highest Percentage of Degrees Awarded:** Business/marketing 22%, education 12%, social sciences 9%, biological/life sciences 8%, computer and information sciences 7%. **Special Study Options:** Cooperative education program, distance learning, double major, honors program, independent study, internships, liberal arts/career combination, teacher certification program, weekend college.

FACILITIES

Housing: Coed dorms, men's dorms, women's dorms, apartments for single students, college-leased housing available. **Special Academic Facilities/Equipment:** Lab school, planetarium, science complex, music engineering station. **Computers:** 90% of public computers are PCs, 2% of public computers are Macs, 8% of public computers are UNIX, network access in dorm rooms, online registration, online administrative functions (other than registration), remote student-access to Web through college's connection.

CAMPUS LIFE

Activities: Choral groups, concert band, dance, drama/theater, jazz band, literary magazine, marching band, music ensembles, musical theater, pep band, radio station, student government, student newspaper, symphony orchestra, television station, yearbook. **Organizations:** 46 registered organizations, 3 honor societies, 4 religious organizations. 4 fraternities (10% men join), 4 sororities (10% women join). **Athletics (Intercollegiate):** *Men:* Baseball, basketball, cheerleading, cross-country, football, golf, softball, tennis, track/field (outdoor), volleyball. *Women:* Baseball, basketball, cheerleading, cross-country, golf, softball, tennis, track/field (outdoor), volleyball.

ADMISSIONS

Freshman Academic Profile: 5% in top 10% of high school class, 21% in top 25% of high school class, 64% in top 50% of high school class. 99% from public high schools. SAT Math middle 50% range 360–450. SAT Critical Reading middle 50% range 360–450. TOEFL required of all international applicants, minimum paper TOEFL 550. **Basis for Candidate Selection:** *Very important factors considered include:* Character/personal qualities, geographical residence, rigor of secondary school record, standardized test scores, state residency. *Important factors considered include:* Class rank, racial/ethnic status, talent/ability. *Other factors considered include:* Alumni/ae relation, application essay, extracurricular activities, interview, recommendation(s), religious affiliation/commitment, work experience. **Freshman Admission Requirements:** High school diploma is required, and GED is accepted. *Academic units required:* 4 English, 3 math, 3 science, 1 social studies, 1 history, 8 academic electives. *Academic units recommended:* 2 foreign language. **Freshman Admission Statistics:** 1,262 applied, 77% admitted, 48% enrolled. **Transfer Admission Requirements:** High school transcript, college transcript(s), statement of good standing from prior institution(s). Minimum college GPA of 2.0 required. Lowest grade transferable C. **General Admission Information:** Application fee $30. Regular application deadline 8/1. Regular notification after 72 hours of receiving all required information. Nonfall registration accepted. Admission may be deferred for a maximum of 1 year. Common Application not accepted. Credit and/or placement offered for CEEB Advanced Placement tests.

COSTS AND FINANCIAL AID

Required Forms and Deadlines: FAFSA, institution's own financial aid form. **Notification of Awards:** Applicants will be notified of awards on or about 4/1. **Types of Aid:** *Need-based scholarships/grants:* Pell, SEOG, state scholarships/grants, private scholarships, the school's own gift aid. *Loans:* FFEL Subsidized

Stafford, FFEL Unsubsidized Stafford, FFEL PLUS, Federal Perkins, college/university loans from institutional funds. **Student Employment:** Federal Work-Study Program available. Off-campus job opportunities are fair. **Financial Aid Statistics:** Highest amount earned per year from on-campus jobs $643.

ELIZABETHTOWN COLLEGE

Leffler House, One Alpha Drive, Elizabethtown, PA 17022
Phone: 717-361-1400 **E-mail:** admissions@etown.edu **CEEB Code:** 2225
Fax: 717-361-1365 **Website:** www.etown.edu **ACT Code:** 3568
Financial Aid Phone: 717-361-1404

This private school, affiliated with the Church of Brethren, was founded in 1899. It has a 193-acre campus.

RATINGS
Admissions Selectivity Rating: 88   **Fire Safety Rating:** 60*   **Green Rating:** 60*

STUDENTS AND FACULTY
Enrollment: 2,096. **Student Body:** 65% female, 35% male, 32% out-of-state, 2% international (17 countries represented). Asian 2%, Caucasian 82%, Hispanic 1%. **Retention and Graduation:** 84% freshmen return for sophomore year. 64% freshmen graduate within 4 years. 20% grads go on to further study within 1 year. **Faculty:** Student/faculty ratio 13:1. 125 full-time faculty, 82% hold PhDs. 100% faculty teach undergrads.

ACADEMICS
Degrees: Associate, bachelor's, certificate, diploma, master's, post-bachelor's certificate. **Academic Requirements:** Arts/fine arts, English (including composition), foreign cultures and international studies, history, humanities, mathematics, philosophy, physical well-being, sciences (biological or physical), social science. **Classes:** Most classes have 10–19 students. Most lab/discussion sections have 10–19 students. **Majors with Highest Enrollment:** Business administration/management; communications, journalism, and related fields. **Disciplines with Highest Percentage of Degrees Awarded:** Business/marketing 22%, health professions and related sciences 16%, education 14%, communication technologies 9%, social sciences 6%. **Special Study Options:** Accelerated program, cooperative education program, distance learning, double major, dual enrollment, English as a second language (ESL), exchange student program (domestic), honors program, independent study, internships, liberal arts/career combination, study abroad, teacher certification program. 2+2, 3+3, and 4+2 (PT doctoral) programs with Thomas Jefferson University in nursing, physical therapy, laboratory sciences, diagnostic imaging; 3+2 in engineering with Penn State University; 3+2 with Duke University in forestry; 3+3 in physical therapy with Widener University and University of Maryland, Baltimore County; 3+1 in invasive cardiovascular technology with Lancaster Institute for Health Education, articulation agreements with Lehigh University, Rutgers University, Loyola College (MD), and Penn State University, Harrisburg, to satisfy 150-hour requirement in accounting.

FACILITIES
Housing: Coed dorms, women's dorms, apartments for single students, special housing for disabled students, special housing for international students, off-campus houses for student service-learning groups. **Special Academic Facilities/Equipment:** Art gallery, Meetinghouse/Center for Anabaptist and Pietist Studies, chapel/performance center, fourier transform multinuclear NMR spectrometer, blood gas analyzer, scanning densitometer, PCR machine, radiometer/data logger, automated ion analyzer, computerized language lab. **Computers:** 90% of public computers are PCs, 10% of public computers are Macs, network access in dorm rooms, network access in dorm lounges, online registration, online administrative functions (other than registration), remote student-access to Web through college's connection.

CAMPUS LIFE
Activities: Choral groups, concert band, dance, drama/theater, jazz band, literary magazine, music ensembles, musical theater, pep band, radio station, student government, student newspaper, student-run film society, symphony orchestra, television station, yearbook. **Organizations:** 80 registered organizations, 16 honor societies, 6 religious organizations. **Athletics (Intercollegiate):** *Men:* Baseball, basketball, cross-country, diving, golf, lacrosse, soccer, swimming, tennis, track/field (indoor), track/field (outdoor), wrestling. *Women:* Basketball, cross-country, diving, field hockey, lacrosse, soccer, softball, swimming, tennis, track/field (indoor), track/field (outdoor), volleyball.

ADMISSIONS
Freshman Academic Profile: 30% in top 10% of high school class, 65% in top 25% of high school class, 93% in top 50% of high school class. 80% from public high schools. SAT Math middle 50% range 510–630. SAT Critical Reading middle 50% range 510–610. ACT middle 50% range 21–26. TOEFL required of all international applicants, minimum paper TOEFL 525, minimum computer TOEFL 200. **Basis for Candidate Selection:** *Very important factors considered include:* Rigor of secondary school record. *Important factors considered include:* Class rank, interview, racial/ethnic status, recommendation(s), standardized test scores, volunteer work. *Other factors considered include:* Alumni/ae relation, application essay, character/personal qualities, extracurricular activities, geographical residence, religious affiliation/commitment, state residency, talent/ability, work experience. **Freshman Admission Requirements:** High school diploma is required, and GED is accepted. *Academic units required:* 4 English, 3 math, 2 science (2 science labs), 2 foreign language, 2 social studies, 2 history. *Academic units recommended:* 4 English, 4 math, 4 science (3 science labs), 2 foreign language, 2 social studies, 2 history, 2 academic electives. **Freshman Admission Statistics:** 2,923 applied, 64% admitted, 29% enrolled. **Transfer Admission Requirements:** High school transcript, college transcript(s), essay or personal statement, standardized test score. Minimum college GPA of 2.5 required. Lowest grade transferable C. **General Admission Information:** Application fee $30. Regular notification is rolling. Nonfall registration accepted. Admission may be deferred for a maximum of 1 year. Common Application accepted. Credit and/or placement offered for CEEB Advanced Placement tests.

COSTS AND FINANCIAL AID
Annual tuition $26,950. Room and board $7,300. Average book expense $700. **Required Forms and Deadlines:** FAFSA, institution's own financial aid form, federal tax records. Financial aid filing deadline 3/15. **Notification of Awards:** Applicants will be notified of awards on a rolling basis beginning on or about 3/1. **Types of Aid:** *Need-based scholarships/grants:* Pell, SEOG, state scholarships/grants, private scholarships, the school's own gift aid. *Loans:* FFEL Subsidized Stafford, FFEL Unsubsidized Stafford, FFEL PLUS, Federal Perkins, state loans. **Financial Aid Statistics:** 71% freshmen, 71% undergrads receive need-based scholarship or grant aid. 59% freshmen, 61% undergrads receive need-based self-help aid. 95% freshmen, 95% undergrads receive any aid.

ELMHURST COLLEGE

190 South Prospect Avenue, Elmhurst, IL 60126
Phone: 630-617-3400 **E-mail:** admit@elmhurst.edu **CEEB Code:** 1204
Fax: 630-617-5501 **Website:** www.elmhurst.edu **ACT Code:** 1020
Financial Aid Phone: 630-617-3075

This private school, affiliated with the United Church of Christ, was founded in 1871. It has a 38-acre campus.

RATINGS
Admissions Selectivity Rating: 60*   **Fire Safety Rating:** 60*   **Green Rating:** 60*

STUDENTS AND FACULTY
Enrollment: 2,717. **Student Body:** 66% female, 34% male, 8% out-of-state, 1% international (29 countries represented). African American 4%, Asian 3%, Caucasian 71%, Hispanic 6%. **Retention and Graduation:** 82% freshmen return for sophomore year. 17% grads go on to further study within 1 year. 8% grads pursue business degrees. 1% grads pursue law degrees. 2% grads pursue medical degrees. **Faculty:** Student/faculty ratio 13:1. 117 full-time faculty, 89% hold PhDs. 100% faculty teach undergrads.

ACADEMICS
Degrees: Bachelor's, master's. **Academic Requirements:** Arts/fine arts, English (including composition), foreign languages, history, humanities, Judeo-Christian Heritage, philosophy, sciences (biological or physical), social science. **Classes:** Most classes have 10–19 students. **Majors with Highest Enrollment:** Business administration and management; elementary education and teaching; nursing/registered nurse training (ASN, BSN, MSN, RN). **Disciplines with Highest Percentage of Degrees Awarded:** Business/marketing 25%, education 16%, health professions and related sciences 8%, social sciences 8%, English 5%, psychology 5%, visual and performing arts 5%, communications/journalism 4%. **Special Study Options:** Accelerated program, cooperative education program, double major, dual enrollment, honors program, independent study, internships, study abroad, teacher certification program.

FACILITIES

Housing: Coed dorms, apartments for single students. **Special Academic Facilities/Equipment:** Accelerator/art space, language lab, recording studio, computer science/technology center, 4 electron microscopes. **Computers:** 90% of public computers are PCs, 9% of public computers are Macs, 1% of public computers are UNIX, network access in dorm rooms, network access in dorm lounges, online registration, online administrative functions (other than registration), support for handheld computing, remote student-access to Web through college's connection.

CAMPUS LIFE

Activities: Choral groups, concert band, drama/theater, jazz band, literary magazine, music ensembles, musical theater, pep band, radio station, student government, student newspaper, yearbook. **Organizations:** 106 registered organizations, 15 honor societies, 6 religious organizations. 3 fraternities (11% men join), 6 sororities (10% women join). **Athletics (Intercollegiate):** *Men:* Baseball, basketball, cross-country, football, golf, soccer, tennis, track/field (outdoor), wrestling. *Women:* Basketball, bowling, cross-country, golf, soccer, softball, tennis, track/field (outdoor), volleyball.

ADMISSIONS

Freshman Academic Profile: 92% from public high schools. SAT Math middle 50% range 480–620. SAT Critical Reading middle 50% range 470–630. SAT Writing middle 50% range 480–630. ACT middle 50% range 22–26. TOEFL required of all international applicants, minimum paper TOEFL 550, minimum computer TOEFL 213. **Basis for Candidate Selection:** *Very important factors considered include:* Academic GPA, class rank, rigor of secondary school record, standardized test scores. *Important factors considered include:* Application essay, interview, recommendation(s). *Other factors considered include:* Alumni/ae relation, character/personal qualities, extracurricular activities, talent/ability. **Freshman Admission Requirements:** High school diploma is required, and GED is accepted. *Academic units required:* 4 English, 2 math, 2 science, (2 science labs), 1 foreign language, 2 social studies, 1 history, 4 academic electives, *Academic units recommended:* 4 English, 3 math, 3 science (3 science labs), 2 foreign language, 3 social studies, 2 history, 4 academic electives. **Freshman Admission Statistics:** 1,952 applied, 72% admitted, 34% enrolled. **Transfer Admission Requirements:** High school transcript, college transcript(s), statement of good standing from prior institution(s). Minimum college GPA of 2.6 required. Lowest grade transferable C. **General Admission Information:** Regular application deadline 7/15. Regular notification is rolling. Nonfall registration accepted. Admission may be deferred for a maximum of 2 years. Credit offered for CEEB Advanced Placement tests.

COSTS AND FINANCIAL AID

Annual tuition $23,100. Room & board $6,825. Required fees $60. Average book expense $1,000. **Required Forms and Deadlines:** FAFSA. Financial aid filing deadline 4/15. **Notification of Awards:** Applicants will be notified of awards on a rolling basis beginning on or about 2/21. **Types of Aid:** *Need-based scholarships/grants:* Pell, SEOG, state scholarships/grants, private scholarships, the school's own gift aid. *Loans:* Direct Subsidized Stafford, Direct Unsubsidized Stafford, Direct PLUS, Federal Perkins. **Student Employment:** Federal Work-Study Program available. Institutional employment available. Off-campus job opportunities are excellent. **Financial Aid Statistics:** 65% freshmen, 62% undergrads receive need-based scholarship or grant aid. 61% freshmen, 63% undergrads receive need-based self-help aid. 95% freshmen, 87% undergrads receive any aid. Highest amount earned per year from on-campus jobs $3,000.

See page 1160.

ELMIRA COLLEGE

One Park Place, Elmira, NY 14901
Phone: 607-735-1724 **E-mail:** admissions@elmira.edu **CEEB Code:** 2226
Fax: 607-735-1718 **Website:** www.elmira.edu **ACT Code:** 2736
Financial Aid Phone: 607-735-1728

This private school was founded in 1855. It has a 50-acre campus.

RATINGS

Admissions Selectivity Rating: 86   **Fire Safety Rating:** 60*   **Green Rating:** 60*

STUDENTS AND FACULTY

Enrollment: 1,363. **Student Body:** 71% female, 29% male, 51% out-of-state, 5% international (20 countries represented). African American 1%, Caucasian 67%, Hispanic 1%. **Retention and Graduation:** 84% freshmen return for sophomore year. 55% freshmen graduate within 4 years. 47% grads go on to further study within 1 year. 35% grads pursue arts and sciences degrees. 9% grads pursue business degrees. 2% grads pursue law degrees. 1% grads pursue medical degrees. **Faculty:** Student/faculty ratio 12:1. 81 full-time faculty, 63% hold PhDs. 100% faculty teach undergrads.

ACADEMICS

Degrees: Bachelor's, master's. **Academic Requirements:** Arts/fine arts, English (including composition), humanities, mathematics, sciences (biological or physical), social science. **Classes:** Most classes have 10–19 students. Most lab/discussion sections have 10–19 students. **Majors with Highest Enrollment:** Business administration/management, elementary education and teaching, psychology. **Disciplines with Highest Percentage of Degrees Awarded:** Business/marketing 24%, education 21%, health professions and related sciences 10%, social sciences 9%, psychology 7%. **Special Study Options:** Accelerated program, double major, English as a second language (ESL), exchange student program (domestic), independent study, internships, liberal arts/career combination, student-designed major, study abroad, teacher certification program.

FACILITIES

Housing: Coed dorms, women's dorms, apartments for single students, special housing for disabled students. **Special Academic Facilities/Equipment:** Center for Mark Twain Studies, American Studies Center. **Computers:** 80% of public computers are PCs, 20% of public computers are Macs, network access in dorm rooms, remote student-access to Web through college's connection.

CAMPUS LIFE

Activities: Choral groups, concert band, dance, drama/theater, literary magazine, music ensembles, musical theater, pep band, radio station, student government, student newspaper, yearbook. **Organizations:** 85 registered organizations, 13 honor societies, 3 religious organizations. **Athletics (Intercollegiate):** *Men:* Basketball, cheerleading, golf, ice hockey, lacrosse, soccer, tennis. *Women:* Basketball, cheerleading, field hockey, golf, ice hockey, lacrosse, soccer, softball, tennis, volleyball.

ADMISSIONS

Freshman Academic Profile: 30% in top 10% of high school class, 65% in top 25% of high school class, 98% in top 50% of high school class. 65% from public high schools. SAT Math middle 50% range 480–590. SAT Critical Reading middle 50% range 480–600. ACT middle 50% range 19–26. TOEFL required of all international applicants, minimum paper TOEFL 500, minimum computer TOEFL 173. **Basis for Candidate Selection:** *Very important factors considered include:* Academic GPA, character/personal qualities, class rank, rigor of secondary school record. *Important factors considered include:* Application essay, extracurricular activities, recommendation(s), standardized test scores. *Other factors considered include:* Alumni/ae relation, first generation, geographical residence, interview, level of applicant's interest, racial/ethnic status, talent/ability, volunteer work, work experience. **Freshman Admission Requirements:** High school diploma is required, and GED is accepted. *Academic units required:* 4 English, 3 math, 3 science (2 science labs), 3 social studies, 1 history, 2 academic electives. *Academic units recommended:* 2 foreign language. **Freshman Admission Statistics:** 2,118 applied, 68% admitted, 25% enrolled. **Transfer Admission Requirements:** College transcript(s), essay or personal statement, statement of good standing from prior institution(s). Minimum college GPA of 2.0 required. Lowest grade transferable C-. **General Admission Information:** Application fee $50. Early decision application deadline 11/15. Regular application deadline 3/1. Regular notification is rolling. Nonfall registration accepted. Admission may be deferred for a maximum of 1 year. Credit and/or placement offered for CEEB Advanced Placement tests.

COSTS AND FINANCIAL AID

Annual tuition $29,000. Room & board $9,100. Required fees $1,050. Average book expense $450. **Required Forms and Deadlines:** FAFSA, state aid form, state aid forms if applicable (NY, VT, RI). Financial aid filing deadline 6/30. **Notification of Awards:** Applicants will be notified of awards on a rolling basis beginning on or about 2/1. **Types of Aid:** *Need-based scholarships/grants:* Pell, SEOG, state scholarships/grants, private scholarships, the school's own gift aid. *Loans:* FFEL Subsidized Stafford, FFEL Unsubsidized Stafford, FFEL PLUS, Federal Perkins, college/university loans from institutional funds, GATE Student Loan, private alternative loans. **Student Employment:** Federal Work-Study Program available. Institutional employment available. Off-campus job opportunities are good. **Financial Aid Statistics:** 82% freshmen, 78% undergrads receive need-based scholarship or grant aid. 69% freshmen, 65% undergrads receive need-based self-help aid. 80% freshmen, 80% undergrads receive any aid. Highest amount earned per year from on-campus jobs $1,000.

ELMS COLLEGE

291 Springfield Street, Chicopee, MA 01013
Phone: 413-592-3189 **E-mail:** admissions@elms.edu **CEEB Code:** 3283
Fax: 413-594-2781 **Website:** www.elms.edu **ACT Code:** 1812
Financial Aid Phone: 413-594-2761

This private school, affiliated with the Roman Catholic Church, was founded in 1928. It has a 32-acre campus.

RATINGS
Admissions Selectivity Rating: 71   **Fire Safety Rating:** 60*   **Green Rating:** 60*

STUDENTS AND FACULTY
Enrollment: 685. **Student Body:** 81% female, 19% male, 17% out-of-state. African American 3%, Asian 1%, Caucasian 53%, Hispanic 2%. **Retention and Graduation:** 62% freshmen return for sophomore year. 48% freshmen graduate within 4 years. **Faculty:** Student/faculty ratio 12:1. 44 full-time faculty, 75% hold PhDs. 100% faculty teach undergrads.

ACADEMICS
Degrees: Associate, bachelor's, certificate, master's. **Academic Requirements:** Arts/fine arts, community service, computer literacy, English (including composition), foreign languages, history, humanities, mathematics, philosophy, sciences (biological or physical), social science. **Classes:** Most classes have fewer than 10 students. **Majors with Highest Enrollment:** Education, nursing/registered nurse training (RN, ASN, BSN, MSN), social work. **Disciplines with Highest Percentage of Degrees Awarded:** Health professions and related sciences 25%, business/marketing 19%, social sciences 12%, psychology 10%, education 7%. **Special Study Options:** Cross-registration, distance learning, double major, English as a second language (ESL), exchange student program (domestic), honors program, independent study, internships, liberal arts/career combination, study abroad, teacher certification program, weekend college.

FACILITIES
Housing: Coed dorms, women's dorms. **Special Academic Facilities/Equipment:** Art gallery, rare book gallery with Edward Bellamy collection of rare manuscripts. **Computers:** 94% of public computers are PCs, 6% of public computers are Macs, network access in dorm rooms, network access in dorm lounges, remote student-access to Web through college's connection.

CAMPUS LIFE
Activities: Choral groups, dance, drama/theater, literary magazine, radio station, student government, student newspaper, yearbook. **Organizations:** 25 registered organizations, 6 honor societies, 1 religious organization. **Athletics (Intercollegiate):** *Men:* Basketball, cross-country, golf, soccer, swimming, volleyball. *Women:* Basketball, cross-country, equestrian sports, field hockey, lacrosse, soccer, softball, swimming, volleyball.

ADMISSIONS
Freshman Academic Profile: 13% in top 10% of high school class, 40% in top 25% of high school class, 67% in top 50% of high school class. 86% from public high schools. SAT Math middle 50% range 430–640. SAT Critical Reading middle 50% range 430–530. TOEFL required of all international applicants, minimum paper TOEFL 450. **Basis for Candidate Selection:** *Very important factors considered include:* Alumni/ae relation, application essay, rigor of secondary school record. *Important factors considered include:* Character/personal qualities, class rank, extracurricular activities, interview, recommendation(s), standardized test scores, volunteer work. *Other factors considered include:* Talent/ability, work experience. **Freshman Admission Requirements:** High school diploma is required, and GED is accepted. *Academic units required:* 4 English, 2 math, 2 science (2 science labs), 2 foreign language, 1 social studies, 1 history. *Academic units recommended:* 4 English, 4 math, 4 science (2 science labs), 4 foreign language, 2 social studies, 2 history. **Freshman Admission Statistics:** 384 applied, 90% admitted, 41% enrolled. **Transfer Admission Requirements:** High school transcript, college transcript(s), essay or personal statement, interview. Minimum college GPA of 2.0 required. Lowest grade transferable C. **General Admission Information:** Application fee $30. Regular notification is rolling. Nonfall registration accepted. Admission may be deferred for a maximum of 1 year. Common Application accepted. Credit and/or placement offered for CEEB Advanced Placement tests.

COSTS AND FINANCIAL AID
Annual tuition $16,490. Room & board $6,490. Required fees $670. Average book expense $600. **Required Forms and Deadlines:** FAFSA, institution's own financial aid form, state aid form. Financial aid filing deadline 3/1. **Notification of Awards:** Applicants will be notified of awards on a rolling basis

beginning on or about 2/15. **Types of Aid:** *Need-based scholarships/grants:* Pell, SEOG, state scholarships/grants, private scholarships, the school's own gift aid. *Loans:* FFEL Subsidized Stafford, FFEL Unsubsidized Stafford, FFEL PLUS, Federal Perkins, state loans, alternative loan sources. **Student Employment:** Federal Work-Study Program available. Institutional employment available. Off-campus job opportunities are good. **Financial Aid Statistics:** 82% freshmen, 84% undergrads receive need-based scholarship or grant aid. 76% freshmen, 79% undergrads receive need-based self-help aid.

ELON UNIVERSITY

100 Campus Drive, 2700 Campus Box, Elon, NC 27244-2010
Phone: 336-278-3566 **E-mail:** admissions@elon.edu **CEEB Code:** 5183
Fax: 336-278-7699 **Website:** www.elon.edu **ACT Code:** 3096
Financial Aid Phone: 336-278-7640

This private school, affiliated with the United Church of Christ, was founded in 1889. It has a 575-acre campus.

RATINGS
Admissions Selectivity Rating: 92   **Fire Safety Rating:** 79   **Green Rating:** 94

STUDENTS AND FACULTY
Enrollment: 4,849. **Student Body:** 60% female, 40% male, 71% out-of-state, 2% international (42 countries represented). African American 7%, Asian 1%, Caucasian 84%, Hispanic 2%. **Retention and Graduation:** 89% freshmen return for sophomore year. 65% freshmen graduate within 4 years. 20% grads go on to further study within 1 year. 10% grads pursue arts and sciences degrees. 2% grads pursue business degrees. 3% grads pursue law degrees. 2% grads pursue medical degrees. **Faculty:** Student/faculty ratio 14:1. 291 full-time faculty, 84% hold PhDs. 100% faculty teach undergrads.

ACADEMICS
Degrees: Bachelor's, doctoral, first professional, master's. **Academic Requirements:** English (including composition), foreign languages, humanities, mathematics, sciences (biological or physical), social science. **Classes:** Most classes have 10–19 students. Most lab/discussion sections have 10–19 students. **Majors with Highest Enrollment:** Business administration/management, education, mass communications/media studies. **Disciplines with Highest Percentage of Degrees Awarded:** Business/marketing 22%, communication technologies 19%, education 12%, psychology 7%, visual and performing arts 6%. **Special Study Options:** Accelerated program, cross-registration, distance learning, double major, dual enrollment, English as a second language (ESL), exchange student program (domestic), honors program, independent study, internships, liberal arts/career combination, student-designed major, study abroad, teacher certification program.

FACILITIES
Housing: Coed dorms, men's dorms, women's dorms, apartments for single students, special housing for international students, fraternity/sorority housing, theme housing. **Special Academic Facilities/Equipment:** Resource center, fine arts center with recital hall, theater, television studios, music rooms, campus center, athletic center, art gallery. **Computers:** 100% of classrooms are wired, 100% of classrooms are wireless, 90% of public computers are PCs, 10% of public computers are Macs, network access in dorm rooms, network access in dorm lounges, online registration, online administrative functions (other than registration), support for handheld computing, remote student-access to Web through college's connection.

CAMPUS LIFE
Activities: Choral groups, concert band, dance, drama/theater, jazz band, literary magazine, marching band, music ensembles, musical theater, pep band, radio station, student government, student newspaper, student-run film society, symphony orchestra, television station. **Organizations:** 140 registered organizations, 24 honor societies, 9 religious organizations. 11 fraternities (18% men join), 11 sororities (31% women join). **Athletics (Intercollegiate):** *Men:* Baseball, basketball, cheerleading, cross-country, football, golf, soccer, tennis. *Women:* Basketball, cheerleading, cross-country, golf, soccer, softball, tennis, track/field (indoor), track/field (outdoor), volleyball. **Environmental initiatives:** Energy reduction campaign of 6%. Recycling campaign with other colleges (RecycleMania). More than $1 million committed to biodiesel transportation.

ADMISSIONS

Freshman Academic Profile: 30% in top 10% of high school class, 64% in top 25% of high school class, 92% in top 50% of high school class. 82% from public high schools. SAT Math middle 50% range 570–660. SAT Critical Reading middle 50% range 560–650. SAT Writing middle 50% range 560–660. ACT middle 50% range 24–28. TOEFL required of all international applicants, minimum paper TOEFL 550, minimum computer TOEFL 213. **Basis for Candidate Selection:** *Very important factors considered include:* Academic GPA, rigor of secondary school record, standardized test scores. *Important factors considered include:* Alumni/ae relation, application essay, extracurricular activities, recommendation(s), talent/ability. *Other factors considered include:* Character/personal qualities, class rank, first generation, level of applicant's interest, racial/ethnic status, state residency, volunteer work, work experience. **Freshman Admission Requirements:** High school diploma is required, and GED is accepted. *Academic units required:* 4 English, 3 math, 3 science (1 science lab), 2 foreign language, 1 social studies, 1 history. *Academic units recommended:* 4 math, 3 foreign language, 2 social studies. **Freshman Admission Statistics:** 9,204 applied, 42% admitted, 33% enrolled. **Transfer Admission Requirements:** High school transcript, college transcript(s), standardized test score, statement of good standing from prior institution(s). Minimum college GPA of 2.5 required. Lowest grade transferable C-. **General Admission Information:** Application fee $40. Early decision application deadline 11/1. Regular application deadline 1/10. Regular notification 12/20. Nonfall registration not accepted. Admission may be deferred for a maximum of 1 year. Credit and/or placement offered for CEEB Advanced Placement tests.

COSTS AND FINANCIAL AID

Annual tuition $21,886. Room and board $7,296. Required fees $280. Average book expense $900. **Required Forms and Deadlines:** FAFSA, institution's own financial aid form, CSS/Financial Aid PROFILE. Financial aid filing deadline 2/15. **Notification of Awards:** Applicants will be notified of awards on a rolling basis beginning on or about 3/30. **Types of Aid:** *Need-based scholarships/grants:* Pell, SEOG, state scholarships/grants, private scholarships, the school's own gift aid. *Loans:* FFEL Subsidized Stafford, FFEL Unsubsidized Stafford, FFEL PLUS, Federal Perkins, state loans, college/university loans from institutional funds, privately funded alternative loans. **Student Employment:** Federal Work-Study Program available. Institutional employment available. Off-campus job opportunities are good. **Financial Aid Statistics:** 28% freshmen, 29% undergrads receive need-based scholarship or grant aid. 28% freshmen, 26% undergrads receive need-based self-help aid. 73 freshmen, 275 undergrads receive athletic scholarships. 69% freshmen, 70% undergrads receive any aid. Highest amount earned per year from on-campus jobs $3,200.

EMBRY RIDDLE AERONAUTICAL UNIVERSITY (AZ)

3700 Willow Creek Road, Prescott, AZ 86301-3720
Phone: 928-777-6600 **E-mail:** pradmit@erau.edu **CEEB Code:** 4305
Fax: 928-777-6606 **Website:** www.embryriddle.edu **ACT Code:** 0725
Financial Aid Phone: 800-888-3728

This private school was founded in 1926. It has a 539-acre campus.

RATINGS

Admissions Selectivity Rating: 82   **Fire Safety Rating:** 60*   **Green Rating:** 60*

STUDENTS AND FACULTY

Enrollment: 1,622. **Student Body:** 17% female, 83% male, 79% out-of-state, 4% international (29 countries represented). African American 2%, Asian 7%, Caucasian 68%, Hispanic 7%. **Retention and Graduation:** 73% freshmen return for sophomore year. 30% freshmen graduate within 4 years. **Faculty:** Student/faculty ratio 14:1. 100 full-time faculty, 67% hold PhDs. 100% faculty teach undergrads.

ACADEMICS

Degrees: Bachelor's, master's. **Academic Requirements:** English (including composition), flight and engineering labs, foreign languages, humanities, mathematics, sciences (biological or physical), social science. **Classes:** Most classes have 10–19 students. Most lab/discussion sections have fewer than 10 students. **Majors with Highest Enrollment:** Aeronautics/aviation/aerospace science and technology; aerospace, aeronautical, and astronautical engineering; airline/commercial/professional pilot and flight crew. **Disciplines with Highest Percentage of Degrees Awarded:** Transportation and materials moving 59%, engineering 26%, social sciences 10%, interdisciplinary studies 3%, computer and information sciences 2%. **Special Study Options:**

Accelerated program, cooperative education program, distance learning, double major, dual enrollment, English as a second language (ESL), flight training, honors program, independent study, internships, student-designed major, study abroad.

FACILITIES

Housing: Coed dorms, apartments for single students. **Special Academic Facilities/Equipment:** Fully equipped aircraft, training simulators, airway science simulation lab, wind tunnel. **Computers:** 80% of public computers are PCs, 10% of public computers are Macs, 10% of public computers are UNIX, network access in dorm rooms, network access in dorm lounges, online administrative functions (other than registration), remote student-access to Web through college's connection.

CAMPUS LIFE

Activities: Dance, literary magazine, music ensembles, radio station, student government, student newspaper. **Organizations:** 82 registered organizations, 2 honor societies, 2 religious organizations. 6 fraternities (12% men join), 3 sororities (15% women join). **Athletics (Intercollegiate):** *Men:* Soccer, wrestling. *Women:* Soccer, volleyball.

ADMISSIONS

Freshman Academic Profile: 27% in top 10% of high school class, 54% in top 25% of high school class, 83% in top 50% of high school class. SAT Math middle 50% range 510–610. SAT Critical Reading middle 50% range 480–590. ACT middle 50% range 22–28. TOEFL required of all international applicants, minimum paper TOEFL 500, minimum computer TOEFL 173. **Basis for Candidate Selection:** *Very important factors considered include:* Academic GPA, class rank, standardized test scores. *Important factors considered include:* Recommendation(s). *Other factors considered include:* Alumni/ae relation, application essay, character/personal qualities, extracurricular activities, interview, level of applicant's interest, rigor of secondary school record, volunteer work, work experience. **Freshman Admission Requirements:** High school diploma is required, and GED is accepted. *Academic units required:* 4 English, 3 math, 2 science (2 science labs), 2 social studies, 1 history, 4 academic electives. *Academic units recommended:* 4 English, 4 math, 3 science (3 science labs), 2 foreign language, 2 social studies, 1 history, 2 academic electives. **Freshman Admission Statistics:** 1,229 applied, 88% admitted, 37% enrolled. **Transfer Admission Requirements:** College transcript(s). Minimum college GPA of 2.0 required. Lowest grade transferable C. **General Admission Information:** Application fee $50. Regular notification is rolling. Nonfall registration accepted. Admission may be deferred for a maximum of 1 year. Credit and/or placement offered for CEEB Advanced Placement tests.

COSTS AND FINANCIAL AID

Annual tuition $25,400. Room & board $7,214. Required fees $730. Average book expense $950. **Required Forms and Deadlines:** FAFSA. **Notification of Awards:** Applicants will be notified of awards on a rolling basis beginning on or about 3/1. **Types of Aid:** *Need-based scholarships/grants:* Pell, SEOG, state scholarships/grants, private scholarships, the school's own gift aid. *Loans:* FFEL Subsidized Stafford, FFEL Unsubsidized Stafford, FFEL PLUS, Federal Perkins. **Financial Aid Statistics:** 70% freshmen, 62% undergrads receive need-based scholarship or grant aid. 53% freshmen, 54% undergrads receive need-based self-help aid. 11 freshmen, 59 undergrads receive athletic scholarships. 70% freshmen, 90% undergrads receive any aid.

See page 1162.

EMBRY RIDDLE AERONAUTICAL UNIVERSITY (FL)

600 South Clyde Morris Boulevard, Daytona Beach, FL 32114-3900
Phone: 386-226-6100 **E-mail:** dbadmit@erau.edu **CEEB Code:** 5190
Fax: 386-226-7070 **Website:** www.erau.edu **ACT Code:** 0725
Financial Aid Phone: 800-226-6307

This private school was founded in 1926. It has a 185-acre campus.

RATINGS

Admissions Selectivity Rating: 80   **Fire Safety Rating:** 60*   **Green Rating:** 60*

STUDENTS AND FACULTY

Enrollment: 4,446. **Student Body:** 16% female, 84% male, 68% out-of-state, 8% international (84 countries represented). African American 6%, Asian 5%, Caucasian 65%, Hispanic 8%. **Retention and Graduation:** 75% freshmen return for sophomore year. 35% freshmen graduate within 4 years. **Faculty:** Student/faculty ratio 16:1. 236 full-time faculty, 65% hold PhDs. 100% faculty teach undergrads.

ACADEMICS

Degrees: Bachelor's, master's. **Academic Requirements:** Computer literacy, English (including composition), humanities, mathematics, sciences (biological or physical), social science. **Classes:** Most classes have 20–29 students. Most lab/discussion sections have 10–19 students. **Majors with Highest Enrollment:** Aeronautics/aviation/aerospace science and technology; aerospace, aeronautical, and astronautical engineering; airline/commercial/professional pilot and flight crew. **Disciplines with Highest Percentage of Degrees Awarded:** Transportation and materials moving 57%, engineering 26%, business/marketing 7%, engineering technologies 4%, psychology 2%, physical sciences 2%. **Special Study Options:** Accelerated program, cooperative education program, distance learning, double major, dual enrollment, English as a second language (ESL), honors program, independent study, internships, student-designed major, study abroad.

FACILITIES

Housing: Coed dorms, apartments for married students, apartments for single students, special housing for disabled students, special units in regular coed dorms. **Special Academic Facilities/Equipment:** Fully equipped aircraft, training simulators, airway science simulation lab, wind tunnel. **Computers:** 94% of public computers are PCs, 1% of public computers are Macs, 5% of public computers are UNIX, network access in dorm rooms, online administrative functions (other than registration), remote student-access to Web through college's connection.

CAMPUS LIFE

Activities: Choral groups, dance, drama/theater, music ensembles, pep band, radio station, student government, student newspaper, yearbook. **Organizations:** 167 registered organizations, 12 honor societies, 7 religious organizations. 13 fraternities (10% men join), 5 sororities (16% women join). **Athletics (Intercollegiate):** *Men:* Baseball, basketball, cheerleading, cross-country, golf, soccer, tennis, track/field (outdoor). *Women:* Cheerleading, cross-country, golf, soccer, tennis, track/field (outdoor), volleyball.

ADMISSIONS

Freshman Academic Profile: 21% in top 10% of high school class, 49% in top 25% of high school class, 80% in top 50% of high school class. SAT Math middle 50% range 500–630. SAT Critical Reading middle 50% range 470–590. ACT middle 50% range 21–27. TOEFL required of all international applicants, minimum paper TOEFL 500, minimum computer TOEFL 173. **Basis for Candidate Selection:** *Very important factors considered include:* Academic GPA, class rank, recommendation(s), standardized test scores. *Other factors considered include:* Alumni/ae relation, application essay, character/personal qualities, extracurricular activities, interview, level of applicant's interest, rigor of secondary school record, volunteer work, work experience. **Freshman Admission Requirements:** High school diploma is required, and GED is accepted. *Academic units required:* 4 English, 3 math, 2 science (2 science labs), 2 social studies, 1 history, 3 academic electives. *Academic units recommended:* 4 English, 4 math, 3 science (2 science labs), 1 foreign language, 2 social studies, 2 history, 3 academic electives. **Freshman Admission Statistics:** 3,757 applied, 82% admitted, 36% enrolled. **Transfer Admission Requirements:** College transcript(s). Minimum college GPA of 2.0 required. Lowest grade transferable C. **General Admission Information:** Application fee $50. Regular notification is rolling. Nonfall registration accepted. Admission may be deferred for a maximum of 1 year. Credit and/or placement offered for CEEB Advanced Placement tests.

COSTS AND FINANCIAL AID

Annual tuition $25,400. Room & board $9,150. Required fees $1,096. Average book expense $950. **Required Forms and Deadlines:** FAFSA. **Notification of Awards:** Applicants will be notified of awards on a rolling basis beginning on or about 3/1. **Types of Aid:** *Need-based scholarships/grants:* Pell, SEOG, state scholarships/grants, private scholarships, the school's own gift aid. *Loans:* Direct Subsidized Stafford, Direct Unsubsidized Stafford, Direct PLUS, FFEL Subsidized Stafford. **Student Employment:** Federal Work-Study Program available. Institutional employment available. Off-campus job opportunities are good. **Financial Aid Statistics:** 72% freshmen, 59% undergrads receive need-based scholarship or grant aid. 63% freshmen, 56% undergrads receive need-based self-help aid. 23 freshmen, 120 undergrads receive athletic scholarships. 72% freshmen, 87% undergrads receive any aid.

120 Boylston Street, Boston, MA 02116-4624
Phone: 617-824-8600 **E-mail:** admission@emerson.edu **CEEB Code:** 3367
Fax: 617-824-8609 **Website:** www.emerson.edu **ACT Code:** 1820
Financial Aid Phone: 617-824-8655

This private school was founded in 1880. It has a 10-acre campus.

RATINGS

Admissions Selectivity Rating: 92   **Fire Safety Rating:** 74   **Green Rating:** 76

STUDENTS AND FACULTY

Enrollment: 3,216. **Student Body:** 55% female, 45% male, 63% out-of-state, 2% international (50 countries represented). African American 3%, Asian 4%, Caucasian 76%, Hispanic 6%. **Retention and Graduation:** 88% freshmen return for sophomore year. 72% freshmen graduate within 4 years. 13% grads go on to further study within 1 year. **Faculty:** Student/faculty ratio 14:1. 149 full-time faculty, 70% hold PhDs. 97% faculty teach undergrads.

ACADEMICS

Degrees: Bachelor's, doctoral, master's. **Academic Requirements:** Arts/fine arts, English (including composition), foreign languages, history, humanities, mathematics, philosophy, sciences (biological or physical), social science. **Classes:** Most classes have 10–19 students. Most lab/discussion sections have 10–19 students. **Majors with Highest Enrollment:** Cinematography and film/video production, creative writing, visual and performing arts. **Disciplines with Highest Percentage of Degrees Awarded:** Communications/journalism 33%, visual and performing arts 33%, English 16%, business/marketing 14%, education 2%, interdisciplinary studies 1%, health professions and related sciences 1%. **Special Study Options:** Cross-registration, double major, honors program, independent study, internships, liberal arts/career combination, student-designed major, study abroad, teacher certification program.

FACILITIES

Housing: Coed dorms, learning/living communities (writers' block and digital culture floor). **Special Academic Facilities/Equipment:** Emerson is home to the historic 1,200-seat Cutler Majestic Theatre and WERS-FM, Boston's oldest noncommercial broadcaster. The college has an 11-story performance and production center, housing rehearsal space, a costume shop, makeup lab, theater design/tech center, and sound-treated TV studios. There are also digital and audio post-production labs, recording studios, a film equipment distribution center, seven clinics/programs to observe speech and hearing therapy, an integrated digital newsroom, and marketing research suite. A new 14-story campus center and residence hall houses a gymnasium and space for student organizations. Current campus construction projects include extensive renovations to the Paramount Theater complex and Colonial Theatre building (both to be completed in 2009). **Computers:** 75% of classrooms are wireless, 56% of public computers are PCs, 44% of public computers are Macs, network access in dorm rooms, network access in dorm lounges, online registration, online administrative functions (other than registration), support for handheld computing, remote student-access to Web through college's connection.

CAMPUS LIFE

Activities: Choral groups, dance, drama/theater, literary magazine, musical theater, radio station, student government, student newspaper, student-run film society, television station, yearbook. **Organizations:** 60 registered organizations, 4 honor societies, 4 religious organizations. 4 fraternities (3% men join), 3 sororities (3% women join). **Athletics (Intercollegiate):** *Men:* Baseball, basketball, cross-country, golf, lacrosse, soccer, tennis, track/field (indoor). *Women:* Basketball, cross-country, golf, lacrosse, soccer, softball, tennis, track/field (indoor), volleyball. **Environmental initiatives:** LEED Certified residence hall (one of only two in Boston). Alternative energy sources. Major recycling programs.

ADMISSIONS

Freshman Academic Profile: 36% in top 10% of high school class, 78% in top 25% of high school class, 98% in top 50% of high school class. 72% from public high schools. SAT Math middle 50% range 550–650. SAT Critical Reading middle 50% range 590–680. SAT Writing middle 50% range 580–670. ACT middle 50% range 25–29. TOEFL required of all international applicants, minimum paper TOEFL 550, minimum computer TOEFL 213. **Basis for Candidate Selection:** *Very important factors considered include:* Academic

GPA, standardized test scores. *Important factors considered include:* Application essay, character/personal qualities, class rank, extracurricular activities, recommendation(s), rigor of secondary school record, talent/ability. *Other factors considered include:* Alumni/ae relation, first generation, geographical residence, racial/ethnic status, volunteer work, work experience. **Freshman Admission Requirements:** High school diploma is required, and GED is accepted. *Academic units required:* 4 English, 3 math, 3 science, 3 foreign language, 3 social studies. *Academic units recommended:* 4 English, 3 math, 3 science, 3 foreign language, 3 social studies, 4 academic electives. **Freshman Admission Statistics:** 4,849 applied, 47% admitted, 32% enrolled. **Transfer Admission Requirements:** High school transcript, college transcript(s), essay or personal statement, statement of good standing from prior institution(s). Minimum college GPA of 3.0 required. Lowest grade transferable C. **General Admission Information:** Application fee $60. Regular application deadline 1/5. Regular notification 4/1. Nonfall registration accepted. Admission may be deferred for a maximum of 1 year. Credit and/or placement offered for CEEB Advanced Placement tests.

COSTS AND FINANCIAL AID

Annual tuition $26,880. Room and board $11,376. Required fees $522. Average book expense $720. **Required Forms and Deadlines:** FAFSA, CSS/Financial Aid PROFILE, Noncustodial PROFILE, Business/Farm Supplement, tax returns, non-custodial statement. Financial aid filing deadline 3/1. **Notification of Awards:** Applicants will be notified of awards on or about 4/1. **Types of Aid:** *Need-based scholarships/grants:* Pell, SEOG, state scholarships/grants, private scholarships, the school's own gift aid. *Loans:* FFEL Subsidized Stafford, FFEL Unsubsidized Stafford, FFEL PLUS, Federal Perkins, state loans. **Student Employment:** Off-campus job opportunities are excellent. **Financial Aid Statistics:** 46% freshmen, 41% undergrads receive need-based scholarship or grant aid. 54% freshmen, 51% undergrads receive need-based self-help aid. 84% freshmen, 71% undergrads receive any aid. Highest amount earned per year from on-campus jobs $2,400.

EMILY CARR INSTITUTE OF ART AND DESIGN

1399 Johnston Street, Granville Island, Vancouver, BC V6H 3R9 Canada
Phone: 604-844-3897 **E-mail:** admissions@eciad.bc.ca
Fax: 604-844-3089 **Website:** www.eciad.ca

This public school was founded in 1925. It has an 80-acre campus.

RATINGS
Admissions Selectivity Rating: 79   **Fire Safety Rating:** 60*   **Green Rating:** 60*

STUDENTS AND FACULTY
Enrollment: 1,293. **Student Body:** 63% female, 37% male, 32% out-of-state. **Retention and Graduation:** 20% grads go on to further study within 1 year. 15% grads pursue arts and sciences degrees. **Faculty:** Student/faculty ratio 22:1. 60 full-time faculty, 30% hold PhDs. 100% faculty teach undergrads.

ACADEMICS
Degrees: Bachelor's. **Academic Requirements:** Arts/fine arts, art history, computer literacy, English (including composition), humanities, social science, theory. **Classes:** Most classes have 10–19 students. Most lab/discussion sections have 10–19 students. **Majors with Highest Enrollment:** Animation, interactive technology, video graphics, special effects, design and visual communications, visual and performing arts. **Disciplines with Highest Percentage of Degrees Awarded:** Visual and performing arts 56%, communication technologies 19%. **Special Study Options:** Cooperative education program, cross-registration, distance learning, exchange student program (domestic), independent study, internships, liberal arts/career combination, student-designed major, study abroad.

FACILITIES
Housing: Off-campus housing assistance. **Special Academic Facilities/Equipment:** Galleries, center for art and technology. **Computers:** Online registration, online administrative functions (other than registration), remote student-access to Web through college's connection.

CAMPUS LIFE
Activities: Radio station, student government, student newspaper, student-run film society, yearbook. **Organizations:** 12 registered organizations.

ADMISSIONS
Freshman Academic Profile: 15% in top 10% of high school class, 35% in top 25% of high school class, 95% in top 50% of high school class. 35% from public high schools. TOEFL required of all international applicants, minimum paper TOEFL 570, minimum computer TOEFL 230. **Basis for Candidate**

Selection: *Very important factors considered include:* Rigor of secondary school record, talent/ability. *Important factors considered include:* Application essay. **Freshman Admission Statistics:** 754 applied, 31% admitted, 94% enrolled. **Transfer Admission Requirements:** College transcript(s), essay or personal statement. **General Admission Information:** Application fee $30. Early decision application deadline 1/30. Regular application deadline 2/1. Regular notification 6/1. Nonfall registration accepted. Admission may be deferred for a maximum of 1 year. Credit and/or placement offered for CEEB Advanced Placement tests.

COSTS AND FINANCIAL AID
Annual in-state tuition $3,500. Average book expense $2,500. Required fees $90. Average book expense $1,500. **Student Employment:** Institutional employment available. Off-campus job opportunities are good. **Financial Aid Statistics:** Highest amount earned per year from on-campus jobs $1,200. **Financial Aid Phone:** 604-844-3844.

EMMANUEL BIBLE COLLEGE

1605 Elizabeth Street, Pasadena, CA 91104
Phone: 626-791-2575 **E-mail:** buildLeaders@EmmanuelBibleCollege.edu
Fax: 626-398-2424 **Website:** www.emmanuel.edu

This private school was founded in 1982. It has a 29-acre campus.

RATINGS
Admissions Selectivity Rating: 60*   **Fire Safety Rating:** 60*   **Green Rating:** 60*

STUDENTS AND FACULTY
Enrollment: 24. **Student Body:** 25% female, 75% male. **Retention and Graduation:** 80% freshmen return for sophomore year. 21% freshmen graduate within 4 years. 10% grads go on to further study within 1 year. **Faculty:** Student/faculty ratio 10:1. 1 full-time faculty, 100% hold PhDs. 100% faculty teach undergrads.

ACADEMICS
Degrees: Associate, bachelor's, certificate, diploma. **Academic Requirements:** Arts/fine arts, English (including composition), history, humanities, mathematics, sciences (biological or physical), social science. **Classes:** Most classes have fewer than 10 students. **Special Study Options:** Independent study, internships, Bible studies.

FACILITIES
Housing: Men's dorms, women's dorms.

CAMPUS LIFE
Activities: Drama/theater, literary magazine, student government, student newspaper.

ADMISSIONS
Freshman Academic Profile: 90% from public high schools. **Basis for Candidate Selection:** *Very important factors considered include:* Rigor of secondary school record. *Important factors considered include:* Class rank, recommendation(s). *Other factors considered include:* Character/personal qualities, extracurricular activities, interview. **Freshman Admission Requirements:** High school diploma is required, and GED is accepted. **Freshman Admission Statistics:** 23 applied, 74% admitted. **Transfer Admission Requirements:** College transcript(s), interview, statement of good standing from prior institution(s). Minimum college GPA of 2.0 required. Lowest grade transferable C. **General Admission Information:** Application fee $25. Regular notification during registration week. Nonfall registration accepted. Admission may be deferred. Common Application not accepted. Neither credit nor placement offered for CEEB Advanced Placement tests.

COSTS AND FINANCIAL AID
Annual tuition $4,800. Average book expense $600. **Required Forms and Deadlines:** FAFSA, institution's own financial aid form. **Types of Aid:** *Need-based scholarships/grants:* Pell. **Student Employment:** Off-campus job opportunities are good. **Financial Aid Statistics:** 100% freshmen, 100% undergrads receive need-based scholarship or grant aid.

EMMANUEL COLLEGE (MA)

400 The Fenway, Boston, MA 02115
Phone: 617-735-9715 **E-mail:** enroll@emmanuel.edu **CEEB Code:** 3368
Fax: 617-735-9801 **Website:** www.emmanuel.edu **ACT Code:** 1822
Financial Aid Phone: 617-735-9938

This private school, affiliated with the Roman Catholic Church, was founded in 1919. It has a 17-acre campus.

RATINGS
Admissions Selectivity Rating: 80   **Fire Safety Rating:** 60*   **Green Rating:** 60*

STUDENTS AND FACULTY
Enrollment: 2,037. **Student Body:** 75% female, 25% male, 36% out-of-state, 2% international (45 countries represented). African American 6%, Asian 3%, Caucasian 68%, Hispanic 3%. **Retention and Graduation:** 80% freshmen return for sophomore year. 50% freshmen graduate within 4 years. **Faculty:** Student/faculty ratio 15:1. 78 full-time faculty, 81% hold PhDs. 100% faculty teach undergrads.

ACADEMICS
Degrees: Bachelor's, master's, post-master's certificate. **Academic Requirements:** Arts/fine arts, computer literacy, English (including composition), foreign languages, history, humanities, mathematics, religious thought and moral reasoning, sciences (biological or physical), social science. **Classes:** Most classes have 10–19 students. Most lab/discussion sections have 10–19 students. **Majors with Highest Enrollment:** Business administration and management, communications studies/speech communication and rhetoric, counseling psychology. **Disciplines with Highest Percentage of Degrees Awarded:** Business/marketing 26%, health professions and related sciences 15%, communications/journalism 8%, education 6%, biological/life sciences 6%, psychology 6%, social sciences 6%, liberal arts/general studies 5%, English 5%, visual and performing arts 5%. **Special Study Options:** Accelerated program, cross-registration, double major, exchange student program (domestic), honors program, independent study, internships, liberal arts/career combination, student-designed major, study abroad, teacher certification program.

FACILITIES
Housing: Coed dorms, apartments for single students, special housing for disabled students. **Special Academic Facilities/Equipment:** Lillian Immig Gallery, Academic Resource Center, Jean Yawkey Center. **Computers:** 2% of classrooms are wired, 90% of public computers are PCs, 10% of public computers are Macs, network access in dorm rooms, network access in dorm lounges, online registration, online administrative functions (other than registration), remote student-access to Web through college's connection.

CAMPUS LIFE
Activities: Choral groups, dance, drama/theater, literary magazine, musical theater, pep band, radio station, student government, student newspaper, symphony orchestra, yearbook. **Organizations:** 49 registered organizations, 6 honor societies. **Athletics (Intercollegiate):** *Men:* Basketball, cross-country, soccer, track/field (outdoor), volleyball. *Women:* Basketball, cross-country, soccer, softball, tennis, track/field (outdoor), volleyball.

ADMISSIONS
Freshman Academic Profile: 11% in top 10% of high school class, 42% in top 25% of high school class, 80% in top 50% of high school class. SAT Math middle 50% range 460–560. SAT Critical Reading middle 50% range 480–580. SAT Writing middle 50% range 490–580. ACT middle 50% range 20–24. TOEFL required of all international applicants, minimum paper TOEFL 550, minimum computer TOEFL 213. **Basis for Candidate Selection:** *Very important factors considered include:* Academic GPA, application essay, recommendation(s). *Important factors considered include:* Alumni/ae relation, extracurricular activities, first generation, level of applicant's interest, standardized test scores, volunteer work. *Other factors considered include:* Character/personal qualities, class rank, geographical residence, religious affiliation/commitment, rigor of secondary school record, talent/ability, work experience. **Freshman Admission Requirements:** High school diploma is required, and GED is accepted. *Academic units required:* 4 English, 3 math, 2 science (2 science labs), 2 foreign language, 2 social studies. **Freshman Admission Statistics:** 3,480 applied, 60% admitted, 23% enrolled. **Transfer Admission Requirements:** High school transcript, college transcript(s), essay or personal statement, standardized test score, statement of good standing from prior institution(s). Minimum college GPA of 2.0 required. Lowest grade transferable C. **General Admission Information:** Application fee $40. Early decision application deadline 11/1. Regular application deadline 3/1. Regular notification is rolling. Nonfall registration accepted. Admission may be deferred

for a maximum of 1 year. Credit and/or placement offered for CEEB Advanced Placement tests.

COSTS AND FINANCIAL AID
Annual tuition $26,100. Room and board $11,200. Required fees $150. **Required Forms and Deadlines:** FAFSA, institution's own financial aid form. Financial aid filing deadline 4/1. **Notification of Awards:** Applicants will be notified of awards on a rolling basis beginning on or about 3/21. **Types of Aid:** *Need-based scholarships/grants:* Pell, SEOG, state scholarships/grants, private scholarships, the school's own gift aid. *Loans:* FFEL Subsidized Stafford, FFEL Unsubsidized Stafford, FFEL PLUS, Federal Perkins, state loans. **Student Employment:** Federal Work-Study Program available. Institutional employment available. Off-campus job opportunities are excellent. **Financial Aid Statistics:** 66% freshmen, 62% undergrads receive need-based scholarship or grant aid. 67% freshmen, 66% undergrads receive need-based self-help aid. 85% freshmen, 81% undergrads receive any aid. Highest amount earned per year from on-campus jobs $7,600.

See page 1164.

EMMANUEL COLLEGE (GA)

PO Box 129, Franklin Springs, GA 30639-0129
Phone: 706-245-7226 **E-mail:** admissions@emmanuelcollege.edu **CEEB Code:** 5184
Fax: 706-245-2876 **Website:** www.emmanuelcollege.edu
Financial Aid Phone: 706-245-2844

This private school, affiliated with the Pentecostal Church, was founded in 1919. It has a 150-acre campus.

RATINGS
Admissions Selectivity Rating: 78   **Fire Safety Rating:** 60*   **Green Rating:** 60*

STUDENTS AND FACULTY
Enrollment: 613. **Student Body:** 54% female, 46% male, 22% out-of-state. African American 16%, Asian 1%, Caucasian 80%, Hispanic 2%. **Retention and Graduation:** 61% freshmen return for sophomore year. 18% freshmen graduate within 4 years. **Faculty:** Student/faculty ratio 13:1. 40 full-time faculty, 65% hold PhDs. 100% faculty teach undergrads.

ACADEMICS
Degrees: Associate, bachelor's. **Academic Requirements:** Bible survey, English (including composition), history, humanities, mathematics, sciences (biological or physical), social science. **Classes:** Most classes have fewer than 10 students. **Majors with Highest Enrollment:** Elementary education and teaching, psychology, theological studies and religious vocations. **Disciplines with Highest Percentage of Degrees Awarded:** Education 35%, business/marketing 14%, theology and religious vocations 10%, psychology 8%, communications/journalism 7%. **Special Study Options:** Dual enrollment, honors program, independent study, internships, teacher certification program.

FACILITIES
Housing: Men's dorms, women's dorms, apartments for married students. **Computers:** 100% of public computers are PCs, network access in dorm rooms, online registration, remote student-access to Web through college's connection.

CAMPUS LIFE
Activities: Choral groups, drama/theater, jazz band, literary magazine, music ensembles, musical theater, student government, student newspaper, yearbook. **Organizations:** 25 registered organizations, 3 honor societies, 15 religious organizations. **Athletics (Intercollegiate):** *Men:* Baseball, basketball, soccer, tennis. *Women:* Basketball, soccer, softball, tennis.

ADMISSIONS
Freshman Academic Profile: 10% in top 10% of high school class, 50% in top 25% of high school class, 60% in top 50% of high school class. 85% from public high schools. SAT Math middle 50% range 400–550. SAT Critical Reading middle 50% range 430–570. TOEFL required of all international applicants, minimum paper TOEFL 550, minimum computer TOEFL 213. **Basis for Candidate Selection:** *Very important factors considered include:* Academic GPA, standardized test scores. *Important factors considered include:* Level of applicant's interest. *Other factors considered include:* Recommendation(s). **Freshman Admission Requirements:** High school diploma is required, and GED is accepted. **Freshman Admission Statistics:** 1,661 applied, 35% admitted, 45% enrolled. **Transfer Admission Requirements:** College transcript(s), standardized test score. Lowest grade transferable D. **General Admission Information:** Application fee $25. Regular application deadline 8/1. Regular notification is rolling. Nonfall registration accepted. Admission may

be deferred for a maximum of 1 year. Credit offered for CEEB Advanced Placement tests.

COSTS AND FINANCIAL AID

Average book expense $600. **Required Forms and Deadlines:** FAFSA, institution's own financial aid form, state aid form. Financial aid filing deadline 3/1. **Notification of Awards:** Applicants will be notified of awards on a rolling basis beginning on or about 3/1. *Types of Aid: Need-based scholarships/grants:* Pell, SEOG, state scholarships/grants. *Loans:* FFEL Subsidized Stafford, FFEL Unsubsidized Stafford, FFEL PLUS. **Student Employment:** Federal Work-Study Program available. Institutional employment available. Off-campus job opportunities are good. **Financial Aid Statistics:** 3 freshmen, 7 undergrads receive athletic scholarships.

EMORY AND HENRY COLLEGE

PO Box 947, Emory, VA 24327
Phone: 800-848-5493 **E-mail:** ehadmiss@ehc.edu **CEEB Code:** 5185
Fax: 276-944-6935 **Website:** www.ehc.edu **ACT Code:** 4350
Financial Aid Phone: 276-944-6884

This private school, affiliated with the Methodist Church, was founded in 1836. It has a 165-acre campus.

RATINGS
Admissions Selectivity Rating: 79 **Fire Safety Rating:** 60* **Green Rating:** 60*

STUDENTS AND FACULTY

Enrollment: 959. **Student Body:** 49% female, 51% male, 29% out-of-state, 1% international (3 countries represented). African American 5%, Caucasian 90%. **Retention and Graduation:** 62% freshmen return for sophomore year. 50% freshmen graduate within 4 years. 20% grads go on to further study within 1 year. 1% grads pursue arts and sciences degrees. 2% grads pursue business degrees. 3% grads pursue law degrees. 6% grads pursue medical degrees. **Faculty:** Student/faculty ratio 11:1. 75 full-time faculty, 84% hold PhDs. 100% faculty teach undergrads.

ACADEMICS

Degrees: Bachelor's, master's. **Academic Requirements:** Computer literacy, English (including composition), history, humanities, mathematics, sciences (biological or physical), social science, religion. All juniors are required to take an ethical inquiry course. All seniors are required to take a global studies course. **Classes:** Most classes have 10–19 students. **Disciplines with Highest Percentage of Degrees Awarded:** Social sciences 15%, education 14%, business/marketing 10%, psychology 9%, biological/life sciences 7%, visual and performing arts 7%, history 7%. **Special Study Options:** Cooperative education program, double major, dual enrollment, honors program, independent study, internships, liberal arts/career combination, student-designed major, study abroad, teacher certification program.

FACILITIES

Housing: Coed dorms, men's dorms, women's dorms, special housing for disabled students, religious life, eco-housing, honors housing. **Special Academic Facilities/Equipment:** Language lab, capillary gas chromatograph, DNA vertical slab gel electrophoretic equipment, infrared spectrophotometer. **Computers:** 75% of public computers are PCs, 25% of public computers are Macs, network access in dorm rooms, remote student-access to Web through college's connection.

CAMPUS LIFE

Activities: Choral groups, concert band, dance, drama/theater, literary magazine, music ensembles, musical theater, pep band, radio station, student government, student newspaper, television station, yearbook. **Organizations:** 53 registered organizations, 7 honor societies, 4 religious organizations, 7 fraternities (13% men join), 6 sororities (26% women join). **Athletics (Intercollegiate):** *Men:* Baseball, basketball, cross-country, football, golf, soccer, tennis. *Women:* Basketball, cross-country, soccer, softball, tennis, volleyball.

ADMISSIONS

Freshman Academic Profile: 20% in top 10% of high school class, 47% in top 25% of high school class, 76% in top 50% of high school class. 92% from public high schools. SAT Math middle 50% range 450–550. SAT Critical Reading middle 50% range 460–575. SAT Writing middle 50% range 440–560. ACT middle 50% range 19–25. TOEFL required of all international applicants, minimum paper TOEFL 550. **Basis for Candidate Selection:** *Very important factors considered include:* Academic GPA, rigor of secondary school record, standardized test scores. *Other factors considered include:* Alumni/ae relation,

character/personal qualities, class rank, extracurricular activities, first generation, interview, level of applicant's interest, recommendation(s), talent/ability, volunteer work, work experience. **Freshman Admission Requirements:** High school diploma is required, and GED is accepted. *Academic units required:* 4 English, 3 math, 2 science (2 science labs), 2 foreign language, 2 social studies. *Academic units recommended:* 1 fine arts. **Freshman Admission Statistics:** 1,309 applied, 75% admitted, 29% enrolled. **Transfer Admission Requirements:** College transcript(s), statement of good standing from prior institution(s). Minimum college GPA of 2.5 required. Lowest grade transferable C. **General Admission Information:** Application fee $30. Early decision application deadline 11/1. Regular notification is rolling. Nonfall registration accepted. Admission may be deferred for a maximum of 1 year. Credit and/or placement offered for CEEB Advanced Placement tests.

COSTS AND FINANCIAL AID

Average book expense $700. **Required Forms and Deadlines:** FAFSA, state aid form. Financial aid filing deadline 4/1. **Notification of Awards:** Applicants will be notified of awards on a rolling basis beginning on or about 2/1. **Types of Aid:** *Need-based scholarships/grants:* Pell, SEOG, state scholarships/grants, private scholarships, the school's own gift aid. *Loans:* FFEL Subsidized Stafford, FFEL Unsubsidized Stafford, FFEL PLUS, Federal Perkins. **Financial Aid Statistics:** 82% freshmen, 75% undergrads receive need-based scholarship or grant aid. 72% freshmen, 65% undergrads receive need-based self-help aid.

See page 1166.

EMORY UNIVERSITY

Boisfeuillet Jones Center, Atlanta, GA 30322
Phone: 404-727-6036 **E-mail:** admiss@emory.edu **CEEB Code:** 5187
Fax: 404-727-4303 **Website:** www.emory.edu **ACT Code:** 0810
Financial Aid Phone: 404-727-6039

This private school, affiliated with the Methodist Church, was founded in 1836. It has a 631-acre campus.

RATINGS
Admissions Selectivity Rating: 98 **Fire Safety Rating:** 68 **Green Rating:** 60*

STUDENTS AND FACULTY

Enrollment: 6,546. **Student Body:** 58% female, 42% male, 71% out-of-state, 5% international (50 countries represented). African American 9%, Asian 18%, Caucasian 57%, Hispanic 3%. **Retention and Graduation:** 94% freshmen return for sophomore year. 83% freshmen graduate within 4 years. 42% grads go on to further study within 1 year. 13% grads pursue arts and sciences degrees. 2% grads pursue business degrees. 8% grads pursue law degrees. 13% grads pursue medical degrees. **Faculty:** Student/faculty ratio 7:1. 1,241 full-time faculty, 100% hold PhDs. 90% faculty teach undergrads.

ACADEMICS

Degrees: Associate, bachelor's, doctoral, first professional, master's. **Academic Requirements:** Arts/fine arts, English (including composition), foreign languages, historical/cultural/international perspectives, history, humanities, mathematics, sciences (biological or physical), social science. Students have to take 1 course on the history of politics, society, or culture in the United States, providing a perspective on American diversity. All students are required to take health and physical education classes. **Classes:** Most classes have 10–19 students. Most lab/discussion sections have fewer than 10 students. **Majors with Highest Enrollment:** Business administration/management, economics, psychology. **Disciplines with Highest Percentage of Degrees Awarded:** Social sciences 25%, business/marketing 15%, psychology 10%, interdisciplinary studies 9%, biological/life sciences 7%. **Special Study Options:** Cooperative education program, cross-registration, double major, dual enrollment, English as a second language (ESL), exchange student program (domestic), honors program, independent study, internships, liberal arts/career combination, study abroad, teacher certification program. Qualified undergraduates may take a semester of off-campus study in Washington, DC.

FACILITIES

Housing: Coed dorms, women's dorms, apartments for married students, apartments for single students, special housing for disabled students, special housing for international students, fraternity/sorority housing. **Special Academic Facilities/Equipment:** Carlos Museum of Art, U.S. Centers for Disease Control, Carter Presidential Center, Yerkes Primate Center. **Computers:** 4% of classrooms are wired, 5% of classrooms are wireless, 80% of public computers are PCs, 19% of public computers are Macs, 1% of public computers are UNIX, network access in dorm rooms, network access in dorm lounges, online registration, online administrative functions (other than registration), remote student-access to Web through college's connection.

CAMPUS LIFE

Activities: Choral groups, concert band, dance, drama/theater, jazz band, literary magazine, music ensembles, musical theater, pep band, radio station, student government, student newspaper, student-run film society, symphony orchestra, television station. **Organizations:** 282 registered organizations, 25 honor societies, 28 religious organizations. 12 fraternities (27% men join), 12 sororities (32% women join). **Athletics (Intercollegiate):** *Men:* Baseball, basketball, cross-country, diving, golf, soccer, swimming, tennis, track/field (outdoor). *Women:* Basketball, cross-country, diving, soccer, softball, swimming, tennis, track/field (outdoor), volleyball.

ADMISSIONS

Freshman Academic Profile: 85% in top 10% of high school class, 95% in top 25% of high school class, 100% in top 50% of high school class. 64% from public high schools. SAT Math middle 50% range 660–740. SAT Critical Reading middle 50% range 640–730. ACT middle 50% range 27–31. **Basis for Candidate Selection:** *Very important factors considered include:* Academic GPA, application essay, extracurricular activities, recommendation(s), rigor of secondary school record, standardized test scores. *Important factors considered include:* Alumni/ae relation, character/personal qualities, talent/ability. *Other factors considered include:* Class rank, first generation, geographical residence, level of applicant's interest, racial/ethnic status, state residency, volunteer work, work experience. **Freshman Admission Requirements:** High school diploma is required, and GED is not accepted. *Academic units required:* 4 English, 3 math, 2 science (2 science labs), 2 foreign language, 2 social studies, 2 history, 2 academic electives. *Academic units recommended:* 4 math, 3 science, 3 foreign language. **Freshman Admission Statistics:** 14,222 applied, 32% admitted, 30% enrolled. **Transfer Admission Requirements:** High school transcript, college transcript(s), essay or personal statement, standardized test score, statement of good standing from prior institution(s). Minimum college GPA of 3.0 required. Lowest grade transferable C. **General Admission Information:** Application fee $50. Early decision application deadline 11/1. Regular application deadline 1/15. Regular notification 4/1. Nonfall registration not accepted. Admission may be deferred for a maximum of 1 year. Credit and/or placement offered for CEEB Advanced Placement tests.

COSTS AND FINANCIAL AID

Annual tuition $32,100. Room & board $9,938. Required fees $406. Average book expense $1,000. **Required Forms and Deadlines:** FAFSA, CSS/Financial Aid PROFILE, Noncustodial PROFILE. Financial aid filing deadline 4/2. **Notification of Awards:** Applicants will be notified of awards on or about 4/2. **Types of Aid:** *Need-based scholarships/grants:* Pell, SEOG, state scholarships/grants, private scholarships, the school's own gift aid. *Loans:* FFEL Subsidized Stafford, FFEL Unsubsidized Stafford, FFEL PLUS, Federal Perkins, Federal Nursing, state loans, college/university loans from institutional funds. **Financial Aid Statistics:** 37% freshmen, 37% undergrads receive need-based scholarship or grant aid. 36% freshmen, 36% undergrads receive need-based self-help aid. 61% freshmen, 60% undergrads receive any aid. Highest amount earned per year from on-campus jobs $18,582.

See page 1168.

EMORY UNIVERSITY—OXFORD COLLEGE

PO Box 1418, Oxford, GA 30054-1418
Phone: 770-784-8328 **E-mail:** oxadmission@learnlink.emory.edu **CEEB Code:** 5186
Fax: 770-784-8359 **Website:** www.emory.edu/oxford **ACT Code:** 0851
Financial Aid Phone: 770-784-8330

This private school, affiliated with the Methodist Church, was founded in 1836. It has a 56-acre campus.

RATINGS

Admissions Selectivity Rating: 60*   **Fire Safety Rating:** 60*   **Green Rating:** 98

STUDENTS AND FACULTY

Enrollment: 569. **Student Body:** 58% female, 42% male, 51% out-of-state, 3% international (7 countries represented). African American 11%, Asian 24%,

Caucasian 49%, Hispanic 4%. **Retention and Graduation:** 89% freshmen return for sophomore year. **Faculty:** Student/faculty ratio 10:1. 44 full-time faculty, 89% hold PhDs. 100% faculty teach undergrads.

ACADEMICS

Degrees: Associate. **Academic Requirements:** English (including composition), foreign languages, history, humanities, mathematics, sciences (biological or physical), social science, physical education. **Classes:** Most classes have 10–19 students. **Majors with Highest Enrollment:** Economics, psychology. **Special Study Options:** Cross-registration, distance learning, double major, dual enrollment, independent study, internships, liberal arts/career combination, study abroad.

FACILITIES

Housing: Coed dorms, women's dorms, special housing for disabled students, arts, diversity, healthy living. **Computers:** 80% of public computers are PCs, 20% of public computers are Macs, network access in dorm rooms, network access in dorm lounges, online registration, online administrative functions (other than registration), support for handheld computing, remote student-access to Web through college's connection.

CAMPUS LIFE

Activities: Choral groups, dance, drama/theater, literary magazine, music ensembles, student government, student newspaper, student-run film society, yearbook. **Organizations:** 51 registered organizations, 2 honor societies, 6 religious organizations. **Athletics (Intercollegiate):** *Men:* Basketball, tennis. *Women:* Soccer, tennis.

ADMISSIONS

Freshman Academic Profile: SAT Math middle 50% range 660–740. SAT Critical Reading middle 50% range 640–730. SAT Writing middle 50% range 640–730. ACT middle 50% range 29–33. TOEFL required of all international applicants, minimum paper TOEFL 600, minimum computer TOEFL 250. **Basis for Candidate Selection:** *Very important factors considered include:* Rigor of secondary school record. *Important factors considered include:* Application essay, extracurricular activities, recommendation(s), standardized test scores. *Other factors considered include:* Alumni/ae relation, talent/ability. **Freshman Admission Requirements:** High school diploma is required, and GED is accepted. *Academic units required:* 4 English, 3 math, 3 science (3 science labs), 2 foreign language, 2 social studies, 5 academic electives. *Academic units recommended:* 4 math. **Freshman Admission Statistics:** 1,336 applied, 78% admitted, 31% enrolled. **Transfer Admission Requirements:** College transcript(s), essay or personal statement, statement of good standing from prior institution(s). Minimum college GPA of 3.0 required. Lowest grade transferable C. **General Admission Information:** Application fee $40. Early decision application deadline 11/1. Regular application deadline 1/15. Regular notification is rolling. Nonfall registration accepted. Admission may be deferred for a maximum of 1 year. Common Application accepted. Credit and/or placement offered for CEEB Advanced Placement tests.

COSTS AND FINANCIAL AID

Annual tuition $33,900. Room and board $10,220. Required fees $436. Average book expense $1,000. **Required Forms and Deadlines:** FAFSA, CSS/Financial Aid PROFILE, signed W-2 statements and tax returns for parents and students. Financial aid filing deadline 3/1. **Notification of Awards:** Applicants will be notified of awards on or about 4/1. **Types of Aid:** *Need-based scholarships/grants:* Pell, SEOG, state scholarships/grants, private scholarships, the school's own gift aid. *Loans:* FFEL Subsidized Stafford, FFEL Unsubsidized Stafford, FFEL PLUS, Federal Perkins. **Student Employment:** Federal Work-Study Program available. Institutional employment available. Off-campus job opportunities are good. **Financial Aid Statistics:** 27% undergrads receive need-based scholarship or grant aid. 27% undergrads receive need-based self-help aid. 77% undergrads receive any aid.

EMPORIA STATE UNIVERSITY

1200 Commercial, Emporia, KS 66801-5087
Phone: 620-341-5465 **E-mail:** go2esu@emporia.edu **CEEB Code:** 6335
Fax: 620-341-5599 **Website:** www.emporia.edu **ACT Code:** 1430
Financial Aid Phone: 620-341-5457

This public school was founded in 1863. It has a 212-acre campus.

RATINGS
Admissions Selectivity Rating: 72   **Fire Safety Rating:** 63   **Green Rating:** 69

STUDENTS AND FACULTY
Enrollment: 4,239. **Student Body:** 61% female, 39% male, 7% out-of-state, 4% international (42 countries represented). African American 4%, Caucasian 82%, Hispanic 5%. **Retention and Graduation:** 74% freshmen return for sophomore year. 24% freshmen graduate within 4 years. 18% grads go on to further study within 1 year. **Faculty:** Student/faculty ratio 18:1. 259 full-time faculty, 83% hold PhDs. 100% faculty teach undergrads.

ACADEMICS
Degrees: Bachelor's, certificate, doctoral, master's, post-bachelor's certificate, post-master's certificate. **Academic Requirements:** Applied science, arts/fine arts, computer literacy, cultural diversity, English (including composition), history, humanities, mathematics, physical education, sciences (biological or physical), social science, speech. **Classes:** Most classes have 20–29 students. Most lab/discussion sections have 10–19 students. **Majors with Highest Enrollment:** Business administration/management, elementary education and teaching, social sciences. **Disciplines with Highest Percentage of Degrees Awarded:** Education 29%, business/marketing 22%, social sciences 9%, health professions and related sciences 9%, visual and performing arts 5%. **Special Study Options:** Continuing education courses, distance learning, double major, dual enrollment, English as a second language (ESL), evening courses, honors program, independent study, interdisciplinary or interdepartmental course of study, internships, learning assistance program, pass-fail grading option, service members opportunity college, student-designed major, study abroad, student exchange program, summer sessions, teacher certification program, trio programs, tutorial programs. Undergrads may take grad-level classes, except 800 level.

FACILITIES
Housing: Coed dorms, apartments for married students, apartments for single students, special housing for disabled students, special housing for international students, fraternity/sorority housing. **Special Academic Facilities/Equipment:** Art gallery, geology and natural history museums, Great Plains Study Center, planetarium. **Computers:** 80% of public computers are PCs, 20% of public computers are Macs, network access in dorm rooms, online administrative functions (other than registration), remote student-access to Web through college's connection.

CAMPUS LIFE
Activities: Choral groups, concert band, dance, drama/theater, jazz band, literary magazine, marching band, music ensembles, musical theater, opera, pep band, student government, student newspaper, student-run film society, symphony orchestra, yearbook. **Organizations:** 121 registered organizations, 15 honor societies, 11 religious organizations. 6 fraternities (12% men join), 4 sororities (9% women join). **Athletics (Intercollegiate):** *Men:* Baseball, basketball, cheerleading, cross-country, football, tennis, track/field (indoor), track/field (outdoor). *Women:* Basketball, cheerleading, cross-country, soccer, softball, tennis, track/field (indoor), track/field (outdoor), volleyball.

ADMISSIONS
Freshman Academic Profile: 9% in top 10% of high school class, 32% in top 25% of high school class, 66% in top 50% of high school class. 96% from public high schools. ACT middle 50% range 19–24. TOEFL required of all international applicants, minimum paper TOEFL 450, minimum computer TOEFL 133. **Basis for Candidate Selection:** *Very important factors considered include:* Academic GPA, class rank, standardized test scores. *Important factors considered include:* Talent/ability. *Other factors considered include:* Application essay, extracurricular activities. **Freshman Admission Requirements:** High school diploma is required, and GED is accepted. *Academic units required:* 4 English, 3 math, 3 science, 3 social studies, 1 computer technology. *Academic units recommended:* 4 English, 3 math, 3 science, 3 social studies, 1 computer

technology. **Freshman Admission Statistics:** 1,333 applied, 80% admitted, 72% enrolled. **Transfer Admission Requirements:** College transcript(s). Minimum college GPA of 2.0 required. Lowest grade transferable D. **General Admission Information:** Application fee $30. Nonfall registration accepted. Admission may be deferred for a maximum of 1 year. Credit and/or placement offered for CEEB Advanced Placement tests.

COSTS AND FINANCIAL AID
Annual in-state tuition $2,862. Out-of-state tuition $10,214. Room & board $5,170. Required fees $724. Average book expense $900. **Required Forms and Deadlines:** FAFSA, state aid form. Financial aid filing deadline 3/15. **Notification of Awards:** Applicants will be notified of awards on a rolling basis beginning on or about 2/2. **Types of Aid:** *Need-based scholarships/grants:* Pell, SEOG, state scholarships/grants, private scholarships, the school's own gift aid, Jones Foundation Grants. *Loans:* FFEL Subsidized Stafford, FFEL Unsubsidized Stafford, FFEL PLUS, Federal Perkins, Alaska Loans, alternative loans. **Financial Aid Statistics:** 40% freshmen, 38% undergrads receive need-based scholarship or grant aid. 48% freshmen, 52% undergrads receive need-based self-help aid. 18 freshmen, 47 undergrads receive athletic scholarships. 58% freshmen, 58% undergrads receive any aid. Highest amount earned per year from on-campus jobs $3,500.

ENDICOTT COLLEGE

376 Hale Street, Beverly, MA 01915
Phone: 978-921-1000 **E-mail:** admissio@endicott.edu **CEEB Code:** 3369
Fax: 978-232-2520 **Website:** www.endicott.edu **ACT Code:** 1824
Financial Aid Phone: 978-232-2060

This private school was founded in 1939. It has a 210-acre campus.

RATINGS
Admissions Selectivity Rating: 78   **Fire Safety Rating:** 92   **Green Rating:** 60*

STUDENTS AND FACULTY
Enrollment: 2,063. **Student Body:** 57% female, 43% male, 50% out-of-state, 2% international (30 countries represented). Caucasian 73%, Hispanic 1%. **Retention and Graduation:** 78% freshmen return for sophomore year. 46% freshmen graduate within 4 years. 22% grads go on to further study within 1 year. **Faculty:** Student/faculty ratio 16:1. 63 full-time faculty, 56% hold PhDs. 100% faculty teach undergrads.

ACADEMICS
Degrees: Associate, bachelor's, master's. **Academic Requirements:** Arts/fine arts, English (including composition), history, humanities, mathematics, sciences (biological or physical), social science. **Classes:** Most classes have 10–19 students. Most lab/discussion sections have fewer than 10 students. **Majors with Highest Enrollment:** Business administration/management, mass communications/media studies, sports and fitness administration/management. **Disciplines with Highest Percentage of Degrees Awarded:** Business/marketing 30%, visual and performing arts 17%, parks and recreation 10%, communications/journalism 8%, psychology 8%. **Special Study Options:** Accelerated program, cross-registration, distance learning, honors program, independent study, internships, liberal arts/career combination, student-designed major, study abroad, teacher certification program.

FACILITIES
Housing: Coed dorms, women's dorms, apartments for single students, special housing for disabled students, special housing for international students, suite type, modular, single parent. **Special Academic Facilities/Equipment:** Endicott Archives Museum (www.endicott.edu/archives/index.htm). **Computers:** 100% of classrooms are wireless, 90% of public computers are PCs, 10% of public computers are Macs, network access in dorm rooms, online registration, online administrative functions (other than registration), remote student-access to Web through college's connection.

CAMPUS LIFE
Activities: Choral groups, dance, drama/theater, jazz band, literary magazine, radio station, student government, student newspaper, television station, yearbook. **Organizations:** 40 registered organizations, 5 honor societies, 3 religious organizations. **Athletics (Intercollegiate):** *Men:* Baseball, basketball, cross-country, equestrian sports, football, golf, lacrosse, soccer, tennis, volleyball. *Women:* Basketball, cross-country, equestrian sports, field hockey, golf, lacrosse, soccer, softball, tennis, volleyball.

ADMISSIONS
Freshman Academic Profile: 12% in top 10% of high school class, 38% in top 25% of high school class, 77% in top 50% of high school class. SAT Math middle

50% range 490–590. SAT Critical Reading middle 50% range 490–580. SAT Writing middle 50% range 490–570. ACT middle 50% range 21–24. TOEFL required of all international applicants, minimum paper TOEFL 550, minimum computer TOEFL 213. **Basis for Candidate Selection:** *Very important factors considered include:* Academic GPA, character/personal qualities, rigor of secondary school record. *Important factors considered include:* Alumni/ae relation, application essay, class rank, extracurricular activities, geographical residence, standardized test scores, talent/ability, volunteer work, work experience. *Other factors considered include:* First generation, interview, level of applicant's interest, racial/ethnic status, recommendation(s), state residency. **Freshman Admission Requirements:** High school diploma is required, and GED is accepted. *Academic units recommended:* 4 English, 3 math, 2 science, 2 social studies, 1 history, 4 academic electives. **Freshman Admission Statistics:** 3,474 applied, 44% admitted, 34% enrolled. **Transfer Admission Requirements:** High school transcript, college transcript(s), essay or personal statement, standardized test score. Minimum college GPA of 2.5 required. Lowest grade transferable C. **General Admission Information:** Application fee $40. Regular application deadline 2/15. Regular notification is rolling. Nonfall registration accepted. Admission may be deferred for a maximum of 1 year. Credit offered for CEEB Advanced Placement tests.

COSTS AND FINANCIAL AID
Annual tuition $24,130. Room and board $11,380. Required fees $400. Average book expense $1,000. **Required Forms and Deadlines:** FAFSA, institution's own financial aid form. Financial aid filing deadline 3/15. **Notification of Awards:** Applicants will be notified of awards on a rolling basis beginning on or about 3/15. **Types of Aid:** *Need-based scholarships/grants:* Pell, SEOG, state scholarships/grants, private scholarships, the school's own gift aid. *Loans:* FFEL Subsidized Stafford, FFEL Unsubsidized Stafford, FFEL PLUS, Federal Perkins, college/university loans from institutional funds. **Student Employment:** Federal Work-Study Program available. Institutional employment available. Off-campus job opportunities are good. **Financial Aid Statistics:** 44% freshmen, 46% undergrads receive need-based scholarship or grant aid. 56% freshmen, 58% undergrads receive need-based self-help aid. 87% freshmen, 81% undergrads receive any aid. Highest amount earned per year from on-campus jobs $1,500.

ERSKINE COLLEGE

Erskine College, 2 Washington Street, Due West, SC 29639
Phone: 864-379-8838 **E-mail:** admissions@erskine.edu
Fax: 864-379-2167 **Website:** www.erskine.edu
Financial Aid Phone: 864-379-8832

This private school, affiliated with the Presbyterian Church, was founded in 1839. It has an 85-acre campus.

RATINGS
Admissions Selectivity Rating: 87   **Fire Safety Rating:** 60*   **Green Rating:** 62

STUDENTS AND FACULTY
Enrollment: 594. **Student Body:** 54% female, 46% male, 32% out-of-state, 2% international (10 countries represented). African American 7%, Caucasian 84%, Hispanic 1%. **Retention and Graduation:** 72% freshmen return for sophomore year. 64% freshmen graduate within 4 years. 29% grads go on to further study within 1 year. **Faculty:** Student/faculty ratio 12:1. 40 full-time faculty, 90% hold PhDs. 100% faculty teach undergrads.

ACADEMICS
Degrees: Bachelor's, doctoral, first professional, master's. **Academic Requirements:** Arts/fine arts, computer literacy, English (including composition), foreign languages, history, humanities, mathematics, sciences (biological or physical). **Classes:** Most classes have 10–19 students. Most lab/discussion sections have fewer than 10 students. **Majors with Highest Enrollment:** Biology/biological sciences, business administration/management, psychology. **Disciplines with Highest Percentage of Degrees Awarded:** Business/marketing 20%, biological/life sciences 16%, philosophy and religious studies 12%, education 11%, physical sciences 7%, psychology 7%. **Special Study Options:** Double major, independent study, internships, study abroad, teacher certification program.

FACILITIES
Housing: Men's dorms, women's dorms. **Special Academic Facilities/Equipment:** Bowie Arts Center. **Computers:** Network access in dorm rooms, network access in dorm lounges, remote student-access to Web through college's connection.

CAMPUS LIFE
Activities: Choral groups, concert band, dance, drama/theater, jazz band, literary magazine, music ensembles, musical theater, radio station, student government, student newspaper, yearbook. **Organizations:** 49 registered organizations, 6 honor societies, 7 religious organizations. 3 fraternities, 4 sororities. **Athletics (Intercollegiate):** *Men:* Baseball, basketball, cross-country, soccer, tennis. *Women:* Basketball, cross-country, soccer, softball, tennis.

ADMISSIONS
Freshman Academic Profile: 34% in top 10% of high school class, 62% in top 25% of high school class, 89% in top 50% of high school class. 85% from public high schools. SAT Math middle 50% range 493–605. SAT Critical Reading middle 50% range 490–600. SAT Writing middle 50% range 480–580. ACT middle 50% range 21–25. TOEFL required of all international applicants, minimum paper TOEFL 550. **Basis for Candidate Selection:** *Very important factors considered include:* Academic GPA, alumni/ae relation, recommendation(s), rigor of secondary school record, standardized test scores. *Other factors considered include:* Application essay, character/personal qualities, class rank, extracurricular activities, interview, level of applicant's interest, talent/ability, volunteer work, work experience. **Freshman Admission Requirements:** High school diploma is required, and GED is accepted. *Academic units required:* 4 English, 2 math. *Academic units recommended:* 4 math, 3 science (2 science labs), 2 foreign language, 2 social studies. **Freshman Admission Statistics:** 945 applied, 68% admitted, 28% enrolled. **Transfer Admission Requirements:** College transcript(s), statement of good standing from prior institution(s). Minimum college GPA of 2.0 required. Lowest grade transferable C. **General Admission Information:** Application fee $25. Nonfall registration accepted. Credit and/or placement offered for CEEB Advanced Placement tests.

COSTS AND FINANCIAL AID
Annual tuition $18,840. Room & board $6,951. Required fees $1,435. Average book expense $900. **Required Forms and Deadlines:** FAFSA, institution's own financial aid form. Financial aid filing deadline 4/1. **Notification of Awards:** Applicants will be notified of awards on a rolling basis beginning on or about 12/15. **Types of Aid:** *Need-based scholarships/grants:* Pell, SEOG, state scholarships/grants, private scholarships, the school's own gift aid. *Loans:* FFEL Subsidized Stafford, FFEL Unsubsidized Stafford, FFEL PLUS, Federal Perkins, college/university loans from institutional funds, teacher loans. **Financial Aid Statistics:** 87% freshmen, 69% undergrads receive need-based scholarship or grant aid. 83% freshmen, 69% undergrads receive need-based self-help aid. 47 freshmen, 139 undergrads receive athletic scholarships. 98% freshmen, 96% undergrads receive any aid. Highest amount earned per year from on-campus jobs $1,000.

EUGENE BIBLE COLLEGE

2155 Bailey Hill Road, Eugene, OR 97405-1194
Phone: 800-322-2638 **E-mail:** admissions@ebc.edu **CEEB Code:** 4274
Fax: 541-343-5801 **Website:** www.ebc.edu **ACT Code:** 3468
Financial Aid Phone: 800-322-2638

This private school, affiliated with the Open Bible (Pentecostal) Church, was founded in 1925. It has a 33-acre campus.

RATINGS
Admissions Selectivity Rating: 79   **Fire Safety Rating:** 60*   **Green Rating:** 60*

STUDENTS AND FACULTY
Enrollment: 180. **Student Body:** 44% female, 56% male, 54% out-of-state. **Retention and Graduation:** 68% freshmen return for sophomore year. 31% freshmen graduate within 4 years. 35% grads go on to further study within 1 year. **Faculty:** Student/faculty ratio 10:1. 10 full-time faculty, 30% hold PhDs. 90% faculty teach undergrads.

ACADEMICS
Degrees: Bachelor's, certificate. **Academic Requirements:** Arts/fine arts, Bible classes, English (including composition), history, mathematics, philosophy, sciences (biological or physical), social science. **Classes:** Most classes have 10–19 students. Most lab/discussion sections have 10–19 students. **Majors with Highest Enrollment:** Bible/biblical studies, pastoral studies/counseling, youth ministry. **Special Study Options:** Cooperative education program, distance learning, double major, dual enrollment, independent study, internships, liberal arts/career combination. One year Bible Certificate obtainable by external studies program.

FACILITIES

Housing: Men's dorms, women's dorms, apartments for married students, apartments for single students. **Special Academic Facilities/Equipment:** Music lab, computer lab. **Computers:** 100% of public computers are PCs, network access in dorm rooms.

CAMPUS LIFE

Activities: Choral groups, drama/theater, music ensembles, student government, yearbook. **Athletics (Intercollegiate):** *Men:* Basketball, soccer. *Women:* Soccer, volleyball.

ADMISSIONS

Freshman Academic Profile: 8% in top 10% of high school class, 29% in top 25% of high school class, 67% in top 50% of high school class. 90% from public high schools. SAT Math middle 50% range 430–610. SAT Critical Reading middle 50% range 450–580. ACT middle 50% range 19–24. TOEFL required of all international applicants, minimum paper TOEFL 500, minimum computer TOEFL 200. **Basis for Candidate Selection:** *Very important factors considered include:* Application essay, character/personal qualities, recommendation(s), religious affiliation/commitment. *Important factors considered include:* Rigor of secondary school record. *Other factors considered include:* Class rank, extracurricular activities, standardized test scores, talent/ability, volunteer work, work experience. **Freshman Admission Requirements:** High school diploma is required, and GED is accepted. **Freshman Admission Statistics:** 217 applied, 47% admitted, 63% enrolled. **Transfer Admission Requirements:** College transcript(s), essay or personal statement. Minimum college GPA of 2.0 required. Lowest grade transferable C. **General Admission Information:** Application fee $30. Regular application deadline 9/1. Regular notification is rolling. Nonfall registration accepted. Admission may be deferred for a maximum of 2 years. Common Application not accepted. Credit offered for CEEB Advanced Placement tests.

COSTS AND FINANCIAL AID

Annual tuition $7,500. Room & board $4,575. Required fees $801. Average book expense $800. **Required Forms and Deadlines:** FAFSA. Financial aid filing deadline 9/1. **Notification of Awards:** Applicants will be notified of awards on a rolling basis beginning on or about 7/15. **Types of Aid:** *Need-based scholarships/grants:* Pell, SEOG, the school's own gift aid. *Loans:* Direct Subsidized Stafford, Direct Unsubsidized Stafford, Direct PLUS, FFEL PLUS. **Financial Aid Statistics:** 73% freshmen, 73% undergrads receive need-based scholarship or grant aid. 73% freshmen, 73% undergrads receive need-based self-help aid.

EUGENE LANG COLLEGE—THE NEW SCHOOL FOR LIBERAL ARTS

65 West Eleventh Street, New York, NY 10011
Phone: 212-229-5665 **E-mail:** lang@newschool.edu **CEEB Code:** 2521
Fax: 212-229-5166 **Website:** www.newschool.edu/lang **ACT Code:** 9384
Financial Aid Phone: 212-229-8930

This private school was founded in 1985. It has a 5-acre campus.

RATINGS

Admissions Selectivity Rating: 85   **Fire Safety Rating:** 60*   **Green Rating:** 60*

STUDENTS AND FACULTY

Enrollment: 1,147. **Student Body:** 68% female, 32% male, 71% out-of-state, 3% international (15 countries represented). African American 3%, Asian 5%, Caucasian 60%, Hispanic 6%. **Retention and Graduation:** 66% freshmen return for sophomore year. 27% freshmen graduate within 4 years. 50% grads go on to further study within 1 year. 66% grads pursue arts and sciences degrees. 2% grads pursue business degrees. 12% grads pursue law degrees. **Faculty:** Student/faculty ratio 15:1. 49 full-time faculty, 78% hold PhDs. 100% faculty teach undergrads.

ACADEMICS

Degrees: Bachelor's. **Academic Requirements:** Arts/fine arts, English (including composition), humanities, sciences (biological or physical), social science. **Classes:** Most classes have 10–19 students. Most lab/discussion sections have 10–19 students. **Majors with Highest Enrollment:** Area,

ethnic, cultural, and gender studies; creative writing; social sciences. **Disciplines with Highest Percentage of Degrees Awarded:** Liberal arts/general studies 100%. **Special Study Options:** Accelerated program, cross-registration, distance learning, dual enrollment, English as a second language (ESL), exchange student program (domestic), independent study, internships, student-designed major, study abroad.

FACILITIES

Housing: Coed dorms, apartments for single students, special housing for disabled students. **Special Academic Facilities/Equipment:** Art gallery, photography gallery, extensive collections of contemporary art. **Computers:** 85% of classrooms are wireless, 50% of public computers are PCs, 50% of public computers are Macs, network access in dorm rooms.

CAMPUS LIFE

Activities: Choral groups, concert band, drama/theater, literary magazine, musical theater, radio station, student government, student newspaper. **Organizations:** 7 registered organizations, 9 honor societies, 1 religious organization.

ADMISSIONS

Freshman Academic Profile: 13% in top 10% of high school class, 58% in top 25% of high school class, 83% in top 50% of high school class. 64% from public high schools. SAT Math middle 50% range 490–610. SAT Critical Reading middle 50% range 555–665. SAT Writing middle 50% range 560–660. ACT middle 50% range 23–28. TOEFL required of all international applicants, minimum paper TOEFL 600, minimum computer TOEFL 250. **Basis for Candidate Selection:** *Very important factors considered include:* Academic GPA, application essay, recommendation(s), rigor of secondary school record. *Important factors considered include:* Character/personal qualities, interview, level of applicant's interest, standardized test scores, volunteer work. *Other factors considered include:* Alumni/ae relation, class rank, extracurricular activities, first generation, geographical residence, work experience. **Freshman Admission Requirements:** High school diploma is required, and GED is accepted. *Academic units required:* 4 English. *Academic units recommended:* 3 math, 2 foreign language, 3 social studies, 2 history. **Freshman Admission Statistics:** 1,458 applied, 66% admitted, 29% enrolled. **Transfer Admission Requirements:** High school transcript, college transcript(s), essay or personal statement, standardized test score. Minimum college GPA of 3.0 required. Lowest grade transferable C. **General Admission Information:** Application fee $50. Early Decision application deadline 11/15. Regular application deadline 2/1. Regular notification is rolling. Nonfall registration accepted. Admission may be deferred for a maximum of 1 year. Credit offered for CEEB Advanced Placement tests.

COSTS AND FINANCIAL AID

Annual tuition $30,660. Room and board $11,750. Required fees $650. Average book expense $2,050. **Required Forms and Deadlines:** FAFSA, state aid form. **Notification of Awards:** Applicants will be notified of awards on or about 3/1. **Types of Aid:** *Need-based scholarships/grants:* Pell, SEOG, state scholarships/grants, private scholarships, the school's own gift aid. *Loans:* FFEL Subsidized Stafford, FFEL Unsubsidized Stafford, Federal Perkins, college/university loans from institutional funds. **Financial Aid Statistics:** Highest amount earned per year from on-campus jobs $2,000.

EUREKA COLLEGE

300 East College Avenue, Eureka, IL 61530-1500
Phone: 309-467-6350 **E-mail:** admissions@eureka.edu **CEEB Code:** 1206
Fax: 309-467-6576 **Website:** www.eureka.edu **ACT Code:** 1022
Financial Aid Phone: 309-467-6311

This private school, affiliated with the Disciples of Christ Church, was founded in 1855. It has a 112-acre campus.

RATINGS

Admissions Selectivity Rating: 75   **Fire Safety Rating:** 76   **Green Rating:** 60*

STUDENTS AND FACULTY

Enrollment: 516. **Student Body:** 56% female, 44% male, 10% out-of-state, 1% international (5 countries represented). African American 9%, Caucasian 88%, Hispanic 1%. **Retention and Graduation:** 80% freshmen return for sophomore year. 24% grads go on to further study within 1 year. 8% grads pursue arts and sciences degrees. 2% grads pursue business degrees. 6% grads pursue law degrees. 3% grads pursue medical degrees. **Faculty:** Student/faculty ratio 12:1. 42 full-time faculty, 83% hold PhDs. 100% faculty teach undergrads.

ACADEMICS

Degrees: Bachelor's, post-bachelor's certificate. **Academic Requirements:** Arts/fine arts, English (including composition), foreign languages, history, humanities, mathematics, philosophy, sciences (biological or physical), social science. **Classes:** Most classes have 10–19 students. Most lab/discussion sections have 10–19 students. **Majors with Highest Enrollment:** Business administration/management, elementary education and teaching, psychology. **Disciplines with Highest Percentage of Degrees Awarded:** Education 22%, business/marketing 21%, social sciences 9%, biological/life sciences 8%, English 7%, communications/journalism 7%. **Special Study Options:** Double major, dual enrollment, English as a second language (ESL), exchange student program (domestic), honors program, independent study, internships, liberal arts/career combination, student-designed major, study abroad, teacher certification program, weekend degree completion cohort program in organizational leadership.

FACILITIES

Housing: Coed dorms, men's dorms, women's dorms, special housing for disabled students, fraternity/sorority housing. **Special Academic Facilities/ Equipment:** Ronald Reagan Museum, electron microscope, peace garden. **Computers:** 50% of classrooms are wired, 50% of classrooms are wireless, 100% of public computers are PCs, network access in dorm rooms, network access in dorm lounges, online administrative functions (other than registration), remote student-access to Web through college's connection.

CAMPUS LIFE

Activities: Choral groups, concert band, dance, drama/theater, jazz band, literary magazine, musical theater, pep band, student government, student newspaper, student-run film society, yearbook. **Organizations:** 41 registered organizations, 15 honor societies, 4 religious organizations. 3 fraternities (36% men join), 3 sororities (33% women join). **Athletics (Intercollegiate):** *Men:* Baseball, basketball, cross-country, football, golf, soccer, swimming, tennis, track/field (outdoor). *Women:* Basketball, cross-country, golf, soccer, softball, swimming, tennis, track/field (outdoor), volleyball.

ADMISSIONS

Freshman Academic Profile: 17% in top 10% of high school class, 44% in top 25% of high school class, 96% in top 50% of high school class. 87% from public high schools. ACT middle 50% range 18–24. TOEFL required of all international applicants, minimum paper TOEFL 500, minimum computer TOEFL 173. **Basis for Candidate Selection:** *Very important factors considered include:* Character/personal qualities, class rank, extracurricular activities, recommendation(s), rigor of secondary school record, standardized test scores, volunteer work. *Important factors considered include:* Talent/ability. *Other factors considered include:* Alumni/ae relation, application essay, interview, work experience. **Freshman Admission Requirements:** High school diploma is required, and GED is accepted. *Academic units recommended:* 4 English, 3 math, 3 science, 2 foreign language, 3 social studies, 2 history. **Freshman Admission Statistics:** 635 applied, 75% admitted, 31% enrolled. **Transfer Admission Requirements:** College transcript(s), statement of good standing from prior institution(s). Minimum college GPA of 2.0 required. Lowest grade transferable C. **General Admission Information:** Regular application deadline 8/1. Regular notification rolling. Nonfall registration accepted. Admission may be deferred for a maximum of 1 year. Common Application accepted. Credit offered for CEEB Advanced Placement tests.

COSTS AND FINANCIAL AID

Annual tuition $15,673. Room and board $7,130. Required fees $580. Average book expense $1,000. **Required Forms and Deadlines:** FAFSA, state aid form, Noncustodial PROFILE, Business/Farm Supplement. Financial aid filing deadline 4/15. **Notification of Awards:** Applicants will be notified of awards on or about 2/15. **Types of Aid:** *Need-based scholarships/grants:* Pell, SEOG, state scholarships/grants, private scholarships, the school's own gift aid. *Loans:* Direct Subsidized Stafford, Direct Unsubsidized Stafford, Direct PLUS, FFEL Subsidized Stafford, FFEL Unsubsidized Stafford, FFEL PLUS, Federal Perkins, state loans, college/university loans from institutional funds. **Student Employment:** Federal Work-Study Program available. Institutional employment available. Off-campus job opportunities are excellent. **Financial Aid Statistics:** 90% freshmen, 88% undergrads receive need-based scholarship or grant aid. 83% freshmen, 83% undergrads receive need-based self-help aid. 100% freshmen, 94% undergrads receive any aid. Highest amount earned per year from on-campus jobs $1,000.

EVANGEL UNIVERSITY

111 North Glenstone, Springfield, MO 65802
Phone: 417-865-2811 **E-mail:** admissions@evangel.edu **CEEB Code:** 6198
Fax: 417-520-0545 **Website:** www.evangel.edu **ACT Code:** 2296
Financial Aid Phone: 417-865-2811

This private school was founded in 1955. It has an 80-acre campus.

RATINGS

Admissions Selectivity Rating: 60*   **Fire Safety Rating:** 60*   **Green Rating:** 60*

STUDENTS AND FACULTY

Enrollment: 1,616. **Student Body:** 56% female, 44% male, 60% out-of-state, 1% international (13 countries represented). African American 2%, Caucasian 64%. **Retention and Graduation:** 77% freshmen return for sophomore year. **Faculty:** 100% faculty teach undergrads.

ACADEMICS

Degrees: Associate, bachelor's, master's. **Academic Requirements:** Arts/fine arts, Bible, computer literacy, English (including composition), history, humanities, mathematics, physical education, sciences (biological or physical), social science. **Special Study Options:** Cooperative education program, double major, dual enrollment, independent study, internships, teacher certification program.

FACILITIES

Housing: Men's dorms, women's dorms, apartments for married students, co-occupancy dorm with men and women in separate wings. **Computers:** 100% of public computers are PCs.

CAMPUS LIFE

Activities: Choral groups, concert band, drama/theater, jazz band, music ensembles, pep band, radio station, student government, student newspaper, television station, yearbook. **Organizations:** 14 registered organizations, 10 honor societies, 3 religious organizations. **Athletics (Intercollegiate):** *Men:* Baseball, basketball, cheerleading, cross-country, football, golf, track/field (indoor), track/field (outdoor). *Women:* Basketball, cheerleading, cross-country, golf, softball, track/field (indoor), track/field (outdoor), volleyball.

ADMISSIONS

Freshman Academic Profile: 76% from public high schools. TOEFL required of all international applicants, minimum paper TOEFL 490. **Basis for Candidate Selection:** *Very important factors considered include:* Class rank, recommendation(s), religious affiliation/commitment, rigor of secondary school record, standardized test scores. *Important factors considered include:* Character/personal qualities. **Freshman Admission Requirements:** High school diploma is required, and GED is accepted. *Academic units recommended:* 3 English, 2 math, 1 science (1 science lab), 2 foreign language, 2 social studies, 3 academic electives. **Freshman Admission Statistics:** 1,254 applied, 78% admitted. **Transfer Admission Requirements:** College transcript(s), statement of good standing from prior institution(s). Minimum college GPA of 2.0 required. Lowest grade transferable C. **General Admission Information:** Application fee $35. Regular application deadline 8/15. Regular notification is rolling. Nonfall registration accepted. Admission may be deferred. Common Application not accepted. Credit offered for CEEB Advanced Placement tests.

COSTS AND FINANCIAL AID

Annual tuition $13,530. Room & board $5,120. Required fees $660. Average book expense $800. **Required Forms and Deadlines:** FAFSA. **Notification of Awards:** Applicants will be notified of awards on a rolling basis beginning on or about 4/1. **Types of Aid:** *Need-based scholarships/grants:* Pell, SEOG, private scholarships. *Loans:* Direct Subsidized Stafford, Direct Unsubsidized Stafford, Direct PLUS, FFEL Subsidized Stafford, FFEL Unsubsidized Stafford, FFEL PLUS, Federal Perkins, college/university loans from institutional funds. **Student Employment:** Federal Work-Study Program available. Institutional employment available. Off-campus job opportunities are excellent.

THE EVERGREEN STATE COLLEGE

2700 Evergreen Parkway NW, Office of Admissions, Olympia, WA 98505
Phone: 360-867-6170 **E-mail:** admissions@evergreen.edu **CEEB Code:** 4292
Fax: 360-867-6576 **Website:** www.evergreen.edu **ACT Code:** 4457
Financial Aid Phone: 360-867-6205

This public school was founded in 1967. It has a 1,000-acre campus.

RATINGS
Admissions Selectivity Rating: 72　　　**Fire Safety Rating:** 60*　　　**Green Rating:** 98

STUDENTS AND FACULTY
Enrollment: 3,931. **Student Body:** 55% female, 45% male, 23% out-of-state. African American 5%, Asian 5%, Caucasian 69%, Hispanic 5%, Native American 4%. **Retention and Graduation:** 68% freshmen return for sophomore year. 45% freshmen graduate within 4 years. 29% grads go on to further study within 1 year. 22% grads pursue arts and sciences degrees. 3% grads pursue business degrees. 1% grads pursue law degrees. 3% grads pursue medical degrees. **Faculty:** Student/faculty ratio 21:1. 158 full-time faculty, 87% hold PhDs. 100% faculty teach undergrads.

ACADEMICS
Degrees: Bachelor's, master's. **Academic Requirements:** Evergreen does not have distribution requirements for specific course work. However, students are expected to work toward the "Expectations of an Evergreen Graduate," which includes a range of interdisciplinary study and student learning outcomes. **Classes:** Most classes have 10–19 students. **Disciplines with Highest Percentage of Degrees Awarded:** Liberal arts/general studies 87%, interdisciplinary studies 13%. **Special Study Options:** Accelerated program, cross-registration, double major, exchange student program (domestic), independent study, internships, learning disabilites, off-campus study, student-designed major, study abroad, summer session for credit, teacher certification program.

FACILITIES
Housing: Coed dorms, apartments for married students, apartments for single students, special housing for disabled students, special housing for international students, first-year experience residence halls, quiet housing, alcohol/drug-free housing, smoke-free house. **Special Academic Facilities/Equipment:** 4 computer music labs, 3 digital studio production studios, 4 analog audio recording studio/control room clusters, digital still imaging lab, 3 non-linear video editing suites, 4 linear analog video editing suites, color and B&W photography labs, 2 digital animation suites, film mixing studio with 5 editing suites, 5 A/V lecture halls, academic sailing fleet (two 45' wooden sailboats), organic farm, scanning electron microscope, gas chromatography mass spectrometer, printmaking studio, ceramics studio, academic wood and metal shops, weaving studio. **Computers:** 70% of public computers are PCs, 20% of public computers are Macs, 10% of public computers are UNIX, network access in dorm rooms, network access in dorm lounges, online registration, online administrative functions (other than registration), support for handheld computing, remote student-access to Web through college's connection.

CAMPUS LIFE
Activities: Choral groups, dance, drama/theater, literary magazine, music ensembles, radio station, student government, student newspaper, student-run film society, television station. **Organizations:** 77 registered organizations, 5 religious organizations. **Athletics (Intercollegiate):** *Men:* Basketball, cross-country, soccer, track/field (outdoor). *Women:* Basketball, cross-country, soccer, track/field (outdoor), volleyball. **Environmental initiatives:** 100% green tags for all electrical use. Annual Carbon Inventory. Hiring of a Director of Sustainability and maintaining a Sustainability Task Force. Serious commitments to sustainability in the college's strategic plan and in the Campus Master Plan. Participation in the AASHE STARS assessment.

ADMISSIONS
Freshman Academic Profile: 10% in top 10% of high school class, 31% in top 25% of high school class, 63% in top 50% of high school class. SAT Math middle 50% range 460–590. SAT Critical Reading middle 50% range 520–640. ACT middle 50% range 21–26. TOEFL required of all international applicants, minimum paper TOEFL 550, minimum computer TOEFL 213. **Basis for Candidate Selection:** *Very important factors considered include:* Academic GPA, application essay, rigor of secondary school record. *Important factors*

considered include: First generation, level of applicant's interest, standardized test scores. *Other factors considered include:* Class rank, extracurricular activities, interview, recommendation(s), volunteer work, work experience. **Freshman Admission Requirements:** High school diploma is required, and GED is accepted. *Academic units required:* 4 English, 3 math, 2 science (1 science lab), 2 foreign language, 3 social studies, 1 academic elective, 1 fine, visual, or performing arts elective or other college prep elective from the areas above. **Freshman Admission Statistics:** 1,602 applied, 95% admitted, 38% enrolled. **Transfer Admission Requirements:** College transcript(s). Minimum college GPA of 2.0 required. Lowest grade transferable C. **General Admission Information:** Application fee $50. Regular notification is rolling. Non-fall registration accepted. Admission may be deferred for a maximum of 1 quarter. Credit offered for CEEB Advanced Placement tests.

COSTS AND FINANCIAL AID
Annual in-state tuition $4,371. Out-of-state tuition $14,562. Room & board $7,140. Required fees $490. Average book expense $924. **Required Forms and Deadlines:** FAFSA, institution's own financial aid form. Financial aid filing deadline 3/15. **Notification of Awards:** Applicants will be notified of awards on a rolling basis beginning on or about 4/15. *Types of Aid: Need-based scholarships/grants:* Pell, SEOG, state scholarships/grants, private scholarships, the school's own gift aid. *Loans:* FFEL Subsidized Stafford, FFEL Unsubsidized Stafford, FFEL PLUS, Federal Perkins. **Student Employment:** Federal Work-Study Program available. Institutional employment available. Off-campus job opportunities are good. **Financial Aid Statistics:** 29% freshmen, 45% undergrads receive need-based scholarship or grant aid. 30% freshmen, 45% undergrads receive need-based self-help aid. 10 freshmen, 27 undergrads receive athletic scholarships. 45% freshmen, 56% undergrads receive any aid. Highest amount earned per year from on-campus jobs $8,000.

EXCELSIOR COLLEGE

7 Columbia Circle, Albany, NY 12203-5159
Phone: 518-464-8500 **E-mail:** admissions@excelsior.edu **CEEB Code:** 0759
Fax: 518-464-8777 **Website:** www.excelsior.edu
Financial Aid Phone: 518-464-8500

This private school was founded in 1970.

RATINGS
Admissions Selectivity Rating: 60*　　　**Fire Safety Rating:** 60*　　　**Green Rating:** 60*

STUDENTS AND FACULTY
Enrollment: 27,426. **Student Body:** 56% female, 44% male, 91% out-of-state, 2% international (56 countries represented). African American 17%, Asian 6%, Caucasian 62%, Hispanic 6%.

ACADEMICS
Degrees: Associate, bachelor's, master's, post-bachelor's certificate. **Academic Requirements:** Computer literacy, English (including composition), mathematics. **Majors with Highest Enrollment:** Business administration and management, liberal arts and sciences/liberal studies, nursing/registered nurse training (RN, ASN, BSN, MSN). **Disciplines with Highest Percentage of Degrees Awarded:** Liberal arts/general studies 72%, business/marketing 10%, computer and information sciences 4%, engineering technologies 3%, psychology 3%, health professions and related sciences 2%. **Special Study Options:** Accelerated program, distance learning, external degree program, honors program, independent study.

FACILITIES
Computers: Online registration, online administrative functions (other than registration).

CAMPUS LIFE
Organizations: 1 honor society.

ADMISSIONS
Freshman Admission Requirements: High school diploma is required, and GED is accepted. **Transfer Admission Requirements:** Lowest grade transferable D. **General Admission Information:** Application fee $75. Regular notification is continuous. Nonfall registration accepted.

COSTS AND FINANCIAL AID
Required Forms and Deadlines: Institution's own financial aid form. **Notification of Awards:** Applicants will be notified of awards on a rolling basis beginning on or about 8/1. **Types of Aid:** *Need-based scholarships/grants:* Private scholarships. **Financial Aid Statistics:** 3% undergrads receive any aid.

FAIRFIELD UNIVERSITY

1073 North Benson Road, Fairfield, CT 06824-5195
Phone: 203-254-4100 **E-mail:** admis@mail.fairfield.edu **CEEB Code:** 3390
Fax: 203-254-4199 **Website:** www.fairfield.edu **ACT Code:** 0560
Financial Aid Phone: 203-254-4125

This private school, affiliated with the Jesuit order of the Roman Catholic Church, was founded in 1942. It has a 200-acre campus.

RATINGS
Admissions Selectivity Rating: 89　　　**Fire Safety Rating:** 92　　　**Green Rating:** 84

STUDENTS AND FACULTY
Enrollment: 3,675. **Student Body:** 57% female, 43% male, 78% out-of-state. African American 2%, Asian 3%, Caucasian 81%, Hispanic 6%. **Retention and Graduation:** 89% freshmen return for sophomore year. 79% freshmen graduate within 4 years. 22% grads go on to further study within 1 year. 5% grads pursue arts and sciences degrees. 8% grads pursue business degrees. 5% grads pursue law degrees. 4% grads pursue medical degrees. **Faculty:** Student/faculty ratio 13:1. 240 full-time faculty, 92% hold PhDs. 100% faculty teach undergrads.

ACADEMICS
Degrees: Associate, bachelor's, master's, post-master's certificate. **Academic Requirements:** Arts/fine arts, computer literacy, diversity course, English (including composition), foreign languages, history, humanities, mathematics, philosophy, sciences (biological or physical), religious studies, social science. **Classes:** Most classes have 20–29 students. Most lab/discussion sections have fewer than 10 students. **Majors with Highest Enrollment:** Communications studies/speech communication and rhetoric, finance, marketing/marketing management. **Disciplines with Highest Percentage of Degrees Awarded:** Business/marketing 33%, social sciences 15%, English 9%, communications/journalism 9%, health professions and related sciences 9%, psychology 7%, biological/life sciences 4%. **Special Study Options:** Distance learning, double major, exchange student program (domestic), honors program, independent study, internships, liberal arts/career combination, student-designed major, study abroad, teacher certification program.

FACILITIES
Housing: Coed dorms, apartments for single students, special housing for disabled students, wellness floor, sophomore college, women in science, freshmen residence halls. **Special Academic Facilities/Equipment:** Center for the arts, media center, TV studio, language labs, computer center for teacher education. **Computers:** 1% of classrooms are wired, 9% of classrooms are wireless, 70% of public computers are PCs, 25% of public computers are Macs, 5% of public computers are UNIX, network access in dorm rooms, network access in dorm lounges, online registration, online administrative functions (other than registration), remote student-access to Web through college's connection.

CAMPUS LIFE
Activities: Choral groups, concert band, dance, drama/theater, jazz band, literary magazine, music ensembles, pep band, radio station, student government, student newspaper, student-run film society, symphony orchestra, television station, yearbook. **Organizations:** 81 registered organizations, 21 honor societies, 1 religious organization. **Athletics (Intercollegiate):** *Men:* Baseball, basketball, cross-country, diving, golf, lacrosse, soccer, swimming, tennis. *Women:* Basketball, crew/rowing, cross-country, diving, field hockey, golf, lacrosse, soccer, softball, swimming, tennis, volleyball. **Environmental initiatives:** Have joined Campus Climate Pact. Built a Co-generation facility providing 90% of campus electricity; 60% campus heating. Large scale recycling and composting/biofuels initiative. Environmental Steering Committees convened in 2006–07 and meets quarterly.

ADMISSIONS
Freshman Academic Profile: 12% in top 10% of high school class, 26% in top 25% of high school class, 98% in top 50% of high school class. 54% from public high schools. SAT Math middle 50% range 550–640. SAT Critical Reading middle 50% range 530–620. ACT middle 50% range 23–28. TOEFL required of all international applicants, minimum paper TOEFL 550, minimum computer TOEFL 213. **Basis for Candidate Selection:** *Very important factors considered include:* Academic GPA, application essay, class rank,

recommendation(s), rigor of secondary school record, standardized test scores. *Important factors considered include:* Character/personal qualities, extracurricular activities, first generation, talent/ability, volunteer work. *Other factors considered include:* Alumni/ae relation, geographical residence, interview, racial/ethnic status, work experience. **Freshman Admission Requirements:** High school diploma is required, and GED is not accepted. *Academic units required:* 4 English, 3 math, 2 science (2 science labs), 2 foreign language, 2 social studies, 2 history, 1 academic elective. *Academic units recommended:* 4 English, 4 math, 3 science (2 science labs), 4 foreign language, 2 social studies, 2 history, 1 academic elective. **Freshman Admission Statistics:** 8,035 applied, 61% admitted; 18% enrolled. **Transfer Admission Requirements:** High school transcript, college transcript(s), essay or personal statement, standardized test score, statement of good standing from prior institution(s). Lowest grade transferable C. **General Admission Information:** Application fee $55. Regular application deadline 1/15. Regular notification 4/1. Nonfall registration not accepted. Admission may be deferred for a maximum of 1 year. Credit offered for CEEB Advanced Placement tests.

COSTS AND FINANCIAL AID
Annual tuition $33,340. Room and board $10,430. Required fees $565. Average book expense $900. **Required Forms and Deadlines:** FAFSA, CSS/Financial Aid PROFILE, Business/Farm Supplement. Financial aid filing deadline 2/15. **Notification of Awards:** Applicants will be notified of awards on or about 4/1. **Types of Aid:** *Need-based scholarships/grants:* Pell, SEOG, state scholarships/grants, private scholarships, the school's own gift aid, United Negro College Fund. *Loans:* FFEL Subsidized Stafford, FFEL Unsubsidized Stafford, FFEL PLUS, Federal Perkins, Federal Nursing, alternative loans. **Financial Aid Statistics:** 49% freshmen, 42% undergrads receive need-based scholarship or grant aid. 44% freshmen, 39% undergrads receive need-based self-help aid. 59 freshmen, 179 undergrads receive athletic scholarships. 76% freshmen, 70% undergrads receive any aid. Highest amount earned per year from on-campus jobs $1,200.

FAIRLEIGH DICKINSON UNIVERSITY—
COLLEGE AT FLORHAM

285 Madison Avenue, Madison, NJ 07940
Phone: 800-338-8803 **E-mail:** globaleducation@fdu.edu **CEEB Code:** 226241
Fax: 973-443-8088 **Website:** www.fdu.edu **ACT Code:** 2554

This private school was founded in 1942. It has a 178-acre campus.

RATINGS
Admissions Selectivity Rating: 71　　　**Fire Safety Rating:** 60*　　　**Green Rating:** 76

STUDENTS AND FACULTY
Enrollment: 2,564. **Student Body:** 53% female, 47% male, 14% out-of-state, 1% international (20 countries represented). African American 8%, Asian 3%, Caucasian 71%, Hispanic 7%. **Retention and Graduation:** 76% freshmen return for sophomore year. **Faculty:** Student/faculty ratio 17:1. 116 full-time faculty, 78% hold PhDs. 100% faculty teach undergrads.

ACADEMICS
Degrees: Bachelor's, master's, post-bachelor's certificate, post-master's certificate. **Academic Requirements:** Arts/fine arts, computer literacy, English (including composition), foreign languages, humanities, mathematics, sciences (biological or physical), social science. **Majors with Highest Enrollment:** Communications studies/speech communication and rhetoric, psychology. **Disciplines with Highest Percentage of Degrees Awarded:** Business/marketing 37%, psychology 16%, communications/journalism 11%, visual and performing arts 9%, liberal arts/general studies 7%. **Special Study Options:** Accelerated program, cooperative education program, cross-registration, distance learning, double major, external degree program, honors program, independent study, internships, liberal arts/career combination, study abroad, teacher certification program, weekend college.

FACILITIES
Housing: Coed dorms, apartments for single students, special housing for disabled students. **Computers:** 100% of classrooms are wireless, 95% of public computers are PCs, 1% of public computers are Macs, 1% of public computers are UNIX, network access in dorm rooms, network access in dorm lounges, online registration, online administrative functions (other than registration), remote student-access to Web through college's connection.

CAMPUS LIFE
Activities: Choral groups, dance, drama/theater, literary magazine, music

ensembles, radio station, student government, student newspaper, student-run film society, yearbook. **Organizations:** 47 registered organizations, 11 honor societies, 4 religious organizations. 6 fraternities (5% men join), 4 sororities (6% women join). **Athletics (Intercollegiate):** *Men:* Baseball, basketball, cross-country, football, golf, lacrosse, soccer, swimming, tennis. *Women:* Basketball, cheerleading, cross-country, field hockey, lacrosse, soccer, softball, swimming, tennis, volleyball. **Environmental initiatives:** RecycleMania. New contruction LEED certification. HVAC upgrades will be energy efficient.

ADMISSIONS

Freshman Academic Profile: 11% in top 10% of high school class, 31% in top 25% of high school class, 66% in top 50% of high school class. SAT Math middle 50% range 460–570. SAT Critical Reading middle 50% range 460–560. SAT Writing middle 50% range 470–560. TOEFL required of all international applicants, minimum paper TOEFL 550, minimum computer TOEFL 213. **Basis for Candidate Selection:** *Very important factors considered include:* Academic GPA, rigor of secondary school record. *Important factors considered include:* Application essay, extracurricular activities, recommendation(s), standardized test scores. *Other factors considered include:* Class rank. **Freshman Admission Requirements:** High school diploma is required, and GED is accepted. *Academic units required:* 4 English, 3 math, 2 science (2 science labs), 2 foreign language, 2 social studies, 2 history, 3 academic electives. *Academic units recommended:* 3 math, 3 science (3 science labs), 2 foreign language, 2 social studies, 2 history, 3 academic electives. **Freshman Admission Statistics:** 3,180 applied, 67% admitted, 31% enrolled. **Transfer Admission Requirements:** College transcript(s), essay or personal statement. Minimum college GPA of 2.0 required. Lowest grade transferable C. **General Admission Information:** Application fee $40. Regular notification is rolling. Nonfall registration accepted. Admission may be deferred for a maximum of 1 year.

COSTS AND FINANCIAL AID

Required Forms and Deadlines: FAFSA. Financial aid filing deadline 2/15. **Notification of Awards:** Applicants will be notified of awards on or about 4/1. **Types of Aid:** *Need-based scholarships/grants:* Pell, SEOG, state scholarships/grants, private scholarships, the school's own gift aid, Federal Nursing Scholarships. *Loans:* FFEL Subsidized Stafford, FFEL Unsubsidized Stafford, FFEL PLUS, Federal Perkins, Federal Nursing, state loans. **Student Employment:** Federal Work-Study Program available. Off-campus job opportunities are good. **Financial Aid Statistics:** 58% freshmen, 56% undergrads receive need-based scholarship or grant aid. 61% freshmen, 61% undergrads receive need-based self-help aid.

FAIRLEIGH DICKINSON UNIVERSITY— METROPOLITAN CAMPUS

1000 River Road, Teaneck, NJ 07666-1966
Phone: 201-692-2553 **E-mail:** globaleducation@fdu.edu **CEEB Code:** 226341
Fax: 201-692-7319 **Website:** www.fdu.edu **ACT Code:** 2552

This private school was founded in 1942. It has an 88-acre campus.

RATINGS
Admissions Selectivity Rating: 73   **Fire Safety Rating:** 60*   **Green Rating:** 75

STUDENTS AND FACULTY

Enrollment: 3,403. **Student Body:** 57% female, 43% male, 14% out-of-state, 7% international (60 countries represented). African American 16%, Asian 6%, Caucasian 42%, Hispanic 18%. **Retention and Graduation:** 70% freshmen return for sophomore year. **Faculty:** Student/faculty ratio 15:1. 185 full-time faculty, 77% hold PhDs. 100% faculty teach undergrads.

ACADEMICS

Degrees: Associate, bachelor's, certificate, doctoral, master's, post-bachelor's certificate, post-master's certificate. **Academic Requirements:** Arts/fine arts, computer literacy, English (including composition), foreign languages, history, humanities, mathematics, philosophy, sciences (biological or physical), social science, university core sequence. **Majors with Highest Enrollment:** Business administration/management, psychology. **Disciplines with Highest Percentage of Degrees Awarded:** Liberal arts/general studies 49%, business/marketing 17%, security and protective services 5%, health professions and related sciences 5%, psychology 5%. **Special Study Options:** Accelerated program, cooperative education program, distance learning, double major, English as a second language (ESL), exchange student program (domestic), honors program, independent study, internships, liberal arts/career combination, student-designed major, study abroad, teacher certification program, weekend college, university core sequence.

FACILITIES

Housing: Coed dorms, men's dorms, women's dorms, special housing for disabled students, special housing for international students, honors and global scholar housing. **Computers:** 100% of classrooms are wireless, 95% of public computers are PCs, 1% of public computers are Macs, 1% of public computers are UNIX, network access in dorm rooms, network access in dorm lounges, online registration, online administrative functions (other than registration), remote student-access to Web through college's connection.

CAMPUS LIFE

Activities: Dance, drama/theater, literary magazine, pep band, radio station, student government, student newspaper, television station, yearbook. **Organizations:** 73 registered organizations, 12 honor societies, 5 religious organizations. 4 fraternities (1% men join), 6 sororities (1% women join). **Athletics (Intercollegiate):** *Men:* Baseball, basketball, cross-country, golf, soccer, swimming, tennis, track/field (indoor), track/field (outdoor). *Women:* Basketball, bowling, cross-country, fencing, golf, soccer, softball, tennis, track/field (indoor), track/field (outdoor), volleyball. **Environmental initiatives:** RecycleMania. Recycling bins.

ADMISSIONS

Freshman Academic Profile: 14% in top 10% of high school class, 40% in top 25% of high school class, 72% in top 50% of high school class. SAT Math middle 50% range 450–560. SAT Critical Reading middle 50% range 440–530. SAT Writing middle 50% range 430–530. TOEFL required of all international applicants, minimum paper TOEFL 550, minimum computer TOEFL 213. **Basis for Candidate Selection:** *Very important factors considered include:* Academic GPA, rigor of secondary school record. *Important factors considered include:* Application essay, extracurricular activities, recommendation(s), standardized test scores. *Other factors considered include:* Class rank. **Freshman Admission Requirements:** High school diploma is required, and GED is accepted. *Academic units required:* 4 English, 3 math, 2 science (2 science labs), 2 foreign language, 2 social studies, 2 history, 3 academic electives. *Academic units recommended:* 3 math, 3 science (3 science labs), 2 foreign language, 2 social studies, 2 history, 3 academic electives. **Freshman Admission Statistics:** 3,247 applied, 59% admitted, 27% enrolled. **Transfer Admission Requirements:** College transcript(s), essay or personal statement. Minimum college GPA of 2.0 required. Lowest grade transferable C. **General Admission Information:** Application fee $40. Regular notification is rolling. Nonfall registration accepted. Admission may be deferred for a maximum of 1 year. Credit offered for CEEB Advanced Placement tests.

COSTS AND FINANCIAL AID

Required Forms and Deadlines: FAFSA. Financial aid filing deadline 2/15. **Notification of Awards:** Applicants will be notified of awards on or about 4/1. **Types of Aid:** *Need-based scholarships/grants:* Pell, SEOG, state scholarships/grants, private scholarships, the school's own gift aid, United Negro College Fund, Federal Nursing Scholarships. *Loans:* FFEL Subsidized Stafford, FFEL Unsubsidized Stafford, FFEL PLUS, Federal Perkins, Federal Nursing, state loans. **Student Employment:** Federal Work-Study Program available. Off-campus job opportunities are good. **Financial Aid Statistics:** 67% freshmen, 59% undergrads receive need-based scholarship or grant aid. 70% freshmen, 64% undergrads receive need-based self-help aid. 47 freshmen, 132 undergrads receive athletic scholarships.

FAIRMONT STATE COLLEGE

1201 Locust Avenue, Fairmont, WV 26554
Phone: 304-367-4141 **E-mail:** admit@mail.fscwv.edu **CEEB Code:** 5211
Fax: 304-367-4789 **Website:** www.fscwv.edu **ACT Code:** 4520
Financial Aid Phone: 304-367-4213

This public school was founded in 1865. It has an 89-acre campus.

RATINGS
Admissions Selectivity Rating: 63   **Fire Safety Rating:** 60*   **Green Rating:** 60*

STUDENTS AND FACULTY

Enrollment: 6,496. **Student Body:** 56% female, 44% male, 6% out-of-state, 1% international (15 countries represented). African American 2%, Caucasian 77%. **Retention and Graduation:** 71% freshmen return for sophomore year. 14% freshmen graduate within 4 years. 22% grads go on to further study within 1 year. 7% grads pursue arts and sciences degrees. 1% grads pursue business degrees. 1% grads pursue law degrees. 1% grads pursue medical degrees. **Faculty:** Student/faculty ratio 17:1. 201 full-time faculty, 46% hold PhDs. 100% faculty teach undergrads.

ACADEMICS

Degrees: Associate, bachelor's, certificate. **Academic Requirements:** Arts/fine arts, English (including composition), foreign languages, history, humanities, mathematics, philosophy, sciences (biological or physical), social science. **Classes:** Most classes have 10–19 students. Most lab/discussion sections have 10–19 students. **Disciplines with Highest Percentage of Degrees Awarded:** Business/marketing 24%, education 21%, engineering 11%, psychology 9%, liberal arts/general studies 6%. **Special Study Options:** Double major, dual enrollment, English as a second language (ESL), honors program, teacher certification program, weekend college.

FACILITIES

Housing: Men's dorms, women's dorms. **Special Academic Facilities/Equipment:** On-campus one-room schoolhouse. **Computers:** Remote student-access to Web through college's connection.

CAMPUS LIFE

Activities: Choral groups, concert band, dance, drama/theater, jazz band, literary magazine, marching band, music ensembles, musical theater, opera, pep band, student government, student newspaper, student-run film society, symphony orchestra, yearbook. **Organizations:** 47 registered organizations, 16 honor societies, 4 religious organizations. 4 fraternities (1% men join), 4 sororities (2% women join). **Athletics (Intercollegiate):** *Men:* Baseball, basketball, cross-country, football, golf, swimming, tennis. *Women:* Basketball, cheerleading, cross-country, golf, softball, swimming, tennis, volleyball.

ADMISSIONS

Freshman Academic Profile: 12% in top 10% of high school class, 25% in top 25% of high school class, 66% in top 50% of high school class. 95% from public high schools. SAT Math middle 50% range 390–500. SAT Critical Reading middle 50% range 400–507.5. ACT middle 50% range 17–22. TOEFL required of all international applicants, minimum paper TOEFL 500. **Basis for Candidate Selection:** *Important factors considered include:* Class rank, extracurricular activities, rigor of secondary school record, standardized test scores. **Freshman Admission Requirements:** High school diploma is required, and GED is accepted. *Academic units required:* 4 English, 2 math, 2 science (2 science labs), 2 social studies, 1 history, 11 academic electives. *Academic units recommended:* 2 foreign language. **Freshman Admission Statistics:** 2,158 applied, 100% admitted, 54% enrolled. **Transfer Admission Requirements:** College transcript(s), statement of good standing from prior institution(s). Minimum college GPA of 2.0 required. Lowest grade transferable D. **General Admission Information:** Regular application deadline 6/15. Regular notification rolling. Nonfall registration accepted. Common Application accepted. Credit and/or placement offered for CEEB Advanced Placement tests.

COSTS AND FINANCIAL AID

Annual in-state tuition $4,656. Annual out-of-state tuition $9,956. Room and board $5,990. Average book expense $900. **Required Forms and Deadlines:** FAFSA. Financial aid filing deadline 3/1. **Notification of Awards:** Applicants will be notified of awards on a rolling basis beginning on or about 4/15. **Types of Aid:** *Need-based scholarships/grants:* Pell, SEOG, state scholarships/grants, private scholarships, the school's own gift aid. *Loans:* Direct Subsidized Stafford, Direct Unsubsidized Stafford, Direct PLUS, Federal Perkins. **Student Employment:** Federal Work-Study Program available. Institutional employment available. Off-campus job opportunities are fair. **Financial Aid Statistics:** 31% freshmen, 37% undergrads receive need-based scholarship or grant aid. 40% freshmen, 38% undergrads receive need-based self-help aid. 13 freshmen, 29 undergrads receive athletic scholarships. Highest amount earned per year from on-campus jobs $800.

Caucasian 96%, Hispanic 2%. **Retention and Graduation:** 64% freshmen return for sophomore year. 51% freshmen graduate within 4 years. 33% grads go on to further study within 1 year. **Faculty:** Student/faculty ratio 10:1. 17 full-time faculty, 65% hold PhDs. 85% faculty teach undergrads.

ACADEMICS

Degrees: Associate, bachelor's, certificate, first professional, master's. **Academic Requirements:** Bible, Computer literacy, English (including composition), history, humanities, mathematics, philosophy, sciences (biological or physical), social science. **Classes:** Most classes have fewer than 10 students. **Majors with Highest Enrollment:** Bible/biblical studies, elementary education and teaching, religious education. **Disciplines with Highest Percentage of Degrees Awarded:** Education 38%, philosophy and religious studies 33%, theology and religious vocations 29%. **Special Study Options:** Independent study, internships, teacher certification program.

FACILITIES

Housing: Men's dorms, women's dorms, apartments for married students, apartments for single students, special housing for disabled students. **Computers:** 80% of classrooms are wireless, 100% of public computers are PCs, network access in dorm rooms, network access in dorm lounges, remote student-access to Web through college's connection.

CAMPUS LIFE

Activities: Choral groups, concert band, drama/theater, music ensembles, pep band, student government, symphony orchestra, yearbook. **Organizations:** 1 registered organization, 1 religious organization. **Athletics (Intercollegiate):** *Men:* Basketball, soccer. *Women:* Basketball, soccer, volleyball.

ADMISSIONS

Freshman Academic Profile: 49% from public high schools. SAT Math middle 50% range 410–500. SAT Critical Reading middle 50% range 450–500. SAT Writing middle 50% range 420–450. ACT middle 50% range 18–21. TOEFL required of all international applicants, minimum paper TOEFL 500, minimum computer TOEFL 197. **Basis for Candidate Selection:** *Very important factors considered include:* Religious affiliation/commitment. *Other factors considered include:* Academic GPA, application essay, character/personal qualities, class rank, extracurricular activities, interview, level of applicant's interest, recommendation(s), standardized test scores, talent/ability, volunteer work. **Freshman Admission Requirements:** High school diploma is required, and GED is accepted. *Academic units recommended:* 4 English, 4 math, 2 science, 2 social studies, 2 history. **Freshman Admission Statistics:** 182 applied, 81% admitted, 59% enrolled. **Transfer Admission Requirements:** College transcript(s), essay or personal statement, statement of good standing from prior institution(s). Minimum college GPA of 2.0 required. Lowest grade transferable C. **General Admission Information:** Application fee $25. Regular application deadline 8/1. Regular notification is rolling. Nonfall registration accepted. Admission may be deferred for a maximum of 1 year. Credit offered for CEEB Advanced Placement tests.

COSTS AND FINANCIAL AID

Annual tuition $12,306. Room and board $5,010. Required fees $400. Average book expense $880. **Required Forms and Deadlines:** FAFSA. Financial aid filing deadline 4/1. **Notification of Awards:** Applicants will be notified of awards on a rolling basis beginning on or about 3/15. **Types of Aid:** *Need-based scholarships/grants:* Pell, state scholarships/grants. *Loans:* Direct Subsidized Stafford, Direct Unsubsidized Stafford, Direct PLUS. **Student Employment:** Institutional employment available. Off-campus job opportunities are excellent. **Financial Aid Statistics:** 94% freshmen, 95% undergrads receive any aid.

FAITH BAPTIST BIBLE COLLEGE AND THEOLOGICAL SEMINARY

1900 Northwest Fourth Street, Ankeny, IA 50021-2152
Phone: 1-888-faith-4-u **E-mail:** admissions@faith.edu **CEEB Code:** 6214
Fax: 515-964-1638 **Website:** www.faith.edu **ACT Code:** 1315
Financial Aid Phone: 515-964-0601

This private school, affiliated with the Baptist Church, was founded in 1921. It has a 52-acre campus.

RATINGS

Admissions Selectivity Rating: 60*   **Fire Safety Rating:** 60*   **Green Rating:** 60*

STUDENTS AND FACULTY

Enrollment: 314. **Student Body:** 50% female, 50% male, 42% out-of-state.

FAULKNER UNIVERSITY

5345 Atlanta Highway, Montgomery, AL 36109-3398
Phone: 334-386-7200 **E-mail:** admissions@faulkner.edu **CEEB Code:** 1034
Fax: 334-386-7137 **Website:** www.faulkner.edu **ACT Code:** 0003
Financial Aid Phone: 334-386-7195

This private school, affiliated with the Church of Christ, was founded in 1942. It has a 78-acre campus.

RATINGS

Admissions Selectivity Rating: 72   **Fire Safety Rating:** 65   **Green Rating:** 60*

STUDENTS AND FACULTY

Enrollment: 1,932. **Student Body:** 65% female, 35% male, 35% out-of-state. African American 30%, Caucasian 47%. **Retention and Graduation:** 59% freshmen return for sophomore year. 11% freshmen graduate within 4 years. 80% grads go on to further study within 1 year. 35% grads pursue arts and sciences degrees. 32% grads pursue business degrees. 12% grads pursue law degrees. 19% grads pursue medical degrees. **Faculty:** Student/faculty ratio 18:1. 97 full-time faculty, 68% hold PhDs. 83% faculty teach undergrads.

ACADEMICS

Degrees: Associate, bachelor's, certificate, diploma, first professional, master's. **Academic Requirements:** Arts/fine arts, computer literacy, English (including composition), foreign languages, history, humanities, mathematics, sciences (biological or physical), social science. **Classes:** Most classes have fewer than 10 students. Most lab/discussion sections have fewer than 10 students. **Majors with Highest Enrollment:** Business administration/management, management information systems. **Disciplines with Highest Percentage of Degrees Awarded:** Business/marketing 50%, law/legal studies 18%, education 2%. **Special Study Options:** Accelerated program, cross-registration, distance learning, double major, dual enrollment, honors program, independent study, internships, study abroad, teacher certification program, weekend college.

FACILITIES

Housing: Men's dorms, women's dorms, apartments for single students, special housing for disabled students. **Computers:** 45% of classrooms are wired, 100% of classrooms are wireless, 100% of public computers are PCs, network access in dorm rooms, network access in dorm lounges, online administrative functions (other than registration), support for handheld computing, remote student-access to Web through college's connection.

CAMPUS LIFE

Activities: Choral groups, drama/theater, music ensembles, musical theater, student government, student newspaper, yearbook. **Organizations:** 12 registered organizations, 1 honor society, 1 religious organization. 4 fraternities, 4 sororities. **Athletics (Intercollegiate):** *Men:* Baseball, basketball, cheerleading, golf, soccer. *Women:* Cheerleading, golf, soccer, softball, volleyball.

ADMISSIONS

Freshman Academic Profile: 11% in top 10% of high school class, 9% in top 25% of high school class, 20% in top 50% of high school class. 75% from public high schools. SAT Math middle 50% range 430–550. SAT Critical Reading middle 50% range 440–560. ACT middle 50% range 18–22. TOEFL required of all international applicants, minimum paper TOEFL 450, minimum computer TOEFL 133. **Basis for Candidate Selection:** *Very important factors considered include:* Character/personal qualities, class rank, extracurricular activities, interview, recommendation(s), rigor of secondary school record, standardized test scores. *Important factors considered include:* Alumni/ae relation, application essay, religious affiliation/commitment, talent/ability. *Other factors considered include:* Volunteer work, work experience. **Freshman Admission Requirements:** High school diploma is required, and GED is accepted. *Academic units recommended:* 12 academic electives. **Freshman Admission Statistics:** 680 applied, 65% admitted, 46% enrolled. **Transfer Admission Requirements:** High school transcript, college transcript(s), standardized test score. Minimum college GPA of 2.0 required. Lowest grade transferable C. **General Admission Information:** Application fee $10. Regular notification is rolling. Nonfall registration accepted. Admission may be deferred for a maximum of 1 year. Placement offered for CEEB Advanced Placement tests.

COSTS AND FINANCIAL AID

Annual tuition $12,000. Room and board $5,850. Required fees $25. Average book expense $1,200. **Required Forms and Deadlines:** FAFSA, institution's own financial aid form, state aid form. Financial aid filing deadline 5/1. **Notification of Awards:** Applicants will be notified of awards on a rolling basis beginning on or about 6/1. **Types of Aid:** *Need-based scholarships/grants:* Pell, SEOG, state scholarships/grants, private scholarships, the school's own gift aid. *Loans:* FFEL Subsidized Stafford, FFEL Unsubsidized Stafford, FFEL PLUS, Federal Perkins. **Financial Aid Statistics:** 55% freshmen, 54% undergrads receive need-based scholarship or grant aid. 64% freshmen, 65% undergrads receive need-based self-help aid. 27 freshmen, 62 undergrads receive athletic scholarships. 95% freshmen, 93% undergrads receive any aid. Highest amount earned per year from on-campus jobs $1,200.

FAYETTEVILLE STATE UNIVERSITY

Newbold Station, Fayetteville, NC 28301
Phone: 910-672-1371 **E-mail:** admissions@uncfsu.edu **CEEB Code:** 5212
Fax: 910-672-1414 **Website:** www.uncfsu.edu **ACT Code:** 3098
Financial Aid Phone: 910-672-1325

This public school was founded in 1867. It has a 136-acre campus.

RATINGS

Admissions Selectivity Rating: 65   **Fire Safety Rating:** 60*   **Green Rating:** 60*

STUDENTS AND FACULTY

Enrollment: 3,660. **Student Body:** 64% female, 36% male, 11% out-of-state. African American 80%, Asian 1%, Caucasian 14%, Hispanic 4%, Native American 1%. **Retention and Graduation:** 74% freshmen return for sophomore year. 14% freshmen graduate within 4 years. 11% grads go on to further study within 1 year. 10% grads pursue arts and sciences degrees. 1% grads pursue business degrees. **Faculty:** Student/faculty ratio 20:1. 202 full-time faculty, 70% hold PhDs. 100% faculty teach undergrads.

ACADEMICS

Degrees: Bachelor's, doctoral, master's. **Academic Requirements:** Arts/fine arts, critical thinking, English (including composition), humanities, mathematics, physical education/health and wellness, sciences (biological or physical), social science, university studies (two-semester freshman seminar course). **Classes:** Most classes have 20–29 students. Most lab/discussion sections have 20–29 students. **Majors with Highest Enrollment:** Business administration/management, criminal justice/police science, elementary education and teaching. **Special Study Options:** Cooperative education program, distance learning, double major, honors program, independent study, internships, liberal arts/career combination, study abroad, teacher certification program, weekend college.

FACILITIES

Housing: Men's dorms, women's dorms, apartments for married students, apartments for single students, special housing for disabled students. **Special Academic Facilities/Equipment:** Planetarium; observatory; distance learning center; science labs; health, physical education, and recreation complex; art gallery.

CAMPUS LIFE

Activities: Choral groups, concert band, dance, drama/theater, jazz band, marching band, music ensembles, musical theater, opera, pep band, radio station, student government, student newspaper, student-run film society, television station, yearbook. **Organizations:** 56 registered organizations, 7 honor societies, 3 religious organizations. 4 fraternities (5% men join), 4 sororities (5% women join). **Athletics (Intercollegiate):** *Men:* Basketball, cheerleading, cross-country, football, golf. *Women:* Basketball, cheerleading, cross-country, softball, tennis, volleyball.

ADMISSIONS

Freshman Academic Profile: 12% in top 10% of high school class, 14% in top 25% of high school class, 48% in top 50% of high school class. SAT Math middle 50% range 360–470. SAT Critical Reading middle 50% range 380–470. Regular application deadline 8/15. **Basis for Candidate Selection:** *Important factors considered include:* Character/personal qualities, class rank, extracurricular activities, rigor of secondary school record, standardized test scores, talent/ability. **Freshman Admission Requirements:** High school diploma is required, and GED is accepted. *Academic units required:* 4 English, 3 math, 3 science, 1 social studies, 1 history, 6 academic electives. *Academic units recommended:* 2 foreign language. **Freshman Admission Statistics:** 1,570 applied, 85% admitted, 58% enrolled. **Transfer Admission Requirements:** College transcript(s), statement of good standing from prior institution(s). Lowest grade transferable C. **General Admission Information:** Application fee $25. Regular application deadline 8/15. Regular notification is rolling. Nonfall registration accepted. Common Application accepted. Credit and/or placement offered for CEEB Advanced Placement tests.

COSTS AND FINANCIAL AID

Annual in-state tuition $1,258. Out-of-state tuition $10,173. Room & board $3,820. Required fees $437. Average book expense $160. **Required Forms and Deadlines:** FAFSA, institution's own financial aid form. **Notification of Awards:** Applicants will be notified of awards on or about 7/15. **Types of Aid:** *Need-based scholarships/grants:* Pell, SEOG, state scholarships/grants, private scholarships, the school's own gift aid. *Loans:* Direct Subsidized Stafford, Direct Unsubsidized Stafford, Direct PLUS, FFEL Subsidized Stafford, FFEL Unsubsidized Stafford, FFEL PLUS, Federal Perkins, Federal Nursing, state loans. **Student Employment:** Federal Work-Study Program available. Off-campus job opportunities are excellent.

FELICIAN COLLEGE

262 South Main Street, Lodi, NJ 07644
Phone: 201-559-6131 **E-mail:** admissions@inet.felician.edu **CEEB Code:** 2321
Fax: 201-559-6138 **Website:** www.felician.edu **ACT Code:** 2559
Financial Aid Phone: 201-559-6010

This private school, affiliated with the Roman Catholic Church, was founded in 1942. It has a 27-acre campus.

RATINGS
Admissions Selectivity Rating: 66   **Fire Safety Rating:** 60*   **Green Rating:** 60*

STUDENTS AND FACULTY
Enrollment: 1,416. **Student Body:** 75% female, 25% male, 2% out-of-state, 2% international. African American 14%, Asian 5%, Caucasian 58%, Hispanic 16%. **Retention and Graduation:** 92% freshmen return for sophomore year. 20% grads go on to further study within 1 year. 40% grads pursue arts and sciences degrees. 12% grads pursue business degrees. 10% grads pursue law degrees. 5% grads pursue medical degrees. **Faculty:** Student/faculty ratio 15:1. 72 full-time faculty, 49% hold PhDs. 100% faculty teach undergrads.

ACADEMICS
Degrees: Associate, bachelor's, certificate, master's, post-bachelor's certificate, post-master's certificate. **Academic Requirements:** Arts/fine arts, computer literacy, English (including composition), humanities, mathematics, philosophy, sciences (biological or physical), social science. **Classes:** Most classes have 10–19 students. **Majors with Highest Enrollment:** Business administration/management, nursing/registered nurse training (RN, ASN, BSN, MSN), psychology. **Disciplines with Highest Percentage of Degrees Awarded:** English 20%, education 20%, psychology 15%, social sciences 10%, health professions and related sciences 10%, biological/life sciences 7%, business/marketing 7%, visual and performing arts 5%. **Special Study Options:** Accelerated program, cooperative education program, cross-registration, distance learning, double major, dual enrollment, English as a second language (ESL), honors program, independent study, internships, liberal arts/career combination, student-designed major, study abroad, teacher certification program, weekend college. Post-baccalaureate certification in elementary and secondary education.

FACILITIES
Housing: Coed dorms, men's dorms, women's dorms, special housing for disabled students. **Special Academic Facilities/Equipment:** On-campus elementary school for exceptional children. **Computers:** 65% of public computers are PCs, 10% of public computers are Macs, network access in dorm rooms, remote student-access to Web through college's connection.

CAMPUS LIFE
Activities: Choral groups, drama/theater, literary magazine, student government. **Organizations:** 25 registered organizations, 2 honor societies, 3 religious organizations. 1 fraternity, 2 sororities (20% women join). **Athletics (Intercollegiate):** *Men:* Baseball, basketball, cheerleading, cross-country, soccer, track/field (outdoor). *Women:* Basketball, cheerleading, cross-country, soccer, softball, track/field (outdoor).

ADMISSIONS
Freshman Academic Profile: 9% in top 10% of high school class, 34% in top 25% of high school class, 50% in top 50% of high school class. 70% from public high schools. SAT Math middle 50% range 400–500. SAT Writing middle 50% range 390–490. **Basis for Candidate Selection:** *Very important factors considered include:* Rigor of secondary school record, standardized test scores. *Other factors considered include:* Alumni/ae relation, application essay, character/personal qualities, class rank, extracurricular activities, interview, racial/ethnic status, recommendation(s), work experience. **Freshman Admission Requirements:** High school diploma is required, and GED is accepted. *Academic units recommended:* 4 English, 3 math, 2 science, 2 foreign language, 2 social studies, 6 academic electives. **Freshman Admission Statistics:** 947 applied, 63% admitted, 73% enrolled. **Transfer Admission Requirements:** College transcript(s), essay or personal statement. Minimum college GPA of 2.5 required. Lowest grade transferable C. **General Admission Information:** Application fee $30. Regular notification 3/15. Nonfall registration accepted. Common Application accepted. Credit and/or placement offered for CEEB Advanced Placement tests.

COSTS AND FINANCIAL AID
Annual tuition $18,900. Room and board $7,432. Required fees $1,050. Average book expense $2,163. **Required Forms and Deadlines:** FAFSA. Financial aid filing deadline 6/2. **Notification of Awards:** Applicants will be notified of awards on a rolling basis beginning on or about 4/2. **Types of Aid:** *Need-based*

scholarships/grants: Pell, SEOG, state scholarships/grants, private scholarships, the school's own gift aid, United Negro College Fund, Federal Nursing Scholarships. *Loans:* Direct Subsidized Stafford, Direct Unsubsidized Stafford, Direct PLUS, FFEL Subsidized Stafford, FFEL Unsubsidized Stafford, FFEL PLUS, state loans. **Student Employment:** Federal Work-Study Program available. Off-campus job opportunities are good. **Financial Aid Statistics:** 36% freshmen, 16% undergrads receive need-based scholarship or grant aid. 44% freshmen, 41% undergrads receive need-based self-help aid. 15 freshmen, 33 undergrads receive athletic scholarships.

See page 1170.

FERRIS STATE UNIVERSITY

1201 South State Street, Center for Student Services, Big Rapids, MI 49307
Phone: 231-591-2100 **E-mail:** admissions@ferris.edu **CEEB Code:** 1222
Fax: 231-591-3944 **Website:** www.ferris.edu **ACT Code:** 1994
Financial Aid Phone: 231-591-2110

This public school was founded in 1884. It has an 880-acre campus.

RATINGS
Admissions Selectivity Rating: 60*   **Fire Safety Rating:** 60*   **Green Rating:** 60*

STUDENTS AND FACULTY
Enrollment: 11,030. **Student Body:** 47% female, 53% male, 5% out-of-state, 1% international. African American 6%, Asian 2%, Caucasian 78%, Hispanic 1%. **Retention and Graduation:** 69% freshmen return for sophomore year. 18% freshmen graduate within 4 years. 11% grads go on to further study within 1 year. **Faculty:** Student/faculty ratio 16:1. 537 full-time faculty, 51% hold PhDs. 100% faculty teach undergrads.

ACADEMICS
Degrees: Associate, bachelor's, certificate, first professional, master's. **Academic Requirements:** Cultural enrichment (history, humanities, forgien language, etc.), English (including composition), humanities, mathematics, sciences (biological or physical), social science. **Classes:** Most classes have 20–29 students. Most lab/discussion sections have 10–19 students. **Majors with Highest Enrollment:** Elementary education and teaching, pharmacy (PharMD, BS/BPharm), pre-pharmacy studies. **Disciplines with Highest Percentage of Degrees Awarded:** Business/marketing 24%, engineering technologies 17%, visual and performing arts 10%, education 9%, security and protective services 9%, health professions and related sciences 7%. **Special Study Options:** Accelerated program, cooperative education program, cross-registration, distance learning, double major, dual enrollment, exchange student program (domestic), external degree program, honors program, independent study, internships, liberal arts/career combination, study abroad, teacher certification program, weekend college.

FACILITIES
Housing: Coed dorms, apartments for married students, apartments for single students, special housing for disabled students, special housing for international students, honors, smoke-free, alcohol-free, quiet residence halls, living/earning communities. **Special Academic Facilities/Equipment:** Rankin Art Gallery, Student Recreation Center, Card Wildlife Museum, Jim Crowe Museum, Elastomer Center. **Computers:** 95% of public computers are PCs, 5% of public computers are Macs, network access in dorm rooms, network access in dorm lounges, online registration, online administrative functions (other than registration), remote student-access to Web through college's connection.

CAMPUS LIFE
Activities: Choral groups, concert band, dance, drama/theater, jazz band, literary magazine, music ensembles, pep band, radio station, student government, student newspaper, symphony orchestra, television station. **Organizations:** 180 registered organizations, 11 honor societies, 14 religious organizations. 8 fraternities (6% men join), 6 sororities (2% women join). **Athletics (Intercollegiate):** *Men:* Basketball, cheerleading, cross-country, football, golf, ice hockey, tennis, track/field (outdoor). *Women:* Basketball, cheerleading, cross-country, golf, soccer, softball, tennis, track/field (outdoor), volleyball.

ADMISSIONS
Freshman Academic Profile: 90% from public high schools. ACT middle 50% range 18–23. TOEFL required of all international applicants, minimum paper TOEFL 500, minimum computer TOEFL 173. **Basis for Candidate Selection:** *Very important factors considered include:* Academic GPA, standardized test scores. *Important factors considered include:* Character/personal qualities. *Other factors considered include:* Alumni/ae relation, extracurricular activities, recommendation(s), rigor of secondary school record,

volunteer work. **Freshman Admission Requirements:** High school diploma is required, and GED is accepted. *Academic units recommended:* 4 English, 4 math, 3 science (1 science lab), 2 foreign language, 2 social studies, 2 history, 3 academic electives. **Freshman Admission Statistics:** 8,623 applied, 76% admitted, 34% enrolled. **Transfer Admission Requirements:** College transcript(s), statement of good standing from prior institution(s). Minimum college GPA of 2.0 required. Lowest grade transferable C. **General Admission Information:** Application fee $30. Regular application deadline 8/4. Regular notification is rolling. Nonfall registration accepted. Credit and/or placement offered for CEEB Advanced Placement tests.

COSTS AND FINANCIAL AID

Annual in-state tuition $7,200. Out-of-state tuition $14,640. Room & board $7,220. Required fees $142. Average book expense $1,000. **Required Forms and Deadlines:** FAFSA. Financial aid filing deadline 8/3. **Notification of Awards:** Applicants will be notified of awards on or about 4/1. **Types of Aid:** *Need-based scholarships/grants:* Pell, SEOG, state scholarships/grants, private scholarships, the school's own gift aid. *Loans:* Direct Subsidized Stafford, Direct Unsubsidized Stafford, Direct PLUS, Federal Perkins, Federal Nursing, college/university loans from institutional funds, Key Loan, MI-Loan, CitiAssist. **Financial Aid Statistics:** 36% freshmen, 40% undergrads receive need-based scholarship or grant aid. 51% freshmen, 57% undergrads receive need-based self-help aid. 667 freshmen, 1,697 undergrads receive athletic scholarships. 68% freshmen, 86% undergrads receive any aid. Highest amount earned per year from on-campus jobs $4,992.

FERRUM COLLEGE

PO Box 1000, Ferrum, VA 24088
Phone: 540-365-4290 **E-mail:** admissions@ferrum.edu **CEEB Code:** 5213
Fax: 540-365-4366 **Website:** www.ferrum.edu **ACT Code:** 4352
Financial Aid Phone: 540-365-4282

This private school, affiliated with the Methodist Church, was founded in 1913. It has a 700-acre campus.

RATINGS

Admissions Selectivity Rating: 70   **Fire Safety Rating:** 60*   **Green Rating:** 60*

STUDENTS AND FACULTY

Enrollment: 951. **Student Body:** 40% female, 60% male, 18% out-of-state. African American 18%, Caucasian 71%, Hispanic 1%. **Retention and Graduation:** 55% freshmen return for sophomore year. 20% freshmen graduate within 4 years. **Faculty:** Student/faculty ratio 13:1. 68 full-time faculty, 65% hold PhDs. 100% faculty teach undergrads.

ACADEMICS

Degrees: Bachelor's. **Academic Requirements:** Arts/fine arts, computer literacy, English (including composition), foreign languages, history, humanities, mathematics, philosophy, religion, sciences (biological or physical), social science. **Classes:** Most classes have 10–19 students. Most lab/discussion sections have 20–29 students. **Majors with Highest Enrollment:** Business administration/management, criminal justice/safety studies, environmental science. **Disciplines with Highest Percentage of Degrees Awarded:** Business/marketing 24%, biological/life sciences 9%, education 8%, psychology 5%, social sciences 5%, computer and information sciences 4%. **Special Study Options:** Cooperative education program, double major, dual enrollment, honors program, independent study, internships, student-designed major, study abroad, teacher certification program.

FACILITIES

Housing: Coed dorms, men's dorms, women's dorms, apartments for married students, apartments for single students. **Special Academic Facilities/ Equipment:** Blue Ridge Institute and Farm Museum. **Computers:** 100% of public computers are PCs, network access in dorm rooms, network access in dorm lounges, remote student-access to Web through college's connection.

CAMPUS LIFE

Activities: Choral groups, dance, drama/theater, jazz band, literary magazine, music ensembles, musical theater, radio station, student government, student newspaper. **Organizations:** 60 registered organizations, 6 honor societies, 2 religious organizations. **Athletics (Intercollegiate):** *Men:* Baseball, basketball, cheerleading, cross-country, football, golf, soccer, tennis. *Women:* Basketball, cheerleading, cross-country, lacrosse, soccer, softball, tennis, volleyball.

ADMISSIONS

Freshman Academic Profile: 6% in top 10% of high school class, 19% in top 25% of high school class, 46% in top 50% of high school class. 85% from public

high schools. SAT Math middle 50% range 400–545. SAT Critical Reading middle 50% range 390–540. TOEFL required of all international applicants, minimum paper TOEFL 550. **Basis for Candidate Selection:** *Very important factors considered include:* Rigor of secondary school record. *Important factors considered include:* Character/personal qualities, extracurricular activities, recommendation(s), standardized test scores, talent/ability. *Other factors considered include:* Class rank, interview, volunteer work, work experience. **Freshman Admission Requirements:** High school diploma is required, and GED is accepted. *Academic units recommended:* 4 English, 3 math, 2 science (1 science lab), 2 foreign language, 3 social studies, 2 academic electives. **Freshman Admission Statistics:** 1,111 applied, 72% admitted, 37% enrolled. **Transfer Admission Requirements:** College transcript(s). Minimum college GPA of 2.0 required. Lowest grade transferable C. **General Admission Information:** Application fee $25. Regular notification 30 days after receipt of completed application. Nonfall registration accepted. Admission may be deferred for a maximum of 1 year. Common Application accepted. Credit and/ or placement offered for CEEB Advanced Placement tests.

COSTS AND FINANCIAL AID

Annual tuition $15,640. Room & board $5,600. Required fees $25. Average book expense $600. **Required Forms and Deadlines:** FAFSA, state aid form. Financial aid filing deadline 3/1. **Notification of Awards:** Applicants will be notified of awards on a rolling basis beginning on or about 3/1. **Types of Aid:** *Need-based scholarships/grants:* Pell, SEOG, state scholarships/grants, private scholarships, the school's own gift aid. *Loans:* FFEL Subsidized Stafford, FFEL Unsubsidized Stafford, FFEL PLUS, Federal Perkins, college/university loans from institutional funds. **Student Employment:** Federal Work-Study Program available. Institutional employment available. Off-campus job opportunities are fair. **Financial Aid Statistics:** 73% freshmen, 76% undergrads receive need-based scholarship or grant aid. 65% freshmen, 67% undergrads receive need-based self-help aid. Highest amount earned per year from on-campus jobs $2,000.

FISK UNIVERSITY

Best 368

1000 Seventeenth Avenue North, Nashville, TN 37208-3051
Phone: 615-329-8665 **E-mail:** admissions@fisk.edu **CEEB Code:** 1224
Fax: 615-329-8774 **Website:** www.fisk.edu **ACT Code:** 3960
Financial Aid Phone: 615-329-8735

This private school was founded in 1866. It has a 40-acre campus.

RATINGS

Admissions Selectivity Rating: 83   **Fire Safety Rating:** 60*   **Green Rating:** 60*

STUDENTS AND FACULTY

Enrollment: 812. **Student Body:** 71% out-of-state, 2% international (5 countries represented). African American 98%. **Retention and Graduation:** 92% freshmen return for sophomore year. 48% freshmen graduate within 4 years. 48% grads go on to further study within 1 year. 30% grads pursue arts and sciences degrees. 20% grads pursue business degrees. 20% grads pursue law degrees. 30% grads pursue medical degrees. **Faculty:** Student/faculty ratio 12:1. 63 full-time faculty, 81% hold PhDs. 100% faculty teach undergrads.

ACADEMICS

Degrees: Bachelor's, master's, post-bachelor's certificate. **Academic Requirements:** African American heritage, arts/fine arts, computer literacy, English (including composition), foreign languages, history, humanities, mathematics, sciences (biological or physical), social science. **Disciplines with Highest Percentage of Degrees Awarded:** Psychology 27%, business/ marketing 21%, biological/life sciences 17%, social sciences 15%, English 9%. **Special Study Options:** Cooperative education program, cross-registration, double major, exchange student program (domestic), honors program, independent study, internships, student-designed major, study abroad, teacher certification program.

FACILITIES

Housing: Men's dorms, women's dorms, apartments for married students. **Special Academic Facilities/Equipment:** Carl Van Vechten Gallery & Museum, Aaron Douglas Gallery, Special Collections of the John Hope and Aurelia Elizabeth Franklin Library. **Computers:** 100% of public computers are

PCs, network access in dorm rooms, network access in dorm lounges, online registration, online administrative functions (other than registration), remote student-access to Web through college's connection.

CAMPUS LIFE

Activities: Choral groups, dance, drama/theater, jazz band, literary magazine, music ensembles, musical theater, radio station, student government, student newspaper, yearbook. **Organizations:** 104 registered organizations, 9 honor societies, 5 religious organizations. 4 fraternities (15% men join), 4 sororities (20% women join). **Athletics (Intercollegiate): Men:** Baseball, basketball, cross-country, golf, soccer, softball, tennis, track/field (outdoor). *Women:* Basketball, cheerleading, cross-country, golf, soccer, softball, tennis, track/field (outdoor), volleyball.

ADMISSIONS

Freshman Academic Profile: 35% in top 10% of high school class, 48% in top 25% of high school class, 73% in top 50% of high school class. 85% from public high schools. SAT Math middle 50% range 365–620. SAT Critical Reading middle 50% range 395–650. ACT middle 50% range 17–29. TOEFL required of all international applicants, minimum paper TOEFL 500, minimum computer TOEFL 250. **Basis for Candidate Selection:** *Very important factors considered include:* Application essay, character/personal qualities, class rank, recommendation(s), rigor of secondary school record, standardized test scores, talent/ability. *Important factors considered include:* Alumni/ae relation, extracurricular activities, interview. *Other factors considered include:* Volunteer work. **Freshman Admission Requirements:** High school diploma is required, and GED is accepted. *Academic units required:* 4 English, 3 math, 2 science (2 science labs), 1 foreign language, 1 history, 4 academic electives. *Academic units recommended:* 4 English, 3 math, 3 science (2 science labs), 2 foreign language, 1 social studies, 1 history, 4 academic electives. **Freshman Admission Statistics:** 1,146 applied, 66% admitted, 29% enrolled. **Transfer Admission Requirements:** High school transcript, college transcript(s), essay or personal statement, statement of good standing from prior institution(s). Minimum college GPA of 2.0 required. Lowest grade transferable C. **General Admission Information:** Application fee $50. Early decision application deadline 12/1. Regular application deadline 3/1. Regular notification is rolling. Nonfall registration accepted. Admission may be deferred for a maximum of 1 semester. Common Application accepted. Credit offered for CEEB Advanced Placement tests.

COSTS AND FINANCIAL AID

Annual tuition $12,480. Room & board $6,730. Required fees $700. Average book expense $1,500. **Required Forms and Deadlines:** FAFSA. Financial aid filing deadline 3/15. **Notification of Awards:** Applicants will be notified of awards on a rolling basis beginning on or about 4/1. **Types of Aid:** *Need-based scholarships/grants:* Pell, SEOG, state scholarships/grants, private scholarships, the school's own gift aid, United Negro College Fund. *Loans:* Direct Subsidized Stafford, Direct Unsubsidized Stafford, Direct PLUS, FFEL PLUS, Federal Perkins. **Student Employment:** Federal Work-Study Program available. Off-campus job opportunities are excellent. **Financial Aid Statistics:** 58% freshmen, 63% undergrads receive need-based scholarship or grant aid. 81% freshmen, 85% undergrads receive need-based self-help aid. Highest amount earned per year from on-campus jobs $1,100.

FITCHBURG STATE COLLEGE

160 Pearl Street, Fitchburg, MA 01420-2697
Phone: 978-665-3144 **E-mail:** admissions@fsc.edu **CEEB Code:** 3518
Fax: 978-665-4540 **Website:** www.fsc.edu **ACT Code:** 1902
Financial Aid Phone: 978-665-3156

This public school was founded in 1894. It has a 78-acre campus.

RATINGS

Admissions Selectivity Rating: 60*   Fire Safety Rating: 92   Green Rating: 74

STUDENTS AND FACULTY

Enrollment: 3,157. **Student Body:** 57% female, 43% male, 5% out-of-state. African American 3%, Asian 2%, Caucasian 83%, Hispanic 3%. **Retention and Graduation:** 70% freshmen return for sophomore year. 10% grads go on to further study within 1 year. 7% grads pursue arts and sciences degrees. 3% grads pursue business degrees. **Faculty:** Student/faculty ratio 13:1. 183 full-time faculty, 87% hold PhDs. 100% faculty teach undergrads.

ACADEMICS

Degrees: Bachelor's, certificate, master's, post-bachelor's certificate, post-master's certificate. **Academic Requirements:** Arts/fine arts, computer

literacy, English (including composition), history, humanities, mathematics, philosophy, sciences (biological or physical), social science. **Classes:** Most classes have 10–19 students. **Majors with Highest Enrollment:** Business administration/management, cinematography and film/video production, education. **Disciplines with Highest Percentage of Degrees Awarded:** Business/marketing 17%, communication technologies 15%, health professions and related sciences 13%, social sciences 9%, English 7%. **Special Study Options:** Accelerated program, cross-registration, distance learning, double major, dual enrollment, honors program, independent study, internships, liberal arts/career combination, student-designed major, study abroad, teacher certification program.

FACILITIES

Housing: Coed dorms, apartments for single students, special housing for disabled students, alcohol- and tobacco-free housing. **Special Academic Facilities/Equipment:** Art gallery, graphics center, on-campus teacher education school, 120-acre conservation area. **Computers:** 90% of public computers are PCs, 10% of public computers are Macs, network access in dorm rooms, online registration, online administrative functions (other than registration), remote student-access to Web through college's connection.

CAMPUS LIFE

Activities: Choral groups, concert band, dance, drama/theater, jazz band, literary magazine, radio station, student government, student newspaper, yearbook. **Organizations:** 66 registered organizations, 7 honor societies, 1 religious organization. 3 fraternities (1% men join), 3 sororities (2% women join). **Athletics (Intercollegiate): Men:** Baseball, basketball, cross-country, football, ice hockey, soccer, track/field (indoor), track/field (outdoor). *Women:* Basketball, cross-country, field hockey, soccer, softball, track/field (indoor), track/field (outdoor). **Environmental initiatives:** Single stream recycling program.

ADMISSIONS

Freshman Academic Profile: 85% from public high schools. SAT Math middle 50% range 460–560. SAT Critical Reading middle 50% range 440–560. SAT Writing middle 50% range 450–540. ACT middle 50% range 17–22. TOEFL required of all international applicants, minimum paper TOEFL 550, minimum computer TOEFL 213. **Basis for Candidate Selection:** *Very important factors considered include:* Rigor of secondary school record. *Important factors considered include:* Application essay, standardized test scores. *Other factors considered include:* Alumni/ae relation, extracurricular activities, recommendation(s), talent/ability, volunteer work, work experience. **Freshman Admission Requirements:** High school diploma is required, and GED is accepted. *Academic units required:* 4 English, 3 math, 3 science (2 science labs), 2 foreign language, 1 social studies, 1 history, 2 academic electives. *Academic units recommended:* 4 math. **Freshman Admission Statistics:** 3,211 applied, 60% admitted, 33% enrolled. **Transfer Admission Requirements:** College transcript(s), essay or personal statement. Minimum college GPA of 2.0 required. Lowest grade transferable C. **General Admission Information:** Application fee $10. Regular notification is rolling. Nonfall registration accepted. Admission may be deferred for a maximum of 1 year. Common Application accepted. Credit offered for CEEB Advanced Placement tests.

COSTS AND FINANCIAL AID

Annual in-state tuition $970. Out-of-state tuition $7,050. Room & board $5,120. Required fees $2,718. Average book expense $600. **Required Forms and Deadlines:** FAFSA, no form required. Financial aid filing deadline 3/1. **Notification of Awards:** Applicants will be notified of awards on a rolling basis beginning on or about 3/15. **Types of Aid:** *Need-based scholarships/grants:* Pell, SEOG, state scholarships/grants, private scholarships, the school's own gift aid. *Loans:* Direct Subsidized Stafford, Direct Unsubsidized Stafford, Direct PLUS, Federal Perkins, Federal Nursing, state loans. **Student Employment:** Federal Work-Study Program available. Institutional employment available. Off-campus job opportunities are good. **Financial Aid Statistics:** 44% freshmen, 39% undergrads receive need-based scholarship or grant aid. 41% freshmen, 41% undergrads receive need-based self-help aid. 50% freshmen, 48% undergrads receive any aid. Highest amount earned per year from on-campus jobs $5,000.

FIVE TOWNS COLLEGE

Five Towns College, 305 North Service Road, Dix Hills, NY 11746
Phone: 631-656-2110 **E-mail:** admissions@ftc.edu **CEEB Code:** 3142
Fax: 631-656-2172 **Website:** www.ftc.edu
Financial Aid Phone: 631-424-7000

This private school was founded in 1972. It has a 35-acre campus.

RATINGS
Admissions Selectivity Rating: 60*   **Fire Safety Rating:** 60*   **Green Rating:** 60*

STUDENTS AND FACULTY
Enrollment: 1,136. **Student Body:** 39% female, 61% male, 6% out-of-state. African American 18%, Asian 2%, Caucasian 53%, Hispanic 13%. **Faculty:** Student/faculty ratio 13:1. 60 full-time faculty. 100% faculty teach undergrads.

ACADEMICS
Degrees: Associate, bachelor's, doctoral, master's. **Academic Requirements:** Computer literacy, English (including composition), humanities, social science. **Classes:** Most classes have 20–29 students. **Disciplines with Highest Percentage of Degrees Awarded:** Business/marketing 69%, visual and performing arts 23%, education 8%. **Special Study Options:** Distance learning, dual enrollment, honors program, independent study, internships, liberal arts/career combination, teacher certification program.

FACILITIES
Housing: Coed dorms. **Computers:** 70% of public computers are PCs, 30% of public computers are Macs, network access in dorm rooms.

CAMPUS LIFE
Activities: Choral groups, concert band, dance, drama/theater, jazz band, music ensembles, musical theater, opera, radio station, student government, student newspaper, symphony orchestra, television station, yearbook. **Organizations:** 1 honor society.

ADMISSIONS
Freshman Academic Profile: 80% from public high schools. SAT Math middle 50% range 410–500. SAT Critical Reading middle 50% range 410–500. SAT Writing middle 50% range 400–490. ACT middle 50% range 19–21. TOEFL required of all international applicants, minimum paper TOEFL 520, minimum computer TOEFL 190. **Basis for Candidate Selection:** *Very important factors considered include:* Academic GPA, character/personal qualities, rigor of secondary school record, standardized test scores, talent/ability. *Important factors considered include:* Application essay, class rank, extracurricular activities, interview, recommendation(s). *Other factors considered include:* Volunteer work, work experience. **Freshman Admission Requirements:** High school diploma is required, and GED is accepted. *Academic units recommended:* 4 English, 3 math, 2 science, 2 foreign language, 3 social studies. **Freshman Admission Statistics:** 1,153 applied, 59% admitted, 57% enrolled. **Transfer Admission Requirements:** High school transcript, college transcript(s), essay or personal statement, minimum college GPA of 2.0 required. Lowest grade transferable C. **General Admission Information:** Application fee $35. Early decision application deadline 12/1. Nonfall registration accepted. Admission may be deferred for a maximum of 1 semester. Placement offered for CEEB Advanced Placement tests.

COSTS AND FINANCIAL AID
Annual tuition $17,400. Room and board $11,850. Required fees $400. Average book expense $1,200. **Required Forms and Deadlines:** FAFSA, institution's own financial aid form, state aid form. Financial aid filing deadline 3/31. **Notification of Awards:** Applicants will be notified of awards on a rolling basis beginning on or about 3/31. **Types of Aid:** *Need-based scholarships/grants:* Pell, SEOG, state scholarships/grants, private scholarships, the school's own gift aid. *Loans:* Direct Subsidized Stafford, Direct Unsubsidized Stafford, Direct PLUS. **Financial Aid Statistics:** 54% freshmen, 64% undergrads receive need-based scholarship or grant aid. 50% freshmen, 59% undergrads receive need-based self-help aid. Highest amount earned per year from on-campus jobs $3,500.

See page 1172.

FLAGLER COLLEGE

74 King Street, PO Box 1027, St. Augustine, FL 32085-1027
Phone: 800-304-4208 **E-mail:** admiss@flagler.edu **CEEB Code:** 5235
Fax: 904-826-0094 **Website:** www.flagler.edu **ACT Code:** 0772
Financial Aid Phone: 904-819-6225

This private school was founded in 1968. It has a 42-acre campus.

RATINGS
Admissions Selectivity Rating: 88   **Fire Safety Rating:** 86   **Green Rating:** 65

STUDENTS AND FACULTY
Enrollment: 2,253. **Student Body:** 61% female, 39% male, 34% out-of-state. African American 2%, Caucasian 90%, Hispanic 4%. **Retention and Graduation:** 76% freshmen return for sophomore year. 41% freshmen graduate within 4 years. 20% grads go on to further study within 1 year. 3% grads pursue arts and sciences degrees. 4% grads pursue business degrees. 2% grads pursue law degrees. **Faculty:** Student/faculty ratio 20:1. 78 full-time faculty, 67% hold PhDs. 100% faculty teach undergrads.

ACADEMICS
Degrees: Bachelor's. **Academic Requirements:** Computer literacy, English (including composition), humanities, mathematics, social science. **Classes:** Most classes have 20–29 students. Most lab/discussion sections have fewer than 10 students. **Majors with Highest Enrollment:** Business administration/management; communications, journalism, and related fields; elementary education and teaching. **Disciplines with Highest Percentage of Degrees Awarded:** Business/marketing 26%, communications/journalism 18%, visual and performing arts 16%, education 16%, psychology 9%. **Special Study Options:** Double major, independent study, internships, liberal arts/career combination, study abroad, teacher certification program.

FACILITIES
Housing: Men's dorms, women's dorms. **Special Academic Facilities/Equipment:** Museum/theater, learning disabilities clinic for student teachers, Northeast Florida Archaeological Association. **Computers:** 10% of classrooms are wireless, 75% of public computers are PCs, 25% of public computers are Macs, network access in dorm rooms, online registration, online administrative functions (other than registration), remote student-access to Web through college's connection.

CAMPUS LIFE
Activities: Choral groups, dance, drama/theater, literary magazine, radio station, student government, student newspaper. **Organizations:** 29 registered organizations, 6 honor societies, 2 religious organizations. **Athletics (Intercollegiate):** *Men:* Baseball, basketball, cross-country, golf, soccer, tennis. *Women:* Basketball, cross-country, golf, soccer, tennis, volleyball. **Environmental initiatives:** Chiller upgrades. Compact flourescents. Green cleaning supplies.

ADMISSIONS
Freshman Academic Profile: 18% in top 10% of high school class, 50% in top 25% of high school class, 84% in top 50% of high school class. 78% from public high schools. SAT Math middle 50% range 510–590. SAT Critical Reading middle 50% range 520–610. SAT Writing middle 50% range 500–600. ACT middle 50% range 21–25. TOEFL required of all international applicants, minimum paper TOEFL 550, minimum computer TOEFL 213. **Basis for Candidate Selection:** *Very important factors considered include:* Academic GPA, rigor of secondary school record, standardized test scores. *Important factors considered include:* Application essay, character/personal qualities, extracurricular activities, recommendation(s). *Other factors considered include:* Alumni/ae relation, class rank, first generation, interview, level of applicant's interest, talent/ability, volunteer work, work experience. **Freshman Admission Requirements:** High school diploma is required, and GED is accepted. *Academic units required:* 4 English, 3 math, 2 science (1 science lab), 2 social studies, 1 history, 1 academic elective. *Academic units recommended:* 4 English, 4 math, 3 science (2 science labs), 2 foreign language, 3 social studies, 2 history, 2 academic electives. **Freshman Admission Statistics:** 2,377 applied, 26% admitted, 76% enrolled. **Transfer Admission Requirements:** College transcript(s), essay or personal statement, standardized test score. Minimum college GPA of 2.7 required. Lowest grade transferable C. **General Admission Information:** Application fee $40. Early decision application deadline 12/1. Regular application deadline 3/1. Regular notification 3/30. Nonfall registration

accepted. Admission may be deferred for a maximum of 1 semester. Credit and/or placement offered for CEEB Advanced Placement tests.

COSTS AND FINANCIAL AID
Annual tuition $13,600. Room and board $6,900. Average book expense $900. **Required Forms and Deadlines:** FAFSA, institution's own financial aid form, state aid form. Financial aid filing deadline 4/1. **Notification of Awards:** Applicants will be notified of awards on a rolling basis beginning on or about 4/1. **Types of Aid:** *Need-based scholarships/grants:* Pell, SEOG, state scholarships/grants, private scholarships, the school's own gift aid. *Loans:* Direct Subsidized Stafford, Direct Unsubsidized Stafford, Direct PLUS, Federal Perkins. **Student Employment:** Federal Work-Study Program available. Institutional employment available. Off-campus job opportunities are excellent. **Financial Aid Statistics:** 16% freshmen, 20% undergrads receive need-based scholarship or grant aid. 25% freshmen, 33% undergrads receive need-based self-help aid. 28 freshmen, 121 undergrads receive athletic scholarships. 70% freshmen, 86% undergrads receive any aid. Highest amount earned per year from on-campus jobs $900.

FLORIDA A&M UNIVERSITY

Suite G-9, Foote-Hilyer Administration Center, Tallahassee, FL 32307
Phone: 850-599-3796 **E-mail:** admission@famu.edu **CEEB Code:** 5215
Fax: 850-599-3069 **Website:** www.famu.edu **ACT Code:** 0726
Financial Aid Phone: 850-599-3730

This public school was founded in 1887. It has a 419-acre campus.

RATINGS
Admissions Selectivity Rating: 60* **Fire Safety Rating:** 87 **Green Rating:** 60*

STUDENTS AND FACULTY
Enrollment: 9,957. **Student Body:** 58% female, 42% male, 27% out-of-state. African American 86%, Caucasian 2%. **Retention and Graduation:** 25% grads go on to further study within 1 year. 25% grads pursue arts and sciences degrees. **Faculty:** Student/faculty ratio 19:1. 610 full-time faculty, 73% hold PhDs. 90% faculty teach undergrads.

ACADEMICS
Degrees: Associate, bachelor's, doctoral, first professional, master's. **Academic Requirements:** Computer literacy, English (including composition), foreign languages, history, humanities, mathematics, sciences (biological or physical), social science. **Classes:** Most classes have fewer than 10 students. **Majors with Highest Enrollment:** Business administration/management, pharmacy (PharMD, BS/BPharm). **Disciplines with Highest Percentage of Degrees Awarded:** Business/marketing 16%, health professions and related sciences 11%, security and protective services 9%, education 8%, psychology 7%, social sciences 7%. **Special Study Options:** Accelerated program, cooperative education program, distance learning, double major, dual enrollment, honors program, independent study, internships, study abroad, teacher certification program, weekend college.

FACILITIES
Housing: Coed dorms, men's dorms, women's dorms, apartments for married students, apartment complex agreement through the university. **Special Academic Facilities/Equipment:** Black Archives and Resource Center, Coleman Memorial Library, Foster Tanner Music/Art Building. **Computers:** Network access in dorm rooms, network access in dorm lounges, remote student-access to Web through college's connection.

CAMPUS LIFE
Activities: Choral groups, concert band, dance, drama/theater, jazz band, marching band, music ensembles, pep band, radio station, student government, student newspaper, symphony orchestra, television station, yearbook. **Organizations:** 9 registered organizations, 16 honor societies, 11 religious organizations. 4 fraternities, 2 sororities. **Athletics (Intercollegiate):** *Men:* Baseball, basketball, cross-country, football, golf, swimming, tennis, track/field (outdoor). *Women:* Basketball, cross-country, golf, softball, swimming, tennis, track/field (outdoor), volleyball.

ADMISSIONS
Freshman Academic Profile: 85% from public high schools. SAT Math middle 50% range 440–550. SAT Critical Reading middle 50% range 440–550. ACT middle 50% range 19–22. TOEFL required of all international applicants, minimum paper TOEFL 500. **Basis for Candidate Selection:** *Very important factors considered include:* Academic GPA, application essay, rigor of secondary school record, standardized test scores. *Other factors considered include:* Alumni/ae relation, character/personal qualities, class rank, extracurricular

activities, racial/ethnic status, state residency, talent/ability, volunteer work, work experience. **Freshman Admission Requirements:** High school diploma is required, and GED is accepted. *Academic units required:* 4 English, 3 math, 3 science (1 science lab), 2 foreign language, 3 social studies, 3 academic electives. *Academic units recommended:* 4 English, 3 math, 3 science, 2 foreign language, 3 social studies, 3 academic electives. **Freshman Admission Statistics:** 4,708 applied, 61% admitted, 61% enrolled. **Transfer Admission Requirements:** College transcript(s). Minimum college GPA of 2.0 required. Lowest grade transferable C. **General Admission Information:** Application fee $20. Regular application deadline 5/9. Regular notification rolling. Nonfall registration accepted. Credit offered for CEEB Advanced Placement tests.

COSTS AND FINANCIAL AID
Annual in-state tuition $3,047. Out-of-state tuition $14,243. Room & board $5,492. Required fees $222. Average book expense $700. **Required Forms and Deadlines:** FAFSA. Financial aid filing deadline 6/30. **Notification of Awards:** Applicants will be notified of awards on or about 5/1. **Types of Aid:** *Need-based scholarships/grants:* Pell, SEOG, state scholarships/grants, private scholarships, the school's own gift aid, United Negro College Fund, Federal Nursing Scholarships. *Loans:* Direct Subsidized Stafford, Direct Unsubsidized Stafford, Direct PLUS, Federal Perkins. **Student Employment:** Federal Work-Study Program available. Off-campus job opportunities are good. **Financial Aid Statistics:** 57% freshmen, 61% undergrads receive need-based scholarship or grant aid. 44% freshmen, 60% undergrads receive need-based self-help aid. 46 freshmen, 254 undergrads receive athletic scholarships. Highest amount earned per year from on-campus jobs $900.

FLORIDA ATLANTIC UNIVERSITY

777 Glades Road, PO Box 3091, Boca Raton, FL 33431-0991
Phone: 561-297-3040 **E-mail:** UGRecruitment@fau.edu **CEEB Code:** 5229
Fax: 561-297-2758 **Website:** www.fau.edu **ACT Code:** 0729
Financial Aid Phone: 561-297-3530

This public school was founded in 1961. It has an 860-acre campus.

RATINGS
Admissions Selectivity Rating: 76 **Fire Safety Rating:** 60* **Green Rating:** 60*

STUDENTS AND FACULTY
Enrollment: 19,951. **Student Body:** 60% female, 40% male, 5% out-of-state, 3% international. African American 18%, Asian 4%, Caucasian 56%, Hispanic 18%. **Retention and Graduation:** 72% freshmen return for sophomore year. 15% freshmen graduate within 4 years. **Faculty:** Student/faculty ratio 18:1. 767 full-time faculty, 88% hold PhDs. 85% faculty teach undergrads.

ACADEMICS
Degrees: Associate, bachelor's, doctoral, master's, post-bachelor's certificate, post-master's certificate. **Academic Requirements:** Arts/fine arts, English (including composition), foreign languages, history, humanities, mathematics, sciences (biological or physical), social science. **Classes:** Most classes have 20–29 students. Most lab/discussion sections have 20–29 students. **Disciplines with Highest Percentage of Degrees Awarded:** Business/marketing 28%, health professions and related sciences 8%, social sciences 8%, psychology 6%, English 6%, security and protective services 5%, public administration and social services 4%, biological/life sciences 4%, engineering 4%. **Special Study Options:** Accelerated program, cooperative education program, cross-registration, distance learning, double major, dual enrollment, English as a second language (ESL), exchange student program (domestic), honors program, independent study, internships, liberal arts/career combination, study abroad, teacher certification program, weekend college.

FACILITIES
Housing: Coed dorms, apartments for married students, apartments for single students. **Special Academic Facilities/Equipment:** Art gallery, on-campus elementary school, robotics lab, marine research facilities. **Computers:** 80% of public computers are PCs, 20% of public computers are Macs, network access in dorm rooms, online registration, online administrative functions (other than registration), remote student-access to Web through college's connection.

CAMPUS LIFE
Activities: Choral groups, dance, drama/theater, jazz band, literary magazine, marching band, music ensembles, musical theater, opera, radio station, student government, student newspaper, television station. **Organizations:** 150 registered organizations, 11 honor societies, 6 religious organizations. 9 fraternities (2% men join), 4 sororities (2% women join). **Athletics (Intercollegiate):** *Men:* Baseball, basketball, cheerleading, cross-country, diving, football,

golf, soccer, swimming, tennis. *Women:* Basketball, cheerleading, cross-country, diving, golf, soccer, softball, swimming, tennis, track/field (outdoor), volleyball.

ADMISSIONS

Freshman Academic Profile: SAT Math middle 50% range 470–560. SAT Critical Reading middle 50% range 260–550. SAT Writing middle 50% range 450–540. ACT middle 50% range 19–23. TOEFL required of all international applicants, minimum paper TOEFL 550, minimum computer TOEFL 300. **Basis for Candidate Selection:** *Very important factors considered include:* Academic GPA, standardized test scores. *Important factors considered include:* Rigor of secondary school record. *Other factors considered include:* Alumni/ae relation, extracurricular activities, recommendation(s), talent/ability. **Freshman Admission Requirements:** High school diploma is required, and GED is accepted. *Academic units required:* 4 English, 3 math, 3 science (2 science labs), 2 foreign language, 3 social studies, 3 academic electives. **Freshman Admission Statistics:** 11,698 applied, 55% admitted, 39% enrolled. **Transfer Admission Requirements:** College transcript(s). Minimum college GPA of 2.0 required. Lowest grade transferable D. **General Admission Information:** Application fee $30. Regular application deadline 6/1. Nonfall registration accepted. Admission may be deferred for a maximum of 2 semesters. Credit offered for CEEB Advanced Placement tests.

COSTS AND FINANCIAL AID

Annual in-state tuition $3,367. Annual out-of-state tuition $16,431. Room and board $8,610. Average book expense $748. **Required Forms and Deadlines:** FAFSA, financial aid transcript. Financial aid filing deadline 3/1. **Notification of Awards:** Applicants will be notified of awards on a rolling basis beginning on or about 5/1. **Types of Aid:** *Need-based scholarships/grants:* Pell, SEOG, state scholarships/grants, private scholarships, the school's own gift aid, Federal Nursing Scholarships. *Loans:* FFEL Subsidized Stafford, FFEL Unsubsidized Stafford, FFEL PLUS, Federal Perkins, college/university loans from institutional funds. **Student Employment:** Off-campus job opportunities are excellent. **Financial Aid Statistics:** 37% freshmen, 39% undergrads receive need-based scholarship or grant aid. 23% freshmen, 32% undergrads receive need-based self-help aid. 41 freshmen, 182 undergrads receive athletic scholarships. Highest amount earned per year from on-campus jobs $1,500.

See page 1174.

FLORIDA COLLEGE

Admissions Office, 119 North Glen Arven Avenue, Temple Terrace, FL 33617-5578
Phone: 813-899-6716 **E-mail:** admissions@FloridaCollege.edu **CEEB Code:** 1562
Fax: 813-899-6722 **Website:** www.floridacollege.edu **ACT Code:** 1482
Financial Aid Phone: 813-899-6774

This private school was founded in 1946.

RATINGS

Admissions Selectivity Rating: 60*   **Fire Safety Rating:** 60*   **Green Rating:** 60*

STUDENTS AND FACULTY

Enrollment: 507. **Student Body:** 51% female, 49% male, 64% out-of-state, 1% international. African American 3%, Caucasian 92%, Hispanic 4%. **Retention and Graduation:** 75% freshmen return for sophomore year. **Faculty:** 31 full-time faculty, 26% hold PhDs. 100% faculty teach undergrads.

ACADEMICS

Degrees: Associate, bachelor's. **Academic Requirements:** Arts/fine arts, computer literacy, English (including composition), history, humanities, mathematics, sciences (biological or physical), social science. **Classes:** Most classes have fewer than 10 students. Most lab/discussion sections have fewer than 10 students. **Disciplines with Highest Percentage of Degrees Awarded:** Theology and religious vocations 28%, liberal arts/general studies 22%.

FACILITIES

Housing: Men's dorms, women's dorms, special housing for disabled students. **Computers:** Network access in dorm rooms.

CAMPUS LIFE

Activities: Choral groups, concert band, drama/theater, jazz band, literary magazine, music ensembles, musical theater, pep band, student government, yearbook. **Athletics (Intercollegiate):** *Men:* Baseball, basketball. *Women:* volleyball.

ADMISSIONS

Freshman Academic Profile: SAT Math middle 50% range 460–590. SAT Critical Reading middle 50% range 430–590. ACT middle 50% range 19–26.

TOEFL required of all international applicants, minimum paper TOEFL 550, minimum computer TOEFL 213. **Basis for Candidate Selection:** *Very important factors considered include:* Recommendation(s), rigor of secondary school record. *Important factors considered include:* Character/personal qualities, standardized test scores. *Other factors considered include:* Alumni/ae relation, application essay, extracurricular activities, interview, religious affiliation/commitment. **Freshman Admission Requirements:** High school diploma is required, and GED is accepted. *Academic units required:* 4 English, 3 math, 2 science (2 science labs), 2 social studies. *Academic units recommended:* 2 foreign language, 3 social studies. **Freshman Admission Statistics:** 342 applied, 67% admitted, 94% enrolled. **Transfer Admission Requirements:** High school transcript, college transcript(s), standardized test score, statement of good standing from prior institution(s). Minimum college GPA of 2.0 required. Lowest grade transferable C. **General Admission Information:** Application fee $25. Regular application deadline 8/1. Regular notification when accepted. Nonfall registration accepted. Credit and/or placement offered for CEEB Advanced Placement tests.

COSTS AND FINANCIAL AID

Average book expense $1,760. **Required Forms and Deadlines:** FAFSA, institution's own financial aid form, state aid form. Financial aid filing deadline 6/1. **Notification of Awards:** Applicants will be notified of awards on a rolling basis beginning on or about 3/2. **Types of Aid:** *Need-based scholarships/grants:* Pell, SEOG, state scholarships/grants, private scholarships, the school's own gift aid. *Loans:* FFEL Subsidized Stafford, FFEL Unsubsidized Stafford, FFEL PLUS, Federal Perkins, alternative loans. **Financial Aid Statistics:** 52% freshmen, 52% undergrads receive need-based scholarship or grant aid. 50% freshmen, 50% undergrads receive need-based self-help aid. 15 freshmen, 36 undergrads receive athletic scholarships.

FLORIDA GULF COAST UNIVERSITY

10501 FGCU Boulevard South, Fort Myers, FL 33965-6565
Phone: 239-590-7878 **E-mail:** admissions@fgcu.edu **CEEB Code:** 5221
Fax: 239-590-7894 **Website:** www.fgcu.edu **ACT Code:** 0733
Financial Aid Phone: 239-590-7920

This public school was founded in 1991. It has a 760-acre campus.

RATINGS

Admissions Selectivity Rating: 77   **Fire Safety Rating:** 94   **Green Rating:** 60*

STUDENTS AND FACULTY

Enrollment: 6,964. **Student Body:** 61% female, 39% male, 9% out-of-state. African American 5%, Asian 2%, Caucasian 78%, Hispanic 11%. **Retention and Graduation:** 73% freshmen return for sophomore year. 15% grads go on to further study within 1 year. **Faculty:** Student/faculty ratio 17:1. 278 full-time faculty, 80% hold PhDs. 100% faculty teach undergrads.

ACADEMICS

Degrees: Associate, bachelor's, certificate, master's. **Academic Requirements:** English (including composition), foreign languages, humanities, mathematics, general education program. **Classes:** Most classes have 20–29 students. **Majors with Highest Enrollment:** Business administration/management, elementary education and teaching, liberal arts and sciences/liberal studies. **Disciplines with Highest Percentage of Degrees Awarded:** Liberal arts/general studies 31%, business/marketing 30%, education 12%, health professions and related sciences 11%, security and protective services 8%. **Special Study Options:** Accelerated program, cooperative education program, cross-registration, distance learning, double major, dual enrollment, honors program, independent study, internships, study abroad, teacher certification program.

FACILITIES

Housing: Coed dorms, apartments for single students, special housing for disabled students. **Special Academic Facilities/Equipment:** Art gallery, observatory. **Computers:** 90% of public computers are PCs, 10% of public computers are Macs, network access in dorm rooms, network access in dorm lounges, online registration, online administrative functions (other than registration), remote student-access to Web through college's connection.

CAMPUS LIFE

Activities: Choral groups, dance, drama/theater, literary magazine, radio station, student government, student newspaper. **Organizations:** 105 registered organizations, 7 honor societies, 8 religious organizations. 4 fraternities (1% men join), 4 sororities (1% women join). **Athletics (Intercollegiate):** *Men:* Baseball, basketball, cross-country, golf, tennis. *Women:* Basketball, cross-country, golf, softball, tennis, volleyball.

ADMISSIONS

Freshman Academic Profile: 16% in top 10% of high school class, 46% in top 25% of high school class, 84% in top 50% of high school class. SAT Math middle 50% range 470–560. SAT Critical Reading middle 50% range 460–550. ACT middle 50% range 20–23. TOEFL required of all international applicants, minimum paper TOEFL 550, minimum computer TOEFL 213. **Basis for Candidate Selection:** *Very important factors considered include:* Academic GPA, rigor of secondary school record, standardized test scores. *Other factors considered include:* Application essay, character/personal qualities, class rank, extracurricular activities, recommendation(s), talent/ability. **Freshman Admission Requirements:** High school diploma is required, and GED is accepted. *Academic units required:* 4 English, 3 math, 3 science (2 science labs), 2 foreign language, 3 social studies, 3 academic electives. **Freshman Admission Statistics:** 4,783 applied, 71% admitted, 48% enrolled. **Transfer Admission Requirements:** College transcript(s). Minimum college GPA of 2.0 required. Lowest grade transferable D. **General Admission Information:** Application fee $30. Regular application deadline 6/2. Regular notification rolling. Nonfall registration accepted. Admission may be deferred for a maximum of 2 semesters. Credit and/or placement offered for CEEB Advanced Placement tests.

COSTS AND FINANCIAL AID

Annual in-state tuition $3,657. Annual out-of-state tuition $16,175. Room and board $8,267. Required fees $2,042. Average book expense $950. **Required Forms and Deadlines:** FAFSA, institution's own financial aid form. Financial aid filing deadline 6/30. **Notification of Awards:** Applicants will be notified of awards on a rolling basis beginning on or about 2/15. **Types of Aid:** *Need-based scholarships/grants:* Pell, SEOG, state scholarships/grants, private scholarships, the school's own gift aid. *Loans:* FFEL Subsidized Stafford, FFEL Unsubsidized Stafford, FFEL PLUS, state loans. **Financial Aid Statistics:** 21% freshmen, 24% undergrads receive need-based scholarship or grant aid. 18% freshmen, 24% undergrads receive need-based self-help aid. 15 freshmen, 93 undergrads receive athletic scholarships. 73% freshmen, 67% undergrads receive any aid. Highest amount earned per year from on-campus jobs $10,530.

FLORIDA INSTITUTE OF TECHNOLOGY

150 West University Boulevard, Melbourne, FL 32901-6975
Phone: 321-674-8030 **E-mail:** admission@fit.edu **CEEB Code:** 5080
Fax: 321-723-9468 **Website:** www.fit.edu **ACT Code:** 0716
Financial Aid Phone: 800-666-4348

This private school was founded in 1958. It has a 130-acre campus.

RATINGS

Admissions Selectivity Rating: 86   **Fire Safety Rating:** 83   **Green Rating:** 67

STUDENTS AND FACULTY

Enrollment: 2,331. **Student Body:** 31% female, 69% male, 62% out-of-state, 16% international (99 countries represented). African American 3%, Asian 3%, Caucasian 55%, Hispanic 7%. **Retention and Graduation:** 77% freshmen return for sophomore year. 39% freshmen graduate within 4 years. 23% grads go on to further study within 1 year. 10% grads pursue arts and sciences degrees. 2% grads pursue business degrees. 1% grads pursue law degrees. 2% grads pursue medical degrees. **Faculty:** Student/faculty ratio 13:1. 214 full-time faculty, 90% hold PhDs. 98% faculty teach undergrads.

ACADEMICS

Degrees: Bachelor's, doctoral, master's, post-master's certificate. **Academic Requirements:** Computer literacy, English (including composition), humanities, mathematics, sciences (biological or physical), social science. **Classes:** Most classes have 10–19 students. Most lab/discussion sections have 10–19 students. **Majors with Highest Enrollment:** Aerospace, aeronautical, and astronautical engineering; aviation/airway management and operations; mechanical engineering. **Disciplines with Highest Percentage of Degrees Awarded:** Engineering 34%, transportation and materials moving 14%, biological/life sciences 12%, physical sciences 12%, business/marketing 8%, computer and information sciences 7%. **Special Study Options:** Cooperative education program, distance learning, double major, dual enrollment, English as a second language (ESL), independent study, internships, study abroad, teacher certification program. Dual degrees in computer engineering/electrical engineering, chemical engineering/chemistry, molecular/marine biology.

FACILITIES

Housing: Coed dorms, special housing for disabled students. **Special Academic Facilities/Equipment:** Medical genetics lab, research vessel, observatory, wind and hurricane impacts research lab, aquaculture lab, Center for Airport Management. **Computers:** 1% of classrooms are wired, 100% of classrooms are wireless, 93% of public computers are PCs, 6% of public computers are Macs, 2% of public computers are UNIX, network access in dorm rooms, network access in dorm lounges, online registration, online administrative functions (other than registration), support for handheld computing, remote student-access to Web through college's connection.

CAMPUS LIFE

Activities: Choral groups, concert band, dance, drama/theater, literary magazine, pep band, radio station, student government, student newspaper, student-run film society, television station. **Organizations:** 94 registered organizations, 10 honor societies, 3 religious organizations. 11 fraternities (16% men join), 8 sororities (15% women join). **Athletics (Intercollegiate):** *Men:* Baseball, basketball, cross-country, golf, soccer, tennis. *Women:* Basketball, crew/rowing, cross-country, golf, soccer, softball, tennis, volleyball.

ADMISSIONS

Freshman Academic Profile: 34% in top 10% of high school class, 60% in top 25% of high school class, 92% in top 50% of high school class. 70% from public high schools. SAT Math middle 50% range 530–640. SAT Critical Reading middle 50% range 510–610. ACT middle 50% range 22–28. TOEFL required of all international applicants, minimum paper TOEFL 550, minimum computer TOEFL 213. **Basis for Candidate Selection:** *Very important factors considered include:* Rigor of secondary school record. *Important factors considered include:* Academic GPA, recommendation(s), standardized test scores. *Other factors considered include:* Character/personal qualities, class rank, work experience. **Freshman Admission Requirements:** High school diploma is required, and GED is accepted. *Academic units required:* 4 English, 4 math, 4 science (2 science labs). *Academic units recommended:* 2 foreign language, 1 social studies, 2 history. **Freshman Admission Statistics:** 5,235 applied, 61% admitted, 19% enrolled. **Transfer Admission Requirements:** College transcript(s). Minimum college GPA of 2.5 required. Lowest grade transferable C. **General Admission Information:** Application fee $50. Regular notification is rolling. Nonfall registration accepted. Admission may be deferred for a maximum of 2 years. Credit and/or placement offered for CEEB Advanced Placement tests.

COSTS AND FINANCIAL AID

Annual tuition $27,540. Room & board $7,400. Average book expense $2,200. **Required Forms and Deadlines:** FAFSA, state aid form. Financial aid filing deadline 3/15. **Notification of Awards:** Applicants will be notified of awards on a rolling basis beginning on or about 2/15. **Types of Aid:** *Need-based scholarships/grants:* Pell, SEOG, state scholarships/grants, private scholarships, the school's own gift aid. *Loans:* FFEL Subsidized Stafford, FFEL Unsubsidized Stafford, FFEL PLUS, Federal Perkins, state loans, college/university loans from institutional funds. **Financial Aid Statistics:** 62% freshmen, 62% undergrads receive need-based scholarship or grant aid. 49% freshmen, 51% undergrads receive need-based self-help aid. 14 freshmen, 53 undergrads receive athletic scholarships. 62% freshmen, 61% undergrads receive any aid. Highest amount earned per year from on-campus jobs $20,000.

FLORIDA INTERNATIONAL UNIVERSITY

University Park, PC 140, Miami, FL 33199
Phone: 305-348-2363 **E-mail:** admiss@fiu.edu **CEEB Code:** 5206
Fax: 305-348-3648 **Website:** www.fiu.edu **ACT Code:** 0776
Financial Aid Phone: 305-348-1500

This public school was founded in 1965. It has a 573-acre campus.

RATINGS

Admissions Selectivity Rating: 91   **Fire Safety Rating:** 60*   **Green Rating:** 60*

STUDENTS AND FACULTY

Enrollment: 28,491. **Student Body:** 57% female, 43% male, 15% out-of-state, 7% international (126 countries represented). African American 13%, Asian 4%, Caucasian 16%, Hispanic 59%. **Retention and Graduation:** 75% freshmen return for sophomore year. 37% grads go on to further study within 1 year. 25% grads pursue arts and sciences degrees. 11% grads pursue business degrees. 4% grads pursue law degrees. 3% grads pursue medical degrees. **Faculty:** Student/faculty ratio 17:1. 757 full-time faculty, 79% hold PhDs.

ACADEMICS

Degrees: Bachelor's, doctoral, first professional, master's, post-bachelor's certificate. **Academic Requirements:** Computer literacy, English (including composition), foreign languages, humanities, mathematics, sciences (biological or physical), social science. **Classes:** Most classes have 20–29 students. Most lab/discussion sections have 20–29 students. **Majors with Highest Enrollment:** Business administration/management, communications studies/speech communication and rhetoric, psychology. **Disciplines with Highest Percentage of Degrees Awarded:** Business/marketing 34%, health professions and related sciences 9%, psychology 8%, social sciences 7%, education 6%, communications/journalism 6%. **Special Study Options:** Distance learning, double major, dual enrollment, exchange student program (domestic), honors program, independent study, internships, study abroad, teacher certification program, weekend college.

FACILITIES

Housing: Coed dorms, apartments for married students, apartments for single students. **Special Academic Facilities/Equipment:** Art gallery, Consumer Affairs Institute, Center for Economic Studies, Women's Studies Center, robotics lab. **Computers:** Network access in dorm rooms, online registration, online administrative functions (other than registration), remote student-access to Web through college's connection.

CAMPUS LIFE

Activities: Drama/theater, jazz band, marching band, music ensembles, musical theater, radio station, student government, student newspaper, yearbook. **Organizations:** 190 registered organizations, 40 honor societies, 2 religious organizations. 13 fraternities (14% men join), 10 sororities (14% women join). **Athletics (Intercollegiate):** *Men:* Baseball, basketball, cross-country, football, soccer, track/field (outdoor). *Women:* Basketball, cross-country, golf, soccer, softball, tennis, track/field (outdoor), volleyball.

ADMISSIONS

Freshman Academic Profile: 42% in top 10% of high school class, 89% in top 25% of high school class, 99% in top 50% of high school class. 52% from public high schools. SAT Math middle 50% range 505–590. SAT Critical Reading middle 50% range 500–600. SAT Writing middle 50% range 400–570. ACT middle 50% range 21–25. TOEFL required of all international applicants, minimum paper TOEFL 500, minimum computer TOEFL 173. **Basis for Candidate Selection:** *Very important factors considered include:* Academic GPA, character/personal qualities, class rank, extracurricular activities, geographical residence, rigor of secondary school record, standardized test scores, state residency, talent/ability. *Other factors considered include:* Interview, recommendation(s). **Freshman Admission Requirements:** High school diploma is required, and GED is accepted. *Academic units required:* 4 English, 3 math, 3 science (2 science labs), 2 foreign language, 3 social studies, 3 academic electives. **Freshman Admission Statistics:** 10,223 applied, 47% admitted, 52% enrolled. **Transfer Admission Requirements:** College transcript(s). Minimum college GPA of 2.0 required. Lowest grade transferable D. **General Admission Information:** Application fee $30. Regular notification rolling. Nonfall registration accepted. Admission may be deferred for a maximum of 1 year. Common Application accepted. Credit offered for CEEB Advanced Placement tests.

COSTS AND FINANCIAL AID

Annual in-state tuition $2,696. Out-of-state tuition $12,162. Room & board $7,180. Required fees $185. Average book expense $1,080. **Required Forms and Deadlines:** FAFSA. Financial aid filing deadline 3/1. **Notification of Awards:** Applicants will be notified of awards on or about 4/15. **Types of Aid:** *Need-based scholarships/grants:* Pell, SEOG, state scholarships/grants, private scholarships, the school's own gift aid. *Loans:* FFEL Subsidized Stafford, FFEL Unsubsidized Stafford, FFEL PLUS, Federal Perkins, college/university loans from institutional funds. **Financial Aid Statistics:** 36% freshmen, 41% undergrads receive need-based scholarship or grant aid. 14% freshmen, 23% undergrads receive need-based self-help aid. 13 freshmen, 77 undergrads receive athletic scholarships.

FLORIDA MEMORIAL COLLEGE

15800 NW Forty-second Avenue, Miami, FL 33054
Phone: 800-822-1362 **E-mail:** pmartin@fmc.edu **CEEB Code:** 5217
Fax: 305-625-4141 **Website:** www.fmc.edu **ACT Code:** 0730
Financial Aid Phone: 305-626-3745

This private school, affiliated with the Baptist Church, was founded in 1879.

RATINGS

Admissions Selectivity Rating: 60*   **Fire Safety Rating:** 60*   **Green Rating:** 60*

STUDENTS AND FACULTY

Student Body: 20% out-of-state.

ACADEMICS

Degrees: Bachelor's. **Special Study Options:** Cooperative education program, exchange student program (domestic), study abroad.

FACILITIES

Housing: Coed dorms, men's dorms, women's dorms, fraternity/sorority housing. **Special Academic Facilities/Equipment:** Reading and study skills labs.

CAMPUS LIFE

Organizations: 1 honor society, 1 religious organization. 4 fraternities, 4 sororities. **Athletics (Intercollegiate):** *Men:* Baseball, basketball, cross-country, soccer, softball, track/field (outdoor), volleyball. *Women:* Basketball, softball, volleyball.

ADMISSIONS

Freshman Academic Profile: 100% from public high schools. **Freshman Admission Requirements:** High school diploma is required, and GED is accepted. *Academic units recommended:* 4 English, 4 math, 3 science, 2 foreign language, 2 social studies. **Transfer Admission Requirements:** Lowest grade transferable C. **General Admission Information:** Early decision application deadline 4/1. Regular application deadline 7/1. Regular notification rolling. Nonfall registration accepted. Common Application not accepted.

COSTS AND FINANCIAL AID

Annual tuition $5,420. Room & board $2,428. Required fees $1,030. Average book expense $550. **Required Forms and Deadlines:** FAFSA. **Types of Aid:** *Need-based scholarships/grants:* United Negro College Fund. *Loans:* FFEL Subsidized Stafford, FFEL PLUS. **Student Employment:** Federal Work-Study Program available. Off-campus job opportunities are excellent. **Financial Aid Statistics:** Highest amount earned per year from on-campus jobs $1,000.

FLORIDA METROPOLITAN UNIVERSITY— MELBOURNE

2401 North Harbor City Boulevard, Melbourne, FL 32935
Phone: 321-253-2929
Fax: 321-255-2017 **Website:** www.fmu.edu
Financial Aid Phone: 321-253-2929

This is a private school.

RATINGS

Admissions Selectivity Rating: 60*   **Fire Safety Rating:** 60*   **Green Rating:** 60*

STUDENTS AND FACULTY

Faculty: 13 full-time faculty, 31% hold PhDs. 90% faculty teach undergrads.

ACADEMICS

Degrees: Associate, bachelor's, master's. **Academic Requirements:** English (including composition), mathematics, strategies for success and critical thinking. **Special Study Options:** Accelerated program, distance learning, internships, weekend college.

CAMPUS LIFE

Activities: Student newspaper.

ADMISSIONS

Freshman Academic Profile: TOEFL required of all international applicants, minimum paper TOEFL 450. **Basis for Candidate Selection:** *Very important factors considered include:* Interview, rigor of secondary school record. *Important factors considered include:* Standardized test scores. *Other factors considered include:* Alumni/ae relation, application essay, character/personal qualities, recommendation(s), talent/ability. **Freshman Admission Requirements:** High school diploma is required, and GED is accepted. **Freshman Admission Statistics:** 241 applied, 60% admitted. **Transfer Admission Requirements:** High school transcript, college transcript(s), interview, standardized test score. Lowest grade transferable C. **General Admission Information:** Application fee $50. Nonfall registration accepted. Common Application not accepted.

COSTS AND FINANCIAL AID

Types of Aid: *Need-based scholarships/grants:* Pell, SEOG, state scholarships/grants, private scholarships, the school's own gift aid, company tuition reimbursement. *Loans:* FFEL Subsidized Stafford, FFEL Unsubsidized Stafford, FFEL PLUS, Federal Perkins, Federal Nursing, state loans, college/university loans from institutional funds, Sallie Mae. **Student Employment:** Federal Work-Study Program available. Off-campus job opportunities are good.

FLORIDA METROPOLITAN UNIVERSITY— ORLANDO NORTH

5421 Diplomat Circle, Orlando, FL 32810
Phone: 407-628-5870
Fax: 407-628-1344 **Website:** www.fmu.edu
Financial Aid Phone: 800-628-5870

This proprietary school was founded in 1890.

RATINGS
Admissions Selectivity Rating: 60* **Fire Safety Rating:** 60* **Green Rating:** 60*

STUDENTS AND FACULTY
Faculty: Student/faculty ratio 25:1.

ACADEMICS
Degrees: Associate, bachelor's, master's. **Academic Requirements:** Computer literacy, English (including composition), history, mathematics. **Majors with Highest Enrollment:** Business administration/management, criminal justice/law enforcement administration, medical/clinical assistant. **Special Study Options:** Cooperative education program, distance learning, English as a second language (ESL), internships.

ADMISSIONS
Transfer Admission Requirements: High school transcript, college transcript(s), interview. Lowest grade transferable C. **General Admission Information:** Nonfall registration not accepted. Common Application not accepted.

COSTS AND FINANCIAL AID
Required fees $200. Average book expense $10,000. **Required Forms and Deadlines:** FAFSA. **Types of Aid:** *Need-based scholarships/grants:* Pell, state scholarships/grants. *Loans:* Direct Subsidized Stafford, Direct Unsubsidized Stafford, Direct PLUS. **Student Employment:** Federal Work-Study Program available. Off-campus job opportunities are excellent.

FLORIDA SOUTHERN COLLEGE

Best 368

111 Lake Hollingworth Drive, Lakeland, FL 33801
Phone: 863-680-4131 **E-mail:** fscadm@flsouthern.edu **CEEB Code:** 5218
Fax: 863-680-4120 **Website:** www.flsouthern.edu **ACT Code:** 0732
Financial Aid Phone: 863-680-4140

This private school, affiliated with the Methodist Church, was founded in 1885. It has a 100-acre campus.

RATINGS
Admissions Selectivity Rating: 83 **Fire Safety Rating:** 81 **Green Rating:** 68

STUDENTS AND FACULTY
Enrollment: 1,753. **Student Body:** 61% female, 39% male, 29% out-of-state, 4% international (31 countries represented). African American 6%, Asian 1%, Caucasian 79%, Hispanic 6%. **Retention and Graduation:** 46% freshmen graduate within 4 years. **Faculty:** Student/faculty ratio 13:1. 106 full-time faculty, 88% hold PhDs. 100% faculty teach undergrads.

ACADEMICS
Degrees: Bachelor's, master's. **Academic Requirements:** Arts/fine arts, computer literacy, English (including composition), history, humanities, mathematics, religion, sciences (biological or physical), social science. **Classes:** Most classes have 10–19 students. Most lab/discussion sections have 10–19 students. **Majors with Highest Enrollment:** Biological and biomedical sciences, elementary education and teaching, marketing/marketing management. **Disciplines with Highest Percentage of Degrees Awarded:** Business/marketing 17%, education 12%, social sciences 10%, visual and performing arts 10%, security and protective services 9%, psychology 6%, biological/life sciences 6%. **Special Study Options:** Double major, dual enrollment, honors program, independent study, internships, liberal arts/career combination, study abroad, teacher certification program.

FACILITIES
Housing: Coed dorms, men's dorms, women's dorms, apartments for married students, apartments for single students, special housing for disabled students, fraternity/sorority housing. **Special Academic Facilities/Equipment:** 12 Frank Lloyd Wright structures (largest collection in the world), Melvin Art Gallery, preschool lab, TV studios, Miller Planetarium, technology center, Nina B. Hollis Wellness Center, Robert A. Davis Performing Arts Center, advanced chemistry lab with nuclear magnetic resonance equipment, Tutu's Cyber Cafe, Frank Lloyd Wright Visitors Center. **Computers:** 2% of classrooms are wired, 5% of classrooms are wireless, 90% of public computers are PCs, 10% of public computers are Macs, network access in dorm rooms, network access in dorm lounges, online registration, online administrative functions (other than registration), remote student-access to Web through college's connection.

CAMPUS LIFE
Activities: Choral groups, concert band, dance, drama/theater, jazz band, literary magazine, music ensembles, musical theater, opera, pep band, student government, student newspaper, symphony orchestra, yearbook. **Organizations:** 80 registered organizations, 18 honor societies, 10 religious organizations. 6 fraternities (5% men join), 5 sororities (18% women join). **Athletics (Intercollegiate):** *Men:* Baseball, basketball, cross-country, golf, soccer, swimming, tennis, track/field (outdoor). *Women:* Basketball, cross-country, golf, soccer, softball, swimming, tennis, track/field (outdoor), volleyball. **Environmental initiatives:** Board approved energy conservation policy. Campus-wide recycling of paper, glass and aluminium. Energy-efficient light bulbs.

ADMISSIONS
Freshman Academic Profile: 19% in top 10% of high school class, 51% in top 25% of high school class, 82% in top 50% of high school class. 75% from public high schools. SAT Math middle 50% range 470–600. SAT Critical Reading middle 50% range 480–600. SAT Writing middle 50% range 460–570. ACT middle 50% range 20–25. TOEFL required of all international applicants, minimum paper TOEFL 550, minimum computer TOEFL 213. **Basis for Candidate Selection:** *Very important factors considered include:* Academic GPA, rigor of secondary school record. *Important factors considered include:* Application essay, character/personal qualities, extracurricular activities, recommendation(s), standardized test scores, talent/ability. *Other factors considered include:* Alumni/ae relation, class rank, first generation, interview, level of applicant's interest, racial/ethnic status, religious affiliation/commit-

ment, volunteer work, work experience. **Freshman Admission Requirements:** High school diploma is required, and GED is accepted. *Academic units required:* 4 English, 3 math, 3 science (2 science labs), 3 social studies, 3 history, 2 academic electives. *Academic units recommended:* 2 foreign language. **Freshman Admission Statistics:** 2,351 applied, 62% admitted, 29% enrolled. **Transfer Admission Requirements:** College transcript(s), essay or personal statement, statement of good standing from prior institution(s). Minimum college GPA of 2.0 required. Lowest grade transferable C. **General Admission Information:** Application fee $30. Early decision application deadline 12/1. Regular application deadline 3/1. Regular notification is rolling. Nonfall registration accepted. Admission may be deferred for a maximum of 1 year. Credit offered for CEEB Advanced Placement tests.

COSTS AND FINANCIAL AID

Annual tuition $20,690. Room & board $7,500. Required fees $500. Average book expense $1,150. **Required Forms and Deadlines:** FAFSA, institution's own financial aid form. Financial aid filing deadline 7/1. **Notification of Awards:** Applicants will be notified of awards on a rolling basis beginning on or about 3/1. **Types of Aid:** *Need-based scholarships/grants:* Pell, SEOG, state scholarships/grants, private scholarships, the school's own gift aid. *Loans:* FFEL Subsidized Stafford, FFEL Unsubsidized Stafford, FFEL PLUS, Federal Perkins. **Financial Aid Statistics:** 58% freshmen, 58% undergrads receive need-based scholarship or grant aid. 56% freshmen, 52% undergrads receive need-based self-help aid. 14 freshmen, 52 undergrads receive athletic scholarships. 98% freshmen, 96% undergrads receive any aid. Highest amount earned per year from on-campus jobs $1,500.

FLORIDA STATE UNIVERSITY

PO Box 3062400, Tallahassee, FL 32306-2400
Phone: 850-644-6200 **E-mail:** admissions@admin.fsu.edu **CEEB Code:** 5219
Fax: 850-644-0197 **Website:** www.fsu.edu **ACT Code:** 0734
Financial Aid Phone: 850-644-5716

This public school was founded in 1851. It has a 452-acre campus.

RATINGS

Admissions Selectivity Rating: 88   **Fire Safety Rating:** 83   **Green Rating:** 83

STUDENTS AND FACULTY

Enrollment: 30,841. **Student Body:** 56% female, 44% male, 12% out-of-state. African American 11%, Asian 3%, Caucasian 73%, Hispanic 11%. **Retention and Graduation:** 88% freshmen return for sophomore year. 42% grads go on to further study within 1 year. **Faculty:** Student/faculty ratio 21:1. 1,309 full-time faculty, 92% hold PhDs. 100% faculty teach undergrads.

ACADEMICS

Degrees: Associate, bachelor's, certificate, doctoral, first professional, master's, post-bachelor's certificate, post-master's certificate. **Academic Requirements:** Arts/fine arts, computer literacy, English (including composition), history, humanities, mathematics, sciences (biological or physical), social science. All students entering the university with fewer than 60 semester hours must complete a cross-cultural course and a diversity in Western culture course. All students entering the university with 60 semester hours or more must complete either a cross-cultural course or a diversity in Western culture course. **Classes:** Most classes have 20–29 students. **Majors with Highest Enrollment:** Criminal justice/safety studies, finance, psychology. **Disciplines with Highest Percentage of Degrees Awarded:** Business/marketing 21%, social sciences 16%, family and consumer sciences 9%, visual and performing arts 6%, education 6%. **Special Study Options:** Accelerated program, cooperative education program, cross-registration, distance learning, double major, dual enrollment, English as a second language (ESL), honors program, independent study, internships, study abroad, teacher certification program.

FACILITIES

Housing: Coed dorms, women's dorms, apartments for married students, apartments for single students, special housing for disabled students, fraternity/sorority housing, honors residences, living learning communities. **Special Academic Facilities/Equipment:** Art gallery, museum, developmental research school, marine lab, oceanographic institute, tandem Van de Graaff accelerator, national high magnetic field lab. **Computers:** 3% of classrooms are wireless, 80% of public computers are PCs, 15% of public computers are Macs,

5% of public computers are UNIX, network access in dorm rooms, network access in dorm lounges, online registration, online administrative functions (other than registration), support for handheld computing, remote student-access to Web through college's connection.

CAMPUS LIFE

Activities: Choral groups, concert band, dance, drama/theater, jazz band, literary magazine, marching band, music ensembles, musical theater, opera, pep band, radio station, student government, student newspaper, student-run film society, symphony orchestra, television station. **Organizations:** 395 registered organizations, 83 honor societies, 31 religious organizations. 28 fraternities (13% men join), 23 sororities (13% women join). **Athletics (Intercollegiate):** *Men:* Baseball, basketball, cheerleading, cross-country, diving, football, golf, swimming, tennis, track/field (indoor), track/field (outdoor). *Women:* Basketball, cheerleading, cross-country, diving, golf, soccer, softball, swimming, tennis, track/field (indoor), track/field (outdoor), volleyball. **Environmental initiatives:** Building LEED certified buildings. Campus-wide recycling program. Campus-wide energy conservation program.

ADMISSIONS

Freshman Academic Profile: 26% in top 10% of high school class, 63% in top 25% of high school class, 94% in top 50% of high school class. 84% from public high schools. SAT Math middle 50% range 550–640. SAT Critical Reading middle 50% range 540–630. ACT middle 50% range 23–28. TOEFL required of all international applicants, minimum paper TOEFL 550, minimum computer TOEFL 213. **Basis for Candidate Selection:** *Very important factors considered include:* Academic GPA, rigor of secondary school record. *Important factors considered include:* Class rank, standardized test scores, state residency, talent/ability. *Other factors considered include:* Alumni/ae relation, application essay, character/personal qualities, extracurricular activities, first generation, geographical residence, recommendation(s), volunteer work, work experience. **Freshman Admission Requirements:** High school diploma is required, and GED is accepted. *Academic units required:* 4 English, 3 math, 3 science (2 science labs), 2 foreign language, 1 social studies, 2 history, 3 academic electives. *Academic units recommended:* 4 English, 4 math, 4 science (2 science labs), 4 foreign language, 1 social studies, 2 history, 3 academic electives. **Freshman Admission Statistics:** 23,687 applied, 59% admitted, 44% enrolled. **Transfer Admission Requirements:** College transcript(s). Minimum college GPA of 3.0 required. Lowest grade transferable D-. **General Admission Information:** Application fee $30. Regular application deadline 2/14. Regular notification 11/1, 12/13, 2/14, 3/28. Nonfall registration accepted. Credit and/or placement offered for CEEB Advanced Placement tests.

COSTS AND FINANCIAL AID

Annual in-state tuition $2,465. Out-of-state tuition $15,596. Room & board $6,778. Required fees $842. Average book expense $856. **Required Forms and Deadlines:** FAFSA. **Notification of Awards:** Applicants will be notified of awards on a rolling basis beginning on or about 3/15. **Types of Aid:** *Need-based scholarships/grants:* Pell, SEOG, state scholarships/grants, private scholarships, the school's own gift aid. *Loans:* FFEL Subsidized Stafford, FFEL Unsubsidized Stafford, FFEL PLUS, Federal Perkins. **Student Employment:** Off-campus job opportunities are excellent. **Financial Aid Statistics:** 18% freshmen, 17% undergrads receive need-based scholarship or grant aid. 22% freshmen, 23% undergrads receive need-based self-help aid. 388 freshmen, 957 undergrads receive athletic scholarships. 35% freshmen, 32% undergrads receive any aid.

FONTBONNE UNIVERSITY

6800 Wydown Boulevard, St. Louis, MO 63105
Phone: 314-889-1400 **E-mail:** fcadmis@fontbonne.edu **CEEB Code:** 6216
Fax: 314-889-1451 **Website:** www.fontbonne.edu **ACT Code:** 2298
Financial Aid Phone: 314-889-1414

This private school, affiliated with the Roman Catholic Church, was founded in 1917. It has a 13-acre campus.

RATINGS

Admissions Selectivity Rating: 60*   **Fire Safety Rating:** 60*   **Green Rating:** 60*

STUDENTS AND FACULTY

Enrollment: 1,981. **Student Body:** 73% female, 27% male, 9% out-of-state. African American 33%, Caucasian 60%, Hispanic 1%. **Retention and Graduation:** 58% freshmen return for sophomore year. 35% freshmen graduate within 4 years. 25% grads go on to further study within 1 year. **Faculty:** Student/faculty ratio 14:1. 76 full-time faculty, 68% hold PhDs. 85% faculty teach undergrads.

ACADEMICS

Degrees: Bachelor's, certificate, master's, post-bachelor's certificate. **Academic Requirements:** Arts/fine arts, computer literacy, English (including composition), history, humanities, mathematics, philosophy, sciences (biological or physical), social science. **Classes:** Most classes have 10–19 students. Most lab/discussion sections have 10–19 students. **Majors with Highest Enrollment:** Business administration and management, elementary education and teaching, special education. **Disciplines with Highest Percentage of Degrees Awarded:** Business/marketing 55%, education 17%, visual and performing arts 5%, health professions and related sciences 4%, family and consumer sciences 3%. **Special Study Options:** Accelerated program, cooperative education program, cross-registration, distance learning, double major, English as a second language (ESL), exchange student program (domestic), honors program, independent study, internships, liberal arts/career combination, student-designed major, study abroad, teacher certification program.

FACILITIES

Housing: Coed dorms, apartments for single students, special housing for international students, off-campus house (13 females). **Special Academic Facilities/Equipment:** Art gallery. **Computers:** 95% of classrooms are wireless, 90% of public computers are PCs, 10% of public computers are Macs, network access in dorm rooms, network access in dorm lounges, online registration, online administrative functions (other than registration), remote student-access to Web through college's connection.

CAMPUS LIFE

Activities: Choral groups, dance, drama/theater, literary magazine, music ensembles, radio station, student government, student newspaper. **Organizations:** 34 registered organizations, 7 honor societies, 4 religious organizations. **Athletics (Intercollegiate):** *Men:* Baseball, basketball, cross-country, golf, lacrosse, soccer, tennis. *Women:* Basketball, bowling, cross-country, golf, lacrosse, soccer, softball, tennis, volleyball.

ADMISSIONS

Freshman Academic Profile: 12% in top 10% of high school class, 26% in top 25% of high school class, 66% in top 50% of high school class. 56% from public high schools. SAT Math middle 50% range 470–625. SAT Critical Reading middle 50% range 500–625. ACT middle 50% range 18–24. TOEFL required of all international applicants, minimum paper TOEFL 525, minimum computer TOEFL 193. **Basis for Candidate Selection:** *Very important factors considered include:* Academic GPA, character/personal qualities, class rank, rigor of secondary school record, standardized test scores. *Other factors considered include:* Alumni/ae relation, application essay, extracurricular activities, first generation, interview, recommendation(s), talent/ability, volunteer work, work experience. **Freshman Admission Requirements:** High school diploma is required, and GED is accepted. *Academic units required:* 4 English, 3 math, 3 science (1 science lab), 3 social studies, 3 academic electives. **Freshman Admission Statistics:** 588 applied, 76% admitted, 45% enrolled. **Transfer Admission Requirements:** College transcript(s), essay or personal statement. Minimum college GPA of 2.0 required. Lowest grade transferable D. **General Admission Information:** Application fee $25. Regular application deadline 8/1. Regular notification is rolling. Nonfall registration accepted. Admission may be deferred for a maximum of 1 year. Credit and/or placement offered for CEEB Advanced Placement tests.

COSTS AND FINANCIAL AID

Annual tuition $19,000. Room and board $6,739. Required fees $320. Average book expense $650. **Required Forms and Deadlines:** FAFSA, institution's own financial aid form. Financial aid filing deadline 7/1. **Types of Aid:** *Need-based scholarships/grants:* Pell, SEOG, state scholarships/grants, private scholarships, the school's own gift aid. *Loans:* FFEL Subsidized Stafford, FFEL Unsubsidized Stafford, FFEL PLUS, Federal Perkins, state loans, college/university loans from institutional funds. **Financial Aid Statistics:** 59% freshmen, 66% undergrads receive need-based scholarship or grant aid. 59% freshmen, 66% undergrads receive need-based self-help aid.

FORDHAM UNIVERSITY

441 East Fordham Road, Duane Library, New York, NY 10458
Phone: 718-817-4000 **E-mail:** enroll@fordham.edu **CEEB Code:** 2259
Fax: 718-367-9404 **Website:** www.fordham.edu **ACT Code:** 2748
Financial Aid Phone: 718-817-3800

This private school, affiliated with the Roman Catholic Church, was founded in 1841. It has a 93-acre campus.

RATINGS

Admissions Selectivity Rating: 92   **Fire Safety Rating:** 60*   **Green Rating:** 60*

STUDENTS AND FACULTY

Enrollment: 7,451. **Student Body:** 58% female, 42% male, 46% out-of-state, 2% international (43 countries represented). African American 5%, Asian 6%, Caucasian 58%, Hispanic 12%. **Retention and Graduation:** 90% freshmen return for sophomore year. 72% freshmen graduate within 4 years. 25% grads go on to further study within 1 year. 10% grads pursue arts and sciences degrees. 1% grads pursue business degrees. 5% grads pursue law degrees. 2% grads pursue medical degrees. **Faculty:** Student/faculty ratio 13:1. 645 full-time faculty, 96% hold PhDs.

ACADEMICS

Degrees: Bachelor's, doctoral, first professional, master's, post-master's certificate. **Academic Requirements:** American pluralism, arts/fine arts, English (including composition), foreign languages, global studies, history, humanities, mathematics, philosophy, religion, sciences (biological or physical), social science. **Classes:** Most classes have 10–19 students. Most lab/discussion sections have 10–19 students. **Majors with Highest Enrollment:** Business administration/management, communications and media studies, social sciences. **Disciplines with Highest Percentage of Degrees Awarded:** Business/marketing 27%, social sciences 20%, communications/journalism 14%, psychology 6%, visual and performing arts 6%. **Special Study Options:** Double major, English as a second language (ESL), exchange student program (domestic), globe program in international business, honors program, independent study, internships, student-designed major, study abroad, teacher certification program. 3-2 engineering cooperative with Columbia University or Case Western Reserve University.

FACILITIES

Housing: Coed dorms, apartments for single students, special housing for disabled students, residential colleges. **Special Academic Facilities/Equipment:** Television station, radio station, theaters, white and black box studio spaces, media and visual arts labs and design space, art gallery, university church, seismic station, 113 biological field station, the Louis Calder Center (Armonk, NY). **Computers:** 85% of public computers are PCs, 15% of public computers are Macs, network access in dorm rooms, network access in dorm lounges, online registration, online administrative functions (other than registration), remote student-access to Web through college's connection.

CAMPUS LIFE

Activities: Choral groups, concert band, dance, drama/theater, jazz band, literary magazine, music ensembles, musical theater, pep band, radio station, student government, student newspaper, student-run film society, symphony orchestra, television station, yearbook. **Organizations:** 133 registered organizations, 12 honor societies, 3 religious organizations. **Athletics (Intercollegiate):** *Men:* Baseball, basketball, cross-country, diving, football, golf, soccer, squash, swimming, tennis, track/field (indoor), track/field (outdoor), water polo. *Women:* Basketball, cheerleading, crew/rowing, cross-country, diving, soccer, softball, swimming, tennis, track/field (indoor), track/field (outdoor), volleyball.

ADMISSIONS

Freshman Academic Profile: 41% in top 10% of high school class, 73% in top 25% of high school class, 96% in top 50% of high school class. 47% from public high schools. SAT Math middle 50% range 550–640. SAT Critical Reading middle 50% range 550–650. SAT Writing middle 50% range 540–590. ACT middle 50% range 24–24. TOEFL required of all international applicants, minimum paper TOEFL 575, minimum computer TOEFL 231. **Basis for Candidate Selection:** *Very important factors considered include:* Class rank, rigor of secondary school record, standardized test scores. *Important factors considered include:* Application essay, character/personal qualities, extracurricular activities, recommendation(s), talent/ability. *Other factors considered include:* Alumni/ae relation, first generation, geographical residence, racial/ethnic status, volunteer work, work experience. **Freshman Admission Requirements:** High school diploma is required, and GED is accepted. *Academic units required:* 4 English, 3 math, 3 science, 2 foreign language, 2 social studies, 2 history, 6 academic electives. *Academic units recommended:* 4 English, 4 math, 4 science, 3 foreign language, 2 social studies, 2 history, 6 academic electives. **Freshman Admission Statistics:** 18,161 applied, 47% admitted, 20% enrolled. **Transfer Admission Requirements:** High school transcript, college transcript(s), essay or personal statement, statement of good standing from prior institution(s). Minimum college GPA of 3.0 required. Lowest grade transferable C. **General Admission Information:** Application fee $50. Regular application deadline 1/15. Regular notification 4/1. Nonfall registration accepted. Admission may be deferred for a maximum of 1 year. Credit and/or placement offered for CEEB Advanced Placement tests.

COSTS AND FINANCIAL AID
Annual tuition $30,000. Room & board $11,780. Required fees $730. Average book expense $500. **Required Forms and Deadlines:** FAFSA, CSS/Financial Aid PROFILE, Noncustodial PROFILE, Business/Farm Supplement. Financial aid filing deadline 2/1. **Notification of Awards:** Applicants will be notified of awards on or about 4/1. *Types of Aid: Need-based scholarships/grants:* Pell, SEOG, state scholarships/grants, private scholarships, the school's own gift aid. *Loans:* FFEL Subsidized Stafford, FFEL Unsubsidized Stafford, FFEL PLUS, Federal Perkins. **Financial Aid Statistics:** 66% freshmen, 62% undergrads receive need-based scholarship or grant aid. 51% freshmen, 52% undergrads receive need-based self-help aid. 31 freshmen, 143 undergrads receive athletic scholarships. 67% freshmen, 62% undergrads receive any aid.

See page 1176.

FORT HAYS STATE UNIVERSITY

600 Park Street, Hays, KS 67601-4099
Phone: 785-628-5666 **E-mail:** tigers@fhsu.edu **CEEB Code:** 6218
Fax: 785-628-4187 **Website:** www.fhsu.edu **ACT Code:** 1408
Financial Aid Phone: 785-628-4408

This public school was founded in 1902. It has a 4,160-acre campus.

RATINGS
Admissions Selectivity Rating: 70 **Fire Safety Rating:** 60* **Green Rating:** 73

STUDENTS AND FACULTY
Enrollment: 7,615. **Student Body:** 55% female, 45% male, 11% out-of-state, 31% international. African American 2%, Caucasian 61%, Hispanic 2%. **Retention and Graduation:** 67% freshmen return for sophomore year. 20% grads go on to further study within 1 year. **Faculty:** Student/faculty ratio 17:1. 265 full-time faculty, 62% hold PhDs. 92% faculty teach undergrads.

ACADEMICS
Degrees: Associate, bachelor's, certificate, master's, post-master's certificate. **Academic Requirements:** Arts/fine arts, computer literacy, English (including composition), humanities, mathematics, sciences (biological or physical), social science. **Classes:** Most classes have 10–19 students. Most lab/discussion sections have fewer than 10 students. **Majors with Highest Enrollment:** Business administration/management, elementary education and teaching, health and physical education. **Disciplines with Highest Percentage of Degrees Awarded:** Liberal arts/general studies 29%, education 16%, business/marketing 13%, health professions and related sciences 8%, security and protective services 5%. **Special Study Options:** Distance learning, double major, dual enrollment, English as a second language (ESL), exchange student program (domestic), external degree program, independent study, internships, liberal arts/career combination, student-designed major, study abroad, teacher certification program.

FACILITIES
Housing: Coed dorms, men's dorms, women's dorms, apartments for married students, apartments for single students, fraternity/sorority housing. **Special Academic Facilities/Equipment:** Paleontology, natural history, visual arts and media center, farm, NMR gas analyzer, telescope (HG). **Computers:** 85% of public computers are PCs, 15% of public computers are Macs, network access in dorm rooms, remote student-access to Web through college's connection.

CAMPUS LIFE
Activities: Choral groups, concert band, dance, drama/theater, jazz band, marching band, music ensembles, musical theater, pep band, radio station, student government, student newspaper, symphony orchestra, television station,

yearbook. **Organizations:** 103 registered organizations, 20 honor societies, 2 religious organizations. 3 fraternities (1% men join), 3 sororities. **Athletics (Intercollegiate):** *Men:* Baseball, basketball, cheerleading, cross-country, football, golf, track/field (indoor), track/field (outdoor), wrestling. *Women:* Basketball, cheerleading, cross-country, golf, softball, tennis, track/field (indoor), track/field (outdoor), volleyball.

ADMISSIONS
Freshman Academic Profile: 9% in top 10% of high school class, 31% in top 25% of high school class, 63% in top 50% of high school class. 95% from public high schools. ACT middle 50% range 18–24. TOEFL required of all international applicants, minimum paper TOEFL 500, minimum computer TOEFL 173. **Basis for Candidate Selection:** *Other factors considered include:* Class rank, rigor of secondary school record, standardized test scores. **Freshman Admission Requirements:** High school diploma is required, and GED is accepted. *Academic units recommended:* 4 English, 3 math, 3 science, 1 foreign language, 3 social studies. **Freshman Admission Statistics:** 1,533 applied, 91% admitted, 58% enrolled. **Transfer Admission Requirements:** College transcript(s). Minimum college GPA of 2.0 required. Lowest grade transferable D. **General Admission Information:** Application fee $30. Regular notification as submitted. Nonfall registration accepted. Admission may be deferred for a maximum of 1 year. Credit offered for CEEB Advanced Placement tests.

COSTS AND FINANCIAL AID
Annual in-state tuition $3,051. Out-of-state tuition $9,575. Room & board $5,450. Average book expense $800. **Required Forms and Deadlines:** FAFSA. *Types of Aid: Need-based scholarships/grants:* Pell, SEOG, state scholarships/grants, private scholarships, the school's own gift aid. *Loans:* FFEL Subsidized Stafford, FFEL Unsubsidized Stafford, FFEL PLUS, Federal Perkins, college/university loans from institutional funds. **Student Employment:** Federal Work-Study Program available. Off-campus job opportunities are fair. **Financial Aid Statistics:** 56% freshmen, 53% undergrads receive need-based scholarship or grant aid. 47% freshmen, 60% undergrads receive need-based self-help aid. 47 freshmen, 165 undergrads receive athletic scholarships. Highest amount earned per year from on-campus jobs $2,000.

FORT LEWIS COLLEGE

1000 Rim Drive, Durango, CO 81301
Phone: 970-247-7184 **E-mail:** admission@fortlewis.edu **CEEB Code:** 4310
Fax: 970-247-7179 **Website:** www.fortlewis.edu **ACT Code:** 0510
Financial Aid Phone: 970-247-7142

This public school was founded in 1911. It has a 362-acre campus.

RATINGS
Admissions Selectivity Rating: 73 **Fire Safety Rating:** 60* **Green Rating:** 81

STUDENTS AND FACULTY
Enrollment: 3,824. **Student Body:** 47% female, 53% male, 28% out-of-state. Caucasian 65%, Hispanic 5%, Native American 18%. **Retention and Graduation:** 57% freshmen return for sophomore year. 14% grads go on to further study within 1 year. **Faculty:** Student/faculty ratio 18:1. 180 full-time faculty, 75% hold PhDs. 100% faculty teach undergrads.

ACADEMICS
Degrees: Bachelor's. **Academic Requirements:** Computer literacy, English (including composition), sciences (biological or physical), social science. Fort Lewis College's commitment to the liberal arts is embodied in its innovative general education program that is relevant for all students in all disciplines. **Classes:** Most classes have 20–29 students. Most lab/discussion sections have 10–19 students. **Majors with Highest Enrollment:** Business administration and management, multi/interdisciplinary studies, psychology. **Disciplines with Highest Percentage of Degrees Awarded:** Business/marketing 26%, liberal arts/general studies 12%, social sciences 9%, psychology 8%, visual and performing arts 8%, parks and recreation 7%, English 7%. **Special Study Options:** Accelerated program, cooperative education program, distance learning, double major, dual enrollment, English as a second language (ESL), exchange student program (domestic), honors program, independent study, internships, liberal arts/career combination, student-designed major, study abroad, teacher certification program.

FACILITIES
Housing: Coed dorms, apartments for married students, apartments for single students, special housing for disabled students, living learning programs. **Special Academic Facilities/Equipment:** Center of Southwest Studies, archaeological dig site, chemistry hall, student life center, community concert hall, nuclear magnetic resonance spectrometer, separations and spectroscopy

lab, mass spectrometer facilities, tissue culture facility, atomic force microscope. **Computers:** 2% of classrooms are wireless, 94% of public computers are PCs, 6% of public computers are Macs, network access in dorm rooms, network access in dorm lounges, online registration, online administrative functions (other than registration), remote student-access to Web through college's connection.

CAMPUS LIFE

Activities: Choral groups, concert band, drama/theater, jazz band, literary magazine, music ensembles, pep band, radio station, student government, student newspaper. **Organizations:** 70 registered organizations, 15 honor societies, 4 religious organizations. **Athletics (Intercollegiate):** *Men:* Basketball, cross-country, football, golf, soccer. *Women:* Basketball, cross-country, soccer, softball, volleyball. **Environmental initiatives:** Green Building—Currently designing three new LEED-certified buildings: a new residence hall (LEED-Silver); a new biology building (LEED-Silver); and a new Student Union Building (LEED-Gold). Creating a Sustainability Action Plan for the college; just completed first-ever campus sustainability assessment. Recycling and Composting: have a didicated staff person who manages the campus recycling program. Recycling includes paper, aluminum, glass, plastic, cardboard, and laser and ink jet cartridges. Have an Earth Tub composter for waste from campus dining services.

ADMISSIONS

Freshman Academic Profile: 8% in top 10% of high school class, 24% in top 25% of high school class, 53% in top 50% of high school class. 88% from public high schools. SAT Math middle 50% range 450–570. SAT Critical Reading middle 50% range 440–570. SAT Writing middle 50% range 430–540. ACT middle 50% range 19–23. TOEFL required of all international applicants, minimum paper TOEFL 500, minimum computer TOEFL 173. **Basis for Candidate Selection:** *Very important factors considered include:* Academic GPA, class rank, standardized test scores. *Important factors considered include:* Rigor of secondary school record. *Other factors considered include:* Alumni/ae relation, application essay, character/personal qualities, extracurricular activities, first generation, geographical residence, interview, level of applicant's interest, racial/ethnic status, recommendation(s), religious affiliation/commitment. **Freshman Admission Requirements:** High school diploma is required, and GED is accepted. *Academic units recommended:* 4 English, 4 math, 3 science, 2 foreign language, 3 social studies, 2 academic electives. **Freshman Admission Statistics:** 2,881 applied, 73% admitted, 43% enrolled. **Transfer Admission Requirements:** College transcript(s). Minimum college GPA of 2.3 required. Lowest grade transferable C-. **General Admission Information:** Application fee $30. Regular application deadline 8/1. Regular notification is rolling. Nonfall registration accepted. Admission may be deferred for a maximum of 1 semester. Credit and/or placement offered for CEEB Advanced Placement tests.

COSTS AND FINANCIAL AID

Annual in-state tuition $5,318. Annual out-of-state tuition $13,848. Room and board $6,876. Required fees $1,146. Average book expense $850. **Required Forms and Deadlines:** FAFSA. Financial aid filing deadline 2/15. **Notification of Awards:** Applicants will be notified of awards on a rolling basis beginning on or about 4/1. **Types of Aid:** *Need-based scholarships/grants:* Pell, SEOG, state scholarships/grants, private scholarships, the school's own gift aid. *Loans:* FFEL Subsidized Stafford, FFEL Unsubsidized Stafford, FFEL PLUS, Federal Perkins, college/university loans from institutional funds. **Student Employment:** Federal Work-Study Program available. Institutional employment available. Off-campus job opportunities are good. **Financial Aid Statistics:** 24% freshmen, 29% undergrads receive need-based scholarship or grant aid. 38% freshmen, 42% undergrads receive need-based self-help aid. 34 freshmen, 152 undergrads receive athletic scholarships. 69% freshmen, 63% undergrads receive any aid. Highest amount earned per year from on-campus jobs $5,340.

FORT VALLEY STATE UNIVERSITY

1005 State University Drive, Fort Valley, GA 31030
Phone: 912-825-6307 **CEEB Code:** 5220
Fax: 912-825-6394 **Website:** www.fvsc.peachnet.edu **ACT Code:** 0814
Financial Aid Phone: 912-825-6363

This public school was founded in 1902. It has a 630-acre campus.

RATINGS

Admissions Selectivity Rating: 60*   **Fire Safety Rating:** 60*   **Green Rating:** 60*

STUDENTS AND FACULTY

Enrollment: 2,088. **Student Body:** 57% female, 43% male, 6% out-of-state,

1% international. African American 95%, Caucasian 3%. **Retention and Graduation:** 67% freshmen return for sophomore year. 9% freshmen graduate within 4 years. 46% grads go on to further study within 1 year. 31% grads pursue arts and sciences degrees. 7% grads pursue business degrees. 1% grads pursue law degrees. 7% grads pursue medical degrees.

ACADEMICS

Degrees: Associate, bachelor's, master's. **Special Study Options:** Cooperative education program, distance learning, dual enrollment, honors program, internships, study abroad. Undergrads may take grad-level classes. Co-op programs also available in fisheries biology and wildlife conservation, and credit for study tours, summer institutes, and work experiences.

FACILITIES

Housing: Coed dorms, men's dorms, women's dorms, apartments for single students. **Special Academic Facilities/Equipment:** Experimental agricultural plots cover most of campus.

CAMPUS LIFE

Activities: Concert band, dance, jazz band, marching band, radio station, student government, student newspaper, television station, yearbook. **Organizations:** 7 honor societies, 2 religious organizations. 4 fraternities, 4 sororities. **Athletics (Intercollegiate):** *Men:* Baseball, basketball, football, golf, soccer, tennis. *Women:* Basketball, tennis, track/field (outdoor), volleyball.

ADMISSIONS

Basis for Candidate Selection: *Very important factors considered include:* Rigor of secondary school record, standardized test scores. *Important factors considered include:* Racial/ethnic status. *Other factors considered include:* Alumni/ae relation, application essay, character/personal qualities, class rank, recommendation(s), state residency. **Freshman Admission Requirements:** High school diploma is required, and GED is accepted. *Academic units required:* 4 English, 3 math, 3 science, 2 foreign language, 3 social studies, 6 academic electives. **Transfer Admission Requirements:** Minimum college GPA of 2.0 required. Lowest grade transferable C-. **General Admission Information:** Application fee $20. Regular application deadline 9/5. Regular notification rolling. Nonfall registration accepted. Common Application not accepted. Credit and/or placement offered for CEEB Advanced Placement tests.

COSTS AND FINANCIAL AID

Annual in-state tuition $2,468. Out-of-state tuition $4,132. Room & board $3,830. Required fees $232. Average book expense $800. **Required Forms and Deadlines:** FAFSA. **Types of Aid:** *Need-based scholarships/grants:* Pell, SEOG, state scholarships/grants, private scholarships. *Loans:* FFEL Subsidized Stafford, FFEL PLUS. **Student Employment:** Institutional employment available. Off-campus job opportunities are good.

FRAMINGHAM STATE COLLEGE

PO Box 9101, 100 State Street, Framingham, MA 01701-9101
Phone: 508-626-4500 **E-mail:** admiss@frc.mass.edu **CEEB Code:** 3519
Fax: 508-626-4017 **Website:** www.framingham.edu **ACT Code:** 1904
Financial Aid Phone: 508-626-4534

This public school was founded in 1839. It has a 73-acre campus.

RATINGS

Admissions Selectivity Rating: 75   **Fire Safety Rating:** 90   **Green Rating:** 89

STUDENTS AND FACULTY

Enrollment: 3,467. **Student Body:** 67% female, 33% male, 4% out-of-state, 1% international. African American 4%, Asian 3%, Caucasian 80%, Hispanic 4%. **Retention and Graduation:** 72% freshmen return for sophomore year. 25% freshmen graduate within 4 years. 15% grads go on to further study within 1 year. **Faculty:** Student/faculty ratio 15:1. 166 full-time faculty, 84% hold PhDs. 100% faculty teach undergrads.

ACADEMICS

Degrees: Bachelor's, master's, post-bachelor's certificate. **Academic Requirements:** Arts/fine arts, English (including composition), foreign languages, history, humanities, mathematics, sciences (biological or physical), social science. **Classes:** Most classes have 10–19 students. Most lab/discussion sections have 10–19 students. **Majors with Highest Enrollment:** Business administration/management; elementary education and teaching; food, nutrition, and wellness studies. **Disciplines with Highest Percentage of Degrees Awarded:** Business/marketing 16%, social sciences 15%, psychology 12%, communications/journalism 11%, English 9%. **Special Study Options:**

Cross-registration, distance learning, double major, honors program, independent study, internships, liberal arts/career combination, study abroad, teacher certification program.

FACILITIES

Housing: Coed dorms, women's dorms. **Special Academic Facilities/ Equipment:** Greenhouse, Early childhood development lab, education curriculum library, McAuliffe Challenger Learning Center. **Computers:** 100% of classrooms are wireless, 80% of public computers are PCs, 20% of public computers are Macs, network access in dorm rooms, network access in dorm lounges, online registration, online administrative functions (other than registration), remote student-access to Web through college's connection. Undergraduates are required to own a computer.

CAMPUS LIFE

Activities: Choral groups, dance, drama/theater, literary magazine, musical theater, radio station, student government, student newspaper, yearbook. **Organizations:** 50 registered organizations, 8 honor societies, 3 religious organizations. **Athletics (Intercollegiate):** *Men:* Baseball, basketball, cross-country, football, ice hockey, soccer. *Women:* Basketball, cross-country, field hockey, lacrosse, soccer, softball, volleyball. **Environmental initiatives:** Developing a Climate Action Plan. Increasing recycling program in residence halls and classromms. Completing capital improvements including re-lighting project in gymnasium to reduce electrical requirement for lighting by 50%.

ADMISSIONS

Freshman Academic Profile: 7% in top 10% of high school class, 33% in top 25% of high school class, 74% in top 50% of high school class. 94% from public high schools. SAT Math middle 50% range 470–560. SAT Critical Reading middle 50% range 470–560. TOEFL required of all international applicants, minimum paper TOEFL 550, minimum computer TOEFL 213. **Basis for Candidate Selection:** *Very important factors considered include:* Academic GPA, rigor of secondary school record. *Important factors considered include:* Class rank, standardized test scores. *Other factors considered include:* Alumni/ ae relation, application essay, character/personal qualities, extracurricular activities, first generation, level of applicant's interest, recommendation(s), state residency, talent/ability, volunteer work, work experience. **Freshman Admission Requirements:** High school diploma is required, and GED is accepted. *Academic units required:* 4 English, 3 math, 3 science (2 science labs), 2 foreign language, 1 social studies, 1 history, 2 academic electives. *Academic units recommended:* 4 English, 4 math, 4 science (3 science labs), 4 foreign language, 1 social studies, 2 history, 2 academic electives. **Freshman Admission Statistics:** 4,261 applied, 60% admitted, 28% enrolled. **Transfer Admission Requirements:** High school transcript, college transcript(s), essay or personal statement. Minimum college GPA of 2.5 required. Lowest grade transferable C-. **General Admission Information:** Application fee $25. Regular application deadline 5/15. Regular notification is rolling. Nonfall registration accepted. Admission may be deferred for a maximum of 1 year. Credit and/or placement offered for CEEB Advanced Placement tests.

COSTS AND FINANCIAL AID

Annual in-state tuition $970. Annual out-of-state tuition $7,050. Room and board $7,127. Required fees $4,829. Average book expense $800. **Required Forms and Deadlines:** FAFSA. Financial aid filing deadline 3/1. **Notification of Awards:** Applicants will be notified of awards on a rolling basis beginning on or about 4/15. **Types of Aid:** *Need-based scholarships/grants:* Pell, SEOG, state scholarships/grants, private scholarships, the school's own gift aid. *Loans:* FFEL Subsidized Stafford, FFEL Unsubsidized Stafford, FFEL PLUS, Federal Perkins, state loans. **Student Employment:** Federal Work-Study Program available. Institutional employment available. Off-campus job opportunities are excellent. **Financial Aid Statistics:** 38% freshmen, 34% undergrads receive need-based scholarship or grant aid. 44% freshmen, 40% undergrads receive need-based self-help aid. 78% freshmen, 58% undergrads receive any aid. Highest amount earned per year from on-campus jobs $982.

FRANCIS MARION UNIVERSITY

Office of Admissions, PO Box 100547, Florence, SC 29501-0547
Phone: 843-661-1231 **E-mail:** admissions@fmarion.edu **CEEB Code:** 5442
Fax: 843-661-4635 **Website:** www.fmarion.edu **ACT Code:** 3856
Financial Aid Phone: 843-661-1190

This public school was founded in 1970. It has a 300-acre campus.

STUDENTS AND FACULTY

Enrollment: 3,068. **Student Body:** 62% female, 38% male, 4% out-of-state, 1% international (24 countries represented). African American 40%, Asian 1%, Caucasian 54%, Hispanic 1%. **Retention and Graduation:** 65% freshmen return for sophomore year. 29% freshmen graduate within 4 years. **Faculty:** Student/faculty ratio 17:1. 170 full-time faculty, 83% hold PhDs. 100% faculty teach undergrads.

ACADEMICS

Degrees: Bachelor's, master's. **Academic Requirements:** Arts/fine arts, computer literacy, English (including composition), foreign languages, history, humanities, mathematics, philosophy, sciences (biological or physical), social science. **Classes:** Most classes have 20–29 students. **Majors with Highest Enrollment:** Business administration/management, elementary education and teaching. **Disciplines with Highest Percentage of Degrees Awarded:** Business/marketing 34%, social sciences 16%, education 13%, biological/life sciences 10%, psychology 7%. **Special Study Options:** Accelerated program, cross-registration, distance learning, double major, dual enrollment, honors program, independent study, internships, study abroad, teacher certification program.

FACILITIES

Housing: Men's dorms, women's dorms, apartments for single students, special housing for disabled students. **Special Academic Facilities/Equipment:** Media center, planetarium, observatory. **Computers:** Network access in dorm rooms, network access in dorm lounges, online registration, remote student-access to Web through college's connection.

CAMPUS LIFE

Activities: Choral groups, drama/theater, jazz band, literary magazine, music ensembles, student government, student newspaper, television station. **Organizations:** 56 registered organizations, 13 honor societies, 5 religious organizations. 7 fraternities (3% men join), 7 sororities (5% women join). **Athletics (Intercollegiate):** *Men:* Baseball, basketball, cross-country, golf, soccer, tennis, track/field (outdoor). *Women:* Basketball, cross-country, soccer, softball, tennis, track/field (outdoor), volleyball.

ADMISSIONS

Freshman Academic Profile: 12% in top 10% of high school class, 34% in top 25% of high school class, 72% in top 50% of high school class. 88% from public high schools. SAT Math middle 50% range 420–520. SAT Critical Reading middle 50% range 420–510. ACT middle 50% range 17–20. TOEFL required of all international applicants, minimum paper TOEFL 500, minimum computer TOEFL 173. **Basis for Candidate Selection:** *Very important factors considered include:* Rigor of secondary school record, standardized test scores. *Important factors considered include:* Class rank. *Other factors considered include:* Recommendation(s). **Freshman Admission Requirements:** High school diploma is required, and GED is accepted. *Academic units required:* 4 English, 3 math, 3 science (3 science labs), 2 foreign language, 2 social studies, 1 history, 4 academic electives, 1 physical education or ROTC. *Academic units recommended:* 4 math, 4 science. **Freshman Admission Statistics:** 2,179 applied, 76% admitted, 45% enrolled. **Transfer Admission Requirements:** High school transcript, college transcript(s), statement of good standing from prior institution(s). Minimum college GPA of 2.0 required. Lowest grade transferable C. **General Admission Information:** Application fee $30. Regular notification is rolling. Nonfall registration accepted. Admission may be deferred for a maximum of 1 semester. Common Application accepted. Credit offered for CEEB Advanced Placement tests.

COSTS AND FINANCIAL AID

Annual in-state tuition $5,849. Out-of-state tuition $11,698. Room & board $5,130. Required fees $135. Average book expense $796. **Required Forms and Deadlines:** FAFSA, institution's own financial aid form. Financial aid filing deadline 6/15. **Notification of Awards:** Applicants will be notified of awards on a rolling basis beginning on or about 4/15. **Types of Aid:** *Need-based scholarships/grants:* Pell, SEOG, state scholarships/grants, private scholarships, the school's own gift aid. *Loans:* FFEL Subsidized Stafford, FFEL Unsubsidized Stafford, FFEL PLUS, Federal Perkins, state loans, college/university loans from institutional funds.

RATINGS

Admissions Selectivity Rating: 73   **Fire Safety Rating:** 60*   **Green Rating:** 60*

THE FRANCISCAN UNIVERSITY

400 North Bluff Blvd, PO Box 2967, Clinton, IA 52733-2967
Phone: 563-242-4153 **E-mail:** admissns@tfu.edu **CEEB Code:** 6418
Fax: 563-243-6102 **Website:** www.tfu.edu **ACT Code:** 1342
Financial Aid Phone: 563-242-4023

This private school was founded in 1918. It has a 25-acre campus.

RATINGS
Admissions Selectivity Rating: 72   **Fire Safety Rating:** 60*   **Green Rating:** 60*

STUDENTS AND FACULTY
Enrollment: 416. **Student Body:** 56% female, 44% male, 46% out-of-state, 3% international (10 countries represented). African American 6%, Caucasian 87%, Hispanic 3%. **Retention and Graduation:** 69% freshmen return for sophomore year. 25% freshmen graduate within 4 years. 25% grads go on to further study within 1 year. **Faculty:** Student/faculty ratio 12:1. 27 full-time faculty, 48% hold PhDs. 100% faculty teach undergrads.

ACADEMICS
Degrees: Associate, bachelor's, master's. **Academic Requirements:** Arts/fine arts, computer literacy, English (including composition), Franciscan course, history, humanities, mathematics, philosophy, sciences (biological or physical), social science. **Areas of required competencies:** Applied ethics, communication, computer, critical thinking, mathematics, writing & speech. **Classes:** Most classes have 10–19 students. Most lab/discussion sections have fewer than 10 students. **Majors with Highest Enrollment:** Education, liberal arts and sciences studies and humanities, social sciences. **Disciplines with Highest Percentage of Degrees Awarded:** Social sciences 23%, education 18%, business/marketing 16%, liberal arts/general studies 13%, visual and performing arts 9%. **Special Study Options:** Advanced placement program, distance learning, double major, dual enrollment, honors program, independent study, internships, off-campus study, senior capstone or culminating academic experiences, student-designed major, study abroad, summer school, teacher certification program, undergraduate research/creative projects, writing in the disciplines.

FACILITIES
Housing: Coed dorms, 2 bedroom suites, single bedrooms. **Special Academic Facilities/Equipment:** On-campus preschool, indoor swimming pool, multipurpose education center. **Computers:** 99% of public computers are PCs, 1% of public computers are Macs, network access in dorm rooms, network access in dorm lounges, online administrative functions (other than registration).

CAMPUS LIFE
Activities: Choral groups, music ensembles, student government, student newspaper. **Organizations:** 20 registered organizations, 2 honor societies. **Athletics (Intercollegiate):** *Men:* Baseball, basketball, cross-country, golf, soccer, track/field (outdoor). *Women:* Basketball, cross-country, soccer, softball, track/field (outdoor), volleyball.

ADMISSIONS
Freshman Academic Profile: 10% in top 10% of high school class, 33% in top 25% of high school class, 62% in top 50% of high school class. ACT middle 50% range 16–22. TOEFL required of all international applicants, minimum paper TOEFL 430, minimum computer TOEFL 213. **Basis for Candidate Selection:** *Very important factors considered include:* Class rank, rigor of secondary school record, standardized test scores. *Other factors considered include:* Recommendation(s). **Freshman Admission Requirements:** High school diploma is required, and GED is accepted. *Academic units recommended:* 4 English, 3 math, 3 science (2 science labs), 2 foreign language, 3 social studies, 3 history. **Freshman Admission Statistics:** 246 applied, 77% admitted, 28% enrolled. **Transfer Admission Requirements:** College transcript(s), statement of good standing from prior institution(s). Minimum college GPA of 2.0 required. Lowest grade transferable C. **General Admission Information:** Application fee $20. Regular application deadline 8/15. Regular notification within 2 weeks of application. Non-fall registration accepted. Admission may be deferred for a maximum of 2 semesters. Common Application accepted. Credit and/or placement offered for CEEB Advanced Placement tests.

COSTS AND FINANCIAL AID
Annual tuition $13,800. Room & board $5,250. Required fees $250. Average book expense $600. **Required Forms and Deadlines:** FAFSA. Financial aid filing deadline 8/1. Financial aid filing deadline 4/1. **Notification of Awards:** Applicants will be notified of awards on a rolling basis beginning on or about 3/15. **Types of Aid:** *Need-based scholarships/grants:* Pell, SEOG, state

scholarships/grants, private scholarships, the school's own gift aid. *Loans:* FFEL Subsidized Stafford, FFEL Unsubsidized Stafford, FFEL PLUS, Federal Perkins, private loan company. **Financial Aid Statistics:** 87% freshmen, 89% undergrads receive need-based scholarship or grant aid. 68% freshmen, 72% undergrads receive need-based self-help aid. 12 freshmen, 43 undergrads receive athletic scholarships.

FRANCISCAN UNIVERSITY OF STEUBENVILLE

1235 University Boulevard, Steubenville, OH 43952-1763
Phone: 740-283-6226 **E-mail:** admissions@franciscan.edu **CEEB Code:** 1133
Fax: 740-284-5456 **Website:** www.franciscan.edu **ACT Code:** 3258
Financial Aid Phone: 740-283-6226

This private school, affiliated with the Roman Catholic Church, was founded in 1946. It has a 124-acre campus.

RATINGS
Admissions Selectivity Rating: 83   **Fire Safety Rating:** 60*   **Green Rating:** 60*

STUDENTS AND FACULTY
Enrollment: 1,883. **Student Body:** 60% female, 40% male, 76% out-of-state. Asian 2%, Caucasian 86%, Hispanic 4%. **Retention and Graduation:** 87% freshmen return for sophomore year. 55% freshmen graduate within 4 years. 13% grads go on to further study within 1 year. 9% grads pursue arts and sciences degrees. 1% grads pursue business degrees. 1% grads pursue medical degrees. **Faculty:** Student/faculty ratio 15:1. 104 full-time faculty, 69% hold PhDs. 90% faculty teach undergrads.

ACADEMICS
Degrees: Associate, bachelor's, master's. **Academic Requirements:** English (including composition), foreign languages, history, humanities, philosophy, sciences (biological or physical), social science, theology. **Classes:** Most classes have 10–19 students. Most lab/discussion sections have 10–19 students. **Majors with Highest Enrollment:** Business administration/management, elementary education and teaching, theology/theological studies. **Disciplines with Highest Percentage of Degrees Awarded:** Business/marketing 12%, health professions and related sciences 12%, education 9%, English 7%, social sciences 7%. **Special Study Options:** Accelerated program, distance learning, double major, honors program, independent study, internships, liberal arts/career combination, study abroad, teacher certification program.

FACILITIES
Housing: Men's dorms, women's dorms. **Special Academic Facilities/Equipment:** Art gallery. **Computers:** 76% of public computers are PCs, 24% of public computers are Macs, online registration, online administrative functions (other than registration), remote student-access to Web through college's connection.

CAMPUS LIFE
Activities: Choral groups, drama/theater, literary magazine, music ensembles, radio station, student government, student newspaper, yearbook. **Organizations:** 31 registered organizations, 3 honor societies, 6 religious organizations. 1 fraternity, 1 sorority.

ADMISSIONS
Freshman Academic Profile: 28% in top 10% of high school class, 51% in top 25% of high school class, 82% in top 50% of high school class. 42% from public high schools. SAT Math middle 50% range 500–620. SAT Critical Reading middle 50% range 520–660. ACT middle 50% range 21–27. TOEFL required of all international applicants, minimum paper TOEFL 550, minimum computer TOEFL 213. **Basis for Candidate Selection:** *Very important factors considered include:* Application essay, character/personal qualities, interview, rigor of secondary school record, standardized test scores. *Important factors considered include:* Extracurricular activities, talent/ability. *Other factors considered include:* Recommendation(s). **Freshman Admission Requirements:** High school diploma is required, and GED is accepted. *Academic units recommended:* 4 English, 3 math, 3 science, 3 foreign language, 2 social studies, 2 history, 1 academic elective. **Freshman Admission Statistics:** 1,002 applied, 86% admitted, 44% enrolled. **Transfer Admission Requirements:** High school transcript, college transcript(s), essay or personal statement. Minimum college GPA of 2.0 required. Lowest grade transferable C. **General Admission Information:** Application fee $20. Regular application deadline 5/1. Regular notification is rolling. Nonfall registration accepted. Admission may be deferred for a maximum of 1 year. Common Application accepted. Credit and/or placement offered for CEEB Advanced Placement tests.

COSTS AND FINANCIAL AID

Average book expense $800. **Required Forms and Deadlines:** FAFSA. Financial aid filing deadline 4/15. **Notification of Awards:** Applicants will be notified of awards on a rolling basis beginning on or about 3/15. **Types of Aid:** *Need-based scholarships/grants:* Pell, SEOG, state scholarships/grants, private scholarships, the school's own gift aid. *Loans:* FFEL Subsidized Stafford, FFEL Unsubsidized Stafford, FFEL PLUS, Federal Perkins, alternative loans. **Student Employment:** Federal Work-Study Program available. Institutional employment available. Off-campus job opportunities are good. **Financial Aid Statistics:** 60% freshmen, 62% undergrads receive need-based scholarship or grant aid. 61% freshmen, 63% undergrads receive need-based self-help aid. 63% freshmen, 62% undergrads receive any aid. Highest amount earned per year from on-campus jobs $3,090.

FRANKLIN & MARSHALL COLLEGE

PO Box 3003, PO Box 3003, Lancaster, PA 17604-3003
Phone: 717-291-3953 **E-mail:** admission@fandm.edu **CEEB Code:** 2261
Fax: 717-291-4389 **Website:** www.fandm.edu **ACT Code:** 3574
Financial Aid Phone: 717-291-3991

This private school was founded in 1787. It has a 125-acre campus.

RATINGS
Admissions Selectivity Rating: 95   **Fire Safety Rating:** 60*   **Green Rating:** 78

STUDENTS AND FACULTY
Enrollment: 1,990. **Student Body:** 49% female, 51% male, 66% out-of-state, 8% international (64 countries represented). African American 3%, Asian 4%, Caucasian 72%, Hispanic 4%. **Retention and Graduation:** 91% freshmen return for sophomore year. 75% freshmen graduate within 4 years. 25% grads go on to further study within 1 year. 10% grads pursue arts and sciences degrees. 1% grads pursue business degrees. 6% grads pursue law degrees. 8% grads pursue medical degrees. **Faculty:** Student/faculty ratio 10:1. 178 full-time faculty, 98% hold PhDs. 100% faculty teach undergrads.

ACADEMICS
Degrees: Bachelor's. **Academic Requirements:** Arts/fine arts, foreign languages, humanities, non-Western cultures, sciences (biological or physical), social science. **Classes:** Most classes have 20–29 students. Most lab/discussion sections have 10–19 students. **Majors with Highest Enrollment:** Business administration/management, economics, political science and government. **Disciplines with Highest Percentage of Degrees Awarded:** Social sciences 27%, business/marketing 12%, interdisciplinary studies 10%, biological/life sciences 8%, English 7%. **Special Study Options:** Accelerated program, cross-registration, double major, dual enrollment, exchange student program (domestic), honors program, independent study, internships, student-designed major, study abroad, teacher certification program.

FACILITIES
Housing: Coed dorms, apartments for single students, special housing for disabled students, special housing for international students, fraternity/sorority housing, arts house, French house, community outreach house. **Special Academic Facilities/Equipment:** Art gallery, associated with natural history museums, bronze casting foundry, retail sales complex, psychology and language labs, TV and radio station, observatory/planetarium, writers' house. **Computers:** 100% of classrooms are wireless, 10% of public computers are PCs, 90% of public computers are Macs, network access in dorm rooms, network access in dorm lounges, online registration, online administrative functions (other than registration), remote student-access to Web through college's connection.

CAMPUS LIFE
Activities: Choral groups, concert band, dance, drama/theater, jazz band, literary magazine, music ensembles, musical theater, opera, radio station, student government, student newspaper, symphony orchestra, yearbook. **Organizations:** 90 registered organizations, 13 honor societies, 8 religious organizations. 7 fraternities (30% men join), 2 sororities (7% women join). **Athletics (Intercollegiate):** *Men:* Baseball, basketball, cross-country, football, golf, lacrosse, soccer, squash, swimming, tennis, track/field (indoor), track/field (outdoor), wrestling. *Women:* Basketball, cross-country, field hockey, golf, lacrosse, soccer, softball, squash, swimming, tennis, track/field (indoor), track/field (outdoor), volleyball.

ADMISSIONS
Freshman Academic Profile: 57% in top 10% of high school class, 84% in top 25% of high school class, 98% in top 50% of high school class. 53% from public high schools. SAT Math middle 50% range 610–690. SAT Critical Reading middle 50% range 600–690. TOEFL required of all international applicants, minimum paper TOEFL 600, minimum computer TOEFL 250. **Basis for Candidate Selection:** *Very important factors considered include:* Academic GPA, character/personal qualities, class rank, rigor of secondary school record. *Important factors considered include:* Application essay, extracurricular activities, interview, recommendation(s), standardized test scores, talent/ability, volunteer work. *Other factors considered include:* Alumni/ae relation, geographical residence, level of applicant's interest, racial/ethnic status, work experience. **Freshman Admission Requirements:** High school diploma is required, and GED is accepted. *Academic units required:* 4 English, 3 math, 2 science (2 science labs), 2 foreign language, 1 social studies, 2 history, 1 art/music/theater. *Academic units recommended:* 4 math, 3 science (3 science labs), 4 foreign language, 3 social studies, 3 history. **Freshman Admission Statistics:** 4,059 applied, 46% admitted, 28% enrolled. **Transfer Admission Requirements:** High school transcript, college transcript(s), essay or personal statement, interview, standardized test score, statement of good standing from prior institution(s). Lowest grade transferable C-. **General Admission Information:** Application fee $50. Early decision application deadline 11/15. Regular application deadline 2/1. Regular notification 4/1. Nonfall registration accepted. Admission may be deferred for a maximum of 1 year. Credit and/or placement offered for CEEB Advanced Placement tests.

COSTS AND FINANCIAL AID
Annual tuition $36,430. Room and board $9,174. Required fees $50. Average book expense $650. **Required Forms and Deadlines:** FAFSA, institution's own financial aid form, CSS/Financial Aid PROFILE, Noncustodial PROFILE, Business/Farm Supplement. Financial aid filing deadline 3/1. **Notification of Awards:** Applicants will be notified of awards on or about 3/15. **Types of Aid:** *Need-based scholarships/grants:* Pell, SEOG, state scholarships/grants, private scholarships, the school's own gift aid. *Loans:* FFEL Subsidized Stafford, FFEL Unsubsidized Stafford, FFEL PLUS, Federal Perkins, college/university loans from institutional funds. **Student Employment:** Federal Work-Study Program available. **Financial Aid Statistics:** 56% freshmen, 42% undergrads receive need-based scholarship or grant aid. 57% freshmen, 43% undergrads receive need-based self-help aid. 59% freshmen, 70% undergrads receive any aid. Highest amount earned per year from on-campus jobs $1,300.

FRANKLIN COLLEGE

101 Branigin Boulevard, Franklin, IN 46131-2623
Phone: 317-738-8062 **E-mail:** admissions@franklincollege.edu **CEEB Code:** 1228
Fax: 317-738-8274 **Website:** www.franklincollege.edu **ACT Code:** 1194
Financial Aid Phone: 317-738-8075

This private school, affiliated with the American Baptist Church, was founded in 1834. It has a 74-acre campus.

RATINGS
Admissions Selectivity Rating: 74   **Fire Safety Rating:** 74   **Green Rating:** 74

STUDENTS AND FACULTY
Enrollment: 1,013. **Student Body:** 49% female, 51% male, 5% out-of-state. African American 2%, Caucasian 60%. **Retention and Graduation:** 71% freshmen return for sophomore year. 51% freshmen graduate within 4 years. 15% grads go on to further study within 1 year. 12% grads pursue arts and sciences degrees. 2% grads pursue law degrees. 1% grads pursue medical degrees. **Faculty:** Student/faculty ratio 16:1. 64 full-time faculty, 80% hold PhDs. 100% faculty teach undergrads.

ACADEMICS
Degrees: Bachelor's. **Academic Requirements:** Arts/fine arts, English (including composition), foreign languages, history, humanities, mathematics, sciences (biological or physical), social science. **Classes:** Most classes have 10–19 students. **Majors with Highest Enrollment:** Elementary education and teaching; journalism; sociology. **Disciplines with Highest Percentage of Degrees Awarded:** Education 18%, communications/journalism 18%, social sciences 12%, business/marketing 12%, biological/life sciences 11%, foreign languages and literature 7%. **Special Study Options:** Double major, dual enrollment, exchange student program (domestic), independent study, internships, study abroad, teacher certification program.

FACILITIES

Housing: Coed dorms, men's dorms, women's dorms, special housing for disabled students, fraternity/sorority housing. **Special Academic Facilities/Equipment:** Pulliam School of Journalism, Dietz Center for Professional Development, leadership center. **Computers:** 10% of classrooms are wired, 90% of public computers are PCs, 10% of public computers are Macs, network access in dorm rooms, network access in dorm lounges, online registration, online administrative functions (other than registration), remote student-access to Web through college's connection.

CAMPUS LIFE

Activities: Choral groups, dance, drama/theater, literary magazine, musical theater, pep band, radio station, student government, student newspaper, yearbook. **Organizations:** 66 registered organizations, 13 honor societies, 3 religious organizations. 4 fraternities (30% men join), 4 sororities (35% women join). **Athletics (Intercollegiate):** *Men:* Baseball, basketball, cross-country, football, golf, soccer, tennis, track/field (outdoor). *Women:* Basketball, cheerleading, cross-country, golf, soccer, softball, tennis, track/field (outdoor), volleyball. **Environmental initiatives:** Completing green hosue car emissions inventory. Star purchase policy. Recycling, composting program.

ADMISSIONS

Freshman Academic Profile: 13% in top 10% of high school class, 31% in top 25% of high school class, 81% in top 50% of high school class. SAT Math middle 50% range 450–560. SAT Critical Reading middle 50% range 440–540. SAT Writing middle 50% range 440–540. ACT middle 50% range 18–23. TOEFL required of all international applicants, minimum paper TOEFL 550, minimum computer TOEFL 213. **Basis for Candidate Selection:** *Very important factors considered include:* Academic GPA, class rank, rigor of secondary school record, standardized test scores. *Important factors considered include:* Alumni/ae relation, application essay, character/personal qualities, extracurricular activities. *Other factors considered include:* First generation, geographical residence, interview, level of applicant's interest, racial/ethnic status, recommendation(s), religious affiliation/commitment, state residency, talent/ability, volunteer work, work experience. **Freshman Admission Requirements:** High school diploma is required, and GED is accepted. *Academic units required:* 4 English, 4 math, 2 science, 3 social studies. **Freshman Admission Statistics:** 1,280 applied, 74% admitted, 33% enrolled. **Transfer Admission Requirements:** High school transcript, college transcript(s), essay or personal statement, statement of good standing from prior institution(s). Minimum college GPA of 2.0 required. Lowest grade transferable C-. **General Admission Information:** Application fee $30. Regular notification 9/1. Nonfall registration accepted. Admission may be deferred for a maximum of 1 year. Credit and/or placement offered for CEEB Advanced Placement tests.

COSTS AND FINANCIAL AID

Required Forms and Deadlines: FAFSA, institution's own financial aid form. Financial aid filing deadline 3/1. **Notification of Awards:** Applicants will be notified of awards on or about 4/1. **Types of Aid:** *Need-based scholarships/grants:* Pell, SEOG, state scholarships/grants, private scholarships, the school's own gift aid. *Loans:* FFEL Subsidized Stafford, FFEL Unsubsidized Stafford, FFEL PLUS, Federal Perkins, college/university loans from institutional funds. **Student Employment:** Federal Work-Study Program available. Institutional employment available. Off-campus job opportunities are good. **Financial Aid Statistics:** 80% freshmen, 81% undergrads receive need-based scholarship or grant aid. 62% freshmen, 63% undergrads receive need-based self-help aid. 100% freshmen, 98% undergrads receive any aid. Highest amount earned per year from on-campus jobs $2,000.

FRANKLIN PIERCE COLLEGE

Admissions Office, Box 60, 20 College Road, Rindge, NH 03461
Phone: 603-899-4050 **E-mail:** admissions@fpc.edu **CEEB Code:** 3395
Fax: 603-889-4394 **Website:** www.fpc.edu **ACT Code:** 2509
Financial Aid Phone: 603-899-4180

This private school was founded in 1962. It has a 1,200-acre campus.

RATINGS

Admissions Selectivity Rating: 73   **Fire Safety Rating:** 86   **Green Rating:** 60*

STUDENTS AND FACULTY

Enrollment: 1,677. **Student Body:** 48% female, 52% male, 78% out-of-state. **Retention and Graduation:** 70% freshmen return for sophomore year. 43% freshmen graduate within 4 years. 21% grads go on to further study within 1 year. 5% grads pursue arts and sciences degrees. 7% grads pursue business degrees. 3% grads pursue law degrees. 1% grads pursue medical degrees.

Faculty: Student/faculty ratio 18:1. 89 full-time faculty, 69% hold PhDs. 100% faculty teach undergrads.

ACADEMICS

Degrees: Associate, bachelor's, doctoral, first professional, master's. **Academic Requirements:** Arts/fine arts, English (including composition), history, humanities, I&C Core Classes, mathematics, sciences (biological or physical), social science. **Classes:** Most classes have 10–19 students. Most lab/discussion sections have 10–19 students. **Majors with Highest Enrollment:** Communications and media studies; criminal justice/safety studies; education. **Disciplines with Highest Percentage of Degrees Awarded:** Business/marketing 25%, security and protective services 12%, visual and performing arts 9%, communications/journalism 8%, area and ethnic studies 6%, liberal arts/general studies 6%, social sciences 6%. **Special Study Options:** Arcadia study abroad, distance learning, double major, dual enrollment, English as a Second Language (ESL), exchange student program (domestic), honors program, independent study, internships, student-designed major, study abroad, teacher certification program, Walk Across Europe program, Washington semester.

FACILITIES

Housing: Coed dorms, apartments for single students, special housing for disabled students, condominiums (townhouses). **Special Academic Facilities/Equipment:** Thoreau Art Gallery; Flynt Center; Fitzwater Communications Center; dance studio; pottery kiln; glass blowing studio; TV station; radio station; Grimshaw-Gudewicz Activities Center. **Computers:** 92% of public computers are PCs, 8% of public computers are Macs, network access in dorm rooms, network access in dorm lounges, remote student-access to Web through college's connection.

CAMPUS LIFE

Activities: Choral groups, dance, drama/theater, literary magazine, music ensembles, musical theater, radio station, student government, student newspaper, television station, yearbook. **Organizations:** 35 registered organizations, 8 honor societies, 3 religious organizations. **Athletics (Intercollegiate):** *Men:* Baseball, basketball, crew/rowing, cross-country, golf, ice hockey, lacrosse, soccer, tennis. *Women:* Basketball, cheerleading, crew/rowing, cross-country, field hockey, golf, lacrosse, soccer, softball, tennis, volleyball.

ADMISSIONS

Freshman Academic Profile: 7% in top 10% of high school class, 20% in top 25% of high school class, 54% in top 50% of high school class. 89% from public high schools. SAT Math middle 50% range 430–540. SAT Critical Reading middle 50% range 440–550. SAT Writing middle 50% range 420–520. TOEFL required of all international applicants, minimum paper TOEFL 500, minimum computer TOEFL 173. **Basis for Candidate Selection:** *Very important factors considered include:* Academic GPA, character/personal qualities, recommendation(s). *Important factors considered include:* Application essay, rigor of secondary school record, standardized test scores. *Other factors considered include:* Class rank, extracurricular activities, interview, talent/ability, volunteer work, work experience. **Freshman Admission Requirements:** High school diploma is required, and GED is accepted. *Academic units required:* 4 English, 3 math, 2 science (2 science labs), 3 social studies, 4 academic electives. **Freshman Admission Statistics:** 4,184 applied, 74% admitted, 19% enrolled. **Transfer Admission Requirements:** College transcript(s), essay or personal statement. Minimum college GPA of 2.0 required. Lowest grade transferable C-. **General Admission Information:** Regular notification is rolling. Nonfall registration accepted. Admission may be deferred for a maximum of 1 year. Credit and/or placement offered for CEEB Advanced Placement tests.

COSTS AND FINANCIAL AID

Annual tuition $27,000. Room and board $9,200. Required fees $1,300. Average book expense $900. **Required Forms and Deadlines:** FAFSA. **Notification of Awards:** Applicants will be notified of awards on a rolling basis beginning on or about 2/1. **Types of Aid:** *Need-based scholarships/grants:* Pell, SEOG, state scholarships/grants, private scholarships, the school's own gift aid. *Loans:* FFEL Subsidized Stafford, FFEL Unsubsidized Stafford, FFEL PLUS, Federal Perkins. **Student Employment:** Federal Work-Study Program available. Institutional employment available. Off-campus job opportunities are good. **Financial Aid Statistics:** 67% freshmen, 73% undergrads receive need-based scholarship or grant aid. 61% freshmen, 67% undergrads receive need-based self-help aid. 15 freshmen, 50 undergrads receive athletic scholarships. 68% freshmen, 74% undergrads receive any aid. Highest amount earned per year from on-campus jobs $2,000.

FRANKLIN UNIVERSITY

201 S Grant Avenue, Columbus, OH 43215
Phone: 614-797-4700 **E-mail:** info@franklin.edu **CEEB Code:** 1229
Fax: 614-224-8027 **Website:** www.franklin.edu **ACT Code:** 3275
Financial Aid Phone: 614-797-4700

This private school was founded in 1902. It has a 14-acre campus.

RATINGS
Admissions Selectivity Rating: 60*   **Fire Safety Rating:** 60*   **Green Rating:** 60*

STUDENTS AND FACULTY
Enrollment: 5,682. **Student Body:** 55% female, 45% male, 26% out-of-state, 5% international. African American 19%, Asian 3%, Caucasian 66%, Hispanic 2%. **Retention and Graduation:** 72% freshmen return for sophomore year. **Faculty:** Student/faculty ratio 19:1. 36 full-time faculty, 64% hold PhDs.

ACADEMICS
Degrees: Associate, bachelor's, master's, post-bachelor's certificate, post-master's certificate. **Academic Requirements:** Computer literacy, English (including composition), history, humanities, mathematics, sciences (biological or physical), social science, speech. **Classes:** Most classes have 10–19 students. **Majors with Highest Enrollment:** Accounting, business administration/management, computer and information sciences. **Disciplines with Highest Percentage of Degrees Awarded:** Business/marketing 82%, computer and information sciences 12%, health professions and related sciences 3%, interdisciplinary studies 2%, communication technologies 1%. **Special Study Options:** Accelerated program, cooperative education program, cross-registration, distance learning, double major, dual enrollment, English as a second language (ESL), independent study, internships, study abroad, weekend college.

FACILITIES
Computers: 100% of public computers are PCs, online registration.

CAMPUS LIFE
Organizations: 6 registered organizations.

ADMISSIONS
Freshman Academic Profile: TOEFL required of all international applicants, minimum paper TOEFL 430, minimum computer TOEFL 117. **Freshman Admission Requirements:** High school diploma is required, and GED is accepted. *Academic units recommended:* 3 math. **Freshman Admission Statistics:** 262 applied, 100% admitted, 47% enrolled. **Transfer Admission Requirements:** College transcript(s). Lowest grade transferable C-. **General Admission Information:** Nonfall registration accepted. Admission may be deferred. Common Application not accepted. Credit and/or placement offered for CEEB Advanced Placement tests.

COSTS AND FINANCIAL AID
Annual tuition $6,990. **Required Forms and Deadlines:** FAFSA. Financial aid filing deadline 6/15. **Types of Aid:** *Need-based scholarships/grants:* Pell, SEOG, state scholarships/grants, private scholarships, the school's own gift aid. *Loans:* FFEL Subsidized Stafford, FFEL Unsubsidized Stafford, FFEL PLUS, college/university loans from institutional funds. **Student Employment:** Federal Work-Study Program available. Institutional employment available. Off-campus job opportunities are good. **Financial Aid Statistics:** 61% freshmen, 40% undergrads receive need-based scholarship or grant aid. 78% freshmen, 59% undergrads receive need-based self-help aid.

FRANKLIN W. OLIN COLLEGE OF ENGINEERING

Olin Way, Needham, MA 02492-1245
Phone: 781-292-2222 **E-mail:** info@olin.edu **CEEB Code:** 2824
Fax: 781-292-2210 **Website:** www.olin.edu **ACT Code:** 1883
Financial Aid Phone: 781-292-2222

This private school was founded in 1997. It has a 70-acre campus.

RATINGS
Admissions Selectivity Rating: 99   **Fire Safety Rating:** 98   **Green Rating:** 60*

STUDENTS AND FACULTY
Enrollment: 304. **Student Body:** 43% female, 57% male, 92% out-of-state. **Retention and Graduation:** 99% freshmen return for sophomore year. **Faculty:** Student/faculty ratio 9:1. 29 full-time faculty, 100% hold PhDs. 100% faculty teach undergrads.

ACADEMICS
Degrees: Bachelor's. **Academic Requirements:** Arts/fine arts, engineering, humanities, mathematics, sciences (biological or physical), social science. **Classes:** Most classes have 20–29 students. Most lab/discussion sections have fewer than 10 students. **Majors with Highest Enrollment:** Electrical, electronics, and communications engineering; engineering; mechanical engineering. **Disciplines with Highest Percentage of Degrees Awarded:** Engineering 66%. **Special Study Options:** Cross-registration, independent study, internships, liberal arts/career combination, Passionate Pursuits Program, student-designed major, study abroad.

FACILITIES
Housing: Coed dorms, special housing for disabled students. **Special Academic Facilities/Equipment:** Student art gallery. **Computers:** 100% of classrooms are wired, 100% of classrooms are wireless, 100% of public computers are PCs, network access in dorm rooms, network access in dorm lounges, online registration, online administrative functions (other than registration), support for handheld computing, remote student-access to Web through college's connection. Undergraduates are required to own a computer.

CAMPUS LIFE
Activities: Choral groups, dance, drama/theater, jazz band, music ensembles, musical theater, student government, student newspaper, student-run film society, symphony orchestra, yearbook. **Organizations:** 54 registered organizations, 2 religious organizations.

ADMISSIONS
Freshman Academic Profile: 71% from public high schools. SAT Math middle 50% range 710–800. SAT Critical Reading middle 50% range 710–770. ACT middle 50% range 31–34. **Basis for Candidate Selection:** *Very important factors considered include:* Academic GPA, application essay, character/personal qualities, extracurricular activities, level of applicant's interest, recommendation(s), rigor of secondary school record, talent/ability. *Important factors considered include:* Class rank, interview, standardized test scores, volunteer work. *Other factors considered include:* First generation, geographical residence, racial/ethnic status, state residency, work experience. **Freshman Admission Requirements:** High school diploma is required, and GED is accepted. *Academic units required:* 4 English, 4 math, 3 science (3 science labs), 2 foreign language, 2 social studies, 2 history. *Academic units recommended:* 2 computing, engineering design. **Freshman Admission Statistics:** 784 applied, 17% admitted, 65% enrolled. **General Admission Information:** Application fee $60. Regular application deadline 1/7. Regular notification 3/21. Nonfall registration not accepted. Admission may be deferred for a maximum of 1 year. Neither credit nor placement offered for CEEB Advanced Placement tests.

COSTS AND FINANCIAL AID
Comprehensive fee $33,600. Room and board $11,800. Required fees $175. Average book expense $750. **Required Forms and Deadlines:** FAFSA. Financial aid filing deadline 4/15. **Notification of Awards:** Applicants will be notified of awards on a rolling basis beginning on or about 3/25. **Types of Aid:** *Need-based scholarships/grants:* State scholarships/grants, private scholarships, the school's own gift aid. **Financial Aid Statistics:** 11% freshmen, 3% undergrads receive need-based scholarship or grant aid. 100% freshmen, 100% undergrads receive any aid.

FREED-HARDEMAN UNIVERSITY

158 East Main Street, Henderson, TN 38340
Phone: 731-989-6651 **E-mail:** admissions@fhu.edu **CEEB Code:** 1230
Fax: 731-989-6047 **Website:** www.fhu.edu **ACT Code:** 3962
Financial Aid Phone: 731-989-6662

This private school, affiliated with the Church of Christ, was founded in 1869. It has a 122-acre campus.

RATINGS
Admissions Selectivity Rating: 77   **Fire Safety Rating:** 60*   **Green Rating:** 69

STUDENTS AND FACULTY
Enrollment: 1,359. **Student Body:** 54% female, 46% male, 50% out-of-state, 3% international (18 countries represented). African American 4%, Caucasian 95%. **Retention and Graduation:** 73% freshmen return for sophomore year. 47% freshmen graduate within 4 years. 40% grads go on to further study within 1 year. **Faculty:** Student/faculty ratio 13:1. 112 full-time faculty, 71% hold PhDs. 97% faculty teach undergrads.

ACADEMICS
Degrees: Associate, bachelor's, first professional, master's, post-bachelor's certificate, post-master's certificate. **Academic Requirements:** Arts/fine arts, computer literacy, English (including composition), history, humanities, mathematics, sciences (biological or physical), social science. Each full-time student is required to take a Bible course and students must take a values class before graduation. **Classes:** Most classes have 10–19 students. Most lab/discussion sections have 10–19 students. **Majors with Highest Enrollment:** Bible/biblical studies; biology/biological sciences; liberal arts and sciences studies and humanities. **Disciplines with Highest Percentage of Degrees Awarded:** Business/marketing 22%, interdisciplinary studies 11%, theology and religious vocations 10%, visual and performing arts 8%, biological/life sciences 7%. **Special Study Options:** Accelerated program, cooperative education program, cross-registration, distance learning, double major, dual enrollment, honors program, independent study, internships, liberal arts/career combination, student-designed major, study abroad, teacher certification program, 3–2 engineering, honors college, study abroad in Belgium and Italy.

FACILITIES
Housing: Men's dorms, women's dorms, apartments for single students. Some student teacher housing is available. **Special Academic Facilities/Equipment:** Child development lab, nursery school. **Computers:** 35% of classrooms are wired, 100% of classrooms are wireless, 92% of public computers are PCs, 8% of public computers are Macs, network access in dorm rooms, network access in dorm lounges, online registration, online administrative functions (other than registration), remote student-access to Web through college's connection.

CAMPUS LIFE
Activities: Choral groups, concert band, drama/theater, jazz band, music ensembles, musical theater, pep band, radio station, student government, student newspaper, television station, yearbook. **Organizations:** 52 registered organizations, 4 honor societies, 5 religious organizations. 6 fraternities, 6 sororities. **Athletics (Intercollegiate):** *Men:* Baseball, basketball, cheerleading, soccer, tennis. *Women:* Basketball, cheerleading, soccer, softball, tennis, volleyball.

ADMISSIONS
Freshman Academic Profile: 25% in top 10% of high school class, 51% in top 25% of high school class, 79% in top 50% of high school class. SAT Math middle 50% range 480–600. SAT Critical Reading middle 50% range 480–640. ACT middle 50% range 20–26. **Basis for Candidate Selection:** *Very important factors considered include:* Rigor of secondary school record, standardized test scores. *Other factors considered include:* Alumni/ae relation, character/personal qualities, extracurricular activities, racial/ethnic status, recommendation(s), religious affiliation/commitment, volunteer work, work experience. **Freshman Admission Requirements:** High school diploma is required, and GED is accepted. *Academic units recommended:* 4 English, 2 math, 2 science, 2 social studies, 10 academic electives. **Freshman Admission Statistics:** 1,040 applied, 99% admitted, 35% enrolled. **Transfer Admission Requirements:** College transcript(s), statement of good standing from prior institution(s). Lowest grade transferable D. **General Admission Information:** Regular notification is rolling. Nonfall registration accepted. Admission may be deferred for a maximum of 2 years. Credit and/or placement offered for CEEB Advanced Placement tests.

COSTS AND FINANCIAL AID
Annual tuition $13,192. Room and board $6,560. Average book expense $1,710. **Required Forms and Deadlines:** FAFSA. Financial aid filing deadline 3/1. **Notification of Awards:** Applicants will be notified of awards on a rolling basis beginning on or about 3/1. **Types of Aid:** *Need-based scholarships/grants:* Pell, SEOG, state scholarships/grants, private scholarships, the school's own gift aid. *Loans:* FFEL Subsidized Stafford, FFEL Unsubsidized Stafford, FFEL PLUS, Federal Perkins, Alternative loan programs. **Student Employment:** Federal Work-Study Program available. Institutional employment available. Off-campus job opportunities are fair. **Financial Aid Statistics:** 74% freshmen, 70% undergrads receive need-based scholarship or grant aid. 56% freshmen, 62% undergrads receive need-based self-help aid. 35 freshmen, 78 undergrads receive athletic scholarships. 86% freshmen, receive any aid.

FRESNO PACIFIC UNIVERSITY

1717 South Chestnut Avenue, Fresno, CA 93702
Phone: 559-453-2039 **E-mail:** ugadmis@fresno.edu
Fax: 559-453-2007 **Website:** www.fresno.edu
Financial Aid Phone: 559-453-2041

This private school, affiliated with the Mennonite Church, was founded in 1944. It has a 42-acre campus.

RATINGS
Admissions Selectivity Rating: 81   **Fire Safety Rating:** 60*   **Green Rating:** 60*

STUDENTS AND FACULTY
Enrollment: 1,459. **Student Body:** 68% female, 32% male, 4% out-of-state, 2% international. African American 4%, Asian 4%, Caucasian 53%, Hispanic 26%, Native American 1%. **Retention and Graduation:** 70% freshmen return for sophomore year. 48% freshmen graduate within 4 years. **Faculty:** Student/faculty ratio 16:1. 84 full-time faculty, 61% hold PhDs.

ACADEMICS
Degrees: Associate, bachelor's, master's. **Academic Requirements:** Arts/fine arts, biblical and religious studies, English (including composition), foreign languages, history, humanities, mathematics, philosophy, sciences (biological or physical), social science. **Classes:** Most classes have fewer than 10 students. Most lab/discussion sections have fewer than 10 students. **Majors with Highest Enrollment:** Bible/biblical studies, business administration/management, education. **Disciplines with Highest Percentage of Degrees Awarded:** Education 41%, theology and religious vocations 9%, psychology 6%, public administration and social services 4%, English 3%, social sciences 3%. **Special Study Options:** Accelerated program, cooperative education program, cross-registration, distance learning, double major, English as a second language (ESL), independent study, internships, liberal arts/career combination, student-designed major, study abroad, teacher certification program.

FACILITIES
Housing: Men's dorms, women's dorms, apartments for single students, special housing for disabled students. **Special Academic Facilities/Equipment:** English Language Training Institute. **Computers:** Network access in dorm rooms, network access in dorm lounges, remote student-access to Web through college's connection.

CAMPUS LIFE
Activities: Choral groups, concert band, dance, drama/theater, jazz band, music ensembles, pep band, student government, student newspaper, yearbook. **Organizations:** 36 registered organizations, 1 honor society, 11 religious organizations. **Athletics (Intercollegiate):** *Men:* Baseball, basketball, cross-country, soccer, tennis, track/field (outdoor). *Women:* Basketball, cross-country, soccer, tennis, track/field (outdoor), volleyball.

ADMISSIONS
Freshman Academic Profile: 27% in top 10% of high school class, 58% in top 25% of high school class, 85% in top 50% of high school class. SAT Math middle 50% range 420–560. SAT Critical Reading middle 50% range 430–580. SAT Writing middle 50% range 410–570. ACT middle 50% range 16–24. **Basis for Candidate Selection:** *Very important factors considered include:* Rigor of secondary school record, standardized test scores. *Important factors considered include:* Academic GPA, application essay, class rank, recommendation(s), religious affiliation/commitment. *Other factors considered include:* Character/personal qualities. **Freshman Admission Requirements:** High school diploma is required, and GED is accepted. *Academic units required:* 4 English, 3 math, 1 science (1 science lab), 2 foreign language, 2 social studies. *Academic units recommended:* 1 visual and performing arts. **Freshman Admission**

Statistics: 672 applied, 68% admitted, 46% enrolled. **Transfer Admission Requirements:** High school transcript, college transcript(s), essay or personal statement. Minimum college GPA of 2.4 required. Lowest grade transferable C. **General Admission Information:** Application fee $40. Regular application deadline 7/31. Regular notification is rolling. Nonfall registration accepted. Credit offered for CEEB Advanced Placement tests.

COSTS AND FINANCIAL AID

Average book expense $1,314. **Required Forms and Deadlines:** FAFSA, institution's own financial aid form. Financial aid filing deadline 3/2. **Notification of Awards:** Applicants will be notified of awards on a rolling basis beginning on or about 3/2. **Types of Aid:** *Need-based scholarships/grants:* Pell, SEOG, state scholarships/grants, private scholarships, the school's own gift aid. *Loans:* FFEL Subsidized Stafford, FFEL Unsubsidized Stafford, FFEL PLUS, Federal Perkins. **Student Employment:** Federal Work-Study Program available. Institutional employment available. Off-campus job opportunities are good. **Financial Aid Statistics:** 80% freshmen, 65% undergrads receive need-based scholarship or grant aid. 62% freshmen, 65% undergrads receive need-based self-help aid. 39 freshmen, 151 undergrads receive athletic scholarships.

FRIENDS UNIVERSITY

2100 University Street., Wichita, KS 67213
Phone: 316-295-5100 **E-mail:** learn@friends.edu
Fax: 316-295-5101 **Website:** www.friends.edu **ACT Code:** 1918
Financial Aid Phone: 316-295-5200

This private school, affiliated with the Society of Friends, was founded in 1898. It has a 45-acre campus.

RATINGS
Admissions Selectivity Rating: 60*   **Fire Safety Rating:** 60*   **Green Rating:** 60*

STUDENTS AND FACULTY
Student Body: 13% out-of-state. **Retention and Graduation:** 63% freshmen return for sophomore year. 33% grads go on to further study within 1 year. **Faculty:** Student/faculty ratio 10:1. 72 full-time faculty, 43% hold PhDs. 95% faculty teach undergrads.

ACADEMICS
Degrees: Bachelor's, master's. **Academic Requirements:** Arts/fine arts, computer literacy, English (including composition), history, humanities, mathematics, religion, sciences (biological or physical). **Special Study Options:** Cooperative education program, cross-registration, double major, dual enrollment, external degree program, honors program, independent study, internships, student-designed major, study abroad, teacher certification program. Degree completion program for working adults.

FACILITIES
Housing: Men's dorms, women's dorms, apartments for married students, apartments for single students, university-owned houses. **Computers:** Network access in dorm rooms, remote student-access to Web through college's connection.

CAMPUS LIFE
Activities: Choral groups, concert band, dance, drama/theater, jazz band, literary magazine, music ensembles, musical theater, pep band, student government, symphony orchestra, yearbook. **Organizations:** 32 registered organizations, 4 honor societies, 3 religious organizations. 2 fraternities, 1 sorority. **Athletics (Intercollegiate):** *Men:* Baseball, basketball, cheerleading, cross-country, football, golf, soccer, tennis, track/field (outdoor). *Women:* Basketball, cheerleading, cross-country, soccer, softball, tennis, track/field (outdoor), volleyball.

ADMISSIONS
Freshman Academic Profile: ACT middle 50% range 17–26. TOEFL required of all international applicants, minimum paper TOEFL 500. **Basis for Candidate Selection:** *Very important factors considered include:* Rigor of secondary school record, standardized test scores. *Important factors considered include:* Interview, recommendation(s). *Other factors considered include:* Alumni/ae relation, extracurricular activities, racial/ethnic status, religious affiliation/commitment, talent/ability. **Freshman Admission Requirements:** High school diploma is required, and GED is accepted. *Academic units recommended:* 3 math, 3 science. **Freshman Admission Statistics:** 668 applied, 93% admitted. **Transfer Admission Requirements:** College transcript(s), statement of good standing from prior institution(s). Minimum college GPA of 2.0 required. Lowest grade transferable C. **General Admission Information:** Application fee $15. Nonfall registration accepted. Common

Application not accepted. Credit and/or placement offered for CEEB Advanced Placement tests.

COSTS AND FINANCIAL AID
Annual tuition $11,050. Room and board $3,420. Required fees $90. Average book expense $750. **Required Forms and Deadlines:** FAFSA, institution's own financial aid form. Financial aid filing deadline 4/1. **Types of Aid:** *Need-based scholarships/grants:* Pell, SEOG, private scholarships. *Loans:* Direct Subsidized Stafford, Direct Unsubsidized Stafford, Direct PLUS, Federal Perkins. **Student Employment:** Federal Work-Study Program available. Institutional employment available. Off-campus job opportunities are excellent.

FROSTBURG STATE UNIVERSITY

FSU, 101 Braddock Road, Frostburg, MD 21532
Phone: 301-687-4201 **E-mail:** fsuadmissions@frostburg.edu **CEEB Code:** 5402
Fax: 301-687-7074 **Website:** www.frostburg.edu **ACT Code:** 1714
Financial Aid Phone: 301-687-4301

This public school was founded in 1898. It has a 260-acre campus.

RATINGS
Admissions Selectivity Rating: 72   **Fire Safety Rating:** 60*   **Green Rating:** 85

STUDENTS AND FACULTY
Enrollment: 4,246. **Student Body:** 49% female, 51% male, 11% out-of-state. African American 15%, Asian 2%, Caucasian 78%, Hispanic 2%. **Retention and Graduation:** 71% freshmen return for sophomore year. 21% freshmen graduate within 4 years. **Faculty:** Student/faculty ratio 17:1. 233 full-time faculty. 100% faculty teach undergrads.

ACADEMICS
Degrees: Bachelor's, certificate, master's, post-bachelor's certificate, post-master's certificate. **Academic Requirements:** Arts/fine arts, English (including composition), history, humanities, mathematics, personal wellness, sciences (biological or physical), social science. **Classes:** Most classes have 10–19 students. Most lab/discussion sections have 10–19 students. **Majors with Highest Enrollment:** Business administration/management, elementary education and teaching, psychology. **Disciplines with Highest Percentage of Degrees Awarded:** Business/marketing 15%, education 14%, social sciences 13%, visual and performing arts 8%, psychology 7%. **Special Study Options:** Accelerated program, cross-registration, distance learning, double major, dual degree program, dual enrollment, honors program, independent study, internships, learning communities, liberal arts/career combination, study abroad, teacher certification program.

FACILITIES
Housing: Coed dorms, men's dorms, women's dorms, leadership hall, honors housing, community service. **Special Academic Facilities/Equipment:** Art gallery, planetarium, electron microscope. **Computers:** 80% of public computers are PCs, 20% of public computers are Macs, network access in dorm rooms, network access in dorm lounges, online registration, online administrative functions (other than registration), remote student-access to Web through college's connection.

CAMPUS LIFE
Activities: Choral groups, concert band, dance, drama/theater, jazz band, literary magazine, marching band, music ensembles, musical theater, radio station, student government, student newspaper, symphony orchestra, television station. **Organizations:** 95 registered organizations, 18 honor societies, 6 religious organizations. 5 fraternities (10% men join), 5 sororities (10% women join). **Athletics (Intercollegiate):** *Men:* Baseball, basketball, cross-country, diving, football, golf, soccer, swimming, tennis, track/field (indoor), track/field (outdoor). *Women:* Basketball, cross-country, diving, field hockey, lacrosse, soccer, softball, swimming, tennis, track/field (indoor), track/field (outdoor), volleyball. **Environmental initiatives:** Adopt an energy-efficient appliance purchasing policy requiring purchase of ENERGY STAR-certified products in all areas for which such ratings exist. Begin purchasing or producing at least 15 percent of institutions electricity consumption from renewable sources within one year of signing the ACUPCC. Participate in the Waste Minimization component of the national RecycleMania competition, and adopt three or more associated measures to reduce waste.

ADMISSIONS
Freshman Academic Profile: 10% in top 10% of high school class, 32% in top 25% of high school class, 73% in top 50% of high school class. SAT Math middle 50% range 430–540. SAT Critical Reading middle 50% range 430–530. SAT Writing middle 50% range 420–520. ACT middle 50% range 17–22. TOEFL

required of all international applicants, minimum paper TOEFL 550, minimum computer TOEFL 213. **Basis for Candidate Selection:** *Very important factors considered include:* Academic GPA, rigor of secondary school record, standardized test scores. *Important factors considered include:* Interview, recommendation(s). *Other factors considered include:* Alumni/ae relation, character/personal qualities, extracurricular activities, talent/ability. **Freshman Admission Requirements:** High school diploma is required, and GED is accepted. *Academic units required:* 4 English, 3 math, 3 science (2 science labs), 2 foreign language, 3 social studies. **Freshman Admission Statistics:** 3,430 applied, 76% admitted, 36% enrolled. **Transfer Admission Requirements:** College transcript(s). Minimum college GPA of 2.0 required. Lowest grade transferable C. **General Admission Information:** Application fee $30. Early decision application deadline 12/15. Regular notification is rolling. Nonfall registration accepted. Common Application not accepted. Credit and/or placement offered for CEEB Advanced Placement tests.

COSTS AND FINANCIAL AID

Annual in-state tuition $5,000. Annual out-of-state tuition $14,612. Room and board $6,746. Required fees $1,550. Average book expense $750. **Required Forms and Deadlines:** FAFSA. Financial aid filing deadline 3/1. **Notification of Awards:** Applicants will be notified of awards on a rolling basis beginning on or about 3/15. **Types of Aid:** *Need-based scholarships/grants:* Pell, SEOG, state scholarships/grants, private scholarships, the school's own gift aid. *Loans:* Direct Subsidized Stafford, Direct Unsubsidized Stafford, Direct PLUS, FFEL PLUS, Federal Perkins, college/university loans from institutional funds. **Financial Aid Statistics:** 42% freshmen, 36% undergrads receive need-based scholarship or grant aid. 36% freshmen, 37% undergrads receive need-based self-help aid. 72% freshmen, 65% undergrads receive any aid. Highest amount earned per year from on-campus jobs $1,000.

See page 1178.

FURMAN UNIVERSITY

Best 368

3300 Poinsett Highway, Greenville, SC 29613
Phone: 864-294-2034 **E-mail:** admissions@furman.edu **CEEB Code:** 5222
Fax: 864-294-3127 **Website:** www.furman.edu **ACT Code:** 3858
Financial Aid Phone: 864-294-2204

This private school was founded in 1826. It has an 800-acre campus.

RATINGS

Admissions Selectivity Rating: 94   **Fire Safety Rating:** 73   **Green Rating:** 97

STUDENTS AND FACULTY

Enrollment: 2,739. **Student Body:** 56% female, 44% male, 71% out-of-state, 2% international (41 countries represented). African American 6%, Asian 2%, Caucasian 85%, Hispanic 1%. **Retention and Graduation:** 94% freshmen return for sophomore year. 81% freshmen graduate within 4 years. 41% grads go on to further study within 1 year. 31% grads pursue arts and sciences degrees. 2% grads pursue business degrees. 4% grads pursue law degrees. 4% grads pursue medical degrees. **Faculty:** Student/faculty ratio 11:1. 228 full-time faculty, 96% hold PhDs. 100% faculty teach undergrads.

ACADEMICS

Degrees: Bachelor's, master's, post-bachelor's certificate. **Academic Requirements:** Arts/fine arts, English (including composition), foreign languages, history, humanities, mathematics, philosophy, sciences (biological or physical), social science, Asian and African courses that emphasize major dimensions of experience from the non-Western two-thirds of humanity. **Classes:** Most classes have 10–19 students. Most lab/discussion sections have fewer than 10 students. **Majors with Highest Enrollment:** Health and physical education, history, political science and government. **Disciplines with Highest Percentage of Degrees Awarded:** Social sciences 20%, business/marketing 10%, history 10%, visual and performing arts 8%, foreign languages and literature 7%, parks and recreation 7%. **Special Study Options:** Double major, independent study, internships, student-designed major, study abroad, teacher certification program.

FACILITIES

Housing: Coed dorms, men's dorms, women's dorms, apartments for single students, special housing for international students, lakeside cottages, language houses, eco-cottage. **Special Academic Facilities/Equipment:** Visual arts gallery and teaching facility, language lab, astronomical lab, Center for Engaged Learning, Center for Collaborative Learning and Communication. **Computers:** 7% of classrooms are wired, 85% of classrooms are wireless, 95% of public computers are PCs, 5% of public computers are Macs, network access in dorm rooms, online registration, online administrative functions (other than registration), remote student-access to Web through college's connection.

CAMPUS LIFE

Activities: Choral groups, concert band, dance, drama/theater, jazz band, literary magazine, marching band, music ensembles, musical theater, opera, pep band, radio station, student government, student newspaper, student-run film society, symphony orchestra, television station. **Organizations:** 152 registered organizations, 29 honor societies, 17 religious organizations. 8 fraternities (35% men join), 8 sororities (40% women join). **Athletics (Intercollegiate):** *Men:* Baseball, basketball, cheerleading, cross-country, football, golf, soccer, tennis, track/field (outdoor). *Women:* Basketball, cheerleading, cross-country, golf, soccer, softball, tennis, track/field (indoor), track/field (outdoor), volleyball. **Environmental initiatives:** LEED certification for campus buildings and renovation required since 2002. Curricular requirement—"Humans in the natural world" with an emphasis on environmental issues. $1,000,000 financial expenditure to restore 30-acre lake and natural surroundings.

ADMISSIONS

Freshman Academic Profile: 64% in top 10% of high school class, 87% in top 25% of high school class, 98% in top 50% of high school class. 63% from public high schools. SAT Math middle 50% range 590–690. SAT Critical Reading middle 50% range 590–690. SAT Writing middle 50% range 580–680. ACT middle 50% range 25–30. TOEFL required of all international applicants, minimum paper TOEFL 570, minimum computer TOEFL 230. **Basis for Candidate Selection:** *Very important factors considered include:* Rigor of secondary school record. *Important factors considered include:* Academic GPA, application essay, character/personal qualities, class rank, extracurricular activities, standardized test scores. *Other factors considered include:* Alumni/ae relation, first generation, racial/ethnic status, recommendation(s), talent/ability, volunteer work, work experience. **Freshman Admission Requirements:** High school diploma is required, and GED is accepted. *Academic units required:* 4 English, 3 math, 2 science (2 science labs), 2 foreign language, 3 social studies. *Academic units recommended:* 4 English, 4 math, 3 science (3 science labs), 3 foreign language, 4 social studies. **Freshman Admission Statistics:** 3,887 applied, 56% admitted, 32% enrolled. **Transfer Admission Requirements:** High school transcript, college transcript(s), essay or personal statement, standardized test score, statement of good standing from prior institution(s). Minimum college GPA of 3.0 required. Lowest grade transferable C. **General Admission Information:** Early decision application deadline 11/15. Regular application deadline 1/15. Regular notification 3/15. Nonfall registration not accepted. Credit offered for CEEB Advanced Placement tests.

COSTS AND FINANCIAL AID

Annual tuition $31,040. Room and board $8,064. Required fees $520. Average book expense $850. **Required Forms and Deadlines:** FAFSA, institution's own financial aid form, state aid form. South Carolina residents must complete required state forms. Financial aid filing deadline 1/15. **Notification of Awards:** Applicants will be notified of awards on or about 3/15. **Types of Aid:** *Need-based scholarships/grants:* Pell, SEOG, state scholarships/grants, private scholarships, the school's own gift aid, Federal SMART and ACG grants. *Loans:* FFEL Subsidized Stafford, FFEL Unsubsidized Stafford, FFEL PLUS, Federal Perkins, state loans, donor sponsored loans for study abroad. **Financial Aid Statistics:** 42% freshmen, 40% undergrads receive need-based scholarship or grant aid. 26% freshmen, 25% undergrads receive need-based self-help aid. 49 freshmen, 168 undergrads receive athletic scholarships. 85% freshmen, 86% undergrads receive any aid. Highest amount earned per year from on-campus jobs $1,200.

GALLAUDET UNIVERSITY

800 Florida Avenue, NE, Washington, DC 20002
Phone: 202-651-5750 **E-mail:** admissions.office@gallaudet.edu **CEEB Code:** 5240
Fax: 202-651-5744 **Website:** www.gallaudet.edu **ACT Code:** 0662
Financial Aid Phone: 202-651-5290

This private school was founded in 1864. It has a 99-acre campus.

RATINGS

Admissions Selectivity Rating: 60*   **Fire Safety Rating:** 60*   **Green Rating:** 60*

STUDENTS AND FACULTY

Enrollment: 1,138. **Student Body:** 53% female, 47% male, 94% out-of-state, 8% international (27 countries represented). African American 11%, Asian 5%, Caucasian 62%, Hispanic 9%, Native American 4%. **Retention and Graduation:** 64% freshmen return for sophomore year. 7% freshmen graduate within 4 years. **Faculty:** Student/faculty ratio 5:1. 227 full-time faculty, 76% hold PhDs.

ACADEMICS

Degrees: Bachelor's, doctoral, master's, post-master's certificate. **Academic Requirements:** English (including composition), foreign languages, humanities, mathematics, sciences (biological or physical), social science. **Classes:** Most classes have 10–19 students. Most lab/discussion sections have 10–19 students. **Majors with Highest Enrollment:** Business administration/management; communications, journalism, and related fields; psychology. **Disciplines with Highest Percentage of Degrees Awarded:** Business/marketing 17%, communications/journalism 13%, visual and performing arts 11%, social sciences 8%, public administration and social services 7%. **Special Study Options:** Accelerated program, cooperative education program, cross-registration, double major, English as a second language (ESL), exchange student program (domestic), honors program, independent study, internships, student-designed major, study abroad, teacher certification program. Experiential programs off-campus include orientation program for employers of deaf students and paraprofessional jobs on campus.

FACILITIES

Housing: Coed dorms, apartments for married students, special housing for disabled students, apartments for students with children. All dorms are equipped for deaf and hard-of-hearing students. Theme community provided for international students. **Special Academic Facilities/Equipment:** Kendall Demonstration Elementary School and Model Secondary School for the Deaf. **Computers:** Network access in dorm rooms, online registration, online administrative functions (other than registration), remote student-access to Web through college's connection.

CAMPUS LIFE

Activities: Dance, drama/theater, literary magazine, student government, student newspaper, student-run film society, television station, yearbook. **Organizations:** 25 registered organizations, 1 honor society, 1 religious organization. 5 fraternities (15% men join), 4 sororities (19% women join). **Athletics (Intercollegiate):** *Men:* Baseball, basketball, cross-country, diving, football, soccer, swimming, tennis, track/field (outdoor), wrestling. *Women:* Basketball, cross-country, diving, soccer, softball, swimming, tennis, track/field (outdoor), volleyball.

ADMISSIONS

Basis for Candidate Selection: *Very important factors considered include:* Recommendation(s), rigor of secondary school record, standardized test scores. *Important factors considered include:* Application essay, character/personal qualities, extracurricular activities, talent/ability. *Other factors considered include:* Class rank, volunteer work, work experience. **Freshman Admission Requirements:** High school diploma is required, and GED is accepted. *Academic units recommended:* 4 English, 4 math, 4 science (2 science labs), 4 social studies, 4 history. **Freshman Admission Statistics:** 411 applied, 73% admitted, 71% enrolled. **Transfer Admission Requirements:** College transcript(s), essay or personal statement, statement of good standing from prior institution(s). Minimum college GPA of 2.0 required. Lowest grade transferable C. **General Admission Information:** Application fee $50. Regular application deadline 8/1. Regular notification is rolling. Nonfall registration accepted. Admission may be deferred for a maximum of 1 year. Credit and/or placement offered for CEEB Advanced Placement tests.

COSTS AND FINANCIAL AID

Required Forms and Deadlines: FAFSA, institution's own financial aid form. Financial aid filing deadline 7/1. **Notification of Awards:** Applicants will be notified of awards on a rolling basis beginning on or about 4/15. **Types of Aid:** *Need-based scholarships/grants:* Pell, SEOG, state scholarships/grants, private scholarships, the school's own gift aid. *Loans:* FFEL Subsidized Stafford, FFEL Unsubsidized Stafford, FFEL PLUS, Federal Perkins. **Student Employment:** Federal Work-Study Program available. Institutional employment available. **Financial Aid Statistics:** 72% freshmen, 69% undergrads receive need-based scholarship or grant aid. 26% freshmen, 34% undergrads receive need-based self-help aid. 84% freshmen, 85% undergrads receive any aid.

GANNON UNIVERSITY

University Square, Erie, PA 16541
Phone: 814-871-7240 **CEEB Code:** 2270
Fax: 814-871-5803 **Website:** www.gannon.edu **ACT Code:** 3576
Financial Aid Phone: 814-871-7337

This private school, affiliated with the Roman Catholic Church, was founded in 1925. It has a 13-acre campus.

RATINGS

Admissions Selectivity Rating: 75   **Fire Safety Rating:** 92   **Green Rating:** 60*

STUDENTS AND FACULTY

Enrollment: 2,457. **Student Body:** 60% female, 40% male, 21% out-of-state, 1% international (23 countries represented). African American 4%, Asian 1%, Caucasian 89%, Hispanic 1%. **Retention and Graduation:** 81% freshmen return for sophomore year. 27% grads go on to further study within 1 year. 19% grads pursue arts and sciences degrees. 2% grads pursue business degrees. 2% grads pursue law degrees. 2% grads pursue medical degrees. **Faculty:** Student/faculty ratio 11:1. 181 full-time faculty, 67% hold PhDs. 80% faculty teach undergrads.

ACADEMICS

Degrees: Associate, bachelor's, certificate, doctoral, master's, post-bachelor's certificate, post-master's certificate. **Academic Requirements:** Arts/fine arts, English (including composition), foreign languages, history, literature, mathematics, philosophy, sciences (biological or physical), social science, theology. **Classes:** Most classes have 10–19 students. Most lab/discussion sections have 10–19 students. **Majors with Highest Enrollment:** Criminal justice/safety studies, nursing/registered nurse training (RN, ASN, BSN, MSN), physician assistant. **Disciplines with Highest Percentage of Degrees Awarded:** Health professions and related sciences 27%, business/marketing 19%, education 11%, security and protective services 6%, biological/life sciences 6%, engineering 4%. **Special Study Options:** Accelerated program, distance learning, double major, dual enrollment, English as a second language (ESL), external degree program, honors program, independent study, internships, liberal arts/career combination, study abroad, teacher certification program, weekend college.

FACILITIES

Housing: Coed dorms, apartments for single students, special housing for disabled students. **Special Academic Facilities/Equipment:** Laser and spectrographic labs, metallurgy institute, computer-integrated manufacturing facilities, Schuster Art Gallery, Schuster Theatres. **Computers:** 3% of classrooms are wired, 100% of classrooms are wireless, 95% of public computers are PCs, 5% of public computers are UNIX, network access in dorm rooms, network access in dorm lounges, online registration, online administrative functions (other than registration), remote student-access to Web through college's connection.

CAMPUS LIFE

Activities: Choral groups, dance, drama/theater, literary magazine, music ensembles, musical theater, pep band, radio station, student government, student newspaper, yearbook. **Organizations:** 65 registered organizations, 16 honor societies, 2 religious organizations. 5 fraternities (8% men join), 5 sororities (8% women join). **Athletics (Intercollegiate):** *Men:* Baseball, basketball, cross-country, football, golf, soccer, swimming, water polo, wrestling. *Women:* Basketball, cross-country, golf, lacrosse, soccer, softball, swimming, volleyball, water polo.

ADMISSIONS

Freshman Academic Profile: 19% in top 10% of high school class, 44% in top 25% of high school class, 75% in top 50% of high school class. 80% from public high schools. SAT Math middle 50% range 470–590. SAT Critical Reading middle 50% range 460–570. ACT middle 50% range 19–25. TOEFL required of all international applicants, minimum paper TOEFL 500, minimum computer TOEFL 173. **Basis for Candidate Selection:** *Very important factors considered include:* Academic GPA, class rank, rigor of secondary school record. *Important factors considered include:* Application essay, character/personal qualities, level of applicant's interest, recommendation(s), standardized test scores. *Other factors considered include:* Alumni/ae relation, extracurricular activities, interview, volunteer work, work experience. **Freshman Admission Requirements:** High school diploma is required, and GED is accepted. *Academic units required:* 4 English, 12 academic units based on planned major. **Freshman Admission Statistics:** 2,526 applied, 86% admitted, 28% enrolled. **Transfer Admission Requirements:** College transcript(s), statement of good standing from prior institution(s). Minimum college GPA of 2.0 required. Lowest grade transferable C. **General Admission Information:** Application fee $25. Regular notification is rolling. Nonfall registration accepted. Admission may be deferred. Credit and/or placement offered for CEEB Advanced Placement tests.

COSTS AND FINANCIAL AID
Average book expense $1,000. **Required Forms and Deadlines:** FAFSA, institution's own financial aid form. Financial aid filing deadline 3/15. **Notification of Awards:** Applicants will be notified of awards on a rolling basis beginning on or about 11/1. **Types of Aid:** *Need-based scholarships/grants:* Pell, SEOG, state scholarships/grants, Federal Nursing Scholarships. *Loans:* FFEL Subsidized Stafford, FFEL Unsubsidized Stafford, FFEL PLUS, Federal Perkins, Federal Nursing, deferred payment. **Student Employment:** Federal Work-Study Program available. Institutional employment available. Off-campus job opportunities are good. **Financial Aid Statistics:** 81% freshmen, 81% undergrads receive need-based scholarship or grant aid. 76% freshmen, 76% undergrads receive need-based self-help aid. 18 freshmen, 82 undergrads receive athletic scholarships. 95% freshmen, 94% undergrads receive any aid. Highest amount earned per year from on-campus jobs $1,700.

GARDNER-WEBB UNIVERSITY

PO Box 817, Boiling Springs, NC 28017
Phone: 704-406-4498 **E-mail:** admissions@gardner-webb.edu **CEEB Code:** 5242
Fax: 704-406-4488 **Website:** www.gardner-webb.edu **ACT Code:** 3102
Financial Aid Phone: 704-406-4243

This private school, affiliated with the Baptist Church, was founded in 1905. It has a 250-acre campus.

RATINGS
Admissions Selectivity Rating: 78   **Fire Safety Rating:** 60*   **Green Rating:** 68

STUDENTS AND FACULTY
Enrollment: 2,620. **Student Body:** 67% female, 33% male, 20% out-of-state. **Retention and Graduation:** 68% freshmen return for sophomore year. 32% freshmen graduate within 4 years. 30% grads go on to further study within 1 year. 12% grads pursue arts and sciences degrees. 20% grads pursue business degrees. 1% grads pursue law degrees. 2% grads pursue medical degrees. **Faculty:** Student/faculty ratio 15:1. 133 full-time faculty, 78% hold PhDs. 100% faculty teach undergrads.

ACADEMICS
Degrees: Associate, bachelor's, doctoral, first professional, master's. **Academic Requirements:** Arts/fine arts, computer literacy, English (including composition), foreign languages, history, mathematics, philosophy, sciences (biological or physical), social science. **Classes:** Most classes have 30–39 students. Most lab/discussion sections have 30-39 students. **Majors with Highest Enrollment:** Business administration/management, mass communications/media studies, social science teacher education. **Disciplines with Highest Percentage of Degrees Awarded:** Business/marketing 38%, social sciences 22%, health professions and related sciences 11%, philosophy and religious studies 5%, education 5%, foreign languages and literature 4%, psychology 4%. **Special Study Options:** Cooperative education program, double major, dual enrollment, English as a second language (ESL), honors program, internships, study abroad, teacher certification program. Spring break in New York, fall break in Washington, summer in Costa Rica.

FACILITIES
Housing: Men's dorms, women's dorms, apartments for single students, special housing for disabled students, housing for honor students. **Special Academic Facilities/Equipment:** Williams Observatory, Millenium Playhouse, Broyhill Adventure Course, Lake Hollifield Complex and Carillon. **Computers:** Network access in dorm rooms, network access in dorm lounges, online registration, online administrative functions (other than registration), support for handheld computing, remote student-access to Web through college's connection.

CAMPUS LIFE
Activities: Choral groups, concert band, dance, drama/theater, jazz band, literary magazine, marching band, music ensembles, musical theater, opera, pep band, radio station, student government, student newspaper, student-run film society, symphony orchestra, television station. **Organizations:** 43 registered organizations, 8 honor societies, 7 religious organizations. **Athletics (Intercollegiate):** *Men:* Baseball, basketball, cheerleading, cross-country, football, golf, soccer, swimming, tennis, track/field (indoor), track/field (outdoor), wrestling. *Women:* Basketball, cheerleading, cross-country, golf, soccer, softball, swimming, tennis, track/field (indoor), track/field (outdoor), volleyball.

Environmental initiatives: recycling programs. environmental science major with student projects.

ADMISSIONS
Freshman Academic Profile: 19% in top 10% of high school class, 42% in top 25% of high school class, 76% in top 50% of high school class. 80% from public high schools. SAT Math middle 50% range 430–550. SAT Critical Reading middle 50% range 440–570. TOEFL required of all international applicants, minimum paper TOEFL 500, minimum computer TOEFL 173. **Basis for Candidate Selection:** *Very important factors considered include:* Academic GPA, rigor of secondary school record. *Important factors considered include:* Class rank, interview, recommendation(s), standardized test scores. *Other factors considered include:* Application essay, character/personal qualities, extracurricular activities, talent/ability. **Freshman Admission Requirements:** High school diploma is required, and GED is accepted. *Academic units recommended:* 4 English, 2 math, 2 science, 2 foreign language, 2 social studies, 1 history. **Freshman Admission Statistics:** 1,876 applied, 70% admitted, 31% enrolled. **Transfer Admission Requirements:** College transcript(s), statement of good standing from prior institution(s). Minimum college GPA of 2.0 required. Lowest grade transferable C. **General Admission Information:** Application fee $40. Regular notification rolling. Nonfall registration accepted. Admission may be deferred for a maximum of 3 semesters. Credit and/or placement offered for CEEB Advanced Placement tests.

COSTS AND FINANCIAL AID
Average book expense $800. **Required Forms and Deadlines:** FAFSA. **Notification of Awards:** Applicants will be notified of awards on a rolling basis beginning on or about 3/1. **Types of Aid:** *Need-based scholarships/grants:* Pell, SEOG, state scholarships/grants, private scholarships, the school's own gift aid. *Loans:* FFEL Subsidized Stafford, FFEL Unsubsidized Stafford, FFEL PLUS, Federal Perkins, state loans. **Financial Aid Statistics:** 62% freshmen, 66% undergrads receive need-based scholarship or grant aid. 61% freshmen, 65% undergrads receive need-based self-help aid. 55 freshmen, 167 undergrads receive athletic scholarships.

GENEVA COLLEGE

3200 College Avenue, Beaver Falls, PA 15010
Phone: 724-847-6500 **E-mail:** admissions@geneva.edu **CEEB Code:** 2273
Fax: 724-847-6776 **Website:** www.geneva.edu
Financial Aid Phone: 724-847-6530

This private school, affiliated with the Reformed Presbyterian Church, was founded in 1848. It has a 55-acre campus.

RATINGS
Admissions Selectivity Rating: 79   **Fire Safety Rating:** 63   **Green Rating:** 60*

STUDENTS AND FACULTY
Enrollment: 1,340. **Student Body:** 54% female, 46% male, 26% out-of-state, 1% international (7 countries represented). African American 15%. **Retention and Graduation:** 78% freshmen return for sophomore year. 45% freshmen graduate within 4 years. 32% grads go on to further study within 1 year. **Faculty:** Student/faculty ratio 13:1. 84 full-time faculty, 76% hold PhDs. 100% faculty teach undergrads.

ACADEMICS
Degrees: Associate, bachelor's, master's. **Academic Requirements:** Arts/fine arts, English (including composition), humanities, sciences (biological or physical), social science. **Classes:** Most classes have 10–19 students. Most lab/discussion sections have fewer than 10 students. **Majors with Highest Enrollment:** Bible/biblical studies, business administration/management, elementary education and teaching. **Disciplines with Highest Percentage of Degrees Awarded:** Business/marketing 36%, theology and religious vocations 15%, education 12%, public administration and social services 6%, psychology 5%. **Special Study Options:** Accelerated program, cooperative education program, cross-registration, double major, dual enrollment, honors program, independent study, internships, student-designed major, study abroad, teacher certification program.

FACILITIES
Housing: Men's dorms, women's dorms, apartments for single students. **Special Academic Facilities/Equipment:** Center for Technology Development. **Computers:** 90% of public computers are PCs, 1% of public computers are Macs, 3% of public computers are UNIX, network access in dorm rooms, network access in dorm lounges, online registration, online administrative

functions (other than registration), remote student-access to Web through college's connection.

CAMPUS LIFE

Activities: Choral groups, concert band, dance, drama/theater, jazz band, literary magazine, marching band, music ensembles, pep band, radio station, student government, student newspaper, yearbook. **Organizations:** 56 registered organizations, 5 honor societies, 11 religious organizations. **Athletics (Intercollegiate):** *Men:* Baseball, basketball, cross-country, football, soccer, track/field (indoor), track/field (outdoor). *Women:* Basketball, cheerleading, cross-country, soccer, softball, tennis, track/field (indoor), track/field (outdoor), volleyball.

ADMISSIONS

Freshman Academic Profile: 16% in top 10% of high school class, 37% in top 25% of high school class, 71% in top 50% of high school class. 72% from public high schools. SAT Math middle 50% range 480–590. SAT Critical Reading middle 50% range 490–610. ACT middle 50% range 20–25. TOEFL required of all international applicants, minimum paper TOEFL 480, minimum computer TOEFL 157. **Basis for Candidate Selection:** *Very important factors considered include:* Academic GPA, application essay, rigor of secondary school record, standardized test scores. *Other factors considered include:* Alumni/ae relation, character/personal qualities, class rank, extracurricular activities, interview, recommendation(s). **Freshman Admission Requirements:** High school diploma is required, and GED is accepted. *Academic units required:* 4 English, 2 math, 1 science, 2 foreign language, 3 social studies, 4 academic electives. **Freshman Admission Statistics:** 1,329 applied, 64% admitted, 35% enrolled. **Transfer Admission Requirements:** High school transcript, college transcript(s), essay or personal statement. Minimum college GPA of 2.0 required. Lowest grade transferable C-. **General Admission Information:** Application fee $40. Regular notification is rolling. Nonfall registration accepted. Admission may be deferred for a maximum of 3 years. Credit and/or placement offered for CEEB Advanced Placement tests.

COSTS AND FINANCIAL AID

Annual tuition $19,430. Room & board $7,200. Average book expense $800. **Required Forms and Deadlines:** FAFSA. Financial aid filing deadline 3/15. **Notification of Awards:** Applicants will be notified of awards on a rolling basis beginning on or about 3/15. **Types of Aid:** *Need-based scholarships/grants:* Pell, SEOG, state scholarships/grants, private scholarships, the school's own gift aid, FSEOG. *Loans:* FFEL Subsidized Stafford, FFEL Unsubsidized Stafford, FFEL PLUS, Federal Perkins. **Student Employment:** Federal Work-Study Program available. Institutional employment available. Off-campus job opportunities are fair. **Financial Aid Statistics:** 83% freshmen, 79% undergrads receive need-based scholarship or grant aid. 70% freshmen, 68% undergrads receive need-based self-help aid. 37 undergrads receive athletic scholarships. 95% freshmen, 92% undergrads receive any aid. Highest amount earned per year from on-campus jobs $2,000.

GEORGE FOX UNIVERSITY

414 North Meridian Street, Newberg, OR 97132
Phone: 503-554-2240 **E-mail:** Admissions@georgefox.edu **CEEB Code:** 4325
Fax: 503-554-3110 **Website:** www.georgefox.edu **ACT Code:** 3462
Financial Aid Phone: 503-554-2290

This private school, affiliated with the Evangelical Friends Church, was founded in 1891. It has an 85-acre campus.

RATINGS

Admissions Selectivity Rating: 79   **Fire Safety Rating:** 76   **Green Rating:** 65

STUDENTS AND FACULTY

Enrollment: 1,836. **Student Body:** 61% female, 39% male, 32% out-of-state, 2% international (11 countries represented). Asian 6%, Caucasian 80%, Hispanic 3%, Native American 2%. **Retention and Graduation:** 78% freshmen return for sophomore year. 57% freshmen graduate within 4 years. 35% grads go on to further study within 1 year. 14% grads pursue arts and sciences degrees. 1% grads pursue business degrees. 2% grads pursue law degrees. 2% grads pursue medical degrees. **Faculty:** Student/faculty ratio 12:1. 158 full-time faculty, 70% hold PhDs. 63% faculty teach undergrads.

ACADEMICS

Degrees: Bachelor's, doctoral, first professional, master's, post-bachelor's certificate, post-master's certificate. **Academic Requirements:** Arts/fine arts, Bible and Religion, Communication, English (including composition), Global and Cultural Understanding, Health and Human Performance, history, humanities, mathematics, sciences (biological or physical), social science.

Classes: Most classes have 10–19 students. Most lab/discussion sections have 10–19 students. **Majors with Highest Enrollment:** Biology/biological sciences; business administration and management; multi/interdisciplinary studies. **Disciplines with Highest Percentage of Degrees Awarded:** Business/marketing 41%, interdisciplinary studies 12%, visual and performing arts 7%, biological/life sciences 5%, psychology 5%, theology and religious vocations 5%, education 5%. **Special Study Options:** Accelerated program, cross-registration, double major, dual enrollment, English as a second language (ESL), exchange student program (domestic), honor program, independent study, internships, student-designed major, study abroad, teacher certification program.

FACILITIES

Housing: Men's dorms, women's dorms, apartments for single students, special housing for disabled students, houses, theme floors, living-learning communities. **Special Academic Facilities/Equipment:** Language lab, electron microscope. **Computers:** 80% of public computers are PCs, 20% of public computers are Macs, 20% of public computers are UNIX, network access in dorm rooms, network access in dorm lounges, online registration, online administrative functions (other than registration), support for handheld computing, remote student-access to Web through college's connection, tuition includes personal computer. Undergraduates are required to own a computer.

CAMPUS LIFE

Activities: Choral groups, concert band, dance, drama/theater, jazz band, literary magazine, music ensembles, musical theater, pep band, radio station, student government, student newspaper, symphony orchestra, yearbook. **Organizations:** 20 registered organizations, 4 honor societies, 3 religious organizations. **Athletics (Intercollegiate):** *Men:* Baseball, basketball, cross-country, soccer, tennis, track/field (outdoor). *Women:* Basketball, cross-country, golf, soccer, softball, tennis, track/field (outdoor), volleyball. **Environmental initiatives:** LEED-certified residence hall. Fleet vehicle hybrid purchases. Progressive recycling program.

ADMISSIONS

Freshman Academic Profile: 31% in top 10% of high school class, 60% in top 25% of high school class, 86% in top 50% of high school class. 80% from public high schools. SAT Math middle 50% range 470–590. SAT Critical Reading middle 50% range 480–600. SAT Writing middle 50% range 460–580. ACT middle 50% range 19–26. TOEFL required of all international applicants, minimum paper TOEFL 500, minimum computer TOEFL 173. **Basis for Candidate Selection:** *Very important factors considered include:* Rigor of secondary school record, *Important factors considered include:* Academic GPA, application essay, recommendation(s), standardized test scores. *Other factors considered include:* Character/personal qualities, extracurricular activities, interview, religious affiliation/commitment, talent/ability, volunteer work, work experience. **Freshman Admission Requirements:** High school diploma is required, and GED is accepted. *Academic units recommended:* 4 English, 3 math, 3 science (3 science labs), 2 foreign language, 2 social studies, 2 history. **Freshman Admission Statistics:** 1,142 applied, 86% admitted, 43% enrolled. **Transfer Admission Requirements:** College transcript(s), essay or personal statement. Minimum college GPA of 2.6 required. Lowest grade transferable C-. **General Admission Information:** Application fee $40. Regular notification is rolling. Nonfall registration accepted. Admission may be deferred for a maximum of 1 year. Credit and/or placement offered for CEEB Advanced Placement tests.

COSTS AND FINANCIAL AID

Annual tuition $24,870. Room and board $8,000. Required fees $320. Average book expense $2,150. **Required Forms and Deadlines:** FAFSA, state aid form. Financial aid filing deadline 2/1. **Notification of Awards:** Applicants will be notified of awards on or about 3/1. **Types of Aid:** *Need-based scholarships/grants:* Pell, SEOG, state scholarships/grants, private scholarships, the school's own gift aid. *Loans:* Direct Subsidized Stafford, Direct Unsubsidized Stafford, Direct PLUS, FFEL Subsidized Stafford, FFEL Unsubsidized Stafford, FFEL PLUS, Federal Perkins, alternative loans. **Student Employment:** Federal Work-Study Program available. Institutional employment available. Off-campus job opportunities are good. **Financial Aid Statistics:** 79% freshmen, 69% undergrads receive need-based scholarship or grant aid. 71% freshmen, 61% undergrads receive need-based self-help aid. 77% freshmen, 80% undergrads receive any aid. Highest amount earned per year from on-campus jobs $2,400.

GEORGE MASON UNIVERSITY

Best 368

Undergraduate Admissions Office, 4400 University Drive MSN 3A4, Fairfax, VA 22030-4444
Phone: 703-993-2400 **E-mail:** admissions@gmu.edu **CEEB Code:** 5827
Fax: 703-993-2392 **Website:** www.gmu.edu **ACT Code:** 4357
Financial Aid Phone: 703-993-2353

This public school was founded in 1957. It has a 667-acre campus.

RATINGS
Admissions Selectivity Rating: 83   **Fire Safety Rating:** 76   **Green Rating:** 91

STUDENTS AND FACULTY
Enrollment: 17,812. **Student Body:** 54% female, 46% male, 12% out-of-state, 4% international (134 countries represented). African American 7%, Asian 17%, Caucasian 49%, Hispanic 8%. **Retention and Graduation:** 86% freshmen return for sophomore year. 38% freshmen graduate within 4 years. **Faculty:** Student/faculty ratio 15:1. 1,055 full-time faculty, 90% hold PhDs. 87% faculty teach undergrads.

ACADEMICS
Degrees: Bachelor's, doctoral, first professional, master's, post-bachelor's certificate. **Academic Requirements:** Arts/fine arts, computer literacy, English (including composition), foreign languages, global understanding, history, humanities, mathematics, philosophy, sciences (biological or physical), social science. **Classes:** Most classes have 20–29 students. Most lab/discussion sections have 20–29 students. **Majors with Highest Enrollment:** Accounting, biology/biological sciences, psychology. **Disciplines with Highest Percentage of Degrees Awarded:** Business/marketing 21%, social sciences 13%, engineering 9%, health professions and related sciences 8%, psychology 8%. **Special Study Options:** Accelerated program, cooperative education program, cross-registration, distance learning, double major, dual enrollment, English as a second language (ESL), exchange student program (domestic), external degree program, honors program, independent study, internships, liberal arts/career combination, student-designed major, study abroad, teacher certification program.

FACILITIES
Housing: Coed dorms, men's dorms, women's dorms, apartments for single students, special housing for disabled students. **Special Academic Facilities/Equipment:** Arts center, science/technology building, television studio, art galleries in Mason Hall and Johnson Center. **Computers:** 9% of classrooms are wired, 25% of classrooms are wireless, 99% of public computers are PCs, 1% of public computers are Macs, network access in dorm rooms, network access in dorm lounges, online registration, online administrative functions (other than registration), support for handheld computing, remote student-access to Web through college's connection.

CAMPUS LIFE
Activities: Choral groups, concert band, dance, drama/theater, jazz band, literary magazine, music ensembles, musical theater, opera, pep band, radio station, student government, student newspaper, student-run film society, symphony orchestra, television station, yearbook. **Organizations:** 150 registered organizations, 10 honor societies, 27 religious organizations. 15 fraternities (5% men join), 12 sororities (5% women join). **Athletics (Intercollegiate):** *Men:* Baseball, basketball, cheerleading, cross-country, diving, golf, soccer, swimming, tennis, track/field (indoor), track/field (outdoor), volleyball, wrestling. *Women:* Basketball, cheerleading, crew/rowing, cross-country, diving, lacrosse, soccer, softball, swimming, tennis, track/field (indoor), track/field (outdoor), volleyball. **Environmental initiatives:** Climate neutrality: Have committed to the American College and University Presidents Climate Commitment. Built environment: Have committed all new buildings to be built to the USGBC LEED Silver standard, and have 6 registered projects in the queue for certification at this time.

ADMISSIONS
Freshman Academic Profile: 15% in top 10% of high school class, 48% in top 25% of high school class, 94% in top 50% of high school class. SAT Math middle 50% range 490–610. SAT Critical Reading middle 50% range 480–600. SAT Writing middle 50% range 470–590. ACT middle 50% range 20–25. TOEFL required of all international applicants, minimum paper TOEFL 570, minimum computer TOEFL 230. **Basis for Candidate Selection:** *Very important*

factors considered include: Academic GPA, rigor of secondary school record. *Important factors considered include:* Alumni/ae relation, application essay, character/personal qualities, class rank, recommendation(s), talent/ability. *Other factors considered include:* Extracurricular activities, first generation, level of applicant's interest, standardized test scores, volunteer work, work experience. **Freshman Admission Requirements:** High school diploma is required, and GED is accepted. *Academic units required:* 4 English, 4 math, 3 science (3 science labs), 3 foreign language, 4 social studies, 5 academic electives. *Academic units recommended:* 4 English, 3 math, 4 science (4 science labs), 2 foreign language, 3 social studies, 3 academic electives. **Freshman Admission Statistics:** 11,015 applied, 61% admitted, 37% enrolled. **Transfer Admission Requirements:** College transcript(s). Lowest grade transferable C. **General Admission Information:** Application fee $70. Regular application deadline 1/15. Regular notification 4/1. Nonfall registration accepted. Admission may be deferred for a maximum of 1 semester. Credit offered for CEEB Advanced Placement tests.

COSTS AND FINANCIAL AID
Annual in-state tuition $5,035. Annual out-of-state tuition $17,923. Room and board $7,020. Required fees $1,805. Average book expense $850. **Required Forms and Deadlines:** FAFSA. Financial aid filing deadline 3/1. **Notification of Awards:** Applicants will be notified of awards on or about 4/1. **Types of Aid:** *Need-based scholarships/grants:* Pell, SEOG, state scholarships/grants, private scholarships, the school's own gift aid. *Loans:* FFEL Subsidized Stafford, FFEL Unsubsidized Stafford, FFEL PLUS, Federal Perkins, Federal Nursing. **Student Employment:** Federal Work-Study Program available. Institutional employment available. Off-campus job opportunities are good. **Financial Aid Statistics:** 27% freshmen, 26% undergrads receive need-based scholarship or grant aid. 27% freshmen, 27% undergrads receive need-based self-help aid. 49 freshmen, 222 undergrads receive athletic scholarships. 56% freshmen, 42% undergrads receive any aid.

THE GEORGE WASHINGTON UNIVERSITY

Best 368

2121 I Street NW, Suite 201, Washington, DC 20052
Phone: 202-994-6040 **E-mail:** gwadm@gwu.edu **CEEB Code:** 5246
Fax: 202-994-0325 **Website:** www.gwu.edu **ACT Code:** 664
Financial Aid Phone: 202-994-6620

This private school was founded in 1821. It has a 45-acre campus.

RATINGS
Admissions Selectivity Rating: 96   **Fire Safety Rating:** 60*   **Green Rating:** 60*

STUDENTS AND FACULTY
Enrollment: 10,563. **Student Body:** 56% female, 44% male, 98% out-of-state, 4% international (101 countries represented). African American 6%, Asian 10%, Caucasian 66%, Hispanic 5%. **Retention and Graduation:** 92% freshmen return for sophomore year. 72% freshmen graduate within 4 years. 19% grads go on to further study within 1 year. 7% grads pursue arts and sciences degrees. 2% grads pursue business degrees. 6% grads pursue law degrees. 4% grads pursue medical degrees. **Faculty:** Student/faculty ratio 13:1. 836 full-time faculty, 95% hold PhDs. 67% faculty teach undergrads.

ACADEMICS
Degrees: Associate, bachelor's, certificate, doctoral, first professional, master's, post-bachelor's certificate, post-master's certificate. **Academic Requirements:** English (including composition), humanities, mathematics, sciences (biological or physical), social science. **Classes:** Most classes have 10–19 students. Most lab/discussion sections have 20–29 students. **Disciplines with Highest Percentage of Degrees Awarded:** Social sciences 28%, business/marketing 18%, psychology 8%, English 7%, communication technologies 4%. **Special Study Options:** Accelerated program, cooperative education program, cross-registration, distance learning, double major, dual enrollment, honors program, independent study, internships, liberal arts/career combination, student-designed major, study abroad.

FACILITIES
Housing: Coed dorms, apartments for single students, fraternity/sorority housing, accommodations for disabled students. **Special Academic Facilities/Equipment:** Art gallery, language lab, word processing center. **Computers:**

Network access in dorm rooms, network access in dorm lounges, online registration, online administrative functions (other than registration), remote student-access to Web through college's connection.

CAMPUS LIFE

Activities: Choral groups, concert band, dance, drama/theater, jazz band, literary magazine, marching band, music ensembles, musical theater, pep band, radio station, student government, student newspaper, student-run film society, television station, yearbook. **Organizations:** 220 registered organizations, 3 honor societies, 5 religious organizations. 12 fraternities (16% men join), 9 sororities (13% women join). **Athletics (Intercollegiate):** *Men:* Baseball, basketball, crew/rowing, cross-country, diving, fencing, golf, rugby, soccer, squash, swimming, tennis, water polo. *Women:* Basketball, crew/rowing, cross-country, fencing, gymnastics, soccer, swimming, tennis, volleyball.

ADMISSIONS

Freshman Academic Profile: 59% in top 10% of high school class, 80% in top 25% of high school class, 99% in top 50% of high school class. 70% from public high schools. SAT Math middle 50% range 590–680. SAT Critical Reading middle 50% range 590–690. ACT middle 50% range 25–30. TOEFL required of all international applicants, minimum paper TOEFL 550, minimum computer TOEFL 300. **Basis for Candidate Selection:** *Very important factors considered include:* Rigor of secondary school record. *Important factors considered include:* Application essay, class rank, extracurricular activities, interview, recommendation(s), standardized test scores, talent/ability, volunteer work. *Other factors considered include:* Alumni/ae relation, character/personal qualities, geographical residence, racial/ethnic status, work experience. **Freshman Admission Requirements:** High school diploma is required, and GED is not accepted. *Academic units required:* 4 English, 2 math, 2 science (1 science lab), 2 foreign language, 2 social studies. *Academic units recommended:* 4 English, 4 math, 4 science, 4 foreign language, 4 social studies. **Freshman Admission Statistics:** 20,159 applied, 38% admitted, 35% enrolled. **Transfer Admission Requirements:** High school transcript, college transcript(s), essay or personal statement, standardized test score. Lowest grade transferable C. **General Admission Information:** Application fee $60. Early decision application deadline 11/10. Regular application deadline 1/10. Regular notification 3/15. Non-fall registration accepted. Admission may be deferred for a maximum of 2 semesters. Common Application accepted. Credit and/or placement offered for CEEB Advanced Placement tests.

COSTS AND FINANCIAL AID

Annual tuition $34,000. Room & board $10,470. Required fees $30. Average book expense $850. **Required Forms and Deadlines:** FAFSA, CSS/Financial Aid Program. Financial aid filing deadline 2/1. Financial aid filing deadline 2/1. **Notification of Awards:** Applicants will be notified of awards on a rolling basis beginning on or about 3/24. **Types of Aid:** *Need-based scholarships/grants:* Pell, SEOG, state scholarships/grants, the school's own gift aid. *Loans:* FFEL Subsidized Stafford, FFEL Unsubsidized Stafford, FFEL PLUS, Federal Perkins. **Student Employment:** Federal Work-Study Program available. Institutional employment available. Off-campus job opportunities are excellent. **Financial Aid Statistics:** 40% freshmen, 38% undergrads receive need-based scholarship or grant aid. 34% freshmen, 35% undergrads receive need-based self-help aid. 50 freshmen, 195 undergrads receive athletic scholarships. Highest amount earned per year from on-campus jobs $3,160.

GEORGETOWN COLLEGE

400 East College Street, Georgetown, KY 40324
Phone: 502-863-8009 **E-mail:** admissions@georgetowncollege.edu **CEEB Code:** 1249
Fax: 502-868-7733 **Website:** www.georgetowncollege.edu **ACT Code:** 1514
Financial Aid Phone: 502-863-8027

This private school, affiliated with the Baptist Church, was founded in 1787. It has a 104-acre campus.

RATINGS

Admissions Selectivity Rating: 76   **Fire Safety Rating:** 73   **Green Rating:** 71

STUDENTS AND FACULTY

Enrollment: 1,316. **Student Body:** 57% female, 43% male, 15% out-of-state. African American 3%, Caucasian 94%. **Retention and Graduation:** 78% freshmen return for sophomore year. 48% freshmen graduate within 4 years. 83% grads go on to further study within 1 year. **Faculty:** Student/faculty ratio 11:1. 106 full-time faculty, 91% hold PhDs. 100% faculty teach undergrads.

ACADEMICS

Degrees: Bachelor's, master's. **Academic Requirements:** Arts/fine arts, computer literacy, English (including composition), foreign languages, history,

humanities, mathematics, philosophy, sciences (biological or physical), social science. **Classes:** Most classes have 20–29 students. Most lab/discussion sections have 10–19 students. **Majors with Highest Enrollment:** Business administration/management, communications studies/speech communication and rhetoric, elementary education and teaching. **Special Study Options:** Accelerated program, cooperative education program, double major, dual enrollment, honors program, independent study, internships, liberal arts/career combination, student-designed major, study abroad, teacher certification program.

FACILITIES

Housing: Men's dorms, women's dorms, fraternity/sorority housing, apartments for upperclassmen. **Computers:** 100% of classrooms are wired, 3% of classrooms are wireless, 98% of public computers are PCs, 2% of public computers are Macs, network access in dorm rooms, network access in dorm lounges, online registration, online administrative functions (other than registration), remote student-access to Web through college's connection.

CAMPUS LIFE

Activities: Choral groups, concert band, dance, drama/theater, literary magazine, music ensembles, musical theater, pep band, radio station, student government, student newspaper, yearbook. **Organizations:** 110 registered organizations, 20 honor societies, 8 religious organizations. 5 fraternities (37% men join), 4 sororities (49% women join). **Athletics (Intercollegiate):** *Men:* Baseball, basketball, cross-country, football, golf, soccer, tennis, track/field (outdoor). *Women:* Basketball, cheerleading, cross-country, golf, soccer, tennis, track/field (outdoor), volleyball.

ADMISSIONS

Freshman Academic Profile: 26% in top 10% of high school class, 57% in top 25% of high school class, 88% in top 50% of high school class. 86% from public high schools. SAT Math middle 50% range 490–610. SAT Critical Reading middle 50% range 500–590. ACT middle 50% range 21–26. TOEFL required of all international applicants, minimum paper TOEFL 520, minimum computer TOEFL 190. **Basis for Candidate Selection:** *Very important factors considered include:* Academic GPA, application essay, rigor of secondary school record. *Important factors considered include:* Character/personal qualities, class rank, extracurricular activities, interview, recommendation(s), standardized test scores, talent/ability. *Other factors considered include:* Alumni/ae relation, geographical residence, level of applicant's interest, religious affiliation/commitment, state residency, volunteer work. **Freshman Admission Requirements:** High school diploma is required, and GED is accepted. *Academic units recommended:* 4 English, 3 math, 3 science, 2 foreign language, 2 social studies. **Freshman Admission Statistics:** 1,215 applied, 76% admitted, 39% enrolled. **Transfer Admission Requirements:** High school transcript, college transcript(s), essay or personal statement, statement of good standing from prior institution(s). Minimum college GPA of 2.5 required. Lowest grade transferable C. **General Admission Information:** Application fee $30. Regular application deadline 8/1. Regular notification is rolling. Nonfall registration accepted. Admission may be deferred for a maximum of 1 year. Credit and/or placement offered for CEEB Advanced Placement tests.

COSTS AND FINANCIAL AID

Annual tuition $22,360. Room & board $6,380. Average book expense $1,050. **Required Forms and Deadlines:** FAFSA, institution's own financial aid form. Financial aid filing deadline 8/1. **Notification of Awards:** Applicants will be notified of awards on a rolling basis beginning on or about 3/1. **Types of Aid:** *Need-based scholarships/grants:* Pell, SEOG, state scholarships/grants, private scholarships, the school's own gift aid. *Loans:* FFEL Subsidized Stafford, FFEL Unsubsidized Stafford, FFEL PLUS, Federal Perkins, college/university loans from institutional funds. **Student Employment:** Federal Work-Study Program available. Institutional employment available. Off-campus job opportunities are good. **Financial Aid Statistics:** 70% freshmen, 68% undergrads receive need-based scholarship or grant aid. 45% freshmen, 48% undergrads receive need-based self-help aid. 22 freshmen, 88 undergrads receive athletic scholarships. 98% freshmen, 98% undergrads receive any aid. Highest amount earned per year from on-campus jobs $2,000.

GEORGETOWN UNIVERSITY

37th and O Streets, Northwest, 103 White-Gravenor, Washington, DC 20057
Phone: 202-687-3600 **CEEB Code:** 5244
Fax: 202-687-5084 **Website:** www.georgetown.edu **ACT Code:** 0668
Financial Aid Phone: 202-687-4547

This private school, affiliated with the Roman Catholic Church, was founded in 1789. It has a 104-acre campus.

RATINGS
Admissions Selectivity Rating: 98   **Fire Safety Rating:** 91   **Green Rating:** 95

STUDENTS AND FACULTY
Enrollment: 6,587. **Student Body:** 54% female, 46% male, 98% out-of-state, 4% international (87 countries represented). African American 7%, Asian 9%, Caucasian 66%, Hispanic 7%. **Retention and Graduation:** 97% freshmen return for sophomore year. 90% freshmen graduate within 4 years. 29% grads go on to further study within 1 year. 15% grads pursue arts and sciences degrees. 1% grads pursue business degrees. 7% grads pursue law degrees. 6% grads pursue medical degrees. **Faculty:** Student/faculty ratio 11:1. 785 full-time faculty, 90% hold PhDs. 100% faculty teach undergrads.

ACADEMICS
Degrees: Bachelor's, certificate, doctoral, first professional, master's. **Academic Requirements:** English (including composition), philosophy, theology. **Classes:** Most classes have 10–19 students. Most lab/discussion sections have fewer than 10 students. **Majors with Highest Enrollment:** Finance, international relations and affairs, political science and government. **Disciplines with Highest Percentage of Degrees Awarded:** Social sciences 31%, business/marketing 26%, English 8%, foreign languages and literature 7%, health professions and related sciences 6%. **Special Study Options:** Cross-registration, double major, English as a second language (ESL), honors program, independent study, internships, student-designed major, study abroad.

FACILITIES
Housing: Coed dorms, apartments for single students, special housing for disabled students, freshmen and sophomores are required to live on campus. **Special Academic Facilities/Equipment:** Language lab, seismological observatory. **Computers:** 2% of classrooms are wired, 40% of classrooms are wireless, 90% of public computers are PCs, 10% of public computers are Macs, network access in dorm rooms, online registration, online administrative functions (other than registration), remote student-access to Web through college's connection.

CAMPUS LIFE
Activities: Choral groups, concert band, dance, drama/theater, jazz band, literary magazine, music ensembles, musical theater, pep band, radio station, student government, student newspaper, student-run film society, symphony orchestra, television station, yearbook. **Organizations:** 103 registered organizations, 14 honor societies, 19 religious organizations. **Athletics (Intercollegiate):** *Men:* Baseball, basketball, crew/rowing, cross-country, diving, football, golf, lacrosse, sailing, soccer, swimming, tennis, track/field (indoor), track/field (outdoor). *Women:* Basketball, crew/rowing, cross-country, diving, field hockey, golf, lacrosse, sailing, soccer, softball, swimming, tennis, track/field (indoor), track/field (outdoor), volleyball. **Environmental initiatives:** Set LEED certification as the standard for new constructions and major renovations. Implemented energy construction programs in utility operations. Expanded recycling program to include construction waste.

ADMISSIONS
Freshman Academic Profile: 84% in top 10% of high school class, 96% in top 25% of high school class, 99% in top 50% of high school class. 52% from public high schools. SAT Math middle 50% range 650–740. SAT Critical Reading middle 50% range 650–750. TOEFL required of all international applicants. **Basis for Candidate Selection:** *Very important factors considered include:* Academic GPA, application essay, character/personal qualities, class rank, recommendation(s), rigor of secondary school record, standardized test scores, talent/ability. *Important factors considered include:* Extracurricular activities, interview, volunteer work. *Other factors considered include:* Alumni/ae relation, geographical residence, racial/ethnic status, state residency, work experience. **Freshman Admission Requirements:** High school diploma is required, and GED is accepted. *Academic units recommended:* 4 English, 2 math, 1 science, 2

foreign language, 2 social studies, 2 history. **Freshman Admission Statistics:** 15,070 applied, 22% admitted, 47% enrolled. **Transfer Admission Requirements:** High school transcript, college transcript(s), essay or personal statement, standardized test score, statement of good standing from prior institution(s). Minimum college GPA of 3.0 required. Lowest grade transferable C. **General Admission Information:** Application fee $65. Regular application deadline 1/10. Regular notification 4/1. Nonfall registration not accepted. Admission may be deferred for a maximum of 1 year. Credit and/or placement offered for CEEB Advanced Placement tests.

COSTS AND FINANCIAL AID
Annual tuition $35,568. Room and board $12,146. Required fees $396. Average book expense $1,060. **Required Forms and Deadlines:** FAFSA, CSS/Financial Aid PROFILE, Noncustodial PROFILE, Business/Farm Supplement, tax returns. Financial aid filing deadline 2/1. **Notification of Awards:** Applicants will be notified of awards on or about 4/1. **Types of Aid:** *Need-based scholarships/grants:* Pell, SEOG, state scholarships/grants, private scholarships, the school's own gift aid. *Loans:* FFEL Subsidized Stafford, FFEL Unsubsidized Stafford, FFEL PLUS, Federal Perkins, Federal Nursing, alternative loans. **Student Employment:** Federal Work-Study Program available. Institutional employment available. Off-campus job opportunities are excellent. **Financial Aid Statistics:** 38% freshmen, 36% undergrads receive need-based scholarship or grant aid. 33% freshmen, 35% undergrads receive need-based self-help aid. 53 freshmen, 189 undergrads receive athletic scholarships. 39% freshmen, 40% undergrads receive any aid. Highest amount earned per year from on-campus jobs $4,120.

GEORGIA BAPTIST COLLEGE OF NURSING

274 Boulevard, NE, Atlanta, GA 30312
Phone: 404-265-4800 **E-mail:** gbcnadm@mindspring.com **CEEB Code:** 6203
Fax: 404-265-6759 **Website:** www.gbcn.edu **ACT Code:** 0819
Financial Aid Phone: 404-265-4801

This private school, affiliated with the Baptist Church, was founded in 1901. It has a 3-acre campus.

RATINGS
Admissions Selectivity Rating: 60*   **Fire Safety Rating:** 60*   **Green Rating:** 60*

STUDENTS AND FACULTY
Enrollment: 310. **Student Body:** 97% female, 3% male, 3% out-of-state. African American 26%, Asian 2%, Caucasian 68%, Hispanic 2%. **Retention and Graduation:** 72% freshmen return for sophomore year. 79% freshmen graduate within 4 years. 5% grads go on to further study within 1 year. 99% grads pursue arts and sciences degrees. 1% grads pursue medical degrees. **Faculty:** Student/faculty ratio 10:1. 27 full-time faculty, 41% hold PhDs. 100% faculty teach undergrads.

ACADEMICS
Degrees: Bachelor's. **Academic Requirements:** Computer literacy, English (including composition), humanities, mathematics, sciences (biological or physical), social science. **Classes:** Most classes have 20–29 students. Most lab/discussion sections have 10–19 students. **Disciplines with Highest Percentage of Degrees Awarded:** Health professions and related sciences 100%. **Special Study Options:** Independent study.

FACILITIES
Housing: Coed dorms. **Computers:** 100% of public computers are PCs, remote student-access to Web through college's connection.

CAMPUS LIFE
Activities: Student government. **Organizations:** 7 registered organizations, 1 honor society, 1 religious organization.

ADMISSIONS
Freshman Academic Profile: 88% from public high schools. SAT Math middle 50% range 420–530. SAT Critical Reading middle 50% range 460–540. TOEFL required of all international applicants, minimum paper TOEFL 550. **Basis for Candidate Selection:** *Very important factors considered include:* Application essay, character/personal qualities, extracurricular activities, rigor of secondary school record, standardized test scores, volunteer work. *Important factors considered include:* Talent/ability, work experience. *Other factors considered include:* Alumni/ae relation, interview, recommendation(s), religious affiliation/commitment. **Freshman Admission Requirements:** High school diploma is required, and GED is not accepted. *Academic units required:* 4 English, 4 math, 3 science (2 science labs), 2 foreign language, 3 history. *Academic units recommended:* 4 science. **Freshman Admission Statistics:** 87

applied, 46% admitted, 80% enrolled. **Transfer Admission Requirements:** College transcript(s), essay or personal statement, statement of good standing from prior institution(s). Minimum college GPA of 2.5 required. Lowest grade transferable C. **General Admission Information:** Application fee $35. Regular application deadline 5/15. Regular notification is rolling. Nonfall registration not accepted. Common Application not accepted. Credit offered for CEEB Advanced Placement tests.

COSTS AND FINANCIAL AID

Annual tuition $10,050. Room & board $5,035. Required fees $539. Average book expense $1,200. **Required Forms and Deadlines:** FAFSA, institution's own financial aid form, state aid form. Financial aid filing deadline 5/1. **Notification of Awards:** Applicants will be notified of awards on a rolling basis beginning on or about 2/15. **Types of Aid:** *Need-based scholarships/grants:* Pell, SEOG, state scholarships/grants, private scholarships, the school's own gift aid. *Loans:* FFEL Subsidized Stafford, FFEL Unsubsidized Stafford, FFEL PLUS, state loans. **Student Employment:** Off-campus job opportunities are good. **Financial Aid Statistics:** 62% freshmen, 74% undergrads receive need-based scholarship or grant aid. 56% freshmen, 60% undergrads receive need-based self-help aid.

GEORGIA COLLEGE & STATE UNIVERSITY

Campus Box 23, Milledgeville, GA 31061
Phone: 478-445-5004 **E-mail:** gcsu@mail.gcsu.edu **CEEB Code:** 5252
Fax: 478-445-1914 **Website:** www.gcsu.edu **ACT Code:** 0828
Financial Aid Phone: 478-445-5149

This public school was founded in 1889. It has a 590-acre campus.

RATINGS

Admissions Selectivity Rating: 82   **Fire Safety Rating:** 98   **Green Rating:** 60*

STUDENTS AND FACULTY

Enrollment: 5,112. **Student Body:** 60% female, 40% male, 2% out-of-state, 2% international (43 countries represented). African American 6%, Asian 1%, Caucasian 88%, Hispanic 1%. **Retention and Graduation:** 84% freshmen return for sophomore year. 23% freshmen graduate within 4 years. 25% grads go on to further study within 1 year. 17% grads pursue arts and sciences degrees. 7% grads pursue business degrees. 8% grads pursue law degrees. 3% grads pursue medical degrees. **Faculty:** 273 full-time faculty, 76% hold PhDs. 100% faculty teach undergrads.

ACADEMICS

Degrees: Bachelor's, master's, post-master's certificate. **Academic Requirements:** Arts/fine arts, English (including composition), foreign languages, history, mathematics, sciences (biological or physical), social science. **Classes:** Most classes have 20–29 students. Most lab/discussion sections have 20–29 students. **Majors with Highest Enrollment:** Business administration/management, nursing/registered nurse training (RN, ASN, BSN, MSN), psychology. **Disciplines with Highest Percentage of Degrees Awarded:** Business/marketing 28%, education 15%, psychology 10%, health professions and related sciences 10%, social sciences 6%. **Special Study Options:** Accelerated program, distance learning, double major, English as a second language (ESL), external degree program, honors program, independent study, internships, study abroad, teacher certification program.

FACILITIES

Housing: Coed dorms, apartments for single students, special housing for international students. **Special Academic Facilities/Equipment:** Education Archives Museum, old governor's mansion. **Computers:** 100% of classrooms are wired, 100% of classrooms are wireless, 90% of public computers are PCs, 10% of public computers are Macs, network access in dorm rooms, network access in dorm lounges, online registration, online administrative functions (other than registration), support for handheld computing, remote student-access to Web through college's connection.

CAMPUS LIFE

Activities: Choral groups, concert band, dance, drama/theater, jazz band, literary magazine, music ensembles, musical theater, radio station, student government, student newspaper, television station. **Organizations:** 106 registered organizations, 12 honor societies, 8 religious organizations. 7

fraternities (2% men join), 7 sororities (2% women join). **Athletics (Intercollegiate):** *Men:* Baseball, basketball, cross-country, golf, tennis. *Women:* Basketball, cross-country, softball, speed skating, tennis.

ADMISSIONS

Freshman Academic Profile: 18% in top 10% of high school class, 56% in top 25% of high school class, 86% in top 50% of high school class. SAT Math middle 50% range 520–610. SAT Critical Reading middle 50% range 520–600. ACT middle 50% range 22–25. TOEFL required of all international applicants, minimum paper TOEFL 500, minimum computer TOEFL 173. **Basis for Candidate Selection:** *Very important factors considered include:* Academic GPA, rigor of secondary school record, standardized test scores. *Important factors considered include:* Application essay, class rank, extracurricular activities, recommendation(s), talent/ability. *Other factors considered include:* Alumni/ae relation, character/personal qualities, first generation, geographical residence, level of applicant's interest, racial/ethnic status, state residency, volunteer work. **Freshman Admission Requirements:** High school diploma is required, and GED is accepted. *Academic units required:* 4 English, 4 math, 3 science (1 science lab), 2 foreign language, 3 social studies. **Freshman Admission Statistics:** 3,608 applied, 55% admitted, 54% enrolled. **Transfer Admission Requirements:** College transcript(s), statement of good standing from prior institution(s). Minimum college GPA of 2.0 required. **General Admission Information:** Application fee $25. Regular application deadline 4/1. Regular notification continuous. Nonfall registration accepted. Admission may be deferred for a maximum of 1 year. Credit offered for CEEB Advanced Placement tests.

COSTS AND FINANCIAL AID

Annual in-state tuition $3,574. Out-of-state tuition $14,296. Room & board $7,116. Required fees $782. Average book expense $800. **Required Forms and Deadlines:** FAFSA. Financial aid filing deadline 3/1. **Notification of Awards:** Applicants will be notified of awards on a rolling basis beginning on or about 3/1. **Types of Aid:** *Need-based scholarships/grants:* Pell, SEOG, state scholarships/grants, private scholarships, the school's own gift aid. *Loans:* Direct PLUS, FFEL Subsidized Stafford, FFEL Unsubsidized Stafford, FFEL PLUS, Federal Perkins, state loans. **Student Employment:** Federal Work-Study Program available. Institutional employment available. Off-campus job opportunities are good. **Financial Aid Statistics:** 12% freshmen, 16% undergrads receive need-based scholarship or grant aid. 16% freshmen, 24% undergrads receive need-based self-help aid. 33 freshmen, 148 undergrads receive athletic scholarships. 35% freshmen, 38% undergrads receive any aid. Highest amount earned per year from on-campus jobs $2,600.

See page 1180.

GEORGIA INSTITUTE OF TECHNOLOGY

Georgia Institute of Technology, Office of Undergraduate Admission, Atlanta, GA 30332-0320
Phone: 404-894-4154 **E-mail:** admission@gatech.edu **CEEB Code:** 5248
Fax: 404-894-9511 **Website:** www.gatech.edu **ACT Code:** 0818
Financial Aid Phone: 404-894-4160

This public school was founded in 1885. It has a 400-acre campus.

RATINGS

Admissions Selectivity Rating: 93   **Fire Safety Rating:** 89   **Green Rating:** 99

STUDENTS AND FACULTY

Enrollment: 12,103. **Student Body:** 28% female, 72% male, 29% out-of-state, 4% international (72 countries represented). African American 7%, Asian 16%, Caucasian 68%, Hispanic 4%. **Retention and Graduation:** 92% freshmen return for sophomore year. 34% freshmen graduate within 4 years. 33% grads go on to further study within 1 year. 3% grads pursue arts and sciences degrees. 2% grads pursue business degrees. 2% grads pursue law degrees. 5% grads pursue medical degrees. **Faculty:** Student/faculty ratio 14:1. 845 full-time faculty, 97% hold PhDs. 100% faculty teach undergrads.

ACADEMICS

Degrees: Bachelor's, doctoral, master's. **Academic Requirements:** Computer literacy, English (including composition), history, humanities, mathematics, sciences (biological or physical), social science. **Classes:** Most classes have 20–29 students. Most lab/discussion sections have 10–19 students. **Majors with**

Highest Enrollment: Business administration and management, industrial engineering, mechanical engineering. **Disciplines with Highest Percentage of Degrees Awarded:** Engineering 56%, business/marketing 14%, computer and information sciences 10%, architecture 4%, interdisciplinary studies 3%, biological/life sciences 3%. **Special Study Options:** Accelerated program, cooperative education program, cross-registration, distance learning, double major, dual enrollment, English as a second language (ESL), honors program, independent study, internships, student-designed major, study abroad. Dual degree program (3-2), Regents' Engineering Transfer Program (RETP) with 14 Georgia colleges; Georgia Tech Regional Engineering Program (GTREP) offers undergraduate and graduate engineering degrees in collaboration with Armstrong Atlantic State University, Georgia Southern University, and Savannah State University.

FACILITIES

Housing: Coed dorms, men's dorms, women's dorms, apartments for married students, apartments for single students, special housing for disabled students, fraternity/sorority housing; first-year housing is guaranteed to all new freshman and transfer students. **Special Academic Facilities/Equipment:** Advanced Technology Development Center, Georgia Tech Research Institute, Ovarian Cancer Institute, electron microscope, Paper Museum, Nanotechnology Research Center (scheduled to open in 2008). **Computers:** 80% of public computers are PCs, 15% of public computers are Macs, 5% of public computers are UNIX, network access in dorm rooms, network access in dorm lounges, online registration, online administrative functions (other than registration), remote student-access to Web through college's connection. Undergraduates are required to own a computer.

CAMPUS LIFE

Activities: Choral groups, concert band, dance, drama/theater, jazz band, literary magazine, marching band, music ensembles, musical theater, pep band, radio station, student government, student newspaper, student-run film society, symphony orchestra, television station. **Organizations:** 357 registered organizations, 28 honor societies, 30 religious organizations. 34 fraternities (22% men join), 14 sororities (27% women join). **Athletics (Intercollegiate):** *Men:* Baseball, basketball, cross-country, diving, football, golf, swimming, tennis, track/field (indoor), track/field (outdoor). *Women:* Basketball, cross-country, diving, softball, swimming, tennis, track/field (indoor), track/field (outdoor), volleyball. **Environmental initiatives:** Recycling. Transportation. Green building (new & renovations/retrofits).

ADMISSIONS

Freshman Academic Profile: 54% in top 10% of high school class, 83% in top 25% of high school class, 98% in top 50% of high school class. SAT SAT Math middle 50% range 650–730. SAT Critical Reading middle 50% range 590–690. SAT Writing middle 50% range 580–670. ACT middle 50% range 27–31. TOEFL required of all international applicants, minimum paper TOEFL 600, minimum computer TOEFL 250. **Basis for Candidate Selection:** *Very important factors considered include:* Academic GPA. *Important factors considered include:* Application essay, extracurricular activities, geographical residence, rigor of secondary school record, standardized test scores, state residency, talent/ability, volunteer work, work experience. **Freshman Admission Requirements:** High school diploma is required, and GED is accepted. *Academic units required:* 4 English, 4 math, 3 science (2 science labs), 2 foreign language, 3 social studies. **Freshman Admission Statistics:** 9,389 applied, 69% admitted, 44% enrolled. **Transfer Admission Requirements:** College transcript(s), statement of good standing from prior institution(s). Lowest grade transferable C. **General Admission Information:** Application fee $50. Regular application deadline 1/15. Regular notification 3/15. Nonfall registration accepted. Credit and/or placement offered for CEEB Advanced Placement tests.

COSTS AND FINANCIAL AID

Required Forms and Deadlines: FAFSA, institution's own financial aid form. Financial aid filing deadline 3/1. **Notification of Awards:** Applicants will be notified of awards on a rolling basis beginning on or about 4/1. **Types of Aid:** *Need-based scholarships/grants:* Pell, SEOG, state scholarships/grants, private scholarships, the school's own gift aid. *Loans:* FFEL Subsidized Stafford, FFEL Unsubsidized Stafford, FFEL PLUS, Federal Perkins, college/university loans from institutional funds. **Student Employment:** Federal Work-Study Program available. Institutional employment available. Off-campus job opportunities are excellent. **Financial Aid Statistics:** 18% freshmen, 18% undergrads receive need-based scholarship or grant aid. 20% freshmen, 22% undergrads receive need-based self-help aid. 63 freshmen, 336 undergrads receive athletic scholarships. 85% freshmen, 74% undergrads receive any aid.

GEORGIA SOUTHERN UNIVERSITY

PO Box 8024, Statesboro, GA 30460
Phone: 912-681-5391 **E-mail:** admissions@georgiasouthern.edu **CEEB Code:** 5253
Fax: 912-486-7240 **Website:** www.georgiasouthern.edu **ACT Code:** 0830
Financial Aid Phone: 912-681-5413

This public school was founded in 1906. It has a 675-acre campus.

RATINGS

Admissions Selectivity Rating: 80   **Fire Safety Rating:** 82   **Green Rating:** 82

STUDENTS AND FACULTY

Enrollment: 13,752. **Student Body:** 49% female, 51% male, 4% out-of-state. African American 21%, Asian 1%, Caucasian 75%, Hispanic 2%. **Retention and Graduation:** 76% freshmen return for sophomore year. 13% freshmen graduate within 4 years. 23% grads go on to further study within 1 year. 4% grads pursue business degrees. **Faculty:** Student/faculty ratio 20:1. 664 full-time faculty, 79% hold PhDs. 91% faculty teach undergrads.

ACADEMICS

Degrees: Bachelor's, doctoral, master's, post-master's certificate. **Academic Requirements:** Arts/fine arts, computer literacy, English (including composition), healthful living, history, humanities, mathematics, physical activity, sciences (biological or physical), social science, university orientation. **Classes:** Most classes have 20–29 students. Most lab/discussion sections have 20–29 students. **Majors with Highest Enrollment:** Biology/biological sciences, elementary education and teaching, nursing/registered nurse training (RN, ASN, BSN, MSN). **Disciplines with Highest Percentage of Degrees Awarded:** Business/marketing 26%, education 15%, engineering technologies 7%, parks and recreation 6%, health professions and related sciences 6%, family and consumer sciences 5%. **Special Study Options:** Cooperative education program, cross-registration, distance learning, double major, dual enrollment, English as a second language (ESL), external degree program, honors program, independent study, internships, student-designed major, study abroad, teacher certification program.

FACILITIES

Housing: Coed dorms, apartments for single students, special housing for disabled students, special housing for international students, fraternity/sorority housing. **Special Academic Facilities/Equipment:** Art galleries, teaching museum, performing arts center, wildlife education center, eagle cinema, broadcasting studios, planetarium, botanical garden, radio station. **Computers:** 10% of classrooms are wired, 10% of classrooms are wireless, 85% of public computers are PCs, 15% of public computers are Macs, network access in dorm rooms, network access in dorm lounges, online registration, online administrative functions (other than registration), remote student-access to Web through college's connection.

CAMPUS LIFE

Activities: Choral groups, concert band, dance, drama/theater, jazz band, literary magazine, marching band, music ensembles, musical theater, opera, pep band, radio station, student government, student newspaper, student-run film society, symphony orchestra, television station. **Organizations:** 208 registered organizations, 12 honor societies, 19 religious organizations. 18 fraternities (10% men join), 7 sororities (11% women join). **Athletics (Intercollegiate):** *Men:* Baseball, basketball, cheerleading, football, golf, soccer, tennis. *Women:* Basketball, cheerleading, cross-country, diving, soccer, softball, swimming, tennis, track/field (outdoor), volleyball. **Environmental initiatives:** Environmental/Coordinator. Recycling. Transit.

ADMISSIONS

Freshman Academic Profile: 14% in top 10% of high school class, 38% in top 25% of high school class, 68% in top 50% of high school class. 90% from public high schools. SAT Math middle 50% range 520–590. SAT Critical Reading middle 50% range 510–590. ACT middle 50% range 21–24. TOEFL required of all international applicants, minimum paper TOEFL 500, minimum computer TOEFL 173. **Basis for Candidate Selection:** *Very important factors considered include:* Academic GPA, rigor of secondary school record, standardized test scores. *Other factors considered include:* Class rank. **Freshman Admission Requirements:** High school diploma is required, and GED is not accepted. *Academic units required:* 4 English, 4 math, 3 science (2 science labs), 2 foreign language, 3 social studies. **Freshman Admission Statistics:** 7,360 applied, 47% admitted, 79% enrolled. **Transfer Admission Requirements:** College transcript(s), statement of good standing from prior institution(s). Minimum college GPA of 2.0 required. Lowest grade transferable D. **General Admission Information:** Application fee $30. Regular application deadline 5/1. Regular notification continuous. Nonfall registration accepted. Admission may be deferred. Credit and/or placement offered for CEEB Advanced Placement tests.

COSTS AND FINANCIAL AID

Annual in-state tuition $2,958. Annual out-of-state tuition $11,830. Room and board $6,860. Required fees $1,124. Average book expense $1,200. **Required Forms and Deadlines:** FAFSA. Financial aid filing deadline 4/20. **Notification of Awards:** Applicants will be notified of awards on a rolling basis beginning on or about 4/20. **Types of Aid:** *Need-based scholarships/grants:* Pell, SEOG, state scholarships/grants, private scholarships, the school's own gift aid, Hope Scholarships, Federal Work Study. *Loans:* Direct Subsidized Stafford, Direct Unsubsidized Stafford, Direct PLUS, Federal Perkins, state loans, service-cancelable state direct student loans, external alternative loans. **Student Employment:** Federal Work-Study Program available. Institutional employment available. Off-campus job opportunities are excellent. **Financial Aid Statistics:** 43% freshmen, 39% undergrads receive need-based scholarship or grant aid. 28% freshmen, 39% undergrads receive need-based self-help aid. 53 freshmen, 163 undergrads receive athletic scholarships. 92% freshmen, 82% undergrads receive any aid. Highest amount earned per year from on-campus jobs $1,636.

GEORGIA SOUTHWESTERN STATE UNIVERSITY

800 Georgia Southwestern State University Drive, Americus, GA 31709-4693
Phone: 912-928-1273 **E-mail:** gswapps@canes.gsw.edu **CEEB Code:** 5250
Fax: 912-931-2983 **Website:** www.gsw.edu **ACT Code:** 0824
Financial Aid Phone: 229-928-1378

This public school was founded in 1906. It has a 325-acre campus.

RATINGS

Admissions Selectivity Rating: 74   **Fire Safety Rating:** 60*   **Green Rating:** 60*

STUDENTS AND FACULTY

Enrollment: 2,183. **Student Body:** 65% female, 35% male, 2% out-of-state, 2% international (22 countries represented). African American 34%, Asian 1%, Caucasian 62%. **Retention and Graduation:** 71% freshmen return for sophomore year. 16% freshmen graduate within 4 years. **Faculty:** Student/faculty ratio 17:1. 96 full-time faculty, 78% hold PhDs. 100% faculty teach undergrads.

ACADEMICS

Degrees: Associate, bachelor's, certificate, master's, post-master's certificate. **Academic Requirements:** English (including composition), humanities, mathematics, sciences (biological or physical), social science. **Classes:** Most classes have 10–19 students. Most lab/discussion sections have 10–19 students. **Majors with Highest Enrollment:** Business administration/management, elementary education and teaching, psychology. **Disciplines with Highest Percentage of Degrees Awarded:** Education 34%, business/marketing 26%, psychology 8%, health professions and related sciences 6%, physical sciences 4%, computer and information sciences 4%, social sciences 4%, history 4%. **Special Study Options:** Accelerated program, cooperative education program, distance learning, double major, dual enrollment, English as a second language (ESL), honors program, independent study, internships, study abroad, teacher certification program. Undergrads may take grad-level classes. Associate degree program in trade and industry with South Georgia Technical College in Americus; Albany Area Technical College in Albany, GA; Middle Georgia in Warner Robbins. 3-2 program in engineering with Georgia Institute of Technology.

FACILITIES

Housing: Coed dorms, men's dorms, women's dorms, special housing for disabled students, special housing for international students, fraternity/sorority housing. **Special Academic Facilities/Equipment:** Observatory, glass-blowing studio. **Computers:** 95% of public computers are PCs, 5% of public computers are Macs, network access in dorm rooms, network access in dorm lounges, online registration, online administrative functions (other than registration).

CAMPUS LIFE

Activities: Choral groups, concert band, drama/theater, jazz band, literary magazine, music ensembles, musical theater, student government, student newspaper, television station. **Organizations:** 12 honor societies, 7 fraternities (17% men join), 6 sororities (10% women join). **Athletics (Intercollegiate):** *Men:* Baseball, basketball, golf, soccer, tennis. *Women:* Basketball, cross-country, soccer, softball, tennis.

ADMISSIONS

Freshman Academic Profile: 14% in top 10% of high school class, 40% in top 25% of high school class, 77% in top 50% of high school class. SAT Math middle

50% range 430–530. SAT Critical Reading middle 50% range 440–530. ACT middle 50% range 18–21. TOEFL required of all international applicants, minimum paper TOEFL 523, minimum computer TOEFL 193. **Basis for Candidate Selection:** *Very important factors considered include:* Academic GPA, rigor of secondary school record, standardized test scores. *Important factors considered include:* Class rank. *Other factors considered include:* Application essay, extracurricular activities, interview, recommendation(s), talent/ability. **Freshman Admission Requirements:** High school diploma is required, and GED is accepted. *Academic units required:* 4 English, 4 math, 3 science (2 science labs), 2 foreign language, 1 social studies, 2 history, 2 academic electives. *Academic units recommended:* 2 academic electives. **Freshman Admission Statistics:** 1,083 applied, 74% admitted, 48% enrolled. **Transfer Admission Requirements:** College transcript(s). Minimum college GPA of 2.0 required. Lowest grade transferable D. **General Admission Information:** Application fee $25. Early decision application deadline 12/15. Regular application deadline 12/21. Regular notification rolling. Nonfall registration accepted. Admission may be deferred for a maximum of 1 year. Common Application accepted. Credit and/or placement offered for CEEB Advanced Placement tests.

COSTS AND FINANCIAL AID

Average book expense $1,000. **Required Forms and Deadlines:** FAFSA, institution's own financial aid form, state aid form. Financial aid filing deadline 6/1. **Notification of Awards:** Applicants will be notified of awards on a rolling basis beginning on or about 3/1. **Types of Aid:** *Need-based scholarships/grants:* Pell, SEOG, state scholarships/grants, the school's own gift aid. *Loans:* FFEL Subsidized Stafford, FFEL Unsubsidized Stafford, FFEL PLUS, Federal Perkins. **Student Employment:** Federal Work-Study Program available. Institutional employment available. Off-campus job opportunities are fair. **Financial Aid Statistics:** 64% freshmen, 59% undergrads receive any aid.

GEORGIA STATE UNIVERSITY

PO Box 4009, Atlanta, GA 30302-4009
Phone: 404-651-2365 **E-mail:** admissions@gsu.edu **CEEB Code:** 5251
Fax: 404-651-4811 **Website:** www.gsu.edu **ACT Code:** 0826
Financial Aid Phone: 404-651-2223

This public school was founded in 1913. It has a 33-acre campus.

RATINGS

Admissions Selectivity Rating: 60*   **Fire Safety Rating:** 89   **Green Rating:** 60*

STUDENTS AND FACULTY

Enrollment: 18,478. **Student Body:** 61% female, 39% male, 7% out-of-state, 3% international (159 countries represented). African American 30%, Asian 10%, Caucasian 36%, Hispanic 4%. **Retention and Graduation:** 80% freshmen return for sophomore year. 15% freshmen graduate within 4 years. **Faculty:** Student/faculty ratio 17:1. 1,046 full-time faculty, 85% hold PhDs.

ACADEMICS

Degrees: Bachelor's, certificate, doctoral, first professional, master's, post-bachelor's certificate, post-master's certificate. **Academic Requirements:** English (including composition), foreign languages, history, humanities, mathematics, philosophy, sciences (biological or physical), social science. **Classes:** Most classes have 20–29 students. **Majors with Highest Enrollment:** Finance, journalism, marketing/marketing management. **Disciplines with Highest Percentage of Degrees Awarded:** Business/marketing 30%, social sciences 14%, psychology 8%, visual and performing arts 7%, education 6%. **Special Study Options:** Accelerated program, cooperative education program, cross-registration, distance learning, double major, dual enrollment, English as a second language (ESL), freshman learning communities, honors program, independent study, internships, student-designed major, study abroad, teacher certification program.

FACILITIES

Housing: Coed dorms, apartments for married students, apartments for single students, special housing for disabled students, special housing for international students, some arrangements for visiting faculty/scholars. **Special Academic Facilities/Equipment:** Cartography Production Laboratory, commuter student services, Cooperative Learning Laboratory, Economic Forecasting Center, Ernest G. Welch School of Art and Design Gallery, Instructional Technology Center, James M. Cox Jr. Multimedia Instructional Lab and Satellite Downlink Facility, Kopleff Recital Hall, Lanette L. Suttles Child Development Center, language acquisition and resource center, mathematics assistance complex, mathematics interactive learning environment, music media center, Rialto Center for the Performing Arts, small business development center, visual resource center, writing studio. **Computers:** 100% of classrooms are wireless, 89% of public computers are PCs, 11% of public computers are Macs, network access in dorm rooms, network access in dorm lounges, online registration, online administrative functions (other than registration), support for handheld computing, remote student-access to Web through college's connection.

CAMPUS LIFE

Activities: Choral groups, concert band, dance, drama/theater, jazz band, literary magazine, music ensembles, pep band, radio station, student government, student newspaper, student-run film society, television station. **Organizations:** 201 registered organizations, 19 honor societies, 21 religious organizations. 9 fraternities (39% men join), 15 sororities (60% women join). **Athletics (Intercollegiate):** *Men:* Baseball, basketball, cross-country, golf, soccer, tennis, track/field (outdoor), volleyball. *Women:* Basketball, cross-country, golf, soccer, softball, tennis, track/field (outdoor), volleyball.

ADMISSIONS

Freshman Academic Profile: 93% from public high schools. SAT Math middle 50% range 500–600. SAT Critical Reading middle 50% range 490–590. ACT middle 50% range 20–25. TOEFL required of all international applicants, minimum paper TOEFL 525, minimum computer TOEFL 213. **Basis for Candidate Selection:** *Very important factors considered include:* Academic GPA, rigor of secondary school record, standardized test scores. *Other factors considered include:* Alumni/ae relation, application essay, character/personal qualities, extracurricular activities, first generation, geographical residence, interview, level of applicant's interest, recommendation(s), state residency, talent/ability, volunteer work, work experience. **Freshman Admission Requirements:** High school diploma is required, and GED is not accepted. *Academic units required:* 4 English, 4 math, 3 science (2 science labs), 2 foreign language, 2 social studies, 1 history. **Freshman Admission Statistics:** 8,346 applied, 52% admitted, 50% enrolled. **Transfer Admission Requirements:** College transcript(s). Minimum college GPA of 2.5 required. Lowest grade transferable D. **General Admission Information:** Application fee $50. Regular application deadline 3/1. Regular notification is rolling. Nonfall registration accepted. Admission may be deferred for a maximum of 2 terms. Credit offered for CEEB Advanced Placement tests.

COSTS AND FINANCIAL AID

Annual in-state tuition $4,202. Out-of-state tuition $16,808. Room & board $7,990. Required fees $1,019. Average book expense $1,000. **Required Forms and Deadlines:** FAFSA. Financial aid filing deadline 11/1. **Notification of Awards:** Applicants will be notified of awards on a rolling basis beginning on or about 3/30. **Types of Aid:** *Need-based scholarships/grants:* Pell, SEOG, state scholarships/grants, private scholarships, the school's own gift aid. *Loans:* Direct Subsidized Stafford, Direct Unsubsidized Stafford, Direct PLUS, FFEL PLUS, Federal Perkins, state loans. **Student Employment:** Federal Work-Study Program available. Institutional employment available. Off-campus job opportunities are good. **Financial Aid Statistics:** 33% freshmen, 20% undergrads receive need-based scholarship or grant aid. 8% freshmen, 11% undergrads receive need-based self-help aid. 20 freshmen, 42 undergrads receive athletic scholarships. 66% freshmen, 42% undergrads receive any aid.

GEORGIAN COURT UNIVERSITY

900 Lakewood Avenue, Lakewood, NJ 08701-2697
Phone: 732-987-2200 **E-mail:** admissions@georgian.edu **CEEB Code:** 2274
Fax: 732-987-2000 **Website:** www.georgian.edu **ACT Code:** 2562
Financial Aid Phone: 732-987-2258

This private school, affiliated with the Roman Catholic Church, was founded in 1908. It has a 155-acre campus.

RATINGS

Admissions Selectivity Rating: 64   **Fire Safety Rating:** 60*   **Green Rating:** 71

STUDENTS AND FACULTY

Enrollment: 1,701. **Student Body:** 93% female, 7% male, 1% out-of-state. African American 7%, Asian 2%, Caucasian 74%, Hispanic 8%. **Retention and Graduation:** 75% freshmen return for sophomore year. 38% freshmen graduate within 4 years. 28% grads go on to further study within 1 year. 83% grads pursue arts and sciences degrees. 13% grads pursue business degrees. 4% grads pursue law degrees. **Faculty:** Student/faculty ratio 13:1. 110 full-time faculty, 85% hold PhDs. 83% faculty teach undergrads.

ACADEMICS

Degrees: Bachelor's, certificate, master's, post-bachelor's certificate, post-master's certificate. **Academic Requirements:** Arts/fine arts, English

(including composition), foreign languages, history, humanities, philosophy, sciences (biological or physical), social science. **Classes:** Most classes have 10–19 students. **Majors with Highest Enrollment:** Business administration/management, elementary education and teaching, psychology. **Disciplines with Highest Percentage of Degrees Awarded:** Education 35%, psychology 14%, business/marketing 12%, liberal arts/general studies 8%, English 6%. **Special Study Options:** Accelerated program, distance learning, double major, dual enrollment, English as a second language (ESL), independent study, internships, liberal arts/career combination, study abroad, teacher certification program. Undergrads may take grad-level classes. Co-op programs include arts, business, health professions, natural science, and social/behavioral science.

FACILITIES

Housing: Women's dorms. **Special Academic Facilities/Equipment:** Art gallery, arboretum, NASA ERC. **Computers:** 68% of public computers are PCs, 7% of public computers are Macs, network access in dorm rooms, online registration, online administrative functions (other than registration), remote student-access to Web through college's connection.

CAMPUS LIFE

Activities: Choral groups, concert band, jazz band, literary magazine, music ensembles, student government, student newspaper, yearbook. **Organizations:** 40 registered organizations, 16 honor societies, 1 religious organization. **Athletics (Intercollegiate):** *Women:* Basketball, cross-country, soccer, softball, tennis, volleyball. **Environmental initiatives:** Have included a sustainability commitment in our strategic plan. Trustees have required all future construction to be LEED certified, level Silver. President was the 8th signatory of ACUPCC in New Jersey.

ADMISSIONS

Freshman Academic Profile: 8% in top 10% of high school class, 27% in top 25% of high school class, 69% in top 50% of high school class. 81% from public high schools. SAT Math middle 50% range 390–490. SAT Critical Reading middle 50% range 400–500. TOEFL required of all international applicants, minimum paper TOEFL 550, minimum computer TOEFL 213. **Basis for Candidate Selection:** *Very important factors considered include:* Academic GPA, rigor of secondary school record. *Important factors considered include:* Standardized test scores. *Other factors considered include:* Alumni/ae relation, application essay, character/personal qualities, class rank, extracurricular activities, first generation, interview, level of applicant's interest, recommendation(s), talent/ability, volunteer work, work experience. **Freshman Admission Requirements:** High school diploma is required, and GED is accepted. *Academic units required:* 4 English, 2 math, 1 science (1 science lab), 2 foreign language, 1 history, 6 academic electives. **Freshman Admission Statistics:** 646 applied, 76% admitted, 42% enrolled. **Transfer Admission Requirements:** College transcript(s), statement of good standing from prior institution(s). Minimum college GPA of 2.0 required. Lowest grade transferable C. **General Admission Information:** Application fee $40. Regular application deadline 8/1. Regular notification is rolling. Nonfall registration accepted. Credit and/or placement offered for CEEB Advanced Placement tests.

COSTS AND FINANCIAL AID

Annual tuition $20,928. Room and board $8,136. Required fees $1,150. Average book expense $1,250. **Required Forms and Deadlines:** FAFSA, institution's own financial aid form. **Notification of Awards:** Applicants will be notified of awards on a rolling basis beginning on or about 2/1. **Types of Aid:** *Need-based scholarships/grants:* Pell, SEOG, state scholarships/grants, private scholarships, the school's own gift aid. *Loans:* FFEL Subsidized Stafford, FFEL Unsubsidized Stafford, FFEL PLUS, Federal Perkins, state loans. **Student Employment:** Federal Work-Study Program available. Institutional employment available. Off-campus job opportunities are good. **Financial Aid Statistics:** 12 freshmen, 23 undergrads receive athletic scholarships. 99% freshmen, 92% undergrads receive any aid. Highest amount earned per year from on-campus jobs $2,000.

GETTYSBURG COLLEGE

Best 368

Admissions Office, Eisenhower House, Gettysburg, PA 17325-1484
Phone: 717-337-6100 **E-mail:** admiss@gettysburg.edu **CEEB Code:** 2275
Fax: 717-337-6145 **Website:** www.gettysburg.edu **ACT Code:** 3580
Financial Aid Phone: 717-337-6611

This private school, affiliated with the Lutheran Church, was founded in 1832. It has a 200-acre campus.

RATINGS
Admissions Selectivity Rating: 95   **Fire Safety Rating:** 85   **Green Rating:** 87

STUDENTS AND FACULTY
Enrollment: 2,511. **Student Body:** 53% female, 47% male, 73% out-of-state, 1% international (27 countries represented). African American 4%, Asian 1%, Caucasian 73%, Hispanic 2%. **Retention and Graduation:** 90% freshmen return for sophomore year. 75% freshmen graduate within 4 years. 40% grads go on to further study within 1 year. **Faculty:** Student/faculty ratio 11:1. 192 full-time faculty, 90% hold PhDs. 100% faculty teach undergrads.

ACADEMICS
Degrees: Bachelor's. **Academic Requirements:** Arts/fine arts, domestic diversity, English (including composition), foreign languages, humanities, non-Western culture, sciences (biological or physical), science and technology, senior capstone project, social science. **Classes:** Most classes have 10–19 students. **Majors with Highest Enrollment:** Business administration/management, political science and government, psychology. **Disciplines with Highest Percentage of Degrees Awarded:** Business/marketing 20%, social sciences 17%, biological/life sciences 11%, psychology 8%, history 8%. **Special Study Options:** Double major, independent study, internships, student-designed major, study abroad, teacher certification program.

FACILITIES
Housing: Coed dorms, women's dorms, apartments for single students, fraternity/sorority housing, special interest and theme housing. **Special Academic Facilities/Equipment:** Art gallery, language lab, child study lab, fine and performing arts facilities, planetarium, observatory, electron microscopes, NMR spectrometer, greenhouse, digital classrooms, wireless network, plasma physics labs, science center. **Computers:** 100% of classrooms are wired, 100% of classrooms are wireless, 99% of public computers are PCs, 1% of public computers are Macs, network access in dorm rooms, network access in dorm lounges, online registration, online administrative functions (other than registration), support for handheld computing, remote student-access to Web through college's connection.

CAMPUS LIFE
Activities: Choral groups, concert band, dance, drama/theater, jazz band, literary magazine, marching band, music ensembles, radio station, student government, student newspaper, student-run film society, symphony orchestra, television station, yearbook. **Organizations:** 100 registered organizations, 16 honor societies, 7 religious organizations. 10 fraternities (40% men join), 6 sororities (26% women join). **Athletics (Intercollegiate):** *Men:* Baseball, basketball, cheerleading, cross-country, football, golf, lacrosse, soccer, swimming, tennis, track/field (indoor), track/field (outdoor), wrestling. *Women:* Basketball, cheerleading, cross-country, field hockey, golf, lacrosse, soccer, softball, swimming, tennis, track/field (indoor), track/field (outdoor), volleyball. **Environmental initiatives:** The Center—a new althetic building which is being built "green." Painted Turtle—an organic garden on campus. Move-Out Day—each May, students donate unwanted clothing, furniture, etc., to the United Way, thus reducing the amount of garbage.

ADMISSIONS
Freshman Academic Profile: 66% in top 10% of high school class, 89% in top 25% of high school class, 100% in top 50% of high school class. 70% from public high schools. SAT Math middle 50% range 610–670. SAT Critical Reading middle 50% range 610–690. TOEFL required of all international applicants, minimum paper TOEFL 570, minimum computer TOEFL 230. **Basis for Candidate Selection:** *Very important factors considered include:* Academic GPA, class rank, recommendation(s), rigor of secondary school record. *Important factors considered include:* Application essay, character/personal qualities, extracurricular activities, interview, standardized test scores, talent/ability, volunteer work. *Other factors considered include:* Alumni/ae

relation, first generation, geographical residence, level of applicant's interest, racial/ethnic status, work experience. **Freshman Admission Requirements:** High school diploma is required, and GED is accepted. *Academic units required:* 4 English, 3 math, 3 science (3 science labs), 3 foreign language, 3 social studies, 3 history. *Academic units recommended:* 4 English, 4 math, 4 science (4 science labs), 4 foreign language, 4 social studies, 4 history. **Freshman Admission Statistics:** 5,310 applied, 41% admitted, 33% enrolled. **Transfer Admission Requirements:** High school transcript, college transcript(s), essay or personal statement, standardized test score, statement of good standing from prior institution(s). Minimum college GPA of 2.5 required. Lowest grade transferable C. **General Admission Information:** Application fee $45. Early decision application deadline 11/15. Regular application deadline 2/1. Regular notification 4/1. Nonfall registration accepted. Admission may be deferred for a maximum of 1 year. Credit and/or placement offered for CEEB Advanced Placement tests.

COSTS AND FINANCIAL AID
Annual tuition $33,700. Room & board $8,260. Required fees $250. Average book expense $500. **Required Forms and Deadlines:** FAFSA, CSS/Financial Aid PROFILE, Business/Farm Supplement. Financial aid filing deadline 2/15. **Notification of Awards:** Applicants will be notified of awards on or about 3/26. **Types of Aid:** *Need-based scholarships/grants:* Pell, SEOG, state scholarships/grants, private scholarships, the school's own gift aid. *Loans:* FFEL Subsidized Stafford, FFEL Unsubsidized Stafford, FFEL PLUS, Federal Perkins, college/university loans from institutional funds. **Student Employment:** Federal Work-Study Program available. Institutional employment available. **Financial Aid Statistics:** 54% freshmen, 56% undergrads receive need-based scholarship or grant aid. 44% freshmen, 49% undergrads receive need-based self-help aid. 70% freshmen, 70% undergrads receive any aid. Highest amount earned per year from on-campus jobs $1,500.

GIBBS COLLEGE

85 Garfield Avenue, Cranston, RI 02920
Phone: 401-824-5300 **E-mail:** psimonin@gibbsRI.edu
Fax: 401-824-5376 **Website:** www.gibbsRI.edu
Financial Aid Phone: 401-824-5327

This proprietary school was founded in 1911. It has a 30-acre campus.

RATINGS
Admissions Selectivity Rating: 60*   **Fire Safety Rating:** 60*   **Green Rating:** 60*

STUDENTS AND FACULTY
Enrollment: 613. **Student Body:** 72% female, 28% male, 5% out-of-state. African American 6%, Asian 5%, Caucasian 57%, Hispanic 22%. **Faculty:** Student/faculty ratio 11:1. 17 full-time faculty, 47% hold PhDs. 100% faculty teach undergrads.

ACADEMICS
Degrees: Associate, certificate. **Academic Requirements:** Arts/fine arts, computer literacy, English (including composition), humanities, mathematics, philosophy, sciences (biological or physical), social science. **Majors with Highest Enrollment:** Computer and information systems security, criminal justice/law enforcement administration, medical/clinical assistant. **Special Study Options:** Internships, liberal arts/career combination.

FACILITIES
Computers: 90% of classrooms are wired, 100% of classrooms are wireless, 100% of public computers are PCs, remote student-access to Web through college's connection.

CAMPUS LIFE
Activities: Student government.

ADMISSIONS
Basis for Candidate Selection: *Very important factors considered include:* Interview, level of applicant's interest. *Important factors considered include:* Character/personal qualities. *Other factors considered include:* Recommendation(s), talent/ability. **Freshman Admission Requirements:** High school diploma is required, and GED is accepted. **Freshman Admission Statistics:** 728 applied, 100% admitted, 59% enrolled. **Transfer Admission Requirements:** High school transcript, college transcript(s), interview. Lowest grade transferable C. **General Admission Information:** Application fee $50. Nonfall registration accepted. Admission may be deferred for a maximum of 1 year. Credit and/or placement offered for CEEB Advanced Placement tests.

COSTS AND FINANCIAL AID
Annual tuition $11,250. Required fees $450.

GLENVILLE STATE COLLEGE

200 High Street, Glenville, WV 26351
Phone: 304-462-4128 **E-mail:** admissions@glenville.edu
Fax: 304-462-8619 **Website:** www.glenville.edu **ACT Code:** 4522
Financial Aid Phone: 304-462-4103

This public school was founded in 1872.

RATINGS
Admissions Selectivity Rating: 60*   **Fire Safety Rating:** 60*   **Green Rating:** 60*

STUDENTS AND FACULTY
Enrollment: 1,374. **Student Body:** 54% female, 46% male. **Retention and Graduation:** 49% freshmen return for sophomore year. **Faculty:** Student/faculty ratio 20:1. 53 full-time faculty, 30% hold PhDs. 100% faculty teach undergrads.

ACADEMICS
Degrees: Associate, bachelor's, certificate. **Special Study Options:** Cooperative education program, double major, honors program, internships, student-designed major, teacher certification program.

FACILITIES
Housing: Coed dorms, men's dorms, women's dorms, apartments for married students, apartments for single students, special housing for disabled students. **Computers:** 100% of public computers are PCs, network access in dorm rooms.

CAMPUS LIFE
Activities: Choral groups, concert band, drama/theater, jazz band, marching band, music ensembles, student government, student newspaper, yearbook. **Organizations:** 30 registered organizations, 2 religious organizations. 2 fraternities, 2 sororities. **Athletics (Intercollegiate):** *Men:* Basketball, cross-country, football, golf, track/field (outdoor). *Women:* Basketball, cross-country, golf, softball, track/field (outdoor), volleyball.

ADMISSIONS
Freshman Academic Profile: TOEFL required of all international applicants, minimum paper TOEFL 550. **Basis for Candidate Selection:** *Very important factors considered include:* Rigor of secondary school record, standardized test scores. *Other factors considered include:* Academic GPA, class rank, recommendation(s), talent/ability. **Freshman Admission Requirements:** High school diploma is required, and GED is accepted. *Academic units required:* 4 English, 3 math, 3 science (2 science labs), 3 social studies. **Freshman Admission Statistics:** 1,132 applied, 100% admitted, 41% enrolled. **Transfer Admission Requirements:** College transcript(s). Minimum college GPA of 2.0 required. Lowest grade transferable C. **General Admission Information:** Nonfall registration accepted. Admission may be deferred for a maximum of 1 year. Credit offered for CEEB Advanced Placement tests.

COSTS AND FINANCIAL AID
Comprehensive fee $4,810. Room & board $3,480. Average book expense $350. **Required Forms and Deadlines:** FAFSA. **Types of Aid:** *Need-based scholarships/grants:* Pell, SEOG, state scholarships/grants, private scholarships, the school's own gift aid. *Loans:* Direct Subsidized Stafford, Direct Unsubsidized Stafford, Direct PLUS, Federal Perkins. **Student Employment:** Federal Work-Study Program available. Off-campus job opportunities are fair. **Financial Aid Statistics:** 64% freshmen, 59% undergrads receive need-based scholarship or grant aid. 48% freshmen, 51% undergrads receive need-based self-help aid. 6 freshmen, 46 undergrads receive athletic scholarships. Highest amount earned per year from on-campus jobs $900.

GLOBAL UNIVERSITY

1211 South Glenstone Avenue, Springfield, MO 65804
Phone: 800-443-1083 **E-mail:** studentinfo@globaluniversity.edu
Fax: 417-862-0863 **Website:** www.globaluniversity.edu

This is a private school.

RATINGS
Admissions Selectivity Rating: 60*   **Fire Safety Rating:** 60*   **Green Rating:** 60*

STUDENTS AND FACULTY
Enrollment: 6,707. **Faculty:** Student/faculty ratio 29:1. 49 full-time faculty.

ACADEMICS
Degrees: Associate, bachelor's, diploma, first professional, master's. **Academic Requirements:** Arts/fine arts, English (including composition), history, humanities, mathematics, sciences (biological or physical), social science, Bible/theology. **Special Study Options:** Distance learning, dual enrollment, external degree program, honors program, independent study.

ADMISSIONS
Basis for Candidate Selection: *Very important factors considered include:* Character/personal qualities. *Important factors considered include:* Religious affiliation/commitment. *Other factors considered include:* Volunteer work, work experience. **Freshman Admission Requirements:** High school diploma is required, and GED is accepted. **Transfer Admission Requirements:** High school transcript, college transcript(s). Lowest grade transferable C. **General Admission Information:** Application fee $35. Regular notification rolling. Nonfall registration accepted. Admission may be deferred for a maximum of 3 months. Common Application not accepted.

COSTS AND FINANCIAL AID
Annual tuition $2,160. **Types of Aid:** *Loans:* Aid provided from Veterans and DANTES.

GLOBE INSTITUTE OF TECHNOLOGY

291 Broadway, New York, NY 10007
Phone: 212-349-4330 **E-mail:** admissions@globe.edu
Fax: 212-227-5920 **Website:** www.globe.edu
Financial Aid Phone: 212-349-4330

This proprietary school was founded in 1984.

RATINGS
Admissions Selectivity Rating: 60*   **Fire Safety Rating:** 60*   **Green Rating:** 60*

STUDENTS AND FACULTY
Enrollment: 876. **Student Body:** 3% international. African American 15%, Asian 21%, Caucasian 49%, Hispanic 10%. **Retention and Graduation:** 70% freshmen return for sophomore year. 35% grads go on to further study within 1 year. **Faculty:** Student/faculty ratio 15:1. 27 full-time faculty. 100% faculty teach undergrads.

ACADEMICS
Degrees: Associate, bachelor's, certificate, diploma. **Academic Requirements:** Computer literacy, English (including composition), mathematics. **Classes:** Most classes have 10–19 students. **Majors with Highest Enrollment:** Accounting and business/management, business administration/management, computer and information sciences. **Disciplines with Highest Percentage of Degrees Awarded:** Business/marketing 40%, computer and information sciences 20%, law/legal studies 10%. **Special Study Options:** Accelerated program, cooperative education program, distance learning, double major, English as a second language (ESL), honors program, independent study, internships, weekend college.

FACILITIES
Housing: Special housing for international students. **Special Academic Facilities/Equipment:** Globe Art Gallery. **Computers:** 95% of public computers are PCs, 5% of public computers are UNIX, network access in dorm rooms, online registration, online administrative functions (other than registration), support for handheld computing, remote student-access to Web through college's connection.

CAMPUS LIFE
Activities: Dance, student government. **Organizations:** 25 registered organizations. **Athletics (Intercollegiate):** *Men:* Baseball, basketball, bowling, cross-country, soccer, track/field (indoor), track/field (outdoor). *Women:* Basketball, bowling, cheerleading, cross-country, track/field (indoor), track/field (outdoor), volleyball.

ADMISSIONS
Freshman Academic Profile: 75% from public high schools. SAT Math middle 50% range 500–600. SAT Critical Reading middle 50% range 500–600. **Basis for Candidate Selection:** *Very important factors considered include:* Class rank, extracurricular activities, rigor of secondary school record. *Important factors considered include:* Application essay, interview, recommendation(s). *Other factors considered include:* Academic GPA, character/personal qualities, level of applicant's interest, standardized test

scores, talent/ability, volunteer work, work experience. **Freshman Admission Requirements:** High school diploma is required, and GED is accepted. **Transfer Admission Requirements:** High school transcript, college transcript(s). Minimum college GPA of 2.0 required. Lowest grade transferable C. **General Admission Information:** Application fee $50. Nonfall registration accepted. Admission may be deferred for a maximum of 1 year.

COSTS AND FINANCIAL AID

Annual tuition $8,930. Required fees $186. Average book expense $800. **Required Forms and Deadlines:** FAFSA, state aid form. **Types of Aid:** *Need-based scholarships/grants:* Pell, SEOG, state scholarships/grants, private scholarships, the school's own gift aid. *Loans:* FFEL Subsidized Stafford, FFEL Unsubsidized Stafford, FFEL PLUS. **Student Employment:** Federal Work-Study Program available. Institutional employment available. Off-campus job opportunities are excellent. **Financial Aid Statistics:** 95% freshmen, 90% undergrads receive need-based scholarship or grant aid. 10% freshmen, 7% undergrads receive need-based self-help aid. 75% freshmen, 75% undergrads receive any aid.

GODDARD COLLEGE

123 Pitkin Road, Plainfield, VT 05667
Phone: 802-454-8311 **E-mail:** admissions@goddard.edu **CEEB Code:** 3416
Fax: 802-454-1029 **Website:** www.goddard.edu **ACT Code:** 4300
Financial Aid Phone: 802-454-8311

This private school was founded in 1938. It has a 250-acre campus.

RATINGS
Admissions Selectivity Rating: 73   **Fire Safety Rating:** 60*   **Green Rating:** 60*

STUDENTS AND FACULTY
Enrollment: 319. **Student Body:** 59% female, 41% male, 87% out-of-state, 2% international (2 countries represented). African American 2%, Asian 1%, Caucasian 73%, Hispanic 2%. **Retention and Graduation:** 73% freshmen return for sophomore year. 8% freshmen graduate within 4 years. 5% grads go on to further study within 1 year. 95% grads pursue arts and sciences degrees. **Faculty:** Student/faculty ratio 11:1. 14 full-time faculty. 100% faculty teach undergrads.

ACADEMICS
Degrees: Bachelor's, master's. **Academic Requirements:** Students must have breadth and depth to their study as well as having to be able to show competency in several areas according to our degree criteria. **Classes:** Most classes have fewer than 10 students. **Majors with Highest Enrollment:** Education, liberal arts and sciences/liberal studies, psychology. **Disciplines with Highest Percentage of Degrees Awarded:** Liberal arts/general studies 51%, English 7%, health professions and related sciences 2%. **Special Study Options:** Cooperative education program, distance learning, double major, exchange student program (domestic), external degree program, independent study, internships, student-designed major, study abroad, teacher certification program.

FACILITIES
Housing: Coed dorms, men's dorms, cooperative housing, students-designated theme dorms. **Special Academic Facilities/Equipment:** Photography lab, radio station. **Computers:** 95% of public computers are PCs, 5% of public computers are Macs, network access in dorm rooms, network access in dorm lounges, remote student-access to Web through college's connection.

CAMPUS LIFE
Activities: Dance, drama/theater, jazz band, literary magazine, music ensembles, radio station, student government, student newspaper.

ADMISSIONS
Freshman Academic Profile: 7% in top 10% of high school class, 27% in top 25% of high school class, 63% in top 50% of high school class. 93% from public high schools. SAT Math middle 50% range 480–590. SAT Critical Reading middle 50% range 550–680. ACT middle 50% range 19–27. TOEFL required of all international applicants, minimum paper TOEFL 550. **Basis for Candidate Selection:** *Very important factors considered include:* Application essay, character/personal qualities, interview. *Important factors considered include:* Talent/ability, volunteer work, work experience. *Other factors considered include:* Class rank, extracurricular activities, recommendation(s), rigor of secondary school record, standardized test scores. **Freshman Admission Requirements:** High school diploma is required, and GED is accepted. **Freshman Admission Statistics:** 128 applied, 93% admitted, 40% enrolled. **Transfer Admission Requirements:** High school transcript, college

transcript(s), essay or personal statement, interview. Lowest grade transferable C-. **General Admission Information:** Application fee $40. Regular notification rolling. Nonfall registration accepted. Admission may be deferred for a maximum of 1 year. Common Application not accepted. Credit offered for CEEB Advanced Placement tests.

COSTS AND FINANCIAL AID
Annual tuition $17,840. Room & board $2,964. Required fees $252. Average book expense $508. **Required Forms and Deadlines:** FAFSA. Financial aid filing deadline 3/1. **Types of Aid:** *Need-based scholarships/grants:* Pell, SEOG, state scholarships/grants, private scholarships, the school's own gift aid. *Loans:* FFEL Subsidized Stafford, FFEL Unsubsidized Stafford, FFEL PLUS, Federal Perkins, college/university loans from institutional funds. **Student Employment:** Federal Work-Study Program available. Off-campus job opportunities are fair. **Financial Aid Statistics:** 90% freshmen, 78% undergrads receive need-based scholarship or grant aid. 90% freshmen, 84% undergrads receive need-based self-help aid.

GOLDEN GATE UNIVERSITY

536 Mission Street, San Francisco, CA 94105
Phone: 415-442-7800 **E-mail:** info@ggu.edu **CEEB Code:** 4329
Fax: 415-442-7807 **Website:** www.ggu.edu **ACT Code:** 0278
Financial Aid Phone: 415-442-7270

This private school was founded in 1901.

RATINGS
Admissions Selectivity Rating: 60*   **Fire Safety Rating:** 60*   **Green Rating:** 60*

STUDENTS AND FACULTY
Enrollment: 513. **Student Body:** 53% female, 47% male. **Retention and Graduation:** 26% freshmen graduate within 4 years. 15% grads go on to further study within 1 year. 30% grads pursue business degrees. **Faculty:** Student/faculty ratio 14:1. 95 full-time faculty, 98% hold PhDs. 100% faculty teach undergrads.

ACADEMICS
Degrees: Bachelor's, certificate, doctoral, first professional, master's, post-bachelor's certificate, post-master's certificate. **Academic Requirements:** Arts/fine arts, computer literacy, English (including composition), history, humanities, mathematics, philosophy, sciences (biological or physical), social science. **Classes:** Most classes have 20–29 students. **Disciplines with Highest Percentage of Degrees Awarded:** Business/marketing 67%, computer and information sciences 27%, liberal arts/general studies 2%. **Special Study Options:** Accelerated program, cooperative education program, distance learning, dual enrollment, English as a second language (ESL), independent study, internships, weekend college.

FACILITIES
Computers: 80% of public computers are PCs, 20% of public computers are Macs, online registration, online administrative functions (other than registration).

CAMPUS LIFE
Activities: Student government, student newspaper. **Organizations:** 16 registered organizations, 5 honor societies.

ADMISSIONS
Freshman Academic Profile: TOEFL required of all international applicants, minimum paper TOEFL 525, minimum computer TOEFL 197. **Basis for Candidate Selection:** *Very important factors considered include:* Rigor of secondary school record. *Other factors considered include:* Application essay, class rank, recommendation(s), standardized test scores. **Freshman Admission Requirements:** High school diploma is required, and GED is accepted. *Academic units recommended:* 4 English, 3 math, 2 science (1 science lab), 2 foreign language, 1 social studies, 1 history. **Freshman Admission Statistics:** 19 applied, 100% admitted, 53% enrolled. **Transfer Admission Requirements:** College transcript(s). Minimum college GPA of 2.0 required. Lowest grade transferable C-. **General Admission Information:** Application fee $55. Regular notification is rolling. Nonfall registration accepted. Admission may be deferred for a maximum of 1 year. Credit offered for CEEB Advanced Placement tests.

COSTS AND FINANCIAL AID
Annual tuition $16,200. Average book expense $1,200. **Required Forms and Deadlines:** FAFSA, institution's own financial aid form. **Notification of**

Awards: Applicants will be notified of awards on a rolling basis beginning on or about 4/1. **Types of Aid:** *Need-based scholarships/grants:* Pell, SEOG, the school's own gift aid. *Loans:* Direct Subsidized Stafford, Direct Unsubsidized Stafford, Federal Perkins, state loans. **Student Employment:** Federal Work-Study Program available. Institutional employment available. Off-campus job opportunities are good. **Financial Aid Statistics:** 8% freshmen, 37% undergrads receive need-based scholarship or grant aid. 17% freshmen, 51% undergrads receive need-based self-help aid. Highest amount earned per year from on-campus jobs $2,480.

GOLDEY-BEACOM COLLEGE

4701 Limestone Road, Wilmington, DE 19808
Phone: 302-998-8814 **E-mail:** admissions@gbc.edu **CEEB Code:** 5255
Fax: 302-996-5408 **Website:** www.goldey.gbc.edu
Financial Aid Phone: 302-998-8814

This private school was founded in 1886. It has a 27-acre campus.

RATINGS
Admissions Selectivity Rating: 72   **Fire Safety Rating:** 60*   **Green Rating:** 60*

STUDENTS AND FACULTY
Enrollment: 385. **Student Body:** 8% international (60 countries represented). African American 6%, Asian 2%, Caucasian 64%, Hispanic 2%. **Retention and Graduation:** 5% grads go on to further study within 1 year. 4% grads pursue business degrees. 1% grads pursue law degrees.

ACADEMICS
Degrees: Associate, bachelor's, master's. **Academic Requirements:** Computer literacy, English (including composition), humanities, mathematics, philosophy, social science. **Special Study Options:** Accelerated program, cooperative education program, distance learning, independent study, internships.

FACILITIES
Housing: Coed dorms, apartments for single students, fraternity/sorority housing.

CAMPUS LIFE
Activities: Drama/theater, student government, student newspaper. **Organizations:** 4 religious organizations. **Athletics (Intercollegiate):** *Men:* Soccer, softball. *Women:* Softball.

ADMISSIONS
Freshman Academic Profile: 12% in top 10% of high school class, 27% in top 25% of high school class, 81% in top 50% of high school class. 90% from public high schools. SAT Math middle 50% range 440–593. SAT Critical Reading middle 50% range 400–512. TOEFL required of all international applicants, minimum paper TOEFL 500. **Basis for Candidate Selection:** *Very important factors considered include:* Rigor of secondary school record, standardized test scores. *Important factors considered include:* Class rank, recommendation(s). *Other factors considered include:* Character/personal qualities, interview. **Freshman Admission Requirements:** High school diploma is required, and GED is accepted. *Academic units required:* 4 English, 3 math, 3 science. *Academic units recommended:* 4 English, 3 math, 3 science. **Freshman Admission Statistics:** 689 applied, 77% admitted, 56% enrolled. **Transfer Admission Requirements:** High school transcript, college transcript(s). Minimum college GPA of 2.0 required. Lowest grade transferable 2.0. **General Admission Information:** Application fee $30. Regular application deadline 8/15. Regular notification is rolling. Nonfall registration accepted. Admission may be deferred for a maximum of 1 year. Common Application accepted. Credit and/or placement offered for CEEB Advanced Placement tests.

COSTS AND FINANCIAL AID
Annual tuition $12,928. Room & board $4,240. Required fees $120. Average book expense $700. **Types of Aid:** *Need-based scholarships/grants:* Pell, SEOG, state scholarships/grants, private scholarships, the school's own gift aid. *Loans:* FFEL Subsidized Stafford, FFEL Unsubsidized Stafford, FFEL PLUS, Federal Perkins, state loans, college/university loans from institutional funds. **Student Employment:** Federal Work-Study Program available. Off-campus job opportunities are excellent.

GONZAGA UNIVERSITY

502 East Boone Avenue, Spokane, WA 99258
Phone: 509-323-6572 **E-mail:** admissions@gonzaga.edu **CEEB Code:** 4330
Fax: 509-324-5780 **Website:** www.gonzaga.edu **ACT Code:** 4458
Financial Aid Phone: 509-323-6582

This private school, affiliated with the Roman Catholic Church, was founded in 1887. It has a 108-acre campus.

RATINGS
Admissions Selectivity Rating: 89   **Fire Safety Rating:** 89   **Green Rating:** 60*

STUDENTS AND FACULTY
Enrollment: 4,186. **Student Body:** 54% female, 46% male, 50% out-of-state, 1% international (36 countries represented). African American 1%, Asian 6%, Caucasian 78%, Hispanic 4%, Native American 1%. **Retention and Graduation:** 92% freshmen return for sophomore year. 67% freshmen graduate within 4 years. 30% grads go on to further study within 1 year. 20% grads pursue arts and sciences degrees. 15% grads pursue business degrees. 5% grads pursue law degrees. 1% grads pursue medical degrees. **Faculty:** Student/faculty ratio 12:1. 335 full-time faculty, 87% hold PhDs. 94% faculty teach undergrads.

ACADEMICS
Degrees: Bachelor's, doctoral, first professional, master's. **Academic Requirements:** English (including composition), history, humanities, mathematics, philosophy, sciences (biological or physical), social science. **Classes:** Most classes have 20–29 students. Most lab/discussion sections have 10–19 students. **Majors with Highest Enrollment:** Business/commerce, political science and government, psychology. **Disciplines with Highest Percentage of Degrees Awarded:** Business/marketing 25%, communications/journalism 10%, engineering 10%, social sciences 10%, psychology 7%, biological/life sciences 6%. **Special Study Options:** Accelerated program, double major, English as a second language (ESL), exchange student program (domestic), honors program, internships, study abroad, teacher certification program, weekend college.

FACILITIES
Housing: Coed dorms, men's dorms, women's dorms, apartments for married students, apartments for single students, special housing for disabled students, special housing for international students. **Special Academic Facilities/Equipment:** Art center, museum, language lab, TV production center, educational center, 2 electron microscopes. **Computers:** 5% of classrooms are wired, 25% of classrooms are wireless, 75% of public computers are PCs, 25% of public computers are Macs, network access in dorm rooms, online registration, online administrative functions (other than registration), remote student-access to Web through college's connection.

CAMPUS LIFE
Activities: Choral groups, concert band, dance, drama/theater, jazz band, literary magazine, music ensembles, radio station, student government, student newspaper, symphony orchestra, television station, yearbook. **Organizations:** 86 registered organizations, 10 honor societies, 4 religious organizations. **Athletics (Intercollegiate):** *Men:* Baseball, basketball, crew/rowing, cross-country, golf, soccer, tennis, track/field (outdoor). *Women:* Basketball, crew/rowing, cross-country, golf, soccer, tennis, track/field (outdoor), volleyball.

ADMISSIONS
Freshman Academic Profile: 44% in top 10% of high school class, 79% in top 25% of high school class, 97% in top 50% of high school class. 65% from public high schools. SAT Math middle 50% range 540–650. SAT Critical Reading middle 50% range 530–640. ACT middle 50% range 24–29. TOEFL required of all international applicants, minimum paper TOEFL 550, minimum computer TOEFL 213. **Basis for Candidate Selection:** *Very important factors considered include:* Academic GPA, character/personal qualities, first generation, rigor of secondary school record. *Important factors considered include:* Application essay, class rank, extracurricular activities, recommendation(s), standardized test scores, talent/ability. *Other factors considered include:* Alumni/ae relation, interview, level of applicant's interest, racial/ethnic status, volunteer work, work experience. **Freshman Admission Requirements:** High school diploma is required, and GED is not accepted. *Academic units required:* 4 English, 3 math, 3 science (3 science labs), 3 foreign language, 2 social studies, 2 history, 2 academic electives. *Academic units*

recommended: 4 English, 4 math, 4 science (4 science labs), 4 foreign language, 3 social studies, 3 history, 3 academic electives. **Freshman Admission Statistics:** 4,965 applied, 67% admitted, 29% enrolled. **Transfer Admission Requirements:** College transcript(s), essay or personal statement, statement of good standing from prior institution(s). Minimum college GPA of 2.7 required. Lowest grade transferable C. **General Admission Information:** Application fee $45. Regular application deadline 2/1. Regular notification 3/15. Nonfall registration accepted. Admission may be deferred for a maximum of 1 year. Credit and/or placement offered for CEEB Advanced Placement tests.

COSTS AND FINANCIAL AID

Annual tuition $26,120. Room and board $7,520. Required fees $438. Average book expense $900. **Required Forms and Deadlines:** FAFSA. Financial aid filing deadline 2/1. **Notification of Awards:** Applicants will be notified of awards on a rolling basis beginning on or about 3/1. **Types of Aid:** *Need-based scholarships/grants:* Pell, SEOG, state scholarships/grants, private scholarships, the school's own gift aid, United Negro College Fund, Federal Nursing Scholarships. *Loans:* FFEL Subsidized Stafford, FFEL Unsubsidized Stafford, FFEL PLUS, Federal Perkins, Federal Nursing, state loans, college/university loans from institutional funds. **Student Employment:** Federal Work-Study Program available. Institutional employment available. Off-campus job opportunities are excellent. **Financial Aid Statistics:** 57% freshmen, 59% undergrads receive need-based scholarship or grant aid. 37% freshmen, 46% undergrads receive need-based self-help aid. 23 freshmen, 147 undergrads receive athletic scholarships. 96% freshmen, 97% undergrads receive any aid. Highest amount earned per year from on-campus jobs $2,900.

See page 1182.

GORDON COLLEGE

255 Grapevine Road, Wenham, MA 01984-1899
Phone: 978-867-4218 **E-mail:** admissions@gordon.edu **CEEB Code:** 3417
Fax: 978-867-4682 **Website:** www.gordon.edu **ACT Code:** 1838
Financial Aid Phone: 978-867-4246

This private school, affiliated with the Protestant Church, was founded in 1889. It has a 500-acre campus.

RATINGS

Admissions Selectivity Rating: 86 | **Fire Safety Rating:** 85 | **Green Rating:** 60*

STUDENTS AND FACULTY

Enrollment: 1,523. **Student Body:** 64% female, 36% male, 71% out-of-state, 2% international (23 countries represented). African American 2%, Asian 2%, Caucasian 88%, Hispanic 3%. **Retention and Graduation:** 84% freshmen return for sophomore year. 61% freshmen graduate within 4 years. 19% grads go on to further study within 1 year. **Faculty:** Student/faculty ratio 14:1. 97 full-time faculty, 82% hold PhDs. 100% faculty teach undergrads.

ACADEMICS

Degrees: Bachelor's, master's. **Academic Requirements:** Arts/fine arts, English (including composition), foreign languages, history, humanities, Old Testament and New Testament courses, philosophy, sciences (biological or physical), social science, Christianity, character and culture. **Classes:** Most classes have 10–19 students. Most lab/discussion sections have 10–19 students. **Majors with Highest Enrollment:** Business administration/management, English language and literature, psychology. **Disciplines with Highest Percentage of Degrees Awarded:** Psychology 10%, philosophy and religious studies 9%, English 9%, education 9%, visual and performing arts 8%, business/marketing 8%, communications/journalism 7%, biological/life sciences 7%, history 7%, foreign languages and literature 5%. **Special Study Options:** Cooperative education program, cross-registration, double major, honors program, independent study, internships, liberal arts/career combination, student-designed major, study abroad, teacher certification program. Gordon-at-Oxford University, England; Gordon-in-France; Italian Semester in Orvieto, Italy; Oregon Extension, LaVida Wilderness Expedition, Boston Urban Semester. Co-op programs also available in arts, business, computer science, education, engineering, health professions, humanities, natural science, social/behavioral science.

FACILITIES

Housing: Coed dorms, men's dorms, apartments for married students, apartments for single students, special housing for disabled students, international hall, mentoring hall, theme houses. Dorms are coed by floors and/or wings. **Special Academic Facilities/Equipment:** Barrington Center for the Arts, Phillips Music Center, Center for Balance and Mobility, electron microscope, gene sequencer, papers of British statesman/reformer William

Wilberforce; East-West Institute, Center for Student Leadership, Center for Christian Studies, international office for Christians in the Visual Arts (CIVA). **Computers:** 3% of classrooms are wired, 10% of classrooms are wireless, 80% of public computers are PCs, 20% of public computers are Macs, network access in dorm rooms, network access in dorm lounges, online administrative functions (other than registration), support for handheld computing, remote student-access to Web through college's connection.

CAMPUS LIFE

Activities: Choral groups, concert band, drama/theater, jazz band, literary magazine, music ensembles, musical theater, student government, student newspaper, student-run film society, symphony orchestra, yearbook. **Organizations:** 35 registered organizations, 17 honor societies, 15 religious organizations. **Athletics (Intercollegiate):** *Men:* Baseball, basketball, cross-country, lacrosse, soccer, swimming, tennis, track/field (indoor), track/field (outdoor). *Women:* Basketball, cross-country, field hockey, lacrosse, soccer, softball, swimming, tennis, track/field (indoor), track/field (outdoor), volleyball.

ADMISSIONS

Freshman Academic Profile: 34% in top 10% of high school class, 60% in top 25% of high school class, 88% in top 50% of high school class. 70% from public high schools. SAT Math middle 50% range 530–640. SAT Critical Reading middle 50% range 540–650. SAT Writing middle 50% range 540–640. ACT middle 50% range 23–28. TOEFL required of all international applicants, minimum paper TOEFL 550, minimum computer TOEFL 213. **Basis for Candidate Selection:** *Very important factors considered include:* Application essay, character/personal qualities, class rank, extracurricular activities, interview, recommendation(s), religious affiliation/commitment, rigor of secondary school record, standardized test scores. *Important factors considered include:* Academic GPA, talent/ability. *Other factors considered include:* Alumni/ae relation, racial/ethnic status, volunteer work, work experience. **Freshman Admission Requirements:** High school diploma is required, and GED is accepted. *Academic units required:* 4 English, 2 math, 2 science (1 science lab), 2 foreign language, 2 social studies, 5 academic electives. *Academic units recommended:* 3 math, 3 science (3 science labs), 4 foreign language, 3 social studies. **Freshman Admission Statistics:** 986 applied, 83% admitted, 47% enrolled. **Transfer Admission Requirements:** College transcript(s), essay or personal statement, interview, statement of good standing from prior institution(s). Minimum college GPA of 2.0 required. Lowest grade transferable C. **General Admission Information:** Application fee $50. Early decision application deadline 11/15. Regular notification is rolling. Nonfall registration accepted. Admission may be deferred for a maximum of 1 year. Credit offered for CEEB Advanced Placement tests.

COSTS AND FINANCIAL AID

Annual tuition $24,652. Room and board $6,906. Required fees $1,096. Average book expense $800. **Required Forms and Deadlines:** FAFSA, CSS/Financial Aid PROFILE, state aid form. Financial aid filing deadline 3/1. **Notification of Awards:** Applicants will be notified of awards on a rolling basis beginning on or about 4/15. **Types of Aid:** *Need-based scholarships/grants:* Pell, SEOG, state scholarships/grants, private scholarships, the school's own gift aid. *Loans:* FFEL Subsidized Stafford, FFEL Unsubsidized Stafford, FFEL PLUS, Federal Perkins, state loans, college/university loans from institutional funds. **Student Employment:** Federal Work-Study Program available. Off-campus job opportunities are good. **Financial Aid Statistics:** 51% freshmen, 65% undergrads receive need-based scholarship or grant aid. 41% freshmen, 57% undergrads receive need-based self-help aid. 93% freshmen, 90% undergrads receive any aid. Highest amount earned per year from on-campus jobs $1,500.

GOSHEN COLLEGE

1700 South Main Street, Goshen, IN 46526-4794
Phone: 574-535-7535 **E-mail:** admission@goshen.edu **CEEB Code:** 1251
Fax: 574-535-7609 **Website:** www.goshen.edu **ACT Code:** 1196
Financial Aid Phone: 574-535-7525

This private school, affiliated with the Mennonite Church, was founded in 1894. It has a 135-acre campus.

RATINGS

Admissions Selectivity Rating: 85 | **Fire Safety Rating:** 98 | **Green Rating:** 75

STUDENTS AND FACULTY

Enrollment: 951. **Student Body:** 60% female, 40% male, 55% out-of-state, 7% international (27 countries represented). African American 3%, Asian 1%, Caucasian 82%, Hispanic 5%. **Retention and Graduation:** 84% freshmen return for sophomore year. 44% freshmen graduate within 4 years. 18% grads go on to further study within 1 year. 9% grads pursue arts and sciences degrees. 2% grads pursue business degrees. 1% grads pursue law degrees. 3% grads pursue medical degrees. **Faculty:** Student/faculty ratio 12:1. 64 full-time faculty, 73% hold PhDs. 100% faculty teach undergrads.

ACADEMICS

Degrees: Bachelor's, certificate, master's. **Academic Requirements:** Arts/fine arts, Bible and religion, English (including composition), foreign languages, history, humanities, international education, mathematics, philosophy, sciences (biological or physical), social science. **Classes:** Most classes have 10–19 students. Most lab/discussion sections have 10–19 students. **Majors with Highest Enrollment:** Business administration/management, elementary education and teaching, nursing/registered nurse training (RN, ASN, BSN, MSN). **Disciplines with Highest Percentage of Degrees Awarded:** Business/marketing 19%, education 9%, visual and performing arts 8%, communications/journalism 6%, interdisciplinary studies 6%, history 5%. **Special Study Options:** Adult degree completion program (1 evening per week, concentrated study), cross-registration, double major, dual enrollment, independent study, internships, liberal arts/career combination, student-designed major, study abroad, teacher certification program.

FACILITIES

Housing: Coed dorms, men's dorms, women's dorms, apartments for single students, special housing for disabled students. **Special Academic Facilities/Equipment:** X-ray precision lab, lab kindergarten, historical library. **Computers:** 90% of classrooms are wireless, 85% of public computers are PCs, 15% of public computers are Macs, network access in dorm rooms, network access in dorm lounges, online registration, online administrative functions (other than registration), support for handheld computing, remote student-access to Web through college's connection.

CAMPUS LIFE

Activities: Choral groups, concert band, drama/theater, jazz band, music ensembles, musical theater, opera, radio station, student government, student newspaper, student-run film society, symphony orchestra, yearbook. **Organizations:** 21 registered organizations, 4 religious organizations. **Athletics (Intercollegiate):** *Men:* Baseball, basketball, cross-country, golf, soccer, tennis, track/field (indoor), track/field (outdoor). *Women:* Basketball, cross-country, soccer, softball, tennis, track/field (indoor), track/field (outdoor), volleyball. **Environmental initiatives:** Built the first Platinum LEED Certified facility in Indiana at Merry Lea Environmental Center. Signing the President's Climate Commitment and the formation of the Ecological Stewardship Committee. Have reduced campus wide gas use by 31% and electric use by 17% over the last six years during a time when actual square footage of buildings increased by 20%.

ADMISSIONS

Freshman Academic Profile: 30% in top 10% of high school class, 60% in top 25% of high school class, 88% in top 50% of high school class. 73% from public high schools. SAT Math middle 50% range 500–650. SAT Critical Reading middle 50% range 510–640. SAT Writing middle 50% range 480–630. ACT middle 50% range 22–28. TOEFL required of all international applicants, minimum paper TOEFL 550, minimum computer TOEFL 213. **Basis for Candidate Selection:** *Very important factors considered include:* Recommendation(s), rigor of secondary school record, standardized test scores. *Important factors considered include:* Character/personal qualities, class rank, interview. *Other factors considered include:* Alumni/ae relation, application essay, extracurricular activities, talent/ability, volunteer work, work experience. **Freshman Admission Requirements:** High school diploma is required, and GED is accepted. *Academic units required:* 4 English, 2 math, 2 science, 2 foreign language, 2 social studies, 2 history. *Academic units recommended:* 4 English, 3 math, 3 science, 2 foreign language, 2 social studies, 2 history. **Freshman Admission Statistics:** 586 applied, 76% admitted, 47% enrolled. **Transfer Admission Requirements:** High school transcript, college transcript(s), essay or personal statement. Lowest grade transferable C. **General Admission Information:** Application fee $25. Regular application deadline 8/1. Regular notification is rolling. Nonfall registration accepted. Admission may be deferred for a maximum of 1 year. Credit and/or placement offered for CEEB Advanced Placement tests.

COSTS AND FINANCIAL AID

Annual tuition $21,300. Room & board $7,000. Average book expense $800. **Required Forms and Deadlines:** FAFSA, institution's own financial aid form. Financial aid filing deadline 2/1. **Notification of Awards:** Applicants will be notified of awards on a rolling basis beginning on or about 3/1. **Types of Aid:** *Need-based scholarships/grants:* Pell, SEOG, state scholarships/grants, private scholarships, the school's own gift aid. *Loans:* Direct Subsidized Stafford, Direct Unsubsidized Stafford, Direct PLUS, Federal Perkins, Federal Nursing, college/university loans from institutional funds. **Financial Aid Statistics:** 77% freshmen, 73% undergrads receive need-based scholarship or grant aid. 60% freshmen, 55% undergrads receive need-based self-help aid. 13 freshmen, 22 undergrads receive athletic scholarships. 100% freshmen, 99% undergrads receive any aid. Highest amount earned per year from on-campus jobs $1,001.

GOUCHER COLLEGE

1021 Dulaney Valley Road, Baltimore, MD 21204-2794
Phone: 410-337-6100 **E-mail:** admissions@goucher.edu **CEEB Code:** 5257
Fax: 410-337-6354 **Website:** www.goucher.edu **ACT Code:** 1696
Financial Aid Phone: 410-337-6141

This private school was founded in 1885. It has a 287-acre campus.

RATINGS

Admissions Selectivity Rating: 85   **Fire Safety Rating:** 80   **Green Rating:** 97

STUDENTS AND FACULTY

Enrollment: 1,414. **Student Body:** 66% female, 34% male, 70% out-of-state. African American 4%, Asian 3%, Caucasian 69%, Hispanic 3%. **Retention and Graduation:** 82% freshmen return for sophomore year. 62% freshmen graduate within 4 years. **Faculty:** Student/faculty ratio 9:1. 133 full-time faculty, 80% hold PhDs. 100% faculty teach undergrads.

ACADEMICS

Degrees: Bachelor's, master's, post-bachelor's certificate. **Academic Requirements:** Arts/fine arts, computer literacy, English (including composition), foreign languages, humanities, mathematics, sciences (biological or physical), social science. **Classes:** Most classes have 10–19 students. **Majors with Highest Enrollment:** English language and literature, mass communications/media studies, psychology. **Disciplines with Highest Percentage of Degrees Awarded:** Visual and performing arts 19%, social sciences 17%, psychology 13%, communications/journalism 10%, English 7%. **Special Study Options:** Cross-registration, distance learning, double major, dual enrollment, independent study, internships, student-designed major, study abroad, teacher certification program.

FACILITIES

Housing: Coed dorms, women's dorms, apartments for single students, special housing for disabled students, healthy living. **Special Academic Facilities/Equipment:** Rosenberg Gallery; Mildred Dunnock Theatre; Center for Teaching, Learning, and Technology; Thorman International Center; Todd Dance Studio; Pilates studio; NMR facility; scientific visualization lab; Kraushaar Auditorium; sports and recreation center. **Computers:** 5% of classrooms are wired, 95% of classrooms are wireless, 86% of public computers are PCs, 14% of public computers are Macs, network access in dorm rooms, network access in dorm lounges, online administrative functions (other than registration), support for handheld computing, remote student-access to Web through college's connection.

CAMPUS LIFE

Activities: Choral groups, dance, drama/theater, jazz band, literary magazine, music ensembles, opera, radio station, student government, student newspaper, student-run film society, symphony orchestra, television station, yearbook. **Organizations:** 70 registered organizations, 1 honor society, 8 religious organizations. **Athletics (Intercollegiate):** *Men:* Basketball, cross-country, equestrian sports, lacrosse, soccer, swimming, tennis, track/field (indoor), track/field (outdoor). *Women:* Basketball, cross-country, equestrian sports, field hockey, lacrosse, soccer, swimming, tennis, track/field (indoor), track/field (outdoor), volleyball. **Environmental initiatives:** Building newest bulding, the Athenaeum, to be LEED certified, and committing that future buildings will also be certified. Signing the American College and University Presidents Climate Commitment. Creating the Goucher Environmental Sustainability Advisory Council The council will research and explore solutions to the environmental issues raised by members of the Goucher Community and report its findings to the president. It will help implement Campus environmental programs and monitor the college's progress in fulfilling the requirements of the climate commitment.

ADMISSIONS

Freshman Academic Profile: 28% in top 10% of high school class, 60% in top 25% of high school class, 93% in top 50% of high school class. 67% from public high schools. SAT Math middle 50% range 510–620. SAT Critical Reading middle 50% range 540–670. SAT Writing middle 50% range 540–650. TOEFL required of all international applicants, minimum paper TOEFL 550, minimum computer TOEFL 230. **Basis for Candidate Selection:** *Very important factors considered include:* Academic GPA, rigor of secondary school record. *Important factors considered include:* Application essay, recommendation(s), standardized test scores, talent/ability. *Other factors considered include:* Alumni/ae relation, character/personal qualities, class rank, extracurricular activities, first generation, interview, level of applicant's interest, racial/ethnic status, volunteer work, work experience. **Freshman Admission Requirements:** High school diploma is required, and GED is accepted. *Academic units required:* 4 English, 3 math, 2 science, 2 foreign language, 3 social studies, 2 academic electives. *Academic units recommended:* 4 English, 4 math, 3 science, 4 foreign language, 3 social studies, 2 academic electives. **Freshman Admission Statistics:** 3,171 applied, 70% admitted, 20% enrolled. **Transfer Admission Requirements:** College transcript(s), essay or personal statement. Minimum college GPA of 2.5 required. Lowest grade transferable C. **General Admission Information:** Application fee $40. Regular application deadline 2/1. Regular notification 4/1. Nonfall registration accepted. Admission may be deferred for a maximum of 1 year. Credit and/or placement offered for CEEB Advanced Placement tests.

COSTS AND FINANCIAL AID

Annual tuition $30,363. Room and board $9,478. Required fees $446. Average book expense $800. **Required Forms and Deadlines:** FAFSA, CSS/Financial Aid PROFILE, Noncustodial PROFILE, Business/Farm Supplement. Financial aid filing deadline 2/15. **Notification of Awards:** Applicants will be notified of awards on or about 4/1. **Types of Aid:** *Need-based scholarships/grants:* Pell, SEOG, state scholarships/grants, private scholarships, the school's own gift aid. *Loans:* FFEL Subsidized Stafford, FFEL Unsubsidized Stafford, FFEL PLUS, Federal Perkins, college/university loans from institutional funds. **Student Employment:** Federal Work-Study Program available. Institutional employment available. Off-campus job opportunities are excellent. **Financial Aid Statistics:** 47% freshmen, 52% undergrads receive need-based scholarship or grant aid. 41% freshmen, 47% undergrads receive need-based self-help aid. 81% freshmen, 86% undergrads receive any aid.

See page 1184.

GOVERNORS STATE UNIVERSITY

1 University Parkway, University Park, IL 60466
Phone: 708-534-4490 **E-mail:** gsunow@govst.edu
Fax: 708-534-1640 **Website:** www.govst.edu
Financial Aid Phone: 708-534-4480

This public school was founded in 1969. It has a 720-acre campus.

RATINGS
Admissions Selectivity Rating: 60*   **Fire Safety Rating:** 60*   **Green Rating:** 60*

STUDENTS AND FACULTY
Enrollment: 2,632. **Student Body:** 3% out-of-state, 1% international (17 countries represented). African American 34%, Asian 2%, Caucasian 52%, Hispanic 6%. **Retention and Graduation:** 34% grads go on to further study within 1 year. 17% grads pursue arts and sciences degrees. 16% grads pursue business degrees. 1% grads pursue law degrees. **Faculty:** Student/faculty ratio 16:1. 203 full-time faculty, 80% hold PhDs. 90% faculty teach undergrads.

ACADEMICS
Degrees: Bachelor's, doctoral, master's. **Academic Requirements:** Arts/fine arts, English (including composition), humanities, mathematics, sciences (biological or physical), social science. **Majors with Highest Enrollment:** Business administration/management, communications and media studies, elementary education and teaching. **Disciplines with Highest Percentage of Degrees Awarded:** Education 19%, liberal arts/general studies 15%, business/marketing 14%, health professions and related sciences 13%. **Special Study Options:** Cross-registration, distance learning, dual enrollment, external degree program, honors program, independent study, internships, student-designed major, study abroad, teacher certification program.

FACILITIES
Special Academic Facilities/Equipment: Manilow Sculpture Park. **Computers:** 100% of public computers are PCs, online registration, online administrative functions (other than registration), remote student-access to Web through college's connection.

CAMPUS LIFE
Activities: Drama/theater, literary magazine, student government, student newspaper, student-run film society. **Organizations:** 7 honor societies.

ADMISSIONS
Transfer Admission Requirements: College transcript(s), statement of good standing from prior institution(s). Minimum college GPA of 2.0 required.

Lowest grade transferable C. **General Admission Information:** Nonfall registration not accepted. Common Application not accepted.

COSTS AND FINANCIAL AID

Annual in-state tuition $4,470. Out-of-state tuition $13,410. Required fees $480. **Types of Aid:** *Need-based scholarships/grants:* Pell, SEOG, state scholarships/grants, private scholarships, the school's own gift aid, Federal Nursing Scholarships. *Loans:* Direct Subsidized Stafford, Federal Perkins, Federal Nursing, state loans, college/university loans from institutional funds. **Student Employment:** Federal Work-Study Program available. Institutional employment available.

GRACE COLLEGE AND SEMINARY

200 Seminary Drive, Winona Lake, IN 46590
Phone: 800-544-7223 **E-mail:** enroll@grace.edu **CEEB Code:** 1252
Fax: 574-372-5120 **Website:** www.grace.edu **ACT Code:** 1198
Financial Aid Phone: 574-372-5100

This private school, affiliated with the Fellowship of Grace Brethren Churches, was founded in 1948. It has a 150-acre campus.

RATINGS
Admissions Selectivity Rating: 83   **Fire Safety Rating:** 60*   **Green Rating:** 60*

STUDENTS AND FACULTY
Enrollment: 1,062. **Student Body:** 45% female, 55% male. African American 10%, Caucasian 86%, Hispanic 2%. **Retention and Graduation:** 73% freshmen return for sophomore year. 58% freshmen graduate within 4 years. **Faculty:** Student/faculty ratio 16:1. 43 full-time faculty, 70% hold PhDs. 100% faculty teach undergrads.

ACADEMICS
Degrees: Associate, bachelor's, certificate, diploma, doctoral, first professional, master's. **Academic Requirements:** Arts/fine arts, biblical studies, English (including composition), history, humanities, mathematics, philosophy, sciences (biological or physical), social science. **Classes:** Most classes have 10–19 students. Most lab/discussion sections have 10–19 students. **Majors with Highest Enrollment:** Business administration/management, counseling psychology, elementary education and teaching. **Disciplines with Highest Percentage of Degrees Awarded:** Business/marketing 22%, education 17%, psychology 15%, communication technologies 7%, visual and performing arts 5%. **Special Study Options:** Cooperative education program, cross-registration, distance learning, double major, dual enrollment, exchange student program (domestic), honors program, independent study, internships, liberal arts/career combination, study abroad, teacher certification program.

FACILITIES
Housing: Men's dorms, women's dorms, apartments for single students. **Special Academic Facilities/Equipment:** Westminster Museum. **Computers:** 100% of public computers are PCs, network access in dorm rooms, network access in dorm lounges, online registration, online administrative functions (other than registration), remote student-access to Web through college's connection.

CAMPUS LIFE
Activities: Choral groups, concert band, drama/theater, music ensembles, musical theater, opera, student government, student newspaper, symphony orchestra, yearbook. **Organizations:** 9 registered organizations, 1 honor society, 8 religious organizations. **Athletics (Intercollegiate):** *Men:* Baseball, basketball, cheerleading, cross-country, golf, soccer, tennis, track/field (outdoor). *Women:* Basketball, cheerleading, cross-country, soccer, softball, tennis, track/field (outdoor), volleyball.

ADMISSIONS
Freshman Academic Profile: 24% in top 10% of high school class, 53% in top 25% of high school class, 76% in top 50% of high school class. 71% from public high schools. SAT Math middle 50% range 465–595. SAT Critical Reading middle 50% range 460–496. ACT middle 50% range 21–28. **Basis for Candidate Selection:** *Very important factors considered include:* Application essay, recommendation(s), religious affiliation/commitment, rigor of secondary school record, standardized test scores. *Important factors considered include:* Academic GPA, character/personal qualities. *Other factors considered include:* Alumni/ae relation, class rank, extracurricular activities, interview, talent/ability. **Freshman Admission Requirements:** High school diploma is required, and GED is accepted. *Academic units recommended:* 4 English, 2 math, 2 science (1 science lab), 2 foreign language, 2 social studies, 1 history. **Freshman Admission Statistics:** 837 applied, 73% admitted, 36% enrolled. **Transfer

Admission Requirements: College transcript(s), essay or personal statement, standardized test score. Minimum college GPA of 2.0 required. Lowest grade transferable C-. **General Admission Information:** Application fee $20. Regular application deadline 8/15. Regular notification is rolling. Nonfall registration accepted. Admission may be deferred for a maximum of 1 semester. Common Application not accepted. Credit offered for CEEB Advanced Placement tests.

COSTS AND FINANCIAL AID

Annual tuition $18,824. Room and board $6,360. Required fees $400. Average book expense $800. **Required Forms and Deadlines:** FAFSA. Financial aid filing deadline 3/10. **Notification of Awards:** Applicants will be notified of awards on a rolling basis beginning on or about 3/1. **Types of Aid:** *Need-based scholarships/grants:* Pell, SEOG, state scholarships/grants, private scholarships, the school's own gift aid. *Loans:* FFEL Subsidized Stafford, FFEL Unsubsidized Stafford, FFEL PLUS, Federal Perkins, alternative educational loan program. **Student Employment:** Off-campus job opportunities are good. **Financial Aid Statistics:** 81% freshmen, 75% undergrads receive need-based scholarship or grant aid. 64% freshmen, 68% undergrads receive need-based self-help aid. 25 freshmen, 71 undergrads receive athletic scholarships.

GRACE UNIVERSITY

1311 South Ninth Street, Omaha, NE 68108
Phone: 402-449-2831 **E-mail:** admissions@graceu.com
Fax: 402-341-9587 **Website:** www.graceuniversity.com **ACT Code:** 2454
Financial Aid Phone: 402-449-2810

This private school, affiliated with the Christian (Nondenominational) Church, was founded in 1943. It has a 20-acre campus.

RATINGS

Admissions Selectivity Rating: 60*   **Fire Safety Rating:** 60*   **Green Rating:** 60*

STUDENTS AND FACULTY

Enrollment: 427. **Student Body:** 57% female, 43% male, 60% out-of-state. **Faculty:** Student/faculty ratio 18:1. 25 full-time faculty, 100% hold PhDs. 100% faculty teach undergrads.

ACADEMICS

Degrees: Associate, bachelor's, certificate, master's. **Academic Requirements:** Bible classes, computer literacy, English (including composition), foreign languages, humanities, mathematics, social science. **Majors with Highest Enrollment:** Bible/biblical studies, education, youth ministry. **Disciplines with Highest Percentage of Degrees Awarded:** Psychology 12%, English 4%, liberal arts/general studies 3%. **Special Study Options:** Accelerated program, cooperative education program, distance learning, double major, dual enrollment, independent study, student-designed major, study abroad, teacher certification program.

FACILITIES

Housing: Men's dorms, women's dorms, apartments for married students. **Computers:** 100% of public computers are PCs, network access in dorm rooms, online administrative functions (other than registration), remote student-access to Web through college's connection.

CAMPUS LIFE

Activities: Choral groups, concert band, drama/theater, music ensembles, musical theater, pep band, radio station, student government, student newspaper, yearbook. **Organizations:** 6 registered organizations, 1 religious organization. **Athletics (Intercollegiate):** *Men:* Basketball, soccer. *Women:* Basketball, volleyball.

ADMISSIONS

Freshman Academic Profile: TOEFL required of all international applicants, minimum paper TOEFL 550, minimum computer TOEFL 213. **Basis for Candidate Selection:** *Very important factors considered include:* Application essay, recommendation(s), religious affiliation/commitment, rigor of secondary school record. *Important factors considered include:* Character/personal qualities, class rank, standardized test scores. *Other factors considered include:* Alumni/ae relation, extracurricular activities, interview, talent/ability, volunteer work, work experience. **Freshman Admission Requirements:** High school diploma is required, and GED is accepted. *Academic units recommended:* 4 English, 4 math, 4 science, 2 foreign language, 4 social studies, 4 history. **Freshman Admission Statistics:** 341 applied, 44% admitted, 77% enrolled. **Transfer Admission Requirements:** High school transcript, college transcript(s), essay or personal statement. Minimum college GPA of 2.0 required. Lowest grade transferable C. **General Admission Information:**

Application fee $35. Nonfall registration accepted. Admission may be deferred for a maximum of 1 year. Common Application not accepted. Credit offered for CEEB Advanced Placement tests.

COSTS AND FINANCIAL AID

Annual tuition $10,500. Room & board $5,000. Required fees $180. Average book expense $800. **Required Forms and Deadlines:** FAFSA, institution's own financial aid form. Financial aid filing deadline 1/31. **Notification of Awards:** Applicants will be notified of awards on or about 4/1. **Types of Aid:** *Need-based scholarships/grants:* Pell, SEOG, state scholarships/grants, private scholarships, the school's own gift aid, United Negro College Fund. *Loans:* FFEL Subsidized Stafford, FFEL Unsubsidized Stafford, FFEL PLUS, alternative loans. **Student Employment:** Federal Work-Study Program available. Institutional employment available. Off-campus job opportunities are excellent. **Financial Aid Statistics:** 57% freshmen, 70% undergrads receive need-based scholarship or grant aid. 50% freshmen, 62% undergrads receive need-based self-help aid. 77% freshmen, 78% undergrads receive any aid. Highest amount earned per year from on-campus jobs $3,750.

GRACELAND UNIVERSITY

Graceland University, 1 University Place, Lamoni, IA 50140
Phone: 641-784-5196 **E-mail:** admissions@graceland.edu **CEEB Code:** 6249
Fax: 641-784-5480 **Website:** www.graceland.edu **ACT Code:** 1314
Financial Aid Phone: 641-784-5136

This private school, affiliated with the Community of Christ Church, was founded in 1895. It has a 169-acre campus.

RATINGS

Admissions Selectivity Rating: 78   **Fire Safety Rating:** 60*   **Green Rating:** 60*

STUDENTS AND FACULTY

Enrollment: 1,878. **Student Body:** 68% female, 32% male, 68% out-of-state, 5% international. African American 3%, Asian 2%, Caucasian 77%, Hispanic 2%. **Retention and Graduation:** 63% freshmen return for sophomore year. 27% freshmen graduate within 4 years. **Faculty:** Student/faculty ratio 16:1. 90 full-time faculty, 58% hold PhDs.

ACADEMICS

Degrees: Bachelor's, master's, post-master's certificate. **Academic Requirements:** Arts/fine arts, computer literacy, English (including composition), foreign languages, history, humanities, mathematics, philosophy, sciences (biological or physical), social science. **Classes:** Most classes have fewer than 10 students. Most lab/discussion sections have 20–29 students. **Disciplines with Highest Percentage of Degrees Awarded:** Health professions and related sciences 28%, business/marketing 21%, education 17%, liberal arts/general studies 10%, biological/life sciences 4%, psychology 4%. **Special Study Options:** Accelerated program, distance learning, double major, dual enrollment, English as a second language (ESL), external degree program, honors program, independent study, internships, liberal arts/career combination, student-designed major, study abroad, teacher certification program. Accelerated program for nursing only.

FACILITIES

Housing: Men's dorms, women's dorms, apartments for married students, students required to live on campus through their sophomore year unless married or living with relatives. **Special Academic Facilities/Equipment:** Electron microscope, cyber café. **Computers:** 85% of public computers are PCs, 35% of public computers are Macs, network access in dorm rooms, remote student-access to Web through college's connection.

CAMPUS LIFE

Activities: Choral groups, concert band, drama/theater, jazz band, marching band, music ensembles, musical theater, pep band, student government, student newspaper, symphony orchestra, yearbook. **Organizations:** 50 registered organizations, 1 religious organization. **Athletics (Intercollegiate):** *Men:* Baseball, basketball, cross-country, football, golf, soccer, tennis, track/field (indoor), track/field (outdoor), volleyball. *Women:* Basketball, cross-country, golf, soccer, softball, tennis, track/field (indoor), track/field (outdoor), volleyball.

ADMISSIONS

Freshman Academic Profile: 20% in top 10% of high school class, 41% in top 25% of high school class, 74% in top 50% of high school class. SAT Math middle 50% range 450–590. SAT Critical Reading middle 50% range 410–610. ACT middle 50% range 19–25. TOEFL required of all international applicants, minimum paper TOEFL 450. **Basis for Candidate Selection:** *Very important factors considered include:* Class rank, rigor of secondary school record, standardized test scores. *Important factors considered include:* Character/personal qualities, extracurricular activities, interview, talent/ability. *Other factors considered include:* Racial/ethnic status, recommendation(s). **Freshman Admission Requirements:** High school diploma is required, and GED is accepted. *Academic units recommended:* 3 English, 2 math, 2 science, 2 foreign language, 2 social studies. **Freshman Admission Statistics:** 1,135 applied, 69% admitted, 53% enrolled. **Transfer Admission Requirements:** High school transcript, college transcript(s). Minimum college GPA of 2.0 required. Lowest grade transferable D. **General Admission Information:** Application fee $30. Regular notification immediately. Nonfall registration accepted. Admission may be deferred for a maximum of 1 semester. Common Application accepted. Credit and/or placement offered for CEEB Advanced Placement tests.

COSTS AND FINANCIAL AID

Annual tuition $16,850. Room & board $5,650. Required fees $200. Average book expense $1,000. **Required Forms and Deadlines:** FAFSA. **Notification of Awards:** Applicants will be notified of awards on a rolling basis beginning on or about 2/1. **Types of Aid:** *Need-based scholarships/grants:* Pell, SEOG, state scholarships/grants, private scholarships, the school's own gift aid. *Loans:* Direct Subsidized Stafford, Direct Unsubsidized Stafford, Direct PLUS, Federal Perkins, state loans, college/university loans from institutional funds. **Student Employment:** Federal Work-Study Program available. Institutional employment available. Off-campus job opportunities are poor. **Financial Aid Statistics:** 68% freshmen, 57% undergrads receive need-based scholarship or grant aid. 50% freshmen, 50% undergrads receive need-based self-help aid. 44 freshmen, 179 undergrads receive athletic scholarships. Highest amount earned per year from on-campus jobs $864.

GRAMBLING STATE UNIVERSITY

PO Box 864, Grambling, LA 71245
Phone: 318-274-6423 **E-mail:** taylorn@gram.edu **CEEB Code:** 6250
Fax: 318-274-3292 **Website:** www.gram.edu **ACT Code:** 1582
Financial Aid Phone: 318-274-6056

This public school was founded in 1901. It has a 340-acre campus.

RATINGS
Admissions Selectivity Rating: 60* **Fire Safety Rating:** 60* **Green Rating:** 60*

STUDENTS AND FACULTY
Enrollment: 4,171. **Student Body:** 57% female, 43% male, 34% out-of-state, 2% international (21 countries represented). **Retention and Graduation:** 68% freshmen return for sophomore year. 20% freshmen graduate within 4 years. 33% grads go on to further study within 1 year. 33% grads pursue arts and sciences degrees. **Faculty:** Student/faculty ratio 17:1. 243 full-time faculty, 57% hold PhDs.

ACADEMICS
Degrees: Associate, bachelor's, doctoral, master's. **Academic Requirements:** Arts/fine arts, computer literacy, English (including composition), history, humanities, mathematics, sciences (biological or physical), social science. **Disciplines with Highest Percentage of Degrees Awarded:** Computer and information sciences 19%, business/marketing 15%, law/legal studies 9%, biological/life sciences 9%, social sciences 9%, parks and recreation 7%, communication technologies 6%. **Special Study Options:** Accelerated program, cooperative education program, distance learning, double major, exchange student program (domestic), honors program, independent study, internships, study abroad, teacher certification program.

FACILITIES
Housing: Men's dorms, women's dorms, fraternity/sorority housing, graduate dorm. **Special Academic Facilities/Equipment:** Audiovisual and TV center, lab schools.

CAMPUS LIFE
Activities: Choral groups, dance, drama/theater, jazz band, marching band, music ensembles, radio station, student government, student newspaper, television station, yearbook. **Organizations:** 50 registered organizations, 11 honor societies, 3 religious organizations. 4 fraternities (2% men join), 5 sororities (7% women join). **Athletics (Intercollegiate):** *Men:* Baseball, basketball, cross-country, football, golf, tennis, track/field (indoor), track/field (outdoor). *Women:* Basketball, cross-country, golf, soccer, softball, tennis, track/field (indoor), track/field (outdoor).

ADMISSIONS
Basis for Candidate Selection: *Very important factors considered include:* Standardized test scores. *Other factors considered include:* Alumni/ae relation, extracurricular activities, recommendation(s), talent/ability. **Freshman Admission Requirements:** High school diploma is required, and GED is accepted. *Academic units required:* 4 English, 3 math, 3 science, 3 social studies, 8 academic electives, 2 health and physical education. **Freshman Admission Statistics:** 2,923 applied, 62% admitted, 57% enrolled. **Transfer Admission Requirements:** College transcript(s), statement of good standing from prior institution(s). Minimum college GPA of 2.0 required. Lowest grade transferable C. **General Admission Information:** Application fee $20. Early decision application deadline 4/15. Regular application deadline 8/1. Nonfall registration accepted. Admission may be deferred for a maximum of 6 months. Common Application not accepted.

COSTS AND FINANCIAL AID
Comprehensive fee $5,652. Out-of-state tuition $8,327. Room & board $2,912. Required fees $60. Average book expense $600. **Required Forms and Deadlines:** FAFSA, Institutional Scholarship Application. Financial aid filing deadline 6/1. **Notification of Awards:** Applicants will be notified of awards on or about 3/1. **Types of Aid:** *Need-based scholarships/grants:* Pell, SEOG, state scholarships/grants. *Loans:* Direct Subsidized Stafford, Direct Unsubsidized Stafford, Direct PLUS, FFEL Subsidized Stafford, FFEL Unsubsidized Stafford, FFEL PLUS, Federal Perkins, college/university loans from institutional funds, non-federal alternative/private loans. **Student Employment:** Federal Work-Study Program available. Institutional employment available. Off-campus job opportunities are good. **Financial Aid Statistics:** 73% freshmen, 68% undergrads receive need-based scholarship or grant aid. 78% freshmen, 69% undergrads receive need-based self-help aid. 35 freshmen, 225 undergrads receive athletic scholarships. 90% freshmen, 92% undergrads receive any aid. Highest amount earned per year from on-campus jobs $4,648.

GRAND CANYON UNIVERSITY

3300 West Camelback Road, Phoenix, AZ 85061-0197
Phone: 602-589-2855 **E-mail:** admissions@grand-canyon.edu **CEEB Code:** 4331
Fax: 602-589-2580 **Website:** www.grand-canyon.edu **ACT Code:** 0092
Financial Aid Phone: 602-589-2885

This private school was founded in 1949. It has a 90-acre campus.

RATINGS
Admissions Selectivity Rating: 60* **Fire Safety Rating:** 60* **Green Rating:** 60*

STUDENTS AND FACULTY
Enrollment: 1,609. **Student Body:** 64% female, 36% male, 19% out-of-state, 3% international. African American 3%, Asian 2%, Caucasian 56%, Hispanic 7%, Native American 1%. **Retention and Graduation:** 76% freshmen return for sophomore year. 32% freshmen graduate within 4 years. **Faculty:** Student/faculty ratio 16:1. 97 full-time faculty, 58% hold PhDs. 100% faculty teach undergrads.

ACADEMICS
Degrees: Bachelor's, diploma, master's. **Academic Requirements:** Arts/fine arts, English (including composition), history, humanities, mathematics, sciences (biological or physical). **Classes:** Most classes have fewer than 10 students. Most lab/discussion sections have 10–19 students. **Disciplines with Highest Percentage of Degrees Awarded:** Business/marketing 25%, health professions and related sciences 18%, education 17%, biological/life sciences 13%, social sciences 6%. **Special Study Options:** Accelerated program, cooperative education program, distance learning, double major, dual enrollment, English as a second language (ESL), exchange student program (domestic), honors program, independent study, internships, study abroad, teacher certification program.

FACILITIES
Housing: Men's dorms, women's dorms, apartments for married students, apartments for single students. **Special Academic Facilities/Equipment:** Art gallery, dynamical systems laboratory. **Computers:** 93% of public computers are PCs, 7% of public computers are Macs.

CAMPUS LIFE
Activities: Choral groups, concert band, drama/theater, jazz band, literary magazine, music ensembles, musical theater, opera, student government, student newspaper. **Organizations:** 20 registered organizations, 3 honor societies, 4 religious organizations. **Athletics (Intercollegiate):** *Men:* Baseball, basketball, golf, soccer. *Women:* Basketball, soccer, tennis, volleyball.

ADMISSIONS

Freshman Academic Profile: 29% in top 10% of high school class, 54% in top 25% of high school class, 78% in top 50% of high school class. TOEFL required of all international applicants, minimum paper TOEFL 500. **Basis for Candidate Selection:** *Very important factors considered include:* Rigor of secondary school record, standardized test scores. *Important factors considered include:* Class rank. *Other factors considered include:* Application essay, character/personal qualities, extracurricular activities, interview, recommendation(s), talent/ability. **Freshman Admission Requirements:** High school diploma is required, and GED is accepted. *Academic units required:* 4 English, 3 math, 2 science (2 science labs), 2 social studies. *Academic units recommended:* 4 English, 3 math, 2 science (2 science labs), 2 social studies. **Freshman Admission Statistics:** 823 applied, 69% admitted, 44% enrolled. **Transfer Admission Requirements:** College transcript(s). Minimum college GPA of 2.0 required. Lowest grade transferable C. **General Admission Information:** Application fee $50. Nonfall registration accepted. Common Application accepted. Credit offered for CEEB Advanced Placement tests.

COSTS AND FINANCIAL AID

Annual tuition $9,750. Room and board $7,130. Average book expense $780. **Required Forms and Deadlines:** FAFSA. **Notification of Awards:** Applicants will be notified of awards on a rolling basis beginning on or about 3/15. **Types of Aid:** *Need-based scholarships/grants:* Pell, SEOG, state scholarships/grants, private scholarships, the school's own gift aid, Bureau of Indian Affairs Grant. *Loans:* FFEL Subsidized Stafford, FFEL Unsubsidized Stafford, FFEL PLUS, Federal Perkins, state loans, alternative loans. **Student Employment:** Federal Work-Study Program available. Institutional employment available. Off-campus job opportunities are excellent. **Financial Aid Statistics:** 23% freshmen, 29% undergrads receive need-based scholarship or grant aid. 39% freshmen, 49% undergrads receive need-based self-help aid. 10 freshmen, 60 undergrads receive athletic scholarships. Highest amount earned per year from on-campus jobs $1,500.

GRAND VALLEY STATE UNIVERSITY

1 Campus Drive, Allendale, MI 49401
Phone: 616-331-2025 **E-mail:** go2gvsu@gvsu.edu **CEEB Code:** 1258
Fax: 616-331-2000 **Website:** www.gvsu.edu **ACT Code:** 2005
Financial Aid Phone: 616-331-3234

This public school was founded in 1960. It has a 1,112-acre campus.

RATINGS

Admissions Selectivity Rating: 80   **Fire Safety Rating:** 79   **Green Rating:** 60*

STUDENTS AND FACULTY

Enrollment: 19,388. **Student Body:** 61% female, 39% male, 4% out-of-state. African American 5%, Asian 3%, Caucasian 86%, Hispanic 3%. **Retention and Graduation:** 83% freshmen return for sophomore year. 20% freshmen graduate within 4 years. 35% grads go on to further study within 1 year. 35% grads pursue arts and sciences degrees. **Faculty:** Student/faculty ratio 18:1. 921 full-time faculty, 73% hold PhDs. 90% faculty teach undergrads.

ACADEMICS

Degrees: Bachelor's, certificate, master's, post-bachelor's certificate, post-master's certificate. **Academic Requirements:** Arts/fine arts, English (including composition), history, humanities, mathematics, philosophy, sciences (biological or physical), social science, thematic studies group requirement. **Classes:** Most classes have 20–29 students. Most lab/discussion sections have 20–29 students. **Majors with Highest Enrollment:** Business administration/management, health services/allied health, psychology. **Disciplines with Highest Percentage of Degrees Awarded:** Business/marketing 19%, health professions and related sciences 14%, psychology 9%, English 9%, social sciences 7%. **Special Study Options:** Distance learning, double major, dual enrollment, English as a second language (ESL), honors program, independent study, internships, student-designed major, study abroad, teacher certification program. Undergrads may take grad-level classes. Co-op programs available in education, engineering, health professions. Off-campus study: Washington, DC.

FACILITIES

Housing: Coed dorms, apartments for married students, apartments for single students, fraternity/sorority housing, honors college building, specialty housing, languages, engineering. **Special Academic Facilities/Equipment:** 2 Great Lakes research vessels, audiovisual center, performance/recital hall, pipe organ, physical therapy/human performance lab. **Computers:** 100% of classrooms are wireless, 90% of public computers are PCs, 9% of public computers are Macs,

1% of public computers are UNIX, network access in dorm rooms, network access in dorm lounges, online registration, online administrative functions (other than registration), support for handheld computing, remote student-access to Web through college's connection.

CAMPUS LIFE

Activities: Choral groups, concert band, dance, drama/theater, jazz band, literary magazine, marching band, music ensembles, musical theater, pep band, radio station, student government, student newspaper, student-run film society, symphony orchestra, television station. **Organizations:** 200 registered organizations, 19 honor societies, 14 religious organizations. 9 fraternities (4% men join), 8 sororities (3% women join). **Athletics (Intercollegiate):** *Men:* Baseball, basketball, cross-country, diving, football, golf, swimming, tennis, track/field (indoor), track/field (outdoor). *Women:* Basketball, cross-country, diving, golf, soccer, softball, swimming, tennis, track/field (indoor), track/field (outdoor), volleyball.

ADMISSIONS

Freshman Academic Profile: 21% in top 10% of high school class, 55% in top 25% of high school class, 90% in top 50% of high school class. 85% from public high schools. ACT middle 50% range 22–26. TOEFL required of all international applicants, minimum paper TOEFL 550, minimum computer TOEFL 213. **Basis for Candidate Selection:** *Very important factors considered include:* Academic GPA, rigor of secondary school record. *Important factors considered include:* Standardized test scores. *Other factors considered include:* Alumni/ae relation, application essay, class rank, extracurricular activities, first generation, recommendation(s), talent/ability, volunteer work, work experience. **Freshman Admission Requirements:** High school diploma is required, and GED is accepted. *Academic units required:* 4 English, 3 math, 3 science (1 science lab), 2 foreign language, 3 social studies. *Academic units recommended:* 4 English, 4 math, 4 science (2 science labs), 2 foreign language, 3 social studies, 1 computer science/fine arts. **Freshman Admission Statistics:** 12,726 applied, 70% admitted, 40% enrolled. **Transfer Admission Requirements:** College transcript(s). Minimum college GPA of 2.5 required. Lowest grade transferable D. **General Admission Information:** Application fee $30. Regular application deadline 5/1. Regular notification is rolling. Nonfall registration accepted. Credit and/or placement offered for CEEB Advanced Placement tests.

COSTS AND FINANCIAL AID

Annual in-state tuition $6,220. Out-of-state tuition $12,721. Comprehensive fee $7,240. Room and board $6,880. Average book expense $900. **Required Forms and Deadlines:** FAFSA. Financial aid filing deadline 3/1. **Notification of Awards:** Applicants will be notified of awards on or about 4/1. **Types of Aid:** *Need-based scholarships/grants:* Pell, SEOG, state scholarships/grants, private scholarships, the school's own gift aid, Federal Nursing Scholarships. *Loans:* Direct Subsidized Stafford, Direct Unsubsidized Stafford, Direct PLUS, Federal Perkins, Federal Nursing, state loans. **Financial Aid Statistics:** 57% freshmen, 54% undergrads receive need-based scholarship or grant aid. 55% freshmen, 52% undergrads receive need-based self-help aid. 108 freshmen, 347 undergrads receive athletic scholarships. 70% freshmen, 70% undergrads receive any aid. Highest amount earned per year from on-campus jobs $2,800.

See page 1186.

GRAND VIEW COLLEGE

1200 Grandview Avenue, Des Moines, IA 50316-1599
Phone: 515-263-2810 **E-mail:** admissions@gvc.edu **CEEB Code:** 6251
Fax: 515-263-2974 **Website:** www.gvc.edu **ACT Code:** 1316
Financial Aid Phone: 515-263-2963

This private school, affiliated with the Lutheran Church, was founded in 1896. It has a 35-acre campus.

RATINGS

Admissions Selectivity Rating: 71   **Fire Safety Rating:** 60*   **Green Rating:** 60*

STUDENTS AND FACULTY

Enrollment: 1,644. **Student Body:** 68% female, 32% male, 6% out-of-state. African American 4%, Asian 3%, Caucasian 72%, Hispanic 2%. **Retention and Graduation:** 65% freshmen return for sophomore year. 28% freshmen graduate within 4 years. **Faculty:** Student/faculty ratio 12:1. 88 full-time faculty, 58% hold PhDs. 100% faculty teach undergrads.

ACADEMICS

Degrees: Associate, bachelor's, certificate, post-bachelor's certificate. **Academic Requirements:** Arts/fine arts, computer literacy, English (including composition), history, humanities, mathematics, sciences (biological or physical), social science. **Classes:** Most classes have 10–19 students. Most lab/discussion sections have fewer than 10 students. **Majors with Highest Enrollment:** Business administration/management, education, nursing/registered nurse training (RN, ASN, BSN, MSN). **Disciplines with Highest Percentage of Degrees Awarded:** Health professions and related sciences 28%, business/marketing 18%, education 11%, communications/journalism 6%, liberal arts/general studies 6%, security and protective services 5%, visual and performing arts 5%. **Special Study Options:** Accelerated program, cooperative education program, cross-registration, distance learning, double major, dual enrollment, honors program, independent study, internships, liberal arts/career combination, student-designed major, study abroad, teacher certification program, weekend college.

FACILITIES

Housing: Coed dorms, apartments for single students, college-owned campus houses. **Special Academic Facilities/Equipment:** Danish American Archives. **Computers:** Network access in dorm rooms, network access in dorm lounges, online administrative functions (other than registration), remote student-access to Web through college's connection.

CAMPUS LIFE

Activities: Choral groups, dance, drama/theater, literary magazine, music ensembles, radio station, student government, student newspaper, television station. **Organizations:** 28 registered organizations, 1 religious organization. **Athletics (Intercollegiate):** *Men:* Baseball, basketball, cross-country, golf, soccer. *Women:* Basketball, cross-country, golf, soccer, softball, volleyball.

ADMISSIONS

Freshman Academic Profile: 14% in top 10% of high school class, 36% in top 25% of high school class, 68% in top 50% of high school class. SAT Math middle 50% range 420–530. SAT Critical Reading middle 50% range 410–540. SAT Writing middle 50% range 440–520. ACT middle 50% range 18–23. TOEFL required of all international applicants, minimum paper TOEFL 550, minimum computer TOEFL 210. **Basis for Candidate Selection:** *Very important factors considered include:* Academic GPA, character/personal qualities, class rank, rigor of secondary school record. *Important factors considered include:* Standardized test scores. *Other factors considered include:* Alumni/ae relation, extracurricular activities, talent/ability, volunteer work, work experience. **Freshman Admission Requirements:** High school diploma is required, and GED is accepted. *Academic units recommended:* 4 English, 3 math, 3 science, 2 foreign language, 3 social studies. **Freshman Admission Statistics:** 418 applied, 99% admitted, 48% enrolled. **Transfer Admission Requirements:** College transcript(s). Minimum college GPA of 2.0 required. Lowest grade transferable D. **General Admission Information:** Application fee $35. Regular application deadline 8/15. Regular notification is rolling. Nonfall registration accepted. Admission may be deferred for a maximum of 1 semester. Credit and/or placement offered for CEEB Advanced Placement tests.

COSTS AND FINANCIAL AID

Annual tuition $18,234. Room and board $6,164. Required fees $320. Average book expense $900. **Required Forms and Deadlines:** FAFSA. Financial aid filing deadline 3/1. **Notification of Awards:** Applicants will be notified of awards on a rolling basis beginning on or about 3/1. **Types of Aid:** *Need-based scholarships/grants:* Pell, SEOG, state scholarships/grants, private scholarships, the school's own gift aid. *Loans:* FFEL Subsidized Stafford, FFEL Unsubsidized Stafford, FFEL PLUS, Federal Perkins, Federal Nursing. **Student Employment:** Federal Work-Study Program available. Institutional employment available. Off-campus job opportunities are excellent. **Financial Aid Statistics:** 77% freshmen, 83% undergrads receive need-based scholarship or grant aid. 62% freshmen, 74% undergrads receive need-based self-help aid. 18 freshmen, 59 undergrads receive athletic scholarships. 97% freshmen, 99% undergrads receive any aid. Highest amount earned per year from on-campus jobs $1,500.

GRANTHAM UNIVERSITY

7200 Northwest Eighty-sixth Street, Kansas City, MO 64153
Phone: 800-955-2527 **E-mail:** Admissions@grantham.edu **CEEB Code:** 2244
Fax: 816-595-5757 **Website:** www.grantham.edu

This proprietary school was founded in 1951.

RATINGS

Admissions Selectivity Rating: 60* **Fire Safety Rating:** 60* **Green Rating:** 60*

STUDENTS AND FACULTY

Faculty: 100% faculty teach undergrads.

ACADEMICS

Degrees: Associate, bachelor's, master's. **Academic Requirements:** Computer literacy, English (including composition), history, humanities, mathematics, philosophy, sciences (biological or physical), social science. **Majors with Highest Enrollment:** Business administration/management; computer and information sciences; criminal justice/police science. **Special Study Options:** Accelerated program, distance learning, external degree program, independent study.

FACILITIES

Computers: Online registration, online administrative functions (other than registration).

CAMPUS LIFE

Organizations: 1 honor society.

ADMISSIONS

Freshman Academic Profile: TOEFL required of all international applicants, minimum paper TOEFL 500, minimum computer TOEFL 500. **Freshman Admission Requirements:** High school diploma is required, and GED is accepted. **Transfer Admission Requirements:** High school transcript, college transcript(s). Minimum college GPA of 2.0 required. Lowest grade transferable C. **General Admission Information:** Nonfall registration accepted.

COSTS AND FINANCIAL AID

Comprehensive fee $7,500. **Types of Aid:** *Need-based scholarships/grants:* The school's own gift aid.

See page 1188.

GRATZ COLLEGE

7605 Old York Road, Melrose Park, PA 19027
Phone: 215-635-7300 **E-mail:** admissions@gratz.edu
Fax: 215-635-7399 **Website:** www.gratzcollege.edu
Financial Aid Phone: 215-635-7300

This private school, affiliated with the Jewish synagogue, was founded in 1895. It has a 28-acre campus.

RATINGS

Admissions Selectivity Rating: 61 **Fire Safety Rating:** 60* **Green Rating:** 60*

STUDENTS AND FACULTY

Enrollment: 12. **Student Body:** 92% female, 8% male, 25% out-of-state. **Retention and Graduation:** 88% freshmen return for sophomore year. **Faculty:** Student/faculty ratio 12:1. 8 full-time faculty, 100% hold PhDs. 100% faculty teach undergrads.

ACADEMICS

Degrees: Bachelor's, master's, post-bachelor's certificate. **Academic Requirements:** Jewish studies and Hebrew language. **Classes:** Most classes have fewer than 10 students. Most lab/discussion sections have fewer than 10 students. **Special Study Options:** Cross-registration, double major, dual enrollment, independent study, internships, liberal arts/career combination, study abroad, teacher certification program. Joint programs with area colleges and universities are offered only at the master's level.

FACILITIES

Housing: The college does not offer housing. All students live off campus. **Computers:** 100% of public computers are PCs.

CAMPUS LIFE

Activities: Choral groups, music ensembles.

ADMISSIONS

Freshman Academic Profile: TOEFL required of all international applicants, minimum paper TOEFL 450, minimum computer TOEFL 133. **Basis for Candidate Selection:** *Very important factors considered include:* Application essay, character/personal qualities, recommendation(s), religious affiliation/commitment, talent/ability. *Important factors considered include:* Interview, rigor of secondary school record, volunteer work. *Other factors considered include:* Alumni/ae relation, class rank, extracurricular activities, racial/ethnic status, standardized test scores, work experience. **Freshman Admission Requirements:** High school diploma is required, and GED is accepted. *Academic units required:* 3 English, 2 math, 2 science (1 science lab), 2 foreign language, 3 social studies, 3 history, 2 academic electives. *Academic units recommended:* 4 English, 2 math, 2 science (1 science lab), 4 foreign language, 4 social studies, 4 history, 2 academic electives. **Freshman Admission**

Statistics: 7 applied, 71% admitted, 100% enrolled. **Transfer Admission Requirements:** High school transcript, college transcript(s), essay or personal statement. Lowest grade transferable C. **General Admission Information:** Application fee $50. Regular notification rolling. Nonfall registration accepted. Admission may be deferred for a maximum of 2 years. Common Application not accepted. Neither credit nor placement offered for CEEB Advanced Placement tests.

COSTS AND FINANCIAL AID

Annual tuition $9,500. Required fees $400. Average book expense $550. **Required Forms and Deadlines:** FAFSA, institution's own financial aid form. **Types of Aid:** *Need-based scholarships/grants:* Pell, private scholarships. *Loans:* FFEL Subsidized Stafford, FFEL Unsubsidized Stafford, FFEL PLUS. **Student Employment:** Institutional employment available. Off-campus job opportunities are good.

GREEN MOUNTAIN COLLEGE

One College Circle, Poultney, VT 05764-1199
Phone: 802-287-8000 **E-mail:** admiss@greenmtn.edu **CEEB Code:** 3418
Fax: 802-287-8099 **Website:** www.greenmtn.edu **ACT Code:** 4302
Financial Aid Phone: 802-287-8210

This private school, affiliated with the Methodist Church, was founded in 1834. It has a 155-acre campus.

RATINGS
Admissions Selectivity Rating: 60*   **Fire Safety Rating:** 60*   **Green Rating:** 60*

STUDENTS AND FACULTY
Enrollment: 721. **Student Body:** 50% female, 50% male, 85% out-of-state. African American 3%, Caucasian 73%, Hispanic 2%, Native American 1%. **Retention and Graduation:** 17% grads go on to further study within 1 year. **Faculty:** Student/faculty ratio 14:1. 43 full-time faculty, 84% hold PhDs. 100% faculty teach undergrads.

ACADEMICS
Degrees: Bachelor's, certificate, master's. **Academic Requirements:** Arts/fine arts, English (including composition), health and well-being, history, humanities, mathematics, philosophy, sciences (biological or physical), social science. **Classes:** Most classes have 10–19 students. Most lab/discussion sections have 10–19 students. **Majors with Highest Enrollment:** Environmental studies; parks, recreation, and leisure studies; psychology. **Disciplines with Highest Percentage of Degrees Awarded:** Natural resources/environmental science 19%, parks and recreation 15%, business/marketing 12%, liberal arts/general studies 8%, education 7%. **Special Study Options:** Cooperative education program, distance learning, double major, exchange student program (domestic), honors program, independent study, internships, liberal arts/career combination, student-designed major, study abroad, teacher certification program.

FACILITIES
Housing: Coed dorms, special housing for disabled students, substance-free, recreation, education, community, honors. **Special Academic Facilities/Equipment:** Welsh Heritage Collection, rare books room, Feick Arts Center. **Computers:** 90% of public computers are PCs, 10% of public computers are Macs, network access in dorm rooms, online registration, online administrative functions (other than registration), remote student-access to Web through college's connection.

CAMPUS LIFE
Activities: Choral groups, concert band, drama/theater, jazz band, literary magazine, music ensembles, radio station, student government, student newspaper, student-run film society, yearbook. **Organizations:** 25 registered organizations, 2 honor societies, 2 religious organizations. **Athletics (Intercollegiate):** *Men:* Basketball, cross-country, golf, lacrosse, skiing (downhill/alpine), soccer, tennis. *Women:* Basketball, cross-country, lacrosse, skiing (downhill/alpine), soccer, softball, tennis, volleyball.

ADMISSIONS
Freshman Academic Profile: 86% from public high schools. SAT Math middle 50% range 430–530. SAT Critical Reading middle 50% range 450–580. SAT Writing middle 50% range 440–550. ACT middle 50% range 17–23. TOEFL required of all international applicants, minimum paper TOEFL 500, minimum computer TOEFL 173. **Basis for Candidate Selection:** *Very important factors considered include:* Academic GPA, application essay, character/personal qualities, rigor of secondary school record, standardized test scores. *Important factors considered include:* Class rank, extracurricular

activities, interview, recommendation(s), volunteer work. *Other factors considered include:* Level of applicant's interest, talent/ability, work experience. **Freshman Admission Requirements:** High school diploma is required, and GED is accepted. *Academic units required:* 4 English, 3 math, 3 science (2 science labs), 2 foreign language, 3 social studies, 1 history, 5 academic electives. *Academic units recommended:* 4 math, 4 science, 3 foreign language, 3 social studies, 2 history. **Freshman Admission Statistics:** 927 applied, 85% admitted, 28% enrolled. **Transfer Admission Requirements:** High school transcript, college transcript(s), essay or personal statement, statement of good standing from prior institution(s). Minimum college GPA of 2.0 required. Lowest grade transferable C-. **General Admission Information:** Application fee $30. Regular notification is rolling. Nonfall registration accepted. Admission may be deferred for a maximum of 1 year. Credit and/or placement offered for CEEB Advanced Placement tests.

COSTS AND FINANCIAL AID

Annual tuition $23,772. Room and board $9,064. Required fees $793. Average book expense $1,000. **Required Forms and Deadlines:** FAFSA, CSS/Financial Aid PROFILE, Noncustodial PROFILE. Financial aid filing deadline 3/1. **Notification of Awards:** Applicants will be notified of awards on a rolling basis beginning on or about 1/1. **Types of Aid:** *Need-based scholarships/grants:* Pell, SEOG, state scholarships/grants, private scholarships, the school's own gift aid. *Loans:* FFEL Subsidized Stafford, FFEL Unsubsidized Stafford, FFEL PLUS, state loans, alternative loans. **Financial Aid Statistics:** 77% freshmen, 83% undergrads receive need-based scholarship or grant aid. 69% freshmen, 78% undergrads receive need-based self-help aid. 80% freshmen, 78% undergrads receive any aid.

GREENSBORO COLLEGE

815 West Market Street, Greensboro, NC 27401-1875
Phone: 800-346-8226 **E-mail:** admissions@gborocollege.edu **CEEB Code:** 5260
Fax: 336-378-0154 **Website:** www.gborocollege.edu **ACT Code:** 3104
Financial Aid Phone: 800-346-8226

This private school, affiliated with the Methodist Church, was founded in 1838. It has a 40-acre campus.

RATINGS
Admissions Selectivity Rating: 70   **Fire Safety Rating:** 60*   **Green Rating:** 60*

STUDENTS AND FACULTY
Enrollment: 1,178. **Student Body:** 54% female, 46% male, 29% out-of-state. 1% international (18 countries represented). African American 15%, Caucasian 80%, Hispanic 2%. **Retention and Graduation:** 65% freshmen return for sophomore year. 27% freshmen graduate within 4 years. 17% grads go on to further study within 1 year. 12% grads pursue arts and sciences degrees. 2% grads pursue business degrees. 1% grads pursue law degrees. 4% grads pursue medical degrees. **Faculty:** Student/faculty ratio 14:1. 56 full-time faculty, 80% hold PhDs. 100% faculty teach undergrads.

ACADEMICS
Degrees: Bachelor's, certificate, master's, post-bachelor's certificate. **Academic Requirements:** Arts/fine arts, computer literacy, English (including composition), foreign languages, history, humanities, mathematics, physical education, religion, sciences (biological or physical), social science. **Classes:** Most classes have 10–19 students. Most lab/discussion sections have 20–29 students. **Majors with Highest Enrollment:** Business/managerial economics, education, health and physical education. **Disciplines with Highest Percentage of Degrees Awarded:** Business/marketing 22%, social sciences 15%, education 14%, biological/life sciences 10%, parks and recreation 9%. **Special Study Options:** Academic development program, accelerated program, cross-registration, double major, dual enrollment, English as a second language (ESL), honors program, independent study, internships, liberal arts/career combination, student-designed major, study abroad, teacher certification program, weekend college.

FACILITIES
Housing: Coed dorms, men's dorms, women's dorms, community service housing. **Special Academic Facilities/Equipment:** Art gallery, historical museum, language lab, computer labs. **Computers:** 90% of public computers are PCs, 10% of public computers are Macs, network access in dorm rooms, online administrative functions (other than registration), remote student-access to Web through college's connection.

CAMPUS LIFE
Activities: Choral groups, dance, drama/theater, jazz band, literary magazine, marching band, music ensembles, musical theater, opera, pep band, student

government, student newspaper, yearbook. **Organizations:** 43 registered organizations, 11 honor societies, 4 religious organizations. 1 fraternity (1% men join). **Athletics (Intercollegiate):** *Men:* Baseball, basketball, cross-country, football, golf, lacrosse, soccer, tennis. *Women:* Basketball, cheerleading, cross-country, lacrosse, soccer, softball, swimming, tennis, volleyball.

ADMISSIONS

Freshman Academic Profile: 5% in top 10% of high school class, 15% in top 25% of high school class, 35% in top 50% of high school class. SAT Math middle 50% range 420–540. SAT Critical Reading middle 50% range 410–530. ACT middle 50% range 17–21. TOEFL required of all international applicants, minimum paper TOEFL 550. **Basis for Candidate Selection:** *Very important factors considered include:* Application essay, class rank, extracurricular activities, rigor of secondary school record. *Important factors considered include:* Alumni/ae relation, character/personal qualities, interview, recommendation(s), standardized test scores, talent/ability. *Other factors considered include:* Religious affiliation/commitment, volunteer work, work experience. **Freshman Admission Requirements:** High school diploma is required, and GED is accepted. *Academic units recommended:* 4 English, 3 math, 2 science (1 science lab), 2 foreign language, 2 history. **Freshman Admission Statistics:** 806 applied, 77% admitted, 39% enrolled. **Transfer Admission Requirements:** College transcript(s), essay or personal statement. Lowest grade transferable C. **General Admission Information:** Application fee $35. Regular notification within 2 weeks of receiving complete application. Nonfall registration accepted. Admission may be deferred for a maximum of 1 year. Common Application accepted. Credit and/or placement offered for CEEB Advanced Placement tests.

COSTS AND FINANCIAL AID

Annual tuition $14,450. Room & board $5,760. Required fees $200. Average book expense $800. **Required Forms and Deadlines:** FAFSA, institution's own financial aid form, state aid form. Financial aid filing deadline 4/15. **Notification of Awards:** Applicants will be notified of awards on a rolling basis beginning on or about 2/15. **Types of Aid:** *Need-based scholarships/grants:* Pell, SEOG, state scholarships/grants, private scholarships, the school's own gift aid. *Loans:* FFEL Subsidized Stafford, FFEL Unsubsidized Stafford, FFEL PLUS, Federal Perkins, college/university loans from institutional funds. **Student Employment:** Federal Work-Study Program available. Institutional employment available. Off-campus job opportunities are excellent. **Financial Aid Statistics:** 70% freshmen, 52% undergrads receive need-based scholarship or grant aid. 68% freshmen, 49% undergrads receive need-based self-help aid. Highest amount earned per year from on-campus jobs $1,000.

GREENVILLE COLLEGE

315 East College Avenue, Greenville, IL 62246-0159
Phone: 618-664-7100 **E-mail:** admissions@greenville.edu **CEEB Code:** 1256
Fax: 618-664-9841 **Website:** www.greenville.edu **ACT Code:** 1032
Financial Aid Phone: 618-664-7110

This private school, affiliated with the Free Methodist Church, was founded in 1892. It has a 40-acre campus.

RATINGS

Admissions Selectivity Rating: 77   **Fire Safety Rating:** 91   **Green Rating:** 60*

STUDENTS AND FACULTY

Enrollment: 1,307. **Student Body:** 55% female, 45% male, 29% out-of-state, 1% international (14 countries represented). African American 7%, Caucasian 83%, Hispanic 2%. **Retention and Graduation:** 67% freshmen return for sophomore year. 39% freshmen graduate within 4 years. **Faculty:** Student/faculty ratio 16:1. 54 full-time faculty, 70% hold PhDs. 100% faculty teach undergrads.

ACADEMICS

Degrees: Bachelor's, master's. **Academic Requirements:** Arts/fine arts, English (including composition), foreign language, history, humanities, mathematics, philosophy, sciences (biological or physical), social science. **Classes:** Most classes have 10–19 students. **Majors with Highest Enrollment:** Elementary education and teaching, organizational behavior studies, visual and performing arts. **Disciplines with Highest Percentage of Degrees Awarded:** Business/marketing 44%, education 10%, visual and performing arts 6%, communication technologies 5%, communications/journalism 4%, biological/life sciences 4%. **Special Study Options:** Accelerated program, cooperative education program, cross-registration, double major, external degree program, honors program, independent study, internships,

liberal arts/career combination, student-designed major, study abroad, teacher certification program.

FACILITIES

Housing: Men's dorms, women's dorms, apartments for single students. All single students not living at home must live in college-approved housing. **Special Academic Facilities/Equipment:** Sculpture museum, sports training annex. **Computers:** 100% of classrooms are wireless, 95% of public computers are PCs, 5% of public computers are Macs, network access in dorm rooms, network access in dorm lounges, online administrative functions (other than registration), remote student-access to Web through college's connection.

CAMPUS LIFE

Activities: Choral groups, concert band, drama/theater, jazz band, music ensembles, musical theater, pep band, radio station, student government, student newspaper, yearbook. **Organizations:** 25 registered organizations, 6 honor societies, 2 religious organizations. **Athletics (Intercollegiate):** *Men:* Baseball, basketball, cross-country, football, soccer, tennis, track/field (indoor), track/field (outdoor). *Women:* Basketball, cross-country, soccer, softball, tennis, track/field (indoor), track/field (outdoor), volleyball.

ADMISSIONS

Freshman Academic Profile: 17% in top 10% of high school class, 48% in top 25% of high school class, 74% in top 50% of high school class. SAT Math middle 50% range 460–570. SAT Critical Reading middle 50% range 480–580. ACT middle 50% range 19–25. TOEFL required of all international applicants, minimum paper TOEFL 500, minimum computer TOEFL 173. **Basis for Candidate Selection:** *Very important factors considered include:* Academic GPA, application essay, character/personal qualities, class rank, religious affiliation/commitment, rigor of secondary school record, talent/ability. *Important factors considered include:* Recommendation(s), standardized test scores. *Other factors considered include:* Alumni/ae relation, extracurricular activities, first generation, geographical residence, interview, level of applicant's interest, racial/ethnic status, volunteer work, work experience. **Freshman Admission Requirements:** High school diploma is required, and GED is accepted. *Academic units recommended:* 4 English, 2 math, 1 science (1 science lab), 2 foreign language, 1 history. **Freshman Admission Statistics:** 879 applied, 82% admitted, 42% enrolled. **Transfer Admission Requirements:** High school transcript, college transcript(s), essay or personal statement. Minimum college GPA of 2.0 required. Lowest grade transferable C. **General Admission Information:** Application fee $25. Regular application deadline 8/1. Regular notification is rolling. Nonfall registration accepted. Admission may be deferred for a maximum of 1 year. Credit and/or placement offered for CEEB Advanced Placement tests.

COSTS AND FINANCIAL AID

Average book expense $900. **Required Forms and Deadlines:** FAFSA. **Notification of Awards:** Applicants will be notified of awards on or about 3/15. **Types of Aid:** *Need-based scholarships/grants:* Pell, SEOG, state scholarships/grants, private scholarships, the school's own gift aid. *Loans:* Direct Subsidized Stafford, Direct Unsubsidized Stafford, Direct PLUS, FFEL Subsidized Stafford, FFEL Unsubsidized Stafford, FFEL PLUS, Federal Perkins, college/university loans from institutional funds. **Student Employment:** Federal Work-Study Program available. Institutional employment available. Off-campus job opportunities are fair. **Financial Aid Statistics:** 82% freshmen, 85% undergrads receive need-based scholarship or grant aid. 74% freshmen, 77% undergrads receive need-based self-help aid. 94% freshmen, 92% undergrads receive any aid. Highest amount earned per year from on-campus jobs $2,407.

GRIGGS UNIVERSITY

PO Box 4437, Silver Spring, MD 20914-4437
Phone: 301-680-6579 **E-mail:** enrollmentservices@griggs.edu
Fax: 301-680-6526 **Website:** www.griggs.edu

This private school, affiliated with the Seventh-Day Adventist Church, was founded in 1909.

RATINGS

Admissions Selectivity Rating: 60*   **Fire Safety Rating:** 60*   **Green Rating:** 60*

STUDENTS AND FACULTY

Enrollment: 1,076. **Student Body:** 50% female, 50% male. **Faculty:** Student/faculty ratio 3:1. 38% faculty teach undergrads.

ACADEMICS

Degrees: Associate, bachelor's. **Academic Requirements:** Arts/fine arts, English (including composition), history, humanities, mathematics, sciences (biological or physical), social science. **Majors with Highest Enrollment:** Pastoral counseling and specialized ministries, religion/religious studies, theology/theological studies. **Disciplines with Highest Percentage of Degrees Awarded:** Business/marketing 2%. **Special Study Options:** Accelerated program, distance learning, independent study.

ADMISSIONS

Basis for Candidate Selection: *Very important factors considered include:* Rigor of secondary school record. *Important factors considered include:* Application essay, religious affiliation/commitment, work experience. *Other factors considered include:* Alumni/ae relation, character/personal qualities, extracurricular activities, interview, recommendation(s), standardized test scores, talent/ability, volunteer work. **Freshman Admission Requirements:** *Academic units required:* 4 English, 3 math, 2 science, 3 social studies, 3 academic electives. **Transfer Admission Requirements:** College transcript(s), essay or personal statement. Minimum college GPA of 2.0 required. Lowest grade transferable C. **General Admission Information:** Application fee $60. Nonfall registration accepted. Common Application not accepted.

COSTS AND FINANCIAL AID

Annual tuition $6,400. Required fees $120. Average book expense $1,000. **Types of Aid:** *Need-based scholarships/grants:* The school's own gift aid.

GRINNELL COLLEGE

Office of Admissions, 1103 Park Street, 2nd Floor, Grinnell, IA 50112-1690
Phone: 641-269-3600 **E-mail:** askgrin@grinnell.edu **CEEB Code:** 6252
Fax: 641-269-4800 **Website:** www.grinnell.edu **ACT Code:** 1318
Financial Aid Phone: 641-269-3250

This private school was founded in 1846. It has a 120-acre campus.

RATINGS
Admissions Selectivity Rating: 95   **Fire Safety Rating:** 60*   **Green Rating:** 60*

STUDENTS AND FACULTY
Enrollment: 1,555. **Student Body:** 54% female, 46% male, 87% out-of-state, 10% international (46 countries represented). African American 5%, Asian 6%, Caucasian 67%, Hispanic 5%. **Retention and Graduation:** 92% freshmen return for sophomore year. 86% freshmen graduate within 4 years. 30% grads go on to further study within 1 year. 40% grads pursue arts and sciences degrees. 5% grads pursue business degrees. 10% grads pursue law degrees. 10% grads pursue medical degrees. **Faculty:** Student/faculty ratio 8:1. 163 full-time faculty, 96% hold PhDs. 100% faculty teach undergrads.

ACADEMICS
Degrees: Bachelor's. **Academic Requirements:** First-semester tutorial focusing on writing. **Classes:** Most classes have 10–19 students. Most lab/discussion sections have 10–19 students. **Majors with Highest Enrollment:** Biological and physical sciences, economics, history. **Disciplines with Highest Percentage of Degrees Awarded:** Social sciences 22%, foreign languages and literature 13%, English 11%, biological/life sciences 11%, physical sciences 8%, history 8%, visual and performing arts 7%. **Special Study Options:** Accelerated program, double major, independent study, internships, liberal arts/career combination, student-designed major, study abroad, teacher certification program. Study abroad available in 32 countries, including Grinnell-in-London. Grinnell-in-Washington program. 3-2 programs available in engineering, architecture, and law.

FACILITIES
Housing: Coed dorms, cooperative housing. **Special Academic Facilities/Equipment:** Art galleries, language lab, nuclear magnetic resonance spectrometer, electron microscope, 24-inch reflecting telescope, 365-acre environmental research area. **Computers:** Network access in dorm rooms, network access in dorm lounges, online administrative functions (other than registration), remote student-access to Web through college's connection.

CAMPUS LIFE
Activities: Choral groups, concert band, dance, drama/theater, jazz band, literary magazine, music ensembles, musical theater, radio station, student government, student newspaper, student-run film society, symphony orchestra, yearbook. **Organizations:** 178 registered organizations, 2 honor societies, 12

---

religious organizations. **Athletics (Intercollegiate):** *Men:* Baseball, basketball, cross-country, diving, football, golf, soccer, swimming, tennis, track/field (indoor), track/field (outdoor). *Women:* Basketball, cross-country, diving, golf, soccer, softball, swimming, tennis, track/field (indoor), track/field (outdoor), volleyball.

ADMISSIONS

Freshman Academic Profile: 64% in top 10% of high school class, 90% in top 25% of high school class, 100% in top 50% of high school class. 30% from public high schools. SAT Math middle 50% range 620–740. SAT Critical Reading middle 50% range 610–750. ACT middle 50% range 29–33. TOEFL required of all international applicants, minimum paper TOEFL 550, minimum computer TOEFL 220. **Basis for Candidate Selection:** *Very important factors considered include:* Academic GPA, class rank, extracurricular activities, recommendation(s), rigor of secondary school record, standardized test scores, talent/ability. *Important factors considered include:* Application essay, interview, racial/ethnic status. *Other factors considered include:* Alumni/ae relation, character/personal qualities, first generation, geographical residence, state residency, volunteer work, work experience. **Freshman Admission Requirements:** High school diploma is required, and GED is accepted. *Academic units recommended:* 4 English, 4 math, 4 science (3 science labs), 4 foreign language, 4 social studies. **Freshman Admission Statistics:** 3,104 applied, 45% admitted, 29% enrolled. **Transfer Admission Requirements:** High school transcript, college transcript(s), essay or personal statement, standardized test score, statement of good standing from prior institution(s). Lowest grade transferable C. **General Admission Information:** Application fee $30. Early decision application deadline 11/20. Regular application deadline 1/20. Regular notification 4/1. Nonfall registration not accepted. Admission may be deferred for a maximum of 1 year. Credit offered for CEEB Advanced Placement tests.

COSTS AND FINANCIAL AID

Annual tuition $29,710. Room and board $8,030. Required fees $482. Average book expense $750. **Required Forms and Deadlines:** FAFSA, institution's own financial aid form, Noncustodial PROFILE. Financial aid filing deadline 2/1. **Notification of Awards:** Applicants will be notified of awards on or about 4/1. **Types of Aid:** *Need-based scholarships/grants:* Pell, SEOG, state scholarships/grants, private scholarships, the school's own gift aid. *Loans:* FFEL Subsidized Stafford, FFEL Unsubsidized Stafford, FFEL PLUS, Federal Perkins, college/university loans from institutional funds. **Financial Aid Statistics:** 57% freshmen, 55% undergrads receive need-based scholarship or grant aid. 45% freshmen, 44% undergrads receive need-based self-help aid. 85% freshmen, 88% undergrads receive any aid. Highest amount earned per year from on-campus jobs $2,500.

GROVE CITY COLLEGE

100 Campus Drive, Grove City, PA 16127-2104
Phone: 724-458-2100 **E-mail:** admissions@gcc.edu **CEEB Code:** 2277
Fax: 724-458-3395 **Website:** www.gcc.edu **ACT Code:** 3582
Financial Aid Phone: 724-458-3300

This private school, affiliated with the Presbyterian Church, was founded in 1876. It has a 150-acre campus.

RATINGS
Admissions Selectivity Rating: 93   **Fire Safety Rating:** 83   **Green Rating:** 63

STUDENTS AND FACULTY
Enrollment: 2,473. **Student Body:** 49% female, 51% male, 52% out-of-state. Asian 2%, Caucasian 94%. **Retention and Graduation:** 93% freshmen return for sophomore year. 74% freshmen graduate within 4 years. 20% grads go on to further study within 1 year. 10% grads pursue arts and sciences degrees. 2% grads pursue business degrees. 1% grads pursue law degrees. 2% grads pursue medical degrees. **Faculty:** Student/faculty ratio 17:1. 131 full-time faculty, 79% hold PhDs. 100% faculty teach undergrads.

ACADEMICS
Degrees: Bachelor's. **Academic Requirements:** Arts/fine arts, foreign languages, history, humanities, mathematics, sciences (biological or physical), social science. **Classes:** Most classes have 20–29 students. Most lab/discussion sections have 10–19 students. **Majors with Highest Enrollment:** Business

administration/management, elementary education and teaching, English language and literature. **Disciplines with Highest Percentage of Degrees Awarded:** Business/marketing 20%, education 12%, biological/life sciences 10%, social sciences 8%, engineering 7%, English 7%, history 7%. **Special Study Options:** Accelerated program, double major, exchange student program (domestic), independent study, internships, student-designed major, study abroad, teacher certification program.

FACILITIES

Housing: Men's dorms, women's dorms, apartments for single students. **Special Academic Facilities/Equipment:** Fine arts center, language lab, on-campus preschool, technological learning center. **Computers:** 52% of classrooms are wired, 76% of classrooms are wireless, 100% of public computers are PCs, 14% of public computers are UNIX, network access in dorm rooms, online registration, online administrative functions (other than registration), remote student-access to Web through college's connection, tuition includes personal computer. Undergraduates are required to own a computer.

CAMPUS LIFE

Activities: Choral groups, concert band, dance, drama/theater, jazz band, literary magazine, marching band, music ensembles, musical theater, opera, pep band, radio station, student government, student newspaper, symphony orchestra, television station, yearbook. **Organizations:** 123 registered organizations, 19 honor societies, 22 religious organizations. 8 fraternities (18% men join), 8 sororities (20% women join). **Athletics (Intercollegiate):** *Men:* Baseball, basketball, cross-country, diving, football, golf, soccer, swimming, tennis, track/field (outdoor). *Women:* Basketball, cheerleading, cross-country, diving, golf, soccer, softball, swimming, tennis, track/field (outdoor), volleyball, water polo.

ADMISSIONS

Freshman Academic Profile: 59% in top 10% of high school class, 86% in top 25% of high school class, 97% in top 50% of high school class. 80% from public high schools. SAT Math middle 50% range 574–691. SAT Critical Reading middle 50% range 566–702. ACT middle 50% range 25–30. TOEFL required of all international applicants, minimum paper TOEFL 550, minimum computer TOEFL 213. **Basis for Candidate Selection:** *Very important factors considered include:* Application essay, character/personal qualities, extracurricular activities, interview, religious affiliation/commitment, rigor of secondary school record, standardized test scores. *Important factors considered include:* Recommendation(s), talent/ability. *Other factors considered include:* Alumni/ae relation, class rank, geographical residence, racial/ethnic status, state residency, volunteer work, work experience. **Freshman Admission Requirements:** High school diploma is required, and GED is accepted. *Academic units recommended:* 4 English, 3 math, 3 science (2 science labs), 3 foreign language, 2 social studies, 2 history. **Freshman Admission Statistics:** 1,918 applied, 57% admitted, 62% enrolled. **Transfer Admission Requirements:** High school transcript, college transcript(s), essay or personal statement, standardized test score, statement of good standing from prior institution(s). Minimum college GPA of 2.0 required. Lowest grade transferable C. **General Admission Information:** Application fee $50. Early decision application deadline 11/15. Regular application deadline 2/1. Regular notification 3/15. Nonfall registration accepted. Admission may be deferred for a maximum of 1 year. Credit offered for CEEB Advanced Placement tests.

COSTS AND FINANCIAL AID

Annual tuition $11,500. Room and board $6,134. Average book expense $900. **Required Forms and Deadlines:** Institution's own financial aid form. Financial aid filing deadline 4/15. **Notification of Awards:** Applicants will be notified of awards on a rolling basis beginning on or about 3/20. **Types of Aid:** *Need-based scholarships/grants:* State scholarships/grants, private scholarships, the school's own gift aid. *Loans:* Private, alternative loans. **Student Employment:** Institutional employment available. Off-campus job opportunities are good. **Financial Aid Statistics:** 42% freshmen, 33% undergrads receive need-based scholarship or grant aid. 22% freshmen, 22% undergrads receive need-based self-help aid. 42% freshmen, 35% undergrads receive any aid. Highest amount earned per year from on-campus jobs $2,500.

GUILFORD COLLEGE

Best 368

5800 West Friendly Avenue, Greensboro, NC 27410
Phone: 336-316-2100 **E-mail:** admission@guilford.edu **CEEB Code:** 5261
Fax: 336-316-2954 **Website:** www.guilford.edu **ACT Code:** 3106
Financial Aid Phone: 336-316-2354

This private school, affiliated with the Society of Friends, was founded in 1837. It has a 340-acre campus.

RATINGS

Admissions Selectivity Rating: 80 **Fire Safety Rating:** 73 **Green Rating:** 60*

STUDENTS AND FACULTY

Enrollment: 2,582. **Student Body:** 62% female, 38% male, 62% out-of-state. **Retention and Graduation:** 74% freshmen return for sophomore year. 50% freshmen graduate within 4 years. **Faculty:** Student/faculty ratio 15:1. 133 full-time faculty, 70% hold PhDs. 100% faculty teach undergrads.

ACADEMICS

Degrees: Bachelor's, certificate. **Academic Requirements:** Arts/fine arts, breadth course in business and policy studies, computer literacy, English (including composition), exploration courses in intercultural studies, first-year experience, foreign languages, historical perspectives, history, humanities, interdisciplinary capstone course, mathematics, philosophy, sciences (biological or physical), social justice/environmental responsibility and diversity in the United States, social science. **Classes:** Most classes have 10–19 students. Most lab/discussion sections have 10–19 students. **Majors with Highest Enrollment:** Biological and biomedical sciences, business administration/management, psychology. **Disciplines with Highest Percentage of Degrees Awarded:** Security and protective services 14%, psychology 9%, biological/life sciences 9%, social sciences 8%, computer and information sciences 6%, visual and performing arts 5%. **Special Study Options:** Accelerated program, cooperative education program, cross-registration, double major, English as a second language (ESL), exchange student program (domestic), honors program, independent study, internships, liberal arts/career combination, student-designed major, study abroad, teacher certification program, weekend college. There are 3-2 degree programs available in forestry and environmental studies with Duke University, and in physician assistant training with Bowman Gray School of Medicine at Wake Forest University. Guilford also offers many internships, a Washington semester, work-study programs, accelerated degree programs in business management, computer information systems, psychology, and biology, dual majors, student-designed majors, study abroad in 9 countries, and cross-registration with members of the Greater Greensboro Consortium (8 colleges/universities).

FACILITIES

Housing: Coed dorms, men's dorms, women's dorms, apartments for single students, special housing for disabled students, special housing for international students, cooperative housing, special interest housing available, alternative houses with themes and communities. **Special Academic Facilities/Equipment:** Friends Historical Collection, Frank Family Science Center, art gallery, language lab, research-grade observatory and planetarium. **Computers:** 25% of classrooms are wired, 15% of classrooms are wireless, 91% of public computers are PCs, 7% of public computers are Macs, 2% of public computers are UNIX, network access in dorm rooms, network access in dorm lounges, online registration, online administrative functions (other than registration), remote student-access to Web through college's connection.

CAMPUS LIFE

Activities: Choral groups, dance, drama/theater, literary magazine, music ensembles, musical theater, radio station, student government, student newspaper, student-run film society, yearbook. **Organizations:** 47 registered organizations, 1 honor society, 8 religious organizations. **Athletics (Intercollegiate):** *Men:* Baseball, basketball, cross-country, football, golf, lacrosse, soccer, tennis. *Women:* Basketball, cross-country, lacrosse, soccer, softball, swimming, tennis, volleyball.

ADMISSIONS

Freshman Academic Profile: 20% in top 10% of high school class, 51% in top 25% of high school class, 83% in top 50% of high school class. 68% from public high schools. SAT Math middle 50% range 500–610. SAT Critical Reading middle 50% range 490–630. ACT middle 50% range 21–26. TOEFL required of all international applicants, minimum paper TOEFL 550, minimum computer TOEFL 213. **Basis for Candidate Selection:** *Very important factors considered include:* Rigor of secondary school record. *Important factors considered include:* Academic GPA, application essay, character/personal qualities, extracurricular activities, level of applicant's interest, standardized test scores, talent/ability. *Other factors considered include:* Alumni/ae relation, class rank, first generation, geographical residence, interview, racial/ethnic status, recommendation(s), religious affiliation/commitment, state residency, volunteer work, work experience. **Freshman Admission Requirements:** High school diploma is required, and GED is accepted. *Academic units recommended:* 4 English, 3 math, 3 science, 2 foreign language. **Freshman Admission Statistics:** 2,603 applied, 73% admitted, 22% enrolled. **Transfer Admission Requirements:** College transcript(s), essay or personal statement, statement of good standing from prior institution(s). Minimum college GPA of 2.0 required. Lowest grade transferable C. **General Admission Information:** Application fee $25. Regular application deadline 2/15. Regular notification is rolling. Nonfall registration accepted. Admission may be deferred for a maximum of 1 year. Credit and/or placement offered for CEEB Advanced Placement tests.

COSTS AND FINANCIAL AID

Annual tuition $24,140. Required fees $330. Average book expense $800. **Required Forms and Deadlines:** FAFSA. Financial aid filing deadline 3/1. **Notification of Awards:** Applicants will be notified of awards on a rolling basis beginning on or about 2/1. **Types of Aid:** *Need-based scholarships/grants:* Pell, SEOG, state scholarships/grants, private scholarships, the school's own gift aid. *Loans:* FFEL Subsidized Stafford, FFEL Unsubsidized Stafford, FFEL PLUS, Federal Perkins, college/university loans from institutional funds. **Student Employment:** Federal Work-Study Program available. Institutional employment available. Off-campus job opportunities are good. **Financial Aid Statistics:** 70% freshmen, 60% undergrads receive need-based scholarship or grant aid. 61% freshmen, 60% undergrads receive need-based self-help aid. 88% freshmen, 92% undergrads receive any aid. Highest amount earned per year from on-campus jobs $11,148.

GUSTAVUS ADOLPHUS COLLEGE

Best 368

800 West College Avenue, Saint Peter, MN 56082
Phone: 507-933-7676 **E-mail:** admission@gustavus.edu **CEEB Code:** 6253
Fax: 507-933-7474 **Website:** www.gustavus.edu **ACT Code:** 2112
Financial Aid Phone: 507-933-7527

This private school, affiliated with the Lutheran Church, was founded in 1862. It has a 340-acre campus.

RATINGS

Admissions Selectivity Rating: 87   **Fire Safety Rating:** 91   **Green Rating:** 90

STUDENTS AND FACULTY

Enrollment: 2,546. **Student Body:** 57% female, 43% male, 17% out-of-state, 1% international (15 countries represented). African American 2%, Asian 4%, Caucasian 93%, Hispanic 2%. **Retention and Graduation:** 89% freshmen return for sophomore year. 79% freshmen graduate within 4 years. 35% grads go on to further study within 1 year. 5% grads pursue arts and sciences degrees. 1% grads pursue business degrees. 3% grads pursue law degrees. 2% grads pursue medical degrees. **Faculty:** Student/faculty ratio 12:1. 192 full-time faculty, 89% hold PhDs. 100% faculty teach undergrads.

ACADEMICS

Degrees: Bachelor's. **Academic Requirements:** Arts/fine arts, English (including composition), foreign languages, history, humanities, mathematics, Northwestern culture, personal fitness, religion, sciences (biological or physical), social science. **Classes:** Most classes have 10–19 students. Most lab/discussion sections have 10–19 students. **Majors with Highest Enrollment:** Business administration/management, communications studies/speech communication and rhetoric, psychology. **Disciplines with Highest Percentage of Degrees Awarded:** Social sciences 15%, business/marketing 15%, biological/life sciences 9%, communications/journalism 9%, education 9%, psychology 6%, visual and performing arts 5%, mathematics 4%, foreign languages and literature 4%, English 4%. **Special Study Options:** Cross-registration, double major, dual enrollment, exchange student program (domestic), honors program, independent study, internships, liberal arts/career

combination, student-designed major, study abroad, teacher certification program. 3-2 engineering programs with University of Minnesota (Institute of Technology) and Minnesota State University—Mankato; 3-2 environmental studies master's degree program with Duke University.

FACILITIES

Housing: Coed dorms, apartments for single students, theme or honors houses. **Special Academic Facilities/Equipment:** Art gallery, mineral museum, electron microscopes, arboretum, 14-inch computer-guided Celestron telescope, artificial intelligence laboratory, materials science laboratory, 300-MHz NMR spectrometer, 5-section greenhouse. **Computers:** 75% of public computers are PCs, 20% of public computers are Macs, 5% of public computers are UNIX, network access in dorm rooms, network access in dorm lounges, online registration, online administrative functions (other than registration), support for handheld computing, remote student-access to Web through college's connection.

CAMPUS LIFE

Activities: Choral groups, concert band, dance, drama/theater, jazz band, literary magazine, music ensembles, musical theater, pep band, radio station, student government, student newspaper, symphony orchestra, yearbook. **Organizations:** 120 registered organizations, 11 honor societies, 8 religious organizations. 3 fraternities (9% men join), 5 sororities (9% women join). **Athletics (Intercollegiate):** *Men:* Baseball, basketball, cross-country, football, golf, ice hockey, skiing (Nordic/cross-country), soccer, swimming, tennis, track/field (indoor), track/field (outdoor). *Women:* Basketball, cross-country, golf, gymnastics, ice hockey, skiing (Nordic/cross-country), soccer, softball, swimming, tennis, track/field (indoor), track/field (outdoor), volleyball. **Environmental initiatives:** Seeking to acquire 5 MW of wind generator capacity. Established the Johnson Center for Environmental Innovation. Strong institutional commitment to recycling & energy conservation.

ADMISSIONS

Freshman Academic Profile: 35% in top 10% of high school class, 70% in top 25% of high school class, 94% in top 50% of high school class. 92% from public high schools. SAT Math middle 50% range 590–680. ACT middle 50% range 24–29. TOEFL required of all international applicants, minimum paper TOEFL 550, minimum computer TOEFL 213. **Basis for Candidate Selection:** *Very important factors considered include:* Application essay, rigor of secondary school record. *Important factors considered include:* Character/personal qualities, class rank, extracurricular activities, interview, recommendation(s), religious affiliation/commitment, talent/ability. *Other factors considered include:* Alumni/ae relation, geographical residence, racial/ethnic status, volunteer work, work experience. **Freshman Admission Requirements:** High school diploma is required, and GED is accepted. *Academic units recommended:* 4 English, 4 math, 3 science (3 science labs). **Freshman Admission Statistics:** 2,663 applied, 78% admitted, 33% enrolled. **Transfer Admission Requirements:** High school transcript, college transcript(s), essay or personal statement, statement of good standing from prior institution(s). Minimum college GPA of 2.4 required. Lowest grade transferable C. **General Admission Information:** Regular application deadline 4/1. Regular notification is rolling. Nonfall registration accepted. Admission may be deferred for a maximum of 1 year. Credit and/or placement offered for CEEB Advanced Placement tests.

COSTS AND FINANCIAL AID

Annual tuition $28,125. Room and board $6,275. Required fees $140. Average book expense $900. **Required Forms and Deadlines:** FAFSA, institution's own financial aid form, students who want to receive an award by 3/1 must file the CSS Financial Aid/PROFILE. Financial aid filing deadline 4/15. **Notification of Awards:** Applicants will be notified of awards on a rolling basis beginning on or about 3/1. **Types of Aid:** *Need-based scholarships/grants:* Pell, SEOG, state scholarships/grants, private scholarships, the school's own gift aid. *Loans:* Direct Subsidized Stafford, Direct Unsubsidized Stafford, Direct PLUS, Federal Perkins, state loans, college/university loans from institutional funds, alternative loans from private lenders. **Financial Aid Statistics:** 67% freshmen, 62% undergrads receive need-based scholarship or grant aid. 58% freshmen, 53% undergrads receive need-based self-help aid. 98% freshmen, 92% undergrads receive any aid. Highest amount earned per year from on-campus jobs $1,800.

GWYNEDD-MERCY COLLEGE

1325 Sumneytown Pike, PO Box 901, Gwynedd Valley, PA 19437-0901
Phone: 215-641-5510 **E-mail:** admissions@gmc.edu **CEEB Code:** 2278
Fax: 215-641-5556 **Website:** www.gmc.edu
Financial Aid Phone: 215-646-7300

This private school, affiliated with the Roman Catholic Church, was founded in 1948. It has a 160-acre campus.

RATINGS
Admissions Selectivity Rating: 60* **Fire Safety Rating:** 60* **Green Rating:** 60*

STUDENTS AND FACULTY
Enrollment: 2,069. **Student Body:** 76% female, 24% male, 8% out-of-state. African American 17%, Asian 2%, Caucasian 77%, Hispanic 2%. **Retention and Graduation:** 75% freshmen return for sophomore year. 55% freshmen graduate within 4 years. **Faculty:** Student/faculty ratio 13:1. 81 full-time faculty, 54% hold PhDs. 96% faculty teach undergrads.

ACADEMICS
Degrees: Associate, bachelor's, certificate, master's, post-bachelor's certificate, post-master's certificate. **Academic Requirements:** Arts/fine arts, English (including composition), foreign languages, history, humanities, philosophy, social science, religious studies. **Classes:** Most classes have 10–19 students. Most lab/discussion sections have 10–19 students. **Majors with Highest Enrollment:** Business administration/management; education; nursing/registered nurse training (ASN, BSN, MSN, RN). **Disciplines with Highest Percentage of Degrees Awarded:** Business/marketing 46%, health professions and related sciences 20%, education 19%, psychology 4%, social sciences 3%, biological/life sciences 3%. **Special Study Options:** Accelerated program, cross-registration, double major, dual enrollment, English as a Second Language (ESL), honors program, independent study, internships, liberal arts/career combination, study abroad, teacher certification program, weekend college.

FACILITIES
Housing: Coed dorms. **Special Academic Facilities/Equipment:** Keiss Hall (Health and Science Center), television production room and small theater, computer labs. **Computers:** 98% of public computers are PCs, 2% of public computers are Macs, network access in dorm rooms, network access in dorm lounges, remote student-access to Web through college's connection.

CAMPUS LIFE
Activities: Choral groups, literary magazine, student government, student newspaper, yearbook. **Organizations:** 20 registered organizations, 10 honor societies, 1 religious organization. **Athletics (Intercollegiate):** *Men:* Baseball, basketball, cross-country, golf, soccer, tennis, track/field (indoor), track/field (outdoor). *Women:* Basketball, cross-country, field hockey, lacrosse, soccer, softball, tennis, track/field (indoor), track/field (outdoor), volleyball.

ADMISSIONS
Freshman Academic Profile: 57% from public high schools. SAT Math middle 50% range 440–540. SAT Critical Reading middle 50% range 440–538. TOEFL required of all international applicants, minimum paper TOEFL 525, minimum computer TOEFL 195. **Basis for Candidate Selection:** *Very important factors considered include:* Rigor of secondary school record. *Important factors considered include:* Academic GPA, class rank, extracurricular activities, recommendation(s), standardized test scores. *Other factors considered include:* Alumni/ae relation, character/personal qualities, interview, religious affiliation/commitment, volunteer work, work experience. **Freshman Admission Requirements:** High school diploma is required, and GED is accepted. *Academic units required:* 4 English, 3 math, 3 science, 1 history, 3 academic electives. **Freshman Admission Statistics:** 1,506 applied, 60% admitted, 31% enrolled. **Transfer Admission Requirements:** High school transcript, college transcript(s), standardized test score. Minimum college GPA of 2.0 required. Lowest grade transferable C. **General Admission Information:** Application fee $25. Regular application deadline 8/20. Regular notification is rolling. Nonfall registration accepted. Admission may be deferred for a maximum of 1 year. Credit and/or placement offered for CEEB Advanced Placement tests.

COSTS AND FINANCIAL AID
Annual tuition $22,340. Room and board $8,600. Required fees $450. Average book expense $600. **Required Forms and Deadlines:** FAFSA, institution's own financial aid form, copies of parent and student federal tax returns. Financial aid filing deadline 7/15. Financial aid filing deadline 3/1. **Notification of Awards:** Applicants will be notified of awards on a rolling basis beginning on or about 3/15. **Types of Aid:** *Need-based scholarships/grants:* Pell, SEOG, state scholarships/grants, private scholarships, the school's own gift aid. *Loans:* FFEL Subsidized Stafford, FFEL Unsubsidized Stafford, FFEL PLUS, Federal Perkins, Federal Nursing. **Student Employment:** Federal Work-Study Program available. Off-campus job opportunities are fair. **Financial Aid Statistics:** 78% freshmen, 72% undergrads receive need-based scholarship or grant aid. 65% freshmen, 61% undergrads receive need-based self-help aid. 71% freshmen, 67% undergrads receive any aid. Highest amount earned per year from on-campus jobs $900.

HAMILTON COLLEGE

Office of Admissions, 198 College Hill Road, Clinton, NY 13323
Phone: 315-859-4421 **E-mail:** admission@hamilton.edu **CEEB Code:** 2286
Fax: 315-859-4457 **Website:** www.hamilton.edu **ACT Code:** 2754
Financial Aid Phone: 315-859-4434

This private school was founded in 1812. It has a 1,300-acre campus.

RATINGS
Admissions Selectivity Rating: 96 **Fire Safety Rating:** 79 **Green Rating:** 95

STUDENTS AND FACULTY
Enrollment: 1,801. **Student Body:** 50% female, 50% male, 65% out-of-state, 5% international (40 countries represented). African American 4%, Asian 7%, Caucasian 71%, Hispanic 4%. **Retention and Graduation:** 93% freshmen return for sophomore year. 83% freshmen graduate within 4 years. 40% grads go on to further study within 1 year. 40% grads pursue arts and sciences degrees. 10% grads pursue business degrees. 15% grads pursue law degrees. 5% grads pursue medical degrees. **Faculty:** Student/faculty ratio 10:1. 147 full-time faculty. 100% faculty teach undergrads.

ACADEMICS
Degrees: Bachelor's. **Academic Requirements:** The Hamilton Plan for Liberal Education provides highly motivated students with both the freedom and responsibility to make educational choices that emphasize breadth and depth. Unique to this plan are two distinct capstone requirements—one prior to declaration of an area of concentration (the sophomore program) and one at the conclusion of the concentration (the senior program)—that serve as integrating and culminating experiences for students at decisive points in their undergraduate careers. As part of the new Hamilton Plan for Liberal Education, the faculty has significantly strengthened the general education sequence by replacing distribution requirements with a series of recommended goals; instituting special first- and second-year seminars; reaffirming the centrality of the three-course writing-intensive program; reinvigorating the advising system; and establishing a multidisciplinary seminar program at the end of the sophomore year that culminates in an integrative project with public presentations. **Classes:** Most classes have 10–19 students. Most lab/discussion sections have 10–19 students. **Majors with Highest Enrollment:** Economics, political science and government, psychology. **Disciplines with Highest Percentage of Degrees Awarded:** Social sciences 34%, foreign languages and literature 11%, English 9%, visual and performing arts 8%, mathematics 7%. **Special Study Options:** Accelerated program, cross-registration, double major, English as a second language (ESL), independent study, internships, student-designed major, study abroad. 3-2 program in engineering with Columbia University, Rensselaer Polytechnic Institute, and Washington University (St. Louis); 3-3 program in law with Columbia University.

FACILITIES
Housing: Coed dorms, apartments for married students, apartments for single students, special housing for disabled students. **Special Academic Facilities/Equipment:** Art gallery, language lab, fitness center, observatory, two electron microscopes, Arthur Levitt Public Affairs Center. **Computers:** 50% of public computers are PCs, 50% of public computers are Macs, network access in dorm rooms, network access in dorm lounges, online registration, online administrative functions (other than registration), support for handheld computing, remote student-access to Web through college's connection.

CAMPUS LIFE
Activities: Choral groups, concert band, dance, drama/theater, jazz band, literary magazine, music ensembles, musical theater, pep band, radio station, student government, student newspaper, student-run film society, symphony

orchestra, yearbook. **Organizations:** 80 registered organizations, 3 honor societies, 4 religious organizations. 7 fraternities (29% men join), 3 sororities (19% women join). **Athletics (Intercollegiate):** *Men:* Baseball, basketball, crew/rowing, cross-country, diving, football, golf, ice hockey, lacrosse, soccer, squash, swimming, tennis, track/field (indoor), track/field (outdoor). *Women:* Basketball, crew/rowing, cross-country, diving, field hockey, golf, ice hockey, lacrosse, soccer, softball, squash, swimming, tennis, track/field (indoor), track/field (outdoor), volleyball. **Environmental initiatives:** Academic initiatives associated with Hamilton's new Environmental Studies major (2005), and various research related projects. Charter signatory to the President's Climate Commitment, which is actively implementing variuos administrative and logistical programs to meet and eventually go beyond the minimum participation requirements. Long standing, regionally superior "Recycling/Reductioin/ Reuse" program, to facilitate environmental responsibility and stewardship.

ADMISSIONS

Freshman Academic Profile: 74% in top 10% of high school class, 92% in top 25% of high school class, 99% in top 50% of high school class. 60% from public high schools. SAT Math middle 50% range 640–720. SAT Critical Reading middle 50% range 640–740. TOEFL required of all international applicants, minimum paper TOEFL 600, minimum computer TOEFL 250. **Basis for Candidate Selection:** *Very important factors considered include:* Academic GPA, class rank, rigor of secondary·school record. *Important factors considered include:* Application essay, character/personal qualities, extracurricular activities, interview, recommendation(s), standardized test scores. *Other factors considered include:* Alumni/ae relation, first generation, geographical residence, level of applicant's interest, racial/ethnic status, talent/ability, volunteer work, work experience. **Freshman Admission Requirements:** High school diploma or equivalent is not required. *Academic units recommended:* 4 English, 3 math, 3 science, 3 foreign language, 3 social studies. **Freshman Admission Statistics:** 4,266 applied, 33% admitted, 35% enrolled. **Transfer Admission Requirements:** High school transcript, college transcript(s), essay or personal statement, standardized test score. Lowest grade transferable C. **General Admission Information:**. Early decision application deadline 11/15. Regular application deadline 1/1. Regular notification 4/1. Nonfall registration accepted. Admission may be deferred for a maximum of 2 years. Credit and/or placement offered for CEEB Advanced Placement tests.

COSTS AND FINANCIAL AID

Annual tuition $36,500. Room and board $9,350. Required fees $360. Average book expense $1,300. **Required Forms and Deadlines:** FAFSA, institution's own financial aid form, CSS/Financial Aid PROFILE, state aid form, Noncustodial PROFILE, Business/Farm Supplement. Financial aid filing deadline 2/8. **Notification of Awards:** Applicants will be notified of awards on or about 5/1. **Types of Aid:** *Need-based scholarships/grants:* Pell, SEOG, state scholarships/grants, private scholarships, the school's own gift aid. *Loans:* FFEL Subsidized Stafford, FFEL Unsubsidized Stafford, FFEL PLUS, Federal Perkins. **Student Employment:** Federal Work-Study Program available. Institutional employment available. **Financial Aid Statistics:** Highest amount earned per year from on-campus jobs $1,600.

HAMLINE UNIVERSITY

1536 Hewitt Avenue, MS-C1930, Saint Paul, MN 55104
Phone: 651-523-2207 **E-mail:** CLA-admis@hamline.edu **CEEB Code:** 6265
Fax: 651-523-2458 **Website:** www.hamline.edu **ACT Code:** 2114
Financial Aid Phone: 651-523-3000

This private school, affiliated with the Methodist Church, was founded in 1854. It has a 77-acre campus.

RATINGS
Admissions Selectivity Rating: 80   **Fire Safety Rating:** 83   **Green Rating:** 70

STUDENTS AND FACULTY
Enrollment: 1,944. **Student Body:** 60% female, 40% male, 15% out-of-state, 3% international (32 countries represented). African American 3%, Asian 6%, Caucasian 80%, Hispanic 2%. **Retention and Graduation:** 84% freshmen return for sophomore year. 63% freshmen graduate within 4 years. 32% grads go on to further study within 1 year. 13% grads pursue arts and sciences degrees. 4% grads pursue business degrees. 8% grads pursue law degrees. 5% grads pursue medical degrees. **Faculty:** Student/faculty ratio 13:1. 174 full-time faculty, 77% hold PhDs. 100% faculty teach undergrads.

ACADEMICS
Degrees: Bachelor's, doctoral, first professional certificate, first professional, master's, post-bachelor's certificate, post-master's certificate. **Academic**

Requirements: Arts/fine arts, computer literacy, cultural breadth, English (including composition), humanities, sciences (biological or physical), social science. **Classes:** Most classes have 10–19 students. Most lab/discussion sections have 20–29 students. **Majors with Highest Enrollment:** Business administration/management, criminal justice/police science, psychology. **Disciplines with Highest Percentage of Degrees Awarded:** Social sciences 25%, psychology 11%, business/marketing 8%, security and protective services 7%, English 6%. **Special Study Options:** Cross-registration, double major, English as a second language (ESL), exchange student program (domestic), honors program, independent study, internships, student-designed major, study abroad, teacher certification program. Undergrads may take grad-level classes. Off-campus study Washington, DC; United Nations; arts program in New York. Co-op programs available in engineering and law. Other special programs include Center for Global Environmental Education, Comprehensive Regional Assistant Center, Center for Literacy and Learning, Center for Women in Government, Upper Midwest Women's History Center, Crossroads Center.

FACILITIES
Housing: Coed dorms, apartments for married students, apartments for single students, special housing for international students, fraternity/sorority housing, PRIDE (African American), Spectrum (GLBT), foreign language interest, theme housing. **Special Academic Facilities/Equipment:** Theater, music hall, art gallery, science center. **Computers:** 97% of public computers are PCs, 3% of public computers are Macs, network access in dorm rooms, network access in dorm lounges, online registration, online administrative functions (other than registration), remote student-access to Web through college's connection.

CAMPUS LIFE
Activities: Choral groups, concert band, dance, drama/theater, jazz band, literary magazine, music ensembles, pep band, radio station, student government, student newspaper, symphony orchestra, television station, yearbook. **Organizations:** 77 registered organizations, 11 honor societies, 9 religious organizations. 1 fraternity (3% men join), 2 sororities. **Athletics (Intercollegiate):** *Men:* Baseball, basketball, cross-country, diving, football, ice hockey, soccer, swimming, tennis, track/field (indoor), track/field (outdoor). *Women:* Basketball, cross-country, diving, gymnastics, ice hockey, soccer, softball, swimming, tennis, track/field (indoor), track/field (outdoor), volleyball.

ADMISSIONS
Freshman Academic Profile: 27% in top 10% of high school class, 51% in top 25% of high school class, 80% in top 50% of high school class. 90% from public high schools. SAT Math middle 50% range 540–640. SAT Critical Reading middle 50% range 512.5–645. SAT Writing middle 50% range 510–615. ACT middle 50% range 21–27. TOEFL required of all international applicants, minimum paper TOEFL 550, minimum computer TOEFL 213. **Basis for Candidate Selection:** *Very important factors considered include:* Class rank, rigor of secondary school record. *Important factors considered include:* Academic GPA, application essay, extracurricular activities, interview, recommendation(s), standardized test scores, talent/ability. *Other factors considered include:* Alumni/ae relation, character/personal qualities, first generation, racial/ethnic status, volunteer work, work experience. **Freshman Admission Requirements:** High school diploma is required, and GED is accepted. *Academic units recommended:* 4 English, 3 math, 3 science (3 science labs), 2 foreign language, 4 social studies, 4 academic electives. **Freshman Admission Statistics:** 1,806 applied, 78% admitted, 33% enrolled. **Transfer Admission Requirements:** College transcript(s), essay or personal statement. Minimum college GPA of 2.0 required. Lowest grade transferable C-. **General Admission Information:** Regular notification is rolling. Nonfall registration accepted. Admission may be deferred for a maximum of 2 years. Common Application accepted. Credit and/or placement offered for CEEB Advanced Placement tests.

COSTS AND FINANCIAL AID
Required Forms and Deadlines: FAFSA. Financial aid filing deadline 3/1. **Notification of Awards:** Applicants will be notified of awards on a rolling basis beginning on or about 3/15. **Types of Aid:** *Need-based scholarships/grants:* Pell, SEOG, state scholarships/grants, private scholarships, the school's own gift aid. *Loans:* FFEL Subsidized Stafford, FFEL Unsubsidized Stafford, FFEL PLUS, Federal Perkins. **Student Employment:** Federal Work-Study Program available. Institutional employment available. Off-campus job opportunities are excellent. **Financial Aid Statistics:** 65% freshmen, 64% undergrads receive need-based scholarship or grant aid. 56% freshmen, 61% undergrads receive need-based self-help aid. 93% freshmen, 92% undergrads receive any aid. Highest amount earned per year from on-campus jobs $3,000.

See page 1190.

HAMPDEN-SYDNEY COLLEGE

PO Box 667, Hampden-Sydney, VA 23943-0667
Phone: 434-223-6120 **E-mail:** hsapp@hsc.edu **CEEB Code:** 5291
Fax: 434-223-6346 **Website:** www.hsc.edu **ACT Code:** 4356
Financial Aid Phone: 434-223-6119

This private school, affiliated with the Presbyterian Church, was founded in 1775. It has a 1,200-acre campus.

RATINGS
Admissions Selectivity Rating: 79   **Fire Safety Rating:** 76   **Green Rating:** 71

STUDENTS AND FACULTY
Enrollment: 1,106. **Student Body:** 100% male, 33% out-of-state. African American 3%, Caucasian 64%. **Retention and Graduation:** 83% freshmen return for sophomore year. 58% freshmen graduate within 4 years. 30% grads go on to further study within 1 year. 20% grads pursue business degrees. 6% grads pursue law degrees. 7% grads pursue medical degrees. **Faculty:** Student/faculty ratio 9:1. 93 full-time faculty. 100% faculty teach undergrads.

ACADEMICS
Degrees: Bachelor's. **Academic Requirements:** Arts/fine arts, English (including composition), foreign languages, history, humanities, mathematics, philosophy, sciences (biological or physical), social science. **Classes:** Most classes have 10–19 students. **Majors with Highest Enrollment:** Economics, history, political science and government. **Disciplines with Highest Percentage of Degrees Awarded:** Social sciences 34%, history 19%, business/marketing 13%, biological/life sciences 10%, physical sciences 7%. **Special Study Options:** Appalachian semester, cross-registration, double major, exchange student program (domestic), honors program, independent study, internships, junior year exchange with members of Virginia consortium, semester at sea, study abroad, Washington semester.

FACILITIES
Housing: Men's dorms, apartments for married students, apartments for single students, fraternity/sorority housing. **Special Academic Facilities/Equipment:** History museum, language lab, international communications center, observatory. **Computers:** 7% of classrooms are wired, 7% of classrooms are wireless, 100% of public computers are PCs, network access in dorm rooms, network access in dorm lounges, online registration, online administrative functions (other than registration), support for handheld computing, remote student-access to Web through college's connection.

CAMPUS LIFE
Activities: Choral groups, drama/theater, literary magazine, music ensembles, pep band, radio station, student government, student newspaper, yearbook. **Organizations:** 45 registered organizations, 14 honor societies, 2 religious organizations. 11 fraternities (22% men join). **Athletics (Intercollegiate):** *Men:* Baseball, basketball, cross-country, football, golf, lacrosse, soccer, tennis.

ADMISSIONS
Freshman Academic Profile: 9% in top 10% of high school class, 20% in top 25% of high school class, 50% in top 50% of high school class. 53% from public high schools. SAT Math middle 50% range 515–630. SAT Critical Reading middle 50% range 510–600. SAT Writing middle 50% range 480–590. ACT middle 50% range 20–26. TOEFL required of all international applicants, minimum paper TOEFL 570, minimum computer TOEFL 230. **Basis for Candidate Selection:** *Very important factors considered include:* Character/personal qualities, recommendation(s), rigor of secondary school record, standardized test scores. *Important factors considered include:* Academic GPA, class rank, extracurricular activities. *Other factors considered include:* Alumni/ae relation, application essay, first generation, interview, level of applicant's interest, racial/ethnic status, talent/ability, volunteer work, work experience. **Freshman Admission Requirements:** High school diploma is required, and GED is accepted. *Academic units required:* 4 English, 3 math, 2 science (1 science lab), 2 foreign language, 1 social studies, 1 history, 3 academic electives. *Academic units recommended:* 4 math, 3 science, 3 foreign language. **Freshman Admission Statistics:** 1,509 applied, 69% admitted, 33% enrolled. **Transfer Admission Requirements:** High school transcript, college transcript(s), standardized test score, statement of good standing from prior institution(s). Minimum college GPA of 2.5 required. Lowest grade transferable C. **General Admission Information:** Application fee $30. Early decision

application deadline 11/15. Regular application deadline 3/1. Regular notification 4/15. Nonfall registration accepted. Credit and/or placement offered for CEEB Advanced Placement tests.

COSTS AND FINANCIAL AID
Annual tuition $28,144. Room and board $9,148. Required fees $1,110. Average book expense $1,000. **Required Forms and Deadlines:** FAFSA, CSS/Financial Aid PROFILE, state aid form. Financial aid filing deadline 5/1. **Notification of Awards:** Applicants will be notified of awards on a rolling basis beginning on or about 12/15. **Types of Aid:** *Need-based scholarships/grants:* Pell, SEOG, state scholarships/grants, private scholarships, the school's own gift aid. *Loans:* FFEL Subsidized Stafford, FFEL Unsubsidized Stafford, FFEL PLUS, Federal Perkins, college/university loans from institutional funds, private loans. **Student Employment:** Federal Work-Study Program available. Institutional employment available. Off-campus job opportunities are fair. **Financial Aid Statistics:** 48% freshmen, 48% undergrads receive need-based scholarship or grant aid. 35% freshmen, 38% undergrads receive need-based self-help aid. 98% freshmen, 97% undergrads receive any aid. Highest amount earned per year from on-campus jobs $4,000.

HAMPSHIRE COLLEGE

Admissions Office, 893 West Street, Amherst, MA 01002
Phone: 413-559-5471 **E-mail:** admissions@hampshire.edu **CEEB Code:** 3447
Fax: 413-559-5631 **Website:** www.hampshire.edu **ACT Code:** 1842
Financial Aid Phone: 413-559-5484

This private school was founded in 1965. It has an 800-acre campus.

RATINGS
Admissions Selectivity Rating: 89   **Fire Safety Rating:** 60*   **Green Rating:** 79

STUDENTS AND FACULTY
Enrollment: 1,434. **Student Body:** 59% female, 41% male, 83% out-of-state, 3% international (28 countries represented). African American 4%, Asian 3%, Caucasian 71%, Hispanic 5%. **Retention and Graduation:** 79% freshmen return for sophomore year. 45% freshmen graduate within 4 years. 12% grads go on to further study within 1 year. 10% grads pursue arts and sciences degrees. 1% grads pursue law degrees. 1% grads pursue medical degrees. **Faculty:** Student/faculty ratio 12:1. 95 full-time faculty, 84% hold PhDs. 100% faculty teach undergrads.

ACADEMICS
Degrees: Bachelor's. **Academic Requirements:** Arts/fine arts, humanities, sciences (biological or physical), social science, Hampshire's School of Cognitive Science (computer science, philosophy, linguistics, animal behavior, cognitive science, education). **Classes:** Most classes have 10–19 students. **Majors with Highest Enrollment:** English language and literature, social sciences, visual and performing arts. **Disciplines with Highest Percentage of Degrees Awarded:** Visual and performing arts 35%, social sciences 22%, English 10%, area and ethnic studies 7%, biological/life sciences 7%, philosophy and religious studies 4%. **Special Study Options:** Exchange student program (domestic), independent study, internships, student-designed major, study abroad, teacher certification program. Member of a 5-college consortium; may take courses at the other colleges.

FACILITIES
Housing: Coed dorms, women's dorms, apartments for single students, special housing for disabled students, special housing for international students. **Special Academic Facilities/Equipment:** Performing and visual arts center, bioshelter (integrated greenhouse/aquaculture facility), farm center, electronic music and TV production studios, extensive film and photography facilities, multimedia center. **Computers:** 27% of public computers are PCs, 70% of public computers are Macs, 3% of public computers are UNIX, network access in dorm rooms, online registration, online administrative functions (other than registration), remote student-access to Web through college's connection.

CAMPUS LIFE
Activities: Choral groups, dance, drama/theater, jazz band, student government, student newspaper, student-run film society. **Organizations:** 114 registered organizations, 4 religious organizations.

ADMISSIONS

Freshman Academic Profile: 25% in top 10% of high school class, 59% in top 25% of high school class, 88% in top 50% of high school class. 49% from public high schools. SAT Math middle 50% range 540–660. SAT Critical Reading middle 50% range 610–710. SAT Writing middle 50% range 590–700. ACT middle 50% range 25–30. TOEFL required of all international applicants, minimum paper TOEFL 577, minimum computer TOEFL 233. **Basis for Candidate Selection:** *Very important factors considered include:* Application essay, character/personal qualities. *Important factors considered include:* Extracurricular activities, level of applicant's interest, recommendation(s), rigor of secondary school record, talent/ability. *Other factors considered include:* Academic GPA, alumni/ae relation, class rank, interview, racial/ethnic status, standardized test scores, volunteer work, work experience. **Freshman Admission Requirements:** High school diploma is required, and GED is accepted. *Academic units required:* 4 English, 4 math, 4 science (2 science labs), 3 foreign language, 2 social studies, 2 history. **Freshman Admission Statistics:** 2,454 applied, 56% admitted, 29% enrolled. **Transfer Admission Requirements:** High school transcript, college transcript(s), essay or personal statement. Lowest grade transferable C. **General Admission Information:** Application fee $55. Early decision application deadline 11/15. Regular application deadline 1/15. Regular notification 4/1. Nonfall registration accepted. Admission may be deferred for a maximum of 1 year. Placement offered for CEEB Advanced Placement tests.

COSTS AND FINANCIAL AID

Annual tuition $33,855. Room & board $9,030. Required fees $750. Average book expense $500. **Required Forms and Deadlines:** FAFSA, CSS/Financial Aid PROFILE, Noncustodial PROFILE. Financial aid filing deadline 2/1. **Notification of Awards:** Applicants will be notified of awards on or about 4/1. **Types of Aid:** *Need-based scholarships/grants:* Pell, SEOG, state scholarships/grants, private scholarships, the school's own gift aid. *Loans:* Direct Subsidized Stafford, Direct Unsubsidized Stafford, FFEL PLUS, Federal Perkins. **Student Employment:** Federal Work-Study Program available. **Financial Aid Statistics:** 56% freshmen, 57% undergrads receive need-based scholarship or grant aid. 56% freshmen, 57% undergrads receive need-based self-help aid. 72% freshmen, 70% undergrads receive any aid. Highest amount earned per year from on-campus jobs $2,400.

HAMPTON UNIVERSITY

Office of Admissions, Hampton University, Hampton, VA 23668
Phone: 757-727-5328 **E-mail:** admit@hamptonu.edu **CEEB Code:** 5292
Fax: 757-727-5095 **Website:** www.hamptonu.edu **ACT Code:** 4358
Financial Aid Phone: 757-727-5332

This private school was founded in 1868. It has a 255-acre campus.

RATINGS

Admissions Selectivity Rating: 87   **Fire Safety Rating:** 60*   **Green Rating:** 60*

STUDENTS AND FACULTY

Enrollment: 5,056. **Student Body:** 64% female, 36% male, 69% out-of-state. **Retention and Graduation:** 85% freshmen return for sophomore year. 40% grads go on to further study within 1 year. 40% grads pursue arts and sciences degrees. 5% grads pursue business degrees. 2% grads pursue law degrees. 10% grads pursue medical degrees. **Faculty:** Student/faculty ratio 16:1. 363 full-time faculty, 75% hold PhDs. 98% faculty teach undergrads.

ACADEMICS

Degrees: Associate, bachelor's, certificate, doctoral, first professional, master's, post-master's certificate. **Academic Requirements:** Arts/fine arts, computer literacy, English (including composition), foreign languages, general education, history, humanities, mathematics, sciences (biological or physical), social science. **Classes:** Most classes have 20–29 students. Most lab/discussion sections have 10–19 students. **Majors with Highest Enrollment:** Business administration/management, journalism, psychology. **Special Study Options:** Accelerated program, cooperative education program, cross-registration, distance learning, double major, dual enrollment, honors program, independent study, internships, study abroad, teacher certification program. Undergrads may take grad-level programs. Co-op programs available in arts, business, education,

engineering, social/behavioral science, pre-college, Army ROTC, Navy ROTC. Member of Tidewater Consortium.

FACILITIES

Housing: Coed dorms, men's dorms, women's dorms, special housing for international students. **Special Academic Facilities/Equipment:** African, Native American, and Oceanic museums; gallery, new student center. **Computers:** 80% of public computers are PCs, 20% of public computers are Macs, 5% of public computers are UNIX, network access in dorm rooms, network access in dorm lounges, online registration, online administrative functions (other than registration), remote student-access to Web through college's connection.

CAMPUS LIFE

Activities: Choral groups, concert band, dance, drama/theater, jazz band, marching band, music ensembles, musical theater, opera, pep band, radio station, student government, student newspaper, symphony orchestra, television station, yearbook. **Organizations:** 85 registered organizations, 16 honor societies, 3 religious organizations. 6 fraternities (5% men join), 3 sororities (4% women join). **Athletics (Intercollegiate):** *Men:* Basketball, cross-country, football, golf, sailing, tennis, track/field (indoor), track/field (outdoor). *Women:* Basketball, bowling, cross-country, golf, sailing, softball, tennis, track/field (indoor), track/field (outdoor), volleyball.

ADMISSIONS

Freshman Academic Profile: 20% in top 10% of high school class, 45% in top 25% of high school class, 90% in top 50% of high school class. 90% from public high schools. SAT Math middle 50% range 464–606. SAT Critical Reading middle 50% range 481–552. ACT middle 50% range 17–26. TOEFL required of all international applicants, minimum paper TOEFL 550, minimum computer TOEFL 214. **Basis for Candidate Selection:** *Very important factors considered include:* Application essay, character/personal qualities, rigor of secondary school record, standardized test scores. *Important factors considered include:* Class rank, recommendation(s). *Other factors considered include:* Alumni/ae relation, extracurricular activities, talent/ability, volunteer work. **Freshman Admission Requirements:** High school diploma is required, and GED is accepted. *Academic units required:* 4 English, 3 math, 2 science (2 science labs), 2 social studies, 6 academic electives. *Academic units recommended:* 2 foreign language. **Freshman Admission Statistics:** 7,120 applied, 37% admitted, 43% enrolled. **Transfer Admission Requirements:** College transcript(s), essay or personal statement, statement of good standing from prior institution(s). Minimum college GPA of 2.3 required. Lowest grade transferable C. **General Admission Information:** Application fee $35. Regular notification rolling 3 weeks after receipt of completed application. Nonfall registration accepted. Admission may be deferred for a maximum of 1 year. Credit and/or placement offered for CEEB Advanced Placement tests.

COSTS AND FINANCIAL AID

Annual tuition $13,358. Room & board $6,746. Required fees $1,460. Average book expense $750. **Required Forms and Deadlines:** FAFSA. Financial aid filing deadline 3/1. **Notification of Awards:** Applicants will be notified of awards on a rolling basis beginning on or about 4/15. **Types of Aid:** *Need-based scholarships/grants:* Pell, SEOG, state scholarships/grants, private scholarships, the school's own gift aid, Federal Nursing Scholarships. *Loans:* Direct Subsidized Stafford, Direct Unsubsidized Stafford, Direct PLUS, FFEL Subsidized Stafford, FFEL Unsubsidized Stafford, FFEL PLUS, Federal Perkins, alternative loans. **Student Employment:** Federal Work-Study Program available. Off-campus job opportunities are excellent. **Financial Aid Statistics:** 96% freshmen, 44% undergrads receive need-based scholarship or grant aid. 79% freshmen, 44% undergrads receive need-based self-help aid. 44% freshmen receive any aid.

HANNIBAL-LAGRANGE COLLEGE

2800 Palmyra Road, Hannibal, MO 63401
Phone: 573-221-3113 **E-mail:** admission@hlg.edu
Fax: 573-221-6594 **Website:** www.hlg.edu **ACT Code:** 2320
Financial Aid Phone: 573-221-3675

This private school, affiliated with the Southern Baptist Church, was founded in 1858. It has a 110-acre campus.

RATINGS

Admissions Selectivity Rating: 60*   **Fire Safety Rating:** 60*   **Green Rating:** 60*

STUDENTS AND FACULTY

Enrollment: 848. **Student Body:** 58% female, 42% male, 25% out-of-state,

4% international (11 countries represented). African American 2%, Caucasian 87%, Hispanic 1%. **Retention and Graduation:** 60% freshmen return for sophomore year. 16% grads go on to further study within 1 year. 10% grads pursue arts and sciences degrees. 5% grads pursue business degrees. **Faculty:** Student/faculty ratio 12:1. 61 full-time faculty, 34% hold PhDs. 100% faculty teach undergrads.

ACADEMICS

Degrees: Associate, bachelor's. **Academic Requirements:** Arts/fine arts, English (including composition), foreign languages, history, humanities, mathematics, Old and New Testament success in education, sciences (biological or physical), social science. **Majors with Highest Enrollment:** Business administration/management, education, social sciences. **Disciplines with Highest Percentage of Degrees Awarded:** Business/marketing 36%, education 23%, social sciences 12%, law/legal studies 6%, psychology 5%. **Special Study Options:** Accelerated program, adult program online courses, cooperative education program, distance learning, double major, dual enrollment, honors program, independent study, internships, liberal arts/career combination, study abroad, teacher certification program, weekend college.

FACILITIES

Housing: Men's dorms, women's dorms, apartments for single students, special housing for disabled students. **Special Academic Facilities/Equipment:** L. A. Foster Library, T. M. Matthews Science Building, Mary Wiehe Science Building. Partee Technology Center, Roland Fine Arts Center. **Computers:** 100% of public computers are PCs, network access in dorm rooms, online registration, remote student-access to Web through college's connection.

CAMPUS LIFE

Activities: Choral groups, concert band, drama/theater, jazz band, music ensembles, musical theater, student government, student newspaper, yearbook. **Organizations:** 22 registered organizations, 1 honor society, 3 religious organizations. **Athletics (Intercollegiate):** *Men:* Baseball, basketball, cheerleading, cross-country, golf, soccer. *Women:* Basketball, cheerleading, cross-country, soccer, softball, volleyball.

ADMISSIONS

Freshman Academic Profile: 22% in top 10% of high school class, 78% in top 50% of high school class. ACT middle 50% range 16–25. TOEFL required of all international applicants, minimum paper TOEFL 520, minimum computer TOEFL 190. **Basis for Candidate Selection:** *Other factors considered include:* Academic GPA, character/personal qualities, class rank, religious affiliation/commitment, rigor of secondary school record, standardized test scores, talent/ability. **Freshman Admission Requirements:** High school diploma is required, and GED is accepted. *Academic units recommended:* 2 English, 1 math, 1 science, 3 history. **Transfer Admission Requirements:** College transcript(s), standardized test score. Minimum college GPA of 2.0 required. Lowest grade transferable D. **General Admission Information:** Application fee $25. Regular application deadline 8/26. Regular notification is rolling. Nonfall registration accepted. Admission may be deferred. Neither credit nor placement offered for CEEB Advanced Placement tests.

COSTS AND FINANCIAL AID

Annual tuition $13,064. Room and board $4,930. Required fees $416. Average book expense $800. **Required Forms and Deadlines:** FAFSA, institution's own financial aid form. Financial aid filing deadline 7/1. **Types of Aid:** *Need-based scholarships/grants:* Pell, SEOG, state scholarships/grants, private scholarships, the school's own gift aid. *Loans:* FFEL Subsidized Stafford, FFEL Unsubsidized Stafford, FFEL PLUS, Federal Perkins. **Student Employment:** Federal Work-Study Program available. Institutional employment available. Off-campus job opportunities are good.

HANOVER COLLEGE

PO Box 108, Hanover, IN 47243-0108
Phone: 812-866-7021 **E-mail:** admission@hanover.edu **CEEB Code:** 1290
Fax: 812-866-7098 **Website:** www.hanover.edu **ACT Code:** 1200
Financial Aid Phone: 812-866-7029

This private school, affiliated with the Presbyterian Church, was founded in 1827. It has a 650-acre campus.

RATINGS

Admissions Selectivity Rating: 89   **Fire Safety Rating:** 76   **Green Rating:** 68

STUDENTS AND FACULTY

Enrollment: 970. **Student Body:** 53% female, 47% male, 34% out-of-state, 4% international (17 countries represented). African American 1%, Asian 3%, Caucasian 85%, Hispanic 1%. **Retention and Graduation:** 85% freshmen return for sophomore year. 63% freshmen graduate within 4 years. 26% grads go on to further study within 1 year. 17% grads pursue arts and sciences degrees. 1% grads pursue business degrees. 5% grads pursue law degrees. 3% grads pursue medical degrees. **Faculty:** Student/faculty ratio 10:1. 96 full-time faculty, 100% hold PhDs. 100% faculty teach undergrads.

ACADEMICS

Degrees: Bachelor's. **Academic Requirements:** Arts/fine arts, English (including composition), foreign languages, history, humanities, mathematics, philosophy, sciences (biological or physical), social science, physical education, theology. **Classes:** Most classes have 10–19 students. **Majors with Highest Enrollment:** Biology/biological sciences, business administration/management, communications studies/speech communication and rhetoric. **Disciplines with Highest Percentage of Degrees Awarded:** Business/marketing 16%, social sciences 16%, communications/journalism 10%, biological/life sciences 10%, psychology 7%, foreign languages and literature 7%, physical sciences 6%, visual and performing arts 6%, English 4%, history 4%. **Special Study Options:** CBP (Center for Business Preparation) Scholar Program, Philadelphia Center, double major, dual enrollment, independent study, internships, student-designed major, study abroad, teacher certification program, and Washington Center Programs.

FACILITIES

Housing: Coed dorms, men's dorms, women's dorms, apartments for single students, fraternity/sorority housing, theme housing. **Special Academic Facilities/Equipment:** Geological museum, electronic language lab, observatory. **Computers:** 10% of classrooms are wired, 20% of classrooms are wireless, 100% of public computers are PCs, network access in dorm rooms, online registration, online administrative functions (other than registration), remote student-access to Web through college's connection.

CAMPUS LIFE

Activities: Choral groups, concert band, dance, drama/theater, jazz band, literary magazine, music ensembles, musical theater, pep band, radio station, student government, student newspaper, student-run film society, symphony orchestra, television station, yearbook. **Organizations:** 56 registered organizations, 5 honor societies, 4 religious organizations. 5 fraternities (38% men join), 4 sororities (42% women join). **Athletics (Intercollegiate):** *Men:* Baseball, basketball, cross-country, football, golf, soccer, tennis, track/field (outdoor). *Women:* Basketball, cross-country, golf, soccer, softball, tennis, track/field (outdoor), volleyball.

ADMISSIONS

Freshman Academic Profile: 34% in top 10% of high school class, 75% in top 25% of high school class, 97% in top 50% of high school class. 85% from public high schools. SAT Math middle 50% range 520–630. SAT Critical Reading middle 50% range 510–630. SAT Writing middle 50% range 490–610. ACT middle 50% range 22–28. TOEFL required of all international applicants, minimum paper TOEFL 550, minimum computer TOEFL 213. **Basis for Candidate Selection:** *Very important factors considered include:* Academic GPA, class rank, rigor of secondary school record. *Important factors considered include:* Recommendation(s), standardized test scores, talent/ability. *Other factors considered include:* Alumni/ae relation, application essay, character/personal qualities, extracurricular activities, first generation, geographical residence, interview, level of applicant's interest, racial/ethnic status, state residency, volunteer work, work experience. **Freshman Admission Require-**

ments: High school diploma is required, and GED is not accepted. *Academic units required:* 4 English, 3 math, 3 science (2 science labs), 2 foreign language, 2 social studies, 2 history, 2 academic electives. *Academic units recommended:* 4 English, 4 math, 4 science (3 science labs), 4 foreign language, 3 social studies, 3 history, 3 academic electives. **Freshman Admission Statistics:** 1,556 applied, 64% admitted, 23% enrolled. **Transfer Admission Requirements:** High school transcript, college transcript(s), essay or personal statement, standardized test score, statement of good standing from prior institution(s). Minimum college GPA of 2.0 required. Lowest grade transferable C-. **General Admission Information:** Application fee $35. Regular application deadline 3/1. Regular notification is rolling. Nonfall registration accepted. Admission may be deferred for a maximum of 1 year. Credit and/or placement offered for CEEB Advanced Placement tests.

COSTS AND FINANCIAL AID

Annual tuition $24,700. Room and board $7,500. Required fees $520. Average book expense $900. **Required Forms and Deadlines:** FAFSA. Financial aid filing deadline 3/1. **Notification of Awards:** Applicants will be notified of awards on or about 3/1. **Types of Aid:** *Need-based scholarships/grants:* Pell, state scholarships/grants, private scholarships, the school's own gift aid. *Loans:* FFEL Subsidized Stafford, FFEL Unsubsidized Stafford, FFEL PLUS. **Student Employment:** Off-campus job opportunities are fair. **Financial Aid Statistics:** 66% freshmen, 76% undergrads receive need-based scholarship or grant aid. 46% freshmen, 47% undergrads receive need-based self-help aid. 97% freshmen, 98% undergrads receive any aid. Highest amount earned per year from on-campus jobs $1,800.

HARDING UNIVERSITY

Box 12255, Searcy, AR 72149
Phone: 501-279-4407 **E-mail:** admissions@harding.edu
Fax: 501-279-4129 **Website:** www.harding.edu **ACT Code:** 0124
Financial Aid Phone: 501-279-4257

This private school, affiliated with the Church of Christ, was founded in 1924. It has a 215-acre campus.

RATINGS
Admissions Selectivity Rating: 87   **Fire Safety Rating:** 60*   **Green Rating:** 60*

STUDENTS AND FACULTY
Enrollment: 3,995. **Student Body:** 53% female, 47% male, 71% out-of-state, 4% international (53 countries represented). African American 4%, Caucasian 87%, Hispanic 2%. **Retention and Graduation:** 81% freshmen return for sophomore year. 37% freshmen graduate within 4 years. 24% grads go on to further study within 1 year. 7% grads pursue arts and sciences degrees. 3% grads pursue business degrees. 1% grads pursue law degrees. 2% grads pursue medical degrees. **Faculty:** Student/faculty ratio 17:1. 228 full-time faculty, 66% hold PhDs. 100% faculty teach undergrads.

ACADEMICS
Degrees: Bachelor's, doctoral, first professional, master's. **Academic Requirements:** Arts/fine arts, Bible and religion, English (including composition), history, humanities, mathematics, philosophy, sciences (biological or physical), social science. **Classes:** Most classes have 10–19 students. Most lab/discussion sections have fewer than 10 students. **Majors with Highest Enrollment:** Business administration/management, early childhood education and teaching, nursing/registered nurse training (RN, ASN, BSN, MSN). **Disciplines with Highest Percentage of Degrees Awarded:** Business/marketing 21%, education 14%, health professions and related sciences 8%, communications/journalism 8%, computer and information sciences 6%. **Special Study Options:** Accelerated program, cooperative education program, distance learning, double major, dual enrollment, English as a second language (ESL), honors program, independent study, internships, liberal arts/career combination, study abroad, teacher certification program.

FACILITIES
Housing: Men's dorms, women's dorms, apartments for married students, apartments for single students, special housing for disabled students, approved off-campus housing. **Special Academic Facilities/Equipment:** On-campus academy (prep school grades K-12). **Computers:** 57% of classrooms are wireless, 80% of public computers are PCs, 20% of public computers are Macs, network access in dorm rooms, online registration, online administrative functions (other than registration), remote student-access to Web through college's connection.

CAMPUS LIFE
Activities: Choral groups, concert band, drama/theater, jazz band, marching band, music ensembles, musical theater, pep band, radio station, student government, student newspaper, symphony orchestra, television station, yearbook. **Organizations:** 52 registered organizations, 13 honor societies, 5 religious organizations. 15 fraternities (41% men join), 14 sororities (43% women join). **Athletics (Intercollegiate):** *Men:* Baseball, basketball, cross-country, football, golf, soccer, tennis, track/field (outdoor). *Women:* Basketball, cheerleading, cross-country, golf, soccer, tennis, track/field (outdoor), volleyball.

ADMISSIONS
Freshman Academic Profile: 27% in top 10% of high school class, 49% in top 25% of high school class, 75% in top 50% of high school class. 89% from public high schools. SAT Math middle 50% range 480–620. SAT Critical Reading middle 50% range 480–620. SAT Writing middle 50% range 450–600. ACT middle 50% range 21–28. TOEFL required of all international applicants, minimum paper TOEFL 500, minimum computer TOEFL 175. **Basis for Candidate Selection:** *Very important factors considered include:* Character/personal qualities, interview, recommendation(s), rigor of secondary school record, standardized test scores. *Important factors considered include:* Academic GPA, class rank, talent/ability. *Other factors considered include:* Alumni/ae relation, application essay, extracurricular activities, first generation, geographical residence, level of applicant's interest, state residency, volunteer work, work experience. **Freshman Admission Requirements:** High school diploma is required, and GED is accepted. *Academic units required:* 4 English, 3 math, 2 science, 3 social studies, 3 academic electives. *Academic units recommended:* 4 English, 4 math, 4 science, 2 foreign language, 4 social studies, 2 academic electives. **Freshman Admission Statistics:** 1,637 applied, 60% admitted, 93% enrolled. **Transfer Admission Requirements:** College transcript(s), essay or personal statement, statement of good standing from prior institution(s). Minimum college GPA of 2 required. Lowest grade transferable C. **General Admission Information:** Application fee $35. Regular application deadline 7/1. Regular notification is rolling. Nonfall registration accepted. Admission may be deferred for a maximum of 1 year. Credit and/or placement offered for CEEB Advanced Placement tests.

COSTS AND FINANCIAL AID
Annual tuition $11,940. Room and board $5,578. Required fees $420. Average book expense $1,200. **Required Forms and Deadlines:** FAFSA. Financial aid filing deadline 4/15. **Notification of Awards:** Applicants will be notified of awards on a rolling basis beginning on or about 2/15. **Types of Aid:** *Need-based scholarships/grants:* Pell, SEOG, state scholarships/grants, private scholarships, the school's own gift aid, Stephens Scholars Program for African-American students. *Loans:* FFEL Subsidized Stafford, FFEL Unsubsidized Stafford, FFEL PLUS, Federal Perkins, Federal Nursing, college/university loans from institutional funds. **Financial Aid Statistics:** 49% freshmen, 48% undergrads receive need-based scholarship or grant aid. 43% freshmen, 48% undergrads receive need-based self-help aid. 19 freshmen, 49 undergrads receive athletic scholarships. 95% freshmen, 91% undergrads receive any aid. Highest amount earned per year from on-campus jobs $9,116.

HARDIN-SIMMONS UNIVERSITY

Box 16050, Abilene, TX 79698
Phone: 325-670-1206 **E-mail:** enroll@hsutx.edu **CEEB Code:** 6268
Fax: 325-671-2115 **Website:** www.hsutx.edu **ACT Code:** 4096
Financial Aid Phone: 325-670-1206

This private school, affiliated with the Baptist Church, was founded in 1891. It has a 120-acre campus.

RATINGS
Admissions Selectivity Rating: 84   **Fire Safety Rating:** 67   **Green Rating:** 66

STUDENTS AND FACULTY
Enrollment: 1,938. **Student Body:** 56% female, 44% male, 4% out-of-state. African American 6%, Caucasian 78%, Hispanic 10%. **Retention and Graduation:** 62% freshmen return for sophomore year. 28% freshmen graduate within 4 years. 44% grads go on to further study within 1 year. 17% grads pursue arts and sciences degrees. 5% grads pursue business degrees. 1% grads pursue law degrees. 15% grads pursue medical degrees. **Faculty:** Student/faculty ratio 14:1. 129 full-time faculty, 80% hold PhDs. 91% faculty teach undergrads.

ACADEMICS
Degrees: Bachelor's, doctoral, first professional, master's, post-bachelor's certificate. **Academic Requirements:** Arts/fine arts, computer literacy,

English (including composition), history, humanities, mathematics, sciences (biological or physical), social science. **Classes:** Most classes have 10–19 students. Most lab/discussion sections have 10–19 students. **Majors with Highest Enrollment:** Biology/biological sciences; business, management, marketing, and related support services; education. **Disciplines with Highest Percentage of Degrees Awarded:** Business/marketing 17%, education 15%, parks and recreation 11%, health professions and related sciences 8%, psychology 8%. **Special Study Options:** Accelerated program, cross-registration, distance learning, double major, dual enrollment, honors program, independent study, internships, study abroad, teacher certification program.

FACILITIES

Housing: Men's dorms, women's dorms, apartments for married students, apartments for single students, special housing for disabled students, single and duplex housing with priority given to families. **Special Academic Facilities/Equipment:** Art center, observatory with 14-inch telescope, rare and fine book room, Six White Horse Facility. **Computers:** 100% of classrooms are wired, 95% of classrooms are wireless, 94% of public computers are PCs, 3% of public computers are Macs, 3% of public computers are UNIX, network access in dorm rooms, network access in dorm lounges, remote student-access to Web through college's connection.

CAMPUS LIFE

Activities: Choral groups, concert band, drama/theater, jazz band, literary magazine, marching band, music ensembles, musical theater, opera, student government, student newspaper, symphony orchestra, yearbook. **Organizations:** 15 honor societies, 1 religious organization. 4 fraternities (8% men join), 4 sororities (13% women join). **Athletics (Intercollegiate):** Men: Baseball, basketball, cheerleading, football, golf, soccer, tennis. Women: Basketball, cheerleading, golf, soccer, softball, tennis, volleyball.

ADMISSIONS

Freshman Academic Profile: 19% in top 10% of high school class, 45% in top 25% of high school class, 77% in top 50% of high school class. 90% from public high schools. SAT Math middle 50% range 470–580. SAT Critical Reading middle 50% range 460–570. SAT Writing middle 50% range 450–550. ACT middle 50% range 19–25. TOEFL required of all international applicants, minimum paper TOEFL 550, minimum computer TOEFL 213. **Basis for Candidate Selection:** *Very important factors considered include:* Academic GPA, class rank, standardized test scores. *Important factors considered include:* Character/personal qualities, recommendation(s), rigor of secondary school record, talent/ability. *Other factors considered include:* Alumni/ae relation, extracurricular activities, level of applicant's interest, religious affiliation/commitment. **Freshman Admission Requirements:** High school diploma is required, and GED is accepted. *Academic units required:* 3 English, 2 math, 2 science, 2 social studies, 7 academic electives. **Freshman Admission Statistics:** 1,374 applied, 55% admitted, 53% enrolled. **Transfer Admission Requirements:** College transcript(s). Minimum college GPA of 2.0 required. Lowest grade transferable C. **General Admission Information:** Application fee $50. Regular notification is rolling. Nonfall registration accepted. Admission may be deferred for a maximum of 1 year. Credit offered for CEEB Advanced Placement tests.

COSTS AND FINANCIAL AID

Annual tuition $17,400. Room and board $5,180. Required fees $980. Average book expense $800. **Required Forms and Deadlines:** FAFSA. Financial aid filing deadline 3/15. **Notification of Awards:** Applicants will be notified of awards on a rolling basis beginning on or about 1/1. **Types of Aid:** *Need-based scholarships/grants:* Pell, SEOG, state scholarships/grants, private scholarships, the school's own gift aid, ACG/SMART (federal grants). *Loans:* FFEL Subsidized Stafford, FFEL Unsubsidized Stafford, FFEL PLUS, Federal Perkins, state loans, college/university loans from institutional funds. **Financial Aid Statistics:** 54% freshmen, 51% undergrads receive need-based scholarship or grant aid. 64% freshmen, 63% undergrads receive need-based self-help aid. 97% freshmen, 91% undergrads receive any aid. Highest amount earned per year from on-campus jobs $3,653.

HARRINGTON COLLEGE OF DESIGN

200 West Madison, Suite 200, Chicago, IL 60606-3433
Phone: 877-939-4975 **E-mail:** hiid@interiordesign.edu
Fax: 312-697-8032 **Website:** www.harringtoncollege.com **ACT Code:** 6641
Financial Aid Phone: 877-939-4975

This proprietary school was founded in 1931.

RATINGS

Admissions Selectivity Rating: 60* **Fire Safety Rating:** 60* **Green Rating:** 60*

STUDENTS AND FACULTY

Student Body: 9% out-of-state. **Faculty:** Student/faculty ratio 17:1.

ACADEMICS

Degrees: Associate, bachelor's, certificate, diploma. **Academic Requirements:** Arts/fine arts, computer literacy, English (including composition), history, humanities, sciences (biological or physical), social science. **Special Study Options:** Accelerated program, internships, study abroad.

FACILITIES

Housing: Apartments for single students, independent referral housing, shared apartment housing. **Computers:** 100% of public computers are PCs, remote student-access to Web through college's connection.

CAMPUS LIFE

Activities: Student government.

ADMISSIONS

Freshman Academic Profile: TOEFL required of all international applicants, minimum paper TOEFL 500. **Basis for Candidate Selection:** *Very important factors considered include:* Interview. *Important factors considered include:* Character/personal qualities, talent/ability. *Other factors considered include:* Application essay, class rank, extracurricular activities, geographical residence, recommendation(s), rigor of secondary school record, standardized test scores, volunteer work, work experience. **Freshman Admission Requirements:** High school diploma is required, and GED is accepted. **Freshman Admission Statistics:** 568 applied, 90% admitted, 7% enrolled. **Transfer Admission Requirements:** College transcript(s), interview. Lowest grade transferable C. **General Admission Information:** Application fee $60. Nonfall registration accepted. Common Application not accepted.

COSTS AND FINANCIAL AID

Annual tuition $6,300. Average book expense $900. **Required Forms and Deadlines:** FAFSA. **Types of Aid:** *Need-based scholarships/grants:* Pell, SEOG. *Loans:* FFEL Subsidized Stafford, FFEL Unsubsidized Stafford, FFEL PLUS. **Student Employment:** Off-campus job opportunities are excellent.

HARRIS-STOWE STATE COLLEGE

3026 Laclede Avenue, St. Louis, MO 63103
Phone: 314-340-3366 **CEEB Code:** 6269
Fax: 314-340-3322 **Website:** www.hssu.edu **ACT Code:** 2302
Financial Aid Phone: 314-340-3500

This public school was founded in 1857.

RATINGS

Admissions Selectivity Rating: 60* **Fire Safety Rating:** 60* **Green Rating:** 60*

STUDENTS AND FACULTY

Student Body: 1% out-of-state.

ACADEMICS

Degrees: Bachelor's. **Special Study Options:** Undergrads may take grad-level classes.

FACILITIES

Special Academic Facilities/Equipment: Education resource center, urban education specialist/multicultural education collection, juvenile literature collection, audiovisual lab.

CAMPUS LIFE

Organizations: 1 honor society, 2 religious organizations. **Athletics (Intercol-**

legiate): *Men:* Baseball, basketball, soccer, track/field (outdoor), volleyball. *Women:* Basketball, track/field (outdoor), volleyball.

ADMISSIONS

Freshman Admission Requirements: High school diploma is required, and GED is accepted. **Transfer Admission Requirements:** Lowest grade transferable C. **General Admission Information:** Regular application deadline rolling. Nonfall registration accepted. Common Application not accepted. Credit and/or placement offered for CEEB Advanced Placement tests.

COSTS AND FINANCIAL AID

Annual in-state tuition $1,992. Out-of-state tuition $3,924. Board $3,000. Required fees $15. Average book expense $750. **Required Forms and Deadlines:** FAFSA, institution's own financial aid form. **Types of Aid:** *Loans:* FFEL Subsidized Stafford, FFEL PLUS. **Student Employment:** Institutional employment available.

HARTWICK COLLEGE

PO Box 4020, Oneonta, NY 13820-4020
Phone: 607-431-4154 **E-mail:** admissions@hartwick.edu **CEEB Code:** 2288
Fax: 607-431-4102 **Website:** www.hartwick.edu
Financial Aid Phone: 607-431-4130

This private school was founded in 1797. It has a 425-acre campus.

RATINGS

Admissions Selectivity Rating: 71   **Fire Safety Rating:** 85   **Green Rating:** 72

STUDENTS AND FACULTY

Enrollment: 1,444. **Student Body:** 57% female, 43% male, 39% out-of-state, 4% international (34 countries represented). African American 5%, Asian 1%, Caucasian 64%, Hispanic 4%. **Retention and Graduation:** 76% freshmen return for sophomore year. 49% freshmen graduate within 4 years. 23% grads go on to further study within 1 year. 19% grads pursue arts and sciences degrees. 1% grads pursue business degrees. 2% grads pursue law degrees. 1% grads pursue medical degrees. **Faculty:** Student/faculty ratio 11:1. 108 full-time faculty, 94% hold PhDs. 100% faculty teach undergrads.

ACADEMICS

Degrees: Bachelor's. **Academic Requirements:** English (including composition), humanities, mathematics, sciences (biological or physical), social science. **Classes:** Most classes have 10–19 students. Most lab/discussion sections have 10–19 students. **Majors with Highest Enrollment:** Business administration/management, nursing/registered nurse training (RN, ASN, BSN, MSN), psychology. **Disciplines with Highest Percentage of Degrees Awarded:** Social sciences 22%, business/marketing 18%, visual and performing arts 12%, psychology 11%, biological/life sciences 7%. **Special Study Options:** Accelerated program, double major, exchange student program (domestic), honors program, independent study, internships, January thematic term, liberal arts/career combination, student-designed major, study abroad, study abroad/international internships, teacher certification program.

FACILITIES

Housing: Coed dorms, women's dorms, apartments for single students, fraternity/sorority housing, housing at Pine Lake environmental campus (lodge and cabins), special-interest housing. **Special Academic Facilities/Equipment:** Art and history museums, Indian artifact collection, environmental center, observatory, electron microscope, tissue culture lab, spectrophotometers. **Computers:** 100% of public computers are PCs, network access in dorm rooms, network access in dorm lounges, online administrative functions (other than registration), remote student-access to Web through college's connection. Undergraduates are required to own a computer.

CAMPUS LIFE

Activities: Choral groups, concert band, dance, drama/theater, jazz band, literary magazine, music ensembles, musical theater, radio station, student government, student newspaper, television station, yearbook. **Organizations:** 60 registered organizations, 30 honor societies, 3 religious organizations. 8 fraternities (4% men join), 3 sororities (7% women join). **Athletics (Intercollegiate):** *Men:* Basketball, cross-country, diving, football, lacrosse, soccer, swimming, tennis. *Women:* Basketball, cheerleading, cross-country, diving, equestrian sports, field hockey, lacrosse, soccer, swimming, tennis, volleyball, water polo.

ADMISSIONS

Freshman Academic Profile: 23% in top 10% of high school class, 80% in top

50% of high school class. 84% from public high schools. SAT Math middle 50% range 510–595. SAT Critical Reading middle 50% range 480–600. SAT Writing middle 50% range 480–590. ACT middle 50% range 21–26. TOEFL required of all international applicants, minimum paper TOEFL 550, minimum computer TOEFL 213. **Basis for Candidate Selection:** *Very important factors considered include:* Academic GPA, class rank, rigor of secondary school record. *Important factors considered include:* Application essay, extracurricular activities, level of applicant's interest, recommendation(s). *Other factors considered include:* Alumni/ae relation, character/personal qualities, geographical residence, interview, racial/ethnic status, standardized test scores, state residency, talent/ability, volunteer work, work experience. **Freshman Admission Requirements:** High school diploma is required, and GED is accepted. *Academic units recommended:* 4 English, 3 math, 3 science (2 science labs), 3 foreign language, 2 social studies, 2 history. **Freshman Admission Statistics:** 2,211 applied, 87% admitted, 21% enrolled. **Transfer Admission Requirements:** High school transcript, college transcript(s), essay or personal statement, statement of good standing from prior institution(s). Minimum college GPA of 2.0 required. Lowest grade transferable C. **General Admission Information:** Application fee $35. Early decision application deadline 11/15. Regular application deadline 2/15. Regular notification 3/7. Nonfall registration accepted. Admission may be deferred for a maximum of 1 year. Common Application accepted. Credit offered for CEEB Advanced Placement tests.

COSTS AND FINANCIAL AID

Annual tuition $26,480. Room & board $7,480. Required fees $530. Average book expense $700. **Required Forms and Deadlines:** FAFSA, institution's own financial aid form. Financial aid filing deadline 2/1. **Notification of Awards:** Applicants will be notified of awards on or about 3/15. **Types of Aid:** *Need-based scholarships/grants:* Pell, SEOG, state scholarships/grants, private scholarships, the school's own gift aid. *Loans:* FFEL Subsidized Stafford, FFEL Unsubsidized Stafford, FFEL PLUS, Federal Perkins, Federal Nursing, alternative loans. **Student Employment:** Federal Work-Study Program available. Off-campus job opportunities are excellent. **Financial Aid Statistics:** 74% freshmen, 70% undergrads receive need-based scholarship or grant aid. 71% freshmen, 69% undergrads receive need-based self-help aid. 3 freshmen, 29 undergrads receive athletic scholarships. 75% freshmen, 82% undergrads receive any aid.

HARVARD COLLEGE

86 Brattle Street, Cambridge, MA 02138
Phone: 617-495-1551 **E-mail:** college@fas.harvard.edu **CEEB Code:** 3434
Fax: 617-495-8821 **Website:** www.harvard.edu **ACT Code:** 1840
Financial Aid Phone: 617-495-1581

This private school was founded in 1636. It has a 380-acre campus.

RATINGS

Admissions Selectivity Rating: 99   **Fire Safety Rating:** 60*   **Green Rating:** 98

STUDENTS AND FACULTY

Enrollment: 6,715. **Student Body:** 49% female, 51% male, 84% out-of-state, 9% international. African American 8%, Asian 14%, Caucasian 47%, Hispanic 7%. **Retention and Graduation:** 98% freshmen return for sophomore year. 25% grads go on to further study within 1 year. 17% grads pursue arts and sciences degrees. 13% grads pursue business degrees. 15% grads pursue law degrees. 20% grads pursue medical degrees. **Faculty:** Student/faculty ratio 7:1. 1,592 full-time faculty, 99% hold PhDs. 100% faculty teach undergrads.

ACADEMICS

Degrees: Associate, bachelor's, certificate, doctoral, first professional certificate, first professional, master's, post-bachelor's certificate, post-master's certificate. **Academic Requirements:** Arts/fine arts, English (including composition), foreign languages, history, humanities, mathematics, philosophy, sciences (biological or physical), social science. **Majors with Highest Enrollment:** Economics, political science and government, psychology. **Disciplines with Highest Percentage of Degrees Awarded:** Social sciences 38%, history 12%, biological/life sciences 9%, psychology 7%, physical sciences 7%. **Special Study Options:** Accelerated program, cross-registration, double major, exchange student program (domestic), honors program, independent study, internships, student-designed major, study abroad, teacher certification program.

The Princeton Review's Complete Book of Colleges

FACILITIES

Housing: Coed dorms, apartments for married students, special housing for disabled students. **Special Academic Facilities/Equipment:** Museums (University Arts Museums, Museums of Cultural History, many others), language labs, observatory, many science and research laboratories and facilities, new state-of-the-art computer science facility. **Computers:** 41% of public computers are PCs, 44% of public computers are Macs, 15% of public computers are UNIX, network access in dorm rooms, online administrative functions (other than registration), remote student-access to Web through college's connection.

CAMPUS LIFE

Activities: Choral groups, concert band, dance, drama/theater, jazz band, literary magazine, marching band, music ensembles, musical theater, opera, radio station, student government, student newspaper, student-run film society, symphony orchestra, television station. **Organizations:** 260 registered organizations, 1 honor society. **Athletics (Intercollegiate):** *Men:* Baseball, basketball, cheerleading, crew/rowing, cross-country, diving, equestrian sports, fencing, football, golf, gymnastics, ice hockey, lacrosse, rugby, sailing, skiing (downhill/alpine), skiing (Nordic/cross-country), soccer, squash, swimming, tennis. *Women:* Basketball, cheerleading, crew/rowing, cross-country, diving, equestrian sports, fencing, field hockey, golf, gymnastics, ice hockey, lacrosse, rugby, sailing, skiing (downhill/alpine), skiing (Nordic/cross-country), soccer, softball, squash, swimming. **Environmental initiatives:** Establishing the Harvard Green Campus Initiative. Adopting Campus wide sustainability Principals and Green Building Guidelines. Establishing a $12 million green campus loan fund.

ADMISSIONS

Freshman Academic Profile: 95% in top 10% of high school class, 100% in top 25% of high school class, 100% in top 50% of high school class. 65% from public high schools. SAT Math middle 50% range 700–790. SAT Critical Reading middle 50% range 700–800. SAT Writing middle 50% range 690–790. ACT middle 50% range 31–35. **Basis for Candidate Selection:** *Very important factors considered include:* Character/personal qualities, extracurricular activities, recommendation(s), rigor of secondary school record, talent/ability. *Important factors considered include:* Application essay, class rank, interview, standardized test scores. *Other factors considered include:* Alumni/ae relation, first generation, geographical residence, racial/ethnic status, volunteer work, work experience. **Freshman Admission Requirements:** High school diploma or equivalent is not required. *Academic units recommended:* 4 English, 4 math, 4 science, 4 foreign language, 3 social studies, 2 history. **Freshman Admission Statistics:** 22,754 applied, 9% admitted, 79% enrolled. **Transfer Admission Requirements:** College transcript(s), essay or personal statement, standardized test score, statement of good standing from prior institution(s). Lowest grade transferable C-. **General Admission Information:** Application fee $60. Regular application deadline 1/1. Regular notification 4/1. Nonfall registration not accepted. Admission may be deferred for a maximum of 1 year. Credit and/or placement offered for CEEB Advanced Placement tests.

COSTS AND FINANCIAL AID

Annual tuition $30,275. Room & board $9,946. Required fees $3,434. Average book expense $1,000. **Required Forms and Deadlines:** FAFSA, CSS/Financial Aid PROFILE, Noncustodial PROFILE, Business/Farm Supplement, tax forms through IDOC. Financial aid filing deadline 2/1. **Notification of Awards:** Applicants will be notified of awards on or about 4/1. **Types of Aid:** *Need-based scholarships/grants:* Pell, SEOG, state scholarships/grants, private scholarships, the school's own gift aid. *Loans:* Direct Subsidized Stafford, Direct Unsubsidized Stafford, Direct PLUS, Federal Perkins, state loans, college/university loans from institutional funds. **Student Employment:** Federal Work-Study Program available. Institutional employment available. Off-campus job opportunities are excellent. **Financial Aid Statistics:** 53% freshmen, 49% undergrads receive need-based scholarship or grant aid. 30% freshmen, 42% undergrads receive need-based self-help aid. Highest amount earned per year from on-campus jobs $1,650.

HARVEY MUDD COLLEGE

301 Platt Boulevard, 301 Platt Boulevard, Claremont, CA 91711-5990
Phone: 909-621-8011 **E-mail:** admission@hmc.edu **CEEB Code:** 4341
Fax: 909-621-8360 **Website:** www.hmc.edu
Financial Aid Phone: 909-621-8055

This private school was founded in 1955. It has a 33-acre campus.

RATINGS

Admissions Selectivity Rating: 99   **Fire Safety Rating:** 74   **Green Rating:** 86

STUDENTS AND FACULTY

Enrollment: 729. **Student Body:** 29% female, 71% male, 51% out-of-state, 4% international (20 countries represented). African American 1%, Asian 19%, Caucasian 48%, Hispanic 8%. **Retention and Graduation:** 93% freshmen return for sophomore year. 78% freshmen graduate within 4 years. 43% grads go on to further study within 1 year. 40% grads pursue arts and sciences degrees. 1% grads pursue medical degrees. **Faculty:** Student/faculty ratio 8:1. 84 full-time faculty, 100% hold PhDs. 100% faculty teach undergrads.

ACADEMICS

Degrees: Bachelor's. **Academic Requirements:** Arts/fine arts, computer literacy, English (including composition), history, humanities, integrative experience looking at the relationship between technology and society, mathematics, philosophy, sciences (biological or physical), social science. **Classes:** Most classes have fewer than 10 students. Most lab/discussion sections have 10–19 students. **Majors with Highest Enrollment:** Computer and information sciences, engineering, physics. **Disciplines with Highest Percentage of Degrees Awarded:** Engineering 36%, physical sciences 20%, computer and information sciences 17%, mathematics 15%, biological/life sciences 6%. **Special Study Options:** Cross-registration, double major, dual enrollment, independent study, study abroad, innovative client-sponsored design projects.

FACILITIES

Housing: Coed dorms, apartments for married students, apartments for single students, housing exchange program with Pomona College, Pitzer College, Scripps College, and Claremont McKenna College. **Computers:** 100% of classrooms are wireless, 60% of public computers are PCs, 30% of public computers are Macs, 10% of public computers are UNIX, network access in dorm rooms, network access in dorm lounges, online administrative functions (other than registration), remote student-access to Web through college's connection.

CAMPUS LIFE

Activities: Choral groups, concert band, dance, drama/theater, jazz band, literary magazine, music ensembles, musical theater, pep band, radio station, student government, student newspaper, student-run film society, symphony orchestra, television station, yearbook. **Organizations:** 109 registered organizations, 4 honor societies, 6 religious organizations. **Athletics (Intercollegiate):** *Men:* Baseball, basketball, cross-country, diving, football, golf, soccer, swimming, tennis, track/field (outdoor), water polo. *Women:* Basketball, cross-country, diving, lacrosse, soccer, softball, swimming, tennis, track/field (outdoor), volleyball, water polo. **Environmental initiatives:** Thorough, publicly available evaluation of all resource and waste streams. Two very active students run sustainability groups. Near total elimination of incandescent light bulbs on campus.

ADMISSIONS

Freshman Academic Profile: 89% in top 10% of high school class, 100% in top 50% of high school class. 75% from public high schools. SAT Math middle 50% range 740–820. SAT Critical Reading middle 50% range 690–760. SAT Writing middle 50% range 680–760. TOEFL required of all international applicants, minimum paper TOEFL 600, minimum computer TOEFL 250. **Basis for Candidate Selection:** *Very important factors considered include:* Application essay, character/personal qualities, class rank, recommendation(s), rigor of secondary school record, standardized test scores. *Important factors considered include:* Alumni/ae relation, interview. *Other factors considered include:* Extracurricular activities, geographical residence, racial/ethnic status, talent/ability, volunteer work, work experience. **Freshman Admission Requirements:** High school diploma is required, and GED is accepted. *Academic units required:* 4 English, 4 math, 3 science (3 science labs).

Academic units recommended: 2 foreign language, 1 social studies, 1 history. **Freshman Admission Statistics:** 2,119 applied, 30% admitted, 28% enrolled. **Transfer Admission Requirements:** High school transcript, college transcript(s), essay or personal statement, standardized test score, statement of good standing from prior institution(s). Minimum college GPA of 3.0 required. Lowest grade transferable C-. **General Admission Information:** Application fee $60. Early decision application deadline 11/15. Regular application deadline 1/2. Regular notification 4/1. Nonfall registration not accepted. Admission may be deferred for a maximum of 1 year. Placement offered for CEEB Advanced Placement tests.

COSTS AND FINANCIAL AID

Annual tuition $34,669. Room and board $11,415. Required fees $222. Average book expense $800. **Required Forms and Deadlines:** FAFSA, CSS/Financial Aid PROFILE, state aid form, Noncustodial PROFILE, Business/Farm Supplement. Financial aid filing deadline 2/1. **Notification of Awards:** Applicants will be notified of awards on or about 4/1. **Types of Aid:** *Need-based scholarships/grants:* Pell, SEOG, state scholarships/grants, private scholarships, the school's own gift aid. *Loans:* FFEL Subsidized Stafford, FFEL Unsubsidized Stafford, FFEL PLUS, Federal Perkins, college/university loans from institutional funds, alternative loans. **Financial Aid Statistics:** 60% freshmen, 51% undergrads receive need-based scholarship or grant aid. 48% freshmen, 45% undergrads receive need-based self-help aid. 84% freshmen, 81% undergrads receive any aid. Highest amount earned per year from on-campus jobs $8,399.

HASTINGS COLLEGE

Hastings College, 710 North Turner Avenue, Hastings, NE 68901
Phone: 402-461-7403 **E-mail:** mmolliconi@hastings.edu **CEEB Code:** 6270
Fax: 402-461-7490 **Website:** www.hastings.edu **ACT Code:** 2456
Financial Aid Phone: 402-461-7431

This private school, affiliated with the Presbyterian Church, was founded in 1882. It has a 109-acre campus.

RATINGS
Admissions Selectivity Rating: 76   **Fire Safety Rating:** 66   **Green Rating:** 60*

STUDENTS AND FACULTY
Enrollment: 1,060. **Student Body:** 49% female, 51% male, 24% out-of-state. African American 2%, Caucasian 93%, Hispanic 2%. **Retention and Graduation:** 69% freshmen return for sophomore year. 48% freshmen graduate within 4 years. 22% grads go on to further study within 1 year. 16% grads pursue arts and sciences degrees. 1% grads pursue business degrees. 2% grads pursue law degrees. 1% grads pursue medical degrees. **Faculty:** Student/faculty ratio 11:1. 84 full-time faculty, 74% hold PhDs. 100% faculty teach undergrads.

ACADEMICS
Degrees: Bachelor's, master's. **Academic Requirements:** Arts/fine arts, computer literacy, English (including composition), foreign languages, health/wellness, history, humanities, mathematics, philosophy, physical education, sciences (biological or physical), social science, speech. **Classes:** Most classes have 10–19 students. Most lab/discussion sections have fewer than 10 students. **Majors with Highest Enrollment:** Business administration/management, education, psychology. **Disciplines with Highest Percentage of Degrees Awarded:** Education 26%, business/marketing 20%, psychology 10%, interdisciplinary studies 7%, physical sciences 5%, security and protective services 5%, communications/journalism 5%, English 5%. **Special Study Options:** Double major, exchange student program (domestic), independent study, internships, student-designed major, study abroad, teacher certification program.

FACILITIES
Housing: Coed dorms, men's dorms, women's dorms, apartments for single students, honors housing; one apartment complex is for quiet and alcohol-free living. **Special Academic Facilities/Equipment:** Center for communication arts, glass-blowing studio, observatory, art gallery. **Computers:** 2% of classrooms are wired, 2% of classrooms are wireless, 73% of public computers are PCs, 27% of public computers are Macs, network access in dorm rooms, network access in dorm lounges, online administrative functions (other than registration), support for handheld computing, remote student-access to Web through college's connection.

CAMPUS LIFE
Activities: Choral groups, concert band, drama/theater, jazz band, literary magazine, marching band, music ensembles, musical theater, radio station,

student government, student newspaper, symphony orchestra, television station, yearbook. **Organizations:** 85 registered organizations, 13 honor societies, 10 religious organizations, 4 fraternities (17% men join), 4 sororities (32% women join). **Athletics (Intercollegiate):** *Men:* Baseball, basketball, cross-country, football, golf, soccer, tennis, track/field (indoor), track/field (outdoor), wrestling. *Women:* Basketball, cheerleading, cross-country, golf, soccer, softball, tennis, track/field (indoor), track/field (outdoor), volleyball.

ADMISSIONS
Freshman Academic Profile: 16% in top 10% of high school class, 40% in top 25% of high school class, 65% in top 50% of high school class. 88% from public high schools. SAT Math middle 50% range 490–605. SAT Critical Reading middle 50% range 500–600. ACT middle 50% range 20–26. TOEFL required of all international applicants, minimum paper TOEFL 600, minimum computer TOEFL 250. **Basis for Candidate Selection:** *Very important factors considered include:* Academic GPA, class rank, recommendation(s), rigor of secondary school record, standardized test scores. *Important factors considered include:* Character/personal qualities, extracurricular activities, talent/ability. *Other factors considered include:* Alumni/ae relation, application essay, interview, level of applicant's interest, racial/ethnic status. **Freshman Admission Requirements:** High school diploma is required, and GED is accepted. *Academic units required:* 3 English, 3 math, 3 science (3 science labs), 4 social studies, 3 history. *Academic units recommended:* 4 English, 4 math, 4 science (4 science labs), 2 foreign language, 4 social studies, 4 history. **Freshman Admission Statistics:** 1,210 applied, 81% admitted, 27% enrolled. **Transfer Admission Requirements:** High school transcript, college transcript(s), statement of good standing from prior institution(s). Minimum college GPA of 2.0 required. Lowest grade transferable C. **General Admission Information:** Application fee $20. Regular notification is rolling. Nonfall registration accepted. Credit and/or placement offered for CEEB Advanced Placement tests.

COSTS AND FINANCIAL AID
Annual tuition $17,572. Room & board $5,148. Required fees $730. Average book expense $730. **Required Forms and Deadlines:** FAFSA, institution's own financial aid form. Financial aid filing deadline 5/1. **Notification of Awards:** Applicants will be notified of awards on a rolling basis beginning on or about 3/1. **Types of Aid:** *Need-based scholarships/grants:* Pell, SEOG, state scholarships/grants, private scholarships, the school's own gift aid. *Loans:* FFEL Subsidized Stafford, FFEL Unsubsidized Stafford, FFEL PLUS, Federal Perkins. **Student Employment:** Federal Work-Study Program available. Institutional employment available. Off-campus job opportunities are good. **Financial Aid Statistics:** 77% freshmen, 71% undergrads receive need-based scholarship or grant aid. 57% freshmen, 56% undergrads receive need-based self-help aid. 58 freshmen, 173 undergrads receive athletic scholarships. 97% freshmen, 98% undergrads receive any aid. Highest amount earned per year from on-campus jobs $600.

HAVERFORD COLLEGE

370 Lancaster Avenue, Haverford, PA 19041
Phone: 610-896-1350 **E-mail:** admitme@haverford.edu **CEEB Code:** 2289
Fax: 610-896-1338 **Website:** www.haverford.edu **ACT Code:** 3409
Financial Aid Phone: 610-896-1350

This private school was founded in 1833. It has a 200-acre campus.

RATINGS
Admissions Selectivity Rating: 98   **Fire Safety Rating:** 70   **Green Rating:** 60*

STUDENTS AND FACULTY
Enrollment: 1,168. **Student Body:** 53% female, 47% male, 86% out-of-state, 4% international (47 countries represented). African American 8%, Asian 11%, Caucasian 69%, Hispanic 7%. **Retention and Graduation:** 96% freshmen return for sophomore year. 92% freshmen graduate within 4 years. 18% grads go on to further study within 1 year. 10% grads pursue arts and sciences degrees. 3% grads pursue law degrees. 4% grads pursue medical degrees. **Faculty:** Student/faculty ratio 8:1. 112 full-time faculty, 94% hold PhDs. 100% faculty teach undergrads.

ACADEMICS

Degrees: Bachelor's. **Academic Requirements:** English (including composition), foreign languages, humanities, mathematics, sciences (biological or physical), social science. **Classes:** Most classes have fewer than 10 students. Most lab/discussion sections have fewer than 10 students. **Majors with Highest Enrollment:** Biology/biological sciences, economics, English language and literature. **Disciplines with Highest Percentage of Degrees Awarded:** Social sciences 29%, biological/life sciences 12%, English 11%, physical sciences 10%, history 10%, psychology 8%. **Special Study Options:** Cross-registration, double major, exchange student program (domestic), independent study, internships, liberal arts/career combination, student-designed major, study abroad, teacher certification program.

FACILITIES

Housing: Coed dorms, men's dorms, women's dorms, apartments for single students, theme houses. **Special Academic Facilities/Equipment:** Art gallery, Center for Cross-Cultural Study of Religion, arboretum, observatory, foundry. **Computers:** 5% of classrooms are wired, 12% of classrooms are wireless, 60% of public computers are PCs, 40% of public computers are Macs, network access in dorm rooms, network access in dorm lounges, online registration, online administrative functions (other than registration), remote student-access to Web through college's connection.

CAMPUS LIFE

Activities: Choral groups, dance, drama/theater, literary magazine, music ensembles, musical theater, radio station, student government, student newspaper, yearbook. **Organizations:** 93 registered organizations, 1 honor society, 6 religious organizations. **Athletics (Intercollegiate):** *Men:* Baseball, basketball, cross-country, fencing, lacrosse, soccer, squash, tennis, track/field (indoor), track/field (outdoor). *Women:* Basketball, cross-country, fencing, field hockey, lacrosse, soccer, softball, squash, tennis, track/field (indoor), track/field (outdoor), volleyball.

ADMISSIONS

Freshman Academic Profile: 88% in top 10% of high school class, 97% in top 25% of high school class, 100% in top 50% of high school class. 55% from public high schools. SAT Math middle 50% range 650–740. SAT Critical Reading middle 50% range 640–760. TOEFL required of all international applicants, minimum paper TOEFL 600, minimum computer TOEFL 250. **Basis for Candidate Selection:** *Very important factors considered include:* Academic GPA, application essay, character/personal qualities, rigor of secondary school record, standardized test scores. *Important factors considered include:* Class rank, extracurricular activities, recommendation(s), talent/ability, volunteer work, work experience. *Other factors considered include:* Alumni/ae relation, first generation, geographical residence, interview, level of applicant's interest, racial/ethnic status. **Freshman Admission Requirements:** High school diploma or equivalent is not required. *Academic units required:* 4 English, 3 math, 1 science (1 science lab), 3 foreign language, 2 social studies. *Academic units recommended:* 4 math, 2 science. **Freshman Admission Statistics:** 3,351 applied, 26% admitted, 36% enrolled. **Transfer Admission Requirements:** High school transcript, college transcript(s), essay or personal statement, standardized test score, statement of good standing from prior institution(s). Minimum college GPA of 3.0 required. Lowest grade transferable C. **General Admission Information:** Application fee $60. Early decision application deadline 11/15. Regular application deadline 1/15. Regular notification 4/15. Nonfall registration not accepted. Admission may be deferred for a maximum of 1 year.

COSTS AND FINANCIAL AID

Annual tuition $33,394. Room & board $10,390. Required fees $316. Average book expense $1,194. **Required Forms and Deadlines:** FAFSA, CSS/Financial Aid PROFILE, Business/Farm Supplement, CSS College Board Noncustodial Parents' Statement is required (not the Noncustodial supplement). Financial aid filing deadline 1/31. **Notification of Awards:** Applicants will be notified of awards on or about 4/1. **Types of Aid:** *Need-based scholarships/grants:* Pell, SEOG, state scholarships/grants, the school's own gift aid. *Loans:* FFEL Subsidized Stafford, FFEL Unsubsidized Stafford, FFEL PLUS, Federal Perkins. **Student Employment:** Federal Work-Study Program available. Institutional employment available. Off-campus job opportunities are good. **Financial Aid Statistics:** 39% freshmen, 40% undergrads receive need-based scholarship or grant aid. 37% freshmen, 38% undergrads receive need-based self-help aid. 41% freshmen, 42% undergrads receive any aid.

See page 1192.

HAWAII PACIFIC UNIVERSITY

1164 Bishop Street, Honolulu, HI 96813
Phone: 808-544-0238 **E-mail:** admissions@hpu.edu **CEEB Code:** 4352
Fax: 808-544-1136 **Website:** www.hpu.edu **ACT Code:** 4352
Financial Aid Phone: 808-544-0253

This private school was founded in 1965. It has a 135-acre campus.

RATINGS

Admissions Selectivity Rating: 76   **Fire Safety Rating:** 77   **Green Rating:** 60+

STUDENTS AND FACULTY

Enrollment: 6,262. **Student Body:** 61% female, 39% male, 52% out-of-state, 10% international (102 countries represented). African American 7%, Asian 31%, Caucasian 34%, Hispanic 7%, Native American 1%. **Retention and Graduation:** 66% freshmen return for sophomore year. 68% grads go on to further study within 1 year. 20% grads pursue arts and sciences degrees. 45% grads pursue business degrees. 5% grads pursue law degrees. 3% grads pursue medical degrees. **Faculty:** Student/faculty ratio 16:1. 264 full-time faculty, 66% hold PhDs. 100% faculty teach undergrads.

ACADEMICS

Degrees: Associate, bachelor's, certificate, master's, post-bachelor's certificate, post-master's certificate. **Academic Requirements:** Communications, computer literacy, economics, English (including composition), geography, history, humanities, mathematics, sciences (biological or physical), social science. **Classes:** Most classes have 10–19 students. Most lab/discussion sections have fewer than 10 students. **Majors with Highest Enrollment:** Business, management, marketing, and related support services; management information systems; nursing/registered nurse training (RN, ASN, BSN, MSN). **Disciplines with Highest Percentage of Degrees Awarded:** Business/marketing 38%, health professions and related sciences 19%, computer and information sciences 8%, law/legal studies 6%, communications/journalism 5%, psychology 5%. **Special Study Options:** Accelerated program, cooperative education program, distance learning, double major, dual enrollment, English as a second language (ESL), honors program, independent study, internships, liberal arts/career combination, student-designed major, study abroad, weekend college.

FACILITIES

Housing: Coed dorms, women's dorms, apartments for married students, apartments for single students, apartment search and referral service. **Special Academic Facilities/Equipment:** Hawaii Pacific University Art Gallery, Hawaii Pacific University Theatre. **Computers:** 44% of classrooms are wired, 35% of classrooms are wireless, 90% of public computers are PCs, 5% of public computers are Macs, 5% of public computers are UNIX, network access in dorm rooms, network access in dorm lounges, online registration, online administrative functions (other than registration), remote student-access to Web through college's connection.

CAMPUS LIFE

Activities: Choral groups, dance, drama/theater, literary magazine, music ensembles, musical theater, pep band, student government, student newspaper, student-run film society. **Organizations:** 80 registered organizations, 18 honor societies, 3 religious organizations. **Athletics (Intercollegiate):** *Men:* Baseball, basketball, cheerleading, cross-country, golf, tennis. *Women:* Cheerleading, cross-country, golf, softball, tennis, volleyball.

ADMISSIONS

Freshman Academic Profile: 20% in top 10% of high school class, 45% in top 25% of high school class, 80% in top 50% of high school class. 60% from public high schools. SAT Math middle 50% range 430–560. SAT Critical Reading middle 50% range 420–550. SAT Writing middle 50% range 350–540. ACT middle 50% range 17–24. TOEFL required of all international applicants, minimum paper TOEFL 550, minimum computer TOEFL 213. **Basis for Candidate Selection:** *Very important factors considered include:* Academic GPA, rigor of secondary school record. *Important factors considered include:* Extracurricular activities, interview, standardized test scores. *Other factors considered include:* Application essay, character/personal qualities, class rank, first generation, recommendation(s), talent/ability, volunteer work, work experience. **Freshman Admission Requirements:** High school diploma is required, and GED is accepted. *Academic units recommended:* 4 English, 3 math, 2 science, 1 foreign language, 4 history. **Freshman Admission Statistics:** 2,991 applied, 80% admitted, 29% enrolled. **Transfer Admission Requirements:** College transcript(s). Minimum college GPA of 2.0 required. Lowest grade transferable C. **General Admission Information:** Application fee $50. Regular notification is rolling. Nonfall registration accepted. Admission may be deferred for a maximum of 2 years. Credit and/or placement offered for

CEEB Advanced Placement tests.

COSTS AND FINANCIAL AID
Annual tuition $13,000. Room & board $10,560. Required fees $80. Average book expense $2,096. **Required Forms and Deadlines:** FAFSA. Financial aid filing deadline 3/1. **Notification of Awards:** Applicants will be notified of awards on a rolling basis beginning on or about 4/1. **Types of Aid:** *Need-based scholarships/grants:* Pell, SEOG, state scholarships/grants, the school's own gift aid, Federal Nursing Scholarships. *Loans:* FFEL Subsidized Stafford, FFEL Unsubsidized Stafford, FFEL PLUS, Federal Perkins, Federal Nursing, alternative loans. **Financial Aid Statistics:** 19% freshmen, 18% undergrads receive need-based scholarship or grant aid. 39% freshmen, 38% undergrads receive need-based self-help aid. 75% freshmen, 67% undergrads receive any aid. Highest amount earned per year from on-campus jobs $3,800.

See page 1194.

HEBREW COLLEGE

160 Herrick Road, Newton Centre, MA 02459
Phone: 617-559-8610 **E-mail:** admissions@hebrewcollege.edu
Fax: 617-559-8601 **Website:** www.hebrewcollege.edu
Financial Aid Phone: 617-559-8642

This private school, affiliated with the Jewish synagogue, was founded in

RATINGS
Admissions Selectivity Rating: 60*   **Fire Safety Rating:** 60*   **Green Rating:** 60*

STUDENTS AND FACULTY
Enrollment: 4. **Student Body:** 50% female, 50% male, 1% out-of-state, 25% international. **Retention and Graduation:** 40% grads go on to further study within 1 year. **Faculty:** 100% faculty teach undergrads.

ACADEMICS
Degrees: Bachelor's, certificate, master's. **Academic Requirements:** Foreign languages, Jewish studies. **Special Study Options:** Cross-registration, distance learning, independent study, internships, student-designed major, semester in Israel (encouraged).

FACILITIES
Computers: 100% of public computers are PCs, remote student-access to Web through college's connection.

CAMPUS LIFE
Activities: Choral groups.

ADMISSIONS
Freshman Academic Profile: TOEFL required of all international applicants, minimum paper TOEFL 400, minimum computer TOEFL 100. **Basis for Candidate Selection:** *Very important factors considered include:* Application essay, religious affiliation/commitment, talent/ability. *Important factors considered include:* Character/personal qualities, class rank, extracurricular activities, interview, recommendation(s), rigor of secondary school record, standardized test scores, volunteer work, work experience. *Other factors considered include:* Alumni/ae relation, geographical residence, state residency. **Transfer Admission Requirements:** College transcript(s), essay or personal statement, interview. Lowest grade transferable C. **General Admission Information:** Regular application deadline 4/15. Regular notification. Nonfall registration accepted. Common Application not accepted.

COSTS AND FINANCIAL AID
Annual tuition $7,920. **Student Employment:** Off-campus job opportunities are good.

HEIDELBERG COLLEGE

310 East Market Street, Tiffin, OH 44883
Phone: 419-448-2330 **E-mail:** adminfo@heidelberg.edu **CEEB Code:** 1292
Fax: 419-448-2334 **Website:** www.heidelberg.edu **ACT Code:** 3278
Financial Aid Phone: 419-448-2293

This private school, affiliated with the United Church of Christ, was founded in 1850. It has a 120-acre campus.

RATINGS
Admissions Selectivity Rating: 75   **Fire Safety Rating:** 60*   **Green Rating:** 60*

STUDENTS AND FACULTY
Enrollment: 1,233. **Student Body:** 51% female, 49% male, 5% out-of-state, 2% international. African American 5%, Caucasian 76%, Hispanic 1%. **Retention and Graduation:** 69% freshmen return for sophomore year. 44% freshmen graduate within 4 years. 25% grads go on to further study within 1 year. 15% grads pursue arts and sciences degrees. 5% grads pursue business degrees. 2% grads pursue law degrees. 3% grads pursue medical degrees. **Faculty:** Student/faculty ratio 14:1. 55 full-time faculty, 84% hold PhDs. 100% faculty teach undergrads.

ACADEMICS
Degrees: Bachelor's, master's. **Academic Requirements:** Arts/fine arts, computer literacy, English (including composition), foreign languages, history, humanities, mathematics, philosophy, sciences (biological or physical), social science. **Classes:** Most classes have fewer than 10 students. Most lab/discussion sections have 10–19 students. **Majors with Highest Enrollment:** Biological and physical sciences, business administration/management, education. **Disciplines with Highest Percentage of Degrees Awarded:** Social sciences 83%, business/marketing 26%, education 21%, psychology 8%, biological/life sciences 7%. **Special Study Options:** Cross-registration, double major, exchange student program (domestic), honors program, independent study, internships, liberal arts/career combination, study abroad, teacher certification program.

FACILITIES
Housing: Coed dorms, women's dorms, apartments for single students, special housing for disabled students, cooperative housing. **Special Academic Facilities/Equipment:** Forest research lots, infant studies lab, water quality lab, Center for Historic and Military Archaeology. **Computers:** 50% of classrooms are wired, 70% of classrooms are wireless, 90% of public computers are PCs, 5% of public computers are Macs, 5% of public computers are UNIX, network access in dorm rooms, network access in dorm lounges, online registration, online administrative functions (other than registration), remote student-access to Web through college's connection.

CAMPUS LIFE
Activities: Choral groups, concert band, dance, drama/theater, jazz band, literary magazine, music ensembles, musical theater, opera, pep band, radio station, student government, student newspaper, student-run film society, symphony orchestra, television station, yearbook. **Organizations:** 75 registered organizations, 6 honor societies, 3 religious organizations. 4 fraternities (18% men join), 4 sororities (24% women join). **Athletics (Intercollegiate):** *Men:* Baseball, basketball, cheerleading, cross-country, football, golf, soccer, tennis, track/field (indoor), track/field (outdoor), wrestling. *Women:* Basketball, cheerleading, cross-country, golf, soccer, softball, tennis, track/field (indoor), track/field (outdoor), volleyball.

ADMISSIONS
Freshman Academic Profile: 14% in top 10% of high school class, 36% in top 25% of high school class, 69% in top 50% of high school class. 61% from public high schools. SAT Math middle 50% range 430–580. SAT Critical Reading middle 50% range 440–580. SAT Writing middle 50% range 400–560. ACT middle 50% range 19–24. TOEFL required of all international applicants, minimum paper TOEFL 550, minimum computer TOEFL 213. **Basis for Candidate Selection:** *Very important factors considered include:* Academic GPA, character/personal qualities, rigor of secondary school record, standardized test scores, talent/ability. *Important factors considered include:* Class rank, extracurricular activities, interview, level of applicant's interest. *Other factors considered include:* Alumni/ae relation, application essay, first generation, geographical residence, recommendation(s), religious affiliation/commitment, state residency, volunteer work, work experience. **Freshman Admission Requirements:** High school diploma is required, and GED is accepted. *Academic units recommended:* 4 English, 3 math, 3 science (1 science lab), 2 foreign language, 3 social studies, 2 history, 3 academic electives. **Freshman Admission Statistics:** 1,802 applied, 72% admitted, 21% enrolled. **Transfer**

Admission Requirements: High school transcript, college transcript(s), standardized test score, statement of good standing from prior institution(s). Minimum college GPA of 2.0 required. Lowest grade transferable C-. **General Admission Information:** Application fee $25. Regular application deadline 8/1. Regular notification is rolling. Nonfall registration accepted. Admission may be deferred for a maximum of 1 year. Credit and/or placement offered for CEEB Advanced Placement tests.

COSTS AND FINANCIAL AID
Average book expense $530. **Required Forms and Deadlines:** FAFSA. Financial aid filing deadline 3/1. **Notification of Awards:** Applicants will be notified of awards on a rolling basis beginning on or about 3/1. **Types of Aid:** *Need-based scholarships/grants:* Pell, SEOG, state scholarships/grants, private scholarships, the school's own gift aid. *Loans:* FFEL Subsidized Stafford, FFEL Unsubsidized Stafford, FFEL PLUS, Federal Perkins. **Student Employment:** Federal Work-Study Program available. Institutional employment available. Off-campus job opportunities are good. **Financial Aid Statistics:** 85% freshmen, 78% undergrads receive need-based scholarship or grant aid. 85% freshmen, 70% undergrads receive need-based self-help aid. 99% freshmen, 97% undergrads receive any aid. Highest amount earned per year from on-campus jobs $1,000.

HELLENIC COLLEGE

50 Goddard Avenue, Brookline, MA 02445
Phone: 617-850-1260 **E-mail:** admissions@hchc.edu
Fax: 617-850-1460 **Website:** www.hchc.edu **ACT Code:** 1843
Financial Aid Phone: 617-850-1297

This private school, affiliated with the Greek Orthodox Church, was founded in 1937. It has a 52-acre campus.

RATINGS
Admissions Selectivity Rating: 60*   **Fire Safety Rating:** 80   **Green Rating:** 60*

STUDENTS AND FACULTY
Enrollment: 82. **Student Body:** 44% female, 56% male, 80% out-of-state, 17% international (11 countries represented). African American 1%, Caucasian 80%, Hispanic 1%. **Retention and Graduation:** 50% grads go on to further study within 1 year. **Faculty:** Student/faculty ratio 9:1. 13 full-time faculty. 50% faculty teach undergrads.

ACADEMICS
Degrees: Bachelor's, master's. **Academic Requirements:** Computer literacy, English (including composition), foreign languages, history, humanities, mathematics, philosophy, religion/theology, sciences (biological or physical), social science. **Classes:** Most classes have 20–29 students. **Disciplines with Highest Percentage of Degrees Awarded:** Philosophy and religious studies 90%, physical sciences 10%. **Special Study Options:** Liberal arts/career combination.

FACILITIES
Housing: Coed dorms, apartments for married students. **Computers:** 75% of classrooms are wired, 90% of public computers are PCs, 10% of public computers are Macs, network access in dorm rooms, network access in dorm lounges, remote student-access to Web through college's connection.

CAMPUS LIFE
Activities: Choral groups, student government, yearbook. **Athletics (Intercollegiate):** *Men:* Basketball. *Women:* Tennis.

ADMISSIONS
Freshman Academic Profile: 100% from public high schools. SAT Math middle 50% range 460–520. SAT Critical Reading middle 50% range 480–620. SAT Writing middle 50% range 430–610. ACT middle 50% range 21–27. TOEFL required of all international applicants, minimum paper TOEFL 500, minimum computer TOEFL 173. **Basis for Candidate Selection:** *Very important factors considered include:* Academic GPA, application essay, interview, recommendation(s), rigor of secondary school record, standardized test scores. *Important factors considered include:* Class rank. *Other factors considered include:* Alumni/ae relation, character/personal qualities, extracurricular activities. **Freshman Admission Requirements:** High school diploma is required, and GED is accepted. *Academic units required:* 4 English, 2 math, 2 science, 2 foreign language, 2 social studies, 2 history. **Freshman Admission Statistics:** 50 applied, 86% admitted, 58% enrolled. **Transfer Admission Requirements:** College transcript(s), essay or personal statement, interview. Minimum college GPA of 2.0 required. Lowest grade transferable C+. **General Admission Information:** Application fee $50. Regular application deadline 8/

15. Regular notification is rolling. Nonfall registration accepted. Admission may be deferred for a maximum of 2 years. Credit offered for CEEB Advanced Placement tests.

COSTS AND FINANCIAL AID
Annual tuition $17,020. Room and board $10,890. Required fees $480. Average book expense $1,000. **Required Forms and Deadlines:** FAFSA, institution's own financial aid form. Financial aid filing deadline 4/1. **Notification of Awards:** Applicants will be notified of awards on or about 4/1. **Types of Aid:** *Need-based scholarships/grants:* Pell, SEOG, state scholarships/grants, private scholarships, the school's own gift aid. *Loans:* FFEL Subsidized Stafford, FFEL Unsubsidized Stafford, FFEL PLUS. **Financial Aid Statistics:** 98% freshmen, 96% undergrads receive any aid. Highest amount earned per year from on-campus jobs $1,670.

HENDERSON STATE UNIVERSITY

1100 Henderson Street, HSU Box 7560, Arkadelphia, AR 71999-0001
Phone: 870-230-5028 **E-mail:** admissions@hsu.edu **CEEB Code:** 6272
Fax: 870-230-5066 **Website:** www.hsu.edu **ACT Code:** 0126
Financial Aid Phone: 870-230-5094

This public school was founded in 1890. It has a 151-acre campus.

RATINGS
Admissions Selectivity Rating: 79   **Fire Safety Rating:** 60*   **Green Rating:** 61

STUDENTS AND FACULTY
Enrollment: 2,681. **Student Body:** 56% female, 44% male, 14% out-of-state, 2% international (25 countries represented). African American 19%, Caucasian 76%, Hispanic 2%. **Retention and Graduation:** 55% freshmen return for sophomore year. 18% freshmen graduate within 4 years. **Faculty:** 98% faculty teach undergrads.

ACADEMICS
Degrees: Associate, bachelor's, master's. **Academic Requirements:** Arts/fine arts, English (including composition), history, humanities, mathematics, non-Western course, sciences (biological or physical), social science. **Classes:** Most classes have fewer than 10 students. Most lab/discussion sections have 10–19 students. **Majors with Highest Enrollment:** Business administration/management, elementary education and teaching, nursing/registered nurse training (RN, ASN, BSN, MSN). **Disciplines with Highest Percentage of Degrees Awarded:** Education 20%, business/marketing 17%, visual and performing arts 9%, English 8%, psychology 8%, health professions and related sciences 7%. **Special Study Options:** Cross-registration, distance learning, English as a second language (ESL), honors program, internships, liberal arts/career combination, teacher certification program.

FACILITIES
Housing: Coed dorms, men's dorms, women's dorms, special housing for international students, honors dorm, on-campus apartments leased by outside firm, floor in dorm dedicated to ACE program students, international student housing. **Special Academic Facilities/Equipment:** Closed-circuit TV studio, planetarium. **Computers:** 90% of public computers are PCs, 10% of public computers are Macs, network access in dorm rooms, online registration, online administrative functions (other than registration).

CAMPUS LIFE
Activities: Choral groups, concert band, dance, drama/theater, jazz band, literary magazine, marching band, music ensembles, radio station, student government, student newspaper, symphony orchestra, television station, yearbook. **Organizations:** 80 registered organizations, 8 fraternities, 7 sororities. **Athletics (Intercollegiate):** *Men:* Baseball, basketball, football, golf, swimming. *Women:* Basketball, cross-country, golf, softball, swimming, tennis, volleyball.

ADMISSIONS
Freshman Academic Profile: 18% in top 10% of high school class, 46% in top 25% of high school class, 79% in top 50% of high school class. SAT Math middle 50% range 460–570. SAT Writing middle 50% range 430–580. ACT middle 50% range 18–25. TOEFL required of all international applicants, minimum paper TOEFL 500, minimum computer TOEFL 300. **Basis for Candidate Selection:** *Very important factors considered include:* Rigor of secondary school record, standardized test scores. *Other factors considered include:* Application essay, character/personal qualities, class rank, interview, recommendation(s). **Freshman Admission Requirements:** High school diploma is required, and GED is accepted. *Academic units required:* 4 English, 2 math, 2 science, 2 social studies, 1 history. *Academic units recommended:* 4

English, 4 math, 3 science, 2 foreign language, 2 social studies, 2 history, 3 academic electives. **Freshman Admission Statistics:** 2,241 applied, 60% admitted, 37% enrolled. **Transfer Admission Requirements:** College transcript(s). Lowest grade transferable C. **General Admission Information:** Regular application deadline 7/15. Regular notification upon receipt. Nonfall registration accepted. Admission may be deferred. Neither credit nor placement offered for CEEB Advanced Placement tests.

COSTS AND FINANCIAL AID

Annual in-state tuition $2,520. Out-of-state tuition $5,040. Room & board $3,272. Required fees $275. Average book expense $800. **Required Forms and Deadlines:** FAFSA. Financial aid filing deadline 6/1. **Notification of Awards:** Applicants will be notified of awards on a rolling basis beginning on or about 3/1. **Types of Aid:** *Need-based scholarships/grants:* Pell, SEOG, state scholarships/grants, private scholarships, the school's own gift aid. *Loans:* Direct Subsidized Stafford, Direct Unsubsidized Stafford, Direct PLUS, FFEL Subsidized Stafford, FFEL Unsubsidized Stafford, FFEL PLUS, Federal Perkins. **Student Employment:** Federal Work-Study Program available. Off-campus job opportunities are good. **Financial Aid Statistics:** 52% freshmen, 67% undergrads receive need-based scholarship or grant aid. 50% freshmen, 66% undergrads receive need-based self-help aid. 70% freshmen, 76% undergrads receive any aid.

HENDRIX COLLEGE

1600 Washington Avenue, Conway, AR 72032
Phone: 501-450-1362 **E-mail:** adm@hendrix.edu **CEEB Code:** 6273
Fax: 501-450-3843 **Website:** www.hendrix.edu **ACT Code:** 0128
Financial Aid Phone: 501-450-1368

This private school, affiliated with the Methodist Church, was founded in 1876. It has a 160-acre campus.

RATINGS

Admissions Selectivity Rating: 88   **Fire Safety Rating:** 65   **Green Rating:** 78

STUDENTS AND FACULTY

Enrollment: 1,087. **Student Body:** 55% female, 45% male, 46% out-of-state. African American 5%, Asian 3%, Caucasian 85%, Hispanic 3%. **Retention and Graduation:** 87% freshmen return for sophomore year. 60% freshmen graduate within 4 years. 60% grads go on to further study within 1 year. 10% grads pursue arts and sciences degrees. 15% grads pursue business degrees. 4% grads pursue law degrees. 21% grads pursue medical degrees. **Faculty:** Student/faculty ratio 11:1. 90 full-time faculty, 97% hold PhDs. 100% faculty teach undergrads.

ACADEMICS

Degrees: Bachelor's, master's. **Academic Requirements:** Arts/fine arts, English (including composition), foreign languages, history, humanities, mathematics, philosophy, sciences (biological or physical), social science. All freshmen are required to take Journeys, a course that is global in its perspective and interdisciplinary in its approach, and Explorations, a course designed to foster an ongoing engagement with the liberal arts experience. All freshmen are required to participate in the academic program entitled Your Hendrix Odyssey: Engaging in Active Learning, designed to encourage students to embark on educational adventures in experiential learning. Graduation requirements include the completion of an approved activity in at least three of the following categories: artistic creativity, global awareness, professional and leadership development, service to the world, undergraduate research, and special projects. **Classes:** Most classes have 10–19 students. Most lab/discussion sections have 10–19 students. **Majors with Highest Enrollment:** Biology/ biological sciences, English language and literature, psychology. **Disciplines with Highest Percentage of Degrees Awarded:** Psychology 15%, social sciences 14%, philosophy and religious studies 13%, biological/life sciences 12%, English 7%, visual and performing arts 7%. **Special Study Options:** Cooperative education program, double major, exchange student program (domestic), Hendrix-in-Oxford, Hendrix-in-London, independent study, internships, programs with Austria and Japan, American University, student-designed major, study abroad, teacher certification program.

FACILITIES

Housing: Coed dorms, men's dorms, women's dorms, apartments for single students, special housing for disabled students, coeducational foreign language house (Spanish, German, French alternating years) available, suite-style small houses, ecology house. **Special Academic Facilities/Equipment:** Herbarium, Wilbur A. Mills Library. **Computers:** 95% of public computers are PCs, 5% of public computers are Macs, network access in dorm rooms, online registration, online administrative functions (other than registration), remote student-access to Web through college's connection.

CAMPUS LIFE

Activities: Choral groups, concert band, dance, drama/theater, jazz band, literary magazine, music ensembles, musical theater, pep band, radio station, student government, student newspaper, symphony orchestra, yearbook. **Organizations:** 72 registered organizations, 5 honor societies, 6 religious organizations. **Athletics (Intercollegiate):** *Men:* Baseball, basketball, cross-country, diving, golf, soccer, swimming, tennis, track/field (outdoor). *Women:* Basketball, cross-country, diving, golf, soccer, softball, swimming, tennis, track/field (outdoor), volleyball. **Environmental initiatives:** Reduction in paper utilization. Maintaining and building environmentally sound buildings. Recycling.

ADMISSIONS

Freshman Academic Profile: 46% in top 10% of high school class, 74% in top 25% of high school class, 95% in top 50% of high school class. 80% from public high schools. SAT Math middle 50% range 550–660. SAT Critical Reading middle 50% range 570–690. ACT middle 50% range 25–31.. TOEFL required of all international applicants, minimum paper TOEFL 550, minimum computer TOEFL 215. **Basis for Candidate Selection:** *Very important factors considered include:* Academic GPA, application essay, rigor of secondary school record, standardized test scores. *Important factors considered include:* Character/personal qualities, class rank, extracurricular activities, interview, recommendation(s). *Other factors considered include:* Racial/ethnic status, talent/ability, volunteer work. **Freshman Admission Requirements:** High school diploma is required, and GED is accepted. *Academic units recommended:* 4 English, 3 math, 2 science, 2 foreign language, 3 social studies. **Freshman Admission Statistics:** 1,263 applied, 85% admitted, 37% enrolled. **Transfer Admission Requirements:** College transcript(s), essay or personal statement, statement of good standing from prior institution(s). Minimum college GPA of 2.5 required. Lowest grade transferable C. **General Admission Information:** Application fee $40. Regular application deadline 8/1. Regular notification is rolling. Nonfall registration accepted. Admission may be deferred for a maximum of 1 year. Credit and/or placement offered for CEEB Advanced Placement tests.

COSTS AND FINANCIAL AID

Annual tuition $24,198. Room and board $7,200. Required fees $300. Average book expense $900. **Required Forms and Deadlines:** FAFSA, state aid form. Financial aid filing deadline 2/15. **Notification of Awards:** Applicants will be notified of awards on a rolling basis beginning on or about 3/1. **Types of Aid:** *Need-based scholarships/grants:* Pell, SEOG, state scholarships/grants, private scholarships, the school's own gift aid. *Loans:* FFEL Subsidized Stafford, FFEL Unsubsidized Stafford, FFEL PLUS, Federal Perkins, Methodist Loan. **Student Employment:** Federal Work-Study Program available. Institutional employment available. Off-campus job opportunities are good. **Financial Aid Statistics:** 57% freshmen, 56% undergrads receive need-based scholarship or grant aid. 41% freshmen, 46% undergrads receive need-based self-help aid. 100% freshmen, 99% undergrads receive any aid. Highest amount earned per year from on-campus jobs $1,500.

HERITAGE BIBLE COLLEGE

PO Box 1628, Dunn, NC 28335
Phone: 910-892-4268
Fax: 910-891-1660 **Website:** www.heritagebiblecollege.org
Financial Aid Phone: 910-892-5266

This private school, affiliated with the Pentecostal Church, was founded in 1971. It has an 80-acre campus.

RATINGS

Admissions Selectivity Rating: 60*   **Fire Safety Rating:** 60*   **Green Rating:** 60*

STUDENTS AND FACULTY

Enrollment: 76. **Student Body:** 25% female, 75% male, 5% international. African American 18%, Asian 1%, Caucasian 70%, Hispanic 5%. **Retention and Graduation:** 71% freshmen return for sophomore year. 100% freshmen graduate within 4 years. **Faculty:** Student/faculty ratio 8:1. 4 full-time faculty, 100% hold PhDs.

ACADEMICS

Degrees: Associate, bachelor's. **Academic Requirements:** Arts/fine arts, Bible/theology, computer literacy, English (including composition), history, humanities, mathematics, philosophy, sciences (biological or physical), social science. **Special Study Options:** Distance learning, independent study.

FACILITIES

Housing: Men's dorms, women's dorms, apartments for married students.

CAMPUS LIFE

Activities: Music ensembles, student government, yearbook.

ADMISSIONS

Basis for Candidate Selection: *Very important factors considered include:* Character/personal qualities, recommendation(s), rigor of secondary school record. *Important factors considered include:* Religious affiliation/commitment, standardized test scores. *Other factors considered include:* Alumni/ae relation, extracurricular activities, interview, talent/ability, work experience. **Freshman Admission Requirements:** High school diploma is required, and GED is accepted. **Freshman Admission Statistics:** 21 applied, 67% admitted, 100% enrolled. **Transfer Admission Requirements:** High school transcript, college transcript(s), essay or personal statement. Lowest grade transferable C. **General Admission Information:** Application fee $20. Nonfall registration not accepted. Common Application not accepted.

COSTS AND FINANCIAL AID

Annual tuition $2,880. Room & board $2,136. Required fees $400. Average book expense $150. **Required Forms and Deadlines:** FAFSA, institution's own financial aid form, verification form, tax form. **Types of Aid:** *Need-based scholarships/grants:* Pell, SEOG, private scholarships. *Loans:* FFEL Subsidized Stafford, FFEL PLUS. **Student Employment:** Federal Work-Study Program available. Institutional employment available.

HERITAGE UNIVERSITY

3240 Fort Road, Toppenish, WA 98948
Phone: 509-865-8508 **E-mail:** 3w_Admissions@heritage.edu **CEEB Code:** 3777
Fax: 509-865-8659 **Website:** www.heritage.edu
Financial Aid Phone: 509-865-8502

This private school was founded in 1982. It has a 20-acre campus.

RATINGS

Admissions Selectivity Rating: 60*   **Fire Safety Rating:** 60*   **Green Rating:** 60*

STUDENTS AND FACULTY

Enrollment: 756. **Student Body:** 73% female, 27% male. African American 1%, Asian 1%, Caucasian 35%, Hispanic 56%, Native American 11%. **Retention and Graduation:** 49% freshmen return for sophomore year. **Faculty:** Student/faculty ratio 10:1. 47 full-time faculty, 38% hold PhDs. 68% faculty teach undergrads.

ACADEMICS

Degrees: Associate, bachelor's, certificate, master's, post-bachelor's certificate, post-master's certificate. **Academic Requirements:** Arts/fine arts, computer literacy, English (including composition), foreign languages, heritage core, history, humanities, mathematics, philosophy, sciences (biological or physical), social science. **Classes:** Most classes have fewer than 10 students. **Majors with Highest Enrollment:** Business administration/management, elementary education and teaching, social work. **Disciplines with Highest Percentage of Degrees Awarded:** Education 38%, public administration and social services 25%, business/marketing 15%, English 6%, natural resources/environmental science 5%, psychology 5%. **Special Study Options:** Cooperative education program, distance learning, double major, English as a second language (ESL), honors program, independent study, internships, liberal arts/career combination, teacher certification program.

FACILITIES

Computers: 20% of classrooms are wired, 99% of public computers are PCs, 1% of public computers are UNIX, support for handheld computing, remote student-access to Web through college's connection.

CAMPUS LIFE

Activities: Drama/theater, literary magazine, music ensembles, student government, student newspaper.

ADMISSIONS

Freshman Academic Profile: 95% from public high schools. TOEFL required of all international applicants, minimum paper TOEFL 500, minimum computer TOEFL 173. **Freshman Admission Requirements:** High school diploma is required, and GED is accepted. *Academic units recommended:* 3 English, 2 math, 1 science (1 science lab), 3 history, 4 academic electives. **Freshman Admission Statistics:** 475 applied, 60% admitted, 31% enrolled. **Transfer Admission Requirements:** College transcript(s). Lowest grade transferable C-. **General Admission Information:** Regular application deadline 9/1. Regular notification on a rolling basis. Nonfall registration accepted. Admission may be deferred for a maximum of 3 years. Common Application accepted. Credit and/or placement offered for CEEB Advanced Placement tests.

COSTS AND FINANCIAL AID

Annual tuition $9,600. Required fees $45. **Required Forms and Deadlines:** FAFSA, institution's own financial aid form. Financial aid filing deadline 2/10. **Types of Aid:** *Need-based scholarships/grants:* Pell, SEOG, state scholarships/grants, private scholarships, the school's own gift aid. *Loans:* FFEL Subsidized Stafford, FFEL Unsubsidized Stafford, FFEL PLUS, Federal Perkins.

HIGH POINT UNIVERSITY

University Station 3598, High Point, NC 27262-3598
Phone: 336-841-9216 **E-mail:** admiss@highpoint.edu **CEEB Code:** 5293
Fax: 336-888-6382 **Website:** www.highpoint.edu **ACT Code:** 3108
Financial Aid Phone: 336-841-9128

This private school, affiliated with the Methodist Church, was founded in 1924. It has a 130-acre campus.

RATINGS

Admissions Selectivity Rating: 77   **Fire Safety Rating:** 60*   **Green Rating:** 60*

STUDENTS AND FACULTY

Enrollment: 2,552. **Student Body:** 62% female, 38% male, 56% out-of-state. **Retention and Graduation:** 78% freshmen return for sophomore year. 44% freshmen graduate within 4 years. 31% grads go on to further study within 1 year. 21% grads pursue arts and sciences degrees. 8% grads pursue business degrees. 1% grads pursue law degrees. **Faculty:** Student/faculty ratio 14:1. 127 full-time faculty, 77% hold PhDs. 100% faculty teach undergrads.

ACADEMICS

Degrees: Bachelor's, master's, post-bachelor's certificate. **Academic Requirements:** Arts/fine arts, computer literacy, English (including composition), ethics, foreign languages, history, humanities, international/interdisciplinary studies, mathematics, philosophy, sciences (biological or physical), physical education, social science. **Classes:** Most classes have 10–19 students. **Majors with Highest Enrollment:** Business administration/management, education, psychology. **Disciplines with Highest Percentage of Degrees Awarded:** Business/marketing 46%, computer and information sciences 8%, education 7%, psychology 6%, health professions and related sciences 6%, security and protective services 4%. **Special Study Options:** Accelerated program, cooperative education program, cross-registration, double major, dual enrollment, English as a second language (ESL), honors program, independent study, internships, liberal arts/career combination, student-designed major, study abroad, teacher certification program. Joint-degree programs in environmental science, forestry, and medical technology.

FACILITIES

Housing: Coed dorms, men's dorms, women's dorms, apartments for married students, apartments for single students, special housing for disabled students, fraternity/sorority housing, cooperative housing, apartments/houses are available for married students. **Special Academic Facilities/Equipment:** Hayworth Chapel, Hayworth Fine Arts Center, Sechrest Gallery, Smith Library, campus television studio, radio studio/station (WHPU). **Computers:** 10% of classrooms are wired, 30% of classrooms are wireless, 81% of public computers are PCs, 8% of public computers are Macs, 11% of public computers are UNIX, network access in dorm rooms, online registration, online administrative functions (other than registration), support for handheld computing, remote student-access to Web through college's connection.

CAMPUS LIFE

Activities: Choral groups, concert band, dance, drama/theater, literary magazine, music ensembles, musical theater, pep band, radio station, student government, student newspaper, television station, yearbook. **Organizations:** 90 registered organizations, 14 honor societies, 8 religious organizations, 4 fraternities (15% men join), 5 sororities (25% women join). **Athletics (Intercollegiate):** *Men:* Baseball, basketball, cheerleading, cross-country, golf, soccer, tennis, track/field (indoor), track/field (outdoor). *Women:* Basketball, cheerleading, cross-country, golf, soccer, tennis, track/field (indoor), track/field (outdoor), volleyball.

ADMISSIONS

Freshman Academic Profile: 13% in top 10% of high school class, 36% in top 25% of high school class, 61% in top 50% of high school class. 86% from public high schools. SAT Math middle 50% range 460–570. SAT Critical Reading middle 50% range 460–570. SAT Writing middle 50% range 460–560. ACT middle 50% range 19–24. TOEFL required of all international applicants, minimum paper TOEFL 500, minimum computer TOEFL 150. **Basis for Candidate Selection:** *Very important factors considered include:* Rigor of secondary school record, standardized test scores. *Important factors considered include:* Academic GPA, character/personal qualities, class rank. *Other factors considered include:* Application essay, extracurricular activities, interview, level of applicant's interest, recommendation(s), talent/ability, volunteer work, work experience. **Freshman Admission Requirements:** High school diploma is required, and GED is accepted. *Academic units required:* 4 English, 3 math, 2 science (2 science labs), 2 social studies, 2 history, 1 academic elective. *Academic units recommended:* 2 foreign language, 2 academic electives. **Freshman Admission Statistics:** 2,289 applied, 71% admitted, 37% enrolled. **Transfer Admission Requirements:** High school transcript, college transcript(s), standardized test score, statement of good standing from prior institution(s). Minimum college GPA of 2.0 required. Lowest grade transferable C. **General Admission Information:** Application fee $40. Early decision application deadline 11/7. Regular application deadline 8/15. Regular notification is rolling. Nonfall registration accepted. Admission may be deferred for a maximum of 1 year. Credit and/or placement offered for CEEB Advanced Placement tests.

COSTS AND FINANCIAL AID

Comprehensive fee $31,000. Average book expense $1,500. **Required Forms and Deadlines:** FAFSA. Financial aid filing deadline 3/1. **Notification of Awards:** Applicants will be notified of awards on a rolling basis beginning on or about 4/1. **Types of Aid:** *Need-based scholarships/grants:* Pell, SEOG, state scholarships/grants, private scholarships, the school's own gift aid. *Loans:* Direct Subsidized Stafford, Direct Unsubsidized Stafford, Direct PLUS, FFEL Subsidized Stafford, FFEL Unsubsidized Stafford, FFEL PLUS, Federal Perkins. **Student Employment:** Federal Work-Study Program available. Institutional employment available. Off-campus job opportunities are good. **Financial Aid Statistics:** 43% freshmen, 76% undergrads receive need-based scholarship or grant aid. 51% freshmen, 79% undergrads receive need-based self-help aid. 19 freshmen, 179 undergrads receive athletic scholarships. 79% freshmen, 88% undergrads receive any aid.

HILBERT COLLEGE

5200 South Park Avenue, Hamburg, NY 14075-1597
Phone: 716-649-7900 **E-mail:** admissions@hilbert.edu **CEEB Code:** 2334
Fax: 716-649-0702 **Website:** www.hilbert.edu **ACT Code:** 2759
Financial Aid Phone: 716-649-7900

This private school, affiliated with the Roman Catholic Church, was founded in 1957. It has a 40-acre campus.

RATINGS

Admissions Selectivity Rating: 64   **Fire Safety Rating:** 89   **Green Rating:** 60*

STUDENTS AND FACULTY

Enrollment: 1,052. **Student Body:** 62% female, 38% male, 10% out-of-state. African American 4%, Caucasian 87%, Hispanic 2%, Native American 1%. **Retention and Graduation:** 60% freshmen return for sophomore year. 41% freshmen graduate within 4 years. 12% grads go on to further study within 1 year. 2% grads pursue arts and sciences degrees. 4% grads pursue business degrees. 3% grads pursue law degrees. **Faculty:** Student/faculty ratio 15:1. 33 full-time faculty, 61% hold PhDs. 100% faculty teach undergrads.

ACADEMICS

Degrees: Associate, bachelor's, certificate. **Academic Requirements:** Computer literacy, English (including composition), history, humanities, mathematics, philosophy, sciences (biological or physical), social science. **Classes:** Most classes have 10–19 students. Most lab/discussion sections have fewer than 10 students. **Majors with Highest Enrollment:** Criminal justice/law enforcement administration, legal assistant/paralegal, protective services. **Disciplines with Highest Percentage of Degrees Awarded:** Business/

marketing 17%, law/legal studies 12%, health professions and related sciences 9%, psychology 6%, English 5%. **Special Study Options:** Cross-registration, distance learning, dual enrollment, honors program, independent study, internships, study abroad. Member of Western New York consortium of colleges.

FACILITIES

Housing: Coed dorms, apartments for single students. **Computers:** 100% of classrooms are wired, 1% of classrooms are wireless, 100% of public computers are PCs, network access in dorm rooms, network access in dorm lounges, online registration, online administrative functions (other than registration), remote student-access to Web through college's connection.

CAMPUS LIFE

Activities: Choral groups, drama/theater, literary magazine, student government, student newspaper. **Organizations:** 20 registered organizations, 2 honor societies, 1 religious organization. **Athletics (Intercollegiate):** *Men:* Baseball, basketball, golf, soccer, volleyball. *Women:* Basketball, cross-country, golf, soccer, softball, volleyball.

ADMISSIONS

Freshman Academic Profile: 5% in top 10% of high school class, 25% in top 25% of high school class, 53% in top 50% of high school class. 85% from public high schools. SAT Math middle 50% range 400–510. SAT Critical Reading middle 50% range 400–510. ACT middle 50% range 17–22. TOEFL required of all international applicants, minimum paper TOEFL 500, minimum computer TOEFL 173. **Basis for Candidate Selection:** *Very important factors considered include:* Rigor of secondary school record. *Important factors considered include:* Recommendation(s). *Other factors considered include:* Application essay, character/personal qualities, class rank, extracurricular activities, interview, standardized test scores, talent/ability, volunteer work, work experience. **Freshman Admission Requirements:** High school diploma is required, and GED is accepted. *Academic units required:* 4 English, 2 math, 2 science (1 science lab), 2 social studies, 2 history, 4 academic electives. *Academic units recommended:* 4 English, 3 math, 3 science, 1 foreign language, 3 social studies. **Freshman Admission Statistics:** 398 applied, 93% admitted, 43% enrolled. **Transfer Admission Requirements:** High school transcript, college transcript(s). Minimum college GPA of 1.5 required. Lowest grade transferable D. **General Admission Information:** Application fee $20. Regular application deadline 9/1. Regular notification is rolling. Nonfall registration accepted. Admission may be deferred for a maximum of 1 year. Common Application not accepted. Credit offered for CEEB Advanced Placement tests.

COSTS AND FINANCIAL AID

Regular application deadline 9/1. Annual tuition $16,000. Room and board $6,600. Required fees $600. Average book expense $700. **Required Forms and Deadlines:** FAFSA, state aid form. Financial aid filing deadline 3/1. **Notification of Awards:** Applicants will be notified of awards on a rolling basis beginning on or about 3/15. **Types of Aid:** *Need-based scholarships/grants:* Pell, SEOG, state scholarships/grants, private scholarships, the school's own gift aid. *Loans:* FFEL Subsidized Stafford, FFEL Unsubsidized Stafford, FFEL PLUS, Federal Perkins. **Student Employment:** Federal Work-Study Program available. Institutional employment available. **Financial Aid Statistics:** 93% freshmen, 85% undergrads receive need-based scholarship or grant aid. 78% freshmen, 76% undergrads receive need-based self-help aid. 94% freshmen, 89% undergrads receive any aid. Highest amount earned per year from on-campus jobs $1,179.

HILLSDALE COLLEGE

33 East College Street, Hillsdale, MI 49242
Phone: 517-607-2327 **E-mail:** admissions@hillsdale.edu **CEEB Code:** 1295
Fax: 517-607-2223 **Website:** www.hillsdale.edu **ACT Code:** 2010
Financial Aid Phone: 517-607-2350

This private school was founded in 1844. It has a 200-acre campus.

RATINGS

Admissions Selectivity Rating: 91   **Fire Safety Rating:** 88   **Green Rating:** 69

STUDENTS AND FACULTY

Enrollment: 1,346. **Student Body:** 52% female, 48% male, 58% out-of-state, 2% international. **Retention and Graduation:** 88% freshmen return for sophomore year. 35% grads go on to further study within 1 year. 8% grads pursue arts and sciences degrees. 14% grads pursue business degrees. 9% grads pursue law degrees. 4% grads pursue medical degrees. **Faculty:** Student/faculty ratio 10:1. 104 full-time faculty, 88% hold PhDs. 100% faculty teach undergrads.

ACADEMICS

Degrees: Bachelor's. **Academic Requirements:** Arts/fine arts, English (including composition), foreign languages, history, humanities, mathematics, philosophy, sciences (biological or physical), social science, 2 1-credit weeklong CCA (Center for Constructive Alternatives) seminars. **Classes:** Most classes have fewer than 10 students. Most lab/discussion sections have 20–29 students. **Majors with Highest Enrollment:** Biology/biological sciences, business administration and management, history. **Disciplines with Highest Percentage of Degrees Awarded:** History 20%, education 12%, business/marketing 12%, social sciences 10%, English 8%, philosophy and religious studies 7%, biological/life sciences 7%. **Special Study Options:** Double major, dual enrollment, honors program, independent study, internships, student-designed major, study abroad, teacher certification program.

FACILITIES

Housing: Men's dorms, women's dorms, apartments for single students, fraternity/sorority housing. **Special Academic Facilities/Equipment:** Early childhood education lab, media center, K-8 private academy, Slayton Arboretum, rare books library. **Computers:** 60% of classrooms are wired, 100% of classrooms are wireless, 80% of public computers are PCs, 20% of public computers are Macs, 10% of public computers are UNIX, network access in dorm rooms, network access in dorm lounges, remote student-access to Web through college's connection.

CAMPUS LIFE

Activities: Choral groups, concert band, dance, drama/theater, jazz band, literary magazine, music ensembles, musical theater, pep band, student government, student newspaper, symphony orchestra, yearbook. **Organizations:** 50 registered organizations, 26 honor societies, 4 religious organizations. 3 fraternities (35% men join), 3 sororities (45% women join). **Athletics (Intercollegiate):** *Men:* Baseball, basketball, cheerleading, cross-country, football, track/field (indoor), track/field (outdoor). *Women:* Basketball, cheerleading, cross-country, diving, equestrian sports, softball, swimming, track/field (indoor), track/field (outdoor), volleyball. **Environmental initiatives:** Central heating and cooling efficiency plan. High efficiency lighting in all new facilities. Environmental controls in all buildings for energy management.

ADMISSIONS

Freshman Academic Profile: 43% in top 10% of high school class, 73% in top 25% of high school class, 97% in top 50% of high school class. 55% from public high schools. SAT Math middle 50% range 570–660. SAT Critical Reading middle 50% range 640–720. SAT Writing middle 50% range 610–690. ACT middle 50% range 25–30. TOEFL required of all international applicants, minimum paper TOEFL 570, minimum computer TOEFL 210. **Basis for Candidate Selection:** *Very important factors considered include:* Academic GPA, character/personal qualities, rigor of secondary school record, standardized test scores. *Important factors considered include:* Application essay, class rank, extracurricular activities, interview, recommendation(s), volunteer work, work experience. *Other factors considered include:* Alumni/ae relation, level of applicant's interest, talent/ability. **Freshman Admission Requirements:** High school diploma is required, and GED is accepted. *Academic units recommended:* 4 English, 4 math, 3 science (1 science lab), 2 foreign language, 1 social studies, 2 history. **Freshman Admission Statistics:** 1,240 applied, 75% admitted, 44% enrolled. **Transfer Admission Requirements:** High school transcript, college transcript(s), essay or personal statement, standardized test score, statement of good standing from prior institution(s). Minimum college GPA of 3.2 required. Lowest grade transferable C. **General Admission Information:** Application fee $35. Early decision application deadline 11/15. Regular application deadline 2/15. Regular notification 12/1, 1/20, 4/1. Nonfall registration accepted. Admission may be deferred for a maximum of 1 year. Credit and/or placement offered for CEEB Advanced Placement tests.

COSTS AND FINANCIAL AID

Annual tuition $18,650. Room and board $7,340. Required fees $490. Average book expense $850. **Required Forms and Deadlines:** FAFSA, institution's own financial aid form, Noncustodial PROFILE, Business/Farm Supplement, FAFSA for state residents only. Financial aid filing deadline 3/15. **Notification of Awards:** Applicants will be notified of awards on or about 4/1. **Types of Aid:** *Need-based scholarships/grants:* State scholarships/grants, private scholarships, the school's own gift aid. *Loans:* College/university loans from institutional funds. **Student Employment:** Institutional employment available. Off-campus job opportunities are good. **Financial Aid Statistics:** 51% freshmen, 40% undergrads receive need-based scholarship or grant aid. 51% freshmen, 40%

undergrads receive need-based self-help aid. 40 freshmen, 201 undergrads receive athletic scholarships. 83% freshmen, 86% undergrads receive any aid. Highest amount earned per year from on-campus jobs $1,300.

HILLSDALE FREE WILL BAPTIST COLLEGE

PO Box 7208, Moore, OK 73153-1208
Phone: 405-912-9005 **E-mail:** schaffin@hc.edu
Fax: 405-912-9050 **Website:** www.hc.edu **ACT Code:** 3413
Financial Aid Phone: 405-912-9006

This private school was founded in 1959. It has a 40-acre campus.

RATINGS

Admissions Selectivity Rating: 60*   **Fire Safety Rating:** 60*   **Green Rating:** 60*

STUDENTS AND FACULTY

Enrollment: 181. **Student Body:** 33% female, 67% male. **Retention and Graduation:** 57% freshmen return for sophomore year. 8% freshmen graduate within 4 years. 16% grads go on to further study within 1 year. 16% grads pursue arts and sciences degrees. **Faculty:** 100% faculty teach undergrads.

ACADEMICS

Degrees: Associate, bachelor's. **Academic Requirements:** Computer literacy, English (including composition), history, humanities, mathematics, philosophy, physical education, religion, sciences (biological or physical), social science. **Special Study Options:** Academic remediation, accelerated program, advanced placement credit, double major, English as a second language (ESL), independent study, internships.

FACILITIES

Housing: Men's dorms, women's dorms, apartments for married students. **Computers:** 100% of public computers are PCs, remote student-access to Web through college's connection.

CAMPUS LIFE

Activities: Choral groups, drama/theater, music ensembles, student government. **Organizations:** 13 registered organizations, 3 religious organizations. 3 fraternities, 3 sororities. **Athletics (Intercollegiate):** *Men:* Baseball, basketball, golf. *Women:* Basketball, softball, volleyball.

ADMISSIONS

Freshman Academic Profile: 12% in top 10% of high school class, 28% in top 25% of high school class, 47% in top 50% of high school class. **Basis for Candidate Selection:** *Very important factors considered include:* Character/personal qualities, recommendation(s), religious affiliation/commitment. *Important factors considered include:* Application essay. *Other factors considered include:* Class rank, extracurricular activities, rigor of secondary school record, standardized test scores, talent/ability. **Freshman Admission Requirements:** High school diploma is required, and GED is accepted. *Academic units recommended:* 4 English, 3 math, 2 science (2 science labs), 1 social studies, 2 history, 3 computer science/language. **Freshman Admission Statistics:** 133 applied, 62% admitted, 98% enrolled. **Transfer Admission Requirements:** College transcript(s), essay or personal statement, **General Admission Information:** Application fee $20. Regular notification nonfall registration accepted. Admission may be deferred for a maximum of 1 year.

COSTS AND FINANCIAL AID

Average book expense $600. **Required Forms and Deadlines:** FAFSA, institution's own financial aid form. Financial aid filing deadline 5/1. **Notification of Awards:** Applicants will be notified of awards on a rolling basis beginning on or about 6/1. **Types of Aid:** *Need-based scholarships/grants:* Pell, SEOG, state scholarships/grants, private scholarships. *Loans:* FFEL Subsidized Stafford, FFEL Unsubsidized Stafford, FFEL PLUS, Federal Perkins. **Student Employment:** Federal Work-Study Program available. Institutional employment available. Off-campus job opportunities are excellent. **Financial Aid Statistics:** 63% undergrads receive need-based scholarship or grant aid. 50% freshmen, 44% undergrads receive need-based self-help aid.

HIRAM COLLEGE

PO Box 96, Hiram, OH 44234
Phone: 330-569-5169 **E-mail:** Admission@hiram.edu **CEEB Code:** 1297
Fax: 330-569-5944 **Website:** www.hiram.edu **ACT Code:** 3280
Financial Aid Phone: 330-569-5107

This private school, affiliated with the Disciples of Christ Church, was founded in 1850. It has a 110-acre campus.

RATINGS

Admissions Selectivity Rating: 76   **Fire Safety Rating:** 60*   **Green Rating:** 60*

STUDENTS AND FACULTY

Enrollment: 1,173. **Student Body:** 56% female, 44% male, 17% out-of-state, 3% international (17 countries represented). African American 9%, Asian 2%, Caucasian 75%, Hispanic 1%. **Retention and Graduation:** 78% freshmen return for sophomore year. 53% freshmen graduate within 4 years. 36% grads go on to further study within 1 year. 30% grads pursue arts and sciences degrees. 1% grads pursue business degrees. 3% grads pursue law degrees. 2% grads pursue medical degrees. **Faculty:** Student/faculty ratio 14:1. 60 full-time faculty. 100% faculty teach undergrads.

ACADEMICS

Degrees: Bachelor's, master's. **Academic Requirements:** Arts/fine arts, humanities, sciences (biological or physical), social science. **Majors with Highest Enrollment:** Business/commerce; education. **Disciplines with Highest Percentage of Degrees Awarded:** Business/marketing 18%, biological/life sciences 13%, education 7%, English 7%, communications/journalism 6%. **Special Study Options:** Accelerated program, cross-registration, double major, English as a second language (ESL), exchange student program (domestic), independent study, internships, student-designed major, study abroad, teacher certification program, weekend college.

FACILITIES

Housing: Coed dorms, women's dorms, special housing for disabled students, cooperative housing. **Special Academic Facilities/Equipment:** Psychology lab, language lab, international center, center for literature and medicine, fitness center, health center, observatory, electron microscope, two field stations for study and research. **Computers:** 100% of public computers are PCs, network access in dorm rooms, network access in dorm lounges, remote student-access to Web through college's connection.

CAMPUS LIFE

Activities: Choral groups, dance, drama/theater, jazz band, marching band, music ensembles, musical theater, radio station, student government, student newspaper, television station, yearbook. **Organizations:** 55 registered organizations, 7 honor societies, 6 religious organizations, 3 fraternities, 3 sororities. **Athletics (Intercollegiate):** *Men:* Baseball, basketball, cheerleading, cross-country, diving, football, golf, soccer, swimming, tennis, track/field (indoor), track/field (outdoor). *Women:* Basketball, cheerleading, cross-country, diving, golf, soccer, softball, swimming, tennis, track/field (indoor), track/field (outdoor), volleyball.

ADMISSIONS

Freshman Academic Profile: 23% in top 10% of high school class, 51% in top 25% of high school class, 81% in top 50% of high school class. 86% from public high schools. SAT Math middle 50% range 490–600. SAT Critical Reading middle 50% range 490–610. ACT middle 50% range 20–25. TOEFL required of all international applicants, minimum paper TOEFL 550. **Basis for Candidate Selection:** *Very important factors considered include:* Academic GPA. *Important factors considered include:* Application essay, character/personal qualities, extracurricular activities, rigor of secondary school record, standardized test scores. *Other factors considered include:* Alumni/ae relation, class rank, first generation, geographical residence, interview, level of applicant's interest, recommendation(s), state residency, talent/ability, volunteer work, work experience. **Freshman Admission Requirements:** High school diploma is required, and GED is accepted. *Academic units required:* 4 English, 3 math, 3 science (2 science labs), 2 foreign language, 3 social studies, 1 history, 2 academic electives. *Academic units recommended:* 3 foreign language. **Freshman Admission Statistics:** 1,058 applied, 88% admitted, 32% enrolled. **Transfer Admission Requirements:** College transcript(s), essay or personal statement, statement of good standing from prior institution(s). Minimum

college GPA of 2.5 required. Lowest grade transferable C. **General Admission Information:** Application fee $25. Regular application deadline 4/15. Regular notification is rolling. Nonfall registration accepted. Admission may be deferred for a maximum of 1 year. Credit and/or placement offered for CEEB Advanced Placement tests.

COSTS AND FINANCIAL AID

Room & board $7,980. Required fees $670. Average book expense $700. **Financial Aid Statistics:** Highest amount earned per year from on-campus jobs $500.

See page 1198.

HOBART AND WILLIAM SMITH COLLEGES

629 South Main Street, Geneva, NY 14456
Phone: 315-781-3472 **E-mail:** admissions@hws.edu **CEEB Code:** 2294
Fax: 315-781-3471 **Website:** www.hws.edu **ACT Code:** 2758
Financial Aid Phone: 315-781-3315

This private school was founded in 1822. It has a 170-acre campus.

RATINGS

Admissions Selectivity Rating: 88   **Fire Safety Rating:** 60*   **Green Rating:** 60*

STUDENTS AND FACULTY

Enrollment: 1,855. **Student Body:** 54% female, 46% male, 55% out-of-state, 2% international (18 countries represented). African American 4%, Asian 2%, Caucasian 88%, Hispanic 4%. **Retention and Graduation:** 85% freshmen return for sophomore year. 30% grads go on to further study within 1 year. 20% grads pursue arts and sciences degrees. 10% grads pursue business degrees. 7% grads pursue law degrees. 4% grads pursue medical degrees. **Faculty:** Student/faculty ratio 11:1. 156 full-time faculty, 94% hold PhDs. 100% faculty teach undergrads.

ACADEMICS

Degrees: Bachelor's, master's. **Academic Requirements:** Arts/fine arts, English (including composition), humanities, mathematics, sciences (biological or physical), social science. Students must meet the 8 goals set by the faculty. **Classes:** Most classes have 10–19 students. **Majors with Highest Enrollment:** Economics, English language and literature, history. **Disciplines with Highest Percentage of Degrees Awarded:** Social sciences 19%, English 10%, history 9%, area and ethnic studies 7%, physical sciences 7%, psychology 7%, visual and performing arts 6%. **Special Study Options:** Cross-registration, double major, dual enrollment, English as a second language (ESL), exchange student program (domestic), honors program, independent study, internships, student-designed major, study abroad, teacher certification program.

FACILITIES

Housing: Coed dorms, men's dorms, women's dorms, apartments for single students, special housing for international students, fraternity/sorority housing, cooperative housing, upperclass town-houses, theme houses, honors houses. **Special Academic Facilities/Equipment:** Houghton Gallery, HWS Explorer (research vessel), 100-acre nature preserve, Melly Academic Center, Rosenberg Science Center. **Computers:** 90% of public computers are PCs, 10% of public computers are Macs, network access in dorm rooms, network access in dorm lounges, online registration, online administrative functions (other than registration), support for handheld computing, remote student-access to Web through college's connection.

CAMPUS LIFE

Activities: Choral groups, dance, drama/theater, jazz band, literary magazine, music ensembles, radio station, student government, student newspaper, student-run film society, symphony orchestra, yearbook. **Organizations:** 77 registered organizations, 12 honor societies, 4 religious organizations, 5 fraternities (15% men join). **Athletics (Intercollegiate):** *Men:* Basketball, crew/rowing, cross-country, football, golf, ice hockey, lacrosse, sailing, soccer, squash, tennis. *Women:* Basketball, crew/rowing, cross-country, diving, field hockey, golf, lacrosse, sailing, soccer, squash, swimming, tennis.

ADMISSIONS

Freshman Academic Profile: 33% in top 10% of high school class, 67% in top 25% of high school class, 95% in top 50% of high school class. 65% from public

high schools. SAT Math middle 50% range 540–630. SAT Critical Reading middle 50% range 530–640. ACT middle 50% range 24–27. TOEFL required of all international applicants, minimum paper TOEFL 550, minimum computer TOEFL 220. **Basis for Candidate Selection:** *Very important factors considered include:* Rigor of secondary school record. *Important factors considered include:* Academic GPA, application essay, character/personal qualities, class rank, extracurricular activities, recommendation(s), standardized test scores, volunteer work, work experience. *Other factors considered include:* Alumni/ae relation, first generation, geographical residence, interview, level of applicant's interest, racial/ethnic status, talent/ability. **Freshman Admission Requirements:** High school diploma is required, and GED is accepted. *Academic units required:* 4 English, 3 math, 3 science (2 science labs), 2 foreign language, 2 social studies, 2 history, 2 academic electives. *Academic units recommended:* 3 foreign language, 3 social studies, 4 academic electives. **Freshman Admission Statistics:** 3,410 applied, 65% admitted, 25% enrolled. **Transfer Admission Requirements:** High school transcript, college transcript(s), essay or personal statement, standardized test score. Minimum college GPA of 2.5 required. Lowest grade transferable C. **General Admission Information:** Application fee $45. Early decision application deadline 11/15. Regular application deadline 2/1. Regular notification 4/1. Nonfall registration not accepted. Admission may be deferred for a maximum of 2 years. Common Application accepted. Credit offered for CEEB Advanced Placement tests.

COSTS AND FINANCIAL AID

Annual tuition $31,850. Room & board $8,386. Required fees $887. Average book expense $850. **Required Forms and Deadlines:** FAFSA, CSS/Financial Aid PROFILE, state aid form, Noncustodial PROFILE, parents' and students' tax return. Financial aid filing deadline 2/1. **Notification of Awards:** Applicants will be notified of awards on or about 4/1. **Types of Aid:** *Need-based scholarships/grants:* Pell, SEOG, state scholarships/grants, private scholarships, the school's own gift aid. *Loans:* FFEL Subsidized Stafford, FFEL Unsubsidized Stafford, FFEL PLUS, Federal Perkins. **Student Employment:** Federal Work-Study Program available. Institutional employment available. Off-campus job opportunities are good. **Financial Aid Statistics:** 58% freshmen, 60% undergrads receive need-based scholarship or grant aid. 48% freshmen, 53% undergrads receive need-based self-help aid. 74% freshmen, 64% undergrads receive any aid. Highest amount earned per year from on-campus jobs $600.

HOFSTRA UNIVERSITY

Best 368

Admissions Center, Bernon Hall, Hempstead, NY 11549
Phone: 516-463-6700 **E-mail:** admitme@hofstra.edu **CEEB Code:** 2295
Fax: 516-463-5100 **Website:** www.hofstra.edu **ACT Code:** 2760
Financial Aid Phone: 516-463-8000

This private school was founded in 1935. It has a 240-acre campus.

RATINGS
Admissions Selectivity Rating: 85   **Fire Safety Rating:** 92   **Green Rating:** 83

STUDENTS AND FACULTY
Enrollment: 8,383. **Student Body:** 53% female, 47% male, 32% out-of-state, 2% international (67 countries represented). African American 10%, Asian 5%, Caucasian 61%, Hispanic 8%. **Retention and Graduation:** 77% freshmen return for sophomore year. 36% freshmen graduate within 4 years. 28% grads go on to further study within 1 year. 2% grads pursue arts and sciences degrees. 2% grads pursue business degrees. 2% grads pursue law degrees. 2% grads pursue medical degrees. **Faculty:** Student/faculty ratio 14:1. 532 full-time faculty. 90% hold PhDs. 84% faculty teach undergrads.

ACADEMICS
Degrees: Bachelor's, certificate, doctoral, first professional, master's, post-bachelor's certificate, post-master's certificate. **Academic Requirements:** English (including composition), foreign languages, humanities, mathematics, sciences (biological or physical), social science. **Classes:** Most classes have 10–19 students. Most lab/discussion sections have 10–19 students. **Majors with Highest Enrollment:** Accounting, marketing/marketing management, psychology. **Disciplines with Highest Percentage of Degrees Awarded:** Business/marketing 31%, communications/journalism 15%, psychology 10%, education 9%, social sciences 6%. **Special Study Options:** Accelerated

program, cross-registration, double major, dual enrollment, English as a second language (ESL), external degree program, honors program, independent study, internships, liberal arts/career combination, student-designed major, study abroad, teacher certification program, weekend college.

FACILITIES
Housing: Coed dorms, women's dorms, apartments for married students, apartments for single students, special housing for disabled students, special housing for international students, learning-living center, honors housing, and quiet floors. **Special Academic Facilities/Equipment:** Financial trading room, comprehensive media production facility including a 24-hour radio station, career center, writing center, Linux Beowolf cluster, digital language lab, technology, science and engineering labs, a rooftop observatory, 6 theaters (with black box teaching theater), assessment centers for child observation and counseling, child care institute, cultural center, museum, arboretum, and bird sanctuary. **Computers:** 11% of classrooms are wired, 30% of classrooms are wireless, 93% of public computers are PCs, 5% of public computers are Macs, 2% of public computers are UNIX, network access in dorm rooms, network access in dorm lounges, online registration, online administrative functions (other than registration), support for handheld computing, remote student-access to Web through college's connection.

CAMPUS LIFE
Activities: Choral groups, concert band, dance, drama/theater, jazz band, literary magazine, music ensembles, musical theater, opera, pep band, radio station, student government, student newspaper, student-run film society, symphony orchestra, television station, yearbook. **Organizations:** 155 registered organizations, 30 honor societies, 6 religious organizations. 18 fraternities (6% men join), 14 sororities (7% women join). **Athletics (Intercollegiate):** *Men:* Baseball, basketball, cross-country, football, golf, lacrosse, soccer, tennis, wrestling. *Women:* Basketball, cross-country, field hockey, golf, lacrosse, soccer, softball, tennis, volleyball. **Environmental initiatives:** Use of Green Products—The University has recently undertaken the purchasing of "Green" products that consider environmental impacts. The university uses only "Green Seal" certified custodial supplies, and purchases "Energy Star Qualified Products" including computers, monitors, copy machines, air conditioners and other appliances. In 2007, the cogeneration plant supplied over 27% of the university's energy demand.

ADMISSIONS
Freshman Academic Profile: 23% in top 10% of high school class, 46% in top 25% of high school class, 80% in top 50% of high school class. SAT Math middle 50% range 550–630. SAT Critical Reading middle 50% range 530–620. ACT middle 50% range 22–26. TOEFL required of all international applicants, minimum paper TOEFL 550, minimum computer TOEFL 213. **Basis for Candidate Selection:** *Very important factors considered include:* Academic GPA, application essay, class rank, recommendation(s), rigor of secondary school record, standardized test scores. *Important factors considered include:* Character/personal qualities, extracurricular activities, interview, talent/ability. *Other factors considered include:* Alumni/ae relation, geographical residence, level of applicant's interest, racial/ethnic status, volunteer work, work experience. **Freshman Admission Requirements:** High school diploma is required, and GED is accepted. *Academic units required:* 4 English, 3 math, 3 science (1 science lab), 2 foreign language, 3 social studies. *Academic units recommended:* 4 math, 4 science (2 science labs), 3 foreign language, 4 social studies. **Freshman Admission Statistics:** 13,493 applied, 62% admitted, 21% enrolled. **Transfer Admission Requirements:** College transcript(s). Lowest grade transferable C-. **General Admission Information:** Application fee $50. Regular notification is rolling. Nonfall registration accepted. Admission may be deferred for a maximum of 1 year. Credit and/or placement offered for CEEB Advanced Placement tests.

COSTS AND FINANCIAL AID
Comprehensive fee $25,700. Room and board $10,300. Required fees $1,030. Average book expense $1,000. **Required Forms and Deadlines:** FAFSA, state aid form. Financial aid filing deadline 2/15. **Notification of Awards:** Applicants will be notified of awards on a rolling basis beginning on or about 3/15. **Types of Aid:** *Need-based scholarships/grants:* Pell, SEOG, state scholarships/grants, private scholarships, the school's own gift aid. *Loans:* FFEL Subsidized Stafford, FFEL Unsubsidized Stafford, FFEL PLUS, Federal Perkins. **Student Employment:** Federal Work-Study Program available. Institutional employment available. Off-campus job opportunities are excellent. **Financial Aid Statistics:** 54% freshmen, 49% undergrads receive need-based scholarship or grant aid. 51% freshmen, 48% undergrads receive need-based self-help aid. 27 freshmen, 146 undergrads receive athletic scholarships. 90% freshmen, 83% undergrads receive any aid. Highest amount earned per year from on-campus jobs $5,500.

See page 1200.

HOLLINS UNIVERSITY

PO Box 9707, Roanoke, VA 24020-1707
Phone: 540-362-6401 **E-mail:** huadm@hollins.edu **CEEB Code:** 5294
Fax: 540-362-6218 **Website:** www.hollins.edu **ACT Code:** 4360
Financial Aid Phone: 540-362-6332

This private school was founded in 1842. It has a 475-acre campus.

RATINGS
Admissions Selectivity Rating: 83   **Fire Safety Rating:** 71   **Green Rating:** 78

STUDENTS AND FACULTY
Enrollment: 781. **Student Body:** 2% international (15 countries represented). African American 8%, Asian 2%, Caucasian 80%, Hispanic 3%. **Retention and Graduation:** 73% freshmen return for sophomore year. 65% freshmen graduate within 4 years. 22% grads go on to further study within 1 year. 1% grads pursue law degrees. 1% grads pursue medical degrees. **Faculty:** Student/faculty ratio 10:1. 67 full-time faculty, 97% hold PhDs. 100% faculty teach undergrads.

ACADEMICS
Degrees: Bachelor's, master's, post-master's certificate. **Academic Requirements:** Arts/fine arts, computer literacy, English (including composition), foreign languages, history, humanities, mathematics, sciences (biological or physical), social science. **Classes:** Most classes have 10–19 students. Most lab/discussion sections have fewer than 10 students. **Majors with Highest Enrollment:** Communications studies/speech communication and rhetoric, English language and literature, psychology. **Disciplines with Highest Percentage of Degrees Awarded:** English 20%, visual and performing arts 16%, social sciences 15%, psychology 13%, business/marketing 6%, history 6%. **Special Study Options:** Accelerated program, cooperative education program, cross-registration, double major, dual enrollment, exchange student program (domestic), independent study, internships, liberal arts/career combination, student-designed major, study abroad, teacher certification program.

FACILITIES
Housing: Women's dorms, apartments for single students, special housing for disabled students, special housing for international students, language/academic/community service, special interest housing. **Special Academic Facilities/Equipment:** Athletic complex, a writing center, language labs, campus-wide computer network, scientific equipment and instrumentation, art museum, state-of-the-art library. **Computers:** 100% of classrooms are wired, 45% of classrooms are wireless, 86% of public computers are PCs, 14% of public computers are Macs, network access in dorm rooms, network access in dorm lounges, online registration, online administrative functions (other than registration), remote student-access to Web through college's connection.

CAMPUS LIFE
Activities: Choral groups, dance, drama/theater, literary magazine, music ensembles, musical theater, student government, student newspaper, television station, yearbook. **Organizations:** 46 registered organizations, 12 honor societies, 5 religious organizations. **Athletics (Intercollegiate):** *Women:* Basketball, equestrian sports, golf, lacrosse, soccer, swimming, tennis.

ADMISSIONS
Freshman Academic Profile: 28% in top 10% of high school class, 56% in top 25% of high school class, 86% in top 50% of high school class. 77% from public high schools. SAT Math middle 50% range 470–600. SAT Critical Reading middle 50% range 500–670. SAT Writing middle 50% range 490–620. ACT middle 50% range 21–28. TOEFL required of all international applicants, minimum paper TOEFL 550, minimum computer TOEFL 213. **Basis for Candidate Selection:** *Very important factors considered include:* Academic GPA, level of applicant's interest, standardized test scores. *Important factors considered include:* Application essay, recommendation(s), talent/ability. *Other factors considered include:* Alumni/ae relation, character/personal qualities, class rank, extracurricular activities, first generation, interview, racial/ethnic status, rigor of secondary school record, volunteer work, work experience. **Freshman Admission Requirements:** High school diploma is required, and GED is accepted. *Academic units required:* 4 English, 3 math, 3 science, 3 foreign language, 3 social studies. **Freshman Admission Statistics:** 651 applied, 84% admitted, 35% enrolled. **Transfer Admission Requirements:** High school transcript, college transcript(s), essay or personal statement.

Minimum college GPA of 2.5 required. Lowest grade transferable C. **General Admission Information:** Application fee $35. Early decision application deadline 12/1. Regular notification is rolling. Nonfall registration accepted. Admission may be deferred for a maximum of usually 1 year. Credit and/or placement offered for CEEB Advanced Placement tests.

COSTS AND FINANCIAL AID
Annual tuition $25,110. Room and board $9,140. Required fees $535. Average book expense $1,000. **Required Forms and Deadlines:** FAFSA, state aid form. Financial aid filing deadline 2/15. **Notification of Awards:** Applicants will be notified of awards on or about 3/1. **Types of Aid:** *Need-based scholarships/grants:* Pell, SEOG, state scholarships/grants, private scholarships, the school's own gift aid. *Loans:* Direct Subsidized Stafford, Direct Unsubsidized Stafford, Direct PLUS, Federal Perkins, college/university loans from institutional funds, PLATO, CitiAssist, SallieMae, Nelnet, Campus Door. **Financial Aid Statistics:** 71% freshmen, 79% undergrads receive need-based scholarship or grant aid. 58% freshmen, 62% undergrads receive need-based self-help aid. 97% freshmen, 93% undergrads receive any aid.

HOLY APOSTLES COLLEGE AND SEMINARY

33 Prospect Hill Road, Cromwell, CT 06416-2005
Phone: 860-632-3033 **E-mail:** admissions@holyapostles.edu
Fax: 860-632-3075 **Website:** www.holyapostles.edu

This is a private school, affiliated with the Roman Catholic Church.

RATINGS
Admissions Selectivity Rating: 60*   **Fire Safety Rating:** 60*   **Green Rating:** 60*

STUDENTS AND FACULTY
Enrollment: 14. **Student Body:** 100% male, 42% out-of-state. African American 7%, Asian 7%, Caucasian 64%, Hispanic 7%, Native American 14%. **Faculty:** Student/faculty ratio 7:1. 14 full-time faculty.

ACADEMICS
Degrees: Associate, bachelor's, certificate, first professional certificate, first professional, master's, post-master's certificate. **Majors with Highest Enrollment:** Philosophy, religious education. **Special Study Options:** Cooperative education program, distance learning, double major, English as a second language (ESL), independent study.

FACILITIES
Housing: Men's dorms. **Computers:** Network access in dorm rooms.

CAMPUS LIFE
Activities: Choral groups, drama/theater, student government, student newspaper, yearbook.

ADMISSIONS
Freshman Academic Profile: TOEFL required of all international applicants, minimum paper TOEFL 540. **Basis for Candidate Selection:** *Very important factors considered include:* Interview. **Freshman Admission Requirements:** High school diploma is required, and GED is accepted. **Transfer Admission Requirements:** High school transcript, college transcript(s). Lowest grade transferable C-. **General Admission Information:** Application fee $50. Regular notification is rolling. Nonfall registration not accepted. Common Application not accepted.

COSTS AND FINANCIAL AID
Annual tuition $8,160. Room & board $6,600. Required fees $80. Average book expense $530.

HOLY FAMILY UNIVERSITY

9801 Frankford Avenue, Philadelphia, PA 19114-2009
Phone: 215-637-3050 **E-mail:** admissions@holyfamily.edu gradstudy@holyfamily.edu
CEEB Code: 2297 **Fax:** 215-281-1022 **Website:** www.holyfamily.edu **ACT Code:** 3592
Financial Aid Phone: 215-637-5538

*This private school, affiliated with the Roman Catholic Church, was
founded in 1954. It has a 46-acre campus.*

RATINGS
Admissions Selectivity Rating: 72   **Fire Safety Rating:** 60*   **Green Rating:** 60*

STUDENTS AND FACULTY
Enrollment: 1,600. **Student Body:** 75% female, 25% male, 11% out-of-state.
African American 3%, Asian 3%, Caucasian 83%, Hispanic 2%. **Retention and
Graduation:** 77% freshmen return for sophomore year. 52% freshmen graduate
within 4 years. 16% grads go on to further study within 1 year. 8% grads pursue
arts and sciences degrees. 2% grads pursue business degrees. 2% grads pursue
law degrees. 2% grads pursue medical degrees. **Faculty:** Student/faculty ratio
11:1. 87 full-time faculty, 64% hold PhDs. 100% faculty teach undergrads.

ACADEMICS
Degrees: Associate, bachelor's, certificate, master's, post-bachelor's certificate.
Academic Requirements: Arts/fine arts, English (including composition),
foreign languages, history, humanities, mathematics, philosophy, sciences
(biological or physical), senior ethics, social science. **Classes:** Most classes have
10–19 students. **Majors with Highest Enrollment:** Accounting, elementary
education and teaching, nursing/registered nurse training (RN, ASN, BSN,
MSN). **Disciplines with Highest Percentage of Degrees Awarded:**
Education 35%, business/marketing 23%, health professions and related
sciences 13%, psychology 5%, liberal arts/general studies 3%, English 3%.
Special Study Options: Accelerated program, cooperative education program,
double major, dual enrollment, independent study, internships, study abroad,
teacher certification program.

FACILITIES
Housing: Coed dorms, housing available for some athletes. **Special Academic
Facilities/Equipment:** On-campus nursery school, language lab. **Computers:**
100% of public computers are PCs, remote student-access to Web through
college's connection.

CAMPUS LIFE
Activities: Drama/theater, literary magazine, student government, student
newspaper, yearbook. **Organizations:** 10 registered organizations, 14 honor
societies, 1 religious organization. **Athletics (Intercollegiate):** *Men:*
Basketball, cross-country, golf, soccer. *Women:* Basketball, cross-country, soccer,
softball, volleyball.

ADMISSIONS
Freshman Academic Profile: 11% in top 10% of high school class, 33% in top
25% of high school class, 73% in top 50% of high school class. 33% from public
high schools. SAT Math middle 50% range 410–520. SAT Critical Reading
middle 50% range 430–510. TOEFL required of all international applicants,
minimum paper TOEFL 550. **Basis for Candidate Selection:** *Very important
factors considered include:* Class rank, interview, rigor of secondary school
record. *Important factors considered include:* Alumni/ae relation, application
essay, character/personal qualities, standardized test scores. *Other factors
considered include:* Extracurricular activities, recommendation(s), talent/ability,
volunteer work, work experience. **Freshman Admission Requirements:** High
school diploma is required, and GED is accepted. *Academic units required:* 4
English, 3 math, 2 science, 2 history, 3 academic electives. *Academic units
recommended:* 2 foreign language. **Freshman Admission Statistics:** 573
applied, 77% admitted, 52% enrolled. **Transfer Admission Requirements:**
High school transcript, college transcript(s), essay or personal statement,
statement of good standing from prior institution(s). Minimum college GPA of
2.5 required. Lowest grade transferable C. **General Admission Information:**
Application fee $25. Regular notification continuous. Nonfall registration not
accepted. Admission may be deferred for a maximum of 1 year. Common
Application accepted. Neither credit nor placement offered for CEEB
Advanced Placement tests.

COSTS AND FINANCIAL AID
Annual tuition $14,990. Required fees $500. **Required Forms and Deadlines:** FAFSA, institution's own financial aid form. Financial aid filing deadline
3/1. **Notification of Awards:** Applicants will be notified of awards on a rolling
basis beginning on or about 4/1. **Types of Aid:** *Need-based scholarships/grants:*
Pell, SEOG, state scholarships/grants, private scholarships, the school's own gift
aid. *Loans:* FFEL Subsidized Stafford, FFEL Unsubsidized Stafford, FFEL

PLUS, Federal Perkins, Federal Nursing, college/university loans from
institutional funds. **Student Employment:** Federal Work-Study Program
available. Institutional employment available. Off-campus job opportunities are
excellent. **Financial Aid Statistics:** 59% freshmen, 24 freshmen, 103
undergrads receive athletic scholarships.

HOLY NAMES UNIVERSITY

3500 Mountain Boulevard, Oakland, CA 94619-1699
Phone: 510-436-1351 **E-mail:** admissions@hnu.edu **CEEB Code:** 4059
Fax: 510-436-1325 **Website:** www.hnu.edu **ACT Code:** 0230
Financial Aid Phone: 510-436-1327

*This private school, affiliated with the Roman Catholic Church, was
founded in 1868. It has a 60-acre campus.*

RATINGS
Admissions Selectivity Rating: 76   **Fire Safety Rating:** 60*   **Green Rating:** 60*

STUDENTS AND FACULTY
Enrollment: 592. **Student Body:** 78% female, 22% male, 4% out-of-state, 3%
international (25 countries represented). African American 32%, Asian 6%,
Caucasian 28%, Hispanic 16%, Native American 1%. **Retention and
Graduation:** 62% freshmen return for sophomore year. 30% freshmen
graduate within 4 years. **Faculty:** Student/faculty ratio 12:1. 31 full-time faculty,
90% hold PhDs. 61% faculty teach undergrads.

ACADEMICS
Degrees: Bachelor's, master's, post-bachelor's certificate. **Academic
Requirements:** Arts/fine arts, computer literacy, English (including composition), foreign languages, history, humanities, mathematics, philosophy, sciences
(biological or physical), social science, oral communication. **Classes:** Most
classes have 10–19 students. Most lab/discussion sections have 10–19 students.
Majors with Highest Enrollment: Business administration/management,
nursing/registered nurse training (RN, ASN, BSN, MSN), psychology.
Disciplines with Highest Percentage of Degrees Awarded: Health
professions and related sciences 27%, business/marketing 22%, psychology
14%, liberal arts/general studies 10%, social sciences 7%. **Special Study
Options:** Academic remediating, accelerated program, cross-registration,
distance learning, double major, English as a second language (ESL), exchange
student program (domestic), independent study, internships, learning disabled
services, liberal arts/career combination, off-campus study, student-designed
major, study abroad, teacher certification program, weekend college.

FACILITIES
Housing: Coed dorms, single-gender floor and wings. **Special Academic
Facilities/Equipment:** Valley Center for the Performing Arts, J. D. Kennedy
Arts Center Gallery. **Computers:** 76% of public computers are PCs, 24% of
public computers are Macs, network access in dorm rooms, network access in
dorm lounges, remote student-access to Web through college's connection.

CAMPUS LIFE
Activities: Choral groups, drama/theater, music ensembles, student government, symphony orchestra. **Organizations:** 16 registered organizations, 11
honor societies, 1 religious organization. **Athletics (Intercollegiate):** *Men:*
Basketball, cross-country, golf, soccer. *Women:* Basketball, cross-country, soccer,
volleyball.

ADMISSIONS
Freshman Academic Profile: 12% in top 10% of high school class, 40% in top
25% of high school class, 79% in top 50% of high school class. 62% from public
high schools. SAT Math middle 50% range 440–540. SAT Critical Reading
middle 50% range 450–510. ACT middle 50% range 16–23. TOEFL required
of all international applicants, minimum paper TOEFL 490, minimum
computer TOEFL 163. **Basis for Candidate Selection:** *Very important
factors considered include:* Rigor of secondary school record. *Important factors
considered include:* Application essay, recommendation(s), standardized test
scores. *Other factors considered include:* Alumni/ae relation, character/personal
qualities, class rank, extracurricular activities, interview, talent/ability, volunteer
work, work experience. **Freshman Admission Requirements:** High school
diploma is required, and GED is accepted. *Academic units required:* 4 English,
3 math, 1 science (1 science lab), 2 foreign language, 1 history, 4 academic
electives. *Academic units recommended:* 3 foreign language. **Freshman
Admission Statistics:** 211 applied, 62% admitted, 44% enrolled. **Transfer
Admission Requirements:** College transcript(s), essay or personal statement,
statement of good standing from prior institution(s). Minimum college GPA of
2.2 required. Lowest grade transferable C-. **General Admission Information:**
Application fee $35. Regular application deadline 8/1. Regular notification is

rolling. Nonfall registration accepted. Admission may be deferred for a maximum of 1 year. Common Application accepted. Credit offered for CEEB Advanced Placement tests.

COSTS AND FINANCIAL AID

Annual tuition $19,970. Room & board $7,800. Required fees $210. Average book expense $946. **Required Forms and Deadlines:** FAFSA, institution's own financial aid form, state aid form. Financial aid filing deadline 3/2. **Notification of Awards:** Applicants will be notified of awards on a rolling basis beginning on or about 4/1. **Types of Aid:** *Need-based scholarships/grants:* Pell, SEOG, state scholarships/grants, private scholarships, the school's own gift aid. *Loans:* FFEL Subsidized Stafford, FFEL Unsubsidized Stafford, FFEL PLUS, Federal Perkins, alternative loans. **Student Employment:** Federal Work-Study Program available. Institutional employment available. Off-campus job opportunities are good. **Financial Aid Statistics:** 74% freshmen, 66% undergrads receive need-based scholarship or grant aid. 79% freshmen, 66% undergrads receive need-based self-help aid. 24 freshmen, 77 undergrads receive athletic scholarships. 79% freshmen, 57% undergrads receive any aid.

HOOD COLLEGE

401 Rosemont Avenue, Frederick, MD 21701
Phone: 301-696-3400 **E-mail:** admissions@hood.edu **CEEB Code:** 5296
Fax: 301-696-3819 **Website:** www.hood.edu **ACT Code:** 1702
Financial Aid Phone: 301-696-3411

This private school was founded in 1893. It has a 50-acre campus.

RATINGS

Admissions Selectivity Rating: 81   **Fire Safety Rating:** 85   **Green Rating:** 68

STUDENTS AND FACULTY

Enrollment: 1,232. **Student Body:** 72% female, 28% male, 18% out-of-state, 2% international (26 countries represented). African American 11%, Asian 3%, Caucasian 75%, Hispanic 3%. **Retention and Graduation:** 80% freshmen return for sophomore year. 69% freshmen graduate within 4 years. 39% grads go on to further study within 1 year. 25% grads pursue arts and sciences degrees. 4% grads pursue business degrees. 4% grads pursue law degrees. 1% grads pursue medical degrees. **Faculty:** Student/faculty ratio 12:1. 80 full-time faculty, 96% hold PhDs. 100% faculty teach undergrads.

ACADEMICS

Degrees: Bachelor's, master's, post-bachelor's certificate. **Academic Requirements:** Arts/fine arts, computer literacy, English (including composition), foreign languages, history, humanities, mathematics, philosophy, sciences (biological or physical), social science, physical education. **Classes:** Most classes have 10–19 students. Most lab/discussion sections have 10–19 students. **Majors with Highest Enrollment:** Biology/biological sciences, business administration and management, psychology. **Disciplines with Highest Percentage of Degrees Awarded:** Education 11%, biological/life sciences 11%, psychology 11%, social sciences 10%, visual and performing arts 8%, communications/journalism 7%, business/marketing 7%, English 6%, mathematics 6%. **Special Study Options:** Accelerated program, distance learning, double major, dual enrollment, honors program, independent study, internships, liberal arts/career combination, student-designed major, study abroad, teacher certification program.

FACILITIES

Housing: Coed dorms, women's dorms, special housing for disabled students, language houses (French, German, and Spanish). **Special Academic Facilities/Equipment:** Art gallery, child development lab, language lab, observatory, science labs. **Computers:** 94% of public computers are PCs, 6% of public computers are UNIX, network access in dorm rooms, network access in dorm lounges, online registration, online administrative functions (other than registration), remote student-access to Web through college's connection.

CAMPUS LIFE

Activities: Choral groups, dance, drama/theater, jazz band, literary magazine, music ensembles, musical theater, radio station, student government, student newspaper, student-run film society, yearbook. **Organizations:** 93 registered organizations, 14 honor societies, 6 religious organizations. **Athletics (Intercollegiate):** *Men:* Basketball, cross-country, golf, lacrosse, soccer, swimming, tennis, track/field (outdoor). *Women:* Basketball, cross-country, field hockey, golf, lacrosse, soccer, softball, swimming, tennis, track/field (outdoor), volleyball.

ADMISSIONS

Freshman Academic Profile: 22% in top 10% of high school class, 57% in top 25% of high school class, 91% in top 50% of high school class. 85% from public high schools. SAT Math middle 50% range 410–590. SAT Critical Reading middle 50% range 490–610. SAT Writing middle 50% range 490–590. ACT middle 50% range 20–26. TOEFL required of all international applicants, minimum paper TOEFL 550, minimum computer TOEFL 215. **Basis for Candidate Selection:** *Very important factors considered include:* Academic GPA, rigor of secondary school record. *Important factors considered include:* Alumni/ae relation, character/personal qualities, class rank, extracurricular activities, level of applicant's interest, standardized test scores, talent/ability. *Other factors considered include:* Application essay, interview, racial/ethnic status, recommendation(s), volunteer work, work experience. **Freshman Admission Requirements:** High school diploma is required, and GED is accepted. *Academic units recommended:* 4 English, 3 math, 3 science (2 science labs), 2 foreign language, 3 social studies, 1 academic elective. **Freshman Admission Statistics:** 1,949 applied, 68% admitted, 21% enrolled. **Transfer Admission Requirements:** College transcript(s), essay or personal statement, statement of good standing from prior institution(s). Minimum college GPA of 2.5 required. Lowest grade transferable C-. **General Admission Information:** Application fee $35. Regular notification is rolling. Nonfall registration accepted. Admission may be deferred for a maximum of 1 year. Credit and/or placement offered for CEEB Advanced Placement tests.

COSTS AND FINANCIAL AID

Average book expense $800. **Required Forms and Deadlines:** FAFSA. Financial aid filing deadline 2/15. **Notification of Awards:** Applicants will be notified of awards on or about 3/1. **Types of Aid:** *Need-based scholarships/grants:* Pell, SEOG, state scholarships/grants, private scholarships, the school's own gift aid. *Loans:* Direct Subsidized Stafford, Direct Unsubsidized Stafford, Direct PLUS, FFEL Subsidized Stafford, FFEL Unsubsidized Stafford, FFEL PLUS, Federal Perkins. **Student Employment:** Federal Work-Study Program available. Institutional employment available. Off-campus job opportunities are good. **Financial Aid Statistics:** 71% freshmen, 78% undergrads receive need-based scholarship or grant aid. 48% freshmen, 57% undergrads receive need-based self-help aid. 98% freshmen, 99% undergrads receive any aid. Highest amount earned per year from on-campus jobs $1,800.

HOPE COLLEGE

69 East 10th, PO Box 9000, Holland, MI 49422-9000
Phone: 616-395-7850 **E-mail:** admissions@hope.edu **CEEB Code:** 1301
Fax: 616-395-7130 **Website:** www.hope.edu **ACT Code:** 2012
Financial Aid Phone: 616-395-7765

This private school, affiliated with the Reformed Church in America, was founded in 1862. It has a 120-acre campus.

RATINGS

Admissions Selectivity Rating: 86   **Fire Safety Rating:** 77   **Green Rating:** 62

STUDENTS AND FACULTY

Enrollment: 3,109. **Student Body:** 60% female, 40% male, 26% out-of-state, 2% international (28 countries represented). African American 2%, Asian 2%, Caucasian 62%, Hispanic 2%. **Retention and Graduation:** 64% freshmen graduate within 4 years. 26% grads go on to further study within 1 year. 9% grads pursue arts and sciences degrees. 1% grads pursue business degrees. 5% grads pursue law degrees. 11% grads pursue medical degrees. **Faculty:** Student/faculty ratio 13:1. 215 full-time faculty, 77% hold PhDs. 100% faculty teach undergrads.

ACADEMICS

Degrees: Bachelor's. **Academic Requirements:** Arts/fine arts, English (including composition), foreign languages, history, humanities, mathematics, sciences (biological or physical), social science. **Classes:** Most classes have 10–19 students. Most lab/discussion sections have 20–29 students. **Majors with Highest Enrollment:** Business administration/management; English language and literature; psychology. **Disciplines with Highest Percentage of Degrees Awarded:** Education 19%, business/marketing 12%, psychology 11%, social sciences 7%, foreign languages and literature 6%. **Special Study Options:** Double major, English as a Second Language (ESL), independent study, internships, student-designed major, study abroad, teacher certification program.

FACILITIES

Housing: Coed dorms, men's dorms, women's dorms, apartments for married students, apartments for single students, special housing for disabled students, fraternity/sorority housing, cottages/houses on or near campus, theme housing. **Special Academic Facilities/Equipment:** Art gallery, particle accelerator, computational chemistry lab, electron microscopes, spectrometers, ultracentrifuge, observatory, new $38M science building. **Computers:** 1% of classrooms are wired, 40% of classrooms are wireless, 100% of public computers are PCs, network access in dorm rooms, network access in dorm lounges, online registration, online administrative functions (other than registration), support for handheld computing, remote student-access to Web through college's connection. **Environmental initiatives:** Replace T12 bulbs with T8s across campus. Replace leaking steam traps on our campus steam system with SteamGuard units to help save energy. Reducing paper use through a new initiative consolidating our copy and print services.

CAMPUS LIFE

Activities: Choral groups, concert band, dance, drama/theater, jazz band, literary magazine, music ensembles, musical theater, pep band, radio station, student government, student newspaper, symphony orchestra, television station, yearbook. **Organizations:** 67 registered organizations, 22 honor societies, 4 religious organizations. 6 fraternities (9% men join), 7 sororities (9% women join). **Athletics (Intercollegiate):** *Men:* Baseball, basketball, cheerleading, cross-country, diving, football, golf, soccer, swimming, tennis, track/field (indoor), track/field (outdoor). *Women:* Basketball, cheerleading, cross-country, diving, golf, soccer, softball, swimming, tennis, track/field (indoor), track/field (outdoor), volleyball.

ADMISSIONS

Freshman Academic Profile: 30% in top 10% of high school class, 58% in top 25% of high school class, 95% in top 50% of high school class. 91% from public high schools. SAT Math middle 50% range 540–650. SAT Critical Reading middle 50% range 530–660. ACT middle 50% range 23–29. TOEFL required of all international applicants, minimum paper TOEFL 550, minimum computer TOEFL 250. **Basis for Candidate Selection:** *Very important factors considered include:* Academic GPA, rigor of secondary school record, standardized test scores. *Important factors considered include:* Application essay, class rank. *Other factors considered include:* Alumni/ae relation, character/personal qualities, extracurricular activities, geographical residence, interview, level of applicant's interest, racial/ethnic status, recommendation(s), state residency, talent/ability, volunteer work, work experience. **Freshman Admission Requirements:** High school diploma is required, and GED is accepted. *Academic units required:* 4 English, 2 math, 1 science (1 science lab), 2 foreign language, 2 social studies, 5 academic electives. *Academic units recommended:* 4 English, 3 math, 3 science, (2 science labs), 3 foreign language, 2 social studies, 1 history, 5 academic electives. **Freshman Admission Statistics:** 2,666 applied, 81% admitted, 35% enrolled. **Transfer Admission Requirements:** High school transcript, college transcript(s), essay or personal statement, standardized test score, statement of good standing from prior institution(s). Minimum college GPA of 2.0 required. Lowest grade transferable C. **General Admission Information:** Application fee $35. Regular notification is rolling. Nonfall registration accepted. Admission may be deferred for a maximum of 1 year. Credit offered for CEEB Advanced Placement tests.

COSTS AND FINANCIAL AID

Annual tuition $24,780. Room and board $7,650. Required fees $140. Average book expense $772. **Required Forms and Deadlines:** FAFSA, institution's own financial aid form. Financial aid filing deadline 3/1. **Notification of Awards:** Applicants will be notified of awards on a rolling basis beginning on or about 3/20. **Types of Aid:** *Need-based scholarships/grants:* Pell, SEOG, state scholarships/grants, private scholarships, the school's own gift aid. *Loans:* Direct Subsidized Stafford, Direct Unsubsidized Stafford, Direct PLUS, Federal Perkins. **Financial Aid Statistics:** 46% freshmen, 49% undergrads receive need-based scholarship or grant aid. 40% freshmen, 44% undergrads receive need-based self-help aid. 84% freshmen, 87% undergrads receive any aid. Highest amount earned per year from on-campus jobs $1,500.

HOPE INTERNATIONAL UNIVERSITY

Undergraduate Admissions, 2500 East Nutwood Avenue, Fullerton, CA 92831
Phone: 866-722-4673 **E-mail:** pccadmissions@hiu.edu
Fax: 714-681-7423 **Website:** www.hiu.edu **ACT Code:** 0356
Financial Aid Phone: 714-879-3901

This private school, affiliated with the Church of Christ, was founded in 1928. It has an 18-acre campus.

RATINGS

Admissions Selectivity Rating: 60*   **Fire Safety Rating:** 61   **Green Rating:** 60*

STUDENTS AND FACULTY

Enrollment: 654. **Student Body:** 51% female, 49% male, 24% out-of-state, 3% international. African American 8%, Asian 4%, Caucasian 62%, Hispanic 16%, Native American 2%. **Retention and Graduation:** 65% freshmen return for sophomore year. 29% freshmen graduate within 4 years. **Faculty:** Student/faculty ratio 26:1. 27 full-time faculty, 70% hold PhDs. 77% faculty teach undergrads.

ACADEMICS

Degrees: Associate, bachelor's, certificate, master's, post-bachelor's certificate. **Academic Requirements:** English (including composition), history, humanities, mathematics, sciences (biological or physical), social science. **Classes:** Most classes have 10–19 students. Most lab/discussion sections have fewer than 10 students. **Majors with Highest Enrollment:** Psychology, teacher education, youth ministry. **Disciplines with Highest Percentage of Degrees Awarded:** Family and consumer sciences 40%, philosophy and religious studies 24%, business/marketing 15%, social sciences 9%, psychology 6%, education 6%. **Special Study Options:** Accelerated program, cross-registration, distance learning, double major, dual enrollment, English as a second language (ESL), independent study, internships, liberal arts/career combination, student-designed major, study abroad, teacher certification program.

FACILITIES

Housing: Men's dorms, women's dorms. **Computers:** Network access in dorm rooms, remote student-access to Web through college's connection.

CAMPUS LIFE

Activities: Choral groups, drama/theater, jazz band, music ensembles, musical theater, student government, student newspaper, yearbook. **Athletics (Intercollegiate):** *Men:* Basketball, soccer, tennis, volleyball. *Women:* Basketball, soccer, softball, tennis, volleyball.

ADMISSIONS

Freshman Academic Profile: 95% from public high schools. SAT Math middle 50% range 430–550. SAT Critical Reading middle 50% range 440–560. ACT middle 50% range 18–27. TOEFL required of all international applicants, minimum paper TOEFL 500, minimum computer TOEFL 173. **Basis for Candidate Selection:** *Very important factors considered include:* Application essay, rigor of secondary school record. *Other factors considered include:* Academic GPA, character/personal qualities, extracurricular activities, interview, level of applicant's interest, recommendation(s), religious affiliation/commitment, standardized test scores, talent/ability. **Freshman Admission Requirements:** High school diploma is required, and GED is accepted. *Academic units recommended:* 4 English, 2 math, 1 science (1 science lab), 1 foreign language, 1 social studies, 1 history, 3 academic electives. **Freshman Admission Statistics:** 62% enrolled. **Transfer Admission Requirements:** College transcript(s), essay or personal statement, statement of good standing from prior institution(s). Minimum college GPA of 2.0 required. Lowest grade transferable C. **General Admission Information:** Application fee $40. Nonfall registration accepted. Credit and/or placement offered for CEEB Advanced Placement tests.

COSTS AND FINANCIAL AID

Annual tuition $18,400. Room & board $7,250. Required fees $300. Average book expense $1,314. **Required Forms and Deadlines:** FAFSA, institution's own financial aid form. Financial aid filing deadline 2/28. **Notification of Awards:** Applicants will be notified of awards on a rolling basis beginning on or about 3/15. **Types of Aid:** *Need-based scholarships/grants:* Pell, SEOG, state scholarships/grants, private scholarships, the school's own gift aid. *Loans:* Direct Subsidized Stafford, Direct Unsubsidized Stafford, Direct PLUS, FFEL Subsidized Stafford, FFEL Unsubsidized Stafford, FFEL PLUS, Federal Perkins, state loans, college/university loans from institutional funds. **Student Employment:** Federal Work-Study Program available. Institutional employment available. Off-campus job opportunities are good. **Financial Aid Statistics:** 42% freshmen, 48% undergrads receive need-based scholarship or

Grant aid. 29% freshmen, 39% undergrads receive need-based self-help aid. 67% freshmen, 73% undergrads receive any aid.

HOUGHTON COLLEGE

PO Box 128, Houghton, NY 14744
Phone: 800-777-2556 **E-mail:** admissions@houghton.edu **CEEB Code:** 2299
Website: www.houghton.edu **ACT Code:** 2766
Financial Aid Phone: 585-567-9328

This private school, affiliated with the Wesleyan Church, was founded in 1883. It has a 1,300-acre campus.

RATINGS
Admissions Selectivity Rating: 82   **Fire Safety Rating:** 73   **Green Rating:** 73

STUDENTS AND FACULTY
Enrollment: 1,378. **Student Body:** 65% female, 35% male, 37% out-of-state, 3% international (23 countries represented). African American 2%, Asian 2%, Caucasian 90%. **Retention and Graduation:** 82% freshmen return for sophomore year. 61% freshmen graduate within 4 years. 25% grads go on to further study within 1 year. 25% grads pursue arts and sciences degrees. 4% grads pursue business degrees. 5% grads pursue law degrees. 6% grads pursue medical degrees. **Faculty:** Student/faculty ratio 13:1. 87 full-time faculty, 80% hold PhDs. 100% faculty teach undergrads.

ACADEMICS
Degrees: Associate, bachelor's, master's. **Academic Requirements:** Arts/fine arts, Bible and theology, communication, English (including composition), foreign languages, history, humanities, library/media research, mathematics, philosophy, sciences (biological or physical), social science. **Classes:** Most classes have 10–19 students. Most lab/discussion sections have 10–19 students. **Majors with Highest Enrollment:** Biology/biological sciences, business administration and management, elementary education and teaching. **Disciplines with Highest Percentage of Degrees Awarded:** Business/marketing 25%, education 14%, English 10%, philosophy and religious studies 9%, biological/life sciences 7%, visual and performing arts 7%. **Special Study Options:** Cross-registration, double major, exchange student program (domestic), honors program, independent study, internships, study abroad, teacher certification program.

FACILITIES
Housing: Men's dorms, women's dorms, apartments for single students, special housing for international students, townhouses for men and women (maximum of 8 males or 8 females per house). **Special Academic Facilities/Equipment:** Electron microscope, art gallery, greenhouse. **Computers:** 26% of classrooms are wired, 25% of classrooms are wireless, 75% of public computers are PCs, 25% of public computers are Macs, network access in dorm rooms, online registration, online administrative functions (other than registration), remote student-access to Web through college's connection, tuition includes personal computer. Undergraduates are required to own a computer.

CAMPUS LIFE
Activities: Choral groups, concert band, drama/theater, jazz band, literary magazine, music ensembles, musical theater, opera, radio station, student government, student newspaper, symphony orchestra, yearbook. **Organizations:** 40 registered organizations, 2 honor societies, 9 religious organizations. **Athletics (Intercollegiate):** *Men:* Basketball, cross-country, soccer, track/field (indoor), track/field (outdoor). *Women:* Basketball, cross-country, field hockey, soccer, track/field (indoor), track/field (outdoor), volleyball.

ADMISSIONS
Freshman Academic Profile: 31% in top 10% of high school class, 64% in top 25% of high school class, 90% in top 50% of high school class. 67% from public high schools. SAT Math middle 50% range 490–620. SAT Critical Reading middle 50% range 510–640. SAT Writing middle 50% range 510–630. ACT middle 50% range 21–28. TOEFL required of all international applicants, minimum paper TOEFL 550, minimum computer TOEFL 213. **Basis for Candidate Selection:** *Very important factors considered include:* Character/ personal qualities, class rank, religious affiliation/commitment, rigor of secondary school record. *Important factors considered include:* Application essay, recommendation(s), standardized test scores. *Other factors considered include:* Alumni/ae relation, extracurricular activities, interview, level of applicant's interest, racial/ethnic status, talent/ability, volunteer work, work experience. **Freshman Admission Requirements:** High school diploma is required, and GED is accepted. *Academic units recommended:* 4 English, 3 math, 2 science (2 science labs), 2 foreign language, 1 social studies, 2 history. **Freshman Admission Statistics:** 983 applied, 93% admitted, 34% enrolled.

Transfer Admission Requirements: College transcript(s), essay or personal statement. Minimum college GPA of 2.7 required. Lowest grade transferable C-. **General Admission Information:** Application fee $40. Regular notification is rolling. Nonfall registration accepted. Admission may be deferred for a maximum of 1 year. Credit and/or placement offered for CEEB Advanced Placement tests.

COSTS AND FINANCIAL AID
Annual tuition $21,620. Room and board $6,860. Average book expense $750. **Required Forms and Deadlines:** FAFSA. Financial aid filing deadline 3/1. **Notification of Awards:** Applicants will be notified of awards on a rolling basis beginning on or about 3/15. **Types of Aid:** *Need-based scholarships/grants:* Pell, SEOG, state scholarships/grants, private scholarships, the school's own gift aid. *Loans:* FFEL Subsidized Stafford, FFEL Unsubsidized Stafford, FFEL PLUS, Federal Perkins, college/university loans from institutional funds, private alternative loans. **Student Employment:** Federal Work-Study Program available. Institutional employment available. Off-campus job opportunities are poor. **Financial Aid Statistics:** 90% freshmen, 89% undergrads receive need-based scholarship or grant aid. 57% freshmen, 73% undergrads receive need-based self-help aid. 2 freshmen, 14 undergrads receive athletic scholarships. 89% freshmen, 89% undergrads receive any aid. Highest amount earned per year from on-campus jobs $2,000.

HOUSTON BAPTIST UNIVERSITY

7502 Fondren Road, Houston, TX 77074
Phone: 281-649-3211 **E-mail:** unadm@hbu.edu **CEEB Code:** 6282
Fax: 281-649-3217 **Website:** www.hbu.edu **ACT Code:** 4101
Financial Aid Phone: 281-649-3471

This private school, affiliated with the Southern Baptist Church, was founded in 1960. It has a 100-acre campus.

RATINGS
Admissions Selectivity Rating: 75   **Fire Safety Rating:** 77   **Green Rating:** 60*

STUDENTS AND FACULTY
Enrollment: 1,916. **Student Body:** 67% female, 33% male, 3% out-of-state, 6% international (36 countries represented). African American 20%, Asian 13%, Caucasian 46%, Hispanic 14%. **Retention and Graduation:** 74% freshmen return for sophomore year. 32% freshmen graduate within 4 years. **Faculty:** Student/faculty ratio 14:1. 103 full-time faculty, 81% hold PhDs. 90% faculty teach undergrads.

ACADEMICS
Degrees: Associate, bachelor's, master's. **Academic Requirements:** Arts/fine arts, Christianity, communications, computer literacy, English (including composition), foreign languages, humanities, kinesiology, mathematics, sciences (biological or physical), social science. **Classes:** Most classes have 10–19 students. Most lab/discussion sections have fewer than 10 students. **Majors with Highest Enrollment:** Biology/biological sciences, business administration/management, psychology. **Disciplines with Highest Percentage of Degrees Awarded:** Business/marketing 32%, biological/life sciences 12%, psychology 11%, education 10%, philosophy and religious studies 6%. **Special Study Options:** Accelerated program, double major, dual enrollment, English as a second language (ESL), independent study, internships, liberal arts/career combination, teacher certification program.

FACILITIES
Housing: Men's dorms, women's dorms, apartments for single students. **Special Academic Facilities/Equipment:** Museum of Architecture/ Decorative Arts, language lab, research center. **Computers:** 100% of public computers are PCs, network access in dorm rooms, network access in dorm lounges, online registration, remote student-access to Web through college's connection.

CAMPUS LIFE
Activities: Choral groups, concert band, drama/theater, music ensembles, pep band, student government, student newspaper, yearbook. **Organizations:** 36 registered organizations, 9 honor societies, 3 religious organizations. 2 fraternities (5% men join), 2 sororities (5% women join). **Athletics (Intercollegiate):** *Men:* Baseball, basketball, cheerleading. *Women:* Basketball, cheerleading, softball, volleyball.

ADMISSIONS
Freshman Academic Profile: 24% in top 10% of high school class, 44% in top 25% of high school class, 79% in top 50% of high school class. 79% from public high schools. SAT Math middle 50% range 500–620. SAT Critical Reading

middle 50% range 500–610. ACT middle 50% range 19–25. TOEFL required of all international applicants, minimum paper TOEFL 550, minimum computer TOEFL 213. **Basis for Candidate Selection:** *Very important factors considered include:* Application essay, recommendation(s), rigor of secondary school record, standardized test scores. *Important factors considered include:* Class rank, extracurricular activities, geographical residence, religious affiliation/commitment, talent/ability, volunteer work. *Other factors considered include:* Alumni/ae relation, character/personal qualities, interview. **Freshman Admission Requirements:** High school diploma is required, and GED is accepted. *Academic units recommended:* 4 English, 3 math, 3 science (1 science lab), 2 foreign language, 2 social studies, 2 history, 2 academic electives. **Freshman Admission Statistics:** 867 applied, 65% admitted, 55% enrolled. **Transfer Admission Requirements:** College transcript(s), essay or personal statement, statement of good standing from prior institution(s). Minimum college GPA of 2.0 required. Lowest grade transferable C. **General Admission Information:** Application fee $25. Regular notification rolling. Nonfall registration accepted. Common Application not accepted. Credit offered for CEEB Advanced Placement tests.

COSTS AND FINANCIAL AID
Required Forms and Deadlines: FAFSA. Financial aid filing deadline 4/15. **Notification of Awards:** Applicants will be notified of awards on a rolling basis beginning on or about 3/10. **Types of Aid:** *Need-based scholarships/grants:* Pell, SEOG, state scholarships/grants, private scholarships, the school's own gift aid. *Loans:* FFEL Subsidized Stafford, FFEL Unsubsidized Stafford, FFEL PLUS, state loans, private, non-federal. **Student Employment:** Federal Work-Study Program available. **Financial Aid Statistics:** 78% freshmen, 84% undergrads receive need-based scholarship or grant aid. 57% freshmen, 72% undergrads receive need-based self-help aid. 4 freshmen, 10 undergrads receive athletic scholarships. 64% freshmen, 85% undergrads receive any aid. Highest amount earned per year from on-campus jobs $1,800.

HOWARD PAYNE UNIVERSITY

Howard Payne Station, Brownwood, TX 76801
Phone: 325-649-8027 **E-mail:** enroll@hputx.edu
Fax: 325-649-8901 **Website:** www.hputx.edu **ACT Code:** 4102
Financial Aid Phone: 325-649-8015

This private school, affiliated with the Baptist Church, was founded in 1889. It has a 30-acre campus.

RATINGS
Admissions Selectivity Rating: 60*   **Fire Safety Rating:** 60*   **Green Rating:** 60*

STUDENTS AND FACULTY
Enrollment: 1,303. **Student Body:** 50% female, 50% male, 3% out-of-state. African American 8%, Asian 1%, Caucasian 75%, Hispanic 12%, Native American 1%. **Retention and Graduation:** 61% freshmen return for sophomore year. 21% freshmen graduate within 4 years. 15% grads go on to further study within 1 year. 2% grads pursue business degrees. 2% grads pursue law degrees. 2% grads pursue medical degrees. **Faculty:** Student/faculty ratio 11:1. 75 full-time faculty, 59% hold PhDs. 100% faculty teach undergrads.

ACADEMICS
Degrees: Associate, bachelor's, certificate. **Academic Requirements:** Arts/fine arts, computer literacy, English (including composition), foreign languages, mathematics, physical education, sciences (biological or physical), social science, speech. **Classes:** Most classes have fewer than 10 students. **Majors with Highest Enrollment:** Bible/biblical studies, business administration/management, education. **Disciplines with Highest Percentage of Degrees Awarded:** Education 19%, business/marketing 17%, communication technologies 9%, social sciences 7%, liberal arts/general studies 6%, parks and recreation 6%. **Special Study Options:** Accelerated program, cooperative education program, distance learning, double major, dual enrollment, English as a second language (ESL), honors program, independent study, internships, liberal arts/career combination, study abroad, teacher certification program. Extension campuses are located in El Paso, Corpus Christi, Weatherford, and Harlingen, Texas.

FACILITIES
Housing: Men's dorms, women's dorms, apartments for single students. **Special Academic Facilities/Equipment:** Douglas MacArthur Academy of Freedom, museum. **Computers:** 90% of public computers are PCs, 10% of public computers are Macs, network access in dorm rooms, network access in dorm lounges, online administrative functions (other than registration), remote student-access to Web through college's connection.

CAMPUS LIFE
Activities: Choral groups, concert band, drama/theater, jazz band, literary magazine, marching band, music ensembles, musical theater, opera, radio station, student government, student newspaper, yearbook. **Organizations:** 32 registered organizations, 3 honor societies, 4 religious organizations. 5 fraternities (11% men join), 5 sororities (11% women join). **Athletics (Intercollegiate):** *Men:* Baseball, basketball, cheerleading, cross-country, football, tennis, track/field (outdoor). *Women:* Basketball, cheerleading, cross-country, softball, tennis, track/field (outdoor), volleyball.

ADMISSIONS
Freshman Academic Profile: 15% in top 10% of high school class, 39% in top 25% of high school class, 71% in top 50% of high school class. 94% from public high schools. SAT Math middle 50% range 440–550. SAT Critical Reading middle 50% range 440–570. ACT middle 50% range 17–23. TOEFL required of all international applicants, minimum paper TOEFL 550, minimum computer TOEFL 213. **Basis for Candidate Selection:** *Very important factors considered include:* Rigor of secondary school record, standardized test scores. *Important factors considered include:* Interview, recommendation(s). *Other factors considered include:* Character/personal qualities, class rank, work experience. **Freshman Admission Requirements:** High school diploma is required, and GED is accepted. *Academic units recommended:* 4 English, 3 math, 2 science (1 science lab), 3 social studies, 10 academic electives. **Freshman Admission Statistics:** 640 applied, 78% admitted, 62% enrolled. **Transfer Admission Requirements:** College transcript(s). Minimum college GPA of 2.0 required. Lowest grade transferable D. **General Admission Information:** Application fee $25. Regular application deadline 8/31. Nonfall registration accepted. Admission may be deferred for a maximum of 1 year. Common Application accepted. Credit and/or placement offered for CEEB Advanced Placement tests.

COSTS AND FINANCIAL AID
Annual tuition $11,500. Room & board $4,615. Required fees $1,000. Average book expense $1,000. **Required Forms and Deadlines:** FAFSA, institution's own financial aid form. Financial aid filing deadline 3/15. **Notification of Awards:** Applicants will be notified of awards on a rolling basis beginning on or about 3/1. **Types of Aid:** *Need-based scholarships/grants:* Pell, SEOG, state scholarships/grants, private scholarships, the school's own gift aid. *Loans:* FFEL Subsidized Stafford, FFEL Unsubsidized Stafford, FFEL PLUS, Federal Perkins, state loans. **Student Employment:** Federal Work-Study Program available. Institutional employment available. Off-campus job opportunities are good. **Financial Aid Statistics:** 79% freshmen, 76% undergrads receive need-based scholarship or grant aid. 58% freshmen, 59% undergrads receive need-based self-help aid.

HOWARD UNIVERSITY

2400 6th Street, NW, Washington, DC 20059
Phone: 202-806-2700 **E-mail:** admission@howard.edu **CEEB Code:** 5297
Fax: 202-806-4467 **Website:** www.howard.edu **ACT Code:** 4102
Financial Aid Phone: 877-577-2575

This private school was founded in 1867. It has an 89-acre campus.

RATINGS
Admissions Selectivity Rating: 87   **Fire Safety Rating:** 97   **Green Rating:** 60*

STUDENTS AND FACULTY
Enrollment: 7,275. **Student Body:** 67% female, 33% male, 77% out-of-state, 7% international (105 countries represented). African American 84%. **Retention and Graduation:** 85% freshmen return for sophomore year. 44% freshmen graduate within 4 years. 58% grads go on to further study within 1 year. 24% grads pursue arts and sciences degrees. 15% grads pursue business degrees. 14% grads pursue law degrees. 12% grads pursue medical degrees. **Faculty:** Student/faculty ratio 8:1. 1069 full-time faculty, 90% hold PhDs. 64% faculty teach undergrads.

ACADEMICS
Degrees: Bachelor's, certificate, doctoral, first professional certificate, first professional, master's, post-master's certificate. **Academic Requirements:** African-American cluster requirement, computer literacy, English (including

composition), foreign languages, mathematics, philosophy, physical education. **Classes:** Most classes have fewer than 10 students. Most lab/discussion sections have fewer than 10 students. **Majors with Highest Enrollment:** Biology/biological sciences; journalism; radio and television. **Disciplines with Highest Percentage of Degrees Awarded:** Visual and performing arts 52%, communication technologies 21%, business/marketing 17%, health professions and related sciences 13%. **Special Study Options:** Accelerated program, cooperative education program, distance learning, double major, English as a Second Language (ESL), exchange student program (domestic), honors program, independent study, internships, study abroad, teacher certification program, tutorial program; advanced placement, continuing education.

FACILITIES

Housing: Coed dorms, men's dorms, women's dorms, apartments for married students, apartments for single students. **Special Academic Facilities/Equipment:** 3 art galleries, language labs, hospital, research center with comprehensive collection on Africa and persons of African descent. **Computers:** 80% of public computers are PCs, 15% of public computers are Macs, online registration, online administrative functions (other than registration), support for handheld computing, remote student-access to Web through college's connection.

CAMPUS LIFE

Activities: Choral groups, concert band, dance, drama/theater, jazz band, literary magazine, marching band, music ensembles, musical theater, opera, pep band, radio station, student government, student newspaper, student-run film society, symphony orchestra, television station, yearbook. **Organizations:** 150 registered organizations, 15 honor societies, 3 religious organizations. 10 fraternities (2% men join), 8 sororities (1% women join). **Athletics (Intercollegiate):** *Men:* Baseball, basketball, cheerleading, cross-country, diving, football, soccer, softball, swimming, tennis, track/field (outdoor), wrestling. *Women:* Basketball, bowling, cheerleading, cross-country, diving, lacrosse, soccer, swimming, tennis, track/field (outdoor), volleyball.

ADMISSIONS

Freshman Academic Profile: 21% in top 10% of high school class, 54% in top 25% of high school class, 84% in top 50% of high school class. 80% from public high schools. SAT Math middle 50% range 440–650. SAT Critical Reading middle 50% range 460–660. SAT Writing middle 50% range 410–650. ACT middle 50% range 20–28. TOEFL required of all international applicants, minimum paper TOEFL 550, minimum computer TOEFL 213. **Basis for Candidate Selection:** *Very important factors considered include:* Class rank, rigor of secondary school record, standardized test scores. *Important factors considered include:* Character/personal qualities, recommendation(s). *Other factors considered include:* Alumni/ae relation, application essay, extracurricular activities, talent/ability, volunteer work, work experience. **Freshman Admission Requirements:** High school diploma is required, and GED is accepted. *Academic units required:* 4 English, 2 math, 2 science, 2 foreign language, 2 social studies, 2 history, *Academic units recommended:* 4 English, 3 math, 4 science (2 science labs), 2 foreign language, 2 social studies, 2 history, 4 any other academic courses counted toward graduation. **Freshman Admission Statistics:** 8,661 applied, 48% admitted, 37% enrolled. **Transfer Admission Requirements:** College transcript(s), statement of good standing from prior institution(s). Minimum college GPA of 2.5 required. Lowest grade transferable C. **General Admission Information:** Application fee $45. Early decision application deadline 11/1. Regular application deadline 2/15. Regular notification rolling basis. Nonfall registration accepted. Admission may be deferred for a maximum of 1 year. Credit and/or placement offered for CEEB Advanced Placement tests.

COSTS AND FINANCIAL AID

Annual tuition $13,215. Room and board $6,976. Required fees $805. Average book expense $1,300. **Required Forms and Deadlines:** FAFSA. Financial aid filing deadline 8/15. **Notification of Awards:** Applicants will be notified of awards on or about 4/1. **Types of Aid:** *Need-based scholarships/grants:* Pell, SEOG, state scholarships/grants, private scholarships, the school's own gift aid, Federal Nursing Scholarships. *Loans:* Direct Subsidized Stafford, Direct Unsubsidized Stafford, Direct PLUS, Federal Perkins, Federal Nursing. **Student Employment:** Federal Work-Study Program available. Institutional employment available. Off-campus job opportunities are excellent. **Financial Aid Statistics:** 65% freshmen, 32% undergrads receive need-based scholarship or grant aid. 17% freshmen, 22% undergrads receive need-based self-help aid. 583 freshmen, 198 undergrads receive athletic scholarships. 67% freshmen, 63% undergrads receive any aid. Highest amount earned per year from on-campus jobs $3,500.

HUMBOLDT STATE UNIVERSITY

1 Harpst Street, Arcata, CA 95521-8299
Phone: 707-826-4402 **E-mail:** hsuinfo@humboldt.edu **CEEB Code:** 4345
Fax: 707-826-6190 **Website:** www.humboldt.edu **ACT Code:** 0286
Financial Aid Phone: 707-826-4321

This public school was founded in 1913. It has a 161-acre campus.

RATINGS

Admissions Selectivity Rating: 72   Fire Safety Rating: 60*   Green Rating: 60*

STUDENTS AND FACULTY

Enrollment: 6,254. **Student Body:** 54% female, 46% male, 4% out-of-state. African American 4%, Asian 4%, Caucasian 57%, Hispanic 11%, Native American 3%. **Retention and Graduation:** 76% freshmen return for sophomore year. 13% freshmen graduate within 4 years. **Faculty:** Student/faculty ratio 18:1. 288 full-time faculty, 81% hold PhDs. 100% faculty teach undergrads.

ACADEMICS

Degrees: Bachelor's, certificate, diploma, master's. **Academic Requirements:** English (including composition), history, humanities, mathematics, sciences (biological or physical). **Classes:** Most classes have 20–29 students. Most lab/discussion sections have 10–19 students. **Majors with Highest Enrollment:** Liberal arts and sciences/liberal studies, social sciences, wildlife and wildlands sciences and management. **Disciplines with Highest Percentage of Degrees Awarded:** Natural resources/environmental science 13%, visual and performing arts 12%, social sciences 11%, liberal arts/general studies 10%, biological/life sciences 9%. **Special Study Options:** Cooperative education program, cross-registration, distance learning, double major, dual enrollment, English as a second language (ESL), exchange student program (domestic), honors program, independent study, internships, student-designed major, study abroad, teacher certification program.

FACILITIES

Housing: Coed dorms, apartments for single students, fraternity/sorority housing, themed residence halls. **Special Academic Facilities/Equipment:** Art and geology museums, marine research lab, fish hatchery, wildlife game pen, observatory, First Street Gallery. **Computers:** Network access in dorm rooms, online registration, remote student-access to Web through college's connection.

CAMPUS LIFE

Activities: Choral groups, concert band, dance, drama/theater, jazz band, literary magazine, marching band, music ensembles, musical theater, radio station, student government, student newspaper, student-run film society. **Organizations:** 160 registered organizations, 6 honor societies, 2 fraternities, 4 sororities. **Athletics (Intercollegiate):** *Men:* Basketball, cross-country, football, soccer, track/field (outdoor). *Women:* Basketball, crew/rowing, cross-country, soccer, softball, track/field (outdoor), volleyball.

ADMISSIONS

Freshman Academic Profile: 3% in top 10% of high school class, 10% in top 25% of high school class, 49% in top 50% of high school class. 90% from public high schools. SAT Math middle 50% range 450–580. SAT Critical Reading middle 50% range 450–590. SAT Writing middle 50% range 440–560. ACT middle 50% range 18–25. TOEFL required of all international applicants, minimum paper TOEFL 500, minimum computer TOEFL 173. **Basis for Candidate Selection:** *Very important factors considered include:* Rigor of secondary school record, standardized test scores. *Other factors considered include:* Application essay, character/personal qualities, extracurricular activities, interview, racial/ethnic status, recommendation(s), talent/ability, volunteer work. **Freshman Admission Requirements:** High school diploma is required, and GED is accepted. *Academic units required:* 4 English, 3 math, 2 science (2 science labs), 2 foreign language, 1 social studies, 1 history, 1 academic elective. **Freshman Admission Statistics:** 7,202 applied, 80% admitted, 17% enrolled. **Transfer Admission Requirements:** College transcript(s). Minimum college GPA of 2.0 required. Lowest grade transferable D-. **General Admission Information:** Application fee $55. Regular application deadline 8/1. Regular notification is rolling. Nonfall registration accepted. Admission may be deferred for a maximum of 1 term. Credit and/or placement offered for CEEB Advanced Placement tests.

COSTS AND FINANCIAL AID

Annual in-state tuition $3,843. Annual out-of-state tuition $11,979. Room and board $8,522. Average book expense $1,142. **Required Forms and Deadlines:** FAFSA. Financial aid filing deadline 3/2. **Notification of Awards:** Applicants will be notified of awards on a rolling basis beginning on or about 4/1. **Types of Aid:** *Need-based scholarships/grants:* Pell, SEOG, state scholarships/grants, private scholarships, the school's own gift aid. *Loans:* Direct Subsidized Stafford, Direct Unsubsidized Stafford, Direct PLUS, Federal Perkins. **Financial Aid Statistics:** 1% freshmen, 36% undergrads receive need-based scholarship or grant aid. 27 freshmen, 88 undergrads receive athletic scholarships. 81% freshmen, 77% undergrads receive any aid.

HUMPHREYS COLLEGE

6650 Inglewood Avenue, Stockton, CA 95207
Phone: 209-478-0800 **E-mail:** slopez@humphreys.edu
Fax: 209-478-0800 **Website:** www.humphreys.edu
Financial Aid Phone: 209-478-0800

This private school was founded in 1896. It has a 10-acre campus.

RATINGS

Admissions Selectivity Rating: 65 **Fire Safety Rating:** 60* **Green Rating:** 60*

STUDENTS AND FACULTY

Enrollment: 692. **Student Body:** 85% female, 15% male. African American 9%, Asian 8%, Caucasian 25%, Hispanic 21%, Native American 2%. **Retention and Graduation:** 64% freshmen return for sophomore year. 100% freshmen graduate within 4 years. 54% grads go on to further study within 1 year. 20% grads pursue arts and sciences degrees. 40% grads pursue business degrees. 30% grads pursue law degrees. 1% grads pursue medical degrees. **Faculty:** Student/faculty ratio 18:1. 18 full-time faculty, 17% hold PhDs. 100% faculty teach undergrads.

ACADEMICS

Degrees: Associate, bachelor's, certificate, first professional. **Academic Requirements:** Arts/fine arts, computer literacy, English (including composition), history, humanities, mathematics, philosophy, sciences (biological or physical), social science. **Classes:** Most classes have more than 100 students. **Disciplines with Highest Percentage of Degrees Awarded:** Law/legal studies 17%, business/marketing 8%, social sciences 6%, liberal arts/general studies 4%, computer and information sciences 1%. **Special Study Options:** Cooperative education program, distance learning, double major, dual enrollment, independent study, internships..

FACILITIES

Housing: Apartments for single students. **Computers:** 25% of classrooms are wired, 25% of classrooms are wireless, 100% of public computers are PCs, remote student-access to Web through college's connection.

CAMPUS LIFE

Activities: Literary magazine, student government, student newspaper. **Organizations:** 3 registered organizations.

ADMISSIONS

Freshman Academic Profile: 15% in top 10% of high school class, 40% in top 25% of high school class. 95% from public high schools. TOEFL required of all international applicants, minimum paper TOEFL 450. **Basis for Candidate Selection:** *Other factors considered include:* Level of applicant's interest. **Freshman Admission Requirements:** High school diploma is required, and GED is accepted. **Freshman Admission Statistics:** 143 applied, 81% admitted, 100% enrolled. **Transfer Admission Requirements:** High school transcript, college transcript(s). Minimum college GPA of 2.0 required. Lowest grade transferable C-. **General Admission Information:** Application fee $35. Nonfall registration accepted. Admission may be deferred. Placement offered for CEEB Advanced Placement tests.

COSTS AND FINANCIAL AID

Annual tuition $11,664. Average book expense $1,386. **Required Forms and Deadlines:** FAFSA. **Types of Aid:** *Need-based scholarships/grants:* Pell, SEOG, state scholarships/grants, private scholarships. *Loans:* FFEL Subsidized Stafford, FFEL Unsubsidized Stafford, FFEL PLUS. **Student Employment:** Off-campus job opportunities are fair. **Financial Aid Statistics:** 81% freshmen, 67% undergrads receive need-based scholarship or grant aid. 18% freshmen, 5% undergrads receive need-based self-help aid. 98% freshmen, 98% undergrads receive any aid. Highest amount earned per year from on-campus jobs $1,603.

HUNTINGDON COLLEGE

1500 East Fairview Avenue, Montgomery, AL 36106-2148
Phone: 334-833-4497 **E-mail:** admiss@huntingdon.edu **CEEB Code:** 1303
Fax: 334-833-4347 **Website:** www.huntingdon.edu **ACT Code:** 0180
Financial Aid Phone: 334-833-4519

This private school, affiliated with the Methodist Church, was founded in 1854. It has a 71-acre campus.

RATINGS

Admissions Selectivity Rating: 82 **Fire Safety Rating:** 60* **Green Rating:** 60*

STUDENTS AND FACULTY

Enrollment: 720. **Student Body:** 50% female, 50% male, 27% out-of-state, 2% international (13 countries represented). African American 12%, Caucasian 80%. **Retention and Graduation:** 66% freshmen return for sophomore year. 50% freshmen graduate within 4 years. 40% grads go on to further study within 1 year. 38% grads pursue arts and sciences degrees. 10% grads pursue business degrees. 15% grads pursue law degrees. 6% grads pursue medical degrees. **Faculty:** Student/faculty ratio 15:1. 32 full-time faculty, 88% hold PhDs. 100% faculty teach undergrads.

ACADEMICS

Degrees: Associate, bachelor's. **Academic Requirements:** Arts/fine arts, English (including composition), foreign languages, history, humanities, mathematics, philosophy, sciences (biological or physical), social science. **Classes:** Most classes have 10–19 students. **Majors with Highest Enrollment:** Kinesiology and exercise science, marketing/marketing management. **Disciplines with Highest Percentage of Degrees Awarded:** Business/marketing 26%, visual and performing arts 13%, communication technologies 11%, social sciences 10%, English 9%. **Special Study Options:** Cross-registration, double major, dual-degree program in engineering with Auburn Uniersity, evening college, honors program, independent study, internships, liberal arts/career combination, member of the Dauphin Island Sea Laboratory, School for Professional Studies, student-designed major, study abroad, teacher certification program.

FACILITIES

Housing: Coed dorms, men's dorms, special housing for disabled students. **Special Academic Facilities/Equipment:** Art gallery, smart classrooms in each academic building (equipped with large touch-screen computers, 20 laptops with wireless Internet connection, capability to project via document cameras, slides, VCR, and other images), theater/performance center, excellent chemistry equipment in Bellingrath Hall (science building), individual studios available for art students in upper-level classes, Top Stage (outdoor stage), Ligon Chapel in Flowers Hall, Smith Music Building, Delchamps Student Center, excellent indoor and outdoor athletic facilities (two gymnasiums), lighted baseball field, new football field and stadium, United Methodist Archives. **Computers:** 75% of public computers are PCs, 24% of public computers are Macs, 1% of public computers are UNIX, network access in dorm rooms, network access in dorm lounges, online administrative functions (other than registration), remote student-access to Web through college's connection. Undergraduates are required to own a computer.

CAMPUS LIFE

Activities: Choral groups, drama/theater, jazz band, literary magazine, music ensembles, musical theater, opera, pep band, student government, student newspaper, yearbook. **Organizations:** 50 registered organizations, 14 honor societies, 4 religious organizations. 2 fraternities (23% men join), 3 sororities (24% women join). **Athletics (Intercollegiate):** *Men:* Baseball, basketball, cross-country, football, golf, soccer, tennis. *Women:* Basketball, cross-country, soccer, softball, tennis, volleyball.

ADMISSIONS

Freshman Academic Profile: 49% in top 10% of high school class, 73% in top 25% of high school class, 93% in top 50% of high school class. 75% from public high schools. SAT Math middle 50% range 470–590. SAT Critical Reading middle 50% range 470–600. ACT middle 50% range 22–24. TOEFL required of all international applicants, minimum paper TOEFL 500, minimum computer TOEFL 173. **Basis for Candidate Selection:** *Very important factors considered include:* Character/personal qualities, rigor of secondary school record, standardized test scores. *Other factors considered include:* Alumni/ae relation, application essay, class rank, extracurricular activities, interview, racial/ethnic status, recommendation(s), talent/ability, volunteer work, work experience. **Freshman Admission Requirements:** High school diploma is required, and GED is accepted. *Academic units recommended:* 4 English, 3 math, 2 science (2 science labs), 2 foreign language, 2 social studies, 2 history. **Freshman Admission Statistics:** 876 applied, 63% admitted, 35% enrolled. **Transfer Admission Requirements:** High school transcript, college transcript(s), standardized test score, statement of good standing from prior institution(s). Minimum college GPA of 2.2 required. Lowest grade transferable C. **General Admission Information:** Application fee $20. Regular notification is rolling. Nonfall registration accepted. Admission may be deferred for a maximum of 1 year. Common Application accepted. Credit and/or placement offered for CEEB Advanced Placement tests.

COSTS AND FINANCIAL AID

Annual tuition $15,990. Room and board $6,720. Required fees $700. Average book expense $900. **Required Forms and Deadlines:** FAFSA, institution's own financial aid form, state aid form. Financial aid filing deadline 4/15. **Notification of Awards:** Applicants will be notified of awards on or about 3/1. **Types of Aid:** *Need-based scholarships/grants:* Pell, SEOG, state scholarships/grants, private scholarships, the school's own gift aid. *Loans:* FFEL Subsidized Stafford, FFEL Unsubsidized Stafford, FFEL PLUS, Federal Perkins, college/university loans from institutional funds, non-parent cosigned loans. **Student Employment:** Federal Work-Study Program available. Institutional employment available. Off-campus job opportunities are excellent. **Financial Aid Statistics:** 57% freshmen, 48% undergrads receive need-based scholarship or grant aid. 61% freshmen, 58% undergrads receive need-based self-help aid. 100% freshmen, 100% undergrads receive any aid. Highest amount earned per year from on-campus jobs $2,500.

HUNTINGTON UNIVERSITY

2303 College Avenue, Huntington, IN 46750
Phone: 260-359-4000 **E-mail:** admissions@huntington.edu **CEEB Code:** 1304
Fax: 260-358-3699 **Website:** www.huntington.edu **ACT Code:** 1202
Financial Aid Phone: 260-359-4015

This private school, affiliated with the Protestant Church, was founded in 1897. It has a 170-acre campus.

RATINGS

Admissions Selectivity Rating: 75   **Fire Safety Rating:** 67   **Green Rating:** 65

STUDENTS AND FACULTY

Enrollment: 955. **Student Body:** 55% female, 45% male, 37% out-of-state, 4% international (13 countries represented). Caucasian 80%. **Retention and Graduation:** 74% freshmen return for sophomore year. 48% freshmen graduate within 4 years. 9% grads go on to further study within 1 year. 7% grads pursue arts and sciences degrees. 1% grads pursue law degrees. 1% grads pursue medical degrees. **Faculty:** Student/faculty ratio 12:1. 58 full-time faculty, 83% hold PhDs. 97% faculty teach undergrads.

ACADEMICS

Degrees: Associate, bachelor's, diploma, master's. **Academic Requirements:** Arts/fine arts, Bible and religion, English (including composition), history, humanities, mathematics, philosophy, sciences (biological or physical), social science. **Classes:** Most classes have 10–19 students. Most lab/discussion sections have 10–19 students. **Majors with Highest Enrollment:** Business/managerial economics, elementary education and teaching, theological and ministerial studies. **Disciplines with Highest Percentage of Degrees Awarded:** Education 25%, business/marketing 22%, visual and performing arts 11%, theology and religious vocations 9%, parks and recreation 8%. **Special Study Options:** Accelerated program, Bible and religion, double major, independent study, internships, study abroad, teacher certification program.

FACILITIES

Housing: Men's dorms, women's dorms, apartments for single students, special housing for disabled students, college-owned houses. **Special Academic Facilities/Equipment:** Thornhill Nature Preserve. **Computers:** 80% of classrooms are wireless, 95% of public computers are PCs, 5% of public computers are Macs, network access in dorm rooms, network access in dorm lounges, online registration, online administrative functions (other than registration), remote student-access to Web through college's connection.

CAMPUS LIFE

Activities: Choral groups, concert band, dance, drama/theater, jazz band, literary magazine, music ensembles, musical theater, opera, pep band, radio station, student government, student newspaper, student-run film society,

television station, yearbook. **Organizations:** 21 registered organizations, 6 honor societies, 4 religious organizations. 1 sorority. **Athletics (Intercollegiate):** *Men:* Baseball, basketball, cheerleading, cross-country, golf, soccer, tennis, track/field (indoor), track/field (outdoor). *Women:* Basketball, cheerleading, cross-country, golf, soccer, softball, tennis, track/field (indoor), track/field (outdoor), volleyball. **Environmental initiatives:** We are working with our contracted custodial service vendor to secure a Green Cleaning certification. Campus recycling program.

ADMISSIONS

Freshman Academic Profile: 27% in top 10% of high school class, 53% in top 25% of high school class, 87% in top 50% of high school class. 85% from public high schools. SAT Math middle 50% range 435–621. SAT Critical Reading middle 50% range 455–631. ACT middle 50% range 21–29. TOEFL required of all international applicants, minimum paper TOEFL 530, minimum computer TOEFL 210. **Basis for Candidate Selection:** *Very important factors considered include:* Academic GPA, religious affiliation/commitment, standardized test scores. *Important factors considered include:* Character/personal qualities, class rank, rigor of secondary school record. *Other factors considered include:* Alumni/ae relation, application essay, extracurricular activities, first generation, interview, level of applicant's interest, racial/ethnic status, recommendation(s), talent/ability, volunteer work, work experience. **Freshman Admission Requirements:** High school diploma is required, and GED is accepted. *Academic units required:* 4 English, 2 math, 2 science (1 science lab), 2 foreign language, 3 social studies, 2 history. *Academic units recommended:* 4 English, 3 math, 3 science (2 science labs), 2 foreign language, 3 social studies, 2 history. **Freshman Admission Statistics:** 759 applied, 91% admitted, 37% enrolled. **Transfer Admission Requirements:** High school transcript, college transcript(s), essay or personal statement, statement of good standing from prior institution(s). Minimum college GPA of 2.0 required. Lowest grade transferable C. **General Admission Information:** Application fee $20. Regular application deadline 8/1. Regular notification is rolling. Nonfall registration accepted. Admission may be deferred for a maximum of 1 year. Credit and/or placement offered for CEEB Advanced Placement tests.

COSTS AND FINANCIAL AID

Comprehensive fee $27,240. Room and board $6,940. **Required Forms and Deadlines:** FAFSA. Financial aid filing deadline 3/1. **Notification of Awards:** Applicants will be notified of awards on a rolling basis beginning on or about 3/1. **Types of Aid:** *Need-based scholarships/grants:* Pell, SEOG, state scholarships/grants, private scholarships, the school's own gift aid. *Loans:* FFEL Subsidized Stafford, FFEL Unsubsidized Stafford, FFEL PLUS, Federal Perkins. **Financial Aid Statistics:** 78% freshmen, 66% undergrads receive need-based scholarship or grant aid. 67% freshmen, 62% undergrads receive need-based self-help aid. 11 freshmen, 32 undergrads receive athletic scholarships. 98% freshmen, 82% undergrads receive any aid. Highest amount earned per year from on-campus jobs $3,500.

HURON UNIVERSITY

333 Ninth Street, SW, Huron, SD 57350
Phone: 605-352-8721 **E-mail:** admissions@huron.edu **CEEB Code:** 6279
Fax: 605-352-7421 **Website:** www.huron.edu **ACT Code:** 3912
Financial Aid Phone: 605-352-8721

This public school was founded in 1883. It has a 15-acre campus.

RATINGS

Admissions Selectivity Rating: 60*   **Fire Safety Rating:** 60*   **Green Rating:** 60*

STUDENTS AND FACULTY

Enrollment: 540. **Student Body:** 49% female, 51% male, 53% out-of-state. African American 11%, Caucasian 80%, Hispanic 6%, Native American 3%. **Retention and Graduation:** 47% freshmen return for sophomore year. 20% grads go on to further study within 1 year. 1% grads pursue arts and sciences degrees. 20% grads pursue business degrees. 1% grads pursue law degrees. **Faculty:** Student/faculty ratio 12:1. 18 full-time faculty, 28% hold PhDs. 100% faculty teach undergrads.

ACADEMICS

Degrees: Associate, bachelor's, master's. **Academic Requirements:** Arts/fine arts, computer literacy, English (including composition), history, humanities, mathematics, philosophy, sciences (biological or physical). **Classes:** Most classes have 10–19 students. Most lab/discussion sections have fewer than 10 students. **Disciplines with Highest Percentage of Degrees Awarded:** Business/marketing 23%, education 13%, parks and recreation 4%, computer and information sciences 2%, liberal arts/general studies 1%, health professions and related sciences 1%. **Special Study Options:** Accelerated program, cooperative education program, double major, independent study, internships, study abroad, teacher certification program.

FACILITIES
Housing: Men's dorms, women's dorms, apartments for single students. **Computers:** 100% of public computers are PCs, network access in dorm rooms, remote student-access to Web through college's connection.

CAMPUS LIFE
Activities: Concert band, dance, jazz band, marching band, pep band, student government, student newspaper. **Organizations:** 10 registered organizations, 8 honor societies, 3 religious organizations. 1 fraternity. **Athletics (Intercollegiate):** *Men:* Baseball, basketball, cheerleading, cross-country, football, soccer, track/field (indoor), track/field (outdoor), wrestling. *Women:* Basketball, cheerleading, cross-country, soccer, softball, track/field (indoor), track/field (outdoor), volleyball.

ADMISSIONS
Freshman Academic Profile: 20% in top 10% of high school class, 40% in top 25% of high school class, 90% in top 50% of high school class. TOEFL required of all international applicants, minimum paper TOEFL 575. **Basis for Candidate Selection:** *Very important factors considered include:* Rigor of secondary school record. *Important factors considered include:* Character/personal qualities, class rank, extracurricular activities, interview, recommendation(s), standardized test scores, talent/ability. *Other factors considered include:* Alumni/ae relation, application essay, racial/ethnic status, state residency, volunteer work, work experience. **Freshman Admission Requirements:** High school diploma is required, and GED is accepted. *Academic units recommended:* 4 English, 4 math, 4 science (2 science labs), 1 foreign language, 4 social studies, 4 history, 2 academic electives. **Freshman Admission Statistics:** 400 applied, 94% admitted, 65% enrolled. **Transfer Admission Requirements:** High school transcript, college transcript(s). Minimum college GPA of 2.0 required. Lowest grade transferable C. **General Admission Information:** Application fee $35. Regular notification rolling. Nonfall registration accepted. Admission may be deferred. Common Application accepted. Credit and/or placement offered for CEEB Advanced Placement tests.

COSTS AND FINANCIAL AID
Comprehensive fee $11,500. Room & board $2,850. Required fees $250. Average book expense $1,000. **Required Forms and Deadlines:** FAFSA. **Types of Aid:** *Need-based scholarships/grants:* Pell, SEOG, the school's own gift aid. *Loans:* FFEL Subsidized Stafford, FFEL Unsubsidized Stafford, FFEL PLUS, Federal Perkins, alternative loans, S.O. State Board of Nursing. **Student Employment:** Federal Work-Study Program available. Institutional employment available. Off-campus job opportunities are good. **Financial Aid Statistics:** 48% freshmen, 52% undergrads receive need-based scholarship or grant aid. 77% freshmen, 77% undergrads receive need-based self-help aid. 70 freshmen, 251 undergrads receive athletic scholarships. Highest amount earned per year from on-campus jobs $1,800.

HUSSON COLLEGE

One College Circle, Bangor, ME 04401
Phone: 207-941-7100 **E-mail:** admit@husson.edu **CEEB Code:** 3440
Fax: 207-941-7935 **Website:** www.husson.edu **ACT Code:** 1646
Financial Aid Phone: 207-941-7156

This private school was founded in 1898. It has a 170-acre campus.

RATINGS
Admissions Selectivity Rating: 69   **Fire Safety Rating:** 95   **Green Rating:** 63

STUDENTS AND FACULTY
Enrollment: 1,710. **Student Body:** 59% female, 41% male, 15% out-of-state, 1% international (15 countries represented). African American 4%, Asian 2%, Caucasian 91%. **Retention and Graduation:** 72% freshmen return for sophomore year. 3% grads go on to further study within 1 year. 1% grads pursue arts and sciences degrees. 2% grads pursue business degrees. 1% grads pursue law degrees. **Faculty:** Student/faculty ratio 19:1. 54 full-time faculty, 61% hold PhDs. 100% faculty teach undergrads.

ACADEMICS
Degrees: Associate, bachelor's, master's, post-master's certificate. **Academic Requirements:** Arts/fine arts, computer literacy, English (including composition), humanities, mathematics, sciences (biological or physical), social science. **Classes:** Most classes have 10–19 students. Most lab/discussion sections have

10–19 students. **Majors with Highest Enrollment:** Business administration/management, computer systems analysis/analyst, nursing/registered nurse training (RN, ASN, BSN, MSN). **Disciplines with Highest Percentage of Degrees Awarded:** Business/marketing 53%, health professions and related sciences 23%, security and protective services 5%, education 5%, computer and information sciences 5%, psychology 4%, natural resources/environmental science 2%, law/legal studies 2%. **Special Study Options:** Cooperative education program, distance learning, double major, English as a second language (ESL), independent study, internships, liberal arts/career combination, student-designed major, teacher certification program, weekend college.

FACILITIES
Housing: Coed dorms, fraternity/sorority housing. **Computers:** 93% of public computers are PCs, 7% of public computers are Macs, network access in dorm rooms, online registration, online administrative functions (other than registration), remote student-access to Web through college's connection.

CAMPUS LIFE
Activities: Drama/theater, literary magazine, pep band, radio station, student government, student newspaper, yearbook. **Organizations:** 26 registered organizations, 1 honor society, 1 religious organization. 1 fraternity (2% men join), 3 sororities (2% women join). **Athletics (Intercollegiate):** *Men:* Baseball, basketball, football, golf, soccer. *Women:* Basketball, field hockey, golf, soccer, softball, swimming, volleyball.

ADMISSIONS
Freshman Academic Profile: 9% in top 10% of high school class, 21% in top 25% of high school class, 44% in top 50% of high school class. 92% from public high schools. SAT Math middle 50% range 400–510. SAT Critical Reading middle 50% range 400–500. SAT Writing middle 50% range 390–500. ACT middle 50% range 17–22. TOEFL required of all international applicants, minimum paper TOEFL 500, minimum computer TOEFL 173. **Basis for Candidate Selection:** *Very important factors considered include:* Interview, recommendation(s), rigor of secondary school record. *Important factors considered include:* Application essay, character/personal qualities, class rank, extracurricular activities, standardized test scores. *Other factors considered include:* Alumni/ae relation, volunteer work, work experience. **Freshman Admission Requirements:** High school diploma is required, and GED is accepted. *Academic units recommended:* 4 English, 3 math, 3 science (2 science labs), 1 social studies, 1 history. **Freshman Admission Statistics:** 943 applied, 89% admitted, 34% enrolled. **Transfer Admission Requirements:** High school transcript, college transcript(s), essay or personal statement. Minimum college GPA of 2.0 required. Lowest grade transferable C. **General Admission Information:** Application fee $25. Regular notification is rolling. Nonfall registration accepted. Admission may be deferred for a maximum of 1 year. Credit and/or placement offered for CEEB Advanced Placement tests.

COSTS AND FINANCIAL AID
Annual tuition $12,450. Room and board $6,790. Required fees $300. Average book expense $970. **Required Forms and Deadlines:** FAFSA. Financial aid filing deadline 4/15. **Notification of Awards:** Applicants will be notified of awards on a rolling basis beginning on or about 3/1. **Types of Aid:** *Need-based scholarships/grants:* Pell, SEOG, state scholarships/grants, private scholarships, the school's own gift aid. *Loans:* FFEL Subsidized Stafford, FFEL Unsubsidized Stafford, FFEL PLUS, Federal Perkins, state loans. **Financial Aid Statistics:** 71% freshmen, 76% undergrads receive need-based scholarship or grant aid. 69% freshmen, 81% undergrads receive need-based self-help aid. 90% freshmen, 85% undergrads receive any aid. Highest amount earned per year from on-campus jobs $1,200.

See page 1202.

HUSTON-TILLOTSON UNIVERSITY

900 Chicon Street, Austin, TX 78702
Phone: 512-505-3028 **E-mail:** thshakir@htc.edu **CEEB Code:** 6280
Fax: 512-505-3192 **Website:** www.htc.edu **ACT Code:** 4104
Financial Aid Phone: 512-505-3030

This private school, affiliated with the United Methodist Church of Christ, was founded in 1875. It has a 35-acre campus.

RATINGS
Admissions Selectivity Rating: 62   **Fire Safety Rating:** 60*   **Green Rating:** 60*

STUDENTS AND FACULTY
Enrollment: 630. **Student Body:** 55% female, 45% male, 14% out-of-state, 3% international (13 countries represented). **Retention and Graduation:** 58%

freshmen return for sophomore year. 9% freshmen graduate within 4 years. **Faculty:** Student/faculty ratio 13:1. 37 full-time faculty, 70% hold PhDs. 100% faculty teach undergrads.

ACADEMICS

Degrees: Bachelor's. **Academic Requirements:** Arts/fine arts, computer literacy, English (including composition), foreign languages, history, humanities, mathematics, philosophy, sciences (biological or physical), social science. **Classes:** Most classes have fewer than 10 students. **Majors with Highest Enrollment:** Business/commerce, computer and information sciences, education. **Disciplines with Highest Percentage of Degrees Awarded:** Business/marketing 22%, computer and information sciences 14%, education 12%, parks and recreation 12%, social sciences 12%, biological/life sciences 9%, psychology 9%, English 5%. **Special Study Options:** Cross-registration, distance learning, double major, dual enrollment, external degree program, honors program, independent study, internships, liberal arts/career combination, study abroad, teacher certification program.

FACILITIES

Housing: Men's dorms, women's dorms. **Computers:** 95% of public computers are PCs, 5% of public computers are Macs, network access in dorm rooms, network access in dorm lounges, remote student-access to Web through college's connection.

CAMPUS LIFE

Activities: Choral groups, literary magazine, music ensembles, student government, student newspaper, yearbook. **Organizations:** 17 registered organizations, 5 honor societies, 5 religious organizations. **Athletics (Intercollegiate):** *Men:* Baseball, basketball, soccer, track/field (outdoor). *Women:* Basketball, track/field (outdoor), volleyball.

ADMISSIONS

Freshman Academic Profile: 7% in top 10% of high school class, 23% in top 25% of high school class, 50% in top 50% of high school class. SAT Math middle 50% range 355–470. SAT Critical Reading middle 50% range 350–435. ACT middle 50% range 14–17. TOEFL required of all international applicants, minimum paper TOEFL 500. **Basis for Candidate Selection:** *Very important factors considered include:* Rigor of secondary school record, standardized test scores. *Important factors considered include:* Application essay, interview, religious affiliation/commitment. *Other factors considered include:* Alumni/ae relation, class rank, extracurricular activities, recommendation(s), talent/ability. **Freshman Admission Requirements:** High school diploma is required, and GED is accepted. *Academic units required:* 4 English, 3 math, 2 science (2 science labs), 2 social studies, 1 academic elective, 2 health. *Academic units recommended:* 2 foreign language. **Freshman Admission Statistics:** 182 applied, 100% admitted, 100% enrolled. **Transfer Admission Requirements:** College transcript(s), essay or personal statement. Minimum college GPA of 2.5 required. Lowest grade transferable C. **General Admission Information:** Application fee $25. Regular application deadline 7/1. Regular notification is rolling. Nonfall registration accepted. Admission may be deferred for a maximum of 1 year. Common Application not accepted. Credit and/or placement offered for CEEB Advanced Placement tests.

COSTS AND FINANCIAL AID

Annual tuition $8,436. Room and board $6,226. Required fees $1,602. Average book expense $800. **Required Forms and Deadlines:** FAFSA, institution's own financial aid form. Financial aid filing deadline 3/15. **Notification of Awards:** Applicants will be notified of awards on a rolling basis beginning on or about 4/1. **Types of Aid:** *Need-based scholarships/grants:* Pell, SEOG, state scholarships/grants, private scholarships, the school's own gift aid, United Negro College Fund. *Loans:* Direct Subsidized Stafford, Direct Unsubsidized Stafford, Direct PLUS, FFEL Subsidized Stafford, FFEL Unsubsidized Stafford, FFEL PLUS, state loans. **Student Employment:** Federal Work-Study Program available. Off-campus job opportunities are good. **Financial Aid Statistics:** 7% freshmen, 3% undergrads receive need-based scholarship or grant aid. 66% freshmen, 49% undergrads receive need-based self-help aid. 14 freshmen, 53 undergrads receive athletic scholarships.

IDAHO STATE UNIVERSITY

Admissions Office, Campus Box 8270, Pocatello, ID 83209-8270
Phone: 208-282-2475 **E-mail:** info@isu.edu **CEEB Code:** 4355
Fax: 208-282-4231 **Website:** www.isu.edu **ACT Code:** 0918
Financial Aid Phone: 208-282-2756

This public school was founded in 1901. It has a 972-acre campus.

RATINGS

Admissions Selectivity Rating: 73 **Fire Safety Rating:** 60* **Green Rating:** 60*

STUDENTS AND FACULTY

Enrollment: 9,670. **Student Body:** 55% female, 45% male, 5% out-of-state, 2% international (65 countries represented). Asian 1%, Caucasian 84%, Hispanic 5%, Native American 2%. **Retention and Graduation:** 54% freshmen return for sophomore year. 5% freshmen graduate within 4 years. **Faculty:** Student/faculty ratio 16:1. 610 full-time faculty, 55% hold PhDs. 85% faculty teach undergrads.

ACADEMICS

Degrees: Associate, bachelor's, certificate, diploma, doctoral, first professional certificate, first professional, master's, post-bachelor's certificate, post-master's certificate. **Academic Requirements:** Arts/fine arts, English (including composition), foreign languages, history, humanities, mathematics, philosophy, sciences (biological or physical), social science. **Classes:** Most classes have fewer than 10 students. Most lab/discussion sections have 10–19 students. **Majors with Highest Enrollment:** Elementary education and teaching, nursing/registered nurse training (RN, ASN, BSN, MSN), secondary education and teaching. **Disciplines with Highest Percentage of Degrees Awarded:** Health professions and related sciences 19%, education 19%, business/marketing 17%, biological/life sciences 9%, social sciences 7%. **Special Study Options:** Accelerated program, cooperative education program, cross-registration, distance learning, double major, dual enrollment, English as a second language (ESL), exchange student program (domestic), honors program, independent study, internships, liberal arts/career combination, student-designed major, study abroad, teacher certification program, weekend college.

FACILITIES

Housing: Coed dorms, men's dorms, women's dorms, apartments for married students, apartments for single students, special housing for disabled students, fraternity/sorority housing, graduate student housing. **Special Academic Facilities/Equipment:** Museum of Natural History, Idaho Accelerator Center. **Computers:** 95% of public computers are PCs, 5% of public computers are Macs, network access in dorm rooms, network access in dorm lounges, online registration, online administrative functions (other than registration), remote student-access to Web through college's connection.

CAMPUS LIFE

Activities: Choral groups, concert band, dance, drama/theater, marching band, musical theater, pep band, radio station, student government, student newspaper, symphony orchestra, television station, yearbook. **Organizations:** 140 registered organizations, 10 honor societies, 6 religious organizations. 3 fraternities (1% men join), 3 sororities (1% women join). **Athletics (Intercollegiate):** *Men:* Basketball, cheerleading, cross-country, football, golf, tennis, track/field (outdoor). *Women:* Basketball, cheerleading, cross-country, golf, soccer, tennis, track/field (outdoor), volleyball.

ADMISSIONS

Freshman Academic Profile: 12% in top 10% of high school class, 31% in top 25% of high school class, 61% in top 50% of high school class. SAT Math middle 50% range 450–590. SAT Critical Reading middle 50% range 460–595. ACT middle 50% range 18–24. TOEFL required of all international applicants, minimum paper TOEFL 500, minimum computer TOEFL 173. **Basis for Candidate Selection:** *Other factors considered include:* Academic GPA, standardized test scores. **Freshman Admission Requirements:** High school diploma is required, and GED is accepted. *Academic units required:* 4 English, 3 math, 3 science (1 science lab), 1 foreign language, 2 social studies, 1 health. *Academic units recommended:* 4 math. **Freshman Admission Statistics:** 2,882 applied, 80% admitted, 80% enrolled. **Transfer Admission Requirements:** High school transcript, college transcript(s), standardized test score. Minimum college GPA of 2.0 required. Lowest grade transferable D. **General Admission Information:** Application fee $40. Regular notification is rolling. Nonfall registration accepted. Admission may be deferred for a maximum of 3 years. Credit and/or placement offered for CEEB Advanced Placement tests.

COSTS AND FINANCIAL AID

Annual in-state tuition $2,882. Annual out-of-state tuition $11,566. Room and board $4,950. Required fees $1,518. Average book expense $900. **Required**

Forms and Deadlines: FAFSA. Financial aid filing deadline 3/1. **Notification of Awards:** Applicants will be notified of awards on or about 4/1. **Types of Aid:** *Need-based scholarships/grants:* Pell, SEOG, state scholarships/grants, private scholarships, the school's own gift aid. *Loans:* Direct Subsidized Stafford, Direct Unsubsidized Stafford, Direct PLUS, Federal Perkins. **Financial Aid Statistics:** 33% freshmen, 48% undergrads receive need-based scholarship or grant aid. 33% freshmen, 57% undergrads receive need-based self-help aid. 49 freshmen, 281 undergrads receive athletic scholarships. 80% freshmen, receive any aid.

ILLINOIS COLLEGE

1101 West College, Jacksonville, IL 62650
Phone: 217-245-3030 **E-mail:** admissions@hilltop.ic.edu **CEEB Code:** 1315
Fax: 217-245-3034 **Website:** www.ic.edu **ACT Code:** 1034
Financial Aid Phone: 217-245-3035

This private school, affiliated with the Presbyterian Church, was founded in 1829. It has a 62-acre campus.

RATINGS
Admissions Selectivity Rating: 79   **Fire Safety Rating:** 60*   **Green Rating:** 60*

STUDENTS AND FACULTY
Enrollment: 903. **Student Body:** 47% female, 53% male, 5% out-of-state, 2% international. African American 4%. **Retention and Graduation:** 70% freshmen return for sophomore year. 41% freshmen graduate within 4 years. 22% grads go on to further study within 1 year. 13% grads pursue arts and sciences degrees. 2% grads pursue business degrees. 5% grads pursue law degrees. 4% grads pursue medical degrees. **Faculty:** Student/faculty ratio 14:1. 55 full-time faculty, 80% hold PhDs. 100% faculty teach undergrads.

ACADEMICS
Degrees: Bachelor's. **Academic Requirements:** Arts/fine arts, English (including composition), history, humanities, mathematics, sciences (biological or physical), social science, speech. **Classes:** Most classes have 10–19 students. Most lab/discussion sections have 10–19 students. **Disciplines with Highest Percentage of Degrees Awarded:** Education 19%, business/marketing 19%, biological/life sciences 11%, social sciences 9%, English 8%, communication technologies 7%. **Special Study Options:** Cross-registration, double major, dual enrollment, independent study, internships, liberal arts/career combination, student-designed major, study abroad, teacher certification program, urban studies program (Chicago), Washington Center (DC).

FACILITIES
Housing: Coed dorms, men's dorms, women's dorms. **Special Academic Facilities/Equipment:** Art gallery, language lab. **Computers:** 95% of public computers are PCs, 5% of public computers are Macs, network access in dorm rooms, remote student-access to Web through college's connection.

CAMPUS LIFE
Activities: Choral groups, concert band, drama/theater, literary magazine, music ensembles, pep band, student government, student newspaper, television station, yearbook. **Organizations:** 72 registered organizations, 12 honor societies, 3 religious organizations. 4 fraternities (20% men join), 3 sororities (18% women join). **Athletics (Intercollegiate):** *Men:* Baseball, basketball, cross-country, football, golf, soccer, tennis, track/field (indoor), track/field (outdoor), wrestling. *Women:* Basketball, cheerleading, cross-country, golf, soccer, softball, tennis, track/field (indoor), track/field (outdoor), volleyball.

ADMISSIONS
Freshman Academic Profile: 15% in top 10% of high school class, 47% in top 25% of high school class, 76% in top 50% of high school class. 80% from public high schools. SAT Math middle 50% range 520–610. SAT Critical Reading middle 50% range 510–630. ACT middle 50% range 20–25. TOEFL required of all international applicants, minimum paper TOEFL 550. **Basis for Candidate Selection:** *Very important factors considered include:* Class rank, rigor of secondary school record. *Important factors considered include:* Character/personal qualities, recommendation(s), standardized test scores. *Other factors considered include:* Application essay, extracurricular activities, geographical residence, interview, racial/ethnic status. **Freshman Admission Requirements:** High school diploma is required, and GED is accepted. *Academic units required:* 3 English, 3 math, 7 academic electives. *Academic units recommended:* 4 English. **Freshman Admission Statistics:** 970 applied, 74% admitted, 33% enrolled. **Transfer Admission Requirements:** High school transcript, college transcript(s), standardized test score. Minimum college GPA of 2.0 required. Lowest grade transferable C. **General Admission Information:** Application fee $10. Regular notification is rolling. Nonfall registration accepted. Admission may be deferred for a maximum of 1 year. Common Application accepted. Credit and/or placement offered for CEEB Advanced Placement tests.

COSTS AND FINANCIAL AID
Annual tuition $10,735. Room & board $4,725. Average book expense $600. **Required Forms and Deadlines:** FAFSA. Financial aid filing deadline 3/15. **Notification of Awards:** Applicants will be notified of awards on a rolling basis beginning on or about 3/15. **Types of Aid:** *Need-based scholarships/grants:* Pell, SEOG, state scholarships/grants, private scholarships, the school's own gift aid. *Loans:* FFEL Subsidized Stafford, FFEL Unsubsidized Stafford, FFEL PLUS, Federal Perkins. **Student Employment:** Federal Work-Study Program available. Institutional employment available. Off-campus job opportunities are good. **Financial Aid Statistics:** 72% freshmen, 70% undergrads receive need-based scholarship or grant aid. 69% freshmen, 68% undergrads receive need-based self-help aid. Highest amount earned per year from on-campus jobs $800.

THE ILLINOIS INSTITUTE OF ART— SCHAUMBURG

1000 Plaza Drive, Suite 100, Schaumburg, IL 60173-4990
Phone: 847-619-3450
Fax: 847-619-3064 **Website:** www.artinstitutes.edu/schaumburg **ACT Code:** 6863
Financial Aid Phone: 847-619-3450

This private school was founded in 1918.

RATINGS
Admissions Selectivity Rating: 60*   **Fire Safety Rating:** 60*   **Green Rating:** 60*

STUDENTS AND FACULTY
Enrollment: 699. **Student Body:** 41% female, 59% male. African American 3%, Asian 8%, Caucasian 66%, Hispanic 6%. **Faculty:** Student/faculty ratio 20:1. 30 full-time faculty, 17% hold PhDs. 100% faculty teach undergrads.

ACADEMICS
Degrees: Bachelor's, certificate. **Academic Requirements:** Arts/fine arts, computer literacy, humanities, mathematics, philosophy, sciences (biological or physical), social science.

FACILITIES
Housing: Apartments for single students.

CAMPUS LIFE
Activities: Student newspaper. **Organizations:** 5 registered organizations.

ADMISSIONS
Freshman Academic Profile: TOEFL required of all international applicants, minimum computer TOEFL 111. **Basis for Candidate Selection:** *Very important factors considered include:* Class rank. *Important factors considered include:* Alumni/ae relation, recommendation(s). *Other factors considered include:* Extracurricular activities, racial/ethnic status, rigor of secondary school record, standardized test scores, talent/ability, work experience. **Freshman Admission Requirements:** High school diploma is required, and GED is accepted. **Freshman Admission Statistics:** 300 applied. **Transfer Admission Requirements:** College transcript(s), essay or personal statement. Lowest grade transferable C. **General Admission Information:** Application fee $50. Regular notification as necessary paperwork is submitted to Admissions. Nonfall registration accepted. Admission may be deferred for a maximum of 6 semesters. Common Application not accepted. Credit and/or placement offered for CEEB Advanced Placement tests.

COSTS AND FINANCIAL AID
Average book expense $75. **Required Forms and Deadlines:** FAFSA. **Notification of Awards:** Applicants will be notified of awards on a rolling basis beginning on or about 1/1. **Types of Aid:** *Need-based scholarships/grants:* Pell, SEOG, the school's own gift aid. *Loans:* Direct Subsidized Stafford, Direct Unsubsidized Stafford, Direct PLUS. **Student Employment:** Institutional employment available. Off-campus job opportunities are excellent.

ILLINOIS INSTITUTE OF TECHNOLOGY

10 West Thirty-third Street, Chicago, IL 60616
Phone: 312-567-3025 **E-mail:** admission@iit.edu **CEEB Code:** 1318
Fax: 312-567-6939 **Website:** www.iit.edu **ACT Code:** 1040
Financial Aid Phone: 312-567-7219

This private school was founded in 1892. It has a 120-acre campus.

RATINGS
Admissions Selectivity Rating: 92   **Fire Safety Rating:** 72   **Green Rating:** 82

STUDENTS AND FACULTY
Enrollment: 2,296. **Student Body:** 25% female, 75% male, 28% out-of-state, 14% international (106 countries represented). African American 4%, Asian 15%, Caucasian 51%, Hispanic 6%. **Retention and Graduation:** 85% freshmen return for sophomore year. 40% freshmen graduate within 4 years. 31% grads go on to further study within 1 year. **Faculty:** Student/faculty ratio 7:1. 363 full-time faculty, 85% hold PhDs. 60% faculty teach undergrads.

ACADEMICS
Degrees: Bachelor's, doctoral, first professional, master's. **Academic Requirements:** Computer literacy, humanities, interprofessional project: multidisciplinary team project, writing and communication courses with significant written and oral communication component, mathematics, sciences (biological or physical), social science. **Classes:** Most classes have 10–19 students. Most lab/discussion sections have 20–29 students. **Majors with Highest Enrollment:** Architecture (BArch, BA/BS, MArch, MA/MS, PhD); computer science; electrical, electronics, and communications engineering. **Disciplines with Highest Percentage of Degrees Awarded:** Engineering 51%, computer and information sciences 16%, architecture 11%, biological/life sciences 7%, business/marketing 4%. **Special Study Options:** Cooperative education program, cross-registration, distance learning, double major, English as a second language (ESL), independent study, liberal arts/career combination, study abroad, teacher certification program.

FACILITIES
Housing: Coed dorms, men's dorms, women's dorms, apartments for married students, apartments for single students, special housing for disabled students, fraternity/sorority housing. **Special Academic Facilities/Equipment:** Environment chamber, wind tunnel, extrusion press, railroad simulator, model railroad, electron microscope, art exhibitions at Galvin Library, Mies van der Rohe Society campus tours, IIT Research Institute, University Technology Park at IIT. **Computers:** 5% of classrooms are wired, 20% of classrooms are wireless, 88% of public computers are PCs, 2% of public computers are Macs, 10% of public computers are UNIX, network access in dorm rooms, network access in dorm lounges, online registration, online administrative functions (other than registration), support for handheld computing.

CAMPUS LIFE
Activities: Dance, drama/theater, literary magazine, musical theater, radio station, student government, student newspaper, student-run film society, television station, yearbook. **Organizations:** 90 registered organizations, 4 honor societies, 12 religious organizations. 7 fraternities (13% men join), 4 sororities (19% women join). **Athletics (Intercollegiate):** *Men:* Baseball, basketball, cross-country, diving, soccer, swimming. *Women:* Basketball, cross-country, diving, soccer, swimming, volleyball. **Environmental initiatives:** Distributed Hot Water System and Infrastructure: Construction started spring 2007 to install a high efficiency hot water/steam plant serving the east side of the IIT Main Campus, the furthest point on the current steam loop. Building Re-Commissioning: Historically, building systems are rarely commissioned to meet the continuous changes inherent to a college environment. The re-commissioning began in an academic building in 2007 and will be performed in two other buildings in 2008. The Downtown Campus is working towards Leadership in Energy and Environmental Design (LEED) certification.

ADMISSIONS
Freshman Academic Profile: 36% in top 10% of high school class, 71% in top 25% of high school class, 96% in top 50% of high school class. 85% from public high schools. SAT Math middle 50% range 620–710. SAT Critical Reading middle 50% range 543–670. SAT Writing middle 50% range 530–640. ACT middle 50% range 25–30. TOEFL required of all international applicants, minimum paper TOEFL 550, minimum computer TOEFL 213. **Basis for**

Candidate Selection: *Very important factors considered include:* Academic GPA, standardized test scores. *Important factors considered include:* Application essay, recommendation(s). *Other factors considered include:* Alumni/ae relation, character/personal qualities, class rank, extracurricular activities, interview, rigor of secondary school record, talent/ability, volunteer work, work experience. **Freshman Admission Requirements:** High school diploma is required, and GED is not accepted. *Academic units required:* 4 English, 4 math, 3 science (2 science labs), 2 social studies, 2 history. *Academic units recommended:* 4 English, 4 math, 3 science (2 science labs), 2 social studies, 2 history. **Freshman Admission Statistics:** 4,966 applied, 54% admitted, 18% enrolled. **Transfer Admission Requirements:** College transcript(s), essay or personal statement, statement of good standing from prior institution(s). Minimum college GPA of 3.0 required. Lowest grade transferable C. **General Admission Information:** Application fee $30. Regular notification is rolling. Nonfall registration accepted. Admission may be deferred for a maximum of 1 year. Credit and/or placement offered for CEEB Advanced Placement tests.

COSTS AND FINANCIAL AID
Annual tuition $24,962. Room and board $8,618. Required fees $784. **Required Forms and Deadlines:** FAFSA. Financial aid filing deadline 4/15. **Notification of Awards:** Applicants will be notified of awards on a rolling basis beginning on or about 3/1. **Types of Aid:** *Need-based scholarships/grants:* Pell, SEOG, state scholarships/grants, private scholarships, the school's own gift aid. *Loans:* FFEL Subsidized Stafford, FFEL Unsubsidized Stafford, FFEL PLUS, Federal Perkins, college/university loans from institutional funds. **Financial Aid Statistics:** 72% freshmen, 58% undergrads receive need-based scholarship or grant aid. 52% freshmen, 46% undergrads receive need-based self-help aid. 25 freshmen, 106 undergrads receive athletic scholarships. 100% freshmen, 92% undergrads receive any aid.

See page 1204.

ILLINOIS STATE UNIVERSITY

Admissions Office, Campus Box 2200, Normal, IL 61790-2200
Phone: 309-438-2181 **E-mail:** admissions@ilstu.edu **CEEB Code:** 1319
Fax: 309-438-3932 **Website:** www.ilstu.edu **ACT Code:** 1042
Financial Aid Phone: 309-438-2231

This public school was founded in 1857. It has an 850-acre campus.

RATINGS
Admissions Selectivity Rating: 71   **Fire Safety Rating:** 61   **Green Rating:** 60*

STUDENTS AND FACULTY
Enrollment: 17,824. **Student Body:** 57% female, 43% male, 2% out-of-state, (63 countries represented). African American 6%, Asian 2%, Caucasian 84%, Hispanic 4%. **Retention and Graduation:** 84% freshmen return for sophomore year. **Faculty:** Student/faculty ratio 19:1. 856 full-time faculty, 82% hold PhDs. 93% faculty teach undergrads.

ACADEMICS
Degrees: Bachelor's, doctoral, master's, post-bachelor's certificate, post-master's certificate. **Academic Requirements:** Arts/fine arts, computer literacy, English (including composition), history, humanities, mathematics, philosophy, sciences (biological or physical), social science. **Classes:** Most classes have 20–29 students. Most lab/discussion sections have 20–29 students. **Majors with Highest Enrollment:** Business administration and management; elementary education and teaching; special education. **Disciplines with Highest Percentage of Degrees Awarded:** Education 22%, business/marketing 18%, social sciences 7%, health professions and related sciences 6%, communications/journalism 6%. **Special Study Options:** Accelerated program, cooperative education program, distance learning, double major, dual enrollment, English as a Second Language (ESL), exchange student program (domestic), honors program, independent study, internships, student-designed major, study abroad, teacher certification program.

FACILITIES
Housing: Coed dorms, women's dorms, apartments for married students, apartments for single students, special housing for disabled students, special housing for international students, fraternity/sorority housing. **Special Academic Facilities/Equipment:** Art gallery, cultural museums, on-campus elementary and secondary schools, greenhouse, farm, planetarium. **Computers:** 90% of public computers are PCs, 8% of public computers are Macs, 2% of public computers are UNIX, network access in dorm rooms, network access in dorm lounges, online registration, online administrative functions (other than registration), remote student-access to Web through college's connection. Undergraduates are required to own a computer.

CAMPUS LIFE

Activities: Choral groups, concert band, dance, drama/theater, jazz band, literary magazine, marching band, music ensembles, musical theater, pep band, radio station, student government, student newspaper, student-run film society, symphony orchestra, television station. **Organizations:** 270 registered organizations, 23 honor societies, 22 religious organizations. 21 fraternities (9% men join), 17 sororities (9% women join). **Athletics (Intercollegiate):** *Men:* Baseball, basketball, cheerleading, cross-country, football, golf, tennis, track/field (indoor), track/field (outdoor). *Women:* Basketball, cheerleading, cross-country, diving, golf, gymnastics, soccer, softball, swimming, tennis, track/field (indoor), track/field (outdoor), volleyball.

ADMISSIONS

Freshman Academic Profile: 11% in top 10% of high school class, 38% in top 25% of high school class, 81% in top 50% of high school class. 87% from public high schools. ACT middle 50% range 22–26. TOEFL required of all international applicants, minimum paper TOEFL 550, minimum computer TOEFL 213. **Basis for Candidate Selection:** *Very important factors considered include:* Academic GPA, rigor of secondary school record, standardized test scores. *Important factors considered include:* Application essay, class rank. *Other factors considered include:* Character/personal qualities, first generation, talent/ability. **Freshman Admission Requirements:** High school diploma is required, and GED is accepted. *Academic units required:* 4 English, 3 math, 2 science (2 science labs), 2 foreign language, 2 social studies, 2 academic electives. **Freshman Admission Statistics:** 12,071 applied, 68% admitted, 39% enrolled. **Transfer Admission Requirements:** College transcript(s), essay or personal statement. Minimum college GPA of 3.0 required. Lowest grade transferable D. **General Admission Information:** Application fee $30. Regular application deadline 3/1. Regular notification is rolling. Nonfall registration accepted. Credit and/or placement offered for CEEB Advanced Placement tests.

COSTS AND FINANCIAL AID

Annual in-state tuition $6,990. Annual out-of-state tuition $14,310. Room and board $6,848. Required fees $2,029. Average book expense $888. **Required Forms and Deadlines:** FAFSA. Financial aid filing deadline 3/1. **Notification of Awards:** Applicants will be notified of awards on a rolling basis beginning on or about 4/1. **Types of Aid:** *Need-based scholarships/grants:* Pell, SEOG, state scholarships/grants, private scholarships, the school's own gift aid, Federal Nursing Scholarships. *Loans:* Direct Subsidized Stafford, Direct Unsubsidized Stafford, Direct PLUS, Federal Perkins, Federal Nursing, college/university loans from institutional funds. **Financial Aid Statistics:** 26% freshmen, 28% undergrads receive need-based scholarship or grant aid. 36% freshmen, 38% undergrads receive need-based self-help aid. 40 freshmen, 235 undergrads receive athletic scholarships. 56% freshmen, 53% undergrads receive any aid. Highest amount earned per year from on-campus jobs $2,416.

ILLINOIS WESLEYAN UNIVERSITY

Best 368

PO Box 2900, Bloomington, IL 61702-2900
Phone: 309-556-3031 **E-mail:** iwuadmit@iwu.edu **CEEB Code:** 1320
Fax: 309-556-3820 **Website:** www.iwu.edu **ACT Code:** 1044
Financial Aid Phone: 309-556-3096

This private school was founded in 1850. It has an 80-acre campus.

RATINGS

Admissions Selectivity Rating: 89   **Fire Safety Rating:** 81   **Green Rating:** 77

STUDENTS AND FACULTY

Enrollment: 2,139. **Student Body:** 58% female, 42% male, 14% out-of-state, 2% international (19 countries represented). African American 5%, Asian 4%, Caucasian 82%, Hispanic 3%. **Retention and Graduation:** 92% freshmen return for sophomore year. 76% freshmen graduate within 4 years. 32% grads go on to further study within 1 year. 15% grads pursue arts and sciences degrees. 1% grads pursue business degrees. 3% grads pursue law degrees. 6% grads pursue medical degrees. **Faculty:** Student/faculty ratio 12:1. 161 full-time faculty, 92% hold PhDs. 100% faculty teach undergrads.

ACADEMICS

Degrees: Bachelor's. **Academic Requirements:** Arts/fine arts, English

(including composition), foreign languages, history, humanities, mathematics, sciences (biological or physical), social science. All students must complete a 2-course requirement on diversity (U.S. and global), a first-year writing seminar, and 2 writing-intensive courses. **Classes:** Most classes have 10–19 students. Most lab/discussion sections have 10–19 students. **Majors with Highest Enrollment:** Biology/biological sciences, business administration/management, psychology. **Disciplines with Highest Percentage of Degrees Awarded:** Business/marketing 25%, visual and performing arts 14%, social sciences 10%, psychology 10%, biological/life sciences 7%. **Special Study Options:** Double major, exchange student program (domestic), honors program, independent study, internships, student-designed major, study abroad, teacher certification program.

FACILITIES

Housing: Coed dorms, special housing for disabled students, fraternity/sorority housing. Groups of students with common curricular or cocurricular interests can propose and implement theme housing consistent with their educational goals. **Special Academic Facilities/Equipment:** Observatory, computerized music lab, graphic design studio, Ames Library Archives and Special Collections, visual anthropology lab, social science lab. **Computers:** 1% of classrooms are wired, 5% of classrooms are wireless, 63% of public computers are PCs, 35% of public computers are Macs, 2% of public computers are UNIX, network access in dorm rooms, network access in dorm lounges, online registration, online administrative functions (other than registration), support for handheld computing, remote student-access to Web through college's connection.

CAMPUS LIFE

Activities: Choral groups, concert band, dance, drama/theater, jazz band, literary magazine, music ensembles, musical theater, opera, pep band, radio station, student government, student newspaper, student-run film society, symphony orchestra, television station, yearbook. **Organizations:** 170 registered organizations, 29 honor societies, 15 religious organizations. 6 fraternities (33% men join), 5 sororities (26% women join). **Athletics (Intercollegiate):** *Men:* Baseball, basketball, cross-country, diving, football, golf, soccer, swimming, tennis, track/field (indoor), track/field (outdoor). *Women:* Basketball, cross-country, diving, golf, soccer, softball, swimming, tennis, track/field (indoor), track/field (outdoor), volleyball. **Environmental initiatives:** IWU has a commitment to environmental sustainability in its mission statement. IWU signed the Talloires Declaration. New Welcome Center will be LEED certified.

ADMISSIONS

Freshman Academic Profile: 46% in top 10% of high school class, 82% in top 25% of high school class, 98% in top 50% of high school class. 80% from public high schools. SAT Math middle 50% range 590–690. SAT Critical Reading middle 50% range 540–680. ACT middle 50% range 26–30. TOEFL required of all international applicants, minimum paper TOEFL 550, minimum computer TOEFL 213. **Basis for Candidate Selection:** *Very important factors considered include:* Academic GPA, interview, rigor of secondary school record. *Important factors considered include:* Application essay, character/personal qualities, class rank, extracurricular activities, standardized test scores, talent/ability. *Other factors considered include:* Alumni/ae relation, first generation, geographical residence, level of applicant's interest, racial/ethnic status, recommendation(s), state residency, volunteer work, work experience. **Freshman Admission Requirements:** High school diploma is required, and GED is accepted. *Academic units recommended:* 4 English, 3 math, 3 science (2 science labs), 3 foreign language, 2 social studies. **Freshman Admission Statistics:** 3,156 applied, 52% admitted, 34% enrolled. **Transfer Admission Requirements:** High school transcript, college transcript(s), essay or personal statement, standardized test score. Minimum college GPA of 2.0 required. Lowest grade transferable C-. **General Admission Information:** Regular notification is rolling. Nonfall registration accepted. Admission may be deferred for a maximum of 1 year. Credit and/or placement offered for CEEB Advanced Placement tests.

COSTS AND FINANCIAL AID

Annual tuition $30,580. Room & board $7,030. Required fees $170. Average book expense $780. **Required Forms and Deadlines:** Institution's own financial aid form, CSS/Financial Aid PROFILE. Financial aid filing deadline 3/1. **Notification of Awards:** Applicants will be notified of awards on a rolling basis beginning on or about 2/15. **Types of Aid:** *Need-based scholarships/grants:* Pell, SEOG, state scholarships/grants, private scholarships, the school's own gift aid. *Loans:* FFEL Subsidized Stafford, FFEL Unsubsidized Stafford, FFEL PLUS, Federal Perkins, Federal Nursing, college/university loans from institutional funds. **Student Employment:** Federal Work-Study Program available. Institutional employment available. Off-campus job opportunities are good. **Financial Aid Statistics:** 61% freshmen, 56% undergrads receive need-based scholarship or grant aid. 50% freshmen, 46% undergrads receive need-based self-help aid. 90% freshmen, 88% undergrads receive any aid. Highest amount earned per year from on-campus jobs $2,225.

IMMACULATA UNIVERSITY COLLEGE OF LIFELONG LEARNING

1145 King Road, P, Immaculata, PA 19345-0642
Phone: 610-647-4400 **E-mail:** cll@immaculata.edu **CEEB Code:** 2320
Fax: 610-647-0215 **Website:** www.immaculata.edu/CLL/home.htm **ACT Code:** 3596
Financial Aid Phone: 877-428-6329

This private school, affiliated with the Roman Catholic Church, was founded in 2000. It has a 400-acre campus.

RATINGS
Admissions Selectivity Rating: 60*   **Fire Safety Rating:** 60*   **Green Rating:** 60*

STUDENTS AND FACULTY
Student Body: 19% out-of-state. **Faculty:** 100% faculty teach undergrads.

ACADEMICS
Degrees: Associate, bachelor's, certificate, post-bachelor's certificate.
Academic Requirements: Arts/fine arts, computer literacy, English (including composition), foreign languages, history, humanities, mathematics, philosophy, sciences (biological or physical), social science, theology. **Majors with Highest Enrollment:** Business administration and management, human resources management and services, nursing/registered nurse training (RN, ASN, BSN, MSN). **Disciplines with Highest Percentage of Degrees Awarded:** Health professions and related sciences 47%, business/marketing 35%, psychology 12%, English 1%, education 1%, computer and information sciences 1%, communications/journalism 1%, theology and religious vocations 1%, interdisciplinary studies 1%. **Special Study Options:** Accelerated program, cooperative education program, cross-registration, distance learning, double major, dual enrollment, external degree program, honors program, independent study, internships, liberal arts/career combination, study abroad, teacher certification program.

FACILITIES
Housing: No housing is available for CLL students. **Special Academic Facilities/Equipment:** Annual art show on-campus. **Computers:** 5% of classrooms are wired, 95% of classrooms are wireless, 100% of public computers are PCs, online administrative functions (other than registration), remote student-access to Web through college's connection.

CAMPUS LIFE
Activities: Choral groups, dance, drama/theater, literary magazine, music ensembles, musical theater, student government, student newspaper, symphony orchestra, yearbook. **Organizations:** 28 registered organizations, 14 honor societies, 1 religious organization. **Athletics (Intercollegiate):** *Men:* Basketball, golf, soccer, tennis. *Women:* Basketball, cross-country, field hockey, golf, lacrosse, soccer, softball, tennis, volleyball.

ADMISSIONS
Freshman Academic Profile: TOEFL required of all international applicants, minimum paper TOEFL 500, minimum computer TOEFL 200. **Basis for Candidate Selection:** *Important factors considered include:* Level of applicant's interest. *Other factors considered include:* Character/personal qualities, interview, work experience. **Freshman Admission Requirements:** High school diploma is required, and GED is accepted. **Transfer Admission Requirements:** High school transcript, college transcript(s). Minimum college GPA of 2.0 required. Lowest grade transferable C. **General Admission Information:** Application fee $50. Regular notification rolling basis no start date. Nonfall registration accepted. Admission may be deferred for a maximum of 1 year. Common Application not accepted. Credit and/or placement offered for CEEB Advanced Placement tests.

COSTS AND FINANCIAL AID
Annual tuition $10,050. **Required Forms and Deadlines:** FAFSA. **Notification of Awards:** Applicants will be notified of awards on a rolling basis beginning on or about 2/1. **Types of Aid:** *Need-based scholarships/grants:* Pell, state scholarships/grants, private scholarships, United Negro College Fund. *Loans:* FFEL Subsidized Stafford, FFEL Unsubsidized Stafford, FFEL PLUS, Federal Perkins. **Student Employment:** Federal Work-Study Program available. Institutional employment available. Off-campus job opportunities are good. **Financial Aid Statistics:** 16% undergrads receive need-based scholarship or grant aid. 33% undergrads receive need-based self-help aid. 34% undergrads receive any aid. Highest amount earned per year from on-campus jobs $1,053.

INDIANA INSTITUTE OF TECHNOLOGY

1600 East Washington Boulevard, Fort Wayne, IN 46803
Phone: 260-422-5561 **E-mail:** admissions@indtech.edu **CEEB Code:** 1805
Fax: 260-422-7696 **Website:** www.indianatech.edu **ACT Code:** 1208
Financial Aid Phone: 800-937-2448

This private school was founded in 1930. It has a 57-acre campus.

RATINGS
Admissions Selectivity Rating: 62   **Fire Safety Rating:** 60*   **Green Rating:** 60*

STUDENTS AND FACULTY
Enrollment: 2,985. **Student Body:** 56% female, 44% male, 35% out-of-state. African American 17%, Caucasian 63%, Hispanic 2%. **Retention and Graduation:** 56% freshmen return for sophomore year. 11% freshmen graduate within 4 years. **Faculty:** Student/faculty ratio 17:1. 40 full-time faculty, 38% hold PhDs. 100% faculty teach undergrads.

ACADEMICS
Degrees: Associate, bachelor's, master's. **Academic Requirements:** Computer literacy, English (including composition), humanities, mathematics, social science. **Classes:** Most classes have 10–19 students. **Majors with Highest Enrollment:** Business administration/management; electrical, electronics, and communications engineering; engineering. **Disciplines with Highest Percentage of Degrees Awarded:** Business/marketing 87%, engineering 8%, computer and information sciences 4%, parks and recreation 1%. **Special Study Options:** Accelerated program, cooperative education program, distance learning, double major, external degree program, independent study, internships.

FACILITIES
Housing: Coed dorms, apartments for single students, fraternity/sorority housing. **Computers:** Network access in dorm rooms, online registration. Undergraduates are required to own a computer.

CAMPUS LIFE
Activities: Choral groups, dance, pep band, student government, student newspaper. **Organizations:** 14 registered organizations, 1 honor society. 3 fraternities (15% men join), 1 sorority (5% women join). **Athletics (Intercollegiate):** *Men:* Baseball, basketball, soccer. *Women:* Basketball, soccer, softball.

ADMISSIONS
Freshman Academic Profile: 8% in top 10% of high school class, 27% in top 25% of high school class, 57% in top 50% of high school class. 80% from public high schools. TOEFL required of all international applicants, minimum paper TOEFL 500. **Basis for Candidate Selection:** *Very important factors considered include:* Alumni/ae relation, rigor of secondary school record. *Important factors considered include:* Class rank, interview, racial/ethnic status, standardized test scores. *Other factors considered include:* Application essay, character/personal qualities, extracurricular activities, recommendation(s), talent/ability, volunteer work, work experience. **Freshman Admission Requirements:** High school diploma is required, and GED is accepted. *Academic units required:* 4 English, 3 math, 2 science. *Academic units recommended:* 4 English, 4 math, 3 science. **Freshman Admission Statistics:** 1,989 applied, 92% admitted, 13% enrolled. **Transfer Admission Requirements:** College transcript(s). Minimum college GPA of 2.0 required. Lowest grade transferable C. **General Admission Information:** Application fee $50. Regular application deadline 9/1. Regular notification is rolling. Nonfall registration accepted. Admission may be deferred for a maximum of 2 years. Common Application not accepted. Credit and/or placement offered for CEEB Advanced Placement tests.

COSTS AND FINANCIAL AID
Annual tuition $16,680. Room & board $6,272. **Required Forms and Deadlines:** FAFSA, institution's own financial aid form. Financial aid filing deadline 3/10. **Notification of Awards:** Applicants will be notified of awards on a rolling basis beginning on or about 2/2. **Types of Aid:** *Need-based scholarships/grants:* Pell, SEOG, state scholarships/grants, private scholarships, the school's own gift aid, United Negro College Fund. *Loans:* FFEL Subsidized Stafford, FFEL Unsubsidized Stafford, FFEL PLUS, Federal Perkins. **Student Employment:** Federal Work-Study Program available. Institutional employment available. Off-campus job opportunities are good. **Financial Aid Statistics:** 64% freshmen, 62% undergrads receive need-based scholarship or grant aid. 62% freshmen, 65% undergrads receive need-based self-help aid. 22 freshmen, 60 undergrads receive athletic scholarships.

INDIANA STATE UNIVERSITY

Office of Admissions, Tirey Hall 134, Terre Haute, IN 47809
Phone: 812-237-2121 **E-mail:** aDMISU@isugw.indstate.edu **CEEB Code:** 1322
Fax: 812-237-8023 **Website:** www.indstate.edu **ACT Code:** 1206
Financial Aid Phone: 812-237-2215

This public school was founded in 1865. It has a 92-acre campus.

RATINGS
Admissions Selectivity Rating: 71   **Fire Safety Rating:** 65   **Green Rating:** 82

STUDENTS AND FACULTY
Enrollment: 8,531. **Student Body:** 52% female, 48% male, 10% out-of-state, 1% international (61 countries represented). African American 11%, Caucasian 82%, Hispanic 1%. **Retention and Graduation:** 67% freshmen return for sophomore year. 17% grads go on to further study within 1 year. **Faculty:** Student/faculty ratio 17:1. 489 full-time faculty, 77% hold PhDs. 86% faculty teach undergrads.

ACADEMICS
Degrees: Associate, bachelor's, certificate, doctoral, master's, post-bachelor's certificate, post-master's certificate. **Academic Requirements:** Arts/fine arts, computer literacy, English (including composition), foreign languages, history, mathematics, physical education, sciences (biological or physical), social science. **Classes:** Most classes have 20–29 students. **Majors with Highest Enrollment:** Criminology, elementary education and teaching, nursing/registered nurse training (RN, ASN, BSN, MSN). **Disciplines with Highest Percentage of Degrees Awarded:** Education 18%, business/marketing 17%, social sciences 12%, engineering technologies 8%, health professions and related sciences 6%. **Special Study Options:** Accelerated program, cooperative education program, distance learning, double major, dual enrollment, English as a second language (ESL), honors program, independent study, internships, study abroad, teacher certification program.

FACILITIES
Housing: Coed dorms, men's dorms, women's dorms, apartments for married students, apartments for single students, special housing for disabled students, fraternity/sorority housing, special housing for freshmen, apartments for students with dependent children. **Special Academic Facilities/Equipment:** Music hall, art gallery, civic center, museum, flight simulator, audiovisual center, observatory, theaters. **Computers:** 91% of public computers are PCs, 9% of public computers are Macs, network access in dorm rooms, network access in dorm lounges, online registration, online administrative functions (other than registration), remote student-access to Web through college's connection.

CAMPUS LIFE
Activities: Choral groups, concert band, dance, drama/theater, jazz band, literary magazine, marching band, music ensembles, musical theater, pep band, radio station, student government, student newspaper, student-run film society, symphony orchestra, yearbook. **Organizations:** 130 registered organizations, 11 honor societies, 11 religious organizations. 19 fraternities (12% men join), 12 sororities (11% women join). **Athletics (Intercollegiate):** *Men:* Baseball, basketball, cross-country, football, tennis, track/field (indoor), track/field (outdoor). *Women:* Basketball, cross-country, golf, soccer, softball, tennis, track/field (indoor), track/field (outdoor), volleyball. **Environmental initiatives:** Signing of the ACUPPC Agrement. President's development of an organizational structure to guide the university through the development of a campus sustainability planning document. Current university and public recycling program has been in operation for over 10 years.

ADMISSIONS
Freshman Academic Profile: 10% in top 10% of high school class, 28% in top 25% of high school class, 62% in top 50% of high school class. SAT Math middle 50% range 420–530. SAT Critical Reading middle 50% range 410–520. SAT Writing middle 50% range 400–500. ACT middle 50% range 17–22. TOEFL required of all international applicants, minimum paper TOEFL 500, minimum computer TOEFL 173. **Basis for Candidate Selection:** *Very important factors considered include:* Academic GPA, class rank, rigor of secondary school record. *Important factors considered include:* Application essay, recommendation(s), standardized test scores. *Other factors considered include:* Character/personal qualities, extracurricular activities, interview, talent/ability. **Freshman Admission Requirements:** High school diploma is required, and GED is accepted. *Academic units recommended:* 2 foreign language, 4 social studies, 2 history, 3 academic electives. **Freshman Admission Statistics:** 5,351 applied, 80% admitted, 38% enrolled. **Transfer Admission Requirements:** College transcript(s). Minimum college GPA of 2.0 required. Lowest grade transferable C. **General Admission Information:** Application fee $25. Regular application deadline 8/15. Regular notification rolling basis beginning

end of the junior year of high school. Nonfall registration accepted. Admission may be deferred for a maximum of 1 year. Common Application not accepted. Credit offered for CEEB Advanced Placement tests.

COSTS AND FINANCIAL AID
Annual in-state tuition $6,106. Out-of-state tuition $13,518. Room & board $5,938. Required fees $334. Average book expense $1,140. **Required Forms and Deadlines:** FAFSA. Financial aid filing deadline 3/1. **Notification of Awards:** Applicants will be notified of awards on a rolling basis beginning on or about 4/15. **Types of Aid:** *Need-based scholarships/grants:* Pell, SEOG, state scholarships/grants, private scholarships, the school's own gift aid. *Loans:* FFEL Subsidized Stafford, FFEL Unsubsidized Stafford, FFEL PLUS, Federal Perkins. **Student Employment:** Federal Work-Study Program available. Institutional employment available. Off-campus job opportunities are good. **Financial Aid Statistics:** 36% freshmen, 35% undergrads receive need-based scholarship or grant aid. 39% freshmen, 42% undergrads receive need-based self-help aid. 57 freshmen, 285 undergrads receive athletic scholarships. 72% freshmen, 78% undergrads receive any aid. Highest amount earned per year from on-campus jobs $14,268.

INDIANA UNIVERSITY—BLOOMINGTON

Best 368

300 North Jordan Avenue, Bloomington, IN 47405-1106
Phone: 812-855-0661 **E-mail:** iuadmit@indiana.edu **CEEB Code:** 1324
Fax: 812-855-5102 **Website:** www.indiana.edu **ACT Code:** 1210
Financial Aid Phone: 812-855-0321

This public school was founded in 1820. It has a 1,931-acre campus.

RATINGS
Admissions Selectivity Rating: 86   **Fire Safety Rating:** 60*   **Green Rating:** 60*

STUDENTS AND FACULTY
Enrollment: 29,258. **Student Body:** 52% female, 48% male, 30% out-of-state, 4% international (132 countries represented). African American 5%, Asian 4%, Caucasian 84%, Hispanic 2%. **Retention and Graduation:** 88% freshmen return for sophomore year. 50% freshmen graduate within 4 years. **Faculty:** Student/faculty ratio 18:1. 1891 full-time faculty, 77% hold PhDs. 46% faculty teach undergrads.

ACADEMICS
Degrees: Associate, bachelor's, certificate, diploma, doctoral, first professional, master's, post-bachelor's certificate, post-master's certificate. **Academic Requirements:** Arts/fine arts, English (including composition), foreign languages, history, sciences (biological or physical), social science. **Classes:** Most classes have 10–19 students. Most lab/discussion sections have 20–29 students. **Majors with Highest Enrollment:** Accounting and finance, biology/biological sciences, marketing/marketing management. **Disciplines with Highest Percentage of Degrees Awarded:** Business/marketing 18%, education 17%, communications/journalism 11%, social sciences 7%, public administration and social services 6%. **Special Study Options:** Accelerated program, cooperative education program, distance learning, double major, dual enrollment, English as a second language (ESL), external degree program, honors program, independent study, internships, liberal arts/career combination, student-designed major, study abroad, teacher certification program.

FACILITIES
Housing: Coed dorms, men's dorms, women's dorms, apartments for married students, apartments for single students, special housing for disabled students, special housing for international students, fraternity/sorority housing, cooperative housing. **Special Academic Facilities/Equipment:** Art gallery, folklore, radio station, natural history museum, TV station, art museum, Mathers Museum of World Cultures, Kirkwood Observatory, Hilltop Garden and Nature Center, arboretum, Student Recreational Sports and Aquatic Center, auditorium, Beck Chapel, golf driving range, musical arts center, health physical education and recreation facilities (HPER), indoor swimming, outdoor swimming, Wildermuth Intramural Center (in HPER complex), cyclotron, Lilly Library, and more than 70 research centers. **Computers:** 1% of classrooms are wired, 100% of classrooms are wireless, 81% of public computers are PCs, 17% of public computers are Macs, 2% of public computers are UNIX, network access in dorm rooms, network access in dorm lounges, online registration,

online administrative functions (other than registration), remote student-access to Web through college's connection.

CAMPUS LIFE

Activities: Choral groups, concert band, dance, drama/theater, jazz band, literary magazine, marching band, music ensembles, musical theater, opera, radio station, student government, student newspaper, symphony orchestra, television station, yearbook. **Organizations:** 9 religious organizations. **Athletics (Intercollegiate):** *Men:* Baseball, basketball, cheerleading, diving, football, golf, soccer, swimming, tennis, track/field (outdoor), wrestling. *Women:* Basketball, cheerleading, cross-country, diving, field hockey, golf, soccer, softball, swimming, tennis, track/field (outdoor), volleyball, water polo.

ADMISSIONS

Freshman Academic Profile: 27% in top 10% of high school class, 61% in top 25% of high school class, 95% in top 50% of high school class. SAT Math middle 50% range 520–640. SAT Critical Reading middle 50% range 510–620. ACT middle 50% range 23–28. **Basis for Candidate Selection:** *Very important factors considered include:* Academic GPA, class rank, rigor of secondary school record. *Important factors considered include:* Standardized test scores. *Other factors considered include:* Alumni/ae relation, application essay, character/personal qualities, extracurricular activities, first generation, geographical residence, interview, level of applicant's interest, racial/ethnic status, recommendation(s), state residency, talent/ability. **Freshman Admission Requirements:** High school diploma is required, and GED is accepted. *Academic units required:* 4 English, 3 math, 1 science (1 science lab), 2 social studies, 4 academic electives. *Academic units recommended:* 4 math, 3 science, 3 foreign language, 3 social studies. **Freshman Admission Statistics:** 24,169 applied, 80% admitted, 38% enrolled. **Transfer Admission Requirements:** College transcript(s). Minimum college GPA of 2.0 required. Lowest grade transferable C. **General Admission Information:** Application fee $50. Nonfall registration accepted. Admission may be deferred for a maximum of 1 year. Credit and/or placement offered for CEEB Advanced Placement tests.

COSTS AND FINANCIAL AID

Annual in-state tuition $5,791. Annual out-of-state tuition $20,200. Room and board $6,676. Required fees $837. Average book expense $758. Average book expense $740. **Required Forms and Deadlines:** FAFSA. Financial aid filing deadline 3/1. **Notification of Awards:** Applicants will be notified of awards on or about 3/10. **Types of Aid:** *Need-based scholarships/grants:* Pell, SEOG, state scholarships/grants, private scholarships, the school's own gift aid. *Loans:* Direct Subsidized Stafford, Direct Unsubsidized Stafford, Direct PLUS, Federal Perkins, Federal Nursing, college/university loans from institutional funds. **Student Employment:** Off-campus job opportunities are good. **Financial Aid Statistics:** 19% freshmen, 19% undergrads receive need-based scholarship or grant aid. 31% freshmen, 31% undergrads receive need-based self-help aid. 115 freshmen, 474 undergrads receive athletic scholarships.

INDIANA UNIVERSITY—EAST

2325 Chester Boulevard, WZ 116, Richmond, IN 47374-1289
Phone: 765-973-8208 **E-mail:** eaadmit@indiana.edu
Fax: 765-973-8288 **Website:** www.iue.edu
Financial Aid Phone: 765-973-8206

This public school was founded in 1971. It has a 174-acre campus.

RATINGS

Admissions Selectivity Rating: 68   **Fire Safety Rating:** 60*   **Green Rating:** 60*

STUDENTS AND FACULTY

Enrollment: 1,924. **Student Body:** 69% female, 31% male, 13% out-of-state. African American 4%, Caucasian 91%, Hispanic 1%. **Retention and Graduation:** 77% freshmen return for sophomore year. 6% freshmen graduate within 4 years. **Faculty:** Student/faculty ratio 13:1. 81 full-time faculty, 52% hold PhDs.

ACADEMICS

Degrees: Associate, bachelor's, post-bachelor's certificate. **Academic Requirements:** Computer literacy, English (including composition), humanities, sciences (biological or physical), social science. **Classes:** Most classes have 10–19 students. Most lab/discussion sections have fewer than 10 students. **Majors with Highest Enrollment:** Business administration/management, elementary education and teaching, nursing/registered nurse training (RN, ASN, BSN, MSN). **Disciplines with Highest Percentage of Degrees Awarded:** Philosophy and religious studies 28%, liberal arts/general studies 18%, education 14%, health professions and related sciences 11%,

security and protective services 5%. **Special Study Options:** Cooperative education program, cross-registration, distance learning, double major, dual enrollment, external degree program, independent study, internships, state-wide technology program with Purdue University, teacher certification program, weekend college.

FACILITIES

Computers: 100% of classrooms are wired, 30% of classrooms are wireless, 85% of public computers are PCs, 7% of public computers are Macs, 7% of public computers are UNIX, online registration, online administrative functions (other than registration), support for handheld computing, remote student-access to Web through college's connection.

CAMPUS LIFE

Activities: Drama/theater, student government, student newspaper, television station. **Athletics (Intercollegiate):** *Men:* Basketball, golf. *Women:* Volleyball.

ADMISSIONS

Freshman Academic Profile: 3% in top 10% of high school class, 23% in top 25% of high school class, 58% in top 50% of high school class. SAT Math middle 50% range 400–510. SAT Critical Reading middle 50% range 400–500. ACT middle 50% range 18–22. **Basis for Candidate Selection:** *Very important factors considered include:* Rigor of secondary school record, standardized test scores. *Important factors considered include:* Academic GPA, class rank. *Other factors considered include:* Geographical residence, state residency. **Freshman Admission Requirements:** High school diploma is required, and GED is accepted. *Academic units required:* 4 English, 3 math, 1 science (1 science lab), 2 social studies. *Academic units recommended:* 3 math, 4 academic electives. **Freshman Admission Statistics:** 404 applied, 84% admitted, 83% enrolled. **Transfer Admission Requirements:** College transcript(s). Minimum college GPA of 2.0 required. Lowest grade transferable C. **General Admission Information:** Application fee $25. Nonfall registration accepted. Admission may be deferred.

COSTS AND FINANCIAL AID

Annual in-state tuition $4,335. Annual out-of-state tuition $11,852. Required fees $360. Average book expense $930. **Required Forms and Deadlines:** FAFSA, institution's own financial aid form. Financial aid filing deadline 3/1. **Notification of Awards:** Applicants will be notified of awards on a rolling basis beginning on or about 5/1. **Types of Aid:** *Need-based scholarships/grants:* Pell, SEOG, state scholarships/grants, private scholarships, the school's own gift aid. *Loans:* FFEL Subsidized Stafford, FFEL Unsubsidized Stafford, FFEL PLUS, Federal Perkins, Federal Nursing, college/university loans from institutional funds. **Financial Aid Statistics:** 48% freshmen, 52% undergrads receive need-based scholarship or grant aid. 35% freshmen, 50% undergrads receive need-based self-help aid.

INDIANA UNIVERSITY—KOKOMO

Office of Admissions, PO Box 9003, KC 230A, Kokomo, IN 46904-9003
Phone: 765-455-9217 **E-mail:** iuadmis@iuk.edu **CEEB Code:** 1337
Fax: 765-455-9537 **Website:** www.iuk.edu **ACT Code:** 1219
Financial Aid Phone: 765-455-9216

This public school was founded in 1945. It has a 51-acre campus.

RATINGS

Admissions Selectivity Rating: 69   **Fire Safety Rating:** 60*   **Green Rating:** 60*

STUDENTS AND FACULTY

Enrollment: 2,368. **Student Body:** 71% female, 29% male. African American 4%, Caucasian 90%, Hispanic 1%. **Retention and Graduation:** 59% freshmen return for sophomore year. 9% freshmen graduate within 4 years. **Faculty:** Student/faculty ratio 15:1. 95 full-time faculty, 67% hold PhDs.

ACADEMICS

Degrees: Associate, bachelor's, certificate, master's, post-bachelor's certificate. **Academic Requirements:** Computer literacy, English (including composition), mathematics, public speaking. **Classes:** Most classes have 10–19 students. Most lab/discussion sections have 20–29 students. **Majors with Highest Enrollment:** Business administration/management, elementary education and teaching, nursing/registered nurse training (RN, ASN, BSN, MSN). **Disciplines with Highest Percentage of Degrees Awarded:** Health professions and related sciences 22%, liberal arts/general studies 20%, education 16%, business/marketing 15%, psychology 6%. **Special Study Options:** Accelerated program, cross-registration, distance learning, double major, dual enrollment, external degree program, honors program, independent study, internships, liberal arts/career combination, Project Success Program, study abroad, teacher certification program.

FACILITIES

Special Academic Facilities/Equipment: Observatory, art gallery. **Computers:** 50% of classrooms are wireless, 100% of public computers are PCs, online registration, online administrative functions (other than registration), remote student-access to Web through college's connection.

CAMPUS LIFE

Activities: Choral groups, drama/theater, music ensembles, student government, student newspaper.

ADMISSIONS

Freshman Academic Profile: 6% in top 10% of high school class, 26% in top 25% of high school class, 61% in top 50% of high school class. SAT Math middle 50% range 430–530. SAT Critical Reading middle 50% range 420–510. ACT middle 50% range 16–23. **Basis for Candidate Selection:** *Very important factors considered include:* Class rank, rigor of secondary school record. *Important factors considered include:* Standardized test scores. *Other factors considered include:* Recommendation(s). **Freshman Admission Requirements:** High school diploma is required, and GED is accepted. *Academic units required:* 4 English, 3 math, 1 science, 2 social studies. *Academic units recommended:* 2 foreign language, 2 history. **Freshman Admission Statistics:** 615 applied, 81% admitted, 77% enrolled. **Transfer Admission Requirements:** College transcript(s). Minimum college GPA of 2.0 required. Lowest grade transferable C. **General Admission Information:** Application fee $30. Regular notification rolling. Nonfall registration accepted. Admission may be deferred. Credit and/or placement offered for CEEB Advanced Placement tests.

COSTS AND FINANCIAL AID

Annual in-state tuition $4,329. Annual out-of-state tuition $11,844. Required fees $397. **Required Forms and Deadlines:** FAFSA, institution's own financial aid form. Financial aid filing deadline 3/1. **Notification of Awards:** Applicants will be notified of awards on a rolling basis beginning on or about 5/1. *Types of Aid: Need-based scholarships/grants:* Pell, SEOG, state scholarships/grants, private scholarships, the school's own gift aid. *Loans:* FFEL Subsidized Stafford, FFEL Unsubsidized Stafford, FFEL PLUS, Federal Perkins, Federal Nursing, college/university loans from institutional funds. **Student Employment:** Federal Work-Study Program available. Institutional employment available. **Financial Aid Statistics:** 29% freshmen, 34% undergrads receive need-based scholarship or grant aid. 36% freshmen, 42% undergrads receive need-based self-help aid.

INDIANA UNIVERSITY—NORTHWEST

3400 Broadway, Hawthorn 100, Gary, IN 46408-1197
Phone: 219-980-6991 **E-mail:** admit@iun.edu
Fax: 219-981-4219 **Website:** www.iun.edu
Financial Aid Phone: 219-980-6778

This public school was founded in 1948. It has a 38-acre campus.

RATINGS

Admissions Selectivity Rating: 70　　**Fire Safety Rating:** 60*　　**Green Rating:** 60*

STUDENTS AND FACULTY

Enrollment: 4,003. **Student Body:** 70% female, 30% male, 1% out-of-state. African American 21%, Asian 2%, Caucasian 61%, Hispanic 13%. **Retention and Graduation:** 61% freshmen return for sophomore year. 8% freshmen graduate within 4 years. **Faculty:** Student/faculty ratio 14:1. 184 full-time faculty, 70% hold PhDs.

ACADEMICS

Degrees: Associate, bachelor's, certificate, master's, post-bachelor's certificate. **Classes:** Most classes have 10–19 students. Most lab/discussion sections have fewer than 10 students. **Majors with Highest Enrollment:** Business administration/management, criminal justice/safety studies, nursing/registered nurse training (RN, ASN, BSN, MSN). **Disciplines with Highest Percentage of Degrees Awarded:** Health professions and related sciences 17%, business/marketing 16%, liberal arts/general studies 15%, security and protective services 14%, education 12%. **Special Study Options:** Accelerated program, cooperative education program, distance learning, double major, dual enrollment, external degree program, honors program, independent study, internships, liberal arts/career combination, off-campus study (Washington semester), student-designed major, study abroad, teacher certification program, weekend college.

FACILITIES

Computers: 52% of public computers are PCs, 48% of public computers are Macs, online registration, online administrative functions (other than registration), remote student-access to Web through college's connection.

CAMPUS LIFE

Activities: Choral groups, drama/theater, literary magazine, student government, student newspaper. **Organizations:** 60 registered organizations, 4 honor societies, 2 religious organizations, 2 fraternities, 3 sororities. **Athletics (Intercollegiate):** *Men:* Baseball, basketball, cheerleading, golf. *Women:* Basketball, cheerleading, volleyball.

ADMISSIONS

Freshman Academic Profile: 8% in top 10% of high school class, 24% in top 25% of high school class, 49% in top 50% of high school class. SAT Math middle 50% range 390–510. SAT Critical Reading middle 50% range 400–510. ACT middle 50% range 16–20. **Basis for Candidate Selection:** *Very important factors considered include:* Academic GPA, class rank, rigor of secondary school record. *Important factors considered include:* Standardized test scores. *Other factors considered include:* Recommendation(s). **Freshman Admission Requirements:** High school diploma is required, and GED is accepted. *Academic units required:* 4 English, 3 math, 1 science, 2 social studies, 4 academic electives. *Academic units recommended:* 1 science lab, 2 foreign language. **Freshman Admission Statistics:** 1,157 applied, 76% admitted, 77% enrolled. **Transfer Admission Requirements:** High school transcript, college transcript(s). Minimum college GPA of 2.0 required. Lowest grade transferable C. **General Admission Information:** Application fee $25. Nonfall registration accepted. Admission may be deferred for a maximum of 2 years. Credit offered for CEEB Advanced Placement tests.

COSTS AND FINANCIAL AID

Annual in-state tuition $4,362. Annual out-of-state tuition $11,850. Required fees $436. Average book expense $864. **Required Forms and Deadlines:** FAFSA, institution's own financial aid form. Financial aid filing deadline 3/1. **Notification of Awards:** Applicants will be notified of awards on a rolling basis beginning on or about 5/1. *Types of Aid: Need-based scholarships/grants:* Pell, SEOG, state scholarships/grants, private scholarships, the school's own gift aid, Federal Nursing Scholarships. *Loans:* FFEL Subsidized Stafford, FFEL Unsubsidized Stafford, FFEL PLUS, Federal Perkins, college/university loans from institutional funds. **Student Employment:** Federal Work-Study Program available. Off-campus job opportunities are good. **Financial Aid Statistics:** 39% freshmen, 43% undergrads receive need-based scholarship or grant aid. 50% freshmen, 53% undergrads receive need-based self-help aid. 2 freshmen, 15 undergrads receive athletic scholarships.

INDIANA UNIVERSITY—PURDUE UNIVERSITY FORT WAYNE

2101 East Coliseum Boulevard, Fort Wayne, IN 46805-1499
Phone: 260-481-6812 **E-mail:** ipfwadms@ipfw.edu **CEEB Code:** 1336
Fax: 260-481-6880 **Website:** www.ipfw.edu **ACT Code:** 1217
Financial Aid Phone: 260-481-6820

This public school was founded in 1917. It has a 565-acre campus.

RATINGS

Admissions Selectivity Rating: 65　　**Fire Safety Rating:** 60*　　**Green Rating:** 60*

STUDENTS AND FACULTY

Enrollment: 10,587. **Student Body:** 58% female, 42% male, 5% out-of-state, 2% international (71 countries represented). African American 5%, Asian 2%, Caucasian 87%, Hispanic 2%. **Retention and Graduation:** 60% freshmen return for sophomore year. **Faculty:** Student/faculty ratio 19:1. 329 full-time faculty, 83% hold PhDs. 99% faculty teach undergrads.

ACADEMICS

Degrees: Associate, bachelor's, certificate, master's, post-bachelor's certificate, post-master's certificate. **Academic Requirements:** Arts/fine arts, English (including composition), humanities, mathematics, sciences (biological or physical), social science. **Classes:** Most classes have 20–29 students. Most lab/discussion sections have 20–29 students. **Majors with Highest Enrollment:** Business/commerce, elementary education and teaching, nursing/registered nurse training (RN, ASN, BSN, MSN). **Disciplines with Highest Percentage of Degrees Awarded:** Education 19%, business/marketing 17%, liberal arts/general studies 14%, engineering 8%, communication technologies 5%, psychology 5%, social sciences 5%, visual and performing arts 5%. **Special Study Options:** Cooperative education program, distance learning, double major, English as a second language (ESL), exchange student program (domestic), honors program, independent study, internships, liberal arts/career combination, student-designed major, study abroad, teacher certification program, weekend college.

FACILITIES
Housing: Coed dorms. **Special Academic Facilities/Equipment:** Williams Theatre, recital hall, anthropology and geology exhibits, art gallery. **Computers:** 97% of public computers are PCs, 3% of public computers are Macs, online registration, online administrative functions (other than registration), remote student-access to Web through college's connection.

CAMPUS LIFE
Activities: Choral groups, concert band, dance, drama/theater, jazz band, literary magazine, music ensembles, musical theater, opera, pep band, student government, student newspaper, symphony orchestra, television station. **Organizations:** 65 registered organizations, 7 honor societies, 3 religious organizations. 2 fraternities (1% men join), 3 sororities (1% women join). **Athletics (Intercollegiate):** *Men:* Baseball, basketball, cross-country, soccer, tennis, track/field (outdoor), volleyball. *Women:* Basketball, cross-country, soccer, softball, tennis, track/field (outdoor), volleyball.

ADMISSIONS
Freshman Academic Profile: 7% in top 10% of high school class, 24% in top 25% of high school class, 57% in top 50% of high school class. 84% from public high schools. SAT Math middle 50% range 430–550. SAT Critical Reading middle 50% range 420–540. ACT middle 50% range 17–23. TOEFL required of all international applicants, minimum paper TOEFL 550, minimum computer TOEFL 213. **Basis for Candidate Selection:** *Very important factors considered include:* Class rank, rigor of secondary school record, standardized test scores. *Other factors considered include:* Recommendation(s), state residency. **Freshman Admission Requirements:** High school diploma is required, and GED is accepted. *Academic units required:* 4 English, 3 math, 1 science, 1 foreign language, 1 social studies. *Academic units recommended:* 3 science (1 science lab), 3 foreign language, 3 social studies. **Freshman Admission Statistics:** 2,471 applied, 97% admitted, 71% enrolled. **Transfer Admission Requirements:** High school transcript, college transcript(s). Minimum college GPA of 2.0 required. Lowest grade transferable C-. **General Admission Information:** Application fee $30. Regular application deadline 8/1. Regular notification is rolling. Nonfall registration accepted. Common Application not accepted. Credit and/or placement offered for CEEB Advanced Placement tests.

COSTS AND FINANCIAL AID
Annual in-state tuition $3,100. Out-of-state tuition $7,728. Required fees $384. Average book expense $800. **Required Forms and Deadlines:** FAFSA. Financial aid filing deadline 3/1. **Notification of Awards:** Applicants will be notified of awards on or about 4/30. **Types of Aid:** *Need-based scholarships/grants:* Pell, SEOG, state scholarships/grants, private scholarships, Federal Nursing Scholarships. *Loans:* FFEL Subsidized Stafford, FFEL Unsubsidized Stafford, FFEL PLUS, Federal Perkins, Federal Nursing. **Student Employment:** Federal Work-Study Program available. Institutional employment available. Off-campus job opportunities are excellent. **Financial Aid Statistics:** 35% freshmen, 57% undergrads receive need-based scholarship or grant aid. 23% freshmen, 33% undergrads receive need-based self-help aid. 48 freshmen, 158 undergrads receive athletic scholarships. Highest amount earned per year from on-campus jobs $1,200.

INDIANA UNIVERSITY—PURDUE UNIVERSITY INDIANAPOLIS

425 University Boulevard, Indianapolis, IN 46202
Phone: 317-274-4591 **E-mail:** apply@iupui.edu
Fax: 317-278-1862 **Website:** www.iupui.edu **ACT Code:** 1214
Financial Aid Phone: 317-274-4162

This public school was founded in 1969. It has a 512-acre campus.

RATINGS
Admissions Selectivity Rating: 74　　　**Fire Safety Rating:** 60*　　　**Green Rating:** 60*

STUDENTS AND FACULTY
Enrollment: 20,221. **Student Body:** 60% female, 40% male, 2% out-of-state, 2% international (131 countries represented). African American 10%, Asian 3%,

Caucasian 80%, Hispanic 2%. **Retention and Graduation:** 65% freshmen return for sophomore year. 8% freshmen graduate within 4 years. 20% grads go on to further study within 1 year. 1% grads pursue arts and sciences degrees. 2% grads pursue business degrees. 1% grads pursue law degrees. 1% grads pursue medical degrees. **Faculty:** Student/faculty ratio 16:1. 2,152 full-time faculty, 82% hold PhDs.

ACADEMICS
Degrees: Associate, bachelor's, certificate, doctoral, first professional, master's, post-bachelor's certificate. **Academic Requirements:** Computer literacy, English (including composition), humanities, mathematics, sciences (biological or physical), social science. **Classes:** Most classes have 20–29 students. Most lab/discussion sections have fewer than 10 students. **Majors with Highest Enrollment:** Business administration/management, elementary education and teaching, nursing/registered nurse training (RN, ASN, BSN, MSN). **Disciplines with Highest Percentage of Degrees Awarded:** Business/marketing 16%, liberal arts/general studies 15%, health professions and related sciences 13%, education 11%, communications/journalism 6%. **Special Study Options:** Accelerated program, cooperative education program, cross-registration, distance learning, double major, dual enrollment, English as a second language (ESL), external degree program, honors program, independent study, internships, liberal arts/career combination, student-designed major, study abroad, teacher certification program, weekend college.

FACILITIES
Housing: Coed dorms, apartments for married students, apartments for single students, special housing for international students. **Special Academic Facilities/Equipment:** Inlow Hall—Law School, Eskenazi Hall—Herron School of Art & Design, Cavanaugh Hall—School of Liberal Arts & IUPUI Enrollment Center, University Library (most high-tech library in North America), IUPUI Sport Complex (host of 11 Olympic Team Trails), White River State Park (Indianapolis' version of the mall in Washington, DC). **Computers:** 1% of classrooms are wired, 100% of classrooms are wireless, 90% of public computers are PCs, 9% of public computers are Macs, 1% of public computers are UNIX, network access in dorm rooms, network access in dorm lounges, online registration, online administrative functions (other than registration), remote student-access to Web through college's connection.

CAMPUS LIFE
Activities: Choral groups, concert band, dance, drama/theater, jazz band, literary magazine, music ensembles, pep band, student government, student newspaper. **Organizations:** 154 registered organizations, 9 honor societies, 10 religious organizations. 2 fraternities (1% men join), 1 sorority (1% women join). **Athletics (Intercollegiate):** *Men:* Basketball, cross-country, diving, golf, soccer, swimming, tennis. *Women:* Basketball, cross-country, diving, golf, soccer, softball, swimming, tennis, volleyball.

ADMISSIONS
Freshman Academic Profile: 12% in top 10% of high school class, 35% in top 25% of high school class, 74% in top 50% of high school class. SAT Math middle 50% range 440–560. SAT Critical Reading middle 50% range 430–540. ACT middle 50% range 18–23. TOEFL required of all international applicants, minimum paper TOEFL 550, minimum computer TOEFL 180. **Basis for Candidate Selection:** *Very important factors considered include:* Rigor of secondary school record. *Important factors considered include:* Academic GPA. *Other factors considered include:* Application essay, character/personal qualities, class rank, interview, recommendation(s), standardized test scores, work experience. **Freshman Admission Requirements:** High school diploma is required, and GED is accepted. *Academic units required:* 4 English, 3 math, 3 science (3 science labs), 2 social studies, 2 history, 4 academic electives. *Academic units recommended:* 4 math, 4 science, 3 foreign language. **Freshman Admission Statistics:** 6,727 applied, 71% admitted, 59% enrolled. **Transfer Admission Requirements:** College transcript(s). Minimum college GPA of 2.0 required. Lowest grade transferable C. **General Admission Information:** Application fee $50. Nonfall registration accepted. Admission may be deferred for a maximum of 1 year. Credit and/or placement offered for CEEB Advanced Placement tests.

COSTS AND FINANCIAL AID
Annual in-state tuition $5,259. Annual out-of-state tuition $17,258. Required fees $630. Average book expense $672. **Required Forms and Deadlines:** FAFSA. Financial aid filing deadline 3/1. **Notification of Awards:** Applicants will be notified of awards on a rolling basis beginning on or about 4/1. **Types of Aid:** *Need-based scholarships/grants:* Pell, SEOG, state scholarships/grants, private scholarships, the school's own gift aid. *Loans:* FFEL Subsidized Stafford, FFEL Unsubsidized Stafford, FFEL PLUS, Federal Perkins, Federal Nursing, college/university loans from institutional funds. **Financial Aid Statistics:** 34% freshmen, 34% undergrads receive need-based scholarship or grant aid. 39% freshmen, 46% undergrads receive need-based self-help aid. 38 freshmen, 187 undergrads receive athletic scholarships.

INDIANA UNIVERSITY—SOUTH BEND

1700 Mishawaka Avenue, PO Box 7111, A169, South Bend, IN 46634-7111
Phone: 574-520-4480 **E-mail:** admissio@iusb.edu **CEEB Code:** 1339
Fax: 574-520-4834 **Website:** www.iusb.edu
Financial Aid Phone: 574-520-4872

This public school was founded in 1922. It has an 80-acre campus.

RATINGS
Admissions Selectivity Rating: 67   **Fire Safety Rating:** 60*   **Green Rating:** 60*

STUDENTS AND FACULTY
Enrollment: 5,714. **Student Body:** 62% female, 38% male, 4% out-of-state, 2% international (75 countries represented). African American 7%, Asian 1%, Caucasian 81%, Hispanic 4%. **Retention and Graduation:** 66% freshmen return for sophomore year. 4% freshmen graduate within 4 years. **Faculty:** Student/faculty ratio 14:1. 275 full-time faculty, 68% hold PhDs.

ACADEMICS
Degrees: Associate, bachelor's, certificate, diploma, master's, post-bachelor's certificate. **Academic Requirements:** Arts/fine arts, computer literacy, English (including composition), humanities, mathematics, sciences (biological or physical), social science. **Classes:** Most classes have 20–29 students. Most lab/discussion sections have 10–19 students. **Majors with Highest Enrollment:** Business administration/management, elementary education and teaching, nursing/registered nurse training (RN, ASN, BSN, MSN). **Disciplines with Highest Percentage of Degrees Awarded:** Education 24%, business/marketing 17%, liberal arts/general studies 14%, health professions and related sciences 12%, security and protective services 6%. **Special Study Options:** Accelerated program, computer technology with Purdue University on Indiana University South Bend campus, cross-registration, distance learning, double major, electrical engineering, English as a second language (ESL), external degree program, honors program, internships, liberal arts/career combination, mechanical engineering, study abroad, teacher certification program, weekend college. Northern Indiana Consortium for Education (NICE): IUSB is one of six member institutions sharing library resources, faculty expertise, and academic strengths resulting in broadened course opportunities to students.

FACILITIES
Housing: Special housing for international students. **Computers:** 100% of classrooms are wired, 100% of classrooms are wireless, 92% of public computers are PCs, 7% of public computers are Macs, 1% of public computers are UNIX, online registration, online administrative functions (other than registration), support for handheld computing, remote student-access to Web through college's connection.

CAMPUS LIFE
Activities: Choral groups, drama/theater, jazz band, literary magazine, music ensembles, musical theater, opera, pep band, student government, student newspaper, student-run film society, symphony orchestra. **Organizations:** 30 registered organizations, 1 religious organization. 2 fraternities, 1 sorority. **Athletics (Intercollegiate):** *Men:* Basketball. *Women:* Basketball.

ADMISSIONS
Freshman Academic Profile: 6% in top 10% of high school class, 23% in top 25% of high school class, 57% in top 50% of high school class. SAT Math middle 50% range 420–530. SAT Critical Reading middle 50% range 410–520. ACT middle 50% range 17–23. TOEFL required of all international applicants, minimum paper TOEFL 550. **Basis for Candidate Selection:** *Very important factors considered include:* Rigor of secondary school record. *Important factors considered include:* Academic GPA, class rank. *Other factors considered include:* Extracurricular activities, interview, recommendation(s), standardized test scores, state residency. **Freshman Admission Requirements:** High school diploma is required, and GED is accepted. *Academic units required:* 4 English, 3 math, 1 science (1 science lab), 2 social studies. *Academic units recommended:* 2 foreign language. **Freshman Admission Statistics:** 1,572 applied, 89% admitted, 71% enrolled. **Transfer Admission Requirements:** College transcript(s). Minimum college GPA of 2.0 required. Lowest grade transferable C. **General Admission Information:** Application fee $45. Regular notification rolling. Nonfall registration accepted. Admission may be deferred. Neither credit nor placement offered for CEEB Advanced Placement tests.

COSTS AND FINANCIAL AID
Annual in-state tuition $4,467. Annual out-of-state tuition $12,869. Required fees $422. **Required Forms and Deadlines:** FAFSA, institution's own financial aid form. Financial aid filing deadline 3/1. **Notification of Awards:**

Applicants will be notified of awards on a rolling basis beginning on or about 5/1. **Types of Aid:** *Need-based scholarships/grants:* Pell, SEOG, state scholarships/grants, private scholarships, the school's own gift aid. *Loans:* Direct Subsidized Stafford, Direct Unsubsidized Stafford, Direct PLUS, Federal Perkins, Federal Nursing, college/university loans from institutional funds. **Student Employment:** Federal Work-Study Program available. Off-campus job opportunities are good. **Financial Aid Statistics:** 36% freshmen, 39% undergrads receive need-based scholarship or grant aid. 40% freshmen, 44% undergrads receive need-based self-help aid. 3 freshmen, 22 undergrads receive athletic scholarships.

INDIANA UNIVERSITY—SOUTHEAST

4201 Grant Line Road, UC-100, New Albany, IN 47150
Phone: 812-941-2212 **E-mail:** admissions@ius.edu **CEEB Code:** 1314
Fax: 812-941-2595 **Website:** www.ius.edu **ACT Code:** 1229
Financial Aid Phone: 812-941-2246

This public school was founded in 1941. It has a 177-acre campus.

RATINGS
Admissions Selectivity Rating: 70   **Fire Safety Rating:** 60*   **Green Rating:** 60*

STUDENTS AND FACULTY
Enrollment: 5,133. **Student Body:** 63% female, 37% male, 23% out-of-state. African American 5%, Caucasian 90%, Hispanic 1%. **Retention and Graduation:** 67% freshmen return for sophomore year. 8% freshmen graduate within 4 years. **Faculty:** Student/faculty ratio 16:1. 192 full-time faculty, 73% hold PhDs.

ACADEMICS
Degrees: Associate, bachelor's, certificate, master's, post-bachelor's certificate. **Academic Requirements:** Computer literacy, English (including composition), humanities, mathematics, sciences (biological or physical), social science. **Classes:** Most classes have 20–29 students. Most lab/discussion sections have 10–19 students. **Majors with Highest Enrollment:** Business administration/management, elementary education and teaching. **Disciplines with Highest Percentage of Degrees Awarded:** Education 25%, business/marketing 20%, liberal arts/general studies 16%, health professions and related sciences 10%, psychology 5%. **Special Study Options:** Accelerated program, cross-registration, double major, dual enrollment, external degree program, independent study, internships, student-designed major, study abroad, teacher certification program, weekend college.

FACILITIES
Special Academic Facilities/Equipment: Paul W. Ogle Center, concert hall, theater, recital hall, Japanese Cultural Center, Ronald L. Barr Art Gallery. **Computers:** 94% of public computers are PCs, 6% of public computers are Macs, online registration, online administrative functions (other than registration), remote student-access to Web through college's connection.

CAMPUS LIFE
Activities: Choral groups, concert band, drama/theater, literary magazine, music ensembles, student government, student newspaper, symphony orchestra. **Organizations:** 76 registered organizations, 1 religious organization. 2 fraternities, 4 sororities. **Athletics (Intercollegiate):** *Men:* Baseball, basketball, cross-country, tennis. *Women:* Basketball, cross-country, softball, tennis, volleyball.

ADMISSIONS
Freshman Academic Profile: 10% in top 10% of high school class, 29% in top 25% of high school class, 69% in top 50% of high school class. SAT Math middle 50% range 420–520. SAT Critical Reading middle 50% range 420–530. ACT middle 50% range 18–22. TOEFL required of all international applicants, minimum paper TOEFL 550. **Basis for Candidate Selection:** *Very important factors considered include:* Class rank, rigor of secondary school record. *Important factors considered include:* Academic GPA, standardized test scores. *Other factors considered include:* Interview, recommendation(s). **Freshman Admission Requirements:** High school diploma is required, and GED is accepted. *Academic units required:* 4 English, 3 math, 1 science (1 science lab), 2 social studies, 4 academic electives. *Academic units recommended:* 4 math, 2 science (2 science labs), 2 foreign language, 1 history. **Freshman Admission Statistics:** 1,260 applied, 88% admitted, 76% enrolled. **Transfer Admission Requirements:** College transcript(s). Lowest grade transferable C. **General Admission Information:** Application fee $30. Regular notification rolling. Nonfall registration accepted. Admission may be deferred. Credit offered for CEEB Advanced Placement tests.

COSTS AND FINANCIAL AID

Annual in-state tuition $4,337. Annual out-of-state tuition $11,853. Required fees $442. **Required Forms and Deadlines:** FAFSA, institution's own financial aid form. Financial aid filing deadline 3/1. **Notification of Awards:** Applicants will be notified of awards on a rolling basis beginning on or about 5/1. **Types of Aid:** *Need-based scholarships/grants:* Pell, SEOG, state scholarships/grants, private scholarships, the school's own gift aid. *Loans:* FFEL Subsidized Stafford, FFEL Unsubsidized Stafford, FFEL PLUS, Federal Perkins, Federal Nursing, college/university loans from institutional funds. **Student Employment:** Federal Work-Study Program available. Institutional employment available. Off-campus job opportunities are excellent. **Financial Aid Statistics:** 32% freshmen, 33% undergrads receive need-based scholarship or grant aid. 38% freshmen, 42% undergrads receive need-based self-help aid. 8 freshmen, 55 undergrads receive athletic scholarships.

INDIANA UNIVERSITY OF PENNSYLVANIA

Best 368

1011 South Drive, Suite 117 Sutton Hall, Indiana, PA 15705
Phone: 724-357-2230 **E-mail:** admissions-inquiry@iup.edu **CEEB Code:** 2652
Fax: 724-357-6281 **Website:** www.iup.edu **ACT Code:** 3704
Financial Aid Phone: 724-357-2218

This public school was founded in 1875. It has a 342-acre campus.

RATINGS
Admissions Selectivity Rating: 66   **Fire Safety Rating:** 94   **Green Rating:** 60*

STUDENTS AND FACULTY
Enrollment: 11,647. **Student Body:** 55% female, 45% male, 4% out-of-state, 1% international (74 countries represented). African American 9%, Caucasian 80%, Hispanic 1%. **Retention and Graduation:** 76% freshmen return for sophomore year. 19% grads go on to further study within 1 year. 11% grads pursue arts and sciences degrees. 1% grads pursue business degrees. 3% grads pursue law degrees. 2% grads pursue medical degrees. **Faculty:** Student/faculty ratio 16:1. 650 full-time faculty. 100% faculty teach undergrads.

ACADEMICS
Degrees: Associate, bachelor's, certificate, doctoral, master's, post-bachelor's certificate, post-master's certificate. **Academic Requirements:** Arts/fine arts, computer literacy, English (including composition), history, humanities, liberal studies, mathematics, philosophy, sciences (biological or physical), social science. **Classes:** Most classes have 20–29 students. Most lab/discussion sections have fewer than 10 students. **Majors with Highest Enrollment:** Communications studies/speech communication and rhetoric, criminology, elementary education and teaching. **Disciplines with Highest Percentage of Degrees Awarded:** Business/marketing 22%, social sciences 16%, communications/journalism 10%, education 9%, visual and performing arts 8%. **Special Study Options:** Accelerated program, cooperative education program, distance learning, double major, English as a second language (ESL), exchange student program (domestic), honors program, independent study, internships, study abroad, teacher certification program, weekend college.

FACILITIES
Housing: Coed dorms, men's dorms, women's dorms, apartments for single students, special housing for disabled students, special housing for international students, fraternity/sorority housing, substance-free, honors college. **Special Academic Facilities/Equipment:** Art museum, natural history museum, on-campus elementary school, lodge, farm, co-generation plant, ski slope, sailing base. **Computers:** 55% of classrooms are wireless, 94% of public computers are PCs, 6% of public computers are Macs, network access in dorm rooms, network access in dorm lounges, online registration, online administrative functions (other than registration), support for handheld computing, remote student-access to Web through college's connection.

CAMPUS LIFE
Activities: Choral groups, concert band, dance, drama/theater, jazz band, literary magazine, marching band, music ensembles, musical theater, opera, pep band, radio station, student government, student newspaper, student-run film society, symphony orchestra, television station. **Organizations:** 200 registered organizations, 21 honor societies, 18 religious organizations. 19 fraternities, 14 sororities. **Athletics (Intercollegiate):** *Men:* Baseball, basketball, cross-country, diving, football, golf, swimming, track/field (indoor), track/field (outdoor). *Women:* Basketball, cross-country, diving, field hockey, lacrosse, soccer, softball, swimming, tennis, track/field (indoor), track/field (outdoor), volleyball.

ADMISSIONS
Freshman Academic Profile: 7% in top 10% of high school class, 22% in top 25% of high school class, 56% in top 50% of high school class. 95% from public high schools. SAT Math middle 50% range 430–540. SAT Critical Reading. middle 50% range 430–530. SAT Writing middle 50% range 420–520. TOEFL required of all international applicants, minimum paper TOEFL 500, minimum computer TOEFL 300. **Basis for Candidate Selection:** *Very important factors considered include:* Academic GPA. *Important factors considered include:* Class rank, rigor of secondary school record, standardized test scores. *Other factors considered include:* Application essay, character/personal qualities, extracurricular activities, interview, level of applicant's interest, recommendation(s), talent/ability, volunteer work, work experience. **Freshman Admission Requirements:** High school diploma is required, and GED is accepted. *Academic units recommended:* 4 English, 3 math, 3 science, 2 foreign language, 3 social studies. **Freshman Admission Statistics:** 8,349 applied, 71% admitted, 43% enrolled. **Transfer Admission Requirements:** High school transcript, college transcript(s). Lowest grade transferable C. **General Admission Information:** Application fee $35. Regular notification is rolling. Nonfall registration accepted. Admission may be deferred for a maximum of 1 year. Credit offered for CEEB Advanced Placement tests.

COSTS AND FINANCIAL AID
Annual in-state tuition $5,178. Annual out-of-state tuition $12,944. Room and board $5,436. Required fees $1,517. Average book expense $1,000. **Required Forms and Deadlines:** FAFSA. Financial aid filing deadline 4/15. **Notification of Awards:** Applicants will be notified of awards on a rolling basis beginning on or about 3/15. **Types of Aid:** *Need-based scholarships/grants:* Pell, SEOG, state scholarships/grants, private scholarships, the school's own gift aid, United Negro College Fund. *Loans:* FFEL Subsidized Stafford, FFEL Unsubsidized Stafford, FFEL PLUS, Federal Perkins, private alternative loans. **Student Employment:** Federal Work-Study Program available. Off-campus job opportunities are good. **Financial Aid Statistics:** 52% freshmen, 47% undergrads receive need-based scholarship or grant aid. 62% freshmen, 58% undergrads receive need-based self-help aid. 39 freshmen, 191 undergrads receive athletic scholarships. 81% freshmen, 77% undergrads receive any aid. Highest amount earned per year from on-campus jobs $1,500.

INDIANA WESLEYAN UNIVERSITY

4201 South Washington Street, Marion, IN 46953-4974
Phone: 765-677-2138 **E-mail:** admissions@indwes.edu **CEEB Code:** 1446
Fax: 317-677-2333 **Website:** www.indwes.edu **ACT Code:** 1226
Financial Aid Phone: 765-677-2137

This private school, affiliated with the Wesleyan Church, was founded in 1920. It has a 130-acre campus.

RATINGS
Admissions Selectivity Rating: 83   **Fire Safety Rating:** 94   **Green Rating:** 60*

STUDENTS AND FACULTY
Enrollment: 2,785. **Student Body:** 62% female, 38% male, 46% out-of-state. African American 1%, Caucasian 91%, Hispanic 1%. **Retention and Graduation:** 83% freshmen return for sophomore year. 50% freshmen graduate within 4 years. **Faculty:** Student/faculty ratio 15:1. 140 full-time faculty, 54% hold PhDs. 100% faculty teach undergrads.

ACADEMICS
Degrees: Associate, bachelor's. **Academic Requirements:** Arts/fine arts, English (including composition), history, humanities, mathematics, philosophy. **Classes:** Most classes have 10–19 students. Most lab/discussion sections have 10–19 students. **Majors with Highest Enrollment:** Business administration and management, elementary education and teaching, nursing/registered nurse training (RN, ASN, BSN, MSN). **Disciplines with Highest Percentage of Degrees Awarded:** Education 19%, theology and religious vocations 13%, health professions and related sciences 13%, business/marketing 12%, psychology 6%. **Special Study Options:** Double major, dual enrollment, honors program, independent study, internships, study abroad, teacher certification program.

FACILITIES
Housing: Men's dorms, women's dorms, apartments for married students,

apartments for single students. **Special Academic Facilities/Equipment:** Lee Howard Art Collection (European artists), Lewis Jackson Library, Tom and Joanne Phillippe Performing Arts Center (1998), bronze statues from Israel (1998-2002), Williams Chapel (medieval replica, 2001), Burns Hall of Science and Nursing (2000), Luckey Recreation and Wellness Center (2001), John Maxwell Business Center (1999). **Computers:** 95% of public computers are PCs, 5% of public computers are Macs, network access in dorm rooms, network access in dorm lounges, online registration, online administrative functions (other than registration), support for handheld computing, remote student-access to Web through college's connection.

CAMPUS LIFE

Activities: Choral groups, concert band, drama/theater, jazz band, literary magazine, music ensembles, musical theater, pep band, radio station, student government, student newspaper, symphony orchestra, television station, yearbook. **Organizations:** 35 registered organizations, 1 honor society, 5 religious organizations. **Athletics (Intercollegiate):** *Men:* Baseball, basketball, cross-country, golf, soccer, tennis, track/field (indoor), track/field (outdoor). *Women:* Basketball, cross-country, soccer, softball, tennis, track/field (indoor), track/field (outdoor), volleyball.

ADMISSIONS

Freshman Academic Profile: 24% in top 10% of high school class, 59% in top 25% of high school class, 86% in top 50% of high school class. SAT Math middle 50% range 480–600. SAT Critical Reading middle 50% range 480–600. ACT middle 50% range 21–27. TOEFL required of all international applicants, minimum paper TOEFL 550, minimum computer TOEFL 213. **Basis for Candidate Selection:** *Very important factors considered include:* Academic GPA, character/personal qualities, recommendation(s), standardized test scores. *Important factors considered include:* Class rank, rigor of secondary school record. *Other factors considered include:* Alumni/ae relation, application essay, extracurricular activities, first generation, interview, level of applicant's interest, religious affiliation/commitment, talent/ability, volunteer work, work experience. **Freshman Admission Requirements:** High school diploma is required, and GED is accepted. *Academic units recommended:* 4 English, 3 math, 3 science, 2 foreign language, 3 social studies, 5 academic electives, 1 health. **Freshman Admission Statistics:** 2,325 applied, 77% admitted, 41% enrolled. **Transfer Admission Requirements:** College transcript(s), statement of good standing from prior institution(s). Minimum college GPA of 2.0 required. Lowest grade transferable C. **General Admission Information:** Application fee $25. Regular application deadline 8/1. Regular notification is rolling. Nonfall registration accepted. Admission may be deferred for a maximum of 1 year. Credit offered for CEEB Advanced Placement tests.

COSTS AND FINANCIAL AID

Annual tuition $19,376. Room and board $6,564. Average book expense $800.**Required Forms and Deadlines:** FAFSA, institution's own financial aid form. Financial aid filing deadline 3/1. **Types of Aid:** *Need-based scholarships/grants:* Pell, SEOG, state scholarships/grants, private scholarships, the school's own gift aid. *Loans:* FFEL Subsidized Stafford, FFEL Unsubsidized Stafford, FFEL PLUS, Federal Perkins, Federal Nursing, college/university loans from institutional funds. **Student Employment:** Off-campus job opportunities are good.

INTER AMERICAN UNIVERSITY OF PUERTO RICO—AGUADILLA CAMPUS

Call Box 20000, Aguadilla, PR 00605
Phone: 787-891-0925 **E-mail:** dperez@aguadilla.inter.edu
Fax: 787-882-3020 **Website:** www.aguadilla.inter.edu
Financial Aid Phone: 787-891-0925

This private school was founded in 1957. It has a 53-acre campus.

RATINGS

Admissions Selectivity Rating: 60*   **Fire Safety Rating:** 60*   **Green Rating:** 60*

STUDENTS AND FACULTY

Enrollment: 4,325. **Student Body:** Hispanic 100%. **Faculty:** 74 full-time faculty, 22% hold PhDs.

ACADEMICS

Degrees: Associate, bachelor's, certificate. **Academic Requirements:** Arts/fine arts, computer literacy, English (including composition), history, humanities, mathematics, philosophy, sciences (biological or physical), social science. **Classes:** Most classes have 20–29 students. **Majors with Highest Enroll-**

ment: Computer and information sciences, criminal justice/law enforcement administration, social work. **Disciplines with Highest Percentage of Degrees Awarded:** Business/marketing 34%, education 16%, psychology 11%, biological/life sciences 8%, engineering 6%. **Special Study Options:** Cross-registration, distance learning, dual enrollment, exchange student program (domestic), honors program, independent study, internships, teacher certification program, weekend college.

FACILITIES

Special Academic Facilities/Equipment: Sala Manuel Méndez Ballester, information and technology building. **Computers:** 100% of public computers are PCs, online registration, online administrative functions (other than registration).

CAMPUS LIFE

Activities: Choral groups, dance, drama/theater, radio station, student government, student newspaper. **Organizations:** 25 registered organizations. **Athletics (Intercollegiate):** *Men:* Baseball, basketball, cross-country, soccer, softball, tennis, track/field (outdoor), volleyball. *Women:* Basketball, cross-country, softball, tennis, track/field (outdoor), volleyball.

ADMISSIONS

Basis for Candidate Selection: *Very important factors considered include:* Rigor of secondary school record, standardized test scores. *Other factors considered include:* Interview, recommendation(s). **Freshman Admission Requirements:** High school diploma is required, and GED is accepted. *Academic units required:* 3 English, 2 math, 2 science, 3 foreign language, 2 history, 6 academic electives. **Transfer Admission Requirements:** College transcript(s), statement of good standing from prior institution(s). Minimum college GPA of 2.0 required. Lowest grade transferable C. **General Admission Information:** Regular application deadline 5/15. Nonfall registration accepted. Common Application not accepted. Credit offered for CEEB Advanced Placement tests.

COSTS AND FINANCIAL AID

Annual tuition $3,750. Required fees $364. **Required Forms and Deadlines:** FAFSA. Financial aid filing deadline 4/30. **Notification of Awards:** Applicants will be notified of awards on or about 6/15. **Types of Aid:** *Need-based scholarships/grants:* Pell, SEOG, state scholarships/grants, private scholarships, the school's own gift aid. *Loans:* Direct Subsidized Stafford, Direct Unsubsidized Stafford, Federal Perkins. **Student Employment:** Federal Work-Study Program available. Off-campus job opportunities are good.

INTER AMERICAN UNIVERSITY OF PUERTO RICO—SAN GERMAN

PO Box 5100, San German, PR 00683-5008
Phone: 787-264-1912 **E-mail:** mi_cama@sg.inter.edu
Fax: 787-892-6350 **Website:** www.sg.inter.edu
Financial Aid Phone: 787-264-1912

This private school was founded in 1912. It has a 260-acre campus.

RATINGS

Admissions Selectivity Rating: 60*   **Fire Safety Rating:** 60*   **Green Rating:** 60*

STUDENTS AND FACULTY

Faculty: 99% faculty teach undergrads.

ACADEMICS

Degrees: Bachelor's, master's. **Academic Requirements:** Arts/fine arts, computer literacy, English (including composition), mathematics, sciences (biological or physical), social science. **Special Study Options:** Accelerated program, cooperative education program, cross-registration, distance learning, double major, dual enrollment, English as a second language (ESL), honors program, independent study, internships, study abroad, teacher certification program.

FACILITIES

Housing: Men's dorms, women's dorms, apartments for married students. **Special Academic Facilities/Equipment:** Arturo Morales Carrion Museum at the library. **Computers:** 7% of public computers are PCs, online registration, online administrative functions (other than registration), remote student-access to Web through college's connection.

CAMPUS LIFE

Activities: Choral groups, concert band, drama/theater, jazz band, music ensembles, pep band, student government, student newspaper. **Organizations:**

50 registered organizations, 2 honor societies, 5 religious organizations. 4 fraternities, 4 sororities. **Athletics (Intercollegiate):** *Men:* Baseball, basketball, cross-country, soccer, softball, swimming, tennis, track/field (outdoor), volleyball, wrestling. *Women:* Cross-country, softball, swimming, tennis, track/field (outdoor), volleyball.

ADMISSIONS

Freshman Academic Profile: 69% from public high schools. **Basis for Candidate Selection:** *Very important factors considered include:* Character/personal qualities, rigor of secondary school record, standardized test scores. *Other factors considered include:* Interview. **Freshman Admission Requirements:** High school diploma is required, and GED is accepted. *Academic units required:* 3 English, 3 math, 3 science, 3 foreign language, 3 history, 3 academic electives. **Freshman Admission Statistics:** 1,656 applied, 94% admitted, 79% enrolled. **Transfer Admission Requirements:** High school transcript, college transcript(s), standardized test score. Minimum college GPA of 2.5 required. Lowest grade transferable C. **General Admission Information:** Application fee $19. Regular application deadline 5/13. Regular notification is rolling. Nonfall registration accepted. Common Application not accepted. Placement offered for CEEB Advanced Placement tests.

COSTS AND FINANCIAL AID

Annual tuition $3,150. Room & board $2,200. Required fees $344. Average book expense $600. **Required Forms and Deadlines:** FAFSA, institution's own financial aid form, state aid form. **Types of Aid:** *Need-based scholarships/grants:* Pell, SEOG, state scholarships/grants, the school's own gift aid, Federal Nursing Scholarships. *Loans:* Direct Subsidized Stafford, Direct Unsubsidized Stafford, Direct PLUS, Federal Perkins. **Student Employment:** Federal Work-Study Program available. Off-campus job opportunities are good. **Financial Aid Statistics:** 75% freshmen, 81% undergrads receive need-based scholarship or grant aid. 49% freshmen, 59% undergrads receive need-based self-help aid.

INTERNATIONAL ACADEMY OF DESIGN & TECHNOLOGY—TAMPA

5225 Memorial Highway, Tampa, FL 33634
Phone: 813-881-0007 **E-mail:** leads@academy.edu
Fax: 813-881-0008 **Website:** www.academy.edu
Financial Aid Phone: 813-881-0007

This proprietary school was founded in 1984. It has a 10-acre campus.

RATINGS

Admissions Selectivity Rating: 60*   **Fire Safety Rating:** 60*   **Green Rating:** 60*

STUDENTS AND FACULTY

Enrollment: 2,043. **Student Body:** 53% female, 47% male, 24% out-of-state, 3% international (17 countries represented). African American 13%, Asian 3%, Caucasian 63%, Hispanic 17%, Native American 1%. **Retention and Graduation:** 72% freshmen return for sophomore year. 21% freshmen graduate within 4 years. 18% grads go on to further study within 1 year. **Faculty:** Student/faculty ratio 16:1. 20 full-time faculty, 25% hold PhDs. 100% faculty teach undergrads.

ACADEMICS

Degrees: Associate, bachelor's. **Academic Requirements:** Arts/fine arts, computer literacy, English (including composition), humanities, mathematics, social science. **Majors with Highest Enrollment:** Design and visual communications, fashion/apparel design, interior design. **Disciplines with Highest Percentage of Degrees Awarded:** Visual and performing arts 84%, business/marketing 16%. **Special Study Options:** Accelerated program, distance learning, independent study, internships, study abroad.

FACILITIES

Housing: Apartments for married students, apartments for single students through outside agency. **Computers:** 60% of public computers are PCs, 30% of public computers are Macs, 10% of public computers are UNIX, remote student-access to Web through college's connection.

CAMPUS LIFE

Organizations: 1 registered organization.

ADMISSIONS

Basis for Candidate Selection: *Very important factors considered include:* Interview. *Other factors considered include:* Character/personal qualities, talent/ability, work experience. **Freshman Admission Requirements:** High school

diploma is required, and GED is accepted. **Freshman Admission Statistics:** 467 applied, 71% admitted, 69% enrolled. **Transfer Admission Requirements:** College transcript(s), interview. Lowest grade transferable C. **General Admission Information:** Application fee $100. Nonfall registration accepted. Admission may be deferred for a maximum of 90 days. Common Application not accepted. Neither credit nor placement offered for CEEB Advanced Placement tests.

COSTS AND FINANCIAL AID

Annual tuition $9,876. Required fees $150. Average book expense $1,300. **Required Forms and Deadlines:** FAFSA. **Types of Aid:** *Need-based scholarships/grants:* Pell, SEOG, state scholarships/grants, private scholarships, the school's own gift aid. *Loans:* FFEL Subsidized Stafford, FFEL Unsubsidized Stafford, FFEL PLUS, Private loans via lenders. **Student Employment:** Federal Work-Study Program available. Off-campus job opportunities are excellent.

INTERNATIONAL COLLEGE

2655 Northbrooke Drive, Naples, FL 34119
Phone: 239-513-1122 **E-mail:** admit@internationalcollege.edu **CEEB Code:** 7113
Fax: 239-598-6254 **Website:** www.internationalcollege.edu **ACT Code:** 4775
Financial Aid Phone: 239-513-1122

This private school was founded in 1990.

RATINGS

Admissions Selectivity Rating: 60*   **Fire Safety Rating:** 60*   **Green Rating:** 60*

STUDENTS AND FACULTY

Enrollment: 1,434. **Student Body:** 70% female, 30% male, 2% international (40 countries represented). African American 16%, Caucasian 58%, Hispanic 20%. **Faculty:** Student/faculty ratio 15:1. 59 full-time faculty, 51% hold PhDs. 100% faculty teach undergrads.

ACADEMICS

Degrees: Associate, bachelor's, master's, post-bachelor's certificate. **Academic Requirements:** Computer literacy, English (including composition), humanities, mathematics, social science. **Classes:** Most classes have 10–19 students. **Majors with Highest Enrollment:** Business administration and management, business/managerial operations, multi/interdisciplinary studies. **Disciplines with Highest Percentage of Degrees Awarded:** Business/marketing 59%, interdisciplinary studies 16%, computer and information sciences 10%, security and protective services 9%, health professions and related sciences 4%. **Special Study Options:** Accelerated program, cooperative education program, distance learning, double major, English as a second language (ESL), internships.

FACILITIES

Computers: 100% of classrooms are wired, 100% of classrooms are wireless, 100% of public computers are PCs.

CAMPUS LIFE

Activities: Literary magazine. **Organizations:** 1 honor society.

ADMISSIONS

Freshman Academic Profile: TOEFL required of all international applicants, minimum paper TOEFL 500, minimum computer TOEFL 173. **Basis for Candidate Selection:** *Important factors considered include:* Application essay, interview, standardized test scores. **Freshman Admission Requirements:** High school diploma is required, and GED is accepted. **Transfer Admission Requirements:** High school transcript, college transcript(s), essay or personal statement. Lowest grade transferable D. **General Admission Information:** Application fee $20. Nonfall registration accepted. Admission may be deferred for a maximum of 1 year. Credit offered for CEEB Advanced Placement tests.

COSTS AND FINANCIAL AID

Annual tuition $9,720. Required fees $380. **Required Forms and Deadlines:** FAFSA. **Types of Aid:** *Need-based scholarships/grants:* Pell, SEOG, state scholarships/grants, private scholarships, the school's own gift aid. *Loans:* FFEL Subsidized Stafford, FFEL Unsubsidized Stafford, FFEL PLUS. **Student Employment:** Federal Work-Study Program available. Institutional employment available. Off-campus job opportunities are good. **Financial Aid Statistics:** 70% freshmen, 69% undergrads receive need-based scholarship or grant aid. 74% freshmen, 76% undergrads receive need-based self-help aid.

IONA COLLEGE

715 North Avenue, New Rochelle, NY 10801
Phone: 914-633-2502 **E-mail:** icad@iona.edu **CEEB Code:** 2324
Fax: 914-633-2642 **Website:** www.iona.edu **ACT Code:** 2770
Financial Aid Phone: 914-633-2497

This private school, affiliated with the Roman Catholic Church, was founded in 1940. It has a 35-acre campus.

RATINGS
Admissions Selectivity Rating: 86　　**Fire Safety Rating:** 86　　**Green Rating:** 83

STUDENTS AND FACULTY
Enrollment: 3,407. **Student Body:** 55% female, 45% male, 20% out-of-state, 2% international (43 countries represented). African American 7%, Asian 2%, Caucasian 67%, Hispanic 11%. **Retention and Graduation:** 83% freshmen return for sophomore year. 47% freshmen graduate within 4 years. 73% grads go on to further study within 1 year. 53% grads pursue arts and sciences degrees. 29% grads pursue business degrees. 8% grads pursue law degrees. 4% grads pursue medical degrees. **Faculty:** Student/faculty ratio 15:1. 176 full-time faculty, 89% hold PhDs. 100% faculty teach undergrads.

ACADEMICS
Degrees: Bachelor's, certificate, master's, post-bachelor's certificate, post-master's certificate. **Academic Requirements:** Arts/fine arts, computer literacy, English (including composition), foreign languages, history, humanities, mathematics, philosophy, sciences (biological or physical), social science. **Classes:** Most classes have 20–29 students. Most lab/discussion sections have 10–19 students. **Majors with Highest Enrollment:** Criminal justice/law enforcement administration, mass communications/media studies, psychology. **Disciplines with Highest Percentage of Degrees Awarded:** Business/marketing 32%, communications/journalism 15%, education 10%, psychology 10%, security and protective services 7%, health professions and related sciences 5%, social sciences 5%. **Special Study Options:** Accelerated program, distance learning, double major, dual enrollment, honors program, independent study, internships, liberal arts/career combination, study abroad, teacher certification program, weekend college.

FACILITIES
Housing: Coed dorms, apartments for single students, special housing for disabled students, housing for honors program students. **Special Academic Facilities/Equipment:** Iona College Art Center, Br. Kenneth Chapman Public Art Gallary, Murphy Science Technology Center, Hynes Natural Science Center, advanced computer laboratory, TV production studio, LaPenta Student Union, Hynes Athletic Center, rowing tank, Arrigoni Center. **Computers:** 100% of classrooms are wired, 100% of classrooms are wireless, 100% of public computers are PCs, network access in dorm rooms, network access in dorm lounges, online registration, online administrative functions (other than registration), support for handheld computing, remote student-access to Web through college's connection.

CAMPUS LIFE
Activities: Choral groups, dance, drama/theater, literary magazine, music ensembles, musical theater, pep band, radio station, student government, student newspaper, student-run film society, television station, yearbook. **Organizations:** 75 registered organizations, 20 honor societies, 4 religious organizations. 4 fraternities (4% men join), 6 sororities (6% women join). **Athletics (Intercollegiate):** *Men:* Baseball, basketball, crew/rowing, cross-country, diving, football, golf, soccer, swimming, track/field (indoor), track/field (outdoor), water polo. *Women:* Basketball, crew/rowing, cross-country, diving, lacrosse, soccer, softball, swimming, track/field (indoor), track/field (outdoor), volleyball, water polo.

ADMISSIONS
Freshman Academic Profile: 31% in top 10% of high school class, 54% in top 25% of high school class, 93% in top 50% of high school class. SAT Math middle 50% range 550–660. SAT Critical Reading middle 50% range 530–640. Regular application deadline 2/15. TOEFL required of all international applicants, minimum paper TOEFL 550, minimum computer TOEFL 213. **Basis for Candidate Selection:** *Very important factors considered include:* Academic GPA, rigor of secondary school record. *Important factors considered include:* Application essay, character/personal qualities, class rank, interview, standardized test scores. *Other factors considered include:* Alumni/ae relation, extracurricular activities, first generation, geographical residence, level of applicant's interest, recommendation(s), talent/ability, volunteer work, work experience. **Freshman Admission Requirements:** High school diploma is required, and GED is accepted. *Academic units required:* 4 English, 3 math, 2 science (2 science labs), 2 foreign language, 1 social studies, 1 history, 1

academic elective. *Academic units recommended:* 4 English, 4 math, 3 science (2 science labs), 2 foreign language, 2 social studies, 2 history, 3 academic electives. **Freshman Admission Statistics:** 5,211 applied, 60% admitted, 29% enrolled. **Transfer Admission Requirements:** High school transcript, college transcript(s), essay or personal statement. Minimum college GPA of 2.5 required. Lowest grade transferable C. **General Admission Information:** Application fee $50. Regular application deadline 2/15. Regular notification 3/20. Nonfall registration accepted. Admission may be deferred for a maximum of 1 year. Credit and/or placement offered for CEEB Advanced Placement tests.

COSTS AND FINANCIAL AID
Annual tuition $24,406. Room and board $10,800. Required fees $1,800. Average book expense $1,500. **Required Forms and Deadlines:** FAFSA, institution's own financial aid form, state aid form. Financial aid filing deadline 4/15. **Notification of Awards:** Applicants will be notified of awards on a rolling basis beginning on or about 12/20. **Types of Aid:** *Need-based scholarships/grants:* Pell, SEOG, state scholarships/grants, private scholarships, the school's own gift aid. *Loans:* FFEL Subsidized Stafford, FFEL Unsubsidized Stafford, FFEL PLUS, Federal Perkins, alternative loans. **Financial Aid Statistics:** 57% freshmen, 34% undergrads receive need-based scholarship or grant aid. 59% freshmen, 57% undergrads receive need-based self-help aid. 51 freshmen, 213 undergrads receive athletic scholarships. 98% freshmen, 89% undergrads receive any aid. Highest amount earned per year from on-campus jobs $4,000.

See page 1206.

IOWA STATE UNIVERSITY

100 Alumni Hall, Ames, IA 50011-2011
Phone: 515-294-5836 **E-mail:** admissions@iastate.edu **CEEB Code:** 6306
Fax: 515-294-2592 **Website:** www.iastate.edu **ACT Code:** 1320
Financial Aid Phone: 515-294-2223

This public school was founded in 1858. It has a 1,788-acre campus.

RATINGS
Admissions Selectivity Rating: 81　　**Fire Safety Rating:** 72　　**Green Rating:** 60*

STUDENTS AND FACULTY
Enrollment: 20,035. **Student Body:** 43% female, 57% male, 21% out-of-state, 3% international (106 countries represented). African American 3%, Asian 3%, Caucasian 84%, Hispanic 2%. **Retention and Graduation:** 83% freshmen return for sophomore year. 31% freshmen graduate within 4 years. 19% grads go on to further study within 1 year. 8% grads pursue arts and sciences degrees. 5% grads pursue business degrees. 2% grads pursue law degrees. 3% grads pursue medical degrees. **Faculty:** Student/faculty ratio 15:1. 1,385 full-time faculty, 92% hold PhDs. 72% faculty teach undergrads.

ACADEMICS
Degrees: Bachelor's, doctoral, first professional, master's. **Academic Requirements:** Diversity, English (including composition), humanities, international perspectives, mathematics, sciences (biological or physical), social science, use of library. **Classes:** Most classes have 20–29 students. Most lab/discussion sections have 20–29 students. **Majors with Highest Enrollment:** Finance; marketing/marketing management; mechanical engineering. **Disciplines with Highest Percentage of Degrees Awarded:** Business/marketing 22%, engineering 17%, agriculture 9%, education 6%, visual and performing arts 6%. **Special Study Options:** Accelerated program, cooperative education program, cross-registration, distance learning, double major, dual enrollment, English as a Second Language (ESL), exchange student program (domestic), external degree program, honors program, independent study, internships, liberal arts/career combination, student-designed major, study abroad, teacher certification program, weekend college.

FACILITIES
Housing: Coed dorms, men's dorms, women's dorms, apartments for married students, apartments for single students, special housing for disabled students, special housing for international students, fraternity/sorority housing, learning communities; family housing; quiet, nonsmoking, or alcohol-free floors; graduate/adult undergraduate housing. **Special Academic Facilities/Equipment:** Brunnier Art Museum, Farm House Museum, observatory, numerous institutes, research centers, college of design gallery, virtual reality

application center, Pappajohn Center for Entrepreneurship. **Computers:** 20% of classrooms are wired, 75% of classrooms are wireless, 75% of public computers are PCs, 20% of public computers are Macs, 5% of public computers are UNIX, network access in dorm rooms, network access in dorm lounges, online registration, online administrative functions (other than registration), support for handheld computing, remote student-access to Web through college's connection.

CAMPUS LIFE

Activities: Choral groups, concert band, dance, drama/theater, jazz band, literary magazine, marching band, music ensembles, musical theater, opera, pep band, radio station, student government, student newspaper, student-run film society, symphony orchestra, television station. **Organizations:** 690 registered organizations, 44 honor societies, 36 religious organizations. 37 fraternities (15% men join), 18 sororities (16% women join). **Athletics (Intercollegiate):** *Men:* Basketball, cross-country, football, golf, track/field (indoor), track/field (outdoor), wrestling. *Women:* Basketball, cross-country, diving, golf, gymnastics, soccer, softball, swimming, tennis, track/field (indoor), track/field (outdoor), volleyball.

ADMISSIONS

Freshman Academic Profile: 27% in top 10% of high school class, 60% in top 25% of high school class, 93% in top 50% of high school class. 93% from public high schools. SAT Math middle 50% range 530–680. SAT Critical Reading middle 50% range 510–640. ACT middle 50% range 22–27. TOEFL required of all international applicants, minimum paper TOEFL 500, minimum computer TOEFL 173. **Basis for Candidate Selection:** *Very important factors considered include:* Academic GPA, class rank, rigor of secondary school record, standardized test scores. *Other factors considered include:* Application essay, character/personal qualities, extracurricular activities, geographical residence, interview, recommendation(s), state residency, talent/ability, volunteer work, work experience. **Freshman Admission Requirements:** High school diploma is required, and GED is accepted. *Academic units required:* 4 English, 3 math, 3 science (2 science labs), 2 foreign language, 2 social studies. *Academic units recommended:* 4 English, 4 math, 4 science (3 science labs), 3 foreign language, 4 social studies. **Freshman Admission Statistics:** 9,634 applied, 90% admitted, 46% enrolled. **Transfer Admission Requirements:** College transcript(s), statement of good standing from prior institution(s). Minimum college GPA of 2.0 required. Lowest grade transferable D-. **General Admission Information:** Application fee $30. Regular application deadline 7/1. Regular notification is rolling. Nonfall registration accepted. Admission may be deferred for a maximum of 1 year. Credit and/or placement offered for CEEB Advanced Placement tests.

COSTS AND FINANCIAL AID

Annual in-state tuition $5,524. Annual out-of-state tuition $16,514. Room and board $6,715. Required fees $836. Average book expense $978. **Required Forms and Deadlines:** FAFSA. Financial aid filing deadline 3/1. **Notification of Awards:** Applicants will be notified of awards on a rolling basis beginning on or about 4/1. **Types of Aid:** *Need-based scholarships/grants:* Pell, SEOG, state scholarships/grants, the school's own gift aid. *Loans:* Direct Subsidized Stafford, Direct Unsubsidized Stafford, Direct PLUS, Federal Perkins, state loans, college/university loans from institutional funds, private alternative loans. **Financial Aid Statistics:** 53% freshmen, 53% undergrads receive need-based scholarship or grant aid. 42% freshmen, 46% undergrads receive need-based self-help aid. 71 freshmen, 334 undergrads receive athletic scholarships. 88% freshmen, 79% undergrads receive any aid. Highest amount earned per year from on-campus jobs $1,686.

IOWA STATE UNIVERSITY OF SCIENCE AND TECHNOLOGY

Office of Admissions, 100 Alumni Hall, Ames, IA 50011-2011
Phone: 515-294-5836 **E-mail:** admissions@iastate.edu **CEEB Code:** 6306
Fax: 515-294-2592 **Website:** www.iastate.edu **ACT Code:** 1320
Financial Aid Phone: 515-294-2223

This public school was founded in 1858. It has a 1,788-acre campus.

RATINGS

Admissions Selectivity Rating: 60*   **Fire Safety Rating:** 60*   **Green Rating:** 60*

STUDENTS AND FACULTY

Enrollment: 21,813. **Student Body:** 44% female, 56% male, 19% out-of-state. African American 3%, Asian 3%, Caucasian 83%, Hispanic 2%. **Retention and Graduation:** 84% freshmen return for sophomore year. 27% freshmen graduate

within 4 years. 17% grads go on to further study within 1 year. 43% grads pursue arts and sciences degrees. 7% grads pursue business degrees. 6% grads pursue law degrees. 14% grads pursue medical degrees. **Faculty:** Student/faculty ratio 16:1. 1,415 full-time faculty, 92% hold PhDs. 75% faculty teach undergrads.

ACADEMICS

Degrees: Bachelor's, doctoral, first professional, master's. **Academic Requirements:** Diversity, English (including composition), humanities, international perspectives, mathematics, sciences (biological or physical), social science. **Classes:** Most classes have 20–29 students. Most lab/discussion sections have 20–29 students. **Disciplines with Highest Percentage of Degrees Awarded:** Engineering 19%, business/marketing 19%, agriculture 11%, education 7%, biological/life sciences 6%, visual and performing arts 6%, social sciences 5%. **Special Study Options:** Accelerated program, cooperative education program, cross-registration, distance learning, double major, dual enrollment, English as a second language (ESL), exchange student program (domestic), external degree program, honors program, independent study, internships, liberal arts/career combination, student-designed major, study abroad, teacher certification program, weekend college.

FACILITIES

Housing: Coed dorms, men's dorms, women's dorms, apartments for married students, apartments for single students, special housing for disabled students, special housing for international students, fraternity/sorority housing, learning communities, family housing. **Special Academic Facilities/Equipment:** Brunnier Art Museum, Farm House Museum, observatory, numerous institutes, research centers, College of Design Gallery. **Computers:** 65% of public computers are PCs, 25% of public computers are Macs, 10% of public computers are UNIX, network access in dorm rooms, network access in dorm lounges, online registration, online administrative functions (other than registration), remote student-access to Web through college's connection.

CAMPUS LIFE

Activities: Choral groups, concert band, dance, drama/theater, jazz band, literary magazine, marching band, music ensembles, musical theater, opera, pep band, radio station, student government, student newspaper, student-run film society, symphony orchestra, television station. **Organizations:** 513 registered organizations, 34 honor societies, 36 religious organizations. 32 fraternities (11% men join), 18 sororities (12% women join). **Athletics (Intercollegiate):** *Men:* Baseball, basketball, cross-country, football, golf, swimming, track/field (indoor), track/field (outdoor), wrestling. *Women:* Basketball, cross-country, golf, gymnastics, soccer, softball, swimming, tennis, track/field (indoor), track/field (outdoor), volleyball.

ADMISSIONS

Freshman Academic Profile: 92% from public high schools. SAT Math middle 50% range 560–680. SAT Critical Reading middle 50% range 520–650. ACT middle 50% range 22–27. TOEFL required of all international applicants, minimum paper TOEFL 500. **Basis for Candidate Selection:** *Very important factors considered include:* Class rank, rigor of secondary school record, standardized test scores. *Other factors considered include:* Application essay, character/personal qualities, extracurricular activities, geographical residence, interview, recommendation(s), religious affiliation/commitment, state residency, talent/ability, work experience. **Freshman Admission Requirements:** High school diploma is required, and GED is accepted. *Academic units required:* 4 English, 3 math, 3 science (2 science labs), 2 foreign language, 2 social studies. *Academic units recommended:* 4 math, 4 science (3 science labs), 4 foreign language, 4 social studies. **Freshman Admission Statistics:** 9,035 applied, 90% admitted, 47% enrolled. **Transfer Admission Requirements:** College transcript(s), statement of good standing from prior institution(s). Minimum college GPA of 2.0 required. Lowest grade transferable D-. **General Admission Information:** Application fee $20. Regular application deadline 8/1. Regular notification is rolling. Nonfall registration accepted. Admission may be deferred for a maximum of 1 year. Common Application accepted. Credit and/or placement offered for CEEB Advanced Placement tests.

COSTS AND FINANCIAL AID

Annual in-state tuition $4,702. Out-of-state tuition $14,404. Room & board $6,121. Required fees $724. Average book expense $843. **Required Forms and Deadlines:** FAFSA. Financial aid filing deadline 3/1. **Notification of Awards:** Applicants will be notified of awards on a rolling basis beginning on or about 4/1. **Types of Aid:** *Need-based scholarships/grants:* Pell, SEOG, state scholarships/grants, the school's own gift aid. *Loans:* Direct Subsidized Stafford, Direct Unsubsidized Stafford, Direct PLUS, Federal Perkins, state loans, college/university loans from institutional funds, private alternative loans. **Student Employment:** Federal Work-Study Program available. Institutional employment available. Off-campus job opportunities are excellent. **Financial Aid Statistics:** 38% freshmen, 40% undergrads receive need-based scholarship or grant aid. 44% freshmen, 53% undergrads receive need-based self-help aid. 38 freshmen, 182 undergrads receive athletic scholarships. Highest amount earned per year from on-campus jobs $3,300.

IOWA WESLEYAN COLLEGE

601 North Main Street, Mt. Pleasant, IA 52641
Phone: 319-385-6231 **E-mail:** admitrwl@iwc.edu **CEEB Code:** 6308
Fax: 319-385-6296 **Website:** www.iwc.edu **ACT Code:** 1324
Financial Aid Phone: 319-385-6242

This private school, affiliated with the Methodist Church, was founded in 1842. It has a 60-acre campus.

RATINGS
Admissions Selectivity Rating: 62   **Fire Safety Rating:** 60*   **Green Rating:** 60*

STUDENTS AND FACULTY
Enrollment: 785. **Student Body:** 61% female, 39% male, 22% out-of-state, 3% international (11 countries represented). African American 5%, Asian 1%, Caucasian 88%, Hispanic 2%. **Retention and Graduation:** 55% freshmen return for sophomore year. 22% freshmen graduate within 4 years. 2% grads go on to further study within 1 year. 1% grads pursue business degrees. 1% grads pursue medical degrees. **Faculty:** Student/faculty ratio 12:1. 44 full-time faculty, 39% hold PhDs. 100% faculty teach undergrads.

ACADEMICS
Degrees: Bachelor's. **Academic Requirements:** Arts/fine arts, computer literacy, English (including composition), history, humanities, mathematics, philosophy, sciences (biological or physical), social science. **Classes:** Most classes have fewer than 10 students. **Disciplines with Highest Percentage of Degrees Awarded:** Education 28%, business/marketing 22%, psychology 7%, biological/life sciences 6%. **Special Study Options:** Cooperative education program, cross-registration, distance learning, double major, dual enrollment, English as a second language (ESL), exchange student program (domestic), independent study, internships, liberal arts/career combination, student-designed major, study abroad, teacher certification program.

FACILITIES
Housing: Men's dorms, women's dorms, special housing for international students. **Special Academic Facilities/Equipment:** Art gallery, biological environment chamber. **Computers:** Network access in dorm lounges, remote student-access to Web through college's connection.

CAMPUS LIFE
Activities: Choral groups, concert band, jazz band, literary magazine, music ensembles, pep band, radio station, student government, student newspaper, symphony orchestra, yearbook. **Organizations:** 42 registered organizations, 2 religious organizations. 1 fraternity (3% men join), 2 sororities (12% women join). **Athletics (Intercollegiate):** *Men:* Baseball, basketball, cross-country, football, golf, soccer, track/field (outdoor). *Women:* Basketball, cross-country, golf, soccer, softball, track/field (outdoor), volleyball.

ADMISSIONS
Freshman Academic Profile: 9% in top 10% of high school class, 18% in top 25% of high school class, 45% in top 50% of high school class. 96% from public high schools. TOEFL required of all international applicants, minimum paper TOEFL 500. **Basis for Candidate Selection:** *Very important factors considered include:* Alumni/ae relation, rigor of secondary school record, volunteer work, work experience. *Important factors considered include:* Class rank, extracurricular activities, geographical residence, standardized test scores, talent/ability. *Other factors considered include:* Application essay, character/personal qualities, recommendation(s), religious affiliation/commitment, state residency. **Freshman Admission Requirements:** High school diploma is required, and GED is accepted. *Academic units recommended:* 4 English, 3 math, 2 science (2 science labs), 3 social studies, 4 academic electives. **Freshman Admission Statistics:** 408 applied, 85% admitted, 33% enrolled. **Transfer Admission Requirements:** College transcript(s). Minimum college GPA of 2.0 required. Lowest grade transferable D. **General Admission Information:** Application fee $15. Early decision application deadline 5/1. Regular application deadline 8/15. Regular notification is rolling. Nonfall registration accepted. Admission may be deferred for a maximum of 1 year. Common Application accepted. Credit and/or placement offered for CEEB Advanced Placement tests.

COSTS AND FINANCIAL AID
Annual tuition $13,200. Room & board $4,250. Average book expense $735. **Required Forms and Deadlines:** FAFSA. Financial aid filing deadline 4/1. **Notification of Awards:** Applicants will be notified of awards on a rolling basis beginning on or about 3/1. **Types of Aid:** *Need-based scholarships/grants:* Pell, SEOG, state scholarships/grants, private scholarships, the school's own gift aid. *Loans:* FFEL Subsidized Stafford, FFEL Unsubsidized Stafford, FFEL PLUS, Federal Perkins, alternative loans. **Student Employment:** Federal Work-Study

Program available. Institutional employment available. Off-campus job opportunities are good. **Financial Aid Statistics:** 89% freshmen, 87% undergrads receive need-based scholarship or grant aid. 79% freshmen, 81% undergrads receive need-based self-help aid. 7 freshmen, 22 undergrads receive athletic scholarships. Highest amount earned per year from on-campus jobs $500.

ITHACA COLLEGE

100 Job Hall, Ithaca, NY 14850-7020
Phone: 607-274-3124 **E-mail:** admission@ithaca.edu **CEEB Code:** 2325
Fax: 607-274-1900 **Website:** www.ithaca.edu **ACT Code:** 2772
Financial Aid Phone: 607-274-3131

This private school was founded in 1892. It has a 757-acre campus.

RATINGS
Admissions Selectivity Rating: 83   **Fire Safety Rating:** 75   **Green Rating:** 91

STUDENTS AND FACULTY
Enrollment: 5,955. **Student Body:** 55% female, 45% male, 53% out-of-state, 2% international (61 countries represented). African American 3%, Asian 3%, Caucasian 82%, Hispanic 4%. **Retention and Graduation:** 85% freshmen return for sophomore year. 69% freshmen graduate within 4 years. 40% grads go on to further study within 1 year. 36% grads pursue arts and sciences degrees. 2% grads pursue business degrees. 1% grads pursue law degrees. 1% grads pursue medical degrees. **Faculty:** Student/faculty ratio 11:1. 460 full-time faculty, 91% hold PhDs. 99% faculty teach undergrads.

ACADEMICS
Degrees: Bachelor's, certificate, doctoral, master's. **Classes:** Most classes have 10–19 students. Most lab/discussion sections have fewer than 10 students. **Majors with Highest Enrollment:** Business administration/management, music/music and performing arts studies, radio and television. **Disciplines with Highest Percentage of Degrees Awarded:** Communications/journalism 19%, visual and performing arts 15%, health professions and related sciences 10%, business/marketing 10%, social sciences 9%. **Special Study Options:** Accelerated program, cross-registration, distance learning, double major, dual enrollment, honors program, independent study, internships, liberal arts/career combination, London Center (London, England), Los Angeles program, student-designed major, study abroad, teacher certification program, Washington, DC semester program, Walkabout Down Under Program (Australia), opportunities to study in more than 50 countries around the world.

FACILITIES
Housing: Coed dorms, women's dorms, apartments for single students, special housing for disabled students, special housing for international students, fraternity/sorority housing, first-year students only, quiet residence hall, music honor fraternity housing. **Special Academic Facilities/Equipment:** Art gallery, radio and TV stations, digital technology throughout communications building, observatory, wellness clinic, fitness center, trading room, speech and hearing handicapped clinic, physical therapy clinic, performing arts centers (music and theater), music recording facility. **Computers:** 100% of classrooms are wired, 5% of classrooms are wireless, 75% of public computers are PCs, 23% of public computers are Macs, 2% of public computers are UNIX, network access in dorm rooms, online registration, online administrative functions (other than registration), support for handheld computing, remote student-access to Web through college's connection.

CAMPUS LIFE
Activities: Choral groups, concert band, dance, drama/theater, jazz band, literary magazine, music ensembles, musical theater, opera, pep band, radio station, student government, student newspaper, student-run film society, symphony orchestra, television station, yearbook. **Organizations:** 154 registered organizations, 8 honor societies, 8 religious organizations. 4 fraternities (1% men join), 1 sorority (1% women join). **Athletics (Intercollegiate):** *Men:* Baseball, basketball, crew/rowing, cross-country, diving, football, lacrosse, soccer, swimming, tennis, track/field (outdoor), wrestling. *Women:* Basketball, crew/rowing, cross-country, diving, field hockey, gymnastics, lacrosse, soccer, softball, swimming, tennis, track/field (outdoor), volleyball. **Environmental initiatives:** Design and construction of a LEED Platinum-

registered facility for our School of Business, and modifying business school curriculum to incorporate sustainability principles and to use the building as a "teaching tool" to model sustainable operations. The design of new Gateway building is also intended to achieve LEED Platinum certification upon completion, making Ithaca the first institution in the world to have two LEED Platinum facilities on its campus. Development of aggressive resource management programs, to engage community to find ways to reduce use of energy, to minimize production of waste, and to support recycling systems.

ADMISSIONS

Freshman Academic Profile: 32% in top 10% of high school class, 70% in top 25% of high school class, 95% in top 50% of high school class. 75% from public high schools. SAT Math middle 50% range 540–630. SAT Critical Reading middle 50% range 530–630. TOEFL required of all international applicants, minimum paper TOEFL 550, minimum computer TOEFL 213. **Basis for Candidate Selection:** *Very important factors considered include:* Academic GPA, rigor of secondary school record, standardized test scores. *Important factors considered include:* Application essay, character/personal qualities, class rank, extracurricular activities, recommendation(s), talent/ability. *Other factors considered include:* Alumni/ae relation, first generation, interview, level of applicant's interest, volunteer work, work experience. **Freshman Admission Requirements:** High school diploma is required, and GED is accepted. *Academic units required:* 4 English, 3 math, 3 science, 2 foreign language, 3 social studies, 1 academic elective. **Freshman Admission Statistics:** 11,312 applied, 69% admitted, 20% enrolled. **Transfer Admission Requirements:** High school transcript, college transcript(s), essay or personal statement, statement of good standing from prior institution(s). Minimum college GPA of 2.8 required. Lowest grade transferable C-. **General Admission Information:** Application fee $60. Regular application deadline 2/1. Regular notification is rolling. Nonfall registration accepted. Admission may be deferred for a maximum of 1 year. Credit and/or placement offered for CEEB Advanced Placement tests.

COSTS AND FINANCIAL AID

Annual tuition $28,670. Room and board $10,728. Average book expense $1,050. **Required Forms and Deadlines:** FAFSA, CSS/Financial Aid PROFILE required of early decision applicants by 11/1. Financial aid filing deadline 2/1. **Notification of Awards:** Applicants will be notified of awards on a rolling basis beginning on or about 2/15. **Types of Aid:** *Need-based scholarships/grants:* Pell, SEOG, state scholarships/grants, private scholarships, the school's own gift aid. *Loans:* FFEL Subsidized Stafford, FFEL Unsubsidized Stafford, FFEL PLUS, Federal Perkins, alternative loans. **Financial Aid Statistics:** 65% freshmen, 64% undergrads receive need-based scholarship or grant aid. 67% freshmen, 64% undergrads receive need-based self-help aid. 85% freshmen, 84% undergrads receive any aid.

level classes. Research semester at Lawrence Berkeley Lab. Co-op programs available in business, computer science, natural science.

FACILITIES

Housing: Men's dorms, women's dorms. **Special Academic Facilities/ Equipment:** Research center. **Computers:** 90% of public computers are PCs, 5% of public computers are Macs, 5% of public computers are UNIX, network access in dorm rooms, network access in dorm lounges, online registration, online administrative functions (other than registration), remote student-access to Web through college's connection.

CAMPUS LIFE

Activities: Choral groups, dance, drama/theater, jazz band, literary magazine, marching band, music ensembles, opera, radio station, student government, student newspaper, television station, yearbook. **Organizations:** 120 registered organizations, 9 honor societies, 4 religious organizations. 4 fraternities, 4 sororities (3% women join). **Athletics (Intercollegiate):** *Men:* Baseball, basketball, cross-country, football, golf, tennis, track/field (indoor), track/field (outdoor), volleyball. *Women:* Basketball, cross-country, golf, softball, tennis, track/field (indoor), track/field (outdoor), volleyball.

ADMISSIONS

Freshman Academic Profile: 5% in top 10% of high school class, 41% in top 25% of high school class, 76% in top 50% of high school class. 85% from public high schools. ACT middle 50% range 16-20. TOEFL required of all international applicants, minimum paper TOEFL 525. **Basis for Candidate Selection:** *Very important factors considered include:* Academic GPA, rigor of secondary school record, standardized test scores. *Important factors considered include:* Level of applicant's interest. **Freshman Admission Requirements:** High school diploma is required, and GED is accepted. *Academic units required:* 4 English, 3 math, 3 science, 3 social studies, 2 academic electives. **Freshman Admission Statistics:** 8,052 applied, 39% admitted, 29% enrolled. **Transfer Admission Requirements:** High school transcript, college transcript(s). Minimum college GPA of 2.0 required. Lowest grade transferable C. **General Admission Information:** Regular notification rolling. Nonfall registration accepted.

COSTS AND FINANCIAL AID

Average book expense $800. **Required Forms and Deadlines:** FAFSA, institution's own financial aid form, state aid form. **Types of Aid:** *Need-based scholarships/grants:* Pell, SEOG, state scholarships/grants, private scholarships, the school's own gift aid. *Loans:* FFEL Subsidized Stafford, FFEL Unsubsidized Stafford, FFEL PLUS, Federal Perkins, college/university loans from institutional funds. **Student Employment:** Federal Work-Study Program available. Institutional employment available. Off-campus job opportunities are good. **Financial Aid Statistics:** Highest amount earned per year from on-campus jobs $2,200.

JACKSON STATE UNIVERSITY

1400 J. R. Lynch Street, PO Box 17330, Jackson, MS 39217
Phone: 601-979-2100 **E-mail:** schatman@ccaix.jsums.edu **CEEB Code:** 1341
Fax: 601-979-3445 **Website:** www.jsums.edu **ACT Code:** 2204
Financial Aid Phone: 601-979-2227

This public school was founded in 1877. It has a 128-acre campus.

RATINGS

Admissions Selectivity Rating: 83   **Fire Safety Rating:** 66   **Green Rating:** 60*

STUDENTS AND FACULTY

Enrollment: 6,509. **Student Body:** 62% female, 38% male, 18% out-of-state. African American 87%, Caucasian 2%. **Retention and Graduation:** 66% freshmen return for sophomore year. 13% grads go on to further study within 1 year. 6% grads pursue law degrees. 7% grads pursue medical degrees. **Faculty:** Student/faculty ratio 18:1. 354 full-time faculty, 76% hold PhDs.

ACADEMICS

Degrees: Bachelor's, doctoral, master's, post-master's certificate. **Academic Requirements:** Arts/fine arts, computer literacy, English (including composition), foreign languages, history, humanities, mathematics, philosophy, sciences (biological or physical), social science. **Disciplines with Highest Percentage of Degrees Awarded:** Business/marketing 21%, education 20%, biological/life sciences 10%, public administration and social services 8%, security and protective services 6%. **Special Study Options:** Cooperative education program, distance learning, double major, dual enrollment, English as a second language (ESL), honors program, independent study, internships, study abroad, teacher certification program, weekend college. Undergrads may take grad-

JACKSONVILLE STATE UNIVERSITY

700 Pelham Road North, Jacksonville, AL 36265
Phone: 256-782-5268 **E-mail:** info@jsu.edu
Fax: 256-782-5953 **Website:** www.jsu.edu **ACT Code:** 0020
Financial Aid Phone: 256-782-5006

This public school was founded in 1883. It has a 459-acre campus.

RATINGS

Admissions Selectivity Rating: 66   **Fire Safety Rating:** 60*   **Green Rating:** 60*

STUDENTS AND FACULTY

Enrollment: 7,096. **Student Body:** 58% female, 42% male, 12% out-of-state. 1% international (73 countries represented). African American 22%, Caucasian 71%, Hispanic 1%. **Retention and Graduation:** 63% freshmen return for sophomore year. 15% freshmen graduate within 4 years. **Faculty:** Student/faculty ratio 21:1. 300 full-time faculty, 66% hold PhDs. 100% faculty teach undergrads.

ACADEMICS

Degrees: Bachelor's, master's, post-master's certificate. **Academic Requirements:** Arts/fine arts, computer literacy, English (including composition), history, humanities, mathematics, sciences (biological or physical), social science. **Classes:** Most classes have 20–29 students. **Majors with Highest Enrollment:** Criminal justice/safety studies, elementary education and teaching, nursing/registered nurse training (RN, ASN, BSN, MSN). **Disciplines with Highest Percentage of Degrees Awarded:** Education 32%, business/marketing 15%, health professions and related sciences 8%, social sciences 6%, visual and performing arts 4%. **Special Study Options:**

The Princeton Review's Complete Book of Colleges

Accelerated program, cooperative education program, distance learning, double major, dual enrollment, honors program, independent study, internships, teacher certification program.

FACILITIES

Housing: Coed dorms, men's dorms, women's dorms, apartments for married students, apartments for single students, special housing for international students, fraternity/sorority housing, apartments for students with dependent children. **Computers:** 98% of public computers are PCs, 2% of public computers are Macs, network access in dorm rooms, network access in dorm lounges, online registration, remote student-access to Web through college's connection.

CAMPUS LIFE

Activities: Choral groups, concert band, dance, drama/theater, jazz band, marching band, music ensembles, musical theater, pep band, radio station, student government, student newspaper, symphony orchestra, yearbook. **Organizations:** 100 registered organizations, 13 honor societies, 8 religious organizations. 11 fraternities (10% men join), 9 sororities (10% women join). **Athletics (Intercollegiate):** *Men:* Baseball, basketball, cheerleading, football, golf, riflery, tennis. *Women:* Basketball, cheerleading, cross-country, golf, riflery, soccer, softball, tennis, track/field (outdoor), volleyball.

ADMISSIONS

Freshman Academic Profile: 3% in top 10% of high school class, 13% in top 25% of high school class, 34% in top 50% of high school class. 99% from public high schools. SAT Math middle 50% range 400–530. SAT Critical Reading middle 50% range 420–530. ACT middle 50% range 17–23. TOEFL required of all international applicants, minimum paper TOEFL 500, minimum computer TOEFL 173. **Basis for Candidate Selection:** *Very important factors considered include:* Rigor of secondary school record, standardized test scores. **Freshman Admission Requirements:** High school diploma is required, and GED is accepted. *Academic units required:* 3 English, 4 academic electives. **Freshman Admission Statistics:** 2,419 applied, 88% admitted, 50% enrolled. **Transfer Admission Requirements:** College transcript(s). Lowest grade transferable D. **General Admission Information:** Application fee $20. Regular notification rolling. Nonfall registration accepted. Admission may be deferred. Common Application not accepted. Credit and/or placement offered for CEEB Advanced Placement tests.

COSTS AND FINANCIAL AID

Annual in-state tuition $4,040. Out-of-state tuition $8,080. Room & board $3,312. Required fees $20. Average book expense $1,008. **Required Forms and Deadlines:** FAFSA, institution's own financial aid form. Financial aid filing deadline 3/15. **Notification of Awards:** Applicants will be notified of awards on a rolling basis beginning on or about 5/15. **Types of Aid:** *Need-based scholarships/grants:* Pell, SEOG, state scholarships/grants, private scholarships, Federal Nursing Scholarships. *Loans:* Direct Subsidized Stafford, Direct Unsubsidized Stafford, Direct PLUS, college/university loans from institutional funds.

JACKSONVILLE UNIVERSITY

Office of Admissions, 2800 University Boulevard North, Jacksonville, FL 32211
Phone: 904-256-7000 **E-mail:** admissions@ju.edu **CEEB Code:** 5331
Fax: 904-256-7012 **Website:** www.ju.edu **ACT Code:** 0740
Financial Aid Phone: 800-558-3467.

This private school was founded in 1934. It has a 198-acre campus.

RATINGS

Admissions Selectivity Rating: 79 **Fire Safety Rating:** 71 **Green Rating:** 60*

STUDENTS AND FACULTY

Enrollment: 2,551. **Student Body:** 56% female, 44% male, 40% out-of-state, 3% international (50 countries represented). African American 20%, Asian 2%, Caucasian 58%, Hispanic 5%. **Retention and Graduation:** 68% freshmen return for sophomore year. 38% freshmen graduate within 4 years. 22% grads go on to further study within 1 year. **Faculty:** Student/faculty ratio 14:1. 137 full-time faculty, 79% hold PhDs. 100% faculty teach undergrads.

ACADEMICS

Degrees: Bachelor's, first professional certificate, master's. **Academic Requirements:** Arts/fine arts, computer literacy, English (including composition), foreign languages, history, humanities, mathematics, philosophy, sciences (biological or physical), social science. **Classes:** Most classes have 10–19 students. **Majors with Highest Enrollment:** Aviation/airway management and operations, business administration/management, nursing/registered nurse

training (RN, ASN, BSN, MSN). **Disciplines with Highest Percentage of Degrees Awarded:** Health professions and related sciences 38%, business/marketing 21%, visual and performing arts 7%, transportation and materials moving 6%, social sciences 6%, education 5%. **Special Study Options:** Accelerated program, cooperative education program, distance learning, double major, dual enrollment, honors program, independent study, internships, liberal arts/career combination, student-designed major, study abroad, teacher certification program.

FACILITIES

Housing: Coed dorms, men's dorms, women's dorms, apartments for single students, special housing for disabled students, fraternity/sorority housing. **Special Academic Facilities/Equipment:** Art museum, dance pavilion, concert hall, on-campus preschool. **Computers:** 95% of public computers are PCs, 5% of public computers are Macs, network access in dorm rooms, network access in dorm lounges, online registration, online administrative functions (other than registration), remote student-access to Web through college's connection.

CAMPUS LIFE

Activities: Choral groups, concert band, dance, drama/theater, jazz band, literary magazine, music ensembles, pep band, radio station, student government, student newspaper, symphony orchestra, television station, yearbook. **Organizations:** 70 registered organizations, 16 honor societies, 7 fraternities (20% men join), 6 sororities (15% women join). **Athletics (Intercollegiate):** *Men:* Baseball, basketball, cross-country, football, golf, soccer, tennis. *Women:* Basketball, crew/rowing, cross-country, golf, soccer, softball, tennis, track/field (indoor), track/field (outdoor), volleyball.

ADMISSIONS

Freshman Academic Profile: 11% in top 10% of high school class, 33% in top 25% of high school class, 70% in top 50% of high school class. SAT Math middle 50% range 448–570. SAT Critical Reading middle 50% range 440–560. ACT middle 50% range 18–23. TOEFL required of all international applicants, minimum paper TOEFL 540, minimum computer TOEFL 207. **Basis for Candidate Selection:** *Very important factors considered include:* Academic GPA, standardized test scores. *Important factors considered include:* Rigor of secondary school record, talent/ability. *Other factors considered include:* Application essay, character/personal qualities, extracurricular activities, interview, recommendation(s), volunteer work, work experience. **Freshman Admission Requirements:** High school diploma is required, and GED is accepted. *Academic units required:* 4 English, 3 math, 3 science (2 science labs), 3 social studies. *Academic units recommended:* 4 English, 4 math, 3 science (2 science labs), 2 foreign language, 3 social studies. **Freshman Admission Statistics:** 4,355 applied, 45% admitted, 25% enrolled. **Transfer Admission Requirements:** college transcript(s), essay or personal statement, statement of good standing from prior institution(s). Minimum college GPA of 2.0 required. Lowest grade transferable C. **General Admission Information:** Application fee $30. Regular notification beg. 12/15. Nonfall registration accepted. Admission may be deferred for a maximum of 1 year. Credit and/or placement offered for CEEB Advanced Placement tests.

COSTS AND FINANCIAL AID

Annual tuition $23,900. Room and board $8,760. Average book expense $600. **Required Forms and Deadlines:** FAFSA. Financial aid filing deadline 3/15. **Notification of Awards:** Applicants will be notified of awards on a rolling basis beginning on or about 2/1. **Types of Aid:** *Need-based scholarships/grants:* Pell, SEOG, state scholarships/grants, private scholarships, the school's own gift aid, Navy ROTC. *Loans:* FFEL Subsidized Stafford, FFEL Unsubsidized Stafford, FFEL PLUS, Federal Perkins, college/university loans from institutional funds, private alternative loans. **Financial Aid Statistics:** 48% freshmen, 48% undergrads receive need-based scholarship or grant aid. 53% freshmen, 56% undergrads receive need-based self-help aid. 9 freshmen, 36 undergrads receive athletic scholarships. 97% freshmen, 87% undergrads receive any aid. Highest amount earned per year from on-campus jobs $4,677.

JAMES MADISON UNIVERSITY

Best 368

Sonner Hall, MSC 0101, Harrisonburg, VA 22807
Phone: 540-568-5681 **E-mail:** admissions@jmu.edu **CEEB Code:** 5392
Fax: 540-568-3332 **Website:** www.jmu.edu **ACT Code:** 4370
Financial Aid Phone: 540-568-7820.

This public school was founded in 1908. It has a 655-acre campus.

RATINGS
Admissions Selectivity Rating: 88   **Fire Safety Rating:** 67   **Green Rating:** 93

STUDENTS AND FACULTY
Enrollment: 15,653. **Student Body:** 61% female, 39% male, 30% out-of-state. African American 4%, Asian 5%, Caucasian 83%, Hispanic 2%. **Retention and Graduation:** 92% freshmen return for sophomore year. 63% freshmen graduate within 4 years. **Faculty:** Student/faculty ratio 16:1. 831 full-time faculty, 79% hold PhDs. 89% faculty teach undergrads.

ACADEMICS
Degrees: Bachelor's, doctoral, master's, post-master's certificate. **Academic Requirements:** Arts/fine arts, computer literacy, English (including composition), history, humanities, mathematics, philosophy, sciences (biological or physical), social science, speech communication, critical thinking, wellness, U.S. history/government. **Classes:** Most classes have 20–29 students. Most lab/discussion sections have 20–29 students. **Majors with Highest Enrollment:** Liberal arts and sciences/liberal studies; marketing/marketing management; psychology. **Disciplines with Highest Percentage of Degrees Awarded:** Business/marketing 22%, social sciences 12%, communications/journalism 8%, visual and performing arts 8%, health professions and related sciences 8%, psychology 7%, liberal arts/general studies 5%, parks and recreation 5%, English 5%. **Special Study Options:** Accelerated program, continuing education, distance learning, double major, honors program, independent study, internships, study abroad, teacher certification program.

FACILITIES
Housing: Coed dorms, apartments for single students, fraternity/sorority housing, international community, learning community, substance-free community. Students must apply. Fraternities are located off-campus. **Special Academic Facilities/Equipment:** Language lab, music and fine arts buildings, herbarium, university farm, planetarium (presently closed for rennovation), arboretum. **Computers:** 79% of classrooms are wireless, 82% of public computers are PCs, 18% of public computers are Macs, network access in dorm rooms, online registration, online administrative functions (other than registration), support for handheld computing, remote student-access to Web through college's connection.

CAMPUS LIFE
Activities: Choral groups, concert band, dance, drama/theater, jazz band, literary magazine, marching band, music ensembles, musical theater, opera, pep band, radio station, student government, student newspaper, symphony orchestra, yearbook. **Organizations:** 308 registered organizations, 13 honor societies, 12 religious organizations. 12 fraternities (8% men join), 8 sororities (10% women join). **Athletics (Intercollegiate):** *Men:* Archery, baseball, basketball, cross-country, diving, football, golf, gymnastics, soccer, swimming, tennis, track/field (outdoor), wrestling. *Women:* Archery, basketball, cross-country, diving, fencing, field hockey, golf, gymnastics, lacrosse, soccer, softball, swimming, tennis, track/field (outdoor), volleyball. Environmental Initiatives: Recycling program is an award-winning program that continues to expand and improve. We have a 10-kilowatt solar photovoltaic array that is tied to the campus power grid, and also have a 2-kilowatt hybrid solar-wind energy installation. 100% of maintenance fleet is rated as alternative fuel vehicles, and public bus service runs on biodiesel. Students helped design and construct a green roof on campus, and won one of MTV's "Break the Addiction Challenge" awards in 2006.

ADMISSIONS
Freshman Academic Profile: 31% in top 10% of high school class, 78% in top 25% of high school class, 98% in top 50% of high school class. SAT Math middle 50% range 530–620. SAT Critical Reading middle 50% range 520–610. SAT Writing middle 50% range 520–610. ACT middle 50% range 21–26. TOEFL required of all international applicants, minimum paper TOEFL 570, minimum computer TOEFL 230. **Basis for Candidate Selection:** *Very important factors considered include:* Academic GPA, rigor of secondary school record.

Important factors considered include: Standardized test scores. *Other factors considered include:* Alumni/ae relation, application essay, character/personal qualities, class rank, extracurricular activities, geographical residence, recommendation(s), state residency, talent/ability, volunteer work, work experience. **Freshman Admission Requirements:** High school diploma is required, and GED is accepted. *Academic units required:* 4 English, 4 math, 4 science (3 science labs), 3 foreign language, 3 social studies. *Academic units recommended:* 4 English, 5 math, 4 science (4 science labs), 4 foreign language, 4 social studies. **Freshman Admission Statistics:** 17,765 applied, 63% admitted, 34% enrolled. **Transfer Admission Requirements:** High school transcript, college transcript(s). Minimum college GPA of 2.0 required. Lowest grade transferable C. **General Admission Information:** Application fee $40. Regular application deadline 1/15. Regular notification 4/1. Nonfall registration not accepted. Admission may be deferred for a maximum of 1 year with approval. Credit offered for CEEB Advanced Placement tests.

COSTS AND FINANCIAL AID
Required Forms and Deadlines: FAFSA. Financial aid filing deadline 3/1. **Notification of Awards:** Applicants will be notified of awards on a rolling basis beginning on or about 4/1. **Types of Aid:** *Need-based scholarships/grants:* Pell, SEOG, state scholarships/grants, private scholarships, the school's own gift aid. *Loans:* FFEL Subsidized Stafford, FFEL Unsubsidized Stafford, FFEL PLUS, Federal Perkins. **Financial Aid Statistics:** 16% freshmen, 12% undergrads receive need-based scholarship or grant aid. 29% freshmen, 23% undergrads receive need-based self-help aid. 79 freshmen, 287 undergrads receive athletic scholarships. 53% freshmen, 51% undergrads receive any aid. Highest amount earned per year from on-campus jobs $3,640.

JAMESTOWN COLLEGE

6081 College Lane, Jamestown, ND 58405-0001
Phone: 701-252-3467 **E-mail:** admissions@jc.edu
Fax: 701-253-4318 **Website:** www.jc.edu **ACT Code:** 3200
Financial Aid Phone: 701-252-3467

This private school, affiliated with the Presbyterian Church, was founded in 1883. It has a 110-acre campus.

RATINGS
Admissions Selectivity Rating: 73   **Fire Safety Rating:** 60*   **Green Rating:** 60*

STUDENTS AND FACULTY
Enrollment: 958. **Student Body:** 55% female, 45% male, 44% out-of-state, 5% international (9 countries represented). African American 1%, Caucasian 90%, Hispanic 1%, Native American 1%. **Retention and Graduation:** 97% freshmen return for sophomore year. 34% freshmen graduate within 4 years. 20% grads go on to further study within 1 year. 9% grads pursue arts and sciences degrees. 2% grads pursue law degrees. 2% grads pursue medical degrees. **Faculty:** Student/faculty ratio 15:1. 57 full-time faculty, 53% hold PhDs. 100% faculty teach undergrads.

ACADEMICS
Degrees: Bachelor's. **Academic Requirements:** Arts/fine arts, computer literacy, English (including composition), foreign languages, history, humanities, mathematics, philosophy, sciences (biological or physical), social science. **Classes:** Most classes have 10–19 students. Most lab/discussion sections have fewer than 10 students. **Majors with Highest Enrollment:** Business administration/management, elementary education and teaching, nursing/registered nurse training (RN, ASN, BSN, MSN). **Disciplines with Highest Percentage of Degrees Awarded:** Education 20%, health professions and related sciences 20%, security and protective services 17%, business/marketing 17%, social sciences 7%, psychology 6%, computer and information sciences 3%. **Special Study Options:** Cooperative education program, double major, dual enrollment, exchange student program (domestic), honors program, independent study, internships, student-designed major, study abroad, teacher certification program.

FACILITIES
Housing: Coed dorms, apartments for single students, special housing for disabled students, houses. **Computers:** 100% of public computers are PCs, network access in dorm rooms, network access in dorm lounges, online registration, online administrative functions (other than registration), remote student-access to Web through college's connection.

CAMPUS LIFE
Activities: Choral groups, concert band, dance, drama/theater, jazz band, literary magazine, music ensembles, musical theater, pep band, student

government, student newspaper, yearbook. **Organizations:** 35 registered organizations, 5 religious organizations. **Athletics (Intercollegiate):** *Men:* Baseball, basketball, cross-country, football, golf, track/field (indoor), track/field (outdoor), wrestling. *Women:* Basketball, cross-country, golf, soccer, softball, track/field (indoor), track/field (outdoor), volleyball.

ADMISSIONS

Freshman Academic Profile: 15% in top 10% of high school class, 35% in top 25% of high school class, 64% in top 50% of high school class. SAT Math middle 50% range 490–530. SAT Critical Reading middle 50% range 410–540. ACT middle 50% range 20–25. TOEFL required of all international applicants, minimum paper TOEFL 525, minimum computer TOEFL 195. **Basis for Candidate Selection:** *Very important factors considered include:* Rigor of secondary school record, standardized test scores. *Important factors considered include:* Class rank. *Other factors considered include:* Alumni/ae relation, application essay, character/personal qualities, extracurricular activities, interview, recommendation(s), talent/ability, volunteer work, work experience. **Freshman Admission Requirements:** High school diploma is required, and GED is accepted. *Academic units recommended:* 4 English, 3 math, 3 science, 2 foreign language, 2 social studies, 1 history. **Freshman Admission Statistics:** 892 applied, 94% admitted, 29% enrolled. **Transfer Admission Requirements:** High school transcript, college transcript(s), statement of good standing from prior institution(s). Minimum college GPA of 2.0 required. Lowest grade transferable C. **General Admission Information:** Application fee $20. Regular notification is rolling. Nonfall registration accepted. Admission may be deferred for a maximum of 1 year. Credit offered for CEEB Advanced Placement tests.

COSTS AND FINANCIAL AID

Annual tuition $11,235. Room & board $4,620. Required fees $100. Average book expense $1,000. **Required Forms and Deadlines:** FAFSA. Financial aid filing deadline 3/1. **Notification of Awards:** Applicants will be notified of awards on a rolling basis beginning on or about 2/1. **Types of Aid:** *Need-based scholarships/grants:* Pell, SEOG, state scholarships/grants, private scholarships, the school's own gift aid, Federal Nursing Scholarships. *Loans:* FFEL Subsidized Stafford, FFEL Unsubsidized Stafford, FFEL PLUS, Federal Perkins, college/university loans from institutional funds, alternative loans (private). **Student Employment:** Federal Work-Study Program available. Institutional employment available. Off-campus job opportunities are good. **Financial Aid Statistics:** 87% freshmen, 83% undergrads receive need-based scholarship or grant aid. 56% freshmen, 60% undergrads receive need-based self-help aid. 41 freshmen, 94 undergrads receive athletic scholarships. 99% freshmen, 99% undergrads receive any aid. Highest amount earned per year from on-campus jobs $2,865.

JARVIS CHRISTIAN COLLEGE

PO Box 1470, Hawkins, TX 75765-1470
Phone: 903-769-5730 **E-mail:** felecia_tyiska@jarvis.edu
Fax: 903-769-1282 **Website:** www.jarvis.edu **ACT Code:** 4110
Financial Aid Phone: 903-769-5740

This private school, affiliated with the Disciples of Christ Church, was founded in 1912. It has a 243-acre campus.

RATINGS
Admissions Selectivity Rating: 61   **Fire Safety Rating:** 83   **Green Rating:** 60*

STUDENTS AND FACULTY
Enrollment: 602. **Student Body:** 50% female, 50% male, 16% out-of-state. Hispanic 3%. **Retention and Graduation:** 43% freshmen return for sophomore year. 18% freshmen graduate within 4 years. 3% grads go on to further study within 1 year. 2% grads pursue business degrees. 1% grads pursue law degrees. **Faculty:** Student/faculty ratio 16:1. 32 full-time faculty, 44% hold PhDs. 100% faculty teach undergrads.

ACADEMICS
Degrees: Bachelor's. **Academic Requirements:** Arts/fine arts, computer literacy, English (including composition), foreign languages, history, humanities, mathematics, sciences (biological or physical), social science. **Classes:** Most classes have 10–19 students. Most lab/discussion sections have 20–29 students. **Majors with Highest Enrollment:** Biology/biological sciences, computer and information sciences, criminal justice/law enforcement administration. **Disciplines with Highest Percentage of Degrees Awarded:** Business/marketing 37%, computer and information sciences 14%, health professions and related sciences 14%, education 9%, history 9%, interdisciplinary studies 5%, visual and performing arts 1%. **Special Study Options:** Cooperative

education program, cross-registration, distance learning, double major, dual enrollment, honors program, internships, liberal arts/career combination, student-designed major, study abroad, teacher certification program.

FACILITIES
Housing: Men's dorms, women's dorms, apartments for married students, apartments for single students, special housing for disabled students. **Special Academic Facilities/Equipment:** Archives. **Computers:** 40% of public computers are PCs, network access in dorm rooms, network access in dorm lounges, remote student-access to Web through college's connection.

CAMPUS LIFE
Activities: Choral groups, drama/theater, music ensembles, student government, yearbook. **Organizations:** 33 registered organizations, 3 honor societies, 5 religious organizations. 4 fraternities (5% men join), 4 sororities (10% women join). **Athletics (Intercollegiate):** *Men:* Baseball, basketball, cheerleading, track/field (outdoor). *Women:* Basketball, cheerleading, track/field (outdoor), volleyball.

ADMISSIONS
Freshman Academic Profile: 3% in top 10% of high school class, 7% in top 25% of high school class, 55% in top 50% of high school class. 99% from public high schools. Annual tuition $7,200. Room and board $4,810. Required fees $770. Average book expense $800. TOEFL required of all international applicants, minimum paper TOEFL 500, minimum computer TOEFL 173. **Basis for Candidate Selection:** *Other factors considered include:* Academic GPA, character/personal qualities, class rank, extracurricular activities, rigor of secondary school record, standardized test scores, talent/ability. **Freshman Admission Requirements:** High school diploma is required, and GED is accepted. *Academic units required:* 3 English, 2 math, 1 science, 3 social studies, 7 academic electives. *Academic units recommended:* 3 English, 2 math, 1 science, 3 social studies, 7 academic electives. **Freshman Admission Statistics:** 398 applied, 59% admitted, 48% enrolled. **Transfer Admission Requirements:** High school transcript, college transcript(s), standardized test score. **General Admission Information:** Application fee $25. Regular application deadline 1/15. Regular notification is rolling. Nonfall registration accepted. Admission may be deferred for a maximum of 1 year. Neither credit nor placement offered for CEEB Advanced Placement tests.

COSTS AND FINANCIAL AID
Annual tuition $7,200. Room & board $4,810. Required fees $770. Average book expense $800. **Required Forms and Deadlines:** FAFSA, institution's own financial aid form. Financial aid filing deadline 5/1. **Notification of Awards:** Applicants will be notified of awards on or about 6/30. **Types of Aid:** *Need-based scholarships/grants:* Pell, SEOG, state scholarships/grants, private scholarships, the school's own gift aid, United Negro College Fund. *Loans:* FFEL Subsidized Stafford, FFEL Unsubsidized Stafford, FFEL PLUS, Federal Perkins, UNCF Institutional. **Student Employment:** Federal Work-Study Program available. Institutional employment available. Off-campus job opportunities are fair. **Financial Aid Statistics:** 78% freshmen, 89% undergrads receive need-based scholarship or grant aid. 81% freshmen, 91% undergrads receive need-based self-help aid. 8 freshmen, 32 undergrads receive athletic scholarships. 98% freshmen, 98% undergrads receive any aid. Highest amount earned per year from on-campus jobs $1,729.

JEWISH THEOLOGICAL SEMINARY— ALBERT A. LIST COLLEGE

3080 Broadway, Box 32, New York, NY 10027
Phone: 212-678-8832 **E-mail:** lcadmissions@jtsa.edu **CEEB Code:** 2339
Fax: 212-678-8947 **Website:** www.jtsa.edu **ACT Code:** 2776
Financial Aid Phone: 212-678-8007

This private school, affiliated with the Jewish synagogue, was founded in 1886. It has a 1-acre campus.

RATINGS
Admissions Selectivity Rating: 60*   **Fire Safety Rating:** 60*   **Green Rating:** 60*

STUDENTS AND FACULTY
Enrollment: 186. **Student Body:** 61% female, 39% male, 75% out-of-state. **Retention and Graduation:** 95% freshmen return for sophomore year. **Faculty:** Student/faculty ratio 6:1. 59 full-time faculty, 100% hold PhDs. 70% faculty teach undergrads.

ACADEMICS
Degrees: Bachelor's, doctoral, first professional, master's. **Academic**

Requirements: Arts/fine arts, English (including composition), foreign languages, history, humanities, mathematics, philosophy, sciences (biological or physical), social science. **Majors with Highest Enrollment:** Bible/biblical studies, Jewish/Judaic studies, philosophy and religion. **Special Study Options:** Accelerated program, cross-registration, distance learning, dual enrollment, honors program, independent study, internships, student-designed major, study abroad.

FACILITIES

Housing: Coed dorms, apartments for married students, apartments for single students. **Special Academic Facilities/Equipment:** The Jewish Museum, rare book room of the library. **Computers:** 100% of public computers are PCs, network access in dorm rooms, remote student-access to Web through college's connection.

CAMPUS LIFE

Activities: Choral groups, concert band, dance, drama/theater, jazz band, literary magazine, music ensembles, musical theater, radio station, student government, student newspaper, yearbook. **Organizations:** 6 honor societies, 8 religious organizations. **Athletics (Intercollegiate):** *Men:* Baseball, basketball, crew/rowing, soccer, tennis, track/field (outdoor), volleyball. *Women:* Baseball, basketball, crew/rowing, soccer, tennis, track/field (outdoor), volleyball.

ADMISSIONS

Freshman Academic Profile: 76% from public high schools. SAT Math middle 50% range 630–690. SAT Critical Reading middle 50% range 650–730. SAT Writing middle 50% range 630–730. ACT middle 50% range 29–31. TOEFL required of all international applicants, minimum paper TOEFL 600. **Basis for Candidate Selection:** *Very important factors considered include:* Application essay, interview, rigor of secondary school record, standardized test scores. *Important factors considered include:* Character/personal qualities, recommendation(s), talent/ability. *Other factors considered include:* Alumni/ae relation, class rank, extracurricular activities, geographical residence, volunteer work, work experience. **Freshman Admission Requirements:** High school diploma is required, and GED is accepted. *Academic units recommended:* 4 English, 3 math, 3 science, 3 foreign language, 3 social studies, 3 history, 3 academic electives. **Freshman Admission Statistics:** 118 applied, 63% admitted, 62% enrolled. **Transfer Admission Requirements:** High school transcript, college transcript(s), essay or personal statement, standardized test score, statement of good standing from prior institution(s). **General Admission Information:** Application fee $65. Early decision application deadline 11/15. Regular application deadline 2/15. Regular notification 4/1. Nonfall registration accepted. Admission may be deferred for a maximum of 1 year. Common Application accepted. Credit and/or placement offered for CEEB Advanced Placement tests.

COSTS AND FINANCIAL AID

Annual tuition $14,200. Room and board $8,630. Required fees $800. **Required Forms and Deadlines:** FAFSA, institution's own financial aid form, CSS/Financial Aid PROFILE. Financial aid filing deadline 3/1. **Notification of Awards:** Applicants will be notified of awards on a rolling basis beginning on or about 3/15. **Types of Aid:** *Loans:* Direct Subsidized Stafford, Direct Unsubsidized Stafford, college/university loans from institutional funds. We meet 100% of a student's demonstrated need; we do this through a minimal amount of loans. **Student Employment:** Federal Work-Study Program available. Institutional employment available. Off-campus job opportunities are excellent.

JOHN BROWN UNIVERSITY

2000 West University Street, Siloam Springs, AR 72761
Phone: 877-528-4636 **E-mail:** jbuinfo@jbu.edu **CEEB Code:** 6321
Fax: 479-524-4196 **Website:** www.jbu.edu **ACT Code:** 0130
Financial Aid Phone: 479-524-7424

This private school, affiliated with the Interdenominational Church, was founded in 1919. It has a 200-acre campus.

RATINGS
Admissions Selectivity Rating: 88   **Fire Safety Rating:** 66   **Green Rating:** 60*

STUDENTS AND FACULTY
Enrollment: 1,647. **Student Body:** 51% female, 49% male, 73% out-of-state, 6% international (45 countries represented). African American 2%, Caucasian 85%, Hispanic 3%, Native American 2%. **Retention and Graduation:** 80% freshmen return for sophomore year. 50% freshmen graduate within 4 years. 28% grads go on to further study within 1 year. **Faculty:** Student/faculty ratio 13:1. 80 full-time faculty, 74% hold PhDs. 90% faculty teach undergrads.

ACADEMICS

Degrees: Bachelor's, master's. **Academic Requirements:** Arts/fine arts, biblical studies, computer literacy, English (including composition), history, humanities, mathematics, philosophy, sciences (biological or physical), social science. **Classes:** Most classes have 10–19 students. Most lab/discussion sections have 10–19 students. **Majors with Highest Enrollment:** Business administration and management, digital communications and media/multimedia, graphic design. **Disciplines with Highest Percentage of Degrees Awarded:** Business/marketing 52%, communications/journalism 7%, communication technologies 7%, theology and religious vocations 7%, education 6%, family and consumer sciences 5%. **Special Study Options:** Accelerated program, distance learning, double major, dual enrollment, English as a second language (ESL), exchange student program (domestic), honors program, independent study, internships, study abroad, teacher certification program.

FACILITIES

Housing: Coed dorms, men's dorms, women's dorms, apartments for married students, apartments for single students. **Special Academic Facilities/Equipment:** Art gallery, human anatomy lab, TV studio, radio station, Outdoor Learning Center, Center for Relationship Enrichment, Soderquist Center for Business and Ethics. **Computers:** 2% of classrooms are wired, 20% of classrooms are wireless, 90% of public computers are PCs, 10% of public computers are Macs, network access in dorm rooms, network access in dorm lounges, online registration, online administrative functions (other than registration), support for handheld computing, remote student-access to Web through college's connection.

CAMPUS LIFE

Activities: Choral groups, drama/theater, music ensembles, musical theater, opera, pep band, radio station, student government, student newspaper, yearbook. **Organizations:** 20 registered organizations, 3 honor societies. **Athletics (Intercollegiate):** *Men:* Basketball, soccer, tennis. *Women:* Basketball, diving, soccer, swimming, tennis, volleyball.

ADMISSIONS

Freshman Academic Profile: 38% in top 10% of high school class, 67% in top 25% of high school class, 91% in top 50% of high school class. 65% from public high schools. SAT Math middle 50% range 510–650. SAT Critical Reading middle 50% range 500–650. ACT middle 50% range 21–28. TOEFL required of all international applicants, minimum paper TOEFL 550, minimum computer TOEFL 173. **Basis for Candidate Selection:** *Very important factors considered include:* Academic GPA, recommendation(s), rigor of secondary school record, standardized test scores. *Important factors considered include:* Application essay, character/personal qualities, interview, religious affiliation/commitment. *Other factors considered include:* Alumni/ae relation, class rank, extracurricular activities, talent/ability. **Freshman Admission Requirements:** High school diploma is required, and GED is accepted. *Academic units recommended:* 4 English, 3 math, 2 science (1 science lab), 2 foreign language, 2 social studies, 1 history. **Freshman Admission Statistics:** 891 applied, 76% admitted, 48% enrolled. **Transfer Admission Requirements:** High school transcript, college transcript(s), essay or personal statement. Minimum college GPA of 2.5 required. Lowest grade transferable C. **General Admission Information:** Application fee $25. Regular notification is rolling. Nonfall registration accepted. Admission may be deferred for a maximum of 1 year. Neither credit nor placement offered for CEEB Advanced Placement tests.

COSTS AND FINANCIAL AID

Annual tuition $15,412. Room and board $5,956. Required fees $746. Average book expense $600. **Required Forms and Deadlines:** FAFSA, institution's own financial aid form. Financial aid filing deadline 3/1. **Notification of Awards:** Applicants will be notified of awards on or about 3/1. **Types of Aid:** *Need-based scholarships/grants:* SEOG, state scholarships/grants, private scholarships, the school's own gift aid. *Loans:* FFEL Subsidized Stafford, FFEL Unsubsidized Stafford, FFEL PLUS, Federal Perkins, state loans. **Student Employment:** Federal Work-Study Program available. Institutional employment available. Off-campus job opportunities are fair. **Financial Aid Statistics:** 57% freshmen, 46% undergrads receive need-based scholarship or grant aid. 55% freshmen, 28% undergrads receive need-based self-help aid. 27 freshmen, 102 undergrads receive athletic scholarships. 90% freshmen, 87% undergrads receive any aid. Highest amount earned per year from on-campus jobs $1,415.

JOHN CARROLL UNIVERSITY

20700 North Park Boulevard, University Heights, OH 44118-4581
Phone: 216-397-4294 **E-mail:** admission@jcu.edu **CEEB Code:** 1342
Fax: 216-397-3098 **Website:** www.jcu.edu **ACT Code:** 3282
Financial Aid Phone: 216-397-4248

This private school, affiliated with the Roman Catholic Church, was founded in 1886. It has a 60-acre campus.

RATINGS
Admissions Selectivity Rating: 81　　　　**Fire Safety Rating:** 60*　　　　**Green Rating:** 60*

STUDENTS AND FACULTY
Enrollment: 3,091. **Student Body:** 53% female, 47% male, 27% out-of-state. African American 4%, Asian 2%, Caucasian 86%, Hispanic 2%. **Retention and Graduation:** 81% freshmen return for sophomore year. **Faculty:** Student/faculty ratio 14:1. 206 full-time faculty, 95% hold PhDs.

ACADEMICS
Degrees: Bachelor's, master's, post-bachelor's certificate. **Academic Requirements:** English (including composition), foreign languages, history, humanities, mathematics, philosophy, religious studies, sciences (biological or physical), single-theme academic first-year seminar, social science. **Classes:** Most classes have 20–29 students. Most lab/discussion sections have 10–19 students. **Special Study Options:** Accelerated program, cooperative education program, cross-registration, double major, dual enrollment, exchange student program (domestic), honors program, independent study, internships, liberal arts/career combination, student-designed major, study abroad, teacher certification program. Undergrads may take grad-level classes.

FACILITIES
Housing: Coed dorms, men's dorms, women's dorms, suite-style housing, homes in neighborhood owned by university and rented to students. **Special Academic Facilities/Equipment:** International Studies Center, closed-circuit TV studio, broadcast archives. **Computers:** 100% of classrooms are wireless, network access in dorm rooms, network access in dorm lounges, online registration, online administrative functions (other than registration), remote student-access to Web through college's connection.

CAMPUS LIFE
Activities: Choral groups, concert band, dance, drama/theater, jazz band, literary magazine, music ensembles, musical theater, pep band, radio station, student government, student newspaper, television station, yearbook. **Organizations:** 68 registered organizations, 3 fraternities (10% men join), 5 sororities (12% women join). **Athletics (Intercollegiate):** *Men:* Baseball, basketball, cross-country, diving, football, golf, sailing, soccer, swimming, tennis, track/field (indoor), track/field (outdoor), wrestling. *Women:* Basketball, cheerleading, cross-country, diving, golf, sailing, soccer, softball, swimming, tennis, track/field (indoor), track/field (outdoor), volleyball.

ADMISSIONS
Freshman Academic Profile: 27% in top 10% of high school class, 55% in top 25% of high school class, 86% in top 50% of high school class. 53% from public high schools. SAT Math middle 50% range 520–630. SAT Critical Reading middle 50% range 520–600. SAT Writing middle 50% range 490–600. ACT middle 50% range 21–25. TOEFL required of all international applicants, minimum paper TOEFL 550, minimum computer TOEFL 213. **Basis for Candidate Selection:** *Very important factors considered include:* Academic GPA, rigor of secondary school record. *Important factors considered include:* Application essay, character/personal qualities, extracurricular activities, recommendation(s), standardized test scores. *Other factors considered include:* Alumni/ae relation, class rank, first generation, interview, level of applicant's interest, talent/ability, volunteer work, work experience. **Freshman Admission Requirements:** High school diploma is required, and GED is accepted. *Academic units required:* 4 English, 3 math, 2 science (2 science labs), 2 foreign language, 2 social studies, 2 history, 3 academic electives. *Academic units recommended:* 4 English, 4 math, 3 science (3 science labs), 3 foreign language, 2 social studies, 2 history. **Freshman Admission Statistics:** 3,213 applied, 82% admitted, 27% enrolled. **Transfer Admission Requirements:** High school transcript, college transcript(s), standardized test score. Minimum college GPA of 2.0 required. **General Admission Information:** Application fee $25. Regular application deadline 2/1. Regular notification is rolling. Nonfall registration accepted. Admission may be deferred for a maximum of 1 year. Credit and/or placement offered for CEEB Advanced Placement tests.

COSTS AND FINANCIAL AID
Annual tuition $24,782. Room & board $7,790. Required fees $290. Average book expense $1,200. **Required Forms and Deadlines:** FAFSA. Financial aid filing deadline 3/1. **Notification of Awards:** Applicants will be notified of awards on a rolling basis beginning on or about 2/1. **Types of Aid:** *Need-based scholarships/grants:* Pell, SEOG, state scholarships/grants, private scholarships, the school's own gift aid, Federal ACG and SMART Grants. *Loans:* FFEL Subsidized Stafford, FFEL Unsubsidized Stafford, FFEL PLUS, Federal Perkins. **Student Employment:** Federal Work-Study Program available. Institutional employment available. Off-campus job opportunities are good. **Financial Aid Statistics:** 63% freshmen, 63% undergrads receive need-based scholarship or grant aid. 52% freshmen, 63% undergrads receive need-based self-help aid.

JOHN F. KENNEDY UNIVERSITY

12 Altarinda Road, Orinda, CA 94563
Phone: 925-258-2213 **E-mail:** proginfo@jfku.edu **CEEB Code:** 4365
Fax: 925-254-6964 **Website:** www.jfku.edu **ACT Code:** 0291
Financial Aid Phone: 925-258-2385

This private school was founded in 1964. It has a 10-acre campus.

RATINGS
Admissions Selectivity Rating: 60*　　　**Fire Safety Rating:** 60*　　　**Green Rating:** 60*

STUDENTS AND FACULTY
Enrollment: 166. **Student Body:** 81% female, 19% male. **Faculty:** Student/faculty ratio 12:1. 33 full-time faculty, 61% hold PhDs.

ACADEMICS
Degrees: Bachelor's, certificate, doctoral, first professional, master's. **Academic Requirements:** English (including composition), humanities, mathematics, sciences (biological or physical), social science. **Classes:** Most classes have 10–19 students. **Disciplines with Highest Percentage of Degrees Awarded:** Liberal arts/general studies 64%, business/marketing 22%, psychology 9%. **Special Study Options:** Independent study, internships, student-designed major, weekend college.

CAMPUS LIFE
Activities: Student government, student newspaper.

ADMISSIONS
Freshman Academic Profile: TOEFL required of all international applicants, minimum paper TOEFL 550, minimum computer TOEFL 213. **Transfer Admission Requirements:** High school transcript, college transcript(s), essay or personal statement, interview, statement of good standing from prior institution(s). **General Admission Information:** Application fee $50. Regular notification rolling. Nonfall registration not accepted. Admission may be deferred for a maximum of 1 year. Common Application not accepted. Credit offered for CEEB Advanced Placement tests.

COSTS AND FINANCIAL AID
Annual tuition $8,568. Required fees $27. **Required Forms and Deadlines:** FAFSA. **Types of Aid:** *Need-based scholarships/grants:* Pell, SEOG, state scholarships/grants, private scholarships, the school's own gift aid. *Loans:* FFEL Subsidized Stafford, FFEL Unsubsidized Stafford, FFEL PLUS, Federal Perkins, college/university loans from institutional funds. **Student Employment:** Off-campus job opportunities are fair. **Financial Aid Statistics:** 8% undergrads receive need-based scholarship or grant aid. 59% undergrads receive need-based self-help aid.

JOHNS HOPKINS UNIVERSITY

Best 368

3400 North Charles Street, 140 Garland Hall, Baltimore, MD 21218
Phone: 410-516-8171 **E-mail:** gotojhu@jhu.edu **CEEB Code:** 5332
Fax: 410-516-6025 **Website:** www.jhu.edu
Financial Aid Phone: 410-516-8028

This private school was founded in 1876. It has a 140-acre campus.

RATINGS
Admissions Selectivity Rating: 98   **Fire Safety Rating:** 70   **Green Rating:** 60*

STUDENTS AND FACULTY
Enrollment: 4,429. **Student Body:** 47% female, 53% male, 86% out-of-state, 5% international (71 countries represented). African American 6%, Asian 22%, Caucasian 61%, Hispanic 6%. **Retention and Graduation:** 97% freshmen return for sophomore year. 83% freshmen graduate within 4 years. 41% grads go on to further study within 1 year. 19% grads pursue arts and sciences degrees. 1% grads pursue business degrees. 5% grads pursue law degrees. 11% grads pursue medical degrees. **Faculty:** Student/faculty ratio 9:1. 451 full-time faculty, 94% hold PhDs. 96% faculty teach undergrads.

ACADEMICS
Degrees: Bachelor's, certificate, diploma, doctoral, first professional, master's, post-bachelor's certificate, post-master's certificate. **Academic Requirements:** English (including composition), humanities, mathematics, sciences (biological or physical), social science. A required core curriculum does not exist at Hopkins. Instead, students complete at least 30 credits in academic areas outside their major. **Classes:** Most classes have 10–19 students. Most lab/discussion sections have 10–19 students. **Majors with Highest Enrollment:** Biomedical/medical engineering, economics, international relations and affairs. **Disciplines with Highest Percentage of Degrees Awarded:** Health professions and related sciences 24%, social sciences 17%, engineering 15%, biological/life sciences 7%, interdisciplinary studies 6%. **Special Study Options:** Cross-registration, double major, dual enrollment, honors programs offered within various departments, independent study, internships, student-designed major, study abroad, 21 combined bachelor's/master's programs.

FACILITIES
Housing: Coed dorms, men's dorms, women's dorms, apartments for single students, special housing for disabled students, fraternity/sorority housing, substance-free floors, vacation housing floors available, available space for disabled students. **Special Academic Facilities/Equipment:** Baltimore Museum of Art, on-campus digital media center, art gallery, electron microscope, Space Telescope Science Institute, 4 major research centers. **Computers:** 15% of classrooms are wired, 100% of classrooms are wireless, network access in dorm rooms, network access in dorm lounges, online registration, online administrative functions (other than registration), support for handheld computing, remote student-access to Web through college's connection.

CAMPUS LIFE
Activities: Choral groups, concert band, dance, drama/theater, jazz band, literary magazine, music ensembles, musical theater, pep band, radio station, student government, student newspaper, student-run film society, symphony orchestra, yearbook. **Organizations:** 250 registered organizations, 17 honor societies, 20 religious organizations. 11 fraternities (21% men join), 7 sororities (22% women join). **Athletics (Intercollegiate):** *Men:* Baseball, basketball, crew/rowing, cross-country, diving, fencing, football, lacrosse, soccer, swimming, tennis, track/field (indoor), track/field (outdoor), water polo, wrestling. *Women:* Basketball, crew/rowing, cross-country, diving, fencing, field hockey, lacrosse, soccer, swimming, tennis, track/field (indoor), track/field (outdoor), volleyball.

ADMISSIONS
Freshman Academic Profile: 80% in top 10% of high school class, 95% in top 25% of high school class, 100% in top 50% of high school class. 69% from public high schools. SAT Math middle 50% range 660–770. SAT Critical Reading middle 50% range 630–730. SAT Writing middle 50% range 630–730. ACT middle 50% range 28–33. TOEFL required of all international applicants, minimum paper TOEFL 600, minimum computer TOEFL 250. **Basis for Candidate Selection:** *Very important factors considered include:* Academic GPA, character/personal qualities, recommendation(s), rigor of secondary school record. *Important factors considered include:* Application essay, class rank, extracurricular activities, standardized test scores, talent/ability, volunteer work, work experience. *Other factors considered include:* Alumni/ae relation, first generation, geographical residence, interview, racial/ethnic status, state residency. **Freshman Admission Requirements:** High school diploma or equivalent is not required. *Academic units recommended:* 4 English, 4 math, 4 science, 4 foreign language, 2 social studies, 2 history, 2 foreign language for engineering majors. **Freshman Admission Statistics:** 13,900 applied, 27% admitted, 32% enrolled. **Transfer Admission Requirements:** High school transcript, college transcript(s), essay or personal statement, statement of good standing from prior institution(s). Minimum college GPA of 3.0 required. Lowest grade transferable C. **General Admission Information:** Application fee $60. Early decision application deadline 11/1. Regular application deadline 1/1. Regular notification 4/1. Nonfall registration not accepted. Admission may be deferred for a maximum of 2 years. Credit offered for CEEB Advanced Placement tests.

COSTS AND FINANCIAL AID
Annual tuition $33,900. Room & board $10,622. Required fees $500. Average book expense $1,000. **Required Forms and Deadlines:** FAFSA, CSS/Financial Aid PROFILE, Noncustodial PROFILE, Business/Farm Supplement, prior and current year federal tax returns. Financial aid filing deadline 2/1. **Notification of Awards:** Applicants will be notified of awards on or about 4/1. **Types of Aid:** *Need-based scholarships/grants:* Pell, SEOG, state scholarships/grants, private scholarships, the school's own gift aid. *Loans:* Direct Subsidized Stafford, Direct Unsubsidized Stafford, FFEL PLUS, Federal Perkins, college/university loans from institutional funds. **Student Employment:** Federal Work-Study Program available. Institutional employment available. **Financial Aid Statistics:** 42% freshmen, 40% undergrads receive need-based scholarship or grant aid. 47% freshmen, 42% undergrads receive need-based self-help aid. 7 freshmen, 30 undergrads receive athletic scholarships. 47% freshmen, 45% undergrads receive any aid.

See page 1210.

JOHNSON & WALES UNIVERSITY

8 Abbott Park Place, Providence, RI 02903-3703
Phone: 401-598-2310 **E-mail:** admissions.pvd@jwu.edu
Fax: 401-598-2948 **Website:** www.jwu.edu **ACT Code:** 3804
Financial Aid Phone: 800-342-5598

This private school was founded in 1914. It has a 50-acre campus.

RATINGS
Admissions Selectivity Rating: 60*   **Fire Safety Rating:** 60*   **Green Rating:** 60*

STUDENTS AND FACULTY
Enrollment: 9,066. **Student Body:** 52% female, 48% male, 69% out-of-state, 3% international. African American 8%, Asian 3%, Caucasian 62%, Hispanic 7%. **Retention and Graduation:** 69% freshmen return for sophomore year. **Faculty:** Student/faculty ratio 27:1. 282 full-time faculty.

ACADEMICS
Degrees: Associate, bachelor's, certificate, doctoral, master's. **Academic Requirements:** Computer literacy, English (including composition), history, mathematics, philosophy, sciences (biological or physical), social science. **Classes:** Most classes have 30–39 students. Most lab/discussion sections have 10–19 students. **Disciplines with Highest Percentage of Degrees Awarded:** Business/marketing 46%, personal and culinary services 15%, family and consumer sciences 15%, computer and information sciences 6%, parks and recreation 6%, security and protective services 4%, communications/journalism 4%, agriculture 1%. **Special Study Options:** Accelerated program, cooperative education program, English as a second language (ESL), exchange student program (domestic), external degree program, honors program, independent study, study abroad, weekend college.

FACILITIES
Housing: Coed dorms, special housing for disabled students. **Special Academic Facilities/Equipment:** Culinary Archives and Museum. **Computers:** Network access in dorm rooms, online registration, online administrative functions (other than registration), remote student-access to Web through college's connection.

CAMPUS LIFE
Activities: Choral groups, dance, drama/theater, pep band, student government, student newspaper, yearbook. **Athletics (Intercollegiate):** *Men:* Baseball, basketball, cheerleading, cross-country, equestrian sports, golf, ice hockey, soccer, tennis, volleyball, wrestling. *Women:* Basketball, cheerleading, cross-country, equestrian sports, golf, ice hockey, soccer, softball, tennis, volleyball.

ADMISSIONS

Basis for Candidate Selection: *Very important factors considered include:* Class rank, interview, rigor of secondary school record. *Important factors considered include:* Extracurricular activities, work experience. *Other factors considered include:* Academic GPA, level of applicant's interest, recommendation(s), standardized test scores, volunteer work. **Freshman Admission Requirements:** High school diploma is required, and GED is accepted. *Academic units recommended:* 4 English, 3 math, 3 science, 2 social studies. **Freshman Admission Statistics:** 15,921 applied, 81% admitted, 23% enrolled. **Transfer Admission Requirements:** High school transcript, college transcript(s). Minimum college GPA of 2.0 required. Lowest grade transferable C. **General Admission Information:** Regular notification is rolling. Nonfall registration accepted. Admission may be deferred for a maximum of 1 year.

COSTS AND FINANCIAL AID

Annual tuition $21,297. Room and board $8,892. Required fees $1,023. Average book expense $1,000. **Required Forms and Deadlines:** FAFSA. **Notification of Awards:** Applicants will be notified of awards on a rolling basis beginning on or about 3/1. **Types of Aid:** *Need-based scholarships/grants:* Pell, SEOG, state scholarships/grants, private scholarships, the school's own gift aid. *Loans:* FFEL Subsidized Stafford, FFEL Unsubsidized Stafford, FFEL PLUS, Federal Perkins, state loans, college/university loans from institutional funds. **Financial Aid Statistics:** 70% freshmen, 54% undergrads receive need-based scholarship or grant aid. 73% freshmen, 62% undergrads receive need-based self-help aid.

See page 1212.

JOHNSON & WALES UNIVERSITY
AT CHARLESTON

701 East Bay Street, Charleston, SC 29403
Phone: 843-727-3000 **E-mail:** admissions@jwu.edu
Fax: 843-763-0318 **Website:** www.jwu.edu
Financial Aid Phone: 800-342-5598

This private school was founded in 1914. It has a 47-acre campus.

RATINGS
Admissions Selectivity Rating: 60*　　**Fire Safety Rating:** 60*　　**Green Rating:** 60*

STUDENTS AND FACULTY

Enrollment: 1,497. **Student Body:** 46% female, 54% male. African American 8%, Caucasian 75%, Hispanic 1%, Native American 1%. **Faculty:** Student/faculty ratio 29:1. 45 full-time faculty, 9% hold PhDs. 100% faculty teach undergrads.

ACADEMICS

Degrees: Associate, bachelor's. **Academic Requirements:** English (including composition), mathematics, professional development, sciences (biological or physical). **Special Study Options:** Accelerated program, cooperative education program, honors program, independent study, internships, study abroad.

FACILITIES

Housing: Coed dorms, apartments for single students. **Computers:** Remote student-access to Web through college's connection.

CAMPUS LIFE

Activities: Choral groups, drama/theater, literary magazine, student government, yearbook.

ADMISSIONS

Freshman Academic Profile: 96% from public high schools. TOEFL required of all international applicants, minimum paper TOEFL 550. **Basis for Candidate Selection:** *Very important factors considered include:* Rigor of secondary school record. *Other factors considered include:* Class rank, extracurricular activities, interview, recommendation(s), standardized test scores. **Freshman Admission Requirements:** High school diploma is required, and GED is accepted. *Academic units recommended:* 4 English, 3 math, 2 science, 1 social studies. **Freshman Admission Statistics:** 1,479 applied, 74% admitted, 33% enrolled. **Transfer Admission Requirements:** High school transcript, college transcript(s). Minimum college GPA of 2.0 required. Lowest grade transferable C. **General Admission Information:** Regular notification is rolling. Nonfall registration accepted. Admission may be deferred for a maximum of 1 year. Common Application accepted.

COSTS AND FINANCIAL AID

Annual tuition $15,222. Room & board $4,860. Required fees $750. Average

book expense $750. **Required Forms and Deadlines:** FAFSA. **Notification of Awards:** Applicants will be notified of awards on a rolling basis beginning on or about 3/1. **Types of Aid:** *Need-based scholarships/grants:* Pell, SEOG, state scholarships/grants, the school's own gift aid. *Loans:* FFEL Subsidized Stafford, FFEL Unsubsidized Stafford, FFEL PLUS, Federal Perkins, college/university loans from institutional funds. **Student Employment:** Federal Work-Study Program available. Off-campus job opportunities are good. **Financial Aid Statistics:** 63% freshmen, 52% undergrads receive need-based scholarship or grant aid. 72% freshmen, 64% undergrads receive need-based self-help aid.

JOHNSON & WALES UNIVERSITY
AT CHARLOTTE

801 West Trade Street, Charlotte, NC 28202
Phone: 980-598-1000 **E-mail:** admissions.clt@jwu.edu
Fax: 980-598-1111 **Website:** www.jwu.edu

This is a private school.

RATINGS
Admissions Selectivity Rating: 60*　　**Fire Safety Rating:** 60*　　**Green Rating:** 60*

STUDENTS AND FACULTY

Enrollment: 2,488. **Student Body:** 53% female, 47% male, 68% out-of-state. African American 26%, Asian 2%, Caucasian 58%, Hispanic 3%. **Retention and Graduation:** 69% freshmen return for sophomore year. **Faculty:** Student/faculty ratio 27:1. 83 full-time faculty.

ACADEMICS

Degrees: Associate, bachelor's. **Academic Requirements:** English (including composition), mathematics, sciences (biological or physical). **Classes:** Most classes have 10–19 students. Most lab/discussion sections have 20–29 students. **Special Study Options:** Accelerated program, cooperative education program, honors program, independent study, study abroad.

FACILITIES

Housing: Coed dorms, special housing for disabled students.

CAMPUS LIFE

Activities: Choral groups, dance, student government, yearbook.

ADMISSIONS

Transfer Admission Requirements: High school transcript, college transcript(s). Lowest grade transferable C.

COSTS AND FINANCIAL AID

Annual tuition $21,297. Room and board $8,892. Required fees $265. Average book expense $1,000. **Required Forms and Deadlines:** FAFSA. **Notification of Awards:** Applicants will be notified of awards on a rolling basis beginning on or about 3/1. **Types of Aid:** *Need-based scholarships/grants:* Pell, SEOG, state scholarships/grants, private scholarships, the school's own gift aid. *Loans:* FFEL Subsidized Stafford, FFEL Unsubsidized Stafford, FFEL PLUS, Federal Perkins, state loans, college/university loans from institutional funds. **Financial Aid Statistics:** 77% freshmen, 62% undergrads receive need-based scholarship or grant aid. 79% freshmen, 69% undergrads receive need-based self-help aid.

JOHNSON & WALES UNIVERSITY—DENVER

7150 Montview Boulevard, Denver, CO 80220
Phone: 303-256-9300 **E-mail:** admissions.den@jwu.edu
Fax: 303-256-9333 **Website:** www.jwu.edu
Financial Aid Phone: 800-342-5598

This private school was founded in 1914.

RATINGS
Admissions Selectivity Rating: 60*　　**Fire Safety Rating:** 60*　　**Green Rating:** 60*

STUDENTS AND FACULTY

Enrollment: 1,539. **Student Body:** 52% female, 48% male, 56% out-of-state, 3% international. African American 5%, Asian 3%, Caucasian 62%, Hispanic

12%. **Retention and Graduation:** 61% freshmen return for sophomore year. **Faculty:** Student/faculty ratio 25:1. 49 full-time faculty.

ACADEMICS

Degrees: Associate, bachelor's. **Academic Requirements:** Computer literacy, English (including composition), history, mathematics, philosophy, sciences (biological or physical), social science. **Classes:** Most classes have 10–19 students. Most lab/discussion sections have 10–19 students. **Majors with Highest Enrollment:** Business administration/management, hotel/motel administration/management, restaurant/food services management. **Disciplines with Highest Percentage of Degrees Awarded:** Business/marketing 62%, family and consumer sciences 38%. **Special Study Options:** Cooperative education program, double major, honors program, independent study, internships, study abroad.

FACILITIES

Housing: Coed dorms.

CAMPUS LIFE

Activities: Choral groups, dance, literary magazine, student government, yearbook.

ADMISSIONS

Basis for Candidate Selection: *Very important factors considered include:* Class rank, interview, rigor of secondary school record. *Important factors considered include:* Extracurricular activities, work experience. *Other factors considered include:* Academic GPA, alumni/ae relation, recommendation(s), standardized test scores, volunteer work. **Freshman Admission Requirements:** High school diploma is required, and GED is accepted. *Academic units recommended:* 4 English, 3 math, 3 science, 2 social studies. **Freshman Admission Statistics:** 3,241 applied, 80% admitted, 20% enrolled. **Transfer Admission Requirements:** High school transcript, college transcript(s). Minimum college GPA of 2.0 required. Lowest grade transferable C. **General Admission Information:** Regular notification is rolling. Nonfall registration accepted.

COSTS AND FINANCIAL AID

Annual tuition $21,297. Room and board $7,956. Required fees $1,023. Average book expense $1,000. **Required Forms and Deadlines:** FAFSA. **Notification of Awards:** Applicants will be notified of awards on a rolling basis beginning on or about 3/1. **Types of Aid:** *Need-based scholarships/grants:* Pell, SEOG, state scholarships/grants, private scholarships, the school's own gift aid. *Loans:* FFEL Subsidized Stafford, FFEL Unsubsidized Stafford, FFEL PLUS, Federal Perkins, state loans, college/university loans from institutional funds. **Financial Aid Statistics:** 63% freshmen, 50% undergrads receive need-based scholarship or grant aid. 68% freshmen, 60% undergrads receive need-based self-help aid.

JOHNSON & WALES UNIVERSITY AT NORFOLK

2428 Almeda Avenue, Suite 316, Norfolk, VA 23513
Phone: 757-853-3508 **E-mail:** admissions@jwu.edu
Fax: 757-857-4869 **Website:** www.jwu.edu

This is a private school.

RATINGS

Admissions Selectivity Rating: 60*   **Fire Safety Rating:** 60*   **Green Rating:** 60*

STUDENTS AND FACULTY

Enrollment: 709. **Student Body:** African American 33%, Asian 2%, Caucasian 59%, Hispanic 5%. **Faculty:** Student/faculty ratio 26:1. 19 full-time faculty.

ACADEMICS

Degrees: Associate, certificate. **Academic Requirements:** Culinary arts, English (including composition), food service management, humanities, mathematics, sciences (biological or physical). **Special Study Options:** Accelerated program, cooperative education program, internships.

FACILITIES

Housing: Coed dorms, apartments for single students.

CAMPUS LIFE

Activities: Choral groups, student newspaper, yearbook.

ADMISSIONS

Freshman Academic Profile: 3% in top 10% of high school class, 11% in top 25% of high school class, 39% in top 50% of high school class. SAT Math middle 50% range 370–480. SAT Critical Reading middle 50% range 400–530. **Basis**

for Candidate Selection: *Very important factors considered include:* Rigor of secondary school record. *Other factors considered include:* Class rank, extracurricular activities, interview, recommendation(s), standardized test scores. **Freshman Admission Requirements:** High school diploma is required, and GED is accepted. *Academic units recommended:* 4 English, 3 math, 2 science, 1 social studies. **Freshman Admission Statistics:** 553 applied, 80% admitted, 40% enrolled. **Transfer Admission Requirements:** High school transcript, college transcript(s). Lowest grade transferable C. **General Admission Information:** Regular application deadline rolling. Regular notification is rolling. Nonfall registration accepted. Admission may be deferred for a maximum of 1 year. Common Application accepted.

COSTS AND FINANCIAL AID

Annual tuition $18,444. Room & board $6,621. Required fees $750. Average book expense $750. **Required Forms and Deadlines:** FAFSA. **Notification of Awards:** Applicants will be notified of awards on a rolling basis beginning on or about 3/1. **Types of Aid:** *Need-based scholarships/grants:* Pell, SEOG, state scholarships/grants, the school's own gift aid. *Loans:* FFEL Subsidized Stafford, FFEL Unsubsidized Stafford, FFEL PLUS, Federal Perkins, college/university loans from institutional funds. **Financial Aid Statistics:** 69% freshmen, 63% undergrads receive need-based scholarship or grant aid. 77% freshmen, 76% undergrads receive need-based self-help aid.

JOHNSON & WALES UNIVERSITY AT NORTH MIAMI

1701 NE 127th Street, North Miami, FL 33181
Phone: 305-892-7600 **E-mail:** admissions.mia@jwu.edu
Fax: 305-892-7020 **Website:** www.jwu.edu

This is a private school.

RATINGS

Admissions Selectivity Rating: 60*   **Fire Safety Rating:** 60*   **Green Rating:** 60*

STUDENTS AND FACULTY

Enrollment: 2,215. **Student Body:** 53% female, 47% male, 69% out-of-state, 7% international. African American 28%, Asian 1%, Caucasian 27%, Hispanic 20%. **Retention and Graduation:** 62% freshmen return for sophomore year. **Faculty:** Student/faculty ratio 30:1. 58 full-time faculty.

ACADEMICS

Degrees: Associate, bachelor's. **Academic Requirements:** Computer literacy, English (including composition), history, mathematics, philosophy, sciences (biological or physical), social science. **Classes:** Most classes have 10–19 students. Most lab/discussion sections have 10–19 students. **Disciplines with Highest Percentage of Degrees Awarded:** Business/marketing 45%, family and consumer sciences 26%, parks and recreation 15%, security and protective services 7%, personal and culinary services 7%. **Special Study Options:** Accelerated program, cooperative education program, honors program, independent study, internships, study abroad, weekend college.

FACILITIES

Housing: Coed dorms, special housing for disabled students.

CAMPUS LIFE

Activities: Dance, drama/theater, student government, student newspaper, yearbook.

ADMISSIONS

Basis for Candidate Selection: *Very important factors considered include:* Class rank, interview, rigor of secondary school record. *Important factors considered include:* Extracurricular activities, work experience. *Other factors considered include:* Academic GPA, alumni/ae relation, recommendation(s), standardized test scores, volunteer work. **Freshman Admission Requirements:** High school diploma is required, and GED is accepted. *Academic units recommended:* 4 English, 3 math, 3 science, 2 social studies. **Freshman Admission Statistics:** 7,255 applied, 76% admitted, 14% enrolled. **Transfer Admission Requirements:** High school transcript, college transcript(s). Minimum college GPA of 2.0 required. Lowest grade transferable C. **General Admission Information:** Regular notification is rolling. Nonfall registration accepted. Admission may be deferred for a maximum of 1 year.

COSTS AND FINANCIAL AID

Annual tuition $21,297. Room and board $7,956. Required fees $1,023. **Required Forms and Deadlines:** FAFSA. **Notification of Awards:** Applicants will be notified of awards on a rolling basis beginning on or about 3/

1. Types of Aid: *Need-based scholarships/grants:* Pell, SEOG, state scholarships/grants, private scholarships, the school's own gift aid. *Loans:* FFEL Subsidized Stafford, FFEL Unsubsidized Stafford, FFEL PLUS, Federal Perkins, state loans, college/university loans from institutional funds. **Financial Aid Statistics:** 73% freshmen, 67% undergrads receive need-based scholarship or grant aid. 75% freshmen, 70% undergrads receive need-based self-help aid.

JOHNSON BIBLE COLLEGE

7900 Johnson Drive, Knoxville, TN 37998
Phone: 800-827-2122 **E-mail:** jbc@jbc.edu **CEEB Code:** 1345
Fax: 865-251-2336 **Website:** www.jbc.edu **ACT Code:** 3968
Financial Aid Phone: 865-251-2303

This private school, affiliated with the Christian (Nondenominational) Church, was founded in 1893. It has a 350-acre campus.

RATINGS
Admissions Selectivity Rating: 77   **Fire Safety Rating:** 60*   **Green Rating:** 60*

STUDENTS AND FACULTY
Enrollment: 776. **Student Body:** 51% female, 49% male, 78% out-of-state, 2% international (12 countries represented). African American 2%, Asian 1%, Caucasian 94%, Hispanic 1%. **Retention and Graduation:** 78% freshmen return for sophomore year. 33% freshmen graduate within 4 years. **Faculty:** Student/faculty ratio 22:1. 27 full-time faculty, 63% hold PhDs. 99% faculty teach undergrads.

ACADEMICS
Degrees: Associate, bachelor's, certificate, master's. **Academic Requirements:** Computer literacy, English (including composition), foreign languages, history, humanities, mathematics, philosophy, sciences (biological or physical). **Classes:** Most classes have 20–29 students. Most lab/discussion sections have 20–29 students. **Disciplines with Highest Percentage of Degrees Awarded:** Education 13%. **Special Study Options:** Accelerated program, cooperative education program, distance learning, double major, English as a second language (ESL), honors program, independent study, internships, teacher certification program.

FACILITIES
Housing: Men's dorms, women's dorms, apartments for married students. **Computers:** Network access in dorm rooms, online registration, online administrative functions (other than registration), remote student-access to Web through college's connection.

CAMPUS LIFE
Activities: Choral groups, music ensembles, musical theater, radio station, student government, yearbook. **Organizations:** 3 honor societies, 3 religious organizations. **Athletics (Intercollegiate):** *Men:* Baseball, basketball, cheerleading, soccer. *Women:* Basketball, cheerleading, volleyball.

ADMISSIONS
Freshman Academic Profile: 20% in top 10% of high school class, 46% in top 25% of high school class, 77% in top 50% of high school class. SAT Math middle 50% range 470–563. SAT Critical Reading middle 50% range 470–580. ACT middle 50% range 20–24. TOEFL required of all international applicants, minimum paper TOEFL 500, minimum computer TOEFL 173. **Basis for Candidate Selection:** *Very important factors considered include:* Character/personal qualities, class rank, recommendation(s), religious affiliation/commitment, rigor of secondary school record, standardized test scores. *Important factors considered include:* Application essay, interview. *Other factors considered include:* Alumni/ae relation, extracurricular activities, talent/ability, volunteer work. **Freshman Admission Requirements:** High school diploma is required, and GED is accepted. **Freshman Admission Statistics:** 296 applied, 95% admitted, 57% enrolled. **Transfer Admission Requirements:** High school transcript, college transcript(s), essay or personal statement, statement of good standing from prior institution(s). Lowest grade transferable C. **General Admission Information:** Application fee $35. Regular application deadline 7/1. Regular notification 9/1. Nonfall registration accepted. Admission may be deferred for a maximum of 1 year. Common Application not accepted.

COSTS AND FINANCIAL AID
Annual tuition $6,200. Room & board $4,490. Required fees $730. Average book expense $1,085. **Required Forms and Deadlines:** FAFSA, institution's own financial aid form. Financial aid filing deadline 8/1. **Notification of Awards:** Applicants will be notified of awards on or about 4/30. **Types of Aid:** *Need-based scholarships/grants:* Pell, SEOG, state scholarships/grants, private scholarships, the school's own gift aid. *Loans:* FFEL Subsidized Stafford, FFEL

Unsubsidized Stafford, FFEL PLUS. **Student Employment:** Federal Work-Study Program available. Institutional employment available. **Financial Aid Statistics:** 83% freshmen, 84% undergrads receive need-based scholarship or grant aid. 57% freshmen, 48% undergrads receive need-based self-help aid. 97% undergrads receive any aid. Highest amount earned per year from on-campus jobs $1,240..

JOHNSON C. SMITH UNIVERSITY

100 Beatties Ford Road, Charlotte, NC 28216-5398
Phone: 704-378-1011 **E-mail:** admissions@jcsu.edu **CEEB Code:** 5333
Fax: 704-378-1242 **Website:** www.jcsu.edu **ACT Code:** 3112
Financial Aid Phone: 704-378-1034

This private school was founded in 1867. It has a 105-acre campus.

RATINGS
Admissions Selectivity Rating: 60*   **Fire Safety Rating:** 60*   **Green Rating:** 60*

STUDENTS AND FACULTY
Student Body: 72% out-of-state. **Retention and Graduation:** 20% grads go on to further study within 1 year. 10% grads pursue arts and sciences degrees. 5% grads pursue business degrees. 2% grads pursue law degrees. 3% grads pursue medical degrees.

ACADEMICS
Degrees: Bachelor's. **Special Study Options:** Cooperative education program, study abroad. Co-op programs available in arts, business, computer science, education, health professions, humanities.

FACILITIES
Housing: Coed dorms. **Special Academic Facilities/Equipment:** Language lab, honors college, banking and finance center.

CAMPUS LIFE
Activities: Student newspaper, yearbook. **Organizations:** 45 registered organizations, 9 honor societies, 4 religious organizations. 4 fraternities (20% men join), 4 sororities (25% women join). **Athletics (Intercollegiate):** *Women:* Basketball, softball, track/field (indoor), track/field (outdoor), volleyball.

ADMISSIONS
Freshman Academic Profile: 6% in top 10% of high school class, 14% in top 25% of high school class, 76% in top 50% of high school class. **Freshman Admission Requirements:** High school diploma is required, and GED is accepted. *Academic units required:* 4 English, 2 math, 2 science, 2 social studies, 7 academic electives. **Transfer Admission Requirements:** Minimum college GPA of 2.0 required. Lowest grade transferable C. **General Admission Information:** Early decision application deadline 4/15. Regular application deadline rolling. Regular notification rolling. Nonfall registration accepted. Common Application not accepted. Credit and/or placement offered for CEEB Advanced Placement tests.

COSTS AND FINANCIAL AID
Annual tuition $8,126. Room & board $3,846. Required fees $100. Average book expense $755. **Required Forms and Deadlines:** FAFSA, state aid form. **Notification of Awards:** Applicants will be notified of awards on or about 4/16. **Types of Aid:** *Need-based scholarships/grants:* State scholarships/grants, United Negro College Fund. *Loans:* FFEL Subsidized Stafford, FFEL PLUS. **Student Employment:** Federal Work-Study Program available. Institutional employment available. Off-campus job opportunities are fair. **Financial Aid Statistics:** Highest amount earned per year from on-campus jobs $2,000.

JOHNSON STATE COLLEGE

337 College Hill, Johnson, VT 05656-9408
Phone: 802-635-1219 **E-mail:** jscadmissions@jsc.vsc.edu **CEEB Code:** 3766
Fax: 802-635-1230 **Website:** www.jsc.vsc.edu **ACT Code:** 4316
Financial Aid Phone: 802-635-2356

This public school was founded in 1828. It has a 350-acre campus.

RATINGS
Admissions Selectivity Rating: 64   **Fire Safety Rating:** 60*   **Green Rating:** 60*

STUDENTS AND FACULTY

Enrollment: 1,554. **Student Body:** 60% female, 40% male, 22% out-of-state. African American 1%, Caucasian 88%, Hispanic 1%. **Faculty:** Student/faculty ratio 13:1. 55 full-time faculty, 65% hold PhDs. 100% faculty teach undergrads.

ACADEMICS

Degrees: Associate, bachelor's, master's, post-bachelor's certificate. **Academic Requirements:** Arts/fine arts, English (including composition), history, humanities, mathematics, philosophy, sciences (biological or physical), social science. **Classes:** Most classes have 10–19 students. **Majors with Highest Enrollment:** Elementary education and teaching, tourism and travel services management, visual and performing arts. **Disciplines with Highest Percentage of Degrees Awarded:** Business/marketing 18%, social sciences 13%, psychology 11%, education 11%, liberal arts/general studies 10%, visual and performing arts 8%. **Special Study Options:** Cross-registration, double major, dual enrollment, English as a second language (ESL), exchange student program (domestic), external degree program, honors program, independent study, internships, study abroad, teacher certification program.

FACILITIES

Housing: Coed dorms, apartments for married students, apartments for single students, apartments for students who have 60 credits and a 3.0 average. **Special Academic Facilities/Equipment:** Art gallery, visual arts center, child development center, human performance lab, 1,000-acre nature preserve, snowboard terrain park, dance studio. **Computers:** Network access in dorm rooms, network access in dorm lounges, online registration, remote student-access to Web through college's connection.

CAMPUS LIFE

Activities: Choral groups, concert band, dance, drama/theater, jazz band, literary magazine, music ensembles, musical theater, pep band, radio station, student government, student newspaper, yearbook. **Organizations:** 40 registered organizations, 1 honor society, 4 religious organizations. **Athletics (Intercollegiate):** *Men:* Basketball, cross-country, lacrosse, soccer, tennis. *Women:* Basketball, cross-country, soccer, softball, tennis. Environmental Initiatives: Owned a 1000 acres preserved land. Bio-Diesel school bus for students transportation.

ADMISSIONS

Freshman Academic Profile: 6% in top 10% of high school class, 24% in top 25% of high school class, 52% in top 50% of high school class. SAT Math middle 50% range 430–550. SAT Critical Reading middle 50% range 430–550. ACT middle 50% range 20–28. TOEFL required of all international applicants, minimum paper TOEFL 500, minimum computer TOEFL 173. **Basis for Candidate Selection:** *Very important factors considered include:* Rigor of secondary school record, standardized test scores. *Important factors considered include:* Application essay, character/personal qualities, class rank, extracurricular activities, interview, recommendation(s), talent/ability. *Other factors considered include:* Volunteer work, work experience. **Freshman Admission Requirements:** High school diploma is required, and GED is accepted. *Academic units required:* 4 English, 3 math, 2 science (1 science lab), 2 social studies, 2 history. *Academic units recommended:* 4 English, 4 math, 3 science (2 science labs), 1 foreign language, 3 social studies, 3 history. **Freshman Admission Statistics:** 1,076 applied, 87% admitted, 43% enrolled. **Transfer Admission Requirements:** College transcript(s), essay or personal statement. Minimum college GPA of 2.0 required. Lowest grade transferable C-. **General Admission Information:** Application fee $34. Regular notification is rolling. Nonfall registration accepted. Admission may be deferred for a maximum of 1 year. Common Application not accepted. Credit and/or placement offered for CEEB Advanced Placement tests.

COSTS AND FINANCIAL AID

Annual in-state tuition $7,409. Annual out-of-state tuition $16,002. Room and board $7,500. Required fees $500. Average book expense $1,000. **Required Forms and Deadlines:** FAFSA. Financial aid filing deadline 3/3. **Notification of Awards:** Applicants will be notified of awards on a rolling basis beginning on or about 4/1. **Types of Aid:** *Need-based scholarships/grants:* Pell, SEOG, state scholarships/grants, private scholarships, the school's own gift aid. *Loans:* Direct Subsidized Stafford, Direct Unsubsidized Stafford, Direct PLUS, Federal Perkins. **Financial Aid Statistics:** 60% freshmen, 58% undergrads receive need-based scholarship or grant aid. 59% freshmen, 59% undergrads receive need-based self-help aid.

JONES INTERNATIONAL UNIVERSITY

9697 East Mineral Avenue, Centennial, CO 80112
Phone: 800-811-5663 **E-mail:** admissions@international.edu
Fax: 303-799-0966 **Website:** www.jonesinternational.edu
Financial Aid Phone: 800-811-5663

This private school was founded in 1993.

RATINGS

Admissions Selectivity Rating: 60* **Fire Safety Rating:** 60* **Green Rating:** 60*

STUDENTS AND FACULTY

Student Body: 50% female, 50% male. **Retention and Graduation:** 97% freshmen return for sophomore year. **Faculty:** Student/faculty ratio 25:1.

ACADEMICS

Degrees: Bachelor's, certificate, master's. **Academic Requirements:** Arts/fine arts, computer literacy, English (including composition), foreign languages, history, humanities, mathematics, sciences (biological or physical), social science. **Majors with Highest Enrollment:** Business administration/management; communications, journalism, and related fields; education. **Disciplines with Highest Percentage of Degrees Awarded:** Communication technologies 100%. **Special Study Options:** Accelerated program, distance learning, external degree program.

FACILITIES

Housing: No housing required. **Computers:** Online registration, online administrative functions (other than registration).

ADMISSIONS

Freshman Academic Profile: TOEFL required of all international applicants, minimum paper TOEFL 550, minimum computer TOEFL 213. **Freshman Admission Requirements:** High school diploma is required, and GED is accepted. **Freshman Admission Statistics:** 22 applied, 100% admitted, 86% enrolled. **Transfer Admission Requirements:** High school transcript, college transcript(s), essay or personal statement. Minimum college GPA of 2.5 required. Lowest grade transferable C. **General Admission Information:** Application fee $75. Nonfall registration accepted. Admission may be deferred for a maximum of 1 year. Common Application not accepted.

COSTS AND FINANCIAL AID

Annual tuition $835. Required fees $75. Average book expense $100.

See page 1214.

JUDSON COLLEGE (AL)

302 Bibb Street, Marion, AL 36756
Phone: 334-683-5110 **E-mail:** admissions@judson.edu **CEEB Code:** 1349
Fax: 334-683-5282 **Website:** www.judson.edu **ACT Code:** 0022
Financial Aid Phone: 334-683-5157

This private school, affiliated with the Baptist Church, was founded in 1838. It has an 80-acre campus.

RATINGS

Admissions Selectivity Rating: 72 **Fire Safety Rating:** 64 **Green Rating:** 60*

STUDENTS AND FACULTY

Enrollment: 305. **Student Body:** 95% female, 5% male, 24% out-of-state, 1% international (3 countries represented). African American 15%, Caucasian 82%. **Retention and Graduation:** 54% freshmen return for sophomore year. 34% freshmen graduate within 4 years. 30% grads go on to further study within 1 year. 84% grads pursue arts and sciences degrees. 11% grads pursue law degrees. 5% grads pursue medical degrees. **Faculty:** Student/faculty ratio 9:1. 20 full-time faculty, 85% hold PhDs. 100% faculty teach undergrads.

ACADEMICS

Degrees: Bachelor's. **Academic Requirements:** Arts/fine arts, computer literacy, English (including composition), health/activity, history, humanities, mathematics, religion, sciences (biological or physical), social science, women's studies. **Classes:** Most classes have fewer than 10 students. Most lab/discussion sections have fewer than 10 students. **Majors with Highest Enrollment:** Biology/biological sciences, elementary education and teaching, psychology.

Disciplines with Highest Percentage of Degrees Awarded: Education 25%, psychology 18%, history 17%, biological/life sciences 15%, visual and performing arts 8%. **Special Study Options:** Accelerated program, cross-registration, distance learning, double major, dual enrollment, independent study, internships, student-designed major, study abroad, teacher certification program.

FACILITIES

Housing: Women's dorms. **Special Academic Facilities/Equipment:** Alabama Women's Hall of Fame. **Computers:** 100% of public computers are PCs, network access in dorm rooms, remote student-access to Web through college's connection.

CAMPUS LIFE

Activities: Choral groups, drama/theater, literary magazine, music ensembles, musical theater, student government, student newspaper, yearbook. **Organizations:** 28 registered organizations, 8 honor societies, 1 religious organization. **Athletics (Intercollegiate):** *Women:* Basketball, equestrian sports, softball, tennis, volleyball.

ADMISSIONS

Freshman Academic Profile: 17% in top 10% of high school class, 43% in top 25% of high school class, 71% in top 50% of high school class. 76% from public high schools. SAT Math middle 50% range 520–640. SAT Critical Reading middle 50% range 570–590. ACT middle 50% range 19–25. TOEFL required of all international applicants, minimum paper TOEFL 500, minimum computer TOEFL 173. **Basis for Candidate Selection:** *Very important factors considered include:* Academic GPA, interview, standardized test scores. *Important factors considered include:* Character/personal qualities. *Other factors considered include:* Class rank, extracurricular activities, recommendation(s), rigor of secondary school record, talent/ability. **Freshman Admission Requirements:** High school diploma is required, and GED is accepted. *Academic units required:* 4 English, 2 math, 2 science, 3 social studies, 5 academic electives. *Academic units recommended:* 4 English, 4 math, 4 science, 2 foreign language, 4 social studies, 2 history. **Freshman Admission Statistics:** 282 applied, 82% admitted, 29% enrolled. **Transfer Admission Requirements:** College transcript(s), interview. Minimum college GPA of 2.0 required. Lowest grade transferable C-. **General Admission Information:** Application fee $30. Regular notification is rolling. Nonfall registration accepted. Admission may be deferred for a maximum of 1 year. Credit and/or placement offered for CEEB Advanced Placement tests.

COSTS AND FINANCIAL AID

Annual tuition $10,920. Room and board $7,120. Required fees $200. Average book expense $800. **Required Forms and Deadlines:** FAFSA, institution's own financial aid form, state aid form. Financial aid filing deadline 3/1. **Notification of Awards:** Applicants will be notified of awards on a rolling basis beginning on or about 11/15. **Types of Aid:** *Need-based scholarships/grants:* Pell, SEOG, state scholarships/grants, private scholarships, the school's own gift aid. *Loans:* FFEL Subsidized Stafford, FFEL Unsubsidized Stafford, FFEL PLUS, Federal Perkins, college/university loans from institutional funds. **Student Employment:** Federal Work-Study Program available. Off-campus job opportunities are poor. **Financial Aid Statistics:** 84% freshmen, 72% undergrads receive need-based scholarship or grant aid. 78% freshmen, 58% undergrads receive need-based self-help aid. 4 freshmen, 6 undergrads receive athletic scholarships. 100% freshmen, 97% undergrads receive any aid. Highest amount earned per year from on-campus jobs $1,750.

ACADEMICS

Degrees: Bachelor's, certificate, master's. **Academic Requirements:** Arts/fine arts, biblical studies and physical education activity course, English (including composition), history, mathematics, sciences (biological or physical), social science. **Classes:** Most classes have 10–19 students. Most lab/discussion sections have fewer than 10 students. **Majors with Highest Enrollment:** Architecture (BArch, BA/BS, MArch, MA/MS, PhD), business administration/management, elementary education and teaching. **Disciplines with Highest Percentage of Degrees Awarded:** Business/marketing 41%, architecture 10%, education 7%, visual and performing arts 6%, psychology 4%. **Special Study Options:** Accelerated program, distance learning, double major, English as a second language (ESL), honors program, independent study, internships, study abroad, teacher certification program.

FACILITIES

Housing: Coed dorms, men's dorms, women's dorms, apartments for married students, special housing for disabled students. **Computers:** 90% of public computers are PCs, 10% of public computers are Macs, network access in dorm lounges, online registration, online administrative functions (other than registration), remote student-access to Web through college's connection.

CAMPUS LIFE

Activities: Choral groups, drama/theater, music ensembles, student government. **Organizations:** 23 registered organizations, 1 honor society. **Athletics (Intercollegiate):** *Men:* Baseball, basketball, cheerleading, soccer. *Women:* Basketball, cheerleading, soccer, softball, volleyball.

ADMISSIONS

Freshman Academic Profile: 7% in top 10% of high school class, 35% in top 25% of high school class, 59% in top 50% of high school class. SAT Math middle 50% range 440–660. SAT Critical Reading middle 50% range 430–600. ACT middle 50% range 20–26. TOEFL required of all international applicants, minimum paper TOEFL 550, minimum computer TOEFL 213. **Basis for Candidate Selection:** *Very important factors considered include:* Rigor of secondary school record, standardized test scores. *Important factors considered include:* Character/personal qualities. *Other factors considered include:* Class rank, recommendation(s), talent/ability. **Freshman Admission Requirements:** High school diploma is required, and GED is accepted. *Academic units recommended:* 4 English, 3 math, 2 science (2 science labs), 2 social studies. **Freshman Admission Statistics:** 520 applied, 73% admitted, 44% enrolled. **Transfer Admission Requirements:** College transcript(s). Minimum college GPA of 2.0 required. Lowest grade transferable C-. **General Admission Information:** Application fee $30. Regular notification is rolling. Nonfall registration accepted. Admission may be deferred for a maximum of 1 semester. Common Application accepted. Credit and/or placement offered for CEEB Advanced Placement tests.

COSTS AND FINANCIAL AID

Annual tuition $13,872. Room & board $5,570. Required fees $550. Average book expense $680. **Required Forms and Deadlines:** FAFSA. **Types of Aid:** *Need-based scholarships/grants:* Pell, SEOG, state scholarships/grants, private scholarships, the school's own gift aid. *Loans:* Direct Subsidized Stafford, Direct Unsubsidized Stafford, Direct PLUS, Federal Perkins. **Student Employment:** Federal Work-Study Program available. Institutional employment available. Off-campus job opportunities are excellent. **Financial Aid Statistics:** 90% freshmen, 90% undergrads receive any aid. Highest amount earned per year from on-campus jobs $1,200.

JUDSON COLLEGE (IL)

1151 North State Street, Elgin, IL 60123
Phone: 847-628-2510 **E-mail:** admission@judsoncollege.edu **CEEB Code:** 1700
Fax: 847-628-2526 **Website:** www.judsoncollege.edu **ACT Code:** 1101
Financial Aid Phone: 847-628-2530

This private school, affiliated with the Baptist Church, was founded in 1963. It has an 84-acre campus.

RATINGS

Admissions Selectivity Rating: 76   **Fire Safety Rating:** 74   **Green Rating:** 60*

STUDENTS AND FACULTY

Enrollment: 1,132. **Student Body:** 58% female, 42% male, 35% out-of-state, 3% international (25 countries represented). African American 4%, Asian 1%, Caucasian 69%, Hispanic 5%. **Retention and Graduation:** 72% freshmen return for sophomore year. 34% freshmen graduate within 4 years. **Faculty:** Student/faculty ratio 16:1. 54 full-time faculty, 74% hold PhDs. 100% faculty teach undergrads.

THE JUILLIARD SCHOOL

60 Lincoln Center Plaza, New York, NY 10023-6588
Phone: 212-799-5000 **E-mail:** admissions@juilliard.edu **CEEB Code:** 2340
Fax: 212-724-0263 **Website:** www.juilliard.edu
Financial Aid Phone: 212-799-5000

This private school was founded in 1905.

RATINGS

Admissions Selectivity Rating: 60*   **Fire Safety Rating:** 60*   **Green Rating:** 60*

STUDENTS AND FACULTY

Enrollment: 482. **Student Body:** 48% female, 52% male, 85% out-of-state, 20% international (40 countries represented). African American 10%, Asian 15%, Caucasian 50%, Hispanic 5%. **Retention and Graduation:** 94% freshmen return for sophomore year. **Faculty:** 114 full-time faculty.

ACADEMICS

Degrees: Bachelor's, diploma, doctoral, first professional, master's, post-master's certificate. **Academic Requirements:** Humanities. **Classes:** Most classes have 10–19 students. Most lab/discussion sections have 10–19 students. **Majors with Highest Enrollment:** Guitar and other stringed instruments, piano and organ, voice and opera, viola, violin. **Disciplines with Highest Percentage of Degrees Awarded:** Visual and performing arts 100%. **Special Study Options:** Accelerated program, cooperative education program, cross-registration, double major, study abroad. Eligible Juilliard students can enroll in courses at Barnard and Columbia Colleges (at Columbia University) to fulfill their liberal arts elective requirement.

FACILITIES

Housing: Coed dorms, single sex floor, quiet floor, graduate-student-only floor, substance-free floor available. **Special Academic Facilities/Equipment:** 2 recital halls, 1 theater (1000 ppl.), 1 drama theater (200 ppl), 15 two-story studios, 35 private teaching studios, 106 practice rooms, organ studios, 200+ pianos, recording studio, the Peter Jay Sharp Special Collections Room. **Computers:** 90% of public computers are PCs, 10% of public computers are Macs, network access in dorm rooms, network access in dorm lounges, online registration, online administrative functions (other than registration), remote student-access to Web through college's connection.

CAMPUS LIFE

Activities: Choral groups, dance, drama/theater, jazz band, music ensembles, opera, student newspaper, symphony orchestra. **Organizations:** 5 registered organizations, 2 religious organizations.

ADMISSIONS

Freshman Academic Profile: TOEFL required of all international applicants, minimum paper TOEFL 533, minimum computer TOEFL 200. **Basis for Candidate Selection:** *Very important factors considered include:* Interview, talent/ability. *Other factors considered include:* Academic GPA, Application essay, recommendation(s). **Freshman Admission Requirements:** High school diploma is required, and GED is accepted. **Freshman Admission Statistics:** 2,314 applied, 7% admitted, 71% enrolled. **Transfer Admission Requirements:** College transcript(s), essay or personal statement, interview. Lowest grade transferable C. **General Admission Information:** Application fee $100. Regular application deadline 12/1. Regular notification 4/1. Non-fall registration not accepted. Neither credit nor placement offered for CEEB Advanced Placement tests.

COSTS AND FINANCIAL AID

Average book expense $700. **Required Forms and Deadlines:** FAFSA, institution's own financial aid form. Financial aid filing deadline 3/1. **Notification of Awards:** Applicants will be notified of awards on or about 4/1. **Types of Aid:** *Need-based scholarships/grants:* Pell, SEOG, state scholarships/grants, private scholarships, the school's own gift aid. *Loans:* Direct Subsidized Stafford, Direct Unsubsidized Stafford, Direct PLUS, FFEL PLUS, Federal Perkins, college/university loans from institutional funds. **Financial Aid Statistics:** 67% freshmen, 73% undergrads receive need-based scholarship or grant aid. 67% freshmen, 73% undergrads receive need-based self-help aid. Highest amount earned per year from on-campus jobs $4,500.

JUNIATA COLLEGE

Best 368

1700 Moore Street, Huntingdon, PA 16652
Phone: 814-641-3420 **E-mail:** admissions@juniata.edu **CEEB Code:** 2341
Fax: 814-641-3100 **Website:** www.juniata.edu **ACT Code:** 3600
Financial Aid Phone: 814-641-3142

> *This private school, affiliated with the Church of Brethren, was founded in 1876. It has an 800-acre campus.*

RATINGS

Admissions Selectivity Rating: 89   **Fire Safety Rating:** 77   **Green Rating:** 85

STUDENTS AND FACULTY

Enrollment: 1,373. **Student Body:** 53% female, 47% male, 31% out-of-state, 3% international (36 countries represented). African American 1%, Asian 1%, Caucasian 92%, Hispanic 1%. **Retention and Graduation:** 86% freshmen

return for sophomore year. 74% freshmen graduate within 4 years. 31% grads go on to further study within 1 year. 17% grads pursue arts and sciences degrees. 4% grads pursue business degrees. 2% grads pursue law degrees. 3% grads pursue medical degrees. **Faculty:** Student/faculty ratio 13:1. 99 full-time faculty, 91% hold PhDs. 100% faculty teach undergrads.

ACADEMICS

Degrees: Bachelor's. **Academic Requirements:** Arts/fine arts, computer literacy, English (including composition), humanities, mathematics, sciences (biological or physical), social science, international studies. **Classes:** Most classes have 10–19 students. Most lab/discussion sections have 10–19 students. **Majors with Highest Enrollment:** Biology/biological sciences, business administration/management. **Disciplines with Highest Percentage of Degrees Awarded:** Biological/life sciences 19%, business/marketing 12%, social sciences 12%, education 11%, interdisciplinary studies 8%, psychology 8%. **Special Study Options:** Accelerated program, cooperative degree programs, double major, dual enrollment, English as a second language (ESL), exchange student program (domestic), honors program, independent study, internships, marine science semester, Philadelphia urban semester, student-designed major, study abroad, teacher certification program, Washington semester.

FACILITIES

Housing: Coed dorms, women's dorms, apartments for single students, special housing for international students, special-interest housing, substance-free housing. **Special Academic Facilities/Equipment:** Environmental Studies Field Station, Juniata Museum of Art, Early Childhood Education Center, ceramics studio and anagama kiln, nature preserve and peace chapel, observatory, electron microscopes, nuclear magnetic resonance spectrometers, human interaction lab, three-story free-form theater. **Computers:** 85% of public computers are PCs, 10% of public computers are Macs, 5% of public computers are UNIX, network access in dorm rooms, network access in dorm lounges, online registration, online administrative functions (other than registration), remote student-access to Web through college's connection.

CAMPUS LIFE

Activities: Choral groups, concert band, dance, drama/theater, jazz band, literary magazine, music ensembles, musical theater, pep band, radio station, student government, student newspaper, student-run film society, symphony orchestra, yearbook. **Organizations:** 92 registered organizations, 12 honor societies, 7 religious organizations. **Athletics (Intercollegiate):** *Men:* Baseball, basketball, cross-country, football, soccer, tennis, track/field (indoor), track/field (outdoor), volleyball. *Women:* Basketball, cross-country, field hockey, soccer, softball, swimming, tennis, track/field (indoor), track/field (outdoor), volleyball. Environmental Initiatives: 5 year contract for Wind REC's to go from 10% of electric consumption in 2007 to 75% in 2012. 2 LEED Certified buildings—New construction at the Raystown Field Station and the renovation of an 1879 building. Signing the President's Climate Commitment and prior to that the creation of a Sustainability Leadership Team and inclusion of specific sustainability related objectives in the soon to be completed strategic plan.

ADMISSIONS

Freshman Academic Profile: 36% in top 10% of high school class, 77% in top 25% of high school class, 95% in top 50% of high school class. 85% from public high schools. SAT Math middle 50% range 540–630. SAT Critical Reading middle 50% range 525–630. TOEFL required of all international applicants, minimum paper TOEFL 550, minimum computer TOEFL 213. **Basis for Candidate Selection:** *Very important factors considered include:* Academic GPA, application essay, character/personal qualities, recommendation(s), rigor of secondary school record, standardized test scores. *Important factors considered include:* Extracurricular activities, first generation, interview, talent/ability, volunteer work. *Other factors considered include:* Alumni/ae relation, geographical residence, level of applicant's interest, state residency. **Freshman Admission Requirements:** High school diploma is required, and GED is accepted. *Academic units required:* 4 English, 3 math, 3 science (2 science labs), 2 foreign language, 1 social studies, 3 history. *Academic units recommended:* 4 English, 4 math, 4 science, 2 foreign language, 1 social studies, 3 history. **Freshman Admission Statistics:** 1,785 applied, 65% admitted, 31% enrolled. **Transfer Admission Requirements:** High school transcript, college transcript(s), essay or personal statement. Minimum college GPA of 2.5 required. Lowest grade transferable C-. **General Admission Information:** Application fee $30. Early decision application deadline 12/1. Regular application deadline 3/15. Regular notification is rolling. Nonfall registration accepted. Admission may be deferred for a maximum of 1 year. Credit and/or placement offered for CEEB Advanced Placement tests.

COSTS AND FINANCIAL AID

Annual tuition $29,610. Room and board $8,420. Required fees $670. Average book expense $600. **Required Forms and Deadlines:** FAFSA. Financial aid filing deadline 3/1. **Notification of Awards:** Applicants will be notified of awards on a rolling basis beginning on or about 2/1. **Types of Aid:** *Need-based scholarships/grants:* Pell, SEOG, state scholarships/grants, private scholarships, the school's own gift aid. *Loans:* FFEL Subsidized Stafford, FFEL Unsubsidized Stafford, FFEL PLUS, Federal Perkins, college/university loans from institutional funds. **Financial Aid Statistics:** 65% freshmen, 71% undergrads receive need-based scholarship or grant aid. 68% freshmen, 71% undergrads receive need-based self-help aid. 99% freshmen, 99% undergrads receive any aid. Highest amount earned per year from on-campus jobs $3,698.

KALAMAZOO COLLEGE

1200 Academy Street, Kalamazoo, MI 49006
Phone: 269-337-7166 **E-mail:** admission@kzoo.edu **CEEB Code:** 1365
Fax: 269-337-7390 **Website:** www.kzoo.edu **ACT Code:** 2018
Financial Aid Phone: 269-337-7192

This private school was founded in 1833. It has a 60-acre campus.

RATINGS
Admissions Selectivity Rating: 89 **Fire Safety Rating:** 60* **Green Rating:** 84

STUDENTS AND FACULTY
Enrollment: 1,306. **Student Body:** 57% female, 43% male, 29% out-of-state. African American 4%, Asian 6%, Caucasian 78%, Hispanic 3%. **Retention and Graduation:** 92% freshmen return for sophomore year. 83% freshmen graduate within 4 years. **Faculty:** Student/faculty ratio 12:1. 101 full-time faculty, 84% hold PhDs. 100% faculty teach undergrads.

ACADEMICS
Degrees: Bachelor's. **Academic Requirements:** Arts/fine arts, English (including composition), foreign languages, history, humanities, mathematics, philosophy, sciences (biological or physical), social science. **Classes:** Most classes have 10–19 students. Most lab/discussion sections have 20–29 students. **Majors with Highest Enrollment:** Economics, English composition, psychology. **Disciplines with Highest Percentage of Degrees Awarded:** Social sciences 24%, psychology 13%, English 10%, physical sciences 9%, biological/life sciences 9%. **Special Study Options:** Cross-registration, double major, dual enrollment, English as a second language (ESL), exchange student program (domestic), independent study, internships, study abroad.

FACILITIES
Housing: Coed dorms, Asian house, wellness house, African American house, nonviolent student organization house, spirituality house, women's resource center. **Special Academic Facilities/Equipment:** Science center. **Computers:** Network access in dorm rooms, online registration, support for handheld computing, remote student-access to Web through college's connection.

CAMPUS LIFE
Activities: Choral groups, concert band, dance, drama/theater, jazz band, literary magazine, music ensembles, musical theater, pep band, radio station, student government, student newspaper, symphony orchestra, yearbook. **Organizations:** 50 registered organizations, 3 honor societies, 3 religious organizations. **Athletics (Intercollegiate):** *Men:* Baseball, basketball, cross-country, diving, football, golf, soccer, swimming, tennis. *Women:* Basketball, cross-country, diving, golf, soccer, softball, swimming, tennis, volleyball. Environmental Initiatives: The College is currently involved in a LEED registered expansion and renovation of Hicks Student Center. The project is expected to receive Silver certification when completed in summer 2008. The College has had an active recycling operation since 1988 and is participating in RecycleMania 2008 for the fourth consecutive year. Kalamazoo College has formed a Sustainability Guild which is overseen by full-time staff and will link students with College alumni who have chosen "green" career paths.

ADMISSIONS
Freshman Academic Profile: 43% in top 10% of high school class, 72% in top 25% of high school class, 96% in top 50% of high school class. 85% from public high schools. SAT Math middle 50% range 570–680. SAT Critical Reading middle 50% range 580–690. ACT middle 50% range 26–30. TOEFL required of all international applicants, minimum paper TOEFL 550, minimum computer TOEFL 213. **Basis for Candidate Selection:** *Very important factors considered include:* Academic GPA, extracurricular activities, rigor of secondary school record, standardized test scores, talent/ability. *Important factors considered include:* Application essay, character/personal qualities, class rank, recommendation(s), volunteer work, work experience. *Other factors*

considered include: Alumni/ae relation, first generation, geographical residence, interview, level of applicant's interest, racial/ethnic status, state residency. **Freshman Admission Requirements:** High school diploma is required, and GED is accepted. *Academic units recommended:* 4 English, 3 math, 3 science, 3 foreign language, 2 social studies, 2 history. **Freshman Admission Statistics:** 1,800 applied, 69% admitted, 31% enrolled. **Transfer Admission Requirements:** High school transcript, college transcript(s), essay or personal statement, interview, standardized test score, statement of good standing from prior institution(s). Minimum college GPA of 3.0 required. Lowest grade transferable B. **General Admission Information:** Application fee $35. Early decision application deadline 11/15. Regular application deadline 2/1. Regular notification 4/1. Nonfall registration not accepted. Admission may be deferred for a maximum of 1 year. Credit and/or placement offered for CEEB Advanced Placement tests.

COSTS AND FINANCIAL AID
Required Forms and Deadlines: FAFSA, institution's own financial aid form. Financial aid filing deadline 2/15. **Notification of Awards:** Applicants will be notified of awards on or about 3/17. **Types of Aid:** *Need-based scholarships/grants:* Pell, SEOG, state scholarships/grants, private scholarships, the school's own gift aid. *Loans:* Direct Subsidized Stafford, Direct Unsubsidized Stafford, Direct PLUS, Federal Perkins, state loans. **Financial Aid Statistics:** 51% freshmen, 51% undergrads receive need-based scholarship or grant aid. 35% freshmen, 47% undergrads receive need-based self-help aid.

KANSAS CITY ART INSTITUTE

4415 Warwick Boulevard, Kansas City, MO 64111-1762
Phone: 816-474-5225 **E-mail:** admiss@kcai.edu **CEEB Code:** 6330
Fax: 816-802-3309 **Website:** www.kcai.edu **ACT Code:** 2277
Financial Aid Phone: 816-802-3337

This private school was founded in 1885. It has a 15-acre campus.

RATINGS
Admissions Selectivity Rating: 78 **Fire Safety Rating:** 60* **Green Rating:** 60*

STUDENTS AND FACULTY
Enrollment: 665. **Student Body:** 57% female, 43% male, 69% out-of-state. African American 3%, Asian 4%, Caucasian 79%, Hispanic 6%. **Retention and Graduation:** 92% freshmen return for sophomore year. 50% freshmen graduate within 4 years. 40% grads go on to further study within 1 year. **Faculty:** Student/faculty ratio 9:1. 50 full-time faculty, 90% hold PhDs. 100% faculty teach undergrads.

ACADEMICS
Degrees: Bachelor's. **Academic Requirements:** Arts/fine arts. **Classes:** Most classes have 10–19 students. **Majors with Highest Enrollment:** Design and visual communications, film/video and photographic arts, painting. **Special Study Options:** Cross-registration, double major, exchange student program (domestic), independent study, internships, student-designed major, study abroad.

FACILITIES
Housing: Coed dorms, apartments for single students. **Special Academic Facilities/Equipment:** H&R Block Artspace at KCAI, student art gallery. **Computers:** 1% of classrooms are wired, 1% of classrooms are wireless, 10% of public computers are PCs, 90% of public computers are Macs, network access in dorm rooms, network access in dorm lounges, online registration, online administrative functions (other than registration), remote student-access to Web through college's connection.

CAMPUS LIFE
Activities: Student government.

ADMISSIONS
Freshman Academic Profile: 11% in top 10% of high school class, 33% in top 25% of high school class, 65% in top 50% of high school class. 80% from public high schools. SAT Math middle 50% range 430–590. SAT Critical Reading middle 50% range 430–580. SAT Writing middle 50% range 420–570. ACT middle 50% range 20–25. TOEFL required of all international applicants, minimum paper TOEFL 550, minimum computer TOEFL 213. **Basis for Candidate Selection:** *Very important factors considered include:* Application essay, character/personal qualities, interview, recommendation(s), rigor of secondary school record, standardized test scores, talent/ability. *Other factors considered include:* Extracurricular activities, volunteer work, work experience. **Freshman Admission Requirements:** High school diploma is required, and GED is accepted. *Academic units recommended:* 4 English, 3 math, 3 science, 3

social studies, 3 academic electives, 4 fine art. **Freshman Admission Statistics:** 603 applied, 72% admitted, 44% enrolled. **Transfer Admission Requirements:** High school transcript, college transcript(s), essay or personal statement, statement of good standing from prior institution(s). Minimum college GPA of 2.5 required. Lowest grade transferable C. **General Admission Information:** Application fee $35. Regular notification is rolling. Nonfall registration accepted. Admission may be deferred for a maximum of 1 year. Credit offered for CEEB Advanced Placement tests.

COSTS AND FINANCIAL AID

Annual tuition $27,220. Room and board $8,294. Average book expense $1,500. **Required Forms and Deadlines:** FAFSA. Financial aid filing deadline 3/15. **Notification of Awards:** Applicants will be notified of awards on or about 4/1. **Types of Aid:** *Need-based scholarships/grants:* Pell, SEOG, state scholarships/grants, the school's own gift aid. *Loans:* FFEL Subsidized Stafford, FFEL Unsubsidized Stafford, FFEL PLUS, Federal Perkins, alternative loans. **Student Employment:** Federal Work-Study Program available. Institutional employment available. Off-campus job opportunities are good. **Financial Aid Statistics:** 73% freshmen, 80% undergrads receive need-based scholarship or grant aid. 59% freshmen, 70% undergrads receive need-based self-help aid. 99% freshmen, 95% undergrads receive any aid. Highest amount earned per year from on-campus jobs $1,000.

KANSAS STATE UNIVERSITY

Best 368

119 Anderson Hall, Manhattan, KS 66506
Phone: 785-532-6250 **E-mail:** kstate@ksu.edu **CEEB Code:** 6334
Fax: 785-532-6393 **Website:** www.ksu.edu **ACT Code:** 1428
Financial Aid Phone: 785-532-6420

This public school was founded in 1863. It has a 668-acre campus.

RATINGS
Admissions Selectivity Rating: 74   **Fire Safety Rating:** 64   **Green Rating:** 60*

STUDENTS AND FACULTY
Enrollment: 18,591. **Student Body:** 49% female, 51% male, 14% out-of-state, 6% international (103 countries represented). **Retention and Graduation:** 81% freshmen return for sophomore year. 22% freshmen graduate within 4 years. 18% grads go on to further study within 1 year. **Faculty:** Student/faculty ratio 21:1. 919 full-time faculty, 83% hold PhDs. 72% faculty teach undergrads.

ACADEMICS
Degrees: Associate, bachelor's, doctoral, first professional, master's. **Academic Requirements:** Arts/fine arts, English (including composition), history, humanities, mathematics, social science. **Classes:** Most classes have 10–19 students. **Majors with Highest Enrollment:** Animal sciences, journalism, mechanical engineering. **Disciplines with Highest Percentage of Degrees Awarded:** Business/marketing 17%, education 10%, agriculture 9%, social sciences 9%, engineering 8%, family and consumer sciences 7%. **Special Study Options:** Accelerated program, cooperative education program, distance learning, double major, English as a second language (ESL), exchange student program (domestic), honors program, independent study, internships, study abroad, teacher certification program.

FACILITIES
Housing: Coed dorms, men's dorms, women's dorms, apartments for married students, apartments for single students, fraternity/sorority housing, cooperative housing. **Special Academic Facilities/Equipment:** South Asian area study center, education communications center, center for cancer research, planetarium, nuclear reactor/accelerator, Beach Art Museum. **Computers:** 1% of classrooms are wired, 67% of classrooms are wireless, 90% of public computers are PCs, 8% of public computers are Macs, 2% of public computers are UNIX, network access in dorm rooms, network access in dorm lounges, online registration, online administrative functions (other than registration), remote student-access to Web through college's connection.

CAMPUS LIFE
Activities: Choral groups, concert band, dance, drama/theater, jazz band, marching band, music ensembles, musical theater, pep band, radio station, student government, student newspaper, symphony orchestra, television station, yearbook. **Organizations:** 594 registered organizations, 36 honor societies, 37

religious organizations. 28 fraternities (20% men join), 16 sororities (20% women join). **Athletics (Intercollegiate):** *Men:* Baseball, basketball, cheerleading, cross-country, football, golf, track/field (indoor), track/field (outdoor). *Women:* Basketball, cheerleading, crew/rowing, cross-country, equestrian sports, golf, tennis, track/field (indoor), track/field (outdoor), volleyball.

ADMISSIONS
Freshman Academic Profile: 23% in top 10% of high school class, 49% in top 25% of high school class, 78% in top 50% of high school class. 81% from public high schools. ACT middle 50% range 27.5–21. **Basis for Candidate Selection:** *Very important factors considered include:* Academic GPA, class rank, rigor of secondary school record, standardized test scores. *Other factors considered include:* Recommendation(s). **Freshman Admission Requirements:** High school diploma is required, and GED is accepted. *Academic units recommended:* 4 English, 3 math, 3 science, 2 social studies, 1 history, 1 computer technology. **Freshman Admission Statistics:** 7,479 applied, 83% admitted, 50% enrolled. **Transfer Admission Requirements:** College transcript(s). Minimum college GPA of 2.0 required. Lowest grade transferable D. **General Admission Information:** Application fee $30. Regular notification is rolling. Nonfall registration accepted. Credit and/or placement offered for CEEB Advanced Placement tests.

COSTS AND FINANCIAL AID
Annual in-state tuition $5,625. Annual out-of-state tuition $15,360. Room and board $6,084. Required fees $610. Average book expense $1,100. **Required Forms and Deadlines:** FAFSA. Financial aid filing deadline 3/1. **Notification of Awards:** Applicants will be notified of awards on a rolling basis beginning on or about 3/15. **Types of Aid:** *Need-based scholarships/grants:* Pell, SEOG, state scholarships/grants, private scholarships, the school's own gift aid. *Loans:* FFEL Subsidized Stafford, FFEL Unsubsidized Stafford, FFEL PLUS, Federal Perkins, college/university loans from institutional funds, alternative student loans. **Financial Aid Statistics:** 41% freshmen, 36% undergrads receive need-based scholarship or grant aid. 40% freshmen, 46% undergrads receive need-based self-help aid. 14 freshmen, 36 undergrads receive athletic scholarships. 53% undergrads receive any aid. Highest amount earned per year from on-campus jobs $2,500.

KANSAS WESLEYAN UNIVERSITY

100 East Claflin, Salina, KS 67401-6196
Phone: 785-827-5541 **E-mail:** admissions@kwu.edu
Fax: 785-827-0927 **Website:** www.kwu.edu
Financial Aid Phone: 785-827-5541

This private school, affiliated with the Methodist Church, was founded in 1886. It has a 10-acre campus.

RATINGS
Admissions Selectivity Rating: 70   **Fire Safety Rating:** 60*   **Green Rating:** 60*

STUDENTS AND FACULTY
Enrollment: 640. **Student Body:** 60% female, 40% male, 39% out-of-state, 5% international (4 countries represented). African American 8%, Caucasian 87%, Hispanic 4%. **Faculty:** 100% faculty teach undergrads.

ACADEMICS
Degrees: Associate, bachelor's, master's. **Academic Requirements:** Arts/fine arts, computer literacy, English (including composition), foreign languages, history, humanities, mathematics, philosophy, sciences (biological or physical), social science. **Special Study Options:** Cooperative education program, cross-registration, distance learning, double major, dual enrollment, English as a second language (ESL), exchange student program (domestic), independent study, internships, liberal arts/career combination, student-designed major, study abroad, teacher certification program.

FACILITIES
Housing: Coed dorms, men's dorms, women's dorms, apartments for married students, apartments for single students. **Computers:** 1% of public computers are PCs, 1% of public computers are UNIX, network access in dorm rooms.

CAMPUS LIFE
Activities: Choral groups, concert band, dance, drama/theater, jazz band, music ensembles, musical theater, pep band, student government, student newspaper, yearbook. **Organizations:** 15 registered organizations, 7 honor societies, 1 religious organization. **Athletics (Intercollegiate):** *Men:* Baseball, basketball, cheerleading, cross-country, football, golf, soccer, track/field (indoor), track/field (outdoor). *Women:* Basketball, cheerleading, cross-country, golf, soccer, softball, track/field (indoor), track/field (outdoor), volleyball.

ADMISSIONS

Freshman Academic Profile: 16% in top 10% of high school class, 27% in top 25% of high school class, 88% in top 50% of high school class. 97% from public high schools. TOEFL required of all international applicants, minimum paper TOEFL 500. **Basis for Candidate Selection:** *Very important factors considered include:* Rigor of secondary school record, standardized test scores. *Important factors considered include:* Class rank. *Other factors considered include:* Application essay, recommendation(s). **Freshman Admission Requirements:** High school diploma is required, and GED is accepted. *Academic units recommended:* 2 English, 3 math, 2 science (2 science labs), 2 foreign language, 1 social studies, 4 history. **Freshman Admission Statistics:** 774 applied, 70% admitted, 21% enrolled. **Transfer Admission Requirements:** College transcript(s). Minimum college GPA of 2.0 required. Lowest grade transferable D. **General Admission Information:** Application fee $15. Regular application deadline rolling. Regular notification is rolling. Nonfall registration accepted. Common Application accepted. Credit and/or placement offered for CEEB Advanced Placement tests.

COSTS AND FINANCIAL AID

Annual tuition $11,000. Room & board $4,000. Average book expense $400. **Required Forms and Deadlines:** FAFSA, institution's own financial aid form. Financial aid filing deadline 3/15. **Notification of Awards:** Applicants will be notified of awards on or about 3/15. **Types of Aid:** *Need-based scholarships/grants:* Pell, SEOG, state scholarships/grants, private scholarships, the school's own gift aid. *Loans:* Direct Subsidized Stafford, Direct Unsubsidized Stafford, Direct PLUS, FFEL Subsidized Stafford, FFEL Unsubsidized Stafford, FFEL PLUS, Federal Perkins, Federal Nursing, college/university loans from institutional funds. **Student Employment:** Federal Work-Study Program available. Institutional employment available. Off-campus job opportunities are excellent. **Financial Aid Statistics:** 71% freshmen, 86% undergrads receive need-based scholarship or grant aid. 71% freshmen, 86% undergrads receive need-based self-help aid. Highest amount earned per year from on-campus jobs $500.

KEAN UNIVERSITY

PO Box 411, 1000 Morris Avenue, Union, NJ 07083-0411
Phone: 908-737-7100 **E-mail:** admitme@kean.edu **CEEB Code:** 2517
Fax: 908-737-7105 **Website:** www.kean.edu **ACT Code:** 2582
Financial Aid Phone: 908-737-3190

This public school was founded in 1855. It has a 150-acre campus.

RATINGS

Admissions Selectivity Rating: 71   **Fire Safety Rating:** 99   **Green Rating:** 60*

STUDENTS AND FACULTY

Enrollment: 9,650. **Student Body:** 63% female, 37% male, 2% out-of-state, 2% international (70 countries represented). African American 20%, Asian 6%, Caucasian 48%, Hispanic 19%. **Retention and Graduation:** 75% freshmen return for sophomore year. 16% freshmen graduate within 4 years. **Faculty:** Student/faculty ratio 15:1. 367 full-time faculty, 89% hold PhDs. 100% faculty teach undergrads.

ACADEMICS

Degrees: Bachelor's, master's, post-bachelor's certificate, post-master's certificate. **Academic Requirements:** Arts/fine arts, computer literacy, English (including composition), health/physical education, history, humanities, mathematics, sciences (biological or physical), social science. **Classes:** Most classes have 20–29 students. **Majors with Highest Enrollment:** Business administration and management, elementary education and teaching, psychology. **Disciplines with Highest Percentage of Degrees Awarded:** Business/marketing 24%, education 19%, psychology 10%, visual and performing arts 6%, social sciences 6%. **Special Study Options:** Accelerated program, cooperative education program, cross-registration, distance learning, double major, English as a second language (ESL), honors program, independent study, internships, liberal arts/career combination, study abroad, teacher certification program. There is a 2-year bachelor's degree program for RNs, foreign transfer programs, Travelearn.

FACILITIES

Housing: Coed dorms, apartments for single students, special housing for disabled students, freshmen housing. **Special Academic Facilities/Equipment:** Holocaust Resource Center, Center for Academic Success, Harwood Arena, Wynona Lipman Ethnic Studies Center, Harwood Arena. **Computers:** 25% of classrooms are wireless, 90% of public computers are PCs, 10% of public computers are Macs, network access

in dorm rooms, network access in dorm lounges, online registration, online administrative functions (other than registration), remote student-access to Web through college's connection.

CAMPUS LIFE

Activities: Choral groups, concert band, dance, drama/theater, jazz band, literary magazine, music ensembles, musical theater, radio station, student government, student newspaper, television station, yearbook. **Organizations:** 127 registered organizations, 20 honor societies, 6 religious organizations. 13 fraternities (3% men join), 17 sororities (3% women join). **Athletics (Intercollegiate):** *Men:* Baseball, basketball, cross-country, football, lacrosse, soccer, track/field (outdoor). *Women:* Basketball, cross-country, field hockey, lacrosse, soccer, softball, tennis, track/field (outdoor), volleyball.

ADMISSIONS

Freshman Academic Profile: 7% in top 10% of high school class, 22% in top 25% of high school class, 59% in top 50% of high school class. SAT Math middle 50% range 410–520. SAT Critical Reading middle 50% range 400–500. **Basis for Candidate Selection:** *Very important factors considered include:* Academic GPA, rigor of secondary school record. *Important factors considered include:* Standardized test scores. *Other factors considered include:* Alumni/ae relation, application essay, character/personal qualities, class rank, extracurricular activities, interview, recommendation(s), talent/ability, volunteer work, work experience. **Freshman Admission Requirements:** High school diploma is required, and GED is accepted. *Academic units required:* 4 English, 3 math, 2 science (2 science labs), 2 history, 5 academic electives. *Academic units recommended:* 2 foreign language, 2 social studies. **Freshman Admission Statistics:** 5,134 applied, 65% admitted, 43% enrolled. **Transfer Admission Requirements:** High school transcript, college transcript(s), statement of good standing from prior institution(s). Minimum college GPA of 2.0 required. Lowest grade transferable C. **General Admission Information:** Application fee $50. Regular application deadline 5/31. Regular notification is rolling. Nonfall registration accepted. Credit and/or placement offered for CEEB Advanced Placement tests.

COSTS AND FINANCIAL AID

Required Forms and Deadlines: FAFSA. Financial aid filing deadline 3/15. **Notification of Awards:** Applicants will be notified of awards on a rolling basis beginning on or about 3/15. **Types of Aid:** *Need-based scholarships/grants:* Pell, SEOG, state scholarships/grants, private scholarships, the school's own gift aid. *Loans:* Direct Subsidized Stafford, Direct Unsubsidized Stafford, Direct PLUS, Federal Perkins. **Financial Aid Statistics:** 59% freshmen, 53% undergrads receive need-based scholarship or grant aid. 59% freshmen, 53% undergrads receive need-based self-help aid. 73% freshmen, 67% undergrads receive any aid. Highest amount earned per year from on-campus jobs $5,610.

See page 1216.

KEENE STATE COLLEGE

229 Main Street, Keene, NH 03435-2604
Phone: 603-358-2276 **E-mail:** admissions@keene.edu **CEEB Code:** 3472
Fax: 603-358-2767 **Website:** www.keene.edu **ACT Code:** 2510
Financial Aid Phone: 603-358-2280

This public school was founded in 1909. It has a 160-acre campus.

RATINGS

Admissions Selectivity Rating: 72   **Fire Safety Rating:** 97   **Green Rating:** 87

STUDENTS AND FACULTY

Enrollment: 4,398. **Student Body:** 58% female, 42% male, 46% out-of-state. Caucasian 95%. **Retention and Graduation:** 76% freshmen return for sophomore year. 29% freshmen graduate within 4 years. 18% grads go on to further study within 1 year. 3% grads pursue arts and sciences degrees. 1% grads pursue business degrees. 2% grads pursue law degrees. **Faculty:** Student/faculty ratio 18:1. 181 full-time faculty, 73% hold PhDs. 100% faculty teach undergrads.

ACADEMICS

Degrees: Associate, bachelor's, certificate, master's, post-bachelor's certificate, post-master's certificate. **Academic Requirements:** Arts/fine arts, English (including composition), history, humanities, mathematics, sciences (biological or physical), social science. Students majoring in the School of Arts and Humanities must complete a foreign language requirement. **Classes:** Most classes have 10–19 students. **Majors with Highest Enrollment:** Business administration and management, elementary education and teaching, occupational safety and health technology/technician. **Disciplines with**

Highest Percentage of Degrees Awarded: Education 22%, social sciences 13%, psychology 11%, engineering technologies 10%, business/marketing 9%. **Special Study Options:** Cooperative education program, double major, English as a second language (ESL), exchange student program (domestic), honors program, independent study, internships, liberal arts/career combination, student-designed major, study abroad, teacher certification program.

FACILITIES

Housing: Coed dorms, women's dorms, apartments for married students, apartments for single students, special housing for disabled students, fraternity/sorority housing, leadership house, substance-free, quiet, music house. **Special Academic Facilities/Equipment:** Thorne-Sagendorph Art Gallery, Redfern Arts Center, recreational center, science center, Mason Library, media arts center, Cohen Center for Holocaust Studies, center for writing. **Computers:** 90% of public computers are PCs, 10% of public computers are Macs, network access in dorm rooms, online registration, online administrative functions (other than registration), support for handheld computing, remote student-access to Web through college's connection.

CAMPUS LIFE

Activities: Choral groups, concert band, dance, drama/theater, jazz band, literary magazine, music ensembles, musical theater, radio station, student government, student newspaper, student-run film society, television station, yearbook. **Organizations:** 80 registered organizations, 21 honor societies, 4 religious organizations. 2 fraternities (3% men join), 4 sororities (3% women join). **Athletics (Intercollegiate):** *Men:* Baseball, basketball, cheerleading, cross-country, diving, lacrosse, soccer, swimming, track/field (indoor), track/field (outdoor), volleyball. *Women:* Basketball, cheerleading, cross-country, diving, field hockey, lacrosse, soccer, softball, swimming, track/field (indoor), track/field (outdoor), volleyball. Environmental Initiatives: LEED building (approval in process). Development of cogeneration capability in steam heat plant (combined heat and power). President's Council for a Sustainable Future.

ADMISSIONS

Freshman Academic Profile: 5% in top 10% of high school class, 23% in top 25% of high school class, 64% in top 50% of high school class. SAT Math middle 50% range 440–540. SAT Critical Reading middle 50% range 440–540. SAT Writing middle 50% range 440–540. TOEFL required of all international applicants, minimum paper TOEFL 500, minimum computer TOEFL 173. **Basis for Candidate Selection:** *Very important factors considered include:* Rigor of secondary school record. *Important factors considered include:* Academic GPA, application essay, interview, recommendation(s), standardized test scores. *Other factors considered include:* Alumni/ae relation, character/personal qualities, class rank, extracurricular activities, first generation, level of applicant's interest, racial/ethnic status, talent/ability, volunteer work, work experience. **Freshman Admission Requirements:** High school diploma is required, and GED is accepted. *Academic units required:* 4 English, 3 math, 3 science, 2 social studies, 2 academic electives. **Freshman Admission Statistics:** 4,150 applied, 75% admitted, 37% enrolled. **Transfer Admission Requirements:** High school transcript, college transcript(s), essay or personal statement, statement of good standing from prior institution(s). Minimum college GPA of 2.0 required. Lowest grade transferable C. **General Admission Information:** Application fee $35. Regular application deadline 4/1. Regular notification is rolling. Nonfall registration accepted. Admission may be deferred for a maximum of 1 year. Credit and/or placement offered for CEEB Advanced Placement tests.

COSTS AND FINANCIAL AID

Annual in-state tuition $6,040. Out-of-state tuition $13,640. Room & board $7,605. Required fees $2,138. Average book expense $800. **Required Forms and Deadlines:** FAFSA. Financial aid filing deadline 3/1. **Notification of Awards:** Applicants will be notified of awards on a rolling basis beginning on or about 12/1. **Types of Aid:** *Need-based scholarships/grants:* Pell, SEOG, state scholarships/grants, private scholarships, the school's own gift aid. *Loans:* FFEL Subsidized Stafford, FFEL Unsubsidized Stafford, FFEL PLUS, Federal Perkins, college/university loans from institutional funds. **Financial Aid Statistics:** 34% freshmen, 34% undergrads receive need-based scholarship or grant aid. 48% freshmen, 48% undergrads receive need-based self-help aid. 67% freshmen, 71% undergrads receive any aid. Highest amount earned per year from on-campus jobs $5,400.

KEISER COLLEGE UNIVERSITY— FORT LAUDERDALE

1500 Northwest 49th Street, Fort Lauderdale, FL 33309
Phone: 954-776-4456 **E-mail:** admissions-ftl@keisercollege.edu
Fax: 954-351-4043 **Website:** www.keisercollege.edu

This private school was founded in 1977.

RATINGS
Admissions Selectivity Rating: 60*   **Fire Safety Rating:** 60*   **Green Rating:** 60*

ACADEMICS

Degrees: Associate, bachelor's, certificate. **Academic Requirements:** Computer literacy, English (including composition), mathematics, social science. **Special Study Options:** Accelerated program, distance learning, double major, independent study, internships.

FACILITIES

Housing: Coed dorms, apartments for single students, college assists students in finding housing close to facilities. **Computers:** Network access in dorm rooms, online registration, online administrative functions (other than registration), remote student-access to Web through college's connection.

CAMPUS LIFE

Activities: Student government, yearbook.

ADMISSIONS

Freshman Academic Profile: TOEFL required of all international applicants, minimum paper TOEFL 500. **Transfer Admission Requirements:** High school transcript, college transcript(s), interview, standardized test score. **General Admission Information:** Application fee $50. Nonfall registration not accepted. Common Application not accepted.

COSTS AND FINANCIAL AID

Annual tuition $5,516. **Required Forms and Deadlines:** FAFSA. **Financial Aid Filing Deadline:** 5/1. **Financial Aid Phone:** 800-749-4456. **Types of Aid:** *Loans:* Direct Subsidized Stafford, Direct Unsubsidized Stafford, Direct PLUS. **Student Employment:** Off-campus job opportunities are fair.

KENDALL COLLEGE

900 North Branch Street, Chicago, IL 60622
Phone: 877-588-8860 **E-mail:** admissions@kendall.edu
Fax: 312-752-2021 **Website:** www.kendall.edu **ACT Code:** 1703
Financial Aid Phone: 866-803-9988

This private school, affiliated with the Methodist Church, was founded in 1934.

RATINGS
Admissions Selectivity Rating: 60*   **Fire Safety Rating:** 60*   **Green Rating:** 60*

STUDENTS AND FACULTY

Student Body: 12% out-of-state. **Faculty:** Student/faculty ratio 19:1. 37 full-time faculty. 80% faculty teach undergrads.

ACADEMICS

Degrees: Associate, bachelor's, certificate. **Academic Requirements:** Computer literacy, English (including composition), foreign languages, humanities, mathematics, social science. **Majors with Highest Enrollment:** Culinary arts and related services, hospitality administration/management, hospitality administration/management. **Special Study Options:** Accelerated program, cooperative education program, distance learning, double major, internships, student-designed major, study abroad, teacher certification program.

FACILITIES

Housing: Coed dorms, special housing for disabled students. **Computers:** Network access in dorm rooms, remote student-access to Web through college's connection.

CAMPUS LIFE

Activities: Student government, student newspaper.

ADMISSIONS

Freshman Academic Profile: TOEFL required of all international applicants, minimum paper TOEFL 525, minimum computer TOEFL 200. **Basis for Candidate Selection:** *Very important factors considered include:* Academic GPA, class rank, recommendation(s), rigor of secondary school record, standardized test scores. *Important factors considered include:* Character/personal qualities. *Other factors considered include:* Application essay, extracurricular activities, geographical residence, interview, talent/ability, work experience. **Freshman Admission Requirements:** High school diploma is required, and GED is accepted. *Academic units required:* 4 English, 2 math, 2 science, 2 foreign language, 2 social studies. **Freshman Admission Statistics:** 78% enrolled. **Transfer Admission Requirements:** College transcript(s), statement of good standing from prior institution(s). Minimum college GPA of 2.0 required. Lowest grade transferable C. **General Admission Information:** Application fee $50. Nonfall registration accepted. Admission may be deferred for a maximum of 2 years. Credit and/or placement offered for CEEB Advanced Placement tests.

COSTS AND FINANCIAL AID

Annual tuition $21,510. Room and board $10,200. Required fees $440. **Required Forms and Deadlines:** FAFSA, institution's own financial aid form, verification form, federal tax return. Financial aid filing deadline 5/1. **Notification of Awards:** Applicants will be notified of awards on or about 4/1. **Types of Aid:** *Need-based scholarships/grants:* Pell, SEOG, state scholarships/grants, private scholarships, the school's own gift aid. *Loans:* Direct Subsidized Stafford, Direct Unsubsidized Stafford, Direct PLUS, FFEL Subsidized Stafford, FFEL Unsubsidized Stafford, FFEL PLUS, Federal Perkins, college/university loans from institutional funds. **Student Employment:** Federal Work-Study Program available. Institutional employment available. Off-campus job opportunities are excellent. **Financial Aid Statistics:** 87% undergrads receive any aid.

KENDALL COLLEGE OF ART AND DESIGN OF FERRIS STATE UNIVERSITY

17 Fountain Street NW, Grand Rapids, MI 49503-3002
Phone: 616-451-2787 **E-mail:** brittons@ferris.edu **CEEB Code:** 1983
Fax: 616-831-9689 **Website:** www.ferris.edu **ACT Code:** 1983
Financial Aid Phone: 616-451-2787

This public school was founded in 1928.

RATINGS

Admissions Selectivity Rating: 63 **Fire Safety Rating:** 60* **Green Rating:** 60*

STUDENTS AND FACULTY

Enrollment: 938. **Student Body:** 10% out-of-state. **Retention and Graduation:** 10% grads go on to further study within 1 year. 10% grads pursue arts and sciences degrees. **Faculty:** Student/faculty ratio 15:1. 47 full-time faculty, 6% hold PhDs. 100% faculty teach undergrads.

ACADEMICS

Degrees: Bachelor's, master's. **Academic Requirements:** Art and design required studio courses, arts/fine arts, English (including composition), history, humanities, mathematics, sciences (biological or physical), social science, studio electives. **Disciplines with Highest Percentage of Degrees Awarded:** Visual and performing arts 100%. **Special Study Options:** Cooperative education program, double major, dual enrollment, independent study, internships, liberal arts/career combination, study abroad, teacher certification program.

FACILITIES

Housing: Apartments for married students, apartments for single students, historic district with rental apartments nearby. **Computers:** 40% of classrooms are wired, 1% of classrooms are wireless, online registration, online administrative functions (other than registration), remote student-access to Web through college's connection.

CAMPUS LIFE

Organizations: 6 registered organizations, 1 religious organization.

ADMISSIONS

Freshman Academic Profile: 10% in top 10% of high school class, 20% in top 25% of high school class, 57% in top 50% of high school class. TOEFL required of all international applicants, minimum paper TOEFL 500, minimum computer TOEFL 173. **Basis for Candidate Selection:** *Very important*

factors considered include: Academic GPA, application essay, rigor of secondary school record, standardized test scores, talent/ability. *Important factors considered include:* Character/personal qualities, interview. *Other factors considered include:* Class rank, extracurricular activities, recommendation(s). **Freshman Admission Requirements:** High school diploma is required, and GED is accepted. **Freshman Admission Statistics:** 338 applied, 78% admitted, 91% enrolled. **Transfer Admission Requirements:** High school transcript, college transcript(s), essay or personal statement. Lowest grade transferable C. **General Admission Information:** Application fee $30. Regular notification rolling. Nonfall registration accepted. Admission may be deferred for a maximum of 1 semester. Credit offered for CEEB Advanced Placement tests.

COSTS AND FINANCIAL AID

Annual in-state tuition $12,674. Annual out-of-state tuition $19,220. Required fees $420. Average book expense $3,604. **Required Forms and Deadlines:** FAFSA. Financial aid filing deadline 2/15. **Notification of Awards:** Applicants will be notified of awards on or about 4/1. **Types of Aid:** *Need-based scholarships/grants:* Pell, SEOG, state scholarships/grants, private scholarships, the school's own gift aid. *Loans:* Direct Subsidized Stafford, Direct Unsubsidized Stafford, Direct PLUS, Federal Perkins, Key Alternative Loan, CitiAssist Student Loan, Michigan Alternative Loan. **Financial Aid Statistics:** Highest amount earned per year from on-campus jobs $2,000.

See page 1218.

KENNESAW STATE UNIVERSITY

1000 Chastain Road, Campus Box 0115, Kennesaw, GA 30144-5591
Phone: 770-423-6300 **E-mail:** ksuadmit@kennesaw.edu **CEEB Code:** 5359
Fax: 770-420-4435 **Website:** www.kennesaw.edu **ACT Code:** 0833
Financial Aid Phone: 770-423-6074

This public school was founded in 1963. It has a 240-acre campus.

RATINGS

Admissions Selectivity Rating: 84 **Fire Safety Rating:** 85 **Green Rating:** 75

STUDENTS AND FACULTY

Enrollment: 17,605. **Student Body:** 61% female, 39% male, 3% international (136 countries represented). African American 9%, Asian 3%, Caucasian 80%, Hispanic 3%. **Retention and Graduation:** 73% freshmen return for sophomore year. 7% freshmen graduate within 4 years. **Faculty:** Student/faculty ratio 22:1. 607 full-time faculty, 73% hold PhDs. 100% faculty teach undergrads.

ACADEMICS

Degrees: Bachelor's, doctoral, master's. **Academic Requirements:** Arts/fine arts, English (including composition), foreign languages, history, humanities, mathematics, sciences (biological or physical), social science. **Classes:** Most classes have 20–29 students. Most lab/discussion sections have 20–29 students. **Majors with Highest Enrollment:** Business administration/management, elementary education and teaching, nursing/registered nurse training (RN, ASN, BSN, MSN). **Disciplines with Highest Percentage of Degrees Awarded:** Business/marketing 27%, education 20%, health professions and related sciences 7%, computer and information sciences 6%, communications/journalism 6%, psychology 6%, social sciences 6%, parks and recreation 5%. **Special Study Options:** Cooperative education program, cross-registration, distance learning, double major, English as a second language (ESL), honors program, internships, study abroad, teacher certification program, weekend college.

FACILITIES

Housing: Apartments for single students. **Computers:** 90% of public computers are PCs, 10% of public computers are Macs, network access in dorm rooms, network access in dorm lounges, online registration, online administrative functions (other than registration), remote student-access to Web through college's connection.

CAMPUS LIFE

Activities: Choral groups, concert band, dance, drama/theater, jazz band, literary magazine, music ensembles, musical theater, student government, student newspaper, symphony orchestra. **Organizations:** 145 registered organizations, 20 honor societies, 18 religious organizations. 8 fraternities (1% men join), 6 sororities (1% women join). **Athletics (Intercollegiate):** *Men:* Baseball, basketball, cross-country, golf, track/field (indoor), track/field (outdoor). *Women:* Basketball, cheerleading, cross-country, golf, soccer, softball, tennis, track/field (indoor), track/field (outdoor), volleyball. Environmental

Initiatives: Commitment by KSU President Daniel S. Papp to reduce the university's carbon footprint, in line with a national coalition of college and university presidents. Naming of a campus Director of Sustainability who will oversee the university's "green" initiatives and teach students as a member of the faculty. Launching a new undergraduate degree program with emphases in environmental science or environmental polity within KSU's existing Interdisciplinary Studies program.

ADMISSIONS

Freshman Academic Profile: 21% in top 10% of high school class, 53% in top 25% of high school class, 81% in top 50% of high school class. 90% from public high schools. SAT Math middle 50% range 490–570. SAT Critical Reading middle 50% range 490–570. SAT Writing middle 50% range 470–560. ACT middle 50% range 20–24. TOEFL required of all international applicants, minimum paper TOEFL 527, minimum computer TOEFL 197. **Basis for Candidate Selection:** *Very important factors considered include:* Academic GPA, class rank, standardized test scores. **Freshman Admission Requirements:** High school diploma is required, and GED is not accepted. *Academic units required:* 4 English, 4 math, 3 science (3 science labs), 2 foreign language, 3 social studies. **Freshman Admission Statistics:** 7,474 applied, 61% admitted, 56% enrolled. **Transfer Admission Requirements:** College transcript(s). Minimum college GPA of 2.0 required. Lowest grade transferable D. **General Admission Information:** Application fee $40. Regular application deadline 5/16. Regular notification is rolling. Nonfall registration accepted. Admission may be deferred for a maximum of 1 year. Credit offered for CEEB Advanced Placement tests.

COSTS AND FINANCIAL AID

Average book expense $1,000. **Required Forms and Deadlines:** FAFSA. Financial aid filing deadline 4/1. **Types of Aid:** *Need-based scholarships/grants:* Pell, SEOG, state scholarships/grants, private scholarships, the school's own gift aid. *Loans:* FFEL Subsidized Stafford, FFEL Unsubsidized Stafford, FFEL PLUS, Federal Perkins, Federal Nursing, state loans. **Financial Aid Statistics:** 14% freshmen, 17% undergrads receive need-based scholarship or grant aid. 30% freshmen, 32% undergrads receive need-based self-help aid. 17 freshmen, 35 undergrads receive athletic scholarships. 71% freshmen, 64% undergrads receive any aid. Highest amount earned per year from on-campus jobs $8,697.

KENT STATE UNIVERSITY—KENT CAMPUS

161 Michael Schwartz Center, Kent, OH 44242-0001
Phone: 330-672-2444 **E-mail:** admissions@kent.edu **CEEB Code:** 1367
Fax: 330-672-2499 **Website:** www.kent.edu **ACT Code:** 3284
Financial Aid Phone: 330-672-2972

This public school was founded in 1910. It has a 1,200-acre campus.

RATINGS

Admissions Selectivity Rating: 72   **Fire Safety Rating:** 60*   **Green Rating:** 60*

STUDENTS AND FACULTY

Enrollment: 17,793. **Student Body:** 59% female, 41% male, 10% out-of-state. African American 8%, Asian 1%, Caucasian 84%, Hispanic 1%. **Retention and Graduation:** 71% freshmen return for sophomore year. 17% freshmen graduate within 4 years. **Faculty:** Student/faculty ratio 18:1. 856 full-time faculty, 69% hold PhDs. 85% faculty teach undergrads.

ACADEMICS

Degrees: Associate, bachelor's, certificate, doctoral, master's, post-bachelor's certificate, post-master's certificate. **Academic Requirements:** Arts/fine arts, diversity and writing intensive, English (including composition), humanities, mathematics, sciences (biological or physical), social science. Mathematics, logic, and foreign language (6-semester hour requirement) students select courses from those disciplines to meet this requirement. **Classes:** Most classes have 10–19 students. **Majors with Highest Enrollment:** Business administration and management, nursing/registered nurse training (RN, ASN, BSN, MSN), psychology. **Disciplines with Highest Percentage of Degrees Awarded:** Business/marketing 20%, education 12%, health professions and related sciences 9%, visual and performing arts 7%, psychology 6%. **Special Study Options:** Accelerated program, cooperative education program, cross-registration, distance learning, double major, dual enrollment, English as a second language (ESL), exchange student program (domestic), external degree program, honors program, independent study, internships, liberal arts/career combination, student-designed major, study abroad, teacher certification program, weekend college.

FACILITIES

Housing: Coed dorms, men's dorms, women's dorms, apartments for married students, special housing for disabled students, fraternity/sorority housing. **Special Academic Facilities/Equipment:** Fashion museum, herbarium, liquid crystal institute, planetarium, airport. **Computers:** 5% of classrooms are wired, 5% of classrooms are wireless, 95% of public computers are PCs, 5% of public computers are Macs, 5% of public computers are UNIX, network access in dorm rooms, network access in dorm lounges, online registration, online administrative functions (other than registration), support for handheld computing, remote student-access to Web through college's connection.

CAMPUS LIFE

Activities: Choral groups, concert band, dance, drama/theater, jazz band, literary magazine, marching band, music ensembles, musical theater, opera, pep band, radio station, student government, student newspaper, student-run film society, television station. **Organizations:** 204 registered organizations, 21 honor societies, 15 religious organizations, 16 fraternities (1% men join), 7 sororities (1% women join). **Athletics (Intercollegiate):** *Men:* Baseball, basketball, cheerleading, cross-country, football, golf, track/field (indoor), track/field (outdoor), wrestling. *Women:* Basketball, cheerleading, cross-country, field hockey, football, golf, gymnastics, soccer, softball, track/field (indoor), track/field (outdoor), volleyball.

ADMISSIONS

Freshman Academic Profile: 12% in top 10% of high school class, 32% in top 25% of high school class, 68% in top 50% of high school class. SAT Math middle 50% range 460–590. SAT Critical Reading middle 50% range 460–580. ACT middle 50% range 18–24. TOEFL required of all international applicants, minimum paper TOEFL 525, minimum computer TOEFL 197. **Basis for Candidate Selection:** *Very important factors considered include:* Academic GPA, standardized test scores. *Important factors considered include:* Rigor of secondary school record. *Other factors considered include:* Class rank, recommendation(s). **Freshman Admission Requirements:** High school diploma is required, and GED is accepted. *Academic units recommended:* 4 English, 3 math, 3 science (2 science labs), 3 foreign language, 3 social studies, 1 arts. **Freshman Admission Statistics:** 10,990 applied, 84% admitted, 40% enrolled. **Transfer Admission Requirements:** College transcript(s). Minimum college GPA of 2.0 required. Lowest grade transferable C. **General Admission Information:** Application fee $30. Regular application deadline 8/1. Regular notification is rolling. Nonfall registration accepted. Admission may be deferred for a maximum of 1 year. Credit and/or placement offered for CEEB Advanced Placement tests.

COSTS AND FINANCIAL AID

Required Forms and Deadlines: FAFSA, University Scholarship Application Form. Financial aid filing deadline 3/1. **Notification of Awards:** Applicants will be notified of awards on or about 3/15. **Types of Aid:** *Need-based scholarships/grants:* Pell, SEOG, state scholarships/grants, private scholarships, the school's own gift aid. *Loans:* Direct Subsidized Stafford, Direct Unsubsidized Stafford, Direct PLUS, Federal Perkins, Federal Nursing, state loans, college/university loans from institutional funds, alternative loans. **Student Employment:** Federal Work-Study Program available. Institutional employment available. Off-campus job opportunities are good. **Financial Aid Statistics:** 50% freshmen, 40% undergrads receive need-based scholarship or grant aid. 55% freshmen, 51% undergrads receive need-based self-help aid. 32 freshmen, 126 undergrads receive athletic scholarships. 63% freshmen, 57% undergrads receive any aid.

KENTUCKY CHRISTIAN COLLEGE

100 Academic Parkway, Grayson, KY 41143
Phone: 606-474-3266 **E-mail:** sdeakins@email.kcc.edu
Fax: 606-474-3155 **Website:** www.kcc.edu

This private school was founded in 1919. It has a 121-acre campus.

RATINGS

Admissions Selectivity Rating: 72   **Fire Safety Rating:** 60*   **Green Rating:** 60*

STUDENTS AND FACULTY

Enrollment: 569. **Student Body:** 55% female, 45% male, 65% out-of-state, 5% international. Caucasian 94%. **Retention and Graduation:** 65% freshmen return for sophomore year. 25% freshmen graduate within 4 years. **Faculty:** Student/faculty ratio 16:1. 30 full-time faculty, 90% hold PhDs. 100% faculty teach undergrads.

ACADEMICS

Degrees: Associate, bachelor's, master's. **Academic Requirements:** Computer literacy, English (including composition), history, mathematics, sciences (biological or physical). **Classes:** Most classes have fewer than 10 students. Most lab/discussion sections have 20–29 students. **Disciplines with Highest Percentage of Degrees Awarded:** Education 35%, business/marketing 12%, psychology 6%, interdisciplinary studies 1%. **Special Study Options:** Accelerated program, cooperative education program, double major, independent study, internships, teacher certification program, learning disabilities studies, off-campus studies.

FACILITIES

Housing: Men's dorms, women's dorms, apartments for married students, honors housing. **Computers:** Network access in dorm rooms.

CAMPUS LIFE

Activities: Choral groups, drama/theater, jazz band, music ensembles, musical theater, pep band, student government, student newspaper, yearbook. **Athletics (Intercollegiate):** *Men:* Basketball, cheerleading, cross-country, soccer, tennis. *Women:* Basketball, cheerleading, cross-country, tennis, volleyball.

ADMISSIONS

Freshman Academic Profile: 10% in top 10% of high school class, 27% in top 25% of high school class, 52% in top 50% of high school class. SAT Math middle 50% range 430–560. SAT Critical Reading middle 50% range 430–580. ACT middle 50% range 18–24. TOEFL required of all international applicants, minimum paper TOEFL 500. **Basis for Candidate Selection:** *Very important factors considered include:* Character/personal qualities, religious affiliation/commitment, rigor of secondary school record, standardized test scores. *Important factors considered include:* Application essay. *Other factors considered include:* Class rank, recommendation(s). **Freshman Admission Requirements:** High school diploma is required, and GED is accepted. **Freshman Admission Statistics:** 268 applied, 90% admitted, 62% enrolled. **Transfer Admission Requirements:** High school transcript, college transcript(s), essay or personal statement, standardized test score. Minimum college GPA of 2.0 required. Lowest grade transferable C. **General Admission Information:** Application fee $25. Nonfall registration accepted. Admission may be deferred for a maximum of 1 year. Common Application accepted.

COSTS AND FINANCIAL AID

Annual tuition $7,360. Room & board $4,070. Average book expense $750. **Required Forms and Deadlines:** FAFSA, institution's own financial aid form. Financial aid filing deadline 4/1. **Notification of Awards:** Applicants will be notified of awards on a rolling basis beginning on or about 5/1. **Types of Aid:** *Need-based scholarships/grants:* Pell, SEOG, state scholarships/grants, private scholarships, the school's own gift aid. *Loans:* FFEL Subsidized Stafford, FFEL Unsubsidized Stafford, FFEL PLUS, Federal Perkins. **Student Employment:** Federal Work-Study Program available. Institutional employment available. Off-campus job opportunities are good. **Financial Aid Statistics:** 40% freshmen, 40% undergrads receive need-based scholarship or grant aid. 51% freshmen, 60% undergrads receive need-based self-help aid.

KENTUCKY STATE UNIVERSITY

400 East Main Street, 3rd Floor, Frankfort, KY 40601
Phone: 502-597-6813 **E-mail:** james.burrell@kysu.edu **CEEB Code:** 1368
Fax: 502-597-5814 **Website:** www.kysu.edu **ACT Code:** 1516
Financial Aid Phone: 502-597-6033

This public school was founded in 1886. It has a 308-acre campus.

RATINGS

Admissions Selectivity Rating: 60*   **Fire Safety Rating:** 60*   **Green Rating:** 60*

STUDENTS AND FACULTY

Enrollment: 2,070. **Student Body:** 56% female, 44% male, 35% out-of-state. African American 69%, Asian 1%, Caucasian 27%. **Retention and Graduation:** 54% freshmen return for sophomore year. 25% freshmen graduate within 4 years. **Faculty:** Student/faculty ratio 12:1. 158 full-time faculty, 70% hold PhDs. 98% faculty teach undergrads.

ACADEMICS

Degrees: Associate, bachelor's, master's, terminal. **Academic Requirements:** Arts/fine arts, English (including composition), foreign languages, history, humanities, mathematics, sciences (biological or physical), social science. **Classes:** Most classes have fewer than 10 students. **Majors with Highest Enrollment:** Business administration/management; computer and information

sciences; nursing—registered nurse training (RN, ASN, BSN, MSN). **Disciplines with Highest Percentage of Degrees Awarded:** Business/marketing 21%, education 14%, liberal arts/general studies 11%, public administration and social services 10%, biological/life sciences 9%. **Special Study Options:** Cooperative education program, distance learning, double major, English as a second language (ESL), honor program, independent study, internships, study abroad, teacher certification program.

FACILITIES

Housing: Men's dorms, women's dorms, special housing for international students. **Special Academic Facilities/Equipment:** Art gallery, school for early childhood education, nutrition lab, agriculture research building, research farm, fish hatchery, electron microscope. **Computers:** 100% of public computers are PCs, network access in dorm rooms, network access in dorm lounges, remote student-access to Web through college's connection.

CAMPUS LIFE

Activities: Choral groups, concert band, dance, drama/theater, jazz band, marching band, music ensembles, musical theater, opera, pep band, student government, student newspaper, symphony orchestra, yearbook. **Organizations:** 40 registered organizations, 1 honor society, 2 religious organizations. 5 fraternities, 4 sororities. **Athletics (Intercollegiate):** *Men:* Baseball, basketball, cheerleading, cross-country, football, golf, tennis, track/field (indoor), track/field (outdoor). *Women:* Basketball, cheerleading, cross-country, softball, tennis, track/field (indoor), track/field (outdoor), volleyball.

ADMISSIONS

Freshman Academic Profile: SAT Math middle 50% range 355–450. SAT Critical Reading middle 50% range 370–465. SAT Writing middle 50% range 330–440. ACT middle 50% range 15–19. TOEFL required of all international applicants, minimum paper TOEFL 525. **Basis for Candidate Selection:** *Very important factors considered include:* Rigor of secondary school record, standardized test scores. *Important factors considered include:* Recommendation(s). *Other factors considered include:* Alumni/ae relation, extracurricular activities, geographical residence. **Freshman Admission Requirements:** High school diploma is required, and GED is accepted. *Academic units required:* 4 English, 3 math, 3 science, 3 social studies, 1 history, 7 academic electives. *Academic units recommended:* 2 foreign language. **Freshman Admission Statistics:** 5,819 applied, 33% admitted, 28% enrolled. **Transfer Admission Requirements:** College transcript(s). Lowest grade transferable C. **General Admission Information:** Application fee $30. Regular notification is rolling. Nonfall registration accepted. Credit and/or placement offered for CEEB Advanced Placement tests.

COSTS AND FINANCIAL AID

Required Forms and Deadlines: FAFSA. Financial aid filing deadline 5/31. Financial aid filing deadline 6/30. **Notification of Awards:** Applicants will be notified of awards on or about 7/1. **Types of Aid:** *Need-based scholarships/grants:* Pell, SEOG, state scholarships/grants, private scholarships, the school's own gift aid, United Negro College Fund. *Loans:* Direct Subsidized Stafford, Direct Unsubsidized Stafford, Direct PLUS, Federal Perkins, Federal Nursing, state loans. **Financial Aid Statistics:** 58% freshmen, 59% undergrads receive need-based scholarship or grant aid. 66% freshmen, 69% undergrads receive need-based self-help aid. 36 freshmen, 153 undergrads receive athletic scholarships. Highest amount earned per year from on-campus jobs $1,000.

KENTUCKY WESLEYAN COLLEGE

3000 Frederica Street, Owensboro, KY 42301
Phone: 270-852-3120 **E-mail:** admitme@kwc.edu **CEEB Code:** 1369
Fax: 270-852-3133 **Website:** www.kwc.edu **ACT Code:** 1518
Financial Aid Phone: 270-852-3130

This private school, affiliated with the Methodist Church, was founded in 1858. It has a 52-acre campus.

RATINGS

Admissions Selectivity Rating: 74   **Fire Safety Rating:** 62   **Green Rating:** 60*

STUDENTS AND FACULTY

Enrollment: 935. **Student Body:** 45% female, 55% male, 20% out-of-state. African American 11%, Caucasian 79%, Hispanic 1%. **Retention and Graduation:** 67% freshmen return for sophomore year. 25% freshmen graduate within 4 years. **Faculty:** Student/faculty ratio 15:1. 42 full-time faculty, 79% hold PhDs. 100% faculty teach undergrads.

ACADEMICS

Degrees: Bachelor's. **Academic Requirements:** Computer literacy, English (including composition), history, humanities, mathematics, philosophy, sciences (biological or physical), social science. **Classes:** Most classes have 10–19 students. Most lab/discussion sections have 10–19 students. **Majors with Highest Enrollment:** Business administration/management, criminal justice/safety studies, psychology. **Disciplines with Highest Percentage of Degrees Awarded:** Education 15%, business/marketing 14%, security and protective services 13%, psychology 10%, physical sciences 7%. **Special Study Options:** Double major, independent study, internships, liberal arts/career combination, study abroad, teacher certification program.

FACILITIES

Housing: Coed dorms, men's dorms, women's dorms, special housing for disabled students, fraternity/sorority housing. **Special Academic Facilities/ Equipment:** President's Hall/Library Learning Center, Ralph Center for Fine Arts, Woodward Health and Recreation Center, Yu Hak Hahn Center for the Sciences. **Computers:** 1% of classrooms are wired, 1% of classrooms are wireless, 100% of public computers are PCs, network access in dorm rooms, network access in dorm lounges, online registration, remote student-access to Web through college's connection.

CAMPUS LIFE

Activities: Choral groups, dance, drama/theater, literary magazine, marching band, music ensembles, pep band, radio station, student government, student newspaper, yearbook. **Organizations:** 42 registered organizations, 6 honor societies, 6 religious organizations. 3 fraternities (13% men join), 2 sororities (16% women join). **Athletics (Intercollegiate):** *Men:* Baseball, basketball, cheerleading, cross-country, football, golf, soccer. *Women:* Basketball, cheerleading, cross-country, golf, soccer, softball, tennis, volleyball.

ADMISSIONS

Freshman Academic Profile: 16% in top 10% of high school class, 38% in top 25% of high school class, 69% in top 50% of high school class. 95% from public high schools. SAT Math middle 50% range 430–530. SAT Critical Reading middle 50% range 430–540. SAT Writing middle 50% range 410–520. ACT middle 50% range 18–23. TOEFL required of all international applicants, minimum paper TOEFL 500, minimum computer TOEFL 173. **Basis for Candidate Selection:** *Very important factors considered include:* Academic GPA, standardized test scores. *Important factors considered include:* Religious affiliation/commitment, talent/ability. **Freshman Admission Requirements:** High school diploma is required, and GED is accepted. *Academic units required:* 4 English, 3 math, 3 science, 3 social studies. *Academic units recommended:* 2 foreign language. **Freshman Admission Statistics:** 1,643 applied, 78% admitted, 26% enrolled. **Transfer Admission Requirements:** College transcript(s). Minimum college GPA of 2.0 required. Lowest grade transferable C. **General Admission Information:** Regular notification is rolling. Nonfall registration accepted. Admission may be deferred for a maximum of 1 year. Credit and/or placement offered for CEEB Advanced Placement tests.

COSTS AND FINANCIAL AID

Annual tuition $13,200. Room & board $5,750. Required fees $400. Average book expense $700. **Required Forms and Deadlines:** FAFSA. Financial aid filing deadline 3/15. **Notification of Awards:** Applicants will be notified of awards on a rolling basis beginning on or about 2/15. **Types of Aid:** *Need-based scholarships/grants:* Pell, SEOG, state scholarships/grants, private scholarships, the school's own gift aid. *Loans:* FFEL Subsidized Stafford, FFEL Unsubsidized Stafford, FFEL PLUS, Federal Perkins, college/university loans from institutional funds, alternative education loans. **Student Employment:** Federal Work-Study Program available. Institutional employment available. Off-campus job opportunities are good. **Financial Aid Statistics:** 83% freshmen, 84% undergrads receive need-based scholarship or grant aid. 62% freshmen, 62% undergrads receive need-based self-help aid. 99% freshmen, 85% undergrads receive any aid.

KENYON COLLEGE

Admissions Office, Ransom Hall, Gambier, OH 43022-9623
Phone: 740-427-5776 **E-mail:** admissions@kenyon.edu **CEEB Code:** 1370
Fax: 740-427-5770 **Website:** www.kenyon.edu **ACT Code:** 3286
Financial Aid Phone: 740-427-5240

This private school, affiliated with the Episcopal Church (but nonde-nominational in practice), was founded in 1824. It has a 1,200-acre campus.

RATINGS

Admissions Selectivity Rating: 97   **Fire Safety Rating:** 64   **Green Rating:** 77

STUDENTS AND FACULTY

Enrollment: 1,629. **Student Body:** 52% female, 48% male, 78% out-of-state, 3% international (28 countries represented). African American 3%, Asian 5%, Caucasian 83%, Hispanic 3%. **Retention and Graduation:** 92% freshmen return for sophomore year. 85% freshmen graduate within 4 years. 23% grads go on to further study within 1 year. **Faculty:** Student/faculty ratio 10:1. 153 full-time faculty, 97% hold PhDs. 100% faculty teach undergrads.

ACADEMICS

Degrees: Bachelor's. **Academic Requirements:** Arts/fine arts, foreign languages, humanities, sciences (biological or physical), social science. Students must demonstrate a level of proficiency in a second language equivalent to 1 full year of college study. They may meet this requirement in any of the following ways: by achieving a satisfactory score on a placement exam administered during orientation; by completing an introductory-level modern or classical language course at Kenyon; by completing a language course elsewhere that is equivalent to an introductory-level Kenyon course, earning a satisfactory grade, and transferring the credit; by earning language credit in a course in the Kenyon Academic Partnership program; by earning a score of 3 or better on the College Board Advanced Placement test in a second language or literature; in the case of Latin, by earning a satisfactory score on the College Board subject examination in Latin; or by earning a score of 540 or higher on an SAT II modern language test. Quantitative-reasoning courses may focus on the organization, analysis, and implementation of numerical and graphical data; or they may involve learning mathematical ideas, understanding their application to the world, and employing them to solve problems. **Classes:** Most classes have 10–19 students. **Majors with Highest Enrollment:** English language and literature, political science and government, psychology. **Disciplines with Highest Percentage of Degrees Awarded:** Social sciences 21%, English 18%, visual and performing arts 11%, psychology 10%, biological/life sciences 10%. **Special Study Options:** Accelerated program, double major, exchange student program (domestic), honors program, independent study, internships, liberal arts/career combination, student-designed major, study abroad.

FACILITIES

Housing: Coed dorms, women's dorms, apartments for single students, special housing for disabled students, fraternity/sorority housing, special-interest housing. **Special Academic Facilities/Equipment:** Horn and Olin Art Galleries, Bolton and Hill Theaters, Black Box Theater, Rosse and Storer Halls for Music, new sciences quadrangle, greenhouse and observatory, environmental center, $70-million fitness/recreation/athletics facility. **Computers:** 100% of classrooms are wireless, 79% of public computers are PCs, 21% of public computers are Macs, network access in dorm rooms, network access in dorm lounges, online administrative functions (other than registration), remote student-access to Web through college's connection.

CAMPUS LIFE

Activities: Choral groups, concert band, dance, drama/theater, jazz band, literary magazine, music ensembles, musical theater, opera, pep band, radio station, student government, student newspaper, student-run film society, symphony orchestra, yearbook. **Organizations:** 120 registered organizations, 4 honor societies, 6 religious organizations. 8 fraternities (27% men join), 4 sororities (19% women join). **Athletics (Intercollegiate):** *Men:* Baseball, basketball, cross-country, diving, football, golf, lacrosse, soccer, swimming, tennis, track/field (indoor), track/field (outdoor). *Women:* Basketball, cross-country, diving, field hockey, lacrosse, soccer, softball, swimming, tennis, track/field (indoor), track/field (outdoor), volleyball. Environmental Initiatives: Food for Thought (purchase of local foods for dining hall and building a countywide

The Princeton Review's Complete Book of Colleges

sustainable food system). Brown Family Environmental Center (academic and public sustainability programs). Paper and plastic recycling program campus wide.

ADMISSIONS

Freshman Academic Profile: 55% in top 10% of high school class, 86% in top 25% of high school class, 99% in top 50% of high school class. 51% from public high schools. SAT Math middle 50% range 630–690. SAT Critical Reading middle 50% range 630–730. SAT Writing middle 50% range 630–710. ACT middle 50% range 28–32. TOEFL required of all international applicants, minimum paper TOEFL 570, minimum computer TOEFL 230. **Basis for Candidate Selection:** *Very important factors considered include:* Academic GPA, application essay, character/personal qualities, recommendation(s), rigor of secondary school record. *Important factors considered:* Class rank, extracurricular activities, first generation, interview, level of applicant's interest, racial/ethnic status, standardized test scores, talent/ability. *Other factors considered include:* Alumni/ae relation, geographical residence, state residency, volunteer work, work experience. **Freshman Admission Requirements:** High school diploma is required, and GED is accepted. *Academic units required:* 4 English, 3 math, 3 science (3 science labs), 3 foreign language, 1 social studies, 1 history, 3 academic electives. *Academic units recommended:* 4 English, 4 math, 4 science (3 science labs), 4 foreign language, 2 social studies, 1 history, 4 academic electives, 1 fine arts. **Freshman Admission Statistics:** 4,368 applied, 32% admitted, 32% enrolled. **Transfer Admission Requirements:** High school transcript, college transcript(s), essay or personal statement, standardized test score, statement of good standing from prior institution(s). Minimum college GPA of 3.0 required. Lowest grade transferable C. **General Admission Information:** Application fee $50. Early decision application deadline 11/15. Regular application deadline 1/15. Regular notification 4/1. Nonfall registration not accepted. Admission may be deferred for a maximum of 1 year. Credit and/or placement offered for CEEB Advanced Placement tests.

COSTS AND FINANCIAL AID

Annual tuition $39,080. Room and board $6,590. Required fees $1,160. Average book expense $1,300. **Required Forms and Deadlines:** FAFSA, CSS/Financial Aid PROFILE, Noncustodial PROFILE. Financial aid filing deadline 2/15. **Notification of Awards:** Applicants will be notified of awards on or about 4/1. **Types of Aid:** *Need-based scholarships/grants:* Pell, SEOG, state scholarships/grants, private scholarships, the school's own gift aid. *Loans:* FFEL Subsidized Stafford, FFEL Unsubsidized Stafford, FFEL PLUS, Federal Perkins, college/university loans from institutional funds. **Student Employment:** Federal Work-Study Program available. Institutional employment available. Off-campus job opportunities are fair. **Financial Aid Statistics:** 38% freshmen, 41% undergrads receive need-based scholarship or grant aid. 32% freshmen, 37% undergrads receive need-based self-help aid. 65% freshmen, 69% undergrads receive any aid. Highest amount earned per year from on-campus jobs $1,000.

KETTERING UNIVERSITY

1700 West Third Avenue, Flint, MI 48504
Phone: 810-762-7865 **E-mail:** admissions@kettering.edu **CEEB Code:** 1246
Fax: 810-762-9837 **Website:** www.kettering.edu **ACT Code:** 1998
Financial Aid Phone: 810-762-7859

This private school was founded in 1919. It has an 85-acre campus.

RATINGS

Admissions Selectivity Rating: 87   Fire Safety Rating: 65   Green Rating: 60*

STUDENTS AND FACULTY

Enrollment: 2,290. **Student Body:** 15% female, 85% male, 33% out-of-state, 2% international (29 countries represented). African American 5%, Asian 5%, Caucasian 75%, Hispanic 2%. **Retention and Graduation:** 90% freshmen return for sophomore year. 7% freshmen graduate within 4 years. 30% grads go on to further study within 1 year. 28% grads pursue arts and sciences degrees. 28% grads pursue business degrees. 1% grads pursue medical degrees. **Faculty:** Student/faculty ratio 9:1. 133 full-time faculty, 89% hold PhDs. 97% faculty teach undergrads.

ACADEMICS

Degrees: Bachelor's, master's. **Academic Requirements:** English (including composition), humanities, mathematics, sciences (biological or physical), social science, written and oral communication. **Classes:** Most classes have 20–29 students. Most lab/discussion sections have 10–19 students. **Majors with Highest Enrollment:** Computer engineering; electrical, electronics, and communications engineering; mechanical engineering. **Disciplines with**

Highest Percentage of Degrees Awarded: Engineering 93%, physical sciences 3%, business/marketing 3%, computer and information sciences 2%. **Special Study Options:** Accelerated program, cooperative education program, distance learning, double major, dual enrollment, independent study, study abroad. Co-op is required of all undergraduate students and typically begins in the first year. Each 24-week semester is divided into 11-weeks of classes and 12–13 weeks of paid professional co-op experience in industry. Students co-op with employers in 43 states and several countries. Income from co-op is a major resource for Kettering students, whose total co-op income throughout their 4.5-year program typically ranges between $40,000 and $65,000. In addition to study abroad some Kettering students also gain experience in foreign locations for their co-op employer. Distance learning is for graduate students only.

FACILITIES

Housing: Coed dorms, apartments for single students, fraternity/sorority housing. **Special Academic Facilities/Equipment:** Art museum, Scharschburg Archives & Industrial History Museum (principal repository for SAE Patents & Technical Papers). Kettering is renowned for the variety and quality of its laboratories for student use and teaching. Labs are required in nearly all science and engineering courses. Of special note are the Bosch Automotive Electronics Systems Lab, Ford Design Simulation Studio, the GM/PACE e-Design and e-Manufacturing Studio, Center for Fuel Cell Systems and Powertrain Integration, the Crash Test Safety, Computer Integrated Manufacturing (CIM), Polymer Processing, and Mechatronics Labs, the Lubrizol Engine Test Center, SAE Project Vehicle facilities, Biomedical, Environmental Scanning Electron Microscopy Lab, and Connie and Jim John Recreation Center and Kettering Park (outdoor recreation). **Computers:** 100% of classrooms are wireless, 100% of public computers are PCs, 34% of public computers are UNIX, network access in dorm rooms, network access in dorm lounges, online registration, online administrative functions (other than registration), remote student-access to Web through college's connection.

CAMPUS LIFE

Activities: Drama/theater, jazz band, music ensembles, radio station, student government, student newspaper, yearbook. **Organizations:** 40 registered organizations, 13 honor societies, 2 religious organizations. 13 fraternities (17% men join), 6 sororities (12% women join).

ADMISSIONS

Freshman Academic Profile: 30% in top 10% of high school class, 70% in top 25% of high school class, 95% in top 50% of high school class. 85% from public high schools. SAT Math middle 50% range 570–680. SAT Critical Reading middle 50% range 500–620. ACT middle 50% range 24–29. TOEFL required of all international applicants, minimum paper TOEFL 550, minimum computer TOEFL 213. **Basis for Candidate Selection:** *Very important factors considered include:* Academic GPA, rigor of secondary school record, standardized test scores. *Important factors considered include:* Class rank. *Other factors considered include:* Extracurricular activities, interview, recommendation(s), talent/ability, volunteer work, work experience. **Freshman Admission Requirements:** High school diploma is required, and GED is not accepted. *Academic units required:* 3 English, 4 math, 2 science (2 science labs), 5 academic electives. *Academic units recommended:* 4 English, 4 math, 4 science (2 science labs), 2 foreign language, 4 social studies, 4 academic electives, 1 drafting/CAD. **Freshman Admission Statistics:** 2,157 applied, 71% admitted, 26% enrolled. **Transfer Admission Requirements:** College transcript(s). Minimum college GPA of 3.0 required. Lowest grade transferable C. **General Admission Information:** Application fee $35. Regular notification is rolling. Nonfall registration accepted. Admission may be deferred for a maximum of 1 year. Credit offered for CEEB Advanced Placement tests.

COSTS AND FINANCIAL AID

Annual tuition $25,248. Room and board $5,798. Required fees $410. Average book expense $1,075. **Required Forms and Deadlines:** FAFSA. Financial aid filing deadline 2/14. **Notification of Awards:** Applicants will be notified of awards on a rolling basis beginning on or about 2/24. **Types of Aid:** *Need-based scholarships/grants:* Pell, SEOG, state scholarships/grants, private scholarships, the school's own gift aid, co-op. *Loans:* FFEL Subsidized Stafford, FFEL Unsubsidized Stafford, FFEL PLUS, state loans, alternative loans. **Student Employment:** Federal Work-Study Program available. Institutional employment available. Off-campus job opportunities are fair. **Financial Aid Statistics:** 75% freshmen, 59% undergrads receive need-based scholarship or grant aid. 72% freshmen, 62% undergrads receive need-based self-help aid. 99% freshmen, 90% undergrads receive any aid. Highest amount earned per year from on-campus jobs $1,200.

See page 1220.

KEUKA COLLEGE

Office of Admissions, Keuka Park, NY 14478-0098
Phone: 315-279-5254 **E-mail:** admissions@mail.keuka.edu **CEEB Code:** 2744
Fax: 315-536-5386 **Website:** www.keuka.edu **ACT Code:** 2782
Financial Aid Phone: 315-279-5646

This private school, affiliated with the American Baptist Church, was founded in 1890. It has a 203-acre campus.

RATINGS
Admissions Selectivity Rating: 70   **Fire Safety Rating:** 60*   **Green Rating:** 60*

STUDENTS AND FACULTY
Enrollment: 1,369. **Student Body:** 70% female, 30% male, 6% out-of-state. African American 4%, Caucasian 61%, Hispanic 1%. **Retention and Graduation:** 70% freshmen return for sophomore year. 30% freshmen graduate within 4 years. 28% grads go on to further study within 1 year. **Faculty:** Student/faculty ratio 14:1. 54 full-time faculty, 85% hold PhDs. 100% faculty teach undergrads.

ACADEMICS
Degrees: Bachelor's, master's. **Academic Requirements:** Arts/fine arts, computer literacy, English (including composition), history, humanities, mathematics, philosophy, sciences (biological or physical), social science, field period (160-hour yearly internship required of all students), integrative studies/institutional courses, physical activity, political science. **Classes:** Most classes have 10–19 students. Most lab/discussion sections have 10–19 students. **Majors with Highest Enrollment:** Business administration and management, occupational therapy/therapist, special education. **Disciplines with Highest Percentage of Degrees Awarded:** Health professions and related sciences 25%, business/marketing 21%, education 18%, social sciences 10%, other 8%. **Special Study Options:** Accelerated program, cooperative education program, cross-registration, double major, dual enrollment, independent study, internships, student-designed major, study abroad, teacher certification program.

FACILITIES
Housing: Coed dorms, men's dorms, women's dorms, special housing for disabled students, cooperative housing, theme housing. **Special Academic Facilities/Equipment:** Bird Museum, Lightner Gallery. **Computers:** 100% of classrooms are wireless, 100% of public computers are PCs, network access in dorm rooms, network access in dorm lounges, remote student-access to Web through college's connection.

CAMPUS LIFE
Activities: Choral groups, concert band, dance, drama/theater, literary magazine, musical theater, radio station, student government, student newspaper, student-run film society, yearbook. **Organizations:** 32 registered organizations, 7 honor societies, 2 religious organizations. **Athletics (Intercollegiate):** *Men:* Baseball, basketball, cross-country, golf, lacrosse, soccer, tennis. *Women:* Basketball, cross-country, golf, lacrosse, soccer, softball, synchronized swimming, tennis, volleyball.

ADMISSIONS
Freshman Academic Profile: 5% in top 10% of high school class, 22% in top 25% of high school class, 58% in top 50% of high school class. 96% from public high schools. SAT Math middle 50% range 425–540. SAT Critical Reading middle 50% range 410–520. TOEFL required of all international applicants, minimum paper TOEFL 500, minimum computer TOEFL 300. **Basis for Candidate Selection:** *Other factors considered include:* Academic GPA, alumni/ae relation, application essay, character/personal qualities, class rank, extracurricular activities, first generation, interview, level of applicant's interest, recommendation(s), rigor of secondary school record, standardized test scores. **Freshman Admission Requirements:** High school diploma is required, and GED is accepted. *Academic units recommended:* 4 English, 3 math, 3 science (2 science labs), 3 foreign language, 3 social studies, 2 history. **Freshman Admission Statistics:** 706 applied, 80% admitted, 41% enrolled. **Transfer Admission Requirements:** College transcript(s), essay or personal statement. Minimum college GPA of 2.0 required. Lowest grade transferable C. **General Admission Information:** Application fee $30. Regular notification is rolling. Nonfall registration accepted. Admission may be deferred for a maximum of 1 year. Credit and/or placement offered for CEEB Advanced Placement tests.

COSTS AND FINANCIAL AID
Annual tuition $19,960. Room and board $8,530. Required fees $590. Average book expense $950. **Required Forms and Deadlines:** FAFSA. **Notification of Awards:** Applicants will be notified of awards on a rolling basis beginning on or about 3/1. **Types of Aid:** *Need-based scholarships/grants:* Pell, SEOG, state scholarships/grants, the school's own gift aid. *Loans:* FFEL Subsidized Stafford, FFEL Unsubsidized Stafford, FFEL PLUS, Federal Perkins. **Financial Aid Statistics:** 90% freshmen, 89% undergrads receive need-based scholarship or grant aid. 77% freshmen, 82% undergrads receive need-based self-help aid. 92% freshmen, 93% undergrads receive any aid. Highest amount earned per year from on-campus jobs $1,800.

KEYSTONE COLLEGE

One College Green, La Plume, PA 18440
Phone: 570-945-8111 **E-mail:** admissions@keystone.edu **CEEB Code:** 2351
Fax: 570-945-7916 **Website:** www.keystone.edu **ACT Code:** 2602
Financial Aid Phone: 570-945-8132

This private school was founded in 1868. It has a 270-acre campus.

RATINGS
Admissions Selectivity Rating: 60*   **Fire Safety Rating:** 60*   **Green Rating:** 60*

STUDENTS AND FACULTY
Enrollment: 1,680. **Student Body:** 62% female, 38% male, 10% out-of-state. African American 3%, Caucasian 59%, Hispanic 2%. **Retention and Graduation:** 66% freshmen return for sophomore year. 18% grads go on to further study within 1 year. **Faculty:** Student/faculty ratio 13:1. 64 full-time faculty, 44% hold PhDs.

ACADEMICS
Degrees: Associate, bachelor's, certificate, post-bachelor's certificate. **Academic Requirements:** Computer literacy, English (including composition), humanities, mathematics, sciences (biological or physical), social science. One ethics course is required of all students, as is one writing intensive course, one diversity awareness course, and one course that requires a service learning component. **Classes:** Most classes have 10–19 students. Most lab/discussion sections have fewer than 10 students. **Disciplines with Highest Percentage of Degrees Awarded:** Business/marketing 27%, education 21%, computer and information sciences 14%, security and protective services 14%, parks and recreation 12%, communications/journalism 8%. **Special Study Options:** Cooperative education program, cross-registration, distance learning, dual enrollment, honors program, independent study, internships, study abroad, teacher certification program, weekend college.

FACILITIES
Housing: Coed dorms, women's dorms, special housing for disabled students. **Special Academic Facilities/Equipment:** Linder Art Gallery, observatory. **Computers:** 100% of classrooms are wired, 100% of classrooms are wireless, network access in dorm rooms, network access in dorm lounges, online registration, online administrative functions (other than registration), remote student-access to Web through college's connection.

CAMPUS LIFE
Activities: Choral groups, drama/theater, literary magazine, musical theater, radio station, student government, student newspaper, yearbook. **Athletics (Intercollegiate):** *Men:* Baseball, basketball, cross-country, golf, tennis, track/field (outdoor). *Women:* Basketball, cross-country, softball, tennis, track/field (outdoor), volleyball. Environmental Initiatives: A recycling program. A policy for purchasing Energy Star compliant products. Purchase of wind derived electricity (10%) and erection of a test tower on campus to evaluate wind energy potential.

ADMISSIONS
Freshman Academic Profile: SAT Writing middle 50% range 390–490. ACT middle 50% range 16–20. TOEFL required of all international applicants, minimum paper TOEFL 550, minimum computer TOEFL 213. **Basis for Candidate Selection:** *Very important factors considered include:* Academic GPA, character/personal qualities, extracurricular activities, interview, rigor of secondary school record. *Important factors considered include:* Application essay, recommendation(s), talent/ability, volunteer work, work experience. *Other factors considered include:* Alumni/ae relation, class rank, first generation, level of applicant's interest, standardized test scores. **Freshman Admission Requirements:** High school diploma is required, and GED is accepted. *Academic units required:* 4 English, 3 math, 2 science (1 science lab), 2 social studies, 3 history, 1 academic elective. *Academic units recommended:* 4 math, 2 foreign language, 3 social studies. **Freshman Admission Statistics:** 945 applied, 79% admitted, 52% enrolled. **Transfer Admission Requirements:** College transcript(s). Minimum college GPA of 2.0 required. Lowest grade transferable C. **General Admission Information:** Application fee $25. Regular application deadline 7/1. Regular notification is rolling. Nonfall

registration accepted. Admission may be deferred for a maximum of 2 years. Credit and/or placement offered for CEEB Advanced Placement tests.

COSTS AND FINANCIAL AID

Annual tuition $16,630. Room and board $8,580. Required fees $1,175. Average book expense $1,400. **Required Forms and Deadlines:** FAFSA, state aid form. Financial aid filing deadline 5/1. **Notification of Awards:** Applicants will be notified of awards on a rolling basis beginning on or about 11/1. **Types of Aid:** *Need-based scholarships/grants:* Pell, SEOG, state scholarships/grants, private scholarships, the school's own gift aid. *Loans:* FFEL Subsidized Stafford, FFEL PLUS, Federal Perkins, alternative loans. **Student Employment:** Federal Work-Study Program available. Institutional employment available. Off-campus job opportunities are good. **Financial Aid Statistics:** 73% freshmen, 88% undergrads receive need-based scholarship or grant aid. 80% freshmen, 100% undergrads receive need-based self-help aid. 86% freshmen, 87% undergrads receive any aid. Highest amount earned per year from on-campus jobs $1,394.

See page 1222.

KING COLLEGE (TN)

1350 King College Road, Bristol, TN 37620-2699
Phone: 423-652-4861 **E-mail:** admissions@king.edu **CEEB Code:** 1371
Fax: 423-652-4727 **Website:** www.king.edu **ACT Code:** 3970
Financial Aid Phone: 423-652-4728

This private school, affiliated with the Presbyterian Church, was founded in 1867. It has a 135-acre campus.

RATINGS
Admissions Selectivity Rating: 78   **Fire Safety Rating:** 62   **Green Rating:** 60*

STUDENTS AND FACULTY
Enrollment: 1,037. **Student Body:** 65% female, 35% male, 43% out-of-state, 3% international (21 countries represented). African American 3%, Caucasian 80%, Hispanic 2%. **Retention and Graduation:** 67% freshmen return for sophomore year. 48% freshmen graduate within 4 years. 25% grads go on to further study within 1 year. 21% grads pursue arts and sciences degrees. 3% grads pursue business degrees. 1% grads pursue law degrees. 2% grads pursue medical degrees. **Faculty:** Student/faculty ratio 14:1. 60 full-time faculty, 67% hold PhDs. 100% faculty teach undergrads.

ACADEMICS
Degrees: Bachelor's, master's. **Academic Requirements:** Arts/fine arts, English (including composition), foreign languages, history, mathematics, sciences (biological or physical), social science. **Classes:** Most classes have 10–19 students. Most lab/discussion sections have 10–19 students. **Majors with Highest Enrollment:** Business administration/management, nursing/registered nurse training (RN, ASN, BSN, MSN), religion/religious studies. **Disciplines with Highest Percentage of Degrees Awarded:** Health professions and related sciences 36%, business/marketing 18%, theology and religious vocations 9%, English 7%, interdisciplinary studies 5%. **Special Study Options:** Accelerated program, cross-registration, double major, dual enrollment, honors program, independent study, internships, student-designed major, study abroad, teacher certification program.

FACILITIES
Housing: Men's dorms, women's dorms, special housing for disabled students. **Special Academic Facilities/Equipment:** Electron microscope, observatory with two reflecting telescopes, solar telescope. **Computers:** 100% of public computers are PCs, network access in dorm rooms, network access in dorm lounges, remote student-access to Web through college's connection, tuition includes personal computer.

CAMPUS LIFE
Activities: Choral groups, dance, drama/theater, literary magazine, music ensembles, musical theater, pep band, student government, student newspaper, yearbook. **Organizations:** 35 registered organizations, 5 honor societies, 9 religious organizations. **Athletics (Intercollegiate):** *Men:* Baseball, basketball, bowling, cheerleading, cross-country, diving, golf, soccer, swimming, tennis, track/field (indoor), track/field (outdoor), wrestling. *Women:* Basketball, bowling, cheerleading, cross-country, diving, golf, soccer, softball, swimming, tennis, track/field (indoor), track/field (outdoor), volleyball.

ADMISSIONS
Freshman Academic Profile: 26% in top 10% of high school class, 56% in top 25% of high school class, 85% in top 50% of high school class. 88% from public

high schools. SAT Math middle 50% range 480–568. SAT Critical Reading middle 50% range 450–540. SAT Writing middle 50% range 440–553. ACT middle 50% range 21–25. TOEFL required of all international applicants, minimum computer TOEFL 523, minimum computer TOEFL 193. **Basis for Candidate Selection:** *Very important factors considered include:* Academic GPA, standardized test scores. *Other factors considered include:* Application essay, class rank, recommendation(s), rigor of secondary school record. **Freshman Admission Requirements:** High school diploma is required, and GED is accepted. *Academic units required:* 4 English, 3 math, 1 science, 2 foreign language, 4 academic electives. **Freshman Admission Statistics:** 645 applied, 95% admitted, 34% enrolled. **Transfer Admission Requirements:** College transcript(s). Minimum college GPA of 2.0 required. Lowest grade transferable C-. **General Admission Information:** Application fee $20. Regular notification year-round. Nonfall registration accepted. Admission may be deferred for a maximum of 2 years. Credit and/or placement offered for CEEB Advanced Placement tests.

COSTS AND FINANCIAL AID
Annual tuition $18,156. Room & board $6,508. Required fees $1,106. Average book expense $850. **Required Forms and Deadlines:** FAFSA. Financial aid filing deadline 3/1. **Notification of Awards:** Applicants will be notified of awards on a rolling basis beginning on or about 4/1. **Types of Aid:** *Need-based scholarships/grants:* Pell, SEOG, state scholarships/grants, private scholarships, the school's own gift aid. *Loans:* FFEL Subsidized Stafford, FFEL Unsubsidized Stafford, FFEL PLUS, Federal Perkins, state loans, college/university loans from institutional funds. **Student Employment:** Off-campus job opportunities are good. **Financial Aid Statistics:** 82% freshmen, 72% undergrads receive need-based scholarship or grant aid. 48% freshmen, 51% undergrads receive need-based self-help aid. 40 freshmen, 123 undergrads receive athletic scholarships. 98% freshmen, 98% undergrads receive any aid.

See page 1224.

THE KING'S COLLEGE

Empire State Building, 350 Fifth Avenue, Lower Level, New York, NY 10118
Phone: 212-659-3610 **E-mail:** info@tkc.edu
Fax: 212-659-3611 **Website:** www.tkc.edu

This is a private school.

RATINGS
Admissions Selectivity Rating: 60*   **Fire Safety Rating:** 60*   **Green Rating:** 60*

STUDENTS AND FACULTY
Enrollment: 231. **Student Body:** 62% female, 38% male, 77% out-of-state, 10% international. African American 4%, Asian 2%, Caucasian 41%, Hispanic 7%. **Retention and Graduation:** 77% freshmen return for sophomore year. **Faculty:** Student/faculty ratio 14:1. 12 full-time faculty, 92% hold PhDs.

ACADEMICS
Degrees: Bachelor's. **Academic Requirements:** Arts/fine arts, English (including composition), history, humanities, mathematics, philosophy, social science. **Classes:** Most classes have fewer than 10 students. **Disciplines with Highest Percentage of Degrees Awarded:** Business/marketing 13%, education 7%. **Special Study Options:** English as a Second Language (ESL), independent study, internships, study abroad.

FACILITIES
Housing: Apartments for single students. **Computers:** 100% of public computers are PCs, network access in dorm rooms, online registration, online administrative functions (other than registration), remote student-access to Web through college's connection. Undergraduates are required to own a computer.

CAMPUS LIFE
Activities: Dance, drama/theater, literary magazine, music ensembles, student government, student newspaper, yearbook.

ADMISSIONS
Freshman Academic Profile: 70% from public high schools. SAT Math middle 50% range 520–640. SAT Critical Reading middle 50% range 570–670. ACT middle 50% range 23–27. TOEFL required of all international applicants, minimum paper TOEFL 580, minimum computer TOEFL 237. **Basis for Candidate Selection:** *Very important factors considered include:* Academic GPA, interview, rigor of secondary school record, standardized test scores. *Important factors considered include:* Character/personal qualities, class rank, extracurricular activities, talent/ability. *Other factors considered include:* Application essay, level of applicant's interest, recommendation(s), religious affiliation/commitment, volunteer work, work experience. **Freshman**

Admission Requirements: High school diploma is required, and GED is accepted. *Academic units required:* 4 English, 4 math, 4 science, 2 foreign language, 2 social studies, 2 history. **Freshman Admission Statistics:** 348 applied, 57% admitted, 41% enrolled. **Transfer Admission Requirements:** College transcript(s), interview. Lowest grade transferable C. **General Admission Information:** Application fee $30. Regular application deadline 2/1. Regular notification 3/8. Non-fall registration accepted. Admission may be deferred for a maximum of 2 semesters. Common Application accepted. Credit and/or placement offered for CEEB Advanced Placement tests.

COSTS AND FINANCIAL AID

Annual tuition $18,590. Room $7,980. Required fees $350. Average book expense $1,000. **Required Forms and Deadlines:** Institution's own financial aid form, federal tax returns. Financial aid filing deadline 3/1. Financial aid filing deadline 12/15. **Notification of Awards:** Applicants will be notified of awards on or about 3/15. **Types of Aid:** *Need-based scholarships/grants:* State scholarships/grants, private scholarships, the school's own gift aid, Veteran's Administration. *Loans:* College/university loans from institutional funds, alternative loans. **Financial Aid Statistics:** 74% freshmen, 80% undergrads receive need-based scholarship or grant aid. 14% freshmen, 5% undergrads receive need-based self-help aid.

KING'S COLLEGE (PA)

133 North River Street, Wilkes-Barre, PA 18711
Phone: 570-208-5858 **E-mail:** admissions@kings.edu **CEEB Code:** 2353
Fax: 570-208-5971 **Website:** www.kings.edu **ACT Code:** 3604
Financial Aid Phone: 570-208-5868

This private school, affiliated with the Roman Catholic Church, was founded in 1946. It has a 48-acre campus.

RATINGS
Admissions Selectivity Rating: 74   **Fire Safety Rating:** 85   **Green Rating:** 79

STUDENTS AND FACULTY

Enrollment: 1,919. **Student Body:** 46% female, 54% male, 24% out-of-state. African American 2%, Caucasian 86%, Hispanic 2%. **Retention and Graduation:** 75% freshmen return for sophomore year. 63% freshmen graduate within 4 years. 21% grads go on to further study within 1 year. 9% grads pursue arts and sciences degrees. 1% grads pursue business degrees. 3% grads pursue law degrees. 8% grads pursue medical degrees. **Faculty:** Student/faculty ratio 16:1. 116 full-time faculty, 82% hold PhDs. 100% faculty teach undergrads.

ACADEMICS

Degrees: Associate, bachelor's, certificate, master's, post-bachelor's certificate. **Academic Requirements:** Arts/fine arts, computer literacy, English (including composition), foreign languages, history, humanities, mathematics, philosophy, sciences (biological or physical), social science, theology. **Classes:** Most classes have 10–19 students. Most lab/discussion sections have 10–19 students. **Majors with Highest Enrollment:** Business administration and management, criminal justice/safety studies, elementary education and teaching. **Disciplines with Highest Percentage of Degrees Awarded:** Business/marketing 25%, education 12%, security and protective services 11%, psychology 9%, health professions and related sciences 8%. **Special Study Options:** Accelerated program, cross-registration, distance learning, double major, dual enrollment, English as a second language (ESL), honors program, independent study, internships, student-designed major, study abroad, teacher certification program, weekend college.

FACILITIES

Housing: Men's dorms, women's dorms, apartments for single students. **Special Academic Facilities/Equipment:** Electron microscope, rooftop greenhouse, molecular biology lab, computer graphics lab. **Computers:** 90% of public computers are PCs, 10% of public computers are Macs, network access in dorm rooms, network access in dorm lounges, online registration, online administrative functions (other than registration), remote student-access to Web through college's connection.

CAMPUS LIFE

Activities: Choral groups, dance, drama/theater, literary magazine, music ensembles, pep band, radio station, student government, student newspaper, yearbook. **Organizations:** 50 registered organizations, 15 honor societies, 2 religious organizations. **Athletics (Intercollegiate):** *Men:* Baseball, basketball, cheerleading, cross-country, football, golf, lacrosse, soccer, swimming, tennis, wrestling. *Women:* Basketball, cheerleading, cross-country, field hockey, lacrosse, soccer, softball, swimming, tennis, volleyball.

ADMISSIONS

Freshman Academic Profile: 15% in top 10% of high school class, 37% in top 25% of high school class, 69% in top 50% of high school class. 71% from public high schools. SAT Math middle 50% range 470–570. SAT Critical Reading middle 50% range 460–560. TOEFL required of all international applicants, minimum paper TOEFL 525, minimum computer TOEFL 210. **Basis for Candidate Selection:** *Very important factors considered include:* Academic GPA, class rank, extracurricular activities, rigor of secondary school record, talent/ability. *Important factors considered include:* Alumni/ae relation, application essay, character/personal qualities, interview, recommendation(s), standardized test scores, volunteer work. **Freshman Admission Requirements:** High school diploma is required, and GED is accepted. *Academic units required:* 4 English, 3 math, 3 science (2 science labs), 2 foreign language, 3 social studies, 1 history. *Academic units recommended:* 4 English, 4 math, 4 science (2 science labs), 4 foreign language, 3 social studies, 1 history, 2 academic electives. **Freshman Admission Statistics:** 1,846 applied, 83% admitted, 31% enrolled. **Transfer Admission Requirements:** High school transcript, college transcript(s), essay or personal statement, standardized test score. Minimum college GPA of 2.0 required. Lowest grade transferable C. **General Admission Information:** Application fee $30. Regular notification is rolling. Nonfall registration accepted. Admission may be deferred for a maximum of 1 year. Neither credit nor placement offered for CEEB Advanced Placement tests.

COSTS AND FINANCIAL AID

Required Forms and Deadlines: FAFSA, institution's own financial aid form. Financial aid filing deadline 2/15. **Notification of Awards:** Applicants will be notified of awards on a rolling basis beginning on or about 3/1. **Types of Aid:** *Need-based scholarships/grants:* Pell, SEOG, state scholarships/grants, private scholarships, the school's own gift aid. *Loans:* FFEL Subsidized Stafford, FFEL Unsubsidized Stafford, FFEL PLUS, Federal Perkins, private loans. **Financial Aid Statistics:** 55% freshmen, 53% undergrads receive need-based scholarship or grant aid. 66% freshmen, 65% undergrads receive need-based self-help aid. 97% freshmen, 95% undergrads receive any aid. Highest amount earned per year from on-campus jobs $2,000.

See page 1226.

KNOX COLLEGE

Box K-148, Galesburg, IL 61401
Phone: 309-341-7100 **E-mail:** admission@knox.edu **CEEB Code:** 1372
Fax: 309-341-7070 **Website:** www.knox.edu **ACT Code:** 1052
Financial Aid Phone: 309-341-7149

This private school was founded in 1837. It has an 82-acre campus.

RATINGS
Admissions Selectivity Rating: 87   **Fire Safety Rating:** 70   **Green Rating:** 68

STUDENTS AND FACULTY

Enrollment: 1,327. **Student Body:** 56% female, 44% male, 49% out-of-state, 7% international (44 countries represented). African American 4%, Asian 6%, Caucasian 74%, Hispanic 4%. **Retention and Graduation:** 90% freshmen return for sophomore year. 69% freshmen graduate within 4 years. 30% grads go on to further study within 1 year. 22% grads pursue arts and sciences degrees. 1% grads pursue business degrees. 4% grads pursue law degrees. 2% grads pursue medical degrees. **Faculty:** Student/faculty ratio 13:1. 97 full-time faculty, 93% hold PhDs. 100% faculty teach undergrads.

ACADEMICS

Degrees: Bachelor's. **Academic Requirements:** Arts/fine arts, foreign languages, humanities, mathematics, sciences (biological or physical), social science. Students must take a 1-term interdisciplinary preceptorial emphasizing writing and discussion skills. In addition to this, 2 writing intensive courses and 1 course emphasizing oral presentation are required. One course focusing on diversity is also required, as well as documentation of a significant experiential learning project outside the classroom. Breadth requirements include 1 course each in the 4 areas of arts, humanities, math and natural science, and an additional field of concentration, minor or major, not in the department of the major. There are also foreign language and quantitative literacy requirements.

Classes: Most classes have 10–19 students. Most lab/discussion sections have 10–19 students. **Majors with Highest Enrollment:** Anthropology, economics, political science and government. **Disciplines with Highest Percentage of Degrees Awarded:** Social sciences 28%, biological/life sciences 11%, visual and performing arts 10%, English 9%, foreign languages and literature 8%. **Special Study Options:** Double major, dual enrollment, honors program, independent study, internships, liberal arts/career combination, student-designed major, study abroad, teacher certification program.

FACILITIES

Housing: Coed dorms, men's dorms, women's dorms, apartments for single students, fraternity/sorority housing. Coed, men's, and women's residence halls consist of bedrooms arranged around a common living area that houses 5-18 students. **Special Academic Facilities/Equipment:** Anthropology; art; and field museums; theater with revolving stage and computerized lighting; ceramics, sculpture, painting, and printmaking studios; 760-acre biological field station; environmental climate chambers; electron microscope. **Computers:** 1% of classrooms are wired, 100% of classrooms are wireless, 77% of public computers are PCs, 11% of public computers are Macs, 12% of public computers are UNIX, network access in dorm rooms, network access in dorm lounges, online registration, online administrative functions (other than registration), remote student-access to Web through college's connection.

CAMPUS LIFE

Activities: Choral groups, concert band, dance, drama/theater, jazz band, literary magazine, music ensembles, radio station, student government, student newspaper, symphony orchestra. **Organizations:** 99 registered organizations, 9 honor societies, 6 religious organizations. 5 fraternities (21% men join), 3 sororities (13% women join). **Athletics (Intercollegiate):** *Men:* Baseball, basketball, cross-country, football, golf, soccer, swimming, tennis, track/field (indoor), track/field (outdoor), wrestling. *Women:* Basketball, cross-country, golf, soccer, softball, swimming, tennis, track/field (indoor), track/field (outdoor), volleyball.

ADMISSIONS

Freshman Academic Profile: 34% in top 10% of high school class, 68% in top 25% of high school class, 94% in top 50% of high school class. 81% from public high schools. SAT Math middle 50% range 580–670. SAT Critical Reading middle 50% range 610–710. SAT Writing middle 50% range 590–690. TOEFL required of all international applicants, minimum paper TOEFL 550, minimum computer TOEFL 213. **Basis for Candidate Selection:** *Very important factors considered include:* Academic GPA, rigor of secondary school record. *Important factors considered include:* Application essay, class rank, recommendation(s). *Other factors considered include:* Alumni/ae relation, character/personal qualities, extracurricular activities, first generation, interview, level of applicant's interest, racial/ethnic status, standardized test scores, talent/ability, volunteer work. **Freshman Admission Requirements:** High school diploma is required, and GED is accepted. *Academic units recommended:* 4 English, 4 math, 3 science (2 science labs), 3 foreign language, 2 social studies, 2 history. **Freshman Admission Statistics:** 2,085 applied, 74% admitted, 27% enrolled. **Transfer Admission Requirements:** High school transcript, college transcript(s), essay or personal statement, statement of good standing from prior institution(s). Minimum college GPA of 3.0 required. Lowest grade transferable C. **General Admission Information:** Application fee $40. Regular application deadline 2/1. Regular notification 3/31. Nonfall registration accepted. Admission may be deferred for a maximum of 1 year. Credit and/or placement offered for CEEB Advanced Placement tests.

COSTS AND FINANCIAL AID

Annual tuition $30,180. Room and board $6,726. Required fees $327. Average book expense $900. **Required Forms and Deadlines:** FAFSA, institution's own financial aid form. Financial aid filing deadline 2/1. **Notification of Awards:** Applicants will be notified of awards on a rolling basis beginning on or about 3/15. **Types of Aid:** *Need-based scholarships/grants:* Pell, SEOG, state scholarships/grants, private scholarships, the school's own gift aid. *Loans:* Direct Subsidized Stafford, Direct Unsubsidized Stafford, Direct PLUS, Federal Perkins, state loans, college/university loans from institutional funds. **Student Employment:** Federal Work-Study Program available. Institutional employment available. Off-campus job opportunities are good. **Financial Aid Statistics:** 69% freshmen, 66% undergrads receive need-based scholarship or grant aid. 62% freshmen, 58% undergrads receive need-based self-help aid. 96% freshmen, 95% undergrads receive any aid. Highest amount earned per year from on-campus jobs $5,740.

KNOXVILLE COLLEGE

901 College Street, Knoxville, TN 37921
Phone: 800-743-5669 **CEEB Code:** 1373
Fax: 615-524-6583 **Website:** www.knoxvillecollege.edu **ACT Code:** 3972
Financial Aid Phone: 615-524-6525

This private school, affiliated with the Presbyterian Church, was founded in 1875. It has a 39-acre campus.

RATINGS

Admissions Selectivity Rating: 60*   **Fire Safety Rating:** 60*   **Green Rating:** 60*

STUDENTS AND FACULTY

Student Body: 72% out-of-state.

ACADEMICS

Degrees: Associate, bachelor's. **Special Study Options:** Cooperative education program, economics, engineering, food and lodging administration, philosophy with the University of Tennessee, teaching training program.

FACILITIES

Housing: Coed dorms. **Special Academic Facilities/Equipment:** Language lab.

CAMPUS LIFE

Organizations: 5 honor societies, 2 religious organizations. 5 fraternities (16% men join), 5 sororities (18% women join). **Athletics (Intercollegiate):** *Women:* Basketball, tennis, track/field (outdoor), volleyball.

ADMISSIONS

Freshman Academic Profile: 90% from public high schools. **Freshman Admission Requirements:** High school diploma is required, and GED is accepted. *Academic units required:* 4 English, 2 math, 2 science, 2 social studies, 4 academic electives. *Academic units recommended:* 3 math. **Transfer Admission Requirements:** Minimum college GPA of 2.0 required. Lowest grade transferable C. **General Admission Information:** Regular application deadline 7/1. Regular notification rolling. Nonfall registration accepted. Common Application not accepted. Credit offered for CEEB Advanced Placement tests.

COSTS AND FINANCIAL AID

Annual tuition $5,400. Room & board $3,450. Required fees $420. Average book expense $600. **Required Forms and Deadlines:** FAFSA, institution's own financial aid form, state aid form. **Types of Aid:** *Need-based scholarships/grants:* Pell, SEOG, state scholarships/grants, private scholarships, the school's own gift aid, United Negro College Fund. *Loans:* FFEL Subsidized Stafford, FFEL Unsubsidized Stafford, FFEL PLUS, Federal Perkins, college/university loans from institutional funds. **Student Employment:** Federal Work-Study Program available. Institutional employment available. Off-campus job opportunities are fair.

KUTZTOWN UNIVERSITY OF PENNSYLVANIA

Admissions Office, PO Box 730, Kutztown, PA 19530-0730
Phone: 610-683-4060 **E-mail:** admission@kutztown.edu **CEEB Code:** 2653
Fax: 610-683-1375 **Website:** www.kutztown.edu **ACT Code:** 3706
Financial Aid Phone: 610-683-4077

This public school was founded in 1866. It has a 326-acre campus.

RATINGS

Admissions Selectivity Rating: 73   **Fire Safety Rating:** 60*   **Green Rating:** 60*

STUDENTS AND FACULTY

Enrollment: 8,616. **Student Body:** 58% female, 42% male, 9% out-of-state. African American 7%, Asian 1%, Caucasian 86%, Hispanic 4%. **Retention and Graduation:** 77% freshmen return for sophomore year. 28% freshmen graduate within 4 years. 6% grads go on to further study within 1 year. 13% grads pursue arts and sciences degrees. 7% grads pursue business degrees. 1% grads pursue law degrees. 6% grads pursue medical degrees. **Faculty:** Student/faculty ratio 20:1. 451 full-time faculty. 61% hold PhDs. 99% faculty teach undergrads.

ACADEMICS

Degrees: Bachelor's, master's, post-bachelor's certificate. **Academic**

Requirements: English (including composition), humanities, mathematics, sciences (biological or physical), social science, physical education, speech. **Classes:** Most classes have 20–29 students. Most lab/discussion sections have 30–39 students. **Majors with Highest Enrollment:** Criminal justice/safety studies, elementary education and teaching, psychology. **Disciplines with Highest Percentage of Degrees Awarded:** Education 18%, business/marketing 16%, visual and performing arts 12%, psychology 9%, English 8%. **Special Study Options:** Cross-registration, distance learning, double major, dual enrollment, honors program, independent study, internships, liberal arts/career combination, student-designed major, study abroad, teacher certification program.

FACILITIES

Housing: Coed dorms, women's dorms, apartments for single students, cooperative housing. **Special Academic Facilities/Equipment:** Art gallery, German Cultural Heritage Center, Early Childhood Learning Center, cartography lab, observatory, planetarium, day care center. **Computers:** 67% of public computers are PCs, 33% of public computers are Macs, network access in dorm rooms, network access in dorm lounges, online registration, online administrative functions (other than registration), remote student-access to Web through college's connection.

CAMPUS LIFE

Activities: Choral groups, concert band, dance, drama/theater, jazz band, literary magazine, marching band, music ensembles, musical theater, radio station, student government, student newspaper, television station, yearbook. **Organizations:** 160 registered organizations, 16 honor societies, 9 religious organizations. 6 fraternities (1% men join), 7 sororities (1% women join). **Athletics (Intercollegiate):** *Men:* Baseball, basketball, cross-country, football, soccer, swimming, tennis, track/field (indoor), track/field (outdoor), wrestling. *Women:* Basketball, cheerleading, cross-country, field hockey, golf, soccer, softball, swimming, tennis, track/field (indoor), track/field (outdoor), volleyball.

ADMISSIONS

Freshman Academic Profile: 6% in top 10% of high school class, 25% in top 25% of high school class, 64% in top 50% of high school class. 99% from public high schools. SAT Math middle 50% range 440–540. SAT Critical Reading middle 50% range 440–530. SAT Writing middle 50% range 430–520. ACT middle 50% range 17–21. TOEFL required of all international applicants, minimum paper TOEFL 500, minimum computer TOEFL 173. **Basis for Candidate Selection:** *Very important factors considered include:* Class rank, rigor of secondary school record, standardized test scores. *Other factors considered include:* Academic GPA, character/personal qualities, extracurricular activities, geographical residence, interview, racial/ethnic status, recommendation(s), state residency, talent/ability, volunteer work, work experience. **Freshman Admission Requirements:** High school diploma is required, and GED is accepted. *Academic units recommended:* 4 English, 3 math, 3 science, 2 foreign language, 4 social studies. **Freshman Admission Statistics:** 8,908 applied, 64% admitted, 34% enrolled. **Transfer Admission Requirements:** College transcript(s), statement of good standing from prior institution(s). Minimum college GPA of 2.0 required. Lowest grade transferable C. **General Admission Information:** Application fee $35. Regular notification is rolling. Nonfall registration accepted. Admission may be deferred for a maximum of 1 year. Credit and/or placement offered for CEEB Advanced Placement tests.

COSTS AND FINANCIAL AID

Annual in-state tuition $5,177. Annual out-of-state tuition $12,944. Room and board $6,960. Required fees $1,696. Average book expense $1,100. **Required Forms and Deadlines:** FAFSA. Financial aid filing deadline 2/15. **Notification of Awards:** Applicants will be notified of awards on a rolling basis beginning on or about 3/30. **Types of Aid:** *Need-based scholarships/grants:* Pell, SEOG, state scholarships/grants, private scholarships, the school's own gift aid. *Loans:* Direct Subsidized Stafford, Direct Unsubsidized Stafford, Direct PLUS, Federal Perkins. **Student Employment:** Federal Work-Study Program available. Institutional employment available. Off-campus job opportunities are fair. **Financial Aid Statistics:** 41% freshmen, 37% undergrads receive need-based scholarship or grant aid. 50% freshmen, 48% undergrads receive need-based self-help aid. 62 freshmen, 213 undergrads receive athletic scholarships. 81% freshmen, 81% undergrads receive any aid. Highest amount earned per year from on-campus jobs $1,002.

LA ROCHE COLLEGE

9000 Babcock Boulevard, Pittsburgh, PA 15237
Phone: 412-536-1271 **E-mail:** admissions@laroche.edu **CEEB Code:** 2379
Fax: 412-536-1048 **Website:** www.laroche.edu **ACT Code:** 3607
Financial Aid Phone: 412-536-1120

This private school, affiliated with the Roman Catholic Church, was founded in 1963. It has an 80-acre campus.

RATINGS

Admissions Selectivity Rating: 70   **Fire Safety Rating:** 90   **Green Rating:** 60*

STUDENTS AND FACULTY

Enrollment: 1,320. **Student Body:** 68% female, 32% male, 7% out-of-state, 10% international (38 countries represented). African American 5%, Caucasian 78%, Hispanic 1%. **Retention and Graduation:** 68% freshmen return for sophomore year. 57% freshmen graduate within 4 years. **Faculty:** Student/faculty ratio 12:1. 64 full-time faculty, 83% hold PhDs. 95% faculty teach undergrads.

ACADEMICS

Degrees: Associate, bachelor's, certificate, master's, post-bachelor's certificate. **Academic Requirements:** Arts/fine arts, computer literacy, English (including composition), foreign languages, history, humanities, mathematics, philosophy, sciences (biological or physical), social science. **Classes:** Most classes have 10–19 students. Most lab/discussion sections have 10–19 students. **Majors with Highest Enrollment:** Design and visual communications, elementary education and teaching, psychology. **Disciplines with Highest Percentage of Degrees Awarded:** Business/marketing 26%, education 15%, visual and performing arts 13%, psychology 10%, security and protective services 5%, computer and information sciences 5%, health professions and related sciences 5%. **Special Study Options:** Accelerated program, cross-registration, distance learning, double major, English as a second language (ESL), independent study, internships, student-designed major, study abroad, teacher certification program.

FACILITIES

Housing: Coed dorms. **Special Academic Facilities/Equipment:** Cantellopes Art Gallery. New College Center extension has state-of-the-art smart classrooms. **Computers:** 70% of public computers are PCs, 30% of public computers are Macs, network access in dorm rooms, network access in dorm lounges, online registration, online administrative functions (other than registration), remote student-access to Web through college's connection.

CAMPUS LIFE

Activities: Choral groups, dance, drama/theater, literary magazine, musical theater, radio station, student government, student newspaper. **Organizations:** 39 registered organizations, 4 honor societies, 1 religious organization. **Athletics (Intercollegiate):** *Men:* Baseball, basketball, cross-country, golf, soccer. *Women:* Basketball, cheerleading, cross-country, soccer, softball, volleyball.

ADMISSIONS

Freshman Academic Profile: 11% in top 10% of high school class, 27% in top 25% of high school class, 59% in top 50% of high school class. 79% from public high schools. SAT Math middle 50% range 410–510. SAT Critical Reading middle 50% range 410–510. SAT Writing middle 50% range 430–510. ACT middle 50% range 15–19. **Basis for Candidate Selection:** *Very important factors considered include:* Academic GPA, rigor of secondary school record, standardized test scores. *Important factors considered include:* Application essay, recommendation(s), talent/ability. *Other factors considered include:* Character/personal qualities, class rank, extracurricular activities, first generation, geographical residence, interview, level of applicant's interest, volunteer work, work experience. **Freshman Admission Requirements:** High school diploma is required, and GED is accepted. *Academic units required:* 4 English, 3 math, 3 science (2 science labs), 3 social studies, 3 history. *Academic units recommended:* 4 English, 3 math, 3 science (2 science labs), 2 foreign language, 3 social studies, 3 history. **Freshman Admission Statistics:** 683 applied, 79% admitted, 49% enrolled. **Transfer Admission Requirements:** College transcript(s). Minimum college GPA of 2.0 required. Lowest grade transferable C. **General Admission Information:** Application fee $50. Regular notification is rolling. Nonfall registration accepted. Admission may be deferred for a maximum of 1 year. Credit offered for CEEB Advanced Placement tests.

COSTS AND FINANCIAL AID

Annual tuition $18,600. Room and board $7,942. Required fees $652. Average book expense $800. **Required Forms and Deadlines:** FAFSA. Financial aid filing deadline 1/15. **Notification of Awards:** Applicants will be notified of awards on a rolling basis beginning on or about 2/15. **Types of Aid:** *Need-based scholarships/grants:* Pell, SEOG, state scholarships/grants, private scholarships, the school's own gift aid. *Loans:* FFEL Subsidized Stafford, FFEL Unsubsidized Stafford, FFEL PLUS, Federal Perkins, private loans. **Financial Aid Statistics:** 62% freshmen, 52% undergrads receive need-based scholarship or grant aid. 68% freshmen, 61% undergrads receive need-based self-help aid. 98% freshmen, 95% undergrads receive any aid.

LA SIERRA UNIVERSITY

4700 Pierce Street, Riverside, CA 92515-8247
Phone: 909-785-2176 **E-mail:** ivy@lasierra.edu **CEEB Code:** 4380
Fax: 909-785-2447 **Website:** www.lasierra.edu **ACT Code:** 4380
Financial Aid Phone: 909-785-2175

This private school, affiliated with the Seventh-Day Adventist Church, was founded in 1922. It has a 147-acre campus.

RATINGS
Admissions Selectivity Rating: 79   **Fire Safety Rating:** 60*   **Green Rating:** 60*

STUDENTS AND FACULTY
Enrollment: 1,148. **Student Body:** 54% female, 46% male, 15% out-of-state, 8% international (59 countries represented). African American 6%, Asian 26%, Caucasian 46%, Hispanic 18%. **Retention and Graduation:** 55% freshmen return for sophomore year. **Faculty:** 100% faculty teach undergrads.

ACADEMICS
Degrees: Bachelor's, doctoral, master's, post-master's certificate. **Academic Requirements:** Arts/fine arts, foreign languages, humanities, mathematics, philosophy, sciences (biological or physical), social science, religion, health and fitness. **Special Study Options:** Accelerated program, cooperative education program, double major, dual enrollment, English as a second language (ESL), honors program, internships, student-designed major, study abroad, teacher certification program.

FACILITIES
Housing: Men's dorms, women's dorms, apartments for married students, apartments for single students, honors residence hall. **Special Academic Facilities/Equipment:** Art gallery, natural history museum, arboretum, observatory. **Computers:** 70% of public computers are PCs, 30% of public computers are Macs, 5% of public computers are UNIX, network access in dorm rooms, online registration, remote student-access to Web through college's connection.

CAMPUS LIFE
Activities: Choral groups, concert band, drama/theater, jazz band, literary magazine, music ensembles, student government, student newspaper, symphony orchestra, yearbook. **Organizations:** 30 registered organizations, 5 religious organizations. **Athletics (Intercollegiate):** *Men:* Football, tennis, volleyball. *Women:* Basketball, football, gymnastics, volleyball.

ADMISSIONS
Freshman Academic Profile: 14% in top 10% of high school class, 34% in top 25% of high school class, 68% in top 50% of high school class. 38% from public high schools. SAT Math middle 50% range 430–600. SAT Critical Reading middle 50% range 430–570. ACT middle 50% range 17–24. TOEFL required of all international applicants, minimum paper TOEFL 550. **Basis for Candidate Selection:** *Very important factors considered include:* Recommendation(s), rigor of secondary school record. *Important factors considered include:* Character/personal qualities, religious affiliation/commitment. *Other factors considered include:* Application essay, interview. **Freshman Admission Requirements:** High school diploma is required, and GED is accepted. *Academic units recommended:* 4 English, 3 math, 3 science (3 science labs), 2 foreign language, 1 social studies, 1 history, 1 computing and health. **Transfer Admission Requirements:** High school transcript, college transcript(s), statement of good standing from prior institution(s). Minimum college GPA of 2.0 required. Lowest grade transferable D. **General Admission Information:** Application fee $30. Early decision application deadline 8/15. Regular notification is rolling. Nonfall registration accepted. Common Application not accepted. Credit offered for CEEB Advanced Placement tests.

COSTS AND FINANCIAL AID
Comprehensive fee $19,101. Room & board $2,496. Average book expense $900. **Required Forms and Deadlines:** FAFSA, institution's own financial aid form, state aid form. Financial aid filing deadline 5/1. **Notification of Awards:** Applicants will be notified of awards on a rolling basis beginning on or about

7/15. **Types of Aid:** *Need-based scholarships/grants:* Pell, SEOG, private scholarships, the school's own gift aid. *Loans:* FFEL Subsidized Stafford, FFEL Unsubsidized Stafford, Federal Perkins. **Student Employment:** Federal Work-Study Program available. Institutional employment available. Off-campus job opportunities are good. **Financial Aid Statistics:** 74% freshmen, 68% undergrads receive need-based scholarship or grant aid. 47% freshmen, 53% undergrads receive need-based self-help aid.

LABORATORY INSTITUTE OF MERCHANDISING

12 East Fifty-third Street, New York, NY 10022
Phone: 212-752-1530 **E-mail:** admissions@limcollege.edu **CEEB Code:** 2380
Fax: 212-317-8602 **Website:** www.limcollege.edu **ACT Code:** 4807
Financial Aid Phone: 212-752-1530

This proprietary school was founded in 1939.

RATINGS
Admissions Selectivity Rating: 72   **Fire Safety Rating:** 60*   **Green Rating:** 60*

STUDENTS AND FACULTY
Enrollment: 970. **Student Body:** 95% female, 5% male, 54% out-of-state, 1% international (8 countries represented). African American 7%, Asian 6%, Caucasian 69%, Hispanic 15%. **Retention and Graduation:** 70% freshmen return for sophomore year. 59% freshmen graduate within 4 years. **Faculty:** Student/faculty ratio 8:1. 16 full-time faculty. 100% faculty teach undergrads.

ACADEMICS
Degrees: Associate, bachelor's. **Academic Requirements:** Arts/fine arts, computer literacy, English (including composition), humanities, mathematics. **Classes:** Most classes have 10–19 students. **Majors with Highest Enrollment:** Fashion merchandising, marketing/marketing management. **Disciplines with Highest Percentage of Degrees Awarded:** Business/marketing 55%, family and consumer sciences 38%, visual and performing arts 7%. **Special Study Options:** Accelerated program, cooperative education program, independent study, internships, study abroad, 3-credit trip in winter/summer to France, England, Germany, Spain, Italy, or China.

FACILITIES
Housing: Coed dorms. LIM is affiliated with a Local Y and YMHA and Educational Housing Services in which students can have a traditional residence life experience. **Computers:** 100% of public computers are PCs, network access in dorm rooms, online administrative functions (other than registration), remote student-access to Web through college's connection.

CAMPUS LIFE
Activities: Student government, student-run film society, yearbook. **Organizations:** 12 registered organizations, 1 honor society.

ADMISSIONS
Freshman Academic Profile: 5% in top 10% of high school class, 17% in top 25% of high school class, 54% in top 50% of high school class. 73% from public high schools. SAT Math middle 50% range 420–500. SAT Critical Reading middle 50% range 430–503. ACT middle 50% range 17–23. TOEFL required of all international applicants, minimum paper TOEFL 550, minimum computer TOEFL 213. **Basis for Candidate Selection:** *Very important factors considered include:* Academic GPA, interview, level of applicant's interest. *Important factors considered include:* Application essay, character/personal qualities, class rank, recommendation(s), standardized test scores, work experience. *Other factors considered include:* Alumni/ae relation, extracurricular activities, rigor of secondary school record, talent/ability, volunteer work. **Freshman Admission Requirements:** High school diploma is required, and GED is accepted. **Freshman Admission Statistics:** 658 applied, 64% admitted, 58% enrolled. **Transfer Admission Requirements:** High school transcript, college transcript(s), essay or personal statement, interview. Minimum college GPA of 2.0 required. Lowest grade transferable C. **General Admission Information:** Application fee $40. Regular notification rolling. Nonfall registration accepted. Admission may be deferred for a maximum of 1 semester. Credit and/or placement offered for CEEB Advanced Placement tests.

COSTS AND FINANCIAL AID
Annual tuition $19,300. Room and board $18,700. Required fees $525. Average book expense $1,100. **Required Forms and Deadlines:** FAFSA, institution's own financial aid form. **Notification of Awards:** Applicants will be notified of awards on a rolling basis beginning on or about 2/15. **Types of Aid:** *Need-based scholarships/grants:* Pell, SEOG, state scholarships/grants, private scholarships, the school's own gift aid. *Loans:* Direct Subsidized Stafford, Direct

Unsubsidized Stafford, Direct PLUS. **Student Employment:** Federal Work-Study Program available. Institutional employment available. Off-campus job opportunities are excellent. **Financial Aid Statistics:** 85% freshmen, 85% undergrads receive any aid.

See page 1228.

LAFAYETTE COLLEGE

118 Markle Hall, Easton, PA 18042
Phone: 610-330-5100 **E-mail:** admissions@lafayette.edu **CEEB Code:** 2361
Fax: 610-330-5355 **Website:** www.lafayette.edu
Financial Aid Phone: 610-330-5055

This private school, affiliated with the Presbyterian Church, was founded in 1826. It has a 340-acre campus.

RATINGS
Admissions Selectivity Rating: 96   **Fire Safety Rating:** 60*   **Green Rating:** 95

STUDENTS AND FACULTY
Enrollment: 2,381. **Student Body:** 48% female, 52% male, 70% out-of-state, 6% international (46 countries represented). African American 5%, Asian 3%, Caucasian 80%, Hispanic 5%. **Retention and Graduation:** 93% freshmen return for sophomore year. 88% freshmen graduate within 4 years. 29% grads go on to further study within 1 year. 12% grads pursue arts and sciences degrees. 5% grads pursue business degrees. 7% grads pursue law degrees. 3% grads pursue medical degrees. **Faculty:** Student/faculty ratio 11:1. 195 full-time faculty, 100% hold PhDs. 100% faculty teach undergrads.

ACADEMICS
Degrees: Bachelor's. **Academic Requirements:** English (including composition), foreign languages, humanities, mathematics, sciences (biological or physical), social science. **Classes:** Most classes have 10–19 students. Most lab/discussion sections have 10–19 students. **Disciplines with Highest Percentage of Degrees Awarded:** Social sciences 31%, English 7%, psychology 7%, biological/life sciences 6%. **Special Study Options:** Accelerated program, cooperative education program, cross-registration, distance learning, double major, honors program, internships, liberal arts/career combination, student-designed major, study abroad.

FACILITIES
Housing: Coed dorms, men's dorms, women's dorms, apartments for married students, apartments for single students, special housing for disabled students, special housing for international students, fraternity/sorority housing, cooperative housing. **Special Academic Facilities/Equipment:** Art and geological museums, center for the arts, engineering labs, INSTRON materials testing machine, electron microscopes, transform nuclear magnetic resonance spectrometer, computerized gas chromatograph/mass spectrometer. **Computers:** 95% of public computers are PCs, 5% of public computers are Macs, network access in dorm rooms, network access in dorm lounges, online registration, online administrative functions (other than registration), remote student-access to Web through college's connection.

CAMPUS LIFE
Activities: Choral groups, concert band, dance, drama/theater, jazz band, literary magazine, music ensembles, musical theater, pep band, radio station, student government, student newspaper, student-run film society, symphony orchestra, yearbook. **Organizations:** 250 registered organizations, 14 honor societies, 7 religious organizations. 7 fraternities (26% men join), 6 sororities (45% women join). **Athletics (Intercollegiate):** *Men:* Baseball, basketball, cheerleading, crew/rowing, cross-country, diving, equestrian sports, fencing, football, golf, gymnastics, ice hockey, lacrosse, soccer, softball, swimming, tennis, track/field (indoor), track/field (outdoor), volleyball, wrestling. *Women:* Basketball, cheerleading, crew/rowing, cross-country, diving, equestrian sports, fencing, field hockey, golf, gymnastics, softball, swimming, tennis, track/field (indoor), track/field (outdoor), volleyball.

ADMISSIONS
Freshman Academic Profile: 62% in top 10% of high school class, 92% in top 25% of high school class, 100% in top 50% of high school class. 68% from public high schools. SAT Math middle 50% range 620–710. SAT Critical Reading middle 50% range 580–670. SAT Writing middle 50% range 580–670.

ACT middle 50% range 24–29. TOEFL required of all international applicants, minimum paper TOEFL 550. **Basis for Candidate Selection:** *Very important factors considered include:* Rigor of secondary school record. *Important factors considered include:* Alumni/ae relation, application essay, character/personal qualities, class rank, extracurricular activities, racial/ethnic status, recommendation(s), standardized test scores, talent/ability, volunteer work. *Other factors considered include:* Geographical residence, interview, work experience. **Freshman Admission Requirements:** High school diploma or equivalent is not required. *Academic units recommended:* 4 English, 3 math, 2 science (2 science labs), 2 foreign language, 5 academic electives. **Freshman Admission Statistics:** 5,875 applied, 37% admitted, 29% enrolled. **Transfer Admission Requirements:** High school transcript, college transcript(s), essay or personal statement. Minimum college GPA of 3.0 required. Lowest grade transferable C. **General Admission Information:** Application fee $60. Early decision application deadline 2/15. Regular application deadline 1/1. Regular notification 4/1. Nonfall registration accepted. Admission may be deferred for a maximum of 1 year. Credit and/or placement offered for CEEB Advanced Placement tests.

COSTS AND FINANCIAL AID
Annual tuition $33,634. Room & board $10,377. Required fees $177. Average book expense $600. **Required Forms and Deadlines:** FAFSA, CSS/Financial Aid PROFILE, Noncustodial PROFILE, Business/Farm Supplement. Financial aid filing deadline 2/1. **Notification of Awards:** Applicants will be notified of awards on or about 4/1. **Types of Aid:** *Need-based scholarships/grants:* Pell, SEOG, state scholarships/grants, private scholarships. *Loans:* FFEL Subsidized Stafford, FFEL Unsubsidized Stafford, FFEL PLUS, Federal Perkins, state loans, college/university loans from institutional funds, HELP loans to parents. **Student Employment:** Federal Work-Study Program available. Institutional employment available. Off-campus job opportunities are good. **Financial Aid Statistics:** 48% freshmen, 48% undergrads receive need-based scholarship or grant aid. 32% freshmen, 38% undergrads receive need-based self-help aid. Highest amount earned per year from on-campus jobs $1,000.

LAGRANGE COLLEGE

Office of Admission, 601 Broad Street, LaGrange, GA 30240
Phone: 706-880-8005 **E-mail:** lgcadmis@lagrange.edu **CEEB Code:** 5362
Fax: 706-880-8010 **Website:** www.lagrange.edu **ACT Code:** 834
Financial Aid Phone: 706-880-8229

This private school, affiliated with the Methodist Church, was founded in 1831. It has a 120-acre campus.

RATINGS
Admissions Selectivity Rating: 71   **Fire Safety Rating:** 60*   **Green Rating:** 84

STUDENTS AND FACULTY
Enrollment: 881. **Student Body:** 61% female, 39% male, 11% out-of-state. African American 13%, Caucasian 70%, Hispanic 1%. **Retention and Graduation:** 76% freshmen return for sophomore year. 33% freshmen graduate within 4 years. 20% grads go on to further study within 1 year. **Faculty:** Student/faculty ratio 10:1. 63 full-time faculty, 79% hold PhDs. 100% faculty teach undergrads.

ACADEMICS
Degrees: Associate, bachelor's, master's. **Academic Requirements:** Arts/fine arts, computer literacy, English (including composition), foreign languages, history, humanities, mathematics, sciences (biological or physical), social science, religion. **Classes:** Most classes have fewer than 10 students. Most lab/discussion sections have fewer than 10 students. **Majors with Highest Enrollment:** Business administration/management, elementary education and teaching, social work. **Disciplines with Highest Percentage of Degrees Awarded:** Business/marketing 30%, education 10%, visual and performing arts 8%, psychology 7%, health professions and related sciences 7%, computer and information sciences 6%, social sciences 6%. **Special Study Options:** Double major, dual enrollment, independent study, internships, liberal arts/career combination, study abroad, teacher certification program.

FACILITIES
Housing: Coed dorms, men's dorms, women's dorms. **Special Academic Facilities/Equipment:** Art center, center for the performing arts, language lab. **Computers:** 82% of public computers are PCs, 18% of public computers are Macs, network access in dorm rooms, network access in dorm lounges, online registration, online administrative functions (other than registration), remote student-access to Web through college's connection.

CAMPUS LIFE

Activities: Choral groups, dance, drama/theater, literary magazine, music ensembles, musical theater, student government, student newspaper, yearbook. **Organizations:** 32 registered organizations, 12 honor societies, 4 religious organizations. 2 fraternities (22% men join), 3 sororities (25% women join). **Athletics (Intercollegiate):** *Men:* Baseball, basketball, cross-country, golf, soccer, swimming, tennis. *Women:* Basketball, cheerleading, cross-country, soccer, softball, swimming, tennis, volleyball.

ADMISSIONS

Freshman Academic Profile: 20% in top 10% of high school class, 48% in top 25% of high school class, 78% in top 50% of high school class. SAT Math middle 50% range 450–550. SAT Critical Reading middle 50% range 450–550. ACT middle 50% range 19–24. TOEFL required of all international applicants, minimum paper TOEFL 500. **Basis for Candidate Selection:** *Very important factors considered include:* Character/personal qualities, rigor of secondary school record, standardized test scores. *Important factors considered include:* Interview, recommendation(s). *Other factors considered include:* Alumni/ae relation, application essay, class rank, extracurricular activities, geographical residence, talent/ability, volunteer work. **Freshman Admission Requirements:** High school diploma is required, and GED is accepted. *Academic units required:* 4 English, 4 math, 2 science, 3 social studies. *Academic units recommended:* 4 English, 4 math, 3 science, 2 foreign language, 3 social studies. **Freshman Admission Statistics:** 563 applied, 90% admitted, 39% enrolled. **Transfer Admission Requirements:** College transcript(s), essay or personal statement. Minimum college GPA of 2.0 required. Lowest grade transferable C. **General Admission Information:** Application fee $20. Regular notification is rolling. Nonfall registration accepted. Admission may be deferred for a maximum of 1 term. Common Application not accepted. Credit and/or placement offered for CEEB Advanced Placement tests.

COSTS AND FINANCIAL AID

Annual tuition $18,500. Room and board $7,598. Average book expense $1,000. **Required Forms and Deadlines:** FAFSA, institution's own financial aid form, state aid form. Financial aid filing deadline 4/1. **Types of Aid:** *Need-based scholarships/grants:* Pell, SEOG, state scholarships/grants, private scholarships, the school's own gift aid. *Loans:* FFEL Subsidized Stafford, FFEL Unsubsidized Stafford, FFEL PLUS, Federal Perkins. **Student Employment:** Federal Work-Study Program available. Institutional employment available. Off-campus job opportunities are excellent. **Financial Aid Statistics:** 66% freshmen, 63% undergrads receive need-based scholarship or grant aid. 44% freshmen, 48% undergrads receive need-based self-help aid. Highest amount earned per year from on-campus jobs $604.

LAKE ERIE COLLEGE

391 West Washington Street, Painesville, OH 44077-3389
Phone: 440-375-7050 **E-mail:** admissions@lec.edu **CEEB Code:** 1391
Fax: 440-375-7005 **Website:** www.lec.edu **ACT Code:** 3288
Financial Aid Phone: 440-375-7100

This private school was founded in 1856. It has a 48-acre campus.

RATINGS

Admissions Selectivity Rating: 77   **Fire Safety Rating:** 60*   **Green Rating:** 60*

STUDENTS AND FACULTY

Enrollment: 903. **Student Body:** 71% female, 29% male, 20% out-of-state. African American 5%, Caucasian 58%, Hispanic 1%. **Retention and Graduation:** 64% freshmen return for sophomore year. 32% freshmen graduate within 4 years. **Faculty:** Student/faculty ratio 12:1. 34 full-time faculty, 76% hold PhDs. 100% faculty teach undergrads.

ACADEMICS

Degrees: Bachelor's, certificate, master's, post-bachelor's certificate. **Academic Requirements:** Arts/fine arts, computer literacy, English (including composition), foreign languages, history, humanities, mathematics, philosophy, sciences (biological or physical), social science, intercultural. **Classes:** Most classes have fewer than 10 students. Most lab/discussion sections have fewer than 10 students. **Disciplines with Highest Percentage of Degrees Awarded:** Education 22%, business/marketing 17%, agriculture 10%, social sciences 10%, interdisciplinary studies 8%, biological/life sciences 7%, communication technologies 7%. **Special Study Options:** Accelerated program, cross-registration, double major, dual enrollment, honors program, independent study, internships, liberal arts/career combination, student-designed major, study abroad, teacher certification program, weekend college.

FACILITIES

Housing: Coed dorms, men's dorms, women's dorms, apartments for single students. **Computers:** 100% of public computers are PCs, network access in dorm rooms, network access in dorm lounges, online registration, online administrative functions (other than registration), remote student-access to Web through college's connection.

CAMPUS LIFE

Activities: Choral groups, dance, drama/theater, pep band, radio station, student government, student newspaper, yearbook. **Organizations:** 15 registered organizations, 3 honor societies, 1 sorority (4% women join). **Athletics (Intercollegiate):** *Men:* Baseball, basketball, cross-country, equestrian sports, golf, soccer. *Women:* Basketball, cross-country, equestrian sports, soccer, softball, volleyball.

ADMISSIONS

Freshman Academic Profile: 15% in top 10% of high school class, 29% in top 25% of high school class, 59% in top 50% of high school class. 83% from public high schools. SAT Math middle 50% range 420–530. SAT Critical Reading middle 50% range 430–550. SAT Writing middle 50% range 420–550. ACT middle 50% range 17–24. TOEFL required of all international applicants, minimum paper TOEFL 550, minimum computer TOEFL 213. **Basis for Candidate Selection:** *Very important factors considered include:* Academic GPA, application essay, character/personal qualities, level of applicant's interest, recommendation(s), rigor of secondary school record, standardized test scores. *Important factors considered include:* Class rank, interview, talent/ability. *Other factors considered include:* Alumni/ae relation, extracurricular activities, first generation, geographical residence, religious affiliation/commitment, state residency, volunteer work, work experience. **Freshman Admission Requirements:** High school diploma is required, and GED is accepted. *Academic units required:* 4 English, 3 math, 3 science (2 science labs), 2 foreign language, 3 social studies, 2 history. *Academic units recommended:* 4 English, 3 math, 3 science (2 science labs), 2 foreign language, 3 social studies, 2 history. **Freshman Admission Statistics:** 768 applied, 53% admitted, 34% enrolled. **Transfer Admission Requirements:** High school transcript, college transcript(s). Minimum college GPA of 2.0 required. Lowest grade transferable C. **General Admission Information:** Application fee $30. Regular notification is rolling. Nonfall registration accepted. Admission may be deferred for a maximum of 1 year. Credit and/or placement offered for CEEB Advanced Placement tests.

COSTS AND FINANCIAL AID

Annual tuition $23,950. Room and board $7,650. Required fees $1,270. Average book expense $900. **Required Forms and Deadlines:** FAFSA. **Notification of Awards:** Applicants will be notified of awards on a rolling basis beginning on or about 1/20. **Types of Aid:** *Need-based scholarships/grants:* Pell, SEOG, state scholarships/grants, private scholarships, the school's own gift aid. *Loans:* FFEL Subsidized Stafford, FFEL Unsubsidized Stafford, FFEL PLUS, Federal Perkins, payment plans. **Financial Aid Statistics:** 100% freshmen, 90% undergrads receive need-based self-help aid. 100% freshmen, 99% undergrads receive any aid. Highest amount earned per year from on-campus jobs $1,200.

See page 1230.

LAKE FOREST COLLEGE

555 North Sheridan Road, Lake Forest, IL 60045
Phone: 847-735-5000 **E-mail:** admissions@lakeforest.edu **CEEB Code:** 1392
Fax: 847-735-6291 **Website:** www.lakeforest.edu **ACT Code:** 1054
Financial Aid Phone: 847-725-5103

This private school was founded in 1857. It has a 107-acre campus.

RATINGS

Admissions Selectivity Rating: 88   **Fire Safety Rating:** 69   **Green Rating:** 60*

STUDENTS AND FACULTY

Enrollment: 1,399. **Student Body:** 58% female, 42% male, 54% out-of-state, 7% international (54 countries represented). African American 4%, Asian 5%, Caucasian 78%, Hispanic 7%. **Retention and Graduation:** 79% freshmen return for sophomore year. 58% freshmen graduate within 4 years. 34% grads go on to further study within 1 year. 54% grads pursue arts and sciences degrees. 17% grads pursue law degrees. 28% grads pursue medical degrees. **Faculty:** Student/faculty ratio 12:1. 88 full-time faculty, 97% hold PhDs. 100% faculty teach undergrads.

ACADEMICS

Degrees: Bachelor's, master's. **Academic Requirements:** English (including composition), humanities, mathematics, sciences (biological or physical), social science. **Classes:** Most classes have 10–19 students. Most lab/discussion sections have 10–19 students. **Majors with Highest Enrollment:** Communications studies/speech communication and rhetoric, economics, English language and literature. **Disciplines with Highest Percentage of Degrees Awarded:** Social sciences 20%, communications/journalism 14%, English 9%, psychology 8%, business/marketing 8%, interdisciplinary studies 7%, foreign languages and literature 7%. **Special Study Options:** Double major, honors program, independent study, internships, liberal arts/career combination, student-designed major, study abroad, teacher certification program.

FACILITIES

Housing: Coed dorms, women's dorms. **Special Academic Facilities/ Equipment:** Center for Chicago Programs, art gallery, language labs, technology resource center, speech and video production room, smart classrooms, music/recording studio with synthesizers, 10 public access computer labs, 24-hour computer lab, wireless network, fiber-optic high-speed wired network, electron microscope, computer molecular modeling equipment, high-resolution FT-IR, NMR spectrometer, neutron howitzer, digital storage oscilloscopes, fluorescence microscope. **Computers:** 50% of classrooms are wired, 15% of classrooms are wireless, 79% of public computers are PCs, 20% of public computers are Macs, 1% of public computers are UNIX, network access in dorm rooms, network access in dorm lounges, online administrative functions (other than registration), support for handheld computing, remote student-access to Web through college's connection.

CAMPUS LIFE

Activities: Choral groups, dance, drama/theater, jazz band, literary magazine, music ensembles, musical theater, pep band, radio station, student government, student newspaper, student-run film society, yearbook. **Organizations:** 90 registered organizations, 11 honor societies, 6 religious organizations. 2 fraternities (8% men join), 5 sororities (17% women join). **Athletics (Intercollegiate):** *Men:* Basketball, cross-country, diving, football, handball, ice hockey, soccer, swimming, tennis. *Women:* Basketball, cross-country, diving, handball, ice hockey, soccer, softball, swimming, tennis, volleyball.

ADMISSIONS

Freshman Academic Profile: 32% in top 10% of high school class, 59% in top 25% of high school class, 88% in top 50% of high school class. 65% from public high schools. SAT Math middle 50% range 540–660. SAT Critical Reading middle 50% range 560–650. SAT Writing middle 50% range 540–640. ACT middle 50% range 24–29. TOEFL required of all international applicants, minimum paper TOEFL 550, minimum computer TOEFL 220. **Basis for Candidate Selection:** *Very important factors considered include:* Academic GPA, interview, rigor of secondary school record. *Important factors considered include:* Application essay, character/personal qualities, extracurricular activities, level of applicant's interest, recommendation(s), talent/ability. *Other factors considered include:* Alumni/ae relation, class rank, first generation, geographical residence, standardized test scores, state residency, volunteer work, work experience. **Freshman Admission Requirements:** High school diploma is required, and GED is accepted. *Academic units required:* 4 English, 3 math, 2 science (2 science labs), 2 social studies, 2 history, 2 academic electives. *Academic units recommended:* 4 English, 4 math, 3 science (3 science labs), 2 foreign language, 3 social studies, 3 history, 3 academic electives, 1 honors or advanced placement course. **Freshman Admission Statistics:** 2,197 applied, 63% admitted, 28% enrolled. **Transfer Admission Requirements:** High school transcript, college transcript(s), essay or personal statement, statement of good standing from prior institution(s). Minimum college GPA of 2.5 required. Lowest grade transferable C-. **General Admission Information:** Application fee $40. Early decision application deadline 12/1. Regular notification 3/15. Nonfall registration accepted. Admission may be deferred for a maximum of 1 year. Credit and/or placement offered for CEEB Advanced Placement tests.

COSTS AND FINANCIAL AID

Annual tuition $30,600. Room and board $7,326. Required fees $364. Average book expense $700. **Required Forms and Deadlines:** FAFSA, institution's own financial aid form, federal income tax return. Financial aid filing deadline 3/1. **Notification of Awards:** Applicants will be notified of awards on a rolling basis beginning on or about 3/1. **Types of Aid:** *Need-based scholarships/grants:* Pell, SEOG, state scholarships/grants, private scholarships, the school's own gift aid. *Loans:* FFEL Subsidized Stafford, FFEL Unsubsidized Stafford, FFEL PLUS, Federal Perkins, college/university loans from institutional funds, private loans. **Financial Aid Statistics:** 78% freshmen, 76% undergrads receive need-based scholarship or grant aid. 50% freshmen, 50% undergrads receive need-

based self-help aid. 90% freshmen, 89% undergrads receive any aid. Highest amount earned per year from on-campus jobs $2,000.

See page 1232.

LAKE REGION STATE COLLEGE

1801 College Drive North, Devils Lake, ND 58301-1598
Phone: 701-662-1514 **E-mail:** lrsc.admissions@lrsc.nodak.edu
Fax: 701-662-1581 **Website:** www.lrsc.nodak.edu **ACT Code:** 3198
Financial Aid Phone: 701-662-1516

This public school was founded in 1941. It has a 120-acre campus.

RATINGS

Admissions Selectivity Rating: 60*   **Fire Safety Rating:** 93   **Green Rating:** 60*

STUDENTS AND FACULTY

Enrollment: 594. **Student Body:** 65% female, 35% male, 10% out-of-state, 2% international (8 countries represented). African American 3%, Caucasian 84%, Hispanic 2%, Native American 6%. **Faculty:** Student/faculty ratio 15:1. 30 full-time faculty, 3% hold PhDs. 100% faculty teach undergrads.

ACADEMICS

Degrees: Associate, certificate, diploma. **Academic Requirements:** Computer literacy, English (including composition), humanities, mathematics, sciences (biological or physical), social science. **Majors with Highest Enrollment:** Business administration and management, criminal justice/police science, liberal arts and sciences/liberal studies. **Special Study Options:** Cooperative education program, distance learning, dual enrollment, English as a second language (ESL), internships, liberal arts/career combination.

FACILITIES

Housing: Men's dorms, women's dorms, apartments for married students, apartments for single students, special housing for disabled students, coed dorms for adult students. **Special Academic Facilities/Equipment:** Paul Hoghaug Library & Law Library. **Computers:** 100% of public computers are PCs, network access in dorm rooms, online registration, online administrative functions (other than registration), remote student-access to Web through college's connection.

CAMPUS LIFE

Activities: Drama/theater, literary magazine, musical theater, student government, symphony orchestra. **Organizations:** 12 registered organizations, 1 religious organization. **Athletics (Intercollegiate):** *Men:* Basketball. *Women:* Basketball.

ADMISSIONS

Freshman Academic Profile: 98% from public high schools. ACT middle 50% range 16–22. TOEFL required of all international applicants, minimum paper TOEFL 525, minimum computer TOEFL 200. **Freshman Admission Requirements:** High school diploma is required, and GED is accepted. *Academic units recommended:* 4 English, 3 math, 3 science (2 science labs), 2 foreign language, 3 social studies. **Freshman Admission Statistics:** 225 applied, 98% admitted, 93% enrolled. **Transfer Admission Requirements:** High school transcript, college transcript(s), statement of good standing from prior institution(s). Minimum college GPA of 2.0 required. Lowest grade transferable D. **General Admission Information:** Application fee $35. Regular notification no set date. Nonfall registration accepted. Admission may be deferred for a maximum of 1 semester.

COSTS AND FINANCIAL AID

Annual in-state tuition $2,780. Out-of-state tuition $2,780. Room & board $4,574. Required fees $783. Average book expense $750. **Required Forms and Deadlines:** FAFSA. Financial aid filing deadline 3/15. **Notification of Awards:** Applicants will be notified of awards on a rolling basis beginning on or about 5/15. **Types of Aid:** *Need-based scholarships/grants:* Pell, SEOG, state scholarships/grants, private scholarships, the school's own gift aid, Academic Competitiveness Grant. *Loans:* FFEL Subsidized Stafford, FFEL Unsubsidized Stafford, FFEL PLUS, Federal Perkins, state loans. **Financial Aid Statistics:** 78% freshmen, 69% undergrads receive need-based scholarship or grant aid. 73% freshmen, 68% undergrads receive need-based self-help aid. 7 freshmen, 16 undergrads receive athletic scholarships. 80% undergrads receive any aid.

LAKE SUPERIOR STATE UNIVERSITY

650 West Easterday Avenue, Sault Ste. Marie, MI 49783-1699
Phone: 906-635-2231 **E-mail:** admissions@lssu.edu **CEEB Code:** 1421
Fax: 906-635-6669 **Website:** www.lssu.edu **ACT Code:** 2031
Financial Aid Phone: 906-635-2678

This public school was founded in 1946. It has a 115-acre campus.

RATINGS
Admissions Selectivity Rating: 70   **Fire Safety Rating:** 60*   **Green Rating:** 60*

STUDENTS AND FACULTY
Enrollment: 2,753. **Student Body:** 51% female, 49% male, 4% out-of-state, 11% international. Caucasian 78%, Native American 9%. **Retention and Graduation:** 61% freshmen return for sophomore year. 18% freshmen graduate within 4 years. **Faculty:** Student/faculty ratio 17:1. 112 full-time faculty, 65% hold PhDs. 100% faculty teach undergrads.

ACADEMICS
Degrees: Associate, bachelor's, certificate, master's. **Academic Requirements:** Computer literacy, English (including composition), humanities, mathematics, sciences (biological or physical), social science, critical thinking, oral communication, aesthetics, ethics, cultural diversity. **Classes:** Most classes have 20–29 students. Most lab/discussion sections have 10–19 students. **Disciplines with Highest Percentage of Degrees Awarded:** Security and protective services 22%, business/marketing 19%, engineering 12%, education 9%, health professions and related sciences 7%. **Special Study Options:** Cooperative education program, cross-registration, distance learning, double major, dual enrollment, honors program, independent study, internships, student-designed major, teacher certification program, weekend college.

FACILITIES
Housing: Coed dorms, men's dorms, women's dorms, apartments for married students, apartments for single students, fraternity/sorority housing. **Special Academic Facilities/Equipment:** Natural Science, Michigan History, and Great Lakes Shipping Museums; planetarium; industrial robots; atomic absorption/flame emission spectrophotometer. **Computers:** Network access in dorm rooms, online registration.

CAMPUS LIFE
Activities: Choral groups, concert band, dance, drama/theater, jazz band, literary magazine, music ensembles, pep band, radio station, student government, student newspaper, symphony orchestra. **Organizations:** 60 registered organizations, 4 fraternities, 4 sororities. **Athletics (Intercollegiate):** *Men:* Basketball, cross-country, ice hockey, tennis, track/field (indoor), track/field (outdoor). *Women:* Basketball, cross-country, softball, tennis, track/field (indoor), track/field (outdoor), volleyball.

ADMISSIONS
Freshman Academic Profile: 9% in top 10% of high school class, 28% in top 25% of high school class, 60% in top 50% of high school class. ACT middle 50% range 18–23. TOEFL required of all international applicants, minimum paper TOEFL 550, minimum computer TOEFL 213. **Basis for Candidate Selection:** *Very important factors considered include:* Academic GPA, rigor of secondary school record, standardized test scores. *Other factors considered include:* Class rank, geographical residence, interview, recommendation(s). **Freshman Admission Requirements:** High school diploma is required, and GED is accepted. *Academic units recommended:* 4 English, 3 math, 3 science (3 science labs), 2 foreign language, 2 social studies, 1 history. **Freshman Admission Statistics:** 1,566 applied, 85% admitted, 41% enrolled. **Transfer Admission Requirements:** College transcript(s). Minimum college GPA of 2.0 required. Lowest grade transferable C-. **General Admission Information:** Application fee $20. Regular application deadline 8/15. Regular notification is rolling. Nonfall registration accepted. Admission may be deferred for a maximum of 1 year. Common Application not accepted. Credit offered for CEEB Advanced Placement tests.

COSTS AND FINANCIAL AID
Annual in-state tuition $5,988. Annual out-of-state tuition $11,976. Room and board $6,536. Required fees $318. Average book expense $750. **Required Forms and Deadlines:** FAFSA. Financial aid filing deadline 2/21. **Notification of Awards:** Applicants will be notified of awards on a rolling basis beginning on or about 11/1. **Types of Aid:** *Need-based scholarships/grants:* Pell, SEOG, state scholarships/grants, private scholarships, the school's own gift aid, Federal Nursing Scholarships, third party payments. *Loans:* Direct Subsidized Stafford, Direct Unsubsidized Stafford, Direct PLUS, Federal Perkins, Federal Nursing, state loans. **Student Employment:** Off-campus job opportunities are good. **Financial Aid Statistics:** 44% freshmen, 39%

undergrads receive need-based scholarship or grant aid. 70% freshmen, 64% undergrads receive need-based self-help aid. 31 freshmen, 142 undergrads receive athletic scholarships. 83% undergrads receive any aid. Highest amount earned per year from on-campus jobs $2,400.

LAKEHEAD UNIVERSITY

955 Oliver Road, Thunder Bay, ON P7B 5E1 Canada
Phone: 807-343-8500 **E-mail:** liaison@lakeheadu.ca
Fax: 807-343-8156 **Website:** www.lakeheadu.ca
Financial Aid Phone: 807-343-8206

This public school was founded in 1965. It has a 345-acre campus.

RATINGS
Admissions Selectivity Rating: 60*   **Fire Safety Rating:** 60*   **Green Rating:** 60*

STUDENTS AND FACULTY
Retention and Graduation: 80% freshmen return for sophomore year. **Faculty:** Student/faculty ratio 19:1. 240 full-time faculty, 81% hold PhDs. 100% faculty teach undergrads.

ACADEMICS
Degrees: Bachelor's, certificate, diploma, doctoral, master's. **Classes:** Most classes have 20–29 students. **Majors with Highest Enrollment:** Business administration/management, engineering, forestry. **Special Study Options:** Cooperative education program, distance learning, double major, exchange student program (domestic), honors program, study abroad, teacher certification program.

FACILITIES
Housing: Coed dorms, women's dorms. **Computers:** 90% of public computers are PCs, 10% of public computers are Macs, 100% of public computers are UNIX, network access in dorm rooms, network access in dorm lounges, remote student-access to Web through college's connection.

CAMPUS LIFE
Activities: Student government, student newspaper. **Athletics (Intercollegiate):** *Men:* Basketball, crew/rowing, cross-country, ice hockey, rugby, skiing (Nordic/cross-country), track/field (outdoor), volleyball, wrestling. *Women:* Basketball, crew/rowing, cross-country, rugby, skiing (Nordic/cross-country), track/field (outdoor), volleyball, wrestling.

ADMISSIONS
Freshman Academic Profile: 70% from public high schools. TOEFL required of all international applicants, minimum paper TOEFL 550. **Basis for Candidate Selection:** *Important factors considered include:* Rigor of secondary school record. **Freshman Admission Requirements:** High school diploma is required, and GED is not accepted. **Freshman Admission Statistics:** 5,759 applied, 35% admitted. **General Admission Information:** Application fee $85. Regular application deadline 9/18. Regular notification is rolling. Nonfall registration accepted. Common Application not accepted. Neither credit nor placement offered for CEEB Advanced Placement tests.

COSTS AND FINANCIAL AID
Room & board $4,917. Required fees $364. Average book expense $700. **Student Employment:** Federal Work-Study Program available. Off-campus job opportunities are fair.

LAKELAND COLLEGE

PO Box 359, Sheboygan, WI 53082-0359
Phone: 920-565-2111 **E-mail:** admissions@lakeland.edu **CEEB Code:** 1393
Fax: 920-565-1206 **Website:** www.lakeland.edu **ACT Code:** 4592
Financial Aid Phone: 920-565-1297

This private school, affiliated with the United Church of Christ, was founded in 1862. It has a 145-acre campus.

RATINGS
Admissions Selectivity Rating: 71   **Fire Safety Rating:** 60*   **Green Rating:** 60*

STUDENTS AND FACULTY

Enrollment: 2,920. **Student Body:** 24% out-of-state, 3% international. African American 5%, Asian 2%, Caucasian 85%, Hispanic 1%. **Retention and Graduation:** 23% freshmen graduate within 4 years. 17% grads go on to further study within 1 year. 5% grads pursue arts and sciences degrees. 8% grads pursue business degrees. 2% grads pursue law degrees. 2% grads pursue medical degrees. **Faculty:** Student/faculty ratio 15:1. 42 full-time faculty, 57% hold PhDs. 42% faculty teach undergrads.

ACADEMICS

Degrees: Bachelor's, master's. **Academic Requirements:** Arts/fine arts. **Disciplines with Highest Percentage of Degrees Awarded:** Business/marketing 71%, computer and information sciences 12%, education 9%, psychology 2%, biological/life sciences 1%. **Special Study Options:** Double major, dual enrollment, English as a second language (ESL), honors program, independent study, internships, study abroad, teacher certification program.

FACILITIES

Housing: Coed dorms, men's dorms, women's dorms, apartments for single students, special housing for disabled students, apartments for honors students, cultural suites available. **Special Academic Facilities/Equipment:** Museum of College History. **Computers:** 100% of public computers are PCs, network access in dorm rooms, network access in dorm lounges, online registration, online administrative functions (other than registration), remote student-access to Web through college's connection.

CAMPUS LIFE

Activities: Choral groups, concert band, drama/theater, jazz band, music ensembles, pep band, student government, student newspaper, television station, yearbook. **Organizations:** 30 registered organizations. 3 fraternities, 3 sororities. **Athletics (Intercollegiate):** *Men:* Baseball, basketball, cross-country, football, golf, ice hockey, skiing (downhill/alpine), skiing (Nordic/cross-country), soccer, softball, tennis, volleyball, wrestling. *Women:* Basketball, cross-country, golf, skiing (downhill/alpine), soccer, softball, tennis, volleyball.

ADMISSIONS

Freshman Academic Profile: 9% in top 10% of high school class, 27% in top 25% of high school class, 53% in top 50% of high school class. 95% from public high schools. ACT middle 50% range 17–22. TOEFL required of all international applicants, minimum paper TOEFL 500. **Basis for Candidate Selection:** *Very important factors considered include:* Class rank, extracurricular activities, rigor of secondary school record, standardized test scores. *Important factors considered include:* Alumni/ae relation, interview, racial/ethnic status, talent/ability. *Other factors considered include:* Application essay, recommendation(s). **Freshman Admission Requirements:** High school diploma is required, and GED is accepted. *Academic units recommended:* 4 English, 2 math, 4 science, 2 foreign language, 1 social studies. **Freshman Admission Statistics:** 584 applied, 68% admitted, 39% enrolled. **Transfer Admission Requirements:** College transcript(s). Minimum college GPA of 2.0 required. Lowest grade transferable C. **General Admission Information:** Application fee $20. Regular application deadline 8/1. Regular notification is rolling. Nonfall registration accepted. Admission may be deferred for a maximum of 1 year. Common Application accepted. Credit and/or placement offered for CEEB Advanced Placement tests.

COSTS AND FINANCIAL AID

Annual tuition $11,980. Room & board $4,860. Required fees $500. Average book expense $500. **Required Forms and Deadlines:** FAFSA, institution's own financial aid form. Financial aid filing deadline 5/1. **Notification of Awards:** Applicants will be notified of awards on a rolling basis beginning on or about 3/1. **Types of Aid:** *Need-based scholarships/grants:* Pell, SEOG, state scholarships/grants, private scholarships, the school's own gift aid. *Loans:* FFEL Subsidized Stafford, FFEL Unsubsidized Stafford, FFEL PLUS, Federal Perkins, college/university loans from institutional funds. **Student Employment:** Federal Work-Study Program available. Institutional employment available. Off-campus job opportunities are good. **Financial Aid Statistics:** 91% freshmen, 63% undergrads receive need-based scholarship or grant aid. 80% freshmen, 58% undergrads receive need-based self-help aid. Highest amount earned per year from on-campus jobs $1,250.

LAMAR UNIVERSITY

PO Box 10009, Beaumont, TX 77710
Phone: 409-880-8888 **E-mail:** admissions@hal.lamar.edu **CEEB Code:** 6360
Fax: 409-880-8463 **Website:** www.lamar.edu **ACT Code:** 4114
Financial Aid Phone: 409-880-8454

This public school was founded in 1923. It has a 200-acre campus.

RATINGS

Admissions Selectivity Rating: 60*   **Fire Safety Rating:** 60*   **Green Rating:** 60*

STUDENTS AND FACULTY

Enrollment: 9,057. **Student Body:** 55% female, 45% male, 1% out-of-state. African American 22%, Asian 3%, Caucasian 74%, Hispanic 5%.

ACADEMICS

Degrees: Bachelor's, doctoral, master's. **Academic Requirements:** Arts/fine arts, computer literacy, English (including composition), history, humanities, mathematics, philosophy, sciences (biological or physical), social science. **Special Study Options:** Cooperative education program, distance learning, double major, dual enrollment, English as a second language (ESL), honors program, internships, study abroad, teacher certification program, Texas Academy for Leadership in the Humanities, a 2-year residential, early admission program for gifted high school students. Students are selected during the sophomore year of high school and enter the university at the end of their junior year.

FACILITIES

Housing: Coed dorms, men's dorms, women's dorms, apartments for single students, fraternity/sorority housing. **Special Academic Facilities/Equipment:** Museum.

CAMPUS LIFE

Activities: Student government, student newspaper. **Organizations:** 145 registered organizations. 11 fraternities (5% men join), 8 sororities (5% women join). **Athletics (Intercollegiate):** *Men:* Baseball, basketball, cross-country, golf, tennis, track/field (outdoor). *Women:* Basketball, cross-country, golf, tennis, track/field (outdoor), volleyball.

ADMISSIONS

Freshman Academic Profile: 10% in top 10% of high school class, 27% in top 25% of high school class, 90% in top 50% of high school class. 96% from public high schools. TOEFL required of all international applicants, minimum paper TOEFL 500. **Freshman Admission Requirements:** High school diploma is required, and GED is accepted. *Academic units recommended:* 4 English, 3 math, 2 science, 2 social studies, 2 academic electives. **Transfer Admission Requirements:** Minimum college GPA of 2.0 required. Lowest grade transferable D. **General Admission Information:** Regular application deadline 8/1. Regular notification rolling. Nonfall registration accepted. Common Application not accepted. Credit and/or placement offered for CEEB Advanced Placement tests.

COSTS AND FINANCIAL AID

Annual in-state tuition $864. Out-of-state tuition $5,976. Room & board $3,040. Required fees $840. Average book expense $587. **Required Forms and Deadlines:** FAFSA, institution's own financial aid form, state aid form. **Types of Aid:** *Loans:* FFEL Subsidized Stafford, FFEL PLUS. **Student Employment:** Federal Work-Study Program available. Institutional employment available. Off-campus job opportunities are good. **Financial Aid Statistics:** Highest amount earned per year from on-campus jobs $1,200.

LAMBUTH UNIVERSITY

705 Lambuth Boulevard, Jackson, TN 38301-5296
Phone: 731-425-3223 **E-mail:** admit@lambuth.edu **CEEB Code:** 1394
Fax: 731-425-3496 **Website:** www.lambuth.edu **ACT Code:** 3974
Financial Aid Phone: 731-425-3444

This private school, affiliated with the Methodist Church, was founded in 1843. It has a 50-acre campus.

RATINGS

Admissions Selectivity Rating: 86   **Fire Safety Rating:** 76   **Green Rating:** 60*

STUDENTS AND FACULTY

Enrollment: 785. **Student Body:** 51% female, 49% male, 20% out-of-state, 2% international (12 countries represented). African American 17%, Caucasian 75%, Hispanic 2%. **Retention and Graduation:** 61% freshmen return for sophomore year. 26% freshmen graduate within 4 years. 20% grads go on to further study within 1 year. 5% grads pursue arts and sciences degrees. 5% grads pursue business degrees. 5% grads pursue law degrees. 5% grads pursue medical degrees. **Faculty:** Student/faculty ratio 12:1. 53 full-time faculty, 75% hold PhDs. 100% faculty teach undergrads.

ACADEMICS

Degrees: Bachelor's. **Academic Requirements:** Arts/fine arts, computer literacy, English (including composition), history, humanities, mathematics, sciences (biological or physical), social science. **Classes:** Most classes have 10–19 students. Most lab/discussion sections have 10–19 students. **Majors with Highest Enrollment:** Business administration/management, elementary education and teaching, social sciences. **Disciplines with Highest Percentage of Degrees Awarded:** Social sciences 29%, business/marketing 11%, psychology 8%, education 8%, biological/life sciences 7%, parks and recreation 6%, visual and performing arts 6%. **Special Study Options:** Accelerated program, cross-registration, double major, English as a second language (ESL), honors program, independent study, internships, liberal arts/career combination, student-designed major, study abroad, teacher certification program, Washington Semester, Tennessee Legislative Internship.

FACILITIES

Housing: Coed dorms, men's dorms, women's dorms, apartments for single students, special housing for disabled students, fraternity/sorority housing. **Special Academic Facilities/Equipment:** Academic support center, interior design lab, planetarium, biological field station, curriculum lab, log cabin museum. **Computers:** 92% of public computers are PCs, 8% of public computers are Macs, network access in dorm rooms, remote student-access to Web through college's connection.

CAMPUS LIFE

Activities: Choral groups, concert band, dance, drama/theater, jazz band, literary magazine, music ensembles, musical theater, pep band, radio station, student government, student newspaper, yearbook. **Organizations:** 28 registered organizations, 6 honor societies, 3 religious organizations. 3 fraternities (30% men join), 4 sororities (29% women join). **Athletics (Intercollegiate):** *Men:* Baseball, basketball, cheerleading, cross-country, football, golf, soccer, swimming, tennis. *Women:* Basketball, cheerleading, cross-country, golf, soccer, softball, swimming, tennis, volleyball.

ADMISSIONS

Freshman Academic Profile: 18% in top 10% of high school class, 41% in top 25% of high school class, 71% in top 50% of high school class. 85% from public high schools. SAT Math middle 50% range 460–570. SAT Critical Reading middle 50% range 450–570. ACT middle 50% range 20–25. TOEFL required of all international applicants, minimum paper TOEFL 425, minimum computer TOEFL 115. **Basis for Candidate Selection:** *Very important factors considered include:* Rigor of secondary school record, standardized test scores. *Other factors considered include:* Application essay, class rank, extracurricular activities, recommendation(s). **Freshman Admission Requirements:** High school diploma is required, and GED is accepted. *Academic units recommended:* 4 English, 4 math, 3 science (2 science labs), 2 foreign language, 2 social studies, 2 history. **Freshman Admission Statistics:** 1,260 applied, 62% admitted, 28% enrolled. **Transfer Admission Requirements:** College transcript(s), statement of good standing from prior institution(s). Minimum college GPA of 2.0 required. Lowest grade transferable D. **General Admission Information:** Application fee $25. Regular notification is rolling. Nonfall registration accepted. Admission may be deferred. Common Application accepted. Credit and/or placement offered for CEEB Advanced Placement tests.

COSTS AND FINANCIAL AID

Annual tuition $17,000. Room and board $7,160. Required fees $400. Average book expense $1,200. **Required Forms and Deadlines:** FAFSA, institution's own financial aid form, admission application. Financial aid filing deadline 2/1. **Notification of Awards:** Applicants will be notified of awards on or about 2/15. **Types of Aid:** *Need-based scholarships/grants:* Pell, SEOG, state scholarships/grants, private scholarships, the school's own gift aid, Tennessee Hope Lottery Programs. *Loans:* FFEL Subsidized Stafford, FFEL Unsubsidized Stafford, FFEL PLUS, Federal Perkins. **Student Employment:** Federal Work-Study Program available. Institutional employment available. Off-campus job opportunities are excellent. **Financial Aid Statistics:** 58% freshmen, 68% undergrads receive need-based scholarship or grant aid. 47% freshmen, 53% undergrads receive need-based self-help aid. 8 freshmen, 36 undergrads receive athletic scholarships. 90% freshmen, 85% undergrads receive any aid. Highest amount earned per year from on-campus jobs $1,000.

LANCASTER BIBLE COLLEGE

PO Box 83403, 901 Eden Road, Lancaster, PA 17608
Phone: 717-560-8271 **E-mail:** Admissions@lbc.edu **CEEB Code:** 2388
Fax: 717-560-8213 **Website:** www.lbc.edu **ACT Code:** 3707
Financial Aid Phone: 717-560-8254

This private school, affiliated with the Christian (nondenominational) Church, was founded in 1933. It has a 100-acre campus.

RATINGS

Admissions Selectivity Rating: 77   **Fire Safety Rating:** 60*   **Green Rating:** 60*

STUDENTS AND FACULTY

Enrollment: 640. **Student Body:** 50% female, 50% male, 23% out-of-state. African American 3%, Caucasian 65%, Hispanic 1%. **Retention and Graduation:** 72% freshmen return for sophomore year. 47% freshmen graduate within 4 years. **Faculty:** Student/faculty ratio 17:1. 48 full-time faculty, 52% hold PhDs. 100% faculty teach undergrads.

ACADEMICS

Degrees: Associate, bachelor's, certificate, master's, post-bachelor's certificate. **Academic Requirements:** Arts/fine arts, English (including composition), history, humanities, mathematics, philosophy, sciences (biological or physical), social science. **Classes:** Most classes have fewer than 10 students. Most lab/discussion sections have 10–19 students. **Majors with Highest Enrollment:** Bible/biblical studies; elementary education and teaching; theological studies and religious vocations. **Disciplines with Highest Percentage of Degrees Awarded:** Theology and religious vocations 91%, education 9%. **Special Study Options:** Accelerated program, double major, independent study, internships, study abroad, teacher certification program.

FACILITIES

Housing: Men's dorms, women's dorms. **Computers:** 100% of public computers are PCs, network access in dorm rooms, network access in dorm lounges, remote student-access to Web through college's connection.

CAMPUS LIFE

Activities: Choral groups, concert band, drama/theater, music ensembles, student government, student newspaper, yearbook. **Organizations:** 20 registered organizations. **Athletics (Intercollegiate):** *Men:* Baseball, basketball, cheerleading, soccer, volleyball. *Women:* Basketball, cheerleading, lacrosse, soccer, volleyball.

ADMISSIONS

Freshman Academic Profile: 15% in top 10% of high school class, 32% in top 25% of high school class, 82% in top 50% of high school class. 60% from public high schools. SAT Math middle 50% range 460–570. SAT Critical Reading middle 50% range 480–580. ACT middle 50% range 17–23. TOEFL required of all international applicants, minimum paper TOEFL 550, minimum computer TOEFL 213. **Basis for Candidate Selection:** *Very important factors considered include:* Application essay, character/personal qualities, recommendation(s), religious affiliation/commitment, rigor of secondary school record, standardized test scores. *Important factors considered include:* Extracurricular activities. *Other factors considered include:* Class rank, interview, talent/ability, volunteer work. **Freshman Admission Requirements:** High school diploma is required, and GED is accepted. **Freshman Admission Statistics:** 239 applied, 67% admitted, 68% enrolled. **Transfer Admission Requirements:** High school transcript, college transcript(s), essay or personal statement, standardized test score, statement of good standing from prior institution(s). Minimum college GPA of 2.0 required. Lowest grade transferable C. **General Admission Information:** Application fee $25. Regular notification is rolling. Nonfall registration accepted. Admission may be deferred for a maximum of 1 year.

COSTS AND FINANCIAL AID

Annual tuition $13,920. Room and board $6,170. Required fees $600. **Required Forms and Deadlines:** FAFSA, state aid form. Financial aid filing deadline 5/4. **Notification of Awards:** Applicants will be notified of awards on a rolling basis beginning on or about 3/15. **Types of Aid:** *Need-based scholarships/grants:* Pell, SEOG, state scholarships/grants, private scholarships, the school's own gift aid, Office of Vocational Rehabilitation Blindness and Visual Services Awards. *Loans:* FFEL Subsidized Stafford, FFEL Unsubsidized Stafford, FFEL PLUS, Federal Perkins, alternative loans. **Student Employment:** Federal Work-Study Program available. Institutional employment available. Off-campus job opportunities are good. **Financial Aid Statistics:** 53% freshmen, 51% undergrads receive need-based scholarship or grant aid. 69% freshmen, 65% undergrads receive need-based self-help aid. Highest amount earned per year from on-campus jobs $1,400.

LANDER UNIVERSITY

320 Stanley Avenue, Greenwood, SC 29649
Phone: 864-388-8307 **E-mail:** admissions@lander.edu **CEEB Code:** 5363
Fax: 864-388-8125 **Website:** www.lander.edu **ACT Code:** 3860
Financial Aid Phone: 864-388-8340

This public school was founded in 1872. It has a 100-acre campus.

RATINGS
Admissions Selectivity Rating: 71   **Fire Safety Rating:** 60*   **Green Rating:** 60*

STUDENTS AND FACULTY
Enrollment: 2,655. **Student Body:** 67% female, 33% male, 3% out-of-state, 2% international (21 countries represented). African American 22%, Caucasian 74%, Hispanic 1%. **Retention and Graduation:** 65% freshmen return for sophomore year. 28% freshmen graduate within 4 years. **Faculty:** Student/faculty ratio 20:1. 117 full-time faculty, 72% hold PhDs. 98% faculty teach undergrads.

ACADEMICS
Degrees: Bachelor's, certificate, master's. **Academic Requirements:** Arts/fine arts, English (including composition), foreign languages, history, humanities, mathematics, sciences (biological or physical), social science, wellness component, global issues. **Classes:** Most classes have 20–29 students. **Majors with Highest Enrollment:** Business administration/management, elementary education and teaching, nursing/registered nurse training (RN, ASN, BSN, MSN). **Disciplines with Highest Percentage of Degrees Awarded:** Business/marketing 30%, education 13%, social sciences 13%, psychology 8%, visual and performing arts 7%, health professions and related sciences 7%, liberal arts/general studies 6%. **Special Study Options:** Cooperative education program, distance learning, double major, dual enrollment, honors program, independent study, internships, liberal arts/career combination, student-designed major, study abroad, teacher certification program, nursing (RN to BSN completion) program courses now offered on the Web. MBA from Clemson U. offered on campus; MEd counseling/school administration from Clemson U. offered on campus; MEd elementary education; MAT master of art in teaching; dual degree in engineering offered in conjunction with Clemson University.

FACILITIES
Housing: Coed dorms, women's dorms, apartments for single students. **Special Academic Facilities/Equipment:** Art gallery, continuing education center, media center, electronic piano instruction facility, amphitheater. **Computers:** Network access in dorm rooms, online registration, online administrative functions (other than registration), remote student-access to Web through college's connection.

CAMPUS LIFE
Activities: Choral groups, concert band, dance, drama/theater, jazz band, literary magazine, music ensembles, student government, student newspaper. **Organizations:** 65 registered organizations, 6 honor societies, 7 religious organizations. 6 fraternities (12% men join), 6 sororities (12% women join). **Athletics (Intercollegiate):** *Men:* Baseball, basketball, golf, soccer, tennis. *Women:* Basketball, cross-country, soccer, softball, tennis, volleyball.

ADMISSIONS
Freshman Academic Profile: 8% in top 10% of high school class, 30% in top 25% of high school class, 68% in top 50% of high school class. SAT Math middle 50% range 440–540. SAT Critical Reading middle 50% range 430–530. ACT middle 50% range 17–22. TOEFL required of all international applicants, minimum paper TOEFL 550, minimum computer TOEFL 213. **Basis for Candidate Selection:** *Very important factors considered include:* Class rank, rigor of secondary school record, standardized test scores. *Other factors considered include:* Alumni/ae relation, application essay, character/personal qualities, extracurricular activities, interview, recommendation(s), talent/ability, volunteer work, work experience. **Freshman Admission Requirements:** High school diploma is required, and GED is accepted. *Academic units required:* 4 English, 3 math, 3 science (3 science labs), 2 foreign language, 2 social studies, 1 history, 4 academic electives, 1 physical education/ROTC. *Academic units recommended:* 4 English, 3 math, 3 science (3 science labs), 2 foreign language, 2 social studies, 1 history, 4 academic electives, 1 physical education/ROTC. **Freshman Admission Statistics:** 1,750 applied, 85% admitted, 45% enrolled. **Transfer Admission Requirements:** College transcript(s), statement of good standing from prior institution(s). Minimum college GPA of 2.0 required. Lowest grade transferable C. **General Admission Information:** Application fee $35. Regular application deadline 8/5. Regular notification rolling. Nonfall registration accepted. Admission may be deferred. Common Application not

accepted. Credit and/or placement offered for CEEB Advanced Placement tests.

COSTS AND FINANCIAL AID
Annual in-state tuition $7,152. Out-of-state tuition $12,024. Room & board $5,176. Required fees $150. Average book expense $840. **Required Forms and Deadlines:** FAFSA. Financial aid filing deadline 4/15. **Notification of Awards:** Applicants will be notified of awards on or about 6/1. **Types of Aid:** *Need-based scholarships/grants:* Pell, SEOG, state scholarships/grants, private scholarships, the school's own gift aid, Federal Nursing Scholarships. *Loans:* FFEL Subsidized Stafford, FFEL Unsubsidized Stafford, FFEL PLUS, Federal Perkins, state loans. **Student Employment:** Federal Work-Study Program available. Off-campus job opportunities are good. **Financial Aid Statistics:** 29% freshmen, 32% undergrads receive need-based scholarship or grant aid. 36% freshmen, 40% undergrads receive need-based self-help aid. 80% freshmen, 80% undergrads receive any aid. Highest amount earned per year from on-campus jobs $4,500.

LANDMARK COLLEGE

PO Box 820, Putney, VT 05346-0820
Phone: 802-387-6718 **E-mail:** admissions@landmark.edu
Fax: 802-387-6868 **Website:** www.landmark.edu **ACT Code:** 4317
Financial Aid Phone: 802-387-6736

This private school was founded in 1984. It has a 128-acre campus.

RATINGS
Admissions Selectivity Rating: 60*   **Fire Safety Rating:** 69   **Green Rating:** 60*

STUDENTS AND FACULTY
Enrollment: 429. **Student Body:** 27% female, 73% male, 96% out-of-state, 3% international (14 countries represented). African American 4%, Asian 2%, Caucasian 64%, Hispanic 4%. **Retention and Graduation:** 95% grads go on to further study within 1 year. **Faculty:** Student/faculty ratio 5:1. 95 full-time faculty. 91% faculty teach undergrads.

ACADEMICS
Degrees: Associate. **Academic Requirements:** English (including composition), humanities, mathematics, sciences (biological or physical), social science. **Classes:** Most classes have 10–19 students. **Special Study Options:** Study abroad.

FACILITIES
Housing: Coed dorms, special housing for disabled students. **Special Academic Facilities/Equipment:** Fine arts building/theater. **Computers:** 100% of classrooms are wireless, 100% of public computers are PCs, network access in dorm rooms, online registration, online administrative functions (other than registration), remote student-access to Web through college's connection. Undergraduates are required to own a computer.

CAMPUS LIFE
Activities: Choral groups, dance, drama/theater, jazz band, literary magazine, music ensembles, student government. **Organizations:** 20 registered organizations, 1 honor society.

ADMISSIONS
Freshman Academic Profile: 70% from public high schools. TOEFL required of all international applicants, minimum paper TOEFL 200, minimum computer TOEFL 40. **Basis for Candidate Selection:** *Very important factors considered include:* Level of applicant's interest, recommendation(s). *Important factors considered include:* Character/personal qualities, extracurricular activities, interview, rigor of secondary school record, talent/ability. *Other factors considered include:* Application essay, standardized test scores, volunteer work, work experience. **Freshman Admission Requirements:** High school diploma is required, and GED is accepted. **Freshman Admission Statistics:** 310 applied, 72% admitted, 47% enrolled. **Transfer Admission Requirements:** High school transcript, college transcript(s), essay or personal statement, interview. Lowest grade transferable C-. **General Admission Information:** Application fee $75. Regular notification is rolling. Nonfall registration accepted. Admission may be deferred for a maximum of 1 calendar year.

COSTS AND FINANCIAL AID
Annual tuition $43,100. Room and board $7,800. Required fees $475. Average book expense $1,200. **Required Forms and Deadlines:** FAFSA, institution's own financial aid form, parent and student federal tax return. Financial aid filing deadline 3/30. **Notification of Awards:** Applicants will be notified of

awards on a rolling basis beginning on or about 4/30. **Types of Aid:** *Need-based scholarships/grants:* Pell, SEOG, state scholarships/grants, private scholarships, the school's own gift aid, Vocational Rehabilitation Grants. *Loans:* FFEL Subsidized Stafford, FFEL Unsubsidized Stafford, FFEL PLUS. **Student Employment:** Federal Work-Study Program available. Institutional employment available. Off-campus job opportunities are good. **Financial Aid Statistics:** 36% undergrads receive need-based scholarship or grant aid. 47% undergrads receive need-based self-help aid. 35% freshmen, 42% undergrads receive any aid. Highest amount earned per year from on-campus jobs $1,500.

See page 1234.

LANE COLLEGE

545 Lane Avenue, Jackson, TN 38301
Phone: 731-426-7532 **E-mail:** admissions@lanecollege.edu
Fax: 731-426-7559 **Website:** www.lanecollege.edu **ACT Code:** 3976
Financial Aid Phone: 731-426-7535

This private school, affiliated with the Methodist Church, was founded in 1882. It has a 25-acre campus.

RATINGS
Admissions Selectivity Rating: 82   **Fire Safety Rating:** 60*   **Green Rating:** 60*

STUDENTS AND FACULTY
Enrollment: 952. **Student Body:** 52% female, 48% male, 42% out-of-state. African American 68%. **Retention and Graduation:** 74% freshmen return for sophomore year. 23% freshmen graduate within 4 years. 52% grads go on to further study within 1 year. 41% grads pursue arts and sciences degrees. 2% grads pursue business degrees. 3% grads pursue law degrees. 5% grads pursue medical degrees. **Faculty:** Student/faculty ratio 19:1. 50 full-time faculty, 60% hold PhDs. 100% faculty teach undergrads.

ACADEMICS
Degrees: Bachelor's. **Academic Requirements:** Arts/fine arts, computer literacy, English (including composition), foreign languages, history, mathematics, sciences (biological or physical), social science, religion. **Classes:** Most classes have 20–29 students. **Majors with Highest Enrollment:** Computer and information sciences, criminal justice/law enforcement administration. **Disciplines with Highest Percentage of Degrees Awarded:** Interdisciplinary studies 21%, computer and information sciences 13%, social sciences 12%, business/marketing 10%, biological/life sciences 8%. **Special Study Options:** Accelerated program, independent study, internships, study abroad, teacher certification program.

FACILITIES
Housing: Men's dorms, women's dorms. **Special Academic Facilities/Equipment:** Williams/Boyd Student Recreational Center. **Computers:** 100% of public computers are PCs, network access in dorm rooms, network access in dorm lounges, remote student-access to Web through college's connection.

CAMPUS LIFE
Activities: Choral groups, concert band, dance, drama/theater, marching band, music ensembles, pep band, student government, student newspaper, yearbook. **Organizations:** 21 registered organizations, 6 honor societies, 4 religious organizations. 2 fraternities (1% men join), 4 sororities (5% women join). **Athletics (Intercollegiate):** *Men:* Baseball, basketball, cross-country, football, tennis, track/field (outdoor). *Women:* Basketball, cross-country, softball, tennis, track/field (outdoor), volleyball.

ADMISSIONS
Freshman Academic Profile: 28% in top 10% of high school class, 53% in top 25% of high school class, 65% in top 50% of high school class. 96% from public high schools. ACT middle 50% range 14–17. TOEFL required of all international applicants, minimum paper TOEFL 339. **Basis for Candidate Selection:** *Very important factors considered include:* Character/personal qualities, recommendation(s), rigor of secondary school record. *Important factors considered include:* Extracurricular activities, standardized test scores, talent/ability. *Other factors considered include:* Alumni/ae relation, class rank, interview. **Freshman Admission Requirements:** High school diploma is required, and GED is accepted. *Academic units required:* 4 English, 2 math, 2 science (1 science lab), 2 social studies, 2 history. *Academic units recommended:* 2 foreign language. **Freshman Admission Statistics:** 2,636 applied, 28% admitted, 40% enrolled. **Transfer Admission Requirements:** College transcript(s), standardized test score, statement of good standing from prior institution(s). Minimum college GPA of 2.0 required. Lowest grade transferable C. **General Admission Information:** Regular application deadline 8/1.

Regular notification is rolling. Nonfall registration accepted. Admission may be deferred for a maximum of 1 semester. Common Application accepted. Credit offered for CEEB Advanced Placement tests.

COSTS AND FINANCIAL AID
Annual tuition $6,262. Room & board $4,366. Required fees $550. Average book expense $550. **Required Forms and Deadlines:** FAFSA. Financial aid filing deadline 4/1. **Notification of Awards:** Applicants will be notified of awards on a rolling basis beginning on or about 3/31. **Types of Aid:** *Need-based scholarships/grants:* Pell, SEOG, state scholarships/grants, private scholarships, the school's own gift aid, United Negro College Fund. *Loans:* Direct Subsidized Stafford, Direct Unsubsidized Stafford, Direct PLUS. **Student Employment:** Federal Work-Study Program available. Off-campus job opportunities are excellent. **Financial Aid Statistics:** 91% freshmen, 87% undergrads receive need-based scholarship or grant aid. 86% freshmen, 84% undergrads receive need-based self-help aid. 1 freshmen, 4 undergrads receive athletic scholarships. 98% freshmen, 79% undergrads receive any aid.

LANGSTON UNIVERSITY

PO Box 728, Langston, OK 73050
Phone: 405-466-2231 **E-mail:** admission@speedy.lunet.edu **CEEB Code:** 6361
Fax: 405-466-3381 **Website:** www.lunet.edu **ACT Code:** 3400
Financial Aid Phone: 405-466-3282

This public school was founded in 1897. It has a 40-acre campus.

RATINGS
Admissions Selectivity Rating: 60*   **Fire Safety Rating:** 60*   **Green Rating:** 60*

STUDENTS AND FACULTY
Student Body: 20% out-of-state.

ACADEMICS
Degrees: Associate, bachelor's, master's.

FACILITIES
Housing: Coed dorms, men's dorms, women's dorms, apartments for married students.

CAMPUS LIFE
Organizations: 9 honor societies, 3 religious organizations. 4 fraternities (10% men join), 4 sororities (15% women join). **Athletics (Intercollegiate):** *Men:* Basketball, cheerleading, cross-country, football, track/field (outdoor). *Women:* Basketball, cheerleading, cross-country, track/field (outdoor).

ADMISSIONS
Freshman Academic Profile: 90% from public high schools. **Freshman Admission Requirements:** High school diploma is required, and GED is accepted. *Academic units required:* 4 English, 3 math, 2 science, 2 history. **Transfer Admission Requirements:** Minimum college GPA of 2.0 required. Lowest grade transferable D. **General Admission Information:** Regular application deadline 8/1. Regular notification rolling. Nonfall registration not accepted. Common Application not accepted.

COSTS AND FINANCIAL AID
Annual in-state tuition $4,700. Out-of-state tuition $7,000. Room & board $2,944. Required fees $1,057. Average book expense $450. **Required Forms and Deadlines:** FAFSA, institution's own financial aid form. **Notification of Awards:** Applicants will be notified of awards on or about 7/15. **Types of Aid:** *Need-based scholarships/grants:* Pell, SEOG, state scholarships/grants, private scholarships, the school's own gift aid. *Loans:* FFEL Subsidized Stafford, FFEL Unsubsidized Stafford, FFEL PLUS, Federal Perkins, college/university loans from institutional funds. **Student Employment:** Institutional employment available. Off-campus job opportunities are poor.

LASALLE UNIVERSITY

1900 West Olney Avenue, Philadelphia, PA 19141-1199
Phone: 215-951-1500 **E-mail:** admiss@lasalle.edu **CEEB Code:** 2363
Fax: 215-951-1656 **Website:** www.lasalle.edu **ACT Code:** 3608
Financial Aid Phone: 215-951-1070

This private school, affiliated with the Roman Catholic Church, was founded in 1863. It has a 120-acre campus.

RATINGS
Admissions Selectivity Rating: 83   **Fire Safety Rating:** 66   **Green Rating:** 60*

STUDENTS AND FACULTY
Enrollment: 4,207. **Student Body:** 61% female, 39% male, 43% out-of-state. African American 16%, Asian 3%, Caucasian 63%, Hispanic 8%. **Retention and Graduation:** 82% freshmen return for sophomore year. 63% freshmen graduate within 4 years. 20% grads go on to further study within 1 year. 15% grads pursue arts and sciences degrees. 3% grads pursue business degrees. 5% grads pursue law degrees. 3% grads pursue medical degrees. **Faculty:** Student/faculty ratio 15:1. 233 full-time faculty, 80% hold PhDs. 100% faculty teach undergrads.

ACADEMICS
Degrees: Associate, bachelor's, certificate, doctoral, master's, post-bachelor's certificate, post-master's certificate. **Academic Requirements:** Arts/fine arts, computer literacy, English (including composition), foreign languages, history, humanities, mathematics, philosophy, sciences (biological or physical), social science, religion. **Classes:** Most classes have 20–29 students. Most lab/discussion sections have fewer than 10 students. **Majors with Highest Enrollment:** Communications, journalism, and related fields; education; public health/community nurse/nursing. **Disciplines with Highest Percentage of Degrees Awarded:** Health professions and related sciences 24%, business/marketing 22%, communication technologies 11%, computer and information sciences 7%, other 7%, education 6%, psychology 6%. **Special Study Options:** Accelerated program, cooperative education program, cross-registration, double major, dual enrollment, English as a second language (ESL), exchange student program (domestic), honors program, independent study, internships, student-designed major, study abroad, teacher certification program. 2+2 with Thomas Jefferson University.

FACILITIES
Housing: Coed dorms, apartments for single students, special housing for disabled students, fraternity/sorority housing. **Special Academic Facilities/Equipment:** Art museum, Japanese tea house, language lab, child development center. **Computers:** 100% of public computers are PCs, network access in dorm rooms, online registration, online administrative functions (other than registration), support for handheld computing, remote student-access to Web through college's connection.

CAMPUS LIFE
Activities: Choral groups, concert band, drama/theater, jazz band, literary magazine, music ensembles, musical theater, pep band, radio station, student government, student newspaper, student-run film society, television station, yearbook. **Organizations:** 100 registered organizations, 10 honor societies, 4 religious organizations. 7 fraternities (6% men join), 5 sororities (13% women join). **Athletics (Intercollegiate):** *Men:* Baseball, basketball, cheerleading, crew/rowing, cross-country, diving, football, golf, soccer, swimming, tennis, track/field (outdoor), wrestling. *Women:* Basketball, cheerleading, crew/rowing, cross-country, diving, field hockey, golf, lacrosse, soccer, softball, swimming, tennis, track/field (outdoor), volleyball.

ADMISSIONS
Freshman Academic Profile: 25% in top 10% of high school class, 55% in top 25% of high school class, 86% in top 50% of high school class. 35% from public high schools. SAT Math middle 50% range 480–580. SAT Critical Reading middle 50% range 480–580. TOEFL required of all international applicants, minimum paper TOEFL 500, minimum computer TOEFL 175. **Basis for Candidate Selection:** *Very important factors considered include:* Rigor of secondary school record. *Important factors considered include:* Application essay, class rank, standardized test scores. *Other factors considered include:* Alumni/ae relation, character/personal qualities, extracurricular activities, interview, recommendation(s), talent/ability, volunteer work, work experience. **Freshman Admission Requirements:** High school diploma is required, and GED is accepted. *Academic units required:* 4 English, 3 math, 1 science (1 science lab), 2 foreign language, 1 history, 5 academic electives. **Freshman Admission Statistics:** 5,205 applied, 64% admitted, 27% enrolled. **Transfer Admission Requirements:** High school transcript, college transcript(s), essay or personal statement, standardized test score, statement of good standing from

prior institution(s). Minimum college GPA of 2.5 required. Lowest grade transferable C. **General Admission Information:** Application fee $35. Regular notification is rolling. Nonfall registration accepted. Admission may be deferred.

COSTS AND FINANCIAL AID
Annual tuition $21,270. Room & board $7,810. Required fees $150. Average book expense $500. **Required Forms and Deadlines:** FAFSA. Financial aid filing deadline 2/15. **Notification of Awards:** Applicants will be notified of awards on a rolling basis beginning on or about 3/15. **Types of Aid:** *Need-based scholarships/grants:* Pell, SEOG, state scholarships/grants, private scholarships, the school's own gift aid. *Loans:* FFEL Subsidized Stafford, FFEL Unsubsidized Stafford, FFEL PLUS, Federal Perkins. **Financial Aid Statistics:** 76% freshmen, 70% undergrads receive need-based scholarship or grant aid. 65% freshmen, 61% undergrads receive need-based self-help aid. 44 freshmen, 160 undergrads receive athletic scholarships. 77% freshmen, 72% undergrads receive any aid.

LASELL COLLEGE

Office of Undergraduate Admissions, 1844 Commonwealth Avenue, Newton, MA 02466
Phone: 617-243-2225 **E-mail:** info@lasell.edu **CEEB Code:** 3481
Fax: 617-243-2380 **Website:** www.lasell.edu **ACT Code:** 1848
Financial Aid Phone: 617-243-2227

This private school was founded in 1851. It has a 55-acre campus.

RATINGS
Admissions Selectivity Rating: 73   **Fire Safety Rating:** 60*   **Green Rating:** 60*

STUDENTS AND FACULTY
Enrollment: 1,154. **Student Body:** 71% female, 29% male, 4% international (15 countries represented). African American 6%, Asian 4%, Caucasian 75%, Hispanic 6%. **Retention and Graduation:** 18% grads go on to further study within 1 year. 13% grads pursue arts and sciences degrees. 5% grads pursue business degrees. **Faculty:** Student/faculty ratio 13:1. 55 full-time faculty, 45% hold PhDs. 100% faculty teach undergrads.

ACADEMICS
Degrees: Bachelor's, master's, post-bachelor's certificate. **Academic Requirements:** Arts/fine arts, computer literacy, English (including composition), history, humanities, mathematics, sciences (biological or physical), social science. **Classes:** Most classes have 10–19 students. Most lab/discussion sections have 10–19 students. **Majors with Highest Enrollment:** Criminology, fashion/apparel design, psychology. **Disciplines with Highest Percentage of Degrees Awarded:** Business/marketing 43%, education 15%, visual and performing arts 13%, social sciences 7%, parks and recreation 4%, liberal arts/general studies 4%, psychology 4%, health professions and related sciences 4%. **Special Study Options:** Double major, honors program, internships, liberal arts/career combination, study abroad.

FACILITIES
Housing: Coed dorms, women's dorms, special interest (human services), some houses alcohol-free, all houses smoke-free. **Special Academic Facilities/Equipment:** Center for Public Service, Yamawaki Art/Cultural Center. **Computers:** 75% of public computers are PCs, 25% of public computers are Macs, network access in dorm rooms, network access in dorm lounges, remote student-access to Web through college's connection.

CAMPUS LIFE
Activities: Choral groups, dance, drama/theater, literary magazine, music ensembles, musical theater, radio station, student government, student newspaper, television station, yearbook. **Organizations:** 30 registered organizations, 1 honor society. **Athletics (Intercollegiate):** *Men:* Basketball, cross-country, lacrosse, soccer, volleyball. *Women:* Basketball, cross-country, field hockey, lacrosse, soccer, softball, volleyball.

ADMISSIONS
Freshman Academic Profile: 6% in top 10% of high school class, 32% in top 25% of high school class, 79% in top 50% of high school class. 85% from public high schools. SAT Math middle 50% range 510–420. SAT Critical Reading middle 50% range 520–430. ACT middle 50% range 21–20. TOEFL required of all international applicants, minimum paper TOEFL 500, minimum computer TOEFL 173. **Basis for Candidate Selection:** *Very important factors considered include:* Recommendation(s), rigor of secondary school record. *Important factors considered include:* Extracurricular activities, interview, standardized test scores. *Other factors considered include:* Alumni/ae

relation, application essay, character/personal qualities, class rank, talent/ability, volunteer work, work experience. **Freshman Admission Requirements:** High school diploma is required, and GED is accepted. *Academic units required:* 4 English, 3 math, 2 science (2 science labs), 2 social studies, 2 history. *Academic units recommended:* 4 English, 3 math, 3 science (2 science labs), 2 foreign language, 3 social studies, 3 history. **Freshman Admission Statistics:** 2,498 applied, 65% admitted, 24% enrolled. **Transfer Admission Requirements:** College transcript(s), statement of good standing from prior institution(s). Minimum college GPA of 2.3 required. Lowest grade transferable C. **General Admission Information:** Application fee $40. Regular notification is rolling. Nonfall registration accepted. Admission may be deferred for a maximum of 1 year. Common Application accepted. Credit offered for CEEB Advanced Placement tests.

COSTS AND FINANCIAL AID

Annual tuition $18,700. Room & board $8,800. Required fees $1,000. Average book expense $1,000. **Required Forms and Deadlines:** FAFSA, institution's own financial aid form. Financial aid filing deadline 3/15. **Notification of Awards:** Applicants will be notified of awards on a rolling basis beginning on or about 2/15. **Types of Aid:** *Need-based scholarships/grants:* Pell, SEOG, state scholarships/grants, private scholarships, the school's own gift aid. *Loans:* FFEL Subsidized Stafford, FFEL Unsubsidized Stafford, FFEL PLUS, Federal Perkins, state loans. **Student Employment:** Federal Work-Study Program available. Institutional employment available. Off-campus job opportunities are excellent. **Financial Aid Statistics:** 81% freshmen, 81% undergrads receive need-based scholarship or grant aid. 72% freshmen, 72% undergrads receive need-based self-help aid. 87% freshmen, 85% undergrads receive any aid.

LAURA AND ALVIN SIEGAL COLLEGE OF JUDAIC STUDIES

26500 Shaker Boulevard, Beachwood, OH 44122-7116
Phone: 216-464-4050 **E-mail:** admissions@siegalcollege.edu
Fax: 216-464-5827 **Website:** www.siegalcollege.edu
Financial Aid Phone: 216-464-4050

This private school, affiliated with the Jewish Synagogue, was founded in 1963.

RATINGS
Admissions Selectivity Rating: 60*   **Fire Safety Rating:** 60*   **Green Rating:** 60*

STUDENTS AND FACULTY
Enrollment: 12. **Student Body:** 67% female, 33% male. Caucasian 100%. **Retention and Graduation:** 100% freshmen return for sophomore year. **Faculty:** Student/faculty ratio 2:1. 11 full-time faculty, 82% hold PhDs. 80% faculty teach undergrads.

ACADEMICS
Degrees: Bachelor's, certificate, master's. **Academic Requirements:** Arts/fine arts, English (including composition), foreign languages, history, humanities, sciences (biological or physical). **Disciplines with Highest Percentage of Degrees Awarded:** Other 100%. **Special Study Options:** Distance learning, double major, independent study, internships.

FACILITIES
Housing: No housing available on campus. **Computers:** 100% of classrooms are wired, 100% of public computers are PCs, online registration.

CAMPUS LIFE
Organizations: 1 registered organization.

ADMISSIONS
Basis for Candidate Selection: *Very important factors considered include:* Application essay, interview, level of applicant's interest, recommendation(s). *Important factors considered include:* Academic GPA, rigor of secondary school record. *Other factors considered include:* Character/personal qualities, class rank, extracurricular activities, standardized test scores, talent/ability, work experience. **Freshman Admission Requirements:** High school diploma is required, and GED is accepted. **Freshman Admission Statistics:** 3 applied, 100% admitted, 100% enrolled. **Transfer Admission Requirements:** College transcript(s), essay or personal statement, interview. Minimum college GPA of 2.7 required. Lowest grade transferable C. **General Admission Information:** Application fee $50. Regular notification rolling admission. Nonfall registration accepted. Admission may be deferred for a maximum of 1 year.

COSTS AND FINANCIAL AID

Annual tuition $12,600. Required fees $25. **Required Forms and Deadlines:** Institution's own financial aid form. **Notification of Awards:** Applicants will be notified of awards on a rolling basis beginning on or about 9/5. **Types of Aid:** *Need-based scholarships/grants:* Pell, the school's own gift aid. *Loans:* FFEL Subsidized Stafford, FFEL Unsubsidized Stafford, FFEL PLUS. **Student Employment:** Off-campus job opportunities are good. **Financial Aid Statistics:** 100% freshmen.

LAWRENCE TECHNOLOGICAL UNIVERSITY

21000 West Ten Mile Road, Southfield, MI 48075-1058
Phone: 248-204-3160 **E-mail:** admissions@ltu.edu **CEEB Code:** 1399
Fax: 248-204-3188 **Website:** www.ltu.edu **ACT Code:** 2020
Financial Aid Phone: 248-204-2120

This private school was founded in 1932. It has a 102-acre campus.

RATINGS
Admissions Selectivity Rating: 81   **Fire Safety Rating:** 76   **Green Rating:** 80

STUDENTS AND FACULTY
Enrollment: 2,368. **Student Body:** 24% female, 76% male, 1% out-of-state, 1% international. African American 11%, Asian 3%, Caucasian 70%, Hispanic 2%. **Retention and Graduation:** 70% freshmen return for sophomore year. **Faculty:** Student/faculty ratio 12:1. 114 full-time faculty, 81% hold PhDs. 100% faculty teach undergrads.

ACADEMICS
Degrees: Associate, bachelor's, certificate, doctoral, master's, post-bachelor's certificate. **Academic Requirements:** Computer literacy, English (including composition), history, humanities, mathematics, sciences (biological or physical), social science. **Classes:** Most classes have 10–19 students. Most lab/discussion sections have 10–19 students. **Majors with Highest Enrollment:** Architecture (BArch, BA/BS, MArch, MA/MS, PhD), computer science, mechanical engineering. **Disciplines with Highest Percentage of Degrees Awarded:** Engineering 54%, architecture 27%, computer and information sciences 11%, visual and performing arts 3%, communication technologies 1%, psychology 1%, mathematics 1%, interdisciplinary studies 1%, liberal arts/general studies 1%. **Special Study Options:** Cooperative education program, cross-registration, distance learning, double major, dual enrollment, English as a second language (ESL), external degree program, honors program, independent study, internships, liberal arts/career combination, study abroad, weekend college.

FACILITIES
Housing: Apartments for single students, special housing for disabled students, fraternity/sorority housing. **Special Academic Facilities/Equipment:** Albert Kahn Library, Center for Innovative Materials Research. **Computers:** 90% of classrooms are wired, 100% of classrooms are wireless, 90% of public computers are PCs, 5% of public computers are Macs, 5% of public computers are UNIX, network access in dorm rooms, network access in dorm lounges, online registration, online administrative functions (other than registration), remote student-access to Web through college's connection, tuition includes personal computer.

CAMPUS LIFE
Activities: Literary magazine, music ensembles, student government, student newspaper. **Organizations:** 50 registered organizations, 6 honor societies, 1 religious organization. 7 fraternities (5% men join), 4 sororities (7% women join). Environmental Initiatives: A. Alfred Taubman Student Services Center is a green building including geothermal wells and a vegetated roof. It serves as a living laboratory for sustainability education of architects and engineers. Establishment of the Center for Sustainability including campus standards for sustainability, a speaker series, and recycling. Academic programming including participation in the Solar Decathlon and Formula Zero international competitions.

ADMISSIONS
Freshman Academic Profile: 27% in top 10% of high school class, 53% in top 25% of high school class, 79% in top 50% of high school class. 65% from public high schools. SAT Math middle 50% range 540–630. SAT Critical Reading middle 50% range 450–600. SAT Writing middle 50% range 420–550. ACT middle 50% range 20–26. TOEFL required of all international applicants, minimum paper TOEFL 550, minimum computer TOEFL 213. **Basis for Candidate Selection:** *Very important factors considered include:* Academic GPA, rigor of secondary school record, standardized test scores. *Other factors*

considered include: Application essay, interview, recommendation(s). **Freshman Admission Requirements:** High school diploma is required, and GED is accepted. *Academic units required:* 4 English, 3 math, 2 science, 3 social studies. *Academic units recommended:* 4 English, 4 math, 4 science (2 science labs), 3 social studies, 2 history. **Freshman Admission Statistics:** 1,420 applied, 66% admitted, 35% enrolled. **Transfer Admission Requirements:** High school transcript, college transcript(s), statement of good standing from prior institution(s). Minimum college GPA of 2.0 required. Lowest grade transferable C. **General Admission Information:** Application fee $30. Regular notification rolling. Nonfall registration accepted. Admission may be deferred for a maximum of 1 year. Credit and/or placement offered for CEEB Advanced Placement tests.

COSTS AND FINANCIAL AID

Annual tuition $20,460. **Required Forms and Deadlines:** FAFSA. Financial aid filing deadline 4/1. **Notification of Awards:** Applicants will be notified of awards on or about 3/1. **Types of Aid:** *Need-based scholarships/grants:* Pell, SEOG, state scholarships/grants, private scholarships, the school's own gift aid. *Loans:* FFEL Subsidized Stafford, FFEL Unsubsidized Stafford, FFEL PLUS, Federal Perkins, state loans, college/university loans from institutional funds, private alternative loans. **Student Employment:** Federal Work-Study Program available. Institutional employment available. Off-campus job opportunities are excellent. **Financial Aid Statistics:** 65% freshmen, 57% undergrads receive need-based scholarship or grant aid. 63% freshmen, 59% undergrads receive need-based self-help aid. 69% freshmen, 54% undergrads receive any aid. Highest amount earned per year from on-campus jobs $8,000.

See page 1236.

LAWRENCE UNIVERSITY

PO Box 599, Appleton, WI 54912-0599
Phone: 920-832-6500 **E-mail:** excel@lawrence.edu **CEEB Code:** 1398
Fax: 920-832-6782 **Website:** www.lawrence.edu **ACT Code:** 4596
Financial Aid Phone: 920-832-6583

This private school was founded in 1847. It has an 84-acre campus.

RATINGS

Admissions Selectivity Rating: 92   **Fire Safety Rating:** 60*   **Green Rating:** 60*

STUDENTS AND FACULTY

Enrollment: 1,429. **Student Body:** 55% female, 45% male, 57% out-of-state. 7% international (42 countries represented). African American 2%, Asian 3%, Caucasian 76%, Hispanic 2%. **Retention and Graduation:** 88% freshmen return for sophomore year. 62% freshmen graduate within 4 years. 22% grads go on to further study within 1 year. 18% grads pursue arts and sciences degrees. 2% grads pursue law degrees. 1% grads pursue medical degrees. **Faculty:** Student/faculty ratio 9:1. 150 full-time faculty, 96% hold PhDs. 100% faculty teach undergrads.

ACADEMICS

Degrees: Bachelor's. **Academic Requirements:** Arts/fine arts, foreign languages, humanities, sciences (biological or physical), social science, music theory, music history, ensemble study, keyboard skills. **Classes:** Most classes have 10–19 students. Most lab/discussion sections have fewer than 10 students. **Majors with Highest Enrollment:** Biology/biological sciences, music performance, psychology. **Disciplines with Highest Percentage of Degrees Awarded:** Visual and performing arts 22%, social sciences 16%, biological/life sciences 9%, foreign languages and literature 8%, psychology 7%. **Special Study Options:** Double major, independent study, internships, student-designed major, study abroad, teacher certification program.

FACILITIES

Housing: Coed dorms, men's dorms, women's dorms, apartments for married students, 14 theme/group houses available. **Special Academic Facilities/ Equipment:** Art galleries, anthropology collection, 425-acre estate on Lake Michigan hosting retreats and seminars for students, electron microscope, laser physics lab, physics/computational graphics lab, nuclear magnetic resonance spectrometer. **Computers:** 80% of public computers are PCs, 20% of public computers are Macs, network access in dorm rooms, network access in dorm lounges, online registration, online administrative functions (other than

registration), remote student-access to Web through college's connection.

CAMPUS LIFE

Activities: Choral groups, concert band, dance, drama/theater, jazz band, literary magazine, music ensembles, musical theater, opera, pep band, radio station, student government, student newspaper, student-run film society, symphony orchestra, yearbook. **Organizations:** 110 registered organizations, 5 honor societies, 4 religious organizations. 5 fraternities (21% men join), 3 sororities (9% women join). **Athletics (Intercollegiate): Men:** Baseball, basketball, cross-country, diving, fencing, football, golf, ice hockey, lacrosse, soccer, swimming, tennis, track/field (indoor), track/field (outdoor), wrestling. *Women:* Basketball, cross-country, diving, fencing, lacrosse, soccer, softball, swimming, tennis, track/field (indoor), track/field (outdoor), volleyball.

ADMISSIONS

Freshman Academic Profile: 34% in top 10% of high school class, 66% in top 25% of high school class, 96% in top 50% of high school class. 77% from public high schools. SAT Math middle 50% range 590–700. SAT Critical Reading middle 50% range 610–730. SAT Writing middle 50% range 600–700. ACT middle 50% range 27–31. TOEFL required of all international applicants, minimum paper TOEFL 575, minimum computer TOEFL 233. **Basis for Candidate Selection:** *Very important factors considered include:* Academic GPA, class rank, rigor of secondary school record. *Important factors considered include:* Application essay, character/personal qualities, extracurricular activities, recommendation(s), talent/ability. *Other factors considered include:* Alumni/ae relation, first generation, interview, racial/ethnic status, standardized test scores, volunteer work, work experience. **Freshman Admission Requirements:** High school diploma is required, and GED is not accepted. *Academic units recommended:* 4 English, 3 math, 3 science, 2 foreign language, 2 social studies, 2 history. **Freshman Admission Statistics:** 2,315 applied, 56% admitted, 29% enrolled. **Transfer Admission Requirements:** High school transcript, college transcript(s), essay or personal statement. Minimum college GPA of 2.7 required. Lowest grade transferable C-. **General Admission Information:** Application fee $40. Early decision application deadline 11/15. Regular application deadline 1/15. Regular notification 4/1. Nonfall registration not accepted. Admission may be deferred for a maximum of 1 year. Credit and/or placement offered for CEEB Advanced Placement tests.

COSTS AND FINANCIAL AID

Annual tuition $29,376. Room & board $6,822. Required fees $222. Average book expense $1,800. **Required Forms and Deadlines:** FAFSA, institution's own financial aid form, parent federal tax returns and W-2 forms, student federal tax returns. Financial aid filing deadline 3/15. **Notification of Awards:** Applicants will be notified of awards on a rolling basis beginning on or about 3/15. **Types of Aid:** *Need-based scholarships/grants:* Pell, SEOG, state scholarships/grants, private scholarships, the school's own gift aid. *Loans:* Direct Subsidized Stafford, Direct Unsubsidized Stafford, Direct PLUS, FFEL PLUS, Federal Perkins. **Financial Aid Statistics:** 68% freshmen, 66% undergrads receive need-based scholarship or grant aid. 58% freshmen, 58% undergrads receive need-based self-help aid. 94% freshmen, 95% undergrads receive any aid. Highest amount earned per year from on-campus jobs $3,730.

See page 1238.

LE MOYNE COLLEGE

1419 Salt Springs Road, Syracuse, NY 13214-1301
Phone: 315-445-4300 **E-mail:** admission@lemoyne.edu **CEEB Code:** 2366
Fax: 315-445-4711 **Website:** www.lemoyne.edu **ACT Code:** 2790
Financial Aid Phone: 315-445-4400.

This private school, affiliated with the Roman Catholic Church, was founded in 1946. It has a 161-acre campus.

RATINGS

Admissions Selectivity Rating: 80   **Fire Safety Rating:** 75   **Green Rating:** 60*

STUDENTS AND FACULTY

Enrollment: 2,416. **Student Body:** 61% female, 39% male, 6% out-of-state. African American 4%, Asian 2%, Caucasian 83%, Hispanic 4%. **Retention and Graduation:** 84% freshmen return for sophomore year. 59% freshmen graduate within 4 years. 30% grads go on to further study within 1 year. 25% grads pursue arts and sciences degrees. 1% grads pursue business degrees. 2% grads pursue law degrees. 2% grads pursue medical degrees. **Faculty:** Student/ faculty ratio 13:1. 161 full-time faculty, 91% hold PhDs. 93% faculty teach undergrads.

ACADEMICS

Degrees: Bachelor's, master's, post-master's certificate. **Academic Requirements:** English (including composition), foreign languages, history, humanities, mathematics, philosophy, sciences (biological or physical), social science, religious studies. **Classes:** Most classes have 20–29 students. Most lab/discussion sections have 10–19 students. **Majors with Highest Enrollment:** Biology/biological sciences, business administration and management, psychology. **Disciplines with Highest Percentage of Degrees Awarded:** Business/marketing 32%, psychology 21%, social sciences 11%, biological/life sciences 9%, English 8%. **Special Study Options:** Accelerated program, double major, dual enrollment, honors program, independent study, internships, study abroad, teacher certification program, certificate of advanced studies in educational leadership and certificate of advanced studies in nursing.

FACILITIES

Housing: Coed dorms, men's dorms, women's dorms, apartments for single students, special housing for disabled students, living/learning communities. **Special Academic Facilities/Equipment:** Art gallery, audiovisual center, electron microscopes, academic support center. **Computers:** 90% of public computers are PCs, 10% of public computers are Macs, network access in dorm rooms, network access in dorm lounges, online registration, online administrative functions (other than registration), support for handheld computing, remote student-access to Web through college's connection.

CAMPUS LIFE

Activities: Choral groups, concert band, dance, drama/theater, jazz band, literary magazine, music ensembles, musical theater, pep band, radio station, student government, student newspaper, yearbook. **Organizations:** 70 registered organizations, 14 honor societies, 10 religious organizations. **Athletics (Intercollegiate):** *Men:* Baseball, basketball, cross-country, diving, golf, lacrosse, soccer, swimming, tennis. *Women:* Basketball, cross-country, diving, lacrosse, soccer, softball, swimming, tennis, volleyball.

ADMISSIONS

Freshman Academic Profile: 21% in top 10% of high school class, 50% in top 25% of high school class, 88% in top 50% of high school class. 80% from public high schools. SAT Math middle 50% range 500–610. SAT Critical Reading middle 50% range 490–600. ACT middle 50% range 21–26. TOEFL required of all international applicants, minimum paper TOEFL 550, minimum computer TOEFL 213. **Basis for Candidate Selection:** *Very important factors considered include:* Academic GPA, rigor of secondary school record. *Important factors considered include:* Application essay, class rank, extracurricular activities, interview, recommendation(s), standardized test scores, talent/ability, work experience. *Other factors considered include:* Alumni/ae relation, character/personal qualities, geographical residence, level of applicant's interest, state residency, volunteer work. **Freshman Admission Requirements:** High school diploma is required, and GED is accepted. *Academic units required:* 4 English, 3 math, 3 science, 4 foreign language, 4 social studies. *Academic units recommended:* 4 math, 4 science (3 science labs). **Freshman Admission Statistics:** 3,608 applied, 70% admitted, 22% enrolled. **Transfer Admission Requirements:** College transcript(s), essay or personal statement, statement of good standing from prior institution(s). Minimum college GPA of 2.6 required. Lowest grade transferable C–. **General Admission Information:** Application fee $35. Early decision application deadline 12/1. Regular notification is rolling. Nonfall registration accepted. Admission may be deferred for a maximum of 1 year. Credit and/or placement offered for CEEB Advanced Placement tests.

COSTS AND FINANCIAL AID

Annual tuition $23,040. Room and board $9,030. Required fees $720. Average book expense $700. **Required Forms and Deadlines:** FAFSA, institution's own financial aid form, state aid form. Financial aid filing deadline 2/1. **Notification of Awards:** Applicants will be notified of awards on or about 3/15. **Types of Aid:** *Need-based scholarships/grants:* Pell, SEOG, state scholarships/grants, private scholarships, the school's own gift aid. *Loans:* FFEL Subsidized Stafford, FFEL Unsubsidized Stafford, FFEL PLUS, Federal Perkins. **Student Employment:** Federal Work-Study Program available. Institutional employment available. Off-campus job opportunities are excellent. **Financial Aid Statistics:** 80% freshmen, 79% undergrads receive need-based scholarship or grant aid. 64% freshmen, 68% undergrads receive need-based self-help aid. 40 freshmen, 166 undergrads receive athletic scholarships. 88% freshmen, 89% undergrads receive any aid. Highest amount earned per year from on-campus jobs $1,200.

101 North College Avenue, Annville, PA 17003-1400
Phone: 717-867-6181 **E-mail:** admission@lvc.edu **CEEB Code:** 2364
Fax: 717-867-6026 **Website:** www.lvc.edu **ACT Code:** 3610
Financial Aid Phone: 717-867-6126

This private school, affiliated with the Methodist Church, was founded in 1866. It has a 340-acre campus.

RATINGS

Admissions Selectivity Rating: 81   **Fire Safety Rating:** 77   **Green Rating:** 65

STUDENTS AND FACULTY

Enrollment: 1,710. **Student Body:** 55% female, 45% male, 20% out-of-state. African American 2%, Asian 2%, Caucasian 89%, Hispanic 2%. **Retention and Graduation:** 83% freshmen return for sophomore year. 63% freshmen graduate within 4 years. 25% grads go on to further study within 1 year. 21% grads pursue arts and sciences degrees. 2% grads pursue business degrees. 1% grads pursue law degrees. 1% grads pursue medical degrees. **Faculty:** Student/faculty ratio 14:1. 98 full-time faculty, 88% hold PhDs. 91% faculty teach undergrads.

ACADEMICS

Degrees: Associate, bachelor's, certificate, doctoral, master's, post-bachelor's certificate. **Academic Requirements:** Arts/fine arts, English (including composition), foreign languages, history, humanities, mathematics, philosophy, sciences (biological or physical), social science, cross-disciplinary studies, cross-cultural studies. **Classes:** Most classes have 10–19 students. Most lab/discussion sections have 10–19 students. **Majors with Highest Enrollment:** Business administration/management, elementary education and teaching, psychology. **Disciplines with Highest Percentage of Degrees Awarded:** Education 20%, business/marketing 13%, psychology 10%, social sciences 10%, English 8%, biological/life sciences 7%. **Special Study Options:** Double major, dual enrollment, independent study, internships, liberal arts/career combination, student-designed major, study abroad, teacher certification program.

FACILITIES

Housing: Coed dorms, men's dorms, women's dorms, apartments for single students, special housing for disabled students, suites, theme housing, substance free, community service. **Special Academic Facilities/Equipment:** Electric pianos, sound recording studio, transmission electron microscope, scanning electron microscope, fourier transform infrared spectrometer, atomic absorption spectrometer, nuclear magnetic resonance spectrometer, molecular modeling lab, campus arboretum, art gallery, therapy pool. **Computers:** 34% of classrooms are wireless, 84% of public computers are PCs, 16% of public computers are Macs, network access in dorm rooms, online registration, online administrative functions (other than registration), remote student-access to Web through college's connection.

CAMPUS LIFE

Activities: Choral groups, concert band, drama/theater, jazz band, literary magazine, marching band, music ensembles, musical theater, radio station, student government, student newspaper, symphony orchestra, yearbook. **Organizations:** 60 registered organizations, 6 honor societies, 12 religious organizations. 4 fraternities (18% men join), 3 sororities (14% women join). **Athletics (Intercollegiate):** *Men:* Baseball, basketball, cross-country, football, golf, ice hockey, soccer, swimming, tennis, track/field (indoor), track/field (outdoor). *Women:* Basketball, cross-country, field hockey, soccer, softball, swimming, tennis, track/field (indoor), track/field (outdoor), volleyball.

ADMISSIONS

Freshman Academic Profile: 36% in top 10% of high school class, 72% in top 25% of high school class, 95% in top 50% of high school class. 95% from public high schools. SAT Math middle 50% range 490–620. SAT Critical Reading middle 50% range 480–600. SAT Writing middle 50% range 480–600. ACT middle 50% range 20–26. TOEFL required of all international applicants, minimum paper TOEFL 550, minimum computer TOEFL 213. **Basis for Candidate Selection:** *Very important factors considered include:* Class rank, rigor of secondary school record. *Important factors considered include:* Academic GPA, character/personal qualities, extracurricular activities, interview, level of applicant's interest, talent/ability. *Other factors considered include:* Alumni/ae relation, application essay, first generation, geographical residence, racial/ethnic status, recommendation(s), standardized test scores, state residency, volunteer work, work experience. **Freshman Admission Requirements:** High school diploma is required, and GED is accepted. *Academic units required:* 4 English, 3 math, 2 science, 2 foreign language, 1 social studies. *Academic units recommended:* 3 science (2 science labs), 3 foreign language, 2 history. **Freshman Admission Statistics:** 2,014 applied, 72% admitted, 31% enrolled. **Transfer Admission Requirements:** High school transcript, college transcript(s), essay or personal statement, statement of good standing from prior institution(s). Minimum college GPA of 2.0 required. Lowest grade transferable C-. **General Admission Information:** Application fee $30. Regular notification is rolling. Nonfall registration accepted. Credit offered for CEEB Advanced Placement tests.

COSTS AND FINANCIAL AID

Annual tuition $27,125. Room and board $7,430. Required fees $675. Average book expense $900. **Required Forms and Deadlines:** FAFSA, institution's own financial aid form. Financial aid filing deadline 3/1. **Notification of Awards:** Applicants will be notified of awards on a rolling basis beginning on or about 3/1. **Types of Aid:** *Need-based scholarships/grants:* Pell, SEOG, state scholarships/grants, private scholarships, the school's own gift aid. *Loans:* FFEL Subsidized Stafford, FFEL Unsubsidized Stafford, FFEL PLUS, Federal Perkins. **Student Employment:** Federal Work-Study Program available. Institutional employment available. Off-campus job opportunities are good. **Financial Aid Statistics:** 80% freshmen, 76% undergrads receive need-based scholarship or grant aid. 66% freshmen, 64% undergrads receive need-based self-help aid. 98% freshmen, 98% undergrads receive any aid. Highest amount earned per year from on-campus jobs $808.

LEE UNIVERSITY

PO Box 3450, Cleveland, TN 37320-3450
Phone: 423-614-8500 **E-mail:** admissions@leeuniversity.edu **CEEB Code:** 1401
Fax: 423-614-8533 **Website:** www.leeuniversity.edu **ACT Code:** 3978
Financial Aid Phone: 423-614-8300

This private school, affiliated with the Church of God, was founded in 1918. It has a 115-acre campus.

RATINGS
Admissions Selectivity Rating: 82   **Fire Safety Rating:** 71   **Green Rating:** 60*

STUDENTS AND FACULTY
Enrollment: 3,580. **Student Body:** 56% female, 44% male, 61% out-of-state, 5% international (51 countries represented). African American 4%, Caucasian 80%, Hispanic 3%, Native American 3%. **Retention and Graduation:** 70% freshmen return for sophomore year. 29% freshmen graduate within 4 years. 20% grads go on to further study within 1 year. **Faculty:** Student/faculty ratio 17:1. 158 full-time faculty, 78% hold PhDs. 100% faculty teach undergrads.

ACADEMICS
Degrees: Bachelor's, master's. **Academic Requirements:** Arts/fine arts, computer literacy, English (including composition), foreign languages, history, humanities, mathematics, sciences (biological or physical), social science, religion. **Classes:** Most classes have 20–29 students. Most lab/discussion sections have 10–19 students. **Majors with Highest Enrollment:** Business administration and management, education, psychology. **Disciplines with Highest Percentage of Degrees Awarded:** Education 22%, theology and religious vocations 17%, business/marketing 14%, psychology 9%, communications/journalism 9%. **Special Study Options:** Distance learning, double major, dual enrollment, English as a second language (ESL), external degree program, honors program, independent study, internships, liberal arts/career combination, study abroad, teacher certification program, religion.

FACILITIES
Housing: Men's dorms, women's dorms, apartments for married students, apartments for single students. Lee University leases apartments and houses for students. **Special Academic Facilities/Equipment:** Curriculum Library in the College of Education. **Computers:** 33% of classrooms are wireless, 95% of public computers are PCs, 5% of public computers are UNIX, network access in dorm rooms, network access in dorm lounges, online registration, online administrative functions (other than registration), remote student-access to Web through college's connection.

CAMPUS LIFE
Activities: Choral groups, concert band, drama/theater, jazz band, literary magazine, music ensembles, musical theater, opera, pep band, student government, student newspaper, symphony orchestra, yearbook. **Organizations:** 72 registered organizations, 16 honor societies, 10 religious organizations. 5 fraternities (10% men join), 5 sororities (8% women join). **Athletics (Intercollegiate):** *Men:* Baseball, basketball, cross-country, golf, soccer, tennis. *Women:* Basketball, cross-country, soccer, softball, tennis, volleyball.

ADMISSIONS
Freshman Academic Profile: 19% in top 10% of high school class, 46% in top 25% of high school class, 74% in top 50% of high school class. 78% from public

high schools. SAT Math middle 50% range 450–600. SAT Critical Reading middle 50% range 470–600. ACT middle 50% range 20–27. TOEFL required of all international applicants, minimum paper TOEFL 450, minimum computer TOEFL 133. **Basis for Candidate Selection:** *Very important factors considered include:* Academic GPA, rigor of secondary school record, standardized test scores. *Important factors considered include:* Character/personal qualities, class rank, level of applicant's interest. *Other factors considered include:* Alumni/ae relation, extracurricular activities, first generation, interview, recommendation(s), talent/ability. **Freshman Admission Requirements:** High school diploma is required, and GED is accepted. *Academic units required:* 4 English, 3 math, 2 science, 1 foreign language, 2 social studies, 1 history. *Academic units recommended:* 4 English, 3 math, 2 science, 1 foreign language, 2 social studies, 1 history, 1 computer skills. **Freshman Admission Statistics:** 1,564 applied, 67% admitted, 78% enrolled. **Transfer Admission Requirements:** College transcript(s). Minimum college GPA of 2.0 required. Lowest grade transferable D. **General Admission Information:** Application fee $25. Regular application deadline 9/1. Regular notification is rolling. Nonfall registration accepted. Admission may be deferred for a maximum of 1 semester. Credit and/or placement offered for CEEB Advanced Placement tests.

COSTS AND FINANCIAL AID
Comprehensive fee $10,824. Room and board $5,470. Required fees $270. Average book expense $900. **Required Forms and Deadlines:** FAFSA. Financial aid filing deadline 3/15. **Notification of Awards:** Applicants will be notified of awards on a rolling basis beginning on or about 2/1. **Types of Aid:** *Need-based scholarships/grants:* Pell, SEOG, state scholarships/grants, private scholarships, the school's own gift aid. *Loans:* FFEL Subsidized Stafford, FFEL Unsubsidized Stafford, FFEL PLUS, Federal Perkins, college/university loans from institutional funds. **Student Employment:** Federal Work-Study Program available. Institutional employment available. Off-campus job opportunities are good. **Financial Aid Statistics:** 50% freshmen, 51% undergrads receive need-based scholarship or grant aid. 34% freshmen, 48% undergrads receive need-based self-help aid. 29 freshmen, 116 undergrads receive athletic scholarships. 62% freshmen, 70% undergrads receive any aid.

LEES-MCRAE COLLEGE

Admissions Office, PO Box 128, Banner Elk, NC 28604
Phone: 828-898-8723 **E-mail:** admissions@lmc.edu **CEEB Code:** 5364
Fax: 828-898-8707 **Website:** www.lmc.edu **ACT Code:** 3116
Financial Aid Phone: 828-898-8793

This private school, affiliated with the Presbyterian Church, was founded in 1900. It has a 400-acre campus.

RATINGS
Admissions Selectivity Rating: 68   **Fire Safety Rating:** 60*   **Green Rating:** 60*

STUDENTS AND FACULTY
Enrollment: 792. **Student Body:** 57% female, 43% male, 35% out-of-state, 4% international. African American 6%, Caucasian 84%, Hispanic 1%. **Retention and Graduation:** 59% freshmen return for sophomore year. 17% freshmen graduate within 4 years. **Faculty:** Student/faculty ratio 14:1. 69 full-time faculty, 71% hold PhDs. 100% faculty teach undergrads.

ACADEMICS
Degrees: Bachelor's. **Academic Requirements:** Arts/fine arts, computer literacy, English (including composition), history, humanities, mathematics, sciences (biological or physical), Bible. **Classes:** Most classes have fewer than 10 students. Most lab/discussion sections have fewer than 10 students. **Majors with Highest Enrollment:** Business administration/management, criminal justice/law enforcement administration, elementary education and teaching. **Disciplines with Highest Percentage of Degrees Awarded:** Education 29%, business/marketing 17%, biological/life sciences 13%, psychology 10%, communication technologies 5%, visual and performing arts 5%. **Special Study Options:** Double major, English as a second language (ESL), honors program, independent study, internships, student-designed major, study abroad, teacher certification program. 3-2 program environmental science, forestry with Duke University.

FACILITIES
Housing: Coed dorms, men's dorms, women's dorms, substance-free. **Special Academic Facilities/Equipment:** Curriculum center for teacher education. **Computers:** 100% of public computers are PCs, network access in dorm rooms, remote student-access to Web through college's connection.

CAMPUS LIFE

Activities: Choral groups, dance, drama/theater, music ensembles, musical theater, student government, student newspaper, yearbook. **Organizations:** 17 registered organizations, 3 honor societies, 4 religious organizations. **Athletics (Intercollegiate):** *Men:* Basketball, cheerleading, cross-country, golf, lacrosse, skiing (downhill/alpine), soccer, tennis, track/field (outdoor). *Women:* Basketball, cheerleading, cross-country, lacrosse, skiing (downhill/alpine), soccer, softball, tennis, track/field (outdoor), volleyball.

ADMISSIONS

Freshman Academic Profile: 7% in top 10% of high school class, 19% in top 25% of high school class, 54% in top 50% of high school class. SAT Math middle 50% range 420–520. SAT Critical Reading middle 50% range 420–530. ACT middle 50% range 17–21. TOEFL required of all international applicants, minimum paper TOEFL 500. **Basis for Candidate Selection:** *Very important factors considered include:* Rigor of secondary school record, standardized test scores. *Other factors considered include:* Alumni/ae relation, application essay, character/personal qualities, class rank, extracurricular activities, interview, recommendation(s), talent/ability, volunteer work, work experience. **Freshman Admission Requirements:** High school diploma is required, and GED is accepted. *Academic units recommended:* 4 English, 3 math, 2 science (1 science lab), 2 foreign language, 2 social studies, 1 history, 6 academic electives. **Freshman Admission Statistics:** 524 applied, 93% admitted, 41% enrolled. **Transfer Admission Requirements:** College transcript(s), statement of good standing from prior institution(s). Minimum college GPA of 2.0 required. Lowest grade transferable C. **General Admission Information:** Application fee $15. Regular notification is rolling. Nonfall registration accepted. Admission may be deferred for a maximum of 1 year. Common Application accepted. Credit and/or placement offered for CEEB Advanced Placement tests.

COSTS AND FINANCIAL AID

Annual tuition $12,292. Room & board $4,664. Required fees $150. Average book expense $760. **Required Forms and Deadlines:** FAFSA. Financial aid filing deadline 3/15. **Notification of Awards:** Applicants will be notified of awards on a rolling basis beginning on or about 3/1. **Types of Aid:** *Need-based scholarships/grants:* Pell, SEOG, state scholarships/grants, private scholarships, the school's own gift aid, Federal Nursing Scholarships. *Loans:* FFEL Subsidized Stafford, FFEL Unsubsidized Stafford, FFEL PLUS, Federal Perkins, Federal Nursing, state loans. **Student Employment:** Federal Work-Study Program available. Institutional employment available. Off-campus job opportunities are excellent. **Financial Aid Statistics:** 44% freshmen, 38% undergrads receive need-based scholarship or grant aid. 51% freshmen, 39% undergrads receive need-based self-help aid. 45 freshmen, 140 undergrads receive athletic scholarships. Highest amount earned per year from on-campus jobs $1,071.

LEHIGH UNIVERSITY

Best 368

27 Memorial Drive West, Bethlehem, PA 18015
Phone: 610-758-3100 **E-mail:** admissions@lehigh.edu **CEEB Code:** 2365
Fax: 610-758-4361 **Website:** www.lehigh.edu **ACT Code:** 3612
Financial Aid Phone: 610-758-3181

This private school was founded in 1865. It has a 1,600-acre campus.

RATINGS

Admissions Selectivity Rating: 97   **Fire Safety Rating:** 60*   **Green Rating:** 84

STUDENTS AND FACULTY

Enrollment: 4,719. **Student Body:** 42% female, 58% male, 73% out-of-state, 2% international (49 countries represented). African American 3%, Asian 6%, Caucasian 78%, Hispanic 3%. **Retention and Graduation:** 94% freshmen return for sophomore year. 75% freshmen graduate within 4 years. 36% grads go on to further study within 1 year. 5% grads pursue arts and sciences degrees. 1% grads pursue business degrees. 2% grads pursue law degrees. 5% grads pursue medical degrees. **Faculty:** Student/faculty ratio 9:1. 443 full-time faculty, 99% hold PhDs. 100% faculty teach undergrads.

ACADEMICS

Degrees: Bachelor's, doctoral, master's, post-bachelor's certificate, post-master's certificate. **Academic Requirements:** Computer literacy, English

(including composition), humanities, mathematics, sciences (biological or physical), social science. **Classes:** Most classes have 10–19 students. Most lab/discussion sections have 20–29 students. **Majors with Highest Enrollment:** Finance, mechanical engineering, psychology. **Disciplines with Highest Percentage of Degrees Awarded:** Business/marketing 28%, engineering 25%, social sciences 11%, computer and information sciences 7%, psychology 6%. **Special Study Options:** Accelerated program, cooperative education program, cross-registration, double major, English as a second language (ESL), exchange student program (domestic), external degree program, honors program, independent study, internships, study abroad.

FACILITIES

Housing: Coed dorms, apartments for married students, apartments for single students, special housing for international students, fraternity/sorority housing. **Special Academic Facilities/Equipment:** Art museum, Zoellner Arts Center, electron optical labs, article accelerator, electron optical labs. **Computers:** 95% of public computers are PCs, 3% of public computers are Macs, 2% of public computers are UNIX, network access in dorm rooms, network access in dorm lounges, online registration, online administrative functions (other than registration), remote student-access to Web through college's connection.

CAMPUS LIFE

Activities: Choral groups, concert band, dance, drama/theater, jazz band, literary magazine, marching band, music ensembles, musical theater, pep band, radio station, student government, student newspaper, student-run film society, symphony orchestra, yearbook. **Organizations:** 130 registered organizations, 18 honor societies, 7 religious organizations. 23 fraternities (35% men join), 9 sororities (38% women join). **Athletics (Intercollegiate):** *Men:* Baseball, basketball, cross-country, diving, football, golf, lacrosse, soccer, swimming, tennis, track/field (indoor), track/field (outdoor), wrestling. *Women:* Basketball, crew/rowing, cross-country, diving, field hockey, golf, lacrosse, soccer, softball, swimming, tennis, track/field (indoor), track/field (outdoor), volleyball. Environmental Initiatives: Environmental Initiative Program. New LEED Building. New LEAG (Lehigh Advisory Group).

ADMISSIONS

Freshman Academic Profile: 90% in top 10% of high school class, 99% in top 25% of high school class, 100% in top 50% of high school class. 64% from public high schools. SAT Math middle 50% range 640–710. SAT Critical Reading middle 50% range 600–680. TOEFL required of all international applicants, minimum paper TOEFL 570, minimum computer TOEFL 230. **Basis for Candidate Selection:** *Very important factors considered include:* Recommendation(s), rigor of secondary school record. *Important factors considered include:* Application essay, character/personal qualities, extracurricular activities, standardized test scores, talent/ability, volunteer work. *Other factors considered include:* Academic GPA, alumni/ae relation, class rank, first generation, geographical residence, level of applicant's interest, racial/ethnic status, work experience. **Freshman Admission Requirements:** High school diploma or equivalent is not required. *Academic units required:* 4 English, 3 math, 2 science (2 science labs), 2 foreign language, 2 social studies, 3 academic electives. **Freshman Admission Statistics:** 10,689 applied, 39% admitted, 29% enrolled. **Transfer Admission Requirements:** High school transcript, college transcript(s), essay or personal statement, statement of good standing from prior institution(s). Minimum college GPA of 3.3 required. Lowest grade transferable C. **General Admission Information:** Application fee $65. Early decision application deadline 11/15. Regular application deadline 1/1. Nonfall registration accepted. Admission may be deferred for a maximum of 1 year. Credit and/or placement offered for CEEB Advanced Placement tests.

COSTS AND FINANCIAL AID

Required Forms and Deadlines: FAFSA, CSS/Financial Aid PROFILE, Noncustodial PROFILE, Business/Farm Supplement. Financial aid filing deadline 2/15. **Notification of Awards:** Applicants will be notified of awards on or about 3/30. **Types of Aid:** *Need-based scholarships/grants:* Pell, SEOG, state scholarships/grants, private scholarships, the school's own gift aid, United Negro College Fund. *Loans:* FFEL Subsidized Stafford, FFEL Unsubsidized Stafford, FFEL PLUS, Federal Perkins, college/university loans from institutional funds, private educational alternative loans. **Student Employment:** Federal Work-Study Program available. Institutional employment available. Off-campus job opportunities are good. **Financial Aid Statistics:** 45% freshmen, 43% undergrads receive need-based scholarship or grant aid. 46% freshmen, 43% undergrads receive need-based self-help aid. 9 freshmen, 41 undergrads receive athletic scholarships. 65% freshmen, 60% undergrads receive any aid.

LEMOYNE-OWEN COLLEGE

807 Walker Avenue, Memphis, TN 38126
Phone: 901-942-7302 **E-mail:** admission@loc.edu **CEEB Code:** 1403
Fax: 901-942-6233 **Website:** www.loc.edu **ACT Code:** 3980
Financial Aid Phone: 901-942-7313

This private school, affiliated with the Baptist and United Church of Christ, was founded in 1862. It has a 15-acre campus.

RATINGS
Admissions Selectivity Rating: 60*   **Fire Safety Rating:** 60*   **Green Rating:** 60*

STUDENTS AND FACULTY
Enrollment: 720. **Student Body:** 100% male, 3% out-of-state, 2% international. African American 98%. **Retention and Graduation:** 38% freshmen graduate within 4 years. **Faculty:** Student/faculty ratio 12:1. 54 full-time faculty, 80% hold PhDs. 100% faculty teach undergrads.

ACADEMICS
Degrees: Bachelor's, post-bachelor's certificate. **Academic Requirements:** Arts/fine arts, computer literacy, English (including composition), foreign languages, history, humanities, mathematics, sciences (biological or physical), social science. **Classes:** Most classes have 20–29 students. **Majors with Highest Enrollment:** Business administration/management, education. **Disciplines with Highest Percentage of Degrees Awarded:** Business/marketing 49%, social sciences 25%, computer and information sciences 7%, biological/life sciences 6%, interdisciplinary studies 3%. **Special Study Options:** Cross-registration, double major, honors program, independent study, internships, student-designed major, study abroad, teacher certification program. Undergrads may take grad-level courses.

FACILITIES
Housing: Coed dorms, men's dorms, women's dorms. **Special Academic Facilities/Equipment:** Museum/gallery, language lab.

CAMPUS LIFE
Activities: Choral groups, drama/theater, jazz band, music ensembles, student government, student newspaper, yearbook. **Organizations:** 5 honor societies, 6 religious organizations. 4 fraternities (35% men join), 3 sororities (55% women join). **Athletics (Intercollegiate):** *Men:* Baseball, basketball, cross-country, tennis. *Women:* Basketball, cross-country, softball, tennis, volleyball.

ADMISSIONS
Freshman Academic Profile: 95% from public high schools. TOEFL required of all international applicants, minimum paper TOEFL 475, minimum computer TOEFL 150. **Basis for Candidate Selection:** *Very important factors considered include:* Standardized test scores. **Freshman Admission Requirements:** High school diploma is required, and GED is accepted. **Freshman Admission Statistics:** 1,118 applied, 17% admitted, 63% enrolled. **Transfer Admission Requirements:** College transcript(s), standardized test score. Minimum college GPA of 2.0 required. Lowest grade transferable C. **General Admission Information:** Application fee $25. Regular application deadline 6/15. Regular notification rolling. Nonfall registration accepted. Common Application accepted. Credit and/or placement offered for CEEB Advanced Placement tests.

COSTS AND FINANCIAL AID
Annual tuition $8,250. Room & board $4,620. Required fees $200. Average book expense $700. **Required Forms and Deadlines:** FAFSA. **Types of Aid:** *Need-based scholarships/grants:* United Negro College Fund. *Loans:* FFEL Subsidized Stafford, FFEL PLUS. **Student Employment:** Federal Work-Study Program available. Institutional employment available.

LENOIR-RHYNE COLLEGE

Admissions Office, LRC Box 7227, Hickory, NC 28603
Phone: 828-328-7300 **E-mail:** admission@lrc.edu **CEEB Code:** 5365
Fax: 828-328-7378 **Website:** www.lrc.edu **ACT Code:** 2941
Financial Aid Phone: 828-328-7304

This private school, affiliated with the Lutheran Church, was founded in 1891. It has a 100-acre campus.

RATINGS
Admissions Selectivity Rating: 77   **Fire Safety Rating:** 60*   **Green Rating:** 60*

STUDENTS AND FACULTY
Enrollment: 1,358. **Student Body:** 64% female, 36% male, 29% out-of-state. African American 7%, Caucasian 91%, Hispanic 1%. **Retention and Graduation:** 80% freshmen return for sophomore year. 40% grads go on to further study within 1 year. 1% grads pursue arts and sciences degrees. 5% grads pursue business degrees. 4% grads pursue law degrees. 4% grads pursue medical degrees. **Faculty:** Student/faculty ratio 12:1. 107 full-time faculty. 100% faculty teach undergrads.

ACADEMICS
Degrees: Bachelor's, certificate, master's. **Academic Requirements:** Arts/fine arts, computer literacy, English (including composition), foreign languages, history, humanities, mathematics, philosophy, sciences (biological or physical), social science, religion, healthful living. **Special Study Options:** Accelerated program, double major, dual enrollment, English as a second language (ESL), honors program, independent study, internships, student-designed major, study abroad, teacher certification program.

FACILITIES
Housing: Coed dorms, men's dorms, women's dorms, special housing for disabled students, fraternity/sorority housing, honors, hearing impaired. **Special Academic Facilities/Equipment:** Language lab. **Computers:** Network access in dorm rooms.

CAMPUS LIFE
Activities: Choral groups, concert band, dance, drama/theater, jazz band, music ensembles, musical theater, pep band, radio station, student government, student newspaper, television station, yearbook. **Organizations:** 54 registered organizations, 10 honor societies, 6 religious organizations. 4 fraternities (23% men join), 4 sororities (27% women join). **Athletics (Intercollegiate):** *Men:* Baseball, basketball, cheerleading, cross-country, football, golf, soccer. *Women:* Basketball, cheerleading, cross-country, golf, soccer, softball, volleyball.

ADMISSIONS
Freshman Academic Profile: 18% in top 10% of high school class, 50% in top 25% of high school class, 82% in top 50% of high school class. 90% from public high schools. SAT Math middle 50% range 470–580. SAT Critical Reading middle 50% range 460–570. ACT middle 50% range 17–24. TOEFL required of all international applicants, minimum paper TOEFL 500. **Basis for Candidate Selection:** *Very important factors considered include:* Rigor of secondary school record, standardized test scores. *Important factors considered include:* Class rank, interview. *Other factors considered include:* Application essay, character/personal qualities, extracurricular activities, recommendation(s), volunteer work, work experience. **Freshman Admission Requirements:** High school diploma is required, and GED is accepted. *Academic units required:* 4 English, 3 math, 1 science (1 science lab), 2 foreign language, 1 social studies, 1 history. **Freshman Admission Statistics:** 915 applied, 85% admitted, 35% enrolled. **Transfer Admission Requirements:** College transcript(s), statement of good standing from prior institution(s). Minimum college GPA of 2.5 required. Lowest grade transferable C. **General Admission Information:** Application fee $25. Regular notification is rolling. Nonfall registration accepted. Admission may be deferred for a maximum of 1 year. Common Application accepted. Credit offered for CEEB Advanced Placement tests.

COSTS AND FINANCIAL AID
Annual tuition $12,870. Room & board $4,920. Required fees $486. Average book expense $700. **Required Forms and Deadlines:** FAFSA, institution's own financial aid form, state aid form. Financial aid filing deadline 3/1. **Types of Aid:** *Need-based scholarships/grants:* Pell, SEOG, state scholarships/grants, the school's own gift aid. *Loans:* Direct Subsidized Stafford, Direct Unsubsidized Stafford, Direct PLUS, Federal Perkins. **Student Employment:** Federal Work-Study Program available. Institutional employment available. Off-campus job opportunities are excellent. **Financial Aid Statistics:** Highest amount earned per year from on-campus jobs $1,000.

LESLEY COLLEGE

Office of Admissions, 29 Everett Street, Cambridge, MA 02138
Phone: 617-349-8800 **E-mail:** lcadmissions@lesley.edu **CEEB Code:** 3777
Fax: 617-349-8810 **Website:** www.lesley.edu
Financial Aid Phone: 617-349-8710

This private school was founded in 1912. It has a 1-acre campus.

RATINGS
Admissions Selectivity Rating: 81 **Fire Safety Rating:** 85 **Green Rating:** 72

STUDENTS AND FACULTY
Enrollment: 1,152. **Student Body:** 76% female, 24% male, 41% out-of-state, 2% international (30 countries represented). African American 5%, Asian 4%, Caucasian 63%, Hispanic 5%. **Retention and Graduation:** 75% freshmen return for sophomore year. 36% freshmen graduate within 4 years. **Faculty:** Student/faculty ratio 10:1. 66 full-time faculty, 71% hold PhDs. 100% faculty teach undergrads.

ACADEMICS
Degrees: Associate, bachelor's, certificate, diploma, doctoral, master's, post-bachelor's certificate, post-master's certificate. **Academic Requirements:** Arts/fine arts, computer literacy, English (including composition), history, humanities, mathematics, philosophy, sciences (biological or physical), social science, multicultural perspectives. **Classes:** Most classes have 10–19 students. **Majors with Highest Enrollment:** Counseling psychology, elementary education and teaching, marketing/marketing management. **Disciplines with Highest Percentage of Degrees Awarded:** Liberal arts/general studies 34%, visual and performing arts 28%, history 11%, psychology 11%, education 7%. **Special Study Options:** Accelerated program, cross-registration, distance learning, double major, dual enrollment, exchange student program (domestic), honors program, independent study, internships, liberal arts/career combination, student-designed major, study abroad, teacher certification program.

FACILITIES
Housing: Coed dorms, women's dorms. **Special Academic Facilities/Equipment:** Kresge Center for Teaching Resources and Educational Software Collection, Marran Art Gallery, Porter Exchange Gallery, AIB Main Gallery. **Computers:** 30% of public computers are PCs, 70% of public computers are Macs, network access in dorm rooms, network access in dorm lounges, online registration, online administrative functions (other than registration), remote student-access to Web through college's connection.

CAMPUS LIFE
Activities: Choral groups, dance, drama/theater, literary magazine, musical theater, student government, student newspaper, yearbook. **Organizations:** 25 registered organizations, 2 honor societies, 2 religious organizations. **Athletics (Intercollegiate):** *Men:* Basketball, crew/rowing, soccer. *Women:* Basketball, crew/rowing, soccer, softball, volleyball. Environmental Initiatives: The continual enhancement of recycling, waste management and composting programs on campus. The formation of sustainability recommendations for faculty, staff and students. Student groups on campus are involved with and sponsor sustainability events.

ADMISSIONS
Freshman Academic Profile: 15% in top 10% of high school class, 49% in top 25% of high school class, 79% in top 50% of high school class. 83% from public high schools. SAT Math middle 50% range 460–560. SAT Critical Reading middle 50% range 450–600. SAT Writing middle 50% range 480–580. ACT middle 50% range 20–26. TOEFL required of all international applicants, minimum paper TOEFL 500, minimum computer TOEFL 173. **Basis for Candidate Selection:** *Very important factors considered include:* Academic GPA, rigor of secondary school record. *Important factors considered include:* Application essay, character/personal qualities, class rank, interview, recommendation(s), standardized test scores, volunteer work. *Other factors considered include:* Alumni/ae relation, extracurricular activities, first generation, geographical residence, level of applicant's interest, racial/ethnic status, talent/ability, work experience. **Freshman Admission Requirements:** High school diploma is required, and GED is accepted. *Academic units required:* 4 English, 3 math, 3 science (2 science labs), 1 social studies, 1 history, 4 academic electives. *Academic units recommended:* 4 English, 4 math, 4 science (2 science labs), 2 foreign language, 2 social studies, 2 history. **Freshman Admission Statistics:** 2,687 applied, 40% admitted, 28% enrolled. **Transfer Admission Requirements:** High school transcript, college transcript(s), essay or personal statement, statement of good standing from prior institution(s). Minimum college GPA of 2.5 required. Lowest grade transferable C. **General Admission Information:** Application fee $50. Regular notification is rolling. Nonfall registration accepted. Admission may be deferred for a maximum of 2 semesters. Credit and/or placement offered for CEEB Advanced Placement tests.

COSTS AND FINANCIAL AID
Annual tuition $27,200. Room and board $12,000. Required fees $310. Average book expense $700. **Required Forms and Deadlines:** FAFSA, institution's own financial aid form. Financial aid filing deadline 2/15. **Notification of Awards:** Applicants will be notified of awards on or about 3/1. **Types of Aid:** *Need-based scholarships/grants:* Pell, SEOG, state scholarships/grants, private scholarships, the school's own gift aid. *Loans:* FFEL Subsidized Stafford, FFEL Unsubsidized Stafford, FFEL PLUS, Federal Perkins, state loans. **Financial Aid Statistics:** 62% freshmen, 62% undergrads receive need-based scholarship or grant aid. 62% freshmen, 68% undergrads receive need-based self-help aid. 92% freshmen, 81% undergrads receive any aid. Highest amount earned per year from on-campus jobs $1,200.

LETOURNEAU UNIVERSITY

PO Box 7001, Longview, TX 75607
Phone: 903-233-3400 **E-mail:** admissions@letu.edu **CEEB Code:** 6365
Fax: 903-233-4301 **Website:** www.letu.edu **ACT Code:** 4120
Financial Aid Phone: 903-233-3430

This private school, affiliated with the Christian (nondenominational) Church, was founded in 1946. It has a 162-acre campus.

RATINGS
Admissions Selectivity Rating: 87 **Fire Safety Rating:** 60* **Green Rating:** 60*

STUDENTS AND FACULTY
Enrollment: 3,619. **Student Body:** 58% female, 42% male, 53% out-of-state. African American 22%, Asian 1%, Caucasian 66%, Hispanic 8%. **Retention and Graduation:** 71% freshmen return for sophomore year. 34% freshmen graduate within 4 years. 19% grads go on to further study within 1 year. **Faculty:** Student/faculty ratio 16:1. 72 full-time faculty, 72% hold PhDs.

ACADEMICS
Degrees: Associate, bachelor's, master's. **Academic Requirements:** English (including composition), history, humanities, mathematics, sciences (biological or physical), social science, Bible. **Classes:** Most classes have 10–19 students. Most lab/discussion sections have 10–19 students. **Majors with Highest Enrollment:** Aviation/airway management and operations, business administration/management, engineering. **Disciplines with Highest Percentage of Degrees Awarded:** Engineering 26%, transportation and materials moving 15%, education 11%, engineering technologies 11%, psychology 6%. **Special Study Options:** Accelerated program, cooperative education program, distance learning, double major, dual enrollment, English as a second language (ESL), honors program, independent study, internships, study abroad, teacher certification program, weekend college.

FACILITIES
Housing: Men's dorms, women's dorms, apartments for married students, apartments for single students, special housing for disabled students, residential societies available. **Special Academic Facilities/Equipment:** Longview Citizens Resource Center; R. G. LeTourneau Memorial Museum. **Computers:** Network access in dorm rooms, network access in dorm lounges, online registration, online administrative functions (other than registration), remote student-access to Web through college's connection.

CAMPUS LIFE
Activities: Choral groups, drama/theater, jazz band, music ensembles, student government, student newspaper, yearbook. **Organizations:** 44 registered organizations, 4 honor societies, 10 religious organizations. **Athletics (Intercollegiate):** *Men:* Baseball, basketball, cross-country, golf, soccer, tennis. *Women:* Basketball, cross-country, golf, soccer, softball, tennis, volleyball.

ADMISSIONS
Freshman Academic Profile: 34% in top 10% of high school class, 59% in top 25% of high school class, 84% in top 50% of high school class. 56% from public high schools. SAT Math middle 50% range 530–670. SAT Critical Reading middle 50% range 500–650. ACT middle 50% range 21–27. TOEFL required of all international applicants, minimum paper TOEFL 500, minimum computer TOEFL 173. **Basis for Candidate Selection:** *Very important factors considered include:* Academic GPA, rigor of secondary school record, standardized test scores. *Important factors considered include:* Application essay, character/personal qualities, class rank, religious affiliation/commitment. *Other factors considered include:* Alumni/ae relation, extracurricular activities, first generation, interview, recommendation(s), talent/ability, volunteer work,

work experience. **Freshman Admission Requirements:** High school diploma is required, and GED is accepted. *Academic units required:* 4 English, 3 math, 3 science (3 science labs), 2 social studies, 1 history. *Academic units recommended:* 1 foreign language, 2 academic electives. **Freshman Admission Statistics:** 885 applied, 73% admitted, 48% enrolled. **Transfer Admission Requirements:** College transcript(s), essay or personal statement, statement of good standing from prior institution(s). Minimum college GPA of 2.0 required. Lowest grade transferable C. **General Admission Information:** Application fee $25. Regular application deadline 8/1. Regular notification is rolling. Nonfall registration accepted. Admission may be deferred for a maximum of 2 years. Credit and/or placement offered for CEEB Advanced Placement tests.

COSTS AND FINANCIAL AID
Annual tuition $8,855. **Required Forms and Deadlines:** FAFSA. Financial aid filing deadline 2/15. **Notification of Awards:** Applicants will be notified of awards on or about 3/1. **Types of Aid:** *Need-based scholarships/grants:* Pell, SEOG, state scholarships/grants, private scholarships, the school's own gift aid. *Loans:* FFEL Subsidized Stafford, FFEL Unsubsidized Stafford, FFEL PLUS, Federal Perkins, state loans. **Student Employment:** Federal Work-Study Program available. Institutional employment available. Off-campus job opportunities are excellent. **Financial Aid Statistics:** 96% undergrads receive any aid.

LEWIS & CLARK COLLEGE

0615 Southwest Palatine Hill Road, Portland, OR 97219-7899
Phone: 503-768-7040 **E-mail:** Admissions@lclark.edu **CEEB Code:** 4384
Fax: 503-768-7055 **Website:** www.lclark.edu **ACT Code:** 3464
Financial Aid Phone: 503-768-7090

This private school was founded in 1867. It has a 137-acre campus.

RATINGS
Admissions Selectivity Rating: 94   **Fire Safety Rating:** 78   **Green Rating:** 80

STUDENTS AND FACULTY
Enrollment: 1,926. **Student Body:** 61% female, 39% male, 77% out-of-state, 4% international (41 countries represented). African American 2%, Asian 6%, Caucasian 65%, Hispanic 4%, Native American 1%. **Retention and Graduation:** 83% freshmen return for sophomore year. 63% freshmen graduate within 4 years. 17% grads go on to further study within 1 year. 14% grads pursue arts and sciences degrees. 1% grads pursue business degrees. 1% grads pursue law degrees. 2% grads pursue medical degrees. **Faculty:** Student/faculty ratio 13:1. 214 full-time faculty, 91% hold PhDs. 100% faculty teach undergrads.

ACADEMICS
Degrees: Bachelor's, certificate, doctoral, first professional, master's, post-master's certificate. **Academic Requirements:** Arts/fine arts, Exploration and Discovery (first-year course), foreign languages, humanities, International Studies (2 semesters), mathematics, sciences (biological or physical). **Classes:** Most classes have 10–19 students. Most lab/discussion sections have 20–29 students. **Majors with Highest Enrollment:** International relations and affairs; psychology; sociology. **Disciplines with Highest Percentage of Degrees Awarded:** Psychology 13%, foreign languages and literature 10%, visual and performing arts 10%, biological/life sciences 8%, philosophy and religious studies 6%, English 6%, history 6%, communications/journalism 3%, natural resources/environmental science 3%, physical sciences 3%. **Special Study Options:** Accelerated program, cross-registration, double major, dual enrollment, English as a second language (ESL), honor program, independent study, internships, student-designed major, study abroad, teacher certification program. Teacher certification is graduate level only.

FACILITIES
Housing: Coed dorms, women's dorms, theme floors, apartment-style residence halls for upperclass students. **Special Academic Facilities/ Equipment:** Art gallery, observatory, world music room, 85 Rank Casavant organ, renovated greenhouse. **Computers:** 20% of classrooms are wired, 50% of classrooms are wireless, 40% of public computers are PCs, 60% of public computers are Macs, 15% of public computers are UNIX, network access in dorm rooms, network access in dorm lounges, online registration, online administrative functions (other than registration), support for handheld computing, remote student-access to Web through college's connection.

CAMPUS LIFE
Activities: Choral groups, concert band, dance, drama/theater, jazz band, literary magazine, music ensembles, musical theater, radio station, student government, student newspaper, symphony orchestra, television station, yearbook. **Organizations:** 70 registered organizations, 5 honor societies, 9 religious organizations. **Athletics (Intercollegiate):** *Men:* Baseball, basketball, crew/rowing, cross-country, football, golf, swimming, tennis, track/field (outdoor). *Women:* Basketball, crew/rowing, cross-country, golf, soccer, softball, swimming, tennis, track/field (outdoor), volleyball. Environmental Initiatives: Lewis & Clark provides students, faculty, and staff with a fare-free shuttle bus system that allows access to downtown Portland, local neighborhoods, and retail stores. Lewis & Clark established an Environmental Council in the late 1990s that has since been renamed as the Sustainability Council. Since 1991 Lewis & Clark has invested in energy conservation projects that have resulted in a current annual reduction in use of 4,000,000 kWh of electricity and 230,000 Therms of natural gas with a corresponding decrease in carbon footprint.

ADMISSIONS
Freshman Academic Profile: 40% in top 10% of high school class, 80% in top 25% of high school class, 96% in top 50% of high school class. 80% from public high schools. SAT Math middle 50% range 590–680. SAT Critical Reading middle 50% range 610–700. SAT Writing middle 50% range 590–680. ACT middle 50% range 26–31. TOEFL required of all international applicants, minimum paper TOEFL 550, minimum computer TOEFL 213. **Basis for Candidate Selection:** *Very important factors considered include:* Academic GPA, racial/ethnic status, rigor of secondary school record. *Important factors considered include:* Alumni/ae relation, application essay, character/personal qualities, class rank, extracurricular activities, first generation, recommendation(s), standardized test scores, talent/ability, volunteer work. *Other factors considered include:* Geographical residence, interview, level of applicant's interest, state residency, work experience. **Freshman Admission Requirements:** High school diploma is required, and GED is accepted. *Academic units recommended:* 4 English, 4 math, 3 science (2 science labs), 3 foreign language, 4 social studies. **Freshman Admission Statistics:** 4,698 applied, 58% admitted, 19% enrolled. **Transfer Admission Requirements:** High school transcript, college transcript(s), essay or personal statement, statement of good standing from prior institution(s). Minimum college GPA of 2.0 required. Lowest grade transferable C. **General Admission Information:** Application fee $50. Regular application deadline 2/1. Regular notification 4/1. Nonfall registration accepted. Admission may be deferred for a maximum of 1 year. Credit and/or placement offered for CEEB Advanced Placement tests.

COSTS AND FINANCIAL AID
Annual tuition $29,340. Room & board $7,776 Required fees $216. Average book expense $1,000. **Required Forms and Deadlines:** FAFSA. Financial aid filing deadline 3/1. **Notification of Awards:** Applicants will be notified of awards on a rolling basis beginning on or about 3/1. **Types of Aid:** *Need-based scholarships/grants:* Pell, SEOG, state scholarships/grants, private scholarships, the school's own gift aid. *Loans:* Direct Subsidized Stafford, Direct Unsubsidized Stafford, Direct PLUS, state loans. **Student Employment:** Federal Work-Study Program available. Institutional employment available. Off-campus job opportunities are fair. **Financial Aid Statistics:** 49% freshmen, 53% undergrads receive need-based scholarship or grant aid. 41% freshmen, 47% undergrads receive need-based self-help aid. 78% freshmen, 80% undergrads receive any aid. Highest amount earned per year from on-campus jobs $1,800.

See page 1240.

LEWIS UNIVERSITY

One University Parkway, Box 297, Romeoville, IL 60446-2200
Phone: 815-836-5250 **E-mail:** admissions@lewisu.edu **CEEB Code:** 1404
Fax: 815-836-5002 **Website:** www.lewisu.edu **ACT Code:** 1058
Financial Aid Phone: 815-836-5135

This private school, affiliated with the Roman Catholic Church, was founded in 1932. It has a 375-acre campus.

RATINGS
Admissions Selectivity Rating: 76   **Fire Safety Rating:** 60*   **Green Rating:** 60*

STUDENTS AND FACULTY
Enrollment: 3,789. **Student Body:** 61% female, 39% male, 3% out-of-state, 3% international (31 countries represented). African American 11%, Asian 4%, Caucasian 69%, Hispanic 10%. **Retention and Graduation:** 81% freshmen return for sophomore year. 30% freshmen graduate within 4 years. **Faculty:**

Student/faculty ratio 12:1. 199 full-time faculty, 55% hold PhDs. 98% faculty teach undergrads.

ACADEMICS

Degrees: Associate, bachelor's, certificate, doctoral, master's, post-master's certificate. **Academic Requirements:** Arts/fine arts, English (including composition), history, humanities, mathematics, philosophy, sciences (biological or physical), social science, university-identified mission-related courses. **Classes:** Most classes have 10–19 students. Most lab/discussion sections have 10–19 students. **Majors with Highest Enrollment:** Business administration/management, criminal justice/police science, nursing/registered nurse training (RN, ASN, BSN, MSN). **Disciplines with Highest Percentage of Degrees Awarded:** Business/marketing 24%, health professions and related sciences 19%, security and protective services 9%, transportation and materials moving 9%, education 8%. **Special Study Options:** Accelerated program, distance learning, double major, dual enrollment, English as a second language (ESL), exchange student program (domestic), honors program, independent study, internships, liberal arts/career combination, student-designed major, study abroad, teacher certification program.

FACILITIES

Housing: Coed dorms. **Special Academic Facilities/Equipment:** Lewis University is located immediately adjacent to the Lewis University airport and contains an aviation complex, which includes a Boeing 737 located on campus for use by students studying aviation maintenance. Special collections on campus include curriculum collection, Eva White Memorial Aviation Collection, Library of American Civilization (ultrafiche), Library of English Literature (ultrafiche), ERIC fiche, government documents (Lewis University has housed a selective Federal Depository since 1952, and possesses a strong collection of the public documents generated during each decennial census), and Canal and Regional History Collection/I & M Canal Archives (one of the largest collections of documents, photographs, and artifacts pertaining to the canal era in the U.S.). **Computers:** 100% of public computers are PCs, network access in dorm rooms, online registration, online administrative functions (other than registration), remote student-access to Web through college's connection.

CAMPUS LIFE

Activities: Choral groups, concert band, dance, drama/theater, jazz band, literary magazine, music ensembles, pep band, radio station, student government, student newspaper, television station. **Organizations:** 45 registered organizations, 10 honor societies, 7 religious organizations. 9 fraternities (1% men join), 5 sororities (2% women join). **Athletics (Intercollegiate):** *Men:* Baseball, basketball, cheerleading, cross-country, golf, soccer, swimming, tennis, track/field (indoor), track/field (outdoor), volleyball. *Women:* Basketball, cheerleading, cross-country, golf, soccer, softball, swimming, tennis, track/field (indoor), track/field (outdoor), volleyball.

ADMISSIONS

Freshman Academic Profile: 12% in top 10% of high school class, 35% in top 25% of high school class, 68% in top 50% of high school class. 75% from public high schools. SAT Math middle 50% range 480–580. SAT Critical Reading middle 50% range 460–570. ACT middle 50% range 19–24. TOEFL required of all international applicants, minimum paper TOEFL 500, minimum computer TOEFL 173. **Basis for Candidate Selection:** *Very important factors considered include:* Academic GPA, rigor of secondary school record, standardized test scores. *Important factors considered include:* Application essay. *Other factors considered include:* Alumni/ae relation, character/personal qualities, class rank, extracurricular activities, first generation, geographical residence, interview, level of applicant's interest, racial/ethnic status, recommendation(s), talent/ability, volunteer work. **Freshman Admission Requirements:** High school diploma is required, and GED is accepted. *Academic units recommended:* 4 English, 3 math, 2 science (1 science lab), 2 foreign language, 2 social studies, 1 history, 4 academic electives. **Freshman Admission Statistics:** 2,325 applied, 68% admitted, 36% enrolled. **Transfer Admission Requirements:** College transcript(s). Minimum college GPA of 2.0 required. Lowest grade transferable D. **General Admission Information:** Application fee $40. Regular notification is rolling. Nonfall registration accepted. Admission may be deferred for a maximum of 2 years. Credit and/or placement offered for CEEB Advanced Placement tests.

COSTS AND FINANCIAL AID

Annual tuition $20,450. Room & board $7,850. Average book expense $800. **Required Forms and Deadlines:** FAFSA. Financial aid filing deadline 5/1. **Notification of Awards:** Applicants will be notified of awards on a rolling basis beginning on or about 2/1. **Types of Aid:** *Need-based scholarships/grants:* Pell, SEOG, state scholarships/grants, private scholarships, the school's own gift aid, Federal Nursing Scholarships. *Loans:* FFEL Subsidized Stafford, FFEL Unsubsidized Stafford, FFEL PLUS, Federal Perkins. **Student Employment:** Federal Work-Study Program available. Institutional employment available. Off-campus job opportunities are good. **Financial Aid Statistics:** 46% freshmen, 55% freshmen, 54 freshmen, 211 undergrads receive athletic scholarships. 85% freshmen, 80% undergrads receive any aid. Highest amount earned per year from on-campus jobs $3,000.

LEWIS-CLARK STATE COLLEGE

500 Eighth Avenue, Lewiston, ID 83501
Phone: 208-792-2210 **E-mail:** admissions@lcsc.edu **CEEB Code:** 4385
Fax: 208-792-2876 **Website:** www.lcsc.edu **ACT Code:** 0920
Financial Aid Phone: 208-792-2224

This public school was founded in 1893. It has a 44-acre campus.

RATINGS

Admissions Selectivity Rating: 74   **Fire Safety Rating:** 60*   **Green Rating:** 60*

STUDENTS AND FACULTY

Enrollment: 2,939. **Student Body:** 62% female, 38% male, 15% out-of-state, 4% international (32 countries represented). Asian 1%, Caucasian 79%, Hispanic 6%, Native American 4%. **Retention and Graduation:** 59% freshmen return for sophomore year. 7% grads go on to further study within 1 year. **Faculty:** Student/faculty ratio 15:1. 155 full-time faculty, 69% hold PhDs. 100% faculty teach undergrads.

ACADEMICS

Degrees: Associate, bachelor's, certificate, diploma. **Academic Requirements:** Arts/fine arts, English (including composition), humanities, mathematics, sciences (biological or physical), social science, communication. **Classes:** Most classes have fewer than 10 students. **Majors with Highest Enrollment:** Business administration/management, elementary education and teaching, nursing/registered nurse training (RN, ASN, BSN, MSN). **Disciplines with Highest Percentage of Degrees Awarded:** Health professions and related sciences 19%, business/marketing 19%, public administration and social services 10%, security and protective services 7%, interdisciplinary studies 5%, biological/life sciences 4%, psychology 4%. **Special Study Options:** Accelerated program, cooperative education program, distance learning, double major, dual enrollment, English as a second language (ESL), honors program, independent study, internships, student-designed major, teacher certification program, weekend college.

FACILITIES

Housing: Coed dorms, apartments for married students, apartments for single students. **Special Academic Facilities/Equipment:** Museum/art gallery, media services. **Computers:** 95% of public computers are PCs, 5% of public computers are Macs, network access in dorm rooms, online registration, online administrative functions (other than registration), remote student-access to Web through college's connection.

CAMPUS LIFE

Activities: Choral groups, dance, drama/theater, jazz band, literary magazine, music ensembles, radio station, student government, student newspaper. **Organizations:** 52 registered organizations, 1 honor society, 3 religious organizations. **Athletics (Intercollegiate):** *Men:* Baseball, basketball, cross-country, golf, tennis. *Women:* Basketball, cross-country, golf, tennis, volleyball.

ADMISSIONS

Freshman Academic Profile: 8% in top 10% of high school class, 28% in top 25% of high school class, 56% in top 50% of high school class. 99% from public high schools. SAT Math middle 50% range 420–550. SAT Critical Reading middle 50% range 390–530. ACT middle 50% range 17–23. TOEFL required of all international applicants, minimum paper TOEFL 500, minimum computer TOEFL 173. **Basis for Candidate Selection:** *Very important factors considered include:* Academic GPA, rigor of secondary school record, standardized test scores. **Freshman Admission Requirements:** High school diploma is required, and GED is accepted. *Academic units required:* 4 English, 3 math, 3 science (2 science labs), 1 academic elective, 1 fine arts. **Freshman Admission Statistics:** 1,211 applied, 62% admitted, 72% enrolled. **Transfer Admission Requirements:** College transcript(s). Minimum college GPA of 2.0 required. Lowest grade transferable D. **General Admission Information:** Application fee $35. Nonfall registration accepted. Admission may be deferred for a maximum of 1 year. Credit and/or placement offered for CEEB Advanced Placement tests.

COSTS AND FINANCIAL AID

Annual in-state tuition $3,897. Annual out-of-state tuition $10,841. Room and board $4,670. Average book expense $1,500. **Required Forms and Deadlines:** FAFSA. Financial aid filing deadline 3/1. **Notification of Awards:** Applicants will be notified of awards on a rolling basis beginning on or about 4/15. **Types of Aid:** *Need-based scholarships/grants:* Pell, SEOG, state scholarships/grants, private scholarships, the school's own gift aid. *Loans:* FFEL Subsidized Stafford, FFEL Unsubsidized Stafford, FFEL PLUS, Federal Perkins, Federal Nursing. **Student Employment:** Federal Work-Study Program available. Institutional employment available. **Financial Aid Statistics:** 42% freshmen, 49% undergrads receive need-based scholarship or grant aid. 50% freshmen, 58% undergrads receive need-based self-help aid. 24 freshmen, 129 undergrads receive athletic scholarships. 85% freshmen, 76% undergrads receive any aid.

LEXINGTON COLLEGE

310 S. Peoria St, Suite 512, Chicago, IL 60607
Phone: 312-226-6294 **E-mail:** admissions@lexingtoncollege.edu
Fax: 312-226-6405 **Website:** www.lexingtoncollege.edu
Financial Aid Phone: 312-226-6294

This private school, affiliated with the Roman Catholic Church, was founded in 1977.

RATINGS
Admissions Selectivity Rating: 60*   **Fire Safety Rating:** 60*   **Green Rating:** 60*

STUDENTS AND FACULTY
Enrollment: 57. **Faculty:** Student/faculty ratio 6:1. 4 full-time faculty.

ACADEMICS
Degrees: Associate, bachelor's. **Academic Requirements:** Arts/fine arts, computer literacy, English (including composition), humanities, mathematics, social science. **Special Study Options:** Independent study, internships, study abroad.

FACILITIES
Housing: Concord residence.

CAMPUS LIFE
Activities: Student government. **Organizations:** 1 registered organization.

ADMISSIONS
Freshman Admission Requirements: High school diploma is required, and GED is accepted. **Freshman Admission Statistics:** 61 applied, 70% admitted, 47% enrolled. **Transfer Admission Requirements:** College transcript(s), essay or personal statement, standardized test score, statement of good standing from prior institution(s). **General Admission Information:** Application fee $30. Nonfall registration accepted. Credit offered for CEEB Advanced Placement tests.

COSTS AND FINANCIAL AID
Average book expense $750. **Student Employment:** Federal Work-Study Program available. Off-campus job opportunities are good. **Financial Aid Statistics:** 82% freshmen, 93% undergrads receive need-based scholarship or grant aid. 39% freshmen, 65% undergrads receive need-based self-help aid.

LIBERTY UNIVERSITY

1971 University Boulevard, Lynchburg, VA 24502
Phone: 434-582-5905 **E-mail:** admissions@liberty.edu **CEEB Code:** 5385
Fax: 800-542-2311 **Website:** www.liberty.edu **ACT Code:** 4364
Financial Aid Phone: 434-582-2270

This private school, affiliated with the Baptist Church, was founded in 1971. It has a 4,400-acre campus.

RATINGS
Admissions Selectivity Rating: 73   **Fire Safety Rating:** 74   **Green Rating:** 60*

STUDENTS AND FACULTY
Enrollment: 13,296. **Student Body:** 52% female, 48% male, 67% out-of-state, 4% international (63 countries represented). African American 11%, Asian 2%, Caucasian 75%, Hispanic 3%. **Retention and Graduation:** 70% freshmen return for sophomore year. 31% freshmen graduate within 4 years. **Faculty:** Student/faculty ratio 20:1. 354 full-time faculty, 66% hold PhDs. 78% faculty teach undergrads.

ACADEMICS
Degrees: Associate, bachelor's, certificate, doctoral, first professional, master's, post-master's certificate. **Academic Requirements:** Computer literacy, English (including composition), history, humanities, mathematics, philosophy, sciences (biological or physical), social science, Bible, theology, history of life. **Classes:** Most classes have 20–29 students. Most lab/discussion sections have

20–29 students. **Majors with Highest Enrollment:** Business administration/management, psychology, religion/religious studies. **Disciplines with Highest Percentage of Degrees Awarded:** Business/marketing 18%, philosophy and religious studies 18%, psychology 13%, interdisciplinary studies 9%, communications/journalism 8%. **Special Study Options:** Accelerated program, cooperative education program, distance learning, double major, dual enrollment, English as a second language (ESL), external degree program, honors program, independent study, internships, student-designed major, teacher certification program, weekend college.

FACILITIES
Housing: Men's dorms, women's dorms, apartments for single students, special housing for disabled students. **Special Academic Facilities/Equipment:** Displays from the Museum of Life and Earth History are located in the library, the Jerry Falwell Museum located in the main lobby of DeMoss Hall. **Computers:** 97% of public computers are PCs, 10% of public computers are Macs, 3% of public computers are UNIX, network access in dorm rooms, network access in dorm lounges, online registration, online administrative functions (other than registration), remote student-access to Web through college's connection.

CAMPUS LIFE
Activities: Choral groups, concert band, drama/theater, marching band, music ensembles, musical theater, pep band, radio station, student government, student newspaper, television station, yearbook. **Organizations:** 25 registered organizations, 8 honor societies, 10 religious organizations. **Athletics (Intercollegiate):** *Men:* Baseball, basketball, cheerleading, cross-country, football, golf, soccer, tennis, track/field (indoor), track/field (outdoor). *Women:* Basketball, cheerleading, cross-country, soccer, softball, tennis, track/field (indoor), track/field (outdoor), volleyball.

ADMISSIONS
Freshman Academic Profile: 4% in top 10% of high school class, 13% in top 25% of high school class, 41% in top 50% of high school class. SAT Math middle 50% range 420–540. SAT Critical Reading middle 50% range 440–550. ACT middle 50% range 18–24. TOEFL required of all international applicants, minimum paper TOEFL 500, minimum computer TOEFL 173. **Basis for Candidate Selection:** *Very important factors considered include:* Rigor of secondary school record, standardized test scores. *Important factors considered include:* Academic GPA, application essay. *Other factors considered include:* Character/personal qualities, class rank, extracurricular activities, level of applicant's interest, recommendation(s), talent/ability. **Freshman Admission Requirements:** High school diploma is required, and GED is accepted. *Academic units recommended:* 4 English, 3 math, 2 science (2 science labs), 2 foreign language, 2 social studies, 4 academic electives. **Freshman Admission Statistics:** 6,874 applied, 71% admitted, 42% enrolled. **Transfer Admission Requirements:** High school transcript, college transcript(s), essay or personal statement, statement of good standing from prior institution(s). Minimum college GPA of 2.0 required. Lowest grade transferable C. **General Admission Information:** Application fee $50. Regular notification continual notification. Nonfall registration accepted. Admission may be deferred for a maximum of 1 year. Credit and/or placement offered for CEEB Advanced Placement tests.

COSTS AND FINANCIAL AID
Annual tuition $14,850. Room & board $5,400. Required fees $950. Average book expense $1,400. **Required Forms and Deadlines:** FAFSA, state aid form. Financial aid filing deadline 3/1. **Notification of Awards:** Applicants will be notified of awards on a rolling basis beginning on or about 3/15. **Types of Aid:** *Need-based scholarships/grants:* Pell, SEOG, state scholarships/grants, private scholarships, the school's own gift aid. *Loans:* FFEL Subsidized Stafford, FFEL Unsubsidized Stafford, FFEL PLUS. **Financial Aid Statistics:** 51% freshmen, 49% undergrads receive need-based scholarship or grant aid. 56% freshmen, 57% undergrads receive need-based self-help aid. 8 freshmen, 67 undergrads receive athletic scholarships. 95% freshmen, 87% undergrads receive any aid.

LIFE PACIFIC COLLEGE

1100 Covina Boulevard, San Dimas, CA 91773
Phone: 909-599-5433 **E-mail:** adm@lifepacific.edu
Fax: 909-599-6690 **Website:** www.lifepacific.edu **ACT Code:** 0489
Financial Aid Phone: 909-599-5433

This private school, affiliated with the Protestant Church, was founded in 1923. It has a 9-acre campus.

RATINGS
Admissions Selectivity Rating: 70　　**Fire Safety Rating:** 60*　　**Green Rating:** 60*

STUDENTS AND FACULTY
Enrollment: 528. **Student Body:** 46% female, 54% male, 48% out-of-state. **Retention and Graduation:** 69% freshmen return for sophomore year. 18% freshmen graduate within 4 years. 48% grads go on to further study within 1 year. **Faculty:** Student/faculty ratio 17:1. 12 full-time faculty, 17% hold PhDs. 100% faculty teach undergrads.

ACADEMICS
Degrees: Associate, bachelor's. **Academic Requirements:** English (including composition), history, humanities, mathematics, philosophy, sciences (biological or physical), social science, theology, Bible, ministry. **Classes:** Most classes have 10–19 students. Most lab/discussion sections have 20–29 students. **Special Study Options:** Accelerated program, distance learning, dual enrollment, external degree program, independent study, internships.

FACILITIES
Housing: Men's dorms, women's dorms. **Special Academic Facilities/ Equipment:** New gymnasium and workout facilities, new computer lab, new student center, new music facilities. **Computers:** 1% of classrooms are wired, 1% of classrooms are wireless, 100% of public computers are PCs, network access in dorm rooms, network access in dorm lounges, online registration, remote student-access to Web through college's connection.

CAMPUS LIFE
Activities: Choral groups, dance, drama/theater, music ensembles, student government, yearbook. **Athletics (Intercollegiate):** *Men:* Basketball. *Women:* Volleyball.

ADMISSIONS
Freshman Academic Profile: 5% in top 10% of high school class, 21% in top 25% of high school class, 38% in top 50% of high school class. SAT Math middle 50% range 410–510. SAT Critical Reading middle 50% range 430–540. ACT middle 50% range 14–23. TOEFL required of all international applicants, minimum paper TOEFL 550, minimum computer TOEFL 213. **Basis for Candidate Selection:** *Very important factors considered include:* Academic GPA, application essay, character/personal qualities, level of applicant's interest, recommendation(s), religious affiliation/commitment, standardized test scores. *Other factors considered include:* Alumni/ae relation, extracurricular activities, talent/ability. **Freshman Admission Requirements:** High school diploma is required, and GED is accepted. **Freshman Admission Statistics:** 102 applied, 87% admitted, 70% enrolled. **Transfer Admission Requirements:** College transcript(s), essay or personal statement, statement of good standing from prior institution(s). Minimum college GPA of 2.0 required. Lowest grade transferable C. **General Admission Information:** Application fee $35. Regular application deadline 6/1. Regular notification within 2 weeks of completing application. Nonfall registration accepted. Admission may be deferred for a maximum of 1 year. Common Application accepted. Credit and/or placement offered for CEEB Advanced Placement tests.

COSTS AND FINANCIAL AID
Annual tuition $9,750. Room & board $5,000. Required fees $350. Average book expense $1,242. **Required Forms and Deadlines:** FAFSA. Financial aid filing deadline 6/1. **Notification of Awards:** Applicants will be notified of awards on a rolling basis beginning on or about 6/1. **Types of Aid:** *Need-based scholarships/grants:* Pell, SEOG, state scholarships/grants, private scholarships, the school's own gift aid. *Loans:* FFEL Subsidized Stafford, FFEL Unsubsidized Stafford, FFEL PLUS. **Student Employment:** Federal Work-Study Program available. Institutional employment available. Off-campus job opportunities are excellent. **Financial Aid Statistics:** 55% freshmen, 51% undergrads receive need-based scholarship or grant aid. 56% freshmen, 49% undergrads receive need-based self-help aid.

LIFE UNIVERSITY

1269 Barclay Circle, Marietta, GA 30060-2903
Phone: 770-426-2884 **E-mail:** admission@life.edu
Fax: 770-426-9886 **Website:** www.life.edu **ACT Code:** 0845

This private school was founded in 1974.

RATINGS
Admissions Selectivity Rating: 60*　　**Fire Safety Rating:** 60*　　**Green Rating:** 60*

STUDENTS AND FACULTY
Enrollment: 823. **Student Body:** 37% female, 63% male. African American 7%, Caucasian 6%. **Faculty:** 100% faculty teach undergrads.

ACADEMICS
Degrees: Associate, bachelor's, certificate, first professional, master's. **Academic Requirements:** Arts/fine arts, computer literacy, English (including composition), foreign languages, history, humanities, mathematics, philosophy, sciences (biological or physical), social science. **Special Study Options:** Accelerated program, cooperative education program, cross-registration, double major, dual enrollment, English as a second language (ESL), honors program, internships, liberal arts/career combination.

FACILITIES
Housing: Apartments for married students, apartments for single students, off-campus living. **Special Academic Facilities/Equipment:** Wellness center.

CAMPUS LIFE
Activities: Choral groups, dance, drama/theater, jazz band, music ensembles, pep band, student government, student newspaper, yearbook. **Organizations:** 50 registered organizations, 1 honor society, 5 religious organizations. 1 sorority. **Athletics (Intercollegiate):** *Men:* Basketball, cheerleading, cross-country, golf, ice hockey, rugby, soccer, track/field (outdoor). *Women:* Basketball, cheerleading, cross-country, golf, track/field (outdoor).

ADMISSIONS
Freshman Academic Profile: TOEFL required of all international applicants, minimum paper TOEFL 500. **Basis for Candidate Selection:** *Important factors considered include:* Rigor of secondary school record, standardized test scores. *Other factors considered include:* Character/personal qualities, class rank, extracurricular activities. **Freshman Admission Requirements:** High school diploma is required, and GED is accepted. **Transfer Admission Requirements:** College transcript(s). Minimum college GPA of 2.0 required. **General Admission Information:** Regular notification. Nonfall registration accepted. Common Application accepted. Credit and/or placement offered for CEEB Advanced Placement tests.

COSTS AND FINANCIAL AID
Required Forms and Deadlines: FAFSA, institution's own financial aid form. Financial aid filing deadline 3/1. **Notification of Awards:** Applicants will be notified of awards on a rolling basis beginning on or about 6/1. **Types of Aid:** *Need-based scholarships/grants:* Pell, SEOG, state scholarships/grants, private scholarships, the school's own gift aid. *Loans:* FFEL Subsidized Stafford, FFEL Unsubsidized Stafford, FFEL PLUS, Federal Perkins.

LIMESTONE COLLEGE

1115 College Drive, Gaffey, SC 29340-3799
Phone: 864-488-4549 **E-mail:** admiss@limestone.edu **CEEB Code:** 5366
Fax: 864-487-8706 **Website:** www.limestone.edu **ACT Code:** 3862
Financial Aid Phone: 864-488-8700

This private school, affiliated with the Christian (nondenominational) Church, was founded in 1845. It has a 115-acre campus.

RATINGS
Admissions Selectivity Rating: 74　　**Fire Safety Rating:** 71　　**Green Rating:** 61

STUDENTS AND FACULTY
Enrollment: 728. **Student Body:** 43% female, 57% male, 42% out-of-state, 4% international (8 countries represented). African American 17%, Caucasian 72%, Hispanic 2%. **Retention and Graduation:** 71% freshmen return for sophomore year. 28% freshmen graduate within 4 years. **Faculty:** Student/faculty ratio 12:1. 54 full-time faculty, 72% hold PhDs. 100% faculty teach undergrads.

ACADEMICS

Degrees: Associate, bachelor's. **Academic Requirements:** Arts/fine arts, computer literacy, English (including composition), history, humanities, mathematics, sciences (biological or physical), social science, foreign languages or art, music or theater, philosophy or religion. **Classes:** Most classes have fewer than 10 students. Most lab/discussion sections have fewer than 10 students. **Majors with Highest Enrollment:** Business/managerial economics, elementary education and teaching, physical education teaching and coaching. **Disciplines with Highest Percentage of Degrees Awarded:** Education 38%, business/marketing 26%, liberal arts/general studies 8%, visual and performing arts 6%, science technologies 4%, public administration and social services 4%, history 4%. **Special Study Options:** Accelerated program, distance learning, double major, honors program, independent study, internships, liberal arts/career combination, student-designed major, teacher certification program.

FACILITIES

Housing: Men's dorms, women's dorms. **Special Academic Facilities/ Equipment:** Graphic Arts Lab. **Computers:** 10% of classrooms are wireless, 99% of public computers are PCs, 1% of public computers are Macs, network access in dorm rooms, online registration, online administrative functions (other than registration), support for handheld computing, remote student-access to Web through college's connection.

CAMPUS LIFE

Activities: Choral groups, concert band, drama/theater, jazz band, literary magazine, music ensembles, musical theater, student government, yearbook. **Organizations:** 23 registered organizations, 6 honor societies, 3 religious organizations. **Athletics (Intercollegiate):** *Men:* Baseball, basketball, cross-country, golf, lacrosse, soccer, swimming, tennis, wrestling. *Women:* Basketball, cross-country, golf, lacrosse, soccer, softball, swimming, tennis, volleyball.

ADMISSIONS

Freshman Academic Profile: 4% in top 10% of high school class, 21% in top 25% of high school class, 56% in top 50% of high school class. 80% from public high schools. SAT Math middle 50% range 460–560. SAT Critical Reading middle 50% range 450–540. ACT middle 50% range 18–23. TOEFL required of all international applicants, minimum paper TOEFL 500, minimum computer TOEFL 173. **Basis for Candidate Selection:** *Very important factors considered include:* Academic GPA, rigor of secondary school record, standardized test scores. *Important factors considered include:* Class rank. *Other factors considered include:* Interview, recommendation(s). **Freshman Admission Requirements:** High school diploma is required, and GED is accepted. *Academic units required:* 4 English, 3 math, 2 science (2 science labs), 3 social studies. **Freshman Admission Statistics:** 984 applied, 61% admitted, 31% enrolled. **Transfer Admission Requirements:** College transcript(s), statement of good standing from prior institution(s). Minimum college GPA of 2.0 required. Lowest grade transferable C. **General Admission Information:** Application fee $25. Regular application deadline 8/26. Regular notification is rolling. Nonfall registration accepted. Admission may be deferred for a maximum of 18 months. Credit offered for CEEB Advanced Placement tests.

COSTS AND FINANCIAL AID

Annual tuition $17,300. Room and board $6,400. Average book expense $1,870. **Required Forms and Deadlines:** FAFSA. Financial aid filing deadline 2/1. **Notification of Awards:** Applicants will be notified of awards on a rolling basis beginning on or about 1/15. **Types of Aid:** *Need-based scholarships/grants:* Pell, SEOG, state scholarships/grants, private scholarships, the school's own gift aid. *Loans:* FFEL Subsidized Stafford, FFEL Unsubsidized Stafford, FFEL PLUS, Federal Perkins. **Financial Aid Statistics:** 79% freshmen, 87% undergrads receive need-based scholarship or grant aid. 62% freshmen, 73% undergrads receive need-based self-help aid. 38 freshmen, 96 undergrads receive athletic scholarships. 90% freshmen, 94% undergrads receive any aid. Highest amount earned per year from on-campus jobs $2,500.

See page 1242.

LINCOLN COLLEGE

300 Keokuk St, Lincoln, IL 62656
Phone: 800-569-0556 **E-mail:** admission@lincolncollege.com
Fax: 217-732-7715 **Website:** www.lincolncollege.edu **ACT Code:** 1062
Financial Aid Phone: 217-732-3155

This private school was founded in 1865. It has a 60-acre campus.

RATINGS

Admissions Selectivity Rating: 60*   **Fire Safety Rating:** 60*   **Green Rating:** 60*

STUDENTS AND FACULTY

Faculty: 90% faculty teach undergrads.

ACADEMICS

Degrees: Associate.

FACILITIES

Computers: 100% of public computers are PCs, online registration, online administrative functions (other than registration), remote student-access to Web through college's connection.

CAMPUS LIFE

Organizations: 10 registered organizations, 1 honor society. **Athletics (Intercollegiate):** *Men:* Baseball, basketball, cheerleading, cross-country, diving, golf, soccer, swimming, wrestling. *Women:* Basketball, cheerleading, cross-country, diving, golf, soccer, softball, swimming, volleyball.

ADMISSIONS

Freshman Academic Profile: 80% from public high schools. TOEFL required of all international applicants, minimum paper TOEFL 480, minimum computer TOEFL 157. **General Admission Information:** Placement offered for CEEB Advanced Placement tests.

COSTS AND FINANCIAL AID

Annual tuition $14,300. Room & board $5,600. Required fees $960. **Student Employment:** Federal Work-Study Program available. Institutional employment available. Off-campus job opportunities are fair. **Financial Aid Statistics:** 92% freshmen, 92% undergrads receive any aid. Highest amount earned per year from on-campus jobs $1,500.

LINCOLN MEMORIAL UNIVERSITY

Cumberland Gap Parkway, Harrogate, TN 37752
Phone: 423-869-6280 **E-mail:** admissions@inetlmu.lmunet.edu **CEEB Code:** 1408
Fax: 423-869-6250 **Website:** www.lmunet.edu **ACT Code:** 3982
Financial Aid Phone: 423-869-6336

This private school was founded in 1897. It has a 1,000-acre campus.

RATINGS

Admissions Selectivity Rating: 60*   **Fire Safety Rating:** 60*   **Green Rating:** 60*

STUDENTS AND FACULTY

Enrollment: 1,048. **Student Body:** 74% female, 26% male, 33% out-of-state, 4% international (14 countries represented). African American 4%, Caucasian 88%. **Faculty:** Student/faculty ratio 9:1. 86 full-time faculty, 55% hold PhDs. 74% faculty teach undergrads.

ACADEMICS

Degrees: Associate, bachelor's, master's, post-bachelor's certificate, post-master's certificate. **Academic Requirements:** Arts/fine arts, computer literacy, English (including composition), history, humanities, mathematics, sciences (biological or physical), social science. **Classes:** Most classes have fewer than 10 students. Most lab/discussion sections have fewer than 10 students. **Disciplines with Highest Percentage of Degrees Awarded:** Education 27%, business/marketing 26%, health professions and related sciences 9%, parks and recreation 8%, computer and information sciences 7%. **Special Study Options:** Accelerated program, double major, English as a second language (ESL), independent study, internships, teacher certification program.

FACILITIES

Housing: Coed dorms, men's dorms, women's dorms, apartments for married students, apartments for single students. **Special Academic Facilities/**

Equipment: Civil War Museum, including Abraham Lincoln memorabilia collection of more than 6,000 books, paintings, and manuscripts. **Computers:** Network access in dorm rooms, remote student-access to Web through college's connection.

CAMPUS LIFE

Activities: Choral groups, drama/theater, literary magazine, radio station, student government, student newspaper, television station, yearbook. **Organizations:** 26 registered organizations, 5 honor societies, 3 religious organizations. 3 fraternities (3% men join), 3 sororities (5% women join). **Athletics (Intercollegiate):** *Men:* Baseball, basketball, cross-country, golf, soccer, tennis. *Women:* Basketball, cross-country, golf, soccer, softball, tennis, volleyball.

ADMISSIONS

Freshman Academic Profile: 36% in top 10% of high school class, 58% in top 25% of high school class, 94% in top 50% of high school class. 90% from public high schools. SAT Math middle 50% range 460–570. SAT Critical Reading middle 50% range 430–540. ACT middle 50% range 18–22. TOEFL required of all international applicants, minimum paper TOEFL 500. **Basis for Candidate Selection:** *Very important factors considered include:* Rigor of secondary school record, standardized test scores. *Important factors considered include:* Alumni/ae relation, character/personal qualities. *Other factors considered include:* Class rank, interview, racial/ethnic status, recommendation(s), volunteer work. **Freshman Admission Requirements:** High school diploma is required, and GED is accepted. *Academic units required:* 4 English, 2 math, 2 science, 1 social studies, 1 history. *Academic units recommended:* 4 English, 3 math, 2 science (2 science labs), 2 foreign language, 2 social studies, 1 history, 7 academic electives. **Freshman Admission Statistics:** 577 applied, 85% admitted, 38% enrolled. **Transfer Admission Requirements:** High school transcript, college transcript(s), standardized test score. Minimum college GPA of 2.0 required. Lowest grade transferable C. **General Admission Information:** Application fee $25. Regular notification is rolling. Nonfall registration accepted. Common Application accepted. Credit offered for CEEB Advanced Placement tests.

COSTS AND FINANCIAL AID

Annual tuition $12,600. Room & board $4,910. Average book expense $800. **Required Forms and Deadlines:** FAFSA. Financial aid filing deadline 4/1. **Notification of Awards:** Applicants will be notified of awards on a rolling basis beginning on or about 4/15. **Types of Aid:** *Need-based scholarships/grants:* Pell, SEOG, state scholarships/grants, private scholarships, the school's own gift aid. *Loans:* FFEL Subsidized Stafford, FFEL Unsubsidized Stafford, FFEL PLUS, Federal Perkins. **Student Employment:** Federal Work-Study Program available. Off-campus job opportunities are fair. **Financial Aid Statistics:** 45% freshmen, 45% undergrads receive need-based scholarship or grant aid. 36% freshmen, 29% undergrads receive need-based self-help aid. 34 freshmen, 139 undergrads receive athletic scholarships. Highest amount earned per year from on-campus jobs $1,500.

LINCOLN UNIVERSITY (CA)

401 Fifteenth Street, Oakland, CA 94612
Phone: 510-628-8010 **E-mail:** admissions@lincolnuca.edu
Fax: 510-628-8012 **Website:** www.lincolnuca.edu

This private school was founded in 1919.

RATINGS

Admissions Selectivity Rating: 60*   **Fire Safety Rating:** 60*   **Green Rating:** 60*

STUDENTS AND FACULTY

Enrollment: 19. **Student Body:** 74% international. African American 21%, Caucasian 5%.

ACADEMICS

Degrees: Associate, bachelor's, certificate, master's. **Academic Requirements:** English (including composition), humanities, mathematics, sciences (biological or physical). **Special Study Options:** Cross-registration, double major, English as a second language (ESL), internships.

ADMISSIONS

Freshman Academic Profile: TOEFL required of all international applicants, minimum paper TOEFL 500, minimum computer TOEFL 173. **Basis for Candidate Selection:** *Very important factors considered include:* Rigor of secondary school record. **Freshman Admission Requirements:** High school diploma is required, and GED is accepted. **Freshman Admission Statistics:** 25 applied, 96% admitted, 42% enrolled. **Transfer Admission Requirements:**

College transcript(s). Minimum college GPA of 2.0 required. Lowest grade transferable C. **General Admission Information:** Application fee $75. Regular application deadline 8/15. Nonfall registration accepted. Admission may be deferred for a maximum of 3 semesters.

COSTS AND FINANCIAL AID

Annual tuition $7,080. Required fees $400. Average book expense $400.

LINCOLN UNIVERSITY (MO)

820 Chestnut Street, B-7 Young Hall, Jefferson City, MO 65102-0029
Phone: 573-681-5599 **E-mail:** enroll@lincolnu.edu
Fax: 573-681-5889 **Website:** www.lincolnu.edu **ACT Code:** 2322
Financial Aid Phone: 573-681-6156

This public school was founded in 1866. It has a 165-acre campus.

RATINGS

Admissions Selectivity Rating: 63   **Fire Safety Rating:** 60*   **Green Rating:** 67

STUDENTS AND FACULTY

Enrollment: 2,447. **Student Body:** 59% female, 41% male, 16% out-of-state, 5% international (26 countries represented). African American 45%, Caucasian 47%, Hispanic 2%. **Retention and Graduation:** 51% freshmen return for sophomore year. 10% freshmen graduate within 4 years. **Faculty:** Student/faculty ratio 17:1. 115 full-time faculty, 59% hold PhDs.

ACADEMICS

Degrees: Associate, bachelor's, master's, post-master's certificate. **Academic Requirements:** Arts/fine arts, English (including composition), history, humanities, mathematics, sciences (biological or physical), social science, cultural diversity, personal and community health, physical activity course, university seminar. **Classes:** Most classes have 20–29 students. **Majors with Highest Enrollment:** Business administration/management, computer and information sciences, criminal justice/law enforcement administration. **Disciplines with Highest Percentage of Degrees Awarded:** Business/marketing 24%, education 15%, computer and information sciences 11%, security and protective services 11%, liberal arts/general studies 9%, psychology 5%, agriculture 5%, social sciences 5%. **Special Study Options:** Accelerated program, distance learning, double major, dual enrollment, exchange student program (domestic), honors program, independent study, internships, teacher certification program, senior citizen program, Learning in Retirement Inc., intersession courses.

FACILITIES

Housing: Coed dorms, men's dorms, women's dorms, honors student housing. **Special Academic Facilities/Equipment:** University Archives/Ethnic Studies Center, media center, student support services, Center for Academic Enrichment, Agriculture and Extension Information Center, education curriculum library. **Computers:** 96% of public computers are PCs, 4% of public computers are Macs, network access in dorm rooms, network access in dorm lounges, online registration, online administrative functions (other than registration), remote student-access to Web through college's connection.

CAMPUS LIFE

Activities: Choral groups, concert band, dance, drama/theater, jazz band, literary magazine, marching band, music ensembles, pep band, radio station, student government, student newspaper, television station, yearbook. **Organizations:** 27 registered organizations, 6 honor societies, 2 religious organizations. 3 fraternities, 2 sororities. **Athletics (Intercollegiate):** *Men:* Baseball, basketball, football, golf, track/field (outdoor). *Women:* Basketball, cheerleading, cross-country, softball, tennis, track/field (outdoor). Environmental Initiatives: Composting cafeteria food waste. Built and are using a cardboard collection bin for recycling from the cafeteria. In the planning stages for developing an integrated and sustainable small firm operation (a microcommunity project).

ADMISSIONS

Freshman Academic Profile: 6% in top 10% of high school class, 18% in top 25% of high school class, 44% in top 50% of high school class. SAT Math middle 50% range 380–490. SAT Critical Reading middle 50% range 350–460. ACT middle 50% range 14–20. TOEFL required of all international applicants, minimum paper TOEFL 500, minimum computer TOEFL 173. **Freshman Admission Requirements:** High school diploma is required, and GED is accepted. *Academic units recommended:* 4 English, 3 math, 2 science (1 science lab), 2 foreign language, 3 social studies, 1 academic elective, 1 visual and performing arts. **Freshman Admission Statistics:** 1,375 applied, 95% admitted, 43% enrolled. **Transfer Admission Requirements:** College transcript(s), statement of good standing from prior institution(s). Minimum college GPA of 2.0 required. Lowest grade transferable C. **General Admission Information:** Application fee $17. Regular application deadline 7/15. Regular notification continuous. Nonfall registration accepted. Credit and/or placement offered for CEEB Advanced Placement tests.

COSTS AND FINANCIAL AID

Annual in-state tuition $21,060. Room and board $7,398. Average book expense $1,300. **Required Forms and Deadlines:** FAFSA. Financial aid filing deadline 3/1. **Notification of Awards:** Applicants will be notified of awards on a rolling basis beginning on or about 2/1. **Types of Aid:** *Need-based scholarships/grants:* Pell, SEOG, state scholarships/grants, private scholarships, the school's own gift aid, Federal Nursing Scholarships. *Loans:* Direct Subsidized Stafford, Direct Unsubsidized Stafford, Direct PLUS, FFEL Subsidized Stafford, FFEL Unsubsidized Stafford, FFEL PLUS. **Student Employment:** Federal Work-Study Program available. Institutional employment available. Off-campus job opportunities are fair. **Financial Aid Statistics:** 80% freshmen, 75% undergrads receive any aid.

LINCOLN UNIVERSITY (PA)

1570 Baltimore Pike, PO Box 179, Lincoln University, PA 19352
Phone: 484-365-7206 **E-mail:** admiss@lincoln.edu **CEEB Code:** 2367
Fax: 484-365-8109 **Website:** www.lincoln.edu **ACT Code:** 3614
Financial Aid Phone: 800-561-2606

This public school was founded in 1854. It has a 422-acre campus.

RATINGS
Admissions Selectivity Rating: 75   **Fire Safety Rating:** 60*   **Green Rating:** 69

STUDENTS AND FACULTY
Enrollment: 1,854. **Student Body:** 61% female, 39% male, 53% out-of-state, 4% international (34 countries represented). African American 95%, Caucasian 1%. **Retention and Graduation:** 67% freshmen return for sophomore year. 20% freshmen graduate within 4 years. **Faculty:** Student/faculty ratio 17:1. 95 full-time faculty, 74% hold PhDs. 78% faculty teach undergrads.

ACADEMICS
Degrees: Bachelor's, master's. **Academic Requirements:** Arts/fine arts, computer literacy, English (including composition), foreign languages, history, humanities, mathematics, philosophy, sciences (biological or physical), social science. **Classes:** Most classes have 20–29 students. Most lab/discussion sections have 10–19 students. **Majors with Highest Enrollment:** Communications studies/speech communication and rhetoric, criminal justice/safety studies, elementary education and teaching. **Disciplines with Highest Percentage of Degrees Awarded:** Business/marketing 20%, education 12%, social sciences 12%, biological/life sciences 9%, security and protective services 9%, communications/journalism 7%. **Special Study Options:** Double major, exchange student program (domestic), honors program, independent study, internships, study abroad, teacher certification program. 3-2 in advanced science/engineering with Drexel University, Pennsylvania State University, Howard University, University of Delaware, Temple University, Widener University, and New Jersey Institute of Technology.

FACILITIES
Housing: Coed dorms, men's dorms, women's dorms, apartments for single students. **Special Academic Facilities/Equipment:** African museum, fine arts center, hall for life sciences, learning resource center. **Computers:** 95% of classrooms are wireless, 90% of public computers are PCs, 10% of public computers are Macs, network access in dorm rooms, network access in dorm lounges, remote student-access to Web through college's connection.

CAMPUS LIFE
Activities: Choral groups, dance, drama/theater, jazz band, music ensembles, radio station, student government, student newspaper, television station, yearbook. **Organizations:** 30 registered organizations, 9 honor societies. 4 fraternities (1% men join), 3 sororities (2% women join). **Athletics (Intercollegiate):** *Men:* Baseball, basketball, cross-country, soccer, tennis, track/field (indoor), track/field (outdoor). *Women:* Basketball, cross-country, soccer, tennis, track/field (indoor), track/field (outdoor), volleyball.

ADMISSIONS
Freshman Academic Profile: 7% in top 10% of high school class, 21% in top 25% of high school class, 51% in top 50% of high school class. SAT Math middle 50% range 360–450. SAT Critical Reading middle 50% range 370–450. ACT middle 50% range 14–18. TOEFL required of all international applicants, minimum paper TOEFL 500. **Basis for Candidate Selection:** *Very important*

factors considered include: Class rank, rigor of secondary school record. *Important factors considered include:* Academic GPA, recommendation(s), standardized test scores, talent/ability. *Other factors considered include:* Alumni/ae relation, application essay, character/personal qualities, extracurricular activities, first generation, geographical residence, interview, level of applicant's interest, religious affiliation/commitment, state residency, volunteer work. **Freshman Admission Requirements:** High school diploma is required, and GED is accepted. *Academic units required:* 4 English, 3 math, 3 science, 3 social studies, 5 academic electives, 2 arts or humanities, 1 health and physical education. **Freshman Admission Statistics:** 5,430 applied, 41% admitted, 29% enrolled. **Transfer Admission Requirements:** College transcript(s), essay or personal statement, statement of good standing from prior institution(s). Minimum college GPA of 2.0 required. Lowest grade transferable C. **General Admission Information:** Application fee $20. Regular notification is rolling. Nonfall registration accepted. Admission may be deferred for a maximum of 1 year. Credit offered for CEEB Advanced Placement tests.

COSTS AND FINANCIAL AID
Annual in-state tuition $5,472. Annual out-of-state tuition $9,312. Room and board $7,278. Required fees $2,290. Average book expense $1,330. **Required Forms and Deadlines:** FAFSA. Financial aid filing deadline 5/1. **Notification of Awards:** Applicants will be notified of awards on a rolling basis beginning on or about 4/1. **Types of Aid:** *Need-based scholarships/grants:* Pell, SEOG, state scholarships/grants, private scholarships, the school's own gift aid, United Negro College Fund. *Loans:* FFEL Subsidized Stafford, FFEL Unsubsidized Stafford, FFEL PLUS, Federal Perkins. **Financial Aid Statistics:** 68% freshmen, 66% undergrads receive need-based scholarship or grant aid. 80% freshmen, 81% undergrads receive need-based self-help aid. 94% freshmen, 93% undergrads receive any aid. Highest amount earned per year from on-campus jobs $3,500.

LINDENWOOD UNIVERSITY

209 South Kings Highway, St. Charles, MO 63301-1695
Phone: 314-949-4949 **E-mail:** admissions@lindenwood.edu **CEEB Code:** 6367
Fax: 314-949-4989 **Website:** www.lindenwood.edu **ACT Code:** 2324
Financial Aid Phone: 314-949-4923

This private school, affiliated with the Presbyterian Church, was founded in 1827. It has a 172-acre campus.

RATINGS
Admissions Selectivity Rating: 75   **Fire Safety Rating:** 60*   **Green Rating:** 60*

STUDENTS AND FACULTY
Enrollment: 5,702. **Student Body:** 56% female, 44% male, 18% out-of-state, 7% international. African American 12%, Caucasian 72%, Hispanic 2%. **Retention and Graduation:** 67% freshmen return for sophomore year. 29% freshmen graduate within 4 years. 20% grads go on to further study within 1 year. 8% grads pursue arts and sciences degrees. 10% grads pursue business degrees. 1% grads pursue law degrees. 1% grads pursue medical degrees. **Faculty:** Student/faculty ratio 21:1. 161 full-time faculty, 55% hold PhDs. 100% faculty teach undergrads.

ACADEMICS
Degrees: Bachelor's, doctoral, master's, post-bachelor's certificate, post-master's certificate. **Academic Requirements:** Arts/fine arts, English (including composition), foreign languages, history, humanities, mathematics, philosophy, sciences (biological or physical), social science, communications. **Classes:** Most classes have 10–19 students. Most lab/discussion sections have fewer than 10 students. **Majors with Highest Enrollment:** Business administration/management, elementary education and teaching, mass communications/media studies. **Disciplines with Highest Percentage of Degrees Awarded:** Business/marketing 40%, education 15%, social sciences 9%, communications/journalism 7%, computer and information sciences 5%, public administration and social services 5%. **Special Study Options:** Accelerated program, cooperative education program, cross-registration, distance learning, double major, dual enrollment, exchange student program (domestic), external degree program, honors program, independent study, internships, liberal arts/career combination, student-designed major, study abroad, teacher certification program. Undergrads with high achievement may apply for early admission to graduate-level program. Co-op programs also available in business and computer science. College for Individualized Education, primarily for adults and other nontraditional students, offers degree programs at regional centers; evening programs; bachelor of engineering with Washington University; 3-2 Lindenwood University/University of MO Columbia dual-degree program in engineering and math or computer science; 3-2

program in engineering; bachelor of science in nursing agreement with Deaconess College of Nursing.

FACILITIES

Housing: Men's dorms, women's dorms, apartments for married students, housing available for students with dependent children. **Special Academic Facilities/Equipment:** Archival museum. **Computers:** Network access in dorm rooms, remote student-access to Web through college's connection.

CAMPUS LIFE

Activities: Choral groups, concert band, dance, drama/theater, jazz band, literary magazine, marching band, music ensembles, musical theater, pep band, radio station, student government, student newspaper, student-run film society, television station. **Organizations:** 72 registered organizations, 11 honor societies, 4 religious organizations. 3 fraternities (2% men join), 1 sorority (2% women join). **Athletics (Intercollegiate):** *Men:* Baseball, basketball, cheerleading, cross-country, diving, football, golf, ice hockey, lacrosse, riflery, soccer, swimming, tennis, track/field (indoor), track/field (outdoor), volleyball, water polo, wrestling. *Women:* Basketball, cheerleading, cross-country, diving, field hockey, golf, ice hockey, lacrosse, riflery, soccer, softball, swimming, tennis, track/field (indoor), track/field (outdoor), volleyball, water polo.

ADMISSIONS

Freshman Academic Profile: 10% in top 10% of high school class, 33% in top 25% of high school class, 62% in top 50% of high school class. 75% from public high schools. SAT Math middle 50% range 460–590. SAT Critical Reading middle 50% range 420–530. SAT Writing middle 50% range 430–520. ACT middle 50% range 20–24. TOEFL required of all international applicants, minimum paper TOEFL 500, minimum computer TOEFL 173. **Basis for Candidate Selection:** *Very important factors considered include:* Academic GPA, character/personal qualities, class rank, extracurricular activities, interview, rigor of secondary school record, talent/ability, volunteer work. *Important factors considered include:* Application essay, standardized test scores, work experience. *Other factors considered include:* Alumni/ae relation, level of applicant's interest, recommendation(s), state residency. **Freshman Admission Requirements:** High school diploma is required, and GED is accepted. *Academic units recommended:* 4 English, 2 math, 2 science, 2 foreign language, 3 social studies, 3 history, 1 fine arts. **Freshman Admission Statistics:** 3,856 applied, 64% admitted, 39% enrolled. **Transfer Admission Requirements:** College transcript(s). Minimum college GPA of 2.3 required. Lowest grade transferable D. **General Admission Information:** Application fee $30. Regular notification continuous. Nonfall registration accepted. Admission may be deferred. Credit and/or placement offered for CEEB Advanced Placement tests.

COSTS AND FINANCIAL AID

Annual tuition $12,700. Room and board $6,500. Required fees $300. Average book expense $3,000. **Required Forms and Deadlines:** FAFSA. Financial aid filing deadline 4/1. **Types of Aid:** *Need-based scholarships/grants:* Pell, SEOG, state scholarships/grants, private scholarships, the school's own gift aid. *Loans:* FFEL Subsidized Stafford, FFEL Unsubsidized Stafford, FFEL PLUS, Federal Perkins. **Student Employment:** Federal Work-Study Program available. Institutional employment available. Off-campus job opportunities are good.

LINDSEY WILSON COLLEGE

210 Lindsey Wilson Street, Columbia, KY 42728
Phone: 800-264-0138 **E-mail:** admissions@lindsey.edu **CEEB Code:** 1409
Fax: 270-384-8591 **Website:** www.lindsey.edu **ACT Code:** 1522
Financial Aid Phone: 270-384-8022

This private school, affiliated with the Methodist Church, was founded in 1903. It has a 43-acre campus.

RATINGS

Admissions Selectivity Rating: 60*   **Fire Safety Rating:** 60*   **Green Rating:** 60*

STUDENTS AND FACULTY

Enrollment: 1,451. **Student Body:** 6% out-of-state, 4% international. African American 7%, Caucasian 84%, Hispanic 1%. **Retention and Graduation:** 49% freshmen return for sophomore year. **Faculty:** Student/faculty ratio 21:1.

ACADEMICS

Degrees: Associate, bachelor's, master's. **Academic Requirements:** Arts/fine arts, English (including composition), humanities, mathematics, sciences

(biological or physical). **Majors with Highest Enrollment:** Elementary education and teaching, social sciences. **Special Study Options:** Cooperative education program, English as a second language (ESL), internships, study abroad.

FACILITIES

Housing: Men's dorms, women's dorms, apartments for single students. **Computers:** Network access in dorm rooms, network access in dorm lounges, online registration, online administrative functions (other than registration), remote student-access to Web through college's connection.

CAMPUS LIFE

Activities: Choral groups, literary magazine, student government, student newspaper, yearbook. **Organizations:** 28 registered organizations. **Athletics (Intercollegiate):** *Men:* Baseball, basketball, cross-country, golf, soccer, tennis, track/field (outdoor). *Women:* Basketball, cross-country, golf, soccer, softball, tennis, track/field (outdoor), volleyball.

ADMISSIONS

Freshman Academic Profile: TOEFL required of all international applicants, minimum paper TOEFL 490. **Freshman Admission Requirements:** High school diploma is required, and GED is accepted. **Freshman Admission Statistics:** 1,335 applied, 57% admitted, 55% enrolled. **Transfer Admission Requirements:** College transcript(s), standardized test score, statement of good standing from prior institution(s). Lowest grade transferable D. **General Admission Information:** Regular notification rolling. Nonfall registration accepted. Common Application accepted. Placement offered for CEEB Advanced Placement tests.

COSTS AND FINANCIAL AID

Annual tuition $12,456. Room & board $5,484. Required fees $146. Average book expense $350. **Required Forms and Deadlines:** FAFSA, institution's own financial aid form, state aid form. **Types of Aid:** *Need-based scholarships/grants:* Pell, SEOG, state scholarships/grants, private scholarships, the school's own gift aid. *Loans:* FFEL Subsidized Stafford, FFEL PLUS, Federal Perkins, college/university loans from institutional funds. **Student Employment:** Federal Work-Study Program available. Institutional employment available. Off-campus job opportunities are good.

LINFIELD COLLEGE

900 South East Baker Street, McMinnville, OR 97128-6894
Phone: 503-883-2213 **E-mail:** admission@linfield.edu **CEEB Code:** 4387
Fax: 503-883-2472 **Website:** www.linfield.edu **ACT Code:** 3466
Financial Aid Phone: 503-883-2225

This private school, affiliated with the American Baptist Church, was founded in 1858. It has a 193-acre campus.

RATINGS

Admissions Selectivity Rating: 86   **Fire Safety Rating:** 86   **Green Rating:** 60*

STUDENTS AND FACULTY

Enrollment: 1,705. **Student Body:** 53% female, 47% male, 43% out-of-state, 2% international (21 countries represented). African American 1%, Asian 7%, Caucasian 80%, Hispanic 3%. **Retention and Graduation:** 86% freshmen return for sophomore year. 65% freshmen graduate within 4 years. 20% grads go on to further study within 1 year. 10% grads pursue arts and sciences degrees. 2% grads pursue business degrees. 2% grads pursue law degrees. 2% grads pursue medical degrees. **Faculty:** Student/faculty ratio 13:1. 104 full-time faculty, 94% hold PhDs. 100% faculty teach undergrads.

ACADEMICS

Degrees: Bachelor's. **Academic Requirements:** Arts/fine arts, English (including composition), foreign languages, history, humanities, mathematics, philosophy, sciences (biological or physical), social science, American diversity, global diversity. **Classes:** Most classes have 10–19 students. **Majors with Highest Enrollment:** Business administration/management, elementary education and teaching, mass communications/media studies. **Disciplines with Highest Percentage of Degrees Awarded:** Business/marketing 25%, parks and recreation 10%, education 9%, social sciences 8%, communications/journalism 7%. **Special Study Options:** Cross-registration, distance learning, double major, English as a second language (ESL), external degree program, independent study, internships, liberal arts/career combination, student-designed major, study abroad, teacher certification program, unique January term courses, widespread participation in off-campus international study.

FACILITIES

Housing: Coed dorms, men's dorms, women's dorms, apartments for single students, special housing for disabled students, fraternity/sorority housing.

Special Academic Facilities/Equipment: New library, new art gallery, anthropology museum, environmental field station, research institute, electron microscope, scanning auger microprobe spectrometer. **Computers:** 90% of classrooms are wireless, 60% of public computers are PCs, 40% of public computers are Macs, network access in dorm rooms, network access in dorm lounges, online registration, online administrative functions (other than registration), remote student-access to Web through college's connection.

CAMPUS LIFE

Activities: Choral groups, concert band, dance, drama/theater, jazz band, literary magazine, music ensembles, musical theater, opera, pep band, radio station, student government, student newspaper, symphony orchestra, yearbook. **Organizations:** 37 registered organizations, 17 honor societies, 5 religious organizations. 4 fraternities (26% men join), 4 sororities (30% women join). **Athletics (Intercollegiate):** *Men:* Baseball, basketball, cross-country, football, golf, soccer, swimming, tennis, track/field (outdoor). *Women:* Basketball, cross-country, golf, lacrosse, soccer, softball, swimming, tennis, track/field (outdoor), volleyball.

ADMISSIONS

Freshman Academic Profile: 37% in top 10% of high school class, 72% in top 25% of high school class, 95% in top 50% of high school class. 85% from public high schools. SAT Math middle 50% range 490–620. SAT Critical Reading middle 50% range 500–610. SAT Writing middle 50% range 490–593. ACT middle 50% range 21–27. TOEFL required of all international applicants, minimum paper TOEFL 550, minimum computer TOEFL 213. **Basis for Candidate Selection:** *Very important factors considered include:* Academic GPA, rigor of secondary school record, standardized test scores. *Important factors considered include:* Application essay, class rank, recommendation(s). *Other factors considered include:* Alumni/ae relation, character/personal qualities, extracurricular activities, first generation, geographical residence, level of applicant's interest, racial/ethnic status, talent/ability, volunteer work, work experience. **Freshman Admission Requirements:** High school diploma is required, and GED is accepted. *Academic units recommended:* 4 English, 4 math, 3 science, 2 foreign language, 3 social studies. **Freshman Admission Statistics:** 2,232 applied, 73% admitted, 27% enrolled. **Transfer Admission Requirements:** College transcript(s), essay or personal statement. Minimum college GPA of 2.0 required. Lowest grade transferable C. **General Admission Information:** Application fee $40. Regular notification 4/1. Nonfall registration accepted. Admission may be deferred for a maximum of 1 year. Credit offered for CEEB Advanced Placement tests.

COSTS AND FINANCIAL AID

Annual tuition $15,986. Room and board $7,070. Required fees $825. Average book expense $1,000. **Required Forms and Deadlines:** FAFSA. Financial aid filing deadline 2/1. **Notification of Awards:** Applicants will be notified of awards on or about 4/1. **Types of Aid:** *Need-based scholarships/grants:* Pell, SEOG, state scholarships/grants, private scholarships, the school's own gift aid. *Loans:* FFEL Subsidized Stafford, FFEL Unsubsidized Stafford, FFEL PLUS, Federal Perkins, private loans from multiple lenders. **Student Employment:** Federal Work-Study Program available. Institutional employment available. Off-campus job opportunities are fair. **Financial Aid Statistics:** 49% freshmen, 53% undergrads receive need-based scholarship or grant aid. 46% freshmen, 54% undergrads receive need-based self-help aid. 90% freshmen, 90% undergrads receive any aid. Highest amount earned per year from on-campus jobs $2,250.

LIPSCOMB UNIVERSITY

3901 Granny White Pike, Nashville, TN 37204-3951
Phone: 615-966-1776 **E-mail:** admissions@lipscomb.edu **CEEB Code:** 1161
Fax: 615-966-1804 **Website:** www.lipscomb.edu **ACT Code:** 3956
Financial Aid Phone: 615-966-1791

This private school, affiliated with the Church of Christ, was founded in 1891. It has a 65-acre campus.

RATINGS

Admissions Selectivity Rating: 81   **Fire Safety Rating:** 95   **Green Rating:** 85

STUDENTS AND FACULTY

Enrollment: 2,269. **Student Body:** 57% female, 43% male, 33% out-of-state, 1% international (24 countries represented). African American 6%, Asian 2%, Caucasian 82%, Hispanic 2%. **Retention and Graduation:** 75% freshmen return for sophomore year. 30% freshmen graduate within 4 years. **Faculty:** Student/faculty ratio 15:1. 109 full-time faculty, 81% hold PhDs. 100% faculty teach undergrads.

ACADEMICS

Degrees: Bachelor's, first professional, master's, post-bachelor's certificate. **Academic Requirements:** Arts/fine arts, computer literacy, English (including composition), history, humanities, mathematics, sciences (biological or physical), social science, Bible. **Classes:** Most classes have 10–19 students. Most lab/discussion sections have 20–29 students. **Majors with Highest Enrollment:** Business administration and management, elementary education and teaching, pre-nursing studies. **Disciplines with Highest Percentage of Degrees Awarded:** Business/marketing 30%, education 11%, communications/journalism 8%, biological/life sciences 8%, mathematics 8%, psychology 6%. **Special Study Options:** Accelerated program, cross-registration, distance learning, double major, dual enrollment, honors program, independent study, internships, study abroad, teacher certification program, weekend college.

FACILITIES

Housing: Men's dorms, women's dorms, out-of-town undergraduates required to live on campus except for seniors, students over 21, and married students. **Special Academic Facilities/Equipment:** On-campus elementary, middle, and secondary schools. **Computers:** 100% of classrooms are wired, 50% of classrooms are wireless, 95% of public computers are PCs, 5% of public computers are Macs, network access in dorm rooms, network access in dorm lounges, online registration, online administrative functions (other than registration), remote student-access to Web through college's connection.

CAMPUS LIFE

Activities: Choral groups, concert band, drama/theater, jazz band, literary magazine, marching band, music ensembles, musical theater, pep band, radio station, student government, student newspaper, yearbook. **Organizations:** 65 registered organizations. **Athletics (Intercollegiate):** *Men:* Baseball, basketball, cross-country, golf, soccer, tennis, track/field (outdoor). *Women:* Basketball, cheerleading, cross-country, soccer, softball, tennis, track/field (indoor), track/field (outdoor), volleyball. Environmental Initiatives: Geothermal field.

ADMISSIONS

Freshman Academic Profile: 25% in top 10% of high school class, 47% in top 25% of high school class, 77% in top 50% of high school class. SAT Math middle 50% range 500–600. SAT Critical Reading middle 50% range 500–620. SAT Writing middle 50% range 490–600, ACT middle 50% range 21–27. TOEFL required of all international applicants, minimum paper TOEFL 550, minimum computer TOEFL 213. **Basis for Candidate Selection:** *Very important factors considered include:* Class rank, standardized test scores. *Important factors considered include:* Academic GPA, character/personal qualities, recommendation(s). *Other factors considered include:* Alumni/ae relation, application essay, extracurricular activities, first generation, interview, rigor of secondary school record, talent/ability, volunteer work. **Freshman Admission Requirements:** High school diploma is required, and GED is accepted. *Academic units required:* 4 English, 2 math, 2 science, 2 foreign language, 2 social studies, 2 academic electives. **Freshman Admission Statistics:** 1,606 applied, 74% admitted, 48% enrolled. **Transfer Admission Requirements:** College transcript(s). Minimum college GPA of 2.0 required. Lowest grade transferable C. **General Admission Information:** Application fee $25. Regular notification continuous. Nonfall registration accepted. Credit and/or placement offered for CEEB Advanced Placement tests.

COSTS AND FINANCIAL AID

Annual tuition $14,896. Room & board $6,730. Required fees $670. Average book expense $1,000. **Required Forms and Deadlines:** FAFSA. Financial aid filing deadline 3/1. **Notification of Awards:** Applicants will be notified of awards on a rolling basis beginning on or about 2/15. **Types of Aid:** *Need-based scholarships/grants:* Pell, SEOG, state scholarships/grants, private scholarships, the school's own gift aid. *Loans:* FFEL Subsidized Stafford, FFEL Unsubsidized Stafford, FFEL PLUS, Federal Perkins, Federal Nursing, alternative. **Financial Aid Statistics:** 25% freshmen, 21% undergrads receive need-based scholarship or grant aid. 49% freshmen, 43% undergrads receive need-based self-help aid. 24 freshmen, 99 undergrads receive athletic scholarships. 64% freshmen, 88% undergrads receive any aid.

LIVINGSTONE COLLEGE

701 West Monroe Street, Salisbury, NC 28144-5213
Phone: 704-216-6001 **E-mail:** admiasions@livingstone.edu
Fax: 704-216-6215 **Website:** www.livingstone.edu
Financial Aid Phone: 704-216-6273

This private school, affiliated with the African Methodist Episcopal Church, was founded in 1879. It has a 272-acre campus.

RATINGS
Admissions Selectivity Rating: 60*   **Fire Safety Rating:** 60*   **Green Rating:** 60*

STUDENTS AND FACULTY
Enrollment: 907. **Student Body:** 43% female, 57% male. African American 67%, Caucasian 1%. **Retention and Graduation:** 61% freshmen return for sophomore year. 50% grads go on to further study within 1 year. 25% grads pursue arts and sciences degrees. 15% grads pursue business degrees. 5% grads pursue law degrees. 5% grads pursue medical degrees. **Faculty:** Student/faculty ratio 15:1. 54 full-time faculty, 50% hold PhDs. 100% faculty teach undergrads.

ACADEMICS
Degrees: Bachelor's. **Academic Requirements:** Arts/fine arts, computer literacy, English (including composition), foreign languages, history, humanities, mathematics, philosophy, sciences (biological or physical), social science. **Classes:** Most classes have fewer than 10 students. Most lab/discussion sections have 10–19 students. **Majors with Highest Enrollment:** Business administration and management; computer and information sciences; criminal justice/safety studies. **Disciplines with Highest Percentage of Degrees Awarded:** Business/marketing 31%, security and protective services 14%, social sciences 10%, public administration and social services 8%, psychology 8%, parks and recreation 7%. **Special Study Options:** Accelerated program, cross-registration, double major, independent study, internships, teacher certification program, community service.

FACILITIES
Housing: Men's dorms, women's dorms, apartments for married students, apartments for single students, special housing for disabled students, special housing for international students. **Special Academic Facilities/Equipment:** Heritage Hall; Poets and Dreamers Garden; NASA SEMAA Lab; and the Elizabeth Koontz Center. **Computers:** 100% of classrooms are wired, 100% of public computers are PCs, network access in dorm rooms, network access in dorm lounges, online registration, online administrative functions (other than registration), remote student-access to Web through college's connection.

CAMPUS LIFE
Activities: Choral groups, concert band, dance, drama/theater, jazz band, marching band, music ensembles, musical theater, pep band, radio station, student government, student-run film society, yearbook. **Organizations:** 16 registered organizations, 4 honor societies, 2 religious organizations. 4 fraternities, 4 sororities. **Athletics (Intercollegiate):** *Men:* Basketball, cross-country, football, track/field (outdoor). *Women:* Basketball, bowling, cheerleading, cross-country, softball, tennis, track/field (outdoor), volleyball.

ADMISSIONS
Freshman Academic Profile: SAT Math middle 50% range 320–430. SAT Critical Reading middle 50% range 323–420. SAT Writing middle 50% range 320–400. ACT middle 50% range 12–16. TOEFL required of all international applicants, minimum paper TOEFL 500, minimum computer TOEFL 250. **Basis for Candidate Selection:** *Important factors considered include:* Academic GPA, recommendation(s). *Other factors considered include:* Alumni/ae relation, application essay, character/personal qualities, class rank, extracurricular activities, first generation, geographical residence, interview, level of applicant's interest, rigor of secondary school record, state residency, talent/ability, volunteer work, work experience. **Freshman Admission Requirements:** High school diploma is required, and GED is accepted. *Academic units required:* 4 English, 3 math, 2 science, 2 foreign language, 2 social studies, 1 history. **Freshman Admission Statistics:** 1,587 applied, 58% admitted, 28% enrolled. **Transfer Admission Requirements:** High school transcript, college transcript(s), statement of good standing from prior institution(s). Minimum college GPA of 2.0 required. Lowest grade transferable C. **General Admission Information:** Application fee $25. Nonfall registration accepted. Credit and/or placement offered for CEEB Advanced Placement tests.

COSTS AND FINANCIAL AID
Required Forms and Deadlines: FAFSA, institution's own financial aid form, state aid form. Financial aid filing deadline 3/15. **Types of Aid:** *Loans:* FFEL Subsidized Stafford, FFEL PLUS. **Financial Aid Statistics:** 88% freshmen, 89% undergrads receive need-based scholarship or grant aid. 70% freshmen, 79% undergrads receive need-based self-help aid. Highest amount earned per year from on-campus jobs $1,200.

LOCK HAVEN UNIVERSITY OF PENNSYLVANIA

Akeley Hall, Lock Haven, PA 17745
Phone: 570-484-2027 **E-mail:** admissions@lhup.edu **CEEB Code:** 2654
Fax: 570-484-2201 **Website:** www.lhup.edu **ACT Code:** 3708
Financial Aid Phone: 877-405-3057

This public school was founded in 1870. It has a 175-acre campus.

RATINGS
Admissions Selectivity Rating: 71   **Fire Safety Rating:** 60*   **Green Rating:** 60*

STUDENTS AND FACULTY
Enrollment: 4,697. **Student Body:** 58% female, 42% male, 10% out-of-state, 1% international (39 countries represented). African American 6%, Caucasian 88%, Hispanic 2%. **Retention and Graduation:** 68% freshmen return for sophomore year. 29% freshmen graduate within 4 years. **Faculty:** Student/faculty ratio 20:1. 236 full-time faculty, 66% hold PhDs. 99% faculty teach undergrads.

ACADEMICS
Degrees: Associate, bachelor's, certificate, master's. **Academic Requirements:** Arts/fine arts, English (including composition), history, humanities, mathematics, philosophy, sciences (biological or physical), social science, wellness. **Classes:** Most classes have 20–29 students. Most lab/discussion sections have 10–19 students. **Majors with Highest Enrollment:** Elementary education and teaching, health and physical education/fitness, health professions and related sciences. **Disciplines with Highest Percentage of Degrees Awarded:** Education 17%, parks and recreation 14%, health professions and related sciences 11%, security and protective services 9%, business/marketing 9%, psychology 6%. **Special Study Options:** Cross-registration, distance learning, double major, dual enrollment, honors program, independent study, internships, student-designed major, study abroad, teacher certification program.

FACILITIES
Housing: Coed dorms, apartments for single students. **Special Academic Facilities/Equipment:** Planetarium, Sloan Art Gallery, Library Archives. **Computers:** Network access in dorm rooms, network access in dorm lounges, online registration, remote student-access to Web through college's connection.

CAMPUS LIFE
Activities: Choral groups, concert band, dance, drama/theater, jazz band, literary magazine, marching band, music ensembles, pep band, radio station, student government, student newspaper, symphony orchestra, television station. **Organizations:** 96 registered organizations, 10 honor societies, 7 religious organizations. 6 fraternities (4% men join), 4 sororities (3% women join). **Athletics (Intercollegiate):** *Men:* Baseball, basketball, football, soccer, track/field (indoor), track/field (outdoor), wrestling. *Women:* Basketball, field hockey, lacrosse, soccer, softball, swimming, track/field (indoor), track/field (outdoor), volleyball.

ADMISSIONS
Freshman Academic Profile: 7% in top 10% of high school class, 25% in top 25% of high school class, 63% in top 50% of high school class. SAT Math middle 50% range 420–520. SAT Critical Reading middle 50% range 420–510. SAT Writing middle 50% range 410–500. ACT middle 50% range 16–22. TOEFL required of all international applicants, minimum paper TOEFL 550. **Basis for Candidate Selection:** *Very important factors considered include:* Character/personal qualities, class rank, rigor of secondary school record, talent/ability. *Important factors considered include:* Racial/ethnic status, standardized test scores. *Other factors considered include:* Application essay, extracurricular activities, first generation, interview, recommendation(s), volunteer work, work experience. **Freshman Admission Requirements:** High school diploma is required, and GED is accepted. *Academic units required:* 4 English, 3 math, 3 science (2 science labs), 2 social studies, 2 history. *Academic units recommended:* 4 English, 4 math, 4 science (3 science labs), 2 foreign language, 2 social studies, 2 history. **Freshman Admission Statistics:** 4,120 applied, 71% admitted, 37% enrolled. **Transfer Admission Requirements:** College transcript(s), statement of good standing from prior institution(s). Minimum college GPA of 2.0 required. Lowest grade transferable C. **General Admission Information:** Application fee $25. Regular notification is rolling. Nonfall registration accepted. Admission may be deferred for a maximum of 1 year. Credit and/or placement offered for CEEB Advanced Placement tests.

COSTS AND FINANCIAL AID
Annual in-state tuition $5,177. Annual out-of-state tuition $10,944. Room and board $6,188. Required fees $1,501. Average book expense $1,100. **Required Forms and Deadlines:** FAFSA, institution's own financial aid form. Financial

aid filing deadline 3/15. **Notification of Awards:** Applicants will be notified of awards on a rolling basis beginning on or about 3/1. **Types of Aid:** *Need-based scholarships/grants:* Pell, SEOG, state scholarships/grants, private scholarships, the school's own gift aid. *Loans:* FFEL Subsidized Stafford, FFEL Unsubsidized Stafford, FFEL PLUS, Federal Perkins, college/university loans from institutional funds. **Student Employment:** Federal Work-Study Program available. Institutional employment available. Off-campus job opportunities are good. **Financial Aid Statistics:** 49% freshmen, 53% undergrads receive need-based scholarship or grant aid. 57% freshmen, 62% undergrads receive need-based self-help aid. 56 freshmen, 223 undergrads receive athletic scholarships. Highest amount earned per year from on-campus jobs $1,200.

LOMA LINDA UNIVERSITY

Office of Admissions, Loma Linda, CA 92350
Phone: 909-824-4599
Fax: 909-824-4291 **Website:** www.llu.edu
Financial Aid Phone: 909-824-4509

This private school, affiliated with the Seventh-Day Adventist Church, was founded in 1905.

RATINGS
Admissions Selectivity Rating: 60*   **Fire Safety Rating:** 60*   **Green Rating:** 60*

ACADEMICS
Degrees: Associate, bachelor's, certificate, doctoral, master's, post-bachelor's certificate. **Academic Requirements:** Sciences (biological or physical). **Special Study Options:** Distance learning, double major.

FACILITIES
Housing: Coed dorms, men's dorms, women's dorms, apartments for single students.

CAMPUS LIFE
Activities: Student government, student newspaper, yearbook. **Organizations:** 1 honor society, 1 religious organization.

ADMISSIONS
Basis for Candidate Selection: *Very important factors considered include:* Application essay, character/personal qualities, interview, recommendation(s), religious affiliation/commitment. *Important factors considered include:* Talent/ability, volunteer work, work experience. *Other factors considered include:* Alumni/ae relation, extracurricular activities. **Freshman Admission Requirements:** High school diploma is required, and GED is accepted. **Transfer Admission Requirements:** High school transcript, college transcript(s), essay or personal statement, interview. Minimum college GPA of 2.0 required. Lowest grade transferable C. **General Admission Information:** Application fee $50. Regular application deadline rolling. Nonfall registration not accepted. Admission may be deferred for a maximum of 1 year.

COSTS AND FINANCIAL AID
Annual tuition $21,825. Room $2,325. Average book expense $975. **Types of Aid:** *Loans:* FFEL Subsidized Stafford, FFEL PLUS.

LONG ISLAND UNIVERSITY— ARNOLD & MARIE SCHWARTZ COLLEGE OF PHARMACY & HEALTH SCIENCE

Long Island University, 75 DeKalb Avenue, Brooklyn, NY 11201
Phone: 718-403-1011 **E-mail:** admissions@brooklyn.liu.edu
Fax: 718-797-2399 **Website:** www.liu.edu

This is a private school.

RATINGS
Admissions Selectivity Rating: 60*   **Fire Safety Rating:** 60*   **Green Rating:** 60*

ACADEMICS
Degrees: Doctoral, first professional, master's. **Academic Requirements:** Sciences (biological or physical). Satisfactory completion of minimum requirements of the Writing Across the Curriculum program or equivalent and full prescribed major curriculum. **Special Study Options:** Honors program.

FACILITIES
Housing: Coed dorms, women's dorms, apartments for single students.

CAMPUS LIFE
Organizations: 3 honor societies, 2 religious organizations. **Athletics (Intercollegiate):** *Men:* Basketball, cross-country, softball, tennis, track/field (indoor), track/field (outdoor).

ADMISSIONS
Freshman Academic Profile: TOEFL required of all international applicants, minimum paper TOEFL 500. **Basis for Candidate Selection:** *Very important factors considered include:* Rigor of secondary school record, standardized test scores. *Important factors considered include:* Character/personal qualities, extracurricular activities, talent/ability. *Other factors considered include:* Class rank, interview, recommendation(s), volunteer work, work experience. **Freshman Admission Requirements:** High school diploma is required, and GED is accepted. *Academic units required:* 2 math, 1 science (1 science lab). *Academic units recommended:* 2 science (2 science labs). **Freshman Admission Statistics:** 813 applied, 64% admitted, 41% enrolled. **Transfer Admission Requirements:** College transcript(s), minimum college GPA of 3.0 required. Lowest grade transferable C. **General Admission Information:** Application fee $30. Regular notification is within 1 month of completion of application file. Nonfall registration not accepted.

COSTS AND FINANCIAL AID
Comprehensive fee $7,900. **Required Forms and Deadlines:** FAFSA. Financial aid filing deadline 3/15. **Types of Aid:** *Need-based scholarships/ grants:* Pell, SEOG, state scholarships/grants, private scholarships, the school's own gift aid. *Loans:* Direct Subsidized Stafford, Direct Unsubsidized Stafford, Direct PLUS, Federal Perkins, Health Professions Student Loan (HPSL). **Student Employment:** Federal Work-Study Program available.

LONG ISLAND UNIVERSITY—BROOKLYN

One University Plaza, Brooklyn, NY 11201
Phone: 800-548-7526 **CEEB Code:** 2369
Fax: 718-797-2399 **Website:** www.liunet.edu
Financial Aid Phone: 718-488-1037

This private school was founded in 1926. It has a 10-acre campus.

RATINGS
Admissions Selectivity Rating: 60*   **Fire Safety Rating:** 60*   **Green Rating:** 60*

STUDENTS AND FACULTY
Student Body: 7% out-of-state. **Retention and Graduation:** 15% grads go on to further study within 1 year. 15% grads pursue arts and sciences degrees.

ACADEMICS
Degrees: Associate, bachelor's, doctoral, master's. **Special Study Options:** Cooperative education program. Undergrads may take grad-level classes. Co-op programs also available in arts, business, computer science, technologies. Off-campus study in the United Nations.

FACILITIES
Housing: Coed dorms, men's dorms, women's dorms, apartments for single students. **Special Academic Facilities/Equipment:** Language lab, instructional resources center.

CAMPUS LIFE
Organizations: 3 fraternities, 3 sororities. **Athletics (Intercollegiate):** *Men:* Basketball, cross-country, softball, tennis, track/field (outdoor). *Women:* Basketball, cross-country, softball, tennis, track/field (outdoor).

ADMISSIONS
Freshman Academic Profile: 82% from public high schools. TOEFL required of all international applicants, minimum paper TOEFL 550. **Freshman Admission Requirements:** High school diploma is required, and GED is accepted. *Academic units required:* 4 English, 2 math, 1 science, 2 foreign language, 3 social studies, 4 academic electives. **Transfer Admission Requirements:** Minimum college GPA of 2.0 required. Lowest grade transferable C. **General Admission Information:** Regular application deadline rolling. Regular notification rolling. Nonfall registration accepted. Common Application not accepted. Credit and/or placement offered for CEEB Advanced Placement tests.

COSTS AND FINANCIAL AID
Comprehensive fee $17,480. Room & board $7,620. Average book expense

$700. **Required Forms and Deadlines:** FAFSA, institution's own financial aid form, state aid form. **Types of Aid:** *Need-based scholarships/grants:* Pell, SEOG, state scholarships/grants, private scholarships, the school's own gift aid. *Loans:* FFEL Subsidized Stafford, FFEL Unsubsidized Stafford, FFEL PLUS, Federal Perkins, college/university loans from institutional funds. **Student Employment:** Federal Work-Study Program available. Institutional employment available. Off-campus job opportunities are good.

LONG ISLAND UNIVERSITY—C.W. POST

720 Northern Boulevard, Brookville, NY 11548
Phone: 516-299-2900 **E-mail:** enroll@cwpost.liu.edu **CEEB Code:** 2070
Fax: 516-299-2137 **Website:** www.liu.edu
Financial Aid Phone: 516-299-2338

This private school was founded in 1954. It has a 308-acre campus.

RATINGS
Admissions Selectivity Rating: 71   **Fire Safety Rating:** 60*   **Green Rating:** 60*

STUDENTS AND FACULTY
Enrollment: 5,748. **Student Body:** 57% female, 43% male, 6% out-of-state, 2% international. African American 7%, Asian 2%, Caucasian 49%, Hispanic 7%. **Faculty:** 100% faculty teach undergrads.

ACADEMICS
Degrees: Associate, bachelor's, certificate, doctoral, master's. **Academic Requirements:** Arts/fine arts, computer literacy, English (including composition), foreign languages, history, humanities, mathematics, philosophy, sciences (biological or physical), social science. **Special Study Options:** Accelerated program, cooperative education program, cross-registration, double major, English as a second language (ESL), honors program, independent study, internships, liberal arts/career combination, student-designed major, study abroad, teacher certification program, weekend college.

FACILITIES
Housing: Coed dorms. **Special Academic Facilities/Equipment:** Art museum, performing arts center, concert theater, television equipment, video production facility, 3 electron microscopes. **Computers:** Network access in dorm rooms, network access in dorm lounges, online administrative functions (other than registration), remote student-access to Web through college's connection.

CAMPUS LIFE
Activities: Choral groups, concert band, dance, drama/theater, jazz band, literary magazine, music ensembles, musical theater, radio station, student government, student newspaper, symphony orchestra, television station, yearbook. **Organizations:** 104 registered organizations, 19 honor societies, 5 fraternities (1% men join), 4 sororities (1% women join). **Athletics (Intercollegiate):** *Men:* Baseball, basketball, cross-country, football, lacrosse, soccer, track/field (outdoor). *Women:* Basketball, cheerleading, cross-country, field hockey, soccer, softball, tennis, track/field (outdoor), volleyball.

ADMISSIONS
Freshman Academic Profile: 10% in top 10% of high school class, 26% in top 25% of high school class, 61% in top 50% of high school class. 80% from public high schools. SAT Math middle 50% range 500–600. SAT Critical Reading middle 50% range 500–550. TOEFL required of all international applicants, minimum paper TOEFL 500. **Basis for Candidate Selection:** *Very important factors considered include:* Rigor of secondary school record. *Important factors considered include:* Class rank, interview, recommendation(s), standardized test scores. *Other factors considered include:* Alumni/ae relation, application essay, character/personal qualities, extracurricular activities, talent/ability, volunteer work, work experience. **Freshman Admission Requirements:** High school diploma is required, and GED is accepted. *Academic units required:* 4 English, 2 math, 2 science (2 science labs), 2 foreign language, 3 social studies, 1 academic elective. *Academic units recommended:* 4 English, 4 math, 4 science (4 science labs), 4 foreign language, 4 social studies. **Freshman Admission Statistics:** 3,315 applied, 85% admitted, 26% enrolled. **Transfer Admission Requirements:** College transcript(s), statement of good standing from prior institution(s). Minimum college GPA of 2.0 required. Lowest grade transferable C. **General Admission Information:** Application fee $30. Regular application deadline rolling. Regular notification is rolling. Nonfall registration accepted. Common Application accepted. Credit offered for CEEB Advanced Placement tests.

COSTS AND FINANCIAL AID
Comprehensive fee $7,900. Annual tuition $18,240. Average book expense

$600. **Required Forms and Deadlines:** FAFSA, CSS/Financial Aid PROFILE, state aid form. Financial aid filing deadline 2/1. **Notification of Awards:** Applicants will be notified of awards on a rolling basis beginning on or about 3/1. **Types of Aid:** *Need-based scholarships/grants:* Pell, SEOG, state scholarships/grants, private scholarships, the school's own gift aid. *Loans:* Direct Subsidized Stafford, Direct Unsubsidized Stafford, Direct PLUS, Federal Perkins, college/university loans from institutional funds. **Student Employment:** Federal Work-Study Program available. Institutional employment available. Off-campus job opportunities are good. **Financial Aid Statistics:** 71% freshmen, 42% undergrads receive need-based scholarship or grant aid. 88% freshmen, 62% undergrads receive need-based self-help aid. 24 freshmen, 150 undergrads receive athletic scholarships. Highest amount earned per year from on-campus jobs $600.

LONG ISLAND UNIVERSITY—SOUTHAMPTON COLLEGE

239 Montauk Highway, Southampton, NY 11968
Phone: 631-287-8200 **E-mail:** admissions@southampton.liunet.edu **CEEB Code:** 2853
Fax: 631-287-8130 **Website:** www.southampton.liu.edu **ACT Code:** 2853
Financial Aid Phone: 631-287-8283

This private school was founded in 1963. It has a 110-acre campus.

RATINGS
Admissions Selectivity Rating: 74   **Fire Safety Rating:** 60*   **Green Rating:** 60*

STUDENTS AND FACULTY
Enrollment: 1,147. **Student Body:** 67% female, 33% male, 35% out-of-state, 5% international (20 countries represented). African American 5%, Asian 1%, Caucasian 62%, Hispanic 5%. **Retention and Graduation:** 68% freshmen return for sophomore year. 20% grads go on to further study within 1 year. 10% grads pursue arts and sciences degrees. **Faculty:** Student/faculty ratio 18:1. 66 full-time faculty. 100% faculty teach undergrads.

ACADEMICS
Degrees: Bachelor's, master's, post-bachelor's certificate. **Academic Requirements:** Arts/fine arts, English (including composition), humanities, sciences (biological or physical), social science. **Classes:** Most classes have 10–19 students. Most lab/discussion sections have 10–19 students. **Majors with Highest Enrollment:** Biopsychology, business administration/management. **Disciplines with Highest Percentage of Degrees Awarded:** Interdisciplinary studies 27%, biological/life sciences 24%, liberal arts/general studies 11%, education 7%, psychology 6%. **Special Study Options:** Accelerated program, cooperative education program, distance learning, double major, dual enrollment, English as a second language (ESL), exchange student program (domestic), friends world program (travel abroad), honors program, independent study, internships, liberal arts/career combination, Semester at Sea, student-designed major, study abroad, teacher certification program, United Nations semester. Undergrads may take grad-level classes.

FACILITIES
Housing: Coed dorms, women's dorms, nonsmoking and substance free, honors, quiet. **Special Academic Facilities/Equipment:** Art galleries, on-campus nursery school, psychobiology lab, marine station and fleet of research vessels, silicon graphics computer lab. **Computers:** 80% of public computers are PCs, 10% of public computers are Macs, 10% of public computers are UNIX, network access in dorm rooms, network access in dorm lounges, online administrative functions (other than registration), remote student-access to Web through college's connection.

CAMPUS LIFE
Activities: Choral groups, drama/theater, literary magazine, music ensembles, musical theater, radio station, student government, student newspaper, student-run film society, yearbook. **Organizations:** 40 registered organizations, 4 honor societies, 2 religious organizations. **Athletics (Intercollegiate):** *Men:* Basketball, cross-country, lacrosse, soccer, tennis, volleyball. *Women:* Basketball, cross-country, soccer, softball, tennis, volleyball.

ADMISSIONS
Freshman Academic Profile: 19% in top 10% of high school class, 40% in top 25% of high school class, 77% in top 50% of high school class. 87% from public high schools. TOEFL required of all international applicants, minimum paper

TOEFL 525, minimum computer TOEFL 197. **Basis for Candidate Selection:** *Very important factors considered include:* Rigor of secondary school record, standardized test scores. *Important factors considered include:* Application essay, character/personal qualities, recommendation(s), talent/ability. *Other factors considered include:* Class rank, extracurricular activities, interview, volunteer work, work experience. **Freshman Admission Requirements:** High school diploma is required, and GED is accepted. *Academic units required:* 4 English, 2 math, 2 science (1 science lab), 2 social studies, 2 history. *Academic units recommended:* 4 English, 3 math, 3 science (1 science lab), 2 foreign language, 2 social studies, 2 history. **Freshman Admission Statistics:** 1,354 applied, 63% admitted, 24% enrolled. **Transfer Admission Requirements:** Minimum college GPA of 2.0 required. Lowest grade transferable C. **General Admission Information:** Application fee $30. Regular notification is rolling. Non-fall registration accepted. Admission may be deferred for a maximum of 1 year. Common Application accepted. Credit and/or placement offered for CEEB Advanced Placement tests.

COSTS AND FINANCIAL AID

Average book expense $600. **Required Forms and Deadlines:** FAFSA, state aid form. Financial aid filing deadline 2/1. **Notification of Awards:** Applicants will be notified of awards on or about 3/1. **Types of Aid:** *Need-based scholarships/grants:* Pell, SEOG, state scholarships/grants, private scholarships, the school's own gift aid. *Loans:* Direct Subsidized Stafford, Direct Unsubsidized Stafford, Direct PLUS, Federal Perkins. **Student Employment:** Federal Work-Study Program available. Institutional employment available. Off-campus job opportunities are good. **Financial Aid Statistics:** 73% freshmen, 74% undergrads receive need-based scholarship or grant aid. 80% freshmen, 86% undergrads receive need-based self-help aid. 2 freshmen, 61 undergrads receive athletic scholarships. 81% freshmen, 77% undergrads receive any aid. Highest amount earned per year from on-campus jobs $1,000.

LONGWOOD UNIVERSITY

Admissions Office, 201 High Street, Farmville, VA 23909
Phone: 434-395-2060 **E-mail:** admissions@longwood.edu **CEEB Code:** 5368
Fax: 434-395-2332 **Website:** www.whylongwood.com **ACT Code:** 4366
Financial Aid Phone: 800-281-4677

This public school was founded in 1839. It has a 160-acre campus.

RATINGS

Admissions Selectivity Rating: 76   **Fire Safety Rating:** 60*   **Green Rating:** 60*

STUDENTS AND FACULTY

Enrollment: 3,718. **Student Body:** 66% female, 34% male, 4% out-of-state. African American 7%, Asian 1%, Caucasian 89%, Hispanic 2%. **Retention and Graduation:** 75% freshmen return for sophomore year. 15% grads go on to further study within 1 year. **Faculty:** Student/faculty ratio 20:1. 201 full-time faculty, 84% hold PhDs. 100% faculty teach undergrads.

ACADEMICS

Degrees: Bachelor's, master's. **Academic Requirements:** Arts/fine arts, computer literacy, English (including composition), foreign languages, history, humanities, mathematics, philosophy, sciences (biological or physical), social science, literature, physical activity, ethics, issues of citizen leadership. **Classes:** Most classes have 20–29 students. Most lab/discussion sections have 10–19 students. **Majors with Highest Enrollment:** Business administration/management, elementary education and teaching, psychology. **Disciplines with Highest Percentage of Degrees Awarded:** Business/marketing 22%, liberal arts/general studies 21%, social sciences 8%, visual and performing arts 8%, psychology 7%. **Special Study Options:** Accelerated program, cross-registration, distance learning, double major, dual enrollment, honors program, independent study, internships, liberal arts/career combination, study abroad, teacher certification program.

FACILITIES

Housing: Coed dorms, women's dorms, apartments for single students, special housing for disabled students, special housing for international students, fraternity/sorority housing, honor student housing. **Special Academic Facilities/Equipment:** Longwood Center for the Visual Arts. **Computers:** 100% of classrooms are wired, 100% of classrooms are wireless, 90% of public computers are PCs, 5% of public computers are Macs, 5% of public computers are UNIX, network access in dorm rooms, network access in dorm lounges, online registration, online administrative functions (other than registration), remote student-access to Web through college's connection. Undergraduates are required to own a computer.

CAMPUS LIFE

Activities: Choral groups, concert band, dance, drama/theater, jazz band, literary magazine, music ensembles, musical theater, opera, radio station, student government, student newspaper, yearbook. **Organizations:** 129 registered organizations, 17 honor societies, 11 religious organizations. 9 fraternities (14% men join), 13 sororities (16% women join). **Athletics (Intercollegiate):** *Men:* Baseball, basketball, cheerleading, cross-country, golf, soccer, tennis. *Women:* Basketball, cheerleading, cross-country, field hockey, golf, lacrosse, soccer, softball, tennis.

ADMISSIONS

Freshman Academic Profile: 9% in top 10% of high school class, 35% in top 25% of high school class, 84% in top 50% of high school class. 92% from public high schools. SAT Math middle 50% range 480–560. SAT Critical Reading middle 50% range 480–570. SAT Writing middle 50% range 460–550. ACT middle 50% range 21–25. TOEFL required of all international applicants, minimum paper TOEFL 550, minimum computer TOEFL 213. **Basis for Candidate Selection:** *Very important factors considered include:* Academic GPA, rigor of secondary school record, standardized test scores. *Important factors considered include:* Application essay. *Other factors considered include:* Alumni/ae relation, character/personal qualities, class rank, extracurricular activities, first generation, geographical residence, level of applicant's interest, racial/ethnic status, recommendation(s), state residency, talent/ability, volunteer work. **Freshman Admission Requirements:** High school diploma is required, and GED is accepted. *Academic units required:* 4 English, 3 math, 3 science (2 science labs), 2 foreign language, 3 history, 3 academic electives. *Academic units recommended:* 4 math, 4 science, 3 foreign language, 1 social studies, 4 academic electives. **Freshman Admission Statistics:** 4,016 applied, 67% admitted, 37% enrolled. **Transfer Admission Requirements:** High school transcript, college transcript(s), essay or personal statement. Minimum college GPA of 2.5 required. Lowest grade transferable C. **General Admission Information:** Application fee $40. Regular notification is rolling. Nonfall registration accepted. Admission may be deferred for a maximum of 1 year. Credit offered for CEEB Advanced Placement tests.

COSTS AND FINANCIAL AID

Annual in-state tuition $3,960. Out-of-state tuition $11,580. Room & board $6,522. Required fees $3,629. Average book expense $800. **Required Forms and Deadlines:** FAFSA. Financial aid filing deadline 3/1. **Notification of Awards:** Applicants will be notified of awards on a rolling basis beginning on or about 4/1. **Types of Aid:** *Need-based scholarships/grants:* Pell, SEOG, state scholarships/grants, private scholarships, the school's own gift aid. *Loans:* FFEL Subsidized Stafford, FFEL Unsubsidized Stafford, FFEL PLUS, Federal Perkins, college/university loans from institutional funds. **Financial Aid Statistics:** 42% freshmen, 38% undergrads receive need-based scholarship or grant aid. 37% freshmen, 37% undergrads receive need-based self-help aid. 34 freshmen, 154 undergrads receive athletic scholarships. 60% freshmen, 66% undergrads receive any aid. Highest amount earned per year from on-campus jobs $1,320.

LORAS COLLEGE

1450 Alta Vista, Dubuque, IA 52004-0178
Phone: 800-245-6727 **E-mail:** admissions@loras.edu **CEEB Code:** 6370
Fax: 563-588-7119 **Website:** www.loras.edu **ACT Code:** 1328
Financial Aid Phone: 563-588-7136

This private school, affiliated with the Roman Catholic Church, was founded in 1839. It has a 60-acre campus.

RATINGS

Admissions Selectivity Rating: 75   **Fire Safety Rating:** 88   **Green Rating:** 60*

STUDENTS AND FACULTY

Enrollment: 1,565. **Student Body:** 50% female, 50% male, 45% out-of-state. 3% international (7 countries represented). African American 1%, Caucasian 93%, Hispanic 1%. **Retention and Graduation:** 78% freshmen return for sophomore year. 55% freshmen graduate within 4 years. 20% grads go on to further study within 1 year. 4% grads pursue arts and sciences degrees. 2% grads pursue business degrees. 1% grads pursue law degrees. 8% grads pursue medical degrees. **Faculty:** Student/faculty ratio 13:1. 111 full-time faculty, 95% hold PhDs. 100% faculty teach undergrads.

ACADEMICS

Degrees: Associate, bachelor's, master's. **Academic Requirements:** Arts/fine arts, computer literacy, English (including composition), history, humanities, mathematics, philosophy, sciences (biological or physical), social science. **Classes:** Most classes have 20–29 students. Most lab/discussion sections have fewer than 10 students. **Majors with Highest Enrollment:** Business administration/management, elementary education and teaching, secondary education and teaching. **Disciplines with Highest Percentage of Degrees Awarded:** Business/marketing 28%, education 25%, security and protective services 9%, social sciences 7%, biological/life sciences 5%, communications/journalism 5%, English 5%. **Special Study Options:** Cooperative education program, cross-registration, double major, dual enrollment, English as a second language (ESL), honors program, independent study, internships, liberal arts/career combination, student-designed major, study abroad, teacher certification program. Undergrads may take graduate-level classes if certain qualifications are met.

FACILITIES

Housing: Coed dorms, men's dorms, women's dorms, apartments for single students. **Special Academic Facilities/Equipment:** Language lab, television studio, observatory, planetarium. **Computers:** 100% of classrooms are wireless, 98% of public computers are PCs, 2% of public computers are Macs, network access in dorm rooms, online registration, online administrative functions (other than registration), remote student-access to Web through college's connection, tuition includes personal computer. Undergraduates are required to own a computer.

CAMPUS LIFE

Activities: Choral groups, concert band, dance, drama/theater, jazz band, music ensembles, musical theater, radio station, student government, student newspaper, television station, yearbook. **Organizations:** 71 registered organizations, 710 honor societies, 5 religious organizations. 2 fraternities, 2 sororities. **Athletics (Intercollegiate): Men:** Baseball, basketball, cross-country, diving, football, golf, soccer, swimming, tennis, track/field (indoor), track/field (outdoor), wrestling. **Women:** Basketball, cross-country, diving, golf, soccer, softball, swimming, tennis, track/field (indoor), track/field (outdoor), volleyball.

ADMISSIONS

Freshman Academic Profile: 13% in top 10% of high school class, 34% in top 25% of high school class, 65% in top 50% of high school class. 57% from public high schools. SAT Math middle 50% range 503–625. SAT Critical Reading middle 50% range 453–575. ACT middle 50% range 20–25. TOEFL required of all international applicants, minimum paper TOEFL 550, minimum computer TOEFL 213. **Basis for Candidate Selection:** *Very important factors considered include:* Academic GPA, rigor of secondary school record, standardized test scores. *Important factors considered include:* Class rank. *Other factors considered include:* Application essay, character/personal qualities, extracurricular activities, racial/ethnic status, recommendation(s), volunteer work. **Freshman Admission Requirements:** High school diploma is required, and GED is accepted. *Academic units recommended:* 4 English, 3 math, 3 science, 3 social studies, 3 history. **Freshman Admission Statistics:** 1,402 applied, 82% admitted, 32% enrolled. **Transfer Admission Requirements:** High school transcript, college transcript(s), standardized test score. Minimum college GPA of 2.0 required. Lowest grade transferable C. **General Admission Information:** Application fee $25. Regular notification rolling. Nonfall registration accepted. Admission may be deferred for a maximum of 2 terms. Common Application not accepted. Credit offered for CEEB Advanced Placement tests.

COSTS AND FINANCIAL AID

Annual tuition $19,990. Room & board $6,095. Required fees $1,108. Average book expense $800. **Required Forms and Deadlines:** FAFSA. Financial aid filing deadline 4/15. **Notification of Awards:** Applicants will be notified of awards on a rolling basis beginning on or about 3/1. **Types of Aid:** *Need-based scholarships/grants:* Pell, SEOG, state scholarships/grants, private scholarships, the school's own gift aid. *Loans:* FFEL Subsidized Stafford, FFEL Unsubsidized Stafford, FFEL PLUS, Federal Perkins, college/university loans from institutional funds. **Financial Aid Statistics:** 76% freshmen, 68% undergrads receive need-based scholarship or grant aid. 76% freshmen, 68% undergrads receive need-based self-help aid. 99% freshmen, 86% undergrads receive any aid. Highest amount earned per year from on-campus jobs $1,500.

LOUISIANA COLLEGE

1140 College Drive, PO Box 560, Pineville, LA 71359-0560
Phone: 318-487-7259 **E-mail:** admissions@lacollege.edu **CEEB Code:** 6371
Fax: 318-487-7550 **Website:** www.lacollege.edu **ACT Code:** 1586
Financial Aid Phone: 318-487-7386

This private school, affiliated with the Baptist Church, was founded in 1906. It has an 81-acre campus.

RATINGS

Admissions Selectivity Rating: 76   **Fire Safety Rating:** 60*   **Green Rating:** 60*

STUDENTS AND FACULTY

Enrollment: 1,014. **Student Body:** 56% female, 44% male, 9% out-of-state. African American 7%, Asian 1%, Caucasian 89%, Hispanic 2%. **Retention and Graduation:** 59% freshmen return for sophomore year. 25% freshmen graduate within 4 years. **Faculty:** Student/faculty ratio 13:1. 68 full-time faculty, 60% hold PhDs. 100% faculty teach undergrads.

ACADEMICS

Degrees: Bachelor's. **Academic Requirements:** Arts/fine arts, computer literacy, English (including composition), foreign languages, history, humanities, mathematics, philosophy, sciences (biological or physical), social science, religion, health and physical education, oral communication, values study. **Classes:** Most classes have fewer than 10 students. Most lab/discussion sections have 10–19 students. **Majors with Highest Enrollment:** Elementary education and teaching, psychology. **Disciplines with Highest Percentage of Degrees Awarded:** Social sciences 19%, education 14%, business/marketing 11%, health professions and related sciences 9%, biological/life sciences 8%. **Special Study Options:** Double major, honors program, independent study, internships, liberal arts/career combination, student-designed major, study abroad, teacher certification program.

FACILITIES

Housing: Men's dorms, women's dorms, apartments for married students, apartments for single students. **Special Academic Facilities/Equipment:** Art gallery, radio station, performing arts center, theater. **Computers:** 76% of public computers are PCs, 24% of public computers are Macs, network access in dorm rooms, remote student-access to Web through college's connection.

CAMPUS LIFE

Activities: Choral groups, concert band, drama/theater, jazz band, literary magazine, music ensembles, musical theater, opera, pep band, radio station, student government, student newspaper, symphony orchestra, yearbook. **Organizations:** 60 registered organizations, 13 honor societies, 8 religious organizations. 4 fraternities (5% men join), 3 sororities (5% women join). **Athletics (Intercollegiate): Men:** Baseball, basketball, cheerleading, football, golf, soccer. **Women:** Basketball, cheerleading, cross-country, soccer, softball, tennis.

ADMISSIONS

Freshman Academic Profile: 23% in top 10% of high school class, 47% in top 25% of high school class, 78% in top 50% of high school class. 82% from public high schools. SAT Math middle 50% range 440–600. SAT Critical Reading middle 50% range 440–570. ACT middle 50% range 21–26. TOEFL required of all international applicants, minimum paper TOEFL 550, minimum computer TOEFL 213. **Basis for Candidate Selection:** *Very important factors considered include:* Class rank, rigor of secondary school record, standardized test scores. *Other factors considered include:* Alumni/ae relation, character/personal qualities, extracurricular activities, geographical residence, interview, racial/ethnic status, recommendation(s), religious affiliation/commitment, state residency, talent/ability, volunteer work, work experience. **Freshman Admission Requirements:** High school diploma is required, and GED is accepted. *Academic units required:* 4 English, 3 math, 3 science (2 science labs), 2 social studies, 1 history, 4 academic electives. *Academic units recommended:* 2 foreign language. **Freshman Admission Statistics:** 727 applied, 85% admitted, 43% enrolled. **Transfer Admission Requirements:** College transcript(s). Minimum college GPA of 2.0 required. Lowest grade transferable D. **General Admission Information:** Application fee $25. Regular application deadline 8/15. Regular notification is rolling. Nonfall registration accepted. Admission may be deferred for a maximum of 1 year. Common Application accepted. Credit and/or placement offered for CEEB Advanced Placement tests.

COSTS AND FINANCIAL AID

Annual tuition $8,850. Room & board $3,740. Required fees $800. Average book expense $750. **Required Forms and Deadlines:** FAFSA, institution's own financial aid form. Financial aid filing deadline 3/31. **Notification of**

Awards: Applicants will be notified of awards on a rolling basis beginning on or about 3/1. **Types of Aid:** *Need-based scholarships/grants:* Pell, SEOG, state scholarships/grants, private scholarships, the school's own gift aid, LEAP. *Loans:* Direct Subsidized Stafford, Direct Unsubsidized Stafford, Direct PLUS, FFEL Subsidized Stafford, FFEL Unsubsidized Stafford, FFEL PLUS, college/university loans from institutional funds. **Student Employment:** Federal Work-Study Program available. Institutional employment available. Off-campus job opportunities are excellent. **Financial Aid Statistics:** 29% freshmen, 27% undergrads receive need-based scholarship or grant aid. 37% freshmen, 34% undergrads receive need-based self-help aid. 98% freshmen, 82% undergrads receive any aid. Highest amount earned per year from on-campus jobs $400.

LOUISIANA STATE UNIVERSITY

Best 368

110 Thomas Boyd Hall, Baton Rouge, LA 70803
Phone: 225-578-1175 **E-mail:** admissions@lsu.edu **CEEB Code:** 6373
Fax: 225-578-4433 **Website:** www.lsu.edu **ACT Code:** 1590
Financial Aid Phone: 225-578-3103

This public school was founded in 1860. It has a 2,000-acre campus.

RATINGS
Admissions Selectivity Rating: 83   **Fire Safety Rating:** 76   **Green Rating:** 60*

STUDENTS AND FACULTY
Enrollment: 25,301. **Student Body:** 52% female, 48% male, 13% out-of-state, 2% international (114 countries represented). African American 9%, Asian 3%, Caucasian 81%, Hispanic 3%. **Retention and Graduation:** 83% freshmen return for sophomore year. 27% freshmen graduate within 4 years. **Faculty:** Student/faculty ratio 22:1. 1277 full-time faculty, 85% hold PhDs. 85% faculty teach undergrads.

ACADEMICS
Degrees: Bachelor's, doctoral, first professional, master's, post-master's certificate. **Academic Requirements:** Arts/fine arts, computer literacy, English (including composition), foreign languages, humanities, mathematics, sciences (biological or physical), social science. **Classes:** Most classes have 20–29 students. Most lab/discussion sections have 10–19 students. **Majors with Highest Enrollment:** Biology/biological sciences, psychology. **Disciplines with Highest Percentage of Degrees Awarded:** Business/marketing 21%, education 10%, engineering 9%, liberal arts/general studies 9%, social sciences 9%. **Special Study Options:** Accelerated program, cooperative education program, cross-registration, distance learning, double major, dual enrollment, English as a second language (ESL), exchange student program (domestic), honors program, independent study, internships, liberal arts/career combination, student-designed major, study abroad, teacher certification program.

FACILITIES
Housing: Coed dorms, men's dorms, women's dorms, apartments for married students, apartments for single students, special housing for disabled students, fraternity/sorority housing. **Special Academic Facilities/Equipment:** Art museum, natural science museum, rural life museum, Lichen/Bryophyte mycological and vascular plant herbariums, on-campus K-12 schools, geoscience and mycological museums, electron microscope, nuclear science center and civil war center. **Computers:** 1% of classrooms are wired, 85% of classrooms are wireless, 95% of public computers are PCs, 5% of public computers are Macs, network access in dorm rooms, network access in dorm lounges, online registration, online administrative functions (other than registration), support for handheld computing, remote student-access to Web through college's connection.

CAMPUS LIFE
Activities: Choral groups, concert band, dance, drama/theater, jazz band, literary magazine, marching band, music ensembles, musical theater, opera, pep band, radio station, student government, student newspaper, student-run film society, symphony orchestra, television studio. **Organizations:** 300 registered organizations, 32 honor societies, 17 religious organizations. 21 fraternities (10% men join), 15 sororities (17% women join). **Athletics (Intercollegiate):** *Men:* Baseball, basketball, cheerleading, cross-country, diving, football, golf, swimming, tennis, track/field (indoor), track/field (outdoor). *Women:* Basketball,

cheerleading, cross-country, diving, golf, gymnastics, soccer, softball, swimming, tennis, track/field (indoor), track/field (outdoor), volleyball.

ADMISSIONS
Freshman Academic Profile: 25% in top 10% of high school class, 53% in top 25% of high school class, 83% in top 50% of high school class. 55% from public high schools. SAT Math middle 50% range 550–650. SAT Critical Reading middle 50% range 520–640. SAT Writing middle 50% range 490–620. ACT middle 50% range 23–28. TOEFL required of all international applicants, minimum paper TOEFL 550, minimum computer TOEFL 213. **Basis for Candidate Selection:** *Very important factors considered include:* Academic GPA, rigor of secondary school record, standardized test scores. *Important factors considered include:* Class rank. *Other factors considered include:* Extracurricular activities, talent/ability. **Freshman Admission Requirements:** High school diploma is required, and GED is accepted. *Academic units required:* 4 English, 3 math, 3 science, 2 foreign language, 3 social studies, 3 academic electives. *Academic units recommended:* 4 math. **Freshman Admission Statistics:** 10,825 applied, 73% admitted, 63% enrolled. **Transfer Admission Requirements:** college transcript(s). Minimum college GPA of 2.5 required. **General Admission Information:** Application fee $40. Regular application deadline 4/15. Nonfall registration accepted. Admission may be deferred for a maximum of 1 year. Common Application not accepted. Credit offered for CEEB Advanced Placement tests.

COSTS AND FINANCIAL AID
Annual in-state tuition $2,981. Out-of-state tuition $11,281. Room & board $6,498. Required fees $1,468. Average book expense $1,500. **Required Forms and Deadlines:** FAFSA, institution's own financial aid form. Financial aid filing deadline 3/1. **Notification of Awards:** Applicants will be notified of awards on or about 3/1. **Types of Aid:** *Need-based scholarships/grants:* Pell, SEOG, state scholarships/grants, private scholarships, the school's own gift aid. *Loans:* FFEL Subsidized Stafford, FFEL Unsubsidized Stafford, FFEL PLUS. **Student Employment:** Federal Work-Study Program available. Institutional employment available. Off-campus job opportunities are excellent. **Financial Aid Statistics:** 45% freshmen, 37% undergrads receive need-based scholarship or grant aid. 26% freshmen, 30% undergrads receive need-based self-help aid. 83 freshmen, 437 undergrads receive athletic scholarships. 94% freshmen, 78% undergrads receive any aid.

See page 1244.

LOUISIANA STATE UNIVERSITY IN SHREVEPORT

One University Place, Shreveport, LA 71115-2399
Phone: 318-797-5061 **E-mail:** admissions@pilot.lsus.edu **CEEB Code:** 6355
Fax: 318-797-5204 **Website:** www.lsus.edu **ACT Code:** 1593
Financial Aid Phone: 318-797-5363

This public school was founded in 1965. It has a 200-acre campus.

RATINGS
Admissions Selectivity Rating: 60*   **Fire Safety Rating:** 60*   **Green Rating:** 60*

STUDENTS AND FACULTY
Enrollment: 3,594. **Student Body:** 62% female, 38% male, 2% out-of-state. African American 22%, Asian 2%, Caucasian 65%, Hispanic 2%. **Retention and Graduation:** 53% freshmen return for sophomore year. **Faculty:** Student/faculty ratio 16:1. 155 full-time faculty, 72% hold PhDs. 100% faculty teach undergrads.

ACADEMICS
Degrees: Bachelor's, master's, post-master's certificate. **Academic Requirements:** Arts/fine arts, English (including composition), humanities, mathematics, sciences (biological or physical), social science. **Classes:** Most classes have 20–29 students. **Majors with Highest Enrollment:** Business administration/management, elementary education and teaching. **Disciplines with Highest Percentage of Degrees Awarded:** Business/marketing 29%, liberal arts/general studies 15%, education 15%, psychology 7%, biological/life sciences 6%, social sciences 6%, communication technologies 5%, computer and information sciences 5%. **Special Study Options:** Cooperative education program, study abroad, teacher certification program. Undergrads may take grad-level courses and evening courses.

FACILITIES
Housing: Apartments for married students, apartments for single students. **Special Academic Facilities/Equipment:** Art center, life science museum, pioneer heritage center. **Computers:** 95% of public computers are PCs, 4% of public computers are Macs, 1% of public computers are UNIX, online

registration, online administrative functions (other than registration), remote student-access to Web through college's connection.

CAMPUS LIFE

Activities: Student government, student newspaper. **Organizations:** 52 registered organizations, 4 honor societies, 3 religious organizations. 5 fraternities (1% men join), 3 sororities (1% women join). **Athletics (Intercollegiate):** *Men:* Baseball.

ADMISSIONS

Freshman Academic Profile: 90% from public high schools. ACT middle 50% range 18–23. TOEFL required of all international applicants, minimum paper TOEFL 500. **Basis for Candidate Selection:** *Other factors considered include:* Rigor of secondary school record, standardized test scores. **Freshman Admission Requirements:** High school diploma is required, and GED is accepted. *Academic units recommended:* 4 English, 3 math, 3 science, 3 social studies. **Freshman Admission Statistics:** 848 applied, 65% admitted. **Transfer Admission Requirements:** College transcript(s). Minimum college GPA of 2.0 required. Lowest grade transferable D. **General Admission Information:** Application fee $10. Regular application deadline 8/1. Regular notification rolling. Nonfall registration accepted. Common Application not accepted. Credit offered for CEEB Advanced Placement tests.

COSTS AND FINANCIAL AID

Annual in-state tuition $2,194. Out-of-state tuition $6,524. Required fees $2,690. **Required Forms and Deadlines:** FAFSA, institution's own financial aid form. **Types of Aid:** *Need-based scholarships/grants:* State scholarships/grants. *Loans:* FFEL Subsidized Stafford, FFEL PLUS. **Student Employment:** Federal Work-Study Program available. Institutional employment available. Off-campus job opportunities are good. **Financial Aid Statistics:** Highest amount earned per year from on-campus jobs $2,000.

LOUISIANA TECH UNIVERSITY

PO Box 3178, Ruston, LA 71272
Phone: 318-257-3036 **E-mail:** bulldog@latech.edu
Fax: 318-257-2499 **Website:** www.latech.edu **ACT Code:** 1588
Financial Aid Phone: 318-257-2641

This public school was founded in 1894. It has a 247-acre campus.

RATINGS

Admissions Selectivity Rating: 72   **Fire Safety Rating:** 60*   **Green Rating:** 60*

STUDENTS AND FACULTY

Enrollment: 8,666. **Student Body:** 47% female, 53% male, 12% out-of-state, 2% international (61 countries represented). African American 15%, Caucasian 75%, Hispanic 2%. **Retention and Graduation:** 72% freshmen return for sophomore year. 32% grads go on to further study within 1 year. **Faculty:** Student/faculty ratio 23:1. 389 full-time faculty, 80% hold PhDs. 100% faculty teach undergrads.

ACADEMICS

Degrees: Associate, bachelor's, doctoral, first professional certificate, master's. **Academic Requirements:** Arts/fine arts, computer literacy, English (including composition), humanities, mathematics, sciences (biological or physical), social science. **Classes:** Most classes have 20–29 students. **Disciplines with Highest Percentage of Degrees Awarded:** Business/marketing 22%, engineering 15%, liberal arts/general studies 12%, education 8%, social sciences 5%. **Special Study Options:** Cooperative education program, cross-registration, distance learning, double major, dual enrollment, English as a second language (ESL), honors program, independent study, internships, study abroad, teacher certification program.

FACILITIES

Housing: Men's dorms, women's dorms, apartments for married students, special housing for disabled students, special housing for international students. **Special Academic Facilities/Equipment:** Art gallery, natural history museum, on-campus elementary school, arboretum, planetarium, Center for Rehabilitation Science and Biomedical Engineering, Institute for Microengineering, water resources center. **Computers:** 45% of public computers are PCs, 10% of public computers are Macs, 45% of public computers are UNIX, network access in dorm rooms, network access in dorm lounges, online administrative functions (other than registration), remote student-access to Web through college's connection.

CAMPUS LIFE

Activities: Choral groups, concert band, dance, drama/theater, jazz band, marching band, music ensembles, musical theater, pep band, radio station, student government, yearbook. **Organizations:** 121 registered organizations, 17 honor societies, 11 religious organizations. 12 fraternities (7% men join), 8 sororities (11% women join). **Athletics (Intercollegiate):** *Men:* Baseball, basketball, cross-country, football, golf, track/field (outdoor). *Women:* Basketball, cross-country, softball, tennis, track/field (outdoor), volleyball.

ADMISSIONS

Freshman Academic Profile: 18% in top 10% of high school class, 43% in top 25% of high school class, 74% in top 50% of high school class. ACT middle 50% range 19–24. TOEFL required of all international applicants, minimum paper TOEFL 500. **Basis for Candidate Selection:** *Very important factors considered include:* Class rank, rigor of secondary school record, standardized test scores. *Important factors considered include:* Talent/ability. *Other factors considered include:* Alumni/ae relation, extracurricular activities, racial/ethnic status, recommendation(s). **Freshman Admission Requirements:** High school diploma is required, and GED is accepted. *Academic units required:* 4 English, 3 math, 3 science, 3 social studies, 5 academic electives. **Freshman Admission Statistics:** 3,607 applied, 92% admitted, 62% enrolled. **Transfer Admission Requirements:** College transcript(s), statement of good standing from prior institution(s). Minimum college GPA of 2.0 required. Lowest grade transferable D. **General Admission Information:** Application fee $20. Regular application deadline 7/31. Regular notification is rolling. Nonfall registration accepted. Common Application not accepted. Credit and/or placement offered for CEEB Advanced Placement tests.

COSTS AND FINANCIAL AID

Annual in-state tuition $3,038. Out-of-state tuition $7,943. Room & board $3,345. Required fees $300. Average book expense $750. **Required Forms and Deadlines:** FAFSA, institution's own financial aid form. **Notification of Awards:** Applicants will be notified of awards on a rolling basis beginning on or about 4/18. **Types of Aid:** *Need-based scholarships/grants:* Pell, SEOG, state scholarships/grants, private scholarships, the school's own gift aid. *Loans:* FFEL Subsidized Stafford, FFEL Unsubsidized Stafford, FFEL PLUS, Federal Perkins, state loans. **Student Employment:** Federal Work-Study Program available. Institutional employment available. Off-campus job opportunities are good. **Financial Aid Statistics:** 43% freshmen, 33% undergrads receive need-based scholarship or grant aid. 32% freshmen, 28% undergrads receive need-based self-help aid. 7 freshmen, 25 undergrads receive athletic scholarships.

LOURDES COLLEGE

6832 Convent Road, Sylvania, OH 43560-2898
Phone: 419-885-5291 **E-mail:** lcadmits@lourdes.edu **CEEB Code:** 1427
Fax: 419-882-3987 **Website:** www.lourdes.edu **ACT Code:** 3598
Financial Aid Phone: 419-824-3732

This private school, affiliated with the Roman Catholic Church, was founded in 1958. It has an 89-acre campus.

RATINGS

Admissions Selectivity Rating: 70   **Fire Safety Rating:** 60*   **Green Rating:** 60*

STUDENTS AND FACULTY

Enrollment: 1,526. **Student Body:** 84% female, 16% male, 10% out-of-state. African American 14%, Caucasian 72%, Hispanic 2%. **Retention and Graduation:** 72% freshmen return for sophomore year. **Faculty:** Student/faculty ratio 12:1. 65 full-time faculty, 43% hold PhDs. 97% faculty teach undergrads.

ACADEMICS

Degrees: Associate, bachelor's, certificate, master's. **Academic Requirements:** Arts/fine arts, computer literacy, English (including composition), history, humanities, mathematics, philosophy, sciences (biological or physical), social science. **Classes:** Most classes have 10–19 students. Most lab/discussion sections have fewer than 10 students. **Majors with Highest Enrollment:** Business administration/management, nursing/registered nurse training (RN, ASN, BSN, MSN). **Disciplines with Highest Percentage of Degrees Awarded:** Business/marketing 27%, health professions and related sciences 26%, education 13%, interdisciplinary studies 11%, public administration and social services 5%, psychology 5%. **Special Study Options:** Accelerated program, cooperative education program, distance learning, double major, dual enrollment, independent study, internships, liberal arts/career combination, student-designed major, teacher certification program, weekend college.

FACILITIES

Computers: 100% of public computers are PCs, online administrative functions (other than registration), remote student-access to Web through college's connection.

CAMPUS LIFE

Activities: Choral groups, literary magazine, student government, student-run film society. **Organizations:** 18 registered organizations, 6 honor societies.

ADMISSIONS

Freshman Academic Profile: 4% in top 10% of high school class, 26% in top 25% of high school class, 64% in top 50% of high school class. SAT Math middle 50% range 430–580. SAT Critical Reading middle 50% range 410–560. ACT middle 50% range 17–21. TOEFL required of all international applicants, minimum paper TOEFL 500, minimum computer TOEFL 173. **Basis for Candidate Selection:** *Very important factors considered include:* Academic GPA, standardized test scores. *Other factors considered include:* Interview, recommendation(s). **Freshman Admission Requirements:** High school diploma is required, and GED is accepted. **Freshman Admission Statistics:** 314 applied, 41% admitted, 100% enrolled. **Transfer Admission Requirements:** College transcript(s). Minimum college GPA of 2.0 required. Lowest grade transferable C. **General Admission Information:** Application fee $25. Regular notification upon completion of file. Nonfall registration accepted. Admission may be deferred for a maximum of 4 years. Common Application accepted. Credit and/or placement offered for CEEB Advanced Placement tests.

COSTS AND FINANCIAL AID

Annual tuition $12,390. Required fees $1,650. **Required Forms and Deadlines:** FAFSA. Financial aid filing deadline 3/1. **Notification of Awards:** Applicants will be notified of awards on a rolling basis beginning on or about 3/1. **Types of Aid:** *Need-based scholarships/grants:* Pell, SEOG, state scholarships/grants, private scholarships, the school's own gift aid. *Loans:* FFEL Subsidized Stafford, FFEL Unsubsidized Stafford, FFEL PLUS, Federal Perkins, state loans, college/university loans from institutional funds. **Student Employment:** Federal Work-Study Program available. Off-campus job opportunities are excellent. **Financial Aid Statistics:** 39% freshmen, 56% undergrads receive need-based scholarship or grant aid. 56% freshmen, 71% undergrads receive need-based self-help aid. 99% freshmen, 95% undergrads receive any aid.

LOYOLA COLLEGE IN MARYLAND

Best 368

4501 North Charles Street, Baltimore, MD 21210
Phone: 410-617-5012 **CEEB Code:** 5370
Fax: 410-617-2176 **Website:** www.loyola.edu
Financial Aid Phone: 410-617-2576

This private school, affiliated with the Roman Catholic Church, was founded in 1852. It has an 89-acre campus.

RATINGS

Admissions Selectivity Rating: 89   **Fire Safety Rating:** 78   **Green Rating:** 60*

STUDENTS AND FACULTY

Enrollment: 3,483. **Student Body:** 60% female, 40% male, 82% out-of-state. African American 5%, Asian 3%, Caucasian 86%, Hispanic 3%. **Retention and Graduation:** 89% freshmen return for sophomore year. 77% freshmen graduate within 4 years. **Faculty:** Student/faculty ratio 12:1. 305 full-time faculty, 83% hold PhDs. 71% faculty teach undergrads.

ACADEMICS

Degrees: Bachelor's, doctoral, master's, post-master's certificate. **Academic Requirements:** Arts/fine arts, English (including composition), foreign languages, history, humanities, mathematics, philosophy, sciences (biological or physical), social science. **Classes:** Most classes have 20–29 students. Most lab/discussion sections have 10–19 students. **Majors with Highest Enrollment:** Biology/biological sciences; business administration and management; communications studies/speech communication and rhetoric. **Disciplines with Highest Percentage of Degrees Awarded:** Business/marketing 36%, communications/journalism 12%, psychology 8%, biological/life sciences 5%,

interdisciplinary studies 5%. **Special Study Options:** Accelerated program, cross-registration, double major, honor program, independent study, internships, liberal arts/career combination, study abroad, teacher certification program.

FACILITIES

Housing: Coed dorms, apartments for single students. **Special Academic Facilities/Equipment:** Art gallery, advanced biology lab, humanities building, speech pathology lab and audiology center. **Computers:** 5% of classrooms are wired, 75% of classrooms are wireless, 95% of public computers are PCs, 5% of public computers are Macs, network access in dorm rooms, network access in dorm lounges, online registration, online administrative functions (other than registration), support for handheld computing, remote student-access to Web through college's connection.

CAMPUS LIFE

Activities: Choral groups, dance, drama/theater, jazz band, literary magazine, music ensembles, musical theater, pep band, radio station, student government, student newspaper, yearbook. **Organizations:** 134 registered organizations, 26 honor societies, 6 religious organizations. **Athletics (Intercollegiate):** *Men:* Basketball, crew/rowing, cross-country, diving, golf, lacrosse, soccer, swimming, tennis. *Women:* Basketball, crew/rowing, cross-country, diving, lacrosse, soccer, swimming, tennis, volleyball.

ADMISSIONS

Freshman Academic Profile: 31% in top 10% of high school class, 66% in top 25% of high school class, 97% in top 50% of high school class. 60% from public high schools. SAT Math middle 50% range 560–650. SAT Critical Reading middle 50% range 540–640. TOEFL required of all international applicants, minimum paper TOEFL 550, minimum computer TOEFL 213. **Basis for Candidate Selection:** *Very important factors considered include:* Academic GPA, rigor of secondary school record. *Important factors considered include:* Standardized test scores. *Other factors considered include:* Alumni/ae relation, application essay, character/personal qualities, class rank, extracurricular activities, racial/ethnic status, recommendation(s), talent/ability, volunteer work, work experience. **Freshman Admission Requirements:** High school diploma is required, and GED is accepted. *Academic units required:* 4 English, 3 math, 3 science, 2 history, *Academic units recommended:* 4 English, 4 math, 4 science, 3 history. **Freshman Admission Statistics:** 7,909 applied, 64% admitted, 19% enrolled. **Transfer Admission Requirements:** High school transcript, college transcript(s), essay or personal statement, standardized test score, statement of good standing from prior institution(s). Minimum college GPA of 2.7 required. Lowest grade transferable C. **General Admission Information:** Application fee $50. Regular application deadline 1/15. Regular notification 4/1. Nonfall registration accepted. Admission may be deferred for a maximum of 1 year. Credit offered for CEEB Advanced Placement tests.

COSTS AND FINANCIAL AID

Annual tuition $33,150. Room and board $9,150. Required fees $1,265. Average book expense $930. **Required Forms and Deadlines:** FAFSA, CSS/Financial Aid PROFILE, Noncustodial PROFILE, Business/Farm Supplement. Financial aid filing deadline 2/15. **Notification of Awards:** Applicants will be notified of awards on or about 4/1. **Types of Aid:** *Need-based scholarships/grants:* Pell, SEOG, state scholarships/grants, private scholarships, the school's own gift aid. *Loans:* Direct Subsidized Stafford, Direct Unsubsidized Stafford, FFEL PLUS, Federal Perkins, college/university loans from institutional funds. **Student Employment:** Off-campus job opportunities are good. **Financial Aid Statistics:** 44% freshmen, 39% undergrads receive need-based scholarship or grant aid. 42% freshmen, 39% undergrads receive need-based self-help aid. 31 freshmen, 121 undergrads receive athletic scholarships. 67% freshmen, 63% undergrads receive any aid. Highest amount earned per year from on-campus jobs $2,290.

LOYOLA MARYMOUNT UNIVERSITY

One LMU Drive, Suite 100, Los Angeles, CA 90045
Phone: 310-338-2750 **E-mail:** admissions@lmu.edu **CEEB Code:** 4403
Fax: 310-338-2797 **Website:** www.lmu.edu **ACT Code:** 0326
Financial Aid Phone: 310-338-2753

This private school, affiliated with the Roman Catholic Church, was founded in 1911. It has a 128-acre campus.

RATINGS

Admissions Selectivity Rating: 88   **Fire Safety Rating:** 60*   **Green Rating:** 78

STUDENTS AND FACULTY

Enrollment: 5,590. **Student Body:** 59% female, 41% male, 23% out-of-state, 1% international (50 countries represented). African American 7%, Asian 13%, Caucasian 56%, Hispanic 19%. **Retention and Graduation:** 90% freshmen return for sophomore year. 62% freshmen graduate within 4 years. **Faculty:** Student/faculty ratio 13:1. 419 full-time faculty, 87% hold PhDs. 100% faculty teach undergrads.

ACADEMICS

Degrees: Bachelor's, first professional certificate, first professional, master's, post-bachelor's certificate, post-master's certificate. **Academic Requirements:** English (including composition), history, mathematics, philosophy, sciences (biological or physical), social science, American cultures, communication or critical thinking, critical and creative arts, literature, theological studies. **Classes:** Most classes have 20–29 students. Most lab/discussion sections have 10–19 students. **Majors with Highest Enrollment:** Business administration/management; communications, journalism, and related fields; psychology. **Disciplines with Highest Percentage of Degrees Awarded:** Biological/life sciences 27%, visual and performing arts 9%, psychology 7%, area and ethnic studies 7%, social sciences 6%, business/marketing 6%, liberal arts/general studies 5%, English 5%. **Special Study Options:** Cross-registration, double major, dual enrollment, honors program, independent study, internships, liberal arts/career combination, student-designed major, study abroad, teacher certification program, encore program for adult students.

FACILITIES

Housing: Coed dorms, men's dorms, women's dorms, apartments for single students, special housing for disabled students. **Special Academic Facilities/Equipment:** Art gallery, theater, TV production labs, computer graphics lab. **Computers:** Network access in dorm rooms, network access in dorm lounges, online registration, online administrative functions (other than registration), remote student-access to Web through college's connection.

CAMPUS LIFE

Activities: Choral groups, dance, drama/theater, literary magazine, music ensembles, musical theater, pep band, radio station, student government, student newspaper, student-run film society, television station, yearbook. **Organizations:** 120 registered organizations, 12 honor societies, 2 religious organizations. 6 fraternities (19% men join), 8 sororities (30% women join). **Athletics (Intercollegiate):** *Men:* Baseball, basketball, crew/rowing, cross-country, golf, soccer, tennis, water polo. *Women:* Basketball, crew/rowing, cross-country, soccer, softball, swimming, tennis, volleyball, water polo. Environmental Initiatives: LEED Building Program: LMU's new $64 million library incorporates state-of-the-art technologies and energy efficiency features, complementing other LEED-certified campus buildings and signifying LMU's commitment ton continued leadership in environmental stewardship. LMU's solar energy program is the largest of its kind in the entire City of Los Angeles.

ADMISSIONS

Freshman Academic Profile: 30% in top 10% of high school class, 66% in top 25% of high school class, 99% in top 50% of high school class. 47% from public high schools. SAT Math middle 50% range 540–640. SAT Critical Reading middle 50% range 530–630. TOEFL required of all international applicants, minimum paper TOEFL 550, minimum computer TOEFL 213. **Basis for Candidate Selection:** *Very important factors considered include:* Academic GPA, rigor of secondary school record. *Important factors considered include:* Application essay, character/personal qualities, class rank, standardized test scores, talent/ability. *Other factors considered include:* Alumni/ae relation, extracurricular activities, first generation, geographical residence, interview, recommendation(s), volunteer work, work experience. **Freshman Admission**

Requirements: High school diploma is required, and GED is accepted. *Academic units recommended:* 4 English, 3 math, 2 science (2 science labs), 3 foreign language, 3 social studies, 1 academic elective. **Freshman Admission Statistics:** 7,730 applied; 56% admitted, 31% enrolled. **Transfer Admission Requirements:** College transcript(s), essay or personal statement, statement of good standing from prior institution(s). Minimum college GPA of 2.8 required. Lowest grade transferable C. **General Admission Information:** Application fee $50. Regular notification is rolling. Nonfall registration accepted. Admission may be deferred for a maximum of 1 year. Common Application not accepted. Credit and/or placement offered for CEEB Advanced Placement tests.

COSTS AND FINANCIAL AID

Annual tuition $27,710. Room & board $8,709. Required fees $430. Average book expense $820. **Required Forms and Deadlines:** FAFSA, CSS/Financial Aid PROFILE, Business/Farm Supplement. Financial aid filing deadline 4/1. **Notification of Awards:** Applicants will be notified of awards on or about 5/1. **Types of Aid:** *Need-based scholarships/grants:* Pell, SEOG, state scholarships/grants, private scholarships, the school's own gift aid. *Loans:* FFEL Subsidized Stafford, FFEL Unsubsidized Stafford, FFEL PLUS, Federal Perkins, college/university loans from institutional funds. **Student Employment:** Federal Work-Study Program available. Institutional employment available. Off-campus job opportunities are excellent. **Financial Aid Statistics:** 46% freshmen, 47% undergrads receive need-based scholarship or grant aid. 42% freshmen, 44% undergrads receive need-based self-help aid. 91 freshmen, 213 undergrads receive athletic scholarships.

LOYOLA UNIVERSITY—CHICAGO

820 North Michigan Avenue, Chicago, IL 60611
Phone: 312-915-6500 **E-mail:** admission@luc.edu **CEEB Code:** 1412
Fax: 312-915-7216 **Website:** www.luc.edu/
Financial Aid Phone: 312-508-7704

This private school, affiliated with the Jesuit order of the Roman Catholic Church, was founded in 1870. It has a 105-acre campus.

RATINGS

Admissions Selectivity Rating: 86   **Fire Safety Rating:** 78   **Green Rating:** 95

STUDENTS AND FACULTY

Enrollment: 9,076. **Student Body:** 65% female, 35% male, 32% out-of-state, 1% international (77 countries represented). African American 6%, Asian 12%, Caucasian 61%, Hispanic 10%. **Retention and Graduation:** 84% freshmen return for sophomore year. 61% freshmen graduate within 4 years. **Faculty:** Student/faculty ratio 13:1. 550 full-time faculty. 97% faculty teach undergrads.

ACADEMICS

Degrees: Bachelor's, certificate, doctoral, first professional, master's, post-bachelor's certificate, post-master's certificate. **Academic Requirements:** Arts/fine arts, English (including composition), foreign languages, history, humanities, mathematics, philosophy, sciences (biological or physical), social science, technical literacy. **Classes:** Most classes have 10–19 students. Most lab/discussion sections have 20–29 students. **Majors with Highest Enrollment:** Biology/biological sciences, nursing/registered nurse training (RN, ASN, BSN, MSN), psychology. **Disciplines with Highest Percentage of Degrees Awarded:** Business/marketing 21%, social sciences 15%, psychology 11%, biological/life sciences 9%, health professions and related sciences 8%. **Special Study Options:** Accelerated program, double major, dual enrollment, exchange student program (domestic), honors program, independent study, internships, study abroad, teacher certification program.

FACILITIES

Housing: Coed dorms, apartments for single students, special housing for disabled students. **Special Academic Facilities/Equipment:** Renaissance art gallery, seismograph station. Loyola University Museum of Art (LUMA), Madonna Della Strada Chapel, Quinlin Life Sciences Building. **Computers:** 5% of classrooms are wired, 65% of classrooms are wireless, 95% of public computers are PCs, 5% of public computers are Macs, network access in dorm rooms, network access in dorm lounges, online registration, online administrative functions (other than registration), support for handheld computing, remote student-access to Web through college's connection.

CAMPUS LIFE

Activities: Choral groups, concert band, drama/theater, jazz band, literary magazine, music ensembles, musical theater, pep band, radio station, student government, student newspaper, student-run film society, yearbook. **Organizations:** 175 registered organizations, 7 honor societies, 13 religious organizations. 6 fraternities (5% men join), 6 sororities (5% women join). **Athletics (Intercollegiate):** *Men:* Basketball, cheerleading, cross-country, golf, soccer, track/field (indoor), track/field (outdoor), volleyball. *Women:* Basketball, cheerleading, cross-country, golf, soccer, softball, track/field (indoor), track/field (outdoor), volleyball. Environmental Initiatives: Green roofs for all new construction (Mundelein Center, Information Commons, Quinlan Life Sciences Building, and Baumhart Hall). Expecting Silver LEED certification for Information Commons. All new construction projects to be LEED certified. All student residences installed with CFLs and available for free to all students. Semi-permeable paving material for all campus roads and pedestrian walks and use of semi-permeable artificial turf to reduce storm water runoff to city sewer system.

ADMISSIONS

Freshman Academic Profile: 32% in top 10% of high school class, 67% in top 25% of high school class, 95% in top 50% of high school class. 65% from public high schools. SAT Math middle 50% range 520–640. SAT Critical Reading middle 50% range 540–640. SAT Writing middle 50% range 510–628. ACT middle 50% range 23–28. TOEFL required of all international applicants, minimum paper TOEFL 550, minimum computer TOEFL 213. **Basis for Candidate Selection:** *Very important factors considered include:* Academic GPA, rigor of secondary school record, standardized test scores. *Important factors considered include:* Application essay, character/personal qualities, extracurricular activities, level of applicant's interest, recommendation(s), volunteer work. *Other factors considered include:* Alumni/ae relation, class rank, first generation, geographical residence, interview, state residency, talent/ability, work experience. **Freshman Admission Requirements:** High school diploma is required, and GED is accepted. *Academic units required:* 4 English, 2 math, 2 science, 2 social studies, 1 history, 1 academic elective. *Academic units recommended:* 4 English, 4 math, 3 science, 2 foreign language, 3 social studies, 2 history, 3 academic electives. **Freshman Admission Statistics:** 15,178 applied, 77% admitted, 18% enrolled. **Transfer Admission Requirements:** College transcript(s). Minimum college GPA of 2.0 required. Lowest grade transferable C. **General Admission Information:** Application fee $25. Regular notification is rolling. Nonfall registration accepted. Credit and/or placement offered for CEEB Advanced Placement tests.

COSTS AND FINANCIAL AID

Annual tuition $28,700. Room and board $10,490. Required fees $786. Average book expense $1,200. **Required Forms and Deadlines:** FAFSA. Financial aid filing deadline 3/1. **Notification of Awards:** Applicants will be notified of awards on a rolling basis beginning on or about 2/15. **Types of Aid:** *Need-based scholarships/grants:* Pell, SEOG, state scholarships/grants, private scholarships, the school's own gift aid. *Loans:* FFEL Subsidized Stafford, FFEL Unsubsidized Stafford, FFEL PLUS, Federal Perkins, Federal Nursing. **Student Employment:** Federal Work-Study Program available. Institutional employment available. Off-campus job opportunities are good. **Financial Aid Statistics:** 71% freshmen, 67% undergrads receive need-based scholarship or grant aid. 64% freshmen, 61% undergrads receive need-based self-help aid. 11 freshmen, 43 undergrads receive athletic scholarships. 97% freshmen, 97% undergrads receive any aid.

See page 1246.

LOYOLA UNIVERSITY—NEW ORLEANS

6363 St. Charles Avenue, Box 18, New Orleans, LA 70118-6195
Phone: 504-865-3240 **E-mail:** admit@loyno.edu **CEEB Code:** 6374
Fax: 504-865-3383 **Website:** www.loyno.edu **ACT Code:** 1592
Financial Aid Phone: 504-865-3231

This private school, affiliated with the Roman Catholic Church, was founded in 1912. It has a 26-acre campus.

RATINGS

Admissions Selectivity Rating: 88   **Fire Safety Rating:** 97   **Green Rating:** 60*

STUDENTS AND FACULTY

Enrollment: 2,938. **Student Body:** 59% female, 41% male, 58% out-of-state, 2% international (48 countries represented). African American 11%, Asian 4%, Caucasian 63%, Hispanic 12%. **Retention and Graduation:** 52% freshmen graduate within 4 years. **Faculty:** Student/faculty ratio 11:1. 259 full-time faculty, 91% hold PhDs. 84% faculty teach undergrads.

ACADEMICS

Degrees: Bachelor's, first professional, master's, post-bachelor's certificate, post-master's certificate. **Academic Requirements:** Arts/fine arts, English (including composition), foreign languages, history, humanities, mathematics, philosophy, sciences (biological or physical), social science, religious studies. **Classes:** Most classes have 10–19 students. Most lab/discussion sections have fewer than 10 students. **Majors with Highest Enrollment:** Biology/biological sciences, communications studies/speech communication and rhetoric, psychology. **Disciplines with Highest Percentage of Degrees Awarded:** Business/marketing 20%, communications/journalism 14%, social sciences 10%, visual and performing arts 9%, psychology 9%. **Special Study Options:** Accelerated program, cross-registration, distance learning, double major, dual enrollment, exchange student program (domestic), external degree program, honors program, independent study, internships, liberal arts/career combination, student-designed major, study abroad, advanced placement credit, limited weekend courses available.

FACILITIES

Housing: Coed dorms, apartments for single students, special housing for disabled students, honors floor available. Counselors live in each hall to provide spiritual/counseling assistance. **Special Academic Facilities/Equipment:** Art gallery, humanities lab with Perseus Project and TLG TV and radio production studios, multimedia classrooms, 24-hour microcomputer labs, computer science lab, graphics lab, visual arts lab, ad club/communications lab, RATHE business computer lab, audio recording studio, multimedia training center, Donnelley Center for Nonprofit Communications. **Computers:** 10% of classrooms are wired, 10% of classrooms are wireless, 85% of public computers are PCs, 15% of public computers are Macs, network access in dorm rooms, network access in dorm lounges, online registration, online administrative functions (other than registration), support for handheld computing, remote student-access to Web through college's connection.

CAMPUS LIFE

Activities: Choral groups, concert band, dance, drama/theater, jazz band, literary magazine, music ensembles, opera, pep band, student government, student newspaper, student-run film society, symphony orchestra, yearbook. **Organizations:** 140 registered organizations, 10 honor societies, 12 religious organizations. 7 fraternities (20% men join), 7 sororities (23% women join). **Athletics (Intercollegiate):** *Men:* Baseball, basketball, cross-country, track/field (outdoor). *Women:* Basketball, cross-country, soccer, track/field (outdoor), volleyball.

ADMISSIONS

Freshman Academic Profile: 26% in top 10% of high school class, 51% in top 25% of high school class, 85% in top 50% of high school class. 41% from public high schools. SAT Math middle 50% range 530–630. SAT Critical Reading middle 50% range 550–690. ACT middle 50% range 23–28. TOEFL required of all international applicants, minimum paper TOEFL 550, minimum computer TOEFL 213. **Basis for Candidate Selection:** *Very important factors considered include:* Rigor of secondary school record, standardized test scores. *Important factors considered include:* Academic GPA, application essay, character/personal qualities, extracurricular activities, first generation, interview, recommendation(s), talent/ability. *Other factors considered include:* Alumni/ae relation, class rank, level of applicant's interest, volunteer work, work experience. **Freshman Admission Requirements:** High school diploma is required, and GED is accepted. *Academic units required:* 4 English, 2 math, 2 science, 2 social studies. *Academic units recommended:* 4 English, 3 math, 3 science, 3 social studies. **Freshman Admission Statistics:** 3,021 applied, 58% admitted, 30% enrolled. **Transfer Admission Requirements:** College transcript(s), essay or personal statement. Minimum college GPA of 2.2 required. Lowest grade transferable C. **General Admission Information:** Application fee $20. Regular notification is rolling. Nonfall registration accepted. Credit and/or placement offered for CEEB Advanced Placement tests.

COSTS AND FINANCIAL AID

Room and board $6,738. Required fees $876. Average book expense $1,000. **Required Forms and Deadlines:** FAFSA. Financial aid filing deadline 6/1. **Notification of Awards:** Applicants will be notified of awards on a rolling basis beginning on or about 3/1. **Types of Aid:** *Need-based scholarships/grants:* Pell, SEOG, private scholarships, the school's own gift aid. *Loans:* FFEL Subsidized Stafford, FFEL Unsubsidized Stafford, FFEL PLUS, Federal Perkins. **Student Employment:** Federal Work-Study Program available. Institutional employment available. Off-campus job opportunities are excellent. **Financial Aid Statistics:** 56% freshmen, 45% undergrads receive need-based scholarship or grant aid. 48% freshmen, 41% undergrads receive need-based self-help aid. 3 freshmen, 15 undergrads receive athletic scholarships. 84% freshmen, 87% undergrads receive any aid. Highest amount earned per year from on-campus jobs $1,483.

See page 1248.

LUBBOCK CHRISTIAN UNIVERSITY

5601 Nineteenth Street, Lubbock, TX 79407
Phone: 800-720-7151 **E-mail:** admissions@lcu.edu **CEEB Code:** 6378
Fax: 806-720-7162 **Website:** www.lcu.edu **ACT Code:** 4123
Financial Aid Phone: 806-720-7176

This private school, affiliated with the Church of Christ, was founded in 1957. It has a 120-acre campus.

RATINGS
Admissions Selectivity Rating: 77　　**Fire Safety Rating:** 60*　　**Green Rating:** 60*

STUDENTS AND FACULTY
Enrollment: 1,728. **Student Body:** 56% female, 44% male, 9% out-of-state. African American 6%, Caucasian 79%, Hispanic 14%. **Retention and Graduation:** 67% freshmen return for sophomore year. 27% freshmen graduate within 4 years. **Faculty:** Student/faculty ratio 15:1. 79 full-time faculty, 59% hold PhDs. 100% faculty teach undergrads.

ACADEMICS
Degrees: Bachelor's, master's. **Academic Requirements:** Arts/fine arts, computer literacy, English (including composition), history, humanities, mathematics, sciences (biological or physical), social science, Bible, kinesiology, communication. **Classes:** Most classes have 10–19 students. Most lab/discussion sections have fewer than 10 students. **Majors with Highest Enrollment:** Elementary education and teaching, humanities/humanistic studies, small business administration/management. **Disciplines with Highest Percentage of Degrees Awarded:** Business/marketing 30%, education 22%, liberal arts/general studies 5%, psychology 5%, biological/life sciences 5%, computer and information sciences 4%, health professions and related sciences 4%. **Special Study Options:** Distance learning, double major, dual enrollment, honors program, internships, liberal arts/career combination, student-designed major, study abroad, teacher certification program, weekend college.

FACILITIES
Housing: Men's dorms, women's dorms, apartments for married students, apartments for single students, special housing for disabled students. **Computers:** 100% of classrooms are wired, 80% of classrooms are wireless, 100% of public computers are PCs, network access in dorm rooms, online registration, remote student-access to Web through college's connection.

CAMPUS LIFE
Activities: Choral groups, drama/theater, music ensembles, student government, student newspaper, yearbook. **Organizations:** 24 registered organizations, 3 honor societies. 4 fraternities, 4 sororities. **Athletics (Intercollegiate):** *Men:* Baseball, basketball, cheerleading, golf. *Women:* Basketball, cheerleading, golf, volleyball.

ADMISSIONS
Freshman Academic Profile: 18% in top 10% of high school class, 44% in top 25% of high school class, 76% in top 50% of high school class. 76% from public high schools. SAT Math middle 50% range 440–572. SAT Critical Reading middle 50% range 450–582. ACT middle 50% range 18–24. TOEFL required of all international applicants, minimum paper TOEFL 500, minimum computer TOEFL 173. **Basis for Candidate Selection:** *Very important factors considered include:* Standardized test scores. *Important factors considered include:* Character/personal qualities, rigor of secondary school record. *Other factors considered include:* Alumni/ae relation, class rank, racial/ethnic status, recommendation(s), religious affiliation/commitment, talent/ability, volunteer work. **Freshman Admission Requirements:** High school diploma is required, and GED is accepted. *Academic units recommended:* 4 English, 3 math, 3 science (2 science labs), 2 foreign language, 2 social studies, 2 history, 4 academic electives. **Freshman Admission Statistics:** 771 applied, 77% admitted, 45% enrolled. **Transfer Admission Requirements:** College transcript(s), statement of good standing from prior institution(s). Lowest grade transferable C. **General Admission Information:** Application fee $20. Regular application deadline 8/15. Regular notification is rolling. Nonfall registration accepted. Common Application accepted. Credit and/or placement offered for CEEB Advanced Placement tests.

COSTS AND FINANCIAL AID
Annual tuition $11,644. Room & board $2,125. Required fees $916. Average book expense $832. **Required Forms and Deadlines:** FAFSA, institution's own financial aid form. Financial aid filing deadline 6/1. **Notification of Awards:** Applicants will be notified of awards on a rolling basis beginning on or about 3/1. **Types of Aid:** *Need-based scholarships/grants:* Pell, SEOG, state scholarships/grants. *Loans:* FFEL Subsidized Stafford, FFEL Unsubsidized Stafford, FFEL PLUS, Federal Perkins. **Student Employment:** Federal Work-Study Program available. Off-campus job opportunities are excellent. **Financial Aid Statistics:** 80% freshmen receive need-based scholarship or grant aid. 68% freshmen receive need-based self-help aid. 14 freshmen, 47 undergrads receive athletic scholarships. 78% freshmen, 72% undergrads receive any aid.

LUTHER COLLEGE

700 College Drive, Decorah, IA 52101-1042
Phone: 563-387-1287 **E-mail:** admissions@luther.edu **CEEB Code:** 6375
Fax: 563-387-2159 **Website:** www.luther.edu **ACT Code:** 1330
Financial Aid Phone: 563-387-1018

This private school, affiliated with the Lutheran Church, was founded in 1861. It has a 175-acre campus.

RATINGS
Admissions Selectivity Rating: 86　　**Fire Safety Rating:** 60*　　**Green Rating:** 60*

STUDENTS AND FACULTY
Enrollment: 2,431. **Student Body:** 58% female, 42% male, 65% out-of-state. 3% international (32 countries represented). Asian 2%, Caucasian 89%, Hispanic 1%. **Retention and Graduation:** 83% freshmen return for sophomore year. 64% freshmen graduate within 4 years. 23% grads go on to further study within 1 year. 17% grads pursue arts and sciences degrees. 1% grads pursue law degrees. 4% grads pursue medical degrees. **Faculty:** Student/faculty ratio 12:1. 181 full-time faculty, 89% hold PhDs. 100% faculty teach undergrads.

ACADEMICS
Degrees: Bachelor's. **Academic Requirements:** Arts/fine arts, English (including composition), foreign languages, history, humanities, mathematics, philosophy, sciences (biological or physical), social science, religion. **Classes:** Most classes have 20–29 students. Most lab/discussion sections have 20–29 students. **Majors with Highest Enrollment:** Biology/biological sciences, business administration and management, elementary education and teaching. **Disciplines with Highest Percentage of Degrees Awarded:** Business/marketing 12%, social sciences 11%, biological/life sciences 10%, visual and performing arts 10%, education 8%. **Special Study Options:** Double major, dual enrollment, honors program, independent study, internships, student-designed major, study abroad, teacher certification program.

FACILITIES
Housing: Coed dorms, apartments for married students, apartments for single students, special housing for disabled students. **Special Academic Facilities/Equipment:** Natural history museum, Norwegian American Museum, 5 art galleries, planetarium, live animal center, archaeological research center, computer music lab, 2 electron microscopes. **Computers:** 77% of public computers are PCs, 15% of public computers are Macs, 8% of public computers are UNIX, network access in dorm rooms, network access in dorm lounges, online registration, online administrative functions (other than registration), remote student-access to Web through college's connection.

CAMPUS LIFE
Activities: Choral groups, concert band, dance, drama/theater, jazz band, literary magazine, music ensembles, musical theater, pep band, radio station, student government, student newspaper, student-run film society, symphony orchestra, yearbook. **Organizations:** 119 registered organizations, 13 honor societies, 5 religious organizations. 2 fraternities (7% men join), 3 sororities (9% women join). **Athletics (Intercollegiate):** *Men:* Baseball, basketball, cross-country, diving, football, golf, soccer, swimming, tennis, track/field (indoor), track/field (outdoor), wrestling. *Women:* Basketball, cross-country, diving, golf, soccer, softball, swimming, tennis, track/field (indoor), track/field (outdoor), volleyball.

ADMISSIONS
Freshman Academic Profile: 30% in top 10% of high school class, 61% in top 25% of high school class, 85% in top 50% of high school class. 96% from public high schools. SAT Math middle 50% range 540–650. SAT Critical Reading

middle 50% range 480–670. SAT Writing middle 50% range 500–650. ACT middle 50% range 22–28. TOEFL required of all international applicants, minimum paper TOEFL 550, minimum computer TOEFL 213. **Basis for Candidate Selection:** *Very important factors considered include:* Academic GPA, class rank, recommendation(s), rigor of secondary school record, standardized test scores. *Important factors considered include:* Application essay, character/personal qualities, extracurricular activities, talent/ability, volunteer work. *Other factors considered include:* Alumni/ae relation, first generation, geographical residence, interview, level of applicant's interest, racial/ethnic status, religious affiliation/commitment. **Freshman Admission Requirements:** High school diploma is required, and GED is accepted. *Academic units recommended:* 4 English, 3 math, 2 science (1 science lab), 2 foreign language, 3 social studies. **Freshman Admission Statistics:** 1,853 applied, 81% admitted, 41% enrolled. **Transfer Admission Requirements:** High school transcript, college transcript(s), essay or personal statement, standardized test score. Minimum college GPA of 2.5 required. Lowest grade transferable C. **General Admission Information:** Application fee $25. Regular notification is rolling. Nonfall registration accepted. Admission may be deferred for a maximum of 1 year. Credit and/or placement offered for CEEB Advanced Placement tests.

COSTS AND FINANCIAL AID

Annual tuition $26,380. Room & board $4,290. Average book expense $830. **Required Forms and Deadlines:** FAFSA, institution's own financial aid form. Financial aid filing deadline 3/1. **Notification of Awards:** Applicants will be notified of awards on a rolling basis beginning on or about 3/1. **Types of Aid:** *Need-based scholarships/grants:* Pell, SEOG, state scholarships/grants, private scholarships, the school's own gift aid. *Loans:* Direct Subsidized Stafford, Direct Unsubsidized Stafford, Direct PLUS, Federal Perkins, college/university loans from institutional funds. **Financial Aid Statistics:** 70% freshmen, 70% undergrads receive need-based scholarship or grant aid. 58% freshmen, 61% undergrads receive need-based self-help aid. 98% freshmen, 97% undergrads receive any aid. Highest amount earned per year from on-campus jobs $3,190.

LUTHER RICE BIBLE COLLEGE AND SEMINARY

3038 Evans Mills Road, Lithonia, GA 30038-2418
Phone: 770-484-1204 **E-mail:** admissions@lrs.edu
Fax: 770-484-1155 **Website:** www.lrs.edu
Financial Aid Phone: 770-484-1204

This private school, affiliated with the Southern Baptist Church, was founded in 1962.

RATINGS

Admissions Selectivity Rating: 60*   **Fire Safety Rating:** 60*   **Green Rating:** 60*

STUDENTS AND FACULTY

Enrollment: 406. **Student Body:** 22% female, 78% male. African American 16%, Asian 10%, Caucasian 47%, Hispanic 2%. **Retention and Graduation:** 88% grads go on to further study within 1 year. **Faculty:** Student/faculty ratio 10:1. 9 full-time faculty, 89% hold PhDs. 90% faculty teach undergrads.

ACADEMICS

Degrees: Bachelor's, doctoral, first professional, master's. **Majors with Highest Enrollment:** Bible/biblical studies, pastoral studies/counseling, theology/theological studies. **Special Study Options:** Distance learning, external degree program, independent study, internships.

FACILITIES

Special Academic Facilities/Equipment: Chapel. **Computers:** 100% of public computers are PCs, online registration, online administrative functions (other than registration).

CAMPUS LIFE

Activities: Student government. **Organizations:** 1 registered organization.

ADMISSIONS

Freshman Academic Profile: 50% from public high schools. **Basis for Candidate Selection:** *Important factors considered include:* Religious affiliation/commitment. **Freshman Admission Requirements:** High school diploma is required, and GED is accepted. **Freshman Admission Statistics:** 67 applied, 100% admitted, 100% enrolled. **Transfer Admission Requirements:** Statement of good standing from prior institution(s). Minimum college GPA of 2.0 required. Lowest grade transferable C. **General Admission Information:** Application fee $50. Nonfall registration accepted. Common Application not accepted.

COSTS AND FINANCIAL AID

Required Forms and Deadlines: FAFSA, institution's own financial aid form. **Student Employment:** Federal Work-Study Program available. Off-campus job opportunities are good.

LYCOMING COLLEGE

700 College Place, Box 164, Williamsport, PA 17701
Phone: 570-321-4026 **E-mail:** admissions@lycoming.edu **CEEB Code:** 2372
Fax: 570-321-4317 **Website:** www.lycoming.edu **ACT Code:** 3622
Financial Aid Phone: 570-433-3068

This private school, affiliated with the Methodist Church, was founded in 1812. It has a 39-acre campus.

RATINGS

Admissions Selectivity Rating: 78   **Fire Safety Rating:** 60*   **Green Rating:** 78

STUDENTS AND FACULTY

Enrollment: 1,399. **Student Body:** 57% female, 43% male, 31% out-of-state. African American 3%, Asian 1%, Caucasian 93%, Hispanic 2%. **Retention and Graduation:** 80% freshmen return for sophomore year. 61% freshmen graduate within 4 years. 20% grads go on to further study within 1 year. 10% grads pursue arts and sciences degrees. 1% grads pursue business degrees. 1% grads pursue law degrees. 6% grads pursue medical degrees. **Faculty:** Student/faculty ratio 13:1. 92 full-time faculty, 84% hold PhDs. 100% faculty teach undergrads.

ACADEMICS

Degrees: Bachelor's. **Academic Requirements:** Arts/fine arts, English (including composition), foreign languages, history, humanities, mathematics, philosophy, sciences (biological or physical), social science. Students are required to complete a cultural diversity course, and the writing across the curriculum program, which consists of 3 writing intensive courses. **Classes:** Most classes have 10–19 students. Most lab/discussion sections have 10–19 students. **Majors with Highest Enrollment:** Biology/biological sciences, business administration/management, psychology. **Disciplines with Highest Percentage of Degrees Awarded:** Social sciences 17%, psychology 16%, business/marketing 14%, biological/life sciences 11%, visual and performing arts 9%. **Special Study Options:** Cross-registration, double major, honors program, independent study, internships, liberal arts/career combination, student-designed major, study abroad, teacher certification program.

FACILITIES

Housing: Coed dorms, women's dorms, apartments for single students, special housing for disabled students, fraternity/sorority housing, substance-free housing, study-intensive housing, creative arts society housing. **Special Academic Facilities/Equipment:** Language lab, tissue culture lab, TV studio, planetarium, video conferencing. **Computers:** 100% of classrooms are wireless, 90% of public computers are PCs, 10% of public computers are Macs, network access in dorm rooms, online registration, online administrative functions (other than registration), support for handheld computing, remote student-access to Web through college's connection.

CAMPUS LIFE

Activities: Choral groups, concert band, dance, drama/theater, jazz band, literary magazine, music ensembles, musical theater, pep band, radio station, student government, student newspaper, student-run film society, symphony orchestra, television station, yearbook. **Organizations:** 70 registered organizations, 19 honor societies, 3 religious organizations. 5 fraternities (16% men join), 5 sororities (26% women join). **Athletics (Intercollegiate):** *Men:* Basketball, cross-country, football, golf, lacrosse, soccer, swimming, tennis, wrestling. *Women:* Basketball, cross-country, lacrosse, soccer, softball, swimming, tennis, volleyball. Environmental Initiatives: The College has replaced older less efficient lighting systems on campus to more energy efficient systems. All residence halls and many of the other campus buildings have been retrofitted to include high EER rated lighting equipment. This has cut our energy costs in half for many buildings. New and renovated buildings are updated to include the latest technology in energy efficiency. The housekeeping staff at Lycoming College now uses green cleaning agents.

ADMISSIONS

Freshman Academic Profile: 19% in top 10% of high school class, 46% in top 25% of high school class, 81% in top 50% of high school class. SAT Math middle 50% range 470–580. SAT Critical Reading middle 50% range 460–570. SAT Writing middle 50% range 450–560. ACT middle 50% range 20–25. TOEFL required of all international applicants, minimum paper TOEFL 500, minimum computer TOEFL 173. **Basis for Candidate Selection:** *Very important* factors considered include: Academic GPA, application essay, character/personal qualities, class rank. *Important factors considered include:* Alumni/ae relation, extracurricular activities, first generation, geographical residence, interview, racial/ethnic status, recommendation(s), rigor of secondary school record, standardized test scores, talent/ability, volunteer work. *Other factors considered include:* Level of applicant's interest, work experience. **Freshman Admission Requirements:** High school diploma is required, and GED is accepted. *Academic units required:* 4 English, 3 math, 2 science (2 science labs), 2 foreign language, 4 social studies, 3 history, 2 academic electives. *Academic units recommended:* 4 English, 4 math, 4 science (2 science labs), 4 foreign language, 4 social studies, 4 history, 2 academic electives. **Freshman Admission Statistics:** 1,532 applied, 76% admitted, 32% enrolled. **Transfer Admission Requirements:** College transcript(s), statement of good standing from prior institution(s). Minimum college GPA of 2.0 required. Lowest grade transferable C-. **General Admission Information:** Application fee $35. Regular application deadline 7/1. Regular notification is rolling. Nonfall registration accepted. Admission may be deferred for a maximum of 1 year. Credit offered for CEEB Advanced Placement tests.

COSTS AND FINANCIAL AID

Annual tuition $28,224. Room and board $7,672. Required fees $540. Average book expense $800. **Required Forms and Deadlines:** FAFSA, institution's own financial aid form. Financial aid filing deadline 3/1. **Notification of Awards:** Applicants will be notified of awards on a rolling basis beginning on or about 3/1. **Types of Aid:** *Need-based scholarships/grants:* Pell, SEOG, state scholarships/grants, private scholarships, the school's own gift aid. *Loans:* FFEL Subsidized Stafford, FFEL Unsubsidized Stafford, FFEL PLUS, Federal Perkins, college/university loans from institutional funds. **Student Employment:** Federal Work-Study Program available. Institutional employment available. Off-campus job opportunities are good. **Financial Aid Statistics:** 81% freshmen, 82% undergrads receive need-based scholarship or grant aid. 74% freshmen, 75% undergrads receive need-based self-help aid. 95% freshmen, 95% undergrads receive any aid. Highest amount earned per year from on-campus jobs $3,792.

LYME ACADEMY OF FINE ARTS

84 Lyme Street, Old Lyme, CT 06371
Phone: 860-434-5232 **E-mail:** admissions@lymeacademy.edu
Fax: 860-434-8725 **Website:** www.lymeacademy.edu
Financial Aid Phone: 860-434-5232

This private school was founded in 1976. It has a 4-acre campus.

RATINGS

Admissions Selectivity Rating: 60*   **Fire Safety Rating:** 60*   **Green Rating:** 60*

STUDENTS AND FACULTY

Enrollment: 75. **Student Body:** 56% female, 44% male, 32% out-of-state. African American 1%, Asian 1%, Caucasian 64%, Hispanic 1%. **Retention and Graduation:** 46% freshmen return for sophomore year. 100% freshmen graduate within 4 years. 21% grads go on to further study within 1 year. 7% grads pursue medical degrees. **Faculty:** Student/faculty ratio 2:1. 9 full-time faculty, 44% hold PhDs. 100% faculty teach undergrads.

ACADEMICS

Degrees: Bachelor's. **Academic Requirements:** Arts/fine arts, English (including composition), humanities, mathematics, social science, sciences: anatomy and linear perspective. **Classes:** Most classes have 10–19 students. **Disciplines with Highest Percentage of Degrees Awarded:** Visual and performing arts 100%. **Special Study Options:** Independent study.

FACILITIES

Housing: All housing is off-campus. **Special Academic Facilities/Equipment:** Sill House Gallery. **Computers:** 100% of public computers are PCs, remote student-access to Web through college's connection.

CAMPUS LIFE

Activities: Student government, student newspaper.

ADMISSIONS

Freshman Academic Profile: 12% in top 25% of high school class, 6% in top 50% of high school class. 60% from public high schools. TOEFL required of all international applicants, minimum paper TOEFL 550, minimum computer TOEFL 213. **Basis for Candidate Selection:** *Very important factors considered include:* Interview, talent/ability. *Important factors considered include:* Application essay, character/personal qualities, recommendation(s). *Other factors considered include:* Class rank, extracurricular activities, rigor of

secondary school record, standardized test scores, volunteer work, work experience. **Freshman Admission Requirements:** High school diploma is required, and GED is accepted. **Freshman Admission Statistics:** 32 applied, 97% admitted, 58% enrolled. **Transfer Admission Requirements:** College transcript(s), essay or personal statement, interview. Lowest grade transferable C. **General Admission Information:** Application fee $35. Regular notification is rolling. Nonfall registration not accepted. Admission may be deferred for a maximum of 1 year. Common Application not accepted.

COSTS AND FINANCIAL AID

Annual tuition $20,256. Required fees $1,200. Average book expense $1,000. **Required Forms and Deadlines:** FAFSA, institution's own financial aid form, CSS/Financial Aid PROFILE, copies of previous year's tax forms and W-2 forms. Financial aid filing deadline 2/15. **Notification of Awards:** Applicants will be notified of awards on or about 4/15. **Types of Aid:** *Need-based scholarships/grants:* Pell, SEOG, state scholarships/grants, private scholarships, the school's own gift aid. *Loans:* FFEL Subsidized Stafford, FFEL Unsubsidized Stafford, FFEL PLUS, state loans. **Student Employment:** Federal Work-Study Program available. Institutional employment available. Off-campus job opportunities are excellent. **Financial Aid Statistics:** 60% freshmen, 19% undergrads receive need-based scholarship or grant aid. 6% undergrads receive need-based self-help aid.

LYNCHBURG COLLEGE

1501 Lakeside Drive, Lynchburg, VA 24501
Phone: 434-544-8300 **E-mail:** admissions@lynchburg.edu **CEEB Code:** 5372
Fax: 434-544-8653 **Website:** www.lynchburg.edu
Financial Aid Phone: 434-544-8229

This private school, affiliated with the Disciples of Christ Church, was founded in 1903. It has a 214-acre campus.

RATINGS

Admissions Selectivity Rating: 77   **Fire Safety Rating:** 75   **Green Rating:** 73

STUDENTS AND FACULTY

Enrollment: 2,021. **Student Body:** 58% female, 42% male, 36% out-of-state. African American 8%, Asian 2%, Caucasian 70%, Hispanic 3%. **Retention and Graduation:** 66% freshmen return for sophomore year. 43% freshmen graduate within 4 years. 25% grads go on to further study within 1 year. 16% grads pursue arts and sciences degrees. 6% grads pursue business degrees. 2% grads pursue law degrees. 1% grads pursue medical degrees. **Faculty:** Student/faculty ratio 12:1. 159 full-time faculty, 74% hold PhDs. 100% faculty teach undergrads.

ACADEMICS

Degrees: Bachelor's, master's. **Academic Requirements:** Arts/fine arts, English (including composition), foreign languages, history, humanities, mathematics, philosophy, sciences (biological or physical), social science. **Classes:** Most classes have 20–29 students. Most lab/discussion sections have 10–19 students. **Majors with Highest Enrollment:** Business administration and management, communications studies/speech communication and rhetoric, teacher education and professional development, specific levels and methods. **Disciplines with Highest Percentage of Degrees Awarded:** Business/marketing 17%, social sciences 13%, education 11%, communications/journalism 9%, health professions and related sciences 9%. **Special Study Options:** Accelerated program, cross-registration, double major, dual enrollment, honors program, independent study, internships, study abroad, teacher certification program.

FACILITIES

Housing: Coed dorms, men's dorms, women's dorms, special housing for disabled students, special housing for international students, fraternity/sorority housing, college-owned houses. **Special Academic Facilities/Equipment:** Daura Art Gallery, Claytor Nature Study Center, Ramsey-Freer Herbarium, forensics cadaver lab, Centennial Hall Audiovisual and Television Studios, Dillard Fine Arts Center. **Computers:** 25% of classrooms are wired, 10% of classrooms are wireless, 90% of public computers are PCs, 10% of public computers are Macs, network access in dorm rooms, network access in dorm lounges, online registration, online administrative functions (other than registration), remote student-access to Web through college's connection.

CAMPUS LIFE

Activities: Choral groups, concert band, dance, drama/theater, jazz band, literary magazine, music ensembles, musical theater, pep band, student government, student newspaper, symphony orchestra, yearbook. **Organizations:** 100 registered organizations, 14 honor societies, 7 religious organizations. 4 fraternities (9% men join), 6 sororities (14% women join). **Athletics (Intercollegiate):** *Men:* Baseball, basketball, cheerleading, cross-country, equestrian sports, golf, lacrosse, soccer, tennis, track/field (outdoor). *Women:* Basketball, cheerleading, cross-country, equestrian sports, field hockey, lacrosse, soccer, softball, tennis, track/field (outdoor), volleyball. Environmental Initiatives: Recovery of College Lake. LC's theme, "A Greener Tomorrow Today," has focused and will continue to focus attention on the need to act now to prevent further degradation of the environment. Dr. Garren (LC President) has signed the American College & University Presidents Climate Commitment, a pledge to reverse the actions that lead to global warming. Lynchburg College is participating in RecycleMania.

ADMISSIONS

Freshman Academic Profile: 12% in top 10% of high school class, 35% in top 25% of high school class, 73% in top 50% of high school class. 81% from public high schools. SAT Math middle 50% range 460–570. SAT Critical Reading middle 50% range 460–560. SAT Writing middle 50% range 450–550. ACT middle 50% range 18–22. TOEFL required of all international applicants, minimum paper TOEFL 525, minimum computer TOEFL 197. **Basis for Candidate Selection:** *Very important factors considered include:* Academic GPA, rigor of secondary school record, standardized test scores. *Important factors considered include:* Class rank, interview. *Other factors considered include:* Application essay, extracurricular activities, level of applicant's interest, recommendation(s), talent/ability, volunteer work. **Freshman Admission Requirements:** High school diploma is required, and GED is accepted. *Academic units required:* 4 English, 3 math, 3 science (2 science labs), 2 foreign language, 2 social studies, 2 history. *Academic units recommended:* 4 English, 4 math, 4 science (2 science labs), 3 foreign language, 2 social studies, 2 history, 1 academic elective. **Freshman Admission Statistics:** 4,277 applied, 69% admitted, 19% enrolled. **Transfer Admission Requirements:** College transcript(s). Minimum college GPA of 2.0 required. Lowest grade transferable C. **General Admission Information:** Application fee $30. Early decision application deadline 11/15. Regular notification is rolling. Nonfall registration accepted. Admission may be deferred for a maximum of 1 year. Credit offered for CEEB Advanced Placement tests.

COSTS AND FINANCIAL AID

Annual tuition $24,860. Room & board $7,000. Required fees $245. Average book expense $600. **Required Forms and Deadlines:** FAFSA, state aid form. Financial aid filing deadline 3/1. **Notification of Awards:** Applicants will be notified of awards on or about 3/5. **Types of Aid:** *Need-based scholarships/grants:* Pell, SEOG, state scholarships/grants, private scholarships, the school's own gift aid. *Loans:* FFEL Subsidized Stafford, FFEL Unsubsidized Stafford, FFEL PLUS, Federal Perkins. **Student Employment:** Federal Work-Study Program available. Institutional employment available. Off-campus job opportunities are good. **Financial Aid Statistics:** 66% freshmen, 63% undergrads receive need-based scholarship or grant aid. 60% freshmen, 59% undergrads receive need-based self-help aid. 98% freshmen, 95% undergrads receive any aid. Highest amount earned per year from on-campus jobs $1,650.

LYNDON STATE COLLEGE

PO Box 919, 1001 College Hill Rd, Lyndonville, VT 05851
Phone: 802-626-6413 **E-mail:** admissions@lyndonstate.edu **CEEB Code:** 3767
Fax: 802-626-6335 **Website:** www.lyndonstate.edu **ACT Code:** 4318
Financial Aid Phone: 802-626-6218

This public school was founded in 1911. It has a 175-acre campus.

RATINGS

Admissions Selectivity Rating: 67   **Fire Safety Rating:** 60*   **Green Rating:** 60*

STUDENTS AND FACULTY

Enrollment: 1,273. **Student Body:** 49% female, 51% male, 40% out-of-state. African American 1%, Caucasian 52%. **Retention and Graduation:** 67% freshmen return for sophomore year. 24% freshmen graduate within 4 years. 10% grads go on to further study within 1 year. **Faculty:** Student/faculty ratio 20:1. 59 full-time faculty, 90% hold PhDs. 100% faculty teach undergrads.

ACADEMICS

Degrees: Associate, bachelor's, certificate, master's. **Academic Requirements:** Arts/fine arts, computer literacy, English (including composition), humanities, mathematics, sciences (biological or physical), social science. **Classes:** Most classes have 10–19 students. Most lab/discussion sections have 10–19 students. **Disciplines with Highest Percentage of Degrees Awarded:** Psychology 16%, liberal arts/general studies 13%, parks and recreation 13%, business/marketing 13%, communication technologies 11%, education 11%, natural resources/environmental science 4%, English 4%, visual and performing arts 4%, mathematics 2%. **Special Study Options:** Accelerated program, cooperative education program, double major, dual enrollment, exchange student program (domestic), independent study, internships, liberal arts/career combination, student-designed major, study abroad, teacher certification program.

FACILITIES

Housing: Coed dorms, women's dorms, special housing for disabled students, substance-free dorms. **Special Academic Facilities/Equipment:** Museum of college history, weather satellite lab, television studio, radio station, geology lab, chemistry lab, physics lab, GIS/GPS lab. **Computers:** 98% of public computers are PCs, 2% of public computers are Macs, network access in dorm rooms, remote student-access to Web through college's connection.

CAMPUS LIFE

Activities: Choral groups, dance, drama/theater, literary magazine, musical theater, radio station, student government, student newspaper, television station. **Organizations:** 26 registered organizations, 1 honor society, 1 religious organization. **Athletics (Intercollegiate):** *Men:* Baseball, basketball, cross-country, soccer, tennis. *Women:* Basketball, cross-country, soccer, softball, tennis.

ADMISSIONS

Freshman Academic Profile: 12% in top 10% of high school class, 22% in top 25% of high school class, 69% in top 50% of high school class. SAT Math middle 50% range 410–530. SAT Critical Reading middle 50% range 418–520. TOEFL required of all international applicants, minimum paper TOEFL 500, minimum computer TOEFL 173. **Basis for Candidate Selection:** *Very important factors considered include:* Rigor of secondary school record. *Important factors considered include:* Character/personal qualities, class rank, interview, recommendation(s), talent/ability. *Other factors considered include:* Alumni/ae relation, application essay, extracurricular activities, standardized test scores, volunteer work, work experience. **Freshman Admission Requirements:** High school diploma is required, and GED is accepted. *Academic units required:* 4 English, 3 math, 2 science (2 science labs), 2 social studies, 2 history. *Academic units recommended:* 4 math, 3 science, 2 foreign language. **Freshman Admission Statistics:** 994 applied, 94% admitted, 36% enrolled. **Transfer Admission Requirements:** College transcript(s), essay or personal statement, statement of good standing from prior institution(s). Minimum college GPA of 2.2 required. Lowest grade transferable C-. **General Admission Information:** Application fee $35. Regular notification is rolling. Nonfall registration accepted. Admission may be deferred for a maximum of 1 year. Common Application accepted. Credit and/or placement offered for CEEB Advanced Placement tests.

COSTS AND FINANCIAL AID

Average book expense $600. **Required Forms and Deadlines:** FAFSA. Financial aid filing deadline 2/13. **Notification of Awards:** Applicants will be notified of awards on a rolling basis beginning on or about 4/1. **Types of Aid:** *Need-based scholarships/grants:* Pell, SEOG, state scholarships/grants, private scholarships, the school's own gift aid. *Loans:* Direct Subsidized Stafford, Direct Unsubsidized Stafford, Direct PLUS, Federal Perkins, state loans. **Student Employment:** Federal Work-Study Program available. Institutional employment available. Off-campus job opportunities are good. **Financial Aid Statistics:** 41% freshmen, 39% undergrads receive need-based scholarship or grant aid. 76% freshmen, 74% undergrads receive need-based self-help aid. Highest amount earned per year from on-campus jobs $700.

LYNN UNIVERSITY

3601 North Military Trail, Boca Raton, FL 33431-5598
Phone: 561-237-7000 **E-mail:** Admission@lynn.edu **CEEB Code:** 5437
Fax: 561-237-7100 **Website:** www.lynn.edu **ACT Code:** 0706
Financial Aid Phone: 561-237-7814

This private school was founded in 1962. It has a 123-acre campus.

RATINGS

Admissions Selectivity Rating: 69   **Fire Safety Rating:** 93   **Green Rating:** 70

STUDENTS AND FACULTY

Enrollment: 2,300. **Student Body:** 50% female, 50% male, 38% out-of-state, 12% international (82 countries represented). African American 5%, Caucasian 53%, Hispanic 7%. **Retention and Graduation:** 63% freshmen return for sophomore year. 27% freshmen graduate within 4 years. **Faculty:** Student/faculty ratio 17:1. 95 full-time faculty, 68% hold PhDs. 92% faculty teach undergrads.

ACADEMICS

Degrees: Bachelor's, certificate, doctoral, master's, post-bachelor's certificate, post-master's certificate. **Academic Requirements:** Arts/fine arts, computer literacy, English (including composition), history, humanities, mathematics, public speaking, sciences (biological or physical), social science. **Classes:** Most classes have 10–19 students. **Majors with Highest Enrollment:** Business administration/management; criminal justice/law enforcement administration; hospitality administration/management. **Disciplines with Highest Percentage of Degrees Awarded:** Business/marketing 43%, physical sciences 14%, communication technologies 13%, communications/journalism 12%, public administration and social services 11%. **Special Study Options:** Accelerated program, cooperative education program, distance learning, double major, dual enrollment, English as a second language (ESL), honor program, independent study, internships, liberal arts/career combination, study abroad, teacher certification program.

FACILITIES

Housing: Coed dorms, women's dorms, special housing for disabled students, special housing for international students. **Computers:** 95% of public computers are PCs, 5% of public computers are Macs, network access in dorm rooms, network access in dorm lounges, online registration, online administrative functions (other than registration), remote student-access to Web through college's connection.

CAMPUS LIFE

Activities: Choral groups, dance, drama/theater, literary magazine, music ensembles, radio station, student government, student newspaper, student-run film society, symphony orchestra, television station, yearbook. **Organizations:** 25 registered organizations, 1 honor society, 2 religious organizations. 1 fraternity, 1 sorority. **Athletics (Intercollegiate):** *Men:* Baseball, basketball, golf, soccer, tennis. *Women:* Basketball, golf, soccer, softball, tennis, volleyball.

ADMISSIONS

Freshman Academic Profile: 2% in top 10% of high school class, 10% in top 25% of high school class, 33% in top 50% of high school class. SAT Math middle 50% range 410–500. SAT Critical Reading middle 50% range 400–490. ACT middle 50% range 16–20. TOEFL required of all international applicants, minimum paper TOEFL 500, minimum computer TOEFL 173. **Basis for Candidate Selection:** *Very important factors considered include:* Rigor of secondary school record, standardized test scores. *Important factors considered include:* Application essay, character/personal qualities, class rank, recommendation(s). *Other factors considered include:* Alumni/ae relation, extracurricular activities, interview, state residency, talent/ability, volunteer work, work experience. **Freshman Admission Requirements:** High school diploma is required, and GED is accepted. *Academic units required:* 4 English, 4 math, 4 science, 2 social studies, 2 history. **Freshman Admission Statistics:** 2,713 applied, 71% admitted, 29% enrolled. **Transfer Admission Requirements:** College transcript(s), essay or personal statement, statement of good standing from prior institution(s). Minimum college GPA of 2.0 required. Lowest grade transferable C. **General Admission Information:** Application fee $35. Regular notification rolling—continuous. Nonfall registration accepted. Admission may be deferred for a maximum of 1 year. Credit offered for CEEB Advanced Placement tests.

COSTS AND FINANCIAL AID

Annual tuition $26,990. Room and board $10,100. Required fees $1,500. Average book expense $1,100. **Required Forms and Deadlines:** FAFSA, institution's own financial aid form. Financial aid filing deadline 3/1. **Notification of Awards:** Applicants will be notified of awards on a rolling basis beginning on or about 2/1. **Types of Aid:** *Need-based scholarships/grants:* Pell, SEOG, state scholarships/grants, private scholarships, the school's own gift aid. *Loans:* FFEL Subsidized Stafford, FFEL Unsubsidized Stafford, FFEL PLUS, Federal Perkins, state loans, college/university loans from institutional funds. **Student Employment:** Off-campus job opportunities are excellent. **Financial Aid Statistics:** 45% freshmen, 55% undergrads receive need-based scholarship or grant aid. 28% freshmen, 29% undergrads receive need-based self-help aid. 8 freshmen, 24 undergrads receive athletic scholarships. 71% freshmen, 72% undergrads receive any aid. Highest amount earned per year from on-campus jobs $6,868.

See page 1250.

LYON COLLEGE

PO Box 2317, Batesville, AR 72503-2317
Phone: 870-698-4250 **E-mail:** admissions@lyon.edu **CEEB Code:** 1088
Fax: 870-793-1791 **Website:** www.lyon.edu **ACT Code:** 0112
Financial Aid Phone: 870-698-4257

This private school, affiliated with the Presbyterian Church, was founded in 1872. It has a 136-acre campus.

RATINGS

Admissions Selectivity Rating: 87   **Fire Safety Rating:** 70   **Green Rating:** 64

STUDENTS AND FACULTY

Enrollment: 476. **Student Body:** 52% female, 48% male, 22% out-of-state, 3% international (13 countries represented). African American 4%, Caucasian 82%, Hispanic 3%, Native American 1%. **Retention and Graduation:** 70% freshmen return for sophomore year. 58% freshmen graduate within 4 years. 25% grads go on to further study within 1 year. 15% grads pursue arts and sciences degrees. 5% grads pursue business degrees. 5% grads pursue medical degrees. **Faculty:** Student/faculty ratio 10:1. 43 full-time faculty, 91% hold PhDs. 100% faculty teach undergrads.

ACADEMICS

Degrees: Bachelor's. **Academic Requirements:** Arts/fine arts, English (including composition), foreign languages, history, humanities, mathematics, philosophy, sciences (biological or physical), social science, physical education. **Classes:** Most classes have 10–19 students. Most lab/discussion sections have 10–19 students. **Majors with Highest Enrollment:** Biology/biological sciences, business administration/management, psychology. **Disciplines with Highest Percentage of Degrees Awarded:** Business/marketing 22%, biological/life sciences 17%, psychology 16%, social sciences 13%, English 11%. **Special Study Options:** Accelerated program, cross-registration, double major, dual enrollment, independent study, internships, student-designed major, study abroad, teacher certification program.

FACILITIES

Housing: Coed dorms, men's dorms, women's dorms, apartments for single students, special housing for disabled students, limited college-owned off-campus housing. **Special Academic Facilities/Equipment:** Ozark Regional Studies Center. **Computers:** 100% of public computers are PCs, network access in dorm rooms, network access in dorm lounges, online registration, online administrative functions (other than registration), remote student-access to Web through college's connection.

CAMPUS LIFE

Activities: Choral groups, drama/theater, literary magazine, music ensembles, student government, student newspaper, yearbook. **Organizations:** 44 registered organizations, 9 honor societies, 7 religious organizations. 3 fraternities (11% men join), 2 sororities (15% women join). **Athletics (Intercollegiate):** *Men:* Baseball, basketball, cheerleading, cross-country, golf, soccer, tennis. *Women:* Basketball, cheerleading, cross-country, golf, soccer, tennis, volleyball.

ADMISSIONS

Freshman Academic Profile: 41% in top 10% of high school class, 72% in top 25% of high school class, 94% in top 50% of high school class. SAT Math middle 50% range 510–600. SAT Critical Reading middle 50% range 505–585. SAT Writing middle 50% range 480–580. ACT middle 50% range 22–27. TOEFL required of all international applicants, minimum paper TOEFL 550, minimum computer TOEFL 213. **Basis for Candidate Selection:** *Very important factors considered include:* Academic GPA, standardized test scores. *Important factors considered include:* Rigor of secondary school record. *Other factors considered include:* Application essay, character/personal qualities, class rank, extracurricular activities, interview, level of applicant's interest, recommendation(s), talent/ability, volunteer work, work experience. **Freshman Admission Requirements:** High school diploma is required, and GED is accepted. *Academic units required:* 4 English, 3 math, 3 science (2 science labs), 2 foreign language, 1 social studies, 2 history, 1 academic elective. *Academic units recommended:* 4 English, 4 math, 4 science (2 science labs), 2 foreign language, 1 social studies, 2 history, 1 academic elective. **Freshman Admission Statistics:** 617 applied, 69% admitted, 30% enrolled. **Transfer Admission Requirements:** College transcript(s), statement of good standing from prior institution(s). Minimum college GPA of 2.8 required. Lowest grade transferable C. **General Admission Information:** Application fee $25. Regular notification 2 weeks after receipt of completed application. Nonfall registration accepted. Admission may be deferred for a maximum of 1 year. Credit and/or placement offered for CEEB Advanced Placement tests.

COSTS AND FINANCIAL AID

Annual tuition $14,420. Room & board $6,270. Required fees $440. Average book expense $1,000. **Required Forms and Deadlines:** FAFSA. Financial aid filing deadline 3/15. **Notification of Awards:** Applicants will be notified of awards on a rolling basis beginning on or about 3/1. **Types of Aid:** *Need-based scholarships/grants:* Pell, SEOG, state scholarships/grants, private scholarships, the school's own gift aid, United Negro College Fund. *Loans:* FFEL Subsidized Stafford, FFEL Unsubsidized Stafford, FFEL PLUS, Federal Perkins. **Financial Aid Statistics:** 70% freshmen, 70% undergrads receive need-based scholarship or grant aid. 41% freshmen, 50% undergrads receive need-based self-help aid. 29 freshmen, 85 undergrads receive athletic scholarships. 100% freshmen, 99% undergrads receive any aid. Highest amount earned per year from on-campus jobs $5,600.

MACALESTER COLLEGE

1600 Grand Avenue, St. Paul, MN 55105
Phone: 651-696-6357 **E-mail:** admissions@macalester.edu **CEEB Code:** 6390
Fax: 651-696-6724 **Website:** www.macalester.edu **ACT Code:** 2122
Financial Aid Phone: 651-696-6214

This private school, affiliated with the Presbyterian Church, was founded in 1874. It has a 53-acre campus.

RATINGS

Admissions Selectivity Rating: 96   **Fire Safety Rating:** 88   **Green Rating:** 85

STUDENTS AND FACULTY

Enrollment: 1,905. **Student Body:** 58% female, 42% male, 77% out-of-state, 11% international (91 countries represented). African American 4%, Asian 8%, Caucasian 72%, Hispanic 4%. **Retention and Graduation:** 93% freshmen return for sophomore year. 82% freshmen graduate within 4 years. 28% grads go on to further study within 1 year. 22% grads pursue arts and sciences degrees. 1% grads pursue business degrees. 4% grads pursue law degrees. 2% grads pursue medical degrees. **Faculty:** Student/faculty ratio 11:1. 154 full-time faculty, 93% hold PhDs. 100% faculty teach undergrads.

ACADEMICS

Degrees: Bachelor's. **Academic Requirements:** Arts/fine arts, foreign languages, humanities, mathematics, sciences (biological or physical), social science, domestic diversity, international diversity. **Classes:** Most classes have 10–19 students. Most lab/discussion sections have 10–19 students. **Majors with Highest Enrollment:** Economics, English language and literature, political science and government. **Disciplines with Highest Percentage of Degrees Awarded:** Social sciences 33%, foreign languages and literature 9%, English 8%, interdisciplinary studies 7%, biological/life sciences 6%, psychology 6%. **Special Study Options:** Cross-registration, double major, honors program, independent study, internships, student-designed major, study abroad, teacher certification program. BA/master's in architecture with Washington University, St. Louis, Missouri; BA/BS in engineering with Washington University, St. Louis, or the University of Minnesota; BA/BS in nursing with Rush University in Chicago, Illinois.

FACILITIES

Housing: Coed dorms, apartments for single students, language houses. **Special Academic Facilities/Equipment:** Humanities learning center, econometrics lab, cartography lab, 250-acre nature preserve, observatory and planetarium, 2 electron microscopes, nuclear magnetic resonance spectrometer, laser spectroscopy lab, X-ray diffractometer, International Center, Center for Scholarship and Teaching. **Computers:** 60% of public computers are PCs, 36% of public computers are Macs, 4% of public computers are UNIX, network access in dorm rooms, network access in dorm lounges, online registration, online administrative functions (other than registration), remote student-access to Web through college's connection.

CAMPUS LIFE

Activities: Choral groups, concert band, dance, drama/theater, jazz band, literary magazine, music ensembles, radio station, student government, student newspaper, symphony orchestra, yearbook. **Organizations:** 80 registered organizations, 15 honor societies, 10 religious organizations. **Athletics (Intercollegiate): Men:** Baseball, basketball, cross-country, diving, football, golf, soccer, swimming, tennis, track/field (indoor), track/field (outdoor). *Women:* Basketball, cross-country, diving, golf, soccer, softball, swimming, tennis, track/field (indoor), track/field (outdoor), volleyball, water polo. Environmental Initiatives: Signed President's Climate Commitment. Hired a sustainability Manager. Building a LEED Platinum Building.

ADMISSIONS

Freshman Academic Profile: 66% in top 10% of high school class, 91% in top 25% of high school class, 99% in top 50% of high school class. 68% from public high schools. SAT Math middle 50% range 620–710. SAT Critical Reading middle 50% range 630–730. SAT Writing middle 50% range 620–720. ACT middle 50% range 28–32. TOEFL required of all international applicants, minimum paper TOEFL 573, minimum computer TOEFL 230. **Basis for Candidate Selection:** *Very important factors considered include:* Academic GPA, rigor of secondary school record. *Important factors considered include:* Application essay, character/personal qualities, extracurricular activities, recommendation(s), standardized test scores. *Other factors considered include:* Alumni/ae relation, class rank, first generation, interview, racial/ethnic status, talent/ability, volunteer work, work experience. **Freshman Admission Requirements:** High school diploma or equivalent is not required. *Academic units recommended:* 4 English, 3 math, 3 science (3 science labs), 3 foreign language, 3 social studies. **Freshman Admission Statistics:** 4,826 applied, 39% admitted, 27% enrolled. **Transfer Admission Requirements:** High school transcript, college transcript(s), essay or personal statement, standardized test score, statement of good standing from prior institution(s). Lowest grade transferable C-. **General Admission Information:** Application fee $40. Early decision application deadline 11/15. Regular application deadline 1/15. Regular notification 3/30. Nonfall registration not accepted. Admission may be deferred for a maximum of 1 year. Credit and/or placement offered for CEEB Advanced Placement tests.

COSTS AND FINANCIAL AID

Annual tuition $33,494. Room and board $8,220. Required fees $200. Average book expense $850. **Required Forms and Deadlines:** FAFSA, CSS/Financial Aid PROFILE, Noncustodial PROFILE, parent and student tax returns. Financial aid filing deadline 3/1. **Notification of Awards:** Applicants will be notified of awards on or about 4/1. **Types of Aid:** *Need-based scholarships/grants:* Pell, SEOG, state scholarships/grants, private scholarships, the school's own gift aid. *Loans:* FFEL Subsidized Stafford, FFEL Unsubsidized Stafford, FFEL PLUS, Federal Perkins, state loans. **Student Employment:** Federal Work-Study Program available. Institutional employment available. Off-campus job opportunities are excellent. **Financial Aid Statistics:** 66% freshmen, 67% undergrads receive need-based scholarship or grant aid. 67% freshmen, 67% undergrads receive need-based self-help aid. 70% freshmen, 73% undergrads receive any aid. Highest amount earned per year from on-campus jobs $2,600.

MACMURRAY COLLEGE

447 East College, Jacksonville, IL 62650
Phone: 217-479-7056 **E-mail:** admissions@mac.edu **CEEB Code:** 1435
Fax: 217-291-0702 **Website:** www.mac.edu **ACT Code:** 1068
Financial Aid Phone: 217-479-7041

This private school, affiliated with the Methodist Church, was founded in 1846. It has a 60-acre campus.

RATINGS

Admissions Selectivity Rating: 72   **Fire Safety Rating:** 60*   **Green Rating:** 60*

STUDENTS AND FACULTY

Enrollment: 685. **Student Body:** 63% female, 37% male, 11% out-of-state. African American 12%, Caucasian 77%, Hispanic 3%. **Retention and Graduation:** 72% freshmen return for sophomore year. 25% grads go on to further study within 1 year. 9% grads pursue arts and sciences degrees. 12% grads pursue business degrees. 1% grads pursue law degrees. 1% grads pursue medical degrees. **Faculty:** Student/faculty ratio 12:1. 44 full-time faculty, 48% hold PhDs. 100% faculty teach undergrads.

ACADEMICS

Degrees: Associate, bachelor's. **Academic Requirements:** Arts/fine arts, English (including composition), history, humanities, mathematics, philosophy, sciences (biological or physical), social science, public speaking. **Classes:** Most classes have 10–19 students. Most lab/discussion sections have 10–19 students. **Majors with Highest Enrollment:** Business/commerce, nursing/registered nurse training (RN, ASN, BSN, MSN), special education. **Disciplines with Highest Percentage of Degrees Awarded:** Education 22%, business/marketing 16%, health professions and related sciences 11%, public administration and social services 8%, history 7%. **Special Study Options:** Accelerated program, cooperative education program, cross-registration, double major, dual enrollment, exchange student program (domestic), independent study, internships, liberal arts/career combination, study abroad, teacher certification program.

FACILITIES

Housing: Coed dorms, women's dorms, special housing for disabled students. **Special Academic Facilities/Equipment:** Art gallery, language lab, music hall, nursing labs. **Computers:** 100% of public computers are PCs, network access in dorm rooms, network access in dorm lounges, remote student-access to Web through college's connection.

CAMPUS LIFE

Activities: Choral groups, dance, drama/theater, literary magazine, music ensembles, musical theater, student government, student newspaper, yearbook. **Organizations:** 37 registered organizations, 2 honor societies, 2 religious organizations. 2 fraternities (3% men join), 1 sorority (6% women join). **Athletics (Intercollegiate):** *Men:* Baseball, basketball, football, golf, soccer, wrestling. *Women:* Basketball, golf, soccer, softball, volleyball.

ADMISSIONS

Freshman Academic Profile: 8% in top 10% of high school class, 18% in top 25% of high school class, 51% in top 50% of high school class. 75% from public high schools. SAT Math middle 50% range 360–550. SAT Critical Reading middle 50% range 350–530. SAT Writing middle 50% range 290–520. ACT middle 50% range 17–22. TOEFL required of all international applicants, minimum paper TOEFL 550, minimum computer TOEFL 213. **Basis for Candidate Selection:** *Very important factors considered include:* Academic GPA, rigor of secondary school record, standardized test scores. *Important factors considered include:* Character/personal qualities, class rank, extracurricular activities. *Other factors considered include:* Application essay, interview, recommendation(s), volunteer work, work experience. **Freshman Admission Requirements:** High school diploma is required, and GED is accepted. *Academic units recommended:* 4 English, 3 math, 3 science (2 science labs), 2 foreign language, 2 social studies, 3 history. **Freshman Admission Statistics:** 1,004 applied, 56% admitted, 31% enrolled. **Transfer Admission Requirements:** College transcript(s). Minimum college GPA of 2.0 required. Lowest grade transferable C. **General Admission Information:** Regular notification is rolling. Nonfall registration accepted. Admission may be deferred for a maximum of 1 year. Credit and/or placement offered for CEEB Advanced Placement tests.

COSTS AND FINANCIAL AID

Annual tuition $15,500. Room and board $5,998. Required fees $250. Average book expense $775. **Required Forms and Deadlines:** FAFSA. Financial aid filing deadline 5/1. **Notification of Awards:** Applicants will be notified of awards on a rolling basis beginning on or about 2/1. **Types of Aid:** *Need-based scholarships/grants:* Pell, SEOG, state scholarships/grants, private scholarships, the school's own gift aid, Federal Nursing Scholarships. *Loans:* FFEL Subsidized Stafford, FFEL Unsubsidized Stafford, FFEL PLUS, Federal Perkins. **Student Employment:** Federal Work-Study Program available. Institutional employment available. **Financial Aid Statistics:** 90% freshmen, 91% undergrads receive need-based scholarship or grant aid. 71% freshmen, 78% undergrads receive need-based self-help aid. 95% freshmen, 97% undergrads receive any aid. Highest amount earned per year from on-campus jobs $945.

MADONNA UNIVERSITY

This private school, affiliated with the Roman Catholic Church, was founded in 1947. It has a 49-acre campus.

RATINGS

Admissions Selectivity Rating: 61   **Fire Safety Rating:** 60*   **Green Rating:** 60*

STUDENTS AND FACULTY

Enrollment: 2,910. **Student Body:** 77% female, 23% male, 3% out-of-state. African American 3%, Caucasian 19%. **Retention and Graduation:** 68% freshmen return for sophomore year. 18% freshmen graduate within 4 years. 48% grads go on to further study within 1 year. **Faculty:** 100% faculty teach undergrads.

ACADEMICS

Degrees: Associate, bachelor's, master's. **Academic Requirements:** Arts/fine arts, computer literacy, English (including composition), history, humanities, mathematics, philosophy, sciences (biological or physical), social science, religious studies. **Special Study Options:** Cooperative education program, cross-registration, distance learning, double major, dual enrollment, English as a second language (ESL), honors program, independent study, internships, liberal arts/career combination, student-designed major, study abroad, teacher certification program, credit for experiential learning.

FACILITIES

Housing: Men's dorms, women's dorms, special housing for disabled students, special housing for international students. **Special Academic Facilities/Equipment:** Paraprofessional training institute, psycho-educational center. **Computers:** Remote student-access to Web through college's connection.

CAMPUS LIFE

Activities: Choral groups, literary magazine, music ensembles, student government, student newspaper, television station. **Organizations:** 18 registered organizations, 8 honor societies, 1 religious organization. **Athletics (Intercollegiate):** *Men:* Baseball, basketball, soccer. *Women:* Basketball, soccer, softball, volleyball.

ADMISSIONS

Freshman Academic Profile: 22% in top 10% of high school class, 47% in top 25% of high school class, 89% in top 50% of high school class. ACT middle 50% range 17–22. TOEFL required of all international applicants, minimum paper TOEFL 540. **Basis for Candidate Selection:** *Very important factors considered include:* Rigor of secondary school record. *Important factors considered include:* Application essay, character/personal qualities, class rank, interview, standardized test scores. *Other factors considered include:* Alumni/ae relation, extracurricular activities, recommendation(s), religious affiliation/commitment, talent/ability, volunteer work, work experience. **Freshman Admission Requirements:** High school diploma is required, and GED is accepted. *Academic units required:* 3 English, 2 math, 2 science, 3 social studies. *Academic units recommended:* 2 foreign language. **Freshman Admission Statistics:** 440 applied, 26% enrolled. **Transfer Admission Requirements:** High school transcript, college transcript(s). Minimum college GPA of 2.0 required. Lowest grade transferable C. **General Admission Information:** Regular application deadline rolling. Regular notification is rolling. Nonfall registration accepted. Common Application accepted. Neither credit nor placement offered for CEEB Advanced Placement tests.

COSTS AND FINANCIAL AID

Annual tuition $6,610. Room & board $4,676. Required fees $100. Average book expense $580. **Required Forms and Deadlines:** FAFSA. Financial aid filing deadline 3/30. **Notification of Awards:** Applicants will be notified of awards on a rolling basis beginning on or about 3/1. **Types of Aid:** *Need-based scholarships/grants:* Pell, SEOG, state scholarships/grants, private scholarships, the school's own gift aid. *Loans:* Direct Subsidized Stafford, Direct Unsubsidized Stafford, Direct PLUS, Federal Perkins. **Student Employment:** Federal Work-Study Program available. Institutional employment available. Off-campus job opportunities are good. **Financial Aid Statistics:** Highest amount earned per year from on-campus jobs $1,200.

MAHARISHI UNIVERSITY OF MANAGEMENT

1000 North Fourth Street, Fairfield, IA 52557
Phone: 641-472-1110 **E-mail:** admissions@mum.edu
Fax: 641-472-1179 **Website:** www.mum.edu **ACT Code:** 1317
Financial Aid Phone: 641-472-1156

This private school was founded in 1971. It has a 242-acre campus.

RATINGS

Admissions Selectivity Rating: 74   **Fire Safety Rating:** 60*   **Green Rating:** 60*

STUDENTS AND FACULTY

Enrollment: 226. **Student Body:** 43% female, 57% male, 44% out-of-state, 44% international. African American 2%, Asian 4%, Caucasian 47%. **Retention and Graduation:** 64% freshmen return for sophomore year. 40% freshmen graduate within 4 years. 84% grads go on to further study within 1 year. **Faculty:** Student/faculty ratio 11:1. 44 full-time faculty, 68% hold PhDs. 100% faculty teach undergrads.

ACADEMICS

Degrees: Associate, bachelor's, certificate, doctoral, master's. **Academic Requirements:** Arts/fine arts, computer literacy, English (including composition), foreign languages, humanities, mathematics, sciences (biological or physical). All new students take a foundation course, the science of creative intelligence. All entering undergraduates take a special series of courses called natural law seminars, which span the full range of human knowledge, from the arts to the sciences to the humanities. Courses are on a block system, each block being 2 to 4 weeks long. **Classes:** Most classes have fewer than 10 students. **Majors with Highest Enrollment:** Alternative and complementary medicine and medical systems, business administration/management, fine/studio arts. **Disciplines with Highest Percentage of Degrees Awarded:** Business/marketing 30%, visual and performing arts 20%, health professions and related sciences 16%, biological/life sciences 7%, mathematics 7%, social sciences 7%, English 5%. **Special Study Options:** Double major, exchange student program (domestic), honors program, independent study, internships, study abroad, teacher certification program. Rotating University: several 1-month blocks out of each academic year, a course is offered abroad (e.g., students spend a month with professor studying art in Italy, literature in Switzerland, or business in Japan).

FACILITIES

Housing: Men's dorms, women's dorms, apartments for married students, apartments for single students, special housing for disabled students, apartments for students with dependent children, quiet dorms. **Special Academic Facilities/Equipment:** Art gallery, scanning electron microscope, real-time cell-imaging computer system, DNA synthesizer, rock-climbing wall. **Computers:** 60% of public computers are PCs, 25% of public computers are Macs, 15% of public computers are UNIX, network access in dorm rooms, remote student-access to Web through college's connection.

CAMPUS LIFE

Activities: Choral groups, dance, drama/theater, music ensembles, musical theater, radio station, student government, student newspaper, yearbook. **Organizations:** 25 registered organizations, 3 honor societies, 1 religious organization. **Athletics (Intercollegiate):** *Men:* Golf. *Women:* Golf.

ADMISSIONS

Freshman Academic Profile: SAT Math middle 50% range 470–620. SAT Critical Reading middle 50% range 510–640. ACT middle 50% range 19–25. TOEFL required of all international applicants, minimum paper TOEFL 550, minimum computer TOEFL 213. **Basis for Candidate Selection:** *Very important factors considered include:* Application essay, character/personal qualities, interview, recommendation(s). *Important factors considered include:* Extracurricular activities, rigor of secondary school record, standardized test scores, volunteer work. *Other factors considered include:* Alumni/ae relation, class rank, state residency, talent/ability, work experience. **Freshman Admission Requirements:** High school diploma is required, and GED is accepted. *Academic units recommended:* 4 English, 3 math, 3 science, 2 foreign language, 3 social studies. **Freshman Admission Statistics:** 51 applied, 67% admitted, 88% enrolled. **Transfer Admission Requirements:** High school transcript, college transcript(s), essay or personal statement, interview. Minimum college GPA of 2.5 required. Lowest grade transferable C. **General Admission Information:** Application fee $25. Regular notification is rolling. Nonfall registration accepted. Admission may be deferred for a maximum of 1 semester. Common Application accepted. Credit offered for CEEB Advanced Placement tests.

COSTS AND FINANCIAL AID

Annual tuition $24,000. Room & board $6,000. Required fees $430. Average book expense $800. **Required Forms and Deadlines:** FAFSA. Financial aid filing deadline 4/15. **Notification of Awards:** Applicants will be notified of awards on a rolling basis beginning on or about 3/1. **Types of Aid:** *Need-based scholarships/grants:* Pell, SEOG, state scholarships/grants, private scholarships, the school's own gift aid, Federal Work Study, Veterans, Benefits. *Loans:* FFEL Subsidized Stafford, FFEL Unsubsidized Stafford, FFEL PLUS, Federal Perkins, college/university loans from institutional funds. **Student Employment:** Federal Work-Study Program available. Off-campus job opportunities are fair. **Financial Aid Statistics:** 86% freshmen, 95% undergrads receive need-based scholarship or grant aid. 86% freshmen, 94% undergrads receive need-based self-help aid. 93% freshmen, 98% undergrads receive any aid.

MAINE COLLEGE OF ART

97 Spring Street, Portland, ME 04101
Phone: 207-775-3052 **E-mail:** admissions@meca.edu **CEEB Code:** 3701
Fax: 207-772-5069 **Website:** www.meca.edu **ACT Code:** 6908
Financial Aid Phone: 207-775-5157

This private school was founded in 1882.

RATINGS

Admissions Selectivity Rating: 75 **Fire Safety Rating:** 60* **Green Rating:** 60*

STUDENTS AND FACULTY

Enrollment: 425. **Student Body:** 62% female, 38% male, 2% international (7 countries represented). Caucasian 49%, Hispanic 2%. **Retention and Graduation:** 73% freshmen return for sophomore year. 32% freshmen graduate within 4 years. **Faculty:** Student/faculty ratio 10:1. 30 full-time faculty, 93% hold PhDs. 100% faculty teach undergrads.

ACADEMICS

Degrees: Bachelor's, master's. **Academic Requirements:** Arts/fine arts, English (including composition), humanities, mathematics, sciences (biological or physical), social science, tool technology. **Classes:** Most classes have 10–19 students. **Disciplines with Highest Percentage of Degrees Awarded:** Visual and performing arts 100%. **Special Study Options:** Cross-registration, double major, exchange student program (domestic), independent study, internships, student-designed major, study abroad, teacher certification program, mobility program with 36 AICAD (Associated Independent Colleges of Art and Design) institutions in U.S.A. and Canada, cross-registration program with 4 other colleges and universities in the greater Portland area, BFA credit available through Provincetown, MA, Fine Arts Work Center.

FACILITIES

Housing: Coed dorms, cooperative housing. **Special Academic Facilities/Equipment:** Institute of Contemporary Art at Maine College of Art, June Fitzpatrick Gallery, ArtMart (art supply store). **Computers:** 10% of public computers are PCs, 90% of public computers are Macs, network access in dorm lounges, remote student-access to Web through college's connection.

CAMPUS LIFE

Activities: Student government, student-run film society.

ADMISSIONS

Freshman Academic Profile: 8% in top 10% of high school class, 19% in top 25% of high school class, 48% in top 50% of high school class. SAT Math middle 50% range 440–560. SAT Critical Reading middle 50% range 480–610. ACT middle 50% range 17–23. TOEFL required of all international applicants, minimum paper TOEFL 500, minimum computer TOEFL 173. **Basis for Candidate Selection:** *Very important factors considered include:* Rigor of secondary school record, talent/ability. *Important factors considered include:* Application essay, character/personal qualities, recommendation(s). *Other factors considered include:* Alumni/ae relation, class rank, extracurricular activities, geographical residence, interview, racial/ethnic status, standardized test scores, state residency, volunteer work, work experience. **Freshman Admission Requirements:** High school diploma is required, and GED is accepted. *Academic units recommended:* 4 English, 3 math, 3 science, 2 foreign language, 4 social studies, 4 history, 3 academic electives, 4 art. **Freshman Admission Statistics:** 440 applied, 64% admitted, 35% enrolled. **Transfer Admission Requirements:** College transcript(s), essay or personal statement, statement of good standing from prior institution(s). Lowest grade transferable C. **General Admission Information:** Application fee $40. Regular notification rolling within 4 weeks of completion. Nonfall registration accepted. Admission may be deferred for a maximum of 1 year. Common Application accepted. Credit and/or placement offered for CEEB Advanced Placement tests.

COSTS AND FINANCIAL AID

Annual tuition $20,600. Room and board $8,550. Required fees $520. **Required Forms and Deadlines:** FAFSA. Financial aid filing deadline 4/15. **Notification of Awards:** Applicants will be notified of awards on a rolling basis beginning on or about 2/15. **Types of Aid:** *Need-based scholarships/grants:* Pell, SEOG, state scholarships/grants, the school's own gift aid. *Loans:* FFEL Subsidized Stafford, FFEL Unsubsidized Stafford, FFEL PLUS, Federal Perkins. **Financial Aid Statistics:** 82% freshmen, 81% undergrads receive need-based scholarship or grant aid. 76% freshmen, 74% undergrads receive need-based self-help aid.

MAINE MARITIME ACADEMY

66 Pleasant Street, Castine, ME 04420
Phone: 207-326-2206 **E-mail:** admissions@mma.edu **CEEB Code:** 3505
Fax: 207-326-2515 **Website:** www.mainemaritime.edu **ACT Code:** 1648
Financial Aid Phone: 207-326-2339

This public school was founded in 1941. It has a 35-acre campus.

RATINGS
Admissions Selectivity Rating: 60*   **Fire Safety Rating:** 60*   **Green Rating:** 60*

STUDENTS AND FACULTY
Enrollment: 814. **Student Body:** 15% female, 85% male, 39% out-of-state. Caucasian 95%, Hispanic 1%. **Retention and Graduation:** 75% freshmen return for sophomore year. 2% grads go on to further study within 1 year. 1% grads pursue arts and sciences degrees. 1% grads pursue law degrees. **Faculty:** Student/faculty ratio 12:1. 55 full-time faculty. 100% faculty teach undergrads.

ACADEMICS
Degrees: Associate, bachelor's, master's. **Academic Requirements:** Computer literacy, English (including composition), humanities, mathematics, sciences (biological or physical). **Classes:** Most classes have 10–19 students. Most lab/discussion sections have 10–19 students. **Disciplines with Highest Percentage of Degrees Awarded:** Transportation and materials moving 44%, engineering technologies 25%, business/marketing 10%, engineering 10%, physical sciences 10%, interdisciplinary studies 2%. **Special Study Options:** Cooperative education program, internships, annual training cruises.

FACILITIES
Housing: Coed dorms, apartments for single students. **Computers:** Network access in dorm rooms, online administrative functions (other than registration), remote student-access to Web through college's connection. Undergraduates are required to own a computer.

CAMPUS LIFE
Activities: Concert band, drama/theater, jazz band, marching band, student government, yearbook. **Organizations:** 28 registered organizations. **Athletics (Intercollegiate):** *Men:* Basketball, cross-country, football, golf, lacrosse, sailing, soccer. *Women:* Basketball, cross-country, golf, sailing, soccer, softball.

ADMISSIONS
Freshman Academic Profile: 28% in top 10% of high school class, 48% in top 25% of high school class, 74% in top 50% of high school class. TOEFL required of all international applicants, minimum paper TOEFL 550, minimum computer TOEFL 213. **Basis for Candidate Selection:** *Very important factors considered include:* Character/personal qualities, rigor of secondary school record. *Important factors considered include:* Interview. *Other factors considered include:* Alumni/ae relation, class rank, extracurricular activities, recommendation(s), talent/ability, volunteer work, work experience. **Freshman Admission Requirements:** High school diploma is required, and GED is accepted. *Academic units required:* 4 English, 3 math, 2 science (2 science labs). *Academic units recommended:* 3 math, 3 science (3 science labs), 2 foreign language, 2 computer literacy. **Freshman Admission Statistics:** 613 applied, 76% admitted, 49% enrolled. **Transfer Admission Requirements:** High school transcript, college transcript(s), standardized test score, statement of good standing from prior institution(s). Minimum college GPA of 2.0 required. Lowest grade transferable C. **General Admission Information:** Application fee $15. Early decision application deadline 12/20. Regular application deadline 7/1. Regular notification is rolling. Nonfall registration accepted. Admission may be deferred for a maximum of 1 year. Common Application not accepted. Credit offered for CEEB Advanced Placement tests.

COSTS AND FINANCIAL AID
Annual in-state tuition $4,739. Out-of-state tuition $8,774. Room & board $5,227. Required fees $715. Average book expense $700. **Types of Aid:** *Loans:* FFEL Subsidized Stafford, FFEL PLUS. **Student Employment:** Federal Work-Study Program available. Institutional employment available. Off-campus job opportunities are fair. **Financial Aid Statistics:** Highest amount earned per year from on-campus jobs $1,200.

MALONE COLLEGE

515 Twenty-fifth Street NW, Canton, OH 44709
Phone: 330-471-8145 **E-mail:** admissions@malone.edu **CEEB Code:** 1439
Fax: 330-471-8149 **Website:** www.malone.edu **ACT Code:** 3289
Financial Aid Phone: 330-471-8162

This private school, affiliated with the Evangelical Friends Church/ Eastern Region Church, was founded in 1892. It has a 78-acre campus.

RATINGS
Admissions Selectivity Rating: 78   **Fire Safety Rating:** 74   **Green Rating:** 61

STUDENTS AND FACULTY
Enrollment: 1,875. **Student Body:** 60% female, 40% male, 12% out-of-state, 1% international (20 countries represented). African American 6%, Caucasian 91%, Hispanic 1%. **Retention and Graduation:** 74% freshmen return for sophomore year. 40% freshmen graduate within 4 years. 18% grads go on to further study within 1 year. 11% grads pursue arts and sciences degrees. 1% grads pursue business degrees. 1% grads pursue law degrees. **Faculty:** Student/faculty ratio 14:1. 108 full-time faculty, 69% hold PhDs. 91% faculty teach undergrads.

ACADEMICS
Degrees: Bachelor's, master's, post-bachelor's certificate. **Academic Requirements:** Arts/fine arts, English (including composition), history, humanities, mathematics, philosophy, sciences (biological or physical), social science, biblical literature/theology, communication skills, health/wellness, cross-cultural studies, global connections. **Classes:** Most classes have 10–19 students. Most lab/discussion sections have 10–19 students. **Majors with Highest Enrollment:** Business administration/management, early childhood education and teaching, nursing/registered nurse training (RN, ASN, BSN, MSN). **Disciplines with Highest Percentage of Degrees Awarded:** Business/marketing 40%, health professions and related sciences 18%, education 15%, theology and religious vocations 6%, parks and recreation 4%, communications/journalism 4%. **Special Study Options:** Accelerated program, cross-registration, distance learning, double major, dual enrollment, exchange student program (domestic), honors program, independent study, internships, student-designed major, study abroad, teacher certification program, weekend college, 2 degree-completion programs for adults, management, nursing. Weekend college is only for degree-completion programs and graduate programs.

FACILITIES
Housing: Men's dorms, women's dorms. **Special Academic Facilities/ Equipment:** Child development center. **Computers:** 100% of classrooms are wired, 80% of classrooms are wireless, 90% of public computers are PCs, 10% of public computers are Macs, network access in dorm rooms, network access in dorm lounges, online registration, online administrative functions (other than registration), remote student-access to Web through college's connection.

CAMPUS LIFE
Activities: Choral groups, concert band, dance, drama/theater, jazz band, literary magazine, marching band, music ensembles, musical theater, radio station, student government, student newspaper, yearbook. **Organizations:** 47 registered organizations, 10 honor societies, 11 religious organizations. **Athletics (Intercollegiate):** *Men:* Baseball, basketball, cheerleading, cross-country, football, golf, soccer, tennis, track/field (indoor), track/field (outdoor). *Women:* Basketball, cheerleading, cross-country, golf, soccer, softball, tennis, track/field (indoor), track/field (outdoor), volleyball. **Environmental Initiatives:** Recycling

ADMISSIONS
Freshman Academic Profile: 23% in top 10% of high school class, 51% in top 25% of high school class, 79% in top 50% of high school class. 80% from public high schools. SAT Math middle 50% range 470–570. SAT Critical Reading middle 50% range 480–580. SAT Writing middle 50% range 490–590. ACT middle 50% range 20–25. TOEFL required of all international applicants, minimum paper TOEFL 550, minimum computer TOEFL 213. **Basis for Candidate Selection:** *Very important factors considered include:* Academic GPA, character/personal qualities, rigor of secondary school record, standardized test scores. *Important factors considered include:* Application essay, class rank, level of applicant's interest, recommendation(s), religious affiliation/ commitment, talent/ability. *Other factors considered include:* Alumni/ae relation, extracurricular activities, interview, racial/ethnic status, volunteer work. **Freshman Admission Requirements:** High school diploma is required, and GED is accepted. *Academic units required:* 4 English, 3 math, 3 science (1 science lab), 2 foreign language, 2 social studies, 1 history, 2 academic electives, 1 fine arts. **Freshman Admission Statistics:** 1,070 applied, 80% admitted,

40% enrolled. **Transfer Admission Requirements:** High school transcript, college transcript(s), essay or personal statement, statement of good standing from prior institution(s). Minimum college GPA of 2.0 required. **General Admission Information:** Application fee $20. Regular application deadline 7/1. Regular notification is rolling. Nonfall registration accepted. Admission may be deferred for a maximum of 2 years. Credit and/or placement offered for CEEB Advanced Placement tests.

COSTS AND FINANCIAL AID

Annual tuition $18,600. Room and board $6,400. Required fees $270. Average book expense $930. **Required Forms and Deadlines:** FAFSA, verification worksheet and tax forms if chosen for verification. Financial aid filing deadline 7/31. **Notification of Awards:** Applicants will be notified of awards on a rolling basis beginning on or about 3/1. **Types of Aid:** *Need-based scholarships/grants:* Pell, SEOG, state scholarships/grants, private scholarships, the school's own gift aid. *Loans:* FFEL Subsidized Stafford, FFEL Unsubsidized Stafford, FFEL PLUS, Federal Perkins, state loans, college/university loans from institutional funds, private loans. **Financial Aid Statistics:** 78% freshmen, 72% undergrads receive need-based scholarship or grant aid. 72% freshmen, 68% undergrads receive need-based self-help aid. 19 freshmen, 69 undergrads receive athletic scholarships. 100% freshmen, 77% undergrads receive any aid. Highest amount earned per year from on-campus jobs $2,500.

MANCHESTER COLLEGE

604 East College Avenue, North Manchester, IN 46962
Phone: 260-982-5055 **E-mail:** Admitinfo@manchester.edu **CEEB Code:** 1440
Fax: 260-982-5239 **Website:** www.manchester.edu **ACT Code:** 1222
Financial Aid Phone: 260-982-5066

This private school, affiliated with the Church of Brethren, was founded in 1889. It has a 124-acre campus.

RATINGS
Admissions Selectivity Rating: 60*   **Fire Safety Rating:** 60*   **Green Rating:** 60*

STUDENTS AND FACULTY
Enrollment: 1,018. **Student Body:** 51% female, 49% male, 12% out-of-state, 4% international (30 countries represented). African American 3%, Asian 1%, Caucasian 87%, Hispanic 2%. **Retention and Graduation:** 25% grads go on to further study within 1 year. 8% grads pursue arts and sciences degrees. 11% grads pursue business degrees. 1% grads pursue law degrees. 2% grads pursue medical degrees. **Faculty:** Student/faculty ratio 14:1. 72 full-time faculty, 89% hold PhDs. 100% faculty teach undergrads.

ACADEMICS
Degrees: Associate, bachelor's, master's. **Academic Requirements:** Arts/fine arts, Christian tradition, cultural studies, English (including composition), history, humanities, mathematics, non-European studies, philosophy, sciences (biological or physical), social science. **Classes:** Most classes have 10–19 students. **Majors with Highest Enrollment:** Accounting and business/management; biochemistry; education. **Disciplines with Highest Percentage of Degrees Awarded:** Education 22%, business/marketing 19%, health professions and related sciences 11%, psychology 7%, history 6%. **Special Study Options:** Cross-registration, double major, dual enrollment, exchange student program (domestic), honor program, independent study, internships, liberal arts/career combination, student-designed major, study abroad, teacher certification program.

FACILITIES
Housing: Coed dorms, women's dorms, apartments for married students, apartments for single students, special housing for disabled students. **Special Academic Facilities/Equipment:** Language lab, observatory, environmental center and labs. **Computers:** 40% of classrooms are wireless, 100% of public computers are PCs, network access in dorm rooms, network access in dorm lounges, remote student-access to Web through college's connection.

CAMPUS LIFE
Activities: Choral groups, concert band, dance, drama/theater, jazz band, literary magazine, music ensembles, musical theater, pep band, radio station, student government, student newspaper, symphony orchestra, yearbook. **Organizations:** 47 registered organizations, 3 honor societies, 5 religious organizations. **Athletics (Intercollegiate):** *Men:* Baseball, basketball, cheerleading, cross-country, football, golf, soccer, tennis, track/field (outdoor), wrestling. *Women:* Basketball, cheerleading, cross-country, golf, soccer, softball, tennis, track/field (outdoor), volleyball.

ADMISSIONS
Freshman Academic Profile: 98% from public high schools. SAT Math middle 50% range 455–578. SAT Critical Reading middle 50% range 440–550. SAT Writing middle 50% range 420–548. ACT middle 50% range 19–24. TOEFL required of all international applicants, minimum paper TOEFL 550, minimum computer TOEFL 213. **Basis for Candidate Selection:** *Very important factors considered include:* Rigor of secondary school record. *Important factors considered include:* Academic GPA, recommendation(s), standardized test scores. *Other factors considered include:* Alumni/ae relation, character/personal qualities, class rank, interview, religious affiliation/commitment, talent/ability. **Freshman Admission Requirements:** High school diploma is required, and GED is accepted. *Academic units required:* 4 English, 2 math, 2 science (2 science labs), 2 foreign language, 2 social studies, 1 history, 1 academic elective, *Academic units recommended:* 4 English, 3 math, 3 science (3 science labs), 2 foreign language, 2 social studies, 2 history, 2 academic electives. **Transfer Admission Requirements:** High school transcript, college transcript(s), standardized test score, statement of good standing from prior institution(s). Minimum college GPA of 2 required. Lowest grade transferable C. **General Admission Information:** Application fee $25. Regular notification is rolling. Nonfall registration accepted. Admission may be deferred for a maximum of 1 year. Credit and/or placement offered for CEEB Advanced Placement tests.

COSTS AND FINANCIAL AID
Annual tuition $22,000. Room and board $8,100. Required fees $720. Average book expense $1,000. **Required Forms and Deadlines:** FAFSA. **Notification of Awards:** Applicants will be notified of awards on a rolling basis beginning on or about 3/1. **Types of Aid:** *Need-based scholarships/grants:* Pell, SEOG, state scholarships/grants, private scholarships, the school's own gift aid. *Loans:* FFEL Subsidized Stafford, FFEL Unsubsidized Stafford, FFEL PLUS, Federal Perkins. **Financial Aid Statistics:** 83% freshmen, 82% undergrads receive need-based scholarship or grant aid. 83% freshmen, 82% undergrads receive need-based self-help aid. 100% freshmen, 98% undergrads receive any aid. Highest amount earned per year from on-campus jobs $2,000.

See page 1252.

MANHATTAN CHRISTIAN COLLEGE

1415 Anderson, Manhattan, KS 66502-4081
Phone: 877-246-4622 **E-mail:** admit@mccks.edu
Fax: 785-776-9251 **Website:** www.mccks.edu **ACT Code:** 1436
Financial Aid Phone: 785-539-3571

This private school, affiliated with the Christian (nondenominational) Church, was founded in 1927. It has a 1-acre campus.

RATINGS
Admissions Selectivity Rating: 74   **Fire Safety Rating:** 60*   **Green Rating:** 60*

STUDENTS AND FACULTY
Enrollment: 310. **Student Body:** 51% female, 49% male, 35% out-of-state. African American 4%, Caucasian 99%, Hispanic 2%. **Retention and Graduation:** 51% freshmen return for sophomore year. 3% grads go on to further study within 1 year. **Faculty:** Student/faculty ratio 15:1. 10 full-time faculty, 40% hold PhDs. 100% faculty teach undergrads.

ACADEMICS
Degrees: Associate, bachelor's, certificate, post-bachelor's certificate. **Academic Requirements:** English (including composition), history, humanities, mathematics, sciences (biological or physical), social science, Bible, leadership. **Classes:** Most classes have 10–19 students. **Majors with Highest Enrollment:** Bible/biblical studies, management science, pastoral counseling and specialized ministries. **Disciplines with Highest Percentage of Degrees Awarded:** Business/marketing 36%. **Special Study Options:** Double major, dual enrollment, internships.

FACILITIES
Housing: Men's dorms, women's dorms, apartments for married students, apartments for single students. **Computers:** 60% of classrooms are wireless, 100% of public computers are PCs, network access in dorm rooms, network access in dorm lounges, support for handheld computing, remote student-access to Web through college's connection.

CAMPUS LIFE
Activities: Dance, music ensembles, student government, yearbook. **Organizations:** 2 honor societies, 10 religious organizations. **Athletics (Intercollegiate):** *Men:* Baseball, basketball, soccer. *Women:* Basketball, soccer, volleyball.

ADMISSIONS

Freshman Academic Profile: 20% in top 10% of high school class, 22% in top 25% of high school class, 94% in top 50% of high school class. 95% from public high schools. ACT middle 50% range 19–25. TOEFL required of all international applicants, minimum paper TOEFL 550, minimum computer TOEFL 213. **Basis for Candidate Selection:** *Very important factors considered include:* Character/personal qualities, recommendation(s), religious affiliation/commitment. *Important factors considered include:* Application essay, rigor of secondary school record, standardized test scores, talent/ability. *Other factors considered include:* Extracurricular activities, interview, volunteer work. **Freshman Admission Requirements:** High school diploma is required, and GED is accepted. *Academic units recommended:* 4 English, 2 math, 2 science. **Freshman Admission Statistics:** 155 applied, 79% admitted, 66% enrolled. **Transfer Admission Requirements:** College transcript(s), essay or personal statement. Minimum college GPA of 2.0 required. Lowest grade transferable C. **General Admission Information:** Application fee $25. Regular application deadline 8/1. Regular notification is rolling. Nonfall registration accepted. Admission may be deferred for a maximum of 1 year. Common Application not accepted. Credit and/or placement offered for CEEB Advanced Placement tests.

COSTS AND FINANCIAL AID

Annual tuition $8,826. Room & board $5,224. Required fees $110. Average book expense $1,150. **Required Forms and Deadlines:** FAFSA. Financial aid filing deadline 4/1. **Notification of Awards:** Applicants will be notified of awards on a rolling basis beginning on or about 5/1. **Types of Aid:** *Need-based scholarships/grants:* Pell, SEOG, state scholarships/grants, private scholarships, the school's own gift aid. *Loans:* Direct Subsidized Stafford, Direct Unsubsidized Stafford, Direct PLUS, Federal Perkins. **Student Employment:** Federal Work-Study Program available. Off-campus job opportunities are good. **Financial Aid Statistics:** 33% freshmen, 70% undergrads receive need-based scholarship or grant aid. 48% freshmen, 76% undergrads receive need-based self-help aid.

MANHATTAN COLLEGE

Manhattan College Parkway, Riverdale, NY 10471
Phone: 718-862-7200 **E-mail:** admit@manhattan.edu **CEEB Code:** 2395
Fax: 718-862-8019 **Website:** www.manhattan.edu
Financial Aid Phone: 718-862-7100

This private school, affiliated with the Roman Catholic Church, was founded in 1853. It has a 22-acre campus.

RATINGS
Admissions Selectivity Rating: 85   **Fire Safety Rating:** 80   **Green Rating:** 67

STUDENTS AND FACULTY

Enrollment: 2,854. **Student Body:** 47% female, 53% male, 15% out-of-state, 2% international (39 countries represented). African American 5%, Asian 4%, Caucasian 59%, Hispanic 8%. **Retention and Graduation:** 15% grads go on to further study within 1 year. 15% grads pursue arts and sciences degrees. 4% grads pursue business degrees. 2% grads pursue law degrees. 4% grads pursue medical degrees. **Faculty:** Student/faculty ratio 13:1. 181 full-time faculty, 93% hold PhDs. 100% faculty teach undergrads.

ACADEMICS

Degrees: Bachelor's, master's. **Academic Requirements:** Arts/fine arts, computer literacy, English (including composition), foreign languages, history, humanities, mathematics, philosophy, sciences (biological or physical). **Classes:** Most classes have 20–29 students. Most lab/discussion sections have 10–19 students. **Majors with Highest Enrollment:** Civil engineering, marketing/marketing management, special education and teaching. **Disciplines with Highest Percentage of Degrees Awarded:** Business/marketing 36%, education 22%, engineering 15%, computer and information sciences 9%, biological/life sciences 6%. **Special Study Options:** Cooperative education program, cross-registration, double major, exchange student program (domestic), honors program, independent study, internships, liberal arts/career combination, student-designed major, study abroad, teacher certification program.

FACILITIES

Housing: Coed dorms, apartments for single students. **Special Academic Facilities/Equipment:** Research and learning center, plant morphogenesis lab, 24-hour Internet cafe. **Computers:** Network access in dorm rooms, network access in dorm lounges, online registration, online administrative functions

(other than registration), remote student-access to Web through college's connection.

CAMPUS LIFE

Activities: Choral groups, concert band, dance, drama/theater, jazz band, literary magazine, music ensembles, musical theater, radio station, student government, student newspaper, symphony orchestra, television station, yearbook. **Organizations:** 64 registered organizations, 30 honor societies, 2 religious organizations. 3 fraternities (8% men join), 2 sororities (7% women join). **Athletics (Intercollegiate):** *Men:* Baseball, basketball, cross-country, golf, lacrosse, soccer, tennis, track/field (indoor), track/field (outdoor). *Women:* Basketball, cross-country, lacrosse, soccer, softball, swimming, tennis, track/field (indoor), track/field (outdoor), volleyball.

ADMISSIONS

Freshman Academic Profile: 19% in top 10% of high school class, 52% in top 25% of high school class, 86% in top 50% of high school class. 60% from public high schools. SAT Math middle 50% range 520–620. SAT Critical Reading middle 50% range 510–600. TOEFL required of all international applicants, minimum paper TOEFL 550, minimum computer TOEFL 213. **Basis for Candidate Selection:** *Very important factors considered include:* Rigor of secondary school record, standardized test scores. *Important factors considered include:* Application essay, class rank, extracurricular activities, interview, recommendation(s). *Other factors considered include:* Alumni/ae relation, character/personal qualities, talent/ability, volunteer work, work experience. **Freshman Admission Requirements:** High school diploma is required, and GED is accepted. *Academic units required:* 4 English, 3 math, 2 science, 2 foreign language, 3 social studies, 2 academic electives. *Academic units recommended:* 4 English, 4 math, 3 science, 3 foreign language, 3 social studies. **Freshman Admission Statistics:** 5,078 applied, 52% admitted, 27% enrolled. **Transfer Admission Requirements:** College transcript(s). Minimum college GPA of 2.5 required. Lowest grade transferable C. **General Admission Information:** Application fee $50. Early decision application deadline 11/15. Regular notification is rolling. Nonfall registration accepted. Admission may be deferred for a maximum of 1 year. Credit and/or placement offered for CEEB Advanced Placement tests.

COSTS AND FINANCIAL AID

Annual tuition $21,640. Room & board $9,625. Required fees $1,600. Average book expense $1,000. **Required Forms and Deadlines:** FAFSA. Financial aid filing deadline 4/1. **Notification of Awards:** Applicants will be notified of awards on or about 3/1. **Types of Aid:** *Need-based scholarships/grants:* Pell, SEOG, state scholarships/grants, private scholarships, the school's own gift aid. *Loans:* Direct Subsidized Stafford, Direct Unsubsidized Stafford, Direct PLUS, FFEL Subsidized Stafford, FFEL Unsubsidized Stafford, FFEL PLUS, Federal Perkins. **Financial Aid Statistics:** 53% freshmen, 52% undergrads receive need-based scholarship or grant aid. 53% freshmen, 51% undergrads receive need-based self-help aid. 14 freshmen, 111 undergrads receive athletic scholarships. 87% freshmen, 76% undergrads receive any aid. Highest amount earned per year from on-campus jobs $1,500.

MANHATTAN SCHOOL OF MUSIC

120 Claremont Avenue, New York, NY 10027
Phone: 212-749-2802 **E-mail:** admission@msmnyc.edu **CEEB Code:** 2396
Fax: 212-749-3025 **Website:** www.msmnyc.edu **ACT Code:** 2809
Financial Aid Phone: 917-493-4463

This private school was founded in 1917. It has a 1-acre campus.

RATINGS
Admissions Selectivity Rating: 60*   **Fire Safety Rating:** 60*   **Green Rating:** 60*

STUDENTS AND FACULTY

Enrollment: 408. **Student Body:** 48% female, 52% male, 67% out-of-state, 20% international (27 countries represented). African American 3%, Asian 9%, Caucasian 44%, Hispanic 4%. **Retention and Graduation:** 82% freshmen return for sophomore year. 90% grads go on to further study within 1 year. 75% grads pursue arts and sciences degrees. 1% grads pursue business degrees. 1% grads pursue law degrees. 1% grads pursue medical degrees. **Faculty:** 95% faculty teach undergrads.

ACADEMICS

Degrees: Bachelor's, diploma, doctoral, master's, post-master's certificate. **Academic Requirements:** Arts/fine arts, history, humanities. **Disciplines with Highest Percentage of Degrees Awarded:** Visual and performing arts 100%. **Special Study Options:** Cross-registration, English as a second language (ESL), study abroad.

FACILITIES

Housing: Coed dorms. **Special Academic Facilities/Equipment:** Electronic music studios, electronic piano lab, recording studio, practice rooms, 1,000-seat auditorium, 3 recital halls. **Computers:** 100% of public computers are PCs, network access in dorm rooms, remote student-access to Web through college's connection.

CAMPUS LIFE

Activities: Choral groups, jazz band, music ensembles, musical theater, opera, student government, student newspaper, symphony orchestra. **Organizations:** 8 registered organizations.

ADMISSIONS

Freshman Academic Profile: 75% from public high schools. TOEFL required of all international applicants, minimum paper TOEFL 550, minimum computer TOEFL 213. **Basis for Candidate Selection:** *Very important factors considered include:* Interview, rigor of secondary school record, talent/ability. *Important factors considered include:* Application essay, character/personal qualities, extracurricular activities, recommendation(s), volunteer work. *Other factors considered include:* Alumni/ae relation, class rank, racial/ethnic status, standardized test scores, work experience. **Freshman Admission Requirements:** High school diploma is required, and GED is accepted. *Academic units required:* 2 English, 2 math, 2 science, 3 social studies, 3 history. *Academic units recommended:* 4 English, 3 math, 3 science, 4 foreign language, 4 social studies, 4 history. **Freshman Admission Statistics:** 794 applied, 40% admitted, 32% enrolled. **Transfer Admission Requirements:** College transcript(s), essay or personal statement, interview. Minimum college GPA of 3 required. Lowest grade transferable C. **General Admission Information:** Application fee $100. Regular application deadline 12/1. Regular notification 4/1. Nonfall registration not accepted. Admission may be deferred for a maximum of 2 semesters. Common Application not accepted. Credit offered for CEEB Advanced Placement tests.

COSTS AND FINANCIAL AID

Annual tuition $26,000. Room and board $14,250. Required fees $460. **Required Forms and Deadlines:** FAFSA, institution's own financial aid form, CSS/Financial Aid PROFILE. Financial aid filing deadline 3/1. **Notification of Awards:** Applicants will be notified of awards on or about 4/1. **Types of Aid:** *Need-based scholarships/grants:* Pell, SEOG, state scholarships/grants, the school's own gift aid. *Loans:* FFEL Subsidized Stafford, FFEL Unsubsidized Stafford, FFEL PLUS, Federal Perkins. **Student Employment:** Federal Work-Study Program available. Institutional employment available. Off-campus job opportunities are excellent. **Financial Aid Statistics:** 30% freshmen, 39% undergrads receive need-based scholarship or grant aid. 26% freshmen, 44% undergrads receive need-based self-help aid. 66% freshmen, 75% undergrads receive any aid. Highest amount earned per year from on-campus jobs $4,000.

MANHATTANVILLE COLLEGE

2900 Purchase Street, Admissions Office, Purchase, NY 10577
Phone: 914-323-5124 **E-mail:** admissions@mville.edu **CEEB Code:** 2397
Fax: 914-694-1732 **Website:** www.mville.edu **ACT Code:** 2800
Financial Aid Phone: 914-323-5357

This private school was founded in 1841. It has a 100-acre campus.

RATINGS

Admissions Selectivity Rating: 80   **Fire Safety Rating:** 60*   **Green Rating:** 88

STUDENTS AND FACULTY

Enrollment: 1,762. **Student Body:** 67% female, 33% male, 36% out-of-state, 8% international (59 countries represented). African American 8%, Asian 3%, Caucasian 59%, Hispanic 15%. **Retention and Graduation:** 74% freshmen return for sophomore year. 53% freshmen graduate within 4 years. **Faculty:** Student/faculty ratio 11:1. 94 full-time faculty, 97% hold PhDs. 100% faculty teach undergrads.

ACADEMICS

Degrees: Bachelor's, master's, post-bachelor's certificate, post-master's certificate. **Academic Requirements:** Arts/fine arts, English (including composition), foreign languages, humanities, sciences (biological or physical), social science, preceptorial, library and information skills, and English writing

competency. **Classes:** Most classes have 10–19 students. Most lab/discussion sections have 10–19 students. **Majors with Highest Enrollment:** Business administration/management, psychology, visual and performing arts. **Disciplines with Highest Percentage of Degrees Awarded:** Business/marketing 22%, psychology 17%, visual and performing arts 15%, social sciences 13%, history 13%, English 5%. **Special Study Options:** Accelerated program, cross-registration, distance learning, double major, English as a second language (ESL), exchange student program (domestic), honors program, independent study, internships, student-designed major, study abroad, teacher certification program, weekend college.

FACILITIES

Housing: Coed dorms, choices for people who prefer a substance-free area, suites for nontraditional and/or graduate students. **Special Academic Facilities/Equipment:** Art gallery, art and music studios, environmental park, English language institute, 2 electron microscopes, library. **Computers:** 7% of classrooms are wired, 96% of public computers are PCs, 3% of public computers are Macs, network access in dorm rooms, network access in dorm lounges, online registration, online administrative functions (other than registration), support for handheld computing, remote student-access to Web through college's connection.

CAMPUS LIFE

Activities: Choral groups, concert band, dance, drama/theater, jazz band, literary magazine, music ensembles, musical theater, opera, radio station, student government, student newspaper, student-run film society, symphony orchestra, television station, yearbook. **Organizations:** 48 registered organizations, 2 honor societies, 5 religious organizations. **Athletics (Intercollegiate):** *Men:* Baseball, basketball, golf, ice hockey, lacrosse, soccer, tennis. *Women:* Basketball, cheerleading, field hockey, ice hockey, lacrosse, soccer, softball, tennis, volleyball.

ADMISSIONS

Freshman Academic Profile: 21% in top 10% of high school class, 47% in top 25% of high school class, 80% in top 50% of high school class. SAT Math middle 50% range 500–610. SAT Critical Reading middle 50% range 500–620. ACT middle 50% range 20–25. TOEFL required of all international applicants, minimum paper TOEFL 550, minimum computer TOEFL 217. **Basis for Candidate Selection:** *Very important factors considered include:* Rigor of secondary school record, standardized test scores. *Important factors considered include:* Application essay, extracurricular activities, interview, recommendation(s). *Other factors considered include:* Alumni/ae relation, character/personal qualities, geographical residence, talent/ability, volunteer work, work experience. **Freshman Admission Requirements:** High school diploma is required, and GED is accepted. *Academic units required:* 4 English, 3 math, 2 science, 2 social studies, 5 academic electives. **Freshman Admission Statistics:** 3,464 applied, 53% admitted, 28% enrolled. **Transfer Admission Requirements:** College transcript(s), statement of good standing from prior institution(s). Minimum college GPA of 2.5 required. Lowest grade transferable C. **General Admission Information:** Application fee $55. Early decision application deadline 12/1. Regular application deadline 3/1. Regular notification is rolling. Nonfall registration accepted. Admission may be deferred for a maximum of 1 year. Credit and/or placement offered for CEEB Advanced Placement tests.

COSTS AND FINANCIAL AID

Annual tuition $30,400. Room and board $13,040. Required fees $1,220. Average book expense $800. Average book expense $850. **Required Forms and Deadlines:** FAFSA, state aid form. Financial aid filing deadline 3/1. **Notification of Awards:** Applicants will be notified of awards on a rolling basis beginning on or about 3/1. **Types of Aid:** *Need-based scholarships/grants:* Pell, SEOG, state scholarships/grants, private scholarships, the school's own gift aid. *Loans:* FFEL Subsidized Stafford, FFEL Unsubsidized Stafford, FFEL PLUS, Federal Perkins. **Student Employment:** Federal Work-Study Program available. Institutional employment available. Off-campus job opportunities are excellent. **Financial Aid Statistics:** 62% freshmen, 57% undergrads receive need-based scholarship or grant aid. 58% freshmen, 54% undergrads receive need-based self-help aid.

MANNES—THE NEW SCHOOL FOR MUSIC

150 West Eighty-fifth Street, New York, NY 10024
Phone: 212-580-0210 **E-mail:** mannesadmissions@newschool.edu **CEEB Code:** 2398
Fax: 212-580-1738 **Website:** www.mannes.edu
Financial Aid Phone: 212-580-0210

This private school was founded in 1916. It has a 1-acre campus.

RATINGS
Admissions Selectivity Rating: 60*   **Fire Safety Rating:** 60*   **Green Rating:** 60*

STUDENTS AND FACULTY
Enrollment: 197. **Student Body:** 57% female, 43% male, 43% out-of-state, 31% international (26 countries represented). African American 3%, Asian 7%, Caucasian 38%, Hispanic 4%. **Retention and Graduation:** 86% freshmen return for sophomore year. 55% freshmen graduate within 4 years. **Faculty:** Student/faculty ratio 2:1. 5 full-time faculty, 20% hold PhDs.

ACADEMICS
Degrees: Bachelor's, diploma, master's, post-bachelor's certificate, post-master's certificate. **Academic Requirements:** Arts/fine arts, English (including composition), humanities. **Classes:** Most classes have fewer than 10 students. **Disciplines with Highest Percentage of Degrees Awarded:** Visual and performing arts 100%. **Special Study Options:** Cross-registration, double major, English as a second language (ESL).

FACILITIES
Housing: Coed dorms, special housing for disabled students. **Computers:** 100% of public computers are PCs.

CAMPUS LIFE
Activities: Choral groups, music ensembles, opera, symphony orchestra.

ADMISSIONS
Freshman Academic Profile: 55% from public high schools. TOEFL required of all international applicants, minimum paper TOEFL 550. **Basis for Candidate Selection:** *Very important factors considered include:* Application essay, interview, level of applicant's interest, talent/ability. *Important factors considered include:* Recommendation(s), rigor of secondary school record. *Other factors considered include:* Character/personal qualities, class rank, extracurricular activities. **Freshman Admission Requirements:** High school diploma is required, and GED is accepted. *Academic units required:* 4 English, 2 math, 2 science (2 science labs), 2 social studies. *Academic units recommended:* 2 foreign language. **Freshman Admission Statistics:** 438 applied, 36% admitted, 21% enrolled. **Transfer Admission Requirements:** High school transcript, college transcript(s), essay or personal statement, interview. Minimum college GPA of 2.0 required. Lowest grade transferable C. **General Admission Information:** Application fee $100. Regular application deadline 12/1. Regular notification is rolling. Nonfall registration not accepted. Credit and/or placement offered for CEEB Advanced Placement tests.

COSTS AND FINANCIAL AID
Annual tuition $29,800. Room and board $11,750. Required fees $610. Average book expense $2,050. **Required Forms and Deadlines:** FAFSA, state aid form. Financial aid filing deadline 3/1. **Notification of Awards:** Applicants will be notified of awards on a rolling basis beginning on or about 3/1. **Types of Aid:** *Need-based scholarships/grants:* Pell, SEOG, state scholarships/grants, private scholarships, the school's own gift aid. *Loans:* FFEL Subsidized Stafford, FFEL Unsubsidized Stafford, FFEL PLUS, Federal Perkins, college/university loans from institutional funds. **Student Employment:** Federal Work-Study Program available. Off-campus job opportunities are good. **Financial Aid Statistics:** 36% freshmen, 22% undergrads receive need-based scholarship or grant aid. 45% freshmen, 28% undergrads receive need-based self-help aid. Highest amount earned per year from on-campus jobs $1,500.

MANSFIELD UNIVERSITY OF PENNSYLVANIA

Office of Admissions, Alumni Hall, Mansfield, PA 16933
Phone: 570-662-4243 **E-mail:** admissions@mansfield.edu **CEEB Code:** 2655
Fax: 570-662-4121 **Website:** www.mansfield.edu **ACT Code:** 3710
Financial Aid Phone: 570-662-4878

This public school was founded in 1857. It has a 174-acre campus.

RATINGS
Admissions Selectivity Rating: 70   **Fire Safety Rating:** 60*   **Green Rating:** 60*

STUDENTS AND FACULTY
Enrollment: 2,870. **Student Body:** 61% female, 39% male, 23% out-of-state. African American 7%, Caucasian 85%, Hispanic 1%. **Retention and Graduation:** 73% freshmen return for sophomore year. 30% freshmen graduate within 4 years. 14% grads go on to further study within 1 year. 1% grads pursue arts and sciences degrees. 1% grads pursue business degrees. 1% grads pursue law degrees. 1% grads pursue medical degrees. **Faculty:** Student/faculty ratio 16:1. 160 full-time faculty, 100% hold PhDs. 100% faculty teach undergrads.

ACADEMICS
Degrees: Associate, bachelor's, certificate, diploma, master's. **Academic Requirements:** Arts/fine arts, computer literacy, English (including composition), foreign languages, history, humanities, mathematics, philosophy, sciences (biological or physical), social science. **Classes:** Most classes have 20–29 students. Most lab/discussion sections have 10–19 students. **Majors with Highest Enrollment:** Criminal justice/law enforcement administration; education; music teacher education. **Disciplines with Highest Percentage of Degrees Awarded:** Security and protective services 11%, education 11%, business/marketing 11%, public administration and social services 9%, visual and performing arts 9%, English 8%, communications/journalism 6%, psychology 6%, health professions and related sciences 6%, biological/life sciences 5%. **Special Study Options:** Cross-registration, distance learning, double major, dual enrollment, exchange student program (domestic), honors program, independent study, internships, liberal arts/career combination, student-designed major, study abroad, teacher certification program.

FACILITIES
Housing: Coed dorms, fraternity/sorority housing. **Special Academic Facilities/Equipment:** Science museum, 2 art galleries, animal collection, planetarium, solar collector. **Computers:** 100% of public computers are PCs, network access in dorm rooms, online registration, remote student-access to Web through college's connection.

CAMPUS LIFE
Activities: Choral groups, concert band, dance, drama/theater, jazz band, literary magazine, marching band, music ensembles, musical theater, pep band, radio station, student government, student newspaper, symphony orchestra, television station. **Organizations:** 108 registered organizations, 10 honor societies, 4 religious organizations. 6 fraternities, 4 sororities. **Athletics (Intercollegiate):** *Men:* Baseball, basketball, cross-country, football, track/field (indoor), track/field (outdoor). *Women:* Basketball, cheerleading, cross-country, diving, field hockey, soccer, softball, swimming, track/field (indoor), track/field (outdoor).

ADMISSIONS
Freshman Academic Profile: 12% in top 10% of high school class, 32% in top 25% of high school class, 66% in top 50% of high school class. SAT Math middle 50% range 430–540. SAT Critical Reading middle 50% range 430–530. SAT Writing middle 50% range 420–510. TOEFL required of all international applicants, minimum paper TOEFL 550, minimum computer TOEFL 230. **Basis for Candidate Selection:** *Very important factors considered include:* Academic GPA, class rank, rigor of secondary school record, standardized test scores. *Other factors considered include:* Alumni/ae relation, application essay, character/personal qualities, extracurricular activities, first generation, geographical residence, interview, racial/ethnic status, recommendation(s), talent/ability, volunteer work, work experience. **Freshman Admission Requirements:** High school diploma is required, and GED is accepted. *Academic units required:* 4 English, 3 math, 2 science (2 science labs), 4 history, 6 academic electives. **Freshman Admission Statistics:** 2,631 applied, 100% admitted, 23% enrolled. **Transfer Admission Requirements:** College transcript(s). Minimum college GPA of 2.0 required. Lowest grade transferable D. **General Admission Information:** Application fee $25. Regular notification is rolling. Nonfall registration accepted. Admission may be deferred for a maximum of 1 year. Credit offered for CEEB Advanced Placement tests.

COSTS AND FINANCIAL AID
Annual in-state tuition $5,177. Annual out-of-state tuition $12,944. Room and board $6,236. Required fees $1,827. Average book expense $1,200. **Required**

Forms and Deadlines: FAFSA, institution's own financial aid form. Financial aid filing deadline 3/15. **Notification of Awards:** Applicants will be notified of awards on a rolling basis beginning on or about 3/15. **Types of Aid:** *Need-based scholarships/grants:* Pell, SEOG, state scholarships/grants, private scholarships, the school's own gift aid, United Negro College Fund, Federal Nursing Scholarships. *Loans:* FFEL Subsidized Stafford, FFEL Unsubsidized Stafford, FFEL PLUS, Federal Perkins, Federal Nursing, state loans. **Student Employment:** Federal Work-Study Program available. Institutional employment available. Off-campus job opportunities are fair. **Financial Aid Statistics:** 47% freshmen, 49% undergrads receive need-based scholarship or grant aid. 3% freshmen, 4% undergrads receive need-based self-help aid. 11 freshmen, 56 undergrads receive athletic scholarships. 85% freshmen, 85% undergrads receive any aid. Highest amount earned per year from on-campus jobs $1,236.

MARIAN COLLEGE

3200 Cold Spring Road, Indianapolis, IN 46222
Phone: 317-955-6300 **E-mail:** admit@marian.edu **CEEB Code:** 1442
Fax: 317-955-6401 **Website:** www.marian.edu **ACT Code:** 1224
Financial Aid Phone: 317-929-0234

This private school, affiliated with the Roman Catholic Church, was founded in 1937. It has a 114-acre campus.

RATINGS
Admissions Selectivity Rating: 72   **Fire Safety Rating:** 60*   **Green Rating:** 60*

STUDENTS AND FACULTY
Enrollment: 1,412. **Student Body:** 69% female, 31% male, 8% out-of-state, 2% international. African American 18%, Asian 1%, Caucasian 66%, Hispanic 2%. **Retention and Graduation:** 71% freshmen return for sophomore year. 5% grads go on to further study within 1 year. 2% grads pursue business degrees. 2% grads pursue law degrees. 1% grads pursue medical degrees. **Faculty:** Student/faculty ratio 12:1. 65 full-time faculty, 55% hold PhDs. 100% faculty teach undergrads.

ACADEMICS
Degrees: Associate, bachelor's, certificate, master's. **Academic Requirements:** Arts/fine arts, English (including composition), foreign languages, history, humanities, mathematics, philosophy, sciences (biological or physical), social science. **Classes:** Most classes have fewer than 10 students. Most lab/discussion sections have fewer than 10 students. **Majors with Highest Enrollment:** Business administration/management, education, nursing/registered nurse training (RN, ASN, BSN, MSN). **Disciplines with Highest Percentage of Degrees Awarded:** Business/marketing 21%, education 15%, health professions and related sciences 14%, parks and recreation 9%, biological/life sciences 6%, social sciences 6%, visual and performing arts 6%. **Special Study Options:** Accelerated program, cross-registration, double major, dual enrollment, honors program, independent study, internships, liberal arts/career combination, study abroad, teacher certification program, mentor leadership training.

FACILITIES
Housing: Coed dorms, men's dorms, women's dorms, apartments for single students, special housing for disabled students. **Computers:** 75% of public computers are PCs, 25% of public computers are Macs, network access in dorm rooms, network access in dorm lounges, remote student-access to Web through college's connection.

CAMPUS LIFE
Activities: Choral groups, dance, drama/theater, jazz band, literary magazine, music ensembles, musical theater, pep band, student government, student newspaper, television station. **Organizations:** 40 registered organizations, 2 honor societies, 2 religious organizations. **Athletics (Intercollegiate):** *Men:* Baseball, basketball, cheerleading, cross-country, golf, soccer, tennis, track/field (indoor), track/field (outdoor), volleyball. *Women:* Basketball, cheerleading, cross-country, golf, soccer, softball, tennis, track/field (indoor), track/field (outdoor), volleyball.

ADMISSIONS
Freshman Academic Profile: 11% in top 10% of high school class, 29% in top 25% of high school class, 61% in top 50% of high school class. 75% from public high schools. SAT Math middle 50% range 430–610. SAT Critical Reading middle 50% range 440–550. ACT middle 50% range 19–25. TOEFL required of all international applicants, minimum paper TOEFL 550. **Basis for Candidate Selection:** *Very important factors considered include:* Class rank, rigor of secondary school record, standardized test scores. *Other factors*

considered include: Alumni/ae relation, application essay, character/personal qualities, extracurricular activities, geographical residence, interview, recommendation(s), state residency, talent/ability, volunteer work, work experience. **Freshman Admission Requirements:** High school diploma is required, and GED is accepted. *Academic units required:* 4 English, 2 math, 1 science, 2 foreign language, 1 social studies, 1 history, 9 academic electives. *Academic units recommended:* 4 English, 3 math, 3 science, 2 foreign language, 2 social studies, 2 history, 4 academic electives. **Freshman Admission Statistics:** 836 applied, 76% admitted, 40% enrolled. **Transfer Admission Requirements:** College transcript(s), statement of good standing from prior institution(s). Minimum college GPA of 2.0 required. Lowest grade transferable C. **General Admission Information:** Application fee $20. Regular application deadline 8/1. Regular notification rolling. Nonfall registration accepted. Common Application not accepted. Credit and/or placement offered for CEEB Advanced Placement tests.

COSTS AND FINANCIAL AID
Annual tuition $16,800. Room & board $5,700. Required fees $580. Average book expense $700. **Required Forms and Deadlines:** FAFSA, institution's own financial aid form, state aid form. Financial aid filing deadline 3/10. **Notification of Awards:** Applicants will be notified of awards on a rolling basis beginning on or about 4/1. **Types of Aid:** *Need-based scholarships/grants:* Pell, state scholarships/grants, private scholarships, the school's own gift aid. *Loans:* Direct Subsidized Stafford, Direct Unsubsidized Stafford, Direct PLUS, FFEL Subsidized Stafford, FFEL PLUS, Federal Perkins, state loans. **Student Employment:** Federal Work-Study Program available. Institutional employment available. Off-campus job opportunities are excellent. **Financial Aid Statistics:** 76% freshmen, 71% undergrads receive need-based scholarship or grant aid. 63% freshmen, 65% undergrads receive need-based self-help aid. 55 freshmen, 189 undergrads receive athletic scholarships. Highest amount earned per year from on-campus jobs $500.

MARIAN COLLEGE OF FOND DU LAC

45 South National Avenue, Fond du Lac, WI 54935
Phone: 920-923-7650 **E-mail:** admissions@mariancollege.edu **CEEB Code:** 1443
Fax: 920-923-8755 **Website:** www.marioncollege.edu **ACT Code:** 4606
Financial Aid Phone: 920-923-7614

This private school, affiliated with the Roman Catholic Church, was founded in 1936. It has a 77-acre campus.

RATINGS
Admissions Selectivity Rating: 70   **Fire Safety Rating:** 60*   **Green Rating:** 60*

STUDENTS AND FACULTY
Enrollment: 1,969. **Student Body:** 73% female, 27% male, 4% out-of-state. African American 4%, Asian 1%, Caucasian 90%, Hispanic 2%. **Retention and Graduation:** 75% freshmen return for sophomore year. 35% freshmen graduate within 4 years. 10% grads go on to further study within 1 year. **Faculty:** Student/faculty ratio 12:1. 81 full-time faculty, 63% hold PhDs. 80% faculty teach undergrads.

ACADEMICS
Degrees: Bachelor's, doctoral, master's. **Academic Requirements:** Arts/fine arts, English (including composition), history, humanities, mathematics, philosophy, sciences (biological or physical), social science, theology. **Classes:** Most classes have fewer than 10 students. Most lab/discussion sections have fewer than 10 students. **Majors with Highest Enrollment:** Business administration/management, nursing/registered nurse training (RN, ASN, BSN, MSN), teacher education and professional development. **Disciplines with Highest Percentage of Degrees Awarded:** Business/marketing 35%, health professions and related sciences 23%, security and protective services 11%, education 7%, public administration and social services 6%. **Special Study Options:** Accelerated program, cooperative education program, distance learning, double major, dual enrollment, honors program, independent study, internships, liberal arts/career combination, student-designed major, study abroad, teacher certification program. Accelerated programs for adults in business, nursing, operation management, and radiologic technology.

FACILITIES
Housing: Coed dorms, apartments for single students, special housing for disabled students, fraternity/sorority housing, townhouses, penthouses, and suites. **Special Academic Facilities/Equipment:** On-campus child-care center, electron microscope. **Computers:** 15% of classrooms are wired, 25% of classrooms are wireless, 94% of public computers are PCs, 6% of public

computers are Macs, network access in dorm rooms, online registration, online administrative functions (other than registration), remote student-access to Web through college's connection.

CAMPUS LIFE

Activities: Choral groups, concert band, dance, drama/theater, jazz band, literary magazine, music ensembles, pep band, student government, student newspaper, symphony orchestra. **Organizations:** 28 registered organizations, 7 honor societies, 1 religious organization. 2 fraternities (5% men join), 3 sororities (5% women join). **Athletics (Intercollegiate):** *Men:* Baseball, basketball, cross-country, golf, ice hockey, soccer, tennis. *Women:* Basketball, cross-country, golf, soccer, softball, tennis, volleyball.

ADMISSIONS

Freshman Academic Profile: 9% in top 10% of high school class, 29% in top 25% of high school class, 66% in top 50% of high school class. 86% from public high schools. ACT middle 50% range 18–22. TOEFL required of all international applicants, minimum paper TOEFL 525, minimum computer TOEFL 193. **Basis for Candidate Selection:** *Very important factors considered include:* Academic GPA, class rank, rigor of secondary school record, standardized test scores. *Important factors considered include:* Character/personal qualities, interview, level of applicant's interest. *Other factors considered include:* Alumni/ae relation, application essay, extracurricular activities, recommendation(s), talent/ability, volunteer work, work experience. **Freshman Admission Requirements:** High school diploma is required, and GED is accepted. *Academic units required:* 4 English, 2 math, 1 science (1 science lab), 1 history. *Academic units recommended:* 3 math, 2 science, 2 foreign language. **Freshman Admission Statistics:** 754 applied, 85% admitted, 38% enrolled. **Transfer Admission Requirements:** High school transcript, college transcript(s). Minimum college GPA of 2.0 required. Lowest grade transferable C. **General Admission Information:** Application fee $25. Regular notification is rolling. Nonfall registration accepted. Admission may be deferred. Credit and/or placement offered for CEEB Advanced Placement tests.

COSTS AND FINANCIAL AID

Annual tuition $17,300. Room & board $5,200. Required fees $330. Average book expense $700. **Required Forms and Deadlines:** FAFSA, institution's own financial aid form. Financial aid filing deadline 3/1. **Notification of Awards:** Applicants will be notified of awards on a rolling basis beginning on or about 3/1. **Types of Aid:** *Need-based scholarships/grants:* Pell, SEOG, state scholarships/grants, private scholarships, the school's own gift aid. *Loans:* FFEL Subsidized Stafford, FFEL Unsubsidized Stafford, FFEL PLUS, Federal Perkins, Federal Nursing. **Student Employment:** Federal Work-Study Program available. Institutional employment available. Off-campus job opportunities are fair. **Financial Aid Statistics:** 86% freshmen, 77% undergrads receive need-based scholarship or grant aid. 78% freshmen, 73% undergrads receive need-based self-help aid. 87% freshmen, 80% undergrads receive any aid. Highest amount earned per year from on-campus jobs $1,200.

MARIETTA COLLEGE

215 Fifth Street, Marietta, OH 45750
Phone: 740-376-4600 **E-mail:** admit@marietta.edu **CEEB Code:** 1444
Fax: 740-376-8888 **Website:** www.marietta.edu **ACT Code:** 3290
Financial Aid Phone: 740-376-4712

This private school was founded in 1835. It has a 120-acre campus.

RATINGS

Admissions Selectivity Rating: 80   **Fire Safety Rating:** 65   **Green Rating:** 71

STUDENTS AND FACULTY

Enrollment: 1,408. **Student Body:** 51% female, 49% male, 37% out-of-state, 4% international (22 countries represented). African American 3%, Asian 2%, Caucasian 77%, Hispanic 2%. **Retention and Graduation:** 67% freshmen return for sophomore year. 51% freshmen graduate within 4 years. 30% grads go on to further study within 1 year. 20% grads pursue arts and sciences degrees. 2% grads pursue business degrees. 3% grads pursue medical degrees. **Faculty:** Student/faculty ratio 12:1. 94 full-time faculty, 81% hold PhDs. 100% faculty teach undergrads.

ACADEMICS

Degrees: Associate, bachelor's, certificate, master's. **Academic Requirements:** Arts/fine arts, computer literacy, English (including composition), history, humanities, mathematics, philosophy, sciences (biological or physical), social science. **Classes:** Most classes have 10–19 students. Most lab/discussion

sections have fewer than 10 students. **Majors with Highest Enrollment:** Athletic training/trainer, education, petroleum engineering. **Disciplines with Highest Percentage of Degrees Awarded:** Business/marketing 22%, communications/journalism 14%, visual and performing arts 10%, education 7%, social sciences 7%, health professions and related sciences 7%. **Special Study Options:** Accelerated program, double major, dual enrollment, English as a second language (ESL), exchange student program (domestic), honors program, independent study, internships, liberal arts/career combination, student-designed major, study abroad, teacher certification program.

FACILITIES

Housing: Coed dorms, men's dorms, women's dorms, apartments for single students, special housing for disabled students, fraternity/sorority housing, theme housing is available. **Special Academic Facilities/Equipment:** Mass media building, fine arts center, natural science field camp, observatory, special collections in library. **Computers:** 100% of classrooms are wireless, 90% of public computers are PCs, 10% of public computers are Macs, network access in dorm rooms, network access in dorm lounges, online registration, online administrative functions (other than registration), remote student-access to Web through college's connection.

CAMPUS LIFE

Activities: Choral groups, concert band, dance, drama/theater, jazz band, literary magazine, music ensembles, musical theater, pep band, radio station, student government, student newspaper, television station, yearbook. **Organizations:** 68 registered organizations, 23 honor societies, 2 religious organizations. 3 fraternities (18% men join), 3 sororities (18% women join). **Athletics (Intercollegiate):** *Men:* Baseball, basketball, crew/rowing, cross-country, football, soccer, tennis, track/field (indoor), track/field (outdoor). *Women:* Basketball, crew/rowing, cross-country, soccer, softball, tennis, track/field (indoor), track/field (outdoor), volleyball. Environmental Initiatives: Environmental Studies and Environmental Science programs. Student run voluntary recycling program. Seek to, where practicable, including energy saving components in new campus construction.

ADMISSIONS

Freshman Academic Profile: 28% in top 10% of high school class, 55% in top 25% of high school class, 84% in top 50% of high school class. 86% from public high schools. SAT Math middle 50% range 470–600. SAT Critical Reading middle 50% range 480–600. ACT middle 50% range 20–26. TOEFL required of all international applicants, minimum paper TOEFL 550, minimum computer TOEFL 213. **Basis for Candidate Selection:** *Very important factors considered include:* Academic GPA, class rank, rigor of secondary school record, standardized test scores. *Important factors considered include:* Character/personal qualities, interview, recommendation(s). *Other factors considered include:* Alumni/ae relation, application essay, extracurricular activities, first generation, geographical residence, racial/ethnic status, talent/ability, volunteer work, work experience. **Freshman Admission Requirements:** High school diploma is required, and GED is accepted. *Academic units required:* 4 English, 3 math, 3 science (2 science labs), 2 foreign language, 2 social studies, 2 history. *Academic units recommended:* 2 foreign language. **Freshman Admission Statistics:** 2,127 applied, 79% admitted, 23% enrolled. **Transfer Admission Requirements:** College transcript(s), essay or personal statement, statement of good standing from prior institution(s). Minimum college GPA of 2.3 required. Lowest grade transferable C. **General Admission Information:** Application fee $25. Regular application deadline rolling. Regular notification is rolling. Nonfall registration accepted. Admission may be deferred for a maximum of 1 year. Credit and/or placement offered for CEEB Advanced Placement tests.

COSTS AND FINANCIAL AID

Annual tuition $24,220. Room and board $7,390. Required fees $622. Average book expense $680. **Required Forms and Deadlines:** FAFSA, institution's own financial aid form. Financial aid filing deadline 4/15. **Notification of Awards:** Applicants will be notified of awards on a rolling basis beginning on or about 3/15. **Types of Aid:** *Need-based scholarships/grants:* Pell, SEOG, state scholarships/grants, private scholarships, the school's own gift aid. *Loans:* Direct Subsidized Stafford, Direct Unsubsidized Stafford, Direct PLUS, FFEL Subsidized Stafford, FFEL Unsubsidized Stafford, FFEL PLUS, Federal Perkins, college/university loans from institutional funds. **Financial Aid Statistics:** 76% freshmen, 73% undergrads receive need-based scholarship or grant aid. 67% freshmen, 63% undergrads receive need-based self-help aid. 98% freshmen, 92% undergrads receive any aid. Highest amount earned per year from on-campus jobs $2,000.

MARIST COLLEGE

3399 North Road, Poughkeepsie, NY 12601-1387
Phone: 845-575-3226 **E-mail:** admissions@marist.edu **CEEB Code:** 2400
Fax: 845-575-3215 **Website:** www.marist.edu **ACT Code:** 2804
Financial Aid Phone: 845-575-3230

This private school was founded in 1929. It has a 180-acre campus.

RATINGS
Admissions Selectivity Rating: 89   **Fire Safety Rating:** 80   **Green Rating:** 81

STUDENTS AND FACULTY
Enrollment: 4,873. **Student Body:** 57% female, 43% male, 40% out-of-state. African American 3%, Asian 2%, Caucasian 78%, Hispanic 5%. **Retention and Graduation:** 90% freshmen return for sophomore year. 69% freshmen graduate within 4 years. 25% grads go on to further study within 1 year. 20% grads pursue arts and sciences degrees. 2% grads pursue business degrees. 2% grads pursue law degrees. 1% grads pursue medical degrees. **Faculty:** Student/faculty ratio 15:1. 204 full-time faculty, 80% hold PhDs. 98% faculty teach undergrads.

ACADEMICS
Degrees: Bachelor's, certificate, master's, post-bachelor's certificate. **Academic Requirements:** Arts/fine arts, computer literacy, English (including composition), history, humanities, mathematics, philosophy, sciences (biological or physical), social science. **Classes:** Most classes have 20–29 students. Most lab/discussion sections have 10–19 students. **Majors with Highest Enrollment:** Business administration and management, mass communications/media studies, special education. **Disciplines with Highest Percentage of Degrees Awarded:** Business/marketing 24%, communications/journalism 21%, education 12%, liberal arts/general studies 8%, psychology 7%. **Special Study Options:** Accelerated program, cooperative education program, cross-registration, distance learning, double major, dual enrollment, English as a second language (ESL), honors program, independent study, internships, liberal arts/career combination, study abroad, teacher certification program, weekend college. Undergrads may take grad-level classes. Co-op programs also available in arts, business, computer science, education, humanities, natural science, social/behavioral science, technologies. Off-campus study in Washington, DC; evening division.

FACILITIES
Housing: Coed dorms, apartments for single students, special housing for disabled students, garden apartments, town-houses, suites. **Special Academic Facilities/Equipment:** Art gallery, language lab, estuarine and environmental studies lab, public opinion institute, audiovisual/TV center, communications center, high-tech classroom, digital state-of-the-art library. **Computers:** 2% of classrooms are wired, 15% of classrooms are wireless, 95% of public computers are PCs, 5% of public computers are UNIX, network access in dorm rooms, network access in dorm lounges, online registration, online administrative functions (other than registration), support for handheld computing, remote student-access to Web through college's connection.

CAMPUS LIFE
Activities: Choral groups, concert band, dance, drama/theater, jazz band, literary magazine, marching band, music ensembles, musical theater, pep band, radio station, student government, student newspaper, student-run film society, television station, yearbook. **Organizations:** 76 registered organizations, 15 honor societies, 6 religious organizations. 3 fraternities (1% men join), 4 sororities (2% women join). **Athletics (Intercollegiate):** *Men:* Baseball, basketball, crew/rowing, cross-country, diving, football, lacrosse, soccer, swimming, tennis, track/field (outdoor). *Women:* Basketball, crew/rowing, cross-country, diving, lacrosse, soccer, softball, swimming, tennis, track/field (outdoor), volleyball, water polo. Environmental Initiatives: Composting / Recycling. Energy efficiency. Sustainable designs for new construction and renovation.

ADMISSIONS
Freshman Academic Profile: 26% in top 10% of high school class, 78% in top 25% of high school class, 95% in top 50% of high school class. 72% from public high schools. SAT Math middle 50% range 540–630. SAT Critical Reading middle 50% range 520–620. SAT Writing middle 50% range 530–630. ACT middle 50% range 22–27. TOEFL required of all international applicants, minimum paper TOEFL 550, minimum computer TOEFL 213. **Basis for**

Candidate Selection: *Very important factors considered include:* Academic GPA, rigor of secondary school record, standardized test scores. *Important factors considered include:* Application essay, character/personal qualities, extracurricular activities, geographical residence, recommendation(s), state residency, talent/ability, volunteer work, work experience. *Other factors considered include:* Alumni/ae relation, class rank, level of applicant's interest, racial/ethnic status. **Freshman Admission Requirements:** High school diploma is required, and GED is accepted. *Academic units required:* 4 English, 3 math, 3 science (2 science labs), 2 foreign language, 2 social studies, 1 history, 2 academic electives. *Academic units recommended:* 4 math, 4 science (3 science labs), 3 foreign language. **Freshman Admission Statistics:** 7,296 applied, 49% admitted, 29% enrolled. **Transfer Admission Requirements:** High school transcript, college transcript(s), essay or personal statement. Minimum college GPA of 2.8 required. Lowest grade transferable C. **General Admission Information:** Application fee $50. Early decision application deadline 11/15. Regular application deadline 2/15. Regular notification 3/15. Nonfall registration accepted. Admission may be deferred for a maximum of 1 year. Credit and/or placement offered for CEEB Advanced Placement tests.

COSTS AND FINANCIAL AID
Annual tuition $23,560. Room and board $10,250. Required fees $480. Average book expense $1,230. **Required Forms and Deadlines:** FAFSA, institution's own financial aid form. Financial aid filing deadline 5/1. **Notification of Awards:** Applicants will be notified of awards on or about 3/15. **Types of Aid:** *Need-based scholarships/grants:* Pell, SEOG, state scholarships/grants, private scholarships, the school's own gift aid. *Loans:* FFEL Subsidized Stafford, FFEL Unsubsidized Stafford, FFEL PLUS, Federal Perkins, alternative loans. **Financial Aid Statistics:** 58% freshmen, 58% undergrads receive need-based scholarship or grant aid. 45% freshmen, 50% undergrads receive need-based self-help aid. 75 freshmen, 269 undergrads receive athletic scholarships. 90% freshmen, 86% undergrads receive any aid. Highest amount earned per year from on-campus jobs $3,380.

MARLBORO COLLEGE

PO Box A, 2582 South Road, Marlboro, VT 05344-0300
Phone: 802-258-9236 **E-mail:** admissions@marlboro.edu **CEEB Code:** 3509
Fax: 802-451-7555 **Website:** www.marlboro.edu **ACT Code:** 4304
Financial Aid Phone: 802-258-9312

This private school was founded in 1946. It has a 350-acre campus.

RATINGS
Admissions Selectivity Rating: 88   **Fire Safety Rating:** 66   **Green Rating:** 72

STUDENTS AND FACULTY
Enrollment: 324. **Student Body:** 53% female, 47% male, 88% out-of-state. Asian 2%, Caucasian 67%, Hispanic 2%. **Retention and Graduation:** 73% freshmen return for sophomore year. **Faculty:** Student/faculty ratio 8:1. 40 full-time faculty, 85% hold PhDs. 100% faculty teach undergrads.

ACADEMICS
Degrees: Bachelor's, master's. **Academic Requirements:** English (including composition), clear writing requirement, plan of concentration completion. **Classes:** Most classes have fewer than 10 students. Most lab/discussion sections have fewer than 10 students. **Majors with Highest Enrollment:** English language and literature, social sciences, visual and performing arts. **Disciplines with Highest Percentage of Degrees Awarded:** Social sciences 13%, English 12%, visual and performing arts 10%, liberal arts/general studies 8%, interdisciplinary studies 8%, biological/life sciences 7%. **Special Study Options:** Double major, dual enrollment, independent study, internships, student-designed major, study abroad. World studies program for students interested in international relations and integrating an internship with study abroad opportunities.

FACILITIES
Housing: Coed dorms, women's dorms, apartments for married students, largest residence hall accommodates about 30 students. **Special Academic Facilities/Equipment:** Art gallery, theater, dance studio, observatory, darkroom, art studios, music practice and performance spaces. **Computers:**

50% of public computers are PCs, 50% of public computers are Macs, network access in dorm rooms, network access in dorm lounges, online administrative functions (other than registration), support for handheld computing, remote student-access to Web through college's connection.

CAMPUS LIFE

Activities: Dance, drama/theater, literary magazine, music ensembles, musical theater, student government, student newspaper, student-run film society. **Organizations:** 22 registered organizations. **Athletics (Intercollegiate):** *Men:* Soccer. *Women:* Soccer.

ADMISSIONS

Freshman Academic Profile: 40% in top 10% of high school class, 60% in top 25% of high school class, 95% in top 50% of high school class. 70% from public high schools. SAT Math middle 50% range 510–650. SAT Critical Reading middle 50% range 590–690. SAT Writing middle 50% range 640–720. ACT middle 50% range 24–32. TOEFL required of all international applicants, minimum paper TOEFL 550, minimum computer TOEFL 213. **Basis for Candidate Selection:** *Very important factors considered include:* Academic GPA, application essay, character/personal qualities, rigor of secondary school record. *Important factors considered include:* Extracurricular activities, interview, talent/ability. *Other factors considered include:* Alumni/ae relation, class rank, first generation, geographical residence, level of applicant's interest, recommendation(s), standardized test scores, state residency, volunteer work, work experience. **Freshman Admission Requirements:** High school diploma is required, and GED is accepted. *Academic units recommended:* 4 English, 3 math, 3 science (1 science lab), 3 foreign language, 3 social studies, 3 history, 3 academic electives. **Freshman Admission Statistics:** 459 applied, 68% admitted, 30% enrolled. **Transfer Admission Requirements:** High school transcript, college transcript(s), essay or personal statement, interview, standardized test score. Minimum college GPA of 2.0 required. Lowest grade transferable C-. **General Admission Information:** Application fee $50. Early decision application deadline 12/1. Regular application deadline 2/15. Regular notification is rolling. Nonfall registration accepted. Admission may be deferred for a maximum of 1 year. Credit offered for CEEB Advanced Placement tests.

COSTS AND FINANCIAL AID

Annual tuition $31,140. Room and board $9,040. Required fees $1,040. Average book expense $1,000. **Required Forms and Deadlines:** FAFSA. Financial aid filing deadline 3/1. **Notification of Awards:** Applicants will be notified of awards on or about 4/1. **Types of Aid:** *Need-based scholarships/grants:* Pell, SEOG, state scholarships/grants, private scholarships, the school's own gift aid. *Loans:* FFEL Subsidized Stafford, FFEL Unsubsidized Stafford, FFEL PLUS, state loans, college/university loans from institutional funds. **Student Employment:** Federal Work-Study Program available. Institutional employment available. Off-campus job opportunities are fair. **Financial Aid Statistics:** 70% freshmen, 77% undergrads receive need-based scholarship or grant aid. 75% freshmen, 76% undergrads receive need-based self-help aid. 75% freshmen, 84% undergrads receive any aid. Highest amount earned per year from on-campus jobs $2,000.

See page 1254.

MARQUETTE UNIVERSITY

PO Box 1881, Milwaukee, WI 53201-1881
Phone: 414-288-7302 **E-mail:** admissions@marquette.edu **CEEB Code:** 1448
Fax: 414-288-3764 **Website:** www.marquette.edu **ACT Code:** 4610
Financial Aid Phone: 414-288-7390

This private school, affiliated with the Jesuit order of the Roman Catholic Church, was founded in 1881. It has an 80-acre campus.

RATINGS

Admissions Selectivity Rating: 84 **Fire Safety Rating:** 73 **Green Rating:** 96

STUDENTS AND FACULTY

Enrollment: 7,812. **Student Body:** 54% female, 46% male, 53% out-of-state, 1% international (77 countries represented). African American 5%, Asian 5%, Caucasian 84%, Hispanic 5%. **Retention and Graduation:** 91% freshmen return for sophomore year. 58% freshmen graduate within 4 years. 31% grads

go on to further study within 1 year. 2% grads pursue business degrees. 4% grads pursue law degrees. 3% grads pursue medical degrees. **Faculty:** Student/faculty ratio 15:1. 600 full-time faculty, 88% hold PhDs. 77% faculty teach undergrads.

ACADEMICS

Degrees: Bachelor's, doctoral, first professional, master's, post-master's certificate. **Academic Requirements:** Arts/fine arts, English (including composition), foreign languages, history, humanities, mathematics, philosophy, sciences (biological or physical), social science, theology, ethics, diverse cultures. **Classes:** Most classes have 10–19 students. Most lab/discussion sections have 10–19 students. **Majors with Highest Enrollment:** Nursing/registered nurse training (RN, ASN, BSN, MSN). **Disciplines with Highest Percentage of Degrees Awarded:** Business/marketing 21%, communication technologies 15%, social sciences 10%, health professions and related sciences 10%, engineering 8%. **Special Study Options:** Accelerated program, cooperative education program, cross-registration, double major, dual enrollment, English as a second language (ESL), honors program, independent study, internships, student-designed major, study abroad, teacher certification program, weekend college.

FACILITIES

Housing: Coed dorms, men's dorms, women's dorms, apartments for married students, apartments for single students, special housing for disabled students, special housing for international students, fraternity/sorority housing, specialty housing for honor students. **Special Academic Facilities/Equipment:** Haggerty Museum of Art, Helfaer Theatre, Al McGuire Center, broadcast facilities, dental school/clinic. **Computers:** 10% of classrooms are wired, 5% of classrooms are wireless, 86% of public computers are PCs, 8% of public computers are Macs, 6% of public computers are UNIX, network access in dorm rooms, network access in dorm lounges, online registration, online administrative functions (other than registration), remote student-access to Web through college's connection.

CAMPUS LIFE

Activities: Choral groups, concert band, dance, drama/theater, jazz band, literary magazine, music ensembles, musical theater, pep band, radio station, student government, student newspaper, symphony orchestra, television station, yearbook. **Organizations:** 230 registered organizations, 21 honor societies, 11 religious organizations. 11 fraternities (2% men join), 11 sororities (4% women join). **Athletics (Intercollegiate):** *Men:* Basketball, cheerleading, cross-country, golf, soccer, tennis, track/field (indoor), track/field (outdoor). *Women:* Basketball, cheerleading, cross-country, soccer, tennis, track/field (indoor), track/field (outdoor), volleyball.

ADMISSIONS

Freshman Academic Profile: 35% in top 10% of high school class, 67% in top 25% of high school class, 92% in top 50% of high school class. 54% from public high schools. SAT Math middle 50% range 550–660. SAT Critical Reading middle 50% range 540–640. SAT Writing middle 50% range 530–630. ACT middle 50% range 24–29. minimum paper TOEFL 520, minimum computer TOEFL 190. **Basis for Candidate Selection:** *Very important factors considered include:* Academic GPA, rigor of secondary school record. *Important factors considered include:* Application essay, class rank, recommendation(s), standardized test scores. *Other factors considered include:* Alumni/ae relation, character/personal qualities, extracurricular activities, first generation, geographical residence, racial/ethnic status, religious affiliation/commitment, state residency, talent/ability. **Freshman Admission Requirements:** High school diploma is required, and GED is accepted. *Academic units required:* 4 English, 2 math, 2 science (2 science labs), 2 foreign language, 2 social studies, 2 academic electives. *Academic units recommended:* 4 English, 4 math, 3 science (3 science labs), 2 foreign language, 3 social studies, 5 academic electives. **Freshman Admission Statistics:** 11,514 applied, 70% admitted, 23% enrolled. **Transfer Admission Requirements:** High school transcript, college transcript(s), essay or personal statement. Lowest grade transferable C. **General Admission Information:** Application fee $30. Regular application deadline 12/1. Regular notification 1/31. Nonfall registration accepted. Admission may be deferred for a maximum of 1 year. Credit and/or placement offered for CEEB Advanced Placement tests.

COSTS AND FINANCIAL AID

Annual tuition $24,670. Room & board $8,120. Required fees $404. Average book expense $900. **Required Forms and Deadlines:** FAFSA, MU Admissions Application. **Notification of Awards:** Applicants will be notified of awards on a rolling basis beginning on or about 3/20. **Types of Aid:** *Need-based scholarships/grants:* Pell, SEOG, state scholarships/grants, private scholarships, the school's own gift aid. *Loans:* Direct Subsidized Stafford, Direct Unsubsidized Stafford, Direct PLUS, Federal Perkins, Federal Nursing, state loans, college/university loans from institutional funds, private educational/alternative loans. **Financial Aid Statistics:** 54% freshmen, 52% undergrads receive need-based scholarship or grant aid. 51% freshmen, 50% undergrads receive need-based self-help aid. 25 freshmen, 116 undergrads receive athletic scholarships. 88% freshmen, 85% undergrads receive any aid. Highest amount earned per year from on-campus jobs $2,500.

See page 1256.

MARS HILL COLLEGE

PO Box 370, Mars Hill, NC 28754
Phone: 828-689-1201 **E-mail:** admissions@mhc.edu **CEEB Code:** 5395
Fax: 828-689-1473 **Website:** www.mhc.edu **ACT Code:** 3124
Financial Aid Phone: 828-689-1123

This private school, affiliated with the Baptist Church, was founded in 1856. It has a 180-acre campus.

RATINGS
Admissions Selectivity Rating: 60*   **Fire Safety Rating:** 60*   **Green Rating:** 60*

STUDENTS AND FACULTY
Enrollment: 1,177. **Student Body:** 56% female, 44% male, 35% out-of-state, 3% international (20 countries represented). African American 8%, Caucasian 99%, Hispanic 1%, Native American 1%. **Retention and Graduation:** 71% freshmen return for sophomore year. **Faculty:** Student/faculty ratio 14:1. 78 full-time faculty, 63% hold PhDs. 100% faculty teach undergrads.

ACADEMICS
Degrees: Bachelor's, diploma. **Academic Requirements:** Arts/fine arts, English (including composition), foreign languages, history, humanities, mathematics, sciences (biological or physical), social science. **Majors with Highest Enrollment:** Biology/biological sciences, business administration/management, elementary education and teaching. **Disciplines with Highest Percentage of Degrees Awarded:** Education 31%, business/marketing 14%, social sciences 9%, communication technologies 7%, parks and recreation 7%, biological/life sciences 6%. **Special Study Options:** Accelerated program, cooperative education program, distance learning, double major, dual enrollment, English as a second language (ESL), honors program, independent study, internships, liberal arts/career combination, study abroad, teacher certification program.

FACILITIES
Housing: Men's dorms, women's dorms, apartments for married students, apartments for single students, special housing for disabled students. **Special Academic Facilities/Equipment:** Language lab, Appalachian artifacts museum, rural life museum. **Computers:** 90% of public computers are PCs, 10% of public computers are Macs, network access in dorm rooms, network access in dorm lounges, online registration, online administrative functions (other than registration), remote student-access to Web through college's connection.

CAMPUS LIFE
Activities: Choral groups, concert band, dance, drama/theater, jazz band, literary magazine, marching band, music ensembles, musical theater, radio station, student government, student newspaper, symphony orchestra, yearbook. **Organizations:** 45 registered organizations, 9 honor societies, 5 religious organizations. 6 fraternities (5% men join), 5 sororities (7% women join). **Athletics (Intercollegiate):** *Men:* Baseball, basketball, cheerleading, cross-country, football, golf, lacrosse, soccer, tennis, track/field (outdoor). *Women:* Basketball, cheerleading, cross-country, golf, soccer, softball, swimming, tennis, track/field (outdoor), volleyball.

ADMISSIONS
Basis for Candidate Selection: *Very important factors considered include:* Rigor of secondary school record, standardized test scores. *Important factors considered include:* Character/personal qualities, class rank, extracurricular activities, interview, recommendation(s), talent/ability. *Other factors considered include:* Alumni/ae relation, religious affiliation/commitment, volunteer work, work experience. **Freshman Admission Requirements:** High school diploma is required, and GED is accepted. *Academic units required:* 4 English, 3 math, 2 science (1 science lab), 2 social studies, 2 history. *Academic units recommended:* 2 foreign language. **Freshman Admission Statistics:** 2,324 applied, 60% admitted, 28% enrolled. **Transfer Admission Requirements:** College transcript(s), statement of good standing from prior institution(s). Minimum college GPA of 2.0 required. Lowest grade transferable C. **General Admission Information:** Application fee $25. Regular notification rolling. Nonfall registration accepted. Common Application not accepted.

COSTS AND FINANCIAL AID
Annual tuition $16,854. Room & board $5,900. Required fees $800. Average book expense $600. **Required Forms and Deadlines:** FAFSA, state aid form. **Types of Aid:** *Need-based scholarships/grants:* state scholarships/grants. *Loans:* FFEL Subsidized Stafford, FFEL PLUS. **Financial Aid Statistics:** 99% freshmen, 90% undergrads receive any aid.

MARSHALL UNIVERSITY

One John Marshall Drive, Huntington, WV 25755
Phone: 304-696-3160 **E-mail:** admissions@marshall.edu **CEEB Code:** 5396
Fax: 304-696-3135 **Website:** www.marshall.edu **ACT Code:** 4526
Financial Aid Phone: 304-696-3162

This public school was founded in 1837. It has a 70-acre campus.

RATINGS
Admissions Selectivity Rating: 60*   **Fire Safety Rating:** 60*   **Green Rating:** 60*

STUDENTS AND FACULTY
Enrollment: 8,931. **Student Body:** 56% female, 44% male, 19% out-of-state. African American 5%, Caucasian 89%. **Retention and Graduation:** 73% freshmen return for sophomore year. 27% grads go on to further study within 1 year. **Faculty:** Student/faculty ratio 19:1. 468 full-time faculty, 81% hold PhDs.

ACADEMICS
Degrees: Associate, bachelor's, doctoral, first professional, master's, post-bachelor's certificate, post-master's certificate. **Academic Requirements:** Arts/fine arts, computer literacy, English (including composition), foreign languages, humanities, mathematics, sciences (biological or physical), social science. **Classes:** Most classes have 20–29 students. **Majors with Highest Enrollment:** Business administration/management, elementary education and teaching, psychology. **Disciplines with Highest Percentage of Degrees Awarded:** Business/marketing 22%, education 18%, liberal arts/general studies 14%, health professions and related sciences 8%, biological/life sciences 6%, psychology 6%. **Special Study Options:** Accelerated program, cooperative education program, cross-registration, distance learning, double major, English as a second language (ESL), exchange student program (domestic), honors program, independent study, internships, study abroad, teacher certification program.

FACILITIES
Housing: Coed dorms, men's dorms, women's dorms, apartments for married students, special housing for disabled students, fraternity/sorority housing. **Special Academic Facilities/Equipment:** Art gallery, audiovisual center, language lab, superconducting nuclear magnetic resonance spectrometer. **Computers:** 95% of public computers are PCs, 5% of public computers are Macs, network access in dorm rooms, network access in dorm lounges, online registration, online administrative functions (other than registration), support for handheld computing, remote student-access to Web through college's connection.

CAMPUS LIFE
Activities: Choral groups, concert band, drama/theater, jazz band, literary magazine, marching band, music ensembles, musical theater, opera, pep band, radio station, student government, student newspaper, symphony orchestra, television station, yearbook. **Organizations:** 100 registered organizations, 11 honor societies, 10 religious organizations. 12 fraternities, 7 sororities. **Athletics (Intercollegiate):** *Men:* Baseball, basketball, cross-country, football, golf, soccer, track/field (outdoor). *Women:* Basketball, cross-country, golf, soccer, softball, swimming, tennis, track/field (outdoor), volleyball.

ADMISSIONS
Freshman Academic Profile: SAT Math middle 50% range 440–560. SAT Critical Reading middle 50% range 450–570. SAT Writing middle 50% range 450–560. ACT middle 50% range 20–25. TOEFL required of all international applicants, minimum paper TOEFL 500, minimum computer TOEFL 173. **Basis for Candidate Selection:** *Very important factors considered include:* Academic GPA, standardized test scores. *Other factors considered include:* Rigor of secondary school record. **Freshman Admission Requirements:** High school diploma is required, and GED is accepted. *Academic units required:* 4 English, 3 math, 3 science (2 science labs), 3 social studies. **Freshman Admission Statistics:** 2,305 applied, 81% admitted, 82% enrolled. **Transfer Admission Requirements:** College transcript(s). Minimum college GPA of 2.0 required. Lowest grade transferable D. **General Admission Information:** Application fee $30. Regular notification is rolling. Nonfall registration accepted. Admission may be deferred for a maximum of 1 year. Credit offered for CEEB Advanced Placement tests.

The Princeton Review's Complete Book of Colleges

COSTS AND FINANCIAL AID

Annual in-state tuition $4,360. Annual out-of-state tuition $11,264. Room and board $6,818. Average book expense $1,000. **Required Forms and Deadlines:** FAFSA, state aid form. Financial aid filing deadline 3/1. **Notification of Awards:** Applicants will be notified of awards on or about 5/1. **Types of Aid:** *Need-based scholarships/grants:* Pell, SEOG, state scholarships/grants, private scholarships, the school's own gift aid. *Loans:* Direct Subsidized Stafford, Direct Unsubsidized Stafford, Direct PLUS, Federal Perkins. **Student Employment:** Off-campus job opportunities are good. **Financial Aid Statistics:** 28% freshmen, 33% undergrads receive need-based scholarship or grant aid. 30% freshmen, 38% undergrads receive need-based self-help aid. 56 freshmen, 374 undergrads receive athletic scholarships.

MARTIN LUTHER COLLEGE

1995 Luther Court, New Ulm, MN 56073-3965
Phone: 507-354-8221 **E-mail:** seboldja-fac@mlc.wels.edu **CEEB Code:** 6435
Fax: 507-354-8225 **Website:** www.mlc-wels.edu **ACT Code:** 2127
Financial Aid Phone: 507-354-8221

This private school, affiliated with the Lutheran Church, was founded in 1995. It has a 50-acre campus.

RATINGS
Admissions Selectivity Rating: 77   **Fire Safety Rating:** 60*   **Green Rating:** 60*

STUDENTS AND FACULTY
Enrollment: 804. **Student Body:** 48% female, 52% male, 80% out-of-state. Caucasian 97%. **Retention and Graduation:** 80% freshmen return for sophomore year. 52% freshmen graduate within 4 years. 2% grads go on to further study within 1 year. **Faculty:** 85% faculty teach undergrads.

ACADEMICS
Degrees: Bachelor's. **Academic Requirements:** Arts/fine arts, computer literacy, English (including composition), history, mathematics, sciences (biological or physical), social science. **Special Study Options:** Double major, English as a second language (ESL).

FACILITIES
Housing: Men's dorms, women's dorms. **Special Academic Facilities/Equipment:** Organ facilities for music students.

CAMPUS LIFE
Activities: Choral groups, concert band, drama/theater, musical theater, student government, student newspaper, yearbook. **Athletics (Intercollegiate):** *Men:* Baseball, basketball, cross-country, football, golf, soccer, tennis, track/field (outdoor), wrestling. *Women:* Basketball, cross-country, soccer, softball, tennis, track/field (outdoor), volleyball.

ADMISSIONS
Freshman Academic Profile: 17% in top 10% of high school class, 38% in top 25% of high school class, 67% in top 50% of high school class. 13% from public high schools. ACT middle 50% range 21–27. TOEFL required of all international applicants, minimum paper TOEFL 500. **Basis for Candidate Selection:** *Very important factors considered include:* Character/personal qualities, recommendation(s), religious affiliation/commitment, rigor of secondary school record. *Important factors considered include:* Class rank, interview, standardized test scores, talent/ability. *Other factors considered include:* extracurricular activities, volunteer work, work experience. **Freshman Admission Requirements:** High school diploma is required, and GED is accepted. *Academic units required:* 4 English, 2 math, 2 science (2 science labs), 2 social studies, 2 academic electives. *Academic units recommended:* 3 math, 3 science. **Freshman Admission Statistics:** 274 applied, 89% admitted, 82% enrolled. **Transfer Admission Requirements:** High school transcript, college transcript(s), statement of good standing from prior institution(s). Minimum college GPA of 2.0 required. Lowest grade transferable C-. **General Admission Information:** Application fee $25. Regular application deadline 5/1. Regular notification is rolling. Nonfall registration accepted. Common Application not accepted. Credit and/or placement offered for CEEB Advanced Placement tests.

COSTS AND FINANCIAL AID
Annual tuition $4,130. Room & board $2,285. Required fees $490. Average book expense $670. **Required Forms and Deadlines:** FAFSA, institution's own financial aid form. Financial aid filing deadline 5/1. **Notification of Awards:** Applicants will be notified of awards on a rolling basis beginning on or about 3/1. **Types of Aid:** *Need-based scholarships/grants:* Pell, SEOG, state scholarships/grants, private scholarships, the school's own gift aid. *Loans:* FFEL

Subsidized Stafford, FFEL Unsubsidized Stafford, FFEL PLUS, Federal Perkins, state loans, college/university loans from institutional funds. **Student Employment:** Federal Work-Study Program available. Institutional employment available. Off-campus job opportunities are good. **Financial Aid Statistics:** 59% freshmen, 58% undergrads receive need-based scholarship or grant aid. 56% freshmen, 58% undergrads receive need-based self-help aid. Highest amount earned per year from on-campus jobs $950.

MARY BALDWIN COLLEGE

PO Box 1500, Staunton, VA 24402
Phone: 540-887-7019 **E-mail:** admit@mbc.edu **CEEB Code:** 5397
Fax: 540-887-7279 **Website:** www.mbc.edu **ACT Code:** 4374
Financial Aid Phone: 540-887-7022

This private school, affiliated with the Presbyterian Church, was founded in 1842. It has a 54-acre campus.

RATINGS
Admissions Selectivity Rating: 75   **Fire Safety Rating:** 60*   **Green Rating:** 60*

STUDENTS AND FACULTY
Enrollment: 1,380. **Student Body:** 95% female, 5% male, 36% out-of-state, 1% international (9 countries represented). African American 20%, Asian 2%, Caucasian 72%, Hispanic 4%. **Retention and Graduation:** 64% freshmen return for sophomore year. 49% freshmen graduate within 4 years. 24% grads go on to further study within 1 year. 10% grads pursue arts and sciences degrees. 4% grads pursue business degrees. 4% grads pursue law degrees. 3% grads pursue medical degrees. **Faculty:** Student/faculty ratio 10:1. 79 full-time faculty, 94% hold PhDs. 100% faculty teach undergrads.

ACADEMICS
Degrees: Bachelor's, certificate, master's. **Academic Requirements:** Arts/fine arts, computer literacy, English (including composition), history, humanities, mathematics, philosophy, sciences (biological or physical), social science, women's studies, physical education, writing emphasis, oral communication, international education, diversity. **Classes:** Most classes have 10–19 students. Most lab/discussion sections have 10–19 students. **Majors with Highest Enrollment:** Business administration/management, psychology, sociology. **Disciplines with Highest Percentage of Degrees Awarded:** Social sciences 18%, psychology 15%, business/marketing 13%, history 12%, visual and performing arts 10%. **Special Study Options:** Accelerated program, cooperative education program, cross-registration, distance learning, double major, dual enrollment, English as a second language (ESL), exchange student program (domestic), external degree program, honors program, independent study, internships, liberal arts/career combination, student-designed major, study abroad, teacher certification program, summer exchange program with Doshisha Women's College in Kyoto.

FACILITIES
Housing: Women's dorms, apartments for single students, special housing for international students, special interest (club) housing, honors, leadership, community services. **Special Academic Facilities/Equipment:** Audiovisual center, TV studio, communications lab, electron microscope, gas chromatoscope, greenhouse. **Computers:** 50% of public computers are PCs, 50% of public computers are Macs, network access in dorm rooms, network access in dorm lounges, online registration, online administrative functions (other than registration), remote student-access to Web through college's connection.

CAMPUS LIFE
Activities: Choral groups, dance, drama/theater, literary magazine, marching band, music ensembles, musical theater, radio station, student government, student newspaper, student-run film society, television station, yearbook. **Organizations:** 34 registered organizations, 9 honor societies, 4 religious organizations. **Athletics (Intercollegiate):** *Women:* Basketball, field hockey, soccer, softball, swimming, tennis, volleyball.

ADMISSIONS
Freshman Academic Profile: 17% in top 10% of high school class, 43% in top 25% of high school class, 77% in top 50% of high school class. 75% from public high schools. SAT Math middle 50% range 450–550. SAT Critical Reading middle 50% range 470–580. SAT Writing middle 50% range 460–570. ACT middle 50% range 20–29. TOEFL required of all international applicants, minimum paper TOEFL 500. **Basis for Candidate Selection:** *Very important factors considered include:* Rigor of secondary school record, standardized test scores. *Important factors considered include:* Character/personal qualities,

extracurricular activities, interview. *Other factors considered include:* Alumni/ae relation, application essay, class rank, recommendation(s), talent/ability, volunteer work, work experience. **Freshman Admission Requirements:** High school diploma is required, and GED is accepted. *Academic units required:* 4 English, 3 math, 2 science (1 science lab), 2 foreign language, 3 social studies. *Academic units recommended:* 3 foreign language, 2 academic electives. **Freshman Admission Statistics:** 1,241 applied, 77% admitted, 27% enrolled. **Transfer Admission Requirements:** High school transcript, college transcript(s), statement of good standing from prior institution(s). Minimum college GPA of 2.0 required. Lowest grade transferable C-. **General Admission Information:** Application fee $35. Early decision application deadline 11/8. Regular notification is rolling. Nonfall registration accepted. Admission may be deferred for a maximum of 1 semester. Credit offered for CEEB Advanced Placement tests.

COSTS AND FINANCIAL AID

Annual tuition $22,530. Room & board $6,470. Required fees $200. Average book expense $900. **Required Forms and Deadlines:** FAFSA, state aid form. Financial aid filing deadline 5/15. **Notification of Awards:** Applicants will be notified of awards on a rolling basis beginning on or about 1/1. **Types of Aid:** *Need-based scholarships/grants:* Pell, SEOG, state scholarships/grants, private scholarships, the school's own gift aid. *Loans:* FFEL Subsidized Stafford, FFEL Unsubsidized Stafford, FFEL PLUS, Federal Perkins, private alternative loans. **Student Employment:** Federal Work-Study Program available. Institutional employment available. Off-campus job opportunities are excellent. **Financial Aid Statistics:** 69% freshmen, 72% undergrads receive need-based scholarship or grant aid. 55% freshmen, 63% undergrads receive need-based self-help aid. Highest amount earned per year from on-campus jobs $1,356.

MARYCREST INTERNATIONAL UNIVERSITY

1607 West Twelfth Street, Davenport, IA 52804
Phone: 563-326-9225 **E-mail:** mfarber@mcrest.edu **CEEB Code:** 6397
Fax: 563-327-9620 **Website:** www.mcrest.edu **ACT Code:** 1334
Financial Aid Phone: 563-326-9524

This private school, affiliated with the Catholic Heritage Church, was founded in 1939. It has a 30-acre campus.

RATINGS
Admissions Selectivity Rating: 60*   **Fire Safety Rating:** 60*   **Green Rating:** 60*

STUDENTS AND FACULTY
Enrollment: 374. **Student Body:** 53% female, 47% male, 45% out-of-state, 6% international. African American 5%, Caucasian 49%, Hispanic 3%. **Retention and Graduation:** 84% freshmen return for sophomore year. 5% grads go on to further study within 1 year. 5% grads pursue arts and sciences degrees. 1% grads pursue law degrees. 1% grads pursue medical degrees. **Faculty:** Student/faculty ratio 12:1. 26 full-time faculty, 54% hold PhDs. 97% faculty teach undergrads.

ACADEMICS
Degrees: Associate, bachelor's, first professional, master's. **Academic Requirements:** Arts/fine arts, computer literacy, English (including composition), foreign languages, history, humanities, mathematics, philosophy, sciences (biological or physical), social science. **Classes:** Most classes have fewer than 10 students. **Disciplines with Highest Percentage of Degrees Awarded:** Computer and information sciences 27%, business/marketing 18%, health professions and related sciences 14%, social sciences 14%, education 12%, psychology 7%. **Special Study Options:** Cooperative education program, double major, English as a second language (ESL), internships, liberal arts/career combination, student-designed major, study abroad, teacher certification program, weekend college.

FACILITIES
Housing: Coed dorms, men's dorms, women's dorms, apartments for single students. **Computers:** Network access in dorm rooms, online registration, remote student-access to Web through college's connection.

CAMPUS LIFE
Activities: Literary magazine, radio station, student government, student newspaper, television station. **Organizations:** 1 religious organization. **Athletics (Intercollegiate):** *Men:* Basketball, soccer, volleyball. *Women:* Basketball, soccer, softball, volleyball.

ADMISSIONS
Freshman Academic Profile: ACT middle 50% range 17–24. TOEFL required of all international applicants, minimum paper TOEFL 530. **Basis for**

Candidate Selection: *Very important factors considered include:* Character/personal qualities, extracurricular activities, geographical residence, interview, racial/ethnic status, recommendation(s), rigor of secondary school record, standardized test scores, talent/ability. *Important factors considered include:* Alumni/ae relation, religious affiliation/commitment, state residency, volunteer work, work experience. *Other factors considered include:* Class rank. **Freshman Admission Requirements:** High school diploma is required, and GED is accepted. *Academic units recommended:* 4 English, 3 math, 2 science, 3 foreign language, 2 social studies, 2 history. **Freshman Admission Statistics:** 399 applied, 98% admitted, 25% enrolled. **Transfer Admission Requirements:** High school transcript, college transcript(s). Minimum college GPA of 2.0 required. Lowest grade transferable C. **General Admission Information:** Application fee $25. Regular notification rolling. Nonfall registration accepted. Common Application not accepted. Credit and/or placement offered for CEEB Advanced Placement tests.

COSTS AND FINANCIAL AID

Annual tuition $13,400. Room & board $5,200. Required fees $370. Average book expense $575. **Required Forms and Deadlines:** FAFSA. **Notification of Awards:** Applicants will be notified of awards on or about 3/1. **Types of Aid:** *Need-based scholarships/grants:* State scholarships/grants. *Loans:* FFEL Subsidized Stafford, FFEL PLUS. **Student Employment:** Federal Work-Study Program available. Institutional employment available. Off-campus job opportunities are good. **Financial Aid Statistics:** Highest amount earned per year from on-campus jobs $1,200.

MARYGROVE COLLEGE

8425 West McNichols Road, Detroit, MI 48221-2599
Phone: 313-927-1240 **E-mail:** info@marygrove.edu **CEEB Code:** 1452
Fax: 313-927-1345 **Website:** www.marygrove.edu **ACT Code:** 2024
Financial Aid Phone: 313-927-1200

This private school, affiliated with the Roman Catholic Church, was founded in 1927. It has a 50-acre campus.

RATINGS
Admissions Selectivity Rating: 81   **Fire Safety Rating:** 60*   **Green Rating:** 60*

STUDENTS AND FACULTY
Enrollment: 662. **Student Body:** 79% female, 21% male, 2% out-of-state, 1% international. African American 70%, Caucasian 5%, Hispanic 2%. **Retention and Graduation:** 61% freshmen return for sophomore year. 30% grads go on to further study within 1 year. 30% grads pursue arts and sciences degrees. **Faculty:** Student/faculty ratio 16:1. 65 full-time faculty, 66% hold PhDs. 100% faculty teach undergrads.

ACADEMICS
Degrees: Associate, bachelor's, certificate, master's, post-bachelor's certificate. **Academic Requirements:** Arts/fine arts, English (including composition), history, humanities, mathematics, philosophy, sciences (biological or physical), social science. **Classes:** Most classes have fewer than 10 students. **Majors with Highest Enrollment:** Business/commerce, computer and information sciences, social work. **Disciplines with Highest Percentage of Degrees Awarded:** Social sciences 23%, education 12%, visual and performing arts 12%, business/marketing 11%, computer and information sciences 10%, English 9%. **Special Study Options:** Cooperative education program, distance learning, double major, honors program, independent study, student-designed major, study abroad, teacher certification program.

FACILITIES
Housing: Coed dorms. **Special Academic Facilities/Equipment:** Conference center, chapel, theater, art gallery. **Computers:** 90% of public computers are PCs, 10% of public computers are Macs, network access in dorm rooms, network access in dorm lounges, online registration, online administrative functions (other than registration), remote student-access to Web through college's connection.

CAMPUS LIFE
Activities: Choral groups, dance, music ensembles, student government. **Organizations:** 17 registered organizations, 6 honor societies.

ADMISSIONS
Freshman Academic Profile: 10% in top 10% of high school class, 75% in top 25% of high school class, 100% in top 50% of high school class. 80% from public high schools. ACT middle 50% range 16–21. TOEFL required of all international applicants, minimum paper TOEFL 520. **Basis for Candidate Selection:** *Important factors considered include:* Character/personal qualities,

interview, rigor of secondary school record, standardized test scores, talent/ability. *Other factors considered include:* Extracurricular activities, recommendation(s), volunteer work, work experience. **Freshman Admission Requirements:** High school diploma is required, and GED is accepted. *Academic units recommended:* 8 English, 4 math, 1 science, 1 foreign language, 4 social studies, 5 history. **Freshman Admission Statistics:** 290 applied, 40% admitted, 36% enrolled. **Transfer Admission Requirements:** College transcript(s), statement of good standing from prior institution(s). Minimum college GPA of 2.7 required. Lowest grade transferable C. **General Admission Information:** Application fee $25. Regular application deadline 8/15. Regular notification 8/15. Nonfall registration accepted. Admission may be deferred for a maximum of 1 year. Common Application not accepted. Credit and/or placement offered for CEEB Advanced Placement tests.

COSTS AND FINANCIAL AID

Annual tuition $12,190. Room & board $6,000. Required fees $250. Average book expense $1,180. **Required Forms and Deadlines:** FAFSA, institution's own financial aid form. Financial aid filing deadline 3/15. **Notification of Awards:** Applicants will be notified of awards on a rolling basis beginning on or about 5/1. **Types of Aid:** *Need-based scholarships/grants:* Pell, SEOG, state scholarships/grants, private scholarships, the school's own gift aid. *Loans:* Direct Subsidized Stafford, Direct Unsubsidized Stafford, Direct PLUS, FFEL Subsidized Stafford, FFEL Unsubsidized Stafford, FFEL PLUS, Federal Perkins, state loans. **Student Employment:** Federal Work-Study Program available. Off-campus job opportunities are good. **Financial Aid Statistics:** Highest amount earned per year from on-campus jobs $2,700.

MARYLAND INSTITUTE COLLEGE OF ART

1300 Mount Royal Avenue, Baltimore, MD 21217
Phone: 410-225-2222 **E-mail:** admissions@mica.edu **CEEB Code:** 5399
Fax: 410-225-2337 **Website:** www.mica.edu **ACT Code:** 1710
Financial Aid Phone: 410-225-2285

This private school was founded in 1826. It has a 12-acre campus.

RATINGS
Admissions Selectivity Rating: 90   **Fire Safety Rating:** 88   **Green Rating:** 65

STUDENTS AND FACULTY

Enrollment: 1,637. **Student Body:** 65% female, 35% male, 80% out-of-state, 5% international (48 countries represented). African American 3%, Asian 9%, Caucasian 67%, Hispanic 4%. **Retention and Graduation:** 86% freshmen return for sophomore year. 59% freshmen graduate within 4 years. 23% grads go on to further study within 1 year. **Faculty:** Student/faculty ratio 10:1. 122 full-time faculty, 81% hold PhDs. 95% faculty teach undergrads.

ACADEMICS

Degrees: Bachelor's, master's, post-bachelor's certificate. **Academic Requirements:** Arts/fine arts, computer literacy, English (including composition), history, humanities, sciences (biological or physical), social science. **Classes:** Most classes have 10–19 students. **Majors with Highest Enrollment:** Illustration, intermedia/multimedia, painting. **Disciplines with Highest Percentage of Degrees Awarded:** Visual and performing arts 94%, education 6%. **Special Study Options:** Accelerated program, cross-registration, distance learning, double major, dual enrollment, exchange student program (domestic), independent study, internships, student-designed major, study abroad, teacher certification program. Cooperative exchange programs with Johns Hopkins University, Goucher College, the Peabody Conservatory of Music, University of Baltimore, Loyola College, Notre Dame College, University of Maryland Baltimore County, Morgan State University, Baltimore Hebrew College, and Towson University.

FACILITIES

Housing: Coed dorms, apartments for married students, apartments for single students, special housing for disabled students, special housing for international students. **Special Academic Facilities/Equipment:** There are 7 art galleries open to the public year-round featuring work by MICA faculty, students, and nationally/internationally known artists; a nature library; and an extensive slide library containing more than 200,000 slides. **Computers:** 25% of classrooms are wired, 90% of classrooms are wireless, 10% of public computers are PCs, 90% of public computers are Macs, network access in dorm rooms, network access in dorm lounges, remote student-access to Web through college's connection.

CAMPUS LIFE

Activities: Choral groups, dance, drama/theater, literary magazine, student government, student-run film society, television station. **Organizations:** 40 registered organizations, 3 religious organizations.

ADMISSIONS

Freshman Academic Profile: 35% in top 10% of high school class, 64% in top 25% of high school class, 86% in top 50% of high school class. 65% from public high schools. SAT Math middle 50% range 500–620. SAT Critical Reading middle 50% range 530–660. SAT Writing middle 50% range 490–630. TOEFL required of all international applicants, minimum paper TOEFL 550, minimum computer TOEFL 213. **Basis for Candidate Selection:** *Very important factors considered include:* Academic GPA, level of applicant's interest, rigor of secondary school record, talent/ability. *Important factors considered include:* Application essay, class rank, extracurricular activities, interview, standardized test scores. *Other factors considered include:* Alumni/ae relation, character/personal qualities, racial/ethnic status, recommendation(s), volunteer work. **Freshman Admission Requirements:** High school diploma is required, and GED is accepted. *Academic units required:* 4 English, 2 math, 2 science (1 science lab), 4 social studies, 3 history, 6 academic electives, 2 studio art, 2 academic electives. *Academic units recommended:* 4 English, 3 math, 3 science, 4 social studies, 4 history, 5 studio art, 2 academic electives. **Freshman Admission Statistics:** 2,313 applied, 43% admitted, 43% enrolled. **Transfer Admission Requirements:** High school transcript, college transcript(s), essay or personal statement. Lowest grade transferable C. **General Admission Information:** Application fee $50. Early decision application deadline 11/15. Regular application deadline 2/15. Regular notification 3/15. Nonfall registration accepted. Admission may be deferred for a maximum of 1 year. Credit and/or placement offered for CEEB Advanced Placement tests.

COSTS AND FINANCIAL AID

Annual tuition $29,700. Room and board $8,390. Required fees $980. Average book expense $1,400. **Required Forms and Deadlines:** FAFSA, institution's own financial aid form. Financial aid filing deadline 3/1. **Notification of Awards:** Applicants will be notified of awards on or about 4/15. **Types of Aid:** *Need-based scholarships/grants:* Pell, SEOG, state scholarships/grants, private scholarships, the school's own gift aid. *Loans:* FFEL Subsidized Stafford, FFEL Unsubsidized Stafford, FFEL PLUS, Federal Perkins. **Student Employment:** Federal Work-Study Program available. Institutional employment available. Off-campus job opportunities are excellent. **Financial Aid Statistics:** 59% freshmen, 62% undergrads receive need-based scholarship or grant aid. 52% freshmen, 55% undergrads receive need-based self-help aid.

MARYLHURST UNIVERSITY

PO Box 261, Marylhurst, OR 97036
Phone: 503-699-6268 **E-mail:** admissions@marylhurst.edu **CEEB Code:** 440
Fax: 503-636-9526 **Website:** www.marylhurst.edu **ACT Code:** 3470
Financial Aid Phone: 503-699-6253

This private school, affiliated with the Roman Catholic Church, was founded in 1893. It has a 68-acre campus.

RATINGS
Admissions Selectivity Rating: 60*   **Fire Safety Rating:** 60*   **Green Rating:** 60*

STUDENTS AND FACULTY

Enrollment: 672. **Student Body:** 78% female, 22% male, 2% out-of-state. **Retention and Graduation:** 50% freshmen return for sophomore year. 17% freshmen graduate within 4 years. **Faculty:** Student/faculty ratio 7:1. 31 full-time faculty, 55% hold PhDs. 100% faculty teach undergrads.

ACADEMICS

Degrees: Bachelor's, certificate, first professional, master's, post-bachelor's certificate, post-master's certificate. **Academic Requirements:** Arts/fine arts, computer literacy, English (including composition), history, humanities, mathematics, philosophy, sciences (biological or physical), social science, interdisciplinary, integrated learning. **Classes:** Most classes have fewer than 10 students. **Majors with Highest Enrollment:** Business administration and management, communications studies/speech communication and rhetoric, multi/interdisciplinary studies. **Disciplines with Highest Percentage of Degrees Awarded:** Communication technologies 25%, business/marketing 21%, liberal arts/general studies 15%, visual and performing arts 15%, interdisciplinary studies 10%, social sciences 6%. **Special Study Options:** Cross-registration, distance learning, double major, dual enrollment, English as a second language (ESL), independent study, internships, student-designed major, study abroad, weekend college. Online BS (business administration and organizational communication) and MBA programs.

FACILITIES

Housing: Temporary housing. **Special Academic Facilities/Equipment:** Art Gym, Streff Gallery. **Computers:** Online registration, online administrative functions (other than registration).

CAMPUS LIFE

Activities: Choral groups, literary magazine, music ensembles, symphony orchestra. **Organizations:** 1 religious organization.

ADMISSIONS

Freshman Academic Profile: TOEFL required of all international applicants, minimum paper TOEFL 550, minimum computer TOEFL 213. **Freshman Admission Requirements:** High school diploma is required, and GED is accepted. **Transfer Admission Requirements:** High school transcript, college transcript(s). Lowest grade transferable C-. **General Admission Information:** Application fee $20. Regular notification continuous. Nonfall registration accepted. Admission may be deferred for a maximum of 1 year. Credit and/or placement offered for CEEB Advanced Placement tests.

COSTS AND FINANCIAL AID

Annual tuition $15,120. Required fees $450. Average book expense $900. **Required Forms and Deadlines:** FAFSA, institution's own financial aid form. **Notification of Awards:** Applicants will be notified of awards on a rolling basis beginning on or about 4/15. **Types of Aid:** *Need-based scholarships/grants:* Pell, SEOG, state scholarships/grants, private scholarships, the school's own gift aid. *Loans:* FFEL Subsidized Stafford, FFEL Unsubsidized Stafford, FFEL PLUS, Federal Perkins. **Financial Aid Statistics:** 56% freshmen, 64% undergrads receive need-based scholarship or grant aid. 44% freshmen, 66% undergrads receive need-based self-help aid.

MARYMOUNT COLLEGE (CA)

Office of Admission, 30800 Palos Verdes Drive East, Rancho Palos Verdes, CA 90275
Phone: 310-377-5501 **E-mail:** admissions@marymountpv.edu or info@marymountpv.edu **CEEB Code:** 4515 **Fax:** 310-265-0962 **Website:** www.marymountpv.edu **ACT Code:** 0316
Financial Aid Phone: 310-377-5501

This private school, affiliated with the Roman Catholic Church, was founded in 1932. It has a 26-acre campus.

RATINGS

Admissions Selectivity Rating: 60*   **Fire Safety Rating:** 60*   **Green Rating:** 60*

STUDENTS AND FACULTY

Enrollment: 723. **Student Body:** 48% female, 52% male, 2% out-of-state, 20% international. African American 5%, Asian 7%, Caucasian 44%, Hispanic 13%. **Retention and Graduation:** 58% freshmen return for sophomore year. **Faculty:** Student/faculty ratio 12:1. 40 full-time faculty, 48% hold PhDs. 100% faculty teach undergrads.

ACADEMICS

Degrees: Associate. **Academic Requirements:** Arts/fine arts, English (including composition), history, humanities, mathematics, philosophy, sciences (biological or physical), social science, religion. **Classes:** Most classes have 10–19 students. Most lab/discussion sections have fewer than 10 students. **Special Study Options:** Cooperative education program, English as a second language (ESL), honors program, independent study, internships, study abroad, weekend college.

FACILITIES

Housing: Apartments for single students, volunteers in community. **Computers:** 100% of public computers are PCs.

CAMPUS LIFE

Activities: Choral groups, dance, drama/theater, literary magazine, music ensembles, musical theater, student government, student newspaper, student-run film society. **Organizations:** 21 registered organizations, 1 honor society, 1 religious organization. **Athletics (Intercollegiate):** *Men:* Tennis. *Women:* Tennis.

ADMISSIONS

Freshman Academic Profile: SAT Math middle 50% range 410–530. SAT Critical Reading middle 50% range 420–530. ACT middle 50% range 17–21. **Basis for Candidate Selection:** *Very important factors considered include:* Rigor of secondary school record. *Other factors considered include:* Alumni/ae relation, application essay, character/personal qualities, class rank, extracurricular activities, interview, recommendation(s), standardized test scores, talent/ability, volunteer work, work experience. **Freshman Admission Requirements:** High school diploma is required, and GED is accepted. *Academic units recommended:* 4 English, 3 math, 2 science, 2 foreign language, 2 social studies. **Freshman Admission Statistics:** 1,303 applied, 68% admitted, 45% enrolled. **Transfer Admission Requirements:** High school transcript, college

transcript(s). Lowest grade transferable C-. **General Admission Information:** Application fee $35. Regular notification is rolling. Nonfall registration accepted. Admission may be deferred for a maximum of 1 year. Common Application accepted. Credit offered for CEEB Advanced Placement tests.

COSTS AND FINANCIAL AID

Annual tuition $15,200. Room & board $7,550. Required fees $230. Average book expense $700. **Required Forms and Deadlines:** FAFSA, institution's own financial aid form. Financial aid filing deadline 3/2. **Notification of Awards:** Applicants will be notified of awards on a rolling basis beginning on or about 5/1. **Types of Aid:** *Need-based scholarships/grants:* Pell, SEOG, state scholarships/grants, private scholarships, the school's own gift aid. *Loans:* FFEL Subsidized Stafford, FFEL Unsubsidized Stafford, FFEL PLUS. **Student Employment:** Federal Work-Study Program available. Institutional employment available. **Financial Aid Statistics:** 26% freshmen, 35% undergrads receive need-based scholarship or grant aid. 26% freshmen, 31% undergrads receive need-based self-help aid. 1 freshmen, 1 undergrads receive athletic scholarships.

MARYMOUNT MANHATTAN COLLEGE

221 East Seventy-first Street, New York, NY 10021
Phone: 212-517-0430 **E-mail:** admissions@mmm.edu **CEEB Code:** 2405
Fax: 212-517-0448 **Website:** www.mmm.edu **ACT Code:** 2810
Financial Aid Phone: 212-517-0500

This private school was founded in 1936. It has a 1-acre campus.

RATINGS

Admissions Selectivity Rating: 60*   **Fire Safety Rating:** 82   **Green Rating:** 88

STUDENTS AND FACULTY

Enrollment: 1,871. **Student Body:** 77% female, 23% male, 51% out-of-state, 3% international (32 countries represented). African American 12%, Asian 4%, Caucasian 71%, Hispanic 10%. **Retention and Graduation:** 69% freshmen return for sophomore year. 30% freshmen graduate within 4 years. 33% grads go on to further study within 1 year. 9% grads pursue arts and sciences degrees. 12% grads pursue business degrees. 7% grads pursue law degrees. 5% grads pursue medical degrees. **Faculty:** Student/faculty ratio 12:1. 91 full-time faculty, 86% hold PhDs. 100% faculty teach undergrads.

ACADEMICS

Degrees: Associate, bachelor's, certificate. **Academic Requirements:** Arts/fine arts, English (including composition), humanities, mathematics, sciences (biological or physical), social science, language, literature, philosophy, psychology, religious studies. **Classes:** Most classes have 10–19 students. **Majors with Highest Enrollment:** Communications studies/speech communication and rhetoric, dance, drama and dramatics/theater arts. **Disciplines with Highest Percentage of Degrees Awarded:** Visual and performing arts 40%, communications/journalism 22%, social sciences 9%, business/marketing 9%, psychology 7%, English 5%. **Special Study Options:** Accelerated program, distance learning, double major, dual enrollment, exchange student program (domestic), independent study, internships, liberal arts/career combination, study abroad, teacher certification program.

FACILITIES

Housing: Coed dorms. **Special Academic Facilities/Equipment:** Gallery, communications and learning center, theater, media center, college skills center, mathematics lab, Samuel Freeman Science Center, communication arts multimedia suite. **Computers:** 45% of classrooms are wired, 33% of classrooms are wireless, 90% of public computers are PCs, 5% of public computers are Macs, 5% of public computers are UNIX, network access in dorm rooms, network access in dorm lounges, online registration, online administrative functions (other than registration), remote student-access to Web through college's connection.

CAMPUS LIFE

Activities: Choral groups, dance, drama/theater, literary magazine, musical theater, opera, radio station, student government, student newspaper, yearbook. **Organizations:** 30 registered organizations, 7 honor societies, 2 religious organizations. Environmental Initiatives: Purchase of renewable energy. recycling of paper and bottles, awareness campaigns to get students and faculty and staff moving in a green direction.

ADMISSIONS

Freshman Academic Profile: 70% from public high schools. SAT Math middle 50% range 470–570. SAT Critical Reading middle 50% range 490–600. ACT middle 50% range 21–25. TOEFL required of all international applicants, minimum paper TOEFL 550, minimum computer TOEFL 213. **Basis for Candidate Selection:** *Very important factors considered include:* Academic GPA, rigor of secondary school record, standardized test scores. *Important factors considered include:* Application essay, character/personal qualities, extracurricular activities, recommendation(s), talent/ability. *Other factors considered include:* Class rank, interview, level of applicant's interest, volunteer work, work experience. **Freshman Admission Requirements:** High school diploma is required, and GED is accepted. *Academic units required:* 4 English, 3 math, 2 science, 3 social studies, 4 academic electives. *Academic units recommended:* 3 science, 2 foreign language. **Freshman Admission Statistics:** 2,255 applied, 76% admitted, 27% enrolled. **Transfer Admission Requirements:** High school transcript, college transcript(s), statement of good standing from prior institution(s). Minimum college GPA of 2.0 required. Lowest grade transferable C-. **General Admission Information:** Application fee $60. Regular notification is rolling. Nonfall registration accepted. Admission may be deferred for a maximum of 1 semester. Credit and/or placement offered for CEEB Advanced Placement tests.

COSTS AND FINANCIAL AID

Annual tuition $19,666. Room and board $12,250. Required fees $934. Average book expense $1,000. **Required Forms and Deadlines:** FAFSA. Financial aid filing deadline 3/15. **Notification of Awards:** Applicants will be notified of awards on a rolling basis beginning on or about 3/15. **Types of Aid:** *Need-based scholarships/grants:* Pell, SEOG, state scholarships/grants, private scholarships, the school's own gift aid. *Loans:* FFEL Subsidized Stafford, FFEL Unsubsidized Stafford, FFEL PLUS. **Student Employment:** Federal Work-Study Program available. Institutional employment available. Off-campus job opportunities are excellent. **Financial Aid Statistics:** 57% freshmen, 56% undergrads receive need-based scholarship or grant aid. 56% freshmen, 56% undergrads receive need-based self-help aid. 81% freshmen, 67% undergrads receive any aid. Highest amount earned per year from on-campus jobs $2,000.

MARYMOUNT UNIVERSITY

2807 North Glebe Road, Arlington, VA 22207
Phone: 703-284-1500 **E-mail:** admissions@marymount.edu **CEEB Code:** 5405
Fax: 703-522-0349 **Website:** www.marymount.edu **ACT Code:** 4378
Financial Aid Phone: 703-284-1530

This private school, affiliated with the Roman Catholic Church, was founded in 1950. It has a 21-acre campus.

RATINGS
Admissions Selectivity Rating: 73　　**Fire Safety Rating:** 60*　　**Green Rating:** 60*

STUDENTS AND FACULTY
Enrollment: 2,260. **Student Body:** 74% female, 26% male, 42% out-of-state, 7% international (76 countries represented). African American 14%, Asian 9%, Caucasian 46%, Hispanic 12%. **Retention and Graduation:** 68% freshmen return for sophomore year. **Faculty:** Student/faculty ratio 13:1. 143 full-time faculty, 85% hold PhDs. 77% faculty teach undergrads.

ACADEMICS
Degrees: Associate, bachelor's, certificate, doctoral, master's, post-bachelor's certificate, post-master's certificate. **Academic Requirements:** English (including composition), history, humanities, mathematics, philosophy, sciences (biological or physical), social science. **Classes:** Most classes have 10–19 students. Most lab/discussion sections have 10–19 students. **Majors with Highest Enrollment:** Business administration and management, interior design, nursing/registered nurse training (RN, ASN, BSN, MSN). **Disciplines with Highest Percentage of Degrees Awarded:** Business/marketing 24%, visual and performing arts 16%, psychology 11%, computer and information sciences 9%, liberal arts/general studies 8%, social sciences 8%. **Special Study Options:** Cross-registration, double major, English as a second language (ESL), honors program, independent study, internships, student-designed major, study abroad, teacher certification program.

FACILITIES
Housing: Coed dorms, women's dorms. **Special Academic Facilities/Equipment:** Art gallery, learning resource center, audiovisual center and studio, computer labs. **Computers:** 85% of public computers are PCs, 15% of public computers are Macs, network access in dorm rooms, network access in dorm lounges, online registration, online administrative functions (other than registration), remote student-access to Web through college's connection.

CAMPUS LIFE
Activities: Choral groups, dance, drama/theater, literary magazine, student

government, student newspaper, yearbook. **Organizations:** 30 registered organizations, 9 honor societies, 1 religious organization. **Athletics (Intercollegiate):** *Men:* Basketball, cross-country, golf, lacrosse, soccer, swimming. *Women:* Basketball, cross-country, lacrosse, soccer, swimming, volleyball. Environmental Initiatives: Recycling program. Public transportation available. Car pool incentives.

ADMISSIONS
Freshman Academic Profile: 7% in top 10% of high school class, 33% in top 25% of high school class, 74% in top 50% of high school class. SAT Math middle 50% range 450–550. SAT Critical Reading middle 50% range 450–560. SAT Writing middle 50% range 450–550. ACT middle 50% range 18–24. TOEFL required of all international applicants, minimum paper TOEFL 550, minimum computer TOEFL 213. **Basis for Candidate Selection:** *Very important factors considered include:* Rigor of secondary school record, standardized test scores. *Important factors considered include:* Class rank, extracurricular activities, recommendation(s), talent/ability, work experience. *Other factors considered include:* Alumni/ae relation, application essay, character/personal qualities, interview. **Freshman Admission Requirements:** High school diploma is required, and GED is accepted. *Academic units recommended:* 4 English, 3 math, 2 science, 3 foreign language, 3 social studies. **Freshman Admission Statistics:** 1,854 applied, 78% admitted, 26% enrolled. **Transfer Admission Requirements:** College transcript(s), statement of good standing from prior institution(s). Minimum college GPA of 2.0 required. Lowest grade transferable C. **General Admission Information:** Application fee $40. Regular notification is rolling. Nonfall registration accepted. Admission may be deferred for a maximum of 1 year. Credit offered for CEEB Advanced Placement tests.

COSTS AND FINANCIAL AID
Annual tuition $20,190. Room and board $8,705. Required fees $220. Average book expense $800. **Required Forms and Deadlines:** FAFSA, state aid form. Financial aid filing deadline 3/1. **Notification of Awards:** Applicants will be notified of awards on a rolling basis beginning on or about 3/15. **Types of Aid:** *Need-based scholarships/grants:* Pell, SEOG, state scholarships/grants, private scholarships, the school's own gift aid, Federal Nursing Scholarships. *Loans:* Direct Subsidized Stafford, Direct Unsubsidized Stafford, FFEL Subsidized Stafford, FFEL Unsubsidized Stafford, FFEL PLUS, Federal Perkins. **Financial Aid Statistics:** 53% freshmen, 42% undergrads receive need-based scholarship or grant aid. 48% freshmen, 46% undergrads receive need-based self-help aid. 78% freshmen, 67% undergrads receive any aid.

See page 1258.

MARYVILLE COLLEGE

502 East Lamar Alexander Parkway, Maryville, TN 37804-5907
Phone: 865-981-8092 **E-mail:** admissions@maryvillecollege.edu **CEEB Code:** 1454
Fax: 865-981-8005 **Website:** www.maryvillecollege.edu **ACT Code:** 3988
Financial Aid Phone: 865-981-8100

This private school, affiliated with the Presbyterian Church, was founded in 1819. It has a 370-acre campus.

RATINGS
Admissions Selectivity Rating: 83　　**Fire Safety Rating:** 88　　**Green Rating:** 81

STUDENTS AND FACULTY
Enrollment: 1,155. **Student Body:** 56% female, 44% male, 21% out-of-state, 5% international (23 countries represented). African American 5%, Asian 1%, Caucasian 86%, Hispanic 2%. **Retention and Graduation:** 72% freshmen return for sophomore year. 45% freshmen graduate within 4 years. 29% grads go on to further study within 1 year. **Faculty:** Student/faculty ratio 13:1. 77 full-time faculty, 83% hold PhDs. 100% faculty teach undergrads.

ACADEMICS
Degrees: Bachelor's. **Academic Requirements:** Arts/fine arts, computer literacy, English (including composition), foreign languages, history, humanities, mathematics, philosophy, sciences (biological or physical), social science, interdisciplinary courses, seminars, religion. **Classes:** Most classes have 10–19 students. Most lab/discussion sections have 10–19 students. **Majors with Highest Enrollment:** Biology/biological sciences, business administration/management, education. **Disciplines with Highest Percentage of Degrees Awarded:** Business/marketing 25%, education 14%, visual and performing arts 14%, psychology 13%, social sciences 11%, biological/life sciences 10%. **Special Study Options:** Double major, English as a second language (ESL), honors program, independent study, internships, liberal arts/career combination, student-designed major, study abroad, teacher certification program.

FACILITIES

Housing: Coed dorms, men's dorms, women's dorms, apartments for single students, special housing for disabled students, special interest groups. **Special Academic Facilities/Equipment:** Art gallery, theater, greenhouse, College Woods. **Computers:** 35% of classrooms are wired, 80% of classrooms are wireless, 92% of public computers are PCs, 8% of public computers are Macs, network access in dorm rooms, online administrative functions (other than registration), remote student-access to Web through college's connection.

CAMPUS LIFE

Activities: Choral groups, concert band, dance, drama/theater, jazz band, literary magazine, music ensembles, musical theater, student government, student newspaper, symphony orchestra, yearbook. **Organizations:** 55 registered organizations, 15 honor societies, 5 religious organizations. **Athletics (Intercollegiate):** *Men:* Baseball, basketball, cross-country, football, soccer, tennis. *Women:* Basketball, cross-country, soccer, softball, tennis, volleyball. Environmental Initiatives: Steam plant boiler is fueled by recycled wood products. Campus-wide recycling program. Purchase of green power for selected campus buildings.

ADMISSIONS

Freshman Academic Profile: 26% in top 10% of high school class, 57% in top 25% of high school class, 86% in top 50% of high school class. 87% from public high schools. SAT Math middle 50% range 480–590. SAT Critical Reading middle 50% range 460–600. SAT Writing middle 50% range 460–600. ACT middle 50% range 21–27. TOEFL required of all international applicants, minimum paper TOEFL 525, minimum computer TOEFL 200. **Basis for Candidate Selection:** *Very important factors considered include:* Class rank, rigor of secondary school record, standardized test scores. *Important factors considered include:* Academic GPA, extracurricular activities, interview, recommendation(s). *Other factors considered include:* Alumni/ae relation, application essay, character/personal qualities, first generation, level of applicant's interest, talent/ability, volunteer work. **Freshman Admission Requirements:** High school diploma is required, and GED is accepted. *Academic units required:* 4 English, 3 math, 2 science (1 science lab), 2 foreign language, 2 social studies, 1 academic elective. *Academic units recommended:* 1 history. **Freshman Admission Statistics:** 1,291 applied, 78% admitted, 30% enrolled. **Transfer Admission Requirements:** College transcript(s), statement of good standing from prior institution(s). Minimum college GPA of 2.0 required. Lowest grade transferable C. **General Admission Information:** Early decision application deadline 11/15. Regular application deadline 3/1. Regular notification is rolling. Nonfall registration accepted. Admission may be deferred for a maximum of 1 year. Credit and/or placement offered for CEEB Advanced Placement tests.

COSTS AND FINANCIAL AID

Annual tuition $24,675. Room and board $7,800. Required fees $675. Average book expense $850. **Required Forms and Deadlines:** FAFSA. Financial aid filing deadline 3/1. **Types of Aid:** *Need-based scholarships/grants:* Pell, SEOG, state scholarships/grants, private scholarships, the school's own gift aid. *Loans:* Direct Subsidized Stafford, Direct Unsubsidized Stafford, Direct PLUS, FFEL Subsidized Stafford, FFEL Unsubsidized Stafford, FFEL PLUS, Federal Perkins, state loans, college/university loans from institutional funds. **Student Employment:** Off-campus job opportunities are good. **Financial Aid Statistics:** 82% freshmen, 76% undergrads receive need-based scholarship or grant aid. 63% freshmen, 61% undergrads receive need-based self-help aid. 99% freshmen, 98% undergrads receive any aid. Highest amount earned per year from on-campus jobs $2,608.

MARYVILLE UNIVERSITY OF SAINT LOUIS

650 Maryville University Drive, St. Louis, MO 63141-7299
Phone: 314-529-9350 **E-mail:** admissions@maryville.edu **CEEB Code:** 6399
Fax: 314-529-9927 **Website:** www.maryville.edu **ACT Code:** 2326
Financial Aid Phone: 314-529-9360

This private school was founded in 1872. It has a 130-acre campus.

RATINGS

Admissions Selectivity Rating: 81   **Fire Safety Rating:** 79   **Green Rating:** 60*

STUDENTS AND FACULTY

Enrollment: 2,656. **Student Body:** 77% female, 23% male, 14% out-of-state. African American 7%, Asian 1%, Caucasian 84%, Hispanic 1%. **Retention and Graduation:** 81% freshmen return for sophomore year. 53% freshmen graduate within 4 years. **Faculty:** Student/faculty ratio 12:1. 106 full-time faculty, 86% hold PhDs. 100% faculty teach undergrads.

ACADEMICS

Degrees: Bachelor's, certificate, master's. **Academic Requirements:** Arts/fine arts, English (including composition), history, humanities, mathematics, sciences (biological or physical), social science, multicultural studies. **Classes:** Most classes have fewer than 10 students. Most lab/discussion sections have 10–19 students. **Majors with Highest Enrollment:** Business administration/management, nursing/registered nurse training (RN, ASN, BSN, MSN), physical therapy/therapist. **Disciplines with Highest Percentage of Degrees Awarded:** Business/marketing 39%, health professions and related sciences 24%, psychology 10%, visual and performing arts 6%, education 5%. **Special Study Options:** Accelerated program, cooperative education program, cross-registration, distance learning, double major, dual enrollment, English as a second language (ESL), honors program, independent study, internships, liberal arts/career combination, student-designed major, study abroad, teacher certification program, weekend college, prior learning assessment program.

FACILITIES

Housing: Coed dorms, apartments for single students. **Special Academic Facilities/Equipment:** University center, art galleries, auditorium, chapel, observatory, teaching lab, clinical labs, art and design labs, videoconferencing facility with downlinking and electronic multimedia capability for presentations. **Computers:** 5% of classrooms are wireless, 90% of public computers are PCs, 10% of public computers are Macs, network access in dorm rooms, network access in dorm lounges, online administrative functions (other than registration), remote student-access to Web through college's connection.

CAMPUS LIFE

Activities: Choral groups, dance, drama/theater, jazz band, literary magazine, music ensembles, pep band, student government, student newspaper. **Organizations:** 40 registered organizations, 3 honor societies, 4 religious organizations. **Athletics (Intercollegiate):** *Men:* Baseball, basketball, cheerleading, cross-country, golf, soccer, tennis. *Women:* Basketball, cheerleading, cross-country, golf, soccer, softball, tennis, volleyball.

ADMISSIONS

Freshman Academic Profile: 23% in top 10% of high school class, 52% in top 25% of high school class, 83% in top 50% of high school class. 77% from public high schools. ACT middle 50% range 22–26. TOEFL required of all international applicants, minimum paper TOEFL 500, minimum computer TOEFL 173. **Basis for Candidate Selection:** *Very important factors considered include:* Academic GPA, standardized test scores. *Important factors considered include:* Extracurricular activities, rigor of secondary school record. *Other factors considered include:* Character/personal qualities, class rank, interview, recommendation(s), talent/ability. **Freshman Admission Requirements:** High school diploma is required, and GED is accepted. *Academic units required:* 4 English, 3 math, 2 science, 2 social studies, 8 academic electives. *Academic units recommended:* 3 foreign language. **Freshman Admission Statistics:** 1,275 applied, 70% admitted, 34% enrolled. **Transfer Admission Requirements:** College transcript(s). Minimum college GPA of 2.0 required. Lowest grade transferable C-. **General Admission Information:** Application fee $25. Regular application deadline 8/15. Regular notification rolling. Nonfall registration accepted. Admission may be deferred for a maximum of 1 year. Credit offered for CEEB Advanced Placement tests.

COSTS AND FINANCIAL AID

Annual tuition $18,600. Average book expense $1,600. **Required Forms and Deadlines:** FAFSA. Financial aid filing deadline 3/1. **Notification of Awards:** Applicants will be notified of awards on or about 3/15. **Types of Aid:** *Need-based scholarships/grants:* Pell, SEOG, state scholarships/grants, private scholarships, the school's own gift aid, Federal Academic Competitiveness Grant, Federal Smart Grant. *Loans:* Direct Subsidized Stafford, Direct Unsubsidized Stafford, Direct PLUS, Federal Perkins. **Financial Aid Statistics:** 76% freshmen, 73% undergrads receive need-based scholarship or grant aid. 72% freshmen, 70% undergrads receive need-based self-help aid. 77% freshmen, 66% undergrads receive any aid.

MARYWOOD UNIVERSITY

Office of Admissions, 2300 Adams Avenue, Scranton, PA 18509
Phone: 570-348-6234 **E-mail:** yourfuture@marywood.edu **CEEB Code:** 2407
Fax: 570-961-4763 **Website:** www.marywood.com **ACT Code:** 3626
Financial Aid Phone: 866-279-9663

This private school, affiliated with the Roman Catholic Church, was founded in 1915. It has a 115-acre campus.

RATINGS

Admissions Selectivity Rating: 78   **Fire Safety Rating:** 90   **Green Rating:** 60*

STUDENTS AND FACULTY

Enrollment: 1,854. **Student Body:** 72% female, 28% male, 24% out-of-state, 1% international (18 countries represented). African American 2%, Asian 2%, Caucasian 83%, Hispanic 3%. **Retention and Graduation:** 76% freshmen return for sophomore year. 39% freshmen graduate within 4 years. 31% grads go on to further study within 1 year. 26% grads pursue arts and sciences degrees. 2% grads pursue business degrees. **Faculty:** Student/faculty ratio 13:1. 140 full-time faculty, 77% hold PhDs. 75% faculty teach undergrads.

ACADEMICS

Degrees: Bachelor's, certificate, doctoral, master's, post-bachelor's certificate, post-master's certificate. **Academic Requirements:** Arts/fine arts, English (including composition), foreign languages, history, humanities, mathematics, philosophy, sciences (biological or physical), social science. **Classes:** Most classes have 10–19 students. Most lab/discussion sections have fewer than 10 students. **Majors with Highest Enrollment:** Design and visual communications; psychology; teacher education and professional development, specific subject areas. **Disciplines with Highest Percentage of Degrees Awarded:** Education 22%, health professions and related sciences 19%, visual and performing arts 15%, business/marketing 10%, psychology 7%. **Special Study Options:** Accelerated program, cross-registration, distance learning, double major, dual enrollment, English as a second language (ESL), honor program, independent study, internships, student-designed major, study abroad, teacher certification program.

FACILITIES

Housing: Coed dorms, men's dorms, women's dorms, apartments for single students, special housing for disabled students, special housing for international students, small house communities. **Special Academic Facilities/Equipment:** Mellow Athletic and Fitness Center, Mahady Gallery, Suraci Gallery, Performing Arts Center, O'Neill Center for Healthy Families, Insalaco Studio Arts Center, Marywood University Arboretum, Curriculum Lab, electronic learning labs, broadcast studios. **Computers:** 74% of public computers are PCs, 26% of public computers are Macs, network access in dorm rooms, network access in dorm lounges, online registration, online administrative functions (other than registration), remote student-access to Web through college's connection.

CAMPUS LIFE

Activities: Choral groups, dance, drama/theater, jazz band, literary magazine, music ensembles, musical theater, radio station, student government, student newspaper, television station. **Organizations:** 53 registered organizations, 26 honor societies, 1 religious organization. 1 sorority. **Athletics (Intercollegiate):** *Men:* Baseball, basketball, cross-country, lacrosse, soccer, tennis. *Women:* Basketball, cross-country, field hockey, lacrosse, soccer, softball, tennis, volleyball.

ADMISSIONS

Freshman Academic Profile: 19% in top 10% of high school class, 45% in top 25% of high school class, 81% in top 50% of high school class. 75% from public high schools. SAT Math middle 50% range 470–560. SAT Critical Reading middle 50% range 470–560. SAT Writing middle 50% range 460–560. ACT middle 50% range 19.25–23. TOEFL required of all international applicants, minimum paper TOEFL 500, minimum computer TOEFL 173. **Basis for Candidate Selection:** *Very important factors considered include:* Character/personal qualities, class rank, rigor of secondary school record, standardized test scores. *Important factors considered include:* Academic GPA, interview, talent/ability. *Other factors considered include:* Application essay, extracurricular activities, level of applicant's interest, recommendation(s), volunteer work. **Freshman Admission Requirements:** High school diploma is required, and GED is accepted. *Academic units required:* 4 English, 2 math, 1 science (1 science lab), 3 social studies, 6 academic electives. **Freshman Admission Statistics:** 1,707 applied, 74% admitted, 31% enrolled. **Transfer Admission Requirements:** High school transcript, college transcript(s). Minimum college GPA of 2.5 required. Lowest grade transferable C. **General Admission Information:** Application fee $30. Regular notification is rolling. Nonfall registration accepted. Admission may be deferred for a maximum of 1 academic year. Credit and/or placement offered for CEEB Advanced Placement tests.

COSTS AND FINANCIAL AID

Average book expense $900. **Required Forms and Deadlines:** FAFSA. **Types of Aid:** *Need-based scholarships/grants:* Pell, SEOG, state scholarships/grants, private scholarships, the school's own gift aid, Federal Nursing Scholarships, Federal AGC, SMART, Disadvantaged Student Scholarship. *Loans:* FFEL Subsidized Stafford, FFEL Unsubsidized Stafford, FFEL PLUS, Federal Perkins, state loans. **Student Employment:** Federal Work-Study Program available. **Financial Aid Statistics:** 83% freshmen, 81% undergrads receive need-based scholarship or grant aid. 67% freshmen, 70% undergrads receive need-based self-help aid. 98% freshmen, 95% undergrads receive any aid.

MASSACHUSETTS COLLEGE OF ART

621 Huntington Avenue, Boston, MA 02115
Phone: 617-879-7222 **E-mail:** Admissions@massart.edu **CEEB Code:** 3516
Fax: 617-879-7250 **Website:** www.massart.edu **ACT Code:** 1846
Financial Aid Phone: 617-232-1555

This public school was founded in 1873. It has a 5-acre campus.

RATINGS

Admissions Selectivity Rating: 82   **Fire Safety Rating:** 60*   **Green Rating:** 89

STUDENTS AND FACULTY

Enrollment: 1,657. **Student Body:** 65% female, 35% male, 29% out-of-state, 3% international. African American 4%, Asian 5%, Caucasian 73%, Hispanic 5%. **Retention and Graduation:** 85% freshmen return for sophomore year. 43% freshmen graduate within 4 years. 10% grads go on to further study within 1 year. 10% grads pursue arts and sciences degrees. **Faculty:** Student/faculty ratio 16:1. 75 full-time faculty, 84% hold PhDs. 100% faculty teach undergrads.

ACADEMICS

Degrees: Bachelor's, certificate, master's, post-bachelor's certificate. **Academic Requirements:** English (including composition), history, humanities, Liberal Arts Studio Foundation, mathematics, sciences (biological or physical), social science, studio electives. **Classes:** Most classes have 10–19 students. **Disciplines with Highest Percentage of Degrees Awarded:** Visual and performing arts 95%, education 5%. **Special Study Options:** Cross-registration, double major, exchange student program (domestic), independent study, internships, liberal arts/career combination, student-designed major, study abroad.

FACILITIES

Housing: Coed dorms. Off-campus housing assistance from school. **Special Academic Facilities/Equipment:** 7 art galleries, foundry, glass furnaces, ceramic kiln, video and film studios, performance spaces, Polaroid 20x24 camera, individual studio spaces, design research unit.

CAMPUS LIFE

Activities: Dance, drama/theater, music ensembles, radio station, student government, student newspaper, student-run film society, television station, yearbook. **Organizations:** 30 registered organizations, 1 honor society, 3 religious organizations.

ADMISSIONS

Freshman Academic Profile: 19% in top 10% of high school class, 47% in top 25% of high school class, 87% in top 50% of high school class. SAT Math middle 50% range 480–570. SAT Critical Reading middle 50% range 490–610. SAT Writing middle 50% range 490–600. TOEFL required of all international applicants, minimum paper TOEFL 530. **Basis for Candidate Selection:** *Very important factors considered include:* Academic GPA, application essay, rigor of secondary school record, talent/ability. *Important factors considered include:* Standardized test scores, state residency. *Other factors considered include:* Character/personal qualities, class rank, extracurricular activities, geographical residence, recommendation(s), volunteer work, work experience. **Freshman Admission Requirements:** High school diploma is required, and GED is accepted. *Academic units required:* 4 English, 2 math, 2 science (2 science labs), 2 foreign language, 2 social studies, 2 academic electives, 2 art electives. *Academic units recommended:* 1 history. **Freshman Admission Statistics:** 1,327 applied, 60% admitted, 43% enrolled. **Transfer Admission Requirements:** College transcript(s), essay or personal statement, statement of good standing from prior institution(s). Minimum college GPA of 2.5 required. Lowest grade transferable C. **General Admission Information:** Application fee $65. Regular notification is rolling. Nonfall registration not accepted. Admission may be deferred for a maximum of 12. Credit and/or placement offered for CEEB Advanced Placement tests.

COSTS AND FINANCIAL AID

Annual in-state tuition $7,200. Out-of-state tuition $20,600. Room & board $11,090. Average book expense $2,000. **Required Forms and Deadlines:** FAFSA. Financial aid filing deadline 3/1. **Notification of Awards:** Applicants will be notified of awards on or about 3/1. **Types of Aid:** *Need-based scholarships/grants:* Pell, SEOG, state scholarships/grants, private scholarships, the school's own gift aid. *Loans:* Direct Subsidized Stafford, Direct Unsubsidized Stafford, Direct PLUS, FFEL Subsidized Stafford, FFEL Unsubsidized Stafford, FFEL PLUS, Federal Perkins, state loans, college/university loans from institutional funds, alternative loans (credit based). **Student Employment:** Federal Work-Study Program available. Institutional employment available. Off-campus job opportunities are good. **Financial Aid Statistics:** 33% freshmen, 35% undergrads receive need-based scholarship or grant aid. 61% freshmen, 59% undergrads receive need-based self-help aid. Highest amount earned per year from on-campus jobs $800.

MASSACHUSETTS COLLEGE OF LIBERAL ARTS

375 Church Street, North Adams, MA 01247
Phone: 413-662-5410 **E-mail:** admissions@mcla.edu **CEEB Code:** 3521
Fax: 413-662-5179 **Website:** www.mcla.edu **ACT Code:** 1908
Financial Aid Phone: 413-662-5219

This public school was founded in 1894. It has a 75-acre campus.

RATINGS
Admissions Selectivity Rating: 60*   **Fire Safety Rating:** 60*   **Green Rating:** 60*

STUDENTS AND FACULTY
Enrollment: 1,246. **Student Body:** 61% female, 39% male, 16% out-of-state. African American 5%, Caucasian 90%, Hispanic 2%. **Retention and Graduation:** 72% freshmen return for sophomore year. 17% freshmen graduate within 4 years. 7% grads go on to further study within 1 year. **Faculty:** Student/faculty ratio 13:1. 84 full-time faculty, 73% hold PhDs. 100% faculty teach undergrads.

ACADEMICS
Degrees: Bachelor's, master's, post-bachelor's certificate. **Academic Requirements:** Arts/fine arts, computer literacy, English (including composition), history, humanities, mathematics, philosophy, sciences (biological or physical), social science, cross-cultural studies. **Classes:** Most classes have 10–19 students. Most lab/discussion sections have fewer than 10 students. **Disciplines with Highest Percentage of Degrees Awarded:** Social sciences 24%, business/marketing 21%, English 16%, psychology 15%, biological/life sciences 6%, computer and information sciences 6%. **Special Study Options:** Cross-registration, distance learning, double major, dual enrollment, exchange student program (domestic), honors program, independent study, internships, liberal arts/career combination, student-designed major, study abroad, teacher certification program.

FACILITIES
Housing: Coed dorms, apartments for single students, special housing for disabled students. **Special Academic Facilities/Equipment:** On-campus day care, cable TV and radio facilities. **Computers:** 82% of public computers are PCs, 18% of public computers are Macs, network access in dorm rooms, remote student-access to Web through college's connection.

CAMPUS LIFE
Activities: Choral groups, concert band, drama/theater, jazz band, literary magazine, music ensembles, radio station, student government, student newspaper, television station, yearbook. **Organizations:** 47 registered organizations, 8 honor societies, 2 religious organizations. 2 fraternities (5% men join), 5 sororities (10% women join). **Athletics (Intercollegiate):** *Men:* Baseball, basketball, cross-country, golf, ice hockey, soccer. *Women:* Basketball, cross-country, soccer, softball, tennis, volleyball.

ADMISSIONS
Freshman Academic Profile: 80% from public high schools. SAT Math middle 50% range 450–560. SAT Critical Reading middle 50% range 480–600. TOEFL required of all international applicants, minimum paper TOEFL 550. **Basis for Candidate Selection:** *Very important factors considered include:* Rigor of secondary school record. *Important factors considered include:* Character/personal qualities, standardized test scores. *Other factors considered include:* Application essay, class rank, extracurricular activities, interview, recommendation(s), talent/ability, volunteer work, work experience. **Freshman Admission Requirements:** High school diploma is required, and GED is accepted. *Academic units required:* 4 English, 3 math, 3 science, 2 foreign language, 2 social studies, 2 academic electives. **Freshman Admission Statistics:** 1,206 applied, 67% admitted, 32% enrolled. **Transfer Admission Requirements:** College transcript(s). Lowest grade transferable D. **General Admission Information:** Application fee $25. Regular notification is rolling. Nonfall registration accepted. Admission may be deferred for a maximum of 1 year. Common Application accepted. Credit offered for CEEB Advanced Placement tests.

COSTS AND FINANCIAL AID
Annual in-state tuition $1,090. Out-of-state tuition $7,050. Room & board $4,290. Required fees $2,267. Average book expense $600. **Required Forms and Deadlines:** FAFSA, institution's own financial aid form. Financial aid filing deadline 4/1. **Notification of Awards:** Applicants will be notified of awards on or about 4/15. **Types of Aid:** *Need-based scholarships/grants:* Pell,

SEOG, state scholarships/grants, private scholarships, the school's own gift aid. *Loans:* FFEL Subsidized Stafford, FFEL Unsubsidized Stafford, FFEL PLUS, Federal Perkins, state loans. **Student Employment:** Federal Work-Study Program available. Institutional employment available. Off-campus job opportunities are fair. **Financial Aid Statistics:** 52% freshmen, 48% undergrads receive need-based scholarship or grant aid. 50% freshmen, 54% undergrads receive need-based self-help aid. Highest amount earned per year from on-campus jobs $3,950.

MASSACHUSETTS COLLEGE OF PHARMACY & HEALTH SCIENCE

Office of Admissions, 179 Longwood Avenue, Boston, MA 02115
Phone: 617-732-2850 **E-mail:** admissions@mcphs.edu **CEEB Code:** 3512
Fax: 617-732-2118 **Website:** www.mcphs.edu **ACT Code:** 1860
Financial Aid Phone: 617-732-2836

This private school was founded in 1823. It has a 3-acre campus.

RATINGS
Admissions Selectivity Rating: 85   **Fire Safety Rating:** 95   **Green Rating:** 60*

STUDENTS AND FACULTY
Enrollment: 2,122. **Student Body:** 68% female, 32% male, 40% out-of-state, 3% international (34 countries represented). African American 5%, Asian 30%, Caucasian 54%, Hispanic 3%. **Retention and Graduation:** 89% freshmen return for sophomore year. **Faculty:** Student/faculty ratio 19:1. 172 full-time faculty, 85% hold PhDs. 100% faculty teach undergrads.

ACADEMICS
Degrees: Bachelor's, certificate, doctoral, first professional, master's, post-bachelor's certificate. **Academic Requirements:** Computer literacy, English (including composition), humanities, mathematics, sciences (biological or physical), social science. **Classes:** Most classes have 20–29 students. Most lab/discussion sections have 10–19 students. **Majors with Highest Enrollment:** Dental hygiene/hygienist, pharmacy (PharMD, BS/BPharm), physician assistant. **Disciplines with Highest Percentage of Degrees Awarded:** Health professions and related sciences 100%. **Special Study Options:** Accelerated program, cross-registration, distance learning, double major, dual enrollment, independent study, internships, liberal arts/career combination. Undergraduates may take graduate-level courses. Accelerated program offered at Worcester and Manchester Campus only for PharmD. degree. Manchester campus offers the physician assistant program.

FACILITIES
Housing: Coed dorms, separate all-women floors. **Special Academic Facilities/Equipment:** Museum of Fine Arts, Gardner Museum. **Computers:** 90% of classrooms are wireless, 100% of public computers are PCs, network access in dorm rooms, network access in dorm lounges, online registration, online administrative functions (other than registration), support for handheld computing, remote student-access to Web through college's connection.

CAMPUS LIFE
Activities: Choral groups, dance, drama/theater, musical theater, student government, student newspaper, symphony orchestra, yearbook. **Organizations:** 67 registered organizations, 2 religious organizations.

ADMISSIONS
Freshman Academic Profile: 27% in top 10% of high school class, 63% in top 25% of high school class, 94% in top 50% of high school class. 80% from public high schools. SAT Math middle 50% range 520–610. SAT Critical Reading middle 50% range 480–570. SAT Writing middle 50% range 490–580. ACT middle 50% range 21–25. TOEFL required of all international applicants, minimum paper TOEFL 550, minimum computer TOEFL 213. **Basis for Candidate Selection:** *Very important factors considered include:* Academic GPA, application essay, recommendation(s), rigor of secondary school record, volunteer work, work experience. *Important factors considered include:* Character/personal qualities, extracurricular activities, level of applicant's interest, standardized test scores, talent/ability. *Other factors considered include:* Alumni/ae relation, class rank, interview. **Freshman Admission Requirements:** High school diploma is required, and GED is accepted. *Academic units required:* 4 English, 3 math, 2 science (2 science labs), 1 social studies, 1 history, 5 academic electives. *Academic units recommended:* 4 English, 4 math, 3 science (3 science labs), 6 academic electives. **Freshman Admission Statistics:** 1,741 applied, 73% admitted, 40% enrolled. **Transfer Admission Requirements:** College transcript(s), essay or personal statement.

Minimum college GPA of 2.5 required. Lowest grade transferable C. **General Admission Information:** Application fee $70. Regular application deadline 2/1. Regular notification is rolling. Nonfall registration not accepted. Admission may be deferred for a maximum of 1 year. Credit and/or placement offered for CEEB Advanced Placement tests.

COSTS AND FINANCIAL AID
Annual tuition $22,000. Room and board $11,800. Required fees $700. Average book expense $800. **Required Forms and Deadlines:** FAFSA. Financial aid filing deadline 3/15. **Notification of Awards:** Applicants will be notified of awards on a rolling basis beginning on or about 2/1. **Types of Aid:** *Need-based scholarships/grants:* Pell, SEOG, state scholarships/grants, private scholarships, the school's own gift aid. *Loans:* FFEL Subsidized Stafford, FFEL Unsubsidized Stafford, FFEL PLUS, Federal Perkins, state loans, health professions student loans. **Student Employment:** Federal Work-Study Program available. Off-campus job opportunities are excellent. **Financial Aid Statistics:** 71% freshmen, 68% undergrads receive need-based scholarship or grant aid. 76% freshmen, 85% undergrads receive need-based self-help aid. 90% freshmen, 90% undergrads receive any aid.

See page 1260.

MASSACHUSETTS INSTITUTE OF TECHNOLOGY

MIT Admissions Office, 77 Massachusetts Avenue, Rm 3-108, Cambridge, MA 02139
Phone: 617-253-4791 **E-mail:** admissions@mit.edu **CEEB Code:** 3514
Fax: 617-258-8304 **Website:** web.mit.edu **ACT Code:** 1858
Financial Aid Phone: 617-253-4971

This private school was founded in 1861. It has a 168-acre campus.

RATINGS
Admissions Selectivity Rating: 99   **Fire Safety Rating:** 75   **Green Rating:** 85

STUDENTS AND FACULTY
Enrollment: 4,114. **Student Body:** 44% female, 56% male, 90% out-of-state, 8% international (86 countries represented). African American 6%, Asian 26%, Caucasian 37%, Hispanic 12%, Native American 1%. **Retention and Graduation:** 98% freshmen return for sophomore year. 82% freshmen graduate within 4 years. **Faculty:** Student/faculty ratio 7:1. 1,191 full-time faculty, 92% hold PhDs. 100% faculty teach undergrads.

ACADEMICS
Degrees: Bachelor's, doctoral, master's. **Academic Requirements:** Arts/fine arts, humanities, mathematics, sciences (biological or physical), social science, physical education requirement, communication requirement, laboratory requirement, restricted electives in science and technology (REST) requirement. **Classes:** Most classes have fewer than 10 students. Most lab/discussion sections have 10–19 students. **Majors with Highest Enrollment:** Chemical engineering, computer science, mechanical engineering. **Disciplines with Highest Percentage of Degrees Awarded:** Engineering 36%, computer and information sciences 15%, physical sciences 11%, biological/life sciences 10%, business/marketing 7%. **Special Study Options:** Cooperative education program, cross-registration, internships, study abroad, teacher certification program. Undergraduate Research Opportunities Program (UROP), Independent Activities Period (IAP), freshman learning communities.

FACILITIES
Housing: Coed dorms, women's dorms, apartments for married students, apartments for single students, special housing for disabled students, fraternity/sorority housing, cooperative housing, independent living group housing, family housing. **Special Academic Facilities/Equipment:** Burndy Library/Dibner Institute; List Visual Arts Center; MIT Museum; Ray and Maria Stata Center for Computer, Information, and Intelligence Sciences; numerous labs and centers. **Computers:** 5% of public computers are PCs, 3% of public computers are Macs, 92% of public computers are UNIX, network access in dorm rooms, network access in dorm lounges, online registration, online administrative functions (other than registration), support for handheld computing, remote student-access to Web through college's connection.

CAMPUS LIFE
Activities: Choral groups, concert band, dance, drama/theater, jazz band,

literary magazine, marching band, music ensembles, musical theater, radio station, student government, student newspaper, student-run film society, symphony orchestra, television station, yearbook. **Organizations:** 400 registered organizations, 11 honor societies, 30 religious organizations. 27 fraternities (55% men join), 5 sororities (26% women join). **Athletics (Intercollegiate):** *Men:* Baseball, basketball, crew/rowing, cross-country, diving, fencing, football, golf, gymnastics, lacrosse, pistol, riflery, sailing, skiing (downhill/alpine), skiing (Nordic/cross-country), soccer, squash, swimming, tennis, track/field (indoor), track/field (outdoor). *Women:* Basketball, crew/rowing, cross-country, diving, fencing, field hockey, gymnastics, ice hockey, lacrosse, pistol, riflery, sailing, skiing (downhill/alpine), skiing (Nordic/cross-country), soccer, softball, swimming, tennis, track/field (indoor), track/field (outdoor). Environmental Initiatives: Campus energy management (conservation, efficiency, renewables). Recycling (40% recycling rate). Green building (LEED) for new and existing buildings.

ADMISSIONS
Freshman Academic Profile: 97% in top 10% of high school class, 100% in top 25% of high school class. 71% from public high schools. SAT Math middle 50% range 720–800. SAT Critical Reading middle 50% range 660–760. SAT Writing middle 50% range 660–750. ACT middle 50% range 31–34. **Basis for Candidate Selection:** *Very important factors considered include:* Character/personal qualities. *Important factors considered include:* Academic GPA, class rank, extracurricular activities, interview, recommendation(s), rigor of secondary school record, standardized test scores, talent/ability. *Other factors considered include:* Alumni/ae relation, application essay, first generation, geographical residence, level of applicant's interest, racial/ethnic status, volunteer work, work experience. **Freshman Admission Requirements:** High school diploma or equivalent is not required. *Academic units recommended:* 4 English, 4 math, 4 science, 2 foreign language, 2 social studies. **Freshman Admission Statistics:** 11,374 applied, 13% admitted, 66% enrolled. **Transfer Admission Requirements:** High school transcript, college transcript(s), essay or personal statement, standardized test score, statement of good standing from prior institution(s). Lowest grade transferable B. **General Admission Information:** Application fee $65. Regular application deadline 1/1. Regular notification 3/25. Nonfall registration not accepted. Admission may be deferred for a maximum of 1 year. Credit and/or placement offered for CEEB Advanced Placement tests.

COSTS AND FINANCIAL AID
Annual tuition $34,750. Room and board $10,400. Required fees $236. Average book expense $1,114. **Required Forms and Deadlines:** FAFSA, CSS/Financial Aid PROFILE, Business/Farm Supplement, parents' complete federal income tax returns from prior year and W-2 forms. Financial aid filing deadline 2/15. **Notification of Awards:** Applicants will be notified of awards on or about 3/15. **Types of Aid:** *Need-based scholarships/grants:* Pell, SEOG, state scholarships/grants, private scholarships, the school's own gift aid. *Loans:* Direct Subsidized Stafford, Direct Unsubsidized Stafford, Direct PLUS, Federal Perkins, college/university loans from institutional funds. **Student Employment:** Federal Work-Study Program available. Institutional employment available. Off-campus job opportunities are excellent. **Financial Aid Statistics:** 61% freshmen, 60% undergrads receive need-based scholarship or grant aid. 53% freshmen, 56% undergrads receive need-based self-help aid. 76% freshmen, 70% undergrads receive any aid. Highest amount earned per year from on-campus jobs $24,583.

MASSACHUSETTS MARITIME ACADEMY

101 Academy Drive, Buzzards Bay, MA 02532
Phone: 800-544-3411 **E-mail:** admissions@maritime.edu
Fax: 508-830-5077 **Website:** www.maritime.edu
Financial Aid Phone: 508-830-5087

This public school was founded in 1891. It has a 55-acre campus.

RATINGS
Admissions Selectivity Rating: 63   **Fire Safety Rating:** 60*   **Green Rating:** 60*

STUDENTS AND FACULTY
Enrollment: 923. **Student Body:** 12% female, 88% male, 28% out-of-state. **Retention and Graduation:** 30% grads go on to further study within 1 year. 10% grads pursue arts and sciences degrees. 15% grads pursue business degrees. 4% grads pursue law degrees. 1% grads pursue medical degrees. **Faculty:** Student/faculty ratio 15:1. 100% faculty teach undergrads.

ACADEMICS
Degrees: Bachelor's, first professional certificate, master's. **Academic Requirements:** Computer literacy, English (including composition), history,

humanities, mathematics, sciences (biological or physical). **Majors with Highest Enrollment:** Environmental science, environmental/environmental health engineering, ocean engineering. **Disciplines with Highest Percentage of Degrees Awarded:** Engineering 65%, natural resources/environmental science 15%, other 15%, business/marketing 5%. **Special Study Options:** Cooperative education program, double major, internships, semester-at-sea.

FACILITIES

Housing: Coed dorms. **Special Academic Facilities/Equipment:** Maritime Ship Model Museum, training ship enterprise. **Computers:** Network access in dorm rooms, remote student-access to Web through college's connection. Undergraduates are required to own a computer.

CAMPUS LIFE

Activities: Drama/theater, jazz band, marching band, music ensembles, student government, student newspaper, yearbook. **Organizations:** 12 registered organizations, 1 honor society, 1 religious organization. **Athletics (Intercollegiate):** *Men:* Baseball, crew/rowing, cross-country, football, lacrosse, riflery, rugby, sailing, soccer. *Women:* Crew/rowing, cross-country, riflery, rugby, sailing, softball, volleyball.

ADMISSIONS

Freshman Academic Profile: 65% from public high schools. TOEFL required of all international applicants, minimum paper TOEFL 500. **Basis for Candidate Selection:** *Very important factors considered include:* Rigor of secondary school record, standardized test scores. *Important factors considered include:* Application essay, character/personal qualities. *Other factors considered include:* Alumni/ae relation, extracurricular activities, interview, recommendation(s), talent/ability, volunteer work, work experience. **Freshman Admission Requirements:** High school diploma is required, and GED is accepted. *Academic units required:* 4 English, 3 math, 3 science (2 science labs), 2 foreign language, 2 history, 2 academic electives. **Freshman Admission Statistics:** 808 applied, 60% admitted, 56% enrolled. **Transfer Admission Requirements:** High school transcript, college transcript(s), essay or personal statement. Minimum college GPA of 2.0 required. Lowest grade transferable C. **General Admission Information:** Application fee $50. Regular notification is rolling. Nonfall registration not accepted. Admission may be deferred for a maximum of 1 year. Common Application not accepted. Credit and/or placement offered for CEEB Advanced Placement tests.

COSTS AND FINANCIAL AID

Annual in-state tuition $9,165. Annual out-of-state tuition $19,500. Room and board $5,500. Required fees $2,600. Average book expense $700. Average book expense $700. **Required Forms and Deadlines:** FAFSA, institution's own financial aid form. Financial aid filing deadline 4/30. **Notification of Awards:** Applicants will be notified of awards on a rolling basis beginning on or about 3/1. **Types of Aid:** *Need-based scholarships/grants:* Pell, SEOG, state scholarships/grants, private scholarships, the school's own gift aid. *Loans:* Direct Subsidized Stafford, Direct Unsubsidized Stafford, Direct PLUS. **Student Employment:** Federal Work-Study Program available. Off-campus job opportunities are good. **Financial Aid Statistics:** 8% freshmen, 8% undergrads receive need-based scholarship or grant aid. 35% freshmen, 26% undergrads receive need-based self-help aid. Highest amount earned per year from on-campus jobs $650.

THE MASTER'S COLLEGE

21726 Placerita Canyon Road, Santa Clarita, CA 91321
Phone: 661-259-3540 **E-mail:** enrollment@masters.edu **CEEB Code:** 4411
Fax: 661-288-1037 **Website:** www.masters.edu **ACT Code:** 303
Financial Aid Phone: 661-259-3540

This private school, affiliated with the Christian (nondenominational) Church, was founded in 1927. It has a 110-acre campus.

RATINGS

Admissions Selectivity Rating: 82   **Fire Safety Rating:** 82   **Green Rating:** 60*

STUDENTS AND FACULTY

Enrollment: 1,125. **Student Body:** 50% female, 50% male, 26% out-of-state, 3% international (21 countries represented). African American 3%, Asian 4%, Caucasian 84%, Hispanic 7%. **Retention and Graduation:** 77% freshmen return for sophomore year. 51% freshmen graduate within 4 years. **Faculty:** Student/faculty ratio 10:1. 72 full-time faculty, 88% hold PhDs. 100% faculty teach undergrads.

ACADEMICS

Degrees: Bachelor's, certificate, doctoral, first professional certificate, first professional, master's. **Academic Requirements:** Arts/fine arts, biblical studies, computer literacy, English (including composition), history, humanities, mathematics, philosophy, sciences (biological or physical), social science. **Classes:** Most classes have fewer than 10 students. **Majors with Highest Enrollment:** Bible/biblical studies, business administration/management, elementary education and teaching. **Disciplines with Highest Percentage of Degrees Awarded:** Philosophy and religious studies 33%, business/marketing 18%, education 16%, history 8%, communications/journalism 6%. **Special Study Options:** Accelerated program, cooperative education program, double major, independent study, internships, Israel semester, liberal arts/career combination, study abroad, teacher certification program.

FACILITIES

Housing: Men's dorms, women's dorms, special housing for international students. **Computers:** 100% of classrooms are wireless, 94% of public computers are PCs, 5% of public computers are Macs, 1% of public computers are UNIX, network access in dorm rooms, network access in dorm lounges, online registration, online administrative functions (other than registration), remote student-access to Web through college's connection. Undergraduates are required to own a computer.

CAMPUS LIFE

Activities: Choral groups, concert band, jazz band, music ensembles, opera, pep band, student government, symphony orchestra. **Organizations:** 15 registered organizations, 1 honor society, 11 religious organizations. **Athletics (Intercollegiate):** *Men:* Baseball, basketball, cross-country, golf, soccer. *Women:* Basketball, cross-country, soccer, softball, volleyball.

ADMISSIONS

Freshman Academic Profile: 33% in top 10% of high school class, 53% in top 25% of high school class, 78% in top 50% of high school class. 51% from public high schools. SAT Math middle 50% range 490–630. SAT Critical Reading middle 50% range 520–620. ACT middle 50% range 19–27. TOEFL required of all international applicants, minimum paper TOEFL 525, minimum computer TOEFL 197. **Basis for Candidate Selection:** *Very important factors considered include:* Academic GPA, application essay, character/personal qualities, interview, recommendation(s), religious affiliation/commitment, rigor of secondary school record, standardized test scores. *Other factors considered include:* Alumni/ae relation, class rank, extracurricular activities, level of applicant's interest, talent/ability. **Freshman Admission Requirements:** High school diploma is required, and GED is accepted. *Academic units required:* 4 English, 3 math, 2 science, 2 history. *Academic units recommended:* 3 academic electives. **Freshman Admission Statistics:** 226 applied, 83% admitted, 100% enrolled. **Transfer Admission Requirements:** High school transcript, college transcript(s), essay or personal statement, interview, statement of good standing from prior institution(s). Minimum college GPA of 2.0 required. Lowest grade transferable C. **General Admission Information:** Application fee $40. Regular notification is rolling. Non-fall registration accepted. Admission may be deferred for a maximum of 2 semesters. Credit and/or placement offered for CEEB Advanced Placement tests.

COSTS AND FINANCIAL AID

Annual tuition $20,700. Room & board $6,900. Average book expense $1,314. **Required Forms and Deadlines:** FAFSA, institution's own financial aid form, state aid form. Financial aid filing deadline 3/2. **Notification of Awards:** Applicants will be notified of awards on a rolling basis beginning on or about 2/18. **Types of Aid:** *Need-based scholarships/grants:* Pell, SEOG, state scholarships/grants, private scholarships, the school's own gift aid. *Loans:* FFEL Subsidized Stafford, FFEL Unsubsidized Stafford, FFEL PLUS, Federal Perkins, alternative private loans. **Student Employment:** Federal Work-Study Program available. Institutional employment available. Off-campus job opportunities are excellent. **Financial Aid Statistics:** 55% freshmen, 67% undergrads receive need-based scholarship or grant aid. 50% freshmen, 64% undergrads receive need-based self-help aid. 15 freshmen, 47 undergrads receive athletic scholarships. 68% freshmen, 85% undergrads receive any aid. Highest amount earned per year from on-campus jobs $6,000.

MAYVILLE STATE UNIVERSITY

330 Third Street Northeast, Mayville, ND 58257-1299
Phone: 701-788-4842 **E-mail:** admit@mayvillestate.edu **CEEB Code:** 6478
Fax: 701-788-4748 **Website:** www.mayvillestate.edu **ACT Code:** 3212
Financial Aid Phone: 701-788-4767

This public school was founded in 1889. It has a 55-acre campus.

RATINGS
Admissions Selectivity Rating: 82   **Fire Safety Rating:** 61   **Green Rating:** 61

STUDENTS AND FACULTY
Enrollment: 832. **Student Body:** 50% female, 50% male, 32% out-of-state, 4% international (16 countries represented). African American 4%, Caucasian 85%, Hispanic 2%, Native American 3%. **Retention and Graduation:** 54% freshmen return for sophomore year. 6% grads go on to further study within 1 year. 3% grads pursue arts and sciences degrees. 1% grads pursue business degrees. 1% grads pursue law degrees. 1% grads pursue medical degrees. **Faculty:** Student/faculty ratio 13:1. 36 full-time faculty, 44% hold PhDs. 100% faculty teach undergrads.

ACADEMICS
Degrees: Bachelor's. **Academic Requirements:** Arts/fine arts, computer literacy, English (including composition), history, humanities, mathematics, sciences (biological or physical), social science. **Classes:** Most classes have 10–19 students. **Majors with Highest Enrollment:** Business administration/management, elementary education and teaching, physical education teaching and coaching. **Disciplines with Highest Percentage of Degrees Awarded:** Education 44%, business/marketing 36%, psychology 5%, mathematics 4%, social sciences 3%. **Special Study Options:** Accelerated program, cooperative education program, distance learning, double major, dual enrollment, honors program, independent study, internships, student-designed major, teacher certification program.

FACILITIES
Housing: Men's dorms, women's dorms, apartments for married students, apartments for single students. **Special Academic Facilities/Equipment:** Art gallery available in the campus center. **Computers:** 100% of public computers are PCs, network access in dorm rooms, network access in dorm lounges, online registration, online administrative functions (other than registration), remote student-access to Web through college's connection, tuition includes personal computer. Undergraduates are required to own a computer.

CAMPUS LIFE
Activities: Choral groups, concert band, drama/theater, jazz band, music ensembles, musical theater, student government. **Organizations:** 18 registered organizations, 1 honor society, 2 religious organizations. **Athletics (Intercollegiate):** *Men:* Baseball, basketball, football. *Women:* Basketball, softball, volleyball.

ADMISSIONS
Freshman Academic Profile: 91% from public high schools. TOEFL required of all international applicants, minimum paper TOEFL 525, minimum computer TOEFL 195. **Basis for Candidate Selection:** *Very important factors considered include:* Academic GPA. *Important factors considered include:* Rigor of secondary school record, standardized test scores. *Other factors considered include:* Character/personal qualities, interview. **Freshman Admission Requirements:** High school diploma is required, and GED is accepted. *Academic units required:* 4 English, 3 math, 3 science (3 science labs), 3 social studies. *Academic units recommended:* 2 foreign language. **Freshman Admission Statistics:** 240 applied, 66% admitted, 86% enrolled. **Transfer Admission Requirements:** College transcript(s), statement of good standing from prior institution(s). Minimum college GPA of 2.0 required. Lowest grade transferable D. **General Admission Information:** Application fee $35. Regular notification is rolling. Nonfall registration accepted. Admission may be deferred. Credit and/or placement offered for CEEB Advanced Placement tests.

COSTS AND FINANCIAL AID
Average book expense $700. **Required Forms and Deadlines:** FAFSA. Financial aid filing deadline 4/15. **Notification of Awards:** Applicants will be notified of awards on a rolling basis beginning on or about 5/1. **Types of Aid:**

Need-based scholarships/grants: Pell, SEOG, state scholarships/grants, private scholarships, the school's own gift aid. *Loans:* FFEL Subsidized Stafford, FFEL Unsubsidized Stafford, FFEL PLUS, Federal Perkins. **Student Employment:** Federal Work-Study Program available. Institutional employment available. Off-campus job opportunities are fair. **Financial Aid Statistics:** 58% undergrads receive need-based scholarship or grant aid. 80% undergrads receive need-based self-help aid. 23 freshmen, 111 undergrads receive athletic scholarships. 95% freshmen, 60% undergrads receive any aid. Highest amount earned per year from on-campus jobs $1,500.

MCDANIEL COLLEGE

2 College Hill, Westminster, MD 21157
Phone: 410-857-2230 **E-mail:** admissions@mcdaniel.edu **CEEB Code:** 5898
Fax: 410-857-2757 **Website:** www.mcdaniel.edu **ACT Code:** 1756
Financial Aid Phone: 410-857-2233

This private school was founded in 1867. It has a 160-acre campus.

RATINGS
Admissions Selectivity Rating: 83   **Fire Safety Rating:** 60*   **Green Rating:** 60*

STUDENTS AND FACULTY
Enrollment: 1,723. **Student Body:** 56% female, 44% male, 29% out-of-state, 1% international (11 countries represented). African American 6%, Asian 2%, Caucasian 83%, Hispanic 2%. **Retention and Graduation:** 86% freshmen return for sophomore year. 66% freshmen graduate within 4 years. **Faculty:** Student/faculty ratio 14:1. 134 full-time faculty, 82% hold PhDs. 98% faculty teach undergrads.

ACADEMICS
Degrees: Bachelor's, master's. **Academic Requirements:** Arts/fine arts, English (including composition), foreign languages, history, humanities, mathematics, sciences (biological or physical), social science. **Classes:** Most classes have 10–19 students. Most lab/discussion sections have 10–19 students. **Majors with Highest Enrollment:** Business administration/management, psychology, sociology. **Disciplines with Highest Percentage of Degrees Awarded:** Social sciences 24%, business/marketing 13%, visual and performing arts 9%, psychology 9%, biological/life sciences 8%. **Special Study Options:** Cross-registration, double major, dual enrollment, honors program, independent study, internships, student-designed major, study abroad, teacher certification program.

FACILITIES
Housing: Coed dorms, men's dorms, women's dorms, apartments for married students, apartments for single students, fraternity/sorority housing, single-family homes shared by 3–10 students. **Special Academic Facilities/Equipment:** Art gallery, computer graphics and physiology labs, electron microscope, math spectrometer. **Computers:** 70% of public computers are PCs, 30% of public computers are Macs, network access in dorm rooms, online registration, online administrative functions (other than registration), remote student-access to Web through college's connection.

CAMPUS LIFE
Activities: Choral groups, concert band, dance, drama/theater, jazz band, literary magazine, music ensembles, musical theater, radio station, student government, student newspaper, symphony orchestra, television station, yearbook. **Organizations:** 136 registered organizations, 22 honor societies, 5 religious organizations. 6 fraternities (18% men join), 4 sororities (22% women join). **Athletics (Intercollegiate):** *Men:* Baseball, basketball, cross-country, football, golf, lacrosse, soccer, swimming, tennis, track/field (indoor), track/field (outdoor), volleyball, wrestling. *Women:* Basketball, cross-country, field hockey, golf, lacrosse, soccer, softball, swimming, tennis, track/field (indoor), track/field (outdoor), volleyball.

ADMISSIONS
Freshman Academic Profile: 29% in top 10% of high school class, 56% in top 25% of high school class, 91% in top 50% of high school class. SAT Math middle 50% range 500–610. SAT Critical Reading middle 50% range 490–600. ACT middle 50% range 20–25. TOEFL required of all international applicants, minimum paper TOEFL 550, minimum computer TOEFL 213. **Basis for Candidate Selection:** *Very important factors considered include:* Academic GPA, rigor of secondary school record. *Important factors considered include:* Application essay, level of applicant's interest, recommendation(s), standardized test scores. *Other factors considered include:* Alumni/ae relation, class rank, extracurricular activities, interview, talent/ability, volunteer work, work experience. **Freshman Admission Requirements:** High school diploma is

required, and GED is accepted. *Academic units required:* 4 English, 3 math, 3 science (3 science labs), 3 foreign language, 3 social studies, 2 history. *Academic units recommended:* 4 English, 4 math, 4 science (3 science labs), 4 foreign language, 3 social studies, 3 history. **Freshman Admission Statistics:** 2,705 applied, 73% admitted, 24% enrolled. **Transfer Admission Requirements:** College transcript(s), statement of good standing from prior institution(s). Minimum college GPA of 2.5 required. Lowest grade transferable C. **General Admission Information:** Application fee $50. Regular application deadline 2/1. Regular notification 4/1. Nonfall registration accepted. Admission may be deferred for a maximum of 1 year. Credit and/or placement offered for CEEB Advanced Placement tests.

COSTS AND FINANCIAL AID

Average book expense $900. **Required Forms and Deadlines:** FAFSA, institution's own financial aid form, copies of parent and student federal tax returns. Financial aid filing deadline 3/1. **Notification of Awards:** Applicants will be notified of awards on a rolling basis beginning on or about 3/1. **Types of Aid:** *Need-based scholarships/grants:* Pell, SEOG, state scholarships/grants, private scholarships, the school's own gift aid. *Loans:* FFEL Subsidized Stafford, FFEL Unsubsidized Stafford, FFEL PLUS, Federal Perkins. **Financial Aid Statistics:** 65% freshmen, 60% undergrads receive need-based scholarship or grant aid. 55% freshmen, 52% undergrads receive need-based self-help aid. 85% undergrads receive any aid.

MCGILL UNIVERSITY

Best 368

845 Sherbrooke St. West, James Administration Bldg., Rm 205, Montreal, QC H3A 2T5 Canada
Phone: 514-398-3910 **E-mail:** admissions@mcgill.ca **CEEB Code:** 935
Fax: 514-398-4193 **Website:** www.mcgill.ca **ACT Code:** 5231
Financial Aid Phone: 514-398-6013

This public school was founded in 1821. It has an 80-acre campus.

RATINGS
Admissions Selectivity Rating: 60*   **Fire Safety Rating:** 67   **Green Rating:** 85

STUDENTS AND FACULTY
Enrollment: 20,271. **Student Body:** 60% female, 40% male, 36% out-of-state, 14% international (153 countries represented). **Faculty:** Student/faculty ratio 16:1. 1,643 full-time faculty, 95% hold PhDs. 100% faculty teach undergrads.

ACADEMICS
Degrees: Bachelor's, certificate, diploma, doctoral, first professional, master's, post-bachelor's certificate. **Academic Requirements:** Requirements vary depending on the program. **Classes:** Most classes have 10–19 students. Most lab/discussion sections have 20–29 students. **Majors with Highest Enrollment:** English/language arts teacher education, political science and government, psychology. **Disciplines with Highest Percentage of Degrees Awarded:** Social sciences 18%, biological/life sciences 11%, engineering 9%, education 7%, psychology 6%. **Special Study Options:** Accelerated program, cooperative education program, cross-registration, distance learning, double major, English as a second language (ESL), exchange student program (domestic), honors program, independent study, internships, study abroad, teacher certification program. The Jewish Teacher Training Program (JTTP) of McGill University prepares students to be teachers of Jewish studies in various formal and informal Jewish educational settings. More than 200 students have graduated from the program since its inception in 1973. While most find employment within the Montreal Jewish community, graduates of the program also teach throughout the United States and Canada. For further information please see: http://www.mcgill.ca/edu-jttp/.

FACILITIES
Housing: Coed dorms, women's dorms, apartments for single students, shared facilities housing. **Special Academic Facilities/Equipment:** McCord Museum of Canadian History, Redpath Museum of Natural History, Lyman Entomological Museum and Research Laboratory, Ecomuseum, Rutherford Museum, Lawrence Lande Collection of Canadiana, Canadian Architecture Collection, Morgan Arboretum, Gault Nature Reserve, herbarium, McGill Archives (Canadian History), Islamic Studies Library, Bellairs Research Institute, McConnell Brain Imaging Centre, McConnell Winter Arena, McGill Sports Centre Gymnasiums, Percival Molson Stadium, memorial pool, Richard

Tomlinson Fieldhouse, outdoor tennis courts, McGill Arctic Research Station, McGill Subarctic Research Station, Phytotron, Schulich School of Music (world-class soundstage, recording studio), McGill Centre for Interdisciplinary Research in Music, Media and Technology, Research Greenhouse, J. S. Marshall Weather Radar Observatory, Mountain and Glen Campuses (McGill University Health Centre Teaching Hospitals), McGill Medical Simulation Centre, McGill Reproductive Centre, McGill University and Genome Quebec Innovation Centre. **Computers:** 38% of classrooms are wired, 23% of classrooms are wireless, 75% of public computers are PCs, 10% of public computers are Macs, 15% of public computers are UNIX, network access in dorm rooms, network access in dorm lounges, online registration, online administrative functions (other than registration), support for handheld computing, remote student-access to Web through college's connection.

CAMPUS LIFE
Activities: Choral groups, concert band, dance, drama/theater, jazz band, literary magazine, marching band, music ensembles, musical theater, opera, pep band, radio station, student government, student newspaper, student-run film society, symphony orchestra, television station. **Organizations:** 134 registered organizations, 2 honor societies, 10 religious organizations. 8 fraternities, 4 sororities. **Athletics (Intercollegiate):** *Men:* Badminton, basketball, crew/rowing, cross-country, football, ice hockey, rugby, soccer, swimming, track/field (indoor), volleyball. *Women:* Badminton, basketball, crew/rowing, cross-country, ice hockey, rugby, soccer, swimming, track/field (indoor), volleyball. Environmental Initiatives: Excellence in environmental research and teaching (e.g. School of Environment, GEC3, Brace, VERT, etc.). Continual investment in energy infrastructure improvements to efficiency and reduce resource consumption. Conservation efforts (including Gault Reserve, Morgan Arboretum, EcoMuseum, etc.).

ADMISSIONS
Freshman Academic Profile: SAT Math middle 50% range 640–720. SAT Critical Reading middle 50% range 640–740. SAT Writing middle 50% range 650–720. ACT middle 50% range 29–31. TOEFL required of all international applicants, minimum paper TOEFL 577, minimum computer TOEFL 233. **Basis for Candidate Selection:** *Very important factors considered include:* Academic GPA, rigor of secondary school record, standardized test scores. *Important factors considered include:* Class rank. *Other factors considered include:* Recommendation(s). **Freshman Admission Requirements:** High school diploma is required, and GED is not accepted. **Freshman Admission Statistics:** 19,406 applied, 56% admitted, 45% enrolled. **Transfer Admission Requirements:** High school transcript, college transcript(s). **General Admission Information:** Application fee $80. Regular application deadline 1/15. Regular notification is rolling. Nonfall registration accepted. Admission may be deferred for a maximum of 1 year. Common Application not accepted. Credit and/or placement offered for CEEB Advanced Placement tests.

COSTS AND FINANCIAL AID
Annual in-state tuition $1,768. Annual out-of-state tuition $5,141. Room and board $10,300. Required fees $1,450. Average book expense $1,000. **Required Forms and Deadlines:** Financial aid filing deadline 6/30. **Student Employment:** Institutional employment available. Off-campus job opportunities are fair.

See page 1262.

MCKENDREE COLLEGE

701 College Road, Lebanon, IL 62254
Phone: 618-537-6831 **E-mail:** inquiry@mckendree.edu **CEEB Code:** 1456
Fax: 618-537-6496 **Website:** www.mckendree.edu **ACT Code:** 1076
Financial Aid Phone: 618-537-6828

This private school, affiliated with the Methodist Church, was founded in 1828. It has a 100-acre campus.

RATINGS
Admissions Selectivity Rating: 81   **Fire Safety Rating:** 60*   **Green Rating:** 60*

STUDENTS AND FACULTY
Enrollment: 2,118. **Student Body:** 57% female, 43% male, 13% out-of-state, 2% international (24 countries represented). African American 12%, Caucasian 81%, Hispanic 2%. **Retention and Graduation:** 73% freshmen return for sophomore year. 37% freshmen graduate within 4 years. 14% grads go on to further study within 1 year. 5% grads pursue arts and sciences degrees. 6% grads pursue business degrees. 3% grads pursue law degrees. 1% grads pursue medical degrees. **Faculty:** Student/faculty ratio 15:1. 70 full-time faculty, 81% hold PhDs. 100% faculty teach undergrads.

ACADEMICS

Degrees: Associate, bachelor's, master's. **Academic Requirements:** Arts/fine arts, computer literacy, English (including composition), history, humanities, mathematics, philosophy, sciences (biological or physical), social science, recreational activities. **Classes:** Most classes have 10–19 students. Most lab/discussion sections have 10–19 students. **Disciplines with Highest Percentage of Degrees Awarded:** Business/marketing 33%, health professions and related sciences 17%, education 13%, computer and information sciences 11%, social sciences 8%. **Special Study Options:** Accelerated program, cooperative education program, double major, external degree program, honors program, independent study, internships, liberal arts/career combination, student-designed major, study abroad, teacher certification program, evening programs in accounting, business administration, organizational communication, 3-2 occupational therapy program with Washington University.

FACILITIES

Housing: Coed dorms, women's dorms, apartments for single students, special housing for disabled students, suite-style apartments are available for both men and women. **Computers:** 50% of public computers are PCs, 10% of public computers are Macs, 5% of public computers are UNIX, network access in dorm rooms, network access in dorm lounges, online registration, online administrative functions (other than registration), remote student-access to Web through college's connection.

CAMPUS LIFE

Activities: Choral groups, concert band, dance, drama/theater, jazz band, literary magazine, marching band, music ensembles, musical theater, pep band, student government, student newspaper, student-run film society, yearbook. **Organizations:** 59 registered organizations, 9 honor societies, 3 religious organizations. 4 fraternities (9% men join), 3 sororities (3% women join). **Athletics (Intercollegiate):** *Men:* Baseball, basketball, bowling, cheerleading, cross-country, football, golf, ice hockey, soccer, tennis, track/field (indoor), track/field (outdoor), wrestling. *Women:* Basketball, bowling, cheerleading, cross-country, golf, ice hockey, soccer, softball, tennis, track/field (indoor), track/field (outdoor), volleyball.

ADMISSIONS

Freshman Academic Profile: 25% in top 10% of high school class, 54% in top 25% of high school class, 91% in top 50% of high school class. 90% from public high schools. SAT Math middle 50% range 430–630. SAT Critical Reading middle 50% range 420–530. ACT middle 50% range 20–27. TOEFL required of all international applicants, minimum paper TOEFL 520, minimum computer TOEFL 190. **Basis for Candidate Selection:** *Very important factors considered include:* Rigor of secondary school record. *Important factors considered include:* Character/personal qualities, class rank, recommendation(s), standardized test scores. *Other factors considered include:* Alumni/ae relation, application essay, extracurricular activities, interview, talent/ability, volunteer work, work experience. **Freshman Admission Requirements:** High school diploma is required, and GED is accepted. *Academic units recommended:* 4 English, 3 math, 3 science, 2 social studies, 1 history. **Freshman Admission Statistics:** 1,150 applied, 69% admitted, 43% enrolled. **Transfer Admission Requirements:** High school transcript, college transcript(s), statement of good standing from prior institution(s). Minimum college GPA of 2.2 required. Lowest grade transferable C. **General Admission Information:** Application fee $40. Regular notification rolling. Nonfall registration accepted. Admission may be deferred. Common Application accepted. Credit and/or placement offered for CEEB Advanced Placement tests.

COSTS AND FINANCIAL AID

Annual tuition $16,400. Room and board $6,480. Required fees $200. Average book expense $1,000. **Required Forms and Deadlines:** FAFSA, institution's own financial aid form. Financial aid filing deadline 5/31. **Notification of Awards:** Applicants will be notified of awards on a rolling basis beginning on or about 3/1. **Types of Aid:** *Need-based scholarships/grants:* Pell, SEOG, state scholarships/grants. *Loans:* FFEL Subsidized Stafford, FFEL Unsubsidized Stafford, FFEL PLUS, Federal Perkins, college/university loans from institutional funds. **Student Employment:** Federal Work-Study Program available. Institutional employment available. Off-campus job opportunities are good. **Financial Aid Statistics:** 78% freshmen, 78% undergrads receive need-based scholarship or grant aid. 58% freshmen, 59% undergrads receive need-based self-help aid. 40 freshmen, 150 undergrads receive athletic scholarships. 99% freshmen, 97% undergrads receive any aid. Highest amount earned per year from on-campus jobs $2,326.

MCMURRY UNIVERSITY

S. 14th and Sayles Boulevard, Abilene, TX 79697
Phone: 915-793-4700 **E-mail:** admissions@mcm.edu **CEEB Code:** 6402
Fax: 915-793-4718 **Website:** www.mcm.edu **ACT Code:** 4130
Financial Aid Phone: 915-793-4713

This private school, affiliated with the Methodist Church, was founded in 1923. It has a 50-acre campus.

RATINGS

Admissions Selectivity Rating: 76   **Fire Safety Rating:** 60*   **Green Rating:** 60*

STUDENTS AND FACULTY

Enrollment: 1,408. **Student Body:** 52% female, 48% male, 3% out-of-state. African American 8%, Asian 1%, Caucasian 76%, Hispanic 12%. **Retention and Graduation:** 70% freshmen return for sophomore year. 15% grads go on to further study within 1 year. 14% grads pursue arts and sciences degrees. 1% grads pursue medical degrees. **Faculty:** Student/faculty ratio 14:1. 76 full-time faculty, 74% hold PhDs. 100% faculty teach undergrads.

ACADEMICS

Degrees: Bachelor's. **Academic Requirements:** Arts/fine arts, computer literacy, English (including composition), foreign languages, history, humanities, mathematics, philosophy, sciences (biological or physical), social science, religion, health fitness. **Classes:** Most classes have 10–19 students. Most lab/discussion sections have 10–19 students. **Disciplines with Highest Percentage of Degrees Awarded:** Education 32%, business/marketing 24%, biological/life sciences 9%, social sciences 6%, visual and performing arts 5%. **Special Study Options:** Accelerated program, cross-registration, double major, dual enrollment, honors program, independent study, internships, liberal arts/career combination, study abroad, teacher certification program, engineering with Texas Tech University.

FACILITIES

Housing: Coed dorms, men's dorms, women's dorms, apartments for single students. **Computers:** 90% of public computers are PCs, 10% of public computers are Macs, network access in dorm rooms, network access in dorm lounges, online administrative functions (other than registration), remote student-access to Web through college's connection.

CAMPUS LIFE

Activities: Choral groups, concert band, drama/theater, jazz band, literary magazine, marching band, music ensembles, musical theater, student government, student newspaper, yearbook. **Organizations:** 45 registered organizations, 13 honor societies, 2 religious organizations. 7 fraternities (29% men join), 6 sororities (20% women join). **Athletics (Intercollegiate):** *Men:* Baseball, basketball, cross-country, diving, football, golf, swimming, tennis, track/field (indoor), track/field (outdoor). *Women:* Basketball, cross-country, diving, golf, swimming, tennis, track/field (indoor), track/field (outdoor), volleyball.

ADMISSIONS

Freshman Academic Profile: 15% in top 10% of high school class, 37% in top 25% of high school class, 72% in top 50% of high school class. 98% from public high schools. SAT Math middle 50% range 460–570. SAT Critical Reading middle 50% range 440–550. ACT middle 50% range 18–23. TOEFL required of all international applicants, minimum paper TOEFL 550. **Basis for Candidate Selection:** *Very important factors considered include:* Class rank, rigor of secondary school record, standardized test scores. *Important factors considered include:* Character/personal qualities, talent/ability. *Other factors considered include:* Alumni/ae relation, application essay, extracurricular activities, geographical residence, interview, recommendation(s), religious affiliation/commitment, state residency, volunteer work, work experience. **Freshman Admission Requirements:** High school diploma is required, and GED is accepted. *Academic units required:* 4 English, 3 math, 2 science, 2 foreign language, 3 social studies. *Academic units recommended:* 4 math, 3 science. **Freshman Admission Statistics:** 911 applied, 70% admitted, 51% enrolled. **Transfer Admission Requirements:** College transcript(s). Minimum college GPA of 2.0 required. Lowest grade transferable C. **General Admission Information:** Application fee $20. Regular notification is rolling. Nonfall registration accepted. Admission may be deferred for a maximum of 1 year. Common Application accepted. Credit and/or placement offered for CEEB Advanced Placement tests.

COSTS AND FINANCIAL AID

Required Forms and Deadlines: FAFSA, institution's own financial aid form. Financial aid filing deadline 3/15. **Notification of Awards:** Applicants will be notified of awards on a rolling basis beginning on or about 3/15. **Types of Aid:**

Need-based scholarships/grants: Pell, SEOG, state scholarships/grants, private scholarships, the school's own gift aid. Loans: FFEL Subsidized Stafford, FFEL Unsubsidized Stafford, FFEL PLUS, Federal Perkins, state loans. **Student Employment:** Federal Work-Study Program available. Institutional employment available. Off-campus job opportunities are excellent. **Financial Aid Statistics:** 75% freshmen, 77% undergrads receive need-based scholarship or grant aid. 66% freshmen, 70% undergrads receive need-based self-help aid. Highest amount earned per year from on-campus jobs $611.

MCNEESE STATE UNIVERSITY

PO Box 92495, Lake Charles, LA 70609-2495
Phone: 318-475-5146 **CEEB Code:** 6403
Fax: 318-475-5189 **Website:** www.mcneese.edu **ACT Code:** 1594
Financial Aid Phone: 318-475-5065

This public school was founded in 1939. It has a 171-acre campus.

RATINGS
Admissions Selectivity Rating: 60*   **Fire Safety Rating:** 60*   **Green Rating:** 60*

STUDENTS AND FACULTY
Enrollment: 7,045. **Student Body:** 58% female, 42% male, 5% out-of-state, 1% international. African American 17%, Caucasian 80%, Hispanic 1%. **Retention and Graduation:** 64% freshmen return for sophomore year. 7% freshmen graduate within 4 years. 5% grads go on to further study within 1 year. 5% grads pursue arts and sciences degrees. **Faculty:** 100% faculty teach undergrads.

ACADEMICS
Degrees: Associate, bachelor's, master's. **Academic Requirements:** Arts/fine arts, computer literacy, English (including composition), history, mathematics, sciences (biological or physical), social science. **Special Study Options:** Cooperative education program, double major, internships, teacher certification program.

FACILITIES
Housing: Coed dorms, men's dorms, women's dorms, apartments for married students, apartments for single students, fraternity/sorority housing. **Special Academic Facilities/Equipment:** Vertebrate museum, art gallery, planetarium.

CAMPUS LIFE
Activities: Choral groups, concert band, dance, drama/theater, jazz band, marching band, music ensembles, pep band, student government, student newspaper, yearbook. **Organizations:** 5 honor societies, 3 religious organizations. 8 fraternities (5% men join), 6 sororities (5% women join). **Athletics (Intercollegiate):** *Men:* Basketball, cross-country, softball, tennis, track/field (outdoor), volleyball.

ADMISSIONS
Freshman Academic Profile: ACT middle 50% range 19–23. TOEFL required of all international applicants, minimum paper TOEFL 450. **Freshman Admission Requirements:** High school diploma is required, and GED is accepted. **Freshman Admission Statistics:** 2,516 applied, 99% admitted, 62% enrolled. **Transfer Admission Requirements:** Minimum college GPA of 2.0 required. Lowest grade transferable C. **General Admission Information:** Application fee $10. Early decision application deadline 4/1. Regular application deadline 8/1. Regular notification rolling. Nonfall registration accepted. Common Application not accepted. Credit and/or placement offered for CEEB Advanced Placement tests.

COSTS AND FINANCIAL AID
Annual in-state tuition $2,226. Annual out-of-state tuition $8,292. Room and board $3,460. Required fees $1,036. Average book expense $1,200. **Required Forms and Deadlines:** FAFSA, institution's own financial aid form, state aid form. **Types of Aid:** *Need-based scholarships/grants:* Pell, SEOG, state scholarships/grants, private scholarships, the school's own gift aid. *Loans:* FFEL Subsidized Stafford, FFEL Unsubsidized Stafford, FFEL PLUS, Federal Perkins, state loans, college/university loans from institutional funds. **Student Employment:** Federal Work-Study Program available. Institutional employment available. Off-campus job opportunities are good. **Financial Aid Statistics:** Highest amount earned per year from on-campus jobs $1,220.

MCPHERSON COLLEGE

PO Box 1402, 1600 East Euclid, McPherson, KS 67460
Phone: 620-241-0731 **E-mail:** admiss@mcpherson.edu **CEEB Code:** 6404
Fax: 620-241-8443 **Website:** www.mcpherson.edu **ACT Code:** 1440
Financial Aid Phone: 800-365-7402

This private school, affiliated with the Church of Brethren, was founded in 1887. It has a 23-acre campus.

RATINGS
Admissions Selectivity Rating: 73   **Fire Safety Rating:** 60*   **Green Rating:** 60*

STUDENTS AND FACULTY
Enrollment: 466. **Student Body:** 38% female, 62% male, 50% out-of-state. African American 6%, Caucasian 86%, Hispanic 6%, Native American 1%. **Retention and Graduation:** 63% freshmen return for sophomore year. 19% freshmen graduate within 4 years. 9% grads go on to further study within 1 year. 9% grads pursue medical degrees. **Faculty:** Student/faculty ratio 12:1. 35 full-time faculty, 63% hold PhDs.

ACADEMICS
Degrees: Bachelor's. **Academic Requirements:** Arts/fine arts, computer literacy, English (including composition), history, humanities, mathematics, philosophy, sciences (biological or physical), social science. **Classes:** Most classes have fewer than 10 students. Most lab/discussion sections have fewer than 10 students. **Disciplines with Highest Percentage of Degrees Awarded:** Education 21%, social sciences 16%, business/marketing 16%, visual and performing arts 13%, biological/life sciences 9%, psychology 5%, English 5%. **Special Study Options:** Accelerated program, cooperative education program, cross-registration, double major, English as a second language (ESL), independent study, internships, liberal arts/career combination, student-designed major, study abroad, teacher certification program.

FACILITIES
Housing: Coed dorms, men's dorms, women's dorms, special housing for disabled students. **Special Academic Facilities/Equipment:** Natural history museum.

CAMPUS LIFE
Activities: Choral groups, concert band, drama/theater, jazz band, music ensembles, musical theater, pep band, student government, student newspaper, yearbook. **Athletics (Intercollegiate):** *Women:* Basketball, cross-country, golf, tennis, track/field (outdoor), volleyball.

ADMISSIONS
Freshman Academic Profile: 26% in top 10% of high school class, 13% in top 25% of high school class, 99% from public high schools. SAT Math middle 50% range 410–580. SAT Critical Reading middle 50% range 410–560. ACT middle 50% range 19–24. **Basis for Candidate Selection:** *Very important factors considered include:* Academic GPA, standardized test scores. *Other factors considered include:* Alumni/ae relation, application essay, character/personal qualities, class rank, extracurricular activities, interview, recommendation(s), rigor of secondary school record, talent/ability, volunteer work, work experience. **Freshman Admission Requirements:** High school diploma is required, and GED is accepted. **Freshman Admission Statistics:** 495 applied, 85% admitted, 26% enrolled. **Transfer Admission Requirements:** High school transcript, college transcript(s), standardized test score. Minimum college GPA of 2.0 required. Lowest grade transferable C. **General Admission Information:** Application fee $25. Regular notification upon acceptance. Nonfall registration accepted. Admission may be deferred for a maximum of 6 months. Common Application not accepted. Credit offered for CEEB Advanced Placement tests.

COSTS AND FINANCIAL AID
Required Forms and Deadlines: FAFSA. Financial aid filing deadline 8/1. **Notification of Awards:** Applicants will be notified of awards on a rolling basis beginning on or about 1/1. **Types of Aid:** *Need-based scholarships/grants:* Pell, SEOG, state scholarships/grants, private scholarships, the school's own gift aid. *Loans:* FFEL Subsidized Stafford, FFEL Unsubsidized Stafford, FFEL PLUS, Federal Perkins. **Student Employment:** Federal Work-Study Program available. Institutional employment available. Off-campus job opportunities are good. **Financial Aid Statistics:** 80% freshmen, 69% undergrads receive need-based scholarship or grant aid. 77% freshmen, 73% undergrads receive need-based self-help aid. Highest amount earned per year from on-campus jobs $400.

MEDAILLE COLLEGE

18 Agassiz Circle, Buffalo, NY 14214
Phone: 716-884-3281 **E-mail:** jmatheny@medaille.edu **CEEB Code:** 2422
Fax: 716-884-0291 **Website:** www.medaille.edu **ACT Code:** 2822
Financial Aid Phone: 716-884-3281

This private school was founded in 1937. It has a 13-acre campus.

RATINGS
Admissions Selectivity Rating: 74   **Fire Safety Rating:** 60*   **Green Rating:** 60*

STUDENTS AND FACULTY
Enrollment: 1,650. **Student Body:** 67% female, 33% male, 1% out-of-state, 3% international (2 countries represented). African American 16%, Caucasian 65%, Hispanic 3%. **Retention and Graduation:** 70% freshmen return for sophomore year. 15% freshmen graduate within 4 years. 24% grads go on to further study within 1 year. 4% grads pursue arts and sciences degrees. 5% grads pursue business degrees. 1% grads pursue law degrees. 1% grads pursue medical degrees. **Faculty:** Student/faculty ratio 15:1. 70 full-time faculty, 56% hold PhDs. 100% faculty teach undergrads.

ACADEMICS
Degrees: Associate, bachelor's, certificate, master's. **Academic Requirements:** Arts/fine arts, computer literacy, English (including composition), history, humanities, mathematics, sciences (biological or physical), social science. **Classes:** Most classes have 10–19 students. Most lab/discussion sections have 10–19 students. **Majors with Highest Enrollment:** Business administration/management, elementary education and teaching, veterinary/animal health technology/technician and veterinary assistant. **Disciplines with Highest Percentage of Degrees Awarded:** Education 54%, business/marketing 27%, liberal arts/general studies 8%, computer and information sciences 3%, social sciences 3%, communication technologies 2%. **Special Study Options:** Accelerated program, cross-registration, double major, honors program, independent study, internships, liberal arts/career combination, student-designed major, teacher certification program, weekend college, module system for full-time evening studies.

FACILITIES
Housing: Coed dorms, men's dorms, women's dorms, apartments for married students, apartments for single students. **Special Academic Facilities/Equipment:** Veterinary technology labs, New Media Institute, children's literature collection. **Computers:** 93% of public computers are PCs, 6% of public computers are Macs, 1% of public computers are UNIX, network access in dorm rooms, network access in dorm lounges, remote student-access to Web through college's connection.

CAMPUS LIFE
Activities: Drama/theater, literary magazine, musical theater, radio station, student government, student newspaper, student-run film society, television station, yearbook. **Organizations:** 18 registered organizations, 2 honor societies. **Athletics (Intercollegiate):** *Men:* Baseball, basketball, cheerleading, lacrosse, soccer, volleyball. *Women:* Basketball, cheerleading, cross-country, lacrosse, soccer, softball, volleyball.

ADMISSIONS
Freshman Academic Profile: 14% in top 10% of high school class, 45% in top 25% of high school class, 75% in top 50% of high school class. 85% from public high schools. SAT Math middle 50% range 410–500. SAT Critical Reading middle 50% range 420–520. ACT middle 50% range 17–21. TOEFL required of all international applicants, minimum paper TOEFL 550, minimum computer TOEFL 213. **Basis for Candidate Selection:** *Very important factors considered include:* Interview, rigor of secondary school record, standardized test scores. *Important factors considered include:* Application essay, extracurricular activities, recommendation(s). *Other factors considered include:* Alumni/ae relation, character/personal qualities, class rank, talent/ability, volunteer work, work experience. **Freshman Admission Requirements:** High school diploma is required, and GED is accepted. *Academic units required:* 4 English, 2 math, 2 science, 4 social studies. *Academic units recommended:* 4 English, 3 math, 3 science (2 science labs), 2 foreign language, 4 social studies, 2 history, 3 mathematics, 3 science. **Freshman Admission Statistics:** 763 applied, 68% admitted, 55% enrolled. **Transfer Admission Requirements:** High school transcript, college transcript(s), essay or personal statement. Minimum college GPA of 2.0 required. Lowest grade transferable C. **General Admission Information:** Application fee $25. Regular notification is rolling. Nonfall registration accepted. Admission may be deferred for a maximum of 1 year. Common Application accepted. Credit and/or placement offered for CEEB Advanced Placement tests.

COSTS AND FINANCIAL AID
Annual tuition $13,350. Room and board $6,400. Required fees $310. Average book expense $930. **Required Forms and Deadlines:** FAFSA, institution's own financial aid form, state aid form. Financial aid filing deadline 4/15. **Notification of Awards:** Applicants will be notified of awards on or about 5/1. **Types of Aid:** *Need-based scholarships/grants:* Pell, SEOG, state scholarships/grants, private scholarships, the school's own gift aid. *Loans:* FFEL Subsidized Stafford, FFEL Unsubsidized Stafford, FFEL PLUS. **Student Employment:** Federal Work-Study Program available. Institutional employment available. Off-campus job opportunities are good. **Financial Aid Statistics:** 84% freshmen, 67% undergrads receive need-based scholarship or grant aid. 87% freshmen, 73% undergrads receive need-based self-help aid. 85% freshmen, 85% undergrads receive any aid. Highest amount earned per year from on-campus jobs $1,500.

MEDCENTER ONE COLLEGE OF NURSING

512 North Seventh Street, Bismarck, ND 58501
Phone: 701-323-6271 **E-mail:** msmith@mohs.org
Fax: 701-323-6967 **Website:** www.college.medcenterone.com **ACT Code:** 3197
Financial Aid Phone: 701-323-6270

This private school was founded in 1988.

RATINGS
Admissions Selectivity Rating: 60*   **Fire Safety Rating:** 60*   **Green Rating:** 60*

STUDENTS AND FACULTY
Enrollment: 88. **Student Body:** 94% female, 6% male, 2% out-of-state. Asian 1%, Caucasian 92%, Hispanic 1%, Native American 6%. **Faculty:** Student/faculty ratio 7:1. 11 full-time faculty. 100% faculty teach undergrads.

ACADEMICS
Degrees: Bachelor's. **Academic Requirements:** Computer literacy, English (including composition), humanities, mathematics, sciences (biological or physical), social science. **Classes:** Most classes have 40–49 students. Most lab/discussion sections have 10–19 students. **Disciplines with Highest Percentage of Degrees Awarded:** Health professions and related sciences 100%. **Special Study Options:** Independent study, internships.

FACILITIES
Housing: Coed dorms. **Special Academic Facilities/Equipment:** Alumni Corner. **Computers:** 100% of public computers are PCs, online administrative functions (other than registration), remote student-access to Web through college's connection.

CAMPUS LIFE
Activities: Student government. **Organizations:** 1 honor society.

ADMISSIONS
Freshman Academic Profile: TOEFL required of all international applicants, minimum paper TOEFL 525. **Freshman Admission Requirements:** High school diploma is required, and GED is accepted. **Transfer Admission Requirements:** High school transcript, college transcript(s), essay or personal statement, interview. Minimum college GPA of 2.5 required. Lowest grade transferable C. **General Admission Information:** Application fee $40. Regular notification is rolling. Nonfall registration not accepted. Common Application not accepted.

COSTS AND FINANCIAL AID
Annual tuition $3,486. Room $900. Required fees $500. Average book expense $1,089. **Required Forms and Deadlines:** FAFSA, institution's own financial aid form. Financial aid filing deadline 4/15. **Notification of Awards:** Applicants will be notified of awards on or about 6/1. **Types of Aid:** *Need-based scholarships/grants:* Pell, SEOG, state scholarships/grants, private scholarships, the school's own gift aid. *Loans:* FFEL Subsidized Stafford, FFEL Unsubsidized Stafford, FFEL PLUS, Federal Perkins, Federal Nursing. **Financial Aid Statistics:** 65% undergrads receive need-based scholarship or grant aid. 61% undergrads receive need-based self-help aid.

MEDICAL COLLEGE OF GEORGIA

Kelly Building-Administration, Room 170, Augusta, GA 30912
Phone: 706-721-2725 **E-mail:** underadm@mail.mcg.edu
Fax: 706-721-7279 **Website:** www.mcg.edu
Financial Aid Phone: 706-721-4901

This public school was founded in 1828. It has a 100-acre campus.

RATINGS
Admissions Selectivity Rating: 60*   **Fire Safety Rating:** 60*   **Green Rating:** 60*

STUDENTS AND FACULTY
Enrollment: 712. **Student Body:** 87% female, 13% male, 11% out-of-state. African American 15%, Asian 2%, Caucasian 80%. **Faculty:** 590 full-time faculty, 87% hold PhDs.

ACADEMICS
Degrees: Bachelor's, doctoral, first professional, master's, post-bachelor's certificate. **Academic Requirements:** Sciences (biological or physical). **Disciplines with Highest Percentage of Degrees Awarded:** Health professions and related sciences 100%. **Special Study Options:** Distance learning, internships, cooperative programs with Augusta State Unviersity.

FACILITIES
Housing: Coed dorms, apartments for married students, apartments for single students. **Computers:** Online registration.

CAMPUS LIFE
Activities: Student government, student newspaper. **Organizations:** 1 religious organization.

ADMISSIONS
Freshman Academic Profile: TOEFL required of all international applicants, minimum paper TOEFL 550. **Transfer Admission Requirements:** College transcript(s), essay or personal statement, standardized test score, statement of good standing from prior institution(s). Minimum college GPA of 2.3 required. Lowest grade transferable C. **General Admission Information:** Application fee $30. Nonfall registration not accepted. Common Application not accepted.

COSTS AND FINANCIAL AID
Annual in-state tuition $2,632. Out-of-state tuition $10,528. Room & board $1,302. Required fees $451. Average book expense $800. **Required Forms and Deadlines:** FAFSA, institution's own financial aid form, Financial Aid Transcript (for mid-year transfers). Financial aid filing deadline 3/31. **Notification of Awards:** Applicants will be notified of awards on a rolling basis beginning on or about 4/30. **Types of Aid:** *Need-based scholarships/grants:* Pell, SEOG, state scholarships/grants, private scholarships, the school's own gift aid. *Loans:* FFEL Subsidized Stafford, FFEL Unsubsidized Stafford, FFEL PLUS, Federal Perkins, Federal Nursing, state loans, college/university loans from institutional funds. **Student Employment:** Federal Work-Study Program available. **Financial Aid Statistics:** 51% undergrads receive need-based scholarship or grant aid. 58% undergrads receive need-based self-help aid.

MEDICAL UNIVERSITY OF SOUTH CAROLINA

PO Box 250203, Charleston, SC 29425
Phone: 843-792-3813 **E-mail:** ohlandt@musc.edu
Fax: 843-792-6615 **Website:** www.musc.edu **ACT Code:** 6440
Financial Aid Phone: 843-792-2536

This public school was founded in 1824. It has a 61-acre campus.

RATINGS
Admissions Selectivity Rating: 60*   **Fire Safety Rating:** 60*   **Green Rating:** 60*

STUDENTS AND FACULTY
Enrollment: 263. **Student Body:** 86% female, 14% male, 28% out-of-state. African American 12%, Asian 1%, Caucasian 76%, Hispanic 2%. **Faculty:** Student/faculty ratio 4:1. 55 full-time faculty, 85% hold PhDs. 12% faculty teach undergrads.

ACADEMICS
Degrees: Bachelor's, doctoral, first professional, master's, post-master's certificate. **Academic Requirements:** Varies with academic program selected.

Classes: Most classes have fewer than 10 students. **Majors with Highest Enrollment:** Cardiovascular technology/technologist, health/health care administration/management, nursing/registered nurse training (RN, ASN, BSN, MSN). **Disciplines with Highest Percentage of Degrees Awarded:** Health professions and related sciences 100%. **Special Study Options:** Accelerated program, distance learning, varies with the academic program selected.

FACILITIES
Housing: No on-campus housing available. Housing available in community. **Special Academic Facilities/Equipment:** Dental museum, medical museum, pharmacy museum. **Computers:** 49% of classrooms are wired, 25% of classrooms are wireless, 48% of public computers are PCs, 52% of public computers are Macs, online registration, online administrative functions (other than registration), remote student-access to Web through college's connection.

CAMPUS LIFE
Activities: Choral groups, literary magazine, student government, student-run film society. **Organizations:** 4 honor societies.

ADMISSIONS
Freshman Academic Profile: Minimum paper TOEFL 600, minimum computer TOEFL 250.

COSTS AND FINANCIAL AID
Annual in-state tuition $10,790. Annual out-of-state tuition $20,588. Required fees $543. Average book expense $600. **Required Forms and Deadlines:** FAFSA, institution's own financial aid form. **Types of Aid:** *Need-based scholarships/grants:* Pell, SEOG, state scholarships/grants, private scholarships, the school's own gift aid, Federal Nursing Scholarships. *Loans:* FFEL Subsidized Stafford, FFEL Unsubsidized Stafford, FFEL PLUS, Federal Perkins, Federal Nursing. **Student Employment:** Federal Work-Study Program available. Off-campus job opportunities are good. **Financial Aid Statistics:** 82% undergrads receive any aid.

MEMORIAL UNIVERSITY OF NEWFOUNDLAND

Admissions Office-Faculty of Medicine, St. Johns, NF A1B 3V6 Canada **Phone:** 709-777-6615 **E-mail:** munmed@mun.ca
Fax: 709-777-6615 **Website:** www.med.mun.ca/admissions
Financial Aid Phone: 709-729-4244

This public school was founded in 1925. It has a 220-acre campus.

RATINGS
Admissions Selectivity Rating: 60*   **Fire Safety Rating:** 60*   **Green Rating:** 60*

STUDENTS AND FACULTY
Enrollment: 13,700. **Faculty:** Student/faculty ratio 16:1. 1,012 full-time faculty. 100% faculty teach undergrads.

ACADEMICS
Degrees: Doctoral. **Academic Requirements:** A combination of arts and science electives. **Disciplines with Highest Percentage of Degrees Awarded:** Other 31%, education 18%, business/marketing 18%, social sciences 7%, psychology 5%, health professions and related sciences 5%, engineering 4%. **Special Study Options:** Accelerated program, cooperative education program, distance learning, double major, English as a second language (ESL), exchange student program (domestic), honors program, internships, liberal arts/career combination, study abroad, teacher certification program.

FACILITIES
Housing: Coed dorms, men's dorms, women's dorms, apartments for married students, apartments for single students, special housing for disabled students. **Special Academic Facilities/Equipment:** Olympic-size swimming pool, complete fitness center, student eating area, indoor aerobics, track and field, soccer field, basketball courts. **Computers:** Online registration, online administrative functions (other than registration), remote student-access to Web through college's connection.

CAMPUS LIFE
Activities: Choral groups, concert band, dance, drama/theater, jazz band, literary magazine, music ensembles, musical theater, radio station, student government, student newspaper, student-run film society, symphony orchestra, yearbook. **Organizations:** 81 registered organizations. **Athletics (Intercollegiate):** *Men:* Basketball, fencing, ice hockey, riflery, rugby, skiing (downhill/alpine), soccer, softball, squash, swimming, track/field (outdoor), volleyball, wrestling. *Women:* Basketball, fencing, ice hockey, riflery, rugby, skiing (downhill/alpine), soccer, softball, squash, swimming, track/field (outdoor), volleyball, wrestling.

ADMISSIONS

Freshman Academic Profile: TOEFL required of all international applicants, minimum paper TOEFL 550. **Freshman Admission Requirements:** High school diploma is required, and GED is accepted. *Academic units required:* 3 English, 4 math, 4 science (4 science labs), 2 social studies, 2 academic electives. **Freshman Admission Statistics:** 3,900 applied, 86% admitted. **Transfer Admission Requirements:** High school transcript, college transcript(s), standardized test score. **General Admission Information:** Application fee $80. Regular application deadline 3/1. Regular notification is rolling. Nonfall registration accepted. Common Application not accepted.

COSTS AND FINANCIAL AID

Room & board $2,153. Required fees $6,600. Average book expense $500. **Student Employment:** Institutional employment available. Off-campus job opportunities are good.

MEMPHIS COLLEGE OF ART

Overton Park, 1930 Poplar Avenue, Memphis, TN 38104-2764
Phone: 901-272-5151 **E-mail:** info@mca.edu **CEEB Code:** 1511
Fax: 901-272-5158 **Website:** www.mca.edu **ACT Code:** 3991
Financial Aid Phone: 901-272-5136

This private school was founded in 1936. It has a 340-acre campus.

RATINGS

Admissions Selectivity Rating: 60*   **Fire Safety Rating:** 75   **Green Rating:** 60*

STUDENTS AND FACULTY

Enrollment: 314. **Student Body:** 50% female, 50% male, 35% out-of-state, 2% international (5 countries represented). African American 15%, Asian 2%, Caucasian 71%, Hispanic 2%. **Retention and Graduation:** 59% freshmen return for sophomore year. 27% freshmen graduate within 4 years. 10% grads go on to further study within 1 year. **Faculty:** 21 full-time faculty, 81% hold PhDs. 99% faculty teach undergrads.

ACADEMICS

Degrees: Bachelor's, master's. **Academic Requirements:** Arts/fine arts, computer literacy, English (including composition), social science. **Classes:** Most classes have 10–19 students. **Disciplines with Highest Percentage of Degrees Awarded:** Visual and performing arts 100%. **Special Study Options:** Cross-registration, double major, exchange student program (domestic), independent study, internships, study abroad, teacher certification program, New York Studies Program. Arts Exchange possible with other AICAD schools.

FACILITIES

Housing: Coed dorms, apartments for single students. **Special Academic Facilities/Equipment:** Art museum, numerous galleries for student exhibition, computer writing lab. **Computers:** 10% of classrooms are wired, 10% of classrooms are wireless, network access in dorm rooms, remote student-access to Web through college's connection.

CAMPUS LIFE

Activities: Student government, student newspaper.

ADMISSIONS

Freshman Academic Profile: 85% from public high schools. ACT middle 50% range 18–24. TOEFL required of all international applicants, minimum paper TOEFL 500, minimum computer TOEFL 195. **Basis for Candidate Selection:** *Very important factors considered include:* Academic GPA, talent/ability. *Important factors considered include:* Interview, rigor of secondary school record, standardized test scores. *Other factors considered include:* Application essay, character/personal qualities, class rank, extracurricular activities, level of applicant's interest, recommendation(s), volunteer work, work experience. **Freshman Admission Requirements:** High school diploma is required, and GED is accepted. **Freshman Admission Statistics:** 617 applied, 55% admitted, 18% enrolled. **Transfer Admission Requirements:** College transcript(s). Minimum college GPA of 2.0 required. Lowest grade transferable C. **General Admission Information:** Application fee $25. Regular notification is rolling. Nonfall registration accepted. Admission may be deferred for a maximum of 1 year. Credit and/or placement offered for CEEB Advanced Placement tests.

COSTS AND FINANCIAL AID

Annual tuition $20,100. Room & board $7,960. Required fees $560. Average book expense $1,600. **Required Forms and Deadlines:** FAFSA. Financial aid filing deadline 3/1. **Notification of Awards:** Applicants will be notified of awards on a rolling basis beginning on or about 1/15. **Types of Aid:** *Need-based scholarships/grants:* Pell, SEOG, state scholarships/grants, private scholarships, the school's own gift aid. *Loans:* Direct Subsidized Stafford, Direct Unsubsidized Stafford, Direct PLUS, FFEL Subsidized Stafford, FFEL Unsubsidized Stafford, FFEL PLUS, Federal Perkins, college/university loans from institutional funds. **Student Employment:** Federal Work-Study Program available. Off-campus job opportunities are good. **Financial Aid Statistics:** 52% freshmen, 48% undergrads receive need-based scholarship or grant aid. 79% freshmen, 78% undergrads receive need-based self-help aid. 95% freshmen, 95% undergrads receive any aid. Highest amount earned per year from on-campus jobs $1,000.

MENLO COLLEGE

1000 El Camino Real, Atherton, CA 94027
Phone: 650-543-3753 **E-mail:** admissions@menlo.edu **CEEB Code:** 4483
Fax: 650-543-4496 **Website:** www.menlo.edu **ACT Code:** 0330
Financial Aid Phone: 650-543-3880

This private school was founded in 1927. It has a 45-acre campus.

RATINGS

Admissions Selectivity Rating: 60*   **Fire Safety Rating:** 61   **Green Rating:** 60*

STUDENTS AND FACULTY

Enrollment: 725. **Student Body:** 42% female, 58% male, 22% out-of-state, 9% international (40 countries represented). African American 9%, Asian 12%, Caucasian 38%, Hispanic 16%. **Retention and Graduation:** 64% freshmen return for sophomore year. **Faculty:** Student/faculty ratio 17:1. 23 full-time faculty, 74% hold PhDs. 100% faculty teach undergrads.

ACADEMICS

Degrees: Bachelor's. **Academic Requirements:** Computer literacy, English (including composition), foreign languages, humanities, mathematics, sciences (biological or physical), economics management. **Classes:** Most classes have 10–19 students. Most lab/discussion sections have 10–19 students. **Disciplines with Highest Percentage of Degrees Awarded:** Business/marketing 78%, communication technologies 16%, liberal arts/general studies 6%. **Special Study Options:** Accelerated program, double major, dual enrollment, English as a Second Language (ESL), honors program, independent study, internships, student-designed major, study abroad, Advanced Placement credit, learning disability services.

FACILITIES

Housing: Coed dorms, men's dorms, special housing for disabled students. **Computers:** 85% of public computers are PCs, 15% of public computers are Macs, online administrative functions (other than registration), remote student-access to Web through college's connection.

CAMPUS LIFE

Activities: Radio station, student government, student newspaper, television station. **Organizations:** 35 registered organizations, 2 honor societies. **Athletics (Intercollegiate):** *Men:* Baseball, basketball, cross-country, football, golf, soccer, tennis, track/field (outdoor). *Women:* Basketball, cross-country, golf, soccer, softball, tennis, track/field (outdoor), volleyball.

ADMISSIONS

Freshman Academic Profile: SAT Math middle 50% range 420–520. SAT Critical Reading middle 50% range 400–510. SAT Writing middle 50% range 400–440. ACT middle 50% range 15–20. TOEFL required of all international applicants, minimum paper TOEFL 500, minimum computer TOEFL 173. **Basis for Candidate Selection:** *Very important factors considered include:* Application essay, class rank, recommendation(s), rigor of secondary school record, standardized test scores. *Important factors considered include:* Character/personal qualities, extracurricular activities. *Other factors considered include:* Alumni/ae relation, interview, talent/ability, volunteer work, work experience. **Freshman Admission Requirements:** High school diploma is required, and GED is accepted. *Academic units recommended:* 4 English, 3 math, 3 science (1 science lab), 2 foreign language, 3 social studies, 3 history. **Freshman Admission Statistics:** 712 applied, 65% admitted, 35% enrolled. **Transfer Admission Requirements:** College transcript(s), essay or personal statement, statement of good standing from prior institution(s). Minimum college GPA of 2.5 required. Lowest grade transferable C-. **General Admission Information:** Application fee $40. Regular notification is rolling. Nonfall registration accepted. Admission may be deferred for a maximum of 2 semesters. Credit and/or placement offered for CEEB Advanced Placement tests.

COSTS AND FINANCIAL AID

Annual tuition $27,550. Room and board $9,980. Required fees $400. Average book expense $1,276. **Required Forms and Deadlines:** FAFSA. Financial aid filing deadline 8/1. **Notification of Awards:** Applicants will be notified of awards on or about 3/10. **Types of Aid:** *Need-based scholarships/grants:* Pell, SEOG, state scholarships/grants, the school's own gift aid, Federal ACG Grant. *Loans:* FFEL Subsidized Stafford, FFEL Unsubsidized Stafford, FFEL PLUS. **Student Employment:** Federal Work-Study Program available. Institutional employment available. Off-campus job opportunities are excellent. **Financial Aid Statistics:** 61% freshmen, 57% undergrads receive need-based scholarship or grant aid. 57% freshmen, 53% undergrads receive need-based self-help aid. 70% freshmen, 82% undergrads receive any aid. Highest amount earned per year from on-campus jobs $2,000.

MERCER UNIVERSITY—MACON

Best 368

Admissions Office, 1400 Coleman Avenue, Macon, GA 31207-0001
Phone: 478-301-2650 **E-mail:** admissions@mercer.edu **CEEB Code:** 5409
Fax: 478-301-2828 **Website:** www.mercer.edu **ACT Code:** 0838
Financial Aid Phone: 478-301-2670

This private school, affiliated with the Baptist Church, was founded in 1833. It has a 150-acre campus.

RATINGS
Admissions Selectivity Rating: 87   **Fire Safety Rating:** 73   **Green Rating:** 60*

STUDENTS AND FACULTY
Enrollment: 2,293. **Student Body:** 54% female, 46% male, 24% out-of-state, 2% international (19 countries represented). African American 17%, Asian 6%, Caucasian 69%, Hispanic 2%. **Retention and Graduation:** 79% freshmen return for sophomore year. 30% freshmen graduate within 4 years. 35% grads go on to further study within 1 year. 8% grads pursue arts and sciences degrees. 5% grads pursue business degrees. 8% grads pursue law degrees. 7% grads pursue medical degrees. **Faculty:** Student/faculty ratio 12:1. 350 full-time faculty, 87% hold PhDs.

ACADEMICS
Degrees: Bachelor's, doctoral, first professional, master's, post-master's certificate. **Academic Requirements:** Arts/fine arts, computer literacy, English (including composition), foreign languages, history, humanities, mathematics, philosophy, sciences (biological or physical), social science, religion/Christianity. **Classes:** Most classes have 10–19 students. Most lab/discussion sections have 10–19 students. **Majors with Highest Enrollment:** Biology/biological sciences, business administration/management, engineering. **Disciplines with Highest Percentage of Degrees Awarded:** Business/marketing 19%, engineering 16%, social sciences 8%, biological/life sciences 7%, communications/journalism 6%. **Special Study Options:** Accelerated program, cooperative education program, cross-registration, double major, dual enrollment, honors program, independent study, internships, liberal arts/career combination, student-designed major, study abroad, teacher certification program, Great Books program.

FACILITIES
Housing: Coed dorms, men's dorms, women's dorms, apartments for married students, apartments for single students, special housing for disabled students, special housing for international students, fraternity/sorority housing. **Special Academic Facilities/Equipment:** McCorkle Music Building. **Computers:** 25% of classrooms are wired, 10% of classrooms are wireless, 97% of public computers are PCs, 2% of public computers are Macs, 1% of public computers are UNIX, network access in dorm rooms, network access in dorm lounges, online registration, online administrative functions (other than registration), support for handheld computing, remote student-access to Web through college's connection.

CAMPUS LIFE
Activities: Choral groups, concert band, dance, drama/theater, jazz band, literary magazine, music ensembles, opera, pep band, student government, student newspaper, student-run film society. **Organizations:** 80 registered organizations, 18 honor societies, 8 religious organizations. 10 fraternities (23% men join), 6 sororities (26% women join). **Athletics (Intercollegiate):** *Men:*

Baseball, basketball, cross-country, golf, riflery, soccer, tennis. *Women:* Basketball, cross-country, golf, riflery, soccer, softball, tennis, volleyball.

ADMISSIONS
Freshman Academic Profile: 42% in top 10% of high school class, 72% in top 25% of high school class, 80% in top 50% of high school class. SAT Math middle 50% range 550–640. SAT Critical Reading middle 50% range 530–630. SAT Writing middle 50% range 520–620. ACT middle 50% range 22–27. TOEFL required of all international applicants, minimum paper TOEFL 550, minimum computer TOEFL 213. **Basis for Candidate Selection:** *Very important factors considered include:* Academic GPA, level of applicant's interest, rigor of secondary school record, standardized test scores. *Important factors considered include:* Character/personal qualities, extracurricular activities, talent/ability, volunteer work. *Other factors considered include:* Alumni/ae relation, class rank, interview, recommendation(s), work experience. **Freshman Admission Requirements:** High school diploma is required, and GED is accepted. *Academic units required:* 4 English, 4 math, 3 science (2 science labs), 2 foreign language, 1 social studies, 2 history. **Freshman Admission Statistics:** 2,857 applied, 79% admitted, 25% enrolled. **Transfer Admission Requirements:** College transcript(s), statement of good standing from prior institution(s). Minimum college GPA of 2.5 required. Lowest grade transferable C. **General Admission Information:** Application fee $50. Regular application deadline 7/1. Regular notification is rolling. Nonfall registration not accepted. Admission may be deferred for a maximum of 1 year. Credit and/or placement offered for CEEB Advanced Placement tests.

COSTS AND FINANCIAL AID
Comprehensive fee $26,760. Room and board $8,015. Required fees $200. Average book expense $900. **Required Forms and Deadlines:** FAFSA, institution's own financial aid form, state aid form. Financial aid filing deadline 4/1. **Notification of Awards:** Applicants will be notified of awards on a rolling basis beginning on or about 3/15. **Types of Aid:** *Need-based scholarships/grants:* Pell, SEOG, state scholarships/grants, the school's own gift aid, Federal Nursing Scholarships. *Loans:* Direct Subsidized Stafford, Direct Unsubsidized Stafford, Direct PLUS, Federal Perkins, Federal Nursing, college/university loans from institutional funds. **Student Employment:** Federal Work-Study Program available. Institutional employment available. Off-campus job opportunities are good. **Financial Aid Statistics:** 68% freshmen, 64% undergrads receive need-based scholarship or grant aid. 40% freshmen, 41% undergrads receive need-based self-help aid. 43 freshmen, 158 undergrads receive athletic scholarships. 99% freshmen, 97% undergrads receive any aid.

MERCY COLLEGE

555 Broadway, Dobbs Ferry, NY 10522
Phone: 914-674-7324 **E-mail:** admissions@mercy.edu **CEEB Code:** 2409
Fax: 914-674-7382 **Website:** www.mercy.edu **ACT Code:** 2814
Financial Aid Phone: 914-693-7600

This private school was founded in 1950. It has a 60-acre campus.

RATINGS
Admissions Selectivity Rating: 60*   **Fire Safety Rating:** 60*   **Green Rating:** 60*

STUDENTS AND FACULTY
Enrollment: 2,312. **Student Body:** 73% female, 27% male, 4% out-of-state, 7% international (100 countries represented). **Retention and Graduation:** 52% freshmen return for sophomore year. 33% grads go on to further study within 1 year. **Faculty:** Student/faculty ratio 17:1. 242 full-time faculty, 57% hold PhDs. 100% faculty teach undergrads.

ACADEMICS
Degrees: Associate, bachelor's, certificate, master's. **Academic Requirements:** Arts/fine arts, computer literacy, English (including composition), foreign languages, history, humanities, mathematics, philosophy, sciences (biological or physical), social science. **Classes:** Most classes have 10–19 students. Most lab/discussion sections have 10–19 students. **Majors with Highest Enrollment:** Business administration/management, computer and information sciences, psychology. **Special Study Options:** Accelerated program, cooperative education program, cross-registration, distance learning, double major, dual enrollment, English as a second language (ESL), honors program, independent study, internships, liberal arts/career combination, student-designed major, study abroad, teacher certification program, weekend college.

FACILITIES
Housing: Coed dorms. **Computers:** 80% of public computers are PCs, 20% of

public computers are Macs, network access in dorm rooms, network access in dorm lounges, online registration, online administrative functions (other than registration), remote student-access to Web through college's connection.

CAMPUS LIFE
Activities: Choral groups, drama/theater, student government, student newspaper. **Organizations:** 31 registered organizations, 1 honor society, 1 religious organization. **Athletics (Intercollegiate):** *Men:* Baseball, basketball, cross-country, golf, soccer, tennis, track/field (outdoor). *Women:* Basketball, cross-country, soccer, softball, track/field (outdoor), volleyball.

ADMISSIONS
Freshman Academic Profile: 6% in top 10% of high school class, 24% in top 25% of high school class, 51% in top 50% of high school class. 75% from public high schools. TOEFL required of all international applicants, minimum paper TOEFL 500, minimum computer TOEFL 173. **Basis for Candidate Selection:** *Very important factors considered include:* Rigor of secondary school record. *Important factors considered include:* Application essay, interview, recommendation(s), standardized test scores. *Other factors considered include:* Alumni/ae relation, character/personal qualities, class rank, racial/ethnic status, talent/ability. **Freshman Admission Requirements:** High school diploma is required, and GED is accepted. *Academic units recommended:* 4 English, 3 math, 2 science, 2 foreign language, 4 social studies. **Freshman Admission Statistics:** 2,282 applied, 47% admitted, 79% enrolled. **Transfer Admission Requirements:** College transcript(s), interview. Minimum college GPA of 3.0 required. Lowest grade transferable C. **General Admission Information:** Application fee $35. Regular notification rolling. Nonfall registration accepted. Common Application not accepted. Credit offered for CEEB Advanced Placement tests.

COSTS AND FINANCIAL AID
Annual tuition $11,230. Room & board $8,755. Required fees $75. Average book expense $1,000. **Required Forms and Deadlines:** FAFSA. Financial aid filing deadline 8/15. **Notification of Awards:** Applicants will be notified of awards on a rolling basis beginning on or about 4/1. **Types of Aid:** *Need-based scholarships/grants:* Pell, SEOG, state scholarships/grants, private scholarships, the school's own gift aid. *Loans:* FFEL Subsidized Stafford, FFEL Unsubsidized Stafford, FFEL PLUS, college/university loans from institutional funds. **Student Employment:** Federal Work-Study Program available. Institutional employment available. Off-campus job opportunities are good. **Financial Aid Statistics:** 70% freshmen, 71% undergrads receive need-based scholarship or grant aid. 44% freshmen, 60% undergrads receive need-based self-help aid. 17 freshmen, 105 undergrads receive athletic scholarships. Highest amount earned per year from on-campus jobs $5,342.

MERCYHURST COLLEGE

Admissions, 501 East Thirty-eighth Street, Erie, PA 16546
Phone: 814-824-2202 **E-mail:** admissions@mercyhurst.edu **CEEB Code:** 2410
Fax: 814-824-2071 **Website:** http://admissions.mercyhurst.edu **ACT Code:** 3629
Financial Aid Phone: 814-824-2000

This private school, affiliated with the Roman Catholic Church, was founded in 1926. It has an 88-acre campus.

RATINGS
Admissions Selectivity Rating: 78   **Fire Safety Rating:** 60*   **Green Rating:** 60*

STUDENTS AND FACULTY
Student Body: 34% out-of-state. **Retention and Graduation:** 79% freshmen return for sophomore year. 16% grads go on to further study within 1 year. 9% grads pursue arts and sciences degrees. 3% grads pursue business degrees. 2% grads pursue law degrees. 2% grads pursue medical degrees. **Faculty:** Student/faculty ratio 19:1. 151 full-time faculty, 41% hold PhDs. 100% faculty teach undergrads.

ACADEMICS
Degrees: Associate, bachelor's, certificate, master's, post-bachelor's certificate. **Academic Requirements:** Arts/fine arts, English (including composition), foreign languages, history, humanities, mathematics, sciences (biological or physical), social science. **Classes:** Most classes have fewer than 10 students. Most lab/discussion sections have 10–19 students. **Disciplines with Highest Percentage of Degrees Awarded:** Business/marketing 26%, education 11%, social sciences 10%, visual and performing arts 7%, biological/life sciences 6%. **Special Study Options:** Accelerated program, cooperative education program, cross-registration, double major, exchange student program (domestic), honors program, independent study, internships, liberal arts/career combination,

student-designed major, study abroad, teacher certification program, weekend college. Co-op programs also available in arts, business, computer science, education, health professions, history, English, home economics, humanities, natural science, social/behavioral science. Off-campus study in Washington, DC. Undergrads may take grad-level classes.

FACILITIES
Housing: Men's dorms, women's dorms, apartments for single students, special housing for disabled students. **Special Academic Facilities/Equipment:** Art gallery, college-owned restaurant for hotel/restaurant management department, observatory, archaeology lab. **Computers:** 5% of public computers are PCs, 5% of public computers are Macs, network access in dorm rooms, network access in dorm lounges, online registration, online administrative functions (other than registration), remote student-access to Web through college's connection.

CAMPUS LIFE
Activities: Choral groups, concert band, dance, drama/theater, literary magazine, music ensembles, musical theater, pep band, radio station, student government, student newspaper, television station, yearbook. **Organizations:** 9 honor societies, 2 religious organizations. **Athletics (Intercollegiate):** *Men:* Baseball, basketball, cheerleading, crew/rowing, cross-country, football, golf, ice hockey, lacrosse, soccer, tennis, volleyball, water polo, wrestling. *Women:* Basketball, cheerleading, crew/rowing, cross-country, field hockey, golf, ice hockey, lacrosse, soccer, softball, tennis, volleyball, water polo.

ADMISSIONS
Freshman Academic Profile: 18% in top 10% of high school class, 43% in top 25% of high school class, 79% in top 50% of high school class. 78% from public high schools. SAT Math middle 50% range 490–590. SAT Critical Reading middle 50% range 480–590. ACT middle 50% range 19–25. TOEFL required of all international applicants, minimum paper TOEFL 550, minimum computer TOEFL 300. **Basis for Candidate Selection:** *Very important factors considered include:* Rigor of secondary school record. *Important factors considered include:* Character/personal qualities, class rank, interview, standardized test scores, talent/ability. *Other factors considered include:* Alumni/ae relation, application essay, extracurricular activities, geographical residence, racial/ethnic status, recommendation(s), religious affiliation/commitment, state residency, volunteer work, work experience. **Freshman Admission Requirements:** High school diploma is required, and GED is accepted. *Academic units recommended:* 4 English, 3 math, 3 science (1 science lab), 2 foreign language, 2 social studies, 2 history. **Freshman Admission Statistics:** 2,650 applied, 81% admitted, 32% enrolled. **Transfer Admission Requirements:** High school transcript, college transcript(s), standardized test score. Minimum college GPA of 2.0 required. Lowest grade transferable C. **General Admission Information:** Application fee $30. Regular notification is rolling. Nonfall registration accepted. Admission may be deferred for a maximum of 1 year. Credit and/or placement offered for CEEB Advanced Placement tests.

COSTS AND FINANCIAL AID
Annual tuition $18,930. Room & board $3,700. Required fees $1,434. Average book expense $750. **Required Forms and Deadlines:** FAFSA, institution's own financial aid form. Financial aid filing deadline 5/1. **Notification of Awards:** Applicants will be notified of awards on a rolling basis beginning on or about 2/15. **Types of Aid:** *Need-based scholarships/grants:* Pell, SEOG, state scholarships/grants, private scholarships, the school's own gift aid. *Loans:* FFEL Subsidized Stafford, FFEL Unsubsidized Stafford, FFEL PLUS, Federal Perkins. **Student Employment:** Federal Work-Study Program available. Institutional employment available. **Financial Aid Statistics:** 76% freshmen, 76% undergrads receive need-based scholarship or grant aid. 75% freshmen, 71% undergrads receive need-based self-help aid. 51 freshmen, 178 undergrads receive athletic scholarships. 93% freshmen receive any aid. Highest amount earned per year from on-campus jobs $1,200.

See page 1264.

MEREDITH COLLEGE

3800 Hillsborough Street, Raleigh, NC 27607
Phone: 919-760-8581 **E-mail:** admissions@meredith.edu **CEEB Code:** 5410
Fax: 919-760-2348 **Website:** www.meredith.edu **ACT Code:** 3126
Financial Aid Phone: 919-760-8565

This private school was founded in 1891. It has a 225-acre campus.

RATINGS
Admissions Selectivity Rating: 75   **Fire Safety Rating:** 80   **Green Rating:** 60*

STUDENTS AND FACULTY

Enrollment: 1,852. **Student Body:** 100% female, 10% out-of-state. African American 11%, Asian 2%, Caucasian 77%, Hispanic 3%. **Retention and Graduation:** 74% freshmen return for sophomore year. **Faculty:** Student/faculty ratio 10:1. 132 full-time faculty, 90% hold PhDs. 99% faculty teach undergrads.

ACADEMICS

Degrees: Bachelor's, master's, post-bachelor's certificate. **Academic Requirements:** Arts/fine arts, computer literacy, English (including composition), foreign languages, history, humanities, mathematics, sciences (biological or physical), social science, religion, health. **Classes:** Most classes have 10–19 students. Most lab/discussion sections have 20–29 students. **Majors with Highest Enrollment:** Business administration/management, interior design, psychology. **Disciplines with Highest Percentage of Degrees Awarded:** Business/marketing 22%, psychology 14%, visual and performing arts 14%, family and consumer sciences 9%, communications/journalism 7%. **Special Study Options:** Accelerated program, cooperative education program, cross-registration, double major, dual enrollment, honors program, independent study, internships, liberal arts/career combination, student-designed major, study abroad, teacher certification program. Semester programs at American University, Drew University, Marymount Manhattan.

FACILITIES

Housing: Women's dorms. **Special Academic Facilities/Equipment:** Art gallery, amphitheater, child-care lab, learning center and fitness center. Experimental and clinical psychology labs including an autism lab. A new Science and Mathematics Building provides a rooftop telescope platform for astronomy observations, an electron microscope suite, greenhouse, and 15 student/faculty research labs. **Computers:** 1% of classrooms are wired, 100% of classrooms are wireless, 95% of public computers are PCs, 5% of public computers are Macs, network access in dorm rooms, network access in dorm lounges, online registration, online administrative functions (other than registration), remote student-access to Web through college's connection, tuition includes personal computer.

CAMPUS LIFE

Activities: Choral groups, concert band, dance, drama/theater, literary magazine, music ensembles, musical theater, student government, student newspaper, symphony orchestra, yearbook. **Organizations:** 90 registered organizations, 21 honor societies, 8 religious organizations. **Athletics (Intercollegiate):** *Women:* Basketball, cross-country, soccer, softball, tennis, volleyball.

ADMISSIONS

Freshman Academic Profile: 21% in top 10% of high school class, 51% in top 25% of high school class, 82% in top 50% of high school class. SAT Math middle 50% range 460–570. SAT Critical Reading middle 50% range 460–580. ACT middle 50% range 19–23. TOEFL required of all international applicants, minimum paper TOEFL 500, minimum computer TOEFL 173. **Basis for Candidate Selection:** *Very important factors considered include:* Academic GPA, class rank, rigor of secondary school record. *Important factors considered include:* Character/personal qualities, recommendation(s), standardized test scores. *Other factors considered include:* Alumni/ae relation, application essay, extracurricular activities, interview, talent/ability, volunteer work, work experience. **Freshman Admission Requirements:** High school diploma is required, and GED is not accepted. *Academic units required:* 4 English, 3 math, 3 science, 2 foreign language. *Academic units recommended:* 1 academic elective. **Freshman Admission Statistics:** 1,135 applied, 94% admitted, 42% enrolled. **Transfer Admission Requirements:** High school transcript, college transcript(s), statement of good standing from prior institution(s). Minimum college GPA of 2.0 required. Lowest grade transferable C. **General Admission Information:** Application fee $40. Early decision application deadline 10/15. Regular notification is rolling. Nonfall registration accepted. Admission may be deferred for a maximum of 1 year. Credit offered for CEEB Advanced Placement tests.

COSTS AND FINANCIAL AID

Annual tuition $22,350. Room and board $6,300. Required fees $50. Average book expense $750. **Required Forms and Deadlines:** FAFSA. Financial aid filing deadline 2/15. **Notification of Awards:** Applicants will be notified of awards on a rolling basis beginning on or about 3/15. **Types of Aid:** *Need-based scholarships/grants:* Pell, SEOG, state scholarships/grants, private scholarships, the school's own gift aid. *Loans:* FFEL Subsidized Stafford, FFEL Unsubsidized Stafford, FFEL PLUS, Federal Perkins, college/university loans from institutional funds. **Financial Aid Statistics:** 65% freshmen, 65% undergrads receive need-based scholarship or grant aid. 53% freshmen, 57% undergrads receive need-based self-help aid.

See page 1266.

MERRIMACK COLLEGE

Office of Admission, Austin Hall, North Andover, MA 01845
Phone: 978-837-5100 **E-mail:** admission@merrimack.edu **CEEB Code:** 3525
Fax: 978-837-5133 **Website:** www.merrimack.edu
Financial Aid Phone: 978-837-5186

This private school, affiliated with the Roman Catholic Church, was founded in 1947. It has a 220-acre campus.

RATINGS

Admissions Selectivity Rating: 79   **Fire Safety Rating:** 60*   **Green Rating:** 60*

STUDENTS AND FACULTY

Enrollment: 2,185. **Student Body:** 53% female, 47% male, 27% out-of-state, 1% international (13 countries represented). African American 1%, Asian 2%, Caucasian 80%, Hispanic 3%. **Retention and Graduation:** 88% freshmen return for sophomore year. 58% freshmen graduate within 4 years. 14% grads go on to further study within 1 year. 9% grads pursue arts and sciences degrees. 3% grads pursue business degrees. 1% grads pursue law degrees. **Faculty:** Student/faculty ratio 13:1. 133 full-time faculty, 82% hold PhDs. 100% faculty teach undergrads.

ACADEMICS

Degrees: Associate, bachelor's, master's. **Academic Requirements:** English (including composition), humanities, mathematics, philosophy, sciences (biological or physical), social science, religious studies, first-year seminar. **Classes:** Most classes have 10–19 students. Most lab/discussion sections have 10–19 students. **Majors with Highest Enrollment:** Business administration/management, English language and literature, psychology. **Disciplines with Highest Percentage of Degrees Awarded:** Business/marketing 37%, social sciences 13%, psychology 11%, English 9%, health professions and related sciences 5%. **Special Study Options:** Accelerated program, cooperative education program, cross-registration, double major, dual enrollment, English as a second language (ESL), internships, liberal arts/career combination, student-designed major, study abroad, teacher certification program. 5-year combined BA/BS program, continuing education program, center for corporate education. ESL available through Kaplan with offices on the college campus. Cross-registration available through college's membership in 10-college consortium.

FACILITIES

Housing: Coed dorms, apartments for single students, special housing for disabled students, special housing for international students, townhouses for single students. **Special Academic Facilities/Equipment:** Observatory, Rogers Center for the Arts. **Computers:** 20% of classrooms are wired, 15% of classrooms are wireless, 80% of public computers are PCs, 10% of public computers are Macs, 10% of public computers are UNIX, network access in dorm rooms, network access in dorm lounges, online registration, online administrative functions (other than registration), remote student-access to Web through college's connection.

CAMPUS LIFE

Activities: Dance, drama/theater, jazz band, student government, student newspaper, television station, yearbook. **Organizations:** 47 registered organizations, 3 honor societies, 5 religious organizations. 3 fraternities (3% men join), 3 sororities (7% women join). **Athletics (Intercollegiate):** *Men:* Baseball, basketball, cross-country, football, ice hockey, lacrosse, soccer, tennis. *Women:* Basketball, cross-country, field hockey, lacrosse, soccer, softball, tennis, volleyball.

ADMISSIONS

Freshman Academic Profile: 20% in top 10% of high school class, 44% in top 25% of high school class, 85% in top 50% of high school class. 65% from public high schools. SAT Math middle 50% range 530–590. SAT Critical Reading middle 50% range 520–580. ACT middle 50% range 21–26. TOEFL required of all international applicants, minimum paper TOEFL 550, minimum computer TOEFL 230. **Basis for Candidate Selection:** *Very important factors considered include:* Academic GPA, application essay, rigor of secondary school record. *Important factors considered include:* Character/personal qualities, class rank, recommendation(s), standardized test scores, talent/ability. *Other factors considered include:* Alumni/ae relation, extracurricular activities, interview, level of applicant's interest, volunteer work, work experience. **Freshman Admission Requirements:** High school diploma is required, and GED is accepted. *Academic units required:* 4 English, 3 math, 3 science (3 science labs), 2 foreign language, 1 social studies, 1 history, 3 academic electives. *Academic units recommended:* 4 English, 4 math, 4 science (4 science labs), 3 foreign language, 2 social studies, 2 history, 3 academic electives. **Freshman Admission Statistics:** 3,424 applied, 72% admitted, 22% enrolled.

Transfer Admission Requirements: College transcript(s), essay or personal statement. Minimum college GPA of 2.5 required. Lowest grade transferable C. **General Admission Information:** Application fee $50. Regular application deadline 2/1. Regular notification 4/1. Nonfall registration accepted. Admission may be deferred for a maximum of 1 year. Credit and/or placement offered for CEEB Advanced Placement tests.

COSTS AND FINANCIAL AID

Annual tuition $29,310. Room and board $11,790. Required fees $500. Average book expense $800. **Required Forms and Deadlines:** FAFSA, Noncustodial PROFILE, Business/Farm Supplement, Sibling Verification. Financial aid filing deadline 2/1. **Notification of Awards:** Applicants will be notified of awards on or about 3/15. **Types of Aid:** *Need-based scholarships/grants:* Pell, SEOG, state scholarships/grants, private scholarships, the school's own gift aid. *Loans:* FFEL Subsidized Stafford, FFEL Unsubsidized Stafford, FFEL PLUS, Federal Perkins, state loans, college/university loans from institutional funds, alternative loans. **Student Employment:** Off-campus job opportunities are good. **Financial Aid Statistics:** 85% freshmen, 60% undergrads receive need-based scholarship or grant aid. 79% freshmen, 58% undergrads receive need-based self-help aid. 35 freshmen, 240 undergrads receive athletic scholarships. 85% freshmen, 69% undergrads receive any aid. Highest amount earned per year from on-campus jobs $1,500.

See page 1268.

MESA STATE COLLEGE

PO Box 2647, Grand Junction, CO 81502-2647
Phone: 970-248-1875 **E-mail:** admissions@mesastate.edu **CEEB Code:** 4484
Fax: 970-248-1973 **Website:** www.mesastate.edu **ACT Code:** 0518
Financial Aid Phone: 970-248-1396

This public school was founded in 1925. It has a 57-acre campus.

RATINGS
Admissions Selectivity Rating: 71   **Fire Safety Rating:** 60*   **Green Rating:** 60*

STUDENTS AND FACULTY
Enrollment: 4,832. **Student Body:** 56% female, 44% male, 9% out-of-state. African American 1%, Asian 1%, Caucasian 86%, Hispanic 7%, Native American 1%. **Retention and Graduation:** 61% freshmen return for sophomore year. 9% freshmen graduate within 4 years. 5% grads go on to further study within 1 year. 4% grads pursue arts and sciences degrees. **Faculty:** 100% faculty teach undergrads.

ACADEMICS
Degrees: Associate, bachelor's, certificate, master's. **Academic Requirements:** Arts/fine arts, English (including composition), foreign languages, humanities, mathematics, sciences (biological or physical), social science. **Special Study Options:** Cooperative education program, distance learning, double major, exchange student program (domestic), external degree program, honors program, independent study, internships, teacher certification program, weekend college.

FACILITIES
Housing: Coed dorms, apartments for single students. **Special Academic Facilities/Equipment:** Art gallery, experimental farm, early childhood education center, electron microscopes, television studio. **Computers:** 40% of public computers are PCs, network access in dorm rooms, network access in dorm lounges, online registration, online administrative functions (other than registration), remote student-access to Web through college's connection.

CAMPUS LIFE
Activities: Choral groups, dance, drama/theater, jazz band, literary magazine, music ensembles, musical theater, pep band, radio station, student government, student newspaper, symphony orchestra, television station. **Organizations:** 50 registered organizations, 10 honor societies, 4 religious organizations. **Athletics (Intercollegiate):** *Men:* Baseball, basketball, football, tennis. *Women:* Basketball, golf, soccer, softball, tennis, volleyball.

ADMISSIONS
Freshman Academic Profile: 18% in top 10% of high school class, 32% in top 25% of high school class, 70% in top 50% of high school class. 98% from public high schools. SAT Math middle 50% range 430–560. SAT Critical Reading middle 50% range 430–550. ACT middle 50% range 18–25. TOEFL required of all international applicants, minimum paper TOEFL 525. **Basis for Candidate Selection:** *Very important factors considered include:* Class rank, recommendation(s), rigor of secondary school record, standardized test scores.

Other factors considered include: Application essay, character/personal qualities, extracurricular activities, geographical residence, interview, state residency, volunteer work. **Freshman Admission Requirements:** High school diploma is required, and GED is accepted. *Academic units recommended:* 1 science lab. **Freshman Admission Statistics:** 1,940 applied, 94% admitted, 57% enrolled. **Transfer Admission Requirements:** College transcript(s), statement of good standing from prior institution(s). Minimum college GPA of 2.0 required. Lowest grade transferable C. **General Admission Information:** Application fee $30. Regular application deadline 8/15. Regular notification. Nonfall registration accepted. Admission may be deferred for a maximum of 1 year. Common Application accepted. Credit and/or placement offered for CEEB Advanced Placement tests.

COSTS AND FINANCIAL AID
Annual in-state tuition $1,576. Out-of-state tuition $5,966. Room & board $5,048. Required fees $546. Average book expense $690. **Required Forms and Deadlines:** FAFSA. Financial aid filing deadline 3/1. **Notification of Awards:** Applicants will be notified of awards on a rolling basis beginning on or about 4/15. **Types of Aid:** *Need-based scholarships/grants:* Pell, SEOG, state scholarships/grants, private scholarships, the school's own gift aid. *Loans:* FFEL Subsidized Stafford, FFEL Unsubsidized Stafford, FFEL PLUS, Federal Perkins. **Student Employment:** Federal Work-Study Program available. Institutional employment available. Off-campus job opportunities are good. **Financial Aid Statistics:** 41% freshmen, 31% undergrads receive need-based scholarship or grant aid. 68% freshmen, 51% undergrads receive need-based self-help aid. Highest amount earned per year from on-campus jobs $1,000.

MESSIAH COLLEGE

PO Box 3005, 1 College Avenue, Grantham, PA 17027
Phone: 717-691-6000 **E-mail:** Admiss@messiah.edu **CEEB Code:** 2411
Fax: 717-796-5374 **Website:** www.messiah.edu **ACT Code:** 3630
Financial Aid Phone: 717-691-6007

This private school, affiliated with the Interdenominational Christian Church, was founded in 1909. It has a 485-acre campus.

RATINGS
Admissions Selectivity Rating: 87   **Fire Safety Rating:** 75   **Green Rating:** 85

STUDENTS AND FACULTY
Enrollment: 2,815. **Student Body:** 63% female, 37% male, 47% out-of-state, 2% international (25 countries represented). African American 2%, Asian 2%, Caucasian 88%, Hispanic 2%. **Retention and Graduation:** 84% freshmen return for sophomore year. 68% freshmen graduate within 4 years. 12% grads go on to further study within 1 year. 10% grads pursue arts and sciences degrees. 1% grads pursue business degrees. 1% grads pursue medical degrees. **Faculty:** Student/faculty ratio 13:1. 173 full-time faculty, 76% hold PhDs. 100% faculty teach undergrads.

ACADEMICS
Degrees: Bachelor's. **Academic Requirements:** Arts/fine arts, computer literacy (built into other course work), English (including composition), foreign languages, history, humanities, mathematics, philosophy, sciences (biological or physical), social science. **Classes:** Most classes have 10–19 students. Most lab/discussion sections have 20–29 students. **Majors with Highest Enrollment:** Elementary education and teaching; nursing—registered nurse training (RN, ASN, BSN, MSN); psychology. **Disciplines with Highest Percentage of Degrees Awarded:** Education 13%, business/marketing 12%, psychology 8%, health professions and related sciences 8%, biological/life sciences 6%, communications/journalism 6%, visual and performing arts 6%, law/legal studies 5%, family and consumer sciences 5%. **Special Study Options:** Accelerated program, double major, dual enrollment, English as a second language (ESL), exchange student program (domestic), honor program, independent study, internships, student-designed major, study abroad, teacher certification program, pass/fail option.

FACILITIES
Housing: Coed dorms, men's dorms, women's dorms, apartments for single students, special housing for disabled students, special housing for international students. **Special Academic Facilities/Equipment:** Boyer Center for Advanced Studies, Brethren in Christ Historical Society & Archives, Oakes Museum of Natural History. **Computers:** 94% of public computers are PCs, 6% of public computers are Macs, network access in dorm rooms, network access in dorm lounges, online registration, online administrative functions (other than registration), remote student-access to Web through college's connection.

CAMPUS LIFE

Activities: Choral groups, concert band, dance, drama/theater, jazz band, literary magazine, music ensembles, musical theater, pep band, radio station, student government, student newspaper, student-run film society, symphony orchestra, yearbook. **Organizations:** 55 registered organizations, 10 honor societies, 9 religious organizations. **Athletics (Intercollegiate):** *Men:* Baseball, basketball, cross-country, golf, lacrosse, soccer, tennis, track/field (indoor), track/field (outdoor), wrestling. *Women:* Basketball, cross-country, field hockey, lacrosse, soccer, softball, tennis, track/field (indoor), track/field (outdoor), volleyball. Environmental Initiatives: Recycling and composting of wastes. Creation Care Community Garden. Digital energy management system across campus buildings which is yielding solid energy savings.

ADMISSIONS

Freshman Academic Profile: 34% in top 10% of high school class, 66% in top 25% of high school class, 90% in top 50% of high school class. 75% from public high schools. SAT Math middle 50% range 520–640. SAT Critical Reading middle 50% range 520–640. SAT Writing middle 50% range 510–630. ACT middle 50% range 22–27. TOEFL required of all international applicants, minimum paper TOEFL 550, minimum computer TOEFL 213. **Basis for Candidate Selection:** *Very important factors considered include:* Academic GPA, character/personal qualities, class rank, extracurricular activities, recommendation(s), religious affiliation/commitment, rigor of secondary school record, standardized test scores, talent/ability. *Important factors considered include:* Application essay, volunteer work. *Other factors considered include:* Alumni/ae relation, interview, level of applicant's interest, racial/ethnic status, work experience. **Freshman Admission Requirements:** High school diploma is required, and GED is accepted. *Academic units required:* 4 English, 2 math, 2 science (2 science labs), 2 foreign language, 2 social studies, 4 academic electives. *Academic units recommended:* 4 English, 3 math, 3 science (3 science labs), 2 foreign language, 2 social studies, 2 history, 4 academic electives. **Freshman Admission Statistics:** 2,569 applied, 76% admitted, 38% enrolled. **Transfer Admission Requirements:** College transcript(s), essay or personal statement, statement of good standing from prior institution(s). Minimum college GPA of 2.5 required. Lowest grade transferable C. **General Admission Information:** Application fee $30. Regular notification is rolling. Nonfall registration accepted. Admission may be deferred for a maximum of 2 years. Credit and/or placement offered for CEEB Advanced Placement tests.

COSTS AND FINANCIAL AID

Annual tuition $23,710. Room and board $7,340. Required fees $710. Average book expense $900. **Required Forms and Deadlines:** FAFSA. Financial aid filing deadline 4/1. **Notification of Awards:** Applicants will be notified of awards on a rolling basis beginning on or about 3/15. **Types of Aid:** *Need-based scholarships/grants:* Pell, SEOG, state scholarships/grants, private scholarships, the school's own gift aid. *Loans:* Direct Subsidized Stafford, Direct Unsubsidized Stafford, Direct PLUS, Federal Perkins, Federal Nursing. **Student Employment:** Federal Work-Study Program available. Institutional employment available. Off-campus job opportunities are good. **Financial Aid Statistics:** 60% freshmen, 60% undergrads receive need-based scholarship or grant aid. 61% freshmen, 64% undergrads receive need-based self-help aid. 99% freshmen, 97% undergrads receive any aid. Highest amount earned per year from on-campus jobs $5,940.

See page 1270.

METHODIST COLLEGE

5400 Ramsey Street, Fayetteville, NC 28311
Phone: 910-630-7027 **E-mail:** admissions@methodist.edu **CEEB Code:** 5426
Fax: 910-630-7285 **Website:** www.methodist.edu **ACT Code:** 3127
Financial Aid Phone: 910-630-7192

This private school, affiliated with the Methodist Church, was founded in 1956. It has a 600-acre campus.

RATINGS

Admissions Selectivity Rating: 75   **Fire Safety Rating:** 60*   **Green Rating:** 60*

STUDENTS AND FACULTY

Enrollment: 2,111. **Student Body:** 43% female, 57% male, 43% out-of-state, 2% international (37 countries represented). African American 21%, Asian 2%, Caucasian 64%, Hispanic 6%. **Retention and Graduation:** 63% freshmen return for sophomore year. 24% freshmen graduate within 4 years. 38% grads go on to further study within 1 year. 8% grads pursue arts and sciences degrees. 12% grads pursue business degrees. 1% grads pursue law degrees. 7% grads

pursue medical degrees. **Faculty:** Student/faculty ratio 15:1. 108 full-time faculty, 59% hold PhDs. 100% faculty teach undergrads.

ACADEMICS

Degrees: Associate, bachelor's, master's. **Academic Requirements:** Arts/fine arts, computer literacy, English (including composition), foreign languages, history, humanities, mathematics, philosophy, sciences (biological or physical), social science, library competency (completed via course work in freshman seminar course required of freshman). **Classes:** Most classes have fewer than 10 students. Most lab/discussion sections have fewer than 10 students. **Majors with Highest Enrollment:** Business administration/management, cell/cellular and molecular biology, secondary education and teaching. **Disciplines with Highest Percentage of Degrees Awarded:** Business/marketing 32%, social sciences 13%, parks and recreation 11%, education 8%, communication technologies 6%, biological/life sciences 6%. **Special Study Options:** Cooperative education program, distance learning, double major, English as a second language (ESL), honors program, independent study, internships, liberal arts/career combination, student-designed major, study abroad, teacher certification program, weekend college, distance learning is online course work available.

FACILITIES

Housing: Coed dorms, men's dorms, women's dorms, apartments for single students, health and wellness hall, first-year experience hall. **Special Academic Facilities/Equipment:** Art gallery, nature trail, 18-hole golf course with practice facilities for PGM students, Academic Development Center. **Computers:** 1% of classrooms are wired, 20% of classrooms are wireless, 80% of public computers are PCs, 20% of public computers are Macs, network access in dorm rooms, remote student-access to Web through college's connection.

CAMPUS LIFE

Activities: Choral groups, concert band, dance, drama/theater, jazz band, literary magazine, music ensembles, musical theater, opera, pep band, student government, student newspaper, symphony orchestra, yearbook. **Organizations:** 72 registered organizations, 15 honor societies, 8 religious organizations. 2 fraternities (1% men join), 3 sororities (1% women join). **Athletics (Intercollegiate):** *Men:* Baseball, basketball, cheerleading, cross-country, football, golf, soccer, tennis, track/field (outdoor). *Women:* Basketball, cheerleading, cross-country, golf, lacrosse, soccer, softball, tennis, track/field (outdoor), volleyball.

ADMISSIONS

Freshman Academic Profile: 11% in top 10% of high school class, 33% in top 25% of high school class, 68% in top 50% of high school class. 88% from public high schools. SAT Math middle 50% range 450–570. SAT Critical Reading middle 50% range 440–530. SAT Writing middle 50% range 410–520. ACT middle 50% range 18–23. TOEFL required of all international applicants, minimum paper TOEFL 500, minimum computer TOEFL 173. **Basis for Candidate Selection:** *Very important factors considered include:* Rigor of secondary school record. *Important factors considered include:* Class rank, interview, standardized test scores. *Other factors considered include:* Alumni/ae relation, application essay, character/personal qualities, extracurricular activities, recommendation(s), talent/ability. **Freshman Admission Requirements:** High school diploma is required, and GED is accepted. *Academic units required:* 4 English, 3 math, 3 science (1 science lab), 1 social studies, 2 history, 4 academic electives. *Academic units recommended:* 4 English, 3 math, 4 science (1 science lab), 2 foreign language, 2 social studies, 2 history. **Freshman Admission Statistics:** 2,691 applied, 51% admitted, 38% enrolled. **Transfer Admission Requirements:** High school transcript, college transcript(s), statement of good standing from prior institution(s). Minimum college GPA of 2.0 required. Lowest grade transferable C. **General Admission Information:** Application fee $25. Regular notification rolling. Nonfall registration accepted. Admission may be deferred for a maximum of 1 academic year. Common Application accepted. Credit and/or placement offered for CEEB Advanced Placement tests.

COSTS AND FINANCIAL AID

Annual tuition $21,520. Room and board $8,046. Required fees $424. Average book expense $1,200. **Required Forms and Deadlines:** FAFSA. **Notification of Awards:** Applicants will be notified of awards on a rolling basis beginning on or about 3/1. **Types of Aid:** *Need-based scholarships/grants:* Pell, SEOG, state scholarships/grants, private scholarships, the school's own gift aid. *Loans:* FFEL Subsidized Stafford, FFEL Unsubsidized Stafford, FFEL PLUS, Federal Perkins. **Student Employment:** Federal Work-Study Program available. Off-campus job opportunities are good. **Financial Aid Statistics:** 76% freshmen, 69% undergrads receive need-based scholarship or grant aid. 76% freshmen, 68% undergrads receive need-based self-help aid. 87% freshmen, 84% undergrads receive any aid. Highest amount earned per year from on-campus jobs $1,600.

METROPOLITAN COLLEGE
OF COURT REPORTING

4640 East Elwood Street, Suite 12, Phoenix, AZ 85040
Phone: 602-955-5900 **E-mail:** metropolitanphx@uswest.net
Fax: 480-894-8999 **Financial Aid Phone:** 602-955-5900

This private school was founded in 1980. It has a 1-acre campus.

RATINGS
Admissions Selectivity Rating: 60*   **Fire Safety Rating:** 60*   **Green Rating:** 60*

STUDENTS AND FACULTY
Enrollment: 132. **Student Body:** 97% female, 3% male. **Retention and Graduation:** 26% freshmen return for sophomore year. **Faculty:** Student/faculty ratio 16:1. 5 full-time faculty. 100% faculty teach undergrads.

ACADEMICS
Degrees: Associate, bachelor's, diploma. **Academic Requirements:** Computer literacy, English (including composition), history, humanities. **Classes:** Most classes have 10–19 students. **Special Study Options:** Accelerated program, independent study, internships.

FACILITIES
Computers: 100% of public computers are PCs.

ADMISSIONS
Freshman Academic Profile: 90% from public high schools. **Freshman Admission Requirements:** High school diploma is required, and GED is accepted. **Freshman Admission Statistics:** 65 applied, 65% admitted, 100% enrolled. **Transfer Admission Requirements:** High school transcript, college transcript(s), interview, standardized test score. Lowest grade transferable C. **General Admission Information:** Application fee $50. Regular notification one week prior to orientation. Nonfall registration accepted. Admission may be deferred for a maximum of 1 trimester. Common Application not accepted. Neither credit nor placement offered for CEEB Advanced Placement tests.

COSTS AND FINANCIAL AID
Annual tuition $5,940. Average book expense $250. **Required Forms and Deadlines:** FAFSA. **Types of Aid:** *Need-based scholarships/grants:* Pell, state scholarships/grants, private scholarships. *Loans:* FFEL Subsidized Stafford, FFEL Unsubsidized Stafford, FFEL PLUS. **Student Employment:** Off-campus job opportunities are excellent. **Financial Aid Statistics:** 48% freshmen, 40% undergrads receive need-based scholarship or grant aid. 76% freshmen, 52% undergrads receive need-based self-help aid.

METROPOLITAN COLLEGE OF NEW YORK

75 Varick Street, New York, NY 10013
Phone: 212-343-1234 **E-mail:** admissions@metropolitan.edu **CEEB Code:** 4802
Fax: 212-343-8470 **Website:** www.metropolitan.edu
Financial Aid Phone: 212-343-1234

This private school was founded in 1964.

RATINGS
Admissions Selectivity Rating: 61   **Fire Safety Rating:** 60*   **Green Rating:** 60*

STUDENTS AND FACULTY
Enrollment: 1,093. **Student Body:** 80% female, 20% male, 10% out-of-state. Asian 1%, Caucasian 5%, Hispanic 18%. **Retention and Graduation:** 72% freshmen return for sophomore year. 60% grads go on to further study within 1 year. 24% grads pursue business degrees. 15% grads pursue law degrees. **Faculty:** Student/faculty ratio 17:1. 26 full-time faculty. 85% faculty teach undergrads.

ACADEMICS
Degrees: Associate, bachelor's, certificate, master's. **Academic Requirements:** Computer literacy, English (including composition), humanities, mathematics, philosophy, sciences (biological or physical), social science, day and evening programs as well. **Classes:** Most classes have 10–19 students. **Disciplines with Highest Percentage of Degrees Awarded:** Other 75%, business/marketing 25%. **Special Study Options:** Accelerated program, cooperative education program, distance learning, honors program, internships, weekend college.

FACILITIES
Computers: 99% of public computers are PCs, 1% of public computers are Macs, online administrative functions (other than registration), remote student-access to Web through college's connection.

CAMPUS LIFE
Activities: Student government, student newspaper. **Organizations:** 10 registered organizations.

ADMISSIONS
Freshman Academic Profile: 70% from public high schools. TOEFL required of all international applicants, minimum paper TOEFL 550. **Basis for Candidate Selection:** *Very important factors considered include:* Interview. *Important factors considered include:* Extracurricular activities, talent/ability, volunteer work, work experience. *Other factors considered include:* Character/personal qualities, recommendation(s). **Freshman Admission Requirements:** High school diploma is required, and GED is accepted. **Freshman Admission Statistics:** 399 applied, 78% admitted, 62% enrolled. **Transfer Admission Requirements:** High school transcript, essay or personal statement, interview. Lowest grade transferable C. **General Admission Information:** Application fee $30. Early decision application deadline 5/2. Regular notification rolling. Nonfall registration accepted. Admission may be deferred for a maximum of 1 year. Common Application not accepted. Neither credit nor placement offered for CEEB Advanced Placement tests.

COSTS AND FINANCIAL AID
Annual tuition $12,960. Required fees $400. Average book expense $1,500. **Required Forms and Deadlines:** FAFSA, state aid form, Noncustodial PROFILE. **Types of Aid:** *Need-based scholarships/grants:* Pell, SEOG, state scholarships/grants, private scholarships, the school's own gift aid. *Loans:* FFEL Subsidized Stafford, FFEL Unsubsidized Stafford, FFEL PLUS, signature loan. **Student Employment:** Federal Work-Study Program available. Off-campus job opportunities are good. **Financial Aid Statistics:** 62% freshmen, 68% undergrads receive need-based scholarship or grant aid. 62% freshmen, 65% undergrads receive need-based self-help aid.

METROPOLITAN STATE COLLEGE OF DENVER

Campus Box 16, PO Box 173362, Denver, CO 80217-3362
Phone: 303-556-3058 **E-mail:** askmetro@mscd.edu **CEEB Code:** 4505
Fax: 303-556-6345 **Website:** www.mscd.edu **ACT Code:** 5190
Financial Aid Phone: 303-575-5880

This public school was founded in 1963. It has a 175-acre campus.

RATINGS
Admissions Selectivity Rating: 69   **Fire Safety Rating:** 60*   **Green Rating:** 60*

STUDENTS AND FACULTY
Enrollment: 18,013. **Student Body:** 57% female, 43% male, 2% out-of-state, 1% international. African American 6%, Asian 4%, Caucasian 70%, Hispanic 12%. **Retention and Graduation:** 61% freshmen return for sophomore year. 4% freshmen graduate within 4 years. 22% grads go on to further study within 1 year. 3% grads pursue arts and sciences degrees. 2% grads pursue business degrees. 2% grads pursue law degrees. 2% grads pursue medical degrees. **Faculty:** Student/faculty ratio 23:1. 393 full-time faculty, 75% hold PhDs. 100% faculty teach undergrads.

ACADEMICS
Degrees: Bachelor's. **Academic Requirements:** English (including composition), history, humanities, mathematics, sciences (biological or physical), social science. **Classes:** Most classes have 20–29 students. Most lab/discussion sections have 10–19 students. **Majors with Highest Enrollment:** Behavioral sciences, criminal justice/safety studies, management information systems. **Disciplines with Highest Percentage of Degrees Awarded:** Business/marketing 24%, social sciences 15%, English 10%, psychology 6%, biological/life sciences 5%. **Special Study Options:** Cooperative education program, cross-registration, distance learning, double major, external degree program, honors program, independent study, internships, student-designed major, study abroad, teacher certification program, weekend college.

FACILITIES
Special Academic Facilities/Equipment: Art gallery, child care center, flight simulators, historic brewery building, on-campus lab school, world indoor airport. **Computers:** 80% of public computers are PCs, 20% of public

computers are Macs, 2% of public computers are UNIX, online registration, online administrative functions (other than registration).

CAMPUS LIFE

Activities: Choral groups, dance, drama/theater, jazz band, literary magazine, music ensembles, student government, student newspaper. **Organizations:** 100 registered organizations, 9 honor societies, 10 religious organizations. **Athletics (Intercollegiate):** *Men:* Baseball, basketball, diving, football, soccer, swimming, tennis. *Women:* Basketball, diving, football, soccer, swimming, tennis, volleyball.

ADMISSIONS

Freshman Academic Profile: 5% in top 10% of high school class, 19% in top 25% of high school class, 49% in top 50% of high school class. 96% from public high schools. SAT Math middle 50% range 420–530. SAT Critical Reading middle 50% range 420–540. ACT middle 50% range 17–22. TOEFL required of all international applicants, minimum paper TOEFL 500, minimum computer TOEFL 173. **Basis for Candidate Selection:** *Important factors considered include:* Rigor of secondary school record, standardized test scores. *Other factors considered include:* Application essay, character/personal qualities, class rank, recommendation(s). **Freshman Admission Requirements:** High school diploma is required, and GED is accepted. **Freshman Admission Statistics:** 4,479 applied, 81% admitted, 63% enrolled. **Transfer Admission Requirements:** College transcript(s). Lowest grade transferable C. **General Admission Information:** Application fee $25. Regular application deadline 8/26. Nonfall registration accepted. Admission may be deferred for a maximum of 1 year. Common Application accepted. Credit and/or placement offered for CEEB Advanced Placement tests.

COSTS AND FINANCIAL AID

Annual in-state tuition $2,130. Out-of-state tuition $8,737. Required fees $538. Average book expense $1,163. **Required Forms and Deadlines:** FAFSA. **Notification of Awards:** Applicants will be notified of awards on a rolling basis beginning on or about 3/15. **Types of Aid:** *Need-based scholarships/grants:* Pell, SEOG, state scholarships/grants, private scholarships, the school's own gift aid. *Loans:* FFEL Subsidized Stafford, FFEL Unsubsidized Stafford, FFEL PLUS, Federal Perkins. **Student Employment:** Federal Work-Study Program available. Institutional employment available. Off-campus job opportunities are good. **Financial Aid Statistics:** 28% freshmen, 32% undergrads receive need-based scholarship or grant aid. 23% freshmen, 34% undergrads receive need-based self-help aid. 23 freshmen, 138 undergrads receive athletic scholarships.

MIAMI UNIVERSITY

Best 368

301 S. Campus Avenue, Oxford, OH 45056
Phone: 513-529-2531 **E-mail:** admissions@muohio.edu **CEEB Code:** 1463
Fax: 513-529-1550 **Website:** www.muohio.edu **ACT Code:** 3294
Financial Aid Phone: 513-529-8734

This public school was founded in 1809. It has a 2,000-acre campus.

RATINGS

Admissions Selectivity Rating: 88   **Fire Safety Rating:** 76   **Green Rating:** 60*

STUDENTS AND FACULTY

Enrollment: 14,471. **Student Body:** 54% female, 46% male, 29% out-of-state. African American 3%, Asian 3%, Caucasian 86%, Hispanic 2%. **Retention and Graduation:** 90% freshmen return for sophomore year. 67% freshmen graduate within 4 years. 52% grads go on to further study within 1 year. 14% grads pursue arts and sciences degrees. 1% grads pursue business degrees. 7% grads pursue law degrees. 8% grads pursue medical degrees. **Faculty:** Student/faculty ratio 16:1. 813 full-time faculty, 90% hold PhDs. 100% faculty teach undergrads.

ACADEMICS

Degrees: Associate, bachelor's, certificate, doctoral, master's, post-master's certificate. **Academic Requirements:** Arts/fine arts, English (including composition), foreign languages, history, humanities, mathematics, philosophy, sciences (biological or physical), social science. **Classes:** Most classes have 20–29 students. Most lab/discussion sections have 20–29 students. **Majors with Highest Enrollment:** Finance, marketing/marketing management, zoology/animal biology. **Disciplines with Highest Percentage of Degrees Awarded:** Business/marketing 28%, education 11%, social sciences 11%,

communications/journalism 6%, biological/life sciences 6%, psychology 5%, English 5%, history 4%. **Special Study Options:** Cooperative education program, cross-registration, double major, exchange student program (domestic), honors program, independent study, internships, liberal arts/career combination, student-designed major, study abroad, teacher certification program.

FACILITIES

Housing: Coed dorms, men's dorms, women's dorms, apartments for married students, apartments for single students, special housing for disabled students, special housing for international students, fraternity/sorority housing. **Special Academic Facilities/Equipment:** Geology, art, anthropology, and zoology museums, performing arts center, herbarium, environmental research center, 400-acre nature preserve, electron microscope center. **Computers:** 5% of classrooms are wired, 100% of classrooms are wireless, 90% of public computers are PCs, 10% of public computers are Macs, network access in dorm rooms, network access in dorm lounges, online registration, online administrative functions (other than registration), support for handheld computing, remote student-access to Web through college's connection.

CAMPUS LIFE

Activities: Choral groups, concert band, dance, drama/theater, jazz band, literary magazine, marching band, music ensembles, musical theater, opera, pep band, radio station, student government, student newspaper, student-run film society, symphony orchestra, television station. **Organizations:** 350 registered organizations, 34 honor societies, 20 religious organizations. 28 fraternities (21% men join), 20 sororities (24% women join). **Athletics (Intercollegiate):** *Men:* Baseball, basketball, cross-country, diving, football, ice hockey, swimming, track/field (outdoor). *Women:* Basketball, cross-country, diving, field hockey, soccer, softball, swimming, tennis, track/field (outdoor), volleyball.

ADMISSIONS

Freshman Academic Profile: 38% in top 10% of high school class, 74% in top 25% of high school class, 98% in top 50% of high school class. SAT Math middle 50% range 570–660. SAT Critical Reading middle 50% range 540–640. ACT middle 50% range 24–29. TOEFL required of all international applicants, minimum paper TOEFL 533, minimum computer TOEFL 200. **Basis for Candidate Selection:** *Very important factors considered include:* Academic GPA, application essay, character/personal qualities, class rank, recommendation(s), rigor of secondary school record, standardized test scores, talent/ability. *Other factors considered include:* Alumni/ae relation, extracurricular activities, first generation, geographical residence, state residency, volunteer work, work experience. **Freshman Admission Requirements:** High school diploma is required, and GED is accepted. *Academic units recommended:* 4 English, 3 math, 3 science, 2 foreign language, 3 social studies, 1 fine arts. **Freshman Admission Statistics:** 15,468 applied, 78% admitted, 30% enrolled. **Transfer Admission Requirements:** High school transcript, college transcript(s), essay or personal statement, statement of good standing from prior institution(s). Minimum college GPA of 2.0 required. Lowest grade transferable C. **General Admission Information:** Application fee $45. Early decision application deadline 11/1. Regular application deadline 1/31. Regular notification 3/15. Nonfall registration accepted. Admission may be deferred for a maximum of 1 year. Credit offered for CEEB Advanced Placement tests.

COSTS AND FINANCIAL AID

Comprehensive fee $8,443. Room and board $8,600. Required fees $2,111. Average book expense $1,140. **Required Forms and Deadlines:** FAFSA. Financial aid filing deadline 2/15. **Notification of Awards:** Applicants will be notified of awards on or about 3/20. **Types of Aid:** *Need-based scholarships/grants:* Pell, SEOG, state scholarships/grants, private scholarships, the school's own gift aid. *Loans:* Direct Subsidized Stafford, Direct Unsubsidized Stafford, Direct PLUS, Federal Perkins, Federal Nursing, college/university loans from institutional funds, bank alternative loans. **Student Employment:** Federal Work-Study Program available. Institutional employment available. Off-campus job opportunities are good. **Financial Aid Statistics:** 16% freshmen, 17% undergrads receive need-based scholarship or grant aid. 28% freshmen, 29% undergrads receive need-based self-help aid. 84 freshmen, 361 undergrads receive athletic scholarships. 87% freshmen, 85% undergrads receive any aid.

MICHIGAN STATE UNIVERSITY

250 Administration Building, East Lansing, MI 48824-1046
Phone: 517-355-8332 **E-mail:** admis@msu.edu **CEEB Code:** 1465
Fax: 517-353-1647 **Website:** www.msu.edu **ACT Code:** 2032
Financial Aid Phone: 517-353-5940

This public school was founded in 1855. It has a 5,200-acre campus.

RATINGS
Admissions Selectivity Rating: 85   **Fire Safety Rating:** 60*   **Green Rating:** 93

STUDENTS AND FACULTY
Enrollment: 35,521. **Student Body:** 54% female, 46% male, 8% out-of-state, 3% international (129 countries represented). African American 8%, Asian 5%, Caucasian 78%, Hispanic 3%. **Retention and Graduation:** 90% freshmen return for sophomore year. **Faculty:** Student/faculty ratio 17:1. 2,567 full-time faculty, 92% hold PhDs.

ACADEMICS
Degrees: Bachelor's, certificate, doctoral, first professional, master's, post-master's certificate. **Academic Requirements:** English (including composition), humanities, mathematics, sciences (biological or physical), social science. **Classes:** Most classes have 20–29 students. Most lab/discussion sections have 20–29 students. **Majors with Highest Enrollment:** Biology/biological sciences, business administration/management, communications studies/speech communication and rhetoric. **Disciplines with Highest Percentage of Degrees Awarded:** Business/marketing 19%, communications/journalism 12%, social sciences 10%, biological/life sciences 8%, engineering 7%. **Special Study Options:** Accelerated program, cooperative education program, distance learning, double major, dual enrollment, English as a second language (ESL), exchange student program (domestic), external degree program, honors program, independent study, internships, liberal arts/career combination, student-designed major, study abroad, teacher certification program, weekend college.

FACILITIES
Housing: Coed dorms, women's dorms, apartments for married students, apartments for single students, special housing for disabled students, fraternity/sorority housing, cooperative housing. **Special Academic Facilities/Equipment:** Art, natural history, Michigan history, anthropology museums, art center, on-campus preschool and elementary school, biological station, experimental farms, botanical garden, planetarium, 2 superconducting cyclotrons, observatory. **Computers:** Network access in dorm rooms, online registration, online administrative functions (other than registration), remote student-access to Web through college's connection. Undergraduates are required to own a computer.

CAMPUS LIFE
Activities: Choral groups, concert band, dance, drama/theater, jazz band, marching band, music ensembles, musical theater, opera, pep band, radio station, student government, student newspaper, student-run film society, symphony orchestra, television station, yearbook. **Organizations:** 500 registered organizations, 33 fraternities, 16 sororities. **Athletics (Intercollegiate):** *Men:* Baseball, basketball, cheerleading, cross-country, diving, football, golf, ice hockey, soccer, swimming, tennis, track/field (indoor), track/field (outdoor), wrestling. *Women:* Basketball, cheerleading, crew/rowing, cross-country, diving, field hockey, golf, gymnastics, soccer, softball, swimming, tennis, track/field (indoor), track/field (outdoor), volleyball. Environmental Initiatives: Chicago Climate Exchange. Implementing Office of Campus Sustainability. Fair Trade Products Preference.

ADMISSIONS
Freshman Academic Profile: 29% in top 10% of high school class, 69% in top 25% of high school class, 95% in top 50% of high school class. SAT Math middle 50% range 520–650. SAT Critical Reading middle 50% range 480–620. SAT Writing middle 50% range 470–600. ACT middle 50% range 23–27. TOEFL required of all international applicants, minimum paper TOEFL 550, minimum computer TOEFL 213. **Basis for Candidate Selection:** *Very important factors considered include:* Academic GPA, rigor of secondary school record, standardized test scores. *Important factors considered include:* Extracurricular activities, first generation. *Other factors considered include:* Alumni/ae relation, application essay, character/personal qualities, class rank, geographical residence, recommendation(s), talent/ability, volunteer work, work experience. **Freshman Admission Requirements:** High school diploma is required, and GED is accepted. *Academic units required:* 4 English, 3 math, 2 science, 2 foreign language, 2 social studies, 1 history. **Freshman Admission Statistics:** 23,247 applied, 73% admitted, 44% enrolled. **Transfer Admission Requirements:** College transcript(s), essay or personal statement, statement of good standing from prior institution(s). Minimum college GPA of 2.0 required. Lowest grade transferable C. **General Admission Information:** Application fee $35. Regular notification rolling 12 to 14 weeks after submission of application. Nonfall registration accepted. Admission may be deferred for a maximum of semester. Credit and/or placement offered for CEEB Advanced Placement tests.

COSTS AND FINANCIAL AID
Annual in-state tuition $8,603. Annual out-of-state tuition $22,343. Room and board $6,676. Required fees $1,240. Average book expense $906.**Required Forms and Deadlines:** FAFSA. **Notification of Awards:** Applicants will be notified of awards on a rolling basis beginning on or about 3/15. *Types of Aid: Need-based scholarships/grants:* Pell, SEOG, state scholarships/grants, private scholarships, the school's own gift aid, United Negro College Fund, Federal Nursing Scholarships. *Loans:* FFEL Subsidized Stafford, FFEL Unsubsidized Stafford, FFEL PLUS, Federal Perkins, Federal Nursing, state loans, college/university loans from institutional funds. **Student Employment:** Off-campus job opportunities are excellent. **Financial Aid Statistics:** 23% freshmen, 24% undergrads receive need-based scholarship or grant aid. 35% freshmen, 35% undergrads receive need-based self-help aid. 103 freshmen, 519 undergrads receive athletic scholarships. 42% freshmen, 40% undergrads receive any aid.

MICHIGAN TECHNOLOGICAL UNIVERSITY

1400 Townsend Drive, Houghton, MI 49931
Phone: 906-487-2335 **E-mail:** mtu4u@mtu.edu **CEEB Code:** 1464
Fax: 906-487-2125 **Website:** www.mtu.edu **ACT Code:** 2030
Financial Aid Phone: 906-487-2622

This public school was founded in 1885. It has a 925-acre campus.

RATINGS
Admissions Selectivity Rating: 85   **Fire Safety Rating:** 95   **Green Rating:** 76

STUDENTS AND FACULTY
Enrollment: 5,534. **Student Body:** 22% female, 78% male, 26% out-of-state, 4% international (72 countries represented). African American 2%, Asian 1%, Caucasian 87%, Hispanic 1%. **Retention and Graduation:** 81% freshmen return for sophomore year. 26% freshmen graduate within 4 years. 15% grads go on to further study within 1 year. 8% grads pursue arts and sciences degrees. 3% grads pursue business degrees. 1% grads pursue law degrees. 3% grads pursue medical degrees. **Faculty:** Student/faculty ratio 12:1. 349 full-time faculty, 87% hold PhDs. 100% faculty teach undergrads.

ACADEMICS
Degrees: Associate, bachelor's, certificate, doctoral, master's, post-bachelor's certificate. **Academic Requirements:** Computer literacy, English (including composition), humanities, mathematics, sciences (biological or physical), social science, physical education. **Classes:** Most classes have 10–19 students. Most lab/discussion sections have 10–19 students. **Majors with Highest Enrollment:** Civil engineering; electrical, electronics, and communications engineering; mechanical engineering. **Disciplines with Highest Percentage of Degrees Awarded:** Engineering 62%, business/marketing 10%, engineering technologies 5%, computer and information sciences 5%, biological/life sciences 5%, mathematics 2%, physical sciences 2%. **Special Study Options:** Cooperative education program, distance learning, double major, dual enrollment, English as a second language (ESL), exchange student program (domestic), honors program, independent study, internships, study abroad, teacher certification program. Dual enrollment with Northwestern MI College, Delta College, Oakland Community College, Adrian College, Albion College, Augsburg College (MN), College of St. Scholastica (MN), Mount Senario College, Lansing Community College, Olivet College, Northland College, University of Wisconsin-Superior.

FACILITIES

Housing: Coed dorms, apartments for married students, apartments for single students, special housing for disabled students, special housing for international students, fraternity/sorority housing. **Special Academic Facilities/Equipment:** Mineralogical museum, 4,700-acre research forest, scanning electron microscope, PUMA robots, X-ray fluorescence spectrometer, process simulation and control center, Rozsa Center for the Performing Arts, cleanrooms, MEMS Fabrication Facility, environmental scanning electron microscope, transmission electron microscope, radio-frequency plasma-assisted deposition chamber, electron lithography equipment. **Computers:** 28% of classrooms are wireless, 80% of public computers are PCs, 5% of public computers are Macs, 15% of public computers are UNIX, network access in dorm rooms, network access in dorm lounges, online registration, online administrative functions (other than registration), remote student-access to Web through college's connection.

CAMPUS LIFE

Activities: Choral groups, concert band, dance, drama/theater, jazz band, literary magazine, music ensembles, musical theater, opera, pep band, radio station, student government, student newspaper, student-run film society, symphony orchestra. **Organizations:** 200 registered organizations, 16 honor societies, 15 religious organizations. 15 fraternities (7% men join), 8 sororities (11% women join). **Athletics (Intercollegiate):** *Men:* Basketball, cross-country, football, ice hockey, skiing (Nordic/cross-country), tennis, track/field (outdoor). *Women:* Basketball, cross-country, skiing (Nordic/cross-country), tennis, track/field (outdoor), volleyball. Environmental Initiatives: Emphasis on multidisciplinary sustainability research, education, and outreach. Commitment of Administration to sustainability in strategic plan and NCA AQIP accreditation project to move toward a carbon-neutral campus.

ADMISSIONS

Freshman Academic Profile: 29% in top 10% of high school class, 57% in top 25% of high school class, 86% in top 50% of high school class. SAT Math middle 50% range 590–690. SAT Critical Reading middle 50% range 530–650. SAT Writing middle 50% range 500–620. ACT middle 50% range 23–28. TOEFL required of all international applicants, minimum paper TOEFL 500, minimum computer TOEFL 173. **Basis for Candidate Selection:** *Very important factors considered include:* Academic GPA, class rank, rigor of secondary school record, standardized test scores. *Other factors considered include:* Alumni/ae relation, application essay, character/personal qualities, extracurricular activities, interview, recommendation(s), talent/ability, volunteer work, work experience. **Freshman Admission Requirements:** High school diploma is required, and GED is accepted. *Academic units required:* 3 English, 3 math, 2 science. *Academic units recommended:* 4 English, 4 math, 3 science, 2 foreign language, 3 social studies, 1 history, 1 academic elective. **Freshman Admission Statistics:** 3,802 applied, 82% admitted, 38% enrolled. **Transfer Admission Requirements:** College transcript(s), statement of good standing from prior institution(s). Minimum college GPA of 2.8 required. Lowest grade transferable C. **General Admission Information:** Application fee $40. Regular notification within 3 weeks of acceptance. Nonfall registration accepted. Admission may be deferred. Credit and/or placement offered for CEEB Advanced Placement tests.

COSTS AND FINANCIAL AID

Required Forms and Deadlines: FAFSA. Financial aid filing deadline 2/16. **Notification of Awards:** Applicants will be notified of awards on or about 5/1. **Types of Aid:** *Need-based scholarships/grants:* Pell, SEOG, state scholarships/grants, private scholarships, the school's own gift aid. *Loans:* Direct Subsidized Stafford, Direct Unsubsidized Stafford, Direct PLUS, Federal Perkins, state loans, college/university loans from institutional funds, external private loans. **Financial Aid Statistics:** 52% freshmen, 50% undergrads receive need-based scholarship or grant aid. 49% freshmen, 53% undergrads receive need-based self-help aid. 14 freshmen, 196 undergrads receive athletic scholarships. 94% freshmen, 86% undergrads receive any aid. Highest amount earned per year from on-campus jobs $3,600.

MID-AMERICA CHRISTIAN UNIVERSITY

3500 SW 119th Street, Oklahoma City, OK 73170
Phone: 405-691-3188 **E-mail:** info@macu.edu **CEEB Code:** 6942
Fax: 405-692-3165 **Website:** www.macu.edu **ACT Code:** 4097

This private school, affiliated with the Church of God, was founded in 1953.

RATINGS

Admissions Selectivity Rating: 60*   **Fire Safety Rating:** 60*   **Green Rating:** 60*

STUDENTS AND FACULTY

Faculty: 95% faculty teach undergrads.

ACADEMICS

Degrees: Associate, bachelor's. **Academic Requirements:** Arts/fine arts, English (including composition), history, humanities, mathematics, philosophy, sciences (biological or physical), social science, Bible/theology. **Majors with Highest Enrollment:** Business administration/management, pastoral studies/counseling, theological studies and religious vocations. **Special Study Options:** Accelerated program, distance learning, double major, external degree program, internships, liberal arts/career combination, student-designed major, teacher certification program.

FACILITIES

Housing: Men's dorms, women's dorms, special housing for disabled students. **Computers:** 100% of public computers are PCs, network access in dorm rooms.

CAMPUS LIFE

Activities: Choral groups, student government, student newspaper, yearbook. **Organizations:** 1 honor society, 5 religious organizations. **Athletics (Intercollegiate):** *Men:* Baseball, basketball, soccer. *Women:* Basketball, softball, volleyball.

ADMISSIONS

Freshman Academic Profile: TOEFL required of all international applicants, minimum paper TOEFL 500. **Transfer Admission Requirements:** College transcript(s). Lowest grade transferable D. **General Admission Information:** Regular application deadline rolling. Credit and/or placement offered for CEEB Advanced Placement tests.

COSTS AND FINANCIAL AID

Comprehensive fee $6,796. Room & board $2,896. Average book expense $500. **Types of Aid:** *Loans:* FFEL Subsidized Stafford, FFEL PLUS. **Student Employment:** Federal Work-Study Program available. Off-campus job opportunities are excellent.

MIDAMERICA NAZARENE UNIVERSITY

2030 College Way, Olathe, KS 66062
Phone: 913-791-3380 **E-mail:** admissions@mnu.edu **CEEB Code:** 6437
Fax: 913-791-3481 **Website:** www.mnu.edu **ACT Code:** 1445
Financial Aid Phone: 913-791-3298

This private school, affiliated with the Nazarene Church, was founded in 1966. It has a 105-acre campus.

RATINGS

Admissions Selectivity Rating: 74   **Fire Safety Rating:** 67   **Green Rating:** 60*

STUDENTS AND FACULTY

Enrollment: 1,287. **Student Body:** 32% out-of-state. African American 7%, Asian 1%, Caucasian 85%, Hispanic 3%. **Retention and Graduation:** 77% freshmen return for sophomore year. **Faculty:** Student/faculty ratio 17:1. 86 full-time faculty, 48% hold PhDs. 75% faculty teach undergrads.

ACADEMICS

Degrees: Associate, bachelor's, master's, post-master's certificate. **Academic Requirements:** Arts/fine arts, computer literacy, English (including composition), foreign languages, history, humanities, mathematics, philosophy, sciences (biological or physical), social science, religion. **Classes:** Most classes have fewer than 10 students. Most lab/discussion sections have 10–19 students. **Majors with Highest Enrollment:** Business administration/management, elementary education and teaching, nursing/registered nurse training (RN, ASN, BSN, MSN). **Disciplines with Highest Percentage of Degrees Awarded:** Business/marketing 42%, other 15%, health professions and related sciences 11%, education 8%, computer and information sciences 5%. **Special Study Options:** Accelerated program, cross-registration, distance learning, double major, dual enrollment, independent study, internships, study abroad, teacher certification program, weekend college.

FACILITIES

Housing: Men's dorms, women's dorms, apartments for single students, special housing for disabled students. **Computers:** 10% of classrooms are wired, 90% of classrooms are wireless, 90% of public computers are PCs, 10% of public computers are Macs, network access in dorm rooms, network access in dorm lounges, online registration, online administrative functions (other than registration), remote student-access to Web through college's connection.

CAMPUS LIFE

Activities: Choral groups, concert band, drama/theater, jazz band, literary magazine, music ensembles, musical theater, pep band, radio station, student government, student newspaper, television station, yearbook. **Organizations:** 43 registered organizations, 6 honor societies, 4 religious organizations. **Athletics (Intercollegiate):** *Men:* Baseball, basketball, cheerleading, cross-country, football, soccer, track/field (indoor), track/field (outdoor). *Women:* Basketball, cheerleading, cross-country, soccer, softball, track/field (indoor), track/field (outdoor), volleyball.

ADMISSIONS

Freshman Academic Profile: 14% in top 10% of high school class, 36% in top 25% of high school class, 88% from public high schools. SAT Math middle 50% range 420–560. SAT Critical Reading middle 50% range 360–590. ACT middle 50% range 20–26. TOEFL required of all international applicants, minimum paper TOEFL 550, minimum computer TOEFL 214. **Basis for Candidate Selection:** *Very important factors considered include:* Character/personal qualities, class rank, rigor of secondary school record, standardized test scores. *Important factors considered include:* Academic GPA, level of applicant's interest, recommendation(s). *Other factors considered include:* Application essay, extracurricular activities, interview, talent/ability. **Freshman Admission Requirements:** High school diploma is required, and GED is accepted. *Academic units recommended:* 4 English, 3 math, 3 science, 1 foreign language, 3 social studies. **Freshman Admission Statistics:** 685 applied, 90% admitted, 39% enrolled. **Transfer Admission Requirements:** College transcript(s). Minimum college GPA of 2.0 required. Lowest grade transferable D. **General Admission Information:** Application fee $25. Regular application deadline 8/1. Nonfall registration not accepted. Admission may be deferred for a maximum of 2 years. Credit offered for CEEB Advanced Placement tests.

COSTS AND FINANCIAL AID

Annual tuition $17,216. Room and board $6,180. Required fees $1,000. Average book expense $1,180. **Required Forms and Deadlines:** FAFSA, institution's own financial aid form. Financial aid filing deadline 3/1. **Types of Aid:** *Need-based scholarships/grants:* Pell, SEOG, state scholarships/grants, private scholarships, the school's own gift aid. *Loans:* FFEL Subsidized Stafford, FFEL Unsubsidized Stafford, FFEL PLUS, Federal Perkins, Federal Nursing. **Financial Aid Statistics:** 77% freshmen, 61% undergrads receive need-based scholarship or grant aid. 66% freshmen, 60% undergrads receive need-based self-help aid. 21 freshmen, 55 undergrads receive athletic scholarships. 92% freshmen, 86% undergrads receive any aid.

MIDDLE TENNESSEE STATE UNIVERSITY

Office of Admissions, Murfreesboro, TN 37132
Phone: 800-433-6878 **E-mail:** admissions@mtsu.edu **CEEB Code:** 1466
Fax: 615-898-5478 **Website:** www.mtsu.edu **Financial Aid Phone:** 615-898-2830

This public school was founded in 1911. It has a 500-acre campus.

RATINGS

Admissions Selectivity Rating: 60*   **Fire Safety Rating:** 60*   **Green Rating:** 60*

STUDENTS AND FACULTY

Student Body: 5% out-of-state. **Retention and Graduation:** 75% freshmen return for sophomore year. **Faculty:** 90% faculty teach undergrads.

ACADEMICS

Special Study Options: Study abroad, study abroad in England and France.

FACILITIES

Housing: Coed dorms, men's dorms, women's dorms. **Special Academic Facilities/Equipment:** On-campus nursery school, kindergarten, elementary school, radio/TV/photography mobile production lab, state-of-the-art recording studios.

CAMPUS LIFE

Activities: Radio station, student government, student newspaper, television station, yearbook. **Organizations:** 155 registered organizations, 1 honor society, 1 religious organization. 14 fraternities (1% men join), 10 sororities (1% women join). **Athletics (Intercollegiate):** *Men:* Basketball, cross-country, tennis, track/field (outdoor), volleyball. *Women:* Basketball, cross-country, tennis, track/field (outdoor), volleyball.

ADMISSIONS

Freshman Academic Profile: 17% in top 10% of high school class, 51% in top 25% of high school class, 64% in top 50% of high school class. TOEFL required of all international applicants, minimum paper TOEFL 525, minimum

---

computer TOEFL 300. **General Admission Information:** Regular application deadline 7/1. Regular notification rolling. Nonfall registration not accepted. Common Application not accepted. Credit offered for CEEB Advanced Placement tests.

COSTS AND FINANCIAL AID

Annual in-state tuition $1,906. Out-of-state tuition $6,732. Room & board $3,030. Required fees $154. Average book expense $600. **Required Forms and Deadlines:** FAFSA, institution's own financial aid form. **Types of Aid:** *Need-based scholarships/grants:* Pell, SEOG, state scholarships/grants, private scholarships, the school's own gift aid. *Loans:* FFEL Subsidized Stafford, FFEL Unsubsidized Stafford, FFEL PLUS, Federal Perkins, college/university loans from institutional funds. **Student Employment:** Federal Work-Study Program available. Off-campus job opportunities are good. **Financial Aid Statistics:** Highest amount earned per year from on-campus jobs $2,720.

MIDDLEBURY COLLEGE

Best 368

The Emma Willard House, Middlebury, VT 05753-6002
Phone: 802-443-3000 **E-mail:** admissions@middlebury.edu **CEEB Code:** 3526
Fax: 802-443-2056 **Website:** www.middlebury.edu **ACT Code:** 4306
Financial Aid Phone: 802-443-5158

This private school was founded in 1800. It has a 350-acre campus.

RATINGS

Admissions Selectivity Rating: 99   **Fire Safety Rating:** 60*   **Green Rating:** 60*

STUDENTS AND FACULTY

Enrollment: 2,376. **Student Body:** 52% female, 48% male, 93% out-of-state. 10% international (70 countries represented). African American 3%, Asian 9%, Caucasian 65%, Hispanic 6%. **Faculty:** Student/faculty ratio 9:1. 254 full-time faculty, 96% hold PhDs. 100% faculty teach undergrads.

ACADEMICS

Degrees: Bachelor's, doctoral, master's. **Academic Requirements:** Arts/fine arts, English (including composition), foreign languages, history, philosophy, sciences (biological or physical), social science. Please see the following Web address for a complete description of degree requirements: www.middlebury.edu/academics/ump/majors/. **Classes:** Most classes have 10–19 students. **Majors with Highest Enrollment:** Economics, English language and literature, psychology. **Disciplines with Highest Percentage of Degrees Awarded:** Social sciences 23%, interdisciplinary studies 12%, English 10%, history 10%, psychology 8%. **Special Study Options:** Accelerated program, double major, exchange student program (domestic), honors program, independent study, internships, student-designed major, study abroad, teacher certification program, Williams College–Mystic Seaport Program in American Maritime Studies, Oxford University summer program, independent scholar programs with Berea College and Swarthmore College, 3-year international major.

FACILITIES

Housing: Coed dorms, apartments for single students, special housing for disabled students, multicultural house, environmental house, foreign language house, 5 coed social houses, commons system organizes residence halls into 5 groups (each with its own budget). **Special Academic Facilities/Equipment:** Art museum, theaters, language lab, observatory, electron microscope, mountain campus, downhill and cross-country ski areas, golf course. **Computers:** Network access in dorm rooms, network access in dorm lounges, online registration, online administrative functions (other than registration), support for handheld computing, remote student-access to Web through college's connection.

CAMPUS LIFE

Activities: Choral groups, dance, drama/theater, jazz band, literary magazine, music ensembles, musical theater, radio station, student government, student newspaper, student-run film society, symphony orchestra, yearbook. **Organizations:** 100 registered organizations. **Athletics (Intercollegiate):** *Men:* Baseball, basketball, cross-country, diving, football, golf, ice hockey, lacrosse, skiing (downhill/alpine), skiing (Nordic/cross-country), soccer, swimming, tennis, track/field (indoor), track/field (outdoor). *Women:* Basketball, cross-country, diving, field hockey, golf, ice hockey, lacrosse, skiing (downhill/alpine), skiing (Nordic/cross-country), soccer, softball, squash, swimming, tennis, track/field (indoor), track/field (outdoor), volleyball.

ADMISSIONS

Freshman Academic Profile: 82% in top 10% of high school class, 96% in top 25% of high school class, 99% in top 50% of high school class. 52% from public high schools. SAT Math middle 50% range 650–740. SAT Critical Reading middle 50% range 650–750. SAT Writing middle 50% range 650–730. ACT middle 50% range 29–33. **Basis for Candidate Selection:** *Very important factors considered include:* Academic GPA, character/personal qualities, class rank, extracurricular activities, rigor of secondary school record, talent/ability. *Important factors considered include:* Application essay, racial/ethnic status, recommendation(s), standardized test scores. *Other factors considered include:* Alumni/ae relation, first generation, geographical residence, level of applicant's interest, volunteer work, work experience. **Freshman Admission Requirements:** High school diploma or equivalent is not required. *Academic units recommended:* 4 English, 4 math, 3 science (3 science labs), 4 foreign language, 3 social studies, 2 history, 1 academic elective, 1 fine arts/music/drama courses recommended. **Freshman Admission Statistics:** 6,205 applied, 22% admitted, 42% enrolled. **Transfer Admission Requirements:** High school transcript, college transcript(s), essay or personal statement, statement of good standing from prior institution(s). Minimum college GPA of 3.0 required. Lowest grade transferable C-. **General Admission Information:** Application fee $65. Early decision application deadline 11/1. Regular application deadline 1/1. Regular notification 4/1. Nonfall registration accepted. Admission may be deferred for a maximum of 1 year. Credit and/or placement offered for CEEB Advanced Placement tests.

COSTS AND FINANCIAL AID

Comprehensive fee $46,910. Average book expense $750. **Required Forms and Deadlines:** FAFSA, CSS/Financial Aid PROFILE, state aid form, Noncustodial PROFILE, Business/Farm Supplement. Financial aid filing deadline 1/1. **Notification of Awards:** Applicants will be notified of awards on or about 4/1. **Types of Aid:** *Need-based scholarships/grants:* Pell, SEOG, state scholarships/grants, private scholarships, the school's own gift aid. *Loans:* Direct Subsidized Stafford, Direct Unsubsidized Stafford, Direct PLUS, Federal Perkins, college/university loans from institutional funds. **Financial Aid Statistics:** 45% freshmen, 43% undergrads receive need-based scholarship or grant aid. 45% freshmen, 43% undergrads receive need-based self-help aid.

MIDLAND LUTHERAN COLLEGE

900 North Clarkson, Fremont, NE 68025
Phone: 402-721-5487 **E-mail:** admissions@admin.mlc.edu
Fax: 402-721-0250 **Website:** www.mlc.edu **Financial Aid Phone:** 402-721-5480

This private school was founded in 1883.

RATINGS
Admissions Selectivity Rating: 73   **Fire Safety Rating:** 60*   **Green Rating:** 60*

STUDENTS AND FACULTY

Enrollment: 1,033. **Student Body:** 24% out-of-state, 1% international (3 countries represented). African American 4%, Caucasian 94%. **Retention and Graduation:** 84% freshmen return for sophomore year. 45% freshmen graduate within 4 years. 19% grads go on to further study within 1 year. 16% grads pursue arts and sciences degrees. 2% grads pursue law degrees. 1% grads pursue medical degrees. **Faculty:** 90% faculty teach undergrads.

ACADEMICS

Degrees: Associate, bachelor's. **Academic Requirements:** Arts/fine arts, computer literacy, English (including composition), foreign languages, history, humanities, mathematics, philosophy, sciences (biological or physical), social science. **Special Study Options:** Cooperative education program, double major, independent study, internships, student-designed major.

FACILITIES

Housing: Coed dorms, apartments for single students.

CAMPUS LIFE

Organizations: 4 fraternities (20% men join), 4 sororities (20% women join). **Athletics (Intercollegiate):** *Men:* Baseball, basketball, cross-country, football, golf, gymnastics, soccer, tennis, track/field (outdoor), volleyball. *Women:* Basketball, cross-country, golf, gymnastics, soccer, softball, tennis, track/field (outdoor), volleyball.

ADMISSIONS

Freshman Academic Profile: 18% in top 10% of high school class, 48% in top

25% of high school class, 81% in top 50% of high school class. 98% from public high schools. ACT middle 50% range 18–25. TOEFL required of all international applicants, minimum paper TOEFL 500. **Freshman Admission Requirements:** High school diploma is required, and GED is accepted. *Academic units required:* 3 English, 2 math. *Academic units recommended:* 4 English, 3 math, 2 science (1 science lab), 2 foreign language, 2 social studies, 10 academic electives. **Freshman Admission Statistics:** 775 applied, 93% admitted, 44% enrolled. **Transfer Admission Requirements:** High school transcript, standardized test score, statement of good standing from prior institution(s). **General Admission Information:** Application fee $20. Regular application deadline 9/1.

COSTS AND FINANCIAL AID

Annual tuition $12,800. Room & board $3,450. Average book expense $500. **Types of Aid:** *Need-based scholarships/grants:* Pell, SEOG, state scholarships/grants, private scholarships, the school's own gift aid. *Loans:* FFEL Subsidized Stafford, FFEL Unsubsidized Stafford, FFEL PLUS, Federal Perkins, college/university loans from institutional funds. **Student Employment:** Federal Work-Study Program available. Off-campus job opportunities are good. **Financial Aid Statistics:** Highest amount earned per year from on-campus jobs $800.

MIDWAY COLLEGE

512 East Stephen Street., Midway, KY 40347-1120
Phone: 859-846-5346 **E-mail:** admissions@midway.edu **CEEB Code:** 1975
Fax: 859-846-5787 **Website:** www.midway.edu **ACT Code:** 1528
Financial Aid Phone: 859-846-5410

This private school, affiliated with the Disciples of Christ Church, was founded in 1847. It has a 105-acre campus.

RATINGS
Admissions Selectivity Rating: 72   **Fire Safety Rating:** 60*   **Green Rating:** 60*

STUDENTS AND FACULTY

Enrollment: 1,284. **Student Body:** 89% female, 11% male, 9% out-of-state. African American 7%, Caucasian 86%. **Retention and Graduation:** 51% freshmen return for sophomore year. 26% freshmen graduate within 4 years. **Faculty:** Student/faculty ratio 13:1. 41 full-time faculty, 44% hold PhDs. 100% faculty teach undergrads.

ACADEMICS

Degrees: Associate, bachelor's. **Academic Requirements:** Computer literacy, English (including composition), history, humanities, mathematics, sciences (biological or physical), social science, women's studies, critical thinking. **Classes:** Most classes have fewer than 10 students. Most lab/discussion sections have 10–19 students. **Majors with Highest Enrollment:** Elementary education and teaching, equestrian/equine studies, nursing/registered nurse training (RN, ASN, BSN, MSN). **Disciplines with Highest Percentage of Degrees Awarded:** Education 45%, business/marketing 38%, agriculture 9%, health professions and related sciences 5%, biological/life sciences 2%. **Special Study Options:** Accelerated program, distance learning, double major, dual enrollment, honors program, study abroad, teacher certification program, weekend college.

FACILITIES

Housing: Women's dorms. **Special Academic Facilities/Equipment:** Anne Hart Raymond Center for Mathematics, Science, and Technology. **Computers:** 100% of public computers are PCs, network access in dorm rooms, network access in dorm lounges, remote student-access to Web through college's connection.

CAMPUS LIFE

Activities: Choral groups, music ensembles, student government, student newspaper, yearbook. **Organizations:** 10 registered organizations, 22 honor societies. **Athletics (Intercollegiate):** *Women:* Basketball, cross-country, equestrian sports, softball, tennis, volleyball.

ADMISSIONS

Freshman Academic Profile: 10% in top 10% of high school class, 34% in top 25% of high school class, 62% in top 50% of high school class. SAT Math middle 50% range 400–560. SAT Critical Reading middle 50% range 420–560. ACT middle 50% range 18–22. TOEFL required of all international applicants, minimum paper TOEFL 500, minimum computer TOEFL 213. **Basis for Candidate Selection:** *Very important factors considered include:* Rigor of secondary school record, standardized test scores. *Important factors considered include:* Alumni/ae relation. *Other factors considered include:* Application essay, character/personal qualities, class rank, extracurricular activities, interview, recommendation(s), talent/ability, volunteer work, work experience. **Freshman Admission Requirements:** High school diploma is required, and GED is accepted. *Academic units required:* 4 English. *Academic units recommended:* 3 math, 2 science, 1 foreign language, 1 social studies. **Freshman Admission Statistics:** 399 applied, 77% admitted, 52% enrolled. **Transfer Admission Requirements:** High school transcript, college transcript(s). Minimum college GPA of 2.0 required. Lowest grade transferable C. **General Admission Information:** Application fee $25. Regular notification is rolling. Nonfall registration accepted. Admission may be deferred. Credit and/or placement offered for CEEB Advanced Placement tests.

COSTS AND FINANCIAL AID

Annual tuition $15,750. Room and board $6,000. Required fees $150. Average book expense $1,200. **Required Forms and Deadlines:** FAFSA, institution's own financial aid form. Financial aid filing deadline 8/1. **Types of Aid:** *Need-based scholarships/grants:* Pell, SEOG, state scholarships/grants, private scholarships. *Loans:* FFEL Subsidized Stafford, FFEL Unsubsidized Stafford, FFEL PLUS, Federal Perkins, college/university loans from institutional funds. **Student Employment:** Federal Work-Study Program available. Institutional employment available. Off-campus job opportunities are good. **Financial Aid Statistics:** 85% freshmen, 77% undergrads receive need-based scholarship or grant aid. 79% freshmen, 73% undergrads receive need-based self-help aid. 2 freshmen, 4 undergrads receive athletic scholarships. 85% freshmen, 81% undergrads receive any aid.

MIDWESTERN STATE UNIVERSITY

3410 Taft Boulevard, Wichita Falls, TX 76308-2099
Phone: 940-397-4334 **E-mail:** admissions@mwsu.edu **CEEB Code:** 6408
Fax: 940-397-4672 **Website:** www.mwsu.edu **ACT Code:** 4132
Financial Aid Phone: 940-397-4119

This public school was founded in 1922. It has a 255-acre campus.

RATINGS

Admissions Selectivity Rating: 76   **Fire Safety Rating:** 90   **Green Rating:** 60*

STUDENTS AND FACULTY

Enrollment: 5,358. **Student Body:** 58% female, 42% male, 5% out-of-state, 5% international (41 countries represented). African American 13%, Asian 4%, Caucasian 67%, Hispanic 9%. **Retention and Graduation:** 66% freshmen return for sophomore year. 9% freshmen graduate within 4 years. **Faculty:** Student/faculty ratio 19:1. 206 full-time faculty, 68% hold PhDs. 94% faculty teach undergrads.

ACADEMICS

Degrees: Associate, bachelor's, master's, post-bachelor's certificate. **Academic Requirements:** Arts/fine arts, computer literacy, English (including composition), foreign languages, history, humanities, mathematics, philosophy, sciences (biological or physical), social science. **Classes:** Most classes have 20–29 students. Most lab/discussion sections have 10–19 students. **Majors with Highest Enrollment:** Multi/interdisciplinary studies, nursing/registered nurse training (RN, ASN, BSN, MSN), radiologic technology/science/radiographer. **Disciplines with Highest Percentage of Degrees Awarded:** Business/marketing 19%, interdisciplinary studies 19%, health professions and related sciences 17%, education 8%, security and protective services 5%. **Special Study Options:** Distance learning, double major, dual enrollment, English as a second language (ESL), honors program, independent study, internships, liberal arts/career combination, study abroad, teacher certification program.

FACILITIES

Housing: Coed dorms, men's dorms, women's dorms, apartments for married students, apartments for single students, special housing for disabled students, housing for honor students, biology cooperative housing. **Special Academic Facilities/Equipment:** Language lab, technology lab, video lab, planetarium, art museum. **Computers:** 98% of public computers are PCs, 2% of public computers are UNIX, network access in dorm rooms, online registration, online administrative functions (other than registration), remote student-access to Web through college's connection.

CAMPUS LIFE

Activities: Choral groups, concert band, dance, drama/theater, jazz band, literary magazine, marching band, music ensembles, pep band, student government, student newspaper, student-run film society, television station, yearbook. **Organizations:** 145 registered organizations, 23 honor societies, 15

religious organizations. 8 fraternities, 8 sororities. **Athletics (Intercollegiate):** *Men:* Basketball, football, golf, soccer, tennis. *Women:* Basketball, cross-country, soccer, softball, tennis, volleyball.

ADMISSIONS

Freshman Academic Profile: 12% in top 10% of high school class, 37% in top 25% of high school class, 73% in top 50% of high school class. 96% from public high schools. SAT Math middle 50% range 450–560. SAT Critical Reading middle 50% range 440–550. SAT Writing middle 50% range 440–540. ACT middle 50% range 18–23. TOEFL required of all international applicants, minimum paper TOEFL 550, minimum computer TOEFL 213. **Basis for Candidate Selection:** *Very important factors considered include:* Academic GPA, class rank, rigor of secondary school record, standardized test scores. *Other factors considered include:* Alumni/ae relation, application essay, character/personal qualities, extracurricular activities, first generation, geographical residence, interview, level of applicant's interest, racial/ethnic status, state residency, talent/ability, volunteer work. **Freshman Admission Requirements:** High school diploma is required, and GED is accepted. *Academic units required:* 4 English, 3 math, 2 science, 6 academic electives. **Freshman Admission Statistics:** 1,407 applied, 69% admitted, 70% enrolled. **Transfer Admission Requirements:** College transcript(s), statement of good standing from prior institution(s). Minimum college GPA of 2.0 required. Lowest grade transferable D. **General Admission Information:** Application fee $25. Regular application deadline 8/7. Regular notification is rolling. Nonfall registration accepted. Credit and/or placement offered for CEEB Advanced Placement tests.

COSTS AND FINANCIAL AID

Required Forms and Deadlines: FAFSA, institution's own financial aid form. Financial aid filing deadline 5/1. **Notification of Awards:** Applicants will be notified of awards on a rolling basis beginning on or about 3/15. **Types of Aid:** *Need-based scholarships/grants:* Pell, SEOG, state scholarships/grants, private scholarships, the school's own gift aid. *Loans:* FFEL Subsidized Stafford, FFEL Unsubsidized Stafford, FFEL PLUS, Federal Perkins, state loans, college/university loans from institutional funds, alternative private loans. **Student Employment:** Federal Work-Study Program available. Institutional employment available. Off-campus job opportunities are good. **Financial Aid Statistics:** 37% freshmen, 40% undergrads receive need-based scholarship or grant aid. 34% freshmen, 40% undergrads receive need-based self-help aid. 35 freshmen, 102 undergrads receive athletic scholarships. 72% freshmen, 76% undergrads receive any aid. Highest amount earned per year from on-campus jobs $9,120.

MILES COLLEGE

5500 Myron Massey Boulevard, Admissions, Fairfield, AL 35064
Phone: 205-929-1656 **E-mail:** admissions@mail.miles.edu
Fax: 205-929-1627 **Website:** http://miles.edu

This private school was founded in 1905. It has a 37-acre campus.

RATINGS

Admissions Selectivity Rating: 73   **Fire Safety Rating:** 60*   **Green Rating:** 60*

STUDENTS AND FACULTY

Enrollment: 1,660. **Student Body:** 57% female, 43% male, 33% out-of-state. African American 98%, Caucasian 1%. **Retention and Graduation:** 70% freshmen return for sophomore year. 26% freshmen graduate within 4 years. **Faculty:** Student/faculty ratio 20:1. 94 full-time faculty, 35% hold PhDs.

ACADEMICS

Degrees: Bachelor's. **Academic Requirements:** Arts/fine arts, computer literacy, English (including composition), history, humanities, mathematics, sciences (biological or physical), social science, speech. **Disciplines with Highest Percentage of Degrees Awarded:** Education 18%, business/marketing 18%, law/legal studies 8%, communication technologies 7%, biological/life sciences 7%, computer and information sciences 3%, English 3%. **Special Study Options:** Cooperative education program, double major, honors program, internships, study abroad, teacher certification program, weekend college.

FACILITIES

Housing: Coed dorms, men's dorms, women's dorms, apartments for single students. **Computers:** remote student-access to Web through college's connection.

CAMPUS LIFE

Activities: Choral groups, concert band, drama/theater, jazz band, marching band, music ensembles, pep band, student government, student newspaper, television station. **Organizations:** 8 honor societies, 1 religious organization. **Athletics (Intercollegiate):** *Men:* Baseball, basketball, cheerleading, football, tennis, track/field (outdoor). *Women:* Basketball, cheerleading, softball, tennis, track/field (outdoor), volleyball.

ADMISSIONS

Freshman Academic Profile: 15% in top 10% of high school class, 31% in top 25% of high school class, 48% in top 50% of high school class. TOEFL required of all international applicants, minimum paper TOEFL 450. **Basis for Candidate Selection:** *Other factors considered include:* Alumni/ae relation, standardized test scores. **Freshman Admission Requirements:** High school diploma is required, and GED is accepted. *Academic units required:* 20 English, 20 math, 20 science, 20 social studies, 20 history, 2 electives. **Freshman Admission Statistics:** 2,146 applied, 39% admitted, 59% enrolled. **Transfer Admission Requirements:** Lowest grade transferable C. **General Admission Information:** Application fee $25. Regular application deadline 8/23. Regular notification no date is determined. Nonfall registration accepted. Admission may be deferred for a maximum of 1 year. Common Application not accepted.

COSTS AND FINANCIAL AID

Annual tuition $5,008. Room & board $2,950. Required fees $350. Average book expense $600. **Required Forms and Deadlines:** FAFSA, state aid form. **Types of Aid:** *Need-based scholarships/grants:* Pell, SEOG, state scholarships/grants, private scholarships, the school's own gift aid, United Negro College Fund. *Loans:* Direct Subsidized Stafford, Direct Unsubsidized Stafford, Direct PLUS, FFEL Subsidized Stafford, FFEL Unsubsidized Stafford, FFEL PLUS, Federal Perkins, state loans, college/university loans from institutional funds. **Student Employment:** Federal Work-Study Program available. **Financial Aid Statistics:** Highest amount earned per year from on-campus jobs $1,000.

MILES COMMUNITY COLLEGE

2715 Dickinson Street, Miles City, MT 59301
Phone: 406-233-3513 **E-mail:** larsonm@po.mcc.cc.mt.us
Fax: 406-233-3599 **Website:** www.mcc.cc.mt.us **ACT Code:** 2421
Financial Aid Phone: 406-233-3525

This public school was founded in 1939.

RATINGS

Admissions Selectivity Rating: 61   **Fire Safety Rating:** 60*   **Green Rating:** 60*

STUDENTS AND FACULTY

Enrollment: 458. **Student Body:** 61% female, 39% male, 2% out-of-state. **Retention and Graduation:** 47% freshmen return for sophomore year. 63% grads go on to further study within 1 year. **Faculty:** 100% faculty teach undergrads.

ACADEMICS

Degrees: Associate, certificate. **Academic Requirements:** Arts/fine arts, English (including composition), history, humanities, mathematics, sciences (biological or physical), social science. **Special Study Options:** Cooperative education program, cross-registration, distance learning, dual enrollment, English as a second language (ESL), independent study, internships, liberal arts/career combination, student-designed major.

FACILITIES

Housing: Coed dorms, apartments for single students. **Computers:** 85% of public computers are PCs, 15% of public computers are Macs, remote student-access to Web through college's connection.

CAMPUS LIFE

Activities: Choral groups, drama/theater, literary magazine, music ensembles, pep band, student government, student newspaper, yearbook. **Organizations:** 3 registered organizations, 2 honor societies, 1 religious organization. **Athletics (Intercollegiate):** *Men:* Baseball, golf, rodeo, soccer. *Women:* Baseball, golf, rodeo, soccer.

ADMISSIONS

Freshman Academic Profile: 10% in top 10% of high school class, 10% in top 25% of high school class, 70% in top 50% of high school class. 83% from public high schools. TOEFL required of all international applicants, minimum paper TOEFL 500. **Freshman Admission Requirements:** High school diploma is required, and GED is accepted. **Freshman Admission Statistics:** 199 applied, 100% admitted, 76% enrolled. **Transfer Admission Requirements:** High school transcript, college transcript(s), standardized test score. Lowest grade transferable C. **General Admission Information:** Application fee $30. Regular notification. Nonfall registration accepted. Admission may be deferred

for a maximum of 2 years. Common Application accepted. Credit offered for CEEB Advanced Placement tests.

COSTS AND FINANCIAL AID

Annual in-state tuition $840. Out-of-state tuition $4,200. Room & board $3,500. Required fees $672. Average book expense $600. **Required Forms and Deadlines:** FAFSA. Financial aid filing deadline 3/1. **Notification of Awards:** Applicants will be notified of awards on or about 4/15. **Types of Aid:** *Need-based scholarships/grants:* Pell, SEOG, state scholarships/grants, private scholarships, the school's own gift aid. *Loans:* FFEL Subsidized Stafford, FFEL Unsubsidized Stafford, FFEL PLUS, Federal Perkins. **Student Employment:** Federal Work-Study Program available. Institutional employment available. Off-campus job opportunities are good. **Financial Aid Statistics:** 73% freshmen, 68% undergrads receive need-based scholarship or grant aid. 93% freshmen, 75% undergrads receive need-based self-help aid. 2 freshmen, 5 undergrads receive athletic scholarships. Highest amount earned per year from on-campus jobs $1,200.

MILLERSVILLE UNIVERSITY OF PENNSYLVANIA

PO Box 1002, Millersville, PA 17551-0302
Phone: 717-872-3371 **E-mail:** admissions@millersville.edu **CEEB Code:** 2656
Fax: 717-871-2147 **Website:** www.millersville.edu **ACT Code:** 3712
Financial Aid Phone: 717-872-3026

This public school was founded in 1855. It has a 220-acre campus.

RATINGS

Admissions Selectivity Rating: 74   **Fire Safety Rating:** 60*   **Green Rating:** 60*

STUDENTS AND FACULTY

Enrollment: 7,998. **Student Body:** 58% female, 42% male, 4% out-of-state. African American 5%, Asian 2%, Caucasian 71%, Hispanic 3%. **Retention and Graduation:** 79% freshmen return for sophomore year. 35% freshmen graduate within 4 years. **Faculty:** Student/faculty ratio 18:1. 320 full-time faculty. 100% faculty teach undergrads.

ACADEMICS

Degrees: Associate, bachelor's, master's, post-bachelor's certificate, post-master's certificate. **Academic Requirements:** English (including composition), humanities, mathematics, sciences (biological or physical), social science, fundamentals of speech, perspectives component (these courses are interdisciplinary and/or multicultural in content), wellness and sport science. **Classes:** Most classes have 20–29 students. Most lab/discussion sections have 20–29 students. **Majors with Highest Enrollment:** Business administration/management, elementary education and teaching. **Disciplines with Highest Percentage of Degrees Awarded:** Education 17%, social sciences 13%, business/marketing 12%, communication technologies 9%, psychology 8%. **Special Study Options:** Accelerated program, cooperative education program, cross-registration, distance learning, double major, dual enrollment, honors program, independent study, internships, study abroad, teacher certification program, academic remediation, advanced placement credit, off-campus study, learning disabilities services, adult and continuing education (ACE) program, Internet courses.

FACILITIES

Housing: Coed dorms, women's dorms, Center for Service Learning and Leadership/Hobbes Hall, freshmen residence hall/Harbold Hall, university-affiliated apartments for single students adjacent to campus. **Special Academic Facilities/Equipment:** Art galleries, early childhood education lab school, language lab, extensive inventory of scientific and technological instrumentation. **Computers:** 100% of classrooms are wired, 58% of public computers are PCs, 37% of public computers are Macs, 5% of public computers are UNIX, network access in dorm rooms, network access in dorm lounges, online registration, online administrative functions (other than registration), remote student-access to Web through college's connection.

CAMPUS LIFE

Activities: Choral groups, concert band, dance, drama/theater, jazz band, literary magazine, marching band, music ensembles, musical theater, pep band, radio station, student government, student newspaper, symphony orchestra, television station, yearbook. **Organizations:** 109 registered organizations, 5 honor societies, 6 religious organizations. 9 fraternities (3% men join), 8 sororities (4% women join). **Athletics (Intercollegiate):** *Men:* Baseball, basketball, cross-country, football, golf, soccer, tennis, track/field (outdoor), wrestling. *Women:* Basketball, cheerleading, cross-country, field hockey, lacrosse, soccer, softball, swimming, tennis, track/field (outdoor), volleyball.

ADMISSIONS

Freshman Academic Profile: 15% in top 10% of high school class, 43% in top 25% of high school class, 82% in top 50% of high school class. SAT Math middle 50% range 480–580. SAT Critical Reading middle 50% range 480–570. ACT middle 50% range 19–23. TOEFL required of all international applicants, minimum paper TOEFL 500, minimum computer TOEFL 183. **Basis for Candidate Selection:** *Very important factors considered include:* Class rank, rigor of secondary school record, standardized test scores. *Important factors considered include:* Application essay, character/personal qualities, extracurricular activities, racial/ethnic status, recommendation(s), talent/ability, volunteer work, work experience. *Other factors considered include:* Alumni/ae relation, geographical residence, interview, state residency. **Freshman Admission Requirements:** High school diploma is required, and GED is accepted. *Academic units required:* 4 English, 3 math, 3 science (1 science lab), 3 social studies, 2 history. *Academic units recommended:* 2 foreign language, 4 academic electives. **Freshman Admission Statistics:** 6,471 applied, 60% admitted, 37% enrolled. **Transfer Admission Requirements:** College transcript(s), statement of good standing from prior institution(s). Minimum college GPA of 2.0 required. Lowest grade transferable C. **General Admission Information:** Application fee $35. Regular notification is rolling. Nonfall registration accepted. Admission may be deferred for a maximum of 1 semester. Common Application accepted. Credit and/or placement offered for CEEB Advanced Placement tests.

COSTS AND FINANCIAL AID

Annual in-state tuition $4,598. Out-of-state tuition $11,496. Room & board $5,450. Required fees $1,221. Average book expense $800. **Required Forms and Deadlines:** FAFSA. Financial aid filing deadline 3/15. **Notification of Awards:** Applicants will be notified of awards on a rolling basis beginning on or about 3/19. **Types of Aid:** *Need-based scholarships/grants:* Pell, SEOG, state scholarships/grants, private scholarships, the school's own gift aid, SICO Scholarship. *Loans:* FFEL Subsidized Stafford, FFEL Unsubsidized Stafford, FFEL PLUS, Federal Perkins, college/university loans from institutional funds. **Financial Aid Statistics:** 43% freshmen, 38% undergrads receive need-based scholarship or grant aid. 47% freshmen, 45% undergrads receive need-based self-help aid. 25 freshmen, 85 undergrads receive athletic scholarships. 76% freshmen, 71% undergrads receive any aid. Highest amount earned per year from on-campus jobs $6,753.

MILLIGAN COLLEGE

PO Box 210, Milligan Coll, TN 37682
Phone: 423-461-8730 **E-mail:** admissions@milligan.edu **CEEB Code:** 1469
Fax: 423-461-8982 **Website:** www.milligan.edu **ACT Code:** 3996
Financial Aid Phone: 423-461-8948

This private school, affiliated with the Christian Churches/Churches of Christ (independent Church), was founded in 1866. It has a 181-acre campus.

RATINGS
Admissions Selectivity Rating: 60*   **Fire Safety Rating:** 74   **Green Rating:** 60*

STUDENTS AND FACULTY
Enrollment: 734. **Student Body:** 61% female, 39% male, 54% out-of-state, 3% international (11 countries represented). African American 3%, Asian 1%, Caucasian 92%, Hispanic 1%. **Retention and Graduation:** 74% freshmen return for sophomore year. **Faculty:** Student/faculty ratio 11:1. 67 full-time faculty, 72% hold PhDs. 96% faculty teach undergrads.

ACADEMICS
Degrees: Bachelor's, master's. **Academic Requirements:** Arts/fine arts, computer literacy, English (including composition), history, humanities, mathematics, philosophy, sciences (biological or physical), social science, foreign language required for BA degree. **Classes:** Most classes have 10–19 students. Most lab/discussion sections have fewer than 10 students. **Majors with Highest Enrollment:** Bible/biblical studies, business administration/management, nursing/registered nurse training (RN, ASN, BSN, MSN). **Disciplines with Highest Percentage of Degrees Awarded:** Business/marketing 33%, philosophy and religious studies 9%, psychology 8%, education 7%, communication technologies 7%, health professions and related sciences 6%. **Special Study Options:** Cross-registration, double major, independent study, internships, study abroad, teacher certification program.

FACILITIES
Housing: Men's dorms, women's dorms, apartments for married students, apartments for single students. **Computers:** 68% of classrooms are wired, 68% of classrooms are wireless, 100% of public computers are PCs, network access in dorm rooms, online administrative functions (other than registration), remote student-access to Web through college's connection.

CAMPUS LIFE
Activities: Choral groups, concert band, drama/theater, jazz band, literary magazine, music ensembles, musical theater, pep band, radio station, student government, student newspaper, symphony orchestra, yearbook. **Organizations:** 36 registered organizations, 5 honor societies, 5 religious organizations. **Athletics (Intercollegiate):** *Men:* Baseball, basketball, cross-country, golf, soccer, tennis, track/field (indoor), track/field (outdoor). *Women:* Basketball, cross-country, soccer, softball, tennis, track/field (indoor), track/field (outdoor), volleyball.

ADMISSIONS
Freshman Academic Profile: 80% from public high schools. SAT Math middle 50% range 480–610. SAT Critical Reading middle 50% range 470–610. SAT Writing middle 50% range 460–600. ACT middle 50% range 20–26. TOEFL required of all international applicants, minimum paper TOEFL 550, minimum computer TOEFL 213. **Basis for Candidate Selection:** *Very important factors considered include:* Academic GPA, application essay, character/personal qualities, religious affiliation/commitment, rigor of secondary school record, standardized test scores. *Important factors considered include:* Extracurricular activities, recommendation(s). *Other factors considered include:* Alumni/ae relation, class rank, interview, racial/ethnic status, talent/ability, volunteer work, work experience. **Freshman Admission Requirements:** High school diploma is required, and GED is accepted. *Academic units recommended:* 4 English, 3 math, 3 science, 2 foreign language, 2 social studies, 3 history. **Freshman Admission Statistics:** 524 applied, 74% admitted, 43% enrolled. **Transfer Admission Requirements:** College transcript(s), essay or personal statement. Minimum college GPA of 2.0 required. Lowest grade transferable C-. **General Admission Information:** Application fee $30. Regular application deadline 8/1. Regular notification is rolling. Nonfall registration accepted. Admission may be deferred for a maximum of 1 year. Credit and/or placement offered for CEEB Advanced Placement tests.

COSTS AND FINANCIAL AID
Average book expense $750. **Required Forms and Deadlines:** FAFSA. Financial aid filing deadline 3/1. **Notification of Awards:** Applicants will be notified of awards on or about 3/15. **Types of Aid:** *Need-based scholarships/grants:* Pell, SEOG, state scholarships/grants, private scholarships, the school's own gift aid. *Loans:* FFEL Subsidized Stafford, FFEL Unsubsidized Stafford, FFEL PLUS, Federal Perkins. **Student Employment:** Federal Work-Study Program available. Institutional employment available. Off-campus job opportunities are excellent. **Financial Aid Statistics:** 27% freshmen, 31% undergrads receive need-based scholarship or grant aid. 46% freshmen, 53% undergrads receive need-based self-help aid. 39 freshmen, 155 undergrads receive athletic scholarships.

MILLIKIN UNIVERSITY

1184 West Main Street, Decatur, IL 62522-2084
Phone: 217-424-6210 **E-mail:** admis@millikin.edu **CEEB Code:** 1470
Fax: 217-425-4669 **Website:** www.millikin.edu **ACT Code:** 1080
Financial Aid Phone: 217-424-6317

This private school, affiliated with the Presbyterian Church, was founded in 1901. It has a 70-acre campus.

RATINGS
Admissions Selectivity Rating: 74   **Fire Safety Rating:** 97   **Green Rating:** 60*

STUDENTS AND FACULTY
Enrollment: 2,435. **Student Body:** 59% female, 41% male, 12% out-of-state. African American 9%, Asian 2%, Caucasian 82%, Hispanic 3%. **Retention and Graduation:** 80% freshmen return for sophomore year. 19% grads go on to further study within 1 year. 13% grads pursue arts and sciences degrees. 2% grads pursue business degrees. 1% grads pursue law degrees. 1% grads pursue medical degrees. **Faculty:** Student/faculty ratio 13:1. 145 full-time faculty, 74% hold PhDs. 99% faculty teach undergrads.

ACADEMICS
Degrees: Bachelor's, master's. **Academic Requirements:** Arts/fine arts, English (including composition), mathematics, sciences (biological or physical), U.S. studies, global studies, off-campus learning, culture or modern language or semiotic systems track. **Classes:** Most classes have 10–19 students. Most lab/discussion sections have 10–19 students. **Majors with Highest Enrollment:** Business/managerial operations, elementary education and teaching, nursing/

registered nurse training (RN, ASN, BSN, MSN). **Disciplines with Highest Percentage of Degrees Awarded:** Business/marketing 27%, visual and performing arts 19%, education 14%, health professions and related sciences 7%, communications/journalism 5%. **Special Study Options:** Accelerated program, double major, exchange student program (domestic), honors program, independent study, internships, student-designed major, study abroad, teacher certification program.

FACILITIES

Housing: Coed dorms, men's dorms, women's dorms, apartments for married students, apartments for single students, special housing for disabled students, fraternity/sorority housing, learning communities. **Special Academic Facilities/Equipment:** Art galleries, art museum, fitness/wellness center, recording studio, indoor sports center, greenhouse, observatory, 2 indoor sports centers, 2,000-seat performance center. **Computers:** 20% of classrooms are wired, 60% of classrooms are wireless, 80% of public computers are PCs, 20% of public computers are Macs, network access in dorm rooms, network access in dorm lounges, online registration, online administrative functions (other than registration), remote student-access to Web through college's connection.

CAMPUS LIFE

Activities: Choral groups, concert band, dance, drama/theater, jazz band, literary magazine, music ensembles, musical theater, opera, pep band, radio station, student government, student newspaper, student-run film society, symphony orchestra. **Organizations:** 91 registered organizations, 9 honor societies, 1 religious organization. 5 fraternities (14% men join), 4 sororities (15% women join). **Athletics (Intercollegiate):** *Men:* Baseball, basketball, cheerleading, cross-country, football, golf, soccer, swimming, track/field (indoor), track/field (outdoor), wrestling. *Women:* Basketball, cheerleading, cross-country, golf, soccer, softball, swimming, tennis, track/field (indoor), track/field (outdoor), volleyball.

ADMISSIONS

Freshman Academic Profile: 17% in top 10% of high school class, 43% in top 25% of high school class, 74% in top 50% of high school class. 91% from public high schools. SAT Math middle 50% range 490–650. SAT Critical Reading middle 50% range 470–630. SAT Writing middle 50% range 450–620. ACT middle 50% range 20–25. TOEFL required of all international applicants, minimum paper TOEFL 550, minimum computer TOEFL 213. **Basis for Candidate Selection:** *Very important factors considered include:* Rigor of secondary school record. *Important factors considered include:* Academic GPA, class rank, interview, recommendation(s), standardized test scores. *Other factors considered include:* Alumni/ae relation, character/personal qualities, extracurricular activities, level of applicant's interest, talent/ability, volunteer work, work experience. **Freshman Admission Requirements:** High school diploma is required, and GED is accepted. *Academic units recommended:* 4 English, 4 math, 3 science, 2 foreign language, 2 social studies, 2 history. **Freshman Admission Statistics:** 2,848 applied, 72% admitted, 23% enrolled. **Transfer Admission Requirements:** College transcript(s). Minimum college GPA of 2.0 required. Lowest grade transferable C-. **General Admission Information:** Regular notification is rolling. Nonfall registration accepted. Admission may be deferred for a maximum of 1 year. Credit and/or placement offered for CEEB Advanced Placement tests.

COSTS AND FINANCIAL AID

Average book expense $1,000. **Required Forms and Deadlines:** FAFSA. Financial aid filing deadline 3/15. **Notification of Awards:** Applicants will be notified of awards on a rolling basis beginning on or about 3/15. **Types of Aid:** *Need-based scholarships/grants:* Pell, SEOG, state scholarships/grants, the school's own gift aid. *Loans:* FFEL Subsidized Stafford, FFEL Unsubsidized Stafford, FFEL PLUS, Federal Perkins. **Student Employment:** Federal Work-Study Program available. Institutional employment available. Off-campus job opportunities are good. **Financial Aid Statistics:** 71% freshmen, 65% undergrads receive need-based scholarship or grant aid. 65% freshmen, 62% undergrads receive need-based self-help aid. 100% freshmen, 98% undergrads receive any aid. Highest amount earned per year from on-campus jobs $6,480.

MILLS COLLEGE

Best 368

5000 MacArthur Boulevard, Oakland, CA 94613
Phone: 510-430-2135 **E-mail:** admission@mills.edu **CEEB Code:** 4485
Fax: 510-430-3314 **Website:** www.mills.edu **ACT Code:** 4485
Financial Aid Phone: 510-430-2000

This private school was founded in 1852. It has a 135-acre campus.

RATINGS

Admissions Selectivity Rating: 86　　**Fire Safety Rating:** 60*　　**Green Rating:** 92

STUDENTS AND FACULTY

Enrollment: 927. **Student Body:** 100% female, 29% out-of-state, 3% international (13 countries represented). African American 8%, Asian 9%, Caucasian 45%, Hispanic 11%. **Retention and Graduation:** 71% freshmen return for sophomore year. 59% freshmen graduate within 4 years. 20% grads go on to further study within 1 year. **Faculty:** Student/faculty ratio 11:1. 89 full-time faculty. 100% faculty teach undergrads.

ACADEMICS

Degrees: Bachelor's, doctoral, master's, post-bachelor's certificate. **Academic Requirements:** Arts/fine arts, computer literacy, English (including composition), history, humanities, mathematics, philosophy, sciences (biological or physical), social science, multicultural course, 2 interdisciplinary courses. **Classes:** Most classes have 10–19 students. **Majors with Highest Enrollment:** English language and literature, political science and government, psychology. **Disciplines with Highest Percentage of Degrees Awarded:** English 18%, social sciences 18%, visual and performing arts 15%, area and ethnic studies 11%, psychology 9%, biological/life sciences 5%. **Special Study Options:** Cross-registration, double major, exchange student program (domestic), honors program, independent study, internships, student-designed major, study abroad, teacher certification program.

FACILITIES

Housing: Coed dorms, women's dorms, apartments for married students, apartments for single students, special housing for disabled students, cooperative housing. **Special Academic Facilities/Equipment:** Art Museum, Center for Contemporary Music, on-campus elementary school, botanical gardens. **Computers:** 100% of classrooms are wired, 100% of classrooms are wireless, 65% of public computers are PCs, 35% of public computers are Macs, network access in dorm rooms, network access in dorm lounges, online administrative functions (other than registration), remote student-access to Web through college's connection.

CAMPUS LIFE

Activities: Choral groups, dance, drama/theater, literary magazine, music ensembles, musical theater, opera, student government, student newspaper, student-run film society, yearbook. **Organizations:** 30 registered organizations, 2 honor societies. **Athletics (Intercollegiate):** *Women:* Crew/rowing, cross-country, soccer, swimming, tennis, volleyball. Environmental Initiatives: Mills recycles, composts and reuses all consumer materials to the extent possible. Students participate in RecycleMania. Mills builds to LEED standards of silver or higher. Mills has been awarded a LEED Platinum for new science building and has just broken ground on a business school designed to achieve LEED Gold. Mills encourages the use and provides access to public and shared transportation by offering a Mills Shuttle service, car share and web based carpool system.

ADMISSIONS

Freshman Academic Profile: 33% in top 10% of high school class, 66% in top 25% of high school class, 95% in top 50% of high school class. 79% from public high schools. SAT Math middle 50% range 490–610. SAT Critical Reading middle 50% range 520–640. SAT Writing middle 50% range 500–630. ACT middle 50% range 19–27. TOEFL required of all international applicants, minimum paper TOEFL 550, minimum computer TOEFL 220. **Basis for Candidate Selection:** *Very important factors considered include:* Rigor of secondary school record. *Important factors considered include:* Academic GPA, application essay, character/personal qualities, class rank, extracurricular activities, recommendation(s), standardized test scores. *Other factors considered include:* Alumni/ae relation, first generation, geographical residence, interview, level of applicant's interest, racial/ethnic status, state residency, talent/ability, volunteer work, work experience. **Freshman Admission Require-**

ments: High school diploma is required, and GED is accepted. *Academic units required:* 3 math, 2 science (2 science labs), 2 foreign language, 2 social studies, 2 history. *Academic units recommended:* 4 English, 4 math, 4 science, 4 foreign language, 4 social studies, 4 history. **Freshman Admission Statistics:** 1,122 applied, 65% admitted, 28% enrolled. **Transfer Admission Requirements:** High school transcript, college transcript(s), essay or personal statement, statement of good standing from prior institution(s). Minimum college GPA of 3.0 required. Lowest grade transferable C-. **General Admission Information:** Application fee $40. Regular application deadline 5/1. Regular notification is rolling. Nonfall registration accepted. Admission may be deferred for a maximum of 1 academic year. Credit and/or placement offered for CEEB Advanced Placement tests.

COSTS AND FINANCIAL AID

Annual tuition $34,170. Room and board $11,270. Required fees $1,018. Average book expense $1,300. **Required Forms and Deadlines:** FAFSA, institution's own financial aid form, state aid form, Noncustodial PROFILE. Financial aid filing deadline 2/15. **Notification of Awards:** Applicants will be notified of awards on a rolling basis beginning on or about 3/1. **Types of Aid:** *Need-based scholarships/grants:* Pell, SEOG, state scholarships/grants, private scholarships, the school's own gift aid. *Loans:* FFEL Subsidized Stafford, FFEL Unsubsidized Stafford, FFEL PLUS, Federal Perkins, college/university loans from institutional funds. **Student Employment:** Federal Work-Study Program available. Off-campus job opportunities are excellent. **Financial Aid Statistics:** 76% freshmen, 82% undergrads receive need-based scholarship or grant aid. 74% freshmen, 68% undergrads receive need-based self-help aid. 96% freshmen, 96% undergrads receive any aid. Highest amount earned per year from on-campus jobs $1,800.

MILLSAPS COLLEGE

1701 North State Street, Jackson, MS 39210
Phone: 601-974-1050 **E-mail:** Admissions@millsaps.edu **CEEB Code:** 1471
Fax: 601-974-1059 **Website:** www.millsaps.edu **ACT Code:** 2212
Financial Aid Phone: 800-352-1050

This private school, affiliated with the Methodist Church, was founded in 1890. It has a 100-acre campus.

RATINGS
Admissions Selectivity Rating: 87   **Fire Safety Rating:** 82   **Green Rating:** 60*

STUDENTS AND FACULTY
Enrollment: 985. **Student Body:** 51% female, 49% male, 51% out-of-state. African American 11%, Asian 4%, Caucasian 82%, Hispanic 2%. **Retention and Graduation:** 78% freshmen return for sophomore year. 60% freshmen graduate within 4 years. 48% grads go on to further study within 1 year. 25% grads pursue arts and sciences degrees. 8% grads pursue business degrees. 6% grads pursue law degrees. 9% grads pursue medical degrees. **Faculty:** Student/faculty ratio 11:1. 92 full-time faculty. 100% faculty teach undergrads.

ACADEMICS
Degrees: Bachelor's, master's. **Academic Requirements:** Arts/fine arts, English (including composition), history, humanities, mathematics, sciences (biological or physical), social science, writing proficiency. **Classes:** Most classes have 10—19 students. Most lab/discussion sections have 10–19 students. **Majors with Highest Enrollment:** Biology/biological sciences; business administration and management; psychology. **Disciplines with Highest Percentage of Degrees Awarded:** Business/marketing 20%, biological/life sciences 12%, psychology 10%, English 9%, education 7%, philosophy and religious studies 7%. **Special Study Options:** Accelerated program, discussion programs with faculty and professionals, double major, fellows programs, honor program, independent study, internships, leadership and service clubs, liberal arts/career combination, public lecture series, service-learning, student-designed major, study abroad, teacher certification program, undergraduate research.

FACILITIES
Housing: Coed dorms, women's dorms, fraternity/sorority housing, community service dormitory, designated alcohol and drug-free hall in a dormitory. **Special Academic Facilities/Equipment:** Special facilities include a state-of-the-art

molecular biology/functional genomics research laboratory, a fluorescence microscopy suite and imaging facility, a GIS workstation with Rockware and Arcview 9.1 GIS Software. **Computers:** 50% of classrooms are wired, 9% of classrooms are wireless, 100% of public computers are PCs, network access in dorm rooms, network access in dorm lounges, online administrative functions (other than registration), support for handheld computing, remote student-access to Web through college's connection.

CAMPUS LIFE
Activities: Choral groups, dance, drama/theater, literary magazine, music ensembles, musical theater, student government, student newspaper, student-run film society, yearbook. **Organizations:** 75 registered organizations, 25 honor societies, 12 religious organizations. 6 fraternities (54% men join), 6 sororities (52% women join). **Athletics (Intercollegiate):** *Men:* Baseball, basketball, cheerleading, cross-country, football, golf, soccer, tennis. *Women:* Basketball, cheerleading, cross-country, golf, soccer, softball, tennis, volleyball.

ADMISSIONS
Freshman Academic Profile: 41% in top 10% of high school class, 65% in top 25% of high school class, 90% in top 50% of high school class. 55% from public high schools. SAT Math middle 50% range 540–650. SAT Critical Reading middle 50% range 550–670. ACT middle 50% range 23–29. TOEFL required of all international applicants, minimum paper TOEFL 550, minimum computer TOEFL 220. **Basis for Candidate Selection:** *Very important factors considered include:* Academic GPA, character/personal qualities, rigor of secondary school record, standardized test scores. *Important factors considered include:* Application essay, class rank, extracurricular activities, interview, recommendation(s), talent/ability, volunteer work. *Other factors considered include:* Work experience. **Freshman Admission Requirements:** High school diploma is required, and GED is accepted. *Academic units required:* 4 English, 3 math, 3 science (1 science lab), 2 social studies, 2 history. *Academic units recommended:* 4 English, 4 math, 4 science (1 science lab), 2 foreign language, 2 social studies, 2 history, 2 academic electives. **Freshman Admission Statistics:** 910 applied, 86% admitted, 29% enrolled. **Transfer Admission Requirements:** College transcript(s), essay or personal statement, standardized test score, statement of good standing from prior institution(s). Minimum college GPA of 2.8 required. Lowest grade transferable C. **General Admission Information:** Application fee $25. Regular application deadline 6/1. Regular notification is rolling. Nonfall registration accepted. Admission may be deferred for a maximum of 1 year. Credit and/or placement offered for CEEB Advanced Placement tests.

COSTS AND FINANCIAL AID
Annual tuition $23,214. Room and board $8,800. Required fees $1,540. Average book expense $1,000. **Required Forms and Deadlines:** FAFSA, institution's own financial aid form. Financial aid filing deadline 3/1. **Notification of Awards:** Applicants will be notified of awards on a rolling basis beginning on or about 3/15. **Types of Aid:** *Need-based scholarships/grants:* Pell, SEOG, state scholarships/grants, private scholarships, the school's own gift aid. *Loans:* FFEL Subsidized Stafford, FFEL Unsubsidized Stafford, FFEL PLUS, Federal Perkins, college/university loans from institutional funds. **Student Employment:** **Financial Aid Statistics:** 55% freshmen, 55% undergrads receive need-based scholarship or grant aid. 37% freshmen, 42% undergrads receive need-based self-help aid. 97% freshmen, 94% undergrads receive any aid. Highest amount earned per year from on-campus jobs $7,693.

MILWAUKEE INSTITUTE OF ART AND DESIGN

273 East Erie Street, 273 E. Erie Street, Milwaukee, WI 53202
Phone: 414-847-3200 **E-mail:** admissions@miad.edu **CEEB Code:** 1506
Fax: 414-291-8077 **Website:** www.miad.edu **ACT Code:** 4701
Financial Aid Phone: 414-291-8272

This private school was founded in 1974. It has a 2-acre campus.

RATINGS
Admissions Selectivity Rating: 64   **Fire Safety Rating:** 60*   **Green Rating:** 60*

STUDENTS AND FACULTY
Enrollment: 643. **Student Body:** 50% female, 50% male, 37% out-of-state, 4% international (3 countries represented). African American 3%, Asian 3%, Caucasian 80%, Hispanic 9%. **Retention and Graduation:** 81% freshmen return for sophomore year. 38% freshmen graduate within 4 years. 6% grads go on to further study within 1 year. 4% grads pursue arts and sciences degrees. **Faculty:** Student/faculty ratio 9:1. 33 full-time faculty, 67% hold PhDs. 100% faculty teach undergrads.

ACADEMICS

Degrees: Bachelor's. **Academic Requirements:** Arts/fine arts, computer literacy, English (including composition), history, humanities, sciences (biological or physical), social science. **Classes:** Most classes have 10–19 students. Most lab/discussion sections have fewer than 10 students. **Majors with Highest Enrollment:** Graphic design, illustration, industrial design. **Disciplines with Highest Percentage of Degrees Awarded:** Visual and performing arts 100%. **Special Study Options:** Double major, exchange student program (domestic), independent study, internships, study abroad.

FACILITIES

Housing: Coed dorms. **Special Academic Facilities/Equipment:** Eisner Museum of Advertisng & Design, Brook Stevens Gallery of Industrial Design, Frederick Layton Gallery. **Computers:** 100% of classrooms are wireless, 15% of public computers are PCs, 85% of public computers are Macs, network access in dorm rooms, network access in dorm lounges, remote student-access to Web through college's connection.

CAMPUS LIFE

Activities: Drama/theater, literary magazine, student government, student newspaper. **Organizations:** 12 registered organizations, 2 honor societies, 1 religious organization.

ADMISSIONS

Freshman Academic Profile: 6% in top 10% of high school class, 25% in top 25% of high school class, 56% in top 50% of high school class. TOEFL required of all international applicants, minimum paper TOEFL 550, minimum computer TOEFL 213. **Basis for Candidate Selection:** *Very important factors considered include:* Academic GPA, application essay, character/personal qualities, interview, level of applicant's interest, talent/ability. *Other factors considered include:* Class rank, extracurricular activities, recommendation(s), rigor of secondary school record, standardized test scores, volunteer work, work experience. **Freshman Admission Requirements:** High school diploma is required, and GED is accepted. **Freshman Admission Statistics:** 416 applied, 75% admitted, 62% enrolled. **Transfer Admission Requirements:** Essay or personal statement, interview. Minimum college GPA of 2.0 required. Lowest grade transferable C. **General Admission Information:** Application fee $25. Regular notification is rolling. Nonfall registration accepted. Admission may be deferred for a maximum of 2 years. Neither credit nor placement offered for CEEB Advanced Placement tests.

COSTS AND FINANCIAL AID

Annual tuition $23,100. Room & board $7,000. Required fees $500. Average book expense $1,825. **Required Forms and Deadlines:** FAFSA. Financial aid filing deadline 3/1. **Notification of Awards:** Applicants will be notified of awards on a rolling basis beginning on or about 4/1. **Types of Aid:** *Need-based scholarships/grants:* Pell, SEOG, state scholarships/grants, private scholarships, the school's own gift aid. *Loans:* Direct Subsidized Stafford, Direct Unsubsidized Stafford, Direct PLUS. **Student Employment:** Federal Work-Study Program available. Institutional employment available. Off-campus job opportunities are good. **Financial Aid Statistics:** 64% freshmen, 80% undergrads receive need-based scholarship or grant aid. 59% freshmen, 76% undergrads receive need-based self-help aid. 95% freshmen, 92% undergrads receive any aid. Highest amount earned per year from on-campus jobs $1,200.

MILWAUKEE SCHOOL OF ENGINEERING

1025 North Broadway, Milwaukee, WI 53202-3109
Phone: 414-277-6763 **E-mail:** explore@msoe.edu **CEEB Code:** 1476
Fax: 414-277-7475 **Website:** www.msoe.edu **ACT Code:** 4616
Financial Aid Phone: 800-778-7223

This private school was founded in 1903. It has a 15-acre campus.

RATINGS

Admissions Selectivity Rating: 60*   **Fire Safety Rating:** 97   **Green Rating:** 86

STUDENTS AND FACULTY

Enrollment: 2,203. **Student Body:** 18% female, 82% male, 27% out-of-state, 2% international (17 countries represented). African American 3%, Asian 3%, Caucasian 80%, Hispanic 3%. **Retention and Graduation:** 76% freshmen return for sophomore year. 35% freshmen graduate within 4 years. 10% grads go on to further study within 1 year. 8% grads pursue business degrees. 1% grads pursue law degrees. **Faculty:** Student/faculty ratio 12:1. 122 full-time faculty, 68% hold PhDs. 99% faculty teach undergrads.

ACADEMICS

Degrees: Bachelor's, master's. **Academic Requirements:** Computer literacy,

English (including composition), humanities, mathematics, sciences (biological or physical), social science. **Classes:** Most classes have 10–19 students. Most lab/discussion sections have 10–19 students. **Majors with Highest Enrollment:** Architectural engineering; electrical, electronics, and communications engineering; mechanical engineering. **Disciplines with Highest Percentage of Degrees Awarded:** Engineering 66%, business/marketing 19%, engineering technologies 10%, health professions and related sciences 4%, communications/journalism 1%. **Special Study Options:** Double major, dual enrollment, English as a second language (ESL), independent study, internships, study abroad, BS in international business and in electrical and mechanical engineering with Fachhochschule Lubeck, Germany. All students may apply to study at Czech Technical University, Prague, Czech Republic.

FACILITIES

Housing: Coed dorms, special housing for disabled students. **Special Academic Facilities/Equipment:** Rader School of Business, Industrial Robotics, Johnson Controls Software Engineering Lab, Fluid Power Institute, Rapid Prototyping Center, Applied Technology Center, Bio-Molecular Modeling Lab, Grohmann Art Gallery, Warren P. Knowles Nursing Lab, Harley-Davidson Design Lab, Johnson Controls Environmental Systems Lab. **Computers:** 70% of classrooms are wired, 70% of classrooms are wireless, 80% of public computers are PCs, 20% of public computers are Macs, network access in dorm rooms, network access in dorm lounges, online registration, online administrative functions (other than registration), remote student-access to Web through college's connection. Undergraduates are required to own a computer.

CAMPUS LIFE

Activities: Choral groups, concert band, dance, drama/theater, jazz band, literary magazine, pep band, radio station, student government, student newspaper, student-run film society, symphony orchestra. **Organizations:** 72 registered organizations, 5 honor societies, 5 religious organizations, 3 fraternities (3% men join), 2 sororities (5% women join). **Athletics (Intercollegiate):** *Men:* Baseball, basketball, cheerleading, crew/rowing, cross-country, golf, ice hockey, soccer, tennis, track/field (indoor), track/field (outdoor), volleyball, wrestling. *Women:* Basketball, cheerleading, crew/rowing, cross-country, golf, soccer, softball, tennis, track/field (indoor), track/field (outdoor), volleyball. Environmental Initiatives: EPA self audit initiative.

ADMISSIONS

Freshman Academic Profile: 88% from public high schools. SAT Math middle 50% range 590–685. SAT Critical Reading middle 50% range 520–630. ACT middle 50% range 25–29. TOEFL required of all international applicants, minimum paper TOEFL 550, minimum computer TOEFL 79. **Basis for Candidate Selection:** *Very important factors considered include:* Academic GPA, standardized test scores. *Important factors considered include:* Rigor of secondary school record. *Other factors considered include:* Application essay, extracurricular activities, interview, recommendation(s), talent/ability, volunteer work, work experience. **Freshman Admission Requirements:** High school diploma is required, and GED is accepted. *Academic units required:* 4 English, 4 math, 2 science. *Academic units recommended:* 4 English, 4 math, 2 science (2 science labs). **Freshman Admission Statistics:** 2,181 applied, 71% admitted, 36% enrolled. **Transfer Admission Requirements:** College transcript(s). Minimum college GPA of 2.5 required. Lowest grade transferable C. **General Admission Information:** Application fee $25. Regular notification rolling. Nonfall registration accepted. Admission may be deferred for a maximum of 2 years. Placement offered for CEEB Advanced Placement tests.

COSTS AND FINANCIAL AID

Annual tuition $27,300. Room and board $6,825. Average book expense $1,500. **Required Forms and Deadlines:** FAFSA, admission application. Financial aid filing deadline 3/15. **Notification of Awards:** Applicants will be notified of awards on a rolling basis beginning on or about 3/1. **Types of Aid:** *Need-based scholarships/grants:* Pell, SEOG, state scholarships/grants, private scholarships, the school's own gift aid. *Loans:* FFEL Subsidized Stafford, FFEL Unsubsidized Stafford, FFEL PLUS, Federal Perkins, state loans. **Student Employment:** Federal Work-Study Program available. Institutional employment available. Off-campus job opportunities are excellent. **Financial Aid Statistics:** 78% freshmen, 79% undergrads receive need-based scholarship or grant aid. 69% freshmen, 70% undergrads receive need-based self-help aid. 100% freshmen, 98% undergrads receive any aid. Highest amount earned per year from on-campus jobs $2,600.

MINNEAPOLIS COLLEGE OF ART AND DESIGN

2501 Stevens Avenue, Minneapolis, MN 55404
Phone: 612-874-3760 **E-mail:** admissions@mcad.edu **CEEB Code:** 6411
Fax: 612-874-3701 **Website:** www.mcad.edu **ACT Code:** 2130
Financial Aid Phone: 612-874-3782

This private school was founded in 1886. It has a 3-acre campus.

RATINGS
Admissions Selectivity Rating: 60*   **Fire Safety Rating:** 60*   **Green Rating:** 60*

STUDENTS AND FACULTY
Enrollment: 697. **Student Body:** 53% female, 47% male, 42% out-of-state, 1% international (10 countries represented). Asian 4%, Caucasian 81%, Hispanic 4%, Native American 1%. **Retention and Graduation:** 90% freshmen return for sophomore year. 10% grads go on to further study within 1 year. 10% grads pursue arts and sciences degrees. **Faculty:** Student/faculty ratio 13:1. 38 full-time faculty, 100% hold PhDs. 100% faculty teach undergrads.

ACADEMICS
Degrees: Bachelor's, master's, post-bachelor's certificate. **Academic Requirements:** Arts/fine arts, computer literacy, English (including composition), history, humanities. **Classes:** Most classes have 10–19 students. **Disciplines with Highest Percentage of Degrees Awarded:** Visual and performing arts 100%. **Special Study Options:** Cooperative education program, cross-registration, distance learning, independent study, internships, study abroad, arts program in New York.

FACILITIES
Housing: Coed dorms, apartments for single students. **Special Academic Facilities/Equipment:** Art gallery. **Computers:** Network access in dorm rooms.

CAMPUS LIFE
Activities: Radio station, student government, student-run film society.

ADMISSIONS
Freshman Academic Profile: 89% from public high schools. TOEFL required of all international applicants, minimum paper TOEFL 550, minimum computer TOEFL 550. **Basis for Candidate Selection:** *Very important factors considered include:* Academic GPA, application essay, recommendation(s), standardized test scores, talent/ability. *Important factors considered include:* Character/personal qualities, interview. **Freshman Admission Requirements:** High school diploma is required, and GED is accepted. *Academic units recommended:* 4 English, 4 social studies, 4 history, 4 art. **Freshman Admission Statistics:** 332 applied, 77% admitted, 44% enrolled. **Transfer Admission Requirements:** High school transcript, college transcript(s), essay or personal statement, standardized test score. Minimum college GPA of 2.5 required. Lowest grade transferable C-. **General Admission Information:** Application fee $35. Regular application deadline 5/1. Regular notification rolling. Nonfall registration accepted. Admission may be deferred for a maximum of 1 semester. Credit offered for CEEB Advanced Placement tests.

COSTS AND FINANCIAL AID
Annual tuition $27,000. Room and board $4,160. Required fees $200. Average book expense $2,300. **Required Forms and Deadlines:** FAFSA. Financial aid filing deadline 3/15. **Notification of Awards:** Applicants will be notified of awards on a rolling basis beginning on or about 3/30. **Types of Aid:** *Need-based scholarships/grants:* Pell, SEOG, state scholarships/grants, private scholarships, the school's own gift aid. *Loans:* FFEL Subsidized Stafford, FFEL Unsubsidized Stafford, FFEL PLUS, Federal Perkins, state loans. **Student Employment:** Federal Work-Study Program available. Institutional employment available. Off-campus job opportunities are good. **Financial Aid Statistics:** 63% freshmen, 71% undergrads receive need-based scholarship or grant aid. 65% freshmen, 72% undergrads receive need-based self-help aid. Highest amount earned per year from on-campus jobs $1,656.

MINNESOTA STATE UNIVERSITY—MANKATO

Room 122, Taylor Center, Mankato, MN 56001
Phone: 507-389-1822 **E-mail:** admissions@mnsu.edu **CEEB Code:** 6677
Fax: 507-389-1511 **Website:** www.mnsu.edu **ACT Code:** 2126
Financial Aid Phone: 507-389-1866

This public school was founded in 1868. It has a 354-acre campus.

RATINGS
Admissions Selectivity Rating: 63   **Fire Safety Rating:** 60*   **Green Rating:** 67

STUDENTS AND FACULTY
Enrollment: 12,048. **Student Body:** 52% female, 48% male, 13% out-of-state, 3% international (68 countries represented). African American 3%, Asian 2%, Caucasian 84%, Hispanic 1%. **Retention and Graduation:** 78% freshmen return for sophomore year. 19% freshmen graduate within 4 years. 11% grads go on to further study within 1 year. **Faculty:** Student/faculty ratio 22:1. 492 full-time faculty, 79% hold PhDs. 96% faculty teach undergrads.

ACADEMICS
Degrees: Associate, bachelor's, certificate, master's, post-master's certificate. **Academic Requirements:** Arts/fine arts, English (including composition), history, mathematics, sciences (biological or physical), social science, cultural diversity. **Classes:** Most classes have 20–29 students. Most lab/discussion sections have 20–29 students. **Majors with Highest Enrollment:** Biology/biological sciences, business administration and management, elementary education and teaching. **Disciplines with Highest Percentage of Degrees Awarded:** Business/marketing 20%, education 15%, health professions and related sciences 11%, security and protective services 7%, social sciences 5%. **Special Study Options:** Cross-registration, distance learning, double major, dual enrollment, English as a second language (ESL), exchange student program (domestic), external degree program, honors program, independent study, internships, student-designed major, study abroad, teacher certification program.

FACILITIES
Housing: Coed dorms, special housing for disabled students, fraternity/sorority housing. **Special Academic Facilities/Equipment:** 2 art galleries, day care facilities, 2 astronomy observatories, black box theater. **Computers:** 100% of classrooms are wired, 100% of classrooms are wireless, 85% of public computers are PCs, 15% of public computers are Macs, network access in dorm rooms, network access in dorm lounges, online registration, online administrative functions (other than registration), support for handheld computing, remote student-access to Web through college's connection.

CAMPUS LIFE
Activities: Choral groups, concert band, dance, drama/theater, jazz band, literary magazine, music ensembles, musical theater, pep band, radio station, student government, student newspaper, symphony orchestra. **Organizations:** 175 registered organizations, 12 honor societies, 14 religious organizations. 7 fraternities (3% men join), 4 sororities (3% women join). **Athletics (Intercollegiate):** *Men:* Baseball, basketball, cross-country, diving, football, golf, ice hockey, swimming, tennis, track/field (indoor), track/field (outdoor), wrestling. *Women:* Basketball, bowling, cross-country, diving, golf, ice hockey, soccer, softball, swimming, tennis, track/field (indoor), track/field (outdoor), volleyball.

ADMISSIONS
Freshman Academic Profile: 8% in top 10% of high school class, 27% in top 25% of high school class, 71% in top 50% of high school class. 95% from public high schools. ACT middle 50% range 20–24. TOEFL required of all international applicants, minimum paper TOEFL 500, minimum computer TOEFL 173. **Basis for Candidate Selection:** *Very important factors considered include:* Class rank, standardized test scores. *Important factors considered include:* Rigor of secondary school record. *Other factors considered include:* Academic GPA, recommendation(s). **Freshman Admission Requirements:** High school diploma is required, and GED is accepted. *Academic units required:* 4 English, 3 math, 3 science (3 science labs), 2 foreign language, 2 social studies, 1 history, 1 world culture/arts elective. **Freshman Admission Statistics:** 5,653 applied, 89% admitted, 43% enrolled. **Transfer Admission Requirements:** College transcript(s). Minimum college GPA of 2.0 required. Lowest grade transferable D. **General Admission Information:** Application fee $20. Regular notification rolling basis beginning after junior year ends. Nonfall registration accepted. Admission may be deferred. Credit offered for CEEB Advanced Placement tests.

COSTS AND FINANCIAL AID
Required Forms and Deadlines: FAFSA, SELF or Alternative Loan Application or PLUS Application. Financial aid filing deadline 3/15. **Notifica-**

tion of Awards: Applicants will be notified of awards on a rolling basis beginning on or about 3/30. **Types of Aid:** *Need-based scholarships/grants:* Pell, SEOG, state scholarships/grants, private scholarships, the school's own gift aid. *Loans:* FFEL Subsidized Stafford, FFEL Unsubsidized Stafford, FFEL PLUS, Federal Perkins, state loans, SELF Loans. **Student Employment:** Federal Work-Study Program available. Institutional employment available. Off-campus job opportunities are good. **Financial Aid Statistics:** 32% freshmen, 33% undergrads receive need-based scholarship or grant aid. 45% freshmen, 45% undergrads receive need-based self-help aid. 60 freshmen, 226 undergrads receive athletic scholarships. 70% freshmen, 65% undergrads receive any aid.

MINNESOTA STATE UNIVERSITY—MOORHEAD

Owens Hall, MSU Moorhead, Moorhead, MN 56563
Phone: 218-477-2161 **E-mail:** dragon@mnstate.edu **CEEB Code:** 6678
Fax: 218-477-4374 **Website:** www.mnstate.edu **ACT Code:** 2134
Financial Aid Phone: 218-477-2251

This public school was founded in 1887. It has a 129-acre campus.

RATINGS
Admissions Selectivity Rating: 68   **Fire Safety Rating:** 60*   **Green Rating:** 60*

STUDENTS AND FACULTY
Enrollment: 6,854. **Student Body:** 59% female, 41% male, 43% out-of-state, 3% international (42 countries represented). African American 1%, Asian 1%, Caucasian 79%, Native American 1%. **Retention and Graduation:** 68% freshmen return for sophomore year. 18% freshmen graduate within 4 years. 15% grads go on to further study within 1 year. **Faculty:** Student/faculty ratio 20:1. 270 full-time faculty. 99% faculty teach undergrads.

ACADEMICS
Degrees: Associate, bachelor's, certificate, master's, post-bachelor's certificate, post-master's certificate. **Academic Requirements:** Arts/fine arts, English (including composition), humanities, mathematics, sciences (biological or physical), social science, multicultural & global studies. **Classes:** Most classes have 20–29 students. Most lab/discussion sections have 20–29 students. **Majors with Highest Enrollment:** Business administration and management, elementary education and teaching, mass communications/media studies. **Disciplines with Highest Percentage of Degrees Awarded:** Education 21%, business/marketing 19%, communications/journalism 8%, visual and performing arts 7%, health professions and related sciences 6%. **Special Study Options:** Cross-registration, distance learning, double major, dual enrollment, exchange student program (domestic), external degree program, honors program, independent study, internships, student-designed major, study abroad, teacher certification program.

FACILITIES
Housing: Coed dorms, men's dorms, women's dorms, apartments for single students, special housing for disabled students, fraternity/sorority housing. **Special Academic Facilities/Equipment:** Art and biology museums on-campus, preschool, planetarium, regional science center, Center for Business, new science building, wellness center. **Computers:** 65% of public computers are PCs, 35% of public computers are Macs, network access in dorm rooms, network access in dorm lounges, online registration, online administrative functions (other than registration), remote student-access to Web through college's connection.

CAMPUS LIFE
Activities: Choral groups, concert band, dance, drama/theater, jazz band, literary magazine, music ensembles, musical theater, radio station, student government, student newspaper, student-run film society, symphony orchestra, television station. **Organizations:** 109 registered organizations, 7 honor societies, 8 religious organizations. 1 fraternity (3% men join), 2 sororities (2% women join). **Athletics (Intercollegiate):** *Men:* Basketball, cross-country, football, track/field (indoor), track/field (outdoor), wrestling. *Women:* Basketball, cross-country, diving, golf, soccer, softball, swimming, tennis, track/field (indoor), track/field (outdoor), volleyball.

ADMISSIONS
Freshman Academic Profile: 10% in top 10% of high school class, 28% in top 25% of high school class, 63% in top 50% of high school class. 98% from public high schools. SAT Math middle 50% range 465–535. SAT Critical Reading middle 50% range 480–580. ACT middle 50% range 19–24. TOEFL required of all international applicants, minimum paper TOEFL 500, minimum computer TOEFL 173. **Basis for Candidate Selection:** *Very important*

factors considered include: Academic GPA, class rank, rigor of secondary school record, standardized test scores. **Freshman Admission Requirements:** High school diploma is required, and GED is accepted. *Academic units required:* 4 English, 3 math, 3 science (1 science lab), 3 social studies, 3 academic electives. **Freshman Admission Statistics:** 2,783 applied, 83% admitted, 49% enrolled. **Transfer Admission Requirements:** College transcript(s), statement of good standing from prior institution(s). Minimum college GPA of 2.0 required. Lowest grade transferable D. **General Admission Information:** Application fee $20. Regular application deadline 8/1. Regular notification is rolling. Nonfall registration accepted. Admission may be deferred. Common Application not accepted. Credit and/or placement offered for CEEB Advanced Placement tests.

COSTS AND FINANCIAL AID
Annual tuition $4,464. Room & board $4,974. Required fees $761. Average book expense $800. **Required Forms and Deadlines:** FAFSA. Financial aid filing deadline 3/1. **Notification of Awards:** Applicants will be notified of awards on or about 6/15. **Types of Aid:** *Need-based scholarships/grants:* Pell, SEOG, state scholarships/grants, the school's own gift aid. *Loans:* Direct Subsidized Stafford, Direct Unsubsidized Stafford, Direct PLUS, Federal Perkins, state loans. **Student Employment:** Federal Work-Study Program available. Institutional employment available. Off-campus job opportunities are excellent. **Financial Aid Statistics:** 30% freshmen, 31% undergrads receive need-based scholarship or grant aid. 42% freshmen, 50% undergrads receive need-based self-help aid. 88% freshmen, 70% undergrads receive any aid. Highest amount earned per year from on-campus jobs $1,550.

MINOT STATE UNIVERSITY

500 University Avenue W, Minot, ND 58707
Phone: 701-858-3350 **E-mail:** msu@minotstateu.edu **CEEB Code:** 2994
Fax: 701-858-3386 **Website:** www.minotstateu.edu **ACT Code:** 3214
Financial Aid Phone: 701-858-3375

This public school was founded in 1913. It has a 103-acre campus.

RATINGS
Admissions Selectivity Rating: 60*   **Fire Safety Rating:** 60*   **Green Rating:** 60*

STUDENTS AND FACULTY
Enrollment: 3,425. **Student Body:** 63% female, 37% male, 8% out-of-state, 5% international (18 countries represented). African American 3%, Asian 1%, Caucasian 85%, Hispanic 2%, Native American 4%. **Retention and Graduation:** 70% freshmen return for sophomore year. 12% grads go on to further study within 1 year. **Faculty:** Student/faculty ratio 16:1. 164 full-time faculty, 50% hold PhDs. 100% faculty teach undergrads.

ACADEMICS
Degrees: Associate, bachelor's, certificate, master's, post-master's certificate. **Academic Requirements:** English (including composition), history, humanities, mathematics, sciences (biological or physical), social science, wellness/personal development. **Classes:** Most classes have 10–19 students. Most lab/discussion sections have fewer than 10 students. **Majors with Highest Enrollment:** Business administration/management, criminal justice/safety studies, elementary education and teaching. **Disciplines with Highest Percentage of Degrees Awarded:** Education 24%, business/marketing 24%, health professions and related sciences 13%, psychology 6%, computer and information sciences 4%, liberal arts/general studies 3%, social sciences 3%. **Special Study Options:** Accelerated program, cooperative education program, distance learning, double major, dual enrollment, external degree program, honors program, independent study, internships, student-designed major, study abroad, teacher certification program.

FACILITIES
Housing: Coed dorms, men's dorms, women's dorms, apartments for married students, apartments for single students, special housing for disabled students. **Special Academic Facilities/Equipment:** Art galleries, natural history museum, North Dakota Center for Persons with Disabilities, Native American collection, observatory. **Computers:** 75% of public computers are PCs, 20% of public computers are Macs, 5% of public computers are UNIX, network access in dorm rooms, network access in dorm lounges, online registration, remote student-access to Web through college's connection.

CAMPUS LIFE
Activities: Choral groups, concert band, drama/theater, jazz band, literary magazine, marching band, music ensembles, musical theater, opera, pep band, radio station, student government, student newspaper, symphony orchestra,

television station, yearbook. **Organizations:** 59 registered organizations, 5 honor societies, 5 religious organizations. **Athletics (Intercollegiate):** *Men:* Baseball, basketball, cross-country, football, golf, track/field (indoor), track/field (outdoor). *Women:* Basketball, cheerleading, cross-country, golf, softball, track/field (indoor), track/field (outdoor), volleyball.

ADMISSIONS

Freshman Academic Profile: 98% from public high schools. ACT middle 50% range 18–23. TOEFL required of all international applicants, minimum paper TOEFL 525, minimum computer TOEFL 195. **Basis for Candidate Selection:** *Very important factors considered include:* Rigor of secondary school record, standardized test scores. **Freshman Admission Requirements:** High school diploma is required, and GED is accepted. *Academic units required:* 4 English, 3 math, 3 science (3 science labs), 3 social studies. *Academic units recommended:* 2 foreign language. **Freshman Admission Statistics:** 743 applied, 86% admitted, 89% enrolled. **Transfer Admission Requirements:** College transcript(s). Minimum college GPA of 2.0 required. Lowest grade transferable D. **General Admission Information:** Application fee $35. Regular notification as soon as application is processed. Nonfall registration accepted. Admission may be deferred. Common Application not accepted. Credit and/or placement offered for CEEB Advanced Placement tests.

COSTS AND FINANCIAL AID

Annual in-state tuition $2,244. Out-of-state tuition $5,991. Room & board $3,000. Required fees $310. Average book expense $700. **Required Forms and Deadlines:** FAFSA, institution's own financial aid form. Financial aid filing deadline 4/15. **Notification of Awards:** Applicants will be notified of awards on or about 6/1. **Types of Aid:** *Need-based scholarships/grants:* Pell, SEOG, state scholarships/grants, private scholarships, the school's own gift aid, Federal Nursing Scholarships. *Loans:* FFEL Subsidized Stafford, FFEL Unsubsidized Stafford, FFEL PLUS, Federal Perkins, Federal Nursing. **Student Employment:** Federal Work-Study Program available. Institutional employment available. Off-campus job opportunities are excellent. **Financial Aid Statistics:** 35% freshmen, 37% undergrads receive need-based scholarship or grant aid. 47% freshmen, 55% undergrads receive need-based self-help aid. 94 undergrads receive athletic scholarships.

MINOT STATE UNIVERSITY— BOTTINEAU CAMPUS

105 Simrall Blvd., Bottineau, ND 58318
Phone: 800-542-6866 **E-mail:** groszk@misu.nodak.edu
Fax: 701-288-5499 **Website:** www.misu-b.nodak.edu **ACT Code:** 2304
Financial Aid Phone: 701-228-5437

This public school was founded in 1907. It has a 36-acre campus.

RATINGS
Admissions Selectivity Rating: 60*   **Fire Safety Rating:** 60*   **Green Rating:** 60*

STUDENTS AND FACULTY
Enrollment: 450. **Student Body:** 52% female, 48% male, 14% out-of-state, 4% international. African American 1%, Caucasian 86%, Native American 8%. **Retention and Graduation:** 65% freshmen return for sophomore year. 50% grads go on to further study within 1 year. **Faculty:** Student/faculty ratio 11:1. 26 full-time faculty, 8% hold PhDs. 100% faculty teach undergrads.

ACADEMICS
Degrees: Associate, certificate, diploma. **Academic Requirements:** Arts/fine arts, computer literacy, English (including composition), history, humanities, mathematics, sciences (biological or physical), social science. **Special Study Options:** Cooperative education program, distance learning, double major, dual enrollment, independent study.

FACILITIES
Housing: Coed dorms, men's dorms, women's dorms. **Computers:** Network access in dorm rooms.

CAMPUS LIFE
Activities: Choral groups, concert band, dance, drama/theater, jazz band, music ensembles, pep band, student government, student newspaper. **Organizations:** 6 registered organizations. **Athletics (Intercollegiate):** *Men:* Baseball, basketball, cheerleading, ice hockey. *Women:* Basketball, cheerleading, volleyball.

ADMISSIONS

Freshman Admission Requirements: High school diploma is required, and GED is accepted. **Freshman Admission Statistics:** 238 applied, 100% admitted, 73% enrolled. **Transfer Admission Requirements:** College transcript(s), **General Admission Information:** Application fee $25. Nonfall registration accepted. Admission may be deferred. Common Application not accepted. Neither credit nor placement offered for CEEB Advanced Placement tests.

COSTS AND FINANCIAL AID

Annual in-state tuition $1,632. Out-of-state tuition $4,357. Room & board $2,816. Required fees $326. Average book expense $600. **Required Forms and Deadlines:** FAFSA. Financial aid filing deadline 4/15. **Notification of Awards:** Applicants will be notified of awards on or about 5/15. **Types of Aid:** *Need-based scholarships/grants:* Pell, SEOG, state scholarships/grants, private scholarships, the school's own gift aid. *Loans:* FFEL Subsidized Stafford, FFEL Unsubsidized Stafford, FFEL PLUS, Federal Perkins. **Student Employment:** Federal Work-Study Program available. Institutional employment available. Off-campus job opportunities are fair.

MISSISSIPPI COLLEGE

Box 4026, Clinton, MS 39058
Phone: 601-925-3800 **E-mail:** enrollment-services@mc.edu **CEEB Code:** 1477
Fax: 601-925-3950 **Website:** www.mc.edu **ACT Code:** 2214
Financial Aid Phone: 601-925-3212

This private school, affiliated with the Southern Baptist Church, was founded in 1826. It has a 320-acre campus.

RATINGS
Admissions Selectivity Rating: 85   **Fire Safety Rating:** 77   **Green Rating:** 60*

STUDENTS AND FACULTY
Enrollment: 2,629. **Student Body:** 61% female, 39% male, 15% out-of-state, 2% international (19 countries represented). African American 24%, Caucasian 70%. **Retention and Graduation:** 68% freshmen return for sophomore year. 46% freshmen graduate within 4 years. 23% grads go on to further study within 1 year. 3% grads pursue law degrees. 3% grads pursue medical degrees. **Faculty:** Student/faculty ratio 15:1. 158 full-time faculty, 79% hold PhDs. 85% faculty teach undergrads.

ACADEMICS
Degrees: Bachelor's, first professional, master's, post-bachelor's certificate. **Academic Requirements:** Arts/fine arts, computer literacy, English (including composition), history, mathematics, sciences (biological or physical), social science, Bible, physical education, foreign language (if in BA degree program). **Classes:** Most classes have 10–19 students. Most lab/discussion sections have fewer than 10 students. **Majors with Highest Enrollment:** Biology/biological sciences, business administration and management, elementary education and teaching. **Disciplines with Highest Percentage of Degrees Awarded:** Business/marketing 23%, health professions and related sciences 18%, education 13%, psychology 6%, communications/journalism 5%, visual and performing arts 5%. **Special Study Options:** Accelerated program, double major, dual enrollment, English as a second language (ESL), honors program, independent study, internships, study abroad, teacher certification program, academic remediation, Advance Placement credit, work-study program, learning disabilities services.

FACILITIES
Housing: Men's dorms, women's dorms, special housing for disabled students. **Computers:** 1% of classrooms are wired, 5% of classrooms are wireless, 94% of public computers are PCs, 4% of public computers are Macs, 2% of public computers are UNIX, network access in dorm rooms, network access in dorm lounges, online registration, online administrative functions (other than registration), remote student-access to Web through college's connection.

CAMPUS LIFE
Activities: Choral groups, concert band, drama/theater, jazz band, literary magazine, marching band, music ensembles, musical theater, opera, radio station, student government, student newspaper, yearbook. **Organizations:** 65 registered organizations, 21 honor societies, 6 religious organizations. 5 fraternities, 4 sororities. **Athletics (Intercollegiate):** *Men:* Baseball, basketball, cross-country, football, golf, soccer, tennis, track/field (outdoor). *Women:* Basketball, cheerleading, cross-country, soccer, softball, tennis, track/field (outdoor), volleyball.

ADMISSIONS

Freshman Academic Profile: 30% in top 10% of high school class, 59% in top 25% of high school class, 84% in top 50% of high school class. SAT Math middle 50% range 450–580. SAT Critical Reading middle 50% range 460–580. ACT middle 50% range 20–26. TOEFL required of all international applicants, minimum paper TOEFL 500, minimum computer TOEFL 173. **Basis for Candidate Selection:** *Very important factors considered include:* Standardized test scores. *Important factors considered include:* Character/personal qualities, extracurricular activities, level of applicant's interest, rigor of secondary school record. *Other factors considered include:* Academic GPA, alumni/ae relation, class rank, interview, recommendation(s), talent/ability, volunteer work, work experience. **Freshman Admission Requirements:** High school diploma is required, and GED is accepted. *Academic units recommended:* 4 English, 3 math, 3 science (1 science lab), 1 foreign language, 3 social studies, 1 history, 5 academic electives. **Freshman Admission Statistics:** 1,685 applied, 54% admitted, 49% enrolled. **Transfer Admission Requirements:** College transcript(s), essay or personal statement, statement of good standing from prior institution(s). Minimum college GPA of 2.0 required. Lowest grade transferable C. **General Admission Information:** Early decision application deadline 12/1. Regular notification as applications are received. Nonfall registration accepted. Admission may be deferred for a maximum of 1 year. Credit offered for CEEB Advanced Placement tests.

COSTS AND FINANCIAL AID

Annual tuition $12,200. Room and board $6,400. Required fees $600. Average book expense $900. **Required Forms and Deadlines:** FAFSA, state aid form. Financial aid filing deadline 3/1. **Notification of Awards:** Applicants will be notified of awards on a rolling basis beginning on or about 3/1. **Types of Aid:** *Need-based scholarships/grants:* Pell, SEOG, state scholarships/grants, private scholarships, the school's own gift aid, Federal Nursing Scholarships. *Loans:* FFEL Subsidized Stafford, FFEL Unsubsidized Stafford, FFEL PLUS, Federal Perkins, Federal Nursing, college/university loans from institutional funds. **Student Employment:** Federal Work-Study Program available. **Financial Aid Statistics:** 25% freshmen, 31% undergrads receive need-based scholarship or grant aid. 32% freshmen, 43% undergrads receive need-based self-help aid. 80% freshmen, 75% undergrads receive any aid. Highest amount earned per year from on-campus jobs $2,100.

MISSISSIPPI STATE UNIVERSITY

PO Box 6334, Mississippi State, MS 39762
Phone: 662-325-2224 **E-mail:** admit@admissions.msstate.edu **CEEB Code:** 1480
Fax: 662-325-1678 **Website:** www.msstate.edu **ACT Code:** 2220
Financial Aid Phone: 662-325-2450

This public school was founded in 1878. It has a 4,200-acre campus.

RATINGS

Admissions Selectivity Rating: 80   Fire Safety Rating: 60*   Green Rating: 60*

STUDENTS AND FACULTY

Enrollment: 11,321. **Student Body:** 48% female, 52% male, 17% out-of-state. African American 19%, Asian 1%, Caucasian 77%. **Retention and Graduation:** 82% freshmen return for sophomore year. **Faculty:** Student/faculty ratio 14:1. 854 full-time faculty, 82% hold PhDs.

ACADEMICS

Degrees: Bachelor's, doctoral, first professional, master's, post-master's certificate. **Academic Requirements:** Arts/fine arts, computer literacy, English (including composition), history, humanities, mathematics, sciences (biological or physical), social science. **Classes:** Most classes have 20–29 students. Most lab/discussion sections have fewer than 10 students. **Majors with Highest Enrollment:** Business administration/management, elementary education and teaching, geology/earth science. **Disciplines with Highest Percentage of Degrees Awarded:** Business/marketing 24%, education 16%, engineering 11%, interdisciplinary studies 6%, agriculture 6%. **Special Study Options:** Cooperative education program, distance learning, double major, dual enrollment, English as a second language (ESL), exchange student program (domestic), honors program, independent study, internships, liberal arts/career combination, student-designed major, study abroad, teacher certification program, weekend college.

FACILITIES

Housing: Coed dorms, men's dorms, women's dorms, apartments for married students, apartments for single students, special housing for disabled students, fraternity/sorority housing. **Special Academic Facilities/Equipment:** Geology, archaeology, music, entomological museums, art gallery, flight research lab. **Computers:** 10% of classrooms are wired, 75% of classrooms are wireless, 94% of public computers are PCs, 5% of public computers are Macs, 1% of public computers are UNIX, network access in dorm rooms, network access in dorm lounges, online registration, online administrative functions (other than registration), remote student-access to Web through college's connection.

CAMPUS LIFE

Activities: Choral groups, concert band, dance, drama/theater, jazz band, literary magazine, marching band, music ensembles, musical theater, pep band, radio station, student government, student newspaper, symphony orchestra, television station, yearbook. **Organizations:** 313 registered organizations, 42 honor societies, 24 religious organizations. 17 fraternities (11% men join), 11 sororities (14% women join). **Athletics (Intercollegiate):** *Men:* Baseball, basketball, cheerleading, cross-country, football, golf, tennis, track/field (outdoor). *Women:* Basketball, cheerleading, cross-country, golf, soccer, softball, tennis, track/field (outdoor), volleyball.

ADMISSIONS

Freshman Academic Profile: 27% in top 10% of high school class, 55% in top 25% of high school class, 82% in top 50% of high school class. SAT Math middle 50% range 500–640. SAT Critical Reading middle 50% range 490–630. ACT middle 50% range 20–27. TOEFL required of all international applicants, minimum paper TOEFL 525, minimum computer TOEFL 197. **Basis for Candidate Selection:** *Very important factors considered include:* Academic GPA, standardized test scores. *Important factors considered include:* Class rank. *Other factors considered include:* Rigor of secondary school record, talent/ability. **Freshman Admission Requirements:** High school diploma is required, and GED is accepted. *Academic units required:* 4 English, 3 math, 3 science (2 science labs), 1 social studies, 2 history, 2 academic electives. *Academic units recommended:* 4 English, 4 math, 4 science (2 science labs), 1 foreign language, 2 social studies, 2 history, 2 academic electives, 1 world geography. **Freshman Admission Statistics:** 5,140 applied, 70% admitted, 54% enrolled. **Transfer Admission Requirements:** College transcript(s), statement of good standing from prior institution(s). Minimum college GPA of 2.0 required. Lowest grade transferable D. **General Admission Information:** Application fee $25. Regular notification is rolling. Nonfall registration accepted. Credit offered for CEEB Advanced Placement tests.

COSTS AND FINANCIAL AID

Annual in-state tuition $4,978. Annual out-of-state tuition $11,469. Room and board $6,951. Average book expense $1,000. **Required Forms and Deadlines:** FAFSA, state grant/scholarship application. Financial aid filing deadline 4/1. **Notification of Awards:** Applicants will be notified of awards on a rolling basis beginning on or about 12/1. **Types of Aid:** *Need-based scholarships/grants:* Pell, SEOG, state scholarships/grants, private scholarships, the school's own gift aid, United Negro College Fund. *Loans:* FFEL Subsidized Stafford, FFEL Unsubsidized Stafford, FFEL PLUS, Federal Perkins, college/university loans from institutional funds. **Student Employment:** Federal Work-Study Program available. Institutional employment available. Off-campus job opportunities are good. **Financial Aid Statistics:** 56% freshmen, 47% undergrads receive need-based scholarship or grant aid. 37% freshmen, 40% undergrads receive need-based self-help aid. 79 freshmen, 328 undergrads receive athletic scholarships. 84% freshmen, 75% undergrads receive any aid.

MISSISSIPPI UNIVERSITY FOR WOMEN

West Box 1613, Columbus, MS 39701
Phone: 662-329-7106 **E-mail:** admissions@muw.edu **CEEB Code:** 1481
Fax: 662-241-7481 **Website:** www.muw.edu **ACT Code:** 2222
Financial Aid Phone: 662-329-7114

This public school was founded in 1884. It has a 104-acre campus.

RATINGS

Admissions Selectivity Rating: 88   Fire Safety Rating: 60*   Green Rating: 60*

STUDENTS AND FACULTY

Enrollment: 3,180. **Student Body:** 81% female, 19% male, 9% out-of-state, 2% international (36 countries represented). African American 28%, Caucasian

69%. **Retention and Graduation:** 64% freshmen return for sophomore year. 21% freshmen graduate within 4 years. **Faculty:** 86% faculty teach undergrads.

ACADEMICS

Degrees: Associate, bachelor's, master's. **Academic Requirements:** Arts/fine arts, computer literacy, English (including composition), history, humanities, mathematics, sciences (biological or physical), social science. **Special Study Options:** Accelerated program, cooperative education program, cross-registration, distance learning, double major, English as a second language (ESL), honors program, internships, study abroad, teacher certification program, weekend college.

FACILITIES

Housing: Men's dorms, women's dorms, apartments for single students with children. **Special Academic Facilities/Equipment:** Museum/gallery, university archives, language lab, TV studio, residential high school for gifted students, elementary school, speech and hearing center. **Computers:** 99% of public computers are PCs, 1% of public computers are Macs, network access in dorm rooms, network access in dorm lounges, online administrative functions (other than registration), remote student-access to Web through college's connection.

CAMPUS LIFE

Activities: Choral groups, dance, drama/theater, literary magazine, music ensembles, radio station, student government, student newspaper, television station, yearbook. **Organizations:** 78 registered organizations, 17 honor societies, 3 religious organizations. 2 fraternities (6% men join), 17 sororities (15% women join). **Athletics (Intercollegiate):** *Women:* Basketball, cheerleading, softball, tennis, volleyball.

ADMISSIONS

Freshman Academic Profile: 79% in top 10% of high school class, 68% in top 25% of high school class, 92% in top 50% of high school class. 65% from public high schools. ACT middle 50% range 21–27. TOEFL required of all international applicants, minimum paper TOEFL 525. **Basis for Candidate Selection:** *Very important factors considered include:* Class rank, rigor of secondary school record, standardized test scores. *Other factors considered include:* Alumni/ae relation, character/personal qualities, extracurricular activities, recommendation(s), talent/ability. **Freshman Admission Requirements:** High school diploma is required, and GED is accepted. *Academic units required:* 4 English, 3 math, 3 science (2 science labs), 3 social studies, 2 academic electives, 1 computer. *Academic units recommended:* 4 math, 1 foreign language. **Freshman Admission Statistics:** 855 applied, 78% admitted, 64% enrolled. **Transfer Admission Requirements:** College transcript(s). Minimum college GPA of 2.0 required. **General Admission Information:** Regular notification. Nonfall registration accepted. Common Application accepted. Credit offered for CEEB Advanced Placement tests.

COSTS AND FINANCIAL AID

Annual in-state tuition $2,556. Out-of-state tuition $5,546. Room & board $2,557. Average book expense $600. **Required Forms and Deadlines:** Financial aid filing deadline 4/1. **Notification of Awards:** Applicants will be notified of awards on a rolling basis beginning on or about 4/15. **Types of Aid:** *Need-based scholarships/grants:* Pell, SEOG, state scholarships/grants, private scholarships, the school's own gift aid, Federal Nursing Scholarships. *Loans:* FFEL Subsidized Stafford, FFEL Unsubsidized Stafford, FFEL PLUS, Federal Perkins. **Student Employment:** Federal Work-Study Program available. Institutional employment available. Off-campus job opportunities are fair. **Financial Aid Statistics:** 36% freshmen, 42% undergrads receive need-based scholarship or grant aid. 34% freshmen, 31% undergrads receive need-based self-help aid. 8 freshmen, 40 undergrads receive athletic scholarships. Highest amount earned per year from on-campus jobs $1,185.

MISSISSIPPI VALLEY STATE UNIVERSITY

14000 Highway 82 West, Itta Bena, MS 38941-1400
Phone: 662-254-3344 **E-mail:** nbtaylor@mvsu.edu **CEEB Code:** 1482
Fax: 662-254-3655 **Website:** www.mvsu.edu **ACT Code:** 2224
Financial Aid Phone: 662-254-3338

This public school was founded in 1950. It has a 250-acre campus.

RATINGS

Admissions Selectivity Rating: 73   **Fire Safety Rating:** 72   **Green Rating:** 60*

STUDENTS AND FACULTY

Enrollment: 2,639. **Student Body:** 66% female, 34% male, 12% out-of-state. African American 94%, Caucasian 5%. **Retention and Graduation:** 62%

---

freshmen return for sophomore year. 13% freshmen graduate within 4 years. **Faculty:** Student/faculty ratio 20:1. 121 full-time faculty, 63% hold PhDs. 100% faculty teach undergrads.

ACADEMICS

Degrees: Bachelor's, master's. **Academic Requirements:** Arts/fine arts, English (including composition), mathematics, sciences (biological or physical), social science, health education, physical education, speech, general psychology. **Classes:** Most classes have 20–29 students. Most lab/discussion sections have 30–39 students. **Majors with Highest Enrollment:** History, kindergarten/preschool education and teaching, social work. **Disciplines with Highest Percentage of Degrees Awarded:** Education 33%, public administration and social services 15%, business/marketing 12%, history 10%, security and protective services 6%, English 6%. **Special Study Options:** Cooperative education program, distance learning, double major, honors program, internships, teacher certification program, weekend college. Co-op programs in business, computer science, natural science, social/behavioral science.

FACILITIES

Housing: Men's dorms, women's dorms, apartments for married students, apartments for single students. **Computers:** 95% of public computers are PCs, 5% of public computers are Macs, network access in dorm rooms, network access in dorm lounges, online registration, remote student-access to Web through college's connection.

CAMPUS LIFE

Activities: Choral groups, concert band, drama/theater, marching band, radio station, student government, student newspaper, yearbook. **Organizations:** 35 registered organizations, 19 honor societies, 6 religious organizations. 5 fraternities, 4 sororities. **Athletics (Intercollegiate):** *Men:* Basketball, cross-country, track/field (outdoor), volleyball. *Women:* Basketball, cross-country, track/field (outdoor), volleyball.

ADMISSIONS

Freshman Academic Profile: 27% in top 25% of high school class, 64% in top 50% of high school class. 96% from public high schools. ACT middle 50% range 15–18. TOEFL required of all international applicants, minimum paper TOEFL 525, minimum computer TOEFL 195. **Basis for Candidate Selection:** *Very important factors considered include:* Class rank, rigor of secondary school record, standardized test scores, state residency. *Other factors considered include:* Extracurricular activities, interview, recommendation(s), talent/ability. **Freshman Admission Requirements:** High school diploma is required, and GED is accepted. *Academic units required:* 4 English, 3 math, 3 science (2 science labs), 3 social studies, 2 academic electives, 1 computer applications. *Academic units recommended:* 1 foreign language. **Freshman Admission Statistics:** 3,739 applied, 32% admitted, 37% enrolled. **Transfer Admission Requirements:** College transcript(s). Minimum college GPA of 2.0 required. Lowest grade transferable C. **General Admission Information:** Nonfall registration accepted.

COSTS AND FINANCIAL AID

Annual in-state tuition $4,417. Annual out-of-state tuition $10,198. Room and board $4,542. Average book expense $1,000. **Required Forms and Deadlines:** FAFSA, institution's own financial aid form. Financial aid filing deadline 4/1. **Notification of Awards:** Applicants will be notified of awards on or about 7/15. **Types of Aid:** *Need-based scholarships/grants:* Pell, SEOG, state scholarships/grants, private scholarships, the school's own gift aid. *Loans:* Direct Unsubsidized Stafford, Direct PLUS. **Financial Aid Statistics:** 95% freshmen, 95% undergrads receive any aid.

MISSOURI BAPTIST COLLEGE

One College Park Drive, St. Louis, MO 63141-8660
Phone: 314-434-1115 **E-mail:** admissions@mobap.edu **CEEB Code:** 2258
Fax: 314-434-7596 **Website:** www.mobap.edu **ACT Code:** 2323
Financial Aid Phone: 314-392-2368

This private school, affiliated with the Southern Baptist Church, was founded in 1964. It has a 65-acre campus.

RATINGS

Admissions Selectivity Rating: 69   **Fire Safety Rating:** 60*   **Green Rating:** 60*

STUDENTS AND FACULTY

Enrollment: 1,151. **Student Body:** 59% female, 41% male, 11% out-of-state, 3% international. African American 5%, Caucasian 84%, Hispanic 2%. **Retention and Graduation:** 61% freshmen return for sophomore year. 29%

freshmen graduate within 4 years. **Faculty:** Student/faculty ratio 16:1. 37 full-time faculty, 59% hold PhDs. 100% faculty teach undergrads.

ACADEMICS

Degrees: Associate, bachelor's, certificate, master's, post-bachelor's certificate. **Academic Requirements:** Arts/fine arts, computer literacy, English (including composition), foreign languages, history, humanities, mathematics, philosophy, sciences (biological or physical), social science. **Classes:** Most classes have 10–19 students. Most lab/discussion sections have 10–19 students. **Disciplines with Highest Percentage of Degrees Awarded:** Education 27%, business/marketing 18%, parks and recreation 6%, interdisciplinary studies 5%, psychology 5%, health professions and related sciences 5%, communication technologies 4%. **Special Study Options:** Accelerated program, cross-registration, distance learning, double major, dual enrollment, independent study, internships, liberal arts/career combination, student-designed major, study abroad, teacher certification program.

FACILITIES

Housing: Men's dorms, women's dorms. **Computers:** 88% of public computers are PCs, 12% of public computers are Macs, network access in dorm rooms, network access in dorm lounges, remote student-access to Web through college's connection.

CAMPUS LIFE

Activities: Choral groups, concert band, drama/theater, jazz band, literary magazine, music ensembles, musical theater, opera, student government, student newspaper. **Organizations:** 13 registered organizations, 5 honor societies, 4 religious organizations. **Athletics (Intercollegiate):** *Men:* Baseball, basketball, cross-country, golf, soccer, track/field (outdoor). *Women:* Cheerleading, cross-country, soccer, softball, track/field (outdoor), volleyball.

ADMISSIONS

Freshman Academic Profile: 12% in top 10% of high school class, 43% in top 25% of high school class, 67% in top 50% of high school class. 74% from public high schools. TOEFL required of all international applicants, minimum paper TOEFL 500, minimum computer TOEFL 500. **Basis for Candidate Selection:** *Very important factors considered include:* Character/personal qualities, class rank, recommendation(s), rigor of secondary school record, standardized test scores. *Important factors considered include:* Interview, religious affiliation/commitment, talent/ability. *Other factors considered include:* Alumni/ae relation, extracurricular activities. **Freshman Admission Requirements:** High school diploma is required, and GED is accepted. *Academic units required:* 4 English, 3 math, 2 science (1 science lab), 2 social studies, 1 history, 3 academic electives, 1 visual and performing arts. *Academic units recommended:* 2 foreign language. **Freshman Admission Statistics:** 370 applied, 75% admitted, 62% enrolled. **Transfer Admission Requirements:** High school transcript, college transcript(s), statement of good standing from prior institution(s). Minimum college GPA of 2.0 required. Lowest grade transferable D. **General Admission Information:** Application fee $25. Regular notification is rolling. Nonfall registration accepted. Admission may be deferred for a maximum of 1 year. Common Application not accepted. Credit and/or placement offered for CEEB Advanced Placement tests.

COSTS AND FINANCIAL AID

Annual tuition $10,290. Room & board $5,080. Required fees $392. Average book expense $1,500. **Required Forms and Deadlines:** FAFSA, institution's own financial aid form. Financial aid filing deadline 4/1. **Notification of Awards:** Applicants will be notified of awards on a rolling basis beginning on or about 4/15. **Types of Aid:** *Need-based scholarships/grants:* Pell, SEOG, state scholarships/grants, private scholarships, the school's own gift aid. *Loans:* FFEL Subsidized Stafford, FFEL Unsubsidized Stafford, FFEL PLUS, state loans, college/university loans from institutional funds. **Student Employment:** Federal Work-Study Program available. Institutional employment available. Off-campus job opportunities are good. **Financial Aid Statistics:** 59% undergrads receive need-based scholarship or grant aid. 52% undergrads receive need-based self-help aid. 152 undergrads receive athletic scholarships. Highest amount earned per year from on-campus jobs $1,779.

MISSOURI SOUTHERN STATE UNIVERSITY— JOPLIN

3950 E. Newman Road, Joplin, MO 64801-1595
Phone: 417-625-9378 **E-mail:** admissions@mssu.edu **CEEB Code:** 6322
Fax: 417-659-4429 **Website:** www.mssu.edu **ACT Code:** 2304
Financial Aid Phone: 417-625-9325

This public school was founded in 1937. It has a 365-acre campus.

RATINGS

Admissions Selectivity Rating: 63   **Fire Safety Rating:** 60*   **Green Rating:** 60*

STUDENTS AND FACULTY

Enrollment: 5,135. **Student Body:** 59% female, 41% male, 15% out-of-state, 1% international (31 countries represented). African American 3%, Asian 1%, Caucasian 89%, Hispanic 2%, Native American 3%. **Retention and Graduation:** 63% freshmen return for sophomore year. 18% freshmen graduate within 4 years. **Faculty:** Student/faculty ratio 19:1. 208 full-time faculty, 64% hold PhDs. 100% faculty teach undergrads.

ACADEMICS

Degrees: Associate, bachelor's, certificate, master's. **Academic Requirements:** Arts/fine arts, computer literacy, English (including composition), foreign languages, history, humanities, mathematics, philosophy, sciences (biological or physical), social science, international cultural studies, health & wellness, communication, economics. **Classes:** Most classes have 20–29 students. Most lab/discussion sections have fewer than 10 students. **Majors with Highest Enrollment:** Business administration/management, criminal justice/law enforcement administration, education. **Disciplines with Highest Percentage of Degrees Awarded:** Business/marketing 27%, education 19%, security and protective services 9%, health professions and related sciences 8%, liberal arts/general studies 7%. **Special Study Options:** Accelerated program, cooperative education program, distance learning, double major, dual enrollment, English as a second language (ESL), exchange student program (domestic), honors program, independent study, internships, liberal arts/career combination, study abroad, teacher certification program, weekend college.

FACILITIES

Housing: Coed dorms, men's dorms, women's dorms, apartments for single students, special housing for disabled students. **Special Academic Facilities/Equipment:** Spiva Art Gallery, biology pond, forensics laboratory, child development center, indoor livefire firearms range, greenhouse, law library, cyber coffee shop, international trade and quality center, graduate center, TV station, radio station, small business development center, Thomas E. Taylor Performing Arts Center, health center. **Computers:** 99% of public computers are PCs, 1% of public computers are Macs, network access in dorm rooms, network access in dorm lounges, online administrative functions (other than registration), remote student-access to Web through college's connection.

CAMPUS LIFE

Activities: Choral groups, concert band, dance, drama/theater, jazz band, literary magazine, marching band, music ensembles, musical theater, pep band, radio station, student government, student newspaper, student-run film society, symphony orchestra, television station. **Organizations:** 82 registered organizations, 12 honor societies, 9 religious organizations. 2 fraternities (1% men join), 2 sororities (1% women join). **Athletics (Intercollegiate):** *Men:* Baseball, basketball, cheerleading, cross-country, football, golf, soccer, track/field (outdoor). *Women:* Basketball, cheerleading, cross-country, soccer, softball, tennis, track/field (outdoor), volleyball.

ADMISSIONS

Freshman Academic Profile: 17% in top 10% of high school class, 40% in top 25% of high school class, 72% in top 50% of high school class. 98% from public high schools. ACT middle 50% range 17–19. TOEFL required of all international applicants, minimum paper TOEFL 535, minimum computer TOEFL 200. **Basis for Candidate Selection:** *Very important factors considered include:* Academic GPA, class rank, rigor of secondary school record, standardized test scores. *Other factors considered include:* Recommendation(s). **Freshman Admission Requirements:** High school diploma is required, and GED is accepted. *Academic units recommended:* 4 English, 3 math, 2 science (1 science lab), 2 foreign language, 3 social studies, 3 academic electives, 1 visual and performing arts. **Freshman Admission Statistics:** 2,669 applied, 98% admitted, 36% enrolled. **Transfer Admission Requirements:** College transcript(s). Minimum college GPA of 2.0 required. Lowest grade transferable D. **General Admission Information:** Application fee $15. Regular notification is rolling. Nonfall registration accepted. Admission may be deferred for a maximum of 1 year. Credit and/or placement offered for CEEB Advanced Placement tests.

COSTS AND FINANCIAL AID

Average book expense $600. **Required Forms and Deadlines:** FAFSA. Financial aid filing deadline 2/15. **Notification of Awards:** Applicants will be notified of awards on a rolling basis beginning on or about 2/15. **Types of Aid:** *Need-based scholarships/grants:* Pell, SEOG, state scholarships/grants, private scholarships. *Loans:* Direct Subsidized Stafford, Direct Unsubsidized Stafford, Direct PLUS, Federal Perkins, state loans.

MISSOURI STATE UNIVERSITY

901 S. National, Springfield, MO 65897
Phone: 417-836-5517 **E-mail:** info@missouristate.edu **CEEB Code:** 6665
Fax: 417-836-6334 **Website:** www.missouristate.edu **ACT Code:** 2370
Financial Aid Phone: 417-835-5262

This public school was founded in 1905. It has a 450-acre campus.

RATINGS

Admissions Selectivity Rating: 78   **Fire Safety Rating:** 83   **Green Rating:** 60*

STUDENTS AND FACULTY

Enrollment: 14,463. **Student Body:** 56% female, 44% male, 7% out-of-state, 2% international. African American 2%, Asian 1%, Caucasian 77%, Hispanic 1%. **Retention and Graduation:** 73% freshmen return for sophomore year. 20% grads go on to further study within 1 year. 2% grads pursue arts and sciences degrees. 10% grads pursue business degrees. 2% grads pursue law degrees. 2% grads pursue medical degrees. **Faculty:** Student/faculty ratio 18:1. 728 full-time faculty, 78% hold PhDs. 94% faculty teach undergrads.

ACADEMICS

Degrees: Bachelor's, doctoral, master's, post-bachelor's certificate, post-master's certificate. **Academic Requirements:** Arts/fine arts, computer literacy, English (including composition), history, humanities, mathematics, sciences (biological or physical), social science. **Classes:** Most classes have 20–29 students. Most lab/discussion sections have 20–29 students. **Majors with Highest Enrollment:** Elementary education and teaching, management information systems, psychology. **Disciplines with Highest Percentage of Degrees Awarded:** Business/marketing 33%, education 16%, communication technologies 8%, psychology 5%, social sciences 5%, visual and performing arts 5%, biological/life sciences 4%. **Special Study Options:** Accelerated program, cooperative education program, distance learning, double major, dual enrollment, English as a second language (ESL), exchange student program (domestic), honors program, independent study, internships, student-designed major, study abroad, teacher certification program.

FACILITIES

Housing: Coed dorms, apartments for married students, apartments for single students, special housing for disabled students, special housing for international students, fraternity/sorority housing, graduate student housing, nontraditional student housing. **Special Academic Facilities** rural Center, Baker Observatory, Bull Shoals Field Station, electron microscope, molecular beam epitaxy laboratory, ion implantation laboratory, art & design gallery, Student Exhibition Center, Coger Theatre, Ellis Recital Hall, Instructional TV Studio, computer animation studio, foundry, Wehr Band Hall, multimedia lab, language lab, Juanita K. Hammons Hall for the Performing Arts. **Computers:** 95% of public computers are PCs, 5% of public computers are Macs, network access in dorm rooms, network access in dorm lounges, online administrative functions (other than registration), remote student-access to Web through college's connection.

CAMPUS LIFE

Activities: Choral groups, concert band, dance, drama/theater, jazz band, literary magazine, marching band, music ensembles, musical theater, pep band, radio station, student government, student newspaper, student-run film society, symphony orchestra, television station. **Organizations:** 280 registered organizations, 40 honor societies, 26 religious organizations. 13 fraternities, 10 sororities. **Athletics (Intercollegiate):** *Men:* Baseball, basketball, cross-country, diving, football, golf, soccer, swimming, tennis, track/field (indoor), track/field (outdoor), volleyball. *Women:* Basketball, cross-country, diving, field hockey, golf, soccer, softball, swimming, tennis, track/field (indoor), track/field (outdoor), volleyball.

ADMISSIONS

Freshman Academic Profile: 22% in top 10% of high school class, 49% in top 25% of high school class, 81% in top 50% of high school class. 93% from public

high schools. ACT middle 50% range 21–26. TOEFL required of all international applicants, minimum paper TOEFL 500, minimum computer TOEFL 173. **Basis for Candidate Selection:** *Very important factors considered include:* Class rank, rigor of secondary school record, standardized test scores. *Other factors considered include:* Alumni/ae relation, application essay, character/personal qualities, extracurricular activities, interview, racial/ethnic status, recommendation(s), talent/ability, volunteer work, work experience. **Freshman Admission Requirements:** High school diploma is required, and GED is accepted. *Academic units required:* 4 English, 3 math, 2 science (1 science lab), 3 social studies, 3 academic electives. **Freshman Admission Statistics:** 6,866 applied, 77% admitted, 50% enrolled. **Transfer Admission Requirements:** College transcript(s). Minimum college GPA of 2.0 required. Lowest grade transferable D. **General Admission Information:** Application fee $30. Regular application deadline 7/20. Nonfall registration accepted. Common Application not accepted. Credit and/or placement offered for CEEB Advanced Placement tests.

COSTS AND FINANCIAL AID

Annual in-state tuition $4,920. Out-of-state tuition $9,840. Room & board $5,294. Required fees $534. Average book expense $800. **Required Forms and Deadlines:** FAFSA. Financial aid filing deadline 3/30. **Notification of Awards:** Applicants will be notified of awards on or about 4/15. **Types of Aid:** *Need-based scholarships/grants:* Pell, SEOG, state scholarships/grants, private scholarships, the school's own gift aid. *Loans:* FFEL Subsidized Stafford, FFEL Unsubsidized Stafford, FFEL PLUS, Federal Perkins, college/university loans from institutional funds. **Student Employment:** Federal Work-Study Program available. Institutional employment available. **Financial Aid Statistics:** 42% freshmen, 41% undergrads receive need-based scholarship or grant aid. 40% freshmen, 48% undergrads receive need-based self-help aid. 75 freshmen, 283 undergrads receive athletic scholarships. 54% freshmen, 58% undergrads receive any aid. Highest amount earned per year from on-campus jobs $2,237.

MISSOURI UNIVERSITY OF SCIENCE AND TECHNOLOGY

106 Parker Hall, Rolla, MO 65409
Phone: 573-341-4165 **E-mail:** admissions@umr.edu **CEEB Code:** 6876
Fax: 573-341-4082 **Website:** www.umr.edu **ACT Code:** 2398
Financial Aid Phone: 573-341-4282

This public school was founded in 1870. It has a 284-acre campus.

RATINGS

Admissions Selectivity Rating: 60*   **Fire Safety Rating:** 60*   **Green Rating:** 60*

STUDENTS AND FACULTY

Enrollment: 4,465. **Student Body:** 22% female, 78% male, 20% out-of-state, 3% international (48 countries represented). African American 4%, Asian 2%, Caucasian 84%, Hispanic 2%. **Retention and Graduation:** 87% freshmen return for sophomore year. 21% freshmen graduate within 4 years. 17% grads go on to further study within 2 semesters. **Faculty:** Student/faculty ratio 14:1. 336 full-time faculty, 86% hold PhDs. 88% faculty teach undergrads.

ACADEMICS

Degrees: Bachelor's, doctoral, master's, post-bachelor's certificate. **Academic Requirements:** Computer literacy, English (including composition), history, humanities, mathematics, sciences (biological or physical), social science. **Classes:** Most classes have fewer than 10 students. Most lab/discussion sections have 10–19 students. **Majors with Highest Enrollment:** Civil engineering, electrical, electronics and communications engineering, mechanical engineering. **Disciplines with Highest Percentage of Degrees Awarded:** Engineering 68%, computer and information sciences 10%, business/marketing 5%, physical sciences 5%, biological/life sciences 3%. **Special Study Options:** Accelerated program, cooperative education program, distance learning, double major, dual enrollment, English as a second language (ESL), honors program, independent study, internships, student-designed major, study abroad, teacher certification program.

FACILITIES

Housing: Coed dorms, men's dorms, women's dorms, apartments for married students, apartments for single students, special housing for disabled students, fraternity/sorority housing, religious-based housing. **Special Academic Facilities/Equipment:** Writing center; student design center; nuclear reactor; observatory; explosives testing lab; underground mine; Museum of Rocks; Minerals, and Gemstones; centers for environmental research; water resources; industrial research; rock mechanics research; geophysical observatory; computerized manufacturing system; Millenium Arch. **Computers:** 25% of classrooms are wired, 85% of classrooms are wireless, 86% of public computers are PCs, 8% of public computers are Macs, 6% of public computers are UNIX, network access in dorm rooms, network access in dorm lounges, online registration, online administrative functions (other than registration), support for handheld computing, remote student-access to Web through college's connection.

CAMPUS LIFE

Activities: Choral groups, concert band, dance, drama/theater, jazz band, literary magazine, marching band, music ensembles, musical theater, pep band, radio station, student government, student newspaper, symphony orchestra, yearbook. **Organizations:** 200 registered organizations, 32 honor societies, 16 religious organizations. 20 fraternities (25% men join), 5 sororities (24% women join). **Athletics (Intercollegiate):** *Men:* Baseball, basketball, cross-country, football, soccer, swimming, track/field (indoor), track/field (outdoor). *Women:* Basketball, cross-country, soccer, softball, track/field (indoor), track/field (outdoor).

ADMISSIONS

Freshman Academic Profile: 39% in top 10% of high school class, 69% in top 25% of high school class, 92% in top 50% of high school class. 85% from public high schools. SAT Math middle 50% range 525–670. SAT Critical Reading middle 50% range 590–690. ACT middle 50% range 25–30. TOEFL required of all international applicants, minimum paper TOEFL 550, minimum computer TOEFL 213. **Basis for Candidate Selection:** *Very important factors considered include:* Academic GPA, class rank, rigor of secondary school record, standardized test scores. *Important factors considered include:* recommendation(s). *Other factors considered include:* Application essay, character/personal qualities, extracurricular activities, interview, talent/ability, volunteer work, work experience. **Freshman Admission Requirements:** High school diploma is required, and GED is accepted. *Academic units required:* 4 English, 4 math, 3 science (1 science lab), 2 foreign language, 3 social studies, 1 fine art. **Freshman Admission Statistics:** 2,257 applied, 90% admitted, 47% enrolled. **Transfer Admission Requirements:** College transcript(s). Minimum college GPA of 2.0 required. Lowest grade transferable D. **General Admission Information:** Application fee $35. Regular application deadline 7/1. Regular notification is rolling. Non-fall registration accepted. Admission may be deferred for a maximum of 4 semesters. Credit and/or placement offered for CEEB Advanced Placement tests.

COSTS AND FINANCIAL AID

Annual in-state tuition $7,077. Annual out-of-state tuition $17,733. Room and board $6,660. Required fees $1,095. Average book expense $900. **Required Forms and Deadlines:** FAFSA, FAFSA not required but strongly recommended. Financial aid filing deadline 3/1. **Notification of Awards:** Applicants will be notified of awards on a rolling basis beginning on or about 4/1. **Types of Aid:** *Need-based scholarships/grants:* Pell, SEOG, state scholarships/grants, private scholarships, the school's own gift aid, ROTC-Army & Air Force. *Loans:* Direct Subsidized Stafford, Direct Unsubsidized Stafford, FFEL PLUS, Federal Perkins, state loans, college/university loans from institutional funds, alternative loans. **Financial Aid Statistics:** 55% freshmen, 45% undergrads receive need-based scholarship or grant aid. 41% freshmen, 41% undergrads receive need-based self-help aid. 32 freshmen, 129 undergrads receive athletic scholarships. Highest amount earned per year from on-campus jobs $1,000.

MISSOURI VALLEY COLLEGE

500 East College Street, Marshall, MO 65340
Phone: 660-831-4114 **E-mail:** admissions@moval.edu
Fax: 660-831-4233 **Website:** www.moval.edu **ACT Code:** 2330
Financial Aid Phone: 660-831-4176

This private school, affiliated with the Presbyterian Church, was founded in 1889. It has a 150-acre campus.

RATINGS

Admissions Selectivity Rating: 74   **Fire Safety Rating:** 60*   **Green Rating:** 60*

STUDENTS AND FACULTY

Enrollment: 1,425. **Student Body:** 43% female, 57% male, 34% out-of-state,

8% international (29 countries represented). African American 13%, Asian 4%, Caucasian 70%, Hispanic 4%. **Retention and Graduation:** 45% freshmen return for sophomore year. 11% freshmen graduate within 4 years. 20% grads go on to further study within 1 year. **Faculty:** Student/faculty ratio 18:1. 66 full-time faculty, 53% hold PhDs. 100% faculty teach undergrads.

ACADEMICS

Degrees: Associate, bachelor's. **Academic Requirements:** Arts/fine arts, computer literacy, English (including composition), history, humanities, mathematics, sciences (biological or physical), social science, religion. **Classes:** Most classes have 20–29 students. Most lab/discussion sections have 20–29 students. **Majors with Highest Enrollment:** Business administration/management, criminal justice/law enforcement administration, elementary education and teaching. **Disciplines with Highest Percentage of Degrees Awarded:** Business/marketing 22%, education 11%, parks and recreation 11%, psychology 9%, health professions and related sciences 7%, biological/life sciences 4%, social sciences 4%. **Special Study Options:** Double major, dual enrollment, internships, teacher certification program.

FACILITIES

Housing: Men's dorms, women's dorms, apartments for married students, apartments for single students, fraternity/sorority housing. **Computers:** 98% of public computers are PCs, 2% of public computers are Macs, network access in dorm rooms, network access in dorm lounges, remote student-access to Web through college's connection.

CAMPUS LIFE

Activities: Choral groups, dance, drama/theater, literary magazine, music ensembles, musical theater, pep band, radio station, student government, student newspaper, television station, yearbook. **Organizations:** 28 registered organizations, 8 honor societies, 7 religious organizations. 4 fraternities (25% men join), 2 sororities (25% women join). **Athletics (Intercollegiate):** *Men:* Baseball, basketball, cheerleading, cross-country, football, golf, rodeo, soccer, tennis, track/field (indoor), track/field (outdoor), volleyball, wrestling. *Women:* Basketball, cheerleading, cross-country, golf, rodeo, soccer, softball, tennis, track/field (indoor), track/field (outdoor), volleyball, wrestling.

ADMISSIONS

Freshman Academic Profile: 4% in top 10% of high school class, 38% in top 25% of high school class, 54% in top 50% of high school class. SAT Math middle 50% range 412–597. SAT Critical Reading middle 50% range 372–537. ACT middle 50% range 19–27. TOEFL required of all international applicants, minimum paper TOEFL 450, minimum computer TOEFL 200. **Basis for Candidate Selection:** *Very important factors considered include:* Character/personal qualities, interview. *Important factors considered include:* Extracurricular activities, talent/ability, volunteer work. *Other factors considered include:* Alumni/ae relation, class rank, recommendation(s), rigor of secondary school record, standardized test scores, work experience. **Freshman Admission Requirements:** High school diploma is required, and GED is accepted. *Academic units recommended:* 4 English, 3 math, 2 science (1 science lab), 2 social studies, 2 history, 3 academic electives. **Freshman Admission Statistics:** 1,345 applied, 67% admitted, 45% enrolled. **Transfer Admission Requirements:** High school transcript, college transcript(s), standardized test score. Minimum college GPA of 2.0 required. Lowest grade transferable C. **General Admission Information:** Application fee $15. Regular application deadline 9/1. Nonfall registration accepted. Common Application accepted.

COSTS AND FINANCIAL AID

Annual tuition $13,000. Room & board $5,200. Required fees $500. Average book expense $1,300. **Required Forms and Deadlines:** FAFSA, state aid form. Financial aid filing deadline 3/1. **Types of Aid:** *Need-based scholarships/grants:* Pell, SEOG, state scholarships/grants, private scholarships, the school's own gift aid. *Loans:* FFEL Subsidized Stafford, FFEL Unsubsidized Stafford, FFEL PLUS, Federal Perkins. **Student Employment:** Federal Work-Study Program available. Institutional employment available. Off-campus job opportunities are excellent. **Financial Aid Statistics:** 95% freshmen, 96% undergrads receive need-based scholarship or grant aid. 83% freshmen, 83% undergrads receive need-based self-help aid. 98% freshmen, 92% undergrads receive any aid..

MISSOURI WESTERN STATE COLLEGE

4525 Downs Drive, Saint Joseph, MO 64507
Phone: 816-271-4266 **E-mail:** admissn@mwsc.edu
Fax: 816-271-5833 **Website:** www.mwsc.edu **ACT Code:** 2344
Financial Aid Phone: 816-271-4361

This public school was founded in 1969. It has a 740-acre campus.

RATINGS
Admissions Selectivity Rating: 62   **Fire Safety Rating:** 60*   **Green Rating:** 60*

STUDENTS AND FACULTY
Enrollment: 4,652. **Student Body:** 61% female, 39% male, 9% out-of-state. African American 11%, Caucasian 85%, Hispanic 2%. **Retention and Graduation:** 55% freshmen return for sophomore year. 16% freshmen graduate within 4 years. 20% grads go on to further study within 1 year. 11% grads pursue arts and sciences degrees. 6% grads pursue business degrees. 1% grads pursue law degrees. 2% grads pursue medical degrees. **Faculty:** Student/faculty ratio 18:1. 180 full-time faculty, 75% hold PhDs. 100% faculty teach undergrads.

ACADEMICS
Degrees: Associate, bachelor's, certificate. **Academic Requirements:** English (including composition), humanities, mathematics, sciences (biological or physical), social science, oral communications physical health. **Classes:** Most classes have 20–29 students. Most lab/discussion sections have 20–29 students. **Majors with Highest Enrollment:** Business administration/management, criminal justice/law enforcement administration, nursing/registered nurse training (RN, ASN, BSN, MSN). **Disciplines with Highest Percentage of Degrees Awarded:** Business/marketing 19%, education 12%, parks and recreation 9%, health professions and related sciences 9%, biological/life sciences 5%, psychology 4%, English 4%, communication technologies 4%, computer and information sciences 4%, social sciences 4%. **Special Study Options:** Distance learning, double major, dual enrollment, honors program, internships, liberal arts/career combination, teacher certification program, weekend college.

FACILITIES
Housing: Coed dorms, apartments for single students, fraternity/sorority housing. **Special Academic Facilities/Equipment:** Multimedia classroom building, planetarium. **Computers:** 90% of public computers are PCs, 10% of public computers are Macs, network access in dorm rooms, network access in dorm lounges.

CAMPUS LIFE
Activities: Choral groups, concert band, dance, drama/theater, jazz band, marching band, music ensembles, pep band, student government, student newspaper, yearbook. **Organizations:** 64 registered organizations, 5 honor societies, 7 religious organizations. 5 fraternities (10% men join), 6 sororities (10% women join). **Athletics (Intercollegiate):** *Men:* Baseball, basketball, football, golf. *Women:* Basketball, golf, softball, tennis, volleyball.

ADMISSIONS
Freshman Academic Profile: 7% in top 10% of high school class, 28% in top 25% of high school class, 61% in top 50% of high school class. 95% from public high schools. ACT middle 50% range 16–22. TOEFL required of all international applicants, minimum paper TOEFL 500. **Freshman Admission Requirements:** High school diploma is required, and GED is accepted. *Academic units required:* 4 English, 3 math, 2 science (1 science lab), 3 social studies, 3 academic electives, 1 visual and performing arts. *Academic units recommended:* 2 foreign language. **Freshman Admission Statistics:** 2,421 applied, 100% admitted, 43% enrolled. **Transfer Admission Requirements:** College transcript(s). Lowest grade transferable D. **General Admission Information:** Application fee $15. Regular application deadline 8/15. Regular notification is rolling. Nonfall registration accepted. Common Application not accepted. Credit offered for CEEB Advanced Placement tests.

COSTS AND FINANCIAL AID
Annual in-state tuition $4,098. Out-of-state tuition $7,674. Room & board $4,058. Required fees $366. Average book expense $700. **Required Forms and Deadlines:** FAFSA, institution's own financial aid form. Financial aid filing deadline 3/1. **Notification of Awards:** Applicants will be notified of awards on or about 4/5. **Types of Aid:** *Need-based scholarships/grants:* Pell, SEOG, state scholarships/grants, private scholarships, the school's own gift aid. *Loans:* FFEL Subsidized Stafford, FFEL Unsubsidized Stafford, FFEL PLUS, Federal Perkins. **Student Employment:** Federal Work-Study Program available. Institutional employment available. Off-campus job opportunities are good. **Financial Aid Statistics:** 39% freshmen, 38% undergrads receive need-based scholarship or grant aid. 39% freshmen, 44% undergrads receive need-

based self-help aid. 32 freshmen, 141 undergrads receive athletic scholarships. Highest amount earned per year from on-campus jobs $1,400.

MITCHELL COLLEGE

437 Pequot Avenue, New London, CT 06320
Phone: 860-701-5011 **E-mail:** admissions@mitchell.edu **CEEB Code:** 3528
Fax: 860-444-1209 **Website:** www.mitchell.edu **ACT Code:** 0572
Financial Aid Phone: 800-443-2811

This private school was founded in 1938. It has a 65-acre campus.

RATINGS
Admissions Selectivity Rating: 71   **Fire Safety Rating:** 60*   **Green Rating:** 60*

STUDENTS AND FACULTY
Enrollment: 762. **Student Body:** 54% female, 46% male, 36% out-of-state. African American 8%, Caucasian 64%, Hispanic 6%, Native American 2%. **Retention and Graduation:** 95% grads go on to further study within 1 year. **Faculty:** Student/faculty ratio 12:1. 27 full-time faculty, 48% hold PhDs. 100% faculty teach undergrads.

ACADEMICS
Degrees: Associate, bachelor's, certificate. **Academic Requirements:** Computer literacy, English (including composition), history, humanities, mathematics, sciences (biological or physical), social science, public speaking. **Majors with Highest Enrollment:** Business administration/management, education, liberal arts and sciences/liberal studies. **Disciplines with Highest Percentage of Degrees Awarded:** Business/marketing 32%, psychology 19%, liberal arts/general studies 16%, other 13%, parks and recreation 8%, social sciences 8%. **Special Study Options:** Dual enrollment, English as a second language (ESL), internships, teacher certification program.

FACILITIES
Housing: Coed dorms, special housing for disabled students, 4 residence halls are Victorian and Colonial houses located on the waterfront, 3 residence halls are of traditional design. **Special Academic Facilities/Equipment:** Private dock with fleet of sailboats, 2 private beaches, 26 acres of woods. **Computers:** 25% of classrooms are wired, 1% of classrooms are wireless, 85% of public computers are PCs, 15% of public computers are Macs, network access in dorm rooms, network access in dorm lounges, remote student-access to Web through college's connection.

CAMPUS LIFE
Activities: Choral groups, dance, drama/theater, literary magazine, student government, student newspaper, yearbook. **Organizations:** 30 registered organizations, 2 honor societies, 2 religious organizations. **Athletics (Intercollegiate):** *Men:* Baseball, basketball, cross-country, golf, lacrosse, soccer, tennis. *Women:* Basketball, cross-country, golf, soccer, softball, tennis, volleyball.

ADMISSIONS
Freshman Academic Profile: 3% in top 10% of high school class, 15% in top 25% of high school class, 35% in top 50% of high school class. 85% from public high schools. SAT Math middle 50% range 460–350. SAT Critical Reading middle 50% range 460–360. ACT middle 50% range 17–15. TOEFL required of all international applicants, minimum paper TOEFL 500. **Basis for Candidate Selection:** *Very important factors considered include:* Interview, recommendation(s), rigor of secondary school record. *Important factors considered include:* Application essay, character/personal qualities, extracurricular activities, standardized test scores, talent/ability. *Other factors considered include:* Alumni/ae relation, class rank, volunteer work, work experience. **Freshman Admission Requirements:** High school diploma is required, and GED is accepted. *Academic units recommended:* 4 English, 3 math, 3 science, 2 social studies, 2 history, 2 academic electives. **Freshman Admission Statistics:** 1,215 applied, 54% admitted, 38% enrolled. **Transfer Admission Requirements:** High school transcript, college transcript(s), essay or personal statement, standardized test score. Minimum college GPA of 2.0 required. Lowest grade transferable C-. **General Admission Information:** Application fee $30. Early decision application deadline 11/15. Regular notification is rolling. Nonfall registration accepted. Admission may be deferred for a maximum of 1 year. Credit and/or placement offered for CEEB Advanced Placement tests.

COSTS AND FINANCIAL AID
Annual tuition $20,382. Room & board $9,795. Required fees $1,355. Average book expense $800. **Required Forms and Deadlines:** FAFSA. Financial aid filing deadline 3/1. **Notification of Awards:** Applicants will be notified of awards on a rolling basis beginning on or about 3/1. **Types of Aid:** *Need-based*

MOLLOY COLLEGE

1000 Hempstead Avenue, Rockville Centre, NY 11570
Phone: 516-678-5000 **E-mail:** Admissions@molloy.edu **CEEB Code:** 2415
Fax: 516-256-2247 **Website:** www.molloy.edu **ACT Code:** 2820
Financial Aid Phone: 516-678-5000

This private school, affiliated with the Roman Catholic Church, was founded in 1955. It has a 35-acre campus.

RATINGS

Admissions Selectivity Rating: 78   **Fire Safety Rating:** 60*   **Green Rating:** 60*

STUDENTS AND FACULTY

Enrollment: 2,748. **Student Body:** 78% female, 22% male. **Retention and Graduation:** 82% freshmen return for sophomore year. **Faculty:** Student/faculty ratio 11:1. 157 full-time faculty, 64% hold PhDs. 100% faculty teach undergrads.

ACADEMICS

Degrees: Associate, bachelor's, master's, post-master's certificate. **Academic Requirements:** Arts/fine arts, English (including composition), foreign languages, history, humanities, mathematics, philosophy, sciences (biological or physical), social science. **Classes:** Most classes have 10–19 students. Most lab/discussion sections have 10–19 students. **Majors with Highest Enrollment:** Business administration/management; education; nursing—registered nurse training (RN, ASN, BSN, MSN). **Disciplines with Highest Percentage of Degrees Awarded:** Health professions and related sciences 38%, education 15%, psychology 7%, business/marketing 7%, visual and performing arts 6%, public administration and social services 5%. **Special Study Options:** Accelerated program, cooperative education program, cross-registration, double major, English as a second language (ESL), honor program, independent study, internships, study abroad, teacher certification program.

FACILITIES

Special Academic Facilities/Equipment: Professional Repertory Theatre Company in residence, dance studio, Institute of Cross-Cultural and Cross-Ethnic Studies, Institute of Gerontology, cablevision studio. **Computers:** 100% of classrooms are wireless, online registration, online administrative functions (other than registration), remote student-access to Web through college's connection.

CAMPUS LIFE

Activities: Choral groups, dance, drama/theater, jazz band, literary magazine, music ensembles, musical theater, student government, student newspaper, yearbook. **Organizations:** 21 registered organizations, 18 honor societies, 1 religious organization. **Athletics (Intercollegiate):** *Men:* Baseball, basketball, cross-country, equestrian sports, lacrosse, soccer. *Women:* Basketball, cross-country, equestrian sports, lacrosse, soccer, softball, tennis, volleyball.

ADMISSIONS

Freshman Academic Profile: 17% in top 10% of high school class, 48% in top 25% of high school class, 89% in top 50% of high school class. 71% from public high schools. SAT Math middle 50% range 450–600. SAT Critical Reading middle 50% range 460–565. TOEFL required of all international applicants, minimum paper TOEFL 500, minimum computer TOEFL 175. **Basis for Candidate Selection:** *Very important factors considered include:* Academic GPA, rigor of secondary school record, standardized test scores. *Important factors considered include:* Class rank. *Other factors considered include:* Alumni/ae relation, application essay, character/personal qualities, extracurricular activities, interview, recommendation(s), talent/ability, volunteer work, work experience. **Freshman Admission Requirements:** High school diploma is required, and GED is accepted. *Academic units required:* 4 English, 3 math, 3 science, 3 foreign language, 4 social studies. **Freshman Admission Statistics:** 1,245 applied, 61% admitted, 38% enrolled. **Transfer Admission Requirements:** College transcript(s), essay or personal statement, statement of good standing from prior institution(s). Minimum college GPA of 2.0 required. Lowest grade transferable C. **General Admission Information:** Application fee $30. Regular notification is rolling. Nonfall registration accepted. Admission may be deferred for a maximum of 1 year. Credit offered for CEEB Advanced Placement tests.

COSTS AND FINANCIAL AID

Annual tuition $17,640. Required fees $930. Average book expense $900. **Required Forms and Deadlines:** FAFSA, state aid form. Financial aid filing deadline 5/1. Financial aid filing deadline 4/15. **Notification of Awards:** Applicants will be notified of awards on a rolling basis beginning on or about 2/15. **Types of Aid:** *Need-based scholarships/grants:* Pell, SEOG, state scholarships/grants, private scholarships, the school's own gift aid, Federal Nursing Scholarships. *Loans:* FFEL Subsidized Stafford, FFEL Unsubsidized Stafford, FFEL PLUS, Federal Perkins. **Financial Aid Statistics:** 75% freshmen, 76% undergrads receive need-based scholarship or grant aid. 67% freshmen, 75% undergrads receive need-based self-help aid. 12 freshmen, 58 undergrads receive athletic scholarships.

See page 1272.

MONMOUTH COLLEGE (IL)

700 East Broadway, Monmouth, IL 61462
Phone: 309-457-2131 **E-mail:** admit@monm.edu **CEEB Code:** 1484
Fax: 309-457-2141 **Website:** www.monm.edu **ACT Code:** 1084
Financial Aid Phone: 309-457-2129

This private school, affiliated with the Presbyterian Church, was founded in 1853. It has an 80-acre campus.

RATINGS

Admissions Selectivity Rating: 76   **Fire Safety Rating:** 60*   **Green Rating:** 67

STUDENTS AND FACULTY

Enrollment: 1,325. **Student Body:** 53% female, 47% male, 8% out-of-state, 1% international (15 countries represented). African American 3%, Caucasian 91%, Hispanic 3%. **Retention and Graduation:** 81% freshmen return for sophomore year. 51% freshmen graduate within 4 years. 25% grads go on to further study within 1 year. 9% grads pursue arts and sciences degrees. 7% grads pursue business degrees. 4% grads pursue law degrees. 5% grads pursue medical degrees. **Faculty:** Student/faculty ratio 13:1. 87 full-time faculty, 76% hold PhDs. 100% faculty teach undergrads.

ACADEMICS

Degrees: Bachelor's. **Academic Requirements:** Arts/fine arts, English (including composition), foreign languages, humanities, sciences (biological or physical), social science, introduction to liberal arts, quantitative analysis, senior ideas and issues. **Classes:** Most classes have 20–29 students. Most lab/discussion sections have 10–19 students. **Majors with Highest Enrollment:** Business administration/management, education, English language and literature. **Disciplines with Highest Percentage of Degrees Awarded:** Business/marketing 25%, education 23%, English 11%, social sciences 10%, history 7%. **Special Study Options:** Double major, honors program, independent study, internships, liberal arts/career combination, student-designed major, study abroad, teacher certification program.

FACILITIES

Housing: Coed dorms, men's dorms, women's dorms, apartments for single students, special housing for disabled students, special housing for international students, fraternity/sorority housing, theme housing, substance-free floors. **Special Academic Facilities/Equipment:** Shields Art Collection, Wackerle Career and Leadership Center. **Computers:** 100% of classrooms are wireless, 92% of public computers are PCs, 8% of public computers are Macs, network access in dorm rooms, network access in dorm lounges, online registration, online administrative functions (other than registration), remote student-access to Web through college's connection.

CAMPUS LIFE

Activities: Choral groups, concert band, dance, drama/theater, jazz band, literary magazine, music ensembles, musical theater, radio station, student government, student newspaper, student-run film society, television station. **Organizations:** 80 registered organizations, 9 honor societies, 5 religious organizations. 3 fraternities (23% men join), 3 sororities (26% women join). **Athletics (Intercollegiate):** *Men:* Baseball, basketball, cheerleading, cross-country, football, golf, soccer, swimming, tennis, track/field (indoor), track/field (outdoor). *Women:* Basketball, cheerleading, cross-country, golf, soccer, softball, swimming, tennis, track/field (indoor), track/field (outdoor), volleyball.

ADMISSIONS

Freshman Academic Profile: 12% in top 10% of high school class, 37% in top 25% of high school class, 79% in top 50% of high school class. 78% from public high schools. SAT Math middle 50% range 560–580. SAT Critical Reading middle 50% range 550–560. ACT middle 50% range 20–26. TOEFL required of all international applicants, minimum paper TOEFL 500, minimum computer TOEFL 213. **Basis for Candidate Selection:** *Very important factors considered include:* Class rank, rigor of secondary school record, standardized test scores. *Important factors considered include:* Recommendation(s). *Other factors considered include:* Application essay, character/personal qualities, extracurricular activities, interview, talent/ability, volunteer work, work experience. **Freshman Admission Requirements:** High school diploma is required, and GED is accepted. *Academic units required:* 4 English, 3 math, 2 science (1 science lab), 1 social studies, 2 history. *Academic units recommended:* 4 English, 4 math, 4 science (2 science labs), 3 foreign language, 3 social studies, 2 history. **Freshman Admission Statistics:** 1,634 applied, 79% admitted, 28% enrolled. **Transfer Admission Requirements:** College transcript(s). Minimum college GPA of 2.5 required. Lowest grade transferable C-. **General Admission Information:** Regular notification is rolling. Nonfall registration accepted. Admission may be deferred for a maximum of 1 year. Common Application accepted. Credit and/or placement offered for CEEB Advanced Placement tests.

COSTS AND FINANCIAL AID
Annual tuition $24,000. Room and board $7,000. Average book expense $650. **Required Forms and Deadlines:** FAFSA. Financial aid filing deadline 3/1. **Notification of Awards:** Applicants will be notified of awards on a rolling basis beginning on or about 2/15. **Types of Aid:** *Need-based scholarships/grants:* Pell, SEOG, state scholarships/grants, private scholarships, the school's own gift aid. *Loans:* FFEL Subsidized Stafford, FFEL Unsubsidized Stafford, FFEL PLUS, Federal Perkins. **Financial Aid Statistics:** 76% freshmen, 81% undergrads receive need-based scholarship or grant aid. 58% freshmen, 58% undergrads receive need-based self-help aid. 98% freshmen, 98% undergrads receive any aid. Highest amount earned per year from on-campus jobs $1,695.

MONMOUTH UNIVERSITY (NJ)

Admission, Monmouth University, 400 Cedar Avenue, West Long Branch, NJ 07764-1898
Phone: 732-571-3456 **E-mail:** admission@monmouth.edu **CEEB Code:** 2416
Fax: 732-263-5166 **Website:** www.monmouth.edu **ACT Code:** 2571
Financial Aid Phone: 732-571-3463

This private school was founded in 1933. It has a 155-acre campus.

RATINGS
Admissions Selectivity Rating: 78   **Fire Safety Rating:** 87   **Green Rating:** 75

STUDENTS AND FACULTY
Enrollment: 4,577. **Student Body:** 58% female, 42% male, 9% out-of-state. African American 4%, Asian 2%, Caucasian 75%, Hispanic 5%. **Retention and Graduation:** 79% freshmen return for sophomore year. 34% freshmen graduate within 4 years. **Faculty:** Student/faculty ratio 15:1. 245 full-time faculty, 79% hold PhDs. 90% faculty teach undergrads.

ACADEMICS
Degrees: Associate, bachelor's, certificate, master's, post-bachelor's certificate, post-master's certificate. **Academic Requirements:** Arts/fine arts, computer literacy, English (including composition), history, humanities, mathematics, sciences (biological or physical), social science, experiential education requirement, aesthetics, cross-cultural, perspectives. **Classes:** Most classes have 20–29 students. **Majors with Highest Enrollment:** Business administration and management, communications and media studies, education. **Disciplines with Highest Percentage of Degrees Awarded:** Business/marketing 28%, communications/journalism 18%, education 18%, security and protective services 6%, psychology 6%. **Special Study Options:** Accelerated program, cooperative education program, cross-registration, distance learning, double major, dual enrollment, honors program, independent study, internships, liberal arts/career combination, student-designed major, study abroad, teacher certification program. Clinical lab science program in collaboration with UMDNJ. Air Force ROTC at Rutgers University. Affiliated with Washington Center providing semester and summer internships and shorter symposia. Monmouth medical scholars program allows 4 incoming freshmen to complete undergraduate degree at Monmouth, including 9-credit clinical requirement at Monmouth Medical Center, and commence medical studies at Drexel University School of Medicine. Study Abroad in London at Regent's College and Sydney, Australia, at Macquarie University.

FACILITIES
Housing: Coed dorms, apartments for single students, honor program housing. **Special Academic Facilities/Equipment:** Art gallery, instructional media center with TV and radio stations, theater. **Computers:** 95% of classrooms are wireless, 90% of public computers are PCs, 5% of public computers are Macs, 5% of public computers are UNIX, network access in dorm rooms, network access in dorm lounges, online registration, online administrative functions (other than registration), remote student-access to Web through college's connection.

CAMPUS LIFE
Activities: Choral groups, concert band, dance, drama/theater, jazz band, literary magazine, music ensembles, musical theater, pep band, radio station, student government, student newspaper, television station, yearbook. **Organizations:** 67 registered organizations, 19 honor societies, 3 religious organizations. 7 fraternities (8% men join), 6 sororities (9% women join). **Athletics (Intercollegiate):** *Men:* Baseball, basketball, cross-country, football, golf, soccer, tennis, track/field (indoor), track/field (outdoor). *Women:* Basketball, cross-country, field hockey, golf, lacrosse, soccer, softball, tennis, track/field (indoor), track/field (outdoor). Environmental Initiatives: Solar power: 454.5 KW solar installation. Wind power. Relamping with compace flourescent bulbs/lights.

ADMISSIONS
Freshman Academic Profile: 9% in top 10% of high school class, 32% in top 25% of high school class, 72% in top 50% of high school class. 83% from public high schools. SAT Math middle 50% range 500–580. SAT Critical Reading middle 50% range 490–560. SAT Writing middle 50% range 480–570. ACT middle 50% range 21–24. TOEFL required of all international applicants, minimum paper TOEFL 550, minimum computer TOEFL 213. **Basis for Candidate Selection:** *Very important factors considered include:* Academic GPA, extracurricular activities, rigor of secondary school record, standardized test scores, volunteer work, work experience. *Other factors considered include:* Alumni/ae relation, application essay, class rank, interview, recommendation(s). **Freshman Admission Requirements:** High school diploma is required, and GED is accepted. *Academic units required:* 4 English, 3 math, 2 science (1 science lab), 2 history, 5 academic electives. *Academic units recommended:* 2 foreign language, 2 social studies. **Freshman Admission Statistics:** 5,952 applied, 61% admitted, 27% enrolled. **Transfer Admission Requirements:** College transcript(s), statement of good standing from prior institution(s). Minimum college GPA of 2.0 required. Lowest grade transferable C. **General Admission Information:** Application fee $50. Early decision application deadline 12/1. Regular application deadline 3/1. Regular notification prior to 4/1. Nonfall registration accepted. Admission may be deferred for a maximum of 2 semesters. Credit and/or placement offered for CEEB Advanced Placement tests.

COSTS AND FINANCIAL AID
Annual tuition $22,406. Room and board $8,904. Required fees $628. Average book expense $1,000. **Required Forms and Deadlines:** FAFSA. Financial aid filing deadline 6/30. **Notification of Awards:** Applicants will be notified of awards on a rolling basis beginning on or about 2/1. **Types of Aid:** *Need-based scholarships/grants:* Pell, SEOG, state scholarships/grants, private scholarships, the school's own gift aid, Federal Nursing Scholarships. *Loans:* Direct Subsidized Stafford, Direct Unsubsidized Stafford, Direct PLUS, FFEL PLUS, Federal Perkins, state loans, college/university loans from institutional funds, alternative loans. **Financial Aid Statistics:** 21% freshmen, 34% undergrads receive need-based scholarship or grant aid. 48% freshmen, 51% undergrads receive need-based self-help aid. 174 freshmen, 260 undergrads receive athletic scholarships. 65% freshmen, 92% undergrads receive any aid. Highest amount earned per year from on-campus jobs $4,000.

MONROE COLLEGE

2501 Jerome Avenue, Bronx, NY 10468
Phone: 718-933-6700 **E-mail:** ejerome@monroecollege.edu **CEEB Code:** 2463
Fax: 718-364-3552 **Website:** www.monroecollege.edu **Financial Aid Phone:** 718-933-6700

This proprietary school was founded in 1933.

RATINGS
Admissions Selectivity Rating: 60*   **Fire Safety Rating:** 60*   **Green Rating:** 60*

STUDENTS AND FACULTY
Enrollment: 5,917. **Student Body:** 71% female, 29% male, 2% out-of-state, 6% international. African American 45%, Asian 1%, Caucasian 2%, Hispanic

43%. **Retention and Graduation:** 72% freshmen return for sophomore year. **Faculty:** Student/faculty ratio 21:1. 70 full-time faculty, 40% hold PhDs. 100% faculty teach undergrads.

ACADEMICS

Degrees: Associate, bachelor's, master's. **Academic Requirements:** Computer literacy, English (including composition), humanities, mathematics, sciences (biological or physical), social science. **Classes:** Most classes have 20–29 students. **Majors with Highest Enrollment:** Business administration/management, criminal justice/law enforcement administration, health/health care administration/management. **Disciplines with Highest Percentage of Degrees Awarded:** Business/marketing 70%, computer and information sciences 23%, security and protective services 4%, health professions and related sciences 3%. **Special Study Options:** Distance learning, honors program, independent study, internships, weekend college.

FACILITIES

Housing: Coed dorms. **Computers:** 95% of classrooms are wireless, 100% of public computers are PCs, network access in dorm rooms, network access in dorm lounges, remote student-access to Web through college's connection.

CAMPUS LIFE

Activities: Literary magazine. **Athletics (Intercollegiate):** *Men:* Basketball, soccer. *Women:* Basketball, softball, volleyball.

ADMISSIONS

Freshman Academic Profile: 99% from public high schools. **Basis for Candidate Selection:** *Very important factors considered include:* Interview. *Important factors considered include:* Application essay. *Other factors considered include:* Alumni/ae relation, character/personal qualities, class rank, extracurricular activities, geographical residence, racial/ethnic status, recommendation(s), religious affiliation/commitment, rigor of secondary school record, standardized test scores. **Freshman Admission Requirements:** High school diploma or equivalent is not required. **Freshman Admission Statistics:** 2,585 applied, 57% admitted, 89% enrolled. **Transfer Admission Requirements:** College transcript(s), essay or personal statement, interview. Lowest grade transferable C. **General Admission Information:** Application fee $35. Nonfall registration accepted. Credit and/or placement offered for CEEB Advanced Placement tests.

COSTS AND FINANCIAL AID

Annual tuition $9,984. Required fees $700. Average book expense $900. **Required Forms and Deadlines:** FAFSA. Financial aid filing deadline 3/31. **Notification of Awards:** Applicants will be notified of awards on or about 7/1. **Types of Aid:** *Need-based scholarships/grants:* Pell, SEOG, the school's own gift aid. *Loans:* Direct Subsidized Stafford, Direct Unsubsidized Stafford, Direct PLUS. **Financial Aid Statistics:** 96% freshmen, 96% undergrads receive need-based scholarship or grant aid. 41% freshmen, 41% undergrads receive need-based self-help aid. 9 freshmen, 19 undergrads receive athletic scholarships. 95% freshmen, 92% undergrads receive any aid.

See page 1274.

MONTANA STATE UNIVERSITY—BILLINGS

1500 University Drive, Billings, MT 59101
Phone: 406-657-2158 **E-mail:** cjohannes@msubillings.edu **CEEB Code:** 4298
Fax: 406-657-2051 **Website:** www.msubillings.edu **ACT Code:** 2416
Financial Aid Phone: 406-657-2288

This public school was founded in 1927. It has a 92-acre campus.

RATINGS

Admissions Selectivity Rating: 69   **Fire Safety Rating:** 60*   **Green Rating:** 60*

STUDENTS AND FACULTY

Enrollment: 4,207. **Student Body:** 63% female, 37% male, 8% out-of-state. Asian 1%, Caucasian 86%, Hispanic 3%, Native American 5%. **Retention and Graduation:** 63% freshmen return for sophomore year. 7% grads go on to further study within 1 year. 80% grads pursue arts and sciences degrees. 13% grads pursue business degrees. **Faculty:** Student/faculty ratio 19:1. 172 full-time faculty, 65% hold PhDs. 100% faculty teach undergrads.

ACADEMICS

Degrees: Associate, bachelor's, certificate, master's, post-bachelor's certificate, post-master's certificate. **Academic Requirements:** Arts/fine arts, English (including composition), history, humanities, mathematics, philosophy, sciences (biological or physical), social science, cultural diversity. **Classes:** Most classes have 20–29 students. Most lab/discussion sections have 10–19 students. **Majors**

---

with Highest Enrollment: Business administration/management, elementary education and teaching, liberal arts and sciences/liberal studies. **Disciplines with Highest Percentage of Degrees Awarded:** Education 28%, business/marketing 22%, liberal arts/general studies 15%, psychology 9%, communications/journalism 6%. **Special Study Options:** Accelerated program, cooperative education program, cross-registration, distance learning, double major, dual enrollment, English as a second language (ESL), external degree program, honors program, independent study, internships, student-designed major, study abroad, teacher certification program, weekend college, online degrees, extensive online course offerings, evening college.

FACILITIES

Housing: Coed dorms, men's dorms, women's dorms, apartments for married students, special housing for disabled students, apartments for students with dependent children. **Special Academic Facilities/Equipment:** Montana Center for Disabilities, business enterprise, Small Business Institute, Urban Institute, public radio, applied economic research, biological station, Northern Plains Studies Center, Montana Business Connections, information commons, academic support center, advising center, TRIO Programs, SOS Programs, Northcutt Steele Gallery, Cisel Recital Hall, Petro Theatre, MSU-Billings Downtown. **Computers:** 30% of classrooms are wired, 20% of classrooms are wireless, 93% of public computers are PCs, 7% of public computers are Macs, network access in dorm rooms, network access in dorm lounges, online registration, online administrative functions (other than registration), support for handheld computing.

CAMPUS LIFE

Activities: Choral groups, concert band, drama/theater, jazz band, literary magazine, music ensembles, pep band, radio station, student government, student newspaper, symphony orchestra. **Organizations:** 53 registered organizations, 10 honor societies, 8 religious organizations. **Athletics (Intercollegiate):** *Men:* Baseball, basketball, cross-country, golf, soccer, tennis. *Women:* Basketball, cross-country, golf, soccer, softball, tennis, volleyball.

ADMISSIONS

Freshman Academic Profile: 8% in top 10% of high school class, 25% in top 25% of high school class, 63% in top 50% of high school class. 96% from public high schools. SAT Math middle 50% range 470–560. SAT Critical Reading middle 50% range 430–570. ACT middle 50% range 19–24. TOEFL required of all international applicants, minimum paper TOEFL 500, minimum computer TOEFL 173. **Basis for Candidate Selection:** *Very important factors considered include:* Class rank, rigor of secondary school record, standardized test scores. *Other factors considered include:* Character/personal qualities. **Freshman Admission Requirements:** High school diploma is required, and GED is accepted. *Academic units required:* 4 English, 3 math, 2 science (2 science labs), 3 social studies, 2 electives. **Freshman Admission Statistics:** 1,285 applied, 100% admitted, 59% enrolled. **Transfer Admission Requirements:** College transcript(s), statement of good standing from prior institution(s). Minimum college GPA of 2.0 required. Lowest grade transferable C-. **General Admission Information:** Application fee $30. Regular application deadline 7/1. Regular notification rolling. Nonfall registration accepted. Credit and/or placement offered for CEEB Advanced Placement tests.

COSTS AND FINANCIAL AID

Annual in-state tuition $3,988. Annual out-of-state tuition $13,707. Room and board $4,882. Required fees $1,144. Average book expense $1,000. **Required Forms and Deadlines:** FAFSA, institution's own financial aid form. Financial aid filing deadline 3/1. **Notification of Awards:** Applicants will be notified of awards on or about 5/1. **Types of Aid:** *Need-based scholarships/grants:* Pell, SEOG, state scholarships/grants, private scholarships, the school's own gift aid, Montana State University-Billings Foundation. *Loans:* FFEL Subsidized Stafford, FFEL Unsubsidized Stafford, FFEL PLUS, Federal Perkins, college/university loans from institutional funds. **Financial Aid Statistics:** 59% freshmen, 64% undergrads receive need-based scholarship or grant aid. 65% freshmen, 71% undergrads receive need-based self-help aid. 60 freshmen, 124 undergrads receive athletic scholarships. 75% freshmen, 67% undergrads receive any aid.

MONTANA STATE UNIVERSITY—BOZEMAN

New Student Services, PO Box 172190, Bozeman, MT 59717-2190
Phone: 406-994-2452 **E-mail:** admissions@montana.edu **CEEB Code:** 4488
Fax: 406-994-1923 **Website:** www.montana.edu **ACT Code:** 2420
Financial Aid Phone: 406-994-2845

This public school was founded in 1893. It has a 1,170-acre campus.

RATINGS
Admissions Selectivity Rating: 80   **Fire Safety Rating:** 87   **Green Rating:** 71

STUDENTS AND FACULTY
Enrollment: 10,748. **Student Body:** 46% female, 54% male, 31% out-of-state, 1% international (69 countries represented). Asian 1%, Caucasian 90%, Hispanic 1%, Native American 3%. **Retention and Graduation:** 71% freshmen return for sophomore year. 19% freshmen graduate within 4 years. 13% grads go on to further study within 1 year. **Faculty:** Student/faculty ratio 17:1. 549 full-time faculty, 81% hold PhDs. 95% faculty teach undergrads.

ACADEMICS
Degrees: Bachelor's, certificate, doctoral, master's, post-master's certificate. **Academic Requirements:** Arts/fine arts, English (including composition), humanities, mathematics, sciences (biological or physical), social science. **Classes:** Most classes have 10–19 students. Most lab/discussion sections have fewer than 10 students. **Majors with Highest Enrollment:** Business administration/management, education. **Disciplines with Highest Percentage of Degrees Awarded:** Business/marketing 12%, engineering 11%, health professions and related sciences 10%, education 9%, biological/life sciences 8%, visual and performing arts 8%. **Special Study Options:** Cooperative education program, cross-registration, distance learning, double major, English as a second language (ESL), exchange student program (domestic), honors program, independent study, internships, student-designed major, study abroad, teacher certification program.

FACILITIES
Housing: Coed dorms, men's dorms, women's dorms, apartments for married students, apartments for single students, fraternity/sorority housing, wellness floors, nonsmoking, older student floors. **Special Academic Facilities/Equipment:** Paleontology and history museums, water resources and planetarium, wind tunnel, electron microscopes, telecommunications center, ag bio-science center. **Computers:** 85% of public computers are PCs, 10% of public computers are Macs, 5% of public computers are UNIX, network access in dorm rooms, network access in dorm lounges, online registration, online administrative functions (other than registration), remote student-access to Web through college's connection.

CAMPUS LIFE
Activities: Choral groups, concert band, dance, drama/theater, jazz band, literary magazine, marching band, music ensembles, musical theater, pep band, radio station, student government, student newspaper, student-run film society, television station. **Organizations:** 140 registered organizations, 18 honor societies, 13 religious organizations. 9 fraternities (3% men join), 4 sororities (3% women join). **Athletics (Intercollegiate):** *Men:* Basketball, cheerleading, cross-country, football, rodeo, skiing (downhill/alpine), skiing (nordic/cross-country), tennis, track/field (indoor), track/field (outdoor). *Women:* Basketball, cheerleading, cross-country, golf, rodeo, skiing (downhill/alpine), skiing (nordic/cross-country), tennis, track/field (indoor), track/field (outdoor), volleyball. Environmental Initiatives: 1) Building Lighting Retrofit projects. 2)Recycling to reduce waste stream. 3)Steam Go-Generation Turbine (generates ~1/7th of campus electrical power need).

ADMISSIONS
Freshman Academic Profile: 18% in top 10% of high school class, 42% in top 25% of high school class, 72% in top 50% of high school class. SAT Math middle 50% range 500–630. SAT Critical Reading middle 50% range 480–610. ACT middle 50% range 21–26. TOEFL required of all international applicants, minimum paper TOEFL 525, minimum computer TOEFL 195. **Basis for Candidate Selection:** *Very important factors considered include:* Class rank, rigor of secondary school record, standardized test scores. **Freshman Admission Requirements:** High school diploma is required, and GED is accepted. *Academic units required:* 4 English, 3 math, 2 science (2 science labs), 3 social studies, 2 electives. **Freshman Admission Statistics:** 6,197 applied, 66% admitted, 54% enrolled. **Transfer Admission Requirements:** College transcript(s), standardized test score, statement of good standing from prior institution(s). Minimum college GPA of 2.0 required. Lowest grade transferable D-. **General Admission Information:** Application fee $30. Nonfall registration accepted. Admission may be deferred for a maximum of 1 year. Credit and/or placement offered for CEEB Advanced Placement tests.

COSTS AND FINANCIAL AID
Annual in-state tuition $5,749. Annual out-of-state tuition $16,274. Room and board $6,780. Average book expense $1,050. **Required Forms and Deadlines:** FAFSA. Financial aid filing deadline 3/1. **Notification of Awards:** Applicants will be notified of awards on a rolling basis beginning on or about 4/1. **Types of Aid:** *Need-based scholarships/grants:* Pell, SEOG, state scholarships/grants, private scholarships, the school's own gift aid, Federal Nursing Scholarships. *Loans:* Direct Subsidized Stafford, Direct Unsubsidized Stafford, Direct PLUS, Federal Perkins, Federal Nursing, college/university loans from institutional funds. **Student Employment:** Institutional employment available. Off-campus job opportunities are good. **Financial Aid Statistics:** 36% freshmen, 36% undergrads receive need-based scholarship or grant aid. 38% freshmen, 44% undergrads receive need-based self-help aid. 12 freshmen, 89 undergrads receive athletic scholarships. 48% freshmen, 51% undergrads receive any aid. Highest amount earned per year from on-campus jobs $2,500.

MONTANA STATE UNIVERSITY—GREAT FALLS COLLEGE OF TECHNOLOGY

PO Box 6010, Great Falls, MT 59406
Phone: 406-771-4300 **E-mail:** information@msugf.edu **CEEB Code:** 4482
Fax: 406-771-4317 **Website:** www.msugf.edu **ACT Code:** 2432
Financial Aid Phone: 406-771-4434

This public school was founded in 1969. It has a 20-acre campus.

RATINGS
Admissions Selectivity Rating: 60*   **Fire Safety Rating:** 60*   **Green Rating:** 60*

STUDENTS AND FACULTY
Enrollment: 1,241. **Student Body:** 71% female, 29% male, 1% out-of-state. African American 2%, Asian 1%, Caucasian 81%, Hispanic 2%, Native American 3%. **Faculty:** Student/faculty ratio 15:1. 40 full-time faculty. 100% faculty teach undergrads.

ACADEMICS
Degrees: Associate, certificate. **Academic Requirements:** Computer literacy, English (including composition), mathematics, sciences (biological or physical), social science. **Majors with Highest Enrollment:** Computer and information sciences, licensed practical nurse training (LPN, CERT, DIPL, AAS). **Special Study Options:** Cooperative education program, distance learning, double major, dual enrollment, independent study, internships.

FACILITIES
Computers: 100% of public computers are PCs, 24% of public computers are UNIX, online registration, online administrative functions (other than registration).

CAMPUS LIFE
Activities: Student government, student newspaper. **Organizations:** 3 registered organizations, 1 honor society.

ADMISSIONS
Freshman Academic Profile: TOEFL required of all international applicants, minimum paper TOEFL 500, minimum computer TOEFL 173. **Freshman Admission Requirements:** High school diploma is required, and GED is accepted. **Freshman Admission Statistics:** 422 applied, 100% admitted, 75% enrolled. **Transfer Admission Requirements:** High school transcript, college transcript(s). Lowest grade transferable C. **General Admission Information:** Application fee $30. Nonfall registration not accepted. Common Application not accepted. Credit offered for CEEB Advanced Placement tests.

COSTS AND FINANCIAL AID
Average book expense $500. **Required Forms and Deadlines:** FAFSA. **Types of Aid:** *Need-based scholarships/grants:* Pell, private scholarships. *Loans:* Direct Subsidized Stafford, Direct Unsubsidized Stafford, Direct PLUS, FFEL Subsidized Stafford, FFEL Unsubsidized Stafford, FFEL PLUS. **Student Employment:** Federal Work-Study Program available. Institutional employment available. Off-campus job opportunities are fair. **Financial Aid Statistics:** 70% freshmen, 69% undergrads receive need-based scholarship or grant aid. 60% freshmen, 64% undergrads receive need-based self-help aid.

MONTANA STATE UNIVERSITY—NORTHERN

PO Box 7751, Havre, MT 59501
Phone: 406-265-3704 **E-mail:** msunadmit@msun.edu **CEEB Code:** 4538
Fax: 406-265-3777 **Website:** www.msun.edu **ACT Code:** 2424
Financial Aid Phone: 406-265-3787

This public school was founded in 1929. It has a 105-acre campus.

RATINGS
Admissions Selectivity Rating: 60*   **Fire Safety Rating:** 60*   **Green Rating:** 60*

STUDENTS AND FACULTY
Enrollment: 1,367. **Student Body:** 4% out-of-state. Caucasian 77%, Native American 10%. **Retention and Graduation:** 4% grads go on to further study within 1 year. 4% grads pursue arts and sciences degrees.

ACADEMICS
Degrees: Associate, bachelor's, certificate, master's. **Academic Requirements:** Computer literacy, English (including composition), mathematics, sciences (biological or physical). **Special Study Options:** Cooperative education program, distance learning, double major, honors program, independent study, teacher certification program, agriculture, business, computer science, humanities, natural science, social/behavioral science, vocational arts.

FACILITIES
Housing: Coed dorms, apartments for married students, apartments for single students.

XTRACURRICULARS
Activities: Music ensembles, radio station, student government, student newspaper, yearbook. **Organizations:** 50 registered organizations, 12 honor societies, 18 religious organizations. **Athletics (Intercollegiate):** *Men:* Basketball, cheerleading, swimming, wrestling. *Women:* Basketball, cheerleading, swimming, volleyball.

ADMISSIONS
Freshman Academic Profile: 98% from public high schools. Minimum paper TOEFL 500. **Basis for Candidate Selection:** *Important factors considered include:* Class rank, rigor of secondary school record, standardized test scores. *Other factors considered include:* State residency. **Freshman Admission Requirements:** High school diploma is required, and GED is accepted. *Academic units required:* 4 English, 3 math, 2 science, 3 social studies, 2 academic electives. **Freshman Admission Statistics:** 629 applied, 100% admitted, 38% enrolled. **Transfer Admission Requirements:** High school transcript, college transcript(s). Minimum college GPA of 2.0 required. Lowest grade transferable C. **General Admission Information:** Application fee $30. Regular notification rolling. Nonfall registration accepted. Common Application not accepted. Credit and/or placement offered for CEEB Advanced Placement tests.

COSTS AND FINANCIAL AID
Annual in-state tuition $2,692. Out-of-state tuition $8,078. Room & board $3,800. Required fees $2,692. Average book expense $800. **Required Forms and Deadlines:** FAFSA. *Types of Aid: Need-based scholarships/grants:* State scholarships/grants. *Loans:* FFEL Subsidized Stafford, FFEL PLUS. **Student Employment:** Federal Work-Study Program available. Institutional employment available. Off-campus job opportunities are fair. **Financial Aid Statistics:** Highest amount earned per year from on-campus jobs $2,250.

MONTANA TECH OF THE UNIVERSITY OF MONTANA

1300 West Park Street, Butte, MT 59701
Phone: 406-496-4178 **E-mail:** Admissions@mtech.edu **CEEB Code:** 4487
Fax: 406-496-4710 **Website:** www.mtech.edu
Financial Aid Phone: 406-496-4212

This public school was founded in 1893. It has a 56-acre campus.

RATINGS
Admissions Selectivity Rating: 73   **Fire Safety Rating:** 89   **Green Rating:** 60*

STUDENTS AND FACULTY
Enrollment: 1,913. **Student Body:** 44% female, 56% male, 12% out-of-state. **Retention and Graduation:** 66% freshmen return for sophomore year. 5% freshmen graduate within 4 years. 14% grads go on to further study within 1 year. **Faculty:** Student/faculty ratio 16:1. 116 full-time faculty, 60% hold PhDs. 100% faculty teach undergrads.

ACADEMICS
Degrees: Associate, bachelor's, certificate, master's, post-bachelor's certificate. **Academic Requirements:** Communications, English (including composition), foreign languages, history, humanities, mathematics, sciences (biological or physical), social science. **Classes:** Most classes have fewer than 10 students. Most lab/discussion sections have 10–19 students. **Majors with Highest Enrollment:** Business administration/management; engineering; petroleum engineering. **Disciplines with Highest Percentage of Degrees Awarded:** Engineering 47%, health professions and related sciences 20%, business/marketing 16%, interdisciplinary studies 4%, biological/life sciences 3%. **Special Study Options:** Cooperative education program, distance learning, double major, dual enrollment, independent study, internships, teacher certification program.

FACILITIES
Housing: Coed dorms, apartments for married students, apartments for single students, special housing for disabled students, special housing for international students, apartments for families (don't have to be married if have children). **Special Academic Facilities/Equipment:** Mineral Museum, World Museum of Mining. **Computers:** 5% of classrooms are wireless, 97% of public computers are PCs, 1% of public computers are Macs, 2% of public computers are UNIX, network access in dorm rooms, network access in dorm lounges, online registration, online administrative functions (other than registration), remote student-access to Web through college's connection.

CAMPUS LIFE
Activities: Concert band, pep band, radio station, student government, student newspaper, yearbook. **Organizations:** 40 registered organizations, 2 honor societies, 3 religious organizations. **Athletics (Intercollegiate):** *Men:* Basketball, football, golf. *Women:* Basketball, golf, volleyball.

ADMISSIONS
Freshman Academic Profile: 14% in top 10% of high school class, 35% in top 25% of high school class, 68% in top 50% of high school class. 92% from public high schools. SAT Math middle 50% range 500–600. SAT Critical Reading middle 50% range 470–590. SAT Writing middle 50% range 430–560. ACT middle 50% range 19–25. TOEFL required of all international applicants, minimum paper TOEFL 525, minimum computer TOEFL 195. **Basis for Candidate Selection:** *Other factors considered include:* Academic GPA, class rank, standardized test scores. **Freshman Admission Requirements:** High school diploma is required, and GED is accepted. *Academic units required:* 4 English, 3 math, 2 science (2 science labs), 3 social studies, 2 combined years of foreign language, visual and performing arts, computer science, or vocational education units. *Academic units recommended:* 4 English, 4 math, 4 science (2 science labs), 2 foreign language. **Freshman Admission Statistics:** 479 applied, 96% admitted, 99% enrolled. **Transfer Admission Requirements:** College transcript(s). Minimum college GPA of 2.0 required. Lowest grade transferable C. **General Admission Information:** Application fee $30. Regular notification is rolling. Nonfall registration accepted. Admission may be deferred for a maximum of 1 year. Credit and/or placement offered for CEEB Advanced Placement tests.

COSTS AND FINANCIAL AID

Annual in-state tuition $5,644. Annual out-of-state tuition $15,076. Room and board $5,860. Average book expense $800. **Required Forms and Deadlines:** FAFSA, institution's own financial aid form. Financial aid filing deadline 3/1. **Notification of Awards:** Applicants will be notified of awards on or about 4/1. **Types of Aid:** *Need-based scholarships/grants:* Pell, SEOG, state scholarships/grants, private scholarships, the school's own gift aid. *Loans:* FFEL Subsidized Stafford, FFEL Unsubsidized Stafford, FFEL PLUS, Federal Perkins, college/university loans from institutional funds. **Student Employment:** Federal Work-Study Program available. Institutional employment available. Off-campus job opportunities are good. **Financial Aid Statistics:** 58% freshmen, 38% undergrads receive need-based scholarship or grant aid. 70% freshmen, 50% undergrads receive need-based self-help aid. 10 freshmen, 35 undergrads receive athletic scholarships. 80% freshmen, 68% undergrads receive any aid. Highest amount earned per year from on-campus jobs $4,200.

MONTCLAIR STATE UNIVERSITY

One Normal Avenue, Montclair, NJ 07043-1624
Phone: 973-655-4444 **E-mail:** undergraduate.admissions@montclair.edu **CEEB Code:** 2520
Fax: 973-655-7700 **Website:** www.montclair.edu
Financial Aid Phone: 973-655-4461

This public school was founded in 1908. It has a 275-acre campus.

RATINGS

Admissions Selectivity Rating: 79 **Fire Safety Rating:** 86 **Green Rating:** 86

STUDENTS AND FACULTY

Enrollment: 12,190. **Student Body:** 60% female, 40% male, 2% out-of-state, 3% international (98 countries represented). African American 10%, Asian 6%, Caucasian 57%, Hispanic 18%. **Retention and Graduation:** 81% freshmen return for sophomore year. 27% freshmen graduate within 4 years. 21% grads go on to further study within 1 year. 13% grads pursue arts and sciences degrees. 12% grads pursue business degrees. **Faculty:** Student/faculty ratio 17:1. 491 full-time faculty, 95% hold PhDs. 100% faculty teach undergrads.

ACADEMICS

Degrees: Bachelor's, certificate, doctoral, master's, post-bachelor's certificate, post-master's certificate. **Academic Requirements:** Arts/fine arts, English (including composition), foreign languages, history, humanities, mathematics, philosophy, sciences (biological or physical), social science. **Classes:** Most classes have 20–29 students. Most lab/discussion sections have fewer than 10 students. **Majors with Highest Enrollment:** Business administration/management, family and consumer sciences/human sciences, psychology. **Disciplines with Highest Percentage of Degrees Awarded:** Business/marketing 22%, family and consumer sciences 12%, psychology 10%, social sciences 7%, visual and performing arts 7%. **Special Study Options:** Cooperative education program, double major, English as a second language (ESL), honors program, independent study, internships, study abroad, teacher certification program.

FACILITIES

Housing: Coed dorms, women's dorms, apartments for single students, special housing for disabled students, special housing for international students. **Special Academic Facilities/Equipment:** The Dumont Television Center, Yogi Berra Museum and Stadium, Floyd Hall Arena **Computers:** 100% of classrooms are wired, 55% of classrooms are wireless, 80% of public computers are PCs, 20% of public computers are Macs, network access in dorm rooms, network access in dorm lounges, online registration, online administrative functions (other than registration), support for handheld computing, remote student-access to Web through college's connection.

CAMPUS LIFE

Activities: Choral groups, concert band, dance, drama/theater, jazz band, literary magazine, music ensembles, musical theater, opera, pep band, radio station, student government, student newspaper, symphony orchestra, television station, yearbook. **Organizations:** 121 registered organizations, 28 honor societies, 7 religious organizations. 14 fraternities (5% men join), 15 sororities (6% women join). **Athletics (Intercollegiate):** *Men:* Baseball, basketball, diving, football, lacrosse, soccer, swimming, track/field (outdoor). *Women:* Basketball, diving, field hockey, lacrosse, soccer, softball, swimming, track/field (outdoor), volleyball. Environmental Initiatives: Recycling Program—campus-wide. Green products used in housekeeping (This was built into the recent contract that was awarded). Food waste composter (Transitions Dining Services food waste into compost that is used by Grounds Services in plantings around campus).

ADMISSIONS

Freshman Academic Profile: 19% in top 10% of high school class, 44% in top 25% of high school class, 83% in top 50% of high school class. SAT Math middle 50% range 460–550. SAT Critical Reading middle 50% range 450–540. SAT Writing middle 50% range 450–540. TOEFL required of all international applicants, minimum paper TOEFL 539, minimum computer TOEFL 189. **Basis for Candidate Selection:** *Very important factors considered include:* Rigor of secondary school record. *Important factors considered include:* Class rank, standardized test scores. *Other factors considered include:* Academic GPA, extracurricular activities, interview, racial/ethnic status, state residency, talent/ability, volunteer work. **Freshman Admission Requirements:** High school diploma is required, and GED is accepted. *Academic units required:* 4 English, 3 math, 2 science (2 science labs), 2 foreign language, 2 social studies, 3 academic electives. **Freshman Admission Statistics:** 9,824 applied, 54% admitted, 38% enrolled. **Transfer Admission Requirements:** College transcript(s), statement of good standing from prior institution(s). Minimum college GPA of 2.0 required. Lowest grade transferable C-. **General Admission Information:** Application fee $55. Regular application deadline 3/1. Regular notification is rolling. Nonfall registration accepted. Admission may be deferred for a maximum of 1 semester. Credit offered for CEEB Advanced Placement tests.

COSTS AND FINANCIAL AID

Annual in-state tuition $6,390. Annual out-of-state tuition $13,659. Room and board $9,500. Required fees $2,505. Average book expense $1,000. **Required Forms and Deadlines:** FAFSA. Financial aid filing deadline 3/1. **Notification of Awards:** Applicants will be notified of awards on a rolling basis beginning on or about 4/1. **Types of Aid:** *Need-based scholarships/grants:* Pell, SEOG, state scholarships/grants, private scholarships, the school's own gift aid. *Loans:* FFEL Subsidized Stafford, FFEL Unsubsidized Stafford, FFEL PLUS, Federal Perkins, state loans. **Financial Aid Statistics:** 19% freshmen, 3% undergrads receive need-based scholarship or grant aid. 39% freshmen, 43% undergrads receive need-based self-help aid. 62% freshmen, 60% undergrads receive any aid. Highest amount earned per year from on-campus jobs $1,256.

MONTEREY INSTITUTE OF INTERNATIONAL STUDIES

425 Van Buren Street, Monterey, CA 93940
Phone: 831-647-4123 **E-mail:** admit@miis.edu
Fax: 831-647-6405 **Website:** www.miis.edu **Financial Aid Phone:** 831-647-4119

This private school was founded in 1955. It has a 5-acre campus.

RATINGS

Admissions Selectivity Rating: 60* **Fire Safety Rating:** 60* **Green Rating:** 60*

STUDENTS AND FACULTY

Enrollment: 20. **Student Body:** 60% female, 40% male, 43% out-of-state, 30% international (50 countries represented). Caucasian 70%. **Retention and Graduation:** 95% grads go on to further study within 1 year. 65% grads pursue arts and sciences degrees. 35% grads pursue business degrees. **Faculty:** Student/faculty ratio 10:1. 30% faculty teach undergrads.

ACADEMICS

Degrees: Bachelor's, master's. **Academic Requirements:** Foreign languages. **Special Study Options:** Cooperative education program, English as a second language (ESL), honors program, study abroad.

FACILITIES

Computers: 100% of public computers are PCs, remote student-access to Web through college's connection.

CAMPUS LIFE

Activities: Choral groups, student government, student newspaper. **Organizations:** 30 registered organizations, 7 honor societies, 5 religious organizations.

ADMISSIONS

Freshman Academic Profile: TOEFL required of all international applicants, minimum paper TOEFL 550. **Transfer Admission Requirements:** College transcript(s), essay or personal statement, statement of good standing from prior institution(s). Minimum college GPA of 3.0 required. Lowest grade transferable B-. **General Admission Information:** Application fee $50. Regular application deadline 8/15. Regular notification rolling. Nonfall registration accepted. Admission may be deferred for a maximum of 1 year. Common Application not accepted.

COSTS AND FINANCIAL AID

Annual tuition $19,500. Required fees $50. **Student Employment:** Federal Work-Study Program available. Institutional employment available. Off-campus job opportunities are good.

MONTREAT COLLEGE

310 Gaither Circle, Montreat, NC 28757-1267
Phone: 828-669-8011 **E-mail:** admissions@montreat.edu **CEEB Code:** 5423
Fax: 828-669-0120 **Website:** www.montreat.edu **ACT Code:** 3130
Financial Aid Phone: 800-545-4656

This private school, affiliated with the Christian (nondenominational) Church, was founded in 1916. It has a 162-acre campus.

RATINGS
Admissions Selectivity Rating: 74 **Fire Safety Rating:** 60* **Green Rating:** 60*

STUDENTS AND FACULTY
Enrollment: 937. **Student Body:** 60% female, 40% male, 20% out-of-state. **Faculty:** Student/faculty ratio 22:1. 46 full-time faculty, 67% hold PhDs. 100% faculty teach undergrads.

ACADEMICS
Degrees: Associate, bachelor's, master's. **Academic Requirements:** Arts/fine arts, computer literacy, English (including composition), history, humanities, mathematics, philosophy, sciences (biological or physical), social science, Bible and religion. **Classes:** Most classes have 10–19 students. Most lab/discussion sections have 10–19 students. **Majors with Highest Enrollment:** Bible/biblical studies, business administration and management, environmental studies. **Disciplines with Highest Percentage of Degrees Awarded:** Business/marketing 52%, liberal arts/general studies 11%, philosophy and religious studies 9%, natural resources/environmental science 7%, parks and recreation 6%. **Special Study Options:** Accelerated program, double major, dual enrollment, independent study, internships, student-designed major, study abroad, teacher certification program, American studies program (Washington, DC), L.A. Film Studies Center (Los Angeles, CA), Martha's Vineyard semester.

FACILITIES
Housing: Men's dorms, women's dorms. **Special Academic Facilities/ Equipment:** Hamilton Art Gallery, Chapel of the Prodigal Son. **Computers:** 95% of public computers are PCs, 5% of public computers are Macs, network access in dorm rooms, network access in dorm lounges, online administrative functions (other than registration), remote student-access to Web through college's connection.

CAMPUS LIFE
Activities: Choral groups, dance, drama/theater, music ensembles, musical theater, student government, student newspaper. **Organizations:** 11 registered organizations, **Athletics (Intercollegiate):** *Men:* Baseball, basketball, cross-country, golf, soccer. *Women:* Basketball, cross-country, golf, soccer, softball, volleyball.

ADMISSIONS
Freshman Academic Profile: 7% in top 10% of high school class, 20% in top 25% of high school class, 59% in top 50% of high school class. SAT Math middle 50% range 430–540. SAT Critical Reading middle 50% range 410–560. ACT middle 50% range 18–22. TOEFL required of all international applicants, minimum paper TOEFL 500, minimum computer TOEFL 173. **Basis for Candidate Selection:** *Very important factors considered include:* Academic GPA, application essay, rigor of secondary school record, standardized test scores. *Important factors considered include:* Character/personal qualities, interview, recommendation(s). *Other factors considered include:* Alumni/ae relation, class rank, extracurricular activities, first generation, level of applicant's interest, talent/ability, volunteer work, work experience. **Freshman Admission Requirements:** High school diploma is required, and GED is accepted. *Academic units required:* 4 English, 3 math, 3 science, 1 foreign language, 3 history. **Freshman Admission Statistics:** 527 applied, 62% admitted, 72% enrolled. **Transfer Admission Requirements:** College transcript(s), essay or personal statement, statement of good standing from prior institution(s). Minimum college GPA of 2.5 required. Lowest grade transferable C. **General Admission Information:** Application fee $30. Regular application deadline 8/1. Regular notification is rolling. Nonfall registration accepted. Admission may be deferred for a maximum of 1 semester. Credit and/or placement offered for CEEB Advanced Placement tests.

COSTS AND FINANCIAL AID

Annual tuition $16,182. Room & board $5,258. Average book expense $1,000. **Required Forms and Deadlines:** FAFSA. Financial aid filing deadline 3/15. **Notification of Awards:** Applicants will be notified of awards on a rolling basis beginning on or about 2/1. **Types of Aid:** *Need-based scholarships/grants:* Pell, SEOG, state scholarships/grants, private scholarships, the school's own gift aid. *Loans:* FFEL Subsidized Stafford, FFEL Unsubsidized Stafford, FFEL PLUS, Federal Perkins. **Financial Aid Statistics:** 78% freshmen, 79% undergrads receive need-based scholarship or grant aid. 59% freshmen, 71% undergrads receive need-based self-help aid. 124 freshmen, 614 undergrads receive athletic scholarships. 98% freshmen, 98% undergrads receive any aid. Highest amount earned per year from on-campus jobs $2,212.

MONTSERRAT COLLEGE OF ART

23 Essex Street, PO Box 26, Beverly, MA 01915
Phone: 978-921-4242 **E-mail:** admiss@montserrat.edu **CEEB Code:** 9101
Fax: 978-921-4241 **Website:** www.montserrat.edu **ACT Code:** 1847
Financial Aid Phone: 978-921-4242

This private school was founded in 1970. It has a 12-acre campus.

RATINGS
Admissions Selectivity Rating: 60* **Fire Safety Rating:** 60* **Green Rating:** 60*

STUDENTS AND FACULTY
Enrollment: 298. **Student Body:** 62% female, 38% male, 50% out-of-state. African American 1%, Asian 2%, Caucasian 76%, Hispanic 2%. **Retention and Graduation:** 51% freshmen return for sophomore year. 45% freshmen graduate within 4 years. **Faculty:** Student/faculty ratio 7:1. 26 full-time faculty, 62% hold PhDs. 100% faculty teach undergrads.

ACADEMICS
Degrees: Bachelor's, certificate, diploma. **Academic Requirements:** Arts/fine arts, computer literacy, English (including composition), humanities, sciences (biological or physical), social science, art history. **Classes:** Most classes have 10–19 students. **Majors with Highest Enrollment:** Graphic design, illustration; painting. **Disciplines with Highest Percentage of Degrees Awarded:** Visual and performing arts 100%. **Special Study Options:** Cross-registration, dual enrollment, exchange student program (domestic), independent study, internships, student-designed major, study abroad, teacher certification program.

FACILITIES
Housing: Special housing for disabled students, apartment style: coed buildings with single-gender apartments. **Special Academic Facilities/Equipment:** Montserrat Gallery, 301 Gallery, Carol Schlosberg Alumni Gallery, 292 Gallery. **Computers:** 5% of public computers are PCs, 95% of public computers are Macs, remote student-access to Web through college's connection.

CAMPUS LIFE
Activities: Literary magazine, student government. **Organizations:** 5 registered organizations.

ADMISSIONS
Freshman Academic Profile: SAT Math middle 50% range 372–589. SAT Critical Reading middle 50% range 416–642. ACT middle 50% range 18–22. TOEFL required of all international applicants, minimum paper TOEFL 550, minimum computer TOEFL 213. **Basis for Candidate Selection:** *Very important factors considered include:* Application essay, character/personal qualities, interview, recommendation(s), rigor of secondary school record, talent/ability. *Important factors considered include:* Standardized test scores. *Other factors considered include:* Class rank, extracurricular activities, volunteer work, work experience. **Freshman Admission Requirements:** High school diploma is required, and GED is accepted. *Academic units recommended:* 4 English, 2 social studies, 2 history, 4 visual arts. **Freshman Admission Statistics:** 326 applied, 85% admitted, 27% enrolled. **Transfer Admission Requirements:** College transcript(s), essay or personal statement. Minimum college GPA of 2.2 required. Lowest grade transferable C. **General Admission Information:** Application fee $40. Regular notification is rolling. Nonfall registration accepted. Admission may be deferred for a maximum of 1 year. Common Application not accepted. Credit offered for CEEB Advanced Placement tests.

COSTS AND FINANCIAL AID
Required Forms and Deadlines: FAFSA, institution's own financial aid form, Noncustodial PROFILE. Financial aid filing deadline 7/1. **Notification of Awards:** Applicants will be notified of awards on a rolling basis beginning on or

about 3/1. **Types of Aid:** *Need-based scholarships/grants:* Pell, SEOG, state scholarships/grants, private scholarships, the school's own gift aid. *Loans:* FFEL Subsidized Stafford, FFEL Unsubsidized Stafford, FFEL PLUS, state loans. **Student Employment:** Federal Work-Study Program available. Institutional employment available. Off-campus job opportunities are good. **Financial Aid Statistics:** 71% freshmen, 69% undergrads receive need-based scholarship or grant aid. 73% freshmen, 76% undergrads receive need-based self-help aid. 96% freshmen, 79% undergrads receive any aid. Highest amount earned per year from on-campus jobs $1,500.

MOORE COLLEGE OF ART & DESIGN

20th Street and The Parkway, Philadelphia, PA 19103-1179
Phone: 215-965-4014 **E-mail:** admiss@moore.edu
Fax: 215-568-3547 **Website:** www.moore.edu **ACT Code:** 2417
Financial Aid Phone: 215-965-4042

This private school was founded in 1848.

RATINGS
Admissions Selectivity Rating: 60*   **Fire Safety Rating:** 60*   **Green Rating:** 60*

STUDENTS AND FACULTY
Enrollment: 507. **Student Body:** 100% female, 38% out-of-state, 2% international (10 countries represented). African American 7%, Asian 4%, Caucasian 71%, Hispanic 5%. **Retention and Graduation:** 79% freshmen return for sophomore year. 55% freshmen graduate within 4 years. 15% grads go on to further study within 1 year. **Faculty:** Student/faculty ratio 8:1. 30 full-time faculty, 70% hold PhDs. 100% faculty teach undergrads.

ACADEMICS
Degrees: Bachelor's, post-bachelor's certificate. **Academic Requirements:** Arts/fine arts, English (including composition), history, humanities, social science. **Classes:** Most classes have 10–19 students. **Majors with Highest Enrollment:** Fashion/apparel design, fine/studio arts, graphic design. **Disciplines with Highest Percentage of Degrees Awarded:** Visual and performing arts 95%, education 5%. **Special Study Options:** Double major, independent study, internships, study abroad, teacher certification program, arts, education, student travel courses.

FACILITIES
Housing: Women's dorms, apartments for single students. **Special Academic Facilities/Equipment:** Paley, Graham, and Levy galleries. **Computers:** 10% of public computers are PCs, 90% of public computers are Macs, network access in dorm rooms, network access in dorm lounges, online registration, online administrative functions (other than registration), remote student-access to Web through college's connection. Undergraduates are required to own a computer.

CAMPUS LIFE
Activities: Literary magazine, student government, student newspaper, yearbook. **Organizations:** 10 registered organizations.

ADMISSIONS
Freshman Academic Profile: 72% from public high schools. TOEFL required of all international applicants, minimum paper TOEFL 527, minimum computer TOEFL 197. **Basis for Candidate Selection:** *Very important factors considered include:* Academic GPA, character/personal qualities, interview, level of applicant's interest, rigor of secondary school record, standardized test scores, talent/ability. *Important factors considered include:* Application essay, extracurricular activities, recommendation(s). *Other factors considered include:* Class rank, volunteer work, work experience. **Freshman Admission Requirements:** High school diploma is required, and GED is accepted. **Freshman Admission Statistics:** 461 applied, 65% admitted, 42% enrolled. **Transfer Admission Requirements:** High school transcript, college transcript(s), essay or personal statement, statement of good standing from prior institution(s). Minimum college GPA of 2.5 required. Lowest grade transferable C. **General Admission Information:** Application fee $40. Early decision application deadline 11/15. Regular application deadline 9/15. Regular notification is rolling. Nonfall registration accepted. Admission may be deferred for a maximum of 1 year. Credit offered for CEEB Advanced Placement tests.

COSTS AND FINANCIAL AID
Annual tuition $22,858. Room & board $9,346. Required fees $816. Average book expense $2,160. **Required Forms and Deadlines:** FAFSA. Financial aid filing deadline 3/1. **Notification of Awards:** Applicants will be notified of awards on a rolling basis beginning on or about 3/1. **Types of Aid:** *Need-based scholarships/grants:* Pell, SEOG, state scholarships/grants, private scholarships,

the school's own gift aid. *Loans:* FFEL Subsidized Stafford, FFEL Unsubsidized Stafford, FFEL PLUS, Federal Perkins, alternative loans. **Student Employment:** Federal Work-Study Program available. Off-campus job opportunities are good. **Financial Aid Statistics:** 65% freshmen, 75% undergrads receive need-based scholarship or grant aid. 57% freshmen, 70% undergrads receive need-based self-help aid. 97% undergrads receive any aid.

MORAVIAN COLLEGE

1200 Main Street, Bethlehem, PA 18018
Phone: 610-861-1320 **E-mail:** admissions@moravian.edu
Fax: 610-625-7930 **Website:** www.moravian.edu **ACT Code:** 2418
Financial Aid Phone: 610-861-1320

This private school, affiliated with the Moravian Church, was founded in 1742. It has a 60-acre campus.

RATINGS
Admissions Selectivity Rating: 79   **Fire Safety Rating:** 82   **Green Rating:** 78

STUDENTS AND FACULTY
Enrollment: 1,625. **Student Body:** 60% female, 40% male, 44% out-of-state. African American 2%, Asian 2%, Caucasian 90%, Hispanic 3%. **Retention and Graduation:** 86% freshmen return for sophomore year. 65% freshmen graduate within 4 years. 17% grads go on to further study within 1 year. 9% grads pursue arts and sciences degrees. 2% grads pursue business degrees. 2% grads pursue law degrees. 3% grads pursue medical degrees. **Faculty:** Student/faculty ratio 11:1. 110 full-time faculty, 88% hold PhDs. 100% faculty teach undergrads.

ACADEMICS
Degrees: Bachelor's, first professional, master's, post-bachelor's certificate. **Academic Requirements:** Arts/fine arts, English (including composition), foreign languages, history, humanities, mathematics, philosophy, sciences (biological or physical), social science. **Classes:** Most classes have 10–19 students. Most lab/discussion sections have 10–19 students. **Majors with Highest Enrollment:** Business administration/management, psychology, sociology. **Disciplines with Highest Percentage of Degrees Awarded:** Social sciences 21%, business/marketing 15%, psychology 12%, visual and performing arts 10%, English 8%. **Special Study Options:** Cross-registration, double major, honors program, independent study, internships, student-designed major, study abroad, teacher certification program.

FACILITIES
Housing: Coed dorms, men's dorms, women's dorms, apartments for single students, fraternity/sorority housing, special interest housing, wellness (substance-free) floors. **Special Academic Facilities/Equipment:** Payne Gallery, Foy Hall, greenhouse, student art studios, observation room for psychology classes, leadership center. **Computers:** 69% of public computers are PCs, 31% of public computers are Macs, network access in dorm rooms, network access in dorm lounges, online administrative functions (other than registration), remote student-access to Web through college's connection.

CAMPUS LIFE
Activities: Choral groups, concert band, dance, drama/theater, jazz band, literary magazine, marching band, music ensembles, musical theater, radio station, student government, student newspaper, symphony orchestra, yearbook. **Organizations:** 80 registered organizations, 16 honor societies, 4 religious organizations. 3 fraternities (15% men join), 4 sororities (22% women join). **Athletics (Intercollegiate):** *Men:* Baseball, basketball, cross-country, football, golf, lacrosse, soccer, tennis, track/field (indoor), track/field (outdoor). *Women:* Basketball, cross-country, field hockey, lacrosse, soccer, softball, tennis, track/field (indoor), track/field (outdoor), volleyball.

ADMISSIONS
Freshman Academic Profile: 24% in top 10% of high school class, 61% in top 25% of high school class, 91% in top 50% of high school class. 82% from public high schools. SAT Math middle 50% range 500–610. SAT Critical Reading middle 50% range 500–600. SAT Writing middle 50% range 490–590. TOEFL required of all international applicants, minimum paper TOEFL 550, minimum computer TOEFL 213. **Basis for Candidate Selection:** *Very important factors considered include:* Academic GPA, character/personal qualities, class

rank, rigor of secondary school record. *Important factors considered include:* Alumni/ae relation, application essay, extracurricular activities, level of applicant's interest, racial/ethnic status, recommendation(s), standardized test scores, talent/ability, volunteer work. *Other factors considered include:* First generation, geographical residence, interview, work experience. **Freshman Admission Requirements:** High school diploma is required, and GED is accepted. *Academic units required:* 4 English, 3 math, 3 science (2 science labs), 2 foreign language, 4 social studies. *Academic units recommended:* 4 math, 3 foreign language. **Freshman Admission Statistics:** 1,871 applied, 65% admitted, 31% enrolled. **Transfer Admission Requirements:** High school transcript, college transcript(s), essay or personal statement, statement of good standing from prior institution(s). Minimum college GPA of 2.8 required. Lowest grade transferable C. **General Admission Information:** Application fee $40. Early decision application deadline 2/1. Regular application deadline 3/1. Regular notification 3/15. Nonfall registration accepted. Admission may be deferred for a maximum of 1 year. Placement offered for CEEB Advanced Placement tests.

COSTS AND FINANCIAL AID

Annual tuition $29,547. Room and board $8,312. Required fees $515. Average book expense $900. **Required Forms and Deadlines:** FAFSA, CSS/Financial Aid PROFILE, Noncustodial PROFILE, Business/Farm Supplement, copies of parent and student W-2 and 1040 forms. Financial aid filing deadline 3/15. **Notification of Awards:** Applicants will be notified of awards on a rolling basis beginning on or about 4/1. **Types of Aid:** *Need-based scholarships/grants:* Pell, SEOG, state scholarships/grants, the school's own gift aid. *Loans:* FFEL Subsidized Stafford, FFEL Unsubsidized Stafford, FFEL PLUS, Federal Perkins. **Financial Aid Statistics:** 74% freshmen, 73% undergrads receive need-based scholarship or grant aid. 67% freshmen, 67% undergrads receive need-based self-help aid. 94% freshmen, 96% undergrads receive any aid. Highest amount earned per year from on-campus jobs $3,000.

MOREHEAD STATE UNIVERSITY

Admissions Center, Morehead, KY 40351
Phone: 606-783-2000 **E-mail:** admissions@morehead-st.edu
Fax: 606-783-5038 **Website:** www.morehead-st.edu **ACT Code:** 1530
Financial Aid Phone: 606-783-2011

This public school was founded in 1922. It has a 1,016-acre campus.

RATINGS

Admissions Selectivity Rating: 76   **Fire Safety Rating:** 86   **Green Rating:** 60*

STUDENTS AND FACULTY

Enrollment: 6,857. **Student Body:** 60% female, 40% male, 16% out-of-state. African American 3%, Caucasian 95%. **Retention and Graduation:** 69% freshmen return for sophomore year. **Faculty:** Student/faculty ratio 16:1. 384 full-time faculty, 60% hold PhDs.

ACADEMICS

Degrees: Associate, bachelor's, master's, post-bachelor's certificate, post-master's certificate. **Academic Requirements:** Computer literacy, English (including composition), history, humanities, mathematics, sciences (biological or physical), social science. **Classes:** Most classes have 10–19 students. Most lab/discussion sections have 10–19 students. **Majors with Highest Enrollment:** Elementary education and teaching, nursing/registered nurse training (RN, ASN, BSN, MSN). **Disciplines with Highest Percentage of Degrees Awarded:** Education 21%, liberal arts/general studies 12%, business/marketing 12%, health professions and related sciences 7%, social sciences 7%, communications/journalism 6%, visual and performing arts 6%, biological/life sciences 5%. **Special Study Options:** Accelerated program, cooperative education program, distance learning, double major, dual enrollment, exchange student program (domestic), honors program, independent study, internships, student-designed major, study abroad, teacher certification program, weekend college.

FACILITIES

Housing: Coed dorms, apartments for married students, apartments for single students, special housing for disabled students, special housing for international students, fraternity/sorority housing. **Special Academic Facilities/Equipment:** Ky. Folk Art Center, 320-acre agricultural complex, Space Science Center, Ky. Center for Traditional Music. **Computers:** 5% of classrooms are wired, 100% of classrooms are wireless, network access in dorm rooms, online registration, online administrative functions (other than registration), remote student-access to Web through college's connection.

CAMPUS LIFE

Activities: Choral groups, concert band, dance, drama/theater, jazz band, literary magazine, marching band, music ensembles, musical theater, opera, pep band, radio station, student government, student newspaper, symphony orchestra, television station, yearbook. **Organizations:** 101 registered organizations, 14 honor societies, 6 religious organizations. 10 fraternities, 8 sororities. **Athletics (Intercollegiate):** *Men:* Baseball, basketball, cheerleading, cross-country, football, golf, riflery, tennis, track/field (outdoor). *Women:* Basketball, cheerleading, cross-country, riflery, soccer, softball, tennis, track/field (indoor), track/field (outdoor), volleyball.

ADMISSIONS

Freshman Academic Profile: 17% in top 10% of high school class, 41% in top 25% of high school class, 71% in top 50% of high school class. SAT Math middle 50% range 440–560. SAT Critical Reading middle 50% range 430–530. ACT middle 50% range 17–24. TOEFL required of all international applicants, minimum paper TOEFL 500, minimum computer TOEFL 173. **Basis for Candidate Selection:** *Very important factors considered include:* Academic GPA, racial/ethnic status, rigor of secondary school record, standardized test scores. *Important factors considered include:* Character/personal qualities, level of applicant's interest, talent/ability. *Other factors considered include:* Class rank, extracurricular activities, interview, recommendation(s), volunteer work, work experience. **Freshman Admission Requirements:** High school diploma is required, and GED is accepted. *Academic units required:* 4 English, 3 math, 3 science (1 science lab), 3 social studies, 7 academic electives. *Academic units recommended:* 2 foreign language. **Freshman Admission Statistics:** 4,757 applied, 69% admitted, 40% enrolled. **Transfer Admission Requirements:** College transcript(s). Minimum college GPA of 2.0 required. Lowest grade transferable C. **General Admission Information:** Regular notification rolling as processed. Nonfall registration accepted. Admission may be deferred for a maximum of 1 semester. Credit and/or placement offered for CEEB Advanced Placement tests.

COSTS AND FINANCIAL AID

Average book expense $600. **Required Forms and Deadlines:** FAFSA, institution's own financial aid form. Financial aid filing deadline 3/15. **Types of Aid:** *Need-based scholarships/grants:* Pell, SEOG, state scholarships/grants, private scholarships, the school's own gift aid. *Loans:* Direct Subsidized Stafford, Direct Unsubsidized Stafford, Direct PLUS, FFEL Subsidized Stafford, FFEL Unsubsidized Stafford, FFEL PLUS, Federal Perkins, college/university loans from institutional funds. **Student Employment:** Federal Work-Study Program available. Institutional employment available. **Financial Aid Statistics:** 93% freshmen, 89% undergrads receive any aid.

MOREHOUSE COLLEGE

830 Westview Drive, SW, Atlanta, GA 30314
Phone: 404-215-2632 **E-mail:** janderso@morehouse.edu **CEEB Code:** 5415
Fax: 404-524-5635 **Website:** www.morehouse.edu **ACT Code:** 0792
Financial Aid Phone: 404-681-2800

This private school was founded in 1867. It has a 61-acre campus.

RATINGS

Admissions Selectivity Rating: 82   **Fire Safety Rating:** 60*   **Green Rating:** 60*

STUDENTS AND FACULTY

Enrollment: 2,891. **Student Body:** 100% male, 70% out-of-state, 3% international. African American 94%. **Retention and Graduation:** 84% freshmen return for sophomore year. 32% freshmen graduate within 4 years. 25% grads go on to further study within 1 year. 22% grads pursue arts and sciences degrees. 10% grads pursue business degrees. 5% grads pursue law degrees. 14% grads pursue medical degrees. **Faculty:** Student/faculty ratio 15:1. 159 full-time faculty, 81% hold PhDs. 100% faculty teach undergrads.

ACADEMICS

Degrees: Bachelor's. **Academic Requirements:** Arts/fine arts, English (including composition), foreign languages, history, humanities, mathematics, philosophy, sciences (biological or physical), social science. **Classes:** Most classes have fewer than 10 students. **Majors with Highest Enrollment:** Business administration/management, computer and information sciences. **Disciplines with Highest Percentage of Degrees Awarded:** Business/marketing 40%, social sciences 15%, psychology 8%, computer and information sciences 7%, biological/life sciences 6%. **Special Study Options:** Cooperative education program, cross-registration, double major, dual enrollment, exchange student program (domestic), honors program, internships, study abroad, dual-degree program in engineering and architecture with other institutions.

FACILITIES

Housing: Men's dorms, apartments for single students. **Special Academic Facilities/Equipment:** Three chapels, meditation room, Olympic arena. **Computers:** 90% of public computers are PCs, 5% of public computers are Macs, 5% of public computers are UNIX, network access in dorm rooms, network access in dorm lounges, online registration, online administrative functions (other than registration), remote student-access to Web through college's connection.

CAMPUS LIFE

Activities: Choral groups, concert band, drama/theater, jazz band, literary magazine, marching band, music ensembles, pep band, student government, student newspaper, yearbook. **Organizations:** 34 registered organizations, 7 honor societies, 4 religious organizations. 6 fraternities (3% men join). **Athletics (Intercollegiate):** *Men:* Basketball, cross-country, football, track/field (outdoor).

ADMISSIONS

Freshman Academic Profile: 20% in top 10% of high school class, 47% in top 25% of high school class, 77% in top 50% of high school class. 80% from public high schools. SAT Math middle 50% range 470–590. SAT Critical Reading middle 50% range 470–580. ACT middle 50% range 19–24. TOEFL required of all international applicants, minimum paper TOEFL 500. **Basis for Candidate Selection:** *Very important factors considered include:* Standardized test scores. *Important factors considered include:* Application essay, class rank, recommendation(s), rigor of secondary school record. *Other factors considered include:* Alumni/ae relation, character/personal qualities, extracurricular activities, geographical residence, interview, racial/ethnic status, talent/ability, volunteer work. **Freshman Admission Requirements:** High school diploma is required, and GED is accepted. *Academic units required:* 4 English, 3 math, 2 science, 2 foreign language, 2 social studies. **Freshman Admission Statistics:** 2,277 applied, 67% admitted, 46% enrolled. **Transfer Admission Requirements:** College transcript(s), essay or personal statement, standardized test score, statement of good standing from prior institution(s). Minimum college GPA of 2.5 required. Lowest grade transferable C. **General Admission Information:** Application fee $45. Early decision application deadline 10/15. Regular application deadline 2/15. Regular notification 4/1. Nonfall registration not accepted. Admission may be deferred for a maximum of 2 years. Common Application accepted.

COSTS AND FINANCIAL AID

Annual tuition $14,318. Room & board $8,748. Required fees $1,422. Average book expense $850. **Required Forms and Deadlines:** FAFSA, institution's own financial aid form, CSS/Financial Aid PROFILE. Financial aid filing deadline 4/1. **Notification of Awards:** Applicants will be notified of awards on or about 5/1. **Types of Aid:** *Need-based scholarships/grants:* Pell, SEOG, state scholarships/grants, private scholarships, the school's own gift aid, United Negro College Fund. *Loans:* Direct Subsidized Stafford, Direct Unsubsidized Stafford, Direct PLUS, FFEL Subsidized Stafford, FFEL Unsubsidized Stafford, FFEL PLUS, Federal Perkins, state loans, college/university loans from institutional funds. **Student Employment:** Federal Work-Study Program available. Institutional employment available. Off-campus job opportunities are good. **Financial Aid Statistics:** 38% freshmen, 37% undergrads receive need-based scholarship or grant aid. 53% freshmen, 56% undergrads receive need-based self-help aid. 21 freshmen, 116 undergrads receive athletic scholarships. Highest amount earned per year from on-campus jobs $1,500.

MORGAN STATE UNIVERSITY

1700 East Cold Spring Lane, Baltimore, MD 21251
Phone: 800-332-6674 **E-mail:** tjenness@moac.morgan.edu **CEEB Code:** 5416
Fax: 410-319-3684 **Website:** www.morgan.edu **ACT Code:** 1722
Financial Aid Phone: 410-319-3170

This public school was founded in 1867. It has a 122-acre campus.

RATINGS

Admissions Selectivity Rating: 60*   **Fire Safety Rating:** 60*   **Green Rating:** 60*

STUDENTS AND FACULTY

Student Body: 40% out-of-state. **Retention and Graduation:** 76% freshmen return for sophomore year.

ACADEMICS

Degrees: Bachelor's, doctoral, master's. **Special Study Options:** Cooperative education program, business, education, engineering, social/behavioral science.

FACILITIES

Housing: Coed dorms, men's dorms, women's dorms, apartments for single students. **Special Academic Facilities/Equipment:** African American collection, new science complex, school of engineering.

CAMPUS LIFE

Activities: Radio station, student government, student newspaper, television station, yearbook. **Organizations:** 250 registered organizations, 1 religious organization. 4 fraternities, 4 sororities. **Athletics (Intercollegiate):** *Men:* Basketball, cross-country, football, tennis, track/field (outdoor), volleyball. *Women:* Basketball, cross-country, tennis, track/field (outdoor), volleyball.

ADMISSIONS

Freshman Academic Profile: 20% in top 10% of high school class, 80% in top 25% of high school class, 96% in top 50% of high school class. TOEFL required of all international applicants, minimum paper TOEFL 550. **Freshman Admission Requirements:** High school diploma is required, and GED is accepted. *Academic units recommended:* 4 English, 3 math, 3 science, 2 foreign language, 3 social studies, 2 history. **Transfer Admission Requirements:** Minimum college GPA of 2.0 required. Lowest grade transferable C. **General Admission Information:** Early decision application deadline 4/15. Regular application deadline 4/15. Regular notification rolling. Nonfall registration accepted. Common Application accepted. Credit offered for CEEB Advanced Placement tests.

COSTS AND FINANCIAL AID

Annual in-state tuition $1,853. Out-of-state tuition $4,405. Room & board $5,296. Required fees $762. Average book expense $1,500. **Required Forms and Deadlines:** FAFSA, institution's own financial aid form, state aid form. **Types of Aid:** *Need-based scholarships/grants:* State scholarships/grants, United Negro College Fund. *Loans:* FFEL Subsidized Stafford, FFEL PLUS. **Student Employment:** Federal Work-Study Program available. Institutional employment available. Off-campus job opportunities are good.

MORNINGSIDE COLLEGE

1501 Morningside Avenue, Sioux City, IA 51106-1751
Phone: 712-274-5511 **E-mail:** mscadm@morningside.edu **CEEB Code:** 6415
Fax: 712-274-5101 **Website:** www.morningside.edu **ACT Code:** 1338
Financial Aid Phone: 712-274-5159

This private school, affiliated with the Methodist Church, was founded in 1894. It has a 68-acre campus.

RATINGS

Admissions Selectivity Rating: 75   **Fire Safety Rating:** 60*   **Green Rating:** 60*

STUDENTS AND FACULTY

Enrollment: 1,191. **Student Body:** 54% female, 46% male, 31% out-of-state, 2% international (7 countries represented). African American 1%, Asian 2%, Caucasian 82%, Hispanic 4%. **Retention and Graduation:** 77% freshmen return for sophomore year. 34% freshmen graduate within 4 years. 14% grads go on to further study within 1 year. 69% grads pursue arts and sciences degrees. 1% grads pursue business degrees. 1% grads pursue law degrees. 25% grads pursue medical degrees. **Faculty:** Student/faculty ratio 17:1. 68 full-time faculty, 76% hold PhDs. 100% faculty teach undergrads.

ACADEMICS

Degrees: Bachelor's, master's. **Academic Requirements:** Arts/fine arts, English (including composition), humanities, mathematics, sciences (biological or physical). **Classes:** Most classes have 20–29 students. Most lab/discussion sections have 10–19 students. **Majors with Highest Enrollment:** Biology/biological sciences, elementary education and teaching, nursing/registered nurse training (RN, ASN, BSN, MSN). **Disciplines with Highest Percentage of Degrees Awarded:** Education 28%, business/marketing 27%, health professions and related sciences 12%, visual and performing arts 8%, communication technologies 5%. **Special Study Options:** Double major, dual enrollment, English as a second language (ESL), honors program, independent study, internships, liberal arts/career combination, student-designed major, study abroad, teacher certification program, health professions.

FACILITIES

Housing: Coed dorms, apartments for married students, apartments for single students. **Special Academic Facilities/Equipment:** media-enhanced smart classroom, high-speed campus Internet connection, art gallery, theater, totally renovated science facility. **Computers:** 100% of classrooms are wireless, 60% of public computers are PCs, 25% of public computers are Macs, 15% of public computers are UNIX, network access in dorm rooms, network access in dorm lounges, online registration, online administrative functions (other than registration), remote student-access to Web through college's connection, tuition includes personal computer. Undergraduates are required to own a computer.

CAMPUS LIFE

Activities: Choral groups, dance, drama/theater, jazz band, literary magazine, music ensembles, pep band, radio station, student government, student newspaper, television station, yearbook. **Organizations:** 40 registered organizations, 15 honor societies, 10 religious organizations. 2 fraternities (7% men join), 1 sorority (3% women join). **Athletics (Intercollegiate):** *Men:* Baseball, basketball, cheerleading, cross-country, football, golf, soccer, swimming, tennis, track/field (indoor), track/field (outdoor), wrestling. *Women:* Basketball, cheerleading, cross-country, golf, soccer, softball, swimming, tennis, track/field (indoor), track/field (outdoor), volleyball.

ADMISSIONS

Freshman Academic Profile: 14% in top 10% of high school class, 43% in top 25% of high school class, 78% in top 50% of high school class. 95% from public high schools. ACT middle 50% range 20–25. TOEFL required of all international applicants, minimum paper TOEFL 450, minimum computer TOEFL 133. **Basis for Candidate Selection:** *Very important factors considered include:* Academic GPA, class rank, recommendation(s), rigor of secondary school record, standardized test scores. *Important factors considered include:* Extracurricular activities, interview, talent/ability. *Other factors considered include:* Application essay. **Freshman Admission Requirements:** High school diploma is required, and GED is accepted. *Academic units recommended:* 3 English, 2 math, 2 science, 3 social studies. **Freshman Admission Statistics:** 1,240 applied, 90% admitted, 30% enrolled. **Transfer Admission Requirements:** High school transcript, college transcript(s), statement of good standing from prior institution(s). Minimum college GPA of 2.3 required. Lowest grade transferable C-. **General Admission Information:** Application fee $25. Regular notification rolling. Nonfall registration accepted. Admission may be deferred. Credit and/or placement offered for CEEB Advanced Placement tests.

COSTS AND FINANCIAL AID

Annual tuition $19,040. Room and board $6,116. Required fees $1,124. Average book expense $800. **Required Forms and Deadlines:** FAFSA. Financial aid filing deadline 3/1. **Notification of Awards:** Applicants will be notified of awards on or about 3/31. **Types of Aid:** *Need-based scholarships/grants:* Pell, SEOG, state scholarships/grants, private scholarships, the school's own gift aid. *Loans:* FFEL Subsidized Stafford, FFEL Unsubsidized Stafford, FFEL PLUS, Federal Perkins, state loans, college/university loans from institutional funds. **Student Employment:** Federal Work-Study Program available. Institutional employment available. Off-campus job opportunities are excellent. **Financial Aid Statistics:** 62% freshmen, 65% undergrads receive need-based scholarship or grant aid. 70% freshmen, 75% undergrads receive need-based self-help aid. 185 freshmen, 526 undergrads receive athletic scholarships. 100% freshmen, 100% undergrads receive any aid. Highest amount earned per year from on-campus jobs $9,536.

MORRIS BROWN COLLEGE

643 Martin Luther King Jr. Drive NW, Atlanta, GA 30314
Phone: 404-739-1560 **E-mail:** admission@morrisbrown.edu **CEEB Code:** 5417
Fax: 404-739-1565 **Website:** www.morrisbrown.edu **ACT Code:** 0844
Financial Aid Phone: 404-739-1050

This private school, affiliated with the African Methodist Episcopal Church, was founded in 1881. It has an 18-acre campus.

RATINGS

Admissions Selectivity Rating: 60*   Fire Safety Rating: 60*   Green Rating: 60*

STUDENTS AND FACULTY

Enrollment: 2,501. **Student Body:** 57% female, 43% male, 35% out-of-state, 2% international. African American 96%. **Retention and Graduation:** 75% freshmen return for sophomore year. **Faculty:** Student/faculty ratio 18:1. 105 full-time faculty, 65% hold PhDs. 100% faculty teach undergrads.

ACADEMICS

Degrees: Bachelor's. **Academic Requirements:** Arts/fine arts, computer literacy, English (including composition), foreign languages, history, humanities, mathematics, sciences (biological or physical), social science. **Classes:** Most classes have 20–29 students. Most lab/discussion sections have fewer than 10 students. **Majors with Highest Enrollment:** Business administration/

management, mass communications/media studies. **Disciplines with Highest Percentage of Degrees Awarded:** Business/marketing 31%, education 14%, social sciences 8%, psychology 7%, communication technologies 6%, visual and performing arts 6%. **Special Study Options:** Accelerated program, cross-registration, honors program, independent study, internships, liberal arts/career combination, study abroad, teacher certification program. Accelerated program is only available through the Adult Education Program.

FACILITIES

Housing: Coed dorms, men's dorms, women's dorms. **Special Academic Facilities/Equipment:** Art gallery, language lab, electron microscope. **Computers:** 100% of public computers are PCs, network access in dorm rooms, network access in dorm lounges, online registration, remote student-access to Web through college's connection.

CAMPUS LIFE

Activities: Choral groups, concert band, dance, drama/theater, jazz band, marching band, music ensembles, opera, student government, student newspaper, yearbook. **Organizations:** 23 registered organizations, 1 honor society, 1 religious organization. 4 fraternities (3% men join), 5 sororities (3% women join). **Athletics (Intercollegiate):** *Men:* Baseball, basketball, cheerleading, cross-country, football, golf, tennis, track/field (outdoor). *Women:* Basketball, cheerleading, cross-country, golf, softball, tennis, track/field (outdoor), volleyball.

ADMISSIONS

Freshman Academic Profile: SAT Math middle 50% range 360–440. SAT Critical Reading middle 50% range 370–450. ACT middle 50% range 15–18. TOEFL required of all international applicants, minimum paper TOEFL 500. **Basis for Candidate Selection:** *Very important factors considered include:* Character/personal qualities, geographical residence, rigor of secondary school record, standardized test scores, state residency. *Important factors considered include:* Alumni/ae relation, class rank, recommendation(s), talent/ability. *Other factors considered include:* Application essay, extracurricular activities, interview, religious affiliation/commitment, volunteer work, work experience. **Freshman Admission Requirements:** High school diploma is required, and GED is accepted. *Academic units required:* 3 English, 3 math, 3 science, 2 social studies, 1 history. *Academic units recommended:* 2 foreign language. **Freshman Admission Statistics:** 2,639 applied, 43% admitted, 40% enrolled. **Transfer Admission Requirements:** College transcript(s), essay or personal statement, statement of good standing from prior institution(s). Minimum college GPA of 2.0 required. Lowest grade transferable C. **General Admission Information:** Application fee $30. Regular application deadline 7/15. Regular notification is rolling. Nonfall registration accepted. Admission may be deferred for a maximum of 1 semester. Common Application not accepted.

COSTS AND FINANCIAL AID

Annual tuition $8,368. Room & board $5,262. Required fees $3,415. Average book expense $800. **Required Forms and Deadlines:** FAFSA. **Notification of Awards:** Applicants will be notified of awards on or about 6/1. **Types of Aid:** *Need-based scholarships/grants:* Pell, SEOG, state scholarships/grants, private scholarships, the school's own gift aid, United Negro College Fund. *Loans:* Direct Subsidized Stafford, Direct Unsubsidized Stafford, Direct PLUS, FFEL Subsidized Stafford, FFEL Unsubsidized Stafford, FFEL PLUS, Federal Perkins, college/university loans from institutional funds. **Student Employment:** Federal Work-Study Program available. Institutional employment available. Off-campus job opportunities are excellent. **Financial Aid Statistics:** 25% freshmen, 24% undergrads receive need-based scholarship or grant aid. 3 freshmen, 7 undergrads receive athletic scholarships.

MORRIS COLLEGE

100 West College Street, Sumter, SC 29150
Phone: 803-934-3225 **E-mail:** gscriven@morris.edu **CEEB Code:** 5418
Fax: 803-773-8241 **Website:** www.morris.edu **ACT Code:** 3868
Financial Aid Phone: 803-934-3238

This private school, affiliated with the Baptist Church, was founded in 1908. It has a 34-acre campus.

RATINGS

Admissions Selectivity Rating: 61   Fire Safety Rating: 63   Green Rating: 60*

STUDENTS AND FACULTY

Enrollment: 822. **Student Body:** 62% female, 38% male, 16% out-of-state. African American 100%. **Retention and Graduation:** 52% freshmen return for sophomore year. 17% freshmen graduate within 4 years. 11% grads go on to further study within 1 year. 8% grads pursue arts and sciences degrees. 2% grads pursue business degrees. 1% grads pursue medical degrees. **Faculty:** Student/faculty ratio 16:1. 46 full-time faculty, 65% hold PhDs. 100% faculty teach undergrads.

ACADEMICS

Degrees: Bachelor's. **Academic Requirements:** Arts/fine arts, computer literacy, English (including composition), foreign languages, history, humanities, mathematics, sciences (biological or physical), social science, speech, religion. **Classes:** Most classes have 10–19 students. Most lab/discussion sections have 10–19 students. **Majors with Highest Enrollment:** Business administration and management, community health services/liaison/counseling, criminal justice/law enforcement administration. **Disciplines with Highest Percentage of Degrees Awarded:** Business/marketing 21%, health professions and related sciences 18%, social sciences 17%, security and protective services 13%, communications/journalism 12%. **Special Study Options:** Accelerated program, cooperative education program, double major, honors program, internships, liberal arts/career combination, teacher certification program. Advanced degree program available for adults 25 and older with 60 earned credit hours.

FACILITIES

Housing: Men's dorms, women's dorms. **Special Academic Facilities/Equipment:** WMMC-640AM student radio station. **Computers:** 3% of public computers are PCs, network access in dorm rooms, network access in dorm lounges, remote student-access to Web through college's connection.

CAMPUS LIFE

Activities: Choral groups, dance, drama/theater, literary magazine, pep band, radio station, student government, student newspaper, yearbook. **Organizations:** 54 registered organizations, 6 honor societies, 2 religious organizations. 4 fraternities (6% men join), 4 sororities (8% women join). **Athletics (Intercollegiate):** *Men:* Baseball, basketball, cheerleading, cross-country, golf, tennis, track/field (outdoor). *Women:* Basketball, cheerleading, cross-country, softball, tennis, track/field (outdoor), volleyball.

ADMISSIONS

Freshman Academic Profile: 3% in top 10% of high school class, 9% in top 25% of high school class, 31% in top 50% of high school class. 98% from public high schools. TOEFL required of all international applicants, minimum paper TOEFL 500, minimum computer TOEFL 300. **Basis for Candidate Selection:** *Very important factors considered include:* Academic GPA. *Important factors considered include:* Class rank. **Freshman Admission Requirements:** High school diploma is required, and GED is accepted. *Academic units required:* 4 English, 4 math, 3 science, 1 foreign language, 2 social studies, 1 history, 7 academic electives. *Academic units recommended:* 2 foreign language. **Freshman Admission Statistics:** 1,068 applied, 100% admitted, 23% enrolled. **Transfer Admission Requirements:** High school transcript, college transcript(s), statement of good standing from prior institution(s). Minimum college GPA of 2.0 required. Lowest grade transferable C. **General Admission Information:** Application fee $20. Regular notification is rolling. Nonfall registration accepted. Admission may be deferred for a maximum of 1 semester. Credit offered for CEEB Advanced Placement tests.

COSTS AND FINANCIAL AID

Average book expense $1,500. **Required Forms and Deadlines:** FAFSA, institution's own financial aid form. Financial aid filing deadline 3/30. **Notification of Awards:** Applicants will be notified of awards on a rolling basis beginning on or about 6/1. **Types of Aid:** *Need-based scholarships/grants:* Pell, SEOG, state scholarships/grants, private scholarships, the school's own gift aid, United Negro College Fund. *Loans:* Direct Subsidized Stafford, Direct Unsubsidized Stafford, Direct PLUS, Federal Perkins. **Financial Aid Statistics:** 94% freshmen, 91% undergrads receive need-based scholarship or grant aid. 97% freshmen, 91% undergrads receive need-based self-help aid. 15 freshmen, 35 undergrads receive athletic scholarships. 97% freshmen, 96% undergrads receive any aid.

MORRISVILLE STATE COLLEGE

PO Box 901, Morrisville, NY 13408
Phone: 315-684-6046 **E-mail:** admissions@morrisville.edu **CEEB Code:** 2527
Fax: 315-684-6427 **Website:** www.morrisville.edu
Financial Aid Phone: 800-626-5844

This public school was founded in 1908. It has a 150-acre campus.

STUDENTS AND FACULTY

Enrollment: 3,016. **Student Body:** 45% female, 55% male, 7% out-of-state, 3% international (8 countries represented). African American 11%, Caucasian 76%, Hispanic 4%. **Retention and Graduation:** 66% freshmen return for sophomore year. 100% freshmen graduate within 4 years. **Faculty:** Student/faculty ratio 19:1. 1,312 full-time faculty, 2% hold PhDs. 100% faculty teach undergrads.

ACADEMICS

Degrees: Associate, bachelor's, certificate. **Academic Requirements:** Computer literacy, English (including composition), humanities, mathematics, sciences (biological or physical), social science. **Classes:** Most classes have 20–29 students. Most lab/discussion sections have 10–19 students. **Majors with Highest Enrollment:** Automobile/automotive mechanics/technology/technician, equestrian/equine studies, nursing/registered nurse training (RN, ASN, BSN, MSN). **Disciplines with Highest Percentage of Degrees Awarded:** Computer and information sciences 26%, agriculture 23%, natural resources/environmental science 5%, mechanic and repair technologies 1%. **Special Study Options:** Cooperative education program, cross-registration, distance learning, double major, dual enrollment, honors program, internships, student-designed major.

FACILITIES

Housing: Coed dorms, special housing for disabled students, special housing for international students. **Special Academic Facilities/Equipment:** Wildlife Museum, Equine Institute, aquaculture center, dairy complex, automotive performance center, IcePlex, recreation building, wood products technology building, greenhouse/horticulture complex. **Computers:** 100% of public computers are PCs, network access in dorm rooms, network access in dorm lounges, online registration, online administrative functions (other than registration), remote student-access to Web through college's connection.

CAMPUS LIFE

Activities: Choral groups, dance, drama/theater, jazz band, music ensembles, musical theater, pep band, radio station, student government, student newspaper, yearbook. **Organizations:** 45 registered organizations, 2 honor societies, 1 religious organization. **Athletics (Intercollegiate):** *Men:* Basketball, diving, equestrian sports, football, ice hockey, lacrosse, soccer, swimming, wrestling. *Women:* Basketball, diving, equestrian sports, field hockey, lacrosse, soccer, softball, swimming, volleyball.

ADMISSIONS

Freshman Academic Profile: 5% in top 10% of high school class, 42% in top 25% of high school class, 84% in top 50% of high school class. 80% from public high schools. SAT Math middle 50% range 470–570. SAT Critical Reading middle 50% range 460–530. TOEFL required of all international applicants, minimum paper TOEFL 450, minimum computer TOEFL 173. **Basis for Candidate Selection:** *Important factors considered include:* Academic GPA, rigor of secondary school record, work experience. *Other factors considered include:* Alumni/ae relation, application essay, character/personal qualities, class rank, extracurricular activities, interview, recommendation(s), standardized test scores, state residency. **Freshman Admission Requirements:** High school diploma is required, and GED is accepted. *Academic units required:* 4 English, 1 foreign language, 4 social studies. *Academic units recommended:* 4 English, 2 math, 2 science (2 science labs). **Freshman Admission Statistics:** 3,541 applied, 75% admitted, 42% enrolled. **Transfer Admission Requirements:** High school transcript, college transcript(s). Minimum college GPA of 2.5 required. Lowest grade transferable C. **General Admission Information:** Application fee $40. Regular notification is rolling. Nonfall registration accepted. Admission may be deferred for a maximum of 1 year. Placement offered for CEEB Advanced Placement tests.

COSTS AND FINANCIAL AID

Annual in-state tuition $4,350. Out-of-state tuition $10,610. Room & board $6,800. Required fees $1,246. Average book expense $1,000. **Required Forms and Deadlines:** FAFSA, state aid form. Financial aid filing deadline 2/1. **Notification of Awards:** Applicants will be notified of awards on or about 3/1. **Types of Aid:** *Need-based scholarships/grants:* Pell, SEOG, state scholarships/grants, the school's own gift aid. *Loans:* Direct Subsidized Stafford, Direct Unsubsidized Stafford, Direct PLUS, Federal Perkins, Federal Nursing. **Student Employment:** Federal Work-Study Program available. Institutional employment available. **Financial Aid Statistics:** 78% freshmen, 77% undergrads receive need-based scholarship or grant aid. 74% freshmen, 71% undergrads receive need-based self-help aid. 90% freshmen, 89% undergrads receive any aid. Highest amount earned per year from on-campus jobs $1,200.

RATINGS

Admissions Selectivity Rating: 72   **Fire Safety Rating:** 60*   **Green Rating:** 60*

MOUNT ALLISON UNIVERSITY

65 York Street, Sackville, NB E4L1E4 Canada
Phone: 506-364-2269 **E-mail:** admissions@mta.ca
Fax: 506-364-2272 **Website:** www.mta.ca
Financial Aid Phone: 506-364-2269

This public school was founded in 1839. It has a 25-acre campus.

RATINGS
Admissions Selectivity Rating: 75 **Fire Safety Rating:** 89 **Green Rating:** 83

STUDENTS AND FACULTY
Enrollment: 2,330. **Student Body:** 61% female, 39% male, 66% out-of-state.
Retention and Graduation: 82% freshmen return for sophomore year. 43% freshmen graduate within 4 years. **Faculty:** Student/faculty ratio 18:1. 124 full-time faculty. 100% faculty teach undergrads.

ACADEMICS
Degrees: Bachelor's, master's. **Academic Requirements:** Arts/fine arts, humanities, sciences (biological or physical), social science. **Classes:** Most classes have fewer than 10 students. **Majors with Highest Enrollment:** Business/commerce, psychology. **Disciplines with Highest Percentage of Degrees Awarded:** Business/marketing 20%, social sciences 16%, interdisciplinary studies 11%, biological/life sciences 9%, psychology 7%, English 7%, liberal arts/general studies 7%. **Special Study Options:** Distance learning, double major, English as a second language (ESL), exchange student program (domestic), honors program, internships, student-designed major, study abroad.

FACILITIES
Housing: Coed dorms, women's dorms, special housing for disabled students, Language Immersion Housing. **Special Academic Facilities/Equipment:** Art gallery. **Computers:** Network access in dorm rooms, online administrative functions (other than registration), remote student-access to Web through college's connection.

CAMPUS LIFE
Activities: Choral groups, concert band, dance, drama/theater, jazz band, literary magazine, music ensembles, musical theater, opera, pep band, radio station, student government, student newspaper, student-run film society, symphony orchestra, yearbook. **Organizations:** 106 registered organizations. **Athletics (Intercollegiate):** *Men:* Basketball, football, rugby, soccer, swimming. *Women:* Basketball, rugby, soccer, swimming, volleyball.

ADMISSIONS
Freshman Academic Profile: 25% in top 10% of high school class, 50% in top 25% of high school class, 95% in top 50% of high school class. TOEFL required of all international applicants, minimum paper TOEFL 550, minimum computer TOEFL 213. **Basis for Candidate Selection:** *Very important factors considered include:* Academic GPA, extracurricular activities, interview, rigor of secondary school record, talent/ability. *Important factors considered include:* Character/personal qualities, recommendation(s), volunteer work. *Other factors considered include:* Application essay, class rank, standardized test scores, work experience. **Freshman Admission Requirements:** High school diploma is required, and GED is accepted. **Freshman Admission Statistics:** 1,960 applied, 82% admitted, 52% enrolled. **Transfer Admission Requirements:** High school transcript, college transcript(s), essay or personal statement, statement of good standing from prior institution(s). **General Admission Information:** Application fee $43. Regular application deadline 5/1. Regular notification any time. Nonfall registration accepted. Admission may be deferred. Common Application not accepted.

COSTS AND FINANCIAL AID
Annual in-state tuition $6,720. Annual out-of-state tuition $6,720. Room and board $5,130. Required fees $116. Average book expense $1,200. **Student Employment:** Off-campus job opportunities are good.

MOUNT ALOYSIUS COLLEGE

7373 Admiral Peary Highway, Cresson, PA 16630
Phone: 814-886-6383 **E-mail:** admissions@mtaloy.edu **CEEB Code:** 2420
Fax: 814-886-6441 **Website:** www.mtaloy.edu **ACT Code:** 3635
Financial Aid Phone: 814-886-6357

This private school was founded in 1939. It has a 125-acre campus.

RATINGS
Admissions Selectivity Rating: 60* **Fire Safety Rating:** 60* **Green Rating:** 60*

STUDENTS AND FACULTY
Enrollment: 1,424. **Student Body:** 72% female, 28% male, 2% out-of-state, 2% international. African American 2%, Caucasian 84%. **Retention and Graduation:** 69% freshmen return for sophomore year. 36% freshmen graduate within 4 years. 22% grads go on to further study within 1 year. **Faculty:** Student/faculty ratio 14:1. 62 full-time faculty, 35% hold PhDs. 100% faculty teach undergrads.

ACADEMICS
Degrees: Associate, bachelor's, diploma, master's. **Academic Requirements:** Arts/fine arts, computer literacy, English (including composition), history, humanities, mathematics, philosophy, sciences (biological or physical), social science, religious studies. **Classes:** Most classes have 10–19 students. Most lab/discussion sections have 10–19 students. **Disciplines with Highest Percentage of Degrees Awarded:** Health professions and related sciences 18%, education 14%, psychology 14%, business/marketing 14%, interdisciplinary studies 11%, foreign languages and literature 5%, law/legal studies 4%. **Special Study Options:** Accelerated program, distance learning, honors program, independent study, internships, student-designed major, teacher certification program.

FACILITIES
Housing: Coed dorms. **Computers:** 100% of public computers are PCs, network access in dorm rooms, network access in dorm lounges.

CAMPUS LIFE
Activities: Choral groups, drama/theater, student government, student newspaper. **Organizations:** 16 registered organizations, 2 honor societies, 1 religious organization. **Athletics (Intercollegiate):** *Men:* Basketball, golf, soccer. *Women:* Basketball, soccer, volleyball.

ADMISSIONS
Freshman Academic Profile: 85% from public high schools. SAT Math middle 50% range 420–508. SAT Math middle 50% range 420–508. SAT Critical Reading middle 50% range 413–520. ACT middle 50% range 16–20. TOEFL required of all international applicants, minimum paper TOEFL 500. **Basis for Candidate Selection:** *Very important factors considered include:* Academic GPA, character/personal qualities, extracurricular activities, first generation, interview, rigor of secondary school record, talent/ability, volunteer work. *Important factors considered include:* Class rank, level of applicant's interest, recommendation(s), standardized test scores. *Other factors considered include:* Application essay. **Freshman Admission Requirements:** High school diploma is required, and GED is accepted. *Academic units required:* 4 English, 3 math, 3 science, 3 social studies, 3 academic electives. *Academic units recommended:* 2 foreign language, 3 history. **Freshman Admission Statistics:** 949 applied, 77% admitted, 41% enrolled. **Transfer Admission Requirements:** High school transcript, college transcript(s). Minimum college GPA of 2.0 required. Lowest grade transferable C. **General Admission Information:** Application fee $30. Regular notification is rolling. Nonfall registration accepted. Admission may be deferred for a maximum of 1 semester. Common Application accepted. Credit and/or placement offered for CEEB Advanced Placement tests.

COSTS AND FINANCIAL AID
Annual tuition $14,220. Room & board $6,190. Required fees $430. Average book expense $1,400. **Required Forms and Deadlines:** FAFSA. Financial aid filing deadline 5/1. **Notification of Awards:** Applicants will be notified of awards on a rolling basis beginning on or about 3/15. **Types of Aid:** *Need-based scholarships/grants:* Pell, SEOG, state scholarships/grants, private scholarships, the school's own gift aid. *Loans:* FFEL Subsidized Stafford, FFEL Unsubsidized Stafford, FFEL PLUS, Federal Perkins, Federal Nursing, alternative loans. **Student Employment:** Federal Work-Study Program available. Institutional employment available. Off-campus job opportunities are poor. **Financial Aid Statistics:** 86% freshmen, 94% undergrads receive need-based scholarship or grant aid. 86% freshmen, 94% undergrads receive need-based self-help aid. 5 undergrads receive athletic scholarships.

MOUNT HOLYOKE COLLEGE

Best 368

Office of Admissions, Newhall Center, South Hadley, MA 01075
Phone: 413-538-2023 **E-mail:** admission@mtholyoke.edu **CEEB Code:** 3529
Fax: 413-538-2409 **Website:** www.mtholyoke.edu **ACT Code:** 1866
Financial Aid Phone: 413-538-2291

This private school was founded in 1837. It has an 800-acre campus.

RATINGS
Admissions Selectivity Rating: 95　　**Fire Safety Rating:** 80　　**Green Rating:** 82

STUDENTS AND FACULTY
Enrollment: 2,134. **Student Body:** 100% female, 75% out-of-state, 17% international (69 countries represented). African American 4%, Asian 11%, Caucasian 52%, Hispanic 6%. **Retention and Graduation:** 92% freshmen return for sophomore year. 78% freshmen graduate within 4 years. 18% grads go on to further study within 1 year. 15% grads pursue arts and sciences degrees. 2% grads pursue law degrees. 1% grads pursue medical degrees. **Faculty:** Student/faculty ratio 10:1. 209 full-time faculty, 93% hold PhDs. 100% faculty teach undergrads.

ACADEMICS
Degrees: Bachelor's, certificate, master's, post-bachelor's certificate. **Academic Requirements:** Foreign languages, humanities, sciences (biological or physical), social science, physical education, multicultural perspectives. **Classes:** Most classes have 10–19 students. Most lab/discussion sections have 10–19 students. **Majors with Highest Enrollment:** Biology/biological sciences; English language and literature; international relations and affairs. **Disciplines with Highest Percentage of Degrees Awarded:** Social sciences 27%, English 11%, psychology 8%, interdisciplinary studies 8%, biological/life sciences 8%, visual and performing arts 8%, foreign languages and literature 6%, area and ethnic studies 6%, philosophy and religious studies 4%, history 4%. **Special Study Options:** Cooperative education program, cross-registration, double major, exchange student program (domestic), independent study, internships, liberal arts/career combination, student-designed major, study abroad, teacher certification program, community-based learning courses.

FACILITIES
Housing: Women's dorms, apartments for single students, special housing for disabled students, Special housing arrangements are available by need. **Special Academic Facilities/Equipment:** Art and historical museums, bronze-casting foundry, child study center, audiovisual center, language learning center, greenhouse, Japanese meditation garden, equestrian center, observatory, linear accelerator, electron microscope, refracting telescope, nuclear magnetic resonance equipment. **Computers:** 9% of classrooms are wired, 34% of classrooms are wireless, 75% of public computers are PCs, 20% of public computers are Macs, 5% of public computers are UNIX, network access in dorm rooms, network access in dorm lounges, online registration, online administrative functions (other than registration), support for handheld computing, remote student-access to Web through college's connection.

CAMPUS LIFE
Activities: Choral groups, dance, drama/theater, jazz band, literary magazine, music ensembles, musical theater, radio station, student government, student newspaper, student-run film society, symphony orchestra, yearbook. **Organizations:** 150 registered organizations, 1 honor society, 10 religious organizations. **Athletics (Intercollegiate):** *Women:* Basketball, crew/rowing, cross-country, diving, equestrian sports, field hockey, golf, horseback riding, lacrosse, soccer, squash, swimming, tennis, track/field (indoor), track/field (outdoor), volleyball. Environmental Initiatives: Green Building and Energy. The College has two LEED certified buildings and a new residence hall under construction will achieve LEED silver certification. Our Greenhouse Gas Inventory indicates that our emissions, primarily associated with building operation, are signifcantly lower per student than many of our peer institutions.

ADMISSIONS
Freshman Academic Profile: 54% in top 10% of high school class, 82% in top 25% of high school class, 99% in top 50% of high school class. 62% from public high schools. SAT Math middle 50% range 590–690. SAT Critical Reading middle 50% range 640–730. SAT Writing middle 50% range 630–710. ACT middle 50% range 26–30. TOEFL required of all international applicants, minimum paper TOEFL 600, minimum computer TOEFL 250. **Basis for**

Candidate Selection: *Very important factors considered include:* Academic GPA, application essay, class rank, recommendation(s), rigor of secondary school record. *Important factors considered include:* Character/personal qualities, extracurricular activities, first generation, interview, talent/ability, volunteer work, work experience. *Other factors considered include:* Alumni/ae relation, geographical residence, level of applicant's interest, racial/ethnic status, standardized test scores. **Freshman Admission Requirements:** High school diploma is required, and GED is accepted. *Academic units recommended:* 4 English, 3 math, 3 science (3 science labs), 3 foreign language, 3 history, 1 academic elective. **Freshman Admission Statistics:** 3,065 applied, 53% admitted, 35% enrolled. **Transfer Admission Requirements:** High school transcript, college transcript(s), essay or personal statement, statement of good standing from prior institution(s). Minimum college GPA of 3.0 required. Lowest grade transferable C-. **General Admission Information:** Application fee $60. Early decision application deadline 11/15. Regular application deadline 1/15. Regular notification 4/1. Nonfall registration accepted. Credit and/or placement offered for CEEB Advanced Placement tests.

COSTS AND FINANCIAL AID
Annual tuition $34,090. Room & board $10,040. Required fees $176. Average book expense $800. **Required Forms and Deadlines:** FAFSA, CSS/Financial Aid PROFILE, Noncustodial PROFILE, Business/Farm Supplement, federal tax returns. Financial aid filing deadline 3/1. Financial aid filing deadline 2/15. **Notification of Awards:** Applicants will be notified of awards on or about 4/1. **Types of Aid:** *Need-based scholarships/grants:* Pell, SEOG, state scholarships/grants, private scholarships, the school's own gift aid. *Loans:* Direct Subsidized Stafford, Direct Unsubsidized Stafford, Direct PLUS, Federal Perkins, college/university loans from institutional funds. **Student Employment:** Federal Work-Study Program available. Institutional employment available. Off-campus job opportunities are fair. **Financial Aid Statistics:** 51% freshmen, 57% undergrads receive need-based scholarship or grant aid. 51% freshmen, 58% undergrads receive need-based self-help aid. 59% freshmen, 66% undergrads receive any aid. Highest amount earned per year from on-campus jobs $1,800.

MOUNT IDA COLLEGE

777 Dedham Street, Newton, MA 02459
Phone: 617-928-4553 **E-mail:** admissions@mountida.edu **CEEB Code:** 3530
Fax: 617-928-4507 **Website:** www.mountida.edu
Financial Aid Phone: 617-928-4785

This private school was founded in 1899. It has a 72-acre campus.

RATINGS
Admissions Selectivity Rating: 60*　　**Fire Safety Rating:** 60*　　**Green Rating:** 60*

STUDENTS AND FACULTY
Enrollment: 439. **Student Body:** 66% female, 34% male, 38% out-of-state, 50% international (46 countries represented). **Retention and Graduation:** 65% freshmen return for sophomore year. **Faculty:** Student/faculty ratio 14:1. 63 full-time faculty, 79% hold PhDs. 100% faculty teach undergrads.

ACADEMICS
Degrees: Associate, bachelor's, certificate. **Academic Requirements:** English (including composition), history, humanities, mathematics, sciences (biological or physical), social science. **Special Study Options:** Distance learning, English as a second language (ESL), internships, liberal arts/career combination, study abroad, teacher certification program.

FACILITIES
Housing: Coed dorms, women's dorms. **Special Academic Facilities/Equipment:** Mount Ida College Art Gallery. **Computers:** Network access in dorm rooms, remote student-access to Web through college's connection.

CAMPUS LIFE
Activities: Choral groups, dance, drama/theater, radio station, student government, student newspaper, yearbook. **Organizations:** 22 registered organizations, 1 honor society, 2 religious organizations. **Athletics (Intercollegiate):** *Men:* Basketball, football, lacrosse, soccer, volleyball. *Women:* Basketball, cross-country, equestrian sports, soccer, softball, volleyball.

ADMISSIONS
Freshman Academic Profile: SAT Math middle 50% range 390–480. SAT Critical Reading middle 50% range 390–480. SAT Writing middle 50% range 380–480. ACT middle 50% range 15–19. TOEFL required of all international applicants, minimum paper TOEFL 525, minimum computer TOEFL 197. **Basis for Candidate Selection:** *Very important factors considered include:* Recommendation(s), rigor of secondary school record. *Important factors*

considered include: Academic GPA, character/personal qualities, class rank, extracurricular activities, standardized test scores, talent/ability, volunteer work. *Other factors considered include:* Alumni/ae relation, application essay, work experience. **Freshman Admission Requirements:** High school diploma is required, and GED is accepted. *Academic units required:* 4 English. *Academic units recommended:* 3 math, 3 science, 2 foreign language, 2 social studies, 2 history. **Freshman Admission Statistics:** 2,381 applied, 77% admitted, 29% enrolled. **Transfer Admission Requirements:** High school transcript, college transcript(s), standardized test score, statement of good standing from prior institution(s). Minimum college GPA of 2.0 required. Lowest grade transferable C. **General Admission Information:** Application fee $35. Regular notification rolling. Nonfall registration accepted. Admission may be deferred for a maximum of 1 year. Credit offered for CEEB Advanced Placement tests.

COSTS AND FINANCIAL AID

Annual tuition $22,275. Room and board $11,100. Required fees $225. Average book expense $1,000. **Required Forms and Deadlines:** FAFSA. Financial aid filing deadline 5/1. **Notification of Awards:** Applicants will be notified of awards on a rolling basis beginning on or about 2/15. **Types of Aid:** *Need-based scholarships/grants:* Pell, SEOG, state scholarships/grants, private scholarships, the school's own gift aid. *Loans:* FFEL Subsidized Stafford, FFEL Unsubsidized Stafford, FFEL PLUS, state loans. **Financial Aid Statistics:** 75% freshmen, 84% undergrads receive need-based scholarship or grant aid. 75% freshmen, 85% undergrads receive need-based self-help aid. Highest amount earned per year from on-campus jobs $1,500.

MOUNT MARTY COLLEGE

1105 West Eighth Street, Yankton, SD 57078-3724
Phone: 605-668-1545 **E-mail:** mmcadmit@mtmc.edu **CEEB Code:** 6416
Fax: 605-668-1607 **Website:** www.mtmc.edu **ACT Code:** 3914
Financial Aid Phone: 605-668-1589

This private school, affiliated with the Roman Catholic Church, was founded in 1936. It has an 80-acre campus.

RATINGS

Admissions Selectivity Rating: 72   **Fire Safety Rating:** 60*   **Green Rating:** 60*

STUDENTS AND FACULTY

Enrollment: 889. **Student Body:** 70% female, 30% male, 22% out-of-state. African American 2%, Caucasian 94%, Hispanic 1%, Native American 1%. **Retention and Graduation:** 72% freshmen return for sophomore year. 35% freshmen graduate within 4 years. **Faculty:** Student/faculty ratio 13:1. 42 full-time faculty, 40% hold PhDs. 97% faculty teach undergrads.

ACADEMICS

Degrees: Associate, bachelor's, certificate, master's. **Academic Requirements:** Arts/fine arts, computer literacy, English (including composition), history, humanities, mathematics, philosophy, sciences (biological or physical), social science, religious studies. **Classes:** Most classes have 10–19 students. Most lab/discussion sections have fewer than 10 students. **Majors with Highest Enrollment:** Business administration/management, education, nursing/registered nurse training (RN, ASN, BSN, MSN). **Disciplines with Highest Percentage of Degrees Awarded:** Business/marketing 28%, education 23%, health professions and related sciences 17%, liberal arts/general studies 8%, psychology 6%. **Special Study Options:** Accelerated program, double major, honors program, independent study, internships, liberal arts/career combination, student-designed major, teacher certification program.

FACILITIES

Housing: Men's dorms, women's dorms, special housing for disabled students, cooperative housing. **Special Academic Facilities/Equipment:** Bede Art Gallery, Laddie E. Cimpl Athletic Arena, Marian Auditorium Theatre. **Computers:** 100% of public computers are PCs, network access in dorm rooms, network access in dorm lounges, online registration, online administrative functions (other than registration), remote student-access to Web through college's connection.

CAMPUS LIFE

Activities: Choral groups, concert band, dance, drama/theater, jazz band, literary magazine, music ensembles, musical theater, pep band, student government, student newspaper. **Organizations:** 40 registered organizations, 7 honor societies, 4 religious organizations. **Athletics (Intercollegiate):** *Men:* Baseball, basketball, cheerleading, cross-country, golf, soccer, track/field (indoor), track/field (outdoor). *Women:* Basketball, cheerleading, cross-country, golf, softball, track/field (indoor), track/field (outdoor), volleyball.

ADMISSIONS

Freshman Academic Profile: 15% in top 10% of high school class, 35% in top 25% of high school class, 69% in top 50% of high school class. 87% from public high schools. ACT middle 50% range 19–24. TOEFL required of all international applicants, minimum paper TOEFL 500, minimum computer TOEFL 173. **Basis for Candidate Selection:** *Very important factors considered include:* Rigor of secondary school record, standardized test scores. *Other factors considered include:* Alumni/ae relation, character/personal qualities, class rank, extracurricular activities, interview, recommendation(s), talent/ability, volunteer work, work experience. **Freshman Admission Requirements:** High school diploma is required, and GED is accepted. **Freshman Admission Statistics:** 315 applied, 90% admitted, 42% enrolled. **Transfer Admission Requirements:** High school transcript, college transcript(s). Minimum college GPA of 2.0 required. Lowest grade transferable C. **General Admission Information:** Application fee $35. Regular application deadline 8/30. Regular notification is rolling. Nonfall registration accepted. Common Application accepted. Credit and/or placement offered for CEEB Advanced Placement tests.

COSTS AND FINANCIAL AID

Annual tuition $11,580. Room & board $4,600. Required fees $1,080. Average book expense $600. **Required Forms and Deadlines:** FAFSA, institution's own financial aid form. Financial aid filing deadline 3/1. **Notification of Awards:** Applicants will be notified of awards on a rolling basis beginning on or about 3/15. **Types of Aid:** *Need-based scholarships/grants:* Pell, SEOG, state scholarships/grants, private scholarships, the school's own gift aid. *Loans:* FFEL Subsidized Stafford, FFEL Unsubsidized Stafford, FFEL PLUS, Federal Perkins, Federal Nursing. **Student Employment:** Federal Work-Study Program available. Institutional employment available. Off-campus job opportunities are good. **Financial Aid Statistics:** 88% freshmen, 86% undergrads receive need-based scholarship or grant aid. 83% freshmen, 83% undergrads receive need-based self-help aid. 15 freshmen, 46 undergrads receive athletic scholarships. Highest amount earned per year from on-campus jobs $800.

MOUNT MARY COLLEGE

2900 North Menomonee River Parkway, Milwaukee, WI 53222-4597
Phone: 414-256-1219 **E-mail:** admiss@mtmary.edu **CEEB Code:** 1490
Fax: 414-256-0180 **Website:** www.mtmary.edu **ACT Code:** 4620

This private school, affiliated with the Roman Catholic Church, was founded in 1913. It has an 80-acre campus.

RATINGS

Admissions Selectivity Rating: 70   **Fire Safety Rating:** 72   **Green Rating:** 60*

STUDENTS AND FACULTY

Enrollment: 1,324. **Student Body:** 98% female, 2% male, 3% out-of-state. African American 17%, Asian 3%, Caucasian 69%, Hispanic 4%, Native American 1%. **Retention and Graduation:** 73% freshmen return for sophomore year. 26% freshmen graduate within 4 years. 15% grads go on to further study within 1 year. 14% grads pursue arts and sciences degrees. 1% grads pursue business degrees. **Faculty:** Student/faculty ratio 9:1. 67 full-time faculty, 64% hold PhDs. 92% faculty teach undergrads.

ACADEMICS

Degrees: Bachelor's, master's, post-bachelor's certificate. **Academic Requirements:** Arts/fine arts, English (including composition), history, humanities, philosophy, sciences (biological or physical), social science. **Classes:** Most classes have 10–19 students. Most lab/discussion sections have 10–19 students. **Majors with Highest Enrollment:** Business administration/management, fashion/apparel design, nursing/registered nurse training (RN, ASN, BSN, MSN). **Disciplines with Highest Percentage of Degrees Awarded:** Health professions and related sciences 34%, visual and performing arts 15%, business/marketing 10%, English 6%, public administration and social services 6%, education 5%. **Special Study Options:** Accelerated program, distance learning, double major, dual enrollment, honors program, independent study, internships, liberal arts/career combination, student-designed major, study abroad, teacher certification program.

FACILITIES

Housing: Women's dorms. **Special Academic Facilities/Equipment:** Hagerty Library, Marian Art Gallery, Walter & Olive Stiemke Memorial Hall & Conference Center. **Computers:** 100% of public computers are PCs, network access in dorm rooms, network access in dorm lounges, remote student-access to Web through college's connection.

CAMPUS LIFE

Activities: Choral groups, dance, drama/theater, literary magazine, music ensembles, student government, student newspaper. **Organizations:** 47 registered organizations, 14 honor societies, 1 religious organization. **Athletics (Intercollegiate):** *Women:* Basketball, soccer, softball, tennis, volleyball.

ADMISSIONS

Freshman Academic Profile: 12% in top 10% of high school class, 35% in top 25% of high school class, 64% in top 50% of high school class. 78% from public high schools. TOEFL required of all international applicants, minimum paper TOEFL 500, minimum computer TOEFL 173. **Basis for Candidate Selection:** *Very important factors considered include:* Academic GPA, rigor of secondary school record, standardized test scores. *Important factors considered include:* Character/personal qualities, class rank, talent/ability. *Other factors considered include:* Alumni/ae relation, application essay, extracurricular activities, first generation, interview, recommendation(s), volunteer work, work experience. **Freshman Admission Requirements:** High school diploma is required, and GED is accepted. *Academic units required:* 4 English, 2 math, 2 science (2 science labs), 2 foreign language, 2 social studies, 2 history, 2 academic electives. *Academic units recommended:* 4 English, 3 math, 2 science (2 science labs), 2 foreign language, 2 social studies, 2 history. **Freshman Admission Statistics:** 495 applied, 60% admitted, 47% enrolled. **Transfer Admission Requirements:** High school transcript, college transcript(s), statement of good standing from prior institution(s). Minimum college GPA of 2.0 required. Lowest grade transferable C. **General Admission Information:** Application fee $25. Regular notification is rolling. Nonfall registration accepted. Admission may be deferred for a maximum of 1 year. Credit and/or placement offered for CEEB Advanced Placement tests.

COSTS AND FINANCIAL AID

Annual tuition $17,938. Room and board $5,990. Required fees $190. Average book expense $1,000. **Required Forms and Deadlines:** FAFSA. Financial aid filing deadline 3/1. **Notification of Awards:** Applicants will be notified of awards on a rolling basis beginning on or about 1/1. **Types of Aid:** *Need-based scholarships/grants:* Pell, SEOG, state scholarships/grants, private scholarships, the school's own gift aid. *Loans:* FFEL Subsidized Stafford, FFEL Unsubsidized Stafford, FFEL PLUS, Federal Perkins. **Student Employment:** Federal Work-Study Program available. Institutional employment available. Off-campus job opportunities are excellent. **Financial Aid Statistics:** 69% freshmen, 68% undergrads receive need-based scholarship or grant aid. 67% freshmen, 64% undergrads receive need-based self-help aid. 72% freshmen, 77% undergrads receive any aid. Highest amount earned per year from on-campus jobs $1,152.

MOUNT MERCY COLLEGE

1330 Elmhurst Drive Northeast, Cedar Rapids, IA 52402-4797
Phone: 319-368-6460 **E-mail:** admission@mtmercy.edu **CEEB Code:** 6417
Fax: 319-363-5270 **Website:** www.mtmercy.edu **ACT Code:** 1340
Financial Aid Phone: 319-368-6467

This private school, affiliated with the Roman Catholic Church, was founded in 1928. It has a 40-acre campus.

RATINGS

Admissions Selectivity Rating: 75   **Fire Safety Rating:** 60*   **Green Rating:** 60*

STUDENTS AND FACULTY

Enrollment: 1,434. **Student Body:** 70% female, 30% male, 6% out-of-state. African American 2%, Asian 1%, Caucasian 87%, Hispanic 1%. **Retention and Graduation:** 77% freshmen return for sophomore year. 49% freshmen graduate within 4 years. 9% grads go on to further study within 1 year. 6% grads pursue arts and sciences degrees. 2% grads pursue business degrees. 1% grads pursue law degrees. **Faculty:** Student/faculty ratio 13:1. 72 full-time faculty, 61% hold PhDs. 100% faculty teach undergrads.

ACADEMICS

Degrees: Bachelor's. **Academic Requirements:** Arts/fine arts, English (including composition), history, humanities, mathematics, philosophy, sciences (biological or physical), social science, religious studies. **Classes:** Most classes have 10–19 students. **Majors with Highest Enrollment:** Business administration/management, education, nursing/registered nurse training (RN, ASN, BSN, MSN). **Disciplines with Highest Percentage of Degrees Awarded:** Business/marketing 41%, education 13%, health professions and related sciences 11%, computer and information sciences 6%, other 6%, social sciences 4%. **Special Study Options:** Accelerated program, cooperative education program, cross-registration, double major, dual enrollment, honors program, independent study, internships, liberal arts/career combination, student-designed major, study abroad, teacher certification program, weekend college.

FACILITIES

Housing: Coed dorms, apartments for single students. **Computers:** 98% of public computers are PCs, 1% of public computers are Macs, 1% of public computers are UNIX, network access in dorm rooms, network access in dorm lounges.

CAMPUS LIFE

Activities: Choral groups, drama/theater, literary magazine, pep band, student government, student newspaper. **Organizations:** 35 registered organizations, 16 honor societies, 7 religious organizations. **Athletics (Intercollegiate):** *Men:* Baseball, basketball, cross-country, golf, soccer, track/field (outdoor). *Women:* Basketball, cross-country, golf, soccer, softball, track/field (outdoor), volleyball.

ADMISSIONS

Freshman Academic Profile: 18% in top 10% of high school class, 44% in top 25% of high school class, 82% in top 50% of high school class. 83% from public high schools. ACT middle 50% range 20–25. TOEFL required of all international applicants, minimum paper TOEFL 550, minimum computer TOEFL 213. **Basis for Candidate Selection:** *Very important factors considered include:* Class rank, rigor of secondary school record, standardized test scores. *Important factors considered include:* Application essay, extracurricular activities, recommendation(s). *Other factors considered include:* Character/personal qualities, interview, talent/ability, volunteer work. **Freshman Admission Requirements:** High school diploma is required, and GED is accepted. *Academic units recommended:* 4 English, 4 math, 3 science, 2 foreign language, 2 social studies, 2 history. **Freshman Admission Statistics:** 488 applied, 84% admitted, 48% enrolled. **Transfer Admission Requirements:** College transcript(s), statement of good standing from prior institution(s). Minimum college GPA of 2.5 required. Lowest grade transferable D. **General Admission Information:** Application fee $20. Regular application deadline 8/30. Regular notification rolling. Nonfall registration accepted. Admission may be deferred for a maximum of 1 year. Common Application accepted. Credit and/or placement offered for CEEB Advanced Placement tests.

COSTS AND FINANCIAL AID

Required Forms and Deadlines: FAFSA. Financial aid filing deadline 3/1. **Notification of Awards:** Applicants will be notified of awards on a rolling basis beginning on or about 3/15. **Types of Aid:** *Need-based scholarships/grants:* Pell, SEOG, state scholarships/grants, the school's own gift aid. *Loans:* Direct Subsidized Stafford, Direct Unsubsidized Stafford, Direct PLUS, Federal Perkins, state loans, college/university loans from institutional funds. **Student Employment:** Federal Work-Study Program available. Institutional employment available. Off-campus job opportunities are excellent. **Financial Aid Statistics:** 87% freshmen, 88% undergrads receive need-based scholarship or grant aid. 73% freshmen, 80% undergrads receive need-based self-help aid.

MOUNT OLIVE COLLEGE

634 Henderson Street, Mount Olive, NC 28365
Phone: 919-658-7164 **E-mail:** admissions@moc.edu **CEEB Code:** 5435
Fax: 919-658-7180 **Website:** www.moc.edu **ACT Code:** 3131
Financial Aid Phone: 919-658-2502

This private school, affiliated with the Baptist Church, was founded in 1951. It has a 138-acre campus.

RATINGS

Admissions Selectivity Rating: 73   **Fire Safety Rating:** 60*   **Green Rating:** 60*

STUDENTS AND FACULTY

Enrollment: 2,474. **Student Body:** 62% female, 38% male, 6% out-of-state. **Retention and Graduation:** 20% grads go on to further study within 1 year. **Faculty:** Student/faculty ratio 11:1. 72 full-time faculty, 81% hold PhDs. 100% faculty teach undergrads.

ACADEMICS

Degrees: Associate, bachelor's. **Academic Requirements:** Arts/fine arts, computer literacy, English (including composition), history, humanities, mathematics, philosophy, sciences (biological or physical), social science. **Disciplines with Highest Percentage of Degrees Awarded:** Business/marketing 55%, security and protective services 15%, psychology 5%, theology and religious vocations 5%, computer and information sciences 4%, visual and performing arts 3%. **Special Study Options:** Accelerated program, cooperative education program, distance learning, double major, dual enrollment, external degree program, honors program, independent study, internships, liberal arts/career combination, teacher certification program.

FACILITIES

Housing: Men's dorms, women's dorms, apartments for single students. **Computers:** 98% of public computers are PCs, 2% of public computers are Macs, network access in dorm rooms, remote student-access to Web through college's connection.

CAMPUS LIFE

Activities: Choral groups, concert band, literary magazine, music ensembles, musical theater, pep band, student government, student newspaper, symphony orchestra, yearbook. **Organizations:** 33 registered organizations, 4 honor societies, 6 religious organizations. **Athletics (Intercollegiate):** *Men:* Baseball, basketball, cross-country, golf, soccer, tennis. *Women:* Basketball, cross-country, soccer, softball, tennis, volleyball.

ADMISSIONS

Freshman Academic Profile: 9% in top 10% of high school class, 36% in top 25% of high school class, 69% in top 50% of high school class. SAT Math middle 50% range 430–530. SAT Critical Reading middle 50% range 420–510. ACT middle 50% range 15–21. TOEFL required of all international applicants, minimum paper TOEFL 500. **Basis for Candidate Selection:** *Very important factors considered include:* Academic GPA, character/personal qualities, rigor of secondary school record. *Important factors considered include:* Class rank, extracurricular activities, interview, level of applicant's interest, standardized test scores, talent/ability. *Other factors considered include:* Alumni/ae relation, geographical residence, recommendation(s), volunteer work. **Freshman Admission Requirements:** High school diploma is required, and GED is accepted. *Academic units required:* 4 English, 3 math, 3 science (1 science lab), 3 social studies, 3 academic electives. **Freshman Admission Statistics:** 807 applied, 71% admitted, 54% enrolled. **Transfer Admission Requirements:** High school transcript, college transcript(s). Minimum college GPA of 2.0 required. Lowest grade transferable C. **General Admission Information:** Application fee $20. Nonfall registration accepted. Admission may be deferred for a maximum of 1 year. Common Application accepted.

COSTS AND FINANCIAL AID

Annual tuition $13,126. Room and board $5,300. Average book expense $1,220. **Required Forms and Deadlines:** FAFSA, state aid form. Financial aid filing deadline 3/1. **Notification of Awards:** Applicants will be notified of awards on a rolling basis beginning on or about 2/14. **Types of Aid:** *Need-based scholarships/grants:* Pell, SEOG, state scholarships/grants, private scholarships, the school's own gift aid. *Loans:* FFEL Subsidized Stafford, FFEL PLUS, Federal Perkins, state loans. **Student Employment:** Federal Work-Study Program available. Off-campus job opportunities are excellent. **Financial Aid Statistics:** 34% freshmen, 49% undergrads receive need-based scholarship or grant aid. 26% freshmen, 40% undergrads receive need-based self-help aid. 26 freshmen, 74 undergrads receive athletic scholarships.

MOUNT SAINT MARY COLLEGE

330 Powell Avenue, Newburgh, NY 12550
Phone: 845-569-3248 **E-mail:** admissions@msmc.edu **CEEB Code:** 2423
Fax: 845-562-6762 **Website:** www.msmc.edu **ACT Code:** 2819
Financial Aid Phone: 845-569-3298

This private school was founded in 1959. It has a 70-acre campus.

RATINGS

Admissions Selectivity Rating: 71   **Fire Safety Rating:** 85   **Green Rating:** 71

STUDENTS AND FACULTY

Enrollment: 2,014. **Student Body:** 74% female, 26% male, 13% out-of-state. African American 10%, Asian 3%, Caucasian 77%, Hispanic 9%. **Retention and Graduation:** 71% freshmen return for sophomore year. 38% freshmen graduate within 4 years. 36% grads go on to further study within 1 year. 33% grads pursue arts and sciences degrees. 3% grads pursue business degrees. **Faculty:** Student/faculty ratio 17:1. 73 full-time faculty, 89% hold PhDs. 92% faculty teach undergrads.

ACADEMICS

Degrees: Bachelor's, certificate, master's, post-bachelor's certificate. **Academic Requirements:** Arts/fine arts, computer literacy, English (including composition), history, humanities, mathematics, philosophy, sciences (biological or physical), social science. **Classes:** Most classes have 10–19 students. Most lab/discussion sections have fewer than 10 students. **Majors with Highest Enrollment:** Business administration and management, English language and literature, nursing/registered nurse training (RN, ASN, BSN, MSN). **Disciplines with Highest Percentage of Degrees Awarded:** Business/marketing

24%, English 13%, psychology 12%, history 10%, health professions and related sciences 9%. **Special Study Options:** Accelerated program, cooperative education program, cross-registration, distance learning, double major, dual enrollment, exchange student program (domestic), honors program, independent study, internships, liberal arts/career combination, student-designed major, study abroad, teacher certification program.

FACILITIES

Housing: Coed dorms, men's dorms, women's dorms, special housing for disabled students. **Special Academic Facilities/Equipment:** On-campus elementary school, television studio and radio station, multimedia lab. **Computers:** 100% of classrooms are wireless, 100% of public computers are PCs, network access in dorm rooms, network access in dorm lounges, online registration, online administrative functions (other than registration).

CAMPUS LIFE

Activities: Choral groups, concert band, dance, drama/theater, literary magazine, music ensembles, musical theater, radio station, student government, student newspaper, student-run film society, yearbook. **Organizations:** 24 registered organizations, 9 honor societies, 1 religious organization. **Athletics (Intercollegiate):** *Men:* Baseball, basketball, soccer, swimming, tennis. *Women:* Basketball, soccer, softball, swimming, tennis, volleyball. **Environmental Initiatives:** Formation of College-wide group: Mount Alliance for Green Initiatives on Campus. Increase Recycling Initiative. Participation in nationwide Focus the Nation event. **Environmental Initiatives:** Formation of College-wide group: Mount Alliance for Green Initiatives on Campus. Increase Recycling Initiative. Participation in nationwide Focus the Nation event.

ADMISSIONS

Freshman Academic Profile: 7% in top 10% of high school class, 27% in top 25% of high school class, 66% in top 50% of high school class. 50% from public high schools. SAT Math middle 50% range 450–550. SAT Critical Reading middle 50% range 460–540. SAT Writing middle 50% range 450–545. ACT middle 50% range 19–23. TOEFL required of all international applicants, minimum paper TOEFL 500, minimum computer TOEFL 200. **Basis for Candidate Selection:** *Very important factors considered include:* Academic GPA, class rank, rigor of secondary school record, standardized test scores. *Important factors considered include:* Interview. *Other factors considered include:* Alumni/ae relation, application essay, character/personal qualities, extracurricular activities, level of applicant's interest, recommendation(s), talent/ability, volunteer work, work experience. **Freshman Admission Requirements:** High school diploma is required, and GED is accepted. *Academic units recommended:* 4 English, 3 math, 3 science, 3 foreign language, 4 social studies, 3 academic electives. **Freshman Admission Statistics:** 1,588 applied, 82% admitted, 31% enrolled. **Transfer Admission Requirements:** High school transcript, college transcript(s). Minimum college GPA of 2.0 required. Lowest grade transferable C. **General Admission Information:** Application fee $35. Regular notification is rolling. Nonfall registration accepted. Admission may be deferred for a maximum of 1 year. Credit and/or placement offered for CEEB Advanced Placement tests.

COSTS AND FINANCIAL AID

Annual tuition $18,900. Room and board $10,400. Required fees $620. Average book expense $1,200. **Required Forms and Deadlines:** FAFSA. Financial aid filing deadline 2/15. **Notification of Awards:** Applicants will be notified of awards on a rolling basis beginning on or about 4/1. **Types of Aid:** *Need-based scholarships/grants:* Pell, SEOG, state scholarships/grants, private scholarships, the school's own gift aid, Federal Nursing Scholarships, Academic Competitiveness Grant (ACG) and National Science and Mathematics Access to Retain Talent Grant (National SMART or NSG). *Loans:* FFEL Subsidized Stafford, FFEL Unsubsidized Stafford, FFEL PLUS, Federal Perkins, Federal Nursing. **Student Employment:** Federal Work-Study Program available. Institutional employment available. Off-campus job opportunities are good. **Financial Aid Statistics:** 66% freshmen, 62% undergrads receive need-based scholarship or grant aid. 64% freshmen, 64% undergrads receive need-based self-help aid. 91% freshmen, 81% undergrads receive any aid. Highest amount earned per year from on-campus jobs $9,324.

MOUNT SAINT MARY'S COLLEGE (CA)

12001 Chalon Road, Los Angeles, CA 90049-1597
Phone: 310-954-4250 **E-mail:** admissions@msmc.la.edu **CEEB Code:** 4493
Fax: 310-954-4259 **Website:** www.msmc.la.edu **ACT Code:** 0338
Financial Aid Phone: 310-954-4190

This private school, affiliated with the Roman Catholic Church, was founded in 1925. It has a 53-acre campus.

RATINGS
Admissions Selectivity Rating: 60*   **Fire Safety Rating:** 60*   **Green Rating:** 60*

STUDENTS AND FACULTY
Enrollment: 1,719. **Student Body:** 95% female, 5% male. African American 10%, Asian 13%, Caucasian 13%, Hispanic 35%. **Retention and Graduation:** 76% freshmen return for sophomore year. 53% freshmen graduate within 4 years. **Faculty:** Student/faculty ratio 16:1. 82 full-time faculty, 41% hold PhDs. 95% faculty teach undergrads.

ACADEMICS
Degrees: Associate, bachelor's, certificate, doctoral, master's, post-bachelor's certificate, terminal. **Academic Requirements:** Arts/fine arts, English (including composition), foreign languages, history, humanities, mathematics, philosophy, sciences (biological or physical), social science. **Classes:** Most classes have 10–19 students. **Majors with Highest Enrollment:** Liberal arts and sciences/liberal studies, nursing/registered nurse training (ASN, BSN, MSN, RN). **Disciplines with Highest Percentage of Degrees Awarded:** Health professions and related sciences 27%, business/marketing 17%, biological/life sciences 14%, social sciences 13%, liberal arts/general studies 12%. **Special Study Options:** Accelerated program, cross-registration, double major, exchange student program (domestic), honors program, independent study, internships, student-designed major, study abroad, teacher certification program, weekend college.

FACILITIES
Housing: Women's dorms, limited men's housing. **Special Academic Facilities/Equipment:** Drudis-Biada Art Gallery. **Computers:** 100% of public computers are PCs, network access in dorm lounges, online administrative functions (other than registration), remote student-access to Web through college's connection.

CAMPUS LIFE
Activities: Choral groups, dance, drama/theater, literary magazine, music ensembles, student government, student newspaper, yearbook. **Organizations:** 29 registered organizations. 1 sorority.

ADMISSIONS
Freshman Academic Profile: 68% from public high schools. SAT Math middle 50% range 470–565. SAT Critical Reading middle 50% range 460–570. TOEFL required of all international applicants, minimum paper TOEFL 550. **Basis for Candidate Selection:** *Very important factors considered include:* Rigor of secondary school record, standardized test scores. *Important factors considered include:* Application essay, interview. *Other factors considered include:* Alumni/ae relation, character/personal qualities, class rank, extracurricular activities, geographical residence, recommendation(s), talent/ability, volunteer work, work experience. **Freshman Admission Requirements:** High school diploma is required, and GED is accepted. *Academic units required:* 4 English, 3 math, 2 science (2 science labs), 2 foreign language, 2 social studies, 2 history. *Academic units recommended:* 4 math, 3 science (3 science labs), 3 foreign language, 3 social studies, 3 history. **Freshman Admission Statistics:** 819 applied, 89% admitted, 41% enrolled. **Transfer Admission Requirements:** College transcript(s), essay or personal statement, statement of good standing from prior institution(s). Minimum college GPA of 2.4 required. Lowest grade transferable C. **General Admission Information:** Application fee $40. Non-fall registration accepted. Admission may be deferred for a maximum of 1 year. Common Application accepted. Credit and/or placement offered for CEEB Advanced Placement tests.

COSTS AND FINANCIAL AID
Annual tuition $18,882. Room & board $7,832. Required fees $892. Average book expense $700. **Required Forms and Deadlines:** FAFSA, institution's own financial aid form, state aid form. Financial aid filing deadline 5/1. **Notification of Awards:** Applicants will be notified of awards on or about 2/1. **Types of Aid:** *Need-based scholarships/grants:* Pell, SEOG, state scholarships/grants, private scholarships, the school's own gift aid. *Loans:* FFEL Subsidized Stafford, FFEL Unsubsidized Stafford, FFEL PLUS, Federal Nursing, college/university loans from institutional funds. **Student Employment:** Federal Work-Study Program available. Institutional employment available. Off-campus job opportunities are good.

MOUNT SAINT VINCENT UNIVERSITY

Admissions Office, 215 Evaristus Hall, Halifax, NS B3M 2J6 Canada
Phone: 902-457-6128 **E-mail:** admissions@msvu.ca
Fax: 902-457-6498 **Website:** www.msvu.ca
Financial Aid Phone: 902-457-6356

This public school was founded in 1873. It has a 45-acre campus.

RATINGS
Admissions Selectivity Rating: 60*   **Fire Safety Rating:** 60*   **Green Rating:** 60*

STUDENTS AND FACULTY
Enrollment: 2,744. **Student Body:** 84% female, 16% male. **Faculty:** Student/faculty ratio 19:1. 140 full-time faculty, 74% hold PhDs. 100% faculty teach undergrads.

ACADEMICS
Degrees: Bachelor's, certificate, diploma, master's. **Academic Requirements:** Arts/fine arts, English (including composition), humanities, social science. All programs incorporate arts & science courses as electives or required components. Students have the opportunity to choose between physical & social sciences when completing science electives. **Majors with Highest Enrollment:** Business/commerce, education, liberal arts and sciences/liberal studies. **Disciplines with Highest Percentage of Degrees Awarded:** Education 29%, business/marketing 17%, communication technologies 12%, liberal arts/general studies 8%, psychology 4%, social sciences 4%. **Special Study Options:** Cooperative education program, distance learning, double major, honors program, independent study, internships, liberal arts/career combination, study abroad, teacher certification program.

FACILITIES
Housing: Coed dorms, women's dorms, apartments for single students, special housing for international students. **Special Academic Facilities/Equipment:** Mount Saint Vincent Art Gallery. **Computers:** 100% of public computers are PCs, network access in dorm rooms, network access in dorm lounges, online registration, online administrative functions (other than registration).

CAMPUS LIFE
Activities: Choral groups, dance, drama/theater, student government, student newspaper. **Organizations:** 30 registered organizations. **Athletics (Intercollegiate):** *Men:* Basketball. *Women:* Basketball, soccer, volleyball.

ADMISSIONS
Freshman Academic Profile: 25% in top 10% of high school class, 70% in top 25% of high school class, 100% in top 50% of high school class. 90% from public high schools. TOEFL required of all international applicants, minimum paper TOEFL 550, minimum computer TOEFL 213. **Basis for Candidate Selection:** *Very important factors considered include:* Rigor of secondary school record. *Important factors considered include:* Class rank, standardized test scores. *Other factors considered include:* Application essay, character/personal qualities, extracurricular activities, recommendation(s), talent/ability, volunteer work, work experience. **Freshman Admission Statistics:** 1,172 applied, 72% admitted, 50% enrolled. **Transfer Admission Requirements:** College transcript(s), statement of good standing from prior institution(s). **General Admission Information:** Application fee $20. Regular application deadline 6/15. Non-fall registration accepted. Admission may be deferred for a maximum of 1 year.

COSTS AND FINANCIAL AID
Annual tuition $2,804. International tuition $4,754. Room & board $4,775. Required fees $124. Average book expense $500. **Student Employment:** Off-campus job opportunities are excellent.

MOUNT SENARIO COLLEGE

College Avenue West, Ladysmith, WI 54848
Phone: 715-532-5511 **E-mail:** admissions@mountsenario.edu
Fax: 715-532-7690 **Website:** www.mountsenario.edu
Financial Aid Phone: 715-532-5511

This private school was founded in 1930.

RATINGS
Admissions Selectivity Rating: 64   **Fire Safety Rating:** 60*   **Green Rating:** 60*

STUDENTS AND FACULTY
Enrollment: 672. **Student Body:** 41% female, 59% male, 13% out-of-state, 3% international (4 countries represented). African American 14%, Asian 2%, Caucasian 74%, Hispanic 3%, Native American 2%. **Retention and Graduation:** 21% freshmen return for sophomore year. 3% freshmen graduate within 4 years. 4% grads go on to further study within 1 year. 2% grads pursue arts and sciences degrees. 1% grads pursue business degrees. 1% grads pursue law degrees. **Faculty:** Student/faculty ratio 14:1. 22 full-time faculty, 36% hold PhDs. 100% faculty teach undergrads.

ACADEMICS
Degrees: Associate, bachelor's. **Academic Requirements:** Arts/fine arts, English (including composition), history, humanities, mathematics, philosophy, sciences (biological or physical), social science. **Classes:** Most classes have fewer than 10 students. Most lab/discussion sections have fewer than 10 students. **Disciplines with Highest Percentage of Degrees Awarded:** Business/marketing 17%, education 11%, parks and recreation 3%, biological/life sciences 2%, visual and performing arts 2%, liberal arts/general studies 1%, psychology 1%, English 1%. **Special Study Options:** Cooperative education program, double major, English as a second language (ESL), independent study, internships, teacher certification program.

FACILITIES
Housing: Coed dorms, modular housing units.

CAMPUS LIFE
Activities: Drama/theater, student government, student newspaper. **Organizations:** 7 honor societies, 2 religious organizations.

ADMISSIONS
Freshman Academic Profile: 5% in top 10% of high school class, 15% in top 25% of high school class, 37% in top 50% of high school class. SAT Math middle 50% range 250–470. SAT Critical Reading middle 50% range 310–380. ACT middle 50% range 15–20, minimum paper TOEFL 420. **Freshman Admission Requirements:** High school diploma is required, and GED is accepted. *Academic units recommended:* 4 English, 2 math, 2 science, 2 social studies, 2 history. **Freshman Admission Statistics:** 314 applied, 70% admitted, 50% enrolled. **Transfer Admission Requirements:** High school transcript, college transcript(s). Lowest grade transferable C-. **General Admission Information:** Application fee $10. Non-fall registration accepted. Common Application not accepted.

COSTS AND FINANCIAL AID
Annual tuition $12,800. Room & board $4,950. Average book expense $650. **Required Forms and Deadlines:** FAFSA. Financial aid filing deadline 4/15. **Types of Aid:** *Need-based scholarships/grants:* Pell, SEOG, state scholarships/grants, private scholarships, the school's own gift aid. *Loans:* FFEL Subsidized Stafford, FFEL Unsubsidized Stafford, FFEL PLUS, Federal Perkins. **Student Employment:** Federal Work-Study Program available. Off-campus job opportunities are fair. **Financial Aid Statistics:** 95% freshmen, 91% undergrads receive need-based scholarship or grant aid. 82% freshmen, 73% undergrads receive need-based self-help aid. Highest amount earned per year from on-campus jobs $800.

MOUNT ST. MARY'S UNIVERSITY

16300 Old Emmitsburg Road, Emmitsburg, MD 21727
Phone: 301-447-5214 **E-mail:** admissions@msmary.edu **CEEB Code:** 5421
Fax: 301-447-5860 **Website:** www.msmary.edu **ACT Code:** 1726
Financial Aid Phone: 301-447-5207

This private school, affiliated with the Roman Catholic Church, was founded in 1808. It has a 1,400-acre campus.

RATINGS
Admissions Selectivity Rating: 77   **Fire Safety Rating:** 77   **Green Rating:** 75

STUDENTS AND FACULTY
Enrollment: 1,695. **Student Body:** 60% female, 40% male, 43% out-of-state. African American 6%, Asian 3%, Caucasian 85%, Hispanic 4%. **Retention and Graduation:** 84% freshmen return for sophomore year. 65% freshmen graduate within 4 years. 40% grads go on to further study within 1 year. 19% grads pursue arts and sciences degrees. 15% grads pursue business degrees. 3% grads pursue law degrees. 3% grads pursue medical degrees. **Faculty:** Student/faculty ratio 13:1. 112 full-time faculty, 87% hold PhDs. 91% faculty teach undergrads.

ACADEMICS
Degrees: Bachelor's, first professional, master's, post-bachelor's certificate, post-master's certificate. **Academic Requirements:** Arts/fine arts, computer literacy, English (including composition), ethics, foreign languages, history, humanities, mathematics, non-Western culture, philosophy, sciences (biological or physical), social science, theology. **Classes:** Most classes have 20–29 students. Most lab/discussion sections have 10–19 students. **Majors with Highest Enrollment:** Business administration/management, elementary education and teaching, psychology. **Disciplines with Highest Percentage of Degrees Awarded:** Business/marketing 37%, education 12%, social sciences 11%, psychology 5%, biological/life sciences 5%. **Special Study Options:** Accelerated program, cross-registration, double major, dual enrollment, honors program, independent study, internships, liberal arts/career combination, student-designed major, study abroad, teacher certification program, weekend college, 3-2 with Johns Hopkins University (BS in biology; BS in nursing), 3–3 with Sacred Heart University (BS in biology; MS in physical therapy), 4–2 with Sacred Heart University (BS in biology; MS in occupational therapy).

FACILITIES
Housing: Coed dorms, apartments for single students, special housing for disabled students, theme houses. **Special Academic Facilities/Equipment:** Historical art collection reflecting Catholic history in America and Marylandia. **Computers:** 100% of classrooms are wireless, 100% of public computers are PCs, network access in dorm rooms, network access in dorm lounges, online registration, online administrative functions (other than registration), remote student-access to Web through college's connection.

CAMPUS LIFE
Activities: Choral groups, concert band, dance, drama/theater, jazz band, literary magazine, music ensembles, musical theater, radio station, student government, student newspaper, television station, yearbook. **Organizations:** 70 registered organizations, 19 honor societies, 10 religious organizations. **Athletics (Intercollegiate):** *Men:* Baseball, basketball, cross-country, golf, lacrosse, soccer, tennis, track/field (indoor), track/field (outdoor). *Women:* Basketball, cross-country, golf, lacrosse, soccer, softball, swimming, tennis, track/field (indoor), track/field (outdoor). **Environmental Initiatives:** ACUPCC. Recycling. Sustainable Purchasing.

ADMISSIONS
Freshman Academic Profile: 21% in top 10% of high school class, 45% in top 25% of high school class, 79% in top 50% of high school class. 52% from public high schools. SAT Math middle 50% range 480–580. SAT Critical Reading middle 50% range 480–590. TOEFL required of all international applicants, minimum paper TOEFL 550, minimum computer TOEFL 213. **Basis for Candidate Selection:** *Very important factors considered include:* Academic GPA, rigor of secondary school record. *Important factors considered include:* Standardized test scores. *Other factors considered include:* Alumni/ae relation, character/personal qualities, class rank, extracurricular activities, recommendation(s), talent/ability, volunteer work, work experience. **Freshman Admission Requirements:** High school diploma is required, and GED is accepted. *Academic units required:* 4 English, 3 math, 3 science (2 science labs), 2 foreign language, 3 social studies, 1 academic elective. **Freshman Admission Statistics:** 2,278 applied, 82% admitted, 23% enrolled. **Transfer Admission Requirements:** College transcript(s), statement of good standing from prior institution(s). Minimum college GPA of 2.0 required. Lowest grade transferable C. **General Admission Information:** Application fee $35. Regular notification is rolling. Non-fall registration accepted. Admission may be

deferred for a maximum of 1 year. Credit and/or placement offered for CEEB Advanced Placement tests.

COSTS AND FINANCIAL AID

Required Forms and Deadlines: FAFSA, institution's own financial aid form. Financial aid filing deadline 3/1. **Notification of Awards:** Applicants will be notified of awards on a rolling basis beginning on or about 2/1. **Types of Aid:** *Need-based scholarships/grants:* Pell, SEOG, state scholarships/grants, private scholarships, the school's own gift aid. *Loans:* FFEL Subsidized Stafford, FFEL Unsubsidized Stafford, FFEL PLUS, Federal Perkins. **Student Employment:** Federal Work-Study Program available. Institutional employment available. Off-campus job opportunities are fair. **Financial Aid Statistics:** 65% freshmen, 59% undergrads receive need-based scholarship or grant aid. 50% freshmen, 45% undergrads receive need-based self-help aid. 35 freshmen, 135 undergrads receive athletic scholarships. 98% freshmen, 97% undergrads receive any aid.

MOUNT UNION COLLEGE

1972 Clark Avenue, Alliance, OH 44601-3993
Phone: 330-823-2590 **E-mail:** admission@muc.edu **CEEB Code:** 1492
Fax: 330-823-5097 **Website:** www.muc.edu
Financial Aid Phone: 330-823-2674

This private school, affiliated with th Methodist Church, was founded in 1846. It has a 115-acre campus.Ratings

---

Admissions Selectivity Rating: 75   **Fire Safety Rating:** 94   **Green Rating:** 72

STUDENTS AND FACULTY

Enrollment: 2,076. **Student Body:** 49% female, 51% male, 10% out-of-state, 2% international. African American 4%, Caucasian 88%. **Retention and Graduation:** 80% freshmen return for sophomore year. 50% freshmen graduate within 4 years. 29% grads go on to further study within 1 year. 22% grads pursue arts and sciences degrees. 3% grads pursue business degrees. 2% grads pursue law degrees. 2% grads pursue medical degrees. **Faculty:** Student/faculty ratio 13:1. 124 full-time faculty, 82% hold PhDs. 100% faculty teach undergrads.

ACADEMICS

Degrees: Bachelor's. **Academic Requirements:** Arts/fine arts, English (including composition), foreign languages, global perspective, history, humanities, mathematics, philosophy, physical education, public speaking, religion, sciences (biological or physical), social science, writing across the curriculum. **Classes:** Most classes have 10–19 students. Most lab/discussion sections have fewer than 10 students. **Majors with Highest Enrollment:** Business administration/management, sociology. **Disciplines with Highest Percentage of Degrees Awarded:** Education 23%, business/marketing 19%, parks and recreation 9%, social sciences 9%, history 6%, biological/life sciences 5%, communications/journalism 5%, communication technologies 5%. **Special Study Options:** Accelerated program, cooperative education program, double major, English as a second language (ESL), honors program, independent study, internships, student-designed major, study abroad, teacher certification program.

FACILITIES

Housing: Coed dorms, men's dorms, women's dorms, special housing for disabled students, special housing for international students, fraternity/sorority housing, small single-sex college-owned residential homes converted to college housing. **Special Academic Facilities/Equipment:** Art gallery, ecological center, observatory, educational media center. **Computers:** 100% of classrooms are wireless, 90% of public computers are PCs, 10% of public computers are Macs, network access in dorm rooms, network access in dorm lounges, online registration, online administrative functions (other than registration), support for handheld computing, remote student-access to Web through college's connection.

CAMPUS LIFE

Activities: Choral groups, concert band, dance, drama/theater, jazz band, literary magazine, marching band, music ensembles, musical theater, pep band, radio station, student government, student newspaper, yearbook. **Organizations:** 80 registered organizations, 16 honor societies, 10 religious organizations. 4 fraternities (15% men join), 4 sororities (26% women join). **Athletics (Intercollegiate):** *Men:* Baseball, basketball, cross-country, diving, football, golf, soccer, swimming, tennis, track/field (indoor), track/field (outdoor), wrestling. *Women:* Basketball, cheerleading, cross-country, diving, golf, soccer, softball, swimming, tennis, track/field (indoor), track/field (outdoor), volleyball. **Environmental Initiatives:** Campus-wide sustainability committee that includes faculty, staff, and students. Campus-wide recycling program for paper and aluminum. Evaluating green initiative with facilities and pursuing LEED certification on new building project.

ADMISSIONS

Freshman Academic Profile: 17% in top 10% of high school class, 40% in top 25% of high school class, 70% in top 50% of high school class. SAT Math middle 50% range 460–570. SAT Critical Reading middle 50% range 450–580. ACT middle 50% range 19–25. TOEFL required of all international applicants, minimum paper TOEFL 550, minimum computer TOEFL 213. **Basis for Candidate Selection:** *Very important factors considered include:* Academic GPA, class rank, rigor of secondary school record, standardized test scores. *Important factors considered include:* Recommendation(s). *Other factors considered include:* Alumni/ae relation, application essay, character/personal qualities, extracurricular activities, racial/ethnic status, talent/ability, volunteer work, work experience. **Freshman Admission Requirements:** High school diploma is required, and GED is accepted. *Academic units recommended:* 4 English, 3 math, 3 science (2 science labs), 2 foreign language, 3 social studies, 1 fine arts. **Freshman Admission Statistics:** 2,067 applied, 79% admitted, 39% enrolled. **Transfer Admission Requirements:** High school transcript, college transcript(s), essay or personal statement, statement of good standing from prior institution(s). Minimum college GPA of 2.0 required. Lowest grade transferable C. **General Admission Information:** Regular notification is rolling. Non-fall registration accepted. Admission may be deferred for a maximum of 1 semester. Credit and/or placement offered for CEEB Advanced Placement tests.

COSTS AND FINANCIAL AID

Required Forms and Deadlines: FAFSA. Financial aid filing deadline 4/1. **Notification of Awards:** Applicants will be notified of awards on a rolling basis beginning on or about 3/15. **Types of Aid:** *Need-based scholarships/grants:* Pell, SEOG, state scholarships/grants, private scholarships, the school's own gift aid. *Loans:* FFEL Subsidized Stafford, FFEL Unsubsidized Stafford, FFEL PLUS, Federal Perkins, college/university loans from institutional funds. **Financial Aid Statistics:** 79% freshmen, 80% undergrads receive need-based scholarship or grant aid. 68% freshmen, 73% undergrads receive need-based self-help aid. 99% freshmen, 95% undergrads receive any aid.

MOUNT VERNON COLLEGE

2100 Foxhall Road NW, Washington, DC 20007-1199
Phone: 800-682-4636 **E-mail:** mvcgw@gwu.edu **CEEB Code:** 5422
Fax: 202-625-4688 **Website:** www.mvc.gwu.edu **ACT Code:** 682
Financial Aid Phone: 202-625-4682

This private school was founded in 1875. It has a 26-acre campus.

RATINGS

Admissions Selectivity Rating: 60*   **Fire Safety Rating:** 60*   **Green Rating:** 60*

STUDENTS AND FACULTY

Student Body: 72% out-of-state. **Retention and Graduation:** 7% grads go on to further study within 1 year. 2% grads pursue arts and sciences degrees. 2% grads pursue business degrees. 3% grads pursue law degrees.

ACADEMICS

Degrees: Bachelor's, doctoral, master's.

FACILITIES

Housing: Coed dorms, men's dorms, women's dorms.

CAMPUS LIFE

Activities: Student government, student newspaper, yearbook. **Organizations:** 20 registered organizations, 1 honor society, 7 religious organizations.

ADMISSIONS

Freshman Academic Profile: 70% from public high schools. TOEFL required of all international applicants, minimum paper TOEFL 500. **Freshman Admission Requirements:** High school diploma is required, and GED is accepted. *Academic units recommended:* 4 English, 3 math, 3 science, 2 foreign language, 1 social studies, 1 history. **Transfer Admission Requirements:** Minimum college GPA of 2.0 required. Lowest grade transferable C-. **General Admission Information:** Early decision application deadline 3/1. Regular application deadline is rolling. Regular notification is rolling. Non-fall registration accepted. Common Application not accepted. Credit and/or placement offered for CEEB Advanced Placement tests.

COSTS AND FINANCIAL AID

Comprehensive fee $22,770. Room & board $7,730. Average book expense $500. **Required Forms and Deadlines:** FAFSA. **Types of Aid:** *Need-based scholarships/grants:* State scholarships/grants. *Loans:* FFEL Subsidized Stafford, FFEL PLUS. **Student Employment:** Federal Work-Study Program available. Institutional employment available. Off-campus job opportunities are excellent. **Financial Aid Statistics:** Highest amount earned per year from on-campus jobs $2,000.

MOUNT VERNON NAZARENE UNIVERSITY

800 Martinsburg Road, Mount Vernon, OH 43050
Phone: 740-392-6868 **E-mail:** admissions@mvnu.edu **CEEB Code:** 1531
Fax: 740-393-0511 **Website:** www.mvnu.edu **ACT Code:** 3372
Financial Aid Phone: 866-686-8243

This private school, affiliated with the Nazarene Church, was founded in 1964. It has a 401-acre campus.

RATINGS
Admissions Selectivity Rating: 77   **Fire Safety Rating:** 62   **Green Rating:** 77

STUDENTS AND FACULTY
Enrollment: 2,046. **Student Body:** 59% female, 41% male, 7% out-of-state. African American 5%, Caucasian 92%, Hispanic 1%. **Retention and Graduation:** 74% freshmen return for sophomore year. 39% freshmen graduate within 4 years. 18% grads go on to further study within 1 year. 4% grads pursue arts and sciences degrees. 5% grads pursue business degrees. 2% grads pursue law degrees. 3% grads pursue medical degrees. **Faculty:** Student/faculty ratio 16:1. 112 full-time faculty, 61% hold PhDs. 100% faculty teach undergrads.

ACADEMICS
Degrees: Associate, bachelor's, master's. **Academic Requirements:** Arts/fine arts, English (including composition), health and physical education, history, humanities, mathematics, philosophy, sciences (biological or physical), social science. **Classes:** Most classes have 10–19 students. **Majors with Highest Enrollment:** Biology/biological sciences, business administration/management, early childhood education and teaching. **Disciplines with Highest Percentage of Degrees Awarded:** Business/marketing 59%, education 12%, philosophy and religious studies 4%, psychology 4%, biological/life sciences 3%, communications/journalism 3%, visual and performing arts 3%, social sciences 3%, family and consumer sciences 2%, parks and recreation. **Special Study Options:** Cooperative education program, cross-registration, distance learning, double major, dual enrollment, honors program, independent study, internships, liberal arts/career combination, study abroad, teacher certification program.

FACILITIES
Housing: Men's dorms, women's dorms, apartments for single students, special housing for disabled students. **Special Academic Facilities/Equipment:** Art gallery, nature reserve. **Computers:** 25% of classrooms are wired, 83% of public computers are PCs, 17% of public computers are Macs, network access in dorm rooms, network access in dorm lounges, online administrative functions (other than registration), support for handheld computing, remote student-access to Web through college's connection.

CAMPUS LIFE
Activities: Choral groups, concert band, drama/theater, jazz band, music ensembles, musical theater, opera, pep band, radio station, student government, student newspaper, yearbook. **Organizations:** 41 registered organizations, 4 honor societies, 18 religious organizations. **Athletics (Intercollegiate):** *Men:* Baseball, basketball, cheerleading, cross-country, golf, soccer. *Women:* Basketball, cheerleading, cross-country, soccer, softball, volleyball. **Environmental Initiatives:** The president has recently made a public commitment for the university to minimize it's "mark" on the environment. Dialogue on how to best develop a university-wide environmental stewardship plan has just begun. The University does have an Environmental Stewardship Committee with faculty, staff, and student representation. Recent efforts to increase campus-wide recycling, and conversation of used vegetable oil into biodisel fuel.

ADMISSIONS
Freshman Academic Profile: 22% in top 10% of high school class, 47% in top 25% of high school class, 77% in top 50% of high school class. 78% from public high schools. SAT Math middle 50% range 460–570. SAT Critical Reading middle 50% range 460–560. ACT middle 50% range 20–25. TOEFL required of all international applicants, minimum paper TOEFL 500, minimum computer TOEFL 173. **Basis for Candidate Selection:** *Very important factors considered include:* Academic GPA, standardized test scores. *Other factors considered include:* Application essay, character/personal qualities, recommendation(s), rigor of secondary school record. **Freshman Admission Requirements:** High school diploma is required, and GED is accepted. *Academic units recommended:* 4 English, 3 math, 3 science (1 science lab), 3

foreign language, 3 social studies, 7 academic electives, 1 health and physical education. **Freshman Admission Statistics:** 798 applied, 81% admitted, 54% enrolled. **Transfer Admission Requirements:** High school transcript, college transcript(s), essay or personal statement, statement of good standing from prior institution(s). Minimum college GPA of 2.0 required. Lowest grade transferable C-. **General Admission Information:** Application fee $25. Regular application deadline 8/1. Regular notification is rolling. Non-fall registration accepted. Admission may be deferred for a maximum of 1 year. Neither credit nor placement offered for CEEB Advanced Placement tests.

COSTS AND FINANCIAL AID
Annual tuition $18,770. Room and board $5,550. Required fees $560. Average book expense $1,000. **Required Forms and Deadlines:** FAFSA, institution's own financial aid form. Financial aid filing deadline 3/15. **Notification of Awards:** Applicants will be notified of awards on a rolling basis beginning on or about 2/15. **Types of Aid:** *Need-based scholarships/grants:* Pell, SEOG, state scholarships/grants, private scholarships, the school's own gift aid. *Loans:* FFEL Subsidized Stafford, FFEL Unsubsidized Stafford, FFEL PLUS, Federal Perkins, college/university loans from institutional funds. **Student Employment:** Federal Work-Study Program available. Institutional employment available. Off-campus job opportunities are good. **Financial Aid Statistics:** 82% freshmen, 52% undergrads receive need-based scholarship or grant aid. 71% freshmen, 47% undergrads receive need-based self-help aid. 12 freshmen, 49 undergrads receive athletic scholarships. 100% freshmen, 94% undergrads receive any aid. Highest amount earned per year from on-campus jobs $6,600.

MOUNTAIN STATE UNIVERSITY

609 South Kanawha Street, Beckley, WV 25801
Phone: 304-929-1433 **E-mail:** gomsu@mountainstate.edu
Fax: 304-253-3463 **Website:** www.mountainstate.edu **ACT Code:** 4510
Financial Aid Phone: 304-929-1595

This private school was founded in 1933. It has a 24-acre campus.

RATINGS
Admissions Selectivity Rating: 60*   **Fire Safety Rating:** 99   **Green Rating:** 60*

STUDENTS AND FACULTY
Enrollment: 3,811. **Student Body:** 66% female, 34% male, 28% out-of-state, 2% international (45 countries represented). African American 9%, Asian 2%, Caucasian 84%, Hispanic 2%. **Retention and Graduation:** 45% freshmen return for sophomore year. 9% freshmen graduate within 4 years. 15% grads go on to further study within 1 year. 5% grads pursue arts and sciences degrees. 5% grads pursue business degrees. 2% grads pursue law degrees. 2% grads pursue medical degrees. **Faculty:** Student/faculty ratio 20:1. 87 full-time faculty, 31% hold PhDs. 97% faculty teach undergrads.

ACADEMICS
Degrees: Associate, bachelor's, certificate, master's, post-bachelor's certificate, post-master's certificate, terminal. **Academic Requirements:** Arts/fine arts, computer literacy, English (including composition), humanities, liberal arts, mathematics, philosophy, sciences (biological or physical), social science. **Classes:** Most classes have fewer than 10 students. Most lab/discussion sections have 10–19 students. **Majors with Highest Enrollment:** Business administration/management, criminal justice/law enforcement administration, health professions and related sciences. **Disciplines with Highest Percentage of Degrees Awarded:** Business/marketing 35%, health professions and related sciences 29%, public administration and social services 22%, interdisciplinary studies 6%, computer and information sciences 4%. **Special Study Options:** Accelerated program, cooperative education program, cross-registration, distance learning, double major, dual enrollment, English as a second language (ESL), honors program, independent study, internships, liberal arts/career combination, student-designed major, weekend college.

FACILITIES
Housing: Coed dorms, off-campus housing for athletes. **Special Academic Facilities/Equipment:** Robert C. Byrd Learning Resources Center, botanical gardens and greenhouse, family practice medical clinic. **Computers:** 10% of classrooms are wired, 50% of classrooms are wireless, 100% of public computers are PCs, network access in dorm rooms, online registration, online administrative functions (other than registration), support for handheld computing, remote student-access to Web through college's connection.

CAMPUS LIFE
Activities: Choral groups, drama/theater, pep band, student government, student newspaper. **Organizations:** 17 registered organizations, 4 honor

societies, 1 religious organization. 1 fraternity. **Athletics (Intercollegiate):** *Men:* Basketball, cheerleading, soccer. *Women:* Cheerleading, soccer, softball, volleyball.

ADMISSIONS

Freshman Academic Profile: SAT Math middle 50% range 138–565. SAT Critical Reading middle 50% range 138–565. SAT Writing middle 50% range 138–565. ACT middle 50% range 17–23. TOEFL required of all international applicants, minimum paper TOEFL 500, minimum computer TOEFL 173. **Basis for Candidate Selection:** *Very important factors considered include:* Academic GPA, alumni/ae relation, application essay, character/personal qualities, class rank, extracurricular activities, first generation, geographical residence, interview, level of applicant's interest, racial/ethnic status, recommendation(s), religion. **Freshman Admission Requirements:** High school diploma is required, and GED is accepted. *Academic units required:* 4 English, 2 math, 2 science (2 science labs), 3 social studies. *Academic units recommended:* 4 English, 2 math, 2 science (2 science labs), 3 social studies, 2 history. **Freshman Admission Statistics:** 1,436 applied, 100% admitted, 29% enrolled. **Transfer Admission Requirements:** College transcript(s). Lowest grade transferable C. **General Admission Information:** Application fee $25. Regular notification is rolling. Non-fall registration accepted. Admission may be deferred for a maximum of 1 semester. Credit offered for CEEB Advanced Placement tests.

COSTS AND FINANCIAL AID

Annual tuition $6,150. Room and board $5,854. Required fees $1,950. Average book expense $1,300. **Required Forms and Deadlines:** FAFSA. Financial aid filing deadline 3/1. **Notification of Awards:** Applicants will be notified of awards on a rolling basis beginning on or about 4/1. **Types of Aid:** *Need-based scholarships/grants:* Pell, SEOG, state scholarships/grants, private scholarships, the school's own gift aid, Federal Nursing Scholarships. *Loans:* FFEL Subsidized Stafford, FFEL Unsubsidized Stafford, FFEL PLUS, private educational loans. **Student Employment:** Federal Work-Study Program available. Institutional employment available. Off-campus job opportunities are good. **Financial Aid Statistics:** 64% freshmen, 43% undergrads receive need-based scholarship or grant aid. 62% freshmen, 60% undergrads receive need-based self-help aid. 6 freshmen, 48 undergrads receive athletic scholarships. 72% freshmen, 67% undergrads receive any aid. Highest amount earned per year from on-campus jobs $15,253.

MUHLENBERG COLLEGE

2400 West Chew Street, Allentown, PA 18104-5596
Phone: 484-664-3200 **E-mail:** admission@muhlenberg.edu **CEEB Code:** 2424
Fax: 484-664-3234 **Website:** www.muhlenberg.edu **ACT Code:** 3640
Financial Aid Phone: 484-664-3175

This private school, affiliated with the Lutheran Church, was founded in 1848. It has an 81-acre campus.

RATINGS

Admissions Selectivity Rating: 94   **Fire Safety Rating:** 89   **Green Rating:** 75

STUDENTS AND FACULTY

Enrollment: 2,443. **Student Body:** 60% female, 40% male, 76% out-of-state. African American 2%, Asian 2%, Caucasian 90%, Hispanic 4%. **Retention and Graduation:** 93% freshmen return for sophomore year. 80% freshmen graduate within 4 years. 29% grads go on to further study within 1 year. 14% grads pursue arts and sciences degrees. 1% grads pursue business degrees. 6% grads pursue law degrees. 8% grads pursue medical degrees. **Faculty:** Student/faculty ratio 12:1. 161 full-time faculty, 88% hold PhDs. 100% faculty teach undergrads.

ACADEMICS

Degrees: Associate, bachelor's, certificate. **Academic Requirements:** Arts/fine arts, English (including composition), foreign languages, history, literature, mathematics, non-Western cultures, philosophy, physical education, sciences (biological or physical), social science, reasoning, religious studies, writing. **Classes:** Most classes have fewer than 10 students. Most lab/discussion sections have 10–19 students. **Majors with Highest Enrollment:** Business administration/management, drama and dramatics/theater arts, psychology. **Disciplines with Highest Percentage of Degrees Awarded:** Business/marketing 20%,

social sciences 16%, visual and performing arts 13%, psychology 12%, biological/life sciences 9%. **Special Study Options:** Accelerated program, cross-registration, double major, exchange student program (domestic), honors program, independent study, internships, student-designed major, study abroad, teacher certification program.

FACILITIES

Housing: Coed dorms, women's dorms, apartments for single students, special housing for disabled students, special housing for international students, fraternity/sorority housing, college-owned houses in the neighborhood surrounding the campus. **Special Academic Facilities/Equipment:** Martin Art Gallery, biology museum, Graver Arboretum, greenhouse, mainstage theater, recital hall, 20-foot boat for marine studies, 40-acre Raker environmental field station, 2 electron microscopes, dance studios, experimental theaters, proscenium theaters. **Computers:** 1% of classrooms are wired, 1% of classrooms are wireless, 98% of public computers are PCs, 1% of public computers are Macs, 1% of public computers are UNIX, network access in dorm rooms, network access in dorm lounges, online administrative functions (other than registration), support for handheld computing.

CAMPUS LIFE

Activities: Choral groups, concert band, dance, drama/theater, jazz band, literary magazine, music ensembles, musical theater, pep band, radio station, student government, student newspaper, student-run film society, television station, yearbook. **Organizations:** 100 registered organizations, 12 honor societies, 7 religious organizations. 4 fraternities (13% men join), 4 sororities (18% women join). **Athletics (Intercollegiate):** *Men:* Baseball, basketball, cheerleading, cross-country, football, golf, lacrosse, soccer, tennis, track/field (indoor), track/field (outdoor), wrestling. *Women:* Basketball, cheerleading, cross-country, field hockey, golf, lacrosse, soccer, softball, tennis, track/field (indoor), track/field (outdoor), volleyball. **Environmental Initiatives:** Strong recycling program. LEED certification for New Science Building. Energy conservation through purchasing policies, replaved light fixtures, and renewable enery credits purchased.

ADMISSIONS

Freshman Academic Profile: 45% in top 10% of high school class, 81% in top 25% of high school class, 98% in top 50% of high school class. 73% from public high schools. SAT Math middle 50% range 560–660. SAT Critical Reading middle 50% range 550–650. SAT Writing middle 50% range 560–660. ACT middle 50% range 24–29. TOEFL required of all international applicants, minimum paper TOEFL 550, minimum computer TOEFL 213. **Basis for Candidate Selection:** *Very important factors considered include:* Academic GPA, rigor of secondary school record. *Important factors considered include:* Application essay, character/personal qualities, class rank, extracurricular activities, interview, recommendation(s), standardized test scores, talent/ability. *Other factors considered include:* Alumni/ae relation, first generation, geographical residence, level of applicant's interest, racial/ethnic status, volunteer work, work experience. **Freshman Admission Requirements:** High school diploma is required, and GED is accepted. *Academic units required:* 4 English, 3 math, 2 science (2 science labs), 2 foreign language, 2 history, 3 academic electives. *Academic units recommended:* 4 math, 3 science (3 science labs), 4 foreign language. **Freshman Admission Statistics:** 4,347 applied, 44% admitted, 32% enrolled. **Transfer Admission Requirements:** High school transcript, college transcript(s), essay or personal statement, interview, standardized test score, statement of good standing from prior institution(s). Minimum college GPA of 2.5 required. Lowest grade transferable C-. **General Admission Information:** Application fee $50. Early decision application deadline 2/1. Regular application deadline 2/15. Regular notification 3/15. Non-fall registration accepted. Admission may be deferred for a maximum of 1 year. Credit and/or placement offered for CEEB Advanced Placement tests.

COSTS AND FINANCIAL AID

Annual tuition $32,850. Room and board $7,790. Required fees $240. Average book expense $800. **Required Forms and Deadlines:** FAFSA, institution's own financial aid form, CSS/Financial Aid PROFILE, Noncustodial PROFILE. Financial aid filing deadline 2/15. **Notification of Awards:** Applicants will be notified of awards on or about 4/1. **Types of Aid:** *Need-based scholarships/grants:* Pell, SEOG, state scholarships/grants, private scholarships, the school's own gift aid. *Loans:* FFEL Subsidized Stafford, FFEL Unsubsidized Stafford, FFEL PLUS, Federal Perkins, private. **Financial Aid Statistics:** 44% freshmen, 42% undergrads receive need-based scholarship or grant aid. 31% freshmen, 31% undergrads receive need-based self-help aid. 75% freshmen, 78% undergrads receive any aid. Highest amount earned per year from on-campus jobs $1,800.

MULTNOMAH BIBLE COLLEGE AND BIBLICAL SEMINARY

8435 Northeast Glisan Street, Portland, OR 97220-5898
Phone: 503-251-6485 **E-mail:** admiss@multnomah.edu
Fax: 503-254-1268 **Website:** www.multnomah.edu
Financial Aid Phone: 503-251-5336

This private school, affiliated with the Christian (nondenominational) Church, was founded in 1936. It has a 25-acre campus.

RATINGS
Admissions Selectivity Rating: 60*   **Fire Safety Rating:** 60*   **Green Rating:** 60*

STUDENTS AND FACULTY
Enrollment: 591. **Student Body:** 45% female, 55% male, 55% out-of-state. African American 1%, Asian 3%, Caucasian 92%, Hispanic 3%. **Retention and Graduation:** 64% freshmen return for sophomore year. 25% freshmen graduate within 4 years. **Faculty:** Student/faculty ratio 19:1. 31 full-time faculty, 68% hold PhDs.

ACADEMICS
Degrees: Bachelor's, first professional, master's, post-bachelor's certificate. **Academic Requirements:** Arts/fine arts, English (including composition), history, humanities, mathematics, philosophy, sciences (biological or physical), social science. Minimum of 56 credit hours in Bible and theology required. **Classes:** Most classes have fewer than 10 students. Most lab/discussion sections have 10–19 students. **Majors with Highest Enrollment:** Bible/biblical studies. **Special Study Options:** Double major, internships, liberal arts/career combination.

FACILITIES
Housing: Men's dorms, women's dorms, apartments for married students, apartments for single students, houses for married students. **Special Academic Facilities/Equipment:** Prayer chapel, weight room, coffee shop. **Computers:** 95% of public computers are PCs, 5% of public computers are Macs, network access in dorm rooms, network access in dorm lounges, online registration, online administrative functions (other than registration), remote student-access to Web through college's connection.

CAMPUS LIFE
Activities: Choral groups, drama/theater, music ensembles, student government, student newspaper, yearbook. **Athletics (Intercollegiate):** *Men:* Basketball. *Women:* Volleyball.

ADMISSIONS
Freshman Academic Profile: SAT Math middle 50% range 460–580. SAT Critical Reading middle 50% range 470–600. SAT Writing middle 50% range 470–580. ACT middle 50% range 18–27. TOEFL required of all international applicants, minimum paper TOEFL 550, minimum computer TOEFL 213. **Basis for Candidate Selection:** *Very important factors considered include:* Academic GPA, recommendation(s), religious affiliation/commitment, rigor of secondary school record, standardized test scores. *Important factors considered include:* Application essay, character/personal qualities. *Other factors considered include:* Alumni/ae relation, class rank, extracurricular activities, talent/ability, volunteer work, work experience. **Freshman Admission Requirements:** High school diploma is required, and GED is accepted. *Academic units recommended:* 4 English, 2 math, 3 science (1 science lab), 2 foreign language, 3 social studies, 2 history. **Freshman Admission Statistics:** 147 applied, 86% admitted, 68% enrolled. **Transfer Admission Requirements:** College transcript(s), essay or personal statement, statement of good standing from prior institution(s). Minimum college GPA of 2.0 required. Lowest grade transferable C-. **General Admission Information:** Application fee $40. Regular application deadline 7/15. Regular notification is rolling. Non-fall registration accepted. Admission may be deferred for a maximum of 1 semester. Credit offered for CEEB Advanced Placement tests.

COSTS AND FINANCIAL AID
Annual tuition $13,480. Room and board $5,750. Average book expense $1,000. **Required Forms and Deadlines:** FAFSA, institution's own financial aid form. Financial aid filing deadline 8/1. **Notification of Awards:** Applicants will be notified of awards on a rolling basis beginning on or about 4/1. **Types of Aid:** *Need-based scholarships/grants:* Pell. *Loans:* Direct Subsidized Stafford, Direct Unsubsidized Stafford, Direct PLUS. **Student Employment:** Federal Work-Study Program available. Institutional employment available. Off-campus job opportunities are good. **Financial Aid Statistics:** 50% freshmen, 67% undergrads receive need-based scholarship or grant aid. 52% freshmen, 69% undergrads receive need-based self-help aid.

MURRAY STATE UNIVERSITY

113 Sparks Hall, Murray, KY 42071-0009
Phone: 270-809-3741 **E-mail:** admissions@murraystate.edu **CEEB Code:** 1494
Fax: 270-809-3780 **Website:** www.murraystate.edu **ACT Code:** 1532
Financial Aid Phone: 270-809-2546

This public school was founded in 1922. It has a 350-acre campus.

RATINGS
Admissions Selectivity Rating: 84   **Fire Safety Rating:** 83   **Green Rating:** 78

STUDENTS AND FACULTY
Enrollment: 7,862. **Student Body:** 58% female, 42% male, 28% out-of-state, 1% international (56 countries represented). African American 6%, Caucasian 89%. **Retention and Graduation:** 77% freshmen return for sophomore year. 39% freshmen graduate within 4 years. **Faculty:** Student/faculty ratio 16:1. 396 full-time faculty, 78% hold PhDs. 100% faculty teach undergrads.

ACADEMICS
Degrees: Associate, bachelor's, master's, post-master's certificate. **Academic Requirements:** Arts/fine arts, computer literacy, English (including composition), history, humanities, mathematics, sciences (biological or physical), social science. Bachelor of art degrees require 12 hours of a foreign language. **Classes:** Most classes have fewer than 10 students. Most lab/discussion sections have 10–19 students. **Majors with Highest Enrollment:** Business administration/management, elementary education and teaching, nursing/registered nurse training (ASN, BSN, MSN, RN). **Disciplines with Highest Percentage of Degrees Awarded:** Education 16%, business/marketing 15%, communications/journalism 10%, health professions and related sciences 10%, engineering technologies 5%, liberal arts/general studies 5%, agriculture 4%, visual and performing arts 4%. **Special Study Options:** Agriculture, arts, accelerated program, business/marketing, biological sciences, communications/communication technologies, computer and information sciences, cooperative education program, cross-registration, distance learning, double major, dual enrollment, education, engineering/engineering technologies, English, English as a second language (ESL), exchange student program (domestic), external degree program, foreign languages, health professions and related sciences, history, home economics, honors program, humanities and liberal arts, independent study, internships, library sciences, mathematics, natural resources and environmental sciences, natural sciences, parks and recreation, philosophy, physical sciences, protective sciences/public administration, psychology, social/behavioral sciences, study abroad, teacher certification program, technologies, trade and industry, visual and performing arts, weekend college.

FACILITIES
Housing: Coed dorms, men's dorms, women's dorms, apartments for married students, apartments for single students, special housing for disabled students, fraternity/sorority housing. All housing is operated under a residential college system. **Special Academic Facilities/Equipment:** State-of-the-art 73,000-square-foot student recreation and wellness center within the residential college housing complex, West Kentucky Museum, 8,500-seat regional special events center. **Computers:** 50% of public computers are PCs, network access in dorm rooms, network access in dorm lounges, online registration, online administrative functions (other than registration), support for handheld computing, remote student-access to Web through college's connection.

CAMPUS LIFE
Activities: Choral groups, concert band, dance, drama/theater, jazz band, literary magazine, marching band, music ensembles, musical theater, pep band, radio station, student government, student newspaper, student-run film society, symphony orchestra, television station. **Organizations:** 210 registered organizations, 30 honor societies, 15 religious organizations. 14 fraternities (16% men join), 8 sororities (12% women join). **Athletics (Intercollegiate):** *Men:* Baseball, basketball, bowling, cheerleading, crew/rowing, cross-country, equestrian sports, football, golf, horseback riding, riflery, rodeo, tennis. *Women:* Basketball, cheerleading, crew/rowing, cross-country, equestrian sports, golf, horseback riding, riflery, rodeo, soccer, tennis, track/field (outdoor), volleyball. **Environmental Initiatives:** Guaranteed Energy performance contracting. Renewable Fuels, BioDiesel, g-35, e-10. Recycling Program.

ADMISSIONS
Freshman Academic Profile: 28% in top 10% of high school class, 60% in top 25% of high school class, 98% in top 50% of high school class. 80% from public high schools. ACT middle 50% range 21–25. TOEFL required of all international applicants, minimum paper TOEFL 500, minimum computer TOEFL 173. **Basis for Candidate Selection:** *Very important factors considered include:* Academic GPA, class rank, rigor of secondary school record, standardized test scores. *Important factors considered include:* Alumni/ae

relation, talent/ability. *Other factors considered include:* Character/personal qualities, extracurricular activities, geographical residence, interview, racial/ethnic status, state residency, volunteer work, work experience. **Freshman Admission Requirements:** High school diploma is required, and GED is accepted. *Academic units required:* 4 English, 3 math, 3 science (1 science lab), 2 foreign language, 3 social studies, 5 academic electives, 2 art appreciation, 1/2 physical education, 1/2 health. *Academic units recommended:* 4 math, 4 science. **Freshman Admission Statistics:** 2,916 applied, 63% admitted, 53% enrolled. **Transfer Admission Requirements:** College transcript(s), statement of good standing from prior institution(s). Minimum college GPA of 2.0 required. Lowest grade transferable D. **General Admission Information:** Application fee $30. Regular application deadline 8/3. Regular notification is rolling. Non-fall registration accepted. Admission may be deferred for a maximum of 1 year. Credit offered for CEEB Advanced Placement tests.

COSTS AND FINANCIAL AID

Annual in-state tuition $4,650. Annual out-of-state tuition $6,728. Room and board $5,670. Required fees $768. Average book expense $700. **Required Forms and Deadlines:** FAFSA, institution's own financial aid form. Financial aid filing deadline 4/1. **Notification of Awards:** Applicants will be notified of awards on a rolling basis beginning on or about 4/15. **Types of Aid:** *Need-based scholarships/grants:* Pell, SEOG, state scholarships/grants, private scholarships, the school's own gift aid, Federal Nursing Scholarships, a wide variety of private and foundation scholarships available. Check out the website www.murraystate.edu. *Loans:* Direct Subsidized Stafford, Direct Unsubsidized Stafford, Direct PLUS, FFEL Subsidized Stafford, FFEL Unsubsidized Stafford, FFEL PLUS, Federal Perkins, Federal Nursing, state loans, college/university loans from institutional funds. **Student Employment:** Federal Work-Study Program available. Institutional employment available. Off-campus job opportunities are good. **Financial Aid Statistics:** 34% freshmen, 30% undergrads receive need-based scholarship or grant aid. 22% freshmen, 43% undergrads receive need-based self-help aid. 59 freshmen, 229 undergrads receive athletic scholarships. 92% freshmen, 87% undergrads receive any aid. Highest amount earned per year from on-campus jobs $3,500.

MUSICIANS INSTITUTE

1655 McCadden Place, Hollywood, CA 90028
Phone: 323-462-1384 **E-mail:** admissions@mi.edu
Fax: 323-462-6978 **Website:** www.mi.edu
Financial Aid Phone: 323-462-1121

This private school was founded in 1977.

RATINGS

Admissions Selectivity Rating: 60*   **Fire Safety Rating:** 60*   **Green Rating:** 60*

STUDENTS AND FACULTY

Enrollment: 489. **Student Body:** 14% female, 86% male, 26% out-of-state. African American 7%, Asian 11%, Caucasian 56%, Hispanic 12%. **Faculty:** 69 full-time faculty.

ACADEMICS

Degrees: Associate, bachelor's, certificate. **Academic Requirements:** Music. **Disciplines with Highest Percentage of Degrees Awarded:** Visual and performing arts 5%.

FACILITIES

Housing: Musicians Institute's Housing Services department assists students and their parents in locating safe, comfortable, affordable, and accessible off-campus housing. MI does not own or operate student housing, but Housing Services manages a vacancy listing.

ADMISSIONS

Basis for Candidate Selection: *Very important factors considered include:* Level of applicant's interest, talent/ability. *Important factors considered include:* Character/personal qualities, extracurricular activities, interview, recommendation(s), work experience. *Other factors considered include:* Academic GPA, alumni/ae relation, application essay, class rank, first generation, rigor of secondary school record, standardized test scores, volunteer work. **Freshman Admission Requirements:** High school diploma is required, and GED is accepted. **Freshman Admission Statistics:** 1,057 applied, 98% admitted, 64% enrolled. **Transfer Admission Requirements:** College transcript(s), essay or personal statement. Minimum college GPA of 2.0 required. Lowest grade transferable C. **General Admission Information:** Application fee $100. Regular notification is rolling. Non-fall registration accepted. Admission may be deferred for a maximum of 1 year.

COSTS AND FINANCIAL AID

Annual tuition $15,250. Required fees $400. **Required Forms and Deadlines:** FAFSA. **Types of Aid:** *Need-based scholarships/grants:* Pell, SEOG, state scholarships/grants, private scholarships. *Loans:* FFEL Subsidized Stafford, FFEL Unsubsidized Stafford, FFEL PLUS, alternative loans. **Financial Aid Statistics:** 11% freshmen, 21% undergrads receive need-based scholarship or grant aid. 7% freshmen, 17% undergrads receive need-based self-help aid.

MUSKINGUM COLLEGE

163 Stormont Drive, New Concord, OH 43762
Phone: 614-826-8137 **E-mail:** adminfo@muskingum.edu **CEEB Code:** 1496
Fax: 614-826-8100 **Website:** www.muskingum.edu **ACT Code:** 3305
Financial Aid Phone: 740-826-8139

This private school, affiliated with the Presbyterian Church, was founded in 1837. It has a 215-acre campus.

RATINGS

Admissions Selectivity Rating: 77   **Fire Safety Rating:** 60*   **Green Rating:** 60*

STUDENTS AND FACULTY

Enrollment: 1,633. **Student Body:** 51% female, 49% male, 10% out-of-state, 2% international (15 countries represented). African American 4%, Caucasian 88%, Hispanic 1%. **Retention and Graduation:** 73% freshmen return for sophomore year. 49% freshmen graduate within 4 years. 20% grads go on to further study within 1 year. 15% grads pursue arts and sciences degrees. 10% grads pursue business degrees. 15% grads pursue law degrees. 10% grads pursue medical degrees. **Faculty:** Student/faculty ratio 15:1. 98 full-time faculty, 87% hold PhDs. 100% faculty teach undergrads.

ACADEMICS

Degrees: Bachelor's, master's. **Academic Requirements:** Arts/fine arts, English (including composition), foreign languages, history, humanities, mathematics, philosophy, physical education, religion, sciences (biological or physical), social science, speech. **Classes:** Most classes have fewer than 10 students. Most lab/discussion sections have fewer than 10 students. **Majors with Highest Enrollment:** Business administration/management, elementary education and teaching, history. **Disciplines with Highest Percentage of Degrees Awarded:** Education 23%, business/marketing 22%, biological/life sciences 10%, psychology 7%, history 6%. **Special Study Options:** Accelerated program, double major, dual enrollment, English as a second language (ESL), independent study, internships, student-designed major, study abroad, teacher certification program, weekend college.

FACILITIES

Housing: Coed dorms, men's dorms, women's dorms, apartments for single students, fraternity/sorority housing, cooperative housing. **Special Academic Facilities/Equipment:** Art gallery, on-campus nursery school, electron microscope, 57-acre biology field station, mobile biology lab. **Computers:** 83% of public computers are PCs, 5% of public computers are Macs, 12% of public computers are UNIX, network access in dorm rooms, network access in dorm lounges, online registration, online administrative functions (other than registration), remote student-access to Web through college's connection.

CAMPUS LIFE

Activities: Choral groups, concert band, dance, drama/theater, jazz band, literary magazine, marching band, music ensembles, musical theater, pep band, radio station, student government, student newspaper, symphony orchestra, television station, yearbook. **Organizations:** 95 registered organizations, 14 honor societies, 4 religious organizations. 5 fraternities (30% men join), 5 sororities (40% women join). **Athletics (Intercollegiate):** *Men:* Baseball, basketball, cheerleading, cross-country, football, golf, soccer, tennis, track/field (indoor), track/field (outdoor), wrestling. *Women:* Basketball, cheerleading, cross-country, golf, soccer, softball, tennis, track/field (indoor), track/field (outdoor), volleyball.

ADMISSIONS

Freshman Academic Profile: 23% in top 10% of high school class, 45% in top 25% of high school class, 72% in top 50% of high school class. 90% from public high schools. SAT Math middle 50% range 450–610. SAT Critical Reading middle 50% range 450–610. SAT Writing middle 50% range 460–590. ACT middle 50% range 19–24. TOEFL required of all international applicants, minimum paper TOEFL 550. **Basis for Candidate Selection:** *Very important factors considered include:* Academic GPA, rigor of secondary school record. *Important factors considered include:* Class rank, recommendation(s), standardized test scores. *Other factors considered include:* Alumni/ae relation, application essay, character/personal qualities, extracurricular activities, geographical residence, interview, racial/ethnic status, talent/ability. **Freshman Admission Requirements:** High school diploma is required, and GED is accepted. *Academic units required:* 4 English, 2 math, 2 science (1 science lab), 2 foreign language, 1 social studies, 2 history. *Academic units recommended:* 4 English, 3 math, 3 science (2 science labs), 2 foreign language, 1 social studies, 2 history. **Freshman Admission Statistics:** 1,759 applied, 79% admitted, 31% enrolled. **Transfer Admission Requirements:** High school transcript, college transcript(s). Minimum college GPA of 2.0 required. Lowest grade transferable C. **General Admission Information:** Regular application deadline 8/1. Regular notification is rolling. Non-fall registration accepted. Admission may be deferred for a maximum of 1 year. Credit and/or placement offered for CEEB Advanced Placement tests.

COSTS AND FINANCIAL AID
Annual tuition $16,600. Room & board $6,740. Required fees $595. Average book expense $1,000. **Required Forms and Deadlines:** FAFSA. Financial aid filing deadline 3/15. **Notification of Awards:** Applicants will be notified of awards on a rolling basis beginning on or about 3/1. **Types of Aid:** *Need-based scholarships/grants:* Pell, SEOG, state scholarships/grants, private scholarships, the school's own gift aid. *Loans:* FFEL Subsidized Stafford, FFEL Unsubsidized Stafford, FFEL PLUS, Federal Perkins, college/university loans from institutional funds. **Student Employment:** Federal Work-Study Program available. Institutional employment available. Off-campus job opportunities are fair. **Financial Aid Statistics:** 78% freshmen, 77% undergrads receive need-based scholarship or grant aid. 66% freshmen, 66% undergrads receive need-based self-help aid. 98% freshmen, 98% undergrads receive any aid. Highest amount earned per year from on-campus jobs $1,500.

NAROPA UNIVERSITY

2130 Araphahoe Avenue, Boulder, CO 80302
Phone: 303-546-3572 **E-mail:** admissions@naropa.edu **CEEB Code:** 0908
Fax: 303-546-3583 **Website:** www.naropa.edu **ACT Code:** 4853
Financial Aid Phone: 303-546-3565

This private school was founded in 1974. It has a 12-acre campus.

RATINGS
Admissions Selectivity Rating: 60*   **Fire Safety Rating:** 60*   **Green Rating:** 97

STUDENTS AND FACULTY
Enrollment: 451. **Student Body:** 60% female, 40% male, 74% out-of-state, 3% international (21 countries represented). Asian 2%, Caucasian 73%, Hispanic 5%. **Retention and Graduation:** 83% freshmen return for sophomore year. 21% freshmen graduate within 4 years. **Faculty:** Student/faculty ratio 9:1. 54 full-time faculty, 54% hold PhDs.

ACADEMICS
Degrees: Bachelor's, certificate, first professional, master's. **Academic Requirements:** Arts/fine arts, contemplative practice (tai chi, meditation, aikido, yoga), English (including composition), humanities, sciences (biological or physical), social science, world wisdom (religious studies). **Classes:** Most classes have 10–19 students. **Majors with Highest Enrollment:** English language and literature, multi/interdisciplinary studies, psychology. **Disciplines with Highest Percentage of Degrees Awarded:** Psychology 28%, philosophy and religious studies 17%, visual and performing arts 15%, English 14%, interdisciplinary studies 9%. **Special Study Options:** Double major, dual enrollment, independent study, internships, student-designed major, study abroad, some courses available online.

FACILITIES
Housing: Apartments for married students, apartments for single students, themed housing (living and learning concept). **Special Academic Facilities/Equipment:** Maitri Rooms, meditation halls, Allen Ginsberg Library, preschool. **Computers:** 95% of public computers are PCs, 5% of public computers are Macs, network access in dorm rooms, network access in dorm lounges, online registration, online administrative functions (other than registration), remote student-access to Web through college's connection.

CAMPUS LIFE
Activities: Choral groups, dance, drama/theater, jazz band, literary magazine, music ensembles, student government. **Organizations:** 22 registered organizations. **Environmental Initiatives:** We compost all of our paper towels in public restrooms diverting 25% of our landfill waste into compost. The cafE composts which will divert 20–25% of organics into compost from the landfill.

CFL installed in the residential halls, and are converting burned out bulbs to green bulbs throughout the campuses.

ADMISSIONS
Freshman Academic Profile: SAT Math middle 50% range 440–550. SAT Critical Reading middle 50% range 490–620. SAT Writing middle 50% range 520–620. ACT middle 50% range 20–26. TOEFL required of all international applicants, minimum paper TOEFL 550, minimum computer TOEFL 213. **Basis for Candidate Selection:** *Very important factors considered include:* Application essay, interview, recommendation(s), rigor of secondary school record. *Important factors considered include:* Academic GPA, character/personal qualities, extracurricular activities, talent/ability, volunteer work. *Other factors considered include:* Alumni/ae relation, first generation, racial/ethnic status, standardized test scores, work experience. **Freshman Admission Requirements:** High school diploma is required, and GED is accepted. *Academic units recommended:* 4 English, 3 math, 3 science (2 science labs), 3 foreign language, 3 social studies, 3 history, 2 academic electives, 2 art/dance/theater and/or creative writing. **Freshman Admission Statistics:** 117 applied, 91% admitted, 51% enrolled. **Transfer Admission Requirements:** College transcript(s), essay or personal statement, interview. Lowest grade transferable C. **General Admission Information:** Application fee $50. Regular notification is rolling. Non-fall registration accepted. Admission may be deferred for a maximum of 1 year. Credit and/or placement offered for CEEB Advanced Placement tests.

COSTS AND FINANCIAL AID
Annual tuition $20,738. Room and board $6,501. Required fees $76. Average book expense $686. **Required Forms and Deadlines:** FAFSA. Financial aid filing deadline 3/1. **Notification of Awards:** Applicants will be notified of awards on a rolling basis beginning on or about 3/1. **Types of Aid:** *Need-based scholarships/grants:* Pell, SEOG, private scholarships, the school's own gift aid. *Loans:* FFEL Subsidized Stafford, FFEL Unsubsidized Stafford, FFEL PLUS, Federal Perkins. **Financial Aid Statistics:** 52% freshmen, 63% undergrads receive need-based scholarship or grant aid. 57% freshmen, 66% undergrads receive need-based self-help aid. 67% freshmen, 72% undergrads receive any aid.

See page 1276.

NATIONAL AMERICAN UNIVERSITY

321 Kansas City Street, Rapid City, SD 57709
Phone: 605-394-4827 **E-mail:** tshea@national.edu **CEEB Code:** 6464
Fax: 605-394-4871 **Website:** www.national.edu **ACT Code:** 3915
Financial Aid Phone: 605-394-4880

This proprietary school was founded in 1941. It has a 7-acre campus.

RATINGS
Admissions Selectivity Rating: 60*   **Fire Safety Rating:** 60*   **Green Rating:** 60*

STUDENTS AND FACULTY
Enrollment: 771. **Student Body:** 53% female, 47% male. **Retention and Graduation:** 50% freshmen return for sophomore year. 24% freshmen graduate within 4 years. 5% grads go on to further study within 1 year. 5% grads pursue business degrees.

ACADEMICS
Degrees: Associate, bachelor's, certificate, diploma, master's. **Academic Requirements:** Computer literacy, English (including composition), history, humanities, mathematics, sciences (biological or physical), social science. **Special Study Options:** Accelerated program, cross-registration, distance learning, English as a second language (ESL), external degree program, independent study, internships, liberal arts/career combination.

FACILITIES
Housing: Coed dorms. **Special Academic Facilities/Equipment:** Medical lab, animal health care center, medical assistant room.

CAMPUS LIFE
Activities: Student government, student newspaper. **Organizations:** 1 fraternity, 1 sorority. **Athletics (Intercollegiate):** *Men:* Rodeo. *Women:* Rodeo, volleyball.

ADMISSIONS
Freshman Academic Profile: TOEFL required of all international applicants, minimum paper TOEFL 490. **Basis for Candidate Selection:** *Important factors considered include:* Application essay, class rank, interview, recommendation(s), rigor of secondary school record, standardized test scores.

The Princeton Review's Complete Book of Colleges

Other factors considered include: Extracurricular activities, talent/ability, volunteer work, work experience. **Freshman Admission Requirements:** High school diploma is required, and GED is accepted. **Freshman Admission Statistics:** 290 applied. **Transfer Admission Requirements:** High school transcript, college transcript(s). Minimum college GPA of 2.0 required. Lowest grade transferable C. **General Admission Information:** Application fee $25. Regular application deadline 2/1. Regular notification is rolling. Non-fall registration accepted. Admission may be deferred for a maximum of 1 year. Common Application not accepted. Credit and/or placement offered for CEEB Advanced Placement tests.

COSTS AND FINANCIAL AID

Room & board $3,630. Required fees $315. Average book expense $1,125. **Required Forms and Deadlines:** FAFSA, institution's own financial aid form. **Types of Aid:** *Need-based scholarships/grants:* Pell, SEOG, state scholarships/grants, private scholarships, the school's own gift aid. *Loans:* Direct Subsidized Stafford, Direct Unsubsidized Stafford, Direct PLUS, FFEL Subsidized Stafford, FFEL Unsubsidized Stafford, FFEL PLUS, Federal Perkins, state loans, college/university loans from institutional funds. **Student Employment:** Federal Work-Study Program available. Institutional employment available. Off-campus job opportunities are good. **Financial Aid Statistics:** Highest amount earned per year from on-campus jobs $2,400.

NATIONAL AMERICAN UNIVERSITY (MN)

1550 West Highway 36, Roseville, MN 55113
Phone: 651-855-6300
Fax: 651-644-0690 **Website:** www.national.edu
Financial Aid Phone: 651-883-0439

This proprietary school was founded in 1941.

RATINGS

Admissions Selectivity Rating: 60*   **Fire Safety Rating:** 60*   **Green Rating:** 60*

STUDENTS AND FACULTY

Enrollment: 393. **Student Body:** 50% female, 50% male. **Retention and Graduation:** 41% freshmen return for sophomore year. 70% freshmen graduate within 4 years. **Faculty:** 100% faculty teach undergrads.

ACADEMICS

Degrees: Associate, bachelor's. **Academic Requirements:** Computer literacy, English (including composition), humanities, mathematics, sciences (biological or physical), social science. **Special Study Options:** Accelerated program, distance learning, double major, independent study.

FACILITIES

Computers: 100% of public computers are PCs, online registration, remote student-access to Web through college's connection.

ADMISSIONS

Freshman Academic Profile: TOEFL required of all international applicants, minimum paper TOEFL 500. **Freshman Admission Requirements:** High school diploma is required, and GED is accepted. **Transfer Admission Requirements:** High school transcript, college transcript(s). Lowest grade transferable C. **General Admission Information:** Application fee $25. Non-fall registration accepted. Admission may be deferred for a maximum of 1 year. Common Application not accepted.

COSTS AND FINANCIAL AID

Annual tuition $7,560. Required fees $135. Average book expense $350. **Types of Aid:** *Need-based scholarships/grants:* Pell, SEOG, state scholarships/grants, private scholarships, the school's own gift aid. *Loans:* Direct Subsidized Stafford, Direct Unsubsidized Stafford, Direct PLUS, FFEL Subsidized Stafford, FFEL Unsubsidized Stafford, FFEL PLUS, Federal Perkins, state loans. **Student Employment:** Federal Work-Study Program available. Institutional employment available. Off-campus job opportunities are good.

NATIONAL AMERICAN UNIVERSITY (MO)

3620 Arrowhead Avenue, Independence, MO 64057
Phone: 816-353-4554
Fax: 816-412-7705 **Website:** www.national.edu
Financial Aid Phone: 816-353-4554

This proprietary school was founded in 1941.

RATINGS

Admissions Selectivity Rating: 60*   **Fire Safety Rating:** 60*   **Green Rating:** 60*

STUDENTS AND FACULTY

Enrollment: 252. **Student Body:** 43% female, 57% male. **Retention and Graduation:** 31% freshmen return for sophomore year. 26% freshmen graduate within 4 years. **Faculty:** 100% faculty teach undergrads.

ACADEMICS

Degrees: Associate, bachelor's, certificate, diploma. **Academic Requirements:** Computer literacy, English (including composition), history, humanities, mathematics, sciences (biological or physical), social science. **Special Study Options:** Accelerated program, distance learning, double major, independent study.

FACILITIES

Computers: 100% of public computers are PCs, online registration, remote student-access to Web through college's connection.

ADMISSIONS

Freshman Academic Profile: TOEFL required of all international applicants, minimum paper TOEFL 500. **Freshman Admission Requirements:** High school diploma is required, and GED is accepted. **Transfer Admission Requirements:** High school transcript, college transcript(s). Lowest grade transferable C. **General Admission Information:** Application fee $25. Non-fall registration accepted. Admission may be deferred for a maximum of 1 year. Common Application not accepted.

COSTS AND FINANCIAL AID

Annual tuition $6,660. Required fees $135. Average book expense $350. **Types of Aid:** *Need-based scholarships/grants:* Pell, SEOG, state scholarships/grants, private scholarships, the school's own gift aid. *Loans:* Direct Subsidized Stafford, Direct Unsubsidized Stafford, Direct PLUS, FFEL Subsidized Stafford, FFEL Unsubsidized Stafford, FFEL PLUS, Federal Perkins, state loans, college/university loans from institutional funds. **Student Employment:** Federal Work-Study Program available. Institutional employment available. Off-campus job opportunities are good.

NATIONAL AMERICAN UNIVERSITY (NM)

4775 Indian School Road, Northeast, Suite 200, Albuquerque, NM 87110
Phone: 505-348-3700 **E-mail:** NPointer@national.edu
Fax: 505-348-3705 **Website:** www.national.edu
Financial Aid Phone: 505-265-7517

This proprietary school was founded in 1941. It has a 15-acre campus.

RATINGS

Admissions Selectivity Rating: 60*   **Fire Safety Rating:** 60*   **Green Rating:** 60*

STUDENTS AND FACULTY

Enrollment: 611. **Student Body:** 42% female, 58% male. African American 5%, Asian 2%, Caucasian 42%, Hispanic 38%, Native American 6%. **Retention and Graduation:** 5% grads go on to further study within 1 year. 5% grads pursue business degrees. 1% grads pursue law degrees. **Faculty:** Student/faculty ratio 10:1. 6 full-time faculty, 33% hold PhDs. 100% faculty teach undergrads.

ACADEMICS

Degrees: Associate, bachelor's, master's. **Academic Requirements:** Computer literacy, English (including composition), humanities, mathematics, sciences (biological or physical), social science. **Classes:** Most classes have fewer than 10 students. Most lab/discussion sections have fewer than 10 students. **Majors with Highest Enrollment:** Accounting, business administration/management, information technology. **Disciplines with Highest Percentage of Degrees Awarded:** Business/marketing 58%, computer and information sciences 42%. **Special Study Options:** Accelerated program, cooperative education program, distance learning, double major, dual enrollment, independent study, weekend college.

FACILITIES
Computers: 100% of public computers are PCs, online registration, online administrative functions (other than registration), remote student-access to Web through college's connection.

CAMPUS LIFE
Activities: Student government. **Organizations:** 1 registered organization, 1 honor society.

ADMISSIONS
Freshman Academic Profile: 99% from public high schools. TOEFL required of all international applicants, minimum paper TOEFL 500, minimum computer TOEFL 173. **Freshman Admission Requirements:** High school diploma is required, and GED is accepted. **Transfer Admission Requirements:** High school transcript, college transcript(s). Lowest grade transferable C. **General Admission Information:** Application fee $25. Regular application deadline 9/13. Regular notification is immediate. Non-fall registration accepted. Admission may be deferred for a maximum of 1 year. Common Application not accepted.

COSTS AND FINANCIAL AID
Annual tuition $8,100. Required fees $315. **Types of Aid:** *Need-based scholarships/grants:* Pell, SEOG, state scholarships/grants, private scholarships, the school's own gift aid. *Loans:* Direct Subsidized Stafford, Direct Unsubsidized Stafford, Direct PLUS, FFEL Subsidized Stafford, FFEL Unsubsidized Stafford, FFEL PLUS, Federal Perkins, state loans, college/university loans from institutional funds. **Student Employment:** Federal Work-Study Program available. Institutional employment available. Off-campus job opportunities are good.

NATIONAL UNIVERSITY

11255 North Torrey Pinos Road, La Jolla, CA 92037
Phone: 858-642-8180 **E-mail:** advisor@nu.edu **CEEB Code:** 4557
Fax: 858-642-8710 **Website:** www.nu.edu **ACT Code:** 0344
Financial Aid Phone: 858-573-7175

This private school was founded in 1971.

RATINGS
Admissions Selectivity Rating: 60*   **Fire Safety Rating:** 60*   **Green Rating:** 60*

STUDENTS AND FACULTY
Enrollment: 4,776. **Student Body:** 57% female, 43% male, 1% international. African American 13%, Asian 9%, Caucasian 52%, Hispanic 18%, Native American 1%. **Retention and Graduation:** 40% freshmen return for sophomore year. **Faculty:** Student/faculty ratio 16:1. 151 full-time faculty, 87% hold PhDs. 100% faculty teach undergrads.

ACADEMICS
Degrees: Associate, bachelor's, certificate, diploma, master's, post-bachelor's certificate, terminal. **Academic Requirements:** Arts/fine arts, computer literacy, English (including composition), humanities, mathematics, sciences (biological or physical), social science. General education policy: The general education curriculum assumes that undergraduates will not concentrate on a major field of study until they have completed a thorough general education program that is writing-intensive and addresses the cultural diversity of contemporary society. Students in the general education program are advised to focus on writing and speech communication first. Students are then counseled to explore mathematical and other formal systems to develop abstract reasoning abilities and are required to take a course in informational literacy and report writing. Finally, all students are required to have a significant exposure to the natural sciences, the humanities and fine arts and the social and behavioral sciences and modern language. **Classes:** Most classes have 10–19 students. **Majors with Highest Enrollment:** Business/commerce, criminal justice/law enforcement administration, multi/interdisciplinary studies. **Disciplines with Highest Percentage of Degrees Awarded:** Business/marketing 24%, computer and information sciences 19%, interdisciplinary studies 18%, psychology 16%, liberal arts/general studies 9%. **Special Study Options:** Accelerated program, distance learning, double major, dual enrollment, English as a second language (ESL), teacher certification program, extensive online offerings are available.

FACILITIES
Computers: 100% of public computers are PCs, online registration, online administrative functions (other than registration), remote student-access to Web through college's connection.

CAMPUS LIFE
Activities: Literary magazine.

ADMISSIONS
Freshman Academic Profile: TOEFL required of all international applicants, minimum paper TOEFL 525, minimum computer TOEFL 197. **Basis for Candidate Selection:** *Important factors considered include:* Interview, work experience. *Other factors considered include:* Application essay, extracurricular activities. **Freshman Admission Requirements:** High school diploma is required, and GED is accepted. **Freshman Admission Statistics:** 156 applied, 100% admitted, 36% enrolled. **Transfer Admission Requirements:** High school transcript, college transcript(s), essay or personal statement, interview, statement of good standing from prior institution(s). Minimum college GPA of 2.0 required. Lowest grade transferable C. **General Admission Information:** Application fee $60. Regular notification is daily. Non-fall registration accepted. Admission may be deferred for a maximum of 1 year. Common Application not accepted. Neither credit nor placement offered for CEEB Advanced Placement tests.

COSTS AND FINANCIAL AID
Annual tuition $7,965. Required fees $60. **Required Forms and Deadlines:** FAFSA, institution's own financial aid form, state aid form. **Types of Aid:** *Need-based scholarships/grants:* Pell, SEOG, state scholarships/grants, private scholarships, the school's own gift aid. *Loans:* Direct Subsidized Stafford, Direct Unsubsidized Stafford, FFEL Subsidized Stafford, FFEL Unsubsidized Stafford, FFEL PLUS, Federal Perkins. **Student Employment:** Institutional employment available. Off-campus job opportunities are good.

NATIONAL UNIVERSITY OF HEALTH SCIENCES

200 East Roosevelt Road, Lombard, IL 60148
Phone: 630-889-6566 **E-mail:** admissions@nuhs.edu
Fax: 630-889-6554 **Website:** www.nuhs.edu
Financial Aid Phone: 630-889-6700

This private school was founded in 1906. It has a 32-acre campus.

RATINGS
Admissions Selectivity Rating: 60*   **Fire Safety Rating:** 60*   **Green Rating:** 60*

STUDENTS AND FACULTY
Retention and Graduation: 99% freshmen return for sophomore year. **Faculty:** Student/faculty ratio 6:1. 46 full-time faculty, 93% hold PhDs.

ACADEMICS
Degrees: Bachelor's, certificate, first professional. **Academic Requirements:** English (including composition), sciences (biological or physical), social science, specific science courses. **Classes:** Most classes have 40–49 students. Most lab/discussion sections have 20–29 students. **Special Study Options:** Internships, accelerated science prerequisite program.

FACILITIES
Housing: Coed dorms, men's dorms, women's dorms, apartments for married students, apartments for single students, studio apartments. **Special Academic Facilities/Equipment:** Museum, fitness center, learning resource center, health care clinic. **Computers:** 50% of public computers are PCs, 50% of public computers are Macs, remote student-access to Web through college's connection.

CAMPUS LIFE
Activities: Student government, student newspaper, yearbook. **Organizations:** 24 registered organizations, 1 religious organization. 2 fraternities, 1 sorority.

ADMISSIONS
Freshman Academic Profile: TOEFL required of all international applicants, minimum paper TOEFL 500, minimum computer TOEFL 172. **Freshman Admission Requirements:** High school diploma is required, and GED is accepted. **Transfer Admission Requirements:** High school transcript, college transcript(s), essay or personal statement, statement of good standing from prior institution(s). Minimum college GPA of 2.5 required. Lowest grade transferable C. **General Admission Information:** Application fee $55. Regular notification is rolling. Non-fall registration accepted. Common Application not accepted. Credit offered for CEEB Advanced Placement tests.

COSTS AND FINANCIAL AID

Types of Aid: *Need-based scholarships/grants:* Pell, SEOG, private scholarships, the school's own gift aid. *Loans:* FFEL Subsidized Stafford, FFEL Unsubsidized Stafford, FFEL PLUS, Federal Perkins. **Student Employment:** Federal Work-Study Program available. Institutional employment available. Off-campus job opportunities are excellent.

NATIONAL-LOUIS UNIVERSITY

2840 Sheridan Road, Evanston, IL 60201
Phone: 847-465-0575 **E-mail:** nlnuinfo@wheeling1.nl.edu
Website: www.nl.edu **ACT Code:** 1094
Financial Aid Phone: 800-443-5522

This private school was founded in 1886.

RATINGS

Admissions Selectivity Rating: 61   **Fire Safety Rating:** 60*   **Green Rating:** 60*

STUDENTS AND FACULTY

Enrollment: 3,545. **Student Body:** 72% female, 28% male, 1% out-of-state. African American 26%, Asian 3%, Caucasian 57%, Hispanic 8%. **Retention and Graduation:** 60% freshmen return for sophomore year. 7% freshmen graduate within 4 years.

ACADEMICS

Degrees: Bachelor's, certificate, doctoral, master's, post-bachelor's certificate, post-master's certificate. **Academic Requirements:** English (including composition), humanities, sciences (biological or physical), social science. **Special Study Options:** Accelerated program, distance learning, English as a second language (ESL), honors program, independent study, internships. General degree completion programs in liberal arts and business for upper level.

FACILITIES

Housing: Coed dorms. **Special Academic Facilities/Equipment:** Pre K-8 elementary demonstration school. **Computers:** 75% of public computers are PCs, 25% of public computers are Macs, network access in dorm lounges, remote student-access to Web through college's connection.

CAMPUS LIFE

Activities: Drama/theater, musical theater, student government, student newspaper. **Organizations:** 15 registered organizations, 1 honor society, 2 religious organizations. **Athletics (Intercollegiate):** *Men:* Soccer, softball, volleyball.

ADMISSIONS

Freshman Academic Profile: 29% in top 25% of high school class, 89% in top 50% of high school class. ACT middle 50% range 15–20. **Basis for Candidate Selection:** *Very important factors considered include:* Rigor of secondary school record. *Important factors considered include:* Standardized test scores. *Other factors considered include:* Application essay, class rank, interview, recommendation(s). **Freshman Admission Requirements:** High school diploma is required, and GED is accepted. *Academic units recommended:* 4 English, 3 math, 2 science (1 science lab), 2 foreign language, 3 social studies. **Freshman Admission Statistics:** 320 applied, 100% admitted, 66% enrolled. **Transfer Admission Requirements:** College transcript(s), statement of good standing from prior institution(s). Minimum college GPA of 2.0 required. Lowest grade transferable C. **General Admission Information:** Application fee $25. Non-fall registration accepted. Admission may be deferred for a maximum of 2 years. Common Application not accepted. Credit offered for CEEB Advanced Placement tests.

COSTS AND FINANCIAL AID

Annual tuition $13,095. Room & board $6,336. Average book expense $250. **Required Forms and Deadlines:** FAFSA, institution's own financial aid form. Financial aid filing deadline 4/15. **Notification of Awards:** Applicants will be notified of awards on or about 5/1. **Types of Aid:** *Need-based scholarships/grants:* Pell, SEOG, state scholarships/grants, the school's own gift aid. *Loans:* Direct Subsidized Stafford, Direct Unsubsidized Stafford, Direct PLUS, Federal Perkins. **Student Employment:** Federal Work-Study Program available. Institutional employment available. Off-campus job opportunities are good.

NAZARETH COLLEGE OF ROCHESTER

4245 East Avenue, Rochester, NY 14618-3790
Phone: 585-389-2860 **E-mail:** admissions@naz.edu **CEEB Code:** 2511
Fax: 585-389-2826 **Website:** www.naz.edu **ACT Code:** 2826
Financial Aid Phone: 585-389-2310

This private school was founded in 1924. It has a 150-acre campus.

RATINGS

Admissions Selectivity Rating: 84   **Fire Safety Rating:** 60*   **Green Rating:** 60*

STUDENTS AND FACULTY

Enrollment: 2,094. **Student Body:** 76% female, 24% male, 5% out-of-state. African American 4%, Asian 2%, Caucasian 84%, Hispanic 3%. **Retention and Graduation:** 87% freshmen return for sophomore year. 61% freshmen graduate within 4 years. **Faculty:** Student/faculty ratio 12:1. 144 full-time faculty, 92% hold PhDs. 97% faculty teach undergrads.

ACADEMICS

Degrees: Bachelor's, doctoral, master's, post-master's certificate. **Academic Requirements:** Arts/fine arts, computer literacy, English (including composition), foreign languages, history, humanities, mathematics, philosophy, sciences (biological or physical), social science. **Classes:** Most classes have 10–19 students. Most lab/discussion sections have 10–19 students. **Majors with Highest Enrollment:** Business administration/management, education, physical therapy/therapist. **Disciplines with Highest Percentage of Degrees Awarded:** Health professions and related sciences 18%, business/marketing 13%, social sciences 12%, psychology 12%, English 9%, visual and performing arts 7%. **Special Study Options:** cross-registration, double major, exchange student program (domestic), honors program, independent study, internships, study abroad, teacher certification program.

FACILITIES

Housing: Coed dorms, women's dorms, apartments for single students, special housing for disabled students, substance free, quiet floors, language house, honors, first-year experience. **Special Academic Facilities/Equipment:** Arts center, speech/hearing/language clinic, reading clinic, psychology center, center for service learning, center for teaching excellence, center for international education. **Computers:** 55% of public computers are PCs, 45% of public computers are Macs, network access in dorm rooms, online registration, remote student-access to Web through college's connection.

CAMPUS LIFE

Activities: Choral groups, concert band, dance, drama/theater, jazz band, literary magazine, music ensembles, musical theater, opera, radio station, student government, student newspaper, symphony orchestra, yearbook. **Organizations:** 50 registered organizations, 19 honor societies, 1 religious organization. **Athletics (Intercollegiate):** *Men:* Basketball, cheerleading, cross-country, diving, equestrian sports, golf, lacrosse, soccer, swimming, tennis, track/field (indoor), track/field (outdoor), volleyball. *Women:* Basketball, cheerleading, cross-country, diving, equestrian sports, field hockey, golf, lacrosse, soccer, softball, swimming, tennis, track/field (indoor), track/field (outdoor), volleyball.

ADMISSIONS

Freshman Academic Profile: 25% in top 10% of high school class, 63% in top 25% of high school class, 93% in top 50% of high school class. 90% from public high schools. SAT Math middle 50% range 530–630. SAT Critical Reading middle 50% range 530–630. SAT Writing middle 50% range 510–610. ACT middle 50% range 23–27. TOEFL required of all international applicants, minimum paper TOEFL 550, minimum computer TOEFL 213. **Basis for Candidate Selection:** *Very important factors considered include:* Academic GPA, application essay, class rank, recommendation(s), rigor of secondary school record. *Important factors considered include:* Character/personal qualities, extracurricular activities, geographical residence, interview, level of applicant's interest, racial/ethnic status, state residency, talent/ability, volunteer work, work experience. *Other factors considered include:* Alumni/ae relation, first generation, standardized test scores. **Freshman Admission Requirements:** High school diploma is required, and GED is accepted. *Academic units required:* 4 English, 3 math, 3 science (2 science labs), 3 foreign language, 3 social studies. *Academic units recommended:* 4 English, 4 math, 4 science, 4 foreign language, 4 social studies. **Freshman Admission Statistics:** 2,001 applied, 76% admitted, 32% enrolled. **Transfer Admission Requirements:** College transcript(s), essay or personal statement. Lowest grade transferable C. **General Admission Information:** Application fee $40. Early decision application deadline 11/15. Regular application deadline 2/15. Regular notification is rolling. Non-fall registration accepted. Admission may be deferred for a maximum of 1 year. Credit and/or placement offered for CEEB Advanced Placement tests.

COSTS AND FINANCIAL AID

Annual tuition $21,900. Room and board $9,500. Required fees $980. Average book expense $900. **Required Forms and Deadlines:** FAFSA. Financial aid filing deadline 5/1. **Types of Aid:** *Need-based scholarships/grants:* Pell, SEOG, state scholarships/grants, private scholarships, the school's own gift aid. *Loans:* FFEL Subsidized Stafford, FFEL Unsubsidized Stafford, FFEL PLUS, Federal Perkins. **Student Employment:** Federal Work-Study Program available. Institutional employment available. Off-campus job opportunities are excellent.

See page 1278.

NEBRASKA CHRISTIAN COLLEGE

1800 Syracuse Avenue, Norfolk, NE 68701
Phone: 402-379-5000 **E-mail:** admissions@nechristian.edu
Fax: 402-379-5100 **Website:** www.nechristian.edu **ACT Code:** 2473
Financial Aid Phone: 402-379-5017

This private school was founded in 1945. It has a 40-acre campus.

RATINGS
Admissions Selectivity Rating: 60*   **Fire Safety Rating:** 60*   **Green Rating:** 60*

STUDENTS AND FACULTY
Enrollment: 146. **Student Body:** 45% female, 55% male. **Faculty:** 100% faculty teach undergrads.

ACADEMICS
Degrees: Associate, bachelor's. **Academic Requirements:** English (including composition), foreign languages, history, humanities, philosophy, sciences (biological or physical), social science. **Special Study Options:** Distance learning, internships, study abroad.

FACILITIES
Housing: Men's dorms, women's dorms, apartments for married students, apartments for single students. **Computers:** 90% of public computers are PCs, 10% of public computers are Macs, network access in dorm rooms, remote student-access to Web through college's connection.

CAMPUS LIFE
Activities: Choral groups, drama/theater, music ensembles, yearbook. **Athletics (Intercollegiate):** *Men:* Basketball, soccer. *Women:* Basketball, volleyball.

ADMISSIONS
Freshman Academic Profile: 5% in top 10% of high school class, 24% in top 25% of high school class, 37% in top 50% of high school class. **Basis for Candidate Selection:** *Very important factors considered include:* Character/personal qualities, recommendation(s), standardized test scores. *Important factors considered include:* Class rank, extracurricular activities, interview, rigor of secondary school record, talent/ability, volunteer work. *Other factors considered include:* Alumni/ae relation, work experience. **Freshman Admission Requirements:** High school diploma is required and GED is accepted. **Freshman Admission Statistics:** 148 applied, 60% admitted, 67% enrolled. **Transfer Admission Requirements:** High school transcript, college transcript(s). **General Admission Information:** Application fee $25. Non-fall registration accepted. Common Application not accepted.

COSTS AND FINANCIAL AID
Annual tuition $4,500. Room & board $2,960. Required fees $450. Average book expense $400. **Required Forms and Deadlines:** FAFSA, institution's own financial aid form. **Types of Aid:** *Need-based scholarships/grants:* Pell, SEOG, state scholarships/grants, private scholarships, the school's own gift aid. *Loans:* FFEL Subsidized Stafford, FFEL Unsubsidized Stafford, FFEL PLUS. **Student Employment:** Federal Work-Study Program available. Institutional employment available. Off-campus job opportunities are excellent. **Financial Aid Statistics:** 93% freshmen, 93% undergrads receive need-based scholarship or grant aid. 59% freshmen, 53% undergrads receive need-based self-help aid. Highest amount earned per year from on-campus jobs $1,625.

NEBRASKA METHODIST COLLEGE

720 North 87th Street, Omaha, NE 68114
Phone: 402-354-7200 **E-mail:** admissions@methodistCollege.edu **CEEB Code:** 6510
Fax: 402-354-7020 **Website:** www.methodistcollege.edu **ACT Code:** 2465
Financial Aid Phone: 402-354-4874

This private school, affiliated with the Methodist Church, was founded in 1891. It has a 6-acre campus.

RATINGS
Admissions Selectivity Rating: 77   **Fire Safety Rating:** 60*   **Green Rating:** 60*

STUDENTS AND FACULTY
Enrollment: 444. **Student Body:** 89% female, 11% male, 35% out-of-state. African American 4%, Asian 2%, Caucasian 93%. **Retention and Graduation:** 83% freshmen return for sophomore year. 70% freshmen graduate within 4 years. 10% grads go on to further study within 1 year. 10% grads pursue arts and sciences degrees. **Faculty:** Student/faculty ratio 10:1. 33 full-time faculty, 39% hold PhDs. 100% faculty teach undergrads.

ACADEMICS
Degrees: Associate, bachelor's, certificate, master's, post-master's certificate. **Academic Requirements:** Computer literacy, English (including composition), humanities, mathematics, sciences (biological or physical), social science. **Classes:** Most classes have 20–29 students. Most lab/discussion sections have fewer than 10 students. **Majors with Highest Enrollment:** Diagnostic medical sonography/sonographer and ultrasound technician, nursing/registered nurse training (ASN, BSN, MSN, RN), radiologic technology/science – radiographer. **Disciplines with Highest Percentage of Degrees Awarded:** Health professions and related sciences 100%. **Special Study Options:** Accelerated program, distance learning, independent study.

FACILITIES
Housing: Coed dorms. **Computers:** 100% of public computers are PCs, network access in dorm lounges, remote student-access to Web through college's connection.

CAMPUS LIFE
Activities: Student government. **Organizations:** 11 registered organizations, 2 honor societies.

ADMISSIONS
Freshman Academic Profile: 20% in top 10% of high school class, 25% in top 25% of high school class, 100% in top 50% of high school class. 90% from public high schools. ACT middle 50% range 19–23. TOEFL required of all international applicants, minimum paper TOEFL 550, minimum computer TOEFL 213. **Basis for Candidate Selection:** *Very important factors considered include:* Rigor of secondary school record, standardized test scores. *Important factors considered include:* Application essay, character/personal qualities, class rank, interview, recommendation(s). *Other factors considered include:* Alumni/ae relation, geographical residence, racial/ethnic status, state residency, volunteer work, work experience. **Freshman Admission Requirements:** High school diploma is required, and GED is accepted. *Academic units required:* 4 English, 3 math, 2 science (2 science labs), 2 social studies. **Freshman Admission Statistics:** 64 applied, 61% admitted, 59% enrolled. **Transfer Admission Requirements:** High school transcript, college transcript(s), essay or personal statement, interview, statement of good standing from prior institution(s). Minimum college GPA of 2.0 required. Lowest grade transferable C. **General Admission Information:** Application fee $25. Regular application deadline 3/1. Regular notification is rolling. Non-fall registration accepted. Admission may be deferred for a maximum of 1 year. Neither credit nor placement offered for CEEB Advanced Placement tests.

COSTS AND FINANCIAL AID
Annual tuition $12,630. Room $2,270. Required fees $600. Average book expense $1,300. **Required Forms and Deadlines:** FAFSA, institution's own financial aid form. Financial aid filing deadline 5/1. **Notification of Awards:** Applicants will be notified of awards on a rolling basis beginning on or about 3/1. **Types of Aid:** *Need-based scholarships/grants:* Pell, SEOG, state scholarships/grants, private scholarships, the school's own gift aid. *Loans:* FFEL Subsidized Stafford, FFEL Unsubsidized Stafford, FFEL PLUS, Federal Perkins, Federal Nursing, state loans, college/university loans from institutional funds, alternative loans. **Student Employment:** Federal Work-Study Program available. Institutional employment available. Off-campus job opportunities are good. **Financial Aid Statistics:** 57% freshmen, 60% undergrads receive need-based scholarship or grant aid. 57% freshmen, 66% undergrads receive need-based self-help aid. 73% freshmen, 65% undergrads receive any aid.

NEBRASKA WESLEYAN UNIVERSITY

Admissions Office, 5000 Saint Paul Avenue, Lincoln, NE 68504
Phone: 402-465-2218 **E-mail:** admissions@nebrwesleyan.edu **CEEB Code:** 6470
Fax: 402-465-2177 **Website:** www.nebrwesleyan.edu **ACT Code:** 2474
Financial Aid Phone: 402-465-2212

This private school, affiliated with the Methodist Church, was founded in 1887. It has a 50-acre campus.

RATINGS
Admissions Selectivity Rating: 75   **Fire Safety Rating:** 60*   **Green Rating:** 76

STUDENTS AND FACULTY
Enrollment: 1,819. **Student Body:** 57% female, 43% male, 8% out-of-state. African American 2%, Asian 1%, Caucasian 93%, Hispanic 1%. **Retention and Graduation:** 80% freshmen return for sophomore year. 56% freshmen graduate within 4 years. **Faculty:** Student/faculty ratio 13:1. 109 full-time faculty, 79% hold PhDs. 99% faculty teach undergrads.

ACADEMICS
Degrees: Bachelor's, certificate, master's, post-bachelor's certificate, post-master's certificate. **Academic Requirements:** Arts/fine arts, English (including composition), foreign language, health and human performance, humanities, liberal arts seminar, mathematics, science (biological or physical), social science. **Classes:** Most classes have 10–19 students. Most lab/discussion sections have 10–19 students. **Majors with Highest Enrollment:** Biology/biological sciences, business administration/management; psychology. **Disciplines with Highest Percentage of Degrees Awarded:** Business/marketing 84%, health professions and related sciences 64%, psychology 37%, English 34%, education 31%. **Special Study Options:** Double major, dual enrollment, independent study, internships, study abroad, teacher certification program, weekend college, 3–2 engineering program with Washington University, Columbia University, or University of Nebraska—Lincoln; Capitol Hill internship program, DC; Urban Life Center, Chicago.

FACILITIES
Housing: Coed dorms, men's dorms, women's dorms, apartments for single students, fraternity/sorority housing, residence hall suites, townhouses. **Special Academic Facilities/Equipment:** Art galleries, psychology/sleep lab, observatory and planetarium, green house, laboratory theater, herbarium, nuclear magnetic resonance laboratory. **Computers:** 60% of public computers are PCs, 40% of public computers are Macs, 5% of public computers are UNIX, network access in dorm rooms, network access in dorm lounges, online administrative functions (other than registration), remote student-access to Web through college's connection.

CAMPUS LIFE
Activities: Choral groups, concert band, drama/theater, jazz band, literary magazine, music ensembles, musical theater, opera, pep band, radio station, student government, student newspaper, yearbook. **Organizations:** 84 registered organizations, 22 honor societies, 5 religious organizations. 4 fraternities (23% men join), 4 sororities (21% women join). **Athletics (Intercollegiate):** *Men:* Baseball, basketball, cross-country, football, golf, soccer, tennis, track/field (indoor), track/field (outdoor). *Women:* Basketball, cross-country, golf, soccer, softball, tennis, track/field (indoor), track/field (outdoor), volleyball. **Environmental Initiatives:** Completed light inventory; retrofitted 80% of all lights. Recycling including cans, plastic bottles, paper, cardboard. Updated central heating plant.

ADMISSIONS
Freshman Academic Profile: 24% in top 10% of high school class, 60% in top 25% of high school class, 89% in top 50% of high school class. ACT middle 50% range 22–27. TOEFL required of all international applicants, minimum paper TOEFL 525, minimum computer TOEFL 195. **Basis for Candidate Selection:** *Very important factors considered include:* Class rank, standardized test scores. *Important factors considered include:* Academic GPA, character/personal qualities, extracurricular activities, talent/ability. *Other factors considered include:* Alumni/ae relation, application essay, first generation, geographical residence, interview, racial/ethnic status, recommendation(s), rigor of secondary school record, volunteer work. **Freshman Admission Requirements:** High school diploma is required, and GED is accepted. *Academic units recommended:* 4 English, 4 math, 4 science, 4 foreign language, 3 social studies. **Freshman Admission Statistics:** 1,409 applied, 84% admitted, 35% enrolled. **Transfer Admission Requirements:** College transcript(s), statement of good standing from prior institution(s). Minimum college GPA of 2.0 required. Lowest grade transferable C-. **General Admission Information:** Application fee $20. Early decision application deadline 11/15. Regular application deadline 8/15. Regular notification is rolling. Nonfall registration accepted. Admission

may be deferred for a maximum of 1 year. Credit offered for CEEB Advanced Placement tests.

COSTS AND FINANCIAL AID
Annual tuition $17,092. Room & board $5,005. Required fees $302. Average book expense $800. **Required Forms and Deadlines:** FAFSA. **Notification of Awards:** Applicants will be notified of awards on a rolling basis beginning on or about 3/15. **Types of Aid:** *Need-based scholarships/grants:* Pell, SEOG, state scholarships/grants, private scholarships, the school's own gift aid. *Loans:* FFEL Subsidized Stafford, FFEL Unsubsidized Stafford, FFEL PLUS, Federal Perkins. **Student Employment:** Federal Work-Study Program available. Institutional employment available. Off-campus job opportunities are good. **Financial Aid Statistics:** 68% freshmen, 67% undergrads receive need-based scholarship or grant aid. 55% freshmen, 58% undergrads receive need-based self-help aid. 97% freshmen, 95% undergrads receive any aid. Highest amount earned per year from on-campus jobs $1,100.

NEUMANN COLLEGE

1 Neumann Drive, Aston, PA 19014
Phone: 610-558-5616 **E-mail:** neumann@neumann.edu **CEEB Code:** 2628
Fax: 610-558-5652 **Website:** www.neumann.edu **ACT Code:** 3649
Financial Aid Phone: 610-558-5532

This private school, affiliated with the Roman Catholic Church, was founded in 1965. It has a 55-acre campus.

RATINGS
Admissions Selectivity Rating: 74   **Fire Safety Rating:** 99   **Green Rating:** 60*

STUDENTS AND FACULTY
Enrollment: 2,418. **Student Body:** 66% female, 34% male, 29% out-of-state, 2% international (7 countries represented). African American 13%, Asian 2%, Caucasian 66%, Hispanic 2%. **Retention and Graduation:** 75% freshmen return for sophomore year. 33% freshmen graduate within 4 years. 20% grads go on to further study within 1 year. 7% grads pursue arts and sciences degrees. 10% grads pursue business degrees. 2% grads pursue law degrees. 1% grads pursue medical degrees. **Faculty:** Student/faculty ratio 15:1. 85 full-time faculty, 56% hold PhDs. 98% faculty teach undergrads.

ACADEMICS
Degrees: Associate, bachelor's, certificate, doctoral, master's, post-bachelor's certificate, post-master's certificate, terminal. **Academic Requirements:** Arts/fine arts, computer literacy, English (including composition), foreign languages, interdisciplinary studies, mathematics, philosophy, religion, sciences (biological or physical), social science. **Classes:** Most classes have 20–29 students. Most lab/discussion sections have 10–19 students. **Majors with Highest Enrollment:** Criminal justice/law enforcement administration, elementary education and teaching, nursing/registered nurse training (ASN, BSN, MSN, RN). **Disciplines with Highest Percentage of Degrees Awarded:** Liberal arts/general studies 34%, education 18%, health professions and related sciences 14%, business/marketing 8%, parks and recreation 6%. **Special Study Options:** Accelerated program, cooperative education program, distance learning, double major, exchange student program (domestic), honors program, independent study, internships, liberal arts/career combination, student-designed major, study abroad, teacher certification program, weekend college.

FACILITIES
Housing: Coed dorms, special housing for disabled students, off-campus housing. **Special Academic Facilities/Equipment:** Child development center. **Computers:** 100% of classrooms are wireless, 100% of public computers are PCs, network access in dorm rooms, network access in dorm lounges, online administrative functions (other than registration), remote student-access to Web through college's connection.

CAMPUS LIFE
Activities: Choral groups, dance, drama/theater, jazz band, literary magazine, music ensembles, musical theater, student government, student newspaper. **Organizations:** 14 registered organizations, 4 honor societies, 2 religious organizations. **Athletics (Intercollegiate):** *Men:* Baseball, basketball, golf, ice hockey, lacrosse, soccer, tennis. *Women:* Basketball, field hockey, ice hockey, lacrosse, soccer, softball, tennis, volleyball.

ADMISSIONS
Freshman Academic Profile: 30% in top 10% of high school class, 50% in top 25% of high school class, 90% in top 50% of high school class. 60% from public high schools. SAT Math middle 50% range 400–490. SAT Critical Reading middle 50% range 400–490. TOEFL required of all international applicants,

minimum paper TOEFL 550, minimum computer TOEFL 213. **Basis for Candidate Selection:** *Very important factors considered include:* Extracurricular activities, recommendation(s), rigor of secondary school record, talent/ability. *Important factors considered include:* Alumni/ae relation, character/personal qualities, class rank, interview, standardized test scores. *Other factors considered include:* Racial/ethnic status, religious affiliation/commitment, volunteer work. **Freshman Admission Requirements:** High school diploma is required, and GED is accepted. *Academic units required:* 4 English, 2 math, 2 science, 2 foreign language, 2 social studies, 4 academic electives. *Academic units recommended:* 4 English, 2 math, 3 science, 2 foreign language, 2 social studies, 4 academic electives. **Freshman Admission Statistics:** 2,135 applied, 94% admitted, 27% enrolled. **Transfer Admission Requirements:** College transcript(s). Minimum college GPA of 2.0 required. Lowest grade transferable C. **General Admission Information:** Application fee $35. Regular notification once info is received. Non-fall registration accepted. Admission may be deferred for a maximum of 1 year. Credit offered for CEEB Advanced Placement tests.

COSTS AND FINANCIAL AID

Annual tuition $18,846. Room and board $8,838. Required fees $640. Average book expense $1,500. **Required Forms and Deadlines:** FAFSA. **Notification of Awards:** Applicants will be notified of awards on a rolling basis beginning on or about 3/1. **Types of Aid:** *Need-based scholarships/grants:* Pell, SEOG, state scholarships/grants, private scholarships, the school's own gift aid, Federal Nursing Scholarships. *Loans:* Direct Subsidized Stafford, Direct Unsubsidized Stafford, Direct PLUS, FFEL Subsidized Stafford, FFEL Unsubsidized Stafford, FFEL PLUS, Federal Nursing. **Student Employment:** Federal Work-Study Program available. Off-campus job opportunities are good. **Financial Aid Statistics:** 77% freshmen, 74% undergrads receive need-based scholarship or grant aid. 77% freshmen, 74% undergrads receive need-based self-help aid. 95% freshmen, 90% undergrads receive any aid. Highest amount earned per year from on-campus jobs $5,000.

NEUMONT UNIVERSITY

10701 South River Front Parkway, Suite 300, South Jordan, UT 84095
Phone: 801-302-2835 **E-mail:** info@neumont.edu
Fax: 801-302-2811 **Website:** www.neumont.edu
Financial Aid Phone: 801-733-2870

This is a proprietary school.

RATINGS

Admissions Selectivity Rating: 60*   **Fire Safety Rating:** 60*   **Green Rating:** 60*

STUDENTS AND FACULTY

Enrollment: 260. **Student Body:** 8% female, 92% male, 60% out-of-state. **Faculty:** Student/faculty ratio 8:1. 25 full-time faculty, 20% hold PhDs. 25% faculty teach undergrads.

ACADEMICS

Degrees: Bachelor's, master's. **Academic Requirements:** English (including composition), humanities, mathematics. **Special Study Options:** Accelerated program.

FACILITIES

Housing: Apartments for married students, apartments for single students. **Computers:** 100% of classrooms are wired, 100% of classrooms are wireless, remote student-access to Web through college's connection.

CAMPUS LIFE

Activities: Student government.

ADMISSIONS

Freshman Academic Profile: 95% from public high schools. TOEFL required of all international applicants, minimum paper TOEFL 550, minimum computer TOEFL 200. **Basis for Candidate Selection:** *Important factors considered include:* Academic GPA, application essay, class rank, interview, level of applicant's interest, recommendation(s), rigor of secondary school record, standardized test scores, talent/ability. *Other factors considered include:* Character/personal qualities, extracurricular activities, work experience. **Freshman Admission Requirements:** High school diploma is required, and GED is accepted. **Freshman Admission Statistics:** 300 applied, 83% admitted, 60% enrolled. **Transfer Admission Requirements:** High school transcript, college transcript(s), essay or personal statement, interview. Minimum college GPA of 2.5 required. Lowest grade transferable C. **General Admission Information:** Application fee $35. Regular notification is rolling. Non-fall registration accepted. Admission may be deferred for a maximum of 1

year. Common Application not accepted. Neither credit nor placement offered for CEEB Advanced Placement tests.

COSTS AND FINANCIAL AID

Annual tuition $21,000. Room $4,500. Required fees $2,500. Average book expense $1,500. **Required Forms and Deadlines:** FAFSA, institution's own financial aid form. **Notification of Awards:** Applicants will be notified of awards on a rolling basis beginning on or about 1/1. **Types of Aid:** *Need-based scholarships/grants:* Pell, SEOG, private scholarships, the school's own gift aid. *Loans:* FFEL Subsidized Stafford, FFEL Unsubsidized Stafford, FFEL PLUS, college/university loans from institutional funds. **Student Employment:** Institutional employment available. Off-campus job opportunities are good. **Financial Aid Statistics:** 37% undergrads receive need-based scholarship or grant aid. 95% freshmen, 95% undergrads receive any aid.

See page 1280.

NEW COLLEGE OF CALIFORNIA

741 Valencia Street, San Francisco, CA 94110
Phone: 415-437-3460 **CEEB Code:** 4555
Fax: 415-861-0461 **Website:** www.newcollege.edu
Financial Aid Phone: 415-241-1300

This private school was founded in 1971. It has a 1-acre campus.

RATINGS

Admissions Selectivity Rating: 60*   **Fire Safety Rating:** 60*   **Green Rating:** 60*

STUDENTS AND FACULTY

Enrollment: 398. **Student Body:** 70% female, 30% male. African American 4%, Asian 1%, Hispanic 3%, Native American 3%. **Retention and Graduation:** 15% grads go on to further study within 1 year. 5% grads pursue law degrees.

ACADEMICS

Degrees: Associate, bachelor's, certificate, diploma, first professional, master's, terminal. **Special Study Options:** Accelerated program, cooperative education program, distance learning, English as a second language (ESL), independent study, internships, liberal arts/career combination, student-designed major, study abroad, summer off-campus field study opportunities, teacher certification program, weekend college.

FACILITIES

Special Academic Facilities/Equipment: Arts studio, video editing lab, letter press lab.

CAMPUS LIFE

Activities: Choral groups, drama/theater, jazz band, literary magazine, musical theater, radio station, student newspaper.

ADMISSIONS

Freshman Academic Profile: TOEFL required of all international applicants. **Basis for Candidate Selection:** *Very important factors considered include:* Rigor of secondary school record. *Important factors considered include:* Geographical residence, interview, racial/ethnic status, state residency, work experience. *Other factors considered include:* Volunteer work. **Freshman Admission Requirements:** High school diploma is required, and GED is accepted. **Freshman Admission Statistics:** 300 applied, 67% admitted, 80% enrolled. **Transfer Admission Requirements:** High school transcript, college transcript(s), essay or personal statement. Lowest grade transferable C. **General Admission Information:** Application fee $50. Early decision application deadline 3/1. Regular application deadline is rolling. Regular notification is rolling. Non-fall registration accepted. Admission may be deferred for a maximum of 1 year.

COSTS AND FINANCIAL AID

Annual tuition $8,200. Average book expense $650. **Required Forms and Deadlines:** FAFSA, institution's own financial aid form, state aid form. Financial aid filing deadline 3/2. **Notification of Awards:** Applicants will be notified of awards on a rolling basis beginning on or about 5/15. **Types of Aid:** *Need-based scholarships/grants:* Pell, SEOG, state scholarships/grants, private scholarships, the school's own gift aid. *Loans:* Direct Subsidized Stafford, Direct Unsubsidized Stafford, FFEL PLUS, Federal Perkins. **Student Employment:** Federal Work-Study Program available. Off-campus job opportunities are good. **Financial Aid Statistics:** Highest amount earned per year from on-campus jobs $3,000.

NEW COLLEGE OF FLORIDA

Best 368

5800 Bay Shore Road, Sarasota, FL 34243-2109
Phone: 941-487-5000 **E-mail:** admissions@ncf.edu **CEEB Code:** 5506
Fax: 941-487-5010 **Website:** www.ncf.edu **ACT Code:** 0750
Financial Aid Phone: 941-487-5001

This public school was founded in 1960. It has a 144-acre campus.

RATINGS
Admissions Selectivity Rating: 94   **Fire Safety Rating:** 64   **Green Rating:** 81

STUDENTS AND FACULTY
Enrollment: 746. **Student Body:** 59% female, 41% male, 27% out-of-state, 1% international (25 countries represented). African American 1%, Asian 3%, Caucasian 82%, Hispanic 10%. **Retention and Graduation:** 80% freshmen return for sophomore year. 54% freshmen graduate within 4 years. **Faculty:** Student/faculty ratio 10:1. 67 full-time faculty, 99% hold PhDs. 100% faculty teach undergrads.

ACADEMICS
Degrees: Bachelor's. **Academic Requirements:** Humanities, sciences (biological or physical), social science. Student must receive credit for the satisfactory completion of 8 courses in the liberal arts curriculum of the college. These courses must include at least 1 course in each of the 3 divisions: Humanities (including fine arts), natural sciences (including mathematics), and social sciences (including behavioral sciences and history). **Classes:** Most classes have 10-19 students. **Majors with Highest Enrollment:** Economics, environmental studies, psychology. **Disciplines with Highest Percentage of Degrees Awarded:** Liberal arts/general studies 100%. **Special Study Options:** Cross-registration, double major, exchange student program (domestic), honors program, independent study, internships, senior thesis, student-designed major, study abroad, tutorials, undergraduate research. Special or unique academic programs: (1) The New College academic contract whereby each student develops her/his individual academic program of coursework, tutorials, field and lab research, study abroad, and so on, in close consultation with a faculty member. See Catalog on the web, www.ncf.edu. Catalog. (2) Non-graded, narrative evaluation, which encourages exploration and mastery. (3) Intensive independent study projects during January, which can be highly individual but can also involve group activities, such as an acting workshop or an ecological tour of Florida. (4) Competitive grants programs to support student research.

FACILITIES
Housing: Coed dorms, apartments for single students, special housing for disabled students, specialized housing options may be arranged in response to student interest. **Special Academic Facilities/Equipment:** Anthropology and psychology labs, electronic music lab, individual studio space for senior art students, marine biology research center with living ecosystem teaching and research aquarium, wet lab, seawater on tap, NMR, scanning electron microscope, inert atmosphere glove box, transparent fume hoods, greenhouse. **Computers:** 1% of classrooms are wired, 10% of classrooms are wireless, 80% of public computers are PCs, 20% of public computers are Macs, network access in dorm rooms, network access in dorm lounges, online registration, online administrative functions (other than registration), support for handheld computing, remote student-access to Web through college's connection.

CAMPUS LIFE
Activities: Choral groups, dance, drama/theater, literary magazine, music ensembles, musical theater, radio station, student government, student newspaper, student-run film society. **Organizations:** 90 registered organizations, 5 religious organizations.

ADMISSIONS
Freshman Academic Profile: 49% in top 10% of high school class, 82% in top 25% of high school class, 96% in top 50% of high school class. 83% from public high schools. SAT Math middle 50% range 600–690. SAT Critical Reading middle 50% range 650–740. SAT Writing middle 50% range 610–690. ACT middle 50% range 26–30. TOEFL required of all international applicants, minimum paper TOEFL 560, minimum computer TOEFL 220. **Basis for Candidate Selection:** *Very important factors considered include:* Academic GPA, application essay, rigor of secondary school record, standardized test scores. *Important factors considered include:* Character/personal qualities, level of applicant's interest, recommendation(s). *Other factors considered include:*

Alumni/ae relation, class rank, extracurricular activities, geographical residence, interview, state residency, talent/ability, volunteer work, work experience. **Freshman Admission Requirements:** High school diploma is required, and GED is accepted. *Academic units required:* 4 English, 3 math, 3 science (2 science labs), 2 foreign language, 3 social studies, 3 academic electives. *Academic units recommended:* 4 English, 3 math, 3 science (2 science labs), 2 foreign language, 3 social studies, 5 academic electives. **Freshman Admission Statistics:** 1,065 applied, 49% admitted, 33% enrolled. **Transfer Admission Requirements:** College transcript(s), essay or personal statement, statement of good standing from prior institution(s). Minimum college GPA of 2.0 required. Lowest grade transferable C. **General Admission Information:** Application fee $30. Regular application deadline 4/15. Regular notification 4/25. Non-fall registration accepted. Admission may be deferred for a maximum of 1 year. Neither credit nor placement offered for CEEB Advanced Placement tests.

COSTS AND FINANCIAL AID
Annual in-state tuition $3,850. Out-of-state tuition $20,575. Room & board $7,080. Average book expense $800. **Required Forms and Deadlines:** FAFSA. Financial aid filing deadline 2/15. **Notification of Awards:** Applicants will be notified of awards on or about 3/15. **Types of Aid:** *Need-based scholarships/grants:* Pell, SEOG, state scholarships/grants, private scholarships, the school's own gift aid, federal academic competitiveness grant. *Loans:* FFEL Subsidized Stafford, FFEL Unsubsidized Stafford, FFEL PLUS, alternative loans. **Student Employment:** Federal Work-Study Program available. Institutional employment available. Off-campus job opportunities are good. **Financial Aid Statistics:** 42% freshmen, 37% undergrads receive need-based scholarship or grant aid. 31% freshmen, 30% undergrads receive need-based self-help aid. 100% freshmen, 88% undergrads receive any aid.

NEW ENGLAND COLLEGE

26 Bridge Street, Henniker, NH 03242
Phone: 603-428-2223 **E-mail:** admission@nec.edu **CEEB Code:** 3657
Fax: 603-428-3155 **Website:** www.nec.edu **ACT Code:** 2513
Financial Aid Phone: 603-428-2226

This private school was founded in 1946. It has a 225-acre campus.

RATINGS
Admissions Selectivity Rating: 68   **Fire Safety Rating:** 94   **Green Rating:** 84

STUDENTS AND FACULTY
Enrollment: 1,039. **Student Body:** 49% female, 51% male, 68% out-of-state, 3% international. African American 2%, Asian 3%, Caucasian 89%, Hispanic 2%. **Retention and Graduation:** 57% freshmen return for sophomore year. 34% freshmen graduate within 4 years. 20% grads go on to further study within 1 year. 5% grads pursue arts and sciences degrees. 15% grads pursue business degrees. 1% grads pursue law degrees. **Faculty:** Student/faculty ratio 14:1. 58 full-time faculty, 76% hold PhDs. 89% faculty teach undergrads.

ACADEMICS
Degrees: Associate, bachelor's, master's. **Academic Requirements:** Arts/fine arts, computer literacy, English (including composition), humanities, mathematics, sciences (biological or physical), social science. **Classes:** Most classes have 10–19 students. Most lab/discussion sections have 10–19 students. **Majors with Highest Enrollment:** Business administration/management, elementary education and teaching, sports and fitness administration/management. **Disciplines with Highest Percentage of Degrees Awarded:** Business/marketing 19%, parks and recreation 16%, education 9%, health professions and related sciences 9%, communications/journalism 7%, psychology 7%, visual and performing arts 7%, security and protective services 5%, English 5%. **Special Study Options:** Cross-registration, distance learning, double major, dual enrollment, English as a second language (ESL), exchange student program (domestic), external degree program, honors program, independent study, internships, liberal arts/career combination, student-designed major, study abroad, teacher certification program.

FACILITIES
Housing: Coed dorms, fraternity/sorority housing, quiet study options, special interest housing. Resident freshmen and sophomores are required to live in college housing. **Special Academic Facilities/Equipment:** New England Art Gallery, graphic design and imaging lab center for educational innovation (high-tech building). **Computers:** 32% of classrooms are wired, 100% of classrooms are wireless, 91% of public computers are PCs, 9% of public computers are Macs, network access in dorm rooms, network access in dorm lounges, online registration, online administrative functions (other than registration), remote student-access to Web through college's connection.

CAMPUS LIFE

Activities: Choral groups, dance, drama/theater, literary magazine, radio station, student government, student newspaper, yearbook. **Organizations:** 40 registered organizations, 1 honor society, 1 religious organization. 3 fraternities (10% men join), 2 sororities (7% women join). **Athletics (Intercollegiate):** *Men:* Baseball, basketball, cross-country, ice hockey, lacrosse, soccer, track/field (outdoor). *Women:* Basketball, cheerleading, cross-country, field hockey, ice hockey, lacrosse, soccer, softball, track/field (outdoor). **Environmental Initiatives:** Addition of sustainability to the mission statement. Environmental Action Committee.

ADMISSIONS

Freshman Academic Profile: 6% in top 10% of high school class, 15% in top 25% of high school class, 37% in top 50% of high school class. 75% from public high schools. SAT Math middle 50% range 380–500. SAT Critical Reading middle 50% range 380–500. SAT Writing middle 50% range 400–500. ACT middle 50% range 14–21. TOEFL required of all international applicants, minimum paper TOEFL 550, minimum computer TOEFL 213. **Basis for Candidate Selection:** *Very important factors considered include:* Application essay, extracurricular activities, interview, level of applicant's interest, recommendation(s), rigor of secondary school record, talent/ability. *Important factors considered include:* Character/personal qualities. *Other factors considered include:* Academic GPA, alumni/ae relation, class rank, standardized test scores, volunteer work, work experience. **Freshman Admission Requirements:** High school diploma is required, and GED is accepted. *Academic units required:* 4 English, 2 math, 2 science (1 science lab), 2 social studies. *Academic units recommended:* 4 English, 3 math, 3 science (2 science labs), 2 foreign language, 3 social studies. **Freshman Admission Statistics:** 2,038 applied, 76% admitted, 21% enrolled. **Transfer Admission Requirements:** High school transcript, college transcript(s), essay or personal statement, statement of good standing from prior institution(s). Lowest grade transferable C-. **General Admission Information:** Application fee $30. Regular application deadline 6/8. Regular notification is rolling. Non-fall registration accepted. Admission may be deferred for a maximum of 1 year. Credit and/or placement offered for CEEB Advanced Placement tests.

COSTS AND FINANCIAL AID

Annual tuition $26,270. Room and board $9,278. Required fees $200. Average book expense $800. **Required Forms and Deadlines:** FAFSA, institution's own financial aid form. Financial aid filing deadline 3/15. **Notification of Awards:** Applicants will be notified of awards on a rolling basis beginning on or about 1/12. **Types of Aid:** *Need-based scholarships/grants:* Pell, SEOG, state scholarships/grants, private scholarships, the school's own gift aid. *Loans:* FFEL Subsidized Stafford, FFEL Unsubsidized Stafford, FFEL PLUS, Federal Perkins, state loans. **Student Employment:** Federal Work-Study Program available. Institutional employment available. Off-campus job opportunities are good. **Financial Aid Statistics:** 72% freshmen, 71% undergrads receive need-based scholarship or grant aid. 58% freshmen, 60% undergrads receive need-based self-help aid. 94% freshmen, 90% undergrads receive any aid. Highest amount earned per year from on-campus jobs $1,500.

NEW ENGLAND CONSERVATORY OF MUSIC

290 Huntington Avenue, Boston, MA 02115
Phone: 617-585-1101 **E-mail:** admissions@newenglandconservatory.edu **CEEB Code:** 3659
Fax: 617-585-1115 **Website:** www.newenglandconservatory.edu **ACT Code:** 1872
Financial Aid Phone: 617-585-1110

This private school was founded in 1867.

RATINGS

Admissions Selectivity Rating: 60*   **Fire Safety Rating:** 60*   **Green Rating:** 60*

STUDENTS AND FACULTY

Enrollment: 378. **Student Body:** 45% female, 55% male, 85% out-of-state, 6% international. Asian 3%, Caucasian 13%, Hispanic 1%. **Retention and Graduation:** 98% freshmen return for sophomore year. 56% freshmen graduate within 4 years. **Faculty:** Student/faculty ratio 4:1. 88 full-time faculty, 26% hold PhDs. 53% faculty teach undergrads.

ACADEMICS

Degrees: Bachelor's, diploma, doctoral, master's. **Academic Requirements:** Arts/fine arts, career skills, English (including composition), history, humanities. **Classes:** Most classes have 10–19 students. Most lab/discussion sections have fewer than 10 students. **Majors with Highest Enrollment:** Jazz/jazz studies; violin, viola, guitar, and other stringed instruments; voice and opera. **Disciplines with Highest Percentage of Degrees Awarded:** Visual and performing arts 100%. **Special Study Options:** Cross-registration, dual enrollment, English as a second language (ESL), independent study, internships, study abroad.

FACILITIES

Housing: Coed dorms. **Special Academic Facilities/Equipment:** Rare instrument collection of over 200 pieces, recording and electronic music studios. Jordan Hall, the main concert hall is a national historic landmark. **Computers:** 1% of classrooms are wired, 1% of classrooms are wireless, 80% of public computers are PCs, 20% of public computers are Macs, network access in dorm lounges.

CAMPUS LIFE

Activities: Choral groups, concert band, jazz band, music ensembles, musical theater, opera, student government, symphony orchestra. **Organizations:** 7 registered organizations, 1 honor society, 1 religious organization. 1 fraternity.

ADMISSIONS

Freshman Academic Profile: TOEFL required of all international applicants, minimum paper TOEFL 500, minimum computer TOEFL 173. **Basis for Candidate Selection:** *Very important factors considered include:* Talent/ability. *Important factors considered include:* Rigor of secondary school record, standardized test scores. *Other factors considered include:* Academic GPA, application essay, character/personal qualities, recommendation(s). **Freshman Admission Requirements:** High school diploma is required, and GED is accepted. **Freshman Admission Statistics:** 1,022 applied, 28% admitted, 28% enrolled. **Transfer Admission Requirements:** College transcript(s), essay or personal statement, interview. Minimum college GPA of 2.7 required. Lowest grade transferable B. **General Admission Information:** Application fee $100. Regular notification is rolling. Non-fall registration accepted. Admission may be deferred for a maximum of 1 year. Credit offered for CEEB Advanced Placement tests.

COSTS AND FINANCIAL AID

Annual tuition $30,650. Room & board $11,300. Required fees $325. Average book expense $700. **Required Forms and Deadlines:** FAFSA, institution's own financial aid form. Financial aid filing deadline 2/1. **Notification of Awards:** Applicants will be notified of awards on or about 4/1. **Types of Aid:** *Need-based scholarships/grants:* Pell, SEOG, state scholarships/grants, private scholarships, the school's own gift aid. *Loans:* FFEL Subsidized Stafford, FFEL Unsubsidized Stafford, FFEL PLUS, Federal Perkins, state loans. **Student Employment:** Federal Work-Study Program available. Institutional employment available. Off-campus job opportunities are good. **Financial Aid Statistics:** 63% freshmen, 61% undergrads receive need-based scholarship or grant aid. 47% freshmen, 48% undergrads receive need-based self-help aid.

NEW ENGLAND CULINARY INSTITUTE

56 College Street, Montpelier, VT 05602
Phone: 877-223-6324 **E-mail:** admissions@neci.edu
Fax: 802-225-3280 **Website:** www.neci.edu

This is a proprietary school.

RATINGS

Admissions Selectivity Rating: 60*   **Fire Safety Rating:** 60*   **Green Rating:** 60*

STUDENTS AND FACULTY

Enrollment: 533. **Student Body:** 35% female, 65% male, 85% out-of-state. African American 3%, Asian 3%, Caucasian 89%, Hispanic 4%. **Retention and Graduation:** 83% freshmen return for sophomore year.

ACADEMICS

Degrees: Associate, bachelor's, certificate, terminal. **Academic Requirements:** English (including composition), mathematics. **Disciplines with Highest Percentage of Degrees Awarded:** Personal and culinary services 100%. **Special Study Options:** Accelerated program, distance learning, dual enrollment, internships.

FACILITIES

Housing: Coed dorms, men's dorms, women's dorms, apartments for married students, special housing for disabled students.

CAMPUS LIFE

Activities: Student government, student newspaper.

ADMISSIONS

60° (out of 100).

COSTS AND FINANCIAL AID
Annual tuition $23,835. Room & board $6,565. Required fees $275. Average book expense $1,350. **Required Forms and Deadlines:** FAFSA, state aid form. **Notification of Awards:** Applicants will be notified of awards on a rolling basis beginning on or about 2/15. **Types of Aid:** *Need-based scholarships/grants:* Pell, SEOG, state scholarships/grants, private scholarships, the school's own gift aid. *Loans:* FFEL Subsidized Stafford, FFEL Unsubsidized Stafford, FFEL PLUS, Federal Perkins.

NEW JERSEY CITY UNIVERSITY

2039 Kennedy Boulevard, Jersey City, NJ 07305
Phone: 888-441-6528 **E-mail:** admissions@njcu.edu **CEEB Code:** 2316
Fax: 201-200-2044 **Website:** www.njcu.edu
Financial Aid Phone: 201-200-3378

This public school was founded in 1927. It has a 17-acre campus.

RATINGS
Admissions Selectivity Rating: 70   **Fire Safety Rating:** 93   **Green Rating:** 60*

STUDENTS AND FACULTY
Enrollment: 6,115. **Student Body:** 63% female, 37% male, 1% out-of-state, 1% international (6 countries represented). African American 19%, Asian 7%, Caucasian 28%, Hispanic 33%. **Retention and Graduation:** 76% freshmen return for sophomore year. 20% grads go on to further study within 1 year. 13% grads pursue arts and sciences degrees. 5% grads pursue business degrees. 1% grads pursue law degrees. 1% grads pursue medical degrees. **Faculty:** Student/faculty ratio 14:1. 243 full-time faculty, 83% hold PhDs. 100% faculty teach undergrads.

ACADEMICS
Degrees: Bachelor's, master's, post-master's certificate. **Academic Requirements:** Arts/fine arts, computer literacy, English (including composition), history, humanities, mathematics, sciences (biological or physical), social science. **Classes:** Most classes have 20–29 students. **Majors with Highest Enrollment:** Business administration and management, computer and information sciences, psychology. **Disciplines with Highest Percentage of Degrees Awarded:** Business/marketing 25%, psychology 11%, education 8%, social sciences 8%, visual and performing arts 5%. **Special Study Options:** Accelerated program, cooperative education program, distance learning, double major, dual enrollment, English as a second language (ESL), honors program, independent study, internships, study abroad, teacher certification program, weekend college.

FACILITIES
Housing: Coed dorms. **Special Academic Facilities/Equipment:** Art galleries, lab school for special education, criminal justice institute, electron microscope, Raimondo Center for Urban Research and Public Policy. **Computers:** 100% of public computers are PCs, network access in dorm rooms, online registration, online administrative functions (other than registration), remote student-access to Web through college's connection.

CAMPUS LIFE
Activities: Choral groups, concert band, dance, drama/theater, jazz band, literary magazine, music ensembles, musical theater, opera, radio station, student government, student newspaper, yearbook. **Organizations:** 50 registered organizations, 2 religious organizations. 7 fraternities (2% men join), 5 sororities (2% women join). **Athletics (Intercollegiate):** *Men:* Baseball, basketball, cross-country, soccer, track/field (indoor), track/field (outdoor), volleyball. *Women:* Basketball, bowling, cross-country, soccer, softball, track/field (indoor), track/field (outdoor), volleyball.

ADMISSIONS
Freshman Academic Profile: 8% in top 10% of high school class, 24% in top 25% of high school class, 62% in top 50% of high school class. 75% from public high schools. SAT Math middle 50% range 410–500. SAT Critical Reading middle 50% range 410–489. SAT Writing middle 50% range 390–470. TOEFL required of all international applicants, minimum paper TOEFL 500, minimum computer TOEFL 150. **Basis for Candidate Selection:** *Very important factors considered include:* Class rank, level of applicant's interest, rigor of secondary school record, standardized test scores, volunteer work. *Important factors considered include:* Academic GPA, application essay, recommendation(s), talent/ability. *Other factors considered include:* Character/personal qualities, extracurricular activities, interview. **Freshman Admission Requirements:** High school diploma is required, and GED is accepted. *Academic units required:* 4 English, 4 math, 4 science (2 science labs), 4 social

studies. *Academic units recommended:* 4 English, 4 math, 4 science (3 science labs), 2 foreign language, 4 social studies. **Freshman Admission Statistics:** 2,401 applied, 49% admitted, 56% enrolled. **Transfer Admission Requirements:** College transcript(s). Minimum college GPA of 2.0 required. **General Admission Information:** Application fee $35. Regular application deadline 4/1. Regular notification is rolling. Non-fall registration accepted. Admission may be deferred for a maximum of 1 year. Credit and/or placement offered for CEEB Advanced Placement tests.

COSTS AND FINANCIAL AID
Annual in-state tuition $5,926. Annual out-of-state tuition $12,540. Room and board $8,558. Required fees $2,218. Average book expense $1,836. **Required Forms and Deadlines:** FAFSA. Financial aid filing deadline 4/15. **Notification of Awards:** Applicants will be notified of awards on or about 4/5. **Types of Aid:** *Need-based scholarships/grants:* Pell, SEOG, state scholarships/grants, private scholarships, the school's own gift aid. *Loans:* FFEL Subsidized Stafford, FFEL Unsubsidized Stafford, FFEL PLUS, Federal Perkins, state loans. **Student Employment:** Federal Work-Study Program available. Institutional employment available. Off-campus job opportunities are good. **Financial Aid Statistics:** 52% freshmen, 54% undergrads receive need-based scholarship or grant aid. 39% freshmen, 49% undergrads receive need-based self-help aid. 70% freshmen, 70% undergrads receive any aid.

NEW JERSEY INSTITUTE OF TECHNOLOGY

University Heights, Newark, NJ 07102
Phone: 973-596-3300 **E-mail:** admissions@njit.edu **CEEB Code:** 2513
Fax: 973-596-3461 **Website:** www.njit.edu **ACT Code:** 2580
Financial Aid Phone: 973-596-3479

This public school was founded in 1881. It has a 48-acre campus.

RATINGS
Admissions Selectivity Rating: 81   **Fire Safety Rating:** 91   **Green Rating:** 60*

STUDENTS AND FACULTY
Enrollment: 5,049. **Student Body:** 20% female, 80% male, 6% out-of-state, 6% international (98 countries represented). African American 10%, Asian 20%, Caucasian 35%, Hispanic 15%. **Retention and Graduation:** 80% freshmen return for sophomore year. 16% freshmen graduate within 4 years. 20% grads go on to further study within 1 year. 9% grads pursue arts and sciences degrees. 3% grads pursue business degrees. 2% grads pursue law degrees. 2% grads pursue medical degrees. **Faculty:** Student/faculty ratio 13:1. 416 full-time faculty, 100% hold PhDs. 70% faculty teach undergrads.

ACADEMICS
Degrees: Bachelor's, doctoral, master's, post-bachelor's certificate. **Academic Requirements:** Computer literacy, English (including composition), humanities, mathematics, sciences (biological or physical). General undergraduate requirements set a broad area of study for students including many humanities and social science courses at Rutgers Newark. **Classes:** Most classes have 20–29 students. **Majors with Highest Enrollment:** Architecture (BArch, BA/BS, MArch, MA/MS, PhD), information technology, mechanical engineering. **Disciplines with Highest Percentage of Degrees Awarded:** Engineering 33%, computer and information sciences 30%, engineering technologies 14%, business/marketing 9%, architecture 9%. **Special Study Options:** Accelerated program, cooperative education program, distance learning, double major, English as a second language (ESL), honors program, independent study, internships, study abroad.

FACILITIES
Housing: Coed dorms, fraternity/sorority housing. Fraternity/sorority housing is self-regulated and self-supervised. NJIT is not responsible for Greek housing. **Special Academic Facilities/Equipment:** New Jersey Literary Hall of Fame, more than 50 research centers and sponsored research laboratories, computer chip manufacturing center, manufacturing systems center. **Computers:** 100% of classrooms are wired, 100% of classrooms are wireless, 75% of public computers are PCs, 25% of public computers are Macs, network access in dorm rooms, network access in dorm lounges, online registration, online administrative functions (other than registration), support for handheld computing, remote student-access to Web through college's connection. Undergraduates are required to own a computer.

CAMPUS LIFE

Activities: Dance, drama/theater, literary magazine, radio station, student government, student newspaper, student-run film society, yearbook. **Organizations:** 60 registered organizations, 8 honor societies, 5 religious organizations. 17 fraternities (7% men join), 8 sororities (5% women join). **Athletics (Intercollegiate):** *Men:* Baseball, basketball, cross-country, fencing, soccer, swimming, tennis, track/field (indoor), track/field (outdoor), volleyball. *Women:* Basketball, cross-country, fencing, soccer, swimming, tennis, track/field (indoor), track/field (outdoor), volleyball.

ADMISSIONS

Freshman Academic Profile: 12% in top 10% of high school class, 60% in top 25% of high school class, 89% in top 50% of high school class. 80% from public high schools. SAT Math middle 50% range 550–650. SAT Critical Reading middle 50% range 480–580. SAT Writing middle 50% range 470–570. TOEFL required of all international applicants, minimum paper TOEFL 550, minimum computer TOEFL 213. **Basis for Candidate Selection:** *Very important factors considered include:* Class rank, rigor of secondary school record, standardized test scores. *Important factors considered include:* Academic GPA. *Other factors considered include:* Alumni/ae relation, application essay, character/personal qualities, extracurricular activities, geographical residence, interview, level of applicant's interest, racial/ethnic status, recommendation(s), religious affiliation/commitment, state residency. **Freshman Admission Requirements:** High school diploma is required, and GED is accepted. *Academic units required:* 4 English, 4 math, 2 science (2 science labs). *Academic units recommended:* 2 foreign language, 1 social studies, 1 history, 2 academic electives. **Freshman Admission Statistics:** 2,891 applied, 53% admitted, 55% enrolled. **Transfer Admission Requirements:** College transcript(s). Minimum college GPA of 2.0 required. Lowest grade transferable C. **General Admission Information:** Application fee $50. Regular application deadline 4/1. Regular notification is rolling. Non-fall registration accepted. Admission may be deferred for a maximum of 1 semester. Credit offered for CEEB Advanced Placement tests.

COSTS AND FINANCIAL AID

Annual in-state tuition $9,700. Annual out-of-state tuition $18,432. Room and board $9,264. Required fees $1,650. Average book expense $1,200. **Required Forms and Deadlines:** FAFSA. Financial aid filing deadline 5/15. **Notification of Awards:** Applicants will be notified of awards on a rolling basis beginning on or about 3/1. **Types of Aid:** *Need-based scholarships/grants:* Pell, SEOG, state scholarships/grants, private scholarships, the school's own gift aid. *Loans:* Direct Subsidized Stafford, Direct Unsubsidized Stafford, Direct PLUS, Federal Perkins, state loans, college/university loans from institutional funds. **Student Employment:** Federal Work-Study Program available. Institutional employment available. Off-campus job opportunities are good. **Financial Aid Statistics:** 51% freshmen, 42% undergrads receive need-based scholarship or grant aid. 38% freshmen, 34% undergrads receive need-based self-help aid. 25 freshmen, 89 undergrads receive athletic scholarships. 70% freshmen, 70% undergrads receive any aid. Highest amount earned per year from on-campus jobs $5,500.

NEW MEXICO HIGHLANDS UNIVERSITY

NMHU Office of Student Recruitment, Box 9000, Las Vegas, NM 87701
Phone: 505-454-3593 **E-mail:** recruitment@nmhu.edu **CEEB Code:** 4532
Fax: 505-454-3511 **Website:** www.nmhu.edu **ACT Code:** 2640
Financial Aid Phone: 505-454-3317

This public school was founded in 1893. It has a 175-acre campus.

RATINGS

Admissions Selectivity Rating: 60*   **Fire Safety Rating:** 60*   **Green Rating:** 60*

STUDENTS AND FACULTY

Student Body: 12% out-of-state. **Retention and Graduation:** 53% freshmen return for sophomore year.

ACADEMICS

Degrees: Bachelor's, master's. **Special Study Options:** Cooperative education program, business, computer science, engineering, natural science.

FACILITIES

Housing: Coed dorms, men's dorms, women's dorms, apartments for married students, apartments for single students.

CAMPUS LIFE

Activities: Literary magazine, radio station, student government, student

newspaper, television station, yearbook. **Organizations:** 13 honor societies, 5 religious organizations. **Athletics (Intercollegiate):** *Men:* Baseball, basketball, cross-country, football. *Women:* Basketball, cross-country, soccer, softball, volleyball.

ADMISSIONS

Freshman Academic Profile: 5% in top 10% of high school class, 20% in top 25% of high school class, 65% in top 50% of high school class. 95% from public high schools. TOEFL required of all international applicants, minimum paper TOEFL 480. **Freshman Admission Requirements:** High school diploma is required, and GED is accepted. *Academic units recommended:* 4 English, 2 math, 3 science, 1 foreign language, 3 social studies, 2 history, 2 academic electives. **Transfer Admission Requirements:** Minimum college GPA of 2.0 required. Lowest grade transferable C. **General Admission Information:** Early decision application deadline 1/1. Regular application deadline 8/1. Regular notification is rolling. Non-fall registration accepted. Common Application not accepted. Credit and/or placement offered for CEEB Advanced Placement tests.

COSTS AND FINANCIAL AID

Annual in-state tuition $1,782. Out-of-state tuition $7,122. Room & board $2,171. Required fees $80. Average book expense $600. **Required Forms and Deadlines:** FAFSA. **Types of Aid:** *Need-based scholarships/grants:* Pell, SEOG, state scholarships/grants, private scholarships, the school's own gift aid. *Loans:* FFEL Subsidized Stafford, FFEL Unsubsidized Stafford, FFEL PLUS, Federal Perkins, state loans, college/university loans from institutional funds. **Student Employment:** Federal Work-Study Program available. Institutional employment available. Off-campus job opportunities are fair.

NEW MEXICO INSTITUTE OF MINING & TECHNOLOGY

Campus Station, 801 Leroy Place, Socorro, NM 87801
Phone: 505-835-5424 **E-mail:** admission@admin.nmt.edu **CEEB Code:** 4533
Fax: 505-835-5989 **Website:** www.nmt.edu **ACT Code:** 2642
Financial Aid Phone: 505-835-5333

This public school was founded in 1889. It has a 320-acre campus.

RATINGS

Admissions Selectivity Rating: 88   **Fire Safety Rating:** 60*   **Green Rating:** 60*

STUDENTS AND FACULTY

Enrollment: 1,170. **Student Body:** 28% female, 72% male, 13% out-of-state, 2% international (30 countries represented). African American 1%, Asian 3%, Caucasian 69%, Hispanic 23%, Native American 3%. **Retention and Graduation:** 68% freshmen return for sophomore year. 30% grads go on to further study within 1 year. **Faculty:** Student/faculty ratio 12:1. 121 full-time faculty, 98% hold PhDs. 85% faculty teach undergrads.

ACADEMICS

Degrees: Associate, bachelor's, certificate, doctoral, master's, terminal. **Academic Requirements:** English (including composition), humanities, mathematics, sciences (biological or physical), social science. **Classes:** Most classes have 10–19 students. Most lab/discussion sections have 10–19 students. **Majors with Highest Enrollment:** Computer and information sciences; electrical, electronics, and communications engineering; mechanical engineering. **Disciplines with Highest Percentage of Degrees Awarded:** Engineering 46%, computer and information sciences 19%, physical sciences 15%, biological/life sciences 9%, mathematics 5%. **Special Study Options:** Accelerated program, cooperative education program, distance learning, double major, dual enrollment, exchange student program (domestic), independent study, internships, student-designed major, teacher certification program.

FACILITIES

Housing: Coed dorms, men's dorms, women's dorms, apartments for married students, apartments for single students. **Special Academic Facilities/Equipment:** Mineral museum, observatory, radio telescope, seismic observatory and library, explosives labs. **Computers:** 90% of public computers are PCs, 10% of public computers are Macs, 8% of public computers are UNIX, network access in dorm rooms, network access in dorm lounges, online registration, online administrative functions (other than registration), remote student-access to Web through college's connection.

CAMPUS LIFE

Activities: Choral groups, concert band, dance, drama/theater, jazz band, music ensembles, musical theater, radio station, student government, student newspaper. **Organizations:** 60 registered organizations, 7 honor societies, 3 religious organizations.

ADMISSIONS

Freshman Academic Profile: 32% in top 10% of high school class, 67% in top 25% of high school class, 91% in top 50% of high school class. 80% from public high schools. SAT Math middle 50% range 560–680. SAT Critical Reading middle 50% range 530–660. ACT middle 50% range 23–29. TOEFL required of all international applicants, minimum paper TOEFL 540, minimum computer TOEFL 207. **Basis for Candidate Selection:** *Very important factors considered include:* Academic GPA, rigor of secondary school record, standardized test scores. *Other factors considered include:* Class rank, extracurricular activities, talent/ability. **Freshman Admission Requirements:** High school diploma is required, and GED is accepted. *Academic units required:* 4 English, 3 math, 2 science (2 science labs), 2 social studies, 1 history, 3 academic electives. *Academic units recommended:* 4 English, 4 math, 4 science (3 science labs), 2 foreign language, 3 social studies, 1 history. **Freshman Admission Statistics:** 834 applied, 61% admitted, 56% enrolled. **Transfer Admission Requirements:** High school transcript, college transcript(s), statement of good standing from prior institution(s). Minimum college GPA of 2.0 required. Lowest grade transferable D. **General Admission Information:** Application fee $15. Regular application deadline 8/1. Regular notification is rolling. Non-fall registration accepted. Admission may be deferred for a maximum of 1 year. Credit and/or placement offered for CEEB Advanced Placement tests.

COSTS AND FINANCIAL AID

Annual in-state tuition $3,543. Annual out-of-state tuition $11,199. Room and board $5,300. Required fees $562. Average book expense $1,000. **Required Forms and Deadlines:** FAFSA, institution's own financial aid form. Financial aid filing deadline 3/1. **Notification of Awards:** Applicants will be notified of awards on a rolling basis beginning on or about 4/1. **Types of Aid:** *Need-based scholarships/grants:* Pell, SEOG, state scholarships/grants, private scholarships, the school's own gift aid. *Loans:* FFEL Subsidized Stafford, FFEL Unsubsidized Stafford, FFEL PLUS, Federal Perkins, state loans. **Student Employment:** Federal Work-Study Program available. Institutional employment available. Off-campus job opportunities are fair. **Financial Aid Statistics:** 19% freshmen, 25% undergrads receive need-based scholarship or grant aid. 16% freshmen, 25% undergrads receive need-based self-help aid. 34% freshmen, 39% undergrads receive any aid. Highest amount earned per year from on-campus jobs $3,500.

NEW MEXICO STATE UNIVERSITY

Box 30001, MSC 3A, Las Cruces, NM 88003-8001
Phone: 505-646-3121 **E-mail:** admissions@nmsu.edu **CEEB Code:** 4531
Fax: 505-646-6330 **Website:** www.nmsu.edu **ACT Code:** 2638
Financial Aid Phone: 505-646-4105

This public school was founded in 1888. It has a 900-acre campus.

RATINGS

Admissions Selectivity Rating: 73 **Fire Safety Rating:** 60* **Green Rating:** 60*

STUDENTS AND FACULTY

Enrollment: 12,157. **Student Body:** 55% female, 45% male, 16% out-of-state. African American 3%, Asian 1%, Caucasian 38%, Hispanic 44%, Native American 3%. **Retention and Graduation:** 70% freshmen return for sophomore year. 12% freshmen graduate within 4 years. **Faculty:** Student/faculty ratio 19:1. 658 full-time faculty, 81% hold PhDs.

ACADEMICS

Degrees: Associate, bachelor's, doctoral, master's, post-master's certificate. **Academic Requirements:** Arts/fine arts, English (including composition), foreign languages, history, humanities, mathematics, philosophy, sciences (biological or physical), social science. **Classes:** Most classes have 10–19 students. Most lab/discussion sections have 10–19 students. **Majors with Highest Enrollment:** Business administration/management; curriculum and instruction; electrical, electronics, and communications engineering. **Disciplines with Highest Percentage of Degrees Awarded:** Business/marketing 22%, education 13%, engineering 7%, security and protective services 6%, health professions and related sciences 6%, social sciences 6%, biological/life

sciences 5%, agriculture 5%. **Special Study Options:** Accelerated program, cooperative education program, cross-registration, distance learning, double major, exchange student program (domestic), honors program, independent study, internships, student-designed major, study abroad, teacher certification program, weekend college.

FACILITIES

Housing: Coed dorms, men's dorms, women's dorms, apartments for married students, apartments for single students, special housing for disabled students, fraternity/sorority housing. **Special Academic Facilities/Equipment:** University and art department museums, theater, horse farm, sports medicine training clinic, observatory, electron microscope, CRAY supercomputer. **Computers:** 90% of public computers are PCs, 10% of public computers are Macs, network access in dorm rooms, network access in dorm lounges, online registration, online administrative functions (other than registration), remote student-access to Web through college's connection.

CAMPUS LIFE

Activities: Choral groups, concert band, dance, drama/theater, jazz band, literary magazine, marching band, music ensembles, musical theater, opera, pep band, radio station, student government, student newspaper, symphony orchestra, television station. **Organizations:** 263 registered organizations, 24 honor societies, 23 religious organizations. 14 fraternities, 5 sororities. **Athletics (Intercollegiate):** *Men:* Baseball, basketball, cross-country, football, golf, tennis. *Women:* Basketball, cross-country, golf, softball, swimming, tennis, track/field (outdoor), volleyball.

ADMISSIONS

Freshman Academic Profile: 17% in top 10% of high school class, 44% in top 25% of high school class, 76% in top 50% of high school class. SAT Math middle 50% range 430–560. SAT Critical Reading middle 50% range 420–550. SAT Writing middle 50% range 420–545. ACT middle 50% range 17–23. TOEFL required of all international applicants, minimum paper TOEFL 500. **Basis for Candidate Selection:** *Very important factors considered include:* Rigor of secondary school record, standardized test scores. **Freshman Admission Requirements:** High school diploma is required, and GED is accepted. *Academic units required:* 4 English, 3 math, 2 science (2 science labs), 1 foreign language. **Freshman Admission Statistics:** 5,434 applied, 87% admitted, 41% enrolled. **Transfer Admission Requirements:** College transcript(s). Minimum college GPA of 2.0 required. Lowest grade transferable C. **General Admission Information:** Application fee $15. Regular notification is rolling basis. Non-fall registration accepted. Admission may be deferred for a maximum of 1 year. Credit offered for CEEB Advanced Placement tests.

COSTS AND FINANCIAL AID

Annual in-state tuition $4,452. Annual out-of-state tuition $14,180. Room and board $5,766. Average book expense $918. **Required Forms and Deadlines:** FAFSA, institution's own financial aid form. **Notification of Awards:** Applicants will be notified of awards on or about 3/1. **Types of Aid:** *Need-based scholarships/grants:* The school's own gift aid. *Loans:* FFEL Subsidized Stafford, FFEL Unsubsidized Stafford, FFEL PLUS, Federal Perkins, college/university loans from institutional funds. **Student Employment:** Federal Work-Study Program available. Institutional employment available. Off-campus job opportunities are good. **Financial Aid Statistics:** 49% freshmen, 45% undergrads receive need-based scholarship or grant aid. 21% freshmen, 28% undergrads receive need-based self-help aid. 27 freshmen, 136 undergrads receive athletic scholarships.

NEW SCHOOL OF ARCHITECTURE AND DESIGN

1249 F Street, San Diego, CA 92101
Phone: 619-235-4100 **E-mail:** pbinnis@newschoolarch.edu
Fax: 619-235-4651 **Website:** www.newschoolarch.edu
Financial Aid Phone: 619-235-4100

This proprietary school was founded in 1980. It has a 10-acre campus.

RATINGS

Admissions Selectivity Rating: 73 **Fire Safety Rating:** 60* **Green Rating:** 60*

STUDENTS AND FACULTY

Faculty: Student/faculty ratio 20:1. 5 full-time faculty, 40% hold PhDs. 100% faculty teach undergrads.

ACADEMICS

Degrees: Associate, bachelor's, first professional, master's. **Academic Requirements:** Arts/fine arts, computer literacy, English (including composition), history, humanities, mathematics, philosophy, social science. **Disciplines**

with **Highest Percentage of Degrees Awarded:** Architecture 5%. **Special Study Options:** Cooperative education program, independent study, internships, study abroad.

FACILITIES

Computers: 100% of public computers are PCs, online administrative functions (other than registration), remote student-access to Web through college's connection.

CAMPUS LIFE

Activities: Student newspaper. **Organizations:** 2 registered organizations.

ADMISSIONS

Freshman Academic Profile: 100% from public high schools. TOEFL required of all international applicants, minimum paper TOEFL 550. **Basis for Candidate Selection:** *Very important factors considered include:* Interview. *Important factors considered include:* Rigor of secondary school record, talent/ability. *Other factors considered include:* Application essay, character/personal qualities, extracurricular activities, recommendation(s), volunteer work. **Freshman Admission Requirements:** High school diploma is required, and GED is accepted. **Freshman Admission Statistics:** 5 applied, 100% admitted, 100% enrolled. **Transfer Admission Requirements:** High school transcript, college transcript(s), interview. Minimum college GPA of 2.0 required. Lowest grade transferable C. **General Admission Information:** Application fee $75. Regular notification is ongoing. Non-fall registration accepted. Admission may be deferred for a maximum of 1 year. Common Application not accepted. Neither credit nor placement offered for CEEB Advanced Placement tests.

COSTS AND FINANCIAL AID

Student Employment: Federal Work-Study Program available. Off-campus job opportunities are good.

See page 1282.

THE NEW SCHOOL FOR JAZZ & CONTEMPORARY MUSIC

55 W 13th Street, New York, NY 10011
Phone: 212-229-5896 **E-mail:** jazzadm@newschool.edu
Fax: 212-229-8936 **Website:** www.jazz.newschool.edu

This is a private school.

RATINGS

Admissions Selectivity Rating: 73   **Fire Safety Rating:** 60*   **Green Rating:** 60*

STUDENTS AND FACULTY

Enrollment: 273. **Student Body:** 21% female, 79% male, 61% out-of-state, 15% international. African American 9%, Asian 3%, Caucasian 39%, Hispanic 5%. **Retention and Graduation:** 70% freshmen return for sophomore year. 37% freshmen graduate within 4 years. **Faculty:** Student/faculty ratio 11:1. 3 full-time faculty.

ACADEMICS

Degrees: Associate, bachelor's, certificate, master's. **Academic Requirements:** Arts/fine arts, English (including composition), history, humanities, philosophy, sciences (biological or physical), social science. **Classes:** Most classes have fewer than 10 students. **Disciplines with Highest Percentage of Degrees Awarded:** Visual and performing arts 100%. **Special Study Options:** Accelerated program, cooperative education program, cross-registration, distance learning, dual enrollment, English as a second language (ESL), exchange student program (domestic), honors program, independent study, internships, liberal arts/career combination, student-designed major, study abroad, teacher certification program.

FACILITIES

Housing: Coed dorms, special housing for disabled students.

CAMPUS LIFE

Activities: Choral groups, concert band, music ensembles, opera, symphony orchestra.

ADMISSIONS

Freshman Academic Profile: 9% in top 10% of high school class, 55% in top 25% of high school class, 82% in top 50% of high school class. **Basis for Candidate Selection:** *Very important factors considered include:* Talent/ability. *Important factors considered include:* Rigor of secondary school record. *Other factors considered include:* Application essay, extracurricular activities, recommendation(s). **Freshman Admission Requirements:** High school

diploma is required, and GED is accepted. **Freshman Admission Statistics:** 212 applied, 71% admitted, 38% enrolled. **Transfer Admission Requirements:** College transcript(s), essay or personal statement, interview. Lowest grade transferable C. **General Admission Information:** Application fee $40. Regular notification within 2 weeks of receiving completed application. Non-fall registration accepted. Common Application not accepted.

COSTS AND FINANCIAL AID

Annual tuition $29,800. Room and board $11,750. Required fees $610. Average book expense $900. Average book expense $918. **Required Forms and Deadlines:** FAFSA, state aid form. Financial aid filing deadline 3/1. **Notification of Awards:** Applicants will be notified of awards on a rolling basis beginning on or about 3/1. **Types of Aid:** *Need-based scholarships/grants:* Pell, SEOG, state scholarships/grants, private scholarships, the school's own gift aid. *Loans:* FFEL Subsidized Stafford, FFEL Unsubsidized Stafford, FFEL PLUS, Federal Perkins, college/university loans from institutional funds. **Financial Aid Statistics:** 9% freshmen, 10% undergrads receive need-based scholarship or grant aid. 47% freshmen, 48% undergrads receive need-based self-help aid.

See page 1282.

NEW WORLD SCHOOL OF THE ARTS

300 NE 2nd Avenue, Miami, FL 33132
Phone: 305-237-7007 **E-mail:** nwsaadm@mdc.edu
Fax: 305-237-3794 **Website:** www.mdc.edu/nwsa
Financial Aid Phone: 305-237-7529

This public school was founded in 1984. It has a 2-acre campus.

RATINGS

Admissions Selectivity Rating: 60*   **Fire Safety Rating:** 60*   **Green Rating:** 60*

STUDENTS AND FACULTY

Enrollment: 359. **Student Body:** 52% female, 48% male, 17% out-of-state. African American 11%, Asian 4%, Caucasian 31%, Hispanic 51%. **Retention and Graduation:** 50% grads pursue arts and sciences degrees. **Faculty:** Student/faculty ratio 10:1. 20 full-time faculty, 100% hold PhDs. 100% faculty teach undergrads.

ACADEMICS

Degrees: Associate, bachelor's. **Academic Requirements:** Arts/fine arts, computer literacy, English (including composition), foreign languages, humanities, mathematics, sciences (biological or physical), social science. **Majors with Highest Enrollment:** Dance, graphic design. **Disciplines with Highest Percentage of Degrees Awarded:** Visual and performing arts 100%. **Special Study Options:** Cooperative education program, distance learning, English as a second language (ESL), independent study, liberal arts/career combination.

FACILITIES

Special Academic Facilities/Equipment: Black box theater, art gallery, dance recital hall. **Computers:** 67% of public computers are PCs, 33% of public computers are Macs, online registration, online administrative functions (other than registration), remote student-access to Web through college's connection.

CAMPUS LIFE

Activities: Dance, drama/theater, music ensembles, musical theater, opera, student government, symphony orchestra.

ADMISSIONS

Freshman Academic Profile: 99% from public high schools. TOEFL required of all international applicants, minimum paper TOEFL 550, minimum computer TOEFL 213. **Basis for Candidate Selection:** *Very important factors considered include:* Talent/ability. *Other factors considered include:* Application essay, character/personal qualities, interview, recommendation(s), rigor of secondary school record. **Freshman Admission Requirements:** High school diploma is required, and GED is accepted. **Freshman Admission Statistics:** 287 applied, 61% admitted, 64% enrolled. **Transfer Admission Requirements:** High school transcript, college transcript(s), essay or personal statement, interview. Lowest grade transferable C. **General Admission Information:** Non-fall registration not accepted. Common Application not accepted. Credit and/or placement offered for CEEB Advanced Placement tests.

COSTS AND FINANCIAL AID

Annual in-state tuition $10,000. Out-of-state tuition $15,000. Average book expense $600. **Required Forms and Deadlines:** FAFSA. **Types of Aid:** *Need-based scholarships/grants:* Pell, SEOG, state scholarships/grants, private scholarships, the school's own gift aid. *Loans:* Direct Subsidized Stafford, Direct Unsubsidized Stafford, Direct PLUS, FFEL PLUS, Federal Perkins, state loans, college/university loans from institutional funds. **Student Employment:** Federal Work-Study Program available. Off-campus job opportunities are excellent.

NEW YORK INSTITUTE OF TECHNOLOGY

PO Box 8000, Northern Boulevard, Old Westbury, NY 11568
Phone: 516-686-7520 **E-mail:** admissions@nyit.edu **CEEB Code:** 2561
Fax: 516-686-7613 **Website:** www.nyit.edu **ACT Code:** 2832
Financial Aid Phone: 516-686-7680

This private school was founded in 1955. It has a 525-acre campus.

RATINGS
Admissions Selectivity Rating: 70   **Fire Safety Rating:** 60*   **Green Rating:** 60*

STUDENTS AND FACULTY
Enrollment: 5,141. **Student Body:** 38% female, 62% male, 10% out-of-state, 7% international. African American 11%, Asian 10%, Caucasian 33%, Hispanic 10%. **Retention and Graduation:** 71% freshmen return for sophomore year. 14% freshmen graduate within 4 years. 29% grads go on to further study within 1 year. 21% grads pursue arts and sciences degrees. 33% grads pursue business degrees. 1% grads pursue law degrees. 2% grads pursue medical degrees. **Faculty:** Student/faculty ratio 16:1. 218 full-time faculty, 89% hold PhDs. 90% faculty teach undergrads.

ACADEMICS
Degrees: Associate, bachelor's, certificate, first professional, master's, post-bachelor's certificate, post-master's certificate, terminal. **Academic Requirements:** Behavioral sciences, computer literacy, economics, English (including composition), history, mathematics, philosophy, sciences (biological or physical), speech. All entering first-year freshman, transfer students with fewer than 12 credits, and students on probation are required to complete the college success seminar. Also, 1 course selected from either social science, fine arts, communication arts, or other liberal arts subject area. **Classes:** Most classes have 10–19 students. Most lab/discussion sections have 10–19 students. **Majors with Highest Enrollment:** Architecture (BArch, BA/BS, MArch, MA/MS, PhD); business, management, marketing, and related support services; communications studies/speech communication and rhetoric. **Disciplines with Highest Percentage of Degrees Awarded:** Business/marketing 21%, architecture 14%, communication technologies 9%, engineering 9%, health professions and related sciences 9%, computer and information sciences 8%, visual and performing arts 8%, interdisciplinary studies 6%. **Special Study Options:** Accelerated program, cooperative education program, cross-registration, distance learning, double major, dual enrollment, English as a second language (ESL), honors program, independent study, internships, liberal arts/career combination, study abroad, teacher certification program, weekend college. Combined bachelor's/professional degree program in life sciences (BS)/osteopathic medicine (DO), architectural technology (BS)/energy management (MS), architectural technology (BS)/MBA, mechanical engineering (BS)/energy management (MS), life sciences (BS)/physical therapy (MS), life sciences (BS)/occupational therapy (MS), behavioral sciences (BS)/law at Touro Law Center (JD).

FACILITIES
Housing: Coed dorms, apartments for single students, special housing for international students, fraternity/sorority housing, housing for graduate, life sciences, first-year experience, student leaders, student government, international, Greek life organizations. **Special Academic Facilities/Equipment:** Center for urban/suburban studies, center for neighborhood revitalization, Parkinson's disease treatment center, center for energy policy & research, academic computing labs, center for labor and industrial relations, Carleton Group (advertising), LI News Tonight, education enterprise zone, center for teaching and learning with technology, production house, motion graphics laboratory, academic health care center, center for business information technologies, de Seversky Culinary Arts Center. **Computers:** 75% of public computers are PCs, 25% of public computers are Macs, 10% of public computers are UNIX, network access in dorm rooms, network access in dorm lounges, online registration, online administrative functions (other than registration), remote student-access to Web through college's connection. Undergraduates are required to own a computer.

CAMPUS LIFE
Activities: Choral groups, dance, drama/theater, literary magazine, musical theater, radio station, student government, student newspaper, student-run film society, television station, yearbook. **Organizations:** 100 registered organizations, 14 honor societies, 4 religious organizations, 5 fraternities (2% men join), 3 sororities (1% women join). **Athletics (Intercollegiate):** *Men:* Baseball, basketball, cross-country, lacrosse, soccer, track/field (outdoor). *Women:* Basketball, cross-country, soccer, softball, track/field (outdoor), volleyball.

ADMISSIONS
Freshman Academic Profile: 60% from public high schools. SAT Math middle 50% range 510–630. SAT Critical Reading middle 50% range 470–580. ACT middle 50% range 20–27. TOEFL required of all international applicants, minimum paper TOEFL 550, minimum computer TOEFL 213. **Basis for Candidate Selection:** *Very important factors considered include:* Rigor of secondary school record. *Important factors considered include:* Application essay, interview, standardized test scores. *Other factors considered include:* Character/personal qualities, class rank, extracurricular activities, recommendation(s), talent/ability, volunteer work, work experience. **Freshman Admission Requirements:** High school diploma is required, and GED is accepted. *Academic units required:* 4 English, 2 math, 1 science (1 science lab), 2 social studies, 7 academic electives. *Academic units recommended:* 4 English, 3 math, 2 science (1 science lab), 2 social studies, 7 academic electives. **Freshman Admission Statistics:** 3,511 applied, 76% admitted, 33% enrolled. **Transfer Admission Requirements:** College transcript(s), essay or personal statement. Minimum college GPA of 2.0 required. Lowest grade transferable C-. **General Admission Information:** Application fee $50. Regular notification is rolling. Non-fall registration accepted. Admission may be deferred for a maximum of 1 year. Common Application accepted. Credit and/or placement offered for CEEB Advanced Placement tests.

COSTS AND FINANCIAL AID
Annual tuition $16,926. Room & board $7,780. Required fees $300. Average book expense $1,200. **Required Forms and Deadlines:** FAFSA. Financial aid filing deadline 3/1. **Notification of Awards:** Applicants will be notified of awards on a rolling basis beginning on or about 3/15. **Types of Aid:** *Need-based scholarships/grants:* Pell, SEOG, state scholarships/grants, private scholarships, the school's own gift aid. *Loans:* FFEL Subsidized Stafford, FFEL Unsubsidized Stafford, FFEL PLUS, Federal Perkins, Federal Nursing, alternative loans. **Student Employment:** Federal Work-Study Program available. Institutional employment available. Off-campus job opportunities are good. **Financial Aid Statistics:** 56% freshmen, 79% undergrads receive need-based scholarship or grant aid. 75% freshmen, 84% undergrads receive need-based self-help aid. 38 freshmen, 186 undergrads receive athletic scholarships. Highest amount earned per year from on-campus jobs $2,200.

NEW YORK SCHOOL OF INTERIOR DESIGN

107 East 70th Street, New York, NY 10021
Phone: 212-472-1500 **E-mail:** admissions@nysid.edu **CEEB Code:** 0333
Fax: 212-472-1867 **Website:** www.nysid.edu **ACT Code:** 2829
Financial Aid Phone: 212-472-1500

This private school was founded in 1916.

RATINGS
Admissions Selectivity Rating: 60*   **Fire Safety Rating:** 60*   **Green Rating:** 60*

STUDENTS AND FACULTY
Enrollment: 614. **Student Body:** 93% female, 7% male, 36% out-of-state, 8% international. African American 3%, Asian 7%, Caucasian 74%, Hispanic 6%. **Retention and Graduation:** 60% freshmen return for sophomore year. **Faculty:** Student/faculty ratio 10:1. 2 full-time faculty. 100% faculty teach undergrads.

ACADEMICS
Degrees: Associate, bachelor's, certificate, first professional, master's, transfer. **Academic Requirements:** Arts/fine arts, computer literacy, English (including composition), foreign languages, history, humanities, mathematics, sciences (biological or physical), social science. **Classes:** Most classes have 10–19 students. **Majors with Highest Enrollment:** Interior design. **Disciplines with Highest Percentage of Degrees Awarded:** Visual and performing arts 100%. **Special Study Options:** Independent study, internships, study abroad.

FACILITIES
Special Academic Facilities/Equipment: 3 galleries, lighting laboratory, student atelier. **Computers:** 50% of classrooms are wired, 100% of public computers are PCs, remote student-access to Web through college's connection.

CAMPUS LIFE
Organizations: 1 registered organization.

ADMISSIONS
Freshman Academic Profile: TOEFL required of all international applicants, minimum paper TOEFL 550, minimum computer TOEFL 213. **Basis for Candidate Selection:** *Very important factors considered include:* Application essay, rigor of secondary school record, talent/ability. *Important factors considered include:* Academic GPA, level of applicant's interest, recommendation(s). *Other factors considered include:* Alumni/ae relation, character/personal qualities, class rank, extracurricular activities, interview, standardized test scores, work experience. **Freshman Admission Requirements:** High school diploma is required, and GED is accepted. *Academic units recommended:* 4 English, 2 math, 2 science, 2 foreign language, 2 social studies, 2 history. **Freshman Admission Statistics:** 38 applied, 76% admitted, 34% enrolled. **Transfer Admission Requirements:** College transcript(s), essay or personal statement. Minimum college GPA of 3.0 required. Lowest grade transferable C. **General Admission Information:** Application fee $50. Regular notification 4/1. Nonfall registration accepted. Admission may be deferred for a maximum of 1 year. Credit offered for CEEB Advanced Placement tests.

COSTS AND FINANCIAL AID
Annual tuition $18,600. Required fees $290. **Required Forms and Deadlines:** FAFSA, institution's own financial aid form, state aid form. Financial aid filing deadline 5/1. **Notification of Awards:** Applicants will be notified of awards on a rolling basis beginning on or about 2/1. **Types of Aid:** *Need-based scholarships/grants:* Pell, SEOG, state scholarships/grants, the school's own gift aid. *Loans:* FFEL Subsidized Stafford, FFEL Unsubsidized Stafford, FFEL PLUS. **Student Employment:** Federal Work-Study Program available. Off-campus job opportunities are excellent. **Financial Aid Statistics:** 44% freshmen, 32% undergrads receive need-based scholarship or grant aid. 23% freshmen, 9% undergrads receive need-based self-help aid.

NEW YORK UNIVERSITY

22 Washington Square North, New York, NY 10011
Phone: 212-998-4500 **E-mail:** admissions@nyu.edu/ **CEEB Code:** 2562
Fax: 212-995-4902 **Website:** www.nyu.edu **ACT Code:** 2838
Financial Aid Phone: 212-998-4444

This private school was founded in 1831.

RATINGS
Admissions Selectivity Rating: 96   **Fire Safety Rating:** 74   **Green Rating:** 96

STUDENTS AND FACULTY
Enrollment: 20,604. **Student Body:** 62% female, 38% male, 66% out-of-state, 5% international (145 countries represented). African American 5%, Asian 17%, Caucasian 50%, Hispanic 8%. **Retention and Graduation:** 92% freshmen return for sophomore year. 74% freshmen graduate within 4 years. 25% grads go on to further study within 1 year. 6% grads pursue arts and sciences degrees. 1% grads pursue business degrees. 12% grads pursue law degrees. 8% grads pursue medical degrees. **Faculty:** Student/faculty ratio 11:1. 2,073 full-time faculty.

ACADEMICS
Degrees: Associate, bachelor's, certificate, diploma, doctoral, first professional certificate, first professional, master's, post-bachelor's certificate, post-master's certificate, terminal. **Academic Requirements:** Arts/fine arts, English (including composition), foreign languages, history, humanities, mathematics, sciences (biological or physical), social science. **Classes:** Most classes have 10–19 students. Most lab/discussion sections have 10–19 students. **Majors with Highest Enrollment:** Drama and dramatics/theater arts, finance, liberal arts and sciences/liberal studies. **Disciplines with Highest Percentage of Degrees Awarded:** Business/marketing 20%, visual and performing arts 18%, social sciences 16%, communications/journalism 9%, liberal arts/general studies 7%. **Special Study Options:** Cross-registration, distance learning, double major, English as a second language (ESL), exchange student program (domestic), independent study, internships, liberal arts/career combination, student-designed major, study abroad, teacher certification program, weekend college.

FACILITIES
Housing: Coed dorms, apartments for single students, special housing for disabled students, fraternity/sorority housing, substance-free communities, FYRE (first-year residential experience), sophomore-year residential experience, explorations learning communities. **Special Academic Facilities/Equipment:** Bobst Library and study center; Grey Art Gallery and study center; special academic facilities for arts, business, culture, education, international relations, language, law, media, music, public service, research; and social policy; Skirball Center for Performing Arts. **Computers:** 5% of classrooms are wired, 25% of classrooms are wireless, 60% of public computers are PCs, 40% of public computers are Macs, network access in dorm rooms, network access in dorm lounges, online registration, online administrative functions (other than registration), remote student-access to Web through college's connection.

CAMPUS LIFE
Activities: Choral groups, concert band, dance, drama/theater, jazz band, literary magazine, music ensembles, musical theater, opera, pep band, radio station, student government, student newspaper, student-run film society, symphony orchestra, television station, yearbook. **Organizations:** 331 registered organizations, 10 honor societies, 29 religious organizations. 17 fraternities (1% men join), 13 sororities (1% women join). **Athletics (Intercollegiate):** *Men:* Basketball, cheerleading, cross-country, diving, fencing, golf, soccer, swimming, tennis, track/field (indoor), track/field (outdoor), volleyball, wrestling. *Women:* Basketball, cheerleading, cross-country, diving, fencing, soccer, swimming, tennis, track/field (indoor), track/field (outdoor), volleyball. **Environmental Initiatives:** 1) Largest university purchaser of renewable energy two years' running. 2) Launched a comprehensive sustainability initiative that has learned from earlier schools' efforts. 3) Committed to an aggressive 10-year, 30% emissions reduction.

ADMISSIONS
Freshman Academic Profile: 67% in top 10% of high school class, 95% in top 25% of high school class, 100% in top 50% of high school class. 68% from public high schools. SAT Math middle 50% range 610–710. SAT Critical Reading middle 50% range 600–700. SAT Writing middle 50% range 600–700. ACT middle 50% range 27–31. TOEFL required of all international applicants, minimum paper TOEFL 600, minimum computer TOEFL 250. **Basis for Candidate Selection:** *Very important factors considered include:* Academic GPA, recommendation(s), rigor of secondary school record, standardized test scores. *Important factors considered include:* Application essay, character/personal qualities, class rank, extracurricular activities, talent/ability. *Other factors considered include:* Alumni/ae relation, first generation, level of applicant's interest, racial/ethnic status, volunteer work, work experience. **Freshman Admission Requirements:** High school diploma is required, and GED is accepted. *Academic units required:* 4 English, 3 math, 3 science (2 science labs), 2 foreign language, 4 history. *Academic units recommended:* 4 math, 3 foreign language. **Freshman Admission Statistics:** 35,448 applied, 36% admitted, 37% enrolled. **Transfer Admission Requirements:** High school transcript, college transcript(s), essay or personal statement, standardized test score, statement of good standing from prior institution(s). Lowest grade transferable C. **General Admission Information:** Application fee $65. Early decision application deadline 11/1. Regular application deadline 1/15. Regular notification 4/1. Non-fall registration accepted. Admission may be deferred for a maximum of 1 year. Credit offered for CEEB Advanced Placement tests.

COSTS AND FINANCIAL AID
Required Forms and Deadlines: FAFSA, state aid form. Early decision applicants may submit an institutional form for an estimated award. Financial aid filing deadline 2/15. **Notification of Awards:** Applicants will be notified of awards on a rolling basis beginning on or about 4/1. **Types of Aid:** *Need-based scholarships/grants:* Pell, SEOG, state scholarships/grants, private scholarships, the school's own gift aid. *Loans:* FFEL Subsidized Stafford, FFEL Unsubsidized Stafford, FFEL PLUS, Federal Perkins, Federal Nursing. **Student Employment:** Federal Work-Study Program available. Institutional employment available. Off-campus job opportunities are excellent. **Financial Aid Statistics:** 48% freshmen, 48% undergrads receive need-based scholarship or grant aid. 49% freshmen, 48% undergrads receive need-based self-help aid. 60% freshmen, 59% undergrads receive any aid.

See page 1286.

NEWBERRY COLLEGE

2100 College Street, Newberry, SC 29108
Phone: 803-321-5127 **E-mail:** admissions@newberry.edu **CEEB Code:** 5493
Fax: 803-321-5138 **Website:** www.newberry.edu **ACT Code:** 3870
Financial Aid Phone: 803-321-5120

This private school, affiliated with the Lutheran Church, was founded in 1856. It has a 60-acre campus.

RATINGS
Admissions Selectivity Rating: 72   **Fire Safety Rating:** 60*   **Green Rating:** 60*

STUDENTS AND FACULTY
Enrollment: 764. **Student Body:** 43% female, 57% male, 25% out-of-state, 2% international (8 countries represented). African American 27%, Caucasian 71%, Hispanic 1%. **Retention and Graduation:** 58% freshmen return for sophomore year. 36% freshmen graduate within 4 years. 15% grads go on to further study within 1 year. **Faculty:** Student/faculty ratio 13:1. 46 full-time faculty, 61% hold PhDs. 100% faculty teach undergrads.

ACADEMICS
Degrees: Bachelor's. **Academic Requirements:** Arts/fine arts, computer literacy, English (including composition), foreign languages, history, humanities, mathematics, religion, sciences (biological or physical), social science, speech. **Classes:** Most classes have fewer than 10 students. Most lab/discussion sections have 20–29 students. **Majors with Highest Enrollment:** Business administration/management, communications studies/speech communication and rhetoric, elementary education and teaching. **Disciplines with Highest Percentage of Degrees Awarded:** Education 17%, parks and recreation 13%, social sciences 13%, psychology 10%, communication technologies 10%, business/marketing 10%, biological/life sciences 7%, interdisciplinary studies 6%. **Special Study Options:** Cooperative education program, double major, dual enrollment, honors program, independent study, internships, liberal arts/career combination, student-designed major, study abroad, teacher certification program.

FACILITIES
Housing: Coed dorms, men's dorms, women's dorms. **Special Academic Facilities/Equipment:** TV studio. **Computers:** 99% of public computers are PCs, 1% of public computers are Macs, network access in dorm rooms, remote student-access to Web through college's connection.

CAMPUS LIFE
Activities: Choral groups, concert band, drama/theater, jazz band, literary magazine, marching band, music ensembles, radio station, student government, student newspaper, television station, yearbook. **Organizations:** 50 registered organizations, 11 honor societies, 4 religious organizations. 5 fraternities (36% men join), 4 sororities (25% women join). **Athletics (Intercollegiate):** *Men:* Baseball, basketball, cross-country, football, golf, soccer, tennis. *Women:* Basketball, cheerleading, cross-country, golf, soccer, softball, tennis, volleyball.

ADMISSIONS
Freshman Academic Profile: 7% in top 10% of high school class, 22% in top 25% of high school class, 61% in top 50% of high school class. 88% from public high schools. SAT Math middle 50% range 460–600. SAT Critical Reading middle 50% range 490–570. ACT middle 50% range 17–22. TOEFL required of all international applicants, minimum paper TOEFL 525, minimum computer TOEFL 197. **Basis for Candidate Selection:** *Very important factors considered include:* Rigor of secondary school record, standardized test scores. *Important factors considered include:* Class rank. *Other factors considered include:* Alumni/ae relation, application essay, character/personal qualities, extracurricular activities, geographical residence, interview, racial/ethnic status, recommendation(s), religious affiliation/commitment, state residency, talent/ability, volunteer work. **Freshman Admission Requirements:** High school diploma is required, and GED is accepted. *Academic units required:* 4 English, 3 math, 2 science (2 science labs), 2 foreign language, 2 social studies, 1 history, 1 academic elective. *Academic units recommended:* 4 English, 3 math, 2 science (2 science labs), 2 foreign language, 2 social studies, 1 history, 1 academic elective. **Freshman Admission Statistics:** 677 applied, 84% admitted, 41% enrolled. **Transfer Admission Requirements:** College transcript(s). Minimum college GPA of 2.0 required. Lowest grade transferable C. **General Admission Information:** Application fee $30. Regular notification is rolling. Non-fall registration accepted. Admission may be deferred for a maximum of 2 years. Common Application accepted. Credit and/or placement offered for CEEB Advanced Placement tests.

COSTS AND FINANCIAL AID
Annual tuition $17,470. Room & board $5,890. Required fees $631. Average book expense $1,195. **Required Forms and Deadlines:** FAFSA, institution's

own financial aid form. Financial aid filing deadline 3/15. **Types of Aid:** *Need-based scholarships/grants:* Pell, SEOG, state scholarships/grants, private scholarships, the school's own gift aid. *Loans:* FFEL Subsidized Stafford, FFEL Unsubsidized Stafford, FFEL PLUS, Federal Perkins, state loans. **Student Employment:** Federal Work-Study Program available. Institutional employment available. Off-campus job opportunities are poor. **Financial Aid Statistics:** 83% freshmen, 84% undergrads receive need-based scholarship or grant aid. 56% freshmen, 59% undergrads receive need-based self-help aid. 33 freshmen, 79 undergrads receive athletic scholarships.

NEWMAN UNIVERSITY

3100 McCormick Avenue, Wichita, KS 67213-2097
Phone: 316-942-4291 **E-mail:** admissions@newmanu.edu **CEEB Code:** 6615
Fax: 316-942-4483 **Website:** www.newmanu.edu **ACT Code:** 1452
Financial Aid Phone: 316-942-4291

This private school was founded in 1933. It has a 53-acre campus.

RATINGS
Admissions Selectivity Rating: 76   **Fire Safety Rating:** 60*   **Green Rating:** 60*

STUDENTS AND FACULTY
Enrollment: 1,843. **Student Body:** 62% female, 38% male, 11% out-of-state, 6% international (26 countries represented). African American 5%, Asian 3%, Caucasian 77%, Hispanic 7%, Native American 2%. **Faculty:** Student/faculty ratio 17:1. 66 full-time faculty. 85% faculty teach undergrads.

ACADEMICS
Degrees: Associate, bachelor's, master's, terminal. **Academic Requirements:** Arts/fine arts, English (including composition), history, humanities, mathematics, philosophy, sciences (biological or physical), social science, theology. **Classes:** Most classes have 10–19 students. Most lab/discussion sections have 10–19 students. **Special Study Options:** Cooperative education program, cross-registration, distance learning, double major, dual enrollment, independent study, internships, liberal arts/career combination, student-designed major, study abroad, teacher certification program, weekend college.

FACILITIES
Housing: Coed dorms, apartments for married students, apartments for single students, special housing for disabled students. Freshmen are required to live in college housing for the first 2 years if not living with parents. **Special Academic Facilities/Equipment:** Cadaver lab, art gallery. **Computers:** 100% of public computers are PCs, network access in dorm rooms, network access in dorm lounges, remote student-access to Web through college's connection.

CAMPUS LIFE
Activities: Choral groups, drama/theater, literary magazine, radio station, student government, student newspaper. **Organizations:** 25 registered organizations, 3 honor societies, 2 religious organizations. **Athletics (Intercollegiate):** *Men:* Baseball, basketball, golf, soccer. *Women:* Basketball, golf, soccer, softball, volleyball.

ADMISSIONS
Freshman Academic Profile: 12% in top 10% of high school class, 26% in top 25% of high school class, 52% in top 50% of high school class. 78% from public high schools. TOEFL required of all international applicants, minimum paper TOEFL 530. **Basis for Candidate Selection:** *Very important factors considered include:* Rigor of secondary school record, standardized test scores. *Other factors considered include:* recommendation(s). **Freshman Admission Requirements:** High school diploma is required, and GED is accepted. *Academic units recommended:* 4 English, 3 math, 3 science, 3 social studies. **Freshman Admission Statistics:** 554 applied, 34% admitted, 100% enrolled. **Transfer Admission Requirements:** College transcript(s). Minimum college GPA of 2.0 required. Lowest grade transferable D. **General Admission Information:** Application fee $20. Regular notification is rolling. Non-fall registration accepted. Admission may be deferred for a maximum of 2 years. Common Application not accepted. Credit offered for CEEB Advanced Placement tests.

COSTS AND FINANCIAL AID
Annual tuition $14,650. Room & board $5,060. Required fees $180. Average book expense $800. **Required Forms and Deadlines:** FAFSA, institution's own financial aid form. Financial aid filing deadline 3/1. **Notification of Awards:** Applicants will be notified of awards on a rolling basis beginning on or about 1/2. **Types of Aid:** *Need-based scholarships/grants:* Pell, SEOG, state scholarships/grants, private scholarships, the school's own gift aid. *Loans:* FFEL Subsidized Stafford, FFEL Unsubsidized Stafford, FFEL PLUS, Federal

Perkins. **Financial Aid Statistics:** 51% freshmen, 60% undergrads receive need-based scholarship or grant aid. 47% freshmen, 60% undergrads receive need-based self-help aid. 70 freshmen, 335 undergrads receive athletic scholarships. Highest amount earned per year from on-campus jobs $1,200.

NIAGARA UNIVERSITY

Bailo Hall, PO Box 2011, Niagara University, NY 14109
Phone: 716-286-8700 **E-mail:** admissions@niagara.edu **CEEB Code:** 2558
Fax: 716-286-8710 **Website:** www.niagara.edu **ACT Code:** 2842
Financial Aid Phone: 716-286-8686

This private school, affiliated with the Roman Catholic Church, was founded in 1856. It has a 160-acre campus.

RATINGS
Admissions Selectivity Rating: 76   **Fire Safety Rating:** 60*   **Green Rating:** 60*

STUDENTS AND FACULTY
Enrollment: 2,915. **Student Body:** 60% female, 40% male, 7% out-of-state, 5% international (12 countries represented). African American 4%, Asian 1%, Caucasian 79%, Hispanic 2%. **Retention and Graduation:** 79% freshmen return for sophomore year. 55% freshmen graduate within 4 years. 33% grads go on to further study within 1 year. 37% grads pursue arts and sciences degrees. 14% grads pursue business degrees. 8% grads pursue law degrees. 4% grads pursue medical degrees. **Faculty:** Student/faculty ratio 16:1. 145 full-time faculty, 94% hold PhDs. 97% faculty teach undergrads.

ACADEMICS
Degrees: Associate, bachelor's, certificate, master's, post-bachelor's certificate, post-master's certificate. **Academic Requirements:** English (including composition), history, humanities, mathematics, philosophy, sciences (biological or physical), social science. **Classes:** Most classes have 10–19 students. Most lab/discussion sections have 10–19 students. **Majors with Highest Enrollment:** Business/commerce, criminal justice/law enforcement administration, teacher education (multiple levels). **Disciplines with Highest Percentage of Degrees Awarded:** Business/marketing 35%, education 20%, security and protective services 8%, social sciences 6%. **Special Study Options:** Accelerated program, cooperative education program, cross-registration, double major, dual enrollment, English as a second language (ESL), exchange student program (domestic), honors program, independent study, internships, liberal arts/career combination, study abroad, teacher certification program.

FACILITIES
Housing: Coed dorms, apartments for single students. **Special Academic Facilities/Equipment:** Castellani Art Museum. **Computers:** Network access in dorm rooms, online registration, remote student-access to Web through college's connection.

CAMPUS LIFE
Activities: Choral groups, dance, drama/theater, musical theater, radio station, student government, student newspaper, yearbook. **Organizations:** 70 registered organizations, 14 honor societies, 2 religious organizations. 3 fraternities (4% men join), 2 sororities (2% women join). **Athletics (Intercollegiate):** *Men:* Baseball, basketball, cross-country, diving, golf, ice hockey, soccer, swimming, tennis. *Women:* Basketball, cross-country, diving, ice hockey, lacrosse, soccer, softball, swimming, tennis, volleyball.

ADMISSIONS
Freshman Academic Profile: 14% in top 10% of high school class, 42% in top 25% of high school class, 77% in top 50% of high school class. SAT Math middle 50% range 470–570. SAT Critical Reading middle 50% range 480–590. ACT middle 50% range 19–25. TOEFL required of all international applicants, minimum paper TOEFL 500, minimum computer TOEFL 173. **Basis for Candidate Selection:** *Very important factors considered include:* Rigor of secondary school record. *Important factors considered include:* Interview, recommendation(s), standardized test scores. *Other factors considered include:* Alumni/ae relation, application essay, character/personal qualities, class rank, extracurricular activities, talent/ability, volunteer work. **Freshman Admission Requirements:** High school diploma is required, and GED is accepted. *Academic units required:* 4 English, 2 math, 2 science, 2 foreign language, 2 social studies, 4 academic electives. **Freshman Admission Statistics:** 3,115 applied, 76% admitted, 30% enrolled. **Transfer Admission Requirements:** High school transcript, college transcript(s). Minimum college GPA of 2.0 required. Lowest grade transferable C. **General Admission Information:** Application fee $30. Regular application deadline 8/1. Regular notification is rolling. Non-fall registration accepted. Admission may be deferred for a

maximum of 1 year. Credit and/or placement offered for CEEB Advanced Placement tests.

COSTS AND FINANCIAL AID
Annual tuition $21,400. Room and board $9,300. Required fees $900. Average book expense $900. **Required Forms and Deadlines:** FAFSA, state aid form. Financial aid filing deadline 2/15. **Notification of Awards:** Applicants will be notified of awards on a rolling basis beginning on or about 3/1. **Types of Aid:** *Need-based scholarships/grants:* Pell, SEOG, state scholarships/grants, private scholarships, the school's own gift aid. *Loans:* Direct Subsidized Stafford, Direct Unsubsidized Stafford, Direct PLUS, Federal Perkins, Federal Nursing, state loans, college/university loans from institutional funds. **Student Employment:** Federal Work-Study Program available. Off-campus job opportunities are excellent. **Financial Aid Statistics:** 81% freshmen, 75% undergrads receive need-based scholarship or grant aid. 69% freshmen, 72% undergrads receive need-based self-help aid. 22 freshmen, 123 undergrads receive athletic scholarships. 82% freshmen, 79% undergrads receive any aid.

See page 1288.

NICHOLLS STATE UNIVERSITY

PO Box 2004, Thibodaux, LA 70310
Phone: 985-448-4507 **E-mail:** nicholls@nicholls.edu **CEEB Code:** 6221
Fax: 985-448-4929 **Website:** www.nicholls.edu **ACT Code:** 1580
Financial Aid Phone: 985-448-4048

This public school was founded in 1948. It has a 210-acre campus.

RATINGS
Admissions Selectivity Rating: 75   **Fire Safety Rating:** 75   **Green Rating:** 60*

STUDENTS AND FACULTY
Enrollment: 6,086. **Student Body:** 62% female, 38% male, 4% out-of-state. African American 18%, Asian 1%, Caucasian 74%, Hispanic 2%, Native American 2%. **Retention and Graduation:** 65% freshmen return for sophomore year. **Faculty:** Student/faculty ratio 20:1. 283 full-time faculty, 56% hold PhDs. 100% faculty teach undergrads.

ACADEMICS
Degrees: Associate, bachelor's, certificate, master's, post-master's certificate. **Academic Requirements:** Arts/fine arts, computer literacy, English (including composition), history, humanities, mathematics, sciences (biological or physical), social science. **Classes:** Most classes have 20–29 students. **Majors with Highest Enrollment:** Business administration and management, general studies, nursing/registered nurse training (ASN, BSN, MSN, RN). **Disciplines with Highest Percentage of Degrees Awarded:** Business/marketing 25%, health professions and related sciences 21%, education 13%, liberal arts/general studies 9%, family and consumer sciences 6%, social sciences 6%. **Special Study Options:** Cooperative education program, cross-registration, distance learning, dual enrollment, honors program, independent study, internships, study abroad, teacher certification program.

FACILITIES
Housing: Men's dorms, women's dorms, apartments for married students, special housing for disabled students, special housing for international students, privatized housing. **Special Academic Facilities/Equipment:** Ameen Art Gallery. **Computers:** 100% of classrooms are wired, 60% of classrooms are wireless, 5% of public computers are PCs, 95% of public computers are Macs, network access in dorm rooms, network access in dorm lounges, online registration, online administrative functions (other than registration), remote student-access to Web through college's connection.

CAMPUS LIFE
Activities: Choral groups, concert band, dance, drama/theater, jazz band, literary magazine, marching band, music ensembles, musical theater, radio station, student government, student newspaper, student-run film society, television station, yearbook. **Organizations:** 76 registered organizations, 11 honor societies, 3 religious organizations. 9 fraternities (3% men join), 7 sororities (3% women join). **Athletics (Intercollegiate):** *Men:* Baseball, basketball, cross-country, football, golf, tennis. *Women:* Basketball, cross-country, golf, soccer, softball, tennis, track/field (indoor), track/field (outdoor), volleyball.

ADMISSIONS
Freshman Academic Profile: 37% in top 10% of high school class, 46% in top 25% of high school class, 61% in top 50% of high school class. 68% from public high schools. ACT middle 50% range 19–23. TOEFL required of all international applicants, minimum paper TOEFL 500, minimum computer TOEFL

173. **Basis for Candidate Selection:** *Very important factors considered include:* Rigor of secondary school record. *Important factors considered include:* Standardized test scores. *Other factors considered include:* Academic GPA, class rank, talent/ability. **Freshman Admission Requirements:** High school diploma is required, and GED is accepted. *Academic units required:* 4 English, 3 math, 3 science, 2 foreign language, 1 social studies, 2 history, 1 academic elective. **Freshman Admission Statistics:** 2,075 applied, 87% admitted, 62% enrolled. **Transfer Admission Requirements:** College transcript(s). Minimum college GPA of 2.0 required. Lowest grade transferable D. **General Admission Information:** Application fee $20. Regular notification is rolling. Non-fall registration accepted. Admission may be deferred for a maximum of 1 semester. Credit and/or placement offered for CEEB Advanced Placement tests.

COSTS AND FINANCIAL AID

Annual in-state tuition $2,231. Out-of-state tuition $7,679. Room & board $4,038. Required fees $1,240. Average book expense $1,000. **Required Forms and Deadlines:** FAFSA, institution's own financial aid form, state aid form, Noncustodial PROFILE. Financial aid filing deadline 6/30. **Types of Aid:** *Need-based scholarships/grants:* Pell, SEOG, state scholarships/grants, private scholarships, the school's own gift aid. *Loans:* FFEL Subsidized Stafford, FFEL Unsubsidized Stafford, FFEL PLUS, Federal Perkins. **Student Employment:** Federal Work-Study Program available. Institutional employment available. Off-campus job opportunities are fair. **Financial Aid Statistics:** 42% freshmen, 41% undergrads receive need-based scholarship or grant aid. 27% freshmen, 37% undergrads receive need-based self-help aid. 31 freshmen, 126 undergrads receive athletic scholarships. 65% freshmen, 46% undergrads receive any aid. Highest amount earned per year from on-campus jobs $7,289.

NICHOLS COLLEGE

PO Box 5000, 124 Center Road, Dudley, MA 01571-5000
Phone: 508-213-2203 **E-mail:** admissions@nichols.edu **CEEB Code:** 3666
Fax: 508-943-9885 **Website:** www.nichols.edu **ACT Code:** 1878
Financial Aid Phone: 508-213-2378

This private school was founded in 1815. It has a 200-acre campus.

RATINGS
Admissions Selectivity Rating: 66   **Fire Safety Rating:** 60*   **Green Rating:** 60*

STUDENTS AND FACULTY
Enrollment: 1,432. **Student Body:** 42% female, 58% male, 35% out-of-state. African American 7%, Asian 2%, Caucasian 88%, Hispanic 4%. **Retention and Graduation:** 7% grads go on to further study within 1 year. 2% grads pursue business degrees. **Faculty:** Student/faculty ratio 20:1. 38 full-time faculty, 87% hold PhDs. 100% faculty teach undergrads.

ACADEMICS
Degrees: Associate, bachelor's, master's. **Academic Requirements:** Arts/fine arts, computer literacy, English (including composition), history, humanities, mathematics, philosophy, sciences (biological or physical), social science. **Majors with Highest Enrollment:** Business administration/management, criminal justice/law enforcement administration, sports and fitness administration/management. **Disciplines with Highest Percentage of Degrees Awarded:** Business/marketing 90%, liberal arts/general studies 10%. **Special Study Options:** Cooperative education program, distance learning, double major, independent study, internships, liberal arts/career combination, study abroad, teacher certification program.

FACILITIES
Housing: Coed dorms. **Computers:** 100% of classrooms are wired, 100% of public computers are PCs, 5% of public computers are UNIX, network access in dorm rooms, network access in dorm lounges, online registration, online administrative functions (other than registration), remote student-access to Web through college's connection.

CAMPUS LIFE
Activities: Drama/theater, literary magazine, musical theater, radio station, student government, student newspaper, yearbook. **Organizations:** 25 registered organizations, 7 honor societies, 1 religious organization. **Athletics (Intercollegiate):** *Men:* Baseball, basketball, football, golf, ice hockey, lacrosse, soccer, tennis. *Women:* Basketball, cheerleading, field hockey, golf, lacrosse, soccer, softball, tennis.

ADMISSIONS
Freshman Academic Profile: 2% in top 10% of high school class, 25% in top 25% of high school class, 49% in top 50% of high school class. 82% from public

high schools. SAT Math middle 50% range 420–520. SAT Critical Reading middle 50% range 400–490. SAT Writing middle 50% range 418–473. TOEFL required of all international applicants, minimum paper TOEFL 550, minimum computer TOEFL 213. **Basis for Candidate Selection:** *Very important factors considered include:* Application essay, rigor of secondary school record. *Important factors considered include:* Interview, recommendation(s), standardized test scores. *Other factors considered include:* Character/personal qualities, class rank, extracurricular activities, talent/ability, volunteer work, work experience. **Freshman Admission Requirements:** High school diploma is required, and GED is accepted. *Academic units required:* 4 English, 3 math, 2 science (2 science labs), 2 social studies, 5 academic electives. *Academic units recommended:* 4 math, 3 science (3 science labs), 2 foreign language. **Freshman Admission Statistics:** 1,155 applied, 86% admitted, 31% enrolled. **Transfer Admission Requirements:** High school transcript, college transcript(s), essay or personal statement. Minimum college GPA of 2.0 required. Lowest grade transferable C. **General Admission Information:** Application fee $25. Regular notification is rolling. Non-fall registration accepted. Admission may be deferred for a maximum of 1 year. Common Application accepted. Neither credit nor placement offered for CEEB Advanced Placement tests.

COSTS AND FINANCIAL AID
Annual tuition $25,400. Room and board $8,960. Required fees $300. Average book expense $1,050. **Required Forms and Deadlines:** FAFSA. Financial aid filing deadline 6/1. **Notification of Awards:** Applicants will be notified of awards on or about 3/15. **Types of Aid:** *Need-based scholarships/grants:* Pell, SEOG, state scholarships/grants, private scholarships. *Loans:* FFEL Subsidized Stafford, FFEL Unsubsidized Stafford, FFEL PLUS, state loans. **Student Employment:** Federal Work-Study Program available. Institutional employment available. Off-campus job opportunities are fair. **Financial Aid Statistics:** 82% freshmen, 76% undergrads receive need-based scholarship or grant aid. 72% freshmen, 69% undergrads receive need-based self-help aid. 70% freshmen, 73% undergrads receive any aid. Highest amount earned per year from on-campus jobs $3,000.

See page 1290.

NORFOLK STATE UNIVERSITY

700 Park Avenue, Norfolk, VA 23504
Phone: 757-823-8396 **E-mail:** admissions@nsu.edu **CEEB Code:** 5864
Fax: 757-823-2078 **Website:** www.nsu.edu **ACT Code:** 4425
Financial Aid Phone: 757-823-8381

This public school was founded in 1935. It has a 134-acre campus.

RATINGS
Admissions Selectivity Rating: 68   **Fire Safety Rating:** 60*   **Green Rating:** 60*

STUDENTS AND FACULTY
Enrollment: 5,810. **Student Body:** 62% female, 38% male, 31% out-of-state. African American 92%, Caucasian 4%, Hispanic 1%. **Retention and Graduation:** 71% freshmen return for sophomore year. 10% freshmen graduate within 4 years. 7% grads go on to further study within 1 year. **Faculty:** Student/faculty ratio 16:1. 314 full-time faculty, 58% hold PhDs. 100% faculty teach undergrads.

ACADEMICS
Degrees: Associate, bachelor's, certificate, doctoral, master's. **Academic Requirements:** Arts/fine arts, computer literacy, cultural electives, English (including composition), health and communication, history, humanities, mathematics, sciences (biological or physical), social science. **Classes:** Most classes have 10–19 students. **Majors with Highest Enrollment:** Business administration/management, computer and information sciences, psychology. **Disciplines with Highest Percentage of Degrees Awarded:** Interdisciplinary studies 21%, business/marketing 18%, social sciences 13%, communication technologies 8%, health professions and related sciences 7%. **Special Study Options:** Accelerated program, cooperative education program, cross-registration, distance learning, double major, dual enrollment, honors program, independent study, internships, study abroad, teacher certification program.

FACILITIES
Housing: Men's dorms, women's dorms. **Special Academic Facilities/Equipment:** Museum, performing arts, center research computer labs, L. Douglas Wilder Fine Arts Center, center for materials research. **Computers:** 100% of public computers are PCs, remote student-access to Web through college's connection.

CAMPUS LIFE

Activities: Choral groups, concert band, dance, drama/theater, jazz band, marching band, music ensembles, radio station, student government, student newspaper, symphony orchestra, television station, yearbook. **Organizations:** 112 registered organizations, 16 honor societies, 4 religious organizations. 12 fraternities (10% men join), 8 sororities (10% women join). **Athletics (Intercollegiate):** *Men:* Baseball, basketball, cross-country, football, tennis, track/field (indoor), track/field (outdoor). *Women:* Basketball, cross-country, softball, tennis, track/field (indoor), track/field (outdoor), volleyball.

ADMISSIONS

Freshman Academic Profile: 4% in top 10% of high school class, 20% in top 25% of high school class, 54% in top 50% of high school class. SAT Math middle 50% range 390–470. SAT Critical Reading middle 50% range 400–470. ACT middle 50% range 16–19. TOEFL required of all international applicants, minimum paper TOEFL 500. **Basis for Candidate Selection:** *Very important factors considered include:* Recommendation(s), rigor of secondary school record, standardized test scores. *Important factors considered include:* Class rank. *Other factors considered include:* Alumni/ae relation, extracurricular activities, interview, state residency, talent/ability. **Freshman Admission Requirements:** High school diploma is required, and GED is accepted. *Academic units recommended:* 4 English, 3 math, 3 science, 3 history, 9 academic electives. **Freshman Admission Statistics:** 4,700 applied, 77% admitted, 32% enrolled. **Transfer Admission Requirements:** College transcript(s), statement of good standing from prior institution(s). Minimum college GPA of 2.0 required. Lowest grade transferable C. **General Admission Information:** Application fee $25. Regular application deadline 7/1. Regular notification within 2 weeks of receipt of credentials. Non-fall registration accepted. Admission may be deferred for a maximum of 1 year. Common Application not accepted. Credit and/or placement offered for CEEB Advanced Placement tests.

COSTS AND FINANCIAL AID

Annual in-state tuition $1,658. Out-of-state tuition $10,065. Room & board $5,588. Required fees $1,638. Average book expense $1,000. **Required Forms and Deadlines:** FAFSA. Financial aid filing deadline 4/15. **Notification of Awards:** Applicants will be notified of awards on a rolling basis beginning on or about 2/1. **Types of Aid:** *Need-based scholarships/grants:* Pell, SEOG, state scholarships/grants, private scholarships, the school's own gift aid. *Loans:* Direct Subsidized Stafford, Direct Unsubsidized Stafford, FFEL PLUS, Federal Perkins, state loans, alternative loans. **Student Employment:** Federal Work-Study Program available. Institutional employment available. Off-campus job opportunities are good. **Financial Aid Statistics:** 68% freshmen, 57% undergrads receive need-based scholarship or grant aid. 57% freshmen, 55% undergrads receive need-based self-help aid.

NORTH CAROLINA AGRICULTURE AND TECHNICAL STATE UNIVERSITY

1601 East Market Street, Greensboro, NC 27411
Phone: 336-334-7946 **E-mail:** uadmit@ncat.edu **CEEB Code:** 5003
Fax: 336-334-7478 **Website:** www.ncat.edu **ACT Code:** 3060
Financial Aid Phone: 800-443-0835

This public school was founded in 1891. It has a 181-acre campus.

RATINGS

Admissions Selectivity Rating: 68   **Fire Safety Rating:** 60*   **Green Rating:** 60*

STUDENTS AND FACULTY

Enrollment: 7,245. **Student Body:** 52% female, 48% male, 19% out-of-state. African American 92%, Caucasian 5%. **Retention and Graduation:** 77% freshmen return for sophomore year. 24% freshmen graduate within 4 years. 10% grads go on to further study within 1 year. 6% grads pursue arts and sciences degrees. 1% grads pursue business degrees. 1% grads pursue law degrees. 2% grads pursue medical degrees. **Faculty:** Student/faculty ratio 16:1. 404 full-time faculty, 90% hold PhDs.

ACADEMICS

Degrees: Bachelor's, doctoral, master's. **Academic Requirements:** Arts/fine arts, computer literacy, English (including composition), foreign languages, history, humanities, mathematics, sciences (biological or physical). **Classes:** Most classes have 20–29 students. **Disciplines with Highest Percentage of Degrees Awarded:** Engineering 22%, business/marketing 18%, education 10%, computer and information sciences 6%, health professions and related sciences 6%, psychology 5%. **Special Study Options:** Cooperative education

program, cross-registration, distance learning, double major, external degree program, honors program, independent study, internships, study abroad, teacher certification program.

FACILITIES

Housing: Coed dorms, men's dorms, women's dorms, honor student housing, graduate housing. **Special Academic Facilities/Equipment:** Art gallery, African heritage center, child development laboratory, microelectronics center of North Carolina, planetarium, herbarium. **Computers:** Network access in dorm rooms.

CAMPUS LIFE

Activities: Choral groups, concert band, dance, drama/theater, jazz band, literary magazine, marching band, music ensembles, musical theater, opera, pep band, radio station, student government, student newspaper, student-run film society, symphony orchestra, television station. **Organizations:** 82 registered organizations, 6 honor societies, 1 religious organization. 4 fraternities (1% men join), 4 sororities (1% women join).

ADMISSIONS

Freshman Academic Profile: 8% in top 10% of high school class, 17% in top 25% of high school class, 49% in top 50% of high school class. SAT Math middle 50% range 510–400. SAT Critical Reading middle 50% range 500–390. ACT middle 50% range 12–18. **Basis for Candidate Selection:** *Very important factors considered include:* Rigor of secondary school record, state residency. *Important factors considered include:* Standardized test scores. *Other factors considered include:* Alumni/ae relation, character/personal qualities, class rank, extracurricular activities, geographical residence, recommendation(s), talent/ ability, volunteer work, work experience. **Freshman Admission Requirements:** High school diploma is required, and GED is accepted. *Academic units required:* 4 English, 3 math, 3 science, 2 social studies, 4 academic electives. **Freshman Admission Statistics:** 4,810 applied, 83% admitted, 44% enrolled. **Transfer Admission Requirements:** High school transcript. Minimum college GPA of 2.0 required. Lowest grade transferable C. **General Admission Information:** Application fee $35. Regular notification is rolling. Non-fall registration accepted. Admission may be deferred for a maximum of 1 semester. Common Application accepted.

COSTS AND FINANCIAL AID

Annual in-state tuition $1,994. Out-of-state tuition $11,436. Room & board $4,470. Required fees $1,017. Average book expense $750. **Required Forms and Deadlines:** FAFSA. Financial aid filing deadline 3/15. **Notification of Awards:** Applicants will be notified of awards on or about 4/15. **Types of Aid:** *Need-based scholarships/grants:* Pell, SEOG, state scholarships/grants, private scholarships, the school's own gift aid, United Negro College Fund, Federal Nursing Scholarships. *Loans:* Direct Subsidized Stafford, Direct Unsubsidized Stafford, Direct PLUS, Federal Perkins, alternative loans. **Student Employment:** Federal Work-Study Program available. Institutional employment available. Off-campus job opportunities are good. **Financial Aid Statistics:** 59% freshmen, 49% undergrads receive need-based scholarship or grant aid. 59% freshmen, 55% undergrads receive need-based self-help aid. 1,512 freshmen, 5,614 undergrads receive athletic scholarships. Highest amount earned per year from on-campus jobs $3,690.

NORTH CAROLINA CENTRAL UNIVERSITY

Fayetteville Street, Durham, NC 27707
Phone: 919-560-6298 **E-mail:** ebridges@wpo.nccu.edu **CEEB Code:** 5495
Fax: 919-530-7625 **Website:** www.nccu.edu **ACT Code:** 3132
Financial Aid Phone: 919-530-6335

This public school was founded in 1910. It has a 130-acre campus.

RATINGS

Admissions Selectivity Rating: 64   **Fire Safety Rating:** 60*   **Green Rating:** 60*

STUDENTS AND FACULTY

Enrollment: 5,439. **Student Body:** 66% female, 34% male, 10% out-of-state. African American 79%, Caucasian 3%. **Retention and Graduation:** 78% freshmen return for sophomore year. **Faculty:** Student/faculty ratio 18:1. 231 full-time faculty, 67% hold PhDs.

ACADEMICS

Degrees: Bachelor's, first professional, master's. **Academic Requirements:** Arts/fine arts, English (including composition), foreign languages, history, humanities, mathematics, sciences (biological or physical), social science. **Classes:** Most classes have fewer than 10 students. Most lab/discussion sections have fewer than 10 students. **Disciplines with Highest Percentage of**

Degrees Awarded: Business/marketing 19%, social sciences 11%, health professions and related sciences 11%, education 10%, English 8%, psychology 5%, biological/life sciences 5%. **Special Study Options:** Cooperative education program, double major, honors program, independent study, internships, study abroad, teacher certification program, weekend college.

FACILITIES

Housing: Coed dorms, men's dorms, women's dorms, coed houses dormitory available. **Special Academic Facilities/Equipment:** Treasury room collection of primary resources on black life and culture, art museum with works of Afro-American culture. **Computers:** 91% of public computers are PCs, 9% of public computers are Macs, 3% of public computers are UNIX, online administrative functions (other than registration), remote student-access to Web through college's connection.

CAMPUS LIFE

Activities: Choral groups, concert band, dance, drama/theater, jazz band, literary magazine, marching band, radio station, student government, student newspaper, yearbook. **Organizations:** 4 fraternities, 4 sororities. **Athletics (Intercollegiate):** *Men:* Basketball, cross-country, football, golf, tennis, track/field (outdoor). *Women:* Basketball, cross-country, golf, softball, tennis, track/field (outdoor), volleyball.

ADMISSIONS

Freshman Academic Profile: 5% in top 10% of high school class, 18% in top 25% of high school class, 49% in top 50% of high school class. SAT Math middle 50% range 380–470. SAT Critical Reading middle 50% range 380–470. ACT middle 50% range 14–18. TOEFL required of all international applicants, minimum paper TOEFL 500, minimum computer TOEFL 173. **Basis for Candidate Selection:** *Very important factors considered include:* Rigor of secondary school record. *Important factors considered include:* Class rank, standardized test scores. *Other factors considered include:* Alumni/ae relation, application essay, extracurricular activities, interview, racial/ethnic status, recommendation(s), state residency, talent/ability. **Freshman Admission Requirements:** High school diploma is required, and GED is accepted. *Academic units required:* 4 English, 3 math, 3 science (1 science lab), 2 social studies, 2 history. *Academic units recommended:* 4 math, 4 science, 2 foreign language, 2 history. **Freshman Admission Statistics:** 2,801 applied, 83% admitted, 50% enrolled. **Transfer Admission Requirements:** High school transcript, college transcript(s), statement of good standing from prior institution(s). Minimum college GPA of 2.0 required. Lowest grade transferable C. **General Admission Information:** Application fee $30. Regular application deadline 7/1. Regular notification is rolling. Non-fall registration accepted. Admission may be deferred for a maximum of 4 semesters. Common Application not accepted. Credit offered for CEEB Advanced Placement tests.

COSTS AND FINANCIAL AID

Annual in-state tuition $1,878. Out-of-state tuition $11,322. Room & board $4,311. Required fees $1,164. Average book expense $1,000. **Required Forms and Deadlines:** FAFSA. Financial aid filing deadline 4/1. **Types of Aid:** *Need-based scholarships/grants:* Pell, SEOG, state scholarships/grants, private scholarships, the school's own gift aid, United Negro College Fund, Federal Nursing Scholarships. *Loans:* Direct Subsidized Stafford, Direct Unsubsidized Stafford, Direct PLUS, Federal Perkins. **Student Employment:** Federal Work-Study Program available. Off-campus job opportunities are fair. **Financial Aid Statistics:** 58% freshmen, 55% undergrads receive need-based scholarship or grant aid. 66% freshmen, 66% undergrads receive need-based self-help aid. 30 freshmen, 74 undergrads receive athletic scholarships.

NORTH CAROLINA SCHOOL OF THE ARTS

1533 South Main Street, PO Box 12189, Winston-Salem, NC 27127-2188
Phone: 336-770-3290 **E-mail:** admissions@ncarts.edu **CEEB Code:** 5512
Fax: 336-770-3370 **Website:** www.ncarts.edu **ACT Code:** 3133
Financial Aid Phone: 336-770-3297

This public school was founded in 1963. It has a 57-acre campus.

RATINGS

Admissions Selectivity Rating: 87   **Fire Safety Rating:** 60*   **Green Rating:** 60*

STUDENTS AND FACULTY

Enrollment: 721. **Student Body:** 41% female, 59% male, 52% out-of-state, 1% international. African American 10%, Asian 3%, Caucasian 83%, Hispanic 2%. **Retention and Graduation:** 75% freshmen return for sophomore year. 40% freshmen graduate within 4 years. **Faculty:** Student/faculty ratio 8:1. 135 full-time faculty. 100% faculty teach undergrads.

ACADEMICS

Degrees: Bachelor's, diploma, master's, post-master's certificate. **Academic Requirements:** Arts/fine arts. **Classes:** Most classes have fewer than 10 students. **Majors with Highest Enrollment:** Cinematography and film/video production, music performance, technical theater/theater design and technology. **Disciplines with Highest Percentage of Degrees Awarded:** Visual and performing arts 100%. **Special Study Options:** Cooperative education program, English as a second language (ESL), independent study, internships, all performing arts.

FACILITIES

Housing: Coed dorms, men's dorms, women's dorms, apartments for single students, special housing for disabled students, non-smoking, 24-hour quiet facility, extended hours practice facility. **Computers:** 80% of public computers are PCs, 20% of public computers are Macs, network access in dorm rooms, network access in dorm lounges, online administrative functions (other than registration), remote student-access to Web through college's connection.

CAMPUS LIFE

Activities: Choral groups, dance, drama/theater, jazz band, literary magazine, music ensembles, musical theater, opera, student government, student-run film society, symphony orchestra, yearbook. **Organizations:** 8 registered organizations, 7 honor societies, 3 religious organizations.

ADMISSIONS

Freshman Academic Profile: 16% in top 10% of high school class, 45% in top 25% of high school class, 78% in top 50% of high school class. SAT Math middle 50% range 500–620. SAT Critical Reading middle 50% range 540–640. ACT middle 50% range 20–25. TOEFL required of all international applicants, minimum paper TOEFL 550, minimum computer TOEFL 213. **Basis for Candidate Selection:** *Very important factors considered include:* Interview, recommendation(s), rigor of secondary school record, talent/ability. *Important factors considered include:* Standardized test scores. *Other factors considered include:* Character/personal qualities, extracurricular activities, racial/ethnic status, work experience. **Freshman Admission Requirements:** High school diploma is required, and GED is accepted. *Academic units required:* 4 English, 3 math, 3 science (1 science lab), 2 social studies, 1 history, 4 academic electives. *Academic units recommended:* 2 foreign language. **Freshman Admission Statistics:** 744 applied, 46% admitted, 59% enrolled. **Transfer Admission Requirements:** High school transcript, college transcript(s), interview, statement of good standing from prior institution(s). Lowest grade transferable C. **General Admission Information:** Application fee $45. Regular application deadline 3/1. Regular notification 4/1. Non-fall registration accepted. Admission may be deferred for a maximum of 1 year. Common Application not accepted. Credit and/or placement offered for CEEB Advanced Placement tests.

COSTS AND FINANCIAL AID

Annual in-state tuition $2,195. Out-of-state tuition $12,795. Room & board $5,115. Required fees $1,255. Average book expense $865. **Required Forms and Deadlines:** FAFSA. Financial aid filing deadline 3/1. **Notification of Awards:** Applicants will be notified of awards on or about 4/15. **Types of Aid:** *Need-based scholarships/grants:* Pell, SEOG, state scholarships/grants, private scholarships, the school's own gift aid. *Loans:* Direct Subsidized Stafford, Direct Unsubsidized Stafford, Direct PLUS, Federal Perkins. **Student Employment:** Federal Work-Study Program available. Institutional employment available. Off-campus job opportunities are good. **Financial Aid Statistics:** 57% freshmen, 43% undergrads receive need-based scholarship or grant aid. 58% freshmen, 43% undergrads receive need-based self-help aid.

NORTH CAROLINA STATE UNIVERSITY

Box 7103, Raleigh, NC 27695
Phone: 919-515-2434 **E-mail:** undergrad_admissions@ncsu.edu **CEEB Code:** 5496
Fax: 919-515-5039 **Website:** www.ncsu.edu **ACT Code:** 3164
Financial Aid Phone: 919-515-2421

This public school was founded in 1887. It has a 2,110-acre campus.

RATINGS

Admissions Selectivity Rating: 89   **Fire Safety Rating:** 84   **Green Rating:** 90

STUDENTS AND FACULTY

Enrollment: 21,438. **Student Body:** 42% female, 58% male, 7% out-of-state. African American 9%, Asian 5%, Caucasian 80%, Hispanic 2%. **Retention and Graduation:** 89% freshmen return for sophomore year. 37% freshmen graduate within 4 years. 31% grads go on to further study within 1 year. 67% grads pursue arts and sciences degrees. 19% grads pursue business degrees. 7% grads pursue law degrees. 7% grads pursue medical degrees. **Faculty:** Student/faculty ratio 16:1. 1,652 full-time faculty, 91% hold PhDs. 100% faculty teach undergrads.

ACADEMICS

Degrees: Associate, bachelor's, doctoral, first professional certificate, first professional, master's, post-bachelor's certificate. **Academic Requirements:** Arts/fine arts, computer literacy, English (including composition), foreign languages, history, humanities, mathematics, sciences (biological or physical), social science. **Classes:** Most classes have 20–29 students. Most lab/discussion sections have 20–29 students. **Majors with Highest Enrollment:** Biology/biological sciences, business, administration and management, mechanical engineering. **Disciplines with Highest Percentage of Degrees Awarded:** Engineering 22%, business/marketing 14%, biological/life sciences 11%, social sciences 9%, communications/journalism 7%. **Special Study Options:** Accelerated program, cooperative education program, cross-registration, distance learning, double major, dual enrollment, exchange student program (domestic), honors program, independent study, internships, liberal arts/career combination, student-designed major, study abroad, teacher certification program.

FACILITIES

Housing: Coed dorms, men's dorms, women's dorms, apartments for married students, apartments for single students, special housing for disabled students, special housing for international students, fraternity/sorority housing, living/learning dormitories. **Special Academic Facilities/Equipment:** Art and arts/crafts galleries; research farms and forest; phytophoton with controlled atmosphere growth chambers; pulp/paper and wood products labs; processing equipment for fiber, fabric, and garment manufacture; electron microscopes; nuclear reactor; stable isotope lab. **Computers:** 2% of classrooms are wired, 70% of classrooms are wireless, 65% of public computers are PCs, 35% of public computers are Macs, 25% of public computers are UNIX, network access in dorm rooms, network access in dorm lounges, online registration, online administrative functions (other than registration), support for handheld computing, remote student-access to Web through college's connection.

CAMPUS LIFE

Activities: Choral groups, concert band, dance, drama/theater, jazz band, literary magazine, marching band, music ensembles, musical theater, pep band, radio station, student government, student newspaper, student-run film society, symphony orchestra, yearbook. **Organizations:** 365 registered organizations, 12 honor societies, 25 religious organizations. 29 fraternities (8% men join), 14 sororities (10% women join). **Athletics (Intercollegiate):** *Men:* Baseball, basketball, cheerleading, cross-country, diving, football, golf, riflery, soccer, swimming, tennis, track/field (indoor), track/field (outdoor), wrestling. *Women:* Basketball, cheerleading, cross-country, diving, golf, gymnastics, riflery, soccer, softball, swimming, tennis, track/field (indoor), track/field (outdoor), volleyball. **Environmental Initiatives:** Signing the President's Climate Commitment engages a large effort at assessing NC State's carbon balance, and at reducing the carbon footprint. The University is in the process of developing the NC State Sustainability Commitment to complement the President's Climate Change Commitment. In addition, an NC State Sustainability Coordinator will accelerate efforts by strengthening existing networkshelp across the NC State Community, guiding assessments to achieve goals, and creating new approaches needed for sustainability.

ADMISSIONS

Freshman Academic Profile: 37% in top 10% of high school class, 79% in top 25% of high school class, 98% in top 50% of high school class. 90% from public high schools. SAT Math middle 50% range 550–650. SAT Critical Reading middle 50% range 520–610. SAT Writing middle 50% range 510–610. ACT middle 50% range 22–27. TOEFL required of all international applicants, minimum paper TOEFL 550, minimum computer TOEFL 213. **Basis for Candidate Selection:** *Very important factors considered include:* Academic GPA, class rank, rigor of secondary school record, standardized test scores. *Other factors considered include:* Alumni/ae relation, application essay, character/personal qualities, extracurricular activities, first generation, geographical residence, racial/ethnic status, recommendation(s), state residency, talent/ability, volunteer work, work experience. **Freshman Admission Requirements:** High school diploma is required, and GED is not accepted. *Academic units required:* 4 English, 4 math, 3 science (1 science lab), 2 foreign language, 1 social studies, 1 history, 1 academic elective. *Academic units recommended:* 4 English, 4 math, 4 science (2 science labs), 2 foreign language, 1 social studies, 1 history, 4 academic electives. **Freshman Admission Statistics:** 15,500 applied, 61% admitted, 48% enrolled. **Transfer Admission Requirements:** College transcript(s). Minimum college GPA of 2.0 required. Lowest grade transferable C-. **General Admission Information:** Application

fee $60. Regular application deadline 2/1. Regular notification is rolling. Non-fall registration accepted. Admission may be deferred for a maximum of 1 year. Credit and/or placement offered for CEEB Advanced Placement tests.

COSTS AND FINANCIAL AID

Annual in-state tuition $3,760. Out-of-state tuition $15,958. Room & board $7,373. Required fees $1,357. Average book expense $930. **Required Forms and Deadlines:** FAFSA, institution's own financial aid form. Financial aid filing deadline 2/1. **Notification of Awards:** Applicants will be notified of awards on a rolling basis beginning on or about 3/15. **Types of Aid:** *Need-based scholarships/grants:* Pell, SEOG, state scholarships/grants, private scholarships, the school's own gift aid, United Negro College Fund. *Loans:* FFEL Subsidized Stafford, FFEL Unsubsidized Stafford, FFEL PLUS, Federal Perkins, state loans, college/university loans from institutional funds. **Financial Aid Statistics:** 39% freshmen, 36% undergrads receive need-based scholarship or grant aid. 29% freshmen, 30% undergrads receive need-based self-help aid. 73 freshmen, 294 undergrads receive athletic scholarships. 68% freshmen, 61% undergrads receive any aid. Highest amount earned per year from on-campus jobs $7,041.

NORTH CAROLINA WESLEYAN COLLEGE

3400 North Wesleyan Boulevard, Rocky Mount, NC 27804
Phone: 252-985-5200 **E-mail:** adm@ncwc.edu
Fax: 252-985-5309 **Website:** www.ncwc.edu
Financial Aid Phone: 800-488-6292

This private school, affiliated with the Methodist Church, was founded in 1956.

RATINGS

Admissions Selectivity Rating: 61   **Fire Safety Rating:** 60*   **Green Rating:** 60*

STUDENTS AND FACULTY

Enrollment: 1,695. **Student Body:** 59% female, 41% male, 12% out-of-state. African American 40%, Caucasian 48%, Hispanic 1%. **Retention and Graduation:** 57% freshmen return for sophomore year. 26% freshmen graduate within 4 years. **Faculty:** Student/faculty ratio 15:1. 45 full-time faculty, 62% hold PhDs. 100% faculty teach undergrads.

ACADEMICS

Degrees: Bachelor's, certificate. **Academic Requirements:** Computer literacy, English (including composition), history, humanities, mathematics, sciences (biological or physical), social science. **Classes:** Most classes have 10–19 students. **Majors with Highest Enrollment:** Business administration/management, computer and information sciences, psychology. **Disciplines with Highest Percentage of Degrees Awarded:** Business/marketing 47%, computer and information sciences 24%, law/legal studies 10%, psychology 7%, biological/life sciences 2%, education 2%, social sciences 2%. **Special Study Options:** Accelerated program, cooperative education program, cross-registration, distance learning, double major, dual enrollment, honors program, independent study, internships, liberal arts/career combination, teacher certification program, weekend college.

FACILITIES

Housing: Coed dorms, men's dorms, women's dorms, special housing for disabled students. **Special Academic Facilities/Equipment:** Mims Gallery, Dunn Center for the Performing Arts. **Computers:** Online administrative functions (other than registration), remote student-access to Web through college's connection.

CAMPUS LIFE

Activities: Choral groups, drama/theater, literary magazine, music ensembles, student government, student newspaper, yearbook. **Organizations:** 30 registered organizations, 2 honor societies, 2 religious organizations. 3 fraternities (2% men join), 3 sororities (2% women join). **Athletics (Intercollegiate):** *Men:* Baseball, basketball, football, golf, soccer, tennis. *Women:* Basketball, soccer, softball, tennis, volleyball.

ADMISSIONS

Freshman Academic Profile: 8% in top 10% of high school class, 18% in top 25% of high school class, 59% in top 50% of high school class. 85% from public high schools. SAT Math middle 50% range 5–23. SAT Critical Reading middle 50% range 4–29. TOEFL required of all international applicants, minimum paper TOEFL 500, minimum computer TOEFL 500. **Basis for Candidate Selection:** *Very important factors considered include:* Recommendation(s), rigor of secondary school record, standardized test scores, talent/ability. *Important factors considered include:* Alumni/ae relation, application essay, character/personal qualities, extracurricular activities, interview, volunteer work, work experience. *Other factors considered include:* Class rank. **Freshman Admission Requirements:** High school diploma is required, and GED is accepted. *Academic units recommended:* 4 English, 3 math, 2 foreign language, 2 social studies. **Freshman Admission Statistics:** 651 applied, 83% admitted, 37% enrolled. **Transfer Admission Requirements:** High school transcript, college transcript(s), standardized test score. Minimum college GPA of 2.0 required. Lowest grade transferable C. **General Admission Information:** Application fee $25. Regular notification is rolling. Non-fall registration accepted. Common Application accepted. Credit and/or placement offered for CEEB Advanced Placement tests.

COSTS AND FINANCIAL AID
Annual tuition $11,225. Room & board $5,555. Required fees $1,218. Average book expense $800. **Required Forms and Deadlines:** FAFSA, state aid form. Financial aid filing deadline 3/15. **Notification of Awards:** Applicants will be notified of awards on or about 2/1. **Types of Aid:** *Need-based scholarships/ grants:* Pell, SEOG, state scholarships/grants, private scholarships, the school's own gift aid. *Loans:* FFEL Subsidized Stafford, FFEL Unsubsidized Stafford, FFEL PLUS, Federal Perkins, alternative loans available. **Student Employment:** Federal Work-Study Program. **Financial Aid Statistics:** Highest amount earned per year from on-campus jobs $800.

NORTH CENTRAL COLLEGE

Office of Admissions, PO Box 3063, Naperville, IL 60566-7063
Phone: 630-637-5800 **E-mail:** admissions@noctrl.edu **CEEB Code:** 1555
Fax: 630-637-5819 **Website:** www.northcentralCollege.edu **ACT Code:** 1096
Financial Aid Phone: 630-637-5600

This private school, affiliated with the Methodist Church, was founded in 1861. It has a 59-acre campus.

RATINGS
Admissions Selectivity Rating: 60*   **Fire Safety Rating:** 74   **Green Rating:** 76

STUDENTS AND FACULTY
Enrollment: 2,136. **Student Body:** 59% female, 41% male, 8% out-of-state. 1% international (31 countries represented). African American 3%, Asian 3%, Caucasian 80%, Hispanic 5%. **Retention and Graduation:** 76% freshmen return for sophomore year. 51% freshmen graduate within 4 years. **Faculty:** Student/faculty ratio 15:1. 111 full-time faculty, 87% hold PhDs. 98% faculty teach undergrads.

ACADEMICS
Degrees: Bachelor's, master's, post-bachelor's certificate. **Academic Requirements:** English (including composition); foreign languages; humanities; intercultural studies; interdisciplinary seminar; leadership, ethics, and values; mathematics; religion and ethics; sciences (biological or physical), social science, speech communication. **Classes:** Most classes have 20–29 students. Most lab/discussion sections have 10–19 students. **Majors with Highest Enrollment:** Business/managerial operations, elementary education and teaching, psychology. **Disciplines with Highest Percentage of Degrees Awarded:** Business/marketing 28%, education 16%, social sciences 10%, communications/journalism 8%, psychology 6%. **Special Study Options:** Accelerated program, cross-registration, double major, dual enrollment, English as a second language (ESL), exchange student program (domestic), honors program, independent study, internships, liberal arts/career combination, student-designed major, study abroad, teacher certification program, 3–2 engineering program with University of Illinois and Washington University in St. Louis, 2–2 or 3–2 nursing program with Rush University, integrated 5-year bachelor's/master's degree programs.

FACILITIES
Housing: Coed dorms, women's dorms, special housing for disabled students, substance-free housing. **Computers:** 63% of public computers are PCs, 36% of public computers are Macs, network access in dorm rooms, online registration, online administrative functions (other than registration), remote student-access to Web through college's connection.

CAMPUS LIFE
Activities: Choral groups, concert band, dance, drama/theater, jazz band, literary magazine, music ensembles, musical theater, opera, pep band, radio station, student government, student newspaper. **Organizations:** 53 registered organizations, 5 honor societies, 7 religious organizations. **Athletics (Intercollegiate):** *Men:* Baseball, basketball, cross-country, football, golf, soccer, swimming, tennis, track/field (indoor), track/field (outdoor), wrestling. *Women:*

Basketball, cheerleading, cross-country, golf, soccer, softball, swimming, tennis, track/field (indoor), track/field (outdoor), volleyball. **Environmental Initiatives:** Development of Sustainabilty Committee. LEED Certification for new construction. Expansion of recycling program.

ADMISSIONS
Freshman Academic Profile: 86% from public high schools. SAT Math middle 50% range 510–650. SAT Critical Reading middle 50% range 545–670. SAT Writing middle 50% range 510–650. ACT middle 50% range 22–27. TOEFL required of all international applicants, minimum paper TOEFL 520, minimum computer TOEFL 190. **Basis for Candidate Selection:** *Very important factors considered include:* Academic GPA, character/personal qualities, rigor of secondary school record, standardized test scores. *Important factors considered include:* Extracurricular activities, talent/ability, volunteer work. *Other factors considered include:* Alumni/ae relation, application essay, first generation, interview, level of applicant's interest, recommendation(s), work experience. **Freshman Admission Requirements:** High school diploma is required, and GED is accepted. *Academic units required:* 4 English, 3 math, 3 science (1 science lab), 2 social studies, 1 history, 3 academic electives. *Academic units recommended:* 4 English, 3 math, 3 science (3 science labs), 3 foreign language, 2 social studies, 1 history, 3 academic electives. **Freshman Admission Statistics:** 2,204 applied, 69% admitted, 31% enrolled. **Transfer Admission Requirements:** College transcript(s). Minimum college GPA of 2.3 required. Lowest grade transferable D. **General Admission Information:** Application fee $25. Regular notification is rolling. Non-fall registration accepted. Admission may be deferred for a maximum of 1 year. Credit and/or placement offered for CEEB Advanced Placement tests.

COSTS AND FINANCIAL AID
Annual tuition $24,159. Room and board $7,677. Required fees $405. Average book expense $1,002. **Required Forms and Deadlines:** FAFSA, institution's own financial aid form, federal income tax returns for both student and parents. **Notification of Awards:** Applicants will be notified of awards on a rolling basis beginning on or about 3/1. **Types of Aid:** *Need-based scholarships/grants:* Pell, SEOG, state scholarships/grants, private scholarships, the school's own gift aid. *Loans:* FFEL Subsidized Stafford, FFEL Unsubsidized Stafford, FFEL PLUS, Federal Perkins, state loans, college/university loans from institutional funds. **Student Employment:** Federal Work-Study Program available. Institutional employment available. Off-campus job opportunities are excellent. **Financial Aid Statistics:** 71% freshmen, 64% undergrads receive need-based scholarship or grant aid. 54% freshmen, 53% undergrads receive need-based self-help aid. 96% freshmen, 90% undergrads receive any aid. Highest amount earned per year from on-campus jobs $8,039.

NORTH CENTRAL UNIVERSITY

Admissions Office, 910 Elliot Ave, Minneapolis, MN 55404
Phone: 612-343-4460 **E-mail:** admissions@northcentral.edu
Fax: 612-343-4146 **Website:** www.northcentral.edu
Financial Aid Phone: 800-289-6222

This private school, affiliated with the Pentecostal Church, was founded in 1930. It has a 9-acre campus.

RATINGS
Admissions Selectivity Rating: 66   **Fire Safety Rating:** 60*   **Green Rating:** 60*

STUDENTS AND FACULTY
Enrollment: 1,217. **Student Body:** 57% female, 43% male, 60% out-of-state. **Retention and Graduation:** 75% freshmen return for sophomore year. 18% freshmen graduate within 4 years. **Faculty:** Student/faculty ratio 18:1. 40 full-time faculty, 42% hold PhDs. 100% faculty teach undergrads.

ACADEMICS
Degrees: Associate, bachelor's, certificate, diploma. **Academic Requirements:** Arts/fine arts, English (including composition), foreign languages, history, mathematics, philosophy, sciences (biological or physical). **Classes:** Most classes have 10–19 students. **Majors with Highest Enrollment:** Education, music/music and performing arts studies, youth ministry. **Disciplines with Highest Percentage of Degrees Awarded:** Psychology 15%, education 14%, visual and performing arts 13%, interdisciplinary studies 7%. **Special Study Options:** Distance learning, double major, exchange student program (domestic), independent study, internships.

FACILITIES
Housing: Men's dorms, women's dorms, apartments for married students, apartments for single students. **Computers:** 80% of public computers are PCs,

20% of public computers are Macs, network access in dorm rooms, network access in dorm lounges, remote student-access to Web through college's connection.

CAMPUS LIFE

Activities: Choral groups, concert band, drama/theater, jazz band, music ensembles, radio station, student government, student newspaper, television station. **Organizations:** 30 registered organizations, 15 religious organizations. **Athletics (Intercollegiate):** *Men:* Basketball, cross-country, soccer, track/field (outdoor). *Women:* Basketball, cross-country, soccer, track/field (outdoor), volleyball.

ADMISSIONS

Freshman Academic Profile: 2% in top 10% of high school class, 11% in top 25% of high school class, 32% in top 50% of high school class. SAT Math middle 50% range 440–300. SAT Critical Reading middle 50% range 480–630. ACT middle 50% range 18–24. TOEFL required of all international applicants, minimum paper TOEFL 500, minimum computer TOEFL 220. **Basis for Candidate Selection:** *Very important factors considered include:* Academic GPA, application essay, character/personal qualities, recommendation(s), religious affiliation/commitment, rigor of secondary school record, standardized test scores. *Important factors considered include:* Extracurricular activities, talent/ability, volunteer work. *Other factors considered include:* Class rank, interview. **Freshman Admission Requirements:** High school diploma is required, and GED is accepted. *Academic units recommended:* 4 English, 2 math, 2 science (1 science lab), 1 foreign language, 2 social studies, 2 history, 4 academic electives. **Freshman Admission Statistics:** 422 applied, 98% admitted, 58% enrolled. **Transfer Admission Requirements:** High school transcript, college transcript(s), essay or personal statement. Minimum college GPA of 2.0 required. Lowest grade transferable C. **General Admission Information:** Application fee $25. Regular application deadline 6/1. Regular notification is rolling. Non-fall registration accepted. Admission may be deferred for a maximum of 1 year. Common Application not accepted.

COSTS AND FINANCIAL AID

Annual tuition $12,060. Room & board $4,612. Required fees $886. Average book expense $600. **Required Forms and Deadlines:** FAFSA, state aid form. Financial aid filing deadline 4/1. **Notification of Awards:** Applicants will be notified of awards on a rolling basis beginning on or about 3/1. **Types of Aid:** *Need-based scholarships/grants:* Pell, SEOG, state scholarships/grants, private scholarships, the school's own gift aid. *Loans:* FFEL Subsidized Stafford, FFEL Unsubsidized Stafford, FFEL PLUS, Federal Perkins, state loans.

NORTH DAKOTA STATE UNIVERSITY

Box 5454, Fargo, ND 58105
Phone: 701-231-8643 **E-mail:** ndsu.admission@ndsu.edu **CEEB Code:** 6474
Fax: 701-231-8802 **Website:** www.ndsu.edu **ACT Code:** 3202
Financial Aid Phone: 800-726-3188

This public school was founded in 1890. It has a 258-acre campus.

RATINGS

Admissions Selectivity Rating: 77   **Fire Safety Rating:** 60*   **Green Rating:** 60*

STUDENTS AND FACULTY

Enrollment: 10,596. **Student Body:** 45% female, 55% male, 46% out-of-state. **Retention and Graduation:** 78% freshmen return for sophomore year. 18% freshmen graduate within 4 years. **Faculty:** Student/faculty ratio 19:1. 541 full-time faculty, 83% hold PhDs.

ACADEMICS

Degrees: Bachelor's, certificate, doctoral, first professional, master's, post-master's certificate. **Academic Requirements:** Arts/fine arts, computer literacy, diversity, English (including composition), global perspectives, humanities, mathematics, sciences (biological or physical), social science, wellness. **Classes:** Most classes have 20–29 students. Most lab/discussion sections have 20–29 students. **Majors with Highest Enrollment:** Business, management, marketing, and related support services; civil engineering; mechanical engineering. **Disciplines with Highest Percentage of Degrees Awarded:** Engineering 15%, business/marketing 15%, health professions and related sciences 11%, architecture 9%, agriculture 7%, biological/life sciences 6%. **Special Study Options:** Cooperative education program, cross-registration, distance learning, double major, dual enrollment, English as a second language (ESL), honors program, independent study, internships, student-designed major, study abroad, teacher certification program, tri-college collaboration and registration with Minnesota State University and Concordia College, collaboration with North Dakota University system institutions.

FACILITIES

Housing: Coed dorms, men's dorms, women's dorms, apartments for married students, apartments for single students, designated floors for engineering and architecture students, learning communities, wellness community. **Special Academic Facilities/Equipment:** Art gallery, language lab, genetics institute, regional studies institute. **Computers:** 70% of public computers are PCs, 30% of public computers are Macs, 3% of public computers are UNIX, network access in dorm rooms, network access in dorm lounges, online registration, online administrative functions (other than registration), remote student-access to Web through college's connection.

CAMPUS LIFE

Activities: Choral groups, concert band, drama/theater, jazz band, marching band, music ensembles, musical theater, pep band, radio station, student government, student newspaper. **Organizations:** 218 registered organizations, 22 honor societies, 18 religious organizations. 10 fraternities (5% men join), 5 sororities (4% women join). **Athletics (Intercollegiate):** *Men:* Baseball, basketball, cross-country, football, golf, track/field (indoor), track/field (outdoor), wrestling. *Women:* Basketball, cross-country, golf, soccer, softball, track/field (indoor), track/field (outdoor), volleyball.

ADMISSIONS

Freshman Academic Profile: 16% in top 10% of high school class, 40% in top 25% of high school class, 74% in top 50% of high school class. SAT Math middle 50% range 490–640. SAT Critical Reading middle 50% range 460–600. ACT middle 50% range 20–25. TOEFL required of all international applicants, minimum paper TOEFL 525, minimum computer TOEFL 193. **Basis for Candidate Selection:** *Very important factors considered include:* Academic GPA, rigor of secondary school record, standardized test scores. *Other factors considered include:* Class rank, recommendation(s). **Freshman Admission Requirements:** High school diploma is required, and GED is accepted. *Academic units required:* 4 English, 3 math, 3 science (3 science labs), 3 social studies. *Academic units recommended:* 2 foreign language. **Freshman Admission Statistics:** 4,120 applied, 87% admitted, 58% enrolled. **Transfer Admission Requirements:** College transcript(s). Minimum college GPA of 2.0 required. Lowest grade transferable D. **General Admission Information:** Application fee $35. Regular application deadline 8/15. Regular notification is rolling. Non-fall registration accepted. Admission may be deferred for a maximum of 3 years. Credit and/or placement offered for CEEB Advanced Placement tests.

COSTS AND FINANCIAL AID

Annual in-state tuition $5,013. Annual out-of-state tuition $13,384. Average book expense $700. **Required Forms and Deadlines:** FAFSA. Financial aid filing deadline 3/15. **Notification of Awards:** Applicants will be notified of awards on a rolling basis beginning on or about 3/15. **Types of Aid:** *Need-based scholarships/grants:* Pell, SEOG, state scholarships/grants, private scholarships, the school's own gift aid, diversity waivers. *Loans:* FFEL Subsidized Stafford, FFEL Unsubsidized Stafford, FFEL PLUS, Federal Perkins, Federal Nursing, private loans from various lending institutions. **Financial Aid Statistics:** 25 freshmen, 72 undergrads receive athletic scholarships.

NORTH GEORGIA COLLEGE & STATE UNIVERSITY

Office of Undergraduate Admissions, 82 College Circle, Dahlonega, GA 30597
Phone: 706-864-1800 **E-mail:** admissions@ngcsu.edu **CEEB Code:** 5497
Fax: 706-864-1478 **Website:** www.ngcsu.edu **ACT Code:** 0848
Financial Aid Phone: 706-864-1412

This public school was founded in 1873. It has a 120-acre campus.

RATINGS

Admissions Selectivity Rating: 82   **Fire Safety Rating:** 60*   **Green Rating:** 60*

STUDENTS AND FACULTY

Enrollment: 3,983. **Student Body:** 60% female, 40% male, 10% out-of-state, 1% international (34 countries represented). African American 1%, Asian 1%, Caucasian 76%, Hispanic 2%. **Retention and Graduation:** 77% freshmen return for sophomore year. 25% freshmen graduate within 4 years. 10% grads go on to further study within 1 year. 1% grads pursue arts and sciences degrees. 5% grads pursue business degrees. 1% grads pursue law degrees. 1% grads pursue medical degrees. **Faculty:** Student/faculty ratio 15:1. 185 full-time faculty, 66% hold PhDs. 90% faculty teach undergrads.

ACADEMICS

Degrees: Associate, bachelor's, certificate, master's, post-bachelor's certificate, post-master's certificate. **Academic Requirements:** Arts/fine arts, computer literacy, English (including composition), foreign languages, history, humanities, mathematics, philosophy, sciences (biological or physical), social science. **Classes:** Most classes have 20–29 students. Most lab/discussion sections have fewer than 10 students. **Majors with Highest Enrollment:** Biology/biological sciences, early childhood education and teaching, marketing/marketing management. **Disciplines with Highest Percentage of Degrees Awarded:** Business/marketing 27%, education 22%, social sciences 9%, biological/life sciences 8%, psychology 7%. **Special Study Options:** Cooperative education program, distance learning, double major, dual enrollment, external degree program, honors program, independent study, internships, study abroad, teacher certification program, dual degree in engineering with GA Institute of Technology and Clemson University.

FACILITIES

Housing: Coed dorms, men's dorms, women's dorms, apartments for single students. **Special Academic Facilities/Equipment:** 2 art galleries, hall of fame, NGCSU museum, planetarium. **Computers:** 90% of public computers are PCs, 10% of public computers are Macs, network access in dorm rooms, network access in dorm lounges, online registration, online administrative functions (other than registration), remote student-access to Web through college's connection.

CAMPUS LIFE

Activities: Choral groups, drama/theater, jazz band, literary magazine, marching band, music ensembles, pep band, student government, student newspaper, symphony orchestra, yearbook. **Organizations:** 60 registered organizations, 8 honor societies, 5 religious organizations. 6 fraternities, 4 sororities (6% women join). **Athletics (Intercollegiate):** *Men:* Baseball, basketball, cross-country, football, golf, riflery, soccer, table tennis, tennis, track/field (outdoor), volleyball, water polo. *Women:* Basketball, cheerleading, cross-country, golf, riflery, soccer, softball, table tennis, tennis, track/field (outdoor), volleyball, water polo.

ADMISSIONS

Freshman Academic Profile: 21% in top 10% of high school class, 53% in top 25% of high school class, 85% in top 50% of high school class. 95% from public high schools. SAT Math middle 50% range 490–580. SAT Critical Reading middle 50% range 500–580. ACT middle 50% range 19–23. TOEFL required of all international applicants, minimum paper TOEFL 550, minimum computer TOEFL 213. **Basis for Candidate Selection:** *Very important factors considered include:* Rigor of secondary school record, standardized test scores. *Other factors considered include:* Alumni/ae relation, character/personal qualities, class rank, extracurricular activities, recommendation(s), talent/ability, volunteer work, work experience. **Freshman Admission Requirements:** High school diploma is required, and GED is accepted. *Academic units required:* 4 English, 4 math, 3 science (1 science lab), 2 foreign language, 3 social studies. **Freshman Admission Statistics:** 2,103 applied, 60% admitted, 60% enrolled. **Transfer Admission Requirements:** College transcript(s), statement of good standing from prior institution(s). Minimum college GPA of 2.0 required. Lowest grade transferable C. **General Admission Information:** Application fee $25. Regular application deadline 7/1. Regular notification is rolling. Non-fall registration accepted. Common Application not accepted. Credit offered for CEEB Advanced Placement tests.

COSTS AND FINANCIAL AID

Annual in-state tuition $2,322. Out-of-state tuition $9,290. Room & board $4,424. Required fees $606. Average book expense $750. **Required Forms and Deadlines:** FAFSA, institution's own financial aid form. Financial aid filing deadline 5/1. **Notification of Awards:** Applicants will be notified of awards on a rolling basis beginning on or about 5/15. **Types of Aid:** *Need-based scholarships/grants:* Pell, SEOG, state scholarships/grants, private scholarships, the school's own gift aid. *Loans:* FFEL Subsidized Stafford, FFEL Unsubsidized Stafford, FFEL PLUS, Federal Perkins, state loans, college/university loans from institutional funds. **Financial Aid Statistics:** 17% freshmen, 19% undergrads receive need-based scholarship or grant aid. 12% freshmen, 10% undergrads receive need-based self-help aid. 13 freshmen, 114 undergrads receive athletic scholarships.

NORTH GREENVILLE COLLEGE

PO Box 1892, Tigerville, SC 29688-1892
Phone: 864-977-7001 **E-mail:** admissions@ngc.edu
Fax: 864-977-7177 **Website:** www.ngc.edu
Financial Aid Phone: 864-977-7056

This private school, affiliated with the Southern Baptist Church, was founded in 1892.

RATINGS
Admissions Selectivity Rating: 74   **Fire Safety Rating:** 60*   **Green Rating:** 60*

STUDENTS AND FACULTY
Enrollment: 1,570. **Student Body:** 49% female, 51% male, 19% out-of-state, 2% international (19 countries represented). African American 10%, Caucasian 90%. **Faculty:** Student/faculty ratio 17:1. 70 full-time faculty.

ACADEMICS
Degrees: Associate, bachelor's. **Academic Requirements:** Arts/fine arts, Christian studies, computer literacy, English (including composition), foreign languages, history, humanities, mathematics, sciences (biological or physical), social science. **Classes:** Most classes have 10–19 students. Most lab/discussion sections have 10–19 students. **Disciplines with Highest Percentage of Degrees Awarded:** Interdisciplinary studies 23%, business/marketing 20%, education 16%, communication technologies 8%, English 6%. **Special Study Options:** Accelerated program, cooperative education program, cross-registration, double major, English as a second language (ESL), external degree program, honors program, independent study, internships, student-designed major, study abroad, teacher certification program.

FACILITIES
Housing: Men's dorms, women's dorms. **Computers:** 73% of public computers are PCs, 27% of public computers are Macs, network access in dorm rooms, network access in dorm lounges, remote student-access to Web through college's connection.

CAMPUS LIFE
Activities: Choral groups, concert band, drama/theater, jazz band, literary magazine, marching band, music ensembles, radio station, student government, student newspaper, television station, yearbook. **Athletics (Intercollegiate):** *Men:* Baseball, basketball, cross-country, football, golf, soccer, softball, tennis. *Women:* Basketball, cross-country, soccer, softball, tennis, volleyball.

ADMISSIONS
Freshman Academic Profile: 20% in top 10% of high school class, 44% in top 25% of high school class, 72% in top 50% of high school class. SAT Math middle 50% range 460–570. SAT Critical Reading middle 50% range 470–580. ACT middle 50% range 20–24. TOEFL required of all international applicants, minimum paper TOEFL 500, minimum computer TOEFL 200. **Basis for Candidate Selection:** *Very important factors considered include:* Class rank, rigor of secondary school record, standardized test scores. *Other factors considered include:* Application essay, recommendation(s). **Freshman Admission Requirements:** High school diploma is required, and GED is accepted. *Academic units recommended:* 4 English, 2 math, 2 science (2 science labs), 2 foreign language, 2 social studies, 2 history, 2 academic electives. **Freshman Admission Statistics:** 769 applied, 95% admitted, 56% enrolled. **Transfer Admission Requirements:** College transcript(s). Minimum college GPA of 2.0 required. Lowest grade transferable C. **General Admission Information:** Application fee $25. Regular application deadline 8/25. Non-fall registration accepted. Admission may be deferred for a maximum of 1 year. Common Application not accepted.

COSTS AND FINANCIAL AID
Required Forms and Deadlines: FAFSA. Financial aid filing deadline 6/1. **Notification of Awards:** Applicants will be notified of awards on a rolling basis beginning on or about 2/1. **Types of Aid:** *Need-based scholarships/grants:* Pell, SEOG, state scholarships/grants, private scholarships, the school's own gift aid. *Loans:* FFEL Subsidized Stafford, FFEL Unsubsidized Stafford, FFEL PLUS, Federal Perkins, state loans, college/university loans from institutional funds. **Financial Aid Statistics:** 71% freshmen, 69% undergrads receive need-based scholarship or grant aid. 18% freshmen, 17% undergrads receive need-based self-help aid. 80 freshmen, 450 undergrads receive athletic scholarships.

NORTH PARK UNIVERSITY

3225 West Foster Avenue, Chicago, IL 60625-4895
Phone: 773-244-5500 **E-mail:** admission@northpark.edu **CEEB Code:** 1556
Fax: 773-244-5243 **Website:** www.northpark.edu **ACT Code:** 1098
Financial Aid Phone: 773-244-5506

This private school, affiliated with the Evangelical Covenant Church, was founded in 1891. It has a 30-acre campus.

RATINGS
Admissions Selectivity Rating: 79   **Fire Safety Rating:** 61   **Green Rating:** 60*

STUDENTS AND FACULTY
Enrollment: 1,973. **Student Body:** 65% female, 35% male, 38% out-of-state, 4% international (22 countries represented). African American 10%, Asian 7%, Caucasian 61%, Hispanic 10%. **Retention and Graduation:** 75% freshmen return for sophomore year. **Faculty:** Student/faculty ratio 11:1. 130 full-time faculty, 87% hold PhDs. 100% faculty teach undergrads.

ACADEMICS
Degrees: Bachelor's, doctoral, master's, post-bachelor's certificate. **Academic Requirements:** Arts/fine arts, English (including composition), foreign languages, history, humanities, mathematics, philosophy, sciences (biological or physical), social science. The North Park Dialogue, interdisciplinary core curriculum required of all undergraduates. **Classes:** Most classes have 20–29 students. Most lab/discussion sections have 20–29 students. **Disciplines with Highest Percentage of Degrees Awarded:** Business/marketing 28%, health professions and related sciences 14%, education 11%, philosophy and religious studies 9%, social sciences 8%. **Special Study Options:** Accelerated program, distance learning, double major, English as a second language (ESL), honors program, independent study, internships, liberal arts/career combination, student-designed major, study abroad, teacher certification program.

FACILITIES
Housing: Men's dorms, women's dorms, apartments for single students, special housing for disabled students. **Special Academic Facilities/Equipment:** Art gallery, language lab, Swedish Historical Society Archives. **Computers:** 20% of classrooms are wired, 4% of classrooms are wireless, 100% of public computers are PCs, network access in dorm rooms, network access in dorm lounges, online registration, online administrative functions (other than registration), remote student-access to Web through college's connection.

CAMPUS LIFE
Activities: Choral groups, concert band, drama/theater, jazz band, literary magazine, music ensembles, musical theater, opera, pep band, student government, student newspaper, symphony orchestra, yearbook. **Organizations:** 4 honor societies, 1 religious organization. **Athletics (Intercollegiate):** *Men:* Baseball, basketball, cross-country, football, golf, soccer, track/field (indoor), track/field (outdoor). *Women:* Basketball, crew/rowing, cross-country, golf, soccer, softball, track/field (indoor), track/field (outdoor), volleyball.

ADMISSIONS
Freshman Academic Profile: 16% in top 10% of high school class, 42% in top 25% of high school class, 77% in top 50% of high school class. 80% from public high schools. SAT Math middle 50% range 480–600. SAT Critical Reading middle 50% range 500–630. ACT middle 50% range 20–25. TOEFL required of all international applicants, minimum paper TOEFL 550, minimum computer TOEFL 213. **Basis for Candidate Selection:** *Very important factors considered include:* Academic GPA, application essay, character/personal qualities, class rank, recommendation(s), rigor of secondary school record, standardized test scores, talent/ability. *Important factors considered include:* Extracurricular activities, first generation, interview, racial/ethnic status, volunteer work. *Other factors considered include:* Alumni/ae relation, geographical residence, level of applicant's interest, work experience. **Freshman Admission Requirements:** High school diploma is required, and GED is accepted. *Academic units recommended:* 4 English, 3 math, 3 science, 2 foreign language, 1 social studies, 1 history. **Freshman Admission Statistics:** 1,304 applied, 70% admitted, 41% enrolled. **Transfer Admission Requirements:** College transcript(s), essay or personal statement, statement of good standing from prior institution(s). Minimum college GPA of 2.0 required. Lowest grade transferable D. **General Admission Information:** Application fee $40. Regular application deadline 7/1. Regular notification is rolling. Non-fall registration accepted. Admission may be deferred for a maximum of 1 year. Credit and/or placement offered for CEEB Advanced Placement tests.

COSTS AND FINANCIAL AID
Annual tuition $17,600. Room and board $7,580. Average book expense $950. **Required Forms and Deadlines:** FAFSA. Financial aid filing deadline 8/1.

Notification of Awards: Applicants will be notified of awards on a rolling basis beginning on or about 3/15. **Types of Aid:** *Need-based scholarships/grants:* Pell, SEOG, state scholarships/grants, private scholarships, the school's own gift aid, Federal Nursing Scholarships. *Loans:* FFEL Subsidized Stafford, FFEL Unsubsidized Stafford, FFEL PLUS, Federal Perkins, Federal Nursing. **Student Employment:** Off-campus job opportunities are excellent. **Financial Aid Statistics:** Highest amount earned per year from on-campus jobs $1,500.

See page 1292.

NORTHCENTRAL UNIVERSITY

505 West Whipple Street, Prescott, AZ 86301
Phone: 928-541-7777 **E-mail:** info@ncu.edu
Fax: 928-541-7817 **Website:** www.ncu.edu

This is a proprietary school.

RATINGS
Admissions Selectivity Rating: 60*   **Fire Safety Rating:** 60*   **Green Rating:** 60*

STUDENTS AND FACULTY
Enrollment: 122. **Student Body:** 45% female, 55% male. African American 16%, Asian 2%, Caucasian 74%, Hispanic 5%, Native American 2%. **Faculty:** Student/faculty ratio 1:1. 9 full-time faculty, 78% hold PhDs.

ACADEMICS
Degrees: Bachelor's, doctoral, master's. **Academic Requirements:** English (including composition), humanities, mathematics, sciences (biological or physical), social science. **Disciplines with Highest Percentage of Degrees Awarded:** Business/marketing 2%, computer and information sciences 1%. **Special Study Options:** Accelerated program, distance learning.

CAMPUS LIFE

ADMISSIONS
Basis for Candidate Selection: *Very important factors considered include:* Application essay. *Other factors considered include:* Work experience. **Freshman Admission Requirements:** High school diploma is required, and GED is accepted. **Transfer Admission Requirements:** High school transcript, college transcript(s), essay or personal statement. Minimum college GPA of 2.0 required. Lowest grade transferable C. **General Admission Information:** Application fee $100. Regular notification is continuous. Non-fall registration accepted. Common Application not accepted.

COSTS AND FINANCIAL AID
Average book expense $400.

NORTHEASTERN ILLINOIS UNIVERSITY

5500 North St. Louis Avenue, Chicago, IL 60625
Phone: 773-442-4000 **E-mail:** admrec@neiu.edu **CEEB Code:** 1090
Fax: 773-442-4020 **Website:** www.neiu.edu **ACT Code:** 0993
Financial Aid Phone: 773-442-5000

This public school was founded in 1961. It has a 63-acre campus.

RATINGS
Admissions Selectivity Rating: 68   **Fire Safety Rating:** 60*   **Green Rating:** 66

STUDENTS AND FACULTY
Enrollment: 9,042. **Student Body:** 61% female, 39% male, 1% out-of-state, 1% international. African American 11%, Asian 10%, Caucasian 43%, Hispanic 30%. **Retention and Graduation:** 66% freshmen return for sophomore year. 3% freshmen graduate within 4 years. 31% grads go on to further study within 1 year. 16% grads pursue arts and sciences degrees. 8% grads pursue business degrees. 1% grads pursue law degrees. 1% grads pursue medical degrees. **Faculty:** Student/faculty ratio 16:1. 411 full-time faculty, 71% hold PhDs. 100% faculty teach undergrads.

ACADEMICS
Degrees: Bachelor's, master's. **Academic Requirements:** Arts/fine arts, computer literacy, English (including composition), humanities, mathematics,

sciences (biological or physical), social science. **Classes:** Most classes have 20–29 students. **Majors with Highest Enrollment:** Computer and information sciences, elementary education and teaching, liberal arts and sciences/liberal studies. **Disciplines with Highest Percentage of Degrees Awarded:** Education 20%, business/marketing 19%, liberal arts/general studies 15%, social sciences 7%, English 6%. **Special Study Options:** Cooperative education program, distance learning, double major, dual enrollment, exchange student program (domestic), honors program, independent study, student-designed major, study abroad, teacher certification program.

FACILITIES

Special Academic Facilities/Equipment: Learning center with audiovisual, TV, multimedia, film, photography, graphic arts, and electronic instructional equipment, listening room. **Computers:** 90% of public computers are PCs, 10% of public computers are Macs, remote student-access to Web through college's connection.

CAMPUS LIFE

Activities: Dance, drama/theater, jazz band, literary magazine, music ensembles, radio station, student government, student newspaper. **Organizations:** 42 registered organizations, 12 honor societies, 6 religious organizations. 3 fraternities, 3 sororities.

ADMISSIONS

Freshman Academic Profile: 7% in top 10% of high school class, 19% in top 25% of high school class, 59% in top 50% of high school class. 81% from public high schools. ACT middle 50% range 16–21. TOEFL required of all international applicants, minimum paper TOEFL 500, minimum computer TOEFL 173. **Basis for Candidate Selection:** *Very important factors considered include:* Class rank, standardized test scores. **Freshman Admission Requirements:** High school diploma is required, and GED is accepted. *Academic units required:* 4 English, 3 math, 3 science, 3 social studies. **Freshman Admission Statistics:** 3,562 applied, 72% admitted, 43% enrolled. **Transfer Admission Requirements:** College transcript(s), statement of good standing from prior institution(s). Minimum college GPA of 2.0 required. Lowest grade transferable D. **General Admission Information:** Application fee $25. Regular application deadline 7/1. Regular notification 9/1. Non-fall registration accepted. Admission may be deferred for a maximum of 1 semester. Credit offered for CEEB Advanced Placement tests.

COSTS AND FINANCIAL AID

Required Forms and Deadlines: FAFSA, institution's own financial aid form. Financial aid filing deadline 2/28. **Notification of Awards:** Applicants will be notified of awards on a rolling basis beginning on or about 4/1. **Types of Aid:** *Need-based scholarships/grants:* Pell, SEOG, state scholarships/grants, private scholarships, the school's own gift aid. *Loans:* FFEL Subsidized Stafford, FFEL Unsubsidized Stafford, FFEL PLUS, Federal Perkins. **Financial Aid Statistics:** 51% freshmen, 43% undergrads receive need-based scholarship or grant aid. 9% freshmen, 18% undergrads receive need-based self-help aid. 54% freshmen, 54% undergrads receive any aid.

NORTHEASTERN STATE UNIVERSITY

Office of Admissions and Records, 600 North Grand, Tahlequah, OK 74464-2399
Phone: 918-444-2200 **E-mail:** nsuinfo@nsuok.edu **CEEB Code:** 6485
Fax: 918-458-2342 **Website:** www.nsuok.edu **ACT Code:** 3408
Financial Aid Phone: 918-444-6402

This public school was founded in 1846. It has a 200-acre campus.

RATINGS

Admissions Selectivity Rating: 60*   **Fire Safety Rating:** 60*   **Green Rating:** 60*

STUDENTS AND FACULTY

Enrollment: 8,485. **Student Body:** 61% female, 39% male, 3% out-of-state, 3% international (41 countries represented). African American 6%, Asian 1%, Caucasian 59%, Hispanic 2%, Native American 29%. **Retention and Graduation:** 64% freshmen return for sophomore year. 12% freshmen graduate within 4 years. **Faculty:** Student/faculty ratio 23:1. 306 full-time faculty, 70% hold PhDs. 90% faculty teach undergrads.

ACADEMICS

Degrees: Bachelor's, first professional, master's, post-bachelor's certificate, post-master's certificate. **Academic Requirements:** Computer literacy, English (including composition), geography, health and physical education, history, humanities, mathematics, sciences (biological or physical), social science, speech communications. **Classes:** Most classes have 20–29 students.

Most lab/discussion sections have 10–19 students. **Majors with Highest Enrollment:** Accounting, business administration and management, elementary education and teaching. **Disciplines with Highest Percentage of Degrees Awarded:** Education 28%, business/marketing 24%, security and protective services 7%, biological/life sciences 5%, psychology 5%. **Special Study Options:** Cooperative education program, distance learning, double major, dual enrollment, honors program, independent study, internships, student-designed major, weekend college.

FACILITIES

Housing: Coed dorms, apartments for married students, apartments for single students, special housing for disabled students, fraternity/sorority housing. **Computers:** 15% of classrooms are wireless, 100% of public computers are PCs, network access in dorm rooms, online administrative functions (other than registration), remote student-access to Web through college's connection.

CAMPUS LIFE

Activities: Choral groups, concert band, dance, drama/theater, jazz band, literary magazine, marching band, music ensembles, musical theater, pep band, student government, student newspaper, symphony orchestra, television station. **Organizations:** 77 registered organizations, 9 honor societies, 5 religious organizations. 7 fraternities (4% men join), 6 sororities (2% women join). **Athletics (Intercollegiate):** *Men:* Baseball, basketball, football, golf, soccer. *Women:* Basketball, golf, soccer, softball, tennis. **Environmental Initiatives:** President's Climate Commitment. LEED Certification for new buildings and major renovations. Aggressive recycling and energy conservation efforts, composting, local produce, fair trade certification, zero transfat, antibiotic free, sustainable seafood, cage free eggs, corporate responsibility partnerships.

ADMISSIONS

Freshman Academic Profile: ACT middle 50% range 18–23. TOEFL required of all international applicants, minimum paper TOEFL 500, minimum computer TOEFL 173. **Basis for Candidate Selection:** *Very important factors considered include:* Academic GPA, class rank, rigor of secondary school record, standardized test scores. *Other factors considered include:* First generation, geographical residence, state residency. **Freshman Admission Requirements:** High school diploma is required, and GED is accepted. *Academic units required:* 4 English, 3 math, 2 science (2 science labs), 2 history, 4 academic electives. *Academic units recommended:* 2 foreign language, 2 social studies. **Freshman Admission Statistics:** 2,186 applied, 74% admitted, 69% enrolled. **Transfer Admission Requirements:** College transcript(s). Minimum college GPA of 2.0 required. Lowest grade transferable D. **General Admission Information:** Regular application deadline 8/1. Non-fall registration accepted. Admission may be deferred for a maximum of 1 semester. Credit offered for CEEB Advanced Placement tests.

COSTS AND FINANCIAL AID

Average book expense $950. **Required Forms and Deadlines:** FAFSA, institution's own financial aid form. Financial aid filing deadline 4/1. **Notification of Awards:** Applicants will be notified of awards on a rolling basis beginning on or about 2/15. **Types of Aid:** *Need-based scholarships/grants:* Pell, SEOG, state scholarships/grants, private scholarships, the school's own gift aid. *Loans:* FFEL Subsidized Stafford, FFEL Unsubsidized Stafford, FFEL PLUS, Federal Perkins. **Student Employment:** Federal Work-Study Program available. Institutional employment available. **Financial Aid Statistics:** 40% freshmen, 46% undergrads receive need-based scholarship or grant aid. 16% freshmen, 41% undergrads receive need-based self-help aid. 38 freshmen, 787 undergrads receive athletic scholarships. 75% freshmen, 75% undergrads receive any aid.

NORTHEASTERN UNIVERSITY

Best 368

360 Huntington Avenue, 150 Richards Hall, Boston, MA 02115
Phone: 617-373-2200 **E-mail:** admissions@neu.edu **CEEB Code:** 3667
Fax: 617-373-8780 **Website:** www.northeastern.edu **ACT Code:** 1880
Financial Aid Phone: 617-373-3190

This private school was founded in 1898. It has a 67-acre campus.

RATINGS
Admissions Selectivity Rating: 91   **Fire Safety Rating:** 87   **Green Rating:** 87

STUDENTS AND FACULTY
Enrollment: 15,195. **Student Body:** 50% female, 50% male, 65% out-of-state, 4% international (94 countries represented). African American 6%, Asian 7%, Caucasian 63%, Hispanic 5%. **Retention and Graduation:** 90% freshmen return for sophomore year. 16% grads go on to further study within 1 year. **Faculty:** Student/faculty ratio 16:1. 873 full-time faculty, 88% hold PhDs. 100% faculty teach undergrads.

ACADEMICS
Degrees: Bachelor's, doctoral, first professional, master's, post-master's certificate. **Academic Requirements:** English (including composition), diversity requirement. **Classes:** Most classes have 10–19 students. **Majors with Highest Enrollment:** Business/commerce, engineering, health services/allied health. **Disciplines with Highest Percentage of Degrees Awarded:** Business/marketing 23%, health professions and related sciences 15%, engineering 11%, social sciences 8%, communications/journalism 7%. **Special Study Options:** Accelerated program, cooperative education program, cross-registration, distance learning, double major, English as a second language (ESL), exchange student program (domestic), honors program, independent study, internships, liberal arts/career combination, student-designed major, study abroad, teacher certification program.

FACILITIES
Housing: Coed dorms, apartments for single students, special housing for disabled students, special housing for international students, honors halls, wellness hall, quiet hall, living and learning halls, international, multicultural, leadership, or by college/program. **Special Academic Facilities/Equipment:** John D. O'Bryant African American Institute, Egan Science/Engineering Research Center, Behrakis Health Sciences Center, marine science center at Nahant, center for subsurfacing sensing and imaging systems (CenSSIS), Barnett Institute of Chemical and Biological Analysis, research vessel *MYSIS*, Marino Recreation Center, Badger-Rosen Squashbusters Center. **Computers:** 3% of classrooms are wired, 12% of classrooms are wireless, 56% of public computers are PCs, 36% of public computers are Macs, 8% of public computers are UNIX, network access in dorm rooms, network access in dorm lounges, online registration, online administrative functions (other than registration), remote student-access to Web through college's connection.

CAMPUS LIFE
Activities: Choral groups, concert band, dance, drama/theater, jazz band, literary magazine, music ensembles, musical theater, pep band, radio station, student government, student newspaper, symphony orchestra, television station, yearbook. **Organizations:** 225 registered organizations, 18 honor societies, 13 religious organizations. 9 fraternities (4% men join), 8 sororities (4% women join). **Athletics (Intercollegiate):** *Men:* Baseball, basketball, crew/rowing, cross-country, football, ice hockey, soccer, track/field (indoor), track/field (outdoor). *Women:* Basketball, crew/rowing, cross-country, diving, field hockey, ice hockey, soccer, swimming, track/field (indoor), track/field (outdoor), volleyball. **Environmental Initiatives:** President's Climate Commitment. LEED Certification for new buildings and major renovations. Aggressive recycling and energy conservation efforts, composting, local produce, fair trade certification, zero transfat, antibiotic free, sustainable seafood, cage free eggs, corporate responsibility partnerships.

ADMISSIONS
Freshman Academic Profile: 38% in top 10% of high school class, 76% in top 25% of high school class, 95% in top 50% of high school class. SAT Math middle 50% range 600–680. SAT Critical Reading middle 50% range 570–660. ACT middle 50% range 25–29. TOEFL required of all international applicants, minimum paper TOEFL 550, minimum computer TOEFL 213. **Basis for Candidate Selection:** *Very important factors considered include:* Academic

GPA, rigor of secondary school record. *Important factors considered include:* Application essay, character/personal qualities, class rank, extracurricular activities, first generation, recommendation(s), standardized test scores, talent/ability. *Other factors considered include:* Alumni/ae relation, geographical residence, racial/ethnic status, state residency, volunteer work, work experience. **Freshman Admission Requirements:** High school diploma is required, and GED is accepted. *Academic units required:* 4 English, 3 math, 3 science (2 science labs), 2 foreign language, 2 social studies, 2 history. *Academic units recommended:* 4 math, 4 science (4 science labs), 4 foreign language. **Freshman Admission Statistics:** 27,168 applied, 45% admitted, 24% enrolled. **Transfer Admission Requirements:** College transcript(s), essay or personal statement, statement of good standing from prior institution(s). Minimum college GPA of 2.0 required. Lowest grade transferable C. **General Admission Information:** Application fee $75. Regular application deadline 1/15. Regular notification decisions released between 3/15 and 4/1. Non-fall registration accepted. Admission may be deferred for a maximum of 1 year. Credit and/or placement offered for CEEB Advanced Placement tests.

COSTS AND FINANCIAL AID
Annual tuition $31,500. Room and board $11,420. Required fees $399. Average book expense $900. **Required Forms and Deadlines:** FAFSA, CSS/Financial Aid PROFILE. Financial aid filing deadline 2/15. **Notification of Awards:** Applicants will be notified of awards on a rolling basis beginning on or about 2/15. **Types of Aid:** *Need-based scholarships/grants:* Pell, SEOG, state scholarships/grants, private scholarships, the school's own gift aid, Federal Nursing Scholarships. *Loans:* FFEL Subsidized Stafford, FFEL Unsubsidized Stafford, FFEL PLUS, Federal Perkins, Federal Nursing, state loans, MEFA, TERI, Signature, Massachusetts No Interest Loan (NIL), CitiAssist. **Student Employment:** Federal Work-Study Program available. Institutional employment available. Off-campus job opportunities are excellent. **Financial Aid Statistics:** 60% freshmen, 55% undergrads receive need-based scholarship or grant aid. 53% freshmen, 50% undergrads receive need-based self-help aid. 47 freshmen, 235 undergrads receive athletic scholarships. 90% freshmen, 83% undergrads receive any aid. Highest amount earned per year from on-campus jobs $2,451.

See page 1294.

NORTHERN ARIZONA UNIVERSITY

PO Box 4084, Flagstaff, AZ 86011-4084
Phone: 928-523-5511 **E-mail:** undergraduate.admissions@nau.edu **CEEB Code:** 4006
Fax: 928-523-0226 **Website:** www.nau.edu **ACT Code:** 0086
Financial Aid Phone: 928-523-4951

This public school was founded in 1899. It has a 740-acre campus.

RATINGS
Admissions Selectivity Rating: 60*   **Fire Safety Rating:** 60*   **Green Rating:** 60*

STUDENTS AND FACULTY
Enrollment: 14,325. **Student Body:** 60% female, 40% male, 19% out-of-state, 2% international (67 countries represented). African American 2%, Asian 2%, Caucasian 71%, Hispanic 12%, Native American 7%. **Retention and Graduation:** 72% freshmen return for sophomore year. 27% freshmen graduate within 4 years. **Faculty:** Student/faculty ratio 16:1. 755 full-time faculty, 77% hold PhDs. 90% faculty teach undergrads.

ACADEMICS
Degrees: Bachelor's, certificate, doctoral, first professional, master's, post-bachelor's certificate. **Academic Requirements:** Computer literacy, English (including composition), mathematics. **Classes:** Most classes have 10–19 students. Most lab/discussion sections have 20–29 students. **Majors with Highest Enrollment:** Business administration/management, elementary education and teaching, psychology. **Disciplines with Highest Percentage of Degrees Awarded:** Education 22%, business/marketing 18%, liberal arts/general studies 8%, psychology 5%, security and protective services 5%, communications/journalism 5%, social sciences 5%, visual and performing arts 5%, biological/life sciences 4%. **Special Study Options:** Accelerated program, cooperative education program, distance learning, double major, dual enrollment, English as a second language (ESL), exchange student program (domestic), external degree program, honors program, independent study, internships, study abroad, teacher certification program.

FACILITIES
Housing: Coed dorms, men's dorms, women's dorms, apartments for married students, apartments for single students, special housing for disabled students,

fraternity/sorority housing. **Special Academic Facilities/Equipment:** Art gallery, art and music studios, observatory, multidisciplinary research center, 4,000-acre experimental forest. **Computers:** 97% of public computers are PCs, 3% of public computers are Macs, network access in dorm rooms, network access in dorm lounges, online registration, online administrative functions (other than registration), remote student-access to Web through college's connection.

CAMPUS LIFE

Activities: Choral groups, dance, drama/theater, jazz band, literary magazine, marching band, music ensembles, pep band, radio station, student government, student newspaper, symphony orchestra, television station, yearbook. **Organizations:** 157 registered organizations, 20 honor societies, 7 religious organizations. 14 fraternities, 9 sororities. **Athletics (Intercollegiate):** *Men:* Basketball, cross-country, football, tennis, track/field (outdoor). *Women:* Basketball, cross-country, diving, golf, soccer, swimming, tennis, track/field (outdoor), volleyball.

ADMISSIONS

Freshman Academic Profile: SAT Math middle 50% range 500–600. SAT Critical Reading middle 50% range 490–590. SAT Writing middle 50% range 480–570. ACT middle 50% range 20–25. TOEFL required of all international applicants, minimum paper TOEFL 525, minimum computer TOEFL 195. **Basis for Candidate Selection:** *Very important factors considered include:* Academic GPA, class rank, rigor of secondary school record, standardized test scores. **Freshman Admission Requirements:** High school diploma is required, and GED is accepted. *Academic units required:* 4 English, 4 math, 3 science (1 science lab), 2 foreign language, 2 social studies, 1 history, 1 fine arts. **Freshman Admission Statistics:** 9,077 applied, 32% admitted, 97% enrolled. **Transfer Admission Requirements:** College transcript(s), statement of good standing from prior institution(s). Minimum college GPA of 2.0 required. Lowest grade transferable C. **General Admission Information:** Application fee $25. Regular notification is rolling. Non-fall registration accepted. Admission may be deferred for a maximum of 2 years. Credit and/or placement offered for CEEB Advanced Placement tests.

COSTS AND FINANCIAL AID

Annual in-state tuition $4,594. Annual out-of-state tuition $14,428. Room and board $6,572. Required fees $250. Average book expense $864. **Required Forms and Deadlines:** FAFSA. Financial aid filing deadline 2/14. **Notification of Awards:** Applicants will be notified of awards on a rolling basis beginning on or about 3/15. **Types of Aid:** *Need-based scholarships/grants:* Pell, SEOG, state scholarships/grants, private scholarships, the school's own gift aid, Federal Nursing Scholarships. *Loans:* Direct Subsidized Stafford, Direct Unsubsidized Stafford, Direct PLUS, Federal Perkins, Federal Nursing, college/university loans from institutional funds. **Student Employment:** Federal Work-Study Program available. Institutional employment available. Off-campus job opportunities are good. **Financial Aid Statistics:** 23% freshmen, 34% undergrads receive need-based scholarship or grant aid. 28% freshmen, 40% undergrads receive need-based self-help aid. 42 freshmen, 240 undergrads receive athletic scholarships. 62% freshmen, 66% undergrads receive any aid. Highest amount earned per year from on-campus jobs $2,097.

NORTHERN ILLINOIS UNIVERSITY

Office of Admissions, Williston Hall 101, NIU, DeKalb, IL 60115-2857
Phone: 815-753-0446 **E-mail:** admissions-info@niu.edu **CEEB Code:** 1559
Fax: 815-753-1783 **Website:** www.niu.edu **ACT Code:** 1102
Financial Aid Phone: 815-753-1395

This public school was founded in 1895. It has a 546-acre campus.

RATINGS

Admissions Selectivity Rating: 71   **Fire Safety Rating:** 60*   **Green Rating:** 60*

STUDENTS AND FACULTY

Enrollment: 18,025. **Student Body:** 53% female, 47% male, 4% out-of-state. African American 12%, Asian 6%, Caucasian 71%, Hispanic 6%. **Retention and Graduation:** 10% grads go on to further study within 1 year. **Faculty:** Student/faculty ratio 17:1. 875 full-time faculty, 83% hold PhDs.

ACADEMICS

Degrees: Bachelor's, doctoral, first professional, master's. **Academic Requirements:** English (including composition), foreign languages, humanities, mathematics, sciences (biological or physical), social science. **Classes:** Most classes have 20–29 students. Most lab/discussion sections have 20–29 students. **Disciplines with Highest Percentage of Degrees Awarded:**

Business/marketing 25%, education 14%, communication technologies 7%, social sciences 7%, health professions and related sciences 7%, visual and performing arts 6%. **Special Study Options:** Cooperative education program, distance learning, double major, dual enrollment, external degree program, honors program, independent study, internships, liberal arts/career combination, student-designed major, study abroad, teacher certification program.

FACILITIES

Housing: Coed dorms, apartments for married students, special housing for disabled students, special housing for international students, fraternity/sorority housing, quiet and alcohol-free lifestyle floors, 21 and over/graduates student floors, honors floors. **Special Academic Facilities/Equipment:** Art and anthropology museums, plant molecular biology center. **Computers:** 95% of public computers are PCs, 5% of public computers are Macs, network access in dorm rooms, online registration, remote student-access to Web through college's connection.

CAMPUS LIFE

Activities: Choral groups, concert band, dance, drama/theater, jazz band, marching band, opera, radio station, student government, student newspaper, student-run film society, symphony orchestra, television station. **Organizations:** 200 registered organizations, 13 religious organizations. 22 fraternities (11% men join), 14 sororities (7% women join). **Athletics (Intercollegiate):** *Men:* Baseball, basketball, diving, football, golf, soccer, swimming, tennis, wrestling. *Women:* Basketball, cross-country, golf, gymnastics, soccer, softball, swimming, tennis, volleyball.

ADMISSIONS

Freshman Academic Profile: 9% in top 10% of high school class, 34% in top 25% of high school class, 74% in top 50% of high school class. ACT middle 50% range 19–24. TOEFL required of all international applicants, minimum paper TOEFL 525. **Basis for Candidate Selection:** *Very important factors considered include:* Class rank, rigor of secondary school record, standardized test scores. *Other factors considered include:* Application essay, extracurricular activities, racial/ethnic status, recommendation(s), talent/ability. **Freshman Admission Requirements:** High school diploma is required, and GED is accepted. *Academic units required:* 4 English, 2 math, 2 science (1 science lab), 1 foreign language, 2 social studies, 1 history. *Academic units recommended:* 4 math, 4 science (2 science labs), 2 foreign language, 3 social studies. **Freshman Admission Statistics:** 18,348 applied, 55% admitted, 29% enrolled. **Transfer Admission Requirements:** College transcript(s). Minimum college GPA of 2.0 required. Lowest grade transferable C. **General Admission Information:** Regular application deadline 8/1. Regular notification is rolling. Non-fall registration accepted. Common Application accepted. Credit and/or placement offered for CEEB Advanced Placement tests.

COSTS AND FINANCIAL AID

Annual in-state tuition $4,347. Room & board $5,010. Average book expense $700. **Required Forms and Deadlines:** FAFSA, institution's own financial aid form, Noncustodial PROFILE. Financial aid filing deadline 3/1. **Notification of Awards:** Applicants will be notified of awards on or about 4/15. **Types of Aid:** *Need-based scholarships/grants:* Pell, SEOG, state scholarships/grants, private scholarships, the school's own gift aid, Federal Nursing Scholarships. *Loans:* FFEL Subsidized Stafford, FFEL Unsubsidized Stafford, FFEL PLUS, Federal Perkins. **Student Employment:** Off-campus job opportunities are good. **Financial Aid Statistics:** 25% freshmen, 21% undergrads receive need-based scholarship or grant aid. 35% freshmen, 37% undergrads receive need-based self-help aid.

NORTHERN KENTUCKY UNIVERSITY

Administrative Center 401, Nunn Drive, Highland Heights, KY 41099
Phone: 859-572-5220 **E-mail:** admitnku@nku.edu **CEEB Code:** 1574
Fax: 859-572-6665 **Website:** www.nku.edu **ACT Code:** 1566
Financial Aid Phone: 859-572-6437

This public school was founded in 1968. It has a 397-acre campus.

RATINGS

Admissions Selectivity Rating: 60*   **Fire Safety Rating:** 90   **Green Rating:** 74

STUDENTS AND FACULTY

Enrollment: 11,611. **Student Body:** 58% female, 42% male, 39% out-of-state, 2% international (63 countries represented). African American 5%, Caucasian 88%, Hispanic 1%. **Retention and Graduation:** 67% freshmen return for sophomore year. **Faculty:** Student/faculty ratio 16:1. 544 full-time faculty, 70% hold PhDs. 95% faculty teach undergrads.

ACADEMICS

Degrees: Associate, bachelor's, certificate, first professional, master's, post-bachelor's certificate. **Academic Requirements:** Arts/fine arts, diversity, English (including composition), history, humanities, mathematics, sciences (biological or physical), social science. **Classes:** Most classes have 20–29 students. Most lab/discussion sections have 10–19 students. **Majors with Highest Enrollment:** Elementary education and teaching, nursing/registered nurse training (ASN, BSN, MSN, RN), psychology. **Disciplines with Highest Percentage of Degrees Awarded:** Business/marketing 24%, education 13%, English 8%, social sciences 8%, visual and performing arts 7%, health professions and related sciences 7%, psychology 6%. **Special Study Options:** Cooperative education program, cross-registration, distance learning, double major, dual enrollment, exchange student program (domestic), honors program, independent study, internships, liberal arts/career combination, study abroad, teacher certification program, Web-based programs, weekend college.

FACILITIES

Housing: Coed dorms, men's dorms, women's dorms, apartments for single students, special housing for disabled students, cooperative housing. One-third of all college housing is accessible to handicapped. **Special Academic Facilities/Equipment:** Art gallery; biology, geology, and anthropology museums; research/technical center; 2 electron microscopes. **Computers:** 10% of classrooms are wired, 80% of classrooms are wireless, 90% of public computers are PCs, 9% of public computers are Macs, 1% of public computers are UNIX, network access in dorm rooms, network access in dorm lounges, online registration, online administrative functions (other than registration), support for handheld computing, remote student-access to Web through college's connection.

CAMPUS LIFE

Activities: Choral groups, concert band, dance, drama/theater, jazz band, literary magazine, music ensembles, musical theater, opera, pep band, radio station, student government, student newspaper, symphony orchestra, television station. **Organizations:** 125 registered organizations, 14 honor societies, 9 religious organizations. 8 fraternities (4% men join), 8 sororities (4% women join). **Athletics (Intercollegiate):** *Men:* Baseball, basketball, cheerleading, cross-country, golf, soccer, tennis. *Women:* Basketball, cheerleading, cross-country, golf, soccer, softball, tennis, volleyball. **Environmental Initiatives:** Energy savings performance contract that is expected to save $4 million in energy over an 11-year period. Highly successful "U-PASS" partnership with the Transit Authority of Northern Kentucky (TANK) to provide free, unlimited bus rides to students and faculty/staff with a valid university ID. The campus recycling program was expanded in 2007 to include recycling of #1 and #2 plastic bottles and cans. In addition, NKU is participating in RecycleMania for the first time during 2008.

ADMISSIONS

Freshman Academic Profile: SAT Math middle 50% range 440–560. SAT Critical Reading middle 50% range 440–540. ACT middle 50% range 18–23. TOEFL required of all international applicants, minimum paper TOEFL 500, minimum computer TOEFL 173. **Basis for Candidate Selection:** *Very important factors considered include:* Academic GPA, class rank, standardized test scores. **Freshman Admission Requirements:** High school diploma is required, and GED is accepted. *Academic units required:* 4 English, 3 math, 3 science (1 science lab), 2 foreign language, 3 social studies, 6 academic electives, 1 health/physical education. **Freshman Admission Statistics:** 4,317 applied, 75% admitted, 55% enrolled. **Transfer Admission Requirements:** College transcript(s). Minimum college GPA of 2.0 required. Lowest grade transferable D. **General Admission Information:** Application fee $30. Regular application deadline 8/1. Regular notification is rolling. Non-fall registration accepted. Common Application not accepted. Credit offered for CEEB Advanced Placement tests.

COSTS AND FINANCIAL AID

Required Forms and Deadlines: FAFSA. Financial aid filing deadline 3/1. **Notification of Awards:** Applicants will be notified of awards on a rolling basis beginning on or about 4/1. **Types of Aid:** *Need-based scholarships/grants:* Pell, SEOG, state scholarships/grants, private scholarships, the school's own gift aid. *Loans:* FFEL Subsidized Stafford, FFEL Unsubsidized Stafford, FFEL PLUS, Federal Perkins, private loans. **Student Employment:** Federal Work-Study Program available. Institutional employment available. Off-campus job opportunities are good. **Financial Aid Statistics:** 46% freshmen, 36% undergrads receive need-based scholarship or grant aid. 36% freshmen, 29% undergrads receive need-based self-help aid. 23 freshmen, 113 undergrads receive athletic scholarships. 90% freshmen, 85% undergrads receive any aid. Highest amount earned per year from on-campus jobs $5,625.

NORTHERN MICHIGAN UNIVERSITY

1401 Presque Isle Avenue, Marquette, MI 49855
Phone: 906-227-2650 **E-mail:** admiss@nmu.edu **CEEB Code:** 1560
Fax: 906-227-1747 **Website:** www.nmu.edu **ACT Code:** 2038
Financial Aid Phone: 800-682-9797

This public school was founded in 1899. It has a 300-acre campus.

RATINGS

Admissions Selectivity Rating: 60* **Fire Safety Rating:** 86 **Green Rating:** 74

STUDENTS AND FACULTY

Enrollment: 8,498. **Student Body:** 53% female, 47% male, 20% out-of-state. African American 2%, Caucasian 89%, Hispanic 1%, Native American 2%. **Retention and Graduation:** 75% freshmen return for sophomore year. 17% freshmen graduate within 4 years. **Faculty:** Student/faculty ratio 22:1. 319 full-time faculty, 62% hold PhDs. 98% faculty teach undergrads.

ACADEMICS

Degrees: Associate, bachelor's, certificate, diploma, master's, post-bachelor's certificate, post-master's certificate, terminal. **Academic Requirements:** Arts/fine arts, computer literacy, English (including composition), humanities, mathematics, sciences (biological or physical), social science, world cultures. **Classes:** Most classes have 20–29 students. Most lab/discussion sections have 20–29 students. **Majors with Highest Enrollment:** Art/art studies, education, nursing/registered nurse training (ASN, BSN, MSN, RN). **Disciplines with Highest Percentage of Degrees Awarded:** Education 16%, business/marketing 15%, health professions and related sciences 8%, social sciences 8%, visual and performing arts 7%. **Special Study Options:** Distance learning, double major, dual enrollment, English as a second language (ESL), exchange student program (domestic), honors program, independent study, internships, liberal arts/career combination, student-designed major, study abroad, teacher certification program, weekend college.

FACILITIES

Housing: Coed dorms, apartments for married students, apartments for single students, special housing for disabled students. **Special Academic Facilities/Equipment:** Seaborg Science Center, new science facility, new and remodeled music and art and design instructional rooms, DeVos Art Gallery. **Computers:** 90% of classrooms are wired, 80% of classrooms are wireless, network access in dorm rooms, network access in dorm lounges, online registration, online administrative functions (other than registration), remote student-access to Web through college's connection, tuition includes personal computer.

CAMPUS LIFE

Activities: Choral groups, concert band, dance, drama/theater, jazz band, literary magazine, marching band, music ensembles, musical theater, opera, pep band, radio station, student government, student newspaper, student-run film society, symphony orchestra, television station. **Organizations:** 202 registered organizations, 18 religious organizations. 4 fraternities, 3 sororities. **Athletics (Intercollegiate):** *Men:* Basketball, cheerleading, football, golf, ice hockey, skiing (Nordic/cross-country). *Women:* Basketball, cheerleading, cross-country, diving, skiing (Nordic/cross-country), soccer, swimming, track/field (indoor), track/field (outdoor), volleyball. **Environmental Initiatives:** Northern is a member of the Association for the Advancement of Sustainability in Higher Education. Reduced energy consumption by providing computer controlled heating and cooling, thermal efficient windows for the dormitories,individual heating controls in dorm rooms, new efficient lighting and controls technology, new energy efficient architectural design components, water efficient fixtures, wells for irrigation and waterless urinals. In 2007 Meyland Hall's renovation received LEED certification.

ADMISSIONS

Freshman Academic Profile: ACT middle 50% range 20–25. TOEFL required of all international applicants, minimum paper TOEFL 500, minimum computer TOEFL 173. **Basis for Candidate Selection:** *Very important factors considered include:* Academic GPA, rigor of secondary school record, standardized test scores. *Other factors considered include:* Application essay, class rank, extracurricular activities, first generation, recommendation(s), talent/ability, volunteer work, work experience. **Freshman Admission Requirements:** High school diploma is required, and GED is accepted. *Academic units recommended:* 4 English, 4 math, 4 science, 3 foreign language, 4 social studies. **Freshman Admission Statistics:** 4,763 applied, 80% admitted, 36% enrolled. **Transfer Admission Requirements:** College transcript(s), statement of good standing from prior institution(s). Minimum college GPA of 2.0 required. Lowest grade transferable C-. **General Admission Information:** Application fee $30. Regular notification is rolling. Non-fall registration accepted. Credit and/or placement offered for CEEB Advanced Placement tests.

COSTS AND FINANCIAL AID

Annual in-state tuition $6,144. Annual out-of-state tuition $10,080. Room and board $7,220. Required fees $565. Average book expense $748. **Required Forms and Deadlines:** FAFSA. Financial aid filing deadline 3/1. **Notification of Awards:** Applicants will be notified of awards on a rolling basis beginning on or about 4/1. **Types of Aid:** *Need-based scholarships/grants:* Pell, SEOG, state scholarships/grants, private scholarships, the school's own gift aid, Federal Nursing Scholarships. *Loans:* Direct Subsidized Stafford, Direct Unsubsidized Stafford, Direct PLUS, Federal Perkins, state loans, private loans. **Financial Aid Statistics:** 35% freshmen, 36% undergrads receive need-based scholarship or grant aid. 43% freshmen, 47% undergrads receive need-based self-help aid. 17 freshmen, 32 undergrads receive athletic scholarships. 90% freshmen, 83% undergrads receive any aid.

NORTHERN STATE UNIVERSITY

1200 South Jay Street, Aberdeen, SD 57401-7198
Phone: 605-626-2544 **E-mail:** admissions1@northern.edu **CEEB Code:** 6487
Fax: 605-626-2431 **Website:** www.northern.edu **ACT Code:** 3916
Financial Aid Phone: 605-626-2640

This public school was founded in 1901. It has a 72-acre campus.

RATINGS

Admissions Selectivity Rating: 60*   Fire Safety Rating: 60*   Green Rating: 86

STUDENTS AND FACULTY

Enrollment: 1,808. **Student Body:** 56% female, 44% male, 19% out-of-state. **Retention and Graduation:** 65% freshmen return for sophomore year. 10% grads go on to further study within 1 year. 7% grads pursue arts and sciences degrees. 1% grads pursue business degrees. 1% grads pursue law degrees. 1% grads pursue medical degrees. **Faculty:** Student/faculty ratio 22:1. 93 full-time faculty, 83% hold PhDs. 100% faculty teach undergrads.

ACADEMICS

Degrees: Associate, bachelor's, certificate, master's. **Academic Requirements:** Arts/fine arts, computer literacy, English (including composition), foreign languages, history, humanities, mathematics, philosophy, sciences (biological or physical), social science. **Classes:** Most classes have 10–19 students. **Majors with Highest Enrollment:** Business administration/management, elementary education and teaching, sociology. **Disciplines with Highest Percentage of Degrees Awarded:** Business/marketing 34%, education 24%, social sciences 16%, biological/life sciences 6%, visual and performing arts 5%. **Special Study Options:** Accelerated program, cooperative education program, distance learning, double major, E-learning certification, English as a second language (ESL), exchange student program (domestic), honors program, international business, internships, student-designed major, study abroad, teacher certification program.

FACILITIES

Housing: Coed dorms, men's dorms, women's dorms, apartments for single students. **Special Academic Facilities/Equipment:** Art galleries. **Computers:** Network access in dorm rooms, network access in dorm lounges, online registration, online administrative functions (other than registration), support for handheld computing, remote student-access to Web through college's connection.

CAMPUS LIFE

Activities: Choral groups, concert band, drama/theater, marching band, pep band, student government, student newspaper, yearbook. **Organizations:** 100 registered organizations, 5 honor societies, 3 religious organizations. **Athletics (Intercollegiate):** *Men:* Baseball, basketball, cheerleading, cross-country, football, golf, track/field (indoor), track/field (outdoor), wrestling. *Women:* Basketball, cheerleading, cross-country, golf, soccer, softball, swimming, tennis, track/field (indoor), track/field (outdoor), volleyball.

ADMISSIONS

Freshman Academic Profile: 8% in top 10% of high school class, 20% in top 25% of high school class, 36% in top 50% of high school class. TOEFL required of all international applicants, minimum paper TOEFL 550, minimum computer TOEFL 173. **Basis for Candidate Selection:** *Very important factors considered include:* Class rank, rigor of secondary school record, standardized test scores. *Other factors considered include:* Interview, talent/ability. **Freshman Admission Requirements:** High school diploma is required, and GED is accepted. *Academic units required:* 4 English, 3 math, 3 science (3 science labs), 3 social studies. **Freshman Admission Statistics:** 844 applied, 94% admitted, 48% enrolled. **Transfer Admission Requirements:** High school transcript, college transcript(s). Minimum college GPA of 2.0

College Directory

---

required. Lowest grade transferable C. **General Admission Information:** Application fee $20. Regular application deadline 8/15. Regular notification is rolling. Non-fall registration accepted. Credit and/or placement offered for CEEB Advanced Placement tests.

COSTS AND FINANCIAL AID

Annual in-state tuition $2,382. Out-of-state tuition $7,569. Room & board $3,679. Required fees $2,580. Average book expense $800. **Required Forms and Deadlines:** FAFSA. **Notification of Awards:** Applicants will be notified of awards on or about 5/1. **Types of Aid:** *Need-based scholarships/grants:* Pell, SEOG, state scholarships/grants, private scholarships, the school's own gift aid. *Loans:* FFEL Subsidized Stafford, FFEL Unsubsidized Stafford, FFEL PLUS, Federal Perkins, college/university loans from institutional funds. **Student Employment:** Federal Work-Study Program available. Institutional employment available. Off-campus job opportunities are excellent. **Financial Aid Statistics:** Highest amount earned per year from on-campus jobs $1,800.

NORTHLAND COLLEGE

1411 Ellis Avenue, Ashland, WI 54806-3999
Phone: 715-682-1224 **E-mail:** admit@northland.edu **CEEB Code:** 1561
Fax: 715-682-1258 **Website:** www.northland.edu **ACT Code:** 4624
Financial Aid Phone: 715-682-1255

This private school, affiliated with the United Church of Christ, was founded in 1892. It has a 130-acre campus.

RATINGS

Admissions Selectivity Rating: 86   Fire Safety Rating: 60*   Green Rating: 98

STUDENTS AND FACULTY

Enrollment: 673. **Student Body:** 57% female, 43% male, 55% out-of-state, 1% international (3 countries represented). African American 2%, Asian 1%, Caucasian 86%, Hispanic 2%, Native American 2%. **Retention and Graduation:** 71% freshmen return for sophomore year. **Faculty:** Student/faculty ratio 12:1. 41 full-time faculty, 85% hold PhDs. 100% faculty teach undergrads.

ACADEMICS

Degrees: Bachelor's. **Academic Requirements:** Arts/fine arts, English (including composition), history, humanities, mathematics, philosophy, sciences (biological or physical), social science. 2 courses in other cultures, which can be in foreign language or other options such as Native American studies, Eastern religions, literature of the third world, study abroad. **Classes:** Most classes have fewer than 10 students. Most lab/discussion sections have 10–19 students. **Majors with Highest Enrollment:** Education, environmental studies, natural resources/conservation. **Disciplines with Highest Percentage of Degrees Awarded:** Natural resources/environmental science 43%, biological/life sciences 29%, education 25%, business/marketing 17%, physical sciences 14%. **Special Study Options:** Distance learning, double major, exchange student program (domestic), independent study, internships, liberal arts/career combination, student-designed major, study abroad, teacher certification program. 3–2 cooperative programs in forestry and engineering with Michigan Technological University and Washington University. Eco league consortium with 6 environmental liberal arts colleges (Prescott, Green Mountain, Alaska Pacific University, Antioch College, College of the Atlantic, Northland College) around the country engaging in student semester exchanges.

FACILITIES

Housing: Coed dorms, men's dorms, women's dorms, apartments for single students, cooperative housing, theme houses. **Special Academic Facilities/Equipment:** Native American museum, language lab, field stations in nearby national forest, observatory. **Computers:** Network access in dorm rooms, network access in dorm lounges, online registration, online administrative functions (other than registration), remote student-access to Web through college's connection.

CAMPUS LIFE

Activities: Choral groups, concert band, dance, drama/theater, jazz band, literary magazine, music ensembles, radio station, student government, student newspaper, symphony orchestra, yearbook. **Organizations:** 30 registered organizations, 1 honor society, 2 religious organizations. **Athletics (Intercollegiate):** *Men:* Baseball, basketball, cross-country, ice hockey, skiing (Nordic/cross-country), soccer. *Women:* Basketball, cross-country, skiing (Nordic/cross-country), soccer, softball, volleyball.

ADMISSIONS

Freshman Academic Profile: 27% in top 10% of high school class, 62% in top 25% of high school class, 86% in top 50% of high school class. 80% from public

high schools. SAT Math middle 50% range 480–620. SAT Critical Reading middle 50% range 530–620. ACT middle 50% range 21–27. TOEFL required of all international applicants, minimum paper TOEFL 550, minimum computer TOEFL 213. **Basis for Candidate Selection:** *Very important factors considered include:* Rigor of secondary school record. *Important factors considered include:* Academic GPA, application essay, class rank, recommendation(s), standardized test scores. *Other factors considered include:* Alumni/ae relation, character/personal qualities, extracurricular activities, first generation, geographical residence, interview, level of applicant's interest, talent/ability, volunteer work, work experience. **Freshman Admission Requirements:** High school diploma is required, and GED is accepted. *Academic units required:* 4 English, 3 math, 3 science (2 science labs), 3 social studies, 3 academic electives. *Academic units recommended:* 4 English, 3 math, 3 science (2 science labs), 2 foreign language, 3 social studies, 4 academic electives. **Freshman Admission Statistics:** 1,697 applied, 57% admitted, 19% enrolled. **Transfer Admission Requirements:** College transcript(s), statement of good standing from prior institution(s). Minimum college GPA of 2.0 required. Lowest grade transferable C-. **General Admission Information:** Application fee $25. Regular notification is rolling. Non-fall registration accepted. Admission may be deferred for a maximum of 2 years. Credit and/or placement offered for CEEB Advanced Placement tests.

COSTS AND FINANCIAL AID

Annual tuition $22,500. Room and board $6,440. Required fees $601. Average book expense $800. **Required Forms and Deadlines:** FAFSA. Financial aid filing deadline 4/15. **Notification of Awards:** Applicants will be notified of awards on a rolling basis beginning on or about 3/1. **Types of Aid:** *Need-based scholarships/grants:* Pell, SEOG, state scholarships/grants, private scholarships, the school's own gift aid, Bureau of Indian Affairs Grants. *Loans:* Direct Subsidized Stafford, Direct Unsubsidized Stafford, Direct PLUS, FFEL Subsidized Stafford, FFEL Unsubsidized Stafford, FFEL PLUS, Federal Perkins. **Student Employment:** Federal Work-Study Program available. Institutional employment available. Off-campus job opportunities are good. **Financial Aid Statistics:** 84% freshmen, 84% undergrads receive need-based scholarship or grant aid. 69% freshmen, 73% undergrads receive need-based self-help aid. 85% freshmen, 78% undergrads receive any aid. Highest amount earned per year from on-campus jobs $1,600.

NORTHWEST CHRISTIAN COLLEGE

828 East 11th Avenue, Eugene, OR 97401
Phone: 541-684-7201 **E-mail:** admissions@nwcc.edu **CEEB Code:** 4543
Fax: 541-628-7317 **Website:** www.nwcc.edu **ACT Code:** 3478
Financial Aid Phone: 541-684-7203

This private school, affiliated with the Christian Churches and Churches of Christ, was founded in 1895. It has an 8-acre campus.

RATINGS
Admissions Selectivity Rating: 78   **Fire Safety Rating:** 60*   **Green Rating:** 60*

STUDENTS AND FACULTY
Enrollment: 380. **Student Body:** 61% female, 39% male, 10% out-of-state. African American 1%, Asian 2%, Caucasian 64%, Hispanic 4%, Native American 2%. **Retention and Graduation:** 66% freshmen return for sophomore year. 23% freshmen graduate within 4 years. **Faculty:** Student/faculty ratio 10:1. 21 full-time faculty, 43% hold PhDs. 100% faculty teach undergrads.

ACADEMICS
Degrees: Associate, bachelor's, certificate, master's, post-bachelor's certificate. **Academic Requirements:** Arts/fine arts, biblical studies, computer literacy, English (including composition), history, humanities, mathematics, philosophy, sciences (biological or physical), social science. **Classes:** Most classes have fewer than 10 students. Most lab/discussion sections have 10–19 students. **Majors with Highest Enrollment:** Business administration/management, teacher education, multiple levels. **Disciplines with Highest Percentage of Degrees Awarded:** Business/marketing 45%, education 26%, theology and religious vocations 9%, psychology 4%, visual and performing arts 4%, public administration and social services 3%, interdisciplinary studies 3%. **Special Study Options:** Accelerated program, distance learning, double major, English as a second language (ESL), independent study, internships, liberal arts/career combination, student-designed major, study abroad, teacher certification program.

FACILITIES
Housing: Coed dorms, apartments for single students. **Special Academic

Facilities/Equipment: Morse Event Center with gym, athletic facilities, weight training room, student life and athletic offices, library museum and rare book collections. **Computers:** 50% of classrooms are wired, 100% of public computers are PCs, network access in dorm rooms, network access in dorm lounges, online administrative functions (other than registration), remote student-access to Web through college's connection.

CAMPUS LIFE
Activities: Choral groups, concert band, drama/theater, literary magazine, music ensembles, student government, student newspaper, yearbook. **Organizations:** 10 registered organizations, 1 honor society, 2 religious organizations. **Athletics (Intercollegiate):** *Men:* Basketball, cross-country, soccer. *Women:* Basketball, cross-country, soccer, softball, volleyball.

ADMISSIONS
Freshman Academic Profile: 11% in top 10% of high school class, 42% in top 25% of high school class, 74% in top 50% of high school class. 89% from public high schools. SAT Math middle 50% range 470–560. SAT Critical Reading middle 50% range 440–540. SAT Writing middle 50% range 410–510. ACT middle 50% range 21–23. TOEFL required of all international applicants, minimum paper TOEFL 500, minimum computer TOEFL 173. **Basis for Candidate Selection:** *Very important factors considered include:* Academic GPA. *Important factors considered include:* Application essay, class rank, recommendation(s), standardized test scores. *Other factors considered include:* Character/personal qualities, rigor of secondary school record, work experience. **Freshman Admission Requirements:** High school diploma is required, and GED is accepted. *Academic units required:* 4 English, 3 math, 2 science (1 science lab), 2 foreign language, 2 social studies, 1 history. **Freshman Admission Statistics:** 232 applied, 61% admitted, 46% enrolled. **Transfer Admission Requirements:** College transcript(s), essay or personal statement, statement of good standing from prior institution(s). Minimum college GPA of 2.2 required. Lowest grade transferable C-. **General Admission Information:** Regular application deadline 8/15. Regular notification is rolling. Non-fall registration accepted. Admission may be deferred for a maximum of 2 years. Credit and/or placement offered for CEEB Advanced Placement tests.

COSTS AND FINANCIAL AID
Annual in-state tuition $2,478. Annual out-of-state tuition $7,872. Room and board $4,042. Required fees $2,802. Average book expense $825. **Required Forms and Deadlines:** FAFSA. Financial aid filing deadline 3/1. **Notification of Awards:** Applicants will be notified of awards on a rolling basis beginning on or about 4/1. **Types of Aid:** *Need-based scholarships/grants:* Pell, SEOG, state scholarships/grants, private scholarships, the school's own gift aid. *Loans:* FFEL Subsidized Stafford, FFEL Unsubsidized Stafford, FFEL PLUS, Federal Perkins. **Student Employment:** Federal Work-Study Program available. Institutional employment available. Off-campus job opportunities are fair. **Financial Aid Statistics:** 85% freshmen, 89% undergrads receive need-based scholarship or grant aid. 64% freshmen, 75% undergrads receive need-based self-help aid. 9 freshmen, 15 undergrads receive athletic scholarships. 97% freshmen, 96% undergrads receive any aid.

NORTHWEST COLLEGE

PO Box 579, Kirkland, WA 98083-0579
Phone: 425-889-5231 **E-mail:** admissions@ncag.edu **CEEB Code:** 4541
Fax: 425-889-5224 **Website:** www.nwcollege.edu **ACT Code:** 4466
Financial Aid Phone: 425-889-5210

This private school, affiliated with the Assemblies of God Church, was founded in 1934. It has a 56-acre campus.

RATINGS
Admissions Selectivity Rating: 60*   **Fire Safety Rating:** 60*   **Green Rating:** 60*

STUDENTS AND FACULTY
Enrollment: 1,054. **Student Body:** 62% female, 38% male, 18% out-of-state, 2% international (9 countries represented). African American 3%, Asian 4%, Caucasian 84%, Hispanic 3%, Native American 1%. **Retention and Graduation:** 66% freshmen return for sophomore year. 35% freshmen graduate within 4 years. **Faculty:** Student/faculty ratio 15:1. 50 full-time faculty, 48% hold PhDs. 100% faculty teach undergrads.

ACADEMICS
Degrees: Associate, bachelor's, certificate, diploma, master's, post-bachelor's certificate. **Academic Requirements:** Arts/fine arts, biblical studies, English (including composition), history, humanities, mathematics, sciences (biological or physical), social science. **Classes:** Most classes have 20–29 students. Most

lab/discussion sections have 10–19 students. **Disciplines with Highest Percentage of Degrees Awarded:** Business/marketing 36%, education 15%, psychology 9%, communication technologies 5%, health professions and related sciences 5%, interdisciplinary studies 4%. **Special Study Options:** Accelerated program, double major, English as a second language (ESL), independent study, internships, liberal arts/career combination, study abroad, teacher certification program.

FACILITIES

Housing: Men's dorms, women's dorms, apartments for married students, apartments for single students, apartments for students with dependent children. **Computers:** 95% of public computers are PCs, network access in dorm rooms, network access in dorm lounges, online registration, remote student-access to Web through college's connection.

CAMPUS LIFE

Activities: Choral groups, concert band, drama/theater, jazz band, music ensembles, musical theater, radio station, student government, student newspaper, symphony orchestra, yearbook. **Organizations:** 15 registered organizations, 9 religious organizations. **Athletics (Intercollegiate):** *Men:* Basketball, cross-country, soccer, track/field (outdoor). *Women:* Basketball, cross-country, track/field (outdoor), volleyball.

ADMISSIONS

Freshman Academic Profile: 75% from public high schools. TOEFL required of all international applicants, minimum paper TOEFL 500, minimum computer TOEFL 173. **Basis for Candidate Selection:** *Very important factors considered include:* Application essay, character/personal qualities, recommendation(s), rigor of secondary school record, standardized test scores. *Important factors considered include:* Class rank, extracurricular activities, religious affiliation/commitment. *Other factors considered include:* Alumni/ae relation, interview, talent/ability, volunteer work. **Freshman Admission Requirements:** High school diploma is required, and GED is accepted. *Academic units recommended:* 4 English, 3 math, 2 science, 2 foreign language, 2 social studies, 2 history, 3 academic electives. **Freshman Admission Statistics:** 308 applied, 90% admitted, 60% enrolled. **Transfer Admission Requirements:** High school transcript, college transcript(s), essay or personal statement, statement of good standing from prior institution(s). Minimum college GPA of 2.3 required. Lowest grade transferable C. **General Admission Information:** Application fee $30. Regular application deadline 8/1. Regular notification is rolling. Non-fall registration accepted. Admission may be deferred for a maximum of 1 year. Common Application accepted. Credit offered for CEEB Advanced Placement tests.

COSTS AND FINANCIAL AID

Annual tuition $13,200. Room & board $6,124. Required fees $324. Average book expense $850. **Required Forms and Deadlines:** FAFSA, institution's own financial aid form. Financial aid filing deadline 3/1. **Notification of Awards:** Applicants will be notified of awards on a rolling basis beginning on or about 4/15. **Types of Aid:** *Need-based scholarships/grants:* Pell, SEOG, state scholarships/grants, private scholarships, the school's own gift aid. *Loans:* FFEL Subsidized Stafford, FFEL Unsubsidized Stafford, FFEL PLUS, Federal Perkins, state loans, alternative (private) loans. **Student Employment:** Federal Work-Study Program available. Institutional employment available. Off-campus job opportunities are excellent. **Financial Aid Statistics:** 73% freshmen, 74% undergrads receive need-based scholarship or grant aid. 63% freshmen, 68% undergrads receive need-based self-help aid. 8 freshmen, 31 undergrads receive athletic scholarships. Highest amount earned per year from on-campus jobs $3,308.

NORTHWEST MISSOURI STATE UNIVERSITY

800 University Drive, Maryville, MO 64468
Phone: 800-633-1175 **E-mail:** admissions@nwmissouri.edu **CEEB Code:** 6488
Fax: 660-562-1121 **Website:** www.nwmissouri.edu **ACT Code:** 2338
Financial Aid Phone: 660-562-1363

This public school was founded in 1905. It has a 240-acre campus.

RATINGS

Admissions Selectivity Rating: 77   **Fire Safety Rating:** 60*   **Green Rating:** 60*

STUDENTS AND FACULTY

Enrollment: 4,956. **Student Body:** 55% female, 45% male, 26% out-of-state, 2% international. African American 4%, Caucasian 86%, Hispanic 2%.
Retention and Graduation: 74% freshmen return for sophomore year.
Faculty: Student/faculty ratio 21:1. 249 full-time faculty, 64% hold PhDs. 100% faculty teach undergrads.

ACADEMICS

Degrees: Bachelor's, master's, post-master's certificate. **Academic Requirements:** Arts/fine arts, computer literacy, English (including composition), history, humanities, mathematics, philosophy, sciences (biological or physical), social science. **Classes:** Most classes have 20–29 students. Most lab/discussion sections have 20–29 students. **Disciplines with Highest Percentage of Degrees Awarded:** Business/marketing 27%, education 18%, communication technologies 9%, psychology 9%, health professions and related sciences 9%, agriculture 7%, family and consumer sciences 5%, parks and recreation 5%. **Special Study Options:** Accelerated program, distance learning, double major, dual enrollment, English as a second language (ESL), honors program, independent study, internships, study abroad, teacher certification program.

FACILITIES

Housing: Coed dorms, apartments for single students, special housing for disabled students, fraternity/sorority housing. **Special Academic Facilities/Equipment:** State history and art collections, earth/science museum, broadcasting museum, on-campus elementary lab school, biomass energy plant. **Computers:** Network access in dorm rooms, network access in dorm lounges, online registration, remote student-access to Web through college's connection.

CAMPUS LIFE

Activities: Choral groups, concert band, dance, drama/theater, jazz band, literary magazine, marching band, music ensembles, musical theater, pep band, radio station, student government, student newspaper, student-run film society, symphony orchestra, television station. **Organizations:** 174 registered organizations, 13 honor societies, 9 religious organizations. 10 fraternities (15% men join), 6 sororities (15% women join). **Athletics (Intercollegiate):** *Men:* Baseball, basketball, cheerleading, cross-country, football, rodeo, tennis, track/field (indoor), track/field (outdoor). *Women:* Basketball, cheerleading, cross-country, rodeo, soccer, softball, tennis, track/field (indoor), track/field (outdoor), volleyball.

ADMISSIONS

Freshman Academic Profile: 13% in top 10% of high school class, 41% in top 25% of high school class, 80% in top 50% of high school class. 90% from public high schools. SAT Math middle 50% range 480–610. SAT Critical Reading middle 50% range 450–600. ACT middle 50% range 19–24. TOEFL required of all international applicants, minimum paper TOEFL 500. **Basis for Candidate Selection:** *Very important factors considered include:* Class rank, rigor of secondary school record, standardized test scores. *Important factors considered include:* Academic GPA. *Other factors considered include:* Application essay, character/personal qualities, extracurricular activities, interview, level of applicant's interest, recommendation(s), state residency. **Freshman Admission Requirements:** High school diploma is required, and GED is accepted. *Academic units required:* 4 English, 3 math, 2 science (1 science lab), 3 social studies, 4 academic electives. *Academic units recommended:* 4 math, 3 science, 2 foreign language. **Freshman Admission Statistics:** 3,759 applied, 75% admitted, 45% enrolled. **Transfer Admission Requirements:** College transcript(s), statement of good standing from prior institution(s). Minimum college GPA of 2.0 required. Lowest grade transferable D. **General Admission Information:** Application fee $25. Non-fall registration accepted.

COSTS AND FINANCIAL AID

Annual in-state tuition $5,835. Out-of-state tuition $10,080. Room & board $5,854. Required fees $295. Average book expense $500. **Required Forms and Deadlines:** FAFSA. Financial aid filing deadline 4/1. **Notification of Awards:** Applicants will be notified of awards on or about 4/15. **Types of Aid:** *Need-based scholarships/grants:* Pell, SEOG, state scholarships/grants, private scholarships, the school's own gift aid. *Loans:* Direct Subsidized Stafford, Direct Unsubsidized Stafford, Direct PLUS, Federal Perkins, college/university loans from institutional funds. **Student Employment:** Federal Work-Study Program available. Institutional employment available. Off-campus job opportunities are fair. **Financial Aid Statistics:** 28% freshmen, 25% undergrads receive need-based scholarship or grant aid. 46% freshmen, 43% undergrads receive need-based self-help aid.

NORTHWEST NAZARENE UNIVERSITY

623 Holly Street, Nampa, ID 83686
Phone: 208-467-8000 **E-mail:** admissions@nnu.edu **CEEB Code:** 4544
Fax: 208-467-8645 **Website:** www.nnu.edu **ACT Code:** 0924
Financial Aid Phone: 208-467-8774

*This private school, affiliated with the Nazarene Church, was founded in
1913. It has an 85-acre campus.*

RATINGS
Admissions Selectivity Rating: 83   **Fire Safety Rating:** 60*   **Green Rating:** 60*

STUDENTS AND FACULTY
Enrollment: 1,162. **Student Body:** 59% female, 41% male. Asian 1%,
Caucasian 52%, Hispanic 1%. **Retention and Graduation:** 72% freshmen
return for sophomore year. **Faculty:** Student/faculty ratio 13:1. 95 full-time
faculty, 68% hold PhDs. 98% faculty teach undergrads.

ACADEMICS
Degrees: Bachelor's, master's. **Academic Requirements:** Arts/fine arts,
computer literacy, English (including composition), history, humanities,
mathematics, philosophy, religion (Bible and theology), sciences (biological or
physical), social science. **Classes:** Most classes have 10–19 students. Most lab/
discussion sections have 20–29 students. **Majors with Highest Enrollment:**
Business administration/management, education, nursing/registered nurse
training (ASN, BSN, MSN, RN). **Disciplines with Highest Percentage of
Degrees Awarded:** Business/marketing 16%, education 11%, communication
technologies 7%, biological/life sciences 7%, liberal arts/general studies 7%,
health professions and related sciences 6%, visual and performing arts 6%,
social sciences 6%, psychology 4%, English 4%. **Special Study Options:**
Cooperative education program, cross-registration, distance learning, double
major, exchange student program (domestic), honors program, independent
study, internships, liberal arts/career combination, service and ministry
programs/opportunities, student-designed major, study abroad, teacher
certification program,

FACILITIES
Housing: Coed dorms, men's dorms, women's dorms, apartments for married
students, apartments for single students. Off-campus housing owned by the
university include rental homes and units. **Computers:** 5% of classrooms are
wired, 100% of classrooms are wireless, 100% of public computers are PCs,
network access in dorm rooms, network access in dorm lounges, online
administrative functions (other than registration), remote student-access to Web
through college's connection.

CAMPUS LIFE
Activities: Choral groups, concert band, drama/theater, jazz band, literary
magazine, music ensembles, musical theater, pep band, student government,
student newspaper, symphony orchestra, yearbook. **Organizations:** 21
registered organizations, 3 honor societies, 8 religious organizations. **Athletics
(Intercollegiate):** *Men:* Baseball, basketball, cross-country, golf, track/field
(indoor), track/field (outdoor). *Women:* Basketball, cross-country, soccer,
softball, track/field (indoor), track/field (outdoor), volleyball.

ADMISSIONS
Freshman Academic Profile: 26% in top 10% of high school class, 53% in top
25% of high school class, 77% in top 50% of high school class. 83% from public
high schools. SAT Math middle 50% range 460–590. SAT Critical Reading
middle 50% range 460–610. ACT middle 50% range 19–26. TOEFL required
of all international applicants, minimum paper TOEFL 500, minimum
computer TOEFL 173. **Basis for Candidate Selection:** *Very important
factors considered include:* Class rank, recommendation(s), rigor of secondary
school record, standardized test scores. *Important factors considered include:*
Character/personal qualities. *Other factors considered include:* Alumni/ae
relation, application essay, extracurricular activities, religious affiliation/
commitment, talent/ability, volunteer work, work experience. **Freshman
Admission Requirements:** High school diploma is required, and GED is
accepted. *Academic units recommended:* 4 English, 3 math, 3 science, 2 foreign
language, 3 social studies, 1 history. **Freshman Admission Statistics:** 806
applied, 68% admitted, 49% enrolled. **Transfer Admission Requirements:**
College transcript(s), essay or personal statement, statement of good standing
from prior institution(s). Minimum college GPA of 2.0 required. Lowest grade
transferable C-. **General Admission Information:** Application fee $25.
Regular application deadline 8/15. Regular notification is rolling. Non-fall
registration accepted. Admission may be deferred for a maximum of 5 years.
Common Application accepted. Credit and/or placement offered for CEEB
Advanced Placement tests.

COSTS AND FINANCIAL AID
Annual tuition $19,700. Room and board $5,300. Required fees $270. Average
book expense $750. **Required Forms and Deadlines:** FAFSA, institution's
own financial aid form. Financial aid filing deadline 3/1. **Notification of
Awards:** Applicants will be notified of awards on a rolling basis beginning on or
about 4/1. **Types of Aid:** *Need-based scholarships/grants:* Pell, SEOG, state
scholarships/grants, private scholarships, the school's own gift aid. *Loans:* FFEL
Subsidized Stafford, FFEL Unsubsidized Stafford, FFEL PLUS, Federal
Perkins, college/university loans from institutional funds, bank loans. **Student
Employment:** Federal Work-Study Program available. Institutional employment available. Off-campus job opportunities are good. **Financial Aid
Statistics:** 58% freshmen, 52% undergrads receive need-based scholarship or
grant aid. 63% freshmen, 57% undergrads receive need-based self-help aid. 7
freshmen, 21 undergrads receive athletic scholarships. 100% freshmen, 99%
undergrads receive any aid. Highest amount earned per year from on-campus
jobs $8,739.

NORTHWESTERN COLLEGE (IA)

101 7th Street SW, Orange City, IA 51041
Phone: 712-707-7130 **E-mail:** admissions@nwciowa.edu **CEEB Code:** 6490
Fax: 712-707-7164 **Website:** www.nwciowa.edu **ACT Code:** 1346
Financial Aid Phone: 712-707-7131

*This private school, affiliated with the Reformed Church, was founded in
1882. It has a 100-acre campus.*

RATINGS
Admissions Selectivity Rating: 81   **Fire Safety Rating:** 82   **Green Rating:** 67

STUDENTS AND FACULTY
Enrollment: 1,288. **Student Body:** 61% female, 39% male, 45% out-of-state,
3% international (16 countries represented). Asian 1%, Caucasian 95%,
Hispanic 1%. **Retention and Graduation:** 81% freshmen return for
sophomore year. 54% freshmen graduate within 4 years. **Faculty:** Student/
faculty ratio 15:1. 77 full-time faculty, 81% hold PhDs. 100% faculty teach
undergrads.

ACADEMICS
Degrees: Bachelor's, certificate. **Academic Requirements:** Arts/fine arts,
English (including composition), foreign languages, history, humanities,
mathematics, philosophy, sciences (biological or physical), social science, 2
courses in biblical/theological studies, 1 course in speech. **Classes:** Most classes
have 10–19 students. **Majors with Highest Enrollment:** Biology/biological
sciences, business administration/management, education. **Disciplines with
Highest Percentage of Degrees Awarded:** Education 20%, business/
marketing 17%, visual and performing arts 10%, psychology 7%, biological/life
sciences 7%, philosophy and religious studies 6%. **Special Study Options:**
Double major, English as a second language (ESL), honors program,
independent study, internships, liberal arts/career combination, student-
designed major, study abroad, teacher certification program. Off-campus study
programs: American studies program (Washington, DC), AuSable Inst of
Environmental Studies Program (Michigan), Chicago metropolitan studies
program (Chicago), China studies program (Xiaman, China), contemporary
music center (Martha's Vineyard, MA), Latin American studies program (Costa
Rica), Los Angeles film studies semester, Middle East studies program (Cairo,
Egypt), Oxford honors program (England), Oxford summer program (Oxford,
England), Romanian studies program, Russian studies program, Trinity
Christian College: Semester in Spain, and creation care study program.

FACILITIES
Housing: Men's dorms, women's dorms, apartments for single students, special
housing for disabled students, theme housing. **Special Academic Facilities/
Equipment:** Thea G Korver Visual Arts Center-art gallery, DeWitt Theatre
Arts Center-proscenium theater, black box theater, costume shop. **Computers:**
100% of classrooms are wired, 65% of classrooms are wireless, 90% of public
computers are PCs, 7% of public computers are Macs, 3% of public computers
are UNIX, network access in dorm rooms, network access in dorm lounges,
online registration, online administrative functions (other than registration),
remote student-access to Web through college's connection.

CAMPUS LIFE
Activities: Choral groups, concert band, dance, drama/theater, jazz band,
literary magazine, music ensembles, musical theater, pep band, student
government, student newspaper, symphony orchestra, television station,
yearbook. **Organizations:** 30 registered organizations, 2 honor societies, 5
religious organizations. **Athletics (Intercollegiate):** *Men:* Baseball, basketball,

cheerleading, cross-country, football, golf, soccer, track/field (indoor), track/field (outdoor), wrestling. *Women:* Basketball, cheerleading, cross-country, golf, soccer, softball, track/field (indoor), track/field (outdoor), volleyball.

ADMISSIONS

Freshman Academic Profile: 28% in top 10% of high school class, 55% in top 25% of high school class, 83% in top 50% of high school class. 79% from public high schools. ACT middle 50% range 21–27. TOEFL required of all international applicants, minimum paper TOEFL 475, minimum computer TOEFL 150. **Basis for Candidate Selection:** *Very important factors considered include:* Class rank, rigor of secondary school record, standardized test scores. *Important factors considered include:* Academic GPA, application essay, character/personal qualities, first generation, interview, level of applicant's interest, recommendation(s), talent/ability. *Other factors considered include:* Extracurricular activities, religious affiliation/commitment. **Freshman Admission Requirements:** High school diploma is required, and GED is accepted. *Academic units recommended:* 4 English, 3 math, 3 science, 3 foreign language, 3 social studies. **Freshman Admission Statistics:** 1,277 applied, 85% admitted, 34% enrolled. **Transfer Admission Requirements:** College transcript(s). Minimum college GPA of 2.2 required. Lowest grade transferable C. **General Admission Information:** Application fee $25. Regular notification is rolling. Non-fall registration accepted. Admission may be deferred for a maximum of 4 years. Credit and/or placement offered for CEEB Advanced Placement tests.

COSTS AND FINANCIAL AID

Annual tuition $21,648. Room and board $5,792. Average book expense $900. **Required Forms and Deadlines:** FAFSA. Financial aid filing deadline 4/1. **Notification of Awards:** Applicants will be notified of awards on a rolling basis beginning on or about 3/15. **Types of Aid:** *Need-based scholarships/grants:* Pell, SEOG, state scholarships/grants, private scholarships, the school's own gift aid, United Negro College Fund. *Loans:* FFEL Subsidized Stafford, FFEL Unsubsidized Stafford, FFEL PLUS, Federal Perkins, college/university loans from institutional funds. **Financial Aid Statistics:** 74% freshmen, 71% undergrads receive need-based scholarship or grant aid. 72% freshmen, 72% undergrads receive need-based self-help aid. 131 freshmen, 323 undergrads receive athletic scholarships. 100% freshmen, 99% undergrads receive any aid. Highest amount earned per year from on-campus jobs $2,100.

NORTHWESTERN COLLEGE (MN)

3003 Snelling Avenue North, Saint Paul, MN 55113-1598
Phone: 651-631-5111 **E-mail:** admissions@nwc.edu **CEEB Code:** 6489
Fax: 651-631-5680 **Website:** www.nwc.edu **ACT Code:** 2138
Financial Aid Phone: 651-631-5212

This private school, affiliated with the Protestant Church, was founded in 1902. It has a 103-acre campus.

RATINGS
Admissions Selectivity Rating: 79   **Fire Safety Rating:** 60*   **Green Rating:** 60*

STUDENTS AND FACULTY
Enrollment: 2,199. **Student Body:** 62% female, 38% male, 39% out-of-state. African American 4%, Asian 2%, Caucasian 91%, Hispanic 1%. **Retention and Graduation:** 80% freshmen return for sophomore year. 44% freshmen graduate within 4 years. 20% grads go on to further study within 1 year. 17% grads pursue arts and sciences degrees. 1% grads pursue business degrees. 1% grads pursue law degrees. 1% grads pursue medical degrees. **Faculty:** Student/faculty ratio 15:1. 78 full-time faculty, 67% hold PhDs. 100% faculty teach undergrads.

ACADEMICS
Degrees: Associate, bachelor's, certificate, terminal. **Academic Requirements:** Arts/fine arts, computer literacy, English (including composition), history, mathematics, sciences (biological or physical), social science. Bible: 30 credits for new freshmen, proportional amount for transfers. General education: Speech, literature or philosophy, physical health and wellness, global perspectives (satisfied by foreign language courses or specified courses with international/cross-cultural/multicultural emphasis). Designated courses in major with written/oral communication emphasis. **Classes:** Most classes have 10–19 students. Most lab/discussion sections have 20–29 students. **Majors with Highest Enrollment:** Business administration/management, elementary education and teaching, psychology. **Disciplines with Highest Percentage of Degrees Awarded:** Education 23%, business/marketing 13%, psychology 9%, visual and performing arts 9%, social sciences 9%, communication technologies 8%, English 5%. **Special Study Options:** Distance learning, double major, English as a second language (ESL), exchange student program (domestic),

honors program, independent study, internships, study abroad, teacher certification program. ESL program is limited to 2 English composition courses.

FACILITIES
Housing: Men's dorms, women's dorms, apartments for married students, apartments for single students, special housing for disabled students. **Special Academic Facilities/Equipment:** Art gallery, radio station, TV studio. **Computers:** 80% of public computers are PCs, 20% of public computers are Macs, network access in dorm rooms, online registration, remote student-access to Web through college's connection. Undergraduates are required to own a computer.

CAMPUS LIFE
Activities: Choral groups, concert band, drama/theater, jazz band, literary magazine, music ensembles, musical theater, opera, pep band, radio station, student government, student newspaper, symphony orchestra, yearbook. **Organizations:** 25 registered organizations, 4 honor societies, 5 religious organizations. **Athletics (Intercollegiate):** *Men:* Baseball, basketball, cross-country, football, golf, soccer, tennis, track/field (outdoor). *Women:* Basketball, cheerleading, cross-country, golf, soccer, softball, tennis, track/field (outdoor), volleyball.

ADMISSIONS
Freshman Academic Profile: 23% in top 10% of high school class, 52% in top 25% of high school class, 80% in top 50% of high school class. 80% from public high schools. SAT Math middle 50% range 490–640. SAT Critical Reading middle 50% range 510–630. ACT middle 50% range 21–26. TOEFL required of all international applicants, minimum paper TOEFL 530, minimum computer TOEFL 197. **Basis for Candidate Selection:** *Very important factors considered include:* Application essay, character/personal qualities, recommendation(s), religious affiliation/commitment. *Important factors considered include:* Extracurricular activities, rigor of secondary school record, standardized test scores. *Other factors considered include:* Class rank, interview, talent/ability. **Freshman Admission Requirements:** High school diploma is required, and GED is accepted. *Academic units recommended:* 4 English, 3 math, 3 science, 2 foreign language, 3 social studies, 1 academic elective. **Freshman Admission Statistics:** 890 applied, 91% admitted, 53% enrolled. **Transfer Admission Requirements:** High school transcript, college transcript(s), essay or personal statement, statement of good standing from prior institution(s). Minimum college GPA of 2.0 required. Lowest grade transferable C-. **General Admission Information:** Application fee $25. Regular application deadline 8/15. Regular notification is rolling. Non-fall registration accepted. Admission may be deferred for a maximum of 1 year. Common Application not accepted. Credit offered for CEEB Advanced Placement tests.

COSTS AND FINANCIAL AID
Annual tuition $17,400. Room & board $5,620. Average book expense $500. **Required Forms and Deadlines:** FAFSA, institution's own financial aid form. Financial aid filing deadline 3/1. **Notification of Awards:** Applicants will be notified of awards on a rolling basis beginning on or about 3/1. **Types of Aid:** *Need-based scholarships/grants:* Pell, SEOG, state scholarships/grants, private scholarships, the school's own gift aid. *Loans:* FFEL Subsidized Stafford, FFEL Unsubsidized Stafford, FFEL PLUS, Federal Perkins, state loans. **Student Employment:** Federal Work-Study Program available. Institutional employment available. Off-campus job opportunities are excellent. **Financial Aid Statistics:** 83% freshmen, 81% undergrads receive need-based scholarship or grant aid. 65% freshmen, 66% undergrads receive need-based self-help aid. Highest amount earned per year from on-campus jobs $1,703.

NORTHWESTERN MICHIGAN COLLEGE

1701 E. Front Street, Traverse City, MI 49686
Phone: 231-995-1154 **E-mail:** welcome@nmc.edu
Fax: 231-995-1339 **Website:** www.nmc.edu

This is a public school.

RATINGS
Admissions Selectivity Rating: 60*   **Fire Safety Rating:** 60*   **Green Rating:** 60*

STUDENTS AND FACULTY
Enrollment: 3,949. **Student Body:** 58% female, 42% male, 2% out-of-state. Hispanic 2%, Native American 3%. **Faculty:** Student/faculty ratio 23:1. 94 full-time faculty.

ACADEMICS
Degrees: Associate, certificate, terminal. **Academic Requirements:** English

(including composition), humanities, mathematics, sciences (biological or physical), social science. **Special Study Options:** Distance learning, dual enrollment, English as a second language (ESL), honors program, independent study, internships.

FACILITIES
Housing: Coed dorms, apartments for married students, apartments for single students, special housing for disabled students, special housing for international students.

CAMPUS LIFE
Activities: Choral groups, concert band, dance, drama/theater, jazz band, literary magazine, music ensembles, radio station, student government, student newspaper, symphony orchestra.

ADMISSIONS
Freshman Admission Requirements: High school diploma is required, and GED is accepted. **Freshman Admission Statistics:** 2,516 applied, 94% admitted. **Transfer Admission Requirements:** College transcript(s). Lowest grade transferable C. **General Admission Information:** Application fee $15. Non-fall registration accepted. Admission may be deferred for a maximum of 1 year. Common Application not accepted.

COSTS AND FINANCIAL AID
Annual in-state tuition $2,426. Annual out-of-state tuition $4,799. Room and board $5,700. Required fees $16. Average book expense $560.

NORTHWESTERN OKLAHOMA STATE UNIVERSITY

709 Oklahoma Boulevard, Alva, OK 73717-2799
Phone: 580-327-8545 **E-mail:** krschroc@ranger1.nmalva.edu **CEEB Code:** 6493
Fax: 580-327-1881 **Website:** www.nwalva.edu **ACT Code:** 3412
Financial Aid Phone: 508-327-8542

This public school was founded in 1897. It has a 70-acre campus.

RATINGS
Admissions Selectivity Rating: 67   **Fire Safety Rating:** 60*   **Green Rating:** 60*

STUDENTS AND FACULTY
Enrollment: 1,648. **Student Body:** 14% out-of-state, 1% international. African American 5%, Caucasian 89%, Hispanic 1%, Native American 3%. **Retention and Graduation:** 54% freshmen return for sophomore year. 12% freshmen graduate within 4 years. **Faculty:** 100% faculty teach undergrads.

ACADEMICS
Degrees: Bachelor's, master's. **Special Study Options:** Accelerated program, cooperative education program, dual enrollment, English as a second language (ESL), honors program, independent study, internships, liberal arts/career combination, teacher certification program.

FACILITIES
Housing: Coed dorms, fraternity/sorority housing. **Special Academic Facilities/Equipment:** Natural history museum, instructional media center, TV production facility.

CAMPUS LIFE
Activities: Choral groups, drama/theater, literary magazine, marching band, radio station, student government, student newspaper, television station, yearbook. **Organizations:** 50 registered organizations, 1 honor society, 2 fraternities, 1 sorority. **Athletics (Intercollegiate):** *Men:* Baseball, basketball, football, golf, softball, tennis, track/field (outdoor). *Women:* Basketball, softball.

ADMISSIONS
Freshman Academic Profile: 8% in top 10% of high school class, 27% in top 25% of high school class, 64% in top 50% of high school class. ACT middle 50% range 18–23. TOEFL required of all international applicants, minimum paper TOEFL 500. **Freshman Admission Requirements:** High school diploma is required, and GED is accepted. *Academic units required:* 4 English, 3 math, 2 science (2 science labs), 1 social studies, 2 history, 3 academic electives. **Freshman Admission Statistics:** 481 applied, 100% admitted, 67% enrolled. **Transfer Admission Requirements:** Minimum college GPA of 2.0 required. Lowest grade transferable D. **General Admission Information:** Application fee $15. Regular application deadline rolling. Regular notification is rolling. Non-fall registration accepted. Common Application not accepted. Credit and/or placement offered for CEEB Advanced Placement tests.

COSTS AND FINANCIAL AID
Annual in-state tuition $1,830. Out-of-state tuition $4,340. Room & board $2,316. Required fees $125. Average book expense $500. **Required Forms and Deadlines:** FAFSA, institution's own financial aid form. **Types of Aid:** *Need-based scholarships/grants:* Pell, SEOG, state scholarships/grants, private scholarships, the school's own gift aid. *Loans:* FFEL Subsidized Stafford, FFEL Unsubsidized Stafford, FFEL PLUS, Federal Perkins, Federal Nursing, college/university loans from institutional funds. **Student Employment:** Federal Work-Study Program available. Institutional employment available. Off-campus job opportunities are good. **Financial Aid Statistics:** Highest amount earned per year from on-campus jobs $1,200.

NORTHWESTERN STATE UNIVERSITY

209 Roy Hall, Natchitoches, LA 71497
Phone: 318-357-6171 **E-mail:** admissions@nsula.edu **CEEB Code:** 6492
Fax: 318-357-4660 **Website:** www.nsula.edu **ACT Code:** 1600
Financial Aid Phone: 800-823-3008

This public school was founded in 1884. It has a 916-acre campus.

RATINGS
Admissions Selectivity Rating: 72   **Fire Safety Rating:** 82   **Green Rating:** 60*

STUDENTS AND FACULTY
Enrollment: 8,034. **Student Body:** 68% female, 32% male, 8% out-of-state. African American 30%, Caucasian 60%, Hispanic 2%, Native American 2%. **Retention and Graduation:** 66% freshmen return for sophomore year. 16% freshmen graduate within 4 years. **Faculty:** Student/faculty ratio 18:1. 313 full-time faculty, 56% hold PhDs. 95% faculty teach undergrads.

ACADEMICS
Degrees: Associate, bachelor's, master's, post-master's certificate. **Academic Requirements:** Arts/fine arts, computer literacy, English (including composition), health and personal fitness, history, humanities, mathematics, sciences (biological or physical), social science. **Classes:** Most classes have 10–19 students. Most lab/discussion sections have 10–19 students. **Majors with Highest Enrollment:** Business administration and management, general studies, nursing/registered nurse training (ASN, BSN, MSN, RN). **Disciplines with Highest Percentage of Degrees Awarded:** Health professions and related sciences 20%, liberal arts/general studies 14%, business/marketing 14%, psychology 9%, education 7%. **Special Study Options:** Cooperative education program, distance learning, double major, dual enrollment, honors program, independent study, internships, study abroad, teacher certification program.

FACILITIES
Housing: Coed dorms, apartments for married students, apartments for single students, special housing for disabled students, fraternity/sorority housing, creative and performing arts wing for CAPA majors. **Special Academic Facilities/Equipment:** Cammie G. Henry Research Center, Louisiana Creole Heritage Center, Louisiana Folklife Center, Louisiana Regional Folk life Center, the Space Science Group, Williamson Museum. **Computers:** 100% of public computers are PCs, network access in dorm rooms, network access in dorm lounges, online registration, online administrative functions (other than registration), remote student-access to Web through college's connection.

CAMPUS LIFE
Activities: Choral groups, concert band, dance, drama/theater, jazz band, literary magazine, marching band, music ensembles, musical theater, opera, pep band, radio station, student government, student newspaper, symphony orchestra, television station, yearbook. **Organizations:** 16 honor societies, 15 religious organizations, 10 fraternities, 8 sororities. **Athletics (Intercollegiate):** *Men:* Baseball, basketball, cross-country, football, track/field (indoor), track/field (outdoor). *Women:* Basketball, cross-country, soccer, softball, tennis, track/field (indoor), track/field (outdoor), volleyball.

ADMISSIONS
Freshman Academic Profile: 14% in top 10% of high school class, 38% in top 25% of high school class, 68% in top 50% of high school class. SAT Math middle 50% range 430–553. SAT Critical Reading middle 50% range 440–560. ACT middle 50% range 18–23. TOEFL required of all international applicants, minimum paper TOEFL 500, minimum computer TOEFL 173. **Basis for Candidate Selection:** *Very important factors considered include:* Rigor of secondary school record, standardized test scores. *Important factors considered include:* Academic GPA, class rank. *Other factors considered include:* Alumni/ae relation, extracurricular activities, geographical residence, state residency, talent/ability. **Freshman Admission Requirements:** High school diploma is

required, and GED is accepted. *Academic units required:* 4 English, 3 math, 3 science (3 science labs), 2 foreign language, 1 social studies, 2 history, 1 academic elective. **Freshman Admission Statistics:** 2,895 applied, 87% admitted, 55% enrolled. **Transfer Admission Requirements:** College transcript(s), statement of good standing from prior institution(s). Minimum college GPA of 2.0 required. Lowest grade transferable D. **General Admission Information:** Application fee $20. Regular application deadline 7/6. Regular notification is rolling. Non-fall registration accepted. Admission may be deferred for a maximum of 3 semesters without a fee. Credit and/or placement offered for CEEB Advanced Placement tests.

COSTS AND FINANCIAL AID

Required Forms and Deadlines: FAFSA, institution's own financial aid form. Financial aid filing deadline 5/1. **Notification of Awards:** Applicants will be notified of awards on a rolling basis beginning on or about 5/1. **Types of Aid:** *Need-based scholarships/grants:* Pell, SEOG, state scholarships/grants, private scholarships, the school's own gift aid, United Negro College Fund, Federal Nursing Scholarships, third-party scholarships. *Loans:* FFEL Subsidized Stafford, FFEL Unsubsidized Stafford, FFEL PLUS, Federal Perkins, alternative loans. **Student Employment:** Federal Work-Study Program available. Institutional employment available. Off-campus job opportunities are fair. **Financial Aid Statistics:** 46% freshmen, 45% undergrads receive need-based scholarship or grant aid. 41% freshmen, 47% undergrads receive need-based self-help aid. 67 freshmen, 249 undergrads receive athletic scholarships. 91% freshmen, 80% undergrads receive any aid. Highest amount earned per year from on-campus jobs $8,034.

NORTHWESTERN UNIVERSITY

PO Box 3060, 1801 Hinman Avenue, Evanston, IL 60204-3060
Phone: 847-491-7271 **E-mail:** ug-admission@northwestern.edu **CEEB Code:** 1565
Website: www.northwestern.edu **ACT Code:** 1106
Financial Aid Phone: 847-491-7400

This private school was founded in 1851. It has a 240-acre campus.

RATINGS
Admissions Selectivity Rating: 98　　**Fire Safety Rating:** 72　　**Green Rating:** 60*

STUDENTS AND FACULTY

Enrollment: 8,060. **Student Body:** 53% female, 47% male, 65% out-of-state, 5% international (95 countries represented). African American 6%, Asian 16%, Caucasian 61%, Hispanic 6%. **Retention and Graduation:** 97% freshmen return for sophomore year. 22% grads go on to further study within 1 year. 1% grads pursue arts and sciences degrees. 4% grads pursue law degrees. 5% grads pursue medical degrees. **Faculty:** Student/faculty ratio 7:1. 938 full-time faculty. 100% faculty teach undergrads.

ACADEMICS

Degrees: Bachelor's, certificate, doctoral, first professional, master's, post-master's certificate. **Academic Requirements:** Arts/fine arts, English (including composition), foreign languages, humanities, mathematics, sciences (biological or physical), social science. **Classes:** Most classes have fewer than 10 students. Most lab/discussion sections have 10–19 students. **Majors with Highest Enrollment:** Economics, engineering, journalism. **Disciplines with Highest Percentage of Degrees Awarded:** Social sciences 20%, communications/journalism 18%, engineering 14%, visual and performing arts 10%, psychology 9%. **Special Study Options:** Accelerated program, cooperative education program, double major, honors program, independent study, internships, liberal arts/career combination, student-designed major, study abroad, teacher certification program.

FACILITIES

Housing: Coed dorms, men's dorms, women's dorms, fraternity/sorority housing, theme residential colleges. **Special Academic Facilities/Equipment:** Art gallery, learning sciences institute, communicative disorders and materials and life sciences buildings, catalysis center, astronomical research center, Ford Motor Company Engineering Design Center. **Computers:** 10% of classrooms are wired, 5% of classrooms are wireless, 80% of public computers are PCs, 10% of public computers are Macs, 10% of public computers are UNIX, network access in dorm rooms, online registration, remote student-access to Web through college's connection.

CAMPUS LIFE

Activities: Choral groups, concert band, dance, drama/theater, jazz band, literary magazine, marching band, music ensembles, musical theater, opera, pep band, radio station, student government, student newspaper, student-run film society, symphony orchestra, television station. **Organizations:** 415 registered organizations, 23 honor societies, 29 religious organizations. 23 fraternities (32% men join), 19 sororities (38% women join). **Athletics (Intercollegiate):** *Men:* Baseball, basketball, cheerleading, diving, football, golf, soccer, swimming, tennis, wrestling. *Women:* Basketball, cheerleading, cross-country, diving, fencing, field hockey, golf, lacrosse, soccer, softball, swimming, tennis, volleyball.

ADMISSIONS

Freshman Academic Profile: 83% in top 10% of high school class, 97% in top 25% of high school class, 100% in top 50% of high school class. 73% from public high schools. SAT Math middle 50% range 680–770. SAT Critical Reading middle 50% range 670–750. SAT Writing middle 50% range 660–750. ACT middle 50% range 30–34. TOEFL required of all international applicants, minimum paper TOEFL 600, minimum computer TOEFL 250. **Basis for Candidate Selection:** *Very important factors considered include:* Academic GPA, application essay, class rank, rigor of secondary school record, standardized test scores. *Important factors considered include:* Character/personal qualities, extracurricular activities, recommendation(s), talent/ability. *Other factors considered include:* Alumni/ae relation, first generation, interview, level of applicant's interest, racial/ethnic status, volunteer work, work experience. **Freshman Admission Requirements:** High school diploma or equivalent is not required. *Academic units recommended:* 4 English, 3 math, 2 science (2 science labs), 2 foreign language, 2 social studies, 1 academic elective. **Freshman Admission Statistics:** 18,385 applied, 30% admitted, 38% enrolled. **Transfer Admission Requirements:** High school transcript, college transcript(s), essay or personal statement, standardized test score, statement of good standing from prior institution(s). Minimum college GPA of 3.0 required. Lowest grade transferable C. **General Admission Information:** Application fee $65. Early decision application deadline 11/1. Regular application deadline 1/1. Regular notification 4/15. Non-fall registration accepted. Admission may be deferred for a maximum of 1 year. Credit and/or placement offered for CEEB Advanced Placement tests.

COSTS AND FINANCIAL AID

Annual tuition $36,756. Room and board $11,295. Required fees $414. Average book expense $1,626. **Required Forms and Deadlines:** FAFSA, CSS/Financial Aid PROFILE, Noncustodial PROFILE, Business/Farm Supplement, parent and student federal tax returns. Financial aid filing deadline 2/15. **Notification of Awards:** Applicants will be notified of awards on or about 4/15. **Types of Aid:** *Need-based scholarships/grants:* Pell, SEOG, state scholarships/grants, private scholarships, the school's own gift aid, United Negro College Fund. *Loans:* FFEL Subsidized Stafford, FFEL Unsubsidized Stafford, FFEL PLUS, Federal Perkins, college/university loans from institutional funds. **Student Employment:** Federal Work-Study Program available. Institutional employment available. **Financial Aid Statistics:** 40% freshmen, 40% undergrads receive need-based scholarship or grant aid. 37% freshmen, 37% undergrads receive need-based self-help aid. 99 freshmen, 358 undergrads receive athletic scholarships. 60% freshmen, 60% undergrads receive any aid.

NORTHWOOD UNIVERSITY

4000 Whiting Drive, Midland, MI 48640
Phone: 989-837-4273 **E-mail:** admissions@northwood.edu **CEEB Code:** 1568
Fax: 989-837-4490 **Website:** www.northwood.edu/mi **ACT Code:** 2041
Financial Aid Phone: 989-837-4320

This private school was founded in 1959. It has a 434-acre campus.

RATINGS
Admissions Selectivity Rating: 71　　**Fire Safety Rating:** 60*　　**Green Rating:** 62

STUDENTS AND FACULTY

Enrollment: 1,968. **Student Body:** 35% female, 65% male, 13% out-of-state, 8% international (26 countries represented). African American 11%, Asian 2%, Caucasian 78%, Hispanic 2%. **Retention and Graduation:** 70% freshmen return for sophomore year. 9% grads go on to further study within 1 year. 5% grads pursue arts and sciences degrees. 85% grads pursue business degrees. 10% grads pursue law degrees. **Faculty:** Student/faculty ratio 33:1. 47 full-time faculty, 28% hold PhDs. 100% faculty teach undergrads.

ACADEMICS

Degrees: Associate, bachelor's, master's, terminal. **Academic Requirements:**

Computer literacy, English (including composition), humanities, mathematics, philosophy, sciences (biological or physical), social science. **Classes:** Most classes have 20–29 students. **Majors with Highest Enrollment:** Business administration and management, sports and fitness administration/management, vehicle parts and accessories marketing operations. **Disciplines with Highest Percentage of Degrees Awarded:** Business/marketing 83%, parks and recreation 10%, communication technologies 7%. **Special Study Options:** Accelerated program, distance learning, double major, dual enrollment, English as a second language (ESL), external degree program, honors program, independent study, internships, study abroad, weekend college.

FACILITIES

Housing: Men's dorms, women's dorms, apartments for single students. **Special Academic Facilities/Equipment:** Hach Student Life Center, Gerstacker Student Union. **Computers:** 100% of classrooms are wired, 100% of public computers are PCs, network access in dorm rooms, network access in dorm lounges, online registration, online administrative functions (other than registration), support for handheld computing, remote student-access to Web through college's connection.

CAMPUS LIFE

Activities: Choral groups, dance, drama/theater, jazz band, pep band, student government, student newspaper, yearbook. **Organizations:** 42 registered organizations, 2 honor societies, 2 religious organizations. 9 fraternities, 3 sororities. **Athletics (Intercollegiate):** *Men:* Baseball, basketball, cheerleading, cross-country, football, golf, soccer, tennis, track/field (indoor), track/field (outdoor). *Women:* Basketball, cheerleading, cross-country, golf, soccer, softball, tennis, track/field (indoor), track/field (outdoor), volleyball.

ADMISSIONS

Freshman Academic Profile: 12% in top 10% of high school class, 27% in top 25% of high school class, 50% in top 50% of high school class. 70% from public high schools. SAT Math middle 50% range 430–550. SAT Critical Reading middle 50% range 410–540. SAT Writing middle 50% range 410–520. ACT middle 50% range 19–23. TOEFL required of all international applicants, minimum paper TOEFL 500, minimum computer TOEFL 173. **Basis for Candidate Selection:** *Very important factors considered include:* Academic GPA, level of applicant's interest, rigor of secondary school record, standardized test scores. *Important factors considered include:* Application essay, class rank. *Other factors considered include:* Alumni/ae relation, character/personal qualities, extracurricular activities, interview, recommendation(s). **Freshman Admission Requirements:** High school diploma is required, and GED is accepted. *Academic units recommended:* 4 English, 3 math, 2 science (1 science lab), 3 foreign language, 3 social studies. **Freshman Admission Statistics:** 1,724 applied, 81% admitted, 36% enrolled. **Transfer Admission Requirements:** High school transcript, college transcript(s). Minimum college GPA of 2.0 required. Lowest grade transferable C. **General Admission Information:** Application fee $25. Regular notification is rolling. Non-fall registration accepted. Admission may be deferred for a maximum of 1 year. Credit and/or placement offered for CEEB Advanced Placement tests.

COSTS AND FINANCIAL AID

Required Forms and Deadlines: FAFSA. **Notification of Awards:** Applicants will be notified of awards on a rolling basis beginning on or about 3/1. **Types of Aid:** *Need-based scholarships/grants:* Pell, SEOG, state scholarships/grants, private scholarships, the school's own gift aid. *Loans:* FFEL Subsidized Stafford, FFEL Unsubsidized Stafford, FFEL PLUS. **Financial Aid Statistics:** 58% freshmen, 50% undergrads receive need-based scholarship or grant aid. 56% freshmen, 49% undergrads receive need-based self-help aid. 30 freshmen, 116 undergrads receive athletic scholarships.

See page 1296.

freshmen return for sophomore year. **Faculty:** Student/faculty ratio 23:1. 19 full-time faculty, 26% hold PhDs. 100% faculty teach undergrads.

ACADEMICS

Degrees: Associate, bachelor's, terminal. **Academic Requirements:** Computer literacy, English (including composition), humanities, mathematics, philosophy, sciences (biological or physical), social science. **Classes:** Most classes have 10–19 students. Most lab/discussion sections have 30–39 students. **Majors with Highest Enrollment:** Business administration/management, sports and fitness administration/management, vehicle parts and accessories marketing operations. **Disciplines with Highest Percentage of Degrees Awarded:** Business/marketing 85%, parks and recreation 8%, communications/journalism 7%. **Special Study Options:** Accelerated program, distance learning, double major, dual enrollment, English as a second language (ESL), external degree program, honors program, independent study, internships, study abroad, weekend college.

FACILITIES

Housing: Men's dorms, women's dorms, special housing for disabled students. **Special Academic Facilities/Equipment:** Art gallery. **Computers:** 100% of classrooms are wired, 100% of public computers are PCs, network access in dorm rooms, network access in dorm lounges, online registration, online administrative functions (other than registration), support for handheld computing, remote student-access to Web through college's connection.

CAMPUS LIFE

Activities: Student government, yearbook. **Organizations:** 23 registered organizations, 1 honor society. **Athletics (Intercollegiate):** *Men:* Baseball, basketball, golf, soccer, tennis. *Women:* Basketball, golf, soccer, softball, tennis, volleyball.

ADMISSIONS

Freshman Academic Profile: 7% in top 10% of high school class, 26% in top 25% of high school class, 60% in top 50% of high school class. 70% from public high schools. SAT Math middle 50% range 420–510. SAT Critical Reading middle 50% range 400–490. SAT Writing middle 50% range 400–490. ACT middle 50% range 17–21. TOEFL required of all international applicants, minimum paper TOEFL 500, minimum computer TOEFL 173. **Basis for Candidate Selection:** *Very important factors considered include:* Academic GPA, level of applicant's interest, rigor of secondary school record, standardized test scores. *Important factors considered include:* Application essay, class rank. *Other factors considered include:* Alumni/ae relation, character/personal qualities, extracurricular activities, interview, recommendation(s). **Freshman Admission Requirements:** High school diploma is required, and GED is accepted. *Academic units recommended:* 4 English, 3 math, 2 science (1 science lab), 3 foreign language, 3 social studies. **Freshman Admission Statistics:** 851 applied, 47% admitted, 32% enrolled. **Transfer Admission Requirements:** High school transcript, college transcript(s). Minimum college GPA of 2.0 required. Lowest grade transferable C. **General Admission Information:** Application fee $25. Regular notification is rolling. Non-fall registration accepted. Admission may be deferred for a maximum of 1 year. Credit and/or placement offered for CEEB Advanced Placement tests.

COSTS AND FINANCIAL AID

Required Forms and Deadlines: FAFSA, state aid form. **Notification of Awards:** Applicants will be notified of awards on a rolling basis beginning on or about 3/1. **Types of Aid:** *Need-based scholarships/grants:* Pell, SEOG, state scholarships/grants, private scholarships, the school's own gift aid. *Loans:* FFEL Subsidized Stafford, FFEL Unsubsidized Stafford, FFEL PLUS. **Financial Aid Statistics:** 38% freshmen, 30% undergrads receive need-based scholarship or grant aid. 41% freshmen, 33% undergrads receive need-based self-help aid. 27 freshmen, 95 undergrads receive athletic scholarships.

NORTHWOOD UNIVERSITY—FLORIDA CAMPUS

2600 North Military Trail, West Palm Beach, FL 33409-2911
Phone: 561-478-5500 **E-mail:** fladmit@northwood.edu **CEEB Code:** 4072
Fax: 561-640-3328 **Website:** www.northwood.edu/fl **ACT Code:** 6736
Financial Aid Phone: 561-478-5590

This private school was founded in 1982. It has a 90-acre campus.

RATINGS
Admissions Selectivity Rating: 78   **Fire Safety Rating:** 60*   **Green Rating:** 62

STUDENTS AND FACULTY
Enrollment: 706. **Student Body:** 35% female, 65% male, 60% out-of-state, 48% international (40 countries represented). African American 9%, Asian 2%, Caucasian 30%, Native American 10%. **Retention and Graduation:** 59%

NORTHWOOD UNIVERSITY—TEXAS CAMPUS

1114 West Fm 1382, Cedar Hill, TX 75104-1204
Phone: 972-293-5400 **E-mail:** txadmit@northwood.edu
Fax: 972-291-3824 **Website:** www.northwood.edu/tx **ACT Code:** 4135
Financial Aid Phone: 972-293-5430

This private school was founded in 1966. It has a 360-acre campus.

RATINGS
Admissions Selectivity Rating: 77   **Fire Safety Rating:** 60*   **Green Rating:** 62

STUDENTS AND FACULTY
Enrollment: 517. **Student Body:** 47% female, 53% male, 6% out-of-state, 4% international (18 countries represented). African American 18%, Asian 3%,

Caucasian 44%, Hispanic 27%. **Retention and Graduation:** 63% freshmen return for sophomore year. **Faculty:** Student/faculty ratio 19:1. 24 full-time faculty, 25% hold PhDs. 100% faculty teach undergrads.

ACADEMICS

Degrees: Associate, bachelor's, terminal. **Academic Requirements:** Computer literacy, English (including composition), humanities, mathematics, philosophy, sciences (biological or physical), social science. **Classes:** Most classes have 10–19 students. Most lab/discussion sections have fewer than 10 students. **Majors with Highest Enrollment:** Entrepreneurship/entrepreneurial studies, international business, marketing/marketing management. **Disciplines with Highest Percentage of Degrees Awarded:** Business/marketing 86%, communications/journalism 9%, parks and recreation 5%. **Special Study Options:** Accelerated program, distance learning, double major, dual enrollment, external degree program, honors program, independent study, internships, study abroad, weekend college.

FACILITIES

Housing: Men's dorms, women's dorms, apartments for single students. **Special Academic Facilities/Equipment:** Butler Gallery, Hopkins Display Cases, Hach Library. **Computers:** 100% of classrooms are wired, 100% of public computers are PCs, network access in dorm rooms, network access in dorm lounges, online registration, online administrative functions (other than registration), support for handheld computing, remote student-access to Web through college's connection.

CAMPUS LIFE

Activities: Choral groups, dance, drama/theater, literary magazine, student newspaper. **Organizations:** 17 registered organizations, 1 honor society, 2 religious organizations. 1 fraternity, 1 sorority. **Athletics (Intercollegiate):** *Men:* Baseball, cross-country, golf, soccer, track/field (indoor), track/field (outdoor). *Women:* Cross-country, golf, soccer, softball, track/field (indoor), track/field (outdoor).

ADMISSIONS

Freshman Academic Profile: 15% in top 10% of high school class, 33% in top 25% of high school class, 69% in top 50% of high school class. 90% from public high schools. SAT Math middle 50% range 410–520. SAT Critical Reading middle 50% range 410–500. SAT Writing middle 50% range 380–500. ACT middle 50% range 18–23. TOEFL required of all international applicants, minimum paper TOEFL 500, minimum computer TOEFL 173. **Basis for Candidate Selection:** *Very important factors considered include:* Academic GPA, level of applicant's interest, rigor of secondary school record, standardized test scores. *Important factors considered include:* Application essay, class rank. *Other factors considered include:* Alumni/ae relation, character/personal qualities, extracurricular activities, interview, recommendation(s). **Freshman Admission Requirements:** High school diploma is required, and GED is accepted. *Academic units recommended:* 4 English, 3 math, 2 science (1 science lab), 3 foreign language, 3 social studies. **Freshman Admission Statistics:** 629 applied, 53% admitted, 39% enrolled. **Transfer Admission Requirements:** High school transcript, college transcript(s). Minimum college GPA of 2.0 required. Lowest grade transferable C. **General Admission Information:** Application fee $25. Regular notification is rolling. Non-fall registration accepted. Admission may be deferred for a maximum of 1 year. Credit and/or placement offered for CEEB Advanced Placement tests.

COSTS AND FINANCIAL AID

Required Forms and Deadlines: FAFSA. **Notification of Awards:** Applicants will be notified of awards on a rolling basis beginning on or about 3/1. **Types of Aid:** *Need-based scholarships/grants:* Pell, SEOG, private scholarships, the school's own gift aid. *Loans:* FFEL Subsidized Stafford, FFEL Unsubsidized Stafford, FFEL PLUS. **Financial Aid Statistics:** 63% freshmen, 65% undergrads receive need-based scholarship or grant aid. 73% freshmen, 64% undergrads receive need-based self-help aid. 10 freshmen, 38 undergrads receive athletic scholarships.

NORWICH UNIVERSITY

Admissions Office, 27 I.D. White Ave, Northfield, VT 05663
Phone: 802-485-2001 **E-mail:** nuadm@norwich.edu
Fax: 802-485-2032 **Website:** www.norwich.edu
Financial Aid Phone: 802-485-2015

This private school was founded in 1819. It has a 1,125-acre campus.

STUDENTS AND FACULTY

Enrollment: 2,099. **Student Body:** 77% out-of-state, 3% international. African American 3%, Asian 2%, Caucasian 79%, Hispanic 4%. **Retention and Graduation:** 74% freshmen return for sophomore year. 10% grads go on to further study within 1 year. 2% grads pursue arts and sciences degrees. 2% grads pursue business degrees. 2% grads pursue law degrees. 1% grads pursue medical degrees. **Faculty:** Student/faculty ratio 13:1. 104 full-time faculty, 77% hold PhDs. 100% faculty teach undergrads.

ACADEMICS

Degrees: Bachelor's, master's, post-bachelor's certificate. **Academic Requirements:** English (including composition), history, humanities, mathematics, sciences (biological or physical), social science. **Classes:** Most classes have 10–19 students. **Majors with Highest Enrollment:** Architecture (BArch, BA/BS, MArch, MA/MS, PhD), criminal justice/law enforcement administration, liberal arts and sciences/liberal studies. **Disciplines with Highest Percentage of Degrees Awarded:** Liberal arts/general studies 39%, social sciences 7%, health professions and related sciences 6%, business/marketing 6%, architecture 5%, computer and information sciences 5%, engineering 5%, communication technologies 3%, biological/life sciences 3%. **Special Study Options:** Cooperative education program, distance learning, double major, English as a second language (ESL), honors program, independent study, internships, study abroad.

FACILITIES

Housing: Coed dorms. **Special Academic Facilities/Equipment:** Museum, architecture and art building with gallery, new library. **Computers:** Network access in dorm rooms, network access in dorm lounges, remote student-access to Web through college's connection.

CAMPUS LIFE

Activities: Choral groups, concert band, drama/theater, jazz band, literary magazine, marching band, pep band, radio station, student government, student newspaper, yearbook. **Organizations:** 40 registered organizations, 8 honor societies, 4 religious organizations. **Athletics (Intercollegiate):** *Men:* Baseball, basketball, cross-country, diving, football, ice hockey, lacrosse, riflery, rugby, soccer, swimming, track/field (outdoor), volleyball, wrestling. *Women:* Basketball, cross-country, diving, riflery, rugby, soccer, softball, swimming, track/field (outdoor), volleyball.

ADMISSIONS

Freshman Academic Profile: 8% in top 10% of high school class, 21% in top 25% of high school class, 43% in top 50% of high school class. 90% from public high schools. SAT Math middle 50% range 440–570. SAT Critical Reading middle 50% range 440–560. TOEFL required of all international applicants, minimum paper TOEFL 500. **Basis for Candidate Selection:** *Very important factors considered include:* Rigor of secondary school record. *Important factors considered include:* Extracurricular activities, talent/ability. *Other factors considered include:* Alumni/ae relation, application essay, character/personal qualities, class rank, interview, recommendation(s), standardized test scores, volunteer work, work experience. **Freshman Admission Requirements:** High school diploma is required, and GED is accepted. *Academic units required:* 4 English, 3 math, 2 science (2 science labs). *Academic units recommended:* 4 English, 4 math, 3 science (2 science labs), 2 foreign language. **Freshman Admission Statistics:** 1,473 applied, 91% admitted, 37% enrolled. **Transfer Admission Requirements:** High school transcript, college transcript(s). Lowest grade transferable C-. **General Admission Information:** Application fee $35. Early decision application deadline 11/15. Regular notification is rolling. Non-fall registration accepted. Admission may be deferred for a maximum of 1 year. Common Application accepted. Credit offered for CEEB Advanced Placement tests.

COSTS AND FINANCIAL AID

Annual tuition $16,710. Room & board $6,372. Required fees $350. Average book expense $500. **Types of Aid:** *Need-based scholarships/grants:* Pell, SEOG. *Loans:* Direct Subsidized Stafford, Direct Unsubsidized Stafford, FFEL Subsidized Stafford, FFEL Unsubsidized Stafford, FFEL PLUS, Federal Perkins. **Student Employment:** Federal Work-Study Program available. Institutional employment available. Off-campus job opportunities are fair.

RATINGS

Admissions Selectivity Rating: 65   **Fire Safety Rating:** 60*   **Green Rating:** 60*

NOTRE DAME COLLEGE

4545 College Road, South Euclid, OH 44121
Phone: 216-381-1680 **E-mail:** admissions@ndc.edu **CEEB Code:** 3085
Fax: 216-373-5278 **Website:** www.NotreDameCollege.edu **ACT Code:** 3302
Financial Aid Phone: 216-373-5213

This private school, affiliated with the Roman Catholic Church, was founded in 1922. It has a 53-acre campus.

RATINGS
Admissions Selectivity Rating: 74 **Fire Safety Rating:** 60* **Green Rating:** 60*

STUDENTS AND FACULTY
Enrollment: 835. **Student Body:** 63% female, 37% male, 3% out-of-state, 4% international. African American 24%, Caucasian 62%, Hispanic 3%. **Retention and Graduation:** 65% freshmen return for sophomore year. 60% grads go on to further study within 1 year. 10% grads pursue arts and sciences degrees. 10% grads pursue business degrees. 5% grads pursue law degrees. 5% grads pursue medical degrees. **Faculty:** Student/faculty ratio 19:1. 36 full-time faculty, 53% hold PhDs. 100% faculty teach undergrads.

ACADEMICS
Degrees: Associate, bachelor's, certificate, master's, post-bachelor's certificate. **Academic Requirements:** Arts/fine arts, computer literacy, English (including composition), foreign languages, history, mathematics, philosophy, sciences (biological or physical), social science, theology. **Classes:** Most classes have 10–19 students. Most lab/discussion sections have 10–19 students. **Majors with Highest Enrollment:** Business administration/management, psychology, secondary education and teaching. **Disciplines with Highest Percentage of Degrees Awarded:** Business/marketing 55%, education 24%, communications/journalism 4%. **Special Study Options:** Cooperative education program, cross-registration, distance learning, double major, independent study, internships, student-designed major, study abroad, teacher certification program, weekend college.

FACILITIES
Housing: Coed dorms, men's dorms, women's dorms. **Special Academic Facilities/Equipment:** Tolerance resource center. **Computers:** 100% of classrooms are wired, 1% of classrooms are wireless, 95% of public computers are PCs, 5% of public computers are Macs, network access in dorm rooms, network access in dorm lounges, remote student-access to Web through college's connection.

CAMPUS LIFE
Activities: Choral groups, dance, drama/theater, literary magazine, pep band, student government, student newspaper, yearbook. **Organizations:** 22 registered organizations, 6 honor societies, 1 religious organization. **Athletics (Intercollegiate):** *Men:* Baseball, basketball, cross-country, golf, soccer, tennis, track/field (outdoor). *Women:* Basketball, cross-country, golf, lacrosse, soccer, softball, track/field (outdoor), volleyball.

ADMISSIONS
Freshman Academic Profile: 4% in top 10% of high school class, 22% in top 25% of high school class, 62% in top 50% of high school class. 60% from public high schools. SAT Math middle 50% range 393–520. SAT Critical Reading middle 50% range 440–528. ACT middle 50% range 17–21. TOEFL required of all international applicants, minimum paper TOEFL 550, minimum computer TOEFL 213. **Basis for Candidate Selection:** *Very important factors considered include:* Academic GPA, rigor of secondary school record, standardized test scores. *Important factors considered include:* Class rank, interview, level of applicant's interest. *Other factors considered include:* Alumni/ae relation, application essay, character/personal qualities, extracurricular activities, recommendation(s), talent/ability, volunteer work, work experience. **Freshman Admission Requirements:** High school diploma is required, and GED is accepted. *Academic units recommended:* 4 English, 3 math, 3 science (3 science labs), 2 foreign language, 3 social studies, 1 fine arts. **Freshman Admission Statistics:** 1,004 applied, 51% admitted, 29% enrolled. **Transfer Admission Requirements:** High school transcript, college transcript(s), interview. Minimum college GPA of 2.5 required. Lowest grade transferable C. **General Admission Information:** Application fee $30. Regular notification is rolling. Non-fall registration accepted. Admission may be deferred for a maximum of 1 year. Common Application accepted. Credit offered for CEEB Advanced Placement tests.

COSTS AND FINANCIAL AID
Annual tuition $18,670. Room & board $6,648. Required fees $550. Average book expense $1,270. **Required Forms and Deadlines:** FAFSA. Financial aid filing deadline 4/1. **Notification of Awards:** Applicants will be notified of awards on a rolling basis beginning on or about 1/1. **Types of Aid:** *Need-based scholarships/grants:* Pell, SEOG, state scholarships/grants, private scholarships, the school's own gift aid. *Loans:* FFEL Subsidized Stafford, FFEL Unsubsidized Stafford, FFEL PLUS, Federal Perkins, state loans, college/university loans from institutional funds. **Student Employment:** Federal Work-Study Program available. Institutional employment available. Off-campus job opportunities are good. **Financial Aid Statistics:** 98% freshmen, 84% undergrads receive need-based scholarship or grant aid. 98% freshmen, 84% undergrads receive need-based self-help aid. 28 undergrads receive athletic scholarships. 93% freshmen, 63% undergrads receive any aid.

See page 1298.

NOTRE DAME DE NAMUR UNIVERSITY

1500 Ralston Avenue, Belmont, CA 94002-1908
Phone: 650-508-3600 **E-mail:** admiss@ndnu.edu **CEEB Code:** 4063
Fax: 650-508-3426 **Website:** www.ndnu.edu **ACT Code:** 0236
Financial Aid Phone: 650-508-3509

This private school, affiliated with the Roman Catholic Church, was founded in 1851. It has an 80-acre campus.

RATINGS
Admissions Selectivity Rating: 72 **Fire Safety Rating:** 60* **Green Rating:** 60*

STUDENTS AND FACULTY
Enrollment: 855. **Student Body:** 64% female, 36% male, 36% out-of-state, 4% international. African American 5%, Asian 17%, Caucasian 44%, Hispanic 20%, Native American 1%. **Retention and Graduation:** 70% freshmen return for sophomore year. 40% freshmen graduate within 4 years. 15% grads go on to further study within 1 year. 8% grads pursue arts and sciences degrees. 5% grads pursue business degrees. 1% grads pursue law degrees. 1% grads pursue medical degrees. **Faculty:** Student/faculty ratio 12:1. 56 full-time faculty. 100% faculty teach undergrads.

ACADEMICS
Degrees: Bachelor's, master's, post-bachelor's certificate. **Academic Requirements:** Arts/fine arts, computer literacy, English (including composition), foreign languages, history, humanities, mathematics, philosophy, sciences (biological or physical), social science, 6 units in religious studies. **Classes:** Most classes have 10–19 students. Most lab/discussion sections have fewer than 10 students. **Disciplines with Highest Percentage of Degrees Awarded:** Business/marketing 35%, public administration and social services 13%, psychology 12%, liberal arts/general studies 12%, visual and performing arts 7%. **Special Study Options:** Accelerated program, double major, English as a second language (ESL), exchange student program (domestic), independent study, internships, liberal arts/career combination, student-designed major, study abroad, teacher certification program.

FACILITIES
Housing: Coed dorms, 2- or 3-person apartments, 4-person suites. **Special Academic Facilities/Equipment:** Student art museum, professional art gallery, archives of modern Christian art, theater, early learning center for Montessori credential training, on-campus elementary school.

CAMPUS LIFE
Activities: Choral groups, dance, literary magazine, music ensembles, musical theater, student government, student newspaper. **Organizations:** 15 registered organizations, 3 honor societies, 1 religious organization. **Athletics (Intercollegiate):** *Men:* Basketball, cheerleading, soccer, tennis, track/field (outdoor). *Women:* Basketball, cheerleading, cross-country, soccer, softball, tennis, track/field (outdoor), volleyball.

ADMISSIONS
Freshman Academic Profile: 17% in top 10% of high school class, 41% in top 25% of high school class, 74% in top 50% of high school class. 62% from public high schools. SAT Math middle 50% range 450–540. SAT Critical Reading middle 50% range 430–530. SAT Writing middle 50% range 430–540. ACT middle 50% range 18–24. TOEFL required of all international applicants, minimum paper TOEFL 450. **Basis for Candidate Selection:** *Very important factors considered include:* Academic GPA, character/personal qualities, rigor of secondary school record. *Important factors considered include:* Application essay, class rank, extracurricular activities, recommendation(s), standardized test scores, talent/ability, volunteer work. *Other factors considered include:* First generation, interview, work experience. **Freshman Admission Requirements:** High school diploma is required, and GED is accepted. *Academic units required:* 4 English, 2 math, 1 science (1 science lab), 2 foreign language, 2

social studies, 1 history, 3 academic electives. *Academic units recommended:* 3 math, 2 science (2 science labs), 3 foreign language. **Freshman Admission Statistics:** 706 applied, 97% admitted, 20% enrolled. **Transfer Admission Requirements:** College transcript(s), essay or personal statement, statement of good standing from prior institution(s). Minimum college GPA of 2.0 required. Lowest grade transferable C. **General Admission Information:** Application fee $40. Regular notification is rolling. Non-fall registration accepted. Admission may be deferred for a maximum of 1 year. Credit offered for CEEB Advanced Placement tests.

COSTS AND FINANCIAL AID

Annual tuition $24,450. Room & board $10,580. Required fees $200. Average book expense $1,330. **Required Forms and Deadlines:** FAFSA. Financial aid filing deadline 3/2. **Types of Aid:** *Need-based scholarships/grants:* Pell, SEOG, state scholarships/grants, private scholarships. *Loans:* FFEL Subsidized Stafford, FFEL Unsubsidized Stafford, FFEL PLUS, Federal Perkins. **Student Employment:** Federal Work-Study Program available. Institutional employment available. Off-campus job opportunities are excellent. **Financial Aid Statistics:** 72% freshmen, 69% undergrads receive need-based scholarship or grant aid. 62% freshmen, 60% undergrads receive need-based self-help aid. Highest amount earned per year from on-campus jobs $1,300.

NOVA SCOTIA COLLEGE OF ART AND DESIGN

5163 Duke Street, Halifax, NS B3J3J6 Canada
Phone: 902-494-8129 **E-mail:** admissions@nscad.ca
Fax: 902-425-2987 **Website:** www.nscad.ca
Financial Aid Phone: 902-494-8130

This public school was founded in 1887. It has a 1-acre campus.

RATINGS
Admissions Selectivity Rating: 60*   **Fire Safety Rating:** 60*   **Green Rating:** 60*

STUDENTS AND FACULTY
Enrollment: 896. **Student Body:** 64% female, 36% male, 54% out-of-state. **Faculty:** Student/faculty ratio 11:1. 68 full-time faculty. 100% faculty teach undergrads.

ACADEMICS
Degrees: Bachelor's, master's. **Academic Requirements:** Arts/fine arts, art history, English (including composition). **Disciplines with Highest Percentage of Degrees Awarded:** Visual and performing arts 100%. **Special Study Options:** Cooperative education program, distance learning, double major, exchange student program (domestic), independent study, internships, study abroad.

FACILITIES
Housing: Coed dorms. **Computers:** 27% of public computers are PCs, 73% of public computers are Macs.

CAMPUS LIFE
Activities: Student government, student newspaper.

ADMISSIONS
Freshman Academic Profile: TOEFL required of all international applicants, minimum paper TOEFL 575, minimum computer TOEFL 233. **Basis for Candidate Selection:** *Very important factors considered include:* Application essay, rigor of secondary school record, talent/ability. *Other factors considered include:* Character/personal qualities, interview, recommendation(s), standardized test scores, volunteer work, work experience. **Freshman Admission Statistics:** 247 applied, 43% admitted. **Transfer Admission Requirements:** College transcript(s), essay or personal statement, statement of good standing from prior institution(s). **General Admission Information:** Application fee $50. Regular application deadline 5/15. Regular notification is rolling. Non-fall registration not accepted. Admission may be deferred for a maximum of 1 year. Placement offered for CEEB Advanced Placement tests.

COSTS AND FINANCIAL AID
Annual tuition $4,436. International tuition $7,884. Required fees $250. Average book expense $1,500.

NOVA SOUTHEASTERN UNIVERSITY

3301 College Avenue, Ft. Lauderdale, FL 33314
Phone: 954-262-8000 **E-mail:** ncsinfo@nova.edu **CEEB Code:** 5514
Fax: 954-262-3811 **Website:** www.nova.edu **ACT Code:** 6706
Financial Aid Phone: 954-262-3380

This private school was founded in 1964. It has a 300-acre campus.

RATINGS
Admissions Selectivity Rating: 60*   **Fire Safety Rating:** 60*   **Green Rating:** 60*

STUDENTS AND FACULTY
Enrollment: 5,236. **Student Body:** 72% female, 28% male, 6% international. African American 26%, Asian 5%, Caucasian 30%, Hispanic 26%. **Retention and Graduation:** 61% freshmen return for sophomore year. 34% freshmen graduate within 4 years. **Faculty:** Student/faculty ratio 26:1. 598 full-time faculty, 91% hold PhDs.

ACADEMICS
Degrees: Associate, bachelor's, doctoral, first professional certificate, first professional, master's, post-bachelor's certificate, post-master's certificate. **Academic Requirements:** English (including composition), mathematics, sciences (biological or physical), social science. General education core may include courses in history, humanities, and philosophy. **Classes:** Most classes have 10–19 students. **Majors with Highest Enrollment:** Biology/biological sciences, business administration/management, elementary education and teaching. **Disciplines with Highest Percentage of Degrees Awarded:** Business/marketing 40%, psychology 13%, biological/life sciences 12%, health professions and related sciences 12%, education 10%, liberal arts/general studies 6%. **Special Study Options:** Accelerated program, distance learning, double major, dual enrollment, English as a second language (ESL), honors program, independent study, internships, study abroad, teacher certification program. Dual admission programs with NSU graduate and professional school.

FACILITIES
Housing: Coed dorms, apartments for married students, apartments for single students, special housing for disabled students, special housing for international students. **Special Academic Facilities/Equipment:** Institute for early childhood studies, university school for pre-kindergarten to grade 12, oceanographic center and lab, biofeedback and learning technology labs, audiology and speech language pathology, psychology clinics. **Computers:** 100% of classrooms are wireless, 98% of public computers are PCs, 2% of public computers are Macs, network access in dorm rooms, network access in dorm lounges, online registration, online administrative functions (other than registration), remote student-access to Web through college's connection.

CAMPUS LIFE
Activities: Choral groups, drama/theater, literary magazine, radio station, student government, student newspaper. **Organizations:** 66 registered organizations, 4 honor societies, 4 religious organizations. 3 fraternities (6% men join), 3 sororities (5% women join). **Athletics (Intercollegiate):** *Men:* Baseball, basketball, cross-country, golf, soccer. *Women:* Basketball, cheerleading, crew/rowing, cross-country, golf, soccer, softball, tennis, volleyball.

ADMISSIONS
Freshman Academic Profile: 20% in top 10% of high school class, 52% in top 25% of high school class, 84% in top 50% of high school class. SAT Math middle 50% range 460–560. SAT Critical Reading middle 50% range 460–530. ACT middle 50% range 19–24. TOEFL required of all international applicants, minimum paper TOEFL 550, minimum computer TOEFL 213. **Basis for Candidate Selection:** *Very important factors considered include:* Academic GPA, rigor of secondary school record, standardized test scores. *Other factors considered include:* Application essay, character/personal qualities, extracurricular activities, interview, level of applicant's interest, recommendation(s), talent/ability, volunteer work, work experience. **Freshman Admission Requirements:** High school diploma is required, and GED is accepted. *Academic units required:* 4 English, 3 math, 3 science, 1 social studies, 2 history. *Academic units recommended:* 2 foreign language, 1 academic elective, 1 computer course. **Freshman Admission Statistics:** 2,766 applied, 50% admitted, 38% enrolled. **Transfer Admission Requirements:** College transcript(s), statement of good standing from prior institution(s). Minimum college GPA of 2.5 required. Lowest grade transferable C. **General Admission Information:** Application fee $50. Regular notification as applications are accepted. Non-fall registration accepted. Admission may be deferred for a maximum of 1 calendar year. Credit and/or placement offered for CEEB Advanced Placement tests.

COSTS AND FINANCIAL AID

Annual tuition $18,150. Room & board $6,012. Required fees $550. Average book expense $1,200. **Required Forms and Deadlines:** FAFSA, institution's own financial aid form. Financial aid filing deadline 4/15. **Notification of Awards:** Applicants will be notified of awards on a rolling basis beginning on or about 3/15. **Types of Aid:** *Need-based scholarships/grants:* Pell, SEOG, the school's own gift aid, Florida Student Assistance Grant (FSAG). *Loans:* Direct Subsidized Stafford, Direct Unsubsidized Stafford, Direct PLUS, FFEL Subsidized Stafford, FFEL Unsubsidized Stafford, FFEL PLUS, Federal Perkins. **Student Employment:** Federal Work-Study Program available. Off-campus job opportunities are good. **Financial Aid Statistics:** 87% freshmen, 92% undergrads receive need-based scholarship or grant aid. 77% freshmen, 85% undergrads receive need-based self-help aid. 5 freshmen, 16 undergrads receive athletic scholarships.

NYACK COLLEGE

1 South Boulevard, Nyack, NY 10960-3698
Phone: 845-358-1710 **E-mail:** enroll@nyack.edu **CEEB Code:** 2560
Fax: 845-358-3047 **Website:** www.nyackcollege.edu **ACT Code:** 2846
Financial Aid Phone: 800-799-6248

This private school, affiliated with the Christian & Missionary Alliance Church, was founded in 1882. It has a 102-acre campus.

RATINGS

Admissions Selectivity Rating: 74   **Fire Safety Rating:** 60*   **Green Rating:** 60*

STUDENTS AND FACULTY

Enrollment: 1,964. **Student Body:** 59% female, 41% male, 36% out-of-state, 4% international (46 countries represented). African American 30%, Asian 6%, Caucasian 35%, Hispanic 22%. **Retention and Graduation:** 64% freshmen return for sophomore year. **Faculty:** Student/faculty ratio 17:1. 83 full-time faculty, 63% hold PhDs. 86% faculty teach undergrads.

ACADEMICS

Degrees: Associate, bachelor's, first professional, master's, terminal. **Academic Requirements:** Arts/fine arts, Bible/theology, English (including composition), foreign languages, history, humanities, mathematics, philosophy, sciences (biological or physical), social science. **Classes:** Most classes have 10–19 students. Most lab/discussion sections have 10–19 students. **Disciplines with Highest Percentage of Degrees Awarded:** Business/marketing 55%, liberal arts/general studies 9%, education 9%, psychology 7%, English 3%, social sciences 3%, computer and information sciences 2%. **Special Study Options:** Accelerated program, distance learning, double major, English as a second language (ESL), honors program, independent study, internships, liberal arts/career combination, study abroad, teacher certification program.

FACILITIES

Housing: Men's dorms, women's dorms, apartments for single students. **Computers:** 100% of public computers are PCs, remote student-access to Web through college's connection.

CAMPUS LIFE

Activities: Choral groups, drama/theater, literary magazine, music ensembles, musical theater, radio station, student government, student newspaper, yearbook. **Organizations:** 1 honor society, 1 religious organization. **Athletics (Intercollegiate):** *Men:* Baseball, basketball, cross-country, golf, soccer. *Women:* Basketball, cross-country, soccer, softball, volleyball.

ADMISSIONS

Freshman Academic Profile: 9% in top 10% of high school class, 23% in top 25% of high school class, 62% in top 50% of high school class. SAT Math middle 50% range 410–550. SAT Critical Reading middle 50% range 430–560. ACT middle 50% range 17–23. TOEFL required of all international applicants, minimum paper TOEFL 550. **Basis for Candidate Selection:** *Very important factors considered include:* Class rank, interview, recommendation(s), religious affiliation/commitment, rigor of secondary school record, standardized test scores. *Important factors considered include:* Application essay, character/personal qualities, extracurricular activities. *Other factors considered include:* Talent/ability, volunteer work, work experience. **Freshman Admission Requirements:** High school diploma is required, and GED is accepted. *Academic units recommended:* 4 English, 2 foreign language, 4 academic electives, 6 additional also recommended: 3 units math/science (any combination), 3 units social studies/history (any combination). **Freshman Admission Statistics:** 944 applied, 63% admitted, 53% enrolled. **Transfer Admission Requirements:** High school transcript, college transcript(s), essay or personal

statement, statement of good standing from prior institution(s). Lowest grade transferable C-. **General Admission Information:** Application fee $15. Regular application deadline 5/15. Non-fall registration accepted. Common Application not accepted. Credit offered for CEEB Advanced Placement tests.

COSTS AND FINANCIAL AID

Annual tuition $12,990. Required fees $800. **Required Forms and Deadlines:** FAFSA. Financial aid filing deadline 3/1. **Notification of Awards:** Applicants will be notified of awards on a rolling basis beginning on or about 3/1. **Types of Aid:** *Need-based scholarships/grants:* Pell, SEOG, state scholarships/grants, private scholarships, the school's own gift aid. *Loans:* FFEL Subsidized Stafford, FFEL Unsubsidized Stafford, FFEL PLUS, Federal Perkins. **Student Employment:** Federal Work-Study Program available. Institutional employment available. Off-campus job opportunities are excellent. **Financial Aid Statistics:** 76% freshmen, 82% undergrads receive need-based scholarship or grant aid. 65% freshmen, 74% undergrads receive need-based self-help aid. 24 freshmen, 47 undergrads receive athletic scholarships.

OAK HILLS CHRISTIAN COLLEGE

1600 Oak Hills Road SW, Bemidji, MN 56601
Phone: 218-751-8670 **E-mail:** admissions@oakhills.edu
Fax: 218-751-8825 **Website:** www.oakhills.edu **ACT Code:** 2167
Financial Aid Phone: 218-751-8670

This private school, affiliated with the Interdenominational Church, was founded in 1946. It has a 180-acre campus.

RATINGS

Admissions Selectivity Rating: 60*   **Fire Safety Rating:** 60*   **Green Rating:** 60*

STUDENTS AND FACULTY

Enrollment: 189. **Student Body:** 48% female, 52% male, 34% out-of-state, 2% international (2 countries represented). African American 1%, Asian 2%, Caucasian 91%, Hispanic 1%, Native American 3%. **Retention and Graduation:** 56% freshmen return for sophomore year. 17% freshmen graduate within 4 years. **Faculty:** Student/faculty ratio 14:1. 6 full-time faculty, 67% hold PhDs. 100% faculty teach undergrads.

ACADEMICS

Degrees: Associate, bachelor's, certificate. **Academic Requirements:** Arts/fine arts, Christian ministries and biblical studies, English (including composition), history, humanities, mathematics, philosophy, sciences (biological or physical), social science. **Classes:** Most classes have fewer than 10 students. **Majors with Highest Enrollment:** General studies, psychology, youth ministry. **Disciplines with Highest Percentage of Degrees Awarded:** Theology and religious vocations 70%, liberal arts/general studies 30%. **Special Study Options:** Double major, independent study, internships.

FACILITIES

Housing: Men's dorms, women's dorms, apartments for married students, apartments for single students, special housing for disabled students. **Special Academic Facilities/Equipment:** American Indian Resource Center. **Computers:** 50% of classrooms are wireless, 100% of public computers are PCs, network access in dorm rooms, remote student-access to Web through college's connection.

CAMPUS LIFE

Activities: Choral groups, music ensembles, yearbook. **Athletics (Intercollegiate):** *Men:* Basketball. *Women:* Basketball, volleyball.

ADMISSIONS

Freshman Academic Profile: 88% from public high schools. ACT middle 50% range 23–17. TOEFL required of all international applicants, minimum paper TOEFL 500, minimum computer TOEFL 173. **Basis for Candidate Selection:** *Very important factors considered include:* Academic GPA, application essay, recommendation(s). *Important factors considered include:* Character/personal qualities. *Other factors considered include:* Class rank, interview, level of applicant's interest, religious affiliation/commitment, standardized test scores. **Freshman Admission Requirements:** High school diploma is required, and GED is accepted. **Freshman Admission Statistics:** 61 applied, 90% admitted, 64% enrolled. **Transfer Admission Requirements:** High school transcript, college transcript(s), essay or personal statement. Minimum college GPA of 2.0 required. Lowest grade transferable C. **General Admission Information:** Application fee $25. Regular notification is rolling. Non-fall registration accepted. Admission may be deferred for a maximum of 2 years. Credit and/or placement offered for CEEB Advanced Placement tests.

COSTS AND FINANCIAL AID

Annual tuition $12,820. Room and board $4,720. Average book expense $730. **Required Forms and Deadlines:** FAFSA, institution's own financial aid form. **Notification of Awards:** Applicants will be notified of awards on a rolling basis beginning on or about 3/1. **Types of Aid:** *Need-based scholarships/grants:* Pell, SEOG, state scholarships/grants, private scholarships, the school's own gift aid. *Loans:* FFEL Subsidized Stafford, FFEL Unsubsidized Stafford, FFEL PLUS, state loans, alternative loan programs. **Student Employment:** Federal Work-Study Program available. Institutional employment available. Off-campus job opportunities are excellent. **Financial Aid Statistics:** 90% freshmen, 91% undergrads receive need-based scholarship or grant aid. 74% freshmen, 77% undergrads receive need-based self-help aid. 100% freshmen, 100% undergrads receive any aid.

OAKLAND CITY UNIVERSITY

143 N. Lucretia Street, Oakland City, IN 47660
Phone: 812-749-4781 **E-mail:** ocuadmit@oak.edu
Fax: 812-749-1233 **Website:** www.oak.edu
Financial Aid Phone: 812-749-1224

This private school, affiliated with the Baptist Church, was founded in 1885.

RATINGS

Admissions Selectivity Rating: 60* **Fire Safety Rating:** 60* **Green Rating:** 60*

STUDENTS AND FACULTY

Enrollment: 1,258. **Student Body:** 50% female, 50% male, 30% out-of-state. African American 15%, Hispanic 2%. **Retention and Graduation:** 50% freshmen graduate within 4 years. 42% grads go on to further study within 1 year. 40% grads pursue arts and sciences degrees. 2% grads pursue business degrees. **Faculty:** Student/faculty ratio 16:1. 36 full-time faculty, 67% hold PhDs. 100% faculty teach undergrads.

ACADEMICS

Degrees: Associate, bachelor's, certificate, doctoral, first professional, master's, terminal. **Academic Requirements:** Arts/fine arts, computer literacy, English (including composition), history, humanities, mathematics, New Testament, philosophy, sciences (biological or physical), social science. **Classes:** Most classes have fewer than 10 students. **Disciplines with Highest Percentage of Degrees Awarded:** Business/marketing 65%, education 21%, computer and information sciences 2%, visual and performing arts 2%, biological/life sciences 1%, liberal arts/general studies 1%, social sciences 1%. **Special Study Options:** Accelerated program, cooperative education program, distance learning, double major, dual enrollment, external degree program, honors program, independent study, internships, teacher certification program.

FACILITIES

Housing: Men's dorms, women's dorms, apartments for married students, apartments for single students, special housing for disabled students. **Computers:** Online registration, online administrative functions (other than registration).

CAMPUS LIFE

Activities: Choral groups, drama/theater, music ensembles, pep band, student government, student newspaper, yearbook. **Organizations:** 18 registered organizations, 5 honor societies, 3 religious organizations. **Athletics (Intercollegiate):** *Men:* Baseball, basketball, cheerleading, cross-country, golf, soccer, volleyball. *Women:* Basketball, cheerleading, cross-country, golf, soccer, softball, volleyball.

ADMISSIONS

Freshman Academic Profile: 7% in top 10% of high school class, 18% in top 25% of high school class, 60% in top 50% of high school class. SAT Math middle 50% range 420–530. SAT Critical Reading middle 50% range 400–510. SAT Writing middle 50% range 398–500. ACT middle 50% range 17–23. TOEFL required of all international applicants, minimum paper TOEFL 500. **Basis for Candidate Selection:** *Very important factors considered include:* Rigor of secondary school record, standardized test scores. *Important factors considered include:* Character/personal qualities, interview. *Other factors considered include:* Application essay, class rank, recommendation(s), talent/ability, volunteer work. **Freshman Admission Requirements:** High school diploma is required, and GED is accepted. *Academic units recommended:* 4 English, 3 math, 3 science, 2 social studies. **Freshman Admission Statistics:** 382 applied, 100% admitted. **Transfer Admission Requirements:** High school transcript, college transcript(s), statement of good standing from prior institution(s).

Minimum college GPA of 2.0 required. Lowest grade transferable C. **General Admission Information:** Application fee $35. Regular application deadline 9/5. Non-fall registration not accepted. Common Application accepted.

COSTS AND FINANCIAL AID

Annual tuition $15,200. Room and board $6,000. Required fees $360. Average book expense $1,500. **Required Forms and Deadlines:** FAFSA. Financial aid filing deadline 3/2. **Notification of Awards:** Applicants will be notified of awards on a rolling basis beginning on or about 6/2. **Student Employment:** Federal Work-Study Program available. Off-campus job opportunities are poor. **Financial Aid Statistics:** Highest amount earned per year from on-campus jobs $1,700.

OAKLAND UNIVERSITY

Office of Admissions, 101 North Foundation Hall, Oakland University, Rochester, MI 48309-4401
Phone: 248-370-3360 **E-mail:** ouinfo@oakland.edu **CEEB Code:** 1497
Fax: 248-370-4462 **Website:** www.oakland.edu **ACT Code:** 2033
Financial Aid Phone: 248-370-2550

This public school was founded in 1957. It has a 1,444-acre campus.

RATINGS

Admissions Selectivity Rating: 60* **Fire Safety Rating:** 60* **Green Rating:** 72

STUDENTS AND FACULTY

Enrollment: 13,195. **Student Body:** 62% female, 38% male, 1% out-of-state. 1% international (75 countries represented). African American 9%, Asian 4%, Caucasian 79%, Hispanic 2%. **Retention and Graduation:** 70% freshmen return for sophomore year. 13% freshmen graduate within 4 years. **Faculty:** Student/faculty ratio 22:1. 471 full-time faculty, 90% hold PhDs. 99% faculty teach undergrads.

ACADEMICS

Degrees: Bachelor's, doctoral, master's, post-bachelor's certificate, post-master's certificate. **Academic Requirements:** Arts/fine arts, computer literacy, English (including composition), ethnic diversity, foreign languages, history, humanities, mathematics, philosophy, sciences (biological or physical), social science. **Classes:** Most classes have 20–29 students. Most lab/discussion sections have fewer than 10 students. **Majors with Highest Enrollment:** Business administration/management, communications studies/speech communication and rhetoric, elementary education and teaching. **Disciplines with Highest Percentage of Degrees Awarded:** Business/marketing 21%, education 13%, health professions and related sciences 12%, communications/journalism 9%, engineering 8%. **Special Study Options:** Accelerated program, cooperative education program, distance learning, double major, English as a second language (ESL), honors program, independent study, internships, student-designed major, study abroad, teacher certification program.

FACILITIES

Housing: Coed dorms, apartments for married students, apartments for single students, special housing for disabled students, special housing for international students, fraternity/sorority housing, cooperative housing, living/learning communities and wellness communities. **Special Academic Facilities/Equipment:** Art gallery, robotics lab, eye research institute, professional theater, Meadowbrook Hall, Meadowbrook Music Festival, 2 golf courses, Pawley Learning Center, Lowry Early Childhood Education Center, Jack's Place for Autism at OU. **Computers:** 10% of classrooms are wired, 10% of classrooms are wireless, 80% of public computers are PCs, 15% of public computers are Macs, 5% of public computers are UNIX, network access in dorm rooms, network access in dorm lounges, online registration, online administrative functions (other than registration), remote student-access to Web through college's connection.

CAMPUS LIFE

Activities: Choral groups, concert band, dance, drama/theater, jazz band, literary magazine, music ensembles, musical theater, pep band, radio station, student government, student newspaper, student-run film society, symphony orchestra, television station. **Organizations:** 140 registered organizations, 4 honor societies, 18 religious organizations. 3 fraternities (2% men join), 7 sororities (2% women join). **Athletics (Intercollegiate):** *Men:* Baseball, basketball, cross-country, diving, golf, soccer, swimming, track/field (outdoor). *Women:* Basketball, cross-country, diving, golf, soccer, softball, swimming, tennis, track/field (outdoor), volleyball.

ADMISSIONS

Freshman Academic Profile: 90% from public high schools. ACT middle 50% range 19–24. TOEFL required of all international applicants, minimum paper TOEFL 550, minimum computer TOEFL 213. **Basis for Candidate Selection:** *Very important factors considered include:* Academic GPA, class rank, rigor of secondary school record. *Important factors considered include:* Character/personal qualities, extracurricular activities, recommendation(s), talent/ability, volunteer work. *Other factors considered include:* Alumni/ae relation, application essay, first generation, interview, level of applicant's interest, standardized test scores, work experience. **Freshman Admission Requirements:** High school diploma is required, and GED is accepted. *Academic units required:* 4 English, 3 math, 3 science, 3 social studies. *Academic units recommended:* 2 foreign language. **Freshman Admission Statistics:** 6,571 applied, 79% admitted, 44% enrolled. **Transfer Admission Requirements:** College transcript(s), statement of good standing from prior institution(s). Minimum college GPA of 2.5 required. Lowest grade transferable C. **General Admission Information:** Application fee $40. Regular notification within 2 weeks of application. Non-fall registration accepted. Admission may be deferred for a maximum of 1 year. Placement offered for CEEB Advanced Placement tests.

COSTS AND FINANCIAL AID

Annual in-state tuition $7,928. Annual out-of-state tuition $18,263. Room and board $6,670. Average book expense $1,178. **Student Employment:** Federal Work-Study Program available. Institutional employment available. Off-campus job opportunities are excellent.

OBERLIN COLLEGE

101 North Professor Street, Oberlin College, Oberlin, OH 44074
Phone: 440-775-8411 **E-mail:** College.admissions@oberlin.edu **CEEB Code:** 1587
Fax: 440-775-6905 **Website:** www.oberlin.edu **ACT Code:** 3304
Financial Aid Phone: 440-775-8142

This private school was founded in 1833. It has a 450-acre campus.

RATINGS

Admissions Selectivity Rating: 97   **Fire Safety Rating:** 60*   **Green Rating:** 60*

STUDENTS AND FACULTY

Enrollment: 2,829. **Student Body:** 55% female, 45% male, 90% out-of-state, 6% international. African American 5%, Asian 8%, Caucasian 76%, Hispanic 5%. **Retention and Graduation:** 92% freshmen return for sophomore year. 71% freshmen graduate within 4 years. 16% grads go on to further study within 1 year. 8% grads pursue arts and sciences degrees. 2% grads pursue business degrees. 3% grads pursue law degrees. 3% grads pursue medical degrees. **Faculty:** Student/faculty ratio 10:1. 274 full-time faculty, 95% hold PhDs. 100% faculty teach undergrads.

ACADEMICS

Degrees: Bachelor's, diploma, master's, post-master's certificate. **Academic Requirements:** Cultural diversity, humanities, quantitative, sciences (biological or physical), social science. **Classes:** Most classes have 10–19 students. Most lab/discussion sections have 10–19 students. **Majors with Highest Enrollment:** English language and literature, history. **Disciplines with Highest Percentage of Degrees Awarded:** Visual and performing arts 26%, social sciences 12%, biological/life sciences 10%, English 9%, area and ethnic studies 8%. **Special Study Options:** Cross-registration, double major, dual enrollment, exchange student program (domestic), honors program, independent study, internships, student-designed major, study abroad, teacher certification program, 5-year double-degree program with Conservatory of Music and College of Arts and Sciences, 3–2 engineering.

FACILITIES

Housing: Coed dorms, women's dorms, cooperative housing. **Special Academic Facilities/Equipment:** Allen Memorial Art museum, theaters, music performance halls. **Computers:** 1% of classrooms are wired, 75% of classrooms are wireless, 45% of public computers are PCs, 55% of public computers are Macs, network access in dorm rooms, network access in dorm lounges, online registration, online administrative functions (other than registration), remote student-access to Web through college's connection.

CAMPUS LIFE

Activities: Choral groups, concert band, dance, drama/theater, jazz band, literary magazine, marching band, music ensembles, musical theater, opera, radio station, student government, student newspaper, student-run film society, symphony orchestra, yearbook. **Organizations:** 125 registered organizations, 3 honor societies, 10 religious organizations. **Athletics (Intercollegiate):** *Men:* Baseball, basketball, cross-country, diving, football, golf, lacrosse, soccer, swimming, tennis, track/field (indoor), track/field (outdoor). *Women:* Basketball, cross-country, diving, field hockey, golf, lacrosse, soccer, softball, swimming, tennis, track/field (indoor), track/field (outdoor), volleyball.

ADMISSIONS

Freshman Academic Profile: 68% in top 10% of high school class, 90% in top 25% of high school class, 97% in top 50% of high school class. 60% from public high schools. SAT Math middle 50% range 610–710. SAT Critical Reading middle 50% range 640–750. SAT Writing middle 50% range 630–730. ACT middle 50% range 26–32. TOEFL required of all international applicants, minimum paper TOEFL 600, minimum computer TOEFL 200. **Basis for Candidate Selection:** *Very important factors considered include:* Academic GPA, class rank, rigor of secondary school record, standardized test scores. *Important factors considered include:* Application essay, character/personal qualities, extracurricular activities, recommendation(s), talent/ability. *Other factors considered include:* Alumni/ae relation, first generation, interview, level of applicant's interest, racial/ethnic status, volunteer work, work experience. **Freshman Admission Requirements:** High school diploma is required, and GED is accepted. *Academic units required:* 4 English, 4 math, 3 science, 3 foreign language, 3 social studies. **Freshman Admission Statistics:** 6,686 applied, 34% admitted, 32% enrolled. **Transfer Admission Requirements:** High school transcript, college transcript(s), essay or personal statement, standardized test score, statement of good standing from prior institution(s). Minimum college GPA of 3.0 required. Lowest grade transferable C-. **General Admission Information:** Application fee $35. Early decision application deadline 11/15. Regular application deadline 1/15. Regular notification 4/1. Non-fall registration not accepted. Admission may be deferred for a maximum of 1 year. Credit and/or placement offered for CEEB Advanced Placement tests.

COSTS AND FINANCIAL AID

Annual tuition $36,064. Room and board $9,280. Required fees $218. Average book expense $830. **Required Forms and Deadlines:** FAFSA, institution's own financial aid form, CSS/Financial Aid PROFILE, Noncustodial PROFILE, Business/Farm Supplement. Financial aid filing deadline 2/15. **Notification of Awards:** Applicants will be notified of awards on or about 4/1. **Types of Aid:** *Need-based scholarships/grants:* Pell, SEOG, state scholarships/grants, private scholarships, the school's own gift aid. *Loans:* FFEL Subsidized Stafford, FFEL Unsubsidized Stafford, FFEL PLUS, Federal Perkins, college/university loans from institutional funds. **Financial Aid Statistics:** 45% freshmen, 51% undergrads receive need-based scholarship or grant aid. 45% freshmen, 48% undergrads receive need-based self-help aid. 61% freshmen, 60% undergrads receive any aid. Highest amount earned per year from on-campus jobs $1,750.

See page 1300.

OCCIDENTAL COLLEGE

1600 Campus Road, Office of Admission, Los Angeles, CA 90041
Phone: 323-259-2700 **E-mail:** admission@oxy.edu **CEEB Code:** 4581
Fax: 323-341-4875 **Website:** www.oxy.edu **ACT Code:** 0350
Financial Aid Phone: 323-259-2548

This private school was founded in 1887. It has a 120-acre campus.

RATINGS

Admissions Selectivity Rating: 94   **Fire Safety Rating:** 60*   **Green Rating:** 60*

STUDENTS AND FACULTY

Enrollment: 1,864. **Student Body:** 56% female, 44% male, 53% out-of-state, 3% international (26 countries represented). African American 6%, Asian 12%, Caucasian 54%, Hispanic 14%. **Retention and Graduation:** 92% freshmen return for sophomore year. 73% freshmen graduate within 4 years. 27% grads go on to further study within 1 year. **Faculty:** Student/faculty ratio 11:1. 145 full-time faculty, 97% hold PhDs. 100% faculty teach undergrads.

ACADEMICS

Degrees: Bachelor's, master's. **Academic Requirements:** Arts/fine arts, English (including composition), foreign languages, history, humanities, sciences (biological or physical). **Classes:** Most classes have 10–19 students. Most lab/discussion sections have 10–19 students. **Majors with Highest Enrollment:** Economics, English language and literature, psychology. **Disciplines with Highest Percentage of Degrees Awarded:** Social sciences 23%, visual and performing arts 11%, business/marketing 11%, biological/life sciences 10%, psychology 9%, English 9%, foreign languages and literature 3%, area and ethnic studies 3%. **Special Study Options:** Cross-registration, double major, exchange student program (domestic), honors program, independent study, internships, student-designed major, study abroad.

FACILITIES

Housing: Coed dorms, women's dorms, fraternity/sorority housing. **Special Academic Facilities/Equipment:** Keck Theater, Mullin Studio & Art Gallery, Moore Ornithology Collection, Smiley Geological Collection, Morse Collection of astronomical instruments, superconducting magnet, vivarium, greenhouses. **Computers:** 100% of classrooms are wireless, 100% of public computers are PCs, network access in dorm rooms, network access in dorm lounges, online registration, online administrative functions (other than registration), remote student-access to Web through college's connection.

CAMPUS LIFE

Activities: Choral groups, concert band, dance, drama/theater, jazz band, literary magazine, music ensembles, musical theater, radio station, student government, student newspaper, student-run film society, symphony orchestra, yearbook. **Organizations:** 98 registered organizations, 8 honor societies, 9 religious organizations. 3 fraternities (6% men join), 3 sororities (13% women join). **Athletics (Intercollegiate):** *Men:* Baseball, basketball, cross-country, diving, football, golf, soccer, swimming, tennis, track/field (outdoor), water polo. *Women:* Basketball, cross-country, diving, golf, soccer, softball, swimming, tennis, track/field (outdoor), volleyball, water polo.

ADMISSIONS

Freshman Academic Profile: 60% in top 10% of high school class, 86% in top 25% of high school class, 100% in top 50% of high school class. 60% from public high schools. SAT Math middle 50% range 600–690. SAT Critical Reading middle 50% range 590–700. SAT Writing middle 50% range 585–690. ACT middle 50% range 26–30. TOEFL required of all international applicants, minimum paper TOEFL 600, minimum computer TOEFL 250. **Basis for Candidate Selection:** *Very important factors considered include:* Extracurricular activities, rigor of secondary school record, volunteer work, work experience. *Important factors considered include:* Application essay, character/personal qualities, class rank, recommendation(s), standardized test scores. *Other factors considered include:* Alumni/ae relation, geographical residence, interview, level of applicant's interest, racial/ethnic status, talent/ability. **Freshman Admission Requirements:** High school diploma is required, and GED is accepted. *Academic units recommended:* 4 English, 4 math, 3 science (2 science labs), 3 foreign language, 2 social studies, 2 history, 2 academic electives. **Freshman Admission Statistics:** 5,121 applied, 41% admitted, 21% enrolled. **Transfer Admission Requirements:** High school transcript, college transcript(s), essay or personal statement, statement of good standing from prior institution(s). Minimum college GPA of 3.0 required. Lowest grade transferable D. **General Admission Information:** Application fee $50. Early decision application deadline 11/15. Regular application deadline 1/10. Regular notification 4/1. Non-fall registration not accepted. Admission may be deferred for a maximum of 1 year. Common Application accepted. Credit and/or placement offered for CEEB Advanced Placement tests.

COSTS AND FINANCIAL AID

Annual tuition $36,160. Room and board $10,270. Required fees $911. Average book expense $988. **Required Forms and Deadlines:** FAFSA, CSS/Financial Aid PROFILE, state aid form, Business/Farm Supplement, Noncustodial Profile. Financial aid filing deadline 2/1. **Notification of Awards:** Applicants will be notified of awards on or about 3/24. **Types of Aid:** *Need-based scholarships/grants:* Pell, SEOG, state scholarships/grants, private scholarships, the school's own gift aid. *Loans:* FFEL Subsidized Stafford, FFEL Unsubsidized Stafford, FFEL PLUS, Federal Perkins, college/university loans from institutional funds. **Student Employment:** Federal Work-Study Program available. Institutional employment available. Off-campus job opportunities are good. **Financial Aid Statistics:** 46% freshmen, 48% undergrads receive need-based scholarship or grant aid. 43% freshmen, 45% undergrads receive need-based self-help aid. 80% freshmen, 73% undergrads receive any aid.

OGLETHORPE UNIVERSITY

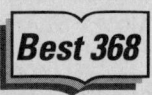

4484 Peachtree Road Northeast, Atlanta, GA 30319
Phone: 404-364-8307 **E-mail:** admission@oglethorpe.edu **CEEB Code:** 5521
Fax: 404-364-8491 **Website:** www.oglethorpe.edu **ACT Code:** 0850
Financial Aid Phone: 404-364-8356

This private school was founded in 1835. It has a 102-acre campus.

RATINGS

Admissions Selectivity Rating: 82   **Fire Safety Rating:** 60*   **Green Rating:** 73

STUDENTS AND FACULTY

Enrollment: 985. **Student Body:** 65% female, 35% male, 23% out-of-state, 5% international (35 countries represented). African American 23%, Asian 4%, Caucasian 55%, Hispanic 3%. **Retention and Graduation:** 87% freshmen return for sophomore year. 51% freshmen graduate within 4 years. 40% grads go on to further study within 1 year. 19% grads pursue arts and sciences degrees. 10% grads pursue business degrees. 9% grads pursue law degrees. 2% grads pursue medical degrees. **Faculty:** Student/faculty ratio 13:1. 57 full-time faculty, 95% hold PhDs. 99% faculty teach undergrads.

ACADEMICS

Degrees: Bachelor's, master's. **Academic Requirements:** Arts/fine arts, computer literacy, English (including composition), foreign languages, history, humanities, mathematics, philosophy, sciences (biological or physical), social science. **Classes:** Most classes have 10–19 students. **Majors with Highest Enrollment:** Business administration/management, English language and literature, psychology. **Disciplines with Highest Percentage of Degrees Awarded:** Business/marketing 24%, English 18%, history 16%, biological/life sciences 10%, psychology 7%. **Special Study Options:** Accelerated program, cooperative education program, cross-registration, double major, dual enrollment, honors program, independent study, internships, liberal arts/career combination, student-designed major, study abroad.

FACILITIES

Housing: Coed dorms, men's dorms, women's dorms, fraternity/sorority housing. **Special Academic Facilities/Equipment:** Art museum, scanning electron microscope. **Computers:** 10% of classrooms are wired, 100% of classrooms are wireless, 95% of public computers are PCs, 5% of public computers are Macs, network access in dorm rooms, network access in dorm lounges, online administrative functions (other than registration), remote student-access to Web through college's connection.

CAMPUS LIFE

Activities: Choral groups, dance, drama/theater, literary magazine, musical theater, radio station, student government, student newspaper, student-run film society, yearbook. **Organizations:** 57 registered organizations, 10 honor societies, 5 religious organizations. 4 fraternities (25% men join), 3 sororities (20% women join). **Athletics (Intercollegiate):** *Men:* Baseball, basketball, cross-country, golf, soccer, tennis, track/field (indoor), track/field (outdoor). *Women:* Basketball, cheerleading, cross-country, golf, soccer, tennis, track/field (indoor), track/field (outdoor), volleyball.

ADMISSIONS

Freshman Academic Profile: 35% in top 10% of high school class, 60% in top 25% of high school class, 84% in top 50% of high school class. 79% from public high schools. SAT Math middle 50% range 500–610. SAT Critical Reading middle 50% range 510–640. SAT Writing middle 50% range 500–610. ACT middle 50% range 21–27. TOEFL required of all international applicants, minimum paper TOEFL 550, minimum computer TOEFL 200. **Basis for Candidate Selection:** *Very important factors considered include:* Academic GPA, rigor of secondary school record, standardized test scores. *Important factors considered include:* Application essay, class rank, extracurricular activities, interview, level of applicant's interest, recommendation(s), volunteer work. *Other factors considered include:* Alumni/ae relation, character/personal qualities, first generation, talent/ability, work experience. **Freshman Admission Requirements:** High school diploma is required, and GED is accepted. *Academic units required:* 4 English, 3 math, 2 science, 3 social studies. *Academic units recommended:* 2 foreign language. **Freshman Admission Statistics:** 1,206 applied, 80% admitted, 20% enrolled. **Transfer Admission Requirements:** College transcript(s), essay or personal statement, statement of good standing from prior institution(s). Minimum college GPA of

2.8 required. Lowest grade transferable C. **General Admission Information:** Application fee $35. Regular notification is rolling. Non-fall registration accepted. Admission may be deferred for a maximum of 1 year. Credit and/or placement offered for CEEB Advanced Placement tests.

COSTS AND FINANCIAL AID

Annual tuition $25,380. Room and board $9,500. Required fees $100. Average book expense $800. **Required Forms and Deadlines:** FAFSA, institution's own financial aid form, state aid form. Financial aid filing deadline 2/1. **Notification of Awards:** Applicants will be notified of awards on a rolling basis beginning on or about 4/1. **Types of Aid:** *Need-based scholarships/grants:* Pell, SEOG, state scholarships/grants, private scholarships, the school's own gift aid, United Negro College Fund. *Loans:* Direct Subsidized Stafford, Direct Unsubsidized Stafford, Direct PLUS, FFEL Subsidized Stafford, FFEL Unsubsidized Stafford, FFEL PLUS, Federal Perkins. **Student Employment:** Federal Work-Study Program available. Institutional employment available. Off-campus job opportunities are excellent. **Financial Aid Statistics:** 72% freshmen, 60% undergrads receive need-based scholarship or grant aid. 62% freshmen, 51% undergrads receive need-based self-help aid. 95% freshmen, 95% undergrads receive any aid.

OHIO DOMINICAN UNIVERSITY

1216 Sunbury Road, Columbus, OH 42319-2099
Phone: 614-251-4500 **E-mail:** admissions@ohiodominican.edu **CEEB Code:** 1131
Fax: 614-251-0156 **Website:** www.ohiodominican.edu **ACT Code:** 3256
Financial Aid Phone: 614-251-4778

This private school, affiliated with the Roman Catholic Church, was founded in 1911. It has a 68-acre campus.

RATINGS
Admissions Selectivity Rating: 72   **Fire Safety Rating:** 69   **Green Rating:** 70

STUDENTS AND FACULTY
Enrollment: 2,243. **Student Body:** 62% female, 38% male, 3% out-of-state. African American 24%, Asian 1%, Caucasian 71%, Hispanic 2%. **Retention and Graduation:** 63% freshmen return for sophomore year. 26% freshmen graduate within 4 years. **Faculty:** Student/faculty ratio 14:1. 70 full-time faculty, 93% hold PhDs. 100% faculty teach undergrads.

ACADEMICS
Degrees: Associate, bachelor's, certificate, master's. **Academic Requirements:** Arts/fine arts, English (including composition), foreign languages, humanities, mathematics, philosophy, sciences (biological or physical), social science. **Classes:** Most classes have 10–19 students. **Majors with Highest Enrollment:** Business administration/management, psychology, secondary education and teaching. **Disciplines with Highest Percentage of Degrees Awarded:** Business/marketing 39%, education 25%, social sciences 7%, liberal arts/general studies 5%, biological/life sciences 3%, philosophy and religious studies 3%, psychology 3%, communications/journalism 3%, communication technologies 3%. **Special Study Options:** Cross-registration, distance learning, double major, dual enrollment, exchange student program (domestic), honors program, independent study, internships, study abroad, teacher certification program, weekend college.

FACILITIES
Housing: Coed dorms, apartments for single students. **Special Academic Facilities/Equipment:** Wehrle Art Gallery. **Computers:** 2% of classrooms are wired, 75% of public computers are PCs, 25% of public computers are Macs, network access in dorm rooms, network access in dorm lounges, online registration, online administrative functions (other than registration), remote student-access to Web through college's connection.

CAMPUS LIFE
Activities: Choral groups, drama/theater, literary magazine, pep band, radio station, student government, student newspaper. **Organizations:** 23 registered organizations, 4 honor societies, 1 religious organization. **Athletics (Intercollegiate):** *Men:* Baseball, basketball, cross-country, football, golf, soccer, tennis. *Women:* Basketball, cross-country, golf, soccer, softball, tennis, volleyball. **Environmental Initiatives:** New buildings are to be LEED silver certified. Recycling program is now in place. Freshmen Sustainability Council.

ADMISSIONS
Freshman Academic Profile: 13% in top 10% of high school class, 30% in top 25% of high school class, 63% in top 50% of high school class. 78% from public high schools. ACT middle 50% range 18–23. TOEFL required of all international applicants, minimum paper TOEFL 550, minimum computer TOEFL

213. **Basis for Candidate Selection:** *Very important factors considered include:* Academic GPA, rigor of secondary school record. *Important factors considered include:* Standardized test scores. *Other factors considered include:* Application essay, character/personal qualities, class rank, extracurricular activities, interview, recommendation(s), talent/ability, volunteer work, work experience. **Freshman Admission Requirements:** High school diploma is required, and GED is accepted. *Academic units recommended:* 4 English, 3 math, 3 science, 3 foreign language, 3 social studies. **Freshman Admission Statistics:** 2,045 applied, 73% admitted, 25% enrolled. **Transfer Admission Requirements:** College transcript(s), essay or personal statement. Lowest grade transferable C. **General Admission Information:** Application fee $25. Regular notification is rolling. Non-fall registration accepted. Admission may be deferred for a maximum of 1 year. Credit and/or placement offered for CEEB Advanced Placement tests.

COSTS AND FINANCIAL AID

Annual tuition $20,500. Room & board $6,800. Required fees $70. Average book expense $900. **Required Forms and Deadlines:** FAFSA. Financial aid filing deadline 4/1. **Notification of Awards:** Applicants will be notified of awards on or about 3/1. **Types of Aid:** *Need-based scholarships/grants:* Pell, SEOG, state scholarships/grants, private scholarships, the school's own gift aid. *Loans:* FFEL Subsidized Stafford, FFEL Unsubsidized Stafford, FFEL PLUS, Federal Perkins. **Financial Aid Statistics:** 98% freshmen, 88% undergrads receive any aid. Highest amount earned per year from on-campus jobs $3,600.

OHIO NORTHERN UNIVERSITY

525 South Main Street, Ada, OH 45810
Phone: 419-772-2260 **E-mail:** admissions-ug@onu.edu **CEEB Code:** 1591
Fax: 419-772-2313 **Website:** www.onu.edu **ACT Code:** 3310
Financial Aid Phone: 419-772-2272

This private school, affiliated with the Methodist Church, was founded in 1871. It has a 300-acre campus.

RATINGS
Admissions Selectivity Rating: 85   **Fire Safety Rating:** 60*   **Green Rating:** 60*

STUDENTS AND FACULTY
Enrollment: 2,543. **Student Body:** 47% female, 53% male, 14% out-of-state. African American 3%, Asian 1%, Caucasian 94%, Hispanic 1%. **Retention and Graduation:** 81% freshmen return for sophomore year. 52% freshmen graduate within 4 years. **Faculty:** Student/faculty ratio 13:1. 225 full-time faculty, 80% hold PhDs. 100% faculty teach undergrads.

ACADEMICS
Degrees: Bachelor's, first professional, master's, post-bachelor's certificate. **Academic Requirements:** Arts/fine arts, computer literacy, English (including composition), history, humanities, mathematics, philosophy, sciences (biological or physical), social science. **Classes:** Most classes have 10–19 students. **Majors with Highest Enrollment:** Business; management, marketing, and related support services; education; engineering. **Disciplines with Highest Percentage of Degrees Awarded:** Engineering 19%, business/marketing 17%, education 10%, biological/life sciences 10%, communications/journalism 5%. **Special Study Options:** Cooperative education program, distance learning, double major, dual enrollment, English as a second language (ESL), exchange student program (domestic), honors program, independent study, internships, liberal arts/career combination, study abroad, teacher certification program.

FACILITIES
Housing: Coed dorms, men's dorms, women's dorms, apartments for married students, apartments for single students, special housing for disabled students, fraternity/sorority housing, honors residence halls. **Special Academic Facilities/Equipment:** Art gallery, performing arts center, language lab, sports center, pharmacy museum. **Computers:** 1% of classrooms are wired, 90% of classrooms are wireless, 95% of public computers are PCs, 5% of public computers are Macs, network access in dorm rooms, online registration, online administrative functions (other than registration), remote student-access to Web through college's connection.

CAMPUS LIFE

Activities: Choral groups, concert band, dance, drama/theater, jazz band, literary magazine, marching band, music ensembles, musical theater, opera, pep band, radio station, student government, student newspaper, symphony orchestra, television station, yearbook. **Organizations:** 150 registered organizations, 39 honor societies, 32 religious organizations. 7 fraternities (13% men join), 4 sororities (16% women join). **Athletics (Intercollegiate):** *Men:* Baseball, basketball, cross-country, diving, football, golf, soccer, swimming, tennis, track/field (indoor), track/field (outdoor), wrestling. *Women:* Basketball, cross-country, diving, golf, soccer, softball, swimming, tennis, track/field (indoor), track/field (outdoor), volleyball.

ADMISSIONS

Freshman Academic Profile: 38% in top 10% of high school class, 66% in top 25% of high school class, 90% in top 50% of high school class. SAT Math middle 50% range 550–660. SAT Critical Reading middle 50% range 510–630. SAT Writing middle 50% range 510–630. ACT middle 50% range 23–29. TOEFL required of all international applicants, minimum paper TOEFL 550, minimum computer TOEFL 213. **Basis for Candidate Selection:** *Very important factors considered include:* Academic GPA, rigor of secondary school record, standardized test scores. *Important factors considered include:* Class rank, extracurricular activities, interview. *Other factors considered include:* Alumni/ae relation, application essay, character/personal qualities, first generation, level of applicant's interest, recommendation(s), talent/ability, volunteer work. **Freshman Admission Requirements:** High school diploma is required, and GED is accepted. *Academic units required:* 4 English, 2 math, 2 science (2 science labs), 2 social studies, 2 history, 4 academic electives. *Academic units recommended:* 4 English, 4 math, 3 science (2 science labs), 2 foreign language, 3 social studies, 2 history, 4 academic electives. **Freshman Admission Statistics:** 3,190 applied, 87% admitted, 27% enrolled. **Transfer Admission Requirements:** High school transcript, college transcript(s), statement of good standing from prior institution(s). Minimum college GPA of 2.0 required. Lowest grade transferable C. **General Admission Information:** Application fee $30. Regular application deadline 8/15. Regular notification is rolling. Non-fall registration accepted. Admission may be deferred for a maximum of 1 year. Credit and/or placement offered for CEEB Advanced Placement tests.

COSTS AND FINANCIAL AID

Annual tuition $30,555. Room and board $7,890. Required fees $210. Average book expense $1,500. **Required Forms and Deadlines:** FAFSA, institution's own financial aid form. Financial aid filing deadline 6/1. **Notification of Awards:** Applicants will be notified of awards on a rolling basis beginning on or about 2/15. **Types of Aid:** *Need-based scholarships/grants:* Pell, SEOG, state scholarships/grants, private scholarships, the school's own gift aid, external scholarships. *Loans:* FFEL Subsidized Stafford, FFEL Unsubsidized Stafford, FFEL PLUS, Federal Perkins, college/university loans from institutional funds, alternative loans, Federal Health Professions Loan. **Financial Aid Statistics:** 86% freshmen, 83% undergrads receive need-based scholarship or grant aid. 86% freshmen, 83% undergrads receive need-based self-help aid. 86% freshmen, 83% undergrads receive any aid.

See page 1302.

THE OHIO STATE UNIVERSITY—COLUMBUS

Best 368

Undergraduate Admissions 110 Enarson Hall, 154 W. 12th Avenue, Columbus, OH 43210
Phone: 614-292-3980 **E-mail:** askabuckeye@osu.edu **CEEB Code:** 1592
Fax: 614-292-4818 **Website:** www.osu.edu **ACT Code:** 3312
Financial Aid Phone: 614-688-5712

This public school was founded in 1870. It has a 6,191-acre campus.

RATINGS

Admissions Selectivity Rating: 86   Fire Safety Rating: 65   Green Rating: 60*

STUDENTS AND FACULTY

Enrollment: 37,239. **Student Body:** 47% female, 53% male, 10% out-of-state, 2% international. African American 7%, Asian 5%, Caucasian 80%, Hispanic 3%. **Retention and Graduation:** 92% freshmen return for sophomore year. 39% freshmen graduate within 4 years. **Faculty:** Student/faculty ratio 13:1. 3012 full-time faculty, 99% hold PhDs.

ACADEMICS

Degrees: Associate, bachelor's, doctoral, first professional, master's, post-bachelor's certificate, post-master's certificate. **Academic Requirements:** Arts/fine arts, data analysis, English (including composition), foreign languages, history, humanities, mathematics, sciences (biological or physical), social science. **Classes:** Most classes have 20–29 students. Most lab/discussion sections have 30–39 students. **Majors with Highest Enrollment:** Biology/biological sciences, political science and government, psychology. **Disciplines with Highest Percentage of Degrees Awarded:** Business/marketing 17%, social sciences 15%, engineering 8%, family and consumer sciences 8%, communications/journalism 6%. **Special Study Options:** Accelerated program, cooperative education program, cross-registration, distance learning, double major, dual enrollment, English as a second language (ESL), exchange student program (domestic), honors program, independent study, internships, liberal arts/career combination, student-designed major, study abroad, teacher certification program.

FACILITIES

Housing: Coed dorms, apartments for married students, apartments for single students, special housing for disabled students, fraternity/sorority housing, cooperative housing, living learning centers. **Special Academic Facilities/Equipment:** Wexner Center for the Arts, zoology museum, geology museum, art and photography galleries, nuclear research reactor, electroscience lab, biomedical engineering center, cartoon art museum. **Computers:** 10% of classrooms are wired, 100% of classrooms are wireless, 70% of public computers are PCs, 30% of public computers are Macs, network access in dorm rooms, network access in dorm lounges, online registration, online administrative functions (other than registration), support for handheld computing, remote student-access to Web through college's connection.

CAMPUS LIFE

Activities: Choral groups, concert band, dance, drama/theater, jazz band, literary magazine, marching band, music ensembles, musical theater, pep band, radio station, student government, student newspaper, student-run film society, symphony orchestra, television station. **Organizations:** 800 registered organizations, 39 honor societies, 60 religious organizations. 39 fraternities (6% men join), 21 sororities (6% women join). **Athletics (Intercollegiate):** *Men:* Baseball, basketball, cheerleading, cross-country, diving, fencing, football, golf, gymnastics, ice hockey, lacrosse, pistol, riflery, soccer, swimming, tennis, track/field (outdoor), volleyball, wrestling. *Women:* Basketball, cheerleading, crew/rowing, cross-country, diving, fencing, field hockey, golf, gymnastics, ice hockey, lacrosse, pistol, riflery, soccer, softball, swimming, synchronized swimming, tennis, track/field (outdoor), volleyball.

ADMISSIONS

Freshman Academic Profile: 43% in top 10% of high school class, 80% in top 25% of high school class, 98% in top 50% of high school class. 88% from public high schools. SAT Math middle 50% range 560–670. SAT Critical Reading middle 50% range 530–640. SAT Writing middle 50% range 520–630. ACT middle 50% range 24–29. TOEFL required of all international applicants, minimum paper TOEFL 527, minimum computer TOEFL 197. **Basis for Candidate Selection:** *Very important factors considered include:* Academic GPA, class rank, rigor of secondary school record, standardized test scores. *Important factors considered include:* Application essay, extracurricular activities, first generation, talent/ability, volunteer work, work experience. *Other factors considered include:* Character/personal qualities, geographical residence, racial/ethnic status, recommendation(s), state residency. **Freshman Admission Requirements:** High school diploma is required, and GED is accepted. *Academic units required:* 4 English, 3 math, 2 science (2 science labs), 2 foreign language, 2 social studies, 1 academic elective, 1 visual and performing art. *Academic units recommended:* 4 English, 4 math, 4 science (3 science labs), 3 foreign language, 3 social studies, 1 academic elective, 1 visual and performing art. **Freshman Admission Statistics:** 18,286 applied, 68% admitted, 51% enrolled. **Transfer Admission Requirements:** College transcript(s). Minimum college GPA of 2.0 required. Lowest grade transferable C-. **General Admission Information:** Application fee $40. Regular application deadline 2/1. Regular notification is rolling. Non-fall registration accepted. Credit and/or placement offered for CEEB Advanced Placement tests.

COSTS AND FINANCIAL AID

Annual in-state tuition $8,298. Out-of-state tuition $20,193. Room & board $6,720. Required fees $261. Average book expense $1,080. **Required Forms and Deadlines:** FAFSA. Financial aid filing deadline 3/1. **Notification of Awards:** Applicants will be notified of awards on or about 4/5. **Types of Aid:** *Need-based scholarships/grants:* Pell, SEOG, state scholarships/grants, private scholarships, the school's own gift aid. *Loans:* Direct Subsidized Stafford, Direct Unsubsidized Stafford, Direct PLUS, Federal Perkins, Federal Nursing, college/university loans from institutional funds. **Financial Aid Statistics:** 52% freshmen, 46% undergrads receive need-based scholarship or grant aid. 46% freshmen, 48% undergrads receive need-based self-help aid. 70 freshmen, 425 undergrads receive athletic scholarships. 54% freshmen, 49% undergrads receive any aid.

THE OHIO STATE UNIVERSITY AT LIMA

4240 Campus Drive, Lima, OH 45804-3596
Phone: 419-995-8434 **E-mail:** admissions@lima.ohio-state.edu **CEEB Code:** 1541
Fax: 419-995-8483 **Website:** www.lima.osu.edu **ACT Code:** 3312
Financial Aid Phone: 419-995-8147

This public school was founded in 1960. It has a 565-acre campus.

RATINGS

Admissions Selectivity Rating: 63   **Fire Safety Rating:** 60*   **Green Rating:** 60*

STUDENTS AND FACULTY

Enrollment: 1,028. **Student Body:** 54% female, 46% male. African American 3%, Caucasian 92%, Hispanic 2%. **Retention and Graduation:** 65% freshmen return for sophomore year. 14% freshmen graduate within 4 years. **Faculty:** Student/faculty ratio 21:1. 37 full-time faculty, 97% hold PhDs. 100% faculty teach undergrads.

ACADEMICS

Degrees: Associate, bachelor's, master's. **Academic Requirements:** Arts/fine arts, data analysis, English (including composition), foreign languages, history, humanities, mathematics, sciences (biological or physical), social science. **Classes:** Most classes have 10–19 students. Most lab/discussion sections have 10–19 students. **Majors with Highest Enrollment:** Business/commerce, elementary education and teaching, psychology. **Special Study Options:** Accelerated program, cooperative education program, cross-registration, distance learning, double major, dual enrollment, English as a second language (ESL), exchange student program (domestic), honors program, independent study, internships, liberal arts/career combination, student-designed major, study abroad, teacher certification program, weekend college.

FACILITIES

Housing: Apartments for married students, apartments for single students. **Special Academic Facilities/Equipment:** Seismological network, geological museum, observatory. **Computers:** 43% of public computers are PCs, 37% of public computers are Macs, 20% of public computers are UNIX, online registration, online administrative functions (other than registration), remote student-access to Web through college's connection.

CAMPUS LIFE

Activities: Choral groups, dance, drama/theater, literary magazine, musical theater, pep band, student government, student-run film society. **Organizations:** 22 registered organizations, 2 honor societies, 1 religious organization.

ADMISSIONS

Freshman Academic Profile: 10% in top 10% of high school class, 28% in top 25% of high school class, 64% in top 50% of high school class. 95% from public high schools. SAT Math middle 50% range 415–570. SAT Critical Reading middle 50% range 463–590. SAT Writing middle 50% range 425–565. ACT middle 50% range 19–24. TOEFL required of all international applicants, minimum paper TOEFL 527, minimum computer TOEFL 197. **Freshman Admission Requirements:** High school diploma is required, and GED is accepted. *Academic units required:* 4 English, 3 math, 2 science (2 science labs), 2 foreign language, 2 social studies, 1 academic elective, 1 visual and performing art. *Academic units recommended:* 4 English, 4 math, 4 science (3 science labs), 3 foreign language, 3 social studies, 1 academic elective, 1 visual and performing art. **Freshman Admission Statistics:** 878 applied, 99% admitted, 42% enrolled. **Transfer Admission Requirements:** College transcript(s). Minimum college GPA of 2.0 required. Lowest grade transferable C-. **General Admission Information:** Application fee $40. Regular notification is rolling.

COSTS AND FINANCIAL AID

Annual in-state tuition $6,240. Out-of-state tuition $18,153. Average book expense $1,080. **Required Forms and Deadlines:** FAFSA. Financial aid filing deadline 3/1. **Notification of Awards:** Applicants will be notified of awards on or about 4/5. **Types of Aid:** *Need-based scholarships/grants:* Pell, SEOG, state scholarships/grants, private scholarships, the school's own gift aid. *Loans:* Direct Subsidized Stafford, Direct Unsubsidized Stafford, Direct PLUS, Federal Perkins, Federal Nursing, college/university loans from institutional funds. **Financial Aid Statistics:** 41% freshmen, 44% undergrads receive need-based scholarship or grant aid. 59% freshmen, 61% undergrads receive need-based self-help aid. Highest amount earned per year from on-campus jobs $1,500.

THE OHIO STATE UNIVERSITY—MANSFIELD

1760 University Drive, Mansfield, OH 44906
Phone: 419-755-4317 **E-mail:** admissions@mansfield.ohio-state.edu **CEEB Code:** 0744
Fax: 419-755-4241 **Website:** www.mansfield.osu.edu **ACT Code:** 3312
Financial Aid Phone: 800-678-6440

This public school was founded in 1958. It has a 644-acre campus.

RATINGS

Admissions Selectivity Rating: 62   **Fire Safety Rating:** 68   **Green Rating:** 60*

STUDENTS AND FACULTY

Enrollment: 1,097. **Student Body:** 58% female, 42% male, 1% out-of-state. African American 8%, Asian 2%, Caucasian 87%, Hispanic 1%. **Retention and Graduation:** 63% freshmen return for sophomore year. 11% freshmen graduate within 4 years. **Faculty:** Student/faculty ratio 19:1. 47 full-time faculty, 98% hold PhDs.

ACADEMICS

Degrees: Associate, bachelor's, master's. **Academic Requirements:** Arts/fine arts, English (including composition), foreign languages, history, humanities, mathematics, sciences (biological or physical), social science, visual or performing arts. **Classes:** Most classes have 10–19 students. Most lab/discussion sections have fewer than 10 students. **Special Study Options:** Accelerated program, cooperative education program, cross-registration, distance learning, double major, dual enrollment, English as a second language (ESL), exchange student program (domestic), honors program, independent study, internships, liberal arts/career combination, student-designed major, study abroad, teacher certification program.

FACILITIES

Housing: Coed dorms. **Computers:** 100% of classrooms are wired, 20% of classrooms are wireless, 60% of public computers are PCs, 40% of public computers are Macs, online registration, online administrative functions (other than registration), remote student-access to Web through college's connection.

CAMPUS LIFE

Activities: Dance, drama/theater. **Organizations:** 16 registered organizations, 1 honor society, 1 religious organization.

ADMISSIONS

Freshman Academic Profile: 8% in top 10% of high school class, 24% in top 25% of high school class, 67% in top 50% of high school class. SAT Math middle 50% range 443–550. SAT Critical Reading middle 50% range 420–530. SAT Writing middle 50% range 448–520. ACT middle 50% range 19–23. TOEFL required of all international applicants, minimum paper TOEFL 527, minimum computer TOEFL 197. **Basis for Candidate Selection:** *Other factors considered include:* Recommendation(s), rigor of secondary school record. **Freshman Admission Requirements:** High school diploma is required, and GED is accepted. *Academic units required:* 4 English, 3 math, 2 science (2 science labs), 2 foreign language, 2 social studies, 1 academic elective, 1 visual and performing art. *Academic units recommended:* 4 English, 4 math, 4 science (3 science labs), 3 foreign language, 3 social studies, 1 academic elective, 1 visual and performing art. **Freshman Admission Statistics:** 1,006 applied, 99% admitted, 39% enrolled. **Transfer Admission Requirements:** College transcript(s). Minimum college GPA of 2.0 required. Lowest grade transferable C-. **General Admission Information:** Application fee $40. Regular application deadline 7/1. Regular notification is rolling. Non-fall registration accepted. Credit and/or placement offered for CEEB Advanced Placement tests.

COSTS AND FINANCIAL AID

Annual in-state tuition $6,240. Out-of-state tuition $18,153. Average book expense $1,080. **Required Forms and Deadlines:** FAFSA. Financial aid filing deadline 3/1. **Notification of Awards:** Applicants will be notified of awards on or about 4/5. **Types of Aid:** *Need-based scholarships/grants:* Pell, SEOG, state scholarships/grants, private scholarships, the school's own gift aid. *Loans:* Direct Subsidized Stafford, Direct Unsubsidized Stafford, Direct PLUS, Federal Perkins, Federal Nursing, college/university loans from institutional funds. **Financial Aid Statistics:** 46% freshmen, 51% undergrads receive need-based scholarship or grant aid. 58% freshmen, 62% undergrads receive need-based self-help aid.

THE OHIO STATE UNIVERSITY AT MARION

1465 Mount Vernon Avenue, Marion, OH 43302
Phone: 740-725-6337 **E-mail:** moreau.1@osu.edu **CEEB Code:** 0752
Website: www.marion.ohio-state.edu **ACT Code:** 3312
Financial Aid Phone: 740-389-6786

This public school was founded in 1957. It has a 180-acre campus.

RATINGS
Admissions Selectivity Rating: 62   **Fire Safety Rating:** 60*   **Green Rating:** 60*

STUDENTS AND FACULTY
Enrollment: 1,327. **Student Body:** 55% female, 45% male. African American 4%, Asian 3%, Caucasian 88%, Hispanic 1%. **Retention and Graduation:** 70% freshmen return for sophomore year. 13% freshmen graduate within 4 years. **Faculty:** Student/faculty ratio 22:1. 36 full-time faculty, 97% hold PhDs.

ACADEMICS
Degrees: Associate, bachelor's, master's. **Academic Requirements:** Arts/fine arts, data analysis, English (including composition), foreign languages, history, humanities, mathematics, sciences (biological or physical), social science. **Classes:** Most classes have 20–29 students. Most lab/discussion sections have 10–19 students. **Special Study Options:** Accelerated program, cooperative education program, cross-registration, distance learning, double major, dual enrollment, English as a second language (ESL), exchange student program (domestic), honors program, independent study, internships, liberal arts/career combination, student-designed major, study abroad, teacher certification program.

FACILITIES
Special Academic Facilities/Equipment: Kuhn Art Gallery. **Computers:** Online registration, online administrative functions (other than registration), remote student-access to Web through college's connection.

CAMPUS LIFE
Activities: Drama/theater, literary magazine, musical theater, student government. **Organizations:** 23 registered organizations, 1 honor society, 2 religious organizations. **Athletics (Intercollegiate):** *Men:* Basketball, cheerleading, golf. *Women:* Basketball, cheerleading, golf, volleyball.

ADMISSIONS
Freshman Academic Profile: 4% in top 10% of high school class, 24% in top 25% of high school class, 65% in top 50% of high school class. 98% from public high schools. SAT Math middle 50% range 450–540. SAT Critical Reading middle 50% range 410–540. SAT Writing middle 50% range 400–515. ACT middle 50% range 18–23. TOEFL required of all international applicants, minimum paper TOEFL 550, minimum computer TOEFL 197. **Basis for Candidate Selection:** *Other factors considered include:* Recommendation(s), rigor of secondary school record. **Freshman Admission Requirements:** High school diploma is required, and GED is accepted. *Academic units required:* 4 English, 3 math, 2 science (2 science labs), 2 foreign language, 2 social studies, 1 academic elective, 1 visual and performing art. *Academic units recommended:* 4 English, 4 math, 4 science (3 science labs), 3 foreign language, 3 social studies, 1 academic elective, 1 visual and performing art. **Freshman Admission Statistics:** 780 applied, 99% admitted, 55% enrolled. **Transfer Admission Requirements:** College transcript(s). Minimum college GPA of 2.0 required. Lowest grade transferable C-. **General Admission Information:** Application fee $40. Regular application deadline 7/1. Regular notification 12/1. Non-fall registration accepted. Credit and/or placement offered for CEEB Advanced Placement tests.

COSTS AND FINANCIAL AID
Annual in-state tuition $6,240. Out-of-state tuition $18,153. Average book expense $1,080. **Required Forms and Deadlines:** FAFSA. Financial aid filing deadline 3/1. **Notification of Awards:** Applicants will be notified of awards on or about 4/5. **Types of Aid:** *Need-based scholarships/grants:* Pell, SEOG, state scholarships/grants, private scholarships, the school's own gift aid. *Loans:* Direct Subsidized Stafford, Direct Unsubsidized Stafford, Direct PLUS, Federal Perkins, Federal Nursing, college/university loans from institutional funds. **Financial Aid Statistics:** 51% freshmen, 47% undergrads receive need-based scholarship or grant aid. 59% freshmen, 60% undergrads receive need-based self-help aid.

THE OHIO STATE UNIVERSITY AT NEWARK

1179 University Drive, Newark, OH 43055
Phone: 740-366-9333 **E-mail:** barclay.3@osu.edu
Fax: 740-364-9645 **Website:** www.newark.osu.edu/osun/index.asp
Financial Aid Phone: 740-366-9435

This public school was founded in 1957. It has a 106-acre campus.

RATINGS
Admissions Selectivity Rating: 62   **Fire Safety Rating:** 78   **Green Rating:** 60*

STUDENTS AND FACULTY
Enrollment: 2,105. **Student Body:** 53% female, 47% male, 1% out-of-state. African American 9%, Asian 2%, Caucasian 86%. **Retention and Graduation:** 64% freshmen return for sophomore year. 13% freshmen graduate within 4 years. **Faculty:** Student/faculty ratio 26:1. 50 full-time faculty, 98% hold PhDs.

ACADEMICS
Degrees: Associate, bachelor's, master's. **Academic Requirements:** Arts/fine arts, English (including composition), foreign languages, history, humanities, mathematics, sciences (biological or physical), social science. **Special Study Options:** Accelerated program, cooperative education program, cross-registration, distance learning, double major, dual enrollment, English as a second language (ESL), exchange student program (domestic), honors program, independent study, internships, liberal arts/career combination, student-designed major, study abroad, teacher certification program.

CAMPUS LIFE
Activities: Choral groups, drama/theater, music ensembles, student government, student-run film society. **Organizations:** 30 registered organizations, 4 honor societies, 2 religious organizations. **Athletics (Intercollegiate):** *Men:* Baseball, basketball, golf, soccer. *Women:* Basketball, golf, soccer, softball, volleyball.

ADMISSIONS
Freshman Academic Profile: 6% in top 10% of high school class, 21% in top 25% of high school class, 61% in top 50% of high school class. SAT Math middle 50% range 450–560. SAT Critical Reading middle 50% range 430–540. SAT Writing middle 50% range 420–520. ACT middle 50% range 18–23. **Basis for Candidate Selection:** *Other factors considered include:* Recommendation(s), rigor of secondary school record. **Freshman Admission Requirements:** High school diploma is required, and GED is accepted. *Academic units required:* 4 English, 3 math, 2 science (2 science labs), 2 foreign language, 2 social studies, 1 academic elective, 1 visual/performing arts. *Academic units recommended:* 4 English, 4 math, 4 science (3 science labs), 3 foreign language, 3 social studies, 1 academic elective, 1 visual/performing arts. **Freshman Admission Statistics:** 1,870 applied, 100% admitted, 50% enrolled. **Transfer Admission Requirements:** College transcript(s). Minimum college GPA of 2.0 required. Lowest grade transferable C-. **General Admission Information:** Application fee $40. Regular application deadline 2/1. Regular notification is rolling. Non-fall registration accepted.

COSTS AND FINANCIAL AID
Annual in-state tuition $6,240. Out-of-state tuition $18,153. Room $4,989. **Types of Aid:** *Loans:* FFEL Subsidized Stafford, FFEL PLUS. Highest amount earned per year from on-campus jobs $1,500.

OHIO UNIVERSITY—ATHENS

120 Chubb Hall, Athens, OH 45701
Phone: 740-593-4100 **E-mail:** admissions@ohio.edu **CEEB Code:** 1593
Fax: 740-593-0560 **Website:** www.ohio.edu **ACT Code:** 3314
Financial Aid Phone: 740-593-4141

This public school was founded in 1804. It has a 1,700-acre campus.

RATINGS
Admissions Selectivity Rating: 75   **Fire Safety Rating:** 67   **Green Rating:** 81

STUDENTS AND FACULTY
Enrollment: 16,872. **Student Body:** 52% female, 48% male, 13% out-of-state, 1% international (111 countries represented). African American 4%, Caucasian 92%, Hispanic 2%. **Retention and Graduation:** 80% freshmen return for sophomore year. 47% freshmen graduate within 4 years. 26% grads go on to further study within 1 year. 8% grads pursue arts and sciences degrees. 1% grads pursue business degrees. 3% grads pursue law degrees. 2% grads pursue medical degrees. **Faculty:** Student/faculty ratio 19:1. 873 full-time faculty, 89% hold PhDs. 100% faculty teach undergrads.

ACADEMICS
Degrees: Associate, bachelor's, doctoral, first professional, master's. **Academic Requirements:** Arts/fine arts, English (including composition), foreign languages, history, humanities, mathematics, philosophy, sciences (biological or physical), social science. **Classes:** Most classes have 10–19 students. Most lab/discussion sections have 10–19 students. **Majors with Highest Enrollment:** Clinical psychology, journalism, kinesiology and exercise science. **Disciplines with Highest Percentage of Degrees Awarded:** Communications/journalism 16%, business/marketing 12%, education 11%, social sciences 9%, family and consumer sciences 7%, liberal arts/general studies 7%. **Special Study Options:** Accelerated program, cooperative education program, cross-registration, distance learning, double major, dual enrollment, English as a second language (ESL), external degree program, honors program, independent study, internships, liberal arts/career combination, student-designed major, study abroad, teacher certification program.

FACILITIES
Housing: Coed dorms, men's dorms, women's dorms, apartments for married students, apartments for single students, special housing for disabled students, special housing for international students, fraternity/sorority housing, cooperative housing. **Special Academic Facilities/Equipment:** Museum of American Art, innovation center, nuclear accelerator, electron microscope, biotech center. **Computers:** 5% of classrooms are wired, 100% of classrooms are wireless, 85% of public computers are PCs, 10% of public computers are Macs, 5% of public computers are UNIX, network access in dorm rooms, network access in dorm lounges, online registration, online administrative functions (other than registration), support for handheld computing, remote student-access to Web through college's connection.

CAMPUS LIFE
Activities: Choral groups, concert band, dance, drama/theater, jazz band, literary magazine, marching band, music ensembles, musical theater, opera, pep band, radio station, student government, student newspaper, student-run film society, symphony orchestra, television station. **Organizations:** 360 registered organizations, 32 honor societies, 18 religious organizations. 19 fraternities (11% men join), 13 sororities (13% women join). **Athletics (Intercollegiate):** *Men:* Baseball, basketball, cross-country, diving, football, golf, swimming, track/field (outdoor), wrestling. *Women:* Basketball, cross-country, diving, field hockey, golf, lacrosse, soccer, softball, swimming, track/field (outdoor), volleyball. **Environmental Initiatives:** Creating Office of Sustainability. Signing Presidents Climate Commitment. Incorporating sustainability objectives into 5-year vision OHIO plan.

ADMISSIONS
Freshman Academic Profile: 15% in top 10% of high school class, 42% in top 25% of high school class, 81% in top 50% of high school class. 92% from public high schools. SAT Math middle 50% range 490–600. SAT Critical Reading middle 50% range 480–600. SAT Writing middle 50% range 480–580. ACT middle 50% range 21–26. **Basis for Candidate Selection:** *Very important factors considered include:* Academic GPA, rigor of secondary school record. *Important factors considered include:* Class rank, standardized test scores.

Other factors considered include: Alumni/ae relation, application essay, character/personal qualities, extracurricular activities, racial/ethnic status, recommendation(s), talent/ability, volunteer work, work experience. **Freshman Admission Requirements:** High school diploma is required, and GED is accepted. *Academic units required:* 4 English, 3 math, 3 science, 2 foreign language, 3 social studies, 1 visual or performing arts. **Freshman Admission Statistics:** 12,684 applied, 85% admitted, 38% enrolled. **Transfer Admission Requirements:** College transcript(s). Minimum college GPA of 2.5 required. Lowest grade transferable C-. **General Admission Information:** Application fee $45. Regular application deadline 2/1. Regular notification is rolling. Non-fall registration accepted. Admission may be deferred for a maximum of 1 year. Credit and/or placement offered for CEEB Advanced Placement tests.

COSTS AND FINANCIAL AID
Annual in-state tuition $8,907. Annual out-of-state tuition $17,871. Room and board $8,427. Average book expense $870. **Required Forms and Deadlines:** FAFSA. Financial aid filing deadline 3/15. **Notification of Awards:** Applicants will be notified of awards on or about 4/1. **Types of Aid:** *Need-based scholarships/grants:* Pell, SEOG, state scholarships/grants, private scholarships, the school's own gift aid. *Loans:* Direct Subsidized Stafford, Direct Unsubsidized Stafford, Direct PLUS, Federal Perkins, institutional short term loans are repaid in 30–60 days. **Financial Aid Statistics:** 20% freshmen, 21% undergrads receive need-based scholarship or grant aid. 36% freshmen, 38% undergrads receive need-based self-help aid. 79 freshmen, 315 undergrads receive athletic scholarships. 50% freshmen, 47% undergrads receive any aid. Highest amount earned per year from on-campus jobs $1,515.

OHIO UNIVERSITY—SOUTHERN

Office of Enrollment Services, 1804 Liberty Avenue, Ironton, OH 45638-2214
Phone: 740-533-4600 **E-mail:** askousc@mail.southern.ohiou.edu
Fax: 740-533-4632 **Website:** www.southern.ohiou.edu

This public school was founded in 1956. It has a 9-acre campus.

RATINGS
Admissions Selectivity Rating: 60*   **Fire Safety Rating:** 60*   **Green Rating:** 60*

STUDENTS AND FACULTY
Enrollment: 2,510. **Student Body:** 11% out-of-state. African American 2%, Caucasian 97%.

ACADEMICS
Degrees: Associate, bachelor's, master's, terminal. **Academic Requirements:** English (including composition), mathematics. **Special Study Options:** Distance learning, double major, independent study, student-designed major, teacher certification program, weekend college.

FACILITIES
Computers: Online registration, online administrative functions (other than registration).

CAMPUS LIFE
Activities: Choral groups, concert band, drama/theater, literary magazine, music ensembles, radio station, student government, television station.

ADMISSIONS
Transfer Admission Requirements: College transcript(s). Lowest grade transferable C. **General Admission Information:** Application fee $20.

COSTS AND FINANCIAL AID
Annual in-state tuition $3,087. Annual out-of-state tuition $3,219. Average book expense $700. **Required Forms and Deadlines:** FAFSA. Financial aid filing deadline 2/15. **Types of Aid:** *Need-based scholarships/grants:* Pell, SEOG, state scholarships/grants, private scholarships, the school's own gift aid. *Loans:* Direct Subsidized Stafford, Direct Unsubsidized Stafford, Direct PLUS, Federal Perkins.

OHIO UNIVERSITY—ZANESVILLE

Office of Admissions, 1425 Newark Road, Zanesville, OH 43701
Phone: 740-588-1439 **E-mail:** tumblin@ohiou.edu **CEEB Code:** 1593
Fax: 740-588-1444 **Website:** www.zanesville.ohiou.edu
Financial Aid Phone: 740-588-1439

This public school was founded in 1946. It has a 146-acre campus.

RATINGS
Admissions Selectivity Rating: 61 **Fire Safety Rating:** 60* **Green Rating:** 60*

STUDENTS AND FACULTY
Enrollment: 1,824. **Student Body:** 5% out-of-state. African American 2%, Caucasian 97%. **Retention and Graduation:** 55% freshmen return for sophomore year. **Faculty:** Student/faculty ratio 20:1. 100% faculty teach undergrads.

ACADEMICS
Degrees: Associate, bachelor's, master's, terminal. **Academic Requirements:** Arts/fine arts, computer literacy, English (including composition), history, humanities, mathematics, sciences (biological or physical), social science. **Majors with Highest Enrollment:** Junior high/intermediate/middle school education and teaching, nursing/registered nurse training (ASN, BSN, MSN, RN). **Special Study Options:** Cooperative education program, cross-registration, distance learning, double major, dual enrollment, external degree program, independent study, internships, liberal arts/career combination, student-designed major, study abroad, teacher certification program, weekend college.

FACILITIES
Housing: Apartments for married students, apartments for single students. **Computers:** Online registration, remote student-access to Web through college's connection.

CAMPUS LIFE
Activities: Music ensembles, radio station, student government. **Organizations:** 10 registered organizations, 3 honor societies. **Athletics (Intercollegiate):** *Men:* Baseball, basketball, golf. *Women:* Basketball, cheerleading, softball, volleyball.

ADMISSIONS
Freshman Academic Profile: 20% in top 10% of high school class, 20% in top 25% of high school class, 50% in top 50% of high school class. **Freshman Admission Requirements:** High school diploma is required, and GED is accepted. *Academic units recommended:* 4 English, 3 math, 3 science (2 science labs), 2 foreign language, 3 social studies, 1 history, 4 academic electives. **Freshman Admission Statistics:** 503 applied, 100% admitted, 96% enrolled. **Transfer Admission Requirements:** College transcript(s), statement of good standing from prior institution(s). Minimum college GPA of 2.0 required. Lowest grade transferable C-. **General Admission Information:** Application fee $20. Regular notification within a week of applying. Non-fall registration accepted. Admission may be deferred for a maximum of 1 year. Common Application not accepted.

COSTS AND FINANCIAL AID
Annual in-state tuition $3,579. Out-of-state tuition $9,150. Required fees $15. Average book expense $400. **Student Employment:** Federal Work-Study Program available. Institutional employment available. Off-campus job opportunities are good. **Financial Aid Statistics:** 85% freshmen receive any aid.

OHIO VALLEY UNIVERSITY

1 Campus View Drive, Vienna, WV 26105
Phone: 304-865-6200 **E-mail:** admissions@ovu.edu
Fax: 304-865-6001 **Website:** www.ovc.edu **ACT Code:** 4548
Financial Aid Phone: 304-865-6075

This private school, affiliated with the Church of Christ, was founded in 1960. It has a 267-acre campus.

RATINGS
Admissions Selectivity Rating: 76 **Fire Safety Rating:** 60* **Green Rating:** 60*

STUDENTS AND FACULTY
Enrollment: 512. **Student Body:** 53% female, 47% male, 6% out-of-state, 7% international (12 countries represented). African American 4%, Caucasian 86%, Hispanic 1%. **Retention and Graduation:** 72% freshmen return for sophomore year. **Faculty:** Student/faculty ratio 14:1. 26 full-time faculty, 38% hold PhDs. 100% faculty teach undergrads.

ACADEMICS
Degrees: Associate, bachelor's. **Academic Requirements:** Arts/fine arts, Bible, computer literacy, English (including composition), history, humanities, mathematics, sciences (biological or physical), social science. **Classes:** Most classes have fewer than 10 students. Most lab/discussion sections have fewer than 10 students. **Majors with Highest Enrollment:** Business administration/management, elementary education and teaching, psychology. **Disciplines with Highest Percentage of Degrees Awarded:** Liberal arts/general studies 33%, business/marketing 20%, education 11%, psychology 7%, philosophy and religious studies 6%. **Special Study Options:** Double major, English as a second language (ESL), study abroad, teacher certification program, weekend college. Adult education: Degree completion program in business administration and Saturday college available.

FACILITIES
Housing: Men's dorms, women's dorms, apartments for married students, apartments for single students. **Computers:** 100% of public computers are PCs, network access in dorm rooms, remote student-access to Web through college's connection.

CAMPUS LIFE
Activities: Choral groups, concert band, drama/theater, jazz band, literary magazine, music ensembles, musical theater, student government, student newspaper, symphony orchestra, yearbook. **Organizations:** 10 registered organizations, 2 honor societies, 3 religious organizations. 4 fraternities (80% men join), 4 sororities (80% women join). **Athletics (Intercollegiate):** *Men:* Baseball, basketball, cross-country, golf, soccer. *Women:* Basketball, cheerleading, cross-country, soccer, softball, volleyball.

ADMISSIONS
Freshman Academic Profile: 10% in top 10% of high school class, 32% in top 25% of high school class, 57% in top 50% of high school class. 95% from public high schools. SAT Math middle 50% range 540–460. SAT Critical Reading middle 50% range 600–510. ACT middle 50% range 23–17. TOEFL required of all international applicants, minimum paper TOEFL 500, minimum computer TOEFL 173. **Basis for Candidate Selection:** *Very important factors considered include:* Character/personal qualities, rigor of secondary school record, standardized test scores. *Important factors considered include:* Alumni/ae relation, recommendation(s), talent/ability. *Other factors considered include:* Application essay, class rank, extracurricular activities, interview, religious affiliation/commitment. **Freshman Admission Requirements:** High school diploma is required, and GED is accepted. *Academic units recommended:* 3 English, 2 math, 3 science (1 science lab), 2 social studies, 1 history. **Freshman Admission Statistics:** 326 applied, 59% admitted, 50% enrolled. **Transfer Admission Requirements:** High school transcript, college transcript(s), standardized test score. Minimum college GPA of 2.0 required. Lowest grade transferable D. **General Admission Information:** Application fee $20. Regular application deadline 8/20. Regular notification is continuous. Non-fall registration accepted. Admission may be deferred for a maximum of 1 year. Credit and/or placement offered for CEEB Advanced Placement tests.

COSTS AND FINANCIAL AID
Annual tuition $12,750. Room & board $5,850. Required fees $1,512. Average book expense $1,000. **Required Forms and Deadlines:** FAFSA. Financial aid filing deadline 2/15. **Notification of Awards:** Applicants will be notified of awards on a rolling basis beginning on or about 3/15. **Types of Aid:** *Need-based scholarships/grants:* Pell, SEOG, state scholarships/grants, private scholarships, the school's own gift aid. *Loans:* FFEL Subsidized Stafford, FFEL Unsubsidized Stafford, FFEL PLUS, Federal Perkins, Signature student loans. **Student Employment:** Federal Work-Study Program available. Institutional employment available. Off-campus job opportunities are good. **Financial Aid Statistics:** 72% freshmen, 63% undergrads receive need-based scholarship or grant aid. 64% freshmen, 63% undergrads receive need-based self-help aid. 16 freshmen, 56 undergrads receive athletic scholarships. 81% freshmen, 89% undergrads receive any aid. Highest amount earned per year from on-campus jobs $800.

OHIO WESLEYAN UNIVERSITY

Best 368

61 South Sandusky Street, Delaware, OH 43015
Phone: 740-368-3020 **E-mail:** owuadmit@owu.edu **CEEB Code:** 1594
Fax: 740-368-3314 **Website:** www.owu.edu **ACT Code:** 3316
Financial Aid Phone: 740-368-3050

This private school, affiliated with the Methodist Church, was founded in 1842. It has a 200-acre campus.

RATINGS
Admissions Selectivity Rating: 86   **Fire Safety Rating:** 60*   **Green Rating:** 60*

STUDENTS AND FACULTY
Enrollment: 1,923. **Student Body:** 52% female, 48% male, 42% out-of-state, 8% international (37 countries represented). African American 5%, Asian 2%, Caucasian 82%, Hispanic 1%. **Retention and Graduation:** 79% freshmen return for sophomore year. 60% freshmen graduate within 4 years. 32% grads go on to further study within 1 year. 14% grads pursue arts and sciences degrees. 2% grads pursue business degrees. 3% grads pursue law degrees. 14% grads pursue medical degrees. **Faculty:** Student/faculty ratio 13:1. 134 full-time faculty, 97% hold PhDs. 100% faculty teach undergrads.

ACADEMICS
Degrees: Bachelor's. **Academic Requirements:** Arts/fine arts, diversity course, English (including composition), foreign languages, humanities, sciences (biological or physical), social science, writing-intensive course. **Classes:** Most classes have 10—19 students. Most lab/discussion sections have 10—19 students. **Majors with Highest Enrollment:** Business/managerial economics; psychology; zoology/animal biology. **Disciplines with Highest Percentage of Degrees Awarded:** Business/marketing 12%, psychology 11%, English 9%, biological/life sciences 9%, visual and performing arts 6%. **Special Study Options:** Double major, dual enrollment, exchange student program (domestic), honor program, independent study, internships, student-designed major, study abroad, teacher certification program.

FACILITIES
Housing: Coed dorms, women's dorms, apartments for single students, special housing for international students, fraternity/sorority housing. Small Living Units (SLUs) are theme houses which offer unique living opportunities to groups of 10–15 OWU students. **Special Academic Facilities/Equipment:** Perkins and Student Observatories, scanning electron microscope, Woltemade Center for Economics, Business, and Entrepreneurship, 9-inch refractor telescope, Ross Art Museum, newly renovated fine arts facilities, newly renovated 150,000-square-foot scien. **Computers:** 10% of classrooms are wireless, 100% of public computers are PCs, network access in dorm rooms, network access in dorm lounges, online administrative functions (other than registration), support for handheld computing, remote student-access to Web through college's connection.

CAMPUS LIFE
Activities: Choral groups, dance, drama/theater, jazz band, literary magazine, music ensembles, musical theater, opera, pep band, radio station, student government, student newspaper, symphony orchestra, yearbook. **Organizations:** 86 registered organizations, 26 honor societies, 10 religious organizations. 11 fraternities (36% men join), 6 sororities (24% women join). **Athletics (Intercollegiate):** *Men:* Baseball, basketball, cross-country, diving, football, golf, lacrosse, sailing, soccer, swimming, tennis, track/field (indoor), track/field (outdoor). *Women:* Basketball, cross-country, diving, field hockey, lacrosse, sailing, soccer, softball, swimming, tennis, track/field (indoor), track/field (outdoor), volleyball.

ADMISSIONS
Freshman Academic Profile: 36% in top 10% of high school class, 59% in top 25% of high school class, 84% in top 50% of high school class. 72% from public high schools. SAT Math middle 50% range 540–650. SAT Critical Reading middle 50% range 530–650. ACT middle 50% range 24–29. TOEFL required of all international applicants, minimum paper TOEFL 550, minimum computer TOEFL 213. **Basis for Candidate Selection:** *Very important factors considered include:* Academic GPA, application essay, character/personal qualities, interview, recommendation(s), rigor of secondary school record. *Important factors considered include:* Class rank, extracurricular activities, standardized test scores, talent/ability. *Other factors considered include:*

Alumni/ae relation, first generation, geographical residence, level of applicant's interest, racial/ethnic status, volunteer work, work experience. **Freshman Admission Requirements:** High school diploma is required, and GED is accepted. *Academic units required:* 4 English, 3 math, 3 science, 2 foreign language, 3 social studies. *Academic units recommended:* 4 math, 4 science, 3 foreign language, 4 social studies. **Freshman Admission Statistics:** 3,579 applied, 63% admitted, 25% enrolled. **Transfer Admission Requirements:** High school transcript, college transcript(s), essay or personal statement, statement of good standing from prior institution(s). Minimum college GPA of 2.5 required. Lowest grade transferable C-. **General Admission Information:** Application fee $35. Early Decision application deadline 12/1. Regular notification is rolling. Nonfall registration accepted. Admission may be deferred for a maximum of 2 years. Credit and/or placement offered for CEEB Advanced Placement tests.

COSTS AND FINANCIAL AID
Annual tuition $31,510. Room and board $8,030. Required fees $420. Average book expense $2,050. **Required Forms and Deadlines:** FAFSA, institution's own financial aid form. Financial aid filing deadline 5/1. Financial aid filing deadline 3/1. **Notification of Awards:** Applicants will be notified of awards on a rolling basis beginning on or about 2/15. **Types of Aid:** *Need-based scholarships/grants:* Pell, SEOG, state scholarships/grants, private scholarships, the school's own gift aid. *Loans:* FFEL Subsidized Stafford, FFEL Unsubsidized Stafford, FFEL PLUS, Federal Perkins, college/university loans from institutional funds. **Student Employment:** Federal Work-Study Program available. Institutional employment available. Off-campus job opportunities are excellent. **Financial Aid Statistics:** 56% freshmen, 54% undergrads receive need-based scholarship or grant aid. 45% freshmen, 45% undergrads receive need-based self-help aid. 99% freshmen, 98% undergrads receive any aid. Highest amount earned per year from on-campus jobs $2,400.

OKANAGAN UNIVERSITY COLLEGE

1000 KLO Road, Kelowna, BC V1Y 4X8 Canada
Phone: 250-862-5417 **E-mail:** N/A@ouc.bc.ca
Fax: 250-862-5466 **Website:** www.ouc.bc.ca/
Financial Aid Phone: 250-862-5419

This public school was founded in 1963.

RATINGS
Admissions Selectivity Rating: 60*   **Fire Safety Rating:** 60*   **Green Rating:** 60*

STUDENTS AND FACULTY
Enrollment: 3,757. **Student Body:** 68% female, 32% male. **Faculty:** Student/faculty ratio 14:1. 247 full-time faculty, 81% hold PhDs.

ACADEMICS
Degrees: Associate, bachelor's, certificate, diploma. **Academic Requirements:** English (including composition), mathematics. **Classes:** Most classes have 20–29 students. Most lab/discussion sections have 10–19 students. **Majors with Highest Enrollment:** Business administration/management, sociology. **Disciplines with Highest Percentage of Degrees Awarded:** Liberal arts/general studies 32%, health professions and related sciences 21%, business/marketing 16%, education 14%, visual and performing arts 4%. **Special Study Options:** Cooperative education program, distance learning, double major, English as a second language (ESL), exchange student program (domestic), honors program, independent study, study abroad, teacher certification program.

FACILITIES
Housing: Coed dorms, special housing for disabled students. **Computers:** Network access in dorm rooms, network access in dorm lounges, online registration, online administrative functions (other than registration), remote student-access to Web through college's connection.

CAMPUS LIFE
Activities: Choral groups, student government, student newspaper. **Athletics (Intercollegiate):** *Men:* Basketball, soccer, volleyball. *Women:* Basketball, soccer, volleyball.

ADMISSIONS
Freshman Academic Profile: TOEFL required of all international applicants, minimum paper TOEFL 550, minimum computer TOEFL 213. **Basis for Candidate Selection:** *Important factors considered include:* Application essay, class rank, recommendation(s), rigor of secondary school record, standardized test scores. *Other factors considered include:* Character/personal qualities, extracurricular activities, interview, talent/ability, volunteer work, work

experience. **Transfer Admission Requirements:** High school transcript, college transcript(s). **General Admission Information:** Application fee $13. Regular application deadline 2/28. Regular notification within 6 weeks of receiving the application. Non-fall registration accepted. Credit and/or placement offered for CEEB Advanced Placement tests.

COSTS AND FINANCIAL AID

Room & board $3,590. Required fees $94. Average book expense $504. **Student Employment:** Federal Work-Study Program available. Institutional employment available. Off-campus job opportunities are good.

OKLAHOMA BAPTIST UNIVERSITY

500 West University, Shawnee, OK 74804
Phone: 800-654-3285 **E-mail:** admissions@okbu.edu **CEEB Code:** 6541
Fax: 405-878-2046 **Website:** www.okbu.edu **ACT Code:** 3414
Financial Aid Phone: 405-878-2016

This private school, affiliated with the Southern Baptist Church, was founded in 1910. It has a 200-acre campus.

RATINGS

Admissions Selectivity Rating: 89   **Fire Safety Rating:** 72   **Green Rating:** 60*

STUDENTS AND FACULTY

Enrollment: 1,438. **Student Body:** 60% female, 40% male, 42% out-of-state, 4% international (25 countries represented). African American 3%, Asian 1%, Caucasian 83%, Hispanic 2%, Native American 6%. **Retention and Graduation:** 71% freshmen return for sophomore year. 48% freshmen graduate within 4 years. 37% grads go on to further study within 1 year. 34% grads pursue arts and sciences degrees. 1% grads pursue business degrees. 1% grads pursue law degrees. 2% grads pursue medical degrees. **Faculty:** Student/faculty ratio 14:1. 112 full-time faculty, 68% hold PhDs. 100% faculty teach undergrads.

ACADEMICS

Degrees: Associate, bachelor's, master's. **Academic Requirements:** Arts/fine arts, computer literacy, English (including composition), foreign languages, health activity, health concepts, history, humanities, mathematics, philosophy, religion, sciences (biological or physical), social science, speech. **Classes:** Most classes have fewer than 10 students. Most lab/discussion sections have fewer than 10 students. **Majors with Highest Enrollment:** Bible/biblical studies, elementary education and teaching, nursing/registered nurse training (ASN, BSN, MSN, RN). **Disciplines with Highest Percentage of Degrees Awarded:** Education 19%, philosophy and religious studies 17%, health professions and related sciences 12%, business/marketing 11%, visual and performing arts 10%. **Special Study Options:** Cooperative education program, double major, English as a second language (ESL), exchange student program (domestic), honors program, independent study, internships, semester-away programs, student-designed major, study abroad, teacher certification program.

FACILITIES

Housing: Men's dorms, women's dorms, apartments for married students, apartments for single students. **Special Academic Facilities/Equipment:** Planetarium, Baptist Historical Society Archives, Avery T. Willis Center for Global Outreach. **Computers:** 45% of classrooms are wireless, 95% of public computers are PCs, 5% of public computers are Macs, network access in dorm rooms, online registration, online administrative functions (other than registration), remote student-access to Web through college's connection.

CAMPUS LIFE

Activities: Choral groups, concert band, drama/theater, jazz band, literary magazine, music ensembles, musical theater, opera, pep band, student government, student newspaper, symphony orchestra, television station, yearbook. **Organizations:** 80 registered organizations, 15 honor societies, 5 religious organizations. 5 fraternities (12% men join), 5 sororities (5% women join). **Athletics (Intercollegiate):** *Men:* Baseball, basketball, cheerleading, cross-country, golf, soccer, tennis, track/field (indoor), track/field (outdoor). *Women:* Basketball, cheerleading, cross-country, golf, soccer, softball, tennis, track/field (indoor), track/field (outdoor).

ADMISSIONS

Freshman Academic Profile: 46% in top 10% of high school class, 73% in top 25% of high school class, 90% in top 50% of high school class. 90% from public high schools. SAT Math middle 50% range 500–630. SAT Critical Reading middle 50% range 510–650. ACT middle 50% range 21–28. TOEFL required of all international applicants, minimum paper TOEFL 500, minimum

computer TOEFL 173. **Basis for Candidate Selection:** *Very important factors considered include:* Academic GPA, rigor of secondary school record. *Important factors considered include:* Character/personal qualities, class rank, extracurricular activities, recommendation(s), standardized test scores. *Other factors considered include:* Alumni/ae relation, application essay, geographical residence, interview, level of applicant's interest, religious affiliation/commitment, state residency, talent/ability, volunteer work, work experience. **Freshman Admission Requirements:** High school diploma is required, and GED is accepted. *Academic units recommended:* 4 English, 3 math, 3 science (2 science labs), 2 foreign language, 1 social studies, 2 history, 2 academic electives, 1 fine arts. **Freshman Admission Statistics:** 1,144 applied, 73% admitted, 43% enrolled. **Transfer Admission Requirements:** College transcript(s). Minimum college GPA of 2.5 required. Lowest grade transferable D. **General Admission Information:** Application fee $25. Regular application deadline 8/1. Regular notification 9/1. Non-fall registration accepted. Admission may be deferred for a maximum of 1 year. Credit and/or placement offered for CEEB Advanced Placement tests.

COSTS AND FINANCIAL AID

Annual tuition $14,732. Room and board $5,000. Required fees $1,262. Average book expense $1,000. **Required Forms and Deadlines:** FAFSA, institution's own financial aid form. Financial aid filing deadline 3/1. **Notification of Awards:** Applicants will be notified of awards on or about 3/15. **Types of Aid:** *Need-based scholarships/grants:* Pell, SEOG, state scholarships/grants, private scholarships, the school's own gift aid, Federal Nursing Scholarships. *Loans:* FFEL Subsidized Stafford, FFEL Unsubsidized Stafford, FFEL PLUS, Federal Perkins, college/university loans from institutional funds. **Financial Aid Statistics:** 63% freshmen, 54% undergrads receive need-based scholarship or grant aid. 49% freshmen, 39% undergrads receive need-based self-help aid. 86 freshmen, 276 undergrads receive athletic scholarships. 87% freshmen, 90% undergrads receive any aid. Highest amount earned per year from on-campus jobs $3,200.

OKLAHOMA CHRISTIAN UNIVERSITY

PO Box 11000, Oklahoma City, OK 73136-1100
Phone: 405-425-5050 **E-mail:** Info@oc.edu
Fax: 405-425-5269 **Website:** www.oc.edu **ACT Code:** 3415
Financial Aid Phone: 405-425-5190

This private school, affiliated with the Church of Christ, was founded in 1950. It has a 200-acre campus.

RATINGS

Admissions Selectivity Rating: 75   **Fire Safety Rating:** 70   **Green Rating:** 60*

STUDENTS AND FACULTY

Enrollment: 1,874. **Student Body:** 59% out-of-state. African American 5%, Asian 2%, Caucasian 83%, Hispanic 3%, Native American 4%. **Retention and Graduation:** 71% freshmen return for sophomore year. 35% freshmen graduate within 4 years. **Faculty:** Student/faculty ratio 11:1. 90 full-time faculty, 69% hold PhDs. 100% faculty teach undergrads.

ACADEMICS

Degrees: Bachelor's, master's. **Academic Requirements:** Arts/fine arts, Bible, English (including composition), history, humanities, mathematics, philosophy, sciences (biological or physical), social science. **Classes:** Most classes have 20–29 students. Most lab/discussion sections have 10–19 students. **Majors with Highest Enrollment:** Business administration/management, elementary education and teaching, mechanical engineering. **Disciplines with Highest Percentage of Degrees Awarded:** Business/marketing 18%, education 11%, engineering 11%, liberal arts/general studies 10%, biological/life sciences 8%, visual and performing arts 7%. **Special Study Options:** Cross-registration, distance learning, double major, English as a second language (ESL), honors program, independent study, internships, student-designed major, study abroad, teacher certification program.

FACILITIES

Housing: Men's dorms, women's dorms, apartments for married students, apartments for single students, special housing for disabled students. **Special Academic Facilities/Equipment:** Art museum. **Computers:** 10% of classrooms are wired, 100% of classrooms are wireless, 99% of public computers are PCs, 1% of public computers are Macs, network access in dorm rooms, network access in dorm lounges, online registration, online administrative functions (other than registration), remote student-access to Web through college's connection, tuition includes personal computer.

CAMPUS LIFE

Activities: Choral groups, concert band, drama/theater, jazz band, music ensembles, musical theater, opera, radio station, student government, student newspaper, symphony orchestra, television station, yearbook. **Organizations:** 20 registered organizations, 5 honor societies, 2 religious organizations. 6 fraternities (32% men join), 6 sororities (34% women join). **Athletics (Intercollegiate):** *Men:* Basketball, cross-country, golf, soccer, tennis, track/field (outdoor). *Women:* Basketball, cheerleading, cross-country, soccer, softball, tennis, track/field (outdoor).

ADMISSIONS

Freshman Academic Profile: 27% in top 10% of high school class, 50% in top 25% of high school class, 77% in top 50% of high school class. SAT Math middle 50% range 480–610. SAT Critical Reading middle 50% range 480–610. SAT Writing middle 50% range 480–590. ACT middle 50% range 20–26. TOEFL required of all international applicants, minimum paper TOEFL 500, minimum computer TOEFL 173. **Basis for Candidate Selection:** *Other factors considered include:* Class rank, rigor of secondary school record, standardized test scores. **Freshman Admission Requirements:** High school diploma is required, and GED is accepted. *Academic units recommended:* 4 English, 4 math, 4 science, 3 social studies. **Freshman Admission Statistics:** 1,459 applied, 100% admitted, 34% enrolled. **Transfer Admission Requirements:** High school transcript, college transcript(s), standardized test score. Lowest grade transferable D. **General Admission Information:** Application fee $25. Regular notification is rolling. Non-fall registration accepted. Admission may be deferred for a maximum of 1 year. Credit offered for CEEB Advanced Placement tests.

COSTS AND FINANCIAL AID

Annual tuition $14,690. Room and board $6,390. Required fees $1,876. Average book expense $1,000. **Required Forms and Deadlines:** FAFSA, institution's own financial aid form. Financial aid filing deadline 3/15. **Notification of Awards:** Applicants will be notified of awards on or about 2/2. **Types of Aid:** *Need-based scholarships/grants:* Pell, SEOG, state scholarships/grants, private scholarships, the school's own gift aid. *Loans:* FFEL Subsidized Stafford, FFEL Unsubsidized Stafford, FFEL PLUS, Federal Perkins. **Student Employment:** Federal Work-Study Program available. Institutional employment available. Off-campus job opportunities are excellent. **Financial Aid Statistics:** 40% freshmen, 34% undergrads receive need-based scholarship or grant aid. 51% freshmen, 52% undergrads receive need-based self-help aid. 103 freshmen, 394 undergrads receive athletic scholarships. 99% freshmen, 98% undergrads receive any aid. Highest amount earned per year from on-campus jobs $6,297.

OKLAHOMA CITY UNIVERSITY

2501 North Blackwelder, Oklahoma City, OK 73106
Phone: 405-208-5050 **E-mail:** uadmission@okcu.edu **CEEB Code:** 6543
Fax: 405-208-5264 **Website:** www.okcu.edu **ACT Code:** 3416
Financial Aid Phone: 405-208-5211

This private school, affiliated with the Methodist Church, was founded in 1904. It has a 76-acre campus.

RATINGS

Admissions Selectivity Rating: 85   **Fire Safety Rating:** 87   **Green Rating:** 77

STUDENTS AND FACULTY

Enrollment: 2,082. **Student Body:** 63% female, 37% male, 36% out-of-state, 20% international (56 countries represented). African American 8%, Asian 3%, Caucasian 57%, Hispanic 4%, Native American 4%. **Retention and Graduation:** 72% freshmen return for sophomore year. 39% freshmen graduate within 4 years. **Faculty:** Student/faculty ratio 13:1. 177 full-time faculty, 75% hold PhDs. 86% faculty teach undergrads.

ACADEMICS

Degrees: Bachelor's, first professional, master's. **Academic Requirements:** Arts/fine arts, computer literacy, English (including composition), foreign languages, history, humanities, mathematics, philosophy, religion, sciences (biological or physical), social science. **Classes:** Most classes have fewer than 10 students. Most lab/discussion sections have fewer than 10 students. **Majors with Highest Enrollment:** Business administration/management, dance, nursing. **Disciplines with Highest Percentage of Degrees Awarded:** Liberal arts/general studies 37%, visual and performing arts 20%, health professions and related sciences 13%, business/marketing 7%, social sciences 5%. **Special Study Options:** Accelerated program, cooperative education program, distance learning, double major, dual enrollment, English as a second language (ESL), exchange student program (domestic), external degree

program, honors program, independent study, internships, student-designed major, study abroad, teacher certification program.

FACILITIES

Housing: Men's dorms, women's dorms, apartments for married students, apartments for single students, special housing for disabled students, fraternity/sorority housing, learning communities. **Special Academic Facilities/Equipment:** Art museum, audiovisual center, language lab. **Computers:** 5% of classrooms are wired, 100% of classrooms are wireless, 90% of public computers are PCs, 10% of public computers are Macs, network access in dorm rooms, network access in dorm lounges, online administrative functions (other than registration), remote student-access to Web through college's connection.

CAMPUS LIFE

Activities: Choral groups, concert band, dance, drama/theater, jazz band, literary magazine, music ensembles, musical theater, opera, pep band, student government, student newspaper, symphony orchestra, television station, yearbook. **Organizations:** 94 registered organizations, 14 honor societies, 6 religious organizations. 3 fraternities (14% men join), 4 sororities (19% women join). **Athletics (Intercollegiate):** *Men:* Baseball, basketball, cheerleading, crew/rowing, golf, soccer, wrestling. *Women:* Basketball, cheerleading, crew/rowing, golf, soccer, softball, volleyball.

ADMISSIONS

Freshman Academic Profile: 30% in top 10% of high school class, 65% in top 25% of high school class, 90% in top 50% of high school class. SAT Math middle 50% range 520–640. SAT Critical Reading middle 50% range 550–640. TOEFL required of all international applicants, minimum paper TOEFL 500, minimum computer TOEFL 173. **Basis for Candidate Selection:** *Very important factors considered include:* Academic GPA, application essay, class rank, rigor of secondary school record, standardized test scores, talent/ability. *Important factors considered include:* Character/personal qualities, extracurricular activities, level of applicant's interest, racial/ethnic status, recommendation(s), volunteer work. *Other factors considered include:* Alumni/ae relation, first generation, interview, religious affiliation/commitment, work experience. **Freshman Admission Requirements:** High school diploma is required, and GED is accepted. *Academic units required:* 4 English, 3 math, 3 science (1 science lab), 2 foreign language, 3 social studies, 3 history. **Freshman Admission Statistics:** 975 applied, 81% admitted, 46% enrolled. **Transfer Admission Requirements:** College transcript(s), essay or personal statement, statement of good standing from prior institution(s). Minimum college GPA of 2.0 required. Lowest grade transferable C-. **General Admission Information:** Application fee $30. Regular application deadline 8/20. Regular notification is rolling. Non-fall registration accepted. Admission may be deferred for a maximum of 1 year. Credit and/or placement offered for CEEB Advanced Placement tests.

COSTS AND FINANCIAL AID

Annual tuition $19,600. Room and board $8,400. Required fees $1,400. Average book expense $1,500. **Required Forms and Deadlines:** FAFSA, institution's own financial aid form, tax returns if selected for verification. Financial aid filing deadline 6/30. **Notification of Awards:** Applicants will be notified of awards on a rolling basis beginning on or about 2/24. **Types of Aid:** *Need-based scholarships/grants:* Pell, SEOG, state scholarships/grants, private scholarships, the school's own gift aid, United Negro College Fund, Native American Grants. *Loans:* FFEL Subsidized Stafford, FFEL Unsubsidized Stafford, FFEL PLUS, Federal Perkins. **Financial Aid Statistics:** 62% freshmen, 48% undergrads receive need-based scholarship or grant aid. 36% freshmen, 36% undergrads receive need-based self-help aid. 45 freshmen, 190 undergrads receive athletic scholarships. 99% freshmen, 84% undergrads receive any aid.

OKLAHOMA PANHANDLE STATE UNIVERSITY

PO Box 430, Goodwell, OK 73939-0430
Phone: 580-349-1312 **E-mail:** opsu@opsu.edu
Fax: 508-349-2302 **Website:** www.opsu.edu **ACT Code:** 34026
Financial Aid Phone: 580-349-1580

This public school was founded in 1909. It has a 120-acre campus.

RATINGS

Admissions Selectivity Rating: 65   **Fire Safety Rating:** 60*   **Green Rating:** 60*

STUDENTS AND FACULTY

Enrollment: 1,226. **Student Body:** 54% female, 46% male, 49% out-of-state, 4% international. African American 4%, Caucasian 79%, Hispanic 10%, Native

American 2%. **Retention and Graduation:** 70% freshmen return for sophomore year. **Faculty:** Student/faculty ratio 15:1. 44 full-time faculty, 43% hold PhDs. 100% faculty teach undergrads.

ACADEMICS

Degrees: Associate, bachelor's, terminal. **Academic Requirements:** Arts/fine arts, computer literacy, English (including composition), history, humanities, mathematics, sciences (biological or physical), social science. **Classes:** Most classes have 20–29 students. Most lab/discussion sections have fewer than 10 students. **Majors with Highest Enrollment:** Agricultural business and management, computer and information sciences, education. **Disciplines with Highest Percentage of Degrees Awarded:** Agriculture 24%, education 22%, business/marketing 15%, computer and information sciences 8%, biological/life sciences 8%, psychology 6%, social sciences 6%. **Special Study Options:** Cooperative education program, distance learning, double major, dual enrollment, independent study, internships, liberal arts/career combination, teacher certification program.

FACILITIES

Housing: Coed dorms, men's dorms, women's dorms, apartments for married students, apartments for single students. **Computers:** 100% of public computers are PCs, remote student-access to Web through college's connection.

CAMPUS LIFE

Activities: Choral groups, concert band, drama/theater, jazz band, literary magazine, marching band, music ensembles, musical theater, radio station, student government, student newspaper, yearbook. **Organizations:** 8 registered organizations, 12 honor societies, 4 religious organizations. **Athletics (Intercollegiate):** *Men:* Baseball, basketball, cheerleading, football, golf, rodeo. *Women:* Basketball, cheerleading, cross-country, golf, rodeo, softball.

ADMISSIONS

Freshman Academic Profile: 9% in top 10% of high school class, 18% in top 25% of high school class, 30% in top 50% of high school class. 99% from public high schools. ACT middle 50% range 27–19. TOEFL required of all international applicants, minimum paper TOEFL 500. **Freshman Admission Requirements:** High school diploma is required, and GED is accepted. *Academic units required:* 4 English, 3 math, 2 science (2 science labs), 1 social studies, 2 history, 3 academic electives. **Freshman Admission Statistics:** 257 applied, 85% admitted, 100% enrolled. **Transfer Admission Requirements:** High school transcript, college transcript(s), standardized test score. **General Admission Information:** Non-fall registration accepted. Common Application not accepted.

COSTS AND FINANCIAL AID

Annual in-state tuition $2,055. Out-of-state tuition $3,840. Room & board $2,670. Required fees $441. Average book expense $180. **Required Forms and Deadlines:** FAFSA. **Types of Aid:** *Need-based scholarships/grants:* Pell, SEOG, state scholarships/grants, private scholarships, the school's own gift aid. *Loans:* FFEL Subsidized Stafford, FFEL Unsubsidized Stafford, FFEL PLUS, Federal Perkins, college/university loans from institutional funds. **Student Employment:** Federal Work-Study Program available. Off-campus job opportunities are good. **Financial Aid Statistics:** Highest amount earned per year from on-campus jobs $1,900.

OKLAHOMA STATE UNIVERSITY

219 Student Union, Stillwater, OK 74078
Phone: 800-233-5019 **E-mail:** admissions@okstate.edu **CEEB Code:** 6546
Fax: 405-744-7092 **Website:** osu.okstate.edu **ACT Code:** 3424
Financial Aid Phone: 405-744-6604

This public school was founded in 1890. It has an 840-acre campus.

RATINGS

Admissions Selectivity Rating: 80   **Fire Safety Rating:** 60*   **Green Rating:** 71

STUDENTS AND FACULTY

Enrollment: 18,600. **Student Body:** 49% female, 51% male, 16% out-of-state, 3% international (117 countries represented). African American 4%, Asian 2%, Caucasian 79%, Hispanic 2%, Native American 9%. **Retention and Graduation:** 79% freshmen return for sophomore year. 28% freshmen graduate within 4 years. **Faculty:** Student/faculty ratio 19:1. 1,020 full-time faculty, 90% hold PhDs. 63% faculty teach undergrads.

ACADEMICS

Degrees: Bachelor's, certificate, doctoral, first professional, master's, post-master's certificate. **Academic Requirements:** American government, English

(including composition), history, humanities, international dimension, mathematics, sciences (biological or physical), social science. **Classes:** Most classes have 20–29 students. Most lab/discussion sections have 10–19 students. **Majors with Highest Enrollment:** Journalism, management science, marketing/marketing management. **Disciplines with Highest Percentage of Degrees Awarded:** Business/marketing 29%, engineering 9%, education 8%, family and consumer sciences 8%, agriculture 8%. **Special Study Options:** Accelerated program, cross-registration, distance learning, double major, dual enrollment, English as a second language (ESL), exchange student program (domestic), honors program, independent study, internships, student-designed major, study abroad, teacher certification program.

FACILITIES

Housing: Coed dorms, men's dorms, women's dorms, apartments for married students, apartments for single students, special housing for disabled students, fraternity/sorority housing, learning communities and special-interest housing. **Special Academic Facilities/Equipment:** Archaeology, art, history, and natural science museums; wellness center; laser research center. **Computers:** 93% of public computers are PCs, 5% of public computers are Macs, 2% of public computers are UNIX, network access in dorm rooms, network access in dorm lounges, online registration, online administrative functions (other than registration), support for handheld computing, remote student-access to Web through college's connection.

CAMPUS LIFE

Activities: Choral groups, concert band, dance, drama/theater, jazz band, literary magazine, marching band, music ensembles, musical theater, opera, pep band, radio station, student government, student newspaper, symphony orchestra, television station. **Organizations:** 404 registered organizations, 32 honor societies, 30 religious organizations. 20 fraternities (14% men join), 15 sororities (16% women join). **Athletics (Intercollegiate):** *Men:* Baseball, basketball, cross-country, football, golf, tennis, track/field (outdoor), wrestling. *Women:* Basketball, cross-country, equestrian sports, golf, soccer, softball, tennis, track/field (outdoor).

ADMISSIONS

Freshman Academic Profile: 27% in top 10% of high school class, 55% in top 25% of high school class, 86% in top 50% of high school class. SAT Math middle 50% range 510–630. SAT Critical Reading middle 50% range 490–610. ACT middle 50% range 22–27. TOEFL required of all international applicants, minimum paper TOEFL 500, minimum computer TOEFL 173. **Basis for Candidate Selection:** *Very important factors considered include:* Academic GPA, class rank, standardized test scores. *Other factors considered include:* Application essay, character/personal qualities, extracurricular activities, interview, recommendation(s), rigor of secondary school record, talent/ability. **Freshman Admission Requirements:** High school diploma is required, and GED is accepted. *Academic units required:* 4 English, 3 math, 2 science (2 science labs), 2 social studies, 1 history, 3 academic electives. *Academic units recommended:* 2 foreign language, 1 computer science. **Freshman Admission Statistics:** 6,730 applied, 87% admitted, 55% enrolled. **Transfer Admission Requirements:** College transcript(s). Minimum college GPA of 2.2 required. Lowest grade transferable D. **General Admission Information:** Application fee $40. Regular notification is rolling. Non-fall registration accepted. Credit offered for CEEB Advanced Placement tests.

COSTS AND FINANCIAL AID

Annual in-state tuition $3,585. Annual out-of-state tuition $13,010. Room and board $6,267. Required fees $1,906. Average book expense $940. **Required Forms and Deadlines:** FAFSA, combined admissions and scholarship application. Financial aid filing deadline 2/1. **Notification of Awards:** Applicants will be notified of awards on a rolling basis beginning on or about 11/1. **Types of Aid:** *Need-based scholarships/grants:* Pell, SEOG, state scholarships/grants, private scholarships, the school's own gift aid. *Loans:* Direct Subsidized Stafford, Direct Unsubsidized Stafford, Direct PLUS, Federal Perkins. **Student Employment:** Off-campus job opportunities are good. **Financial Aid Statistics:** 33% freshmen, 36% undergrads receive need-based scholarship or grant aid. 27% freshmen, 38% undergrads receive need-based self-help aid. 38 freshmen, 219 undergrads receive athletic scholarships.

OKLAHOMA WESLEYAN UNIVERSITY

2201 Silver Lake Road, Bartlesville, OK 74006
Phone: 918-335-6219 **E-mail:** admissions@okwu.edu **CEEB Code:** 6135
Fax: 918-335-6229 **Website:** www.okwu.edu **ACT Code:** 3387
Financial Aid Phone: 918-335-6282

This private school was founded in 1972. It has a 127-acre campus.

RATINGS
Admissions Selectivity Rating: 81   **Fire Safety Rating:** 60*   **Green Rating:** 60*

STUDENTS AND FACULTY
Enrollment: 539. **Student Body:** 43% out-of-state, 6% international (12 countries represented). African American 3%, Caucasian 80%, Hispanic 3%, Native American 8%. **Retention and Graduation:** 10% grads go on to further study within 1 year. 2% grads pursue arts and sciences degrees. 5% grads pursue business degrees. 2% grads pursue law degrees. 2% grads pursue medical degrees. **Faculty:** 100% faculty teach undergrads.

ACADEMICS
Degrees: Associate, bachelor's, certificate, master's. **Academic Requirements:** Computer literacy, English (including composition), history, humanities, mathematics, philosophy, religion, sciences (biological or physical), social science. **Special Study Options:** Double major, English as a second language (ESL), independent study, internships, student-designed major, study abroad.

FACILITIES
Housing: Men's dorms, women's dorms. **Special Academic Facilities/ Equipment:** La Quinta Mansion. **Computers:** Undergraduates are required to own a computer.

CAMPUS LIFE
Activities: Choral groups, music ensembles, pep band, student government, student newspaper, yearbook. **Organizations:** 10 registered organizations, 2 honor societies, 3 religious organizations. **Athletics (Intercollegiate):** *Men:* Baseball, basketball, cheerleading, golf, soccer. *Women:* Basketball, cheerleading, soccer, softball, volleyball.

ADMISSIONS
Freshman Academic Profile: 20% in top 10% of high school class, 40% in top 25% of high school class, 80% in top 50% of high school class. 90% from public high schools. ACT middle 50% range 19–25. TOEFL required of all international applicants, minimum paper TOEFL 500. **Basis for Candidate Selection:** *Very important factors considered include:* Character/personal qualities, class rank, recommendation(s), religious affiliation/commitment, rigor of secondary school record, standardized test scores, state residency. *Important factors considered include:* Alumni/ae relation, geographical residence, interview, racial/ethnic status. *Other factors considered include:* Extracurricular activities, talent/ability. **Freshman Admission Requirements:** High school diploma is required, and GED is accepted. *Academic units required:* 4 English, 2 math, 1 science (1 science lab), 1 social studies, 1 history, 6 academic electives. **Freshman Admission Statistics:** 317 applied, 60% admitted, 62% enrolled. **Transfer Admission Requirements:** High school transcript, college transcript(s), essay or personal statement, statement of good standing from prior institution(s). Minimum college GPA of 2.0 required. Lowest grade transferable D. **General Admission Information:** Application fee $25. Regular application deadline rolling. Non-fall registration accepted. Admission may be deferred for a maximum of 1 year. Common Application accepted. Credit and/or placement offered for CEEB Advanced Placement tests.

COSTS AND FINANCIAL AID
Annual tuition $8,200. Room & board $3,800. Required fees $500. **Types of Aid:** *Need-based scholarships/grants:* Pell, SEOG, state scholarships/grants, private scholarships, the school's own gift aid. *Loans:* Direct Subsidized Stafford, Direct Unsubsidized Stafford, Direct PLUS, Federal Perkins. **Student Employment:** Federal Work-Study Program available. Institutional employment available. Off-campus job opportunities are excellent. **Financial Aid Statistics:** Highest amount earned per year from on-campus jobs $1,913.

OLD DOMINION UNIVERSITY

108 Rollins Hall, 5115 Hampton Boulevard, Norfolk, VA 23529-0050
Phone: 757-683-3685 **E-mail:** admit@odu.edu **CEEB Code:** 5126
Fax: 757-683-3255 **Website:** www.odu.edu
Financial Aid Phone: 757-683-3683

This public school was founded in 1930. It has a 188-acre campus.

RATINGS
Admissions Selectivity Rating: 78   **Fire Safety Rating:** 60*   **Green Rating:** 70

STUDENTS AND FACULTY
Enrollment: 14,845. **Student Body:** 59% female, 41% male, 9% out-of-state, 2% international (114 countries represented). African American 22%, Asian 6%, Caucasian 61%, Hispanic 4%. **Retention and Graduation:** 76% freshmen return for sophomore year. 23% freshmen graduate within 4 years. 28% grads go on to further study within 1 year. 3% grads pursue arts and sciences degrees. 3% grads pursue business degrees. 6% grads pursue law degrees. **Faculty:** Student/faculty ratio 17:1. 663 full-time faculty, 81% hold PhDs. 70% faculty teach undergrads.

ACADEMICS
Degrees: Bachelor's, doctoral, master's, post-master's certificate. **Academic Requirements:** Arts/fine arts, computer literacy, English (including composition), foreign languages, history, humanities, literature, mathematics, oral communication, philosophy, sciences (biological or physical), social science. **Classes:** Most classes have 20–29 students. Most lab/discussion sections have 20–29 students. **Majors with Highest Enrollment:** Criminology, engineering-related technologies/technicians, psychology. **Disciplines with Highest Percentage of Degrees Awarded:** Business/marketing 21%, health professions and related sciences 17%, social sciences 12%, English 8%, interdisciplinary studies 7%. **Special Study Options:** Accelerated program, cooperative education program, cross-registration, distance learning, double major, dual enrollment, English as a second language (ESL), exchange student program (domestic), experiential learning, honors program, independent study, internships, liberal arts/career combination, student-designed major, study abroad, teacher certification program, weekend college.

FACILITIES
Housing: Coed dorms, apartments for single students, special housing for disabled students, special housing for international students, off-campus apartments. **Special Academic Facilities/Equipment:** Centers for urban research/service, economic education, and child study; planetarium; marine science research vessel; random wave pool. **Computers:** 10% of classrooms are wired, 100% of classrooms are wireless, 95% of public computers are PCs, 5% of public computers are Macs, network access in dorm rooms, network access in dorm lounges, online registration, online administrative functions (other than registration), support for handheld computing, remote student-access to Web through college's connection.

CAMPUS LIFE
Activities: Choral groups, concert band, dance, drama/theater, jazz band, literary magazine, music ensembles, musical theater, pep band, radio station, student government, student newspaper, television station, yearbook. **Organizations:** 191 registered organizations, 18 honor societies, 16 religious organizations. 14 fraternities (5% men join), 10 sororities (3% women join). **Athletics (Intercollegiate):** *Men:* Baseball, basketball, diving, golf, sailing, swimming, tennis, wrestling. *Women:* Basketball, diving, field hockey, golf, lacrosse, sailing, soccer, swimming, tennis. **Environmental Initiatives:** Created Environmental Advisory Council. Recycling Efforts. Incorporate Low-Impact Development Techniques for Storm Water Management.

ADMISSIONS
Freshman Academic Profile: 14% in top 10% of high school class, 46% in top 25% of high school class, 87% in top 50% of high school class. 85% from public high schools. SAT Math middle 50% range 480–580. SAT Critical Reading middle 50% range 480–570. SAT Writing middle 50% range 470–560. ACT middle 50% range 18–22. TOEFL required of all international applicants, minimum paper TOEFL 550, minimum computer TOEFL 213. **Basis for Candidate Selection:** *Very important factors considered include:* Academic GPA, extracurricular activities, rigor of secondary school record, standardized test scores. *Important factors considered include:* Application essay, class rank, recommendation(s), volunteer work, work experience. *Other factors considered include:* Alumni/ae relation, character/personal qualities, first generation, interview, level of applicant's interest, talent/ability. **Freshman Admission Requirements:** High school diploma is required, and GED is accepted. *Academic units recommended:* 4 English, 3 math, 3 science, 3 foreign language, 3 social studies, 3 history. **Freshman Admission Statistics:** 7,350 applied, 69%

admitted, 41% enrolled. **Transfer Admission Requirements:** College transcript(s). Minimum college GPA of 2.2 required. Lowest grade transferable C. **General Admission Information:** Application fee $40. Regular application deadline 3/15. Regular notification is rolling. Non-fall registration accepted. Admission may be deferred for a maximum of 1 year. Credit and/or placement offered for CEEB Advanced Placement tests.

COSTS AND FINANCIAL AID

Annual in-state tuition $6,330. Annual out-of-state tuition $17,550. Room and board $7,100. Required fees $198. Average book expense $1,000. **Required Forms and Deadlines:** FAFSA. Financial aid filing deadline 3/15. **Notification of Awards:** Applicants will be notified of awards on a rolling basis beginning on or about 2/1. **Types of Aid:** *Need-based scholarships/grants:* Pell, SEOG, state scholarships/grants, private scholarships, the school's own gift aid, United Negro College Fund, Federal Nursing Scholarships. *Loans:* Direct Subsidized Stafford, Direct Unsubsidized Stafford, Direct PLUS, Federal Perkins, Federal Nursing, college/university loans from institutional funds. **Student Employment:** Federal Work-Study Program available. Institutional employment available. Off-campus job opportunities are excellent. **Financial Aid Statistics:** 30% freshmen, 29% undergrads receive need-based scholarship or grant aid. 30% freshmen, 34% undergrads receive need-based self-help aid. 52 freshmen, 208 undergrads receive athletic scholarships. 83% freshmen, 85% undergrads receive any aid. Highest amount earned per year from on-campus jobs $3,910.

See page 1304.

OLIVET COLLEGE

320 South Main Street, Olivet, MI 49076
Phone: 269-749-7635 **E-mail:** admissions@olivetcollege.edu **CEEB Code:** 1595
Fax: 269-749-6617 **Website:** www.olivetcollege.edu **ACT Code:** 2042
Financial Aid Phone: 269-749-7102

This private school, affiliated with the United Church of Christ, was founded in 1844. It has a 45-acre campus.

RATINGS

Admissions Selectivity Rating: 60*   **Fire Safety Rating:** 60*   **Green Rating:** 60*

STUDENTS AND FACULTY

Enrollment: 1,070. **Student Body:** 42% female, 58% male, 5% out-of-state, 3% international. African American 16%, Caucasian 76%, Hispanic 2%, Native American 1%. **Retention and Graduation:** 65% grads go on to further study within 1 year. 72% grads pursue arts and sciences degrees. 45% grads pursue business degrees. 20% grads pursue law degrees. 10% grads pursue medical degrees. **Faculty:** Student/faculty ratio 14:1. 46 full-time faculty, 46% hold PhDs. 99% faculty teach undergrads.

ACADEMICS

Degrees: Bachelor's, master's. **Academic Requirements:** Arts/fine arts, English (including composition), humanities, mathematics, philosophy, sciences (biological or physical), social science. **Special Study Options:** Cooperative education program, dual enrollment, freshman-year experience, honors program, independent study, internships, liberal arts/career combination, portfolio assessment, senior experience, service learning programs, student-designed major, study abroad, teacher certification program.

FACILITIES

Housing: Coed dorms, men's dorms, women's dorms, apartments for married students, apartments for single students, special housing for international students, fraternity/sorority housing. **Computers:** 98% of public computers are PCs, 2% of public computers are Macs, network access in dorm rooms, online registration, online administrative functions (other than registration), remote student-access to Web through college's connection.

CAMPUS LIFE

Activities: Choral groups, concert band, drama/theater, jazz band, music ensembles, musical theater, pep band, radio station, student government, student newspaper, yearbook. **Organizations:** 12 registered organizations, 1 honor society, 1 religious organization. 3 fraternities (38% men join), 3 sororities (29% women join). **Athletics (Intercollegiate):** *Men:* Baseball, basketball, cross-country, diving, football, golf, soccer, swimming, track/field (outdoor), wrestling. *Women:* Basketball, cheerleading, cross-country, diving, golf, soccer, softball, swimming, tennis, track/field (outdoor), volleyball.

ADMISSIONS

Freshman Academic Profile: 93% from public high schools. TOEFL required of all international applicants, minimum paper TOEFL 500, minimum

computer TOEFL 173. **Basis for Candidate Selection:** *Very important factors considered include:* Alumni/ae relation, character/personal qualities, extracurricular activities, rigor of secondary school record, standardized test scores, volunteer work, work experience. *Important factors considered include:* Racial/ethnic status, recommendation(s). *Other factors considered include:* Application essay, class rank, geographical residence, interview, religious affiliation/commitment, state residency, talent/ability. **Freshman Admission Requirements:** High school diploma is required, and GED is accepted. *Academic units recommended:* 4 English, 2 math, 2 science, 3 social studies, 2 academic electives. **Freshman Admission Statistics:** 1,065 applied, 50% admitted, 42% enrolled. **Transfer Admission Requirements:** High school transcript, college transcript(s). Minimum college GPA of 2.0 required. Lowest grade transferable C-. **General Admission Information:** Application fee $25. Regular notification is rolling. Non-fall registration accepted. Admission may be deferred for a maximum of 1 year. Credit and/or placement offered for CEEB Advanced Placement tests.

COSTS AND FINANCIAL AID

Annual tuition $17,994. Room and board $6,346. Required fees $664. Average book expense $800. **Required Forms and Deadlines:** FAFSA. **Notification of Awards:** Applicants will be notified of awards on a rolling basis beginning on or about 2/1. **Types of Aid:** *Need-based scholarships/grants:* Pell, SEOG, state scholarships/grants, private scholarships, the school's own gift aid. *Loans:* FFEL Subsidized Stafford, FFEL Unsubsidized Stafford, FFEL PLUS, Federal Perkins, state loans. **Student Employment:** Federal Work-Study Program available. Institutional employment available. Off-campus job opportunities are fair. **Financial Aid Statistics:** 71% freshmen, 84% undergrads receive need-based scholarship or grant aid. 66% freshmen, 78% undergrads receive need-based self-help aid. Highest amount earned per year from on-campus jobs $850.

OLIVET NAZARENE UNIVERSITY

1 University Avenue, Bourbonnais, IL 60914
Phone: 815-939-5603 **E-mail:** admissions@olivet.edu **CEEB Code:** 32
Fax: 815-935-4998 **Website:** www.olivet.edu **ACT Code:** 1112
Financial Aid Phone: 815-939-5249

This private school, affiliated with the Nazarene Church, was founded in 1907. It has a 225-acre campus.

RATINGS

Admissions Selectivity Rating: 83   **Fire Safety Rating:** 60*   **Green Rating:** 60*

STUDENTS AND FACULTY

Enrollment: 2,633. **Student Body:** 60% female, 40% male, 55% out-of-state, 1% international (18 countries represented). African American 9%, Asian 1%, Caucasian 86%, Hispanic 3%. **Retention and Graduation:** 79% freshmen return for sophomore year. 39% grads go on to further study within 1 year. 27% grads pursue arts and sciences degrees. 13% grads pursue business degrees. 3% grads pursue law degrees. 9% grads pursue medical degrees. **Faculty:** Student/faculty ratio 20:1. 94 full-time faculty, 68% hold PhDs. 100% faculty teach undergrads.

ACADEMICS

Degrees: Associate, bachelor's, master's. **Academic Requirements:** Arts/fine arts, English (including composition), foreign languages, history, humanities, mathematics, religion/biblical literature, sciences (biological or physical), social science. **Classes:** Most classes have 20–29 students. **Majors with Highest Enrollment:** Business administration/management, education, health/medical preparatory programs. **Disciplines with Highest Percentage of Degrees Awarded:** Education 16%, business/marketing 15%, social sciences 12%, psychology 7%, biological/life sciences 7%, health professions and related sciences 6%. **Special Study Options:** Accelerated program, distance learning, double major, honors program, independent study, internships, student-designed major, study abroad, teacher certification program.

FACILITIES

Housing: Men's dorms, women's dorms, apartments for married students, apartments for single students, special housing for disabled students. **Special Academic Facilities/Equipment:** Planetarium, smart classrooms, radio station. **Computers:** 100% of classrooms are wireless, 91% of public computers are PCs, 9% of public computers are Macs, 8% of public computers are UNIX, network access in dorm rooms, network access in dorm lounges, online registration, online administrative functions (other than registration), remote student-access to Web through college's connection.

CAMPUS LIFE

Activities: Choral groups, concert band, dance, drama/theater, jazz band, literary magazine, marching band, music ensembles, musical theater, opera, pep band, radio station, student government, student newspaper, student-run film society, symphony orchestra, television station. **Organizations:** 79 registered organizations, 8 honor societies, 23 religious organizations. **Athletics (Intercollegiate):** *Men:* Baseball, basketball, cheerleading, cross-country, football, golf, soccer, tennis, track/field (indoor), track/field (outdoor). *Women:* Basketball, cheerleading, cross-country, soccer, softball, tennis, track/field (indoor), track/field (outdoor), volleyball.

ADMISSIONS

Freshman Academic Profile: 22% in top 10% of high school class, 45% in top 25% of high school class, 75% in top 50% of high school class. 85% from public high schools. SAT Math middle 50% range 480–590. SAT Critical Reading middle 50% range 490–620. ACT middle 50% range 20–26. TOEFL required of all international applicants, minimum paper TOEFL 500, minimum computer TOEFL 173. **Basis for Candidate Selection:** *Very important factors considered include:* Character/personal qualities, class rank, recommendation(s), rigor of secondary school record, standardized test scores. *Important factors considered include:* Application essay, extracurricular activities, interview, talent/ability. *Other factors considered include:* Religious affiliation/commitment, volunteer work, work experience. **Freshman Admission Requirements:** High school diploma is required, and GED is accepted. *Academic units required:* 4 English, 3 math, 3 science, 3 social studies, 2 history. *Academic units recommended:* 4 English, 3 math, 3 science, 2 foreign language, 3 social studies, 2 history. **Freshman Admission Statistics:** 2,747 applied, 64% admitted, 40% enrolled. **Transfer Admission Requirements:** College transcript(s), essay or personal statement, statement of good standing from prior institution(s). Minimum college GPA of 2.0 required. Lowest grade transferable D-. **General Admission Information:** Regular application deadline 5/15. Regular notification is rolling. Non-fall registration accepted. Common Application not accepted. Credit and/or placement offered for CEEB Advanced Placement tests.

COSTS AND FINANCIAL AID

Annual tuition $16,750. Room & board $6,400. Required fees $840. Average book expense $800. **Required Forms and Deadlines:** FAFSA, institution's own financial aid form. Financial aid filing deadline 3/1. **Notification of Awards:** Applicants will be notified of awards on a rolling basis beginning on or about 2/1. **Types of Aid:** *Need-based scholarships/grants:* Pell, SEOG, state scholarships/grants, private scholarships, the school's own gift aid. *Loans:* Direct Subsidized Stafford, Direct Unsubsidized Stafford, Direct PLUS, FFEL Subsidized Stafford, FFEL Unsubsidized Stafford, FFEL PLUS, Federal Perkins. **Student Employment:** Federal Work-Study Program available. **Financial Aid Statistics:** 76% freshmen, 73% undergrads receive need-based scholarship or grant aid. 63% freshmen, 64% undergrads receive need-based self-help aid. 83 freshmen, 296 undergrads receive athletic scholarships. 96% undergrads receive any aid.

ORAL ROBERTS UNIVERSITY

7777 South Lewis Avenue, Tulsa, OK 74171
Phone: 918-495-6518 **E-mail:** admissions@oru.edu **CEEB Code:** 6552
Fax: 918-495-6222 **Website:** www.oru.edu **ACT Code:** 3427
Financial Aid Phone: 918-495-6510

This is a private school. It has a 500-acre campus.

RATINGS

Admissions Selectivity Rating: 81   **Fire Safety Rating:** 60*   **Green Rating:** 60*

STUDENTS AND FACULTY

Enrollment: 3,303. **Student Body:** 58% female, 42% male, 61% out-of-state, 5% international. African American 16%, Asian 2%, Caucasian 64%, Hispanic 6%, Native American 2%. **Retention and Graduation:** 82% freshmen return for sophomore year. 38% freshmen graduate within 4 years. 50% grads go on to further study within 1 year. 25% grads pursue arts and sciences degrees. 10% grads pursue business degrees. 1% grads pursue law degrees. 5% grads pursue medical degrees. **Faculty:** Student/faculty ratio 16:1. 179 full-time faculty, 41% hold PhDs. 85% faculty teach undergrads.

ACADEMICS

Degrees: Bachelor's, doctoral, first professional, master's. **Academic Requirements:** English (including composition), foreign languages, history, humanities, mathematics, sciences (biological or physical), social science. **Classes:** Most classes have 10–19 students. Most lab/discussion sections have

---

20–29 students. **Majors with Highest Enrollment:** Marketing/marketing management, mass communications/media studies, theology/theological studies. **Disciplines with Highest Percentage of Degrees Awarded:** Business/marketing 21%, communication technologies 16%, education 8%, visual and performing arts 7%, psychology 6%. **Special Study Options:** Distance learning, double major, dual enrollment, English as a second language (ESL), external degree program, honors program, independent study, internships, liberal arts/career combination, student-designed major, study abroad, teacher certification program, weekend college.

FACILITIES

Housing: Men's dorms, women's dorms, special housing for disabled students. **Special Academic Facilities/Equipment:** Dial access information retrieval system, programmed learning facilities, early learning center, TV production studio.

CAMPUS LIFE

Activities: Choral groups, concert band, drama/theater, jazz band, literary magazine, music ensembles, musical theater, opera, pep band, radio station, student government, student newspaper, student-run film society, symphony orchestra, television station, yearbook. **Athletics (Intercollegiate):** *Men:* Baseball, basketball, cheerleading, cross-country, soccer, swimming, tennis, track/field (outdoor). *Women:* Basketball, cheerleading, cross-country, soccer, swimming, tennis, track/field (outdoor), volleyball.

ADMISSIONS

Freshman Academic Profile: 27% in top 10% of high school class, 53% in top 25% of high school class, 80% in top 50% of high school class. 75% from public high schools. SAT Math middle 50% range 440–580. SAT Critical Reading middle 50% range 480–600. ACT middle 50% range 20–25. TOEFL required of all international applicants, minimum paper TOEFL 500, minimum computer TOEFL 150. **Basis for Candidate Selection:** *Very important factors considered include:* Application essay, rigor of secondary school record, standardized test scores. *Important factors considered include:* Class rank, recommendation(s). *Other factors considered include:* Alumni/ae relation, character/personal qualities, religious affiliation/commitment. **Freshman Admission Requirements:** High school diploma is required, and GED is accepted. *Academic units required:* 4 English, 2 math, 1 science (1 science lab), 2 foreign language, 2 social studies. **Freshman Admission Statistics:** 1,244 applied, 70% admitted, 61% enrolled. **Transfer Admission Requirements:** High school transcript, college transcript(s), essay or personal statement. Minimum college GPA of 2.0 required. Lowest grade transferable C. **General Admission Information:** Application fee $35. Regular notification is rolling. Non-fall registration accepted. Admission may be deferred for a maximum of 2 years. Common Application not accepted. Credit and/or placement offered for CEEB Advanced Placement tests.

COSTS AND FINANCIAL AID

Annual tuition $17,000. Room and board $7,350. Required fees $400. Average book expense $1,500. **Required Forms and Deadlines:** FAFSA. Financial aid filing deadline 3/15. **Types of Aid:** *Need-based scholarships/grants:* Pell, SEOG, state scholarships/grants, private scholarships, the school's own gift aid. *Loans:* FFEL Subsidized Stafford, FFEL Unsubsidized Stafford, FFEL PLUS, Federal Perkins. **Financial Aid Statistics:** 67% freshmen, 64% undergrads receive need-based scholarship or grant aid. 63% freshmen, 65% undergrads receive need-based self-help aid. 11 freshmen, 105 undergrads receive athletic scholarships. Highest amount earned per year from on-campus jobs $1,800.

OREGON COLLEGE OF ART AND CRAFT

8245 SW Barnes Road, Portland, OR 97225
Phone: 503-297-5544 **E-mail:** dspencer@ocac.edu **CEEB Code:** 4236
Fax: 503-297-9651 **Website:** www.ocac.edu **ACT Code:** 3471
Financial Aid Phone: 503-297-5544

This private school was founded in 1907. It has a 9-acre campus.

RATINGS

Admissions Selectivity Rating: 60*   **Fire Safety Rating:** 61   **Green Rating:** 60*

STUDENTS AND FACULTY

Enrollment: 117. **Student Body:** 67% female, 33% male, 48% out-of-state. Asian 2%, Caucasian 88%, Hispanic 3%, Native American 3%. **Retention and Graduation:** 60% freshmen return for sophomore year. 15% grads pursue arts and sciences degrees. **Faculty:** Student/faculty ratio 5:1. 10 full-time faculty, 90% hold PhDs. 100% faculty teach undergrads.

ACADEMICS

Degrees: Bachelor's, certificate, post-bachelor's certificate. **Academic Requirements:** Arts/fine arts, art history, English (including composition), humanities, mathematics, sciences (biological or physical), social science. **Classes:** Most classes have fewer than 10 students. **Majors with Highest Enrollment:** Drawing, fine arts and art studies, metal and jewelry arts. **Disciplines with Highest Percentage of Degrees Awarded:** Visual and performing arts 100%. **Special Study Options:** Cross-registration, exchange student program (domestic), independent study, internships, study abroad.

FACILITIES

Housing: Cooperative housing. The college offers a small number of on-campus housing for new students straight from high school. In addition, the college has contract with 2 apartment complexes across the street from the college. **Special Academic Facilities/Equipment:** Hoffman Gallery, Centrum Gallery, and 7 specialized studios for art making. **Computers:** 6% of public computers are PCs, 94% of public computers are Macs, remote student-access to Web through college's connection.

CAMPUS LIFE

Activities: Student government, student newspaper. **Organizations:** 1 registered organization.

ADMISSIONS

Freshman Academic Profile: 85% from public high schools. SAT Math middle 50% range 383–700. SAT Critical Reading middle 50% range 400–675. ACT middle 50% range 21–25. TOEFL required of all international applicants, minimum paper TOEFL 550, minimum computer TOEFL 213. **Basis for Candidate Selection:** *Very important factors considered include:* Academic GPA, application essay, interview, talent/ability. *Important factors considered include:* Character/personal qualities, level of applicant's interest, recommendation(s), rigor of secondary school record. *Other factors considered include:* Alumni/ae relation, extracurricular activities, first generation, standardized test scores, volunteer work, work experience. **Freshman Admission Requirements:** High school diploma is required, and GED is accepted. *Academic units recommended:* 4 English, 3 math, 4 science, 2 foreign language, 1 social studies, 3 history, 2 visual arts. **Freshman Admission Statistics:** 40 applied, 82% admitted, 27% enrolled. **Transfer Admission Requirements:** High school transcript, college transcript(s), essay or personal statement. Minimum college GPA of 2.0 required. Lowest grade transferable C. **General Admission Information:** Application fee $35. Regular notification is rolling. Non-fall registration accepted. Admission may be deferred for a maximum of 1 year. Credit and/or placement offered for CEEB Advanced Placement tests.

COSTS AND FINANCIAL AID

Annual tuition $16,900. Room & board $3,600. Required fees $950. **Required Forms and Deadlines:** FAFSA. Financial aid filing deadline 3/1. **Notification of Awards:** Applicants will be notified of awards on or about 7/31. **Types of Aid:** *Need-based scholarships/grants:* Pell, SEOG, state scholarships/grants, private scholarships, the school's own gift aid. *Loans:* FFEL Subsidized Stafford, FFEL Unsubsidized Stafford, FFEL PLUS, state loans. **Student Employment:** Federal Work-Study Program available. Institutional employment available. **Financial Aid Statistics:** 50% freshmen, 73% undergrads receive need-based scholarship or grant aid. 75% freshmen, 78% undergrads receive need-based self-help aid. 65% freshmen, 80% undergrads receive any aid.

OREGON HEALTH SCIENCES UNIVERSITY

3181 SW Sam Jackson Park Road, L-109, Portland, OR 97201-3098
Phone: 503-494-7800 **E-mail:** finaid@ohsu.edu
Fax: 503-494-4629 **Website:** www.ohsu.edu
Financial Aid Phone: 503-494-7800

This is a public school.

RATINGS

Admissions Selectivity Rating: 60*   **Fire Safety Rating:** 60*   **Green Rating:** 60*

STUDENTS AND FACULTY

Enrollment: 609. **Student Body:** 1% international. Asian 6%, Caucasian 87%, Hispanic 2%, Native American 2%.

ACADEMICS

Degrees: Associate, bachelor's, certificate, doctoral, first professional, first professional certificate, master's, post-master's certificate. **Special Study Options:** Distance learning.

FACILITIES

Housing: Single dorm (coed), dorm capacity 85, considerable housing for rent available in the local community.

CAMPUS LIFE

Organizations: 2 religious organizations.

ADMISSIONS

General Admission Information: Application fee $60. Regular application deadline 1/15.

COSTS AND FINANCIAL AID

Annual in-state tuition $4,939. Annual out-of-state tuition $20,176. Room $3,420. Required fees $2,668. Average book expense $1,444. **Types of Aid:** *Need-based scholarships/grants:* Pell, SEOG, state scholarships/grants, private scholarships, the school's own gift aid. *Loans:* Direct Subsidized Stafford, Direct Unsubsidized Stafford, Direct PLUS, Federal Perkins, Federal Nursing, college/university loans from institutional funds. **Student Employment:** Federal Work-Study Program available.

OREGON INSTITUTE OF TECHNOLOGY

3201 Campus Drive, Klamath Falls, OR 97601
Phone: 541-885-1150 **E-mail:** oit@oit.edu **CEEB Code:** 4587
Fax: 541-885-1115 **Website:** www.oit.edu **ACT Code:** 3484
Financial Aid Phone: 541-885-1280

This public school was founded in 1947. It has a 173-acre campus.

RATINGS

Admissions Selectivity Rating: 77   **Fire Safety Rating:** 60*   **Green Rating:** 60*

STUDENTS AND FACULTY

Enrollment: 2,663. **Student Body:** 44% female, 56% male, 15% out-of-state. African American 1%, Asian 5%, Caucasian 81%, Hispanic 4%, Native American 2%. **Retention and Graduation:** 69% freshmen return for sophomore year. **Faculty:** Student/faculty ratio 16:1. 126 full-time faculty, 33% hold PhDs. 100% faculty teach undergrads.

ACADEMICS

Degrees: Associate, bachelor's, certificate, master's. **Academic Requirements:** Computer literacy, English (including composition), humanities, mathematics, sciences (biological or physical), social science. **Classes:** Most classes have 10–19 students. Most lab/discussion sections have 10–19 students. **Majors with Highest Enrollment:** Computer engineering technology/technician, computer software technology/technician, mechanical engineering/mechanical technology/technician. **Disciplines with Highest Percentage of Degrees Awarded:** Health professions and related sciences 31%, engineering technologies 28%, business/marketing 17%, psychology 11%, engineering 5%. **Special Study Options:** Cooperative education program, cross-registration, distance learning, double major, dual enrollment, external degree program, internships, study abroad.

FACILITIES

Housing: Coed dorms. **Special Academic Facilities/Equipment:** Shaw Historical Library. **Computers:** 75% of public computers are PCs, network access in dorm rooms, network access in dorm lounges, online registration, online administrative functions (other than registration), remote student-access to Web through college's connection.

CAMPUS LIFE

Activities: Choral groups, pep band, radio station, student government, student newspaper, symphony orchestra, television station. **Organizations:** 30 registered organizations, 5 honor societies, 1 religious organization. 1 fraternity, 1 sorority. **Athletics (Intercollegiate):** *Men:* Baseball, basketball, cross-country, track/field (outdoor). *Women:* Basketball, cross-country, soccer, softball, track/field (outdoor), volleyball.

ADMISSIONS

Freshman Academic Profile: 25% in top 10% of high school class, 56% in top 25% of high school class, 92% in top 50% of high school class. SAT Math middle 50% range 480–600. SAT Critical Reading middle 50% range 460–570. ACT middle 50% range 21–26. TOEFL required of all international applicants, minimum paper TOEFL 520, minimum computer TOEFL 190. **Basis for Candidate Selection:** *Very important factors considered include:* Rigor of secondary school record, standardized test scores. *Other factors considered include:* Application essay, character/personal qualities, class rank, interview, recommendation(s), work experience. **Freshman Admission Requirements:** High school diploma is required, and GED is accepted. *Academic units* *required:* 4 English, 3 math, 2 science (1 science lab), 2 foreign language, 3 social studies. **Freshman Admission Statistics:** 651 applied, 88% admitted, 46% enrolled. **Transfer Admission Requirements:** College transcript(s). Minimum college GPA of 2.0 required. Lowest grade transferable D. **General Admission Information:** Application fee $50. Regular application deadline 10/1. Regular notification is rolling. Non-fall registration accepted. Admission may be deferred for a maximum of 2 years. Credit and/or placement offered for CEEB Advanced Placement tests.

COSTS AND FINANCIAL AID

Annual in-state tuition $4,590. Out-of-state tuition $14,760. Room & board $6,480. Required fees $1,329. Average book expense $1,000. **Required Forms and Deadlines:** FAFSA. Financial aid filing deadline 3/1. **Notification of Awards:** Applicants will be notified of awards on a rolling basis beginning on or about 4/1. *Types of Aid: Need-based scholarships/grants:* Pell, SEOG, state scholarships/grants, private scholarships, the school's own gift aid. *Loans:* FFEL Subsidized Stafford, FFEL Unsubsidized Stafford, FFEL PLUS, Federal Perkins, college/university loans from institutional funds. **Financial Aid Statistics:** 34% freshmen, 43% undergrads receive need-based scholarship or grant aid. 55% freshmen, 64% undergrads receive need-based self-help aid. 1 freshmen, 16 undergrads receive athletic scholarships. 89% freshmen, 86% undergrads receive any aid.

OREGON STATE UNIVERSITY

104 Kerr Administration Building, Corvallis, OR 97331-2106
Phone: 541-737-4411 **E-mail:** osuadmit@oregonstate.edu **CEEB Code:** 4586
Fax: 541-737-2482 **Website:** http://oregonstate.edu
Financial Aid Phone: 541-737-2241

This public school was founded in 1858. It has a 573-acre campus.

RATINGS

Admissions Selectivity Rating: 76   **Fire Safety Rating:** 77   **Green Rating:** 97

STUDENTS AND FACULTY

Enrollment: 15,196. **Student Body:** 46% female, 54% male, 14% out-of-state, 1% international. African American 1%, Asian 8%, Caucasian 76%, Hispanic 4%, Native American 1%. **Retention and Graduation:** 81% freshmen return for sophomore year. 29% freshmen graduate within 4 years. **Faculty:** Student/faculty ratio 19:1. 766 full-time faculty, 75% hold PhDs. 100% faculty teach undergrads.

ACADEMICS

Degrees: Bachelor's, certificate, doctoral, first professional, master's, post-bachelor's certificate, post-master's certificate. **Academic Requirements:** Difference, power, and discrimination; English (including composition); fitness; humanities; mathematics; sciences (biological or physical); social science. **Classes:** Most classes have 20–29 students. Most lab/discussion sections have 20–29 students. **Majors with Highest Enrollment:** Business administration/management, health and physical education, natural sciences. **Disciplines with Highest Percentage of Degrees Awarded:** Engineering 15%, business/marketing 14%, family and consumer sciences 11%, biological/life sciences 7%, agriculture 6%. **Special Study Options:** Accelerated program, cooperative education program, cross-registration, distance learning, double major, dual enrollment, English as a second language (ESL), exchange student program (domestic), external degree program, honors program, internships, liberal arts/career combination, student-designed major, study abroad, teacher certification program.

FACILITIES

Housing: Coed dorms, apartments for married students, apartments for single students, special housing for disabled students, special housing for international students, fraternity/sorority housing, cooperative housing. **Special Academic Facilities/Equipment:** Museums, galleries, collections, exhibits of cultural and scientific materials, language lab. **Computers:** 85% of public computers are PCs, 15% of public computers are Macs, network access in dorm rooms, network access in dorm lounges, online registration, online administrative functions (other than registration), remote student-access to Web through college's connection.

CAMPUS LIFE

Activities: Choral groups, concert band, dance, drama/theater, jazz band, literary magazine, marching band, music ensembles, musical theater, opera, pep band, radio station, student government, student newspaper, student-run film society, symphony orchestra, television studio. **Organizations:** 350 registered organizations, 29 honor societies, 23 religious organizations. 24 fraternities (9% men join), 13 sororities (9% women join). **Athletics (Intercollegiate):** *Men:* Baseball, basketball, crew/rowing, football, golf, soccer, wrestling. *Women:* Basketball, crew/rowing, cross-country, golf, gymnastics, soccer, softball, swimming, track/field (outdoor), volleyball. **Environmental Initiatives:** Many areas of OSU research have large impacts on sustainability state- and nation-wide. Particularly the climate change research center (opening 2008) and the wave and wind research make global impacts. A student fee, combined with donations and administrative money, offsets about 73% of campus electrical use with a green tags purchase. Will also install large scale solar equipment summer and fall 2008. Completed in 2008, a new cogeneration facility will reduce our stationary source GHG emmissions by 38%. Signed the President's Climate Commitment.

ADMISSIONS

Freshman Academic Profile: 19% in top 10% of high school class, 47% in top 25% of high school class, 83% in top 50% of high school class. SAT Math middle 50% range 490–610. SAT Critical Reading middle 50% range 460–580. ACT middle 50% range 20–26. TOEFL required of all international applicants, minimum paper TOEFL 550, minimum computer TOEFL 213. **Basis for Candidate Selection:** *Very important factors considered include:* Academic GPA, application essay, rigor of secondary school record. *Important factors considered include:* Character/personal qualities, class rank, talent/ability, volunteer work. *Other factors considered include:* Extracurricular activities, first generation, interview, level of applicant's interest, recommendation(s), standardized test scores, work experience. **Freshman Admission Requirements:** High school diploma is required, and GED is accepted. *Academic units required:* 4 English, 3 math, 2 science (1 science lab), 2 foreign language, 3 social studies. **Freshman Admission Statistics:** 9,077 applied, 92% admitted, 35% enrolled. **Transfer Admission Requirements:** College transcript(s), statement of good standing from prior institution(s). Minimum college GPA of 2.3 required. Lowest grade transferable D. **General Admission Information:** Application fee $50. Regular application deadline 9/1. Regular notification is rolling. Non-fall registration accepted. Admission may be deferred for a maximum of 1 year. Credit and/or placement offered for CEEB Advanced Placement tests.

COSTS AND FINANCIAL AID

Required Forms and Deadlines: FAFSA. Financial aid filing deadline 2/28. **Notification of Awards:** Applicants will be notified of awards on a rolling basis beginning on or about 4/1. *Types of Aid: Need-based scholarships/grants:* Pell, SEOG, state scholarships/grants, private scholarships, the school's own gift aid. *Loans:* Direct Subsidized Stafford, Direct Unsubsidized Stafford, Direct PLUS, Federal Perkins, college/university loans from institutional funds. **Student Employment:** Federal Work-Study Program available. Institutional employment available. Off-campus job opportunities are good. **Financial Aid Statistics:** 37% freshmen, 35% undergrads receive need-based scholarship or grant aid. 43% freshmen, 45% undergrads receive need-based self-help aid. 85 freshmen, 446 undergrads receive athletic scholarships.

OTIS COLLEGE OF ART & DESIGN

9045 Lincoln Boulevard, Los Angeles, CA 90045
Phone: 310-665-6820 **E-mail:** admissions@otis.edu **CEEB Code:** 4394
Fax: 310-665-6821 **Website:** www.otis.edu **ACT Code:** 0359
Financial Aid Phone: 310-665-6880

This private school was founded in 1918. It has a 5-acre campus.

RATINGS

Admissions Selectivity Rating: 60*   **Fire Safety Rating:** 60*   **Green Rating:** 60*

STUDENTS AND FACULTY

Enrollment: 900. **Student Body:** 63% female, 37% male, 13% international. African American 3%, Asian 32%, Caucasian 36%, Hispanic 14%. **Retention and Graduation:** 75% freshmen return for sophomore year. 36% freshmen graduate within 4 years. 80% grads pursue arts and sciences degrees. **Faculty:** Student/faculty ratio 8:1. 43 full-time faculty, 63% hold PhDs.

ACADEMICS

Degrees: Bachelor's, master's. **Academic Requirements:** Arts/fine arts, computer literacy, English (including composition), mathematics, sciences (biological or physical), social science. **Classes:** Most classes have 10–19 students. **Majors with Highest Enrollment:** Animation, interactive technology, video graphics and special effects, fashion/apparel design, graphic design. **Disciplines with Highest Percentage of Degrees Awarded:** Visual and performing arts 100%. **Special Study Options:** English as a second language (ESL), exchange student program (domestic), honors program, independent study, internships, study abroad.

FACILITIES
Housing: Apartments for single students. **Special Academic Facilities/ Equipment:** Art gallery, student gallery, woodshop, metal shop, photo lab, digital media lab, printmaking lab, letterpress lab. **Computers:** 20% of public computers are PCs, 80% of public computers are Macs, online administrative functions (other than registration).

CAMPUS LIFE
Activities: Literary magazine, student government, student newspaper. **Organizations:** 7 registered organizations.

ADMISSIONS
Freshman Academic Profile: SAT Math middle 50% range 440–580. SAT Critical Reading middle 50% range 420–550. ACT middle 50% range 17–22. TOEFL required of all international applicants, minimum paper TOEFL 550, minimum computer TOEFL 213. **Basis for Candidate Selection:** *Very important factors considered include:* Rigor of secondary school record, talent/ability. *Important factors considered include:* Application essay, standardized test scores. *Other factors considered include:* Alumni/ae relation, character/personal qualities, extracurricular activities, interview, recommendation(s), volunteer work, work experience. **Freshman Admission Requirements:** High school diploma is required, and GED is accepted. *Academic units required:* 4 English, 3 math, 2 science (1 science lab), 1 social studies, 2 history. *Academic units recommended:* 4 English, 4 math, 4 science (4 science labs), 2 foreign language, 2 social studies, 3 history. **Freshman Admission Statistics:** 695 applied, 58% admitted, 30% enrolled. **Transfer Admission Requirements:** High school transcript, college transcript(s), essay or personal statement, statement of good standing from prior institution(s). Minimum college GPA of 2.5 required. Lowest grade transferable C. **General Admission Information:** Application fee $50. Regular notification is rolling. Non-fall registration accepted. Common Application not accepted. Credit offered for CEEB Advanced Placement tests.

COSTS AND FINANCIAL AID
Annual tuition $25,710. Required fees $600. Average book expense $2,400. **Required Forms and Deadlines:** FAFSA, state aid form. Financial aid filing deadline 2/15. **Notification of Awards:** Applicants will be notified of awards on or about 3/1. **Types of Aid:** *Need-based scholarships/grants:* Pell, SEOG, state scholarships/grants, private scholarships, the school's own gift aid. *Loans:* FFEL Subsidized Stafford, FFEL Unsubsidized Stafford, FFEL PLUS. **Student Employment:** Federal Work-Study Program available. Institutional employment available. Off-campus job opportunities are excellent. **Financial Aid Statistics:** 87% freshmen, 69% undergrads receive need-based scholarship or grant aid. 72% freshmen, 61% undergrads receive need-based self-help aid. 42% freshmen, 44% undergrads receive any aid.

OTTAWA UNIVERSITY

1001 S. Cedar Street #17, Ottawa, KS 66067-3399
Phone: 785-242-5200 **E-mail:** admiss@ottawa.edu **CEEB Code:** 6547
Fax: 785-229-1008 **Website:** www.ottawa.edu **ACT Code:** 1446
Financial Aid Phone: 785-242-5200

This private school was founded in 1865. It has a 64-acre campus.

RATINGS
Admissions Selectivity Rating: 75   **Fire Safety Rating:** 60*   **Green Rating:** 60*

STUDENTS AND FACULTY
Enrollment: 490. **Student Body:** 42% female, 58% male, 41% out-of-state, 7% international (11 countries represented). African American 11%, Asian 1%, Caucasian 84%, Hispanic 2%, Native American 2%. **Retention and Graduation:** 68% freshmen return for sophomore year. 17% freshmen graduate within 4 years. 15% grads go on to further study within 1 year. 13% grads pursue arts and sciences degrees. 26% grads pursue business degrees. 1% grads pursue law degrees. 2% grads pursue medical degrees. **Faculty:** 100% faculty teach undergrads.

ACADEMICS
Degrees: Bachelor's. **Academic Requirements:** Arts/fine arts, English (including composition), history, mathematics, sciences (biological or physical), social science. **Special Study Options:** Double major, English as a second language (ESL), internships, student-designed major, teacher certification program.

FACILITIES
Housing: Men's dorms, women's dorms, apartments for married students. **Special Academic Facilities/Equipment:** Art collection, FM radio station. **Computers:** 100% of public computers are PCs, network access in dorm rooms, network access in dorm lounges, online registration, remote student-access to Web through college's connection.

CAMPUS LIFE
Activities: Choral groups, concert band, dance, drama/theater, jazz band, music ensembles, pep band, radio station, student government, student newspaper, yearbook. **Organizations:** 33 registered organizations, 3 honor societies, 4 religious organizations. 2 fraternities, 3 sororities. **Athletics (Intercollegiate):** *Men:* Baseball, basketball, cheerleading, football, golf, soccer, track/field (indoor), track/field (outdoor). *Women:* Basketball, cheerleading, soccer, softball, track/field (indoor), track/field (outdoor), volleyball.

ADMISSIONS
Freshman Academic Profile: 7% in top 10% of high school class, 23% in top 25% of high school class, 73% in top 50% of high school class. 98% from public high schools. SAT Math middle 50% range 500–600. SAT Critical Reading middle 50% range 500–600. ACT middle 50% range 18–23. TOEFL required of all international applicants, minimum paper TOEFL 550. **Basis for Candidate Selection:** *Very important factors considered include:* Class rank, rigor of secondary school record, standardized test scores. *Other factors considered include:* Alumni/ae relation, application essay, character/personal qualities, extracurricular activities, interview, recommendation(s), religious affiliation/commitment, talent/ability. **Freshman Admission Requirements:** High school diploma is required, and GED is accepted. *Academic units recommended:* 4 English, 3 math, 2 science, 2 foreign language, 1 social studies, 2 history, 2 academic electives. **Freshman Admission Statistics:** 630 applied, 68% admitted, 32% enrolled. **Transfer Admission Requirements:** College transcript(s). Minimum college GPA of 2.5 required. Lowest grade transferable D. **General Admission Information:** Application fee $15. Regular application deadline 7/15. Regular notification is rolling. Non-fall registration accepted. Common Application accepted. Credit and/or placement offered for CEEB Advanced Placement tests.

COSTS AND FINANCIAL AID
Annual tuition $10,750. Room & board $4,640. Required fees $210. Average book expense $600. **Required Forms and Deadlines:** FAFSA, institution's own financial aid form, state aid form. **Types of Aid:** *Need-based scholarships/grants:* Pell, SEOG, state scholarships/grants, private scholarships, the school's own gift aid. *Loans:* FFEL Subsidized Stafford, FFEL Unsubsidized Stafford, FFEL PLUS, Federal Perkins, Federal Nursing, college/university loans from institutional funds. **Student Employment:** Federal Work-Study Program available. Institutional employment available. Off-campus job opportunities are excellent. **Financial Aid Statistics:** Highest amount earned per year from on-campus jobs $1,500.

OTTERBEIN COLLEGE

Office of Admission, One Otterbein College, Westerville, OH 43081
Phone: 614-823-1500 **E-mail:** uotterb@otterbein.edu **CEEB Code:** 1597
Fax: 614-823-1200 **Website:** www.otterbein.edu **ACT Code:** 3318
Financial Aid Phone: 614-823-1502

This private school, affiliated with the Methodist Church, was founded in 1847. It has a 140-acre campus.

RATINGS
Admissions Selectivity Rating: 73   **Fire Safety Rating:** 60*   **Green Rating:** 60*

STUDENTS AND FACULTY
Enrollment: 2,804. **Student Body:** 8% out-of-state. African American 7%, Asian 2%, Caucasian 88%, Hispanic 2%. **Retention and Graduation:** 92% freshmen return for sophomore year. **Faculty:** Student/faculty ratio 12:1. 159 full-time faculty, 91% hold PhDs. 100% faculty teach undergrads.

ACADEMICS
Degrees: Bachelor's, master's. **Academic Requirements:** Arts/fine arts,

computer literacy, English (including composition), foreign languages, history, humanities, mathematics, philosophy, sciences (biological or physical), social science. **Majors with Highest Enrollment:** Business administration/management, education, radio and television. **Disciplines with Highest Percentage of Degrees Awarded:** Business/marketing 18%, education 15%, communications/journalism 14%, visual and performing arts 13%, health professions and related sciences 10%. **Special Study Options:** Accelerated program, cooperative education program, cross-registration, double major, dual enrollment, exchange student program (domestic), honors program, internships, liberal arts/career combination, student-designed major, study abroad, teacher certification program, weekend college.

FACILITIES

Housing: Coed dorms, men's dorms, women's dorms, apartments for single students, fraternity/sorority housing, theme housing. **Special Academic Facilities/Equipment:** Language lab, horse stable, observatory and planetarium, Celestron 8-inch and 14-inch telescopes, 3 art galleries. **Computers:** 100% of public computers are PCs, network access in dorm rooms, network access in dorm lounges, online registration, online administrative functions (other than registration), remote student-access to Web through college's connection.

CAMPUS LIFE

Activities: Choral groups, concert band, dance, drama/theater, jazz band, literary magazine, marching band, music ensembles, musical theater, opera, pep band, radio station, student government, student newspaper, symphony orchestra, television station, yearbook. **Organizations:** 100 registered organizations. 7 fraternities (28% men join), 6 sororities (28% women join). **Athletics (Intercollegiate):** *Men:* Baseball, basketball, cheerleading, cross-country, equestrian sports, football, golf, soccer, tennis, track/field (indoor), track/field (outdoor). *Women:* Basketball, cheerleading, cross-country, equestrian sports, golf, soccer, softball, tennis, track/field (indoor), track/field (outdoor), volleyball.

ADMISSIONS

Freshman Academic Profile: 24% in top 10% of high school class, 55% in top 25% of high school class, 85% in top 50% of high school class. TOEFL required of all international applicants, minimum paper TOEFL 500, minimum computer TOEFL 193. **Basis for Candidate Selection:** *Important factors considered include:* Class rank, rigor of secondary school record, standardized test scores. *Other factors considered include:* Alumni/ae relation, application essay, character/personal qualities, extracurricular activities, interview, racial/ethnic status, recommendation(s), talent/ability, volunteer work, work experience. **Freshman Admission Requirements:** High school diploma is required, and GED is accepted. *Academic units recommended:* 4 English, 3 math, 3 science, 2 foreign language, 3 social studies, 2 performing arts. **Freshman Admission Statistics:** 2,776 applied, 77% admitted, 31% enrolled. **Transfer Admission Requirements:** College transcript(s). Minimum college GPA of 2.5 required. Lowest grade transferable C-. **General Admission Information:** Application fee $25. Regular notification is rolling. Non-fall registration accepted. Admission may be deferred for a maximum of 1 year. Credit and/or placement offered for CEEB Advanced Placement tests.

COSTS AND FINANCIAL AID

Annual tuition $26,319. Room and board $7,461. Average book expense $700. **Required Forms and Deadlines:** FAFSA. Financial aid filing deadline 4/1. **Types of Aid:** *Need-based scholarships/grants:* Pell, SEOG, state scholarships/grants, private scholarships, the school's own gift aid. *Loans:* Direct Subsidized Stafford, Direct Unsubsidized Stafford, Direct PLUS, Federal Perkins. **Student Employment:** Federal Work-Study Program available. Institutional employment available. Off-campus job opportunities are excellent. **Financial Aid Statistics:** Highest amount earned per year from on-campus jobs $1,800.

See page 1306.

OUACHITA BAPTIST UNIVERSITY

410 Ouachita Street, Arkadelphia, AR 71998-0001
Phone: 870-245-5110 **E-mail:** admissions@alpha.obu.edu **CEEB Code:** 6549
Fax: 870-245-5500 **Website:** www.obu.edu **ACT Code:** 0134
Financial Aid Phone: 870-245-5570

This private school, affiliated with the Southern Baptist Church, was founded in 1886. It has a 200-acre campus.

RATINGS

Admissions Selectivity Rating: 86   **Fire Safety Rating:** 83   **Green Rating:** 66

STUDENTS AND FACULTY

Enrollment: 1,420. **Student Body:** 55% female, 45% male, 44% out-of-state, 4% international. African American 6%, Caucasian 88%, Hispanic 2%. **Retention and Graduation:** 75% freshmen return for sophomore year. 41% freshmen graduate within 4 years. 33% grads go on to further study within 1 year. 8% grads pursue arts and sciences degrees. 4% grads pursue business degrees. 4% grads pursue law degrees. 9% grads pursue medical degrees. **Faculty:** 100% faculty teach undergrads.

ACADEMICS

Degrees: Bachelor's, terminal. **Academic Requirements:** Arts/fine arts, English (including composition), foreign languages, history, humanities, kinesiology, mathematics, philosophy, religion, sciences (biological or physical), social science. **Special Study Options:** Cross-registration, distance learning, double major, English as a second language (ESL), honors program, independent study, internships, study abroad, teacher certification program.

FACILITIES

Housing: Men's dorms, women's dorms, apartments for married students, apartments for single students. **Special Academic Facilities/Equipment:** Historical archives, Senator John McClellan collection, language lab, TV studio.

CAMPUS LIFE

Activities: Choral groups, concert band, drama/theater, jazz band, literary magazine, marching band, music ensembles, musical theater, opera, pep band, student government, student newspaper, yearbook. **Organizations:** 60 registered organizations, 8 honor societies, 4 religious organizations. 5 fraternities (20% men join), 4 sororities (30% women join). **Athletics (Intercollegiate):** *Men:* Baseball, basketball, cross-country, diving, football, golf, soccer, softball, swimming, tennis. *Women:* Basketball, cross-country, diving, soccer, softball, swimming, tennis, volleyball. **Environmental Initiatives:** Faculty and staff initiatives for reduction of utility use. Recycling.

ADMISSIONS

Freshman Academic Profile: 32% in top 10% of high school class, 63% in top 25% of high school class, 88% in top 50% of high school class. 95% from public high schools. SAT Math middle 50% range 480–610. SAT Critical Reading middle 50% range 480–630. ACT middle 50% range 20–27. TOEFL required of all international applicants, minimum paper TOEFL 550. **Basis for Candidate Selection:** *Very important factors considered include:* Academic GPA, rigor of secondary school record, standardized test scores. **Freshman Admission Requirements:** High school diploma is required, and GED is accepted. *Academic units required:* 4 English, 2 math, 2 science, 1 social studies, 2 history, 4 academic electives. *Academic units recommended:* 4 English, 3 math, 3 science, 2 foreign language, 1 social studies, 2 history, 4 academic electives. **Freshman Admission Statistics:** 1,058 applied, 58% admitted, 60% enrolled. **Transfer Admission Requirements:** College transcript(s), statement of good standing from prior institution(s). Minimum college GPA of 2.0 required. Lowest grade transferable C. **General Admission Information:** Application fee $50. Regular notification is rolling. Non-fall registration accepted. Admission may be deferred for a maximum of 1 year. Common Application not accepted. Credit offered for CEEB Advanced Placement tests.

COSTS AND FINANCIAL AID

Annual tuition $17,560. Room and board $5,400. Required fees $390. Average book expense $950. **Required Forms and Deadlines:** Institution's own financial aid form. Financial aid filing deadline 6/1. **Notification of Awards:** Applicants will be notified of awards on a rolling basis beginning on or about 12/1. **Types of Aid:** *Need-based scholarships/grants:* Pell, SEOG, state scholarships/grants, private scholarships, the school's own gift aid. *Loans:* FFEL Subsidized Stafford, FFEL Unsubsidized Stafford, FFEL PLUS, Federal Perkins, college/university loans from institutional funds. **Student Employment:** Federal Work-Study Program available. Off-campus job opportunities are fair. **Financial Aid Statistics:** 47% freshmen, 45% undergrads receive need-based scholarship or grant aid. 25% freshmen, 32% undergrads receive need-based self-help aid. 25 freshmen, 83 undergrads receive athletic scholarships. Highest amount earned per year from on-campus jobs $1,400.

OUR LADY OF HOLY CROSS COLLEGE

4123 Woodland Drive, New Orleans, LA 70131
Phone: 504-398-2175 **E-mail:** kkopecky@olhcc.edu **CEEB Code:** 6002
Fax: 504-391-2421 **Website:** www.olhcc.edu **ACT Code:** 1574
Financial Aid Phone: 504-398-216

This private school, affiliated with the Roman Catholic Church, was founded in 1916. It has a 40-acre campus.

RATINGS
Admissions Selectivity Rating: 60*   **Fire Safety Rating:** 60*   **Green Rating:** 60*

STUDENTS AND FACULTY
Enrollment: 1,199. **Student Body:** 78% female, 22% male. African American 13%, Asian 3%, Caucasian 73%, Hispanic 5%. **Retention and Graduation:** 63% freshmen return for sophomore year. **Faculty:** Student/faculty ratio 19:1. 38 full-time faculty, 61% hold PhDs.

ACADEMICS
Degrees: Associate, bachelor's, master's, post-bachelor's certificate. **Academic Requirements:** Arts/fine arts, computer literacy, English (including composition), foreign languages, history, humanities, mathematics, philosophy, sciences (biological or physical), social science. **Classes:** Most classes have 20–29 students. **Majors with Highest Enrollment:** Education, nursing/registered nurse training (ASN, BSN, MSN, RN). **Disciplines with Highest Percentage of Degrees Awarded:** Health professions and related sciences 30%, education 25%, business/marketing 18%, psychology 12%, liberal arts/general studies 6%. **Special Study Options:** Cross-registration, distance learning, double major, dual enrollment, exchange student program (domestic), independent study, internships, liberal arts/career combination, study abroad, teacher certification program.

FACILITIES
Computers: 100% of public computers are PCs.

CAMPUS LIFE
Activities: Choral groups, drama/theater, literary magazine, student government, student newspaper, yearbook. **Organizations:** 18 registered organizations, 5 honor societies.

ADMISSIONS
Freshman Academic Profile: 38% from public high schools. TOEFL required of all international applicants, minimum paper TOEFL 500. **Basis for Candidate Selection:** *Very important factors considered include:* Rigor of secondary school record, standardized test scores. *Important factors considered include:* Class rank, recommendation(s). *Other factors considered include:* Racial/ethnic status. **Freshman Admission Requirements:** High school diploma is required, and GED is accepted. *Academic units required:* 4 English, 2 math, 2 science, 2 foreign language, 3 social studies, 3 academic electives. **Freshman Admission Statistics:** 320 applied, 97% admitted, 42% enrolled. **Transfer Admission Requirements:** College transcript(s). Minimum college GPA of 2.0 required. Lowest grade transferable C. **General Admission Information:** Application fee $15. Non-fall registration accepted. Admission may be deferred for a maximum of 1 year. Common Application accepted. Placement offered for CEEB Advanced Placement tests.

COSTS AND FINANCIAL AID
Annual tuition $5,160. Required fees $400. **Required Forms and Deadlines:** FAFSA, institution's own financial aid form. Financial aid filing deadline 4/15. **Notification of Awards:** Applicants will be notified of awards on or about 7/2. **Types of Aid:** *Need-based scholarships/grants:* Pell, SEOG, state scholarships/grants, private scholarships, the school's own gift aid. *Loans:* FFEL Subsidized Stafford, FFEL Unsubsidized Stafford, FFEL PLUS. **Student Employment:** Federal Work-Study Program available. Off-campus job opportunities are good. **Financial Aid Statistics:** 29% freshmen, 41% undergrads receive need-based scholarship or grant aid. 10% freshmen, 36% undergrads receive need-based self-help aid. Highest amount earned per year from on-campus jobs $1,238. 4.

OUR LADY OF THE LAKE UNIVERSITY (OLLU)

Admissions Office, 411 South West 24th Street, San Antonio, TX 78207-4689
Phone: 210-434-6711 **E-mail:** admission@lake.ollusa.edu **CEEB Code:** 6550
Fax: 210-431-4036 **Website:** www.ollusa.edu **ACT Code:** 4140
Financial Aid Phone: 210-434-3960

This private school was founded in 1895. It has a 75-acre campus.

RATINGS
Admissions Selectivity Rating: 60*   **Fire Safety Rating:** 60*   **Green Rating:** 60*

STUDENTS AND FACULTY
Enrollment: 1,792. **Student Body:** 76% female, 24% male, 2% out-of-state. African American 8%, Caucasian 15%, Hispanic 71%. **Retention and Graduation:** 62% freshmen return for sophomore year. 14% freshmen graduate within 4 years. 30% grads go on to further study within 1 year. **Faculty:** 118 full-time faculty, 76% hold PhDs.

ACADEMICS
Degrees: Bachelor's, doctoral, master's. **Academic Requirements:** Arts/fine arts, computer literacy, English (including composition), history, humanities, mathematics, philosophy, religion, sciences (biological or physical), social science. **Classes:** Most classes have fewer than 10 students. **Disciplines with Highest Percentage of Degrees Awarded:** Business/marketing 22%, psychology 16%, public administration and social services 8%, liberal arts/general studies 8%, education 8%, computer and information sciences 7%, social sciences 7%, family and consumer sciences 5%, biological/life sciences 5%. **Special Study Options:** Cooperative education program, cross-registration, distance learning, double major, dual enrollment, English as a second language (ESL), independent study, internships, liberal arts/career combination, service learning, study abroad, teacher certification program, weekend college.

FACILITIES
Housing: Coed dorms, men's dorms, women's dorms, special housing for disabled students. **Special Academic Facilities/Equipment:** Lab school for children with language and learning disabilities, elementary demonstration school, intercultural institute for training and research, language lab. **Computers:** 10% of public computers are PCs, network access in dorm lounges, remote student-access to Web through college's connection.

CAMPUS LIFE
Activities: Choral groups, dance, drama/theater, jazz band, marching band, music ensembles, musical theater, student government, student newspaper, symphony orchestra, television station.

ADMISSIONS
Freshman Academic Profile: 75% from public high schools. SAT Math middle 50% range 400–490. SAT Critical Reading middle 50% range 410–500. ACT middle 50% range 17–20. TOEFL required of all international applicants, minimum paper TOEFL 525. **Basis for Candidate Selection:** *Very important factors considered include:* Academic GPA, rigor of secondary school record, standardized test scores. *Important factors considered include:* Class rank. *Other factors considered include:* Alumni/ae relation, application essay, character/personal qualities, extracurricular activities, first generation, interview, recommendation(s), talent/ability, volunteer work, work experience. **Freshman Admission Requirements:** High school diploma is required, and GED is accepted. *Academic units required:* 4 English, 2 math, 2 science (2 science labs), 3 foreign language, 3 social studies, 3 academic electives. *Academic units recommended:* 3 math, 2 academic electives. **Freshman Admission Statistics:** 2,214 applied, 53% admitted, 23% enrolled. **Transfer Admission Requirements:** College transcript(s). Minimum college GPA of 2.0 required. Lowest grade transferable D. **General Admission Information:** Application fee $25. Regular application deadline 7/15. Admission may be deferred for a maximum of 1 year. Common Application accepted. Credit and/or placement offered for CEEB Advanced Placement tests.

COSTS AND FINANCIAL AID
Annual tuition $17,048. Room & board $5,384. Required fees $258. Average book expense $1,000. **Required Forms and Deadlines:** FAFSA. **Notification of Awards:** Applicants will be notified of awards on a rolling basis beginning on or about 4/1. **Types of Aid:** *Need-based scholarships/grants:* Pell, SEOG, state scholarships/grants, private scholarships, the school's own gift aid. *Loans:* FFEL Subsidized Stafford, FFEL Unsubsidized Stafford, FFEL PLUS, Federal Perkins, state loans, private loans. **Student Employment:** Federal Work-Study Program available. Institutional employment available. Off-campus job opportunities are good. **Financial Aid Statistics:** Highest amount earned per year from on-campus jobs $1,206.

OZARK CHRISTIAN COLLEGE

1111 North Main Street, Joplin, MO 64801
Phone: 417-624-2518 **E-mail:** occadmin@occ.edu
Fax: 417-624-0090 **Website:** www.occ.edu **ACT Code:** 2279
Financial Aid Phone: 800-299-4622

This private school, affiliated with the Christian (nondenominational) Church, was founded in 1942. It has a 122-acre campus.

RATINGS

Admissions Selectivity Rating: 60*   **Fire Safety Rating:** 60*   **Green Rating:** 60*

STUDENTS AND FACULTY

Enrollment: 772. **Student Body:** 48% female, 52% male, 2% international. African American 2%, Caucasian 92%, Hispanic 2%, Native American 2%. **Retention and Graduation:** 66% freshmen return for sophomore year. 12% freshmen graduate within 4 years. **Faculty:** Student/faculty ratio 19:1. 29 full-time faculty, 17% hold PhDs.

ACADEMICS

Degrees: Associate, bachelor's, certificate. **Academic Requirements:** English (including composition), history, humanities, philosophy. **Majors with Highest Enrollment:** Bible/biblical studies, pastoral studies/counseling, youth ministry. **Special Study Options:** Distance learning, double major, internships.

FACILITIES

Housing: Men's dorms, women's dorms. **Computers:** 100% of public computers are PCs, network access in dorm rooms, remote student-access to Web through college's connection.

CAMPUS LIFE

Activities: Choral groups, drama/theater, music ensembles, radio station, yearbook. **Athletics (Intercollegiate):** *Men:* Basketball, cheerleading, soccer. *Women:* Basketball, cheerleading.

ADMISSIONS

Freshman Academic Profile: TOEFL required of all international applicants, minimum paper TOEFL 550. **Basis for Candidate Selection:** *Very important factors considered include:* Character/personal qualities. *Important factors considered include:* Recommendation(s). *Other factors considered include:* Religious affiliation/commitment, rigor of secondary school record, standardized test scores, talent/ability, volunteer work. **Freshman Admission Requirements:** High school diploma is required, and GED is accepted. *Academic units required:* 3 English, 2 math, 2 science, 1 history, 7 academic electives. **Freshman Admission Statistics:** 332 applied, 100% admitted, 65% enrolled. **Transfer Admission Requirements:** College transcript(s), essay or personal statement, standardized test score, statement of good standing from prior institution(s). Lowest grade transferable C. **General Admission Information:** Application fee $30. Regular notification after full acceptance. Non-fall registration accepted. Common Application not accepted.

COSTS AND FINANCIAL AID

Annual tuition $10,920. Room & board $3,970. Required fees $590. Average book expense $300. **Student Employment:** Federal Work-Study Program available. Institutional employment available. Off-campus job opportunities are excellent. **Financial Aid Statistics:** Highest amount earned per year from on-campus jobs $1,236.

PACE UNIVERSITY

1 Pace Plaza, New York, NY 10038
Phone: 212-346-1323 **E-mail:** Infoctr@pace.edu **CEEB Code:** 2635
Fax: 212-346-1040 **Website:** www.pace.edu **ACT Code:** 2852
Financial Aid Phone: 212-346-1300

This private school was founded in 1906. It has a 1-acre campus.

RATINGS

Admissions Selectivity Rating: 77   **Fire Safety Rating:** 82   **Green Rating:** 71

STUDENTS AND FACULTY

Enrollment: 7,407. **Student Body:** 61% female, 39% male, 28% out-of-state, 3% international (113 countries represented). African American 11%, Asian 10%, Caucasian 47%, Hispanic 11%. **Retention and Graduation:** 73% freshmen return for sophomore year. 39% freshmen graduate within 4 years. **Faculty:** Student/faculty ratio 13:1. 460 full-time faculty, 88% hold PhDs. 76% faculty teach undergrads.

ACADEMICS

Degrees: Associate, bachelor's, certificate, doctoral, first professional certificate, master's, post-bachelor's certificate, post-master's certificate. **Academic Requirements:** Arts/fine arts, computer literacy, English (including composition), foreign languages, history, humanities, mathematics, philosophy, sciences (biological or physical), social science, public speaking and civic engagement. **Classes:** Most classes have 10–19 students. Most lab/discussion sections have fewer than 10 students. **Majors with Highest Enrollment:** Accounting; finance; information science/studies. **Disciplines with Highest Percentage of Degrees Awarded:** Business/marketing 43%, health professions and related sciences 11%, communications/journalism 10%, psychology 6%, social sciences 4%, education 4%. **Special Study Options:** Accelerated program, cooperative education program, cross-registration, distance learning, double major, dual enrollment, English as a second language (ESL), honors program, independent study, internships, study abroad, teacher certification program, evening and freshman studies programs, pre-freshman summer program, learning communities and service learning.

FACILITIES

Housing: Coed dorms, apartments for single students, apartment style for 3–4 upperclassmen. **Special Academic Facilities/Equipment:** Laboratory theater, communication center, language center, center for the arts, art gallery, English language institute. **Computers:** 99% of public computers are PCs, 1% of public computers are Macs, network access in dorm rooms, online registration, remote student-access to Web through college's connection.

CAMPUS LIFE

Activities: Choral groups, dance, drama/theater, literary magazine, musical theater, radio station, student government, student newspaper, student-run film society, television station, yearbook. **Organizations:** 74 registered organizations, 15 honor societies, 4 religious organizations. 7 fraternities (5% men join), 7 sororities (5% women join). **Athletics (Intercollegiate):** *Men:* Baseball, basketball, cross-country, football, golf, lacrosse, swimming, tennis, track/field (indoor), track/field (outdoor). *Women:* Basketball, cheerleading, cross-country, equestrian sports, golf, soccer, softball, swimming, tennis, track/field (indoor), track/field (outdoor), volleyball. **Environmental Initiatives:** Successfully building a community commitment to sustainability that encompasses students, faculty, and staff in part through sustainability fellowships. Including environmental goals for waste diversion, reduction of water and electricity consumption, LEED building and carbon neutrality into the campus master plan. PLU is in the leadership circle for the President's Climate Commitment and is planning to meet all goals and deadlines of that commitment. **Environmental Initiatives:** Environmental Law Program—Pace Law School. Environmental Sciences Program at Dyson College of Arts & Science.

ADMISSIONS

Freshman Academic Profile: 19% in top 10% of high school class, 47% in top 25% of high school class, 86% in top 50% of high school class. 70% from public high schools. SAT Math middle 50% range 490–590. SAT Critical Reading middle 50% range 480–580. ACT middle 50% range 20–26. TOEFL required of all international applicants, minimum paper TOEFL 570, minimum computer TOEFL 230. **Basis for Candidate Selection:** *Very important factors considered include:* Rigor of secondary school record, standardized test scores. *Important factors considered include:* Academic GPA, class rank. *Other factors considered include:* Alumni/ae relation, application essay, character/personal qualities, extracurricular activities, recommendation(s), talent/ability, volunteer work, work experience. **Freshman Admission Requirements:** High school diploma is required, and GED is accepted. *Academic units required:* 4 English, 3 math, 2 science, (2 science labs), 2 foreign language, 1 social studies, 2 history, 2 academic electives. *Academic units recommended:* 4 English, 4 math, 2 science (2 science labs), 3 foreign language, 2 social studies, 3 history, 2 academic electives. **Freshman Admission Statistics:** 8,167 applied, 75% admitted, 19% enrolled. **Transfer Admission Requirements:** College transcript(s), statement of good standing from prior institution(s). Minimum college GPA of 2.5 required. Lowest grade transferable C. **General Admission Information:** Application fee $45. Regular notification is rolling. Nonfall registration accepted. Admission may be deferred for a maximum of 1 year. Credit offered for CEEB Advanced Placement tests.

COSTS AND FINANCIAL AID

Annual tuition $30,632. Room and board $11,180. Required fees $743. Average book expense $800. **Required Forms and Deadlines:** FAFSA, state aid form. Financial aid filing deadline 2/15. **Notification of Awards:** Applicants will be notified of awards on a rolling basis beginning on or about 2/28. **Types of Aid:** *Need-based scholarships/grants:* Pell, SEOG, state scholarships/grants, private scholarships, the school's own gift aid. *Loans:* Direct Subsidized Stafford, Direct Unsubsidized Stafford, Direct PLUS, Federal Perkins, Federal Nursing.

Financial Aid Statistics: 67% freshmen, 64% undergrads receive need-based scholarship or grant aid. 62% freshmen, 64% undergrads receive need-based self-help aid. 8 freshmen, 18 undergrads receive athletic scholarships. 90% freshmen, 91% undergrads receive any aid. Highest amount earned per year from on-campus jobs $3,600.

PACE UNIVERSITY— PLEASANTVILLE/BRIARCLIFF

861 Bedford Road, Pleasantville, NY 10570
Phone: 914-773-3746 **E-mail:** infoctr@pace.edu **CEEB Code:** 2685
Fax: 914-773-3851 **Website:** www.pace.edu **ACT Code:** 2855
Financial Aid Phone: 914-773-3486

This private school was founded in 1906. It has a 198-acre campus.

RATINGS
Admissions Selectivity Rating: 70   **Fire Safety Rating:** 60*   **Green Rating:** 60*

STUDENTS AND FACULTY
Enrollment: 2,760. **Student Body:** 59% female, 41% male, 11% out-of-state, 3% international (42 countries represented). African American 9%, Asian 5%, Caucasian 56%, Hispanic 9%. **Retention and Graduation:** 75% freshmen return for sophomore year. 37% freshmen graduate within 4 years. **Faculty:** Student/faculty ratio 15:1. 151 full-time faculty, 79% hold PhDs.

ACADEMICS
Degrees: Associate, bachelor's, certificate, diploma, doctoral, first professional certificate, first professional, master's, post-bachelor's certificate, post-master's certificate. **Academic Requirements:** Arts/fine arts, computer literacy, English (including composition), foreign languages, history, humanities, mathematics, philosophy, sciences (biological or physical), social science, speech. **Classes:** Most classes have 20–29 students. Most lab/discussion sections have fewer than 10 students. **Majors with Highest Enrollment:** Accounting, computer and information sciences, finance. **Disciplines with Highest Percentage of Degrees Awarded:** Business/marketing 42%, computer and information sciences 17%, health professions and related sciences 9%, psychology 5%, communication technologies 4%, education 4%, social sciences 4%. **Special Study Options:** Accelerated program, cooperative education program, cross-registration, distance learning, double major, dual enrollment, English as a second language (ESL), evening and freshman studies program, honors program, independent study, internships, pre-freshman summer program, study abroad, teacher certification program

FACILITIES
Housing: Coed dorms, apartments for single students, apartment style for upperclassmen. **Special Academic Facilities/Equipment:** Center for the arts, art gallery, laboratory theater, communication center, language center, environmental center, English language institute. **Computers:** 20% of public computers are PCs, network access in dorm rooms, remote student-access to Web through college's connection.

CAMPUS LIFE
Activities: Choral groups, dance, drama/theater, literary magazine, musical theater, radio station, student government, student newspaper, student-run film society, television station, yearbook. **Organizations:** 40 registered organizations, 7 honor societies, 4 religious organizations. 7 fraternities (4% men join), 6 sororities (4% women join). **Athletics (Intercollegiate):** *Men:* Baseball, basketball, cross-country, equestrian sports, football, golf, lacrosse, tennis, track/field (indoor), track/field (outdoor). *Women:* Basketball, cross-country, equestrian sports, golf, soccer, softball, tennis, track/field (indoor), track/field (outdoor), volleyball.

ADMISSIONS
Freshman Academic Profile: 20% in top 10% of high school class, 52% in top 25% of high school class, 86% in top 50% of high school class. 70% from public high schools. SAT Math middle 50% range 460–580. SAT Critical Reading middle 50% range 450–550. ACT middle 50% range 19–23. TOEFL required of all international applicants, minimum paper TOEFL 450. **Basis for Candidate Selection:** *Very important factors considered include:* Rigor of secondary school record, standardized test scores. *Important factors considered include:* Class rank. *Other factors considered include:* Alumni/ae relation, application essay, character/personal qualities, extracurricular activities, recommendation(s), talent/ability, volunteer work, work experience. **Freshman Admission Requirements:** High school diploma is required, and GED is accepted. *Academic units required:* 4 English, 3 math, 2 science (2 science labs), 2 foreign language, 1 social studies, 2 history, 2 academic electives.

Academic units recommended: 4 English, 4 math, 2 science (2 science labs), 3 foreign language, 2 social studies, 2 history, 3 academic electives. **Freshman Admission Statistics:** 2,051 applied, 92% admitted, 30% enrolled. **Transfer Admission Requirements:** High school transcript, college transcript(s). Minimum college GPA of 2.5 required. Lowest grade transferable C. **General Admission Information:** Application fee $45. Regular notification is rolling. Non-fall registration accepted. Admission may be deferred for a maximum of 1 year. Common Application accepted. Credit offered for CEEB Advanced Placement tests.

COSTS AND FINANCIAL AID
Annual tuition $16,650. Room & board $7,070. Required fees $380. Average book expense $720. **Required Forms and Deadlines:** FAFSA, state aid form. Financial aid filing deadline 2/15. **Notification of Awards:** Applicants will be notified of awards on a rolling basis beginning on or about 4/1. **Types of Aid:** *Need-based scholarships/grants:* Pell, SEOG, state scholarships/grants, private scholarships, the school's own gift aid, Federal Nursing Scholarships. *Loans:* Direct Subsidized Stafford, Direct Unsubsidized Stafford, Direct PLUS, Federal Perkins, Federal Nursing. **Student Employment:** Off-campus job opportunities are excellent. **Financial Aid Statistics:** 72% freshmen, 81% undergrads receive need-based scholarship or grant aid. 68% freshmen, 59% undergrads receive need-based self-help aid. 33 freshmen, 96 undergrads receive athletic scholarships. Highest amount earned per year from on-campus jobs $3,600.

PACE UNIVERSITY—WHITE PLAINS

78 North Broadway, White Plains, NY 10603
Phone: 914-422-4000 **E-mail:** wpgrad@pace.edu **CEEB Code:** 2635
Fax: 914-773-3851 **Website:** www.pace.edu **ACT Code:** 2852
Financial Aid Phone: 914-773-3486

This private school was founded in 1906. It has a 13-acre campus.

RATINGS
Admissions Selectivity Rating: 60*   **Fire Safety Rating:** 60*   **Green Rating:** 60*

STUDENTS AND FACULTY
Faculty: Student/faculty ratio 12:1. 66 full-time faculty, 59% hold PhDs.

ACADEMICS
Degrees: Doctoral, first professional, master's, post-bachelor's certificate, post-master's certificate. **Special Study Options:** Cross-registration, distance learning, double major, independent study, teacher certification program.

FACILITIES
Special Academic Facilities/Equipment: Center for the arts, lab theater, communication center, language center. **Computers:** 20% of public computers are PCs, network access in dorm rooms, network access in dorm lounges, remote student-access to Web through college's connection.

CAMPUS LIFE
Organizations: 106 registered organizations, 8 honor societies, 4 religious organizations. 5 fraternities, 4 sororities. **Athletics (Intercollegiate):** *Women:* Basketball, cross-country, softball, tennis, volleyball.

ADMISSIONS
Freshman Academic Profile: 25% in top 10% of high school class, 57% in top 25% of high school class, 87% in top 50% of high school class. **General Admission Information:** Application fee $35. Non-fall registration accepted. Common Application accepted.

COSTS AND FINANCIAL AID
Student Employment: Federal Work-Study Program available. Off-campus job opportunities are excellent.

PACIFIC LUTHERAN UNIVERSITY

Office of Admission, Tacoma, WA 98447-0003
Phone: 253-535-7151 **E-mail:** admission@plu.edu **CEEB Code:** 4597
Fax: 253-536-5136 **Website:** www.plu.edu **ACT Code:** 4470
Financial Aid Phone: 253-535-7134

This private school, affiliated with the Lutheran Church, was founded in 1890. It has a 126-acre campus.

RATINGS
Admissions Selectivity Rating: 86   **Fire Safety Rating:** 84   **Green Rating:** 91

STUDENTS AND FACULTY
Enrollment: 3,331. **Student Body:** 64% female, 36% male, 21% out-of-state, 6% international (24 countries represented). African American 2%, Asian 6%, Caucasian 75%, Hispanic 2%. **Retention and Graduation:** 82% freshmen return for sophomore year. 47% freshmen graduate within 4 years. 20% grads go on to further study within 1 year. **Faculty:** Student/faculty ratio 15:1. 236 full-time faculty, 86% hold PhDs. 100% faculty teach undergrads.

ACADEMICS
Degrees: Bachelor's, master's, post-bachelor's certificate, post-master's certificate. **Academic Requirements:** Arts/fine arts, English (including composition), foreign languages, history, humanities, mathematics, philosophy, sciences (biological or physical), social science. **Classes:** Most classes have 10–19 students. Most lab/discussion sections have 10–19 students. **Majors with Highest Enrollment:** Business administration/management, education. **Disciplines with Highest Percentage of Degrees Awarded:** Education 16%, business/marketing 14%, social sciences 13%, health professions and related sciences 8%, psychology 7%. **Special Study Options:** Cooperative education program, cross-registration, double major, dual enrollment, English as a second language (ESL), exchange student program (domestic), independent study, internships, liberal arts/career combination, student-designed major, study abroad, teacher certification program.

FACILITIES
Housing: Coed dorms, women's dorms, apartments for married students, apartments for single students, special housing for disabled students, special housing for international students, cooperative housing, foreign languages learning housing. **Special Academic Facilities/Equipment:** Mary Baker Russell Music Center, Wekell Art Gallery, Keck Observatory, Rieke Science Center, Scandinavian Cultural Center. **Computers:** 90% of public computers are PCs, 10% of public computers are Macs, network access in dorm rooms, online registration, remote student-access to Web through college's connection.

CAMPUS LIFE
Activities: Choral groups, concert band, dance, drama/theater, jazz band, literary magazine, music ensembles, musical theater, opera, pep band, radio station, student government, student newspaper, student-run film society, symphony orchestra, television station, yearbook. **Organizations:** 58 registered organizations, 4 honor societies, 8 religious organizations. **Athletics (Intercollegiate):** *Men:* Baseball, basketball, cheerleading, crew/rowing, cross-country, football, golf, soccer, swimming, tennis, track/field (outdoor), volleyball. *Women:* Basketball, cheerleading, crew/rowing, cross-country, golf, soccer, softball, swimming, tennis, track/field (outdoor), volleyball. **Environmental initiatives:** Successfully building a community commitment to sustainability that encompasses students, faculty, and staff in part through sustainability fellowships. Including environmental goals for waste diversion, reduction of water and electricity consumption, LEED building and carbon neutrality into the campus master plan. PLU is in the leadership circle for the President's Climate Commitment and is planning to meet all goals and deadlines of that commitment.

ADMISSIONS
Freshman Academic Profile: 33% in top 10% of high school class, 65% in top 25% of high school class, 89% in top 50% of high school class. SAT Math middle 50% range 490–610. SAT Critical Reading middle 50% range 500–620. SAT Writing middle 50% range 480–600. ACT middle 50% range 22–28. TOEFL required of all international applicants, minimum paper TOEFL 550, minimum computer TOEFL 213. **Basis for Candidate Selection:** *Very important factors considered include:* Application essay, rigor of secondary school record. *Important factors considered include:* Academic GPA, character/personal qualities, class rank, extracurricular activities, recommendation(s), standardized test scores, talent/ability, volunteer work. *Other factors considered include:* Interview, work experience. **Freshman Admission Requirements:** High school diploma is required, and GED is accepted. *Academic units required:* 4 English, 2 math, 2 science (2 science labs), 2 foreign language, 3 academic electives. *Academic units recommended:* 3 math, 3 foreign language. **Freshman**

Admission Statistics: 2,112 applied, 76% admitted, 43% enrolled. **Transfer Admission Requirements:** High school transcript, college transcript(s), essay or personal statement, statement of good standing from prior institution(s). Minimum college GPA of 2.5 required. Lowest grade transferable C-. **General Admission Information:** Application fee $40. Regular notification is rolling. Non-fall registration accepted. Admission may be deferred for a maximum of 2 years. Common Application accepted. Credit and/or placement offered for CEEB Advanced Placement tests.

COSTS AND FINANCIAL AID
Annual tuition $25,088. Room and board $7,712. Average book expense $900. **Required Forms and Deadlines:** FAFSA. Financial aid filing deadline 1/31. **Notification of Awards:** Applicants will be notified of awards on a rolling basis beginning on or about 4/1. **Types of Aid:** *Need-based scholarships/grants:* Pell, SEOG, state scholarships/grants, private scholarships, the school's own gift aid, Federal Nursing Scholarships. *Loans:* FFEL Subsidized Stafford, FFEL Unsubsidized Stafford, FFEL PLUS, Federal Perkins, Federal Nursing, state loans. **Student Employment:** Federal Work-Study Program available. Institutional employment available. Off-campus job opportunities are excellent. **Financial Aid Statistics:** 56% freshmen, 54% undergrads receive need-based scholarship or grant aid. 64% freshmen, 65% undergrads receive need-based self-help aid. 96% freshmen, 95% undergrads receive any aid. Highest amount earned per year from on-campus jobs $1,972.

PACIFIC NORTHWEST COLLEGE OF ART

1241 NW Johnson Street, Portland, OR 97209
Phone: 503-821-8972 **E-mail:** admissions@pnca.edu **CEEB Code:** 4504
Fax: 503-821-8978 **Website:** www.pnca.edu **ACT Code:** 3477
Financial Aid Phone: 503-821-8972

This private school was founded in 1909. It has a 1-acre campus.

RATINGS
Admissions Selectivity Rating: 60*   **Fire Safety Rating:** 60*   **Green Rating:** 60*

STUDENTS AND FACULTY
Enrollment: 288. **Student Body:** 59% female, 41% male, 24% out-of-state. Asian 3%, Caucasian 92%, Hispanic 3%, Native American 1%. **Retention and Graduation:** 66% freshmen return for sophomore year. 18% freshmen graduate within 4 years. **Faculty:** Student/faculty ratio 11:1. 13 full-time faculty, 85% hold PhDs. 100% faculty teach undergrads.

ACADEMICS
Degrees: Bachelor's. **Academic Requirements:** Art history, Arts/fine arts, computer literacy, English (including composition), humanities, mathematics, sciences (biological or physical), social science. **Classes:** Most classes have 10–19 students. **Majors with Highest Enrollment:** Design and visual communications, painting, photography. **Disciplines with Highest Percentage of Degrees Awarded:** Visual and performing arts 100%. **Special Study Options:** Cross-registration, exchange student program (domestic), independent study, internships, student-designed major, study abroad.

FACILITIES
Housing: Apartments for single students, housing/student dorm. **Special Academic Facilities/Equipment:** Student galleries, darkrooms, student painting studios, printmaking studio, computer labs. **Computers:** 1% of public computers are PCs, 99% of public computers are Macs, online administrative functions (other than registration), remote student-access to Web through college's connection.

CAMPUS LIFE
Activities: Student government. **Organizations:** 2 registered organizations.

ADMISSIONS
Freshman Academic Profile: 89% from public high schools. SAT Math middle 50% range 370–590. SAT Critical Reading middle 50% range 440–650. ACT middle 50% range 16–26. TOEFL required of all international applicants, minimum paper TOEFL 550, minimum computer TOEFL 213. **Basis for Candidate Selection:** *Very important factors considered include:* Academic GPA, talent/ability. *Important factors considered include:* Application essay, extracurricular activities, interview, rigor of secondary school record. *Other factors considered include:* Character/personal qualities, level of applicant's interest, recommendation(s), standardized test scores. **Freshman Admission Requirements:** High school diploma is required, and GED is accepted. *Academic units recommended:* 4 English, 3 math, 3 science, 3 social studies, 4 art. **Freshman Admission Statistics:** 120 applied, 72% admitted, 31% enrolled. **Transfer Admission Requirements:** College transcript(s), essay or

personal statement. Minimum college GPA of 2.0 required. Lowest grade transferable C. **General Admission Information:** Application fee $35. Regular notification is rolling. Non-fall registration accepted. Admission may be deferred for a maximum of 2 years. Common Application accepted. Credit and/or placement offered for CEEB Advanced Placement tests.

COSTS AND FINANCIAL AID

Annual tuition $16,490. Room and board $4,500. Required fees $806. Average book expense $98,500. **Required Forms and Deadlines:** FAFSA. Financial aid filing deadline 3/1. **Notification of Awards:** Applicants will be notified of awards on a rolling basis beginning on or about 4/1. **Types of Aid:** *Need-based scholarships/grants:* Pell, SEOG, state scholarships/grants, private scholarships, the school's own gift aid. *Loans:* FFEL Subsidized Stafford, FFEL Unsubsidized Stafford, FFEL PLUS. **Financial Aid Statistics:** 65% freshmen, 97% undergrads receive need-based scholarship or grant aid. 65% freshmen, 97% undergrads receive need-based self-help aid. Highest amount earned per year from on-campus jobs $1,000.

PACIFIC OAKS COLLEGE

5 Westmoreland Place, Pasadena, CA 91103
Phone: 626-397-1349 **E-mail:** admissions@pacificoaks.edu
Fax: 626-685-2531 **Website:** www.pacificoaks.edu
Financial Aid Phone: 626-397-1350

This private school was founded in 1945.

RATINGS
Admissions Selectivity Rating: 60*   **Fire Safety Rating:** 60*   **Green Rating:** 60*

STUDENTS AND FACULTY
Enrollment: 258. **Student Body:** 93% female, 7% male, 19% out-of-state. African American 12%, Asian 4%, Caucasian 40%, Hispanic 29%, Native American 2%. **Faculty:** Student/faculty ratio 7:1. 29 full-time faculty, 59% hold PhDs. 100% faculty teach undergrads.

ACADEMICS
Degrees: Bachelor's, master's, post-bachelor's certificate, post-master's certificate. **Academic Requirements:** Social science. **Classes:** Most classes have 10–19 students. **Disciplines with Highest Percentage of Degrees Awarded:** Social sciences 100%. **Special Study Options:** Accelerated program, distance learning, dual enrollment, independent study, student-designed major, teacher certification program, weekend college.

FACILITIES
Computers: 50% of public computers are PCs, 50% of public computers are Macs.

CAMPUS LIFE
Activities: Student government. **Organizations:** 3 registered organizations.

ADMISSIONS
Freshman Academic Profile: TOEFL required of all international applicants, minimum paper TOEFL 550. **Freshman Admission Requirements:** High school diploma is required, and GED is accepted. **Transfer Admission Requirements:** College transcript(s), essay or personal statement. Minimum college GPA of 2.0 required. Lowest grade transferable C. **General Admission Information:** Application fee $55. Regular application deadline 6/1. Regular notification is rolling. Non-fall registration not accepted. Admission may be deferred for a maximum of 2 years. Common Application not accepted.

COSTS AND FINANCIAL AID
Annual tuition $13,800. Required fees $60. **Required Forms and Deadlines:** FAFSA, institution's own financial aid form, state aid form, Noncustodial PROFILE. Financial aid filing deadline 4/15. **Notification of Awards:** Applicants will be notified of awards on a rolling basis beginning on or about 5/1. **Types of Aid:** *Need-based scholarships/grants:* Pell, SEOG, state scholarships/grants, private scholarships, the school's own gift aid. *Loans:* FFEL Subsidized Stafford, FFEL Unsubsidized Stafford, FFEL PLUS, Federal Perkins. **Student Employment:** Federal Work-Study Program available. Institutional employment available. Off-campus job opportunities are good.

PACIFIC STATES UNIVERSITY

Admissions Office, 1516 South Western Avenue, Los Angeles, CA 90006
Phone: 323-731-2383 **E-mail:** admission@psuca.edu
Fax: 323-731-7276 **Website:** www.psuca.edu

This private school was founded in 1923.

RATINGS
Admissions Selectivity Rating: 60*   **Fire Safety Rating:** 60*   **Green Rating:** 60*

STUDENTS AND FACULTY
Enrollment: 28. **Student Body:** 100% male, 100% international. Asian 100%. **Faculty:** Student/faculty ratio 5:1. 4 full-time faculty.

ACADEMICS
Degrees: Bachelor's, certificate, master's. **Disciplines with Highest Percentage of Degrees Awarded:** Business/marketing 70%, computer and information sciences 30%.

ADMISSIONS
Basis for Candidate Selection: *Important factors considered include:* Application essay, rigor of secondary school record, standardized test scores. **Freshman Admission Requirements:** High school diploma is required, and GED is accepted. **Freshman Admission Statistics:** 40 applied, 100% admitted, 100% enrolled. **Transfer Admission Requirements:** College transcript(s). Minimum college GPA of 2.5 required. Lowest grade transferable C. **General Admission Information:** Non-fall registration not accepted. Common Application not accepted.

COSTS AND FINANCIAL AID
Annual tuition $40,320. Average book expense $400. **Required Forms and Deadlines:** FAFSA. **Types of Aid:** *Need-based scholarships/grants:* Pell. *Loans:* Direct Subsidized Stafford, Direct Unsubsidized Stafford.

PACIFIC UNION COLLEGE

Enrollment Services, 1 Angwin Avenue, Angwin, CA 94508
Phone: 800-862-7080 **E-mail:** enroll@puc.edu **CEEB Code:** 4600
Fax: 707-965-6432 **Website:** www.puc.edu **ACT Code:** 0362
Financial Aid Phone: 707-965-7200

This private school, affiliated with the Seventh Day Adventist Church, was founded in 1882. It has a 200-acre campus.

RATINGS
Admissions Selectivity Rating: 60*   **Fire Safety Rating:** 67   **Green Rating:** 60*

STUDENTS AND FACULTY
Enrollment: 1,294. **Student Body:** 54% female, 46% male, 19% out-of-state, 7% international (24 countries represented). African American 4%, Asian 22%, Caucasian 44%, Hispanic 12%. **Retention and Graduation:** 75% freshmen return for sophomore year. 21% freshmen graduate within 4 years. **Faculty:** Student/faculty ratio 15:1. 81 full-time faculty, 53% hold PhDs. 100% faculty teach undergrads.

ACADEMICS
Degrees: Associate, bachelor's, master's. **Academic Requirements:** Arts/fine arts, computer literacy, English (including composition), history, mathematics, philosophy, sciences (biological or physical), social science. **Classes:** Most classes have fewer than 10 students. Most lab/discussion sections have fewer than 10 students. **Majors with Highest Enrollment:** Business administration/management, nursing/registered nurse training (ASN, BSN, MSN, RN), teacher education, multiple levels. **Disciplines with Highest Percentage of Degrees Awarded:** Business/marketing 16%, education 11%, health professions and related sciences 11%, biological/life sciences 10%, philosophy and religious studies 7%, communications/journalism 7%, visual and performing arts 6%. **Special Study Options:** Cooperative education program, double major, external degree program, honors program, independent study, internships, study abroad, teacher certification program.

FACILITIES
Housing: Men's dorms, women's dorms, apartments for married students. **Special Academic Facilities/Equipment:** Art gallery, natural history

collection, Pitcairn Island studies center, on-campus elementary and high schools, airport, flight training facility, observatory. **Computers:** 9% of classrooms are wireless, 100% of public computers are PCs, network access in dorm rooms, network access in dorm lounges, online registration, online administrative functions (other than registration), support for handheld computing, remote student-access to Web through college's connection.

CAMPUS LIFE

Activities: Choral groups, concert band, drama/theater, jazz band, literary magazine, music ensembles, musical theater, radio station, student government, student newspaper, student-run film society, symphony orchestra, yearbook. **Organizations:** 24 registered organizations, 8 honor societies. **Athletics (Intercollegiate):** *Men:* Basketball, cross-country, volleyball. *Women:* Basketball, cross-country, volleyball.

ADMISSIONS

Freshman Academic Profile: SAT Math middle 50% range 440–570. SAT Critical Reading middle 50% range 460–580. SAT Writing middle 50% range 460–580. ACT middle 50% range 17–24. TOEFL required of all international applicants, minimum paper TOEFL 525, minimum computer TOEFL 195. **Basis for Candidate Selection:** *Very important factors considered include:* Recommendation(s), rigor of secondary school record. *Important factors considered include:* Academic GPA, character/personal qualities, level of applicant's interest. *Other factors considered include:* Extracurricular activities, interview, religious affiliation/commitment, standardized test scores. **Freshman Admission Requirements:** High school diploma is required, and GED is accepted. *Academic units required:* 4 English, 2 math, 1 science, 1 history. *Academic units recommended:* 3 math, 3 science, 2 foreign language, 2 history, 1 computer literacy. **Freshman Admission Statistics:** 1,867 applied, 41% admitted, 33% enrolled. **Transfer Admission Requirements:** High school transcript, college transcript(s). Minimum college GPA of 2.0 required. Lowest grade transferable C-. **General Admission Information:** Application fee $30. Regular notification is rolling. Non-fall registration accepted. Admission may be deferred for a maximum of 1 year. Credit offered for CEEB Advanced Placement tests.

COSTS AND FINANCIAL AID

Annual tuition $20,300. Room and board $5,955. Required fees $135. Average book expense $1,385. **Required Forms and Deadlines:** FAFSA, institution's own financial aid form, state aid form, Business/Farm Supplement, federal tax returns. **Types of Aid:** *Need-based scholarships/grants:* Pell, SEOG, state scholarships/grants, the school's own gift aid. *Loans:* FFEL Subsidized Stafford, FFEL Unsubsidized Stafford, FFEL PLUS, Federal Perkins, college/university loans from institutional funds. **Student Employment:** Federal Work-Study Program available. Institutional employment available. Off-campus job opportunities are fair. **Financial Aid Statistics:** 93% undergrads receive need-based scholarship or grant aid. 48% freshmen, 48% undergrads receive need-based self-help aid. Highest amount earned per year from on-campus jobs $1,200.

PACIFIC UNIVERSITY

2043 College Way, Forest Grove, OR 97116
Phone: 503-352-2218 **E-mail:** admissions@pacificu.edu **CEEB Code:** 4601
Fax: 503-352-2975 **Website:** www.pacificu.edu
Financial Aid Phone: 503-352-2222

This private school, affiliated with the United Church of Christ, was founded in 1849. It has a 60-acre campus.

RATINGS

Admissions Selectivity Rating: 86   **Fire Safety Rating:** 72   **Green Rating:** 77

STUDENTS AND FACULTY

Enrollment: 1,323. **Student Body:** 61% female, 39% male, 50% out-of-state. African American 1%, Asian 23%, Caucasian 63%, Hispanic 4%, Native American 1%. **Retention and Graduation:** 80% freshmen return for sophomore year. 51% freshmen graduate within 4 years. 35% grads go on to further study within 1 year. 10% grads pursue arts and sciences degrees. 2% grads pursue business degrees. 2% grads pursue law degrees. 2% grads pursue medical degrees. **Faculty:** Student/faculty ratio 13:1. 89 full-time faculty, 89% hold PhDs. 100% faculty teach undergrads.

ACADEMICS

Degrees: Bachelor's, doctoral, first professional, master's. **Academic Requirements:** Arts/fine arts, cross-cultural studies, English (including composition), foreign languages, humanities, mathematics, sciences (biological

or physical), social science. **Classes:** Most classes have 10–19 students. Most lab/discussion sections have 10–19 students. **Majors with Highest Enrollment:** Kinesiology and exercise science. **Disciplines with Highest Percentage of Degrees Awarded:** Parks and recreation 13%, business/marketing 11%, biological/life sciences 9%, psychology 8%, education 8%, foreign languages and literature 7%, social sciences 7%, health professions and related sciences 7%. **Special Study Options:** Cross-registration, double major, English as a second language (ESL), independent study, internships, liberal arts/career combination, study abroad, teacher certification program.

FACILITIES

Housing: Coed dorms, apartments for single students, special housing for disabled students, cooperative housing, houses (limited number) available for married students. **Special Academic Facilities/Equipment:** State history museum, performing arts center, media center, humanitarian center, Holocaust resource center, politics/law forum, Berglund Center for Internet Studies, electron microscopes. **Computers:** 100% of classrooms are wired, 100% of classrooms are wireless, 64% of public computers are PCs, 36% of public computers are Macs, network access in dorm rooms, network access in dorm lounges, support for handheld computing, remote student-access to Web through college's connection.

CAMPUS LIFE

Activities: Choral groups, concert band, dance, drama/theater, jazz band, literary magazine, music ensembles, musical theater, radio station, student government, student newspaper, student-run film society, symphony orchestra, yearbook. **Organizations:** 45 registered organizations, 2 honor societies, 4 religious organizations. 3 fraternities (4% men join), 4 sororities (5% women join). **Athletics (Intercollegiate):** *Men:* Baseball, basketball, cross-country, golf, soccer, swimming, tennis, track/field (outdoor), wrestling. *Women:* Basketball, cross-country, golf, lacrosse, soccer, softball, swimming, tennis, track/field (outdoor), volleyball, wrestling. **Environmental Initiatives:** Sustainability Committee. New LEED-certified buildings. B-Street Permaculture Project.

ADMISSIONS

Freshman Academic Profile: 30% in top 10% of high school class, 60% in top 25% of high school class, 88% in top 50% of high school class. 88% from public high schools. SAT Math middle 50% range 490–610. SAT Critical Reading middle 50% range 510–600. ACT middle 50% range 21–28. TOEFL required of all international applicants, minimum paper TOEFL 550, minimum computer TOEFL 213. **Basis for Candidate Selection:** *Very important factors considered include:* Academic GPA, level of applicant's interest, recommendation(s), rigor of secondary school record, standardized test scores. *Important factors considered include:* Application essay, class rank, interview, volunteer work. *Other factors considered include:* Alumni/ae relation, character/personal qualities, extracurricular activities, talent/ability, work experience. **Freshman Admission Requirements:** High school diploma is required, and GED is accepted. *Academic units recommended:* 4 English, 3 math, 3 science (1 science lab), 2 foreign language, 3 social studies, 1 history, 4 academic electives. **Freshman Admission Statistics:** 1,292 applied, 82% admitted, 34% enrolled. **Transfer Admission Requirements:** College transcript(s), essay or personal statement. Minimum college GPA of 2.7 required. Lowest grade transferable C-. **General Admission Information:** Application fee $40. Regular application deadline 8/15. Regular notification is rolling. Non-fall registration not accepted. Admission may be deferred for a maximum of 3 years. Credit and/or placement offered for CEEB Advanced Placement tests.

COSTS AND FINANCIAL AID

Annual tuition $21,954. Room & board $6,468. Required fees $580. **Required Forms and Deadlines:** FAFSA. Financial aid filing deadline 2/15. **Notification of Awards:** Applicants will be notified of awards on a rolling basis beginning on or about 3/1. **Types of Aid:** *Need-based scholarships/grants:* Pell, SEOG, state scholarships/grants, private scholarships, the school's own gift aid. *Loans:* FFEL Subsidized Stafford, FFEL Unsubsidized Stafford, FFEL PLUS, Federal Perkins, private alternative loans. **Financial Aid Statistics:** 76% freshmen, 70% undergrads receive need-based scholarship or grant aid. 68% freshmen, 66% undergrads receive need-based self-help aid. 99% freshmen, 98% undergrads receive any aid. Highest amount earned per year from on-campus jobs $3,520.

PAINE COLLEGE

1235 15th Street, Augusta, GA 30901-3182
Phone: 800-476-7703 **E-mail:** simpkins@mail.paine.edu
Fax: 706-821-8691 **Website:** www.paine.edu

This private school was founded in 1882.

RATINGS
Admissions Selectivity Rating: 60* **Fire Safety Rating:** 60* **Green Rating:** 60*

STUDENTS AND FACULTY
Enrollment: 863. **Student Body:** 23% out-of-state. African American 97%, Caucasian 2%. **Retention and Graduation:** 67% freshmen return for sophomore year. 6% grads go on to further study within 1 year. 6% grads pursue arts and sciences degrees.

ACADEMICS
Degrees: Bachelor's. **Special Study Options:** Accelerated program, cooperative education program, honors program, independent study, internships, study abroad.

FACILITIES
Housing: Coed dorms.

CAMPUS LIFE
Activities: Literary magazine, student government, student newspaper, yearbook. **Organizations:** 1 honor society, 1 religious organization. **Athletics (Intercollegiate):** *Women:* Basketball, cross-country, track/field (outdoor), volleyball.

ADMISSIONS
Freshman Academic Profile: TOEFL required of all international applicants, minimum paper TOEFL 500. **Freshman Admission Requirements:** High school diploma is required, and GED is accepted. *Academic units required:* 4 English, 2 math, 2 science (2 science labs), 1 social studies, 1 history, 6 academic electives. *Academic units recommended:* 3 math, 2 foreign language. **General Admission Information:** Application fee $10. Regular application deadline 8/1. Regular notification is rolling.

COSTS AND FINANCIAL AID
Comprehensive fee $9,240. Room & board $3,020. Required fees $420. Average book expense $500. **Types of Aid:** *Loans:* FFEL Subsidized Stafford, FFEL PLUS. **Student Employment:** Federal Work-Study Program available.

PALM BEACH ATLANTIC UNIVERSITY

PO Box 24708, 901 South Flagler Drive, West Palm Beach, FL 33416-4708
Phone: 561-803-2100 **E-mail:** admit@pba.edu **CEEB Code:** 5553
Fax: 561-803-2115 **Website:** www.pba.edu **ACT Code:** 0739
Financial Aid Phone: 561-803-2125

This private school, affiliated with the Christian (nondenominational) Church, was founded in 1968. It has a 25-acre campus.

RATINGS
Admissions Selectivity Rating: 79 **Fire Safety Rating:** 60* **Green Rating:** 60*

STUDENTS AND FACULTY
Enrollment: 2,355. **Student Body:** 62% female, 38% male, 24% out-of-state, 3% international (25 countries represented). African American 15%, Asian 1%, Caucasian 69%, Hispanic 8%. **Retention and Graduation:** 67% freshmen return for sophomore year. 22% freshmen graduate within 4 years. **Faculty:** Student/faculty ratio 14:1. 140 full-time faculty, 74% hold PhDs. 90% faculty teach undergrads.

ACADEMICS
Degrees: Associate, bachelor's, first professional, master's. **Academic Requirements:** Arts/fine arts, English (including composition), humanities, mathematics, sciences (biological or physical), social science. **Classes:** Most classes have 10–19 students. Most lab/discussion sections have fewer than 10 students. **Majors with Highest Enrollment:** Communications studies/speech communication and rhetoric, psychology. **Disciplines with Highest Percentage of Degrees Awarded:** Business/marketing 50%, education 10%, communication technologies 8%, psychology 8%, visual and performing arts

5%, biological/life sciences 3%. **Special Study Options:** Accelerated program, cooperative education program, cross-registration, double major, dual enrollment, exchange student program (domestic), honors program, independent study, internships, study abroad, teacher certification program.

FACILITIES
Housing: Men's dorms, women's dorms, off-campus apartments. **Special Academic Facilities/Equipment:** DeSantis Family Chapel, Greene Sports Complex (Cafe), Helen K. Persson Recital Hall. **Computers:** 100% of public computers are PCs, network access in dorm rooms, network access in dorm lounges, online registration, online administrative functions (other than registration), remote student-access to Web through college's connection.

CAMPUS LIFE
Activities: Choral groups, concert band, dance, drama/theater, jazz band, literary magazine, music ensembles, musical theater, pep band, student government, student newspaper, student-run film society, symphony orchestra, yearbook. **Organizations:** 55 registered organizations, 29 honor societies, 6 religious organizations. **Athletics (Intercollegiate):** *Men:* Baseball, basketball, cheerleading, cross-country, soccer, tennis, volleyball. *Women:* Basketball, cheerleading, cross-country, soccer, softball, tennis, volleyball.

ADMISSIONS
Freshman Academic Profile: 19% in top 10% of high school class, 47% in top 25% of high school class, 74% in top 50% of high school class. SAT Math middle 50% range 490–590. SAT Critical Reading middle 50% range 490–590. ACT middle 50% range 21–26. TOEFL required of all international applicants, minimum paper TOEFL 550, minimum computer TOEFL 213. **Basis for Candidate Selection:** *Very important factors considered include:* Application essay, class rank, rigor of secondary school record, standardized test scores. *Important factors considered include:* Character/personal qualities, interview, recommendation(s), talent/ability, volunteer work. *Other factors considered include:* Alumni/ae relation, extracurricular activities, geographical residence, racial/ethnic status, religious affiliation/commitment, state residency, work experience. **Freshman Admission Requirements:** High school diploma is required, and GED is accepted. *Academic units required:* 4 English, 3 math, 3 science, 3 social studies, 5 academic electives. *Academic units recommended:* 2 foreign language, 3 academic electives. **Freshman Admission Statistics:** 2,111 applied, 44% admitted, 48% enrolled. **Transfer Admission Requirements:** High school transcript, college transcript(s), essay or personal statement, interview, statement of good standing from prior institution(s). Minimum college GPA of 2.5 required. Lowest grade transferable C. **General Admission Information:** Application fee $25. Regular notification as soon as all required items are received. Non-fall registration accepted. Common Application accepted. Credit offered for CEEB Advanced Placement tests.

COSTS AND FINANCIAL AID
Annual tuition $19,950. Room and board $8,086. Required fees $260. Average book expense $1,200. **Required Forms and Deadlines:** FAFSA. Financial aid filing deadline 8/1. **Notification of Awards:** Applicants will be notified of awards on a rolling basis beginning on or about 2/15. **Types of Aid:** *Need-based scholarships/grants:* Pell, SEOG, state scholarships/grants, private scholarships, the school's own gift aid. *Loans:* FFEL Subsidized Stafford, FFEL Unsubsidized Stafford, FFEL PLUS, Federal Perkins, college/university loans from institutional funds. **Student Employment:** Federal Work-Study Program available. Institutional employment available. Off-campus job opportunities are excellent. **Financial Aid Statistics:** 38% freshmen, 44% undergrads receive need-based scholarship or grant aid. 53% freshmen, 58% undergrads receive need-based self-help aid. 88 undergrads receive athletic scholarships. 98% freshmen, 95% undergrads receive any aid.

PARK UNIVERSITY

8700 River Park Drive, Campus Box 1, Parkville, MO 64152
Phone: 816-584-6214 **E-mail:** admissions@mail.park.edu **CEEB Code:** 6574
Fax: 816-741-4462 **Website:** www.park.edu **ACT Code:** 2340
Financial Aid Phone: 816-548-6290

This private school was founded in 1875. It has a 700-acre campus.

RATINGS
Admissions Selectivity Rating: 76 **Fire Safety Rating:** 60* **Green Rating:** 60*

STUDENTS AND FACULTY
Enrollment: 11,451. **Student Body:** 49% female, 51% male, 81% out-of-state, 2% international (93 countries represented). African American 21%, Asian 2%, Caucasian 57%, Hispanic 16%. **Retention and Graduation:** 48% freshmen

return for sophomore year. 15% freshmen graduate within 4 years. 7% grads go on to further study within 1 year. 6% grads pursue arts and sciences degrees. 1% grads pursue business degrees. **Faculty:** Student/faculty ratio 14:1. 107 full-time faculty, 59% hold PhDs. 100% faculty teach undergrads.

ACADEMICS

Degrees: Associate, bachelor's, master's. **Academic Requirements:** Computer literacy, English (including composition), foreign languages, humanities, mathematics, sciences (biological or physical), social science. **Majors with Highest Enrollment:** Business administration/management, human resources management/personnel administration, management information systems. **Disciplines with Highest Percentage of Degrees Awarded:** Business/marketing 66%, psychology 16%, security and protective services 9%, computer and information sciences 3%. **Special Study Options:** Accelerated program, cross-registration, distance learning, double major, dual enrollment, English as a second language (ESL), honors program, independent study, internships, student-designed major, study abroad, teacher certification program, weekend college.

FACILITIES

Housing: Coed dorms, apartments for married students. **Computers:** 100% of public computers are PCs, network access in dorm rooms, network access in dorm lounges, online registration, online administrative functions (other than registration), remote student-access to Web through college's connection.

CAMPUS LIFE

Activities: Choral groups, drama/theater, literary magazine, radio station, student government, student newspaper, symphony orchestra, yearbook. **Organizations:** 15 registered organizations, 4 honor societies, 13 religious organizations. **Athletics (Intercollegiate):** *Men:* Baseball, basketball, cross-country, soccer, track/field (indoor), track/field (outdoor), volleyball. *Women:* Basketball, cross-country, golf, soccer, softball, track/field (indoor), track/field (outdoor), volleyball.

ADMISSIONS

Freshman Academic Profile: 12% in top 10% of high school class, 38% in top 25% of high school class, 68% in top 50% of high school class. 80% from public high schools. ACT middle 50% range 19–26. TOEFL required of all international applicants, minimum paper TOEFL 500, minimum computer TOEFL 173. **Basis for Candidate Selection:** *Very important factors considered include:* Class rank, rigor of secondary school record, standardized test scores. *Other factors considered include:* Application essay, recommendation(s). **Freshman Admission Requirements:** High school diploma is required, and GED is accepted. *Academic units recommended:* 3 English, 2 math, 2 science (1 science lab), 2 foreign language, 3 social studies, 1 history, 6 academic electives. **Freshman Admission Statistics:** 528 applied, 76% admitted, 48% enrolled. **Transfer Admission Requirements:** High school transcript, college transcript(s). Minimum college GPA of 2.0 required. Lowest grade transferable C. **General Admission Information:** Application fee $25. Regular application deadline 7/1. Non-fall registration accepted. Admission may be deferred for a maximum of 1 year. Credit and/or placement offered for CEEB Advanced Placement tests.

COSTS AND FINANCIAL AID

Average book expense $1,200. **Required Forms and Deadlines:** FAFSA, institution's own financial aid form. Financial aid filing deadline 4/1. **Types of Aid:** *Need-based scholarships/grants:* Pell, SEOG, state scholarships/grants, private scholarships, the school's own gift aid. *Loans:* FFEL Subsidized Stafford, FFEL Unsubsidized Stafford, FFEL PLUS, Federal Perkins, college/university loans from institutional funds. **Financial Aid Statistics:** 26% freshmen, 7% undergrads receive need-based scholarship or grant aid. 50% freshmen, 28% undergrads receive need-based self-help aid. 5 freshmen, 31 undergrads receive athletic scholarships. 78% freshmen receive any aid.

PARKS COLLEGE OF SAINT LOUIS UNIVERSITY

500 Falling Springs Road, Cahokia, IL 62206
Phone: 618-337-7500 **E-mail:** admitme@sluca.slu.edu **CEEB Code:** 1621
Fax: 618-332-6802 **Website:** www.slu.edu **ACT Code:** 1114
Financial Aid Phone: 618-337-7500

This private school was founded in 1927. It has a 113-acre campus.

RATINGS

Admissions Selectivity Rating: 60* **Fire Safety Rating:** 60* **Green Rating:** 60*

STUDENTS AND FACULTY

Student Body: 77% out-of-state. **Retention and Graduation:** 70% freshmen return for sophomore year.

FACILITIES

Housing: Coed dorms, apartments for single students. **Special Academic Facilities/Equipment:** Aerodynamics, aircraft maintenance engineering, meteorology, and other labs; fleet of single- and twin-engine planes.

CAMPUS LIFE

Activities: Student government, student newspaper. **Organizations:** 12 registered organizations, 2 honor societies, 4 religious organizations. 5 fraternities (30% men join), 2 sororities (50% women join).

ADMISSIONS

Freshman Academic Profile: 16% in top 10% of high school class, 44% in top 25% of high school class, 84% in top 50% of high school class. ACT middle 50% range 21–26. **Freshman Admission Requirements:** High school diploma is required, and GED is accepted. *Academic units required:* 4 English. *Academic units recommended:* 4 English, 2 math, 2 science, 2 social studies, 2 academic electives. **Transfer Admission Requirements:** Minimum college GPA of 2.0 required. Lowest grade transferable C. **General Admission Information:** Early decision application deadline 12/1. Regular application deadline rolling. Regular notification is rolling. Non-fall registration accepted. Common Application not accepted. Credit and/or placement offered for CEEB Advanced Placement tests.

COSTS AND FINANCIAL AID

Comprehensive fee $19,010. Room & board $5,110. Average book expense $800. **Required Forms and Deadlines:** FAFSA, institution's own financial aid form, CSS/Financial Aid PROFILE. **Notification of Awards:** Applicants will be notified of awards on or about rolling. **Types of Aid:** *Need-based scholarships/grants:* State scholarships/grants. *Loans:* FFEL Subsidized Stafford, FFEL PLUS. **Student Employment:** Federal Work-Study Program available. Institutional employment available. Off-campus job opportunities are good. **Financial Aid Statistics:** Highest amount earned per year from on-campus jobs $1,000.

PARSONS—THE NEW SCHOOL FOR DESIGN

65 Fifth Avenue, New York, NY 10011
Phone: 877-528-3321 **E-mail:** studentinfo@newschool.edu **CEEB Code:** 2638
Fax: 212-229-5166 **Website:** www.parsons.newschool.edu **ACT Code:** 2854
Financial Aid Phone: 212-229-8930

This private school was founded in 1896. It has a 2-acre campus.

RATINGS

Admissions Selectivity Rating: 85 **Fire Safety Rating:** 60* **Green Rating:** 60*

STUDENTS AND FACULTY

Enrollment: 3,180. **Student Body:** 79% female, 21% male, 47% out-of-state, 34% international. African American 3%, Asian 17%, Caucasian 30%, Hispanic 6%. **Retention and Graduation:** 84% freshmen return for sophomore year. 52% freshmen graduate within 4 years. **Faculty:** 92 full-time faculty, 54% hold PhDs. 100% faculty teach undergrads.

ACADEMICS

Degrees: Associate, bachelor's, certificate, master's. **Academic Requirements:** Arts/fine arts, computer literacy, English (including composition), humanities, social science. History of decorative arts majors are required to take courses in history. **Classes:** Most classes have 10–19 students. Most lab/discussion sections have 10–19 students. **Majors with Highest Enrollment:** Design and visual communications, fashion/apparel design, illustration. **Disciplines with Highest Percentage of Degrees Awarded:** Visual and performing arts 100%. **Special Study Options:** Accelerated program, cooperative education program, cross-registration, distance learning, dual enrollment, English as a second language (ESL), exchange student program (domestic), independent study, internships, liberal arts/career combination, student-designed major, study abroad, 5-year combined BA/BFA NY studio program.

FACILITIES

Housing: Coed dorms, apartments for single students, special housing for disabled students. **Special Academic Facilities/Equipment:** Fashion education center in New York's garment district with labs and studios for fashion design students. **Computers:** Online registration, remote student-access to Web through college's connection.

CAMPUS LIFE

Activities: Concert band, dance, drama/theater, jazz band, literary magazine, music ensembles, musical theater, radio station, student government, student-run film society. **Organizations:** 3 registered organizations.

ADMISSIONS

Freshman Academic Profile: 16% in top 10% of high school class, 48% in top 25% of high school class, 77% in top 50% of high school class. SAT Math middle 50% range 490–610. SAT Critical Reading middle 50% range 480–600. SAT Writing middle 50% range 480–590. ACT middle 50% range 20–26. TOEFL required of all international applicants, minimum paper TOEFL 550, minimum computer TOEFL 213. **Basis for Candidate Selection:** *Very important factors considered include:* Academic GPA, level of applicant's interest, rigor of secondary school record, standardized test scores, talent/ability. *Important factors considered include:* Interview. *Other factors considered include:* Application essay, class rank, extracurricular activities, recommendation(s). **Freshman Admission Requirements:** High school diploma is required, and GED is accepted. **Freshman Admission Statistics:** 2,394 applied, 46% admitted, 45% enrolled. **Transfer Admission Requirements:** College transcript(s). Minimum college GPA of 2.0 required. Lowest grade transferable C. **General Admission Information:** Application fee $50. Regular application deadline 3/1. Non-fall registration accepted. Neither credit nor placement offered for CEEB Advanced Placement tests.

COSTS AND FINANCIAL AID

Annual tuition $31,940. Room and board $11,750. Required fees $700. Average book expense $2,050. **Required Forms and Deadlines:** FAFSA. **Notification of Awards:** Applicants will be notified of awards on a rolling basis beginning on or about 3/1. **Types of Aid:** *Need-based scholarships/grants:* Pell, SEOG, state scholarships/grants, private scholarships, the school's own gift aid. *Loans:* FFEL Subsidized Stafford, FFEL Unsubsidized Stafford, FFEL PLUS, Federal Perkins, college/university loans from institutional funds. **Student Employment:** Federal Work-Study Program available. Institutional employment available. Off-campus job opportunities are excellent. **Financial Aid Statistics:** 45% freshmen, 44% undergrads receive need-based scholarship or grant aid. 40% freshmen, 40% undergrads receive need-based self-help aid. Highest amount earned per year from on-campus jobs $2,500.

See page 1282.

PEACE COLLEGE

15 East Peace Street, Raleigh, NC 27604-1194
Phone: 800-732-2306 **E-mail:** mmccleery@peace.edu
Fax: 919-508-2306 **Website:** www.peace.edu
Financial Aid Phone: 919-508-2000

This private school was founded in 1857. It has a 15-acre campus.

RATINGS

Admissions Selectivity Rating: 60*   **Fire Safety Rating:** 60*   **Green Rating:** 60*

STUDENTS AND FACULTY

Retention and Graduation: 69% freshmen return for sophomore year. **Faculty:** Student/faculty ratio 13:1. 37 full-time faculty, 73% hold PhDs. 100% faculty teach undergrads.

ACADEMICS

Degrees: Associate, bachelor's. **Academic Requirements:** Arts/fine arts, computer literacy, English (including composition), foreign languages, history, humanities, mathematics, philosophy, sciences (biological or physical), social science. **Classes:** Most classes have 10–19 students. **Disciplines with Highest Percentage of Degrees Awarded:** Liberal arts/general studies 27%, business/marketing 27%, communication technologies 20%, psychology 16%, biological/life sciences 5%, visual and performing arts 2%. **Special Study Options:** Cross-registration, double major, dual enrollment, honors program, independent study, internships, liberal arts/career combination, study abroad.

FACILITIES

Housing: Women's dorms, special housing for disabled students. **Special Academic Facilities/Equipment:** Macintosh laboratories for biology, music, visual communication; student laboratories for chemistry, general biology, molecular ad cellular biology; recital hall, theater, dance studio are available; academic building features $500,000 of new technology to support instruction in business/human resources laboratory, communication media laboratory, language laboratory, psychology/anthropology laboratory, psychology observation room. **Computers:** Network access in dorm rooms, online administrative functions (other than registration).

CAMPUS LIFE

Activities: Choral groups, dance, drama/theater, literary magazine, music ensembles, musical theater, student government, student newspaper, yearbook. **Organizations:** 15 registered organizations, 3 honor societies. **Athletics (Intercollegiate):** *Women:* Basketball, softball, tennis, volleyball.

ADMISSIONS

Freshman Academic Profile: SAT Math middle 50% range 410–520. SAT Critical Reading middle 50% range 520–430. ACT middle 50% range 16–20. **Basis for Candidate Selection:** *Very important factors considered include:* Character/personal qualities, rigor of secondary school record. *Important factors considered include:* Extracurricular activities, interview, recommendation(s). *Other factors considered include:* Application essay, class rank, geographical residence, racial/ethnic status, state residency, talent/ability, volunteer work, work experience. **Freshman Admission Requirements:** High school diploma is required, and GED is accepted. *Academic units required:* 4 English, 3 math, 2 science (1 science lab), 2 foreign language, 2 social studies. *Academic units recommended:* 3 math, 3 science. **Freshman Admission Statistics:** 348 applied, 86% admitted, 57% enrolled. **Transfer Admission Requirements:** College transcript(s). Minimum college GPA of 2.0 required. Lowest grade transferable C. **General Admission Information:** Application fee $25. Regular notification is rolling. Non-fall registration accepted. Admission may be deferred for a maximum of 1 year. Common Application accepted. Credit offered for CEEB Advanced Placement tests.

COSTS AND FINANCIAL AID

Annual tuition $9,727. Room & board $5,000. Required fees $200. Average book expense $750. **Required Forms and Deadlines:** FAFSA, institution's own financial aid form, state aid form. Financial aid filing deadline 4/1. **Notification of Awards:** Applicants will be notified of awards on a rolling basis beginning on or about 2/1. **Types of Aid:** *Need-based scholarships/grants:* Pell, SEOG, state scholarships/grants, private scholarships, the school's own gift aid. *Loans:* FFEL Subsidized Stafford, FFEL Unsubsidized Stafford, FFEL PLUS, alternative loans. **Student Employment:** Federal Work-Study Program available. Institutional employment available. Off-campus job opportunities are excellent. **Financial Aid Statistics:** 39% freshmen, 38% undergrads receive need-based scholarship or grant aid. 39% freshmen, 38% undergrads receive need-based self-help aid. Highest amount earned per year from on-campus jobs $1,472.

PENNSYLVANIA COLLEGE OF ART & DESIGN

204 North Prince Street, PO Box 59, Lancaster, PA 17608-0059
Phone: 717-396-7833 **E-mail:** admissions@pcad.edu **CEEB Code:** 2681
Fax: 717-396-1339 **Website:** www.pcad.edu **ACT Code:** 3569
Financial Aid Phone: 717-396-7833

This private school was founded in 1982.

RATINGS

Admissions Selectivity Rating: 60*   **Fire Safety Rating:** 60*   **Green Rating:** 60*

STUDENTS AND FACULTY

Faculty: Student/faculty ratio 11:1. 10 full-time faculty, 70% hold PhDs. 100% faculty teach undergrads.

ACADEMICS

Degrees: Bachelor's, certificate. **Academic Requirements:** Art history, arts/fine arts, English (including composition), humanities, mathematics, sciences (biological or physical). **Special Study Options:** Internships.

FACILITIES

Special Academic Facilities/Equipment: Main gallery library. **Computers:** 100% of public computers are Macs. Undergraduates are required to own a computer.

CAMPUS LIFE

Activities: Student government, yearbook. **Organizations:** 2 registered organizations.

ADMISSIONS

Freshman Academic Profile: TOEFL required of all international applicants, minimum paper TOEFL 500, minimum computer TOEFL 173. **Basis for Candidate Selection:** *Very important factors considered include:* Application essay, interview, rigor of secondary school record, talent/ability. *Important factors considered include:* Class rank, recommendation(s). *Other factors considered include:* Character/personal qualities, extracurricular activities, volunteer work, work experience. **Freshman Admission Requirements:** High school diploma is required, and GED is accepted. **Freshman Admission Statistics:** 169 applied, 58% admitted, 66% enrolled. **Transfer Admission Requirements:** High school transcript, college transcript(s), essay or personal statement, interview. Minimum college GPA of 2.0 required. Lowest grade transferable C. **General Admission Information:** Application fee $35. Regular notification is rolling. Non-fall registration not accepted. Admission may be deferred for a maximum of up to 1 year. Common Application not accepted. Credit offered for CEEB Advanced Placement tests.

COSTS AND FINANCIAL AID

Annual tuition $11,100. Required fees $400. Average book expense $1,100. **Required Forms and Deadlines:** FAFSA. **Student Employment:** Federal Work-Study Program available. Institutional employment available. Off-campus job opportunities are good.

PENNSYLVANIA COLLEGE OF TECHNOLOGY

1 College Avenue, Williamsport, PA 17701
Phone: 570-327-4761 **E-mail:** Admissions@pct.edu
Fax: 570-321-5551 **Website:** www.pct.edu/princeton
Financial Aid Phone: 570-327-4766

This public school was founded in 1989. It has a 981-acre campus

RATINGS
Admissions Selectivity Rating: 60*   **Fire Safety Rating:** 60*   **Green Rating:** 60*

STUDENTS AND FACULTY
Enrollment: 6,458. **Student Body:** 34% female, 66% male. **Retention and Graduation:** Faculty: Student/faculty ratio 19:1. 288 full-time faculty.

ACADEMICS
Degrees: Associate, bachelor's, certificate. **Academic Requirements:** Arts/fine arts, computer literacy, English (including composition), humanities, mathematics, sciences (biological or physical), social science. **Classes:** Most classes have 10—19 students. **Majors with Highest Enrollment:** Building/construction management/manager; business administration/management; information technology. **Disciplines with Highest Percentage of Degrees Awarded:** Engineering technologies 41%, business/marketing 18%, health professions and related sciences 11%, mechanic and repair technologies 4%, visual and performing arts 3%. **Special Study Options:** Cooperative education program, cross-registration, distance learning, double major, dual enrollment, honor program, independent study, internships, study abroad.

FACILITIES
Housing: Coed dorms, apartments for single students, special housing for disabled students, special interest housing for the following groups: first-year students and school of health sciences. **Computers:** 95% of classrooms are wireless, 50% of public computers are PCs, 50% of public computers are Macs, network access in dorm rooms, online registration, online administrative functions (other than registration), support for handheld computing, remote student-access to Web through college's connection.

CAMPUS LIFE
Activities: Dance, radio station, student government, television station. **Organizations:** 50 registered organizations, 3 honor societies, 4 religious organizations. **Athletics (Intercollegiate):** *Men:* Archery, baseball, basketball, bowling, cross-country, golf, soccer, tennis, volleyball. *Women:* Archery, basketball, bowling, cross-country, golf, soccer, softball, tennis, volleyball.

ADMISSIONS
Freshman Academic Profile: TOEFL required of all international applicants, minimum paper TOEFL 500, minimum computer TOEFL 125. **Freshman Admission Requirements:** High school diploma is required, and GED is accepted. **Freshman Admission Statistics:** 2,793 applied, 97% admitted, 62% enrolled. **Transfer Admission Requirements:** College transcript(s). Lowest grade transferable C. **General Admission Information:** Application fee $50. Regular application deadline 7/1. Nonfall registration accepted. Admission may be deferred for a maximum of 1 year. Credit and/or placement offered for CEEB Advanced Placement tests.

COSTS AND FINANCIAL AID
Annual in-state tuition $11,260. Out-of-state tuition $14,150. Room & board $7,083. Average book expense $1,000. **Required Forms and Deadlines:** FAFSA, institution's own financial aid form. Financial aid filing deadline 4/1. **Notification of Awards:** Applicants will be notified of awards on or about 6/1. **Types of Aid:** *Need-based scholarships/grants:* Pell, SEOG, state scholarships/grants, private scholarships. *Loans:* FFEL Subsidized Stafford, FFEL

Unsubsidized Stafford, FFEL PLUS. **Student Employment: Financial Aid Statistics:** 76% undergrads receive any aid. Highest amount earned per year from on-campus jobs $2,300.

See page 1308.

PENNSYLVANIA STATE UNIVERSITY— ABINGTON

106 Sutherland, Abington, PA 19001
Phone: 215-881-7600 **E-mail:** abingtonadmissions@psu.edu
Fax: 215-881-7655 **Website:** www.abington.psu.edu

This public school was founded in 1950. It has a 45-acre campus.

RATINGS
Admissions Selectivity Rating: 71   **Fire Safety Rating:** 60*   **Green Rating:** 60*

STUDENTS AND FACULTY
Enrollment: 2,660. **Student Body:** 49% female, 51% male, 4% out-of-state. African American 12%, Asian 15%, Caucasian 67%, Hispanic 6%. **Retention and Graduation:** 77% freshmen return for sophomore year. **Faculty:** Student/faculty ratio 18:1. 108 full-time faculty, 59% hold PhDs.

ACADEMICS
Degrees: Bachelor's, terminal. **Academic Requirements:** Arts/fine arts, computer literacy, English (including composition), foreign languages, humanities, international cultures, mathematics, sciences (biological or physical), social science, United States cultures. **Classes:** Most classes have 20–29 students. Most lab/discussion sections have fewer than 10 students. **Disciplines with Highest Percentage of Degrees Awarded:** English 40%, business/marketing 39%, psychology 16%, security and protective services 16%, computer and information sciences 6%. **Special Study Options:** Accelerated program, cooperative education program, distance learning, double major, dual enrollment, English as a second language (ESL), exchange student program (domestic), external degree program, honors program, independent study, internships, liberal arts/career combination, student-designed major, study abroad.

CAMPUS LIFE
Activities: Dance, drama/theater, literary magazine, student government, student newspaper, student-run film society. **Athletics (Intercollegiate):** *Men:* Basketball, soccer, softball, tennis. *Women:* Basketball, field hockey, softball, tennis, volleyball.

ADMISSIONS
Freshman Academic Profile: 10% in top 10% of high school class, 28% in top 25% of high school class, 61% in top 50% of high school class. SAT Math middle 50% range 420–540. SAT Critical Reading middle 50% range 400–520. TOEFL required of all international applicants, minimum paper TOEFL 550. **Basis for Candidate Selection:** *Very important factors considered include:* Academic GPA, standardized test scores. *Important factors considered include:* Rigor of secondary school record. *Other factors considered include:* Alumni/ae relation, application essay, character/personal qualities, class rank, extracurricular activities, recommendation(s), talent/ability, volunteer work, work experience. **Freshman Admission Requirements:** High school diploma is required, and GED is accepted. *Academic units required:* 4 English, 3 math, 3 science, 2 foreign language, 3 social studies. **Freshman Admission Statistics:** 3,284 applied, 76% admitted, 35% enrolled. **Transfer Admission Requirements:** High school transcript, college transcript(s). Lowest grade transferable C. **General Admission Information:** Application fee $50. Regular notification is rolling. Non-fall registration accepted. Admission may be deferred for a maximum of 1 year.

COSTS AND FINANCIAL AID
Annual in-state tuition $10,454. Annual out-of-state tuition $15,954. Room and board $3,360. Required fees $552. Average book expense $1,168. **Required Forms and Deadlines:** FAFSA. Financial aid filing deadline 2/15. **Types of Aid:** *Need-based scholarships/grants:* Pell, SEOG, state scholarships/grants, private scholarships, the school's own gift aid. *Loans:* FFEL Subsidized Stafford, FFEL Unsubsidized Stafford, FFEL PLUS, Federal Perkins, college/university loans from institutional funds, private loans. **Financial Aid Statistics:** 55% freshmen, 51% undergrads receive need-based scholarship or grant aid. 53% freshmen, 53% undergrads receive need-based self-help aid.

PENNSYLVANIA STATE UNIVERSITY—ALTOONA

E108 Raymond Smith Building, Altoona, PA 16601-3760
Phone: 814-949-5466 **E-mail:** aaadmit@psu.edu
Fax: 814-949-5564 **Website:** www.aa.psu.edu

This public school was founded in 1929.

RATINGS
Admissions Selectivity Rating: 71   **Fire Safety Rating:** 60*   **Green Rating:** 60*

STUDENTS AND FACULTY
Enrollment: 3,705. **Student Body:** 50% female, 50% male, 14% out-of-state. African American 8%, Asian 2%, Caucasian 87%, Hispanic 2%. **Retention and Graduation:** 83% freshmen return for sophomore year. **Faculty:** Student/faculty ratio 18:1. 154 full-time faculty, 72% hold PhDs.

ACADEMICS
Degrees: Bachelor's, terminal. **Academic Requirements:** Arts/fine arts, computer literacy, English (including composition), foreign languages, humanities, international cultures, mathematics, sciences (biological or physical), social science, United States cultures. **Classes:** Most classes have 10–19 students. Most lab/discussion sections have 20–29 students. **Disciplines with Highest Percentage of Degrees Awarded:** Business/marketing 19%, education 14%, security and protective services 13%, engineering 11%, family and consumer sciences 10%. **Special Study Options:** Cooperative education program, cross-registration, distance learning, double major, dual enrollment, English as a second language (ESL), honors program, independent study, internships, liberal arts/career combination, student-designed major, study abroad, teacher certification program.

FACILITIES
Housing: Coed dorms, suites, special-interest housing.

CAMPUS LIFE
Activities: Choral groups, dance, drama/theater, jazz band, literary magazine, music ensembles, pep band, student government, student newspaper, student-run film society. **Athletics (Intercollegiate):** *Men:* Basketball, diving, skiing (downhill/alpine), soccer, swimming, tennis, volleyball. *Women:* Basketball, diving, skiing (downhill/alpine), swimming, tennis, volleyball.

ADMISSIONS
Freshman Academic Profile: 7% in top 10% of high school class, 28% in top 25% of high school class, 72% in top 50% of high school class. SAT Math middle 50% range 460–570. SAT Critical Reading middle 50% range 450–550. TOEFL required of all international applicants. **Basis for Candidate Selection:** *Very important factors considered include:* Academic GPA, rigor of secondary school record, standardized test scores. *Other factors considered include:* Alumni/ae relation, application essay, character/personal qualities, class rank, extracurricular activities, recommendation(s), talent/ability, volunteer work, work experience. **Freshman Admission Requirements:** High school diploma is required, and GED is accepted. *Academic units required:* 4 English, 3 math, 3 science, 2 foreign language, 3 social studies. **Freshman Admission Statistics:** 5,151 applied, 79% admitted, 37% enrolled. **Transfer Admission Requirements:** High school transcript, college transcript(s). Lowest grade transferable C. **General Admission Information:** Application fee $50. Regular notification is rolling. Non-fall registration accepted. Admission may be deferred for a maximum of 1 year.

COSTS AND FINANCIAL AID
Annual in-state tuition $10,912. Annual out-of-state tuition $16,694. Room and board $7,180. Required fees $552. Average book expense $1,168. **Required Forms and Deadlines:** FAFSA. Financial aid filing deadline 2/15. **Types of Aid:** *Need-based scholarships/grants:* Pell, SEOG, state scholarships/grants, private scholarships, the school's own gift aid. *Loans:* FFEL Subsidized Stafford, FFEL Unsubsidized Stafford, FFEL PLUS, Federal Perkins, college/university loans from institutional funds, private loans. **Financial Aid Statistics:** 46% freshmen, 49% undergrads receive need-based scholarship or grant aid. 61% freshmen, 62% undergrads receive need-based self-help aid.

PENNSYLVANIA STATE UNIVERSITY—BEAVER

100 University Drive, Monaca, PA 15061-2799
Phone: 877-564-3800 **E-mail:** br-admissions@psu.edu
Fax: 724-773-3658 **Website:** www.beaver.psu.edu

This public school was founded in 1964. It has a 90-acre campus.

RATINGS
Admissions Selectivity Rating: 68   **Fire Safety Rating:** 60*   **Green Rating:** 60*

STUDENTS AND FACULTY
Enrollment: 615. **Student Body:** 40% female, 60% male, 4% out-of-state. African American 7%, Asian 2%, Caucasian 90%. **Retention and Graduation:** 75% freshmen return for sophomore year. **Faculty:** Student/faculty ratio 16:1. 32 full-time faculty, 66% hold PhDs.

ACADEMICS
Degrees: Bachelor's, terminal. **Academic Requirements:** Arts/fine arts, computer literacy, English (including composition), foreign languages, humanities, international cultures, mathematics, sciences (biological or physical), social science, United States cultures. **Classes:** Most classes have 10–19 students. Most lab/discussion sections have 10–19 students. **Disciplines with Highest Percentage of Degrees Awarded:** Business/marketing 55%, computer and information sciences 21%, psychology 14%, communications/journalism 10%. **Special Study Options:** Accelerated program, cross-registration, distance learning, double major, dual enrollment, English as a second language (ESL), honors program, independent study, internships, study abroad.

FACILITIES
Housing: Coed dorms, townhouses.

CAMPUS LIFE
Activities: Drama/theater, literary magazine, radio station, student government, student newspaper, student-run film society. **Athletics (Intercollegiate):** *Men:* Baseball, basketball, fencing, ice hockey, tennis, track/field (outdoor), volleyball. *Women:* Basketball, fencing, ice hockey, softball, tennis, track/field (outdoor), volleyball.

ADMISSIONS
Freshman Academic Profile: 6% in top 10% of high school class, 29% in top 25% of high school class, 61% in top 50% of high school class. SAT Math middle 50% range 430–560. SAT Critical Reading middle 50% range 420–530. TOEFL required of all international applicants, minimum paper TOEFL 550. **Basis for Candidate Selection:** *Very important factors considered include:* Academic GPA, standardized test scores. *Important factors considered include:* Rigor of secondary school record. *Other factors considered include:* Alumni/ae relation, application essay, character/personal qualities, class rank, extracurricular activities, recommendation(s), talent/ability, volunteer work, work experience. **Freshman Admission Requirements:** High school diploma is required, and GED is accepted. *Academic units required:* 4 English, 3 math, 3 science, 2 foreign language, 3 social studies. **Freshman Admission Statistics:** 677 applied, 91% admitted, 40% enrolled. **Transfer Admission Requirements:** High school transcript, college transcript(s). Lowest grade transferable C. **General Admission Information:** Application fee $50. Regular notification is rolling. Non-fall registration accepted. Admission may be deferred for a maximum of 1 year.

COSTS AND FINANCIAL AID
Annual in-state tuition $10,454. Annual out-of-state tuition $15,954. Room and board $7,180. Required fees $552. Average book expense $1,168. **Required Forms and Deadlines:** FAFSA. Financial aid filing deadline 2/15. **Types of Aid:** *Need-based scholarships/grants:* Pell, SEOG, state scholarships/grants, private scholarships, the school's own gift aid. *Loans:* FFEL Subsidized Stafford, FFEL Unsubsidized Stafford, FFEL PLUS, Federal Perkins, college/university loans from institutional funds, private loans. **Financial Aid Statistics:** 49% freshmen, 52% undergrads receive need-based scholarship or grant aid. 63% freshmen, 63% undergrads receive need-based self-help aid.

PENNSYLVANIA STATE UNIVERSITY—BERKS

14 Perkins Student Center, Reading, PA 19610-6009
Phone: 610-396-6060 **E-mail:** admissionsbk@psu.edu
Fax: 610-396-6077 **Website:** www.bk.psu.edu

This public school was founded in 1924. It has a 241-acre campus.

RATINGS
Admissions Selectivity Rating: 70   **Fire Safety Rating:** 60*   **Green Rating:** 60*

STUDENTS AND FACULTY
Enrollment: 2,486. **Student Body:** 43% female, 57% male, 8% out-of-state. African American 8%, Asian 4%, Caucasian 84%, Hispanic 4%. **Retention and Graduation:** 82% freshmen return for sophomore year. **Faculty:** Student/faculty ratio 19:1. 105 full-time faculty, 68% hold PhDs.

ACADEMICS
Degrees: Bachelor's, terminal. **Academic Requirements:** Arts/fine arts, computer literacy, English (including composition), foreign languages, humanities, international cultures, mathematics, sciences (biological or physical), social science, United States cultures. **Classes:** Most classes have 20–29 students. Most lab/discussion sections have 10–19 students. **Disciplines with Highest Percentage of Degrees Awarded:** Business/marketing 38%, computer and information sciences 21%, psychology 12%, engineering 9%, parks and recreation 6%. **Special Study Options:** Accelerated program, cooperative education program, cross-registration, distance learning, dual enrollment, honors program, independent study, internships, study abroad.

FACILITIES
Housing: Coed dorms, special housing for disabled students, honor students, suites, special-interest houses.

CAMPUS LIFE
Activities: Choral groups, dance, drama/theater, pep band, radio station, student government, student newspaper, yearbook. **Athletics (Intercollegiate):** *Men:* Baseball, basketball, fencing, soccer, tennis, volleyball. *Women:* Fencing, softball, tennis, volleyball.

ADMISSIONS
Freshman Academic Profile: 4% in top 10% of high school class, 20% in top 25% of high school class, 56% in top 50% of high school class. SAT Math middle 50% range 430–560. SAT Critical Reading middle 50% range 420–540. TOEFL required of all international applicants, minimum paper TOEFL 550. **Basis for Candidate Selection:** *Very important factors considered include:* Academic GPA, standardized test scores. *Important factors considered include:* Rigor of secondary school record. *Other factors considered include:* Alumni/ae relation, application essay, character/personal qualities, class rank, extracurricular activities, recommendation(s), talent/ability, volunteer work, work experience. **Freshman Admission Requirements:** High school diploma is required, and GED is accepted. *Academic units required:* 4 English, 3 math, 3 science, 2 foreign language, 3 social studies. **Freshman Admission Statistics:** 3,069 applied, 79% admitted, 40% enrolled. **Transfer Admission Requirements:** High school transcript, college transcript(s). Lowest grade transferable C. **General Admission Information:** Application fee $50. Regular notification is rolling. Non-fall registration accepted. Admission may be deferred for a maximum of 1 year.

COSTS AND FINANCIAL AID
Annual in-state tuition $10,912. Annual out-of-state tuition $16,694. Room and board $7,850. Required fees $552. Average book expense $1,168. **Required Forms and Deadlines:** FAFSA. Financial aid filing deadline 2/15. **Types of Aid:** *Need-based scholarships/grants:* Pell, SEOG, state scholarships/grants, private scholarships, the school's own gift aid. *Loans:* Direct Subsidized Stafford, FFEL Subsidized Stafford, FFEL Unsubsidized Stafford, FFEL PLUS, Federal Perkins, college/university loans from institutional funds, private loans. **Financial Aid Statistics:** 35% freshmen, 37% undergrads receive need-based scholarship or grant aid. 50% freshmen, 49% undergrads receive need-based self-help aid.

PENNSYLVANIA STATE UNIVERSITY— DELAWARE COUNTY

25 Yearsley Mill Road, Media, PA 19063-5596
Phone: 610-892-1200 **E-mail:** admissions-delco@psu.edu
Fax: 610-892-1320 **Website:** www.de.psu.edu

This public school was founded in 1966. It has an 87-acre campus.

RATINGS
Admissions Selectivity Rating: 70   **Fire Safety Rating:** 60*   **Green Rating:** 60*

STUDENTS AND FACULTY
Enrollment: 1,440. **Student Body:** 45% female, 55% male, 3% out-of-state. African American 16%, Asian 7%, Caucasian 74%, Hispanic 2%. **Retention and Graduation:** 69% freshmen return for sophomore year. **Faculty:** Student/faculty ratio 18:1. 62 full-time faculty, 58% hold PhDs.

ACADEMICS
Degrees: Bachelor's, terminal. **Academic Requirements:** Arts/fine arts, computer literacy, English (including composition), foreign languages, humanities, international cultures, mathematics, sciences (biological or physical), social science, United States cultures. **Classes:** Most classes have 20–29 students. Most lab/discussion sections have fewer than 10 students. **Disciplines with Highest Percentage of Degrees Awarded:** Business/marketing 46%, family and consumer sciences 13%, computer and information sciences 10%, communications/journalism 9%, liberal arts/general studies 7%. **Special Study Options:** Distance learning, double major, dual enrollment, English as a second language (ESL), honors program, independent study, internships, study abroad, teacher certification program.

CAMPUS LIFE
Activities: Choral groups, dance, drama/theater, literary magazine, student government, student newspaper, student-run film society. **Athletics (Intercollegiate):** *Men:* Baseball, basketball, ice hockey, riflery, soccer, tennis, volleyball. *Women:* Basketball, ice hockey, riflery, soccer, tennis, volleyball.

ADMISSIONS
Freshman Academic Profile: 6% in top 10% of high school class, 22% in top 25% of high school class, 54% in top 50% of high school class. SAT Math middle 50% range 410–540. SAT Critical Reading middle 50% range 400–520. TOEFL required of all international applicants, minimum paper TOEFL 550. **Basis for Candidate Selection:** *Very important factors considered include:* Academic GPA, standardized test scores. *Important factors considered include:* Rigor of secondary school record. *Other factors considered include:* Alumni/ae relation, application essay, character/personal qualities, class rank, extracurricular activities, recommendation(s), talent/ability, volunteer work, work experience. **Freshman Admission Requirements:** High school diploma is required, and GED is accepted. *Academic units required:* 4 English, 3 math, 3 science, 2 foreign language, 3 social studies. **Freshman Admission Statistics:** 1,724 applied, 75% admitted, 36% enrolled. **Transfer Admission Requirements:** High school transcript, college transcript(s). Lowest grade transferable C. **General Admission Information:** Application fee $50. Regular notification is rolling. Non-fall registration accepted. Admission may be deferred for a maximum of 1 year.

COSTS AND FINANCIAL AID
Annual in-state tuition $10,008. Out-of-state tuition $15,284. Room & board $3,230. Required fees $512. Average book expense $1,088. **Required Forms and Deadlines:** FAFSA. Financial aid filing deadline 2/15. **Types of Aid:** *Need-based scholarships/grants:* Pell, SEOG, state scholarships/grants, private scholarships, the school's own gift aid. *Loans:* FFEL Subsidized Stafford, FFEL Unsubsidized Stafford, FFEL PLUS, Federal Perkins, college/university loans from institutional funds, private loans. **Financial Aid Statistics:** 46% freshmen, 45% undergrads receive need-based scholarship or grant aid. 50% freshmen, 48% undergrads receive need-based self-help aid.

PENNSYLVANIA STATE UNIVERSITY—DUBOIS

108 Hiller, Dubois, PA 15801-3199
Phone: 814-375-4720 **E-mail:** duboisinfo@psu.edu
Fax: 814-375-4784 **Website:** www.ds.psu.edu

This public school was founded in 1935. It has a 13-acre campus.

RATINGS
Admissions Selectivity Rating: 67   **Fire Safety Rating:** 60*   **Green Rating:** 60*

STUDENTS AND FACULTY
Enrollment: 667. **Student Body:** 53% female, 47% male, 1% out-of-state. African American 1%, Caucasian 98%. **Retention and Graduation:** 81% freshmen return for sophomore year. **Faculty:** Student/faculty ratio 12:1. 42 full-time faculty, 57% hold PhDs.

ACADEMICS
Degrees: Bachelor's, terminal. **Academic Requirements:** Arts/fine arts, computer literacy, English (including composition), foreign languages, humanities, international cultures, mathematics, sciences (biological or physical), social science, United States cultures. **Classes:** Most classes have 10–19 students. Most lab/discussion sections have fewer than 10 students. **Disciplines with Highest Percentage of Degrees Awarded:** Business/marketing 45%, family and consumer sciences 39%, liberal arts/general studies 16%. **Special Study Options:** Accelerated program, cross-registration, distance learning, double major, dual enrollment, honors program, independent study, internships, student-designed major, study abroad.

FACILITIES
Housing: Independently owned housing nearby.

CAMPUS LIFE
Activities: Choral groups, drama/theater, literary magazine, student government, student newspaper, student-run film society. **Athletics (Intercollegiate):** *Men:* Basketball. *Women:* Volleyball.

ADMISSIONS
Freshman Academic Profile: 9% in top 10% of high school class, 25% in top 25% of high school class, 59% in top 50% of high school class. SAT Math middle 50% range 415–545. SAT Critical Reading middle 50% range 410–500. SAT Critical Reading middle 50% range 400–510. TOEFL required of all international applicants, minimum paper TOEFL 550. **Basis for Candidate Selection:** *Very important factors considered include:* Academic GPA, standardized test scores. *Important factors considered include:* Rigor of secondary school record. *Other factors considered include:* Alumni/ae relation, application essay, character/personal qualities, class rank, extracurricular activities, recommendation(s), talent/ability, volunteer work, work experience. **Freshman Admission Requirements:** High school diploma is required, and GED is accepted. *Academic units required:* 4 English, 3 math, 3 science, 2 foreign language, 3 social studies. **Freshman Admission Statistics:** 424 applied, 89% admitted, 51% enrolled. **Transfer Admission Requirements:** High school transcript, college transcript(s). Lowest grade transferable C. **General Admission Information:** Application fee $50. Regular notification is rolling. Non-fall registration accepted. Admission may be deferred for a maximum of 1 year.

COSTS AND FINANCIAL AID
Annual in-state tuition $10,454. Annual out-of-state tuition $15,954. Room and board $3,360. Required fees $542. Average book expense $1,168. **Required Forms and Deadlines:** FAFSA. Financial aid filing deadline 2/15. **Types of Aid:** *Need-based scholarships/grants:* Pell, SEOG, state scholarships/grants, private scholarships, the school's own gift aid. *Loans:* FFEL Subsidized Stafford, FFEL Unsubsidized Stafford, FFEL PLUS, Federal Perkins, college/university loans from institutional funds, private loans. **Financial Aid Statistics:** 70% freshmen, 71% undergrads receive need-based scholarship or grant aid. 72% freshmen, 76% undergrads receive need-based self-help aid.

PENNSYLVANIA STATE UNIVERSITY— ERIE, THE BEHREND COLLEGE

5091 Station Road, Erie, PA 16563-0105
Phone: 814-898-6100 **E-mail:** behrend.admissions@psu.edu
Fax: 814-898-6044 **Website:** www.erie.psu.edu **ACT Code:** 3656
Financial Aid Phone: 814-898-6162

This public school was founded in 1948. It has a 732-acre campus.

RATINGS
Admissions Selectivity Rating: 74   **Fire Safety Rating:** 60*   **Green Rating:** 60*

STUDENTS AND FACULTY
Enrollment: 3,494. **Student Body:** 35% female, 65% male, 7% out-of-state, 1% international. African American 4%, Asian 2%, Caucasian 91%, Hispanic 1%. **Retention and Graduation:** 84% freshmen return for sophomore year. **Faculty:** Student/faculty ratio 16:1. 198 full-time faculty, 60% hold PhDs. 100% faculty teach undergrads.

ACADEMICS
Degrees: Bachelor's, master's, terminal. **Academic Requirements:** Arts/fine arts, computer literacy, English (including composition), foreign languages, humanities, international cultures, mathematics, sciences (biological or physical), social science, United States cultures. **Classes:** Most classes have 20–29 students. Most lab/discussion sections have 10–19 students. **Disciplines with Highest Percentage of Degrees Awarded:** Business/marketing 37%, engineering 20%, engineering technologies 8%, psychology 6%, communications/journalism 6%. **Special Study Options:** Accelerated program, cooperative education program, distance learning, double major, dual enrollment, honors program, independent study, internships, liberal arts/career combination, study abroad, teacher certification program.

FACILITIES
Housing: Coed dorms, men's dorms, women's dorms, apartments for single students, special housing for disabled students, suites, special-interest housing. **Special Academic Facilities/Equipment:** Observatory, plastics lab. **Computers:** 95% of public computers are PCs, 5% of public computers are UNIX, network access in dorm rooms, network access in dorm lounges, online registration, online administrative functions (other than registration), remote student-access to Web through college's connection.

CAMPUS LIFE
Activities: Choral groups, concert band, dance, drama/theater, jazz band, literary magazine, music ensembles, pep band, radio station, student government, student newspaper, student-run film society. **Organizations:** 75 registered organizations, 46 honor societies, 26 religious organizations. 6 fraternities (3% men join), 4 sororities (1% women join). **Athletics (Intercollegiate):** *Men:* Baseball, basketball, cheerleading, cross-country, golf, soccer, swimming, tennis, track/field (outdoor), water polo, wrestling. *Women:* Basketball, cheerleading, cross-country, golf, soccer, softball, swimming, tennis, track/field (outdoor), volleyball, water polo.

ADMISSIONS
Freshman Academic Profile: 11% in top 10% of high school class, 37% in top 25% of high school class, 81% in top 50% of high school class. SAT Math middle 50% range 480–590. SAT Critical Reading middle 50% range 460–560. TOEFL required of all international applicants, minimum paper TOEFL 550. **Basis for Candidate Selection:** *Very important factors considered include:* Academic GPA, standardized test scores. *Important factors considered include:* Rigor of secondary school record. *Other factors considered include:* Alumni/ae relation, application essay, character/personal qualities, class rank, extracurricular activities, recommendation(s), talent/ability, volunteer work, work experience. **Freshman Admission Requirements:** High school diploma is required, and GED is accepted. *Academic units required:* 4 English, 3 math, 3 science, 2 foreign language, 3 social studies. **Freshman Admission Statistics:** 2,948 applied, 82% admitted, 43% enrolled. **Transfer Admission Requirements:** High school transcript, college transcript(s). Lowest grade transferable C. **General Admission Information:** Application fee $50. Regular notification is rolling. Non-fall registration accepted. Admission may be deferred for a maximum of 1 year. Credit offered for CEEB Advanced Placement tests.

COSTS AND FINANCIAL AID
Annual in-state tuition $10,912. Annual out-of-state tuition $16,694. Room and board $7,180. Required fees $552. Average book expense $1,168. **Required Forms and Deadlines:** FAFSA. Financial aid filing deadline 2/15. **Types of Aid:** *Need-based scholarships/grants:* Pell, SEOG, state scholarships/grants, private scholarships, the school's own gift aid. *Loans:* FFEL Subsidized

Stafford, FFEL Unsubsidized Stafford, FFEL PLUS, Federal Perkins, college/university loans from institutional funds, private loans. **Student Employment:** Federal Work-Study Program available. Institutional employment available. Off-campus job opportunities are good. **Financial Aid Statistics:** 48% freshmen, 49% undergrads receive need-based scholarship or grant aid. 64% freshmen, 63% undergrads receive need-based self-help aid. Highest amount earned per year from on-campus jobs $656.

PENNSYLVANIA STATE UNIVERSITY— FAYETTE, THE EBERLY CAMPUS

PO Box 519, Route 119 North, 108 Williams Building, Uniontown, PA 15401-0519
Phone: 724-430-4130 **E-mail:** feadm@psu.edu
Fax: 724-430-4175 **Website:** www.fe.psu.edu

This public school was founded in 1934. It has a 193-acre campus.

RATINGS
Admissions Selectivity Rating: 71   **Fire Safety Rating:** 60*   **Green Rating:** 60*

STUDENTS AND FACULTY
Enrollment: 903. **Student Body:** 61% female, 39% male, 1% out-of-state. African American 5%, Caucasian 94%. **Retention and Graduation:** 77% freshmen return for sophomore year. **Faculty:** Student/faculty ratio 14:1. 53 full-time faculty, 49% hold PhDs.

ACADEMICS
Degrees: Bachelor's, terminal. **Academic Requirements:** Arts/fine arts, computer literacy, English (including composition), foreign languages, humanities, international cultures, mathematics, sciences (biological or physical), social science, United States cultures. **Classes:** Most classes have 10–19 students. Most lab/discussion sections have fewer than 10 students. **Disciplines with Highest Percentage of Degrees Awarded:** Business/marketing 43%, security and protective services 40%, family and consumer sciences 14%, liberal arts/general studies 4%. **Special Study Options:** Accelerated program, cross-registration, distance learning, double major, dual enrollment, honors program, independent study, internships, student-designed major, study abroad, weekend college.

CAMPUS LIFE
Activities: Choral groups, drama/theater, student government, student newspaper.

ADMISSIONS
Freshman Academic Profile: 12% in top 10% of high school class, 38% in top 25% of high school class, 72% in top 50% of high school class. SAT Math middle 50% range 400–520. SAT Critical Reading middle 50% range 400–510. TOEFL required of all international applicants, minimum paper TOEFL 550. **Basis for Candidate Selection:** *Very important factors considered include:* Academic GPA, standardized test scores. *Important factors considered include:* Rigor of secondary school record. *Other factors considered include:* Alumni/ae relation, application essay, character/personal qualities, class rank, extracurricular activities, recommendation(s), talent/ability, volunteer work, work experience. **Freshman Admission Requirements:** High school diploma is required, and GED is accepted. *Academic units required:* 4 English, 3 math, 3 science, 2 foreign language, 3 social studies. **Freshman Admission Statistics:** 537 applied, 85% admitted, 46% enrolled. **Transfer Admission Requirements:** High school transcript, college transcript(s). Lowest grade transferable C. **General Admission Information:** Application fee $50. Regular notification is rolling. Non-fall registration accepted. Admission may be deferred for a maximum of 1 year.

COSTS AND FINANCIAL AID
Annual in-state tuition $10,454. Annual out-of-state tuition $15,954. Room and board $3,360. Required fees $542. Average book expense $1,168. **Required Forms and Deadlines:** FAFSA. Financial aid filing deadline 2/15. **Types of Aid:** *Need-based scholarships/grants:* Pell, SEOG, state scholarships/grants, private scholarships, the school's own gift aid. *Loans:* FFEL Subsidized Stafford, FFEL Unsubsidized Stafford, FFEL PLUS, Federal Perkins, college/university loans from institutional funds, private loans. **Financial Aid Statistics:** 68% freshmen, 71% undergrads receive need-based scholarship or grant aid. 76% freshmen, 78% undergrads receive need-based self-help aid. 1 undergrad receives athletic scholarship.

PENNSYLVANIA STATE UNIVERSITY— GREATER ALLEGHENY

101 Frable Building, 4000 University Drive, McKeesport, PA 15132
Phone: 412-675-9010 **E-mail:** psumk@psu.edu
Fax: 412-675-9056 **Website:** www.ga.psu.edu

This is a public school.

RATINGS
Admissions Selectivity Rating: 70   **Fire Safety Rating:** 60*   **Green Rating:** 60*

STUDENTS AND FACULTY
Enrollment: 643. **Student Body:** 40% female, 60% male, 6% out-of-state. African American 17%, Asian 2%, Caucasian 77%, Hispanic 2%. **Retention and Graduation:** 78% freshmen return for sophomore year. **Faculty:** Student/faculty ratio 14:1. 38 full-time faculty, 74% hold PhDs.

ACADEMICS
Degrees: Bachelor's, terminal. **Academic Requirements:** Arts/fine arts, English (including composition), foreign languages, humanities, international cultures, mathematics, sciences (biological or physical), social science, United States cultures. **Classes:** Most classes have fewer than 10 students. Most lab/discussion sections have 10–19 students. **Disciplines with Highest Percentage of Degrees Awarded:** Business/marketing 43%, computer and information sciences 33%, psychology 15%, communications/journalism 9%. **Special Study Options:** Accelerated program, cross-registration, distance learning, double major, dual enrollment, honors program, independent study, internships, study abroad.

FACILITIES
Housing: Coed dorms.

CAMPUS LIFE
Activities: Choral groups, dance, drama/theater, jazz band, literary magazine, radio station, student government, student newspaper. **Athletics (Intercollegiate):** *Men:* Basketball, diving, fencing, ice hockey, skiing (downhill/alpine), soccer, squash, swimming, tennis, track/field (outdoor), volleyball. *Women:* Diving, fencing, skiing (downhill/alpine), squash, swimming, tennis, track/field (outdoor), volleyball.

ADMISSIONS
Freshman Academic Profile: 7% in top 10% of high school class, 33% in top 25% of high school class, 68% in top 50% of high school class. SAT Math middle 50% range 400–540. SAT Critical Reading middle 50% range 400–520. TOEFL required of all international applicants, minimum paper TOEFL 550, minimum computer TOEFL 213. **Basis for Candidate Selection:** *Very important factors considered include:* Academic GPA, standardized test scores. *Important factors considered include:* Rigor of secondary school record. *Other factors considered include:* Alumni/ae relation, application essay, character/personal qualities, class rank, extracurricular activities, recommendation(s), talent/ability, volunteer work, work experience. **Freshman Admission Requirements:** High school diploma is required, and GED is accepted. *Academic units required:* 4 English, 3 math, 3 science, 2 foreign language, 3 social studies. **Freshman Admission Statistics:** 540 applied, 84% admitted, 51% enrolled. **Transfer Admission Requirements:** High school transcript, college transcript(s). Lowest grade transferable C. **General Admission Information:** Application fee $50. Non-fall registration accepted. Admission may be deferred for a maximum of 1 year. Credit and/or placement offered for CEEB Advanced Placement tests.

COSTS AND FINANCIAL AID
Annual in-state tuition $10,454. Annual out-of-state tuition $15,954. Room and board $7,180. Required fees $552. Average book expense $1,168. **Required Forms and Deadlines:** FAFSA. Financial aid filing deadline 2/15. **Types of Aid:** *Need-based scholarships/grants:* Pell, SEOG, state scholarships/grants, private scholarships, the school's own gift aid. *Loans:* Direct Subsidized Stafford, Direct Unsubsidized Stafford, Direct PLUS, FFEL Subsidized Stafford, FFEL Unsubsidized Stafford, FFEL PLUS, Federal Perkins, college/university loans from institutional funds, private loans. **Financial Aid Statistics:** 58% freshmen, 55% undergrads receive need-based scholarship or grant aid. 63% freshmen, 66% undergrads receive need-based self-help aid.

PENNSYLVANIA STATE UNIVERSITY— HARRISBURG

Swatapa Building, 777 West Harrisburg Pike, Middletown, PA 17057-4898
Phone: 717-948-6250 **E-mail:** hbgadmit@psu.edu
Fax: 717-948-6325 **Website:** www.hbg.psu.edu

This public school was founded in 1966.

RATINGS
Admissions Selectivity Rating: 74   **Fire Safety Rating:** 60*   **Green Rating:** 60*

STUDENTS AND FACULTY
Enrollment: 2,137. **Student Body:** 47% female, 53% male, 7% out-of-state, 2% international. African American 9%, Asian 7%, Caucasian 79%, Hispanic 4%. **Retention and Graduation:** 85% freshmen return for sophomore year. **Faculty:** Student/faculty ratio 12:1. 179 full-time faculty, 83% hold PhDs.

ACADEMICS
Degrees: Bachelor's, doctoral, master's, post-bachelor's certificate, terminal. **Academic Requirements:** Arts/fine arts, computer literacy, English (including composition), foreign languages, humanities, international cultures, mathematics, sciences (biological or physical), social science, United States cultures. **Classes:** Most classes have 20–29 students. Most lab/discussion sections have fewer than 10 students. **Disciplines with Highest Percentage of Degrees Awarded:** Business/marketing 33%, engineering 16%, education 11%, computer and information sciences 10%, psychology 8%. **Special Study Options:** Accelerated program, cooperative education program, cross-registration, distance learning, double major, dual enrollment, honors program, independent study, internships, student-designed major, study abroad, teacher certification program, weekend college.

FACILITIES
Housing: Apartments for single students, special housing for disabled students, special-interest housing.

CAMPUS LIFE
Activities: Choral groups, dance, drama/theater, literary magazine, radio station, student government, student newspaper. **Organizations:** 2 honor societies, 1 religious organization. **Athletics (Intercollegiate):** *Men:* Basketball, skiing (downhill/alpine), soccer, tennis, track/field (outdoor), volleyball. *Women:* skiing (downhill/alpine), soccer, track/field (outdoor), volleyball.

ADMISSIONS
Freshman Academic Profile: 6% in top 10% of high school class, 32% in top 25% of high school class, 80% in top 50% of high school class. SAT Math middle 50% range 475–580. SAT Critical Reading middle 50% range 460–570. TOEFL required of all international applicants. **Basis for Candidate Selection:** *Very important factors considered include:* Academic GPA, standardized test scores. *Important factors considered include:* Rigor of secondary school record. *Other factors considered include:* Alumni/ae relation, application essay, character/personal qualities, class rank, extracurricular activities, recommendation(s), talent/ability, volunteer work, work experience. **Freshman Admission Requirements:** High school diploma is required, and GED is accepted. *Academic units required:* 4 English, 3 math, 3 science, 2 foreign language, 3 social studies. **Freshman Admission Statistics:** 2,271 applied, 68% admitted, 22% enrolled. **Transfer Admission Requirements:** High school transcript, college transcript(s). **General Admission Information:** Application fee $50. Regular notification is rolling. Non-fall registration accepted. Admission may be deferred for a maximum of 1 year.

COSTS AND FINANCIAL AID
Annual in-state tuition $10,912. Annual out-of-state tuition $16,694. Room and board $8,610. Required fees $542. Average book expense $1,168. **Required Forms and Deadlines:** FAFSA. Financial aid filing deadline 2/15. **Types of Aid:** *Need-based scholarships/grants:* Pell, SEOG, state scholarships/grants, private scholarships, the school's own gift aid. *Loans:* FFEL Subsidized Stafford, FFEL Unsubsidized Stafford, FFEL PLUS, Federal Perkins, college/university loans from institutional funds, private loans. **Financial Aid Statistics:** 42% freshmen, 47% undergrads receive need-based scholarship or grant aid. 54% freshmen, 57% undergrads receive need-based self-help aid.

PENNSYLVANIA STATE UNIVERSITY— HAZLETON

110 Administration Building, 76 University Drive, Hazleton, PA 18202
Phone: 570-450-3142 **E-mail:** admissions-hn@psu.edu
Fax: 570-450-3182 **Website:** www.hn.psu.edu

This public school was founded in 1934. It has a 73-acre campus.

RATINGS
Admissions Selectivity Rating: 69   **Fire Safety Rating:** 60*   **Green Rating:** 60*

STUDENTS AND FACULTY
Enrollment: 1,103. **Student Body:** 39% female, 61% male, 25% out-of-state. African American 8%, Asian 6%, Caucasian 78%, Hispanic 7%. **Retention and Graduation:** 82% freshmen return for sophomore year. **Faculty:** Student/faculty ratio 18:1. 50 full-time faculty, 60% hold PhDs.

ACADEMICS
Degrees: Bachelor's, terminal. **Academic Requirements:** Arts/fine arts, computer literacy, English (including composition), foreign languages, humanities, international cultures, mathematics, sciences (biological or physical), social science, United States cultures. **Classes:** Most classes have 10–19 students. Most lab/discussion sections have fewer than 10 students. **Disciplines with Highest Percentage of Degrees Awarded:** Computer and information sciences 42%, business/marketing 31%, liberal arts/general studies 28%. **Special Study Options:** Accelerated program, cross-registration, distance learning, double major, dual enrollment, English as a second language (ESL), honors program, independent study, internships, student-designed major, study abroad.

FACILITIES
Housing: Coed dorms, townhouses, suites.

CAMPUS LIFE
Activities: Choral groups, dance, drama/theater, literary magazine, radio station, student government, student newspaper. **Athletics (Intercollegiate):** *Men:* Baseball, basketball, soccer, tennis. *Women:* Softball, tennis, volleyball.

ADMISSIONS
Freshman Academic Profile: 4% in top 10% of high school class, 24% in top 25% of high school class, 62% in top 50% of high school class. SAT Math middle 50% range 420–540. SAT Critical Reading middle 50% range 420–530. TOEFL required of all international applicants, minimum paper TOEFL 550. **Basis for Candidate Selection:** *Very important factors considered include:* Academic GPA, standardized test scores. *Important factors considered include:* Rigor of secondary school record. *Other factors considered include:* Alumni/ae relation, application essay, character/personal qualities, class rank, extracurricular activities, recommendation(s), talent/ability, volunteer work, work experience. **Freshman Admission Requirements:** High school diploma is required, and GED is accepted. *Academic units required:* 4 English, 3 math, 3 science, 2 foreign language, 3 social studies. **Freshman Admission Statistics:** 1,296 applied, 89% admitted, 47% enrolled. **Transfer Admission Requirements:** High school transcript, college transcript(s). Lowest grade transferable C. **General Admission Information:** Application fee $50. Regular notification is rolling. Non-fall registration accepted. Admission may be deferred for a maximum of 1 year.

COSTS AND FINANCIAL AID
Annual in-state tuition $10,454. Annual out-of-state tuition $15,954. Room and board $7,180. Required fees $552. Average book expense $1,168. **Required Forms and Deadlines:** FAFSA. Financial aid filing deadline 2/15. **Types of Aid:** *Need-based scholarships/grants:* Pell, SEOG, state scholarships/grants, private scholarships, the school's own gift aid. *Loans:* FFEL Subsidized Stafford, FFEL Unsubsidized Stafford, FFEL PLUS, Federal Perkins, college/university loans from institutional funds, private loans. **Financial Aid Statistics:** 52% freshmen, 52% undergrads receive need-based scholarship or grant aid. 65% freshmen, 63% undergrads receive need-based self-help aid.

PENNSYLVANIA STATE UNIVERSITY— LEHIGH VALLEY

8380 Mohr Lane, Academic Building, Fogelsville, PA 18051
Phone: 610-285-5035 **E-mail:** epg2@psu.edu
Fax: 610-285-5220 **Website:** www.lv.psu.edu

This public school was founded in 1912. It has a 42-acre campus.

RATINGS
Admissions Selectivity Rating: 71 **Fire Safety Rating:** 60* **Green Rating:** 60*

STUDENTS AND FACULTY
Enrollment: 628. **Student Body:** 41% female, 59% male, 3% out-of-state. African American 4%, Asian 4%, Caucasian 84%, Hispanic 8%. **Retention and Graduation:** 83% freshmen return for sophomore year. **Faculty:** Student/faculty ratio 15:1. 28 full-time faculty, 75% hold PhDs.

ACADEMICS
Degrees: Bachelor's, terminal. **Academic Requirements:** Arts/fine arts, computer literacy, English (including composition), foreign languages, humanities, international cultures, mathematics, sciences (biological or physical), social science, United States cultures. **Classes:** Most classes have 10–19 students. Most lab/discussion sections have 10–19 students. **Disciplines with Highest Percentage of Degrees Awarded:** Business/marketing 64%, psychology 17%, computer and information sciences 14%, English 3%, interdisciplinary studies 3%. **Special Study Options:** Accelerated program, cooperative education program, cross-registration, distance learning, dual enrollment, honors program, independent study, internships, study abroad.

CAMPUS LIFE
Activities: Drama/theater, student government, student newspaper. **Athletics (Intercollegiate):** *Men:* Basketball, cross-country, golf, soccer, tennis, volleyball. *Women:* Basketball, golf, tennis, volleyball.

ADMISSIONS
Freshman Academic Profile: 9% in top 10% of high school class, 26% in top 25% of high school class, 72% in top 50% of high school class. SAT Math middle 50% range 450–570. SAT Critical Reading middle 50% range 420–530. TOEFL required of all international applicants, minimum paper TOEFL 550. **Basis for Candidate Selection:** *Very important factors considered include:* Academic GPA, standardized test scores. *Important factors considered include:* Rigor of secondary school record. *Other factors considered include:* Alumni/ae relation, application essay, character/personal qualities, class rank, extracurricular activities, recommendation(s), talent/ability, volunteer work, work experience. **Freshman Admission Requirements:** High school diploma is required, and GED is accepted. *Academic units required:* 4 English, 3 math, 3 science, 2 foreign language, 3 social studies. **Freshman Admission Statistics:** 982 applied, 78% admitted, 26% enrolled. **Transfer Admission Requirements:** High school transcript, college transcript(s). Lowest grade transferable C. **General Admission Information:** Application fee $50. Regular notification is rolling. Non-fall registration accepted. Admission may be deferred for a maximum of 1 year.

COSTS AND FINANCIAL AID
Annual in-state tuition $10,454. Annual out-of-state tuition $15,954. Room and board $3,360. Required fees $552. Average book expense $1,168. **Required Forms and Deadlines:** FAFSA. Financial aid filing deadline 2/15. **Types of Aid:** *Need-based scholarships/grants:* Pell, SEOG, state scholarships/grants, private scholarships, the school's own gift aid. *Loans:* FFEL Subsidized Stafford, FFEL Unsubsidized Stafford, FFEL PLUS, Federal Perkins, college/university loans from institutional funds, private loans. **Financial Aid Statistics:** 53% freshmen, 48% undergrads receive need-based scholarship or grant aid. 54% freshmen, 51% undergrads receive need-based self-help aid.

PENNSYLVANIA STATE UNIVERSITY— MONT ALTO

1 Campus Drive, Mont Alto, PA 17237-9703
Phone: 717-749-6130 **E-mail:** psuma@psu.edu
Fax: 717-749-6132 **Website:** www.ma.psu.edu

This public school was founded in 1929. It has a 62-acre campus.

RATINGS
Admissions Selectivity Rating: 70 **Fire Safety Rating:** 60* **Green Rating:** 60*

STUDENTS AND FACULTY
Enrollment: 910. **Student Body:** 60% female, 40% male, 12% out-of-state. African American 14%, Asian 3%, Caucasian 80%, Hispanic 3%. **Retention and Graduation:** 76% freshmen return for sophomore year. 22% grads go on to further study within 1 year. **Faculty:** Student/faculty ratio 13:1. 53 full-time faculty, 49% hold PhDs.

ACADEMICS
Degrees: Bachelor's, terminal. **Academic Requirements:** Arts/fine arts, computer literacy, English (including composition), foreign languages, humanities, international cultures, mathematics, sciences (biological or physical), social science, United States cultures. **Classes:** Most classes have 10–19 students. Most lab/discussion sections have fewer than 10 students. **Disciplines with Highest Percentage of Degrees Awarded:** Health professions and related sciences 50%, business/marketing 25%, family and consumer sciences 19%. **Special Study Options:** Accelerated program, cross-registration, distance learning, double major, dual enrollment, honors program, independent study, internships, study abroad.

FACILITIES
Housing: Coed dorms, special housing for disabled students, suites, special-interest housing, townhouses.

CAMPUS LIFE
Activities: Dance, drama/theater, jazz band, student government, student newspaper. **Athletics (Intercollegiate):** *Men:* Basketball, soccer, tennis. *Women:* Basketball, tennis.

ADMISSIONS
Freshman Academic Profile: 9% in top 10% of high school class, 28% in top 25% of high school class, 67% in top 50% of high school class. SAT Math middle 50% range 430–560. SAT Critical Reading middle 50% range 440–545. **Basis for Candidate Selection:** *Very important factors considered include:* Academic GPA, standardized test scores. *Important factors considered include:* Rigor of secondary school record. *Other factors considered include:* Alumni/ae relation, application essay, character/personal qualities, class rank, extracurricular activities, recommendation(s), talent/ability, volunteer work, work experience. **Freshman Admission Requirements:** High school diploma is required, and GED is accepted. *Academic units required:* 4 English, 3 math, 3 science, 2 foreign language, 3 social studies. **Freshman Admission Statistics:** 827 applied, 86% admitted, 56% enrolled. **Transfer Admission Requirements:** High school transcript, college transcript(s). Lowest grade transferable C. **General Admission Information:** Application fee $50. Regular notification is rolling. Non-fall registration accepted. Admission may be deferred for a maximum of 1 year.

COSTS AND FINANCIAL AID
Annual in-state tuition $10,454. Annual out-of-state tuition $15,954. Room and board $7,180. Required fees $552. Average book expense $1,168. **Required Forms and Deadlines:** FAFSA. Financial aid filing deadline 2/15. **Types of Aid:** *Need-based scholarships/grants:* Pell, SEOG, state scholarships/grants, private scholarships, the school's own gift aid. *Loans:* FFEL Subsidized Stafford, FFEL Unsubsidized Stafford, FFEL PLUS, Federal Perkins, college/university loans from institutional funds, private loans. **Financial Aid Statistics:** 50% freshmen, 52% undergrads receive need-based scholarship or grant aid. 62% freshmen, 63% undergrads receive need-based self-help aid.

PENNSYLVANIA STATE UNIVERSITY— NEW KENSINGTON

3550 7th Street Road, Route 780, New Kensington, PA 15068-1798
Phone: 724-334-5466 **E-mail:** nkadmissions@psu.edu
Fax: 724-334-6111 **Website:** www.nk.psu.edu

This public school was founded in 1958. It has a 71-acre campus.

RATINGS
Admissions Selectivity Rating: 70   **Fire Safety Rating:** 60*   **Green Rating:** 60*

STUDENTS AND FACULTY
Enrollment: 720. **Student Body:** 45% female, 55% male, 2% out-of-state. African American 2%, Caucasian 96%, Hispanic 1%. **Retention and Graduation:** 72% freshmen return for sophomore year. **Faculty:** Student/faculty ratio 13:1. 41 full-time faculty, 61% hold PhDs.

ACADEMICS
Degrees: Bachelor's, terminal. **Academic Requirements:** Arts/fine arts, computer literacy, English (including composition), foreign languages, humanities, international cultures, mathematics, sciences (biological or physical), social science, United States cultures. **Classes:** Most classes have 10–19 students. Most lab/discussion sections have fewer than 10 students. **Disciplines with Highest Percentage of Degrees Awarded:** Business/marketing 32%, computer and information sciences 29%, engineering 28%, psychology 11%. **Special Study Options:** Cross-registration, distance learning, double major, dual enrollment, external degree program, honors program, independent study, internships, study abroad.

CAMPUS LIFE
Activities: Choral groups, dance, drama/theater, jazz band, literary magazine, musical theater, student government, student newspaper. **Athletics (Intercollegiate):** *Men:* Baseball, basketball, ice hockey, tennis, volleyball. *Women:* Basketball, ice hockey, tennis, volleyball.

ADMISSIONS
Freshman Academic Profile: 7% in top 10% of high school class, 29% in top 25% of high school class, 68% in top 50% of high school class. SAT Math middle 50% range 440–570. SAT Critical Reading middle 50% range 430–540. TOEFL required of all international applicants, minimum paper TOEFL 550. **Basis for Candidate Selection:** *Very important factors considered include:* Academic GPA, standardized test scores. *Important factors considered include:* Rigor of secondary school record. *Other factors considered include:* Alumni/ae relation, application essay, character/personal qualities, class rank, extracurricular activities, recommendation(s), talent/ability, volunteer work, work experience. **Freshman Admission Requirements:** High school diploma is required, and GED is accepted. *Academic units required:* 4 English, 3 math, 3 science, 2 foreign language, 3 social studies. **Freshman Admission Statistics:** 475 applied, 83% admitted, 52% enrolled. **Transfer Admission Requirements:** High school transcript, college transcript(s). Lowest grade transferable C. **General Admission Information:** Application fee $50. Regular notification is rolling. Non-fall registration accepted. Admission may be deferred for a maximum of 1 year.

COSTS AND FINANCIAL AID
Annual in-state tuition $10,454. Annual out-of-state tuition $15,954. Room and board $3,360. Required fees $552. Average book expense $1,168. **Required Forms and Deadlines:** FAFSA. Financial aid filing deadline 2/15. **Types of Aid:** *Need-based scholarships/grants:* Pell, SEOG, state scholarships/grants, private scholarships, the school's own gift aid. *Loans:* FFEL Subsidized Stafford, FFEL Unsubsidized Stafford, FFEL PLUS, Federal Perkins, college/university loans from institutional funds, private loans. **Financial Aid Statistics:** 52% freshmen, 53% undergrads receive need-based scholarship or grant aid. 59% freshmen, 61% undergrads receive need-based self-help aid.

PENNSYLVANIA STATE UNIVERSITY— SCHUYLKILL

200 University Drive, A102 Administration Building, Schuylkill Haven, PA 17972-2208
Phone: 570-385-6252 **E-mail:** sl-admissions@psu.edu
Fax: 570-385-6272 **Website:** www.sl.psu.edu

This public school was founded in 1934. It has a 42-acre campus.

RATINGS
Admissions Selectivity Rating: 67   **Fire Safety Rating:** 60*   **Green Rating:** 60*

STUDENTS AND FACULTY
Enrollment: 790. **Student Body:** 54% female, 46% male, 12% out-of-state. African American 30%, Asian 2%, Caucasian 65%, Hispanic 3%. **Retention and Graduation:** 78% freshmen return for sophomore year. **Faculty:** Student/faculty ratio 17:1. 41 full-time faculty, 73% hold PhDs.

ACADEMICS
Degrees: Bachelor's, terminal. **Academic Requirements:** Arts/fine arts, computer literacy, English (including composition), foreign languages, humanities, international cultures, mathematics, sciences (biological or physical), social science, United States cultures. **Classes:** Most classes have 20–29 students. Most lab/discussion sections have 10–19 students. **Disciplines with Highest Percentage of Degrees Awarded:** Psychology 40%, security and protective services 31%, business/marketing 22%, computer and information sciences 5%, public administration and social services 2%. **Special Study Options:** Accelerated program, cooperative education program, distance learning, double major, dual enrollment, honors program, independent study, internships, student-designed major, study abroad.

FACILITIES
Housing: Apartments for single students, special housing for disabled students.

CAMPUS LIFE
Activities: Choral groups, dance, drama/theater, musical theater, student government, student newspaper. **Athletics (Intercollegiate):** *Men:* Basketball, cross-country, softball, tennis, volleyball. *Women:* Basketball, cross-country, softball, tennis, volleyball.

ADMISSIONS
Freshman Academic Profile: 4% in top 10% of high school class, 20% in top 25% of high school class, 59% in top 50% of high school class. SAT Math middle 50% range 380–520. SAT Critical Reading middle 50% range 380–500. TOEFL required of all international applicants, minimum paper TOEFL 550. **Basis for Candidate Selection:** *Very important factors considered include:* Academic GPA, standardized test scores. *Important factors considered include:* Rigor of secondary school record. *Other factors considered include:* Alumni/ae relation, application essay, character/personal qualities, class rank, extracurricular activities, recommendation(s), talent/ability, volunteer work, work experience. **Freshman Admission Requirements:** High school diploma is required, and GED is accepted. *Academic units required:* 4 English, 3 math, 3 science, 2 foreign language, 3 social studies. **Freshman Admission Statistics:** 878 applied, 76% admitted, 44% enrolled. **Transfer Admission Requirements:** High school transcript, college transcript(s). Lowest grade transferable C. **General Admission Information:** Application fee $50. Regular notification is rolling. Non-fall registration accepted. Admission may be deferred for a maximum of 1 year.

COSTS AND FINANCIAL AID
Annual in-state tuition $10,454. Annual out-of-state tuition $15,954. Room and board $8,480. Required fees $542. Average book expense $1,168. **Required Forms and Deadlines:** FAFSA. Financial aid filing deadline 2/15. **Types of Aid:** *Need-based scholarships/grants:* Pell, SEOG, state scholarships/grants, private scholarships, the school's own gift aid. *Loans:* FFEL Subsidized Stafford, FFEL Unsubsidized Stafford, FFEL PLUS, Federal Perkins, college/university loans from institutional funds, private loans. **Financial Aid Statistics:** 73% freshmen, 66% undergrads receive need-based scholarship or grant aid. 79% freshmen, 75% undergrads receive need-based self-help aid.

PENNSYLVANIA STATE UNIVERSITY— SHENANGO

147 Shenango Avenue, Sharon, PA 16146-1597
Phone: 724-983-2800 **E-mail:** psushenango@psu.edu
Fax: 724-983-2820 **Website:** www.shenango.psu.edu

This public school was founded in 1965. It has a 14-acre campus.

RATINGS
Admissions Selectivity Rating: 65   **Fire Safety Rating:** 60*   **Green Rating:** 60*

STUDENTS AND FACULTY
Enrollment: 655. **Student Body:** 66% female, 34% male, 11% out-of-state. African American 9%, Caucasian 89%. **Retention and Graduation:** 65% freshmen return for sophomore year. **Faculty:** Student/faculty ratio 14:1. 29 full-time faculty, 48% hold PhDs.

ACADEMICS
Degrees: Bachelor's, terminal. **Academic Requirements:** Arts/fine arts, computer literacy, English (including composition), foreign languages, humanities, international cultures, mathematics, sciences (biological or physical), social science, United States cultures. **Classes:** Most classes have 10–19 students. Most lab/discussion sections have 10–19 students. **Disciplines with Highest Percentage of Degrees Awarded:** Business/marketing 62%, family and consumer sciences 35%, liberal arts/general studies 3%. **Special Study Options:** Accelerated program, cross-registration, distance learning, double major, dual enrollment, honors program, independent study, internships, student-designed major, study abroad.

CAMPUS LIFE
Activities: Drama/theater, literary magazine, student government.

ADMISSIONS
Freshman Academic Profile: 5% in top 10% of high school class, 15% in top 25% of high school class, 53% in top 50% of high school class. SAT Math middle 50% range 400–520. SAT Critical Reading middle 50% range 400–490. TOEFL required of all international applicants, minimum paper TOEFL 550. **Basis for Candidate Selection:** *Very important factors considered include:* Academic GPA, standardized test scores. *Important factors considered include:* Rigor of secondary school record. *Other factors considered include:* Alumni/ae relation, application essay, character/personal qualities, class rank, extracurricular activities, recommendation(s), talent/ability, volunteer work, work experience. **Freshman Admission Requirements:** High school diploma is required, and GED is accepted. *Academic units required:* 4 English, 3 math, 3 science, 2 foreign language, 3 social studies. **Freshman Admission Statistics:** 258 applied, 84% admitted, 62% enrolled. **Transfer Admission Requirements:** High school transcript, college transcript(s). Lowest grade transferable C. **General Admission Information:** Application fee $50. Regular notification is rolling. Non-fall registration accepted. Admission may be deferred for a maximum of 1 year.

COSTS AND FINANCIAL AID
Annual in-state tuition $10,454. Annual out-of-state tuition $15,954. Room and board $3,360. Required fees $552. Average book expense $1,168. **Required Forms and Deadlines:** FAFSA. Financial aid filing deadline 2/15. **Types of Aid:** *Need-based scholarships/grants:* Pell, SEOG, state scholarships/grants, private scholarships, the school's own gift aid. *Loans:* FFEL Subsidized Stafford, FFEL Unsubsidized Stafford, FFEL PLUS, Federal Perkins, college/university loans from institutional funds, private loans. **Financial Aid Statistics:** 61% freshmen, 70% undergrads receive need-based scholarship or grant aid. 71% freshmen, 80% undergrads receive need-based self-help aid.

PENNSYLVANIA STATE UNIVERSITY— UNIVERSITY PARK

201 Shields Building, Box 3000, University Park, PA 16802-3000
Phone: 814-865-5471 **E-mail:** admissions@psu.edu **CEEB Code:** 2660
Fax: 814-863-7590 **Website:** www.psu.edu **ACT Code:** 3656
Financial Aid Phone: 814-865-6301

This public school was founded in 1855. It has a 15,984-acre campus.

RATINGS
Admissions Selectivity Rating: 91   **Fire Safety Rating:** 94   **Green Rating:** 97

STUDENTS AND FACULTY
Enrollment: 35,711. **Student Body:** 45% female, 55% male, 23% out-of-state, 2% international (121 countries represented). African American 4%, Asian 6%, Caucasian 85%, Hispanic 3%. **Retention and Graduation:** 93% freshmen return for sophomore year. 22% grads go on to further study within 1 year. **Faculty:** Student/faculty ratio 17:1. 2,290 full-time faculty, 78% hold PhDs.

ACADEMICS
Degrees: Bachelor's, certificate, doctoral, first professional, master's, post-bachelor's certificate, terminal. **Academic Requirements:** Arts/fine arts, computer literacy, English (including composition), foreign languages, humanities, international cultures, mathematics, sciences (biological or physical), social science, United States cultures. **Classes:** Most classes have 20–29 students. Most lab/discussion sections have 20–29 students. **Disciplines with Highest Percentage of Degrees Awarded:** Business/marketing 18%, engineering 13%, communications/journalism 10%, social sciences 6%, education 6%. **Special Study Options:** Accelerated program, cooperative education program, cross-registration, distance learning, double major, dual enrollment, English as a second language (ESL), exchange student program (domestic), external degree program, honors program, independent study, internships, liberal arts/career combination, student-designed major, study abroad, teacher certification program.

FACILITIES
Housing: Coed dorms, men's dorms, women's dorms, apartments for married students, apartments for single students, special housing for disabled students, special housing for international students, fraternity/sorority housing, suites, special interest housing. **Special Academic Facilities/Equipment:** Museums, theaters, language labs, weather station, nuclear reactor. **Computers:** 30% of classrooms are wired, 30% of classrooms are wireless, 75% of public computers are PCs, 25% of public computers are Macs, 2% of public computers are UNIX, network access in dorm rooms, network access in dorm lounges, online registration, online administrative functions (other than registration), support for handheld computing, remote student-access to Web through college's connection.

CAMPUS LIFE
Activities: Choral groups, concert band, dance, drama/theater, jazz band, literary magazine, marching band, music ensembles, musical theater, opera, pep band, radio station, student government, student newspaper, student-run film society, symphony orchestra, television station. **Organizations:** 600 registered organizations, 32 honor societies, 53 religious organizations. 54 fraternities (12% men join), 31 sororities (11% women join). **Athletics (Intercollegiate):** *Men:* Baseball, basketball, cheerleading, cross-country, diving, fencing, football, golf, gymnastics, lacrosse, soccer, swimming, tennis, track/field (outdoor), volleyball, wrestling. *Women:* Basketball, cheerleading, cross-country, diving, fencing, field hockey, golf, gymnastics, lacrosse, soccer, softball, swimming, tennis, track/field (outdoor), volleyball. **Environmental Initiatives:** Penn State has finalized its Greenhouse gas inventory and has committed to make a 17% reduction in overall greenhouse gas emissions by 2012. Penn State is currently listed in the top five Universities in the country by the EPA for renewable energy purchases. The University has established a goal that all new buildings will be LEED certified (like the Stuckeman Family Building).

ADMISSIONS
Freshman Academic Profile: 37% in top 10% of high school class, 77% in top 25% of high school class, 98% in top 50% of high school class. SAT Math middle 50% range 560–670. SAT Critical Reading middle 50% range 530–630. TOEFL required of all international applicants, minimum paper TOEFL 550, minimum

computer TOEFL 213. **Basis for Candidate Selection:** *Very important factors considered include:* Academic GPA, standardized test scores. *Important factors considered include:* Rigor of secondary school record. *Other factors considered include:* Alumni/ae relation, application essay, character/personal qualities, class rank, extracurricular activities, recommendation(s), talent/ability, volunteer work, work experience. **Freshman Admission Requirements:** High school diploma is required, and GED is accepted. *Academic units required:* 4 English, 3 math, 3 science, 2 foreign language, 3 social studies. **Freshman Admission Statistics:** 34,813 applied, 58% admitted, 40% enrolled. **Transfer Admission Requirements:** High school transcript, college transcript(s). Lowest grade transferable C. **General Admission Information:** Application fee $50. Regular notification is rolling. Non-fall registration accepted. Admission may be deferred for a maximum of 1 year. Credit and/or placement offered for CEEB Advanced Placement tests.

COSTS AND FINANCIAL AID

Annual in-state tuition $12,284. Annual out-of-state tuition $23,152. Room and board $7,180. Required fees $560. Average book expense $1,168. **Required Forms and Deadlines:** FAFSA. Financial aid filing deadline 2/15. **Types of Aid:** *Need-based scholarships/grants:* Pell, SEOG, state scholarships/grants, private scholarships, the school's own gift aid. *Loans:* FFEL Subsidized Stafford, FFEL Unsubsidized Stafford, FFEL PLUS, Federal Perkins, college/university loans from institutional funds, private loans. **Student Employment:** Federal Work-Study Program available. Institutional employment available. Off-campus job opportunities are good. **Financial Aid Statistics:** 26% freshmen, 29% undergrads receive need-based scholarship or grant aid. 41% freshmen, 43% undergrads receive need-based self-help aid. 117 freshmen, 485 undergrads receive athletic scholarships. 77% freshmen, 73% undergrads receive any aid.

PENNSYLVANIA STATE UNIVERSITY— WILKES-BARRE

PO Box PSU, Lehman, PA 18627
Phone: 570-675-9238 **E-mail:** wbadmissions@psu.edu
Fax: 570-675-9113 **Website:** www.wb.psu.edu

This public school was founded in 1916. It has a 58-acre campus.

RATINGS

Admissions Selectivity Rating: 70   **Fire Safety Rating:** 60*   **Green Rating:** 60*

STUDENTS AND FACULTY

Enrollment: 601. **Student Body:** 31% female, 69% male, 4% out-of-state. African American 2%, Asian 1%, Caucasian 95%, Hispanic 2%. **Retention and Graduation:** 80% freshmen return for sophomore year. **Faculty:** Student/faculty ratio 15:1. 35 full-time faculty, 57% hold PhDs.

ACADEMICS

Degrees: Bachelor's, post-bachelor's certificate, terminal. **Academic Requirements:** Arts/fine arts, English (including composition), foreign languages, humanities, international cultures, mathematics, sciences (biological or physical), social science, United States cultures. **Classes:** Most classes have 10–19 students. Most lab/discussion sections have fewer than 10 students. **Disciplines with Highest Percentage of Degrees Awarded:** Business/marketing 48%, computer and information sciences 24%, security and protective services 23%, English 4%, engineering technologies 1%. **Special Study Options:** Accelerated program, cross-registration, distance learning, double major, dual enrollment, honors program, independent study, internships, student-designed major, study abroad.

CAMPUS LIFE

Activities: Radio station, student government, student newspaper. **Athletics (Intercollegiate):** *Men:* Baseball, soccer, volleyball. *Women:* Volleyball.

ADMISSIONS

Freshman Academic Profile: 5% in top 10% of high school class, 28% in top 25% of high school class, 69% in top 50% of high school class. SAT Math middle 50% range 440–560. SAT Critical Reading middle 50% range 430–530. TOEFL required of all international applicants, minimum paper TOEFL 550. **Basis for Candidate Selection:** *Very important factors considered include:* Academic GPA, standardized test scores. *Important factors considered include:* Rigor of secondary school record. *Other factors considered include:* Alumni/ae relation, application essay, character/personal qualities, class rank, extracurricular activities, recommendation(s), talent/ability, volunteer work, work experience. **Freshman Admission Requirements:** High school diploma is required, and

GED is accepted. *Academic units required:* 4 English, 3 math, 3 science, 2 foreign language, 3 social studies. **Freshman Admission Statistics:** 540 applied, 84% admitted, 41% enrolled. **Transfer Admission Requirements:** High school transcript, college transcript(s). Lowest grade transferable C. **General Admission Information:** Application fee $50. Regular notification is rolling. Non-fall registration accepted. Admission may be deferred for a maximum of 1 year.

COSTS AND FINANCIAL AID

Annual in-state tuition $10,454. Annual out-of-state tuition $15,954. Room and board $3,360. Required fees $552. Average book expense $1,168. **Required Forms and Deadlines:** FAFSA. Financial aid filing deadline 2/15. **Types of Aid:** *Need-based scholarships/grants:* Pell, SEOG, state scholarships/grants, private scholarships, the school's own gift aid. *Loans:* FFEL Subsidized Stafford, FFEL Unsubsidized Stafford, FFEL PLUS, Federal Perkins, college/university loans from institutional funds, private loans. **Financial Aid Statistics:** 59% freshmen, 52% undergrads receive need-based scholarship or grant aid. 64% freshmen, 58% undergrads receive need-based self-help aid.

PENNSYLVANIA STATE UNIVERSITY— WORTHINGTON SCRANTON

120 Ridge View Drive, Dunmore, PA 18512-1699
Phone: 570-963-2500 **E-mail:** wsadmissions@psu.edu
Fax: 570-963-2524 **Website:** www.sn.psu.edu

This public school was founded in 1923. It has a 43-acre campus.

RATINGS

Admissions Selectivity Rating: 67   **Fire Safety Rating:** 60*   **Green Rating:** 60*

STUDENTS AND FACULTY

Enrollment: 1,111. **Student Body:** 51% female, 49% male, 1% out-of-state. African American 1%, Asian 2%, Caucasian 95%, Hispanic 2%. **Retention and Graduation:** 77% freshmen return for sophomore year. **Faculty:** Student/faculty ratio 16:1. 52 full-time faculty, 60% hold PhDs.

ACADEMICS

Degrees: Bachelor's, terminal. **Academic Requirements:** Arts/fine arts, computer literacy, English (including composition), foreign languages, humanities, international cultures, mathematics, sciences (biological or physical), social science, United States cultures. **Classes:** Most classes have 10–19 students. Most lab/discussion sections have fewer than 10 students. **Disciplines with Highest Percentage of Degrees Awarded:** Business/marketing 56%, family and consumer sciences 29%, computer and information sciences 14%, security and protective services 1%. **Special Study Options:** Accelerated program, cooperative education program, cross-registration, distance learning, double major, dual enrollment, honors program, independent study, internships, study abroad.

CAMPUS LIFE

Activities: Choral groups, drama/theater, jazz band, literary magazine, music ensembles, student government, student newspaper. **Athletics (Intercollegiate):** *Men:* Baseball, basketball, cross-country, soccer. *Women:* Volleyball.

ADMISSIONS

Freshman Academic Profile: 7% in top 10% of high school class, 23% in top 25% of high school class, 62% in top 50% of high school class. TOEFL required of all international applicants, minimum paper TOEFL 550. **Basis for Candidate Selection:** *Very important factors considered include:* Academic GPA, standardized test scores. *Important factors considered include:* Rigor of secondary school record. *Other factors considered include:* Alumni/ae relation, application essay, character/personal qualities, class rank, extracurricular activities, recommendation(s), talent/ability, volunteer work, work experience. **Freshman Admission Requirements:** High school diploma is required, and GED is accepted. *Academic units required:* 4 English, 3 math, 3 science, 2 foreign language, 3 social studies. **Freshman Admission Statistics:** 785 applied, 84% admitted, 48% enrolled. **Transfer Admission Requirements:** High school transcript, college transcript(s). Lowest grade transferable C. **General Admission Information:** Application fee $50. Regular notification is rolling. Non-fall registration accepted. Admission may be deferred for a maximum of 1 year.

COSTS AND FINANCIAL AID

Annual in-state tuition $10,454. Annual out-of-state tuition $15,954. Room and board $3,360. Required fees $532. Average book expense $1,168. **Required**

Forms and Deadlines: FAFSA. Financial aid filing deadline 2/15. Types of Aid: *Need-based scholarships/grants:* Pell, SEOG, state scholarships/grants, private scholarships, the school's own gift aid. *Loans:* FFEL Subsidized Stafford, FFEL Unsubsidized Stafford, FFEL PLUS, Federal Perkins, college/university loans from institutional funds, private loans. Financial Aid Statistics: 58% freshmen, 59% undergrads receive need-based scholarship or grant aid. 63% freshmen, 66% undergrads receive need-based self-help aid.

PENNSYLVANIA STATE UNIVERSITY—YORK

1031 Edgecomb Avenue, York, PA 17403-3398
Phone: 717-771-4040 **E-mail:** ykadmission@psu.edu
Fax: 717-771-4005 **Website:** www.yk.psu.edu

This public school was founded in 1926. It has a 52-acre campus.

RATINGS
Admissions Selectivity Rating: 70   Fire Safety Rating: 60*   Green Rating: 60*

STUDENTS AND FACULTY
Enrollment: 1,068. **Student Body:** 44% female, 56% male, 2% out-of-state. African American 5%, Asian 6%, Caucasian 84%, Hispanic 4%. **Retention and Graduation:** 68% freshmen return for sophomore year. **Faculty:** Student/faculty ratio 14:1. 62 full-time faculty, 63% hold PhDs.

ACADEMICS
Degrees: Bachelor's, terminal. **Academic Requirements:** Arts/fine arts, computer literacy, English (including composition), foreign languages, humanities, international cultures, mathematics, sciences (biological or physical), social science, United States cultures. **Classes:** Most classes have 10–19 students. Most lab/discussion sections have fewer than 10 students. **Disciplines with Highest Percentage of Degrees Awarded:** Business/marketing 40%, computer and information sciences 18%, interdisciplinary studies 14%, engineering 11%, liberal arts/general studies 8%. **Special Study Options:** Accelerated program, cross-registration, distance learning, double major, English as a second language (ESL), honors program, independent study, internships, student-designed major, study abroad.

CAMPUS LIFE
Activities: Dance, drama/theater, literary magazine, student government, student newspaper. **Athletics (Intercollegiate):** *Men:* Basketball, soccer, tennis. *Women:* Tennis, volleyball.

ADMISSIONS
Freshman Academic Profile: 8% in top 10% of high school class, 24% in top 25% of high school class, 52% in top 50% of high school class. SAT Math middle 50% range 440–550. SAT Critical Reading middle 50% range 410–530. TOEFL required of all international applicants, minimum paper TOEFL 550. **Basis for Candidate Selection:** *Very important factors considered include:* Academic GPA, standardized test scores. *Important factors considered include:* Rigor of secondary school record. *Other factors considered include:* Alumni/ae relation, application essay, character/personal qualities, class rank, extracurricular activities, recommendation(s), talent/ability, volunteer work, work experience. **Freshman Admission Requirements:** High school diploma is required, and GED is accepted. *Academic units required:* 4 English, 3 math, 3 science, 2 foreign language, 3 social studies. **Freshman Admission Statistics:** 1,039 applied, 80% admitted, 36% enrolled. **Transfer Admission Requirements:** High school transcript, college transcript(s). Lowest grade transferable C. **General Admission Information:** Application fee $50. Regular notification is rolling. Non-fall registration accepted. Admission may be deferred for a maximum of 1 year.

COSTS AND FINANCIAL AID
Annual in-state tuition $10,454. Annual out-of-state tuition $15,954. Room and board $3,360. Required fees $532. Average book expense $1,168. **Required Forms and Deadlines:** FAFSA. Financial aid filing deadline 2/15. **Types of Aid:** *Need-based scholarships/grants:* Pell, SEOG, state scholarships/grants, private scholarships, the school's own gift aid. *Loans:* FFEL Subsidized Stafford, FFEL Unsubsidized Stafford, FFEL PLUS, Federal Perkins, college/university loans from institutional funds, private loans. **Financial Aid Statistics:** 43% freshmen, 47% undergrads receive need-based scholarship or grant aid. 44% freshmen, 52% undergrads receive need-based self-help aid.

PEPPERDINE UNIVERSITY

24255 Pacific Coast Highway, Malibu, CA 90263
Phone: 310-506-4392 **E-mail:** admission-seaver@pepperdine.edu **CEEB Code:** 4630
Fax: 310-506-4861 **Website:** www.pepperdine.edu **ACT Code:** 0373
Financial Aid Phone: 310-506-4301

This private school, affiliated with the Church of Christ, was founded in 1937. It has an 830-acre campus.

RATINGS
Admissions Selectivity Rating: 94   Fire Safety Rating: 70   Green Rating: 80

STUDENTS AND FACULTY
Enrollment: 3,281. **Student Body:** 57% female, 43% male, 50% out-of-state, 6% international. African American 8%, Asian 10%, Caucasian 58%, Hispanic 11%, Native American 2%. **Retention and Graduation:** 89% freshmen return for sophomore year. 53% grads go on to further study within 1 year. 14% grads pursue arts and sciences degrees. 12% grads pursue business degrees. 9% grads pursue law degrees. 5% grads pursue medical degrees. **Faculty:** Student/faculty ratio 12:1. 395 full-time faculty, 98% hold PhDs. 100% faculty teach undergrads.

ACADEMICS
Degrees: Bachelor's, doctoral, first professional, master's. **Academic Requirements:** Arts/fine arts, English (including composition), foreign languages, history, humanities, mathematics, sciences (biological or physical), social science. **Classes:** Most classes have 10–19 students. Most lab/discussion sections have fewer than 10 students. **Majors with Highest Enrollment:** Advertising, business administration and management, psychology. **Disciplines with Highest Percentage of Degrees Awarded:** Business/marketing 34%, communications/journalism 18%, social sciences 10%, psychology 10%, interdisciplinary studies 6%. **Special Study Options:** Double major, honors program, independent study, internships, student-designed major, study abroad, teacher certification program, weekend college, 3-2 programming engineering with University of Southern California, Washington University(MO), Boston University(MA).

FACILITIES
Housing: Men's dorms, women's dorms, apartments for married students, apartments for single students, special housing for disabled students. Freshman and sophomores must live on campus or at home with parent or guardian if single and under age 21. **Special Academic Facilities/Equipment:** Art museum. **Computers:** 50% of public computers are PCs, 50% of public computers are Macs, network access in dorm rooms, network access in dorm lounges, online registration, online administrative functions (other than registration), remote student-access to Web through college's connection.

CAMPUS LIFE
Activities: Choral groups, concert band, dance, drama/theater, jazz band, literary magazine, music ensembles, musical theater, opera, pep band, radio station, student government, student newspaper, student-run film society, symphony orchestra, television station, yearbook. **Organizations:** 50 registered organizations, 5 honor societies, 8 religious organizations. 5 fraternities (25% men join), 7 sororities (25% women join). **Athletics (Intercollegiate):** *Men:* Baseball, basketball, cross-country, golf, tennis, volleyball, water polo. *Women:* Basketball, cheerleading, cross-country, golf, soccer, swimming, tennis, track/field (outdoor), volleyball. **Environmental Initiatives:** Pepperdine uses recycled water to irrigate over 90% of the University's managed grounds. Pepperdine University recycles all refuse disposed of on campus. Pepperdine University promotes a Rideshare program that provides incentives and subsidies for participating in carpools.

ADMISSIONS
Freshman Academic Profile: SAT Math middle 50% range 570–680. SAT Critical Reading middle 50% range 560–670. SAT Writing middle 50% range 560–670. ACT middle 50% range 24–29. TOEFL required of all international applicants, minimum paper TOEFL 550, minimum computer TOEFL 220. **Basis for Candidate Selection:** *Very important factors considered include:* Academic GPA, application essay, character/personal qualities, extracurricular activities, recommendation(s), rigor of secondary school record, standardized test scores, talent/ability. *Important factors considered include:* Religious

affiliation/commitment, volunteer work. *Other factors considered include:* Alumni/ae relation, first generation, racial/ethnic status, work experience. **Freshman Admission Requirements:** High school diploma is required, and GED is accepted. *Academic units recommended:* 4 English, 4 math, 4 science (3 science labs), 3 foreign language, 3 social studies, 3 history, 3 academic electives, 1 speech. **Freshman Admission Statistics:** 7,483 applied, 28% admitted, 34% enrolled. **Transfer Admission Requirements:** High school transcript, college transcript(s), essay or personal statement. Minimum college GPA of 3.0 required. Lowest grade transferable C. **General Admission Information:** Application fee $65. Regular application deadline 1/15. Regular notification 4/1. Non-fall registration accepted. Credit and/or placement offered for CEEB Advanced Placement tests.

COSTS AND FINANCIAL AID

Required Forms and Deadlines: FAFSA, institution's own financial aid form. Financial aid filing deadline 2/15. **Notification of Awards:** Applicants will be notified of awards on or about 4/15. **Types of Aid:** *Need-based scholarships/grants:* Pell, SEOG, state scholarships/grants, private scholarships, the school's own gift aid. *Loans:* FFEL Subsidized Stafford, FFEL Unsubsidized Stafford, FFEL PLUS, Federal Perkins, college/university loans from institutional funds. **Financial Aid Statistics:** 35% freshmen, 45% undergrads receive need-based scholarship or grant aid. 36% freshmen, 47% undergrads receive need-based self-help aid. 34 freshmen, 132 undergrads receive athletic scholarships. Highest amount earned per year from on-campus jobs $2,000.

PERU STATE COLLEGE

PO Box 10, Peru, NE 68421-0010
Phone: 402-872-2221 **E-mail:** admissions@oakmail.peru.edu **CEEB Code:** 6468
Fax: 402-872-2296 **Website:** www.peru.edu **ACT Code:** 2470
Financial Aid Phone: 402-872-2228

This public school was founded in 1867. It has a 103-acre campus.

RATINGS
Admissions Selectivity Rating: 66   **Fire Safety Rating:** 60*   **Green Rating:** 60*

STUDENTS AND FACULTY
Enrollment: 1,482. **Student Body:** 58% female, 42% male, 15% out-of-state. African American 3%, Asian 1%, Caucasian 81%, Hispanic 2%. **Retention and Graduation:** 55% freshmen return for sophomore year. 8% freshmen graduate within 4 years. 10% grads go on to further study within 1 year. 6% grads pursue arts and sciences degrees. 1% grads pursue business degrees. 1% grads pursue law degrees. 1% grads pursue medical degrees. **Faculty:** Student/faculty ratio 16:1. 41 full-time faculty, 73% hold PhDs. 100% faculty teach undergrads.

ACADEMICS
Degrees: Bachelor's, master's. **Academic Requirements:** Arts/fine arts, computer literacy, English (including composition), history, humanities, mathematics, sciences (biological or physical), social science. **Majors with Highest Enrollment:** Business administration/management, criminology, education. **Disciplines with Highest Percentage of Degrees Awarded:** Education 28%, biological/life sciences 25%, interdisciplinary studies 24%, business/marketing 16%, social sciences 3%. **Special Study Options:** Accelerated program, cooperative education program, distance learning, double major, dual enrollment, honors program, independent study, internships, teacher certification program. Accelerated teacher education program is offered at our Offutt air force base facility.

FACILITIES
Housing: Coed dorms, men's dorms, women's dorms, apartments for married students, apartments for single students. **Special Academic Facilities/Equipment:** TV studio, TV distance learning classroom. **Computers:** 90% of public computers are PCs, 10% of public computers are Macs, network access in dorm rooms, remote student-access to Web through college's connection.

CAMPUS LIFE
Activities: Choral groups, concert band, drama/theater, jazz band, literary magazine, marching band, music ensembles, musical theater, pep band, student government, student newspaper, yearbook. **Organizations:** 50 registered organizations, 8 honor societies. **Athletics (Intercollegiate):** *Men:* Baseball, basketball, cheerleading, football. *Women:* Basketball, cheerleading, softball, volleyball.

ADMISSIONS
Freshman Academic Profile: 6% in top 10% of high school class, 23% in top 25% of high school class, 53% in top 50% of high school class. 95% from public

---

high schools. TOEFL required of all international applicants, minimum paper TOEFL 550, minimum computer TOEFL 213. **Basis for Candidate Selection:** *Very important factors considered include:* Rigor of secondary school record, standardized test scores. *Important factors considered include:* Class rank, recommendation(s). **Freshman Admission Requirements:** High school diploma is required, and GED is accepted. *Academic units recommended:* 4 English, 3 math, 2 science (2 science labs), 2 foreign language, 3 social studies, 3 history, 2 academic electives. **Freshman Admission Statistics:** 504 applied, 62% admitted, 57% enrolled. **Transfer Admission Requirements:** College transcript(s). Minimum college GPA of 2.0 required. Lowest grade transferable C. **General Admission Information:** Application fee $10. Regular notification is rolling. Non-fall registration accepted. Common Application accepted. Credit and/or placement offered for CEEB Advanced Placement tests.

COSTS AND FINANCIAL AID
Annual in-state tuition $2,288. Out-of-state tuition $4,575. Room & board $4,010. Required fees $600. Average book expense $600. **Required Forms and Deadlines:** FAFSA, institution's own financial aid form. Financial aid filing deadline 3/3. **Notification of Awards:** Applicants will be notified of awards on a rolling basis beginning on or about 4/3. **Types of Aid:** *Need-based scholarships/grants:* Pell, SEOG, state scholarships/grants, the school's own gift aid. *Loans:* FFEL Subsidized Stafford, FFEL Unsubsidized Stafford, FFEL PLUS, Federal Perkins. **Student Employment:** Federal Work-Study Program available. Institutional employment available. Off-campus job opportunities are good. **Financial Aid Statistics:** Highest amount earned per year from on-campus jobs $1,000.

PFEIFFER UNIVERSITY

PO Box 960, Misenheimer, NC 28109
Phone: 800-338-2060 **E-mail:** admissions@pfeiffer.edu **CEEB Code:** 5536
Fax: 704-463-1363 **Website:** www.pfeiffer.edu **ACT Code:** 3140
Financial Aid Phone: 704-463-1360

This private school, affiliated with the Methodist Church, was founded in 1885.

RATINGS
Admissions Selectivity Rating: 74   **Fire Safety Rating:** 60*   **Green Rating:** 60*

STUDENTS AND FACULTY
Enrollment: 1,188. **Student Body:** 58% female, 42% male, 19% out-of-state, 5% international (13 countries represented). African American 16%, Caucasian 59%. **Retention and Graduation:** 77% freshmen return for sophomore year. 41% freshmen graduate within 4 years. 23% grads go on to further study within 1 year. 15% grads pursue arts and sciences degrees. 20% grads pursue business degrees. 5% grads pursue law degrees. 2% grads pursue medical degrees. **Faculty:** Student/faculty ratio 13:1. 65 full-time faculty, 66% hold PhDs. 81% faculty teach undergrads.

ACADEMICS
Degrees: Bachelor's, master's, post-master's certificate. **Academic Requirements:** Arts/fine arts, computer literacy, English (including composition), history, humanities, mathematics, religion, sciences (biological or physical), social science, 60 earned credits in the cultural program. **Classes:** Most classes have fewer than 10 students. **Majors with Highest Enrollment:** Business administration/management, criminal justice/law enforcement administration, elementary education and teaching. **Disciplines with Highest Percentage of Degrees Awarded:** Business/marketing 32%, parks and recreation 8%, education 8%, social sciences 7%, communication technologies 4%, liberal arts/general studies 4%, biological/life sciences 3%, visual and performing arts 3%. **Special Study Options:** Accelerated program, Capitol Hill internship program, cross-registration, distance learning, double major, dual enrollment, honors program, independent study, internships, study abroad, teacher certification program.

FACILITIES
Housing: Coed dorms, men's dorms, women's dorms. **Special Academic Facilities/Equipment:** Beth Haltiwanger Retreat Center, Francis Center for Servant Leadership, new science building. **Computers:** 100% of public computers are PCs, network access in dorm rooms, network access in dorm lounges, online administrative functions (other than registration), remote student-access to Web through college's connection.

CAMPUS LIFE
Activities: Choral groups, concert band, drama/theater, jazz band, literary

---

magazine, music ensembles, musical theater, pep band, student government, student newspaper, yearbook. **Organizations:** 60 registered organizations, 6 honor societies, 1 religious organization. **Athletics (Intercollegiate):** *Men:* Baseball, basketball, cheerleading, cross-country, golf, lacrosse, soccer, tennis. *Women:* Basketball, cheerleading, cross-country, golf, lacrosse, soccer, softball, swimming, tennis, volleyball.

ADMISSIONS

Freshman Academic Profile: 11% in top 10% of high school class, 30% in top 25% of high school class, 62% in top 50% of high school class. 90% from public high schools. SAT Math middle 50% range 450–570. SAT Critical Reading middle 50% range 430–540. ACT middle 50% range 18–24. TOEFL required of all international applicants, minimum paper TOEFL 500, minimum computer TOEFL 173. **Basis for Candidate Selection:** *Very important factors considered include:* Character/personal qualities, rigor of secondary school record, standardized test scores, volunteer work. *Important factors considered include:* Extracurricular activities, recommendation(s), talent/ability. *Other factors considered include:* Alumni/ae relation, application essay, class rank, interview, religious affiliation/commitment, work experience. **Freshman Admission Requirements:** High school diploma is required, and GED is accepted. *Academic units required:* 4 English, 3 math, 2 science (1 science lab), 2 social studies, 2 history. *Academic units recommended:* 2 foreign language. **Freshman Admission Statistics:** 586 applied, 72% admitted, 41% enrolled. **Transfer Admission Requirements:** College transcript(s), statement of good standing from prior institution(s). Minimum college GPA of 2.0 required. Lowest grade transferable D. **General Admission Information:** Application fee $25. Regular notification is rolling. Non-fall registration accepted. Common Application not accepted. Credit offered for CEEB Advanced Placement tests.

COSTS AND FINANCIAL AID

Annual tuition $13,550. Room & board $5,430. Average book expense $500. **Required Forms and Deadlines:** FAFSA. **Notification of Awards:** Applicants will be notified of awards on a rolling basis beginning on or about 2/15. **Types of Aid:** *Need-based scholarships/grants:* Pell, SEOG, state scholarships/grants, the school's own gift aid. *Loans:* FFEL Subsidized Stafford, FFEL Unsubsidized Stafford, FFEL PLUS, Federal Perkins. **Student Employment:** Federal Work-Study Program available. Off-campus job opportunities are good. **Financial Aid Statistics:** 77% freshmen, 62% undergrads receive need-based scholarship or grant aid. 65% freshmen, 55% undergrads receive need-based self-help aid. 90% freshmen, 90% undergrads receive any aid.

PHILADELPHIA BIBLICAL UNIVERSITY

200 Manor Avenue, Langhorne, PA 19047
Phone: 215-702-4235 **E-mail:** admissions@pbu.edu
Fax: 215-702-4248 **Website:** www.pbu.edu **ACT Code:** 3658
Financial Aid Phone: 215-702-4247

This private school, affiliated with the Protestant Church, was founded in 1913. It has a 105-acre campus.

RATINGS

Admissions Selectivity Rating: 79   **Fire Safety Rating:** 60*   **Green Rating:** 69

STUDENTS AND FACULTY

Enrollment: 1,018. **Student Body:** 55% female, 45% male, 49% out-of-state, 2% international (37 countries represented). African American 10%, Asian 2%, Caucasian 83%, Hispanic 2%. **Retention and Graduation:** 18% freshmen graduate within 4 years. **Faculty:** Student/faculty ratio 14:1. 67 full-time faculty, 57% hold PhDs. 89% faculty teach undergrads.

ACADEMICS

Degrees: Bachelor's, certificate, first professional, master's. **Academic Requirements:** Arts/fine arts, Bible, computer literacy, cultural diversity, English (including composition), foreign languages, history, humanities, ministry, philosophy, physical education, sciences (biological or physical), social science. **Classes:** Most classes have 10–19 students. **Majors with Highest Enrollment:** Bible/biblical studies, elementary education and teaching, social work. **Disciplines with Highest Percentage of Degrees Awarded:** Education 12%, social sciences 8%, business/marketing 4%, visual and performing arts 2%. **Special Study Options:** Accelerated program, double major, dual enrollment, honors program, independent study, internships, study abroad, teacher certification program.

FACILITIES

Housing: Men's dorms, women's dorms, special housing for disabled students,

special housing for international students. **Computers:** 100% of public computers are PCs, network access in dorm rooms, network access in dorm lounges, online registration, online administrative functions (other than registration).

CAMPUS LIFE

Activities: Choral groups, concert band, drama/theater, music ensembles, student government, student newspaper, symphony orchestra, yearbook. **Organizations:** 17 registered organizations, 4 honor societies, 3 religious organizations. **Athletics (Intercollegiate):** *Men:* Baseball, basketball, golf, soccer, tennis, volleyball. *Women:* Basketball, field hockey, soccer, softball, tennis, volleyball.

ADMISSIONS

Freshman Academic Profile: 17% in top 10% of high school class, 46% in top 25% of high school class, 75% in top 50% of high school class. 60% from public high schools. SAT Math middle 50% range 460–580. SAT Critical Reading middle 50% range 488–600. ACT middle 50% range 20–25. TOEFL required of all international applicants, minimum paper TOEFL 550, minimum computer TOEFL 213. **Basis for Candidate Selection:** *Very important factors considered include:* Application essay, character/personal qualities, recommendation(s), religious affiliation/commitment, rigor of secondary school record, standardized test scores. *Important factors considered include:* Class rank. *Other factors considered include:* Extracurricular activities, interview, volunteer work. **Freshman Admission Requirements:** High school diploma is required, and GED is accepted. *Academic units recommended:* 4 English, 1 math, 2 science, 2 foreign language, 3 social studies. **Freshman Admission Statistics:** 412 applied, 76% admitted, 60% enrolled. **Transfer Admission Requirements:** College transcript(s), essay or personal statement. Minimum college GPA of 2.0 required. Lowest grade transferable C. **General Admission Information:** Application fee $25. Regular notification is rolling. Non-fall registration accepted. Admission may be deferred for a maximum of 1 year. Common Application accepted. Neither credit nor placement offered for CEEB Advanced Placement tests.

COSTS AND FINANCIAL AID

Annual tuition $13,190. Room & board $5,855. Required fees $305. Average book expense $800. **Required Forms and Deadlines:** FAFSA. Financial aid filing deadline 5/1. **Notification of Awards:** Applicants will be notified of awards on a rolling basis beginning on or about 3/15. **Types of Aid:** *Need-based scholarships/grants:* Pell, SEOG, state scholarships/grants, private scholarships, the school's own gift aid. *Loans:* FFEL Subsidized Stafford, FFEL Unsubsidized Stafford, FFEL PLUS. **Student Employment:** Federal Work-Study Program available. Institutional employment available. Off-campus job opportunities are excellent. **Financial Aid Statistics:** 73% freshmen, 76% undergrads receive need-based scholarship or grant aid. 56% freshmen, 53% undergrads receive need-based self-help aid. 85% freshmen, 81% undergrads receive any aid. Highest amount earned per year from on-campus jobs $800.

PHILADELPHIA UNIVERSITY

School House Lane and Henry Avenue, Philadelphia, PA 19144-5497
Phone: 215-951-2800 **E-mail:** admissions@philau.edu **CEEB Code:** 2666
Fax: 215-951-2907 **Website:** www.PhilaU.edu **ACT Code:** 3668
Financial Aid Phone: 215-951-2940

This private school was founded in 1884. It has a 100-acre campus.

RATINGS

Admissions Selectivity Rating: 80   **Fire Safety Rating:** 60*   **Green Rating:** 60*

STUDENTS AND FACULTY

Enrollment: 2,736. **Student Body:** 70% female, 30% male, 48% out-of-state, 2% international (26 countries represented). African American 10%, Asian 4%, Caucasian 73%, Hispanic 3%. **Retention and Graduation:** 73% freshmen return for sophomore year. 36% freshmen graduate within 4 years. 19% grads go on to further study within 1 year. 8% grads pursue arts and sciences degrees. 10% grads pursue business degrees. 1% grads pursue law degrees. 1% grads pursue medical degrees. **Faculty:** Student/faculty ratio 14:1. 108 full-time faculty, 74% hold PhDs. 100% faculty teach undergrads.

ACADEMICS

Degrees: Associate, bachelor's, certificate, doctoral, master's, post-bachelor's certificate, post-master's certificate. **Academic Requirements:** Arts/fine arts, computer literacy, English (including composition), history, humanities, mathematics, sciences (biological or physical), social science. **Classes:** Most classes have 10–19 students. Most lab/discussion sections have 10–19 students.

Majors with Highest Enrollment: Architecture (BArch, BA/BS, MArch, MA/MS, PhD), fashion merchandising, fashion/apparel design. **Disciplines with Highest Percentage of Degrees Awarded:** Business/marketing 42%, architecture 20%, visual and performing arts 20%, psychology 4%, health professions and related sciences 4%, computer and information sciences 3%, communications/journalism 2%, physical sciences 2%, biological/life sciences 2%. **Special Study Options:** Distance learning, double major, honors program, independent study, internships, liberal arts/career combination, study abroad.

FACILITIES

Housing: Coed dorms, women's dorms, apartments for single students, special housing for disabled students, town houses. **Special Academic Facilities/Equipment:** The Design Center; industrial design studios; graphic design studios; architecture design studios; CAD labs in fashion design, interior design, and architecture. **Computers:** 25% of classrooms are wired, 20% of classrooms are wireless, 70% of public computers are PCs, 30% of public computers are Macs, network access in dorm rooms, network access in dorm lounges, online registration, online administrative functions (other than registration), remote student-access to Web through college's connection.

CAMPUS LIFE

Activities: Choral groups, dance, drama/theater, student government, student newspaper, yearbook. **Organizations:** 32 registered organizations, 3 religious organizations. 1 fraternity (1% men join), 1 sorority (1% women join). **Athletics (Intercollegiate):** *Men:* Baseball, basketball, crew/rowing, cross-country, golf, soccer, tennis. *Women:* Basketball, crew/rowing, cross-country, field hockey, lacrosse, soccer, softball, tennis, volleyball.

ADMISSIONS

Freshman Academic Profile: 11% in top 10% of high school class, 38% in top 25% of high school class, 80% in top 50% of high school class. 80% from public high schools. SAT Math middle 50% range 490–590. SAT Critical Reading middle 50% range 480–560. SAT Writing middle 50% range 470–560. TOEFL required of all international applicants, minimum paper TOEFL 500, minimum computer TOEFL 170. **Basis for Candidate Selection:** *Very important factors considered include:* Academic GPA, rigor of secondary school record, standardized test scores. *Important factors considered include:* Class rank, extracurricular activities, interview, recommendation(s). *Other factors considered include:* Application essay. **Freshman Admission Requirements:** High school diploma is required, and GED is accepted. *Academic units required:* 4 English, 3 math, 3 science (2 science labs), 2 social studies, 1 history, 2 academic electives. *Academic units recommended:* 4 English, 4 math, 4 science, 2 foreign language, 3 social studies, 2 history. **Freshman Admission Statistics:** 4,307 applied, 61% admitted, 27% enrolled. **Transfer Admission Requirements:** College transcript(s). Minimum college GPA of 2.5 required. Lowest grade transferable C. **General Admission Information:** Application fee $35. Regular notification is rolling. Non-fall registration accepted. Admission may be deferred for a maximum of 1 year. Credit and/or placement offered for CEEB Advanced Placement tests.

COSTS AND FINANCIAL AID

Annual tuition $23,748. Average book expense $1,400. **Required Forms and Deadlines:** FAFSA. Financial aid filing deadline 4/15. **Notification of Awards:** Applicants will be notified of awards on a rolling basis beginning on or about 2/10. **Types of Aid:** *Need-based scholarships/grants:* Pell, SEOG, state scholarships/grants, private scholarships, the school's own gift aid. Gift scholarships from outside sources (non-endowed) for which the university chooses recipient and may involve a need component. *Loans:* FFEL Subsidized Stafford, FFEL Unsubsidized Stafford, FFEL PLUS, Federal Perkins, private loan programs. **Student Employment:** Federal Work-Study Program available. Institutional employment available. Off-campus job opportunities are good. **Financial Aid Statistics:** 72% freshmen, 68% undergrads receive need-based scholarship or grant aid. 67% freshmen, 63% undergrads receive need-based self-help aid. 18 freshmen, 73 undergrads receive athletic scholarships. 99% freshmen, 97% undergrads receive any aid.

PHILANDER SMITH COLLEGE

812 West Thirteenth Street, Little Rock, AR 72202
Phone: 501-370-5221 **E-mail:** admission@philander.edu **CEEB Code:** 6578
Fax: 501-370-5225 **Website:** www.philander.edu **ACT Code:** 0136
Financial Aid Phone: 501-370-5350

This private school was founded in 1877. It has a 25-acre campus.

RATINGS

Admissions Selectivity Rating: 63   **Fire Safety Rating:** 60*   **Green Rating:** 60*

STUDENTS AND FACULTY

Enrollment: 918. **Student Body:** 64% female, 36% male, 7% out-of-state, 3% international. African American 79%. **Retention and Graduation:** 61% freshmen return for sophomore year. 6% freshmen graduate within 4 years. **Faculty:** Student/faculty ratio 26:1. 42 full-time faculty, 57% hold PhDs. 100% faculty teach undergrads.

ACADEMICS

Degrees: Bachelor's. **Academic Requirements:** Arts/fine arts, computer literacy, English (including composition), foreign languages, history, humanities, mathematics, philosophy, sciences (biological or physical), social science. **Classes:** Most classes have fewer than 10 students. Most lab/discussion sections have fewer than 10 students. **Disciplines with Highest Percentage of Degrees Awarded:** Business/marketing 35%, social sciences 23%, psychology 18%, education 12%, computer and information sciences 4%, biological/life sciences 4%. **Special Study Options:** Cooperative education program, double major, independent study, internships, teacher certification program.

FACILITIES

Housing: Men's dorms, women's dorms. **Computers:** 1% of public computers are PCs, network access in dorm rooms, network access in dorm lounges.

CAMPUS LIFE

Activities: Choral groups, drama/theater, student government, student newspaper, yearbook. **Organizations:** 25 registered organizations, 3 honor societies, 3 religious organizations. 4 fraternities (8% men join), 4 sororities (8% women join). **Athletics (Intercollegiate):** *Men:* Basketball, cheerleading. *Women:* Basketball, cheerleading, volleyball.

ADMISSIONS

Freshman Academic Profile: 4% in top 10% of high school class, 23% in top 25% of high school class, 55% in top 50% of high school class. 80% from public high schools. SAT Math middle 50% range 380–450. SAT Critical Reading middle 50% range 330–450. ACT middle 50% range 16–22. TOEFL required of all international applicants, minimum paper TOEFL 500. **Basis for Candidate Selection:** *Very important factors considered include:* Rigor of secondary school record, standardized test scores. **Freshman Admission Requirements:** High school diploma is required, and GED is accepted. *Academic units required:* 3 English, 2 math, 2 science, 2 foreign language, 2 social studies. **Freshman Admission Statistics:** 368 applied, 55% admitted, 84% enrolled. **Transfer Admission Requirements:** High school transcript, college transcript(s), standardized test score, statement of good standing from prior institution(s). Lowest grade transferable D. **General Admission Information:** Application fee $10. Regular notification is rolling. Non-fall registration accepted. Common Application not accepted.

COSTS AND FINANCIAL AID

Annual tuition $3,360. Room & board $2,746. Required fees $175. Average book expense $600. **Required Forms and Deadlines:** FAFSA, institution's own financial aid form. Financial aid filing deadline 4/15. **Notification of Awards:** Applicants will be notified of awards on or about 4/1. **Types of Aid:** *Need-based scholarships/grants:* Pell, SEOG, state scholarships/grants, private scholarships, the school's own gift aid, United Negro College Fund. *Loans:* Direct Subsidized Stafford, Direct Unsubsidized Stafford, Direct PLUS, FFEL Subsidized Stafford, FFEL PLUS, Federal Perkins. **Student Employment:** Federal Work-Study Program available. Institutional employment available. Off-campus job opportunities are good. **Financial Aid Statistics:** 72% freshmen, 70% undergrads receive need-based scholarship or grant aid. 27% freshmen, 51% undergrads receive need-based self-help aid. 2 freshmen, 2 undergrads receive athletic scholarships. Highest amount earned per year from on-campus jobs $2,318.

PHILLIPS UNIVERSITY

100 South University Avenue, Enid, OK 73701-6439
Phone: 888-477-6887 **E-mail:** phillipa@fullnet.net **CEEB Code:** 6579
Fax: 405-237-1607 **Website:** www.phillips.edu **ACT Code:** 3428
Financial Aid Phone: 405-548-2201

This private school was founded in 1906. It has a 35-acre campus.

RATINGS

Admissions Selectivity Rating: 84   **Fire Safety Rating:** 60*   **Green Rating:** 60*

STUDENTS AND FACULTY

Student Body: 32% out-of-state. **Retention and Graduation:** 64% freshmen return for sophomore year. 23% grads go on to further study within 1 year. 8% grads pursue arts and sciences degrees. 5% grads pursue business degrees. 5%

grads pursue law degrees. 5% grads pursue medical degrees. **Faculty:** 70% faculty teach undergrads.

ACADEMICS

Degrees: Associate, bachelor's, master's. **Special Study Options:** Study abroad.

FACILITIES

Housing: Coed dorms, men's dorms, women's dorms, apartments for married students, apartments for single students.

CAMPUS LIFE

Activities: Student government, student newspaper, yearbook. **Organizations:** 1 honor society, 1 religious organization. 3 fraternities (25% men join), 4 sororities (30% women join). **Athletics (Intercollegiate):** *Men:* Baseball, basketball, cheerleading, soccer, tennis. *Women:* Basketball, cheerleading, tennis.

ADMISSIONS

Freshman Academic Profile: 16% in top 10% of high school class, 42% in top 25% of high school class, 72% in top 50% of high school class. 92% from public high schools. SAT Math middle 50% range 460–680. SAT Critical Reading middle 50% range 450–660. ACT middle 50% range 18–25. TOEFL required of all international applicants, minimum paper TOEFL 500. **Freshman Admission Requirements:** High school diploma is required, and GED is accepted. *Academic units required:* 4 English, 3 math, 3 science, 2 social studies, 2 history. *Academic units recommended:* 2 foreign language. **Transfer Admission Requirements:** Minimum college GPA of 2.0 required. Lowest grade transferable C. **General Admission Information:** Regular application deadline 8/15. Regular notification is rolling. Non-fall registration accepted. Common Application not accepted. Credit and/or placement offered for CEEB Advanced Placement tests.

COSTS AND FINANCIAL AID

Annual tuition $6,685. Room & board $3,900. Required fees $550. Average book expense $400. **Required Forms and Deadlines:** FAFSA. **Types of Aid:** *Need-based scholarships/grants:* Pell, SEOG, state scholarships/grants, private scholarships, the school's own gift aid. *Loans:* FFEL Subsidized Stafford, FFEL Unsubsidized Stafford, FFEL PLUS, Federal Perkins, college/university loans from institutional funds. **Student Employment:** Federal Work-Study Program available. Institutional employment available. Off-campus job opportunities are good. **Financial Aid Statistics:** Highest amount earned per year from on-campus jobs $450.

PIEDMONT BAPTIST COLLEGE

716 Franklin Street, Winston-Salem, NC 27101-5197
Phone: 336-725-8344 **E-mail:** admissions@pbc.edu
Fax: 336-725-5522 **Website:** www.pbc.edu

This private school was founded in 1945.

RATINGS

Admissions Selectivity Rating: 60*   **Fire Safety Rating:** 60*   **Green Rating:** 60*

STUDENTS AND FACULTY

Enrollment: 275. **Student Body:** 47% female, 53% male. **Retention and Graduation:** 6% freshmen return for sophomore year. 38% freshmen graduate within 4 years.

ACADEMICS

Degrees: Associate, bachelor's, certificate, diploma, post-bachelor's certificate. **Academic Requirements:** Arts/fine arts, computer literacy, English (including composition), history, mathematics, philosophy, sciences (biological or physical), social science. **Disciplines with Highest Percentage of Degrees Awarded:** Education 22%. **Special Study Options:** Double major, dual enrollment, teacher certification program.

FACILITIES

Housing: Men's dorms, women's dorms, apartments for married students.

CAMPUS LIFE

Activities: Choral groups, drama/theater, music ensembles, student government, yearbook. **Athletics (Intercollegiate):** *Men:* Basketball. *Women:* Volleyball.

ADMISSIONS

Freshman Academic Profile: 16% in top 10% of high school class, 16% in top 25% of high school class, 37% in top 50% of high school class. TOEFL required

of all international applicants. **Freshman Admission Requirements:** High school diploma is required, and GED is accepted. **Freshman Admission Statistics:** 78 applied, 100% admitted, 65% enrolled. **Transfer Admission Requirements:** High school transcript, college transcript(s), essay or personal statement, standardized test score. Lowest grade transferable C. **General Admission Information:** Application fee $30. Non-fall registration accepted. Common Application not accepted.

COSTS AND FINANCIAL AID

Required Forms and Deadlines: FAFSA, institution's own financial aid form. **Notification of Awards:** Applicants will be notified of awards on a rolling basis beginning on or about 3/1. **Types of Aid:** *Need-based scholarships/grants:* Pell, SEOG, private scholarships, the school's own gift aid. *Loans:* FFEL Subsidized Stafford, FFEL Unsubsidized Stafford, FFEL PLUS. **Student Employment:** Off-campus job opportunities are excellent. **Financial Aid Statistics:** 81% freshmen, 89% undergrads receive need-based scholarship or grant aid.

PIEDMONT COLLEGE

PO Box 10, Demorest, GA 30535
Phone: 706-776-0103 **E-mail:** ugrad@piedmont.edu **CEEB Code:** 5537
Fax: 706-776-6635 **Website:** www.piedmont.edu **ACT Code:** 0853
Financial Aid Phone: 706-778-3000

This private school, affiliated with the Congregational Church, was founded in 1897. It has a 115-acre campus.

RATINGS

Admissions Selectivity Rating: 78   **Fire Safety Rating:** 60*   **Green Rating:** 60*

STUDENTS AND FACULTY

Enrollment: 939. **Student Body:** 64% female, 36% male, 5% out-of-state. African American 6%, Caucasian 88%, Hispanic 2%. **Retention and Graduation:** 69% freshmen return for sophomore year. 26% freshmen graduate within 4 years. **Faculty:** Student/faculty ratio 13:1. 98 full-time faculty, 77% hold PhDs. 90% faculty teach undergrads.

ACADEMICS

Degrees: Bachelor's, master's, post-master's certificate. **Academic Requirements:** Arts/fine arts, computer literacy, English (including composition), foreign languages, history, humanities, mathematics, philosophy, sciences (biological or physical), social science. **Classes:** Most classes have fewer than 10 students. Most lab/discussion sections have 10–19 students. **Majors with Highest Enrollment:** Business administration/management, elementary education and teaching, sociology. **Disciplines with Highest Percentage of Degrees Awarded:** Education 32%, business/marketing 23%, social sciences 11%, health professions and related sciences 8%, psychology 6%. **Special Study Options:** Accelerated program, distance learning, double major, dual enrollment, honors program, independent study, internships, student-designed major, study abroad, teacher certification program.

FACILITIES

Housing: Coed dorms, men's dorms, women's dorms, apartments for single students, special housing for disabled students. **Special Academic Facilities/Equipment:** Art gallery, 4 NE Georgia youth and tech center, botanical center, fitness center. **Computers:** 50% of classrooms are wired, 30% of classrooms are wireless, 90% of public computers are PCs, 10% of public computers are Macs, network access in dorm rooms, network access in dorm lounges, online administrative functions (other than registration), remote student-access to Web through college's connection.

CAMPUS LIFE

Activities: Choral groups, concert band, drama/theater, music ensembles, opera, radio station, student government, student newspaper, student-run film society, television station, yearbook. **Organizations:** 20 registered organizations, 7 honor societies, 1 religious organization. **Athletics (Intercollegiate):** *Men:* Baseball, basketball, cross-country, golf, soccer, tennis. *Women:* Basketball, cross-country, golf, soccer, softball, tennis, volleyball.

ADMISSIONS

Freshman Academic Profile: 19% in top 10% of high school class, 41% in top 25% of high school class, 79% in top 50% of high school class. SAT Math middle 50% range 460–570. SAT Critical Reading middle 50% range 480–570. ACT middle 50% range 18–23. TOEFL required of all international applicants, minimum paper TOEFL 550, minimum computer TOEFL 213. **Basis for Candidate Selection:** *Very important factors considered include:* Academic GPA, rigor of secondary school record, standardized test scores. *Important factors considered include:* Application essay, character/personal qualities, class rank, extracurricular activities, first generation, interview, recommendation(s), talent/ability. *Other factors considered include:* Alumni/ae relation, geographical residence, level of applicant's interest, state residency, volunteer work, work experience. **Freshman Admission Requirements:** High school diploma is required, and GED is accepted. *Academic units recommended:* 4 English, 3 math, 3 science, 2 foreign language, 1 social studies, 2 history. **Freshman Admission Statistics:** 485 applied, 66% admitted, 52% enrolled. **Transfer Admission Requirements:** College transcript(s), statement of good standing from prior institution(s). Minimum college GPA of 2.0 required. Lowest grade transferable C. **General Admission Information:** Regular application deadline 7/11. Regular notification 7/1. Non-fall registration accepted. Admission may be deferred for a maximum of 1 year. Common Application not accepted. Neither credit nor placement offered for CEEB Advanced Placement tests.

COSTS AND FINANCIAL AID

Annual tuition $15,500. Room & board $5,000. Average book expense $850. **Required Forms and Deadlines:** FAFSA, institution's own financial aid form, state aid form. Financial aid filing deadline 5/5. **Types of Aid:** *Need-based scholarships/grants:* Pell, SEOG, state scholarships/grants, private scholarships, the school's own gift aid. *Loans:* Direct Subsidized Stafford, Direct Unsubsidized Stafford, Direct PLUS. **Student Employment:** Federal Work-Study Program available. Institutional employment available. Off-campus job opportunities are good. **Financial Aid Statistics:** 45% freshmen, 52% undergrads receive need-based scholarship or grant aid. 54% freshmen, 48% undergrads receive need-based self-help aid. 96% freshmen, 87% undergrads receive any aid. Highest amount earned per year from on-campus jobs $3,530.

PIKEVILLE COLLEGE

Admissions Office, 147 Sycamore Street, Pikeville, KY 41501
Phone: 606-218-5251 **E-mail:** wewantyou@pc.edu **CEEB Code:** 1980
Fax: 606-218-5255 **Website:** www.pc.edu **ACT Code:** 1540
Financial Aid Phone: 606-218-5251

This private school, affiliated with the Presbyterian Church, was founded in 1889. It has a 25-acre campus.

RATINGS

Admissions Selectivity Rating: 73 **Fire Safety Rating:** 60* **Green Rating:** 60*

STUDENTS AND FACULTY

Enrollment: 794. **Student Body:** 53% female, 47% male, 21% out-of-state. African American 9%, Caucasian 89%. **Retention and Graduation:** 47% freshmen return for sophomore year. 17% freshmen graduate within 4 years. 10% grads go on to further study within 1 year. 5% grads pursue arts and sciences degrees. 2% grads pursue business degrees. 1% grads pursue law degrees. 2% grads pursue medical degrees. **Faculty:** Student/faculty ratio 12:1. 59 full-time faculty, 51% hold PhDs. 100% faculty teach undergrads.

ACADEMICS

Degrees: Associate, bachelor's, first professional, post-bachelor's certificate, terminal. **Academic Requirements:** Computer literacy, English (including composition), history, humanities, mathematics, public speaking, religion, sciences (biological or physical), social science. **Classes:** Most classes have 10–19 students. **Majors with Highest Enrollment:** Business administration/management, nursing/registered nurse training (ASN, BSN, MSN, RN), psychology. **Disciplines with Highest Percentage of Degrees Awarded:** Business/marketing 24%, psychology 14%, education 11%, English 8%, communications/journalism 8%, biological/life sciences 8%, social sciences 7%, history 7%. **Special Study Options:** Double major, independent study, internships, liberal arts/career combination, study abroad, teacher certification program.

FACILITIES

Housing: Coed dorms, men's dorms, women's dorms, apartments for married students. **Computers:** 100% of public computers are PCs, network access in dorm rooms, network access in dorm lounges, remote student-access to Web through college's connection.

CAMPUS LIFE

Activities: Choral groups, concert band, dance, drama/theater, jazz band, pep band, student government, student newspaper, yearbook. **Organizations:** 40 registered organizations, 6 honor societies, 2 religious organizations. **Athletics (Intercollegiate):** *Men:* Baseball, basketball, bowling, cheerleading, cross-country, football, golf, soccer, tennis, track/field (outdoor). *Women:* Basketball, bowling, cheerleading, cross-country, golf, soccer, softball, tennis, track/field (outdoor), volleyball.

ADMISSIONS

Freshman Academic Profile: 45% in top 25% of high school class, 85% in top 50% of high school class. 99% from public high schools. ACT middle 50% range 17–23. **Freshman Admission Requirements:** High school diploma is required, and GED is accepted. *Academic units recommended:* 4 English, 3 math, 3 science, 2 social studies, 1 history. **Freshman Admission Statistics:** 547 applied, 100% admitted, 41% enrolled. **Transfer Admission Requirements:** High school transcript, college transcript(s), standardized test score, statement of good standing from prior institution(s). Lowest grade transferable C. **General Admission Information:** Regular application deadline 8/15. Regular notification is continuous. Non-fall registration accepted. Admission may be deferred for a maximum of 3 semesters. Credit and/or placement offered for CEEB Advanced Placement tests.

COSTS AND FINANCIAL AID

Annual tuition $13,750. Room and board $5,250. Average book expense $2,000. **Required Forms and Deadlines:** FAFSA, institution's own financial aid form. Financial aid filing deadline 3/15. **Notification of Awards:** Applicants will be notified of awards on a rolling basis beginning on or about 1/15. **Types of Aid:** *Need-based scholarships/grants:* Pell, SEOG, state scholarships/grants, private scholarships, the school's own gift aid. *Loans:* FFEL Subsidized Stafford, FFEL Unsubsidized Stafford, FFEL PLUS, Federal Perkins, college/university loans from institutional funds. **Student Employment:** Federal Work-Study Program available. Off-campus job opportunities are good. **Financial Aid Statistics:** 98% freshmen, 97% undergrads receive need-based scholarship or grant aid. 66% freshmen, 66% undergrads receive need-based self-help aid. 99% freshmen, 98% undergrads receive any aid.

PINE MANOR COLLEGE

400 Heath Street, Chestnut Hill, MA 02467-2332
Phone: 617-731-7104 **E-mail:** admission@pmc.edu **CEEB Code:** 3689
Fax: 617-731-7102 **Website:** www.pmc.edu **ACT Code:** 1882
Financial Aid Phone: 800-762-1357

This private school was founded in 1911. It has a 60-acre campus.

RATINGS

Admissions Selectivity Rating: 65 **Fire Safety Rating:** 60* **Green Rating:** 60*

STUDENTS AND FACULTY

Enrollment: 477. **Student Body:** 100% female, 24% out-of-state, 8% international (24 countries represented). African American 32%, Asian 4%, Caucasian 25%, Hispanic 21%. **Retention and Graduation:** 58% freshmen return for sophomore year. 31% freshmen graduate within 4 years. 27% grads go on to further study within 1 year. 11% grads pursue arts and sciences degrees. 11% grads pursue business degrees. 1% grads pursue law degrees. 4% grads pursue medical degrees. **Faculty:** Student/faculty ratio 10:1. 30 full-time faculty, 80% hold PhDs. 100% faculty teach undergrads.

ACADEMICS

Degrees: Associate, bachelor's, certificate. **Academic Requirements:** Arts/fine arts, computer literacy, English (including composition), history, humanities, mathematics, sciences (biological or physical), social science. Portfolio and completion of 12 outcomes. **Classes:** Most classes have 10–19 students. Most lab/discussion sections have 10–19 students. **Majors with Highest Enrollment:** Business administration/management, communications and media studies, psychology. **Disciplines with Highest Percentage of Degrees Awarded:** Business/marketing 28%, communication technologies 19%, psychology 15%, biological/life sciences 11%, visual and performing arts 11%, social sciences 10%. **Special Study Options:** Cross-registration, double major, English as a second language (ESL), honors program, independent study, internships, liberal arts/career combination, student-designed major, study abroad, teacher certification program.

FACILITIES

Housing: Women's dorms, special housing for disabled students. **Special Academic Facilities/Equipment:** Hess Art Gallery, Annenberg Library and Communications Center, Ann Pappajohn Child Study Center. **Computers:** 100% of public computers are PCs, network access in dorm rooms, network access in dorm lounges, online administrative functions (other than registration), remote student-access to Web through college's connection.

CAMPUS LIFE

Activities: Choral groups, dance, drama/theater, literary magazine, radio station, student government, yearbook. **Organizations:** 25 registered organizations, 1 honor society, 1 religious organization. **Athletics (Intercolle-**

giate): *Women:* Basketball, cross-country, lacrosse, soccer, softball, tennis, volleyball.

ADMISSIONS

Freshman Academic Profile: 23% in top 25% of high school class, 49% in top 50% of high school class. 89% from public high schools. SAT Math middle 50% range 340–450. SAT Critical Reading middle 50% range 360–480. ACT middle 50% range 15–19. TOEFL required of all international applicants, minimum paper TOEFL 475, minimum computer TOEFL 150. **Basis for Candidate Selection:** *Very important factors considered include:* Application essay, recommendation(s), rigor of secondary school record. *Important factors considered include:* Interview, standardized test scores. *Other factors considered include:* Alumni/ae relation, character/personal qualities, class rank, extracurricular activities, talent/ability, volunteer work, work experience. **Freshman Admission Requirements:** High school diploma is required, and GED is accepted. *Academic units recommended:* 4 English, 3 math, 3 science, 2 foreign language, 2 social studies. **Freshman Admission Statistics:** 478 applied, 75% admitted, 42% enrolled. **Transfer Admission Requirements:** College transcript(s), essay or personal statement, statement of good standing from prior institution(s). Minimum college GPA of 2.0 required. Lowest grade transferable C-. **General Admission Information:** Application fee $25. Non-fall registration accepted. Admission may be deferred for a maximum of 1 year. Common Application accepted. Credit and/or placement offered for CEEB Advanced Placement tests.

COSTS AND FINANCIAL AID

Annual tuition $3,234. Room and board $5,088. Required fees $826. Average book expense $900. **Required Forms and Deadlines:** FAFSA. Financial aid filing deadline 5/1. **Notification of Awards:** Applicants will be notified of awards on a rolling basis beginning on or about 3/1. **Types of Aid:** *Need-based scholarships/grants:* Pell, SEOG, state scholarships/grants, private scholarships, the school's own gift aid. *Loans:* FFEL Subsidized Stafford, FFEL Unsubsidized Stafford, FFEL PLUS, state loans. **Student Employment:** Federal Work-Study Program available. Institutional employment available. Off-campus job opportunities are excellent. **Financial Aid Statistics:** 84% freshmen, 85% undergrads receive any aid.

PITTSBURG STATE UNIVERSITY

1701 South Broadway, Pittsburg, KS 66762
Phone: 620-235-4251 **E-mail:** psuadmit@pittstate.edu **CEEB Code:** 6336
Fax: 620-235-6003 **Website:** www.pittstate.edu **ACT Code:** 1449
Financial Aid Phone: 800-854-7488

This public school was founded in 1903. It has a 233-acre campus.

RATINGS

Admissions Selectivity Rating: 73   **Fire Safety Rating:** 78   **Green Rating:** 76

STUDENTS AND FACULTY

Enrollment: 5,517. **Student Body:** 49% female, 51% male, 23% out-of-state, 3% international (37 countries represented). African American 3%, Caucasian 88%, Hispanic 2%, Native American 2%. **Retention and Graduation:** 26% freshmen graduate within 4 years. **Faculty:** Student/faculty ratio 18:1. 300 full-time faculty, 78% hold PhDs. 100% faculty teach undergrads.

ACADEMICS

Degrees: Associate, bachelor's, certificate, master's. **Academic Requirements:** Arts/fine arts, computer literacy, cultural studies, English (including composition), foreign languages, health and well-being, history, humanities, mathematics, philosophy, producing and consuming, sciences (biological or physical), social science. **Classes:** Most classes have 10–19 students. Most lab/discussion sections have 10–19 students. **Disciplines with Highest Percentage of Degrees Awarded:** Business/marketing 16%, education 10%, mechanic and repair technologies 5%, biological/life sciences 5%, psychology 5%. **Special Study Options:** Accelerated program, cooperative education program, distance learning, double major, dual enrollment, English as a second language (ESL), exchange student program (domestic), external degree program, honors program, independent study, internships, liberal arts/career combination, student-designed major, study abroad, teacher certification program.

FACILITIES

Housing: Coed dorms, apartments for married students, special housing for disabled students, substance-free and academic excellence floors. **Special Academic Facilities/Equipment:** Planetarium, observatory, field biology reserve, nature reach, herbarium, technology center, mammal collection, greenhouse, art gallery, polymer research center, cadaver lab, veterans memorial amphitheater, broadcasting lab, public radio station. **Computers:** 100% of classrooms are wireless, 90% of public computers are PCs, 10% of public computers are Macs, network access in dorm rooms, network access in dorm lounges, online registration, online administrative functions (other than registration), remote student-access to Web through college's connection.

CAMPUS LIFE

Activities: Choral groups, concert band, dance, drama/theater, jazz band, literary magazine, marching band, music ensembles, musical theater, opera, pep band, radio station, student government, student newspaper, student-run-film society, symphony orchestra, television station. **Organizations:** 140 registered organizations, 7 fraternities (3% men join), 3 sororities (3% women join). **Athletics (Intercollegiate):** *Men:* Baseball, basketball, cheerleading, cross-country, football, golf, track/field (indoor), track/field (outdoor). *Women:* Basketball, cheerleading, cross-country, softball, track/field (indoor), track/field (outdoor), volleyball. **Environmental Initiatives:** Establishment of recycling center on campus. Installation of energy efficient lighting. Installation of water saving fixtures.

ADMISSIONS

Freshman Academic Profile: 13% in top 10% of high school class, 36% in top 25% of high school class, 67% in top 50% of high school class. ACT middle 50% range 19–24. TOEFL required of all international applicants, minimum paper TOEFL 520, minimum computer TOEFL 190. **Basis for Candidate Selection:** *Very important factors considered include:* Academic GPA, class rank, rigor of secondary school record, standardized test scores. **Freshman Admission Requirements:** High school diploma is required, and GED is accepted. *Academic units recommended:* 4 English, 3 math, 3 science, 3 social studies, 1 computer technology. **Freshman Admission Statistics:** 1,973 applied, 88% admitted, 57% enrolled. **Transfer Admission Requirements:** College transcript(s). Minimum college GPA of 2.0 required. Lowest grade transferable D. **General Admission Information:** Application fee $30. Non-fall registration accepted. Credit and/or placement offered for CEEB Advanced Placement tests.

COSTS AND FINANCIAL AID

Annual in-state tuition $3,036. Out-of-state tuition $10,366. Room & board $4,844. Required fees $754. Average book expense $1,000. **Required Forms and Deadlines:** FAFSA, institution's own financial aid form, state aid form. Financial aid filing deadline 3/1. **Notification of Awards:** Applicants will be notified of awards on a rolling basis beginning on or about 2/15. **Types of Aid:** *Need-based scholarships/grants:* Pell, SEOG, state scholarships/grants, private scholarships, the school's own gift aid. *Loans:* FFEL Subsidized Stafford, FFEL Unsubsidized Stafford, FFEL PLUS, Federal Perkins, Federal Nursing, college/university loans from institutional funds. **Student Employment:** Federal Work-Study Program available. Institutional employment available. Off-campus job opportunities are good. **Financial Aid Statistics:** 47% freshmen, 43% undergrads receive need-based scholarship or grant aid. 42% freshmen, 51% undergrads receive need-based self-help aid. 24 freshmen, 118 undergrads receive athletic scholarships. 83% freshmen, 84% undergrads receive any aid. Highest amount earned per year from on-campus jobs $4,944.

PITZER COLLEGE

1050 North Mills Avenue, Claremont, CA 91711-6101
Phone: 909-621-8129 **E-mail:** admission@pitzer.edu **CEEB Code:** 4619
Fax: 909-621-8770 **Website:** www.pitzer.edu **ACT Code:** 0363
Financial Aid Phone: 909-621-8208

This private school was founded in 1963. It has a 35-acre campus.

RATINGS

Admissions Selectivity Rating: 90   **Fire Safety Rating:** 65   **Green Rating:** 75

STUDENTS AND FACULTY

Enrollment: 970. **Student Body:** 59% female, 41% male, 43% out-of-state, 2% international (10 countries represented). African American 6%, Asian 10%, Caucasian 42%, Hispanic 14%. **Retention and Graduation:** 89% freshmen return for sophomore year. 68% freshmen graduate within 4 years. 8% grads pursue business degrees. 9% grads pursue law degrees. 5% grads pursue medical degrees. **Faculty:** Student/faculty ratio 11:1. 68 full-time faculty, 99% hold PhDs. 100% faculty teach undergrads.

ACADEMICS

Degrees: Bachelor's. **Academic Requirements:** English (including composition), humanities, interdisciplinary and intercultural, mathematics, sciences (biological or physical), social responsibility, social science exploration. **Classes:** Most classes have 10–19 students. **Majors with Highest Enrollment:** Political science and government, psychology, sociology. **Disciplines with Highest Percentage of Degrees Awarded:** Social sciences 23%, English 11%, psychology 10%, visual and performing arts 10%, area and ethnic studies 8%, communications/journalism 6%, business/marketing 6%. **Special Study Options:** Cooperative education program, cross-registration, double major, English as a second language (ESL), exchange student program (domestic), honors program, independent study, internships, liberal arts/career combination, new resources program for nontraditional age students (over age 25), student-designed major, study abroad.

FACILITIES

Housing: Coed dorms, special housing for disabled students, friendship suites, thematic corridors, food cooperative. **Special Academic Facilities/Equipment:** Theater arts center; Black, Asian American, and Chicano study centers; film, TV, and videotape studios; arboretum; biological field station; student health services; Gold Student Center. **Computers:** 10% of classrooms are wired, 75% of classrooms are wireless, 75% of public computers are PCs, 25% of public computers are Macs, network access in dorm rooms, network access in dorm lounges, online administrative functions (other than registration), remote student-access to Web through college's connection.

CAMPUS LIFE

Activities: Choral groups, dance, drama/theater, literary magazine, music ensembles, radio station, student government, student newspaper, symphony orchestra. **Organizations:** 120 registered organizations, 1 honor society. **Athletics (Intercollegiate):** *Men:* Baseball, basketball, cross-country, diving, football, golf, soccer, swimming, tennis, track/field (outdoor), water polo. *Women:* Basketball, cross-country, diving, soccer, softball, swimming, tennis, track/field (outdoor), volleyball, water polo. **Environmental Initiatives:** New 'Green' dorms. Costa Rica Firestone Center. Campus Climate challenge through Eco Center.

ADMISSIONS

Freshman Academic Profile: 38% in top 10% of high school class, 73% in top 25% of high school class, 96% in top 50% of high school class. SAT Math middle 50% range 550–650. SAT Critical Reading middle 50% range 570–680. TOEFL required of all international applicants, minimum paper TOEFL 587, minimum computer TOEFL 240. **Basis for Candidate Selection:** *Very important factors considered include:* Academic GPA, application essay, character/personal qualities, class rank, extracurricular activities, recommendation(s), rigor of secondary school record, talent/ability. *Important factors considered include:* Alumni/ae relation, first generation, geographical residence, interview, level of applicant's interest, racial/ethnic status, volunteer work, work experience. *Other factors considered include:* Standardized test scores, state residency. **Freshman Admission Requirements:** High school diploma is required, and GED is accepted. *Academic units required:* 4 English, 3 math, 3 science (3 science labs), 3 foreign language, 3 social studies. **Freshman Admission Statistics:** 3,437 applied, 37% admitted, 18% enrolled. **Transfer Admission Requirements:** College transcript(s), essay or personal statement, statement of good standing from prior institution(s). Minimum college GPA of 2.0 required. Lowest grade transferable C. **General Admission Information:** Application fee $50. Early decision application deadline 11/15. Regular application deadline 1/1. Regular notification 4/1. Non-fall registration not accepted. Admission may be deferred for a maximum of 1 year. Placement offered for CEEB Advanced Placement tests.

COSTS AND FINANCIAL AID

Average book expense $900. **Required Forms and Deadlines:** FAFSA, CSS/Financial Aid PROFILE, state aid form, Noncustodial PROFILE, Business/Farm Supplement. Financial aid filing deadline 2/1. **Notification of Awards:** Applicants will be notified of awards on or about 4/1. **Types of Aid:** *Need-based scholarships/grants:* Pell, SEOG, state scholarships/grants, private scholarships, the school's own gift aid, ACG & National SMART. *Loans:* FFEL Subsidized Stafford, FFEL Unsubsidized Stafford, FFEL PLUS, Federal Perkins, college/university loans from institutional funds. **Student Employment:** Federal Work-Study Program available. Institutional employment available. Off-campus job opportunities are fair. **Financial Aid Statistics:** 34% freshmen, 36% undergrads receive need-based scholarship or grant aid. 34% freshmen, 35% undergrads receive need-based self-help aid. 48% freshmen, 46% undergrads receive any aid.

See page 1310.

PLYMOUTH STATE UNIVERSITY

17 High Street, MSC 52, Plymouth, NH 03264
Phone: 603-535-2237 **E-mail:** plymouthadmit@plymouth.edu **CEEB Code:** 3690
Fax: 603-535-2714 **Website:** www.plymouth.edu **ACT Code:** 2518
Financial Aid Phone: 877-846-5755

This public school was founded in 1871. It has a 170-acre campus.

RATINGS

Admissions Selectivity Rating: 70   **Fire Safety Rating:** 80   **Green Rating:** 85

STUDENTS AND FACULTY

Enrollment: 4,081. **Student Body:** 49% female, 51% male, 40% out-of-state. Caucasian 90%. **Retention and Graduation:** 76% freshmen return for sophomore year. 28% freshmen graduate within 4 years. 16% grads go on to further study within 1 year. **Faculty:** Student/faculty ratio 17:1. 175 full-time faculty, 87% hold PhDs. 80% faculty teach undergrads.

ACADEMICS

Degrees: Bachelor's, master's, post-bachelor's certificate, post-master's certificate. **Academic Requirements:** First-year seminar, composition, math foundations, quantitative reasoning, technology, writing in the discipline. 6 credits each in creative thought, past and present, scientific inquiry, self and society. 3 credits each in diversity, global awareness, integration, wellness. **Classes:** Most classes have 20–29 students. Most lab/discussion sections have 10–19 students. **Majors with Highest Enrollment:** Business administration and management, criminal justice/safety studies, elementary education and teaching. **Disciplines with Highest Percentage of Degrees Awarded:** Education 21%, business/marketing 17%, visual and performing arts 9%, parks and recreation 9%, communication technologies 8%. **Special Study Options:** Distance learning, double major, exchange student program (domestic), honors program, independent study, internships, student-designed major, study abroad, teacher certification program.

FACILITIES

Housing: Coed dorms, apartments for married students, apartments for single students, fraternity/sorority housing, nontraditional student apartments. **Special Academic Facilities/Equipment:** Karl Drerup Art Gallery, Silver Cultural Arts Center, Sylvestre Planetarium, Child Development & Family Center (NAEYC accredited lab school for children 2–6 years old), meteorology lab, geographic information system lab, psychology lab, graphic design computer lab. **Computers:** 10% of classrooms are wired, 40% of classrooms are wireless, 100% of public computers are PCs, network access in dorm rooms, network access in dorm lounges, online registration, online administrative functions (other than registration), remote student-access to Web through college's connection.

CAMPUS LIFE

Activities: Choral groups, concert band, dance, drama/theater, jazz band, literary magazine, music ensembles, musical theater, radio station, student government, student newspaper, student-run film society, yearbook. **Organizations:** 90 registered organizations, 8 honor societies, 6 religious organizations. 2 fraternities (1% men join), 2 sororities (1% women join). **Athletics (Intercollegiate):** *Men:* Baseball, basketball, football, ice hockey, lacrosse, skiing (downhill/alpine), soccer, wrestling. *Women:* Basketball, diving, field hockey, ice hockey, lacrosse, skiing (downhill/alpine), soccer, softball, swimming, tennis, volleyball. **Environmental Initiatives:** New degree program. All new campus construction must achieve LEED Silver Standard or the Equivalent. Establish a purchasing policy that requires Energy Star certified.

ADMISSIONS

Freshman Academic Profile: 4% in top 10% of high school class, 16% in top 25% of high school class, 52% in top 50% of high school class. 95% from public high schools. SAT Math middle 50% range 430–530. SAT Critical Reading middle 50% range 420–520. ACT middle 50% range 18–21. TOEFL required of all international applicants, minimum paper TOEFL 520, minimum computer TOEFL 190. **Basis for Candidate Selection:** *Very important factors considered include:* Rigor of secondary school record. *Important factors considered include:* Academic GPA, application essay, character/personal qualities, class rank, recommendation(s), standardized test scores, talent/ability. *Other factors considered include:* Alumni/ae relation, extracurricular activities, racial/ethnic status, volunteer work, work experience. **Freshman Admission**

Requirements: High school diploma is required, and GED is accepted. *Academic units required:* 4 English, 3 math, 2 science (1 science lab), 2 social studies, 1 history. *Academic units recommended:* 4 English, 3 math, 3 science (1 science lab), 2 foreign language, 3 social studies, 2 history. **Freshman Admission Statistics:** 3,655 applied, 77% admitted, 36% enrolled. **Transfer Admission Requirements:** High school transcript, college transcript(s). Minimum college GPA of 2.0 required. Lowest grade transferable C. **General Admission Information:** Application fee $35. Regular application deadline 4/1. Regular notification is rolling. Non-fall registration accepted. Admission may be deferred for a maximum of 1 year. Common Application not accepted. Credit offered for CEEB Advanced Placement tests.

COSTS AND FINANCIAL AID

Annual in-state tuition $5,410. Out-of-state tuition $12,250. Room & board $6,780. Required fees $1,618. Average book expense $786. **Required Forms and Deadlines:** FAFSA. Financial aid filing deadline 3/1. **Notification of Awards:** Applicants will be notified of awards on a rolling basis beginning on or about 3/1. **Types of Aid:** *Need-based scholarships/grants:* Pell, SEOG, state scholarships/grants, private scholarships, the school's own gift aid. *Loans:* FFEL Subsidized Stafford, FFEL Unsubsidized Stafford, FFEL PLUS, Federal Perkins. **Student Employment:** Federal Work-Study Program available. Institutional employment available. Off-campus job opportunities are good. **Financial Aid Statistics:** 37% freshmen, 30% undergrads receive need-based scholarship or grant aid. 58% freshmen, 30% undergrads receive need-based self-help aid. 59% freshmen, 52% undergrads receive any aid. Highest amount earned per year from on-campus jobs $1,000.

POINT LOMA NAZARENE UNIVERSITY

3900 Lomaland Drive, San Diego, CA 92106
Phone: 619-849-2273 **E-mail:** admissions@pointloma.edu **CEEB Code:** 4605
Fax: 619-849-2601 **Website:** www.pointloma.edu **ACT Code:** 0370
Financial Aid Phone: 619-849-2296

This private school, affiliated with the Nazarene Church, was founded in 1902. It has a 90-acre campus.

RATINGS
Admissions Selectivity Rating: 89   **Fire Safety Rating:** 60*   **Green Rating:** 60*

STUDENTS AND FACULTY

Enrollment: 2,369. **Student Body:** 61% female, 39% male, 21% out-of-state. African American 2%, Asian 5%, Caucasian 79%, Hispanic 11%. **Retention and Graduation:** 86% freshmen return for sophomore year. 51% freshmen graduate within 4 years. **Faculty:** Student/faculty ratio 15:1. 141 full-time faculty, 76% hold PhDs. 100% faculty teach undergrads.

ACADEMICS

Degrees: Bachelor's, master's. **Academic Requirements:** Arts/fine arts, Bible and theology, English (including composition), foreign languages, history, humanities, mathematics, philosophy, physical fitness, sciences (biological or physical), social science. **Classes:** Most classes have 10–19 students. **Majors with Highest Enrollment:** Business administration/management, liberal arts and sciences/liberal studies, psychology. **Disciplines with Highest Percentage of Degrees Awarded:** Education 29%, business/marketing 14%, health professions and related sciences 8%, liberal arts/general studies 6%, psychology 6%. **Special Study Options:** Double major, honors program, independent study, internships, study abroad, teacher certification program.

FACILITIES

Housing: Men's dorms, women's dorms, apartments for married students, apartments for single students. **Special Academic Facilities/Equipment:** Language lab, on-campus preschool, electron microscope. **Computers:** Network access in dorm rooms, network access in dorm lounges, online registration, online administrative functions (other than registration), remote student-access to Web through college's connection.

CAMPUS LIFE

Activities: Choral groups, concert band, drama/theater, jazz band, music ensembles, radio station, student government, student newspaper, television station, yearbook. **Organizations:** 30 registered organizations, 2 honor societies, 7 religious organizations. 3 fraternities, 3 sororities. **Athletics (Intercollegiate):** *Men:* Baseball, basketball, cross-country, golf, soccer, tennis, track/field (outdoor). *Women:* Basketball, cross-country, softball, tennis, track/field (outdoor), volleyball.

ADMISSIONS

Freshman Academic Profile: 65% in top 10% of high school class, 69% in top 25% of high school class, 89% in top 50% of high school class. SAT Math middle 50% range 500–620. SAT Critical Reading middle 50% range 510–620. TOEFL required of all international applicants, minimum paper TOEFL 550, minimum computer TOEFL 213. **Basis for Candidate Selection:** *Very important factors considered include:* Academic GPA, character/personal qualities, rigor of secondary school record, standardized test scores. *Important factors considered include:* Application essay, class rank, interview, recommendation(s). *Other factors considered include:* Alumni/ae relation, extracurricular activities, first generation, religious affiliation/commitment, talent/ability. **Freshman Admission Requirements:** High school diploma is required, and GED is accepted. *Academic units recommended:* 4 English, 3 math, 2 science (2 science labs), 2 foreign language, 2 social studies, 2 history, 1 academic elective. **Freshman Admission Statistics:** 1,942 applied, 65% admitted, 42% enrolled. **Transfer Admission Requirements:** College transcript(s), essay or personal statement, interview. Minimum college GPA of 2.0 required. Lowest grade transferable D. **General Admission Information:** Application fee $50. Regular notification 4/1. Non-fall registration not accepted. Credit and/or placement offered for CEEB Advanced Placement tests.

COSTS AND FINANCIAL AID

Annual tuition $24,580. Room and board $8,170. Required fees $540. Average book expense $1,566. **Required Forms and Deadlines:** FAFSA, institution's own financial aid form. Financial aid filing deadline 3/2. **Notification of Awards:** Applicants will be notified of awards on or about 3/1. **Types of Aid:** *Need-based scholarships/grants:* Pell, SEOG, state scholarships/grants, private scholarships, the school's own gift aid. *Loans:* FFEL Subsidized Stafford, FFEL Unsubsidized Stafford, FFEL PLUS, Federal Perkins, Federal Nursing, state loans. **Financial Aid Statistics:** 61% freshmen, 58% undergrads receive need-based scholarship or grant aid. 48% freshmen, 51% undergrads receive need-based self-help aid. 10 freshmen, 66 undergrads receive athletic scholarships.

See page 1312.

POINT PARK UNIVERSITY

201 Wood Street, Pittsburgh, PA 15222
Phone: 412-392-3430 **E-mail:** enroll@pointpark.edu **CEEB Code:** 2676
Fax: 412-391-1980 **Website:** www.pointpark.edu **ACT Code:** 3530
Financial Aid Phone: 412-392-3930

This private school was founded in 1960.

RATINGS
Admissions Selectivity Rating: 74   **Fire Safety Rating:** 97   **Green Rating:** 73

STUDENTS AND FACULTY

Enrollment: 3,049. **Student Body:** 59% female, 41% male, 16% out-of-state, 1% international (25 countries represented). African American 19%, Caucasian 77%, Hispanic 2%. **Retention and Graduation:** 71% freshmen return for sophomore year. 36% freshmen graduate within 4 years. **Faculty:** Student/faculty ratio 14:1. 100 full-time faculty, 54% hold PhDs. 95% faculty teach undergrads.

ACADEMICS

Degrees: Associate, bachelor's, certificate, master's. **Academic Requirements:** Arts/fine arts, computer literacy, English (including composition), foreign languages, history, humanities, mathematics, philosophy, sciences (biological or physical), social science. **Classes:** Most classes have 10–19 students. **Majors with Highest Enrollment:** Dance, drama and dramatics/theater arts, teacher education and professional development, specific subject areas. **Disciplines with Highest Percentage of Degrees Awarded:** Business/marketing 22%, visual and performing arts 20%, security and protective services 13%, education 11%, communications/journalism 10%. **Special Study Options:** Accelerated program, cross-registration, double major, English as a second language (ESL), exchange student program (domestic), honors program, independent study, internships, liberal arts/career combination, student-designed major, study abroad, teacher certification program, weekend college.

FACILITIES

Housing: Coed dorms, men's dorms, women's dorms, special housing for disabled students, quiet floors, single gender floors. **Special Academic Facilities/Equipment:** Theater, day care center and elementary school, engineering technology labs, television and radio studios, digital film editing suites, dance studios. **Computers:** 1% of classrooms are wireless, 90% of public computers are PCs, 10% of public computers are Macs, network access in dorm rooms, network access in dorm lounges, support for handheld computing, remote student-access to Web through college's connection.

CAMPUS LIFE

Activities: Choral groups, dance, drama/theater, literary magazine, musical theater, opera, radio station, student government, student newspaper, student-run film society, television station. **Organizations:** 25 registered organizations, 3 honor societies, 2 religious organizations. **Athletics (Intercollegiate):** *Men:* Baseball, basketball, cross-country, soccer. *Women:* Basketball, cross-country, softball, volleyball.

ADMISSIONS

Freshman Academic Profile: 12% in top 10% of high school class, 38% in top 25% of high school class, 72% in top 50% of high school class. SAT Math middle 50% range 430–540. SAT Critical Reading middle 50% range 460–570. SAT Writing middle 50% range 440–560. ACT middle 50% range 19–24. TOEFL required of all international applicants, minimum paper TOEFL 500, minimum computer TOEFL 173. **Basis for Candidate Selection:** *Other factors considered include:* Academic GPA, class rank, extracurricular activities, rigor of secondary school record, standardized test scores, talent/ability, work experience. **Freshman Admission Requirements:** High school diploma is required, and GED is accepted. *Academic units recommended:* 4 English, 4 math, 4 science, 2 foreign language, 4 social studies, 4 history, 2 academic electives. **Freshman Admission Statistics:** 2,348 applied, 78% admitted, 27% enrolled. **Transfer Admission Requirements:** College transcript(s). Minimum college GPA of 2.0 required. Lowest grade transferable C. **General Admission Information:** Application fee $40. Regular notification is rolling. Non-fall registration accepted. Admission may be deferred for a maximum of 1 year. Neither credit nor placement offered for CEEB Advanced Placement tests.

COSTS AND FINANCIAL AID

Annual tuition $17,260. Room & board $7,880. Required fees $510. Average book expense $1,000. **Required Forms and Deadlines:** FAFSA. Financial aid filing deadline 5/1. **Notification of Awards:** Applicants will be notified of awards on a rolling basis beginning on or about 2/15. **Types of Aid:** *Need-based scholarships/grants:* Pell, SEOG, state scholarships/grants, private scholarships, the school's own gift aid. *Loans:* FFEL Subsidized Stafford, FFEL Unsubsidized Stafford, FFEL PLUS, Federal Perkins. **Financial Aid Statistics:** 68% freshmen, 79% undergrads receive need-based scholarship or grant aid. 63% freshmen, 74% undergrads receive need-based self-help aid. 4 freshmen, 29 undergrads receive athletic scholarships. 97% freshmen, 88% undergrads receive any aid. Highest amount earned per year from on-campus jobs $4,000.

See page 1314.

POLYTECHNIC UNIVERSITY—BROOKLYN

6 Metrotech Center, Brooklyn, NY 11201-2999
Phone: 718-260-3100 **E-mail:** uadmit@poly.edu **CEEB Code:** 2668
Fax: 718-260-3446 **Website:** www.poly.edu **ACT Code:** 2860
Financial Aid Phone: 718-260-3300

This private school was founded in 1854. It has a 3-acre campus.

RATINGS

Admissions Selectivity Rating: 84　　　**Fire Safety Rating:** 60*　　　**Green Rating:** 60*

STUDENTS AND FACULTY

Enrollment: 1,453. **Student Body:** 20% female, 80% male, 7% out-of-state, 10% international (44 countries represented). African American 11%, Asian 31%, Caucasian 29%, Hispanic 12%. **Retention and Graduation:** 76% freshmen return for sophomore year. 29% freshmen graduate within 4 years. 22% grads go on to further study within 1 year. **Faculty:** Student/faculty ratio 13:1. 138 full-time faculty, 90% hold PhDs. 100% faculty teach undergrads.

ACADEMICS

Degrees: Bachelor's, certificate, doctoral, master's. **Academic Requirements:** Computer literacy, English (including composition), history, humanities, mathematics, sciences (biological or physical), social science. **Classes:** Most classes have 20–29 students. Most lab/discussion sections have 10–19 students. **Majors with Highest Enrollment:** Computer and information sciences; computer engineering; electrical, electronics, and communications engineering. **Disciplines with Highest Percentage of Degrees Awarded:** Engineering 59%, computer and information sciences 24%, business/marketing 9%, liberal

arts/general studies 4%, physical sciences 2%, mathematics 2%. **Special Study Options:** Accelerated program, cooperative education program, distance learning, double major, dual enrollment, honors program, independent study, internships.

FACILITIES

Housing: Coed dorms, fraternity/sorority housing. **Special Academic Facilities/Equipment:** Electron microscope, supersonic wind tunnel, art displays in student center. **Computers:** 82% of public computers are PCs, 2% of public computers are Macs, 16% of public computers are UNIX, network access in dorm rooms, network access in dorm lounges, online registration, online administrative functions (other than registration), remote student-access to Web through college's connection. Undergraduates are required to own a computer.

CAMPUS LIFE

Activities: Drama/theater, literary magazine, student government, student newspaper, student-run film society, yearbook. **Organizations:** 46 registered organizations, 9 honor societies, 3 religious organizations. 3 fraternities (3% men join), 1 sorority (4% women join). **Athletics (Intercollegiate):** *Men:* Baseball, basketball, cross-country, soccer, tennis, track/field (outdoor), volleyball. *Women:* Basketball, cross-country, softball, tennis, track/field (outdoor), volleyball.

ADMISSIONS

Freshman Academic Profile: 35% in top 10% of high school class, 61% in top 25% of high school class, 95% in top 50% of high school class. 82% from public high schools. SAT Math middle 50% range 560–675. SAT Critical Reading middle 50% range 470–600. SAT Writing middle 50% range 480–590. TOEFL required of all international applicants, minimum paper TOEFL 550, minimum computer TOEFL 217. **Basis for Candidate Selection:** *Very important factors considered include:* Rigor of secondary school record, standardized test scores. *Important factors considered include:* Class rank. *Other factors considered include:* Application essay, interview, recommendation(s). **Freshman Admission Requirements:** High school diploma is required, and GED is accepted. *Academic units required:* 4 English, 4 math, 4 science, 3 social studies, 2 academic electives. *Academic units recommended:* 2 foreign language. **Freshman Admission Statistics:** 1,356 applied, 73% admitted, 38% enrolled. **Transfer Admission Requirements:** College transcript(s). Minimum college GPA of 2.5 required. Lowest grade transferable C. **General Admission Information:** Application fee $50. Regular notification is rolling. Non-fall registration accepted. Credit and/or placement offered for CEEB Advanced Placement tests.

COSTS AND FINANCIAL AID

Annual tuition $28,745. Room & board $8,500. Required fees $1,044. Average book expense $1,000. **Required Forms and Deadlines:** FAFSA, institution's own financial aid form, CSS/Financial Aid PROFILE, state aid form. **Notification of Awards:** Applicants will be notified of awards on a rolling basis beginning on or about 2/15. **Types of Aid:** *Need-based scholarships/grants:* Pell, SEOG, state scholarships/grants, private scholarships, the school's own gift aid, United Negro College Fund. *Loans:* FFEL Subsidized Stafford, FFEL Unsubsidized Stafford, FFEL PLUS, Federal Perkins, college/university loans from institutional funds, alternative loans. **Financial Aid Statistics:** 83% freshmen, 75% undergrads receive need-based scholarship or grant aid. 59% freshmen, 63% undergrads receive need-based self-help aid. 99% freshmen, 92% undergrads receive any aid. Highest amount earned per year from on-campus jobs $10,500.

See page 1316.

POMONA COLLEGE

333 North College Way, Claremont, CA 91711-6312
Phone: 909-621-8134 **E-mail:** admissions@pomona.edu **CEEB Code:** 4607
Fax: 909-621-8952 **Website:** www.pomona.edu **ACT Code:** 0372
Financial Aid Phone: 909-621-8205

This private school was founded in 1887. It has a 140-acre campus.

RATINGS

Admissions Selectivity Rating: 99　　　**Fire Safety Rating:** 80　　　**Green Rating:** 60*

STUDENTS AND FACULTY

Enrollment: 1,545. **Student Body:** 50% female, 50% male, 65% out-of-state, 3% international (24 countries represented). African American 8%, Asian 14%, Caucasian 50%, Hispanic 11%. **Retention and Graduation:** 98% freshmen return for sophomore year. 87% freshmen graduate within 4 years. 33% grads go on to further study within 1 year. 12% grads pursue arts and sciences degrees. 11% grads pursue law degrees. 11% grads pursue medical degrees. **Faculty:** Student/faculty ratio 8:1. 177 full-time faculty, 98% hold PhDs. 100% faculty teach undergrads.

ACADEMICS

Degrees: Bachelor's. **Academic Requirements:** Arts/fine arts, computer literacy, English (including composition), foreign languages, history, humanities, mathematics, philosophy, sciences (biological or physical), social science. **Classes:** Most classes have 10–19 students. Most lab/discussion sections have 10–19 students. **Majors with Highest Enrollment:** Biology/biological sciences, economics, English language and literature. **Disciplines with Highest Percentage of Degrees Awarded:** Social sciences 26%, biological/life sciences 13%, psychology 9%, communications/journalism 6%, English 6%, foreign languages and literature 5%, physical sciences 5%, history 5%. **Special Study Options:** Cross-registration, double major, exchange student program (domestic), independent study, internships, student-designed major, study abroad.

FACILITIES

Housing: Coed dorms, language residence hall. **Special Academic Facilities/Equipment:** Oldenborg Center for Foreign Languages, museum of art, Brackett Observatory. **Computers:** 100% of classrooms are wireless, 70% of public computers are PCs, 30% of public computers are Macs, 11% of public computers are UNIX, network access in dorm rooms, network access in dorm lounges, online administrative functions (other than registration), remote student-access to Web through college's connection.

CAMPUS LIFE

Activities: Choral groups, concert band, dance, drama/theater, jazz band, literary magazine, music ensembles, musical theater, pep band, radio station, student government, student newspaper, student-run film society, symphony orchestra, television station, yearbook. **Organizations:** 280 registered organizations, 3 honor societies, 5 religious organizations. 3 fraternities (3% men join). **Athletics (Intercollegiate):** *Men:* Baseball, basketball, cross-country, diving, football, golf, soccer, swimming, tennis, track/field (outdoor), water polo. *Women:* Basketball, cross-country, diving, golf, lacrosse, soccer, softball, swimming, tennis, track/field (outdoor), volleyball, water polo.

ADMISSIONS

Freshman Academic Profile: 87% in top 10% of high school class, 98% in top 25% of high school class, 100% in top 50% of high school class. 60% from public high schools. SAT Math middle 50% range 680–760. SAT Critical Reading middle 50% range 690–760. SAT Writing middle 50% range 680–760. ACT middle 50% range 29–34. TOEFL required of all international applicants, minimum paper TOEFL 600, minimum computer TOEFL 250. **Basis for Candidate Selection:** *Very important factors considered include:* Academic GPA, application essay, character/personal qualities, class rank, extracurricular activities, recommendation(s), rigor of secondary school record, standardized test scores, talent/ability. *Important factors considered include:* Interview. *Other factors considered include:* Alumni/ae relation, first generation, geographical residence, racial/ethnic status, volunteer work, work experience. **Freshman Admission Requirements:** High school diploma or equivalent is not required. *Academic units required:* 4 English, 3 math, 3 science (2 science labs), 2 foreign language, 2 social studies, 3 history. *Academic units recommended:* 4 math, 3 science (3 science labs), 3 foreign language, 2 social studies, 3 history. **Freshman Admission Statistics:** 5,440 applied, 18% admitted, 39% enrolled. **Transfer Admission Requirements:** High school transcript, college transcript(s), essay or personal statement, standardized test score, statement of good standing from prior institution(s). Minimum college GPA of 3.0 required. Lowest grade transferable C. **General Admission Information:** Application fee $65. Early decision application deadline 11/15. Regular application deadline 1/2. Regular notification 4/10. Non-fall registration not accepted. Admission may be deferred for a maximum of 1 year. Credit and/or placement offered for CEEB Advanced Placement tests.

COSTS AND FINANCIAL AID

Annual tuition $33,635. Room and board $11,748. Required fees $297. Average book expense $850. **Required Forms and Deadlines:** FAFSA, CSS/Financial Aid PROFILE, state aid form, Noncustodial PROFILE, Business/Farm Supplement, tax returns for both the student and parents. Financial aid filing deadline 2/1. **Notification of Awards:** Applicants will be notified of awards on or about 4/1. **Types of Aid:** *Need-based scholarships/grants:* Pell, SEOG, state scholarships/grants, the school's own gift aid. *Loans:* FFEL Subsidized Stafford, FFEL Unsubsidized Stafford, FFEL PLUS, Federal Perkins, college/university loans from institutional funds. **Student Employment:** Federal Work-Study Program available. Institutional employment available. Off-campus job

opportunities are good. **Financial Aid Statistics:** 54% freshmen, 53% undergrads receive need-based scholarship or grant aid. 54% freshmen, 53% undergrads receive need-based self-help aid. 53% freshmen, 50% undergrads receive any aid.

PONTIFICAL COLLEGE JOSEPHINUM

7625 North High Street, Columbus, OH 43235-1498
Phone: 614-885-5585 **E-mail:** admissions@pcj.edu
Fax: 614-885-2307 **Website:** www.pc.edu
Financial Aid Phone: 614-885-5585

This private school, affiliated with the Roman Catholic Church, was founded in 1888.

RATINGS

Admissions Selectivity Rating: 60*   **Fire Safety Rating:** 60*   **Green Rating:** 60*

STUDENTS AND FACULTY

Enrollment: 80. **Student Body:** 100% male, 70% out-of-state, 8% international. Asian 1%, Caucasian 80%, Hispanic 9%. **Retention and Graduation:** 95% freshmen return for sophomore year. 33% freshmen graduate within 4 years. 95% grads go on to further study within 1 year. 50% grads pursue arts and sciences degrees. **Faculty:** Student/faculty ratio 4:1. 20 full-time faculty, 85% hold PhDs.

ACADEMICS

Degrees: Bachelor's, first professional, master's. **Academic Requirements:** Arts/fine arts, English (including composition), foreign languages, history, humanities, mathematics, philosophy, sciences (biological or physical), social science, theology. **Classes:** Most classes have fewer than 10 students. **Disciplines with Highest Percentage of Degrees Awarded:** Philosophy and religious studies 80%, English 10%, area and ethnic studies 5%, history 5%. **Special Study Options:** Cross-registration, double major, honors program.

FACILITIES

Housing: Men's dorms. **Computers:** Network access in dorm rooms, remote student-access to Web through college's connection.

CAMPUS LIFE

Activities: Choral groups, drama/theater. **Organizations:** 1 religious organization.

ADMISSIONS

Freshman Academic Profile: 25% in top 10% of high school class, 35% in top 25% of high school class, 60% in top 50% of high school class. SAT Math middle 50% range 340–700. SAT Critical Reading middle 50% range 510–670. SAT Writing middle 50% range 450–560. ACT middle 50% range 17–31. TOEFL required of all international applicants, minimum paper TOEFL 550, minimum computer TOEFL 173. **Basis for Candidate Selection:** *Very important factors considered include:* Recommendation(s), religious affiliation/commitment, rigor of secondary school record, standardized test scores. *Important factors considered include:* Academic GPA, application essay, interview. *Other factors considered include:* Character/personal qualities, class rank, extracurricular activities, talent/ability. **Freshman Admission Requirements:** High school diploma is required, and GED is accepted. *Academic units required:* 4 English, 2 math, 1 science, 1 foreign language, 2 social studies. *Academic units recommended:* 4 math, 4 science, 2 foreign language, 4 social studies. **Freshman Admission Statistics:** 23 applied, 91% admitted, 100% enrolled. **Transfer Admission Requirements:** High school transcript, college transcript(s), essay or personal statement, interview, standardized test score. Lowest grade transferable C. **General Admission Information:** Application fee $25. Regular notification is rolling. Non-fall registration not accepted.

COSTS AND FINANCIAL AID

Annual tuition $14,997. Room and board $7,498. Required fees $680. Average book expense $950. **Required Forms and Deadlines:** FAFSA, institution's own financial aid form. **Types of Aid:** *Need-based scholarships/grants:* Pell, SEOG, state scholarships/grants, private scholarships, the school's own gift aid. *Loans:* FFEL Subsidized Stafford, FFEL Unsubsidized Stafford, FFEL PLUS, Federal Perkins. **Student Employment:** Federal Work-Study Program available. **Financial Aid Statistics:** 24% freshmen, 19% undergrads receive need-based scholarship or grant aid. 35% freshmen, 14% undergrads receive need-based self-help aid. Highest amount earned per year from on-campus jobs $1,200.

PORTLAND STATE UNIVERSITY

Office of Admissions and Records, PO Box 751, Portland, OR 97207-0751
Phone: 503-725-3511 **E-mail:** Admissions@pdx.edu **CEEB Code:** 4610
Fax: 503-725-5525 **Website:** www.pdx.edu **ACT Code:** 3492
Financial Aid Phone: 800-547-8887

This public school was founded in 1946. It has a 49-acre campus.

RATINGS
Admissions Selectivity Rating: 60* **Fire Safety Rating:** 60* **Green Rating:** 60*

STUDENTS AND FACULTY
Enrollment: 15,915. **Student Body:** 54% female, 46% male, 15% out-of-state, 4% international. African American 4%, Asian 10%, Caucasian 65%, Hispanic 5%, Native American 2%. **Retention and Graduation:** 68% freshmen return for sophomore year. 10% freshmen graduate within 4 years. **Faculty:** Student/faculty ratio 18:1. 739 full-time faculty, 75% hold PhDs. 88% faculty teach undergrads.

ACADEMICS
Degrees: Bachelor's, certificate, doctoral, master's, post-bachelor's certificate. **Academic Requirements:** University Studies, a general education program, is required of all undergraduates: Freshman Inquiry (15 credits), Sophomore Inquiry (12 credits), Upper Division Cluster (12 credits), and Senior Capstone (6 credits). **Classes:** Most classes have 20–29 students. Most lab/discussion sections have 10–19 students. **Majors with Highest Enrollment:** Business administration/management; fine/studio arts; psychology. **Disciplines with Highest Percentage of Degrees Awarded:** Business/marketing 24%, physical sciences 8%, psychology 7%, liberal arts/general studies 6%, engineering 4%. **Special Study Options:** Accelerated program, cooperative education program, cross-registration, distance learning, double major, English as a second language (ESL), exchange student program (domestic), honor program, independent study, internships, study abroad, teacher certification program, Haystack Summer Program in the Arts and Sciences.

FACILITIES
Housing: Coed dorms, apartments for married students, apartments for single students, special housing for disabled students, fraternity/sorority housing, special housing for new students. Apartments for students with dependent children. **Special Academic Facilities/Equipment:** Art galleries, audiovisual resources, classroom multimedia computer systems, learning lab, child development center, Native American Center. **Computers:** 85% of public computers are PCs, 15% of public computers are Macs, network access in dorm rooms, network access in dorm lounges, online registration, online administrative functions (other than registration), support for handheld computing, remote student-access to Web through college's connection.

CAMPUS LIFE
Activities: Choral groups, concert band, dance, drama/theater, jazz band, literary magazine, music ensembles, musical theater, opera, pep band, radio station, student government, student newspaper, student-run film society, symphony orchestra. **Organizations:** 148 registered organizations, 8 religious organizations. 4 fraternities (2% men join), 4 sororities **Athletics (Intercollegiate):** *Men:* Basketball, cross-country, football, track/field (indoor), track/field (outdoor), wrestling. *Women:* Basketball, cross-country, golf, soccer, softball, track/field (indoor), track/field (outdoor), volleyball.

ADMISSIONS
Freshman Academic Profile: SAT Math middle 50% range 460–580. SAT Critical Reading middle 50% range 460–600. SAT Writing middle 50% range 440–560. ACT middle 50% range 18–25. TOEFL required of all international applicants, minimum paper TOEFL 525, minimum computer TOEFL 197. **Basis for Candidate Selection:** *Very important factors considered include:* Rigor of secondary school record. *Other factors considered include:* Standardized test scores. **Freshman Admission Requirements:** High school diploma is required, and GED is accepted. *Academic units required:* 4 English, 3 math, 2 science, 2 foreign language, 2 social studies, 1 history. *Academic units recommended:* 1 science lab. **Freshman Admission Statistics:** 3,160 applied, 91% admitted, 52% enrolled. **Transfer Admission Requirements:** College transcript(s). Minimum college GPA of 2.0 required. Lowest grade transferable C-. **General Admission Information:** Application fee $50. Regular notification is rolling. Nonfall registration accepted. Admission may be deferred for a maximum of 1 year. Credit and/or placement offered for CEEB Advanced Placement tests.

COSTS AND FINANCIAL AID
Annual in-state tuition $4,450. Annual out-of-state tuition $16,380. Room and board $8,940. Required fees $1,451. Average book expense $1,800. **Types of**

Aid: *Need-based scholarships/grants:* Pell, SEOG, state scholarships/grants, private scholarships, the school's own gift aid, United Negro College Fund. *Loans:* Direct Subsidized Stafford, Direct Unsubsidized Stafford, Direct PLUS, FFEL Subsidized Stafford, FFEL Unsubsidized Stafford, FFEL PLUS, Federal Perkins, state loans. **Student Employment:** Federal Work-Study Program available. Institutional employment available. Off-campus job opportunities are excellent. **Financial Aid Statistics:** 31% freshmen, 35% undergrads receive need-based scholarship or grant aid. 43% freshmen, 50% undergrads receive need-based self-help aid. 48 freshmen, 205 undergrads receive athletic scholarships.

POST UNIVERSITY

PO Box 2540, Waterbury, CT 06723
Phone: 203-596-4520 **E-mail:** admissions@post.edu **CEEB Code:** 3698
Fax: 203-756-5810 **Website:** www.post.edu **ACT Code:** 0580
Financial Aid Phone: 204-596-4526

This proprietary school was founded in 1890. It has a 58-acre campus.

RATINGS
Admissions Selectivity Rating: 60* **Fire Safety Rating:** 60* **Green Rating:** 70

STUDENTS AND FACULTY
Enrollment: 1,198. **Student Body:** 62% female, 38% male, 24% out-of-state, 5% international (15 countries represented). African American 18%, Asian 2%, Caucasian 62%, Hispanic 11%. **Retention and Graduation:** 64% freshmen return for sophomore year. 24% freshmen graduate within 4 years. 25% grads go on to further study within 1 year. 20% grads pursue arts and sciences degrees. 25% grads pursue business degrees. 5% grads pursue law degrees. **Faculty:** Student/faculty ratio 15:1. 31 full-time faculty, 65% hold PhDs. 100% faculty teach undergrads.

ACADEMICS
Degrees: Associate, bachelor's, certificate, master's, post-bachelor's certificate, terminal. **Academic Requirements:** Computer literacy, English (including composition), history, humanities, interdisciplinary leadership core, mathematics, sciences (biological or physical), social science. **Majors with Highest Enrollment:** Accounting, business administration/management, criminal justice/law enforcement administration. **Disciplines with Highest Percentage of Degrees Awarded:** Business/marketing 60%, liberal arts/general studies 8%, psychology 6%, law/legal studies 5%, social sciences 4%. **Special Study Options:** Accelerated program, cooperative education program, cross-registration, distance learning, double major, honors program, independent study, internships, liberal arts/career combination, study abroad, weekend college.

FACILITIES
Housing: Coed dorms, apartments for single students, learning communities. **Computers:** 98% of classrooms are wired, 100% of public computers are PCs, network access in dorm rooms, network access in dorm lounges, online registration, online administrative functions (other than registration), remote student-access to Web through college's connection.

CAMPUS LIFE
Activities: Choral groups, drama/theater, literary magazine, musical theater, student government, student newspaper. **Organizations:** 30 registered organizations. **Athletics (Intercollegiate):** *Men:* Baseball, basketball, cross-country, equestrian sports, golf, soccer, tennis. *Women:* Basketball, cross-country, equestrian sports, soccer, softball, tennis, volleyball.

ADMISSIONS
Freshman Academic Profile: 90% from public high schools. TOEFL required of all international applicants, minimum paper TOEFL 500, minimum computer TOEFL 170. **Basis for Candidate Selection:** *Very important factors considered include:* Academic GPA, interview, level of applicant's interest. *Important factors considered include:* Character/personal qualities, extracurricular activities, standardized test scores, talent/ability, volunteer work. *Other factors considered include:* Alumni/ae relation, application essay, first generation, recommendation(s). **Freshman Admission Requirements:** High school diploma is required, and GED is accepted. *Academic units required:* 4 English, 2 math, 2 science (1 science lab), 2 foreign language, 1 social studies, 2 history, 2 academic electives. *Academic units recommended:* 4 English, 2 math, 2 science (1 science lab), 2 foreign language, 1 social studies, 2 history, 2 academic electives. **Transfer Admission Requirements:** College transcript(s). Minimum college GPA of 2.0 required. Lowest grade transferable C-. **General Admission Information:** Application fee $40. Regular notification is rolling.

Non-fall registration accepted. Admission may be deferred for a maximum of 1 year. Common Application accepted. Credit and/or placement offered for CEEB Advanced Placement tests.

COSTS AND FINANCIAL AID

Annual tuition $22,500. Room and board $9,000. Average book expense $1,000. **Required Forms and Deadlines:** FAFSA, institution's own financial aid form. Financial aid filing deadline 2/15. **Types of Aid:** *Need-based scholarships/grants:* Pell, SEOG, state scholarships/grants, private scholarships, the school's own gift aid. *Loans:* FFEL Subsidized Stafford, FFEL Unsubsidized Stafford, FFEL PLUS, Federal Perkins, state loans, college/university loans from institutional funds. **Student Employment:** Federal Work-Study Program available. **Financial Aid Statistics:** 80% freshmen, 75% undergrads receive any aid. Highest amount earned per year from on-campus jobs $2,100.

See page 1318.

PRAIRIE VIEW A&M UNIVERSITY

PO Box 519, MS# 1009, Prairie View, TX 77446
Phone: 936-261-1066 **E-mail:** megooch@pvamu.edu **CEEB Code:** 6580
Fax: 936-857-2699 **Website:** www.pvamu.edu **ACT Code:** 4202
Financial Aid Phone: 936-857-2422

This public school was founded in 1878. It has a 1,440-acre campus.

RATINGS

Admissions Selectivity Rating: 75   **Fire Safety Rating:** 60*   **Green Rating:** 60*

STUDENTS AND FACULTY

Enrollment: 5,813. **Student Body:** 57% female, 43% male, 2% international (21 countries represented). African American 88%, Asian 1%, Caucasian 3%, Hispanic 4%. **Faculty:** Student/faculty ratio 17:1. 378 full-time faculty.

ACADEMICS

Degrees: Bachelor's, doctoral, master's. **Academic Requirements:** Arts/fine arts, computer literacy, English (including composition), foreign languages, history, humanities, mathematics, philosophy, sciences (biological or physical), social science. **Majors with Highest Enrollment:** Biology/biological sciences, multi/interdisciplinary studies, nursing/registered nurse training (ASN, BSN, MSN, RN). **Disciplines with Highest Percentage of Degrees Awarded:** Engineering technologies 16%, engineering 16%, business/marketing 16%, health professions and related sciences 15%, interdisciplinary studies 8%, security and protective services 8%, public administration and social services 8%, biological/life sciences 7%. **Special Study Options:** Accelerated program, cooperative education program, distance learning, double major, dual enrollment, English as a second language (ESL), honors program, independent study, internships, liberal arts/career combination, teacher certification program, weekend college.

FACILITIES

Housing: Coed dorms, apartments for single students, special housing for disabled students. **Computers:** 20% of classrooms are wired, 70% of classrooms are wireless, network access in dorm rooms, online registration, remote student-access to Web through college's connection.

CAMPUS LIFE

Activities: Choral groups, concert band, dance, drama/theater, jazz band, marching band, music ensembles, radio station, student government, student newspaper, symphony orchestra, television station, yearbook. **Organizations:** 21 registered organizations, 15 honor societies, 6 religious organizations. 9 fraternities (3% men join), 9 sororities (4% women join). **Athletics (Intercollegiate):** *Men:* Baseball, basketball, cross-country, football, golf, tennis, track/field (indoor), track/field (outdoor). *Women:* Basketball, boxing, cross-country, golf, soccer, softball, tennis, track/field (indoor), track/field (outdoor), volleyball.

ADMISSIONS

Freshman Academic Profile: 8% in top 10% of high school class, 25% in top 25% of high school class, 60% in top 50% of high school class. SAT Math middle 50% range 380–480. SAT Critical Reading middle 50% range 370–460. ACT middle 50% range 15–19. TOEFL required of all international applicants, minimum paper TOEFL 500, minimum computer TOEFL 173. **Basis for Candidate Selection:** *Very important factors considered include:* Academic GPA, class rank, rigor of secondary school record, standardized test scores. *Other factors considered include:* Character/personal qualities, extracurricular activities, first generation, volunteer work, work experience. **Freshman Admission Requirements:** High school diploma is required, and GED is accepted. *Academic units required:* 4 English, 3 math, 3 science, 2 social studies, 4 academic electives. *Academic units recommended:* 4 math, 2 foreign

language. **Freshman Admission Statistics:** 4,541 applied, 51% admitted, 49% enrolled. **Transfer Admission Requirements:** College transcript(s), statement of good standing from prior institution(s). Minimum college GPA of 2.0 required. Lowest grade transferable C. **General Admission Information:** Application fee $25. Regular application deadline 6/1. Regular notification is rolling. Non-fall registration accepted. Credit and/or placement offered for CEEB Advanced Placement tests.

COSTS AND FINANCIAL AID

Annual in-state tuition $3,765. Annual out-of-state tuition $12,690. Room and board $7,226. Required fees $6,477. Average book expense $1,000. **Required Forms and Deadlines:** FAFSA, institution's own financial aid form. Financial aid filing deadline 3/1. **Notification of Awards:** Applicants will be notified of awards on or about 6/1. **Types of Aid:** *Need-based scholarships/grants:* Pell, SEOG, state scholarships/grants, the school's own gift aid, United Negro College Fund. *Loans:* Direct Subsidized Stafford, Direct Unsubsidized Stafford, Direct PLUS, FFEL Subsidized Stafford, FFEL Unsubsidized Stafford, FFEL PLUS, Federal Perkins, college/university loans from institutional funds. **Financial Aid Statistics:** 80% freshmen, 74% undergrads receive need-based scholarship or grant aid. 80% freshmen, 74% undergrads receive need-based self-help aid. 74 freshmen, 186 undergrads receive athletic scholarships. 90% freshmen, 88% undergrads receive any aid. Highest amount earned per year from on-campus jobs $3,050.

PRATT INSTITUTE

200 Willoughby Avenue, Brooklyn, NY 11205
Phone: 718-636-3514 **E-mail:** admissions@pratt.edu **CEEB Code:** 2669
Fax: 718-636-3670 **Website:** www.pratt.edu **ACT Code:** 2862
Financial Aid Phone: 718-636-3599

This private school was founded in 1887. It has a 25-acre campus.

RATINGS

Admissions Selectivity Rating: 60*   **Fire Safety Rating:** 60*   **Green Rating:** 89

STUDENTS AND FACULTY

Enrollment: 3,103. **Student Body:** 59% female, 41% male, 63% out-of-state, 9% international (56 countries represented). African American 7%, Asian 13%, Caucasian 60%, Hispanic 9%. **Retention and Graduation:** 88% freshmen return for sophomore year. 43% freshmen graduate within 4 years. 13% grads pursue arts and sciences degrees. 6% grads pursue business degrees. 1% grads pursue law degrees. **Faculty:** Student/faculty ratio 12:1. 124 full-time faculty, 44% hold PhDs. 100% faculty teach undergrads.

ACADEMICS

Degrees: Associate, bachelor's, first professional, master's, post-master's certificate, terminal. **Academic Requirements:** Arts/fine arts, English (including composition), history, humanities, mathematics, philosophy, sciences (biological or physical), social science. **Classes:** Most classes have 10–19 students. **Majors with Highest Enrollment:** Architecture (BArch, BA/BS, MArch, MA/MS, PhD), design and visual communications, fashion/apparel design. **Disciplines with Highest Percentage of Degrees Awarded:** Visual and performing arts 74%, architecture 15%, communication technologies 4%, education 3%, English 2%. **Special Study Options:** Accelerated program, double major, English as a second language (ESL), exchange student program (domestic), independent study, internships, liberal arts/career combination, student-designed major, study abroad.

FACILITIES

Housing: Coed dorms, apartments for married students, apartments for single students, special housing for disabled students, special housing for international students. **Special Academic Facilities/Equipment:** 5 art galleries, fine arts center, printmaking center, computer graphics lab. **Computers:** 75% of classrooms are wired, 75% of classrooms are wireless, 50% of public computers are PCs, 50% of public computers are Macs, network access in dorm rooms, network access in dorm lounges, remote student-access to Web through college's connection. Undergraduates are required to own a computer.

CAMPUS LIFE

Activities: Dance, drama/theater, jazz band, literary magazine, musical theater, radio station, student government, student newspaper, student-run film society, yearbook. **Organizations:** 50 registered organizations, 4 honor societies, 3 religious organizations. 3 fraternities, 1 sorority. **Athletics (Intercollegiate):** *Men:* Basketball, cross-country, soccer, tennis, track/field (indoor), track/field (outdoor). *Women:* Basketball, cross-country, soccer, tennis, track/field (outdoor), volleyball. **Environmental Initiatives:** New building will be LEED gold. Received a $475K FIPSE "Green by Design" grant to embed sustainable best practices into every program, create interdisciplinary programs that center around environmental projects and create a "living laboratory" that links greening our facilities with greening our academic programs and provide educational programs to our city. Have a new Center for Sustainable Design and Research that centers faculty and students from various programs around environmental projects and research.

ADMISSIONS

Freshman Academic Profile: 70% from public high schools. SAT Math middle 50% range 520–630. SAT Critical Reading middle 50% range 510–640. ACT middle 50% range 22–27. TOEFL required of all international applicants, minimum paper TOEFL 530, minimum computer TOEFL 213. **Basis for Candidate Selection:** *Very important factors considered include:* Academic GPA, rigor of secondary school record, standardized test scores, talent/ability. *Important factors considered include:* Alumni/ae relation, application essay, character/personal qualities, interview, level of applicant's interest, recommendation(s). *Other factors considered include:* Class rank, extracurricular activities, volunteer work, work experience. **Freshman Admission Requirements:** High school diploma is required, and GED is accepted. *Academic units recommended:* 4 English, 3 math, 2 science, 2 social studies. **Freshman Admission Statistics:** 4,453 applied, 43% admitted, 31% enrolled. **Transfer Admission Requirements:** College transcript(s), essay or personal statement, statement of good standing from prior institution(s). Lowest grade transferable C. **General Admission Information:** Application fee $40. Regular application deadline 2/1. Regular notification 1/6. Non-fall registration accepted. Admission may be deferred by request for a maximum of 1 year. Credit and/or placement offered for CEEB Advanced Placement tests.

COSTS AND FINANCIAL AID

Annual tuition $31,700. Room and board $9,476. Required fees $1,290. Average book expense $3,000. **Required Forms and Deadlines:** FAFSA, institution's own financial aid form. Financial aid filing deadline 2/1. **Notification of Awards:** Applicants will be notified of awards on a rolling basis beginning on or about 4/15. **Types of Aid:** *Need-based scholarships/grants:* Pell, SEOG, state scholarships/grants, the school's own gift aid. *Loans:* FFEL Subsidized Stafford, FFEL Unsubsidized Stafford, FFEL PLUS, Federal Perkins, college/university loans from institutional funds. **Student Employment:** Federal Work-Study Program available. Institutional employment available. Off-campus job opportunities are excellent. **Financial Aid Statistics:** Highest amount earned per year from on-campus jobs $2,250.

PRESBYTERIAN COLLEGE

503 South Broad Street, Clinton, SC 29325
Phone: 864-833-8230 **E-mail:** admissions@presby.edu **CEEB Code:** 5540
Fax: 864-833-8195 **Website:** www.presby.edu **ACT Code:** 3874
Financial Aid Phone: 864-833-8287

This private school, affiliated with the Presbyterian Church, was founded in 1880. It has a 215-acre campus.

RATINGS

Admissions Selectivity Rating: 82   **Fire Safety Rating:** 89   **Green Rating:** 74

STUDENTS AND FACULTY

Enrollment: 1,171. **Student Body:** 52% female, 48% male, 37% out-of-state. African American 5%, Caucasian 92%, Hispanic 1%. **Retention and Graduation:** 84% freshmen return for sophomore year. 72% freshmen graduate within 4 years. 25% grads go on to further study within 1 year. 3% grads pursue business degrees. 2% grads pursue law degrees. 4% grads pursue medical degrees. **Faculty:** Student/faculty ratio 12:1. 83 full-time faculty. 90% hold PhDs. 100% faculty teach undergrads.

ACADEMICS

Degrees: Bachelor's. **Academic Requirements:** Arts/fine arts, English (including composition), foreign languages, history, humanities, mathematics, religion, sciences (biological or physical), social science. **Classes:** Most classes have 10–19 students. **Majors with Highest Enrollment:** Biology/biological sciences, business administration and management, political science and government. **Disciplines with Highest Percentage of Degrees Awarded:** Business/marketing 19%, education 12%, philosophy and religious studies 11%,

biological/life sciences 11%, social sciences 11%, history 10%, psychology 7%. **Special Study Options:** Accelerated program, double major, dual enrollment, exchange student program (domestic), forestry and environmental science program, honors program, independent study, internships, study abroad, teacher certification program, 3-2 engineering program.

FACILITIES

Housing: Coed dorms, men's dorms, women's dorms, apartments for single students, special housing for international students, fraternity/sorority housing, sorority housing not available. **Special Academic Facilities/Equipment:** Art gallery, recital hall, media center, marine/ecological center, scanning and transmission electron microscopes, visible spectrophotometer. **Computers:** 50% of public computers are PCs, 50% of public computers are Macs, network access in dorm rooms, network access in dorm lounges, online registration, online administrative functions (other than registration), remote student-access to Web through college's connection.

CAMPUS LIFE

Activities: Choral groups, dance, drama/theater, jazz band, literary magazine, music ensembles, musical theater, pep band, radio station, student government, student newspaper, symphony orchestra, yearbook. **Organizations:** 48 registered organizations, 11 honor societies, 7 religious organizations. 6 fraternities (44% men join), 3 sororities (36% women join). **Athletics (Intercollegiate):** *Men:* Baseball, basketball, cheerleading, cross-country, football, golf, lacrosse, soccer, tennis. *Women:* Basketball, cheerleading, cross-country, golf, lacrosse, soccer, softball, tennis, volleyball. **Environmental Initiatives:** Energy conservation. Use of alternate fuels. Recyling Center.

ADMISSIONS

Freshman Academic Profile: 30% in top 10% of high school class, 54% in top 25% of high school class, 86% in top 50% of high school class. 71% from public high schools. SAT Math middle 50% range 530–640. SAT Critical Reading middle 50% range 500–610. ACT middle 50% range 22–27. TOEFL required of all international applicants, minimum paper TOEFL 550, minimum computer TOEFL 200. **Basis for Candidate Selection:** *Very important factors considered include:* Academic GPA, character/personal qualities, class rank, rigor of secondary school record, standardized test scores. *Important factors considered include:* Alumni/ae relation, application essay, extracurricular activities, recommendation(s), state residency. *Other factors considered include:* First generation, talent/ability, volunteer work. **Freshman Admission Requirements:** High school diploma is required, and GED is accepted. *Academic units required:* 4 English, 3 math, 2 science (2 science labs), 2 foreign language, 2 history, 2 academic electives. *Academic units recommended:* 3 foreign language. **Freshman Admission Statistics:** 1,194 applied, 78% admitted, 39% enrolled. **Transfer Admission Requirements:** High school transcript, college transcript(s), essay or personal statement, standardized test score. Minimum college GPA of 2.5 required. Lowest grade transferable C. **General Admission Information:** Application fee $35. Early decision application deadline 11/15. Regular application deadline 1/2. Regular notification is rolling. Non-fall registration accepted. Admission may be deferred for a maximum of 1 year. Credit and/or placement offered for CEEB Advanced Placement tests.

COSTS AND FINANCIAL AID

Annual tuition $25,472. Room and board $8,064. Required fees $2,430. Average book expense $850. **Required Forms and Deadlines:** FAFSA, institution's own financial aid form. Financial aid filing deadline 3/1. **Notification of Awards:** Applicants will be notified of awards on a rolling basis beginning on or about 3/25. **Types of Aid:** *Need-based scholarships/grants:* Pell, SEOG, state scholarships/grants, private scholarships, the school's own gift aid. *Loans:* FFEL Subsidized Stafford, FFEL Unsubsidized Stafford, FFEL PLUS, Federal Perkins. **Student Employment:** Federal Work-Study Program available. Institutional employment available. **Financial Aid Statistics:** 67% freshmen, 61% undergrads receive need-based scholarship or grant aid. 31% freshmen, 32% undergrads receive need-based self-help aid. 29 freshmen, 105 undergrads receive athletic scholarships. 93% freshmen, 95% undergrads receive any aid. Highest amount earned per year from on-campus jobs $1,200.

See page 1320.

PRESCOTT COLLEGE

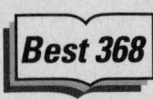

220 Grove Avenue, Attention: Admissions, Prescott, AZ 86301
Phone: 928-350-2100 **E-mail:** admissions@prescott.edu **CEEB Code:** 9295
Fax: 928-776-5242 **Website:** www.prescott.edu **ACT Code:** 5022
Financial Aid Phone: 928-350-1111

This private school was founded in 1966. It has a 4-acre campus.

RATINGS
Admissions Selectivity Rating: 77   **Fire Safety Rating:** 60*   **Green Rating:** 79

STUDENTS AND FACULTY
Enrollment: 711. **Student Body:** 62% female, 38% male, 57% out-of-state.
Asian 1%, Caucasian 86%, Hispanic 7%, Native American 3%. **Retention and Graduation:** 85% freshmen return for sophomore year. 20% freshmen graduate within 4 years. **Faculty:** Student/faculty ratio 7:1. 41 full-time faculty, 59% hold PhDs. 81% faculty teach undergrads.

ACADEMICS
Degrees: Bachelor's, doctoral, master's, post-bachelor's certificate. **Academic Requirements:** English (including composition), mathematics. **Classes:** Most classes have fewer than 10 students. **Majors with Highest Enrollment:** Counseling psychology, elementary education and teaching, political science and government. **Disciplines with Highest Percentage of Degrees Awarded:** Education 43%, psychology 11%, natural resources/environmental science 10%, social sciences 8%, public administration and social services 5%, visual and performing arts 5%. **Special Study Options:** Cross-registration, distance learning, double major, exchange student program (domestic), external degree program, independent study, internships, liberal arts/career combination, student-designed major, teacher certification program.

FACILITIES
Housing: Coed dorms. **Special Academic Facilities/Equipment:** Wolfberry Farm, an experimental agroecology farm; Kino Bay Center; MX, a field station on the Gulf of California; Sam Hill Warehouse (visual arts center); GIS Lab (geographic information systems); several computer labs; multimedia center. **Computers:** 75% of classrooms are wired, 25% of classrooms are wireless, 95% of public computers are PCs, 5% of public computers are Macs, network access in dorm rooms, network access in dorm lounges, remote student-access to Web through college's connection.

CAMPUS LIFE
Activities: Dance, drama/theater, literary magazine, music ensembles, radio station, student government, student newspaper, student-run film society. **Organizations:** 10 registered organizations. **Environmental Initiatives:** Local food initiatives (campus Community Supported Agriculture, college farm and gardens). Progress toward carbon neutrality. Student HUB (Helping Understand Bicycles) organization.

ADMISSIONS
Freshman Academic Profile: 11% in top 10% of high school class, 32% in top 25% of high school class, 57% in top 50% of high school class. 73% from public high schools. SAT Math middle 50% range 500–610. SAT Critical Reading middle 50% range 510–660. SAT Writing middle 50% range 490–600. ACT middle 50% range 21–27. TOEFL required of all international applicants, minimum paper TOEFL 500, minimum computer TOEFL 173. **Basis for Candidate Selection:** *Very important factors considered include:* Application essay, recommendation(s), rigor of secondary school record. *Important factors considered include:* Academic GPA, character/personal qualities, extracurricular activities, interview, level of applicant's interest, standardized test scores, talent/ability. *Other factors considered include:* First generation, volunteer work, work experience. **Freshman Admission Requirements:** High school diploma is required, and GED is accepted. *Academic units recommended:* 4 English, 3 math, 2 science, 3 foreign language, 1 social studies, 2 history, 1 arts. **Freshman Admission Statistics:** 233 applied, 82% admitted, 29% enrolled. **Transfer Admission Requirements:** College transcript(s), essay or personal statement. Lowest grade transferable C. **General Admission Information:** Application fee $25. Early decision application deadline 12/1. Regular application deadline 8/15. Regular notification is rolling. Non-fall registration accepted. Admission may be deferred for a maximum of 2 terms. Credit offered for CEEB Advanced Placement tests.

COSTS AND FINANCIAL AID
Annual tuition $21,492. Required fees $1,250. Average book expense $650. **Required Forms and Deadlines:** FAFSA, institution's own financial aid form. Financial aid filing deadline 4/1. **Notification of Awards:** Applicants will be notified of awards on a rolling basis beginning on or about 3/15. **Types of Aid:** *Need-based scholarships/grants:* Pell, SEOG, state scholarships/grants, private scholarships, the school's own gift aid. *Loans:* FFEL Subsidized Stafford, FFEL Unsubsidized Stafford, FFEL PLUS, state loans. **Financial Aid Statistics:** 16% freshmen, 42% undergrads receive need-based scholarship or grant aid. 30% freshmen, 66% undergrads receive need-based self-help aid. 56% freshmen, 64% undergrads receive any aid. Highest amount earned per year from on-campus jobs $3,500.

PRESENTATION COLLEGE

1500 North Main Street, Aberdeen, SD 57401
Phone: 800-437-6060 **CEEB Code:** 6582
Fax: 605-229-8332 **Website:** www.presentation.edu **ACT Code:** 3918
Financial Aid Phone: 605-229-8427

This private school was founded in 1951. It has a 100-acre campus.

RATINGS
Admissions Selectivity Rating: 71   **Fire Safety Rating:** 60*   **Green Rating:** 60*

STUDENTS AND FACULTY
Enrollment: 303. **Student Body:** 77% female, 23% male, 19% out-of-state. African American 4%, Native American 18%. **Faculty:** 100% faculty teach undergrads.

ACADEMICS
Degrees: Associate, bachelor's, certificate. **Academic Requirements:** Arts/fine arts, English (including composition), humanities, mathematics, sciences (biological or physical), social science. **Special Study Options:** Accelerated program, distance learning, dual enrollment, external degree program.

FACILITIES
Housing: Coed dorms.

CAMPUS LIFE
Activities: Drama/theater, student government. **Organizations:** 2 honor societies, 1 religious organization. **Athletics (Intercollegiate):** *Men:* Basketball. *Women:* Basketball.

ADMISSIONS
Freshman Academic Profile: 5% in top 10% of high school class, 19% in top 25% of high school class, 49% in top 50% of high school class. ACT middle 50% range 17–21. TOEFL required of all international applicants, minimum paper TOEFL 500. **Basis for Candidate Selection:** *Very important factors considered include:* Class rank. *Important factors considered include:* Rigor of secondary school record, standardized test scores. **Freshman Admission Requirements:** High school diploma is required, and GED is accepted. *Academic units recommended:* 4 English, 3 math, 2 science, 2 social studies. **Transfer Admission Requirements:** High school transcript, college transcript(s), standardized test score. Lowest grade transferable C. **General Admission Information:** Application fee $15. Regular application deadline is rolling. Regular notification is rolling. Non-fall registration accepted. Common Application not accepted.

COSTS AND FINANCIAL AID
Annual tuition $6,820. Room & board $3,100. Required fees $148. Average book expense $800. **Required Forms and Deadlines:** FAFSA. Financial aid filing deadline 4/1. **Notification of Awards:** Applicants will be notified of awards on a rolling basis beginning on or about 5/1. **Types of Aid:** *Loans:* Direct Subsidized Stafford, Direct Unsubsidized Stafford, Direct PLUS, Federal Perkins, college/university loans from institutional funds. **Student Employment:** Federal Work-Study Program available. Off-campus job opportunities are good.

PRINCETON UNIVERSITY

Best 368

PO Box 430, Admission Office, Princeton, NJ 08544-0430
Phone: 609-258-3060 **CEEB Code:** 2672
Fax: 609-258-6743 **Website:** www.princeton.edu **ACT Code:** 2588
Financial Aid Phone: 609-258-3330

This private school was founded in 1746. It has a 600-acre campus.

RATINGS
Admissions Selectivity Rating: 99   **Fire Safety Rating:** 60*   **Green Rating:** 94

STUDENTS AND FACULTY
Enrollment: 4,775. **Student Body:** 46% female, 54% male, 85% out-of-state, 9% international. African American 9%, Asian 14%, Caucasian 58%, Hispanic 7%. **Retention and Graduation:** 98% freshmen return for sophomore year. 89% freshmen graduate within 4 years. **Faculty:** Student/faculty ratio 5:1. 827 full-time faculty, 93% hold PhDs.

ACADEMICS
Degrees: Bachelor's, doctoral, master's. **Academic Requirements:** English (including composition), foreign languages, history, humanities, mathematics, philosophy, sciences (biological or physical), social science. **Classes:** Most classes have 10–19 students. Most lab/discussion sections have 10–19 students. **Disciplines with Highest Percentage of Degrees Awarded:** Social sciences 26%, engineering 16%, history 10%, biological/life sciences 9%, public administration and social services 7%, English 7%. **Special Study Options:** Cross-registration, exchange student program (domestic), independent study, student-designed major, study abroad, teacher certification program.

FACILITIES
Housing: Coed dorms, men's dorms, women's dorms, special housing for disabled students. **Special Academic Facilities/Equipment:** Art museum, natural history museum, energy and environmental studies center, plasma physics lab, Center for Jewish Life, center for human values, Woodrow Wilson School of Public and International Affairs. **Computers:** 70% of public computers are PCs, 30% of public computers are Macs, network access in dorm rooms, network access in dorm lounges, online registration, online administrative functions (other than registration), remote student-access to Web through college's connection, tuition includes personal computer.

CAMPUS LIFE
Activities: Choral groups, concert band, dance, drama/theater, jazz band, literary magazine, marching band, music ensembles, musical theater, opera, pep band, radio station, student government, student newspaper, student-run film society, symphony orchestra, yearbook. **Organizations:** 250 registered organizations, 30 honor societies, 24 religious organizations. **Athletics (Intercollegiate):** *Men:* Baseball, basketball, cheerleading, crew/rowing, cross-country, diving, equestrian sports, fencing, football, golf, ice hockey, lacrosse, rugby, sailing, skiing (Nordic/cross-country), soccer, squash, swimming, tennis, track/field (indoor), track/field (outdoor). *Women:* Basketball, cheerleading, crew/rowing, cross-country, diving, equestrian sports, fencing, field hockey, golf, ice hockey, lacrosse, rugby, sailing, skiing (Nordic/cross-country), soccer, softball, squash, swimming, tennis, track/field (indoor), track/field (outdoor). **Environmental Initiatives:** Greenhouse gas reduction goal: 1990 levels by 2020, while adding 2 million gross square feet of built area, and without the use of off-campus offsets. Sustainable Building Guidelines: requiring all new buildings and major renovations to be 50% more energy efficient than code requires, 95% demolition and construction debris recycling, and use of sustainable materials. Implementation of transportation demand management program to reduce by 10% the number of cars coming to campus by 2020.

ADMISSIONS
Freshman Academic Profile: 94% in top 10% of high school class, 99% in top 25% of high school class, 100% in top 50% of high school class. 58% from public high schools. SAT Math middle 50% range 700–790. SAT Critical Reading middle 50% range 690–790. SAT Writing middle 50% range 690–780. ACT middle 50% range 30–34. TOEFL required of all international applicants, minimum paper TOEFL 600, minimum computer TOEFL 250. **Basis for Candidate Selection:** *Very important factors considered include:* Academic GPA, application essay, character/personal qualities, class rank, extracurricular activities, recommendation(s), rigor of secondary school record, standardized test scores, talent/ability. *Important factors considered include:* Volunteer work, work experience. *Other factors considered include:* Alumni/ae relation, geographical residence, interview, racial/ethnic status. **Freshman Admission Requirements:** High school diploma is required, and GED is accepted. *Academic units recommended:* 4 English, 4 math, 3 science, 4 foreign language, 2 social studies, 2 history. **Freshman Admission Statistics:** 17,564 applied, 10% admitted, 69% enrolled. **General Admission Information:** Application fee $65. Regular application deadline 1/1. Regular notification 4/10. Non-fall registration not accepted. Admission may be deferred for a maximum of 1 year. Credit and/or placement offered for CEEB Advanced Placement tests.

COSTS AND FINANCIAL AID
Annual tuition $34,290. Room and board $11,405. Average book expense $1,200. **Required Forms and Deadlines:** FAFSA, institution's own financial aid form, college Noncustodial form. Financial aid filing deadline 2/1. **Notification of Awards:** Applicants will be notified of awards on or about 4/1. **Types of Aid:** *Need-based scholarships/grants:* Pell, SEOG, state scholarships/grants, private scholarships, the school's own gift aid. *Loans:* FFEL Subsidized Stafford, FFEL Unsubsidized Stafford, FFEL PLUS, Federal Perkins, college/university loans from institutional funds. **Financial Aid Statistics:** 55% freshmen, 51% undergrads receive need-based scholarship or grant aid. 55% freshmen, 51% undergrads receive need-based self-help aid. 55% freshmen, 52% undergrads receive any aid. Highest amount earned per year from on-campus jobs $3,000.

See page 1322.

PRINCIPIA COLLEGE

1 Maybeck Place, Elsah, IL 62028
Phone: 618-374-5181 **E-mail:** Collegeadmissions@prin.edu **CEEB Code:** 1630
Fax: 618-374-4000 **Website:** www.prin.edu/College **ACT Code:** 1118
Financial Aid Phone: 800-277-4648

This private school, affiliated with the Christian Science Church, was founded in 1898. It has a 2,600-acre campus.

RATINGS
Admissions Selectivity Rating: 86   **Fire Safety Rating:** 66   **Green Rating:** 60*

STUDENTS AND FACULTY
Enrollment: 542. **Student Body:** 52% female, 48% male, 88% out-of-state, 13% international (28 countries represented). African American 1%, Caucasian 81%, Hispanic 1%. **Retention and Graduation:** 79% freshmen return for sophomore year. 73% freshmen graduate within 4 years. 27% grads go on to further study within 1 year. 15% grads pursue arts and sciences degrees. 6% grads pursue business degrees. 3% grads pursue law degrees. **Faculty:** Student/faculty ratio 8:1. 55 full-time faculty, 45% hold PhDs. 100% faculty teach undergrads.

ACADEMICS
Degrees: Bachelor's. **Academic Requirements:** Arts/fine arts, Bible, English (including composition), foreign languages, history, humanities, mathematics, philosophy, physical education, sciences (biological or physical), social science. **Classes:** Most classes have 10–19 students. **Majors with Highest Enrollment:** Business administration/management, fine/studio arts, mass communications/media studies. **Disciplines with Highest Percentage of Degrees Awarded:** Social sciences 26%, visual and performing arts 14%, business/marketing 10%, liberal arts/general studies 8%, computer and information sciences 7%. **Special Study Options:** Double major, independent study, internships, liberal arts/career combination, student-designed major, study abroad, teacher certification program, 3-2 engineering with Washington University (St. Louis, MO), USC (Los Angeles), and Southern Illinois University (SIU) in Edwardsville, IL.

FACILITIES
Housing: Men's dorms, women's dorms, apartments for married students. Houses with single-gender wings (1 side for men and 1 side for women) with a common living room. This is not really considered coed because there are no shared bathrooms or men and women living together. **Special Academic Facilities/Equipment:** Science center with indoor aviary, school of nations museum and classrooms, Voney Art Studio, school of government, Merrick Wing for Performing Arts. **Computers:** 80% of public computers are PCs, 20% of public computers are Macs, network access in dorm rooms.

CAMPUS LIFE
Activities: Choral groups, dance, drama/theater, jazz band, music ensembles, musical theater, radio station, student government, student newspaper, television station, yearbook. **Organizations:** 29 registered organizations, 1

honor society, 1 religious organization. **Athletics (Intercollegiate):** *Men:* Baseball, basketball, cross-country, diving, football, soccer, swimming, tennis, track/field (indoor), track/field (outdoor). *Women:* Basketball, cross-country, diving, soccer, swimming, tennis, track/field (indoor), track/field (outdoor), volleyball.

ADMISSIONS

Freshman Academic Profile: 38% in top 10% of high school class, 63% in top 25% of high school class, 79% in top 50% of high school class. 61% from public high schools. SAT Math middle 50% range 500–620. SAT Critical Reading middle 50% range 510–650. ACT middle 50% range 21–30. TOEFL required of all international applicants, minimum paper TOEFL 550, minimum computer TOEFL 213. **Basis for Candidate Selection:** *Very important factors considered include:* Application essay, character/personal qualities, religious affiliation/commitment, rigor of secondary school record. *Important factors considered include:* Class rank, extracurricular activities, interview, recommendation(s), standardized test scores, talent/ability. *Other factors considered include:* Alumni/ae relation, racial/ethnic status, volunteer work, work experience. **Freshman Admission Requirements:** High school diploma is required, and GED is accepted. *Academic units required:* 4 English, 4 math, 2 science (2 science labs), 2 foreign language, 2 social studies, 1 history, 1 academic elective. *Academic units recommended:* 4 English, 4 math, 3 science (2 science labs), 3 foreign language, 2 social studies, 2 history, 2 academic electives. **Freshman Admission Statistics:** 221 applied, 87% admitted, 61% enrolled. **Transfer Admission Requirements:** High school transcript, college transcript(s), essay or personal statement. Minimum college GPA of 2.0 required. Lowest grade transferable C-. **General Admission Information:** Regular application deadline 3/1. Regular notification is rolling. Non-fall registration accepted. Admission may be deferred for a maximum of 1 year. Common Application not accepted. Credit and/or placement offered for CEEB Advanced Placement tests.

COSTS AND FINANCIAL AID

Annual tuition $21,150. Room & board $7,896. Required fees $300. Average book expense $900. **Required Forms and Deadlines:** Institution's own financial aid form, CSS/Financial Aid PROFILE. Financial aid filing deadline 3/1. **Notification of Awards:** Applicants will be notified of awards on or about 4/1. **Types of Aid:** *Need-based scholarships/grants:* Private scholarships, the school's own gift aid. *Loans:* College/university loans from institutional funds. **Financial Aid Statistics:** 55% freshmen, 54% undergrads receive need-based scholarship or grant aid. 46% freshmen, 45% undergrads receive need-based self-help aid. 87% freshmen, 79% undergrads receive any aid. Highest amount earned per year from on-campus jobs $1,310.

PROVIDENCE COLLEGE

Harkins 222, 549 River Avenue, Providence, RI 02918
Phone: 401-865-2535 **E-mail:** pcadmiss@providence.edu **CEEB Code:** 3693
Fax: 401-865-2826 **Website:** www.providence.edu **ACT Code:** 3806
Financial Aid Phone: 401-865-2286

This private school, affiliated with the Roman Catholic Church, was founded in 1917. It has a 105-acre campus.

RATINGS

Admissions Selectivity Rating: 93   **Fire Safety Rating:** 97   **Green Rating:** 75

STUDENTS AND FACULTY

Enrollment: 3,990. **Student Body:** 56% female, 44% male, 88% out-of-state, 1% international (16 countries represented). African American 2%, Asian 2%, Caucasian 84%, Hispanic 2%. **Retention and Graduation:** 91% freshmen return for sophomore year. **Faculty:** Student/faculty ratio 12:1. 295 full-time faculty, 88% hold PhDs. 100% faculty teach undergrads.

ACADEMICS

Degrees: Associate, bachelor's, certificate, master's, post-bachelor's certificate, terminal. **Academic Requirements:** Arts/fine arts, development of Western civilization, English (including composition), mathematics, philosophy, sciences (biological or physical), social science, theology. **Classes:** Most classes have 20–29 students. Most lab/discussion sections have 10–19 students. **Majors with Highest Enrollment:** Biology/biological sciences, business administration and

management, marketing/marketing management. **Disciplines with Highest Percentage of Degrees Awarded:** Business/marketing 27%, social sciences 16%, education 10%, history 7%, psychology 6%. **Special Study Options:** Cooperative education program, cross-registration, double major, dual enrollment, honors program, independent study, internships, student-designed major, study abroad, teacher certification program.

FACILITIES

Housing: Coed dorms, men's dorms, women's dorms, apartments for single students, special housing for disabled students. **Special Academic Facilities/Equipment:** Hunt-Cavanaugh Art Gallery, Blackfriar Theatre, science center complex, computer and language labs, Smith Center for the Arts. **Computers:** 1% of classrooms are wired, 1% of classrooms are wireless, 95% of public computers are PCs, 5% of public computers are Macs, network access in dorm rooms, online registration, online administrative functions (other than registration), support for handheld computing, remote student-access to Web through college's connection.

CAMPUS LIFE

Activities: Choral groups, concert band, dance, drama/theater, jazz band, literary magazine, music ensembles, musical theater, pep band, radio station, student government, student newspaper, television station, yearbook. **Organizations:** 112 registered organizations, 18 honor societies, 2 religious organizations. **Athletics (Intercollegiate):** *Men:* Basketball, cross-country, diving, ice hockey, lacrosse, soccer, swimming, track/field (indoor), track/field (outdoor). *Women:* Basketball, cross-country, diving, field hockey, ice hockey, soccer, softball, swimming, tennis, track/field (indoor), track/field (outdoor), volleyball.

ADMISSIONS

Freshman Academic Profile: 45% in top 10% of high school class, 83% in top 25% of high school class, 97% in top 50% of high school class. 63% from public high schools. SAT Math middle 50% range 540–640. SAT Critical Reading middle 50% range 530–630. SAT Writing middle 50% range 540–650. ACT middle 50% range 23–28. TOEFL required of all international applicants, minimum paper TOEFL 550, minimum computer TOEFL 213. **Basis for Candidate Selection:** *Very important factors considered include:* Academic GPA, rigor of secondary school record. *Important factors considered include:* Application essay, character/personal qualities, extracurricular activities, recommendation(s). *Other factors considered include:* Alumni/ae relation, class rank, first generation, geographical residence, level of applicant's interest, racial/ethnic status, standardized test scores, talent/ability, volunteer work, work experience. **Freshman Admission Requirements:** High school diploma is required, and GED is not accepted. *Academic units required:* 4 English, 4 math, 3 science (2 science labs), 3 foreign language, 2 social studies, 2 history. *Academic units recommended:* 4 English, 4 math, 4 science (2 science labs), 3 foreign language, 2 social studies, 2 history. **Freshman Admission Statistics:** 8,799 applied, 48% admitted, 25% enrolled. **Transfer Admission Requirements:** High school transcript, college transcript(s), essay or personal statement, statement of good standing from prior institution(s). Minimum college GPA of 3.0 required. Lowest grade transferable C. **General Admission Information:** Application fee $55. Regular application deadline 1/15. Regular notification 4/1. Non-fall registration accepted. Admission may be deferred for a maximum of 1 year. Credit and/or placement offered for CEEB Advanced Placement tests.

COSTS AND FINANCIAL AID

Annual tuition $28,920. Room and board $10,335. Required fees $579. Average book expense $800. **Required Forms and Deadlines:** FAFSA, CSS/Financial Aid PROFILE, Business/Farm Supplement. Financial aid filing deadline 2/1. **Notification of Awards:** Applicants will be notified of awards on or about 4/1. **Types of Aid:** *Need-based scholarships/grants:* Pell, SEOG, state scholarships/grants, private scholarships, the school's own gift aid, Federal Academic Competitive Grant/Smart Grant. *Loans:* Direct Subsidized Stafford, Direct Unsubsidized Stafford, Direct PLUS, FFEL Subsidized Stafford, FFEL Unsubsidized Stafford, FFEL PLUS, Federal Perkins. **Student Employment:** Federal Work-Study Program available. Institutional employment available. Off-campus job opportunities are good. **Financial Aid Statistics:** 52% freshmen, 56% undergrads receive need-based scholarship or grant aid. 55% freshmen, 46% undergrads receive need-based self-help aid. 59 freshmen, 125 undergrads receive athletic scholarships. 82% freshmen, 80% undergrads receive any aid. Highest amount earned per year from on-campus jobs $2,500.

PURDUE UNIVERSITY—CALUMET

Office of Admissions, 2200 169th Street, Hammond, IN 46323-2094
Phone: 219-989-2213 **E-mail:** adms@calumet.purdue.edu **CEEB Code:** 1638
Fax: 219-989-2775 **Website:** www.calumet.purdue.edu **ACT Code:** 1233
Financial Aid Phone: 219-989-2301

This public school was founded in 1946. It has a 194-acre campus.

RATINGS
Admissions Selectivity Rating: 63   **Fire Safety Rating:** 91   **Green Rating:** 60*

STUDENTS AND FACULTY
Enrollment: 7,948. **Student Body:** 57% female, 43% male, 11% out-of-state, 1% international (26 countries represented). African American 17%, Asian 1%, Caucasian 65%, Hispanic 14%. **Retention and Graduation:** 60% freshmen return for sophomore year. 4% freshmen graduate within 4 years. **Faculty:** Student/faculty ratio 18:1. 288 full-time faculty, 64% hold PhDs.

ACADEMICS
Degrees: Associate, bachelor's, certificate, master's, post-bachelor's certificate. **Academic Requirements:** Computer literacy, English (including composition), freshman experience course, humanities, mathematics, sciences (biological or physical), social science, speech communication. **Classes:** Most classes have 20–29 students. Most lab/discussion sections have 20–29 students. **Majors with Highest Enrollment:** Elementary education and teaching, finance, marketing/marketing management. **Disciplines with Highest Percentage of Degrees Awarded:** Social sciences 95%, computer and information sciences 59%, engineering technologies 51%, engineering 51%, communications/journalism 49%. **Special Study Options:** Cooperative education program, distance learning, double major, English as a second language (ESL), honors program, independent study, internships, teacher certification program, weekend college.

FACILITIES
Housing: Apartments for single students. **Special Academic Facilities/ Equipment:** Audiovisual services, urban development institute. **Computers:** Online registration, online administrative functions (other than registration), remote student-access to Web through college's connection.

CAMPUS LIFE
Activities: Choral groups, dance, drama/theater, literary magazine, radio station, student government, student newspaper, television station. **Organizations:** 25 honor societies, 3 religious organizations. 2 fraternities, 3 sororities. **Athletics (Intercollegiate):** *Men:* Basketball. *Women:* Basketball.

ADMISSIONS
Freshman Academic Profile: 6% in top 10% of high school class, 20% in top 25% of high school class, 49% in top 50% of high school class. SAT Math middle 50% range 380–510. SAT Critical Reading middle 50% range 400–510. SAT Writing middle 50% range 380–480. TOEFL required of all international applicants, minimum paper TOEFL 550, minimum computer TOEFL 213. **Basis for Candidate Selection:** *Important factors considered include:* Academic GPA, class rank, rigor of secondary school record, standardized test scores. **Freshman Admission Requirements:** High school diploma is required, and GED is accepted. *Academic units recommended:* 4 English, 2 math, 2 science (2 science labs), 2 foreign language, 2 social studies, 1 history. **Freshman Admission Statistics:** 2,763 applied, 81% admitted, 57% enrolled. **Transfer Admission Requirements:** High school transcript. Minimum college GPA of 2.0 required. Lowest grade transferable C. **General Admission Information:** Regular notification is rolling. Non-fall registration accepted. Admission may be deferred for a maximum of 1 semester. Credit offered for CEEB Advanced Placement tests.

COSTS AND FINANCIAL AID
Annual in-state tuition $2,262. Out-of-state tuition $5,688. Required fees $228. Average book expense $1,000. **Required Forms and Deadlines:** FAFSA. Financial aid filing deadline 6/30. **Notification of Awards:** Applicants will be notified of awards on or about 6/1. **Types of Aid:** *Need-based scholarships/ grants:* Pell, SEOG, state scholarships/grants, private scholarships. *Loans:* Direct Subsidized Stafford, Direct Unsubsidized Stafford, Direct PLUS, Federal Perkins. **Financial Aid Statistics:** 40% freshmen, 37% undergrads receive need-based scholarship or grant aid. 37% freshmen, 39% undergrads receive need-based self-help aid. 22 undergrads receive athletic scholarships. 55% freshmen, 50% undergrads receive any aid.

PURDUE UNIVERSITY—NORTH CENTRAL

1401 South U.S. Highway 421, Westville, IN 46391-9528
Phone: 219-785-5458 **E-mail:** admissions@purduenc.edu **CEEB Code:** 1640
Fax: 219-785-5538 **Website:** www.pnc.edu **ACT Code:** 1826
Financial Aid Phone: 219-785-5493

This public school was founded in 1948. It has a 296-acre campus.

RATINGS
Admissions Selectivity Rating: 65   **Fire Safety Rating:** 60*   **Green Rating:** 60*

STUDENTS AND FACULTY
Enrollment: 3,434. **Student Body:** 59% female, 41% male, 1% out-of-state. African American 3%, Caucasian 88%, Hispanic 3%, Native American 1%. **Retention and Graduation:** 63% freshmen return for sophomore year. **Faculty:** Student/faculty ratio 18:1. 96 full-time faculty, 58% hold PhDs. 100% faculty teach undergrads.

ACADEMICS
Degrees: Associate, bachelor's, certificate, master's. **Academic Requirements:** Computer literacy, English (including composition), humanities, mathematics, sciences (biological or physical), social science. **Classes:** Most classes have 20–29 students. Most lab/discussion sections have 10–19 students. **Majors with Highest Enrollment:** Business administration/management, elementary education and teaching, liberal arts and sciences/liberal studies. **Disciplines with Highest Percentage of Degrees Awarded:** Liberal arts/ general studies 51%, business/marketing 24%, education 15%, English 5%, engineering 3%. **Special Study Options:** Distance learning, dual enrollment, independent study, internships, teacher certification program.

FACILITIES
Computers: 88% of public computers are PCs, 12% of public computers are Macs, online registration, online administrative functions (other than registration), remote student-access to Web through college's connection.

CAMPUS LIFE
Activities: Student government, student newspaper. **Organizations:** 13 registered organizations, 2 honor societies, 1 religious organization. **Athletics (Intercollegiate):** *Men:* Baseball, basketball, cheerleading. *Women:* Cheerleading.

ADMISSIONS
Freshman Academic Profile: 5% in top 10% of high school class, 18% in top 25% of high school class, 49% in top 50% of high school class. 95% from public high schools. SAT Math middle 50% range 410–530. SAT Critical Reading middle 50% range 410–530. ACT middle 50% range 17–22. TOEFL required of all international applicants, minimum paper TOEFL 213. **Basis for Candidate Selection:** *Very important factors considered include:* Rigor of secondary school record. *Important factors considered include:* Class rank, standardized test scores. *Other factors considered include:* Character/personal qualities, extracurricular activities, interview, recommendation(s), talent/ability, volunteer work, work experience. **Freshman Admission Requirements:** High school diploma is required, and GED is accepted. *Academic units required:* 4 English, 3 math, 2 science (2 science labs), 1 social studies, 5 academic electives. *Academic units recommended:* 4 English, 4 math, 3 science (3 science labs), 4 foreign language, 2 social studies, 1 history, 5 academic electives. **Freshman Admission Statistics:** 1,089 applied, 91% admitted, 70% enrolled. **Transfer Admission Requirements:** High school transcript, college transcript(s). Minimum college GPA of 2.0 required. Lowest grade transferable C. **General Admission Information:** Regular notification is rolling. Non-fall registration accepted. Admission may be deferred for a maximum of 1 year. Common Application not accepted. Credit and/or placement offered for CEEB Advanced Placement tests.

COSTS AND FINANCIAL AID
Annual in-state tuition $2,878. Out-of-state tuition $7,735. Required fees $280. Average book expense $800. **Required Forms and Deadlines:** FAFSA, state aid form. Financial aid filing deadline 3/1. **Notification of Awards:** Applicants will be notified of awards on a rolling basis beginning on or about 5/1. **Types of Aid:** *Need-based scholarships/grants:* Pell, SEOG, state scholarships/grants, private scholarships, the school's own gift aid. *Loans:* FFEL Subsidized Stafford, FFEL Unsubsidized Stafford, FFEL PLUS, Federal Perkins, college/ university loans from institutional funds. **Student Employment:** Federal Work-Study Program available. Institutional employment available. Off-campus job opportunities are good. **Financial Aid Statistics:** 33% freshmen, 35% undergrads receive need-based scholarship or grant aid. 27% freshmen, 34% undergrads receive need-based self-help aid.

PURDUE UNIVERSITY—WEST LAFAYETTE

Best 368

1080 Schleman Hall, West Lafayette, IN 47907
Phone: 765-494-1776 **E-mail:** admissions@purdue.edu **CEEB Code:** 1631
Fax: 765-494-0544 **Website:** www.purdue.edu **ACT Code:** 1230
Financial Aid Phone: 765-494-0998

This public school was founded in 1869. It has a 1,579-acre campus.

RATINGS
Admissions Selectivity Rating: 83   **Fire Safety Rating:** 89   **Green Rating:** 75

STUDENTS AND FACULTY
Enrollment: 30,545. **Student Body:** 41% female, 59% male, 29% out-of-state, 6% international (126 countries represented). African American 4%, Asian 5%, Caucasian 82%, Hispanic 3%. **Retention and Graduation:** 86% freshmen return for sophomore year. **Faculty:** Student/faculty ratio 14:1. 1,960 full-time faculty, 98% hold PhDs. 76% faculty teach undergrads.

ACADEMICS
Degrees: Bachelor's, certificate, doctoral, first professional, master's, terminal. **Academic Requirements:** Computer literacy, English (including composition), humanities, mathematics, sciences (biological or physical), social science. **Classes:** Most classes have 20–29 students. Most lab/discussion sections have 10–19 students. **Majors with Highest Enrollment:** Business administration and management, engineering, humanities/humanistic studies. **Disciplines with Highest Percentage of Degrees Awarded:** Engineering 20%, business/marketing 16%, engineering technologies 8%, education 7%, family and consumer sciences 6%. **Special Study Options:** Accelerated program, cooperative education program, distance learning, double major, dual enrollment, exchange student program (domestic), honors program, independent study, internships, study abroad, teacher certification program, weekend college.

FACILITIES
Housing: Coed dorms, men's dorms, women's dorms, apartments for married students, apartments for single students, special housing for disabled students, fraternity/sorority housing, cooperative housing. **Special Academic Facilities/Equipment:** Hall of music, child development lab, speech and hearing clinic, small animal veterinary clinic, horticulture park, linear accelerator, tornado simulator, nuclear accelerator. **Computers:** 100% of classrooms are wired, 100% of classrooms are wireless, 85% of public computers are PCs, 5% of public computers are Macs, 7% of public computers are UNIX, network access in dorm rooms, network access in dorm lounges, online administrative functions (other than registration), support for handheld computing, remote student-access to Web through college's connection.

CAMPUS LIFE
Activities: Choral groups, concert band, dance, jazz band, literary magazine, marching band, music ensembles, musical theater, pep band, radio station, student government, student newspaper, symphony orchestra, yearbook. **Organizations:** 747 registered organizations, 59 honor societies, 64 religious organizations. 49 fraternities (18% men join), 29 sororities (17% women join). **Athletics (Intercollegiate):** *Men:* Baseball, basketball, cross-country, diving, football, golf, swimming, tennis, track/field (indoor), track/field (outdoor), wrestling. *Women:* Basketball, cross-country, diving, golf, soccer, softball, swimming, tennis, track/field (indoor), track/field (outdoor), volleyball.

ADMISSIONS
Freshman Academic Profile: 27% in top 10% of high school class, 58% in top 25% of high school class, 90% in top 50% of high school class. SAT Math middle 50% range 530–660. SAT Critical Reading middle 50% range 490–610. ACT middle 50% range 23–28. TOEFL required of all international applicants, minimum paper TOEFL 550, minimum computer TOEFL 213. **Basis for Candidate Selection:** *Very important factors considered include:* Academic GPA, class rank, rigor of secondary school record, standardized test scores. *Other factors considered include:* Alumni/ae relation, application essay, character/personal qualities, extracurricular activities, first generation, geographical residence, level of applicant's interest, racial/ethnic status, recommendation(s), state residency, volunteer work, work experience. **Freshman Admission Requirements:** High school diploma is required, and GED is accepted. *Academic units required:* 4 English, 3 math, 2 science (2 science labs), 2 foreign language. *Academic units recommended:* 4 English, 3 math, 3 science (3 science labs), 2 foreign language. **Freshman Admission Statistics:** 24,052 applied, 85% admitted, 35% enrolled. **Transfer Admission Requirements:** College transcript(s). Minimum college GPA of 2.8 required. Lowest grade transferable C. **General Admission Information:** Application fee $30. Regular notification is rolling. Non-fall registration accepted. Admission may be deferred for a maximum of 1 year. Common Application not accepted. Credit and/or placement offered for CEEB Advanced Placement tests.

COSTS AND FINANCIAL AID
Annual in-state tuition $7,317. Annual out-of-state tuition $22,791. Room and board $7,530. Required fees $433. Average book expense $1,050. **Required Forms and Deadlines:** FAFSA. Financial aid filing deadline 3/1. **Notification of Awards:** Applicants will be notified of awards on or about 4/15. **Types of Aid:** *Need-based scholarships/grants:* Pell, SEOG, state scholarships/grants, private scholarships, the school's own gift aid. *Loans:* FFEL Subsidized Stafford, FFEL Unsubsidized Stafford, FFEL PLUS, Federal Perkins, college/university loans from institutional funds. **Financial Aid Statistics:** 15% freshmen, 13% undergrads receive need-based scholarship or grant aid. 36% freshmen, 36% undergrads receive need-based self-help aid. 52 freshmen, 336 undergrads receive athletic scholarships. 80% freshmen, 76% undergrads receive any aid. Highest amount earned per year from on-campus jobs $5,000.

QUEEN'S UNIVERSITY

Admission Services, Gordon Hall, 74 Union Street, Kingston, ON K7L3N6 Canada
Phone: 613-533-2218 **E-mail:** admission@queensu.ca **CEEB Code:** 0949
Fax: 613-533-6810 **Website:** www.queensu.ca **ACT Code:** 5236
Financial Aid Phone: 613-533-2216

This public school was founded in 1841. It has a 160-acre campus.

RATINGS
Admissions Selectivity Rating: 60*   **Fire Safety Rating:** 60*   **Green Rating:** 60*

STUDENTS AND FACULTY
Enrollment: 14,130. **Student Body:** 59% female, 41% male, 18% out-of-state. **Faculty:** Student/faculty ratio 16:1. 1,032 full-time faculty, 94% hold PhDs.

ACADEMICS
Degrees: Bachelor's, doctoral, master's. **Classes:** Most classes have 20–29 students. Most lab/discussion sections have 20–29 students. **Disciplines with Highest Percentage of Degrees Awarded:** Social sciences 18%, education 17%, engineering 14%, biological/life sciences 12%, psychology 5%, health professions and related sciences 5%, business/marketing 5%. **Special Study Options:** Cooperative education program, distance learning, double major, dual enrollment, English as a second language (ESL), exchange student program (domestic), honors program, independent study, internships, study abroad, teacher certification program. The university owns and operates an International Study Centre (ISC) at Herstmonceux, East Sussex, England.

FACILITIES
Housing: Coed dorms, men's dorms, women's dorms, apartments for married students, apartments for single students, special housing for international students, cooperative housing. **Special Academic Facilities/Equipment:** Agnes Etherington Art Centre, Miller Museum of Geology. **Computers:** 90% of public computers are PCs, 10% of public computers are Macs, 10% of public computers are UNIX, network access in dorm rooms, online registration, online administrative functions (other than registration), remote student-access to Web through college's connection.

CAMPUS LIFE
Activities: Choral groups, concert band, dance, drama/theater, jazz band, literary magazine, marching band, music ensembles, musical theater, opera, pep band, radio station, student government, student newspaper, student-run film society, symphony orchestra, television studio. **Organizations:** 18 religious organizations. **Athletics (Intercollegiate):** *Men:* Baseball, basketball, cheerleading, crew/rowing, cross-country, curling, fencing, football, golf, ice hockey, lacrosse, mountain biking, rodeo, rugby, sailing, skiing (Nordic/cross-country), soccer, squash, swimming, tennis, track/field (outdoor). *Women:* Basketball, cheerleading, crew/rowing, cross-country, curling, fencing, field hockey, ice hockey, lacrosse, mountain biking, rodeo, rugby, sailing, skiing (Nordic/cross-country), soccer, squash, swimming, synchronized swimming, tennis, track/field (outdoor).

ADMISSIONS
Freshman Academic Profile: TOEFL required of all international applicants, minimum paper TOEFL 580, minimum computer TOEFL 237. **Basis for**

Candidate Selection: *Very important factors considered include:* Academic GPA, standardized test scores. *Important factors considered include:* Extracurricular activities, rigor of secondary school record, talent/ability, volunteer work. *Other factors considered include:* Class rank, recommendation(s), work experience. **Freshman Admission Requirements:** High school diploma is required, and GED is accepted. **Freshman Admission Statistics:** 25,403 applied, 42% admitted, 31% enrolled. **Transfer Admission Requirements:** High school transcript, college transcript(s), **General Admission Information:** Application fee $135. Regular application deadline 2/16. Regular notification is rolling. Non-fall registration not accepted. Admission may be deferred for a maximum of 1 year. Common Application not accepted.

COSTS AND FINANCIAL AID

In-province tuition $4,296–$8,149. Out-of-province tuition $4,296–$8,149. Room & board $7,600. Required fees $640. Average book expense $1,100. **Required Forms and Deadlines:** Financial aid filing deadline 1/31.

QUEENS UNIVERSITY OF CHARLOTTE

1900 Selwyn Avenue, Charlotte, NC 28274
Phone: 704-337-2212 **E-mail:** admissions@queens.edu **CEEB Code:** 5560
Fax: 704-337-2403 **Website:** www.queens.edu **ACT Code:** 3148
Financial Aid Phone: 704-337-2225

This private school, affiliated with the Presbyterian Church, was founded in 1857. It has a 30-acre campus.

RATINGS

Admissions Selectivity Rating: 77   **Fire Safety Rating:** 60*   **Green Rating:** 60*

STUDENTS AND FACULTY

Enrollment: 1,536. **Student Body:** 76% female, 24% male, 5% international. African American 21%, Asian 3%, Caucasian 70%, Hispanic 4%. **Retention and Graduation:** 75% freshmen return for sophomore year. 46% freshmen graduate within 4 years. **Faculty:** Student/faculty ratio 14:1. 74 full-time faculty, 78% hold PhDs.

ACADEMICS

Degrees: Associate, bachelor's, master's, post-bachelor's certificate, terminal. **Academic Requirements:** English (including composition), foreign languages, history, humanities, mathematics, sciences (biological or physical), social science. **Classes:** Most classes have 10–19 students. Most lab/discussion sections have 10–19 students. **Majors with Highest Enrollment:** Business administration/management, communications studies/speech communication and rhetoric, nursing/registered nurse training (ASN, BSN, MSN, RN). **Disciplines with Highest Percentage of Degrees Awarded:** Business/marketing 27%, communications/journalism 20%, psychology 12%, health professions and related sciences 12%, visual and performing arts 6%, public administration and social services 4%, philosophy and religious studies 4%, education 4%. **Special Study Options:** Cross-registration, double major, dual enrollment, honors program, independent study, internships, liberal arts/career combination, student-designed major, study abroad, teacher certification program, weekend college.

FACILITIES

Housing: Coed dorms, special housing for disabled students. **Special Academic Facilities/Equipment:** 3 art galleries, rare books museum. **Computers:** 95% of public computers are PCs, 5% of public computers are Macs, network access in dorm rooms, remote student-access to Web through college's connection.

CAMPUS LIFE

Activities: Choral groups, dance, drama/theater, literary magazine, music ensembles, musical theater, pep band, student government, student newspaper, yearbook. **Organizations:** 27 registered organizations, 9 honor societies, 2 religious organizations. 2 fraternities (22% men join), 4 sororities (11% women join). **Athletics (Intercollegiate):** *Men:* Basketball, cheerleading, cross-country, golf, lacrosse, soccer, tennis, track/field (outdoor). *Women:* Basketball, cheerleading, cross-country, golf, lacrosse, soccer, softball, tennis, track/field (outdoor), volleyball.

ADMISSIONS

Freshman Academic Profile: 16% in top 10% of high school class, 37% in top 25% of high school class, 76% in top 50% of high school class. 85% from public high schools. SAT Math middle 50% range 570–460. SAT Critical Reading middle 50% range 570–470. SAT Writing middle 50% range 570–450. ACT middle 50% range 24–20. TOEFL required of all international applicants, minimum paper TOEFL 550, minimum computer TOEFL 213. **Basis for**

Candidate Selection: *Very important factors considered include:* Academic GPA, character/personal qualities, extracurricular activities, rigor of secondary school record, standardized test scores. *Important factors considered include:* Class rank, interview, volunteer work. *Other factors considered include:* Alumni/ae relation, application essay, first generation, recommendation(s), talent/ability, work experience. **Freshman Admission Requirements:** High school diploma is required, and GED is accepted. *Academic units required:* 4 English, 3 math, 2 science (1 science lab), 2 foreign language, 2 social studies. **Freshman Admission Statistics:** 1,038 applied, 78% admitted, 29% enrolled. **Transfer Admission Requirements:** High school transcript, college transcript(s), essay or personal statement, statement of good standing from prior institution(s). Minimum college GPA of 2.0 required. Lowest grade transferable C. **General Admission Information:** Application fee $40. Regular notification is rolling. Non-fall registration accepted. Admission may be deferred for a maximum of 1 year. Credit and/or placement offered for CEEB Advanced Placement tests.

COSTS AND FINANCIAL AID

Comprehensive fee $26,430. Room & board $6,980. **Required Forms and Deadlines:** FAFSA, state aid form. Financial aid filing deadline 3/1. **Notification of Awards:** Applicants will be notified of awards on a rolling basis beginning on or about 3/1. **Types of Aid:** *Need-based scholarships/grants:* Pell, SEOG, state scholarships/grants, private scholarships, the school's own gift aid. *Loans:* FFEL Subsidized Stafford, FFEL Unsubsidized Stafford, FFEL PLUS, Federal Perkins, state loans. **Financial Aid Statistics:** 71% freshmen, 58% undergrads receive need-based scholarship or grant aid. 58% freshmen, 49% undergrads receive need-based self-help aid. 24 freshmen, 102 undergrads receive athletic scholarships. Highest amount earned per year from on-campus jobs $1,500.

QUINCY UNIVERSITY

1800 College Avenue, Quincy, IL 62301
Phone: 217-228-5215 **E-mail:** admissions@quincy.edu **CEEB Code:** 1645
Fax: 217-228-5479 **Website:** www.quincy.edu **ACT Code:** 1120
Financial Aid Phone: 217-228-5260

This private school, affiliated with the Roman Catholic Church, was founded in 1860. It has a 75-acre campus.

RATINGS

Admissions Selectivity Rating: 71   **Fire Safety Rating:** 60*   **Green Rating:** 60*

STUDENTS AND FACULTY

Enrollment: 925. **Student Body:** 58% female, 42% male, 29% out-of-state, 1% international (6 countries represented). African American 6%, Asian 1%, Caucasian 75%, Hispanic 2%. **Retention and Graduation:** 70% freshmen return for sophomore year. 33% freshmen graduate within 4 years. 25% grads go on to further study within 1 year. 10% grads pursue arts and sciences degrees. 2% grads pursue business degrees. 3% grads pursue law degrees. 2% grads pursue medical degrees. **Faculty:** Student/faculty ratio 13:1. 52 full-time faculty, 81% hold PhDs. 100% faculty teach undergrads.

ACADEMICS

Degrees: Associate, bachelor's, master's, terminal. **Academic Requirements:** Arts/fine arts, computer literacy, English (including composition), history, humanities, mathematics, philosophy, sciences (biological or physical), social science, theology. **Classes:** Most classes have 10–19 students. Most lab/discussion sections have fewer than 10 students. **Majors with Highest Enrollment:** Business administration/management, elementary education and teaching, psychology. **Disciplines with Highest Percentage of Degrees Awarded:** Business/marketing 28%, education 14%, health professions and related sciences 9%, liberal arts/general studies 7%, psychology 5%, security and protective services 5%. **Special Study Options:** Accelerated program, distance learning, double major, dual enrollment, English as a second language (ESL), honors program, independent study, internships, student-designed major, study abroad, teacher certification program, 3-2 program in pre-engineering with Washington University, 3-1 program in medical technology with various hospitals.

FACILITIES

Housing: Coed dorms, men's dorms, women's dorms, apartments for married students, apartments for single students, special housing for international students, fraternity/sorority housing. **Special Academic Facilities/Equipment:** On-campus reading center for student teachers, television studio, computer art lab, computer writing lab, environmental field station, NPR radio station. **Computers:** 98% of public computers are PCs, 2% of public computers are UNIX, network access in dorm rooms, online registration, online administrative functions (other than registration), remote student-access to Web through college's connection.

CAMPUS LIFE

Activities: Choral groups, concert band, dance, drama/theater, jazz band, literary magazine, music ensembles, musical theater, opera, pep band, radio station, student government, student newspaper, symphony orchestra, television station, yearbook. **Organizations:** 45 registered organizations, 6 honor societies, 4 religious organizations. 1 fraternity (4% men join), 2 sororities (11% women join). **Athletics (Intercollegiate):** *Men:* Baseball, basketball, football, golf, soccer, tennis, volleyball. *Women:* Basketball, golf, soccer, softball, tennis, volleyball. **Environmental Initiatives:** Have partnered with local "end market" recycler (Quincy Recycle Paper, Inc.) to implement on ongoing recycling program for paper, plastic, and metal. The University co-sponsored a solid waste recycling drive that included over 300 participants and 40 tons of recycled electronics in November of 2007. University does have in place a program for the recycling of used computer ink cartridges.

ADMISSIONS

Freshman Academic Profile: 9% in top 10% of high school class, 31% in top 25% of high school class, 60% in top 50% of high school class. 75% from public high schools. SAT Math middle 50% range 440–590. SAT Critical Reading middle 50% range 440–570. ACT middle 50% range 19–24. TOEFL required of all international applicants, minimum paper TOEFL 500, minimum computer TOEFL 173. **Basis for Candidate Selection:** *Very important factors considered include:* Academic GPA, application essay, recommendation(s), rigor of secondary school record, standardized test scores. *Important factors considered include:* Class rank, interview. *Other factors considered include:* Alumni/ae relation, character/personal qualities, extracurricular activities, geographical residence, racial/ethnic status, religious affiliation/commitment, state residency, talent/ability, volunteer work, work experience. **Freshman Admission Requirements:** High school diploma is required, and GED is accepted. *Academic units required:* 4 English. *Academic units recommended:* 4 English, 3 math, 3 science, 2 foreign language, 2 social studies, 2 history. **Freshman Admission Statistics:** 527 applied, 93% admitted, 33% enrolled. **Transfer Admission Requirements:** College transcript(s), statement of good standing from prior institution(s). Minimum college GPA of 2.0 required. Lowest grade transferable D. **General Admission Information:** Application fee $25. Regular notification is rolling. Non-fall registration accepted. Admission may be deferred for a maximum of 1 year. Credit offered for CEEB Advanced Placement tests.

COSTS AND FINANCIAL AID

Annual tuition $20,100. Room and board $7,900. Required fees $690. Average book expense $1,250. **Required Forms and Deadlines:** FAFSA. Financial aid filing deadline 4/15. **Notification of Awards:** Applicants will be notified of awards on a rolling basis beginning on or about 2/15. **Types of Aid:** *Need-based scholarships/grants:* Pell, SEOG, state scholarships/grants, private scholarships, the school's own gift aid. *Loans:* FFEL Subsidized Stafford, FFEL Unsubsidized Stafford, FFEL PLUS, Federal Perkins. **Student Employment:** Federal Work-Study Program available. Institutional employment available. Off-campus job opportunities are fair. **Financial Aid Statistics:** 77% freshmen, 75% undergrads receive need-based scholarship or grant aid. 67% freshmen, 58% undergrads receive need-based self-help aid. 22 freshmen, 52 undergrads receive athletic scholarships. 99% freshmen, 95% undergrads receive any aid. Highest amount earned per year from on-campus jobs $2,000.

QUINNIPIAC UNIVERSITY

Best 368

275 Mount Carmel Avenue, Hamden, CT 06518
Phone: 203-582-8600 **E-mail:** admissions@quinnipiac.edu **CEEB Code:** 3712
Fax: 203-582-8906 **Website:** www.quinnipiac.edu **ACT Code:** 0582
Financial Aid Phone: 203-582-8750

This private school was founded in 1929. It has a 600-acre campus.

RATINGS

Admissions Selectivity Rating: 88   **Fire Safety Rating:** 86   **Green Rating:** 60*

STUDENTS AND FACULTY

Enrollment: 5,676. **Student Body:** 61% female, 39% male, 70% out-of-state,

1% international (20 countries represented). African American 3%, Asian 2%, Caucasian 79%, Hispanic 4%. **Retention and Graduation:** 88% freshmen return for sophomore year. 64% freshmen graduate within 4 years. 37% grads go on to further study within 1 year. 12% grads pursue arts and sciences degrees. 20% grads pursue business degrees. 2% grads pursue law degrees. 3% grads pursue medical degrees. **Faculty:** Student/faculty ratio 15:1. 280 full-time faculty, 88% hold PhDs. 88% faculty teach undergrads.

ACADEMICS

Degrees: Bachelor's, doctoral, first professional certificate, first professional, master's, post-bachelor's certificate. **Academic Requirements:** Arts/fine arts, English (including composition), foreign languages, history, humanities, mathematics, sciences (biological or physical), social science. **Classes:** Most classes have 10–19 students. Most lab/discussion sections have 10–19 students. **Majors with Highest Enrollment:** Business administration/management, physical therapy/therapist, psychology. **Disciplines with Highest Percentage of Degrees Awarded:** Health professions and related sciences 25%, business/marketing 22%, communications/journalism 17%, psychology 8%, social sciences 6%. **Special Study Options:** Distance learning, double major, dual enrollment, English as a second language (1 course only), exchange student program (domestic), honors program, independent study, internships, liberal arts/career combination, online option for summer course offerings, online/on ground hybrid offerings for degree completion program in the college of professional studies for adult students, BS and MS in organizational leadership, student-designed major, study abroad, teacher certification program.

FACILITIES

Housing: Coed dorms, apartments for single students, university-owned houses near campus. **Special Academic Facilities/Equipment:** Quinnipiac Polling Institute, financial technology center, motion analysis lab, Albert Schweitzer Institute, critical care nursing lab, fully digital/high definition TV production studio, editing labs, news technology center, Lender Family Special Collection Room in the library on the Irish Famine (An Gorta Mor). **Computers:** 80% of classrooms are wired, 100% of classrooms are wireless, 85% of public computers are PCs, 15% of public computers are Macs, network access in dorm rooms, network access in dorm lounges, online registration, online administrative functions (other than registration), remote student-access to Web through college's connection. Undergraduates are required to own a computer.

CAMPUS LIFE

Activities: Choral groups, dance, drama/theater, literary magazine, pep band, radio station, student government, student newspaper, television station, yearbook. **Organizations:** 70 registered organizations, 8 honor societies, 3 religious organizations. 2 fraternities (6% men join), 3 sororities (8% women join). **Athletics (Intercollegiate):** *Men:* Baseball, basketball, cross-country, golf, ice hockey, lacrosse, soccer, tennis, track/field (indoor), track/field (outdoor). *Women:* Basketball, cross-country, field hockey, ice hockey, lacrosse, soccer, softball, tennis, track/field (indoor), track/field (outdoor), volleyball.

ADMISSIONS

Freshman Academic Profile: 22% in top 10% of high school class, 60% in top 25% of high school class, 95% in top 50% of high school class. 70% from public high schools. SAT Math middle 50% range 560–630. SAT Critical Reading middle 50% range 540–610. ACT middle 50% range 23–27. TOEFL required of all international applicants, minimum paper TOEFL 550, minimum computer TOEFL 213. **Basis for Candidate Selection:** *Very important factors considered include:* Rigor of secondary school record. *Important factors considered include:* Academic GPA, application essay, class rank, recommendation(s), standardized test scores. *Other factors considered include:* Alumni/ae relation, character/personal qualities, extracurricular activities, interview, level of applicant's interest, racial/ethnic status, talent/ability, volunteer work, work experience. **Freshman Admission Requirements:** High school diploma is required, and GED is accepted. *Academic units required:* 4 English, 3 math, 3 science (2 science labs), 2 foreign language, 2 social studies, 4 years of science and math required for physical therapy, occupational therapy, nursing. *Academic units recommended:* 4 English, 4 math, 4 science (3 science labs), 2 foreign language, 3 social studies. **Freshman Admission Statistics:** 10,313 applied, 58% admitted, 24% enrolled. **Transfer Admission Requirements:** College transcript(s), essay or personal statement. Minimum college GPA of 2.5 required. Lowest grade transferable C. **General Admission Information:** Application fee $45. Regular notification is rolling. Non-fall registration accepted. Admission may be deferred for a maximum of 1 year. Credit and/or placement offered for CEEB Advanced Placement tests.

COSTS AND FINANCIAL AID

Annual tuition $29,700. Room and board $12,200. Required fees $1,200. Average book expense $800. **Required Forms and Deadlines:** FAFSA. Financial aid filing deadline 3/1. **Notification of Awards:** Applicants will be notified of awards on a rolling basis beginning on or about 2/15. **Types of Aid:** *Need-based scholarships/grants:* Pell, SEOG, state scholarships/grants, private scholarships, the school's own gift aid, Federal Nursing Scholarships. *Loans:* FFEL Subsidized Stafford, FFEL Unsubsidized Stafford, FFEL PLUS,

The Princeton Review's Complete Book of Colleges

Federal Perkins, Federal Nursing, state loans. **Student Employment:** Federal Work-Study Program available. Institutional employment available. Off-campus job opportunities are excellent. **Financial Aid Statistics:** 59% freshmen, 56% undergrads receive need-based scholarship or grant aid. 49% freshmen, 51% undergrads receive need-based self-help aid. 66 freshmen, 236 undergrads receive athletic scholarships. 70% freshmen, 68% undergrads receive any aid. Highest amount earned per year from on-campus jobs $2,100.

See page 1324.

RADFORD UNIVERSITY

PO Box 6903, RU, Radford, VA 24142-6903
Phone: 540-831-5371 **E-mail:** ruadmiss@radford.edu **CEEB Code:** 5565
Fax: 540-831-5038 **Website:** www.radford.edu **ACT Code:** 4422
Financial Aid Phone: 540-831-5408

This public school was founded in 1910. It has a 177-acre campus.

RATINGS
Admissions Selectivity Rating: 71   **Fire Safety Rating:** 87   **Green Rating:** 60*

STUDENTS AND FACULTY
Enrollment: 8,089. **Student Body:** 58% female, 42% male, 7% out-of-state. African American 6%, Asian 2%, Caucasian 89%, Hispanic 2%. **Retention and Graduation:** 74% freshmen return for sophomore year. 25% freshmen graduate within 4 years. 18% grads go on to further study within 1 year. **Faculty:** Student/faculty ratio 19:1. 383 full-time faculty, 83% hold PhDs. 86% faculty teach undergrads.

ACADEMICS
Degrees: Bachelor's, master's, post-bachelor's certificate, post-master's certificate. **Academic Requirements:** Arts/fine arts, computer literacy, English (including composition), history, humanities, mathematics, philosophy, sciences (biological or physical), social science. **Classes:** Most classes have 20–29 students. Most lab/discussion sections have 20–29 students. **Majors with Highest Enrollment:** Criminal justice/safety studies, multi/interdisciplinary studies, physical education teaching and coaching. **Disciplines with Highest Percentage of Degrees Awarded:** Business/marketing 20%, interdisciplinary studies 13%, security and protective services 8%, communications/journalism 8%, visual and performing arts 8%, social sciences 8%, education 5%, psychology 5%, health professions and related sciences 5%. **Special Study Options:** Accelerated program, cross-registration, distance learning, double major, dual enrollment, English as a second language (ESL), honors program, independent study, internships, student-designed major, study abroad, teacher certification program.

FACILITIES
Housing: Coed dorms, apartments for single students, special housing for disabled students, special housing for international students. **Special Academic Facilities/Equipment:** Language lab, art gallery with sculpture garden, planetarium, Selu Conservancy, on-campus speech/language/hearing clinic. **Computers:** 100% of classrooms are wireless, 80% of public computers are PCs, 15% of public computers are Macs, 5% of public computers are UNIX, network access in dorm rooms, network access in dorm lounges, online registration, online administrative functions (other than registration), support for handheld computing, remote student-access to Web through college's connection.

CAMPUS LIFE
Activities: Choral groups, concert band, dance, drama/theater, jazz band, literary magazine, music ensembles, musical theater, pep band, radio station, student government, student newspaper, television station, yearbook. **Organizations:** 159 registered organizations, 26 honor societies, 18 religious organizations. 13 fraternities (11% men join), 11 sororities (10% women join). **Athletics (Intercollegiate):** *Men:* Baseball, basketball, cross-country, golf, soccer, tennis, track/field (outdoor). *Women:* Basketball, cross-country, field hockey, golf, soccer, softball, swimming, tennis, track/field (outdoor), volleyball.

ADMISSIONS
Freshman Academic Profile: 6% in top 10% of high school class, 23% in top 25% of high school class, 72% in top 50% of high school class. 96% from public high schools. SAT Math middle 50% range 460–550. SAT Critical Reading middle 50% range 450–550. SAT Writing middle 50% range 450–540. ACT middle 50% range 20–24. TOEFL required of all international applicants,

minimum paper TOEFL 520, minimum computer TOEFL 190. **Basis for Candidate Selection:** *Very important factors considered include:* Rigor of secondary school record. *Other factors considered include:* Academic GPA, alumni/ae relation, application essay, character/personal qualities, class rank, extracurricular activities, first generation, geographical residence, racial/ethnic status, recommendation(s), standardized test scores, state residency, talent. **Freshman Admission Requirements:** High school diploma is required, and GED is accepted. *Academic units recommended:* 4 English, 4 math, 4 science (3 science labs), 3 foreign language, 2 social studies, 2 history, 5 academic electives. **Freshman Admission Statistics:** 6,201 applied, 78% admitted, 36% enrolled. **Transfer Admission Requirements:** College transcript(s). Minimum college GPA of 2.0 required. Lowest grade transferable C. **General Admission Information:** Application fee $50. Regular application deadline 2/1. Regular notification 3/20. Non-fall registration accepted. Credit and/or placement offered for CEEB Advanced Placement tests.

COSTS AND FINANCIAL AID
Annual in-state tuition $4,026. Annual out-of-state tuition $12,360. Room and board $6,490. Required fees $2,150. Average book expense $877. **Required Forms and Deadlines:** FAFSA. Financial aid filing deadline 3/1. **Notification of Awards:** Applicants will be notified of awards on a rolling basis beginning on or about 4/15. **Types of Aid:** *Need-based scholarships/grants:* Pell, SEOG, state scholarships/grants, private scholarships, the school's own gift aid. *Loans:* FFEL Subsidized Stafford, FFEL Unsubsidized Stafford, FFEL PLUS, Federal Perkins, Federal Nursing, state loans, college/university loans from institutional funds. **Financial Aid Statistics:** 22% freshmen, 24% undergrads receive need-based scholarship or grant aid. 29% freshmen, 33% undergrads receive need-based self-help aid. 41 freshmen, 210 undergrads receive athletic scholarships. 60% freshmen, 69% undergrads receive any aid. Highest amount earned per year from on-campus jobs $1,627.

See page 1326.

RAMAPO COLLEGE OF NEW JERSEY

505 Ramapo Valley Road, Mahwah, NJ 07430-1680
Phone: 201-684-7300 **E-mail:** admissions@ramapo.edu **CEEB Code:** 2884
Fax: 201-684-7964 **Website:** www.ramapo.edu **ACT Code:** 2591
Financial Aid Phone: 201-684-7550

This public school was founded in 1971. It has a 300-acre campus.

RATINGS
Admissions Selectivity Rating: 89   **Fire Safety Rating:** 90   **Green Rating:** 72

STUDENTS AND FACULTY
Enrollment: 4,906. **Student Body:** 59% female, 41% male, 6% out-of-state, 3% international (51 countries represented). African American 6%, Asian 4%, Caucasian 78%, Hispanic 8%. **Retention and Graduation:** 88% freshmen return for sophomore year. 45% freshmen graduate within 4 years. **Faculty:** Student/faculty ratio 17:1. 192 full-time faculty, 96% hold PhDs. 100% faculty teach undergrads.

ACADEMICS
Degrees: Bachelor's, certificate, master's. **Academic Requirements:** Computer literacy; English (including composition); foreign languages; global/multicultural disciplines; history; humanities; mathematics; sciences (biological or physical); senior seminar; social science; values, ethics, and aesthetics. **Classes:** Most classes have 20–29 students. Most lab/discussion sections have 10–19 students. **Majors with Highest Enrollment:** Business administration/management, communications studies/speech communication and rhetoric, psychology. **Disciplines with Highest Percentage of Degrees Awarded:** Business/marketing 20%, psychology 15%, communications/journalism 15%, social sciences 9%, visual and performing arts 7%. **Special Study Options:** Accelerated program, cooperative education program, cross-registration, distance learning, double major, dual enrollment, English as a second language (ESL), exchange student program (domestic), external degree program, honors program, independent study, internships, liberal arts/career combination, student-designed major, study abroad, teacher certification program.

FACILITIES
Housing: Coed dorms, apartments for single students, special housing for disabled students, special housing for international students, cooperative housing, special arrangements are made from time to time. **Special Academic**

Facilities/Equipment: Art museum, media center, international telecommunications center, electron microscope, Holocaust Studies Center, new sports/fitness complex. A new center for science, education, and technology is underway, as well as a sustainability education center. **Computers:** 1% of classrooms are wired, 100% of classrooms are wireless, 85% of public computers are PCs, 15% of public computers are Macs, network access in dorm rooms, network access in dorm lounges, online registration, online administrative functions (other than registration), remote student-access to Web through college's connection.

CAMPUS LIFE

Activities: Choral groups, dance, drama/theater, literary magazine, music ensembles, musical theater, radio station, student government, student newspaper, television station, yearbook. **Organizations:** 80 registered organizations, 18 honor societies, 7 religious organizations. 10 fraternities (8% men join), 7 sororities (5% women join). **Athletics (Intercollegiate):** *Men:* Baseball, basketball, bowling, cross-country, light weight football, soccer, tennis, track/field (indoor), track/field (outdoor), volleyball. *Women:* Basketball, bowling, cheerleading, cross-country, field hockey, lacrosse, soccer, softball, tennis, track/field (indoor), track/field (outdoor), volleyball.

ADMISSIONS

Freshman Academic Profile: 29% in top 10% of high school class, 71% in top 25% of high school class, 97% in top 50% of high school class. SAT Math middle 50% range 540–630. SAT Critical Reading middle 50% range 520–620. SAT Writing middle 50% range 530–620. TOEFL required of all international applicants, minimum paper TOEFL 550, minimum computer TOEFL 213. **Basis for Candidate Selection:** *Very important factors considered include:* Academic GPA, class rank, rigor of secondary school record, standardized test scores. *Important factors considered include:* Application essay, character/personal qualities, extracurricular activities, recommendation(s), talent/ability. *Other factors considered include:* Alumni/ae relation, geographical residence, state residency, volunteer work, work experience. **Freshman Admission Requirements:** High school diploma is required, and GED is accepted. *Academic units required:* 4 English, 3 math, 3 science (3 science labs), 3 foreign language, 3 social studies, 2 academic electives. **Freshman Admission Statistics:** 4,430 applied, 46% admitted, 40% enrolled. **Transfer Admission Requirements:** College transcript(s), essay or personal statement. Minimum college GPA of 2.5 required. Lowest grade transferable C. **General Admission Information:** Application fee $55. Regular application deadline 3/1. Regular notification rolls 11/15 through 3/1. Non-fall registration accepted. Admission may be deferred for a maximum of 1 year. Credit offered for CEEB Advanced Placement tests.

COSTS AND FINANCIAL AID

Annual in-state tuition $6,904. Annual out-of-state tuition $12,475. Room and board $10,310. Required fees $3,061. Average book expense $1,200. **Required Forms and Deadlines:** FAFSA. Financial aid filing deadline 3/1. **Notification of Awards:** Applicants will be notified of awards on or about 4/1. **Types of Aid:** *Need-based scholarships/grants:* Pell, SEOG, state scholarships/grants, private scholarships, the school's own gift aid. *Loans:* Direct Subsidized Stafford, Direct Unsubsidized Stafford, Direct PLUS, Federal Perkins, state loans. **Financial Aid Statistics:** 25% freshmen, 24% undergrads receive need-based scholarship or grant aid. 43% freshmen, 39% undergrads receive need-based self-help aid. 81% freshmen, 76% undergrads receive any aid.

RANDOLPH COLLEGE

2500 Rivermont Avenue, Lynchburg, VA 24503-1526
Phone: 434-947-8100 **E-mail:** admissions@randolphCollege.edu **CEEB Code:** 5567
Fax: 434-947-8996 **Website:** www.randolphcollege.edu **ACT Code:** 4388
Financial Aid Phone: 434-947-8128

This private school, affiliated with the Methodist Church, was founded in 1891. It has a 100-acre campus.

RATINGS

Admissions Selectivity Rating: 81   **Fire Safety Rating:** 88   **Green Rating:** 72

STUDENTS AND FACULTY

Enrollment: 668. **Student Body:** 100% female, 61% out-of-state, 11%

international (46 countries represented). African American 9%, Asian 4%, Caucasian 69%, Hispanic 5%, Native American 1%. **Retention and Graduation:** 78% freshmen return for sophomore year. 65% freshmen graduate within 4 years. 31% grads go on to further study within 1 year. 25% grads pursue arts and sciences degrees. 2% grads pursue business degrees. 6% grads pursue law degrees. 5% grads pursue medical degrees. **Faculty:** Student/faculty ratio 8:1. 74 full-time faculty, 95% hold PhDs. 100% faculty teach undergrads.

ACADEMICS

Degrees: Bachelor's, master's. **Academic Requirements:** Arts/fine arts, English (including composition), foreign languages, history, humanities, mathematics, philosophy, sciences (biological or physical), social science, wellness/physical education. **Classes:** Most classes have fewer than 10 students. Most lab/discussion sections have 10–19 students. **Majors with Highest Enrollment:** Biology/biological sciences, political science and government, psychology. **Disciplines with Highest Percentage of Degrees Awarded:** Social sciences 21%, biological/life sciences 11%, psychology 11%, visual and performing arts 11%, foreign languages and literature 8%, history 8%, philosophy and religious studies 7%, English 6%. **Special Study Options:** Accelerated program, American culture program, cross-registration, double major, dual enrollment, exchange student program (domestic), honors program, independent study, internships, junior year abroad program, liberal arts/career combination, student-designed major, study abroad, teacher certification program. 7-college exchange with Washington and Lee University, Hollins University, Hampden-Sydney College, Mary Baldwin College, Sweet Briar College, and Randolph-Macon College.

FACILITIES

Housing: Coed dorms, women's dorms, shared housing for nontraditional age students. **Special Academic Facilities/Equipment:** Maier Museum of American Art, computer-equipped classrooms (including wireless computer networks and smart boards), 100-acre equestrian center, language lab, science and math resource center, learning resources center, writing lab, nursery school, nature preserves, observatory, electron microscope. **Computers:** 100% of classrooms are wired, 25% of classrooms are wireless, 94% of public computers are PCs, 6% of public computers are Macs, network access in dorm rooms, network access in dorm lounges, online registration, online administrative functions (other than registration), remote student-access to Web through college's connection.

CAMPUS LIFE

Activities: Choral groups, dance, drama/theater, literary magazine, music ensembles, radio station, student government, student newspaper, student-run film society, yearbook. **Organizations:** 40 registered organizations, 7 honor societies, 6 religious organizations. **Athletics (Intercollegiate):** *Men:* Basketball, cross-country, equestrian sports, soccer, tennis. *Women:* Basketball, cross-country, equestrian sports, field hockey, horseback riding, soccer, softball, swimming, tennis, volleyball. **Environmental Initiatives:** Instead of a sustainability coordinator, the College has an Environmental Issues Council, composed of faculty, staff and students, who coordinate sustainability initiatives on campus. The College is conducting a comprehensive Greenhouse Gas Inventory and is participating the the STARS pilot program. These will be components of a Green Master Plan that is being developed this year in conjunction with our overall Facilities Master Plan. Environmental Studies faculty and students promote sustainability in the local community by participating in city planning. One member of the faculty chairs the city's Natural Resources Advisory Council, and another serves on the local Planning Commission. One honors students is developing an environmental checklist to evaluate the sustainability of development proposals.

ADMISSIONS

Freshman Academic Profile: 38% in top 10% of high school class, 70% in top 25% of high school class, 90% in top 50% of high school class. 78% from public high schools. SAT Math middle 50% range 500–610. SAT Critical Reading middle 50% range 510–640. ACT middle 50% range 23–27. TOEFL required of all international applicants, minimum paper TOEFL 550, minimum computer TOEFL 213. **Basis for Candidate Selection:** *Very important factors considered include:* Academic GPA, character/personal qualities, rigor of secondary school record. *Important factors considered include:* Application essay, extracurricular activities, recommendation(s), standardized test scores, talent/ability, volunteer work. *Other factors considered include:* Alumni/ae relation, class rank, first generation, interview, level of applicant's interest, work experience. **Freshman Admission Requirements:** High school diploma is required, and GED is accepted. *Academic units required:* 4 English, 3 math, 2 science (2 science labs), 3 foreign language, 2 history, 2 academic electives. **Freshman Admission Statistics:** 745 applied, 89% admitted, 28% enrolled. **Transfer Admission Requirements:** High school transcript, college transcript(s), essay or personal statement. Minimum college GPA of 2.5 required. Lowest grade transferable C-. **General Admission Information:** Application fee $35. Early decision application deadline 11/15. Regular application deadline 3/1. Regular notification is rolling. Non-fall registration accepted. Admission may be deferred for a maximum of 1 year. Credit and/or placement offered for CEEB Advanced Placement tests.

COSTS AND FINANCIAL AID

Annual tuition $25,350. Room and board $9,000. Required fees $510. Average book expense $800. **Required Forms and Deadlines:** FAFSA, state aid form. Financial aid filing deadline 3/1. **Notification of Awards:** Applicants will be notified of awards on a rolling basis beginning on or about 3/1. **Types of Aid:** *Need-based scholarships/grants:* Pell, SEOG, state scholarships/grants, private scholarships, the school's own gift aid. *Loans:* FFEL Subsidized Stafford, FFEL Unsubsidized Stafford, FFEL PLUS, Federal Perkins, college/university loans from institutional funds, private. **Financial Aid Statistics:** 68% freshmen, 65% undergrads receive need-based scholarship or grant aid. 57% freshmen, 57% undergrads receive need-based self-help aid. 99% freshmen, 96% undergrads receive any aid.

RANDOLPH-MACON COLLEGE

PO Box 5005, Ashland, VA 23005
Phone: 804-752-7305 **E-mail:** admissions@rmc.edu **CEEB Code:** 5566
Fax: 804-752-4707 **Website:** www.rmc.edu **ACT Code:** 4386
Financial Aid Phone: 804-752-7259

This private school, affiliated with the Methodist Church, was founded in 1830. It has a 120-acre campus.

RATINGS

Admissions Selectivity Rating: 82   **Fire Safety Rating:** 67   **Green Rating:** 68

STUDENTS AND FACULTY

Enrollment: 1,127. **Student Body:** 54% female, 46% male, 30% out-of-state, 2% international (21 countries represented). African American 7%, Asian 2%, Caucasian 87%, Hispanic 1%. **Retention and Graduation:** 74% freshmen return for sophomore year. 15% freshmen graduate within 4 years. 27% grads go on to further study within 1 year. 10% grads pursue arts and sciences degrees. 2% grads pursue business degrees. 2% grads pursue law degrees. 2% grads pursue medical degrees. **Faculty:** Student/faculty ratio 11:1. 90 full-time faculty, 93% hold PhDs. 100% faculty teach undergrads.

ACADEMICS

Degrees: Bachelor's. **Academic Requirements:** Arts/fine arts, computer literacy, English (including composition), first-year seminar, foreign languages, history, humanities, mathematics, philosophy or religion, sciences (biological or physical), social science. **Classes:** Most classes have 10–19 students. Most lab/discussion sections have fewer than 10 students. **Majors with Highest Enrollment:** Business/managerial economics, psychology, sociology. **Disciplines with Highest Percentage of Degrees Awarded:** Social sciences 25%, business/marketing 21%, English 9%, history 7%, psychology 6%, biological/life sciences 6%, visual and performing arts 6%. **Special Study Options:** Accelerated program, cross-registration, double major, dual enrollment, exchange student program (domestic), honors program, independent study, internships, liberal arts/career combination, study abroad, teacher certification program.

FACILITIES

Housing: Coed dorms, men's dorms, women's dorms, apartments for single students, special housing for disabled students, special housing for international students, fraternity/sorority housing, honors house, substance-free housing, special interest housing. **Special Academic Facilities/Equipment:** Language lab, learning center, media center, greenhouse, observatory with telescope, electron microscopes, nuclear magnetic resonator, art gallery, fine arts center. **Computers:** 30% of classrooms are wired, 15% of classrooms are wireless, 85% of public computers are PCs, 10% of public computers are Macs, 5% of public computers are UNIX, network access in dorm rooms, online registration, online administrative functions (other than registration), support for handheld computing, remote student-access to Web through college's connection.

CAMPUS LIFE

Activities: Choral groups, dance, drama/theater, jazz band, literary magazine, music ensembles, musical theater, pep band, radio station, student government, student newspaper, student-run film society, television station, yearbook. **Organizations:** 104 registered organizations, 18 honor societies, 4 religious

organizations. 6 fraternities (33% men join), 4 sororities (33% women join). **Athletics (Intercollegiate):** *Men:* Baseball, basketball, football, golf, lacrosse, soccer, tennis. *Women:* Basketball, field hockey, lacrosse, soccer, softball, swimming, tennis, volleyball.

ADMISSIONS

Freshman Academic Profile: 18% in top 10% of high school class, 44% in top 25% of high school class, 79% in top 50% of high school class. 71% from public high schools. SAT Math middle 50% range 500–590. SAT Critical Reading middle 50% range 490–580. SAT Writing middle 50% range 490–580. TOEFL required of all international applicants, minimum paper TOEFL 550, minimum computer TOEFL 213. **Basis for Candidate Selection:** *Very important factors considered include:* Academic GPA, rigor of secondary school record. *Important factors considered include:* Application essay, class rank, recommendation(s), standardized test scores. *Other factors considered include:* Alumni/ae relation, character/personal qualities, extracurricular activities, first generation, interview, racial/ethnic status, talent/ability, volunteer work, work experience. **Freshman Admission Requirements:** High school diploma is required, and GED is accepted. *Academic units required:* 4 English, 3 math, 3 science (2 science labs), 2 foreign language, 1 social studies, 2 history, 1 academic elective. *Academic units recommended:* 4 English, 4 math, 4 science (4 science labs), 4 foreign language, 4 social studies, 2 history. **Freshman Admission Statistics:** 2,878 applied, 58% admitted, 24% enrolled. **Transfer Admission Requirements:** High school transcript, college transcript(s), essay or personal statement, statement of good standing from prior institution(s). Minimum college GPA of 2.0 required. Lowest grade transferable C-. **General Admission Information:** Application fee $30. Early decision application deadline 11/15. Regular application deadline 3/1. Regular notification 4/1. Non-fall registration accepted. Admission may be deferred for a maximum of 1 year. Credit and/or placement offered for CEEB Advanced Placement tests.

COSTS AND FINANCIAL AID

Annual tuition $26,195. Room and board $8,180. Required fees $635. Average book expense $1,000. **Required Forms and Deadlines:** FAFSA, state aid form, R-MC entitlement eligibility form, college prepaid education program form. Financial aid filing deadline 3/1. **Notification of Awards:** Applicants will be notified of awards on or about 3/15. **Types of Aid:** *Need-based scholarships/grants:* Pell, SEOG, state scholarships/grants, private scholarships, the school's own gift aid. *Loans:* FFEL Subsidized Stafford, FFEL Unsubsidized Stafford, FFEL PLUS, Federal Perkins, college/university loans from institutional funds. **Student Employment:** Federal Work-Study Program available. Institutional employment available. Off-campus job opportunities are excellent. **Financial Aid Statistics:** 58% freshmen, 58% undergrads receive need-based scholarship or grant aid. 46% freshmen, 49% undergrads receive need-based self-help aid. 100% freshmen, 95% undergrads receive any aid. Highest amount earned per year from on-campus jobs $1,500.

REED COLLEGE

3203 SE Woodstock Boulevard, Portland, OR 97202-8199
Phone: 503-777-7511 **E-mail:** admission@reed.edu **CEEB Code:** 4654
Fax: 503-777-7553 **Website:** www.reed.edu **ACT Code:** 3494
Financial Aid Phone: 503-777-7223

This private school was founded in 1908. It has a 110-acre campus.

RATINGS

Admissions Selectivity Rating: 97   **Fire Safety Rating:** 60*   **Green Rating:** 79

STUDENTS AND FACULTY

Enrollment: 1,372. **Student Body:** 55% female, 45% male, 87% out-of-state, 4% international (39 countries represented). African American 1%, Asian 5%, Caucasian 44%, Hispanic 4%. **Retention and Graduation:** 90% freshmen return for sophomore year. 57% freshmen graduate within 4 years. 65% grads go on to further study within 1 year. 48% grads pursue arts and sciences degrees. 4% grads pursue business degrees. 6% grads pursue law degrees. 5% grads pursue medical degrees. **Faculty:** Student/faculty ratio 10:1. 119 full-time faculty, 88% hold PhDs. 100% faculty teach undergrads.

ACADEMICS

Degrees: Bachelor's, master's. **Academic Requirements:** Arts/fine arts,

English (including composition), foreign languages, humanities, mathematics, philosophy, sciences (biological or physical), social science. **Classes:** Most classes have 10–19 students. Most lab/discussion sections have 10–19 students. **Majors with Highest Enrollment:** Biology/biological sciences, English language and literature, psychology. **Disciplines with Highest Percentage of Degrees Awarded:** Social sciences 17%, English 15%, biological/life sciences 13%, physical sciences 9%, foreign languages and literature 9%, psychology 8%. **Special Study Options:** Computer science, cooperative education program, cross-registration, double major, dual enrollment, exchange student program (domestic), independent study, internships, liberal arts/career combination, study abroad. Dual degrees: BA from Reed and a BS computer science from the University of Washington; BA from Reed and MS computer science and engineering from the Oregon Graduate Institute School of Science and Engineering (OGI) in Portland (matriculation for 5 years); BA from Reed and bachelor's degree in engineering (alternatively, computer science or certain earth and planetary sciences) in California Institute of Technology (Caltech), Columbia University School of Engineering and Applied Sciences, or Rensselaer Polytechnic Institute; BA from Reed and a professional master's degree from the Nicholas School of the Environment in Duke (master of forestry or master of environmental management); pre-medical and pre-veterinary; exchange programs and summer internships at other institutions for visual arts (programs in painting and sculpture, architecture, art history, archaeology, conservation, historic preservation, and museum work), a joint 5-year program is also available with the Pacific Northwest College of Art. These programs are described in more detail in the art department section of the website.

FACILITIES

Housing: Coed dorms, apartments for single students, special housing for disabled students, cooperative housing, Reed language houses accommodate upper-division students studying Chinese, French, German, Russian, and Spanish. First-year students required to live on campus. **Special Academic Facilities/Equipment:** Art gallery, studio art building, language labs, computerized music listening lab, nuclear research reactor, 20 music practice rooms and midi lab, 800-seat auditorium, quantitative skills center, educational technology center. **Computers:** 100% of classrooms are wireless, 16% of public computers are PCs, 83% of public computers are Macs, 1% of public computers are UNIX, network access in dorm rooms, network access in dorm lounges, online registration, online administrative functions (other than registration), remote student-access to Web through college's connection.

CAMPUS LIFE

Activities: Choral groups, dance, drama/theater, literary magazine, music ensembles, radio station, student government, student newspaper, student-run film society, symphony orchestra. **Organizations:** 83 registered organizations, 1 honor society, 5 religious organizations. **Environmental Initiatives:** LEED construction. recycling. installation for energy efficiency across campus, i.e., lighting, windows, heating.

ADMISSIONS

Freshman Academic Profile: 67% in top 10% of high school class, 89% in top 25% of high school class, 98% in top 50% of high school class. 60% from public high schools. SAT Math middle 50% range 630–710. SAT Critical Reading middle 50% range 680–760. SAT Writing middle 50% range 650–730. ACT middle 50% range 28–32. TOEFL required of all international applicants, minimum paper TOEFL 600, minimum computer TOEFL 259. **Basis for Candidate Selection:** *Very important factors considered include:* Academic GPA, application essay, rigor of secondary school record. *Important factors considered include:* Class rank, interview, level of applicant's interest, recommendation(s), standardized test scores. *Other factors considered include:* Alumni/ae relation, character/personal qualities, extracurricular activities, first generation, racial/ethnic status, talent/ability, volunteer work, work experience. **Freshman Admission Requirements:** High school diploma is required, and GED is accepted. *Academic units recommended:* 4 English, 4 math, 3 science, 3 foreign language, 1 social studies, 3 history. **Freshman Admission Statistics:** 3,049 applied, 40% admitted, 31% enrolled. **Transfer Admission Requirements:** High school transcript, college transcript(s), essay or personal statement, standardized test score, statement of good standing from prior institution(s). Lowest grade transferable C-. **General Admission Information:** Application fee $40. Early decision application deadline 11/15. Regular application deadline 1/15. Regular notification 4/1. Non-fall registration not accepted. Admission may be deferred for a maximum of 1 year. Credit and/or placement offered for CEEB Advanced Placement tests.

COSTS AND FINANCIAL AID

Annual tuition $36,190. Room and board $9,460. Required fees $230. Average book expense $950. **Required Forms and Deadlines:** FAFSA, institution's own financial aid form, CSS/Financial Aid PROFILE, Noncustodial PROFILE. Financial aid filing deadline 1/15. **Notification of Awards:** Applicants will be notified of awards on or about 4/1. **Types of Aid:** *Need-based scholarships/grants:* Pell, SEOG, state scholarships/grants, private scholarships, the school's own gift aid. *Loans:* FFEL Subsidized Stafford, FFEL Unsubsidized Stafford,

FFEL PLUS, Federal Perkins. **Student Employment:** Federal Work-Study Program available. Institutional employment available. **Financial Aid Statistics:** 43% freshmen, 46% undergrads receive need-based scholarship or grant aid. 41% freshmen, 45% undergrads receive need-based self-help aid. 45% freshmen, 50% undergrads receive any aid. Highest amount earned per year from on-campus jobs $700.

See page 1328.

REEDLEY COLLEGE

995 North, Reed Avenue, Reedley, CA 93654
Phone: 559-638-3641 **E-mail:** emerzian@scccd.org
Fax: 559-638-5040 **Website:** www.reedleyCollege.com

This is a public school.

RATINGS
Admissions Selectivity Rating: 60*   **Fire Safety Rating:** 60*   **Green Rating:** 60*

STUDENTS AND FACULTY
Enrollment: 7,434. **Student Body:** 1% out-of-state. African American 3%, Asian 4%, Caucasian 40%, Hispanic 41%, Native American 2%. **Faculty:** Student/faculty ratio 25:1. 83 full-time faculty.

ACADEMICS
Degrees: Associate, certificate, diploma, terminal. **Special Study Options:** Academic remediation, advanced placement credit, cooperative education program, distance learning, English as a second language (ESL), freshman honors college, honors program, independent study, learning disabilities services.

FACILITIES
Computers: Network access in dorm rooms, online registration, remote student-access to Web through college's connection.

ADMISSIONS
Freshman Admission Requirements: High school diploma is required, and GED is accepted. **Freshman Admission Statistics:** 303 applied, 100% admitted. **General Admission Information:** Regular notification is continuous. Non-fall registration not accepted. Common Application not accepted.

COSTS AND FINANCIAL AID
Annual in-state tuition $330. Out-of-state tuition $3,830. Room & board $3,820. Average book expense $300.

REFORMED BIBLE COLLEGE

3333 East Beltline, NE, Grand Rapids, MI 49525-9749
Phone: 616-222-3000 **E-mail:** admissions@reformed.edu
Fax: 616-222-3045 **Website:** www.reformed.edu
Financial Aid Phone: 616-222-3000

This private school was founded in 1939. It has a 201-acre campus.

RATINGS
Admissions Selectivity Rating: 60*   **Fire Safety Rating:** 60*   **Green Rating:** 60*

ACADEMICS
Degrees: Associate, bachelor's, certificate. **Academic Requirements:** English (including composition), history, mathematics, philosophy, religion/theology and Bible, sciences (biological or physical), social science. **Special Study Options:** Cooperative education program, double major, English as a second language (ESL), internships, study abroad.

FACILITIES
Housing: Coed dorms, apartments for married students, apartments for single students. **Computers:** Network access in dorm rooms.

CAMPUS LIFE
Activities: Choral groups, drama/theater, student government, yearbook. **Athletics (Intercollegiate):** *Men:* Basketball, soccer, volleyball. *Women:* Soccer, volleyball.

ADMISSIONS

Freshman Academic Profile: TOEFL required of all international applicants, minimum paper TOEFL 550. **Basis for Candidate Selection:** *Very important factors considered include:* Application essay, character/personal qualities, recommendation(s), religious affiliation/commitment. *Important factors considered include:* Volunteer work. *Other factors considered include:* Extracurricular activities, racial/ethnic status, standardized test scores, talent/ability, work experience. **Freshman Admission Requirements:** High school diploma is required, and GED is accepted. **Transfer Admission Requirements:** High school transcript, college transcript(s), essay or personal statement. Lowest grade transferable C. **General Admission Information:** Non-fall registration accepted. Credit and/or placement offered for CEEB Advanced Placement tests.

COSTS AND FINANCIAL AID

Student Employment: Off-campus job opportunities are good.

REGENT UNIVERSITY

1000 Regent University Drive, SC 218, Virginia Beach, VA 23464
Phone: 800-373-5504 **E-mail:** admissions@regent.edu
Fax: 757-226-4381 **Website:** www.regent.edu
Financial Aid Phone: 757-226-4125

This private school, affiliated with the Christian (nondenominational) Church, was founded in 1978.

RATINGS

Admissions Selectivity Rating: 60*   **Fire Safety Rating:** 60*   **Green Rating:** 60*

STUDENTS AND FACULTY

Enrollment: 987. **Student Body:** 70% female, 30% male, 46% out-of-state. African American 5%, Caucasian 14%. **Retention and Graduation:** 57% freshmen return for sophomore year. **Faculty:** Student/faculty ratio 7:1. 162 full-time faculty.

ACADEMICS

Degrees: Bachelor's, doctoral, first professional, master's, post-master's certificate. **Academic Requirements:** Arts/fine arts, computer literacy, English (including composition), humanities, mathematics, sciences (biological or physical), social science. **Classes:** Most classes have 10–19 students. **Majors with Highest Enrollment:** Business administration/management, psychology, religion/religious studies. **Disciplines with Highest Percentage of Degrees Awarded:** Business/marketing 45%, philosophy and religious studies 21%, education 18%, psychology 10%. **Special Study Options:** Distance learning, independent study, internships, study abroad, teacher certification program.

FACILITIES

Special Academic Facilities/Equipment: The 31,000-square-foot student center on Regent's Virginia Beach Campus, opened in 2003, includes the university bookstore; student organizations and meeting rooms; a cafe/coffee shop; computer lab; student lounge; offices for the registrar, admissions, and financial aid. The 135,000-square-foot communication and performing arts center, opened in 2002, includes film and animation studios, a state-of-the-art main theater, screening rooms and editing suites in one of the most technologically advanced communication buildings on the East coast. **Computers:** 20% of classrooms are wired, 100% of classrooms are wireless, 100% of public computers are PCs, online registration, online administrative functions (other than registration), support for handheld computing, remote student-access to Web through college's connection.

CAMPUS LIFE

Activities: Choral groups, concert band, drama/theater, student government. **Organizations:** 25 registered organizations.

ADMISSIONS

Freshman Academic Profile: SAT Math middle 50% range 450–570. SAT Critical Reading middle 50% range 480–640. SAT Writing middle 50% range 470–560. ACT middle 50% range 20–24. TOEFL required of all international applicants, minimum paper TOEFL 577, minimum computer TOEFL 233. **Basis for Candidate Selection:** *Very important factors considered include:* Academic GPA, application essay, standardized test scores. **Freshman Admission Requirements:** High school diploma is required, and GED is accepted. **Freshman Admission Statistics:** 1,105 applied, 56% admitted, 39% enrolled. **Transfer Admission Requirements:** College transcript(s), essay or personal statement. Minimum college GPA of 2.5 required. Lowest grade transferable C. **General Admission Information:** Application fee $50. Regular application deadline 8/13. Non-fall registration accepted.

COSTS AND FINANCIAL AID

Required Forms and Deadlines: FAFSA, institution's own financial aid form. **Notification of Awards:** Applicants will be notified of awards on a rolling basis beginning on or about 3/1. **Types of Aid:** *Need-based scholarships/grants:* Pell, state scholarships/grants, private scholarships, the school's own gift aid. *Loans:* FFEL Subsidized Stafford, FFEL Unsubsidized Stafford, FFEL PLUS. **Financial Aid Statistics:** 43% freshmen, 46% undergrads receive need-based scholarship or grant aid. 60% freshmen, 63% undergrads receive need-based self-help aid. 84% freshmen, 84% undergrads receive any aid.

REGIS COLLEGE

235 Wellesley Street, Weston, MA 02493-1571
Phone: 781-768-7100 **E-mail:** admission@regisCollege.edu **CEEB Code:** 3723
Fax: 781-768-7071 **Website:** www.regiscollege.edu **ACT Code:** 1886
Financial Aid Phone: 781-768-7180

This private school, affiliated with the Roman Catholic Church, was founded in 1927. It has a 131-acre campus.

RATINGS

Admissions Selectivity Rating: 67   **Fire Safety Rating:** 83   **Green Rating:** 60*

STUDENTS AND FACULTY

Enrollment: 859. **Student Body:** 98% female, 2% male, 10% out-of-state, 1% international (31 countries represented). African American 17%, Asian 7%, Caucasian 39%, Hispanic 9%. **Retention and Graduation:** 76% freshmen return for sophomore year. 25% grads go on to further study within 1 year. 23% grads pursue arts and sciences degrees. 1% grads pursue business degrees. 1% grads pursue law degrees. **Faculty:** Student/faculty ratio 14:1. 55 full-time faculty, 75% hold PhDs. 88% faculty teach undergrads.

ACADEMICS

Degrees: Associate, bachelor's, doctoral, master's, post-master's certificate, terminal. **Academic Requirements:** English (including composition), first year seminar, humanities, mathematics, religious studies, sciences (biological or physical), social science. **Classes:** Most classes have 10–19 students. Most lab/discussion sections have 10–19 students. **Majors with Highest Enrollment:** Biology/biological sciences, communications studies/speech communication and rhetoric, nursing/registered nurse training (ASN, BSN, MSN, RN). **Disciplines with Highest Percentage of Degrees Awarded:** Health professions and related sciences 43%, business/marketing 14%, communications/journalism 9%, social sciences 7%, psychology 5%, visual and performing arts 5%, history 5%. **Special Study Options:** Accelerated program, cross-registration, double major, dual enrollment, exchange student program (domestic), honors program, independent study, internships, student-designed major, study abroad, teacher certification program.

FACILITIES

Housing: Coed dorms, women's dorms. **Special Academic Facilities/Equipment:** Fine arts center, philatelic museum. **Computers:** 10% of classrooms are wired, 15% of classrooms are wireless, 75% of public computers are PCs, 25% of public computers are Macs, network access in dorm rooms, network access in dorm lounges, online registration, online administrative functions (other than registration), support for handheld computing, remote student-access to Web through college's connection.

CAMPUS LIFE

Activities: Choral groups, dance, drama/theater, literary magazine, music ensembles, musical theater, radio station, student government, yearbook. **Organizations:** 28 registered organizations, 9 honor societies, 1 religious organization. **Athletics (Intercollegiate):** *Women:* Basketball, diving, field hockey, lacrosse, soccer, softball, swimming, tennis, track/field (indoor), track/field (outdoor), volleyball.

ADMISSIONS

Freshman Academic Profile: 21% in top 10% of high school class, 49% in top 25% of high school class, 75% in top 50% of high school class. 67% from public high schools. SAT Math middle 50% range 400–500. SAT Critical Reading middle 50% range 400–500. SAT Writing middle 50% range 400–510. ACT middle 50% range 16–20. TOEFL required of all international applicants, minimum paper TOEFL 550, minimum computer TOEFL 213. **Basis for Candidate Selection:** *Very important factors considered include:* Application essay, character/personal qualities, recommendation(s), rigor of secondary school record, standardized test scores. *Important factors considered include:* Academic GPA, class rank, extracurricular activities, interview, talent/ability, volunteer work, work experience. *Other factors considered include:* Alumni/ae relation, first generation, level of applicant's interest. **Freshman Admission**

Requirements: High school diploma is required, and GED is accepted. *Academic units required:* 4 English, 3 math, 2 science (1 science lab), 2 foreign language, 2 social studies, 3 academic electives. **Freshman Admission Statistics:** 674 applied, 82% admitted, 31% enrolled. **Transfer Admission Requirements:** High school transcript, college transcript(s), essay or personal statement, standardized test score, statement of good standing from prior institution(s). Minimum college GPA of 2.5 required. Lowest grade transferable C. **General Admission Information:** Application fee $50. Regular notification is rolling. Non-fall registration accepted. Admission may be deferred for a maximum of 1 year. Credit and/or placement offered for CEEB Advanced Placement tests.

COSTS AND FINANCIAL AID

Required Forms and Deadlines: FAFSA, institution's own financial aid form. Financial aid filing deadline 2/15. **Notification of Awards:** Applicants will be notified of awards on a rolling basis beginning on or about 3/15. **Types of Aid:** *Need-based scholarships/grants:* Pell, SEOG, state scholarships/grants, private scholarships, the school's own gift aid, Federal Nursing Scholarships. *Loans:* FFEL Subsidized Stafford, FFEL Unsubsidized Stafford, FFEL PLUS, Federal Perkins, state loans. **Financial Aid Statistics:** 76% freshmen, 73% undergrads receive need-based scholarship or grant aid. 84% freshmen, 79% undergrads receive need-based self-help aid. 85% freshmen, 81% undergrads receive any aid. Highest amount earned per year from on-campus jobs $3,900.

REGIS UNIVERSITY

3333 Regis Boulevard, A-12, Denver, CO 80221-1099
Phone: 303-458-4900 **E-mail:** regisadm@regis.edu/college.asp **CEEB Code:** 4656
Fax: 303-964-5534 **Website:** www.regis.edu **ACT Code:** 0526
Financial Aid Phone: 303-458-4066

This private school, affiliated with the Roman Catholic Church, was founded in 1877. It has a 90-acre campus.

RATINGS
Admissions Selectivity Rating: 77 **Fire Safety Rating:** 60* **Green Rating:** 60*

STUDENTS AND FACULTY
Enrollment: 5,430. **Student Body:** 62% female, 38% male, 24% out-of-state. African American 5%, Asian 3%, Caucasian 64%, Hispanic 8%. **Faculty:** Student/faculty ratio 10:1. 240 full-time faculty, 29% hold PhDs. 100% faculty teach undergrads.

ACADEMICS
Degrees: Bachelor's, doctoral, master's. **Academic Requirements:** Arts/fine arts, English (including composition), foreign languages, history, humanities, mathematics, philosophy, sciences (biological or physical), social science. **Classes:** Most classes have fewer than 10 students. Most lab/discussion sections have 10–19 students. **Disciplines with Highest Percentage of Degrees Awarded:** Business/marketing 40%, health professions and related sciences 19%, computer and information sciences 13%, interdisciplinary studies 13%, communication technologies 6%. **Special Study Options:** Accelerated program, cooperative education program, cross-registration, distance learning, double major, dual enrollment, exchange student program (domestic), honors program, independent study, internships, liberal arts/career combination, student-designed major, study abroad, teacher certification program, weekend college.

FACILITIES
Housing: Coed dorms, apartments for single students, special housing for disabled students. **Special Academic Facilities/Equipment:** Language lab, wellness center. **Computers:** Network access in dorm lounges, online administrative functions (other than registration), remote student-access to Web through college's connection.

CAMPUS LIFE
Activities: Choral groups, drama/theater, literary magazine, music ensembles, musical theater, radio station, student government, student newspaper, yearbook. **Organizations:** 40 registered organizations, 1 honor society, 1 religious organization. **Athletics (Intercollegiate):** *Men:* Baseball, basketball, cross-country, golf, soccer. *Women:* Basketball, cross-country, lacrosse, soccer, softball, volleyball.

ADMISSIONS
Freshman Academic Profile: 21% in top 10% of high school class, 47% in top 25% of high school class, 79% in top 50% of high school class. 65% from public high schools. SAT Math middle 50% range 480–600. SAT Critical Reading middle 50% range 490–590. ACT middle 50% range 21–26. TOEFL required

of all international applicants, minimum paper TOEFL 550. **Basis for Candidate Selection:** *Very important factors considered include:* Rigor of secondary school record, standardized test scores. *Important factors considered include:* Application essay, recommendation(s). *Other factors considered include:* Character/personal qualities, class rank, extracurricular activities, interview, talent/ability, volunteer work, work experience. **Freshman Admission Requirements:** High school diploma is required, and GED is accepted. *Academic units recommended:* 4 English, 2 math, 2 science, 2 foreign language, 2 social studies, 1 history. **Freshman Admission Statistics:** 1,327 applied, 84% admitted, 27% enrolled. **Transfer Admission Requirements:** College transcript(s), essay or personal statement. Minimum college GPA of 2.0 required. **General Admission Information:** Application fee $40. Regular notification is rolling. Non-fall registration accepted. Common Application accepted. Credit and/or placement offered for CEEB Advanced Placement tests.

COSTS AND FINANCIAL AID
Annual tuition $18,400. Room & board $7,150. Required fees $170. Average book expense $1,187. **Required Forms and Deadlines:** FAFSA. Financial aid filing deadline 3/5. **Notification of Awards:** Applicants will be notified of awards on or about rolling. **Types of Aid:** *Need-based scholarships/grants:* Pell, SEOG, state scholarships/grants, private scholarships, the school's own gift aid, Federal Nursing Scholarships. *Loans:* FFEL Subsidized Stafford, FFEL Unsubsidized Stafford, FFEL PLUS, Federal Perkins, Federal Nursing. **Student Employment:** Federal Work-Study Program available. Off-campus job opportunities are good. **Financial Aid Statistics:** 58% freshmen, 41% undergrads receive need-based scholarship or grant aid. 51% freshmen, 49% undergrads receive need-based self-help aid. 48 freshmen, 170 undergrads receive athletic scholarships. Highest amount earned per year from on-campus jobs $1,800.

See page 1330.

REINHARDT COLLEGE

7300 Reinhardt College Circle, Waleska, GA 30183
Phone: 770-720-5526 **E-mail:** admissions@reinhardt.edu
Fax: 770-720-5899 **Website:** www.reinhardt.edu **ACT Code:** 856
Financial Aid Phone: 770-720-5667

This private school, affiliated with the Methodist Church, was founded in 1883. It has a 600-acre campus.

RATINGS
Admissions Selectivity Rating: 60* **Fire Safety Rating:** 81 **Green Rating:** 60*

STUDENTS AND FACULTY
Enrollment: 1,008. **Student Body:** 58% female, 42% male, 12% out-of-state. African American 6%, Caucasian 75%, Hispanic 2%. **Retention and Graduation:** 62% freshmen return for sophomore year. 19% freshmen graduate within 4 years. 35% grads go on to further study within 1 year. 20% grads pursue arts and sciences degrees. 45% grads pursue business degrees. 5% grads pursue law degrees. 5% grads pursue medical degrees. **Faculty:** Student/faculty ratio 10:1. 53 full-time faculty, 57% hold PhDs. 100% faculty teach undergrads.

ACADEMICS
Degrees: Associate, bachelor's. **Academic Requirements:** Arts/fine arts, English (including composition), foreign languages, history, humanities, mathematics, philosophy, sciences (biological or physical), social science, religion. **Classes:** Most classes have 10–19 students. **Majors with Highest Enrollment:** Business/commerce, elementary education and teaching, management information systems. **Disciplines with Highest Percentage of Degrees Awarded:** Business/marketing 31%, education 24%, communication technologies 17%, liberal arts/general studies 9%, biological/life sciences 6%, computer and information sciences 6%. **Special Study Options:** Accelerated program, double major, dual enrollment, external degree program, honors program, independent study, internships, study abroad, teacher certification program.

FACILITIES
Housing: Coed dorms, men's dorms, women's dorms, honors house. **Special Academic Facilities/Equipment:** Funk Heritage Center. **Computers:** 80% of classrooms are wireless, 100% of public computers are PCs, network access in dorm rooms, network access in dorm lounges, online registration, remote student-access to Web through college's connection.

CAMPUS LIFE

Activities: Choral groups, concert band, music ensembles, student government, student newspaper, student-run film society, television station, yearbook. **Organizations:** 5 registered organizations, 3 honor societies, 3 religious organizations. **Athletics (Intercollegiate):** *Men:* Baseball, basketball, cheerleading, cross-country, golf, soccer. *Women:* Basketball, cheerleading, cross-country, soccer, softball, volleyball.

ADMISSIONS

Freshman Academic Profile: 75% in top 50% of high school class. 98% from public high schools. SAT Math middle 50% range 430–540. SAT Critical Reading middle 50% range 450–550. ACT middle 50% range 17–21. TOEFL required of all international applicants, minimum paper TOEFL 500, minimum computer TOEFL 150. **Basis for Candidate Selection:** *Very important factors considered include:* Rigor of secondary school record, standardized test scores. *Important factors considered include:* Interview. *Other factors considered include:* Application essay, character/personal qualities, class rank, extracurricular activities, recommendation(s), talent/ability. **Freshman Admission Requirements:** High school diploma is required, and GED is accepted. *Academic units required:* 4 English, 4 math, 3 science, 3 social studies. *Academic units recommended:* 2 foreign language. **Freshman Admission Statistics:** 3,807 applied, 17% admitted, 46% enrolled. **Transfer Admission Requirements:** College transcript(s), statement of good standing from prior institution(s). Minimum college GPA of 2.0 required. Lowest grade transferable C. **General Admission Information:** Application fee $25. Non-fall registration accepted. Admission may be deferred for a maximum of 2 years. Common Application not accepted. Credit and/or placement offered for CEEB Advanced Placement tests.

COSTS AND FINANCIAL AID

Annual tuition $12,000. Room & board $5,270. Required fees $35. Average book expense $300. **Required Forms and Deadlines:** FAFSA, state aid form. Financial aid filing deadline 5/1. **Notification of Awards:** Applicants will be notified of awards on or about 4/1. **Types of Aid:** *Need-based scholarships/grants:* Pell, SEOG, state scholarships/grants, private scholarships, the school's own gift aid. *Loans:* FFEL Subsidized Stafford, FFEL Unsubsidized Stafford, FFEL PLUS. **Student Employment:** Federal Work-Study Program available. Off-campus job opportunities are good. **Financial Aid Statistics:** 65% freshmen, 65% undergrads receive any aid. Highest amount earned per year from on-campus jobs $2,800.

RENSSELAER POLYTECHNIC INSTITUTE

Best 368

110 Eighth Street, Troy, NY 12180-3590
Phone: 518-276-6216 **E-mail:** admissions@rpi.edu **CEEB Code:** 2757
Fax: 518-276-4072 **Website:** www.rpi.edu **ACT Code:** 2866
Financial Aid Phone: 518-276-6816

This private school was founded in 1824. It has a 284-acre campus.

RATINGS

Admissions Selectivity Rating: 93   **Fire Safety Rating:** 73   **Green Rating:** 88

STUDENTS AND FACULTY

Enrollment: 5,148. **Student Body:** 25% female, 75% male, 55% out-of-state, 3% international (67 countries represented). African American 4%, Asian 11%, Caucasian 74%, Hispanic 6%. **Retention and Graduation:** 94% freshmen return for sophomore year. 64% freshmen graduate within 4 years. 24% grads go on to further study within 1 year. 17% grads pursue arts and sciences degrees. 13% grads pursue business degrees. 2% grads pursue law degrees. 7% grads pursue medical degrees. **Faculty:** Student/faculty ratio 15:1. 393 full-time faculty, 98% hold PhDs. 100% faculty teach undergrads.

ACADEMICS

Degrees: Bachelor's, doctoral, master's. **Academic Requirements:** Computer literacy, English (including composition), humanities, mathematics, sciences (biological or physical), social science. **Classes:** Most classes have 20–29 students. Most lab/discussion sections have 20–29 students. **Majors with Highest Enrollment:** Business; management, marketing, and related support services; computer and information sciences; electrical, electronics, and communications engineering. **Disciplines with Highest Percentage of**

Degrees Awarded: Engineering 53%, computer and information sciences 18%, business/marketing 7%, biological/life sciences 5%, communications/journalism 4%. **Special Study Options:** Accelerated program, cooperative education program, cross-registration, distance learning, double major, dual enrollment, English as a second language (ESL), exchange student program (domestic), honors program, independent study, internships, liberal arts/career combination, student-designed major, study abroad.

FACILITIES

Housing: Coed dorms, apartments for married students, apartments for single students, special housing for disabled students, fraternity/sorority housing, living/learning. **Special Academic Facilities/Equipment:** Shelnutt Art Gallery in the student union, The George M. Low Gallery (museum), Center for Terahertz Research, Nanoscale Science and Engineering Centers (NSEC), center for biotechnology and interdisciplinary studies, Gaerttner Linear Accelerator (LINAC) Laboratory, Hirsch Observatory, RPIdeaLab and Incubator Program (supports student business ventures), Rensselaer Technology Park, Darrin Fresh Water Institute at Lake George, Experimental Media and Performing Arts Center (EMPAC, under construction), lighting research center, social and behavioral research laboratory, O.T. Swanson Multidisciplinary Laboratory, and other research centers and laboratories as described at www.rpi.edu/research/research_centers.html. **Computers:** 46% of classrooms are wired, 33% of classrooms are wireless, 96% of public computers are PCs, 1% of public computers are Macs, 4% of public computers are UNIX, network access in dorm rooms, network access in dorm lounges, online registration, online administrative functions (other than registration), remote student-access to Web through college's connection. Undergraduates are required to own a computer.

CAMPUS LIFE

Activities: Choral groups, concert band, dance, drama/theater, jazz band, literary magazine, music ensembles, musical theater, pep band, radio station, student government, student newspaper, student-run film society, symphony orchestra, television station, yearbook. **Organizations:** 160 registered organizations, 40 honor societies, 10 religious organizations. 32 fraternities (33% men join), 5 sororities (21% women join). **Athletics (Intercollegiate):** *Men:* Baseball, basketball, cross-country, diving, football, golf, ice hockey, lacrosse, soccer, swimming, tennis, track/field (indoor), track/field (outdoor). *Women:* Basketball, cross-country, diving, field hockey, ice hockey, lacrosse, soccer, softball, swimming, tennis, track/field (indoor), track/field (outdoor). **Environmental Initiatives:** Student Sustainability Taskforce. Energy Conservation Program Purchase of Wind Certificates. Sustainability Initiatives in New Construction.

ADMISSIONS

Freshman Academic Profile: 62% in top 10% of high school class, 95% in top 25% of high school class, 100% in top 50% of high school class. 80% from public high schools. SAT Math middle 50% range 650–730. SAT Critical Reading middle 50% range 600–690. SAT Writing middle 50% range 580–670. ACT middle 50% range 25–29. TOEFL required of all international applicants, minimum paper TOEFL 570, minimum computer TOEFL 230. **Basis for Candidate Selection:** *Very important factors considered include:* Academic GPA, class rank, rigor of secondary school record, standardized test scores. *Important factors considered include:* Application essay, character/personal qualities, extracurricular activities, recommendation(s). *Other factors considered include:* Alumni/ae relation, geographical residence, level of applicant's interest, racial/ethnic status, talent/ability, volunteer work, work experience. **Freshman Admission Requirements:** High school diploma is required, and GED is accepted. *Academic units required:* 4 English, 4 math, 3 science, 2 social studies. *Academic units recommended:* 4 science, 3 social studies. **Freshman Admission Statistics:** 6,875 applied, 28% admitted, 28% enrolled. **Transfer Admission Requirements:** College transcript(s), statement of good standing from prior institution(s). Minimum college GPA of 3.0 required. Lowest grade transferable C. **General Admission Information:** Application fee $70. Early decision application deadline 11/1. Regular application deadline 1/15. Regular notification 3/15. Non-fall registration accepted. Admission may be deferred for a maximum of 1 year. Credit and/or placement offered for CEEB Advanced Placement tests.

COSTS AND FINANCIAL AID

Annual tuition $36,950. Room and board $10,730. Required fees $1,040. Average book expense $1,802. **Required Forms and Deadlines:** FAFSA, state aid form. Financial aid filing deadline 2/15. **Notification of Awards:** Applicants will be notified of awards on or about 3/25. **Types of Aid:** *Need-based scholarships/grants:* Pell, SEOG, state scholarships/grants, private scholarships, the school's own gift aid, Gates Millennium Scholarship. *Loans:* FFEL Subsidized Stafford, FFEL Unsubsidized Stafford, FFEL PLUS, Federal Perkins, college/university loans from institutional funds. **Financial Aid Statistics:** 66% freshmen, 67% undergrads receive need-based scholarship or grant aid. 42% freshmen, 42% undergrads receive need-based self-help aid. 7 freshmen, 28 undergrads receive athletic scholarships. 99% freshmen, 92%

undergrads receive any aid. Highest amount earned per year from on-campus jobs $2,000.

See page 1332.

RHODE ISLAND COLLEGE

Office of Undergraduate Admissions, 600 Mount Pleasant Avenue, Providence, RI 02908
Phone: 401-456-8234 **E-mail:** admissions@ric.edu **CEEB Code:** 3724
Fax: 401-456-8817 **Website:** www.ric.edu
Financial Aid Phone: 401-456-8033

This public school was founded in 1854. It has a 170-acre campus.

RATINGS
Admissions Selectivity Rating: 60*   **Fire Safety Rating:** 60*   **Green Rating:** 60*

STUDENTS AND FACULTY
Enrollment: 6,531. **Student Body:** 68% female, 32% male. African American 4%, Asian 2%, Caucasian 77%, Hispanic 5%. **Retention and Graduation:** 74% freshmen return for sophomore year. 14% freshmen graduate within 4 years. **Faculty:** Student/faculty ratio 14:1. 306 full-time faculty, 85% hold PhDs. 90% faculty teach undergrads.

ACADEMICS
Degrees: Bachelor's, doctoral, master's, post-master's certificate. **Academic Requirements:** Arts/fine arts, English (including composition), history, mathematics, sciences (biological or physical), social science. **Classes:** Most classes have 20–29 students. **Majors with Highest Enrollment:** Communications studies/speech commnnication and rhetoric, history, psychology. **Disciplines with Highest Percentage of Degrees Awarded:** Education 33%, psychology 12%, business/marketing 10%, health professions and related sciences 8%, social sciences 7%. **Special Study Options:** Double major, exchange student program (domestic), honors program, independent study, internships, student-designed major, study abroad, teacher certification program, weekend college.

FACILITIES
Housing: Coed dorms, women's dorms, special housing for disabled students. **Special Academic Facilities/Equipment:** Art gallery, curriculum resource center, center for economic education, on-campus elementary school, closed-circuit TV studios.
Computers: Network access in dorm rooms.

CAMPUS LIFE
Activities: Choral groups, concert band, dance, drama/theater, jazz band, literary magazine, music ensembles, musical theater, radio station, student government, student newspaper, symphony orchestra, television station, yearbook. **Organizations:** 60 registered organizations, 4 honor societies, 3 religious organizations. 1 fraternity, 1 sorority. **Athletics (Intercollegiate):** *Men:* Baseball, basketball, cross-country, soccer, tennis, track/field (outdoor), wrestling. *Women:* Basketball, cross-country, gymnastics, soccer, softball, tennis, track/field (outdoor), volleyball.

ADMISSIONS
Freshman Academic Profile: SAT Math middle 50% range 430–540. SAT Critical Reading middle 50% range 440–550. TOEFL required of all international applicants, minimum paper TOEFL 550. **Basis for Candidate Selection:** *Very important factors considered include:* Class rank, rigor of secondary school record. *Important factors considered include:* Application essay, recommendation(s). *Other factors considered include:* Alumni/ae relation, extracurricular activities, interview, standardized test scores, talent/ability, volunteer work, work experience. **Freshman Admission Requirements:** High school diploma is required, and GED is accepted. *Academic units required:* 4 English, 3 math, 2 science (2 science labs), 2 foreign language, 2 social studies, 4 academic electives, 0.5 art, 0.5 computer literacy. **Freshman Admission Statistics:** 2,901 applied, 72% admitted, 46% enrolled. **Transfer Admission Requirements:** College transcript(s). Lowest grade transferable C. **General Admission Information:** Application fee $25. Regular application deadline 5/1. Regular notification is rolling. Non-fall registration accepted. Admission may be deferred for a maximum of 1 semester. Common Application accepted. Credit and/or placement offered for CEEB Advanced Placement tests.

COSTS AND FINANCIAL AID
Annual in-state tuition $3,700. Out-of-state tuition $9,500. Room & board $6,136. Required fees $675. Average book expense $650. **Required Forms and Deadlines:** FAFSA, institution's own financial aid form. Financial aid filing deadline 3/1. **Notification of Awards:** Applicants will be notified of awards on a rolling basis beginning on or about 3/15. **Types of Aid:** *Need-based*

scholarships/grants: Pell, SEOG, state scholarships/grants, private scholarships, the school's own gift aid. *Loans:* FFEL Subsidized Stafford, FFEL Unsubsidized Stafford, FFEL PLUS, Federal Perkins, state loans. **Student Employment:** Federal Work-Study Program available. Institutional employment available. Off-campus job opportunities are good. **Financial Aid Statistics:** Highest amount earned per year from on-campus jobs $1,000.

RHODE ISLAND SCHOOL OF DESIGN

2 College Street, Providence, RI 02903
Phone: 401-454-6300 **E-mail:** admissions@risd.edu **CEEB Code:** 3726
Fax: 401-454-6309 **Website:** www.risd.edu **ACT Code:** 3812
Financial Aid Phone: 401-454-6661

This private school was founded in 1877. It has a 13-acre campus.

RATINGS
Admissions Selectivity Rating: 90   **Fire Safety Rating:** 60*   **Green Rating:** 60*

STUDENTS AND FACULTY
Enrollment: 1,882. **Student Body:** 66% female, 34% male, 12% international (44 countries represented). African American 2%, Asian 14%, Caucasian 51%, Hispanic 5%. **Faculty:** Student/faculty ratio 11:1. 146 full-time faculty. 100% faculty teach undergrads.

ACADEMICS
Degrees: Bachelor's, master's. **Academic Requirements:** Arts/fine arts, English (including composition), history, philosophy, social science. **Majors with Highest Enrollment:** Graphic design, illustration, industrial design. **Disciplines with Highest Percentage of Degrees Awarded:** Visual and performing arts 90%, architecture 10%. **Special Study Options:** Continuing education program, cross-registration, exchange student program (domestic), independent study, internships, study abroad. 6-week pre-college summer program for secondary school students, summer workshops for undergraduate credit, 6-week winter session study abroad courses.

FACILITIES
Housing: Coed dorms, apartments for single students. **Special Academic Facilities/Equipment:** Art museum with over 45 galleries; extensive facilities for glassblowing, metalsmithing, lithography, sculpture, painting, and other art disciplines; nature lab. **Computers:** 35% of public computers are PCs, 65% of public computers are Macs, network access in dorm rooms, network access in dorm lounges, online administrative functions (other than registration), remote student-access to Web through college's connection.

CAMPUS LIFE
Activities: Drama/theater, literary magazine, student government, student newspaper, student-run film society, yearbook. **Organizations:** 35 registered organizations, 5 religious organizations.

ADMISSIONS
Freshman Academic Profile: 28% in top 10% of high school class, 54% in top 25% of high school class, 91% in top 50% of high school class. 60% from public high schools. SAT Math middle 50% range 550–670. SAT Critical Reading middle 50% range 530–660. TOEFL required of all international applicants, minimum paper TOEFL 580, minimum computer TOEFL 237. **Basis for Candidate Selection:** *Very important factors considered include:* Rigor of secondary school record, talent/ability. *Important factors considered include:* Application essay, character/personal qualities, recommendation(s), standardized test scores. *Other factors considered include:* Alumni/ae relation, class rank, extracurricular activities, racial/ethnic status, volunteer work, work experience. **Freshman Admission Requirements:** High school diploma is required, and GED is accepted. **Freshman Admission Statistics:** 2,511 applied, 34% admitted, 47% enrolled. **Transfer Admission Requirements:** College transcript(s), essay or personal statement. Lowest grade transferable C. **General Admission Information:** Application fee $50. Regular application deadline 2/15. Regular notification 4/1. Non-fall registration accepted. Admission may be deferred for a maximum of 1 year. Common Application not accepted. Credit and/or placement offered for CEEB Advanced Placement tests.

COSTS AND FINANCIAL AID
Annual tuition $27,510. Room & board $7,709. Required fees $465. Average book expense $2,200. **Required Forms and Deadlines:** FAFSA, CSS/Financial Aid PROFILE. Financial aid filing deadline 2/15. **Notification of Awards:** Applicants will be notified of awards on or about 4/1. **Types of Aid:** *Need-based scholarships/grants:* Pell, SEOG, state scholarships/grants, private scholarships, the school's own gift aid. *Loans:* FFEL Subsidized Stafford, FFEL

Unsubsidized Stafford, FFEL PLUS, Federal Perkins. **Student Employment:** Federal Work-Study Program available. Institutional employment available. Off-campus job opportunities are good. **Financial Aid Statistics:** 27% freshmen, 44% undergrads receive need-based scholarship or grant aid. 42% freshmen, 48% undergrads receive need-based self-help aid. Highest amount earned per year from on-campus jobs $1,100.

RHODES COLLEGE

Office of Admissions, 2000 North Parkway, Memphis, TN 38112
Phone: 901-843-3700 **E-mail:** adminfo@rhodes.edu **CEEB Code:** 1730
Fax: 901-843-3631 **Website:** www.rhodes.edu **ACT Code:** 4008
Financial Aid Phone: 901-843-3810

This private school, affiliated with the Presbyterian Church, was founded in 1848. It has a 100-acre campus.

RATINGS
Admissions Selectivity Rating: 94   **Fire Safety Rating:** 81   **Green Rating:** 82

STUDENTS AND FACULTY
Enrollment: 1,672. **Student Body:** 59% female, 41% male, 73% out-of-state. African American 6%, Asian 4%, Caucasian 84%, Hispanic 2%. **Retention and Graduation:** 86% freshmen return for sophomore year. 75% freshmen graduate within 4 years. 45% grads go on to further study within 1 year. 24% grads pursue arts and sciences degrees. 5% grads pursue business degrees. 9% grads pursue law degrees. 5% grads pursue medical degrees. **Faculty:** Student/faculty ratio 11:1. 144 full-time faculty, 94% hold PhDs. 100% faculty teach undergrads.

ACADEMICS
Degrees: Bachelor's, master's. **Academic Requirements:** Arts/fine arts, cultural perspective, English (including composition), foreign languages, history, human interaction and contemporary institutions, humanities, literature, mathematics, meaning and value, natural science, philosophy, physical education, sciences (biological or physical), senior seminar in the major, social science, writing. Engage in 1 for-credit activity broadening connections between the classroom and the world. **Classes:** Most classes have 10–19 students. Most lab/discussion sections have 20–29 students. **Majors with Highest Enrollment:** Biology/biological sciences, business administration/management, English language and literature. **Disciplines with Highest Percentage of Degrees Awarded:** Social sciences 29%, biological/life sciences 11%, English 11%, history 10%, business/marketing 10%. **Special Study Options:** Cooperative education program, cross-registration, double major, dual enrollment, exchange student program (domestic), honors program, independent study, internships, liberal arts/career combination, student-designed major, study abroad. Dual degree: Master of education, master of science in nursing, master of science in biomedical engineering.

FACILITIES
Housing: Coed dorms, men's dorms, women's dorms, apartments for single students, substance-free, quiet study, restricted visitation, nonsmoking, special interest, town houses. **Special Academic Facilities/Equipment:** Art gallery, anthropology museum, 2 reflecting telescopes, electron microscopes, cell culture lab, nuclear magnetic resonance instrument. **Computers:** 1% of classrooms are wired, 95% of classrooms are wireless, 98% of public computers are PCs, 2% of public computers are Macs, network access in dorm rooms, network access in dorm lounges, online registration, online administrative functions (other than registration), remote student-access to Web through college's connection.

CAMPUS LIFE
Activities: Choral groups, dance, drama/theater, literary magazine, music ensembles, musical theater, pep band, student government, student newspaper, student-run film society, symphony orchestra, yearbook. **Organizations:** 90 registered organizations, 14 honor societies, 8 religious organizations. 7 fraternities (48% men join), 6 sororities (52% women join). **Athletics (Intercollegiate):** *Men:* Baseball, basketball, cross-country, football, golf, soccer, swimming, tennis, track/field (outdoor). *Women:* Basketball, cross-country, field hockey, golf, soccer, softball, swimming, tennis, track/field (outdoor), volleyball. **Environmental Initiatives:** $500,000 Andrew W. Mellon Foundation grant to expand Environmental Studies initiatives through

community partnerships. Comprehensive campus-wide recycling program. Centralized energy management system and Green Power Switch.

ADMISSIONS
Freshman Academic Profile: 47% in top 10% of high school class, 78% in top 25% of high school class, 95% in top 50% of high school class. 50% from public high schools. SAT Math middle 50% range 590–690. SAT Critical Reading middle 50% range 590–690. ACT middle 50% range 26–30. TOEFL required of all international applicants, minimum paper TOEFL 550, minimum computer TOEFL 213. **Basis for Candidate Selection:** *Very important factors considered include:* Academic GPA, class rank, rigor of secondary school record. *Important factors considered include:* Alumni/ae relation, application essay, character/personal qualities, racial/ethnic status, recommendation(s), standardized test scores. *Other factors considered include:* Extracurricular activities, first generation, geographical residence, interview, level of applicant's interest, state residency, talent/ability, volunteer work, work experience. **Freshman Admission Requirements:** High school diploma is required, and GED is accepted. *Academic units required:* 4 English, 3 math, 2 science (2 science labs), 2 foreign language, 2 social studies, 3 academic electives. *Academic units recommended:* 4 math. **Freshman Admission Statistics:** 3,786 applied, 49% admitted, 24% enrolled. **Transfer Admission Requirements:** High school transcript, college transcript(s), essay or personal statement, standardized test score, statement of good standing from prior institution(s). Minimum college GPA of 2.5 required. Lowest grade transferable C-. **General Admission Information:** Application fee $45. Early decision application deadline 11/1. Regular notification 4/1. Regular decision 12/1 for spring semester. Non-fall registration accepted. Admission may be deferred for a maximum of 1 year. Credit and/or placement offered for CEEB Advanced Placement tests.

COSTS AND FINANCIAL AID
Annual tuition $28,232. Room and board $7,468. Required fees $310. Average book expense $904. **Required Forms and Deadlines:** FAFSA, CSS/Financial Aid PROFILE, Noncustodial PROFILE. Financial aid filing deadline 3/1. **Types of Aid:** *Need-based scholarships/grants:* Pell, SEOG, state scholarships/grants, private scholarships, the school's own gift aid. *Loans:* FFEL Subsidized Stafford, FFEL Unsubsidized Stafford, FFEL PLUS, Federal Perkins. **Student Employment:** Federal Work-Study Program available. Institutional employment available. Off-campus job opportunities are good. **Financial Aid Statistics:** 46% freshmen, 39% undergrads receive need-based scholarship or grant aid. 29% freshmen, 25% undergrads receive need-based self-help aid.

RICE UNIVERSITY

MS 17 PO Box 1892, Houston, TX 77251-1892
Phone: 713-348-7423 **CEEB Code:** 6609
Fax: 713-348-5952 **Website:** www.rice.edu **ACT Code:** 4152
Financial Aid Phone: 713-348-4958

This private school was founded in 1912. It has a 300-acre campus.

RATINGS
Admissions Selectivity Rating: 98   **Fire Safety Rating:** 60*   **Green Rating:** 60*

STUDENTS AND FACULTY
Enrollment: 2,988. **Student Body:** 48% female, 52% male, 47% out-of-state, 3% international (32 countries represented). African American 7%, Asian 16%, Caucasian 54%, Hispanic 12%. **Retention and Graduation:** 96% freshmen return for sophomore year. 76% freshmen graduate within 4 years. 43% grads go on to further study within 1 year. 13% grads pursue arts and sciences degrees. 2% grads pursue business degrees. 6% grads pursue law degrees. 13% grads pursue medical degrees. **Faculty:** Student/faculty ratio 5:1. 567 full-time faculty, 95% hold PhDs. 91% faculty teach undergrads.

ACADEMICS
Degrees: Bachelor's, doctoral, master's. **Academic Requirements:** 12 semester hours are required in each of 3 areas of study: Humanities, social sciences, natural sciences/engineering. **Classes:** Most classes have 10–19 students. **Majors with Highest Enrollment:** Biology/biological sciences, economics, political science and government. **Disciplines with Highest Percentage of Degrees Awarded:** Social sciences 20%, engineering 13%, biological/life sciences 8%, visual and performing arts 7%, English 6%. **Special**

Study Options: Cross-registration, double major, dual enrollment, honors program, independent study, internships, liberal arts/career combination, student-designed major, study abroad, teacher certification program. 8-year guaranteed medical school program with The Baylor College of Medicine.

FACILITIES

Housing: Coed dorms, special housing for disabled students. All undergraduate students are automatically assigned to 1 of 9 (coed) residential colleges and keep this affiliation regardless of whether they live in the colleges or not. **Special Academic Facilities/Equipment:** Art gallery, museum, media center, language labs, computer labs, civil engineering lab, observatory and NASA equipment for students in space physics courses. **Computers:** 10% of classrooms are wired, 19% of classrooms are wireless, 60% of public computers are PCs, 14% of public computers are Macs, 26% of public computers are UNIX, network access in dorm rooms, network access in dorm lounges, online registration, online administrative functions (other than registration), support for handheld computing, remote student-access to Web through college's connection.

CAMPUS LIFE

Activities: Choral groups, concert band, dance, drama/theater, jazz band, literary magazine, marching band, music ensembles, musical theater, opera, pep band, radio station, student government, student newspaper, student-run film society, symphony orchestra, television station. **Organizations:** 208 registered organizations, 11 honor societies, 14 religious organizations. **Athletics (Intercollegiate):** *Men:* Baseball, basketball, cross-country, football, golf, tennis, track/field (indoor), track/field (outdoor). *Women:* Basketball, cross-country, soccer, swimming, tennis, track/field (indoor), track/field (outdoor), volleyball.

ADMISSIONS

Freshman Academic Profile: 88% in top 10% of high school class, 96% in top 25% of high school class, 99% in top 50% of high school class. 71% from public high schools. SAT Math middle 50% range 680–780. SAT Critical Reading middle 50% range 650–760. SAT Writing middle 50% range 640–740. ACT middle 50% range 30–34. TOEFL required of all international applicants, minimum paper TOEFL 600, minimum computer TOEFL 250. **Basis for Candidate Selection:** *Very important factors considered include:* Academic GPA, application essay, character/personal qualities, class rank, extracurricular activities, recommendation(s), rigor of secondary school record, standardized test scores, talent/ability. *Other factors considered include:* Alumni/ae relation, first generation, geographical residence, interview, level of applicant's interest, racial/ethnic status, state residency, volunteer work, work experience. **Freshman Admission Requirements:** High school diploma or equivalent is not required. *Academic units required:* 4 English, 3 math, 2 science (2 science labs), 2 foreign language, 2 social studies, 3 academic electives. *Academic units recommended:* 4 English, 4 math, 4 science (3 science labs), 4 foreign language, 2 social studies, 2 academic electives. **Freshman Admission Statistics:** 7,890 applied, 25% admitted, 37% enrolled. **Transfer Admission Requirements:** High school transcript, college transcript(s), essay or personal statement, standardized test score, statement of good standing from prior institution(s). Minimum college GPA of 3.2 required. Lowest grade transferable C-. **General Admission Information:** Application fee $50. Early decision application deadline 11/1. Regular application deadline 1/10. Regular notification 4/1. Non-fall registration not accepted. Admission may be deferred for a maximum of 2 years. Common Application accepted. Credit offered for CEEB Advanced Placement tests.

COSTS AND FINANCIAL AID

Annual tuition $25,606. Room and board $10,250. Required fees $500. Average book expense $800. **Required Forms and Deadlines:** FAFSA, CSS/Financial Aid PROFILE, Noncustodial PROFILE, Business/Farm Supplement. Financial aid filing deadline 3/1. **Notification of Awards:** Applicants will be notified of awards on or about 4/15. **Types of Aid:** *Need-based scholarships/grants:* Pell, SEOG, state scholarships/grants, private scholarships, the school's own gift aid. *Loans:* FFEL Subsidized Stafford, FFEL Unsubsidized Stafford, FFEL PLUS, Federal Perkins, college/university loans from institutional funds. **Financial Aid Statistics:** 40% freshmen, 34% undergrads receive need-based scholarship or grant aid. 23% freshmen, 26% undergrads receive need-based self-help aid. 58 freshmen, 286 undergrads receive athletic scholarships. 65% freshmen, 63% undergrads receive any aid.

THE RICHARD STOCKTON COLLEGE OF NEW JERSEY

Jim Leeds Road, PO Box 195, Pomona, NJ 08240-0195
Phone: 609-652-4261 **E-mail:** admissions@stockton.edu **CEEB Code:** 2889
Fax: 609-748-5541 **Website:** www.stockton.edu
Financial Aid Phone: 609-652-4201

This public school was founded in 1969. It has a 1,600-acre campus.

RATINGS

Admissions Selectivity Rating: 81   **Fire Safety Rating:** 89   **Green Rating:** 60*

STUDENTS AND FACULTY

Enrollment: 6,560. **Student Body:** 58% female, 42% male, 1% out-of-state, (36 countries represented). African American 8%, Asian 5%, Caucasian 80%, Hispanic 7%. **Retention and Graduation:** 83% freshmen return for sophomore year. 36% freshmen graduate within 4 years. 20% grads go on to further study within 1 year. 38% grads pursue arts and sciences degrees. 15% grads pursue business degrees. 3% grads pursue law degrees. 11% grads pursue medical degrees. **Faculty:** Student/faculty ratio 19:1. 242 full-time faculty, 90% hold PhDs. 97% faculty teach undergrads.

ACADEMICS

Degrees: Bachelor's, doctoral, master's, post-bachelor's certificate. **Academic Requirements:** Arts/fine arts, English (including composition), history, mathematics, values/ethics, international/multicultural general studies core. **Classes:** Most classes have 20–29 students. Most lab/discussion sections have fewer than 10 students. **Majors with Highest Enrollment:** Business administration and management; criminology; psychology. **Disciplines with Highest Percentage of Degrees Awarded:** Business/marketing 18%, social sciences 16%, psychology 12%, biological/life sciences 11%, education 10%. **Special Study Options:** Cross-registration, distance learning, double major, dual enrollment, honors program, independent study, internships, liberal arts/career combination, service learning, student-designed major, study abroad, teacher certification program.

FACILITIES

Housing: Coed dorms, special housing for disabled students, wellness (substance-free) housing, academic units. **Special Academic Facilities/Equipment:** Observatory, Nacote Creek field station, Holocaust Resource Center. **Computers:** 100% of classrooms are wired, 90% of classrooms are wireless, 90% of public computers are PCs, 5% of public computers are Macs, 5% of public computers are UNIX, network access in dorm rooms, online registration, online administrative functions (other than registration), remote student-access to Web through college's connection.

CAMPUS LIFE

Activities: Choral groups, concert band, dance, drama/theater, literary magazine, music ensembles, musical theater, pep band, radio station, student government, student newspaper, television station, yearbook. **Organizations:** 86 registered organizations, 5 honor societies, 4 religious organizations. 9 fraternities (5% men join), 9 sororities (5% women join). **Athletics (Intercollegiate):** *Men:* Baseball, basketball, cheerleading, cross-country, lacrosse, soccer, track/field (indoor), track/field (outdoor). *Women:* Basketball, cheerleading, crew/rowing, cross-country, field hockey, soccer, softball, tennis, track/field (indoor), track/field (outdoor), volleyball.

ADMISSIONS

Freshman Academic Profile: 19% in top 10% of high school class, 52% in top 25% of high school class, 93% in top 50% of high school class. 74% from public high schools. SAT Math middle 50% range 500–580. SAT Critical Reading middle 50% range 480–570. SAT Writing middle 50% range 471–560. ACT middle 50% range 18–21. TOEFL required of all international applicants, minimum paper TOEFL 550, minimum computer TOEFL 217. **Basis for Candidate Selection:** *Very important factors considered include:* Class rank, rigor of secondary school record, standardized test scores. *Important factors considered include:* Academic GPA, extracurricular activities. *Other factors considered include:* Alumni/ae relation, application essay, character/personal qualities, first generation, racial/ethnic status, recommendation(s), talent/ability, volunteer work, work experience. **Freshman Admission Requirements:** High school diploma is required, and GED is accepted. *Academic units required:* 4 English, 3 math, 2 science (2 science labs), 2 social studies, 2 history, 5 academic electives. *Academic units recommended:* 2 foreign language, 2 social studies, 2 history. **Freshman Admission Statistics:** 3,731 applied, 53% admitted, 41% enrolled. **Transfer Admission Requirements:** College transcript(s), minimum college GPA of 2.5 required. Lowest grade transferable C. **General Admission Information:** Application fee $50. Regular application deadline 5/1. Regular notification is rolling. Nonfall registration accepted. Credit and/or placement offered for CEEB Advanced Placement tests.

COSTS AND FINANCIAL AID

Annual in-state tuition $5,956. Annual out-of-state tuition $10,550. Room and board $9,077. Required fees $3,135. Average book expense $1,200. **Required Forms and Deadlines:** FAFSA. Financial aid filing deadline 3/1. **Notification of Awards:** Applicants will be notified of awards on a rolling basis beginning on or about 4/1. **Types of Aid:** *Need-based scholarships/grants:* Pell, SEOG, state scholarships/grants. *Loans:* FFEL Subsidized Stafford, FFEL Unsubsidized Stafford, FFEL PLUS, Federal Perkins, state loans. **Student Employment:** Federal Work-Study Program available. Institutional employment available. Off-campus job opportunities are excellent. **Financial Aid Statistics:** 30% freshmen, 30% undergrads receive need-based scholarship or grant aid. 57% freshmen, 52% undergrads receive need-based self-help aid. 80% freshmen, 77% undergrads receive any aid. Highest amount earned per year from on-campus jobs $1,393.

See page 1334.

RICHMOND—THE AMERICAN INTERNATIONAL UNIVERSITY IN LONDON

US Office of Admissions, 343 Congress Street Suite 3100, Boston, MA 02210
Phone: 617-450-5617 **E-mail:** us_admissions@richmond.ac.uk **CEEB Code:** 0823
Fax: 617-450-5601 **Website:** www.richmond.ac.uk **ACT Code:** 5244
Financial Aid Phone: 011-44-20-8332-8244

This private school was founded in 1972. It has a 6-acre campus.

RATINGS

Admissions Selectivity Rating: 86   **Fire Safety Rating:** 60*   **Green Rating:** 60*

STUDENTS AND FACULTY

Enrollment: 874. **Student Body:** 55% female, 45% male. **Retention and Graduation:** 72% freshmen return for sophomore year. 35% grads go on to further study within 1 year. **Faculty:** Student/faculty ratio 12:1. 41 full-time faculty, 85% hold PhDs. 100% faculty teach undergrads.

ACADEMICS

Degrees: Associate, bachelor's, master's, post-bachelor's certificate, terminal. **Academic Requirements:** Arts/fine arts, computer literacy, English (including composition), foreign languages, history, humanities, mathematics, philosophy, sciences (biological or physical), social science. **Classes:** Most classes have 10–19 students. **Majors with Highest Enrollment:** Business administration/management, communications studies/speech communication and rhetoric, international relations and affairs. **Disciplines with Highest Percentage of Degrees Awarded:** Business/marketing 44%, social sciences 19%, communication technologies 16%, computer and information sciences 8%, psychology 6%. **Special Study Options:** English as a second language (ESL), independent study, internships, joint engineering program with George Washington University, liberal arts/career combination, study abroad.

FACILITIES

Housing: Coed dorms, men's dorms, women's dorms. **Computers:** 100% of classrooms are wired, 100% of classrooms are wireless, 85% of public computers are PCs, 10% of public computers are Macs, 5% of public computers are UNIX, network access in dorm rooms, network access in dorm lounges, online administrative functions (other than registration), remote student-access to Web through college's connection.

CAMPUS LIFE

Activities: Choral groups, dance, drama/theater, literary magazine, music ensembles, musical theater, student government, student newspaper, yearbook. **Organizations:** 1 honor society. **Athletics (Intercollegiate):** *Men:* Rugby, soccer. *Women:* Rugby.

ADMISSIONS

Freshman Academic Profile: 29% in top 10% of high school class, 40% in top 25% of high school class, 94% in top 50% of high school class. 60% from public high schools. SAT Math middle 50% range 488–610. SAT Critical Reading middle 50% range 495–625. ACT middle 50% range 24–28. TOEFL required of all international applicants, minimum paper TOEFL 550, minimum computer TOEFL 230. **Basis for Candidate Selection:** *Very important factors considered include:* Academic GPA, application essay, recommendation(s), rigor of secondary school record. *Important factors considered include:* Extracurricular activities. *Other factors considered include:* Alumni/ae relation, character/personal qualities, interview, standardized test

scores, talent/ability. **Freshman Admission Requirements:** High school diploma is required, and GED is accepted. *Academic units required:* 4 English, 3 math, 3 science. **Freshman Admission Statistics:** 1,232 applied, 52% admitted, 32% enrolled. **Transfer Admission Requirements:** College transcript(s), essay or personal statement, statement of good standing from prior institution(s). Minimum college GPA of 2.5 required. Lowest grade transferable C. **General Admission Information:** Application fee $50. Regular application deadline 8/1. Regular notification is rolling. Non-fall registration accepted. Admission may be deferred for a maximum of 1 year. Credit and/or placement offered for CEEB Advanced Placement tests.

COSTS AND FINANCIAL AID

Annual tuition $27,000. Room and board $12,900. Average book expense $1,000. **Required Forms and Deadlines:** FAFSA. Financial aid filing deadline 3/15. **Notification of Awards:** Applicants will be notified of awards on or about 3/15. **Types of Aid:** *Need-based scholarships/grants:* Private scholarships, the school's own gift aid. *Loans:* FFEL Subsidized Stafford, FFEL Unsubsidized Stafford, FFEL PLUS, college/university loans from institutional funds. **Student Employment:** Off-campus job opportunities are good. **Financial Aid Statistics:** 80% freshmen, 70% undergrads receive any aid. Highest amount earned per year from on-campus jobs $1,500.

RIDER UNIVERSITY

2083 Lawrenceville Road, Lawrenceville, NJ 08648-3099
Phone: 609-896-5042 **E-mail:** admissions@rider.edu **CEEB Code:** 2758
Fax: 609-895-6645 **Website:** www.rider.edu **ACT Code:** 2590
Financial Aid Phone: 609-896-5360

This private school was founded in 1865. It has a 280-acre campus.

RATINGS

Admissions Selectivity Rating: 75   **Fire Safety Rating:** 60*   **Green Rating:** 71

STUDENTS AND FACULTY

Enrollment: 4,369. **Student Body:** 60% female, 40% male, 25% out-of-state, 1% international (46 countries represented). African American 9%, Asian 4%, Caucasian 56%, Hispanic 5%. **Retention and Graduation:** 79% freshmen return for sophomore year. 46% freshmen graduate within 4 years. 17% grads go on to further study within 1 year. 6% grads pursue arts and sciences degrees. 11% grads pursue business degrees. 10% grads pursue law degrees. 6% grads pursue medical degrees. **Faculty:** Student/faculty ratio 13:1. 236 full-time faculty, 96% hold PhDs. 84% faculty teach undergrads.

ACADEMICS

Degrees: Associate, bachelor's, master's, post-master's certificate. **Academic Requirements:** Computer literacy, English (including composition), history, humanities, mathematics, sciences (biological or physical), social science. **Classes:** Most classes have 10–19 students. Most lab/discussion sections have 10–19 students. **Majors with Highest Enrollment:** Accounting, business administration/management, elementary education and teaching. **Disciplines with Highest Percentage of Degrees Awarded:** Business/marketing 32%, education 18%, English 13%, visual and performing arts 7%, psychology 6%. **Special Study Options:** Cross-registration, double major, English as a second language (ESL), honors program, independent study, internships, liberal arts/career combination, study abroad, teacher certification program, weekend college, learning community.

FACILITIES

Housing: Coed dorms, women's dorms, apartments for single students, special housing for disabled students, fraternity/sorority housing, suites, wellness, quite, first-year experience, science, learning community. **Special Academic Facilities/Equipment:** Art gallery, Holocaust/Genocide Resource Center. **Computers:** 75% of public computers are PCs, 25% of public computers are Macs, network access in dorm rooms, network access in dorm lounges, online registration, online administrative functions (other than registration), remote student-access to Web through college's connection.

CAMPUS LIFE

Activities: Choral groups, concert band, dance, drama/theater, literary magazine, music ensembles, musical theater, opera, pep band, radio station, student government, student newspaper, student-run film society, television station, yearbook. **Organizations:** 87 registered organizations, 24 honor societies, 6 religious organizations. 7 fraternities (10% men join), 7 sororities (9% women join). **Athletics (Intercollegiate):** *Men:* Baseball, basketball, cheerleading, cross-country, diving, golf, soccer, swimming, tennis, track/field (outdoor), wrestling. *Women:* Basketball, cheerleading, cross-country, diving, field hockey, soccer, softball, swimming, tennis, track/field (outdoor), volleyball. **Environmental Initiatives:** Signing the American College & University Presidents Climate Commitment. Energy and Sustainability Steering Committee established to implement strategic plan establishing sustainability initiatives for the university. Building LEED Certified new residence hall.

ADMISSIONS

Freshman Academic Profile: 13% in top 10% of high school class, 40% in top 25% of high school class, 75% in top 50% of high school class. 85% from public high schools. SAT Math middle 50% range 480–590. SAT Critical Reading middle 50% range 470–570. SAT Writing middle 50% range 470–570. ACT middle 50% range 20–24. TOEFL required of all international applicants, minimum paper TOEFL 563, minimum computer TOEFL 202. **Basis for Candidate Selection:** *Very important factors considered include:* Academic GPA, application essay, recommendation(s), rigor of secondary school record, standardized test scores. *Important factors considered include:* Level of applicant's interest. *Other factors considered include:* Alumni/ae relation, character/personal qualities, class rank, extracurricular activities, geographical residence, interview, state residency, talent/ability, volunteer work, work experience. **Freshman Admission Requirements:** High school diploma is required, and GED is accepted. *Academic units required:* 4 English, 3 math. *Academic units recommended:* 4 math, 4 science (2 science labs), 2 foreign language, 2 social studies, 2 history. **Freshman Admission Statistics:** 5,006 applied, 79% admitted, 26% enrolled. **Transfer Admission Requirements:** College transcript(s), essay or personal statement. Minimum college GPA of 2.5 required. Lowest grade transferable C. **General Admission Information:** Application fee $45. Early decision application deadline 11/15. Regular notification within 3 to 4 weeks of receipt of application. Non-fall registration accepted. Admission may be deferred for a maximum of 1 year. Credit and/or placement offered for CEEB Advanced Placement tests.

COSTS AND FINANCIAL AID

Annual tuition $24,220. Room & board $9,280. Required fees $570. Average book expense $1,400. **Required Forms and Deadlines:** FAFSA. Financial aid filing deadline 3/1. **Notification of Awards:** Applicants will be notified of awards on a rolling basis beginning on or about 3/15. **Types of Aid:** *Need-based scholarships/grants:* Pell, SEOG, state scholarships/grants, private scholarships, the school's own gift aid. *Loans:* FFEL Subsidized Stafford, FFEL Unsubsidized Stafford, FFEL PLUS, Federal Perkins, state loans, college/university loans from institutional funds, alternative loans. **Financial Aid Statistics:** 67% freshmen, 64% undergrads receive need-based scholarship or grant aid. 54% freshmen, 50% undergrads receive need-based self-help aid. 68 freshmen, 243 undergrads receive athletic scholarships. 85% freshmen, 66% undergrads receive any aid. Highest amount earned per year from on-campus jobs $6,195.

RINGLING SCHOOL OF ART & DESIGN

2700 North Tamiami Trail, Sarasota, FL 34234-5895
Phone: 941-351-5100 **E-mail:** admissions@ringling.edu **CEEB Code:** 5573
Fax: 941-359-7517 **Website:** www.ringling.edu **ACT Code:** 6724
Financial Aid Phone: 941-359-7534

This private school was founded in 1931. It has a 34-acre campus.

RATINGS

Admissions Selectivity Rating: 60*   **Fire Safety Rating:** 77   **Green Rating:** 76

STUDENTS AND FACULTY

Enrollment: 1,090. **Student Body:** 51% female, 49% male, 45% out-of-state, 5% international (23 countries represented). African American 3%, Asian 4%, Caucasian 77%, Hispanic 11%, Native American 1%. **Retention and Graduation:** 83% freshmen return for sophomore year. 51% freshmen graduate within 4 years. 7% grads go on to further study within 1 year. 7% grads pursue arts and sciences degrees. **Faculty:** Student/faculty ratio 13:1. 63 full-time faculty, 63% hold PhDs. 100% faculty teach undergrads.

ACADEMICS

Degrees: Bachelor's, certificate. **Academic Requirements:** Arts/fine arts, computer literacy, English (including composition), environmental studies, history, humanities, mathematics, philosophy, social science. **Classes:** Most classes have 10–19 students. Most lab/discussion sections have fewer than 10

---

students. **Majors with Highest Enrollment:** Animation, interactive technology, video graphics and special effects, graphic design, illustration. **Disciplines with Highest Percentage of Degrees Awarded:** Visual and performing arts 100%. **Special Study Options:** Dual enrollment, exchange student program (domestic), independent study, internships, study abroad.

FACILITIES

Housing: Men's dorms, women's dorms, apartments for single students. All housing accommodations are ADA compliant. **Special Academic Facilities/ Equipment:** William G. and Marie Selby Gallery, Crossley Gallery, Verman Kimbrough Memorial Library. **Computers:** 100% of classrooms are wireless, 45% of public computers are PCs, 60% of public computers are Macs, 60% of public computers are UNIX, network access in dorm rooms, network access in dorm lounges, online registration, online administrative functions (other than registration), support for handheld computing, remote student-access to Web through college's connection, tuition includes personal computer.

CAMPUS LIFE

Activities: Dance, student government. **Organizations:** 24 registered organizations, 2 religious organizations. 2 fraternities (1% men join), 1 sorority (1% women join).

ADMISSIONS

Freshman Academic Profile: TOEFL required of all international applicants, minimum paper TOEFL 500, minimum computer TOEFL 173. **Basis for Candidate Selection:** *Very important factors considered include:* Academic GPA, rigor of secondary school record, talent/ability. *Important factors considered include:* Application essay, character/personal qualities, recommendation(s). *Other factors considered include:* Alumni/ae relation, extracurricular activities, geographical residence, interview, level of applicant's interest, volunteer work, work experience. **Freshman Admission Requirements:** High school diploma is required, and GED is accepted. **Freshman Admission Statistics:** 826 applied, 73% admitted, 40% enrolled. **Transfer Admission Requirements:** High school transcript, college transcript(s), essay or personal statement. Minimum college GPA of 2.0 required. Lowest grade transferable C. **General Admission Information:** Application fee $35. Regular notification is rolling. Non-fall registration accepted. Admission may be deferred for a maximum of 2 years. Credit and/or placement offered for CEEB Advanced Placement tests.

COSTS AND FINANCIAL AID

Required Forms and Deadlines: FAFSA. Financial aid filing deadline 3/1. **Notification of Awards:** Applicants will be notified of awards on or about 4/1. **Types of Aid:** *Need-based scholarships/grants:* Pell, SEOG, state scholarships/grants, private scholarships, the school's own gift aid. *Loans:* FFEL Subsidized Stafford, FFEL Unsubsidized Stafford, FFEL PLUS. **Student Employment:** Federal Work-Study Program available. Institutional employment available. Off-campus job opportunities are excellent. **Financial Aid Statistics:** 54% freshmen, 57% undergrads receive need-based scholarship or grant aid. 58% freshmen, 63% undergrads receive need-based self-help aid. 68% freshmen, 79% undergrads receive any aid. Highest amount earned per year from on-campus jobs $2,345.

RIPON COLLEGE

Best 368

PO Box 248, Ripon, WI 54971
Phone: 920-748-8114 **E-mail:** adminfo@ripon.edu **CEEB Code:** 1664
Fax: 920-748-8335 **Website:** www.ripon.edu **ACT Code:** 4336
Financial Aid Phone: 920-748-8101

This private school was founded in 1851. It has a 250-acre campus.

RATINGS

Admissions Selectivity Rating: 79   **Fire Safety Rating:** 62   **Green Rating:** 70

STUDENTS AND FACULTY

Enrollment: 963. **Student Body:** 54% female, 46% male, 26% out-of-state. African American 2%, Asian 1%, Caucasian 63%, Hispanic 2%. **Retention and Graduation:** 87% freshmen return for sophomore year. 10% grads go on to further study within 1 year. 19% grads pursue arts and sciences degrees. 1% grads pursue business degrees. 2% grads pursue law degrees. 2% grads pursue medical degrees. **Faculty:** Student/faculty ratio 13:1. 49 full-time faculty, 94% hold PhDs. 100% faculty teach undergrads.

ACADEMICS

Degrees: Bachelor's. **Academic Requirements:** Arts/fine arts, English (including composition), foreign languages, global studies, humanities, mathematics, physical education, sciences (biological or physical), social science. **Classes:** Most classes have 10–19 students. Most lab/discussion sections have 10–19 students. **Majors with Highest Enrollment:** Business administration/management, history, kinesiology and exercise science. **Disciplines with Highest Percentage of Degrees Awarded:** Business/marketing 27%, social sciences 26%, education 25%, psychology 19%, history 17%. **Special Study Options:** Double major, exchange student program (domestic), internships, student-designed major, study abroad, teacher certification program. Semester-away programs: Argonne Science Semester (Illinois), Newberry Library Program in the humanities (Illinois), urban studies program (Chicago), wilderness field station program (Minnesota).

FACILITIES

Housing: Coed dorms, men's dorms, women's dorms, fraternity/sorority housing. **Special Academic Facilities/Equipment:** Art gallery, language labs. **Computers:** Network access in dorm rooms, remote student-access to Web through college's connection.

CAMPUS LIFE

Activities: Choral groups, concert band, dance, drama/theater, jazz band, literary magazine, music ensembles, musical theater, radio station, student government, student newspaper, symphony orchestra, yearbook. **Organizations:** 45 registered organizations, 13 honor societies, 2 religious organizations. 5 fraternities (37% men join), 3 sororities (19% women join). **Athletics (Intercollegiate):** *Men:* Baseball, basketball, cross-country, football, golf, soccer, swimming, tennis, track/field (indoor), track/field (outdoor). *Women:* Basketball, cross-country, golf, soccer, softball, swimming, tennis, track/field (indoor), track/field (outdoor), volleyball.

ADMISSIONS

Freshman Academic Profile: 26% in top 10% of high school class, 56% in top 25% of high school class, 86% in top 50% of high school class. 75% from public high schools. SAT Math middle 50% range 480–650. SAT Critical Reading middle 50% range 440–610. ACT middle 50% range 21–27. TOEFL required of all international applicants, minimum paper TOEFL 550, minimum computer TOEFL 220. **Basis for Candidate Selection:** *Very important factors considered include:* Interview, rigor of secondary school record. *Important factors considered include:* Academic GPA, character/personal qualities, class rank, extracurricular activities, recommendation(s), standardized test scores. *Other factors considered include:* Application essay, talent/ability, volunteer work. **Freshman Admission Requirements:** High school diploma is required, and GED is accepted. *Academic units required:* 4 English, 2 math, 2 science, 2 social studies. *Academic units recommended:* 4 math, 4 science, 2 foreign language, 4 social studies. **Freshman Admission Statistics:** 979 applied, 78% admitted, 35% enrolled. **Transfer Admission Requirements:** High school transcript, college transcript(s), essay or personal statement, standardized test score, statement of good standing from prior institution(s). Minimum college GPA of 2.0 required. Lowest grade transferable C. **General Admission Information:** Application fee $30. Regular notification is rolling. Non-fall registration accepted. Admission may be deferred for a maximum of 1 year. Credit and/or placement offered for CEEB Advanced Placement tests.

COSTS AND FINANCIAL AID

Annual tuition $23,970. Room and board $6,770. Required fees $275. Average book expense $800. **Required Forms and Deadlines:** FAFSA. Financial aid filing deadline 3/1. **Notification of Awards:** Applicants will be notified of awards on a rolling basis beginning on or about 3/1. **Types of Aid:** *Need-based scholarships/grants:* Pell, SEOG, state scholarships/grants, private scholarships, the school's own gift aid. *Loans:* FFEL Subsidized Stafford, FFEL Unsubsidized Stafford, FFEL PLUS, Federal Perkins. **Student Employment:** Federal Work-Study Program available. Institutional employment available. Off-campus job opportunities are good. **Financial Aid Statistics:** 84% freshmen, 78% undergrads receive need-based scholarship or grant aid. 64% freshmen, 65% undergrads receive need-based self-help aid. 100% freshmen, 98% undergrads receive any aid. Highest amount earned per year from on-campus jobs $1,200.

See page 1336.

RIVIER COLLEGE

420 South Main Street, Nashua, NH 03060
Phone: 603-897-8219 **E-mail:** rivadmit@rivier.edu **CEEB Code:** 3728
Fax: 603-891-1799 **Website:** www.rivier.edu **ACT Code:** 2520
Financial Aid Phone: 603-897-8510

This private school, affiliated with the Roman Catholic Church, was founded in 1933. It has a 68-acre campus.

RATINGS

Admissions Selectivity Rating: 67   **Fire Safety Rating:** 60*   **Green Rating:** 60*

STUDENTS AND FACULTY

Enrollment: 1,387. **Student Body:** 78% female, 22% male. African American 1%, Asian 2%, Caucasian 73%, Hispanic 2%. **Retention and Graduation:** 79% freshmen return for sophomore year. 41% freshmen graduate within 4 years. 21% grads go on to further study within 1 year. 12% grads pursue arts and sciences degrees. 7% grads pursue business degrees. 1% grads pursue law degrees. 1% grads pursue medical degrees. **Faculty:** Student/faculty ratio 11:1. 71 full-time faculty, 68% hold PhDs. 88% faculty teach undergrads.

ACADEMICS

Degrees: Associate, bachelor's, certificate, master's, post-bachelor's certificate, post-master's certificate. **Academic Requirements:** Arts/fine arts, English (including composition), foreign languages, history, humanities, mathematics, philosophy, sciences (biological or physical), service learning, social science. **Classes:** Most classes have 10–19 students. Most lab/discussion sections have 10–19 students. **Disciplines with Highest Percentage of Degrees Awarded:** Education 24%, health professions and related sciences 22%, business/marketing 14%, psychology 12%, visual and performing arts 7%. **Special Study Options:** Accelerated program, cross-registration, double major, honors program, independent study, internships, liberal arts/career combination, student-designed major, teacher certification program.

FACILITIES

Housing: Coed dorms, coed wellness dorm (substance-free). **Special Academic Facilities/Equipment:** Art gallery, early childhood center/laboratory school, language lab, TV microscope, video/laser disk system, photo spectrometer, high-performance liquid chromatograph, digital imaging lab, several art studios including a photography darkroom. **Computers:** 98% of public computers are PCs, 2% of public computers are Macs, network access in dorm rooms, online administrative functions (other than registration), remote student-access to Web through college's connection.

CAMPUS LIFE

Activities: Choral groups, dance, drama/theater, music ensembles, student government, student newspaper, television station, yearbook. **Organizations:** 30 registered organizations, 2 honor societies, 2 religious organizations. **Athletics (Intercollegiate):** *Men:* Baseball, basketball, cross-country, soccer, volleyball. *Women:* Basketball, cross-country, soccer, softball, volleyball.

ADMISSIONS

Freshman Academic Profile: 80% in top 50% of high school class. 80% from public high schools. SAT Math middle 50% range 420–530. SAT Critical Reading middle 50% range 420–530. SAT Writing middle 50% range 430–520. TOEFL required of all international applicants, minimum paper TOEFL 500, minimum computer TOEFL 173. **Basis for Candidate Selection:** *Very important factors considered include:* Academic GPA, rigor of secondary school record. *Important factors considered include:* Application essay, class rank, extracurricular activities, standardized test scores, talent/ability, volunteer work, work experience. *Other factors considered include:* Character/personal qualities, interview, recommendation(s). **Freshman Admission Requirements:** High school diploma is required, and GED is accepted. *Academic units recommended:* 4 English, 3 math, 1 science (1 science lab), 2 foreign language, 2 social studies, 1 history, 3 academic electives. **Freshman Admission Statistics:** 1,095 applied, 77% admitted, 41% enrolled. **Transfer Admission Requirements:** College transcript(s). Minimum college GPA of 2.5 required. Lowest grade transferable C. **General Admission Information:** Application fee $25. Regular notification is rolling. Non-fall registration accepted. Admission may be deferred for a maximum of 1 year. Credit and/or placement offered for CEEB Advanced Placement tests.

COSTS AND FINANCIAL AID

Annual tuition $20,970. Room & board $7,942. Required fees $725. Average book expense $800. **Required Forms and Deadlines:** FAFSA. **Notification of Awards:** Applicants will be notified of awards on a rolling basis beginning on or about 3/1. **Types of Aid:** *Need-based scholarships/grants:* Pell, SEOG, state scholarships/grants, private scholarships, the school's own gift aid. *Loans:* FFEL Subsidized Stafford, FFEL Unsubsidized Stafford, FFEL PLUS, Federal Perkins, Federal Nursing, state loans. **Financial Aid Statistics:** 88% freshmen, 87% undergrads receive need-based scholarship or grant aid. 82% freshmen, 82% undergrads receive need-based self-help aid. Highest amount earned per year from on-campus jobs $800.

ROANOKE BIBLE COLLEGE

715 North Poindexter Street, Elizabeth City, NC 27909-4054
Phone: 252-334-2028 **E-mail:** admissions@roanokeBible.edu
Fax: 252-334-2064 **Website:** www.roanokebible.edu **ACT Code:** 3153
Financial Aid Phone: 252-334-2020

This private school, affiliated with the Christian Church of Christ, was founded in 1948. It has a 20-acre campus.

RATINGS
Admissions Selectivity Rating: 64   **Fire Safety Rating:** 63   **Green Rating:** 76

STUDENTS AND FACULTY
Enrollment: 147. **Student Body:** 49% female, 51% male, 72% out-of-state. African American 6%, Caucasian 91%, Hispanic 1%. **Retention and Graduation:** 60% freshmen return for sophomore year. 33% freshmen graduate within 4 years. **Faculty:** Student/faculty ratio 8:1. 11 full-time faculty, 36% hold PhDs. 100% faculty teach undergrads.

ACADEMICS
Degrees: Associate, bachelor's, certificate, terminal. **Academic Requirements:** Arts/fine arts, biblical and theological studies, computer literacy, English (including composition), history, humanities, mathematics, sciences (biological or physical), social science. **Classes:** Most classes have fewer than 10 students. Most lab/discussion sections have fewer than 10 students. **Majors with Highest Enrollment:** Bible/biblical studies. **Disciplines with Highest Percentage of Degrees Awarded:** Philosophy and religious studies 100%. **Special Study Options:** Cross-cultural semester abroad, cross-registration, distance learning, double major, dual enrollment, independent study, internships.

FACILITIES
Housing: Men's dorms, women's dorms, apartments for married students, apartments for single students. **Computers:** 100% of public computers are PCs, network access in dorm rooms, network access in dorm lounges, remote student-access to Web through college's connection.

CAMPUS LIFE
Activities: Choral groups, music ensembles, musical theater, student government. **Organizations:** 1 honor society. **Athletics (Intercollegiate):** *Men:* Basketball. *Women:* Basketball, volleyball. **Environmental Initiatives:** Geothermal heating and cooling. Solar hot water. Recycle program.

ADMISSIONS
Freshman Academic Profile: 6% in top 10% of high school class, 17% in top 25% of high school class, 72% in top 50% of high school class. 68% from public high schools. SAT Math middle 50% range 410–575. SAT Critical Reading middle 50% range 403–528. ACT middle 50% range 19–24. TOEFL required of all international applicants, minimum paper TOEFL 500, minimum computer TOEFL 222. **Basis for Candidate Selection:** *Very important factors considered include:* Academic GPA, character/personal qualities, class rank, recommendation(s), religious affiliation/commitment, standardized test scores. *Important factors considered include:* Application essay, rigor of secondary school record. *Other factors considered include:* Extracurricular activities, interview, level of applicant's interest, talent/ability, volunteer work, work experience. **Freshman Admission Requirements:** High school diploma is required, and GED is accepted. *Academic units required:* 4 English, 3 math, 3 science (2 science labs), 2 social studies, 2 history, 4 academic electives. *Academic units recommended:* 6 foreign language. **Freshman Admission Statistics:** 45 applied, 44% enrolled. **Transfer Admission Requirements:** College transcript(s), essay or personal statement, statement of good standing from prior institution(s). Minimum college GPA of 2.0 required. Lowest grade transferable C. **General Admission Information:** Application fee $25. Regular notification is rolling. Non-fall registration accepted. Admission may be deferred for a maximum of 1 semester. Credit and/or placement offered for CEEB Advanced Placement tests.

COSTS AND FINANCIAL AID
Annual tuition $8,850. Room & board $5,720. Required fees $475. Average book expense $400. **Required Forms and Deadlines:** FAFSA, institution's own financial aid form. Financial aid filing deadline 3/15. **Notification of Awards:** Applicants will be notified of awards on a rolling basis beginning on or about 5/1. **Types of Aid:** *Need-based scholarships/grants:* Pell, SEOG, state scholarships/grants, private scholarships, the school's own gift aid. *Loans:* FFEL Subsidized Stafford, FFEL Unsubsidized Stafford, FFEL PLUS, alternative loans. **Student Employment:** Federal Work-Study Program available. Institutional employment available. Off-campus job opportunities are good. **Financial Aid Statistics:** 83% freshmen, 85% undergrads receive need-based scholarship or grant aid. 67% freshmen, 70% undergrads receive need-based self-help aid. 95% freshmen, 95% undergrads receive any aid.

ROANOKE COLLEGE

221 College Lane, Salem, VA 24153-3794
Phone: 540-375-2270 **E-mail:** admissions@roanoke.edu **CEEB Code:** 5571
Fax: 540-375-2267 **Website:** web.roanoke.edu **ACT Code:** 4392
Financial Aid Phone: 540-375-2235

This private school, affiliated with the Lutheran Church, was founded in 1842. It has a 68-acre campus.

RATINGS
Admissions Selectivity Rating: 82   **Fire Safety Rating:** 75   **Green Rating:** 60*

STUDENTS AND FACULTY
Enrollment: 1,877. **Student Body:** 56% female, 44% male, 43% out-of-state, 1% international (25 countries represented). African American 4%, Asian 2%, Caucasian 83%, Hispanic 2%. **Retention and Graduation:** 77% freshmen return for sophomore year. 57% freshmen graduate within 4 years. 20% grads go on to further study within 1 year. **Faculty:** Student/faculty ratio 14:1. 146 full-time faculty, 83% hold PhDs. 100% faculty teach undergrads.

ACADEMICS
Degrees: Bachelor's. **Academic Requirements:** Arts/fine arts, co-curricular learning and service course, computer literacy, English (including composition), foreign languages, history, humanities, mathematics, May intensive learning course, philosophy, sciences (biological or physical), social science. **Classes:** Most classes have 20–29 students. Most lab/discussion sections have 10–19 students. **Majors with Highest Enrollment:** Business administration/management, English language and literature, psychology. **Disciplines with Highest Percentage of Degrees Awarded:** Business/marketing 22%, social sciences 15%, psychology 10%, history 10%, English 7%, biological/life sciences 7%. **Special Study Options:** Accelerated program, cross-registration, double major, dual enrollment, English as a second language (ESL), honors program, independent study, internships, liberal arts/career combination, study abroad, teacher certification program.

FACILITIES
Housing: Coed dorms, men's dorms, women's dorms, apartments for single students, fraternity/sorority housing, theme housing. **Special Academic Facilities/Equipment:** Fine arts center, community research center, language lab, church and society center. **Computers:** 91% of public computers are PCs, 1% of public computers are Macs, 8% of public computers are UNIX, network access in dorm rooms, network access in dorm lounges, online registration, online administrative functions (other than registration), remote student-access to Web through college's connection.

CAMPUS LIFE
Activities: Choral groups, dance, drama/theater, jazz band, literary magazine, music ensembles, musical theater, pep band, radio station, student government, student newspaper, student-run film society, yearbook. **Organizations:** 85 registered organizations, 30 honor societies, 5 religious organizations. 4 fraternities (22% men join), 4 sororities (27% women join). **Athletics (Intercollegiate):** *Men:* Baseball, basketball, cross-country, golf, lacrosse, soccer, tennis, track/field (indoor), track/field (outdoor). *Women:* Basketball, cross-country, field hockey, lacrosse, soccer, softball, tennis, track/field (indoor), track/field (outdoor), volleyball.

ADMISSIONS
Freshman Academic Profile: 21% in top 10% of high school class, 50% in top 25% of high school class, 83% in top 50% of high school class. 70% from public high schools. SAT Math middle 50% range 500–590. SAT Critical Reading middle 50% range 500–600. SAT Writing middle 50% range 480–570. TOEFL

required of all international applicants, minimum paper TOEFL 520, minimum computer TOEFL 190. **Basis for Candidate Selection:** *Very important factors considered include:* Academic GPA, character/personal qualities, class rank, rigor of secondary school record, standardized test scores. *Important factors considered include:* Extracurricular activities, interview, recommendation(s). *Other factors considered include:* Alumni/ae relation, application essay, racial/ethnic status, talent/ability, volunteer work, work experience. **Freshman Admission Requirements:** High school diploma is required, and GED is accepted. *Academic units required:* 4 English, 3 math, 2 science (2 science labs), 2 social studies, 5 academic electives. *Academic units recommended:* 4 foreign language. **Freshman Admission Statistics:** 3,166 applied, 74% admitted, 21% enrolled. **Transfer Admission Requirements:** High school transcript, college transcript(s), statement of good standing from prior institution(s). Minimum college GPA of 2.2 required. Lowest grade transferable C-. **General Admission Information:** Application fee $30. Early decision application deadline 12/1. Regular application deadline 3/15. Regular notification 4/1. Non-fall registration accepted. Admission may be deferred for a maximum of 2 years. Credit and/or placement offered for CEEB Advanced Placement tests.

COSTS AND FINANCIAL AID

Annual tuition $25,550. Room and board $8,726. Required fees $700. Average book expense $850. **Required Forms and Deadlines:** FAFSA, state aid form. Financial aid filing deadline 3/1. **Notification of Awards:** Applicants will be notified of awards on a rolling basis beginning on or about 11/1. **Types of Aid:** *Need-based scholarships/grants:* Pell, SEOG, state scholarships/grants, private scholarships, the school's own gift aid. *Loans:* FFEL Subsidized Stafford, FFEL Unsubsidized Stafford, FFEL PLUS, Federal Perkins, college/university loans from institutional funds, alternative loans. **Student Employment:** Federal Work-Study Program available. Institutional employment available. Off-campus job opportunities are good. **Financial Aid Statistics:** 57% freshmen, 61% undergrads receive need-based scholarship or grant aid. 41% freshmen, 44% undergrads receive need-based self-help aid. 96% freshmen, 96% undergrads receive any aid. Highest amount earned per year from on-campus jobs $3,000.

ROBERT MORRIS COLLEGE (IL)

401 South State Street, Chicago, IL 60605
Phone: 800-762-5960 **E-mail:** enroll@robertmorris.edu **CEEB Code:** 1670
Fax: 312-935-6819 **Website:** www.robertmorris.edu **ACT Code:** 1121
Financial Aid Phone: 312-935-4075

This private school was founded in 1913.

RATINGS
Admissions Selectivity Rating: 62   **Fire Safety Rating:** 60*   **Green Rating:** 60*

STUDENTS AND FACULTY
Enrollment: 4,847. **Student Body:** 65% female, 35% male, 1% out-of-state. African American 37%, Asian 2%, Caucasian 34%, Hispanic 24%. **Retention and Graduation:** 56% freshmen return for sophomore year. 40% freshmen graduate within 4 years. **Faculty:** Student/faculty ratio 20:1. 134 full-time faculty, 19% hold PhDs. 100% faculty teach undergrads.

ACADEMICS
Degrees: Associate, bachelor's, diploma, master's. **Academic Requirements:** Arts/fine arts, behavioral science, computer literacy, English (including composition), history, humanities, mathematics, philosophy, sciences (biological or physical), social science. **Classes:** Most classes have 20–29 students. **Majors with Highest Enrollment:** Business administration/management, computer systems networking and telecommunications, medical/clinical assistant. **Disciplines with Highest Percentage of Degrees Awarded:** Business/marketing 79%, computer and information sciences 13%, visual and performing arts 8%. **Special Study Options:** Accelerated program, cooperative education program, distance learning, dual enrollment, honors program, internships, study abroad.

FACILITIES
Housing: Coed dorms. **Computers:** 40% of public computers are PCs, 8% of public computers are Macs, online administrative functions (other than registration), remote student-access to Web through college's connection.

CAMPUS LIFE
Activities: Choral groups, dance, drama/theater, literary magazine, student newspaper. **Organizations:** 30 registered organizations, 1 honor society. **Athletics (Intercollegiate):** *Men:* Baseball, basketball, cross-country, golf, soccer. *Women:* Basketball, bowling, cross-country, golf, soccer, softball, tennis, track/field (indoor), track/field (outdoor), volleyball.

ADMISSIONS
Freshman Academic Profile: 7% in top 10% of high school class, 23% in top 25% of high school class, 50% in top 50% of high school class. TOEFL required of all international applicants, minimum paper TOEFL 500, minimum computer TOEFL 173. **Basis for Candidate Selection:** *Very important factors considered include:* Class rank, interview, rigor of secondary school record. *Other factors considered include:* Application essay, character/personal qualities, extracurricular activities, recommendation(s), standardized test scores, talent/ability, volunteer work, work experience. **Freshman Admission Requirements:** High school diploma is required, and GED is accepted. **Freshman Admission Statistics:** 2,714 applied, 80% admitted, 45% enrolled. **Transfer Admission Requirements:** High school transcript, college transcript(s). Minimum college GPA of 2.0 required. Lowest grade transferable C. **General Admission Information:** Application fee $30. Regular notification is weekly. Non-fall registration accepted. Admission may be deferred. Common Application accepted. Neither credit nor placement offered for CEEB Advanced Placement tests.

COSTS AND FINANCIAL AID
Annual tuition $16,800. Room and board $8,700. Average book expense $1,350. **Required Forms and Deadlines:** FAFSA. **Types of Aid:** *Need-based scholarships/grants:* Pell, SEOG, state scholarships/grants, private scholarships, the school's own gift aid. *Loans:* FFEL Subsidized Stafford, FFEL Unsubsidized Stafford, FFEL PLUS, Federal Perkins. **Student Employment:** Federal Work-Study Program available. Institutional employment available. Off-campus job opportunities are excellent. **Financial Aid Statistics:** 83% freshmen, 90% undergrads receive need-based scholarship or grant aid. 73% freshmen, 77% undergrads receive need-based self-help aid. 12 freshmen, 62 undergrads receive athletic scholarships. 85% freshmen, 92% undergrads receive any aid.

See page 1338.

ROBERT MORRIS UNIVERSITY

6001 University Boulevard, Moon Township, PA 15108-1189
Phone: 412-262-8206 **E-mail:** enrollmentoffice@rmu.edu **CEEB Code:** 2769
Fax: 412-397-2425 **Website:** www.rmu.edu **ACT Code:** 3674
Financial Aid Phone: 412-262-8212

This private school was founded in 1921. It has a 230-acre campus.

RATINGS
Admissions Selectivity Rating: 72   **Fire Safety Rating:** 80   **Green Rating:** 72

STUDENTS AND FACULTY
Enrollment: 3,844. **Student Body:** 45% female, 55% male, 11% out-of-state, 2% international (27 countries represented). African American 8%, Caucasian 83%, Hispanic 1%. **Retention and Graduation:** 74% freshmen return for sophomore year. 32% freshmen graduate within 4 years. 5% grads go on to further study within 1 year. **Faculty:** Student/faculty ratio 16:1. 166 full-time faculty, 82% hold PhDs. 100% faculty teach undergrads.

ACADEMICS
Degrees: Bachelor's, certificate, doctoral, master's, post-bachelor's certificate. **Academic Requirements:** Computer literacy, English (including composition), history, humanities, mathematics, sciences (biological or physical), social science. **Classes:** Most classes have 10–19 students. Most lab/discussion sections have fewer than 10 students. **Majors with Highest Enrollment:** Accounting, business administration/management, information science/studies. **Disciplines with Highest Percentage of Degrees Awarded:** Business/marketing 60%, communications/journalism 8%, computer and information sciences 6%, parks and recreation 4%, education 4%. **Special Study Options:** Cooperative education program, cross-registration, distance learning, double major, evening, honors program, independent study, internships, study abroad, teacher certification program, weekend college, 5-week/8-week programs.

FACILITIES
Housing: Coed dorms, men's dorms, women's dorms, apartments for single students. **Special Academic Facilities/Equipment:** Learning factory, an automated manufacturing facility for engineering students. **Computers:** 10% of classrooms are wired, 65% of classrooms are wireless, 95% of public computers are PCs, 5% of public computers are Macs, network access in dorm rooms, network access in dorm lounges, online registration, online administrative functions (other than registration), support for handheld computing, remote student-access to Web through college's connection.

CAMPUS LIFE

Activities: Drama/theater, marching band, musical theater, pep band, student government, student newspaper, television station. **Organizations:** 50 registered organizations, 2 honor societies, 2 religious organizations. 6 fraternities (3% men join), 2 sororities (3% women join). **Athletics (Intercollegiate):** *Men:* Basketball, cheerleading, football, golf, ice hockey, lacrosse, soccer, tennis, track/field (indoor), track/field (outdoor). *Women:* Basketball, cheerleading, crew/rowing, field hockey, golf, ice hockey, lacrosse, soccer, softball, tennis, track/field (indoor), track/field (outdoor), volleyball. **Environmental Initiatives:** Recycling paper, cardboard, plastic, bottles and cans, and flourescent bulbs.

ADMISSIONS

Freshman Academic Profile: 8% in top 10% of high school class, 29% in top 25% of high school class, 64% in top 50% of high school class. 81% from public high schools. SAT Math middle 50% range 440–560. SAT Critical Reading middle 50% range 430–530. ACT middle 50% range 18–22. TOEFL required of all international applicants, minimum paper TOEFL 500, minimum computer TOEFL 173. **Basis for Candidate Selection:** *Very important factors considered include:* Academic GPA, standardized test scores. *Important factors considered include:* Character/personal qualities, class rank, extracurricular activities, interview, recommendation(s), rigor of secondary school record. *Other factors considered include:* Application essay, geographical residence, level of applicant's interest, talent/ability, volunteer work, work experience. **Freshman Admission Requirements:** High school diploma is required, and GED is accepted. *Academic units required:* 4 English, 3 math, 2 science, 4 social studies, 3 academic electives. *Academic units recommended:* 2 foreign language. **Freshman Admission Statistics:** 2,622 applied, 78% admitted, 32% enrolled. **Transfer Admission Requirements:** College transcript(s), statement of good standing from prior institution(s). Minimum college GPA of 2.0 required. Lowest grade transferable C. **General Admission Information:** Application fee $30. Regular application deadline 7/1. Regular notification is rolling. Non-fall registration accepted. Admission may be deferred for a maximum of 1 year. Credit and/or placement offered for CEEB Advanced Placement tests.

COSTS AND FINANCIAL AID

Average book expense $1,100. **Required Forms and Deadlines:** FAFSA. **Notification of Awards:** Applicants will be notified of awards on a rolling basis beginning on or about 3/15. **Types of Aid:** *Need-based scholarships/grants:* Pell, SEOG, state scholarships/grants, private scholarships, the school's own gift aid. *Loans:* FFEL Subsidized Stafford, FFEL Unsubsidized Stafford, FFEL PLUS, Federal Perkins, alternative private loans. **Student Employment:** Federal Work-Study Program available. Institutional employment available. Off-campus job opportunities are excellent. **Financial Aid Statistics:** 76% freshmen, 71% undergrads receive need-based scholarship or grant aid. 71% freshmen, 72% undergrads receive need-based self-help aid. 23 freshmen, 111 undergrads receive athletic scholarships. 78% freshmen, 77% undergrads receive any aid.

See page 1340.

ROBERTS WESLEYAN COLLEGE

2301 Westside Drive, Rochester, NY 14624-1997
Phone: 585-594-6400 **E-mail:** admissions@roberts.edu **CEEB Code:** 2805
Fax: 585-594-6371 **Website:** www.roberts.edu **ACT Code:** 2759
Financial Aid Phone: 585-594-6150

This private school, affiliated with the Methodist Church, was founded in 1866. It has a 75-acre campus.

RATINGS

Admissions Selectivity Rating: 77   **Fire Safety Rating:** 60*   **Green Rating:** 60*

STUDENTS AND FACULTY

Enrollment: 1,408. **Student Body:** 69% female, 31% male, 12% out-of-state, 2% international. African American 4%, Caucasian 60%, Hispanic 1%. **Retention and Graduation:** 51% freshmen graduate within 4 years. 30% grads go on to further study within 1 year. 20% grads pursue arts and sciences degrees. 5% grads pursue business degrees. 5% grads pursue medical degrees. **Faculty:** Student/faculty ratio 13:1. 104 full-time faculty, 62% hold PhDs. 84% faculty teach undergrads.

ACADEMICS

Degrees: Bachelor's, master's. **Academic Requirements:** Arts/fine arts, English (including composition), foreign languages, history, humanities,

mathematics, Old and New Testament, philosophy, physical education, sciences (biological or physical), social science. **Classes:** Most classes have 10–19 students. Most lab/discussion sections have 10–19 students. **Disciplines with Highest Percentage of Degrees Awarded:** Business/marketing 27%, education 23%, health professions and related sciences 14%, psychology 6%, visual and performing arts 5%. **Special Study Options:** Cross-registration, double major, honors program, internships, study abroad, teacher certification program.

FACILITIES

Housing: Coed dorms, men's dorms, women's dorms, apartments for married students, apartments for single students, special housing for disabled students. **Special Academic Facilities/Equipment:** Davison Art Gallery. **Computers:** 15% of classrooms are wired, 100% of classrooms are wireless, 90% of public computers are PCs, 10% of public computers are Macs, network access in dorm rooms, network access in dorm lounges, online registration, online administrative functions (other than registration), support for handheld computing, remote student-access to Web through college's connection.

CAMPUS LIFE

Activities: Choral groups, concert band, dance, drama/theater, jazz band, music ensembles, musical theater, opera, radio station, student government, student newspaper, symphony orchestra, yearbook. **Organizations:** 28 registered organizations, 11 religious organizations. **Athletics (Intercollegiate):** *Men:* Basketball, cross-country, golf, soccer, tennis, track/field (indoor), track/field (outdoor). *Women:* Basketball, cross-country, soccer, tennis, track/field (indoor), track/field (outdoor), volleyball.

ADMISSIONS

Freshman Academic Profile: 23% in top 10% of high school class, 50% in top 25% of high school class, 81% in top 50% of high school class. SAT Math middle 50% range 470–600. SAT Critical Reading middle 50% range 470–580. SAT Writing middle 50% range 450–500. ACT middle 50% range 19–25. TOEFL required of all international applicants, minimum paper TOEFL 550, minimum computer TOEFL 213. **Basis for Candidate Selection:** *Very important factors considered include:* Academic GPA, application essay, character/personal qualities, recommendation(s), standardized test scores. *Important factors considered include:* Class rank, religious affiliation/commitment, rigor of secondary school record. *Other factors considered include:* Alumni/ae relation, extracurricular activities, interview, level of applicant's interest, talent/ability, volunteer work, work experience. **Freshman Admission Requirements:** High school diploma is required, and GED is accepted. *Academic units required:* 4 English, 3 math, 3 science (1 science lab), 3 social studies. *Academic units recommended:* 3 foreign language. **Freshman Admission Statistics:** 652 applied, 83% admitted, 48% enrolled. **Transfer Admission Requirements:** College transcript(s), essay or personal statement. Minimum college GPA of 2.5 required. Lowest grade transferable C. **General Admission Information:** Application fee $35. Regular application deadline rolling. Regular notification is rolling. Non-fall registration accepted. Admission may be deferred for a maximum of 1 year. Credit and/or placement offered for CEEB Advanced Placement tests.

COSTS AND FINANCIAL AID

Annual tuition $19,264. Room & board $7,448. Required fees $738. Average book expense $800. **Required Forms and Deadlines:** FAFSA, state aid form. Financial aid filing deadline 3/15. **Notification of Awards:** Applicants will be notified of awards on a rolling basis beginning on or about 3/1. **Types of Aid:** *Need-based scholarships/grants:* Pell, SEOG, state scholarships/grants, private scholarships, the school's own gift aid. *Loans:* FFEL Subsidized Stafford, FFEL Unsubsidized Stafford, FFEL PLUS, Federal Perkins. **Student Employment:** Federal Work-Study Program available. Institutional employment available. Off-campus job opportunities are fair. **Financial Aid Statistics:** 88% freshmen, 85% undergrads receive need-based scholarship or grant aid. 83% freshmen, 80% undergrads receive need-based self-help aid. 5 freshmen, 41 undergrads receive athletic scholarships. 96% freshmen, 94% undergrads receive any aid. Highest amount earned per year from on-campus jobs $3,000.

ROCHESTER COLLEGE

800 West Avon Road, Rochester Hills, MI 48307
Phone: 248-218-2031 **E-mail:** admissions@rc.edu **CEEB Code:** 1516
Fax: 248-218-2035 **Website:** www.rc.edu **ACT Code:** 2072
Financial Aid Phone: 248-218-2028

This private school, affiliated with the Church of Christ, was founded in 1959. It has an 83-acre campus.

RATINGS

Admissions Selectivity Rating: 60*   **Fire Safety Rating:** 60*   **Green Rating:** 60*

STUDENTS AND FACULTY

Enrollment: 927. **Student Body:** 14% out-of-state, 3% international (10 countries represented). African American 11%, Caucasian 83%. **Retention and Graduation:** 69% freshmen return for sophomore year. 8% freshmen graduate within 4 years. **Faculty:** Student/faculty ratio 15:1. 32 full-time faculty, 28% hold PhDs. 100% faculty teach undergrads.

ACADEMICS

Degrees: Associate, bachelor's, master's. **Academic Requirements:** Arts/fine arts, communication, computer literacy, English (including composition), history, literature, mathematics, physical education, sciences (biological or physical), social science. **Majors with Highest Enrollment:** Business administration/management, communications studies/speech communication and rhetoric. **Disciplines with Highest Percentage of Degrees Awarded:** Business/marketing 47%, education 11%, psychology 10%, interdisciplinary studies 6%, communication technologies 5%. **Special Study Options:** Accelerated program, cross-registration, double major, dual enrollment, independent study, internships, liberal arts/career combination, study abroad, teacher certification program, weekend college.

FACILITIES

Housing: Men's dorms, women's dorms, apartments for married students, special housing for disabled students. **Computers:** 100% of public computers are PCs, network access in dorm rooms, network access in dorm lounges, remote student-access to Web through college's connection.

CAMPUS LIFE

Activities: Choral groups, drama/theater, jazz band, music ensembles, student government, student newspaper, yearbook. **Organizations:** 19 registered organizations, 3 honor societies, 1 religious organization. **Athletics (Intercollegiate):** *Men:* Baseball, basketball, cross-country, soccer, track/field (outdoor). *Women:* Basketball, cross-country, softball, track/field (outdoor), volleyball.

ADMISSIONS

Freshman Academic Profile: TOEFL required of all international applicants, minimum paper TOEFL 500, minimum computer TOEFL 173. **Basis for Candidate Selection:** *Important factors considered include:* Rigor of secondary school record, standardized test scores. *Other factors considered include:* Interview. **Freshman Admission Requirements:** High school diploma is required, and GED is accepted. **Freshman Admission Statistics:** 277 applied, 83% admitted, 65% enrolled. **Transfer Admission Requirements:** High school transcript, college transcript(s). Minimum college GPA of 2.0 required. Lowest grade transferable C. **General Admission Information:** Application fee $25. Regular notification is rolling. Non-fall registration accepted. Admission may be deferred for a maximum of 2 years. Common Application not accepted. Credit and/or placement offered for CEEB Advanced Placement tests.

COSTS AND FINANCIAL AID

Annual tuition $9,462. Room & board $5,342. Required fees $600. Average book expense $600. **Required Forms and Deadlines:** FAFSA, institution's own financial aid form. Financial aid filing deadline 8/1. **Notification of Awards:** Applicants will be notified of awards on a rolling basis beginning on or about 6/1. **Types of Aid:** *Need-based scholarships/grants:* Pell, SEOG, state scholarships/grants, private scholarships, the school's own gift aid. *Loans:* Direct Subsidized Stafford, Direct Unsubsidized Stafford, Direct PLUS, Federal Perkins. **Student Employment:** Federal Work-Study Program available. Institutional employment available. Off-campus job opportunities are excellent.

ROCHESTER INSTITUTE OF TECHNOLOGY

Best 368

60 Lomb Memorial Drive, Rochester, NY 14623-5604
Phone: 585-475-6631 **E-mail:** admissions@rit.edu **CEEB Code:** 2760
Fax: 585-475-7424 **Website:** www.rit.edu **ACT Code:** 2870
Financial Aid Phone: 585-475-2186

This private school was founded in 1829. It has a 1,300-acre campus.

RATINGS

Admissions Selectivity Rating: 83   **Fire Safety Rating:** 60*   **Green Rating:** 60*

STUDENTS AND FACULTY

Enrollment: 12,532. **Student Body:** 31% female, 69% male, 45% out-of-state. **Retention and Graduation:** 89% freshmen return for sophomore year. 15% grads go on to further study within 1 year. **Faculty:** Student/faculty ratio 14:1. 783 full-time faculty, 73% hold PhDs. 95% faculty teach undergrads.

ACADEMICS

Degrees: Associate, bachelor's, certificate, diploma, doctoral, master's, post-bachelor's certificate, terminal. **Academic Requirements:** Arts/fine arts, computer literacy, English (including composition), humanities, mathematics, sciences (biological or physical), social science. **Classes:** Most classes have 10–19 students. Most lab/discussion sections have 10–19 students. **Majors with Highest Enrollment:** Business administration/management, information technology, photography. **Disciplines with Highest Percentage of Degrees Awarded:** Computer and information sciences 18%, engineering 15%, visual and performing arts 15%, business/marketing 10%, engineering technologies 8%, interdisciplinary studies 8%. **Special Study Options:** Accelerated program, cooperative education program, cross-registration, distance learning, double major, English as a second language (ESL), exchange student program (domestic), honors program, independent study, internships, liberal arts/career combination, student-designed major, study abroad, weekend college.

FACILITIES

Housing: Coed dorms, apartments for married students, apartments for single students, special housing for disabled students, special housing for international students, fraternity/sorority housing, special interest floors for selected majors/groups, men's floors. **Special Academic Facilities/Equipment:** Art galleries, microelectronic engineering center, RIT inn and conference center, observatory, student-managed restaurant, packaging testing facility, media resource center, Sunday 2000 Printing Press, center for manufacturing studies, 2 OC3 connections to Internet and Internet2, laser optics laboratory, observatory, animal care facility, more than 100 color and black-and-white photography darkrooms, electronic prepress and publishing equipment, ceramic kilns, glass furnaces, blacksmithing area, computer graphics and robotic labs. **Computers:** 100% of classrooms are wired, 30% of classrooms are wireless, 78% of public computers are PCs, 20% of public computers are Macs, 2% of public computers are UNIX, network access in dorm rooms, network access in dorm lounges, online registration, online administrative functions (other than registration), support for handheld computing, remote student-access to Web through college's connection.

CAMPUS LIFE

Activities: Choral groups, concert band, dance, drama/theater, jazz band, literary magazine, music ensembles, musical theater, pep band, radio station, student government, student newspaper, student-run film society, symphony orchestra, yearbook. **Organizations:** 170 registered organizations, 9 honor societies, 5 religious organizations. 19 fraternities (5% men join), 10 sororities (5% women join). **Athletics (Intercollegiate):** *Men:* Baseball, basketball, crew/rowing, cross-country, diving, ice hockey, lacrosse, soccer, swimming, tennis, track/field (indoor), track/field (outdoor), wrestling. *Women:* Basketball, cheerleading, crew/rowing, cross-country, diving, ice hockey, lacrosse, soccer, softball, swimming, tennis, track/field (indoor), track/field (outdoor), volleyball.

ADMISSIONS

Freshman Academic Profile: 30% in top 10% of high school class, 62% in top 25% of high school class, 89% in top 50% of high school class. 85% from public high schools. SAT Math middle 50% range 560–670. SAT Critical Reading middle 50% range 530–630. ACT middle 50% range 24–29. TOEFL required of all international applicants, minimum paper TOEFL 550, minimum computer TOEFL 215. **Basis for Candidate Selection:** *Very important*

factors considered include: Academic GPA, rigor of secondary school record. *Important factors considered include:* Class rank, standardized test scores. *Other factors considered include:* Alumni/ae relation, application essay, character/personal qualities, extracurricular activities, first generation, geographical residence, interview, level of applicant's interest, racial/ethnic status, recommendation(s), talent/ability, volunteer work. **Freshman Admission Requirements:** High school diploma is required, and GED is accepted. *Academic units required:* 4 English, 2 math, 2 science (1 science lab), 4 social studies, 10 academic electives. *Academic units recommended:* 4 English, 3 math, 3 science (2 science labs), 3 foreign language, 4 social studies, 5 academic electives. **Freshman Admission Statistics:** 10,219 applied, 65% admitted, 36% enrolled. **Transfer Admission Requirements:** College transcript(s), essay or personal statement. Minimum college GPA of 2.5 required. Lowest grade transferable C-. **General Admission Information:** Application fee $50. Early decision application deadline 12/1. Regular application deadline 2/1. Regular notification is rolling. Non-fall registration accepted. Admission may be deferred for a maximum of 1 year. Credit and/or placement offered for CEEB Advanced Placement tests.

COSTS AND FINANCIAL AID

Annual tuition $26,085. Room and board $9,054. Required fees $396. Average book expense $900. **Required Forms and Deadlines:** FAFSA, state aid form. Financial aid filing deadline 3/1. **Notification of Awards:** Applicants will be notified of awards on a rolling basis beginning on or about 3/15. **Types of Aid:** *Need-based scholarships/grants:* Pell, SEOG, state scholarships/grants, private scholarships, the school's own gift aid, NACME. *Loans:* Direct Subsidized Stafford, Direct Unsubsidized Stafford, Direct PLUS, Federal Perkins, RIT Loan program, alternative loans. **Student Employment:** Federal Work-Study Program available. Institutional employment available. Off-campus job opportunities are excellent. **Financial Aid Statistics:** 68% freshmen, 62% undergrads receive need-based scholarship or grant aid. 63% freshmen, 59% undergrads receive need-based self-help aid. 81% freshmen, 75% undergrads receive any aid. Highest amount earned per year from on-campus jobs $2,500.

See page 1342.

ROCKFORD COLLEGE

Admission, 5050 E. State Street, Rockford, IL 61108-2393
Phone: 815-226-4050 **E-mail:** RCAdmissions@rockford.edu **CEEB Code:** 1665
Fax: 815-226-2822 **Website:** www.rockford.edu **ACT Code:** 1122
Financial Aid Phone: 815-226-4062

This private school was founded in 1847. It has a 130-acre campus.

RATINGS
Admissions Selectivity Rating: 78   **Fire Safety Rating:** 62   **Green Rating:** 60*

STUDENTS AND FACULTY
Enrollment: 866. **Student Body:** 65% female, 35% male, 7% out-of-state. African American 7%, Asian 2%, Caucasian 75%, Hispanic 6%. **Retention and Graduation:** 62% freshmen return for sophomore year. 32% freshmen graduate within 4 years. **Faculty:** Student/faculty ratio 11:1. 62 full-time faculty, 74% hold PhDs. 100% faculty teach undergrads.

ACADEMICS
Degrees: Bachelor's, master's. **Academic Requirements:** Arts/fine arts, English (including composition), humanities, mathematics, sciences (biological or physical), social science. **Classes:** Most classes have 10–19 students. Most lab/discussion sections have fewer than 10 students. **Majors with Highest Enrollment:** Business administration/management, education, nursing/registered nurse training (ASN, BSN, MSN, RN). **Disciplines with Highest Percentage of Degrees Awarded:** Education 32%, business/marketing 24%, psychology 7%, health professions and related sciences 6%, social sciences 6%, visual and performing arts 6%, biological/life sciences 4%, mathematics 4%, English 4%. **Special Study Options:** Accelerated program, cooperative education program, double major, English as a second language (ESL), honors program, independent study, internships, liberal arts/career combination, student-designed major, study abroad, teacher certification program.

FACILITIES
Housing: Coed dorms, special housing for disabled students. **Special Academic Facilities/Equipment:** Language lab, art gallery, sculpture garden. **Computers:** 100% of classrooms are wireless, 94% of public computers are PCs, 6% of public computers are Macs, network access in dorm rooms, network

access in dorm lounges, online administrative functions (other than registration), support for handheld computing, remote student-access to Web through college's connection.

CAMPUS LIFE
Activities: Choral groups, dance, drama/theater, music ensembles, musical theater, opera, student government, student newspaper. **Organizations:** 25 registered organizations, 6 honor societies, 1 religious organization. **Athletics (Intercollegiate):** *Men:* Baseball, basketball, cross-country, football, golf, soccer, tennis, track/field (indoor), track/field (outdoor). *Women:* Basketball, cross-country, golf, soccer, softball, tennis, track/field (indoor), track/field (outdoor), volleyball.

ADMISSIONS
Freshman Academic Profile: 6% in top 10% of high school class, 27% in top 25% of high school class, 56% in top 50% of high school class. 87% from public high schools. SSAT Math middle 50% range 440–470. SAT Critical Reading middle 50% range 450–500. SAT Writing middle 50% range 445–513. ACT middle 50% range 18–24. TOEFL required of all international applicants, minimum paper TOEFL 550, minimum computer TOEFL 213. **Basis for Candidate Selection:** *Very important factors considered include:* Academic GPA, rigor of secondary school record, standardized test scores. *Important factors considered include:* Character/personal qualities, class rank, extracurricular activities, interview, level of applicant's interest, recommendation(s). *Other factors considered include:* Application essay, talent/ability, volunteer work, work experience. **Freshman Admission Requirements:** High school diploma is required, and GED is accepted. *Academic units required:* 4 English, 3 math, 3 science (3 science labs), 3 social studies, 2 academic electives. *Academic units recommended:* 4 English, 3 math, 3 science (3 science labs), 2 foreign language, 3 social studies, 1 history, 2 academic electives. **Freshman Admission Statistics:** 711 applied, 47% admitted, 30% enrolled. **Transfer Admission Requirements:** College transcript(s). Minimum college GPA of 2.3 required. Lowest grade transferable C. **General Admission Information:** Application fee $35. Regular application deadline 8/15. Non-fall registration accepted. Admission may be deferred for a maximum of 2 years. Credit and/or placement offered for CEEB Advanced Placement tests.

COSTS AND FINANCIAL AID
Annual tuition $22,950. Room & board $6,580. Average book expense $1,200. **Required Forms and Deadlines:** FAFSA. Financial aid filing deadline 3/15. **Types of Aid:** *Need-based scholarships/grants:* Pell, SEOG, state scholarships/grants, private scholarships, the school's own gift aid. *Loans:* Direct Subsidized Stafford, Direct Unsubsidized Stafford, Direct PLUS, FFEL Subsidized Stafford, FFEL Unsubsidized Stafford, FFEL PLUS, Federal Perkins. **Financial Aid Statistics:** Highest amount earned per year from on-campus jobs $2,000.

See page 1344.

ROCKHURST UNIVERSITY

1100 Rockhurst Road, Kansas City, MO 64110
Phone: 816-501-4100 **E-mail:** admission@rockhurst.edu **CEEB Code:** 6611
Fax: 816-501-4241 **Website:** www.rockhurst.edu **ACT Code:** 2342
Financial Aid Phone: 816-501-4100

This private school, affiliated with the Roman Catholic Church, was founded in 1910. It has a 55-acre campus.

RATINGS
Admissions Selectivity Rating: 83   **Fire Safety Rating:** 63   **Green Rating:** 60*

STUDENTS AND FACULTY
Enrollment: 1,528. **Student Body:** 59% female, 41% male, 37% out-of-state. African American 6%, Asian 3%, Caucasian 83%, Hispanic 6%. **Retention and Graduation:** 86% freshmen return for sophomore year. 51% freshmen graduate within 4 years. 21% grads go on to further study within 1 year. 4% grads pursue arts and sciences degrees. 11% grads pursue business degrees. 4% grads pursue law degrees. 3% grads pursue medical degrees. **Faculty:** Student/faculty ratio 11:1. 125 full-time faculty, 84% hold PhDs. 98% faculty teach undergrads.

ACADEMICS
Degrees: Bachelor's, certificate, doctoral, master's, post-bachelor's certificate. **Academic Requirements:** Arts/fine arts, computer literacy, English (including composition), history, humanities, mathematics, philosophy, sciences (biological

or physical), theology. **Classes**: Most classes have 20–29 students. Most lab/discussion sections have 10–19 students. **Majors with Highest Enrollment**: Business administration/management, nursing/registered nurse training (ASN, BSN, MSN, RN), psychology. **Disciplines with Highest Percentage of Degrees Awarded**: Business/marketing 26%, health professions and related sciences 25%, psychology 8%, social sciences 7%, biological/life sciences 6%, communications/journalism 6%, English 6%. **Special Study Options**: Accelerated program, cooperative education program, cross-registration, double major, dual enrollment, exchange student program (domestic), honors program, independent study, internships, study abroad, teacher certification program.

FACILITIES

Housing: Coed dorms, men's dorms, women's dorms, apartments for single students, special housing for disabled students, RU on-campus housing. **Special Academic Facilities/Equipment**: Greenlease Art Gallery, Richardson Science Center. **Computers**: 100% of classrooms are wired, 100% of classrooms are wireless, 100% of public computers are PCs, network access in dorm rooms, network access in dorm lounges, online registration, online administrative functions (other than registration), remote student-access to Web through college's connection.

CAMPUS LIFE

Activities: Choral groups, drama/theater, literary magazine, musical theater, student government, student newspaper, yearbook. **Organizations**: 44 registered organizations, 4 honor societies, 6 religious organizations. 3 fraternities (13% men join), 3 sororities (26% women join). **Athletics (Intercollegiate)**: *Men*: Baseball, basketball, golf, soccer, tennis. *Women*: Basketball, golf, soccer, softball, tennis, volleyball.

ADMISSIONS

Freshman Academic Profile: 22% in top 10% of high school class, 55% in top 25% of high school class, 82% in top 50% of high school class. 45% from public high schools. SAT Math middle 50% range 510–610. SAT Critical Reading middle 50% range 480–630. ACT middle 50% range 22–27. TOEFL required of all international applicants, minimum paper TOEFL 550, minimum computer TOEFL 234. **Basis for Candidate Selection**: *Very important factors considered include*: Academic GPA, standardized test scores. *Important factors considered include*: Character/personal qualities, class rank, recommendation(s), rigor of secondary school record. *Other factors considered include*: Alumni/ae relation, extracurricular activities, interview, level of applicant's interest, religious affiliation/commitment, talent/ability, volunteer work. **Freshman Admission Requirements**: High school diploma is required, and GED is accepted. *Academic units recommended*: 4 English, 3 math, 3 science (1 science lab), 4 academic electives, 3 foreign language/social studies. **Freshman Admission Statistics**: 1,767 applied, 75% admitted, 30% enrolled. **Transfer Admission Requirements**: College transcript(s). Minimum college GPA of 2.5 required. Lowest grade transferable C-. **General Admission Information**: Application fee $25. Regular notification 9/15. Non-fall registration accepted. Admission may be deferred for a maximum of 1 year. Credit and/or placement offered for CEEB Advanced Placement tests.

COSTS AND FINANCIAL AID

Annual tuition $22,000. Room & board $6,200. Required fees $840. Average book expense $1,400. **Required Forms and Deadlines**: FAFSA. Financial aid filing deadline 6/30. **Notification of Awards**: Applicants will be notified of awards on a rolling basis beginning on or about 1/30. **Types of Aid**: *Need-based scholarships/grants*: Pell, SEOG, state scholarships/grants, private scholarships, the school's own gift aid. *Loans*: FFEL Subsidized Stafford, FFEL Unsubsidized Stafford, FFEL PLUS, Federal Perkins, alternative loans. **Student Employment**: Federal Work-Study Program available. Institutional employment available. Off-campus job opportunities are fair. **Financial Aid Statistics**: 56% freshmen, 50% undergrads receive need-based scholarship or grant aid. 48% freshmen, 43% undergrads receive need-based self-help aid. 39 freshmen, 157 undergrads receive athletic scholarships. 89% freshmen, 92% undergrads receive any aid. Highest amount earned per year from on-campus jobs $1,650.

ROCKY MOUNTAIN COLLEGE

1511 Poly Drive, Billings, MT 59102-1796
Phone: 406-657-1026 **E-mail**: admissions@rocky.edu **CEEB Code**: 4660
Fax: 406-657-1189 **Website**: www.rocky.edu **ACT Code**: 2426
Financial Aid Phone: 406-657-1031

This private school, affiliated with the Methodist Church, was founded in 1878. It has a 60-acre campus.

RATINGS

Admissions Selectivity Rating: 79   **Fire Safety Rating**: 60*   **Green Rating**: 60*

STUDENTS AND FACULTY

Enrollment: 817. **Student Body**: 55% female, 45% male, 38% out-of-state, 5% international (15 countries represented). Asian 1%, Caucasian 84%, Hispanic 2%, Native American 7%. **Retention and Graduation**: 67% freshmen return for sophomore year. 28% freshmen graduate within 4 years. 19% grads go on to further study within 1 year. 15% grads pursue arts and sciences degrees. 3% grads pursue business degrees. 1% grads pursue law degrees. 2% grads pursue medical degrees. **Faculty**: Student/faculty ratio 13:1. 48 full-time faculty, 65% hold PhDs. 100% faculty teach undergrads.

ACADEMICS

Degrees: Associate, bachelor's, master's, terminal. **Academic Requirements**: Arts/fine arts, English (including composition), health and wellness, history, humanities, mathematics, philosophy, public speaking, sciences (biological or physical), social science. **Classes**: Most classes have 10–19 students. Most lab/discussion sections have fewer than 10 students. **Majors with Highest Enrollment**: Biology/biological sciences, business administration/management, physician assistant. **Disciplines with Highest Percentage of Degrees Awarded**: Business/marketing 30%, education 11%, visual and performing arts 8%, psychology 7%, biological/life sciences 6%. **Special Study Options**: Accelerated program, distance learning, double major, dual enrollment, English as a second language (ESL), honors program, independent study, internships, student-designed major, study abroad, teacher certification program.

FACILITIES

Housing: Coed dorms, apartments for married students, apartments for single students, suites. **Special Academic Facilities/Equipment**: Billings Studio Theater, equestrian facilities, flight simulator/flight school, geology collection, museum, studio. **Computers**: 20% of classrooms are wireless, 100% of public computers are PCs, 10% of public computers are UNIX, network access in dorm rooms, network access in dorm lounges, online registration, online administrative functions (other than registration), support for handheld computing, remote student-access to Web through college's connection.

CAMPUS LIFE

Activities: Choral groups, concert band, drama/theater, jazz band, literary magazine, music ensembles, musical theater, pep band, student government, student newspaper, yearbook. **Organizations**: 28 registered organizations, 1 honor society, 4 religious organizations. **Athletics (Intercollegiate)**: *Men*: Basketball, cheerleading, football, golf, skiing (downhill/alpine). *Women*: Basketball, cheerleading, golf, skiing (downhill/alpine), soccer, volleyball.

ADMISSIONS

Freshman Academic Profile: 21% in top 10% of high school class, 43% in top 25% of high school class, 78% in top 50% of high school class. SAT Math middle 50% range 450–570. SAT Critical Reading middle 50% range 460–590. ACT middle 50% range 19–24. TOEFL required of all international applicants, minimum paper TOEFL 525, minimum computer TOEFL 197. **Basis for Candidate Selection**: *Very important factors considered include*: Academic GPA, rigor of secondary school record, standardized test scores. *Important factors considered include*: Class rank. *Other factors considered include*: Alumni/ae relation, application essay, character/personal qualities, extracurricular activities, interview, level of applicant's interest, recommendation(s), talent/ability, volunteer work, work experience. **Freshman Admission Requirements**: High school diploma is required, and GED is accepted. *Academic units required*: 4 English, 2 math, 2 science (1 science lab), 1 foreign language, 2 social studies, 2 history. *Academic units recommended*: 4 English, 3 math, 2 science (1 science lab), 2 foreign language, 2 social studies, 2 history. **Freshman Admission Statistics**: 596 applied, 72% admitted, 36% enrolled. **Transfer Admission Requirements**: College transcript(s). Minimum college GPA of 2.0 required. Lowest grade transferable C-. **General Admission Information**: Application fee $25. Regular notification is rolling. Non-fall registration accepted. Admission may be deferred for a maximum of 1 year. Credit and/or placement offered for CEEB Advanced Placement tests.

COSTS AND FINANCIAL AID

Annual tuition $16,389. Room & board $5,608. Required fees $253. Average book expense $900. **Required Forms and Deadlines**: FAFSA, institution's own financial aid form. Financial aid filing deadline 3/1. **Notification of Awards**: Applicants will be notified of awards on a rolling basis beginning on or about 2/1. **Types of Aid**: *Need-based scholarships/grants*: Pell, SEOG, state scholarships/grants, private scholarships, the school's own gift aid. *Loans*: FFEL Subsidized Stafford, FFEL Unsubsidized Stafford, FFEL PLUS, Federal Perkins. **Student Employment**: Federal Work-Study Program available. Institutional employment available. Off-campus job opportunities are good. **Financial Aid Statistics**: 67% freshmen, 73% undergrads receive need-based scholarship or grant aid. 52% freshmen, 55% undergrads receive need-based self-help aid. 17 freshmen, 31 undergrads receive athletic scholarships. 90% freshmen, 90% undergrads receive any aid. Highest amount earned per year from on-campus jobs $3,985..

ROCKY MOUNTAIN COLLEGE OF ART & DESIGN

1600 Pierce Street, Lakewood, CO 80214
Phone: 303-753-6046 **E-mail**: admissions@rmcad.edu
Fax: 303-567-7281 **Website**: www.rmcad.edu **ACT Code**: 5359
Financial Aid Phone: 303-753-6046

This proprietary school was founded in 1963. It has a 23-acre campus.

RATINGS

Admissions Selectivity Rating: 60*   **Fire Safety Rating**: 60*   **Green Rating**: 60*

STUDENTS AND FACULTY

Enrollment: 450. **Faculty**: Student/faculty ratio 19:1.

ACADEMICS

Degrees: Bachelor's. **Majors with Highest Enrollment**: Graphic design, illustration, interior design.

FACILITIES

Special Academic Facilities/Equipment: Drive-up gallery, fine arts exhibit space, Philip Steele Gallery.

ADMISSIONS

Freshman Academic Profile: TOEFL required of all international applicants, minimum paper TOEFL 500, minimum computer TOEFL 173. **Basis for Candidate Selection**: *Very important factors considered include*: Extracurricular activities. *Important factors considered include*: Academic GPA. **Freshman Admission Requirements**: High school diploma is required, and GED is accepted. **Freshman Admission Statistics**: 420 applied. **Transfer Admission Requirements**: College transcript(s). Minimum college GPA of 2.0 required. **General Admission Information**: Non-fall registration accepted. Admission may be deferred for a maximum of 1 semester.

COSTS AND FINANCIAL AID

Annual tuition $19,752. Average book expense $600. **Student Employment**: Federal Work-Study Program available. Off-campus job opportunities are good.

See page 1346.

ROGER WILLIAMS UNIVERSITY

1 Old Ferry Road, Bristol, RI 02809
Phone: 401-254-3500 **E-mail**: admit@rwu.edu **CEEB Code**: 3729
Fax: 401-254-3557 **Website**: www.rwu.edu **ACT Code**: 3814
Financial Aid Phone: 401-254-3100

This private school was founded in 1956. It has a 140-acre campus.

RATINGS

Admissions Selectivity Rating: 80   **Fire Safety Rating**: 89   **Green Rating**: 60*

STUDENTS AND FACULTY

Enrollment: 4,343. **Student Body**: 49% female, 51% male, 86% out-of-state, 2% international (39 countries represented). African American 1%, Asian 1%,

Caucasian 78%, Hispanic 2%. **Retention and Graduation**: 77% freshmen return for sophomore year. 20% grads go on to further study within 1 year. **Faculty**: Student/faculty ratio 15:1. 182 full-time faculty, 82% hold PhDs. 100% faculty teach undergrads.

ACADEMICS

Degrees: Associate, bachelor's, certificate, first professional, master's, post-bachelor's certificate, terminal. **Academic Requirements**: Arts/fine arts, English (including composition), history, humanities, mathematics, philosophy, sciences (biological or physical), social science. **Classes**: Most classes have 20–29 students. Most lab/discussion sections have 20–29 students. **Majors with Highest Enrollment**: Architecture (BArch, BA/BS, MArch, MA/MS, PhD), business administration/management, criminal justice/law enforcement administration. **Disciplines with Highest Percentage of Degrees Awarded**: Business/marketing 21%, security and protective services 15%, architecture 10%, psychology 10%, biological/life sciences 6%. **Special Study Options**: Cooperative education program, distance learning, double major, dual enrollment, English as a second language (ESL), exchange student program (domestic), external degree program, honors program, independent study, internships, liberal arts/career combination, student-designed major, study abroad, teacher certification program.

FACILITIES

Housing: Coed dorms, apartments for single students, special housing for disabled students, special interest, academic theme housing, honors, wellness, nonsmoking. **Special Academic Facilities/Equipment**: Marine and natural sciences building, school of law and law library, main library, architecture building and architecture library, performing arts center, Thomas J. Paolino Recreation Center. **Computers**: 25% of classrooms are wired, 75% of classrooms are wireless, 90% of public computers are PCs, 10% of public computers are Macs, network access in dorm rooms, online registration, online administrative functions (other than registration), remote student-access to Web through college's connection.

CAMPUS LIFE

Activities: Choral groups, dance, drama/theater, literary magazine, musical theater, radio station, student government, student newspaper, student-run film society, yearbook. **Organizations**: 93 registered organizations, 8 honor societies, 4 religious organizations. **Athletics (Intercollegiate)** *Men*: Baseball, basketball, cross-country, diving, equestrian sports, lacrosse, sailing, soccer, swimming, tennis, wrestling. *Women*: Basketball, cross-country, diving, equestrian sports, lacrosse, sailing, soccer, softball, swimming, tennis, volleyball.

ADMISSIONS

Freshman Academic Profile: 12% in top 10% of high school class, 30% in top 25% of high school class, 75% in top 50% of high school class. 85% from public high schools. SAT Math middle 50% range 510–600. SAT Critical Reading middle 50% range 490–580. ACT middle 50% range 21–25. **Basis for Candidate Selection**: *Very important factors considered include*: Academic GPA, application essay, recommendation(s), rigor of secondary school record, standardized test scores. *Important factors considered include*: Class rank, extracurricular activities. *Other factors considered include*: Alumni/ae relation, character/personal qualities, first generation, interview, talent/ability, volunteer work, work experience. **Freshman Admission Requirements**: High school diploma is required, and GED is accepted. *Academic units required*: 4 English, 3 math, 2 science (2 science labs), 2 social studies, 2 history, 2 academic electives. *Academic units recommended*: 4 English, 4 math, 4 science (2 science labs), 2 foreign language, 3 social studies, 3 history, 3 academic electives. **Freshman Admission Statistics**: 7,200 applied, 68% admitted, 21% enrolled. **Transfer Admission Requirements**: College transcript(s), essay or personal statement. Minimum college GPA of 2.5 required. Lowest grade transferable C. **General Admission Information**: Application fee $50. Early decision application deadline 11/1. Regular application deadline 2/1. Regular notification 3/15. Non-fall registration accepted. Admission may be deferred for a maximum of 1 year. Credit and/or placement offered for CEEB Advanced Placement tests.

COSTS AND FINANCIAL AID

Annual tuition $24,312. Room and board $11,490. Required fees $1,630. Average book expense $900. **Required Forms and Deadlines**: FAFSA, CSS/Financial Aid PROFILE. Financial aid filing deadline 2/1. **Notification of Awards**: Applicants will be notified of awards on a rolling basis beginning on or about 3/20. **Types of Aid**: *Need-based scholarships/grants*: Pell, SEOG, state scholarships/grants, private scholarships, the school's own gift aid. *Loans*: FFEL Subsidized Stafford, FFEL Unsubsidized Stafford, FFEL PLUS, Federal Perkins. **Student Employment**: Federal Work-Study Program available. Institutional employment available. Off-campus job opportunities are excellent. **Financial Aid Statistics**: 43% freshmen, 40% undergrads receive need-based scholarship or grant aid. 50% freshmen, 49% undergrads receive need-based self-help aid. 85% freshmen, 78% undergrads receive any aid.

ROLLINS COLLEGE

Best 368

1000 Holt Avenue, #2720, Winter Park, FL 32789-4499
Phone: 407-646-2161 **E-mail:** admission@rollins.edu **CEEB Code:** 5572
Fax: 407-646-1502 **Website:** www.rollins.edu **ACT Code:** 0748
Financial Aid Phone: 407-646-2395

This private school was founded in 1885. It has a 70-acre campus.

RATINGS
Admissions Selectivity Rating: 91   **Fire Safety Rating:** 87   **Green Rating:** 72

STUDENTS AND FACULTY
Enrollment: 1,720. **Student Body:** 60% female, 40% male, 47% out-of-state, 3% international (33 countries represented). African American 5%, Asian 4%, Caucasian 71%, Hispanic 10%. **Retention and Graduation:** 84% freshmen return for sophomore year. 59% freshmen graduate within 4 years. 33% grads go on to further study within 1 year. 19% grads pursue arts and sciences degrees. 6% grads pursue business degrees. 6% grads pursue law degrees. 2% grads pursue medical degrees. **Faculty:** Student/faculty ratio 10:1. 188 full-time faculty, 93% hold PhDs. 100% faculty teach undergrads.

ACADEMICS
Degrees: Bachelor's, master's. **Academic Requirements:** Arts/fine arts, communication across the curriculum, computer literacy, English (including composition), foreign languages, history, humanities, mathematics, non-Western cultures, personal fitness, philosophy, sciences (biological or physical), social science, values. **Classes:** Most classes have 10–19 students. **Majors with Highest Enrollment:** Economics, international business, psychology. **Disciplines with Highest Percentage of Degrees Awarded:** Social sciences 27%, psychology 15%, visual and performing arts 14%, business/marketing 11%, biological/life sciences 8%. **Special Study Options:** Accelerated program, cross-registration, double major, dual enrollment, exchange student program (domestic), honors program, independent study, internships, student-designed major, study abroad, teacher certification program.

FACILITIES
Housing: Coed dorms, men's dorms, women's dorms, apartments for single students, special housing for disabled students, fraternity/sorority housing. **Special Academic Facilities/Equipment:** Art museum, child development center, fine arts center, language lab, psychology center, skills development building, state-of-the-art IT classroom, theaters. **Computers:** 33% of classrooms are wired, 98% of classrooms are wireless, 90% of public computers are PCs, 10% of public computers are Macs, network access in dorm rooms, network access in dorm lounges, online registration, online administrative functions (other than registration), remote student-access to Web through college's connection.

CAMPUS LIFE
Activities: Choral groups, dance, drama/theater, literary magazine, music ensembles, musical theater, pep band, radio station, student government, student newspaper, student-run film society, television station, yearbook. **Organizations:** 88 registered organizations, 5 honor societies, 5 religious organizations. 6 fraternities (20% men join), 7 sororities (23% women join). **Athletics (Intercollegiate):** *Men:* Baseball, basketball, crew/rowing, cross-country, golf, sailing, soccer, swimming, tennis, water skiing. *Women:* Basketball, cheerleading, crew/rowing, cross-country, golf, sailing, soccer, softball, swimming, tennis, volleyball, water skiing. Environmental Initiatives: Recycling throughout campus including dorms and dining service areas. Planting of native and drought resistant foliage throughout campus. An ongoing commitment is in the works for using biodegradable plates and cups in dining service area. Next step is to use them for catering events.

ADMISSIONS
Freshman Academic Profile: 35% in top 10% of high school class, 65% in top 25% of high school class, 90% in top 50% of high school class. 53% from public high schools. SAT Math middle 50% range 555–640. SAT Critical Reading middle 50% range 555–640. ACT middle 50% range 23–28. TOEFL required of all international applicants, minimum paper TOEFL 550, minimum computer TOEFL 213. **Basis for Candidate Selection:** *Very important factors considered include:* Academic GPA, rigor of secondary school record. *Important factors considered include:* Application essay, extracurricular

activities, recommendation(s), standardized test scores, talent/ability. *Other factors considered include:* Alumni/ae relation, character/personal qualities, class rank, first generation, interview, level of applicant's interest, racial/ethnic status, volunteer work, work experience. **Freshman Admission Requirements:** High school diploma is required, and GED is accepted. *Academic units required:* 4 English, 3 math, 2 science, 2 foreign language, 2 social studies, 2 history, 2 academic electives. *Academic units recommended:* 4 English, 4 math, 4 science, 3 foreign language, 3 social studies, 3 history, 3 academic electives. **Freshman Admission Statistics:** 2,998 applied, 55% admitted, 30% enrolled. **Transfer Admission Requirements:** High school transcript, college transcript(s), essay or personal statement, standardized test score, statement of good standing from prior institution(s). Lowest grade transferable C. **General Admission Information:** Application fee $40. Early decision application deadline 11/15. Regular application deadline 2/15. Regular notification 4/1. Non-fall registration accepted. Credit and/or placement offered for CEEB Advanced Placement tests.

COSTS AND FINANCIAL AID
Average book expense $676. **Required Forms and Deadlines:** FAFSA, institution's own financial aid form. Financial aid filing deadline 3/1. **Notification of Awards:** Applicants will be notified of awards on or about 3/1. **Types of Aid:** *Need-based scholarships/grants:* Pell, SEOG, state scholarships/grants, private scholarships, the school's own gift aid. *Loans:* Direct Subsidized Stafford, Direct Unsubsidized Stafford, Direct PLUS, Federal Perkins, college/university loans from institutional funds. **Financial Aid Statistics:** 40% freshmen, 41% undergrads receive need-based scholarship or grant aid. 38% freshmen, 38% undergrads receive need-based self-help aid. 12 freshmen, 84 undergrads receive athletic scholarships. 70% freshmen, 70% undergrads receive any aid.

ROOSEVELT UNIVERSITY

430 South Michigan Avenue, Chicago, IL 60605
Phone: 312-341-3515 **E-mail:** applyRU@roosevelt.edu **CEEB Code:** 1666
Fax: 312-341-3523 **Website:** www.roosevelt.edu **ACT Code:** 1124
Financial Aid Phone: 312-341-2195

This private school was founded in 1945. It has a 34-acre campus.

RATINGS
Admissions Selectivity Rating: 73   **Fire Safety Rating:** 60*   **Green Rating:** 60*

STUDENTS AND FACULTY
Enrollment: 3,907. **Student Body:** 67% female, 33% male, 8% out-of-state, 2% international (65 countries represented). African American 24%, Asian 5%, Caucasian 49%, Hispanic 11%. **Retention and Graduation:** 70% freshmen return for sophomore year. **Faculty:** Student/faculty ratio 12:1. 121 full-time faculty. 95% faculty teach undergrads.

ACADEMICS
Degrees: Bachelor's, diploma, doctoral, master's, post-bachelor's certificate, post-master's certificate. **Academic Requirements:** English (including composition), history, humanities, mathematics, sciences (biological or physical), social science. **Classes:** Most classes have 10–19 students. **Majors with Highest Enrollment:** Business administration/management, elementary education and teaching, psychology. **Disciplines with Highest Percentage of Degrees Awarded:** Business/marketing 32%, psychology 12%, computer and information sciences 9%, education 8%, social sciences 8%. **Special Study Options:** Accelerated program, distance learning, double major, dual enrollment, English as a second language (ESL), honors program, independent study, internships, student-designed major, study abroad, teacher certification program.

FACILITIES
Housing: Coed dorms, apartments for single students, traditional residence hall, high-rise residence hall. **Special Academic Facilities/Equipment:** The Chicago campus is approximately 1 mile from the Museum of Natural History, aquarium, planetarium, contemporary art museums; and 2 blocks from the Art Institute of Chicago. **Computers:** 95% of public computers are PCs, 5% of public computers are Macs, 1% of public computers are UNIX, online registration, online administrative functions (other than registration), remote student-access to Web through college's connection.

CAMPUS LIFE
Activities: Dance, literary magazine, radio station, student government, student newspaper. **Organizations:** 48 registered organizations, 3 honor societies, 4

religious organizations. 1 fraternity (1% men join), 2 sororities (1% women join).

ADMISSIONS

Freshman Academic Profile: 3% in top 10% of high school class, 11% in top 25% of high school class, 33% in top 50% of high school class. 80% from public high schools. SAT Math middle 50% range 455–610. SAT Critical Reading middle 50% range 512–628. ACT middle 50% range 20–26. TOEFL required of all international applicants, minimum paper TOEFL 525, minimum computer TOEFL 197. **Basis for Candidate Selection**: *Very important factors considered include*: Rigor of secondary school record. *Important factors considered include*: Application essay, character/personal qualities, class rank, interview, recommendation(s), standardized test scores. *Other factors considered include*: Alumni/ae relation, extracurricular activities, talent/ability, volunteer work, work experience. **Freshman Admission Requirements**: High school diploma is required, and GED is accepted. *Academic units required*: 4 English, 3 math, 3 science (2 science labs), 2 social studies, 1 history, 2 academic electives. *Academic units recommended*: 4 English, 4 math, 3 science (2 science labs), 2 foreign language, 2 social studies, 2 history, 2 academic electives. **Freshman Admission Statistics**: 1,390 applied, 60% admitted, 39% enrolled. **Transfer Admission Requirements**: College transcript(s), essay or personal statement, statement of good standing from prior institution(s). Minimum college GPA of 2.3 required. Lowest grade transferable D. **General Admission Information**: Application fee $25. Regular application deadline 9/1. Regular notification is rolling. Non-fall registration accepted. Admission may be deferred for a maximum of 1 year. Common Application accepted. Credit and/or placement offered for CEEB Advanced Placement tests.

COSTS AND FINANCIAL AID

Annual tuition $16,680. Room and board $9,848. Required fees $300. Average book expense $1,200. **Required Forms and Deadlines**: FAFSA, institution's own financial aid form. Financial aid filing deadline 4/1. **Notification of Awards**: Applicants will be notified of awards on a rolling basis beginning on or about 3/15. **Types of Aid**: *Need-based scholarships/grants*: Pell, SEOG, state scholarships/grants, private scholarships, the school's own gift aid. *Loans*: FFEL Subsidized Stafford, FFEL Unsubsidized Stafford, FFEL PLUS, Federal Perkins. **Financial Aid Statistics**: 43% freshmen, 52% undergrads receive need-based scholarship or grant aid. 43% freshmen, 50% undergrads receive need-based self-help aid.

ROSE-HULMAN INSTITUTE OF TECHNOLOGY

5500 Wabash Avenue-CM 1, Terre Haute, IN 47803-3999
Phone: 812-877-8213 **E-mail**: admis.ofc@rose-hulman.edu **CEEB Code**: 1668
Fax: 812-877-8941 **Website**: www.rose-hulman.edu **ACT Code**: 1232
Financial Aid Phone: 812-877-8259

This private school was founded in 1874. It has a 200-acre campus.

RATINGS

Admissions Selectivity Rating: 91   **Fire Safety Rating**: 93   **Green Rating**: 77

STUDENTS AND FACULTY

Enrollment: 1,851. **Student Body**: 19% female, 81% male, 57% out-of-state, 2% international (20 countries represented). African American 2%, Asian 4%, Caucasian 91%, Hispanic 1%. **Retention and Graduation**: 92% freshmen return for sophomore year. 71% freshmen graduate within 4 years. 20% grads go on to further study within 1 year. 17% grads pursue arts and sciences degrees. 1% grads pursue business degrees. 1% grads pursue law degrees. 1% grads pursue medical degrees. **Faculty**: Student/faculty ratio 12:1. 154 full-time faculty, 100% hold PhDs. 100% faculty teach undergrads.

ACADEMICS

Degrees: Bachelor's, master's. **Academic Requirements**: Computer literacy, English (including composition), humanities, mathematics, sciences (biological or physical), social science. **Classes**: Most classes have 20–29 students. Most lab/discussion sections have 20–29 students. **Majors with Highest Enrollment**: Chemical engineering; electrical, electronics, and communications engineering; mechanical engineering. **Disciplines with Highest Percentage of Degrees Awarded**: Engineering 77%, computer and information sciences 11%, mathematics 5%, physical sciences 4%, biological/life sciences 2%. **Special Study Options**: Accelerated program, cooperative education program, cross-registration, double major, independent study, study abroad.

FACILITIES

Housing: Coed dorms, men's dorms, apartments for single students, fraternity/sorority housing. **Special Academic Facilities/Equipment**: Union Building has a collection of British watercolors; Moench Hall section A: Western sculpture, all sections: Eclectic Art; Hadley Hall: Hadley Pottery and Salty Seamon Paintings; Oakley Observatory. **Computers**: 100% of classrooms are wired, 100% of classrooms are wireless, 95% of public computers are PCs, 5% of public computers are UNIX, network access in dorm rooms, network access in dorm lounges, online registration, online administrative functions (other than registration), support for handheld computing, remote student-access to Web through college's connection. Undergraduates are required to own a computer. Environmental Initiatives: Signing of the American College & University President's Climate Commitment. Formation of a Sustainability Team responsible for instilling a culture of sustainability integrating sustainability with programs in education, operations, and communtiy service. Serving as a pilot campus for the Sustainability Tracking and Assessment Rating System (STARS) Project through the Association for the Advancement of Sustainability in Higher Education.

CAMPUS LIFE

Activities: Choral groups, concert band, dance, drama/theater, jazz band, literary magazine, music ensembles, musical theater, pep band, radio station, student government, student newspaper, yearbook. **Organizations**: 60 registered organizations, 13 honor societies, 3 religious organizations. 8 fraternities (37% men join), 3 sororities (50% women join). **Athletics (Intercollegiate)**: *Men*: Baseball, basketball, cheerleading, cross-country, diving, football, golf, riflery, soccer, swimming, tennis, track/field (indoor), track/field (outdoor), wrestling. *Women*: Basketball, cheerleading, cross-country, diving, golf, riflery, soccer, softball, swimming, tennis, track/field (indoor), track/field (outdoor), volleyball.

ADMISSIONS

Freshman Academic Profile: 63% in top 10% of high school class, 93% in top 25% of high school class, 100% in top 50% of high school class. 84% from public high schools. SAT Math middle 50% range 630–710. SAT Critical Reading middle 50% range 560–680. SAT Writing middle 50% range 550–650. ACT middle 50% range 27–31. TOEFL required of all international applicants, minimum paper TOEFL 550, minimum computer TOEFL 210. **Basis for Candidate Selection**: *Very important factors considered include*: Class rank, rigor of secondary school record, standardized test scores. *Important factors considered include*: Character/personal qualities, racial/ethnic status, recommendation(s). *Other factors considered include*: Alumni/ae relation, extracurricular activities, interview, talent/ability, volunteer work, work experience. **Freshman Admission Requirements**: High school diploma is required, and GED is not accepted. *Academic units required*: 4 English, 4 math, 2 science (2 science labs), 2 social studies, 4 academic electives. *Academic units recommended*: 5 math, 3 science. **Freshman Admission Statistics**: 3,059 applied, 72% admitted, 24% enrolled. **Transfer Admission Requirements**: College transcript(s), essay or personal statement, statement of good standing from prior institution(s). Minimum college GPA of 3.0 required. Lowest grade transferable C. **General Admission Information**: Application fee $40. Regular application deadline 3/1. Regular notification is rolling. Non-fall registration not accepted. Admission may be deferred for a maximum of 1 year. Credit and/or placement offered for CEEB Advanced Placement tests.

COSTS AND FINANCIAL AID

Annual tuition $30,243. Room and board $8,343. Required fees $480. Average book expense $1,500. **Required Forms and Deadlines**: FAFSA. Financial aid filing deadline 3/1. **Notification of Awards**: Applicants will be notified of awards on or about 3/10. **Types of Aid**: *Need-based scholarships/grants*: Pell, SEOG, state scholarships/grants, the school's own gift aid. *Loans*: Direct Subsidized Stafford, Direct Unsubsidized Stafford, Direct PLUS, Federal Perkins. **Financial Aid Statistics**: 73% freshmen, 67% undergrads receive need-based scholarship or grant aid. 65% freshmen, 59% undergrads receive need-based self-help aid. 100% freshmen, 99% undergrads receive any aid. Highest amount earned per year from on-campus jobs $1,500.

ROSEMONT COLLEGE

1400 Montgomery Avenue, Rosemont, PA 19010
Phone: 610-526-2966 **E-mail:** admissions@rosemont.edu **CEEB Code:** 2763
Fax: 610-520-4399 **Website:** www.rosemont.edu **ACT Code:** 3676
Financial Aid Phone: 610-527-0200

This private school, affiliated with the Roman Catholic Church, was founded in 1921. It has a 56-acre campus.

RATINGS
Admissions Selectivity Rating: 79   **Fire Safety Rating:** 82   **Green Rating:** 79

STUDENTS AND FACULTY
Enrollment: 578. **Student Body:** 95% female, 5% male, 35% out-of-state, 2% international (21 countries represented). African American 33%, Asian 5%, Caucasian 48%, Hispanic 7%. **Retention and Graduation:** 81% freshmen return for sophomore year. 58% freshmen graduate within 4 years. 36% grads go on to further study within 1 year. 35% grads pursue arts and sciences degrees. 5% grads pursue business degrees. 2% grads pursue law degrees. 9% grads pursue medical degrees. **Faculty:** Student/faculty ratio 8:1. 32 full-time faculty, 91% hold PhDs. 100% faculty teach undergrads.

ACADEMICS
Degrees: Bachelor's, master's, post-bachelor's certificate. **Academic Requirements:** Arts/fine arts, computer literacy, English (including composition), experiential component (choice of: internship, service learning, study abroad/study away), foreign languages, history, humanities, mathematics, philosophy, religious studies, sciences (biological or physical), social science. **Classes:** Most classes have 10–19 students. **Majors with Highest Enrollment:** English language and literature, psychology, social sciences. **Disciplines with Highest Percentage of Degrees Awarded:** Business/marketing 49%, social sciences 11%, psychology 9%, visual and performing arts 7%, communication technologies 4%, English 4%, foreign languages and literature 4%. **Special Study Options:** Accelerated program, cross-registration, double major, honors program, independent study, internships, liberal arts/career combination, student-designed major, study abroad, teacher certification program.

FACILITIES
Housing: Women's dorms, redesigned Cornelia Connelly Hall in the center of campus is now a state-of-the-art residence hall. **Special Academic Facilities/Equipment:** McShain Performing Arts Center, Conwell Learning Center. **Computers:** 70% of public computers are PCs, 30% of public computers are Macs, network access in dorm rooms, network access in dorm lounges, remote student-access to Web through college's connection.

CAMPUS LIFE
Activities: Choral groups, concert band, dance, drama/theater, jazz band, literary magazine, marching band, music ensembles, musical theater, opera, pep band, radio station, student government, student newspaper, yearbook. **Organizations:** 23 registered organizations, 6 honor societies, 1 religious organization. **Athletics (Intercollegiate):** *Women:* Basketball, field hockey, lacrosse, softball, tennis, volleyball. Environmental Initiatives: Energy Star Procurement Policy. Waste Minimization Policy. Indoor Space Temperature Policy.

ADMISSIONS
Freshman Academic Profile: 57% in top 10% of high school class, 43% in top 25% of high school class, 83% in top 50% of high school class. 61% from public high schools. SAT Math middle 50% range 415–500. SAT Critical Reading middle 50% range 410–500. SAT Writing middle 50% range 410–505. TOEFL required of all international applicants, minimum paper TOEFL 500. **Basis for Candidate Selection:** *Very important factors considered include:* Class rank, interview, rigor of secondary school record. *Important factors considered include:* Application essay, extracurricular activities, recommendation(s), standardized test scores, talent/ability, volunteer work. *Other factors considered include:* Alumni/ae relation, character/personal qualities, work experience. **Freshman Admission Requirements:** High school diploma is required, and GED is accepted. *Academic units required:* 4 English, 3 math, 3 science (2 science labs), 1 social studies, 1 history, 7 academic electives. *Academic units recommended:* 4 English, 3 math, 3 science (2 science labs), 2 foreign language, 2 social studies, 2 history, 4 academic electives. **Freshman Admission Statistics:** 450 applied, 58% admitted, 27% enrolled. **Transfer Admission Requirements:** College transcript(s). Minimum college GPA of 2.5 required. Lowest grade transferable C. **General Admission Information:** Application fee $35. Regular application deadline 8/1. Regular notification is rolling. Non-fall registration accepted. Admission may be deferred for a maximum of 1 year. Credit and/or placement offered for CEEB Advanced Placement tests.

COSTS AND FINANCIAL AID
Annual tuition $20,600. Room & board $9,200. Required fees $875. Average book expense $1,000. **Required Forms and Deadlines:** FAFSA. Financial aid filing deadline 2/15. **Notification of Awards:** Applicants will be notified of awards on a rolling basis beginning on or about 2/15. **Types of Aid:** *Need-based scholarships/grants:* Pell, SEOG, state scholarships/grants, private scholarships, the school's own gift aid. *Loans:* FFEL Subsidized Stafford, FFEL Unsubsidized Stafford, FFEL PLUS, Federal Perkins, alternative loans offered, payment plans offered. **Student Employment:** Federal Work-Study Program available. Institutional employment available. Off-campus job opportunities are good. **Financial Aid Statistics:** 73% freshmen, 77% undergrads receive need-based scholarship or grant aid. 56% freshmen, 60% undergrads receive need-based self-help aid. Highest amount earned per year from on-campus jobs $2,000.

ROWAN UNIVERSITY

201 Mullica Hill Road, Glassboro, NJ 08028
Phone: 856-256-4200 **E-mail:** admissions@rowan.edu **CEEB Code:** 2515
Fax: 856-256-4430 **Website:** www.rowan.edu **ACT Code:** 2560
Financial Aid Phone: 856-256-4250

This public school was founded in 1923. It has a 200-acre campus.

RATINGS
Admissions Selectivity Rating: 84   **Fire Safety Rating:** 87   **Green Rating:** 87

STUDENTS AND FACULTY
Enrollment: 8,018. **Student Body:** 53% female, 47% male, 3% out-of-state. African American 9%, Asian 3%, Caucasian 79%, Hispanic 7%. **Retention and Graduation:** 84% freshmen return for sophomore year. 42% freshmen graduate within 4 years. **Faculty:** Student/faculty ratio 12:1. 451 full-time faculty, 78% hold PhDs. 95% faculty teach undergrads.

ACADEMICS
Degrees: Bachelor's, doctoral, master's. **Academic Requirements:** Arts/fine arts, computer literacy, English (including composition), history, humanities, information literacy, mathematics, multicultural/global, philosophy, public speaking, sciences (biological or physical), writing intensive. **Classes:** Most classes have 20–29 students. Most lab/discussion sections have 20–29 students. **Majors with Highest Enrollment:** Business administration/management; communications, journalism, and related fields; elementary education and teaching. **Disciplines with Highest Percentage of Degrees Awarded:** Education 23%, communications/journalism 15%, business/marketing 14%, visual and performing arts 7%, law/legal studies 6%. **Special Study Options:** Cross-registration, double major, dual enrollment, English as a second language (ESL), honors program, independent study, internships, study abroad, teacher certification program.

FACILITIES
Housing: Coed dorms, men's dorms, women's dorms, apartments for married students, apartments for single students, special housing for disabled students, special housing for international students, town houses, unmarried students under age 21 not living with parents must live on campus. **Special Academic Facilities/Equipment:** Concert hall, glass collection, student recreation center, on-campus early childhood demonstration center, greenhouse for biological studies, observatory, art gallery. **Computers:** 1% of classrooms are wired, 95% of classrooms are wireless, 79% of public computers are PCs, 18% of public computers are Macs, 3% of public computers are UNIX, network access in dorm rooms, network access in dorm lounges, online registration, online administrative functions (other than registration), support for handheld computing, remote student-access to Web through college's connection.

CAMPUS LIFE
Activities: Choral groups, concert band, dance, drama/theater, jazz band, literary magazine, music ensembles, musical theater, opera, pep band, radio station, student government, student newspaper, student-run film society, television station, yearbook. **Organizations:** 111 registered organizations, 7 honor societies, 4 religious organizations. 13 fraternities (12% men join), 12 sororities (8% women join). **Athletics (Intercollegiate):** *Men:* Baseball, basketball, cross-country, diving, football, soccer, swimming, track/field (indoor), track/field (outdoor). *Women:* Basketball, cross-country, diving, field hockey, lacrosse, soccer, softball, swimming, track/field (indoor), track/field (outdoor), volleyball. Environmental Initiatives: Purchase 25% of electricity from renewable resources. First installation of higher education in NJ to sign the ACUPCC. Energy Star procurement policy for appliances and equipment.

ADMISSIONS

Freshman Academic Profile: 18% in top 10% of high school class, 52% in top 25% of high school class, 89% in top 50% of high school class. SAT Math middle 50% range 510–620. SAT Critical Reading middle 50% range 490–590. SAT Writing middle 50% range 480–580. TOEFL required of all international applicants, minimum paper TOEFL 550, minimum computer TOEFL 213. **Basis for Candidate Selection**: *Very important factors considered include*: Academic GPA, class rank, rigor of secondary school record, standardized test scores. *Important factors considered include*: Extracurricular activities, recommendation(s), talent/ability. *Other factors considered include*: Alumni/ae relation, character/personal qualities, level of applicant's interest, racial/ethnic status, volunteer work, work experience. **Freshman Admission Requirements**: High school diploma is required, and GED is accepted. *Academic units required*: 4 English, 3 math, 2 science (2 science labs), 2 social studies, 5 academic electives. **Freshman Admission Statistics**: 7,816 applied, 46% admitted, 34% enrolled. **Transfer Admission Requirements**: College transcript(s). Minimum college GPA of 2.0 required. Lowest grade transferable D-. **General Admission Information**: Application fee $50. Regular application deadline 3/1. Regular notification is rolling. Non-fall registration accepted. Admission may be deferred for a maximum of 1 year. Credit and/or placement offered for CEEB Advanced Placement tests.

COSTS AND FINANCIAL AID

Annual in-state tuition $7,308. Annual out-of-state tuition $14,616. Room and board $9,242. Required fees $2,760. Average book expense $900. **Required Forms and Deadlines**: FAFSA. Financial aid filing deadline 3/15. **Notification of Awards**: Applicants will be notified of awards on or about 3/1. **Types of Aid**: *Need-based scholarships/grants*: Pell, SEOG, state scholarships/grants, private scholarships, the school's own gift aid. *Loans*: Direct Subsidized Stafford, Direct Unsubsidized Stafford, Direct PLUS. **Student Employment**: Off-campus job opportunities are good. **Financial Aid Statistics**: 53% freshmen, 46% undergrads receive need-based scholarship or grant aid. 44% freshmen, 53% undergrads receive need-based self-help aid. 82% freshmen, 83% undergrads receive any aid. Highest amount earned per year from on-campus jobs $2,000.

RUSH UNIVERSITY

600 South Paulina, Suite 440, Chicago, IL 60612-3878
Phone: 312-942-7100 **E-mail**: Rush_Admissions@rush.edu
Fax: 312-942-2219 **Website**: www.rushu.rush.edu **ACT Code**: 1617
Financial Aid Phone: 312-942-6256

This private school was founded in 1972. It has a 35-acre campus.

RATINGS
Admissions Selectivity Rating: 60*   **Fire Safety Rating**: 60*   **Green Rating**: 60*

STUDENTS AND FACULTY

Enrollment: 258. **Student Body**: 87% female, 13% male, 15% out-of-state, 2% international. African American 7%, Asian 18%, Caucasian 69%, Hispanic 3%. **Retention and Graduation**: 25% grads go on to further study within 1 year. 5% grads pursue medical degrees. **Faculty**: Student/faculty ratio 8:1. 305 full-time faculty. 15% faculty teach undergrads.

ACADEMICS

Degrees: Bachelor's, doctoral, first professional, master's. **Academic Requirements**: Sciences (biological or physical). **Classes**: Most classes have 10–19 students. **Majors with Highest Enrollment**: Audiology/audiologist and speech-language pathology/pathologist, medicine (MD), nursing/registered nurse training (ASN, BSN, MSN, RN). **Disciplines with Highest Percentage of Degrees Awarded**: Health professions and related sciences 100%. **Special Study Options**: Accelerated program, distance learning.

FACILITIES

Housing: Apartments for married students, apartments for single students. **Computers**: 10% of classrooms are wired, 100% of classrooms are wireless, 95% of public computers are PCs, 5% of public computers are Macs, remote student-access to Web through college's connection.

CAMPUS LIFE

Activities: Yearbook. **Organizations**: 15 registered organizations, 2 honor societies, 1 religious organization.

ADMISSIONS

Freshman Academic Profile: 100% in top 50% of high school class. TOEFL

required of all international applicants, minimum paper TOEFL 550, minimum computer TOEFL 213. **Transfer Admission Requirements**: College transcript(s), essay or personal statement. Minimum college GPA of 2.7 required. Lowest grade transferable C. **General Admission Information**: Non-fall registration not accepted. Neither credit nor placement offered for CEEB Advanced Placement tests.

COSTS AND FINANCIAL AID

Annual tuition $21,060. Room and board $7,398. Average book expense $1,300. **Required Forms and Deadlines**: FAFSA, institution's own financial aid form, Business/Farm Supplement. Financial aid filing deadline 4/1. **Notification of Awards**: Applicants will be notified of awards on a rolling basis beginning on or about 4/1. **Types of Aid**: *Need-based scholarships/grants*: Pell, SEOG, state scholarships/grants, private scholarships, the school's own gift aid. *Loans*: FFEL Subsidized Stafford, FFEL Unsubsidized Stafford, FFEL PLUS, Federal Perkins, Federal Nursing, college/university loans from institutional funds, credit-based loans. **Student Employment**: Federal Work-Study Program available. Institutional employment available. Off-campus job opportunities are fair. **Financial Aid Statistics**: 84% undergrads receive any aid. Highest amount earned per year from on-campus jobs $2,000.

RUSSELL SAGE COLLEGE

Office of Admissions, 45 Ferry Street, Troy, NY 12180
Phone: 518-244-2217 **E-mail**: rscadm@sage.edu **CEEB Code**: 2764
Fax: 518-244-6880 **Website**: www.sage.edu/RSC **ACT Code**: 2876
Financial Aid Phone: 518-244-4525

This private school was founded in 1916. It has an 8-acre campus.

RATINGS
Admissions Selectivity Rating: 82   **Fire Safety Rating**: 60*   **Green Rating**: 60*

STUDENTS AND FACULTY

Enrollment: 801. **Student Body**: 100% female, 9% out-of-state. African American 4%, Asian 2%, Caucasian 77%, Hispanic 3%. **Retention and Graduation**: 79% freshmen return for sophomore year. 46% freshmen graduate within 4 years. 48% grads go on to further study within 1 year. 24% grads pursue arts and sciences degrees. 5% grads pursue business degrees. **Faculty**: Student/faculty ratio 12:1. 61 full-time faculty, 87% hold PhDs. 100% faculty teach undergrads.

ACADEMICS

Degrees: Bachelor's. **Academic Requirements**: Arts/fine arts, computer literacy, 3 cross-cultural courses (2 pre-determined), English (including composition), foreign languages, humanities, sciences (biological or physical), social science, 1 technology intensive. **Classes**: Most classes have 10–19 students. Most lab/discussion sections have fewer than 10 students. **Majors with Highest Enrollment**: Education, nursing, psychology. **Disciplines with Highest Percentage of Degrees Awarded**: Health professions and related sciences 17%, psychology 16%, biological/life sciences 11%, English 11%, interdisciplinary studies 10%, social sciences 10%, security and protective services 8%. **Special Study Options**: Accelerated program, cooperative education program, cross-registration, distance learning, double major, honors program, independent study, internships, liberal arts/career combination, student-designed major, study abroad, teacher certification program.

FACILITIES

Housing: Women's dorms, honors housing, over-21 senior housing, Spanish and French housing, returning adult housing. **Special Academic Facilities/Equipment**: Schacht Fine Arts Center (home of NYS Theatre Institute), Robinson Athletic and Recreational Center, state-of-the-art lab and research facilities in biology, historic 19th century brownstones. **Computers**: 1% of classrooms are wired, 1% of classrooms are wireless, 100% of public computers are PCs, network access in dorm rooms, network access in dorm lounges, online registration, online administrative functions (other than registration), remote student-access to Web through college's connection.

CAMPUS LIFE

Activities: Choral groups, dance, drama/theater, literary magazine, music ensembles, musical theater, student government, student newspaper, yearbook. **Organizations**: 40 registered organizations, 14 honor societies, 4 religious organizations. **Athletics (Intercollegiate)**: *Women*: Basketball, soccer, softball, tennis, volleyball.

ADMISSIONS

Freshman Academic Profile: 30% in top 10% of high school class, 67% in top 25% of high school class, 95% in top 50% of high school class. SAT Math middle 50% range 480–590. SAT Critical Reading middle 50% range 490–620. ACT middle 50% range 21–25. TOEFL required of all international applicants, minimum paper TOEFL 550, minimum computer TOEFL 213. **Basis for Candidate Selection**: *Very important factors considered include:* Rigor of secondary school record, standardized test scores. *Important factors considered include*: Class rank, interview, recommendation(s). *Other factors considered include*: Academic GPA, alumni/ae relation, application essay, character/personal qualities, extracurricular activities, talent/ability, volunteer work, work experience. **Freshman Admission Requirements**: High school diploma is required, and GED is accepted. *Academic units required*: 4 English, 3 math, 3 science (3 science labs), 2 foreign language, 4 social studies. *Academic units recommended*: 4 math, 4 science, 4 foreign language. **Freshman Admission Statistics**: 394 applied, 81% admitted, 36% enrolled. **Transfer Admission Requirements**: High school transcript, college transcript(s), statement of good standing from prior institution(s). Minimum college GPA of 2.5 required. Lowest grade transferable C-. **General Admission Information**: Application fee $30. Early decision application deadline 12/1. Regular notification is rolling. Non-fall registration accepted. Admission may be deferred for a maximum of 1 year. Common Application accepted. Credit and/or placement offered for CEEB Advanced Placement tests.

COSTS AND FINANCIAL AID

Annual tuition $23,800. Room & board $8,370. Required fees $870. Average book expense $900. **Required Forms and Deadlines**: FAFSA, state aid form. Financial aid filing deadline 3/6. **Notification of Awards**: Applicants will be notified of awards on a rolling basis beginning on or about 3/12. **Types of Aid**: *Need-based scholarships/grants*: Pell, SEOG, state scholarships/grants, private scholarships, the school's own gift aid, Federal Nursing Scholarships. *Loans*: FFEL Subsidized Stafford, FFEL Unsubsidized Stafford, FFEL PLUS, Federal Perkins. **Student Employment**: Off-campus job opportunities are good. **Financial Aid Statistics**: 60% freshmen, 56% undergrads receive need-based scholarship or grant aid. 93% freshmen, 91% undergrads receive need-based self-help aid. 94% freshmen, 89% undergrads receive any aid. Highest amount earned per year from on-campus jobs $3,000.

RUST COLLEGE

150 Rust Avenue, Holly Springs, MS 38635
Phone: 662-252-8000 **E-mail**: jbmcdonald@rustcollege.edu
Fax: 662-252-8895 **Website**: www.rustcollege.edu **ACT Code**: 2240
Financial Aid Phone: 662-252-8000

This private school, affiliated with the Moravian Church, was founded in 1866. It has a 126-acre campus.

RATINGS
Admissions Selectivity Rating: 60*   **Fire Safety Rating**: 60*   **Green Rating**: 60*

STUDENTS AND FACULTY
Enrollment: 911. **Student Body**: 63% female, 37% male. **Retention and Graduation**: 54% freshmen return for sophomore year. 18% freshmen graduate within 4 years. 19% grads go on to further study within 1 year. 12% grads pursue arts and sciences degrees. 7% grads pursue medical degrees. **Faculty**: Student/faculty ratio 20:1. 42 full-time faculty. 100% faculty teach undergrads.

ACADEMICS
Degrees: Associate, bachelor's. **Academic Requirements**: Arts/fine arts, computer literacy, English (including composition), history, humanities, mathematics, philosophy, religion, sciences (biological or physical), social science. **Classes**: Most classes have 10–19 students. Most lab/discussion sections have 10–19 students. **Majors with Highest Enrollment**: Biology/biological sciences, business administration/management, computer and information sciences. **Disciplines with Highest Percentage of Degrees Awarded**: Biological/life sciences 27%, business/marketing 14%, computer and information sciences 12%, social sciences 9%, public administration and social services 8%. **Special Study Options**: Adult pathway program, advanced placement program, double major, honors program, independent study, internships, liberal arts/career combination, study abroad, teacher certification program, weekend college. Dual enrollment includes 3 dual degree programs with other institutions and 1 cooperative program with another institution.

FACILITIES

Housing: Men's dorms, women's dorms, honors. **Special Academic Facilities/Equipment**: Dr. Ron Trojcak collection of African tribal art, which includes fabrics, masks, and statues used for religious ceremonies, weddings, ritual dance, and funerals. **Computers**: 99% of public computers are PCs, 1% of public computers are Macs, network access in dorm rooms, network access in dorm lounges, remote student-access to Web through college's connection.

CAMPUS LIFE

Activities: Choral groups, concert band, dance, drama/theater, marching band, music ensembles, pep band, radio station, student government, student newspaper, television station, yearbook. **Organizations**: 35 registered organizations, 7 honor societies, 5 religious organizations. 3 fraternities (6% men join), 4 sororities (2% women join). **Athletics (Intercollegiate)**: *Men*: Baseball, basketball, cheerleading, cross-country, soccer, tennis, track/field (outdoor). *Women*: Basketball, cheerleading, cross-country, softball, tennis, track/field (outdoor), volleyball.

ADMISSIONS

Freshman Academic Profile: 98% from public high schools. ACT middle 50% range 14–17. TOEFL required of all international applicants, minimum paper TOEFL 540. **Basis for Candidate Selection**: *Very important factors considered include:* Recommendation(s), talent/ability. *Important factors considered include*: Academic GPA, standardized test scores. *Other factors considered include*: Character/personal qualities, class rank, extracurricular activities, interview, rigor of secondary school record, state residency. **Freshman Admission Requirements**: High school diploma is required, and GED is accepted. *Academic units required*: 4 English, 3 math, 3 science, 3 social studies, 6 academic electives. **Freshman Admission Statistics**: 1,482 applied, 48% admitted, 35% enrolled. **Transfer Admission Requirements**: High school transcript, college transcript(s), statement of good standing from prior institution(s). Minimum college GPA of 2.0 required. Lowest grade transferable C. **General Admission Information**: Application fee $10. Regular notification is rolling. Non-fall registration accepted. Admission may be deferred for a maximum of 1 year. Credit offered for CEEB Advanced Placement tests.

COSTS AND FINANCIAL AID

Annual tuition $6,000. Room & board $2,600. Average book expense $500. **Required Forms and Deadlines**: FAFSA, institution's own financial aid form, state aid form. Financial aid filing deadline 5/1. **Notification of Awards**: Applicants will be notified of awards on a rolling basis beginning on or about 6/1. **Types of Aid**: *Need-based scholarships/grants*: Pell, SEOG, state scholarships/grants, private scholarships, United Negro College Fund. *Loans*: FFEL Subsidized Stafford, FFEL Unsubsidized Stafford, FFEL PLUS, United Methodist. **Financial Aid Statistics**: 95% freshmen, 76% undergrads receive need-based scholarship or grant aid. 83% freshmen, 69% undergrads receive need-based self-help aid. Highest amount earned per year from on-campus jobs $1,600.

RUTGERS, THE STATE UNIVERSITY OF NEW JERSEY— CAMDEN COLLEGE OF ARTS & SCIENCES

406 Penn Street, Camden, NJ 08102
Phone: 856-225-6104 **E-mail**: admissions@asb-ugadm.rutgers.edu **CEEB Code**: 2765
Fax: 856-225-6498 **Website**: www.rutgers.edu **ACT Code**: 2592
Financial Aid Phone: 609-225-6039

This public school was founded in 1927. It has a 25-acre campus.

RATINGS
Admissions Selectivity Rating: 78   **Fire Safety Rating**: 73   **Green Rating**: 60*

STUDENTS AND FACULTY
Enrollment: 3,635. **Student Body**: 59% female, 41% male, 3% out-of-state. African American 16%, Asian 7%, Caucasian 66%, Hispanic 6%. **Retention and Graduation**: 86% freshmen return for sophomore year. **Faculty**: Student/

faculty ratio 12:1. 219 full-time faculty, 98% hold PhDs. 70% faculty teach undergrads.

ACADEMICS

Degrees: Bachelor's, first professional, master's. **Academic Requirements**: Arts/fine arts, English (including composition), foreign languages, history, humanities, interdisciplinary course, mathematics, sciences (biological or physical), social science. **Classes**: Most classes have 20–29 students. Most lab/discussion sections have 10–19 students. **Disciplines with Highest Percentage of Degrees Awarded**: Business/marketing 26%, psychology 17%, social sciences 15%, biological/life sciences 6%, English 6%, health professions and related sciences 6%, computer and information sciences 5%. **Special Study Options**: Accelerated program, cooperative education program, cross-registration, distance learning, double major, dual enrollment, English as a second language (ESL), honors program, independent study, liberal arts/career combination, student-designed major, study abroad, teacher certification program, 8 year BA/MD with UMDNJ, 5 year BA or BS/MA in criminal justice with school of criminal justice—Newark Campus, 2–3 dual bachelor's degree with school of engineering, BA in political science/MPA.

FACILITIES

Housing: Coed dorms, apartments for single students, special housing for disabled students. **Special Academic Facilities/Equipment**: Art gallery, electron microscope, music synthesizer, poetry center, school of law, theater. **Computers**: Network access in dorm rooms, remote student-access to Web through college's connection.

CAMPUS LIFE

Activities: Drama/theater, literary magazine, radio station, student government, student newspaper, yearbook. **Organizations**: 50 registered organizations, 11 honor societies, 4 fraternities, 4 sororities. **Athletics (Intercollegiate)**: *Men*: Baseball, basketball, cross-country, golf, soccer, track/field (outdoor). *Women*: Basketball, cross-country, soccer, softball, track/field (outdoor), volleyball.

ADMISSIONS

Freshman Academic Profile: 15% in top 10% of high school class, 51% in top 25% of high school class, 89% in top 50% of high school class. SAT Math middle 50% range 500–620. SAT Critical Reading middle 50% range 490–590. TOEFL required of all international applicants, minimum paper TOEFL 550. **Basis for Candidate Selection**: *Very important factors considered include*: Class rank, rigor of secondary school record, standardized test scores. *Other factors considered include*: Application essay, extracurricular activities, geographical residence, racial/ethnic status, recommendation(s), state residency, volunteer work, work experience. **Freshman Admission Requirements**: High school diploma is required, and GED is accepted. *Academic units required*: 4 English, 3 math, 2 science, 2 foreign language, 5 academic electives. *Academic units recommended*: 4 math. **Freshman Admission Statistics**: 5,414 applied, 59% admitted, 13% enrolled. **Transfer Admission Requirements**: High school transcript, college transcript(s). Lowest grade transferable C. **General Admission Information**: Application fee $50. Regular notification 2/28. Non-fall registration accepted. Admission may be deferred for a maximum of 1 year. Common Application not accepted. Credit and/or placement offered for CEEB Advanced Placement tests.

COSTS AND FINANCIAL AID

Annual in-state tuition $4,762. Out-of-state tuition $9,692. Room & board $5,322. Required fees $1,112. Average book expense $700. **Required Forms and Deadlines**: FAFSA. Financial aid filing deadline 3/15. **Notification of Awards**: Applicants will be notified of awards on a rolling basis beginning on or about 2/15. **Types of Aid**: *Need-based scholarships/grants*: Pell, SEOG, state scholarships/grants, private scholarships, the school's own gift aid. *Loans*: Direct Subsidized Stafford, Direct Unsubsidized Stafford, Direct PLUS, Federal Perkins, state loans, college/university loans from institutional funds. **Student Employment**: Federal Work-Study Program available. Institutional employment available. Off-campus job opportunities are good. **Financial Aid Statistics**: 47% freshmen, 49% undergrads receive need-based scholarship or grant aid. 41% freshmen, 49% undergrads receive need-based self-help aid.

RUTGERS, THE STATE UNIVERSITY OF NEW JERSEY—COLLEGE OF NURSING

249 University Avenue, Newark, NJ 07102-1896
Phone: 973-353-5205 **E-mail**: admissions@asb-ugadm.rutgers.edu **CEEB Code**: 2765 **Fax**: 973-353-1189 **Website**: www.nursing.rutgers.edu **ACT Code**: 2592
Financial Aid Phone: 973-353-5152

This public school was founded in 1956. It has a 36-acre campus.

RATINGS

Admissions Selectivity Rating: 86   **Fire Safety Rating**: 60*   **Green Rating**: 60*

STUDENTS AND FACULTY

Enrollment: 443. **Student Body**: 92% female, 8% male, 4% out-of-state, 1% international (2 countries represented). African American 17%, Asian 16%, Caucasian 47%, Hispanic 12%. **Faculty**: Student/faculty ratio 11:1. 36 full-time faculty, 97% hold PhDs. 70% faculty teach undergrads.

ACADEMICS

Degrees: Bachelor's. **Academic Requirements**: English (including composition), humanities, nursing curriculum, sciences (biological or physical), social science. **Disciplines with Highest Percentage of Degrees Awarded**: Health professions and related sciences 100%. **Special Study Options**: Distance learning, dual enrollment, English as a second language (ESL), honors program, internships.

FACILITIES

Housing: Coed dorms, apartments for single students, special housing for disabled students, fraternity/sorority housing. **Special Academic Facilities/Equipment**: Center for molecular and behavioral neuroscience, center for nursing research. **Computers**: 72% of public computers are PCs, 27% of public computers are Macs, 1% of public computers are UNIX, network access in dorm rooms, online registration, online administrative functions (other than registration), remote student-access to Web through college's connection.

CAMPUS LIFE

Activities: Choral groups, concert band, drama/theater, literary magazine, radio station, student government, student newspaper, symphony orchestra, yearbook. **Organizations**: 80 registered organizations, 1 honor society. 7 fraternities, 7 sororities. **Athletics (Intercollegiate)**: *Men*: Baseball, basketball, soccer, tennis, volleyball. *Women*: Basketball, softball, tennis, volleyball.

ADMISSIONS

Freshman Academic Profile: 20% in top 10% of high school class, 67% in top 25% of high school class, 96% in top 50% of high school class. SAT Math middle 50% range 500–580. SAT Critical Reading middle 50% range 480–570. TOEFL required of all international applicants, minimum paper TOEFL 600. **Basis for Candidate Selection**: *Very important factors considered include*: Class rank, rigor of secondary school record, standardized test scores. *Other factors considered include*: Application essay, extracurricular activities, geographical residence, racial/ethnic status, recommendation(s), state residency, talent/ability, volunteer work, work experience. **Freshman Admission Requirements**: High school diploma is required, and GED is accepted. *Academic units required*: 4 English, 3 math, 2 science, 7 academic electives. *Academic units recommended*: 4 math. **Freshman Admission Statistics**: 711 applied, 26% admitted, 31% enrolled. **Transfer Admission Requirements**: High school transcript, college transcript(s). Lowest grade transferable C. **General Admission Information**: Application fee $50. Regular notification 2/27. Non-fall registration not accepted. Admission may be deferred for a maximum of 1 year. Common Application not accepted. Credit and/or placement offered for CEEB Advanced Placement tests.

COSTS AND FINANCIAL AID

Annual in-state tuition $4,762. Annual out-of-state tuition $9,692. Room and board $6,090. Required fees $1,030. Average book expense $800. **Required Forms and Deadlines**: FAFSA. Financial aid filing deadline 3/15. **Notification of Awards**: Applicants will be notified of awards on a rolling basis beginning on or about 2/15. **Types of Aid**: *Need-based scholarships/grants*: Pell, SEOG, state scholarships/grants, the school's own gift aid. *Loans*: Direct Subsidized Stafford, Direct Unsubsidized Stafford, Direct PLUS, Federal Perkins, state loans, college/university loans from institutional funds. **Student Employment**: Federal Work-Study Program available. Institutional employment available. Off-campus job opportunities are good. **Financial Aid Statistics**: 53% freshmen, 43% undergrads receive need-based scholarship or grant aid. 49% freshmen, 48% undergrads receive need-based self-help aid.

RUTGERS, THE STATE UNIVERSITY OF NEW JERSEY—COLLEGE OF PHARMACY

Office of Admissions, 65 Davidson Road, New Brunswick, NJ 08903-2101
Phone: 732-932-4636 **E-mail:** admissions@asb-ugadm.rutgers.edu **CEEB Code:** 2765
Fax: 732-445-0237 **Website:** www.rutgers.edu **ACT Code:** 2592
Financial Aid Phone: 732-932-7057

This public school was founded in 1892. It has a 2,695-acre campus.

RATINGS
Admissions Selectivity Rating: 94   **Fire Safety Rating:** 60*   **Green Rating:** 60*

STUDENTS AND FACULTY
Enrollment: 825. **Student Body:** 64% female, 36% male, 15% out-of-state, 2% international (9 countries represented). African American 6%, Asian 47%, Caucasian 31%, Hispanic 7%. **Retention and Graduation:** 92% freshmen return for sophomore year. **Faculty:** Student/faculty ratio 11:1. 63 full-time faculty, 98% hold PhDs. 70% faculty teach undergrads.

ACADEMICS
Degrees: Doctoral, first professional. **Academic Requirements:** English (including composition), humanities, mathematics, pharmacy curriculum, sciences (biological or physical), social science. **Disciplines with Highest Percentage of Degrees Awarded:** Health professions and related sciences 100%. **Special Study Options:** Distance learning, English as a second language (ESL), honors program, independent study, internships, study abroad.

FACILITIES
Housing: Coed dorms, men's dorms, women's dorms, apartments for single students, special housing for disabled students, fraternity/sorority housing, language and cultural houses, math/science house for women, substance-free/wellness house, first-year and transfer. **Special Academic Facilities/Equipment:** Controlled drug-delivery research center, institute for environmental and occupational health sciences. **Computers:** 45% of public computers are PCs, 35% of public computers are Macs, 20% of public computers are UNIX, network access in dorm rooms, remote student-access to Web through college's connection.

CAMPUS LIFE
Activities: Choral groups, concert band, dance, drama/theater, jazz band, literary magazine, marching band, music ensembles, opera, pep band, radio station, student government, student newspaper, student-run film society, symphony orchestra, television station, yearbook. **Organizations:** 400 registered organizations, 3 honor societies. 29 fraternities, 15 sororities. **Athletics (Intercollegiate):** *Men:* Baseball, basketball, cheerleading, crew/rowing, cross-country, diving, fencing, football, golf, lacrosse, soccer, swimming, tennis, track/field (indoor), track/field (outdoor), wrestling. *Women:* Basketball, cheerleading, crew/rowing, cross-country, diving, fencing, field hockey, golf, gymnastics, lacrosse, soccer, softball, swimming, tennis, track/field (indoor), track/field (outdoor), volleyball.

ADMISSIONS
Freshman Academic Profile: 67% in top 10% of high school class, 100% in top 25% of high school class, 100% in top 50% of high school class. SAT Math middle 50% range 620–710. SAT Critical Reading middle 50% range 580–650. TOEFL required of all international applicants, minimum paper TOEFL 550. **Basis for Candidate Selection:** *Very important factors considered include:* Class rank, rigor of secondary school record, standardized test scores. *Other factors considered include:* Application essay, extracurricular activities, geographical residence, racial/ethnic status, recommendation(s), state residency, talent/ability, volunteer work, work experience. **Freshman Admission Requirements:** High school diploma is required, and GED is accepted. *Academic units required:* 4 English, 3 math, 2 science, 2 foreign language, 5 academic electives. *Academic units recommended:* 4 math. **Freshman Admission Statistics:** 1,401 applied, 45% admitted, 29% enrolled. **Transfer Admission Requirements:** High school transcript, college transcript(s). Lowest grade transferable C. **General Admission Information:** Application fee $50. Regular notification 2/27. Non-fall registration not accepted. Admission may be deferred for a maximum of 1 year. Common Application not accepted. Credit and/or placement offered for CEEB Advanced Placement tests.

COSTS AND FINANCIAL AID
Annual in-state tuition $5,286. Out-of-state tuition $10,754. Room & board $6,098. Required fees $1,290. Average book expense $800. **Required Forms and Deadlines:** FAFSA. Financial aid filing deadline 3/15. **Notification of Awards:** Applicants will be notified of awards on a rolling basis beginning on or about 2/15. **Types of Aid:** *Need-based scholarships/grants:* Pell, SEOG, state scholarships/grants, the school's own gift aid. *Loans:* Direct Subsidized Stafford, Direct Unsubsidized Stafford, Direct PLUS, Federal Perkins, state loans, college/university loans from institutional funds, educational loans. **Student Employment:** Federal Work-Study Program available. Institutional employment available. Off-campus job opportunities are good. **Financial Aid Statistics:** 28% freshmen, 31% undergrads receive need-based scholarship or grant aid. 33% freshmen, 38% undergrads receive need-based self-help aid. 2 undergrads receive athletic scholarships. Highest amount earned per year from on-campus jobs $1,374.

RUTGERS, THE STATE UNIVERSITY OF NEW JERSEY—COOK COLLEGE

65 Davidson Road, Piscataway, NJ 08854-8097
Phone: 732-932-4326 **E-mail:** admissions@asb-ugadm.rutgers.edu **CEEB Code:** 2765
Fax: 732-445-0237 **Website:** www.rutgers.edu **ACT Code:** 2592
Financial Aid Phone: 732-932-7057

This public school was founded in 1864. It has a 2,695-acre campus.

RATINGS
Admissions Selectivity Rating: 82   **Fire Safety Rating:** 60*   **Green Rating:** 60*

STUDENTS AND FACULTY
Enrollment: 3,175. **Student Body:** 50% female, 50% male, 9% out-of-state, 2% international (23 countries represented). African American 6%, Asian 13%, Caucasian 67%, Hispanic 6%. **Retention and Graduation:** 91% freshmen return for sophomore year. 42% freshmen graduate within 4 years. **Faculty:** Student/faculty ratio 11:1. 256 full-time faculty, 98% hold PhDs. 70% faculty teach undergrads.

ACADEMICS
Degrees: Bachelor's. **Academic Requirements:** Computer literacy, economic and political systems, English (including composition), human diversity, humanities, interdisciplinary/ethical analysis, sciences (biological or physical). **Disciplines with Highest Percentage of Degrees Awarded:** Natural resources/environmental science 25%, area and ethnic studies 25%, agriculture 15%, education 9%, social sciences 9%, architecture 7%, communication technologies 4%. **Special Study Options:** Cooperative education program, distance learning, double major, dual enrollment, English as a second language (ESL), honors program, independent study, internships, student-designed major, study abroad, teacher certification program, 8-year BA or BS/MD, 5-year dual degree in bio-resource engineering with the college of engineering, BA or BS/MPP with school of planning and public policy.

FACILITIES
Housing: Coed dorms, men's dorms, apartments for single students, special housing for disabled students, fraternity/sorority housing, cooperative housing, substance-free/wellness housing, transfer center, first-year residence. **Special Academic Facilities/Equipment:** Center for advanced food technology, agricultural experiment station, center for agricultural molecular biology, institute of marine and coastal sciences, center for remote sensing and spatial analysis, ecopolicy center, center for theoretical and applied genetics, center for advanced biotechnology and medicine. **Computers:** 45% of public computers are PCs, 35% of public computers are Macs, 20% of public computers are UNIX, network access in dorm rooms, remote student-access to Web through college's connection.

CAMPUS LIFE
Activities: Choral groups, concert band, dance, drama/theater, jazz band, literary magazine, marching band, music ensembles, opera, pep band, radio station, student government, student newspaper, student-run film society, symphony orchestra, television station, yearbook. **Organizations:** 400 registered organizations, 9 honor societies. 29 fraternities (8% men join), 15 sororities (5% women join). **Athletics (Intercollegiate):** *Men:* Baseball, basketball, cheerleading, crew/rowing, cross-country, diving, fencing, football, golf, lacrosse, soccer, swimming, tennis, track/field (indoor), track/field (outdoor), wrestling. *Women:* Basketball, cheerleading, crew/rowing, cross-country, diving, fencing, field hockey, golf, gymnastics, lacrosse, soccer, softball, swimming, tennis, track/field (indoor), track/field (outdoor), volleyball.

ADMISSIONS

Freshman Academic Profile: 28% in top 10% of high school class, 71% in top 25% of high school class, 97% in top 50% of high school class. SAT Math middle 50% range 540–630. SAT Critical Reading middle 50% range 510–610. TOEFL required of all international applicants, minimum paper TOEFL 550. **Basis for Candidate Selection**: *Very important factors considered include*: Class rank, rigor of secondary school record, standardized test scores. *Other factors considered include*: Application essay, extracurricular activities, geographical residence, racial/ethnic status, recommendation(s), state residency, talent/ability, volunteer work, work experience. **Freshman Admission Requirements**: High school diploma is required, and GED is accepted. *Academic units required*: 4 English, 3 math, 2 science, 7 academic electives. *Academic units recommended*: 4 math. **Freshman Admission Statistics**: 6,673 applied, 64% admitted, 15% enrolled. **Transfer Admission Requirements**: High school transcript, college transcript(s). Lowest grade transferable C. **General Admission Information**: Application fee $50. Regular notification 2/27. Non-fall registration not accepted. Admission may be deferred for a maximum of 1 year. Common Application not accepted. Credit and/or placement offered for CEEB Advanced Placement tests.

COSTS AND FINANCIAL AID

Annual in-state tuition $5,286. Out-of-state tuition $10,754. Room & board $6,098. Required fees $1,258. Average book expense $800. **Required Forms and Deadlines**: FAFSA. Financial aid filing deadline 3/15. **Notification of Awards**: Applicants will be notified of awards on a rolling basis beginning on or about 2/15. **Types of Aid**: *Need-based scholarships/grants*: Pell, SEOG, state scholarships/grants, the school's own gift aid. *Loans*: Direct Subsidized Stafford, Direct Unsubsidized Stafford, Direct PLUS, Federal Perkins, state loans, college/university loans from institutional funds, educational loans. **Student Employment**: Federal Work-Study Program available. Institutional employment available. Off-campus job opportunities are good. **Financial Aid Statistics**: 35% freshmen, 32% undergrads receive need-based scholarship or grant aid. 50% freshmen, 41% undergrads receive need-based self-help aid. 12 freshmen, 31 undergrads receive athletic scholarships. Highest amount earned per year from on-campus jobs $1,374.

RUTGERS, THE STATE UNIVERSITY OF NEW JERSEY—DOUGLASS COLLEGE

---

65 Davidson Road, Room 202, Piscataway, NJ 08854-8097
Phone: 732-932-4636 **E-mail**: admissions@asb-ugadm.rutgers.edu **CEEB Code**: 2765
Fax: 732-445-0237 **Website**: www.rutgers.edu **ACT Code**: 2592
Financial Aid Phone: 732-932-7057

This public school was founded in 1918. It has a 2,695-acre campus.

RATINGS
Admissions Selectivity Rating: 75   **Fire Safety Rating**: 60*   **Green Rating**: 60*

STUDENTS AND FACULTY
Enrollment: 3,094. **Student Body**: 100% female, 7% out-of-state, 2% international (25 countries represented). African American 12%, Asian 14%, Caucasian 56%, Hispanic 8%. **Faculty**: Student/faculty ratio 15:1. 1,051 full-time faculty, 98% hold PhDs. 70% faculty teach undergrads.

ACADEMICS
Degrees: Bachelor's. **Academic Requirements**: Cross-cultural perspectives, English (including composition), foreign languages, history, humanities, mathematics, sciences (biological or physical), social science, experience of women courses. **Disciplines with Highest Percentage of Degrees Awarded**: Social sciences 20%, psychology 20%, biological/life sciences 10%, communication technologies 10%, English 9%, foreign languages and literature 6%, area and ethnic studies 5%, business/marketing 5%. **Special Study Options**: Cross-registration, distance learning, double major, dual enrollment, English as a second language (ESL), honors program, independent study, internships, liberal arts/career combination, student-designed major, study abroad, teacher certification program, Washington semester, 8-year BA or BS/MD UMDNJ, 5-year dual degree with the school of engineering, 5-year BA/MBA with graduate school of management, 5-year BA or BS/MPP with school of planning and public policy, 5-year BA or BS/MEd in conjunction with the graduate school of education, BA or BS/MPH with school of planning and public policy.

FACILITIES

Housing: Women's dorms, apartments for single students, special housing for disabled students, fraternity/sorority housing, language and cultural houses, special house for women in math/sciences/engineering, cooperative community house for single mothers with children. **Special Academic Facilities/Equipment**: Center for women and work, institute for research on women, center for women's global leadership, center for American women and politics, center for public interest pulling, Douglass Project for Women in Math, Science, and Engineering, Walt Whitman Center for the Culture and Politics of Democracy. **Computers**: 45% of public computers are PCs, 35% of public computers are Macs, 20% of public computers are UNIX, network access in dorm rooms, remote student-access to Web through college's connection.

CAMPUS LIFE

Activities: Choral groups, concert band, dance, drama/theater, jazz band, literary magazine, marching band, music ensembles, opera, pep band, radio station, student government, student newspaper, student-run film society, symphony orchestra, television station, yearbook. **Organizations**: 400 registered organizations, 15 sororities. **Athletics (Intercollegiate)**: *Women*: Basketball, cheerleading, crew/rowing, cross-country, diving, fencing, field hockey, golf, gymnastics, lacrosse, soccer, softball, swimming, tennis, track/field (indoor), track/field (outdoor), volleyball.

ADMISSIONS

Freshman Academic Profile: 19% in top 10% of high school class, 53% in top 25% of high school class, 98% in top 50% of high school class. SAT Math middle 50% range 490–590. SAT Critical Reading middle 50% range 500–590. TOEFL required of all international applicants, minimum paper TOEFL 550. **Basis for Candidate Selection**: *Very important factors considered include*: Class rank, rigor of secondary school record, standardized test scores. *Other factors considered include*: Application essay, extracurricular activities, geographical residence, racial/ethnic status, recommendation(s), state residency, talent/ability, volunteer work, work experience. **Freshman Admission Requirements**: High school diploma is required, and GED is accepted. *Academic units required*: 4 English, 3 math, 2 science, 2 foreign language, 5 academic electives. *Academic units recommended*: 4 math. **Freshman Admission Statistics**: 6,453 applied, 68% admitted, 15% enrolled. **Transfer Admission Requirements**: High school transcript, college transcript(s). Lowest grade transferable C. **General Admission Information**: Application fee $50. Regular notification 2/27. Non-fall registration not accepted. Admission may be deferred for a maximum of 1 year. Common Application not accepted. Credit and/or placement offered for CEEB Advanced Placement tests.

COSTS AND FINANCIAL AID

Annual in-state tuition $4,762. Out-of-state tuition $9,692. Room & board $6,098. Required fees $1,255. Average book expense $700. **Required Forms and Deadlines**: FAFSA. Financial aid filing deadline 3/15. **Notification of Awards**: Applicants will be notified of awards on a rolling basis beginning on or about 2/15. **Types of Aid**: *Need-based scholarships/grants*: Pell, SEOG, state scholarships/grants, the school's own gift aid. *Loans*: Direct Subsidized Stafford, Direct Unsubsidized Stafford, Direct PLUS, Federal Perkins, state loans, college/university loans from institutional funds, educational loans. **Student Employment**: Federal Work-Study Program available. Institutional employment available. Off-campus job opportunities are good. **Financial Aid Statistics**: 36% freshmen, 35% undergrads receive need-based scholarship or grant aid. 48% freshmen, 43% undergrads receive need-based self-help aid. 2 freshmen, 13 undergrads receive athletic scholarships. Highest amount earned per year from on-campus jobs $1,374.

RUTGERS, THE STATE UNIVERSITY OF NEW JERSEY—LIVINGSTON COLLEGE

---

65 Davidson Road, Piscataway, NJ 00854-8097
Phone: 732-932-4636 **E-mail**: admissions@asb-ugadm.rutgers.edu **CEEB Code**: 2765
Fax: 732-445-0237 **Website**: www.rutgers.edu **ACT Code**: 2592
Financial Aid Phone: 732-932-7057

This public school was founded in 1969. It has a 2,695-acre campus.

RATINGS
Admissions Selectivity Rating: 74   **Fire Safety Rating**: 60*   **Green Rating**: 60*

STUDENTS AND FACULTY
Enrollment: 3,527. **Student Body**: 52% female, 48% male, 8% out-of-state, 2% international (30 countries represented). African American 10%, Asian 18%,

Caucasian 55%, Hispanic 8%. **Faculty**: Student/faculty ratio 15:1. 1,051 full-time faculty, 98% hold PhDs. 70% faculty teach undergrads.

ACADEMICS

Degrees: Bachelor's. **Academic Requirements**: Arts/fine arts, areas of cultural perspectives and contemporary issues, English (including composition), humanities, mathematics, sciences (biological or physical), social science. **Disciplines with Highest Percentage of Degrees Awarded**: Social sciences 30%, psychology 13%, communication technologies 10%, English 6%, biological/life sciences 6%, business/marketing 6%, computer and information sciences 4%. **Special Study Options**: Cross-registration, distance learning, double major, dual enrollment, English as a second language (ESL), honors program, independent study, internships, liberal arts/career combination, student-designed major, study abroad, Washington semester, 5-year BA/MEd offered in conjunction with the graduate school of education, 8-year BA/MD, 6-year bachelors in biology/masters in physician assistance, 5-year dual degree in liberal arts and engineering.

FACILITIES

Housing: Coed dorms, apartments for single students, special housing for disabled students, fraternity/sorority housing, special interest housing, leadership house, first-year residence, wellness/substance-free housing, transfer center. **Special Academic Facilities/Equipment**: Art and geology museums, Center for International Business Education, Bureau of Government Research, Center for Urban Policy Research, Center for International Business Education, Bureau of Government Research, Institute for Criminological Research, American Affordable Housing Institute, Institute for Ethnic Studies in Social Work, Center for Negotiation and Conflict Resolution. **Computers**: 45% of public computers are PCs, 35% of public computers are Macs, 20% of public computers are UNIX, network access in dorm rooms, remote student-access to Web through college's connection.

CAMPUS LIFE

Activities: Choral groups, concert band, dance, drama/theater, jazz band, literary magazine, marching band, music ensembles, opera, pep band, radio station, student government, student newspaper, student-run film society, symphony orchestra, television station, yearbook. **Organizations**: 400 registered organizations, 1 honor society. 29 fraternities, 15 sororities. **Athletics (Intercollegiate)**: *Men*: Baseball, basketball, cheerleading, crew/rowing, cross-country, diving, fencing, football, golf, lacrosse, soccer, swimming, tennis, track/field (indoor), track/field (outdoor), wrestling. *Women*: Basketball, cheerleading, crew/rowing, cross-country, diving, fencing, field hockey, golf, gymnastics, lacrosse, soccer, softball, swimming, tennis, track/field (indoor), track/field (outdoor), volleyball.

ADMISSIONS

Freshman Academic Profile: 9% in top 10% of high school class, 42% in top 25% of high school class, 95% in top 50% of high school class. SAT Math middle 50% range 520–610. SAT Critical Reading middle 50% range 500–580. TOEFL required of all international applicants, minimum paper TOEFL 550. **Basis for Candidate Selection**: *Very important factors considered include*: Class rank, rigor of secondary school record, standardized test scores. *Other factors considered include*: Application essay, extracurricular activities, geographical residence, racial/ethnic status, recommendation(s), state residency, talent/ability, volunteer work, work experience. **Freshman Admission Requirements**: High school diploma is required, and GED is accepted. *Academic units required*: 4 English, 3 math, 2 science, 2 foreign language, 5 academic electives. *Academic units recommended*: 4 math. **Freshman Admission Statistics**: 14,995 applied, 60% admitted, 9% enrolled. **Transfer Admission Requirements**: High school transcript, college transcript(s). Lowest grade transferable C. **General Admission Information**: Application fee $50. Regular notification 2/27. Non-fall registration not accepted. Admission may be deferred for a maximum of 1 year. Common Application not accepted. Credit and/or placement offered for CEEB Advanced Placement tests.

COSTS AND FINANCIAL AID

Annual in-state tuition $4,762. Out-of-state tuition $9,692. Room & board $6,098. Required fees $1,276. Average book expense $700. **Required Forms and Deadlines**: FAFSA. Financial aid filing deadline 3/15. **Notification of Awards**: Applicants will be notified of awards on a rolling basis beginning on or about 2/15. **Types of Aid**: *Need-based scholarships/grants*: Pell, SEOG, state scholarships/grants, the school's own gift aid. *Loans*: Direct Subsidized Stafford, Direct Unsubsidized Stafford, Direct PLUS, Federal Perkins, state loans, college/university loans from institutional funds, educational loans. **Student Employment**: Federal Work-Study Program available. Institutional employment available. Off-campus job opportunities are good. **Financial Aid Statistics**: 37% freshmen, 35% undergrads receive need-based scholarship or grant aid. 46% freshmen, 43% undergrads receive need-based self-help aid. 8 freshmen, 37 undergrads receive athletic scholarships. Highest amount earned per year from on-campus jobs $1,374.

RUTGERS, THE STATE UNIVERSITY OF NEW JERSEY—MASON GROSS SCHOOL OF THE ARTS

65 Davidson Road, #202, Piscataway, NJ 08854-8097
Phone: 732-932-4636 **E-mail**: admissions@asb-ugadm.rutgers.edu **CEEB Code**: 2765
Fax: 732-445-0237 **Website**: www.rutgers.edu **ACT Code**: 2592
Financial Aid Phone: 732-932-7057

This public school was founded in 1976. It has a 2,695-acre campus.

RATINGS

Admissions Selectivity Rating: 86 **Fire Safety Rating**: 60* **Green Rating**: 60*

STUDENTS AND FACULTY

Enrollment: 617. **Student Body**: 58% female, 42% male, 18% out-of-state, 1% international (6 countries represented). African American 5%, Asian 6%, Caucasian 76%, Hispanic 4%. **Faculty**: Student/faculty ratio 6:1. 79 full-time faculty, 97% hold PhDs. 70% faculty teach undergrads.

ACADEMICS

Degrees: Bachelor's, doctoral, master's. **Academic Requirements**: Arts/fine arts, English (including composition), humanities, mathematics, sciences (biological or physical), social science. **Disciplines with Highest Percentage of Degrees Awarded**: Visual and performing arts 100%. **Special Study Options**: Cross-registration, distance learning, English as a second language (ESL), honors program, internships, study abroad, teacher certification program.

FACILITIES

Housing: Coed dorms, freshman dorms, men's dorms, women's dorms, apartments for single students, special housing for disabled students, fraternity/sorority housing, language and cultural houses for women, substance-free/wellness house. **Special Academic Facilities/Equipment**: Agricultural, art, and geology museums; dance, music, and art studios; concert and recital halls; theaters; institute of jazz studies; music library. **Computers**: 45% of public computers are PCs, 35% of public computers are Macs, 20% of public computers are UNIX, network access in dorm rooms, remote student-access to Web through college's connection.

CAMPUS LIFE

Activities: Choral groups, concert band, dance, drama/theater, jazz band, literary magazine, marching band, music ensembles, opera, pep band, radio station, student government, student newspaper, student-run film society, symphony orchestra, television station, yearbook. **Organizations**: 400 registered organizations. 29 fraternities, 15 sororities. **Athletics (Intercollegiate)**: *Men*: Baseball, basketball, cheerleading, crew/rowing, cross-country, diving, fencing, football, golf, lacrosse, soccer, swimming, tennis, track/field (indoor), track/field (outdoor), wrestling. *Women*: Basketball, cheerleading, crew/rowing, cross-country, diving, fencing, field hockey, golf, gymnastics, lacrosse, soccer, softball, swimming, tennis, track/field (indoor), track/field (outdoor), volleyball.

ADMISSIONS

Freshman Academic Profile: 24% in top 10% of high school class, 48% in top 25% of high school class, 85% in top 50% of high school class. SAT Math middle 50% range 490–620. SAT Critical Reading middle 50% range 510–620. TOEFL required of all international applicants, minimum paper TOEFL 550. **Basis for Candidate Selection**: *Very important factors considered include*: Class rank, interview, rigor of secondary school record, standardized test scores, talent/ability. *Other factors considered include*: Application essay, extracurricular activities, geographical residence, racial/ethnic status, recommendation(s), state residency, volunteer work, work experience. **Freshman Admission Requirements**: High school diploma is required, and GED is accepted. *Academic units required*: 4 English, 3 math, 9 academic electives. *Academic units recommended*: 2 foreign language. **Freshman Admission Statistics**: 1,603 applied, 22% admitted, 37% enrolled. **Transfer Admission Requirements**: High school transcript, college transcript(s), interview. Lowest grade transferable C. **General Admission Information**: Application fee $50. Regular notification 2/27. Non-fall registration not accepted. Admission may be deferred for a maximum of 1 year. Common Application not accepted. Credit and/or placement offered for CEEB Advanced Placement tests.

COSTS AND FINANCIAL AID

Annual in-state tuition $4,762. Out-of-state tuition $9,692. Room & board $6,098. Required fees $1,290. Average book expense $700. **Required Forms** and **Deadlines**: FAFSA. Financial aid filing deadline 3/15. **Notification of Awards**: Applicants will be notified of awards on a rolling basis beginning on or about 2/15. **Types of Aid**: *Need-based scholarships/grants*: Pell, SEOG, state scholarships/grants, the school's own gift aid. *Loans*: Direct Subsidized Stafford, Direct Unsubsidized Stafford, Direct PLUS, Federal Perkins, state loans, college/university loans from institutional funds, education loans. **Student Employment**: Federal Work-Study Program available. Institutional employment available. Off-campus job opportunities are good. **Financial Aid Statistics**: 21% freshmen, 25% undergrads receive need-based scholarship or grant aid. 32% freshmen, 37% undergrads receive need-based self-help aid. 2 undergrads receive athletic scholarships. Highest amount earned per year from on-campus jobs $1,374.

RUTGERS, THE STATE UNIVERSITY OF NEW JERSEY— NEWARK COLLEGE OF ARTS & SCIENCES

249 University Avenue, Newark, NJ 07102-1896
Phone: 973-353-1440 **CEEB Code**: 2765
Fax: 973-353-1440 **Website**: www.rutgers.edu **ACT Code**: 2592
Financial Aid Phone: 973-353-5357

This public school was founded in 1930. It has a 36-acre campus.

RATINGS
Admissions Selectivity Rating: 84   **Fire Safety Rating**: 72   **Green Rating**: 60*

STUDENTS AND FACULTY
Enrollment: 6,276. **Student Body**: 59% female, 41% male, 8% out-of-state, 3% international. African American 20%, Asian 22%, Caucasian 30%, Hispanic 17%. **Retention and Graduation**: 86% freshmen return for sophomore year. **Faculty**: Student/faculty ratio 12:1. 386 full-time faculty, 99% hold PhDs. 70% faculty teach undergrads.

ACADEMICS
Degrees: Bachelor's, doctoral, first professional, master's. **Academic Requirements**: Arts/fine arts, English (including composition), humanities, mathematics, sciences (biological or physical), social science. **Classes**: Most classes have 10–19 students. Most lab/discussion sections have 10–19 students. **Disciplines with Highest Percentage of Degrees Awarded**: Business/marketing 28%, computer and information sciences 13%, social sciences 11%, psychology 10%, health professions and related sciences 10%, biological/life sciences 7%. **Special Study Options**: Accelerated program, cooperative education program, cross-registration, distance learning, double major, dual enrollment, English as a second language (ESL), honors college (by-invitation-only 4-year program), honors program, independent study, liberal arts/career combination, student-designed major, study abroad, teacher certification program, 8-year BA/MD with University of Medicine and Dentistry of New Jersey, 5-year BA or BS/MA in criminal justice, 2+2 and 2+3 in engineering, 5-year BA/MBA, dual admission to School of Law, BA in physics/BS in industrial engineering with New Jersey Institute of Technology, articulated bachelor's/dentistry program with University of Medicine and Dentistry of New Jersey.

FACILITIES
Housing: Coed dorms, apartments for single students, special housing for disabled students, fraternity/sorority housing. **Special Academic Facilities/Equipment**: Institute of jazz studies, TV/radio media center, animal behavior institute, molecular and behavioral neuroscience, center for crime prevention studies, center for negotiation and conflict resolution. **Computers**: 72% of public computers are PCs, 27% of public computers are Macs, 1% of public computers are UNIX, network access in dorm rooms, online registration, online administrative functions (other than registration), remote student-access to Web through college's connection.

CAMPUS LIFE
Activities: Choral groups, drama/theater, radio station, student government, student newspaper, yearbook. **Organizations**: 13 honor societies. 7 fraternities, 7 sororities. **Athletics (Intercollegiate)**: *Men*: Baseball, basketball, soccer, tennis, volleyball. *Women*: Basketball, softball, tennis, volleyball.

ADMISSIONS
Freshman Academic Profile: 29% in top 10% of high school class, 63% in top 25% of high school class, 97% in top 50% of high school class. SAT Math middle 50% range 510–620. SAT Critical Reading middle 50% range 480–570. SAT

Writing middle 50% range 490–580. TOEFL required of all international applicants, minimum paper TOEFL 550. **Basis for Candidate Selection**: *Very important factors considered include*: Class rank, rigor of secondary school record, standardized test scores. *Other factors considered include*: Application essay, extracurricular activities, geographical residence, racial/ethnic status, recommendation(s), state residency, volunteer work, work experience. **Freshman Admission Requirements**: High school diploma is required, and GED is accepted. *Academic units required*: 4 English, 3 math, 2 science, 2 foreign language, 5 academic electives. *Academic units recommended*: 4 math. **Freshman Admission Statistics**: 8,413 applied, 48% admitted, 25% enrolled. **Transfer Admission Requirements**: High school transcript, college transcript(s). **General Admission Information**: Application fee $50. Regular notification 2/28. Non-fall registration accepted. Common Application not accepted. Credit and/or placement offered for CEEB Advanced Placement tests.

COSTS AND FINANCIAL AID
Annual in-state tuition $4,762. Out-of-state tuition $9,692. Room & board $6,110. Required fees $1,052. Average book expense $700. **Required Forms and Deadlines**: Priority financial aid filing date 3/15. **Notification of Awards**: Applicants will be notified of awards on a rolling basis beginning on or about 2/1. **Types of Aid**: *Need-based scholarships/grants*: Pell, SEOG, state scholarships/grants, private scholarships, the school's own gift aid, outside scholarships. *Loans*: Direct Subsidized Stafford, Direct Unsubsidized Stafford, Direct PLUS, Federal Perkins, state loans, college/university loans from institutional funds, educational loans. **Student Employment**: Federal Work-Study Program available. Institutional employment available. Off-campus job opportunities are good. **Financial Aid Statistics**: 53% freshmen, 50% undergrads receive need-based scholarship or grant aid. 48% freshmen, 46% undergrads receive need-based self-help aid. 5 undergrads receive athletic scholarships.

RUTGERS, THE STATE UNIVERSITY OF NEW JERSEY—RUTGERS COLLEGE

65 Davidson Road, Piscataway, NJ 08854-8097
Phone: 732-932-4636 **E-mail**: admissions@asb-ugadm.rutgers.edu **CEEB Code**: 2765
Fax: 732-445-0237 **Website**: www.rutgers.edu **ACT Code**: 2592
Financial Aid Phone: 732-932-7057

This public school was founded in 1766. It has a 2,695-acre campus.

RATINGS
Admissions Selectivity Rating: 89   **Fire Safety Rating**: 60*   **Green Rating**: 60*

STUDENTS AND FACULTY
Enrollment: 10,894. **Student Body**: 51% female, 49% male, 10% out-of-state, 3% international (70 countries represented). African American 7%, Asian 20%, Caucasian 55%, Hispanic 9%. **Faculty**: Student/faculty ratio 15:1. 1,051 full-time faculty, 98% hold PhDs. 70% faculty teach undergrads.

ACADEMICS
Degrees: Bachelor's. **Academic Requirements**: English (including composition), humanities, mathematics, non-Western world, sciences (biological or physical), social science. **Disciplines with Highest Percentage of Degrees Awarded**: Social sciences 24%, psychology 13%, biological/life sciences 12%, business/marketing 10%, communication technologies 7%, English 7%. **Special Study Options**: Accelerated program, cross-registration, distance learning, double major, dual enrollment, English as a second language (ESL), honors program, independent study, internships, liberal arts/career combination, student-designed major, study abroad, teacher certification program, Washington semester, 8-year BA or BS/MD, 5-year BA or BS/MBA, 5-year dual degree with school of engineering, 5-year BA or BS/MEd with graduate school of education, BA or BS/MA in criminal justice, BA or BS/MPH, BA or BS/MPP with Edward J. Bloustein School of Planning and Public Policy.

FACILITIES
Housing: Coed dorms, apartments for single students, special housing for disabled students, fraternity/sorority housing, special interest housing, substance-free house, first-year residence, transfer center. **Special Academic Facilities/Equipment**: Waksman Institute of Microbiology, center for the critical analysis of contemporary culture, Eagleton Institute of Politics, center for historical analysis, Center for the study of Jewish Life, center for mathematical sciences research, center for molecular biophysics and biophysical chemistry. **Computers**: 45% of public computers are PCs, 35% of public

computers are Macs, 20% of public computers are UNIX, network access in dorm rooms, remote student-access to Web through college's connection.

CAMPUS LIFE
Activities: Choral groups, concert band, dance, drama/theater, jazz band, literary magazine, marching band, music ensembles, opera, pep band, radio station, student government, student newspaper, student-run film society, symphony orchestra, television station, yearbook. **Organizations**: 400 registered organizations, 1 honor society, 22 religious organizations. 25 fraternities, 15 sororities. **Athletics (Intercollegiate)**: *Men*: Baseball, basketball, cheerleading, crew/rowing, cross-country, diving, fencing, football, golf, lacrosse, soccer, swimming, tennis, track/field (indoor), track/field (outdoor), wrestling. *Women*: Basketball, cheerleading, crew/rowing, cross-country, diving, fencing, field hockey, golf, gymnastics, lacrosse, soccer, softball, swimming, tennis, track/field (indoor), track/field (outdoor), volleyball.

ADMISSIONS
Freshman Academic Profile: 43% in top 10% of high school class, 82% in top 25% of high school class, 99% in top 50% of high school class. SAT Math middle 50% range 560–670. SAT Critical Reading middle 50% range 540–640. TOEFL required of all international applicants, minimum paper TOEFL 550. **Basis for Candidate Selection**: *Very important factors considered include*: Class rank, rigor of secondary school record, standardized test scores. *Other factors considered include*: Extracurricular activities, geographical residence, racial/ethnic status, state residency, talent/ability, volunteer work, work experience. **Freshman Admission Requirements**: High school diploma is required, and GED is accepted. *Academic units required*: 4 English, 3 math, 2 science, 2 foreign language, 5 academic electives. *Academic units recommended*: 4 math. **Freshman Admission Statistics**: 20,441 applied, 48% admitted, 25% enrolled. **Transfer Admission Requirements**: High school transcript, college transcript(s). Lowest grade transferable C. **General Admission Information**: Application fee $50. Regular notification 2/27. Non-fall registration not accepted. Admission may be deferred for a maximum of 1 year. Common Application not accepted. Credit and/or placement offered for CEEB Advanced Placement tests.

COSTS AND FINANCIAL AID
Annual in-state tuition $4,762. Out-of-state tuition $9,692. Room & board $6,098. Required fees $1,290. Average book expense $700. **Required Forms and Deadlines**: FAFSA. Financial aid filing deadline 3/15. **Notification of Awards**: Applicants will be notified of awards on a rolling basis beginning on or about 2/15. **Types of Aid**: *Need-based scholarships/grants*: Pell, SEOG, state scholarships/grants, the school's own gift aid. *Loans*: Direct Subsidized Stafford, Direct Unsubsidized Stafford, Direct PLUS, Federal Perkins, state loans, college/university loans from institutional funds, educational loans. **Student Employment**: Federal Work-Study Program available. Institutional employment available. Off-campus job opportunities are good. **Financial Aid Statistics**: 33% freshmen, 30% undergrads receive need-based scholarship or grant aid. 41% freshmen, 37% undergrads receive need-based self-help aid. 71 freshmen, 317 undergrads receive athletic scholarships.

RUTGERS, THE STATE UNIVERSITY OF NEW JERSEY—SCHOOL OF ENGINEERING

65 Davidson Road, Piscataway, NJ 08854-8097
Phone: 732-932-4636 **E-mail**: admissions@asb-ugadm.rutgers.edu **CEEB Code**: 2765
Fax: 732-445-0237 **Website**: www.rutgers.edu **ACT Code**: 2592
Financial Aid Phone: 732-932-7057

This public school was founded in 1914. It has a 2,695-acre campus.

RATINGS
Admissions Selectivity Rating: 85   **Fire Safety Rating**: 60*   **Green Rating**: 60*

STUDENTS AND FACULTY
Enrollment: 2,181. **Student Body**: 22% female, 78% male, 9% out-of-state, 6% international (39 countries represented). African American 7%, Asian 27%, Caucasian 48%, Hispanic 6%. **Faculty**: Student/faculty ratio 15:1. 139 full-time faculty, 98% hold PhDs. 70% faculty teach undergrads.

ACADEMICS
Degrees: Bachelor's. **Academic Requirements**: English (including composition), humanities, mathematics, sciences (biological or physical), social science. **Disciplines with Highest Percentage of Degrees Awarded**: Engineering 100%. **Special Study Options**: Cooperative education program, distance learning, double major, dual enrollment, English as a second language

(ESL), honors program, internships, liberal arts/career combination, student-designed major, study abroad, 5-year BS/MBA, 8-year BS/MD with University of Dentistry of New Jersey, 5-year dual degree in bioresource engineering with Cook College, 5-year BA/BS.

FACILITIES
Housing: Coed dorms, men's dorms, women's dorms, apartments for single students, special housing for disabled students, fraternity/sorority housing, cooperative housing. For students who affiliate with Cook College: Language and cultural houses, math/science/ engineering houses. **Special Academic Facilities/Equipment**: Agricultural, art, and geology museums; center for fiber optics materials research; center for ceramics research; center for advanced biotechnology and medicine; center for computer aids to industrial productivity; draw tower lab; Massively Parrell Processor (MPP). **Computers**: 45% of public computers are PCs, 35% of public computers are Macs, 20% of public computers are UNIX, network access in dorm rooms, remote student-access to Web through college's connection.

CAMPUS LIFE
Activities: Choral groups, concert band, dance, drama/theater, jazz band, literary magazine, concert band, dance, drama/theater, jazz band, literary magazine, music ensembles, opera, pep band, radio station, student government, student newspaper, student-run film society, symphony orchestra, television station, yearbook. **Organizations**: 400 registered organizations, 7 honor societies. 29 fraternities, 15 sororities. **Athletics (Intercollegiate)**: *Men*: Baseball, basketball, cheerleading, crew/rowing, cross-country, diving, fencing, football, golf, lacrosse, soccer, swimming, tennis, track/field (indoor), track/field (outdoor), wrestling. *Women*: Basketball, cheerleading, crew/rowing, cross-country, diving, fencing, field hockey, golf, gymnastics, lacrosse, soccer, softball, swimming, tennis, track/field (indoor), track/field (outdoor), volleyball.

ADMISSIONS
Freshman Academic Profile: 35% in top 10% of high school class, 73% in top 25% of high school class, 98% in top 50% of high school class. SAT Math middle 50% range 610–710. SAT Critical Reading middle 50% range 530–630. TOEFL required of all international applicants, minimum paper TOEFL 550. **Basis for Candidate Selection**: *Very important factors considered include*: Class rank, rigor of secondary school record, standardized test scores. *Other factors considered include*: Application essay, extracurricular activities, racial/ethnic status, recommendation(s), state residency, talent/ability, volunteer work, work experience. **Freshman Admission Requirements**: High school diploma is required, and GED is accepted. *Academic units required*: 4 English, 4 math, 2 science (2 science labs), 6 academic electives. **Freshman Admission Statistics**: 3,806 applied, 68% admitted, 22% enrolled. **Transfer Admission Requirements**: High school transcript, college transcript(s). Lowest grade transferable C. **General Admission Information**: Application fee $50. Regular notification 2/27. Non-fall registration not accepted. Admission may be deferred for a maximum of 2 years. Common Application not accepted. Credit and/or placement offered for CEEB Advanced Placement tests.

COSTS AND FINANCIAL AID
Annual in-state tuition $5,286. Out-of-state tuition $10,754. Room & board $6,098. Required fees $1,290. Average book expense $800. **Required Forms and Deadlines**: FAFSA. Financial aid filing deadline 3/15. **Notification of Awards**: Applicants will be notified of awards on a rolling basis beginning on or about 2/15. **Types of Aid**: *Need-based scholarships/grants*: Pell, SEOG, state scholarships/grants, the school's own gift aid. *Loans*: Direct Subsidized Stafford, Direct Unsubsidized Stafford, Direct PLUS, Federal Perkins, state loans, college/university loans from institutional funds, educational loan. **Student Employment**: Federal Work-Study Program available. Institutional employment available. Off-campus job opportunities are good. **Financial Aid Statistics**: 36% freshmen, 32% undergrads receive need-based scholarship or grant aid. 43% freshmen, 39% undergrads receive need-based self-help aid. 5 freshmen, 11 undergrads receive athletic scholarships.

SACRED HEART UNIVERSITY

5151 Park Avenue, Fairfield, CT 06825
Phone: 203-371-7880 **E-mail**: enroll@sacredheart.edu **CEEB Code**: 3780
Fax: 203-365-7607 **Website**: www.sacredheart.edu **ACT Code**: 0589
Financial Aid Phone: 203-371-7980

This private school, affiliated with the Roman Catholic Church, was founded in 1963. It has a 65-acre campus.

RATINGS
Admissions Selectivity Rating: 83   **Fire Safety Rating**: 82   **Green Rating**: 70

STUDENTS AND FACULTY
Enrollment: 4,136. **Student Body**: 62% female, 38% male, 68% out-of-state, 1% international (41 countries represented). African American 5%, Asian 2%, Caucasian 85%, Hispanic 6%. **Retention and Graduation**: 80% freshmen return for sophomore year. 56% freshmen graduate within 4 years. 39% grads go on to further study within 1 year. 22% grads pursue arts and sciences degrees. 13% grads pursue business degrees. 2% grads pursue law degrees. 2% grads pursue medical degrees. **Faculty**: Student/faculty ratio 13:1. 189 full-time faculty, 76% hold PhDs. 96% faculty teach undergrads.

ACADEMICS
Degrees: Associate, bachelor's, certificate, doctoral, master's, post-bachelor's certificate, post-master's certificate. **Academic Requirements**: Arts/fine arts, English (including composition), history, humanities, mathematics, philosophy, sciences (biological or physical), social science. **Classes**: Most classes have 10–19 students. **Majors with Highest Enrollment**: Business administration/management, kinesiology and exercise science, psychology. **Disciplines with Highest Percentage of Degrees Awarded**: Business/marketing 33%, psychology 18%, health professions and related sciences 9%, security and protective services 5%, communications/journalism 5%, English 4%, social sciences 4%. **Special Study Options**: Accelerated program (5th year MBA program, MSCIS: Computer Information Systems), combined degree programs in physical therapy (doctoral) and occupational therapy (masters), cooperative education program, cross-registration, distance learning, double major, English as a second language (ESL), exchange student program (domestic), honors program, independent study, internships, liberal arts/career combination, semester in Ireland, semester in Luxembourg, student-designed major, study abroad, teacher certification program, weekend college.

FACILITIES
Housing: Coed dorms, apartments for single students, special housing for disabled students, thematic floors. **Special Academic Facilities/Equipment**: WHRT student radio station, WSHU National Public Radio, Edgerton Center for the Performing Arts, gallery of contemporary art. **Computers**: 11% of classrooms are wired, 86% of classrooms are wireless, 86% of public computers are PCs, 15% of public computers are Macs, network access in dorm rooms, network access in dorm lounges, online registration, online administrative functions (other than registration), remote student-access to Web through college's connection, tuition includes personal computer. Undergraduates are required to own a computer.

CAMPUS LIFE
Activities: Choral groups, concert band, dance, drama/theater, jazz band, literary magazine, marching band, music ensembles, musical theater, pep band, radio station, student government, student newspaper, student-run film society, television station, yearbook. **Organizations**: 85 registered organizations, 13 honor societies, 4 religious organizations. 4 fraternities (5% men join), 6 sororities (5% women join). **Athletics (Intercollegiate)**: *Men*: Baseball, basketball, bowling, cross-country, fencing, football, golf, ice hockey, lacrosse, soccer, tennis, track/field (indoor), track/field (outdoor), volleyball, wrestling. *Women*: Basketball, bowling, crew/rowing, cross-country, diving, equestrian sports, fencing, field hockey, golf, ice hockey, lacrosse, soccer, softball, swimming, tennis, track/field (indoor), track/field (outdoor), volleyball. Environmental Initiatives: Lighting renewal for all new construction and renovations, as well as low energy bulbs and motion detection systems. Transfer from 28 chemicals to 6 green chemicals for custodial work. Free shuttle service for students to reduce the number of cars traveling between campuses.

ADMISSIONS
Freshman Academic Profile: 14% in top 10% of high school class, 43% in top 25% of high school class, 80% in top 50% of high school class. 70% from public high schools. SAT Math middle 50% range 500–580. SAT Critical Reading middle 50% range 490–570. ACT middle 50% range 21–25. TOEFL required of all international applicants, minimum paper TOEFL 500, minimum computer TOEFL 270. **Basis for Candidate Selection**: *Very important factors considered include*: Academic GPA, rigor of secondary school record. *Important factors considered include*: Character/personal qualities, class rank, extracurricular activities, geographical residence, interview, recommendation(s), standardized test scores, state residency, volunteer work. *Other factors considered include*: Alumni/ae relation, application essay, first generation, level of applicant's interest, racial/ethnic status, religious affiliation/commitment, talent/ability, work experience. **Freshman Admission Requirements**: High school diploma is required, and GED is accepted. *Academic units required*: 4 English, 3 math, 3 science (1 science lab), 2 foreign language, 3 social studies, 3 history, 3 academic electives. *Academic units recommended*: 4 English, 4 math, 4 science (2 science labs), 4 foreign language, 4 social studies, 4 history, 4 academic electives. **Freshman Admission Statistics**: 6,219 applied, 62% admitted, 24% enrolled. **Transfer Admission Requirements**: High school transcript, college transcript(s), essay or personal statement, standardized test score. Minimum college GPA of 3.0 required. Lowest grade transferable C-. **General Admission Information**: Application fee $50. Early decision application deadline 11/15. Regular notification is rolling. Non-fall registration accepted. Admission may be deferred for a maximum of 1 year. Credit and/or placement offered for CEEB Advanced Placement tests.

COSTS AND FINANCIAL AID
Annual tuition $26,950. Room and board $10,816. Required fees $200. Average book expense $700. **Required Forms and Deadlines**: FAFSA, CSS/Financial Aid PROFILE, Noncustodial PROFILE. Financial aid filing deadline 2/15. **Notification of Awards**: Applicants will be notified of awards on a rolling basis beginning on or about 3/1. **Types of Aid**: *Need-based scholarships/grants*: Pell, SEOG, state scholarships/grants, private scholarships, the school's own gift aid, Federal Nursing Scholarships. *Loans*: FFEL Subsidized Stafford, FFEL Unsubsidized Stafford, FFEL PLUS, Federal Perkins, state loans, alternative loans. **Student Employment**: Federal Work-Study Program available. Institutional employment available. Off-campus job opportunities are excellent. **Financial Aid Statistics**: 65% freshmen, 64% undergrads receive need-based scholarship or grant aid. 59% freshmen, 58% undergrads receive need-based self-help aid. 54 freshmen, 173 undergrads receive athletic scholarships. 83% freshmen, 88% undergrads receive any aid. Highest amount earned per year from on-campus jobs $7,684.

SAGINAW VALLEY STATE UNIVERSITY

7400 Bay Road, University Center, MI 48710
Phone: 989-964-4200 **E-mail**: admissions@svsu.edu **CEEB Code**: 1766
Fax: 989-790-0180 **Website**: www.svsu.edu **ACT Code**: 2057
Financial Aid Phone: 989-964-4103

This public school was founded in 1963. It has a 782-acre campus.

RATINGS
Admissions Selectivity Rating: 72   **Fire Safety Rating**: 85   **Green Rating**: 65

STUDENTS AND FACULTY
Enrollment: 7,678. **Student Body**: 60% female, 40% male, 3% international (48 countries represented). African American 7%, Caucasian 82%, Hispanic 2%. **Retention and Graduation**: 68% freshmen return for sophomore year. 6% freshmen graduate within 4 years. 21% grads go on to further study within 1 year. **Faculty**: Student/faculty ratio 20:1. 270 full-time faculty, 77% hold PhDs. 100% faculty teach undergrads.

ACADEMICS
Degrees: Bachelor's, master's, post-master's certificate. **Academic Requirements**: Arts/fine arts, communications, English (including composition), history, mathematics, philosophy, sciences (biological or physical), social science. **Classes**: Most classes have 20–29 students. Most lab/discussion sections have 10–19 students. **Majors with Highest Enrollment**: Criminal justice/safety studies, elementary education and teaching, nursing/registered nurse training (ASN, BSN, MSN, RN). **Disciplines with Highest Percentage of Degrees Awarded**: Education 34%, business/marketing 13%, health professions and related sciences 9%, security and protective services 7%, public administration and social services 7%. **Special Study Options**: Accelerated program, cooperative education program, distance learning, double major, dual enrollment, English as a second

language (ESL), honors program, independent study, internships, student-designed major, study abroad, teacher certification program.

FACILITIES

Housing: Coed dorms, apartments for single students, special housing for disabled students. **Special Academic Facilities/Equipment**: Sculpture gallery, fine arts center, center for health and physical education, independent testing lab, center for economic and business research, applied technology research center. **Computers**: 100% of public computers are PCs, network access in dorm rooms, network access in dorm lounges, online registration, online administrative functions (other than registration), remote student-access to Web through college's connection.

CAMPUS LIFE

Activities: Choral groups, concert band, dance, drama/theater, jazz band, literary magazine, marching band, music ensembles, musical theater, pep band, student government, student newspaper, student-run film society. **Organizations**: 90 registered organizations, 8 religious organizations. 4 fraternities, 5 sororities. **Athletics (Intercollegiate)**: *Men*: Baseball, basketball, bowling, cheerleading, cross-country, football, golf, soccer, track/field (indoor), track/field (outdoor). *Women*: Basketball, cheerleading, cross-country, soccer, softball, tennis, track/field (indoor), track/field (outdoor), volleyball. Environmental Initiatives: Building buildings with energy savings in mind for many years. Spending consistently through the years for energy and utility conservation measures. Recycling upgrades, cutting down on areas mowed, etc.

ADMISSIONS

Freshman Academic Profile: 23% in top 10% of high school class, 44% in top 25% of high school class, 76% in top 50% of high school class. ACT middle 50% range 18–24. TOEFL required of all international applicants, minimum paper TOEFL 500, minimum computer TOEFL 173. **Basis for Candidate Selection**: *Very important factors considered include:* Academic GPA, rigor of secondary school record, standardized test scores. *Other factors considered include:* Recommendation(s). **Freshman Admission Requirements**: High school diploma is required, and GED is accepted. *Academic units required:* 4 English, 3 math, 2 science, 3 social studies. *Academic units recommended:* 4 English, 4 math, 4 science, 2 foreign language, 4 social studies, 1 communications. **Freshman Admission Statistics**: 4,346 applied, 89% admitted, 37% enrolled. **Transfer Admission Requirements**: College transcript(s). Minimum college GPA of 2.0 required. Lowest grade transferable C-. **General Admission Information**: Application fee $25. Regular notification is rolling. Non-fall registration accepted. Credit and/or placement offered for CEEB Advanced Placement tests.

COSTS AND FINANCIAL AID

Annual in-state tuition $5,832. Annual out-of-state tuition $13,857. Room and board $6,630. Required fees $426. Average book expense $900. **Required Forms and Deadlines**: FAFSA. Financial aid filing deadline 2/14. **Notification of Awards**: Applicants will be notified of awards on a rolling basis beginning on or about 3/20. **Types of Aid**: *Need-based scholarships/grants:* Pell, SEOG, state scholarships/grants, private scholarships, the school's own gift aid. *Loans:* Direct Subsidized Stafford, Direct Unsubsidized Stafford, Direct PLUS, state loans, CitiAssist Loans, Signature Student Loans. **Student Employment**: Federal Work-Study Program available. Institutional employment available. Off-campus job opportunities are good. **Financial Aid Statistics**: 41% freshmen, 36% undergrads receive need-based scholarship or grant aid. 41% freshmen, 46% undergrads receive need-based self-help aid. 81 freshmen, 266 undergrads receive athletic scholarships. 90% freshmen, 72% undergrads receive any aid.

SAINT ANSELM COLLEGE

Best 368

100 Saint Anselm Drive, Manchester, NH 03102-1310
Phone: 603-641-7500 **E-mail**: admission@anselm.edu **CEEB Code**: 3748
Fax: 603-641-7550 **Website**: www.anselm.edu **ACT Code**: 2522
Financial Aid Phone: 603-641-7110

This private school, affiliated with the Roman Catholic Church, was founded in 1889. It has a 404-acre campus.

RATINGS

Admissions Selectivity Rating: 84   **Fire Safety Rating**: 60*   **Green Rating**: 60*

STUDENTS AND FACULTY

Enrollment: 1,922. **Student Body**: 58% female, 42% male, 78% out-of-state, (18 countries represented). Asian 1%, Caucasian 75%. **Retention and Graduation**: 82% freshmen return for sophomore year. 71% freshmen graduate within 4 years. 14% grads go on to further study within 1 year. 9% grads pursue arts and sciences degrees. 1% grads pursue business degrees. 3% grads pursue law degrees. 1% grads pursue medical degrees. **Faculty**: Student/faculty ratio 12:1. 137 full-time faculty, 93% hold PhDs. 100% faculty teach undergrads.

ACADEMICS

Degrees: Bachelor's. **Academic Requirements**: English (including composition), foreign languages, humanities, philosophy, sciences (biological or physical), theology. **Classes**: Most classes have 10–19 students. Most lab/discussion sections have 10–19 students. **Majors with Highest Enrollment**: Business administration/management; nursing; psychology. **Disciplines with Highest Percentage of Degrees Awarded**: Social sciences 29%, business/marketing 19%, health professions and related sciences 12%, psychology 8%, English 8%. **Special Study Options**: Cross-registration, dual enrollment, exchange student program (domestic), honors program, independent study, internships, liberal arts/career combination, study abroad, teacher certification program.

FACILITIES

Housing: Coed dorms, men's dorms, women's dorms, apartments for single students, special housing for disabled students, substance-free housing. **Special Academic Facilities/Equipment**: Chapel Art Center, New Hampshire Institute of Politics, Izart Observatory, Koonz Theater, Comisky Studio (Fine Arts), Poisson Hall. **Computers**: 64% of classrooms are wireless, 90% of public computers are PCs, 10% of public computers are Macs, network access in dorm rooms, network access in dorm lounges, online administrative functions (other than registration), remote student-access to Web through college's connection.

CAMPUS LIFE

Activities: Choral groups, dance, drama/theater, jazz band, literary magazine, music ensembles, musical theater, pep band, radio station, student government, student newspaper, television station, yearbook. **Organizations**: 120 registered organizations, 11 honor societies, 7 religious organizations. **Athletics (Intercollegiate)**: *Men:* Baseball, basketball, cross-country, football, golf, ice hockey, lacrosse, skiing (downhill/alpine), soccer, tennis. *Women:* Basketball, cross-country, field hockey, lacrosse, skiing (downhill/alpine), soccer, softball, tennis, volleyball.

ADMISSIONS

Freshman Academic Profile: 23% in top 10% of high school class, 56% in top 25% of high school class, 91% in top 50% of high school class. 45% from public high schools. SAT Math middle 50% range 510–600. SAT Critical Reading middle 50% range 510–600. SAT Writing middle 50% range 510–610. ACT middle 50% range 22–26. TOEFL required of all international applicants, minimum paper TOEFL 550, minimum computer TOEFL 213. **Basis for Candidate Selection**: *Very important factors considered include:* Academic GPA, character/personal qualities, rigor of secondary school record. *Important factors considered include:* Application essay, class rank, recommendation(s), standardized test scores, talent/ability. *Other factors considered include:* Alumni/ae relation, extracurricular activities, geographical residence, level of applicant's interest, racial/ethnic status, volunteer work, work experience. **Freshman Admission Requirements**: High school diploma is required, and GED is accepted. *Academic units required:* 4 English, 3 math, 3 science (3 science labs), 2 foreign language, 2 social studies, 1 history, 3 academic electives. *Academic units recommended:* 4 math, 4 science, 4 foreign language, 2 history. **Freshman Admission Statistics**: 3,163 applied, 71% admitted, 25% enrolled. **Transfer Admission Requirements**: High school transcript, college transcript(s), essay or personal statement, standardized test score, statement of good standing from prior institution(s). Minimum college GPA of 2.5 required. Lowest grade transferable C. **General Admission Information**: Application fee $55. Early decision application deadline 11/15. Regular notification is rolling. Nonfall registration accepted. Admission may be deferred for a maximum of 1 year. Credit and/or placement offered for CEEB Advanced Placement tests.

COSTS AND FINANCIAL AID

Annual tuition $26,960. Room and board $10,200. Required fees $750. Average book expense $750. **Required Forms and Deadlines**: FAFSA, CSS/Financial Aid PROFILE. Financial aid filing deadline 3/15. Financial aid filing deadline 3/15. **Notification of Awards**: Applicants will be notified of awards on or about 3/15. **Types of Aid**: *Need-based scholarships/grants:* Pell, SEOG, state scholarships/grants, private scholarships, the school's own gift aid. *Loans:* FFEL Subsidized Stafford, FFEL Unsubsidized Stafford, FFEL PLUS, Federal Perkins, GATE student loans. **Student Employment**: Federal Work-Study Program available. Institutional employment available. **Financial Aid Statistics**: 71% freshmen, 70% undergrads receive need-based scholarship or grant aid. 62% freshmen, 63% undergrads receive need-based self-help aid. 4 freshmen, 16 undergrads receive athletic scholarships.

See page 1348.

SAINT ANTHONY COLLEGE OF NURSING

5658 East State Street, Rockford, IL 61108-2468
Phone: 815-395-5100 **E-mail:** cheryldelgado@sacn.edu
Fax: 815-395-2275 **Website:** www.sacn.edu
Financial Aid Phone: 815-395-5089

This private school, affiliated with the Roman Catholic Church, was founded in 1915.

RATINGS
Admissions Selectivity Rating: 60*   **Fire Safety Rating:** 60*   **Green Rating:** 60*

STUDENTS AND FACULTY
Enrollment: 86. **Student Body:** 93% female, 7% male. **Retention and Graduation:** 10% grads go on to further study within 1 year. **Faculty:** 83% faculty teach undergrads.

ACADEMICS
Degrees: Bachelor's, master's. **Academic Requirements:** 59 credits in nursing, 2 credits in religion, 3 credits in philosophy. **Disciplines with Highest Percentage of Degrees Awarded:** Health professions and related sciences 100%. **Special Study Options:** Distance learning, independent study.

FACILITIES
Computers: 1% of classrooms are wired, 1% of classrooms are wireless, 100% of public computers are PCs, remote student-access to Web through college's connection.

CAMPUS LIFE
Activities: Student government. **Organizations:** 1 registered organization.

ADMISSIONS
Freshman Academic Profile: TOEFL required of all international applicants, minimum paper TOEFL 550, minimum computer TOEFL 213. **Basis for Candidate Selection:** *Important factors considered include:* Application essay, interview, recommendation(s). *Other factors considered include:* Extracurricular activities, volunteer work, work experience. **Freshman Admission Requirements:** High school diploma or equivalent is not required. *Academic units recommended:* 4 English, 3 math, 4 science. **Transfer Admission Requirements:** College transcript(s), essay or personal statement, interview. Minimum college GPA of 2.5 required. Lowest grade transferable C. **General Admission Information:** Application fee $50. Regular application deadline 1/15. Credit offered for CEEB Advanced Placement tests.

COSTS AND FINANCIAL AID
Annual tuition $17,220. Required fees $192. **Types of Aid:** *Need-based scholarships/grants:* Pell, state scholarships/grants, private scholarships, the school's own gift aid. *Loans:* FFEL Subsidized Stafford, FFEL Unsubsidized Stafford, FFEL PLUS. **Financial Aid Statistics:** 93% undergrads receive need-based scholarship or grant aid. 85% undergrads receive need-based self-help aid. 86% undergrads receive any aid.

SAINT AUGUSTINE'S COLLEGE

1315 Oakwood Avenue, Raleigh, NC 27610
Phone: 919-516-4016 **E-mail:** admissions@st-aug.edu
Fax: 919-516-5805 **Website:** www.st-aug.edu **ACT Code:** 3152
Financial Aid Phone: 919-516-4133

This private school, affiliated with the Episcopal Church, was founded in 1867. It has a 105-acre campus.

RATINGS
Admissions Selectivity Rating: 70   **Fire Safety Rating:** 60*   **Green Rating:** 60*

STUDENTS AND FACULTY
Enrollment: 1,493. **Student Body:** 52% female, 48% male, 44% out-of-state, 6% international (22 countries represented). African American 60%. **Retention and Graduation:** 62% freshmen return for sophomore year. 13% freshmen graduate within 4 years. 27% grads go on to further study within 1 year. 21% grads pursue arts and sciences degrees. 4% grads pursue business degrees. 2% grads pursue law degrees. **Faculty:** Student/faculty ratio 16:1. 76 full-time faculty, 66% hold PhDs. 100% faculty teach undergrads.

ACADEMICS
Degrees: Bachelor's. **Academic Requirements:** Arts/fine arts, computer literacy, English (including composition), foreign languages, history, humanities, mathematics, philosophy, sciences (biological or physical), social science. **Classes:** Most classes have 10–19 students. Most lab/discussion sections have 10–19 students. **Majors with Highest Enrollment:** Business administration/management, computer and information sciences, criminal justice/law enforcement administration. **Disciplines with Highest Percentage of Degrees Awarded:** Business/marketing 43%, social sciences 10%, parks and recreation 9%, computer and information sciences 8%, communication technologies 8%, psychology 7%. **Special Study Options:** Accelerated program, cooperative education program, cross-registration, double major, honors program, independent study, internships, liberal arts/career combination, teacher certification program, weekend college.

FACILITIES
Housing: Men's dorms, women's dorms. **Special Academic Facilities/Equipment:** Radio and TV station. **Computers:** 100% of public computers are PCs, network access in dorm rooms, online administrative functions (other than registration), remote student-access to Web through college's connection.

CAMPUS LIFE
Activities: Choral groups, concert band, dance, drama/theater, jazz band, music ensembles, musical theater, pep band, radio station, student government, student newspaper, student-run film society, symphony orchestra, television station, yearbook. **Organizations:** 45 registered organizations, 8 honor societies, 1 religious organization. 4 fraternities (6% men join), 4 sororities (12% women join). **Athletics (Intercollegiate):** *Men:* Baseball, basketball, cross-country, football, golf, tennis, track/field (indoor), track/field (outdoor). *Women:* Basketball, cheerleading, cross-country, softball, tennis, track/field (indoor), track/field (outdoor), volleyball.

ADMISSIONS
Freshman Academic Profile: 4% in top 10% of high school class, 16% in top 25% of high school class, 37% in top 50% of high school class. 95% from public high schools. SAT Math middle 50% range 210–690. SAT Critical Reading middle 50% range 260–670. ACT middle 50% range 15–23. TOEFL required of all international applicants, minimum paper TOEFL 500. **Basis for Candidate Selection:** *Very important factors considered include:* Rigor of secondary school record. *Important factors considered include:* Character/personal qualities, racial/ethnic status, recommendation(s), state residency, talent/ability. *Other factors considered include:* Alumni/ae relation, application essay, class rank, extracurricular activities, geographical residence, interview, religious affiliation/commitment, standardized test scores, volunteer work, work experience. **Freshman Admission Requirements:** High school diploma is required, and GED is accepted. *Academic units required:* 4 English, 3 math, 2 science, 2 social studies, 9 academic electives. 1 algebra. **Freshman Admission Statistics:** 1,287 applied, 66% admitted, 53% enrolled. **Transfer Admission Requirements:** High school transcript, college transcript(s), standardized test score, statement of good standing from prior institution(s). Minimum college GPA of 2.0 required. Lowest grade transferable C. **General Admission Information:** Application fee $25. Regular application deadline 7/1. Regular notification is rolling. Non-fall registration accepted. Admission may be deferred for a maximum of 2 years. Common Application not accepted. Credit offered for CEEB Advanced Placement tests.

COSTS AND FINANCIAL AID
Annual tuition $6,030. Room & board $4,960. Required fees $2,250. Average book expense $700. **Required Forms and Deadlines:** FAFSA, institution's own financial aid form, state aid form. Financial aid filing deadline 6/1. **Types of Aid:** *Need-based scholarships/grants:* Pell, SEOG, state scholarships/grants, private scholarships, the school's own gift aid, United Negro College Fund. *Loans:* FFEL Subsidized Stafford, FFEL Unsubsidized Stafford, FFEL PLUS, Federal Perkins. **Student Employment:** Federal Work-Study Program available. Institutional employment available. Off-campus job opportunities are excellent. **Financial Aid Statistics:** 29% freshmen, 23% undergrads receive need-based self-help aid. Highest amount earned per year from on-campus jobs $1,000.

SAINT CHARLES BORROMEO SEMINARY

100 East Wynnewood Road, Wynnewood, PA 19096
Phone: 610-785-6271 **E-mail:** dandrassy@adphila.org **CEEB Code:** 2794
Fax: 610-617-9267 **Website:** www.scs.edu **ACT Code:** 5923
Financial Aid Phone: 610-785-6582

*This private school, affiliated with the Roman Catholic Church, was
founded in 1832. It has a 77-acre campus.*

RATINGS
Admissions Selectivity Rating: 71   **Fire Safety Rating:** 60*   **Green Rating:** 60*

STUDENTS AND FACULTY
Enrollment: 53. **Student Body:** 100% male, 42% out-of-state, 4% international (3 countries represented). Asian 4%, Caucasian 92%. **Retention and Graduation:** 75% freshmen return for sophomore year. 33% freshmen graduate within 4 years. 90% grads go on to further study within 1 year. **Faculty:** Student/faculty ratio 7:1. 21 full-time faculty, 67% hold PhDs. 60% faculty teach undergrads.

ACADEMICS
Degrees: Bachelor's, first professional, master's. **Academic Requirements:** English (including composition), foreign languages, history, humanities, mathematics, philosophy, sciences (biological or physical), social science, theology. **Classes:** Most classes have 10–19 students. Most lab/discussion sections have fewer than 10 students. **Disciplines with Highest Percentage of Degrees Awarded:** Philosophy and religious studies 100%. **Special Study Options:** Accelerated program, English as a second language (ESL), independent study.

FACILITIES
Housing: Men's dorms, men's and women's dorms available during summer sessions. **Computers:** 80% of classrooms are wired, 100% of public computers are PCs, online registration, remote student-access to Web through college's connection.

CAMPUS LIFE
Activities: Choral groups, drama/theater, music ensembles, student government, student newspaper. **Organizations:** 3 registered organizations, 1 honor society, 2 religious organizations.

ADMISSIONS
Freshman Academic Profile: 22% in top 10% of high school class, 44% in top 25% of high school class, 67% in top 50% of high school class. 40% from public high schools. SAT Math middle 50% range 470–590. SAT Critical Reading middle 50% range 460–710. TOEFL required of all international applicants, minimum paper TOEFL 450, minimum computer TOEFL 150. **Basis for Candidate Selection:** *Very important factors considered include:* Application essay, character/personal qualities, interview, recommendation(s), religious affiliation/commitment, rigor of secondary school record. *Important factors considered include:* Class rank, standardized test scores. *Other factors considered include:* Extracurricular activities, talent/ability, work experience. **Freshman Admission Requirements:** High school diploma is required, and GED is accepted. *Academic units recommended:* 4 English, 3 math, 3 science, 2 foreign language, 3 social studies. **Freshman Admission Statistics:** 11 applied, 100% admitted, 91% enrolled. **Transfer Admission Requirements:** High school transcript, college transcript(s), essay or personal statement. Minimum college GPA of 2.0 required. Lowest grade transferable C. **General Admission Information:** Regular application deadline 7/15. Non-fall registration accepted. Credit and/or placement offered for CEEB Advanced Placement tests.

COSTS AND FINANCIAL AID
Annual tuition $11,734. Room & board $7,875. Average book expense $1,000. **Required Forms and Deadlines:** FAFSA, institution's own financial aid form. **Student Employment:** Federal Work-Study Program available. Institutional employment available. Off-campus job opportunities are poor. **Financial Aid Statistics:** 100% freshmen, 100% undergrads receive any aid.

SAINT CLOUD STATE UNIVERSITY

720 South Fourth Avenue, Saint Cloud, MN 56301-4498
Phone: 320-308-2244 **E-mail:** scsu4u@stcloudstate.edu **CEEB Code:** 6679
Fax: 320-308-2243 **Website:** www.stcloudstate.edu **ACT Code:** 2144
Financial Aid Phone: 320-308-2047

This public school was founded in 1869. It has a 920-acre campus.

RATINGS
Admissions Selectivity Rating: 64   **Fire Safety Rating:** 60*   **Green Rating:** 60*

STUDENTS AND FACULTY
Enrollment: 13,120. **Student Body:** 53% female, 47% male, 8% out-of-state, 4% international (85 countries represented). African American 2%, Asian 2%, Caucasian 72%. **Retention and Graduation:** 71% freshmen return for sophomore year. **Faculty:** Student/faculty ratio 17:1. 650 full-time faculty, 80% hold PhDs. 100% faculty teach undergrads.

ACADEMICS
Degrees: Associate, bachelor's, master's, post-bachelor's certificate, post-master's certificate. **Academic Requirements:** Computer literacy, English (including composition), history, humanities, mathematics, philosophy, sciences (biological or physical), social science. **Classes:** Most classes have 20–29 students. **Majors with Highest Enrollment:** Elementary education and teaching, marketing/marketing management, mass communications/media studies. **Disciplines with Highest Percentage of Degrees Awarded:** Business/marketing 24%, education 18%, social sciences 9%, psychology 5%. **Special Study Options:** Accelerated program, cooperative education program, cross-registration, distance learning, double major, dual enrollment, English as a second language (ESL), honors program, independent study, internships, student-designed major, study abroad, teacher certification program.

FACILITIES
Housing: Coed dorms, special housing for international students. **Special Academic Facilities/Equipment:** Art and anthropology museums, electron microscope, planetarium, GIS and weather labs. **Computers:** 76% of public computers are PCs, 24% of public computers are Macs, network access in dorm rooms, network access in dorm lounges, online registration, online administrative functions (other than registration), remote student-access to Web through college's connection.

CAMPUS LIFE
Activities: Choral groups, concert band, dance, drama/theater, music ensembles, musical theater, opera, radio station, student government, student newspaper, symphony orchestra, television station. **Organizations:** 240 registered organizations, 6 honor societies, 12 religious organizations. 5 fraternities, 4 sororities. **Athletics (Intercollegiate):** *Men:* Baseball, basketball, cheerleading, cross-country, diving, football, golf, ice hockey, rugby, swimming, tennis, track/field (indoor), track/field (outdoor), wrestling. *Women:* Basketball, cheerleading, cross-country, diving, golf, ice hockey, rugby, skiing (downhill/alpine), soccer, softball, swimming, tennis, track/field (indoor), track/field (outdoor), volleyball.

ADMISSIONS
Freshman Academic Profile: 7% in top 10% of high school class, 29% in top 25% of high school class, 76% in top 50% of high school class. 99% from public high schools. ACT middle 50% range 19–24. TOEFL required of all international applicants, minimum paper TOEFL 500, minimum computer TOEFL 173. **Basis for Candidate Selection:** *Very important factors considered include:* Class rank, rigor of secondary school record. *Other factors considered include:* Academic GPA, application essay, extracurricular activities, recommendation(s), standardized test scores, talent/ability. **Freshman Admission Requirements:** High school diploma is required, and GED is accepted. *Academic units required:* 4 English, 3 math, 3 science (1 science lab), 2 foreign language, 3 social studies, 1 history, 1 fine arts. **Freshman Admission Statistics:** 5,912 applied, 78% admitted, 47% enrolled. **Transfer Admission Requirements:** College transcript(s), statement of good standing from prior institution(s). Minimum college GPA of 2.0 required. Lowest grade transferable C. **General Admission Information:** Application fee $20. Regular application deadline 6/1. Regular notification is rolling. Non-fall registration accepted. Admission may be deferred for a maximum of 2 years. Common Application not accepted. Credit offered for CEEB Advanced Placement tests.

COSTS AND FINANCIAL AID
Annual in-state tuition $4,760. Out-of-state tuition $10,332. Room & board $4,688. Required fees $562. Average book expense $1,000. **Required Forms**

and **Deadlines**: FAFSA, institution's own financial aid form. Financial aid filing deadline 6/30. **Notification of Awards**: Applicants will be notified of awards on a rolling basis beginning on or about 6/3. **Types of Aid**: *Need-based scholarships/grants*: Pell, SEOG, state scholarships/grants, private scholarships, the school's own gift aid. *Loans*: FFEL Subsidized Stafford, FFEL Unsubsidized Stafford, FFEL PLUS, Federal Perkins, state loans. **Student Employment**: Federal Work-Study Program available. Institutional employment available. **Financial Aid Statistics**: 39% freshmen, 34% undergrads receive need-based scholarship or grant aid. 47% freshmen, 44% undergrads receive need-based self-help aid. 43 freshmen, 199 undergrads receive athletic scholarships.

SAINT FRANCIS COLLEGE (NY)

180 Remsen Street, Brooklyn Heights, NY 11201
Phone: 718-489-5200 **E-mail**: admissions@stfranciscollege.edu **CEEB Code**: 2796
Fax: 718-522-1274 **Website**: www.stfranciscollege.edu **ACT Code**: 2884
Financial Aid Phone: 718-489-5255

This private school, affiliated with the Roman Catholic Church, was founded in 1884. It has a 1-acre campus.

RATINGS
Admissions Selectivity Rating: 60*   **Fire Safety Rating**: 60*   **Green Rating**: 60*

STUDENTS AND FACULTY
Enrollment: 2,294. **Student Body**: 57% female, 43% male, 1% out-of-state, 13% international (52 countries represented). African American 20%, Asian 2%, Caucasian 49%, Hispanic 14%. **Retention and Graduation**: 76% freshmen return for sophomore year. 21% freshmen graduate within 4 years. **Faculty**: Student/faculty ratio 18:1. 69 full-time faculty, 77% hold PhDs. 100% faculty teach undergrads.

ACADEMICS
Degrees: Associate, bachelor's. **Academic Requirements**: Arts/fine arts, communications (phonetics, diction, extemporaneous speaking), English (including composition), history, humanities, mathematics, philosophy, religious studies, sciences (biological or physical), social science. **Classes**: Most classes have 10–19 students. Most lab/discussion sections have 10–19 students. **Majors with Highest Enrollment**: Business administration/management, liberal arts and sciences/liberal studies, psychology. **Disciplines with Highest Percentage of Degrees Awarded**: Business/marketing 22%, liberal arts/general studies 15%, social sciences 13%, psychology 11%, biological/life sciences 7%, health professions and related sciences 7%. **Special Study Options**: Accelerated program, cooperative education program, cross-registration, double major, dual enrollment, honors program, independent study, internships, study abroad, teacher certification program. Accelerated biomedical science program with New York College of Podiatric Medicine, medical technology program with St. Vincent's Catholic Medical Centers of New York and New York Methodist Hospital, joint program in radiological sciences with St. Vincent's Catholic Medical Centers of New York, 7-year cooperative program with the New York University College of Dentistry, can complete BA at St. Francis and master of science in computer science from Polytechnic University.

FACILITIES
Housing: Students may apply for housing in the recently opened dormitory at Polytechnic University, a few minutes walk from St. Francis College. **Computers**: 100% of public computers are PCs, support for handheld computing, remote student-access to Web through college's connection.

CAMPUS LIFE
Activities: Choral groups, drama/theater, literary magazine, student government, student newspaper, yearbook. **Organizations**: 25 registered organizations, 1 honor society, 1 religious organization. 1 fraternity, 1 sorority. **Athletics (Intercollegiate)**: *Men*: Baseball, basketball, cross-country, diving, football, soccer, softball, swimming, tennis, track/field (outdoor), volleyball, water polo. *Women*: Basketball, cross-country, soccer, softball, swimming, tennis, track/field (outdoor), volleyball, water polo.

ADMISSIONS
Freshman Academic Profile: 44% from public high schools. SAT Math middle 50% range 400–550. SAT Critical Reading middle 50% range 410–540. TOEFL required of all international applicants, minimum paper TOEFL 500. **Basis for Candidate Selection**: *Very important factors considered include*: Rigor of secondary school record, standardized test scores. *Important factors considered include*: Alumni/ae relation, application essay, character/personal

qualities, class rank, interview, recommendation(s), talent/ability. *Other factors considered include*: Extracurricular activities, volunteer work. **Freshman Admission Requirements**: High school diploma is required, and GED is accepted. *Academic units required*: 4 English, 3 math, 2 science (1 science lab), 2 foreign language, 4 social studies, 1 academic elective. 1 music/art. **Freshman Admission Statistics**: 1,304 applied, 88% admitted, 38% enrolled. **Transfer Admission Requirements**: High school transcript, college transcript(s), essay or personal statement, statement of good standing from prior institution(s). Minimum college GPA of 2.0 required. Lowest grade transferable C. **General Admission Information**: Application fee $35. Regular notification is rolling. Non-fall registration accepted. Admission may be deferred for a maximum of 1 year. Common Application not accepted. Placement offered for CEEB Advanced Placement tests.

COSTS AND FINANCIAL AID
Annual tuition: $13,500. **Required Forms and Deadlines**: FAFSA, institution's own financial aid form, state aid form. Priority Financial aid filing deadline 2/15. **Types of Aid**: *Need-based scholarships/grants*: Pell, SEOG, state scholarships/grants, private scholarships, the school's own gift aid. *Loans*: FFEL Subsidized Stafford, FFEL Unsubsidized Stafford, FFEL PLUS, Federal Perkins. **Student Employment**: Federal Work-Study Program available. Institutional employment available. Off-campus job opportunities are good. **Financial Aid Statistics**: 50% undergrads receive need-based scholarship or grant aid. 28% undergrads receive need-based self-help aid. 132 undergrads receive athletic scholarships.

SAINT FRANCIS MEDICAL CENTER
COLLEGE OF NURSING

511 NE Greenleaf Street, Peoria, IL 61603-3783
Phone: 309-655-2596 **E-mail**: janice.farquharson@osfhealthcare.org
Fax: 309-624-8973 **Website**: www.sfmccon.edu

This is a private school.

RATINGS
Admissions Selectivity Rating: 60*   **Fire Safety Rating**: 60*   **Green Rating**: 60*

STUDENTS AND FACULTY
Enrollment: 154. **Student Body**: African American 2%, Asian 1%, Caucasian 95%, Hispanic 1%. **Retention and Graduation**: 97% freshmen return for sophomore year. 100% freshmen graduate within 4 years.

ACADEMICS
Degrees: Bachelor's, master's. **Academic Requirements**: Arts/fine arts, computer literacy, English (including composition), history, humanities, mathematics, nursing major courses, philosophy, sciences (biological or physical), social science. **Disciplines with Highest Percentage of Degrees Awarded**: Health professions and related sciences 100%. **Special Study Options**: Distance learning, independent study. Advanced placement credit for RNs returning to complete the BSN; some online courses offered.

FACILITIES
Housing: Coed dorms.

CAMPUS LIFE
Activities: Student government.

ADMISSIONS
Transfer Admission Requirements: High school transcript, college transcript(s), essay or personal statement. Minimum college GPA of 2.5 required. Lowest grade transferable C. **General Admission Information**: Common Application accepted.

COSTS AND FINANCIAL AID
Annual tuition $13,650. Room and board $2,000. Required fees $440.

SAINT FRANCIS UNIVERSITY (PA)

PO Box 600, Loretto, PA 15940
Phone: 814-472-3000 **E-mail**: admissions@francis.edu **CEEB Code**: 2797
Fax: 814-472-3335 **Website**: www.francis.edu **ACT Code**: 3682
Financial Aid Phone: 814-472-3010

This private school, affiliated with the Roman Catholic Church, was founded in 1847. It has a 600-acre campus.

RATINGS
Admissions Selectivity Rating: 74   **Fire Safety Rating**: 64   **Green Rating**: 60*

STUDENTS AND FACULTY
Enrollment: 1,360. **Student Body**: 61% female, 39% male, 31% out-of-state.
Retention and Graduation: 83% freshmen return for sophomore year. 48% freshmen graduate within 4 years. 29% grads go on to further study within 1 year. 5% grads pursue arts and sciences degrees. 9% grads pursue business degrees. 3% grads pursue law degrees. 3% grads pursue medical degrees.
Faculty: Student/faculty ratio 14:1. 90 full-time faculty. 99% faculty teach undergrads.

ACADEMICS
Degrees: Associate, bachelor's, doctoral, master's, post-bachelor's certificate.
Academic Requirements: Arts/fine arts, computer literacy, English (including composition), foreign languages, history, humanities, mathematics, philosophy, religious studies, sciences (biological or physical), social science, speech.
Classes: Most classes have 10–19 students. Most lab/discussion sections have 10–19 students. **Majors with Highest Enrollment**: Business administration/management, health professions and related sciences, physician assistant.
Disciplines with Highest Percentage of Degrees Awarded: Business/marketing 32%, health professions and related sciences 24%, education 7%, computer and information sciences 5%, psychology 5%, social sciences 5%, public administration and social services 4%. **Special Study Options**: Cooperative education program, distance learning, double major, honors program, independent study, internships, liberal arts/career combination, student-designed major, study abroad, teacher certification program.

FACILITIES
Housing: Coed dorms, men's dorms, women's dorms, apartments for single students, fraternity/sorority housing, special housing for honors students, special housing for campus ministry. **Special Academic Facilities/Equipment**: Art museum, center of excellence for remote and medically underserved areas, elementary-level library for education majors, physician assistant practice facilities, cadaver lab, physical therapy lab. **Computers**: 100% of classrooms are wired, 100% of classrooms are wireless, 100% of public computers are PCs, network access in dorm rooms, online administrative functions (other than registration), remote student-access to Web through college's connection, tuition includes personal computer. Undergraduates are required to own a computer.

CAMPUS LIFE
Activities: Choral groups, dance, drama/theater, literary magazine, music ensembles, pep band, radio station, student government, student newspaper, student-run film society, television station, yearbook. **Organizations**: 60 registered organizations, 9 honor societies, 10 religious organizations. 3 fraternities (7% men join), 3 sororities (12% women join). **Athletics (Intercollegiate)**: *Men*: Basketball, cross-country, football, golf, soccer, swimming, tennis, track/field (indoor), track/field (outdoor), volleyball. *Women*: Basketball, cross-country, field hockey, golf, lacrosse, soccer, softball, swimming, tennis, track/field (indoor), track/field (outdoor), volleyball.

ADMISSIONS
Freshman Academic Profile: 23% in top 10% of high school class, 28% in top 25% of high school class, 78% in top 50% of high school class. 78% from public high schools. SAT Math middle 50% range 480–580. SAT Critical Reading middle 50% range 470–570. ACT middle 50% range 19–26. TOEFL required of all international applicants, minimum paper TOEFL 500, minimum computer TOEFL 220. **Basis for Candidate Selection**: *Very important factors considered include*: Academic GPA, class rank, extracurricular activities, rigor of secondary school record, standardized test scores. *Important factors considered include*: Application essay, character/personal qualities, interview, level of applicant's interest, recommendation(s), talent/ability, volunteer work. *Other factors considered include*: Alumni/ae relation, work experience.
Freshman Admission Requirements: High school diploma is required, and GED is accepted. *Academic units required*: 4 English, 2 math, 1 science (1 science lab), 2 social studies, 7 academic electives. *Academic units recommended*: 2 science, 1 foreign language. **Freshman Admission Statistics**: 1,246

applied, 91% admitted, 32% enrolled. **Transfer Admission Requirements**: High school transcript, college transcript(s), standardized test score, statement of good standing from prior institution(s). Minimum college GPA of 2.0 required. Lowest grade transferable C. **General Admission Information**: Application fee $30. Regular notification is rolling. Non-fall registration accepted. Admission may be deferred for a maximum of 1 year. Credit offered for CEEB Advanced Placement tests.

COSTS AND FINANCIAL AID
Annual tuition $20,360. Room & board $7,568. Required fees $1,050. Average book expense $500. **Required Forms and Deadlines**: FAFSA. Financial aid filing deadline 5/1. **Notification of Awards**: Applicants will be notified of awards on a rolling basis beginning on or about 10/1. **Types of Aid**: *Need-based scholarships/grants*: Pell, SEOG, state scholarships/grants, private scholarships, the school's own gift aid. *Loans*: FFEL Subsidized Stafford, FFEL Unsubsidized Stafford, FFEL PLUS, Federal Perkins. **Student Employment**: Federal Work-Study Program available. Institutional employment available. Off-campus job opportunities are fair. **Financial Aid Statistics**: 83% freshmen, 84% undergrads receive need-based scholarship or grant aid. 64% freshmen, 70% undergrads receive need-based self-help aid. 46 freshmen, 120 undergrads receive athletic scholarships. 94% freshmen, receive any aid. Highest amount earned per year from on-campus jobs $1,000.

SAINT JOHN FISHER COLLEGE

3690 East Avenue, Rochester, NY 14618-3597
Phone: 585-385-8064 **E-mail**: admissions@sjfc.edu **CEEB Code**: 2798
Fax: 585-385-8386 **Website**: www.sjfc.edu **ACT Code**: 2798
Financial Aid Phone: 585-385-8042

This private school, affiliated with the in the Catholic Tradition Church, was founded in 1948. It has a 140-acre campus.

RATINGS
Admissions Selectivity Rating: 81   **Fire Safety Rating**: 78   **Green Rating**: 60*

STUDENTS AND FACULTY
Enrollment: 2,738. **Student Body**: 58% female, 42% male, 1% out-of-state. African American 4%, Asian 2%, Caucasian 87%, Hispanic 3%. **Retention and Graduation**: 83% freshmen return for sophomore year. 54% freshmen graduate within 4 years. 19% grads go on to further study within 1 year. 17% grads pursue arts and sciences degrees. 1% grads pursue business degrees. 1% grads pursue medical degrees. **Faculty**: Student/faculty ratio 14:1. 167 full-time faculty, 83% hold PhDs. 87% faculty teach undergrads.

ACADEMICS
Degrees: Bachelor's, doctoral, first professional, master's, post-bachelor's certificate, post-master's certificate. **Academic Requirements**: English (including composition), humanities, mathematics, philosophy, sciences (biological or physical), social science. **Classes**: Most classes have 20–29 students. Most lab/discussion sections have 10–19 students. **Majors with Highest Enrollment**: Business administration and management, communications studies/speech communication and rhetoric, elementary education and teaching. **Disciplines with Highest Percentage of Degrees Awarded**: Business/marketing 22%, education 19%, social sciences 10%, communications/journalism 9%, health professions and related sciences 7%. **Special Study Options**: Accelerated program, cross-registration, distance learning, double major, honors program, independent study, internships, liberal arts/career combination, student-designed major, study abroad, teacher certification program, weekend college.

FACILITIES
Housing: Coed dorms, women's dorms, special housing for disabled students. **Special Academic Facilities/Equipment**: TV studio, language labs, 2 electron microscopes, multimedia computer lab, video and recording, child care center (for observation and development), cyber cafe, biotechnology lab, field station. **Computers**: 17% of classrooms are wireless, 100% of public computers are PCs, network access in dorm rooms, network access in dorm lounges, online registration, online administrative functions (other than registration), support for handheld computing, remote student-access to Web through college's connection.

CAMPUS LIFE
Activities: Choral groups, dance, drama/theater, literary magazine, musical theater, pep band, radio station, student government, student newspaper, television station, yearbook. **Organizations**: 60 registered organizations, 7

honor societies, 2 religious organizations. **Athletics (Intercollegiate)**: *Men*: Baseball, basketball, football, golf, lacrosse, soccer, tennis. *Women*: Basketball, lacrosse, soccer, softball, tennis, volleyball.

ADMISSIONS

Freshman Academic Profile: 19% in top 10% of high school class, 53% in top 25% of high school class, 90% in top 50% of high school class. 93% from public high schools. SAT Math middle 50% range 520–610. SAT Critical Reading middle 50% range 490–580. ACT middle 50% range 21–24. TOEFL required of all international applicants, minimum paper TOEFL 550, minimum computer TOEFL 213. **Basis for Candidate Selection**: *Very important factors considered include*: Academic GPA, alumni/ae relation, character/ personal qualities, recommendation(s), rigor of secondary school record. *Important factors considered include*: Class rank, extracurricular activities, interview, racial/ethnic status, standardized test scores, talent/ability, volunteer work, work experience. *Other factors considered include*: Application essay, first generation, geographical residence, level of applicant's interest, state residency. **Freshman Admission Requirements**: High school diploma is required, and GED is accepted. *Academic units recommended*: 4 English, 3 math, 3 science, 3 foreign language, 4 social studies. **Freshman Admission Statistics**: 2,968 applied, 62% admitted, 31% enrolled. **Transfer Admission Requirements**: College transcript(s), statement of good standing from prior institution(s). Minimum college GPA of 2.0 required. Lowest grade transferable C. **General Admission Information**: Application fee $30. Early decision application deadline 12/1. Regular notification 2–3 weeks after application is complete. Non-fall registration accepted. Admission may be deferred for a maximum of 2 semesters. Credit offered for CEEB Advanced Placement tests.

COSTS AND FINANCIAL AID

Annual tuition $20,450. Room & board $8,888. Required fees $260. Average book expense $900. **Required Forms and Deadlines**: FAFSA, state aid form. Financial aid filing deadline 2/15. **Notification of Awards**: Applicants will be notified of awards on a rolling basis beginning on or about 3/22. **Types of Aid**: *Need-based scholarships/grants*: Pell, SEOG, state scholarships/grants, private scholarships, the school's own gift aid. *Loans*: FFEL Subsidized Stafford, FFEL Unsubsidized Stafford, FFEL PLUS, Federal Perkins, Bureau of Indian Affairs, adult vocational training program, Federal College Work Study. **Financial Aid Statistics**: 79% freshmen, 80% undergrads receive need-based scholarship or grant aid. 67% freshmen, 70% undergrads receive need-based self-help aid. 80% freshmen, 66% undergrads receive any aid. Highest amount earned per year from on-campus jobs $1,800.

SAINT JOSEPH COLLEGE (CT)

1678 Asylum Avenue, West Hartford, CT 06117
Phone: 860-231-5216 **E-mail**: admissions@sjc.edu
Fax: 860-231-5744 **Website**: www.sjc.edu
Financial Aid Phone: 860-231-5223

This private school, affiliated with the Roman Catholic Church, was founded in 1932. It has an 84-acre campus.

RATINGS
Admissions Selectivity Rating: 75   **Fire Safety Rating**: 60*   **Green Rating**: 60*

STUDENTS AND FACULTY
Enrollment: 973. **Student Body**: 99% female, 1% male, 8% out-of-state. African American 12%, Asian 2%, Caucasian 69%, Hispanic 8%. **Retention and Graduation**: 71% freshmen return for sophomore year. 39% freshmen graduate within 4 years. **Faculty**: Student/faculty ratio 10:1. 78 full-time faculty.

ACADEMICS
Degrees: Bachelor's, master's. **Academic Requirements**: Computer literacy, English (including composition), foreign languages, humanities, mathematics, philosophy, sciences (biological or physical), social science. **Classes**: Most classes have 10–19 students. Most lab/discussion sections have 10–19 students. **Disciplines with Highest Percentage of Degrees Awarded**: Psychology 18%, public administration and social services 11%, family and consumer sciences 10%, education 8%, English 5%. **Special Study Options**: Accelerated program, cross-registration, distance learning, double major, honors program, independent study, internships, liberal arts/career combination, student-designed major, study abroad, teacher certification program, weekend college.

FACILITIES
Housing: Women's dorms, special housing for disabled students, single rooms available for nontraditional students, medical singles with private bathrooms

available on a limited basis. **Computers**: Network access in dorm rooms, online registration.

CAMPUS LIFE
Activities: Choral groups, dance, drama/theater, literary magazine, music ensembles, opera, student government, student newspaper, yearbook.

ADMISSIONS
Freshman Academic Profile: 15% in top 10% of high school class, 86% in top 50% of high school class. SAT Math middle 50% range 418–530. SAT Critical Reading middle 50% range 430–530. **Basis for Candidate Selection**: *Very important factors considered include*: Academic GPA, rigor of secondary school record, standardized test scores. *Other factors considered include*: Alumni/ae relation, application essay, character/personal qualities, class rank, extracurricular activities, first generation, geographical residence, interview, level of applicant's interest, racial/ethnic status, recommendation(s), religious affiliation. **Freshman Admission Requirements**: High school diploma is required, and GED is accepted. *Academic units required*: 4 English, 3 math, 3 science, 3 foreign language, 3 social studies. **Freshman Admission Statistics**: 821 applied, 73% admitted, 22% enrolled. **Transfer Admission Requirements**: High school transcript, college transcript(s). Lowest grade transferable C. **General Admission Information**: Application fee $50. Regular notification is rolling. Non-fall registration accepted.

COSTS AND FINANCIAL AID
Annual tuition $24,040. Room and board $11,880. Required fees $650. Average book expense $1,000. **Required Forms and Deadlines**: FAFSA. **Types of Aid**: *Need-based scholarships/grants*: Pell, SEOG, state scholarships/grants, private scholarships, the school's own gift aid. *Loans*: FFEL Subsidized Stafford, FFEL Unsubsidized Stafford, FFEL PLUS, Federal Perkins, state loans. **Financial Aid Statistics**: 93% freshmen, 83% undergrads receive need-based scholarship or grant aid. 71% freshmen, 76% undergrads receive need-based self-help aid.

SAINT JOSEPH SEMINARY COLLEGE

75376 River Road, Saint Benedict, LA 70457
Phone: 985-867-2248 **E-mail**: georgebinderregistrar@sjasc.edu **CEEB Code**: 6689
Fax: 985-867-2270 **Website**: www.seminary.saintjosephabbey.com **ACT Code**: 1604
Financial Aid Phone: 985-867-2229

This private school, affiliated with the Roman Catholic Church, was founded in 1891. It has a 1,200-acre campus.

RATINGS
Admissions Selectivity Rating: 60*   **Fire Safety Rating**: 60*   **Green Rating**: 60*

STUDENTS AND FACULTY
Enrollment: 60. **Student Body**: 34% out-of-state. African American 3%, Asian 5%, Caucasian 72%, Hispanic 20%. **Faculty**: Student/faculty ratio 5:1. 16 full-time faculty, 31% hold PhDs. 100% faculty teach undergrads.

ACADEMICS
Degrees: Bachelor's. **Academic Requirements**: Arts/fine arts, English (including composition), foreign languages, history, humanities, mathematics, philosophy, sciences (biological or physical), social science, undergraduate theology. **Classes**: Most classes have 10–19 students. **Special Study Options**: Distance learning, English as a second language (ESL), independent study, study abroad.

FACILITIES
Housing: Men's dorms. **Computers**: 95% of public computers are PCs, 5% of public computers are Macs, network access in dorm rooms, network access in dorm lounges, remote student-access to Web through college's connection.

CAMPUS LIFE
Activities: Choral groups, drama/theater, literary magazine, student government, student newspaper, yearbook. **Organizations**: 1 religious organization.

ADMISSIONS
Freshman Academic Profile: TOEFL required of all international applicants, minimum paper TOEFL 520, minimum computer TOEFL 190. **Basis for Candidate Selection**: *Very important factors considered include*: Character/ personal qualities, religious affiliation/commitment, rigor of secondary school record. *Important factors considered include*: Recommendation(s), standardized test scores. *Other factors considered include*: Class rank, extracurricular activities, interview, volunteer work. **Freshman Admission Requirements**:

666

High school diploma is required, and GED is accepted. *Academic units required*: 3 English, 2 math, 2 science, 2 foreign language, 1 history. *Academic units recommended*: 3 English, 2 math, 2 science, 2 foreign language, 1 history. **Freshman Admission Statistics**: 9 applied, 100% admitted, 100% enrolled. **Transfer Admission Requirements**: High school transcript, college transcript(s), standardized test score. Lowest grade transferable C. **General Admission Information**: Regular notification is open. Non-fall registration accepted. Common Application not accepted. Neither credit nor placement offered for CEEB Advanced Placement tests.

COSTS AND FINANCIAL AID

Annual tuition $17,500. Room & board $7,415. Required fees $1,165. Average book expense $1,000. **Required Forms and Deadlines**: FAFSA, institution's own financial aid form, state aid form. **Notification of Awards**: Applicants will be notified of awards on a rolling basis beginning on or about 8/3. **Types of Aid**: *Need-based scholarships/grants*: Pell, SEOG, state scholarships/grants, private scholarships, the school's own gift aid. *Loans*: FFEL Subsidized Stafford, FFEL Unsubsidized Stafford, FFEL PLUS, Federal Perkins. **Financial Aid Statistics**: 44% freshmen, 43% undergrads receive need-based scholarship or grant aid. 44% freshmen, 43% undergrads receive need-based self-help aid.

SAINT JOSEPH'S COLLEGE (IN)

PO Box 890, Rensselaer, IN 47978
Phone: 219-866-6170 **E-mail**: admissions@saintjoe.edu **CEEB Code**: 1697
Fax: 219-866-6122 **Website**: www.saintjoe.edu **ACT Code**: 1240
Financial Aid Phone: 219-866-6163

This private school, affiliated with the Roman Catholic Church, was founded in 1889. It has a 180-acre campus.

RATINGS

Admissions Selectivity Rating: 74   **Fire Safety Rating**: 72   **Green Rating**: 63

STUDENTS AND FACULTY

Enrollment: 1,015. **Student Body**: 59% female, 41% male, 27% out-of-state, 1% international (6 countries represented). African American 7%, Caucasian 87%, Hispanic 4%. **Retention and Graduation**: 76% freshmen return for sophomore year. 49% freshmen graduate within 4 years. 13% grads go on to further study within 1 year. 38% grads pursue arts and sciences degrees. 13% grads pursue law degrees. 13% grads pursue medical degrees. **Faculty**: Student/faculty ratio 15:1. 59 full-time faculty, 71% hold PhDs. 100% faculty teach undergrads.

ACADEMICS

Degrees: Associate, bachelor's, certificate, diploma, master's, terminal. **Academic Requirements**: Arts/fine arts, computer literacy, English (including composition), history, humanities, philosophy, sciences (biological or physical), social science. **Classes**: Most classes have 10–19 students. Most lab/discussion sections have 10–19 students. **Majors with Highest Enrollment**: Business administration/management, elementary education and teaching, nursing/registered nurse training (ASN, BSN, MSN, RN). **Disciplines with Highest Percentage of Degrees Awarded**: Education 24%, business/marketing 17%, biological/life sciences 15%, security and protective services 7%, psychology 6%. **Special Study Options**: Accelerated program, cross-registration, double major, dual enrollment, honors program, independent study, internships, liberal arts/career combination, student-designed major, study abroad, teacher certification program.

FACILITIES

Housing: Coed dorms, men's dorms, women's dorms, apartments for single students, special housing for disabled students. **Computers**: 98% of classrooms are wireless, 100% of public computers are PCs, 70% of public computers are UNIX, network access in dorm rooms, network access in dorm lounges, remote student-access to Web through college's connection.

CAMPUS LIFE

Activities: Choral groups, concert band, dance, drama/theater, jazz band, literary magazine, marching band, music ensembles, musical theater, pep band, radio station, student government, student newspaper, student-run film society, television station. **Organizations**: 41 registered organizations, 4 honor societies, 7 religious organizations. **Athletics (Intercollegiate)**: *Men*: Baseball, basketball, cross-country, football, golf, soccer, tennis, track/field (indoor), track/field (outdoor). *Women*: Basketball, cross-country, golf, soccer, softball, tennis, track/field (indoor), track/field (outdoor), volleyball.

ADMISSIONS

Freshman Academic Profile: 17% in top 10% of high school class, 34% in top 25% of high school class, 61% in top 50% of high school class. SAT Math middle 50% range 440–560. SAT Critical Reading middle 50% range 420–530. ACT middle 50% range 19–24. TOEFL required of all international applicants, minimum paper TOEFL 550, minimum computer TOEFL 213. **Basis for Candidate Selection**: *Very important factors considered include*: Academic GPA, rigor of secondary school record, standardized test scores. *Important factors considered include*: Character/personal qualities, class rank, extracurricular activities, interview, volunteer work. *Other factors considered include*: Alumni/ae relation, application essay, recommendation(s), talent/ability, work experience. **Freshman Admission Requirements**: High school diploma is required, and GED is accepted. *Academic units recommended*: 4 English, 3 math, 3 science (2 science labs), 2 foreign language, 3 social studies. **Freshman Admission Statistics**: 1,111 applied, 74% admitted, 29% enrolled. **Transfer Admission Requirements**: College transcript(s). Minimum college GPA of 2.0 required. Lowest grade transferable C-. **General Admission Information**: Application fee $25. Regular notification is rolling. Non-fall registration accepted. Credit offered for CEEB Advanced Placement tests.

COSTS AND FINANCIAL AID

Annual tuition $23,000. Room and board $7,170. Required fees $180. Average book expense $800. **Required Forms and Deadlines**: FAFSA. Financial aid filing deadline 3/1. **Notification of Awards**: Applicants will be notified of awards on a rolling basis beginning on or about 3/1. **Types of Aid**: *Need-based scholarships/grants*: Pell, SEOG, state scholarships/grants, private scholarships, the school's own gift aid. *Loans*: FFEL Subsidized Stafford, FFEL Unsubsidized Stafford, FFEL PLUS, Federal Perkins. **Student Employment**: Federal Work-Study Program available. Institutional employment available. Off-campus job opportunities are poor. **Financial Aid Statistics**: 84% freshmen, 71% undergrads receive need-based scholarship or grant aid. 58% freshmen, 50% undergrads receive need-based self-help aid. 10 freshmen, 53 undergrads receive athletic scholarships. 97% freshmen, 97% undergrads receive any aid. Highest amount earned per year from on-campus jobs $1,500.

SAINT JOSEPH'S COLLEGE OF MAINE

278 Whites Bridge Road, Standish, ME 04084-5263
Phone: 207-893-7746 **E-mail**: admission@sjcme.edu **CEEB Code**: 3755
Fax: 207-893-7862 **Website**: www.sjcme.edu **ACT Code**: 1659
Financial Aid Phone: 207-893-6612

This private school, affiliated with the Roman Catholic Church, was founded in 1912. It has a 350-acre campus.

RATINGS

Admissions Selectivity Rating: 60*   **Fire Safety Rating**: 60*   **Green Rating**: 60*

STUDENTS AND FACULTY

Enrollment: 1,034. **Student Body**: 65% female, 35% male, 44% out-of-state. African American 2%, Caucasian 83%. **Retention and Graduation**: 78% freshmen return for sophomore year. 56% freshmen graduate within 4 years. 15% grads go on to further study within 1 year. 1% grads pursue arts and sciences degrees. 3% grads pursue business degrees. 2% grads pursue medical degrees. **Faculty**: Student/faculty ratio 15:1. 68 full-time faculty, 82% hold PhDs. 100% faculty teach undergrads.

ACADEMICS

Degrees: Bachelor's. **Academic Requirements**: Arts/fine arts, English (including composition), foreign languages, history, humanities, mathematics, philosophy, sciences (biological or physical), social science, theology. **Classes**: Most classes have 10–19 students. Most lab/discussion sections have 10–19 students. **Majors with Highest Enrollment**: Business administration/management, elementary education and teaching, nursing/registered nurse training (ASN, BSN, MSN, RN). **Disciplines with Highest Percentage of Degrees Awarded**: Health professions and related sciences 21%, business/marketing 20%, education 13%, communication technologies 8%, biological/life sciences 6%, parks and recreation 6%, social sciences 6%. **Special Study Options**: Cross-registration, distance learning, double major, dual enrollment, honors program, independent study, internships, student-designed major, study abroad, teacher certification program.

FACILITIES

Housing: Coed dorms, men's dorms, women's dorms, substance-free housing. **Special Academic Facilities/Equipment**: Radio studio, telescope. **Computers: 100% of classrooms are wired, 100% of classrooms are wireless, 90% of public computers are PCs, 10% of public computers are Macs, network access in dorm rooms, online administrative functions (other than registration), remote student-access to Web through college's connection.

CAMPUS LIFE

Activities: Choral groups, dance, drama/theater, literary magazine, radio station, student government, student newspaper, yearbook. **Organizations**: 25 registered organizations, 2 honor societies, 1 religious organization. **Athletics (Intercollegiate)**: *Men*: Baseball, basketball, cross-country, golf, lacrosse, soccer, swimming. *Women*: Basketball, cross-country, field hockey, lacrosse, soccer, softball, swimming, volleyball.

ADMISSIONS

Freshman Academic Profile: 80% from public high schools. SAT Math middle 50% range 440–540. SAT Critical Reading middle 50% range 440–520. TOEFL required of all international applicants, minimum paper TOEFL 500, minimum computer TOEFL 250. **Basis for Candidate Selection**: *Very important factors considered include*: Application essay, character/personal qualities, recommendation(s), rigor of secondary school record. *Important factors considered include*: Academic GPA, class rank, standardized test scores, talent/ability, volunteer work. *Other factors considered include*: Extracurricular activities, interview, level of applicant's interest, work experience. **Freshman Admission Requirements**: High school diploma is required, and GED is accepted. *Academic units recommended*: 4 English, 3 math, 2 science (2 science labs), 2 foreign language, 2 social studies, 2 history. **Freshman Admission Statistics**: 1,094 applied, 82% admitted, 41% enrolled. **Transfer Admission Requirements**: College transcript(s), essay or personal statement. Minimum college GPA of 2.0 required. Lowest grade transferable C. **General Admission Information**: Application fee $50. Regular application deadline 8/1. Early action notification 12/15. Regular notification after 12/15. Non-fall registration accepted. Admission may be deferred for a maximum of 1 year. Credit and/or placement offered for CEEB Advanced Placement tests.

COSTS AND FINANCIAL AID

Annual tuition $21,000. Room & board $9,030. Required fees $760. Average book expense $800. **Required Forms and Deadlines**: FAFSA, institution's own financial aid form. Financial aid filing deadline 3/1. **Notification of Awards**: Applicants will be notified of awards on a rolling basis beginning on or about 3/1. **Types of Aid**: *Need-based scholarships/grants*: Pell, SEOG, state scholarships/grants, private scholarships, the school's own gift aid, Federal Nursing Scholarships. *Loans*: FFEL Subsidized Stafford, FFEL Unsubsidized Stafford, FFEL PLUS, Federal Perkins, Federal Nursing, state loans. **Student Employment**: Federal Work-Study Program available. Institutional employment available. Off-campus job opportunities are good. **Financial Aid Statistics**: 84% freshmen, 80% undergrads receive need-based scholarship or grant aid. 72% freshmen, 70% undergrads receive need-based self-help aid. 98% freshmen, 95% undergrads receive any aid. Highest amount earned per year from on-campus jobs $1,275.

SAINT JOSEPH'S UNIVERSITY (PA)

5600 City Avenue, Philadelphia, PA 19131
Phone: 610-660-1300 **E-mail**: admit@sju.edu **CEEB Code**: 2801
Fax: 610-660-1314 **Website**: www.sju.edu **ACT Code**: 3684
Financial Aid Phone: 610-660-1556

This private school, affiliated with the Jesuit order of the Roman Catholic Church, was founded in 1851. It has a 65-acre campus.

RATINGS

Admissions Selectivity Rating: 86   **Fire Safety Rating**: 92   **Green Rating**: 78

STUDENTS AND FACULTY

Enrollment: 4,782. **Student Body**: 53% female, 47% male, 48% out-of-state, 1% international (60 countries represented). African American 8%, Asian 2%, Caucasian 82%, Hispanic 3%. **Retention and Graduation**: 87% freshmen return for sophomore year. 68% freshmen graduate within 4 years. 19% grads go on to further study within 1 year. 11% grads pursue arts and sciences degrees. 3% grads pursue business degrees. 2% grads pursue law degrees. 3% grads pursue medical degrees. **Faculty**: Student/faculty ratio 13:1. 281 full-time faculty, 86% hold PhDs. 81% faculty teach undergrads.

ACADEMICS

Degrees: Associate, bachelor's, certificate, doctoral, master's, post-bachelor's certificate, post-master's certificate. **Academic Requirements**: Arts/fine arts,

English (including composition), foreign languages, history, humanities, mathematics, philosophy, sciences (biological or physical), social science, theology. **Classes**: Most classes have 10–19 students. Most lab/discussion sections have 10–19 students. **Majors with Highest Enrollment**: Accounting; marketing/marketing management; specialized merchandising, sales, and related marketing operations. **Disciplines with Highest Percentage of Degrees Awarded**: Business/marketing 45%, social sciences 15%, education 9%, psychology 6%, English 6%. **Special Study Options**: Accelerated program, cooperative education program, distance learning, double major, dual enrollment, English as a second language (ESL), honors program, independent study, internships, off campus study in Jesuit student exchange, student-designed major, study abroad, teacher certification program, weekend college.

FACILITIES

Housing: Coed dorms, men's dorms, women's dorms, apartments for single students, special accommodations upon need for disabled students. **Special Academic Facilities/Equipment**: Wall Street Trading Room, Claver House, Mandeville Hall, Moot Board Room, university gallery. **Computers**: 47% of classrooms are wired, 95% of classrooms are wireless, 83% of public computers are PCs, 13% of public computers are Macs, 4% of public computers are UNIX, network access in dorm rooms, network access in dorm lounges, online registration, online administrative functions (other than registration), support for handheld computing, remote student-access to Web through college's connection.

CAMPUS LIFE

Activities: Choral groups, concert band, dance, drama/theater, jazz band, literary magazine, music ensembles, musical theater, pep band, radio station, student government, student newspaper, student-run film society, yearbook. **Organizations**: 94 registered organizations, 20 honor societies. 3 fraternities (7% men join), 4 sororities (13% women join). **Athletics (Intercollegiate)**: *Men*: Baseball, basketball, cheerleading, crew/rowing, cross-country, golf, lacrosse, soccer, tennis, track/field (indoor), track/field (outdoor). *Women*: Basketball, cheerleading, crew/rowing, cross-country, field hockey, lacrosse, soccer, softball, tennis, track/field (indoor), track/field (outdoor). Environmental Initiatives: EPA/DEP Code Compliance & OSHA. Recycling. OSHA environmentally clean air and workspace.

ADMISSIONS

Freshman Academic Profile: 21% in top 10% of high school class, 54% in top 25% of high school class, 88% in top 50% of high school class. 47% from public high schools. SAT Math middle 50% range 540–630. SAT Critical Reading middle 50% range 530–620. ACT middle 50% range 23–28. TOEFL required of all international applicants, minimum paper TOEFL 550, minimum computer TOEFL 213. **Basis for Candidate Selection**: *Very important factors considered include*: Academic GPA, rigor of secondary school record, standardized test scores. *Important factors considered include*: Application essay, class rank, recommendation(s). *Other factors considered include*: Alumni/ae relation, character/personal qualities, extracurricular activities, first generation, geographical residence, level of applicant's interest, talent/ability, volunteer work, work experience. **Freshman Admission Requirements**: High school diploma is required, and GED is not accepted. *Academic units required*: 4 English, 3 math, 2 science (1 science lab), 2 foreign language, 1 history. *Academic units recommended*: 4 math, 3 science (1 science lab). **Freshman Admission Statistics**: 8,777 applied, 56% admitted, 21% enrolled. **Transfer Admission Requirements**: High school transcript, college transcript(s), statement of good standing from prior institution(s). Minimum college GPA of 2.5 required. Lowest grade transferable C. **General Admission Information**: Application fee $55. Regular application deadline 2/1. Regular notification 3/15. Non-fall registration accepted. Admission may be deferred for a maximum of 2 semesters. Credit offered for CEEB Advanced Placement tests.

COSTS AND FINANCIAL AID

Required Forms and Deadlines: FAFSA. Financial aid filing deadline 5/1. **Notification of Awards**: Applicants will be notified of awards on a rolling basis beginning on or about 2/15. **Types of Aid**: *Need-based scholarships/grants*: Pell, SEOG, state scholarships/grants, private scholarships, the school's own gift aid. *Loans*: FFEL Subsidized Stafford, FFEL Unsubsidized Stafford, FFEL PLUS, Federal Perkins. **Student Employment**: Federal Work-Study Program available. Institutional employment available. Off-campus job opportunities are excellent. **Financial Aid Statistics**: 36% freshmen, 33% undergrads receive need-based scholarship or grant aid. 48% freshmen, 45% undergrads receive need-based self-help aid. 24 freshmen, 147 undergrads receive athletic scholarships.

SAINT LEO UNIVERSITY

Saint Leo University Office of Admission, MC 2008 PO Box 6665, Saint Leo, FL 33574-6665
Phone: 352-588-8283 **E-mail:** admission@saintleo.edu **CEEB Code:** 5638
Fax: 352-588-8257 **Website:** www.saintleo.edu **ACT Code:** 0755
Financial Aid Phone: 800-240-7658

This private school, affiliated with the Roman Catholic Church, was founded in 1889. It has a 186-acre campus.

RATINGS
Admissions Selectivity Rating: 79   **Fire Safety Rating:** 60*   **Green Rating:** 60*

STUDENTS AND FACULTY
Enrollment: 1,510. **Student Body:** 54% female, 46% male, 37% out-of-state, 8% international (45 countries represented). African American 8%, Asian 1%, Caucasian 65%, Hispanic 9%. **Retention and Graduation:** 70% freshmen return for sophomore year. 31% freshmen graduate within 4 years. **Faculty:** Student/faculty ratio 16:1. 74 full-time faculty, 84% hold PhDs. 100% faculty teach undergrads.

ACADEMICS
Degrees: Associate, bachelor's, certificate, master's. **Academic Requirements:** Arts/fine arts, computer literacy, English (including composition), history, humanities, mathematics, philosophy, physical education, religion, sciences (biological or physical), social science. **Classes:** Most classes have 20–29 students. Most lab/discussion sections have 10–19 students. **Majors with Highest Enrollment:** Business administration/management, criminal justice/safety studies, elementary education and teaching. **Disciplines with Highest Percentage of Degrees Awarded:** Business/marketing 23%, education 18%, social sciences 11%, psychology 9%, security and protective services 9%, parks and recreation 6%. **Special Study Options:** Distance learning, double major, dual enrollment, honors program, independent study, internships, Internet based instruction, liberal arts/career combination, study abroad, teacher certification program, weekend college.

FACILITIES
Housing: Coed dorms, men's dorms, women's dorms, apartments for single students, special housing for disabled students, freshmen only housing. **Computers:** 10% of classrooms are wired, 100% of classrooms are wireless, 100% of public computers are PCs, network access in dorm rooms, network access in dorm lounges, online registration, online administrative functions (other than registration), remote student-access to Web through college's connection.

CAMPUS LIFE
Activities: Choral groups, concert band, dance, drama/theater, literary magazine, music ensembles, musical theater, radio station, student government, student newspaper, student-run film society, television station, yearbook. **Organizations:** 44 registered organizations, 9 honor societies, 5 religious organizations. 8 fraternities (18% men join), 4 sororities (13% women join). **Athletics (Intercollegiate):** *Men:* Baseball, basketball, cheerleading, cross-country, golf, lacrosse, soccer, swimming, tennis. *Women:* Basketball, cheerleading, cross-country, golf, soccer, softball, swimming, tennis, volleyball.

ADMISSIONS
Freshman Academic Profile: 8% in top 10% of high school class, 27% in top 25% of high school class, 66% in top 50% of high school class. 70% from public high schools. SAT Math middle 50% range 540–670. SAT Critical Reading middle 50% range 540–650. ACT middle 50% range 24–29. TOEFL required of all international applicants, minimum paper TOEFL 550, minimum computer TOEFL 213. **Basis for Candidate Selection:** *Very important factors considered include:* Academic GPA, character/personal qualities, recommendation(s), rigor of secondary school record, standardized test scores. *Important factors considered include:* Alumni/ae relation, extracurricular activities, interview, level of applicant's interest, talent/ability, volunteer work. *Other factors considered include:* Application essay, class rank, first generation, racial/ethnic status, work experience. **Freshman Admission Requirements:** High school diploma is required, and GED is accepted. *Academic units recommended:* 4 English, 3 math, 2 science, 2 foreign language, 3 social studies, 2 academic electives. **Freshman Admission Statistics:** 4,091 applied, 39% admitted, 26% enrolled. **Transfer Admission Requirements:** College transcript(s), essay or personal statement, statement of good standing from prior institution(s). Minimum college GPA of 2.0 required. Lowest grade transferable D. **General Admission Information:** Application fee $35. Regular application deadline 8/1. Regular notification is rolling. Non-fall registration accepted. Admission may be deferred for a maximum of 1 year. Credit and/or placement offered for CEEB Advanced Placement tests.

COSTS AND FINANCIAL AID
Annual tuition $28,480. Room and board $8,550. Required fees $398. Average book expense $1,040. **Required Forms and Deadlines:** FAFSA. Financial aid filing deadline 4/1. **Notification of Awards:** Applicants will be notified of awards on a rolling basis beginning on or about 1/31. **Types of Aid:** *Need-based scholarships/grants:* Pell, SEOG, state scholarships/grants, private scholarships, the school's own gift aid, United Negro College Fund. *Loans:* FFEL Subsidized Stafford, FFEL Unsubsidized Stafford, FFEL PLUS, Federal Perkins. **Student Employment:** Federal Work-Study Program available. Institutional employment available. Off-campus job opportunities are fair. **Financial Aid Statistics:** 65% freshmen, 64% undergrads receive need-based scholarship or grant aid. 54% freshmen, 53% undergrads receive need-based self-help aid. 12 freshmen, 49 undergrads receive athletic scholarships. 99% freshmen, 92% undergrads receive any aid. Highest amount earned per year from on-campus jobs $3,796.

SAINT LOUIS UNIVERSITY

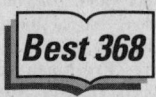

221 North Grand Boulevard, DuBourg Hall Room 100, Saint Louis, MO 63103
Phone: 314-977-2500 **E-mail:** admitme@slu.edu **CEEB Code:** 6629
Fax: 314-977-7136 **Website:** www.slu.edu **ACT Code:** 2352
Financial Aid Phone: 314-977-2350.

This private school, affiliated with the Roman Catholic Church, was founded in 1818. It has a 244-acre campus.

RATINGS
Admissions Selectivity Rating: 89   **Fire Safety Rating:** 87   **Green Rating:** 75

STUDENTS AND FACULTY
Enrollment: 7,279. **Student Body:** 58% female, 42% male, 53% out-of-state, 2% international (80 countries represented). African American 8%, Asian 6%, Caucasian 71%, Hispanic 3%. **Retention and Graduation:** 83% freshmen return for sophomore year. 63% freshmen graduate within 4 years. 30% grads go on to further study within 1 year. 3% grads pursue business degrees. 7% grads pursue law degrees. 7% grads pursue medical degrees. **Faculty:** Student/faculty ratio 12:1. 615 full-time faculty, 92% hold PhDs. 78% faculty teach undergrads.

ACADEMICS
Degrees: Bachelor's, certificate, doctoral, first professional, master's, post-bachelor's certificate, post-master's certificate. **Academic Requirements:** English (including composition), history, mathematics, philosophy, sciences (biological or physical), social science, theology. **Classes:** Most classes have 10–19 students. Most lab/discussion sections have 20–29 students. **Majors with Highest Enrollment:** Biology/biological sciences, business administration and management, nursing/registered nurse training (ASN, BSN, MSN, RN), **Disciplines with Highest Percentage of Degrees Awarded:** Business/marketing 25%, health professions and related sciences 18%, psychology 8%, social sciences 6%, communications/journalism 6%. **Special Study Options:** Accelerated program, cooperative education program, cross-registration, distance learning, double major, dual enrollment, English as a second language (ESL), honors program, independent study, internships, liberal arts/career combination, student-designed major, study abroad, teacher certification program.

FACILITIES
Housing: Coed dorms, men's dorms, women's dorms, apartments for married students, apartments for single students, fraternity/sorority housing, theme housing. MICAH House with the social justice floor. **Special Academic Facilities/Equipment:** Saint Louis University Museum of Art (SLUMA), McNamee Gallery of Samuel Cupples House, Museum of Contemporary Religious Art (MOCRA). **Computers:** 10% of classrooms are wired, 15% of classrooms are wireless, 85% of public computers are PCs, 15% of public computers are Macs, network access in dorm rooms, network access in dorm lounges, online registration, online administrative functions (other than registration), remote student-access to Web through college's connection.

CAMPUS LIFE
Activities: Choral groups, dance, drama/theater, jazz band, literary magazine, music ensembles, musical theater, pep band, radio station, student government,

student newspaper, television station, yearbook. **Organizations**: 100 registered organizations, 25 honor societies, 36 religious organizations. 13 fraternities (16% men join), 6 sororities (24% women join). **Athletics (Intercollegiate)**: *Men*: Baseball, basketball, cross-country, diving, golf, soccer, swimming, tennis. *Women*: Basketball, cross-country, diving, field hockey, golf, soccer, softball, swimming, tennis, volleyball. Environmental Initiatives: Recycling. Lamp Refitting. LEED Silver Certification on the new Edward A. Doisy Research Building.

ADMISSIONS

Freshman Academic Profile: 34% in top 10% of high school class, 62% in top 25% of high school class, 88% in top 50% of high school class. SAT Math middle 50% range 550–660. SAT Critical Reading middle 50% range 530–640. ACT middle 50% range 24–29. TOEFL required of all international applicants, minimum paper TOEFL 525, minimum computer TOEFL 194. **Basis for Candidate Selection**: *Very important factors considered include*: Academic GPA, standardized test scores. *Important factors considered include*: Application essay, extracurricular activities, rigor of secondary school record. *Other factors considered include*: Alumni/ae relation, character/personal qualities, first generation, interview, level of applicant's interest, recommendation(s), talent/ability, volunteer work. **Freshman Admission Requirements**: High school diploma is required, and GED is accepted. *Academic units required*: 4 English, 4 math, 3 science, 2 foreign language, 3 social studies, 3 academic electives. *Academic units recommended*: 4 English, 4 math, 3 science, 2 foreign language, 3 social studies, 3 academic electives. **Freshman Admission Statistics**: 12,120 applied, 67% admitted, 19% enrolled. **Transfer Admission Requirements**: College transcript(s), statement of good standing from prior institution(s). Minimum college GPA of 2.0 required. Lowest grade transferable C. **General Admission Information**: Application fee $25. Regular application deadline 8/1. Regular notification is rolling. Non-fall registration accepted. Admission may be deferred for a maximum of 1 year. Credit and/or placement offered for CEEB Advanced Placement tests.

COSTS AND FINANCIAL AID

Annual tuition $26,250. Room & board $8,230. Required fees $398. Average book expense $1,040. **Required Forms and Deadlines**: FAFSA. Financial aid filing deadline 3/1. **Notification of Awards**: Applicants will be notified of awards on or about 3/1. **Types of Aid**: *Need-based scholarships/grants*: Pell, SEOG, state scholarships/grants, private scholarships, the school's own gift aid, Federal Nursing Scholarships. *Loans*: FFEL Subsidized Stafford, FFEL Unsubsidized Stafford, FFEL PLUS, Federal Perkins, Federal Nursing. **Financial Aid Statistics**: 61% freshmen, 57% undergrads receive need-based scholarship or grant aid. 49% freshmen, 47% undergrads receive need-based self-help aid. 31 freshmen, 139 undergrads receive athletic scholarships. 99% freshmen, 86% undergrads receive any aid.

See page 1356.

SAINT MARTIN'S UNIVERSITY

5300 Pacific Avenue SE, Lacey, WA 98503-1297
Phone: 360-438-4596 **E-mail**: admissions@stmartin.edu **CEEB Code**: 4674
Fax: 360-412-6189 **Website**: www.stmartin.edu **ACT Code**: 4474
Financial Aid Phone: 360-438-4397

This private school, affiliated with the Roman Catholic Church, was founded in 1895. It has a 280-acre campus.

RATINGS
Admissions Selectivity Rating: 68   **Fire Safety Rating**: 78   **Green Rating**: 60*

STUDENTS AND FACULTY

Enrollment: 1,217. **Student Body**: 58% female, 42% male, 11% out-of-state, 7% international (7 countries represented). African American 7%, Asian 9%, Caucasian 65%, Hispanic 6%, Native American 1%. **Retention and Graduation**: 76% freshmen return for sophomore year. 33% freshmen graduate within 4 years. 14% grads go on to further study within 1 year. 2% grads pursue arts and sciences degrees. 8% grads pursue business degrees. 2% grads pursue law degrees. 2% grads pursue medical degrees. **Faculty**: Student/faculty ratio 14:1. 76 full-time faculty, 67% hold PhDs. 95% faculty teach undergrads.

ACADEMICS

Degrees: Bachelor's, master's, post-bachelor's certificate, post-master's certificate. **Academic Requirements**: Arts/fine arts, computer literacy, English (including composition), foreign languages, history, humanities, mathematics, philosophy, religious studies, sciences (biological or physical),

social science. **Classes**: Most classes have 10–19 students. Most lab/discussion sections have 10–19 students. **Majors with Highest Enrollment**: Biology/biological sciences, business administration/management, elementary education and teaching. **Disciplines with Highest Percentage of Degrees Awarded**: Business/marketing 28%, psychology 17%, social sciences 11%, education 9%, engineering 7%. **Special Study Options**: Double major, English as a second language (ESL), exchange student program (domestic), independent study, internships, study abroad, teacher certification program.

FACILITIES

Housing: Coed dorms, apartments for single students, special housing for disabled students, new residence hall and apartments for juniors and seniors opened in fall 2005. **Special Academic Facilities/Equipment**: Arts education building, Waynick Museum. **Computers**: 100% of classrooms are wired, 100% of classrooms are wireless, 100% of public computers are PCs, network access in dorm rooms, network access in dorm lounges, online registration, online administrative functions (other than registration), support for handheld computing, remote student-access to Web through college's connection.

CAMPUS LIFE

Activities: Choral groups, concert band, dance, drama/theater, jazz band, musical theater, pep band, student government, student newspaper. **Organizations**: 33 registered organizations, 3 honor societies, 2 religious organizations. **Athletics (Intercollegiate)**: *Men*: Baseball, basketball, cross-country, golf, track/field (indoor), track/field (outdoor). *Women*: Basketball, cross-country, golf, softball, track/field (indoor), track/field (outdoor), volleyball.

ADMISSIONS

Freshman Academic Profile: 5% in top 25% of high school class, 20% in top 50% of high school class. 77% from public high schools. SAT Math middle 50% range 440–560. SAT Critical Reading middle 50% range 440–540. SAT Writing middle 50% range 420–540. ACT middle 50% range 19–23. TOEFL required of all international applicants, minimum paper TOEFL 525, minimum computer TOEFL 193. **Basis for Candidate Selection**: *Very important factors considered include*: Academic GPA, rigor of secondary school record. *Important factors considered include*: Application essay, character/personal qualities, extracurricular activities, recommendation(s), standardized test scores, volunteer work. *Other factors considered include*: Alumni/ae relation, class rank, interview, talent/ability, work experience. **Freshman Admission Requirements**: High school diploma is required, and GED is accepted. *Academic units recommended*: 4 English, 3 math, 3 science (1 science lab), 2 foreign language, 2 social studies, 3 academic electives. **Freshman Admission Statistics**: 586 applied, 82% admitted, 43% enrolled. **Transfer Admission Requirements**: College transcript(s), essay or personal statement. Minimum college GPA of 2.5 required. Lowest grade transferable C. **General Admission Information**: Application fee $35. Regular notification is rolling. Non-fall registration accepted. Credit offered for CEEB Advanced Placement tests.

COSTS AND FINANCIAL AID

Annual tuition $23,810. Room and board $8,630. Required fees $302. Average book expense $1,000. **Required Forms and Deadlines**: FAFSA. Financial aid filing deadline 3/1. **Notification of Awards**: Applicants will be notified of awards on a rolling basis beginning on or about 2/25. **Types of Aid**: *Need-based scholarships/grants*: Pell, SEOG, state scholarships/grants, private scholarships, the school's own gift aid. *Loans*: Direct Subsidized Stafford, Direct Unsubsidized Stafford, FFEL PLUS, Federal Perkins, state loans, college/university loans from institutional funds. **Student Employment**: Federal Work-Study Program available. Institutional employment available. Off-campus job opportunities are good. **Financial Aid Statistics**: 81% freshmen, 85% undergrads receive need-based scholarship or grant aid. 70% freshmen, 75% undergrads receive need-based self-help aid. 9 freshmen, 36 undergrads receive athletic scholarships. 78% freshmen, 86% undergrads receive any aid.

SAINT MARY-OF-THE-WOODS COLLEGE

Office of Admission, Guerin Hall, Saint Mary-of-the-Woods, IN 47876-0068
Phone: 812-535-5106 **E-mail**: smwcadms@smwc.edu **CEEB Code**: 1704
Fax: 812-535-5010 **Website**: www.smwc.edu **ACT Code**: 1242
Financial Aid Phone: 812-535-5100

This private school, affiliated with the Roman Catholic Church, was founded in 1840. It has a 67-acre campus.

RATINGS
Admissions Selectivity Rating: 76   **Fire Safety Rating**: 96   **Green Rating**: 60*

STUDENTS AND FACULTY

Enrollment: 1,595. **Student Body**: 100% female, 17% out-of-state. African American 3%, Caucasian 92%, Hispanic 1%. **Retention and Graduation**: 64% freshmen return for sophomore year. 18% grads go on to further study within 1 year. 15% grads pursue arts and sciences degrees. 1% grads pursue business degrees. 1% grads pursue law degrees. 1% grads pursue medical degrees. **Faculty**: Student/faculty ratio 11:1. 58 full-time faculty, 57% hold PhDs. 98% faculty teach undergrads.

ACADEMICS

Degrees: Associate, bachelor's, certificate, master's, post-bachelor's certificate, post-master's certificate. **Academic Requirements**: Arts/fine arts, computer literacy, English (including composition), foreign languages, history, humanities, integrative studies, mathematics, philosophy, sciences (biological or physical), social science. **Classes**: Most classes have fewer than 10 students. **Majors with Highest Enrollment**: Elementary education and teaching, equestrian/equine studies, pre-medicine/pre-medical studies. **Disciplines with Highest Percentage of Degrees Awarded**: Education 33%, business/marketing 14%, communication technologies 10%, visual and performing arts 8%, social sciences 6%. **Special Study Options**: Accelerated program, cross-registration, distance learning, double major, external degree program, independent study, internships, student-designed major, study abroad, teacher certification program.

FACILITIES

Housing: Women's dorms, special housing for disabled students. **Special Academic Facilities/Equipment**: Cecilian Auditorium and Conservatory of Music, SMWC Art Gallery. **Computers**: 90% of classrooms are wired, 80% of classrooms are wireless, 90% of public computers are PCs, 10% of public computers are Macs, network access in dorm rooms, online registration, online administrative functions (other than registration), support for handheld computing, remote student-access to Web through college's connection.

CAMPUS LIFE

Activities: Choral groups, drama/theater, jazz band, literary magazine, music ensembles, musical theater, student government, student newspaper. **Organizations**: 30 registered organizations, 6 honor societies, 1 religious organization. **Athletics (Intercollegiate)**: *Women*: Basketball, equestrian sports, soccer, softball.

ADMISSIONS

Freshman Academic Profile: 15% in top 10% of high school class, 41% in top 25% of high school class, 80% in top 50% of high school class. 85% from public high schools. SAT Math middle 50% range 440–560. SAT Critical Reading middle 50% range 450–580. ACT middle 50% range 19–25. TOEFL required of all international applicants, minimum paper TOEFL 500, minimum computer TOEFL 173. **Basis for Candidate Selection**: *Important factors considered include*: Academic GPA, application essay, class rank, recommendation(s), rigor of secondary school record, standardized test scores. *Other factors considered include*: Alumni/ae relation, character/personal qualities, extracurricular activities, first generation, geographical residence, interview, level of applicant's interest, state residency, talent/ability, volunteer work. **Freshman Admission Requirements**: High school diploma is required, and GED is accepted. *Academic units required*: 8 English, 6 math, 6 science (2 science labs), 4 foreign language, 4 social studies, 2 history, 10 academic electives. *Academic units recommended*: 8 English, 8 math, 8 science (4 science labs), 6 foreign language, 6 social studies, 4 history, 7 academic electives. **Freshman Admission Statistics**: 268 applied, 78% admitted, 38% enrolled. **Transfer Admission Requirements**: College transcript(s), essay or personal statement. Minimum college GPA of 2.0 required. Lowest grade transferable C. **General Admission Information**: Application fee $30. Regular application deadline 8/1. Regular notification is rolling. Non-fall registration accepted. Admission may be deferred for a maximum of 1 year. Common Application not accepted. Credit and/or placement offered for CEEB Advanced Placement tests.

COSTS AND FINANCIAL AID

Annual tuition $19,530. Room and board $7,380. Required fees $650. Average book expense $900. **Required Forms and Deadlines**: FAFSA. **Notification of Awards**: Applicants will be notified of awards on a rolling basis beginning on or about 12/1. **Types of Aid**: *Need-based scholarships/grants*: Pell, SEOG, state scholarships/grants, private scholarships, the school's own gift aid. *Loans*: FFEL Subsidized Stafford, FFEL Unsubsidized Stafford, FFEL PLUS, Federal Perkins. **Financial Aid Statistics**: 48% freshmen, 41% undergrads receive need-based scholarship or grant aid. 47% freshmen, 38% undergrads receive need-based self-help aid. 8 freshmen, 54 undergrads receive athletic scholarships. 96% freshmen, 92% undergrads receive any aid. Highest amount earned per year from on-campus jobs $600.

SAINT MARY'S COLLEGE (IN)

Admission Office, Notre Dame, IN 46556
Phone: 574-284-4587 **E-mail**: admission@saintmarys.edu **CEEB Code**: 1702
Fax: 574-284-4841 **Website**: www.saintmarys.edu **ACT Code**: 1244
Financial Aid Phone: 574-284-4557

This private school, affiliated with the Roman Catholic Church, was founded in 1844. It has a 275-acre campus.

RATINGS

Admissions Selectivity Rating: 87   **Fire Safety Rating**: 84   **Green Rating**: 76

STUDENTS AND FACULTY

Enrollment: 1,366. **Student Body**: 100% female, 75% out-of-state. Asian 2%, Caucasian 92%, Hispanic 4%. **Retention and Graduation**: 87% freshmen return for sophomore year. 69% freshmen graduate within 4 years. 44% grads go on to further study within 1 year. 18% grads pursue arts and sciences degrees. 3% grads pursue business degrees. 13% grads pursue law degrees. 10% grads pursue medical degrees. **Faculty**: Student/faculty ratio 10:1. 125 full-time faculty, 77% hold PhDs. 100% faculty teach undergrads.

ACADEMICS

Degrees: Bachelor's. **Academic Requirements**: Arts/fine arts, computer literacy, English (including composition), foreign languages, history, humanities, mathematics, philosophy, religious studies, sciences (biological or physical), social science. **Classes**: Most classes have 10–19 students. Most lab/discussion sections have 10–19 students. **Majors with Highest Enrollment**: Business administration/management, communications studies/speech communication and rhetoric, elementary education and teaching. **Disciplines with Highest Percentage of Degrees Awarded**: Education 15%, business/marketing 14%, communications/journalism 11%, English 9%, social sciences 8%. **Special Study Options**: Accelerated program, cooperative education program, cross-registration, double major, exchange student program (domestic), independent study, internships, liberal arts/career combination, student-designed major, study abroad, teacher certification program.

FACILITIES

Housing: Women's dorms, apartments for single students. **Special Academic Facilities/Equipment**: Art gallery, early childhood development center, language lab, electron microscope. **Computers**: 100% of classrooms are wired, 100% of classrooms are wireless, 54% of public computers are PCs, 46% of public computers are Macs, network access in dorm rooms, network access in dorm lounges, online registration, online administrative functions (other than registration), remote student-access to Web through college's connection.

CAMPUS LIFE

Activities: Choral groups, dance, drama/theater, literary magazine, marching band, music ensembles, musical theater, opera, radio station, student government, student newspaper, television station, yearbook. **Organizations**: 101 registered organizations, 14 honor societies, 8 religious organizations. **Athletics (Intercollegiate)**: *Women*: Basketball, cross-country, diving, golf, soccer, softball, swimming, tennis, volleyball. Environmental Initiatives: Campus Recycling Program. Environmental considerations in building projects—Spes Unica. Hybrid fleet vehicle.

ADMISSIONS

Freshman Academic Profile: 32% in top 10% of high school class, 66% in top 25% of high school class, 94% in top 50% of high school class. 47% from public high schools. SAT Math middle 50% range 510–620. SAT Critical Reading middle 50% range 510–620. SAT Writing middle 50% range 520–630. ACT middle 50% range 22–27. TOEFL required of all international applicants, minimum paper TOEFL 550, minimum computer TOEFL 213. **Basis for Candidate Selection**: *Very important factors considered include*: Academic GPA, application essay, rigor of secondary school record, standardized test scores. *Important factors considered include*: Character/personal qualities, class rank, extracurricular activities, recommendation(s), talent/ability. *Other factors considered include*: Alumni/ae relation, first generation, geographical residence, interview, level of applicant's interest, racial/ethnic status, volunteer work, work experience. **Freshman Admission Requirements**: High school diploma is required, and GED is accepted. *Academic units required*: 4 English, 3 math, 2 science (2 science labs), 2 foreign language, 2 social studies, 4 academic electives. *Academic units recommended*: 4 English, 4 math, 4 science, 4 foreign language. **Freshman Admission Statistics**: 997 applied, 81% admitted, 47% enrolled. **Transfer Admission Requirements**: High school transcript, college transcript(s), essay or personal statement. Minimum college GPA of 3.0 required. Lowest grade transferable C. **General Admission Information**: Application fee $30. Early decision application deadline 11/15. Regular notification is rolling. Non-fall registration accepted. Admission may be deferred for a maximum of 1 year. Common Application accepted. Credit and/ or placement offered for CEEB Advanced Placement tests.

COSTS AND FINANCIAL AID
Annual tuition $26,285. Room and board $8,675. Required fees $590. Average book expense $1,150. **Required Forms and Deadlines**: FAFSA, CSS/ Financial Aid PROFILE. Financial aid filing deadline 3/1. **Notification of Awards**: Applicants will be notified of awards on a rolling basis beginning on or about 12/15. **Types of Aid**: *Need-based scholarships/grants*: Pell, SEOG, state scholarships/grants, private scholarships, the school's own gift aid. *Loans*: FFEL Subsidized Stafford, FFEL Unsubsidized Stafford, FFEL PLUS, Federal Perkins, college/university loans from institutional funds. **Financial Aid Statistics**: 57% freshmen, 61% undergrads receive need-based scholarship or grant aid. 49% freshmen, 53% undergrads receive need-based self-help aid. 92% freshmen, 88% undergrads receive any aid. Highest amount earned per year from on-campus jobs $3,307.

SAINT MARY'S COLLEGE OF AVE MARIA UNIVERSITY (MI)

3535 Indian Trail, Orchard Lake, MI 48324
Phone: 248-683-1757 **E-mail**: info@stmarys.avemaria.edu **CEEB Code**: 1753
Fax: 248-683-1756 **Website**: www.stmarys.avemaria.edu **ACT Code**: 2053
Financial Aid Phone: 248-683-0508

This private school was founded in 1885. It has a 100-acre campus.

RATINGS
Admissions Selectivity Rating: 63   **Fire Safety Rating**: 60*   **Green Rating**: 60*

STUDENTS AND FACULTY
Enrollment: 381. **Student Body**: 40% female, 60% male, 1% out-of-state, 29% international (17 countries represented). African American 8%, Asian 1%, Caucasian 56%. **Retention and Graduation**: 89% freshmen graduate within 4 years. **Faculty**: Student/faculty ratio 14:1. 11 full-time faculty. 100% faculty teach undergrads.

ACADEMICS
Degrees: Bachelor's, certificate. **Academic Requirements**: Arts/fine arts, computer literacy, English (including composition), foreign languages, history, humanities, mathematics, philosophy, sciences (biological or physical), social science, theology. **Classes**: Most lab/discussion sections have fewer than 10 students. **Disciplines with Highest Percentage of Degrees Awarded**: Communication technologies 32%, social sciences 21%, psychology 14%, biological/life sciences 7%, English 7%, health professions and related sciences 7%, computer and information sciences 4%, business/marketing 4%. **Special Study Options**: Double major, English as a second language (ESL), independent study, internships.

FACILITIES
Housing: Men's dorms, women's dorms. **Computers**: 100% of public computers are PCs, remote student-access to Web through college's connection.

CAMPUS LIFE
Activities: Choral groups, drama/theater, student government. **Organizations**: 3 registered organizations, 1 religious organization. **Athletics (Intercollegiate)**: *Men*: Baseball, basketball, soccer. *Women*: Cheerleading, soccer.

ADMISSIONS
Freshman Academic Profile: 15% in top 10% of high school class, 30% in top 25% of high school class, 51% in top 50% of high school class. 80% from public high schools. TOEFL required of all international applicants, minimum paper TOEFL 500. **Basis for Candidate Selection**: *Important factors considered include*: Rigor of secondary school record, standardized test scores. *Other factors considered include*: Character/personal qualities, extracurricular activities, interview, talent/ability. **Freshman Admission Requirements**: High school diploma is required, and GED is accepted. *Academic units recommended*: 2 math, 2 science (2 science labs), 3 social studies. **Freshman Admission Statistics**: 120 applied, 80% admitted, 47% enrolled. **Transfer Admission Requirements**: High school transcript, college transcript(s). Minimum college GPA of 2.0 required. Lowest grade transferable C. **General Admission Information**: Application fee $25. Regular application deadline 8/ 15. Regular notification is continuous. Non-fall registration accepted. Admission may be deferred for a maximum of 1 year. Common Application accepted.

COSTS AND FINANCIAL AID
Annual tuition $7,380. Room & board $4,900. Required fees $72. **Required Forms and Deadlines**: FAFSA, institution's own financial aid form. Financial aid filing deadline 4/30. **Notification of Awards**: Applicants will be notified of awards on or about 5/30. **Types of Aid**: *Need-based scholarships/grants*: Pell, SEOG, state scholarships/grants, private scholarships, the school's own gift aid. *Loans*: FFEL Subsidized Stafford, FFEL Unsubsidized Stafford, FFEL PLUS, state loans. **Student Employment**: Federal Work-Study Program available. Institutional employment available. Off-campus job opportunities are good. **Financial Aid Statistics**: 61% freshmen, 68% undergrads receive need-based scholarship or grant aid. 23% freshmen, 49% undergrads receive need-based self-help aid. Highest amount earned per year from on-campus jobs $2,663.

SAINT MARY'S COLLEGE OF CALIFORNIA

Best 368

PO Box 4800, Moraga, CA 94575-4800
Phone: 925-631-4224 **E-mail**: smcadmit@stmarys-ca.edu **CEEB Code**: 4675
Fax: 925-376-7193 **Website**: www.stmary-ca.edu **ACT Code**: 0386
Financial Aid Phone: 925-631-4686

This private school, affiliated with the Roman Catholic Church, was founded in 1863. It has a 420-acre campus.

RATINGS
Admissions Selectivity Rating: 60*   **Fire Safety Rating**: 86   **Green Rating**: 79

STUDENTS AND FACULTY
Enrollment: 2,835. **Student Body**: 63% female, 37% male, 11% out-of-state, 2% international (31 countries represented). African American 5%, Asian 10%, Caucasian 47%, Hispanic 18%. **Retention and Graduation**: 82% freshmen return for sophomore year. 59% freshmen graduate within 4 years. 18% grads go on to further study within 1 year. **Faculty**: Student/faculty ratio 11:1. 200 full-time faculty, 91% hold PhDs. 100% faculty teach undergrads.

ACADEMICS
Degrees: Associate, bachelor's, doctoral, master's. **Academic Requirements**: Arts/fine arts, collegiate seminar, English (including composition), foreign languages, humanities, mathematics, sciences (biological or physical), social science. **Classes**: Most classes have 10–19 students. **Majors with Highest Enrollment**: Business administration/management, communications studies/ speech communication and rhetoric, liberal arts and sciences/liberal studies. **Disciplines with Highest Percentage of Degrees Awarded**: Business/ marketing 28%, social sciences 15%, liberal arts/general studies 11%, communications/journalism 9%, psychology 9%. **Special Study Options**: Double major, exchange student program (domestic), independent study, internships, student-designed major, study abroad.

FACILITIES
Housing: Coed dorms, apartments for single students, special housing for disabled students. **Special Academic Facilities/Equipment**: Hearst Art Gallery. **Computers**: 20% of classrooms are wired, 100% of classrooms are wireless, 62% of public computers are PCs, 38% of public computers are Macs, network access in dorm rooms, network access in dorm lounges, online registration, online administrative functions (other than registration), remote student-access to Web through college's connection.

CAMPUS LIFE
Activities: Choral groups, dance, drama/theater, jazz band, music ensembles, pep band, radio station, student government, student newspaper, yearbook. **Organizations**: 42 registered organizations, 1 religious organization. **Athletics (Intercollegiate)**: *Men*: Baseball, basketball, cross-country, golf, soccer, tennis. *Women*: Basketball, crew/rowing, cross-country, golf, lacrosse, soccer, softball, tennis, volleyball. Environmental Initiatives: 2007 Summer reading program for incoming students focuses on global warming. Energy conservation program (phase 2) reduces consumption by 71KW. College Strategic Plan sets goals for environmental awareness and campus stewardship.

ADMISSIONS
Freshman Academic Profile: 56% from public high schools. SAT Math middle 50% range 480–590. SAT Critical Reading middle 50% range 480–590.

TOEFL required of all international applicants, minimum paper TOEFL 525, minimum computer TOEFL 197. **Basis for Candidate Selection**: *Very important factors considered include:* Academic GPA, rigor of secondary school record, standardized test scores. *Important factors considered include*: Application essay, first generation, recommendation(s). *Other factors considered include*: Alumni/ae relation, character/personal qualities, class rank, extracurricular activities, geographical residence, interview, level of applicant's interest, racial/ethnic status, religious affiliation/commitment, talent/ability, volunteer work, work experience. **Freshman Admission Requirements**: High school diploma is required, and GED is accepted. *Academic units required*: 4 English, 3 math, 2 science (1 science lab), 2 foreign language, 1 social studies, 1 history, 2 academic electives. *Academic units recommended*: 4 English, 4 math, 3 science (1 science lab), 3 foreign language, 1 social studies, 1 history, 2 academic electives. **Freshman Admission Statistics**: 4,991 applied, 70% admitted, 17% enrolled. **Transfer Admission Requirements**: High school transcript, college transcript(s), essay or personal statement. Minimum college GPA of 2.3 required. Lowest grade transferable C-. **General Admission Information**: Application fee $55. Regular application deadline 2/1. Regular notification 3/15. Non-fall registration accepted. Admission may be deferred for a maximum of 1 year. Credit and/or placement offered for CEEB Advanced Placement tests.

COSTS AND FINANCIAL AID

Annual tuition $30,930. Room and board $11,090. Required fees $150. Average book expense $1,206. **Required Forms and Deadlines**: FAFSA, state aid form. Regular application deadline 2/1. **Notification of Awards**: Applicants will be notified of awards on or about 3/15. **Types of Aid**: *Need-based scholarships/grants*: Pell, SEOG, state scholarships/grants, private scholarships, the school's own gift aid. *Loans*: FFEL Subsidized Stafford, FFEL Unsubsidized Stafford, FFEL PLUS, Federal Perkins, state loans, college/university loans from institutional funds. **Student Employment**: Federal Work-Study Program available. Institutional employment available. Off-campus job opportunities are good. **Financial Aid Statistics**: 66% freshmen, 52% undergrads receive need-based scholarship or grant aid. 72% freshmen, 55% undergrads receive need-based self-help aid. 26 freshmen, 97 undergrads receive athletic scholarships. 75% freshmen, 73% undergrads receive any aid. Highest amount earned per year from on-campus jobs $17,140.

See page 1358.

SAINT MARY'S UNIVERSITY OF MINNESOTA

700 Terrace Heights #2, Winona, MN 55987-1399
Phone: 507-457-1600 **E-mail**: admissions@smumn.edu **CEEB Code**: 6632
Fax: 507-457-1722 **Website**: www.smumn.edu **ACT Code**: 2148
Financial Aid Phone: 507-457-1437

This private school, affiliated with the Roman Catholic Church, was founded in 1912. It has a 400-acre campus.

RATINGS

Admissions Selectivity Rating: 76   **Fire Safety Rating**: 60*   **Green Rating**: 60*

STUDENTS AND FACULTY

Enrollment: 1,635. **Student Body**: 52% female, 48% male, 29% out-of-state, 1% international (21 countries represented). African American 4%, Asian 2%, Caucasian 76%, Hispanic 2%. **Retention and Graduation**: 75% freshmen return for sophomore year. 52% freshmen graduate within 4 years. 20% grads go on to further study within 1 year. 19% grads pursue arts and sciences degrees. 2% grads pursue business degrees. 3% grads pursue law degrees. 1% grads pursue medical degrees. **Faculty**: Student/faculty ratio 12:1. 101 full-time faculty, 80% hold PhDs. 100% faculty teach undergrads.

ACADEMICS

Degrees: Bachelor's, certificate, diploma, doctoral, master's, post-bachelor's certificate, post-master's certificate. **Academic Requirements**: Arts/fine arts, English (including composition), history, mathematics, philosophy, sciences (biological or physical), social science, theology. **Classes**: Most classes have 20–29 students. Most lab/discussion sections have 10–19 students. **Majors with Highest Enrollment**: Marketing/marketing management. **Disciplines with Highest Percentage of Degrees Awarded**: Business/marketing 33%, computer and information sciences 7%, visual and performing arts 7%, security and protective services 6%, communications/journalism 6%, education 6%. **Special Study Options**: Cooperative education program, cross-registration, double major, dual enrollment, English as a second language (ESL), honors program, independent study, internships, student-designed major, study abroad, teacher certification program.

FACILITIES

Housing: Coed dorms, men's dorms, women's dorms, apartments for single students, special housing for disabled students. **Special Academic Facilities/Equipment**: Art gallery, performance center, technology center, laboratories, observatory. **Computers**: 65% of public computers are PCs, 35% of public computers are Macs, network access in dorm rooms, network access in dorm lounges, online registration, online administrative functions (other than registration), remote student-access to Web through college's connection.

CAMPUS LIFE

Activities: Choral groups, concert band, dance, drama/theater, jazz band, literary magazine, music ensembles, musical theater, radio station, student government, student newspaper, yearbook. **Organizations**: 80 registered organizations, 13 honor societies, 5 religious organizations. **Athletics (Intercollegiate)**: *Men*: Baseball, basketball, cross-country, diving, golf, ice hockey, skiing (Nordic/cross-country), soccer, swimming, tennis, track/field (indoor), track/field (outdoor). *Women*: Basketball, cross-country, diving, golf, ice hockey, skiing (Nordic/cross-country), soccer, softball, swimming, tennis, track/field (indoor), track/field (outdoor), volleyball.

ADMISSIONS

Freshman Academic Profile: 19% in top 10% of high school class, 47% in top 25% of high school class, 70% in top 50% of high school class. 67% from public high schools. SAT Math middle 50% range 470–590. SAT Critical Reading middle 50% range 475–600. SAT Writing middle 50% range 490–650. ACT middle 50% range 19–25. TOEFL required of all international applicants, minimum paper TOEFL 520. **Basis for Candidate Selection**: *Very important factors considered include:* Academic GPA, rigor of secondary school record, standardized test scores. *Important factors considered include*: Character/personal qualities, class rank, interview, talent/ability. *Other factors considered include*: Alumni/ae relation, application essay, extracurricular activities, level of applicant's interest, recommendation(s), volunteer work. **Freshman Admission Requirements**: High school diploma is required, and GED is accepted. *Academic units required*: 4 English, 3 math, 3 science (2 science labs), 2 social studies, 6 academic electives. *Academic units recommended*: 2 foreign language. **Freshman Admission Statistics**: 1,048 applied, 83% admitted, 36% enrolled. **Transfer Admission Requirements**: High school transcript, college transcript(s), statement of good standing from prior institution(s). Minimum college GPA of 2.0 required. Lowest grade transferable C. **General Admission Information**: Application fee $25. Regular application deadline 5/1. Regular notification 5/1. Non-fall registration accepted. Admission may be deferred for a maximum of 1 year. Common Application accepted. Credit and/or placement offered for CEEB Advanced Placement tests.

COSTS AND FINANCIAL AID

Annual tuition $21,918. Room and board $6,130. Required fees $480. Average book expense $1,186. **Required Forms and Deadlines**: FAFSA. Financial aid filing deadline 3/15. **Notification of Awards**: Applicants will be notified of awards on a rolling basis beginning on or about 2/1. **Types of Aid**: *Need-based scholarships/grants*: Pell, SEOG, state scholarships/grants, the school's own gift aid. *Loans*: FFEL Subsidized Stafford, FFEL Unsubsidized Stafford, FFEL PLUS, Federal Perkins, state loans. **Student Employment**: Federal Work-Study Program available. Institutional employment available. Off-campus job opportunities are good. **Financial Aid Statistics**: 68% freshmen, 79% undergrads receive need-based scholarship or grant aid. 68% freshmen, 79% undergrads receive need-based self-help aid.

SAINT MICHAEL'S COLLEGE

One Winooski Park, Box 7, Colchester, VT 05439
Phone: 802-654-3000 **E-mail:** admission@smcvt.edu **CEEB Code:** 3757
Fax: 802-654-2906 **Website:** www.smcvt.edu **ACT Code:** 4312
Financial Aid Phone: 802-654-3244

This private school, affiliated with the Roman Catholic Church, was founded in 1904. It has a 440-acre campus.

RATINGS
Admissions Selectivity Rating: 84   **Fire Safety Rating:** 74   **Green Rating:** 89

STUDENTS AND FACULTY
Enrollment: 1,940. **Student Body:** 55% female, 45% male, 79% out-of-state, 1% international (13 countries represented). Asian 1%, Caucasian 94%, Hispanic 1%. **Retention and Graduation:** 91% freshmen return for sophomore year. 70% freshmen graduate within 4 years. 15% grads go on to further study within 1 year. 55% grads pursue arts and sciences degrees. 13% grads pursue business degrees. 4% grads pursue law degrees. 4% grads pursue medical degrees. **Faculty:** Student/faculty ratio 13:1. 154 full-time faculty, 86% hold PhDs. 100% faculty teach undergrads.

ACADEMICS
Degrees: Bachelor's, master's, post-bachelor's certificate, post-master's certificate. **Academic Requirements:** Arts/fine arts, English (including composition), foreign languages, history, humanities, philosophy, religious studies (2 courses, 1 100-level, and 1 200-level), sciences (biological or physical), social science. **Classes:** Most classes have 10–19 students. Most lab/discussion sections have 20–29 students. **Majors with Highest Enrollment:** Business administration/management, English language and literature, psychology. **Disciplines with Highest Percentage of Degrees Awarded:** Business/marketing 24%, social sciences 15%, psychology 13%, English 11%, education 6%. **Special Study Options:** Double major, English as a second language (ESL), honors program, independent research with faculty (no credit), independent study, internships, liberal arts/career combination, senior seminar (credit), student-designed major, study abroad, teacher certification program.

FACILITIES
Housing: Coed dorms, men's dorms, women's dorms, apartments for single students, special housing for disabled students, special housing for international students, substance-free housing, theme housing. **Special Academic Facilities/Equipment:** Holcomb Observatory, McCarthy Arts Center Gallery. **Computers:** 1% of classrooms are wired, 25% of classrooms are wireless, 100% of public computers are PCs, 1% of public computers are UNIX, network access in dorm rooms, network access in dorm lounges, online registration, online administrative functions (other than registration), remote student-access to Web through college's connection.

CAMPUS LIFE
Activities: Choral groups, concert band, dance, drama/theater, jazz band, literary magazine, music ensembles, musical theater, radio station, student government, student newspaper, yearbook. **Organizations:** 50 registered organizations, 11 honor societies, 1 religious organization. **Athletics (Intercollegiate):** *Men:* Baseball, basketball, cross-country, diving, golf, ice hockey, lacrosse, skiing (downhill/alpine), skiing (Nordic/cross-country), soccer, swimming, tennis. *Women:* Basketball, cross-country, diving, field hockey, ice hockey, lacrosse, skiing (downhill/alpine), skiing (Nordic/cross-country), soccer, softball, swimming, tennis, volleyball. Environmental Initiatives: Three Degree Challenge to further reduce campus wide building temperatures by turning down thermostats to reduce energy consumption. LEED certification for new alumni center to be constucted during the next year. Campus wide recycling program.

ADMISSIONS
Freshman Academic Profile: 22% in top 10% of high school class, 53% in top 25% of high school class, 86% in top 50% of high school class. 68% from public high schools. SAT Math middle 50% range 520–610. SAT Critical Reading middle 50% range 520–620. SAT Writing middle 50% range 520–620. ACT middle 50% range 22–26. TOEFL required of all international applicants, minimum paper TOEFL 550, minimum computer TOEFL 213. **Basis for Candidate Selection:** *Very important factors considered include:* Academic

GPA, class rank, rigor of secondary school record. *Important factors considered include:* Application essay, character/personal qualities, extracurricular activities, recommendation(s), standardized test scores, talent/ability. *Other factors considered include:* Alumni/ae relation, first generation, geographical residence, interview, level of applicant's interest, racial/ethnic status, volunteer work, work experience. **Freshman Admission Requirements:** High school diploma is required, and GED is accepted. *Academic units required:* 4 English, 3 math, 3 science (2 science labs), 3 foreign language, 3 social studies. *Academic units recommended:* 4 English, 4 math, 4 science (3 science labs), 4 foreign language, 4 social studies. **Freshman Admission Statistics:** 3,073 applied, 73% admitted, 26% enrolled. **Transfer Admission Requirements:** High school transcript, college transcript(s), essay or personal statement, standardized test score. Lowest grade transferable C-. **General Admission Information:** Application fee $50. Regular application deadline 2/1. Regular notification 4/1. Non-fall registration accepted. Admission may be deferred for a maximum of 1 year. Credit and/or placement offered for CEEB Advanced Placement tests.

COSTS AND FINANCIAL AID
Annual tuition $31,675. Room and board $7,960. Required fees $265. Average book expense $1,200. **Required Forms and Deadlines:** FAFSA, parent and student federal tax forms and W-2 forms. Financial aid filing deadline 3/15. **Notification of Awards:** Applicants will be notified of awards on or about 4/1. **Types of Aid:** *Need-based scholarships/grants:* Pell, SEOG, state scholarships/grants, private scholarships, the school's own gift aid. *Loans:* FFEL Subsidized Stafford, FFEL Unsubsidized Stafford, FFEL PLUS, Federal Perkins. **Student Employment:** Federal Work-Study Program available. Institutional employment available. Off-campus job opportunities are excellent. **Financial Aid Statistics:** 66% freshmen, 63% undergrads receive need-based scholarship or grant aid. 59% freshmen, 58% undergrads receive need-based self-help aid. 4 freshmen, 17 undergrads receive athletic scholarships. 94% freshmen, 85% undergrads receive any aid. Highest amount earned per year from on-campus jobs $7,081.

SAINT OLAF COLLEGE

1520 St. Olaf Avenue, Northfield, MN 55057
Phone: 507-786-3025 **E-mail:** admissions@stolaf.edu **CEEB Code:** 6638
Fax: 507-786-3832 **Website:** www.stolaf.edu **ACT Code:** 2150
Financial Aid Phone: 507-786-3019

This private school, affiliated with the Lutheran Church, was founded in 1874. It has a 300-acre campus.

RATINGS
Admissions Selectivity Rating: 93   **Fire Safety Rating:** 61   **Green Rating:** 87

STUDENTS AND FACULTY
Enrollment: 2,993. **Student Body:** 56% female, 44% male, 42% out-of-state. African American 1%, Asian 5%, Caucasian 84%, Hispanic 2%. **Retention and Graduation:** 93% freshmen return for sophomore year. 80% freshmen graduate within 4 years. 29% grads go on to further study within 1 year. 14% grads pursue arts and sciences degrees. 2% grads pursue business degrees. 3% grads pursue law degrees. 5% grads pursue medical degrees. **Faculty:** Student/faculty ratio 13:1. 195 full-time faculty, 94% hold PhDs. 100% faculty teach undergrads.

ACADEMICS
Degrees: Bachelor's. **Academic Requirements:** Arts/fine arts, English (including composition), foreign languages, history, humanities, mathematics, philosophy, physical activity, religion, sciences (biological or physical), social science. **Classes:** Most classes have 10–19 students. Most lab/discussion sections have 20–29 students. **Majors with Highest Enrollment:** Biology/biological sciences, English language and literature, mathematics. **Disciplines with Highest Percentage of Degrees Awarded:** Visual and performing arts 15%, social sciences 12%, biological/life sciences 11%, English 8%, foreign languages and literature 7%. **Special Study Options:** Cross-registration, double major, dual enrollment, independent study, internships, student-designed major, study abroad, teacher certification program.

FACILITIES

Housing: Coed dorms, special housing for disabled students, honor houses, language houses, quiet halls, first-year only dorms. Disabled students accommodated in dorm of their choice. **Special Academic Facilities/Equipment**: Finstad Office for Entrepreneurial Studies, Kierkegaard Library, Flaten Art Museum, Norwegian American Historical Association Archives. **Computers**: 5% of classrooms are wired, 85% of classrooms are wireless, 65% of public computers are PCs, 35% of public computers are Macs, 2% of public computers are UNIX, network access in dorm rooms, network access in dorm lounges, online registration, online administrative functions (other than registration), support for handheld computing, remote student-access to Web through college's connection.

CAMPUS LIFE

Activities: Choral groups, concert band, dance, drama/theater, jazz band, literary magazine, music ensembles, musical theater, opera, pep band, radio station, student government, student newspaper, student-run film society, symphony orchestra, television station, yearbook. **Organizations**: 122 registered organizations, 18 honor societies, 17 religious organizations. **Athletics (Intercollegiate)**: *Men*: Baseball, basketball, cross-country, diving, football, golf, ice hockey, skiing (downhill/alpine), skiing (Nordic/cross-country), soccer, swimming, tennis, track/field (indoor), track/field (outdoor), wrestling. *Women*: Basketball, cross-country, diving, golf, ice hockey, skiing (downhill/alpine), skiing (Nordic/cross-country), soccer, softball, swimming, tennis, track/field (indoor), track/field (outdoor), volleyball. **Environmental Initiatives**: Self-generating renewable power. A 1.65 wind turbine that feeds the campus distribution directly, with provisions for flowing excess power to the "grid." Infrastructure is in place to add two identical units which would produce kwh equal to all those consumed in 2007. Weekly diversion of 3.5 tons of food waste to on-campus composting, and incorporation of compost into grounds and student food producing operations. Adoption of St. Olaf Sustainable Design Guidelines that we incorporate into design and construction contracts, and that will yield a LEED gold building.

ADMISSIONS

Freshman Academic Profile: 51% in top 10% of high school class, 83% in top 25% of high school class, 99% in top 50% of high school class. 84% from public high schools. SAT Math middle 50% range 600–700. SAT Critical Reading middle 50% range 600–720. ACT middle 50% range 26–31. TOEFL required of all international applicants, minimum paper TOEFL 550, minimum computer TOEFL 213. **Basis for Candidate Selection**: *Very important factors considered include*: Academic GPA, application essay, rigor of secondary school record. *Important factors considered include*: Character/personal qualities, extracurricular activities, recommendation(s), standardized test scores, talent/ability. *Other factors considered include*: Alumni/ae relation, class rank, first generation, geographical residence, interview, level of applicant's interest, racial/ethnic status, religious affiliation/commitment, state residency, volunteer work, work experience. **Freshman Admission Requirements**: High school diploma is required, and GED is accepted. *Academic units required*: 4 English, 2 math, 2 science (1 science lab), 2 foreign language, 1 social studies, 1 history, 2 academic electives. *Academic units recommended*: 4 English, 4 math, 4 science (2 science labs), 4 foreign language, 2 social studies, 2 history, 4 academic electives. **Freshman Admission Statistics**: 3,529 applied, 65% admitted, 35% enrolled. **Transfer Admission Requirements**: High school transcript, college transcript(s), essay or personal statement, standardized test score. Minimum college GPA of 3.0 required. Lowest grade transferable C. **General Admission Information**: Application fee $40. Early decision application deadline 11/1. Regular notification is rolling. Non-fall registration not accepted. Admission may be deferred for a maximum of 1 year. Credit and/or placement offered for CEEB Advanced Placement tests.

COSTS AND FINANCIAL AID

Annual tuition $30,600. Room and board $7,900. Average book expense $900. **Required Forms and Deadlines**: FAFSA, CSS/Financial Aid PROFILE, Saint Olaf non-custodial parent statement. Financial aid filing deadline 4/15. **Notification of Awards**: Applicants will be notified of awards on a rolling basis beginning on or about 3/1. **Types of Aid**: *Need-based scholarships/grants*: Pell, SEOG, state scholarships/grants, private scholarships, the school's own gift aid. *Loans*: FFEL Subsidized Stafford, FFEL Unsubsidized Stafford, FFEL PLUS, Federal Perkins, Federal Nursing, state loans, college/university loans from institutional funds. **Student Employment**: Federal Work-Study Program available. Off-campus job opportunities are fair. **Financial Aid Statistics**: 64% freshmen, 65% undergrads receive need-based scholarship or grant aid. 64% freshmen, 65% undergrads receive need-based self-help aid. 90% freshmen, 89% undergrads receive any aid.

SAINT PAUL UNIVERSITY

223 Main Street, Ottawa, ON K1S 1C4 Canada
Phone: 613-236-1393 **E-mail**: info@ustpaul.ca
Fax: 613-782 3014 **Website**: www.ustpaul.ca
Financial Aid Phone: 613-236-1393

This private school, affiliated with the Roman Catholic Church, was founded in 1848.

RATINGS
Admissions Selectivity Rating: 60*   **Fire Safety Rating**: 60*   **Green Rating**: 60*

STUDENTS AND FACULTY
Enrollment: 438. **Student Body**: 61% female, 39% male, 21% out-of-state. **Retention and Graduation**: 30% grads pursue arts and sciences degrees. **Faculty**: Student/faculty ratio 12:1.

ACADEMICS
Degrees: Bachelor's, certificate, diploma, doctoral, master's, post-bachelor's certificate, post-master's certificate. **Special Study Options**: Distance learning, double major, honors program, weekend college. Bachelor in ethics, bachelor of arts with major in ethics, bachelor of arts with major in pastoral studies, bachelor of arts with major in theology, bachelor of arts with honors in mission studies and inter-religious dialogue, bachelor of arts with joint honors in philosophy and theology, bachelor of theology, master of arts in conflict studies, master of arts in theology, master of arts in pastoral counseling, master of arts in mission studies.

FACILITIES
Housing: Apartments for married students, apartments for single students, special housing for international students, cooperative housing. **Special Academic Facilities/Equipment**: Located near the Rideau Canal, the Parliament buildings, and library network. Endowed with largest religious studies library in Canada and has one of the world's major collections in Canon Law. **Computers**: Remote student-access to Web through college's connection.

CAMPUS LIFE
Activities: Student government.

ADMISSIONS
60° (out of 100).

COSTS AND FINANCIAL AID
In-province tuition $453–$1,650. Out-of-province tuition $453–$1,650. International tuition $951–$3,730. Average book expense $200. **Student Employment**: Federal Work-Study Program available. Off-campus job opportunities are excellent. **Financial Aid Statistics**: Highest amount earned per year from on-campus jobs $2,000.

SAINT PAUL'S COLLEGE

115 College Drive, Lawrenceville, VA 23868
Phone: 434-848-1856 **E-mail**: admissions@saintpauls.edu
Fax: 804-848-6407 **Website**: www.saintpauls.edu **ACT Code**: 4394
Financial Aid Phone: 434-848-6495

This private school, affiliated with the Episcopal Church, was founded in 1888. It has a 185-acre campus.

RATINGS
Admissions Selectivity Rating: 64   **Fire Safety Rating**: 60*   **Green Rating**: 60*

STUDENTS AND FACULTY
Enrollment: 707. **Student Body**: 52% female, 48% male, 31% out-of-state. African American 99%, Caucasian 2%. **Retention and Graduation**: 100% freshmen return for sophomore year. 16% freshmen graduate within 4 years. 10% grads go on to further study within 1 year. **Faculty**: Student/faculty ratio 17:1. 30 full-time faculty, 53% hold PhDs. 100% faculty teach undergrads.

ACADEMICS
Degrees: Bachelor's. **Academic Requirements**: Arts/fine arts, computer literacy, English (including composition), foreign languages, history, humanities, mathematics, philosophy, sciences (biological or physical), social science.

Classes: Most classes have fewer than 10 students. Most lab/discussion sections have fewer than 10 students. **Majors with Highest Enrollment**: Business administration/management; criminal justice/police science; sociology. **Disciplines with Highest Percentage of Degrees Awarded**: Business/marketing 67%, social sciences 9%, English 5%, education 2%, liberal arts/general studies 1%, biological/life sciences 1%. **Special Study Options**: Accelerated program, cooperative education program, double major, honors program, independent study, internships, liberal arts/career combination, study abroad, teacher certification program, U.S. Army ROTC.

FACILITIES

Housing: Men's dorms, women's dorms, apartments for single students. **Special Academic Facilities/Equipment**: The Saul Building (1888, the first classroom built on SPC campus). **Computers**: 100% of public computers are PCs, network access in dorm rooms, network access in dorm lounges.

CAMPUS LIFE

Activities: Choral groups, dance, drama/theater, student government, yearbook. **Organizations**: 30 registered organizations, 2 honor societies, 2 religious organizations. 3 fraternities (7% men join), 3 sororities (7% women join). **Athletics (Intercollegiate)**: *Men*: Baseball, basketball, cross-country, golf, tennis, track/field (indoor), track/field (outdoor). *Women*: Basketball, cross-country, golf, softball, tennis, track/field (indoor), track/field (outdoor), volleyball.

ADMISSIONS

Freshman Academic Profile: 3% in top 10% of high school class, 8% in top 25% of high school class, 23% in top 50% of high school class. 95% from public high schools. SAT Math middle 50% range 330–410. SAT Critical Reading middle 50% range 330–410. ACT middle 50% range 13–17. **Basis for Candidate Selection**: *Important factors considered include*: Application essay, character/personal qualities, class rank, extracurricular activities, interview, recommendation(s), rigor of secondary school record, standardized test scores, talent/ability. *Other factors considered include*: Volunteer work, work experience. **Freshman Admission Requirements**: High school diploma is required, and GED is accepted. *Academic units required*: 4 English, 2 math, 2 science. *Academic units recommended*: 4 English, 2 math, 2 science, 2 social studies. **Freshman Admission Statistics**: 641 applied, 71% admitted, 64% enrolled. **Transfer Admission Requirements**: High school transcript, college transcript(s), essay or personal statement, statement of good standing from prior institution(s). Minimum college GPA of 2.0 required. Lowest grade transferable C. **General Admission Information**: Application fee $20. Regular notification 2–4 weeks upon receiving the application. Nonfall registration accepted. Neither credit nor placement offered for CEEB Advanced Placement tests.

COSTS AND FINANCIAL AID

Annual tuition $10,400. Room & board $5,890. Required fees $681. Average book expense $600. **Required Forms and Deadlines**: FAFSA, state aid form. Financial aid filing deadline 6/30. Financial aid filing deadline 3/30. **Notification of Awards**: Applicants will be notified of awards on a rolling basis beginning on or about 1/7. **Types of Aid**: *Need-based scholarships/grants*: Pell, SEOG, state scholarships/grants, private scholarships, the school's own gift aid, United Negro College Fund. *Loans*: Direct Subsidized Stafford, Direct Unsubsidized Stafford, Direct PLUS, Federal Perkins. **Student Employment**: Federal Work-Study Program available. Off-campus job opportunities are fair. **Financial Aid Statistics**: 80% freshmen, 76% undergrads receive need-based scholarship or grant aid. 87% freshmen, 82% undergrads receive need-based self-help aid. 6 freshmen, 50 undergrads receive athletic scholarships. 91% freshmen, 59% undergrads receive any aid. Highest amount earned per year from on-campus jobs $1,300.

SAINT PETER'S COLLEGE

2641 Kennedy Boulevard, Jersey City, NJ 07306
Phone: 201-915-9213 **E-mail**: admissions@spc.edu **CEEB Code**: 2806
Fax: 201-432-5860 **Website**: www.spc.edu **ACT Code**: 2604
Financial Aid Phone: 201-915-9308

This private school was founded in 1872. It has a 10-acre campus.

RATINGS

Admissions Selectivity Rating: 74   **Fire Safety Rating**: 60*   **Green Rating**: 60*

STUDENTS AND FACULTY

Enrollment: 2,095. **Student Body**: 52% female, 48% male, 19% out-of-state, 3% international (9 countries represented). African American 22%, Asian 7%,

Caucasian 30%, Hispanic 24%. **Retention and Graduation**: 72% freshmen return for sophomore year. 27% grads go on to further study within 1 year. 9% grads pursue arts and sciences degrees. 6% grads pursue business degrees. 5% grads pursue law degrees. 7% grads pursue medical degrees. **Faculty**: Student/faculty ratio 15:1. 104 full-time faculty. 100% faculty teach undergrads.

ACADEMICS

Degrees: Associate, bachelor's, certificate, diploma, master's, post-bachelor's certificate, terminal. **Academic Requirements**: Arts/fine arts, computer literacy, English (including composition), foreign languages, history, humanities, mathematics, philosophy, sciences (biological or physical), social science, theology. **Classes**: Most classes have 10–19 students. **Disciplines with Highest Percentage of Degrees Awarded**: Business/marketing 52%, education 34%, security and protective services 26%, computer and information sciences 24%, social sciences 21%. **Special Study Options**: Accelerated program, cooperative education program, double major, dual enrollment, exchange student program (domestic), honors program, independent study, internships, liberal arts/career combination, student-designed major, study abroad, teacher certification program, weekend college. Joint degree in clinical and laboratory sciences with the University of Medicine and Dentistry of New Jersey (UMDNJ), joint degree in pharmacy with Rutgers University.

FACILITIES

Housing: Coed dorms, men's dorms, women's dorms, apartments for single students. **Special Academic Facilities/Equipment**: TV production facilities, center for government affairs.

CAMPUS LIFE

Activities: Choral groups, drama/theater, literary magazine, radio station, student government, student newspaper, yearbook. **Organizations**: 50 registered organizations, 13 honor societies. **Athletics (Intercollegiate)**: *Men*: Baseball, basketball, cheerleading, cross-country, diving, football, golf, soccer, swimming, tennis, track/field (outdoor). *Women*: Basketball, cheerleading, cross-country, diving, soccer, softball, swimming, tennis, track/field (outdoor), volleyball.

ADMISSIONS

Freshman Academic Profile: 14% in top 10% of high school class, 36% in top 25% of high school class, 69% in top 50% of high school class. SAT Math middle 50% range 440–530. SAT Critical Reading middle 50% range 420–520. TOEFL required of all international applicants, minimum paper TOEFL 500. **Basis for Candidate Selection**: *Very important factors considered include:* Academic GPA, rigor of secondary school record, standardized test scores. *Important factors considered include*: Application essay, class rank, recommendation(s). *Other factors considered include*: Character/personal qualities, extracurricular activities, interview, talent/ability, volunteer work, work experience. **Freshman Admission Requirements**: High school diploma is required, and GED is accepted. *Academic units required*: 4 English, 3 math, 2 science (1 science lab), 2 foreign language, 2 history, 3 academic electives. *Academic units recommended*: 4 math, 3 science, 3 history. **Freshman Admission Statistics**: 2,863 applied, 69% admitted, 26% enrolled. **Transfer Admission Requirements**: College transcript(s), essay or personal statement. Minimum college GPA of 2.0 required. Lowest grade transferable C. **General Admission Information**: Regular notification is rolling. Non-fall registration accepted. Admission may be deferred for a maximum of 2 years. Common Application accepted. Credit offered for CEEB Advanced Placement tests.

COSTS AND FINANCIAL AID

Required Forms and Deadlines: FAFSA. Financial aid filing deadline 3/15. **Notification of Awards**: Applicants will be notified of awards on or about 3/4. **Types of Aid**: *Need-based scholarships/grants*: Pell, SEOG, state scholarships/grants, the school's own gift aid. *Loans*: FFEL Subsidized Stafford, FFEL Unsubsidized Stafford, FFEL PLUS, Federal Perkins, state loans. **Student Employment**: Federal Work-Study Program available. Institutional employment available. Off-campus job opportunities are excellent. **Financial Aid Statistics**: Highest amount earned per year from on-campus jobs $1,500.

See page 1362.

SAINT THOMAS AQUINAS COLLEGE

125 Route 340, Sparkill, NY 10976
Phone: 845-398-4100 **E-mail:** admissions@stac.edu **CEEB Code:** 2807
Fax: 845-398-4114 **Website:** www.stac.edu **ACT Code:** 2897
Financial Aid Phone: 845-398-4098

This private school was founded in 1952. It has a 47-acre campus.

RATINGS

Admissions Selectivity Rating: 70   **Fire Safety Rating:** 87   **Green Rating:** 60*

STUDENTS AND FACULTY

Enrollment: 1,416. **Student Body:** 55% female, 45% male, 29% out-of-state. African American 6%, Asian 3%, Caucasian 70%, Hispanic 14%. **Retention and Graduation:** 68% freshmen return for sophomore year. 36% grads go on to further study within 1 year. 25% grads pursue arts and sciences degrees. 5% grads pursue business degrees. 5% grads pursue law degrees. 5% grads pursue medical degrees. **Faculty:** Student/faculty ratio 16:1. 62 full-time faculty, 89% hold PhDs. 100% faculty teach undergrads.

ACADEMICS

Degrees: Associate, bachelor's, master's, post-master's certificate, terminal. **Academic Requirements:** Arts/fine arts, computer literacy, English (including composition), foreign languages, freshman seminar, history, humanities, mathematics, philosophy, sciences (biological or physical), social science. **Classes:** Most classes have 20–29 students. **Majors with Highest Enrollment:** Business administration/management, criminal justice/law enforcement administration, elementary education and teaching. **Disciplines with Highest Percentage of Degrees Awarded:** Business/marketing 23%, social sciences 15%, education 14%, psychology 8%, communications/journalism 7%. **Special Study Options:** Accelerated program, cross-registration, double major, dual enrollment, exchange student program (domestic), honors program, independent study, internships, liberal arts/career combination, study abroad, teacher certification program. Undergrads may take grad level classes. Cooperative education programs: Combined BS/MSW in social work in partnership with NYU; engineering combined degree programs: 3-2 engineering programs with George Washington University and Manhattan College; foreign exchange program(s): Study abroad in England.

FACILITIES

Housing: Men's dorms, women's dorms, apartments for single students. **Special Academic Facilities/Equipment:** Azarian-McCullough Art Gallery, Sullivan Theatre, Spellman Technology Corridor, Costello Hall Science & Technology Center. **Computers:** 100% of classrooms are wireless, 24% of public computers are PCs, 7% of public computers are Macs, 3% of public computers are UNIX, network access in dorm rooms, network access in dorm lounges, online registration, remote student-access to Web through college's connection.

CAMPUS LIFE

Activities: Choral groups, dance, drama/theater, literary magazine, musical theater, opera, radio station, student government, student newspaper, yearbook. **Organizations:** 35 registered organizations, 8 honor societies, 1 religious organization. **Athletics (Intercollegiate):** *Men:* Baseball, basketball, cross-country, golf, soccer, tennis, track/field (indoor), track/field (outdoor). *Women:* Basketball, cross-country, lacrosse, soccer, softball, tennis, track/field (outdoor).

ADMISSIONS

Freshman Academic Profile: 5% in top 10% of high school class, 35% in top 25% of high school class, 50% in top 50% of high school class. 70% from public high schools. SAT Math middle 50% range 410–530. SAT Critical Reading middle 50% range 420–510. SAT Writing middle 50% range 420–520. ACT middle 50% range 17–22. TOEFL required of all international applicants, minimum paper TOEFL 530, minimum computer TOEFL 173. **Basis for Candidate Selection:** *Very important factors considered include:* Rigor of secondary school record. *Important factors considered include:* Application essay, character/personal qualities, extracurricular activities, interview, recommendation(s), standardized test scores, talent/ability. *Other factors considered include:* Alumni/ae relation, class rank, volunteer work, work experience. **Freshman Admission Requirements:** High school diploma is required, and GED is accepted. *Academic units required:* 4 English, 3 math, 3 science (2 science labs), 3 foreign language, 4 social studies, 1 history. *Academic units recommended:* 3 academic electives. **Freshman Admission Statistics:** 1,226 applied, 82% admitted, 32% enrolled. **Transfer Admission Requirements:** College transcript(s), statement of good standing from prior institution(s). Minimum college GPA of 2.0 required. Lowest grade transferable C. **General Admission Information:** Application fee $30. Early decision

application deadline 12/15. Regular notification is rolling. Non-fall registration accepted. Admission may be deferred for a maximum of 1 year. Credit and/or placement offered for CEEB Advanced Placement tests.

COSTS AND FINANCIAL AID

Annual tuition $19,500. Room and board $9,730. Required fees $500. Average book expense $750. **Required Forms and Deadlines:** FAFSA. Financial aid filing deadline 2/15. **Notification of Awards:** Applicants will be notified of awards on a rolling basis beginning on or about 3/1. **Types of Aid:** *Need-based scholarships/grants:* Pell, SEOG, state scholarships/grants, private scholarships, the school's own gift aid. *Loans:* Direct Subsidized Stafford, Direct Unsubsidized Stafford, Direct PLUS, FFEL Subsidized Stafford, FFEL Unsubsidized Stafford, FFEL PLUS, Federal Perkins, private alternative loans from lending institutions. **Student Employment:** Federal Work-Study Program available. Institutional employment available. Off-campus job opportunities are good. **Financial Aid Statistics:** 56% freshmen, 57% undergrads receive need-based scholarship or grant aid. 44% freshmen, 46% undergrads receive need-based self-help aid. 8 freshmen, 35 undergrads receive athletic scholarships. 66% freshmen, 72% undergrads receive any aid.

SAINT VINCENT COLLEGE

Office of Admission & Financial Aid, 300 Fraser Purchase Road, Latrobe, PA 15650-2690
Phone: 724-537-4540 **E-mail:** admission@stvincent.edu **CEEB Code:** 2808
Fax: 724-532-5069 **Website:** www.stvincent.edu **ACT Code:** 3686
Financial Aid Phone: 800-782-5549

This private school, affiliated with the Roman Catholic Church, was founded in 1846. It has a 200-acre campus.

RATINGS

Admissions Selectivity Rating: 78   **Fire Safety Rating:** 60*   **Green Rating:** 72

STUDENTS AND FACULTY

Enrollment: 1,568. **Student Body:** 51% female, 49% male, 12% out-of-state, 1% international (13 countries represented). African American 2%, Caucasian 65%. **Retention and Graduation:** 86% freshmen return for sophomore year. 64% freshmen graduate within 4 years. 30% grads go on to further study within 1 year. **Faculty:** Student/faculty ratio 13:1. 97 full-time faculty, 75% hold PhDs. 100% faculty teach undergrads.

ACADEMICS

Degrees: Bachelor's, certificate, master's, post-bachelor's certificate. **Academic Requirements:** Arts/fine arts, English (including composition), foreign languages, history, mathematics, philosophy, religious studies, sciences (biological or physical), social science. **Classes:** Most classes have 20–29 students. Most lab/discussion sections have 10–19 students. **Majors with Highest Enrollment:** Accounting, biology/biological sciences, history. **Disciplines with Highest Percentage of Degrees Awarded:** Business/marketing 20%, social sciences 13%, psychology 12%, biological/life sciences 10%, history 8%. **Special Study Options:** Accelerated program, cooperative education program, cross-registration, double major, dual enrollment, external degree program, honors program, independent study, internships, liberal arts/career combination, study abroad, teacher certification program.

FACILITIES

Housing: Coed dorms. **Special Academic Facilities/Equipment:** Art gallery, life sciences research center, spectrophotometer, spectrometer, physiograph work stations, data acquisition work station, planetarium, observatory, radio telescope, instructional technology resource center. **Computers:** 6% of classrooms are wired, 23% of classrooms are wireless, 94% of public computers are PCs, 6% of public computers are Macs, network access in dorm rooms, network access in dorm lounges, online registration, online administrative functions (other than registration), remote student-access to Web through college's connection.

CAMPUS LIFE

Activities: Choral groups, dance, drama/theater, literary magazine, music ensembles, pep band, radio station, student government, student newspaper, television station, yearbook. **Organizations:** 43 registered organizations, 11 honor societies, 2 religious organizations. **Athletics (Intercollegiate):** *Men:* Baseball, basketball, cross-country, football, golf, lacrosse, soccer, swimming, tennis, track/field (outdoor). *Women:* Basketball, cross-country, field hockey, golf, lacrosse, soccer, softball, swimming, tennis, volleyball. Environmental Initiatives: New construction on-campus, including a current building project, will be green. Environmental Education Center provides education opportunities to students.

ADMISSIONS

Freshman Academic Profile: 20% in top 10% of high school class, 50% in top 25% of high school class, 82% in top 50% of high school class. SAT Math middle 50% range 490–600. SAT Critical Reading middle 50% range 480–590. SAT Writing middle 50% range 470–570. ACT middle 50% range 20–26. TOEFL required of all international applicants, minimum paper TOEFL 550, minimum computer TOEFL 213. **Basis for Candidate Selection**: *Very important factors considered include:* Academic GPA, class rank, rigor of secondary school record. *Important factors considered include:* Application essay, character/ personal qualities, standardized test scores. *Other factors considered include:* Alumni/ae relation, extracurricular activities, interview, recommendation(s), talent/ability. **Freshman Admission Requirements**: High school diploma is required, and GED is accepted. *Academic units required:* 4 English, 3 math, 1 science (1 science lab), 3 social studies, 5 academic electives. *Academic units recommended:* 4 English, 3 math, 3 science (1 science lab), 2 foreign language, 3 social studies, 5 academic electives. **Freshman Admission Statistics**: 1,383 applied, 78% admitted, 41% enrolled. **Transfer Admission Requirements**: High school transcript, college transcript(s), essay or personal statement, statement of good standing from prior institution(s). Minimum college GPA of 2.5 required. Lowest grade transferable C-. **General Admission Information**: Application fee $25. Regular application deadline 5/1. Regular notification is rolling. Non-fall registration accepted. Admission may be deferred for a maximum of 1 year. Credit and/or placement offered for CEEB Advanced Placement tests.

COSTS AND FINANCIAL AID

Annual tuition $22,350. Room & board $7,242. Required fees $650. Average book expense $650. **Required Forms and Deadlines**: FAFSA, state aid form. Financial aid filing deadline 5/1. **Notification of Awards**: Applicants will be notified of awards on or about 3/1. **Types of Aid**: *Need-based scholarships/ grants*: Pell, SEOG, state scholarships/grants, private scholarships, the school's own gift aid, United Negro College Fund. *Loans*: FFEL Subsidized Stafford, FFEL Unsubsidized Stafford, FFEL PLUS, Federal Perkins. **Financial Aid Statistics**: 80% freshmen, 74% undergrads receive need-based scholarship or grant aid. 41% freshmen, 39% undergrads receive need-based self-help aid. 271 undergrads receive athletic scholarships. 100% freshmen, 98% undergrads receive any aid. Highest amount earned per year from on-campus jobs $1,800.

SAINT XAVIER UNIVERSITY

3700 West 103rd Street., Chicago, IL 60655
Phone: 773-298-3050 **E-mail**: admissions@sxu.edu **CEEB Code**: 1708
Fax: 773-298-3076 **Website**: www.sxu.edu **ACT Code**: 1134
Financial Aid Phone: 773-298-3070

This private school, affiliated with the Roman Catholic Church, was founded in 1847. It has a 70-acre campus.

RATINGS

Admissions Selectivity Rating: 60*   **Fire Safety Rating**: 60*   **Green Rating**: 60*

STUDENTS AND FACULTY

Enrollment: 3,269. **Student Body**: 72% female, 28% male, 5% out-of-state. African American 17%, Asian 3%, Caucasian 61%, Hispanic 13%. **Retention and Graduation**: 76% freshmen return for sophomore year. 32% freshmen graduate within 4 years. 10% grads go on to further study within 1 year. **Faculty**: Student/faculty ratio 14:1. 190 full-time faculty, 84% hold PhDs.

ACADEMICS

Degrees: Bachelor's, certificate, master's, post-bachelor's certificate, post-master's certificate. **Academic Requirements**: English (including composition), history, humanities, mathematics, philosophy, sciences (biological or physical), social science. **Classes**: Most classes have 20–29 students. Most lab/ discussion sections have 10–19 students. **Majors with Highest Enrollment**: Business administration/management, elementary education and teaching, nursing/registered nurse training (ASN, BSN, MSN, RN). **Disciplines with Highest Percentage of Degrees Awarded**: Education 21%, health professions and related sciences 21%, business/marketing 20%, liberal arts/ general studies 7%, psychology 7%, biological/life sciences 6%, security and protective services 3%, communications/journalism 3%. **Special Study Options**: Accelerated program, cooperative education program, distance learning, dual enrollment, English as a second language (ESL), external degree program, honors program, independent study, internships, liberal arts/career combination, student-designed major, study abroad, teacher certification program, weekend college.

FACILITIES

Housing: Coed dorms. **Computers**: 50% of public computers are PCs, 50% of public computers are Macs, network access in dorm rooms, network access in dorm lounges, online registration, online administrative functions (other than registration), remote student-access to Web through college's connection.

CAMPUS LIFE

Activities: Choral groups, concert band, jazz band, literary magazine, marching band, music ensembles, pep band, radio station, student government, student newspaper, student-run film society, symphony orchestra, yearbook. **Organizations**: 41 registered organizations, 2 honor societies, 2 religious organizations. **Athletics (Intercollegiate)**: *Men*: Baseball, basketball, football, soccer. *Women*: Basketball, cross-country, soccer, softball, volleyball.

ADMISSIONS

Freshman Academic Profile: 55% from public high schools. SAT Math middle 50% range 470–570. SAT Critical Reading middle 50% range 470–570. SAT Writing middle 50% range 460–540. ACT middle 50% range 20–24. TOEFL required of all international applicants, minimum paper TOEFL 550, minimum computer TOEFL 550. **Basis for Candidate Selection**: *Very important factors considered include:* Academic GPA, application essay, standardized test scores. *Important factors considered include:* Rigor of secondary school record. *Other factors considered include:* Character/personal qualities, extracurricular activities, interview, level of applicant's interest, recommendation(s), talent/ability, volunteer work, work experience. **Freshman Admission Requirements**: High school diploma is required, and GED is accepted. *Academic units recommended:* 4 English, 3 math, 2 foreign language, 3 academic electives, 4 science and social science combined. **Freshman Admission Statistics**: 2,230 applied, 73% admitted, 33% enrolled. **Transfer Admission Requirements**: College transcript(s). Minimum college GPA of 2.5 required. Lowest grade transferable C. **General Admission Information**: Application fee $25. Regular notification is 2 weeks after file is complete. Non-fall registration accepted. Credit offered for CEEB Advanced Placement tests.

COSTS AND FINANCIAL AID

Annual tuition $21,016. Room and board $7,626. Required fees $220. Average book expense $900. **Required Forms and Deadlines**: FAFSA. Financial aid filing deadline 3/1. **Notification of Awards**: Applicants will be notified of awards on a rolling basis beginning on or about 2/15. **Types of Aid**: *Need-based scholarships/grants*: Pell, SEOG, state scholarships/grants, private scholarships, the school's own gift aid. *Loans*: FFEL Subsidized Stafford, FFEL Unsubsidized Stafford, FFEL PLUS, Federal Perkins. **Student Employment**: Federal Work-Study Program available. Institutional employment available. Off-campus job opportunities are excellent. **Financial Aid Statistics**: 83% freshmen, 82% undergrads receive need-based scholarship or grant aid. 70% freshmen, 72% undergrads receive need-based self-help aid. 46 freshmen, 205 undergrads receive athletic scholarships.

SALEM COLLEGE

PO Box 10548, Winston-Salem, NC 27108
Phone: 336-721-2621 **E-mail**: admissions@salem.edu **CEEB Code**: 5607
Fax: 336-917-5572 **Website**: www.salem.edu **ACT Code**: 3156
Financial Aid Phone: 336-721-2808

This private school, affiliated with the Moravian Church, was founded in 1772. It has a 57-acre campus.

RATINGS

Admissions Selectivity Rating: 87   **Fire Safety Rating**: 78   **Green Rating**: 64

STUDENTS AND FACULTY

Enrollment: 809. **Student Body**: 97% female, 3% male, 42% out-of-state, 11% international (22 countries represented). African American 17%, Asian 1%, Caucasian 64%, Hispanic 3%. **Retention and Graduation**: 79% freshmen return for sophomore year. 49% freshmen graduate within 4 years. 29% grads go on to further study within 1 year. 23% grads pursue arts and sciences degrees. 3% grads pursue business degrees. 3% grads pursue law degrees. **Faculty**: Student/faculty ratio 13:1. 61 full-time faculty, 89% hold PhDs. 96% faculty teach undergrads.

ACADEMICS

Degrees: Bachelor's, master's. **Academic Requirements**: Arts/fine arts, English (including composition), foreign languages, history, humanities, mathematics, sciences (biological or physical), social science. **Classes**: Most classes have 10–19 students. Most lab/discussion sections have 10–19 students.

Majors with Highest Enrollment: Business administration/management; communications, journalism, and related fields; sociology. **Disciplines with Highest Percentage of Degrees Awarded**: Social sciences 18%, visual and performing arts 13%, psychology 12%, English 11%, business/marketing 11%. **Special Study Options**: Cross-registration, double major, dual enrollment, honors program, independent study, internships, liberal arts/career combination, student-designed major, study abroad, teacher certification program.

FACILITIES

Housing: Women's dorms, apartments for single students. **Special Academic Facilities/Equipment**: Art gallery, fine arts center, center for women writers, videoconferencing center. **Computers**: 100% of classrooms are wired, 80% of public computers are PCs, 20% of public computers are Macs, network access in dorm rooms, online administrative functions (other than registration), remote student-access to Web through college's connection.

CAMPUS LIFE

Activities: Choral groups, dance, drama/theater, literary magazine, marching band, music ensembles, musical theater, student government, student newspaper, yearbook. **Organizations**: 26 registered organizations, 14 honor societies, 7 religious organizations. **Athletics (Intercollegiate)**: *Women*: Basketball, cross-country, field hockey, softball, swimming, tennis, volleyball.

ADMISSIONS

Freshman Academic Profile: 36% in top 10% of high school class, 57% in top 25% of high school class, 92% in top 50% of high school class. SAT Math middle 50% range 480–630. SAT Critical Reading middle 50% range 490–650. ACT middle 50% range 21–31. TOEFL required of all international applicants, minimum paper TOEFL 550, minimum computer TOEFL 213. **Basis for Candidate Selection**: *Very important factors considered include:* Academic GPA, rigor of secondary school record. *Important factors considered include*: Application essay, character/personal qualities, extracurricular activities, recommendation(s), standardized test scores. *Other factors considered include*: Alumni/ae relation, class rank, interview, level of applicant's interest, talent/ability, volunteer work, work experience. **Freshman Admission Requirements**: High school diploma is required, and GED is accepted. *Academic units recommended*: 4 English, 3 math, 3 science, 2 foreign language, 2 history, 3 academic electives. **Freshman Admission Statistics**: 435 applied, 69% admitted, 51% enrolled. **Transfer Admission Requirements**: High school transcript, college transcript(s), essay or personal statement, statement of good standing from prior institution(s). Minimum college GPA of 2.0 required. Lowest grade transferable C-. **General Admission Information**: Application fee $30. Regular notification is rolling. Non-fall registration accepted. Admission may be deferred for a maximum of 1 year. Credit and/or placement offered for CEEB Advanced Placement tests.

COSTS AND FINANCIAL AID

Annual tuition $18,850. Room and board $10,050. Required fees $340. Average book expense $900. **Required Forms and Deadlines**: FAFSA, CSS/Financial Aid PROFILE, state aid form. Financial aid filing deadline 3/1. **Notification of Awards**: Applicants will be notified of awards on or about 3/15. **Types of Aid**: *Need-based scholarships/grants*: Pell, SEOG, state scholarships/grants, private scholarships, the school's own gift aid. *Loans*: FFEL Subsidized Stafford, FFEL Unsubsidized Stafford, FFEL PLUS, Federal Perkins. **Financial Aid Statistics**: 56% freshmen, 59% undergrads receive need-based scholarship or grant aid. 68% freshmen, 67% undergrads receive need-based self-help aid.

SALEM INTERNATIONAL UNIVERSITY

223 West Main Street, Salem, WV 26426-0500
Phone: 304-782-5336 **E-mail**: admissions@salemiu.edu **CEEB Code**: 5608
Fax: 304-782-5592 **Website**: www.salemiu.edu **ACT Code**: 4530
Financial Aid Phone: 304-782-5205

This private school was founded in 1888. It has a 300-acre campus.

RATINGS

Admissions Selectivity Rating: 70   **Fire Safety Rating**: 60*   **Green Rating**: 60*

STUDENTS AND FACULTY

Enrollment: 439. **Student Body**: 47% female, 53% male, 56% out-of-state, 39% international (20 countries represented). African American 8%, Caucasian 46%, Hispanic 2%, Native American 1%. **Retention and Graduation**: 69% freshmen return for sophomore year. 3% grads go on to further study within 1 year. 2% grads pursue arts and sciences degrees. 2% grads pursue business degrees. 1% grads pursue law degrees. 1% grads pursue medical degrees.

Faculty: Student/faculty ratio 14:1. 33 full-time faculty, 70% hold PhDs. 100% faculty teach undergrads.

ACADEMICS

Degrees: Associate, bachelor's, master's, post-master's certificate. **Academic Requirements**: Arts/fine arts, computer literacy, English (including composition), foreign languages, global business and international perspectives, global issues, history, humanities, international courses, mathematics, sciences (biological or physical), social science. **Classes**: Most classes have fewer than 10 students. **Majors with Highest Enrollment**: Business administration/management, computer and information sciences. **Disciplines with Highest Percentage of Degrees Awarded**: Communication technologies 16%, business/marketing 11%, English 10%, agriculture 9%, biological/life sciences 8%. **Special Study Options**: Combined bachelor's/graduate degree in molecular biology, distance learning, double major, English as a second language (ESL), foreign exchange programs abroad in Japan (Teikyo University, Hachioji) and Germany (Teikyo University, Berlin), independent study, internships, liberal arts/career combination, study abroad. Undergrads may take grad level classes.

FACILITIES

Housing: Coed dorms, men's dorms, women's dorms. **Special Academic Facilities/Equipment**: Living museum of culture and crafts of West Virginia settlers, Fort New Salem, biotechnology labs, equestrian center. **Computers**: 100% of public computers are PCs, network access in dorm rooms, network access in dorm lounges, remote student-access to Web through college's connection.

CAMPUS LIFE

Activities: Choral groups, dance, student government, student newspaper, television station, yearbook. **Organizations**: 20 registered organizations, 1 honor society, 2 religious organizations. 4 fraternities (5% men join), 4 sororities (7% women join). **Athletics (Intercollegiate)**: *Men*: Baseball, basketball, cheerleading, equestrian sports, golf, soccer, swimming, tennis, water polo. *Women*: Basketball, cheerleading, equestrian sports, soccer, softball, swimming, tennis, volleyball, water polo.

ADMISSIONS

Freshman Academic Profile: 7% in top 10% of high school class, 27% in top 25% of high school class, 47% in top 50% of high school class. SAT Math middle 50% range 420–570. SAT Critical Reading middle 50% range 380–550. ACT middle 50% range 16–22. TOEFL required of all international applicants, minimum paper TOEFL 500, minimum computer TOEFL 173. **Basis for Candidate Selection**: *Very important factors considered include*: Rigor of secondary school record, standardized test scores. *Important factors considered include*: Extracurricular activities, recommendation(s). *Other factors considered include*: Alumni/ae relation, application essay, character/personal qualities, interview, talent/ability. **Freshman Admission Requirements**: High school diploma is required, and GED is accepted. *Academic units recommended*: 4 English, 2 math, 2 science, 2 foreign language, 3 social studies. **Freshman Admission Statistics**: 251 applied, 99% admitted, 24% enrolled. **Transfer Admission Requirements**: High school transcript, college transcript(s), statement of good standing from prior institution(s). Minimum college GPA of 2.5 required. Lowest grade transferable C. **General Admission Information**: Application fee $25. Regular notification is rolling. Non-fall registration accepted. Admission may be deferred for a maximum of 1 year. Common Application accepted. Credit and/or placement offered for CEEB Advanced Placement tests.

COSTS AND FINANCIAL AID

Annual tuition $13,770. Room & board $4,632. Required fees $280. Average book expense $550. **Required Forms and Deadlines**: FAFSA, institution's own financial aid form. Financial aid filing deadline 4/15. **Notification of Awards**: Applicants will be notified of awards on a rolling basis beginning on or about 2/15. **Types of Aid**: *Need-based scholarships/grants*: Pell, SEOG, state scholarships/grants, private scholarships, the school's own gift aid. *Loans*: Direct Subsidized Stafford, Direct Unsubsidized Stafford, Direct PLUS, FFEL Subsidized Stafford, FFEL Unsubsidized Stafford, FFEL PLUS, Federal Perkins, college/university loans from institutional funds. **Student Employment**: Federal Work-Study Program available. Institutional employment available. Off-campus job opportunities are fair. **Financial Aid Statistics**: 43% freshmen, 39% undergrads receive need-based scholarship or grant aid. 61% freshmen, 54% undergrads receive need-based self-help aid. 16 freshmen, 23 undergrads receive athletic scholarships. Highest amount earned per year from on-campus jobs $2,000.

SALEM STATE COLLEGE

352 Lafayette Street, Salem, MA 01970
Phone: 978-542-6210 **E-mail:** admissions@salemstate.edu **CEEB Code:** 3522
Fax: 978-542-6893 **Website:** www.salemstate.edu
Financial Aid Phone: 978-542-6112

This public school was founded in 1854. It has a 108-acre campus.

RATINGS
Admissions Selectivity Rating: 60*   **Fire Safety Rating:** 60*   **Green Rating:** 60*

STUDENTS AND FACULTY
Enrollment: 6,834. **Student Body:** 64% female, 36% male, 4% international.
African American 7%, Asian 3%, Caucasian 76%, Hispanic 6%. **Retention and
Graduation:** 76% freshmen return for sophomore year. **Faculty:** Student/
faculty ratio 16:1. 320 full-time faculty.

ACADEMICS
Degrees: Bachelor's, certificate, master's, post-master's certificate. **Academic
Requirements:** Arts/fine arts, computer literacy, English (including composition), foreign languages, health, history, humanities, mathematics, sciences
(biological or physical), SFL, social science, speech. **Classes:** Most classes have
10–19 students. Most lab/discussion sections have 10–19 students. **Majors with
Highest Enrollment:** Business administration/management, criminal justice/
law enforcement administration, education. **Disciplines with Highest
Percentage of Degrees Awarded:** Business/marketing 18%, education 13%,
health professions and related sciences 11%, security and protective services
9%, psychology 7%. **Special Study Options:** Accelerated program, cooperative
education program, cross-registration, distance learning, double major, English
as a second language (ESL), honors program, independent study, internships,
student-designed major, study abroad, teacher certification program.

FACILITIES
Housing: Coed dorms, men's dorms, women's dorms, special housing for
disabled students, cooperative housing, substance-free housing, scholar-in-
residence, academic achievement. **Special Academic Facilities/Equipment:**
Aquaculture center, on-campus elementary school, color TV studio, instructional media center. **Computers:** Network access in dorm rooms, network
access in dorm lounges, remote student-access to Web through college's
connection.

CAMPUS LIFE
Activities: Choral groups, concert band, dance, drama/theater, music
ensembles, musical theater, radio station, student government, student
newspaper, student-run film society, yearbook. **Organizations:** 149 registered
organizations, 13 honor societies, 3 religious organizations. **Athletics
(Intercollegiate):** *Men:* Baseball, basketball, cross-country, diving, golf, ice
hockey, lacrosse, soccer, swimming, tennis, track/field (outdoor). *Women:*
Basketball, cross-country, diving, field hockey, lacrosse, soccer, softball,
swimming, tennis, track/field (outdoor), volleyball.

ADMISSIONS
Freshman Academic Profile: SAT Math middle 50% range 430–540. SAT
Critical Reading middle 50% range 430–530. TOEFL required of all
international applicants, minimum paper TOEFL 500, minimum computer
TOEFL 173. **Basis for Candidate Selection:** *Very important factors
considered include:* Academic GPA, rigor of secondary school record,
standardized test scores. *Other factors considered include:* Character/personal
qualities, extracurricular activities, interview, level of applicant's interest,
recommendation(s), talent/ability, volunteer work. **Freshman Admission
Requirements:** High school diploma is required, and GED is accepted.
Academic units required: 4 English, 3 math, 3 science (2 science labs), 2 foreign
language, 2 social studies, 1 history, 2 academic electives. *Academic units
recommended:* 4 English, 3 math, 3 science (2 science labs), 2 foreign language,
2 social studies, 3 history, 2 academic electives. **Freshman Admission
Statistics:** 4,608 applied, 84% admitted, 29% enrolled. **Transfer Admission
Requirements:** College transcript(s). Minimum college GPA of 2.0 required.
Lowest grade transferable C–. **General Admission Information:** Application
fee $25. Regular notification is rolling. Non-fall registration accepted.
Admission may be deferred for a maximum of 1 semester. Credit and/or
placement offered for CEEB Advanced Placement tests.

COSTS AND FINANCIAL AID
Average book expense $900. **Required Forms and Deadlines:** FAFSA.
Financial aid filing deadline 2/28. **Financial Aid Statistics:** 73% freshmen,
75% undergrads receive any aid.

SALISBURY UNIVERSITY

Admissions Office, 1101 Camden Avenue, Salisbury, MD 21801
Phone: 410-543-6161 **E-mail:** admissions@salisbury.edu **CEEB Code:** 5403
Fax: 410-546-6016 **Website:** www.salisbury.edu **ACT Code:** 1716
Financial Aid Phone: 406-675-4800
Financial Aid Phone: 410-543-6165

This public school was founded in 1925. It has a 154-acre campus.

RATINGS
Admissions Selectivity Rating: 86   **Fire Safety Rating:** 72   **Green Rating:** 77

STUDENTS AND FACULTY
Enrollment: 6,520. **Student Body:** 55% female, 45% male, 14% out-of-state.
African American 10%, Asian 3%, Caucasian 80%, Hispanic 3%. **Retention
and Graduation:** 81% freshmen return for sophomore year. 27% grads go on
to further study within 1 year. 23% grads pursue arts and sciences degrees. 2%
grads pursue business degrees. 1% grads pursue law degrees. 1% grads pursue
medical degrees. **Faculty:** Student/faculty ratio 16:1. 337 full-time faculty, 80%
hold PhDs. 100% faculty teach undergrads.

ACADEMICS
Degrees: Bachelor's, master's, post-bachelor's certificate. **Academic
Requirements:** Arts/fine arts, computer literacy, English (including composition), foreign languages, history, humanities, mathematics, physical education,
sciences (biological or physical), social science. **Classes:** Most classes have 20–
29 students. Most lab/discussion sections have 20–29 students. **Majors with
Highest Enrollment:** Business administration and management, communications studies/speech communication and rhetoric, elementary education and
teaching. **Disciplines with Highest Percentage of Degrees Awarded:**
Business/marketing 19%, education 14%, communications/journalism 10%,
health professions and related sciences 8%, biological/life sciences 6%. **Special
Study Options:** Accelerated program, cross-registration, distance learning,
double major, dual enrollment, English as a second language (ESL), honors
program, independent study, internships, liberal arts/career combination,
student-designed major, study abroad, teacher certification program.

FACILITIES
Housing: Coed dorms, men's dorms, women's dorms, apartments for single
students, wellness housing, affiliated off-campus apartments, quiet/study
housing available, world living/learning option-community of international and
American students. **Special Academic Facilities/Equipment:** Arboretum,
University Galleries, Scarborough Student Leadership Center, Research Center
for Delmarva History and Culture, small business development center, Ward
Museum of Wildfowl Art. **Computers:** 43% of classrooms are wired, 18% of
classrooms are wireless, 93% of public computers are PCs, 7% of public
computers are Macs, network access in dorm rooms, network access in dorm
lounges, online registration, online administrative functions (other than
registration), remote student-access to Web through college's connection.

CAMPUS LIFE
Activities: Choral groups, concert band, dance, drama/theater, jazz band,
literary magazine, music ensembles, musical theater, pep band, radio station,
student government, student newspaper, student-run film society, symphony
orchestra, television station. **Organizations:** 104 registered organizations, 20
honor societies, 8 religious organizations. 6 fraternities (5% men join), 5
sororities (6% women join). **Athletics (Intercollegiate):** *Men:* Baseball,
basketball, football, lacrosse, soccer, swimming, tennis, track/field (indoor),
track/field (outdoor). *Women:* Basketball, field hockey, lacrosse, soccer,
swimming, tennis, track/field (indoor), track/field (outdoor), volleyball.

ADMISSIONS
Freshman Academic Profile: 26% in top 10% of high school class, 58% in top
25% of high school class, 90% in top 50% of high school class. 85% from public
high schools. SAT Math middle 50% range 520–610. SAT Critical Reading
middle 50% range 510–590. SAT Writing middle 50% range 520–589. ACT
middle 50% range 20–24. TOEFL required of all international applicants,
minimum paper TOEFL 550, minimum computer TOEFL 213. **Basis for
Candidate Selection:** *Very important factors considered include:* Academic
GPA, extracurricular activities, rigor of secondary school record, talent/ability.

Important factors considered include: Alumni/ae relation, class rank, geographical residence, standardized test scores, volunteer work. *Other factors considered include*: Application essay, character/personal qualities, racial/ethnic status, recommendation(s), work experience. **Freshman Admission Requirements**: High school diploma is required, and GED is accepted. *Academic units required*: 4 English, 3 math, 3 science (2 science labs), 2 foreign language, 3 social studies. *Academic units recommended*: 4 English, 4 math, 4 science (3 science labs), 3 foreign language, 3 social studies, 3 academic electives. **Freshman Admission Statistics**: 5,910 applied, 55% admitted, 32% enrolled. **Transfer Admission Requirements**: College transcript(s). Minimum college GPA of 2.0 required. Lowest grade transferable C. **General Admission Information**: Application fee $45. Regular notification 3/15. Non-fall registration accepted. Credit offered for CEEB Advanced Placement tests.

COSTS AND FINANCIAL AID

Average book expense $100. **Required Forms and Deadlines**: FAFSA. Financial aid filing deadline 12/31. **Notification of Awards**: Applicants will be notified of awards on or about 3/15. **Types of Aid**: *Need-based scholarships/grants*: Pell, SEOG, state scholarships/grants, private scholarships, the school's own gift aid. *Loans*: Direct Subsidized Stafford, Direct Unsubsidized Stafford, Direct PLUS, Federal Perkins. **Financial Aid Statistics**: 32% freshmen, 28% undergrads receive need-based scholarship or grant aid. 30% freshmen, 33% undergrads receive need-based self-help aid. 65% freshmen, 66% undergrads receive any aid. Highest amount earned per year from on-campus jobs $2,000.

SALISH-KOOTENAI COLLEGE

Attn: Jackie Moran, PO Box 117, Pablo, MT 59855
Phone: 406-275-4866 **E-mail**: jackie_moran@skc.edu
Fax: 406-275-4810 **Website**: www.skc.edu

This private school was founded in 1977.

RATINGS
Admissions Selectivity Rating: 60*   **Fire Safety Rating**: 60*   **Green Rating**: 60*

STUDENTS AND FACULTY
Enrollment: 108. **Student Body**: 62% female, 38% male, 27% out-of-state. African American 2%, Caucasian 202%, Hispanic 3%. **Faculty**: Student/faculty ratio 35:1.

ACADEMICS
Degrees: Associate, bachelor's, certificate. **Special Study Options**: Cooperative education program, distance learning.

FACILITIES
Housing: Apartments for married students, apartments for single students. **Computers**: 95% of public computers are PCs, 5% of public computers are Macs, remote student-access to Web through college's connection.

CAMPUS LIFE
Activities: Student government. **Athletics (Intercollegiate)**: *Men*: Baseball, basketball. *Women*: Basketball.

ADMISSIONS
Freshman Admission Requirements: High school diploma is required, and GED is accepted. **Freshman Admission Statistics**: 133 applied, 81% admitted, 100% enrolled. **Transfer Admission Requirements**: High school transcript, college transcript(s). Lowest grade transferable C. **General Admission Information**: Regular notification is rolling. Non-fall registration accepted. Common Application not accepted.

COSTS AND FINANCIAL AID
Annual tuition $1,620. Required fees $687. Average book expense $750. **Financial Aid Statistics**: 24% freshmen, 48% undergrads receive need-based scholarship or grant aid. 4% freshmen, 16% undergrads receive need-based self-help aid.

SALVE REGINA UNIVERSITY

100 Ochre Point Avenue, Newport, RI 02840-4192
Phone: 401-341-2908 **E-mail**: sruadmis@salve.edu **CEEB Code**: 3759
Fax: 401-848-2823 **Website**: www.salve.edu **ACT Code**: 3816
Financial Aid Phone: 401-341-2901

This private school, affiliated with the Roman Catholic Church, was founded in 1947. It has a 70-acre campus.

RATINGS
Admissions Selectivity Rating: 87   **Fire Safety Rating**: 87   **Green Rating**: 80

STUDENTS AND FACULTY
Enrollment: 2,079. **Student Body**: 71% female, 29% male, 84% out-of-state, 1% international (17 countries represented). African American 1%, Asian 1%, Caucasian 82%, Hispanic 2%. **Retention and Graduation**: 80% freshmen return for sophomore year. 53% freshmen graduate within 4 years. 26% grads go on to further study within 1 year. 10% grads pursue arts and sciences degrees. 12% grads pursue business degrees. 4% grads pursue law degrees. **Faculty**: Student/faculty ratio 13:1. 121 full-time faculty, 79% hold PhDs. 95% faculty teach undergrads.

ACADEMICS
Degrees: Associate, bachelor's, certificate, doctoral, master's, post-bachelor's certificate, post-master's certificate. **Academic Requirements**: Arts/fine arts, English (including composition), foreign languages, history, humanities, mathematics, philosophy, sciences (biological or physical), social science. **Classes**: Most classes have 10–19 students. Most lab/discussion sections have 20–29 students. **Majors with Highest Enrollment**: Business administration/management, criminal justice/law enforcement administration, elementary education and teaching. **Disciplines with Highest Percentage of Degrees Awarded**: Education 22%, business/marketing 19%, security and protective services 11%, health professions and related sciences 11%, English 7%, psychology 5%. **Special Study Options**: Accelerated program, distance learning, double major, dual enrollment, English as a second language (ESL), exchange student program (domestic), honors program, independent study, internships, liberal arts/career combination, study abroad, teacher certification program.

FACILITIES
Housing: Coed dorms, men's dorms, women's dorms, apartments for single students, special housing for disabled students, both unique housing and traditional style dormitories options in Newport's historic buildings, off-campus downtown housing. **Special Academic Facilities/Equipment**: Art gallery, theater, technology center. **Computers**: 10% of classrooms are wired, 85% of classrooms are wireless, 81% of public computers are PCs, 19% of public computers are Macs, network access in dorm rooms, network access in dorm lounges, online registration, online administrative functions (other than registration), remote student-access to Web through college's connection. Undergraduates are required to own a computer.

CAMPUS LIFE
Activities: Choral groups, concert band, dance, drama/theater, jazz band, literary magazine, music ensembles, radio station, student government, student newspaper, student-run film society, yearbook. **Organizations**: 42 registered organizations, 16 honor societies, 2 religious organizations. **Athletics (Intercollegiate)**: *Men*: Baseball, basketball, cross-country, football, ice hockey, lacrosse, sailing, soccer, tennis. *Women*: Basketball, cross-country, field hockey, ice hockey, lacrosse, sailing, soccer, softball, tennis, track/field (outdoor), volleyball. Environmental Initiatives: Recycling. Energy conservation. Water conservation.

ADMISSIONS
Freshman Academic Profile: 15% in top 10% of high school class, 54% in top 25% of high school class, 89% in top 50% of high school class. 65% from public high schools. SAT Math middle 50% range 510–590. SAT Critical Reading middle 50% range 510–600. SAT Writing middle 50% range 510–600. ACT middle 50% range 22–26. TOEFL required of all international applicants, minimum paper TOEFL 500, minimum computer TOEFL 173. **Basis for Candidate Selection**: *Very important factors considered include*: Academic GPA, class rank, rigor of secondary school record. *Important factors considered include*: Application essay, recommendation(s), standardized test scores. *Other factors considered include*: Alumni/ae relation, character/personal qualities, extracurricular activities, level of applicant's interest, racial/ethnic status, talent/ability, volunteer work, work experience. **Freshman Admission Requirements**: High school diploma is required, and GED is accepted. *Academic units required*: 4 English, 3 math, 2 science (2 science labs), 2 foreign language, 1

social studies, 4 academic electives. **Freshman Admission Statistics**: 5,231 applied, 56% admitted, 19% enrolled. **Transfer Admission Requirements**: High school transcript, college transcript(s), essay or personal statement, statement of good standing from prior institution(s). Minimum college GPA of 2.7 required. Lowest grade transferable C. **General Admission Information**: Application fee $40. Regular notification is rolling. Non-fall registration accepted. Admission may be deferred for a maximum of 1 year. Credit and/or placement offered for CEEB Advanced Placement tests.

COSTS AND FINANCIAL AID

Annual tuition $26,750. Room and board $10,200. Required fees $200. Average book expense $900. **Required Forms and Deadlines**: FAFSA, CSS/Financial Aid PROFILE, Noncustodial PROFILE, Business/Farm Supplement. Financial aid filing deadline 3/1. **Notification of Awards**: Applicants will be notified of awards on or about 2/15. **Types of Aid**: *Need-based scholarships/grants*: Pell, SEOG, state scholarships/grants, private scholarships, the school's own gift aid. *Loans*: FFEL Subsidized Stafford, FFEL Unsubsidized Stafford, FFEL PLUS, Federal Perkins, Federal Nursing, state loans, college/university loans from institutional funds, private loans. **Student Employment**: Federal Work-Study Program available. Institutional employment available. Off-campus job opportunities are excellent. **Financial Aid Statistics**: 69% freshmen, 64% undergrads receive need-based scholarship or grant aid. 68% freshmen, 64% undergrads receive need-based self-help aid. 72% freshmen, 68% undergrads receive any aid. Highest amount earned per year from on-campus jobs $1,200.

SAM HOUSTON STATE UNIVERSITY

Box 2418, SHSU, Huntsville, TX 77341-2418
Phone: 936-294-1828 **E-mail**: admissions@shsu.edu **CEEB Code**: 6643
Fax: 936-294-3758 **Website**: www.shsu.edu **ACT Code**: 4162
Financial Aid Phone: 936-294-1724

This public school was founded in 1879. It has a 272-acre campus.

RATINGS
Admissions Selectivity Rating: 70   **Fire Safety Rating**: 83   **Green Rating**: 72

STUDENTS AND FACULTY
Enrollment: 12,270. **Student Body**: 58% female, 42% male, 1% out-of-state. African American 15%, Asian 1%, Caucasian 72%, Hispanic 11%. **Retention and Graduation**: 68% freshmen return for sophomore year. 15% freshmen graduate within 4 years. 18% grads go on to further study within 1 year. 16% grads pursue arts and sciences degrees. 2% grads pursue business degrees. **Faculty**: Student/faculty ratio 22:1. 417 full-time faculty. 90% faculty teach undergrads.

ACADEMICS
Degrees: Bachelor's, certificate, diploma, doctoral, master's, post-bachelor's certificate. **Academic Requirements**: Arts/fine arts, computer literacy, cultural studies, English (including composition), history, humanities, mathematics, philosophy, sciences (biological or physical), social science. **Classes**: Most classes have 20–29 students. Most lab/discussion sections have 20–29 students. **Majors with Highest Enrollment**: Business administration/management, criminal justice/safety studies, multi/interdisciplinary studies. **Disciplines with Highest Percentage of Degrees Awarded**: Business/marketing 29%, interdisciplinary studies 11%, visual and performing arts 6%, agriculture 6%, psychology 6%. **Special Study Options**: Combined 3-2 engineering degree programs with Texas A&M University, distance learning, double major, dual enrollment, English as a second language (ESL), honors program, independent study, internships, study abroad, teacher certification program. Undergrads may take grad level classes, weekend college.

FACILITIES
Housing: Coed dorms, men's dorms, women's dorms, apartments for married students, apartments for single students, fraternity/sorority housing. **Special Academic Facilities/Equipment**: Sam Houston Memorial Museum; on-campus elementary school; communications center for photography, radio, TV, and film; agricultural complex and university farm. **Computers**: 90% of classrooms are wired, 90% of classrooms are wireless, 90% of public computers are PCs, 10% of public computers are Macs, network access in dorm rooms, network access in dorm lounges, online registration, online administrative functions (other than registration), remote student-access to Web through college's connection.

CAMPUS LIFE
Activities: Choral groups, concert band, dance, drama/theater, jazz band, marching band, music ensembles, musical theater, pep band, radio station, student government, student newspaper, symphony orchestra, television station, yearbook. **Organizations**: 185 registered organizations, 12 honor societies, 17 religious organizations. 16 fraternities, 10 sororities. **Athletics (Intercollegiate)**: *Men*: Baseball, basketball, cheerleading, cross-country, equestrian sports, football, golf, rodeo, soccer, softball, tennis, track/field (indoor), track/field (outdoor). *Women*: Basketball, cheerleading, cross-country, equestrian sports, golf, rodeo, soccer, softball, tennis, track/field (indoor), track/field (outdoor), volleyball.

ADMISSIONS
Freshman Academic Profile: 13% in top 10% of high school class, 43% in top 25% of high school class, 81% in top 50% of high school class. SAT Math middle 50% range 430–540. SAT Critical Reading middle 50% range 420–530. ACT middle 50% range 17–22. TOEFL required of all international applicants, minimum paper TOEFL 550, minimum computer TOEFL 213. **Basis for Candidate Selection**: *Very important factors considered include*: Class rank, rigor of secondary school record, standardized test scores. *Other factors considered include*: Application essay, recommendation(s). **Freshman Admission Requirements**: High school diploma is required, and GED is accepted. *Academic units required*: 4 English, 3 math, 2 science, 3 social studies, 1 academic elective, 10 health/physical education. *Academic units recommended*: 4 English, 3 math, 3 science, 2 foreign language, 4 social studies, 4 academic electives, 5 health/physical education. **Freshman Admission Statistics**: 5,598 applied, 79% admitted, 49% enrolled. **Transfer Admission Requirements**: College transcript(s), statement of good standing from prior institution(s). Minimum college GPA of 2.0 required. Lowest grade transferable C. **General Admission Information**: Application fee $35. Regular application deadline 8/1. Regular notification is rolling. Non-fall registration accepted. Common Application accepted. Credit and/or placement offered for CEEB Advanced Placement tests.

COSTS AND FINANCIAL AID
Annual in-state tuition $5,566. Annual out-of-state tuition $13,906. Room and board $6,046. Required fees $4,406. Average book expense $1,016. **Required Forms and Deadlines**: FAFSA, institution's own financial aid form. Financial aid filing deadline 5/31. **Notification of Awards**: Applicants will be notified of awards on a rolling basis beginning on or about 5/1. **Types of Aid**: *Need-based scholarships/grants*: Pell, SEOG, state scholarships/grants, the school's own gift aid. *Loans*: FFEL Subsidized Stafford, FFEL Unsubsidized Stafford, FFEL PLUS, Federal Perkins, state loans, college/university loans from institutional funds. **Financial Aid Statistics**: 37% freshmen, 36% undergrads receive need-based scholarship or grant aid. 36% freshmen, 37% undergrads receive need-based self-help aid. 62 freshmen, 292 undergrads receive athletic scholarships. 32% freshmen, 43% undergrads receive any aid. Highest amount earned per year from on-campus jobs $2,500.

SAMFORD UNIVERSITY

Best 368

800 Lakeshore Drive, Birmingham, AL 35229
Phone: 205-726-3673 **E-mail**: admiss@samford.edu **CEEB Code**: 1302
Fax: 205-726-2171 **Website**: www.samford.edu **ACT Code**: 0016
Financial Aid Phone: 205-726-2860

This private school, affiliated with the Baptist Church, was founded in 1841. It has a 180-acre campus.

RATINGS
Admissions Selectivity Rating: 84   **Fire Safety Rating**: 88   **Green Rating**: 74

STUDENTS AND FACULTY
Enrollment: 2,846. **Student Body**: 63% female, 37% male, 57% out-of-state. African American 7%, Caucasian 89%, Hispanic 1%. **Retention and Graduation**: 83% freshmen return for sophomore year. **Faculty**: Student/faculty ratio 12:1. 280 full-time faculty, 82% hold PhDs.

ACADEMICS

Degrees: Associate, bachelor's, certificate, doctoral, first professional, master's, post-master's certificate, terminal. **Academic Requirements**: Arts/fine arts, English (including composition), foreign languages, history, humanities, mathematics, physical education, sciences (biological or physical), social science, religion. **Classes**: Most classes have 10-19 students. Most lab/discussion sections have fewer than 10 students. **Majors with Highest Enrollment**: Law (LLB, JD), nursing/registered nurse training (ASN, BSN, MSN, RN), pharmacy (PharmD, BS/BPharm). **Disciplines with Highest Percentage of Degrees Awarded**: Business/marketing 15%, health professions and related sciences 12%, visual and performing arts 9%, psychology 8%, education 8%, communications/journalism 8%. **Special Study Options**: Accelerated program, cooperative education program, distance learning, double major, dual enrollment, exchange student program (domestic), honors program, independent study, internships, liberal arts/career combination, semester offered at Samford London Study Center, study abroad, teacher certification program.

FACILITIES

Housing: Men's dorms, women's dorms, special housing for disabled students, fraternity/sorority housing, several houses are occupied by students. **Special Academic Facilities/Equipment**: Language lab, reflective telescope, geographic information systems lab, global center, planetarium, conservatory. **Computers**: 90% of public computers are PCs, 10% of public computers are Macs, network access in dorm rooms, online administrative functions (other than registration), support for handheld computing, remote student-access to Web through college's connection.

CAMPUS LIFE

Activities: Choral groups, concert band, dance, drama/theater, jazz band, literary magazine, marching band, music ensembles, musical theater, radio station, student government, student newspaper, symphony orchestra, yearbook. **Organizations**: 102 registered organizations, 28 honor societies, 20 religious organizations. 7 fraternities (27% men join), 7 sororities (39% women join). **Athletics (Intercollegiate)**: *Men*: Baseball, basketball, cross-country, football, golf, tennis, track/field (outdoor). *Women*: Basketball, cross-country, golf, soccer, softball, tennis, track/field (outdoor), volleyball.

ADMISSIONS

Freshman Academic Profile: 40% in top 10% of high school class, 65% in top 25% of high school class, 90% in top 50% of high school class. 56% from public high schools. SAT Math middle 50% range 490–630. SAT Critical Reading middle 50% range 510–620. ACT middle 50% range 22–28. TOEFL required of all international applicants, minimum paper TOEFL 550, minimum computer TOEFL 213. **Basis for Candidate Selection**: *Very important factors considered include*: Academic GPA, application essay, character/personal qualities, recommendation(s), religious affiliation/commitment, rigor of secondary school record, standardized test scores. *Important factors considered include*: Alumni/ae relation, class rank, extracurricular activities, interview. *Other factors considered include*: Geographical residence, level of applicant's interest, racial/ethnic status, state residency, talent/ability, volunteer work, work experience. **Freshman Admission Requirements**: High school diploma is required, and GED is accepted. *Academic units required*: 4 English, 3 math, 3 science (2 science labs), 2 social studies, 2 history. *Academic units recommended*: 2 foreign language. **Freshman Admission Statistics**: 1,837 applied, 86% admitted, 41% enrolled. **Transfer Admission Requirements**: College transcript(s), essay or personal statement, statement of good standing from prior institution(s). Minimum college GPA of 2.5 required. Lowest grade transferable C-. **General Admission Information**: Application fee $35. Regular notification is rolling. Non-fall registration accepted. Admission may be deferred for a maximum of 1 year. Credit and/or placement offered for CEEB Advanced Placement tests.

COSTS AND FINANCIAL AID

Required Forms and Deadlines: FAFSA. Financial aid filing deadline 3/1. **Notification of Awards**: Applicants will be notified of awards on or about 4/1. **Types of Aid**: *Need-based scholarships/grants*: Pell, SEOG, state scholarships/grants, private scholarships, the school's own gift aid. *Loans*: FFEL Subsidized Stafford, FFEL Unsubsidized Stafford, FFEL PLUS, Federal Perkins, college/university loans from institutional funds. **Financial Aid Statistics**: 35% freshmen, 34% undergrads receive need-based scholarship or grant aid. 31% freshmen, 34% undergrads receive need-based self-help aid. 58 freshmen, 204 undergrads receive athletic scholarships. 35% freshmen, 34% undergrads receive any aid.

SAMUEL MERRITT COLLEGE

370 Hawthorne Avenue, Oakland, CA 94609
Phone: 510-869-6576 **E-mail**: admission@samuelmerritt.edu **CEEB Code**: 0412
Fax: 510-869-6525 **Website**: www.samuelmerritt.edu **ACT Code**: 4750
Financial Aid Phone: 510-869-6131

This private school was founded in 1909. It has a 1-acre campus.

RATINGS

Admissions Selectivity Rating: 60*   **Fire Safety Rating**: 60*   **Green Rating**: 60*

STUDENTS AND FACULTY

Enrollment: 256. **Student Body**: 87% female, 13% male, 1% out-of-state. African American 11%, Asian 21%, Caucasian 65%, Hispanic 8%, Native American 2%. **Retention and Graduation**: 67% freshmen return for sophomore year. 81% freshmen graduate within 4 years. 1% grads go on to further study within 1 year. **Faculty**: 48% faculty teach undergrads.

ACADEMICS

Degrees: Bachelor's, master's, post-master's certificate. **Academic Requirements**: English (including composition), humanities, mathematics, philosophy, sciences (biological or physical), social science. **Special Study Options**: Accelerated program, double major, dual enrollment, independent study, internships, study abroad.

FACILITIES

Housing: Coed dorms.

CAMPUS LIFE

Activities: Student government, student newspaper. **Organizations**: 11 registered organizations, 1 honor society. **Athletics (Intercollegiate)**: *Men*: Baseball, basketball, crew/rowing, cross-country, football, golf, rugby, soccer, tennis, volleyball. *Women*: Basketball, crew/rowing, cross-country, soccer, tennis, volleyball.

ADMISSIONS

Freshman Academic Profile: SAT Math middle 50% range 435–570. SAT Critical Reading middle 50% range 415–525. ACT middle 50% range 17–23. TOEFL required of all international applicants, minimum paper TOEFL 550. **Basis for Candidate Selection**: *Very important factors considered include*: Rigor of secondary school record, standardized test scores. *Important factors considered include*: Character/personal qualities, recommendation(s), volunteer work. *Other factors considered include*: Application essay, extracurricular activities, interview, talent/ability, work experience. **Freshman Admission Requirements**: High school diploma is required, and GED is accepted. *Academic units required*: 3 English, 2 math, 2 science (2 science labs), 2 social studies. **Freshman Admission Statistics**: 43 applied, 63% admitted, 33% enrolled. **Transfer Admission Requirements**: College transcript(s), essay or personal statement. Minimum college GPA of 2.5 required. Lowest grade transferable C-. **General Admission Information**: Application fee $35. Regular application deadline 5/1. Non-fall registration accepted. Admission may be deferred for a maximum of 1 year. Common Application accepted. Credit offered for CEEB Advanced Placement tests.

COSTS AND FINANCIAL AID

Annual tuition $14,560. Room $3,330. Required fees $65. Average book expense $864. **Required Forms and Deadlines**: FAFSA. Financial aid filing deadline 3/2. **Notification of Awards**: Applicants will be notified of awards on a rolling basis beginning on or about 4/15. **Types of Aid**: *Need-based scholarships/grants*: Pell, SEOG, state scholarships/grants, private scholarships, the school's own gift aid. *Loans*: FFEL Subsidized Stafford, FFEL Unsubsidized Stafford, FFEL PLUS, Federal Nursing, college/university loans from institutional funds. **Student Employment**: Federal Work-Study Program available. Institutional employment available. Off-campus job opportunities are excellent. **Financial Aid Statistics**: 89% freshmen, 78% undergrads receive need-based scholarship or grant aid. 67% freshmen, 94% undergrads receive need-based self-help aid. Highest amount earned per year from on-campus jobs $1,000.

SAN DIEGO STATE UNIVERSITY

5500 Campanile Drive, San Diego, CA 92182-7455
Phone: 619-594-6336 **CEEB Code:** 4682
Fax: 619-594-1250 **Website:** www.sdsu.edu **ACT Code:** 0398
Financial Aid Phone: 619-594-6323

This public school was founded in 1897. It has a 300-acre campus.

RATINGS
Admissions Selectivity Rating: 60*   **Fire Safety Rating:** 73   **Green Rating:** 60*

STUDENTS AND FACULTY
Enrollment: 28,527. **Student Body:** 58% female, 42% male, 5% out-of-state, 2% international (79 countries represented). African American 4%, Asian 15%, Caucasian 45%, Hispanic 23%. **Retention and Graduation:** 82% freshmen return for sophomore year. 17% freshmen graduate within 4 years. **Faculty:** Student/faculty ratio 19:1. 985 full-time faculty. 100% faculty teach undergrads.

ACADEMICS
Degrees: Bachelor's, doctoral, master's, post-bachelor's certificate, post-master's certificate. **Academic Requirements:** Arts/fine arts, English (including composition), foreign languages, history, humanities, mathematics, philosophy, sciences (biological or physical), social science. **Classes:** Most classes have 20–29 students. Most lab/discussion sections have 20–29 students. **Majors with Highest Enrollment:** Business administration/management, liberal arts and sciences/liberal studies, psychology. **Disciplines with Highest Percentage of Degrees Awarded:** Business/marketing 18%, social sciences 12%, psychology 9%, liberal arts/general studies 8%, English 6%, visual and performing arts 6%. **Special Study Options:** Cross-registration, distance learning, double major, dual enrollment, English as a second language (ESL), exchange student program (domestic), honors program, independent study, internships, student-designed major, study abroad, teacher certification program.

FACILITIES
Housing: Coed dorms, apartments for single students, special housing for international students, fraternity/sorority housing. The Housing and Residential Life office has a website to assist students and families to find off-campus housing. **Special Academic Facilities/Equipment:** Art gallery, theater, recital hall, research bureaus for labor economics, marine studies and social science, audiovisual center, electronic boardroom, multimedia interactive fine arts technology lab, Palomar Observatory (off-campus), field studies stations (off-campus). **Computers:** 70% of public computers are PCs, 16% of public computers are Macs, 14% of public computers are UNIX, network access in dorm rooms, online registration, online administrative functions (other than registration), remote student-access to Web through college's connection.

CAMPUS LIFE
Activities: Choral groups, concert band, dance, drama/theater, jazz band, literary magazine, marching band, music ensembles, musical theater, opera, pep band, radio station, student government, student newspaper, student-run film society, symphony orchestra, television station. **Organizations:** 180 registered organizations, 6 honor societies, 11 religious organizations. 25 fraternities (11% men join), 23 sororities (8% women join). **Athletics (Intercollegiate):** *Men:* Baseball, basketball, football, golf, soccer, tennis. *Women:* Basketball, crew/rowing, cross-country, diving, golf, soccer, softball, swimming, tennis, track/field (outdoor), volleyball, water polo.

ADMISSIONS
Freshman Academic Profile: 85% from public high schools. SAT Math middle 50% range 480–590. SAT Critical Reading middle 50% range 460–570. ACT middle 50% range 19–25. TOEFL required of all international applicants, minimum paper TOEFL 550, minimum computer TOEFL 213. **Basis for Candidate Selection:** *Very important factors considered include:* Academic GPA, rigor of secondary school record, standardized test scores. *Important factors considered include:* Geographical residence, state residency. **Freshman Admission Requirements:** High school diploma is required, and GED is accepted. *Academic units required:* 4 English, 3 math, 2 science (2 science labs), 2 foreign language, 1 social studies, 1 history, 1 academic elective, 1 visual and performing arts. *Academic units recommended:* 4 math. **Freshman Admission Statistics:** 40,959 applied, 48% admitted, 26% enrolled. **Transfer Admission Requirements:** College transcript(s). Lowest grade transferable D-. **General Admission Information:** Application fee $55. Regular application deadline 11/30. Regular notification 3/1. Nonfall registration not accepted. Credit offered for CEEB Advanced Placement tests.

COSTS AND FINANCIAL AID
Annual in-state tuition $2,046. Out-of-state tuition $8,460. Room and board $10,904. Required fees $3,428. Average book expense $1,332. **Required Forms and Deadlines:** FAFSA, state aid form. Financial aid filing deadline 3/2. **Notification of Awards:** Applicants will be notified of awards on a rolling basis beginning on or about 2/14. **Types of Aid:** *Need-based scholarships/grants:* Pell, SEOG, state scholarships/grants, private scholarships, the school's own gift aid, Federal Nursing Scholarships. *Loans:* Direct Subsidized Stafford, Direct Unsubsidized Stafford, Direct PLUS, Federal Perkins, college/university loans from institutional funds. **Student Employment:** Federal Work-Study Program available. Institutional employment available. Off-campus job opportunities are good. **Financial Aid Statistics:** 28% freshmen, 35% undergrads receive need-based scholarship or grant aid. 39% freshmen, 44% undergrads receive need-based self-help aid. 60 freshmen, 240 undergrads receive athletic scholarships.

SAN FRANCISCO ART INSTITUTE

800 Chestnut Street, San Francisco, CA 94133
Phone: 415-749-4500 **E-mail:** admissions@sfai.edu **CEEB Code:** 4036
Fax: 415-749-4592 **Website:** www.sfai.edu
Financial Aid Phone: 415-749-4520

This private school was founded in 1871. It has a 4-acre campus.

RATINGS
Admissions Selectivity Rating: 60*   **Fire Safety Rating:** 60*   **Green Rating:** 60*

STUDENTS AND FACULTY
Enrollment: 412. **Student Body:** 55% female, 45% male. **Faculty:** Student/faculty ratio 8:1. 39 full-time faculty.

ACADEMICS
Degrees: Bachelor's, certificate, master's, post-bachelor's certificate. **Academic Requirements:** Arts/fine arts, English (including composition), history, humanities, mathematics, sciences (biological or physical), social science. **Classes:** Most classes have 10–19 students. **Majors with Highest Enrollment:** Intermedia/multimedia, painting, photography. **Disciplines with Highest Percentage of Degrees Awarded:** Visual and performing arts 100%. **Special Study Options:** Accelerated program, double major, English as a second language (ESL), exchange student program (domestic), independent study, internships, study abroad.

FACILITIES
Housing: SFAI has an extended lease on 9 apartments in the San Francisco Presidio, housing 45 students in a neighborhood of students from several local colleges and universities. SFAI housing is staffed by resident advisors who are upper-division students at SF. **Special Academic Facilities/Equipment:** Art gallery.

CAMPUS LIFE
Activities: Student government, student newspaper, student-run film society.

ADMISSIONS
Freshman Academic Profile: TOEFL required of all international applicants, minimum paper TOEFL 500, minimum computer TOEFL 173. **Basis for Candidate Selection:** *Very important factors considered include:* Application essay, interview, talent/ability. *Important factors considered include:* Recommendation(s). *Other factors considered include:* Rigor of secondary school record, standardized test scores. **Freshman Admission Requirements:** High school diploma is required, and GED is accepted. **Freshman Admission Statistics:** 248 applied, 87% admitted, 24% enrolled. **Transfer Admission Requirements:** College transcript(s), essay or personal statement, interview. Lowest grade transferable C. **General Admission Information:** Application fee $65. Regular application deadline 9/1. Regular notification is rolling. Non-fall registration accepted. Admission may be deferred for a maximum of 1 year. Common Application not accepted. Credit offered for CEEB Advanced Placement tests.

COSTS AND FINANCIAL AID
Annual tuition $22,176. Average book expense $1,800. **Required Forms and Deadlines:** FAFSA, California residents must submit Cal Grant GPA Verification Form to CA Student Aid Commission (CSAC). Financial aid filing deadline 3/1. **Notification of Awards:** Applicants will be notified of awards on a rolling basis beginning on or about 3/31. **Types of Aid:** *Need-based scholarships/grants:* Pell, SEOG, state scholarships/grants, the school's own gift

aid. *Loans*: Direct Subsidized Stafford, Direct Unsubsidized Stafford, Direct PLUS, alternative educational loans. **Student Employment**: Federal Work-Study Program available. Off-campus job opportunities are good. **Financial Aid Statistics**: 50% freshmen, 68% undergrads receive need-based scholarship or grant aid. 50% freshmen, 67% undergrads receive need-based self-help aid.

SAN FRANCISCO CONSERVATORY OF MUSIC

1201 Ortega Street, San Francisco, CA 94122
Phone: 415-759-3431 **E-mail**: sed@sfcm.edu **CEEB Code**: 4744
Fax: 417-759-3499 **Website**: www.sfcm.edu
Financial Aid Phone: 415-759-3422

This private school was founded in 1917. It has a 5-acre campus.

RATINGS
Admissions Selectivity Rating: 60*   **Fire Safety Rating**: 60*   **Green Rating**: 60*

STUDENTS AND FACULTY
Enrollment: 131. **Student Body**: 56% female, 44% male, 41% out-of-state, 17% international. African American 4%, Asian 11%, Caucasian 46%, Hispanic 6%. **Retention and Graduation**: 85% freshmen return for sophomore year. 60% freshmen graduate within 4 years. 50% grads go on to further study within 1 year. 50% grads pursue arts and sciences degrees. 5% grads pursue law degrees. **Faculty**: Student/faculty ratio 7:1. 26 full-time faculty, 23% hold PhDs. 100% faculty teach undergrads.

ACADEMICS
Degrees: Bachelor's, diploma, master's, post-master's certificate. **Academic Requirements**: Arts/fine arts, English (including composition), history. **Classes**: Most classes have fewer than 10 students. **Disciplines with Highest Percentage of Degrees Awarded**: Visual and performing arts 100%. **Special Study Options**: Independent study.

FACILITIES
Special Academic Facilities/Equipment: Performance hall, electronic composition studio. **Computers**: 100% of public computers are PCs.

CAMPUS LIFE
Activities: Choral groups, music ensembles, musical theater, opera, student government, symphony orchestra.

ADMISSIONS
Freshman Academic Profile: 71% from public high schools. SAT Math middle 50% range 530–630. SAT Critical Reading middle 50% range 490–700. TOEFL required of all international applicants, minimum paper TOEFL 500. **Basis for Candidate Selection**: *Very important factors considered include*: Talent/ability. *Important factors considered include*: Rigor of secondary school record. *Other factors considered include*: Application essay, character/personal qualities, class rank, extracurricular activities, recommendation(s), standardized test scores. **Freshman Admission Requirements**: High school diploma is required, and GED is accepted. *Academic units recommended*: 3 English, 3 foreign language. **Freshman Admission Statistics**: 110 applied, 64% admitted, 30% enrolled. **Transfer Admission Requirements**: High school transcript, college transcript(s). Minimum college GPA of 2.0 required. Lowest grade transferable C. **General Admission Information**: Application fee $70. Regular notification is rolling. Non-fall registration accepted. Common Application not accepted. Credit offered for CEEB Advanced Placement tests.

COSTS AND FINANCIAL AID
Annual tuition $20,500. Required fees $280. Average book expense $850. **Required Forms and Deadlines**: FAFSA, institution's own financial aid form. Financial aid filing deadline 3/1. **Notification of Awards**: Applicants will be notified of awards on a rolling basis beginning on or about 3/15. **Types of Aid**: *Need-based scholarships/grants*: Pell, SEOG, state scholarships/grants, the school's own gift aid. *Loans*: FFEL Subsidized Stafford, FFEL Unsubsidized Stafford, FFEL PLUS, Federal Perkins. **Student Employment**: Federal Work-Study Program available. Institutional employment available. Off-campus job opportunities are excellent. **Financial Aid Statistics**: 70% freshmen, 69% undergrads receive need-based scholarship or grant aid. 55% freshmen, 56% undergrads receive need-based self-help aid. Highest amount earned per year from on-campus jobs $1,000.

SAN FRANCISCO STATE UNIVERSITY

1600 Holloway Avenue, San Francisco, CA 94132
Phone: 415-338-6486 **E-mail**: ugadmit@sfsu.edu **CEEB Code**: 4684
Fax: 415-338-7196 **Website**: www.sfsu.edu
Financial Aid Phone: 415-338-7000

This public school was founded in 1899. It has a 136-acre campus.

RATINGS
Admissions Selectivity Rating: 60*   **Fire Safety Rating**: 83   **Green Rating**: 60*

STUDENTS AND FACULTY
Enrollment: 23,843. **Student Body**: 59% female, 41% male, 6% international (149 countries represented). African American 6%, Asian 31%, Caucasian 29%, Hispanic 15%. **Retention and Graduation**: 77% freshmen return for sophomore year. **Faculty**: Student/faculty ratio 21:1. 884 full-time faculty, 77% hold PhDs. 74% faculty teach undergrads.

ACADEMICS
Degrees: Bachelor's, certificate, doctoral, master's, post-bachelor's certificate. **Academic Requirements**: Arts/fine arts, English (including composition), history, humanities, mathematics, sciences (biological or physical), social science. **Classes**: Most classes have 20–29 students. Most lab/discussion sections have 20–29 students. **Majors with Highest Enrollment**: Business administration and management, film/cinema studies, psychology. **Disciplines with Highest Percentage of Degrees Awarded**: Business/marketing 23%, social sciences 10%, visual and performing arts 9%, psychology 8%, English 7%. **Special Study Options**: Cooperative education program, cross-registration, distance learning, double major, dual enrollment, English as a second language (ESL), exchange student program (domestic), honors program, independent study, internships, liberal arts/career combination, student-designed major, study abroad, teacher certification program.

FACILITIES
Housing: Coed dorms, apartments for married students, apartments for single students, special housing for disabled students, special housing for international students, women-only floors. **Special Academic Facilities/Equipment**: Treganza Anthropology Museum, Moss Landing Marine Laboratories, Romberg Tiburon Center for Environmental Studies, Sierra Nevada Field Campus, Sutro Egyptian Collection. **Computers**: 100% of classrooms are wireless, 57% of public computers are PCs, 42% of public computers are Macs, 2% of public computers are UNIX, network access in dorm rooms, network access in dorm lounges, online registration, online administrative functions (other than registration), support for handheld computing, remote student-access to Web through college's connection.

CAMPUS LIFE
Activities: Choral groups, concert band, dance, drama/theater, jazz band, literary magazine, marching band, music ensembles, musical theater, opera, pep band, radio station, student government, student newspaper, student-run film society, symphony orchestra, television studio. **Organizations**: 213 registered organizations, 7 honor societies, 10 religious organizations. 13 fraternities (1% men join), 14 sororities (1% women join). **Athletics (Intercollegiate)**: *Men*: Baseball, basketball, cross-country, soccer, tennis, track/field (outdoor), wrestling. *Women*: Basketball, cross-country, soccer, softball, track/field (indoor), track/field (outdoor).

ADMISSIONS
Freshman Academic Profile: 79% from public high schools. SAT Math middle 50% range 440–560. SAT Critical Reading middle 50% range 440–560. SAT Writing middle 50% range 440–550. ACT middle 50% range 18–23. TOEFL required of all international applicants, minimum paper TOEFL 550, minimum computer TOEFL 173. **Basis for Candidate Selection**: *Very important factors considered include:* Academic GPA, rigor of secondary school record, standardized test scores. *Important factors considered include*: Geographical residence. *Other factors considered include*: Recommendation(s), state residency, talent/ability. **Freshman Admission Requirements**: High school diploma is required, and GED is accepted. *Academic units required*: 4 English, 3 math, 2 science (2 science labs), 2 foreign language, 1 social studies, 1 history, 1 visual and performing arts. *Academic units recommended*: 1 academic elective. **Freshman Admission Statistics**: 26,031 applied, 66% admitted, 19% enrolled. **Transfer Admission Requirements**: College transcript(s), statement of good standing from prior institution(s). Minimum college GPA of 2.0 required. Lowest grade transferable D. **General Admission Information**: Application fee $55. Regular notification is rolling. Non-fall registration accepted. Credit offered for CEEB Advanced Placement tests.

COSTS AND FINANCIAL AID

Annual in-state tuition $2,520. Out-of-state tuition $12,690. Room & board $9,544. Required fees $646. Average book expense $1,400. **Required Forms and Deadlines**: FAFSA. Financial aid filing deadline 3/2. **Notification of Awards**: Applicants will be notified of awards on a rolling basis beginning on or about 1/1. **Types of Aid**: *Need-based scholarships/grants*: Pell, SEOG, state scholarships/grants, private scholarships, the school's own gift aid. *Loans*: Direct Subsidized Stafford, Direct Unsubsidized Stafford, FFEL PLUS, Federal Perkins. **Student Employment**: Federal Work-Study Program available. Institutional employment available. **Financial Aid Statistics**: 33% freshmen, 36% undergrads receive need-based scholarship or grant aid. 46% freshmen, 47% undergrads receive need-based self-help aid. 24 freshmen, 71 undergrads receive athletic scholarships. 60% freshmen, 55% undergrads receive any aid.

SAN JOSE STATE UNIVERSITY

1 Washington Square, San Jose, CA 95112-0001
Phone: 408-283-7500 **E-mail**: contact@sjsu.edu **CEEB Code**: 4687
Fax: 408-924-2050 **Website**: www.sjsu.edu
Financial Aid Phone: 408-283-7500

This public school was founded in 1857. It has a 154-acre campus.

RATINGS

Admissions Selectivity Rating: 60*   **Fire Safety Rating**: 60*   **Green Rating**: 60*

STUDENTS AND FACULTY

Enrollment: 22,521. **Student Body**: 51% female, 49% male. **Retention and Graduation**: 7% freshmen graduate within 4 years.

ACADEMICS

Degrees: Bachelor's, master's. **Academic Requirements**: Arts/fine arts, English (including composition), history, humanities, mathematics, sciences (biological or physical), social science. **Classes**: Most classes have 20–29 students. Most lab/discussion sections have 10–19 students. **Disciplines with Highest Percentage of Degrees Awarded**: Business/marketing 31%, engineering 10%, visual and performing arts 8%, health professions and related sciences 7%, communications/journalism 6%, social sciences 6%. **Special Study Options**: Accelerated program, cooperative education program, cross-registration, distance learning, double major, dual enrollment, English as a second language (ESL), honors program, independent study, internships, liberal arts/career combination, student-designed major, study abroad, teacher certification program, weekend college.

FACILITIES

Housing: Coed dorms, special housing for international students, fraternity/sorority housing, cooperative housing. **Special Academic Facilities/Equipment**: Martin Luther King Jr. Library (joint with city), child development lab, Chicano Resource Center, Beethoven Studies Center, John Steinbeck Research Center, art metal foundry, Natural History Living Museum (science education), Science Resource Center, deep-sea research ship, electro-acoustical/recording studios, nuclear science and engineering labs. **Computers**: Network access in dorm rooms, online registration, online administrative functions (other than registration), remote student-access to Web through college's connection.

CAMPUS LIFE

Activities: Choral groups, dance, drama/theater, literary magazine, marching band, music ensembles, musical theater, radio station, student government, student newspaper, student-run film society. **Organizations**: 20 fraternities, 15 sororities. **Athletics (Intercollegiate)**: *Men*: Baseball, basketball, cheerleading, cross-country, football, golf, softball, swimming, volleyball, water polo. *Women*: Basketball, cheerleading, cross-country, diving, golf, gymnastics, softball, swimming, tennis, volleyball, water polo.

ADMISSIONS

Freshman Academic Profile: SAT Math middle 50% range 440–570. ACT middle 50% range 16–23. TOEFL required of all international applicants, minimum paper TOEFL 550, minimum computer TOEFL 213. **Freshman Admission Requirements**: High school diploma is required, and GED is accepted. *Academic units required*: 4 English, 3 math, 2 science (2 science labs), 2 foreign language, 1 social studies, 1 history, 1 academic elective, 1 visual and performing arts. *Academic units recommended*: 4 math, 3 science. **Freshman Admission Statistics**: 20,443 applied, 65% admitted, 21% enrolled. **General Admission Information**: Application fee $55. Regular application deadline 3/1. Regular notification 10/1. Non-fall registration accepted.

COSTS AND FINANCIAL AID

Out-of-state tuition $11,187. Required fees $3,609. Average book expense $1,242. **Required Forms and Deadlines**: FAFSA. Financial aid filing deadline 5/15. **Notification of Awards**: Applicants will be notified of awards on or about 5/1. **Types of Aid**: *Need-based scholarships/grants*: Pell, SEOG, state scholarships/grants, private scholarships, the school's own gift aid. *Loans*: FFEL Subsidized Stafford, FFEL Unsubsidized Stafford, FFEL PLUS, Federal Perkins, college/university loans from institutional funds. **Financial Aid Statistics**: 33% freshmen, 35% undergrads receive need-based scholarship or grant aid. 15% freshmen, 20% undergrads receive need-based self-help aid. 10 undergrads receive athletic scholarships.

SANTA CLARA UNIVERSITY

Best 368

500 El Camino Real, Santa Clara, CA 95053
Phone: 408-554-4700 **E-mail**: Ugadmissions@scu.edu **CEEB Code**: 4851
Fax: 408-554-5255 **Website**: www.scu.edu
Financial Aid Phone: 408-554-4505

This private school, affiliated with the Roman Catholic Church, was founded in 1851. It has a 104-acre campus.

RATINGS

Admissions Selectivity Rating: 89   **Fire Safety Rating**: 94   **Green Rating**: 96

STUDENTS AND FACULTY

Enrollment: 4,592. **Student Body**: 55% female, 45% male, 36% out-of-state, 3% international (34 countries represented). African American 3%, Asian 18%, Caucasian 55%, Hispanic 13%. **Retention and Graduation**: 94% freshmen return for sophomore year. 79% freshmen graduate within 4 years. 32% grads go on to further study within 1 year. **Faculty**: Student/faculty ratio 12:1. 476 full-time faculty, 91% hold PhDs. 82% faculty teach undergrads.

ACADEMICS

Degrees: Bachelor's, doctoral, first professional certificate, first professional, master's, post-bachelor's certificate, post-master's certificate. **Academic Requirements**: Arts/fine arts, computer literacy, English (including composition), ethics, foreign languages, history, humanities, mathematics, philosophy, sciences (biological or physical), social science. **Classes**: Most classes have 20–29 students. Most lab/discussion sections have 10–19 students. **Majors with Highest Enrollment**: Communications and media studies, finance, psychology. **Disciplines with Highest Percentage of Degrees Awarded**: Business/marketing 32%, social sciences 13%, psychology 9%, engineering 8%, communications/journalism 7%. **Special Study Options**: Cooperative education program, double major, exchange student program (domestic), honors program, independent study, internships, student-designed major, study abroad, teacher certification program.

FACILITIES

Housing: Coed dorms, apartments for single students. **Special Academic Facilities/Equipment**: Art and history museum; mission church; theater; media lab; retail management institute; computer design center, engineering labs; Markkula Center for Applied Ethics, center for science, technology, and society. **Computers**: 5% of classrooms are wired, 10% of classrooms are wireless, 90% of public computers are PCs, 6% of public computers are Macs, 4% of public computers are UNIX, network access in dorm rooms, network access in dorm lounges, online registration, online administrative functions (other than registration), support for handheld computing, remote student-access to Web through college's connection.

CAMPUS LIFE

Activities: Choral groups, dance, drama/theater, jazz band, literary magazine, music ensembles, musical theater, opera, pep band, radio station, student government, student newspaper, symphony orchestra, yearbook. **Organizations**: 85 registered organizations, 26 honor societies, 5 religious organizations. **Athletics (Intercollegiate)**: *Men*: Baseball, basketball, crew/rowing, cross-country, golf, soccer, tennis, track/field (outdoor), water polo. *Women*: Basketball, crew/rowing, cross-country, golf, soccer, softball, tennis, track/field (outdoor), volleyball, water polo. Environmental Initiatives: Designing new buildings for energy efficiency (new library will consume the same amount of

The Princeton Review's Complete Book of Colleges

energy as the previous library, though twice the size), the University is increasing its support of and dependence on renewable energy. University installed a 50-kilowatt photovoltaic (PV) system, projected to produce an average of 80,300 kilowatt-hours annually. SCU is also the second largest contributor to Silicon Valley Power's (SVP) Green Power program.

ADMISSIONS

Freshman Academic Profile: 45% from public high schools. SAT Math middle 50% range 570–670. SAT Critical Reading middle 50% range 540–650. ACT middle 50% range 24–29. TOEFL required of all international applicants, minimum paper TOEFL 550, minimum computer TOEFL 213. **Basis for Candidate Selection**: *Very important factors considered include:* Academic GPA, application essay, recommendation(s), rigor of secondary school record. *Important factors considered include:* Extracurricular activities, racial/ethnic status, standardized test scores, talent/ability, volunteer work. *Other factors considered include:* Alumni/ae relation, character/personal qualities, class rank, first generation, geographical residence, level of applicant's interest, religious affiliation/commitment, state residency, work experience. **Freshman Admission Requirements**: High school diploma is required, and GED is accepted. *Academic units required:* 4 English, 3 math, 2 science, 2 foreign language, 3 social studies, 1 academic elective. *Academic units recommended:* 4 English, 4 math, 3 science, 3 foreign language, 3 social studies, 1 academic elective. **Freshman Admission Statistics**: 8,670 applied, 66% admitted, 23% enrolled. **Transfer Admission Requirements**: College transcript(s), essay or persojnal statement. Lowest grade transferable C. **General Admission Information**: Application fee $55. Regular application deadline 1/7. Regular notification is rolling. Nonfall registration not accepted. Admission may be deferred for a maximum of 1 year. Credit and/or placement offered for CEEB Advanced Placement tests.

COSTS AND FINANCIAL AID

Annual tuition $33,000. Room and board $10,644. Average book expense $1,386. **Required Forms and Deadlines**: FAFSA, CSS/Financial Aid PROFILE. Financial aid filing deadline 2/1. **Notification of Awards**: Applicants will be notified of awards on a rolling basis beginning on or about 11/6. **Types of Aid**: *Need-based scholarships/grants:* Pell, SEOG, state scholarships/grants, private scholarships, the school's own gift aid. *Loans:* Direct Subsidized Stafford, Direct Unsubsidized Stafford, Direct PLUS, Federal Perkins, Private alternative loans. **Financial Aid Statistics**: 28% freshmen, 33% undergrads receive need-based scholarship or grant aid. 23% freshmen, 25% undergrads receive need-based self-help aid. 54 freshmen, 197 undergrads receive athletic scholarships. 83% freshmen, 69% undergrads receive any aid.

SARAH LAWRENCE COLLEGE

Best 368

1 Mead Way, Bronxville, NY 10708-5999
Phone: 914-395-2510 **E-mail**: slcadmit@slc.edu **CEEB Code**: 2810
Fax: 914-395-2676 **Website**: www.sarahlawrence.edu **ACT Code**: 2904
Financial Aid Phone: 914-395 2570

This private school was founded in 1926. It has a 41-acre campus.

RATINGS

Admissions Selectivity Rating: 89   **Fire Safety Rating**: 81   **Green Rating**: 86

STUDENTS AND FACULTY

Enrollment: 1,306. **Student Body**: 74% female, 26% male, 77% out-of-state, 2% international (32 countries represented). African American 6%, Asian 5%, Caucasian 72%, Hispanic 5%. **Retention and Graduation**: 81% freshmen return for sophomore year. 70% freshmen graduate within 4 years. **Faculty**: Student/faculty ratio 6:1. 199 full-time faculty. 87% faculty teach undergrads.

ACADEMICS

Degrees: Bachelor's, certificate, master's. **Academic Requirements**: 120 credit hours and meet distribution requirements in 3 of 4 areas: History and social sciences, natural sciences and math, humanities, creative and performing arts. **Classes**: Most classes have 10–19 students. **Disciplines with Highest Percentage of Degrees Awarded**: Liberal arts/general studies 100%. **Special Study Options**: Double major, exchange student program (domestic), independent study, internships, student-designed major, study abroad, teacher

certification program, 3–2 program BA/MSEd art of teaching. Sarah Lawrence College has no formal majors, but students may concentrate in subject areas. All students design their own educational programs (with faculty advisement), so the equivalent of a double major is available.

FACILITIES

Housing: Coed dorms, men's dorms, women's dorms. **Special Academic Facilities/Equipment**: Performing arts center including a concert hall, dance studios, and theaters; visual arts center including studios; gallery; film theater; sound stage; visual resources library; music building including music library; science center; early childhood center; greenhouse. **Computers**: 80% of public computers are PCs, 20% of public computers are Macs, network access in dorm rooms, online administrative functions (other than registration), remote student-access to Web through college's connection.

CAMPUS LIFE

Activities: Choral groups, dance, drama/theater, jazz band, literary magazine, music ensembles, musical theater, radio station, student government, student newspaper, student-run film society, symphony orchestra, yearbook. **Organizations**: 56 registered organizations, 3 religious organizations. **Athletics (Intercollegiate)**: *Men:* Basketball, crew/rowing, equestrian sports, tennis. *Women:* Crew/rowing, equestrian sports, softball, swimming, tennis, volleyball.

ADMISSIONS

Freshman Academic Profile: 33% in top 10% of high school class, 70% in top 25% of high school class, 97% in top 50% of high school class. 54% from public high schools. TOEFL required of all international applicants, minimum paper TOEFL 600, minimum computer TOEFL 250. **Basis for Candidate Selection**: *Very important factors considered include:* Application essay, recommendation(s), rigor of secondary school record. *Important factors considered include:* Academic GPA, character/personal qualities, extracurricular activities, talent/ability. *Other factors considered include:* Alumni/ae relation, class rank, first generation, geographical residence, interview, level of applicant's interest, racial/ethnic status, volunteer work, work experience. **Freshman Admission Requirements**: High school diploma is required, and GED is accepted. *Academic units required:* 4 English, 2 math, 2 science, 2 foreign language, 2 history. *Academic units recommended:* 4 math, 4 science, 4 foreign language, 4 history. **Freshman Admission Statistics**: 2,727 applied, 46% admitted, 30% enrolled. **Transfer Admission Requirements**: High school transcript, college transcript(s), essay or personal statement, statement of good standing from prior institution(s). Minimum college GPA of 3.0 required. Lowest grade transferable C. **General Admission Information**: Application fee $60. Early decision application deadline 11/15. Regular application deadline 1/1. Regular notification 4/1. Non-fall registration not accepted. Admission may be deferred for a maximum of 1 year. Credit offered for CEEB Advanced Placement tests.

COSTS AND FINANCIAL AID

Annual tuition $37,230. Room and board $12,720. Required fees $860. **Required Forms and Deadlines**: FAFSA, CSS/Financial Aid PROFILE, state aid form, Noncustodial PROFILE. Financial aid filing deadline 2/1. **Notification of Awards**: Applicants will be notified of awards on or about 4/1. **Types of Aid**: *Need-based scholarships/grants:* Pell, SEOG, state scholarships/grants, private scholarships, the school's own gift aid. *Loans:* FFEL Subsidized Stafford, FFEL Unsubsidized Stafford, FFEL PLUS, Federal Perkins. **Financial Aid Statistics**: 45% freshmen, 45% undergrads receive need-based scholarship or grant aid. 48% freshmen, 47% undergrads receive need-based self-help aid. 50% freshmen, 52% undergrads receive any aid. Highest amount earned per year from on-campus jobs $1,500.

SAVANNAH COLLEGE OF ART AND DESIGN

PO Box 3146, Savannah, GA 31402-3146
Phone: 912-525-5100 **E-mail**: admission@scad.edu **CEEB Code**: 5631
Fax: 912-525-5986 **Website**: www.scad.edu **ACT Code**: 0855
Financial Aid Phone: 912-525-6104

This private school was founded in 1978.

RATINGS

Admissions Selectivity Rating: 60*   **Fire Safety Rating**: 60*   **Green Rating**: 63

STUDENTS AND FACULTY

Enrollment: 6,835. **Student Body**: 53% female, 47% male, 80% out-of-state, 4% international (77 countries represented). African American 6%, Asian 3%, Caucasian 44%, Hispanic 4%. **Retention and Graduation**: 81% freshmen return for sophomore year. 43% freshmen graduate within 4 years. 10% grads go on to further study within 1 year. 10% grads pursue arts and sciences degrees. **Faculty**: Student/faculty ratio 16:1. 409 full-time faculty, 75% hold PhDs. 98% faculty teach undergrads.

ACADEMICS

Degrees: Bachelor's, certificate, master's, post-bachelor's certificate. **Academic Requirements**: Arts/fine arts, computer literacy, English (including composition), humanities, mathematics, social science. **Classes**: Most classes have 10–19 students. **Majors with Highest Enrollment**: Digital communications and media/multimedia, graphic design, photography. **Disciplines with Highest Percentage of Degrees Awarded**: Visual and performing arts 74%, communication technologies 16%, architecture 7%, communications/journalism 2%, interdisciplinary studies 1%. **Special Study Options**: Distance learning, double major, dual enrollment, English as a second language (ESL), independent study, internships, study abroad, summer quarter programs in New York City and Europe. Apprenticeships with artists or designers and internships with museums, agencies, media production companies, architectural firms, and other companies in the United States or abroad.

FACILITIES

Housing: Coed dorms, apartments for single students, themed housing, accommodations for disabled students are handled on an individual basis. **Special Academic Facilities/Equipment**: Art galleries; computer, video, photography, and design labs; SCAD Museum of Art. **Computers**: 25% of classrooms are wireless, 90% of public computers are PCs, 10% of public computers are Macs, network access in dorm rooms, network access in dorm lounges, online registration, online administrative functions (other than registration), support for handheld computing, remote student-access to Web through college's connection.

CAMPUS LIFE

Activities: Choral groups, dance, drama/theater, music ensembles, musical theater, radio station, student government, student newspaper, television station. **Organizations**: 45 registered organizations, 3 honor societies, 3 religious organizations. **Athletics (Intercollegiate)**: *Men*: Baseball, basketball, cheerleading, crew/rowing, cross-country, equestrian sports, golf, soccer, swimming, tennis. *Women*: Basketball, cheerleading, crew/rowing, cross-country, equestrian sports, golf, soccer, softball, swimming, tennis, volleyball.

ADMISSIONS

Freshman Academic Profile: SAT Math middle 50% range 480–590. SAT Critical Reading middle 50% range 500–600. SAT Writing middle 50% range 480–590. ACT middle 50% range 21–26. TOEFL required of all international applicants, minimum paper TOEFL 500, minimum computer TOEFL 133. **Basis for Candidate Selection**: *Very important factors considered include*: Academic GPA, class rank, interview, level of applicant's interest, recommendation(s), rigor of secondary school record, talent/ability. *Important factors considered include*: Character/personal qualities, standardized test scores. *Other factors considered include*: Alumni/ae relation, application essay, extracurricular activities. **Freshman Admission Requirements**: High school diploma is required, and GED is accepted. **Freshman Admission Statistics**: 5,701 applied, 58% admitted, 45% enrolled. **Transfer Admission Requirements**: College transcript(s), essay or personal statement. Minimum college GPA of 2.0 required. Lowest grade transferable.C. **General Admission Information**: Application fee $50. Regular notification is ongoing. Non-fall registration accepted. Admission may be deferred for a maximum of 2 quarters. Credit and/or placement offered for CEEB Advanced Placement tests.

COSTS AND FINANCIAL AID

Annual tuition $25,965. Room and board $10,360. Average book expense $1,560. **Required Forms and Deadlines**: FAFSA, institution's own financial aid form, state aid form. Financial aid filing deadline 2/15. **Notification of Awards**: Applicants will be notified of awards on a rolling basis beginning on or about 4/1. **Types of Aid**: *Need-based scholarships/grants*: SEOG, state scholarships/grants, private scholarships, the school's own gift aid. *Loans*: Direct Subsidized Stafford, Direct Unsubsidized Stafford, Direct PLUS, Federal Perkins. **Student Employment**: Federal Work-Study Program available. Institutional employment available. Off-campus job opportunities are excellent. **Financial Aid Statistics**: 13% freshmen, 18% undergrads receive need-based scholarship or grant aid. 48% freshmen, 49% undergrads receive need-based self-help aid. 37 freshmen, 219 undergrads receive athletic scholarships. 52% freshmen, 52% undergrads receive any aid. Highest amount earned per year from on-campus jobs $2,500.

See page 1364.

College Station, PO Box 20209, Savannah, GA 31404
Phone: 912-356-2181 **E-mail**: SSUAdmissions@savstate.edu **CEEB Code**: 5609
Fax: 912-356-2256 **Website**: www.savstate.edu **ACT Code**: 0858
Financial Aid Phone: 912-356-2253

This public school was founded in 1890. It has a 165-acre campus.

RATINGS

Admissions Selectivity Rating: 60*   **Fire Safety Rating**: 60*   **Green Rating**: 60*

STUDENTS AND FACULTY

Enrollment: 2,635. **Student Body**: 15% out-of-state. African American 96%, Caucasian 3%. **Retention and Graduation**: 7% grads go on to further study within 1 year. 7% grads pursue arts and sciences degrees.

ACADEMICS

Degrees: Bachelor's, master's. **Special Study Options**: Foreign exchange study abroad program(s) in England, France, Germany, Italy, and Spain; internships; off-campus summer quarter study programs in New York City and Europe. Undergrads may take grad level classes. Apprenticeships with artists or designers and internships with museums, agencies, media production companies, architectural firms, and other companies in the United States or abroad.

FACILITIES

Housing: Coed dorms, men's dorms, women's dorms, fraternity/sorority housing.

CAMPUS LIFE

Organizations: 8 honor societies, 3 religious organizations. 5 fraternities (38% men join), 4 sororities (39% women join).

ADMISSIONS

Freshman Academic Profile: 12% in top 10% of high school class, 39% in top 25% of high school class, 77% in top 50% of high school class. 94% from public high schools. **Freshman Admission Requirements**: High school diploma is required, and GED is accepted. *Academic units recommended*: 4 English, 3 math, 3 science, 2 foreign language, 3 social studies, 3 academic electives. **Transfer Admission Requirements**: Minimum college GPA of 2.0 required. Lowest grade transferable D. **General Admission Information**: Early decision application deadline 3/1. Regular application deadline 9/1. Regular notification is rolling. Non-fall registration accepted. Common Application not accepted. Credit and/or placement offered for CEEB Advanced Placement tests.

COSTS AND FINANCIAL AID

Comprehensive fee $5,100. Room & board $3,495. Average book expense $750. **Required Forms and Deadlines**: FAFSA, institution's own financial aid form. **Types of Aid**: *Need-based scholarships/grants*: State scholarships/grants. *Loans*: FFEL Subsidized Stafford, FFEL PLUS. **Student Employment**: Off-campus job opportunities are good.

101 Murray Street, New York, NY 10007
Phone: 212-815-9232 **E-mail**: admissions@tci.edu
Fax: 212-964-3381 **Website**: www.tci.edu
Financial Aid Phone: 212-815-9222

This private school was founded in 1901.

RATINGS

Admissions Selectivity Rating: 60*   **Fire Safety Rating**: 60*   **Green Rating**: 60*

STUDENTS AND FACULTY

Enrollment: 181. **Student Body**: 49% female, 51% male, 20% international (17 countries represented). African American 14%, Asian 7%, Caucasian 49%, Hispanic 9%. **Retention and Graduation**: 94% freshmen return for sophomore year. 20% freshmen graduate within 4 years. **Faculty**: 100% faculty teach undergrads.

ACADEMICS

Academic Requirements: English (including composition), foreign languages, history. **Special Study Options**: Distance learning, double major, English as a second language (ESL), internships, weekend college.

FACILITIES

Housing: Coed dorms.

CAMPUS LIFE

Activities: Drama/theater, student government, student newspaper. **Organizations**: 10 honor societies, 1 religious organization. 1 fraternity.

ADMISSIONS

Freshman Academic Profile: TOEFL required of all international applicants, minimum paper TOEFL 550. **Basis for Candidate Selection**: *Very important factors considered include:* Rigor of secondary school record, standardized test scores. *Important factors considered include*: Application essay, extracurricular activities, interview, recommendation(s). *Other factors considered include*: Alumni/ae relation, character/personal qualities, talent/ability, volunteer work, work experience. **Freshman Admission Requirements**: High school diploma is required, and GED is accepted. *Academic units required*: 4 English, 3 math, 3 science (1 science lab), 1 foreign language, 1 social studies, 1 history, 4 academic electives. *Academic units recommended*: 3 math. **Freshman Admission Statistics**: 62 applied, 60% admitted, 27% enrolled. **Transfer Admission Requirements**: High school transcript, college transcript(s), essay or personal statement, interview. Minimum college GPA of 2.5 required. Lowest grade transferable C. **General Admission Information**: Application fee $30. Early decision application deadline 12/1. Regular application deadline 8/1. Regular notification is rolling. Non-fall registration accepted. Common Application accepted. Credit offered for CEEB Advanced Placement tests.

COSTS AND FINANCIAL AID

Annual tuition $14,252. Room & board $9,140. Required fees $360. Average book expense $900. **Required Forms and Deadlines**: FAFSA, institution's own financial aid form, state aid form. **Types of Aid**: *Need-based scholarships/grants*: Pell, SEOG, state scholarships/grants, private scholarships, the school's own gift aid, Co-op Education Sponsorship tuition payments. *Loans*: FFEL Subsidized Stafford, FFEL Unsubsidized Stafford, FFEL PLUS, Federal Perkins, college/university loans from institutional funds, private loans. **Student Employment**: Institutional employment available. Off-campus job opportunities are excellent. **Financial Aid Statistics**: 40% freshmen, 42% undergrads receive need-based scholarship or grant aid. 47% freshmen, 37% undergrads receive need-based self-help aid. Highest amount earned per year from on-campus jobs $4,500.

SCHOOL OF THE ART INSTITUTE OF CHICAGO

37 South Wabash Avenue, Chicago, IL 60603
Phone: 312-629-6100 **E-mail**: admiss@saic.edu **CEEB Code**: 1713
Fax: 312-629-6101 **Website**: www.saic.edu **ACT Code**: 1136
Financial Aid Phone: 312-629-6600

This private school was founded in 1866.

RATINGS

Admissions Selectivity Rating: 60*   **Fire Safety Rating**: 84   **Green Rating**: 60*

STUDENTS AND FACULTY

Enrollment: 2,194. **Student Body**: 65% female, 35% male, 70% out-of-state, 17% international (21 countries represented). African American 3%, Asian 12%, Caucasian 58%, Hispanic 8%. **Retention and Graduation**: 80% freshmen return for sophomore year. 40% freshmen graduate within 4 years. **Faculty**: Student/faculty ratio 11:1. 132 full-time faculty, 88% hold PhDs.

ACADEMICS

Degrees: Bachelor's, master's, post-bachelor's certificate. **Academic Requirements**: Arts/fine arts, art history, English (including composition), humanities, sciences (biological or physical), social science. **Classes**: Most classes have 10–19 students. **Disciplines with Highest Percentage of Degrees Awarded**: Visual and performing arts 99%. **Special Study Options**: Cooperative education program, cross-registration, double major, dual enrollment, English as a second language (ESL), exchange student program (domestic), credit/no credit grading option, independent study, internships, multi-disciplinary curriculum, student-designed major, study abroad, teacher

certification program, 6 credit off-campus requirement.

FACILITIES

Housing: Coed dorms, special housing for disabled students. **Special Academic Facilities/Equipment**: The School is directly affiliated with The Art Institute of Chicago. The Gene Siskel Film Center, fashion resource center, John M. Flaxman Library and Screening Room, galleries (Betty Rymer, Gallery 2 and project space, student union galleries), Joan Flasch Artists' Book Collection, Roger Brown Resources, video data bank, poetry center, visiting artists' program, media center. **Computers**: 15% of classrooms are wired, 75% of classrooms are wireless, 1% of public computers are PCs, 99% of public computers are Macs, network access in dorm rooms, network access in dorm lounges, online registration, online administrative functions (other than registration), remote student-access to Web through college's connection. Undergraduates are required to own a computer.

CAMPUS LIFE

Activities: Dance, drama/theater, literary magazine, music ensembles, radio station, student government, student newspaper, student-run film society. **Organizations**: 37 registered organizations, 2 religious organizations.

ADMISSIONS

Freshman Academic Profile: TOEFL required of all international applicants, minimum paper TOEFL 550, minimum computer TOEFL 213. **Basis for Candidate Selection**: *Very important factors considered include:* Application essay, character/personal qualities, level of applicant's interest, recommendation(s), talent/ability. *Important factors considered include*: Academic GPA, class rank, extracurricular activities, interview, racial/ethnic status, standardized test scores. *Other factors considered include*: Alumni/ae relation, geographical residence, rigor of secondary school record, state residency, volunteer work, work experience. **Freshman Admission Requirements**: High school diploma is required, and GED is accepted. **Freshman Admission Statistics**: 1,769 applied, 81% admitted, 31% enrolled. **Transfer Admission Requirements**: High school transcript, college transcript(s), essay or personal statement. Lowest grade transferable C. **General Admission Information**: Application fee $65. Regular application deadline 3/15. Regular notification is rolling. Non-fall registration accepted. Admission may be deferred for a maximum of 1 year. Credit offered for CEEB Advanced Placement tests.

COSTS AND FINANCIAL AID

Annual tuition $30,750. Room and board $8,900. Average book expense $2,340. **Required Forms and Deadlines**: FAFSA. Financial aid filing deadline 3/15. **Notification of Awards**: Applicants will be notified of awards on a rolling basis beginning on or about 3/1. **Types of Aid**: *Need-based scholarships/grants*: Pell, SEOG, state scholarships/grants, private scholarships, the school's own gift aid. *Loans*: FFEL Subsidized Stafford, FFEL Unsubsidized Stafford, FFEL PLUS, Federal Perkins, alternative/private loans. **Financial Aid Statistics**: 39% freshmen, 48% undergrads receive need-based scholarship or grant aid. 46% freshmen, 54% undergrads receive need-based self-help aid.

See page 1366.

SCHOOL OF THE MUSEUM OF FINE ARTS

230 The Fenway, Boston, MA 02115
Phone: 617-369-3626 **E-mail**: admissions@smfa.edu **CEEB Code**: 3794
Fax: 617-369-4264 **Website**: www.smfa.edu **ACT Code**: 1895
Financial Aid Phone: 617-369-3645

This private school was founded in 1876. It has a 14-acre campus.

RATINGS

Admissions Selectivity Rating: 60*   **Fire Safety Rating**: 60*   **Green Rating**: 60*

STUDENTS AND FACULTY

Enrollment: 620. **Student Body**: 65% female, 35% male, 63% out-of-state, 7% international (32 countries represented). African American 2%, Asian 3%, Caucasian 70%, Hispanic 5%. **Retention and Graduation**: 79% freshmen return for sophomore year. 34% freshmen graduate within 4 years. **Faculty**: Student/faculty ratio 9:1. 51 full-time faculty, 67% hold PhDs. 100% faculty teach undergrads.

ACADEMICS

Degrees: Bachelor's, certificate, diploma, master's, post-bachelor's certificate. **Academic Requirements**: Arts/fine arts, art history, English (including composition), foreign languages, humanities, sciences (biological or physical), social science. Culture can be substituted for language. Mathematics can be substituted for science/technology. Diploma students are only required to take studio art, but are strongly encouraged to take art history. **Classes**: Most classes have 10–19 students. **Majors with Highest Enrollment**: Art teacher education, fine arts and art studies, fine/studio arts. **Disciplines with Highest Percentage of Degrees Awarded**: Visual and performing arts 89%, education 3%. **Special Study Options**: Combined Degree (BFA or BFE + BS or BA), cross-registration, double major, English as a second language (ESL), exchange student program (domestic), independent study, internships, liberal arts/career combination, student-designed major, study abroad, teacher certification program. All-studio elective program (diploma).

FACILITIES

Housing: Coed dorms, professional off-campus housing assistance. **Special Academic Facilities/Equipment**: Museum of Fine Arts, Boston, art galleries. **Computers**: 5% of public computers are PCs, 95% of public computers are Macs, network access in dorm rooms, network access in dorm lounges, online registration, online administrative functions (other than registration), remote student-access to Web through college's connection.

CAMPUS LIFE

Activities: Student government, student-run film society. **Organizations**: 10 registered organizations

ADMISSIONS

Freshman Academic Profile: SAT Math middle 50% range 480–590. SAT Critical Reading middle 50% range 520–635. SAT Writing middle 50% range 493–600. ACT middle 50% range 19.7–26.3. TOEFL required of all international applicants, minimum paper TOEFL 550, minimum computer TOEFL 213. **Basis for Candidate Selection**: *Very important factors considered include*: Rigor of secondary school record, talent/ability. *Important factors considered include*: Academic GPA, application essay, interview, level of applicant's interest, standardized test scores. *Other factors considered include*: Alumni/ae relation, character/personal qualities, class rank, extracurricular activities, first generation, geographical residence, recommendation(s), volunteer work, work experience. **Freshman Admission Requirements**: High school diploma is required, and GED is accepted. **Freshman Admission Statistics**: 918 applied, 77% admitted, 16% enrolled. **Transfer Admission Requirements**: College transcript(s), essay or personal statement. Minimum college GPA of 2.0 required. Lowest grade transferable C-. **General Admission Information**: Application fee $65. Regular notification is rolling. Non-fall registration accepted. Admission may be deferred for a maximum of 1 year. Neither credit nor placement offered for CEEB Advanced Placement tests.

COSTS AND FINANCIAL AID

Annual tuition $26,950. Required fees $2,810. Average book expense $1,500. **Required Forms and Deadlines**: FAFSA, institution's own financial aid form. Financial aid filing deadline 3/15. **Notification of Awards**: Applicants will be notified of awards on a rolling basis beginning on or about 4/1. **Types of Aid**: *Need-based scholarships/grants*: Pell, SEOG, state scholarships/grants, private scholarships, the school's own gift aid. *Loans*: FFEL Subsidized Stafford, FFEL Unsubsidized Stafford, FFEL PLUS, state loans. **Financial Aid Statistics**: 58% freshmen, 67% undergrads receive need-based scholarship or grant aid. 54% freshmen, 60% undergrads receive need-based self-help aid. 57% freshmen, 66% undergrads receive any aid. Highest amount earned per year from on-campus jobs $3,000.

See page 1368.

SCHOOL OF VISUAL ARTS

209 East Twenty-third Street, New York, NY 10010
Phone: 212-592-2100 **E-mail**: admissions@sva.edu **CEEB Code**: 2835
Fax: 212-592-2116 **Website**: www.schoolofvisualarts.edu **ACT Code**: 2895
Financial Aid Phone: 212-592-2030

This proprietary school was founded in 1947. It has a 14-acre campus.

RATINGS

Admissions Selectivity Rating: 60*   **Fire Safety Rating**: 98   **Green Rating**: 62

STUDENTS AND FACULTY

Enrollment: 3,093. **Student Body**: 53% female, 47% male, 48% out-of-state, 14% international (43 countries represented). African American 4%, Asian 13%,

Caucasian 56%, Hispanic 10%. **Retention and Graduation**: 85% freshmen return for sophomore year. 58% freshmen graduate within 4 years. 10% grads go on to further study within 1 year. 4% grads pursue arts and sciences degrees. **Faculty**: Student/faculty ratio 4:1. 102 full-time faculty, 55% hold PhDs. 87% faculty teach undergrads.

ACADEMICS

Degrees: Bachelor's, master's. **Academic Requirements**: Arts/fine arts, computer literacy, English (including composition), history, humanities, mathematics, philosophy, sciences (biological or physical), social science. **Classes**: Most classes have 10–19 students. **Majors with Highest Enrollment**: Film/video and photographic arts, graphic design, photography. **Disciplines with Highest Percentage of Degrees Awarded**: Visual and performing arts 100%. **Special Study Options**: English as a second language (ESL), exchange student program (domestic), honors program, internships, liberal arts/career combination, teacher certification program.

FACILITIES

Housing: Coed dorms, women's dorms. **Special Academic Facilities/ Equipment**: Art museum, student galleries, animation studio, amphitheater. **Computers**: 25% of classrooms are wired, 100% of classrooms are wireless, 5% of public computers are PCs, 95% of public computers are Macs, network access in dorm rooms, network access in dorm lounges, online registration, online administrative functions (other than registration), remote student-access to Web through college's connection.

CAMPUS LIFE

Activities: Literary magazine, radio station, student government, student newspaper, student-run film society, yearbook. **Organizations**: 21 registered organizations, 3 religious organizations. Environmental Initiatives: Recycle. SVA also recycles batteries used in electronic equipment as well as computers, monitors printers and other consumer electronics. SVA monitors waste water that comes from areas like the Photo Labs, Printmaking and the Sculpture Labs. The waste water is tested to make sure that it is in compliance with all city, state and federal regulations.

ADMISSIONS

Freshman Academic Profile: 60% from public high schools. SAT Math middle 50% range 440–560. SAT Critical Reading middle 50% range 460–580. SAT Writing middle 50% range 458–570. ACT middle 50% range 20–25. TOEFL required of all international applicants, minimum paper TOEFL 550, minimum computer TOEFL 213. **Basis for Candidate Selection**: *Very important factors considered include:* Academic GPA, application essay, interview, level of applicant's interest, rigor of secondary school record, talent/ability. *Important factors considered include*: Character/personal qualities. *Other factors considered include*: Alumni/ae relation, extracurricular activities, recommendation(s), standardized test scores, volunteer work, work experience. **Freshman Admission Requirements**: High school diploma is required, and GED is accepted. *Academic units recommended*: 4 English, 4 social studies, 4 history, 2 art. **Freshman Admission Statistics**: 2,530 applied, 69% admitted, 38% enrolled. **Transfer Admission Requirements**: College transcript(s), essay or personal statement, statement of good standing from prior institution(s). Minimum college GPA of 2.0 required. Lowest grade transferable C. **General Admission Information**: Application fee $50. Early decision application deadline 12/1. Regular notification is rolling. Non-fall registration not accepted. Admission may be deferred for a maximum of 1 year. Credit offered for CEEB Advanced Placement tests.

COSTS AND FINANCIAL AID

Annual tuition $23,520. Room and board $11,350. Average book expense $2,100. **Required Forms and Deadlines**: FAFSA, state aid form. Financial aid filing deadline 3/1. **Notification of Awards**: Applicants will be notified of awards on a rolling basis beginning on or about 2/15. **Types of Aid**: *Need-based scholarships/grants*: Pell, SEOG, state scholarships/grants, private scholarships, the school's own gift aid, alternate loans. *Loans*: FFEL Subsidized Stafford, FFEL Unsubsidized Stafford, Federal Perkins. **Student Employment**: Federal Work-Study Program available. Off-campus job opportunities are fair. **Financial Aid Statistics**: 35% freshmen, 37% undergrads receive need-based scholarship or grant aid. 54% freshmen, 55% undergrads receive need-based self-help aid. 57% freshmen, 56% undergrads receive any aid. Highest amount earned per year from on-campus jobs $5,000.

See page 1370.

SCHREINER UNIVERSITY

2100 Memorial Boulevard, Kerrville, TX 78028-5697
Phone: 830-792-7217 **E-mail:** admissions@schreiner.edu **CEEB Code:** 6647
Fax: 830-792-7226 **Website:** www.schreiner.edu **ACT Code:** 4168
Financial Aid Phone: 830-792-7230

This private school, affiliated with the Presbyterian Church, was founded in 1923. It has a 175-acre campus.

RATINGS
Admissions Selectivity Rating: 78 **Fire Safety Rating:** 60* **Green Rating:** 60*

STUDENTS AND FACULTY
Enrollment: 876. **Student Body:** 58% female, 42% male, 2% out-of-state. African American 3%, Asian 2%, Caucasian 73%, Hispanic 20%. **Retention and Graduation:** 66% freshmen return for sophomore year. 24% freshmen graduate within 4 years. 7% grads go on to further study within 1 year. 1% grads pursue arts and sciences degrees. **Faculty:** Student/faculty ratio 14:1. 52 full-time faculty, 69% hold PhDs. 99% faculty teach undergrads.

ACADEMICS
Degrees: Associate, bachelor's, certificate, master's, post-bachelor's certificate, post-master's certificate. **Academic Requirements:** Arts/fine arts, computer literacy, English (including composition), foreign languages, history, humanities, mathematics, philosophy, sciences (biological or physical), social science. **Classes:** Most classes have 10–19 students. Most lab/discussion sections have 20–29 students. **Majors with Highest Enrollment:** Business administration/management, kinesiology and exercise science, psychology. **Disciplines with Highest Percentage of Degrees Awarded:** Business/marketing 24%, education 18%, psychology 15%, biological/life sciences 9%, interdisciplinary studies 8%. **Special Study Options:** Accelerated program, double major, dual enrollment, honors program, independent study, internships, liberal arts/career combination, student-designed major, study abroad, teacher certification program, weekend college.

FACILITIES
Housing: Coed dorms, apartments for married students, apartments for single students. **Computers:** 93% of public computers are PCs, 7% of public computers are Macs, network access in dorm rooms, network access in dorm lounges, remote student-access to Web through college's connection.

CAMPUS LIFE
Activities: Choral groups, dance, drama/theater, literary magazine, music ensembles, musical theater, pep band, student government, student newspaper, symphony orchestra. **Organizations:** 35 registered organizations, 5 honor societies, 6 religious organizations. 2 fraternities, 2 sororities. **Athletics (Intercollegiate):** *Men:* Baseball, basketball, golf, soccer, tennis. *Women:* Basketball, cheerleading, golf, soccer, softball, tennis, volleyball.

ADMISSIONS
Freshman Academic Profile: 11% in top 10% of high school class, 40% in top 25% of high school class, 72% in top 50% of high school class. 87% from public high schools. SAT Math middle 50% range 450–560. SAT Critical Reading middle 50% range 430–540. SAT Writing middle 50% range 420–430. ACT middle 50% range 18–23. TOEFL required of all international applicants, minimum paper TOEFL 550, minimum computer TOEFL 213. **Basis for Candidate Selection:** *Important factors considered include:* Academic GPA, application essay, class rank, interview, rigor of secondary school record, standardized test scores. *Other factors considered include:* Character/personal qualities, extracurricular activities, level of applicant's interest, recommendation(s), talent/ability, volunteer work, work experience. **Freshman Admission Requirements:** High school diploma is required, and GED is accepted. *Academic units recommended:* 4 English, 3 math, 2 science (2 science labs), 2 social studies. **Freshman Admission Statistics:** 872 applied, 58% admitted, 50% enrolled. **Transfer Admission Requirements:** College transcript(s). Minimum college GPA of 2.0 required. **General Admission Information:** Application fee $25. Regular application deadline 8/1. Non-fall registration accepted. Admission may be deferred for a maximum of 1 year. Credit and/or placement offered for CEEB Advanced Placement tests.

COSTS AND FINANCIAL AID
Annual tuition $16,408. Room and board $7,910. Required fees $300. Average book expense $1,000. **Required Forms and Deadlines:** FAFSA. Financial aid filing deadline 8/1. **Notification of Awards:** Applicants will be notified of awards on or about 2/1. **Types of Aid:** *Need-based scholarships/grants:* Pell, SEOG, state scholarships/grants, private scholarships, the school's own gift aid, academic competitiveness, SMART Grant. *Loans:* FFEL Subsidized Stafford, FFEL Unsubsidized Stafford, FFEL PLUS, state loans, alternative loans. **Student Employment:** Federal Work-Study Program available. Institutional employment available. Off-campus job opportunities are good. **Financial Aid Statistics:** 72% freshmen, 67% undergrads receive need-based scholarship or grant aid. 61% freshmen, 57% undergrads receive need-based self-help aid. Highest amount earned per year from on-campus jobs $995.

SCRIPPS COLLEGE

1030 Columbia Avenue, Claremont, CA 91711
Phone: 909-621-8149 **E-mail:** admission@scrippscollege.edu **CEEB Code:** 4693
Fax: 909-607-7508 **Website:** www.scrippscollege.edu **ACT Code:** 0426
Financial Aid Phone: 909-621-8275

This private school was founded in 1926. It has a 30-acre campus.

RATINGS
Admissions Selectivity Rating: 96 **Fire Safety Rating:** 71 **Green Rating:** 77

STUDENTS AND FACULTY
Enrollment: 859. **Student Body:** 100% female, 58% out-of-state. African American 3%, Asian 10%, Caucasian 41%, Hispanic 4%. **Retention and Graduation:** 89% freshmen return for sophomore year. 68% freshmen graduate within 4 years. 21% grads go on to further study within 1 year. 60% grads pursue arts and sciences degrees. 13% grads pursue law degrees. 7% grads pursue medical degrees. **Faculty:** Student/faculty ratio 11:1. 67 full-time faculty, 100% hold PhDs. 100% faculty teach undergrads.

ACADEMICS
Degrees: Bachelor's, post-bachelor's certificate. **Academic Requirements:** Arts/fine arts, English (including composition), foreign languages, humanities, interdisciplinary core (women's studies, race and ethnic studies), mathematics, sciences (biological or physical), social science. **Classes:** Most classes have 10–19 students. Most lab/discussion sections have 10–19 students. **Majors with Highest Enrollment:** English language and literature, fine/studio arts, psychology. **Disciplines with Highest Percentage of Degrees Awarded:** Visual and performing arts 18%, area and ethnic studies 15%, social sciences 12%, psychology 9%, interdisciplinary studies 8%, biological/life sciences 8%, English 8%. **Special Study Options:** Accelerated program, cross-registration, double major, exchange student program (domestic), independent study, internships, student-designed major, study abroad.

FACILITIES
Housing: Women's dorms, apartments for single students, special housing for disabled students. **Special Academic Facilities/Equipment:** Art center, music complex, dance studio, humanities museum and institute, science center, biological field station. **Computers:** 50% of classrooms are wireless, 50% of public computers are PCs, 50% of public computers are Macs, network access in dorm rooms, network access in dorm lounges, remote student-access to Web through college's connection.

CAMPUS LIFE
Activities: Choral groups, dance, drama/theater, literary magazine, music ensembles, radio station, student government, student newspaper, symphony orchestra, yearbook. **Organizations:** 200 registered organizations, 5 honor societies, 7 religious organizations. **Athletics (Intercollegiate):** *Women:* Basketball, cross-country, diving, golf, lacrosse, soccer, softball, swimming, tennis, track/field (outdoor), volleyball, water polo. **Environmental Initiatives:** Publication of current practices on the web. Working with students on recycling/composting programs. Requesting information from building contractors on sustainability practices/materials.

ADMISSIONS
Freshman Academic Profile: 75% in top 10% of high school class, 95% in top 25% of high school class, 100% in top 50% of high school class. 61% from public high schools. SAT Math middle 50% range 630–700. SAT Critical Reading middle 50% range 650–740. SAT Writing middle 50% range 640–720. ACT middle 50% range 28–31. TOEFL required of all international applicants, minimum paper TOEFL 600, minimum computer TOEFL 250. **Basis for Candidate Selection:** *Very important factors considered include:* Academic GPA, alumni/ae relation, application essay, character/personal qualities, class

rank, extracurricular activities, first generation, interview, racial/ethnic status, recommendation(s), rigor of secondary school record, standardized test scores, talent/ability. *Important factors considered include*: Geographical residence. **Freshman Admission Requirements**: High school diploma is required, and GED is accepted. *Academic units required*: 4 English, 3 math, 3 science, 3 foreign language, 3 social studies. *Academic units recommended*: 4 English, 4 math, 4 science, 4 foreign language, 4 social studies and history. **Freshman Admission Statistics**: 1,873 applied, 45% admitted, 26% enrolled. **Transfer Admission Requirements**: High school transcript, college transcript(s), essay or personal statement, standardized test score, statement of good standing from prior institution(s). Minimum college GPA of 3.0 required. Lowest grade transferable C. **General Admission Information**: Application fee $50. Early decision application deadline 11/1. Regular application deadline 1/1. Regular notification 4/1. Non-fall registration accepted. Admission may be deferred for a maximum of 1 year. Credit offered for CEEB Advanced Placement tests.

COSTS AND FINANCIAL AID

Annual tuition $35,636. Room and board $10,800. Required fees $214. Average book expense $800. **Required Forms and Deadlines**: FAFSA, CSS/Financial Aid PROFILE, Noncustodial PROFILE, Business/Farm Supplement, verification worksheet, parent and student federal tax returns. Financial aid filing deadline 2/1. **Notification of Awards**: Applicants will be notified of awards on or about 4/1. **Types of Aid**: *Need-based scholarships/grants*: Pell, SEOG, state scholarships/grants, private scholarships, the school's own gift aid, Federal work-study. *Loans*: FFEL Subsidized Stafford, FFEL Unsubsidized Stafford, FFEL PLUS, Federal Perkins, college/university loans from institutional funds. **Student Employment**: Federal Work-Study Program available. Institutional employment available. Off-campus job opportunities are good. **Financial Aid Statistics**: 42% freshmen, 41% undergrads receive need-based scholarship or grant aid. 33% freshmen, 37% undergrads receive need-based self-help aid. 57% freshmen, 61% undergrads receive any aid.

See page 1372.

SEATTLE PACIFIC UNIVERSITY

3307 Third Avenue West, Seattle, WA 98119-1997
Phone: 206-281-2021 **E-mail**: admissions@spu.edu **CEEB Code**: 4694
Fax: 206-281-2669 **Website**: www.spu.edu **ACT Code**: 4476
Financial Aid Phone: 206-281-2061

This private school, affiliated with the Methodist Church, was founded in 1891. It has a 35-acre campus.

RATINGS
Admissions Selectivity Rating: 87   **Fire Safety Rating**: 60*   **Green Rating**: 60*

STUDENTS AND FACULTY
Enrollment: 2,954. **Student Body**: 67% female, 33% male, 34% out-of-state. African American 2%, Asian 6%, Caucasian 80%, Hispanic 3%, Native American 1%. **Retention and Graduation**: 87% freshmen return for sophomore year. 48% freshmen graduate within 4 years. **Faculty**: Student/faculty ratio 14:1. 183 full-time faculty, 88% hold PhDs. 99% faculty teach undergrads.

ACADEMICS
Degrees: Bachelor's, diploma, doctoral, master's, post-master's certificate. **Academic Requirements**: Arts/fine arts, biblical literature and Christian perspectives, English (including composition), foreign languages, history, humanities, mathematics, philosophy, sciences (biological or physical), social science. **Classes**: Most classes have 10–19 students. Most lab/discussion sections have fewer than 10 students. **Majors with Highest Enrollment**: Business administration/management, nursing/registered nurse training (ASN, BSN, MSN, RN), psychology. **Disciplines with Highest Percentage of Degrees Awarded**: Business/marketing 14%, social sciences 11%, psychology 9%, family and consumer sciences 8%, health professions and related sciences 8%, communications/journalism 7%. **Special Study Options**: Cross-registration, distance learning, double major, English as a second language (ESL), exchange student program (domestic), external degree program, honors program, independent study, internships, liberal arts/career combination, student-designed major, study abroad, teacher certification program, weekend college.

FACILITIES
Housing: Coed dorms, apartments for married students, apartments for single students, theme housing. **Special Academic Facilities/Equipment**: Art

gallery, language lab, instructional media center, performing arts theater, science learning center, island campus used for seminars, summer workshops, field work in botany and marine biology. **Computers**: 80% of public computers are PCs, 20% of public computers are Macs, network access in dorm rooms, network access in dorm lounges, online registration, online administrative functions (other than registration), remote student-access to Web through college's connection.

CAMPUS LIFE
Activities: Choral groups, drama/theater, jazz band, literary magazine, music ensembles, pep band, radio station, student government, student newspaper, symphony orchestra, yearbook. **Organizations**: 37 registered organizations, 1 honor society, 1 religious organization. **Athletics (Intercollegiate)**: *Men*: Basketball, crew/rowing, cross-country, soccer, track/field (indoor), track/field (outdoor). *Women*: Basketball, crew/rowing, cross-country, gymnastics, soccer, track/field (indoor), track/field (outdoor), volleyball.

ADMISSIONS
Freshman Academic Profile: 37% in top 10% of high school class, 65% in top 25% of high school class, 90% in top 50% of high school class. 60% from public high schools. SAT Math middle 50% range 510–640. SAT Critical Reading middle 50% range 520–640. SAT Writing middle 50% range 620–620. ACT middle 50% range 22–28. TOEFL required of all international applicants, minimum paper TOEFL 550, minimum computer TOEFL 213. **Basis for Candidate Selection**: *Very important factors considered include*: Academic GPA, application essay, recommendation(s), rigor of secondary school record, standardized test scores. *Important factors considered include*: Character/personal qualities, extracurricular activities, first generation, interview, level of applicant's interest, racial/ethnic status, religious affiliation/commitment, talent/ability, volunteer work, work experience. *Other factors considered include*: Alumni/ae relation, class rank, geographical residence. **Freshman Admission Requirements**: High school diploma is required, and GED is accepted. *Academic units required*: 4 English, 3 math, 2 science, 3 social studies, 2 history. *Academic units recommended*: 4 English, 3 math, 3 science, 3 foreign language, 2 history. **Freshman Admission Statistics**: 2,001 applied, 80% admitted, 39% enrolled. **Transfer Admission Requirements**: College transcript(s), essay or personal statement. Minimum college GPA of 2.5 required. Lowest grade transferable C. **General Admission Information**: Application fee $45. Regular application deadline 2/1. Regular notification 3/1. Non-fall registration accepted. Credit offered for CEEB Advanced Placement tests.

COSTS AND FINANCIAL AID
Annual tuition $24,783. Room and board $8,082. Required fees $345. Average book expense $849. **Required Forms and Deadlines**: FAFSA. Financial aid filing deadline 4/1. **Notification of Awards**: Applicants will be notified of awards on a rolling basis beginning on or about 3/15. **Types of Aid**: *Need-based scholarships/grants*: Pell, SEOG, state scholarships/grants, private scholarships, the school's own gift aid. *Loans*: FFEL Subsidized Stafford, FFEL Unsubsidized Stafford, FFEL PLUS, Federal Perkins, Federal Nursing, college/university loans from institutional funds. **Student Employment**: Federal Work-Study Program available. **Financial Aid Statistics**: 61% freshmen, 61% undergrads receive need-based scholarship or grant aid. 57% freshmen, 58% undergrads receive need-based self-help aid. 7 freshmen, 42 undergrads receive athletic scholarships. 93% freshmen, 91% undergrads receive any aid. **Financial Aid Phone**: 206-281-2061.

SEATTLE UNIVERSITY

Admissions Office, 900 Broadway, Seattle, WA 98122-4340
Phone: 206-296-2000 **E-mail**: admissions@seattleu.edu **CEEB Code**: 4695
Fax: 206-296-5656 **Website**: www.seattleu.edu **ACT Code**: 4478
Financial Aid Phone: 206-296-2000

This private school, affiliated with the Jesuit order of the Roman Catholic Church, was founded in 1891. It has a 46-acre campus.

RATINGS
Admissions Selectivity Rating: 87   **Fire Safety Rating**: 60*   **Green Rating**: 97

The Princeton Review's Complete Book of Colleges

STUDENTS AND FACULTY

Enrollment: 4,134. **Student Body**: 61% female, 39% male, 41% out-of-state, 6% international (74 countries represented). African American 6%, Asian 21%, Caucasian 52%, Hispanic 7%, Native American 2%. **Retention and Graduation**: 84% freshmen return for sophomore year. 51% freshmen graduate within 4 years. **Faculty**: Student/faculty ratio 13:1. 401 full-time faculty, 79% hold PhDs. 73% faculty teach undergrads.

ACADEMICS

Degrees: Bachelor's, doctoral, first professional certificate, first professional, master's, post-bachelor's certificate, post-master's certificate. **Academic Requirements**: Arts/fine arts, English (including composition), ethics, history, mathematics, philosophy, religious studies, sciences (biological or physical), social science, theology. **Classes**: Most classes have 10–19 students. Most lab/discussion sections have 10–19 students. **Majors with Highest Enrollment**: Finance, marketing/marketing management, nursing/registered nurse training (ASN, BSN, MSN, RN). **Disciplines with Highest Percentage of Degrees Awarded**: Business/marketing 25%, health professions and related sciences 11%, engineering 7%, communications/journalism 5%, social sciences 5%. **Special Study Options**: Cooperative education program, double major, English as a second language (ESL), honors program, independent study, internships, liberal arts/career combination, student-designed major, study abroad.

FACILITIES

Housing: Coed dorms, apartments for single students, special housing for disabled students, single-gender floors. **Special Academic Facilities/Equipment**: Observatory, electron microscope, St. Ignatius Chapel. **Computers**: 70% of public computers are PCs, 30% of public computers are Macs, network access in dorm rooms, network access in dorm lounges, online registration, online administrative functions (other than registration), remote student-access to Web through college's connection.

CAMPUS LIFE

Activities: Choral groups, concert band, drama/theater, jazz band, literary magazine, music ensembles, musical theater, radio station, student government, student newspaper. **Organizations**: 65 registered organizations. **Athletics (Intercollegiate)**: *Men*: Basketball, cross-country, soccer, swimming, track/field (indoor), track/field (outdoor). *Women*: Basketball, cross-country, soccer, softball, swimming, track/field (indoor), track/field (outdoor), volleyball. Environmental Initiatives: The 48 acres have been maintained pesticide-free since 1986 by using Integrated Pest Management methods. The on-site composting facility annually turns 16 tons of kitchen food waste generated by on-campus restaurants and cafÈs into compost—which is applied on our landscape. The pre-consumer food waste includes: fruit and veggie trimmings, old bread, expired grains, all the coffee grounds from the cafÈs and waxed cardboard. There are 12 electric vehicles in the Facilities maintenance staff fleet.

ADMISSIONS

Freshman Academic Profile: 32% in top 10% of high school class, 64% in top 25% of high school class, 93% in top 50% of high school class. 63% from public high schools. SAT Math middle 50% range 530–630. SAT Critical Reading middle 50% range 520–640. SAT Writing middle 50% range 510–620. ACT middle 50% range 23–28. TOEFL required of all international applicants, minimum paper TOEFL 520, minimum computer TOEFL 190. **Basis for Candidate Selection**: *Very important factors considered include*: Academic GPA, application essay, recommendation(s), rigor of secondary school record, standardized test scores. *Important factors considered include*: Character/personal qualities, extracurricular activities, first generation, talent/ability, volunteer work. *Other factors considered include*: Alumni/ae relation, class rank, geographical residence, interview, level of applicant's interest, racial/ethnic status, state residency, work experience. **Freshman Admission Requirements**: High school diploma is required, and GED is accepted. *Academic units required*: 4 English, 3 math, 2 science (2 science labs), 2 foreign language, 3 social studies, 2 academic electives. *Academic units recommended*: 4 science (3 science labs), 4 social studies. **Freshman Admission Statistics**: 4,532 applied, 65% admitted, 27% enrolled. **Transfer Admission Requirements**: College transcript(s), essay or personal statement. Minimum college GPA of 2.5 required. Lowest grade transferable C. **General Admission Information**: Application fee $45. Regular application deadline 2/1. Regular notification is rolling. Non-fall registration accepted. Credit and/or placement offered for CEEB Advanced Placement tests.

COSTS AND FINANCIAL AID

Annual tuition $28,260. Room and board $8,340. Average book expense $1,350. **Required Forms and Deadlines**: FAFSA. Financial aid filing deadline 2/1. **Notification of Awards**: Applicants will be notified of awards on or about 3/21. **Types of Aid**: *Need-based scholarships/grants*: Pell, SEOG, state scholarships/grants, private scholarships, the school's own gift aid. *Loans*: Direct Subsidized Stafford, Direct Unsubsidized Stafford, Direct PLUS, Federal Perkins, Federal Nursing. **Financial Aid Statistics**: 34% freshmen, 35% undergrads receive need-based scholarship or grant aid. 45% freshmen, 45% undergrads receive need-based self-help aid. 27 freshmen, 131 undergrads receive athletic scholarships. 88% freshmen, 76% undergrads receive any aid.

See page 1374.

SETON HALL UNIVERSITY

Enrollment Services, 400 South Orange Avenue, South Orange, NJ 07079
Phone: 973-761-9332 **E-mail**: thehall@shu.edu **CEEB Code**: 2811
Fax: 973-275-2040 **Website**: www.shu.edu **ACT Code**: 2606
Financial Aid Phone: 973-761-9332

This private school, affiliated with the Roman Catholic Church, was founded in 1856. It has a 58-acre campus.

RATINGS

Admissions Selectivity Rating: 81   **Fire Safety Rating**: 84   **Green Rating**: 60*

STUDENTS AND FACULTY

Enrollment: 4,951. **Student Body**: 55% female, 45% male, 26% out-of-state, 1% international (71 countries represented). African American 11%, Asian 6%, Caucasian 51%, Hispanic 11%. **Retention and Graduation**: 83% freshmen return for sophomore year. 41% freshmen graduate within 4 years. 30% grads go on to further study within 1 year. 9% grads pursue arts and sciences degrees. 5% grads pursue business degrees. 7% grads pursue law degrees. 9% grads pursue medical degrees. **Faculty**: Student/faculty ratio 14:1. 441 full-time faculty, 90% hold PhDs. 75% faculty teach undergrads.

ACADEMICS

Degrees: Bachelor's, doctoral, first professional, master's, post-master's certificate. **Academic Requirements**: English (including composition), humanities, mathematics, philosophy, sciences (biological or physical), social science. **Classes**: Most classes have 10–19 students. Most lab/discussion sections have 10–19 students. **Majors with Highest Enrollment**: Communications studies/speech communication and rhetoric, criminal justice/safety studies, nursing/registered nurse training (ASN, BSN, MSN, RN). **Disciplines with Highest Percentage of Degrees Awarded**: Security and protective services 84%. **Special Study Options**: Accelerated program, cooperative education program, cross-registration, distance learning, double major, dual enrollment, English as a second language (ESL), honors program, independent study, internships, study abroad, teacher certification program.

FACILITIES

Housing: Coed dorms, apartments for single students, special housing for disabled students. **Special Academic Facilities/Equipment**: Art and natural history museums, theater-in-the-round, archaeological research center, TV studio, radio station. **Computers**: 50% of classrooms are wired, 100% of classrooms are wireless, 95% of public computers are PCs, 3% of public computers are Macs, 2% of public computers are UNIX, network access in dorm rooms, network access in dorm lounges, online registration, online administrative functions (other than registration), support for handheld computing, remote student-access to Web through college's connection, tuition includes personal computer. Undergraduates are required to own a computer.

CAMPUS LIFE

Activities: Choral groups, drama/theater, pep band, radio station, student government, student newspaper, television station. **Organizations**: 100 registered organizations, 13 honor societies, 3 religious organizations. 11 fraternities, 12 sororities. **Athletics (Intercollegiate)**: *Men*: Baseball, basketball, cross-country, diving, golf, soccer, swimming, track/field (outdoor). *Women*: Basketball, cross-country, diving, soccer, softball, swimming, tennis, track/field (outdoor), volleyball.

ADMISSIONS

Freshman Academic Profile: 28% in top 10% of high school class, 60% in top 25% of high school class, 88% in top 50% of high school class. 70% from public high schools. SAT Math middle 50% range 500–600. SAT Critical Reading middle 50% range 480–590. TOEFL required of all international applicants, minimum paper TOEFL 550, minimum computer TOEFL 213. **Basis for**

Candidate Selection: *Very important factors considered include:* Academic GPA, application essay, recommendation(s), rigor of secondary school record, standardized test scores. *Important factors considered include:* Extracurricular activities, volunteer work, work experience. *Other factors considered include:* Character/personal qualities, class rank, interview, talent/ability. **Freshman Admission Requirements:** High school diploma is required, and GED is accepted. *Academic units required:* 4 English, 3 math, 1 science, 2 foreign language, 2 social studies, 4 academic electives. **Freshman Admission Statistics:** 5,365 applied, 77% admitted, 25% enrolled. **Transfer Admission Requirements:** High school transcript, college transcript(s), essay or personal statement. Minimum college GPA of 2.5 required. Lowest grade transferable C. **General Admission Information:** Application fee $55. Regular notification is rolling. Non-fall registration accepted. Admission may be deferred for a maximum of 1 year. Credit and/or placement offered for CEEB Advanced Placement tests.

COSTS AND FINANCIAL AID

Annual tuition $22,770. Room & board $10,466. Required fees $1,950. **Required Forms and Deadlines:** FAFSA. Financial aid filing deadline 2/15. **Notification of Awards:** Applicants will be notified of awards on a rolling basis beginning on or about 3/1. **Types of Aid:** *Need-based scholarships/grants:* Pell, SEOG, state scholarships/grants, private scholarships, the school's own gift aid. *Loans:* FFEL Subsidized Stafford, FFEL Unsubsidized Stafford, FFEL PLUS, Federal Perkins, state loans. **Student Employment:** Federal Work-Study Program available. Institutional employment available. Off-campus job opportunities are good. **Financial Aid Statistics:** 54% freshmen, 38% undergrads receive need-based scholarship or grant aid. 45% freshmen, 45% undergrads receive need-based self-help aid. 48 freshmen, 207 undergrads receive athletic scholarships. 91% freshmen, 86% undergrads receive any aid. Highest amount earned per year from on-campus jobs $2,700.

See page 1376.

SETON HILL UNIVERSITY

1 Seton Hill Drive, Greensburg, PA 15601
Phone: 724-838-4255 **E-mail:** admit@setonhill.edu **CEEB Code:** 2812
Fax: 724-830-1294 **Website:** www.setonhill.edu **ACT Code:** 3688
Financial Aid Phone: 724-838-4293

This private school, affiliated with the Roman Catholic Church, was founded in 1883. It has a 200-acre campus.

RATINGS

Admissions Selectivity Rating: 82   **Fire Safety Rating:** 79   **Green Rating:** 61

STUDENTS AND FACULTY

Enrollment: 1,374. **Student Body:** 62% female, 38% male, 20% out-of-state, 2% international (15 countries represented). African American 9%, Caucasian 84%, Hispanic 2%. **Retention and Graduation:** 65% freshmen return for sophomore year. 44% freshmen graduate within 4 years. 31% grads go on to further study within 1 year. 12% grads pursue arts and sciences degrees. 9% grads pursue business degrees. 2% grads pursue law degrees. 2% grads pursue medical degrees. **Faculty:** Student/faculty ratio 14:1. 67 full-time faculty, 85% hold PhDs. 100% faculty teach undergrads.

ACADEMICS

Degrees: Bachelor's, certificate, master's, post-bachelor's certificate, post-master's certificate. **Academic Requirements:** Arts/fine arts, computer literacy, English (including composition), foreign languages, history, humanities, mathematics, philosophy, religious studies, sciences (biological or physical). **Classes:** Most classes have 10–19 students. **Majors with Highest Enrollment:** Business administration/management, fine/studio arts, psychology. **Disciplines with Highest Percentage of Degrees Awarded:** Business/marketing 28%, public administration and social services 10%, social sciences 10%, psychology 9%, visual and performing arts 6%. **Special Study Options:** Accelerated program, cross-registration, distance learning, double major, English as a second language (ESL), exchange student program (domestic), honors program, independent study, internships, liberal arts/career combination, student-designed major, study abroad, teacher certification program, weekend college.

FACILITIES

Housing: Coed dorms, men's dorms, women's dorms, special housing for honors students. **Special Academic Facilities/Equipment:** Art gallery, concert hall, theater, nursery school, kindergarten, smart classrooms.

Computers: 20% of classrooms are wired, 10% of classrooms are wireless, 95% of public computers are PCs, 5% of public computers are Macs, network access in dorm rooms, network access in dorm lounges, online registration, online administrative functions (other than registration), support for handheld computing, remote student-access to Web through college's connection.

CAMPUS LIFE

Activities: Choral groups, concert band, dance, drama/theater, jazz band, literary magazine, music ensembles, musical theater, pep band, student government, student newspaper, symphony orchestra. **Organizations:** 40 registered organizations, 8 honor societies, 2 religious organizations. **Athletics (Intercollegiate):** *Men:* Baseball, basketball, cross-country, football, golf, lacrosse, soccer, tennis, track/field (outdoor), wrestling. *Women:* Basketball, cross-country, equestrian sports, field hockey, golf, lacrosse, soccer, softball, tennis, track/field (outdoor), volleyball. Environmental Initiatives: Association of Independent Colleges and Universities of Pennsylvania self/peer assessment program.

ADMISSIONS

Freshman Academic Profile: 18% in top 10% of high school class, 40% in top 25% of high school class, 73% in top 50% of high school class. SAT Math middle 50% range 450–570. SAT Critical Reading middle 50% range 450–550. TOEFL required of all international applicants, minimum paper TOEFL 550, minimum computer TOEFL 213. **Basis for Candidate Selection:** *Very important factors considered include:* Academic GPA, interview, rigor of secondary school record. *Important factors considered include:* Character/personal qualities, class rank, extracurricular activities, standardized test scores, talent/ability. *Other factors considered include:* Alumni/ae relation, application essay, level of applicant's interest, recommendation(s), volunteer work, work experience. **Freshman Admission Requirements:** High school diploma is required, and GED is accepted. *Academic units required:* 4 English, 2 math, 1 science (1 science lab), 2 social studies, 4 academic electives. *Academic units recommended:* 4 English, 2 math, 1 science (1 science lab), 2 foreign language, 2 social studies, 4 academic electives. **Freshman Admission Statistics:** 1,961 applied, 54% admitted, 30% enrolled. **Transfer Admission Requirements:** High school transcript, college transcript(s), statement of good standing from prior institution(s). Minimum college GPA of 2.0 required. Lowest grade transferable C-. **General Admission Information:** Application fee $35. Regular application deadline 8/15. Regular notification is rolling. Non-fall registration accepted. Admission may be deferred for a maximum of 1 year. Credit and/or placement offered for CEEB Advanced Placement tests.

COSTS AND FINANCIAL AID

Annual tuition $23,180. Room & board $7,230. Required fees $200. Average book expense $1,000. **Required Forms and Deadlines:** FAFSA, institution's own financial aid form, state aid form. Financial aid filing deadline 6/1. **Notification of Awards:** Applicants will be notified of awards on a rolling basis beginning on or about 11/15. **Types of Aid:** *Need-based scholarships/grants:* Pell, SEOG, state scholarships/grants, private scholarships, the school's own gift aid. *Loans:* FFEL Subsidized Stafford, FFEL Unsubsidized Stafford, FFEL PLUS, Federal Perkins, college/university loans from institutional funds, alternative loans. **Student Employment:** Federal Work-Study Program available. Institutional employment available. Off-campus job opportunities are good. **Financial Aid Statistics:** 91% freshmen, 75% undergrads receive need-based scholarship or grant aid. 91% freshmen, 75% undergrads receive need-based self-help aid. 19 freshmen, 27 undergrads receive athletic scholarships. 97% freshmen, 83% undergrads receive any aid. Highest amount earned per year from on-campus jobs $1,800.

SHASTA BIBLE COLLEGE

2951 Goodwater Avenue, Redding, CA 96002
Phone: 530-221-4275 **E-mail:** admissions@shasta.edu
Fax: 530-221-6929 **Website:** www.shasta.edu **ACT Code:** 0427
Financial Aid Phone: 530-221-4275

This private school, affiliated with the Baptist Church, was founded in 1970. It has a 63-acre campus.

RATINGS

Admissions Selectivity Rating: 60*   **Fire Safety Rating:** 60*   **Green Rating:** 60*

STUDENTS AND FACULTY

Enrollment: 89. **Student Body:** 44% female, 56% male, 25% out-of-state, 3% international (5 countries represented). African American 1%, Caucasian 73%, Hispanic 1%. **Retention and Graduation:** 40% freshmen return for sophomore year. 20% grads pursue arts and sciences degrees. **Faculty**: Student/faculty ratio 12:1. 7 full-time faculty, 71% hold PhDs. 80% faculty teach undergrads.

ACADEMICS

Degrees: Associate, bachelor's, certificate, diploma, master's. **Academic Requirements**: Arts/fine arts, computer literacy, English (including composition), foreign languages, history, humanities, mathematics, philosophy, sciences (biological or physical), social science. **Classes**: Most classes have 10–19 students. **Disciplines with Highest Percentage of Degrees Awarded**: Education 50%. **Special Study Options**: Distance learning, double major, external degree program, independent study, master's in school administration, teacher certification program, weekend college.

FACILITIES

Housing: Men's dorms, women's dorms, apartments for married students, apartments for single students. **Computers**: 100% of public computers are PCs, network access in dorm lounges, remote student-access to Web through college's connection.

CAMPUS LIFE

Activities: Choral groups, music ensembles, radio station, student government, student newspaper, yearbook.

ADMISSIONS

Freshman Academic Profile: 30% from public high schools. TOEFL required of all international applicants, minimum paper TOEFL 500, minimum computer TOEFL 173. **Basis for Candidate Selection**: *Very important factors considered include*: Application essay, character/personal qualities, recommendation(s), religious affiliation/commitment, volunteer work. *Important factors considered include*: Extracurricular activities, work experience. *Other factors considered include*: Alumni/ae relation, class rank, interview, standardized test scores, talent/ability. **Freshman Admission Requirements**: High school diploma is required, and GED is accepted. **Freshman Admission Statistics**: 38 applied, 100% admitted, 100% enrolled. **Transfer Admission Requirements**: High school transcript, college transcript(s). Minimum college GPA of 2.0 required. Lowest grade transferable C. **General Admission Information**: Application fee $35. Regular notification after approval of the staff and file is complete. Non-fall registration accepted. Admission may be deferred for a maximum of 1 semester. Common Application not accepted. Neither credit nor placement offered for CEEB Advanced Placement tests.

COSTS AND FINANCIAL AID

Annual tuition $5,300. Room & board $1,200. Required fees $135. Average book expense $250. **Notification of Awards**: Applicants will be notified of awards on a rolling basis beginning on or about 1/2. **Types of Aid**: *Need-based scholarships/grants*: Pell, state scholarships/grants. **Student Employment**: Federal Work-Study Program available. Off-campus job opportunities are excellent. **Financial Aid Statistics**: Highest amount earned per year from on-campus jobs $700.

SHAW UNIVERSITY

118 East South Street, Raleigh, NC 27601
Phone: 919-546-8275 **E-mail**: admissions@shawu.edu **CEEB Code**: 5612
Fax: 919-546-8271 **Website**: www.shawu.edu **ACT Code**: 3158
Financial Aid Phone: 919-546-8240

This private school, affiliated with the Baptist Church, was founded in 1865. It has a 30-acre campus.

RATINGS

Admissions Selectivity Rating: 69   **Fire Safety Rating**: 60*   **Green Rating**: 60*

STUDENTS AND FACULTY

Enrollment: 2,649. **Student Body**: 64% female, 36% male, 36% out-of-state, 2% international (11 countries represented). African American 85%, Caucasian 1%. **Retention and Graduation**: 11% freshmen graduate within 4 years. **Faculty**: Student/faculty ratio 15:1. 112 full-time faculty, 63% hold PhDs. 94% faculty teach undergrads.

ACADEMICS

Degrees: Associate, bachelor's, first professional, master's. **Academic Requirements**: Computer literacy, English (including composition), ethics, humanities, mathematics, public speaking, sciences (biological or physical), social science. **Classes**: Most classes have fewer than 10 students. **Majors with**

Highest Enrollment: Business administration/management, criminal justice/safety studies, psychology. **Disciplines with Highest Percentage of Degrees Awarded**: Business/marketing 26%, security and protective services 15%, social sciences 10%, public administration and social services 9%, psychology 8%, philosophy and religious studies 8%. **Special Study Options**: Accelerated program, cross-registration, distance learning, double major, dual enrollment, honors program, independent study, internships, student-designed major, study abroad, teacher certification program, weekend college.

FACILITIES

Housing: Men's dorms, women's dorms. **Special Academic Facilities/Equipment**: TV and film production facilities, curriculum and materials center. **Computers**: 98% of public computers are PCs, 2% of public computers are Macs, network access in dorm rooms, network access in dorm lounges, online registration, online administrative functions (other than registration), remote student-access to Web through college's connection.

CAMPUS LIFE

Activities: Choral groups, concert band, dance, drama/theater, jazz band, marching band, music ensembles, musical theater, pep band, radio station, student government, student newspaper, yearbook. **Organizations**: 4 honor societies. 4 fraternities (4% men join), 4 sororities (5% women join). **Athletics (Intercollegiate)**: *Men*: Baseball, basketball, cross-country, football, golf, tennis, track/field (indoor), track/field (outdoor). *Women*: Basketball, bowling, cross-country, softball, tennis, track/field (indoor), track/field (outdoor), volleyball.

ADMISSIONS

Freshman Academic Profile: 2% in top 10% of high school class, 9% in top 25% of high school class, 33% in top 50% of high school class. 90% from public high schools. SAT Math middle 50% range 310–420. SAT Critical Reading middle 50% range 320–420. SAT Writing middle 50% range 330–420. ACT middle 50% range 12–17. **Basis for Candidate Selection**: *Very important factors considered include*: Academic GPA, first generation, geographical residence, level of applicant's interest, recommendation(s). *Important factors considered include*: Application essay, character/personal qualities, class rank, extracurricular activities, rigor of secondary school record, standardized test scores, state residency, volunteer work, work experience. *Other factors considered include*: Alumni/ae relation, talent/ability. **Freshman Admission Requirements**: High school diploma is required, and GED is accepted. *Academic units required*: 3 English, 2 math, 2 science, 2 social studies, 9 academic electives. **Freshman Admission Statistics**: 5,361 applied, 49% admitted, 28% enrolled. **Transfer Admission Requirements**: College transcript(s). Lowest grade transferable C. **General Admission Information**: Application fee $25. Regular application deadline 7/30. Regular notification is rolling. Non-fall registration accepted. Admission may be deferred indefinitely. Credit and/or placement offered for CEEB Advanced Placement tests.

COSTS AND FINANCIAL AID

Required Forms and Deadlines: FAFSA, institution's own financial aid form, state aid form. Financial aid filing deadline 6/1. **Notification of Awards**: Applicants will be notified of awards on a rolling basis beginning on or about 2/1. **Types of Aid**: *Need-based scholarships/grants*: Pell, SEOG, state scholarships/grants, private scholarships, the school's own gift aid, United Negro College Fund. *Loans*: FFEL Subsidized Stafford, FFEL Unsubsidized Stafford, FFEL PLUS, Federal Perkins. **Student Employment**: Federal Work-Study Program available. Institutional employment available. Off-campus job opportunities are excellent.

SHAWNEE STATE UNIVERSITY

940 Second Street, Portsmouth, OH 45662
Phone: 740-351-4778 **E-mail**: to_ssu@shawnee.edu **CEEB Code**: 1790
Fax: 740-351-3111 **Website**: www.shawnee.edu **ACT Code**: 3336
Financial Aid Phone: 740-351-4243

This public school was founded in 1986. It has a 50-acre campus.

RATINGS

Admissions Selectivity Rating: 62   **Fire Safety Rating**: 76   **Green Rating**: 79

STUDENTS AND FACULTY

Enrollment: 3,101. **Student Body**: 59% female, 41% male, 8% out-of-state. African American 3%, Caucasian 87%. **Retention and Graduation**: 60% freshmen return for sophomore year. **Faculty**: Student/faculty ratio 17:1. 143 full-time faculty, 56% hold PhDs. 100% faculty teach undergrads.

ACADEMICS

Degrees: Associate, bachelor's, certificate, master's. **Academic Requirements**: Arts/fine arts, cultural perspectives, capstone, English (including composition), ethics, history, humanities, mathematics, philosophy, sciences (biological or physical), social science. **Classes**: Most classes have 10–19 students. Most lab/discussion sections have 10–19 students. **Majors with Highest Enrollment**: Business administration/management, early childhood education and teaching, social sciences. **Disciplines with Highest Percentage of Degrees Awarded**: Business/marketing 19%, social sciences 17%, education 16%, biological/life sciences 9%, visual and performing arts 7%. **Special Study Options**: Cross-registration, distance learning, double major, dual enrollment, English as a second language (ESL), honors program, independent study, internships, student-designed major, study abroad, teacher certification program.

FACILITIES

Housing: Coed dorms, list of housing in community available. **Special Academic Facilities/Equipment**: Vern Riffe Center for the Arts. **Computers**: 95% of public computers are PCs, 5% of public computers are Macs, network access in dorm rooms, network access in dorm lounges, online registration, remote student-access to Web through college's connection.

CAMPUS LIFE

Activities: Choral groups, drama/theater, literary magazine, music ensembles, musical theater, student government, student newspaper. **Organizations**: 30 registered organizations, 2 honor societies, 2 religious organizations. 3 fraternities (5% men join), 3 sororities (3% women join). **Athletics (Intercollegiate)**: *Men*: Baseball, basketball, cross-country, golf, soccer. *Women*: Basketball, cross-country, soccer, softball, tennis, volleyball.

ADMISSIONS

Freshman Academic Profile: 13% in top 10% of high school class, 33% in top 25% of high school class, 59% in top 50% of high school class. ACT middle 50% range 18–22. TOEFL required of all international applicants, minimum paper TOEFL 500, minimum computer TOEFL 250. **Freshman Admission Requirements**: High school diploma is required, and GED is accepted. *Academic units recommended*: 4 English, 3 math, 3 science, 2 foreign language, 3 social studies, 1 academic elective. **Freshman Admission Statistics**: 2,904 applied, 100% admitted, 17% enrolled. **Transfer Admission Requirements**: High school transcript, college transcript(s). Minimum college GPA of 2.0 required. Lowest grade transferable C. **General Admission Information**: Regular notification is rolling. Non-fall registration accepted. Admission may be deferred for a maximum of 1 year. Credit and/or placement offered for CEEB Advanced Placement tests.

COSTS AND FINANCIAL AID

Annual in-state tuition $5,184. Annual out-of-state tuition $9,324. Room and board $7,410. Required fees $648. Average book expense $1,440. **Required Forms and Deadlines**: FAFSA, institution's own financial aid form. Financial aid filing deadline 6/15. **Notification of Awards**: Applicants will be notified of awards on a rolling basis beginning on or about 5/1. **Types of Aid**: *Need-based scholarships/grants*: Pell, SEOG, state scholarships/grants, private scholarships, the school's own gift aid. *Loans*: FFEL Subsidized Stafford, FFEL Unsubsidized Stafford, FFEL PLUS, state loans. **Student Employment**: Off-campus job opportunities are fair. **Financial Aid Statistics**: 58% freshmen, 65% undergrads receive need-based scholarship or grant aid. 31% freshmen, 45% undergrads receive need-based self-help aid. 10 freshmen, 34 undergrads receive athletic scholarships.

SHELDON JACKSON COLLEGE

801 Lincoln Street, Sitka, AK 99835
Phone: 800-478-4556 **E-mail**: elower@sj-alaska.edu **CEEB Code**: 4742
Fax: 907-747-6366 **Website**: www.sj-alaska.edu **ACT Code**: 0074
Financial Aid Phone: 800-478-4556

This private school, affiliated with the Presbyterian Church, was founded in 1878. It has a 300-acre campus.

RATINGS

Admissions Selectivity Rating: 60*   **Fire Safety Rating**: 60*   **Green Rating**: 60*

STUDENTS AND FACULTY

Enrollment: 158. **Student Body**: 58% female, 42% male, 70% out-of-state. Asian 3%, Caucasian 58%, Hispanic 2%, Native American 18%. **Retention and Graduation**: 42% freshmen return for sophomore year. 20% grads go on to

---

further study within 1 year. 90% grads pursue arts and sciences degrees. 10% grads pursue law degrees. **Faculty**: Student/faculty ratio 10:1. 30 full-time faculty, 53% hold PhDs. 100% faculty teach undergrads.

ACADEMICS

Degrees: Associate, bachelor's, certificate. **Academic Requirements**: Arts/fine arts, computer literacy, English (including composition), history, humanities, mathematics, philosophy, sciences (biological or physical), social science. **Classes**: Most classes have fewer than 10 students. **Disciplines with Highest Percentage of Degrees Awarded**: Education 58%, natural resources/environmental science 33%, interdisciplinary studies 8%. **Special Study Options**: Consortium agreement with University of Alaska Southeast and Alaska Public Safety Academy, cooperative education program, cross-registration, double major, exchange student program (domestic), exchange program with Warren Wilson College, independent study, internships, liberal arts/career combination, student-designed major, teacher certification program.

FACILITIES

Housing: Coed dorms, apartments for married students, housing for students over 21 off-campus. **Special Academic Facilities/Equipment**: Sheldon Jackson Museum. **Computers**: 100% of public computers are PCs, network access in dorm rooms, remote student-access to Web through college's connection.

CAMPUS LIFE

Activities: Choral groups, concert band, music ensembles, student government. **Organizations**: 10 registered organizations, 2 honor societies, 1 religious organization.

ADMISSIONS

Freshman Academic Profile: 90% from public high schools. TOEFL required of all international applicants, minimum paper TOEFL 550. **Basis for Candidate Selection**: *Factors considered include*: Alumni/ae relation, character/personal qualities, extracurricular activities, geographical residence, racial/ethnic status, religious affiliation/commitment, rigor of secondary school record, state residency, volunteer work, work experience. **Freshman Admission Requirements**: High school diploma is required, and GED is accepted. *Academic units recommended*: 4 English, 4 math, 4 science (2 science labs), 4 social studies. **Freshman Admission Statistics**: 150 applied, 100% admitted, 29% enrolled. **Transfer Admission Requirements**: College transcript(s). Minimum college GPA of 2.0 required. Lowest grade transferable C. **General Admission Information**: Application fee $25. Non-fall registration accepted. Admission may be deferred for a maximum of 1 year. Common Application accepted. Credit offered for CEEB Advanced Placement tests.

COSTS AND FINANCIAL AID

Annual tuition $9,400. Room & board $6,920. Required fees $370. Average book expense $750. **Required Forms and Deadlines**: FAFSA. Financial aid filing deadline 5/2. **Notification of Awards**: Applicants will be notified of awards on a rolling basis beginning on or about 4/2. **Types of Aid**: *Need-based scholarships/grants*: Pell, SEOG, state scholarships/grants, private scholarships, the school's own gift aid, endowments. *Loans*: FFEL Subsidized Stafford, FFEL Unsubsidized Stafford, Federal Perkins, state loans, endowments. **Student Employment**: Federal Work-Study Program available. Institutional employment available. Off-campus job opportunities are excellent. **Financial Aid Statistics**: 85% freshmen, 82% undergrads receive need-based scholarship or grant aid. 82% freshmen, 81% undergrads receive need-based self-help aid. Highest amount earned per year from on-campus jobs $2,000.

SHENANDOAH UNIVERSITY

1460 University Drive, Winchester, VA 22601-5195
Phone: 540-665-4581 **E-mail**: admit@su.edu **CEEB Code**: 5613
Fax: 540-665-4627 **Website**: www.su.edu **ACT Code**: 5613
Financial Aid Phone: 540-665-4538

This private school, affiliated with the Methodist Church, was founded in 1875. It has a 100-acre campus.

RATINGS

Admissions Selectivity Rating: 77   **Fire Safety Rating**: 79   **Green Rating**: 60*

STUDENTS AND FACULTY

Enrollment: 1,562. **Student Body**: 60% female, 40% male, 43% out-of-state, 4% international (46 countries represented). African American 2%, Caucasian 93%. **Retention and Graduation**: 75% freshmen return for sophomore year. 28% freshmen graduate within 4 years. 42% grads go on to further study within

1 year. 34% grads pursue arts and sciences degrees. 13% grads pursue business degrees. 1% grads pursue law degrees. 1% grads pursue medical degrees. **Faculty**: Student/faculty ratio 9:1. 181 full-time faculty, 74% hold PhDs. 70% faculty teach undergrads.

ACADEMICS

Degrees: Associate, bachelor's, certificate, doctoral, first professional, master's, post-bachelor's certificate, post-master's certificate, terminal. **Academic Requirements**: Computer literacy, English (including composition), foreign languages, history, humanities, mathematics, philosophy, sciences (biological or physical), social science. **Classes**: Most classes have 10–19 students. Most lab/discussion sections have fewer than 10 students. **Majors with Highest Enrollment**: Business administration/management, drama and dramatics/theater arts, nursing/registered nurse training (ASN, BSN, MSN, RN). **Disciplines with Highest Percentage of Degrees Awarded**: Visual and performing arts 29%, business/marketing 17%, education 15%, health professions and related sciences 13%, biological/life sciences 6%. **Special Study Options**: Accelerated program, cooperative education program, distance learning, double major, English as a second language (ESL), independent study, internships, liberal arts/career combination, student-designed major, study abroad, teacher certification program, weekend college.

FACILITIES

Housing: Coed dorms, special housing for disabled students, special housing for international students. **Computers**: 100% of classrooms are wired, 100% of classrooms are wireless, 30% of public computers are PCs, 10% of public computers are Macs, network access in dorm rooms, network access in dorm lounges, online registration, online administrative functions (other than registration), support for handheld computing, remote student-access to Web through college's connection.

CAMPUS LIFE

Activities: Choral groups, concert band, dance, drama/theater, jazz band, music ensembles, musical theater, opera, radio station, student government, student newspaper, symphony orchestra, television station. **Organizations**: 65 registered organizations, 2 honor societies, 2 religious organizations. 7 fraternities (2% men join), 1 sorority. **Athletics (Intercollegiate)**: *Men*: Baseball, basketball, cross-country, football, golf, lacrosse, soccer, tennis. *Women*: Basketball, cross-country, field hockey, lacrosse, soccer, softball, tennis, volleyball.

ADMISSIONS

Freshman Academic Profile: 15% in top 10% of high school class, 37% in top 25% of high school class, 68% in top 50% of high school class. SAT Math middle 50% range 432–579. SAT Critical Reading middle 50% range 400–639. ACT middle 50% range 20–26. TOEFL required of all international applicants, minimum paper TOEFL 450, minimum computer TOEFL 133. **Basis for Candidate Selection**: *Very important factors considered include*: Academic GPA, interview, rigor of secondary school record, talent/ability. *Important factors considered include*: Extracurricular activities, recommendation(s), standardized test scores, volunteer work. *Other factors considered include*: Application essay, character/personal qualities, level of applicant's interest, work experience. **Freshman Admission Requirements**: High school diploma is required, and GED is accepted. *Academic units required*: 4 English, 3 math, 2 science (1 science lab), 2 foreign language, 2 social studies, 2 history, 2 academic electives. *Academic units recommended*: 4 math, 4 science, 3 foreign language, 4 academic electives. **Freshman Admission Statistics**: 1,479 applied, 70% admitted, 36% enrolled. **Transfer Admission Requirements**: College transcript(s), statement of good standing from prior institution(s). Minimum college GPA of 2.0 required. Lowest grade transferable C. **General Admission Information**: Application fee $30. Regular notification is rolling. Non-fall registration accepted. Admission may be deferred for a maximum of 1 year. Common Application accepted. Credit and/or placement offered for CEEB Advanced Placement tests.

COSTS AND FINANCIAL AID

Annual tuition $19,900. Room and board $7,550. Required fees $150. Average book expense $1,000. **Required Forms and Deadlines**: FAFSA, state aid form. Financial aid filing deadline 2/15. **Notification of Awards**: Applicants will be notified of awards on a rolling basis beginning on or about 3/15. **Types of Aid**: *Need-based scholarships/grants*: Pell, SEOG, state scholarships/grants, private scholarships, the school's own gift aid, Federal Nursing Scholarships. *Loans*: Direct Subsidized Stafford, Direct Unsubsidized Stafford, Direct PLUS, Federal Perkins, Federal Nursing, college/university loans from institutional funds. **Financial Aid Statistics**: 39% freshmen, 55% undergrads receive need-based scholarship or grant aid. 48% freshmen, 52% undergrads receive need-based self-help aid. 91% freshmen, 80% undergrads receive any aid. Highest amount earned per year from on-campus jobs $1,500.

See page 1378.

SHEPHERD UNIVERSITY

Office of Admissions, PO Box 3210, Shepherdstown, WV 25443-3210
Phone: 304-876-5212 **E-mail**: admissions@shepherd.edu **CEEB Code**: 5615
Fax: 304-876-5165 **Website**: www.shepherd.edu **ACT Code**: 4532
Financial Aid Phone: 304-876-5470

This public school was founded in 1871. It has a 320-acre campus.

RATINGS

Admissions Selectivity Rating: 60* **Fire Safety Rating**: 75 **Green Rating**: 71

STUDENTS AND FACULTY

Enrollment: 3,970. **Student Body**: 57% female, 43% male, 39% out-of-state. African American 4%, Asian 1%, Caucasian 80%, Hispanic 2%. **Retention and Graduation**: 70% freshmen return for sophomore year. 18% freshmen graduate within 4 years. 16% grads go on to further study within 1 year. 12% grads pursue arts and sciences degrees. 2% grads pursue business degrees. 2% grads pursue law degrees. 1% grads pursue medical degrees. **Faculty**: Student/faculty ratio 19:1. 116 full-time faculty, 83% hold PhDs. 100% faculty teach undergrads.

ACADEMICS

Degrees: Bachelor's, master's. **Academic Requirements**: Arts/fine arts, computer literacy, English (including composition), history, humanities, mathematics, physical education, sciences (biological or physical), social science. **Classes**: Most classes have 20–29 students. Most lab/discussion sections have 20–29 students. **Majors with Highest Enrollment**: Business administration/management, nursing/registered nurse training (ASN, BSN, MSN, RN), teacher education (multiple levels). **Disciplines with Highest Percentage of Degrees Awarded**: Liberal arts/general studies 18%, business/marketing 18%, education 13%, health professions and related sciences 7%, social sciences 6%. **Special Study Options**: Cooperative education program, double major, dual enrollment, honors program, independent study, internships, study abroad, teacher certification program.

FACILITIES

Housing: Coed dorms, apartments for single students, special housing for disabled students, suites, first-year housing, living-learning programs. **Special Academic Facilities/Equipment**: Nursery school, elementary education lab, art gallery, theaters, Fazioli concert grand piano, George Tyler Moore Center for the Study of the Civil War, Robert C. Byrd Center for Legislative Studies. **Computers**: 90% of public computers are PCs, 9% of public computers are Macs, 1% of public computers are UNIX, network access in dorm rooms, network access in dorm lounges, online registration, online administrative functions (other than registration), remote student-access to Web through college's connection.

CAMPUS LIFE

Activities: Choral groups, concert band, drama/theater, jazz band, literary magazine, marching band, music ensembles, musical theater, pep band, radio station, student government, student newspaper, symphony orchestra. **Organizations**: 57 registered organizations, 8 honor societies, 3 religious organizations. 4 fraternities (4% men join), 3 sororities (4% women join). **Athletics (Intercollegiate)**: *Men*: Baseball, basketball, football, golf, soccer, tennis. *Women*: Basketball, soccer, softball, tennis, volleyball.

ADMISSIONS

Freshman Academic Profile: 94% from public high schools. SAT Math middle 50% range 460–540. SAT Critical Reading middle 50% range 450–560. ACT middle 50% range 19–24. TOEFL required of all international applicants, minimum paper TOEFL 550, minimum computer TOEFL 213. **Basis for Candidate Selection**: *Very important factors considered include*: Academic GPA, rigor of secondary school record, standardized test scores. *Important factors considered include*: talent/ability. *Other factors considered include*: Alumni/ae relation, application essay, character/personal qualities, class rank, extracurricular activities, interview, level of applicant's interest, recommendation(s). **Freshman Admission Requirements**: High school diploma is required, and GED is accepted. *Academic units required*: 4 English, 3 math, 3 science (2 science labs), 2 social studies, 1 history, 12 academic electives. *Academic units recommended*: 2 foreign language. **Freshman Admission Statistics**: 1,853 applied, 83% admitted, 45% enrolled. **Transfer Admission Requirements**: College transcript(s). Minimum college GPA of 2.0 required. Lowest grade transferable D. **General Admission Information**: Application fee $35. Regular application deadline 8/15. Regular notification is rolling. Non-fall registration accepted. Admission may be deferred for a maximum of 1 year. Credit and/or placement offered for CEEB Advanced Placement tests.

COSTS AND FINANCIAL AID

Annual in-state tuition $4,564. Annual out-of-state tuition $12,036. Room and board $6,714. Average book expense $1,100. **Required Forms and Deadlines**: FAFSA, state aid form. Financial aid filing deadline 3/1. **Notification of Awards**: Applicants will be notified of awards on or about 3/10. **Types of Aid**: *Need-based scholarships/grants*: Pell, SEOG, state scholarships/grants, private scholarships, the school's own gift aid. *Loans*: Direct Subsidized Stafford, Direct Unsubsidized Stafford, Direct PLUS, Federal Perkins. **Student Employment**: Federal Work-Study Program available. Institutional employment available. **Financial Aid Statistics**: 21% freshmen, 26% undergrads receive need-based scholarship or grant aid. 33% freshmen, 39% undergrads receive need-based self-help aid. 38 freshmen, 141 undergrads receive athletic scholarships. 75% freshmen, 65% undergrads receive any aid. Highest amount earned per year from on-campus jobs $8,663.

SHIMER COLLEGE

Shimer College, 3424 S. State Street, Chicago, IL 60616
Phone: 312-235-3500 **E-mail**: admission@shimer.edu **CEEB Code**: 1717
Fax: 312-235-3501 **Website**: www.shimer.edu **ACT Code**: 1142
Financial Aid Phone: 312-235-3507

This private school was founded in 1853. It has a 140-acre campus.

RATINGS
Admissions Selectivity Rating: 60*   **Fire Safety Rating**: 60*   **Green Rating**: 60*

STUDENTS AND FACULTY
Enrollment: 81. **Student Body**: 49% female, 51% male, 60% out-of-state, 2% international (4 countries represented). African American 9%, Asian 6%, Caucasian 80%, Hispanic 2%. **Retention and Graduation**: 50% grads go on to further study within 1 year. 40% grads pursue arts and sciences degrees. 10% grads pursue law degrees. **Faculty**: Student/faculty ratio 7:1. 11 full-time faculty, 91% hold PhDs. 100% faculty teach undergrads.

ACADEMICS
Degrees: Bachelor's. **Academic Requirements**: Arts/fine arts, English (including composition), history, humanities, mathematics, philosophy, sciences (biological or physical), social science. **Classes**: Most classes have fewer than 10 students. **Majors with Highest Enrollment**: Humanities/humanistic studies, natural sciences, social sciences. **Disciplines with Highest Percentage of Degrees Awarded**: Liberal arts/general studies 55%, social sciences 35%. **Special Study Options**: Cross-registration, double major, dual enrollment, independent study, internships, study abroad, weekend college.

FACILITIES
Housing: Coed dorms, apartments for married students, apartments for single students. **Special Academic Facilities/Equipment**: The Galvin Library (1 million volumes and 120 digital databases), the MTCC (student center). **Computers**: 100% of classrooms are wireless, 100% of public computers are PCs, network access in dorm rooms, network access in dorm lounges, remote student-access to Web through college's connection.

CAMPUS LIFE
Activities: Choral groups, drama/theater, literary magazine, music ensembles, radio station, student government, student newspaper. **Organizations**: 10 religious organizations.

ADMISSIONS
Freshman Academic Profile: 50% from public high schools. SAT Writing middle 50% range 2–4. TOEFL required of all international applicants, minimum paper TOEFL 625, minimum computer TOEFL 263. **Basis for Candidate Selection**: *Very important factors considered include:* Application essay, interview, level of applicant's interest, recommendation(s). *Important factors considered include:* Character/personal qualities, rigor of secondary school record, talent/ability. *Other factors considered include:* Academic GPA, alumni/ae relation, class rank, extracurricular activities, standardized test scores, volunteer work, work experience. **Freshman Admission Requirements**: High school diploma or equivalent is not required. *Academic units recommended:* 4 English, 4 math, 3 science (1 science lab), 3 foreign language, 1 social studies, 2 history, 3 academic electives. **Freshman Admission Statistics**: 31 applied, 74% admitted, 70% enrolled. **Transfer Admission Requirements**: College transcript(s), essay or personal statement, interview. Lowest grade transferable C. **General Admission Information**: Application fee $25. Regular application deadline 8/1. Regular notification is rolling. Non-fall registration accepted. Admission may be deferred for a maximum of 2 years. Neither credit nor placement offered for CEEB Advanced Placement tests.

COSTS AND FINANCIAL AID

Annual tuition $22,600. Room and board $8,000. Required fees $750. Average book expense $900. **Required Forms and Deadlines**: FAFSA, institution's own financial aid form. Financial aid filing deadline 3/1. **Notification of Awards**: Applicants will be notified of awards on a rolling basis beginning on or about 2/1. **Types of Aid**: *Need-based scholarships/grants*: Pell, SEOG, state scholarships/grants, private scholarships, the school's own gift aid. *Loans*: FFEL Subsidized Stafford, FFEL Unsubsidized Stafford, FFEL PLUS, Federal Perkins. **Student Employment**: Federal Work-Study Program available. Institutional employment available. Off-campus job opportunities are excellent. **Financial Aid Statistics**: 78% freshmen, 80% undergrads receive need-based scholarship or grant aid. 78% freshmen, 82% undergrads receive need-based self-help aid. Highest amount earned per year from on-campus jobs $1,500.

SHIPPENSBURG UNIVERSITY OF PENNSYLVANIA

Old Main 105, 1871 Old Main Drive, Shippensburg, PA 17257-2299
Phone: 717-477-1231 **E-mail**: admiss@ship.edu **CEEB Code**: 2657
Fax: 717-477-4016 **Website**: www.ship.edu **ACT Code**: 3714
Financial Aid Phone: 717-477-1131

This public school was founded in 1871. It has a 200-acre campus.

RATINGS
Admissions Selectivity Rating: 74   **Fire Safety Rating**: 81   **Green Rating**: 79

STUDENTS AND FACULTY
Enrollment: 6,363. **Student Body**: 52% female, 48% male, 6% out-of-state. African American 5%, Asian 2%, Caucasian 85%, Hispanic 1%. **Retention and Graduation**: 77% freshmen return for sophomore year. 45% freshmen graduate within 4 years. **Faculty**: Student/faculty ratio 19:1. 331 full-time faculty, 90% hold PhDs. 93% faculty teach undergrads.

ACADEMICS
Degrees: Bachelor's, certificate, master's, post-master's certificate. **Academic Requirements**: Diversity requirement, economic and geographic sciences, English (including composition), history, humanities, mathematics, political, sciences (biological or physical), social science. **Classes**: Most classes have 20–29 students. Most lab/discussion sections have 10–19 students. **Majors with Highest Enrollment**: Criminal justice/safety studies, elementary education and teaching, psychology. **Disciplines with Highest Percentage of Degrees Awarded**: Business/marketing 22%, education 15%, communications/journalism 8%, security and protective services 8%, psychology 7%, English 7%, computer and information sciences 5%, social sciences 5%, biological/life sciences 5%, history 5%. **Special Study Options**: Accelerated program, cooperative education program, distance learning, double major, dual enrollment, honors program, independent study, internships, Raider plan, study abroad, teacher certification program.

FACILITIES
Housing: Coed dorms, women's dorms, suites, apartment complex off-campus. **Special Academic Facilities/Equipment**: Art gallery, vertebrate museum, on-campus elementary school, planetarium, electron microscope, NMR spectrometer, greenhouse, herbarium, fashion archives, women's center, closed-circuit TV. **Computers**: 90% of classrooms are wireless, 90% of public computers are PCs, 10% of public computers are Macs, network access in dorm rooms, network access in dorm lounges, online registration, online administrative functions (other than registration), remote student-access to Web through college's connection.

CAMPUS LIFE
Activities: Choral groups, concert band, dance, drama/theater, jazz band, literary magazine, marching band, music ensembles, musical theater, radio station, student government, student newspaper, symphony orchestra, television station, yearbook. **Organizations**: 244 registered organizations, 23 honor societies, 6 religious organizations. 10 fraternities (5% men join), 10 sororities (8% women join). **Athletics (Intercollegiate)**: *Men*: Baseball, basketball, cross-country, football, soccer, swimming, track/field (outdoor), wrestling. *Women*: Basketball, cross-country, field hockey, lacrosse, soccer, softball, swimming, tennis, track/field (outdoor), volleyball. Environmental Initiatives: Focus the Nation Climate Day. Biodiesel Project. Burd Run Watershed Project.

ADMISSIONS
Freshman Academic Profile: 9% in top 10% of high school class, 29% in top

25% of high school class, 68% in top 50% of high school class. 90% from public high schools. SAT Math middle 50% range 440–550. SAT Critical Reading middle 50% range 450–540. TOEFL required of all international applicants, minimum paper TOEFL 550, minimum computer TOEFL 213. **Basis for Candidate Selection**: *Very important factors considered include*: Academic GPA, class rank, rigor of secondary school record, standardized test scores. *Other factors considered include*: Application essay, character/personal qualities, extracurricular activities, interview, level of applicant's interest, recommendation(s), talent/ability, volunteer work, work experience. **Freshman Admission Requirements**: High school diploma is required, and GED is accepted. *Academic units recommended*: 4 English, 3 math, 3 science (3 science labs), 2 foreign language, 3 social sciences. **Freshman Admission Statistics**: 6,263 applied, 70% admitted, 34% enrolled. **Transfer Admission Requirements**: College transcript(s), statement of good standing from prior institution(s). Minimum college GPA of 2.2 required. Lowest grade transferable C. **General Admission Information**: Application fee $30. Regular notification is rolling. Non-fall registration accepted. Admission may be deferred for a maximum of 1 year. Credit and/or placement offered for CEEB Advanced Placement tests.

COSTS AND FINANCIAL AID

Annual in-state tuition $5,178. Annual out-of-state tuition $12,944. Room and board $6,272. Required fees $1,671. Average book expense $1,080. **Required Forms and Deadlines**: FAFSA. Financial aid filing deadline 3/15. **Notification of Awards**: Applicants will be notified of awards on a rolling basis beginning on or about 2/15. **Types of Aid**: *Need-based scholarships/grants*: Pell, SEOG, state scholarships/grants, private scholarships, the school's own gift aid. *Loans*: FFEL Subsidized Stafford, FFEL Unsubsidized Stafford, FFEL PLUS, Federal Perkins, college/university loans from institutional funds, alternative loans. **Student Employment**: Federal Work-Study Program available. Off-campus job opportunities are good. **Financial Aid Statistics**: 38% freshmen, 36% undergrads receive need-based scholarship or grant aid. 46% freshmen, 42% undergrads receive need-based self-help aid. 78 freshmen, 237 undergrads receive athletic scholarships. 77% freshmen, 74% undergrads receive any aid. Highest amount earned per year from on-campus jobs $1,500.

SHORTER COLLEGE

315 Shorter Avenue, Box 1, Rome, GA 30165
Phone: 706-233-7319 **E-mail**: admissions@shorter.edu **CEEB Code**: 5616
Fax: 706-233-7224 **Website**: www.shorter.edu **ACT Code**: 0860
Financial Aid Phone: 706-233-7227

This private school, affiliated with the Southern Baptist Church, was founded in 1873. It has a 150-acre campus.

RATINGS
Admissions Selectivity Rating: 76   **Fire Safety Rating**: 71   **Green Rating**: 68

STUDENTS AND FACULTY
Enrollment: 1,033. **Student Body**: 50% female, 50% male, 8% out-of-state, 5% international (26 countries represented). African American 10%, Caucasian 78%, Hispanic 2%. **Retention and Graduation**: 68% freshmen return for sophomore year. 35% freshmen graduate within 4 years. 30% grads go on to further study within 1 year. **Faculty**: Student/faculty ratio 12:1. 64 full-time faculty, 73% hold PhDs. 100% faculty teach undergrads.

ACADEMICS
Degrees: Bachelor's. **Academic Requirements**: Arts/fine arts, computer literacy, English (including composition), history, mathematics, religion, sciences (biological or physical), social science. **Classes**: Most classes have 10–19 students. Most lab/discussion sections have 20–29 students. **Majors with Highest Enrollment**: Biology/biological sciences, business/commerce, elementary education and teaching. **Disciplines with Highest Percentage of Degrees Awarded**: Business/marketing 20%, education 17%, visual and performing arts 13%, biological/life sciences 10%, communications/journalism 8%. **Special Study Options**: Cross-registration, double major, dual enrollment, honors program, independent study, internships, student-designed major, study abroad, teacher certification program, weekend college.

FACILITIES
Housing: Men's dorms, women's dorms, apartments for single students. **Special Academic Facilities/Equipment**: Shorter History Museum. **Computers**: 75% of classrooms are wireless, 100% of public computers are PCs, network access in dorm rooms, network access in dorm lounges, online registration, online administrative functions (other than registration), remote student-access to Web through college's connection.

CAMPUS LIFE
Activities: Choral groups, concert band, drama/theater, literary magazine, music ensembles, musical theater, opera, pep band, radio station, student government, student newspaper, student-run film society, television station, yearbook. **Organizations**: 32 registered organizations, 10 honor societies, 3 religious organizations. 2 fraternities (6% men join), 2 sororities (28% women join). **Athletics (Intercollegiate)**: *Men*: Baseball, basketball, cheerleading, cross-country, football, golf, soccer, tennis, track/field (outdoor). *Women*: Basketball, cheerleading, cross-country, golf, soccer, softball, tennis, track/field (outdoor), volleyball.

ADMISSIONS
Freshman Academic Profile: 16% in top 10% of high school class, 42% in top 25% of high school class, 71% in top 50% of high school class. 95% from public high schools. SAT Math middle 50% range 440–550. SAT Critical Reading middle 50% range 440–550. SAT Writing middle 50% range 430–540. ACT middle 50% range 17–22. TOEFL required of all international applicants, minimum paper TOEFL 500, minimum computer TOEFL 173. **Basis for Candidate Selection**: *Very important factors considered include*: Academic GPA, standardized test scores. *Important factors considered include*: Application essay, class rank, rigor of secondary school record, talent/ability. *Other factors considered include*: Alumni/ae relation, character/personal qualities, extracurricular activities, first generation, interview, level of applicant's interest, recommendation(s), volunteer work, work experience. **Freshman Admission Requirements**: High school diploma is required, and GED is accepted. *Academic units required*: 4 English, 4 math, 3 science, 2 foreign language, 3 history. **Freshman Admission Statistics**: 1,185 applied, 76% admitted, 33% enrolled. **Transfer Admission Requirements**: College transcript(s), statement of good standing from prior institution(s). Minimum college GPA of 2.0 required. **General Admission Information**: Application fee $25. Regular notification is rolling. Non-fall registration accepted. Admission may be deferred for a maximum of 2 years. Credit and/or placement offered for CEEB Advanced Placement tests.

COSTS AND FINANCIAL AID
Annual tuition $14,850. Room and board $7,000. Required fees $310. Average book expense $1,000. **Required Forms and Deadlines**: FAFSA, institution's own financial aid form, state aid form. Financial aid filing deadline 4/15. **Types of Aid**: *Need-based scholarships/grants*: Pell, SEOG, private scholarships, the school's own gift aid. *Loans*: FFEL Subsidized Stafford, FFEL Unsubsidized Stafford, FFEL PLUS, Federal Perkins. **Financial Aid Statistics**: 75% freshmen, 67% undergrads receive need-based scholarship or grant aid. 52% freshmen, 47% undergrads receive need-based self-help aid. 43 freshmen, 117 undergrads receive athletic scholarships. 99% freshmen, 99% undergrads receive any aid. Highest amount earned per year from on-campus jobs $1,500.

SIENA COLLEGE

515 Loudon Road, Loudonville, NY 12211
Phone: 518-783-2423 **E-mail**: admit@siena.edu **CEEB Code**: 2814
Fax: 518-783-2436 **Website**: www.siena.edu **ACT Code**: 2878
Financial Aid Phone: 888-287-4362

This private school, affiliated with the Roman Catholic Church, was founded in 1937. It has a 164-acre campus.

RATINGS
Admissions Selectivity Rating: 86   **Fire Safety Rating**: 60*   **Green Rating**: 60*

STUDENTS AND FACULTY
Enrollment: 3,156. **Student Body**: 56% female, 44% male, 12% out-of-state. African American 2%, Asian 4%, Caucasian 85%, Hispanic 4%. **Retention and Graduation**: 85% freshmen return for sophomore year. 72% freshmen graduate within 4 years. 24% grads go on to further study within 1 year. 35% grads pursue arts and sciences degrees. 10% grads pursue business degrees. 7% grads pursue law degrees. 19% grads pursue medical degrees. **Faculty**: Student/faculty ratio 14:1. 180 full-time faculty, 93% hold PhDs. 100% faculty teach undergrads.

ACADEMICS

Degrees: Bachelor's, certificate. **Academic Requirements**: Arts/fine arts, English (including composition), history, humanities, mathematics, philosophy, religious studies, sciences (biological or physical), social science. **Classes**: Most classes have 20–29 students. Most lab/discussion sections have 10–19 students. **Majors with Highest Enrollment**: Biology/biological sciences, marketing/marketing management, psychology. **Disciplines with Highest Percentage of Degrees Awarded**: Business/marketing 40%, psychology 11%, social sciences 10%, biological/life sciences 10%, English 10%, history 6%. **Special Study Options**: Accelerated program, cross-registration, double major, English as a second language (ESL), honors program, independent study, internships, liberal arts/career combination, semester in Washington, DC, study abroad, teacher certification program

FACILITIES

Housing: Coed dorms, special housing for disabled students, on-campus town houses (men and women). **Special Academic Facilities/Equipment**: Hickey Financial Center. **Computers**: 2% of classrooms are wired, 1% of classrooms are wireless, 95% of public computers are PCs, 5% of public computers are Macs, network access in dorm rooms, network access in dorm lounges, online registration, online administrative functions (other than registration), remote student-access to Web through college's connection.

CAMPUS LIFE

Activities: Dance, drama/theater, literary magazine, musical theater, pep band, radio station, student government, student newspaper, television station, yearbook. **Organizations**: 68 registered organizations, 19 honor societies, 2 religious organizations. **Athletics (Intercollegiate)**: *Men*: Baseball, basketball, cross-country, golf, lacrosse, soccer, tennis. *Women*: Basketball, cross-country, diving, field hockey, golf, lacrosse, soccer, softball, swimming, tennis, volleyball, water polo.

ADMISSIONS

Freshman Academic Profile: 23% in top 10% of high school class, 60% in top 25% of high school class, 92% in top 50% of high school class. SAT Math middle 50% range 520–620. SAT Critical Reading middle 50% range 500–590. SAT Writing middle 50% range 490–590. ACT middle 50% range 20–24. TOEFL required of all international applicants, minimum paper TOEFL 550, minimum computer TOEFL 213. **Basis for Candidate Selection**: *Very important factors considered include*: Academic GPA, rigor of secondary school record. *Important factors considered include*: Recommendation(s), standardized test scores. *Other factors considered include*: Alumni/ae relation, application essay, character/personal qualities, class rank, extracurricular activities, first generation, interview, level of applicant's interest, racial/ethnic status, talent/ability, volunteer work, work experience. **Freshman Admission Requirements**: High school diploma is required, and GED is accepted. *Academic units required*: 4 English, 3 math, 3 science (3 science labs), 1 social studies, 2 history. *Academic units recommended*: 4 English, 4 math, 4 science (4 science labs), 3 foreign language, 1 social studies, 3 history. **Freshman Admission Statistics**: 5,094 applied, 55% admitted, 25% enrolled. **Transfer Admission Requirements**: College transcript(s), statement of good standing from prior institution(s). Minimum college GPA of 2.5 required. Lowest grade transferable C-. **General Admission Information**: Application fee $50. Early decision application deadline 12/1. Regular application deadline 3/1. Regular notification 3/15. Non-fall registration accepted. Admission may be deferred for a maximum of 1 year. Credit and/or placement offered for CEEB Advanced Placement tests.

COSTS AND FINANCIAL AID

Annual tuition $22,510. Room and board $8,875. Required fees $175. Average book expense $930. **Required Forms and Deadlines**: FAFSA, state aid form. Financial aid filing deadline 2/15. **Notification of Awards**: Applicants will be notified of awards on or about 4/1. **Types of Aid**: *Need-based scholarships/grants*: Pell, SEOG, state scholarships/grants, private scholarships, the school's own gift aid, Siena Grants, St. Francis Community Grants. *Loans*: FFEL Subsidized Stafford, FFEL Unsubsidized Stafford, FFEL PLUS, Federal Perkins. **Financial Aid Statistics**: 71% freshmen, 66% undergrads receive need-based scholarship or grant aid. 56% freshmen, 53% undergrads receive need-based self-help aid. 71 freshmen, 234 undergrads receive athletic scholarships. 84% freshmen, 84% undergrads receive any aid. Highest amount earned per year from on-campus jobs $1,000.

See page 1380.

1247 East Siena Heights Drive, Adrian, MI 49221
Phone: 517-263-0731 **E-mail**: admissions@alpha.sienahts.edu **CEEB Code**: 1719
Fax: 517-264-7704 **Website**: www.sienahts.edu **ACT Code**: 2052
Financial Aid Phone: 916-781-0568

This private school was founded in 1919. It has a 140-acre campus.

RATINGS
Admissions Selectivity Rating: 60*   **Fire Safety Rating**: 60*   **Green Rating**: 60*

STUDENTS AND FACULTY

Student Body: 16% out-of-state. **Retention and Graduation**: 68% freshmen return for sophomore year. 14% grads go on to further study within 1 year. 11% grads pursue arts and sciences degrees. 2% grads pursue law degrees. 1% grads pursue medical degrees.

ACADEMICS

Degrees: Associate, bachelor's, master's. **Special Study Options**: Combined pre-engineering degree 2-2 programs with University of Detroit and University of Michigan, continuing education classes, cooperative education program, foreign study abroad exchange program in Italy, study abroad, undergrads may take grad level classes. Cooperative Education Programs: Arts, business, computer science, education, health professions, humanities, natural science, social/behavioral science.

FACILITIES

Housing: Coed dorms, fraternity/sorority housing. **Special Academic Facilities/Equipment**: Art gallery, Montessori school, language lab.

CAMPUS LIFE

Organizations: 2 fraternities (5% men join), 2 sororities (5% women join). **Athletics (Intercollegiate)**: *Men*: Baseball, basketball, cross-country, soccer, tennis, track/field (outdoor), wrestling. *Women*: Basketball, cross-country, softball, tennis, track/field (outdoor), volleyball.

ADMISSIONS

Freshman Academic Profile: 78% from public high schools. Minimum paper TOEFL 500. **Freshman Admission Requirements**: High school diploma is required, and GED is accepted. *Academic units recommended*: 4 English, 2 math, 1 science, 2 foreign language, 2 social studies, 2 history. **Transfer Admission Requirements**: Minimum college GPA of 2.0 required. Lowest grade transferable C. **General Admission Information**: Regular application deadline 8/15. Regular notification is rolling. Non-fall registration accepted. Common Application not accepted. Credit and/or placement offered for CEEB Advanced Placement tests.

COSTS AND FINANCIAL AID

Comprehensive fee $14,190. Room & board $4,630. Average book expense $575. **Required Forms and Deadlines**: FAFSA. **Notification of Awards**: Applicants will be notified of awards on or about 3/1. **Types of Aid**: *Need-based scholarships/grants*: Pell, SEOG, state scholarships/grants, private scholarships, the school's own gift aid. *Loans*: FFEL Subsidized Stafford, FFEL Unsubsidized Stafford, FFEL PLUS, Federal Perkins, state loans, college/university loans from institutional funds. **Student Employment**: Federal Work-Study Program available. Institutional employment available. Off-campus job opportunities are good. **Financial Aid Statistics**: Highest amount earned per year from on-campus jobs $1,275. **Financial Aid Phone**: 517-264-7130.

SIERRA COLLEGE

5000 Rocklin Road, Rocklin, CA 95677
Phone: 916-781-0430 **E-mail**: gmodder@sierracollege.edu
Fax: 916-789-2878 **Website**: www.sierracollege.edu

This public school was founded in 1914.

RATINGS
Admissions Selectivity Rating: 60*   **Fire Safety Rating**: 60*   **Green Rating**: 60*

STUDENTS AND FACULTY
Enrollment: 20,173. **Student Body**: African American 1%, Asian 4%,

Caucasian 78%, Hispanic 7%, Native American 2%. **Faculty**: Student/faculty ratio 16:1.

ACADEMICS

Degrees: Associate, certificate. **Academic Requirements**: Arts/fine arts, English (including composition), history, humanities, mathematics, sciences (biological or physical), social science. **Special Study Options**: Cooperative education program, distance learning, dual enrollment, English as a second language (ESL), independent study, internships, study abroad, weekend college.

FACILITIES

Housing: Coed dorms. **Special Academic Facilities/Equipment**: Ridley Art Gallery, Dietrich Theater, gymnasium, weight room, cardio room. **Computers**: Online registration.

CAMPUS LIFE

Activities: Choral groups, concert band, dance, drama/theater, jazz band, music ensembles, musical theater, student government, student newspaper, television station. **Athletics (Intercollegiate)**: *Men*: Baseball, basketball, cheerleading, cross-country, football, golf, skiing (downhill/alpine), swimming, tennis, track/field (outdoor), water polo, wrestling. *Women*: Basketball, cheerleading, cross-country, golf, skiing (downhill/alpine), soccer, softball, swimming, tennis, track/field (outdoor), volleyball, water polo.

ADMISSIONS

81 (out of 100).

COSTS AND FINANCIAL AID

Annual in-state tuition $132. Out-of-state tuition $132. Room & board $2,895. Required fees $12. Average book expense $250. **Student Employment**: Off-campus job opportunities are good.

SIERRA NEVADA COLLEGE

999 Tahoe Boulevard, Incline Village, NV 89451
Phone: 775-831-1314 **E-mail**: admissions@sierraneveda.edu
Fax: 702-831-1347 **Website**: www.sierraneveda.edu
Financial Aid Phone: 775-831-7799

This private school was founded in 1969. It has a 25-acre campus.

RATINGS

Admissions Selectivity Rating: 80   **Fire Safety Rating**: 60*   **Green Rating**: 60*

STUDENTS AND FACULTY

Enrollment: 302. **Student Body**: 51% female, 49% male, 70% out-of-state, 3% international. African American 1%, Asian 3%, Caucasian 75%, Hispanic 3%. **Retention and Graduation**: 70% freshmen return for sophomore year. 13% freshmen graduate within 4 years. 33% grads go on to further study within 1 year. **Faculty**: Student/faculty ratio 8:1. 19 full-time faculty. 100% faculty teach undergrads.

ACADEMICS

Degrees: Bachelor's, post-bachelor's certificate. **Academic Requirements**: Arts/fine arts, computer literacy, English (including composition), entrepreneurship, foreign languages, history, humanities, mathematics, sciences (biological or physical). **Majors with Highest Enrollment**: Business, management, marketing, and related support services, environmental science, humanities/humanistic studies. **Disciplines with Highest Percentage of Degrees Awarded**: Business/marketing 31%, interdisciplinary studies 29%, visual and performing arts 16%, computer and information sciences 8%, psychology 5%. **Special Study Options**: Double major, honors program, internships, study abroad, teacher certification program.

FACILITIES

Housing: Coed dorms. **Special Academic Facilities/Equipment**: McLean Observatory. **Computers**: 100% of public computers are PCs, network access in dorm rooms, network access in dorm lounges, remote student-access to Web through college's connection.

CAMPUS LIFE

Activities: Literary magazine, student government, student newspaper. **Organizations**: 10 registered organizations, 1 honor society, 2 religious organizations. **Athletics (Intercollegiate)**: *Men*: Equestrian sports, skiing (downhill/alpine). *Women*: Equestrian sports, skiing (downhill/alpine).

ADMISSIONS

Freshman Academic Profile: 10% in top 10% of high school class, 35% in top 25% of high school class, 70% in top 50% of high school class. 60% from public high schools. SAT Math middle 50% range 480–560. SAT Critical Reading middle 50% range 480–560. ACT middle 50% range 20–26. TOEFL required of all international applicants, minimum paper TOEFL 500. **Basis for Candidate Selection**: *Important factors considered include*: Application essay, recommendation(s), rigor of secondary school record. *Other factors considered include*: Alumni/ae relation, character/personal qualities, class rank, extracurricular activities, geographical residence, interview, racial/ethnic status, standardized test scores, talent/ability, volunteer work, work experience. **Freshman Admission Requirements**: High school diploma is required, and GED is accepted. *Academic units recommended*: 4 English, 3 math, 2 science, 2 foreign language, 2 social studies, 2 history. **Freshman Admission Statistics**: 497 applied, 53% admitted, 26% enrolled. **Transfer Admission Requirements**: College transcript(s), essay or personal statement. Lowest grade transferable C. **General Admission Information**: Regular notification is rolling. Non-fall registration accepted. Admission may be deferred for a maximum of 1 year. Common Application accepted. Credit and/or placement offered for CEEB Advanced Placement tests.

COSTS AND FINANCIAL AID

Annual tuition $19,500. Room & board $7,450. Required fees $150. Average book expense $700. **Required Forms and Deadlines**: FAFSA. Financial aid filing deadline 4/1. **Notification of Awards**: Applicants will be notified of awards on a rolling basis beginning on or about 3/1. **Types of Aid**: *Need-based scholarships/grants*: Pell, SEOG, state scholarships/grants, private scholarships, the school's own gift aid. *Loans*: Direct Subsidized Stafford, Direct PLUS. **Student Employment**: Federal Work-Study Program available. Institutional employment available. Off-campus job opportunities are excellent. **Financial Aid Statistics**: 67% freshmen, 67% undergrads receive need-based scholarship or grant aid. 67% freshmen, 67% undergrads receive need-based self-help aid.

SILVER LAKE COLLEGE

2406 South Alverno Road, Manitowoc, WI 54220
Phone: 920-686-6175 **E-mail**: admslc@silver.sl.edu **CEEB Code**: 1300
Fax: 920-684-7082 **Website**: www.sl.edu **ACT Code**: 4586
Financial Aid Phone: 920-686-6122

This private school, affiliated with the Roman Catholic Church, was founded in 1935. It has a 30-acre campus.

RATINGS

Admissions Selectivity Rating: 71   **Fire Safety Rating**: 60*   **Green Rating**: 60*

STUDENTS AND FACULTY

Enrollment: 489. **Student Body**: 73% female, 27% male, 2% out-of-state. Asian 2%, Caucasian 88%, Hispanic 2%, Native American 5%. **Retention and Graduation**: 64% freshmen return for sophomore year. 10% freshmen graduate within 4 years. 15% grads go on to further study within 1 year. **Faculty**: Student/faculty ratio 9:1. 44 full-time faculty, 50% hold PhDs. 98% faculty teach undergrads.

ACADEMICS

Degrees: Associate, bachelor's, certificate, master's, post-bachelor's certificate. **Academic Requirements**: Arts/fine arts, computer literacy, English (including composition), history, humanities, mathematics, philosophy, sciences (biological or physical), social science. **Classes**: Most classes have fewer than 10 students. **Disciplines with Highest Percentage of Degrees Awarded**: Business/marketing 50%, education 26%, psychology 10%, engineering 4%, computer and information sciences 2%, visual and performing arts 2%, social sciences 2%. **Special Study Options**: Accelerated program, double major, independent study, internships, student-designed major, teacher certification program.

FACILITIES

Housing: Apartments for single students. **Computers**: 75% of public computers are PCs.

CAMPUS LIFE

Activities: Choral groups, concert band, dance, jazz band, literary magazine, music ensembles, student government, student newspaper. **Organizations**: 14 registered organizations, 6 honor societies, 1 religious organization. **Athletics (Intercollegiate)**: *Women*: Basketball.

ADMISSIONS

Freshman Academic Profile: 4% in top 10% of high school class, 4% in top 25% of high school class, 64% in top 50% of high school class. 75% from public high schools. ACT middle 50% range 17–20. TOEFL required of all international applicants, minimum paper TOEFL 550, minimum computer TOEFL 213. **Basis for Candidate Selection**: *Very important factors considered include:* Rigor of secondary school record, standardized test scores. *Important factors considered include:* Character/personal qualities. *Other factors considered include:* Alumni/ae relation, class rank, interview, recommendation(s). **Freshman Admission Requirements**: High school diploma is required, and GED is accepted. *Academic units required:* 3 English, 2 math, 1 science (1 science lab), 1 social studies, 1 history, 7 academic electives. **Freshman Admission Statistics**: 86 applied, 47% admitted. **Transfer Admission Requirements**: College transcript(s). Minimum college GPA of 2.0 required. Lowest grade transferable C. **General Admission Information**: Application fee $35. Non-fall registration accepted. Common Application accepted.

COSTS AND FINANCIAL AID

Annual tuition $14,350. Room $4,100. Average book expense $600. **Required Forms and Deadlines**: FAFSA, institution's own financial aid form. Financial aid filing deadline 4/15. **Notification of Awards**: Applicants will be notified of awards on a rolling basis beginning on or about 5/1. **Types of Aid**: *Need-based scholarships/grants:* Pell, SEOG, state scholarships/grants, private scholarships, the school's own gift aid. *Loans:* FFEL Subsidized Stafford, FFEL Unsubsidized Stafford, FFEL PLUS, state loans. **Student Employment**: Federal Work-Study Program available. Off-campus job opportunities are good. **Financial Aid Statistics**: 97% freshmen, 61% undergrads receive need-based scholarship or grant aid. 88% freshmen, 54% undergrads receive need-based self-help aid. 9 undergrads receive athletic scholarships.

SIMMONS COLLEGE

300 The Fenway, Boston, MA 02115
Phone: 617-521-2051 **E-mail:** ugadm@simmons.edu **CEEB Code:** 3761
Fax: 617-521-3190 **Website:** www.simmons.edu **ACT Code:** 1892
Financial Aid Phone: 617-521-2001

This private school was founded in 1899. It has a 12-acre campus.

RATINGS

Admissions Selectivity Rating: 84   **Fire Safety Rating:** 89   **Green Rating:** 90

STUDENTS AND FACULTY

Enrollment: 2,009. **Student Body:** 100% female, 45% out-of-state, 2% international (26 countries represented). African American 6%, Asian 8%, Caucasian 76%, Hispanic 3%. **Retention and Graduation:** 84% freshmen return for sophomore year. 65% freshmen graduate within 4 years. 30% grads go on to further study within 1 year. 6% grads pursue arts and sciences degrees. 5% grads pursue business degrees. 2% grads pursue law degrees. 1% grads pursue medical degrees. **Faculty:** Student/faculty ratio 12:1. 193 full-time faculty, 59% hold PhDs. 100% faculty teach undergrads.

ACADEMICS

Degrees: Bachelor's, diploma, doctoral, master's, post-bachelor's certificate, post-master's certificate. **Academic Requirements:** Arts/fine arts, computer literacy, English (including composition), foreign languages, history, humanities, mathematics, multidisciplinary core course, philosophy, sciences (biological or physical), social science. **Classes:** Most classes have 10–19 students. **Majors with Highest Enrollment:** Communications studies/speech communication and rhetoric; nursing—registered nurse training (RN, ASN, BSN, MSN); psychology. **Disciplines with Highest Percentage of Degrees Awarded:** Health professions and related sciences 27%, communications/journalism 9%, biological/life sciences 9%, public administration and social services 7%, business/marketing 7%. **Special Study Options:** Accelerated program, cooperative education program, cross-registration, double major, dual enrollment, English as a second language (ESL), exchange student program (domestic), honor program, independent study, internships, liberal arts/career combination, student-designed major, study abroad, teacher certification program. Exhange program with Mills College (CA), Spellman College (GA),

Fisk University (TN), American University (DC), Colleges of the Fenway. Double-degree programs with Massachusetts College of Pharmacy and Health Sciences, and with Hebrew College.

FACILITIES

Housing: Coed dorms, women's dorms, special housing for disabled students, special interest housing options (limited visitation floor, quiet floor, community service floor, wellness residence), off-campus townhouse. **Special Academic Facilities/Equipment:** Art gallery, media center, science center with dream/sleep analysis lab, physical therapy clinic areas, sports center with pool and spa. **Computers:** 75% of classrooms are wired, 75% of classrooms are wireless, 70% of public computers are PCs, 30% of public computers are Macs, network access in dorm rooms, network access in dorm lounges, online registration, online administrative functions (other than registration), support for handheld computing, remote student-access to Web through college's connection.

CAMPUS LIFE

Activities: Choral groups, concert band, dance, drama/theater, literary magazine, music ensembles, student government, student newspaper, student-run film society, yearbook. **Organizations:** 70 registered organizations, 1 honor society, 4 religious organizations. **Athletics (Intercollegiate):** *Women:* Basketball, crew/rowing, cross-country, diving, field hockey, soccer, softball, swimming, tennis, track/field (outdoor), volleyball. Environmental Initiatives: Recycling Program. Mechanical equipment upgrades to improvement efficiency and performance. LEED certified new building.

ADMISSIONS

Freshman Academic Profile: 26% in top 10% of high school class, 59% in top 25% of high school class, 92% in top 50% of high school class. SAT Math middle 50% range 480–590. SAT Critical Reading middle 50% range 500–600. SAT Writing middle 50% range 510–610. ACT middle 50% range 21–26. TOEFL required of all international applicants, minimum paper TOEFL 560, minimum computer TOEFL 220. **Basis for Candidate Selection:** *Very important factors considered include:* Academic GPA, rigor of secondary school record. *Important factors considered include:* Application essay, character/personal qualities, class rank, recommendation(s), standardized test scores. *Other factors considered include:* Extracurricular activities, interview, talent/ability, volunteer work, work experience. **Freshman Admission Requirements:** High school diploma or equivalent is not required. *Academic units required:* 4 English, 3 math, 3 science, 3 foreign language, 3 social studies, 3 history. *Academic units recommended:* 4 English, 4 math, 3 science, 4 foreign language, 4 social studies, 3 history. **Freshman Admission Statistics:** 2,537 applied, 59% admitted, 29% enrolled. **Transfer Admission Requirements:** High school transcript, college transcript(s), essay or personal statement, standardized test score, statement of good standing from prior institution(s). Minimum college GPA of 2.8 required. Lowest grade transferable C+. **General Admission Information:** Application fee $35. Regular application deadline 2/1. Regular notification 4/15. Nonfall registration accepted. Admission may be deferred for a maximum of 1 year. Credit and/or placement offered for CEEB Advanced Placement tests.

COSTS AND FINANCIAL AID

Annual tuition $27,468. Room and board $11,138. Required fees $834. Average book expense $800. **Required Forms and Deadlines:** FAFSA. Financial aid filing deadline 3/1. Financial aid filing deadline 2/15. **Notification of Awards:** Applicants will be notified of awards on or about 3/15. **Types of Aid:** *Need-based scholarships/grants:* Pell, SEOG, state scholarships/grants, private scholarships, the school's own gift aid. *Loans:* FFEL Subsidized Stafford, FFEL Unsubsidized Stafford, FFEL PLUS, Federal Perkins, state loans, college/university loans from institutional funds. **Student Employment:** Financial **Aid Statistics:** 59% freshmen, 61% undergrads receive need-based scholarship or grant aid. 63% freshmen, 61% undergrads receive need-based self-help aid. 74% freshmen, 70% undergrads receive any aid. Highest amount earned per year from on-campus jobs $2,000.

See page 1382.

SIMON FRASER UNIVERSITY

Office of the Registrar, 8888 University Drive, Burnaby, BC V5A 1S6 Canada
Phone: 604-291-3224 **E-mail:** undergraduate-admissions@sfu.ca
Fax: 604-291-4969 **Website:** www.sfu.ca

This is a public school. It has a 400-acre campus.

RATINGS

Admissions Selectivity Rating: 60*   **Fire Safety Rating:** 60*   **Green Rating:** 60*

STUDENTS AND FACULTY

Enrollment: 16,399. **Student Body:** 56% female, 44% male, 7% out-of-state. **Faculty:** Student/faculty ratio 22:1.

ACADEMICS

Degrees: Bachelor's, certificate, diploma, doctoral, master's, post-master's certificate. **Classes:** Most classes have 10–19 students. Most lab/discussion sections have 10–19 students. **Majors with Highest Enrollment:** Business administration/management, communications and media studies, psychology. **Disciplines with Highest Percentage of Degrees Awarded:** Social sciences 28%, business/marketing 14%, psychology 8%, biological/life sciences 7%, liberal arts/general studies 7%, communication technologies 6%. **Special Study Options:** Cooperative education program, distance learning, double major, exchange student program (domestic), honors program, independent study, study abroad, teacher certification program.

FACILITIES

Housing: Coed dorms, women's dorms, apartments for married students, special housing for disabled students.

CAMPUS LIFE

Activities: Dance, drama/theater, radio station, student government, student newspaper, student-run film society.

ADMISSIONS

Basis for Candidate Selection: *Very important factors considered include:* Class rank, rigor of secondary school record, standardized test scores. **Freshman Admission Statistics:** 37% enrolled. **Transfer Admission Requirements:** High school transcript, college transcript(s). **General Admission Information:** Application fee $25. Early decision application deadline 5/1. Regular application deadline 4/30. Non-fall registration accepted.

COSTS AND FINANCIAL AID

In-province tuition $2,195. Out-of-province tuition $2,195. International tuition $6,930. Room $2,712. Required fees $209. Average book expense $540.

SIMON'S ROCK COLLEGE OF BARD

84 Alford Road, Great Barrington, MA 01230
Phone: 413-528-7312 **E-mail:** admit@simons-rock.edu **CEEB Code:** 3795
Fax: 413-528-7334 **Website:** www.simons-rock.edu **ACT Code:** 1893
Financial Aid Phone: 413-528-7249

This private school was founded in 1964. It has a 275-acre campus.

RATINGS

Admissions Selectivity Rating: 90   **Fire Safety Rating:** 60*   **Green Rating:** 60*

STUDENTS AND FACULTY

Enrollment: 368. **Student Body:** 57% female, 43% male, 80% out-of-state, 4% international. African American 7%, Asian 4%, Caucasian 58%, Hispanic 6%. **Retention and Graduation:** 82% freshmen return for sophomore year. 73% freshmen graduate within 4 years. **Faculty:** Student/faculty ratio 8:1. 37 full-time faculty, 95% hold PhDs. 100% faculty teach undergrads.

ACADEMICS

Degrees: Associate, bachelor's. **Academic Requirements:** Arts/fine arts, English (including composition), foreign languages, history, humanities, mathematics, sciences (biological or physical), social science, year long first-year seminar, sophomore year seminar, BA seminar in their area of concentration. **Classes:** Most classes have 10–19 students. Most lab/discussion sections have 10–19 students. **Majors with Highest Enrollment:** Cell/cellular biology and histology, creative writing, psychology. **Disciplines with Highest Percentage of Degrees Awarded:** Visual and performing arts 26%, English 14%, social sciences 13%, foreign languages and literature 11%, psychology 8%. **Special Study Options:** Accelerated program, cooperative education program, cross-registration, dual enrollment, exchange student program (domestic), independent study, internships, student-designed major, study abroad. Study abroad program(s) in the last 2 years: Honduras, Spain, England, Germany, Thailand, South Africa, Japan, China.

FACILITIES

Housing: Coed dorms, men's dorms, women's dorms, apartments for single students. If students propose a plan for cooperative housing it will be considered by Dean of Student Life. **Special Academic Facilities/Equipment:** Daniel Arts Center, Fisher Science & Academic Center. **Computers:** 2% of classrooms are wired, 1% of classrooms are wireless, 50% of public computers are PCs, 50% of public computers are Macs, 15% of public computers are UNIX, network access in dorm rooms, network access in dorm lounges, online administrative functions (other than registration), support for handheld computing, remote student-access to Web through college's connection.

CAMPUS LIFE

Activities: Choral groups, dance, drama/theater, jazz band, literary magazine, music ensembles, radio station, student government, student newspaper, student-run film society, yearbook. **Organizations:** 21 registered organizations, 3 religious organizations. **Athletics (Intercollegiate):** *Men:* Basketball, soccer, swimming, tennis. *Women:* Basketball, soccer, swimming, tennis.

ADMISSIONS

Freshman Academic Profile: 60% in top 10% of high school class, 82% in top 25% of high school class, 94% in top 50% of high school class. SAT Math middle 50% range 530–680. SAT Critical Reading middle 50% range 560–690. ACT middle 50% range 25–30. TOEFL required of all international applicants, minimum paper TOEFL 550, minimum computer TOEFL 200. **Basis for Candidate Selection:** *Very important factors considered include:* Application essay, character/personal qualities, interview, recommendation(s), rigor of secondary school record, talent/ability. *Important factors considered include:* Academic GPA, class rank, level of applicant's interest. *Other factors considered include:* Alumni/ae relation, extracurricular activities, first generation, racial/ethnic status, standardized test scores, volunteer work, work experience. **Freshman Admission Requirements:** High school diploma or equivalent is not required. *Academic units recommended:* 2 English, 2 math, 2 science (1 science lab), 2 foreign language, 2 social studies, 2 history. **Freshman Admission Statistics:** 204 applied, 84% admitted, 74% enrolled. **Transfer Admission Requirements:** College transcript(s), essay or personal statement, interview. Minimum college GPA of 2.0 required. Lowest grade transferable C. **General Admission Information:** Application fee $50. Regular application deadline 5/31. Regular notification is rolling. Non-fall registration accepted. Admission may be deferred for a maximum of 1 year. Credit and/or placement offered for CEEB Advanced Placement tests.

COSTS AND FINANCIAL AID

Annual tuition $34,804. Room & board $9,260. Required fees $530. Average book expense $1,000. **Required Forms and Deadlines:** FAFSA, CSS/Financial Aid PROFILE, Business/Farm Supplement, parent and student federal taxes, federal verification worksheet. Financial aid filing deadline 4/15. **Notification of Awards:** Applicants will be notified of awards on a rolling basis beginning on or about 4/15. **Types of Aid:** *Need-based scholarships/grants:* Pell, SEOG, state scholarships/grants, private scholarships, the school's own gift aid. *Loans:* FFEL Subsidized Stafford, FFEL Unsubsidized Stafford, FFEL PLUS, Federal Perkins, state loans, alternative educational loans. **Student Employment:** Federal Work-Study Program available. Institutional employment available. Off-campus job opportunities are good. **Financial Aid Statistics:** 51% freshmen, 39% undergrads receive need-based scholarship or grant aid. 47% freshmen, 43% undergrads receive need-based self-help aid. 78% freshmen, 71% undergrads receive any aid. Highest amount earned per year from on-campus jobs $1,300.

SIMPSON COLLEGE (IA)

701 North C Street, Indianola, IA 50125
Phone: 515-961-1624 **E-mail:** admiss@simpson.edu **CEEB Code:** 6650
Fax: 515-961-1870 **Website:** www.simpson.edu **ACT Code:** 1354
Financial Aid Phone: 515-961-1630

This private school, affiliated with the Methodist Church, was founded in 1860. It has a 63-acre campus.

RATINGS
Admissions Selectivity Rating: 75   **Fire Safety Rating:** 60*   **Green Rating:** 60*

STUDENTS AND FACULTY
Enrollment: 1,758. **Student Body:** 60% female, 40% male, 10% out-of-state, 2% international (13 countries represented). Asian 1%, Caucasian 93%, Hispanic 1%. **Retention and Graduation:** 78% freshmen return for sophomore year. 57% freshmen graduate within 4 years. 11% grads go on to further study within 1 year. 6% grads pursue arts and sciences degrees. 1% grads pursue business degrees. 2% grads pursue law degrees. 2% grads pursue medical degrees. **Faculty:** Student/faculty ratio 14:1. 84 full-time faculty, 87% hold PhDs. 100% faculty teach undergrads.

ACADEMICS
Degrees: Bachelor's, post-bachelor's certificate. **Academic Requirements:** Arts/fine arts, English (including composition), history, humanities, mathematics, minority perspective, sciences (biological or physical), senior colloquium, social science. **Classes:** Most classes have 10–19 students. Most lab/discussion sections have 10–19 students. **Disciplines with Highest Percentage of Degrees Awarded:** Business/marketing 20%, education 13%, social sciences 10%, computer and information sciences 7%, liberal arts/general studies 7%, visual and performing arts 6%. **Special Study Options:** Accelerated program, cooperative education program, double major, English as a second language (ESL), honors program, independent study, international program, internships, liberal arts/career combination, student-designed major, study abroad, teacher certification program, weekend college.

FACILITIES
Housing: Coed dorms, men's dorms, women's dorms, apartments for single students, fraternity/sorority housing, Simpson College owns several homes surrounding the campus known as theme houses. **Special Academic Facilities/Equipment:** The biology department hosts a human cadaver lab, while Dunn library boasts the Avery O. Craven Room which houses an extensive antebellum collection. **Computers:** 38% of public computers are PCs, 62% of public computers are Macs, network access in dorm rooms, network access in dorm lounges, remote student-access to Web through college's connection.

CAMPUS LIFE
Activities: Choral groups, concert band, dance, drama/theater, jazz band, literary magazine, music ensembles, opera, pep band, radio station, student government, student newspaper, yearbook. **Organizations:** 89 registered organizations, 15 honor societies, 17 religious organizations. 4 fraternities (27% men join), 4 sororities (25% women join). **Athletics (Intercollegiate):** *Men:* Baseball, basketball, cheerleading, cross-country, football, golf, soccer, tennis, track/field (indoor), track/field (outdoor), wrestling. *Women:* Basketball, cheerleading, cross-country, golf, soccer, softball, swimming, tennis, track/field (indoor), track/field (outdoor), volleyball.

ADMISSIONS
Freshman Academic Profile: 21% in top 10% of high school class, 57% in top 25% of high school class, 90% in top 50% of high school class. 96% from public high schools. ACT middle 50% range 22–27. TOEFL required of all international applicants, minimum paper TOEFL 550. **Basis for Candidate Selection:** *Very important factors considered include:* Class rank, rigor of secondary school record, standardized test scores. *Important factors considered include:* Character/personal qualities, recommendation(s). *Other factors considered include:* Alumni/ae relation, extracurricular activities, interview, volunteer work. **Freshman Admission Requirements:** High school diploma is required, and GED is accepted. *Academic units recommended:* 4 English, 3 math, 3 science (3 science labs), 3 foreign language, 3 social studies. **Freshman Admission Statistics:** 1,442 applied, 76% admitted, 38% enrolled. **Transfer Admission Requirements:** High school transcript, college transcript(s), standardized test score. Minimum college GPA of 2.5 required. Lowest grade transferable C-. **General Admission Information:** Non-fall registration accepted. Admission may be deferred for a maximum of 2 years. Common Application not accepted. Credit and/or placement offered for CEEB Advanced Placement tests.

COSTS AND FINANCIAL AID
Annual tuition $17,908. Room & board $6,062. Required fees $189. Average book expense $800. **Required Forms and Deadlines:** FAFSA. Financial aid filing deadline 4/1. **Notification of Awards:** Applicants will be notified of awards on a rolling basis beginning on or about 3/15. **Types of Aid:** *Need-based scholarships/grants:* Pell, SEOG, state scholarships/grants, private scholarships, the school's own gift aid. *Loans:* FFEL Subsidized Stafford, FFEL Unsubsidized Stafford, FFEL PLUS, Federal Perkins, state loans, college/university loans from institutional funds, private educational loans. **Student Employment:** Federal Work-Study Program available. Institutional employment available. Off-campus job opportunities are fair. **Financial Aid Statistics:** 87% freshmen, 86% undergrads receive need-based scholarship or grant aid. 72% freshmen, 75% undergrads receive need-based self-help aid. Highest amount earned per year from on-campus jobs $735.

SIMPSON UNIVERSITY

2211 College View Drive, Redding, CA 96003
Phone: 530-226-4606 **E-mail:** admissions@simpsonuniversity.edu
Fax: 530-226-4861 **Website:** www.simpsonuniversity.edu **ACT Code:** 0430
Financial Aid Phone: 530-224-5600

This private school, affiliated with the Christian & Missionary Alliance Church, was founded in 1921. It has a 92-acre campus.

RATINGS
Admissions Selectivity Rating: 82   **Fire Safety Rating:** 60*   **Green Rating:** 60*

STUDENTS AND FACULTY
Enrollment: 953. **Student Body:** African American 1%, Asian 6%, Caucasian 75%, Hispanic 4%. **Retention and Graduation:** 61% freshmen return for sophomore year. **Faculty:** Student/faculty ratio 17:1. 38 full-time faculty, 55% hold PhDs. 87% faculty teach undergrads.

ACADEMICS
Degrees: Associate, bachelor's, certificate, master's. **Academic Requirements:** Arts/fine arts, English (including composition), foundational studies in biblical Christianity, history, humanities, mathematics, philosophy, sciences (biological or physical), social science. **Classes:** Most classes have 10–19 students. Most lab/discussion sections have 10–19 students. **Majors with Highest Enrollment:** Elementary education and teaching, organizational behavior studies, psychology. **Disciplines with Highest Percentage of Degrees Awarded:** Liberal arts/general studies 33%, psychology 22%, business/marketing 15%, education 7%, communication technologies 3%. **Special Study Options:** Accelerated program, distance learning, double major, honors program, independent study, internships, student-designed major, study abroad, teacher certification program, weekend college.

FACILITIES
Housing: Men's dorms, women's dorms, apartments for married students, special housing for disabled students, special housing for international students. **Computers:** 20% of public computers are PCs, 15% of public computers are Macs, network access in dorm rooms, network access in dorm lounges, online registration, online administrative functions (other than registration), remote student-access to Web through college's connection.

CAMPUS LIFE
Activities: Choral groups, drama/theater, jazz band, music ensembles, pep band, student government, student newspaper, yearbook. **Organizations:** 17 registered organizations, 1 honor society, 20 religious organizations. **Athletics (Intercollegiate):** *Men:* Baseball, basketball. *Women:* Basketball.

ADMISSIONS
Freshman Academic Profile: 19% in top 10% of high school class, 47% in top 25% of high school class, 79% in top 50% of high school class. 63% from public high schools. SAT Math middle 50% range 430–560. SAT Critical Reading middle 50% range 450–590. ACT middle 50% range 18–23. TOEFL required of all international applicants, minimum paper TOEFL 500, minimum computer TOEFL 180. **Basis for Candidate Selection:** *Very important factors considered include:* Character/personal qualities, recommendation(s), religious affiliation/commitment, rigor of secondary school record, standardized test scores. *Important factors considered include:* Class rank, volunteer work. *Other factors considered include:* Application essay, extracurricular activities, interview, talent/ability. **Freshman Admission Requirements:** High school diploma is required, and GED is accepted. *Academic units recommended:* 4 English, 3 math, 2 science, 2 foreign language, 3 social studies. **Freshman**

Admission Statistics: 938 applied, 59% admitted, 34% enrolled. **Transfer Admission Requirements**: High school transcript, college transcript(s), essay or personal statement, statement of good standing from prior institution(s). Minimum college GPA of 2.0 required. Lowest grade transferable C. **General Admission Information**: Application fee $20. Non-fall registration accepted. Admission may be deferred for a maximum of 2 years. Common Application not accepted. Credit and/or placement offered for CEEB Advanced Placement tests.

COSTS AND FINANCIAL AID

Annual tuition $17,000. Room & board $5,900. Average book expense $1,200. **Required Forms and Deadlines**: FAFSA, institution's own financial aid form. Financial aid filing deadline 3/2. **Notification of Awards**: Applicants will be notified of awards on a rolling basis beginning on or about 3/16. **Types of Aid**: *Need-based scholarships/grants*: Pell, SEOG, state scholarships/grants, private scholarships, the school's own gift aid. *Loans*: FFEL Subsidized Stafford, FFEL Unsubsidized Stafford, FFEL PLUS, Federal Perkins, alternative loans. **Student Employment**: Federal Work-Study Program available. Institutional employment available. Off-campus job opportunities are good. **Financial Aid Statistics**: 84% freshmen, 91% undergrads receive need-based scholarship or grant aid. 82% freshmen, 89% undergrads receive need-based self-help aid. 96% freshmen, 96% undergrads receive any aid.

SKIDMORE COLLEGE

815 North Broadway, Saratoga Springs, NY 12866-1632
Phone: 518-580-5570 **E-mail**: admissions@skidmore.edu **CEEB Code**: 2815
Fax: 518-580-5584 **Website**: www.skidmore.edu **ACT Code**: 2906
Financial Aid Phone: 518-580-5750

This private school was founded in 1903. It has an 850-acre campus.

RATINGS
Admissions Selectivity Rating: 94   **Fire Safety Rating**: 60*   **Green Rating**: 60*

STUDENTS AND FACULTY
Enrollment: 2,727. **Student Body**: 61% female, 39% male, 70% out-of-state. African American 3%, Asian 6%, Caucasian 72%, Hispanic 4%. **Retention and Graduation**: 92% freshmen return for sophomore year. 73% freshmen graduate within 4 years. 15% grads go on to further study within 1 year. 7% grads pursue arts and sciences degrees. 1% grads pursue business degrees. 3% grads pursue law degrees. 1% grads pursue medical degrees. **Faculty**: Student/faculty ratio 9:1. 228 full-time faculty, 82% hold PhDs. 100% faculty teach undergrads.

ACADEMICS
Degrees: Bachelor's, master's. **Academic Requirements**: Arts/fine arts, cultural diversity, English (including composition), foreign languages, history, humanities, interdisciplinary study, mathematics, non-Western culture, sciences (biological or physical), social science. **Classes**: Most classes have 10–19 students. Most lab/discussion sections have 10–19 students. **Majors with Highest Enrollment**: Business administration/management, English language and literature, fine arts and art studies. **Disciplines with Highest Percentage of Degrees Awarded**: Visual and performing arts 19%, social sciences 15%, business/marketing 12%, English 10%, psychology 8%. **Special Study Options**: Accelerated program, cross-registration, distance learning, double major, dual enrollment, external degree program, honors program, independent study, internships, liberal arts/career combination, student-designed major, study abroad, teacher certification program.

FACILITIES
Housing: Coed dorms, men's dorms, women's dorms, apartments for single students, special housing for disabled students, special housing for international students, honors floors, substance-free floors. **Special Academic Facilities/Equipment**: Tang Teaching Museum and Art Gallery; center for child study; art, music, dance, and theater facilities; electron microscope; spectrometer. **Computers**: 50% of public computers are PCs, 50% of public computers are Macs, 100% of public computers are UNIX, network access in dorm rooms, online registration, online administrative functions (other than registration), remote student-access to Web through college's connection.

CAMPUS LIFE
Activities: Choral groups, concert band, dance, drama/theater, jazz band, literary magazine, music ensembles, musical theater, opera, radio station, student government, student newspaper, student-run film society, symphony orchestra, television station, yearbook. **Organizations**: 80 registered organizations, 10 honor societies, 3 religious organizations. **Athletics (Intercollegiate)**: *Men*: Baseball, basketball, crew/rowing, diving, golf, ice hockey, lacrosse, soccer, swimming, tennis. *Women*: Basketball, crew/rowing, diving, equestrian sports, field hockey, lacrosse, soccer, softball, swimming, tennis, volleyball.

ADMISSIONS
Freshman Academic Profile: 46% in top 10% of high school class, 78% in top 25% of high school class, 96% in top 50% of high school class. 61% from public high schools. SAT Math middle 50% range 580–670. SAT Critical Reading middle 50% range 580–680. SAT Writing middle 50% range 590–690. ACT middle 50% range 26–30. TOEFL required of all international applicants, minimum paper TOEFL 590, minimum computer TOEFL 243. **Basis for Candidate Selection**: *Very important factors considered include*: Rigor of secondary school record. *Important factors considered include*: Academic GPA, application essay, character/personal qualities, class rank, extracurricular activities, recommendation(s), talent/ability, volunteer work, work experience. *Other factors considered include*: Alumni/ae relation, first generation, geographical residence, interview, racial/ethnic status, standardized test scores. **Freshman Admission Requirements**: High school diploma is required, and GED is accepted. *Academic units recommended*: 4 English, 4 math, 4 science (3 science labs), 4 foreign language, 4 social studies. **Freshman Admission Statistics**: 6,055 applied, 44% admitted, 26% enrolled. **Transfer Admission Requirements**: High school transcript, college transcript(s), essay or personal statement, standardized test score, statement of good standing from prior institution(s). Minimum college GPA of 2.7 required. Lowest grade transferable C. **General Admission Information**: Application fee $60. Early decision application deadline 11/15. Regular application deadline 1/15. Regular notification 4/1. Non-fall registration accepted. Admission may be deferred for a maximum of 2 years. Common Application accepted. Credit and/or placement offered for CEEB Advanced Placement tests.

COSTS AND FINANCIAL AID
Annual tuition $34,224. Room and board $9,556. Required fees $470. Average book expense $1,000. **Required Forms and Deadlines**: FAFSA, CSS/Financial Aid PROFILE. Financial aid filing deadline 1/15. **Notification of Awards**: Applicants will be notified of awards on or about 4/1. **Types of Aid**: *Need-based scholarships/grants*: Pell, SEOG, state scholarships/grants, the school's own gift aid. *Loans*: FFEL Subsidized Stafford, FFEL Unsubsidized Stafford, FFEL PLUS, Federal Perkins. **Financial Aid Statistics**: 40% freshmen, 41% undergrads receive need-based scholarship or grant aid. 40% freshmen, 41% undergrads receive need-based self-help aid. 40% freshmen, 41% undergrads receive any aid. Highest amount earned per year from on-campus jobs $2,100.

See page 1384.

SLIPPERY ROCK UNIVERSITY OF PENNSYLVANIA

Office of Admissions, 146 North Hall Welcome Center, Slippery Rock, PA 16057
Phone: 724-738-2015 **E-mail**: Asktherock@sru.edu **CEEB Code**: 2658
Fax: 724-738-2913 **Website**: www.sru.edu **ACT Code**: 3716
Financial Aid Phone: 724-738-2044

This public school was founded in 1889. It has a 600-acre campus.

RATINGS
Admissions Selectivity Rating: 75   **Fire Safety Rating**: 95   **Green Rating**: 84

STUDENTS AND FACULTY
Enrollment: 7,506. **Student Body**: 56% female, 44% male, 8% out-of-state, 1% international (45 countries represented). African American 5%, Caucasian 88%. **Retention and Graduation**: 76% freshmen return for sophomore year.

28% freshmen graduate within 4 years. 14% grads go on to further study within 1 year. 25% grads pursue arts and sciences degrees. 10% grads pursue business degrees. 2% grads pursue law degrees. 1% grads pursue medical degrees. **Faculty:** Student/faculty ratio 20:1. 329 full-time faculty, 86% hold PhDs. 100% faculty teach undergrads.

ACADEMICS

Degrees: Bachelor's, certificate, doctoral, master's, post-bachelor's certificate, post-master's certificate. **Academic Requirements:** Arts/fine arts, computer literacy, English (including composition), history, humanities, mathematics, sciences (biological or physical), social science. **Classes:** Most classes have 20–29 students. Most lab/discussion sections have 20–29 students. **Majors with Highest Enrollment:** Elementary education and teaching; physical therapy/therapist; rehabilitation and therapeutic professions. **Disciplines with Highest Percentage of Degrees Awarded:** Education 25%, business/marketing 14%, health professions and related sciences 12%, parks and recreation 11%, psychology 5%. **Special Study Options:** Distance learning, double major, exchange student program (domestic), honor program, independent study, internships, liberal arts/career combination, study abroad, teacher certification program.

FACILITIES

Housing: Coed dorms, women's dorms, apartments for single students, special housing for disabled students. Both traditional halls and newly constructed residential suites. **Special Academic Facilities/Equipment:** Special education school for student teachers, physical therapy clinic, microvideo system, planetarium, electron microscope. **Computers:** 1% of classrooms are wired, 5% of classrooms are wireless, 90% of public computers are PCs, 10% of public computers are Macs, network access in dorm rooms, network access in dorm lounges, online registration, online administrative functions (other than registration), remote student-access to Web through college's connection.

CAMPUS LIFE

Activities: Choral groups, concert band, dance, drama/theater, jazz band, literary magazine, marching band, music ensembles, musical theater, radio station, student government, student newspaper, symphony orchestra, television station, yearbook. **Organizations:** 170 registered organizations, 35 honor societies, 7 religious organizations. 12 fraternities, 9 sororities. **Athletics (Intercollegiate):** *Men:* Baseball, basketball, cheerleading, cross-country, diving, football, soccer, track/field (indoor), track/field (outdoor). *Women:* Basketball, cheerleading, cross-country, diving, field hockey, lacrosse, soccer, softball, swimming, tennis, track/field (indoor), track/field (outdoor), volleyball, water polo. Environmental Initiatives: Recycling. Green building designs and renovations. Green procurement practices.

ADMISSIONS

Freshman Academic Profile: 10% in top 10% of high school class, 33% in top 25% of high school class, 70% in top 50% of high school class. 80% from public high schools. SAT Math middle 50% range 460–550. SAT Critical Reading middle 50% range 450–530. ACT middle 50% range 19–23. TOEFL required of all international applicants, minimum paper TOEFL 500, minimum computer TOEFL 173. **Basis for Candidate Selection:** *Important factors considered include:* Academic GPA, class rank, rigor of secondary school record, standardized test scores. *Other factors considered include:* Alumni/ae relation, application essay, character/personal qualities, extracurricular activities, first generation, geographical residence, interview, level of applicant's interest, racial/ethnic status, recommendation(s), state residency, talent/ability. **Freshman Admission Requirements:** High school diploma is required, and GED is accepted. *Academic units recommended:* 4 English, 3 math, 3 science (1 science lab), 2 foreign language, 3 social studies, 3 history. **Freshman Admission Statistics:** 4,848 applied, 71% admitted, 42% enrolled. **Transfer Admission Requirements:** College transcript(s). Minimum college GPA of 2.0 required. Lowest grade transferable C. **General Admission Information:** Application fee $30. Nonfall registration accepted. Admission may be deferred for a maximum of 1 year. Credit and/or placement offered for CEEB Advanced Placement tests.

COSTS AND FINANCIAL AID

Annual in-state tuition $5,178. Annual out-of-state tuition $7,767. Room and board $7,862. Required fees $1,493. Average book expense $1,278. **Required Forms and Deadlines:** FAFSA. Financial aid filing deadline 5/1. **Notification of Awards:** Applicants will be notified of awards on a rolling basis beginning on or about 3/15. **Types of Aid:** *Need-based scholarships/grants:* Pell, SEOG, state scholarships/grants, private scholarships, the school's own gift aid. *Loans:* FFEL Subsidized Stafford, FFEL Unsubsidized Stafford, FFEL PLUS, Federal Perkins. **Student Employment: Financial Aid Statistics:** 47% freshmen, 46% undergrads receive need-based scholarship or grant aid. 62% freshmen, 58% undergrads receive need-based self-help aid. 53 freshmen, 227 undergrads receive athletic scholarships. 89% freshmen, 83% undergrads receive any aid. Highest amount earned per year from on-campus jobs $3,600.

SMITH COLLEGE

7 College Lane, Northampton, MA 01063
Phone: 413-585-2500 **E-mail:** admission@smith.edu **CEEB Code:** 3762
Fax: 413-585-2527 **Website:** www.smith.edu **ACT Code:** 1894
Financial Aid Phone: 413-585-2530

This private school was founded in 1871. It has a 125-acre campus.

RATINGS
Admissions Selectivity Rating: 95   **Fire Safety Rating:** 74   **Green Rating:** 96

STUDENTS AND FACULTY

Enrollment: 2,598. **Student Body:** 100% female, 78% out-of-state, 7% international (56 countries represented). African American 7%, Asian 12%, Caucasian 50%, Hispanic 7%. **Retention and Graduation:** 91% freshmen return for sophomore year. 81% freshmen graduate within 4 years. 20% grads go on to further study within 1 year. 7% grads pursue arts and sciences degrees. 2% grads pursue law degrees. 1% grads pursue medical degrees. **Faculty:** 285 full-time faculty, 98% hold PhDs. 100% faculty teach undergrads.

ACADEMICS

Degrees: Bachelor's, doctoral, master's, post-bachelor's certificate, post-master's certificate. **Academic Requirements:** Writing intensive course. **Classes:** Most classes have 10–19 students. Most lab/discussion sections have fewer than 10 students. **Majors with Highest Enrollment:** Political science and government, psychology, visual and performing arts. **Disciplines with Highest Percentage of Degrees Awarded:** Social sciences 23%, foreign languages and literature 14%, visual and performing arts 10%, psychology 8%, area and ethnic studies 8%. **Special Study Options:** Accelerated program, cross-registration, double major, exchange student program (domestic), honors program, independent study, internships, student-designed major, study abroad, teacher certification program.

FACILITIES

Housing: Women's dorms, cooperative housing, apartment complex for a limited number of juniors and seniors, a senior house, French house, Ada Comstock (nontraditional age) house. **Special Academic Facilities/Equipment:** Art museum; printing, darkroom, and sculpture facilities; dance, electronic music, television, and theater studios; recital hall; rehearsal rooms; multimedia language lab; early childhood/elementary education campus school; 2 electronic classrooms; physiology and horticultural labs; animal care facilities; 2 electron microscopes; greenhouses; observatories. **Computers:** 98% of classrooms are wired, 15% of classrooms are wireless, 65% of public computers are PCs, 31% of public computers are Macs, 4% of public computers are UNIX, network access in dorm rooms, network access in dorm lounges, online registration, online administrative functions (other than registration), remote student-access to Web through college's connection.

CAMPUS LIFE

Activities: Choral groups, concert band, dance, drama/theater, jazz band, literary magazine, music ensembles, musical theater, radio station, student government, student newspaper, television station, yearbook. **Organizations:** 133 registered organizations, 3 honor societies, 9 religious organizations. **Athletics (Intercollegiate):** *Women:* Basketball, crew/rowing, cross-country, diving, equestrian sports, field hockey, lacrosse, skiing (downhill/alpine), soccer, softball, squash, swimming, tennis, track/field (indoor), track/field (outdoor), volleyball. Environmental Initiatives: Presently constructing cogeneration facility that will generate 2/3 of campus electricity use and 1/2 of steam for heat. System will decrease use of #6 fuel oil and greatly reduce greenhouse gas emissions. Created shared Energy Manager and Recycling Manager positions (collaboration w/ Five Colleges Inc.). Hiring full-time Sustainability Coordinator in progress. Implemented 14 energy efficiency projects and 7 conservation programs over past 3 years, these have generated substantial financial and environmental savings.

ADMISSIONS

Freshman Academic Profile: 61% in top 10% of high school class, 91% in top 25% of high school class, 100% in top 50% of high school class. 67% from public high schools. SAT Math middle 50% range 560–670. SAT Critical Reading middle 50% range 580–700. SAT Writing middle 50% range 640–730. ACT middle 50% range 25–29. TOEFL required of all international applicants,

minimum paper TOEFL 600, minimum computer TOEFL 250. **Basis for Candidate Selection**: *Very important factors considered include:* Academic GPA, character/personal qualities, recommendation(s), rigor of secondary school record. *Important factors considered include:* Application essay, class rank, extracurricular activities, interview, standardized test scores, talent/ability. *Other factors considered include:* Alumni/ae relation, first generation, racial/ethnic status, volunteer work, work experience. **Freshman Admission Requirements**: High school diploma or equivalent is not required. *Academic units recommended:* 4 English, 4 math, 3 science (3 science labs), 3 foreign language, 2 history. **Freshman Admission Statistics**: 3,427 applied, 53% admitted, 37% enrolled. **Transfer Admission Requirements**: High school transcript, college transcript(s), essay or personal statement, statement of good standing from prior institution(s). Lowest grade transferable C. **General Admission Information**: Application fee $60. Early decision application deadline 11/15. Regular application deadline 1/15. Regular notification 4/1. Non-fall registration not accepted. Admission may be deferred for a maximum of 1 year. Credit and/or placement offered for CEEB Advanced Placement tests.

COSTS AND FINANCIAL AID

Annual tuition $32,320. Room & board $10,880. Required fees $238. Average book expense $600. **Required Forms and Deadlines**: FAFSA, CSS/Financial Aid PROFILE, Noncustodial PROFILE, Business/Farm Supplement. Financial aid filing deadline 2/1. **Notification of Awards**: Applicants will be notified of awards on or about 4/1. **Types of Aid**: *Need-based scholarships/grants:* Pell, SEOG, state scholarships/grants, the school's own gift aid. *Loans:* Direct Subsidized Stafford, Direct Unsubsidized Stafford, FFEL PLUS, Federal Perkins, state loans, college/university loans from institutional funds. **Student Employment**: Federal Work-Study Program available. Institutional employment available. Off-campus job opportunities are excellent. **Financial Aid Statistics**: 59% freshmen, 59% undergrads receive need-based scholarship or grant aid. 58% freshmen, 58% undergrads receive need-based self-help aid. 66% freshmen, 65% undergrads receive any aid. Highest amount earned per year from on-campus jobs $2,500.

SOKA UNIVERSITY OF AMERICA

1 University Drive, Enrollment Services, Aliso Viejo, CA 92656-4105
Phone: 949-480-4150 **E-mail**: admission@soka.edu **CEEB Code**: 4066
Fax: 949-480-4151 **Website**: www.soka.edu **ACT Code**: 0467
Financial Aid Phone: 949-480-4048

This private school was founded in 2001. It has a 103-acre campus.

RATINGS
Admissions Selectivity Rating: 60*   **Fire Safety Rating**: 82   **Green Rating**: 60*

STUDENTS AND FACULTY
Enrollment: 360. **Student Body**: 62% female, 38% male, 61% out-of-state, 53% international (28 countries represented). African American 3%, Asian 19%, Caucasian 10%, Hispanic 4%. **Retention and Graduation**: 91% freshmen return for sophomore year. 40% grads go on to further study within 1 year. 34% grads pursue arts and sciences degrees. 2% grads pursue business degrees. 2% grads pursue law degrees. 2% grads pursue medical degrees. **Faculty**: Student/faculty ratio 8:1. 38 full-time faculty, 95% hold PhDs. 100% faculty teach undergrads.

ACADEMICS
Degrees: Bachelor's, master's. **Academic Requirements**: Arts/fine arts, computer literacy, English (including composition), foreign languages, history, humanities, mathematics, philosophy, sciences (biological or physical), social science. Our courses stress multicultural, ethnic, and/or gender-related content. **Classes**: Most classes have 10–19 students. Most lab/discussion sections have 10–19 students. **Disciplines with Highest Percentage of Degrees Awarded**: Liberal arts/general studies 100%. **Special Study Options**: English as a second language (ESL), independent study, internships, liberal arts/career combination, study abroad.

FACILITIES
Housing: Coed dorms, special housing for disabled students. **Special Academic Facilities/Equipment**: Art gallery, Athenaeum (reception center). **Computers**: 75% of classrooms are wired, 100% of classrooms are wireless, 100% of public computers are PCs, network access in dorm rooms, network access in dorm lounges, online registration, online administrative functions (other than registration), support for handheld computing, remote student-access to Web through college's connection, tuition includes personal computer. Undergraduates are required to own a computer.

CAMPUS LIFE
Activities: Choral groups, concert band, dance, drama/theater, jazz band, literary magazine, music ensembles, student government, student newspaper, student-run film society, symphony orchestra, yearbook. **Organizations**: 38 registered organizations, 1 religious organization. **Athletics (Intercollegiate)**: *Men:* Cross-country, diving, soccer, swimming, track/field (outdoor). *Women:* Cross-country, diving, soccer, swimming, track/field (outdoor).

ADMISSIONS
Freshman Academic Profile: 60% from public high schools. SAT Math middle 50% range 570–680. SAT Critical Reading middle 50% range 460–640. SAT Writing middle 50% range 490–630. ACT middle 50% range 23–24. **Basis for Candidate Selection**: *Very important factors considered include:* Academic GPA, application essay, character/personal qualities, class rank, extracurricular activities, level of applicant's interest, recommendation(s), rigor of secondary school record. *Important factors considered include:* Standardized test scores, talent/ability, volunteer work. *Other factors considered include:* Geographical residence, interview, racial/ethnic status, work experience. **Freshman Admission Requirements**: High school diploma is required, and GED is accepted. *Academic units recommended:* 4 English, 3 math, 2 science (2 science labs), 2 foreign language, 2 social studies, 2 history. **Freshman Admission Statistics**: 321 applied, 40% admitted, 68% enrolled. **General Admission Information**: Application fee $45. Regular application deadline 1/6. Regular notification 3/15. Non-fall registration not accepted. Admission may be deferred for a maximum of 1 year. Neither credit nor placement offered for CEEB Advanced Placement tests.

COSTS AND FINANCIAL AID
Annual tuition $22,108. Room & board $8,600. Average book expense $1,000. **Required Forms and Deadlines**: FAFSA. Financial aid filing deadline 5/1. **Notification of Awards**: Applicants will be notified of awards on a rolling basis beginning on or about 3/15. **Types of Aid**: *Need-based scholarships/grants:* Pell, SEOG, state scholarships/grants, private scholarships, the school's own gift aid, Hispanic Educational Endowment Fund (HEEF). *Loans:* FFEL Subsidized Stafford, FFEL Unsubsidized Stafford, FFEL PLUS, college/university loans from institutional funds. **Financial Aid Statistics**: 35% freshmen, 84% undergrads receive need-based scholarship or grant aid. 34% freshmen, 61% undergrads receive need-based self-help aid. 100% freshmen, 100% undergrads receive any aid. Highest amount earned per year from on-campus jobs $5,400.

SONOMA STATE UNIVERSITY

Best 368

1801 East Cotati Avenue, Rohnert Park, CA 94928
Phone: 707-664-2778 **E-mail**: admitme@sonoma.edu **CEEB Code**: 4723
Fax: 707-664-2060 **Website**: www.sonoma.edu **ACT Code**: 431
Financial Aid Phone: 707-664-2389

This public school was founded in 1960. It has a 269-acre campus.

RATINGS
Admissions Selectivity Rating: 60*   **Fire Safety Rating**: 60*   **Green Rating**: 98

STUDENTS AND FACULTY
Enrollment: 7,112. **Student Body**: 63% female, 37% male, 1% out-of-state. African American 2%, Caucasian 67%, Hispanic 11%. **Retention and Graduation**: 79% freshmen return for sophomore year. 22% freshmen graduate within 4 years. **Faculty**: Student/faculty ratio 22:1. 268 full-time faculty, 90% hold PhDs. 98% faculty teach undergrads.

ACADEMICS
Degrees: Bachelor's, master's. **Academic Requirements**: Arts/fine arts, English (including composition), ethnic studies, history, humanities, mathematics, sciences (biological or physical), social science, U.S. and California government. **Classes**: Most classes have 20–29 students. **Majors with Highest Enrollment**: Business administration/management; liberal arts, sciences studies, and humanities; psychology. **Disciplines with Highest Percentage of Degrees Awarded**: Business/marketing 17%, social sciences 11%, liberal arts/general studies 10%, psychology 10%, communication technologies 6%, English 5%. **Special Study Options**: Accelerated program, combined degree programs

(bachelor's/MBA, bachelor's/MPA), cooperative education program, cross-registration, distance learning, double major, dual enrollment, English as a second language (ESL), exchange student program (domestic), external degree program, honors program, independent study, internships, liberal arts/career combination, student-designed major, study abroad, teacher certification program.

FACILITIES

Housing: Coed dorms, apartments for single students, special housing for international students, housing for focused learning communities (freshman seminar dorms, healthy living dorms, women in math/science dorms). **Special Academic Facilities/Equipment**: Performing arts center, observatory, electron microscope, seismograph, information technology center, environmental technology center, high technology high school, nature preserve. **Computers**: 5% of classrooms are wired, 95% of classrooms are wireless, 80% of public computers are PCs, 20% of public computers are Macs, network access in dorm rooms, network access in dorm lounges, online registration, online administrative functions (other than registration), support for handheld computing, remote student-access to Web through college's connection. Undergraduates are required to own a computer.

CAMPUS LIFE

Activities: Choral groups, dance, drama/theater, jazz band, literary magazine, music ensembles, musical theater, opera, pep band, radio station, student government, student newspaper, symphony orchestra. **Organizations**: 109 registered organizations, 6 honor societies, 4 religious organizations. 4 fraternities (6% men join), 4 sororities (5% women join). **Athletics (Intercollegiate)**: *Men*: Baseball, basketball, soccer, tennis. *Women*: Basketball, cross-country, soccer, softball, tennis, track/field (outdoor), volleyball. Environmental Initiatives: The Student Recreation Center sustainable design features increase energy efficiency and strive to lessen impact on the environment. The Environmental Technology Center (ETC) incorporates a wide range of sustainable building techniques and features that minimize energy use, consuming less than 50% of the energy allowed by state code for similar buildings. The former university library is now one of the most energy efficient public buildings in northern California and has one of the largest solar panel grids in the region, covering 9,500 square feet with 1200 panels.

ADMISSIONS

Freshman Academic Profile: 87% from public high schools. SAT Math middle 50% range 460–550. SAT Critical Reading middle 50% range 460–560. ACT middle 50% range 19–24. TOEFL required of all international applicants, minimum paper TOEFL 500, minimum computer TOEFL 173. **Basis for Candidate Selection**: *Very important factors considered include*: Rigor of secondary school record, standardized test scores. *Important factors considered include*: Geographical residence, racial/ethnic status, state residency. **Freshman Admission Requirements**: High school diploma is required, and GED is accepted. *Academic units required*: 4 English, 3 math, 2 science (1 science lab), 2 foreign language, 1 history, 3 academic electives, 1 visual and performing arts, 1 U.S. government. **Freshman Admission Statistics**: 10,398 applied, 69% admitted, 21% enrolled. **Transfer Admission Requirements**: College transcript(s). Minimum college GPA of 2.0 required. Lowest grade transferable D. **General Admission Information**: Application fee $55. Regular application deadline 1/31. Regular notification is rolling. Non-fall registration accepted. Credit and/or placement offered for CEEB Advanced Placement tests.

COSTS AND FINANCIAL AID

Annual out-of-state tuition $8,136. Room and board $8,820. Required fees $3,946. Average book expense $1,386. **Required Forms and Deadlines**: FAFSA. Financial aid filing deadline 1/31. **Notification of Awards**: Applicants will be notified of awards on a rolling basis beginning on or about 4/15. **Types of Aid**: *Need-based scholarships/grants*: Pell, SEOG, state scholarships/grants, private scholarships, the school's own gift aid. *Loans*: Direct Subsidized Stafford, Direct Unsubsidized Stafford, Direct PLUS, Federal Perkins. **Financial Aid Statistics**: 12% freshmen, 23% undergrads receive need-based scholarship or grant aid. 12% freshmen, 25% undergrads receive need-based self-help aid. 12 freshmen, 81 undergrads receive athletic scholarships. 26% freshmen, 37% undergrads receive any aid. Highest amount earned per year from on-campus jobs $2,200.

SOUTH CAROLINA STATE UNIVERSITY

300 College Street Northeast, Orangeburg, SC 29117-0001
Phone: 800-260-5956 **CEEB Code**: 5618
Fax: 803-536-8990 **Website**: www.scsu.edu **ACT Code**: 3876
Financial Aid Phone: 803-536-7067

This public school was founded in 1896. It has a 147-acre campus.

RATINGS
Admissions Selectivity Rating: 60*   **Fire Safety Rating**: 60*   **Green Rating**: 60*

STUDENTS AND FACULTY
Student Body: 8% out-of-state.

ACADEMICS
Degrees: Associate, bachelor's, master's. **Special Study Options**: Cooperative education program (business, engineering), foreign study abroad exchange program(s) in Italy and Spain (University of Madrid), study abroad.

FACILITIES
Housing: Coed dorms, apartments for married students. **Special Academic Facilities/Equipment**: Museum, planetarium, language lab.

CAMPUS LIFE
Organizations: 1 religious organization. 4 fraternities, 4 sororities.

ADMISSIONS
Freshman Academic Profile: 7% in top 10% of high school class, 16% in top 25% of high school class, 60% in top 50% of high school class. 98% from public high schools. TOEFL required of all international applicants, minimum paper TOEFL 550. **Freshman Admission Requirements**: High school diploma is required, and GED is accepted. *Academic units required*: 4 English, 3 math, 2 science, 2 foreign language, 2 social studies, 1 history, 2 academic electives. **Transfer Admission Requirements**: Minimum college GPA of 2.0 required. Lowest grade transferable C. **General Admission Information**: Regular application deadline 7/31. Regular notification is rolling. Non-fall registration accepted. Common Application accepted. Credit and/or placement offered for CEEB Advanced Placement tests.

COSTS AND FINANCIAL AID
Comprehensive fee $5,256. Room & board $4,100. Required fees $75. Average book expense $1,000. **Required Forms and Deadlines**: FAFSA. **Notification of Awards**: Applicants will be notified of awards on or about 6/15. **Types of Aid**: *Loans*: FFEL Subsidized Stafford, FFEL PLUS. **Student Employment**: Institutional employment available.

SOUTH COLLEGE

709 Mall Boulevard, Savannah, GA 31406-4881
Phone: 912-691-6000 **E-mail**: southcollege@southcolege.edu **CEEB Code**: 4200
Fax: 912-691-6070 **Website**: www.southcollege.edu **ACT Code**: 0866
Financial Aid Phone: 912-691-6000

This private school was founded in 1899. It has a 7-acre campus.

RATINGS
Admissions Selectivity Rating: 60*   **Fire Safety Rating**: 60*   **Green Rating**: 60*

STUDENTS AND FACULTY
Enrollment: 445. **Student Body**: 81% female, 19% male. **Retention and Graduation**: 9% grads go on to further study within 1 year. **Faculty**: 100% faculty teach undergrads.

ACADEMICS
Degrees: Associate, bachelor's, certificate. **Academic Requirements**: Computer literacy, English (including composition), mathematics, sciences (biological or physical), social science. **Special Study Options**: Accelerated program, double major, dual enrollment, internships.

FACILITIES
Computers: 100% of public computers are PCs, online administrative functions (other than registration).

ADMISSIONS

Freshman Academic Profile: TOEFL required of all international applicants, minimum paper TOEFL 550. **Basis for Candidate Selection**: *Very important factors considered include*: Application essay, interview, recommendation(s), standardized test scores, work experience. *Other factors considered include*: Extracurricular activities, rigor of secondary school record, talent/ability. **Freshman Admission Requirements**: High school diploma is required, and GED is accepted. **Transfer Admission Requirements**: High school transcript, college transcript(s), interview, standardized test score. Minimum college GPA of 1.5 required. Lowest grade transferable C. **General Admission Information**: Application fee $25. Regular application deadline is rolling. Non-fall registration accepted. Admission may be deferred for a maximum of 1 year. Common Application not accepted.

COSTS AND FINANCIAL AID

Annual tuition $6,885. Required fees $25. Average book expense $700. **Required Forms and Deadlines**: FAFSA, state aid form. **Types of Aid**: *Need-based scholarships/grants*: Pell, SEOG, state scholarships/grants, private scholarships, the school's own gift aid. *Loans*: Direct Subsidized Stafford, Direct Unsubsidized Stafford, Direct PLUS, FFEL Subsidized Stafford, FFEL Unsubsidized Stafford, FFEL PLUS, Federal Perkins, college/university loans from institutional funds. **Student Employment**: Federal Work-Study Program available. Off-campus job opportunities are good. **Financial Aid Statistics**: 56% freshmen, 65% undergrads receive need-based scholarship or grant aid. 11% freshmen, 3% undergrads receive need-based self-help aid.

SOUTH DAKOTA SCHOOL
OF MINES & TECHNOLOGY

501 East Saint Joseph Street, Rapid City, SD 57701-3995
Phone: 605-394-2414 **E-mail**: admissions@sdsmt.edu **CEEB Code**: 6652
Fax: 605-394-6131 **Website**: www.sdsmt.edu **ACT Code**: 3922
Financial Aid Phone: 605-394-2274

This public school was founded in 1885. It has a 120-acre campus.

RATINGS

Admissions Selectivity Rating: 82   **Fire Safety Rating**: 60*   **Green Rating**: 60*

STUDENTS AND FACULTY

Enrollment: 1,564. **Student Body**: 23% female, 77% male, 34% out-of-state. Asian 1%, Caucasian 87%, Hispanic 1%, Native American 3%. **Retention and Graduation**: 74% freshmen return for sophomore year. 13% freshmen graduate within 4 years. **Faculty**: Student/faculty ratio 15:1. 108 full-time faculty, 86% hold PhDs. 95% faculty teach undergrads.

ACADEMICS

Degrees: Associate, bachelor's, doctoral, master's, terminal. **Academic Requirements**: Arts/fine arts, English (including composition), humanities, mathematics, sciences (biological or physical), social science. **Classes**: Most classes have 10–19 students. Most lab/discussion sections have fewer than 10 students. **Majors with Highest Enrollment**: Civil engineering, mechanical engineering, multi/interdisciplinary studies. **Disciplines with Highest Percentage of Degrees Awarded**: Engineering 76%, interdisciplinary studies 9%, computer and information sciences 8%, physical sciences 5%, mathematics 2%. **Special Study Options**: Accelerated program, distance learning, dual enrollment, English as a second language (ESL), honors program, student-designed major, study abroad. SDSMT offers an MS degree in technology management via the Internet. Our BS in interdisciplinary sciences is essentially a student-designed majors. SDSMT students utilize the CSL program offered by National American University, a private college in Rapid City.

FACILITIES

Housing: Coed dorms, special housing for disabled students, fraternity/sorority housing. **Special Academic Facilities/Equipment**: Museum of geology and paleontology, electron microscope, engineering/mining experiment station, supersonic wind tunnel, 3-D visualization lab, polymer processing lab, friction stir welding lab, high-frequency microwave lab, tech development lab, fluid computational dynamics lab, robotics lab, clean manufacturing lab, institute atmospheric science and other research institutes. **Computers**: 100% of classrooms are wired, 100% of classrooms are wireless, 95% of public computers are PCs, 5% of public computers are UNIX, network access in dorm rooms, network access in dorm lounges, online registration, online administrative functions (other than registration), remote student-access to Web through college's connection.

CAMPUS LIFE

Activities: Choral groups, drama/theater, music ensembles, radio station, student government, student newspaper. **Organizations**: 73 registered organizations, 6 honor societies, 9 religious organizations. 4 fraternities (19% men join), 2 sororities (21% women join). **Athletics (Intercollegiate)**: *Men*: Basketball, cross-country, football, golf, track/field (indoor), track/field (outdoor). *Women*: Basketball, cross-country, golf, track/field (indoor), track/field (outdoor), volleyball.

ADMISSIONS

Freshman Academic Profile: 24% in top 10% of high school class, 54% in top 25% of high school class, 85% in top 50% of high school class. 93% from public high schools. SAT Math middle 50% range 540–630. SAT Critical Reading middle 50% range 480–600. ACT middle 50% range 23–28. TOEFL required of all international applicants, minimum paper TOEFL 530, minimum computer TOEFL 200. **Basis for Candidate Selection**: *Very important factors considered include*: Rigor of secondary school record, standardized test scores. *Important factors considered include*: Academic GPA, class rank. *Other factors considered include*: Character/personal qualities, extracurricular activities, level of applicant's interest, talent/ability, volunteer work, work experience. **Freshman Admission Requirements**: High school diploma is required, and GED is accepted. *Academic units required*: 4 English, 3 math, 3 science (3 science labs), 3 social studies, 2 fine arts, .5 computer skills. *Academic units recommended*: 2 foreign language. **Freshman Admission Statistics**: 711 applied, 82% admitted, 49% enrolled. **Transfer Admission Requirements**: College transcript(s), statement of good standing from prior institution(s). Minimum college GPA of 2.0 required. Lowest grade transferable D. **General Admission Information**: Application fee $20. Regular notification is rolling. Non-fall registration accepted. Admission may be deferred for a maximum of 1 year. Credit and/or placement offered for CEEB Advanced Placement tests.

COSTS AND FINANCIAL AID

Annual in-state tuition $2,480. Annual out-of-state tuition $3,720. Room and board $4,600. Required fees $3,190. Average book expense $1,200. **Required Forms and Deadlines**: FAFSA, freshman scholarship application form. Financial aid filing deadline 3/15. **Notification of Awards**: Applicants will be notified of awards on a rolling basis beginning on or about 5/1. **Types of Aid**: *Need-based scholarships/grants*: Pell, SEOG, state scholarships/grants, private scholarships, the school's own gift aid, SMART grants, ACG grants. *Loans*: FFEL Subsidized Stafford, FFEL Unsubsidized Stafford, FFEL PLUS, Federal Perkins, private alternative loans. **Student Employment**: Federal Work-Study Program available. Institutional employment available. Off-campus job opportunities are good. **Financial Aid Statistics**: 34% freshmen, 31% undergrads receive need-based scholarship or grant aid. 47% freshmen, 50% undergrads receive need-based self-help aid. 17 freshmen, 61 undergrads receive athletic scholarships.

SOUTH DAKOTA STATE UNIVERSITY

SAD 200, BOX 2201, Brookings, SD 57007-0649
Phone: 605-688-4121 **E-mail**: sdsu.admissions@sdstate.edu **CEEB Code**: 6653
Fax: 605-688-6891 **Website**: www3.sdstate.edu **ACT Code**: 3924
Financial Aid Phone: 605-688-4695

This public school was founded in 1881. It has a 272-acre campus.

RATINGS

Admissions Selectivity Rating: 72   **Fire Safety Rating**: 79   **Green Rating**: 66

STUDENTS AND FACULTY

Enrollment: 9,003. **Student Body**: 50% female, 50% male, 30% out-of-state. Caucasian 91%, Native American 2%. **Retention and Graduation**: 77% freshmen return for sophomore year. 23% freshmen graduate within 4 years. **Faculty**: Student/faculty ratio 18:1. 423 full-time faculty, 72% hold PhDs. 78% faculty teach undergrads.

ACADEMICS

Degrees: Associate, bachelor's, doctoral, first professional, master's, post-bachelor's certificate, post-master's certificate, terminal. **Academic Requirements**: Arts/fine arts, citizenship, computer literacy, cultural diversity, English (including composition), history, humanities, mathematics, sciences (biological or physical), social science, wellness. **Classes**: Most classes have 20–29 students. Most lab/discussion sections have 20–29 students. **Majors with Highest Enrollment**: Biology/biological sciences; economics; nursing—registered nurse training (RN, ASN, BSN, MSN). **Disciplines with Highest**

Percentage of Degrees Awarded: Health professions and related sciences 23%, engineering 11%, agriculture 11%, family and consumer sciences 6%, biological/life sciences 5%. **Special Study Options**: Accelerated program, cooperative education program, cross-registration, distance learning, double major, dual enrollment, exchange student program (domestic), honor program, independent study, internships, study abroad, teacher certification program. Help and courses in English as a second language (ESL) are available, but it is not an official program.

FACILITIES

Housing: Coed dorms, apartments for married students, apartments for single students, special housing for disabled students, special housing for international students, fraternity/sorority housing, limited single rooms with optional meal plan for upperclassmen. Students out of high school fewer than 2 years are required to live in campus housing unless living with family. **Special Academic Facilities/Equipment**: SD Art Museum; SD Agricultural Heritage Museum; Northern Plains Bio-stress Laboratory; Animal Disease Research and Diagnostic Lab; McCrory Gardens; new Center for Infectious Disease, Research, and Vaccinology; EROS-SDSU GISc Center of Excellence. **Computers**: 20% of classrooms are wireless, 85% of public computers are PCs, 10% of public computers are Macs, 5% of public computers are UNIX, network access in dorm rooms, network access in dorm lounges, online registration, online administrative functions (other than registration), support for handheld computing, remote student-access to Web through college's connection.

CAMPUS LIFE

Activities: Choral groups, concert band, dance, drama/theater, jazz band, literary magazine, marching band, music ensembles, musical theater, pep band, radio station, student government, student newspaper, symphony orchestra, yearbook. **Organizations**: 200 registered organizations, 32 honor societies, 15 religious organizations. 7 fraternities, 3 sororities **Athletics (Intercollegiate)**: *Men*: Baseball, basketball, cross-country, diving, football, golf, swimming, tennis, track/field (indoor), track/field (outdoor), wrestling. *Women*: Basketball, cross-country, diving, equestrian sports, golf, soccer, softball, swimming, tennis, track/field (indoor), track/field (outdoor), volleyball.

ADMISSIONS

Freshman Academic Profile: 13% in top 10% of high school class, 35% in top 25% of high school class, 68% in top 50% of high school class. ACT middle 50% range 20-25. TOEFL required of all international applicants, minimum paper TOEFL 500, minimum computer TOEFL 173. **Basis for Candidate Selection**: *Very important factors considered include*: Academic GPA, class rank, rigor of secondary school record, standardized test scores. *Other factors considered include*: Recommendation(s). **Freshman Admission Requirements**: High school diploma is required, and GED is accepted. *Academic units required*: 4 English, 3 math, 3 science (3 science labs), 3 social studies, 1 fine arts **Freshman Admission Statistics**: 3,597 applied, 94% admitted, 57% enrolled. **Transfer Admission Requirements**: High school transcript, college transcript(s), statement of good standing from prior institution(s). Minimum college GPA of 2.0 required. Lowest grade transferable D. **General Admission Information**: Application fee $20. Regular notification is rolling. Nonfall registration accepted. Admission may be deferred for a maximum of 1 year. Credit and/or placement offered for CEEB Advanced Placement tests.

COSTS AND FINANCIAL AID

Annual in-state tuition $2,478. Annual out-of-state tuition $3,716. Room and board $5,240. Required fees $2,895. Average book expense $976. **Required Forms and Deadlines**: FAFSA. Financial aid filing deadline 3/11. **Notification of Awards**: Applicants will be notified of awards on a rolling basis beginning on or about 4/1. **Types of Aid**: *Need-based scholarships/grants*: Pell, SEOG, state scholarships/grants, private scholarships, the school's own gift aid, United Negro College Fund, Federal Nursing Scholarships, Federal SMART grants; Federal Academic Comp Grants. *Loans*: FFEL Subsidized Stafford, FFEL Unsubsidized Stafford, FFEL PLUS, Federal Perkins, Federal Nursing, college/university loans from institutional funds, Health Profession loans. **Student Employment**: Federal Work-Study Program available. Institutional employment available. Off-campus job opportunities are good. **Financial Aid Statistics**: 40% freshmen, 39% undergrads receive need-based scholarship or grant aid. 72% freshmen, 77% undergrads receive need-based self-help aid. 82 freshmen, 238 undergrads receive athletic scholarships. 94% freshmen, 85% undergrads receive any aid. Highest amount earned per year from on-campus jobs $5,400.

See page 1386.

SOUTHEAST MISSOURI STATE UNIVERSITY

One University Plaza, Mail Stop 3550, Cape Girardeau, MO 63701
Phone: 573-651-2590 **E-mail**: admissions@semo.edu **CEEB Code**: 6655
Fax: 573-651-5936 **Website**: www.semo.edu **ACT Code**: 2366
Financial Aid Phone: 573-651-2253

This public school was founded in 1873. It has a 400-acre campus.

RATINGS

Admissions Selectivity Rating: 77   **Fire Safety Rating**: 75   **Green Rating**: 60*

STUDENTS AND FACULTY

Enrollment: 8,280. **Student Body**: 60% female, 40% male, 10% out-of-state, 2% international (33 countries represented). African American 9%, Caucasian 83%, Hispanic 1%. **Retention and Graduation**: 69% freshmen return for sophomore year. 26% freshmen graduate within 4 years. **Faculty**: Student/faculty ratio 18:1. 396 full-time faculty, 79% hold PhDs. 97% faculty teach undergrads.

ACADEMICS

Degrees: Associate, bachelor's, certificate, master's, post-master's certificate. **Academic Requirements**: Arts/fine arts, English (including composition), history, humanities, mathematics, sciences (biological or physical). **Classes**: Most classes have 20–29 students. **Majors with Highest Enrollment**: Communications studies/speech communication and rhetoric, elementary education and teaching, nursing/registered nurse training (ASN, BSN, MSN, RN). **Disciplines with Highest Percentage of Degrees Awarded**: Education 20%, business/marketing 16%, liberal arts/general studies 11%, family and consumer sciences 6%, communications/journalism 6%. **Special Study Options**: Accelerated program, distance learning, double major, dual enrollment, English as a second language (ESL), honors program, independent study, internships, liberal arts/career combination, student-designed major, study abroad, teacher certification program.

FACILITIES

Housing: Coed dorms; fraternity/sorority housing; apartments for students with dependents, who are married or graduate students over the age of 25. **Special Academic Facilities/Equipment**: University Museum, Center for Faulkner Studies, center for earthquake studies, center for scholarship in teaching & learning, clinical education lab, writing center, university demonstration farm, 4 corporate video studios, 2 radio stations, Southeast Explorer, SHOW (Southeast Health on Wheels). **Computers**: 8% of classrooms are wireless, 99% of public computers are PCs, 1% of public computers are Macs, network access in dorm rooms, online registration, online administrative functions (other than registration), remote student-access to Web through college's connection.

CAMPUS LIFE

Activities: Choral groups, concert band, dance, drama/theater, jazz band, literary magazine, marching band, music ensembles, musical theater, opera, pep band, radio station, student government, student newspaper, symphony orchestra. **Organizations**: 118 registered organizations, 7 honor societies, 10 religious organizations. 6 fraternities (12% men join), 7 sororities (8% women join). **Athletics (Intercollegiate)**: *Men*: Baseball, basketball, cheerleading, cross-country, football, track/field (indoor), track/field (outdoor). *Women*: Basketball, cheerleading, cross-country, gymnastics, soccer, softball, tennis, track/field (indoor), track/field (outdoor), volleyball.

ADMISSIONS

Freshman Academic Profile: 15% in top 10% of high school class, 39% in top 25% of high school class, 67% in top 50% of high school class. 47% from public high schools. SAT Math middle 50% range 460–600. SAT Critical Reading middle 50% range 460–610. SAT Writing middle 50% range 493–643. ACT middle 50% range 19–25. TOEFL required of all international applicants, minimum paper TOEFL 500, minimum computer TOEFL 173. **Basis for Candidate Selection**: *Very important factors considered include*: Academic GPA, rigor of secondary school record, standardized test scores. *Other factors considered include*: Class rank. **Freshman Admission Requirements**: High school diploma is required, and GED is accepted. *Academic units required*: 4 English, 3 math, 3 science (1 science lab), 2 social studies, 1 history, 3 academic electives, 1 visual or performing arts. **Freshman Admission Statistics**: 4,849 applied, 69% admitted, 45% enrolled. **Transfer Admission Requirements**: College transcript(s). Minimum college GPA of 2.0 required. Lowest grade transferable D. **General Admission Information**: Application fee $20. Regular application deadline 5/1. Regular notification is rolling. Non-fall registration accepted. Credit offered for CEEB Advanced Placement tests.

COSTS AND FINANCIAL AID

Annual in-state tuition $5,034. Out-of-state tuition $9,159. Room & board $5,647. Required fees $471. Average book expense $413. **Required Forms and Deadlines**: FAFSA. Financial aid filing deadline 3/1. **Notification of Awards**: Applicants will be notified of awards on a rolling basis beginning on or about 4/1. **Types of Aid**: *Need-based scholarships/grants*: Pell, SEOG, state scholarships/grants, private scholarships, the school's own gift aid. *Loans*: FFEL Subsidized Stafford, FFEL Unsubsidized Stafford, FFEL PLUS, Federal Perkins, state loans. **Student Employment**: Federal Work-Study Program available. Institutional employment available. **Financial Aid Statistics**: 46% freshmen, 40% undergrads receive need-based scholarship or grant aid. 41% freshmen, 43% undergrads receive need-based self-help aid. 37 freshmen, 168 undergrads receive athletic scholarships. 48% freshmen, 61% undergrads receive any aid. Highest amount earned per year from on-campus jobs $7,763.

SOUTHEASTERN BIBLE COLLEGE

3001 Highway 280 East, Birmingham, AL 35243
Phone: 205-970-9209 **E-mail**: admissions@sebc.edu
Fax: 205-970-9207 **Website**: www.sebc.edu **ACT Code**: 0038
Financial Aid Phone: 205-970-9215

This private school was founded in 1935. It has a 10-acre campus.

RATINGS
Admissions Selectivity Rating: 60*   **Fire Safety Rating**: 60*   **Green Rating**: 60*

STUDENTS AND FACULTY

Enrollment: 228. **Student Body**: 38% female, 62% male, 30% out-of-state. African American 18%, Asian 1%, Caucasian 79%. **Retention and Graduation**: 62% freshmen return for sophomore year. 38% freshmen graduate within 4 years. **Faculty**: Student/faculty ratio 13:1. 11 full-time faculty, 64% hold PhDs. 100% faculty teach undergrads.

ACADEMICS

Degrees: Associate, bachelor's, diploma, terminal. **Academic Requirements**: 32 hours of Bible, computer literacy, English (including composition), history, mathematics, philosophy, sciences (biological or physical). **Classes**: Most classes have fewer than 10 students. **Majors with Highest Enrollment**: Bible/biblical studies, elementary education and teaching, youth ministry. **Special Study Options**: Independent study, internships.

FACILITIES

Housing: Men's dorms, women's dorms, apartments for married students. **Computers**: 100% of public computers are PCs, remote student-access to Web through college's connection.

CAMPUS LIFE

Activities: Choral groups, music ensembles, student government.

ADMISSIONS

Freshman Academic Profile: 60% from public high schools. TOEFL required of all international applicants, minimum paper TOEFL 500, minimum computer TOEFL 173. **Basis for Candidate Selection**: *Very important factors considered include*: Character/personal qualities, recommendation(s), religious affiliation/commitment, rigor of secondary school record, standardized test scores. *Important factors considered include*: Application essay. *Other factors considered include*: Alumni/ae relation, interview. **Freshman Admission Requirements**: High school diploma is required, and GED is accepted. *Academic units required*: 4 English, 4 math, 4 science. **Freshman Admission Statistics**: 279 applied, 52% admitted, 32% enrolled. **Transfer Admission Requirements**: High school transcript, college transcript(s), essay or personal statement. Minimum college GPA of 2.0 required. Lowest grade transferable C. **General Admission Information**: Application fee $20. Regular application deadline 8/1. Regular notification is rolling. Non-fall registration accepted. Admission may be deferred for a maximum of 1 year. Common Application not accepted. Credit offered for CEEB Advanced Placement tests.

COSTS AND FINANCIAL AID

Annual tuition $7,500. Room & board $3,450. Required fees $25. Average book expense $500. **Required Forms and Deadlines**: FAFSA, institution's own financial aid form. Financial aid filing deadline 5/1. **Notification of Awards**: Applicants will be notified of awards on or about 6/1. **Types of Aid**: *Need-based scholarships/grants*: Pell, SEOG, state scholarships/grants. *Loans*: FFEL Subsidized Stafford, FFEL Unsubsidized Stafford, FFEL PLUS. **Student Employment**: Federal Work-Study Program available. Off-campus job

opportunities are excellent. **Financial Aid Statistics**: 57% freshmen, 56% undergrads receive need-based scholarship or grant aid. 57% freshmen, 66% undergrads receive need-based self-help aid. 8 freshmen, 38 undergrads receive athletic scholarships. 80% freshmen, 85% undergrads receive any aid. Highest amount earned per year from on-campus jobs $2,000.

SOUTHEASTERN COLLEGE OF THE ASSEMBLIES OF GOD

1000 Longfellow Boulevard, Lakeland, FL 33801-6099
Phone: 863-667-5081 **E-mail**: admission@secollege.edu **CEEB Code**: 5621
Fax: 863-667-5200 **Website**: www.secollege.edu **ACT Code**: 0754
Financial Aid Phone: 863-667-5026

This private school, affiliated with the Assemblies of God Church, was founded in 1935. It has a 60-acre campus.

RATINGS
Admissions Selectivity Rating: 60*   **Fire Safety Rating**: 60*   **Green Rating**: 60*

STUDENTS AND FACULTY

Enrollment: 1,078. **Student Body**: 52% female, 48% male, 44% out-of-state, 1% international (18 countries represented). African American 4%, Asian 1%, Caucasian 85%, Hispanic 8%. **Retention and Graduation**: 65% freshmen return for sophomore year. 17% freshmen graduate within 4 years. **Faculty**: Student/faculty ratio 28:1. 44 full-time faculty, 59% hold PhDs. 100% faculty teach undergrads.

ACADEMICS

Degrees: Bachelor's. **Academic Requirements**: English (including composition), foreign languages, humanities, mathematics, religion, sciences (biological or physical), social science. **Classes**: Most classes have 10–19 students. **Majors with Highest Enrollment**: Psychology, theological studies and religious vocations, youth ministry. **Disciplines with Highest Percentage of Degrees Awarded**: Education 27%, psychology 15%, business/marketing 8%, communication technologies 7%, visual and performing arts 6%. **Special Study Options**: Accelerated program, double major, dual enrollment, independent study, internships, learning disabilities services, study abroad, teacher certification program.

FACILITIES

Housing: Coed dorms, men's dorms, women's dorms. **Special Academic Facilities/Equipment**: Art museum, environmental studies institute, center for teaching and learning, writing center, clinical education lab, farm. **Computers**: 99% of public computers are PCs, 1% of public computers are Macs, network access in dorm rooms, online administrative functions (other than registration), remote student-access to Web through college's connection.

CAMPUS LIFE

Activities: Choral groups, concert band, drama/theater, jazz band, literary magazine, marching band, music ensembles, opera, radio station, student government, student newspaper, television station, yearbook. **Organizations**: 18 registered organizations, 3 honor societies. **Athletics (Intercollegiate)**: *Men*: Baseball, basketball, golf, soccer. *Women*: Basketball, volleyball.

ADMISSIONS

Freshman Academic Profile: TOEFL required of all international applicants, minimum paper TOEFL 500. **Freshman Admission Requirements**: High school diploma is required, and GED is accepted. **Freshman Admission Statistics**: 361 applied, 83% admitted, 78% enrolled. **Transfer Admission Requirements**: High school transcript, college transcript(s), essay or personal statement, standardized test score, statement of good standing from prior institution(s). Lowest grade transferable C. **General Admission Information**: Application fee $40. Regular application deadline 8/1. Regular notification 8/1. Non-fall registration accepted. Common Application not accepted. Credit offered for CEEB Advanced Placement tests.

COSTS AND FINANCIAL AID

Required Forms and Deadlines: FAFSA, institution's own financial aid form, state aid form. Financial aid filing deadline 5/1. **Notification of Awards**: Applicants will be notified of awards on a rolling basis beginning on or about 5/10. **Types of Aid**: *Need-based scholarships/grants*: Pell, SEOG, state scholarships/grants, private scholarships, the school's own gift aid. *Loans*: FFEL Subsidized Stafford, FFEL Unsubsidized Stafford, FFEL PLUS, Federal Perkins. **Student Employment**: Federal Work-Study Program available. Institutional employment available. Off-campus job opportunities are excellent.

Financial Aid Statistics: 80% freshmen, 83% undergrads receive need-based scholarship or grant aid. 74% freshmen, 77% undergrads receive need-based self-help aid.

SOUTHEASTERN LOUISIANA UNIVERSITY

SLU 10752, Hammond, LA 70402
Phone: 985-549-2066 **E-mail:** admissions@selu.edu
Fax: 985-549-5632 **Website:** www.selu.edu **ACT Code:** 1608
Financial Aid Phone: 985-549-2244

This public school was founded in 1925. It has a 365-acre campus.

RATINGS
Admissions Selectivity Rating: 67   **Fire Safety Rating:** 93   **Green Rating:** 67

STUDENTS AND FACULTY
Enrollment: 13,542. **Student Body:** 62% female, 38% male, 3% out-of-state. African American 17%, Caucasian 76%, Hispanic 2%. **Retention and Graduation:** 66% freshmen return for sophomore year. 6% freshmen graduate within 4 years. **Faculty:** Student/faculty ratio 27:1. 502 full-time faculty, 60% hold PhDs. 95% faculty teach undergrads.

ACADEMICS
Degrees: Associate, bachelor's, master's. **Academic Requirements:** Arts/fine arts, computer literacy, English (including composition), history, humanities, mathematics, sciences (biological or physical), social science. **Classes:** Most classes have 20–29 students. **Majors with Highest Enrollment:** Biology/biological sciences, business administration and management, nursing/registered nurse training (ASN, BSN, MSN, RN). **Disciplines with Highest Percentage of Degrees Awarded:** Business/marketing 32%, education 13%, liberal arts/general studies 11%, health professions and related sciences 10%, psychology 4%. **Special Study Options:** Cross-registration, distance learning, double major, English as a second language (ESL), honors program, independent study, internships, liberal arts/career combination, study abroad, teacher certification program.

FACILITIES
Housing: Coed dorms, women's dorms, apartments for single students, fraternity/sorority housing. **Special Academic Facilities/Equipment:** Contemporary art gallery, radio station, television station, Columbia Theatre, maritime museum. **Computers:** 5% of classrooms are wired, 5% of classrooms are wireless, 99% of public computers are PCs, 1% of public computers are Macs, network access in dorm rooms, network access in dorm lounges, online registration, online administrative functions (other than registration), support for handheld computing, remote student-access to Web through college's connection.

CAMPUS LIFE
Activities: Choral groups, concert band, dance, drama/theater, jazz band, literary magazine, marching band, music ensembles, musical theater, opera, pep band, radio station, student government, student newspaper, student-run film society, symphony orchestra, television studio. **Organizations:** 97 registered organizations, 15 honor societies, 9 religious organizations. 10 fraternities, 9 sororities. **Athletics (Intercollegiate):** *Men:* Baseball, basketball, cheerleading, cross-country, football, golf, tennis, track/field (outdoor). *Women:* Basketball, cheerleading, cross-country, soccer, softball, tennis, track/field (outdoor), volleyball. Environmental Initiatives: Computer recycling program. Campus shuttle. Ponchartrain wetland environmental research.

ADMISSIONS
Freshman Academic Profile: 8% in top 10% of high school class, 27% in top 25% of high school class, 58% in top 50% of high school class. 72% from public high schools. ACT middle 50% range 19–23. TOEFL required of all international applicants, minimum paper TOEFL 500, minimum computer TOEFL 173. **Basis for Candidate Selection:** *Very important factors considered include:* Rigor of secondary school record, standardized test scores. *Important factors considered include:* Academic GPA. *Other factors considered include:* Class rank. **Freshman Admission Requirements:** High school diploma is required, and GED is accepted. *Academic units required:* 4 English, 3 math, 3 science, 2 foreign language, 3 social studies, 1 computer. **Freshman Admission Statistics:** 3,761 applied, 93% admitted, 83% enrolled. **Transfer Admission Requirements:** College transcript(s). Minimum college GPA of 2.0 required. Lowest grade transferable D. **General Admission Information:** Application fee $20. Regular application deadline 8/1. Regular notification is rolling. Non-fall registration accepted. Admission may be deferred for a maximum of 1 year. Credit and/or placement offered for CEEB Advanced Placement tests.

COSTS AND FINANCIAL AID
Annual in-state tuition $2,216. Out-of-state tuition $7,544. Room & board $5,750. Required fees $1,207. Average book expense $1,000. **Required Forms and Deadlines:** FAFSA. Financial aid filing deadline 5/1. **Notification of Awards:** Applicants will be notified of awards on a rolling basis beginning on or about 5/1. **Types of Aid:** *Need-based scholarships/grants:* Pell, SEOG, state scholarships/grants, private scholarships, the school's own gift aid, Federal Nursing Scholarships. *Loans:* FFEL Subsidized Stafford, FFEL Unsubsidized Stafford, FFEL PLUS, Federal Perkins, college/university loans from institutional funds. **Student Employment:** Federal Work-Study Program available. Institutional employment available. Off-campus job opportunities are good. **Financial Aid Statistics:** 33% freshmen, 37% undergrads receive need-based scholarship or grant aid. 31% freshmen, 38% undergrads receive need-based self-help aid. 5 freshmen, 15 undergrads receive athletic scholarships. 74% freshmen, 72% undergrads receive any aid. Highest amount earned per year from on-campus jobs $7,615.

SOUTHEASTERN OKLAHOMA STATE UNIVERSITY

1405 North Fourth Avenue, PMB 4225, Durant, OK 74701-0609
Phone: 580-745-2060 **E-mail:** admissions@sosu.edu **CEEB Code:** 6657
Fax: 580-745-4502 **Website:** www.sosu.edu **ACT Code:** 3438
Financial Aid Phone: 580-745-2186

This public school was founded in 1909. It has a 177-acre campus.

RATINGS
Admissions Selectivity Rating: 73   **Fire Safety Rating:** 72   **Green Rating:** 60*

STUDENTS AND FACULTY
Enrollment: 3,498. **Student Body:** 56% female, 44% male, 22% out-of-state. African American 4%, Caucasian 50%, Hispanic 2%, Native American 24%. **Retention and Graduation:** 58% freshmen return for sophomore year. 12% freshmen graduate within 4 years. **Faculty:** Student/faculty ratio 19:1. 141 full-time faculty, 74% hold PhDs. 100% faculty teach undergrads.

ACADEMICS
Degrees: Bachelor's, master's, post-master's certificate. **Academic Requirements:** Computer literacy, English (including composition), history, mathematics, sciences (biological or physical), social science. **Classes:** Most classes have 20–29 students. Most lab/discussion sections have 10–19 students. **Majors with Highest Enrollment:** Elementary education and teaching, occupational safety and health technology/technician, psychology. **Disciplines with Highest Percentage of Degrees Awarded:** Education 22%, business/marketing 12%, engineering technologies 9%, liberal arts/general studies 8%, communications/journalism 6%, parks and recreation 6%. **Special Study Options:** Distance learning, double major, honors program, independent study, internships, teacher certification program.

FACILITIES
Housing: Coed dorms, apartments for single students. **Special Academic Facilities/Equipment:** Visual and performing arts gallery. **Computers:** 14% of classrooms are wired, 1% of classrooms are wireless, 97% of public computers are PCs, 1% of public computers are Macs, 2% of public computers are UNIX, network access in dorm rooms, network access in dorm lounges, online registration, online administrative functions (other than registration), remote student-access to Web through college's connection.

CAMPUS LIFE
Activities: Choral groups, concert band, dance, drama/theater, jazz band, literary magazine, marching band, music ensembles, musical theater, opera, pep band, radio station, student government, student newspaper, yearbook. **Organizations:** 40 registered organizations, 12 honor societies, 8 religious organizations. 2 fraternities (1% men join), 2 sororities (1% women join). **Athletics (Intercollegiate):** *Men:* Baseball, basketball, football, golf, tennis. *Women:* Basketball, cross-country, softball, tennis, volleyball.

ADMISSIONS
Freshman Academic Profile: 17% in top 10% of high school class, 45% in top 25% of high school class, 77% in top 50% of high school class. 99% from public high schools. ACT middle 50% range 18–23. TOEFL required of all international applicants, minimum paper TOEFL 500, minimum computer TOEFL

173. **Basis for Candidate Selection**: *Very important factors considered include:* Academic GPA, class rank, standardized test scores. *Other factors considered include:* Character/personal qualities, interview, level of applicant's interest, recommendation(s), rigor of secondary school record, state residency, talent/ability. **Freshman Admission Requirements**: High school diploma is required, and GED is accepted. *Academic units required:* 4 English, 3 math, 2 science (2 science labs), 2 history, 3 academic electives, 1 citizenship. *Academic units recommended:* 1 foreign language. **Freshman Admission Statistics**: 922 applied, 88% admitted, 76% enrolled. **Transfer Admission Requirements**: College transcript(s). Minimum college GPA of 2.0 required. Lowest grade transferable D. **General Admission Information**: Application fee $20. Regular notification when admitted. Non-fall registration accepted. Credit offered for CEEB Advanced Placement tests.

COSTS AND FINANCIAL AID

Annual in-state tuition $3,249. Annual out-of-state tuition $9,044. Room and board $2,005. Required fees $677. Average book expense $800. **Required Forms and Deadlines**: FAFSA, institution's own financial aid form. Financial aid filing deadline 3/1. **Notification of Awards**: Applicants will be notified of awards on or about 4/15. **Types of Aid**: *Need-based scholarships/grants:* Pell, SEOG, state scholarships/grants, private scholarships, the school's own gift aid. *Loans:* FFEL Subsidized Stafford, FFEL Unsubsidized Stafford, FFEL PLUS, Federal Perkins, college/university loans from institutional funds. **Student Employment**: Federal Work-Study Program available. Institutional employment available. Off-campus job opportunities are good. **Financial Aid Statistics**: 50% freshmen, 46% undergrads receive need-based scholarship or grant aid. 35% freshmen, 48% undergrads receive need-based self-help aid. 37 freshmen, 128 undergrads receive athletic scholarships. 81% freshmen, 71% undergrads receive any aid. Highest amount earned per year from on-campus jobs $11,214.

SOUTHEASTERN UNIVERSITY

501 Eye Street, Southwest, Washington, DC 20024
Phone: 202-265-5343 **E-mail**: admissions@admin.seu.edu
Fax: 202-488-8093 **Website**: www.seu.edu
Financial Aid Phone: 202-488-8162

This private school was founded in 1879. It has a 1-acre campus.

RATINGS
Admissions Selectivity Rating: 60* **Fire Safety Rating**: 60* **Green Rating**: 60*

STUDENTS AND FACULTY
Enrollment: 490. **Student Body**: 70% female, 30% male, 44% out-of-state, 14% international (51 countries represented). African American 78%, Asian 3%, Caucasian 2%, Hispanic 9%. **Retention and Graduation**: 50% freshmen return for sophomore year. 8% freshmen graduate within 4 years. **Faculty**: Student/faculty ratio 11:1. 16 full-time faculty, 56% hold PhDs. 100% faculty teach undergrads.

ACADEMICS
Degrees: Associate, bachelor's, certificate, master's. **Academic Requirements**: Arts/fine arts, computer literacy, English (including composition), humanities, mathematics, social science. **Classes**: Most classes have fewer than 10 students. **Disciplines with Highest Percentage of Degrees Awarded**: Business/marketing 38%, computer and information sciences 30%, liberal arts/general studies 28%. **Special Study Options**: Accelerated program, cooperative education program, double major, English as a second language (ESL), honors program, independent study, internships, weekend college.

FACILITIES
Computers: 100% of public computers are PCs.

CAMPUS LIFE
Activities: Student government, student newspaper. **Organizations**: 6 registered organizations. 2 fraternities (2% men join), 2 sororities (2% women join).

ADMISSIONS
Freshman Academic Profile: 99% from public high schools. TOEFL required of all international applicants, minimum paper TOEFL 500. **Basis for Candidate Selection**: *Factors considered include:* Alumni/ae relation, application essay, character/personal qualities, class rank, interview, recommendation(s), rigor of secondary school record, standardized test scores, talent/ability. **Freshman Admission Requirements**: High school diploma is required, and GED is accepted. *Academic units recommended:* 4 English, 3

math, 2 science, 2 foreign language, 2 social studies, 2 history. **Transfer Admission Requirements**: High school transcript, college transcript(s). Minimum college GPA of 2.0 required. Lowest grade transferable C. **General Admission Information**: Application fee $45. Non-fall registration accepted. Admission may be deferred for a maximum of 1 year. Common Application not accepted. Credit and/or placement offered for CEEB Advanced Placement tests.

COSTS AND FINANCIAL AID
Annual tuition $8,100. Required fees $525. **Required Forms and Deadlines**: FAFSA, institution's own financial aid form. Financial aid filing deadline 8/15. **Notification of Awards**: Applicants will be notified of awards on a rolling basis beginning on or about 8/15. **Types of Aid**: *Need-based scholarships/grants:* Pell, SEOG, state scholarships/grants, private scholarships, the school's own gift aid. *Loans:* FFEL Subsidized Stafford, FFEL Unsubsidized Stafford, FFEL PLUS, Federal Perkins. **Student Employment**: Federal Work-Study Program available. Institutional employment available. Off-campus job opportunities are excellent. **Financial Aid Statistics**: 53% freshmen, 28% undergrads receive need-based scholarship or grant aid. 18% freshmen, 10% undergrads receive need-based self-help aid. 1 freshmen, 8 undergrads receive athletic scholarships.

SOUTHERN ADVENTIST UNIVERSITY

PO Box 370, Collegedale, TN 37315
Phone: 423-236-2844 **E-mail**: admissions@southern.edu **CEEB Code**: 3518
Fax: 423-236-1844 **Website**: www.southern.edu **ACT Code**: 4006
Financial Aid Phone: 423-236-2894

This private school, affiliated with the Seventh-Day Adventist Church, was founded in 1892. It has a 1,000-acre campus.

RATINGS
Admissions Selectivity Rating: 60* **Fire Safety Rating**: 88 **Green Rating**: 68

STUDENTS AND FACULTY
Enrollment: 2,335. **Student Body**: 55% female, 45% male, 68% out-of-state, 6% international. African American 11%, Asian 5%, Caucasian 71%, Hispanic 13%. **Retention and Graduation**: 69% freshmen return for sophomore year. 22% freshmen graduate within 4 years. 15% grads go on to further study within 1 year. 10% grads pursue arts and sciences degrees. 1% grads pursue business degrees. 3% grads pursue medical degrees. **Faculty**: Student/faculty ratio 16:1. 134 full-time faculty, 68% hold PhDs. 100% faculty teach undergrads.

ACADEMICS
Degrees: Associate, bachelor's, certificate, master's. **Academic Requirements**: Arts/fine arts, computer literacy, English (including composition), foreign language, history, humanities, mathematics, philosophy, sciences (biological or physical), social science. **Majors with Highest Enrollment**: Business administration/management, education, nursing/registered nurse training (ASN, BSN, MSN, RN). **Disciplines with Highest Percentage of Degrees Awarded**: Business/marketing 15%, health professions and related sciences 13%, visual and performing arts 10%, education 9%, communications/journalism 7%, biological/life sciences 7%. **Special Study Options**: Double major, dual enrollment, English as a second language (ESL), honors program, independent study, internships, study abroad, teacher certification program.

FACILITIES
Housing: Men's dorms, women's dorms, apartments for married students. **Special Academic Facilities/Equipment**: Near-Eastern archaeology teaching collection. **Computers**: 25% of classrooms are wired, 100% of classrooms are wireless, 80% of public computers are PCs, 20% of public computers are Macs, network access in dorm rooms, network access in dorm lounges, online registration, online administrative functions (other than registration), support for handheld computing, remote student-access to Web through college's connection.

CAMPUS LIFE
Activities: Choral groups, concert band, drama/theater, music ensembles, radio station, student government, student newspaper, student-run film society, symphony orchestra, television station, yearbook. **Organizations**: 30 registered organizations, 8 honor societies, 3 religious organizations. Environmental Initiatives: Energy-saving light bulbs. Campus-wide chemical cleanout. Battery and aerosol collection. ¡

ADMISSIONS

Freshman Academic Profile: 17% from public high schools. SAT Math middle 50% range 438–560. ACT middle 50% range 19–25. TOEFL required of all international applicants, minimum paper TOEFL 550, minimum computer TOEFL 213. **Basis for Candidate Selection**: *Very important factors considered include:* Academic GPA, rigor of secondary school record, standardized test scores. **Freshman Admission Requirements**: High school diploma is required, and GED is accepted. *Academic units required:* 3 English, 2 math, 2 science, 1 social studies, 1 history, 9 academic electives. *Academic units recommended:* 4 English, 3 math, 3 science, 2 foreign language, 1 social studies, 2 history, 9 academic electives, 1 computer competency. **Freshman Admission Statistics**: 1,471 applied, 69% admitted, 59% enrolled. **Transfer Admission Requirements**: College transcript(s). Minimum college GPA of 2 required. Lowest grade transferable D. **General Admission Information**: Application fee $25. Regular application deadline 9/8. Regular notification is rolling as soon as decision is made. Non-fall registration accepted. Admission may be deferred for a maximum of 1 year. Credit and/or placement offered for CEEB Advanced Placement tests.

COSTS AND FINANCIAL AID

Annual tuition $15,820. Room and board $4,900. Required fees $740. Average book expense $1,000. **Required Forms and Deadlines**: FAFSA. Financial aid filing deadline 3/1. **Notification of Awards**: Applicants will be notified of awards on a rolling basis beginning on or about 4/15. **Types of Aid**: *Need-based scholarships/grants*: Pell, SEOG, state scholarships/grants, private scholarships, the school's own gift aid. *Loans*: FFEL Subsidized Stafford, FFEL Unsubsidized Stafford, FFEL PLUS, Federal Perkins, Federal Nursing, college/university loans from institutional funds. **Student Employment**: Federal Work-Study Program available. Institutional employment available. Off-campus job opportunities are good. **Financial Aid Statistics**: 33% freshmen, 25% undergrads receive need-based scholarship or grant aid. 36% freshmen, 36% undergrads receive need-based self-help aid. 95% undergrads receive any aid. Highest amount earned per year from on-campus jobs $2,000.

SOUTHERN ARKANSAS UNIVERSITY

PO Box 9382, Magnolia, AR 71754
Phone: 870-235-4040 **E-mail**: muleriders@saumag.edu **CEEB Code**: 0142
Fax: 870-235-5072 **Website**: www.saumag.edu **ACT Code**: 0142
Financial Aid Phone: 870-235-4023

This public school was founded in 1909. It has a 1,418-acre campus.

RATINGS

Admissions Selectivity Rating: 74   **Fire Safety Rating**: 60*   **Green Rating**: 60*

STUDENTS AND FACULTY

Enrollment: 2,671. **Student Body**: 57% female, 43% male, 21% out-of-state, 6% international (29 countries represented). African American 29%, Caucasian 62%, Hispanic 1%. **Retention and Graduation**: 62% freshmen return for sophomore year. 19% freshmen graduate within 4 years. **Faculty**: Student/faculty ratio 16:1. 148 full-time faculty. 100% faculty teach undergrads.

ACADEMICS

Degrees: Associate, bachelor's, master's. **Academic Requirements**: Arts/fine arts, English (including composition), history, humanities, mathematics, sciences (biological or physical), social science. **Classes**: Most classes have fewer than 10 students. Most lab/discussion sections have 20–29 students. **Disciplines with Highest Percentage of Degrees Awarded**: Business/marketing 32%, education 18%, psychology 6%, security and protective services 6%, biological/life sciences 6%, agriculture 6%. **Special Study Options**: Cross-registration, distance learning, double major, dual enrollment, honors program, internships, teacher certification program.

FACILITIES

Housing: Coed dorms, men's dorms, women's dorms, apartments for married students, apartments for single students. **Computers**: 97% of public computers are PCs, 3% of public computers are Macs, network access in dorm rooms, network access in dorm lounges, online registration, online administrative functions (other than registration), remote student-access to Web through college's connection.

CAMPUS LIFE

Activities: Choral groups, concert band, drama/theater, jazz band, marching band, music ensembles, musical theater, pep band, radio station, student government, student newspaper, yearbook. **Organizations**: 80 registered

organizations, 10 honor societies, 7 religious organizations. 5 fraternities (10% men join), 6 sororities (10% women join). **Athletics (Intercollegiate)**: *Men*: Baseball, basketball, cheerleading, cross-country, football, golf, rodeo, track/field (outdoor). *Women*: Basketball, cheerleading, cross-country, rodeo, softball, tennis, track/field (outdoor), volleyball.

ADMISSIONS

Freshman Academic Profile: 38% in top 25% of high school class, 70% in top 50% of high school class. 99% from public high schools. ACT middle 50% range 17–23. TOEFL required of all international applicants, minimum paper TOEFL 500, minimum computer TOEFL 173. **Basis for Candidate Selection**: *Very important factors considered include:* Class rank, rigor of secondary school record, standardized test scores. *Other factors considered include:* Application essay, recommendation(s). **Freshman Admission Requirements**: High school diploma is required, and GED is accepted. *Academic units recommended:* 4 English, 4 math, 3 science (3 science labs), 2 foreign language, 3 social studies. **Freshman Admission Statistics**: 1,417 applied, 100% admitted, 42% enrolled. **Transfer Admission Requirements**: College transcript(s), statement of good standing from prior institution(s). Lowest grade transferable C. **General Admission Information**: Regular application deadline 8/27. Regular notification On a continuous rolling basis. Non-fall registration accepted. Credit offered for CEEB Advanced Placement tests.

COSTS AND FINANCIAL AID

Annual in-state tuition $4,260. Out-of-state tuition $6,450. Room & board $3,980. Required fees $630. Average book expense $1,000. **Required Forms and Deadlines**: FAFSA. Financial aid filing deadline 7/2. **Notification of Awards**: Applicants will be notified of awards on a rolling basis beginning on or about 4/15. **Types of Aid**: *Need-based scholarships/grants*: Pell, SEOG, state scholarships/grants, private scholarships, the school's own gift aid. *Loans*: FFEL Subsidized Stafford, FFEL Unsubsidized Stafford, FFEL PLUS, Federal Perkins. **Financial Aid Statistics**: 53% freshmen, 52% undergrads receive need-based scholarship or grant aid. 45% freshmen, 45% undergrads receive need-based self-help aid. 26 freshmen, 144 undergrads receive athletic scholarships. 85% freshmen, 82% undergrads receive any aid. Highest amount earned per year from on-campus jobs $4,900.

SOUTHERN CALIFORNIA COLLEGE OF OPTOMETRY

2575 Yorba Linda Boulevard, Fullerton, CA 92631
Phone: 714-870-7226 **E-mail**: admissions@scco.edu
Fax: 714-992-7878 **Website**: www.scco.edu
Financial Aid Phone: 714-449-7448

This private school was founded in 1904. It has an 8-acre campus.

RATINGS

Admissions Selectivity Rating: 60*   **Fire Safety Rating**: 60*   **Green Rating**: 60*

STUDENTS AND FACULTY

Retention and Graduation: 90% grads go on to further study within 1 year. 90% grads pursue arts and sciences degrees. **Faculty**: Student/faculty ratio 8:1. 42 full-time faculty, 100% hold PhDs.

ACADEMICS

Degrees: First professional.

FACILITIES

Computers: 75% of public computers are PCs, 25% of public computers are Macs, remote student-access to Web through college's connection.

CAMPUS LIFE

Activities: Student government, yearbook. **Organizations**: 1 honor society, 2 religious organizations. 2 fraternities.

ADMISSIONS

Freshman Admission Requirements: High school diploma is required, and GED is accepted. **General Admission Information**: Application fee $50. Regular application deadline 3/15. Regular notification is rolling. Non-fall registration not accepted. Common Application not accepted.

COSTS AND FINANCIAL AID

Types of Aid: *Loans*: FFEL Subsidized Stafford, FFEL PLUS. **Student Employment**: Federal Work-Study Program available. Institutional employment available.

SOUTHERN CALIFORNIA INSTITUTE OF ARCHITECTURE

SCI-Arc Admissions Office, 960 East Third Street, Los Angeles, CA 90013-1822
Phone: 213-613-2200 **E-mail:** admissions@sciarc.edu
Fax: 213-613-2260 **Website:** www.sciarc.edu

This is a private school.

RATINGS
Admissions Selectivity Rating: 60*   **Fire Safety Rating:** 60*   **Green Rating:** 60*

STUDENTS AND FACULTY
Student Body: 15% out-of-state.

ACADEMICS
Degrees: Bachelor's, first professional, master's. **Academic Requirements:** Arts/fine arts, computer literacy, English (including composition), history, humanities, mathematics, philosophy, sciences (biological or physical). **Special Study Options:** Cooperative education program, study abroad.

CAMPUS LIFE
Activities: Literary magazine, student government.

ADMISSIONS
Basis for Candidate Selection: *Very important factors considered include:* Application essay, character/personal qualities, recommendation(s), rigor of secondary school record, talent/ability. *Important factors considered include:* Interview, standardized test scores. *Other factors considered include:* Extracurricular activities, work experience. **Freshman Admission Requirements:** High school diploma is required, and GED is accepted. **Transfer Admission Requirements:** High school transcript, college transcript(s), essay or personal statement, statement of good standing from prior institution(s). Lowest grade transferable C. **General Admission Information:** Application fee $60. Regular application deadline 2/1. Regular notification 4/1. Non-fall registration not accepted. Admission may be deferred for a maximum of 1 year. Common Application not accepted.

COSTS AND FINANCIAL AID
Annual tuition $10,772. Required fees $70.

SOUTHERN CHRISTIAN UNIVERSITY

PO Box 240240, Montgomery, Al 36124-0240
Phone: 334-387-3877 **E-mail:** rickjohnson@southernchristian.edu
Fax: 334-387-3878 **Website:** www.southernchristian.edu
Financial Aid Phone: 334-387-3877

This private school was founded in 1967. It has a 9-acre campus.

RATINGS
Admissions Selectivity Rating: 60*   **Fire Safety Rating:** 60*   **Green Rating:** 60*

STUDENTS AND FACULTY
Enrollment: 134. **Student Body:** 25% female, 75% male. African American 25%, Caucasian 67%, Hispanic 1%. **Retention and Graduation:** 60% grads go on to further study within 1 year. **Faculty:** Student/faculty ratio 20:1. 18 full-time faculty, 61% hold PhDs. 80% faculty teach undergrads.

ACADEMICS
Degrees: Bachelor's, certificate, doctoral, first professional, master's. **Academic Requirements:** Computer literacy, humanities. **Special Study Options:** Accelerated program, distance learning, dual enrollment, independent study, internships.

FACILITIES
Computers: Online registration, online administrative functions (other than registration).

CAMPUS LIFE
Activities: Student government.

ADMISSIONS
Transfer Admission Requirements: High school transcript, college transcript(s), standardized test score. Lowest grade transferable C. **General Admission Information:** Application fee $50. Non-fall registration not accepted. Common Application not accepted.

COSTS AND FINANCIAL AID
Annual tuition $7,200. Required fees $750. Average book expense $700. **Types of Aid:** *Need-based scholarships/grants:* Pell, SEOG, state scholarships/grants, private scholarships, the school's own gift aid. *Loans:* FFEL Subsidized Stafford, FFEL Unsubsidized Stafford, FFEL PLUS. **Student Employment:** Federal Work-Study Program available. Institutional employment available. Off-campus job opportunities are excellent. **Financial Aid Statistics:** 65% undergrads receive need-based scholarship or grant aid. 5% undergrads receive need-based self-help aid.

SOUTHERN CONNECTICUT STATE UNIVERSITY

SCSU-Admissions House, 131 Farnham Avenue, New Haven, CT 06515-1202
Phone: 203-392-5656 **E-mail:** adminfo@scsu.ctstateu.edu **CEEB Code:** 3662
Fax: 203-392-5727 **Website:** www.southernct.edu
Financial Aid Phone: 203-392-5222

This public school was founded in 1893. It has a 168-acre campus.

RATINGS
Admissions Selectivity Rating: 70   **Fire Safety Rating:** 60*   **Green Rating:** 60*

STUDENTS AND FACULTY
Enrollment: 8,309. **Student Body:** 62% female, 38% male, 6% out-of-state. African American 10%, Asian 2%, Caucasian 57%, Hispanic 5%. **Retention and Graduation:** 75% freshmen return for sophomore year. 12% freshmen graduate within 4 years. 27% grads go on to further study within 1 year. **Faculty:** Student/faculty ratio 17:1. 403 full-time faculty, 90% hold PhDs. 85% faculty teach undergrads.

ACADEMICS
Degrees: Bachelor's, doctoral, master's, post-master's certificate. **Academic Requirements:** Arts/fine arts, English (including composition), foreign languages, history, humanities, mathematics, philosophy, sciences (biological or physical), social science. **Classes:** Most classes have 20–29 students. Most lab/discussion sections have 10–19 students. **Disciplines with Highest Percentage of Degrees Awarded:** Psychology 14%, business/marketing 13%, education 11%, communications/journalism 10%, liberal arts/general studies 8%, social sciences 8%, health professions and related sciences 8%. **Special Study Options:** Accelerated program, cooperative education programs (arts, business, computer science, education, health professions, humanities, natural science, social/behavioral science, technologies), cross-registration, distance learning, double major, evening division, foreign study abroad exchange program(s) (England, France, and Spain), exchange student program (domestic, members of state university system), external degree program, honors program, independent study, internships, liberal arts/career combination, student-designed major, study abroad, teacher certification program. Undergrads may take grad level classes.

FACILITIES
Housing: Coed dorms, apartments for single students, special housing for disabled students, freshmen have their own residence halls. Students must be 19 or older to live in upper-classman residence halls. **Special Academic Facilities/Equipment:** Art gallery, language lab, child development center, communication disorders center, planetarium and observatory, closed-circuit TV center.

CAMPUS LIFE
Activities: Choral groups, concert band, drama/theater, literary magazine, marching band, music ensembles, pep band, radio station, student government, student newspaper, yearbook. **Organizations:** 63 registered organizations, 3 religious organizations. 2 fraternities (1% men join), 4 sororities (1% women join). **Athletics (Intercollegiate):** *Men:* Baseball, basketball, cross-country, football, golf, gymnastics, ice hockey, rugby, soccer, softball, swimming, track/field (indoor), track/field (outdoor), volleyball, wrestling. *Women:* Basketball, cheerleading, cross-country, field hockey, golf, gymnastics, rugby, soccer, softball, swimming, track/field (indoor), track/field (outdoor), volleyball.

ADMISSIONS
Freshman Academic Profile: 5% in top 10% of high school class, 22% in top

25% of high school class, 57% in top 50% of high school class. 88% from public high schools. SAT Math middle 50% range 420–520. SAT Critical Reading middle 50% range 430–530. TOEFL required of all international applicants, minimum paper TOEFL 525. **Basis for Candidate Selection**: *Very important factors considered include:* Rigor of secondary school record. *Important factors considered include*: Academic GPA, application essay, recommendation(s), standardized test scores. *Other factors considered include*: Alumni/ae relation, character/personal qualities, class rank, extracurricular activities, first generation, racial/ethnic status, talent/ability, volunteer work, work experience. **Freshman Admission Requirements**: High school diploma is required, and GED is accepted. *Academic units required*: 4 English, 3 math, 2 science (1 science lab), 2 foreign language, 2 social studies, 2 history. *Academic units recommended*: 4 math, 3 foreign language. **Freshman Admission Statistics**: 5,037 applied, 54% admitted, 49% enrolled. **Transfer Admission Requirements**: College transcript(s), statement of good standing from prior institution(s). Minimum college GPA of 2.0 required. Lowest grade transferable C-. **General Admission Information**: Application fee $50. Regular application deadline 7/1. Regular notification is rolling. Non-fall registration accepted. Admission may be deferred for a maximum of 2 years. Common Application accepted. Credit offered for CEEB Advanced Placement tests.

COSTS AND FINANCIAL AID

Annual in-state tuition $3,187. Out-of-state tuition $10,315. Room & board $8,101. Required fees $3,255. Average book expense $750. **Required Forms and Deadlines**: FAFSA. Financial aid filing deadline 3/10. **Types of Aid**: *Need-based scholarships/grants*: Pell, SEOG, state scholarships/grants, the school's own gift aid. *Loans*: FFEL Subsidized Stafford, FFEL Unsubsidized Stafford, FFEL PLUS, Federal Perkins. **Student Employment**: Federal Work-Study Program available. Institutional employment available. Off-campus job opportunities are good. **Financial Aid Statistics**: 37% freshmen, 37% undergrads receive need-based scholarship or grant aid. 37% freshmen, 41% undergrads receive need-based self-help aid. 15 freshmen, 151 undergrads receive athletic scholarships. Highest amount earned per year from on-campus jobs $1,400.

SOUTHERN ILLINOIS UNIVERSITY— CARBONDALE

Southern Illinois University Carbondale MC 4710, Carbondale, IL 62901-4512
Phone: 618-536-4405 **E-mail**: joinsiuc@siu.edu **CEEB Code**: 1726
Fax: 618-453-4609 **Website**: www.siuc.edu **ACT Code**: 1144
Financial Aid Phone: 618-453-4334

This public school was founded in 1869. It has a 1139-acre campus.

RATINGS

Admissions Selectivity Rating: 70 **Fire Safety Rating**: 84 **Green Rating**: 60*

STUDENTS AND FACULTY

Enrollment: 16,217. **Student Body**: 43% female, 57% male, 14% out-of-state, 2% international (107 countries represented). African American 17%, Asian 2%, Caucasian 71%, Hispanic 3%. **Retention and Graduation**: 67% freshmen return for sophomore year. 21% freshmen graduate within 4 years. 30% grads go on to further study within 1 year. **Faculty**: Student/faculty ratio 17:1. 904 full-time faculty, 85% hold PhDs. 80% faculty teach undergrads.

ACADEMICS

Degrees: Associate, bachelor's, doctoral, first professional certificate, first professional, master's, post-bachelor's certificate. **Academic Requirements**: Arts/fine arts, English (including composition), Human Health, mathematics, sciences (biological or physical), social science. **Classes**: Most classes have 20–29 students. Most lab/discussion sections have 10–19 students. **Majors with Highest Enrollment**: Industrial technology/technician; occupational safety and health technology/technician; trade and industrial teacher education. **Disciplines with Highest Percentage of Degrees Awarded**: Education 22%, engineering technologies 9%, business/marketing 9%, health professions and related sciences 7%, visual and performing arts 5%. **Special Study Options**: Cooperative education program, distance learning, double major, English as a second language (ESL), honor program, independent study, internships, student-designed major, study abroad, teacher certification program. After a student completes the core curriculum, all courses to complete a degree in Workforce Education and Development are offered on weeekends.

FACILITIES

Housing: Coed dorms, men's dorms, women's dorms, apartments for married students, apartments for single students, special housing for disabled students, fraternity/sorority housing. **Special Academic Facilities/Equipment**: Art, natural history, and science museums; outdoor education center; center for crime studies; advertising and public relations agencies, child development lab, community human services center, airport training facility; archaeological research center. **Computers**: 5% of classrooms are wired, 50% of classrooms are wireless, 80% of public computers are PCs, 15% of public computers are Macs, 5% of public computers are UNIX, network access in dorm rooms, online registration, online administrative functions (other than registration), remote student-access to Web through college's connection.

CAMPUS LIFE

Activities: Choral groups, concert band, dance, drama/theater, jazz band, literary magazine, marching band, music ensembles, musical theater, opera, pep band, radio station, student government, student newspaper, student-run film society, symphony orchestra, television station, yearbook. **Organizations**: 402 registered organizations, 26 honor societies, 29 religious organizations. 20 fraternities (5% men join), 11 sororities (5% women join). **Athletics (Intercollegiate)**: *Men*: Baseball, basketball, cheerleading, cross-country, diving, football, golf, swimming, tennis, track/field (indoor), track/field (outdoor). *Women*: Basketball, cheerleading, cross-country, diving, golf, softball, swimming, tennis, track/field (indoor), track/field (outdoor), volleyball.

ADMISSIONS

Freshman Academic Profile: 9% in top 10% of high school class, 28% in top 25% of high school class, 61% in top 50% of high school class. SAT Math middle 50% range 460–610. SAT Critical Reading middle 50% range 460–610. SAT Writing middle 50% range 340–550. ACT middle 50% range 19–24. TOEFL required of all international applicants, minimum paper TOEFL 520, minimum computer TOEFL 190. **Basis for Candidate Selection**: *Very important factors considered include:* Class rank, standardized test scores. *Important factors considered include*: Academic GPA. *Other factors considered include*: Extracurricular activities, recommendation(s), rigor of secondary school record, talent/ability, volunteer work, work experience. **Freshman Admission Requirements**: High school diploma is required, and GED is accepted. *Academic units required*: 4 English, 3 math, 3 science (3 science labs), 3 social studies, 2 academic electives. **Freshman Admission Statistics**: 9,013 applied, 71% admitted, 37% enrolled. **Transfer Admission Requirements**: College transcript(s), statement of good standing from prior institution(s). Minimum college GPA of 2.0 required. Lowest grade transferable D. **General Admission Information**: Application fee $30. Nonfall registration accepted. Admission may be deferred for a maximum of 1 semester. Credit and/or placement offered for CEEB Advanced Placement tests.

COSTS AND FINANCIAL AID

Annual in-state tuition $5,808. Annual out-of-state tuition $14,520. Room and board $6,666. Required fees $2,263. Average book expense $900. **Required Forms and Deadlines**: FAFSA. Financial aid filing deadline 4/1. **Notification of Awards**: Applicants will be notified of awards on a rolling basis beginning on or about 3/15. **Types of Aid**: *Need-based scholarships/grants*: Pell, SEOG, state scholarships/grants, private scholarships, the school's own gift aid. *Loans*: Direct Subsidized Stafford, Direct Unsubsidized Stafford, Direct PLUS, Federal Perkins, college/university loans from institutional funds, alternative loans. **Student Employment**: Federal Work-Study Program available. Institutional employment available. Off-campus job opportunities are good. **Financial Aid Statistics**: 43% freshmen, 42% undergrads receive need-based scholarship or grant aid. 52% freshmen, 49% undergrads receive need-based self-help aid. 31 freshmen, 155 undergrads receive athletic scholarships. 78% freshmen, 77% undergrads receive any aid. Highest amount earned per year from on-campus jobs $9,122.

SOUTHERN ILLINOIS UNIVERSITY—EDWARDSVILLE

PO Box 1600, Edwardsville, IL 62026-1080
Phone: 618-650-3705 **E-mail:** admissions@siue.edu **CEEB Code:** 1759
Fax: 618-650-5013 **Website:** www.siue.edu **ACT Code:** 1147
Financial Aid Phone: 618-650-3880

This public school was founded in 1957. It has a 2,660-acre campus.

RATINGS
Admissions Selectivity Rating: 60*   **Fire Safety Rating:** 60*   **Green Rating:** 60*

STUDENTS AND FACULTY
Enrollment: 10,886. **Student Body:** 55% female, 45% male. African American 9%, Asian 2%, Caucasian 86%, Hispanic 2%. **Retention and Graduation:** 75% freshmen return for sophomore year. 20% freshmen graduate within 4 years. 31% grads go on to further study within 1 year. 1% grads pursue law degrees. 1% grads pursue medical degrees. **Faculty:** Student/faculty ratio 17:1. 578 full-time faculty, 81% hold PhDs. 100% faculty teach undergrads.

ACADEMICS
Degrees: Bachelor's, first professional certificate, first professional, master's, post-bachelor's certificate, post-master's certificate. **Academic Requirements:** Arts/fine arts, computer literacy, English (including composition), history, humanities, interdisciplinary studies, mathematics, philosophy, sciences (biological or physical), social science. **Classes:** Most classes have 20–29 students. Most lab/discussion sections have fewer than 10 students. **Majors with Highest Enrollment:** Business/managerial economics. **Disciplines with Highest Percentage of Degrees Awarded:** Business/marketing 21%, education 10%, health professions and related sciences 9%, social sciences 9%, psychology 7%, public administration and social services 6%, biological/life sciences 6%. **Special Study Options:** Accelerated program, cooperative education program, cross-registration, distance learning, double major, English as a second language (ESL), honors program, independent study, internships, student-designed major, study abroad, teacher certification program, weekend college. Independent study: elementary and secondary teacher certificate programs in art, music, social studies, English, kinesiology, biology, chemistry, foreign languages, history, math, physics, speech communication.

FACILITIES
Housing: Coed dorms, apartments for married students, apartments for single students, special housing for disabled students, fraternity/sorority housing, focused interest communities. **Special Academic Facilities/Equipment:** Art gallery, anthropology museum, language lab, center for advanced manufacturing and production, technology commercialization center, electron microscope, psychomotorskills lab, new engineering building and lab. **Computers:** 95% of public computers are PCs, 4% of public computers are Macs, 1% of public computers are UNIX, network access in dorm rooms, network access in dorm lounges, online administrative functions (other than registration), remote student-access to Web through college's connection.

CAMPUS LIFE
Activities: Choral groups, concert band, dance, drama/theater, jazz band, literary magazine, music ensembles, musical theater, opera, pep band, radio station, student government, student newspaper, symphony orchestra. **Organizations:** 140 registered organizations, 15 honor societies, 9 religious organizations. 10 fraternities, 7 sororities. **Athletics (Intercollegiate):** *Men:* Baseball, basketball, cross-country, golf, soccer, tennis, track/field (indoor), track/field (outdoor), wrestling. *Women:* Basketball, cross-country, golf, soccer, softball, tennis, track/field (indoor), track/field (outdoor), volleyball.

ADMISSIONS
Freshman Academic Profile: 18% in top 10% of high school class, 44% in top 25% of high school class, 79% in top 50% of high school class. ACT middle 50% range 19–25. TOEFL required of all international applicants, minimum paper TOEFL 550, minimum computer TOEFL 213. **Basis for Candidate Selection:** *Very important factors considered include:* Class rank, rigor of secondary school record, standardized test scores. **Freshman Admission Requirements:** High school diploma is required, and GED is accepted. *Academic units required:* 4 English, 3 math, 3 science (3 science labs), 3 social studies, 2 academic electives, *Academic units recommended:* 2 foreign language. **Freshman Admission Statistics:** 5,807 applied, 75% admitted, 41% enrolled. **Transfer Admission Requirements:** College transcript(s). Minimum college GPA of 2 required. Lowest grade transferable D. **General Admission Information:** Application fee $30. Regular application deadline 5/31. Regular notification is rolling. Nonfall registration accepted. Admission may be deferred for a maximum of 1 year. Credit and/or placement offered for CEEB Advanced Placement tests.

COSTS AND FINANCIAL AID
Annual in-state tuition $4,758. Out-of-state tuition $11,895. Room & board $6,500. Required fees $1,180. Average book expense $652. **Required Forms and Deadlines:** FAFSA. Financial aid filing deadline 6/1. Financial aid filing deadline 3/1. **Notification of Awards:** Applicants will be notified of awards on a rolling basis beginning on or about 3/15. **Types of Aid:** *Need-based scholarships/grants:* Pell, SEOG, state scholarships/grants, private scholarships, the school's own gift aid, Federal Nursing Scholarships, Presidential Scholars Program, Chancellor's Scholars Program, Johnetta Haley Scholarship Program, Provost Scholarship. *Loans:* Direct Subsidized Stafford, Direct Unsubsidized Stafford, Direct PLUS, FFEL PLUS, Federal Perkins, college/university loans from institutional funds, HPL. **Financial Aid Statistics:** 36% freshmen, 37% undergrads receive need-based scholarship or grant aid. 39% freshmen, 41% undergrads receive need-based self-help aid. 21 freshmen, 101 undergrads receive athletic scholarships. Highest amount earned per year from on-campus jobs $1,348.

SOUTHERN MAINE COMMUNITY COLLEGE

2 Fort Road, South Portland, ME 04106
Phone: 207-741-5800 **E-mail:** enrollmentservices@smccme.edu
Fax: 207-741-5760 **Website:** www.smccme.edu
Financial Aid Phone: 207-767-9518

This is a public school.

RATINGS
Admissions Selectivity Rating: 60*   **Fire Safety Rating:** 60*   **Green Rating:** 60*

STUDENTS AND FACULTY
Enrollment: 4,689. **Student Body:** 51% female, 49% male, 3% out-of-state. **Faculty:** 102 full-time faculty.

ACADEMICS
Degrees: Associate, certificate, terminal. **Academic Requirements:** English (including composition), humanities, mathematics, sciences (biological or physical), social science. **Special Study Options:** Cross-registration, distance learning, double major, dual enrollment, English as a second language (ESL), independent study, internships, liberal arts/career combination, study abroad.

FACILITIES
Housing: Coed dorms.

CAMPUS LIFE
Activities: Choral groups, drama/theater, student government, student newspaper.

ADMISSIONS
Basis for Candidate Selection: *Factors considered include:* State residency. **Freshman Admission Requirements:** High school diploma is required, and GED is accepted. **Transfer Admission Requirements:** High school transcript, college transcript(s). Lowest grade transferable C. **General Admission Information:** Application fee $20. Non-fall registration accepted.

COSTS AND FINANCIAL AID
Annual in-state tuition $2,200. Out-of-state tuition $4,650.

SOUTHERN METHODIST UNIVERSITY

PO Box 750181, Dallas, TX 75275-0181
Phone: 214-768-3417 **E-mail**: enrol_serv@smu.edu **CEEB Code**: 6660
Fax: 214-768-0202 **Website**: www.smu.edu **ACT Code**: 4171
Financial Aid Phone: 214-768-3417

This private school, affiliated with the Methodist Church, was founded in 1911. It has a 175-acre campus.

RATINGS
Admissions Selectivity Rating: 91   **Fire Safety Rating**: 60*   **Green Rating**: 69

STUDENTS AND FACULTY
Enrollment: 6,199. **Student Body**: 54% female, 46% male, 35% out-of-state, 5% international (94 countries represented). African American 5%, Asian 6%, Caucasian 75%, Hispanic 8%. **Retention and Graduation**: 86% freshmen return for sophomore year. 58% freshmen graduate within 4 years. **Faculty**: Student/faculty ratio 12:1. 609 full-time faculty, 84% hold PhDs. 89% faculty teach undergrads.

ACADEMICS
Degrees: Bachelor's, certificate, doctoral, first professional, master's, post-bachelor's certificate. **Academic Requirements**: Arts/fine arts, computer literacy, English (including composition), history, humanities, mathematics, philosophy, sciences (biological or physical), social science. **Classes**: Most classes have 10–19 students. Most lab/discussion sections have 10–19 students. **Majors with Highest Enrollment**: Business administration and management, communications, journalism, and related fields, social sciences. **Disciplines with Highest Percentage of Degrees Awarded**: Business/marketing 26%, social sciences 18%, communications/journalism 14%, psychology 8%, visual and performing arts 8%, engineering 4%. **Special Study Options**: Accelerated program, cooperative education program, distance learning, double major, English as a second language (ESL), exchange student program (domestic), honors program, independent study, internships, student-designed major, study abroad, teacher certification program.

FACILITIES
Housing: Coed dorms, apartments for married students, apartments for single students, fraternity/sorority housing, theme residence halls. **Special Academic Facilities/Equipment**: Art, natural history, and paleontology museums; Southwest film/video archives; sculpture garden; performing arts theaters; pollen analysis and geothermal labs; electron microbe lab; microscopy lab; seismological observatory; institute of technology services; TV studio. **Computers**: 10% of classrooms are wireless, 90% of public computers are PCs, 10% of public computers are Macs, network access in dorm rooms, network access in dorm lounges, online registration, online administrative functions (other than registration), support for handheld computing, remote student-access to Web through college's connection.

CAMPUS LIFE
Activities: Choral groups, concert band, dance, drama/theater, jazz band, literary magazine, marching band, music ensembles, musical theater, opera, pep band, radio station, student government, student newspaper, student-run film society, symphony orchestra, yearbook. **Organizations**: 200 registered organizations, 15 honor societies, 27 religious organizations. 15 fraternities (29% men join), 13 sororities (40% women join). **Athletics (Intercollegiate)**: *Men*: Basketball, cross-country, diving, football, golf, soccer, swimming, tennis, track/field (outdoor). *Women*: Basketball, crew/rowing, cross-country, diving, equestrian sports, golf, soccer, swimming, tennis, track/field (outdoor), volleyball. Environmental Initiatives: Developing a masters certificate program and a masters degree program in sustainability. The Embrey Engineering building is LEED Gold. Purchase 2,100,000 KWh of wind power each year and plan to purchase more with each new LEED building.

ADMISSIONS
Freshman Academic Profile: 35% in top 10% of high school class, 70% in top 25% of high school class, 91% in top 50% of high school class. 61% from public high schools. SAT Math middle 50% range 570–670. SAT Critical Reading middle 50% range 560–660. SAT Writing middle 50% range 560–650. ACT middle 50% range 25–29. TOEFL required of all international applicants, minimum paper TOEFL 550, minimum computer TOEFL 213. **Basis for**

Candidate Selection: *Very important factors considered include*: Academic GPA, application essay, class rank, recommendation(s), rigor of secondary school record, standardized test scores. *Important factors considered include*: Character/personal qualities, extracurricular activities, talent/ability, volunteer work, work experience. *Other factors considered include*: Alumni/ae relation, first generation, interview, level of applicant's interest. **Freshman Admission Requirements**: High school diploma is required, and GED is not accepted. *Academic units required*: 4 English, 3 math, 3 science (2 science labs), 2 foreign language, 1 social studies, 2 history. *Academic units recommended*: 4 English, 4 math, 4 science (3 science labs), 3 foreign language, 2 social studies, 3 history. **Freshman Admission Statistics**: 7,648 applied, 54% admitted, 33% enrolled. **Transfer Admission Requirements**: College transcript(s), essay or personal statement. Minimum college GPA of 2.7 required. Lowest grade transferable C-. **General Admission Information**: Application fee $60. Regular application deadline 3/15. Regular notification is rolling. Non-fall registration accepted. Admission may be deferred for a maximum of 1 year. Credit and/or placement offered for CEEB Advanced Placement tests.

COSTS AND FINANCIAL AID
Annual tuition $29,430. Room and board $11,875. Required fees $3,740. Average book expense $800. **Required Forms and Deadlines**: FAFSA, CSS/Financial Aid PROFILE, Noncustodial PROFILE, Business/Farm Supplement. Financial aid filing deadline 2/15. **Notification of Awards**: Applicants will be notified of awards on a rolling basis beginning on or about 3/15. **Types of Aid**: *Need-based scholarships/grants*: Pell, SEOG, state scholarships/grants, private scholarships, the school's own gift aid. *Loans*: FFEL Subsidized Stafford, FFEL Unsubsidized Stafford, FFEL PLUS, Federal Perkins, state loans, college/university loans from institutional funds. **Student Employment**: Federal Work-Study Program available. Institutional employment available. Off-campus job opportunities are good. **Financial Aid Statistics**: 24% freshmen, 29% undergrads receive need-based scholarship or grant aid. 27% freshmen, 32% undergrads receive need-based self-help aid. 55 freshmen, 263 undergrads receive athletic scholarships. 82% freshmen, 65% undergrads receive any aid.

SOUTHERN NAZARENE UNIVERSITY

6729 Northwest Thirty-ninth Expressway, Bethany, OK 73008-2694
Phone: 800-648-9899 **E-mail**: rmeek@snu.edu **CEEB Code**: 6036
Fax: 405-491-6320 **Website**: www.snu.edu **ACT Code**: 3384
Financial Aid Phone: 405-491-6310

This private school was founded in 1899. It has a 40-acre campus.

RATINGS
Admissions Selectivity Rating: 60*   **Fire Safety Rating**: 60*   **Green Rating**: 60*

STUDENTS AND FACULTY
Student Body: 55% out-of-state. **Retention and Graduation**: 37% grads go on to further study within 1 year. 15% grads pursue arts and sciences degrees. 14% grads pursue business degrees. 5% grads pursue law degrees. 3% grads pursue medical degrees.

ACADEMICS
Degrees: Bachelor's, master's. **Special Study Options**: American Studies Program (Washington, DC), Los Angeles Film Studies Program (California), study abroad in Costa Rica and England (may be arranged elsewhere). Undergrads may take grad level classes.

FACILITIES
Housing: Coed dorms, men's dorms, women's dorms, apartments for married students. **Special Academic Facilities/Equipment**: On-campus lab school, recital hall, concert grand piano, tracker pipe organ, 7-foot double French harpsichord, media center, anatomy lab, laser labs.

CAMPUS LIFE
Activities: Student government, student newspaper, yearbook. **Organizations**: 50 registered organizations, 3 religious organizations. **Athletics (Intercollegiate)**: *Men*: Basketball, cheerleading, cross-country, golf, soccer, softball, tennis, track/field (outdoor), volleyball. *Women*: Basketball, cheerleading, cross-country, golf, soccer, softball, tennis, track/field (outdoor), volleyball.

ADMISSIONS
Freshman Academic Profile: 14% in top 10% of high school class, 43% in top 25% of high school class, 91% in top 50% of high school class. 90% from public high schools. TOEFL required of all international applicants, minimum paper

TOEFL 500. **Freshman Admission Requirements**: High school diploma is required, and GED is accepted. *Academic units required*: 4 English, 3 math, 2 science, 2 foreign language, 1 social studies, 2 history, 7 academic electives. **Transfer Admission Requirements**: Minimum college GPA of 2.0 required. Lowest grade transferable D. **General Admission Information**: Regular application deadline 8/15. Regular notification is rolling. Non-fall registration accepted. Common Application not accepted. Credit and/or placement offered for CEEB Advanced Placement tests.

COSTS AND FINANCIAL AID
Comprehensive fee $11,134. Room & board $4,028. Required fees $348. Average book expense $350. **Required Forms and Deadlines**: FAFSA, institution's own financial aid form. **Types of Aid**: *Need-based scholarships/ grants*: Pell, SEOG, state scholarships/grants, private scholarships, the school's own gift aid. *Loans*: FFEL Subsidized Stafford, FFEL Unsubsidized Stafford, FFEL PLUS, Federal Perkins, college/university loans from institutional funds. **Student Employment**: Federal Work-Study Program available. Institutional employment available. Off-campus job opportunities are good. **Financial Aid Statistics**: Highest amount earned per year from on-campus jobs $2,000.

SOUTHERN NEW HAMPSHIRE UNIVERSITY

2500 North River Road, Manchester, NH 03108
Phone: 603-645-9611 **E-mail**: admission@snhu.edu **CEEB Code**: 3649
Fax: 603-645-9693 **Website**: www.snhu.edu **ACT Code**: 2514
Financial Aid Phone: 603-645-9645

This private school was founded in 1932. It has a 280-acre campus.

RATINGS
Admissions Selectivity Rating: 74   **Fire Safety Rating**: 94   **Green Rating**: 93

STUDENTS AND FACULTY
Enrollment: 1,706. **Student Body**: 55% female, 45% male, 54% out-of-state, 4% international (70 countries represented). African American 1%, Asian 2%, Caucasian 80%, Hispanic 1%. **Retention and Graduation**: 71% freshmen return for sophomore year. 34% freshmen graduate within 4 years. **Faculty**: Student/faculty ratio 15:1. 126 full-time faculty, 63% hold PhDs. 90% faculty teach undergrads.

ACADEMICS
Degrees: Associate, bachelor's, certificate, doctoral, master's, post-bachelor's certificate. **Academic Requirements**: Arts/fine arts, computer literacy, English (including composition), history, humanities, mathematics, philosophy, sciences (biological or physical), social science. **Classes**: Most classes have 20–29 students. **Majors with Highest Enrollment**: Business administration and management, culinary arts/chef training, psychology. **Disciplines with Highest Percentage of Degrees Awarded**: Business/marketing 73%, personal and culinary services 16%, psychology 3%, communications/journalism 2%, English 2%, communication technologies 1%, social sciences 1%. **Special Study Options**: Accelerated program, cooperative education program, distance learning, double major, English as a second language (ESL), honors program, independent study, internships, study abroad, teacher certification program, weekend college.

FACILITIES
Housing: Coed dorms, apartments for single students, special housing for disabled students, townhouses, wellness housing, single-gender areas in residence halls are also available. **Special Academic Facilities/Equipment**: Art gallery. **Computers**: 8% of classrooms are wired, 100% of classrooms are wireless, 97% of public computers are PCs, 3% of public computers are Macs, network access in dorm rooms, network access in dorm lounges, online registration, support for handheld computing, remote student-access to Web through college's connection.

CAMPUS LIFE
Activities: Choral groups, dance, drama/theater, musical theater, radio station, student government, student newspaper, yearbook. **Organizations**: 45 registered organizations, 6 honor societies, 1 religious organization. 3 fraternities (4% men join), 4 sororities (5% women join). **Athletics (Intercollegiate)**: *Men*: Baseball, basketball, cheerleading, cross-country, golf, ice hockey, lacrosse, soccer, tennis. *Women*: Basketball, cheerleading, cross-country, golf, lacrosse, soccer, softball, tennis, volleyball. Environmental Initiatives: Renewable Energy Hedge from 2007–2022 based on 17,500 megawatt hours of wind power output with PPM Energy Inc. Establishment of the SNHU School of Liberal Arts Bachelor of Arts in Environment, Ethics and Public Policy.

Under development are initiatives including use of sawdust for wood gasification for cogeneration units to supply electricity and heat; the use of geothermal systems based on innovative use of ground water near the Merrimack River for heat pumps; real time price control for optimization of energy use based on 5-minte ISO-NE price signals.

ADMISSIONS
Freshman Academic Profile: 6% in top 10% of high school class, 26% in top 25% of high school class, 64% in top 50% of high school class. SAT Math middle 50% range 440–540. SAT Critical Reading middle 50% range 440–530. SAT Writing middle 50% range 440–530. ACT middle 50% range 19–22. TOEFL required of all international applicants, minimum paper TOEFL 500, minimum computer TOEFL 173. **Basis for Candidate Selection**: *Very important factors considered include:* Academic GPA, rigor of secondary school record. *Important factors considered include*: Application essay, extracurricular activities, recommendation(s), standardized test scores. *Other factors considered include*: Alumni/ae relation, character/personal qualities, class rank, first generation, geographical residence, interview, level of applicant's interest, talent/ability, volunteer work, work experience. **Freshman Admission Requirements**: High school diploma is required, and GED is accepted. *Academic units recommended*: 4 English, 3 math, 3 science (2 science labs), 2 foreign language, 2 social studies, 2 history. **Freshman Admission Statistics**: 2,295 applied, 72% admitted, 29% enrolled. **Transfer Admission Requirements**: High school transcript, college transcript(s), essay or personal statement. Minimum college GPA of 2.5 required. Lowest grade transferable C-. **General Admission Information**: Application fee $35. Regular notification within 30 days. Non-fall registration accepted. Admission may be deferred for a maximum of 1 year. Credit and/or placement offered for CEEB Advanced Placement tests.

COSTS AND FINANCIAL AID
Annual tuition $30,194. Room & board $8,480. Required fees $330. Average book expense $850. **Required Forms and Deadlines**: FAFSA. Financial aid filing deadline 3/15. **Notification of Awards**: Applicants will be notified of awards on a rolling basis beginning on or about 3/1. **Types of Aid**: *Need-based scholarships/grants*: Pell, SEOG, state scholarships/grants, private scholarships, the school's own gift aid. *Loans*: FFEL Subsidized Stafford, FFEL Unsubsidized Stafford, FFEL PLUS, Federal Perkins. **Student Employment**: Federal Work-Study Program available. Institutional employment available. Off-campus job opportunities are good. **Financial Aid Statistics**: 71% freshmen, 67% undergrads receive need-based scholarship or grant aid. 68% freshmen, 65% undergrads receive need-based self-help aid. 19 freshmen, 71 undergrads receive athletic scholarships. 94% freshmen, 93% undergrads receive any aid.

SOUTHERN OREGON UNIVERSITY

Office of Admissions, 1250 Siskiyou Boulevard, Ashland, OR 97520-5032
Phone: 541-552-6411 **E-mail**: admissions@sou.edu **CEEB Code**: 4702
Fax: 541-552-6614 **Website**: www.sou.edu **ACT Code**: 3496
Financial Aid Phone: 541-552-6161

This public school was founded in 1926. It has a 175-acre campus.

RATINGS
Admissions Selectivity Rating: 60*   **Fire Safety Rating**: 77   **Green Rating**: 60*

STUDENTS AND FACULTY
Enrollment: 4,130. **Student Body**: 58% female, 42% male, 21% out-of-state, 2% international (32 countries represented). African American 2%, Asian 4%, Caucasian 79%, Hispanic 5%, Native American 3%. **Faculty**: Student/faculty ratio 21:1. 207 full-time faculty, 81% hold PhDs. 100% faculty teach undergrads.

ACADEMICS
Degrees: Bachelor's, master's, post-bachelor's certificate. **Academic Requirements**: Arts/fine arts, computer literacy, English (including composition), foreign languages, humanities, mathematics, sciences (biological or physical), social science. **Classes**: Most classes have 20–29 students. Most lab/ discussion sections have 20–29 students. **Majors with Highest Enrollment**: Business administration/management, criminology, psychology. **Disciplines with Highest Percentage of Degrees Awarded**: Business/marketing 19%, communications/journalism 10%, communication technologies 10%, social sciences 10%, psychology 9%, visual and performing arts 9%, English 8%. **Special Study Options**: Accelerated program, cooperative education program, cross-registration, distance learning, double major, dual enrollment, English as a

second language (ESL), external degree program, honors program, independent study, internships, liberal arts/career combination, student-designed major, teacher certification program. Undergrads may take grad level classes. Concurrent enrollment with Rogue Community College. Nursing programs with Oregon Health Sciences University. Exchange programs with College of the Redwoods, College of the Siskiyous, and Shasta College Member of National Student Exchange (NSE). Exchange programs abroad in Korea (Dankook University) and Mexico (University of Guanajuato). Study abroad also in Asian, European, and South American countries.

FACILITIES

Housing: Coed dorms, apartments for married students, apartments for single students, special housing for disabled students, special housing for international students, special quiet, substance-free, nonsmoking, older students or freshman-only residence halls. **Special Academic Facilities/Equipment**: Art and history museums, art galleries, on-campus preschool and kindergarten, National Guard armory, United States Wildlife Forensics Lab. **Computers**: Network access in dorm rooms, online registration, online administrative functions (other than registration), remote student-access to Web through college's connection.

CAMPUS LIFE

Activities: Choral groups, concert band, dance, drama/theater, jazz band, literary magazine, music ensembles, musical theater, opera, pep band, radio station, student government, student newspaper, symphony orchestra, television station. **Organizations**: 52 registered organizations, 13 honor societies, 5 religious organizations. **Athletics (Intercollegiate)**: *Men*: Basketball, cross-country, football, track/field (outdoor), wrestling. *Women*: Basketball, cross-country, soccer, softball, tennis, track/field (outdoor), volleyball.

ADMISSIONS

Freshman Academic Profile: 90% from public high schools. TOEFL required of all international applicants, minimum paper TOEFL 520, minimum computer TOEFL 190. **Basis for Candidate Selection**: *Very important factors considered include*: Rigor of secondary school record, standardized test scores. *Other factors considered include*: Application essay, character/personal qualities, extracurricular activities, recommendation(s), talent/ability, volunteer work, work experience. **Freshman Admission Requirements**: High school diploma is required, and GED is accepted. *Academic units required*: 4 English, 3 math, 2 science, 2 foreign language, 3 social studies. **Freshman Admission Statistics**: 1,871 applied, 93% admitted, 44% enrolled. **Transfer Admission Requirements**: College transcript(s). Minimum college GPA of 2.2 required. Lowest grade transferable D-. **General Admission Information**: Application fee $50. Regular notification is rolling. Non-fall registration accepted. Admission may be deferred for a maximum of 1 year. Credit and/or placement offered for CEEB Advanced Placement tests.

COSTS AND FINANCIAL AID

Required Forms and Deadlines: FAFSA, Institutional scholarship application. Financial aid filing deadline 3/1. **Notification of Awards**: Applicants will be notified of awards on a rolling basis beginning on or about 4/1. **Types of Aid**: *Need-based scholarships/grants*: Pell, SEOG, state scholarships/grants, private scholarships, the school's own gift aid. *Loans*: Direct Subsidized Stafford, Direct Unsubsidized Stafford, Direct PLUS, Federal Perkins, state loans, college/university loans from institutional funds. **Student Employment**: Federal Work-Study Program available. Institutional employment available. Off-campus job opportunities are excellent. **Financial Aid Statistics**: 69% freshmen, 68% undergrads receive need-based scholarship or grant aid. 57% freshmen, 70% undergrads receive need-based self-help aid. 4 freshmen, 26 undergrads receive athletic scholarships. 67% freshmen, 67% undergrads receive any aid.

SOUTHERN POLYTECHNIC STATE UNIVERSITY

1100 South Marietta Parkway, Marietta, GA 30060-2896
Phone: 678-915-4188 **E-mail**: admiss@spsu.edu **CEEB Code**: 5626
Fax: 678-915-7292 **Website**: www.spsu.edu **ACT Code**: 0865
Financial Aid Phone: 678-915-7290

This public school was founded in 1948. It has a 200-acre campus.

RATINGS

Admissions Selectivity Rating: 60*   **Fire Safety Rating**: 89   **Green Rating**: 71

STUDENTS AND FACULTY

Enrollment: 3,619. **Student Body**: 17% female, 83% male, 2% out-of-state, 6% international (89 countries represented). African American 19%, Asian 6%, Caucasian 65%, Hispanic 3%. **Retention and Graduation**: 72% freshmen return for sophomore year. **Faculty**: Student/faculty ratio 22:1. 129 full-time faculty, 55% hold PhDs. 100% faculty teach undergrads.

ACADEMICS

Degrees: Associate, bachelor's, certificate, master's, post-bachelor's certificate, transfer. **Academic Requirements**: Arts/fine arts, English (including composition), humanities, mathematics, sciences (biological or physical), social science, speech and science, technology and society, science/math/technology. **Classes**: Most classes have 20–29 students. Most lab/discussion sections have fewer than 10 students. **Majors with Highest Enrollment**: Architecture (BArch, BA/BS, MArch, MA/MS, PhD); construction management, mechanical engineering/mechanical technology/technician. **Disciplines with Highest Percentage of Degrees Awarded**: Engineering technologies 47%, business/marketing 17%, architecture 8%, communications/journalism 3%, mathematics 3%, engineering 1%, social sciences 1%. **Special Study Options**: Cooperative education program, cross-registration, distance learning, double major, dual enrollment, honors program, independent study, internships, student-designed major, study abroad.

FACILITIES

Housing: Coed dorms, men's dorms, apartments for single students, special housing for disabled students. **Computers**: 10% of classrooms are wireless, 100% of public computers are PCs, network access in dorm rooms, network access in dorm lounges, online registration, online administrative functions (other than registration), support for handheld computing, remote student-access to Web through college's connection.

CAMPUS LIFE

Activities: Jazz band, pep band, radio station, student government, student newspaper. **Organizations**: 64 registered organizations, 3 honor societies, 2 religious organizations. 8 fraternities (5% men join), 2 sororities (2% women join). **Athletics (Intercollegiate)**: *Men:* Baseball, basketball. *Women:* Basketball. Environmental Initiatives: Recycling. Purchase of "green" cleaning supplies. Reducing the university's carbon footprint by using EMS green building materials and voluntary recycling.

ADMISSIONS

Freshman Academic Profile: 95% from public high schools. SAT Math middle 50% range 520–610. SAT Critical Reading middle 50% range 490–570. ACT middle 50% range 20–24. TOEFL required of all international applicants, minimum paper TOEFL 550, minimum computer TOEFL 213. **Basis for Candidate Selection**: *Very important factors considered include*: Academic GPA, rigor of secondary school record, standardized test scores. **Freshman Admission Requirements**: High school diploma is required, and GED is not accepted. *Academic units required*: 4 English, 4 math, 3 science (2 science labs), 2 foreign language, 3 social studies, 2 history, 2 academic electives. **Freshman Admission Statistics**: 1,228 applied, 60% admitted, 61% enrolled. **Transfer Admission Requirements**: College transcript(s). Minimum college GPA of 2.0 required. Lowest grade transferable C. **General Admission Information**: Application fee $20. Regular application deadline 8/1. Regular notification is rolling. Nonfall registration accepted. Credit and/or placement offered for CEEB Advanced Placement tests.

COSTS AND FINANCIAL AID

Annual in-state tuition $2,780. Out-of-state tuition $11,115. Room & board $5,610. Required fees $568. Average book expense $1,500. **Required Forms and Deadlines**: FAFSA. Financial aid filing deadline 3/15. **Notification of Awards**: Applicants will be notified of awards on a rolling basis beginning on or about 6/1. **Types of Aid**: *Need-based scholarships/grants*: Pell, SEOG, state scholarships/grants, private scholarships, the school's own gift aid. *Loans*: FFEL Subsidized Stafford, FFEL Unsubsidized Stafford, FFEL PLUS, state loans. **Financial Aid Statistics**: 22% freshmen, 25% undergrads receive need-based scholarship or grant aid. 27% freshmen, 35% undergrads receive need-based self-help aid. 3 freshmen, 52 undergrads receive athletic scholarships. 83% freshmen, 44% undergrads receive any aid.

SOUTHERN UNIVERSITY AND A&M COLLEGE

PO Box 9901, Baton Rouge, LA 70813
Phone: 225-771-2430 **E-mail:** admit@subr.edu **CEEB Code:** 6663
Fax: 225-771-2500 **Website:** www.subr.edu **ACT Code:** 1610
Financial Aid Phone: 225-771-2790

This public school was founded in 1880. It has an 884-acre campus.

RATINGS
Admissions Selectivity Rating: 71   **Fire Safety Rating:** 72   **Green Rating:** 64

STUDENTS AND FACULTY
Enrollment: 8,493. **Student Body:** 61% female, 39% male, 19% out-of-state, 1% international (29 countries represented). African American 97%, Caucasian 2%. **Retention and Graduation:** 68% freshmen return for sophomore year. 7% freshmen graduate within 4 years. 15% grads go on to further study within 1 year. 4% grads pursue arts and sciences degrees. 1% grads pursue law degrees. **Faculty:** Student/faculty ratio 19:1. 406 full-time faculty, 67% hold PhDs. 90% faculty teach undergrads.

ACADEMICS
Degrees: Associate, bachelor's, doctoral, master's, post-master's certificate. **Academic Requirements:** African American experience course, arts/fine arts, community service component, computer literacy, English (including composition), freshman studies, health or physical education, history, humanities, mathematics, sciences (biological or physical), social science. **Classes:** Most classes have 30–39 students. Most lab/discussion sections have 20–29 students. **Majors with Highest Enrollment:** Biology/biological sciences, business administration and management, nursing/registered nurse training (ASN, BSN, MSN, RN). **Disciplines with Highest Percentage of Degrees Awarded:** Health professions and related sciences 17%, business/marketing 17%, engineering 8%, computer and information sciences 7%, security and protective services 6%, family and consumer sciences 6%. **Special Study Options:** Cooperative education program, cross-registration, distance learning, double major, dual enrollment, engineering combined degree programs, exchange student program (domestic), honors program, independent study, internships, study abroad, teacher certification program, weekend college. Undergrads may take grad level classes. Dual degree programs with Jackson State University and Xavier University.

FACILITIES
Housing: Men's dorms, women's dorms, special housing for disabled students. **Special Academic Facilities/Equipment:** Jazz institute, Southern Museum of Art. **Computers:** 10% of classrooms are wired, 70% of classrooms are wireless, 95% of public computers are PCs, 4% of public computers are Macs, 1% of public computers are UNIX, network access in dorm rooms, network access in dorm lounges, online registration, online administrative functions (other than registration), remote student-access to Web through college's connection.

CAMPUS LIFE
Activities: Choral groups, concert band, dance, drama/theater, jazz band, literary magazine, marching band, music ensembles, musical theater, pep band, student government, student newspaper, yearbook. **Organizations:** 80 registered organizations, 11 honor societies, 7 religious organizations. 5 fraternities (1% men join), 4 sororities (2% women join). **Athletics (Intercollegiate):** *Men:* Baseball, basketball, cross-country, football, golf, tennis, track/field (outdoor). *Women:* Basketball, cross-country, golf, softball, tennis, track/field (outdoor), volleyball. **Environmental Initiatives:** MS4-Stormwater Permit with the Parish of East Baton Rouge. Full-time Environmental, Safety and Health Director. Storm Water Plan (Debris Management).

ADMISSIONS
Freshman Academic Profile: 3% in top 10% of high school class, 12% in top 25% of high school class, 38% in top 50% of high school class. 75% from public high schools. SAT Math middle 50% range 380–460. ACT middle 50% range 15–18. TOEFL required of all international applicants, minimum paper TOEFL 500, minimum computer TOEFL 125. **Basis for Candidate Selection:** *Very important factors considered include:* Rigor of secondary school record, standardized test scores. *Important factors considered include:* Academic GPA, class rank. *Other factors considered include:* Talent/ability. **Freshman Admission Requirements:** High school diploma is required, and GED is accepted. *Academic units required:* 4 English, 3 math, 3 science, 2 foreign language, 2 social studies, 1 history, 1 computer science, arts (1.5 credits). **Freshman Admission Statistics:** 4,703 applied, 53% admitted, 60% enrolled. **Transfer Admission Requirements:** High school transcript, college transcript(s), standardized test score, statement of good standing from prior

institution(s). Minimum college GPA of 2.0 required. Lowest grade transferable C. **General Admission Information:** Application fee $20. Regular application deadline 7/1. Regular notification is rolling. Non-fall registration accepted. Admission may be deferred for a maximum of 2 semesters. Common Application not accepted. Credit offered for CEEB Advanced Placement tests.

COSTS AND FINANCIAL AID
Annual in-state tuition $3,666. Annual out-of-state tuition $9,458. Room and board $5,784. Average book expense $1,200. **Required Forms and Deadlines:** FAFSA, institution's own financial aid form. Financial aid filing deadline 5/15. **Notification of Awards:** Applicants will be notified of awards on a rolling basis beginning on or about 6/30. **Types of Aid:** *Need-based scholarships/grants:* Pell, SEOG, state scholarships/grants, private scholarships, the school's own gift aid. *Loans:* Direct Subsidized Stafford, Direct Unsubsidized Stafford, Direct PLUS, FFEL Subsidized Stafford, FFEL Unsubsidized Stafford, FFEL PLUS, college/university loans from institutional funds, TOPS, TH Harris, LEAP. **Financial Aid Statistics:** 57% freshmen, 55% undergrads receive need-based scholarship or grant aid. 64% freshmen, 72% undergrads receive need-based self-help aid. 63 freshmen, 244 undergrads receive athletic scholarships. Highest amount earned per year from on-campus jobs $1,000.

SOUTHERN UNIVERSITY AND AGRICULTURAL AND MECHANICAL COLLEGE

3050 Martin Luther King Jr. Drive, Shreveport, LA 71107
Phone: 318-674-3342
Fax: 318-674-3338 **Website:** www.susla.edu **ACT Code:** 1613
Financial Aid Phone: 318-674-3494

This public school was founded in 1967. It has a 101-acre campus.

RATINGS
Admissions Selectivity Rating: 60*   **Fire Safety Rating:** 60*   **Green Rating:** 60*

STUDENTS AND FACULTY
Enrollment: 1,342. **Student Body:** 69% female, 31% male, 2% out-of-state. African American 91%, Caucasian 9%. **Faculty:** 100% faculty teach undergrads.

ACADEMICS
Degrees: Associate, certificate, diploma. **Academic Requirements:** Arts/fine arts, computer literacy, English (including composition), humanities, mathematics, sciences (biological or physical), social science. **Special Study Options:** Cooperative education program, cross-registration, double major, dual enrollment, honors program, independent study, internships, teacher certification program, weekend college.

FACILITIES
Special Academic Facilities/Equipment: Academic Career Enhancement Lab (ACE), aerospace technology center, Rad Tech Lab/CAD Lab.

CAMPUS LIFE
Activities: Choral groups, student government, student newspaper. **Organizations:** 17 registered organizations, 1 honor society, 2 religious organizations. **Athletics (Intercollegiate):** *Men:* Basketball. *Women:* Basketball.

ADMISSIONS
Freshman Academic Profile: 90% from public high schools. ACT middle 50% range 13–16. TOEFL required of all international applicants, minimum paper TOEFL 500. **Basis for Candidate Selection:** *Very important factors considered include:* Rigor of secondary school record. *Other factors considered include:* Standardized test scores, state residency. **Freshman Admission Requirements:** High school diploma is required, and GED is accepted. *Academic units required:* 4 English, 3 math, 3 science, 1 foreign language, 1 social studies, 3 history, 9 academic electives. *Academic units recommended:* 4 English, 3 math, 3 science, 1 foreign language, 1 social studies, 3 history, 9 academic electives. **Freshman Admission Statistics:** 458 applied, 100% admitted, 100% enrolled. **Transfer Admission Requirements:** College transcript(s). Minimum college GPA of 2.0 required. Lowest grade transferable C. **General Admission Information:** Regular application deadline is rolling. Non-fall registration accepted. Common Application not accepted.

COSTS AND FINANCIAL AID
Annual in-state tuition $1,104. Out-of-state tuition $2,394. Average book expense $300. **Required Forms and Deadlines:** FAFSA, institution's own financial aid form. Financial aid filing deadline 4/1. **Types of Aid:** *Need-based*

scholarships/grants: Pell, SEOG, state scholarships/grants, private scholarships, the school's own gift aid. *Loans*: Direct Subsidized Stafford, Direct Unsubsidized Stafford, Direct PLUS. **Student Employment**: Federal Work-Study Program available. Off-campus job opportunities are fair. **Financial Aid Statistics**: 99% freshmen, 99% undergrads receive need-based scholarship or grant aid. 39% freshmen, 11% undergrads receive need-based self-help aid.

SOUTHERN UTAH UNIVERSITY

Southern Utah University, Admissions Office, 351 West University Boulevard, Cedar City, UT 84720
Phone: 435-586-7740 **E-mail**: adminfo@suu.edu **CEEB Code**: 4092
Fax: 435-865-8223 **Website**: www.suu.edu **ACT Code**: 4271
Financial Aid Phone: 801-586-7735

This public school was founded in 1897. It has a 113-acre campus.

RATINGS
Admissions Selectivity Rating: 79   **Fire Safety Rating**: 60*   **Green Rating**: 60*

STUDENTS AND FACULTY
Enrollment: 5,268. **Student Body**: 57% female, 43% male, 14% out-of-state, 1% international (7 countries represented). Asian 2%, Caucasian 88%, Hispanic 3%, Native American 2%. **Retention and Graduation**: 64% freshmen return for sophomore year. 19% freshmen graduate within 4 years. **Faculty**: Student/faculty ratio 23:1. 220 full-time faculty, 77% hold PhDs.

ACADEMICS
Degrees: Associate, bachelor's, certificate, diploma, master's, terminal. **Academic Requirements**: Arts/fine arts, computer literacy, English (including composition), history, humanities, mathematics, philosophy, sciences (biological or physical), social science. **Classes**: Most classes have 20–29 students. Most lab/discussion sections have fewer than 10 students. **Disciplines with Highest Percentage of Degrees Awarded**: Education 23%, business/marketing 15%, psychology 8%, biological/life sciences 7%, social sciences 7%, communications/journalism 6%. **Special Study Options**: Cooperative education program, distance learning, double major, English as a second language (ESL), honors program, independent study, internships, liberal arts/career combination, teacher certification program, weekend college.

FACILITIES
Housing: Coed dorms, men's dorms, women's dorms, apartments for single students, special housing for disabled students, fraternity/sorority housing. **Special Academic Facilities/Equipment**: Art gallery, natural history museum, farm and ranch, TV studio.

CAMPUS LIFE
Activities: Choral groups, concert band, dance, drama/theater, jazz band, literary magazine, marching band, music ensembles, musical theater, opera, pep band, radio station, student government, student newspaper, symphony orchestra, television station, yearbook. **Organizations**: 3 religious organizations. 2 fraternities (4% men join), 3 sororities (4% women join). **Athletics (Intercollegiate)**: *Men*: Baseball, basketball, cross-country, football, golf, track/field (outdoor). *Women*: Basketball, cross-country, gymnastics, softball, tennis, track/field (outdoor).

ADMISSIONS
Freshman Academic Profile: 28% in top 10% of high school class, 55% in top 25% of high school class, 82% in top 50% of high school class. 95% from public high schools. SAT Math middle 50% range 450–570. SAT Critical Reading middle 50% range 440–590. ACT middle 50% range 18–24. TOEFL required of all international applicants, minimum paper TOEFL 500. **Basis for Candidate Selection**: *Very important factors considered include:* Academic GPA, standardized test scores. *Other factors considered include*: First generation, racial/ethnic status. **Freshman Admission Requirements**: High school diploma is required, and GED is accepted. *Academic units recommended*: 4 English, 3 math, 3 science (1 science lab), 2 foreign language, 3 social studies. **Freshman Admission Statistics**: 3,134 applied, 80% admitted, 51% enrolled. **Transfer Admission Requirements**: College transcript(s). Minimum college GPA of 2.3 required. Lowest grade transferable D. **General Admission Information**: Application fee $40. Regular application deadline 8/

1. Regular notification decision sent immediately. Non-fall registration accepted. Admission may be deferred for a maximum of 2 semesters. Credit and/or placement offered for CEEB Advanced Placement tests.

COSTS AND FINANCIAL AID
Annual in-state tuition $3,060. Out-of-state tuition $10,098. Room & board $4,124. Required fees $505. Average book expense $1,036. **Required Forms and Deadlines**: FAFSA, institution's own financial aid form. **Notification of Awards**: Applicants will be notified of awards on a rolling basis beginning on or about 2/1. **Types of Aid**: *Need-based scholarships/grants*: Pell, SEOG, state scholarships/grants, private scholarships, the school's own gift aid. *Loans*: FFEL Subsidized Stafford, FFEL Unsubsidized Stafford, FFEL PLUS, Federal Perkins, college/university loans from institutional funds. **Student Employment**: Federal Work-Study Program available. Institutional employment available. Off-campus job opportunities are good. **Financial Aid Statistics**: 48% freshmen, 64% undergrads receive need-based scholarship or grant aid. 25% freshmen, 38% undergrads receive need-based self-help aid. 58 freshmen, 228 undergrads receive athletic scholarships. Highest amount earned per year from on-campus jobs $2,000.

SOUTHERN VERMONT COLLEGE

982 Mansion Drive, Bennington, VT 05201
Phone: 802-447-6304 **E-mail**: admis@svc.edu **CEEB Code**: 3796
Fax: 802-447-4695 **Website**: www.svc.edu **ACT Code**: 4310
Financial Aid Phone: 800-660-3561

This private school was founded in 1974. It has a 371-acre campus.

RATINGS
Admissions Selectivity Rating: 69   **Fire Safety Rating**: 60*   **Green Rating**: 60*

STUDENTS AND FACULTY
Enrollment: 464. **Student Body**: 64% female, 36% male, 66% out-of-state. **Retention and Graduation**: 61% freshmen return for sophomore year. **Faculty**: Student/faculty ratio 11:1. 16 full-time faculty, 25% hold PhDs. 100% faculty teach undergrads.

ACADEMICS
Degrees: Associate, bachelor's, terminal. **Academic Requirements**: Arts/fine arts, computer literacy, English (including composition), environmental studies elective, history, humanities, mathematics, philosophy, sciences (biological or physical), social science. **Disciplines with Highest Percentage of Degrees Awarded**: Business/marketing 28%, health professions and related sciences 11%, liberal arts/general studies 10%, communication technologies 10%, natural resources/environmental science 10%, psychology 8%, interdisciplinary studies 1%. **Special Study Options**: Accelerated program, cooperative education program, distance learning, double major, dual enrollment, honors program, independent study, internships, liberal arts/career combination, student-designed major, study abroad.

FACILITIES
Housing: Coed dorms, quiet, substance-free and nonsmoking, freshmen and upperclassmen residence halls. **Special Academic Facilities/Equipment**: Mountaineers field house and fitness center, apartment style resident halls and courtyard, dining hall and student center, Everett Mansion. **Computers**: Network access in dorm rooms, remote student-access to Web through college's connection.

CAMPUS LIFE
Activities: Drama/theater, literary magazine, music ensembles, radio station, student government, student newspaper, yearbook. **Organizations**: 14 registered organizations, 1 honor society. **Athletics (Intercollegiate)**: *Men*: Baseball, basketball, cross-country, rugby, soccer, volleyball. *Women*: Basketball, cross-country, rugby, soccer, softball, volleyball.

ADMISSIONS
Freshman Academic Profile: 5% in top 25% of high school class, 35% in top 50% of high school class. 85% from public high schools. SAT Math middle 50% range 390–490. SAT Critical Reading middle 50% range 420–510. TOEFL required of all international applicants, minimum paper TOEFL 500, minimum computer TOEFL 173. **Basis for Candidate Selection**: *Very important factors considered include:* Application essay, interview, recommendation(s), rigor of secondary school record. *Important factors considered include*: Character/personal qualities, extracurricular activities, standardized test scores, volunteer work. *Other factors considered include*: Class rank, work experience. **Freshman Admission Requirements**: High school diploma is required, and

The Princeton Review's Complete Book of Colleges

GED is accepted. *Academic units required*: 4 English, 2 math. *Academic units recommended*: 4 science, 2 foreign language, 4 social studies, 4 history. **Freshman Admission Statistics**: 373 applied, 71% admitted, 37% enrolled. **Transfer Admission Requirements**: High school transcript, college transcript(s), essay or personal statement. Minimum college GPA of 2.0 required. Lowest grade transferable C. **General Admission Information**: Application fee $30. Regular notification is rolling. Non-fall registration accepted. Admission may be deferred for a maximum of 1 year. Common Application accepted. Credit offered for CEEB Advanced Placement tests.

COSTS AND FINANCIAL AID

Annual tuition $14,374. Room & board $6,948. Average book expense $500. **Required Forms and Deadlines**: FAFSA, institution's own financial aid form. Financial aid filing deadline 5/1. **Notification of Awards**: Applicants will be notified of awards on or about 3/1. **Types of Aid**: *Need-based scholarships/grants*: Pell, SEOG, state scholarships/grants, private scholarships, the school's own gift aid, Southern Vermont College Opportunity Grant, Everett Scholarship, Leadership Scholarship, Vermont Resident Scholarship, TRIO Scholarship. *Loans*: Direct Subsidized Stafford, Direct Unsubsidized Stafford, Direct PLUS. **Student Employment**: Federal Work-Study Program available. Off-campus job opportunities are good. **Financial Aid Statistics**: 64% freshmen, 73% undergrads receive need-based scholarship or grant aid. 67% freshmen, 76% undergrads receive need-based self-help aid. 75% freshmen, 75% undergrads receive any aid.

SOUTHERN WESLEYAN UNIVERSITY

Wesleyan Drive, PO Box 1020, Central, SC 29630-1020
Phone: 864-644-5550 **E-mail**: admissions@swu.edu **CEEB Code**: 5896
Fax: 864-644-5972 **Website**: www.swu.edu **ACT Code**: 3837
Financial Aid Phone: 864-644-5500

This private school, affiliated with the Wesleyan Church, was founded in 1906. It has a 210-acre campus.

RATINGS

Admissions Selectivity Rating: 72   **Fire Safety Rating**: 64   **Green Rating**: 64

STUDENTS AND FACULTY

Enrollment: 1,783. **Student Body**: 64% female, 36% male, 33% out-of-state. African American 34%, Caucasian 58%, Hispanic 1%. **Retention and Graduation**: 62% freshmen return for sophomore year. 36% freshmen graduate within 4 years. **Faculty**: Student/faculty ratio 23:1. 50 full-time faculty, 74% hold PhDs. 100% faculty teach undergrads.

ACADEMICS

Degrees: Associate, bachelor's, master's. **Academic Requirements**: Arts/fine arts, computer literacy, English (including composition), history, mathematics, philosophy, sciences (biological or physical), social science. To graduate, students must complete 128 credit hours with a minimum GPA of 2.0. All students must take 12 hours each of English and religion, 6 of history, 3 of social sciences, and 3 of math or statistics, plus 2 science lab courses. Specific required courses include aesthetics, introduction to computer science, physical education, and interdisciplinary seminars. **Classes**: Most classes have 10–19 students. Most lab/discussion sections have 10–19 students. **Majors with Highest Enrollment**: Business administration/management, elementary education and teaching, religion/religious studies. **Disciplines with Highest Percentage of Degrees Awarded**: Business/marketing 60%, education 26%, philosophy and religious studies 3%, psychology 3%, English 2%. **Special Study Options**: Cross-registration, distance learning, double major, dual enrollment, English as a second language (ESL), honors program, independent study, internships, student-designed major, study abroad, teacher certification program.

FACILITIES

Housing: Coed dorms, women's dorms, apartments for single students, special housing for disabled students. **Computers**: 100% of classrooms are wired, 100% of classrooms are wireless, 100% of public computers are PCs, network access in dorm rooms, network access in dorm lounges, online registration, online administrative functions (other than registration), remote student-access to Web through college's connection.

CAMPUS LIFE

Activities: Choral groups, concert band, drama/theater, jazz band, literary magazine, music ensembles, musical theater, student government, yearbook. **Organizations**: 11 registered organizations, 1 honor society, 3 religious organizations. **Athletics (Intercollegiate)**: *Men*: Baseball, basketball, cross-country, golf, soccer. *Women*: Basketball, cross-country, soccer, softball, volleyball.

ADMISSIONS

Freshman Academic Profile: 14% in top 10% of high school class, 33% in top 25% of high school class, 69% in top 50% of high school class. SAT Math middle 50% range 450–570. SAT Critical Reading middle 50% range 430–560. SAT Writing middle 50% range 430–550. ACT middle 50% range 17–23. TOEFL required of all international applicants, minimum paper TOEFL 500, minimum computer TOEFL 173. **Basis for Candidate Selection**: *Very important factors considered include*: Academic GPA, rigor of secondary school record, standardized test scores. *Important factors considered include*: Class rank, recommendation(s). *Other factors considered include*: Character/personal qualities, extracurricular activities, interview, talent/ability, volunteer work, work experience. **Freshman Admission Requirements**: High school diploma is required, and GED is accepted. *Academic units required*: 4 English, 2 math, 2 science, 2 social studies. **Freshman Admission Statistics**: 434 applied, 58% admitted, 54% enrolled. **Transfer Admission Requirements**: College transcript(s). Minimum college GPA of 2.0 required. Lowest grade transferable C. **General Admission Information**: Application fee $25. Regular application deadline 8/1. Non-fall registration accepted. Admission may be deferred for a maximum of 1 semester. Credit and/or placement offered for CEEB Advanced Placement tests.

COSTS AND FINANCIAL AID

Comprehensive fee $17,500. Room and board $7,450. Required fees $500. Average book expense $950. **Required Forms and Deadlines**: FAFSA, institution's own financial aid form. Financial aid filing deadline 6/30. **Notification of Awards**: Applicants will be notified of awards on a rolling basis beginning on or about 2/1. **Types of Aid**: *Need-based scholarships/grants*: Pell, SEOG, state scholarships/grants, private scholarships, the school's own gift aid. *Loans*: FFEL Subsidized Stafford, FFEL Unsubsidized Stafford, FFEL PLUS, Federal Perkins. **Financial Aid Statistics**: 47% freshmen, 39% undergrads receive need-based scholarship or grant aid. 40% freshmen, 39% undergrads receive need-based self-help aid. 15 freshmen, 57 undergrads receive athletic scholarships. 86% freshmen, 85% undergrads receive any aid.

SOUTHWEST BAPTIST UNIVERSITY

1600 University Avenue, Bolivar, MO 65613-2597
Phone: 417-328-1810 **E-mail**: admitme@sbuniv.edu **CEEB Code**: 6664
Fax: 417-328-1808 **Website**: www.sbuniv.edu **ACT Code**: 2368
Financial Aid Phone: 417-328-1823

This private school, affiliated with the Southern Baptist Church, was founded in 1878. It has a 180-acre campus.

RATINGS

Admissions Selectivity Rating: 80   **Fire Safety Rating**: 66   **Green Rating**: 60*

STUDENTS AND FACULTY

Enrollment: 2,441. **Student Body**: 66% female, 34% male, 29% out-of-state. African American 3%, Caucasian 90%, Hispanic 1%. **Retention and Graduation**: 72% freshmen return for sophomore year. 35% freshmen graduate within 4 years. 25% grads go on to further study within 1 year. **Faculty**: Student/faculty ratio 14:1. 105 full-time faculty, 63% hold PhDs. 81% faculty teach undergrads.

ACADEMICS

Degrees: Associate, bachelor's, certificate, doctoral, master's, post-master's certificate. **Academic Requirements**: Arts/fine arts, Bible, computer literacy, cultural studies, English (including composition), history, humanities, mathematics, physical fitness, sciences (biological or physical), social science. **Classes**: Most classes have 10–19 students. Most lab/discussion sections have 10–19 students. **Majors with Highest Enrollment**: Elementary education and teaching, psychology. **Disciplines with Highest Percentage of Degrees Awarded**: Education 19%, business/marketing 15%, psychology 13%, theology and religious vocations 10%, health professions and related sciences 6%, social sciences 6%. **Special Study Options**: Cooperative education program, distance learning, double major, dual enrollment, exchange student program (domestic), honors program, independent study, internships, study abroad, teacher certification program.

FACILITIES

Housing: Men's dorms, women's dorms. **Special Academic Facilities/ Equipment**: The Driskell Art Gallery, Jester Learning and Performance Center, Meyer Wellness and Sports Center. **Computers**: 2% of classrooms are wired, 100% of classrooms are wireless, 99% of public computers are PCs, 1% of public computers are Macs, network access in dorm rooms, network access in dorm lounges, online administrative functions (other than registration), remote student-access to Web through college's connection.

CAMPUS LIFE

Activities: Choral groups, concert band, drama/theater, jazz band, music ensembles, musical theater, opera, pep band, student government, student newspaper, symphony orchestra, yearbook. **Organizations**: 34 registered organizations, 4 honor societies, 10 religious organizations. **Athletics (Intercollegiate)**: *Men*: Baseball, basketball, cheerleading, cross-country, football, golf, tennis, track/field (outdoor). *Women*: Basketball, cheerleading, cross-country, soccer, softball, tennis, track/field (outdoor), volleyball.

ADMISSIONS

Freshman Academic Profile: 26% in top 10% of high school class, 56% in top 25% of high school class, 83% in top 50% of high school class. 90% from public high schools. SAT Math middle 50% range 400–590. SAT Critical Reading middle 50% range 430–600. ACT middle 50% range 20–26. TOEFL required of all international applicants, minimum paper TOEFL 550, minimum computer TOEFL 213. **Basis for Candidate Selection**: *Very important factors considered include*: Academic GPA, class rank, standardized test scores. *Important factors considered include*: Application essay, recommendation(s), rigor of secondary school record. *Other factors considered include*: Character/personal qualities, interview, talent/ability. **Freshman Admission Requirements**: High school diploma is required, and GED is accepted. *Academic units recommended*: 4 English, 3 math, 2 science, 2 social studies, 2 additional units from foreign language, computer science, English, mathematics, social studies, or natural sciences. **Freshman Admission Statistics**: 1,311 applied, 75% admitted, 47% enrolled. **Transfer Admission Requirements**: High school transcript, college transcript(s), standardized test score. Minimum college GPA of 2.0 required. Lowest grade transferable D. **General Admission Information**: Application fee $30. Regular notification is rolling. Non-fall registration accepted. Admission may be deferred for a maximum of 1 year. Credit and/or placement offered for CEEB Advanced Placement tests.

COSTS AND FINANCIAL AID

Annual tuition $14,100. Room & board $4,550. Required fees $850. Average book expense $1,000. **Required Forms and Deadlines**: FAFSA, institution's own financial aid form. Financial aid filing deadline 3/15. **Notification of Awards**: Applicants will be notified of awards on a rolling basis beginning on or about 3/1. **Types of Aid**: *Need-based scholarships/grants*: Pell, SEOG, state scholarships/grants, private scholarships, the school's own gift aid. *Loans*: FFEL Subsidized Stafford, FFEL Unsubsidized Stafford, FFEL PLUS, Federal Perkins, Federal Nursing, alternative loans. **Financial Aid Statistics**: 26% freshmen, 35% undergrads receive need-based scholarship or grant aid. 54% freshmen, 58% undergrads receive need-based self-help aid. 79 freshmen, 236 undergrads receive athletic scholarships. 71% freshmen, 69% undergrads receive any aid.

SOUTHWEST MINNESOTA STATE UNIVERSITY

Admission Office, 1501 State Street, Marshall, MN 56258
Phone: 800-642-0684 **E-mail**: shearerr@southwest.msus.edu **CEEB Code**: 6703
Fax: 507-537-7154 **Website**: www.southwest.msus.edu **ACT Code**: 2151

This public school was founded in 1963. It has a 216-acre campus.

RATINGS
Admissions Selectivity Rating: 60*   **Fire Safety Rating**: 60*   **Green Rating**: 60*

STUDENTS AND FACULTY

Student Body: 17% out-of-state. **Retention and Graduation**: 66% freshmen return for sophomore year. 8% freshmen graduate within 4 years.

ACADEMICS

Degrees: Associate, bachelor's, master's. **Special Study Options**: Exchange program abroad in Japan, study abroad also in Chile and China.

FACILITIES

Housing: Apartments for single students. **Special Academic Facilities/ Equipment**: Art gallery, natural history museum, science museum, planetarium, greenhouse, wildlife area.

CAMPUS LIFE

Activities: Literary magazine, radio station, student government, student newspaper, television station, yearbook. **Organizations**: 65 registered organizations, 1 honor society, 5 religious organizations. **Athletics (Intercollegiate)**: *Men*: Cross-country. *Women*: Basketball, cross-country, softball, tennis, volleyball.

ADMISSIONS

Freshman Academic Profile: 17% in top 10% of high school class, 41% in top 25% of high school class, 81% in top 50% of high school class. ACT middle 50% range 19–24. Minimum paper TOEFL 500. **Freshman Admission Requirements**: High school diploma is required, and GED is accepted. *Academic units recommended*: 4 English, 3 math, 3 science, 2 foreign language, 3 social studies, 1 history. **Transfer Admission Requirements**: Minimum college GPA of 2.0 required. Lowest grade transferable C. **General Admission Information**: Application fee $20. Regular application deadline is rolling. Regular notification is rolling. Non-fall registration accepted. Common Application accepted. Credit offered for CEEB Advanced Placement tests.

COSTS AND FINANCIAL AID

Annual in-state tuition $2,648. Out-of-state tuition $5,965. Room & board $3,000. Required fees $484. Average book expense $800. **Required Forms and Deadlines**: FAFSA, institution's own financial aid form. **Types of Aid**: *Need-based scholarships/grants*: Pell, SEOG, state scholarships/grants, private scholarships, the school's own gift aid. *Loans*: FFEL Subsidized Stafford, FFEL Unsubsidized Stafford, FFEL PLUS, Federal Perkins, college/university loans from institutional funds. **Student Employment**: Federal Work-Study Program available. Institutional employment available. Off-campus job opportunities are excellent. **Financial Aid Statistics**: Highest amount earned per year from on-campus jobs $2,602. **Financial Aid Phone**: 507-537-6281.

SOUTHWESTERN ADVENTIST UNIVERSITY

PO Box 567, Keene, TX 76059
Phone: 800-433-2240 **E-mail**: illingworth@swac.edu
Fax: 817-645-3921 **Website**: www.swac.edu
Financial Aid Phone: 817-645-3921

This private school was founded in 1893.

RATINGS
Admissions Selectivity Rating: 81   **Fire Safety Rating**: 60*   **Green Rating**: 60*

STUDENTS AND FACULTY

Student Body: 46% out-of-state. **Retention and Graduation**: 63% freshmen return for sophomore year. 28% grads go on to further study within 1 year. 10% grads pursue arts and sciences degrees. 5% grads pursue business degrees. 3% grads pursue law degrees. 10% grads pursue medical degrees. **Faculty**: 100% faculty teach undergrads.

FACILITIES

Housing: Coed dorms, men's dorms, women's dorms.

CAMPUS LIFE

Organizations: 2 honor societies, 2 religious organizations.

ADMISSIONS

Freshman Academic Profile: 15% in top 10% of high school class, 37% in top 25% of high school class, 65% in top 50% of high school class. 30% from public high schools. SAT Math middle 50% range 400–540. SAT Critical Reading middle 50% range 450–570. ACT middle 50% range 18–23. Minimum paper TOEFL 520. **General Admission Information**: Regular application deadline 9/10. Credit and/or placement offered for CEEB Advanced Placement tests.

COSTS AND FINANCIAL AID

Comprehensive fee $11,918. Room & board $4,084. Required fees $100. Average book expense $536. **Types of Aid**: *Loans*: FFEL Subsidized Stafford, FFEL PLUS. **Student Employment**: Federal Work-Study Program available. Off-campus job opportunities are fair. **Financial Aid Statistics**: Highest amount earned per year from on-campus jobs $2,140.

SOUTHWESTERN CHRISTIAN UNIVERSITY

PO Box 340, Bethany, OK 73008
Phone: 405-789-7661 **E-mail:** admissions@swcu.edu
Fax: 405-495-0078 **Website:** www.swcu.edu **ACT Code:** 3439
Financial Aid Phone: 405-789-7661

This private school was founded in 1946. It has an 11-acre campus.

RATINGS
Admissions Selectivity Rating: 73   **Fire Safety Rating:** 60*   **Green Rating:** 60*

STUDENTS AND FACULTY
Enrollment: 637. **Student Body:** 89% female, 11% male, 30% out-of-state. Caucasian 14%. **Retention and Graduation:** 42% freshmen return for sophomore year. 16% freshmen graduate within 4 years. **Faculty:** Student/faculty ratio 8:1. 5 full-time faculty, 20% hold PhDs.

ACADEMICS
Degrees: Associate, bachelor's, certificate, diploma, master's. **Academic Requirements:** Bible, computer literacy, English (including composition), history, humanities, mathematics, sciences (biological or physical), social science. **Classes:** Most classes have fewer than 10 students. **Special Study Options:** Cooperative education program, double major, internships.

FACILITIES
Housing: Men's dorms, women's dorms.

CAMPUS LIFE
Activities: Choral groups, music ensembles, musical theater, student government. **Organizations:** 10 honor societies, 4 religious organizations. **Athletics (Intercollegiate):** *Men:* Basketball, golf. *Women:* Basketball, volleyball.

ADMISSIONS
Freshman Academic Profile: 11% in top 10% of high school class, 30% in top 25% of high school class, 55% in top 50% of high school class. ACT middle 50% range 19–21. TOEFL required of all international applicants, minimum paper TOEFL 550. **Basis for Candidate Selection:** *Very important factors considered include:* Recommendation(s), rigor of secondary school record. *Important factors considered include:* Character/personal qualities, class rank, standardized test scores. *Other factors considered include:* Application essay, extracurricular activities, interview, religious affiliation/commitment, talent/ability. **Freshman Admission Requirements:** High school diploma is required, and GED is accepted. **Freshman Admission Statistics:** 81 applied, 77% admitted. **Transfer Admission Requirements:** College transcript(s), statement of good standing from prior institution(s). Minimum college GPA of 2.5 required. Lowest grade transferable C. **General Admission Information:** Application fee $30. Early decision application deadline 3/15. Regular application deadline 7/15. Regular notification is 20 days after receiving application. Non-fall registration accepted. Admission may be deferred for a maximum of 2 semesters. Common Application accepted.

COSTS AND FINANCIAL AID
Comprehensive fee $5,926. Room and board $2,208. Required fees $300. Average book expense $300. **Types of Aid:** *Loans:* FFEL Subsidized Stafford, FFEL PLUS. **Student Employment:** Federal Work-Study Program available. Off-campus job opportunities are excellent. **Financial Aid Statistics:** Highest amount earned per year from on-campus jobs $800.

SOUTHWESTERN COLLEGE (AZ)

2625 East Cactus Road, Phoenix, AZ 85032
Phone: 602-992-6101 **E-mail:** admissions@swcaz.edu
Fax: 602-404-2159 **Website:** www.swcaz.edu
Financial Aid Phone: 602-992-6160

This private school, affiliated with the Baptist Church, was founded in 1960. It has a 17-acre campus.

RATINGS
Admissions Selectivity Rating: 60*   **Fire Safety Rating:** 60*   **Green Rating:** 60*

STUDENTS AND FACULTY
Enrollment: 257. **Student Body:** 43% female, 57% male, 14% out-of-state, 1% international. African American 4%, Asian 2%, Caucasian 84%, Hispanic 5%, Native American 2%. **Retention and Graduation:** 67% freshmen return for sophomore year. 70% freshmen graduate within 4 years. **Faculty:** Student/faculty ratio 16:1. 9 full-time faculty, 33% hold PhDs. 100% faculty teach undergrads.

ACADEMICS
Degrees: Associate, bachelor's, certificate. **Academic Requirements:** Arts/fine arts, computer literacy, English (including composition), history, humanities, mathematics, philosophy, sciences (biological or physical), social science. **Disciplines with Highest Percentage of Degrees Awarded:** Education 50%.

FACILITIES
Housing: Men's dorms, women's dorms, apartments for single students. **Computers:** Network access in dorm rooms, remote student-access to Web through college's connection.

CAMPUS LIFE
Activities: Choral groups, drama/theater, music ensembles, student government, student newspaper, yearbook. **Athletics (Intercollegiate):** *Men:* Basketball. *Women:* Basketball, volleyball.

ADMISSIONS
Freshman Academic Profile: 72% from public high schools. ACT middle 50% range 17–23. TOEFL required of all international applicants, minimum paper TOEFL 500. **Basis for Candidate Selection:** *Very important factors considered include:* Application essay, recommendation(s), religious affiliation/commitment, rigor of secondary school record, standardized test scores. *Important factors considered include:* Character/personal qualities. *Other factors considered include:* Extracurricular activities, interview. **Freshman Admission Requirements:** High school diploma is required, and GED is accepted. **Freshman Admission Statistics:** 95 applied, 86% admitted, 71% enrolled. **Transfer Admission Requirements:** High school transcript, college transcript(s), essay or personal statement, statement of good standing from prior institution(s). Minimum college GPA of 2.0 required. Lowest grade transferable C. **General Admission Information:** Application fee $25. Non-fall registration accepted. Admission may be deferred for a maximum of 1 semester. Common Application not accepted.

COSTS AND FINANCIAL AID
Annual tuition $8,600. Room & board $3,400. Required fees $8,600. Average book expense $700. **Required Forms and Deadlines:** FAFSA. Financial aid filing deadline 4/15. **Notification of Awards:** Applicants will be notified of awards on or about 5/1. **Types of Aid:** *Need-based scholarships/grants:* Pell, SEOG, state scholarships/grants. *Loans:* FFEL Subsidized Stafford, FFEL Unsubsidized Stafford, FFEL PLUS, Federal Perkins. **Student Employment:** Federal Work-Study Program available. Institutional employment available. **Financial Aid Statistics:** 92% freshmen, 91% undergrads receive need-based self-help aid.

SOUTHWESTERN COLLEGE (KS)

100 College Street, Winfield, KS 67156
Phone: 620-229-6236 **E-mail:** scadmit@sckans.edu **CEEB Code:** 6670
Fax: 620-229-6344 **Website:** www.sckans.edu **ACT Code:** 1464
Financial Aid Phone: 620-229-6215

This private school, affiliated with the Methodist Church, was founded in 1885. It has an 85-acre campus.

RATINGS
Admissions Selectivity Rating: 75   **Fire Safety Rating:** 75   **Green Rating:** 60*

STUDENTS AND FACULTY
Enrollment: 1,252. **Student Body:** 49% female, 51% male, 1% international (10 countries represented). African American 10%, Asian 2%, Caucasian 68%, Hispanic 4%, Native American 2%. **Retention and Graduation:** 71% freshmen return for sophomore year. 42% freshmen graduate within 4 years. 16% grads go on to further study within 1 year. **Faculty:** Student/faculty ratio 10:1. 47 full-time faculty, 57% hold PhDs. 100% faculty teach undergrads.

ACADEMICS
Degrees: Bachelor's, master's. **Academic Requirements:** Computer literacy, English (including composition), mathematics. **Classes:** Most classes have fewer than 10 students. Most lab/discussion sections have fewer than 10 students. **Majors with Highest Enrollment:** Business administration and management, elementary education and teaching, nursing/registered nurse training (ASN, BSN, MSN, RN). **Disciplines with Highest Percentage of Degrees Awarded:** Business/marketing 45%, computer and information sciences 13%, security and protective services 12%, health professions and related sciences 8%, education 4%. **Special Study Options:** Accelerated program, distance learning, double major, honors program, independent study, internships, student-designed major, study abroad, teacher certification program.

FACILITIES
Housing: Coed dorms, men's dorms, women's dorms, apartments for married students, apartments for single students, special housing for disabled students. **Special Academic Facilities/Equipment:** Ruth Warren Abbott Horticulture Lab, Floyd and Ethel Moore Biological Field Station. **Computers:** 98% of public computers are PCs, 2% of public computers are Macs, network access in dorm rooms, network access in dorm lounges, online registration, remote student-access to Web through college's connection.

CAMPUS LIFE
Activities: Choral groups, concert band, dance, drama/theater, jazz band, literary magazine, music ensembles, musical theater, pep band, radio station, student government, student newspaper, symphony orchestra, television station, yearbook. **Organizations:** 17 registered organizations, 3 honor societies, 10 religious organizations. 2 fraternities (5% men join), 1 sorority (8% women join). **Athletics (Intercollegiate):** *Men:* Basketball, cheerleading, cross-country, football, golf, soccer, tennis, track/field (indoor), track/field (outdoor). *Women:* Basketball, cheerleading, cross-country, golf, soccer, softball, tennis, track/field (indoor), track/field (outdoor), volleyball.

ADMISSIONS
Freshman Academic Profile: 13% in top 10% of high school class, 34% in top 25% of high school class, 68% in top 50% of high school class. 90% from public high schools. SAT Math middle 50% range 430–560. SAT Critical Reading middle 50% range 400–520. ACT middle 50% range 19–25 TOEFL required of all international applicants, minimum paper TOEFL 550, minimum computer TOEFL 213. **Basis for Candidate Selection:** *Very important factors considered include:* Academic GPA, rigor of secondary school record, standardized test scores. *Important factors considered include:* Application essay. *Other factors considered include:* Alumni/ae relation, character/personal qualities, class rank, extracurricular activities, interview, recommendation(s), talent/ability. **Freshman Admission Requirements:** High school diploma is required, and GED is accepted. *Academic units required:* 4 English, 3 math, 2 science (1 science lab), 2 social studies, 1 history. **Freshman Admission Statistics:** 457 applied, 67% admitted, 46% enrolled. **Transfer Admission Requirements:** College transcript(s), essay or personal statement. Minimum college GPA of 2.5 required. Lowest grade transferable C. **General Admission Information:** Application fee $20. Regular application deadline 8/25. Regular notification is rolling. Non-fall registration accepted. Credit and/or placement offered for CEEB Advanced Placement tests.

COSTS AND FINANCIAL AID
Annual tuition $18,600. Room and board $5,698. Required fees $100. Average book expense $600. **Required Forms and Deadlines:** FAFSA, institution's own financial aid form. Financial aid filing deadline 8/15. **Types of Aid:** *Need-based scholarships/grants:* Pell, SEOG, state scholarships/grants, the school's own gift aid. *Loans:* FFEL Subsidized Stafford, FFEL Unsubsidized Stafford, FFEL PLUS, Federal Perkins. **Financial Aid Statistics:** 84% freshmen, 78% undergrads receive need-based scholarship or grant aid. 69% freshmen, 65% undergrads receive need-based self-help aid. 15 freshmen, 31 undergrads receive athletic scholarships. Highest amount earned per year from on-campus jobs $730.

SOUTHWESTERN OKLAHOMA STATE UNIVERSITY

100 Campus Drive, Weatherford, OK 73096
Phone: 580-774-3782 **E-mail:** admissions@swosu.edu **CEEB Code:** 6673
Fax: 580-774-7131 **Website:** www.swosu.edu **ACT Code:** 3340
Financial Aid Phone: 405-774-3786

This public school was founded in 1901. It has a 73-acre campus.

RATINGS
Admissions Selectivity Rating: 73   **Fire Safety Rating:** 60*   **Green Rating:** 60*

STUDENTS AND FACULTY
Enrollment: 4,247. **Student Body:** 58% female, 42% male, 12% out-of-state, 3% international. African American 5%, Asian 1%, Caucasian 79%, Hispanic 4%, Native American 7%. **Retention and Graduation:** 65% freshmen return for sophomore year. **Faculty:** Student/faculty ratio 21:1. 211 full-time faculty, 59% hold PhDs.

ACADEMICS
Degrees: Associate, bachelor's, first professional, master's. **Academic Requirements:** Arts/fine arts, computer literacy, English (including composition), history, humanities, international and cultural studies, mathematics, sciences (biological or physical), social science, wellness. **Classes:** Most classes have 10–819 students. Most lab/discussion sections have 20–29 students. **Disciplines with Highest Percentage of Degrees Awarded:** Education 21%, business/marketing 20%, health professions and related sciences 17%, visual and performing arts 7%, parks and recreation 6%. **Special Study Options:** Accelerated program, distance learning, double major, independent study, internships, student-designed major, teacher certification program, weekend college.

FACILITIES
Housing: Men's dorms, women's dorms, apartments for married students, apartments for single students. **Special Academic Facilities/Equipment:** Writing lab, museum.

CAMPUS LIFE
Activities: Choral groups, concert band, drama/theater, jazz band, literary magazine, marching band, music ensembles, musical theater, pep band, student government, student newspaper, symphony orchestra, television station, yearbook. **Organizations:** 3 religious organizations. 3 fraternities, 3 sororities. **Athletics (Intercollegiate):** *Men:* Baseball, basketball, football, golf, tennis, track/field (outdoor). *Women:* Basketball, tennis.

ADMISSIONS
Freshman Academic Profile: 18% in top 10% of high school class, 41% in top 25% of high school class, 71% in top 50% of high school class. 98% from public high schools. ACT middle 50% range 18–24. TOEFL required of all international applicants, minimum paper TOEFL 500. **Basis for Candidate Selection:** *Very important factors considered include:* Academic GPA, class rank, standardized test scores. **Freshman Admission Requirements:** High school diploma is required, and GED is accepted. *Academic units required:* 4 English, 3 math, 2 science (2 science labs), 1 social studies, 2 history, 3 computer science or foreign language. *Academic units recommended:* 4 English, 3 math, 2 science (2 science labs), 1 social studies, 2 history, 2 academic electives, 3 computer science or foreign language. **Freshman Admission Statistics:** 1,301 applied, 89% admitted, 74% enrolled. **Transfer Admission Requirements:** College transcript(s). Minimum college GPA of 2.0 required. Lowest grade transferable D. **General Admission Information:** Application fee $15. Non-fall registration accepted. Admission may be deferred for a maximum of 1 year. Credit and/or placement offered for CEEB Advanced Placement tests.

COSTS AND FINANCIAL AID

Annual in-state tuition $2,700. Out-of-state tuition $7,200. Room & board $3,550. Required fees $750. Average book expense $1,200. **Required Forms and Deadlines**: FAFSA, institution's own financial aid form. Financial aid filing deadline 3/1. **Notification of Awards**: Applicants will be notified of awards on or about 3/20. **Types of Aid**: *Need-based scholarships/grants*: Pell, SEOG, state scholarships/grants, private scholarships, the school's own gift aid. *Loans*: FFEL Subsidized Stafford, FFEL Unsubsidized Stafford, FFEL PLUS, alternative loans through various institutions. **Student Employment**: Federal Work-Study Program available. Institutional employment available. Off-campus job opportunities are fair. **Financial Aid Statistics**: 39% freshmen, 43% undergrads receive need-based scholarship or grant aid. 47% freshmen, 51% undergrads receive need-based self-help aid. 38 freshmen, 135 undergrads receive athletic scholarships.

SOUTHWESTERN UNIVERSITY

Admission Office, PO Box 770, Georgetown, TX 78627-0770
Phone: 512-863-1200 **E-mail**: admission@southwestern.edu **CEEB Code**: 6674
Fax: 512-863-9601 **Website**: www.southwestern.edu **ACT Code**: 4186
Financial Aid Phone: 512-863-1259

This private school, affiliated with the Methodist Church, was founded in 1840. It has a 703-acre campus.

RATINGS

Admissions Selectivity Rating: 88   **Fire Safety Rating**: 76   **Green Rating**: 74

STUDENTS AND FACULTY

Enrollment: 1,267. **Student Body**: 59% female, 41% male, 7% out-of-state. African American 3%, Asian 5%, Caucasian 79%, Hispanic 13%. **Retention and Graduation**: 86% freshmen return for sophomore year. 65% freshmen graduate within 4 years. 26% grads go on to further study within 1 year. 6% grads pursue law degrees. 5% grads pursue medical degrees. **Faculty**: Student/faculty ratio 10:1. 120 full-time faculty, 98% hold PhDs. 100% faculty teach undergrads.

ACADEMICS

Degrees: Bachelor's. **Academic Requirements**: Arts/fine arts, computer literacy, English (including composition), foreign languages, humanities, mathematics, sciences (biological or physical), social science. **Classes**: Most classes have 10–19 students. Most lab/discussion sections have fewer than 10 students. **Majors with Highest Enrollment**: Business administration/management, communications studies/speech communication and rhetoric, psychology. **Disciplines with Highest Percentage of Degrees Awarded**: Social sciences 16%, business/marketing 12%, biological/life sciences 11%, communications/journalism 10%, education 10%. **Special Study Options**: Double major, honors program, independent study, internships, liberal arts/career combination, student-designed major, study abroad, teacher certification program.

FACILITIES

Housing: Coed dorms, men's dorms, women's dorms, apartments for married students, apartments for single students, special housing for disabled students, special housing for international students, fraternity/sorority housing. **Special Academic Facilities/Equipment**: Alma Thomas Fine Arts Center, Red and Charline McCombs Campus Center, Corbin J. Robertson Center for Fitness and Wellness, Fountainwood Astronomical Observatory. **Computers**: 20% of classrooms are wired, 100% of classrooms are wireless, 64% of public computers are PCs, 35% of public computers are Macs, 1% of public computers are UNIX, network access in dorm rooms, network access in dorm lounges, online registration, online administrative functions (other than registration), support for handheld computing, remote student-access to Web through college's connection.

CAMPUS LIFE

Activities: Choral groups, concert band, dance, drama/theater, jazz band, literary magazine, music ensembles, musical theater, student government, student newspaper, student-run film society. **Organizations**: 107 registered organizations, 14 honor societies, 11 religious organizations. 4 fraternities (28%

men join), 4 sororities (31% women join). **Athletics (Intercollegiate)**: *Men*: Baseball, basketball, cross-country, diving, golf, soccer, swimming, tennis, track/field (outdoor). *Women*: Basketball, cross-country, diving, golf, soccer, swimming, tennis, track/field (outdoor), volleyball. Environmental Initiatives: Signed Talloires Declaration in Spring 2007. Participated in "e-recycling" event—campus community encouraged to bring in old computers, monitors, printers, telephones, cameras, scanners and other "e-waste" to campus for recycling. Creating native plant nursery.

ADMISSIONS

Freshman Academic Profile: 50% in top 10% of high school class, 85% in top 25% of high school class, 99% in top 50% of high school class. 84% from public high schools. SAT Math middle 50% range 570–660. SAT Critical Reading middle 50% range 560–680. ACT middle 50% range 24–29. TOEFL required of all international applicants, minimum paper TOEFL 570, minimum computer TOEFL 230. **Basis for Candidate Selection**: *Very important factors considered include*: Academic GPA, application essay, class rank, recommendation(s), rigor of secondary school record, standardized test scores. *Important factors considered include*: Alumni/ae relation, character/personal qualities, extracurricular activities, first generation, geographical residence, interview, level of applicant's interest, racial/ethnic status, talent/ability, volunteer work, work experience. **Freshman Admission Requirements**: High school diploma is required, and GED is accepted. *Academic units required*: 4 English, 4 math, 3 science (2 science labs), 2 foreign language, 2 social studies, 2 history, *Academic units recommended*: 4 English, 4 math, 4 science (2 science labs), 3 foreign language, 2 social studies, 2 history. **Freshman Admission Statistics**: 1,955 applied, 65% admitted, 27% enrolled. **Transfer Admission Requirements**: High school transcript, college transcript(s), essay or personal statement, standardized test score, statement of good standing from prior institution(s). Minimum college GPA of 3.0 required. **General Admission Information**: Application fee $40. Early decision application deadline 11/1. Regular application deadline 2/15. Regular notification 4/1. Non-fall registration accepted. Admission may be deferred for a maximum of 1 year. Credit offered for CEEB Advanced Placement tests.

COSTS AND FINANCIAL AID

Annual tuition $25,740. Room and board $8,440. Average book expense $1,000. **Required Forms and Deadlines**: FAFSA. Financial aid filing deadline 3/1. **Notification of Awards**: Applicants will be notified of awards on a rolling basis beginning on or about 3/25. **Types of Aid**: *Need-based scholarships/grants*: Pell, SEOG, state scholarships/grants, private scholarships, the school's own gift aid. *Loans*: FFEL Subsidized Stafford, FFEL Unsubsidized Stafford, FFEL PLUS, Federal Perkins, state loans, college/university loans from institutional funds. **Financial Aid Statistics**: 54% freshmen, 50% undergrads receive need-based scholarship or grant aid. 49% freshmen, 46% undergrads receive need-based self-help aid. 82% freshmen, 84% undergrads receive any aid. Highest amount earned per year from on-campus jobs $4,840.

SPALDING UNIVERSITY

851 South Fourth Street, Louisville, KY 40203
Phone: 502-585-7111 **E-mail**: admission@spalding.edu **CEEB Code**: 1552
Fax: 502-992-2418 **Website**: www.spalding.edu **ACT Code**: 1534
Financial Aid Phone: 502-585-9911

This private school, affiliated with the Roman Catholic Church, was founded in 1814. It has a 6-acre campus.

RATINGS

Admissions Selectivity Rating: 72   **Fire Safety Rating**: 60*   **Green Rating**: 60*

STUDENTS AND FACULTY

Enrollment: 1,128. **Student Body**: 18% out-of-state, 5% international (36 countries represented). African American 13%, Asian 1%, Caucasian 80%. **Retention and Graduation**: 90% freshmen return for sophomore year. 35% freshmen graduate within 4 years. **Faculty**: Student/faculty ratio 12:1. 82 full-time faculty, 76% hold PhDs. 80% faculty teach undergrads.

ACADEMICS

Degrees: Associate, bachelor's, certificate, doctoral, master's. **Academic Requirements**: Arts/fine arts, computer literacy, English (including composition), history, humanities, mathematics, philosophy, sciences (biological or physical), social science. **Classes**: Most classes have 10–19 students. **Majors with Highest Enrollment**: Business administration/management, nursing/registered nurse training (ASN, BSN, MSN, RN), social work. **Disciplines with Highest Percentage of Degrees Awarded**: Health professions and related sciences 24%, business/marketing 21%, psychology 10%, education 8%, liberal arts/general studies 5%. **Special Study Options**: Accelerated program, cooperative education program, cross-registration, double major, independent study, internships, liberal arts/career combination, study abroad, teacher certification program, weekend college.

FACILITIES
Housing: Men's dorms, women's dorms. **Special Academic Facilities/ Equipment**: Huff Gallery. **Computers**: 18% of classrooms are wired, 72% of classrooms are wireless, 100% of public computers are PCs, network access in dorm lounges, remote student-access to Web through college's connection.

CAMPUS LIFE
Activities: Choral groups, drama/theater, student government, student newspaper. **Organizations**: 30 registered organizations, 7 honor societies, 2 religious organizations. **Athletics (Intercollegiate)**: *Men*: Baseball, basketball, soccer. *Women*: Basketball, soccer, softball, volleyball.

ADMISSIONS
Freshman Academic Profile: 15% in top 10% of high school class, 25% in top 25% of high school class, 19% in top 50% of high school class. SAT Math middle 50% range 390–595. SAT Critical Reading middle 50% range 350–590. ACT middle 50% range 19–23. TOEFL required of all international applicants, minimum paper TOEFL 535, minimum computer TOEFL 203. **Basis for Candidate Selection**: *Very important factors considered include*: Rigor of secondary school record, standardized test scores. *Important factors considered include*: Application essay, class rank, extracurricular activities, interview, recommendation(s). *Other factors considered include*: Character/personal qualities, talent/ability. **Freshman Admission Requirements**: High school diploma is required, and GED is accepted. *Academic units recommended*: 4 English, 3 math, 4 science, 2 foreign language. **Freshman Admission Statistics**: 373 applied, 74% admitted, 33% enrolled. **Transfer Admission Requirements**: College transcript(s), statement of good standing from prior institution(s). Minimum college GPA of 2.5 required. Lowest grade transferable C. **General Admission Information**: Application fee $20. Regular application deadline 8/1. Regular notification is rolling. Non-fall registration not accepted. Admission may be deferred for a maximum of 2 semesters. Common Application accepted. Credit and/or placement offered for CEEB Advanced Placement tests.

COSTS AND FINANCIAL AID
Required Forms and Deadlines: FAFSA, institution's own financial aid form. Financial aid filing deadline 3/1. **Notification of Awards**: Applicants will be notified of awards on a rolling basis beginning on or about 3/1. **Types of Aid**: *Need-based scholarships/grants*: Pell, SEOG, state scholarships/grants, private scholarships, the school's own gift aid. *Loans*: FFEL Subsidized Stafford, FFEL Unsubsidized Stafford, FFEL PLUS, Federal Perkins, Federal Nursing. **Financial Aid Statistics**: 23% freshmen, 44% undergrads receive need-based self-help aid. 90% freshmen, 90% undergrads receive any aid. Highest amount earned per year from on-campus jobs $1,400.

SPELMAN COLLEGE

Best 368

350 Spelman Lane, S.W. Box 277, Atlanta, GA 30314-4399
Phone: 404-270-5193 **E-mail**: admiss@spelman.edu **CEEB Code**: 5628
Fax: 404-270-5201 **Website**: www.spelman.edu **ACT Code**: 0794
Financial Aid Phone: 404-270-5212

This private school was founded in 1881. It has a 32-acre campus.

RATINGS
Admissions Selectivity Rating: 92   **Fire Safety Rating**: 60*   **Green Rating**: 60*

STUDENTS AND FACULTY
Enrollment: 2,284. **Student Body**: 100% female, 70% out-of-state, 1% international (18 countries represented). African American 98%. **Retention and Graduation**: 92% freshmen return for sophomore year. 67% freshmen graduate within 4 years. **Faculty**: Student/faculty ratio 11:1. 167 full-time faculty, 81% hold PhDs. 100% faculty teach undergrads.

ACADEMICS
Degrees: Bachelor's. **Academic Requirements**: Arts/fine arts, computer literacy, English (including composition), foreign languages, history, humanities, mathematics, philosophy, sciences (biological or physical), social science. An African diaspora class must be taken by all students. **Classes**: Most classes have 20–29 students. Most lab/discussion sections have 20–29 students. **Majors with Highest Enrollment**: Political science and government, psychology. **Disciplines with Highest Percentage of Degrees Awarded**: Social sciences 24%, psychology 20%, biological/life sciences 12%, English 10%, interdisciplinary studies 7%. **Special Study Options**: Cross-registration, double major, exchange student program (domestic), honors program, independent study, internships, student-designed major, study abroad, teacher certification program.

FACILITIES
Housing: Women's dorms. **Special Academic Facilities/Equipment**: Nursery-elementary school for child development majors, language lab, electron microscope. **Computers**: 100% of classrooms are wired, 1% of classrooms are wireless, 80% of public computers are PCs, 15% of public computers are Macs, 5% of public computers are UNIX, network access in dorm rooms, network access in dorm lounges, online registration, online administrative functions (other than registration), remote student-access to Web through college's connection.

CAMPUS LIFE
Activities: Choral groups, dance, drama/theater, jazz band, music ensembles, student government, student newspaper, yearbook. **Organizations**: 17 registered organizations, 18 honor societies, 9 religious organizations. 4 sororities. **Athletics (Intercollegiate)**: *Women*: Basketball, cross-country, golf, soccer, softball, tennis, volleyball.

ADMISSIONS
Freshman Academic Profile: 32% in top 10% of high school class, 71% in top 25% of high school class, 94% in top 50% of high school class. 84% from public high schools. SAT Math middle 50% range 490–570. SAT Critical Reading middle 50% range 500–580. ACT middle 50% range 21–25. TOEFL required of all international applicants, minimum paper TOEFL 500, minimum computer TOEFL 250. **Basis for Candidate Selection**: *Very important factors considered include*: Academic GPA, application essay, character/personal qualities, rigor of secondary school record, standardized test scores. *Important factors considered include*: Extracurricular activities, recommendation(s). *Other factors considered include*: Alumni/ae relation, class rank, first generation, geographical residence, level of applicant's interest, volunteer work, work experience. **Freshman Admission Requirements**: High school diploma is required, and GED is accepted. *Academic units required*: 4 English, 3 math, 3 science (2 science labs), 2 foreign language, 3 social studies, 2 history, 2 academic electives. *Academic units recommended*: 4 English, 4 math, 4 science (3 science labs), 4 foreign language, 4 social studies, 3 history, 2 academic electives. **Freshman Admission Statistics**: 5,428 applied, 36% admitted, 29% enrolled. **Transfer Admission Requirements**: High school transcript, college transcript(s), essay or personal statement, statement of good standing from prior institution(s). Minimum college GPA of 2.0 required. Lowest grade transferable C. **General Admission Information**: Application fee $35. Early decision application deadline 11/1. Regular application deadline 2/1. Regular notification 4/1. Non-fall registration not accepted. Admission may be deferred for a maximum of 1 year. Credit offered for CEEB Advanced Placement tests.

COSTS AND FINANCIAL AID
Annual tuition $14,470. Room & board $8,750. Required fees $2,535. Average book expense $1,150. **Required Forms and Deadlines**: Institution's own financial aid form, CSS/Financial Aid PROFILE. Financial aid filing deadline 3/1. **Types of Aid**: *Need-based scholarships/grants*: Pell, SEOG, state scholarships/grants, private scholarships, the school's own gift aid, United Negro College Fund. *Loans*: FFEL Subsidized Stafford, FFEL Unsubsidized Stafford, FFEL PLUS. **Financial Aid Statistics**: 61% freshmen, 57% undergrads receive need-based scholarship or grant aid. 82% freshmen, 75% undergrads receive need-based self-help aid. 82% freshmen, 75% undergrads receive any aid.

SPRING ARBOR UNIVERSITY

106 East Main Street, Spring Arbor, MI 49283-9799
Phone: 517-750-6458 **E-mail:** admissions@admin.arbor.edu **CEEB Code:** 1732
Fax: 517-750-6620 **Website:** www.arbor.edu **ACT Code:** 2056
Financial Aid Phone: 517-750-6468

This private school, affiliated with the Free Methodist Church, was founded in 1873. It has a 113-acre campus.

RATINGS

Admissions Selectivity Rating: 77   **Fire Safety Rating:** 60*   **Green Rating:** 60*

STUDENTS AND FACULTY

Enrollment: 2,447. **Student Body:** 67% female, 33% male, 17% out-of-state. **Retention and Graduation:** 72% freshmen return for sophomore year. 38% freshmen graduate within 4 years. 30% grads go on to further study within 1 year. 8% grads pursue arts and sciences degrees. 15% grads pursue business degrees. 5% grads pursue law degrees. 5% grads pursue medical degrees. **Faculty:** Student/faculty ratio 15:1. 82 full-time faculty, 62% hold PhDs. 100% faculty teach undergrads.

ACADEMICS

Degrees: Associate, bachelor's, certificate, master's. **Academic Requirements:** Arts/fine arts, computer literacy, CORE courses (Christian perspective in the liberal arts), cross-cultural experience, English (including composition), history, humanities, mathematics, oral communication, philosophy, sciences (biological or physical), social science. **Classes:** Most classes have 10–19 students. **Majors with Highest Enrollment:** Business/managerial operations, education, family systems. **Disciplines with Highest Percentage of Degrees Awarded:** Business/marketing 32%, family and consumer sciences 19%, education 15%, health professions and related sciences 6%, social sciences 4%. **Special Study Options:** Accelerated program, cross-registration, distance learning, double major, dual enrollment, English as a second language (ESL), honors program, independent study, internships, student-designed major, study abroad, teacher certification program, weekend college. Undergraduates may take grad level classes. Off-campus study: Washington, DC, AuSable Inst. of Environmental Studies Program (Michigan). Study programs available: China, Latin America, Middle East, Oxford Honors, Russian, Jerusalem University, Russia at St. Petersburg, People's Republic of China at Sichuan College.

FACILITIES

Housing: Men's dorms, women's dorms, apartments for married students, apartments for single students, special housing for disabled students, special housing for international students. **Special Academic Facilities/Equipment:** Radio and TV studios, commercial writing/computer graphics lab, science center, art gallery. **Computers:** 85% of public computers are PCs, 15% of public computers are Macs, network access in dorm rooms, network access in dorm lounges, online registration, online administrative functions (other than registration), remote student-access to Web through college's connection.

CAMPUS LIFE

Activities: Choral groups, concert band, drama/theater, jazz band, music ensembles, musical theater, pep band, radio station, student government, student newspaper, student-run film society, symphony orchestra, television station, yearbook. **Organizations:** 7 religious organizations. **Athletics (Intercollegiate):** *Men:* Baseball, basketball, cross-country, golf, soccer, tennis, track/field (indoor), track/field (outdoor). *Women:* Basketball, cross-country, soccer, softball, tennis, track/field (indoor), track/field (outdoor), volleyball.

ADMISSIONS

Freshman Academic Profile: 19% in top 10% of high school class, 42% in top 25% of high school class, 69% in top 50% of high school class. SAT Math middle 50% range 460–600. SAT Critical Reading middle 50% range 470–600. SAT Writing middle 50% range 430–580. ACT middle 50% range 19–25. TOEFL required of all international applicants, minimum paper TOEFL 525, minimum computer TOEFL 197. **Basis for Candidate Selection:** *Very important factors considered include:* Academic GPA, character/personal qualities, religious affiliation/commitment, rigor of secondary school record, standardized test scores. *Other factors considered include:* Application essay, class rank, extracurricular activities, interview, racial/ethnic status, recommendation(s), talent/ability. **Freshman Admission Requirements:** High school diploma is required, and GED is accepted. *Academic units required:* 4 English, 3 math, 2 science (2 science labs), 2 social studies, 1 physical education or health related course required and computer science course recommended. *Academic units recommended:* 2 foreign language. **Freshman Admission Statistics:** 1,594 applied, 74% admitted, 28% enrolled. **Transfer Admission Requirements:** High school transcript, college transcript(s), essay or personal statement.

Minimum college GPA of 2.0 required. Lowest grade transferable C. **General Admission Information:** Application fee $30. Regular application deadline 8/1. Regular notification is rolling. Non-fall registration accepted. Admission may be deferred for indefinitely. Credit offered for CEEB Advanced Placement tests.

COSTS AND FINANCIAL AID

Annual tuition $16,990. Room & board $6,070. Required fees $396. Average book expense $640. **Required Forms and Deadlines:** FAFSA. Financial aid filing deadline 3/1. **Notification of Awards:** Applicants will be notified of awards on a rolling basis beginning on or about 4/1. **Types of Aid:** *Need-based scholarships/grants:* Pell, SEOG, state scholarships/grants, private scholarships, the school's own gift aid. *Loans:* FFEL Subsidized Stafford, FFEL Unsubsidized Stafford, FFEL PLUS, Federal Perkins, state loans, alternative loans. **Student Employment:** Federal Work-Study Program available. Institutional employment available. Off-campus job opportunities are fair. **Financial Aid Statistics:** 76% freshmen, 64% undergrads receive need-based scholarship or grant aid. 56% freshmen, 54% undergrads receive need-based self-help aid. 55 freshmen, 167 undergrads receive athletic scholarships. 79% freshmen, 68% undergrads receive any aid. Highest amount earned per year from on-campus jobs $1,100.

SPRING HILL COLLEGE

4000 Dauphin Street, Mobile, AL 36608
Phone: 251-380-3030 **E-mail:** admit@shc.edu **CEEB Code:** 1733
Fax: 251-460-2186 **Website:** www.shc.edu **ACT Code:** 0042
Financial Aid Phone: 251-380-3460

This private school, affiliated with the Roman Catholic Church, was founded in 1830. It has a 450-acre campus.

RATINGS

Admissions Selectivity Rating: 88   **Fire Safety Rating:** 85   **Green Rating:** 65

STUDENTS AND FACULTY

Enrollment: 1,210. **Student Body:** 65% female, 35% male, 53% out-of-state. African American 16%, Caucasian 71%, Hispanic 6%. **Retention and Graduation:** 82% freshmen return for sophomore year. 55% freshmen graduate within 4 years. 33% grads go on to further study within 1 year. 19% grads pursue arts and sciences degrees. 3% grads pursue business degrees. 6% grads pursue law degrees. 5% grads pursue medical degrees. **Faculty:** Student/faculty ratio 12:1. 77 full-time faculty, 81% hold PhDs. 91% faculty teach undergrads.

ACADEMICS

Degrees: Associate, bachelor's, certificate, master's, post-bachelor's certificate, terminal. **Academic Requirements:** Arts/fine arts, cultural diversity, English (including composition), foreign languages, history, mathematics, philosophy, sciences (biological or physical), social science, theology, writing across the curriculum. **Classes:** Most classes have 10–19 students. Most lab/discussion sections have 10–19 students. **Majors with Highest Enrollment:** Biology/biological sciences, business administration/management, nursing/registered nurse training (ASN, BSN, MSN, RN). **Disciplines with Highest Percentage of Degrees Awarded:** Business/marketing 19%, biological/life sciences 10%, education 10%, health professions and related sciences 8%, psychology 8%. **Special Study Options:** Accelerated program, distance learning, double major, dual enrollment, honors program, independent study, internships, student-designed major, study abroad, teacher certification program.

FACILITIES

Housing: Coed dorms, men's dorms, women's dorms, apartments for single students. **Special Academic Facilities/Equipment:** Public radio broadcasting station, theater. **Computers:** 2% of classrooms are wired, 90% of public computers are PCs, 10% of public computers are Macs, network access in dorm rooms, network access in dorm lounges, online registration, online administrative functions (other than registration), remote student-access to Web through college's connection.

CAMPUS LIFE

Activities: Choral groups, dance, drama/theater, literary magazine, student government, student newspaper, yearbook. **Organizations:** 44 registered organizations, 8 honor societies, 10 religious organizations. 2 fraternities (14% men join), 3 sororities (23% women join). **Athletics (Intercollegiate):** *Men:* Baseball, basketball, cross-country, golf, soccer, tennis. *Women:* Basketball, cross-country, golf, soccer, softball, tennis, volleyball. Environmental Initiatives:

Central cooling loop. Design of LEED campus center. Initiation of recycling program.

ADMISSIONS

Freshman Academic Profile: 32% in top 10% of high school class, 60% in top 25% of high school class, 87% in top 50% of high school class. 53% from public high schools. SAT Math middle 50% range 480–570. SAT Critical Reading middle 50% range 490–608. SAT Writing middle 50% range 490–598. ACT middle 50% range 21–26. TOEFL required of all international applicants, minimum paper TOEFL 550, minimum computer TOEFL 213. **Basis for Candidate Selection**: *Very important factors considered include*: Academic GPA, rigor of secondary school record, standardized test scores. *Important factors considered include*: Class rank, interview, recommendation(s). *Other factors considered include*: Alumni/ae relation, application essay, character/personal qualities, extracurricular activities, talent/ability, volunteer work. **Freshman Admission Requirements**: High school diploma is required, and GED is accepted. *Academic units recommended*: 4 English, 3 math, 3 science (1 science lab), 2 foreign language, 2 social studies, 1 history, 1 academic elective. **Freshman Admission Statistics**: 2,937 applied, 53% admitted, 22% enrolled. **Transfer Admission Requirements**: College transcript(s), statement of good standing from prior institution(s). Minimum college GPA of 2.5 required. Lowest grade transferable C-. **General Admission Information**: Application fee $25. Regular application deadline 7/15. Regular notification is rolling. Non-fall registration accepted. Admission may be deferred for a maximum of 1 year. Credit and/or placement offered for CEEB Advanced Placement tests.

COSTS AND FINANCIAL AID

Required Forms and Deadlines: FAFSA, state aid form. Financial aid filing deadline 3/1. **Notification of Awards**: Applicants will be notified of awards on a rolling basis beginning on or about 2/15. **Types of Aid**: *Need-based scholarships/grants*: Pell, SEOG, state scholarships/grants, private scholarships, the school's own gift aid, ACG and SMART grants. *Loans*: FFEL Subsidized Stafford, FFEL Unsubsidized Stafford, FFEL PLUS, Federal Perkins, alternative loans (CitiAssist, Signature). **Student Employment**: Federal Work-Study Program available. Institutional employment available. Off-campus job opportunities are good. **Financial Aid Statistics**: 66% freshmen, 61% undergrads receive need-based scholarship or grant aid. 50% freshmen, 50% undergrads receive need-based self-help aid. 23 freshmen, 93 undergrads receive athletic scholarships. 96% freshmen, 94% undergrads receive any aid. Highest amount earned per year from on-campus jobs $3,056.

SPRINGFIELD COLLEGE

263 Alden Street, Springfield, MA 01109
Phone: 413-748-3136 **E-mail**: admissions@spfldcol.edu **CEEB Code**: 3763
Fax: 413-748-3694 **Website**: www.spfldcol.edu
Financial Aid Phone: 413-748-3108

This private school was founded in 1885. It has an 80-acre campus.

RATINGS

Admissions Selectivity Rating: 75   **Fire Safety Rating**: 60*   **Green Rating**: 60*

STUDENTS AND FACULTY

Student Body: 66% out-of-state. **Retention and Graduation**: 82% freshmen return for sophomore year. 58% freshmen graduate within 4 years. 20% grads go on to further study within 1 year. **Faculty**: 85% faculty teach undergrads.

ACADEMICS

Degrees: Bachelor's, doctoral, master's. **Academic Requirements**: Arts/fine arts, computer literacy, English (including composition), foreign languages, history, humanities, mathematics, philosophy, sciences (biological or physical), social science, physical education. **Special Study Options**: Cooperative education program, cross-registration, distance learning, double major, English as a second language (ESL), independent study, internships, liberal arts/career combination, study abroad, teacher certification program, weekend college.

FACILITIES

Housing: Coed dorms, men's dorms, women's dorms, apartments for single students. **Special Academic Facilities/Equipment**: International center; college-operated summer day camp; hypermedia lab; centers for allied health sciences, emergency medical services management, occupational therapy, and physician assistant. **Computers**: Network access in dorm rooms.

CAMPUS LIFE

Activities: Dance, drama/theater, literary magazine, musical theater, radio station, student government, student newspaper, yearbook. **Athletics**

(Intercollegiate): *Men*: Baseball, basketball, cross-country, diving, football, golf, gymnastics, lacrosse, soccer, swimming, tennis, track/field (outdoor), volleyball, wrestling. *Women*: Basketball, cross-country, diving, field hockey, golf, gymnastics, lacrosse, soccer, softball, swimming, tennis, track/field (outdoor), volleyball.

ADMISSIONS

Freshman Academic Profile: 14% in top 10% of high school class, 35% in top 25% of high school class, 76% in top 50% of high school class. 84% from public high schools. SAT Math middle 50% range 450–550. SAT Critical Reading middle 50% range 440–550. TOEFL required of all international applicants, minimum paper TOEFL 525. **Basis for Candidate Selection**: *Factors considered include*: Alumni/ae relation, application essay, character/personal qualities, class rank, extracurricular activities, geographical residence, interview, racial/ethnic status, recommendation(s), religious affiliation/commitment, rigor of secondary school record, talent/ability. **Freshman Admission Requirements**: High school diploma is required, and GED is accepted. *Academic units recommended*: 4 English, 2 math, 2 science, 2 foreign language, 2 social studies, 4 academic electives. **Freshman Admission Statistics**: 2,249 applied, 59% admitted, 38% enrolled. **Transfer Admission Requirements**: College transcript(s), essay or personal statement, interview, statement of good standing from prior institution(s). Minimum college GPA of 2.5 required. Lowest grade transferable C. **General Admission Information**: Application fee $40. Early decision application deadline 12/1. Regular application deadline 4/11. Regular notification is rolling. Non-fall registration accepted. Admission may be deferred for a maximum of 1 year. Common Application not accepted. Credit and/or placement offered for CEEB Advanced Placement tests.

COSTS AND FINANCIAL AID

Annual tuition $20,360. Room & board $7,350. Average book expense $950. **Required Forms and Deadlines**: FAFSA, CSS/Financial Aid PROFILE. **Types of Aid**: *Need-based scholarships/grants*: Pell, SEOG, state scholarships/grants, private scholarships, the school's own gift aid. *Loans*: FFEL Subsidized Stafford, FFEL Unsubsidized Stafford, FFEL PLUS, Federal Perkins, college/university loans from institutional funds. **Student Employment**: Federal Work-Study Program available. Institutional employment available. Off-campus job opportunities are good. **Financial Aid Statistics**: Highest amount earned per year from on-campus jobs $1,100.

ST. AMBROSE UNIVERSITY

518 West Locust Street, Davenport, IA 52803-2898
Phone: 563-333-6300 **E-mail**: admit@sau.edu **CEEB Code**: 6617
Fax: 563-333-6297 **Website**: www.sau.edu **ACT Code**: 1352
Financial Aid Phone: 563-333-6314

This private school, affiliated with the Roman Catholic Church, was founded in 1882. It has a 52-acre campus.

RATINGS

Admissions Selectivity Rating: 76   **Fire Safety Rating**: 74   **Green Rating**: 60*

STUDENTS AND FACULTY

Enrollment: 2,728. **Student Body**: 61% female, 39% male, 46% out-of-state, 1% international (22 countries represented). African American 3%, Caucasian 91%, Hispanic 4%. **Retention and Graduation**: 76% freshmen return for sophomore year. 51% freshmen graduate within 4 years. 29% grads go on to further study within 1 year. 22% grads pursue arts and sciences degrees. 12% grads pursue business degrees. 3% grads pursue law degrees. 2% grads pursue medical degrees. **Faculty**: Student/faculty ratio 12:1. 162 full-time faculty, 75% hold PhDs. 98% faculty teach undergrads.

ACADEMICS

Degrees: Bachelor's, certificate, doctoral, master's, post-bachelor's certificate, post-master's certificate. **Academic Requirements**: Arts/fine arts, communication, English (including composition), foreign languages, history, humanities, information literacy, mathematics, philosophy, sciences (biological or physical), social science, theology. **Classes**: Most classes have 10–19 students. Most lab/discussion sections have fewer than 10 students. **Majors with Highest Enrollment**: Business administration/management, elementary education and teaching, psychology. **Disciplines with Highest Percentage of Degrees Awarded**: Business/marketing 33%, education 12%, psychology 9%, social sciences 8%, communications/journalism 7%. **Special Study Options**: Accelerated program, cooperative education program, distance learning, double major, independent study, internships, liberal arts/career combination, student-designed major, study abroad, teacher certification program. Overseas academic experiences in England, Ireland, Lithuania, and Ecuador. Students can also take advantage of the overseas experiences through Central College in Iowa.

FACILITIES

Housing: Coed dorms, men's dorms, women's dorms, apartments for single students, special housing for disabled students. The university owns several houses next to campus and will rent them out to graduate or married students. **Special Academic Facilities/Equipment**: Art gallery, observatory, language lab, distance learning classrooms (5). **Computers**: 90% of classrooms are wired, 5% of classrooms are wireless, network access in dorm rooms, online registration, online administrative functions (other than registration), remote student-access to Web through college's connection.

CAMPUS LIFE

Activities: Choral groups, concert band, dance, drama/theater, jazz band, literary magazine, music ensembles, musical theater, opera, pep band, radio station, student government, student newspaper, symphony orchestra, television station. **Organizations**: 42 registered organizations, 11 honor societies, 3 religious organizations. **Athletics (Intercollegiate)**: *Men*: Baseball, basketball, cheerleading, cross-country, football, golf, soccer, tennis, track/field (indoor), track/field (outdoor), volleyball. *Women*: Basketball, cheerleading, cross-country, golf, soccer, softball, tennis, track/field (indoor), track/field (outdoor), volleyball.

ADMISSIONS

Freshman Academic Profile: 16% in top 10% of high school class, 35% in top 25% of high school class, 61% in top 50% of high school class. 54% from public high schools. ACT middle 50% range 19–24. TOEFL required of all international applicants, minimum paper TOEFL 500, minimum computer TOEFL 213. **Basis for Candidate Selection**: *Very important factors considered include*: Academic GPA, class rank, level of applicant's interest, rigor of secondary school record, standardized test scores. *Important factors considered include*: Alumni/ae relation, character/personal qualities, recommendation(s). *Other factors considered include*: Application essay, extracurricular activities, first generation, interview, talent/ability, volunteer work. **Freshman Admission Requirements**: High school diploma is required, and GED is accepted. *Academic units recommended*: 4 English, 3 math, 2 science (2 science labs), 1 foreign language, 1 social studies, 1 history, 4 academic electives. **Freshman Admission Statistics**: 1,709 applied, 84% admitted, 35% enrolled. **Transfer Admission Requirements**: High school transcript, college transcript(s), standardized test score, statement of good standing from prior institution(s). Minimum college GPA of 2.0 required. Lowest grade transferable D. **General Admission Information**: Application fee $25. Regular notification is rolling. Non-fall registration accepted. Admission may be deferred for a maximum of 1 semester. Credit and/or placement offered for CEEB Advanced Placement tests.

COSTS AND FINANCIAL AID

Annual tuition $21,610. Room and board $7,825. Average book expense $1,000. **Required Forms and Deadlines**: FAFSA. Financial aid filing deadline 3/15. **Notification of Awards**: Applicants will be notified of awards on a rolling basis beginning on or about 2/1. **Types of Aid**: *Need-based scholarships/grants*: Pell, SEOG, state scholarships/grants, private scholarships, the school's own gift aid. *Loans*: FFEL Subsidized Stafford, FFEL Unsubsidized Stafford, FFEL PLUS, Federal Perkins, state loans. **Student Employment**: Federal Work-Study Program available. Institutional employment available. Off-campus job opportunities are excellent. **Financial Aid Statistics**: 70% freshmen, 69% undergrads receive need-based scholarship or grant aid. 58% freshmen, 62% undergrads receive need-based self-help aid. 45 freshmen, 169 undergrads receive athletic scholarships. 80% freshmen, 77% undergrads receive any aid. Highest amount earned per year from on-campus jobs $1,866.

ST. ANDREWS PRESBYTERIAN COLLEGE

1700 Dogwood Mile, Laurinburg, NC 28352
Phone: 910-277-5555 **E-mail**: admissions@sapc.edu **CEEB Code**: 5214
Fax: 910-277-5087 **Website**: www.sapc.edu **ACT Code**: 3146
Financial Aid Phone: 910-277-5560

This private school, affiliated with the Presbyterian Church, was founded in 1958. It has a 600-acre campus.

RATINGS

Admissions Selectivity Rating: 60*   **Fire Safety Rating**: 60*   **Green Rating**: 60*

STUDENTS AND FACULTY

Enrollment: 768. **Student Body**: 60% female, 40% male, 48% out-of-state, 3% international (20 countries represented). African American 7%, Caucasian 62%, Hispanic 2%. **Retention and Graduation**: 65% freshmen return for sophomore year. 30% freshmen graduate within 4 years. 40% grads go on to further study within 1 year. **Faculty**: Student/faculty ratio 15:1. 42 full-time faculty, 83% hold PhDs. 100% faculty teach undergrads.

ACADEMICS

Degrees: Bachelor's. **Academic Requirements**: Arts/fine arts, computer literacy, English (including composition), foreign languages, history, humanities, mathematics, sciences (biological or physical), social science. **Classes**: Most classes have fewer than 10 students. **Majors with Highest Enrollment**: Business administration/management, elementary education and teaching, English language and literature. **Disciplines with Highest Percentage of Degrees Awarded**: Business/marketing 26%, education 13%, English 10%, social sciences 9%, parks and recreation 8%. **Special Study Options**: Double major, honors program, internships, student-designed major, study abroad, teacher certification program, weekend college. Weekend college is also a night college at our branch campus called St. Andrews at Sandhills Community College.

FACILITIES

Housing: Coed dorms, men's dorms, women's dorms, special housing for disabled students, alcohol-free residence halls available, adaptive living environment for disabled students. **Special Academic Facilities/Equipment**: Art gallery, anthropology museum, science lab, electron microscopy center with 3 electron microscopes, psychology lab, artronics graphics computer, Scottish Heritage Foundation. **Computers**: 2% of classrooms are wired, 100% of public computers are PCs, network access in dorm rooms, online administrative functions (other than registration), remote student-access to Web through college's connection.

CAMPUS LIFE

Activities: Choral groups, drama/theater, literary magazine, music ensembles, student government, student newspaper, yearbook. **Organizations**: 30 registered organizations, 3 honor societies, 1 religious organization. **Athletics (Intercollegiate)**: *Men*: Baseball, basketball, cross-country, equestrian sports, golf, horseback riding, lacrosse, soccer, tennis, track/field (outdoor). *Women*: Basketball, cross-country, equestrian sports, horseback riding, lacrosse, soccer, softball, tennis, track/field (outdoor), volleyball.

ADMISSIONS

Annual tuition $18,192. Average book expense $1,000. **Freshman Academic Profile**: TOEFL required of all international applicants, minimum paper TOEFL 550, minimum computer TOEFL 280. **Basis for Candidate Selection**: *Important factors considered include*: Academic GPA, character/personal qualities, extracurricular activities, level of applicant's interest, standardized test scores, talent/ability. *Other factors considered include*: Application essay, class rank, interview, recommendation(s), rigor of secondary school record. **Freshman Admission Requirements**: High school diploma is required, and GED is accepted. *Academic units recommended*: 4 English, 3 math, 3 science, 2 foreign language, 2 social studies, 2 academic electives. **Freshman Admission Statistics**: 918 applied, 73% admitted, 29% enrolled. **Transfer Admission Requirements**: College transcript(s). Minimum college GPA of 2.0 required. Lowest grade transferable C-. **General Admission Information**: Application fee $30. Regular notification is rolling. Non-fall registration accepted. Admission may be deferred for a maximum of 1 year. Credit offered for CEEB Advanced Placement tests.

COSTS AND FINANCIAL AID

Annual tuition $17,162. Average book expense $1,000. **Required Forms and Deadlines**: FAFSA, state aid form. **Notification of Awards**: Applicants will be notified of awards on a rolling basis beginning on or about 10/6. **Types of Aid**: *Need-based scholarships/grants*: Pell, SEOG, state scholarships/grants, private scholarships, the school's own gift aid. *Loans*: FFEL Subsidized Stafford, FFEL Unsubsidized Stafford, FFEL PLUS. **Student Employment**: Federal Work-Study Program available. Institutional employment available. **Financial Aid Statistics**: 58% freshmen, 59% undergrads receive need-based scholarship or grant aid. 44% freshmen, 47% undergrads receive need-based self-help aid. 35 freshmen, 119 undergrads receive athletic scholarships. 98% freshmen, 97% undergrads receive any aid. Highest amount earned per year from on-campus jobs $2,000.

ST. BONAVENTURE UNIVERSITY

PO Box D, St. Bonaventure, NY 14778
Phone: 716-375-2400 **E-mail**: admissions@sbu.edu **CEEB Code**: 2793
Fax: 716-375-4005 **Website**: www.sbu.edu **ACT Code**: 2882
Financial Aid Phone: 800-462-5050

This private school, affiliated with the Roman Catholic Church, was founded in 1858. It has a 500-acre campus.

RATINGS

Admissions Selectivity Rating: 73   **Fire Safety Rating**: 60*   **Green Rating**: 60*

STUDENTS AND FACULTY

Enrollment: 2,072. **Student Body**: 49% female, 51% male, 24% out-of-state. **Retention and Graduation**: 76% freshmen return for sophomore year. 54% freshmen graduate within 4 years. 33% grads go on to further study within 1 year. 8% grads pursue arts and sciences degrees. 17% grads pursue business degrees. 6% grads pursue law degrees. 2% grads pursue medical degrees. **Faculty**: Student/faculty ratio 15:1. 153 full-time faculty, 79% hold PhDs. 93% faculty teach undergrads.

ACADEMICS

Degrees: Bachelor's, master's, post-bachelor's certificate, post-master's certificate. **Academic Requirements**: Arts/fine arts, English (including composition), foreign languages, history, humanities, mathematics, philosophy, sciences (biological or physical), social science, theology/Franciscan studies. **Classes**: Most classes have 10–19 students. Most lab/discussion sections have 10–19 students. **Majors with Highest Enrollment**: Business administration/management, elementary education and teaching, journalism. **Disciplines with Highest Percentage of Degrees Awarded**: Business/marketing 29%, communications/journalism 17%, education 14%, social sciences 14%, psychology 6%, English 4%, history 4%. **Special Study Options**: Accelerated program, cross-registration, distance learning, double major, dual enrollment, exchange student program (domestic), honors program, independent study, internships, liberal arts/career combination, student-designed major, study abroad, teacher certification program, weekend college.

FACILITIES

Housing: Men's dorms, women's dorms, apartments for single students, special housing for disabled students. **Special Academic Facilities/Equipment**: Quick Center for the Arts, digital conferencing and media center, Franciscan Center for Social Concern, Franciscan Institute. **Computers**: 15% of classrooms are wired, 90% of classrooms are wireless, 97% of public computers are PCs, 3% of public computers are Macs, network access in dorm rooms, network access in dorm lounges, online registration, remote student-access to Web through college's connection.

CAMPUS LIFE

Activities: Choral groups, concert band, dance, drama/theater, jazz band, literary magazine, music ensembles, pep band, radio station, student government, student newspaper, television station, yearbook. **Organizations**: 47 registered organizations, 7 honor societies, 6 religious organizations. **Athletics (Intercollegiate)**: *Men*: Baseball, basketball, cross-country, diving, golf, soccer, swimming, tennis. *Women*: Basketball, cross-country, diving, lacrosse, soccer, softball, swimming, tennis.

ADMISSIONS

Freshman Academic Profile: 11% in top 10% of high school class, 31% in top 25% of high school class, 68% in top 50% of high school class. 70% from public high schools. SAT Math middle 50% range 470–570. SAT Critical Reading middle 50% range 480–570. ACT middle 50% range 19–23. TOEFL required of all international applicants, minimum paper TOEFL 550, minimum computer TOEFL 213. **Basis for Candidate Selection**: *Very important factors considered include*: Academic GPA, character/personal qualities, interview, recommendation(s), rigor of secondary school record. *Important factors considered include*: Application essay, extracurricular activities, level of applicant's interest, standardized test scores, talent/ability, volunteer work. *Other factors considered include*: Alumni/ae relation, class rank, first generation, work experience. **Freshman Admission Requirements**: High school diploma is required, and GED is accepted. *Academic units required*: 4 English, 3 math, 3 science, 2 foreign language, 4 social studies. *Academic units recommended*: 4 English, 3 math, 3 science (3 science labs), 2 foreign language, 4 social studies. **Freshman Admission Statistics**: 1,730 applied, 86% admitted, 32% enrolled. **Transfer Admission Requirements**: High school transcript, college transcript(s), statement of good standing from prior institution(s). Minimum college GPA of 2.0 required. Lowest grade transferable C. **General Admission Information**: Application fee $30. Regular application deadline 4/15. Regular notification is rolling. Non-fall registration accepted. Admission may be deferred for a maximum of 1 year. Common Application accepted. Credit and/or placement offered for CEEB Advanced Placement tests.

COSTS AND FINANCIAL AID

Annual tuition $21,650. Room & board $7,760. Required fees $865. Average book expense $650. **Required Forms and Deadlines**: FAFSA, institution's own financial aid form, state aid form. Financial aid filing deadline 2/1. **Notification of Awards**: Applicants will be notified of awards on a rolling basis beginning on or about 4/1. **Types of Aid**: *Need-based scholarships/grants*: Pell, SEOG, state scholarships/grants, private scholarships, the school's own gift aid. *Loans*: FFEL Subsidized Stafford, FFEL Unsubsidized Stafford, FFEL PLUS, Federal Perkins, college/university loans from institutional funds. **Financial Aid Statistics**: 73% freshmen, 71% undergrads receive need-based scholarship or grant aid. 60% freshmen, 59% undergrads receive need-based self-help aid. 15 freshmen, 72 undergrads receive athletic scholarships. Highest amount earned per year from on-campus jobs $815.

ST. EDWARD'S UNIVERSITY

3001 South Congress Avenue, Austin, TX 78704
Phone: 512-448-8500 **E-mail**: seu.admit@stewards.edu **CEEB Code**: 6619
Fax: 512-464-8877 **Website**: www.gotostedwards.com **ACT Code**: 4156
Financial Aid Phone: 512-448-8523

This private school, affiliated with the Roman Catholic Church, was founded in 1885. It has a 160-acre campus.

RATINGS

Admissions Selectivity Rating: 76   **Fire Safety Rating**: 80   **Green Rating**: 60*

STUDENTS AND FACULTY

Enrollment: 4,200. **Student Body**: 60% female, 40% male, 6% out-of-state, 2% international (37 countries represented). African American 5%, Asian 3%, Caucasian 55%, Hispanic 30%. **Retention and Graduation**: 85% freshmen return for sophomore year. 30% freshmen graduate within 4 years. **Faculty**: Student/faculty ratio 15:1. 166 full-time faculty, 87% hold PhDs. 85% faculty teach undergrads.

ACADEMICS

Degrees: Bachelor's, master's, post-bachelor's certificate. **Academic Requirements**: Arts/fine arts, computer literacy, English (including composition), foreign languages, history, humanities, mathematics, philosophy, sciences (biological or physical), social science. **Classes**: Most classes have 20–29 students. **Majors with Highest Enrollment**: Biology/biological sciences, communications and media studies, psychology. **Disciplines with Highest Percentage of Degrees Awarded**: Business/marketing 38%, psychology 9%, communications/journalism 9%, social sciences 8%, visual and performing arts 6%. **Special Study Options**: Double major, honors program, internships, liberal arts/career combination, study abroad, teacher certification program.

FACILITIES

Housing: Coed dorms, women's dorms, apartments for single students, special housing for disabled students, community style living casitas. **Special**

Academic Facilities/Equipment: Fine arts building; photography labs; new 61,000 square foot natural sciences center including state-of-the-art labs, classrooms, and seminar rooms (Phase 1 opened fall 2006). **Computers**: 100% of classrooms are wired, 100% of classrooms are wireless, 76% of public computers are PCs, 24% of public computers are Macs, network access in dorm rooms, network access in dorm lounges, online registration, online administrative functions (other than registration), support for handheld computing, remote student-access to Web through college's connection.

CAMPUS LIFE

Activities: Choral groups, dance, drama/theater, literary magazine, music ensembles, musical theater, student government, student newspaper. **Organizations**: 60 registered organizations, 5 honor societies, 4 religious organizations. **Athletics (Intercollegiate)**: *Men*: Baseball, basketball, cross-country, golf, soccer, tennis. *Women*: Basketball, cross-country, golf, soccer, softball, tennis, volleyball.

ADMISSIONS

Freshman Academic Profile: 16% in top 10% of high school class, 52% in top 25% of high school class, 81% in top 50% of high school class. 72% from public high schools. SAT Math middle 50% range 510–600. SAT Critical Reading middle 50% range 520–620. SAT Writing middle 50% range 510–610. ACT middle 50% range 21–26. TOEFL required of all international applicants, minimum paper TOEFL 500, minimum computer TOEFL 173. **Basis for Candidate Selection**: *Very important factors considered include*: Academic GPA, class rank, rigor of secondary school record, standardized test scores. *Important factors considered include*: Application essay, extracurricular activities. *Other factors considered include*: Alumni/ae relation, character/personal qualities, first generation, geographical residence, interview, level of applicant's interest, racial/ethnic status, recommendation(s), religious affiliation/commitment, state residency, talent/ability, volunteer work. **Freshman Admission Requirements**: High school diploma is required, and GED is accepted. *Academic units required*: 4 English, 3 math, 2 science (2 science labs), 2 foreign language, 1 social studies, 2 history. *Academic units recommended*: 4 English, 4 math, 3 science (3 science labs), 3 foreign language, 1 social studies, 3 history, 1 academic elective. **Freshman Admission Statistics**: 2,397 applied, 64% admitted, 45% enrolled. **Transfer Admission Requirements**: College transcript(s), essay or personal statement. Minimum college GPA of 2.3 required. Lowest grade transferable C. **General Admission Information**: Application fee $45. Regular application deadline 5/1. Regular notification is rolling. Non-fall registration accepted. Admission may be deferred for a maximum of 1 year. Credit and/or placement offered for CEEB Advanced Placement tests.

COSTS AND FINANCIAL AID

Annual tuition $22,150. Room and board $8,158. Average book expense $1,100. **Required Forms and Deadlines**: FAFSA. Financial aid filing deadline 4/15. **Notification of Awards**: Applicants will be notified of awards on a rolling basis beginning on or about 2/15. **Types of Aid**: *Need-based scholarships/grants*: Pell, SEOG, state scholarships/grants, private scholarships, the school's own gift aid, endowed scholarships. *Loans*: FFEL Subsidized Stafford, FFEL Unsubsidized Stafford, FFEL PLUS, Federal Perkins, state loans, alternative educational loans. **Student Employment**: Federal Work-Study Program available. Institutional employment available. Off-campus job opportunities are excellent. **Financial Aid Statistics**: 57% freshmen, 54% undergrads receive need-based scholarship or grant aid. 32% freshmen, 41% undergrads receive need-based self-help aid. 38 freshmen, 165 undergrads receive athletic scholarships. 94% freshmen, 84% undergrads receive any aid. Highest amount earned per year from on-campus jobs $3,800.

See page 1350.

ST. JOHN'S COLLEGE (MD)

PO Box 2800, Annapolis, MD 21404
Phone: 410-626-2522 **E-mail**: admissions@sjca.edu **CEEB Code**: 5598
Fax: 410-269-7916 **Website**: www.stjohnscollege.edu **ACT Code**: 1732
Financial Aid Phone: 410-626-2502

This private school was founded in 1696. It has a 36-acre campus.

RATINGS

Admissions Selectivity Rating: 86   **Fire Safety Rating**: 84   **Green Rating**: 78

STUDENTS AND FACULTY

Enrollment: 474. **Student Body**: 46% female, 54% male, 85% out-of-state. African American 1%, Asian 3%, Caucasian 89%, Hispanic 3%. **Retention and Graduation**: 82% freshmen return for sophomore year. 65% freshmen graduate within 4 years. 10% grads go on to further study within 1 year. 5% grads pursue arts and sciences degrees. 1% grads pursue business degrees. 2% grads pursue law degrees. **Faculty**: Student/faculty ratio 8:1. 70 full-time faculty, 76% hold PhDs. 100% faculty teach undergrads.

ACADEMICS

Degrees: Bachelor's, master's. **Academic Requirements**: English (including composition), foreign languages, history, humanities, mathematics, philosophy, sciences (biological or physical). **Classes**: Most classes have 10–19 students. **Majors with Highest Enrollment**: Liberal arts, sciences studies, humanities. **Disciplines with Highest Percentage of Degrees Awarded**: Liberal arts/general studies 100%. **Special Study Options**: Students may spend 1 or more years at the college's Santa Fe, New Mexico, campus.

FACILITIES

Housing: Coed dorms, special housing for disabled students. **Special Academic Facilities/Equipment**: Art gallery, planetarium, pendulum, Ptolemy stone, laboratories. **Computers**: 1% of classrooms are wired, 1% of classrooms are wireless, 95% of public computers are PCs, 5% of public computers are Macs, network access in dorm rooms, network access in dorm lounges, online administrative functions (other than registration), remote student-access to Web through college's connection.

CAMPUS LIFE

Activities: Choral groups, dance, drama/theater, literary magazine, music ensembles, student government, student newspaper, student-run film society, yearbook. **Organizations**: 60 registered organizations, 3 religious organizations. Environmental Initiatives: Purchasing renewable energy credits for 100% of electric consumption. Installing a new central heating plant and disttribution system that will reduce fossil fuel consumption for heating by approximately 25%, as well as smokestack emissions. Stabilization of 800'+ of waterfront with removal of bulkhead and installation/ restoration of natural wetland.

ADMISSIONS

Freshman Academic Profile: 28% in top 10% of high school class, 57% in top 25% of high school class, 87% in top 50% of high school class. 61% from public high schools. SAT Math middle 50% range 570–680. SAT Critical Reading middle 50% range 620–730. ACT middle 50% range 25–31. TOEFL required of all international applicants, minimum paper TOEFL 600, minimum computer TOEFL 250. **Basis for Candidate Selection**: *Very important factors considered include*: Application essay. *Important factors considered include*: Character/personal qualities, recommendation(s), rigor of secondary school record. *Other factors considered include*: Academic GPA, alumni/ae relation, class rank, extracurricular activities, first generation, interview, racial/ethnic status, standardized test scores, talent/ability. **Freshman Admission Requirements**: High school diploma is required, and GED is accepted. *Academic units required*: 3 math, 2 foreign language. *Academic units recommended*: 4 English, 4 math, 3 science (3 science labs), 4 foreign language, 2 social studies, 2 history. **Freshman Admission Statistics**: 426 applied, 81% admitted, 44% enrolled. **Transfer Admission Requirements**: High school transcript, college transcript(s), essay or personal statement. **General Admission Information**: Regular notification 2 weeks after completed application. Non-fall registration accepted. Admission may be deferred for a maximum of 1 year. Neither credit nor placement offered for CEEB Advanced Placement tests.

COSTS AND FINANCIAL AID

Annual tuition $36,346. Room and board $8,684. Required fees $250. Average book expense $275. **Required Forms and Deadlines**: FAFSA, CSS/Financial Aid PROFILE, state aid form, Noncustodial PROFILE, Business/Farm Supplement. Financial aid filing deadline 2/15. **Notification of Awards**: Applicants will be notified of awards on a rolling basis beginning on or about 12/1. **Types of Aid**: *Need-based scholarships/grants*: Pell, SEOG, state scholarships/grants, the school's own gift aid. *Loans*: FFEL Subsidized Stafford, FFEL Unsubsidized Stafford, FFEL PLUS, Federal Perkins, college/university loans from institutional funds. **Financial Aid Statistics**: 55% freshmen, 55% undergrads receive need-based scholarship or grant aid. 58% freshmen, 58% undergrads receive need-based self-help aid. 60% freshmen, 59% undergrads receive any aid. Highest amount earned per year from on-campus jobs $3,320.

ST. JOHN'S COLLEGE (NM)

1160 Camino Cruz Blanca, Santa Fe, NM 87505
Phone: 505-984-6060 **E-mail**: admissions@sjcsf.edu **CEEB Code**: 4737
Fax: 505-984-6162 **Website**: www.stjohnscollege.edu **ACT Code**: 2649
Financial Aid Phone: 505-984-6058

This private school was founded in 1696. It has a 250-acre campus.

RATINGS

Admissions Selectivity Rating: 85 **Fire Safety Rating**: 60* **Green Rating**: 81

STUDENTS AND FACULTY

Enrollment: 433. **Student Body**: 44% female, 56% male, 95% out-of-state, 2% international (10 countries represented). Asian 4%, Caucasian 87%, Hispanic 5%. **Retention and Graduation**: 74% freshmen return for sophomore year. 75% grads go on to further study within 1 year. 42% grads pursue arts and sciences degrees. 7% grads pursue business degrees. 10% grads pursue law degrees. 6% grads pursue medical degrees. **Faculty**: Student/faculty ratio 8:1. 69 full-time faculty, 80% hold PhDs. 100% faculty teach undergrads.

ACADEMICS

Degrees: Bachelor's, master's. **Academic Requirements**: Arts/fine arts, English (including composition), foreign languages, history, humanities, mathematics, philosophy, sciences (biological or physical), social science. **Classes**: Most classes have 10–19 students. Most lab/discussion sections have fewer than 10 students. **Disciplines with Highest Percentage of Degrees Awarded**: Liberal arts/general studies 100%. **Special Study Options**: Internships, the great books program—reading and discussion of the seminal texts of Western civilization in the humanities, mathmatics, and science. Also, students may spend a year or more on the Maryland campus.

FACILITIES

Housing: Coed dorms, men's dorms, women's dorms, apartments for married students, apartments for single students, special housing for disabled students. **Special Academic Facilities/Equipment**: Art gallery. **Computers**: 50% of public computers are PCs, 50% of public computers are Macs, network access in dorm rooms, online administrative functions (other than registration), remote student-access to Web through college's connection.

CAMPUS LIFE

Activities: Choral groups, dance, drama/theater, jazz band, literary magazine, music ensembles, musical theater, student newspaper, student-run film society. **Organizations**: 27 registered organizations. Environmental Initiatives: Paper, Glass, Plastic, Cardboard Recycling. Compost Food from Cafeteria. Rainwater Collection from Roofs.

ADMISSIONS

Freshman Academic Profile: 33% in top 10% of high school class, 61% in top 25% of high school class, 84% in top 50% of high school class. 71% from public high schools. SAT Math middle 50% range 600–670. SAT Critical Reading middle 50% range 660–740. ACT middle 50% range 27–31. TOEFL required of all international applicants, minimum paper TOEFL 550, minimum computer TOEFL 213. **Basis for Candidate Selection**: *Very important factors considered include*: Application essay, character/personal qualities, interview, talent/ability. *Important factors considered include*: Extracurricular activities, recommendation(s), rigor of secondary school record. *Other factors*

considered include: Class rank, standardized test scores, volunteer work, work experience. **Freshman Admission Requirements**: High school diploma or equivalent is not required. *Academic units required*: 3 math, 2 foreign language. *Academic units recommended*: 4 English, 1 math, 3 science (3 science labs), 3 foreign language, 2 social studies, 2 history. **Freshman Admission Statistics**: 318 applied, 80% admitted, 48% enrolled. **Transfer Admission Requirements**: High school transcript, college transcript(s), essay or personal statement, statement of good standing from prior institution(s). **General Admission Information**: Regular notification is rolling. Nonfall registration accepted. Admission may be deferred for a maximum of 1 year. Neither credit nor placement offered for CEEB Advanced Placement tests.

COSTS AND FINANCIAL AID

Annual tuition $36,346. Room & board $8,864. Required fees $250. Average book expense $275. **Required Forms and Deadlines**: FAFSA, CSS/Financial Aid PROFILE, Noncustodial PROFILE, Business/Farm Supplement. Financial aid filing deadline 2/15. **Notification of Awards**: Applicants will be notified of awards on a rolling basis beginning on or about 12/1. **Types of Aid**: *Need-based scholarships/grants*: Pell, SEOG, state scholarships/grants, the school's own gift aid. *Loans*: FFEL Subsidized Stafford, FFEL Unsubsidized Stafford, FFEL PLUS, Federal Perkins, college/university loans from institutional funds. **Student Employment**: Federal Work-Study Program available. Institutional employment available. Off-campus job opportunities are excellent. **Financial Aid Statistics**: 47% freshmen, 63% undergrads receive need-based scholarship or grant aid. 52% freshmen, 63% undergrads receive need-based self-help aid. Highest amount earned per year from on-campus jobs $2,015.

ST. JOHN'S COLLEGE— DEPARTMENT OF NURSING (IL)

421 North Ninth Street, Springfield, IL 62702-5317
Phone: 217-525-5628 **E-mail**: College@st-johns.org
Fax: 217-757-6870 **Website**: www.st-johns.org/collegeofnursing

This private school, affiliated with the Roman Catholic Church, was founded in 1992.

RATINGS

Admissions Selectivity Rating: 60* **Fire Safety Rating**: 60* **Green Rating**: 60*

STUDENTS AND FACULTY

Enrollment: 83. **Student Body**: 93% female, 7% male, 1% international (1 country represented). African American 1%, Caucasian 98%. **Faculty**: Student/faculty ratio 4:1. 12 full-time faculty, 17% hold PhDs. 100% faculty teach undergrads.

ACADEMICS

Degrees: Bachelor's. **Academic Requirements**: Arts/fine arts, computer literacy, English (including composition), foreign languages, history, humanities, mathematics, nursing, philosophy, sciences (biological or physical), social science. **Classes**: Most classes have 30–39 students. Most lab/discussion sections have fewer than 10 students. **Majors with Highest Enrollment**: Nursing/registered nurse training (ASN, BSN, MSN, RN). **Disciplines with Highest Percentage of Degrees Awarded**: Health professions and related sciences 100%.

FACILITIES

Computers: 100% of public computers are PCs, remote student-access to Web through college's connection.

CAMPUS LIFE

Activities: Student government. **Organizations**: 1 registered organization.

ADMISSIONS

Freshman Academic Profile: TOEFL required of all international applicants, minimum paper TOEFL 500, minimum computer TOEFL 200. **Basis for Candidate Selection**: *Very important factors considered include*: Academic GPA, alumni/ae relation, application essay, character/personal qualities, class rank, extracurricular activities, interview, level of applicant's interest, recommendation(s), rigor of secondary school record, standardized test scores, volunteer. *Other factors considered include*: Talent/ability, work experience. **Freshman Admission Requirements**: High school diploma is required, and GED is accepted. *Academic units required*: 4 English, 3 math, 3 science (3 science labs), 3 social studies, 2 academic electives. **Transfer Admission Requirements**: High school transcript, college transcript(s), interview, statement of good standing from prior institution(s). Minimum college GPA of 2.5 required. Lowest grade transferable C. **General Admission Information**: Application fee $50. Regular notification is open. Non-fall registration not accepted. Neither credit nor placement offered for CEEB Advanced Placement tests.

COSTS AND FINANCIAL AID

Annual tuition $11,708. Required fees $444. Average book expense $750.

ST. JOHN'S UNIVERSITY

Best 368

8000 Utopia Parkway, Queens, NY 11439
Phone: 718-990-2000 **E-mail**: admissions@stjohns.edu **CEEB Code**: 2799
Fax: 718-990-5728 **Website**: www.stjohns.edu **ACT Code**: 2888
Financial Aid Phone: 718-990-2000

This private school, affiliated with the Roman Catholic Church, was founded in 1870. It has a 131-acre campus.

RATINGS

Admissions Selectivity Rating: 81   **Fire Safety Rating**: 92   **Green Rating**: 89

STUDENTS AND FACULTY

Enrollment: 12,326. **Student Body**: 56% female, 44% male, 13% out-of-state, 3% international (126 countries represented). African American 16%, Asian 16%, Caucasian 38%, Hispanic 15%. **Retention and Graduation**: 78% freshmen return for sophomore year. 39% freshmen graduate within 4 years. 21% grads go on to further study within 1 year. 5% grads pursue arts and sciences degrees. 3% grads pursue business degrees. 2% grads pursue law degrees. 1% grads pursue medical degrees. **Faculty**: Student/faculty ratio 17:1. 627 full-time faculty, 89% hold PhDs. 93% faculty teach undergrads.

ACADEMICS

Degrees: Associate, bachelor's, certificate, diploma, doctoral, first professional, master's, post-bachelor's certificate, post-master's certificate, terminal. **Academic Requirements**: Arts/fine arts, English (including composition), foreign languages, history, mathematics, philosophy, sciences (biological or physical), social science. **Classes**: Most classes have 20–29 students. Most lab/discussion sections have 20–29 students. **Majors with Highest Enrollment**: Biology/biological sciences, pharmacy (PharmD, BS/BPharm), psychology. **Disciplines with Highest Percentage of Degrees Awarded**: Business/marketing 24%, communications/journalism 11%, education 9%, security and protective services 7%, health professions and related sciences 7%, psychology 7%. **Special Study Options**: Accelerated program, cross-registration, distance learning, double major, dual enrollment, English as a second language (ESL), honors program, independent study, internships, liberal arts/career combination, study abroad, teacher certification program, weekend college.

FACILITIES

Housing: Coed dorms. Some off-campus apartments are available on a limited basis on the Staten Island campus. **Special Academic Facilities/Equipment**: University gallery; instructional media center; Institute of Asian Studies; health education resource center; center for psychological services, TV center, speech and hearing center; reading and writing education center. **Computers**: 75% of classrooms are wired, 100% of classrooms are wireless, 90% of public computers are PCs, 10% of public computers are Macs, 90% of public computers are UNIX, network access in dorm rooms, network access in dorm lounges, online registration, online administrative functions (other than registration), support for handheld computing, remote student-access to Web through college's connection, tuition includes personal computer. Undergraduates are required to own a computer.

CAMPUS LIFE

Activities: Choral groups, dance, drama/theater, jazz band, literary magazine, musical theater, pep band, radio station, student government, student newspaper, student-run film society, television station, yearbook. **Organizations**: 180 registered organizations, 19 honor societies, 7 religious organizations. 22 fraternities (6% men join), 24 sororities (6% women join). **Athletics (Intercollegiate)**: *Men*: Baseball, basketball, fencing, golf, lacrosse, soccer, tennis. *Women*: Basketball, cross-country, fencing, golf, soccer, softball, tennis, track/field (indoor), track/field (outdoor), volleyball.

ADMISSIONS

Freshman Academic Profile: 14% in top 10% of high school class, 41% in top 25% of high school class, 74% in top 50% of high school class. 63% from public high schools. SAT Math middle 50% range 480–600. SAT Critical Reading middle 50% range 480–580. TOEFL required of all international applicants, minimum paper TOEFL 500, minimum computer TOEFL 173. **Basis for Candidate Selection**: *Very important factors considered include*: Academic GPA, standardized test scores. *Important factors considered include*: Class rank, recommendation(s), rigor of secondary school record. *Other factors considered include*: Alumni/ae relation, application essay, character/personal qualities, extracurricular activities, first generation, interview, talent/ability, volunteer work, work experience. **Freshman Admission Requirements**: High school diploma is required, and GED is accepted. *Academic units required*: 4 English. *Academic units recommended*: 3 math, 2 science (2 science labs), 2 foreign language, 2 history, 1 academic elective. **Freshman Admission Statistics**: 25,594 applied, 59% admitted, 22% enrolled. **Transfer Admission Requirements**: High school transcript, college transcript(s). Lowest grade transferable C. **General Admission Information**: Application fee $30. Non-fall registration accepted. Admission may be deferred for a maximum of 1 semester. Credit and/or placement offered for CEEB Advanced Placement tests.

COSTS AND FINANCIAL AID

Annual tuition $26,200. Room and board $12,070. Required fees $690. Average book expense $1,000. **Required Forms and Deadlines**: FAFSA. Financial aid filing deadline 2/1. **Notification of Awards**: Applicants will be notified of awards on a rolling basis beginning on or about 3/15. **Types of Aid**: *Need-based scholarships/grants*: Pell, SEOG, state scholarships/grants, private scholarships, the school's own gift aid. *Loans*: FFEL Subsidized Stafford, FFEL Unsubsidized Stafford, FFEL PLUS, Federal Perkins. **Financial Aid Statistics**: 73% freshmen, 70% undergrads receive need-based scholarship or grant aid. 60% freshmen, 64% undergrads receive need-based self-help aid. 44 freshmen, 209 undergrads receive athletic scholarships. 98% freshmen, 94% undergrads receive any aid. Highest amount earned per year from on-campus jobs $5,000.

See page 1352.

ST. JOSEPH'S COLLEGE— NEW YORK (BROOKLYN)

245 Clinton Avenue, Brooklyn, NY 11205
Phone: 718-636-6868 **E-mail**: brooklynas@sjcny.edu **CEEB Code**: 2802
Fax: 718-636-8303 **Website**: www.sjcny.edu **ACT Code**: 2890
Financial Aid Phone: 718-636-6808

This private school was founded in 1916. It has a 2-acre campus.

RATINGS

Admissions Selectivity Rating: 60*   **Fire Safety Rating**: 60*   **Green Rating**: 60*

STUDENTS AND FACULTY

Enrollment: 1,194. **Student Body**: 78% female, 22% male, 1% out-of-state. African American 39%, Asian 4%, Caucasian 49%, Hispanic 8%. **Retention and Graduation**: 86% freshmen return for sophomore year. 54% freshmen graduate within 4 years. 40% grads go on to further study within 1 year. 22% grads pursue arts and sciences degrees. 1% grads pursue business degrees. 3% grads pursue law degrees. 3% grads pursue medical degrees. **Faculty**: Student/faculty ratio 13:1. 46 full-time faculty, 70% hold PhDs. 100% faculty teach undergrads.

ACADEMICS

Degrees: Bachelor's, certificate, master's. **Academic Requirements**: Arts/fine arts, computer literacy, English (including composition), foreign languages, history, humanities, mathematics, philosophy, sciences (biological or physical), social science. **Classes**: Most classes have 10–19 students. Most lab/discussion sections have 10–19 students. **Disciplines with Highest Percentage of Degrees Awarded**: Health professions and related sciences 50%, education 18%, business/marketing 17%, biological/life sciences 3%, psychology 3%, social sciences 2%, English 2%, liberal arts/general studies 2%. **Special Study Options**: Accelerated program, double major, honors program, independent study, internships, liberal arts/career combination, teacher certification program. 5-year affiliated program: BA/BS + MS program St. Joseph's College/MS in computer science from Polytechnic University. 6-year affiliated program: BS/DPM with N.Y. College of Podiatric Medicine.

FACILITIES

Special Academic Facilities/Equipment: Child study center, on-campus laboratory preschool, videoconferencing center, Internet access. **Computers**: 100% of public computers are PCs.

CAMPUS LIFE

Activities: Choral groups, drama/theater, musical theater, student government, student newspaper, yearbook. **Organizations**: 24 registered organizations, 5 honor societies, 1 religious organization. 1 fraternity (1% men join), 1 sorority (6% women join). **Athletics (Intercollegiate)**: *Men*: Basketball, cross-country. *Women*: Basketball, cheerleading, cross-country, softball, volleyball.

ADMISSIONS

Freshman Academic Profile: 16% in top 10% of high school class, 49% in top 25% of high school class, 67% in top 50% of high school class. 18% from public high schools. TOEFL required of all international applicants, minimum paper TOEFL 550. **Basis for Candidate Selection**: *Very important factors considered include*: Rigor of secondary school record, standardized test scores. *Important factors considered include*: Class rank. *Other factors considered include*: Alumni/ae relation, application essay, character/personal qualities, extracurricular activities, interview, recommendation(s), volunteer work, work experience. **Freshman Admission Requirements**: High school diploma is required, and GED is accepted. *Academic units required*: 4 English, 3 math, 2 science, 2 foreign language, 4 social studies, 3 academic electives. **Freshman Admission Statistics**: 460 applied, 49% admitted, 40% enrolled. **Transfer Admission Requirements**: College transcript(s), interview. Minimum college GPA of 2.0 required. **General Admission Information**: Application fee $25. Regular notification is rolling. Non-fall registration accepted. Admission may be deferred for a maximum of 1 year. Common Application not accepted. Credit and/or placement offered for CEEB Advanced Placement tests.

COSTS AND FINANCIAL AID

Annual tuition $10,050. Required fees $322. Average book expense $600. **Required Forms and Deadlines**: FAFSA, institution's own financial aid form, state aid form. Financial aid filing deadline 2/25. **Notification of Awards**: Applicants will be notified of awards on a rolling basis beginning on or about 4/15. **Types of Aid**: *Need-based scholarships/grants*: Pell, SEOG, state scholarships/grants, private scholarships, the school's own gift aid. *Loans*: FFEL Subsidized Stafford, FFEL Unsubsidized Stafford, FFEL PLUS, Federal Perkins. **Student Employment**: Federal Work-Study Program available. Institutional employment available. Off-campus job opportunities are excellent. **Financial Aid Statistics**: 68% freshmen, 59% undergrads receive need-based scholarship or grant aid. 68% freshmen, 62% undergrads receive need-based self-help aid. Highest amount earned per year from on-campus jobs $1,200.

ST. JOSEPH'S COLLEGE— NEW YORK (PATCHOGUE)

155 West Roe Boulevard, Patchogue, NY 11772
Phone: 631-447-3219 **E-mail**: suffolkas@sjcny.edu **CEEB Code**: 2802
Fax: 631-447-1734 **Website**: www.sjcny.edu **ACT Code**: 2923
Financial Aid Phone: 631-447-3214

This private school was founded in 1916. It has a 27-acre campus.

RATINGS
Admissions Selectivity Rating: 85   **Fire Safety Rating**: 60*   **Green Rating**: 60*

STUDENTS AND FACULTY

Enrollment: 3,703. **Student Body**: 74% female, 26% male. African American 4%, Asian 1%, Caucasian 84%, Hispanic 6%. **Retention and Graduation**: 81% freshmen return for sophomore year. 61% grads go on to further study within 1 year. 5% grads pursue arts and sciences degrees. 3% grads pursue business degrees. 2% grads pursue law degrees. 1% grads pursue medical degrees. **Faculty**: Student/faculty ratio 17:1. 104 full-time faculty, 65% hold PhDs. 100% faculty teach undergrads.

ACADEMICS

Degrees: Bachelor's, certificate, master's. **Academic Requirements**: Arts/fine arts, English (including composition), humanities, sciences (biological or physical), social science. **Classes**: Most classes have 20–29 students. Most lab/discussion sections have fewer than 10 students. **Majors with Highest Enrollment**: Early childhood education and teaching, education, mathematics and computer science. **Disciplines with Highest Percentage of Degrees Awarded**: Education 47%, business/marketing 15%, health professions and related sciences 8%, psychology 6%, social sciences 6%. **Special Study Options**: Accelerated program, cross-registration, double major, honors program, internships, liberal arts/career combination, study abroad, teacher certification program, weekend college.

FACILITIES

Computers: 100% of public computers are PCs, online registration, remote student-access to Web through college's connection.

CAMPUS LIFE

Activities: Choral groups, dance, drama/theater, jazz band, literary magazine, music ensembles, musical theater, student government, student newspaper, yearbook. **Organizations**: 34 registered organizations, 8 honor societies, 2 religious organizations. 1 fraternity (1% men join), 1 sorority (2% women join). **Athletics (Intercollegiate)**: *Men*: Baseball, basketball, cross-country, golf, soccer, tennis, track/field (outdoor). *Women*: Basketball, cheerleading, cross-country, equestrian sports, soccer, softball, swimming, tennis, track/field (outdoor), volleyball.

ADMISSIONS

Freshman Academic Profile: 19% in top 10% of high school class, 55% in top 25% of high school class, 87% in top 50% of high school class. 88% from public high schools. SAT Math middle 50% range 500–590. SAT Critical Reading middle 50% range 490–560. SAT Writing middle 50% range 450–550. ACT middle 50% range 20–24. TOEFL required of all international applicants, minimum paper TOEFL 500, minimum computer TOEFL 213. **Basis for Candidate Selection**: *Very important factors considered include*: Academic GPA, class rank, rigor of secondary school record, standardized test scores. *Important factors considered include*: Application essay, character/personal qualities, interview, recommendation(s). *Other factors considered include*: Alumni/ae relation, extracurricular activities, first generation, level of applicant's interest, talent/ability, volunteer work, work experience. **Freshman Admission Requirements**: High school diploma is required, and GED is accepted. *Academic units required*: 4 English, 3 math, 3 science, 2 foreign language, 4 social studies, 2 academic electives. **Freshman Admission Statistics**: 1,267 applied, **Transfer Admission Requirements**: College transcript(s). Minimum college GPA of 2.0 required. **General Admission Information**: Application fee $25. Non-fall registration accepted. Admission may be deferred for a maximum of 2 years. Credit offered for CEEB Advanced Placement tests.

COSTS AND FINANCIAL AID

Annual tuition $14,000. Required fees $532. **Required Forms and Deadlines**: FAFSA, institution's own financial aid form, state aid form. Financial aid filing deadline 2/25. **Notification of Awards**: Applicants will be notified of awards on or about 3/15. **Types of Aid**: *Need-based scholarships/grants*: Pell, SEOG, state scholarships/grants, private scholarships, the school's own gift aid. *Loans*: FFEL Subsidized Stafford, FFEL Unsubsidized Stafford, FFEL PLUS, Federal Perkins. **Student Employment**: Federal Work-Study Program available. Institutional employment available. Off-campus job opportunities are good. **Financial Aid Statistics**: 85% freshmen, 74% undergrads receive need-based scholarship or grant aid. 39% freshmen, 38% undergrads receive need-based self-help aid.

ST. LAWRENCE UNIVERSITY

Payson Hall, Canton, NY 13617
Phone: 315-229-5261 **E-mail**: admissions@stlawu.edu **CEEB Code**: 2805
Fax: 315-229-5818 **Website**: www.stlawu.edu **ACT Code**: 2896
Financial Aid Phone: 315-229-5265

This private school was founded in 1856. It has a 1,000-acre campus.

RATINGS
Admissions Selectivity Rating: 89   **Fire Safety Rating**: 68   **Green Rating**: 87

STUDENTS AND FACULTY

Enrollment: 2,145. **Student Body**: 52% female, 48% male, 53% out-of-state, 5% international (40 countries represented). African American 3%, Asian 2%, Caucasian 71%, Hispanic 3%. **Retention and Graduation**: 89% freshmen return for sophomore year. 71% freshmen graduate within 4 years. 24% grads go on to further study within 1 year. 10% grads pursue arts and sciences degrees. 3% grads pursue business degrees. 2% grads pursue law degrees. 3% grads pursue medical degrees. **Faculty**: Student/faculty ratio 11:1. 167 full-time faculty, 98% hold PhDs. 98% faculty teach undergrads.

ACADEMICS

Degrees: Bachelor's, master's, post-master's certificate. **Academic Requirements**: Arts/fine arts, humanities, sciences (biological or physical), social science, 1 course in mathematics or foreign language, 2 courses (from 2 different departments) on diversity issues. **Classes**: Most classes have 10–19 students. Most lab/discussion sections have 10–19 students. **Majors with Highest Enrollment**: Economics, English language and literature, psychology. **Disciplines with Highest Percentage of Degrees Awarded**: Social sciences 30%, psychology 12%, English 12%, visual and performing arts 9%, biological/life sciences 8%. **Special Study Options**: Community-based learning, cross-registration, double major, exchange student program (domestic), independent study, internships, student-designed major, study abroad, teacher certification program.

FACILITIES

Housing: Coed dorms, apartments for single students, special housing for disabled students, special housing for international students, fraternity/sorority housing, theme cottages and theme areas/halls. **Special Academic Facilities/Equipment**: Art gallery, arts technology center, language lab, center for international education, environmental research facility, 76-acre forest preserve, 2 electron microscopes, microscopy and sleep labs, neuroscience lab. **Computers**: 27% of classrooms are wireless, 99% of public computers are PCs, 1% of public computers are Macs, network access in dorm rooms, online registration, online administrative functions (other than registration), remote student-access to Web through college's connection.

CAMPUS LIFE

Activities: Choral groups, dance, drama/theater, literary magazine, music ensembles, radio station, student government, student newspaper, student-run film society, television station, yearbook. **Organizations**: 117 registered organizations, 22 honor societies, 3 religious organizations. 1 fraternity (6% men join), 4 sororities (20% women join). **Athletics (Intercollegiate)**: *Men*: Baseball, basketball, crew/rowing, cross-country, diving, equestrian sports, football, golf, ice hockey, lacrosse, skiing (downhill/alpine), skiing (Nordic/cross-country), soccer, squash, swimming, tennis, track/field (indoor), track/field (outdoor). *Women*: Basketball, crew/rowing, cross-country, diving, equestrian sports, field hockey, golf, ice hockey, lacrosse, skiing (downhill/alpine), skiing (Nordic/cross-country), soccer, softball, squash, swimming, tennis, track/field (indoor), track/field (outdoor). Environmental Initiatives: Pledge of climate neutrality. Energy audits of all on- and off-campus buildings and appropriate retrofits of energy and water efficiency measures. Beginning to re-source electricity to renewable sources (10% currently) and analyzing a renewable source for heat.

ADMISSIONS

Freshman Academic Profile: 33% in top 10% of high school class, 67% in top 25% of high school class, 91% in top 50% of high school class. 68% from public high schools. SAT Math middle 50% range 560–640. SAT Critical Reading middle 50% range 560–640. SAT Writing middle 50% range 560–640. ACT middle 50% range 25–29. TOEFL required of all international applicants, minimum paper TOEFL 600, minimum computer TOEFL 250. **Basis for Candidate Selection**: *Very important factors considered include*: Academic GPA, application essay, character/personal qualities, recommendation(s). *Important factors considered include*: Class rank, extracurricular activities, interview, racial/ethnic status, rigor of secondary school record. *Other factors considered include*: Alumni/ae relation, first generation, geographical residence, level of applicant's interest, standardized test scores, talent/ability, volunteer work, work experience. **Freshman Admission Requirements**: High school diploma is required, and GED is accepted. *Academic units recommended*: 4 English, 4 math, 4 science, 4 foreign language, 2 social studies, 2 history. **Freshman Admission Statistics**: 3,192 applied, 59% admitted, 33% enrolled. **Transfer Admission Requirements**: High school transcript, college transcript(s), essay or personal statement, statement of good standing from prior institution(s). Lowest grade transferable C. **General Admission Information**: Application fee $60. Early decision application deadline 11/15 Regular application deadline 2/1. Regular notification 3/30. Non-fall registration accepted. Admission may be deferred for a maximum of 1 year. Credit offered for CEEB Advanced Placement tests.

COSTS AND FINANCIAL AID

Required Forms and Deadlines: FAFSA, institution's own financial aid form, Noncustodial PROFILE, income tax returns/W-2 forms. Financial aid filing deadline 2/1. **Notification of Awards**: Applicants will be notified of awards on or about 3/30. **Types of Aid**: *Need-based scholarships/grants*: Pell, SEOG, state scholarships/grants, the school's own gift aid. *Loans*: FFEL Subsidized Stafford, FFEL Unsubsidized Stafford, FFEL PLUS, Federal Perkins, college/university

loans from institutional funds, Gate Student Loan Program. **Student Employment**: Federal Work-Study Program available. Institutional employment available. Off-campus job opportunities are poor. **Financial Aid Statistics**: 62% freshmen, 64% undergrads receive need-based scholarship or grant aid. 56% freshmen, 60% undergrads receive need-based self-help aid. 7 freshmen, 34 undergrads receive athletic scholarships. 80% freshmen, 82% undergrads receive any aid.

See page 1354.

ST. LOUIS COLLEGE OF PHARMACY

4588 Parkview Place, St. Louis, MO 63110
Phone: 314-367-8700 **E-mail**: pkulage@stlcop.edu **CEEB Code**: 6626
Fax: 314-446-8310 **Website**: www.stlcop.edu **ACT Code**: 2346
Financial Aid Phone: 314-367-8700

This private school was founded in 1864. It has a 7-acre campus.

RATINGS

Admissions Selectivity Rating: 80   **Fire Safety Rating**: 60*   **Green Rating**: 60*

STUDENTS AND FACULTY

Faculty: Student/faculty ratio 13:1. 64 full-time faculty, 91% hold PhDs.

ACADEMICS

Degrees: First professional, master's. **Academic Requirements**: English (including composition), history, humanities, mathematics, sciences (biological or physical), social science. **Disciplines with Highest Percentage of Degrees Awarded**: Health professions and related sciences 100%.

FACILITIES

Housing: Coed dorms, apartments for single students, fraternity/sorority housing. **Computers**: Network access in dorm rooms, network access in dorm lounges, remote student-access to Web through college's connection.

CAMPUS LIFE

Activities: Choral groups, concert band, drama/theater, literary magazine, musical theater, student government, student newspaper, yearbook. **Organizations**: 2 honor societies, 6 religious organizations. 5 fraternities. **Athletics (Intercollegiate)**: *Men*: Basketball, cheerleading, cross-country. *Women*: Cheerleading, cross-country, volleyball.

ADMISSIONS

Freshman Academic Profile: 20% in top 10% of high school class, 35% in top 25% of high school class, 98% in top 50% of high school class. SAT Math middle 50% range 628–687. SAT Critical Reading middle 50% range 536–562. ACT middle 50% range 25–26. TOEFL required of all international applicants, minimum paper TOEFL 550. **Basis for Candidate Selection**: *Very important factors considered include*: Rigor of secondary school record, standardized test scores. *Important factors considered include*: Class rank. *Other factors considered include*: Alumni/ae relation, application essay, character/personal qualities, extracurricular activities, recommendation(s), volunteer work, work experience. **Freshman Admission Requirements**: High school diploma is required, and GED is accepted. *Academic units required*: 4 English, 3 math, 2 science (2 science labs). *Academic units recommended*: 3 science. **Freshman Admission Statistics**: 356 applied, 80% admitted, 59% enrolled. **Transfer Admission Requirements**: College transcript(s), essay or personal statement, standardized test score. Minimum college GPA of 3.0 required. Lowest grade transferable C. **General Admission Information**: Application fee $35. Regular application deadline 4/2. Regular notification is rolling. Non-fall registration accepted. Common Application not accepted. Credit offered for CEEB Advanced Placement tests.

COSTS AND FINANCIAL AID

Average book expense $1,000. **Required Forms and Deadlines**: FAFSA, institution's own financial aid form. Financial aid filing deadline 3/2. **Notification of Awards**: Applicants will be notified of awards on a rolling basis beginning on or about 2/19. **Types of Aid**: *Need-based scholarships/grants*: Pell, SEOG, state scholarships/grants, private scholarships, the school's own gift aid. *Loans*: FFEL Subsidized Stafford, FFEL Unsubsidized Stafford, FFEL PLUS, Federal Perkins, health professions loan. **Student Employment**: Federal Work-Study Program available. Institutional employment available. Off-campus job opportunities are excellent. **Financial Aid Statistics**: Highest amount earned per year from on-campus jobs $800.

ST. MARY'S COLLEGE OF MARYLAND

Best 368

Admissions Office, 18952 East Fisher Road, St. Mary's City, MD 20686-3001
Phone: 240-895-5000 **E-mail:** admissions@smcm.edu **CEEB Code:** 5601
Fax: 240-895-5001 **Website:** www.smcm.edu **ACT Code:** 1736
Financial Aid Phone: 240-895-3000

This public school was founded in 1840. It has a 319-acre campus.

RATINGS
Admissions Selectivity Rating: 90   **Fire Safety Rating:** 79   **Green Rating:** 84

STUDENTS AND FACULTY
Enrollment: 1,892. **Student Body:** 57% female, 43% male, 17% out-of-state, 1% international (34 countries represented). African American 8%, Asian 4%, Caucasian 76%, Hispanic 4%. **Retention and Graduation:** 87% freshmen return for sophomore year. 70% freshmen graduate within 4 years. 34% grads go on to further study within 1 year. 28% grads pursue arts and sciences degrees. 1% grads pursue business degrees. 3% grads pursue law degrees. 2% grads pursue medical degrees. **Faculty:** Student/faculty ratio 12:1. 128 full-time faculty, 95% hold PhDs. 100% faculty teach undergrads.

ACADEMICS
Degrees: Bachelor's, master's. **Academic Requirements:** Arts/fine arts, English (including composition), foreign languages, history, humanities, mathematics, philosophy, sciences (biological or physical), social science. **Classes:** Most classes have 10–19 students. Most lab/discussion sections have 10–19 students. **Majors with Highest Enrollment:** Economics, political science and government, psychology. **Disciplines with Highest Percentage of Degrees Awarded:** Social sciences 25%, psychology 20%, biological/life sciences 11%, English 10%, visual and performing arts 7%. **Special Study Options:** Double major, dual enrollment, exchange student program (domestic), honors program, independent study, internships, student-designed major, study abroad, teacher certification program.

FACILITIES
Housing: Coed dorms, men's dorms, women's dorms, apartments for single students, special housing for disabled students, town houses. **Special Academic Facilities/Equipment:** Art gallery, archaeological sites, historic St. Mary's City, historic state house of early Maryland settlers, electron microscope, freshwater and saltwater research facilities, research boat. **Computers:** 50% of classrooms are wired, 100% of classrooms are wireless, 70% of public computers are PCs, 25% of public computers are Macs, 5% of public computers are UNIX, network access in dorm rooms, network access in dorm lounges, online registration, online administrative functions (other than registration), support for handheld computing, remote student-access to Web through college's connection.

CAMPUS LIFE
Activities: Choral groups, dance, drama/theater, jazz band, literary magazine, music ensembles, musical theater, radio station, student government, student newspaper, student-run film society, symphony orchestra, television station, yearbook. **Organizations:** 90 registered organizations, 8 honor societies, 2 religious organizations. **Athletics (Intercollegiate):** *Men:* Baseball, basketball, lacrosse, sailing, soccer, swimming, tennis. *Women:* Basketball, field hockey, lacrosse, sailing, soccer, swimming, tennis, volleyball. Environmental Initiatives: SMCM now has 100% elect RCC's. Future buildings are certified LEED Silver. There is student funding of geothermal energy for the River Center.

ADMISSIONS
Freshman Academic Profile: 41% in top 10% of high school class, 78% in top 25% of high school class, 96% in top 50% of high school class. 78% from public high schools. SAT Math middle 50% range 560–660. SAT Critical Reading middle 50% range 570–670. SAT Writing middle 50% range 560–670. TOEFL required of all international applicants, minimum paper TOEFL 550, minimum computer TOEFL 250. **Basis for Candidate Selection:** *Very important factors considered include:* Academic GPA, application essay, rigor of secondary school record. *Important factors considered include:* Recommendation(s), standardized test scores. *Other factors considered include:* Alumni/ae relation, character/personal qualities, class rank, extracurricular activities, first generation, talent/ability, volunteer work. **Freshman Admission Requirements:** High school diploma is required, and GED is accepted. *Academic units*

required: 4 English, 3 math, 3 science (2 science labs), 3 social studies, 7 academic electives. **Freshman Admission Statistics:** 2,255 applied, 56% admitted, 34% enrolled. **Transfer Admission Requirements:** College transcript(s), essay or personal statement. Minimum college GPA of 3.0 required. Lowest grade transferable D. **General Admission Information:** Application fee $40. Early decision application deadline 12/1. Regular application deadline 1/15. Regular notification 4/1. Admission may be deferred for a maximum of 1 year. Credit and/or placement offered for CEEB Advanced Placement tests.

COSTS AND FINANCIAL AID
Annual in-state tuition $10,472. Annual out-of-state tuition $21,322. Room and board $9,225. Required fees $2,132. Average book expense $1,000. **Required Forms and Deadlines:** FAFSA. Financial aid filing deadline 3/1. **Notification of Awards:** Applicants will be notified of awards on or about 4/1. **Types of Aid:** *Need-based scholarships/grants:* Pell, SEOG, state scholarships/grants, private scholarships, the school's own gift aid. *Loans:* FFEL Subsidized Stafford, FFEL Unsubsidized Stafford, FFEL PLUS, Federal Perkins. **Student Employment:** Federal Work-Study Program available. Institutional employment available. Off-campus job opportunities are good. **Financial Aid Statistics:** 17% freshmen, 19% undergrads receive need-based scholarship or grant aid. 17% freshmen, 19% undergrads receive need-based self-help aid. 59% freshmen, 61% undergrads receive any aid.

See page 1360.

ST. MARY'S UNIVERSITY

1 Camino Santa Maria, San Antonio, TX 78228
Phone: 210-436-3126 **E-mail:** uadm@stmarytx.edu **CEEB Code:** 6637
Fax: 210-431-6742 **Website:** www.stmarytx.edu **ACT Code:** 4158
Financial Aid Phone: 210-436-3141

This private school, affiliated with the Roman Catholic Church, was founded in 1852. It has a 135-acre campus.

RATINGS
Admissions Selectivity Rating: 82   **Fire Safety Rating:** 60*   **Green Rating:** 60*

STUDENTS AND FACULTY
Enrollment: 2,394. **Student Body:** 60% female, 40% male, 5% out-of-state, 4% international. African American 4%, Asian 3%, Caucasian 19%, Hispanic 69%. **Retention and Graduation:** 80% freshmen return for sophomore year. 31% freshmen graduate within 4 years. 62% grads go on to further study within 1 year. 19% grads pursue arts and sciences degrees. 14% grads pursue business degrees. 10% grads pursue law degrees. 5% grads pursue medical degrees. **Faculty:** Student/faculty ratio 13:1. 183 full-time faculty, 92% hold PhDs.

ACADEMICS
Degrees: Bachelor's, doctoral, first professional, master's. **Academic Requirements:** Arts/fine arts, computer literacy, English (including composition), foreign languages, history, humanities, mathematics, philosophy, sciences (biological or physical), social science. **Classes:** Most classes have 20–29 students. Most lab/discussion sections have 10–19 students. **Majors with Highest Enrollment:** Biology/biological sciences, political science and government, psychology. **Disciplines with Highest Percentage of Degrees Awarded:** Business/marketing 27%, social sciences 13%, biological/life sciences 12%, psychology 8%, communications/journalism 7%. **Special Study Options:** Cooperative education program, cross-registration, distance learning, double major, honors program, independent study, internships, liberal arts/career combination, study abroad, teacher certification program.

FACILITIES
Housing: Coed dorms, women's dorms, 22 years old or above/nontraditional dorms. **Computers:** Network access in dorm rooms, network access in dorm lounges, support for handheld computing, remote student-access to Web through college's connection, tuition includes personal computer. Undergraduates are required to own a computer.

CAMPUS LIFE
Activities: Choral groups, concert band, dance, drama/theater, jazz band, literary magazine, music ensembles, musical theater, pep band, student government, student newspaper. **Organizations:** 55 registered organizations, 10 honor societies, 12 religious organizations. 5 fraternities (13% men join), 4 sororities (13% women join). **Athletics (Intercollegiate):** *Men:* Baseball,

basketball, golf, soccer, tennis. *Women*: Basketball, soccer, softball, tennis, volleyball.

ADMISSIONS

Freshman Academic Profile: 32% in top 10% of high school class, 64% in top 25% of high school class, 86% in top 50% of high school class. 74% from public high schools.SAT Math middle 50% range 490–590. SAT Critical Reading middle 50% range 460–570. SAT Writing middle 50% range 460–560. ACT middle 50% range 21–26. TOEFL required of all international applicants, minimum paper TOEFL 550, minimum computer TOEFL 215. **Basis for Candidate Selection**: *Very important factors considered include:* Class rank. *Important factors considered include*: Academic GPA, rigor of secondary school record, standardized test scores. *Other factors considered include*: Application essay, character/personal qualities, extracurricular activities, interview, recommendation(s), talent/ability, volunteer work, work experience. **Freshman Admission Requirements**: High school diploma is required, and GED is accepted. *Academic units required*: 4 English, 3 math, 3 science (1 science lab), 2 foreign language, 3 social studies, 1 academic elective. *Academic units recommended*: 4 English, 4 math, 4 science, 3 foreign language, 4 social studies. **Freshman Admission Statistics**: 1,998 applied, 73% admitted, 38% enrolled. **Transfer Admission Requirements**: College transcript(s), essay or personal statement, statement of good standing from prior institution(s). Minimum college GPA of 2.5 required. Lowest grade transferable C. **General Admission Information**: Application fee $30. Regular notification is rolling. Non-fall registration accepted. Admission may be deferred for a maximum of 2 years. Credit and/or placement offered for CEEB Advanced Placement tests.

COSTS AND FINANCIAL AID

Annual tuition $9,137. Room & board $6,796. Required fees $500. Average book expense $1,000. **Required Forms and Deadlines**: FAFSA. Financial aid filing deadline 2/15. **Notification of Awards**: Applicants will be notified of awards on a rolling basis beginning on or about 3/15. **Types of Aid**: *Need-based scholarships/grants*: Pell, SEOG, state scholarships/grants, private scholarships, the school's own gift aid. *Loans*: FFEL Subsidized Stafford, FFEL Unsubsidized Stafford, FFEL PLUS, Federal Perkins, state loans. **Student Employment**: Federal Work-Study Program available. Institutional employment available. Off-campus job opportunities are good. **Financial Aid Statistics**: 67% freshmen, 61% undergrads receive need-based scholarship or grant aid. 64% freshmen, 57% undergrads receive need-based self-help aid. 26 freshmen, 146 undergrads receive athletic scholarships. 78% freshmen, 73% undergrads receive any aid.

ST. NORBERT COLLEGE

100 Grant Street, De Pere, WI 54115-2099
Phone: 920-403-3005 **E-mail:** admit@snc.edu **CEEB Code:** 1706
Fax: 920-403-4072 **Website:** www.snc.edu **ACT Code:** 4644
Financial Aid Phone: 920-403-3071

This private school, affiliated with the Roman Catholic Church, was founded in 1898. It has a 93-acre campus.

RATINGS
Admissions Selectivity Rating: 80   **Fire Safety Rating:** 72   **Green Rating:** 76

STUDENTS AND FACULTY
Enrollment: 1,966. **Student Body**: 56% female, 44% male, 26% out-of-state, 2% international (27 countries represented). Asian 2%, Caucasian 92%, Hispanic 2%, Native American 1%. **Retention and Graduation**: 80% freshmen return for sophomore year. 66% freshmen graduate within 4 years. 16% grads go on to further study within 1 year. **Faculty**: Student/faculty ratio 14:1. 109 full-time faculty, 92% hold PhDs. 99% faculty teach undergrads.

ACADEMICS
Degrees: Bachelor's, master's. **Academic Requirements**: Arts/fine arts, English (including composition), history, humanities, mathematics, philosophy, religion or theology, sciences (biological or physical), social science. **Majors with Highest Enrollment**: Business administration/management, communications studies/speech communication and rhetoric, elementary education and teaching. **Disciplines with Highest Percentage of Degrees Awarded**: Business/marketing 22%, education 18%, communications/journalism 12%, social sciences 9%, biological/life sciences 7%. **Special Study Options**: Double major, English as a second language (ESL), Foundation for International Education (London) Internships, honors program, independent study, internships, student-designed major, study abroad, teacher certification program, Washington semester.

FACILITIES

Housing: Coed dorms, women's dorms, apartments for single students, special housing for disabled students, fraternity/sorority housing, town houses, off-campus college owned housing. **Special Academic Facilities/Equipment**: Center for leadership and service, Bush Art Center with 3 art galleries, scanning electron microscope, center for adaptive education and assistive technology, visual and performing arts center, center for international education, riverfront campus center with marina, peace and justice center, career services, children's center in cooperation with early childhood education, center of economic education, survey center, Kress Inn, conference services, academic support services, St. Joseph Church, chapels in residence halls, women's center, Journey-Men (men's center). **Computers**: 50% of classrooms are wireless, 70% of public computers are PCs, 30% of public computers are Macs, network access in dorm rooms, network access in dorm lounges, online registration, remote student-access to Web through college's connection.

CAMPUS LIFE

Activities: Choral groups, concert band, drama/theater, jazz band, literary magazine, music ensembles, musical theater, radio station, student government, student newspaper, student-run film society, television station. **Organizations**: 63 registered organizations, 8 honor societies, 4 religious organizations. 3 fraternities (7% men join), 5 sororities (7% women join). **Athletics (Intercollegiate)**: *Men*: Baseball, basketball, cross-country, football, golf, ice hockey, soccer, tennis, track/field (indoor), track/field (outdoor). *Women*: Basketball, cross-country, golf, soccer, softball, swimming, tennis, track/field (indoor), track/field (outdoor), volleyball.

ADMISSIONS

Freshman Academic Profile: 29% in top 10% of high school class, 56% in top 25% of high school class, 85% in top 50% of high school class. 75% from public high schools. ACT middle 50% range 22–27. TOEFL required of all international applicants, minimum paper TOEFL 550, minimum computer TOEFL 213. **Basis for Candidate Selection**: *Very important factors considered include*: Rigor of secondary school record. *Important factors considered include*: Academic GPA, standardized test scores. *Other factors considered include*: Alumni/ae relation, application essay, character/personal qualities, class rank, extracurricular activities, first generation, interview, recommendation(s), talent/ability, volunteer work, work experience. **Freshman Admission Requirements**: High school diploma is required, and GED is accepted. *Academic units recommended*: 4 English, 3 math, 3 science (3 science labs), 2 foreign language, 2 social studies, 2 history. **Freshman Admission Statistics**: 1,725 applied, 88% admitted, 36% enrolled. **Transfer Admission Requirements**: High school transcript, college transcript(s), essay or personal statement, standardized test score. Minimum college GPA of 2.5 required. Lowest grade transferable C. **General Admission Information**: Application fee $25. Early decision application deadline 12/1. Regular notification is rolling. Non-fall registration accepted. Admission may be deferred for a maximum of 1 year. Credit and/or placement offered for CEEB Advanced Placement tests.

COSTS AND FINANCIAL AID

Annual tuition $24,253. Room and board $6,579. Required fees $400. Average book expense $500. **Required Forms and Deadlines**: FAFSA. Financial aid filing deadline 3/1. **Notification of Awards**: Applicants will be notified of awards on a rolling basis beginning on or about 3/15. **Types of Aid**: *Need-based scholarships/grants*: Pell, SEOG, state scholarships/grants, private scholarships, the school's own gift aid. *Loans*: Direct Subsidized Stafford, Direct Unsubsidized Stafford, Direct PLUS, Federal Perkins, college/university loans from institutional funds. **Student Employment**: Federal Work-Study Program available. Institutional employment available. Off-campus job opportunities are good. **Financial Aid Statistics**: 66% freshmen, 64% undergrads receive need-based scholarship or grant aid. 54% freshmen, 53% undergrads receive need-based self-help aid. 98% freshmen, 96% undergrads receive any aid. Highest amount earned per year from on-campus jobs $5,868.

ST. THOMAS UNIVERSITY

1540 Northwest Thirty-second Avenue, Miami, FL 33054
Phone: 305-628-6546 **E-mail:** signup@stu.edu **CEEB Code:** 5076
Fax: 305-628-6591 **Website:** www.stu.edu **ACT Code:** 0719
Financial Aid Phone: 305-628-6547

This private school, affiliated with the Roman Catholic Church, was founded in 1961. It has a 140-acre campus.

RATINGS
Admissions Selectivity Rating: 64   **Fire Safety Rating:** 60*   **Green Rating:** 63

STUDENTS AND FACULTY

Enrollment: 1,155. **Student Body**: 60% female, 40% male, 8% out-of-state, 6% international (57 countries represented). African American 21%, Caucasian 13%, Hispanic 34%. **Retention and Graduation**: 71% freshmen return for sophomore year. 21% freshmen graduate within 4 years. **Faculty**: Student/faculty ratio 14:1. 102 full-time faculty, 89% hold PhDs. 90% faculty teach undergrads.

ACADEMICS

Degrees: Bachelor's, first professional, master's, post-bachelor's certificate, post-master's certificate. **Academic Requirements**: Computer literacy, English (including composition), history, mathematics, philosophy, religious studies, sciences (biological or physical), social science. **Classes**: Most classes have 10–19 students. Most lab/discussion sections have 10–19 students. **Majors with Highest Enrollment**: Business administration/management, organizational behavior studies, psychology. **Disciplines with Highest Percentage of Degrees Awarded**: Business/marketing 51%, psychology 11%, education 8%, security and protective services 5%, communications/journalism 5%. **Special Study Options**: Distance learning, double major, dual enrollment, honors program, independent study, internships, liberal arts/career combination, teacher certification program.

FACILITIES

Housing: Men's dorms, women's dorms. **Special Academic Facilities/Equipment**: Multimedia computer equipment, TV studio, art atrium gallery. **Computers**: 80% of classrooms are wireless, 95% of public computers are PCs, 5% of public computers are Macs, network access in dorm rooms, online registration, online administrative functions (other than registration), remote student-access to Web through college's connection.

CAMPUS LIFE

Activities: Choral groups, literary magazine, music ensembles, student government, television station, yearbook. **Organizations**: 26 registered organizations, 4 honor societies, 2 religious organizations. **Athletics (Intercollegiate)**: *Men*: Baseball, basketball, cross-country, golf, soccer, tennis. *Women*: Cross-country, soccer, softball, tennis, volleyball. Environmental Initiatives: Recycle bins in all areas. Reduction of plastic and styrofoam products in cafeteria. Promotion of reduced energy usage.

ADMISSIONS

Freshman Academic Profile: 3% in top 10% of high school class, 17% in top 25% of high school class, 48% in top 50% of high school class. SAT Math middle 50% range 390–490. SAT Critical Reading middle 50% range 400–490. SAT Writing middle 50% range 400–480. ACT middle 50% range 16–20. TOEFL required of all international applicants, minimum paper TOEFL 525, minimum computer TOEFL 193. **Basis for Candidate Selection**: *Very important factors considered include:* Academic GPA, class rank, standardized test scores. *Important factors considered include:* Alumni/ae relation, application essay, level of applicant's interest, recommendation(s), rigor of secondary school record. *Other factors considered include:* Character/personal qualities, extracurricular activities, talent/ability, volunteer work, work experience. **Freshman Admission Requirements**: High school diploma is required, and GED is accepted. *Academic units required:* 4 English, 3 math, 2 science, 3 social studies, 6 academic electives. **Freshman Admission Statistics**: 601 applied, 91% admitted, 46% enrolled. **Transfer Admission Requirements**: College transcript(s), essay or personal statement, statement of good standing from prior institution(s). Minimum college GPA of 2.0 required. Lowest grade transferable C-. **General Admission Information**: Application fee $40. Regular application deadline 8/31. Regular notification after admission decision. Non-fall registration accepted. Admission may be deferred for a maximum of 1 year. Credit and/or placement offered for CEEB Advanced Placement tests.

COSTS AND FINANCIAL AID

Annual tuition $17,000. Room & board $4,400. Required fees $630. Average book expense $1,000. **Required Forms and Deadlines**: FAFSA, state aid form. Financial aid filing deadline 3/31. **Notification of Awards**: Applicants will be notified of awards on a rolling basis beginning on or about 3/1. **Types of Aid**: *Need-based scholarships/grants*: Pell, SEOG, state scholarships/grants, private scholarships, the school's own gift aid. *Loans*: Direct Subsidized Stafford, Direct Unsubsidized Stafford, Direct PLUS, FFEL Subsidized Stafford, Federal Perkins. **Student Employment**: Federal Work-Study Program available. Institutional employment available. Off-campus job opportunities are good. **Financial Aid Statistics**: 76% freshmen, 61% undergrads receive need-based scholarship or grant aid. 75% freshmen, 62% undergrads receive need-based self-help aid. 14 freshmen, 27 undergrads receive athletic scholarships. 98% freshmen, 98% undergrads receive any aid.

STANFORD UNIVERSITY

Best 368

Undergraduate Admission, Montag Hall, Stanford, CA 94305-3020
Phone: 650-723-2091 **E-mail**: admission@stanford.edu **CEEB Code**: 4704
Fax: 650-723-6050 **Website**: www.stanford.edu **ACT Code**: 0434
Financial Aid Phone: 650-723-3058

This private school was founded in 1885. It has an 8,180-acre campus.

RATINGS

Admissions Selectivity Rating: 99   **Fire Safety Rating**: 83   **Green Rating**: 92

STUDENTS AND FACULTY

Enrollment: 6,391. **Student Body**: 48% female, 52% male, 54% out-of-state, 6% international (68 countries represented). African American 10%, Asian 24%, Caucasian 40%, Hispanic 11%, Native American 2%. **Retention and Graduation**: 98% freshmen return for sophomore year. 76% freshmen graduate within 4 years. 35% grads go on to further study within 1 year. **Faculty**: Student/faculty ratio 6:1. 1,019 full-time faculty, 98% hold PhDs. 98% faculty teach undergrads.

ACADEMICS

Degrees: Bachelor's, doctoral, first professional, master's. **Academic Requirements**: English (including composition), foreign languages, humanities, mathematics, sciences (biological or physical), social science. Undergrads complete at least 180 units, including requirements for the major, writing and rhetoric requirements, 1 year of a foreign language, and courses in the following areas: Introduction to the humanities (1 course each quarter of the freshman year), disciplinary breadth (5 courses required, at least 1 in engineering and applied sciences, humanities, mathematics, natural sciences, and social sciences), education for citizenship (2 courses in at least 2 subject areas of ethical reasoning, the global community, American cultures, and gender studies). **Classes**: Most classes have fewer than 10 students. Most lab/discussion sections have 10–19 students. **Majors with Highest Enrollment**: Biology/biological sciences, economics, political science and government. **Disciplines with Highest Percentage of Degrees Awarded**: Social sciences 24%, engineering 13%, interdisciplinary studies 13%, biological/life sciences 8%, psychology 5%. **Special Study Options**: Double major; exchange student program (domestic); honors program; independent study; internships; student-designed major; study abroad; Marine Research Center; Bing Stanford in Washington program; exchange programs with Dartmouth, Howard, Morehouse, and Spelman; undergraduate research opportunities; honors college, summer research college; overseas study.

FACILITIES

Housing: Coed dorms, women's dorms, apartments for married students, apartments for single students, special housing for disabled students, fraternity/sorority housing, cooperative housing, academic, cross-cultural, language theme and ethnic theme houses. **Special Academic Facilities/Equipment**: Art museum, marine station, observatory, biological preserve, linear accelerator. **Computers**: 100% of classrooms are wireless, 40% of public computers are PCs, 40% of public computers are Macs, 20% of public computers are UNIX, network access in dorm rooms, network access in dorm lounges, online registration, online administrative functions (other than registration), remote student-access to Web through college's connection.

CAMPUS LIFE

Activities: Choral groups, concert band, dance, drama/theater, jazz band, literary magazine, marching band, music ensembles, musical theater, opera, pep band, radio station, student government, student newspaper, student-run film society, symphony orchestra, television studio. **Organizations**: 600 registered organizations, 50 religious organizations. 17 fraternities, 11 sororities. **Athletics (Intercollegiate)**: *Men*: Baseball, basketball, crew/rowing, cross-country, diving, fencing, football, golf, gymnastics, sailing, soccer, swimming, tennis, track/field (outdoor), volleyball, water polo, wrestling. *Women*: Basketball, crew/rowing, cross-country, diving, fencing, field hockey, golf, gymnastics, lacrosse, sailing, soccer, softball, squash, swimming, synchronized swimming, tennis, track/field (outdoor), volleyball, water polo. Environmental Initiatives: Stanford's award-winning Transportation Demand Management program has been recognized by the EPA. Stanford's recycling program, recognized by the EPA, diverts 60 percent of waste from landfills. In 2007, Stanford placed second

---

in RecycleMania. Over the past decade, an energy retrofit program has reduced campus energy use by 195 million kWh—enough to run Stanford for a year.

ADMISSIONS

Freshman Academic Profile: 89% in top 10% of high school class, 98% in top 25% of high school class, 100% in top 50% of high school class. 62% from public high schools. SAT Math middle 50% range 680–790. SAT Critical Reading middle 50% range 660–760. SAT Writing middle 50% range 660–760. ACT middle 50% range 29–33. **Basis for Candidate Selection**: *Very important factors considered include*: Academic GPA, application essay, character/personal qualities, class rank, extracurricular activities, recommendation(s), rigor of secondary school record, standardized test scores, talent/ability. *Other factors considered include*: Alumni/ae relation, first generation, geographical residence, racial/ethnic status, volunteer work, work experience. **Freshman Admission Requirements**: High school diploma is required, and GED is accepted. *Academic units recommended*: 4 English, 4 math, 3 science (3 science labs), 3 foreign language, 2 social studies, 1 history. **Freshman Admission Statistics**: 22,333 applied, 11% admitted, 67% enrolled. **Transfer Admission Requirements**: High school transcript, college transcript(s), essay or personal statement, standardized test score, statement of good standing from prior institution(s). Lowest grade transferable C-. **General Admission Information**: Application fee $75. Regular application deadline 1/15. Regular notification 4/1. Non-fall registration not accepted. Admission may be deferred for a maximum of 2 years. Credit and/or placement offered for CEEB Advanced Placement tests.

COSTS AND FINANCIAL AID

Annual tuition $34,800. Room and board $10,808. Average book expense $1,335. **Required Forms and Deadlines**: FAFSA, CSS/Financial Aid PROFILE. Financial aid filing deadline 2/1. **Notification of Awards**: Applicants will be notified of awards on a rolling basis beginning on or about 4/3. **Types of Aid**: *Need-based scholarships/grants*: Pell, SEOG, state scholarships/grants, private scholarships, the school's own gift aid. *Loans*: FFEL Subsidized Stafford, FFEL Unsubsidized Stafford, FFEL PLUS, Federal Perkins, GATE Loans. **Student Employment**: Federal Work-Study Program available. Institutional employment available. Off-campus job opportunities are excellent. **Financial Aid Statistics**: 42% freshmen, 43% undergrads receive need-based scholarship or grant aid. 25% freshmen, 30% undergrads receive need-based self-help aid. 120 freshmen, 427 undergrads receive athletic scholarships. 77% undergrads receive any aid.

STATE UNIVERSITY OF NEW YORK— ALFRED STATE COLLEGE

Huntington Administration Building, Alfred, NY 14802
Phone: 607-587-4215 **E-mail**: admissions@alfredstate.edu **CEEB Code**: 2522
Fax: 607-587-4299 **Website**: www.alfredstate.edu **ACT Code**: 2910
Financial Aid Phone: 607-587-4253

This public school was founded in 1908. It has an 840-acre campus.

RATINGS
Admissions Selectivity Rating: 60*   **Fire Safety Rating**: 60*   **Green Rating**: 60*

STUDENTS AND FACULTY
Enrollment: 3,231. **Student Body**: 36% female, 64% male, 11% out-of-state. African American 6%, Asian 3%, Caucasian 87%, Hispanic 2%. **Retention and Graduation**: 38% grads go on to further study within 1 year. **Faculty**: Student/faculty ratio 20:1. 148 full-time faculty. 100% faculty teach undergrads.

ACADEMICS
Degrees: Associate, bachelor's, certificate, terminal. **Academic Requirements**: English (including composition), humanities, mathematics, sciences (biological or physical), social science. **Classes**: Most classes have 10–19 students. Most lab/discussion sections have 10–19 students. **Majors with Highest Enrollment**: Architecture (BArch, BA/BS, MArch, MA/MS, PhD), information technology, mechanical engineering/mechanical technology/technician. **Disciplines with Highest Percentage of Degrees Awarded**: Engineering technologies 64%, computer and information sciences 30%, business/marketing 6%. **Special Study Options**: Cooperative education program, cross-registration, distance learning, honors program, independent study, internships, student-designed major. Internet courses.

FACILITIES
Housing: Coed dorms, special housing for disabled students, suite, corridor,

singles, smoke-free, over 21 years, over 24 years, wellness living, quiet study, same curriculum housing, baccalaureate, single-room options, computer life style opening in fall 2007. **Computers**: 100% of classrooms are wired, 100% of classrooms are wireless, network access in dorm rooms, network access in dorm lounges, online registration, online administrative functions (other than registration), remote student-access to Web through college's connection.

CAMPUS LIFE

Activities: Choral groups, concert band, drama/theater, jazz band, literary magazine, music ensembles, musical theater, radio station, student government, student newspaper, symphony orchestra, yearbook. **Organizations**: 60 registered organizations, 4 honor societies. 3 fraternities (10% men join), 2 sororities (10% women join). **Athletics (Intercollegiate)**: *Men*: Baseball, basketball, cheerleading, cross-country, football, lacrosse, soccer, swimming, track/field (outdoor), wrestling. *Women*: Basketball, cheerleading, cross-country, soccer, softball, swimming, track/field (outdoor), volleyball.

ADMISSIONS

Freshman Academic Profile: SAT Math middle 50% range 440–560. SAT Critical Reading middle 50% range 410–510. ACT middle 50% range 18–24. TOEFL required of all international applicants, minimum paper TOEFL 500, minimum computer TOEFL 173. **Basis for Candidate Selection**: *Very important factors considered include:* Academic GPA, rigor of secondary school record. *Important factors considered include:* Class rank. *Other factors considered include:* Alumni/ae relation, application essay, character/personal qualities, extracurricular activities, interview, recommendation(s), standardized test scores, talent/ability, volunteer work, work experience. **Freshman Admission Requirements**: High school diploma is required, and GED is accepted. *Academic units recommended:* 4 English, 4 math, 4 science, 4 social studies. **Freshman Admission Statistics**: 4,414 applied, 65% admitted, 45% enrolled. **Transfer Admission Requirements**: High school transcript, college transcript(s), statement of good standing from prior institution(s). Minimum college GPA of 2.4 required. Lowest grade transferable C. **General Admission Information**: Application fee $40. Regular notification is rolling. Non-fall registration accepted. Admission may be deferred for a maximum of 1 semester. Credit and/or placement offered for CEEB Advanced Placement tests.

COSTS AND FINANCIAL AID

Annual in-state tuition $4,350. Out-of-state tuition $7,210. Room & board $8,040. Required fees $1,056. Average book expense $1,000. **Required Forms and Deadlines**: FAFSA, state aid form. Financial aid filing deadline 1/7. **Notification of Awards**: Applicants will be notified of awards on a rolling basis beginning on or about 3/3. **Types of Aid**: *Need-based scholarships/grants*: Pell, SEOG, state scholarships/grants, private scholarships, the school's own gift aid. *Loans*: FFEL Subsidized Stafford, FFEL Unsubsidized Stafford, FFEL PLUS, Federal Perkins, Federal Nursing. **Student Employment**: Federal Work-Study Program available. Institutional employment available. **Financial Aid Statistics**: 97% undergrads receive any aid.

STATE UNIVERSITY OF NEW YORK AT BINGHAMTON

Best 368

PO Box 6001, Binghamton, NY 13902-6001
Phone: 607-777-2171 **E-mail**: admit@binghamton.edu **CEEB Code**: 2535
Fax: 607-777-4445 **Website**: www.binghamton.edu **ACT Code**: 2956
Financial Aid Phone: 607-777-2428

This public school was founded in 1946. It has a 930-acre campus.

RATINGS
Admissions Selectivity Rating: 94   **Fire Safety Rating**: 72   **Green Rating**: 98

STUDENTS AND FACULTY
Enrollment: 11,470. **Student Body**: 48% female, 52% male, 7% out-of-state, 7% international (93 countries represented). African American 5%, Asian 14%, Caucasian 47%, Hispanic 7%. **Retention and Graduation**: 89% freshmen return for sophomore year. 66% freshmen graduate within 4 years. 38% grads go on to further study within 1 year. 10% grads pursue arts and sciences degrees. 2% grads pursue business degrees. 7% grads pursue law degrees. 9%

grads pursue medical degrees. **Faculty**: Student/faculty ratio 20:1. 551 full-time faculty, 93% hold PhDs. 90% faculty teach undergrads.

ACADEMICS

Degrees: Bachelor's, doctoral, master's, post-master's certificate. **Academic Requirements**: Arts/fine arts, English (including composition), humanities, mathematics, physical education, sciences (biological or physical), social science. **Classes**: Most classes have 20–29 students. Most lab/discussion sections have 20–29 students. **Majors with Highest Enrollment**: Business administration/management, English language and literature, psychology. **Disciplines with Highest Percentage of Degrees Awarded**: Social sciences 17%, business/marketing 14%, psychology 12%, English 9%, health professions and related sciences 9%, biological/life sciences 8%. **Special Study Options**: Accelerated program, cross-registration, distance learning, double major, dual enrollment, English as a second language (ESL), exchange student program (domestic), honors program, independent study, internships, liberal arts/career combination, student-designed major, study abroad, teacher certification program is a graduate study only.

FACILITIES

Housing: Coed dorms, apartments for single students, special housing for disabled students, special interest housing available. Extensive bus system, both school operated and public transportation with free access. **Special Academic Facilities/Equipment**: Art gallery, performing arts center, indoor/outdoor theater, multi-climate greenhouse, teaching greenhouse, sculpture foundry, events center. **Computers**: 10% of classrooms are wired, 90% of classrooms are wireless, 90% of public computers are PCs, 8% of public computers are Macs, 2% of public computers are UNIX, network access in dorm rooms, online registration, online administrative functions (other than registration), remote student-access to Web through college's connection.

CAMPUS LIFE

Activities: Choral groups, concert band, dance, drama/theater, jazz band, literary magazine, music ensembles, musical theater, opera, pep band, radio station, student government, student newspaper, student-run film society, symphony orchestra, television station, yearbook. **Organizations**: 160 registered organizations, 23 honor societies, 12 religious organizations. 22 fraternities (8% men join), 17 sororities (9% women join). **Athletics (Intercollegiate)**: *Men*: Baseball, basketball, cross-country, diving, golf, lacrosse, soccer, swimming, tennis, track/field (indoor), track/field (outdoor). *Women*: Basketball, cross-country, diving, lacrosse, soccer, softball, swimming, tennis, track/field (indoor), track/field (outdoor), volleyball. Environmental Initiatives: Nearly 70% of Binghamton University's 900-acre campus is in its natural state. Binghamton University's goal is to design, construct, operate and maintain all new buildings following guidelines set forth by the U.S. Green Building Council's LEED rating system. Since 2004, Binghamton has obtained LEED certification on two buildings and is in the process of applying for LEED Silver certification for a recently constructed building.

ADMISSIONS

Freshman Academic Profile: 49% in top 10% of high school class, 84% in top 25% of high school class, 98% in top 50% of high school class. 87% from public high schools. SAT Math middle 50% range 610–690. SAT Critical Reading middle 50% range 570–660. ACT middle 50% range 25–29. TOEFL required of all international applicants, minimum paper TOEFL 550, minimum computer TOEFL 213. **Basis for Candidate Selection**: *Very important factors considered include:* Academic GPA, rigor of secondary school record, standardized test scores. *Important factors considered include:* Application essay, extracurricular activities, first generation, recommendation(s), volunteer work. *Other factors considered include:* Alumni/ae relation, character/personal qualities, class rank, geographical residence, level of applicant's interest, racial/ethnic status, state residency, talent/ability, work experience. **Freshman Admission Requirements**: High school diploma is required, and GED is accepted. *Academic units required*: 4 English, 3 math, 2 science, 3 foreign language, 2 social studies. *Academic units recommended*: 4 math, 4 science, 3 foreign language, 3 history. **Freshman Admission Statistics**: 22,853 applied, 43% admitted, 24% enrolled. **Transfer Admission Requirements**: College transcript(s). Lowest grade transferable C-. **General Admission Information**: Application fee $40. Regular notification 4/1. Non-fall registration accepted. Admission may be deferred for a maximum of 1 year. Credit offered for CEEB Advanced Placement tests.

COSTS AND FINANCIAL AID

Annual in-state tuition $4,350. Out-of-state tuition $10,610. Room & board $8,588. Required fees $1,560. Average book expense $800. **Required Forms and Deadlines**: FAFSA, state aid form. Financial aid filing deadline 3/1. **Notification of Awards**: Applicants will be notified of awards on a rolling basis beginning on or about 3/15. **Types of Aid**: *Need-based scholarships/grants*: Pell, SEOG, state scholarships, private scholarships, the school's own gift aid. *Loans*: Direct Subsidized Stafford, Direct Unsubsidized Stafford, FFEL PLUS, Federal Perkins, Federal Nursing, college/university loans from institutional funds. **Student Employment**: Federal Work-Study Program available. Institutional employment available. Off-campus job opportunities are excellent. **Financial Aid Statistics**: 38% freshmen, 40% undergrads receive need-based scholarship or grant aid. 40% freshmen, 43% undergrads receive need-based self-help aid. 57 freshmen, 218 undergrads receive athletic scholarships. 79% freshmen, 69% undergrads receive any aid. Highest amount earned per year from on-campus jobs $3,400.

STATE UNIVERSITY OF NEW YORK— BROCKPORT

350 New Campus Drive, Brockport, NY 14420
Phone: 585-395-2751 **E-mail**: admit@brockport.edu **CEEB Code**: 2537
Fax: 585-395-5452 **Website**: www.brockport.edu **ACT Code**: 2928
Financial Aid Phone: 585-395-2501

This public school was founded in 1867. It has a 435-acre campus.

RATINGS

Admissions Selectivity Rating: 85 **Fire Safety Rating**: 79 **Green Rating**: 87

STUDENTS AND FACULTY

Enrollment: 6,848. **Student Body**: 57% female, 43% male, 1% out-of-state. African American 6%, Asian 1%, Caucasian 76%, Hispanic 3%. **Retention and Graduation**: 83% freshmen return for sophomore year. 32% freshmen graduate within 4 years. 28% grads go on to further study within 1 year. 29% grads pursue arts and sciences degrees. 2% grads pursue business degrees. 2% grads pursue law degrees. 2% grads pursue medical degrees. **Faculty**: Student/faculty ratio 18:1. 321 full-time faculty, 78% hold PhDs. 95% faculty teach undergrads.

ACADEMICS

Degrees: Bachelor's, master's, post-master's certificate. **Academic Requirements**: Arts/fine arts, computer literacy, English (including composition), foreign languages, history, humanities, mathematics, sciences (biological or physical), social science. **Classes**: Most classes have 20–29 students. Most lab/discussion sections have fewer than 10 students. **Majors with Highest Enrollment**: Business administration and management, history, physical education teaching and coaching. **Disciplines with Highest Percentage of Degrees Awarded**: Business/marketing 15%, education 12%, health professions and related sciences 11%, psychology 9%, security and protective services 9%, communications/journalism 7%. **Special Study Options**: Accelerated program, cross-registration, distance learning, double major, dual enrollment, honors program, independent study, internships, student-designed major, study abroad, teacher certification program.

FACILITIES

Housing: Coed dorms, special housing for disabled students, special housing for international students, first-year experience, transfer student housing, academic interest floors. **Special Academic Facilities/Equipment**: Theater, leadership development institute, greenhouse, planetarium, electron microscope, art galleries, aquaculture ponds, newly-renovated science building, environmental science deciduous woodlot, new meteorology lab with on campus Doppler radar station, state-of-the-art dance facilities, student computing center, student learning center, fitness centers and weight rooms. **Computers**: 15% of classrooms are wired, 95% of classrooms are wireless, 90% of public computers are PCs, 7% of public computers are Macs, 3% of public computers are UNIX, network access in dorm rooms, network access in dorm lounges, online registration, online administrative functions (other than registration), support for handheld computing, remote student-access to Web through college's connection.

CAMPUS LIFE

Activities: Choral groups, dance, drama/theater, literary magazine, radio station, student government, student newspaper, television station. **Organizations**: 68 registered organizations, 20 honor societies, 21 religious organizations. 6 fraternities (1% men join), 3 sororities (1% women join). **Athletics (Intercollegiate)**: *Men*: Baseball, basketball, cross-country, diving, football, ice hockey, lacrosse, soccer, swimming, track/field (indoor), track/field (outdoor), wrestling. *Women*: Basketball, cross-country, diving, field hockey, gymnastics, lacrosse, soccer, softball, swimming, tennis, track/field (indoor), track/field (outdoor), volleyball. Environmental Initiatives: New 208 bed townhomes that are LEED certifiable including: geothermal HVAC, recycled materials, energy efficient systems, etc. Roughly 12 million dollars of investments in a diverse spectrum of energy related facility projects. High recycling rates and alternative energy fuels program including bio-diesels and alternative energy vehicles.

ADMISSIONS

Freshman Academic Profile: 16% in top 10% of high school class, 51% in top 25% of high school class, 90% in top 50% of high school class. SAT Math middle 50% range 480–580. SAT Critical Reading middle 50% range 500–600. SAT Writing middle 50% range 460–560. ACT middle 50% range 21–25. TOEFL required of all international applicants, minimum paper TOEFL 530, minimum computer TOEFL 197. **Basis for Candidate Selection**: *Very important factors considered include*: Academic GPA, class rank, rigor of secondary school record, standardized test scores. *Important factors considered include*: Application essay, extracurricular activities, recommendation(s), talent/ability. *Other factors considered include*: Character/personal qualities, interview, volunteer work, work experience. **Freshman Admission Requirements**: High school diploma is required, and GED is accepted. *Academic units required*: 4 English, 3 math, 3 science (1 science lab), 4 social studies, 4 academic electives. *Academic units recommended*: 3 foreign language. **Freshman Admission Statistics**: 8,149 applied, 44% admitted, 28% enrolled. **Transfer Admission Requirements**: College transcript(s). Minimum college GPA of 2.5 required. Lowest grade transferable D. **General Admission Information**: Application fee $40. Regular notification is rolling. Non-fall registration accepted. Admission may be deferred for a maximum of 1 year. Credit and/or placement offered for CEEB Advanced Placement tests.

COSTS AND FINANCIAL AID

Annual in-state tuition $4,350. Out-of-state tuition $10,610. Room & board $7,830. Required fees $1,006. Average book expense $1,000. **Required Forms and Deadlines**: FAFSA, state aid form. Financial aid filing deadline 2/15. **Notification of Awards**: Applicants will be notified of awards on a rolling basis beginning on or about 4/15. **Types of Aid**: *Need-based scholarships/grants*: Pell, SEOG, state scholarships/grants, private scholarships, the school's own gift aid. *Loans*: Direct Subsidized Stafford, Direct Unsubsidized Stafford, Direct PLUS, Federal Perkins, Federal Nursing, alternative education loans. **Financial Aid Statistics**: 62% freshmen, 61% undergrads receive need-based scholarship or grant aid. 55% freshmen, 58% undergrads receive need-based self-help aid. 70% freshmen, 69% undergrads receive any aid. Highest amount earned per year from on-campus jobs $12,298.

STATE UNIVERSITY OF NEW YORK—BROOME COMMUNITY COLLEGE

Admissions Office, Box 1017, Binghamton, NY 13902
Phone: 607-778-5001 **E-mail**: Fiorelli_a@sunybroome.edu **CEEB Code**: 2048
Fax: 607-778-5310 **Website**: www.sunybroome.edu
Financial Aid Phone: 607-778-5028

This public school was founded in 1946. It has a 223-acre campus.

RATINGS

Admissions Selectivity Rating: 62   **Fire Safety Rating**: 60*   **Green Rating**: 60*

STUDENTS AND FACULTY

Enrollment: 4,519. **Student Body**: 56% female, 44% male, 22% out-of-state, 2% international (30 countries represented). African American 1%, Caucasian 118%. **Retention and Graduation**: 42% grads go on to further study within 1 year. **Faculty**: 100% faculty teach undergrads.

ACADEMICS

Degrees: Associate, certificate. **Academic Requirements**: English (including composition). **Special Study Options**: Cooperative education program, distance learning, double major, English as a second language (ESL), honors program, independent study, internships, liberal arts/career combination, student-designed major, study abroad, weekend college.

FACILITIES

Computers: 28% of public computers are PCs, online administrative functions (other than registration), remote student-access to Web through college's connection.

CAMPUS LIFE

Activities: Choral groups, concert band, drama/theater, jazz band, music ensembles, student government, student newspaper. **Organizations**: 50 registered organizations, 1 honor society, 2 religious organizations. **Athletics (Intercollegiate)**: *Men*: Baseball, basketball, cheerleading, cross-country, golf, ice hockey, lacrosse, soccer, tennis. *Women*: Basketball, cheerleading, cross-country, soccer, softball, volleyball.

ADMISSIONS

Freshman Academic Profile: 5% in top 10% of high school class, 9% in top 25% of high school class, 40% in top 50% of high school class. 95% from public high schools. TOEFL required of all international applicants, minimum paper TOEFL 400. **Freshman Admission Requirements**: High school diploma is required, and GED is accepted. *Academic units recommended*: 4 English, 3 math, 3 science (2 science labs), 2 foreign language, 4 social studies, 4 history. **Freshman Admission Statistics**: 3,840 applied, 82% admitted, 49% enrolled. **General Admission Information**: Nonfall registration accepted. Admission may be deferred for a maximum of 1 year. Common Application accepted. Neither credit nor placement offered for CEEB Advanced Placement tests.

COSTS AND FINANCIAL AID

Annual in-state tuition $2,338. Out-of-state tuition $4,676. Required fees $170. Average book expense $600.

STATE UNIVERSITY OF NEW YORK— BUFFALO STATE COLLEGE

1300 Elmwood Avenue, Buffalo, NY 14222
Phone: 716-878-4017 **E-mail**: admissions@buffalostate.edu **CEEB Code**: 2533
Fax: 716-878-6100 **Website**: www.buffalostate.edu **ACT Code**: 2930
Financial Aid Phone: 716-878-4902

This public school was founded in 1871. It has a 115-acre campus.

RATINGS

Admissions Selectivity Rating: 76   **Fire Safety Rating**: 60*   **Green Rating**: 75

STUDENTS AND FACULTY

Enrollment: 9,023. **Student Body**: 59% female, 41% male, 1% out-of-state. African American 14%, Asian 2%, Caucasian 66%, Hispanic 4%. **Retention and Graduation**: 76% freshmen return for sophomore year. 14% freshmen graduate within 4 years. 27% grads go on to further study within 1 year. 2% grads pursue arts and sciences degrees. 1% grads pursue business degrees. 1% grads pursue law degrees. **Faculty**: Student/faculty ratio 19:1. 416 full-time faculty, 80% hold PhDs. 100% faculty teach undergrads.

ACADEMICS

Degrees: Bachelor's, master's, post-master's certificate. **Academic Requirements**: Arts/fine arts, computer literacy, English (including composition), foreign languages, history, humanities, mathematics, philosophy, sciences (biological or physical), social science. **Majors with Highest Enrollment**: Business administration/management, elementary education and teaching, mass communications/media studies. **Disciplines with Highest Percentage of Degrees Awarded**: Education 33%, business/marketing 9%, communications/journalism 8%, social sciences 8%, visual and performing arts 7%, security and protective services 6%. **Special Study Options**: Cooperative education program, cross-registration, distance learning, double major, dual enrollment, English as a second language (ESL), exchange student program (domestic), honors program, independent study, internships, liberal arts/career combination, study abroad, teacher certification program.

FACILITIES

Housing: Coed dorms, special housing for international students, apartments for students with dependent children. **Special Academic Facilities/Equipment**: Art center, anthropology museum, concert hall with pipe organ, nature preserve. **Computers**: 80% of public computers are PCs, 20% of public computers are Macs, network access in dorm rooms, network access in dorm lounges, online registration, online administrative functions (other than registration), support for handheld computing, remote student-access to Web through college's connection.

CAMPUS LIFE

Activities: Choral groups, concert band, dance, drama/theater, jazz band, literary magazine, music ensembles, radio station, student government, student newspaper, student-run film society, television station, yearbook. **Organizations**: 75 registered organizations, 5 religious organizations. 10 fraternities (1% men join), 10 sororities (1% women join). **Athletics (Intercollegiate)**: *Men*: Basketball, cross-country, diving, football, ice hockey, soccer, swimming, track/field (indoor), track/field (outdoor). *Women*: Basketball, cheerleading, cross-country, diving, ice hockey, lacrosse, soccer, softball, swimming, tennis, track/field (indoor), track/field (outdoor), volleyball.

ADMISSIONS

Freshman Academic Profile: 6% in top 10% of high school class, 25% in top 25% of high school class, 73% in top 50% of high school class. SAT Math middle 50% range 450–540. SAT Critical Reading middle 50% range 440–530. TOEFL required of all international applicants, minimum paper TOEFL 500, minimum computer TOEFL 173. **Basis for Candidate Selection**: *Very important factors considered include*: Academic GPA, rigor of secondary school record, standardized test scores. *Important factors considered include*: Class rank. *Other factors considered include*: Application essay, character/personal qualities, extracurricular activities, first generation, interview, recommendation(s), talent/ability, volunteer work, work experience. **Freshman Admission Requirements**: High school diploma is required, and GED is accepted. *Academic units required*: 2 math, 2 science. *Academic units recommended*: 4 English, 3 math, 3 science, 3 foreign language, 4 history. **Freshman Admission Statistics**: 9,791 applied, 46% admitted, 33% enrolled. **Transfer Admission Requirements**: College transcript(s), statement of good standing from prior institution(s). Minimum college GPA of 2.0 required. **General Admission Information**: Application fee $40. Early decision application deadline 11/15. Regular notification is rolling. Non-fall registration accepted. Admission may be deferred for a maximum of 1 year. Credit offered for CEEB Advanced Placement tests.

COSTS AND FINANCIAL AID

Annual in-state tuition $4,350. Out-of-state tuition $10,610. Room & board $7,482. Required fees $935. Average book expense $900. **Required Forms and Deadlines**: FAFSA. Financial aid filing deadline 5/1. **Notification of Awards**: Applicants will be notified of awards on a rolling basis beginning on or about 5/1. **Types of Aid**: *Need-based scholarships/grants*: Pell, SEOG, state scholarships/grants. *Loans*: FFEL Subsidized Stafford, FFEL Unsubsidized Stafford, FFEL PLUS, Federal Perkins.

STATE UNIVERSITY OF NEW YORK—CANTON

French Hall, SUNY Canton, Canton, NY 13617
Phone: 315-386-7123 **E-mail**: admissions@canton.edu **CEEB Code**: 2523
Fax: 315-386-7929 **Website**: www.canton.edu **ACT Code**: 2912
Financial Aid Phone: 315-386-7616

This public school was founded in 1906. It has a 555-acre campus.

RATINGS

Admissions Selectivity Rating: 60*   **Fire Safety Rating**: 60*   **Green Rating**: 60*

STUDENTS AND FACULTY

Enrollment: 2,119. **Student Body**: 48% female, 52% male. African American 8%, Caucasian 86%, Hispanic 3%, Native American 2%. **Retention and Graduation**: 81% freshmen return for sophomore year. 45% grads go on to further study within 1 year. **Faculty**: Student/faculty ratio 23:1. 83 full-time faculty, 20% hold PhDs. 100% faculty teach undergrads.

ACADEMICS

Degrees: Associate, bachelor's, certificate, terminal. **Academic Requirements**: computer literacy, English (including composition), mathematics, sciences (biological or physical), social science. **Classes**: Most classes have 20–29 students. Most lab/discussion sections have 10–19 students. **Majors with Highest Enrollment**: Computer/information technology services administration and management, criminal justice/law enforcement administration. **Special Study Options**: Cooperative education program, cross-registration, distance learning, dual enrollment, internships, liberal arts/career combination, student-designed major.

FACILITIES

Housing: Coed dorms, single-gender wings, intensive quiet atmosphere, relaxed atmosphere, suites, private rooms, computer floors, 21+ floor, Grasse River Community (pet floor), Umoja Ahora Community (multicultural), North Country experience, alcohol-free, smoke-free. **Special Academic Facilities/Equipment**: Criminal investigation labs, radio station, distance learning classrooms. **Computers**: 100% of public computers are PCs, network access in dorm rooms, remote student-access to Web through college's connection.

CAMPUS LIFE

Activities: Choral groups, literary magazine, radio station, student government, student newspaper, yearbook. **Organizations**: 50 registered organizations, 2 honor societies, 1 religious organization. 3 fraternities, 3 sororities. **Athletics (Intercollegiate)**: *Men*: Basketball, football, ice hockey, lacrosse, soccer. *Women*: Basketball, soccer, softball, volleyball.

ADMISSIONS

Freshman Academic Profile: TOEFL required of all international applicants, minimum paper TOEFL 550, minimum computer TOEFL 213. **Basis for Candidate Selection**: *Very important factors considered include*: Rigor of secondary school record. *Other factors considered include*: Character/personal qualities, class rank, extracurricular activities, interview, recommendation(s), standardized test scores, talent/ability, work experience. **Freshman Admission Requirements**: High school diploma is required, and GED is accepted. *Academic units recommended*: 4 English, 2 math, 2 science, 4 social studies. **Freshman Admission Statistics**: 1,830 applied, 98% admitted, 45% enrolled. **Transfer Admission Requirements**: High school transcript, college transcript(s). Lowest grade transferable C. **General Admission Information**: Application fee $40. Regular notification is rolling. Non-fall registration accepted. Admission may be deferred for a maximum of 1 year. Common Application not accepted.

COSTS AND FINANCIAL AID

Annual in-state tuition $3,200. Out-of-state tuition $5,000. Room & board $6,490. Required fees $980. Average book expense $800. **Required Forms and Deadlines**: FAFSA, state aid form. Financial aid filing deadline 3/15. **Notification of Awards**: Applicants will be notified of awards on a rolling basis beginning on or about 2/3. **Types of Aid**: *Need-based scholarships/grants*: Pell, SEOG, private scholarships. *Loans*: Direct Subsidized Stafford, Direct Unsubsidized Stafford, Direct PLUS, Federal Perkins. **Student Employment**: Federal Work-Study Program available. Institutional employment available. Off-campus job opportunities are fair.

STATE UNIVERSITY OF NEW YORK— COBLESKILL

Office of Admissions, Cobleskill, NY 12043
Phone: 518-255-5525 **E-mail**: admissions@cobleskill.edu **CEEB Code**: 2524
Fax: 518-255-6769 **Website**: www.cobleskill.edu **ACT Code**: 2914
Financial Aid Phone: 518-255-5623

This public school was founded in 1916. It has a 750-acre campus.

RATINGS

Admissions Selectivity Rating: 65   **Fire Safety Rating**: 76   **Green Rating**: 83

STUDENTS AND FACULTY

Enrollment: 2,475. **Student Body**: 48% female, 52% male, 10% out-of-state, 2% international (9 countries represented). African American 3%, Caucasian 49%, Hispanic 2%. **Retention and Graduation**: 87% freshmen return for sophomore year. 63% grads go on to further study within 1 year. **Faculty**: Student/faculty ratio 18:1. 104 full-time faculty. 100% faculty teach undergrads.

ACADEMICS

Degrees: Associate, bachelor's, certificate, terminal. **Academic Requirements**: Arts/fine arts, English (including composition), foreign languages, history, humanities, mathematics, sciences (biological or physical), social science. The SUNY trustees general education requirements include the above areas, plus Western civilization and world cultures. For associate, a student must take 3 credits in 7 of the 10 areas; for the bachelor's, a student must take 3 credits in 8 of the 10 areas. **Classes**: Most classes have 20–29 students. Most lab/discussion sections have 10–19 students. **Disciplines with Highest Percentage of Degrees Awarded**: Agriculture 65%, business/marketing 17%, family and consumer sciences 2%. **Special Study Options**: Distance learning, English as a second language (ESL), honors program, independent study, internships, study abroad, weekend college.

FACILITIES

Housing: Coed dorms, men's dorms, women's dorms, special housing for disabled students, housing options for bachelor degree seeking students. **Special Academic Facilities/Equipment**: Art museum, 650-acre agricultural campus, distance learning classrooms, ski area, adult study center. **Computers**: 2% of classrooms are wired, 2% of classrooms are wireless, 97% of public computers are PCs, 3% of public computers are Macs, network access in dorm rooms, network access in dorm lounges, online registration, online administrative functions (other than registration), remote student-access to Web through college's connection.

CAMPUS LIFE

Activities: Choral groups, drama/theater, jazz band, music ensembles, musical theater, student government, student newspaper. **Organizations**: 40 registered organizations, 1 honor society, 1 religious organization. **Athletics (Intercollegiate)**: *Men:* Baseball, basketball, cross-country, diving, equestrian sports, golf, lacrosse, soccer, swimming, tennis, track/field (outdoor), volleyball. *Women:* Basketball, cross-country, diving, equestrian sports, golf, soccer, softball, swimming, tennis, track/field (outdoor), volleyball.

ADMISSIONS

Freshman Academic Profile: 3% in top 10% of high school class, 12% in top 25% of high school class, 40% in top 50% of high school class. 98% from public high schools. SAT Math middle 50% range 400–510. SAT Critical Reading middle 50% range 400–510. ACT middle 50% range 16–21. TOEFL required of all international applicants, minimum paper TOEFL 500. **Basis for Candidate Selection**: *Very important factors considered include:* Rigor of secondary school record. *Important factors considered include:* Academic GPA, class rank, level of applicant's interest. *Other factors considered include:* Alumni/ae relation, application essay, character/personal qualities, extracurricular activities, first generation, interview, recommendation(s), standardized test scores, talent/ability, volunteer work, work experience. **Freshman Admission Requirements**: High school diploma is required, and GED is accepted. *Academic units required:* 4 English, 1 math, 1 science, 12 academic electives. *Academic units recommended:* 3 math, 3 science (2 science labs), 3 social studies. **Freshman Admission Statistics**: 3,489 applied, 73% admitted, 38% enrolled. **Transfer Admission Requirements**: College transcript(s), statement of good standing from prior institution(s). Lowest grade transferable C-. **General Admission Information**: Application fee $40. Regular notification is rolling. Nonfall registration accepted. Admission may be deferred for a maximum of 2 semesters. Credit offered for CEEB Advanced Placement tests.

COSTS AND FINANCIAL AID

Annual in-state tuition $4,350. Out-of-state tuition $10,610. Room & board $8,630. Required fees $1,034. Average book expense $1,200. **Required Forms and Deadlines**: FAFSA, CSS/Financial Aid PROFILE. Financial aid filing deadline 3/15. **Notification of Awards**: Applicants will be notified of awards on or about 4/15. **Types of Aid**: *Need-based scholarships/grants:* Pell, SEOG, state scholarships/grants, private scholarships, the school's own gift aid. *Loans:* FFEL Subsidized Stafford, FFEL Unsubsidized Stafford, FFEL PLUS, Federal Perkins. **Student Employment**: Federal Work-Study Program available. Institutional employment available. Off-campus job opportunities are fair. **Financial Aid Statistics**: 77% freshmen, 68% undergrads receive any aid. Highest amount earned per year from on-campus jobs $800.

STATE UNIVERSITY OF NEW YORK—COLLEGE OF ENVIRONMENTAL SCIENCE AND FORESTRY

106 Bray Hall, SUNY-ESF, Syracuse, NY 13210
Phone: 315-470-6600 **E-mail:** esfinfo@esf.edu **CEEB Code:** 2530
Fax: 315-470-6933 **Website:** www.esf.edu **ACT Code:** 2948
Financial Aid Phone: 315-470-6706

This public school was founded in 1911. It has a 12-acre campus.

RATINGS

Admissions Selectivity Rating: 84   **Fire Safety Rating:** 60*   **Green Rating:** 97

STUDENTS AND FACULTY

Enrollment: 1,372. **Student Body**: 37% female, 63% male, 7% out-of-state. African American 1%, Asian 2%, Caucasian 92%, Hispanic 3%. **Retention and Graduation**: 83% freshmen return for sophomore year. 44% freshmen graduate within 4 years. **Faculty**: 100% faculty teach undergrads.

ACADEMICS

Degrees: Associate, bachelor's, doctoral, master's, terminal. **Academic Requirements**: Arts/fine arts, English (including composition), history, humanities, mathematics, sciences (biological or physical), social science. **Disciplines with Highest Percentage of Degrees Awarded**: Natural resources/environmental science 49%, biological/life sciences 34%, engineering 8%, architecture 6%, physical sciences 3%. **Special Study Options**: Cooperative education program, cross-registration, English as a second language (ESL), honors program, internships, study abroad, teacher certification program.

FACILITIES

Housing: Coed dorms, apartments for married students, apartments for single students, fraternity/sorority housing. **Special Academic Facilities/Equip-**

ment: Museums, art galleries, plant growth & animal environmental simulation chambers, wildlife collection, electron microscope, paper machine, photogrammetric and geodetic facilities. **Computers**: Network access in dorm rooms, network access in dorm lounges, online registration, online administrative functions (other than registration), remote student-access to Web through college's connection.

CAMPUS LIFE

Activities: Choral groups, concert band, dance, drama/theater, jazz band, literary magazine, marching band, music ensembles, musical theater, pep band, radio station, student government, student newspaper, symphony orchestra, television station, yearbook. **Organizations**: 300 registered organizations, 1 honor society. Environmental Initiatives: The College uses a 250 kilowatt carbonate fuel cell to generate approximately 17% of the College's electrical power. Faculty at SUNY-ESF are conducting nationally recognized and government supported research in the development of ethanol and other renewable products from wood. Have partnered with the NY State government and private industry to develop the state's first "biorefinery" aimed at producing ethanol and other chemical products from wood sugars. The College has also developed a genetically engineered species of fast growth willow that is being grown as an alternative to corn use in ethanol production.

ADMISSIONS

Freshman Academic Profile: 22% in top 10% of high school class, 53% in top 25% of high school class, 92% in top 50% of high school class. SAT Math middle 50% range 530–610. SAT Critical Reading middle 50% range 510–610. ACT middle 50% range 22–27. TOEFL required of all international applicants, minimum paper TOEFL 550, minimum computer TOEFL 213. **Basis for Candidate Selection**: *Very important factors considered include:* Academic GPA, application essay, rigor of secondary school record. *Important factors considered include:* Character/personal qualities, class rank, extracurricular activities, recommendation(s), standardized test scores, volunteer work. *Other factors considered include:* Alumni/ae relation, first generation, interview, level of applicant's interest, work experience. **Freshman Admission Requirements**: High school diploma is required, and GED is accepted. *Academic units required:* 4 English, 3 math, 3 science (3 science labs), 4 social studies. *Academic units recommended:* 4 math, 4 science (4 science labs). **Freshman Admission Statistics**: 921 applied, 66% admitted, 43% enrolled. **Transfer Admission Requirements**: High school transcript, college transcript(s). Minimum college GPA of 2.0 required. Lowest grade transferable C. **General Admission Information**: Application fee $40. Regular notification is rolling. Non-fall registration accepted. Admission may be deferred for a maximum of 1 year. Common Application not accepted. Credit offered for CEEB Advanced Placement tests.

COSTS AND FINANCIAL AID

Annual in-state tuition $4,350. Out-of-state tuition $10,610. Room & board $10,180. Required fees $641. Average book expense $1,050. **Required Forms and Deadlines**: FAFSA, state aid form. Financial aid filing deadline 3/1. **Notification of Awards**: Applicants will be notified of awards on a rolling basis beginning on or about 3/15. **Types of Aid**: *Need-based scholarships/grants:* Pell, SEOG, state scholarships/grants, private scholarships, the school's own gift aid. *Loans:* FFEL Subsidized Stafford, FFEL Unsubsidized Stafford, FFEL PLUS, Federal Perkins. **Student Employment**: Federal Work-Study Program available. Institutional employment available. Off-campus job opportunities are excellent. **Financial Aid Statistics**: 56% freshmen, 67% undergrads receive need-based scholarship or grant aid. 56% freshmen, 67% undergrads receive need-based self-help aid.

See page 1388.

STATE UNIVERSITY OF NEW YORK— THE COLLEGE AT OLD WESTBURY

PO Box 307, Old Westbury, NY 11568-0307
Phone: 516-876-3073 **E-mail:** enroll@oldwestbury.edu **CEEB Code:** 2866
Fax: 516-876-3307 **Website:** www.oldwestbury.edu **ACT Code:** 2939
Financial Aid Phone: 516-876-3222

This public school was founded in 1968. It has a 605-acre campus.

RATINGS

Admissions Selectivity Rating: 72   **Fire Safety Rating:** 85   **Green Rating:** 72

STUDENTS AND FACULTY

Enrollment: 3,282. **Student Body**: 61% female, 39% male, 1% out-of-state, 2% international (31 countries represented). African American 29%, Asian 6%, Caucasian 29%, Hispanic 17%. **Retention and Graduation**: 72% freshmen return for sophomore year. 15% freshmen graduate within 4 years. 74% grads go on to further study within 1 year. 13% grads pursue arts and sciences degrees. 43% grads pursue business degrees. 7% grads pursue law degrees. 5% grads pursue medical degrees. **Faculty**: Student/faculty ratio 17:1. 133 full-time faculty, 77% hold PhDs. 100% faculty teach undergrads.

ACADEMICS

Degrees: Bachelor's, certificate, master's. **Academic Requirements**: Arts/fine arts, computer literacy, English (including composition), foreign languages, history, humanities, mathematics, philosophy, sciences (biological or physical), social science. **Classes**: Most classes have 20–29 students. Most lab/discussion sections have 20–29 students. **Majors with Highest Enrollment**: Accounting, elementary education and teaching, psychology. **Disciplines with Highest Percentage of Degrees Awarded**: Business/marketing 32%, education 15%, social sciences 14%, psychology 11%, computer and information sciences 7%. **Special Study Options**: Cross-registration, distance learning, double major, English as a second language (ESL), exchange student program (domestic), honors program, independent study, internships, liberal arts/career combination, study abroad, teacher certification program, disabled student services, minority access to research centers, minority biomedical research.

FACILITIES

Housing: Coed dorms. **Special Academic Facilities/Equipment**: Art gallery, language lab, TV studio, radio station, recital hall, physical recreation center, Maguire Theatre. **Computers**: 50% of classrooms are wired, 100% of classrooms are wireless, 100% of public computers are PCs, network access in dorm rooms, network access in dorm lounges, online registration, online administrative functions (other than registration), remote student-access to Web through college's connection.

CAMPUS LIFE

Activities: Choral groups, dance, drama/theater, radio station, student government, student newspaper, student-run film society, yearbook. **Organizations**: 55 registered organizations, 5 honor societies, 2 religious organizations. 6 fraternities (2% men join), 4 sororities (2% women join). **Athletics (Intercollegiate)**: *Men*: Baseball, basketball, cross-country, soccer, swimming. *Women*: Basketball, cross-country, softball, swimming, volleyball. Environmental Initiatives: SEMPRA Energy Contract. Energy STAR purchases.

ADMISSIONS

Freshman Academic Profile: 2% in top 10% of high school class, 20% in top 25% of high school class, 62% in top 50% of high school class. 88% from public high schools. SAT Math middle 50% range 450–530. SAT Critical Reading middle 50% range 440–510. SAT Writing middle 50% range 420–500. ACT middle 50% range 18–22. TOEFL required of all international applicants, minimum paper TOEFL 513, minimum computer TOEFL 183. **Basis for Candidate Selection**: *Very important factors considered include*: Academic GPA, application essay, rigor of secondary school record. *Important factors considered include*: Recommendation(s), standardized test scores. *Other factors considered include*: Character/personal qualities, extracurricular activities, interview, talent/ability, volunteer work, work experience. **Freshman Admission Requirements**: High school diploma is required, and GED is accepted. *Academic units required*: 4 English, 3 math, 3 science (3 science labs), 2 foreign language, 2 social studies, 2 history, 2 academic electives. *Academic units recommended*: 4 English, 3 math, 3 science (3 science labs), 3 foreign language, 2 social studies, 2 history, 3 academic electives. **Freshman Admission Statistics**: 3,357 applied, 55% admitted, 23% enrolled. **Transfer Admission Requirements**: College transcript(s), essay or personal statement. Minimum college GPA of 2.0 required. Lowest grade transferable C. **General Admission Information**: Application fee $40. Regular notification is rolling. Non-fall registration accepted. Admission may be deferred for a maximum of 1 year. Credit and/or placement offered for CEEB Advanced Placement tests.

COSTS AND FINANCIAL AID

Annual in-state tuition $4,350. Out-of-state tuition $10,610. Room & board $8,083. Required fees $726. Average book expense $800. **Required Forms and Deadlines**: FAFSA, institution's own financial aid form, state aid form. Financial aid filing deadline 4/1. **Notification of Awards**: Applicants will be notified of awards on or about 4/15. **Types of Aid**: *Need-based scholarships/grants*: Pell, SEOG, state scholarships/grants, private scholarships, the school's own gift aid. *Loans*: FFEL Subsidized Stafford, FFEL Unsubsidized Stafford, FFEL PLUS, Federal Perkins, Federal College Work Study Grants, Federal Pell Grants, Federal Supplemental Education Opportunity Grants, State Educational Opportunity Program Grants. **Financial Aid Statistics**: 77% freshmen, 63% undergrads receive need-based scholarship or grant aid. 53% freshmen, 44% undergrads receive need-based self-help aid. 79% freshmen, 68% undergrads receive any aid. Highest amount earned per year from on-campus jobs $952.

STATE UNIVERSITY OF NEW YORK— COLLEGE AT ONEONTA

116 Alumni Hall, State University College, Oneonta, NY 13820
Phone: 607-432-2524 **E-mail**: admissions@oneonta.edu **CEEB Code**: 2542
Fax: 607-436-3074 **Website**: www.oneonta.edu **ACT Code**: 2940
Financial Aid Phone: 607-436-2532

This public school was founded in 1889. It has a 250-acre campus.

RATINGS

Admissions Selectivity Rating: 85   **Fire Safety Rating**: 71   **Green Rating**: 92

STUDENTS AND FACULTY

Enrollment: 5,541. **Student Body**: 58% female, 42% male, 2% out-of-state, 2% international (19 countries represented). African American 3%, Asian 2%, Caucasian 83%, Hispanic 4%. **Retention and Graduation**: 82% freshmen return for sophomore year. 37% freshmen graduate within 4 years. 46% grads go on to further study within 1 year. 13% grads pursue business degrees. **Faculty**: Student/faculty ratio 17:1. 259 full-time faculty, 78% hold PhDs. 99% faculty teach undergrads.

ACADEMICS

Degrees: Bachelor's, master's, post-bachelor's certificate, post-master's certificate. **Academic Requirements**: Arts/fine arts, computer literacy, English (including composition), foreign languages, history, humanities, mathematics, philosophy, sciences (biological or physical), social science. **Classes**: Most classes have 10–19 students. **Majors with Highest Enrollment**: Business/managerial economics, elementary education and teaching, music management and merchandising. **Disciplines with Highest Percentage of Degrees Awarded**: Education 20%, visual and performing arts 15%, English 12%, family and consumer sciences 9%, business/marketing 8%. **Special Study Options**: Cross-registration, distance learning, double major, English as a second language (ESL), honors program, independent study, internships, liberal arts/career combination, study abroad, teacher certification program. Variety of 3–1, 3–2, and 2–2 programs with other colleges and universities.

FACILITIES

Housing: Coed dorms, special housing for international students, special interest wings in residence halls, apartment-style suites in new hall. **Special Academic Facilities/Equipment**: Science discovery center, biological field station, weather station, planetarium, observatory, college camp, children's center. **Computers**: 12% of classrooms are wired, 100% of classrooms are wireless, 90% of public computers are PCs, 10% of public computers are Macs, network access in dorm rooms, network access in dorm lounges, online registration, online administrative functions (other than registration), remote student-access to Web through college's connection.

CAMPUS LIFE

Activities: Choral groups, concert band, dance, drama/theater, jazz band, literary magazine, music ensembles, musical theater, opera, pep band, radio station, student government, student newspaper, student-run film society, symphony orchestra, television station, yearbook. **Organizations**: 70 registered organizations, 14 honor societies, 4 religious organizations. 4 fraternities (5% men join), 6 sororities (5% women join). **Athletics (Intercollegiate)**: *Men*: Baseball, basketball, cross-country, lacrosse, soccer, swimming, tennis, track/field (indoor), track/field (outdoor), wrestling. *Women*: Basketball, cross-country, diving, field hockey, lacrosse, soccer, softball, swimming, tennis, track/field (indoor), track/field (outdoor), volleyball. Environmental Initiatives: Recycling program. Green construction standards. Protect Your Environment organization.

ADMISSIONS

Freshman Academic Profile: 12% in top 10% of high school class, 50% in top 25% of high school class, 94% in top 50% of high school class. 92% from public high schools. SAT Math middle 50% range 530–610. SAT Critical Reading middle 50% range 510–590. ACT middle 50% range 22–25. TOEFL required of all international applicants, minimum paper TOEFL 500, minimum computer TOEFL 173. **Basis for Candidate Selection**: *Very important factors considered include*: Rigor of secondary school record. *Important factors considered include*: Academic GPA, application essay, character/personal qualities, extracurricular activities, interview, standardized test scores, talent/ability, volunteer work. *Other factors considered include*: Alumni/ae relation, class rank, level of applicant's interest, racial/ethnic status, recommendation(s), work experience. **Freshman Admission Requirements**: High school diploma is required, and GED is accepted. *Academic units required*: 4 English, 2 math, 2 science (2 science labs), 2 foreign language, 3 social studies. *Academic units recommended*: 3 math, 3 science, 3 foreign language. **Freshman Admission Statistics**: 11,347 applied, 43% admitted, 23% enrolled. **Transfer Admission Requirements**: College transcript(s). Minimum college GPA of 2.0 required. Lowest grade transferable C-. **General Admission Information**: Application fee $40. Regular notification is rolling. Non-fall registration accepted. Admission may be deferred for a maximum of 1 year. Credit offered for CEEB Advanced Placement tests.

COSTS AND FINANCIAL AID

Annual in-state tuition $4,350. Out-of-state tuition $10,610. Room & board $7,696. Required fees $1,097. Average book expense $850. **Required Forms and Deadlines**: FAFSA, state aid form. Financial aid filing deadline 2/15. **Notification of Awards**: Applicants will be notified of awards on a rolling basis beginning on or about 3/1. **Types of Aid**: *Need-based scholarships/grants*: Pell, SEOG, state scholarships/grants, private scholarships, the school's own gift aid. *Loans*: FFEL Subsidized Stafford, FFEL Unsubsidized Stafford, FFEL PLUS, Federal Perkins. **Financial Aid Statistics**: 44% freshmen, 49% undergrads receive need-based scholarship or grant aid. 43% freshmen, 47% undergrads receive need-based self-help aid. 2 undergrads receive athletic scholarships. 61% freshmen, 70% undergrads receive any aid. Highest amount earned per year from on-campus jobs $1,800.

STATE UNIVERSITY OF NEW YORK—CORTLAND

PO Box 2000, Cortland, NY 13045-0900
Phone: 607-753-4712 **E-mail**: admissions@cortland.edu **CEEB Code**: 2538
Fax: 607-753-5998 **Website**: www.cortland.edu **ACT Code**: 2932
Financial Aid Phone: 607-753-4717

This public school was founded in 1868. It has a 191-acre campus.

RATINGS
Admissions Selectivity Rating: 60*   **Fire Safety Rating**: 60*   **Green Rating**: 60*

STUDENTS AND FACULTY
Enrollment: 5,770. **Student Body**: 57% female, 43% male, 3% out-of-state. African American 3%, Asian 2%, Caucasian 79%, Hispanic 5%. **Retention and Graduation**: 78% freshmen return for sophomore year. **Faculty**: Student/faculty ratio 17:1. 299 full-time faculty, 77% hold PhDs. 97% faculty teach undergrads.

ACADEMICS
Degrees: Bachelor's, master's, post-bachelor's certificate, post-master's certificate. **Classes**: Most classes have 20–29 students. Most lab/discussion sections have 20–29 students. **Disciplines with Highest Percentage of Degrees Awarded**: Education 50%, communications/journalism 12%, parks and recreation 12%, social sciences 10% 9%, health professions and related sciences 4%. **Special Study Options**: Cooperative education program, cross-registration, distance learning, double major, dual enrollment, exchange student program (domestic), honors program, independent study, internships, liberal arts/career combination, student-designed major, study abroad, teacher certification program. Students eligible to participate in more than 400 international study programs offered via SUNY.

FACILITIES
Housing: Coed dorms, apartments for single students, special housing for international students, fraternity/sorority housing. **Special Academic Facilities/Equipment**: Natural science museum, greenhouse, center for speech and hearing disorders, classrooms with integrated technologies, specialized labs to support various program offerings. **Computers**: 20% of classrooms are wired, 42% of classrooms are wireless, 75% of public computers are PCs, 25% of public computers are Macs, network access in dorm rooms, network access in dorm lounges, online registration, online administrative functions (other than registration), remote student-access to Web through college's connection.

CAMPUS LIFE
Activities: Choral groups, concert band, dance, drama/theater, jazz band, literary magazine, music ensembles, musical theater, radio station, student government, student newspaper, student-run film society, symphony orchestra, television station, yearbook. **Organizations**: 100 registered organizations, 16 honor societies, 3 religious organizations. 2 fraternities, 5 sororities. **Athletics (Intercollegiate)**: *Men*: Baseball, basketball, cheerleading, cross-country, diving, football, gymnastics, ice hockey, lacrosse, soccer, swimming, track/field (indoor), track/field (outdoor), wrestling. *Women*: Basketball, cheerleading,

cross-country, diving, field hockey, golf, gymnastics, ice hockey, lacrosse, soccer, softball, swimming, tennis, track/field (indoor), track/field (outdoor), volleyball.

ADMISSIONS
Freshman Academic Profile: 9% in top 10% of high school class, 45% in top 25% of high school class, 87% in top 50% of high school class. 91% from public high schools. SAT Math middle 50% range 550–480. TOEFL required of all international applicants, minimum paper TOEFL 550. **Basis for Candidate Selection**: *Very important factors considered include*: Rigor of secondary school record, standardized test scores. *Important factors considered include*: Application essay, extracurricular activities, recommendation(s), talent/ability. *Other factors considered include*: Alumni/ae relation, class rank, geographical residence, interview, racial/ethnic status, state residency, volunteer work, work experience. **Freshman Admission Requirements**: High school diploma is required, and GED is accepted. *Academic units required*: 4 English, 3 math, 3 science (3 science labs), 3 foreign language, 4 social studies. *Academic units recommended*: 4 math, 4 science, 4 foreign language. **Freshman Admission Statistics**: 10,096 applied, 47% admitted, 23% enrolled. **Transfer Admission Requirements**: High school transcript, college transcript(s). Minimum college GPA of 2.5 required. Lowest grade transferable C-. **General Admission Information**: Application fee $40. Early decision application deadline 11/15. Regular notification is rolling. Admission may be deferred for a maximum of 1 year. Credit offered for CEEB Advanced Placement tests.

COSTS AND FINANCIAL AID
Average book expense $800. **Required Forms and Deadlines**: FAFSA. Financial aid filing deadline 4/1. **Notification of Awards**: Applicants will be notified of awards on a rolling basis beginning on or about 3/1. **Financial Aid Statistics**: 45% freshmen, 50% undergrads receive need-based scholarship or grant aid. 46% freshmen, 51% undergrads receive need-based self-help aid.

STATE UNIVERSITY OF NEW YORK—DELHI

Bush Hall, 2 Main Street, Delhi, NY 13753
Phone: 607-746-4550 **E-mail**: enroll@Delhi.edu
Fax: 607-746-4104 **Website**: www.delhi.edu

This is a public school.

RATINGS
Admissions Selectivity Rating: 60*   **Fire Safety Rating**: 60*   **Green Rating**: 60*

STUDENTS AND FACULTY
Enrollment: 1,791. **Student Body**: 44% female, 56% male, 4% out-of-state. African American 11%, Asian 2%, Caucasian 84%, Hispanic 7%. **Faculty**: Student/faculty ratio 15:1.

ACADEMICS
Degrees: Associate, bachelor's, certificate, terminal. **Special Study Options**: Distance learning, English as a second language (ESL), honors program, internships, student-designed major, weekend college.

FACILITIES
Housing: Coed dorms.

CAMPUS LIFE
Activities: Choral groups, dance, drama/theater, music ensembles, musical theater, radio station, student government, student newspaper, yearbook. **Athletics (Intercollegiate)**: *Men*: Basketball, cross-country, diving, golf, lacrosse, soccer, swimming, tennis, track/field (indoor), track/field (outdoor), wrestling. *Women*: Basketball, cross-country, diving, golf, soccer, softball, swimming, tennis, track/field (indoor), track/field (outdoor), volleyball.

ADMISSIONS
Basis for Candidate Selection: *Very important factors considered include*: Rigor of secondary school record. *Important factors considered include*: Character/personal qualities, recommendation(s), talent/ability. *Other factors considered include*: Alumni/ae relation, application essay, class rank, extracurricular activities, geographical residence, interview, standardized test scores, state residency, volunteer work, work experience. **Freshman Admission Requirements**: High school diploma is required, and GED is accepted. *Academic units required*: 4 English, 1 math, 1 science, 3 social studies, 1 history. *Academic units recommended*: 2 math, 2 science (1 science lab). **Transfer Admission Requirements**: High school transcript, college transcript(s). Lowest grade transferable C. **General Admission Information**: Application fee $30. Regular notification is rolling. Non-fall registration accepted. Admission may be deferred for a maximum of 1 year.

COSTS AND FINANCIAL AID

Annual in-state tuition $4,350. Out-of-state tuition $10,610. Room & board $6,830. Average book expense $650. **Financial Aid Statistics**: 66% undergrads receive need-based scholarship or grant aid. 68% undergrads receive need-based self-help aid.

STATE UNIVERSITY OF NEW YORK— EMPIRE STATE COLLEGE

111 West Avenue, Saratoga, NY 12866
Phone: 518-587-2100 **E-mail**: admissions@esc.edu **CEEB Code**: 2214
Fax: 518-587-9759 **Website**: www.esc.edu **ACT Code**: 2737
Financial Aid Phone: 518-587-2100

This public school was founded in 1971.

RATINGS
Admissions Selectivity Rating: 60*   **Fire Safety Rating**: 60*   **Green Rating**: 60*

STUDENTS AND FACULTY

Enrollment: 7,881. **Student Body**: 79% female, 21% male, 8% out-of-state, 8% international. African American 18%, Asian 2%, Caucasian 86%, Hispanic 8%. **Faculty**: Student/faculty ratio 11:1. 155 full-time faculty, 96% hold PhDs. 99% faculty teach undergrads.

ACADEMICS

Degrees: Associate, bachelor's, master's. **Academic Requirements**: Arts/fine arts, computer literacy, English (including composition), foreign languages, history, humanities, mathematics, philosophy, sciences (biological or physical), social science. Students must satisfy the general education requirements set forth by the State University of New York (including but not limited to the areas selected above). **Majors with Highest Enrollment**: Business/commerce, community organization and advocacy, multi/interdisciplinary studies. **Disciplines with Highest Percentage of Degrees Awarded**: Business/marketing 40%, public administration and social services 19%, interdisciplinary studies 8%, English 8%, psychology 7%, physical sciences 6%. **Special Study Options**: Cross-registration, distance learning, double major, dual enrollment, external degree program, independent study, internships, student-designed major, student-designed courses of study.

FACILITIES

Computers: Online registration, online administrative functions (other than registration).

CAMPUS LIFE

Activities: Literary magazine.

ADMISSIONS

Freshman Academic Profile: TOEFL required of all international applicants, minimum paper TOEFL 550, minimum computer TOEFL 213. **Basis for Candidate Selection**: *Very important factors considered include*: Application essay, character/personal qualities. *Other factors considered include*: Recommendation(s), rigor of secondary school record, talent/ability. **Freshman Admission Requirements**: High school diploma is required, and GED is accepted. **Freshman Admission Statistics**: 1,360 applied, 76% admitted, 49% enrolled. **Transfer Admission Requirements**: High school transcript, essay or personal statement. Lowest grade transferable C. **General Admission Information**: Non-fall registration accepted. Admission may be deferred for a maximum of 3 years.

COSTS AND FINANCIAL AID

Annual in-state tuition $4,350. Out-of-state tuition $10,610. Required fees $556. **Required Forms and Deadlines**: FAFSA, state aid form. Financial aid filing deadline 4/1. **Types of Aid**: *Need-based scholarships/grants*: Pell, SEOG, state scholarships/grants, private scholarships, the school's own gift aid. *Loans*: FFEL Subsidized Stafford, FFEL Unsubsidized Stafford, FFEL PLUS, Federal Perkins. **Student Employment**: Federal Work-Study Program available. **Financial Aid Statistics**: 8% undergrads receive need-based scholarship or grant aid. 30% undergrads receive need-based self-help aid. 43% undergrads receive any aid.

STATE UNIVERSITY OF NEW YORK— ERIE COMMUNITY COLLEGE, CITY CAMPUS

121 Ellicott Street, Buffalo, NY 14203-2698
Phone: 716-851-1155 **E-mail**: hannen@ecc.edu
Fax: 716-851-1129 **Website**: www.ecc.edu **ACT Code**: 2742
Financial Aid Phone: 716-851-1177

This public school was founded in 1971.

RATINGS
Admissions Selectivity Rating: 60*   **Fire Safety Rating**: 60*   **Green Rating**: 60*

STUDENTS AND FACULTY

Enrollment: 1,982. **Student Body**: 64% female, 36% male. African American 39%, Asian 2%, Caucasian 48%, Hispanic 9%, Native American 2%. **Retention and Graduation**: 41% grads go on to further study within 1 year. **Faculty**: Student/faculty ratio 16:1. 101 full-time faculty. 100% faculty teach undergrads.

ACADEMICS

Degrees: Associate, certificate. **Academic Requirements**: Computer literacy, English (including composition), humanities, mathematics, sciences (biological or physical), social science. **Special Study Options**: Cooperative education program, cross-registration, distance learning, double major, dual admission with 4-year institution, dual enrollment, English as a second language (ESL), exchange student program (domestic), honors program, independent study, internships, liberal arts/career combination, student-designed major, study abroad, teacher certification program, weekend college.

FACILITIES

Housing: An up-to-date listing of housing options in the local area is available from the campus Dean of Students office. **Computers**: Remote student-access to Web through college's connection.

CAMPUS LIFE

Activities: Choral groups, dance, music ensembles, student government, student newspaper, yearbook. **Organizations**: 34 registered organizations, 3 honor societies, 1 religious organization. **Athletics (Intercollegiate)**: *Men*: Baseball, basketball, cross-country, diving, golf, ice hockey, soccer, swimming, track/field (outdoor). *Women*: Basketball, cross-country, diving, golf, soccer, softball, swimming, track/field (outdoor).

ADMISSIONS

Freshman Academic Profile: TOEFL required of all international applicants. **Basis for Candidate Selection**: *Other factors considered include*: Class rank, rigor of secondary school record, standardized test scores. **Freshman Admission Requirements**: High school diploma is required, and GED is accepted. **Transfer Admission Requirements**: College transcript(s), standardized test score. Lowest grade transferable C. **General Admission Information**: Nonfall registration accepted. Common Application accepted. Credit and/or placement offered for CEEB Advanced Placement tests.

COSTS AND FINANCIAL AID

Annual in-state tuition $2,475. Out-of-state tuition $4,950. Required fees $100. **Required Forms and Deadlines**: FAFSA, institution's own financial aid form, state aid form. Financial aid filing deadline 4/30. **Notification of Awards**: Applicants will be notified of awards on a rolling basis beginning on or about 5/1. **Types of Aid**: *Need-based scholarships/grants*: Pell, SEOG, state scholarships/grants, ECC Foundation. *Loans*: FFEL Subsidized Stafford, FFEL Unsubsidized Stafford, FFEL PLUS. **Student Employment**: Federal Work-Study Program available. Off-campus job opportunities are excellent.

STATE UNIVERSITY OF NEW YORK—
ERIE COMMUNITY COLLEGE, NORTH CAMPUS

6205 Main street, Williamsville, NY 14221-7095
Phone: 716-851-1455 **E-mail:** smith-br@ecc.edu
Fax: 716-851-1429 **Website:** www.ecc.edu **ACT Code:** 2740
Financial Aid Phone: 716-851-1477

This public school was founded in 1946. It has a 120-acre campus.

RATINGS
Admissions Selectivity Rating: 60*   **Fire Safety Rating:** 60*   **Green Rating:** 60*

STUDENTS AND FACULTY
Enrollment: 4,301. **Student Body:** 51% female, 49% male, 1% international (17 countries represented). African American 10%, Asian 2%, Caucasian 85%, Hispanic 2%. **Retention and Graduation:** 37% grads go on to further study within 1 year. **Faculty:** Student/faculty ratio 19:1. 169 full-time faculty. 100% faculty teach undergrads.

ACADEMICS
Degrees: Associate, certificate. **Academic Requirements:** Computer literacy, English (including composition), humanities, mathematics, sciences (biological or physical), social science. **Special Study Options:** Cooperative education program, cross-registration, distance learning, double major, dual enrollment, English as a second language (ESL), exchange student program (domestic), honors program, independent study, internships, liberal arts/career combination, student-designed major, study abroad, teacher certification program, weekend college. Dual admissions with 4-year institutions and bilingual education.

FACILITIES
Housing: An up-to-date listing of housing options in the local area is available from the campus Dean of Students office. **Computers:** Remote student-access to Web through college's connection.

CAMPUS LIFE
Activities: Dance, drama/theater, jazz band, literary magazine, music ensembles, musical theater, radio station, student government, student newspaper, yearbook. **Organizations:** 29 registered organizations, 3 honor societies, 1 religious organization. **Athletics (Intercollegiate):** *Men:* Baseball, basketball, cross-country, diving, golf, ice hockey, soccer, swimming, track/field (outdoor). *Women:* Basketball, cross-country, diving, golf, soccer, softball, swimming, track/field (outdoor).

ADMISSIONS
Freshman Academic Profile: TOEFL required of all international applicants. **Basis for Candidate Selection:** *Other factors considered include:* Class rank, rigor of secondary school record, standardized test scores. **Freshman Admission Requirements:** High school diploma is required, and GED is accepted. **Transfer Admission Requirements:** College transcript(s), standardized test score. Lowest grade transferable C. **General Admission Information:** Nonfall registration accepted. Common Application accepted. Credit and/or placement offered for CEEB Advanced Placement tests.

COSTS AND FINANCIAL AID
Annual in-state tuition $2,475. Out-of-state tuition $4,950. Required fees $100. **Required Forms and Deadlines:** FAFSA, institution's own financial aid form, state aid form. Financial aid filing deadline 4/30. **Notification of Awards:** Applicants will be notified of awards on a rolling basis beginning on or about 6/15. **Types of Aid:** *Need-based scholarships/grants:* Pell, SEOG, state scholarships/grants, ECC Foundation. *Loans:* FFEL Subsidized Stafford, FFEL Unsubsidized Stafford, FFEL PLUS. **Student Employment:** Federal Work-Study Program available. Off-campus job opportunities are excellent.

STATE UNIVERSITY OF NEW YORK—
ERIE COMMUNITY COLLEGE, SOUTH CAMPUS

4041 Southwestern Boulevard, Orchard Park, NY 14127-2199
Phone: 716-851-1655 **E-mail:** rosinskip@ecc.edu
Fax: 716-851-1629 **Website:** www.ecc.edu. **ACT Code:** 2741
Financial Aid Phone: 716-851-1677

This public school was founded in 1974.

RATINGS
Admissions Selectivity Rating: 60*   **Fire Safety Rating:** 60*   **Green Rating:** 60*

STUDENTS AND FACULTY
Enrollment: 2,660. **Student Body:** 46% female, 54% male. African American 2%, Caucasian 96%. **Retention and Graduation:** 37% grads go on to further study within 1 year. **Faculty:** Student/faculty ratio 17:1. 111 full-time faculty. 100% faculty teach undergrads.

ACADEMICS
Degrees: Associate, certificate. **Academic Requirements:** Computer literacy, English (including composition), humanities, mathematics, sciences (biological or physical), social science. **Special Study Options:** Cooperative education program, cross-registration, distance learning, double major, dual admissions with 4-year insitutions, dual enrollment, English as a second language (ESL), exchange student program (domestic), honors program, independent study, internships, liberal arts/career combination, student-designed major, study abroad, teacher certification program, weekend college.

FACILITIES
Housing: An up-to-date listing of housing options in the local area is available from the campus Dean of Students office. **Computers:** Remote student-access to Web through college's connection.

CAMPUS LIFE
Activities: Choral groups, dance, drama/theater, literary magazine, music ensembles, radio station, student government, student newspaper, yearbook. **Organizations:** 18 registered organizations, 2 honor societies, 1 religious organization. **Athletics (Intercollegiate):** *Men:* Baseball, basketball, cross-country, diving, golf, ice hockey, soccer, swimming, track/field (outdoor). *Women:* Basketball, cross-country, diving, golf, soccer, softball, swimming, track/field (outdoor).

ADMISSIONS
Freshman Academic Profile: TOEFL required of all international applicants. **Basis for Candidate Selection:** *Other factors considered include:* Class rank, rigor of secondary school record, standardized test scores. **Freshman Admission Requirements:** High school diploma is required, and GED is accepted. **Transfer Admission Requirements:** College transcript(s), standardized test score. Lowest grade transferable C. **General Admission Information:** Nonfall registration accepted. Common Application accepted. Credit and/or placement offered for CEEB Advanced Placement tests.

COSTS AND FINANCIAL AID
Annual in-state tuition $2,475. Out-of-state tuition $4,950. Required fees $100. **Required Forms and Deadlines:** FAFSA, institution's own financial aid form, state aid form. Financial aid filing deadline 4/30. **Notification of Awards:** Applicants will be notified of awards on a rolling basis beginning on or about 6/15. **Types of Aid:** *Need-based scholarships/grants:* Pell, SEOG, state scholarships/grants, ECC Foundation. *Loans:* FFEL Subsidized Stafford, FFEL Unsubsidized Stafford, FFEL PLUS. **Student Employment:** Federal Work-Study Program available. Off-campus job opportunities are excellent.

STATE UNIVERSITY OF NEW YORK—FARMINGDALE

Admissions Office, 2350 Broadhollow Road, Farmingdale, NY 11735
Phone: 631-420-2200 **E-mail:** admissions@farmingdale.edu
Fax: 631-420-2633 **Website:** www.farmingdale.edu

This public school was founded in 1912. It has a 380-acre campus.

RATINGS
Admissions Selectivity Rating: 60*   **Fire Safety Rating:** 60*   **Green Rating:** 60*

STUDENTS AND FACULTY
Enrollment: 3,909. **Student Body:** African American 15%, Asian 4%, Caucasian 62%, Hispanic 9%. **Faculty:** Student/faculty ratio 21:1. 187 full-time faculty, 50% hold PhDs. 100% faculty teach undergrads.

ACADEMICS
Degrees: Associate, bachelor's, certificate, terminal. **Academic Requirements:** English (including composition), humanities, mathematics, sciences (biological or physical), social science. **Classes:** Most classes have 20–29 students. **Disciplines with Highest Percentage of Degrees Awarded:** Engineering 47%, business/marketing 37%. **Special Study Options:** Distance learning, double major, dual enrollment, internships, study abroad.

FACILITIES
Housing: Coed dorms. **Computers:** 85% of public computers are PCs, 10% of public computers are Macs, 5% of public computers are UNIX, online registration, online administrative functions (other than registration), remote student-access to Web through college's connection.

CAMPUS LIFE
Activities: Drama/theater, radio station, student government, student newspaper, yearbook. **Athletics (Intercollegiate):** *Men:* Baseball, basketball, cross-country, golf, lacrosse, soccer, track/field (indoor), track/field (outdoor). *Women:* Basketball, cross-country, soccer, softball, track/field (indoor), track/field (outdoor), volleyball.

ADMISSIONS
Freshman Academic Profile: TOEFL required of all international applicants, minimum paper TOEFL 500, minimum computer TOEFL 173. **Basis for Candidate Selection:** *Very important factors considered include:* Class rank, rigor of secondary school record. *Important factors considered include:* Talent/ability. *Other factors considered include:* Alumni/ae relation, application essay, character/personal qualities, extracurricular activities, interview, recommendation(s), standardized test scores, volunteer work, work experience. **Freshman Admission Requirements:** High school diploma is required, and GED is accepted. *Academic units required:* 4 English, 2 math, 1 science (1 science lab), 4 social studies. *Academic units recommended:* 4 English, 4 math, 3 science (3 science labs), 4 social studies. **Freshman Admission Statistics:** 2,382 applied, 68% admitted, 56% enrolled. **Transfer Admission Requirements:** High school transcript, college transcript(s), statement of good standing from prior institution(s). Minimum college GPA of 2.0 required. Lowest grade transferable C. **General Admission Information:** Application fee $30. Regular notification is rolling. Non-fall registration accepted. Admission may be deferred for a maximum of 1 year. Common Application not accepted. Credit and/or placement offered for CEEB Advanced Placement tests.

COSTS AND FINANCIAL AID
Out-of-state tuition $10,300. Room & board $6,810. Required fees $710. Average book expense $800. **Required Forms and Deadlines:** FAFSA, institution's own financial aid form. **Types of Aid:** *Need-based scholarships/grants:* Pell, SEOG, state scholarships/grants. *Loans:* Direct Subsidized Stafford, Direct Unsubsidized Stafford, Direct PLUS, FFEL Subsidized Stafford, FFEL Unsubsidized Stafford, FFEL PLUS, Federal Perkins, Federal Nursing, state loans. **Student Employment:** Federal Work-Study Program available. Institutional employment available. Off-campus job opportunities are good.

STATE UNIVERSITY OF NEW YORK—FASHION INSTITUTE OF TECHNOLOGY

Seventh Avenue at Twenty-seventh Street, New York, NY 10001
Phone: 212-217-7675 **E-mail:** fitinfo@fitsuny.edu
Website: www.fitnyc.suny.edu

This public school was founded in 1944.

RATINGS
Admissions Selectivity Rating: 60*   **Fire Safety Rating:** 60*   **Green Rating:** 60*

STUDENTS AND FACULTY
Student Body: 17% out-of-state.

FACILITIES
Housing: Coed dorms, men's dorms, women's dorms, apartments for single students.

CAMPUS LIFE
Activities: Literary magazine, radio station, student government, student newspaper, yearbook. **Organizations:** 70 registered organizations, 7 honor societies, 1 religious organization.

ADMISSIONS
Freshman Academic Profile: 11% in top 10% of high school class, 32% in top 25% of high school class, 68% in top 50% of high school class. **General Admission Information:** Regular application deadline 1/15.

COSTS AND FINANCIAL AID
Annual in-state tuition $2,500. Out-of-state tuition $5,950. Room & board $5,600. Required fees $210. Average book expense $1,200. **Required Forms and Deadlines:** FAFSA, institution's own financial aid form, state aid form. **Types of Aid:** *Loans:* FFEL Subsidized Stafford, FFEL PLUS. **Student Employment:** Federal Work-Study Program available. **Financial Aid Statistics:** Highest amount earned per year from on-campus jobs $1,400.

STATE UNIVERSITY OF NEW YORK—FREDONIA

178 Central Avenue, Fredonia, NY 14063
Phone: 716-673-3251 **E-mail:** admissions.office@fredonia.edu **CEEB Code:** 2539
Fax: 716-673-3249 **Website:** www.fredonia.edu **ACT Code:** 2934
Financial Aid Phone: 716-673-3253

This public school was founded in 1826. It has a 249-acre campus.

RATINGS
Admissions Selectivity Rating: 82   **Fire Safety Rating:** 77   **Green Rating:** 60*

STUDENTS AND FACULTY
Enrollment: 5,026. **Student Body:** 56% female, 44% male, 2% out-of-state. African American 2%, Asian 2%, Caucasian 85%, Hispanic 3%. **Retention and Graduation:** 84% freshmen return for sophomore year. 50% freshmen graduate within 4 years. 32% grads go on to further study within 1 year. **Faculty:** Student/faculty ratio 16:1. 244 full-time faculty, 80% hold PhDs. 100% faculty teach undergrads.

ACADEMICS
Degrees: Bachelor's, master's, post-master's certificate. **Academic Requirements:** Arts/fine arts, English (including composition), foreign languages, history, humanities, mathematics, sciences (biological or physical), social science. **Classes:** Most classes have 10–19 students. Most lab/discussion sections have 20–29 students. **Majors with Highest Enrollment:** Business administration/management, elementary education and teaching, music. **Disciplines with Highest Percentage of Degrees Awarded:** Education 34%, business/marketing 12%, communications/journalism 10%, social sciences 9%, psychology 7%, visual and performing arts 7%. **Special Study Options:** Accelerated program, cross-registration, distance learning, double major, exchange student program (domestic), honors program, independent study, internships, liberal arts/career combination, student-designed major, study abroad, teacher certification program. Off-campus study opportunities.

FACILITIES

Housing: Coed dorms, men's dorms, women's dorms, apartments for single students, special housing for disabled students, smoke-free residence hall options. **Special Academic Facilities/Equipment**: Art center, education and local history museums, teacher education research center, developmental reading center, Sheldon Communications Lab, SMART classrooms, greenhouse. **Computers**: 25% of classrooms are wired, 25% of classrooms are wireless, 70% of public computers are PCs, 30% of public computers are Macs, network access in dorm rooms, network access in dorm lounges, online registration, online administrative functions (other than registration), support for handheld computing, remote student-access to Web through college's connection.

CAMPUS LIFE

Activities: Choral groups, concert band, dance, drama/theater, jazz band, literary magazine, music ensembles, musical theater, opera, radio station, student government, student newspaper, symphony orchestra, television station. **Organizations**: 152 registered organizations, 22 honor societies, 5 religious organizations. 3 fraternities (5% men join), 3 sororities (3% women join). **Athletics (Intercollegiate)**: *Men*: Baseball, basketball, cheerleading, cross-country, diving, ice hockey, soccer, swimming, track/field (indoor), track/field (outdoor). *Women*: Basketball, cheerleading, cross-country, diving, lacrosse, soccer, softball, swimming, tennis, track/field (indoor), track/field (outdoor), volleyball. Environmental Initiatives: Campus owned gas well. RecycleMania. Sustainability Committee.

ADMISSIONS

Freshman Academic Profile: 14% in top 10% of high school class, 50% in top 25% of high school class, 90% in top 50% of high school class. 75% from public high schools. SAT Math middle 50% range 510–600. SAT Critical Reading middle 50% range 500–590. ACT middle 50% range 21–26. TOEFL required of all international applicants, minimum paper TOEFL 500, minimum computer TOEFL 173. **Basis for Candidate Selection**: *Very important factors considered include*: Academic GPA, rigor of secondary school record. *Important factors considered include*: Class rank, extracurricular activities, recommendation(s), standardized test scores. *Other factors considered include*: Alumni/ae relation, application essay, character/personal qualities, first generation, level of applicant's interest, racial/ethnic status, talent/ability, volunteer work, work experience. **Freshman Admission Requirements**: High school diploma is required, and GED is accepted. *Academic units required*: 4 English, 3 math, 3 science, 3 foreign language, 4 social studies. *Academic units recommended*: 4 English, 4 math, 4 science, 3 foreign language, 4 social studies. **Freshman Admission Statistics**: 5,988 applied, 54% admitted, 31% enrolled. **Transfer Admission Requirements**: College transcript(s). Minimum college GPA of 2.0 required. Lowest grade transferable D. **General Admission Information**: Application fee $40. Early decision application deadline 11/1. Regular notification is rolling. Non-fall registration accepted. Admission may be deferred for a maximum of 1 year. Credit and/or placement offered for CEEB Advanced Placement tests.

COSTS AND FINANCIAL AID

Annual in-state tuition $4,350. Out-of-state tuition $10,610. Room & board $7,880. Required fees $1,132. Average book expense $1,000. **Required Forms and Deadlines**: FAFSA, state aid form. Financial aid filing deadline 5/15. **Notification of Awards**: Applicants will be notified of awards on a rolling basis beginning on or about 3/10. **Types of Aid**: *Need-based scholarships/grants*: Pell, SEOG, state scholarships/grants, private scholarships, the school's own gift aid. *Loans*: FFEL Subsidized Stafford, FFEL Unsubsidized Stafford, FFEL PLUS, Federal Perkins. **Student Employment**: Federal Work-Study Program available. Off-campus job opportunities are good. **Financial Aid Statistics**: 54% freshmen, 55% undergrads receive need-based scholarship or grant aid. 51% freshmen, 53% undergrads receive need-based self-help aid. 81% freshmen, 85% undergrads receive any aid. Highest amount earned per year from on-campus jobs $1,000.

STATE UNIVERSITY OF NEW YORK AT GENESEO

Best 368

1 College Circle, Geneseo, NY 14454-1401
Phone: 585-245-5571 **E-mail**: admissions@geneseo.edu **CEEB Code**: 2540
Fax: 585-245-5550 **Website**: www.geneseo.edu **ACT Code**: 2936
Financial Aid Phone: 585-245-5731

This public school was founded in 1871. It has a 220-acre campus.

RATINGS

Admissions Selectivity Rating: 94   **Fire Safety Rating**: 84   **Green Rating**: 77

STUDENTS AND FACULTY

Enrollment: 5,344. **Student Body**: 59% female, 41% male, 1% out-of-state, 3% international (30 countries represented). African American 2%, Asian 6%, Caucasian 76%, Hispanic 3%. **Retention and Graduation**: 92% freshmen return for sophomore year. 62% freshmen graduate within 4 years. 39% grads go on to further study within 1 year. 46% grads pursue arts and sciences degrees. 13% grads pursue business degrees. 2% grads pursue law degrees. 3% grads pursue medical degrees. **Faculty**: Student/faculty ratio 19:1. 245 full-time faculty, 86% hold PhDs. 100% faculty teach undergrads.

ACADEMICS

Degrees: Bachelor's, master's. **Academic Requirements**: Arts/fine arts, critical writing and reading, English (including composition), foreign languages, history, humanities, mathematics, non-Western traditions, numeric and symbolic reasoning, sciences (biological or physical), social science, U.S. history. **Classes**: Most classes have 20–29 students. **Majors with Highest Enrollment**: Biology/biological sciences, business administration/management, elementary education and teaching. **Disciplines with Highest Percentage of Degrees Awarded**: Education 19%, business/marketing 15%, social sciences 12%, psychology 9%, biological/life sciences 9%, English 7%. **Special Study Options**: Cross-registration, double major, honors program, independent study, internships, study abroad, teacher certification program. Albany semester, Washington semester, 3/2 engineering, 3/2 MBA, 4/1 MBA, 3/3 physical therapy, 3/4 dentistry, 3/4 optometry, 3/4 osteopathic medicine, 2/4 program with Upstate Medical University.

FACILITIES

Housing: Coed dorms, town houses and special-interest housing are available (e.g., math and science). Some fraternities and sororities have housing independent of college. **Special Academic Facilities/Equipment**: 3 theaters, electron microscopes, new technology building. **Computers**: 100% of classrooms are wired, 100% of classrooms are wireless, 85% of public computers are PCs, 13% of public computers are Macs, 2% of public computers are UNIX, network access in dorm rooms, network access in dorm lounges, online registration, online administrative functions (other than registration), support for handheld computing, remote student-access to Web through college's connection.

CAMPUS LIFE

Activities: Choral groups, dance, drama/theater, jazz band, literary magazine, music ensembles, musical theater, radio station, student government, student newspaper, symphony orchestra, television station, yearbook. **Organizations**: 169 registered organizations, 14 honor societies, 5 religious organizations. 9 fraternities (9% men join), 12 sororities (13% women join). **Athletics (Intercollegiate)**: *Men*: Basketball, cross-country, diving, ice hockey, lacrosse, soccer, swimming, track/field (indoor), track/field (outdoor). *Women*: Basketball, cross-country, diving, equestrian sports, field hockey, lacrosse, soccer, softball, swimming, tennis, track/field (indoor), track/field (outdoor), volleyball. **Environmental Initiatives**: Signing of the Presidents Climate Commitment. Establishment of Geneseo's Environmental Impact and Sustainability Task Force. Gold Lecture Series—Live Green Task Force Work/Initiatives.

ADMISSIONS

Freshman Academic Profile: 54% in top 10% of high school class, 89% in top 25% of high school class, 99% in top 50% of high school class. 81% from public high schools. SAT Math middle 50% range 620–690. SAT Critical Reading middle 50% range 600–690. ACT middle 50% range 28–30. TOEFL required of all international applicants, minimum paper TOEFL 525, minimum computer TOEFL 197. **Basis for Candidate Selection**: *Very important factors considered include*: Rigor of secondary school record, standardized test scores. *Important factors considered include*: Academic GPA, application essay, extracurricular activities, racial/ethnic status, recommendation(s), talent/ability. *Other factors considered include*: Character/personal qualities, class rank, volunteer work. **Freshman Admission Requirements**: High school diploma is required, and GED is accepted. *Academic units recommended*: 4 English, 4 math, 4 science, 4 foreign language, 4 social studies. **Freshman Admission Statistics**: 9,043 applied, 41% admitted, 29% enrolled. **Transfer Admission Requirements**: College transcript(s). Minimum college GPA of 2.0 required. Lowest grade transferable D. **General Admission Information**: Application fee $40. Early decision application deadline 11/15. Regular application deadline 1/15. Regular notification is rolling. Non-fall registration accepted. Admission may be deferred for a maximum of 1 year. Credit offered for CEEB Advanced Placement tests.

COSTS AND FINANCIAL AID

Annual in-state tuition $4,350. Out-of-state tuition $10,610. Room & board $7,788. Required fees $1,210. Average book expense $800. **Required Forms and Deadlines**: FAFSA, state aid form. Financial aid filing deadline 2/15. **Notification of Awards**: Applicants will be notified of awards on a rolling basis beginning on or about 3/15. **Types of Aid**: *Need-based scholarships/grants*: Pell, SEOG, state scholarships/grants, private scholarships, the school's own gift aid. *Loans*: FFEL Subsidized Stafford, FFEL Unsubsidized Stafford, FFEL PLUS, Federal Perkins, state loans, alternative loans. **Financial Aid Statistics**: 31% freshmen, 37% undergrads receive need-based scholarship or grant aid. 34% freshmen, 39% undergrads receive need-based self-help aid. 70% freshmen, 75% undergrads receive any aid. Highest amount earned per year from on-campus jobs $2,100.

STATE UNIVERSITY OF NEW YORK— HERKIMER COUNTY COMMUNITY COLLEGE

Admissions Office, 100 Reservoir Road, Herkimer, NY 13350
Phone: 315-866-0300 **E-mail**: hughessj@herkimer.edu
Fax: 315-866-0062 **Website**: www.herkimer.edu
Financial Aid Phone: 315-866-0300

This public school was founded in 1966. It has a 268-acre campus.

RATINGS
Admissions Selectivity Rating: 60*   **Fire Safety Rating**: 60*   **Green Rating**: 60*

STUDENTS AND FACULTY
Enrollment: 2,745. **Student Body**: 48% female, 52% male, 11% out-of-state, 2% international. African American 2%, Caucasian 73%, Hispanic 2%. **Faculty**: Student/faculty ratio 28:1. 84 full-time faculty. 100% faculty teach undergrads.

ACADEMICS
Degrees: Associate, certificate. **Academic Requirements**: Arts/fine arts, computer literacy, English (including composition), foreign languages, history, humanities, mathematics, philosophy, sciences (biological or physical), social science. **Special Study Options**: Distance learning, English as a second language (ESL), honors program, independent study, teacher certification program.

FACILITIES
Housing: Coed dorms, apartments for single students, special housing for international students. **Special Academic Facilities/Equipment**: Radio station, cable TV public access station, Lummel Co., professional education center, Cogar Gallery. **Computers**: Online registration, online administrative functions (other than registration).

CAMPUS LIFE
Activities: Dance, drama/theater, literary magazine, radio station, student government, student newspaper, television station. **Organizations**: 37 registered organizations, 1 honor society, 1 religious organization. **Athletics (Intercollegiate)**: *Men*: Baseball, basketball, cross-country, golf, lacrosse, soccer, swimming, tennis, track/field (outdoor), volleyball. *Women*: Basketball, cross-country, field hockey, golf, soccer, softball, swimming, tennis, track/field (outdoor), volleyball.

ADMISSIONS
Freshman Admission Requirements: High school diploma is required, and GED is accepted. *Academic units required*: 4 English, 3 math, 3 science (2

science labs), 3 social studies, 1 history. *Academic units recommended*: 4 English, 3 math, 3 science, 2 foreign language, 3 social studies, 1 history. **Freshman Admission Statistics**: 2,635 applied, 100% admitted, 38% enrolled. **Transfer Admission Requirements**: High school transcript. Lowest grade transferable C. **General Admission Information**: Regular application deadline 8/25. Regular notification is rolling. Nonfall registration accepted. Admission may be deferred for a maximum of 1 year. Common Application accepted.

COSTS AND FINANCIAL AID

Annual in-state tuition $2,500. Out-of-state tuition $5,000. Room & board $5,800. Required fees $185. Average book expense $700. **Required Forms and Deadlines**: FAFSA, state aid form. Financial aid filing deadline 4/1. **Types of Aid**: *Need-based scholarships/grants*: Pell, SEOG, state scholarships/grants. *Loans*: Direct Subsidized Stafford, Direct Unsubsidized Stafford, Direct PLUS, Federal Perkins. **Student Employment**: Federal Work-Study Program available. Institutional employment available. Off-campus job opportunities are fair. **Financial Aid Statistics**: 33% freshmen, 32% undergrads receive need-based scholarship or grant aid.

STATE UNIVERSITY OF NEW YORK—INSTITUTE OF TECHNOLOGY AT UTICA/ROME

PO Box 3050, Utica, NY 13504
Phone: 315-792-7500 **E-mail**: admissions@sunyit.edu **CEEB Code**: 2896
Fax: 315-792-7837 **Website**: www.sunyit.edu **ACT Code**: 2953
Financial Aid Phone: 315-792-7210

This public school was founded in 1966. It has an 850-acre campus.

RATINGS
Admissions Selectivity Rating: 60*   **Fire Safety Rating**: 60*   **Green Rating**: 60*

STUDENTS AND FACULTY
Enrollment: 1,747. **Student Body**: 47% female, 53% male, 1% out-of-state, 2% international. African American 6%, Asian 3%, Caucasian 82%, Hispanic 3%. **Faculty**: Student/faculty ratio 19:1. 85 full-time faculty.

ACADEMICS
Degrees: Bachelor's, master's, post-master's certificate. **Academic Requirements**: Arts/fine arts, computer literacy, English (including composition), foreign languages, history, humanities, mathematics, sciences (biological or physical), social science. **Majors with Highest Enrollment**: Business administration/management, computer and information sciences, nursing/registered nurse training (ASN, BSN, MSN, RN). **Disciplines with Highest Percentage of Degrees Awarded**: Business/marketing 26%, engineering 21%, computer and information sciences 17%, health professions and related sciences 13%, communication technologies 8%, psychology 8%. **Special Study Options**: Accelerated program, cross-registration, distance learning, double major, English as a second language (ESL), independent study, internships.

FACILITIES
Housing: Coed dorms, special housing for disabled students. **Special Academic Facilities/Equipment**: Gannett Gallery, New York State Telecommunications Museum. **Computers**: 34% of public computers are PCs, 40% of public computers are UNIX, network access in dorm rooms, network access in dorm lounges, online registration, online administrative functions (other than registration), remote student-access to Web through college's connection.

CAMPUS LIFE
Activities: Jazz band, radio station, student government, student newspaper, television station, yearbook. **Organizations**: 30 registered organizations, 4 honor societies, 1 religious organization. **Athletics (Intercollegiate)**: *Men*: Baseball, basketball, golf, lacrosse, soccer. *Women*: Basketball, cross-country, golf, soccer, softball, volleyball.

ADMISSIONS
Freshman Academic Profile: TOEFL required of all international applicants, minimum paper TOEFL 550, minimum computer TOEFL 213. **Transfer Admission Requirements**: College transcript(s). Minimum college GPA of 2.0 required. Lowest grade transferable D. **General Admission Information**: Application fee $30. Non-fall registration not accepted. Admission may be deferred for a maximum of 1 year. Common Application not accepted. Neither credit nor placement offered for CEEB Advanced Placement tests.

COSTS AND FINANCIAL AID

Annual in-state tuition $3,400. Out-of-state tuition $8,300. Room & board $6,560. Required fees $764. Average book expense $750. **Required Forms and Deadlines**: FAFSA, institution's own financial aid form. **Types of Aid**: *Need-based scholarships/grants*: Pell, SEOG, state scholarships/grants, private scholarships. *Loans*: Direct Subsidized Stafford, Direct Unsubsidized Stafford, Direct PLUS, Federal Perkins, Federal Nursing. **Student Employment**: Federal Work-Study Program available. Institutional employment available. Off-campus job opportunities are good. **Financial Aid Statistics**: 73% undergrads receive need-based scholarship or grant aid. 65% undergrads receive need-based self-help aid.

STATE UNIVERSITY OF NEW YORK— MARITIME COLLEGE

6 Pennyfield Avenue, Throggs Neck, NY 10465
Phone: 718-409-2221 **E-mail**: admissions@sunymaritime.edu
Fax: 718-409-7465 **Website**: www.sunymaritime.edu **ACT Code**: 2954
Financial Aid Phone: 718-409-7254

This public school was founded in 1874. It has a 56-acre campus.

RATINGS
Admissions Selectivity Rating: 73   **Fire Safety Rating**: 81   **Green Rating**: 74

STUDENTS AND FACULTY
Enrollment: 1,186. **Student Body**: 10% female, 90% male, 26% out-of-state, 6% international. African American 6%, Asian 5%, Caucasian 73%, Hispanic 10%. **Retention and Graduation**: 77% freshmen return for sophomore year. 34% freshmen graduate within 4 years. **Faculty**: Student/faculty ratio 15:1. 63 full-time faculty, 49% hold PhDs. 100% faculty teach undergrads.

ACADEMICS
Degrees: Associate, bachelor's, diploma, master's. **Academic Requirements**: Computer literacy, English (including composition), history, humanities, mathematics, sciences (biological or physical). **Classes**: Most classes have 10–19 students. Most lab/discussion sections have 10–19 students. **Majors with Highest Enrollment**: Business/commerce, engineering, transportation/transportation management. **Disciplines with Highest Percentage of Degrees Awarded**: Engineering 50%, business/marketing 43%, physical sciences 7%. **Special Study Options**: Cooperative education program, distance learning, double major, dual enrollment, English as a second language (ESL), honors program, independent study, internships, student-designed major, United States Coast Guard issued deck and engine license program.

FACILITIES
Housing: Coed dorms, special housing for disabled students. **Special Academic Facilities/Equipment**: Maritime Industry Museum, Fort Schuyler (National Historic Landmark), bridge simulator, liquid cargo simulator, 565-foot training ship Empire State VI, diesel simulator, 2 research ships, state-of-the-art electrical engineering lab, NY State Strategic Center for Port and Maritime Security (224 foot USS Stalwart), computerized weather station, maritime college waterfront sailboat fleet (20 Vanguard 420's, 6 Vanguard FJ's, 1 Laser, J-105, J-35, J-24, Colgate 26). **Computers**: 40% of classrooms are wired, 40% of classrooms are wireless, 100% of public computers are PCs, network access in dorm rooms, network access in dorm lounges, online registration, remote student-access to Web through college's connection.

CAMPUS LIFE
Activities: Choral groups, jazz band, marching band, music ensembles, student government, yearbook. **Organizations**: 25 registered organizations, 4 religious organizations. **Athletics (Intercollegiate)**: *Men*: Baseball, basketball, crew/rowing, cross-country, football, lacrosse, riflery, rugby, sailing, soccer, softball, swimming, tennis, wrestling. *Women*: Basketball, crew/rowing, cross-country, lacrosse, riflery, sailing, soccer, softball, swimming, tennis, volleyball.

ADMISSIONS
Freshman Academic Profile: 10% in top 10% of high school class, 25% in top 25% of high school class, 69% in top 50% of high school class. SAT Math middle 50% range 490–590. SAT Critical Reading middle 50% range 460–560. ACT middle 50% range 18–22. TOEFL required of all international applicants, minimum paper TOEFL 500, minimum computer TOEFL 213. **Basis for Candidate Selection**: *Very important factors considered include*: Academic GPA, application essay, character/personal qualities, class rank, extracurricular activities, interview, recommendation(s), rigor of secondary school record,

---

standardized test scores, talent/ability. *Important factors considered include*: Level of applicant's interest, volunteer work, work experience. *Other factors considered include*: Alumni/ae relation, racial/ethnic status. **Freshman Admission Requirements**: High school diploma is required, and GED is accepted. *Academic units required*: 3 English, 3 math, 3 science, 3 foreign language, 3 social studies, 3 history. *Academic units recommended*: 4 math, 4 science. **Freshman Admission Statistics**: 954 applied, 72% admitted, 36% enrolled. **Transfer Admission Requirements**: High school transcript, college transcript(s), standardized test score. Minimum college GPA of 2.5 required. Lowest grade transferable C. **General Admission Information**: Application fee $40. Early decision application deadline 11/15. Regular application deadline 9/1. Regular notification is rolling. Non-fall registration accepted. Admission may be deferred for a maximum of 1 year. Credit offered for CEEB Advanced Placement tests.

COSTS AND FINANCIAL AID

Annual in-state tuition $4,350. Out-of-state tuition $10,610. Room & board $8,450. Required fees $989. Average book expense $900. **Required Forms and Deadlines**: FAFSA, institution's own financial aid form. Financial aid filing deadline 3/15. **Notification of Awards**: Applicants will be notified of awards on a rolling basis beginning on or about 1/15. **Types of Aid**: *Need-based scholarships/grants*: Pell, SEOG, state scholarships/grants, private scholarships. *Loans*: FFEL Subsidized Stafford, FFEL Unsubsidized Stafford, FFEL PLUS, Federal Perkins. **Student Employment**: Federal Work-Study Program available. Institutional employment available. Off-campus job opportunities are excellent. **Financial Aid Statistics**: Highest amount earned per year from on-campus jobs $800.

STATE UNIVERSITY OF NEW YORK— MOHAWK VALLEY COMMUNITY COLLEGE

1101 Sherman Drive, Utica, NY 13501-5394
Phone: 315-792-5354 **E-mail**: admissions@mvcc.edu
Fax: 315-792-5527 **Website**: www.mvcc.edu
Financial Aid Phone: 315-792-5415

This public school was founded in 1946.

RATINGS
Admissions Selectivity Rating: 60*   **Fire Safety Rating**: 60*   **Green Rating**: 60*

STUDENTS AND FACULTY
Enrollment: 4,410. **Student Body**: 53% female, 47% male, 2% out-of-state, 2% international. African American 6%, Asian 2%, Hispanic 3%. **Retention and Graduation**: 8% grads go on to further study within 1 year. 7% grads pursue arts and sciences degrees. 9% grads pursue business degrees. **Faculty**: 134 full-time faculty, 16% hold PhDs. 100% faculty teach undergrads.

ACADEMICS
Degrees: Associate. **Academic Requirements**: English (including composition), humanities, mathematics, sciences (biological or physical), social science. **Classes**: Most classes have 10–19 students. Most lab/discussion sections have 10–19 students. **Special Study Options**: Cross-registration, distance learning, double major, English as a second language (ESL), honors program, independent study, internships, liberal arts/career combination, student-designed major.

FACILITIES
Housing: Coed dorms, special housing for disabled students, special housing for international students. **Computers**: 80% of public computers are PCs, 20% of public computers are Macs, remote student-access to Web through college's connection.

CAMPUS LIFE
Activities: Choral groups, concert band, drama/theater, jazz band, music ensembles, musical theater, radio station, student government, student newspaper, yearbook. **Organizations**: 45 registered organizations, 2 honor societies, 4 fraternities. **Athletics (Intercollegiate)**: *Men*: Baseball, basketball, cross-country, golf, ice hockey, lacrosse, soccer, tennis, track/field (outdoor). *Women*: Basketball, cross-country, golf, soccer, softball, tennis, track/field (outdoor), volleyball.

ADMISSIONS
Freshman Academic Profile: 3% in top 10% of high school class, 15% in top 25% of high school class, 40% in top 50% of high school class. **Basis for Candidate Selection**: *Very important factors considered include*: Rigor of

secondary school record. *Other factors considered include:* Recommendation(s). **Freshman Admission Requirements**: High school diploma or equivalent is not required. *Academic units recommended:* 4 English, 2 math, 1 science (1 science lab), 1 foreign language, 2 social studies, 1 history. **Freshman Admission Statistics**: 2,851 applied, 91% admitted, 52% enrolled. **Transfer Admission Requirements**: College transcript(s). Lowest grade transferable C. **General Admission Information**: Regular notification is rolling. Nonfall registration accepted. Admission may be deferred. Common Application not accepted.

COSTS AND FINANCIAL AID

Annual in-state tuition $2,500. Out-of-state tuition $3,750. Room & board $4,696. Required fees $100. Average book expense $800. **Required Forms and Deadlines**: FAFSA, institution's own financial aid form. **Notification of Awards**: Applicants will be notified of awards on a rolling basis beginning on or about 3/1. **Types of Aid**: *Need-based scholarships/grants:* Pell, SEOG, state scholarships/grants. *Loans:* Direct Subsidized Stafford, Direct Unsubsidized Stafford, Direct PLUS, Federal Perkins. **Student Employment**: Federal Work-Study Program available. Institutional employment available. Off-campus job opportunities are fair. **Financial Aid Statistics**: 12% freshmen receive need-based self-help aid.

STATE UNIVERSITY OF NEW YORK—NEW PALTZ

75 South Manheim Boulevard, Suite 1, New Paltz, NY 12561-2499
Phone: 845-257-3200 **E-mail:** admissions@newpaltz.edu **CEEB Code:** 2541
Fax: 914-257-3209 **Website:** www.newpaltz.edu **ACT Code:** 2938
Financial Aid Phone: 845-257-3250

This public school was founded in 1828. It has a 216-acre campus.

RATINGS
Admissions Selectivity Rating: 87   **Fire Safety Rating:** 69   **Green Rating:** 60*

STUDENTS AND FACULTY

Enrollment: 6,169. **Student Body**: 67% female, 33% male, 3% out-of-state, 3% international (39 countries represented). African American 6%, Asian 3%, Caucasian 61%, Hispanic 10%. **Retention and Graduation**: 38% grads go on to further study within 1 year. **Faculty**: Student/faculty ratio 16:1. 294 full-time faculty. 98% faculty teach undergrads.

ACADEMICS

Degrees: Bachelor's, master's, post-master's certificate. **Academic Requirements**: Arts/fine arts, computer literacy, English (including composition), foreign languages, history, humanities, mathematics, philosophy, sciences (biological or physical), social science. **Classes**: Most classes have 10–19 students. Most lab/discussion sections have 10–19 students. **Majors with Highest Enrollment**: Accounting, education, psychology. **Disciplines with Highest Percentage of Degrees Awarded**: Education 20%, business/marketing 14%, English 11%, visual and performing arts 11%, social sciences 10%, psychology 7%, communication technologies 7%. **Special Study Options**: Cooperative education program, cross-registration, distance learning, double major, English as a second language (ESL), exchange student program (domestic), honors program, independent study, internships, liberal arts/career combination, student-designed major, study abroad, teacher certification program.

FACILITIES

Housing: Coed dorms, special housing for disabled students. **Special Academic Facilities/Equipment**: Samuel Dorsky Museum of Art, Resnick Engineering Hall, Coykendall Media Center, communication disorders training center and clinic, music therapy training center & clinic, Shepherd Recitial Hall, honors center, Martin Luther King Jr. Study Center, Fournier Mass Spectrometer, Raymond Kurdt Theatre Collection. **Computers**: 89% of public computers are PCs, 10% of public computers are Macs, 1% of public computers are UNIX, network access in dorm rooms, online registration, online administrative functions (other than registration), remote student-access to Web through college's connection.

CAMPUS LIFE

Activities: Choral groups, concert band, dance, drama/theater, jazz band, music ensembles, musical theater, radio station, student government, student newspaper, symphony orchestra, television station, yearbook. **Organizations**: 135 registered organizations, 8 honor societies, 10 religious organizations. 10 fraternities (3% men join), 12 sororities (2% women join). **Athletics (Intercollegiate)**: *Men:* Baseball, basketball, cheerleading, cross-country, diving, soccer,

swimming, tennis, track/field (outdoor), volleyball. *Women:* Basketball, cheerleading, cross-country, diving, field hockey, lacrosse, soccer, softball, swimming, tennis, track/field (outdoor), volleyball.

ADMISSIONS

Freshman Academic Profile: 15% in top 10% of high school class, 56% in top 25% of high school class, 94% in top 50% of high school class. 92% from public high schools. SAT Math middle 50% range 520–605. SAT Critical Reading middle 50% range 520–600. TOEFL required of all international applicants, minimum paper TOEFL 550, minimum computer TOEFL 213. **Basis for Candidate Selection**: *Very important factors considered include:* Academic GPA, rigor of secondary school record, standardized test scores. *Other factors considered include:* Application essay, class rank, extracurricular activities, recommendation(s), talent/ability, volunteer work, work experience. **Freshman Admission Requirements**: High school diploma is required, and GED is accepted. *Academic units required:* 4 English, 3 math, 3 science (3 science labs), 2 foreign language, 3 social studies. *Academic units recommended:* 4 English, 4 math, 4 science (4 science labs), 4 foreign language, 4 social studies. **Freshman Admission Statistics**: 11,358 applied, 44% admitted, 21% enrolled. **Transfer Admission Requirements**: College transcript(s), statement of good standing from prior institution(s). Minimum college GPA of 2.5 required. Lowest grade transferable C. **General Admission Information**: Application fee $40. Regular application deadline 4/1. Regular notification is rolling. Non-fall registration not accepted. Admission may be deferred for a maximum of 1 year. Common Application not accepted. Credit and/or placement offered for CEEB Advanced Placement tests.

COSTS AND FINANCIAL AID

Annual in-state tuition $4,350. Out-of-state tuition $10,610. Room & board $7,220. Required fees $910. Average book expense $1,100. **Required Forms and Deadlines**: FAFSA, state aid form. Financial aid filing deadline 4/1. **Notification of Awards**: Applicants will be notified of awards on or about 3/15. **Types of Aid**: *Need-based scholarships/grants:* Pell, SEOG, state scholarships/grants, private scholarships, the school's own gift aid. *Loans:* FFEL Subsidized Stafford, FFEL Unsubsidized Stafford, FFEL PLUS, Federal Perkins, private alternative loans. **Student Employment**: Federal Work-Study Program available. Institutional employment available. Off-campus job opportunities are good. **Financial Aid Statistics**: 50% freshmen, 48% undergrads receive need-based scholarship or grant aid. 48% freshmen, 47% undergrads receive need-based self-help aid. 60% freshmen, 65% undergrads receive any aid. Highest amount earned per year from on-campus jobs $800.

STATE UNIVERSITY OF NEW YORK— NIAGARA COUNTY COMMUNITY COLLEGE

3111 Saunders Settlement Road, Sanborn, NY 14132-9460
Phone: 716-614-6200 **E-mail:** admiss@alpha.sunyniagara.cc.ny.us
Fax: 716-731-4053 **Website:** www.ntripc.org **ACT Code:** 2843
Financial Aid Phone: 716-614-6200

This public school was founded in 1962. It has a 287-acre campus.

RATINGS
Admissions Selectivity Rating: 61   **Fire Safety Rating:** 60*   **Green Rating:** 60*

STUDENTS AND FACULTY

Enrollment: 3,707. **Student Body**: 57% female, 43% male, 51% out-of-state. African American 5%, Caucasian 87%, Native American 2%. **Retention and Graduation**: 40% grads go on to further study within 1 year. **Faculty**: 100% faculty teach undergrads.

ACADEMICS

Degrees: Associate, certificate, terminal. **Academic Requirements**: English (including composition), health and physical education, social science. **Special Study Options**: Cooperative education program, cross-registration, double major, dual enrollment, honors program, independent study, internships, student-designed major, study abroad.

FACILITIES

Special Academic Facilities/Equipment: Art gallery. **Computers**: 10% of public computers are Macs, remote student-access to Web through college's connection.

CAMPUS LIFE

Activities: Choral groups, dance, drama/theater, jazz band, music ensembles, musical theater, radio station, student government, student newspaper, television station. **Organizations**: 1 honor society. **Athletics (Intercollegiate)**: *Men*: Baseball, basketball, golf, soccer, volleyball, wrestling. *Women*: Basketball, golf, soccer, softball.

ADMISSIONS

Freshman Academic Profile: 2% in top 10% of high school class, 11% in top 25% of high school class, 42% in top 50% of high school class. 90% from public high schools. TOEFL required of all international applicants, minimum paper TOEFL 450. **Freshman Admission Requirements**: High school diploma is required, and GED is accepted. **Freshman Admission Statistics**: 2,001 applied, 100% admitted, 60% enrolled. **Transfer Admission Requirements**: High school transcript, college transcript(s). Lowest grade transferable D. **General Admission Information**: Regular notification is rolling. Non-fall registration accepted. Common Application not accepted.

COSTS AND FINANCIAL AID

Annual in-state tuition $1,250. Out-of-state tuition $1,875. Required fees $60. **Types of Aid**: *Need-based scholarships/grants*: Pell, SEOG, state scholarships/grants, private scholarships, the school's own gift aid. *Loans*: FFEL Subsidized Stafford, FFEL Unsubsidized Stafford, FFEL PLUS, Federal Perkins, college/university loans from institutional funds. **Student Employment**: Federal Work-Study Program available. Institutional employment available. Off-campus job opportunities are good. **Financial Aid Statistics**: 10% undergrads receive need-based scholarship or grant aid. 4% undergrads receive need-based self-help aid. Highest amount earned per year from on-campus jobs $1,100.

STATE UNIVERSITY OF NEW YORK— ONONDAGA COMMUNITY COLLEGE

4941, Onondaga Road, Syracuse, NY 13215
Phone: 315-498-2201 **E-mail**: occinfo@sunyocc.edu
Fax: 315-469-2107 **Website**: www.sunyocc.edu
Financial Aid Phone: 315-498-2291

This public school was founded in 1961. It has a 181-acre campus.

RATINGS
Admissions Selectivity Rating: 60*   **Fire Safety Rating**: 60*   **Green Rating**: 60*

STUDENTS AND FACULTY
Enrollment: 5,097. **Student Body**: 54% female, 46% male. **Faculty**: Student/faculty ratio 17:1. 179 full-time faculty.

ACADEMICS
Degrees: Associate, certificate. **Academic Requirements**: Health professions humanities, mathematics, social science. **Classes**: Most classes have 10–19 students. **Special Study Options**: Cooperative education program, double major, dual enrollment, English as a second language (ESL), honors program, independent study, internships, liberal arts/career combination, study abroad.

FACILITIES
Computers: 17% of public computers are PCs, 8% of public computers are Macs.

CAMPUS LIFE
Activities: Choral groups, music ensembles, radio station, student government, student newspaper, television station. **Organizations**: 1 honor society. **Athletics (Intercollegiate)**: *Men*: Baseball, basketball, cross-country, lacrosse, tennis. *Women*: Basketball, cross-country, softball, tennis, volleyball.

ADMISSIONS
Freshman Academic Profile: 95% from public high schools. TOEFL required of all international applicants, minimum paper TOEFL 500, minimum computer TOEFL 173. **Basis for Candidate Selection**: *Very important factors considered include:* Rigor of secondary school record. *Other factors considered include*: Character/personal qualities, interview, recommendation(s). **Freshman Admission Requirements**: High school diploma is required, and GED is accepted. *Academic units recommended*: 4 English, 2 math, 3 science (2 science labs), 2 foreign language, 4 social studies, 4 history. **Freshman Admission Statistics**: 2,899 applied, 79% admitted. **Transfer Admission Requirements**: High school transcript, college transcript(s). Lowest grade transferable C. **General Admission Information**: Application fee $30. Non-fall registration accepted. Admission may be deferred for a maximum of 2 semesters. Common Application accepted.

COSTS AND FINANCIAL AID

Annual in-state tuition $3,180. Out-of-state tuition $9,540. Required fees $155. **Required Forms and Deadlines**: FAFSA, state aid form. Financial aid filing deadline 2/15. **Notification of Awards**: Applicants will be notified of awards on or about 4/15. **Types of Aid**: *Need-based scholarships/grants*: Pell, SEOG, state scholarships/grants, Federal work study. *Loans*: FFEL Subsidized Stafford, FFEL Unsubsidized Stafford, FFEL PLUS. **Student Employment**: Federal Work-Study Program available. Off-campus job opportunities are excellent. **Financial Aid Statistics**: 36% freshmen, 41% undergrads receive need-based scholarship or grant aid. 44% freshmen, 49% undergrads receive need-based self-help aid.

STATE UNIVERSITY OF NEW YORK—OSWEGO

229 Sheldon Hall, Oswego, NY 13126-3599
Phone: 315-312-2250 **E-mail**: admiss@oswego.edu **CEEB Code**: 2543
Fax: 315-312-3260 **Website**: www.oswego.edu **ACT Code**: 2942
Financial Aid Phone: 315-312-2248

This public school was founded in 1861. It has a 696-acre campus.

RATINGS
Admissions Selectivity Rating: 82   **Fire Safety Rating**: 67   **Green Rating**: 70

STUDENTS AND FACULTY
Enrollment: 6,998. **Student Body**: 54% female, 46% male, 3% out-of-state, 1% international (27 countries represented). African American 4%, Asian 2%, Caucasian 88%, Hispanic 4%. **Retention and Graduation**: 78% freshmen return for sophomore year. 35% freshmen graduate within 4 years. 19% grads go on to further study within 1 year. 22% grads pursue arts and sciences degrees. 6% grads pursue business degrees. 4% grads pursue law degrees. 5% grads pursue medical degrees. **Faculty**: Student/faculty ratio 19:1. 319 full-time faculty, 83% hold PhDs. 93% faculty teach undergrads.

ACADEMICS
Degrees: Bachelor's, master's, post-master's certificate. **Academic Requirements**: Arts/fine arts, computer literacy, English (including composition), foreign languages, history, humanities, mathematics, philosophy, sciences (biological or physical), social science. Students possibly will take all depending on major and degree for the campus wide general education requirements. **Classes**: Most classes have 10–19 students. Most lab/discussion sections have 10–19 students. **Majors with Highest Enrollment**: Business administration/management, communications studies/speech communication and rhetoric, elementary education and teaching. **Disciplines with Highest Percentage of Degrees Awarded**: Education 28%, business/marketing 20%, communications/journalism 10%, psychology 10%, visual and performing arts 7%. **Special Study Options**: Accelerated program, cross-registration, distance learning, double major, dual enrollment, English as a second language (ESL), exchange student program (domestic), external degree program, honors program, independent study, internships, liberal arts/career combination, study abroad, teacher certification program.

FACILITIES
Housing: Coed dorms, global living and learning center, suites for upperclassmen, nontraditional student housing, first-year experience residence hall for incoming freshmen only, housing for 21 and over single suites, several rooms equipped with special equipment. **Special Academic Facilities/Equipment**: Tyler Hall Art Galleries, Rice Creek Biological Field Station, curriculum materials center, electron microscopy lab, planetarium. **Computers**: 35% of classrooms are wireless, 80% of public computers are PCs, 15% of public computers are Macs, 5% of public computers are UNIX, network access in dorm rooms, network access in dorm lounges, online registration, online administrative functions (other than registration), remote student-access to Web through college's connection.

CAMPUS LIFE
Activities: Choral groups, concert band, dance, drama/theater, jazz band, literary magazine, music ensembles, musical theater, radio station, student government, student newspaper, student-run film society, symphony orchestra, television station, yearbook. **Organizations**: 127 registered organizations, 21 honor societies, 6 religious organizations. 12 fraternities (7% men join), 9 sororities (6% women join). **Athletics (Intercollegiate)**: *Men*: Baseball, basketball, cross-country, diving, golf, ice hockey, lacrosse, soccer, swimming, tennis, track/field (indoor), track/field (outdoor), wrestling. *Women*: Basketball, cross-country, diving, field hockey, ice hockey, lacrosse, soccer, softball, swimming, tennis, track/field (indoor), track/field (outdoor), volleyball.

Environmental Initiatives: Meet LEED silver or better on all building projects. Established organization to implement green policy and strategy. Selected enviroment reading as freshman reading initiative.

ADMISSIONS

Freshman Academic Profile: 10% in top 10% of high school class, 50% in top 25% of high school class, 84% in top 50% of high school class. SAT Math middle 50% range 520–580. SAT Critical Reading middle 50% range 510–590. ACT middle 50% range 21–25. TOEFL required of all international applicants, minimum paper TOEFL 550, minimum computer TOEFL 213. **Basis for Candidate Selection**: *Very important factors considered include:* Academic GPA, rigor of secondary school record. *Important factors considered include:* Application essay. *Other factors considered include:* Character/personal qualities, class rank, extracurricular activities, first generation, interview, racial/ethnic status, recommendation(s), standardized test scores, talent/ability, volunteer work, work experience. **Freshman Admission Requirements**: High school diploma is required, and GED is accepted. *Academic units required:* 4 English, 3 math, 3 science (2 science labs), 2 foreign language, 4 social studies. *Academic units recommended:* 4 English, 4 math, 4 science (3 science labs), 4 foreign language, 4 social studies. **Freshman Admission Statistics**: 8,500 applied, 52% admitted, 31% enrolled. **Transfer Admission Requirements**: College transcript(s). Minimum college GPA of 2.5 required. Lowest grade transferable D. **General Admission Information**: Application fee $40. Early decision application deadline 11/15. Regular notification is rolling. Non-fall registration accepted. Admission may be deferred for a maximum of 1 year. Credit offered for CEEB Advanced Placement tests.

COSTS AND FINANCIAL AID

Annual in-state tuition $4,350. Out-of-state tuition $10,610. Room & board $8,940. Required fees $1,010. Average book expense $800. **Required Forms and Deadlines**: FAFSA, state aid form. Financial aid filing deadline 4/1. **Notification of Awards**: Applicants will be notified of awards on a rolling basis beginning on or about 3/1. **Types of Aid**: *Need-based scholarships/grants:* Pell, SEOG, state scholarships/grants. *Loans:* FFEL Subsidized Stafford, FFEL Unsubsidized Stafford, FFEL PLUS, Federal Perkins. **Financial Aid Statistics**: 58% freshmen, 58% undergrads receive need-based scholarship or grant aid. 52% freshmen, 57% undergrads receive need-based self-help aid. 62% freshmen, 64% undergrads receive any aid. Highest amount earned per year from on-campus jobs $1,100.

STATE UNIVERSITY OF NEW YORK— PLATTSBURGH

1001 Kehoe Building, Plattsburgh, NY 12901
Phone: 518-564-2040 **E-mail**: admissions@plattsburgh.edu **CEEB Code**: 2544
Fax: 518-564-2045 **Website**: www.plattsburgh.edu **ACT Code**: 2944
Financial Aid Phone: 518-564-4076

This public school was founded in 1889. It has a 300-acre campus.

RATINGS
Admissions Selectivity Rating: 71   **Fire Safety Rating**: 60*   **Green Rating**: 60*

STUDENTS AND FACULTY
Enrollment: 5,328. **Student Body**: 58% female, 42% male, 4% out-of-state, 7% international (56 countries represented). African American 5%, Asian 2%, Caucasian 76%, Hispanic 3%. **Retention and Graduation**: 75% freshmen return for sophomore year. 37% freshmen graduate within 4 years. 34% grads go on to further study within 1 year. 31% grads pursue arts and sciences degrees. 2% grads pursue business degrees. 1% grads pursue law degrees. 1% grads pursue medical degrees. **Faculty**: Student/faculty ratio 18:1. 250 full-time faculty, 90% hold PhDs. 100% faculty teach undergrads.

ACADEMICS
Degrees: Bachelor's, master's, post-bachelor's certificate, post-master's certificate. **Academic Requirements**: Arts/fine arts, computer literacy, English (including composition), foreign languages, humanities, mathematics, sciences (biological or physical), social science. **Classes**: Most classes have 10–19 students. Most lab/discussion sections have 20–29 students. **Majors with Highest Enrollment**: Business administration/management, special education. **Disciplines with Highest Percentage of Degrees Awarded**: Education 22%, business/marketing 17%, social sciences 9%, communication technologies 7%, English 6%, health professions and related sciences 6%. **Special Study Options**: Cooperative education program, cross-registration, distance learning, double major, dual enrollment, English as a second language (ESL), exchange

student program (domestic), honors program, independent study, internships, liberal arts/career combination, student-designed major, study abroad, teacher certification program.

FACILITIES
Housing: Coed dorms, special housing for disabled students, special housing for international students, wellness floor, substance free building and floors, quiet floors, men's floor, women's floors, extended lodging. **Special Academic Facilities/Equipment**: Art galleries, sculpture courtyard, theater and concert halls, communications/lecture hall, interactive video for telecourses, radio and TV broadcasting facilities, planetarium, on-site research center for biotechnology and environmental science, enzymology lab, electron microscope, remote sensing lab, NMR spectrophotometer, computer-operated infrared spectrophotometer, gas chromatograph, mass spectrometer, computerized liquid scintillation counter, facility for analysis of environmental pollutants in lake water, sediments and biota, lake research/sampling vessel with differential GPS navigation equipment, ubductively coupled plasma/mass spectrometer, ion chromatograph/high performance liquid chromatograph, mercury detector. **Computers**: 6% of public computers are PCs, network access in dorm rooms, online registration, online administrative functions (other than registration), remote student-access to Web through college's connection.

CAMPUS LIFE
Activities: Choral groups, concert band, drama/theater, jazz band, literary magazine, music ensembles, radio station, student government, student newspaper, student-run film society, symphony orchestra, television station, yearbook. **Organizations**: 97 registered organizations, 26 honor societies, 3 religious organizations. 6 fraternities (6% men join), 7 sororities (5% women join). **Athletics (Intercollegiate)**: *Men:* Basketball, cross-country, golf, ice hockey, lacrosse, rugby, soccer, track/field (indoor), track/field (outdoor). *Women:* Basketball, cross-country, golf, ice hockey, rugby, soccer, softball, tennis, track/field (indoor), track/field (outdoor), volleyball.

ADMISSIONS
Freshman Academic Profile: 10% in top 10% of high school class, 30% in top 25% of high school class, 75% in top 50% of high school class. 98% from public high schools. SAT Math middle 50% range 480–560. SAT Critical Reading middle 50% range 480–560. ACT middle 50% range 19–24. TOEFL required of all international applicants, minimum paper TOEFL 450, minimum computer TOEFL 133. **Basis for Candidate Selection**: *Very important factors considered include:* Interview, rigor of secondary school record, standardized test scores. *Important factors considered include:* Alumni/ae relation, application essay, character/personal qualities, class rank, extracurricular activities, racial/ethnic status, recommendation(s), talent/ability. *Other factors considered include:* volunteer work, work experience. **Freshman Admission Requirements**: High school diploma is required, and GED is accepted. *Academic units required:* 4 English, 3 math, 3 science, 3 foreign language, 3 social studies, 1 history. *Academic units recommended:* 4 English, 4 math, 4 science, 3 foreign language, 3 social studies, 1 history, 2 academic electives. **Freshman Admission Statistics**: 6,798 applied, 62% admitted, 23% enrolled. **Transfer Admission Requirements**: College transcript(s). Minimum college GPA of 2.3 required. Lowest grade transferable D. **General Admission Information**: Application fee $40. Early decision application deadline 11/15. Regular application deadline 8/1. Regular notification is rolling. Non-fall registration accepted. Admission may be deferred for a maximum of 1 year. Common Application not accepted. Credit and/or placement offered for CEEB Advanced Placement tests.

COSTS AND FINANCIAL AID
Annual in-state tuition $4,350. Out-of-state tuition $10,300. Room & board $6,500. Required fees $850. Average book expense $850. **Required Forms and Deadlines**: FAFSA, state aid form. Financial aid filing deadline 3/1. **Notification of Awards**: Applicants will be notified of awards on a rolling basis beginning on or about 3/15. **Types of Aid**: *Need-based scholarships/grants:* Pell, SEOG, state scholarships/grants, private scholarships, the school's own gift aid, Scholarships for disavantaged students, State Educational Opportunity Program. *Loans:* Direct Subsidized Stafford, Direct Unsubsidized Stafford, Direct PLUS, Federal Perkins, Federal Nursing. Grace Appleton Loan, privately endowed administered by a Trust Company, awarded by the college. **Student Employment**: Federal Work-Study Program available. Institutional employment available. Off-campus job opportunities are good. **Financial Aid Statistics**: 55% freshmen, 55% undergrads receive need-based scholarship or grant aid. 52% freshmen, 52% undergrads receive need-based self-help aid. Highest amount earned per year from on-campus jobs $1,540.

STATE UNIVERSITY OF NEW YORK—POTSDAM

44 Pierrepont Avenue, Potsdam, NY 13676
Phone: 315-267-2180 **E-mail:** admissions@potsdam.edu **CEEB Code:** 2545
Fax: 315-267-2163 **Website:** www.potsdam.edu **ACT Code:** 2946
Financial Aid Phone: 315-267-2162

This public school was founded in 1816. It has a 240-acre campus.

RATINGS

Admissions Selectivity Rating: 75   **Fire Safety Rating:** 75   **Green Rating:** 81

STUDENTS AND FACULTY

Enrollment: 3,610. **Student Body:** 56% female, 44% male, 2% out-of-state, 3% international (10 countries represented). African American 2%, Asian 1%, Caucasian 75%, Hispanic 2%, Native American 1%. **Retention and Graduation:** 76% freshmen return for sophomore year. 28% freshmen graduate within 4 years. 33% grads go on to further study within 1 year. 27% grads pursue arts and sciences degrees. 13% grads pursue business degrees. 1% grads pursue law degrees. 3% grads pursue medical degrees. **Faculty:** Student/faculty ratio 14:1. 259 full-time faculty, 91% hold PhDs. 95% faculty teach undergrads.

ACADEMICS

Degrees: Bachelor's, master's. **Academic Requirements:** Arts/fine arts, English (including composition), foreign languages, history, humanities, mathematics, philosophy, physical education, sciences (biological or physical), social science. **Classes:** Most classes have fewer than 10 students. Most lab/discussion sections have fewer than 10 students. **Majors with Highest Enrollment:** Business/managerial economics, elementary education and teaching, music teacher education. **Disciplines with Highest Percentage of Degrees Awarded:** Education 26%, visual and performing arts 13%, social sciences 11%, business/marketing 11%, psychology 9%, English 8%. **Special Study Options:** Cross-registration, distance learning, double major, dual enrollment, exchange student program (domestic), honors program, independent study, internships, liberal arts/career combination, student-designed major, study abroad, teacher certification program. Combined degree options in engineering with Clarkson University and SUNY Binghamton; accounting, engineering, or management with SUNY Utica/Rome.

FACILITIES

Housing: Coed dorms, apartments for single students, special housing for disabled students, special housing for international students, first-year experience, substance-free, study intensive, honors house, arts house. **Special Academic Facilities/Equipment:** Art gallery, anthropology museum, ecology museum, 3 performance halls, theater, synthesizer music studios, planetarium, electron microscope, nuclear magnetic resonator, seismograph. **Computers:** 100% of classrooms are wired, 10% of classrooms are wireless, 60% of public computers are PCs, 40% of public computers are Macs, network access in dorm rooms, network access in dorm lounges, online registration, online administrative functions (other than registration), support for handheld computing, remote student-access to Web through college's connection.

CAMPUS LIFE

Activities: Choral groups, concert band, dance, drama/theater, jazz band, literary magazine, music ensembles, musical theater, opera, radio station, student government, student newspaper, symphony orchestra, yearbook. **Organizations:** 100 registered organizations, 23 honor societies, 3 religious organizations. 6 fraternities (5% men join), 8 sororities (6% women join). **Athletics (Intercollegiate):** *Men:* Basketball, cross-country, diving, golf, ice hockey, lacrosse, soccer, swimming. *Women:* Basketball, cheerleading, cross-country, diving, equestrian sports, lacrosse, soccer, softball, swimming, tennis, volleyball. Environmental Initiatives: Increase recycle efforts. Increase purchase of green products and energy star equipment. Increase purchase of renewable energy.

ADMISSIONS

Freshman Academic Profile: 13% in top 10% of high school class, 35% in top 25% of high school class, 70% in top 50% of high school class. SAT Math middle 50% range 480–590. SAT Critical Reading middle 50% range 470–580. ACT middle 50% range 20–24. TOEFL required of all international applicants, minimum paper TOEFL 550, minimum computer TOEFL 213. **Basis for Candidate Selection:** *Very important factors considered include:* Academic GPA, rigor of secondary school record, standardized test scores. *Important factors considered include:* Talent/ability. *Other factors considered include:* Alumni/ae relation, application essay, character/personal qualities, class rank, extracurricular activities, interview, level of applicant's interest, recommendation(s), volunteer work, work experience. **Freshman Admission Requirements:** High school diploma is required, and GED is accepted.

Academic units required: 4 English, 2 math, 2 science (1 science lab), 4 social studies, 1 fine arts. *Academic units recommended:* 4 English, 4 math, 4 science (2 science labs), 4 foreign language, 4 social studies, 1 fine arts. **Freshman Admission Statistics:** 3,539 applied, 71% admitted, 30% enrolled. **Transfer Admission Requirements:** College transcript(s). Minimum college GPA of 2.0 required. Lowest grade transferable D. **General Admission Information:** Application fee $40. Regular notification is rolling. Non-fall registration accepted. Admission may be deferred for a maximum of 1 year. Credit and/or placement offered for CEEB Advanced Placement tests.

COSTS AND FINANCIAL AID

Annual in-state tuition $4,350. Out-of-state tuition $10,610. Room & board $8,170. Required fees $1,007. Average book expense $1,000. **Required Forms and Deadlines:** FAFSA, state aid form. Financial aid filing deadline 3/1. **Notification of Awards:** Applicants will be notified of awards on a rolling basis beginning on or about 2/15. **Types of Aid:** *Need-based scholarships/grants:* Pell, SEOG, state scholarships/grants, private scholarships, the school's own gift aid, VESIS, Veteran Benefits, BIA, Native American. *Loans:* Direct Subsidized Stafford, Direct Unsubsidized Stafford, Direct PLUS, Federal Perkins, college/university loans from institutional funds, alternative loans. **Student Employment:** Federal Work-Study Program available. Institutional employment available. Off-campus job opportunities are good. **Financial Aid Statistics:** 62% freshmen, 60% undergrads receive need-based scholarship or grant aid. 55% freshmen, 55% undergrads receive need-based self-help aid. 83% freshmen, 86% undergrads receive any aid.

STATE UNIVERSITY OF NEW YORK— PURCHASE COLLEGE

Best 368

Admissions Office, 735 Anderson Hill Road, Purchase, NY 10577
Phone: 914-251-6300 **E-mail:** admissn@purchase.edu **CEEB Code:** 2878
Fax: 914-251-6314 **Website:** www.purchase.edu **ACT Code:** 2931
Financial Aid Phone: 914-251-6350

This public school was founded in 1967. It has a 550-acre campus.

RATINGS

Admissions Selectivity Rating: 84   **Fire Safety Rating:** 60*   **Green Rating:** 60*

STUDENTS AND FACULTY

Enrollment: 3,480. **Student Body:** 53% female, 47% male, 18% out-of-state, 2% international (33 countries represented). African American 9%, Asian 4%, Caucasian 57%, Hispanic 10%. **Retention and Graduation:** 76% freshmen return for sophomore year. 35% freshmen graduate within 4 years. **Faculty:** Student/faculty ratio 15:1. 146 full-time faculty. 100% faculty teach undergrads.

ACADEMICS

Degrees: Bachelor's, certificate, master's, post-master's certificate. **Academic Requirements:** Critical thinking, English (including composition), foreign languages, history, humanities, information management, mathematics, sciences (biological or physical), social science. Some art majors are exempt. **Classes:** Most classes have fewer than 10 students. Most lab/discussion sections have 10–19 students. **Majors with Highest Enrollment:** Liberal arts and sciences/liberal studies, psychology, visual and performing arts. **Disciplines with Highest Percentage of Degrees Awarded:** Visual and performing arts 41%, liberal arts/general studies 23%, English 7%, social sciences 7%, psychology 5%, communications/journalism 4%. **Special Study Options:** Cross-registration, distance learning, double major, English as a second language (ESL), independent study, internships, liberal arts/career combination, student-designed major, study abroad.

FACILITIES

Housing: Coed dorms, apartments for single students, special housing for disabled students, special housing for international students. **Special Academic Facilities/Equipment:** Museum, 4 theater performing arts center, visual arts facility, children's center, recording studio, electron microscopes. **Computers:** 90% of public computers are PCs, 10% of public computers are Macs, 1% of public computers are UNIX, network access in dorm rooms, network access in dorm lounges, remote student-access to Web through college's connection.

CAMPUS LIFE

Activities: Choral groups, dance, drama/theater, jazz band, literary magazine, music ensembles, musical theater, radio station, student government, student newspaper, student-run film society, television station. **Organizations**: 30 registered organizations. **Athletics (Intercollegiate)**: *Men*: Baseball, basketball, cross-country, soccer, tennis, volleyball. *Women*: Basketball, cross-country, soccer, softball, tennis, volleyball.

ADMISSIONS

Freshman Academic Profile: 10% in top 10% of high school class, 32% in top 25% of high school class, 72% in top 50% of high school class. SAT Math middle 50% range 480–590. SAT Critical Reading middle 50% range 510–620. TOEFL required of all international applicants, minimum paper TOEFL 550, minimum computer TOEFL 213. **Basis for Candidate Selection**: *Very important factors considered include*: Academic GPA, application essay, talent/ability. *Important factors considered include*: Standardized test scores. *Other factors considered include*: Character/personal qualities, extracurricular activities, interview, recommendation(s), rigor of secondary school record. **Freshman Admission Requirements**: High school diploma is required, and GED is accepted. **Freshman Admission Statistics**: 7,388 applied, 30% admitted, 31% enrolled. **Transfer Admission Requirements**: College transcript(s). Minimum college GPA of 3.0 required. Lowest grade transferable D. **General Admission Information**: Application fee $40. Early decision application deadline 11/1. Regular application deadline 7/15. Regular notification 5/1. Non-fall registration accepted. Admission may be deferred for a maximum of 1 year. Credit and/or placement offered for CEEB Advanced Placement tests.

COSTS AND FINANCIAL AID

Annual in-state tuition $4,350. Out-of-state tuition $10,610. Room & board $9,028. Required fees $1,359. Average book expense $1,500. **Required Forms and Deadlines**: FAFSA, state aid form. Financial aid filing deadline 3/1. **Notification of Awards**: Applicants will be notified of awards on a rolling basis beginning on or about 3/1. **Types of Aid**: *Need-based scholarships/grants*: Pell, SEOG, state scholarships/grants, private scholarships, the school's own gift aid. *Loans*: FFEL Subsidized Stafford, FFEL Unsubsidized Stafford, FFEL PLUS, Federal Perkins. **Student Employment**: Federal Work-Study Program available. Institutional employment available. Off-campus job opportunities are excellent. **Financial Aid Statistics**: 80% freshmen, 66% undergrads receive any aid. Highest amount earned per year from on-campus jobs $1,073.

See page 1390.

STATE UNIVERSITY OF NEW YORK— SCHENECTADY COUNTY COMMUNITY COLLEGE

Office of Admissions, 78 Washington Avenue, Schenectady, NY 12305
Phone: 518-381-1366 **E-mail**: dinellre@gw.sunysccc.edu
Fax: 518-381-1477 **Website**: www.sunysccc.edu
Financial Aid Phone: 518-381-1352

This public school was founded in 1967. It has a 50-acre campus.

RATINGS

Admissions Selectivity Rating: 60*   **Fire Safety Rating**: 60*   **Green Rating**: 60*

STUDENTS AND FACULTY

Enrollment: 2,532. **Student Body**: 56% female, 44% male. African American 10%, Asian 2%, Hispanic 4%. **Faculty**: Student/faculty ratio 20:1. 64 full-time faculty, 20% hold PhDs. 100% faculty teach undergrads.

ACADEMICS

Degrees: Associate, certificate, diploma, terminal. **Academic Requirements**: English (including composition), humanities, mathematics, sciences (biological or physical), social science. **Special Study Options**: Cooperative education program, cross-registration, distance learning, dual enrollment, English as a second language (ESL), internships, liberal arts/career combination.

FACILITIES

Computers: Remote student-access to Web through college's connection.

CAMPUS LIFE

Athletics (Intercollegiate): *Men*: Baseball, basketball, soccer. *Women*: Basketball, softball.

ADMISSIONS

Freshman Academic Profile: TOEFL required of all international applicants, minimum paper TOEFL 213. **Freshman Admission Requirements**: High school diploma is required, and GED is accepted. **Transfer Admission Requirements**: High school transcript. Lowest grade transferable C. **General Admission Information**: Regular notification is rolling. Non-fall registration accepted. Common Application not accepted. Credit and/or placement offered for CEEB Advanced Placement tests.

COSTS AND FINANCIAL AID

Annual in-state tuition $2,340. Out-of-state tuition $4,680. Required fees $115. Average book expense $700. **Required Forms and Deadlines**: FAFSA, state aid form. **Types of Aid**: *Need-based scholarships/grants*: Pell, SEOG, state scholarships/grants, the school's own gift aid, Veteran's Benefits Federal Aid to Native Americans. *Loans*: Direct Subsidized Stafford, Direct Unsubsidized Stafford, Direct PLUS. **Student Employment**: Federal Work-Study Program available. Off-campus job opportunities are excellent.

STATE UNIVERSITY OF NEW YORK— STONY BROOK UNIVERSITY

Office of Admissions, Stony Brook, NY 11794-1901
Phone: 631-632-6868 **E-mail**: enroll@stonybrook.edu **CEEB Code**: 2548
Fax: 631-632-9898 **Website**: www.stonybrook.edu/ **ACT Code**: 2952
Financial Aid Phone: 631-632-6840

This public school was founded in 1957. It has a 1,100-acre campus.

RATINGS

Admissions Selectivity Rating: 60*   **Fire Safety Rating**: 60*   **Green Rating**: 84

STUDENTS AND FACULTY

Enrollment: 14,639. **Student Body**: 50% female, 50% male, 4% out-of-state, 5% international (100 countries represented). African American 9%, Asian 22%, Caucasian 35%, Hispanic 9%. **Retention and Graduation**: 87% freshmen return for sophomore year. 37% freshmen graduate within 4 years. **Faculty**: Student/faculty ratio 17:1. 909 full-time faculty, 97% hold PhDs. 88% faculty teach undergrads.

ACADEMICS

Degrees: Bachelor's, doctoral, first professional certificate, first professional, master's, post-bachelor's certificate, post-master's certificate. **Academic Requirements**: Arts/fine arts, English (including composition), foreign languages, history, humanities, mathematics, philosophy, sciences (biological or physical), social science. **Classes**: Most classes have 20–29 students. Most lab/discussion sections have 20–29 students. **Majors with Highest Enrollment**: Biology/biological sciences, business administration/management, psychology. **Disciplines with Highest Percentage of Degrees Awarded**: Social sciences 17%, health professions and related sciences 17%, psychology 12%, biological/life sciences 11%, business/marketing 8%, engineering 6%, computer and information sciences 6%. **Special Study Options**: Cross-registration, distance learning, double major, English as a second language (ESL), exchange student program (domestic), honors program, independent study, internships, student-designed major, study abroad, teacher certification program. Albany semester. Undergrads may take grad level courses. BS/MS programs, BE/MS, BS/MA - living learning centers in residence halls, honors college, undergraduate research and creative activities program where undergraduates work with faculty on research projects, university learning communities and (WISE) Women in Science and Engineering.

FACILITIES

Housing: Coed dorms, apartments for married students, apartments for single students, special housing for disabled students, single sex floors in coed dorms, living learning centers, first-year resident members of each college are housed together in the same residence hall. **Special Academic Facilities/Equipment**: Fine arts center, natural sciences museum, federated learning center, curriculum development center, economic research bureau, instructional resource center, marine sciences research center, Van de Graaff accelerator. **Computers**: 89% of public computers are PCs, 8% of public computers are

Macs, 3% of public computers are UNIX, network access in dorm rooms, network access in dorm lounges, online registration, online administrative functions (other than registration), remote student-access to Web through college's connection.

CAMPUS LIFE

Activities: Choral groups, concert band, dance, drama/theater, jazz band, literary magazine, music ensembles, musical theater, pep band, radio station, student government, student newspaper, student-run film society, symphony orchestra, yearbook. **Organizations**: 261 registered organizations, 6 honor societies, 13 religious organizations. 15 fraternities (1% men join), 18 sororities (1% women join). **Athletics (Intercollegiate)**: *Men*: Baseball, basketball, cross-country, diving, football, lacrosse, soccer, swimming, tennis, track/field (indoor), track/field (outdoor). *Women*: Basketball, cross-country, diving, lacrosse, soccer, softball, swimming, tennis, track/field (indoor), track/field (outdoor), volleyball. Environmental Initiatives: Signing of ACUPCC. Creation of Environmental Stewardship Department. President's 5 Year Plan.

ADMISSIONS

Freshman Academic Profile: 90% from public high schools. SAT Math middle 50% range 570–670. SAT Critical Reading middle 50% range 510–610. TOEFL required of all international applicants, minimum paper TOEFL 550, minimum computer TOEFL 213. **Basis for Candidate Selection**: *Very important factors considered include:* Rigor of secondary school record, standardized test scores. *Important factors considered include:* Class rank. *Other factors considered include:* Alumni/ae relation, application essay, character/personal qualities, extracurricular activities, interview, recommendation(s), talent/ability, volunteer work, work experience. **Freshman Admission Requirements**: High school diploma is required, and GED is accepted. *Academic units required:* 4 English, 3 math, 3 science, 2 foreign language, 4 social studies. *Academic units recommended:* 4 math, 4 science, 3 foreign language. **Freshman Admission Statistics**: 21,292 applied, 47% admitted, 27% enrolled. **Transfer Admission Requirements**: High school transcript, college transcript(s), standardized test score, statement of good standing from prior institution(s). Minimum college GPA of 2.5 required. Lowest grade transferable C. **General Admission Information**: Application fee $40. Regular notification 2/1. Non-fall registration accepted. Admission may be deferred for a maximum of 1 year. Credit and/or placement offered for CEEB Advanced Placement tests.

COSTS AND FINANCIAL AID

Annual in-state tuition $4,350. Out-of-state tuition $10,610. Room & board $8,394. Required fees $1,281. Average book expense $900. **Required Forms and Deadlines**: FAFSA. Financial aid filing deadline 3/1. **Notification of Awards**: Applicants will be notified of awards on a rolling basis beginning on or about 3/1. **Types of Aid**: *Need-based scholarships/grants:* Pell, SEOG, state scholarships/grants, the school's own gift aid. *Loans:* FFEL Subsidized Stafford, FFEL Unsubsidized Stafford, FFEL PLUS, Federal Perkins. **Financial Aid Statistics**: 52% freshmen, 51% undergrads receive need-based scholarship or grant aid. 41% freshmen, 42% undergrads receive need-based self-help aid. 46 freshmen, 222 undergrads receive athletic scholarships. 75% freshmen, 68% undergrads receive any aid. Highest amount earned per year from on-campus jobs $16,488.

STATE UNIVERSITY OF NEW YORK—STONY BROOK UNIVERSITY HEALTH SCIENCE CENTER

Office of Admissions, Stony Brook, NY 11794-1901
Phone: 631-632-6868 **E-mail**: ugadmissions@notes.cc.sunysb.edu **CEEB Code**: 2548
Fax: 631-632-9898 **Website**: www.sunysb.edu **ACT Code**: 2952
Financial Aid Phone: 631-632-6840

This public school was founded in 1957. It has a 1,100-acre campus.

RATINGS

Admissions Selectivity Rating: 84   **Fire Safety Rating**: 60*   **Green Rating**: 60*

STUDENTS AND FACULTY

Enrollment: 12,479. **Student Body**: 50% female, 50% male, 2% out-of-state, 3% international. African American 9%, Asian 30%, Caucasian 7%, Hispanic 7%. **Retention and Graduation**: 81% freshmen return for sophomore year. 31% freshmen graduate within 4 years. **Faculty**: Student/faculty ratio 14:1. 1,282 full-time faculty.

ACADEMICS

Degrees: Bachelor's, doctoral, first professional, master's, post-master's certificate. **Academic Requirements**: Arts/fine arts, English (including composition), foreign languages, history, humanities, mathematics, philosophy, sciences (biological or physical), social science. **Disciplines with Highest Percentage of Degrees Awarded**: Social sciences 23%, psychology 14%, biological/life sciences 12%, health professions and related sciences 11%, interdisciplinary studies 6%, computer and information sciences 6%. **Special Study Options**: Cross-registration, distance learning, double major, independent study, teacher certification program. Albany semester. Undergrads may take grad level courses BSMS programs, BE/MS, BS/MA-living learning centers in residence halls, honors college, undergraduate research and creative activities, program where UG work with faculty on research projects, university learning communities and women in science and engineering.

FACILITIES

Housing: Coed dorms, apartments for married students, apartments for single students, special housing for disabled students. **Special Academic Facilities/Equipment**: Fine arts center, natural sciences museum, federated learning center, curriculum development center, economic research bureau, instructional resource center, marine sciences research center, Van de Graaff accelerator. **Computers**: 40% of public computers are PCs, network access in dorm rooms, network access in dorm lounges, online registration, online administrative functions (other than registration), remote student-access to Web through college's connection.

CAMPUS LIFE

Activities: Choral groups, concert band, dance, drama/theater, jazz band, literary magazine, music ensembles, musical theater, opera, pep band, radio station, student government, student newspaper, student-run film society, symphony orchestra, television station, yearbook. **Organizations**: 200 registered organizations, 26 honor societies, 27 religious organizations. 15 fraternities, 11 sororities. **Athletics (Intercollegiate)**: *Men*: Baseball, basketball, cross-country, diving, equestrian sports, football, golf, lacrosse, soccer, swimming, tennis, track/field (indoor), track/field (outdoor). *Women*: Basketball, cross-country, diving, equestrian sports, soccer, softball, swimming, tennis, track/field (indoor), track/field (outdoor), volleyball.

ADMISSIONS

Freshman Academic Profile: 24% in top 10% of high school class, 63% in top 25% of high school class, 98% in top 50% of high school class. 85% from public high schools. SAT Math middle 50% range 520–640. SAT Critical Reading middle 50% range 490–590. TOEFL required of all international applicants, minimum paper TOEFL 550. **Basis for Candidate Selection**: *Very important factors considered include:* Interview, rigor of secondary school record, standardized test scores. *Important factors considered include:* Alumni/ae relation, character/personal qualities, class rank, recommendation(s), talent/ability. *Other factors considered include:* Application essay, extracurricular activities, volunteer work, work experience. **Freshman Admission Requirements**: High school diploma is required, and GED is accepted. *Academic units required:* 4 English, 3 math, 3 science, 4 social studies. *Academic units recommended:* 4 English, 4 math, 4 science, 3 foreign language, 4 social studies. **Freshman Admission Statistics**: 14,892 applied, 58% admitted, 26% enrolled. **Transfer Admission Requirements**: College transcript(s), statement of good standing from prior institution(s). Minimum college GPA of 2.5 required. **General Admission Information**: Application fee $30. Early decision application deadline 10/1. Regular application deadline 7/10. Regular notification is rolling. Non-fall registration accepted. Admission may be deferred for a maximum of 1 year. Common Application not accepted. Credit and/or placement offered for CEEB Advanced Placement tests.

COSTS AND FINANCIAL AID

Annual in-state tuition $3,400. Out-of-state tuition $8,300. Room & board $6,230. Required fees $741. Average book expense $750. **Student Employment**: Federal Work-Study Program available. Institutional employment available. Off-campus job opportunities are excellent.

STATE UNIVERSITY OF NEW YORK—SULLIVAN COUNTY COMMUNITY COLLEGE

112 College Road, Loch Sheldrake, NY 12759
Phone: 845-434-5750 **E-mail:** admissions@sullivan.suny.edu
Fax: 845-434-4806 **Website:** www.sullivan.suny.edu
Financial Aid Phone: 845-434-5750

This public school was founded in 1962. It has a 405-acre campus.

RATINGS
Admissions Selectivity Rating: 60*   **Fire Safety Rating:** 60*   **Green Rating:** 60*

STUDENTS AND FACULTY
Enrollment: 1,552. **Student Body:** 29% out-of-state. African American 20%, Asian 2%, Caucasian 65%, Hispanic 12%. **Faculty:** Student/faculty ratio 15:1. 40 full-time faculty. 100% faculty teach undergrads.

ACADEMICS
Degrees: Associate, certificate, terminal. **Academic Requirements:** English (including composition), history, humanities, mathematics, sciences (biological or physical), social science. **Special Study Options:** Distance learning, double major, honors program, internships.

FACILITIES
Housing: Approved dorm and apartment style off-campus housing. **Computers:** 88% of public computers are PCs, 12% of public computers are Macs, remote student-access to Web through college's connection.

CAMPUS LIFE
Activities: Student government, student newspaper. **Organizations:** 1 honor society. **Athletics (Intercollegiate):** *Men:* Basketball, golf. *Women:* Basketball, softball, volleyball.

ADMISSIONS
Freshman Admission Statistics: 1,183 applied, 95% admitted, 54% enrolled. **Transfer Admission Requirements:** High school transcript, college transcript(s). Lowest grade transferable C. **General Admission Information:** Regular notification is continuous. Non-fall registration accepted. Admission may be deferred for a maximum of 2 years. Common Application not accepted.

COSTS AND FINANCIAL AID
Annual in-state tuition $2,500. Out-of-state tuition $5,000. Required fees $156. Average book expense $700. **Required Forms and Deadlines:** FAFSA, institution's own financial aid form, state aid form. Financial aid filing deadline 4/15. **Notification of Awards:** Applicants will be notified of awards on or about 5/15. **Types of Aid:** *Need-based scholarships/grants:* Pell, SEOG, state scholarships/grants, the school's own gift aid. *Loans:* FFEL Subsidized Stafford, FFEL Unsubsidized Stafford, FFEL PLUS, Federal Perkins. **Student Employment:** Federal Work-Study Program available. Off-campus job opportunities are fair.

STATE UNIVERSITY OF NEW YORK— ULSTER COMMUNITY COLLEGE

Admissions Office, SUNY at Ulster, Stone Ridge, NY 12484
Phone: 914-687-5018 **E-mail:** admissions@sunyulster.edu
Fax: 914-687-5090 **Website:** www.sunyulster.edu
Financial Aid Phone: 914-687-5058

This public school was founded in 1962. It has a 160-acre campus.

RATINGS
Admissions Selectivity Rating: 60*   **Fire Safety Rating:** 60*   **Green Rating:** 60*

STUDENTS AND FACULTY
Enrollment: 2,048. **Student Body:** 58% female, 42% male. **Faculty:** Student/faculty ratio 11:1. 60 full-time faculty, 12% hold PhDs. 100% faculty teach undergrads.

ACADEMICS
Degrees: Associate, certificate, diploma, terminal. **Academic Requirements:** Computer literacy, English (including composition), history, humanities, mathematics, sciences (biological or physical), social science. **Classes:** Most classes have 10–19 students. Most lab/discussion sections have fewer than 10 students. **Special Study Options:** Cooperative education program, cross registration, distance learning, English as a second language (ESL), honors program, independent study, internships, liberal arts/career combination, student-designed major.

FACILITIES
Computers: 95% of public computers are PCs, 5% of public computers are Macs, online registration, online administrative functions (other than registration), remote student-access to Web through college's connection.

CAMPUS LIFE
Activities: Choral groups, drama/theater, radio station, student government, student newspaper. **Organizations:** 16 registered organizations, 1 honor society, 1 religious organization. **Athletics (Intercollegiate):** *Men:* Baseball, basketball, golf, soccer, tennis. *Women:* basketball, softball, tennis, volleyball.

ADMISSIONS
Freshman Academic Profile: 99% from public high schools.

COSTS AND FINANCIAL AID
Student Employment: Federal Work-Study Program available. Institutional employment available. Off-campus job opportunities are good.

STATE UNIVERSITY OF NEW YORK— UNIVERSITY AT ALBANY

Office of Undergraduate Admissions, UAB 101, 1400 Washington Avenue, Albany, NY 12222
Phone: 518-442-5435 **E-mail:** ugadmissions@albany.edu **CEEB Code:** 2532
Fax: 518-442-5383 **Website:** www.albany.edu **ACT Code:** 2926
Financial Aid Phone: 518-442-5757

This public school was founded in 1844. It has a 560-acre campus.

RATINGS
Admissions Selectivity Rating: 83   **Fire Safety Rating:** 60*   **Green Rating:** 88

STUDENTS AND FACULTY
Enrollment: 11,680. **Student Body:** 50% female, 50% male, 6% out-of-state, 2% international (87 countries represented). African American 8%, Asian 6%, Caucasian 60%, Hispanic 7%. **Retention and Graduation:** 85% freshmen return for sophomore year. 50% freshmen graduate within 4 years. **Faculty:** Student/faculty ratio 19:1. 631 full-time faculty, 98% hold PhDs. 93% faculty teach undergrads.

ACADEMICS
Degrees: Bachelor's, doctoral, master's, post-bachelor's certificate, post-master's certificate. **Academic Requirements:** Arts/fine arts, computer literacy, foreign languages, history, humanities, mathematics, sciences (biological or physical), social science. 30 credits of coursework in the above mentioned as well as in: national and international perspectives, pluralism and diversity, communication and reasoning competencies, and information literacy. For details see www.albany.edu/gened. **Classes:** Most classes have 20–29 students. Most lab/discussion sections have 10–19 students. **Majors with Highest Enrollment:** Business administration/management, English language and literature, psychology, **Disciplines with Highest Percentage of Degrees Awarded:** Social sciences 24%, business/marketing 14%, psychology 14%, communications/journalism 9%, English 9%. **Special Study Options:** Accelerated program, cross-registration, distance learning, double major, dual enrollment, English as a second language (ESL), honors program, independent study, internships, liberal arts/career combination, student-designed major, study abroad. Accelerated 5 year bachelor's/master's programs in 40 fields; internships with New York State Legislature; combined bachelor's/law degree with Albany Law school; 3+2 engineering program with RPI, Clarkson, and others; biology/dental program with Boston University Goldman School of Dental Medicine; bachelor's/doctor of optometry with SUNY state college.

FACILITIES

Housing: Coed dorms, men's dorms, women's dorms, apartments for married students, apartments for single students, special housing for international students. Disabled Student Services provides individualized services including information on accessible housing. **Special Academic Facilities/Equipment**: Performing arts center, art museum, art and dance studios, sculpture foundry, nuclear accelerator and advanced materials facilities, a peptide synthesis facility, recombinant DNA sequencing laboratories, atmospheric science's Whiteface Mountain observational facility. **Computers**: Network access in dorm rooms, network access in dorm lounges, online registration, online administrative functions (other than registration), remote student-access to Web through college's connection.

CAMPUS LIFE

Activities: Choral groups, concert band, dance, drama/theater, jazz band, literary magazine, music ensembles, musical theater, pep band, radio station, student government, student newspaper, symphony orchestra, yearbook. **Organizations**: 160 registered organizations, 20 honor societies, 17 religious organizations. 19 fraternities (2% men join), 15 sororities (5% women join). **Athletics (Intercollegiate)**: *Men*: Baseball, basketball, crew/rowing, cross-country, football, lacrosse, rugby, skiing (downhill/alpine), soccer, track/field (indoor), track/field (outdoor). *Women*: Basketball, crew/rowing, cross-country, field hockey, golf, lacrosse, rugby, skiing (downhill/alpine), soccer, softball, tennis, track/field (indoor), track/field (outdoor), volleyball. Environmental Initiatives: Recycling, energy campaign, farmers market.

ADMISSIONS

Freshman Academic Profile: 14% in top 10% of high school class, 31% in top 25% of high school class, 87% in top 50% of high school class. SAT Math middle 50% range 540–620. SAT Critical Reading middle 50% range 520–600. ACT middle 50% range 23–26. TOEFL required of all international applicants, minimum paper TOEFL 550, minimum computer TOEFL 213. **Basis for Candidate Selection**: *Very important factors considered include*: Academic GPA, character/personal qualities, class rank, rigor of secondary school record, standardized test scores. *Important factors considered include*: Application essay, recommendation(s). *Other factors considered include*: Alumni/ae relation, extracurricular activities, first generation, geographical residence, talent/ability, volunteer work, work experience. **Freshman Admission Requirements**: High school diploma is required, and GED is accepted. *Academic units required*: 4 English, 2 math, 2 science (2 science labs), 1 foreign language, 3 social studies, 2 history, 4 academic electives. *Academic units recommended*: 4 math, 3 science (3 science labs), 3 foreign language. **Freshman Admission Statistics**: 16,725 applied, 63% admitted, 24% enrolled. **Transfer Admission Requirements**: College transcript(s), essay or personal statement, statement of good standing from prior institution(s). Minimum college GPA of 2.0 required. Lowest grade transferable C. **General Admission Information**: Application fee $40. Regular application deadline 3/1. Regular notification is rolling. Non-fall registration accepted. Admission may be deferred for a maximum of 1 year. Common Application accepted. Credit and/or placement offered for CEEB Advanced Placement tests.

COSTS AND FINANCIAL AID

Annual in-state tuition $4,350. Out-of-state tuition $10,610. Room & board $8,604. Required fees $1,589. Average book expense $1,000. **Required Forms and Deadlines**: FAFSA, NY State residents should apply for TAP on-line at www.tapWeb.org. Financial aid filing deadline 4/15. **Notification of Awards**: Applicants will be notified of awards on a rolling basis beginning on or about 3/15. **Types of Aid**: *Need-based scholarships/grants*: Pell, SEOG, state scholarships/grants. *Loans*: FFEL Subsidized Stafford, FFEL Unsubsidized Stafford, FFEL PLUS, Federal Perkins. **Student Employment**: Federal Work-Study Program available. Institutional employment available. Off-campus job opportunities are excellent. **Financial Aid Statistics**: 51% freshmen, 51% undergrads receive need-based scholarship or grant aid. 47% freshmen, 46% undergrads receive need-based self-help aid. 31 freshmen, 131 undergrads receive athletic scholarships. 63% freshmen, 60% undergrads receive any aid. Highest amount earned per year from on-campus jobs $4,560.

STATE UNIVERSITY OF NEW YORK— UNIVERSITY AT BUFFALO

17 Capen Hall, Buffalo, NY 14260-1660
Phone: 716-645-6900 **E-mail**: admissions@buffalo.edu **CEEB Code**: 2925
Fax: 716-645-6411 **Website**: www.buffalo.edu **ACT Code**: 2978
Financial Aid Phone: 866-838-7257

This public school was founded in 1846. It has a 1,346-acre campus.

RATINGS

Admissions Selectivity Rating: 85   **Fire Safety Rating**: 60*   **Green Rating**: 60*

STUDENTS AND FACULTY

Enrollment: 17,509. **Student Body**: 46% female, 54% male, 2% out-of-state, 6% international (113 countries represented). African American 7%, Asian 9%, Caucasian 65%, Hispanic 4%. **Retention and Graduation**: 85% freshmen return for sophomore year. 34% freshmen graduate within 4 years. 36% grads go on to further study within 1 year. 35% grads pursue arts and sciences degrees. **Faculty**: Student/faculty ratio 15:1. 1,142 full-time faculty, 98% hold PhDs. 73% faculty teach undergrads.

ACADEMICS

Degrees: Bachelor's, doctoral, first professional certificate, first professional, master's, post-master's certificate. **Academic Requirements**: American pluralism, Arts/fine arts, computer literacy, depth requirements English (including composition), foreign language, history, humanities, library sciences, mathematics, sciences (biology or physical), social science, world civilizations. **Classes**: Most classes have 20-29 students. Most lab/discussion sections have 20-29 students. **Majors with Highest Enrollment**: Business administration/management, mechanical engineering, psychology. **Disciplines with Highest Percentage of Degrees Awarded**: Business/marketing 18%, social sciences 13%, engineering 11%, communication technologies 10%, psychology 9%. **Special Study Options**: Accelerated program, cooperative education program, cross-registration, distance learning, double major, dual enrollment, English as a second language (ESL), exchange student program (domestic), honors program, independent study, internships, liberal arts/career combination, student-designed major, study abroad, teacher certification program. Early Assurance Program with School of Medicine & Dentistry.

FACILITIES

Housing: Coed dorms, apartments for married students, special housing for disabled students, shared interest, cultural interest, and academic interest housing, freshman housing, honors housing. See website: www.ub-housing.buffalo.edu/special. **Special Academic Facilities/Equipment**: UB Center for the Arts, Slee Concert Hall, The Anthropology Research Museum, Multidisciplinary Center for Earthquake Engineering Research (MCEER), University at Buffalo Center of Excellence in Bioinformatics, Center for Computational Research (CCR), University at Buffalo Poetry and Rare Books Collection, pharmacy museum, the virtual site museum. **Computers**: 12% of classrooms are wired, 50% of classrooms are wireless, 80% of public computers are PCs, 10% of public computers are Macs, 10% of public computers are UNIX, network access in dorm rooms, network access in dorm lounges, online registration, online administrative functions (other than registration), support for handheld computing, remote student-access to Web through college's connection.

CAMPUS LIFE

Activities: Choral groups, concert band, dance, drama/theater, jazz band, marching band, music ensembles, musical theater, pep band, radio station, student government, student newspaper, student-run film society, symphony orchestra, television station. **Organizations**: 300 registered organizations, 29 honor societies, 17 religious organizations. 19 fraternities (2% men join), 14 sororities (4% women join). **Athletics (Intercollegiate)**: *Men*: Baseball, basketball, cross-country, football, soccer, swimming, tennis, track/field (outdoor), wrestling. *Women*: Basketball, crew/rowing, cross-country, soccer, softball, swimming, tennis, track/field (outdoor), volleyball.

ADMISSIONS

Freshman Academic Profile: 24% in top 10% of high school class, 62% in top 25% of high school class, 94% in top 50% of high school class. SAT Math middle

50% range 550–640. SAT Critical Reading middle 50% range 520–610. ACT middle 50% range 24–28. TOEFL required of all international applicants, minimum paper TOEFL 550, minimum computer TOEFL 213. **Basis for Candidate Selection**: *Very important factors considered include:* Class rank, rigor of secondary school record, standardized test scores. *Other factors considered include:* Application essay, character/personal qualities, extracurricular activities, geographical residence, racial/ethnic status, recommendation(s), talent/ability, volunteer work, work experience. **Freshman Admission Requirements**: High school diploma is required, and GED is accepted. *Academic units recommended:* 4 English, 3 math, 3 science, 3 foreign language, 4 social studies. **Freshman Admission Statistics**: 18,207 applied, 56% admitted, 31% enrolled. **Transfer Admission Requirements**: High school transcript, college transcript(s). Minimum college GPA of 2.0 required. Lowest grade transferable D. **General Admission Information**: Application fee $40. Early decision application deadline 11/1. Regular notification is rolling. Non-fall registration accepted. Common Application not accepted. Credit and/or placement offered for CEEB Advanced Placement tests.

COSTS AND FINANCIAL AID
Annual in-state tuition $4,350. Out-of-state tuition $10,610. Room & board $8,086. Required fees $1,616. Average book expense $795. **Required Forms and Deadlines**: FAFSA. Financial aid filing deadline 3/1. **Notification of Awards**: Applicants will be notified of awards on a rolling basis beginning on or about 2/1. **Types of Aid**: *Need-based scholarships/grants:* Pell, SEOG, state scholarships/grants, private scholarships, the school's own gift aid, Federal Nursing Scholarships. *Loans:* Direct Subsidized Stafford, Direct Unsubsidized Stafford, Direct PLUS, Federal Perkins, Federal Nursing, college/university loans from institutional funds. **Financial Aid Statistics**: 35% freshmen, 33% undergrads receive need-based scholarship or grant aid. 52% freshmen, 50% undergrads receive need-based self-help aid. 26 freshmen, 124 undergrads receive athletic scholarships. 67% freshmen, 75% undergrads receive any aid.

STATE UNIVERSITY OF NEW YORK— UPSTATE MEDICAL UNIVERSITY

766 Irving Avenue, Syracuse, NY 13210
Phone: 315-464-4570 **E-mail**: admiss@upstate.edu **CEEB Code**: 2547
Fax: 315-464-8867 **Website**: www.upstate.edu **ACT Code**: 2981
Financial Aid Phone: 315-464-4329

This public school was founded in 1850. It has a 25-acre campus.

RATINGS
Admissions Selectivity Rating: 60*   **Fire Safety Rating**: 60*   **Green Rating**: 60*

STUDENTS AND FACULTY
Enrollment: 262. **Student Body**: 77% female, 23% male, 2% out-of-state, 1% international. African American 5%, Asian 3%, Caucasian 67%.

ACADEMICS
Degrees: Bachelor's, doctoral, first professional, master's, post-master's certificate. **Academic Requirements**: Health sciences. **Disciplines with Highest Percentage of Degrees Awarded**: Health professions and related sciences 100%.

FACILITIES
Housing: Coed dorms, apartments for married students, apartments for single students. **Special Academic Facilities/Equipment**: 350-bed tertiary care hospital. **Computers**: Network access in dorm rooms, remote student-access to Web through college's connection.

CAMPUS LIFE
Activities: Student government, yearbook. **Organizations**: 45 registered organizations.

ADMISSIONS
Freshman Academic Profile: TOEFL required of all international applicants, minimum paper TOEFL 500, minimum computer TOEFL 250. **Basis for Candidate Selection**: *Very important factors considered include:* Interview, volunteer work, work experience. *Important factors considered include:* Extracurricular activities, geographical residence, racial/ethnic status. *Other factors considered include:* Application essay, character/personal qualities, class rank, recommendation(s), rigor of secondary school record, standardized test scores, state residency. **Freshman Admission Requirements**: High school diploma is required, and GED is accepted. *Academic units recommended:* 4

English, 3 math, 3 science, 3 social studies. **Transfer Admission Requirements**: College transcript(s), essay or personal statement, interview, statement of good standing from prior institution(s). Minimum college GPA of 2.0 required. Lowest grade transferable C-. **General Admission Information**: Application fee $40. Non-fall registration not accepted. Admission may be deferred for a maximum of 1 year. Common Application not accepted.

COSTS AND FINANCIAL AID
Annual in-state tuition $8,700. Annual out-of-state tuition $21,200. Room and board $88,000. Required fees $536. Average book expense $900. **Required Forms and Deadlines**: FAFSA. Financial aid filing deadline 4/1. **Notification of Awards**: Applicants will be notified of awards on a rolling basis beginning on or about 6/1. **Types of Aid**: *Need-based scholarships/grants:* Pell, SEOG, state scholarships/grants, the school's own gift aid. *Loans:* FFEL Subsidized Stafford, FFEL Unsubsidized Stafford, FFEL PLUS, Federal Perkins. **Student Employment**: Federal Work-Study Program available. Institutional employment available. Off-campus job opportunities are excellent. **Financial Aid Statistics**: 30% undergrads receive need-based scholarship or grant aid. 50% undergrads receive need-based self-help aid.

STEPHEN F. AUSTIN STATE UNIVERSITY

PO Box 13051, SFA Station, Nacogdoches, TX 75962
Phone: 936-468-2504 **E-mail**: admissions@sfasu.edu **CEEB Code**: 6682
Fax: 936-468-3849 **Website**: www.sfasu.edu **ACT Code**: 4188
Financial Aid Phone: 936-468-2403

This public school was founded in 1923. It has a 401-acre campus.

RATINGS
Admissions Selectivity Rating: 71   **Fire Safety Rating**: 60*   **Green Rating**: 60*

STUDENTS AND FACULTY
Enrollment: 9,568. **Student Body**: 59% female, 41% male, 2% out-of-state. African American 16%, Asian 1%, Caucasian 74%, Hispanic 7%. **Retention and Graduation**: 66% freshmen return for sophomore year. 17% freshmen graduate within 4 years. **Faculty**: Student/faculty ratio 18:1. 434 full-time faculty, 76% hold PhDs. 98% faculty teach undergrads.

ACADEMICS
Degrees: Bachelor's, doctoral, master's. **Academic Requirements**: Arts/fine arts, communication, computer literacy, English (including composition), history, humanities, mathematics, sciences (biological or physical), social science. **Classes**: Most classes have 20–29 students. Most lab/discussion sections have 10–19 students. **Majors with Highest Enrollment**: Health and physical education, multi/interdisciplinary studies, nursing/registered nurse training (ASN, BSN, MSN, RN). **Disciplines with Highest Percentage of Degrees Awarded**: Business/marketing 22%, interdisciplinary studies 16%, social sciences 8%, health professions and related sciences 7%, parks and recreation 6%. **Special Study Options**: Accelerated program, distance learning, double major, dual enrollment, honors program, independent study, internships, liberal arts/career combination, student-designed major, study abroad, teacher certification program.

FACILITIES
Housing: Coed dorms, men's dorms, women's dorms, apartments for married students, apartments for single students, special housing for disabled students, fraternity/sorority housing, apartments for students with dependent children. **Special Academic Facilities/Equipment**: Stone Fort Museum, planetarium, arboretum, observatory, GIS Lab, forest resources institute, soils analysis lab, East Texas Historical Association, East Texas Research Center, science research center, research feed mill. **Computers**: 60% of public computers are PCs, 35% of public computers are Macs, 5% of public computers are UNIX, network access in dorm rooms, online registration, online administrative functions (other than registration), remote student-access to Web through college's connection.

CAMPUS LIFE
Activities: Choral groups, concert band, dance, drama/theater, jazz band, literary magazine, marching band, music ensembles, musical theater, opera, pep band, radio station, student government, student newspaper, student-run film society, symphony orchestra, television studio. **Organizations**: 21 registered organizations, 15 honor societies, 25 religious organizations. 25 fraternities (13% men join), 14 sororities (9% women join). **Athletics (Intercollegiate)**: *Men:* Basketball, cross-country, football, golf, track/field (indoor), track/field (outdoor). *Women:* Basketball, cross-country, soccer, softball, tennis, track/field (indoor), track/field (outdoor), volleyball.

ADMISSIONS

Freshman Academic Profile: 16% in top 10% of high school class, 44% in top 25% of high school class, 83% in top 50% of high school class. 90% from public high schools. SAT Math middle 50% range 450–550. SAT Critical Reading middle 50% range 450–560. ACT middle 50% range 18–23. TOEFL required of all international applicants, minimum paper TOEFL 550, minimum computer TOEFL 213. **Basis for Candidate Selection**: *Very important factors considered include:* Class rank, rigor of secondary school record, standardized test scores. *Other factors considered include*: Extracurricular activities, geographical residence, talent/ability, volunteer work, work experience. **Freshman Admission Requirements**: High school diploma is required, and GED is accepted. *Academic units required:* 4 English, 3 math, 3 science, 2 foreign language. *Academic units recommended*: 1 social studies, 2 history, 3 fine arts/computer/government economic. **Freshman Admission Statistics**: 5,873 applied, 75% admitted, 38% enrolled. **Transfer Admission Requirements**: College transcript(s). Minimum college GPA of 2.0 required. Lowest grade transferable D. **General Admission Information**: Application fee $25. Regular notification is rolling. Non-fall registration accepted. Common Application not accepted. Credit and/or placement offered for CEEB Advanced Placement tests.

COSTS AND FINANCIAL AID

Annual in-state tuition $3,360. Out-of-state tuition $11,100. Room & board $5,012. Required fees $938. Average book expense $905. **Required Forms and Deadlines**: FAFSA. Financial aid filing deadline 4/1. **Notification of Awards**: Applicants will be notified of awards on a rolling basis beginning on or about 5/1. **Types of Aid**: *Need-based scholarships/grants*: Pell, SEOG, state scholarships/grants, private scholarships, the school's own gift aid. *Loans*: FFEL Subsidized Stafford, FFEL Unsubsidized Stafford, FFEL PLUS, Federal Perkins, state loans, college/university loans from institutional funds, alternative loans. **Financial Aid Statistics**: 39% freshmen, 43% undergrads receive need-based scholarship or grant aid. 37% freshmen, 44% undergrads receive need-based self-help aid. 51 freshmen, 248 undergrads receive athletic scholarships. 46% freshmen, 47% undergrads receive any aid. Highest amount earned per year from on-campus jobs $4,100.

STEPHENS COLLEGE

1200 East Broadway, Box 2121, Columbia, MO 65215
Phone: 573-876-7207 **E-mail**: apply@wc.stephens.edu **CEEB Code**: 6683
Fax: 573-876-7237 **Website**: www.stephens.edu **ACT Code**: 2374
Financial Aid Phone: 573-876-7106

This private school was founded in 1833. It has an 86-acre campus.

RATINGS

Admissions Selectivity Rating: 79   **Fire Safety Rating**: 74   **Green Rating**: 65

STUDENTS AND FACULTY

Enrollment: 824. **Student Body**: 97% female, 3% male, 55% out-of-state. African American 8%, Asian 3%, Caucasian 81%, Hispanic 3%, Native American 1%. **Retention and Graduation**: 71% freshmen return for sophomore year. 49% freshmen graduate within 4 years. **Faculty**: Student/faculty ratio 12:1. 44 full-time faculty, 43% hold PhDs. 100% faculty teach undergrads.

ACADEMICS

Degrees: Associate, bachelor's, master's, post-bachelor's certificate. **Academic Requirements**: Arts/fine arts, computer literacy, English (including composition), history, humanities, mathematics, philosophy, sciences (biological or physical), social science. **Classes**: Most classes have 10–19 students. Most lab/discussion sections have 10–19 students. **Majors with Highest Enrollment**: Dance, drama, and dramatics/theater arts; fashion/apparel design. **Disciplines with Highest Percentage of Degrees Awarded**: Visual and performing arts 35%, communication technologies 7%, psychology 7%, education 6%, health professions and related sciences 5%, business/marketing 5%. **Special Study Options**: Cross-registration, distance learning, double major, dual enrollment, external degree program, independent study, internships, liberal arts/career combination, student-designed major, study abroad, teacher certification program.

FACILITIES

Housing: Women's dorms, apartments for married students, apartments for single students. **Special Academic Facilities/Equipment**: Art gallery and historical costume collections; on-campus preschool, kindergarten, and elementary school; language lab. **Computers**: 50% of classrooms are wireless, 70% of public computers are PCs, 30% of public computers are Macs, network access in dorm rooms, network access in dorm lounges, online administrative functions (other than registration), remote student-access to Web through college's connection.

CAMPUS LIFE

Activities: Choral groups, dance, drama/theater, literary magazine, music ensembles, musical theater, radio station, student government, student newspaper, television station, yearbook. **Organizations**: 45 registered organizations, 10 honor societies, 5 religious organizations. 2 sororities (10% women join). **Athletics (Intercollegiate)**: *Women*: Basketball, cross-country, softball, swimming, tennis, volleyball. Environmental Initiatives: Recycling. Decreased energy usage. Meeting LEED criteria on building projects and operations.

ADMISSIONS

Freshman Academic Profile: 21% in top 10% of high school class, 67% in top 25% of high school class, 93% in top 50% of high school class. 76% from public high schools. SAT Math middle 50% range 480–580. SAT Critical Reading middle 50% range 540–610. ACT middle 50% range 21–26. TOEFL required of all international applicants, minimum paper TOEFL 550, minimum computer TOEFL 213. **Basis for Candidate Selection**: *Very important factors considered include:* Application essay, character/personal qualities, recommendation(s), rigor of secondary school record, standardized test scores. *Important factors considered include*: Extracurricular activities, talent/ability. *Other factors considered include*: Class rank, interview, volunteer work, work experience. **Freshman Admission Requirements**: High school diploma is required, and GED is accepted. *Academic units recommended*: 4 English, 2 math, 2 science, 2 foreign language, 2 social studies. **Freshman Admission Statistics**: 633 applied, 76% admitted, 51% enrolled. **Transfer Admission Requirements**: High school transcript, college transcript(s), statement of good standing from prior institution(s). Minimum college GPA of 2.0 required. Lowest grade transferable C. **General Admission Information**: Application fee $25. Regular notification is rolling. Non-fall registration accepted. Admission may be deferred for a maximum of 1 year. Credit offered for CEEB Advanced Placement tests.

COSTS AND FINANCIAL AID

Annual tuition $23,000. Room and board $8,730. Average book expense $1,000. **Required Forms and Deadlines**: FAFSA. Financial aid filing deadline 3/15. **Notification of Awards**: Applicants will be notified of awards on a rolling basis beginning on or about 3/1. **Types of Aid**: *Need-based scholarships/grants*: Pell, SEOG, state scholarships/grants, private scholarships, the school's own gift aid. *Loans*: FFEL Subsidized Stafford, FFEL Unsubsidized Stafford, FFEL PLUS, Federal Perkins. **Financial Aid Statistics**: 64% freshmen, 54% undergrads receive need-based scholarship or grant aid. 62% freshmen, 58% undergrads receive need-based self-help aid. 16 freshmen, 51 undergrads receive athletic scholarships. 98% freshmen, 83% undergrads receive any aid. Highest amount earned per year from on-campus jobs $1,400.

STERLING COLLEGE

125 W. Cooper, Sterling, KS 67579
Phone: 620-278-4275 **E-mail**: admissions@sterling.edu **CEEB Code**: 6684
Fax: 620-278-4416 **Website**: www.sterling.edu **ACT Code**: 1466
Financial Aid Phone: 620-278-4207

This private school, affiliated with the Presbyterian Church, was founded in 1887. It has a 42-acre campus.

RATINGS

Admissions Selectivity Rating: 76   **Fire Safety Rating**: 60*   **Green Rating**: 60*

STUDENTS AND FACULTY

Enrollment: 545. **Student Body**: 44% female, 56% male, 54% out-of-state. African American 11%, Asian 1%, Caucasian 79%, Hispanic 6%, Native American 2%. **Retention and Graduation**: 64% freshmen return for sophomore year. 38% freshmen graduate within 4 years. 10% grads go on to further study within 1 year. 5% grads pursue arts and sciences degrees. 2% grads pursue business degrees. 1% grads pursue law degrees. 2% grads pursue medical degrees. **Faculty**: Student/faculty ratio 15:1. 35 full-time faculty, 43% hold PhDs. 100% faculty teach undergrads.

ACADEMICS

Degrees: Bachelor's. **Academic Requirements**: Arts/fine arts, computer literacy, English (including composition), exercise science, history, humanities, mathematics, philosophy, religion, sciences (biological or physical), social science. **Classes**: Most classes have 10–19 students. Most lab/discussion sections have 10–19 students. **Majors with Highest Enrollment**: Business administration/management, elementary education and teaching, health and physical education. **Disciplines with Highest Percentage of Degrees Awarded**: Business/marketing 21%, theology and religious vocations 12%, education 11%, biological/life sciences 8%, parks and recreation 7%, English 7%. **Special Study Options**: Distance learning, double major, dual enrollment, honors program, independent study, internships, liberal arts/career combination, student-designed major, study abroad, teacher certification program.

FACILITIES

Housing: Men's dorms, women's dorms. **Special Academic Facilities/ Equipment**: History/cultural museum. **Computers**: 10% of classrooms are wireless, 99% of public computers are PCs, 1% of public computers are Macs, network access in dorm rooms, network access in dorm lounges, remote student-access to Web through college's connection.

CAMPUS LIFE

Activities: Choral groups, concert band, drama/theater, jazz band, literary magazine, music ensembles, musical theater, pep band, radio station, student government, student newspaper, television station, yearbook. **Organizations**: 12 registered organizations, 4 honor societies, 2 religious organizations. **Athletics (Intercollegiate)**: *Men*: Baseball, basketball, cross-country, football, soccer, track/field (outdoor). *Women*: Basketball, cheerleading, cross-country, soccer, softball, track/field (outdoor), volleyball.

ADMISSIONS

Freshman Academic Profile: 5% in top 10% of high school class, 30% in top 25% of high school class, 60% in top 50% of high school class. 80% from public high schools. SAT Math middle 50% range 420–510. SAT Critical Reading middle 50% range 420–490. SAT Writing middle 50% range 410–490. ACT middle 50% range 18–23. TOEFL required of all international applicants, minimum paper TOEFL 520, minimum computer TOEFL 190. **Basis for Candidate Selection**: *Very important factors considered include:* Character/ personal qualities, rigor of secondary school record, standardized test scores. *Important factors considered include:* Academic GPA, application essay, extracurricular activities, interview, level of applicant's interest, recommendation(s), religious affiliation/commitment, volunteer work. *Other factors considered include:* Alumni/ae relation, class rank, first generation, talent/ability, work experience. **Freshman Admission Requirements**: High school diploma is required, and GED is accepted. *Academic units recommended:* 4 English, 3 math, 3 science (1 science lab), 2 foreign language, 1 social studies, 2 history, 1 academic elective, 2 computer info/tech, 1 physical education. **Freshman Admission Statistics**: 932 applied, 65% admitted, 33% enrolled. **Transfer Admission Requirements**: College transcript(s), essay or personal statement. Minimum college GPA of 2.2 required. Lowest grade transferable C-. **General Admission Information**: Application fee $25. Regular notification is rolling. Non-fall registration accepted. Admission may be deferred for a maximum of 1 semester. Credit offered for CEEB Advanced Placement tests.

COSTS AND FINANCIAL AID

Annual tuition $15,500. Room and board $6,230. Average book expense $600. **Required Forms and Deadlines**: FAFSA. Financial aid filing deadline 4/1. **Notification of Awards**: Applicants will be notified of awards on a rolling basis beginning on or about 1/1. **Types of Aid**: *Need-based scholarships/grants*: Pell, SEOG, state scholarships/grants, private scholarships, the school's own gift aid. *Loans*: FFEL Subsidized Stafford, FFEL Unsubsidized Stafford, FFEL PLUS, Federal Perkins. **Student Employment**: Federal Work-Study Program available. Institutional employment available. Off-campus job opportunities are fair. **Financial Aid Statistics**: 86% freshmen, 82% undergrads receive need-based scholarship or grant aid. 74% freshmen, 73% undergrads receive need-based self-help aid. 9 freshmen, 37 undergrads receive athletic scholarships. 100% freshmen, 96% undergrads receive any aid. Highest amount earned per year from on-campus jobs $1,100.

STERLING COLLEGE (VT)

PO Box 72, Craftsbury Common, VT 05827
Phone: 802-586-7711 **E-mail**: admissions@sterlingcollege.edu **CEEB Code**: 3752
Fax: 802-586-2596 **Website**: www.sterlingcollege.edu **ACT Code**: 6946
Financial Aid Phone: 802-586-7711

This private school was founded in 1958. It has a 430-acre campus.

RATINGS

Admissions Selectivity Rating: 65   **Fire Safety Rating**: 60*   **Green Rating**: 60*

STUDENTS AND FACULTY

Enrollment: 102. **Student Body**: 43% female, 57% male, 78% out-of-state. Caucasian 69%, Hispanic 2%. **Retention and Graduation**: 76% freshmen return for sophomore year. **Faculty**: Student/faculty ratio 4:1. 17 full-time faculty, 29% hold PhDs. 100% faculty teach undergrads.

ACADEMICS

Degrees: Bachelor's. **Academic Requirements**: Arts/fine arts, English (including composition), humanities, mathematics, sciences (biological or physical), social science. **Classes**: Most classes have fewer than 10 students. **Majors with Highest Enrollment**: Agriculture, environmental studies, natural resources/conservation. **Disciplines with Highest Percentage of Degrees Awarded**: Natural resources/environmental science 33%, parks and recreation 25%, agriculture 21%, area and ethnic studies 8%. **Special Study Options**: Exchange student program (domestic), independent study, internships, liberal arts/career combination, student-designed major, study abroad.

FACILITIES

Housing: Coed dorms, apartments for married students. **Special Academic Facilities/Equipment**: Library serves as art gallery. There is a 6–8 week rotation of Vermont artist displays. Campus also includes a wind and solar-powered barn that serves as an instructional facility and lab, a heated greenhouse provides a working lab for plant and soil studies. Other facilities include: A woodshop, logging shop, sugarhouse, root cellar, darkroom, certified organic gardens, and a 32' tall climbing tower provides students with the ability to develop leadership and technical rock-climbing skills. The Center for Northern Studies at Sterling College includes a 300-acre boreal forest. **Computers**: 90% of classrooms are wired, 60% of classrooms are wireless, 100% of public computers are PCs, online administrative functions (other than registration), remote student-access to Web through college's connection.

CAMPUS LIFE

Activities: Choral groups, dance, music ensembles, student government, yearbook.

ADMISSIONS

Freshman Academic Profile: 8% in top 10% of high school class, 17% in top 25% of high school class, 58% in top 50% of high school class. 67% from public high schools. TOEFL required of all international applicants, minimum paper TOEFL 500, minimum computer TOEFL 173. **Basis for Candidate Selection**: *Very important factors considered include:* Recommendation(s), rigor of secondary school record. *Important factors considered include:* Academic GPA, application essay, character/personal qualities, extracurricular activities, level of applicant's interest, talent/ability, volunteer work. *Other factors considered include:* Alumni/ae relation, class rank, interview, work experience. **Freshman Admission Requirements**: High school diploma is required, and GED is accepted. *Academic units required:* 4 English, 3 math, 2 science (1 science lab), 2 social studies, 2 history. *Academic units recommended:* 4 English, 4 math, 3 science (2 science labs), 2 foreign language, 2 social studies, 2 history. **Freshman Admission Statistics**: 78 applied, 76% admitted, 36% enrolled. **Transfer Admission Requirements**: High school transcript, college transcript(s), essay or personal statement. Minimum college GPA of 2.0 required. Lowest grade transferable C. **General Admission Information**: Application fee $35. Regular application deadline 2/15. Regular notification is rolling. Non-fall registration not accepted. Admission may be deferred for a maximum of 1 year. Credit and/or placement offered for CEEB Advanced Placement tests.

COSTS AND FINANCIAL AID

Annual tuition $21,280. Room and board $7,192. Required fees $375. Average book expense $900. **Required Forms and Deadlines**: FAFSA, institution's own financial aid form, state aid form. Financial aid filing deadline 3/1. **Notification of Awards**: Applicants will be notified of awards on a rolling basis beginning on or about 2/1. **Types of Aid**: *Need-based scholarships/grants*: Pell,

SEOG, state scholarships/grants, private scholarships, the school's own gift aid. *Loans*: FFEL Subsidized Stafford, FFEL Unsubsidized Stafford, FFEL PLUS. **Student Employment**: Federal Work-Study Program available. Institutional employment available. Off-campus job opportunities are fair. **Financial Aid Statistics**: 71% freshmen, 74% undergrads receive need-based scholarship or grant aid. 71% freshmen, 74% undergrads receive need-based self-help aid. 71% freshmen, 74% undergrads receive any aid. Highest amount earned per year from on-campus jobs $1,450.

STETSON UNIVERSITY

421 North Woodland Boulevard, Unit 8378, DeLand, FL 32723
Phone: 386-822-7100 **E-mail:** admissions@stetson.edu **CEEB Code:** 5630
Fax: 386-822-7112 **Website:** www.stetson.edu **ACT Code:** 0756
Financial Aid Phone: 800-688-7120

This private school was founded in 1883. It has a 170-acre campus.

RATINGS
Admissions Selectivity Rating: 89 **Fire Safety Rating:** 60* **Green Rating:** 60*

STUDENTS AND FACULTY
Enrollment: 2,235. **Student Body:** 58% female, 42% male, 20% out-of-state, 3% international (32 countries represented). African American 5%, Asian 2%, Caucasian 76%, Hispanic 8%. **Retention and Graduation:** 80% freshmen return for sophomore year. 53% freshmen graduate within 4 years. 48% grads go on to further study within 1 year. 24% grads pursue arts and sciences degrees. 11% grads pursue business degrees. 8% grads pursue law degrees. 5% grads pursue medical degrees. **Faculty:** Student/faculty ratio 11:1. 236 full-time faculty, 93% hold PhDs. 96% faculty teach undergrads.

ACADEMICS
Degrees: Bachelor's, first professional certificate, first professional, master's, post-master's certificate. **Academic Requirements:** Arts/fine arts, computer literacy, English (including composition), foreign languages, history, humanities, mathematics, religious studies, sciences (biological or physical), social science. **Classes:** Most classes have 10–19 students. Most lab/discussion sections have 10–19 students. **Majors with Highest Enrollment:** Business administration/management, elementary education and teaching, psychology. **Disciplines with Highest Percentage of Degrees Awarded:** Business/marketing 33%, social sciences 10%, visual and performing arts 9%, education 8%, psychology 8%. **Special Study Options:** Accelerated program, double major, honors program, independent study, internships, liberal arts/career combination, student-designed major, study abroad, teacher certification program, weekend college.

FACILITIES
Housing: Coed dorms, men's dorms, women's dorms, apartments for single students, fraternity/sorority housing, foreign language house, French house, the Service Station (community service house). **Special Academic Facilities/Equipment:** Language lab, art gallery, greenhouse with growth chambers, mineral museum, electron microscopes. **Computers:** 85% of public computers are PCs, 15% of public computers are Macs, network access in dorm rooms, network access in dorm lounges, online registration, online administrative functions (other than registration), remote student-access to Web through college's connection.

CAMPUS LIFE
Activities: Choral groups, concert band, dance, drama/theater, jazz band, literary magazine, music ensembles, musical theater, opera, pep band, radio station, student government, student newspaper, student-run film society, symphony orchestra. **Organizations:** 124 registered organizations, 24 honor societies, 11 religious organizations. 7 fraternities (22% men join), 6 sororities (19% women join). **Athletics (Intercollegiate):** *Men:* Baseball, basketball, crew/rowing, cross-country, golf, soccer, tennis. *Women:* Basketball, crew/rowing, cross-country, golf, soccer, softball, tennis, volleyball.

ADMISSIONS
Freshman Academic Profile: 41% in top 10% of high school class, 82% in top 25% of high school class, 100% in top 50% of high school class. 70% from public high schools. SAT Math middle 50% range 500–610. SAT Critical Reading middle 50% range 500–620. ACT middle 50% range 21–27. TOEFL required of all international applicants, minimum paper TOEFL 550, minimum computer TOEFL 213. **Basis for Candidate Selection:** *Very important factors considered include:* Academic GPA, rigor of secondary school record. *Important factors considered include:* Application essay, character/personal

qualities, class rank, extracurricular activities, interview, recommendation(s), standardized test scores, talent/ability, volunteer work, work experience. *Other factors considered include:* Alumni/ae relation, geographical residence, racial/ethnic status, state residency. **Freshman Admission Requirements:** High school diploma is required, and GED is accepted. *Academic units required:* 4 English, 3 math, 3 science, 2 foreign language, 2 social studies. **Freshman Admission Statistics:** 2,919 applied, 65% admitted, 30% enrolled. **Transfer Admission Requirements:** High school transcript, college transcript(s), essay or personal statement, standardized test score, statement of good standing from prior institution(s). Minimum college GPA of 2.0 required. Lowest grade transferable C. **General Admission Information:** Application fee $40. Early decision application deadline 11/1. Regular notification is rolling. Non-fall registration accepted. Credit and/or placement offered for CEEB Advanced Placement tests.

COSTS AND FINANCIAL AID
Annual tuition $27,100. Room and board $7,968. Required fees $1,680. Average book expense $1,000. **Required Forms and Deadlines:** FAFSA, institution's own financial aid form. Financial aid filing deadline 3/15. **Notification of Awards:** Applicants will be notified of awards on a rolling basis beginning on or about 2/15. **Types of Aid:** *Need-based scholarships/grants:* Pell, SEOG, state scholarships/grants, private scholarships, the school's own gift aid. *Loans:* FFEL Subsidized Stafford, FFEL Unsubsidized Stafford, FFEL PLUS, Federal Perkins, state loans, college/university loans from institutional funds. **Student Employment:** Federal Work-Study Program available. Institutional employment available. Off-campus job opportunities are good. **Financial Aid Statistics:** 60% freshmen, 52% undergrads receive need-based scholarship or grant aid. 42% freshmen, 40% undergrads receive need-based self-help aid. 31 freshmen, 110 undergrads receive athletic scholarships. 99% freshmen, 95% undergrads receive any aid.

STEVENS INSTITUTE OF TECHNOLOGY

Castle Point on Hudson, Hoboken, NJ 07030
Phone: 201-216-5194 **E-mail:** admissions@stevens.edu **CEEB Code:** 2819
Fax: 201-216-8348 **Website:** www.stevens.edu **ACT Code:** 2610
Financial Aid Phone: 201-216-5555

This private school was founded in 1870. It has a 55-acre campus.

RATINGS
Admissions Selectivity Rating: 93 **Fire Safety Rating:** 60* **Green Rating:** 60*

STUDENTS AND FACULTY
Enrollment: 1,843. **Student Body:** 24% female, 76% male, 32% out-of-state, 5% international (65 countries represented). African American 4%, Asian 12%, Caucasian 52%, Hispanic 9%. **Retention and Graduation:** 90% freshmen return for sophomore year. 36% freshmen graduate within 4 years. 11% grads go on to further study within 1 year. 3% grads pursue arts and sciences degrees. 1% grads pursue business degrees. 1% grads pursue law degrees. 2% grads pursue medical degrees. **Faculty:** Student/faculty ratio 8:1. 189 full-time faculty. 100% faculty teach undergrads.

ACADEMICS
Degrees: Bachelor's, doctoral, first professional certificate, first professional, master's, post-bachelor's certificate. **Academic Requirements:** Computer literacy, English (including composition), humanities, mathematics, sciences (biological or physical). See website for corresponding core curriculum which varies by major. **Classes:** Most classes have 20–29 students. Most lab/discussion sections have 10–19 students. **Majors with Highest Enrollment:** Computer and information sciences, computer engineering, mechanical engineering. **Disciplines with Highest Percentage of Degrees Awarded:** Engineering 55%, business/marketing 12%, computer and information sciences 11%, biological/life sciences 8%, engineering technologies 6%. **Special Study Options:** Accelerated program, cooperative education program, cross-registration, distance learning, double major, dual enrollment, honors program, independent study, internships, study abroad. Dual enrollment program with NYU.

FACILITIES

Housing: Coed dorms, women's dorms, apartments for married students, apartments for single students, fraternity/sorority housing, freshmen not living at home must live on campus. **Special Academic Facilities/Equipment**: Art museum, electron microscope, ocean engineering lab, HDTV research facility, advanced telecommunications institute, environmental lab, design/manufacturing institute, wind tunnel, robotics lab, product management center, polymer processing institute, DeBaun Theater, a multimedia facility, wireless campus network. **Computers**: 31% of classrooms are wired, 93% of classrooms are wireless, 80% of public computers are PCs, 5% of public computers are Macs, 15% of public computers are UNIX, network access in dorm rooms, network access in dorm lounges, online registration, online administrative functions (other than registration), support for handheld computing, remote student-access to Web through college's connection, tuition includes personal computer. Undergraduates are required to own a computer.

CAMPUS LIFE

Activities: Choral groups, concert band, dance, drama/theater, jazz band, literary magazine, music ensembles, musical theater, pep band, radio station, student government, student newspaper, television station, yearbook. **Organizations**: 70 registered organizations, 8 honor societies, 9 religious organizations. 10 fraternities (25% men join), 3 sororities (23% women join). **Athletics (Intercollegiate)**: *Men*: Baseball, basketball, cross-country, fencing, lacrosse, soccer, swimming, tennis, track/field (indoor), track/field (outdoor), volleyball, wrestling. *Women*: Basketball, cross-country, equestrian sports, fencing, field hockey, lacrosse, soccer, swimming, tennis, track/field (indoor), track/field (outdoor), volleyball.

ADMISSIONS

Freshman Academic Profile: 53% in top 10% of high school class, 82% in top 25% of high school class, 96% in top 50% of high school class. 80% from public high schools. SAT Math middle 50% range 620–710. SAT Critical Reading middle 50% range 540–650. TOEFL required of all international applicants, minimum paper TOEFL 550, minimum computer TOEFL 213. **Basis for Candidate Selection**: *Very important factors considered include*: Academic GPA, application essay, character/personal qualities, extracurricular activities, interview, recommendation(s), rigor of secondary school record, standardized test scores, volunteer work, work experience. *Important factors considered include*: Class rank, talent/ability. *Other factors considered include*: Alumni/ae relation. **Freshman Admission Requirements**: High school diploma is required, and GED is not accepted. *Academic units required*: 4 English, 4 math, 3 science (3 science labs). *Academic units recommended*: 4 science (4 science labs), 2 foreign language, 2 social studies, 2 history, 4 academic electives. **Freshman Admission Statistics**: 2,278 applied, 54% admitted, 39% enrolled. **Transfer Admission Requirements**: High school transcript, college transcript(s), essay or personal statement, interview. Minimum college GPA of 3.0 required. Lowest grade transferable C. **General Admission Information**: Application fee $55. Early decision application deadline 11/15. Regular application deadline 2/15. Regular notification 4/1. Non-fall registration not accepted. Credit and/or placement offered for CEEB Advanced Placement tests.

COSTS AND FINANCIAL AID

Annual tuition $33,300. Room and board $10,500. Required fees $1,800. Average book expense $900. **Required Forms and Deadlines**: FAFSA. Financial aid filing deadline 2/15. **Notification of Awards**: Applicants will be notified of awards on a rolling basis beginning on or about 3/30. **Types of Aid**: *Need-based scholarships/grants*: Pell, SEOG, state scholarships/grants, private scholarships, the school's own gift aid. *Loans*: Direct Subsidized Stafford, Direct Unsubsidized Stafford, Direct PLUS, FFEL Subsidized Stafford, Federal Perkins, state loans, Signature Loans, TERI Loans, NJ CLASS, CitiAssist. **Student Employment**: Federal Work-Study Program available. Off-campus job opportunities are excellent. **Financial Aid Statistics**: 58% freshmen, 54% undergrads receive need-based scholarship or grant aid. 57% freshmen, 56% undergrads receive need-based self-help aid. 83% freshmen, 76% undergrads receive any aid. Highest amount earned per year from on-campus jobs $1,300.

See page 1392.

STONEHILL COLLEGE

320 Washington Street, Easton, MA 02357-5610
Phone: 508-565-1373 **E-mail**: admissions@stonehill.edu **CEEB Code**: 3770
Fax: 508-565-1545 **Website**: www.stonehill.edu **ACT Code**: 1918
Financial Aid Phone: 508-565-1088

This private school, affiliated with the Roman Catholic Church, was founded in 1948. It has a 375-acre campus.

RATINGS

Admissions Selectivity Rating: 93   **Fire Safety Rating**: 60*   **Green Rating**: 60*

STUDENTS AND FACULTY

Enrollment: 2,341. **Student Body**: 60% female, 40% male, 43% out-of-state. African American 3%, Asian 2%, Caucasian 91%, Hispanic 4%. **Retention and Graduation**: 86% freshmen return for sophomore year. 82% freshmen graduate within 4 years. 31% grads go on to further study within 1 year. 28% grads pursue arts and sciences degrees. 1% grads pursue business degrees. 1% grads pursue law degrees. 1% grads pursue medical degrees. **Faculty**: Student/faculty ratio 13:1. 134 full-time faculty, 85% hold PhDs. 100% faculty teach undergrads.

ACADEMICS

Degrees: Bachelor's, certificate, master's. **Academic Requirements**: English (including composition), foreign languages, history, learning communities (2 courses with an integrative seminar), philosophy, religious studies, sciences (biological or physical), senior year capstone course (connects major to general education), social science, statistical reasoning. **Classes**: Most classes have 20–29 students. Most lab/discussion sections have 20–29 students. **Majors with Highest Enrollment**: Biology/biological sciences, English language and literature, psychology. **Disciplines with Highest Percentage of Degrees Awarded**: Business/marketing 21%, social sciences 15%, psychology 15%, education 8%, communications/journalism 7%. **Special Study Options**: Cross-registration, double major, dual enrollment, honors program, independent study, internships, liberal arts/career combination, student-designed major, study abroad, teacher certification program. Full-time international internship sites in London, Brussels, Zaragoza, Dublin, Paris, Stonehill Quebec exchange program, 3–2 computer engineering BA/BS program with University of Notre Dame, Indiana, Stonehill Undergraduate Research Experience (SURE) Program.

FACILITIES

Housing: Coed dorms, women's dorms, special housing for disabled students, special interest housing. **Special Academic Facilities/Equipment**: Institute for law and society, observatory, Stonehill Industrial History Center.

CAMPUS LIFE

Activities: Choral groups, dance, drama/theater, literary magazine, music ensembles, musical theater, pep band, radio station, student government, student newspaper, student-run film society, yearbook. **Organizations**: 72 registered organizations, 16 honor societies, 1 religious organization. **Athletics (Intercollegiate)**: *Men*: Baseball, basketball, cross-country, football, ice hockey, soccer, tennis, track/field (indoor), track/field (outdoor). *Women*: Basketball, cross-country, equestrian sports, field hockey, lacrosse, soccer, softball, tennis, track/field (indoor), track/field (outdoor), volleyball.

ADMISSIONS

Freshman Academic Profile: 50% in top 10% of high school class, 91% in top 25% of high school class, 100% in top 50% of high school class. 67% from public high schools. SAT Math middle 50% range 550–640. SAT Critical Reading middle 50% range 540–630. ACT middle 50% range 24–27. TOEFL required of all international applicants, minimum paper TOEFL 550, minimum computer TOEFL 213. **Basis for Candidate Selection**: *Very important factors considered include*: Academic GPA, class rank, rigor of secondary school record, standardized test scores. *Important factors considered include*: Application essay, character/personal qualities, extracurricular activities, recommendation(s), talent/ability. *Other factors considered include*: Alumni/ae relation, first generation, geographical residence, level of applicant's interest, racial/ethnic status, volunteer work, work experience. **Freshman Admission Requirements**: High school diploma is required, and GED is accepted. *Academic units required*: 4 English, 3 math, 1 science (1 science lab), 2 foreign language, 3 history, 3 academic electives. *Academic units recommended*: 4 English, 4 math, 3 science (2 science labs), 3 foreign language, 3 history, 3 academic electives. **Freshman Admission Statistics**: 5,243 applied, 54% admitted, 21% enrolled. **Transfer Admission Requirements**: High school transcript, college transcript(s), essay or personal statement. Minimum college

GPA of 2.0 required. Lowest grade transferable C. **General Admission Information**: Application fee $55. Early decision application deadline 11/1. Regular application deadline 1/15. Regular notification 4/1. Non-fall registration accepted. Admission may be deferred for a maximum of 1 year. Credit and/or placement offered for CEEB Advanced Placement tests.

COSTS AND FINANCIAL AID

Average book expense $1,200. **Required Forms and Deadlines**: FAFSA, CSS/Financial Aid PROFILE, Noncustodial PROFILE, Business/Farm Supplement, Verification Form provided by Institution. Financial aid filing deadline 2/1. **Notification of Awards**: Applicants will be notified of awards on or about 4/1. **Types of Aid**: *Need-based scholarships/grants*: Pell, SEOG, state scholarships/grants, private scholarships, the school's own gift aid. *Loans*: Direct Subsidized Stafford, Direct Unsubsidized Stafford, Direct PLUS, Federal Perkins, state loans, private education loans. **Financial Aid Statistics**: 64% freshmen, 61% undergrads receive need-based scholarship or grant aid. 57% freshmen, 58% undergrads receive need-based self-help aid. 14 freshmen, 51 undergrads receive athletic scholarships. 93% freshmen, 89% undergrads receive any aid. Highest amount earned per year from on-campus jobs $2,509.

See page 1394.

STRAYER UNIVERSITY

1025 Fifteenth Street, NW, Washington, DC 20005
Phone: 202-408-2400 **E-mail**: washington@strayer.edu
Fax: 202-289-1831 **Website**: www.strayer.edu **ACT Code**: 0694
Financial Aid Phone: 202-408-2400

This proprietary school was founded in 1892.

RATINGS

Admissions Selectivity Rating: 60*   **Fire Safety Rating**: 60*   **Green Rating**: 60*

STUDENTS AND FACULTY

Enrollment: 12,703. **Student Body**: 58% female, 42% male, 5% out-of-state, 5% international (110 countries represented). African American 40%, Asian 5%, Caucasian 32%, Hispanic 4%. **Faculty**: Student/faculty ratio 20:1. 137 full-time faculty, 34% hold PhDs. 100% faculty teach undergrads.

ACADEMICS

Degrees: Associate, bachelor's, diploma, master's, post-bachelor's certificate. **Academic Requirements**: Arts/fine arts, computer literacy, English (including composition), humanities, mathematics, social science. **Disciplines with Highest Percentage of Degrees Awarded**: Computer and information sciences 61%, business/marketing 39%. **Special Study Options**: Accelerated program, cooperative education program, distance learning, double major, internships, weekend college.

FACILITIES

Computers: Online administrative functions (other than registration), remote student-access to Web through college's connection.

CAMPUS LIFE

Activities: Student newspaper. Organizations: 9 registered organizations, 2 honor societies.

ADMISSIONS

Freshman Academic Profile: TOEFL required of all international applicants, minimum paper TOEFL 400. Basis for Candidate Selection: Very important factors considered include: Rigor of secondary school record, work experience. Important factors considered include: Alumni/ae relation, interview, recommendation(s), talent/ability. Other factors considered include: Character/personal qualities, extracurricular activities, standardized test scores. Freshman Admission Requirements: High school diploma is required, and GED is accepted. Academic units recommended: 3 English, 3 math, 2 foreign language, 1 social studies, 1 history, 4 academic electives. Freshman Admission Statistics: 71% enrolled. Transfer Admission Requirements: College transcript(s). Lowest grade transferable C. General Admission Information: Application fee $25. Regular application deadline is rolling. Non-fall registration accepted. Common Application not accepted. Credit and/or placement offered for CEEB Advanced Placement tests.

COSTS AND FINANCIAL AID

Annual tuition $7,695. Required Forms and Deadlines: FAFSA. Types of Aid: Need-based scholarships/grants: Pell, SEOG, the school's own gift aid.

Loans: Direct Subsidized Stafford, Direct Unsubsidized Stafford, Direct PLUS, FFEL Subsidized Stafford, FFEL Unsubsidized Stafford, FFEL PLUS, Federal Perkins. Student Employment: Federal Work-Study Program available. Institutional employment available. Off-campus job opportunities are excellent.

SUFFOLK UNIVERSITY

Best 368

8 Ashburton Place, Boston, MA 02108
Phone: 617-573-8460 E-mail: admission@suffolk.edu CEEB Code: 3771
Fax: 617-742-4291 Website: www.suffolk.edu ACT Code: 1920
Financial Aid Phone: 617-573-8470

This private school was founded in 1906.

RATINGS

Admissions Selectivity Rating: 72   **Fire Safety Rating**: 99   **Green Rating**: 91

STUDENTS AND FACULTY

Enrollment: 4,985. Student Body: 57% female, 43% male, 25% out-of-state, 9% international (99 countries represented). African American 3%, Asian 6%, Caucasian 64%, Hispanic 5%. Retention and Graduation: 71% freshmen return for sophomore year. 38% freshmen graduate within 4 years. 39% grads go on to further study within 1 year. 13% grads pursue arts and sciences degrees. 14% grads pursue business degrees. 8% grads pursue law degrees. 1% grads pursue medical degrees. Faculty: Student/faculty ratio 13:1. 393 full-time faculty, 90% hold PhDs. 90% faculty teach undergrads.

ACADEMICS

Degrees: Associate, bachelor's, certificate, diploma, doctoral, first professional, master's, post-bachelor's certificate, post-master's certificate. Academic Requirements: Computer literacy, English (including composition), foreign languages, humanities, mathematics, philosophy, sciences (biological or physical), social science. Classes: Most classes have 20–29 students. Most lab/discussion sections have 10–19 students. Majors with Highest Enrollment: Communications studies/speech communication and rhetoric, sociology. Disciplines with Highest Percentage of Degrees Awarded: Business/marketing 43%, social sciences 17%, communications/journalism 14%, visual and performing arts 6%, psychology 5%. Special Study Options: Accelerated program, cooperative education program, cross-registration, distance learning, double major, English as a second language (ESL), exchange student program (domestic), honors program, independent study, internships, liberal arts/career combination, study abroad, weekend college.

FACILITIES

Housing: Coed dorms. Special Academic Facilities/Equipment: Marine biology field station in Maine, NESAD art gallery, Adams Art Gallery, and C. Walsh Theatre. Computers: 30% of classrooms are wired, 75% of public computers are PCs, 15% of public computers are Macs, 10% of public computers are UNIX, network access in dorm rooms, network access in dorm lounges, online registration, online administrative functions (other than registration), support for handheld computing, remote student-access to Web through college's connection.

CAMPUS LIFE

Activities: Choral groups, dance, drama/theater, literary magazine, music ensembles, musical theater, radio station, student government, student newspaper, television station, yearbook. Organizations: 75 registered organizations, 3 honor societies, 3 religious organizations. 1 fraternity, 1 sorority. Athletics (Intercollegiate): Men: Baseball, basketball, cross-country, golf, ice hockey, soccer, tennis. Women: Basketball, cross-country, softball, tennis, volleyball. Environmental Initiatives: Commitment to LEED Silver for building projects (first LEED Silver application being completed now for newly opened residence hall). Lighting Efficiency and Water Conservation. Waste Reduction and Recycling.

ADMISSIONS

Freshman Academic Profile: 9% in top 10% of high school class, 29% in top 25% of high school class, 68% in top 50% of high school class. 69% from public high schools. SAT Math middle 50% range 450–570. SAT Critical Reading middle 50% range 460–560. SAT Writing middle 50% range 460–560. ACT middle 50% range 20–24. TOEFL required of all international applicants, minimum paper TOEFL 525, minimum computer TOEFL 197. Basis for Candidate Selection: Very important factors considered include: Academic GPA, rigor of secondary school record. Important factors considered include: Application essay, class rank, standardized test scores. Other factors considered include: Alumni/ae relation, character/personal qualities, extracurricular activities, first generation, geographical residence, interview, level of applicant's interest, recommendation(s), talent/ability, volunteer work, work experience. Freshman Admission Requirements: High school diploma is required, and GED is accepted. Academic units required: 4 English, 3 math, 2 science (1 science lab), 2 foreign language, 1 social studies, 1 history, 4 academic electives. Academic units recommended: 4 English, 4 math, 3 science (1 science lab), 3 foreign language, 1 social studies, 1 history, 4 academic electives. Freshman Admission Statistics: 7,106 applied, 83% admitted, 22% enrolled. Transfer Admission Requirements: College transcript(s), essay or personal statement. Minimum college GPA of 2.5 required. Lowest grade transferable C. General Admission Information: Application fee $50. Regular application deadline 3/1. Regular notification is rolling. Non-fall registration accepted. Admission may be deferred for a maximum of 1 year. Credit and/or placement offered for CEEB Advanced Placement tests.

COSTS AND FINANCIAL AID

Required Forms and Deadlines: FAFSA, institution's own financial aid form. Financial aid filing deadline 3/1. Notification of Awards: Applicants will be notified of awards on a rolling basis beginning on or about 3/1. Types of Aid: Need-based scholarships/grants: Pell, SEOG, state scholarships/grants, private scholarships, the school's own gift aid. Loans: Direct Subsidized Stafford, Direct Unsubsidized Stafford, Direct PLUS, Federal Perkins. Financial Aid Statistics: 53% freshmen, 50% undergrads receive need-based scholarship or grant aid. 57% freshmen, 54% undergrads receive need-based self-help aid. 68% freshmen, 63% undergrads receive any aid. Highest amount earned per year from on-campus jobs $1,860.

SUL ROSS STATE UNIVERSITY

Box C-2, Alpine, TX 79832
Phone: 915-837-8050 **E-mail:** admissions@sulross.edu **CEEB Code:** 6685
Fax: 915-837-8431 **Website:** www.sulross.edu **ACT Code:** 4190
Financial Aid Phone: 915-837-8055

This public school was founded in 1917. It has a 650-acre campus.

RATINGS

Admissions Selectivity Rating: 62   **Fire Safety Rating:** 60*   **Green Rating:** 60*

STUDENTS AND FACULTY

Enrollment: 1,402. **Student Body:** 48% female, 52% male, 2% out-of-state. African American 4%, Caucasian 44%, Hispanic 48%. **Retention and Graduation:** 48% freshmen return for sophomore year. 7% freshmen graduate within 4 years. 10% grads go on to further study within 1 year. 1% grads pursue arts and sciences degrees. 1% grads pursue business degrees. 1% grads pursue law degrees. 1% grads pursue medical degrees. **Faculty:** Student/faculty ratio 13:1. 88 full-time faculty, 72% hold PhDs. 99% faculty teach undergrads.

ACADEMICS

Degrees: Associate, bachelor's, certificate, master's. **Academic Requirements:** Arts/fine arts, English (including composition), history, humanities, mathematics, sciences (biological or physical), social science, political science. **Classes:** Most classes have 10–19 students. Most lab/discussion sections have fewer than 10 students. **Majors with Highest Enrollment:** Criminal justice/safety studies, health and physical education, multi/interdisciplinary studies. **Disciplines with Highest Percentage of Degrees Awarded:** Education 16%, interdisciplinary studies 15%, business/marketing 10%, agriculture 9%, communication technologies 6%. **Special Study Options:** Distance learning, honors program, internships, teacher certification program.

FACILITIES

Housing: Coed dorms, men's dorms, women's dorms, apartments for married students, apartments for single students, special housing for disabled students. **Special Academic Facilities/Equipment:** Museum, range animal science ranch, planetarium, observatory, scanning electron microscope, automated electron probe microanalyzer, computer-controlled X-ray fluorescence analyzer, archives of the Big Bend. **Computers:** 99% of public computers are PCs, 1% of public computers are Macs, network access in dorm rooms, online registration, online administrative functions (other than registration), remote student-access to Web through college's connection.

CAMPUS LIFE

Activities: Choral groups, concert band, drama/theater, jazz band, literary magazine, music ensembles, pep band, radio station, student government, student newspaper, yearbook. **Organizations:** 30 registered organizations, 10 honor societies, 3 religious organizations. **Athletics (Intercollegiate):** *Men:* Baseball, basketball, cheerleading, football, rodeo, tennis, track/field (outdoor). *Women:* Basketball, cheerleading, cross-country, rodeo, softball, tennis, track/field (outdoor), volleyball.

ADMISSIONS

Freshman Academic Profile: 5% in top 10% of high school class, 18% in top 25% of high school class, 55% in top 50% of high school class. 95% from public high schools. ACT middle 50% range 15–19. TOEFL required of all international applicants, minimum paper TOEFL 520, minimum computer TOEFL 190. **Basis for Candidate Selection:** *Very important factors considered include:* Class rank, standardized test scores. *Other factors considered include:* Extracurricular activities, rigor of secondary school record. **Freshman Admission Requirements:** High school diploma is required, and GED is accepted. *Academic units required:* 4 English, 3 math 2 science (2 science labs), 2 social studies, 1 history, 2 fine arts, 1 computer science, 2 physical education and health education. *Academic units recommended:* 4 English, 4 math 4 science (4 science labs), 3 foreign language, 2 social studies, 2 history, 2 academic electives, 4 fine arts, 1 computer science, 2 physical education and health education. **Freshman Admission Statistics:** 1,021 applied, 73% admitted, 43% enrolled. **Transfer Admission Requirements:** College transcript(s). Lowest grade transferable D. **General Admission Information:** Regular notification is rolling. Non-fall registration accepted. Admission may be deferred for a maximum of 1 year. Common Application accepted. Credit and/or placement offered for CEEB Advanced Placement tests.

COSTS AND FINANCIAL AID

Annual in-state tuition $2,040. Out-of-state tuition $8,580. Room & board $3,850. Required fees $992. Average book expense $692. **Required Forms and Deadlines:** FAFSA, institution's own financial aid form. **Notification of Awards:** Applicants will be notified of awards on a rolling basis beginning on or about 4/1. **Types of Aid:** *Need-based scholarships/grants:* Pell, SEOG, state scholarships/grants, the school's own gift aid, Federal Nursing Scholarships. *Loans:* FFEL Subsidized Stafford, FFEL Unsubsidized Stafford, FFEL PLUS, college/university loans from institutional funds. **Student Employment:** Federal Work-Study Program available. Institutional employment available. Off-campus job opportunities are poor. **Financial Aid Statistics:** 71% freshmen, 65% undergrads receive need-based scholarship or grant aid. 40% freshmen, 47% undergrads receive need-based self-help aid. Highest amount earned per year from on-campus jobs $2,000.

SUSQUEHANNA UNIVERSITY

514 University Avenue, Selinsgrove, PA 17870
Phone: 570-372-4260 **E-mail:** Suadmiss@susqu.edu **CEEB Code:** 2820
Fax: 570-372-2722 **Website:** www.susqu.edu **ACT Code:** 3720
Financial Aid Phone: 570-372-4450

This private school, affiliated with the Lutheran Church, was founded in 1858. It has a 220-acre campus.

RATINGS

Admissions Selectivity Rating: 79   **Fire Safety Rating:** 84   **Green Rating:** 79

STUDENTS AND FACULTY

Enrollment: 1,928. **Student Body:** 54% female, 46% male, 41% out-of-state, (8 countries represented). African American 3%, Asian 2%, Caucasian 92%, Hispanic 2%. **Retention and Graduation:** 86% freshmen return for sophomore year. 77% freshmen graduate within 4 years. 24% grads go on to further study within 1 year. 18% grads pursue arts and sciences degrees. 3% grads pursue law degrees. 1% grads pursue medical degrees. **Faculty:** Student/faculty ratio 14:1. 122 full-time faculty, 92% hold PhDs. 100% faculty teach undergrads.

ACADEMICS

Degrees: Associate, bachelor's, terminal. **Academic Requirements**: Arts/fine arts, computer literacy, English (including composition), foreign languages, history, humanities, sciences (biological or physical), social science, philosophy or religion, mathematics or logic. **Classes**: Most classes have 10–19 students. Most lab/discussion sections have fewer than 10 students. **Majors with Highest Enrollment**: Biology/biological sciences, business administration/management, communications studies/speech communication and rhetoric. **Disciplines with Highest Percentage of Degrees Awarded**: Business/marketing 26%, education 12%, communications/journalism 11%, social sciences 10%, psychology 8%. **Special Study Options**: Accelerated program, cross-registration, double major, dual enrollment, exchange student program (domestic), honors program, independent study, internships, student-designed major, study abroad, teacher certification program. The United Nations semester, the Boston semester, the Washington semester, the Philadelphia center program, semester in London for junior business majors, Denmark international program. Lutheran College Washington consortium semester in Washington, SU en Provence, consortium semester in Washington. Susquehanna's Focus Program offers students the opportunity to go on a 2-week study seminar in Australia after having taken interdisciplinary coursework the previous semesterrelated to Australia.

FACILITIES

Housing: Coed dorms, apartments for single students, special housing for international students, fraternity/sorority housing, Scholars' House. Student volunteers in Susquehanna's nationally recognized project house system have the privilege of living together in university-owned houses, in Shobrt Hall apartment-suites, or in the upper level of Seibert hall, one of the landmark historic buildings on campus. Seibert hall is also home to international students and student volunteers in the student association for cultural awareness, and includes dedicated space for multicultural and international programming. **Special Academic Facilities/Equipment**: Art gallery, electronic music lab, child development center, foreign language broadcast system, teaching theater, greenhouse, rare book room, ecological field station, electron microscope, reflecting telescope, fluorescent microscopes, video conference center, and the new business and communications building featuring 3 multimedia classrooms, 3 computer laboratories/classrooms, conference and seminar rooms, student team study rooms and alcoves, 2 video studios, seminar/observation rooms and a room for faculty instructional development. The building facilitates use of laptop computers by offering informational technology dataports for every seat in the classrooms, team study areas, student lounges, faculty offices. **Computers**: 2% of classrooms are wired, 35% of classrooms are wireless, 97% of public computers are PCs, 3% of public computers are Macs, network access in dorm rooms, network access in dorm lounges, online registration, online administrative functions (other than registration), support for handheld computing, remote student-access to Web through college's connection.

CAMPUS LIFE

Activities: Choral groups, concert band, dance, drama/theater, jazz band, literary magazine, music ensembles, musical theater, opera, pep band, radio station, student government, student newspaper, student-run film society, symphony orchestra, yearbook. **Organizations**: 121 registered organizations, 24 honor societies, 12 religious organizations. 5 fraternities (13% men join), 4 sororities (20% women join). **Athletics (Intercollegiate)**: *Men*: Baseball, basketball, crew/rowing, cross-country, football, golf, lacrosse, soccer, swimming, tennis, track/field (indoor), track/field (outdoor). *Women*: Basketball, crew/rowing, cross-country, field hockey, golf, lacrosse, soccer, softball, swimming, tennis, track/field (indoor), track/field (outdoor), volleyball. Environmental Initiatives: New science facility and new student housing will be LEED certified. This housing and two units built last year utilize geo-thermal energy for heating and cooling. Actively pursuing alternative sources of fuel to replace coal-fired power plant. Cut fuel usage 25% last year by installing highly-efficient insulated steam lines. Susquehanna University is a flagship member of the Graduation Pledge Alliance, a national student organization whose mission is to promote socially and environmentally responsible actions by graduating seniors.

ADMISSIONS

Freshman Academic Profile: 32% in top 10% of high school class, 64% in top 25% of high school class, 92% in top 50% of high school class. 85% from public high schools. SAT Math middle 50% range 530–610. SAT Critical Reading middle 50% range 520–610. SAT Writing middle 50% range 510–610. ACT middle 50% range 22–27. TOEFL required of all international applicants, minimum paper TOEFL 550, minimum computer TOEFL 213. **Basis for Candidate Selection**: *Very important factors considered include*: Academic GPA, rigor of secondary school record. *Important factors considered include*: Application essay, character/personal qualities, class rank, extracurricular activities, interview, recommendation(s), standardized test scores, talent/ability, volunteer work, work experience. *Other factors considered include*: Alumni/ae relation, first generation, geographical residence, level of applicant's interest, racial/ethnic status, religious affiliation/commitment, state residency. **Freshman Admission Requirements**: High school diploma is required, and GED is accepted. *Academic units required*: 4 English, 3 math, 3 science (2 science labs), 2 foreign language, 1 social studies, 1 history, 2 academic electives. *Academic units recommended*: 4 English, 4 math, 4 science (3 science labs), 4 foreign language, 4 social studies, 1 history, 4 academic electives. **Freshman Admission Statistics**: 2,292 applied, 79% admitted, 30% enrolled. **Transfer Admission Requirements**: High school transcript, college transcript(s), essay or personal statement, statement of good standing from prior institution(s). Minimum college GPA of 2.0 required. Lowest grade transferable C-. **General Admission Information**: Application fee $35. Early decision application deadline 11/15. Regular application deadline 8/1. Regular notification is rolling. Nonfall registration accepted. Admission may be deferred for a maximum of 1 year. Credit and/or placement offered for CEEB Advanced Placement tests.

COSTS AND FINANCIAL AID

Annual tuition $27,300. Room & board $7,600. Required fees $320. Average book expense $750. **Required Forms and Deadlines**: FAFSA, CSS/Financial Aid PROFILE, Business/Farm Supplement. Financial aid filing deadline 5/1. Financial aid filing deadline 3/1. **Notification of Awards**: Applicants will be notified of awards on a rolling basis beginning on or about 2/15. **Types of Aid**: *Need-based scholarships/grants*: Pell, SEOG, state scholarships/grants, private scholarships, the school's own gift aid. *Loans*: FFEL Subsidized Stafford, FFEL Unsubsidized Stafford, FFEL PLUS, Federal Perkins, college/university loans from institutional funds. **Financial Aid Statistics**: 65% freshmen, 64% undergrads receive need-based scholarship or grant aid. 55% freshmen, 53% undergrads receive need-based self-help aid. 92% freshmen, 92% undergrads receive any aid. Highest amount earned per year from on-campus jobs $4,035.

See page 1396.

SWARTHMORE COLLEGE

500 College Avenue, Swarthmore, PA 19081
Phone: 610-328-8300 **E-mail**: admissions@swarthmore.edu **CEEB Code**: 2821
Fax: 610-328-8580 **Website**: www.swarthmore.edu **ACT Code**: 3722
Financial Aid Phone: 610-328-8358

This private school was founded in 1864. It has a 357-acre campus.

RATINGS

Admissions Selectivity Rating: 99   **Fire Safety Rating**: 88   **Green Rating**: 83

STUDENTS AND FACULTY

Enrollment: 1,472. **Student Body**: 52% female, 48% male, 83% out-of-state, 6% international (40 countries represented). African American 9%, Asian 16%, Caucasian 45%, Hispanic 10%. **Retention and Graduation**: 96% freshmen return for sophomore year. 86% freshmen graduate within 4 years. 21% grads go on to further study within 1 year. 15% grads pursue arts and sciences degrees. 3% grads pursue law degrees. 3% grads pursue medical degrees. **Faculty**: Student/faculty ratio 8:1. 169 full-time faculty, 99% hold PhDs. 100% faculty teach undergrads.

ACADEMICS

Degrees: Bachelor's. **Academic Requirements**: Foreign languages, humanities, sciences (biological or physical), social science. **Classes**: Most classes have 10–19 students. Most lab/discussion sections have fewer than 10 students. **Majors with Highest Enrollment**: Biology/biological sciences, economics, political science and government. **Disciplines with Highest Percentage of Degrees Awarded**: Social sciences 23%, biological/life sciences 13%, English 8%, foreign languages and literature 8%, history 7%, mathematics 6%, philosophy and religious studies 6%. **Special Study Options**: Accelerated program, cross-registration, double major, exchange student program (domestic), honors program, independent study, internships, student-designed major, study abroad, teacher certification program.

FACILITIES

Housing: Coed dorms, men's dorms, women's dorms, special housing for disabled students, fraternity/sorority housing, special housing for disabled students available on individual basis. Fraternity/sorority housing has only 2 beds available in 2 fraternities. New 75-bed dorm with 6 loft-style doubles and generous lounge space to facilitate dorm social life. **Special Academic Facilities/Equipment**: 330-acre arboretum, observatory, Lang Performing Arts Center with art gallery and dance studios, outdoor amphitheater, solar energy laboratory, Friends Historical Library, Peace Collection in library, a stadium complex including lights, a 400-meter dual durometer track, and a synthetic grass field for soccer, lacrosse, and field hockey, a state-of-the-art fitness center and 3 indoor tennis courts on a Rebound Ace surface, new $77 million environmentally friendly science center, specially designed for interdisciplinary and student-faculty collaboration. **Computers**: 100% of classrooms are wired, 100% of classrooms are wireless, 50% of public computers are PCs, 40% of public computers are Macs, 10% of public computers are UNIX, network access in dorm rooms, network access in dorm lounges, online registration, online administrative functions (other than registration), support for handheld computing, remote student-access to Web through college's connection.

CAMPUS LIFE

Activities: Choral groups, dance, drama/theater, jazz band, literary magazine, music ensembles, opera, radio station, student government, student newspaper, student-run film society, symphony orchestra, yearbook. **Organizations**: 110 registered organizations, 3 honor societies, 7 religious organizations. 2 fraternities (7% men join). **Athletics (Intercollegiate)**: *Men*: Baseball, basketball, cross-country, golf, lacrosse, soccer, swimming, tennis, track/field (indoor), track/field (outdoor). *Women*: Badminton, basketball, cross-country, field hockey, lacrosse, soccer, softball, swimming, tennis, track/field (indoor), track/field (outdoor), volleyball. Environmental Initiatives: Wind Power. LEED Certified Science Center. Environmental Task Force.

ADMISSIONS

Freshman Academic Profile: 83% in top 10% of high school class, 89% in top 25% of high school class, 100% in top 50% of high school class. 66% from public high schools. SAT Math middle 50% range 680–760. SAT Critical Reading middle 50% range 680–780. SAT Writing middle 50% range 680–760. ACT middle 50% range 27–33. **Basis for Candidate Selection**: *Very important factors considered include*: Academic GPA, application essay, character/personal qualities, class rank, recommendation(s), rigor of secondary school record. *Important factors considered include*: Extracurricular activities, standardized test scores. *Other factors considered include*: Alumni/ae relation, first generation, geographical residence, interview, level of applicant's interest, racial/ethnic status, talent/ability, volunteer work, work experience. **Freshman Admission Requirements**: High school diploma or equivalent is not required. **Freshman Admission Statistics**: 4,852 applied, 19% admitted, 40% enrolled. **Transfer Admission Requirements**: High school transcript, college transcript(s), essay or personal statement, standardized test score, statement of good standing from prior institution(s). Lowest grade transferable C. **General Admission Information**: Application fee $60. Early decision application deadline 11/15. Regular application deadline 1/2. Regular notification 4/1. Non-fall registration not accepted. Admission may be deferred for a maximum of 1 year. Credit and/or placement offered for CEEB Advanced Placement tests.

COSTS AND FINANCIAL AID

Annual tuition $34,564. Room and board $10,816. Required fees $320. Average book expense $1,080. **Required Forms and Deadlines**: FAFSA, institution's own financial aid form, CSS/Financial Aid PROFILE, state aid form, Noncustodial PROFILE, Business/Farm Supplement, federal tax return, W-2 forms, year-end paycheck stub. Financial aid filing deadline 2/15. **Notification of Awards**: Applicants will be notified of awards on or about 4/1. **Types of Aid**: *Need-based scholarships/grants*: Pell, SEOG, state scholarships/grants, private scholarships, the school's own gift aid. *Loans*: FFEL Subsidized Stafford, FFEL Unsubsidized Stafford, FFEL PLUS, Federal Perkins, state loans, college/university loans from institutional funds. **Financial Aid Statistics**: 49% freshmen, 49% undergrads receive need-based scholarship or grant aid. 47% freshmen, 47% undergrads receive need-based self-help aid. 49% freshmen, 52% undergrads receive any aid. Highest amount earned per year from on-campus jobs $1,660.

See page 1398.

SWEET BRIAR COLLEGE

PO Box B, Sweet Briar, VA 24595
Phone: 434-381-6142 **E-mail**: admissions@sbc.edu **CEEB Code**: 5634
Fax: 434-381-6152 **Website**: www.sbc.edu **ACT Code**: 4406
Financial Aid Phone: 434-381-6156

This private school was founded in 1901. It has a 3,250-acre campus.

RATINGS

Admissions Selectivity Rating: 82 **Fire Safety Rating**: 93 **Green Rating**: 60*

STUDENTS AND FACULTY

Enrollment: 580. **Student Body**: 100% female, 52% out-of-state, 1% international (12 countries represented). African American 3%, Asian 1%, Caucasian 88%, Hispanic 2%. **Retention and Graduation**: 80% freshmen return for sophomore year. 66% freshmen graduate within 4 years. 20% grads go on to further study within 1 year. 8% grads pursue arts and sciences degrees. 2% grads pursue law degrees. 2% grads pursue medical degrees. **Faculty**: Student/faculty ratio 9:1. 66 full-time faculty, 95% hold PhDs. 100% faculty teach undergrads.

ACADEMICS

Degrees: Bachelor's, master's. **Academic Requirements**: Arts/fine arts, English (including composition), foreign languages, humanities, physical activity, sciences (biological or physical), social science, Western and non-Western cultures. **Classes**: Most classes have fewer than 10 students. **Majors with Highest Enrollment**: Biology/biological sciences, business administration/management, psychology. **Disciplines with Highest Percentage of Degrees Awarded**: Social sciences 24%, biological/life sciences 12%, visual and performing arts 10%, English 9%, business/marketing 8%. **Special Study Options**: Accelerated program, cross-registration, double major, dual enrollment, exchange student program (domestic), honors program, independent study, internships, liberal arts/career combination, student-designed major, study abroad, teacher certification program.

FACILITIES

Housing: Women's dorms, substance-free housing available. **Special Academic Facilities/Equipment**: Art museum and galleries, college and local history museums, environmental education/nature center, kindergarten/nursery school, riding center, electron microscope, DNA sequencing equipment, 400MHz nuclear magnetic resonance spectrometer. **Computers**: 100% of classrooms are wired, 80% of classrooms are wireless, 40% of public computers are PCs, 60% of public computers are Macs, network access in dorm rooms, network access in dorm lounges, online registration, online administrative functions (other than registration), remote student-access to Web through college's connection.

CAMPUS LIFE

Activities: Choral groups, dance, drama/theater, literary magazine, music ensembles, musical theater, radio station, student government, student newspaper, student-run film society, symphony orchestra, television station, yearbook. **Organizations**: 54 registered organizations, 12 honor societies, 2 religious organizations. **Athletics (Intercollegiate)**: *Women*: Field hockey, lacrosse, soccer, softball, swimming, tennis, volleyball.

ADMISSIONS

Freshman Academic Profile: 24% in top 10% of high school class, 55% in top 25% of high school class, 88% in top 50% of high school class. 70% from public high schools. SAT Math middle 50% range 470–595. SAT Critical Reading middle 50% range 510–640. SAT Writing middle 50% range 500–600. ACT middle 50% range 21–26. TOEFL required of all international applicants, minimum paper TOEFL 550, minimum computer TOEFL 213. **Basis for Candidate Selection**: *Very important factors considered include*: Academic GPA, rigor of secondary school record. *Important factors considered include*: Application essay, class rank, interview, recommendation(s), standardized test scores. *Other factors considered include*: Alumni/ae relation, character/personal qualities, extracurricular activities, first generation, talent/ability, volunteer work, work experience. **Freshman Admission Requirements**: High school diploma is required, and GED is accepted. *Academic units required*: 4 English, 3 math, 3 science (2 science labs), 2 foreign language, 3 social studies. *Academic units recommended*: 4 English, 4 math, 4 science (3 science labs), 4 foreign language, 4 social studies. **Freshman Admission Statistics**: 585 applied, 80% admitted, 40% enrolled. **Transfer Admission Requirements**: High school transcript, college transcript(s), essay or personal statement, standardized test score, statement of good standing from prior institution(s). Minimum college GPA of 2.5 required. Lowest grade transferable C-. **General Admission Information**: Application fee $40. Early decision application deadline 12/1. Regular application deadline 12/1. Regular notification 2/1. Non-fall registration accepted. Admission may be deferred for a maximum of 1 year. Credit and/or placement offered for CEEB Advanced Placement tests.

COSTS AND FINANCIAL AID

Annual tuition $24,470. Room & board $10,040. Required fees $275. Average book expense $600. **Required Forms and Deadlines**: FAFSA, state aid form. Financial aid filing deadline 3/1. **Notification of Awards**: Applicants will be notified of awards on a rolling basis beginning on or about 3/1. **Types of Aid**: *Need-based scholarships/grants*: Pell, SEOG, state scholarships/grants, private scholarships, the school's own gift aid. *Loans*: Direct Subsidized Stafford, Direct Unsubsidized Stafford, Direct PLUS, Federal Perkins, college/university loans from institutional funds. **Student Employment**: Federal Work-Study Program available. Institutional employment available. Off-campus job opportunities are fair. **Financial Aid Statistics**: 53% freshmen, 42% undergrads receive need-based scholarship or grant aid. 49% freshmen, 39% undergrads receive need-based self-help aid. 93% freshmen, 91% undergrads receive any aid.

See page 1400.

SYRACUSE UNIVERSITY

200 Crouse-Hinds Hall, Office of Admissions, Syracuse, NY 13244-2130
Phone: 315-443-3611 **E-mail**: orange@syr.edu **CEEB Code**: 2823
Website: www.syr.edu **ACT Code**: 2968
Financial Aid Phone: 315-443-1513

This private school was founded in 1870. It has a 200-acre campus.

RATINGS

Admissions Selectivity Rating: 92   **Fire Safety Rating**: 60*   **Green Rating**: 89

STUDENTS AND FACULTY

Enrollment: 11,546. **Student Body**: 55% female, 45% male, 57% out-of-state. **Retention and Graduation**: 92% freshmen return for sophomore year. 18% grads go on to further study within 1 year. 6% grads pursue arts and sciences degrees. 3% grads pursue business degrees. 2% grads pursue law degrees. 1% grads pursue medical degrees. **Faculty**: Student/faculty ratio 12:1. 896 full-time faculty, 88% hold PhDs. 95% faculty teach undergrads.

ACADEMICS

Degrees: Bachelor's, doctoral, first professional, master's, post-bachelor's certificate, post-master's certificate. **Academic Requirements**: English (including composition), foreign languages, humanities, mathematics, sciences (biological or physical), social science. **Classes**: Most classes have fewer than 10 students. Most lab/discussion sections have 20–29 students. **Majors with Highest Enrollment**: Architecture (BArch, BA/BS, MArch, MA/MS, PhD), political science and government, psychology. **Disciplines with Highest Percentage of Degrees Awarded**: Business/marketing 16%, visual and performing arts 13%, social sciences 13%, communications/journalism 10%, psychology 7%. **Special Study Options**: Accelerated program, cooperative education program, distance learning, double major, dual enrollment, English as a second language (ESL), honors program, independent study, internships, liberal arts/career combination, pre-professional programs and minors, student-designed major, study abroad, teacher certification program, undergraduate research.

FACILITIES

Housing: Coed dorms, apartments for married students, apartments for single students, special housing for disabled students, special housing for international students, fraternity/sorority housing, international living center and language groups within residence. **Special Academic Facilities/Equipment**: Ballentine Investment Institute, institute for sensory research, center for public and community service, child care & child development laboratory school, center for undergraduate research and innovative learning, audio archives, global collaboratory multimedia classroom, center for science and technology, community darkrooms, Lowe Art Gallery, Syracuse Stage Theater Complex, computer applications center, CAD Studio, laser spectroscopy labs, gerentology center and a speech/hearing clinic. **Computers**: 68% of classrooms are wired, 40% of classrooms are wireless, 90% of public computers are PCs, 8% of public computers are Macs, 2% of public computers are UNIX, network access in dorm rooms, network access in dorm lounges, online registration, online administrative functions (other than registration), support for handheld computing, remote student-access to Web through college's connection.

CAMPUS LIFE

Activities: Choral groups, concert band, dance, drama/theater, jazz band, literary magazine, marching band, music ensembles, musical theater, pep band, radio station, student government, student newspaper, student-run film society, symphony orchestra, television station. **Organizations**: 300 registered organizations, 34 honor societies. 27 fraternities (18% men join), 18 sororities (21% women join). **Athletics (Intercollegiate)**: *Men*: Basketball, crew/rowing, cross-country, diving, football, lacrosse, soccer, swimming, track/field (indoor), track/field (outdoor). *Women*: Basketball, crew/rowing, cross-country, diving, field hockey, lacrosse, soccer, softball, swimming, tennis, track/field (indoor), track/field (outdoor), volleyball. Environmental Initiatives: 20% renewable energy purchases. Create a sustainability department. Making a multi-million dollar investment in temperature controls.

ADMISSIONS

Freshman Academic Profile: 45% in top 10% of high school class, 78% in top 25% of high school class, 97% in top 50% of high school class. 80% from public high schools. SAT Math middle 50% range 570–680. SAT Critical Reading middle 50% range 550–650. ACT middle 50% range 24–29. TOEFL required of all international applicants, minimum paper TOEFL 560, minimum computer TOEFL 217. **Basis for Candidate Selection**: *Very important factors considered include*: Academic GPA, application essay, character/personal qualities, class rank, level of applicant's interest, recommendation(s), rigor of secondary school record, standardized test scores. *Important factors considered include*: Extracurricular activities, interview, talent/ability, volunteer work, work experience. *Other factors considered include*: Alumni/ae relation, first generation, racial/ethnic status. **Freshman Admission Requirements**: High school diploma is required, and GED is accepted. *Academic units required*: 4 English, 3 math, 3 science (3 science labs), 2 foreign language, 3 social studies, 5 academic electives. *Academic units recommended*: 4 English, 3 math, 3 science (3 science labs), 3 foreign language, 3 social studies, 5 academic electives. **Freshman Admission Statistics**: 19,744 applied, 51% admitted, 30% enrolled. **Transfer Admission Requirements**: College transcript(s), essay or personal statement. Minimum college GPA of 3.0 required. Lowest grade transferable C. **General Admission Information**: Application fee $70. Early decision application deadline 11/15. Regular application deadline 1/1. Regular notification is rolling. Non-fall registration accepted. Admission may be deferred for a maximum of 1 year. Credit and/or placement offered for CEEB Advanced Placement tests.

COSTS AND FINANCIAL AID

Annual tuition $30,470. Room and board $10,940. Required fees $1,216. Average book expense $1,230. **Required Forms and Deadlines**: FAFSA, CSS/Financial Aid PROFILE, Noncustodial PROFILE, Business/Farm Supplement. Financial aid filing deadline 2/1. **Notification of Awards**: Applicants will be notified of awards on or about 4/1. **Types of Aid**: *Need-based scholarships/grants*: Pell, SEOG, state scholarships/grants, the school's own gift aid. *Loans*: FFEL Subsidized Stafford, FFEL Unsubsidized Stafford, FFEL PLUS, Federal Perkins. **Student Employment**: Federal Work-Study Program available. Institutional employment available. Off-campus job opportunities are good. **Financial Aid Statistics**: 54% freshmen, 52% undergrads receive need-based scholarship or grant aid. 50% freshmen, 50% undergrads receive need-based self-help aid. 78 freshmen, 345 undergrads receive athletic scholarships. 72% freshmen, 72% undergrads receive any aid.

TABOR COLLEGE

400 South Jefferson, Hillsboro, KS 67063
Phone: 620-947-3121 **E-mail:** admissions@tabor.edu
Fax: 620-947-6276 **Website:** www.tabor.edu **ACT Code:** 1468
Financial Aid Phone: 800-822-6799

This private school, affiliated with the Mennonite Church, was founded in 1908. It has a 30-acre campus.

RATINGS
Admissions Selectivity Rating: 75   **Fire Safety Rating:** 60*   **Green Rating:** 60*

STUDENTS AND FACULTY
Enrollment: 544. **Student Body:** 46% female, 54% male, 40% out-of-state, 1% international. African American 4%, Asian 9%, Caucasian 90%, Hispanic 2%. **Retention and Graduation:** 72% freshmen return for sophomore year. 36% freshmen graduate within 4 years. 15% grads go on to further study within 1 year. **Faculty:** 100% faculty teach undergrads.

ACADEMICS
Degrees: Associate, bachelor's, diploma, master's. **Academic Requirements:** Arts/fine arts, Bible, computer literacy, cross-cultural experience, English (including composition), history, humanities, mathematics, philosophy, sciences (biological or physical), social science. **Disciplines with Highest Percentage of Degrees Awarded:** Business/marketing 32%, education 20%, communication technologies 6%, biological/life sciences 5%, parks and recreation 4%, interdisciplinary studies 4%. **Special Study Options:** Accelerated program, cross-registration, distance learning, double major, exchange student program (domestic), honors program, independent study, internships, student-designed major, study abroad, teacher certification program.

FACILITIES
Housing: Men's dorms, women's dorms, Off-campus housing. **Special Academic Facilities/Equipment:** Center for Mennonite Brethren Studies, historic church. **Computers:** 90% of public computers are PCs, 10% of public computers are Macs, network access in dorm rooms, remote student-access to Web through college's connection.

CAMPUS LIFE
Activities: Choral groups, concert band, dance, drama/theater, jazz band, music ensembles, pep band, student government, student newspaper, yearbook. **Organizations:** 27 registered organizations, 9 religious organizations. **Athletics (Intercollegiate) Men:** Baseball, basketball, cheerleading, cross-country, football, golf, soccer, tennis, track/field (indoor), track/field (outdoor). *Women:* Basketball, cheerleading, cross-country, golf, soccer, softball, tennis, track/field (indoor), track/field (outdoor), volleyball.

ADMISSIONS
Freshman Academic Profile: 18% in top 10% of high school class, 40% in top 25% of high school class, 71% in top 50% of high school class. 83% from public high schools. TOEFL required of all international applicants, minimum paper TOEFL 525, minimum computer TOEFL 195. **Basis for Candidate Selection:** *Very important factors considered include:* Application essay, character/personal qualities, recommendation(s), rigor of secondary school record, standardized test scores. *Important factors considered include:* Interview, religious affiliation/commitment. *Other factors considered include:* Class rank, volunteer work. **Freshman Admission Requirements:** High school diploma is required, and GED is accepted. *Academic units recommended:* 4 English, 2 math, 2 science (1 science lab), 2 foreign language, 1 social studies, 2 history. **Freshman Admission Statistics:** 280 applied, 59% admitted, 60% enrolled. **Transfer Admission Requirements:** College transcript(s), essay or personal statement, standardized test score, statement of good standing from prior institution(s). Minimum college GPA of 2.0 required. Lowest grade transferable C-. **General Admission Information:** Application fee $20. Regular application deadline 8/1. Regular notification is rolling. Non-fall registration accepted. Common Application accepted.

COSTS AND FINANCIAL AID
Annual tuition $13,314. Room & board $4,900. Required fees $320. Average book expense $600. **Required Forms and Deadlines:** FAFSA, institution's own financial aid form. Financial aid filing deadline 3/1. **Notification of Awards:** Applicants will be notified of awards on or about 3/1. **Types of Aid:** *Need-based scholarships/grants:* Pell, SEOG, state scholarships/grants, private scholarships, the school's own gift aid. *Loans:* FFEL Subsidized Stafford, FFEL Unsubsidized Stafford, FFEL PLUS, Federal Perkins. **Student Employment:** Federal Work-Study Program available. Institutional employment available.

Off-campus job opportunities are good. **Financial Aid Statistics:** 73% freshmen, 67% undergrads receive need-based scholarship or grant aid. 68% freshmen, 66% undergrads receive need-based self-help aid. 80 freshmen, 240 undergrads receive athletic scholarships. Highest amount earned per year from on-campus jobs $1,500.

TALLADEGA COLLEGE

627 West Battle Street, Talladega, AL 35160
Phone: 205-761-6235 **E-mail:** admissions@talladega.edu
Fax: 205-362-0274 **Website:** www.talladega.edu
Financial Aid Phone: 256-761-6341

This private school, affiliated with the United Church of Christ, was founded in 1867. It has a 350-acre campus.

RATINGS
Admissions Selectivity Rating: 60*   **Fire Safety Rating:** 60*   **Green Rating:** 60*

STUDENTS AND FACULTY
Enrollment: 368. **Student Body:** 61% female, 39% male, 48% out-of-state. African American 92%, Caucasian 1%. **Retention and Graduation:** 43% freshmen return for sophomore year. 27% freshmen graduate within 4 years. 10% grads go on to further study within 1 year. 10% grads pursue arts and sciences degrees. 5% grads pursue business degrees. 5% grads pursue law degrees. 5% grads pursue medical degrees. **Faculty:** Student/faculty ratio 47:1. 35 full-time faculty, 60% hold PhDs. 100% faculty teach undergrads.

ACADEMICS
Degrees: Bachelor's. **Academic Requirements:** Foreign languages, humanities, mathematics, philosophy, physical education, sciences (biological or physical), social science. **Classes:** Most classes have fewer than 10 students. Most lab/discussion sections have fewer than 10 students. **Majors with Highest Enrollment:** Biology/biological sciences, business administration/management, psychology. **Disciplines with Highest Percentage of Degrees Awarded:** Business/marketing 25%, biological/life sciences 23%, social sciences 13%, psychology 10%, public administration and social services 7%, English 7%. **Special Study Options:** Cooperative education program, double major, dual enrollment, independent study, internships, teacher certification program.

FACILITIES
Housing: Men's dorms, women's dorms. **Special Academic Facilities/ Equipment:** Savery Library, Swayne Hall, DeForest Chapel, Goodnow Art Building. **Computers:** 5% of classrooms are wired, 5% of classrooms are wireless, 100% of public computers are PCs, network access in dorm rooms, network access in dorm lounges, online administrative functions (other than registration), remote student-access to Web through college's connection.

CAMPUS LIFE
Activities: Choral groups, concert band, dance, drama/theater, student government. **Organizations:** 40 registered organizations, 8 honor societies, 1 religious organization. 4 fraternities, 4 sororities.

ADMISSIONS
Freshman Academic Profile: 75% from public high schools. SAT Math middle 50% range 340–410. SAT Critical Reading middle 50% range 320–460. ACT middle 50% range 16–19. TOEFL required of all international applicants, minimum paper TOEFL 500, minimum computer TOEFL 250. **Basis for Candidate Selection:** *Very important factors considered include:* Application essay, character/personal qualities, extracurricular activities, recommendation(s), rigor of secondary school record, standardized test scores, talent/ability, volunteer work, work experience. *Important factors considered include:* Class rank. *Other factors considered include:* Interview. **Freshman Admission Requirements:** High school diploma is required, and GED is accepted. *Academic units required:* 4 English, 2 math, 2 science, 3 social studies, 2 physical education or health. **Freshman Admission Statistics:** 1,960 applied, 38% admitted, 24% enrolled. **Transfer Admission Requirements:** High school transcript, college transcript(s), essay or personal statement, standardized test score, statement of good standing from prior institution(s). Minimum college GPA of 2.0 required. Lowest grade transferable C. **General Admission Information:** Application fee $25. Non-fall registration accepted. Admission may be deferred for a maximum of 2 years. Common Application not accepted. Credit and/or placement offered for CEEB Advanced Placement tests.

COSTS AND FINANCIAL AID
Annual tuition $6,720. Room & board $4,290. Required fees $408. Average

book expense $1,000. **Required Forms and Deadlines**: FAFSA, institution's own financial aid form, CSS/Financial Aid PROFILE, state aid form. Financial aid filing deadline 6/30. Financial aid filing deadline 6/30. **Notification of Awards**: Applicants will be notified of awards on or about 4/1. **Types of Aid**: *Need-based scholarships/grants*: Pell, SEOG, state scholarships/grants, private scholarships, the school's own gift aid, United Negro College Fund. *Loans*: FFEL Subsidized Stafford, FFEL Unsubsidized Stafford, FFEL PLUS, Federal Perkins. **Financial Aid Statistics**: 75% freshmen, 86% undergrads receive need-based scholarship or grant aid. 75% freshmen, 86% undergrads receive need-based self-help aid. 90% freshmen, 90% undergrads receive any aid.

TARLETON STATE UNIVERSITY

PO Box T-0030, Tarleton Station, Stephenville, TX 76402
Phone: 254-968-9125 **E-mail**: uadm@tarleton.edu **CEEB Code**: 6817
Fax: 254-968-9951 **Website**: www.tarleton.edu **ACT Code**: 4204
Financial Aid Phone: 254-968-9070

This public school was founded in 1899. It has a 125-acre campus.

RATINGS
Admissions Selectivity Rating: 70   **Fire Safety Rating**: 86   **Green Rating**: 60*

STUDENTS AND FACULTY
Enrollment: 7,829. **Student Body**: 56% female, 44% male, 3% out-of-state. African American 8%, Asian 1%, Caucasian 80%, Hispanic 9%. **Retention and Graduation**: 62% freshmen return for sophomore year. 15% freshmen graduate within 4 years. **Faculty**: Student/faculty ratio 19:1. 265 full-time faculty, 68% hold PhDs. 100% faculty teach undergrads.

ACADEMICS
Degrees: Associate, bachelor's, doctoral, master's, terminal. **Academic Requirements**: Arts/fine arts, English (including composition), foreign languages, history, humanities, mathematics, sciences (biological or physical), social science, wellness health course. **Classes**: Most classes have 20–29 students. Most lab/discussion sections have 10–19 students. **Majors with Highest Enrollment**: Agricultural, agricultural operations, and related sciences, business administration/management, education. **Disciplines with Highest Percentage of Degrees Awarded**: Business/marketing 29%, agriculture 11%, interdisciplinary studies 11%, parks and recreation 8%, security and protective services 5%. **Special Study Options**: Accelerated program, distance learning, double major, dual enrollment, honors program, internships, study abroad, teacher certification program. Undergrads may take grad level classes.

FACILITIES
Housing: Coed dorms, men's dorms, women's dorms, apartments for married students, apartments for single students. **Special Academic Facilities/Equipment**: Planetarium in science building, W. K. Gordon Center for Industrial History of Texas. **Computers**: 80% of classrooms are wired, 70% of classrooms are wireless, network access in dorm rooms, online registration, online administrative functions (other than registration), remote student-access to Web through college's connection.

CAMPUS LIFE
Activities: Choral groups, concert band, dance, drama/theater, jazz band, literary magazine, marching band, music ensembles, musical theater, pep band, radio station, student government, student newspaper, symphony orchestra, yearbook. **Organizations**: 125 registered organizations, 12 honor societies, 9 religious organizations. 10 fraternities (8% men join), 7 sororities (7% women join). **Athletics (Intercollegiate)**: *Men*: Baseball, basketball, cheerleading, cross-country, football, rodeo, track/field (outdoor). *Women*: Basketball, cheerleading, cross-country, golf, rodeo, softball, tennis, track/field (outdoor), volleyball.

ADMISSIONS
Freshman Academic Profile: 9% in top 10% of high school class, 34% in top 25% of high school class, 77% in top 50% of high school class. 99% from public high schools. SAT Math middle 50% range 440–540. SAT Critical Reading middle 50% range 430–530. SAT Writing middle 50% range 420–510. ACT middle 50% range 18–23. TOEFL required of all international applicants, minimum paper TOEFL 520, minimum computer TOEFL 190. **Basis for Candidate Selection**: *Very important factors considered include*: Class rank, rigor of secondary school record, standardized test scores. *Important factors considered include*: Academic GPA. *Other factors considered include*: First

generation. **Freshman Admission Requirements**: High school diploma is required, and GED is accepted. *Academic units required*: 4 English, 3 math, 2 science (2 science labs), 2 social studies, 1 history, 2 academic electives. *Academic units recommended*: 3 science, 2 foreign language, 4 academic electives. **Freshman Admission Statistics**: 3,429 applied, 66% admitted, 56% enrolled. **Transfer Admission Requirements**: College transcript(s). Minimum college GPA of 2.0 required. Lowest grade transferable D. **General Admission Information**: Application fee $25. Regular application deadline 8/1. Non-fall registration accepted. Credit offered for CEEB Advanced Placement tests.

COSTS AND FINANCIAL AID
Annual in-state tuition $3,600. Out-of-state tuition $9,100. Room & board $5,802. Required fees $1,026. Average book expense $1,050. **Required Forms and Deadlines**: FAFSA. Financial aid filing deadline 11/1. **Notification of Awards**: Applicants will be notified of awards on a rolling basis beginning on or about 2/1. **Types of Aid**: *Need-based scholarships/grants*: Pell, SEOG, state scholarships/grants, private scholarships, the school's own gift aid. *Loans*: FFEL Subsidized Stafford, FFEL Unsubsidized Stafford, FFEL PLUS, state loans, college/university loans from institutional funds. **Financial Aid Statistics**: 35% freshmen, 39% undergrads receive need-based scholarship or grant aid. 33% freshmen, 40% undergrads receive need-based self-help aid. 50 freshmen, 213 undergrads receive athletic scholarships. 69% freshmen, 69% undergrads receive any aid.

TAYLOR UNIVERSITY

236 West Reade Avenue, Upland, IN 46989-1001
Phone: 765-998-5134 **E-mail**: admissions_u@tayloru.edu **CEEB Code**: 1802
Fax: 765-998-4925 **Website**: www.tayloru.edu **ACT Code**: 1248
Financial Aid Phone: 765-998-5358

This private school, affiliated with the Evangelical Christian Interdenominational Church, was founded in 1846. It has a 250-acre campus.

RATINGS
Admissions Selectivity Rating: 87   **Fire Safety Rating**: 76   **Green Rating**: 60*

STUDENTS AND FACULTY
Enrollment: 1,840. **Student Body**: 55% female, 45% male, 68% out-of-state, 1% international (23 countries represented). African American 2%, Asian 2%, Caucasian 93%, Hispanic 1%. **Retention and Graduation**: 87% freshmen return for sophomore year. 71% freshmen graduate within 4 years. 15% grads go on to further study within 1 year. **Faculty**: Student/faculty ratio 9:1. 127 full-time faculty, 80% hold PhDs. 100% faculty teach undergrads.

ACADEMICS
Degrees: Associate, bachelor's, certificate, master's. **Academic Requirements**: Arts/fine arts, computer literacy, English (including composition), history, humanities, mathematics, philosophy, sciences (biological or physical), social science. BA degree candidates must complete a foreign language requirement. **Classes**: Most classes have 10–19 students. Most lab/discussion sections have 10–19 students. **Majors with Highest Enrollment**: Bible/biblical studies, business/managerial operations, elementary education and teaching. **Disciplines with Highest Percentage of Degrees Awarded**: Education 19%, business/marketing 14%, psychology 11%, theology and religious vocations 7%, communications/journalism 7%, computer and information sciences 7%. **Special Study Options**: Cooperative education program, double major, dual enrollment, English as a second language (ESL), exchange student program (domestic), honors program, independent study, internships, liberal arts/career combination, student-designed major, study abroad, teacher certification program.

FACILITIES
Housing: Men's dorms, women's dorms, apartments for married students, apartments for single students, some off-campus apartments available to upperclassmen with special permission. **Special Academic Facilities/Equipment**: Compton Art Gallery, Edwin W. Brown Collection/CS Lewis and Friends. **Computers**: 99% of classrooms are wireless, 89% of public computers are PCs, 10% of public computers are Macs, 1% of public computers are UNIX, network access in dorm rooms, network access in dorm lounges, online registration, online administrative functions (other than registration), remote student-access to Web through college's connection.

CAMPUS LIFE
Activities: Choral groups, concert band, drama/theater, jazz band, literary magazine, music ensembles, musical theater, opera, pep band, radio station,

student government, student newspaper, student-run film society, symphony orchestra, television station, yearbook. **Organizations**: 100 registered organizations, 6 honor societies, 30 religious organizations. **Athletics (Intercollegiate)**: *Men*: Baseball, basketball, cross-country, football, golf, soccer, tennis, track/field (indoor), track/field (outdoor). *Women*: Basketball, cross-country, soccer, softball, tennis, track/field (indoor), track/field (outdoor), volleyball.

ADMISSIONS

Freshman Academic Profile: 38% in top 10% of high school class, 68% in top 25% of high school class, 90% in top 50% of high school class. SAT Math middle 50% range 520–670. SAT Critical Reading middle 50% range 520–670. SAT Writing middle 50% range 510–640. ACT middle 50% range 23–30. TOEFL required of all international applicants, minimum paper TOEFL 550, minimum computer TOEFL 213. **Basis for Candidate Selection**: *Very important factors considered include*: Academic GPA, application essay, character/personal qualities, interview, recommendation(s), rigor of secondary school record, standardized test scores. *Important factors considered include*: Class rank, extracurricular activities, volunteer work. *Other factors considered include*: Alumni/ae relation, racial/ethnic status, religious affiliation/commitment, work experience. **Freshman Admission Requirements**: High school diploma is required, and GED is accepted. *Academic units required*: 4 English, 3 math, 3 science (3 science labs), 2 social studies, 3 academic electives. *Academic units recommended*: 4 math, 4 science (4 science labs), 2 foreign language, 3 social studies. **Freshman Admission Statistics**: 1,529 applied, 86% admitted, 37% enrolled. **Transfer Admission Requirements**: High school transcript, college transcript(s), essay or personal statement, standardized test score, statement of good standing from prior institution(s). Minimum college GPA of 2.5 required. Lowest grade transferable C+. **General Admission Information**: Application fee $25. Regular application deadline 8/1. Regular notification is rolling. Non-fall registration accepted. Admission may be deferred for a maximum of 1 year. Credit and/or placement offered for CEEB Advanced Placement tests.

COSTS AND FINANCIAL AID

Annual tuition $24,314. Room and board $4,556. Required fees $160. Average book expense $900. **Required Forms and Deadlines**: FAFSA, institution's own financial aid form. Financial aid filing deadline 3/10. **Notification of Awards**: Applicants will be notified of awards on a rolling basis beginning on or about 3/1. **Types of Aid**: *Need-based scholarships/grants*: Pell, SEOG, state scholarships/grants, private scholarships, the school's own gift aid. *Loans*: FFEL Subsidized Stafford, FFEL Unsubsidized Stafford, FFEL PLUS, Federal Perkins, college/university loans from institutional funds. **Financial Aid Statistics**: 58% freshmen, 53% undergrads receive need-based scholarship or grant aid. 51% freshmen, 50% undergrads receive need-based self-help aid. 16 freshmen, 63 undergrads receive athletic scholarships. Highest amount earned per year from on-campus jobs $850.

TAYLOR UNIVERSITY—FORT WAYNE CAMPUS

1025 West Rudisill Boulevard, Fort Wayne, IN 46807
Phone: 260-744-8689 **E-mail**: admissions_f@tayloru.edu **CEEB Code**: 1227
Fax: 260-744-8660 **Website**: www.tayloru.edu/fw **ACT Code**: 1192
Financial Aid Phone: 260-744-8644

This private school, affiliated with the Protestant Church, was founded in 1846. It has a 32-acre campus.

RATINGS
Admissions Selectivity Rating: 72   **Fire Safety Rating**: 60*   **Green Rating**: 60*

STUDENTS AND FACULTY
Enrollment: 521. **Student Body**: 60% female, 40% male, 25% out-of-state. African American 6%, Caucasian 86%, Hispanic 2%. **Retention and Graduation**: 71% freshmen return for sophomore year. 32% freshmen graduate within 4 years. **Faculty**: Student/faculty ratio 14:1. 26 full-time faculty, 62% hold PhDs. 100% faculty teach undergrads.

ACADEMICS
Degrees: Associate, bachelor's, certificate, master's, terminal. **Academic Requirements**: Arts/fine arts, biblical studies, communications, computer literacy, cross cultural studies, English (including composition), history, humanities, mathematics, philosophy, physical fitness, sciences (biological or physical), social science. **Classes**: Most classes have fewer than 10 students. Most lab/discussion sections have 10–19 students. **Majors with Highest Enrollment**: Elementary education and teaching, pastoral studies/counseling, psychology. **Disciplines with Highest Percentage of Degrees Awarded**:

Education 15%, communication technologies 14%, psychology 14%, business/marketing 9%, English 8%. **Special Study Options**: Accelerated program, cooperative education program, distance learning, double major, exchange student program (domestic), independent study, internships, student-designed major, study abroad, teacher certification program, weekend college.

FACILITIES
Housing: Men's dorms, women's dorms, apartments for single students. **Computers**: 60% of public computers are PCs, 30% of public computers are Macs, network access in dorm rooms, online registration, remote student-access to Web through college's connection.

CAMPUS LIFE
Activities: Choral groups, drama/theater, jazz band, music ensembles, student government, student newspaper, yearbook. **Organizations**: 11 registered organizations, 1 religious organization. **Athletics (Intercollegiate)**: *Men*: Basketball, cheerleading, soccer. *Women*: Basketball, cheerleading, volleyball.

ADMISSIONS
Freshman Academic Profile: 12% in top 10% of high school class, 31% in top 25% of high school class, 65% in top 50% of high school class. 65% from public high schools. SAT Math middle 50% range 418–563. SAT Critical Reading middle 50% range 445–580. ACT middle 50% range 19–26. TOEFL required of all international applicants, minimum paper TOEFL 550, minimum computer TOEFL 213. **Basis for Candidate Selection**: *Very important factors considered include*: Religious affiliation/commitment, rigor of secondary school record. *Important factors considered include*: Application essay, character/personal qualities, interview, recommendation(s), standardized test scores. *Other factors considered include*: Class rank, extracurricular activities, volunteer work, work experience. **Freshman Admission Requirements**: High school diploma is required, and GED is accepted. *Academic units required*: 4 English, 3 math, 3 science (3 science labs), 2 social studies, 2 history. *Academic units recommended*: 2 foreign language. **Freshman Admission Statistics**: 313 applied, 83% admitted, 46% enrolled. **Transfer Admission Requirements**: High school transcript, college transcript(s), essay or personal statement, statement of good standing from prior institution(s). Minimum college GPA of 2.5 required. Lowest grade transferable C-. **General Admission Information**: Application fee $20. Regular application deadline 8/15. Regular notification is rolling. Non-fall registration accepted. Admission may be deferred for a maximum of 2 years. Common Application accepted. Neither credit nor placement offered for CEEB Advanced Placement tests.

COSTS AND FINANCIAL AID
Comprehensive fee $20,470. **Required Forms and Deadlines**: FAFSA, institution's own financial aid form. Financial aid filing deadline 3/1. **Notification of Awards**: Applicants will be notified of awards on or about 3/1. **Types of Aid**: *Need-based scholarships/grants*: Pell, SEOG, state scholarships/grants, private scholarships, the school's own gift aid, endowed-donor scholarships. *Loans*: FFEL Subsidized Stafford, FFEL Unsubsidized Stafford, FFEL PLUS, Federal Perkins. **Student Employment**: Federal Work-Study Program available. Institutional employment available. Off-campus job opportunities are excellent. **Financial Aid Statistics**: 83% freshmen, 85% undergrads receive need-based scholarship or grant aid. 76% freshmen, 79% undergrads receive need-based self-help aid. 2 undergrads receive athletic scholarships.

TEMPLE UNIVERSITY

1801 North Broad Street, Philadelphia, PA 19122-6096
Phone: 215-204-7200 **E-mail**: Tuadm@temple.edu **CEEB Code**: 2906
Fax: 215-204-5694 **Website**: www.temple.edu **ACT Code**: 3724
Financial Aid Phone: 215-204-8760

This public school was founded in 1884. It has a 362-acre campus.

RATINGS
Admissions Selectivity Rating: 83   **Fire Safety Rating**: 85   **Green Rating**: 75

STUDENTS AND FACULTY
Enrollment: 24,070. **Student Body**: 55% female, 45% male, 22% out-of-state, 3% international (133 countries represented). African American 18%, Asian 9%, Caucasian 58%, Hispanic 3%. **Retention and Graduation**: 87% freshmen

return for sophomore year. 29% freshmen graduate within 4 years. **Faculty**: Student/faculty ratio 17:1. 1,225 full-time faculty, 77% hold PhDs.

ACADEMICS

Degrees: Associate, bachelor's, certificate, diploma, doctoral, first professional certificate, first professional, master's, post-master's certificate, terminal. **Academic Requirements**: Arts/fine arts, computer literacy, English (including composition), foreign languages, history, humanities, mathematics, philosophy, sciences (biological or physical), social science, intellectual heritage, general education. **Classes**: Most classes have 10–19 students. Most lab/discussion sections have 20–29 students. **Majors with Highest Enrollment**: Biology/biological sciences, elementary education and teaching, psychology. **Disciplines with Highest Percentage of Degrees Awarded**: Business/marketing 21%, education 12%, visual and performing arts 12%, communications/journalism 11%, public administration and social services 7%, social sciences 5%, psychology 5%, health professions and related sciences 5%. **Special Study Options**: Cooperative education program, cross-registration, distance learning, double major, dual enrollment, English as a second language (ESL), exchange student program (domestic), honors program, independent study, internships, liberal arts/career combination, student-designed major, study abroad, teacher certification program.

FACILITIES

Housing: Coed dorms, apartments for single students, special housing for disabled students, Living/Learning Centers. **Special Academic Facilities/Equipment**: Blockson collection, urban archieves, observatory. **Computers**: 1% of classrooms are wired, 25% of classrooms are wireless, 82% of public computers are PCs, 14% of public computers are Macs, 4% of public computers are UNIX, network access in dorm rooms, network access in dorm lounges, online registration, online administrative functions (other than registration), support for handheld computing, remote student-access to Web through college's connection.

CAMPUS LIFE

Activities: Choral groups, concert band, dance, drama/theater, jazz band, literary magazine, marching band, music ensembles, opera, pep band, radio station, student government, student newspaper, student-run film society, symphony orchestra, yearbook. **Organizations**: 182 registered organizations, 24 honor societies, 14 religious organizations. 13 fraternities (1% men join), 12 sororities (1% women join). **Athletics (Intercollegiate)**: *Men*: Baseball, basketball, cheerleading, crew/rowing, cross-country, football, golf, gymnastics, soccer, tennis, track/field (indoor), track/field (outdoor). *Women*: Basketball, cheerleading, crew/rowing, cross-country, fencing, field hockey, gymnastics, lacrosse, soccer, softball, tennis, track/field (indoor), track/field (outdoor), volleyball. Environmental Initiatives: The Sustainability Action Plan was developed in the Fall 2007. A transportation survey is underway. The Office of Sustainability is being established to operate by Fall 2009.

ADMISSIONS

Freshman Academic Profile: 18% in top 10% of high school class, 50% in top 25% of high school class, 88% in top 50% of high school class. 83% from public high schools. SAT Math middle 50% range 490–590. SAT Critical Reading middle 50% range 490–590. ACT middle 50% range 20–25. TOEFL required of all international applicants, minimum paper TOEFL 527, minimum computer TOEFL 197. **Basis for Candidate Selection**: *Very important factors considered include*: Academic GPA, class rank, rigor of secondary school record. *Important factors considered include*: Standardized test scores. *Other factors considered include*: Alumni/ae relation, application essay, character/personal qualities, extracurricular activities, recommendation(s), talent/ability, volunteer work, work experience. **Freshman Admission Requirements**: High school diploma is required, and GED is accepted. *Academic units required*: 4 English, 3 math, 2 science (1 science lab), 2 foreign language, 2 social studies, 1 history, 1 academic elective. *Academic units recommended*: 4 English, 4 math, 3 science, (2 science labs), 2 foreign language, 2 social studies, 2 history, 3 academic electives. **Freshman Admission Statistics**: 18,140 applied, 60% admitted, 36% enrolled. **Transfer Admission Requirements**: High school transcript, college transcript(s), essay or personal statement, statement of good standing from prior institution(s). Minimum college GPA of 2.4 required. Lowest grade transferable C. **General Admission Information**: Application fee $50. Regular application deadline 3/1. Regular notification is rolling. Nonfall registration accepted. Admission may be deferred for a maximum of 1 year. Credit and/or placement offered for CEEB Advanced Placement tests.

COSTS AND FINANCIAL AID

Annual in-state tuition $10,252. Annual out-of-state tuition $18,770. Room and board $8,518. Required fees $550. Average book expense $1,000. **Required Forms and Deadlines**: FAFSA. Financial aid filing deadline 3/1. **Notification of Awards**: Applicants will be notified of awards on a rolling basis beginning on or about 2/15. **Types of Aid**: *Need-based scholarships/grants*: Pell, SEOG, state scholarships/grants, private scholarships, the school's own gift aid, Federal Nursing Scholarships. *Loans*: FFEL Subsidized Stafford, FFEL Unsubsidized Stafford, FFEL PLUS, Federal Perkins, Federal Nursing, college/university

loans from institutional funds. **Student Employment**: Federal Work-Study Program available. Institutional employment available. Off-campus job opportunities are excellent. **Financial Aid Statistics**: 67% freshmen, 64% undergrads receive need-based scholarship or grant aid. 57% freshmen, 56% undergrads receive need-based self-help aid. 37 freshmen, 205 undergrads receive athletic scholarships. 88% freshmen, 89% undergrads receive any aid.

See page 1402.

TENNESSEE STATE UNIVERSITY

3500 John Merritt Boulevard, Nashville, TN 37209-1561
Phone: 615-963-3101 **E-mail**: jcade@tnstate.edu **CEEB Code**: 1803
Fax: 615-963-5108 **Website**: www.tnstate.edu **ACT Code**: 4010
Financial Aid Phone: 615-963-5701

This public school was founded in 1912. It has a 465-acre campus.

RATINGS

Admissions Selectivity Rating: 60*   **Fire Safety Rating**: 60*   **Green Rating**: 60*

STUDENTS AND FACULTY

Enrollment: 7,000. **Student Body**: 63% female, 37% male, 49% out-of-state, 1% international (54 countries represented). African American 83%, Asian 1%, Caucasian 15%. **Retention and Graduation**: 77% freshmen return for sophomore year. 14% freshmen graduate within 4 years. 20% grads go on to further study within 1 year. **Faculty**: Student/faculty ratio 22:1. 383 full-time faculty, 74% hold PhDs. 83% faculty teach undergrads.

ACADEMICS

Degrees: Associate, bachelor's, doctoral, master's. **Academic Requirements**: Arts/fine arts, English (including composition), foreign languages, history, humanities, mathematics, philosophy, sciences (biological or physical), social science. **Classes**: Most classes have fewer than 10 students. Most lab/discussion sections have 10–19 students. **Majors with Highest Enrollment**: Business/managerial economics, liberal arts and sciences studies and humanities, nursing/registered nurse training (ASN, BSN, MSN, RN). **Disciplines with Highest Percentage of Degrees Awarded**: Interdisciplinary studies 20%, health professions and related sciences 10%, psychology 9%, business/marketing 9%, engineering 8%, education 7%, computer and information sciences 7%, social sciences 7%. **Special Study Options**: Cooperative education program, cross-registration, double major, exchange student program (domestic), honors program, independent study, internships, liberal arts/career combination, teacher certification program. Online degree (courses offered via computer approved by Tennessee Board of Regents).

FACILITIES

Housing: Coed dorms, men's dorms, women's dorms, apartments for single students. **Special Academic Facilities/Equipment**: 8 structural buildings on the national register of historic places, Hiran V. Gordon Art Gallery. **Computers**: Network access in dorm rooms, network access in dorm lounges, online registration, online administrative functions (other than registration), remote student-access to Web through college's connection.

CAMPUS LIFE

Activities: Choral groups, drama/theater, jazz band, marching band, music ensembles, radio station, student government, student newspaper, yearbook. **Organizations**: 82 registered organizations, 8 honor societies, 4 religious organizations. 4 fraternities (29% men join), 5 sororities (12% women join). **Athletics (Intercollegiate)**: *Men*: Basketball, cheerleading, cross-country, football, golf, tennis, track/field (indoor), track/field (outdoor). *Women*: Basketball, cheerleading, cross-country, softball, tennis, track/field (indoor), track/field (outdoor), volleyball.

ADMISSIONS

Freshman Academic Profile: 96% from public high schools. SAT Math middle 50% range 430–510. SAT Critical Reading middle 50% range 430–510. ACT middle 50% range 18–21. TOEFL required of all international applicants, minimum paper TOEFL 500. **Basis for Candidate Selection**: *Very important factors considered include*: Standardized test scores, state residency. *Important factors considered include*: Class rank, geographical residence, recommendation(s), rigor of secondary school record. *Other factors considered include*: Alumni/ae relation, character/personal qualities, extracurricular activities, talent/ability. **Freshman Admission Requirements**: High school diploma is required, and GED is accepted. *Academic units required*: 4 English, 3 math, 2 science (1 science lab), 2 foreign language, 1 social studies, 1 history,

1 academic elective. **Freshman Admission Statistics**: 6,344 applied, 35% admitted, 59% enrolled. **Transfer Admission Requirements**: College transcript(s). Minimum college GPA of 2.9 required. Lowest grade transferable C. **General Admission Information**: Application fee $15. Regular application deadline 8/1. Non-fall registration accepted. Common Application not accepted. Credit offered for CEEB Advanced Placement tests.

COSTS AND FINANCIAL AID
Annual in-state tuition $3,272. Out-of-state tuition $10,230. Room & board $3,060. Required fees $150. Average book expense $850. **Required Forms and Deadlines**: FAFSA, CSS/Financial Aid PROFILE, Noncustodial PROFILE. **Types of Aid**: *Need-based scholarships/grants*: Pell, SEOG. *Loans*: Direct Subsidized Stafford, Direct Unsubsidized Stafford, Direct PLUS, FFEL Subsidized Stafford, FFEL Unsubsidized Stafford, FFEL PLUS, Federal Perkins. **Student Employment**: Federal Work-Study Program available. Off-campus job opportunities are good. **Financial Aid Statistics**: 29% freshmen, 33% freshmen, 10 freshmen, 118 undergrads receive athletic scholarships.

TENNESSEE TECHNOLOGICAL UNIVERSITY

Best Value

PO Box 5006, Cookeville, TN 38505
Phone: 931-372-3888 **E-mail**: admissions@tntech.edu **CEEB Code**: 1804
Fax: 931-372-6250 **Website**: www.tntech.edu **ACT Code**: 4012
Financial Aid Phone: 931-372-3073

This public school was founded in 1915. It has a 235-acre campus.

RATINGS
Admissions Selectivity Rating: 77   **Fire Safety Rating**: 68   **Green Rating**: 60*

STUDENTS AND FACULTY
Enrollment: 7,446. **Student Body**: 46% female, 54% male, 4% out-of-state. African American 4%, Asian 1%, Caucasian 88%, Hispanic 1%. **Retention and Graduation**: 74% freshmen return for sophomore year. 18% freshmen graduate within 4 years. **Faculty**: Student/faculty ratio 18:1. 389 full-time faculty, 82% hold PhDs. 99% faculty teach undergrads.

ACADEMICS
Degrees: Bachelor's, doctoral, master's, post-master's certificate. **Academic Requirements**: Computer literacy, English (including composition), history, humanities, mathematics, sciences (biological or physical), social science, speech or professional communication. **Classes**: Most classes have 10–19 students. Most lab/discussion sections have 10–19 students. **Majors with Highest Enrollment**: Business administration/management, elementary education and teaching, mechanical engineering. **Disciplines with Highest Percentage of Degrees Awarded**: Education 22%, business/marketing 21%, engineering 14%, liberal arts/general studies 5%, family and consumer sciences 4%, agriculture 4%, health professions and related sciences 4%, social sciences 4%. **Special Study Options**: Cooperative education program, distance learning, double major, dual enrollment, honors program, internships, study abroad, teacher certification program.

FACILITIES
Housing: Coed dorms, men's dorms, women's dorms, apartments for married students, apartments for single students, special housing for disabled students, special housing for international students. **Special Academic Facilities/ Equipment**: 300-acre farm lab, electric power center, water resources center, manufacturing center. **Computers**: 95% of public computers are PCs, 5% of public computers are Macs, network access in dorm rooms, network access in dorm lounges, online registration, online administrative functions (other than registration), remote student-access to Web through college's connection.

CAMPUS LIFE
Activities: Choral groups, concert band, dance, drama/theater, jazz band, literary magazine, marching band, music ensembles, musical theater, opera, pep band, radio station, student government, student newspaper, symphony orchestra, television station, yearbook. **Organizations**: 182 registered organizations, 14 honor societies, 16 religious organizations. 16 fraternities (9% men join), 6 sororities (7% women join). **Athletics (Intercollegiate)**: *Men*: Baseball, basketball, cheerleading, cross-country, football, golf, riflery, tennis.

Women: Basketball, cheerleading, cross-country, golf, riflery, soccer, softball, tennis, track/field (indoor), track/field (outdoor), volleyball.

ADMISSIONS
Freshman Academic Profile: 22% in top 10% of high school class, 52% in top 25% of high school class, 82% in top 50% of high school class. 80% from public high schools. SAT Math middle 50% range 530–640. SAT Critical Reading middle 50% range 500–630. ACT middle 50% range 20–25. TOEFL required of all international applicants, minimum paper TOEFL 500, minimum computer TOEFL 173. **Basis for Candidate Selection**: *Very important factors considered include*: Academic GPA, rigor of secondary school record, standardized test scores. *Other factors considered include*: Alumni/ae relation, application essay, character/personal qualities, extracurricular activities, interview, recommendation(s). **Freshman Admission Requirements**: High school diploma is required, and GED is accepted. *Academic units required*: 4 English, 3 math, 2 science (1 science lab), 2 foreign language, 1 social studies, 1 history, 1 visual and performing art. **Freshman Admission Statistics**: 2,937 applied, 92% admitted, 56% enrolled. **Transfer Admission Requirements**: College transcript(s). Minimum college GPA of 2.0 required. Lowest grade transferable D. **General Admission Information**: Application fee $15. Regular application deadline 8/1. Regular notification is rolling. Non-fall registration accepted. Admission may be deferred for a maximum of 1 semester. Credit and/or placement offered for CEEB Advanced Placement tests.

COSTS AND FINANCIAL AID
Annual in-state tuition $4,058. Annual out-of-state tuition $14,334. Room and board $6,630. Required fees $922. Average book expense $1,200. **Required Forms and Deadlines**: FAFSA. Financial aid filing deadline 3/15. **Notification of Awards**: Applicants will be notified of awards on a rolling basis beginning on or about 3/15. **Types of Aid**: *Need-based scholarships/grants*: Pell, SEOG, state scholarships/grants, private scholarships, the school's own gift aid, United Negro College Fund. *Loans*: Direct Subsidized Stafford, Direct Unsubsidized Stafford, FFEL PLUS, Federal Perkins, state loans, college/university loans from institutional funds. **Financial Aid Statistics**: 14% freshmen, 25% undergrads receive need-based scholarship or grant aid. 13% freshmen, 28% undergrads receive need-based self-help aid. 31 freshmen, 253 undergrads receive athletic scholarships. 91% freshmen, 89% undergrads receive any aid.

TENNESSEE WESLEYAN COLLEGE

PO Box 40, Athens, TN 37371-0040
Phone: 423-745-7504 **E-mail**: twilliams@twcnet.edu
Fax: 423-745-9335 **Website**: www.twcnet.edu **ACT Code**: 4014
Financial Aid Phone: 423-746-5209

This private school, affiliated with the United Methodist Church, was founded in 1857. It has a 40-acre campus.

RATINGS
Admissions Selectivity Rating: 60*   **Fire Safety Rating**: 72   **Green Rating**: 60*

STUDENTS AND FACULTY
Enrollment: 847. **Student Body**: 68% female, 32% male, 6% out-of-state, 3% international (13 countries represented). African American 3%, Caucasian 75%, Hispanic 2%. **Retention and Graduation**: 65% freshmen return for sophomore year. 16% freshmen graduate within 4 years. **Faculty**: Student/faculty ratio 13:1. 46 full-time faculty, 59% hold PhDs. 100% faculty teach undergrads.

ACADEMICS
Degrees: Bachelor's. **Academic Requirements**: Arts/fine arts, computer literacy, English (including composition), history, mathematics, philosophy, sciences (biological or physical), social science. For the bachelor of arts degree, the student must complete 12 semester hours of a foreign language. **Classes**: Most classes have 10–19 students. Most lab/discussion sections have 10–19 students. **Majors with Highest Enrollment**: Business administration/ management, education, nursing/registered nurse training (ASN, BSN, MSN, RN). **Disciplines with Highest Percentage of Degrees Awarded**: Business/ marketing 30%, health professions and related sciences 16%, education 11%, public administration and social services 11%, parks and recreation 11%, computer and information sciences 6%, English 4%. **Special Study Options**: Accelerated program, double major, honors program, independent study, internships, student-designed major, study abroad, teacher certification program.

FACILITIES

Housing: Men's dorms, women's dorms, apartments for single students. Residency exemption policy: All students are required to live on campus unless they are married, have custody of a child, are a military veteran eligible for benefits under Public Law 358 GI Bill. **Special Academic Facilities/Equipment**: Old College (building is on historical registry). **Computers**: 100% of public computers are PCs, network access in dorm rooms, network access in dorm lounges, remote student-access to Web through college's connection.

CAMPUS LIFE

Activities: Choral groups, drama/theater, literary magazine, musical theater, student government, student newspaper, yearbook. **Organizations**: 19 registered organizations, 5 honor societies, 3 religious organizations. 2 sororities (9% women join). **Athletics (Intercollegiate)**: *Men*: Baseball, basketball, cheerleading, cross-country, golf, soccer, tennis. *Women*: Basketball, cheerleading, cross-country, golf, soccer, softball, tennis, volleyball.

ADMISSIONS

Freshman Academic Profile: 96% from public high schools. ACT middle 50% range 18–24. TOEFL required of all international applicants, minimum paper TOEFL 500, minimum computer TOEFL 173. **Basis for Candidate Selection**: *Very important factors considered include:* Academic GPA, rigor of secondary school record, standardized test scores. *Important factors considered include:* Application essay, level of applicant's interest, recommendation(s). *Other factors considered include:* Alumni/ae relation, class rank, extracurricular activities, first generation, interview. **Freshman Admission Requirements**: High school diploma is required, and GED is accepted. *Academic units recommended*: 4 English, 2 math, 2 science, 1 social studies, 1 history. **Freshman Admission Statistics**: 515 applied, 77% admitted, 42% enrolled. **Transfer Admission Requirements**: College transcript(s). Minimum college GPA of 2.0 required. Lowest grade transferable D. **General Admission Information**: Application fee $25. Regular application deadline 8/20. Regular notification is rolling. Non-fall registration accepted. Admission may be deferred for a maximum of 1 semester. Common Application not accepted. Credit and/or placement offered for CEEB Advanced Placement tests.

COSTS AND FINANCIAL AID

Annual tuition $14,000. Room & board $5,500. Required fees $550. Average book expense $1,000. **Required Forms and Deadlines**: FAFSA, institution's own financial aid form. **Notification of Awards**: Applicants will be notified of awards on a rolling basis beginning on or about 2/1. **Types of Aid**: *Need-based scholarships/grants*: Pell, SEOG, state scholarships/grants, private scholarships, the school's own gift aid. *Loans*: FFEL Subsidized Stafford, FFEL Unsubsidized Stafford, FFEL PLUS, Federal Perkins, United Methodist. **Financial Aid Statistics**: 83% freshmen, 80% undergrads receive need-based scholarship or grant aid. 55% freshmen, 61% undergrads receive need-based self-help aid. 34 freshmen, 85 undergrads receive athletic scholarships. 99% freshmen, 99% undergrads receive any aid. Highest amount earned per year from on-campus jobs $2,800.

TEXAS A&M UNIVERSITY—COLLEGE STATION

Admissions Counseling, College Station, TX 77843-1265
Phone: 979-845-3741 **E-mail**: admissions@tamu.edu **CEEB Code**: 6003
Fax: 979-847-8737 **Website**: www.tamu.edu **ACT Code**: 4198
Financial Aid Phone: 979-845-3236

This public school was founded in 1876. It has a 5,200-acre campus.

RATINGS

Admissions Selectivity Rating: 83   **Fire Safety Rating**: 60*   **Green Rating**: 86

STUDENTS AND FACULTY

Enrollment: 36,473. **Student Body**: 48% female, 52% male, 3% out-of-state, 1% international (125 countries represented). African American 3%, Asian 4%, Caucasian 79%, Hispanic 12%. **Retention and Graduation**: 92% freshmen return for sophomore year. 37% freshmen graduate within 4 years. **Faculty**: Student/faculty ratio 20:1. 2,117 full-time faculty, 92% hold PhDs. 75% faculty teach undergrads.

ACADEMICS

Degrees: Bachelor's, doctoral, first professional, master's, post-bachelor's certificate. **Academic Requirements**: Arts/fine arts, computer literacy, English (including composition), foreign languages, history, humanities, mathematics, philosophy, sciences (biological or physical), social science. **Classes**: Most classes have 20–29 students. Most lab/discussion sections have 20–29 students. **Majors with Highest Enrollment**: Biological and physical sciences, multi/interdisciplinary studies, operations management and supervision. **Disciplines with Highest Percentage of Degrees Awarded**: Business/marketing 17%, agriculture 13%, engineering 12%, interdisciplinary studies 10%, biological/life sciences 9%. **Special Study Options**: Accelerated program, cooperative education program, cross-registration, distance learning, double major, dual enrollment, English as a second language (ESL), exchange student program (domestic), honors program, independent study, internships, study abroad, teacher certification program.

FACILITIES

Housing: Coed dorms, men's dorms, women's dorms, apartments for married students, apartments for single students, special housing for disabled students, fraternity/sorority housing, honors dorm. **Special Academic Facilities/Equipment**: Bush Library/Museum, Jordan International Collection, Corps of Cadets Center/Museum, Forsyth Center Gallery, MSC Visual Arts Gallery, J. Wayne Stark University Center Galleries, Oran W. Nicks Low Speed Wind Tunnel, astronomical observatory, ocean drilling program building. **Computers**: 70% of classrooms are wired, 68% of classrooms are wireless, 96% of public computers are PCs, 2% of public computers are Macs, 2% of public computers are UNIX, network access in dorm rooms, network access in dorm lounges, online registration, online administrative functions (other than registration), remote student-access to Web through college's connection.

CAMPUS LIFE

Activities: Choral groups, concert band, dance, drama/theater, jazz band, literary magazine, marching band, music ensembles, musical theater, radio station, student government, student newspaper, student-run film society, symphony orchestra, television station, yearbook. **Organizations**: 725 registered organizations, 34 honor societies, 77 religious organizations. 33 fraternities (6% men join), 23 sororities (12% women join). **Athletics (Intercollegiate)**: *Men*: Baseball, basketball, cross-country, diving, football, golf, riflery, swimming, tennis, track/field (indoor), track/field (outdoor). *Women*: Basketball, cross-country, diving, equestrian sports, golf, riflery, soccer, softball, swimming, tennis, track/field (indoor), track/field (outdoor), volleyball. Environmental Initiatives: LEED. Paper Recycling. Transportation Fuel.

ADMISSIONS

Freshman Academic Profile: 46% in top 10% of high school class, 77% in top 25% of high school class, 90% in top 50% of high school class. SAT Math middle 50% range 560–670. SAT Critical Reading middle 50% range 520–630. SAT Writing middle 50% range 500–610. ACT middle 50% range 23–28. TOEFL required of all international applicants, minimum paper TOEFL 550. **Basis for Candidate Selection**: *Very important factors considered include:* Academic GPA, class rank, extracurricular activities, rigor of secondary school record, standardized test scores, state residency, talent/ability. *Important factors considered include:* Application essay, volunteer work, work experience. *Other factors considered include:* Character/personal qualities, first generation, geographical residence, recommendation(s). **Freshman Admission Requirements**: High school diploma is required, and GED is accepted. *Academic units required*: 4 English, 3 math, 3 science (2 science labs), 2 foreign language, 2 social studies, 1 history. *Academic units recommended*: 4 English, 3 math, 3 science (2 science labs), 2 foreign language, 2 social studies, 1 history, 1 computer course. **Freshman Admission Statistics**: 17,410 applied, 77% admitted, 59% enrolled. **Transfer Admission Requirements**: High school transcript, college transcript(s). Minimum college GPA of 2.5 required. Lowest grade transferable D. **General Admission Information**: Application fee $60. Regular application deadline 2/1. Regular notification is rolling. Non-fall registration accepted. Credit offered for CEEB Advanced Placement tests.

COSTS AND FINANCIAL AID

Annual in-state tuition $4,680. Annual out-of-state tuition $13,020. Room and board $6,480. Required fees $2,655. Average book expense $1,156. **Required Forms and Deadlines**: FAFSA, institution's own financial aid form, Financial aid transcripts (for transfer students). Financial aid filing deadline 4/1. **Notification of Awards**: Applicants will be notified of awards on or about 3/15. **Types of Aid**: *Need-based scholarships/grants*: Pell, SEOG, state scholarships/grants, private scholarships, the school's own gift aid. *Loans*: FFEL Subsidized Stafford, FFEL Unsubsidized Stafford, FFEL PLUS, Federal Perkins, state loans, college/university loans from institutional funds. **Student Employment**: Off-campus job opportunities are excellent. **Financial Aid Statistics**: 34% freshmen, 29% undergrads receive need-based scholarship or grant aid. 22% freshmen, 25% undergrads receive need-based self-help aid. 64 freshmen, 288 undergrads receive athletic scholarships. Highest amount earned per year from on-campus jobs $1,934.

TEXAS A&M UNIVERSITY—COMMERCE

PO Box 3011, Commerce, TX 75429
Phone: 903-886-5106 **E-mail:** admissions@tamu-commerce.edu
Fax: 903-886-5888 **Website:** www.tamu-commerce.edu **ACT Code:** 6188
Financial Aid Phone: 903-886-5096

This public school was founded in 1889. It has a 140-acre campus.

RATINGS
Admissions Selectivity Rating: 77   **Fire Safety Rating:** 60*   **Green Rating:** 60*

STUDENTS AND FACULTY
Student Body: 4% out-of-state. **Faculty:** Student/faculty ratio 16:1. 294 full-time faculty, 64% hold PhDs. 17% faculty teach undergrads.

ACADEMICS
Degrees: Bachelor's, doctoral, master's. **Academic Requirements:** Arts/fine arts, English (including composition), foreign languages, government, history, humanities, mathematics, sciences (biological or physical), social science. **Classes:** Most classes have 10-19 students. **Majors with Highest Enrollment:** Business administration/management, computer and information sciences, criminal justice/safety studies. **Disciplines with Highest Percentage of Degrees Awarded:** Visual and performing arts 5%, social sciences 4%, agriculture 2%, communication technologies 1%, computer and information sciences 1%, English 1%, law/legal studies 1%, foreign languages and literature 1%, psychology 1%, parks and recreation 1%. **Special Study Options:** Cooperative education program, distance learning, double major, dual enrollment, honors program, independent study, internships, study abroad, teacher certification program, weekend college (for graduate students only). Selected courses available online.

FACILITIES
Housing: Coed dorms, men's dorms, women's dorms, apartments for married students, apartments for single students, special housing for disabled students, special housing for international students, fraternity/sorority housing. **Computers:** 90% of public computers are PCs, 10% of public computers are Macs, network access in dorm lounges, online registration, online administrative functions (other than registration), remote student-access to Web through college's connection.

CAMPUS LIFE
Activities: Choral groups, concert band, dance, drama/theater, jazz band, literary magazine, marching band, music ensembles, musical theater, pep band, radio station, student government, student newspaper, student-run film society, television station, yearbook. **Organizations:** 110 registered organizations, 12 honor societies, 10 religious organizations. 9 fraternities (11% men join), 9 sororities (8% women join). **Athletics (Intercollegiate):** *Men:* Basketball, cheerleading, cross-country, football, golf, track/field (outdoor). *Women:* Basketball, cheerleading, cross-country, golf, soccer, track/field (outdoor), volleyball.

ADMISSIONS
Freshman Academic Profile: 13% in top 10% of high school class, 26% in top 25% of high school class, 33% in top 50% of high school class. 98% from public high schools. SAT Math middle 50% range 460–560. SAT Critical Reading middle 50% range 440–540. ACT middle 50% range 17–23. TOEFL required of all international applicants, minimum paper TOEFL 500. **Basis for Candidate Selection:** *Very important factors considered include:* Class rank, rigor of secondary school record, standardized test scores. *Other factors considered include:* Work experience. **Freshman Admission Requirements:** High school diploma is required, and GED is accepted. *Academic units required:* 4 English, 3 math, 2 science, 2 history and social studies. *Academic units recommended:* 2 foreign language. **Freshman Admission Statistics:** 1,899 applied, 51% admitted, 58% enrolled. **Transfer Admission Requirements:** College transcript(s), standardized test score, statement of good standing from prior institution(s). Minimum college GPA of 2.0 required. Lowest grade transferable D. **General Admission Information:** Application fee $25. Regular application deadline 8/1. Regular notification is rolling. Non-fall registration accepted. Admission may be deferred for a maximum of 1 year. Credit and/or placement offered for CEEB Advanced Placement tests.

COSTS AND FINANCIAL AID
Annual in-state tuition $9,232. Out-of-state tuition $25,732. Room & board $6,220. Required fees $1,106. Average book expense $1,010. **Required Forms and Deadlines:** FAFSA. Financial aid filing deadline 5/1. **Notification of Awards:** Applicants will be notified of awards on or about 6/1. **Types of Aid:**

Need-based scholarships/grants: Pell, SEOG, state scholarships/grants, private scholarships, the school's own gift aid. *Loans:* Direct Subsidized Stafford, Direct Unsubsidized Stafford, FFEL Subsidized Stafford, FFEL Unsubsidized Stafford, FFEL PLUS, Federal Perkins. **Student Employment:** Federal Work-Study Program available. Institutional employment available. Off-campus job opportunities are good. **Financial Aid Statistics:** 60% freshmen, 60% undergrads receive need-based scholarship or grant aid. 47% freshmen, 53% undergrads receive need-based self-help aid. 19 freshmen, 72 undergrads receive athletic scholarships. Highest amount earned per year from on-campus jobs $2,500.

TEXAS A&M UNIVERSITY—CORPUS CHRISTI

6300 Ocean Drive, Corpus Christi, TX 78412
Phone: 361-825-2624 **E-mail:** Judith.Perales@mail.tamucc.edu **CEEB Code:** 366
Fax: 361-825-5887 **Website:** www.tamucc.edu **ACT Code:** 4045
Financial Aid Phone: 361-825-2338

This public school was founded in 1947. It has a 240-acre campus.

RATINGS
Admissions Selectivity Rating: 68   **Fire Safety Rating:** 60*   **Green Rating:** 60*

STUDENTS AND FACULTY
Enrollment: 6,017. **Student Body:** 61% female, 39% male, 3% out-of-state. African American 2%, Asian 2%, Caucasian 58%, Hispanic 37%. **Retention and Graduation:** 65% freshmen return for sophomore year. 13% freshmen graduate within 4 years. **Faculty:** Student/faculty ratio 16:1. 141 full-time faculty. 87% faculty teach undergrads.

ACADEMICS
Degrees: Bachelor's, doctoral, master's. **Academic Requirements:** Arts/fine arts, computer literacy, English (including composition), foreign languages, history, mathematics, philosophy, sciences (biological or physical), social science. **Classes:** Most classes have 20–29 students. Most lab/discussion sections have 20–29 students. **Disciplines with Highest Percentage of Degrees Awarded:** Business/marketing 20%, interdisciplinary studies 18%, psychology 9%, parks and recreation 6%, social sciences 6%, biological/life sciences 5%, health professions and related sciences 5%. **Special Study Options:** Cooperative education program, distance learning, double major, independent study, internships, teacher certification program.

FACILITIES
Housing: Coed dorms, apartments for single students. **Special Academic Facilities/Equipment:** Weil Gallery, S. Texas Institute for the Arts. **Computers:** 85% of public computers are PCs, 15% of public computers are Macs, 12% of public computers are UNIX, network access in dorm rooms, online registration, online administrative functions (other than registration), remote student-access to Web through college's connection.

CAMPUS LIFE
Activities: Choral groups, concert band, dance, drama/theater, jazz band, literary magazine, marching band, music ensembles, musical theater, opera, pep band, student government, student newspaper, student-run film society, symphony orchestra, yearbook. **Organizations:** 50 registered organizations, 15 honor societies, 4 religious organizations, 5 fraternities, 5 sororities. **Athletics (Intercollegiate):** *Men:* Baseball, basketball, cross-country, tennis, track/field (outdoor). *Women:* Basketball, cross-country, golf, softball, tennis, track/field (outdoor), volleyball.

ADMISSIONS
Freshman Academic Profile: 15% in top 10% of high school class, 45% in top 25% of high school class, 83% in top 50% of high school class. SAT Math middle 50% range 410–527. SAT Critical Reading middle 50% range 530–518. ACT middle 50% range 17–23. TOEFL required of all international applicants, minimum paper TOEFL 550, minimum computer TOEFL 213. **Basis for Candidate Selection:** *Very important factors considered include:* Class rank, rigor of secondary school record. *Important factors considered include:* Standardized test scores. *Other factors considered include:* Character/personal qualities, extracurricular activities, recommendation(s), talent/ability, volunteer work, work experience. **Freshman Admission Requirements:** High school diploma is required, and GED is accepted. *Academic units required:* 4 English, 3 math, 3 science, 2 foreign language, 3 social studies. **Freshman Admission Statistics:** 3,114 applied, 85% admitted, 38% enrolled. **Transfer Admission Requirements:** College transcript(s), statement of good standing from prior institution(s). Minimum college GPA of 2.0 required. Lowest grade transferable

D. General Admission Information: Application fee $20. Regular application deadline 7/1. Regular notification is rolling. Non-fall registration accepted. Common Application not accepted. Credit offered for CEEB Advanced Placement tests.

COSTS AND FINANCIAL AID

Required Forms and Deadlines: FAFSA, institution's own financial aid form. Financial aid filing deadline 4/1. **Notification of Awards**: Applicants will be notified of awards on a rolling basis beginning on or about 5/1. **Types of Aid**: *Need-based scholarships/grants*: Pell, SEOG, state scholarships/grants, the school's own gift aid. *Loans*: FFEL Subsidized Stafford, FFEL Unsubsidized Stafford, FFEL PLUS, Federal Perkins, college/university loans from institutional funds. **Student Employment**: Federal Work-Study Program available. Institutional employment available. Off-campus job opportunities are good. **Financial Aid Statistics**: 42% freshmen, 42% undergrads receive need-based scholarship or grant aid. 28% freshmen, 33% undergrads receive need-based self-help aid. 33 freshmen, 161 undergrads receive athletic scholarships.

TEXAS A&M UNIVERSITY AT GALVESTON

Admissions Office, PO Box 1675, Galveston, TX 77553
Phone: 409-740-4414 **E-mail**: seaaggie@tamug.edu **CEEB Code**: 6835
Fax: 409-740-4731 **Website**: www.tamug.edu **ACT Code**: 6592
Financial Aid Phone: 409-740-4500

This public school was founded in 1963. It has a 150-acre campus.

RATINGS
Admissions Selectivity Rating: 66   **Fire Safety Rating**: 81   **Green Rating**: 60*

STUDENTS AND FACULTY
Enrollment: 1,520. **Student Body**: 42% female, 58% male, 20% out-of-state. African American 3%, Asian 3%, Caucasian 54%, Hispanic 10%. **Retention and Graduation**: 78% freshmen return for sophomore year. 60% grads go on to further study within 1 year. 35% grads pursue arts and sciences degrees. 5% grads pursue business degrees. 3% grads pursue law degrees. 2% grads pursue medical degrees. **Faculty**: Student/faculty ratio 14:1. 92 full-time faculty, 65% hold PhDs. 99% faculty teach undergrads.

ACADEMICS
Degrees: Bachelor's, master's. **Academic Requirements**: Computer literacy, English (including composition), foreign languages, history, humanities, mathematics, sciences (biological or physical), social science. **Classes**: Most classes have 10–19 students. **Majors with Highest Enrollment**: Business, management, marketing, and related support services, marine biology and biological oceanography, naval architecture and marine engineering. **Disciplines with Highest Percentage of Degrees Awarded**: Biological/life sciences 31%, business/marketing 21%, engineering 13%, transportation and materials moving 12%, natural resources/environmental science 11%. **Special Study Options**: Accelerated program, cooperative education program, double major, dual enrollment, independent study, internships, study abroad, teacher certification program, merchant marine certification, NROTC, naval sciences.

FACILITIES
Housing: Coed dorms, women's dorms, special housing for disabled students, privatized apartment housing available next to campus. **Special Academic Facilities/Equipment**: USTS Texas Clipper II, Radar School/Ship Bridge Simulator, Engineering Laboratory Building, Sea Camp, Center for Bioacoustics, Center for Marine Training and Safety/TEEX, Laboratory for Oceanographic and Environmental Research, Galveston Bay Information Center, Center for Ports and Waterways, Coastal Zone Laboratory, GulfCet, Marine Mammal Research Program, Naval Science, Texas State Maritime Academy, Texas Institute of Oceanography, Texas Marine Mammal Stranding Network, Sea Turtle/Fisheries Ecology Lab. **Computers**: 99% of public computers are PCs, 1% of public computers are Macs, network access in dorm rooms, online registration, online administrative functions (other than registration), remote student-access to Web through college's connection.

CAMPUS LIFE
Activities: Choral groups, dance, drama/theater, literary magazine, student government, student newspaper, television station, yearbook. **Organizations**: 37 registered organizations, 16 honor societies, 4 religious organizations. **Athletics (Intercollegiate)**: *Men*: Crew/rowing, sailing. *Women*: Crew/rowing, sailing.

ADMISSIONS
Freshman Academic Profile: 11% in top 10% of high school class, 40% in top 25% of high school class, 73% in top 50% of high school class. 82% from public high schools. SAT Math middle 50% range 490–600. SAT Critical Reading middle 50% range 460–590. ACT middle 50% range 20–25. TOEFL required of all international applicants, minimum paper TOEFL 550, minimum computer TOEFL 220. **Basis for Candidate Selection**: *Very important factors considered include*: Class rank, rigor of secondary school record, standardized test scores. *Important factors considered include*: Academic GPA, application essay, character/personal qualities, extracurricular activities, recommendation(s), talent/ability, volunteer work, work experience. *Other factors considered include*: Alumni/ae relation, interview, level of applicant's interest. **Freshman Admission Requirements**: High school diploma is required, and GED is accepted. *Academic units required*: 4 English, 3 math, 3 science (2 science labs), 3 social studies, 1 computer. *Academic units recommended*: 4 English, 4 math, 4 science, 3 foreign language, 3 social studies, 1 computer. **Freshman Admission Statistics**: 1,088 applied, 95% admitted, 41% enrolled. **Transfer Admission Requirements**: High school transcript, college transcript(s), essay or personal statement. Minimum college GPA of 2.5 required. Lowest grade transferable C. **General Admission Information**: Application fee $45. Regular notification is rolling. Non-fall registration accepted. Admission may be deferred for a maximum of 1 semester. Credit offered for CEEB Advanced Placement tests.

COSTS AND FINANCIAL AID
Annual in-state tuition $4,680. Annual out-of-state tuition $13,020. Room and board $5,203. Required fees $1,375. Average book expense $1,381. **Required Forms and Deadlines**: FAFSA. **Notification of Awards**: Applicants will be notified of awards on or about 3/15. **Types of Aid**: *Need-based scholarships/grants*: Pell, SEOG, state scholarships/grants, private scholarships, the school's own gift aid. *Loans*: Direct Subsidized Stafford, Direct Unsubsidized Stafford, Direct PLUS, FFEL Subsidized Stafford, FFEL Unsubsidized Stafford, FFEL PLUS, Federal Perkins, college/university loans from institutional funds. **Student Employment**: Federal Work-Study Program available. Institutional employment available. Off-campus job opportunities are good. **Financial Aid Statistics**: 25% freshmen, 29% undergrads receive need-based scholarship or grant aid. 1% undergrads receive need-based self-help aid. 46% freshmen, 48% undergrads receive any aid. Highest amount earned per year from on-campus jobs $2,100.

TEXAS A&M UNIVERSITY—KINGSVILLE

MSC 105, Kingsville, TX 78363
Phone: 361-593-2315 **E-mail**: ksossrx@tamuk.edu
Fax: 361-593-2195 **Website**: www.tamuk.edu

This is a public school.

RATINGS
Admissions Selectivity Rating: 60*   **Fire Safety Rating**: 60*   **Green Rating**: 60*

STUDENTS AND FACULTY
Enrollment: 4,373. **Student Body**: 2% out-of-state, 1% international. African American 5%, Caucasian 27%, Hispanic 66%. **Retention and Graduation**: 59% freshmen return for sophomore year. 6% freshmen graduate within 4 years. **Faculty**: Student/faculty ratio 15:1. 276 full-time faculty, 70% hold PhDs.

ACADEMICS
Degrees: Bachelor's, doctoral, master's, post-bachelor's certificate, post-master's certificate. **Academic Requirements**: Arts/fine arts, computer literacy, English (including composition), history, humanities, mathematics, sciences (biological or physical), social science. **Classes**: Most classes have 10–19 students. Most lab/discussion sections have 10–19 students. **Disciplines with Highest Percentage of Degrees Awarded**: Engineering 17%, business/marketing 15%, interdisciplinary studies 14%, parks and recreation 10%, social sciences 10%, agriculture 6%. **Special Study Options**: Accelerated program, cooperative education program, distance learning, double major, English as a second language (ESL), honors program, internships, study abroad, teacher certification program.

FACILITIES
Housing: Coed dorms, men's dorms, women's dorms, apartments for married students.

CAMPUS LIFE

Activities: Choral groups, concert band, dance, drama/theater, jazz band, marching band, music ensembles, musical theater, pep band, radio station, student government, student newspaper, television station.

ADMISSIONS

Basis for Candidate Selection: *Important factors considered include*: Class rank, rigor of secondary school record, standardized test scores. **Freshman Admission Requirements**: High school diploma is required, and GED is accepted. *Academic units recommended*: 4 English, 3 math, 3 science, 3 foreign language, 4 social studies, 3 history, 3 academic electives. **Freshman Admission Statistics**: 2,105 applied, 99% admitted, 43% enrolled. **Transfer Admission Requirements**: Minimum college GPA of 2.0 required. Lowest grade transferable D. **General Admission Information**: Application fee $15. Regular notification open. Non-fall registration not accepted. Common Application accepted.

COSTS AND FINANCIAL AID

Annual in-state tuition $1,380. Out-of-state tuition $7,590. Room & board $3,966. Required fees $1,602. Average book expense $614. **Required Forms and Deadlines**: FAFSA. Financial aid filing deadline 4/15. **Financial Aid Statistics**: 59% freshmen, 92% undergrads receive need-based scholarship or grant aid. 56% freshmen, 76% undergrads receive need-based self-help aid.

TEXAS A&M UNIVERSITY—TEXARKANA

PO Box 5518, Texarkana, TX 75505
Phone: 903-223-3069 **E-mail**: admissions@tamut.edu
Fax: 903-223-3140 **Website**: www.tamut.edu
Financial Aid Phone: 903-223-3060

This public school was founded in 1971. It has a 1-acre campus.

RATINGS

Admissions Selectivity Rating: 60* **Fire Safety Rating**: 60* **Green Rating**: 60*

STUDENTS AND FACULTY

Enrollment: 995. **Student Body**: 74% female, 26% male, 25% out-of-state. African American 13%, Caucasian 81%, Hispanic 5%, Native American 1%. **Faculty**: Student/faculty ratio 14:1.

ACADEMICS

Degrees: Bachelor's, master's. **Academic Requirements**: Arts/fine arts, computer literacy, English (including composition), history, humanities, mathematics, sciences (biological or physical), social science. **Majors with Highest Enrollment**: Accounting, general studies, multi/interdisciplinary studies. **Disciplines with Highest Percentage of Degrees Awarded**: Interdisciplinary studies 34%, business/marketing 22%, liberal arts/general studies 15%, psychology 7%, history 5%. **Special Study Options**: Distance learning, independent study, internships, liberal arts/career combination, teacher certification program.

FACILITIES

Computers: Online registration, online administrative functions (other than registration).

CAMPUS LIFE

Activities: Student government, student newspaper. **Organizations**: 20 registered organizations, 5 honor societies, 1 religious organization.

ADMISSIONS

Freshman Academic Profile: TOEFL required of all international applicants, minimum paper TOEFL 550. **Transfer Admission Requirements**: College transcript(s). Minimum college GPA of 2.0 required. Lowest grade transferable D. **General Admission Information**: Non-fall registration not accepted. Credit offered for CEEB Advanced Placement tests.

COSTS AND FINANCIAL AID

Required Forms and Deadlines: FAFSA, institution's own financial aid form. Other documents may be required upon review of student aid reports. **Types of Aid**: *Need-based scholarships/grants*: Pell, SEOG, state scholarships/grants, private scholarships, the school's own gift aid. *Loans*: FFEL Subsidized Stafford, FFEL Unsubsidized Stafford, FFEL PLUS, college/university loans from institutional funds. **Student Employment**: Federal Work-Study Program available. Off-campus job opportunities are good.

TEXAS CHRISTIAN UNIVERSITY

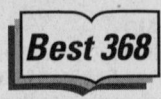

Office of Admissions, TCU Box 297013, Fort Worth, TX 76129
Phone: 817-257-7490 **E-mail**: frogmail@tcu.edu **CEEB Code**: 6820
Fax: 817-257-7268 **Website**: www.tcu.edu **ACT Code**: 4206
Financial Aid Phone: 817-257-7858

This private school, affiliated with the Disciples of Christ Church, was founded in 1873. It has a 300-acre campus.

RATINGS

Admissions Selectivity Rating: 86 **Fire Safety Rating**: 91 **Green Rating**: 78

STUDENTS AND FACULTY

Enrollment: 7,140. **Student Body**: 59% female, 41% male, 21% out-of-state, 4% international (75 countries represented). African American 5%, Asian 2%, Caucasian 77%, Hispanic 7%. **Retention and Graduation**: 84% freshmen return for sophomore year. **Faculty**: Student/faculty ratio 14:1. 478 full-time faculty, 87% hold PhDs. 97% faculty teach undergrads.

ACADEMICS

Degrees: Bachelor's, certificate, doctoral, first professional certificate, first professional, master's, post-bachelor's certificate. **Academic Requirements**: Arts/fine arts, English (including composition), foreign languages, history, humanities, mathematics, sciences (biological or physical), social science. **Classes**: Most classes have 10–19 students. Most lab/discussion sections have 20–29 students. **Majors with Highest Enrollment**: Advertising, communications studies/speech communication and rhetoric. **Disciplines with Highest Percentage of Degrees Awarded**: Business/marketing 22%, communications/journalism 19%, health professions and related sciences 13%, education 8%, social sciences 7%. **Special Study Options**: Accelerated program, cross-registration, distance learning, double major, English as a second language (ESL), honors program, independent study, internships, liberal arts/career combination, study abroad, teacher certification program.

FACILITIES

Housing: Coed dorms, men's dorms, women's dorms, apartments for married students, apartments for single students, fraternity/sorority housing, designated rooms available for ADA needs. **Special Academic Facilities/Equipment**: Art exhibition hall, Tandy film library, speech/hearing clinic, TV studios, computer labs, observatory, Moncrief Meteorite, special collections, alumni and visitors center, cable TV, radio station, performance hall, variety of athletic facilities. **Computers**: 31% of classrooms are wired, 100% of classrooms are wireless, 70% of public computers are PCs, 30% of public computers are Macs, network access in dorm rooms, network access in dorm lounges, online registration, online administrative functions (other than registration), support for handheld computing, remote student-access to Web through college's connection.

CAMPUS LIFE

Activities: Choral groups, concert band, dance, drama/theater, jazz band, literary magazine, marching band, music ensembles, musical theater, opera, pep band, radio station, student government, student newspaper, television station, yearbook. **Organizations**: 165 registered organizations, 29 honor societies. 13 fraternities (37% men join), 16 sororities (39% women join). **Athletics (Intercollegiate)**: *Men*: Baseball, basketball, cross-country, diving, football, golf, swimming, tennis, track/field (indoor), track/field (outdoor). *Women*: Basketball, cross-country, diving, golf, riflery, soccer, swimming, tennis, track/field (indoor), track/field (outdoor), volleyball. Environmental Initiatives: TCU Purple Bike Program. Water Chilled Plant. Food Service—biodegradable products.

ADMISSIONS

Freshman Academic Profile: 32% in top 10% of high school class, 64% in top 25% of high school class, 93% in top 50% of high school class. 74% from public high schools. SAT Math middle 50% range 530–640. SAT Critical Reading middle 50% range 530–620. SAT Writing middle 50% range 530–620. ACT middle 50% range 23–28. TOEFL required of all international applicants, minimum paper TOEFL 550, minimum computer TOEFL 213. **Basis for Candidate Selection**: *Very important factors considered include*: Academic GPA, application essay, character/personal qualities, class rank, recommendation(s), rigor of secondary school record, standardized test scores.

Important factors considered include: Extracurricular activities, geographical residence, level of applicant's interest, racial/ethnic status, religious affiliation/commitment, talent/ability, volunteer work, work experience. *Other factors considered include*: Alumni/ae relation, first generation, interview. **Freshman Admission Requirements**: High school diploma is required, and GED is not accepted. *Academic units required*: 4 English, 3 math, 3 science, 2 foreign language, 3 social studies, 2 academic electives. *Academic units recommended*: 4 English, 4 math, 4 science, 4 foreign language, 4 social studies, 4 academic electives. **Freshman Admission Statistics**: 8,677 applied, 63% admitted, 30% enrolled. **Transfer Admission Requirements**: College transcript(s), essay or personal statement. Minimum college GPA of 2.0 required. Lowest grade transferable C. **General Admission Information**: Application fee $40. Regular application deadline 2/15. Regular notification 4/1. Non-fall registration accepted. Admission may be deferred for a maximum of 1 year. Credit offered for CEEB Advanced Placement tests.

COSTS AND FINANCIAL AID

Required Forms and Deadlines: FAFSA. Financial aid filing deadline 5/1. **Notification of Awards**: Applicants will be notified of awards on a rolling basis beginning on or about 3/1. **Types of Aid**: *Need-based scholarships/grants*: Pell, SEOG, state scholarships/grants, private scholarships, the school's own gift aid, Federal Nursing Scholarships. *Loans*: FFEL Subsidized Stafford, FFEL Unsubsidized Stafford, FFEL PLUS, Federal Perkins, Federal Nursing, state loans. **Financial Aid Statistics**: 33% freshmen, 37% undergrads receive need-based scholarship or grant aid. 29% freshmen, 38% undergrads receive need-based self-help aid. 56 freshmen, 261 undergrads receive athletic scholarships. 73% freshmen, 72% undergrads receive any aid. Highest amount earned per year from on-campus jobs $8,054.

TEXAS COLLEGE

2404 North Grand Avenue, Tyler, TX 75702
Phone: 903-593-8311 **E-mail**: afrancis@texascollege.edu
Fax: 903-593-0588 **Website**: www.texascollege.edu **ACT Code**: 4210
Financial Aid Phone: 903-593-8311

This private school, affiliated with the Methodist Church, was founded in 1894. It has a 25-acre campus.

RATINGS

Admissions Selectivity Rating: 60*   **Fire Safety Rating**: 60*   **Green Rating**: 60*

STUDENTS AND FACULTY

Enrollment: 1,035. **Student Body**: 49% female, 51% male, 15% out-of-state. African American 95%, Caucasian 2%, Hispanic 2%. **Retention and Graduation**: 5% grads go on to further study within 1 year. 5% grads pursue arts and sciences degrees. 2% grads pursue business degrees. 1% grads pursue medical degrees. **Faculty**: Student/faculty ratio 10:1. 28 full-time faculty, 46% hold PhDs. 100% faculty teach undergrads.

ACADEMICS

Degrees: Associate, bachelor's. **Academic Requirements**: Arts/fine arts, computer literacy, English (including composition), foreign languages, health, history, humanities, mathematics, physical education, religion, sciences (biological or physical), social science, speech. **Classes**: Most classes have 30–39 students. **Majors with Highest Enrollment**: Business administration/management, social work, sociology. **Disciplines with Highest Percentage of Degrees Awarded**: Business/marketing 61%, social sciences 9%, English 4%, biological/life sciences 4%, visual and performing arts 4%, computer and information sciences 3%. **Special Study Options**: Accelerated program, distance learning, dual enrollment, independent study, internships, teacher certification program.

FACILITIES

Housing: Men's dorms, women's dorms, apartments for single students. **Special Academic Facilities/Equipment**: Moody Science-Business Center, D. R. Glass Library, Willie Lee Glass Community Development Services Center. **Computers**: 100% of public computers are PCs, network access in dorm lounges, support for handheld computing.

CAMPUS LIFE

Activities: Choral groups, jazz band, marching band, student government, yearbook. **Organizations**: 31 registered organizations, 3 religious organizations. 3 fraternities (4% men join), 3 sororities (8% women join). **Athletics (Intercollegiate)**: *Men*: Baseball, basketball, cheerleading, football, track/field (outdoor). *Women*: Basketball, cheerleading, softball, track/field (outdoor), volleyball.

ADMISSIONS

Freshman Academic Profile: 98% from public high schools. TOEFL required of all international applicants, minimum paper TOEFL 500. **Basis for Candidate Selection**: *Very important factors considered include*: Rigor of secondary school record. **Freshman Admission Requirements**: High school diploma is required, and GED is accepted. *Academic units required*: 4 English, 2 math, 2 science, 2 social studies, 2 history, 4 academic electives. **Freshman Admission Statistics**: 1,066 applied, 98% admitted, 32% enrolled. **Transfer Admission Requirements**: College transcript(s), statement of good standing from prior institution(s). Lowest grade transferable C. **General Admission Information**: Application fee $20. Regular notification is rolling. Non-fall registration accepted. Admission may be deferred for a maximum of 1 year. Common Application accepted.

COSTS AND FINANCIAL AID

Annual tuition $6,305. Room & board $4,730. Required fees $20. Average book expense $800. **Required Forms and Deadlines**: FAFSA, institution's own financial aid form. Financial aid filing deadline 4/15. **Notification of Awards**: Applicants will be notified of awards on a rolling basis beginning on or about 4/15. **Types of Aid**: *Need-based scholarships/grants*: Pell, SEOG, state scholarships/grants, private scholarships, the school's own gift aid, United Negro College Fund. *Loans*: state loans. **Student Employment**: Federal Work-Study Program available. Off-campus job opportunities are good. **Financial Aid Statistics**: 100% freshmen, 83% undergrads receive need-based scholarship or grant aid. 100% freshmen, 87% undergrads receive need-based self-help aid. 50 freshmen, 145 undergrads receive athletic scholarships. 100% freshmen, 90% undergrads receive any aid.

TEXAS LUTHERAN UNIVERSITY

1000 West Court Street, Seguin, TX 78155
Phone: 830-372-8050 **E-mail**: admissions@tlu.edu **CEEB Code**: 6823
Fax: 830-372-8096 **Website**: www.tlu.edu **ACT Code**: 4214
Financial Aid Phone: 830-372-8078

This private school, affiliated with the Lutheran Church, was founded in 1891. It has a 161-acre campus.

RATINGS

Admissions Selectivity Rating: 79   **Fire Safety Rating**: 80   **Green Rating**: 69

STUDENTS AND FACULTY

Enrollment: 1,375. **Student Body**: 53% female, 47% male, 3% out-of-state. African American 7%, Caucasian 52%, Hispanic 13%. **Retention and Graduation**: 68% freshmen return for sophomore year. 42% freshmen graduate within 4 years. 17% grads go on to further study within 1 year. 4% grads pursue arts and sciences degrees. 5% grads pursue business degrees. 3% grads pursue law degrees. 5% grads pursue medical degrees. **Faculty**: Student/faculty ratio 15:1. 70 full-time faculty, 73% hold PhDs. 100% faculty teach undergrads.

ACADEMICS

Degrees: Bachelor's. **Academic Requirements**: Arts/fine arts, English (including composition), history, humanities, mathematics, sciences (biological or physical), social science, theology. **Classes**: Most classes have 10–19 students. **Majors with Highest Enrollment**: Accounting, business administration/management, education. **Disciplines with Highest Percentage of Degrees Awarded**: Business/marketing 23%, education 14%, parks and recreation 13%, biological/life sciences 8%, communications/journalism 8%. **Special Study Options**: Double major, dual enrollment, honors program, independent study, internships, senior seminars, student-designed major, study abroad, teacher certification program.

FACILITIES

Housing: Coed dorms, men's dorms, women's dorms, apartments for married students, apartments for single students, special housing for disabled students. **Special Academic Facilities/Equipment**: Mexican-American Studies Center, geological museum. **Computers**: 90% of public computers are PCs, 5% of public computers are Macs, 5% of public computers are UNIX, network access in dorm rooms, network access in dorm lounges, online registration, online administrative functions (other than registration), remote student-access to Web through college's connection.

CAMPUS LIFE

Activities: Choral groups, concert band, dance, drama/theater, jazz band, literary magazine, music ensembles, musical theater, pep band, student government, student newspaper, symphony orchestra, yearbook. **Organizations**: 55 registered organizations, 10 honor societies, 3 religious organizations. 5 fraternities (5% men join), 4 sororities (12% women join). **Athletics (Intercollegiate)**: *Men*: Baseball, basketball, football, golf, soccer, tennis. *Women*: Basketball, cross-country, golf, soccer, softball, tennis, track/field (outdoor), volleyball.

ADMISSIONS

Freshman Academic Profile: 22% in top 10% of high school class, 54% in top 25% of high school class, 84% in top 50% of high school class. 88% from public high schools. SAT Math middle 50% range 460–580. SAT Critical Reading middle 50% range 450–550. ACT middle 50% range 19–24. TOEFL required of all international applicants, minimum paper TOEFL 550, minimum computer TOEFL 213. **Basis for Candidate Selection**: *Very important factors considered include*: Academic GPA, application essay, rigor of secondary school record, standardized test scores. *Important factors considered include*: Class rank, recommendation(s), volunteer work. *Other factors considered include*: Character/personal qualities, extracurricular activities, interview, level of applicant's interest, work experience. **Freshman Admission Requirements**: High school diploma is required, and GED is accepted. *Academic units recommended*: 4 English, 3 math, 3 science, 2 foreign language, 3 social studies, 3 history, 4 academic electives. **Freshman Admission Statistics**: 1,138 applied, 71% admitted, 48% enrolled. **Transfer Admission Requirements**: High school transcript, college transcript(s), essay or personal statement, statement of good standing from prior institution(s). Minimum college GPA of 2.3 required. Lowest grade transferable C. **General Admission Information**: Application fee $25. Regular application deadline 8/1. Regular notification is rolling. Non-fall registration accepted. Credit and/or placement offered for CEEB Advanced Placement tests.

COSTS AND FINANCIAL AID

Annual tuition $19,940. Room and board $6,780. Required fees $120. Average book expense $800. **Required Forms and Deadlines**: FAFSA. Financial aid filing deadline 4/1. **Notification of Awards**: Applicants will be notified of awards on a rolling basis beginning on or about 3/1. **Types of Aid**: *Need-based scholarships/grants*: Pell, SEOG, state scholarships/grants, private scholarships, the school's own gift aid. *Loans*: FFEL Subsidized Stafford, FFEL Unsubsidized Stafford, FFEL PLUS, Federal Perkins, state loans, Key, Signature. **Student Employment**: Federal Work-Study Program available. Institutional employment available. Off-campus job opportunities are good. **Financial Aid Statistics**: 67% freshmen, 63% undergrads receive need-based scholarship or grant aid. 54% freshmen, 56% undergrads receive need-based self-help aid. 97% freshmen, 97% undergrads receive any aid.

TEXAS SOUTHERN UNIVERSITY

3100 Cleburne Street, Houston, TX 77004
Phone: 713-313-7420 **CEEB Code**: 6824
Fax: 713-313-4317 **Website**: www.tsu.edu **ACT Code**: 4216
Financial Aid Phone: 713-527-7530

This public school was founded in 1949. It has a 125-acre campus.

RATINGS
Admissions Selectivity Rating: 60*   **Fire Safety Rating**: 60*   **Green Rating**: 60*

STUDENTS AND FACULTY
Student Body: 9% out-of-state. **Retention and Graduation**: 46% grads go on to further study within 1 year. 17% grads pursue arts and sciences degrees. 11% grads pursue business degrees. 15% grads pursue law degrees. 3% grads pursue medical degrees.

ACADEMICS
Degrees: Bachelor's, master's. **Special Study Options**: Cooperative education program.

FACILITIES
Housing: Coed dorms, men's dorms, women's dorms, apartments for single students. **Special Academic Facilities/Equipment**: Excellence in Education Center, Hunger and World Peace Center, Minority Institute Reserve Center.

CAMPUS LIFE
Activities: Radio station, student government, television station, yearbook. **Organizations**: 64 registered organizations, 10 honor societies, 15 religious organizations. 4 fraternities (15% men join), 4 sororities (15% women join).

ADMISSIONS

Freshman Academic Profile: 15% in top 10% of high school class, 85% in top 25% of high school class, 95% in top 50% of high school class. 90% from public high schools. TOEFL required of all international applicants. **Freshman Admission Requirements**: High school diploma is required, and GED is accepted. *Academic units recommended*: 4 English, 2 math, 2 science, 2 social studies. **Transfer Admission Requirements**: Minimum college GPA of 2.0 required. Lowest grade transferable D. **General Admission Information**: Early decision application deadline 6/15. Regular application deadline 8/15. Regular notification 8/31. Non-fall registration accepted. Common Application not accepted.

COSTS AND FINANCIAL AID

Annual in-state tuition $2,058. Out-of-state tuition $7,180. Room & board $4,000. Required fees $152. Average book expense $600. **Required Forms and Deadlines**: FAFSA, institution's own financial aid form. **Types of Aid**: *Need-based scholarships/grants*: state scholarships/grants. *Loans*: FFEL Subsidized Stafford, FFEL PLUS. **Student Employment**: Federal Work-Study Program available. Institutional employment available. Off-campus job opportunities are good. **Financial Aid Statistics**: Highest amount earned per year from on-campus jobs $900.

TEXAS STATE UNIVERSITY—SAN MARCOS

429 North Guadalupe Street, San Marcos, TX 78666
Phone: 512-245-2364 **E-mail**: admissions@txstate.edu **CEEB Code**: 6667
Fax: 512-245-9020 **Website**: www.txstate.edu **ACT Code**: 4178
Financial Aid Phone: 512-245-2315

This public school was founded in 1899. It has a 455-acre campus.

RATINGS
Admissions Selectivity Rating: 73   **Fire Safety Rating**: 86   **Green Rating**: 60*

STUDENTS AND FACULTY
Enrollment: 23,568. **Student Body**: 55% female, 45% male, 1% out-of-state, 1% international (83 countries represented). African American 5%, Asian 2%, Caucasian 69%, Hispanic 21%. **Retention and Graduation**: 76% freshmen return for sophomore year. 21% freshmen graduate within 4 years. 30% grads go on to further study within 1 year. **Faculty**: Student/faculty ratio 21:1. 841 full-time faculty, 75% hold PhDs. 88% faculty teach undergrads.

ACADEMICS
Degrees: Bachelor's, doctoral, master's, post-bachelor's certificate. **Academic Requirements**: English (including composition), foreign languages, history, humanities, mathematics, philosophy, sciences (biological or physical), social science. **Classes**: Most classes have 20–29 students. Most lab/discussion sections have 10–19 students. **Majors with Highest Enrollment**: Mass communications/media studies, multi/interdisciplinary studies, psychology. **Disciplines with Highest Percentage of Degrees Awarded**: Business/marketing 19%, interdisciplinary studies 14%, visual and performing arts 10%, social sciences 8%, English 7%. **Special Study Options**: Accelerated program, distance learning, double major, dual enrollment, English as a second language (ESL), exchange student program (domestic), honors program, independent study, internships, study abroad, teacher certification program, weekend college. English as a second language is offered to international students or any students, for that matter, who wish to improve their command of the English language. It is not offered as a degree program.

FACILITIES
Housing: Coed dorms, men's dorms, women's dorms, apartments for married students, apartments for single students, fraternity/sorority housing, non-smoking, honors. Access for the disabled, but not separate housing. **Special Academic Facilities/Equipment**: Child development center, aquifer research center, 2 demonstration farms, physical anthropology and archaeology laboratories, Southwestern writer's collection, observatory with a 17-inch telescope. **Computers**: Network access in dorm rooms, network access in dorm lounges, online registration, online administrative functions (other than registration), remote student-access to Web through college's connection.

CAMPUS LIFE
Activities: Choral groups, concert band, dance, drama/theater, jazz band, literary magazine, marching band, music ensembles, musical theater, opera, pep band, radio station, student government, student newspaper, student-run film society, symphony orchestra, yearbook. **Organizations**: 308 registered organizations, 24 honor societies, 32 religious organizations. 18 fraternities (5% men join), 14 sororities (5% women join). **Athletics (Intercollegiate)**: *Men*:

Baseball, basketball, cheerleading, cross-country, football, golf, track/field (outdoor). *Women:* Basketball, cheerleading, cross-country, golf, soccer, softball, tennis, track/field (outdoor), volleyball. **Environmental Initiatives:** Established the Texas Rivers Systems Institute. The James and Marilyn Lovell Center for Environmental Geography and Hazards Research located within Texas State University—San Marcos' Department of Geography (one of the largest such departments in the United States), the JMLC provides a focal point around which its scholars can gather to share ideas and mentor students. Full-time position of coordinator of recycling and waste management for a campus wide recycling program.

ADMISSIONS

Freshman Academic Profile: 14% in top 10% of high school class, 52% in top 25% of high school class, 95% in top 50% of high school class. 98% from public high schools. SAT Math middle 50% range 500–590. SAT Critical Reading middle 50% range 480–580. SAT Writing middle 50% range 470–560. ACT middle 50% range 21–25. TOEFL required of all international applicants, minimum paper TOEFL 550, minimum computer TOEFL 213. **Basis for Candidate Selection**: *Very important factors considered include:* Class rank, standardized test scores. *Other factors considered include*: Application essay, rigor of secondary school record, talent/ability. **Freshman Admission Requirements**: High school diploma is required, and GED is accepted. *Academic units required*: 4 English, 3 math, 3 science (2 science labs), 2 foreign language, 3 social studies, 3 academic electives. 5 computer literacy 1, physical education 1.5, economics 0.5, health education 0.5, speech 0.5. *Academic units recommended*: 4 English, 3 math, 3 science (2 science labs), 2 foreign language, 3 social studies, 3 academic electives. 5 computer literacy 1, physical education 1.5, economics 0.5, health education 0.5, speech 0.5. **Freshman Admission Statistics**: 10,062 applied, 73% admitted, 40% enrolled. **Transfer Admission Requirements**: College transcript(s), statement of good standing from prior institution(s). Minimum college GPA of 2.2 required. Lowest grade transferable D. **General Admission Information**: Application fee $40. Regular application deadline 5/1. Regular notification is rolling. Non-fall registration accepted. Admission may be deferred, fee required. Credit offered for CEEB Advanced Placement tests.

COSTS AND FINANCIAL AID

Annual in-state tuition $4,140. Out-of-state tuition $12,390. Room & board $5,610. Required fees $1,512. Average book expense $978. **Required Forms and Deadlines**: FAFSA. Financial aid filing deadline 4/1. **Notification of Awards**: Applicants will be notified of awards on a rolling basis beginning on or about 5/1. **Types of Aid**: *Need-based scholarships/grants*: Pell, SEOG, state scholarships/grants, private scholarships. *Loans*: Direct Subsidized Stafford, Direct Unsubsidized Stafford, Direct PLUS, FFEL Subsidized Stafford, FFEL Unsubsidized Stafford, FFEL PLUS, Federal Perkins, state loans, college/university loans from institutional funds, alternative loans. **Student Employment**: Federal Work-Study Program available. Institutional employment available. Off-campus job opportunities are good. **Financial Aid Statistics**: 32% freshmen, 32% undergrads receive need-based scholarship or grant aid. 39% freshmen, 39% undergrads receive need-based self-help aid. 65 freshmen, 291 undergrads receive athletic scholarships. 39% freshmen, 39% undergrads receive any aid. Highest amount earned per year from on-campus jobs $12,000.

TEXAS TECH UNIVERSITY

Box 45005, Lubbock, TX 79409-5005
Phone: 806-742-1480 **E-mail:** admissions@ttu.edu **CEEB Code:** 6827
Fax: 806-742-0062 **Website:** www.ttu.edu **ACT Code:** 4220
Financial Aid Phone: 806-742-3681

This public school was founded in 1923. It has a 1,839-acre campus.

RATINGS

Admissions Selectivity Rating: 76   Fire Safety Rating: 90   Green Rating: 60*

STUDENTS AND FACULTY

Enrollment: 22,838. **Student Body**: 45% female, 55% male, 4% out-of-state. African American 3%, Asian 3%, Caucasian 80%, Hispanic 12%. **Retention and Graduation**: 83% freshmen return for sophomore year. 25% freshmen graduate within 4 years. **Faculty**: Student/faculty ratio 18:1. 1,078 full-time faculty, 87% hold PhDs. 100% faculty teach undergrads.

ACADEMICS

Degrees: Bachelor's, doctoral, first professional, master's, post-bachelor's certificate. **Academic Requirements**: Arts/fine arts, English (including composition), foreign languages, history, humanities, mathematics,

multicultural, philosophy, sciences (biological or physical), social science. **Classes**: Most classes have 20–29 students. Most lab/discussion sections have 20–29 students. **Majors with Highest Enrollment**: Health and physical education, mechanical engineering, psychology. **Disciplines with Highest Percentage of Degrees Awarded**: Business/marketing 26%, family and consumer sciences 12%, engineering 7%, communications/journalism 6%, English 6%. **Special Study Options**: Accelerated program, cooperative education program, cross-registration, distance learning, double major, dual enrollment, English as a second language (ESL), exchange student program (domestic), external degree program, honors program, independent study, internships, liberal arts/career combination, student-designed major, study abroad, teacher certification program.

FACILITIES

Housing: Coed dorms, men's dorms, women's dorms, apartments for single students, special housing for disabled students, special housing for international students. **Special Academic Facilities/Equipment**: Museum, child development center, textile research center, agricultural research center, planetarium, ranching heritage center semi-arid land studies center, ranching heritage center, seismological observatory. **Computers**: 73% of classrooms are wired, 98% of classrooms are wireless, 84% of public computers are PCs, 12% of public computers are Macs, 4% of public computers are UNIX, network access in dorm rooms, network access in dorm lounges, online registration, online administrative functions (other than registration), support for handheld computing, remote student-access to Web through college's connection.

CAMPUS LIFE

Activities: Choral groups, concert band, dance, drama/theater, jazz band, literary magazine, marching band, music ensembles, musical theater, opera, pep band, radio station, student government, student newspaper, student-run film society, symphony orchestra, television studio. **Organizations**: 411 registered organizations, 31 honor societies, 37 religious organizations. 28 fraternities, 21 sororities. **Athletics (Intercollegiate)**: *Men*: Baseball, basketball, cross-country, football, golf, tennis, track/field (indoor), track/field (outdoor). *Women*: Basketball, cross-country, golf, soccer, softball, tennis, track/field (indoor), track/field (outdoor), volleyball.

ADMISSIONS

Freshman Academic Profile: 22% in top 10% of high school class, 54% in top 25% of high school class, 88% in top 50% of high school class. SAT Math middle 50% range 520–620. SAT Critical Reading middle 50% range 500–590. SAT Writing middle 50% range 470–570. ACT middle 50% range 21–26. TOEFL required of all international applicants, minimum paper TOEFL 550, minimum computer TOEFL 213. **Basis for Candidate Selection**: *Very important factors considered include:* Academic GPA, class rank, rigor of secondary school record, standardized test scores. *Important factors considered include*: Alumni/ae relation, application essay, character/personal qualities, extracurricular activities, talent/ability, volunteer work, work experience. *Other factors considered include*: First generation, level of applicant's interest, racial/ethnic status, recommendation(s). **Freshman Admission Requirements**: High school diploma is required, and GED is accepted. *Academic units required*: 4 English, 3 math, 2 science (2 science labs), 2 foreign language. **Freshman Admission Statistics**: 13,809 applied, 70% admitted, 40% enrolled. **Transfer Admission Requirements**: College transcript(s), statement of good standing from prior institution(s). Minimum college GPA of 2.2 required. Lowest grade transferable D-. **General Admission Information**: Application fee $50. Regular application deadline 5/1. Non-fall registration accepted. Credit offered for CEEB Advanced Placement tests.

COSTS AND FINANCIAL AID

Annual in-state tuition $4,310. Annual out-of-state tuition $12,650. Room and board $7,460. Required fees $2,473. **Required Forms and Deadlines**: FAFSA. Financial aid filing deadline 4/15. **Types of Aid**: *Need-based scholarships/grants*: Pell, SEOG, state scholarships/grants, private scholarships, the school's own gift aid. *Loans*: FFEL Subsidized Stafford, FFEL Unsubsidized Stafford, FFEL PLUS, Federal Perkins, state loans, college/university loans from institutional funds. **Student Employment**: Federal Work-Study Program available. Institutional employment available. Off-campus job opportunities are excellent. **Financial Aid Statistics**: 17% freshmen, 27% undergrads receive need-based scholarship or grant aid. 32% freshmen, 35% undergrads receive need-based self-help aid. 82 freshmen, 354 undergrads receive athletic scholarships. 45% freshmen, 44% undergrads receive any aid. Highest amount earned per year from on-campus jobs $4,466.

TEXAS WESLEYAN UNIVERSITY

1201 Wesleyan, Fort Worth, TX 76105-1536
Phone: 817-531-4422 **E-mail:** info@txwesleyan.edu **CEEB Code:** 6828
Fax: 817-531-7515 **Website:** www.txwesleyan.edu **ACT Code:** 4222
Financial Aid Phone: 817-531-4420

This private school, affiliated with the Methodist Church, was founded in 1890. It has a 75-acre campus.

RATINGS
Admissions Selectivity Rating: 78   **Fire Safety Rating:** 60*   **Green Rating:** 60*

STUDENTS AND FACULTY
Enrollment: 1,407. **Student Body:** 64% female, 36% male, 1% out-of-state, 2% international (32 countries represented). African American 20%, Asian 2%, Caucasian 58%, Hispanic 18%, Native American 1%. **Retention and Graduation:** 58% freshmen return for sophomore year. **Faculty:** Student/faculty ratio 15:1. 110 full-time faculty, 83% hold PhDs.

ACADEMICS
Degrees: Bachelor's, first professional, master's. **Academic Requirements:** Arts/fine arts, English (including composition), history, humanities, mathematics, religion, sciences (biological or physical), social science. **Classes:** Most classes have 10–19 students. **Majors with Highest Enrollment:** Business administration/management, psychology, radio and television. **Disciplines with Highest Percentage of Degrees Awarded:** Business/marketing 31%, education 26%, interdisciplinary studies 8%, psychology 6%, visual and performing arts 4%. **Special Study Options:** English as a second language (ESL), independent study, internships, study abroad, teacher certification program, weekend college.

FACILITIES
Housing: Coed dorms, men's dorms, women's dorms. **Special Academic Facilities/Equipment:** Art gallery. **Computers:** 99% of public computers are PCs, 1% of public computers are Macs.

CAMPUS LIFE
Activities: Choral groups, concert band, drama/theater, jazz band, literary magazine, music ensembles, musical theater, opera, pep band, student government, student newspaper. **Organizations:** 55 registered organizations, 7 honor societies, 5 religious organizations. 3 fraternities, 2 sororities. **Athletics (Intercollegiate):** *Men:* Baseball, basketball, cheerleading, golf, soccer, tennis. *Women:* Basketball, cheerleading, soccer, softball, tennis, volleyball.

ADMISSIONS
Freshman Academic Profile: 14% in top 10% of high school class, 37% in top 25% of high school class, 68% in top 50% of high school class. 94% from public high schools. SAT Math middle 50% range 430–550. SAT Critical Reading middle 50% range 450–550. ACT middle 50% range 17–23. TOEFL required of all international applicants, minimum paper TOEFL 550, minimum computer TOEFL 190. **Basis for Candidate Selection:** *Very important factors considered include:* Character/personal qualities, rigor of secondary school record. *Important factors considered include:* Application essay, class rank, interview, recommendation(s), standardized test scores. *Other factors considered include:* Alumni/ae relation, extracurricular activities, talent/ability, volunteer work, work experience. **Freshman Admission Requirements:** High school diploma is required, and GED is accepted. *Academic units recommended:* 4 English, 4 math, 2 science, 2 social studies, 1 history, 7 academic electives. **Freshman Admission Statistics:** 335 applied, 55% admitted, 76% enrolled. **Transfer Admission Requirements:** College transcript(s). Minimum college GPA of 2.0 required. Lowest grade transferable D. **General Admission Information:** Application fee $25. Regular notification. Non-fall registration accepted. Admission may be deferred for a maximum of 1 year. Common Application accepted. Credit offered for CEEB Advanced Placement tests.

COSTS AND FINANCIAL AID
Annual tuition $10,306. Room & board $3,990. Required fees $970. Average book expense $675. **Required Forms and Deadlines:** FAFSA, institution's own financial aid form. Financial aid filing deadline 4/15. **Notification of Awards:** Applicants will be notified of awards on a rolling basis beginning on or about 4/15. **Types of Aid:** *Need-based scholarships/grants:* Pell, SEOG, state scholarships/grants, private scholarships, the school's own gift aid. *Loans:* FFEL Subsidized Stafford, FFEL Unsubsidized Stafford, FFEL PLUS, state loans, college/university loans from institutional funds. **Student Employment:** Federal Work-Study Program available. Institutional employment available. Off-campus job opportunities are excellent. **Financial Aid Statistics:** 85%

TEXAS WOMAN'S UNIVERSITY

PO Box 425589, Denton, TX 76204-5589
Phone: 940-898-3188 **E-mail:** admissions@twu.edu **CEEB Code:** 6826
Fax: 940-898-3081 **Website:** www.twu.edu **ACT Code:** 4224
Financial Aid Phone: 940-898-3050

This public school was founded in 1901. It has a 270-acre campus.

RATINGS
Admissions Selectivity Rating: 74   **Fire Safety Rating:** 98   **Green Rating:** 60*

STUDENTS AND FACULTY
Enrollment: 6,623. **Student Body:** 93% female, 7% male, 1% out-of-state, 3% international (62 countries represented). African American 21%, Asian 6%, Caucasian 54%, Hispanic 15%. **Retention and Graduation:** 68% freshmen return for sophomore year. 19% freshmen graduate within 4 years. 4% grads go on to further study within 1 year. **Faculty:** Student/faculty ratio 16:1. 366 full-time faculty. 74% faculty teach undergrads.

ACADEMICS
Degrees: Bachelor's, doctoral, master's, post-bachelor's certificate, post-master's certificate. **Academic Requirements:** Arts/fine arts, English (including composition), history, humanities, mathematics, sciences (biological or physical), social science, women's studies and multicultural studies. **Classes:** Most classes have 10–19 students. **Majors with Highest Enrollment:** Multi/interdisciplinary studies, nursing/registered nurse training (ASN, BSN, MSN, RN), psychology. **Disciplines with Highest Percentage of Degrees Awarded:** Health professions and related sciences 39%, interdisciplinary studies 12%, psychology 6%, visual and performing arts 6%, business/marketing 6%, liberal arts/general studies 5%, family and consumer sciences 5%, biological/life sciences 3%, parks and recreation 3%, public administration and social services 3%. **Special Study Options:** Cross-registration, distance learning, double major, dual enrollment, honors program, independent study, internships, study abroad, teacher certification program.

FACILITIES
Housing: Coed dorms, women's dorms, apartments for married students, apartments for single students, special housing for disabled students, special housing for international students. **Special Academic Facilities/Equipment:** Museum, radiation lab, language lab. **Computers:** 80% of classrooms are wired, 10% of classrooms are wireless, 95% of public computers are PCs, 5% of public computers are Macs, network access in dorm rooms, network access in dorm lounges, online registration, online administrative functions (other than registration), support for handheld computing, remote student-access to Web through college's connection.

CAMPUS LIFE
Activities: Choral groups, dance, drama/theater, jazz band, music ensembles, musical theater, opera, student government, student newspaper, television station. **Organizations:** 94 registered organizations, 16 honor societies, 10 religious organizations. 9 sororities (1% women join). **Athletics (Intercollegiate):** *Women:* Basketball, gymnastics, soccer, softball, volleyball.

ADMISSIONS
Freshman Academic Profile: 17% in top 10% of high school class, 30% in top 25% of high school class, 76% in top 50% of high school class. 93% from public high schools. SAT Math middle 50% range 420–530. SAT Critical Reading middle 50% range 420–520. ACT middle 50% range 18–22. TOEFL required of all international applicants, minimum paper TOEFL 550, minimum computer TOEFL 213. **Basis for Candidate Selection:** *Very important factors considered include:* Class rank, rigor of secondary school record, standardized test scores. **Freshman Admission Requirements:** High school diploma is required, and GED is accepted. *Academic units required:* 4 English, 3 math, 2 science, 2 social studies, 3 academic electives. *Academic units recommended:* 4 English, 3 math, 3 science, 3 social studies, 5 academic electives. **Freshman Admission Statistics:** 2,804 applied, 61% admitted, 45% enrolled. **Transfer Admission Requirements:** College transcript(s). Minimum college GPA of 2.0 required. Lowest grade transferable D. **General Admission Information:** Application fee $30. Regular notification rolling. Nonfall registration accepted. Admission may be deferred for a maximum of 2 years. Credit and/or placement offered for CEEB Advanced Placement tests.

COSTS AND FINANCIAL AID

Annual in-state tuition $3,840. Out-of-state tuition $12,120. Room & board $5,598. Required fees $1,320. Average book expense $930. **Required Forms and Deadlines:** FAFSA, institution's own financial aid form. Financial aid filing deadline 4/1. **Notification of Awards:** Applicants will be notified of awards on a rolling basis beginning on or about 3/1. **Types of Aid:** *Need-based scholarships/grants:* Pell, SEOG, state scholarships/grants, private scholarships, the school's own gift aid, Federal Nursing Scholarships. *Loans:* FFEL Subsidized Stafford, FFEL Unsubsidized Stafford, FFEL PLUS, Federal Perkins, Federal Nursing, state loans, college/university loans from institutional funds. **Financial Aid Statistics:** 42% freshmen, 44% undergrads receive need-based scholarship or grant aid. 43% freshmen, 48% undergrads receive need-based self-help aid. 7 freshmen, 78 undergrads receive athletic scholarships. 85% freshmen, 81% undergrads receive any aid. Highest amount earned per year from on-campus jobs $3,520.

THIEL COLLEGE

75 College Avenue, Greenville, PA 16125
Phone: 724-589-2345 **E-mail:** admissions@thiel.edu **CEEB Code:** 2910
Fax: 724-589-2013 **Website:** www.thiel.edu **ACT Code:** 3730
Financial Aid Phone: 724-589-2178

This private school, affiliated with the Lutheran Church, was founded in 1866. It has a 135-acre campus.

RATINGS

Admissions Selectivity Rating: 71   **Fire Safety Rating:** 60*   **Green Rating:** 60*

STUDENTS AND FACULTY

Enrollment: 1,242. **Student Body:** 47% female, 53% male, 28% out-of-state, 4% international (14 countries represented). African American 6%, Caucasian 63%. **Retention and Graduation:** 62% freshmen return for sophomore year. 41% freshmen graduate within 4 years. 13% grads go on to further study within 1 year. 86% grads pursue arts and sciences degrees. 12% grads pursue business degrees. 1% grads pursue law degrees. 1% grads pursue medical degrees. **Faculty:** Student/faculty ratio 16:1. 65 full-time faculty, 63% hold PhDs. 100% faculty teach undergrads.

ACADEMICS

Degrees: Associate, bachelor's. **Academic Requirements:** Arts/fine arts, English (including composition), foreign languages, humanities, mathematics, sciences (biological or physical), social science. **Classes:** Most classes have 20–29 students. Most lab/discussion sections have 10–19 students. **Majors with Highest Enrollment:** Biology/biological sciences, business administration/management, elementary education and teaching. **Disciplines with Highest Percentage of Degrees Awarded:** Business/marketing 30%, education 12%, social sciences 10%, biological/life sciences 9%, psychology 7%, security and protective services 7%. **Special Study Options:** Cooperative education program, double major, dual enrollment, English as a second language (ESL), honors program, independent study, internships, liberal arts/career combination, study abroad, teacher certification program.

FACILITIES

Housing: Coed dorms, apartments for single students, fraternity/sorority housing. **Special Academic Facilities/Equipment:** Art gallery, blackbox theater. **Computers:** 100% of classrooms are wired, 100% of classrooms are wireless, 100% of public computers are PCs, network access in dorm rooms, network access in dorm lounges, online registration, remote student-access to Web through college's connection, tuition includes personal computer.undergraduates are required to own a computer.

CAMPUS LIFE

Activities: Choral groups, concert band, dance, drama/theater, literary magazine, music ensembles, musical theater, pep band, radio station, student government, student newspaper, symphony orchestra, television station, yearbook. **Organizations:** 40 registered organizations, 8 honor societies, 4 religious organizations. 3 fraternities (15% men join), 4 sororities (18% women join). **Athletics (Intercollegiate):** *Men:* Baseball, basketball, cheerleading, football, soccer, track/field (indoor), track/field (outdoor), wrestling. *Women:* Basketball, cheerleading, soccer, softball, track/field (indoor), track/field (outdoor), volleyball.

ADMISSIONS

Freshman Academic Profile: 8% in top 10% of high school class, 26% in top 25% of high school class, 58% in top 50% of high school class. 88% from public high schools. SAT Math middle 50% range 410–530. SAT Critical Reading

middle 50% range 410–530. ACT middle 50% range 17–23. TOEFL required of all international applicants, minimum paper TOEFL 450, minimum computer TOEFL 140. **Basis for Candidate Selection:** *Very important factors considered include:* Academic GPA, application essay, interview, level of applicant's interest, recommendation(s), rigor of secondary school record, standardized test scores. *Important factors considered include:* Character/personal qualities, class rank. *Other factors considered include:* Extracurricular activities, talent/ability, volunteer work, work experience. **Freshman Admission Requirements:** High school diploma is required, and GED is accepted. *Academic units recommended:* 4 English, 2 math, 2 science (2 science labs), 2 foreign language, 3 social studies, 1 academic elective. **Freshman Admission Statistics:** 1,578 applied, 76% admitted, 30% enrolled. **Transfer Admission Requirements:** High school transcript, college transcript(s), essay or personal statement, interview, standardized test score, statement of good standing from prior institution(s). Minimum college GPA of 2.0 required. Lowest grade transferable C. **General Admission Information:** Application fee $35. Regular application deadline 6/30. Regular notification is rolling. Non-fall registration accepted. Admission may be deferred for a maxiumum of 2 semesters. Credit and/or placement offered for CEEB Advanced Placement tests.

COSTS AND FINANCIAL AID

Annual tuition $17,160. Room & board $7,574. Required fees $1,560. Average book expense $800. **Required Forms and Deadlines:** FAFSA, state aid form. Financial aid filing deadline 3/15. **Notification of Awards:** Applicants will be notified of awards on a rolling basis beginning on or about 2/15. **Types of Aid:** *Need-based scholarships/grants:* Pell, SEOG, state scholarships/grants, private scholarships, the school's own gift aid. *Loans:* FFEL Subsidized Stafford, FFEL Unsubsidized Stafford, FFEL PLUS, Federal Perkins, college/university loans from institutional funds. **Student Employment:** Federal Work-Study Program available. Institutional employment available. Off-campus job opportunities are fair. **Financial Aid Statistics:** 85% freshmen, 89% undergrads receive need-based scholarship or grant aid. 85% freshmen, 89% undergrads receive need-based self-help aid. 90% freshmen, 91% undergrads receive any aid. Highest amount earned per year from on-campus jobs $350.

THOMAS AQUINAS COLLEGE

10000 North Ojai Road, Santa Paula, CA 93060
Phone: 805-525-4417 **E-mail:** admissions@thomasaquinas.edu **CEEB Code:** 4828
Fax: 805-525-9342 **Website:** www.thomasaquinas.edu **ACT Code:** 425
Financial Aid Phone: 800-634-9797

This private school, affiliated with the Roman Catholic Church, was founded in 1971. It has a 131-acre campus.

RATINGS

Admissions Selectivity Rating: 91   **Fire Safety Rating:** 88   **Green Rating:** 61

STUDENTS AND FACULTY

Enrollment: 351. **Student Body:** 50% female, 50% male, 58% out-of-state, 8% international (8 countries represented). Asian 3%, Caucasian 78%, Hispanic 6%, Native American 1%. **Retention and Graduation:** 84% freshmen return for sophomore year. 78% freshmen graduate within 4 years. 20% grads go on to further study within 1 year. 12% grads pursue arts and sciences degrees. 1% grads pursue business degrees. 6% grads pursue law degrees. 1% grads pursue medical degrees. **Faculty:** Student/faculty ratio 11:1. 31 full-time faculty, 61% hold PhDs. 100% faculty teach undergrads.

ACADEMICS

Degrees: Bachelor's. **Academic Requirements:** English (including composition), foreign languages, history, humanities, logic, mathematics, music, philosophy, rhetoric, sciences (biological or physical), social science, theology. **Classes:** Most classes have 10–19 students. **Disciplines with Highest Percentage of Degrees Awarded:** Liberal arts/general studies 100%. **Special Study Options:** The sole academic program offered is a "cross-disciplinary" curriculum of liberal education through reading and analyzing the "Great Books." There is special emphasis on theology, philosophy, mathematics, laboratory science, and literature.

FACILITIES

Housing: Men's dorms, women's dorms. **Special Academic Facilities/ Equipment:** St. Bernardine Library. **Computers:** 100% of public computers are PCs, remote student-access to Web through college's connection.

CAMPUS LIFE

Activities: Choral groups, dance, drama/theater, literary magazine, music ensembles, musical theater. **Organizations:** 2 registered organizations, 4 religious organizations. **Environmental Initiatives:** The College recycles recyclable material.

ADMISSIONS

Freshman Academic Profile: 75% in top 10% of high school class, 75% in top 25% of high school class, 100% in top 50% of high school class. 19% from public high schools. SAT Math middle 50% range 570–660. SAT Critical Reading middle 50% range 600–740. ACT middle 50% range 25–29. TOEFL required of all international applicants, minimum paper TOEFL 570, minimum computer TOEFL 230. **Basis for Candidate Selection:** *Very important factors considered include:* Application essay, character/personal qualities, level of applicant's interest, recommendation(s), rigor of secondary school record, standardized test scores. *Important factors considered include:* Academic GPA, religious affiliation/commitment. *Other factors considered include:* Class rank, extracurricular activities, interview, talent/ability, volunteer work, work experience. **Freshman Admission Requirements:** High school diploma is required, and GED is accepted. *Academic units required:* 4 English, 3 math, 2 foreign language, 2 history. *Academic units recommended:* 4 English, 4 math, 3 science (2 science labs), 2 foreign language, 2 history, 3 academic electives. **Freshman Admission Statistics:** 207 applied, 83% admitted, 60% enrolled. **General Admission Information:** Regular notification is rolling. Non-fall registration not accepted. Admission may be deferred for a maximum of 2 semesters. Neither credit nor placement offered for CEEB Advanced Placement tests.

COSTS AND FINANCIAL AID

Annual tuition $21,400. Room and board $6,950. Average book expense $450. **Required Forms and Deadlines:** FAFSA, institution's own financial aid form, state aid form, tax return, noncustodial parent statement. Financial aid filing deadline 3/2. **Notification of Awards:** Applicants will be notified of awards on a rolling basis beginning on or about 1/1. **Types of Aid:** *Need-based scholarships/grants:* Pell, state scholarships/grants, private scholarships, the school's own gift aid. *Loans:* FFEL Subsidized Stafford, FFEL Unsubsidized Stafford, FFEL PLUS, college/university loans from institutional funds, Canadian student loans. **Student Employment:** Off-campus job opportunities are fair. **Financial Aid Statistics:** 60% freshmen, 60% undergrads receive need-based scholarship or grant aid. 69% freshmen, 67% undergrads receive need-based self-help aid. 69% freshmen, 68% undergrads receive any aid.

THOMAS COLLEGE

180 West River Road, Waterville, ME 04901
Phone: 207-859-1101 **E-mail:** admiss@thomas.edu **CEEB Code:** 2052
Fax: 207-859-1114 **Website:** www.thomas.edu **ACT Code:** 1663
Financial Aid Phone: 207-859-1105

This private school was founded in 1894. It has a 70-acre campus.

RATINGS

Admissions Selectivity Rating: 70 **Fire Safety Rating:** 60* **Green Rating:** 60*

STUDENTS AND FACULTY

Enrollment: 730. **Student Body:** 50% female, 50% male, 14% out-of-state. African American 2%, Caucasian 85%, Hispanic 1%. **Retention and Graduation:** 64% freshmen return for sophomore year. 7% grads go on to further study within 1 year. 7% grads pursue business degrees. **Faculty:** Student/faculty ratio 19:1. 22 full-time faculty, 50% hold PhDs. 100% faculty teach undergrads.

ACADEMICS

Degrees: Associate, bachelor's, master's. **Academic Requirements:** Computer literacy, English (including composition), history, humanities, mathematics, philosophy, sciences (biological or physical), social science. **Classes:** Most classes have 20–29 students. **Majors with Highest Enrollment:** Accounting and business/management, accounting, computer and information sciences. **Disciplines with Highest Percentage of Degrees Awarded:** Business/marketing 66%, computer and information sciences 12%, education 8%, psychology 4%, liberal arts/general studies 1%. **Special Study**

Options: Cooperative education program, cross registration, double major, internships, study abroad, teacher certification program.

FACILITIES

Housing: Coed dorms, apartments for single students, residence halls are designated coed male or female by floor or suite, not by building. **Computers:** 98% of public computers are PCs, 1% of public computers are Macs, 1% of public computers are UNIX, network access in dorm rooms, network access in dorm lounges, online registration, online administrative functions (other than registration), remote student-access to Web through college's connection.

CAMPUS LIFE

Activities: Choral groups, dance, drama/theater, student government, student newspaper, yearbook. **Organizations:** 20 registered organizations, 3 honor societies, 1 fraternity (2% men join), 2 sororities (1% women join). **Athletics (Intercollegiate):** *Men:* Baseball, basketball, golf, lacrosse, soccer, tennis. *Women:* Basketball, field hockey, lacrosse, soccer, softball, volleyball.

ADMISSIONS

Freshman Academic Profile: 13% in top 10% of high school class, 13% in top 25% of high school class, 58% in top 50% of high school class. SAT Math middle 50% range 390–510. SAT Critical Reading middle 50% range 400–500. SAT Writing middle 50% range 380–500. ACT middle 50% range 13–22. TOEFL required of all international applicants, minimum paper TOEFL 530, minimum computer TOEFL 197. **Basis for Candidate Selection:** *Very important factors considered include:* Recommendation(s), rigor of secondary school record. *Important factors considered include:* Academic GPA, application essay, class rank, standardized test scores. *Other factors considered include:* Alumni/ae relation, character/personal qualities, extracurricular activities, interview, talent/ ability, volunteer work, work experience. **Freshman Admission Requirements:** High school diploma is required, and GED is accepted. *Academic units recommended:* 4 English, 3 math, 3 science, 2 foreign language, 2 social studies, 2 academic electives. **Freshman Admission Statistics:** 483 applied, 83% admitted, 48% enrolled. **Transfer Admission Requirements:** High school transcript, college transcript(s), essay or personal statement. Minimum college GPA of 2.0 required. Lowest grade transferable C. **General Admission Information:** Application fee $50. Regular notification is rolling. Non-fall registration accepted. Admission may be deferred for a maximum of 2 years. Credit and/or placement offered for CEEB Advanced Placement tests.

COSTS AND FINANCIAL AID

Annual tuition $17,280. Room & board $7,430. Required fees $450. Average book expense $800. **Required Forms and Deadlines:** FAFSA. Financial aid filing deadline 2/15. **Notification of Awards:** Applicants will be notified of awards on a rolling basis beginning on or about 3/15. **Types of Aid:** *Need-based scholarships/grants:* Pell, SEOG, state scholarships/grants, private scholarships, the school's own gift aid. *Loans:* Direct Subsidized Stafford, Direct Unsubsidized Stafford, Direct PLUS, Federal Perkins. **Student Employment:** Federal Work-Study Program available. Institutional employment available. Off-campus job opportunities are excellent. **Financial Aid Statistics:** 96% freshmen, 90% undergrads receive need-based scholarship or grant aid. 90% freshmen, 83% undergrads receive need-based self-help aid.

THOMAS EDISON STATE COLLEGE

101 West State Street, Trenton, NJ 08608-1176
Phone: 888-442-8372 **E-mail:** admissions@tesc.edu **CEEB Code:** 2612
Fax: 609-984-8447 **Website:** www.tesc.edu **ACT Code:** 274872
Financial Aid Phone: 609-633-9658

This public school was founded in 1972. It has a 2-acre campus.

RATINGS

Admissions Selectivity Rating: 60* **Fire Safety Rating:** 60* **Green Rating:** 60*

STUDENTS AND FACULTY

Enrollment: 12,229. **Student Body:** 41% female, 59% male, 62% out-of-state, 2% international (70 countries represented). African American 15%, Asian 2%, Caucasian 67%, Hispanic 7%, Native American 1%.

ACADEMICS

Degrees: Associate, bachelor's, certificate, master's, post-bachelor's certificate, post-master's certificate. **Academic Requirements:** English (including composition), humanities, mathematics, sciences (biological or physical), social science. **Majors with Highest Enrollment:** Business administration and management, liberal arts and sciences/liberal studies, nuclear engineering technologies/technician. **Disciplines with Highest Percentage of Degrees Awarded:** Liberal arts/general studies 29%, engineering technologies 18%, business/marketing 13%, health professions and related sciences 7%, social sciences 7%. **Special Study Options:** Distance learning, dual enrollment, external degree program, independent study, joint degree program with the University of Medicine and Dentistry of New Jersey for bachelor of science in health sciences. Graduates of associate degree and diploma programs of nursing may enroll for a BSN degree only (RN-BSN program), or both a BSN and a MSN degree (RN-BSN/MSN program) with preparation as a nurse educator at the master's level.

FACILITIES

Computers: Online registration, online administrative functions (other than registration), support for handheld computing.

CAMPUS LIFE

Environmental Initiatives: Only recycled paper to be used. Purchased hybrid vehicle for Vice Presidents to use. Adopted recycling programs.

ADMISSIONS

Freshman Academic Profile: TOEFL required of all international applicants, minimum paper TOEFL 500, minimum computer TOEFL 173. **Freshman Admission Requirements:** High school diploma is required, and GED is accepted. **Transfer Admission Requirements:** College transcript(s). Lowest grade transferable D. **General Admission Information:** Application fee $75. Regular notification is rolling. Credit offered for CEEB Advanced Placement tests.

COSTS AND FINANCIAL AID

Required Forms and Deadlines: FAFSA, institution's own financial aid form. **Types of Aid:** *Need-based scholarships/grants:* Pell, state scholarships/grants, private scholarships. *Loans:* FFEL Subsidized Stafford, FFEL Unsubsidized Stafford, FFEL PLUS, state loans, Private Educational Loans. **Financial Aid Statistics:** 11% undergrads receive any aid.

THOMAS JEFFERSON UNIVERSITY

130 South NinthStreet, Suite 100, Philadelphia, PA 19107
Phone: 215-503-8890 **E-mail:** jchp@jefferson.edu **CEEB Code:** 2903
Fax: 215-503-7241 **Website:** www.jefferson.edu/jchp

This is a private school.

RATINGS

Admissions Selectivity Rating: 60* **Fire Safety Rating:** 60* **Green Rating:** 60*

STUDENTS AND FACULTY

Enrollment: 656. **Student Body:** 83% female, 17% male, 27% out-of-state, 7% international. African American 11%, Asian 6%, Caucasian 74%, Hispanic 2%.

ACADEMICS

Degrees: Associate, bachelor's, doctoral, master's, post-bachelor's certificate, post-master's certificate. **Special Study Options:** Independent study, internships, study abroad.

FACILITIES

Housing: Coed dorms, apartments for married students, apartments for single students, special housing for disabled students.

CAMPUS LIFE

Activities: Choral groups, student government, student newspaper, student-run film society, yearbook.

ADMISSIONS

Freshman Admission Statistics: 1,170 applied, 57% admitted. **Transfer Admission Requirements:** College transcript(s), essay or personal statement, statement of good standing from prior institution(s). Minimum college GPA of 2.5 required. Lowest grade transferable C. **General Admission Information:** Regular notification is rolling. Non-fall registration not accepted. Common Application not accepted.

COSTS AND FINANCIAL AID

Annual tuition $23,685. Room and board $8,280. Required fees $400. Average book expense $1,495. **Required Forms and Deadlines:** Financial aid filing deadline 5/1.

THOMAS MORE COLLEGE

333 Thomas More Parkway, Crestview Hill, KY 41017-3495
Phone: 859-344-3332 **E-mail:** admissions@thomasmore.edu **CEEB Code:** 3892
Fax: 859-344-3444 **Website:** www.thomasmore.edu **ACT Code:** 1560
Financial Aid Phone: 859-344-3319

This private school, affiliated with the Roman Catholic Church, was founded in 1921. It has a 100-acre campus.

RATINGS

Admissions Selectivity Rating: 77 **Fire Safety Rating:** 60* **Green Rating:** 60*

STUDENTS AND FACULTY

Enrollment: 1,371. **Student Body:** 51% female, 49% male, 66% out-of-state, 1% international. African American 5%, Asian 1%, Caucasian 79%. **Retention and Graduation:** 62% freshmen return for sophomore year. 39% freshmen graduate within 4 years. 25% grads go on to further study within 1 year. 44% grads pursue arts and sciences degrees. 5% grads pursue business degrees. 6% grads pursue law degrees. 5% grads pursue medical degrees. **Faculty:** Student/faculty ratio 15:1. 71 full-time faculty, 66% hold PhDs. 100% faculty teach undergrads.

ACADEMICS

Degrees: Associate, bachelor's, certificate, master's, terminal. **Academic Requirements:** Arts/fine arts, computer literacy, English (including composition), foreign languages, history, humanities, mathematics, philosophy, sciences (biological or physical), social science. **Classes:** Most classes have 10–19 students. Most lab/discussion sections have 10–19 students. **Majors with Highest Enrollment:** Business administration/management, teacher education and professional development, specific subject areas. **Disciplines with Highest Percentage of Degrees Awarded:** Business/marketing 54%, social sciences 8%, biological/life sciences 6%, liberal arts/general studies 5%, education 4%, computer and information sciences 4%. **Special Study Options:** Accelerated program, cooperative education program, cross registration, double major, dual enrollment, English as a second language (ESL), honors program, independent study, internships, liberal arts/career combination, student-designed major, study abroad, teacher certification program, weekend college.

FACILITIES

Housing: Coed dorms, men's dorms, women's dorms. **Special Academic Facilities/Equipment:** See webssite. **Computers:** 99% of public computers are PCs, 1% of public computers are UNIX, network access in dorm rooms, network access in dorm lounges, online registration, online administrative functions (other than registration), remote student-access to Web through college's connection.

CAMPUS LIFE

Activities: Choral groups, drama/theater, literary magazine, student government, yearbook. **Organizations:** 29 registered organizations, 5 honor societies, 1 religious organization. 1 fraternity. **Athletics (Intercollegiate):** *Men:* Baseball, basketball, cross-country, football, golf, soccer, tennis. *Women:* Basketball, cross-country, golf, soccer, softball, tennis, volleyball.

ADMISSIONS

Freshman Academic Profile: 7% in top 10% of high school class, 31% in top 25% of high school class, 85% in top 50% of high school class. 69% from public high schools. SAT Math middle 50% range 460–600. SAT Critical Reading middle 50% range 460–580. ACT middle 50% range 19–24. TOEFL required of all international applicants, minimum paper TOEFL 515, minimum computer TOEFL 187. **Basis for Candidate Selection:** *Very important factors considered include:* Rigor of secondary school record, standardized test scores. *Important factors considered include:* Class rank. *Other factors considered include:* Application essay, character/personal qualities, extracurricular activities, interview, recommendation(s), talent/ability, volunteer work. **Freshman Admission Requirements:** High school diploma is required, and GED is accepted. *Academic units required:* 4 English, 3 math, 3 science (1 science lab), 2 foreign language, 3 social studies. *Academic units recommended:* 2 arts appreciation, computer literacy. **Freshman Admission Statistics:** 1,363 applied, 61% admitted, 31% enrolled. **Transfer Admission Requirements:** College transcript(s), statement of good standing from prior institution(s). Minimum college GPA of 2.0 required. Lowest grade transferable C. **General Admission Information:** Application fee $25. Regular notification is rolling. Non-fall registration accepted. Admission may be deferred for a maxiumum of 2 semesters. Common Application not accepted. Credit and/or placement offered for CEEB Advanced Placement tests.

COSTS AND FINANCIAL AID

Annual tuition $19,500. Room & board $5,400. Required fees $450. Average book expense $800. **Required Forms and Deadlines:** FAFSA, institution's own financial aid form. Financial aid filing deadline 3/15. **Notification of Awards:** Applicants will be notified of awards on a rolling basis beginning on or about 3/1. **Types of Aid:** *Need-based scholarships/grants:* Pell, SEOG, private scholarships, the school's own gift aid, United Negro College Fund. *Loans:* FFEL Subsidized Stafford, FFEL Unsubsidized Stafford, FFEL PLUS, Federal Perkins, Federal Nursing, college/university loans from institutional funds. **Financial Aid Statistics:** 94% freshmen, 89% undergrads receive need-based scholarship or grant aid. 65% freshmen, 61% undergrads receive need-based self-help aid. 90% freshmen, 74% undergrads receive any aid. Highest amount earned per year from on-campus jobs $1,400.

See page 1404.

THOMAS MORE COLLEGE OF LIBERAL ARTS

6 Manchester Street, Merrimack, NH 03054-4818
Phone: 603-880-8308 **E-mail:** admissions@thomasmorecollege.edu
Fax: 603-880-9280 **Website:** www.thomasmorecollege.edu **ACT Code:** 3892
Financial Aid Phone: 603-880-8308

This private school, affiliated with the Roman Catholic Church, was founded in 1978. It has a 13-acre campus.

RATINGS
Admissions Selectivity Rating: 60*   **Fire Safety Rating:** 60*   **Green Rating:** 60*

STUDENTS AND FACULTY
Enrollment: 92. **Student Body:** 48% female, 52% male, 85% out-of-state, 4% international. Caucasian 52%, Hispanic 1%. **Retention and Graduation:** 60% freshmen return for sophomore year. 52% grads go on to further study within 1 year. 48% grads pursue arts and sciences degrees. 2% grads pursue business degrees. 8% grads pursue law degrees. 2% grads pursue medical degrees. **Faculty:** Student/faculty ratio 12:1. 5 full-time faculty, 100% hold PhDs. 100% faculty teach undergrads.

ACADEMICS
Degrees: Bachelor's. **Academic Requirements:** Arts/fine arts, English (including composition), foreign languages, history, humanities, mathematics, philosophy, sciences (biological or physical), social science, theology. **Classes:** Most classes have 10–19 students. **Disciplines with Highest Percentage of Degrees Awarded:** English 40%, philosophy and religious studies 34%, biological/life sciences 6%. **Special Study Options:** Study abroad, spring semester in Rome for all sophomores.

FACILITIES
Housing: Men's dorms, women's dorms. **Computers:** Remote student-access to Web through college's connection.

CAMPUS LIFE
Activities: Choral groups.

ADMISSIONS
Freshman Academic Profile: 12% from public high schools. **Basis for Candidate Selection:** *Very important factors considered include:* Application essay, character/personal qualities, interview, recommendation(s). *Important factors considered include:* Talent/ability. *Other factors considered include:* Academic GPA, class rank, extracurricular activities, level of applicant's interest, religious affiliation/commitment, rigor of secondary school record, standardized test scores. **Freshman Admission Requirements:** High school diploma is required, and GED is accepted. *Academic units required:* 4 English, 3 math, 2 science (2 science labs), 2 foreign language, 2 social studies, 2 history. *Academic units recommended:* 2 music, art. **Freshman Admission Statistics:** 75% applied, 55% admitted, 63% enrolled. **Transfer Admission Requirements:** College transcript(s), essay or personal statement. Lowest grade transferable C. **General Admission Information:** Regular notification is rolling. Non-fall registration accepted. Admission may be deferred. Neither credit nor placement offered for CEEB Advanced Placement tests.

COSTS AND FINANCIAL AID
Annual tuition $11,100. Room & board $8,000. Average book expense $525. **Required Forms and Deadlines:** FAFSA. Financial aid filing deadline 5/1. **Notification of Awards:** Applicants will be notified of awards on a rolling basis beginning on or about 5/15. **Types of Aid:** *Need-based scholarships/grants:* Pell, SEOG, state scholarships/grants, the school's own gift aid. *Loans:* FFEL

Subsidized Stafford, FFEL Unsubsidized Stafford, FFEL PLUS. **Student Employment:** Off-campus job opportunities are good. **Financial Aid Statistics:** 47% freshmen, 36% undergrads receive need-based scholarship or grant aid. 47% freshmen, 34% undergrads receive need-based self-help aid.

THOMAS UNIVERSITY (GA)

1501 Millpond Road, Thomasville, GA 31792-7499
Phone: 912-227-6934 **E-mail:** gferrell@thomasu.edu
Fax: 912-226-1653 **Website:** www.thomasu.edu
Financial Aid Phone: 912-227-6931

This private school was founded in 1950. It has a 25-acre campus.

RATINGS
Admissions Selectivity Rating: 60*   **Fire Safety Rating:** 60*   **Green Rating:** 60*

STUDENTS AND FACULTY
Enrollment: 530. **Student Body:** 64% female, 36% male. **Retention and Graduation:** 66% freshmen return for sophomore year. 18% freshmen graduate within 4 years. 28% grads go on to further study within 1 year. **Faculty:** Student/faculty ratio 10:1. 100% faculty teach undergrads.

ACADEMICS
Degrees: Associate, bachelor's, master's, terminal. **Academic Requirements:** Arts/fine arts, computer literacy, English (including composition), history, humanities, mathematics, sciences (biological or physical), social science. **Disciplines with Highest Percentage of Degrees Awarded:** Education 32%, health professions and related sciences 22%, business/marketing 14%, parks and recreation 4%, social sciences 3%. **Special Study Options:** Accelerated program, double major, dual enrollment, honors program, internships.

FACILITIES
Housing: Special housing for international students. **Computers:** 100% of public computers are PCs, remote student-access to Web through college's connection.

CAMPUS LIFE
Activities: Choral groups, drama/theater, jazz band, literary magazine, music ensembles, student government, student newspaper. **Organizations:** 16 registered organizations, 5 honor societies, 2 religious organizations. **Athletics (Intercollegiate):** *Men:* Baseball, basketball, golf, soccer. *Women:* Equestrian sports, soccer, softball, tennis.

ADMISSIONS
Freshman Academic Profile: 98% from public high schools. TOEFL required of all international applicants, minimum paper TOEFL 550. **Freshman Admission Requirements:** High school diploma is required, and GED is accepted. **Freshman Admission Statistics:** 173 applied, 100% admitted, 62% enrolled. **Transfer Admission Requirements:** High school transcript, college transcript(s). **General Admission Information:** Application fee $25. Regular notification. Non-fall registration accepted. Common Application not accepted. Neither credit nor placement offered for CEEB Advanced Placement tests.

COSTS AND FINANCIAL AID
Annual tuition $7,500. $1,500 Required fees $370. **Required Forms and Deadlines:** FAFSA, institution's own financial aid form, state aid form. **Types of Aid:** *Need-based scholarships/grants:* Pell, SEOG, state scholarships/grants, private scholarships, the school's own gift aid. *Loans:* FFEL Subsidized Stafford, FFEL Unsubsidized Stafford, FFEL PLUS, college/university loans from institutional funds. **Student Employment:** Federal Work-Study Program available. Institutional employment available. Off-campus job opportunities are fair. **Financial Aid Statistics:** 65% undergrads receive need-based scholarship or grant aid. 43% undergrads receive need-based self-help aid. Highest amount earned per year from on-campus jobs $1,000.

THOMPSON RIVERS UNIVERISTY

UCC Admissions, PO Box 3010, Kamloops, BC V2C 5N3 Canada
Phone: 250-828-5071 **E-mail:** admissions@cariboo.bc.ca
Fax: 250-371-5513 **Website:** www.cariboo.bc.ca
Financial Aid Phone: 250-828-5000

This public school was founded in 1970. It has a 200-acre campus.

RATINGS
Admissions Selectivity Rating: 60*   **Fire Safety Rating:** 60*   **Green Rating:** 60*

STUDENTS AND FACULTY
Enrollment: 4,497. **Student Body:** 61% female, 39% male, 7% out-of-province. **Faculty:** Student/faculty ratio 20:1. 375 full-time faculty, 28% hold PhDs. 100% faculty teach undergrads.

ACADEMICS
Degrees: Associate, bachelor's, certificate, diploma, post-bachelor's certificate, terminal. **Academic Requirements:** Arts/fine arts, computer literacy, English (including composition), humanities, mathematics, sciences (biological or physical), social science. **Classes:** Most classes have 20–29 students. Most lab/discussion sections have 10–19 students. **Majors with Highest Enrollment:** Business administration/management, education, English language and literature, **Disciplines with Highest Percentage of Degrees Awarded:** Liberal arts/general studies 15%, business/marketing 13%, education 10%, English 9%, natural resources/environmental science 9%, health professions and related sciences 8%. **Special Study Options:** cooperative education program, distance learning, double major, English as a second language (ESL), honors program, internships, liberal arts/career combination, study abroad.

FACILITIES
Housing: Coed dorms. **Computers:** 100% of public computers are PCs, network access in dorm rooms, online registration, online administrative functions (other than registration), remote student-access to Web through college's connection.

CAMPUS LIFE
Activities: Choral groups, drama/theater, literary magazine, radio station, student government, student newspaper. **Organizations:** 5 religious organizations. **Athletics (Intercollegiate):** *Men:* Baseball, basketball, soccer, volleyball. *Women:* Basketball, soccer, volleyball.

ADMISSIONS
Freshman Academic Profile: 95% from public high schools. **Basis for Candidate Selection:** *Very important factors considered include:* Rigor of secondary school record. *Important factors considered include:* Standardized test scores. *Other factors considered include:* Character/personal qualities, interview, racial/ethnic status, recommendation(s), talent/ability, volunteer work, work experience. **Freshman Admission Statistics:** 3,900 applied, 64% admitted, 64% enrolled. **Transfer Admission Requirements:** High school transcript, college transcript(s). **General Admission Information:** Application fee $60. Regular application deadline 3/1. Regular notification is rolling. Non-fall registration accepted. Admission may be deferred for a maxiumum of 2 semesters. Neither credit nor placement offered for CEEB Advanced Placement tests.

COSTS AND FINANCIAL AID
Room and board $2,100. Required fees $200. Average book expense $1,000. **Student Employment:** Off-campus job opportunities are good.

TIFFIN UNIVERSITY

155 Miami Street, Tiffin, OH 44883
Phone: 419-448-3423 **E-mail:** Admiss@tiffin.edu **CEEB Code:** 1817
Fax: 419-443-5006 **Website:** www.tiffin.edu **ACT Code:** 3334
Financial Aid Phone: 419-448-3415

This private school was founded in 1888. It has a 110-acre campus.

RATINGS
Admissions Selectivity Rating: 60*   **Fire Safety Rating:** 71   **Green Rating:** 74

STUDENTS AND FACULTY
Enrollment: 1,376. **Student Body:** 52% female, 48% male, 2% international (16 countries represented). African American 13%, Caucasian 57%, Hispanic 1%. **Retention and Graduation:** 23% freshmen graduate within 4 years. **Faculty:** Student/faculty ratio 15:1. 53 full-time faculty, 74% hold PhDs. 100% faculty teach undergrads.

ACADEMICS
Degrees: Associate, bachelor's, master's. **Academic Requirements:** Arts/fine arts, computer literacy, English (including composition), history, humanities, mathematics, philosophy, sciences (biological or physical), social science. **Classes:** Most classes have fewer than 10 students. Most lab/discussion sections have fewer than 10 students. **Majors with Highest Enrollment:** Business administration/management; criminal justice/law enforcement administration; forensic science and technology. **Disciplines with Highest Percentage of Degrees Awarded:** Business/marketing 58%, security and protective services 19%, psychology 13%, parks and recreation 6%, communications/journalism 1%. **Special Study Options:** Accelerated program, cross-registration, distance learning, double major, English as a second language (ESL), exchange student program (domestic), external degree program, honor program, independent study, internships, study abroad, teacher certification program.

FACILITIES
Housing: Coed dorms, men's dorms, women's dorms, apartments for married students, special housing for disabled students, special housing for international students, fraternity/sorority housing, themed housing (e.g., performing arts). **Special Academic Facilities/Equipment:** University art gallery, multimedia lab. **Computers:** 80% of classrooms are wireless, 100% of public computers are PCs, network access in dorm rooms, online registration, online administrative functions (other than registration), remote student-access to Web through college's connection.

CAMPUS LIFE
Activities: Choral groups, concert band, dance, drama/theater, jazz band, marching band, music ensembles, musical theater, pep band, student government, student newspaper. **Organizations:** 32 registered organizations, 1 honor society, 1 religious organization. 2 fraternities (3% men join), 2 sororities (2% women join). **Athletics (Intercollegiate):** *Men:* Baseball, basketball, cheerleading, cross-country, football, golf, soccer, tennis, track/field (indoor), track/field (outdoor). *Women:* Basketball, cheerleading, cross-country, golf, soccer, softball, tennis, track/field (indoor), track/field (outdoor), volleyball. **Environmental Initiatives:** Establishment of a green committee. All future buildings will be LEED certified (silver level). Paper, aluminum, and plastic recycling is to be established.

ADMISSIONS
Freshman Academic Profile: SAT Math middle 50% range 450–540. SAT Critical Reading middle 50% range 430–560. ACT middle 50% range 18–23. **Basis for Candidate Selection:** *Very important factors considered include:* Academic GPA, standardized test scores, *Important factors considered include:* Rigor of secondary school record. *Other factors considered include:* Alumni/ae relation, application essay, character/personal qualities, class rank, extracurricular activities, first generation, interview, level of applicant's interest, recommendation(s), talent/ability, volunteer work, work experience. **Freshman Admission Requirements:** High school diploma is required, and GED is accepted. *Academic units required:* 4 English, 3 math, 3 science, 3 social studies, **Freshman Admission Statistics:** 1,795 applied, 74% admitted, 25% enrolled. **Transfer Admission Requirements:** High school transcript, college transcript(s). Minimum college GPA of 2.0 required. Lowest grade transferable C. **General Admission Information:** Application fee $20. Nonfall registration accepted. Credit offered for CEEB Advanced Placement tests.

COSTS AND FINANCIAL AID
Annual tuition $16,800. Room and board $7,170. Average book expense $1,200. **Required Forms and Deadlines:** FAFSA. Financial aid filing deadline 1/1. **Notification of Awards:** Applicants will be notified of awards on a rolling basis beginning on or about 2/15. **Types of Aid:** *Need-based scholarships/grants:* Pell, SEOG, state scholarships/grants, private scholarships, the school's own gift aid. *Loans:* FFEL Subsidized Stafford, FFEL Unsubsidized Stafford, FFEL PLUS, Federal Perkins, college/university loans from institutional funds. **Student Employment:** Federal Work-Study Program available. Institutional employment available. **Financial Aid Statistics:** 41% freshmen, 55% undergrads receive need-based scholarship or grant aid. 66% freshmen, 75% undergrads receive need-based self-help aid. 34 freshmen, 112 undergrads receive athletic scholarships. 94% freshmen, 97% undergrads receive any aid. Highest amount earned per year from on-campus jobs $1,600.

TOCCOA FALLS COLLEGE

Toccoa Falls College, Office of Admissions, Toccoa Falls, GA 30598
Phone: 888-785-5624 **E-mail:** Admissions@tfc.edu
Fax: 706-282-6012 **Website:** www.tfc.edu
Financial Aid Phone: 706-886-6831

This private school, affiliated with the Christian and Missionary Alliance Church, was founded in 1907. It has a 1,100-acre campus.

RATINGS
Admissions Selectivity Rating: 79   **Fire Safety Rating:** 61   **Green Rating:** 60*

STUDENTS AND FACULTY
Enrollment: 920. **Student Body:** 57% female, 42% male, 56% out-of-state. African American 3%, Asian 6%, Caucasian 88%, Hispanic 2%. **Retention and Graduation:** 71% freshmen return for sophomore year. 32% freshmen graduate within 4 years. **Faculty:** Student/faculty ratio 12:1. 47 full-time faculty, 57% hold PhDs. 100% faculty teach undergrads.

ACADEMICS
Degrees: Associate, bachelor's. **Academic Requirements:** Computer literacy, Bible and Doctrine (30 hours), English (including composition), humanities, mathematics, social science. **Disciplines with Highest Percentage of Degrees Awarded:** Education 19%, psychology 18%, communication technologies 6%, business/marketing 5%, visual and performing arts 3%. **Special Study Options:** Distance learning, double major, dual enrollment, independent study, internships, teacher certification program.

FACILITIES
Housing: Men's dorms, women's dorms, apartments for married students, apartments for single students, special housing for international students, trailer-court living available for married students. **Computers:** 100% of public computers are PCs, network access in dorm rooms, online registration, remote student-access to Web through college's connection.

CAMPUS LIFE
Activities: Choral groups, concert band, drama/theater, music ensembles, radio station, student government, student newspaper, television station, yearbook. **Organizations:** Athletics (Intercollegiate): *Men:* Baseball, basketball, football, golf, soccer, softball, tennis, volleyball. *Women:* Basketball, cheerleading, golf, soccer, softball, tennis, volleyball.

ADMISSIONS
Freshman Academic Profile: 12% in top 10% of high school class, 38% in top 25% of high school class, 70% in top 50% of high school class. SAT Math middle 50% range 430–550. SAT Critical Reading middle 50% range 460–570. ACT middle 50% range 18–25. TOEFL required of all international applicants, minimum paper TOEFL 500, minimum computer TOEFL 173. **Basis for Candidate Selection:** *Very important factors considered include:* Application essay, character/personal qualities, recommendation(s), religious affiliation/commitment, rigor of secondary school record, standardized test scores. *Other factors considered include:* Extracurricular activities, interview, talent/ability, volunteer work, work experience. **Freshman Admission Requirements:** High school diploma is required, and GED is accepted. *Academic units recommended:* 4 English, 3 math, 3 science (2 science labs), 6 academic electives. **Freshman Admission Statistics:** 1,196 applied, 60% admitted, 46% enrolled. **Transfer Admission Requirements:** College transcript(s), essay or personal statement. Minimum college GPA of 2.0 required. Lowest grade transferable C-. **General Admission Information:** Application fee $20. Regular application deadline 8/1. Regular notification 3/1. Nonfall registration accepted. Admission may be deferred for a maximum of 2 years. Credit and/or placement offered for CEEB Advanced Placement tests.

COSTS AND FINANCIAL AID
Annual tuition $13,700. Room & board $5,050. Required fees $125. Average book expense $908. **Required Forms and Deadlines:** FAFSA, institution's own financial aid form. Financial aid filing deadline 5/1. **Notification of Awards:** Applicants will be notified of awards on a rolling basis beginning on or about 3/1. **Types of Aid:** *Need-based scholarships/grants:* Pell, SEOG, state scholarships/grants, private scholarships, the school's own gift aid. *Loans:* FFEL Subsidized Stafford, FFEL Unsubsidized Stafford, FFEL PLUS, Federal Perkins, state loans, college/university loans from institutional funds. **Financial Aid Statistics:** 85% freshmen, 87% undergrads receive need-based scholarship or grant aid. 79% freshmen, 77% undergrads receive need-based self-help aid. 100% freshmen, 98% undergrads receive any aid. Highest amount earned per year from on-campus jobs $6,000.

TOUGALOO COLLEGE

500 West Country Line Road, Tougaloo, MS 39174
Phone: 888-424-2566 **E-mail:** slaterJa@mail.tougaloo.edu
Fax: 601-977-6185 **Website:** http://tougaloo.edu
Financial Aid Phone: 601-977-6134

This private school was founded in 1869.

RATINGS
Admissions Selectivity Rating: 60*   **Fire Safety Rating:** 87   **Green Rating:** 60*

STUDENTS AND FACULTY
Enrollment: 967. **Student Body:** 72% female, 28% male, 14% out-of-state. African American 100%. **Retention and Graduation:** 78% freshmen return for sophomore year. 63% freshmen graduate within 4 years. 55% grads go on to further study within 1 year. 35% grads pursue arts and sciences degrees. 5% grads pursue business degrees. 10% grads pursue law degrees. 10% grads pursue medical degrees. **Faculty:** Student/faculty ratio 14:1. 60 full-time faculty, 63% hold PhDs. 100% faculty teach undergrads.

ACADEMICS
Degrees: Associate, bachelor's, certificate. **Academic Requirements:** Computer literacy, English (including composition), foreign languages, history, humanities, mathematics, sciences (biological or physical), social science. **Classes:** Most classes have 20–29 students. Most lab/discussion sections have 10–19 students. **Disciplines with Highest Percentage of Degrees Awarded:** Psychology 23%, social sciences 20%, biological/life sciences 12%, English 10%, education 6%. **Special Study Options:** Cooperative education program, double major, dual enrollment, exchange student program (domestic), independent study, internships, liberal arts/career combination, study abroad, teacher certification program.

FACILITIES
Housing: Men's dorms, women's dorms. **Special Academic Facilities/Equipment:** Art collection, Bailey-Ward Black Collection. **Computers:** 95% of public computers are PCs, 4% of public computers are Macs, 1% of public computers are UNIX.

CAMPUS LIFE
Activities: Choral groups, drama/theater, literary magazine, student government, student newspaper, yearbook. **Organizations:** 20 registered organizations, 2 honor societies, 7 religious organizations. 4 fraternities (10% men join), 4 sororities (10% women join). **Athletics (Intercollegiate):** *Men:* Basketball, cross-country, golf. *Women:* Basketball, cross-country, golf, softball.

ADMISSIONS
Freshman Academic Profile: 95% from public high schools. ACT middle 50% range 16–21. TOEFL required of all international applicants, minimum paper TOEFL 500. **Basis for Candidate Selection:** *Important factors considered include:* Character/personal qualities, recommendation(s), rigor of secondary school record, standardized test scores, talent/ability. *Other factors considered include:* Alumni/ae relation, application essay, class rank, extracurricular activities, interview. **Freshman Admission Requirements:** High school diploma is required, and GED is accepted. *Academic units required:* 3 English, 2 math, 2 science, 1 social studies, 1 history, 7 academic electives. *Academic units recommended:* 4 English, 3 math, 3 science, 2 foreign language, 2 social studies, 2 history, 7 academic electives. **Freshman Admission Statistics:** 646 applied, 99% admitted, 39% enrolled. **Transfer Admission Requirements:** High school transcript, college transcript(s), standardized test score, statement of good standing from prior institution(s). Lowest grade transferable C. **General Admission Information:** Application fee $5. Regular notification 6/15. Non-fall registration accepted. Common Application not accepted.

COSTS AND FINANCIAL AID
Annual tuition $9,240. Room and board $6,330. Required fees $470. Average book expense $1,200. **Required Forms and Deadlines:** FAFSA, institution's own financial aid form, CSS/Financial Aid PROFILE. **Types of Aid:** *Need-based scholarships/grants:* Pell, SEOG, state scholarships/grants, private scholarships, the school's own gift aid, United Negro College Fund. *Loans:* Direct Subsidized Stafford, Federal Perkins. **Student Employment:** Federal Work-Study Program available. Off-campus job opportunities are good.

TOURO COLLEGE

1602 Avenue J, Brooklyn, NY 11230
Phone: 718-252-7800 **E-mail:** lasadmit@touro.edu **CEEB Code:** 2902
Fax: 718-253-6479 **Website:** www.touro.edu **ACT Code:** 2961
Financial Aid Phone: 212-463-0400

This private school was founded in 1971.

RATINGS
Admissions Selectivity Rating: 60*   **Fire Safety Rating:** 60*   **Green Rating:** 60*

STUDENTS AND FACULTY
Enrollment: 8,741. **Student Body:** 69% female, 31% male. African American 12%, Asian 4%, Caucasian 48%, Hispanic 9%. **Faculty:** Student/faculty ratio 12:1. 282 full-time faculty.

ACADEMICS
Degrees: Associate, bachelor's, certificate, doctoral, first professional, master's, post-bachelor's certificate. **Academic Requirements:** Computer literacy, English (including composition), humanities, mathematics, sciences (biological or physical). **Special Study Options:** Accelerated program, distance learning, double major, dual enrollment, English as a second language (ESL), honors program, independent study, internships, student-designed major, study abroad, teacher certification program. Undergrads may take grad level classes.

FACILITIES
Housing: Men's dorms, women's dorms.

CAMPUS LIFE
Activities: Literary magazine, student government, student newspaper, yearbook. **Organizations:** 33 honor societies, 18 religious organizations.

ADMISSIONS
Freshman Academic Profile: Minimum paper TOEFL 500. **Basis for Candidate Selection:** *Very important factors considered include:* Rigor of secondary school record. *Important factors considered include:* Application essay, interview, recommendation(s), standardized test scores. *Other factors considered include:* Alumni/ae relation, extracurricular activities, racial/ethnic status. **Freshman Admission Requirements:** High school diploma is required, and GED is accepted. *Academic units required:* 4 English, 2 math, 2 science, 2 foreign language, 2 history. **Freshman Admission Statistics:** 5,891 applied, 45% admitted, 83% enrolled. **Transfer Admission Requirements:** College transcript(s). Minimum college GPA of 2.5 required. Lowest grade transferable C. **General Admission Information:** Application fee $35. Regular notification rolling. Non-fall registration accepted. Common Application not accepted. Credit and/or placement offered for CEEB Advanced Placement tests.

COSTS AND FINANCIAL AID
Annual tuition $9,900. Board $4,700. Required fees $300. Average book expense $778. **Required Forms and Deadlines:** FAFSA, institution's own financial aid form, state aid form. Financial aid filing deadline 5/15. **Notification of Awards:** Applicants will be notified of awards on or about 8/15. **Types of Aid:** *Need-based scholarships/grants:* Pell, SEOG, state scholarships/grants, the school's own gift aid. *Loans:* FFEL Subsidized Stafford, FFEL Unsubsidized Stafford, FFEL PLUS, Federal Perkins. **Student Employment:** Federal Work-Study Program available. Institutional employment available. Off-campus job opportunities are excellent.

TOWSON UNIVERSITY

8000 York Road, Towson, MD 21252-0001
Phone: 410-704-2113 **E-mail:** admissions@towson.edu **CEEB Code:** 5404
Fax: 410-704-3030 **Website:** www.towson.edu **ACT Code:** 1718
Financial Aid Phone: 410-704-4236

This public school was founded in 1866. It has a 321-acre campus.

RATINGS
Admissions Selectivity Rating: 80   **Fire Safety Rating:** 95   **Green Rating:** 79

STUDENTS AND FACULTY
Enrollment: 14,760. **Student Body:** 61% female, 39% male, 17% out-of-state, 3% international. African American 11%, Asian 4%, Caucasian 70%, Hispanic 2%. **Retention and Graduation:** 80% freshmen return for sophomore year. 35% freshmen graduate within 4 years. **Faculty:** Student/faculty ratio 18:1. 694 full-time faculty, 76% hold PhDs.

ACADEMICS
Degrees: Bachelor's, doctoral, master's, post-bachelor's certificate, post-master's certificate. **Academic Requirements:** Arts/fine arts, computer literacy, English (including composition), history, humanities, mathematics, sciences (biological or physical), social science. **Classes:** Most classes have 20–29 students. Most lab/discussion sections have 10–19 students. **Majors with Highest Enrollment:** Business administration/management, elementary education and teaching, mass communications/media studies, **Disciplines with Highest Percentage of Degrees Awarded:** Business/marketing 16%, education 14%, social sciences 10%, communications/journalism 9%, psychology 8%. **Special Study Options:** Cooperative education program, cross registration, distance learning, double major, dual enrollment, English as a second language (ESL), exchange student program (domestic), honors program, independent study, internships, liberal arts/career combination, student-designed major, study abroad, teacher certification program.

FACILITIES
Housing: Coed dorms, apartments for single students, special housing for disabled students, special housing for international students, honors hall, alcohol free floors, academic emphasis floors, smoke-free floors, nontraditional aged areas. **Special Academic Facilities/Equipment:** Art galleries, animal museum, Asian art collection, elementary school, media center, speech/language clinic, planetarium/observatory, herbarium, electron microscope, argon laser. **Computers:** 100% of classrooms are wireless, network access in dorm rooms, network access in dorm lounges, online registration, online administrative functions (other than registration), support for handheld computing, remote student-access to Web through college's connection.

CAMPUS LIFE
Activities: Choral groups, concert band, dance, drama/theater, jazz band, literary magazine, marching band, music ensembles, musical theater, opera, pep band, radio station, student government, student newspaper, student-run film society, symphony orchestra, television station. **Organizations:** 150 registered organizations, 15 honor societies, 12 religious organizations. 12 fraternities (7% men join), 10 sororities (6% women join). **Athletics (Intercollegiate):** *Men:* Baseball, basketball, cheerleading, cross-country, diving, football, golf, lacrosse, soccer, swimming, tennis. *Women:* Basketball, cheerleading, cross-country, diving, field hockey, gymnastics, lacrosse, soccer, softball, swimming, tennis, track/field (outdoor), volleyball. **Environmental Initiatives:** Recycle Mania. Stream Clean-Up. Earth Week Plus.

ADMISSIONS
Freshman Academic Profile: 23% in top 10% of high school class, 54% in top 25% of high school class, 89% in top 50% of high school class. SAT Math middle 50% range 500–590. SAT Critical Reading middle 50% range 490–580. SAT Writing middle 50% range 500–580. ACT middle 50% range 20–24. TOEFL required of all international applicants, minimum paper TOEFL 500, minimum computer TOEFL 173. **Basis for Candidate Selection:** *Very important factors considered include:* Academic GPA. *Important factors considered include:* Rigor of secondary school record, standardized test scores. *Other factors considered include:* Application essay, class rank, first generation, recommendation(s), talent/ability. **Freshman Admission Requirements:** High school diploma is required, and GED is accepted. *Academic units required:* 4 English, 3 math, 3 science (2 science labs), 2 foreign language, 3

social studies, 6 academic electives. *Academic units recommended:* 4 English, 4 math, 3 science (3 science labs), 4 foreign language, 4 social studies. **Freshman Admission Statistics:** 13,470 applied, 69% admitted, 29% enrolled. **Transfer Admission Requirements:** College transcript(s). Minimum college GPA of 2.0 required. Lowest grade transferable D. **General Admission Information:** Application fee $45. Regular application deadline 2/15. Regular notification is rolling. Non-fall registration accepted. Admission may be deferred for a maxiumum of 2 semesters.

COSTS AND FINANCIAL AID

Annual in-state tuition $5,180. Out-of-state tuition $14,538. Room & board $7,506. Required fees $1,984. Average book expense $912. **Required Forms and Deadlines:** FAFSA. Financial aid filing deadline 1/31. **Notification of Awards:** Applicants will be notified of awards on a rolling basis beginning on or about 3/21. **Types of Aid:** *Need-based scholarships/grants:* Pell, SEOG, state scholarships/grants, private scholarships, the school's own gift aid. *Loans:* Direct Subsidized Stafford, Direct Unsubsidized Stafford, Direct PLUS, Federal Perkins. **Financial Aid Statistics:** 29% freshmen, 27% undergrads receive need-based scholarship or grant aid. 29% freshmen, 29% undergrads receive need-based self-help aid. 24 freshmen, 163 undergrads receive athletic scholarships. 65% freshmen, 72% undergrads receive any aid.

TRANSYLVANIA UNIVERSITY

300 North Broadway, Lexington, KY 40508-1797
Phone: 859-233-8242 **E-mail:** Admissions@transy.edu **CEEB Code:** 1808
Fax: 859-233-8797 **Website:** www.transy.edu **ACT Code:** 1550
Financial Aid Phone: 859-233-8239

This private school, affiliated with the Disciples of Christ Church, was founded in 1780. It has a 36-acre campus.

RATINGS

Admissions Selectivity Rating: 86   **Fire Safety Rating:** 85   **Green Rating:** 60*

STUDENTS AND FACULTY

Enrollment: 1,108. **Student Body:** 59% female, 41% male, 18% out-of-state. African American 2%, Asian 2%, Caucasian 86%, Hispanic 2%. **Retention and Graduation:** 79% freshmen return for sophomore year. 67% freshmen graduate within 4 years. 41% grads go on to further study within 1 year. 26% grads pursue arts and sciences degrees. 5% grads pursue business degrees. 6% grads pursue law degrees. 4% grads pursue medical degrees. **Faculty:** Student/faculty ratio 13:1. 82 full-time faculty, 89% hold PhDs. 100% faculty teach undergrads.

ACADEMICS

Degrees: Bachelor's. **Academic Requirements:** Arts/fine arts, English (including composition), foreign languages, humanities, mathematics, non-Western cultural traditions, sciences (biological or physical), social science, Western cultural traditions. **Classes:** Most classes have 10–19 students. Most lab/discussion sections have 10–19 students. **Majors with Highest Enrollment:** Biology/biological sciences; business/commerce; psychology. **Disciplines with Highest Percentage of Degrees Awarded:** Business/marketing 24%, biological/life sciences 12%, psychology 8%, parks and recreation 5%, visual and performing arts 5%, physical sciences 4%, English 4%, foreign languages and literature 4%. **Special Study Options:** Double major, independent study, internships, liberal arts/career combination, student-designed major, study abroad, teacher certification program.

FACILITIES

Housing: Coed dorms, men's dorms, women's dorms, apartments for single students, special housing for disabled students, efficiency apartment option for upperclassmen. Units with facilities for disabled students. **Special Academic Facilities/Equipment:** Art gallery, museum of early scientific apparatus, medical museum, language lab, transmission electron microscope. **Computers:** 100% of classrooms are wired, 100% of classrooms are wireless, 100% of public computers are PCs, 30% of public computers are UNIX, network access in dorm rooms, online administrative functions (other than registration), remote student-access to Web through college's connection.

CAMPUS LIFE

Activities: Choral groups, concert band, dance, drama/theater, jazz band,

literary magazine, music ensembles, musical theater, opera, pep band, radio station, student government, student newspaper, yearbook. **Organizations:** 55 registered organizations, 10 honor societies, 7 religious organizations. 4 fraternities (50% men join), 4 sororities (50% women join). **Athletics (Intercollegiate):** *Men:* Baseball, basketball, cheerleading, cross-country, diving, golf, soccer, swimming, tennis. *Women:* Basketball, cheerleading, cross-country, diving, field hockey, golf, soccer, softball, swimming, tennis, volleyball.

ADMISSIONS

Freshman Academic Profile: 41% in top 10% of high school class, 73% in top 25% of high school class, 96% in top 50% of high school class. 82% from public high schools. SAT Math middle 50% range 520–650. SAT Critical Reading middle 50% range 540–660. ACT middle 50% range 23–28. TOEFL required of all international applicants, minimum paper TOEFL 550, minimum computer TOEFL 213. **Basis for Candidate Selection:** *Very important factors considered include:* Academic GPA, rigor of secondary school record, standardized test scores. *Important factors considered include:* Application essay, extracurricular activities, recommendation(s). *Other factors considered include:* Alumni/ae relation, character/personal qualities, class rank, first generation, geographical residence, interview, talent/ability, volunteer work, work experience. **Freshman Admission Requirements:** High school diploma is required, and GED is accepted. *Academic units required:* 4 English, 3 math, 3 science, 2 social studies. *Academic units recommended:* 4 English, 4 math, 4 science (2 science labs), 2 foreign language, 2 social studies, 1 history, 1 academic elective. **Freshman Admission Statistics:** 1,286 applied, 83% admitted, 27% enrolled. **Transfer Admission Requirements:** High school transcript, college transcript(s), essay or personal statement. Minimum college GPA of 2.7 required. Lowest grade transferable C-. **General Admission Information:** Application fee $30. Regular application deadline 2/1. Regular notification 3/1. Nonfall registration accepted. Admission may be deferred for a maximum of 1 year. Credit and/or placement offered for CEEB Advanced Placement tests.

COSTS AND FINANCIAL AID

Annual tuition $21,400. Room and board $7,130. Required fees $900. Average book expense $750. **Required Forms and Deadlines:** FAFSA. Financial aid filing deadline 3/1. **Notification of Awards:** Applicants will be notified of awards on a rolling basis beginning on or about 3/15. **Types of Aid:** *Need-based scholarships/grants:* Pell, SEOG, state scholarships/grants, private scholarships, the school's own gift aid. *Loans:* Direct Subsidized Stafford, Direct Unsubsidized Stafford, Direct PLUS, FFEL Subsidized Stafford, FFEL Unsubsidized Stafford, FFEL PLUS, Federal Perkins, college/university loans from institutional funds. **Student Employment:** Federal Work-Study Program available. Institutional employment available. Off-campus job opportunities are excellent. **Financial Aid Statistics:** 69% freshmen, 61% undergrads receive need-based scholarship or grant aid. 52% freshmen, 49% undergrads receive need-based self-help aid. 99% freshmen, 98% undergrads receive any aid.

See page 1406.

TRENT UNIVERSITY

1600 West Bank street, Peterborough, ON K9J 7B8 Canada
Phone: 705-748-1215 **E-mail:** registrar@trentu.ca
Fax: 705-748-1629 **Website:** www.trentu.ca
Financial Aid Phone: 705-748-1524

This public school was founded in 1963. It has a 580-acre campus.

RATINGS

Admissions Selectivity Rating: 60*   **Fire Safety Rating:** 60*   **Green Rating:** 60*

STUDENTS AND FACULTY

Retention and Graduation: 85% freshmen return for sophomore year. **Faculty:** Student/faculty ratio 18:1. 240 full-time faculty.

ACADEMICS

Degrees: Bachelor's, certificate, diploma, doctoral, master's. **Academic Requirements:** Must study one credit minimum in 3 different areas. **Majors with Highest Enrollment:** Business administration/management, nursing/registered nurse training (RN, ASN, BSN, MSN), psychology. **Special Study Options:** Accelerated program, cooperative education program, double major, English as a second language (ESL), exchange student program (domestic), honors program, independent study, internships, student-designed major, study abroad.

FACILITIES

Housing: Coed dorms, men's dorms, women's dorms, special housing for disabled students, coed town houses. **Special Academic Facilities/Equip-ment:** Theater, archives, nature preserve **Computers:** Network access in dorm rooms, online administrative functions (other than registration).

CAMPUS LIFE

Activities: Choral groups, dance, drama/theater, jazz band, marching band, music ensembles, musical theater, radio station, student government, student newspaper, student-run film society, yearbook. **Organizations:** 60 registered organizations, 5 religious organizations. **Athletics (Intercollegiate):** *Men:* Crew/rowing, cross-country, fencing, rugby, soccer, swimming. *Women:* crew/rowing, cross-country, fencing, field hockey, rugby, soccer, swimming.

ADMISSIONS

Freshman Academic Profile: TOEFL required of all international applicants, minimum paper TOEFL 550, minimum computer TOEFL 213. **Basis for Candidate Selection:** *Very important factors considered include:* Rigor of secondary school record, standardized test scores, *Other factors considered include:* Class rank, interview, recommendation(s). **Freshman Admission Requirements:** High school diploma is required, and GED is accepted. *Academic units recommended:* 3 math, 3 science, **Freshman Admission Statistics:** 6,893 applied, 79% admitted, 28% enrolled. **Transfer Admission Requirements:** High school transcript, college transcript(s), standardized test score, statement of good standing from prior institution(s). **General Admission Information:** Application fee $35. Regular application deadline 6/11. Non-fall registration accepted. Admission may be deferred for a maxiumum of 2 semesters.

COSTS AND FINANCIAL AID

Annual in-state tuition $5,000. Average book expense $1,000. In-province tuition $3,951. Out-of-province tuition $3,951. International tuition·$10,516. Room & board $6,996. Required fees $840. Average book expense $750. **Required Forms and Deadlines:** Financial aid filing deadline 3/1. **Student Employment:** Off-campus job opportunities are good.

TREVECCA NAZARENE UNIVERSITY

333 Murfreesboro Road, Nashville, TN 37210
Phone: 615-248-1320 **E-mail:** admissions_und@trevecca.edu
Fax: 615-248-7406 **Website:** www.trevecca.edu **ACT Code:** 4016
Financial Aid Phone: 615-248-1242

This private school, affiliated with the Nazarene Church, was founded in 1901. It has a 65-acre campus.

RATINGS

Admissions Selectivity Rating: 79   **Fire Safety Rating:** 60*   **Green Rating:** 60*

STUDENTS AND FACULTY

Enrollment: 1,195. **Student Body:** 55% female, 45% male, 40% out-of-state, 2% international (12 countries represented). African American 8%, Asian 2%, Caucasian 84%, Hispanic 2%. **Retention and Graduation:** 68% freshmen return for sophomore year. 37% freshmen graduate within 4 years. **Faculty:** Student/faculty ratio 17:1. 82 full-time faculty, 76% hold PhDs. 64% faculty teach undergrads.

ACADEMICS

Degrees: Associate, bachelor's, doctoral, master's. **Academic Requirements:** Arts/fine arts, computer literacy, English (including composition), foreign languages, history, humanities, mathematics, philosophy, religion, sciences (biological or physical), social science. **Classes:** Most classes have 10–19 students. **Majors with Highest Enrollment:** Business administration and management, elementary education and teaching, religion/religious studies. **Disciplines with Highest Percentage of Degrees Awarded:** Business/marketing 62%, education 7%, visual and performing arts 7%, philosophy and religious studies 6%, communications/journalism 4%. **Special Study Options:** Adult degree completion program, double major, internships, study abroad, teacher certification program.

FACILITIES

Housing: Men's dorms, women's dorms, apartments for married students, apartments for single students. **Computers:** Network access in dorm rooms, network access in dorm lounges, online administrative functions (other than registration), remote student-access to Web through college's connection.

CAMPUS LIFE

Activities: Choral groups, concert band, drama/theater, jazz band, literary magazine, marching band, music ensembles, musical theater, pep band, radio station, student government, student newspaper, symphony orchestra,

yearbook. **Organizations:** 26 registered organizations. **Athletics (Intercollegiate):** *Men:* Baseball, basketball, golf, soccer. *Women:* Basketball, golf, soccer, softball, volleyball.

ADMISSIONS

Freshman Academic Profile: 21% in top 10% of high school class, 45% in top 25% of high school class, 74% in top 50% of high school class. SAT Math middle 50% range 460–580. SAT Critical Reading middle 50% range 480–600. ACT middle 50% range 19–25. TOEFL required of all international applicants, minimum paper TOEFL 500, minimum computer TOEFL 173. **Basis for Candidate Selection:** *Very important factors considered include:* Academic GPA, character/personal qualities, standardized test scores. *Important factors considered include:* Level of applicant's interest. *Other factors considered include:* Application essay, class rank, extracurricular activities, interview, recommendation(s), talent/ability. **Freshman Admission Requirements:** High school diploma is required, and GED is accepted. *Academic units recommended:* 4 English, 2 math, 1 science, 2 foreign language, 1 social studies, 1 history, 4 academic electives. **Freshman Admission Statistics:** 803 applied, 69% admitted, 45% enrolled. **Transfer Admission Requirements:** College transcript(s). Lowest grade transferable D. **General Admission Information:** Application fee $25. Non-fall registration accepted. Credit offered for CEEB Advanced Placement tests.

COSTS AND FINANCIAL AID

Required Forms and Deadlines: FAFSA. Financial aid filing deadline 3/1. **Notification of Awards:** Applicants will be notified of awards on a rolling basis beginning on or about 3/15. **Types of Aid:** *Need-based scholarships/grants:* Pell, SEOG, state scholarships/grants, private scholarships, the school's own gift aid. *Loans:* FFEL Subsidized Stafford, FFEL Unsubsidized Stafford, FFEL PLUS, Federal Perkins. **Student Employment:** Federal Work-Study Program available. Off-campus job opportunities are excellent. **Financial Aid Statistics:** 41% freshmen, 53% undergrads receive need-based scholarship or grant aid. 28% freshmen, 48% undergrads receive need-based self-help aid. 6 freshmen, 8 undergrads receive athletic scholarships. 95% undergrads receive any aid.

TRINITY BIBLE COLLEGE

50 South Sixth Avenue, Ellendale, ND 58436-7150
Phone: 701-349-5403 **E-mail:** admissions@trinitybiblecollege.edu
Fax: 701-349-5443 **Website:** www.trinitybiblecollege.edu

This is a private school.

RATINGS

Admissions Selectivity Rating: 60*   **Fire Safety Rating:** 60*   **Green Rating:** 60*

STUDENTS AND FACULTY

Enrollment: 305. **Student Body:** 54% female, 46% male. African American 3%, Caucasian 91%, Hispanic 2%, Native American 4%. **Retention and Graduation:** 77% freshmen return for sophomore year.

ACADEMICS

Degrees: Associate, bachelor's, certificate. **Academic Requirements:** Bible, English (including composition), history, humanities, mathematics, philosophy, sciences (biological or physical), social science, theology. **Disciplines with Highest Percentage of Degrees Awarded:** Education 13%, business/marketing 5%. **Special Study Options:** Distance learning, double major, dual enrollment, independent study, teacher certification program.

FACILITIES

Housing: Men's dorms, women's dorms.

CAMPUS LIFE

Activities: Choral groups, drama/theater, jazz band, music ensembles, radio station, student government, yearbook.

ADMISSIONS

Basis for Candidate Selection: *Very important factors considered include:* Character/personal qualities, recommendation(s), standardized test scores. *Important factors considered include:* Application essay. *Other factors considered include:* Religious affiliation/commitment, rigor of secondary school record. **Freshman Admission Requirements:** High school diploma is required, and GED is accepted. **Freshman Admission Statistics:** 228 applied, 100% admitted, 64% enrolled. **Transfer Admission Requirements:** High school transcript, college transcript(s), essay or personal statement, statement of good standing from prior institution(s). Lowest grade transferable C. **General Admission Information:** Application fee $25. Regular notification is rolling. Non-fall registration accepted. Admission may be deferred. Common Application not accepted.

COSTS AND FINANCIAL AID

Annual tuition $9,680. Room & board $4,370. Required fees $1,478. Average book expense $700. **Required Forms and Deadlines:** FAFSA, Information provided on student application for admission. Financial aid filing deadline 3/1. **Notification of Awards:** Applicants will be notified of awards on a rolling basis beginning on or about 3/1. **Types of Aid:** *Need-based scholarships/grants:* Pell, SEOG, state scholarships/grants, private scholarships, the school's own gift aid. *Loans:* FFEL Subsidized Stafford, FFEL Unsubsidized Stafford, FFEL PLUS, Federal Perkins. **Financial Aid Statistics:** 94% freshmen, 95% undergrads receive need-based scholarship or grant aid. 93% freshmen, 93% undergrads receive need-based self-help aid.

TRINITY CHRISTIAN COLLEGE

6601 West College Drive, Palos Heights, IL 60463
Phone: 708-239-4708 **E-mail:** admissions@trnty.edu **CEEB Code:** 1820
Fax: 708-239-4826 **Website:** www.trnty.edu **ACT Code:** 1165
Financial Aid Phone: 708-239-4706

This private school, affiliated with the Reformed Church, was founded in 1959. It has a 56-acre campus.

RATINGS

Admissions Selectivity Rating: 73   **Fire Safety Rating:** 70   **Green Rating:** 61

STUDENTS AND FACULTY

Enrollment: 1,198. **Student Body:** 67% female, 33% male, 51% out-of-state, 1% international (13 countries represented). African American 8%, Asian 2%, Caucasian 78%, Hispanic 5%. **Retention and Graduation:** 77% freshmen return for sophomore year. 52% freshmen graduate within 4 years. 13% grads go on to further study within 1 year. 3% grads pursue arts and sciences degrees. 1% grads pursue business degrees. 2% grads pursue law degrees. 2% grads pursue medical degrees. **Faculty:** Student/faculty ratio 12:1. 74 full-time faculty, 64% hold PhDs. 100% faculty teach undergrads.

ACADEMICS

Degrees: Bachelor's. **Academic Requirements:** Arts/fine arts, English (including composition), history, humanities, mathematics, philosophy, sciences (biological or physical), social science. **Classes:** Most classes have 10–19 students. **Majors with Highest Enrollment:** Business administration/management, elementary education and teaching, nursing/registered nurse training (RN, ASN, BSN, MSN). **Disciplines with Highest Percentage of Degrees Awarded:** Education 32%, business/marketing 16%, theology and religious vocations 10%, health professions and related sciences 8%, psychology 5%, visual and performing arts 5%. **Special Study Options:** Cooperative education program, double major, honors program, independent study, internships, liberal arts/career combination, study abroad, teacher certification program.

FACILITIES

Housing: Coed dorms, apartments for married students, apartments for single students. **Special Academic Facilities/Equipment:** Dutch Heritage Center. **Computers:** 10% of classrooms are wired, 10% of classrooms are wireless, 100% of public computers are PCs, network access in dorm rooms, network access in dorm lounges, online administrative functions (other than registration), remote student-access to Web through college's connection.

CAMPUS LIFE

Activities: Choral groups, concert band, dance, drama/theater, jazz band, literary magazine, music ensembles, student government, student newspaper, yearbook. **Organizations:** 15 registered organizations, 2 honor societies, 1 religious organization. **Athletics (Intercollegiate):** *Men:* Baseball, basketball, cross-country, soccer, track/field (outdoor). *Women:* Basketball, cross-country, soccer, softball, track/field (outdoor), volleyball. **Environmental Initiatives:** Recycling of paper, aluminum, and glass. Maintenance of a nature trail on campus.

ADMISSIONS

Freshman Academic Profile: 16% in top 10% of high school class, 22% in top 25% of high school class, 34% in top 50% of high school class. 48% from public high schools. SAT Math middle 50% range 450–630. SAT Critical Reading middle 50% range 470–600. ACT middle 50% range 19–26. TOEFL required of all international applicants, minimum paper TOEFL 550, minimum computer TOEFL 213. **Basis for Candidate Selection:** *Very important factors considered include:* Academic GPA, rigor of secondary school record, standardized test scores. *Important factors considered include:* Application essay, character/personal qualities, class rank, extracurricular activities,

interview, level of applicant's interest, recommendation(s), religious affiliation/commitment, talent/ability. *Other factors considered include:* Alumni/ae relation, volunteer work, work experience. **Freshman Admission Requirements:** High school diploma is required, and GED is accepted. *Academic units required:* 3 English, 3 math, 2 science, 2 social studies. *Academic units recommended:* 4 English, 4 math, 3 science, 2 foreign language, 3 social studies, 2 history. **Freshman Admission Statistics:** 566 applied, 92% admitted, 43% enrolled. **Transfer Admission Requirements:** College transcript(s), essay or personal statement, interview. Minimum college GPA of 2.0 required. Lowest grade transferable C. **General Admission Information:** Application fee $20. Regular notification is rolling. Non-fall registration accepted. Admission may be deferred for a maxiumum of 2 semesters. Credit and/or placement offered for CEEB Advanced Placement tests.

COSTS AND FINANCIAL AID

Annual tuition $17,920. Room & board $7,010. Average book expense $925. **Required Forms and Deadlines:** FAFSA, institution's own financial aid form. Financial aid filing deadline 2/15. **Notification of Awards:** Applicants will be notified of awards on a rolling basis beginning on or about 4/1. **Types of Aid:** *Need-based scholarships/grants:* Pell, SEOG, state scholarships/grants, private scholarships, the school's own gift aid. *Loans:* FFEL Subsidized Stafford, FFEL Unsubsidized Stafford, FFEL PLUS, Federal Perkins, Federal Nursing. **Student Employment:** Federal Work-Study Program available. Institutional employment available. Off-campus job opportunities are fair. **Financial Aid Statistics:** 61% freshmen, 59% undergrads receive need-based scholarship or grant aid. 66% freshmen, 53% undergrads receive need-based self-help aid. 26 freshmen, 32 undergrads receive athletic scholarships. 90% freshmen, 78% undergrads receive any aid. Highest amount earned per year from on-campus jobs $6,520.

TRINITY COLLEGE (CT)

300 Summit Street, Hartford, CT 06016
Phone: 860-297-2180 **E-mail:** admissions.office@trincoll.edu **CEEB Code:** 3899
Fax: 860-297-2287 **Website:** www.trincoll.edu **ACT Code:** 598
Financial Aid Phone: 860-297-2047

This private school was founded in 1823. It has a 100-acre campus.

RATINGS

Admissions Selectivity Rating: 95   **Fire Safety Rating:** 86   **Green Rating:** 60*

STUDENTS AND FACULTY

Enrollment: 2,203. **Student Body:** 49% female, 51% male, 82% out-of-state, 3% international (29 countries represented). African American 6%, Asian 6%, Caucasian 60%, Hispanic 5%. **Retention and Graduation:** 92% freshmen return for sophomore year. 80% freshmen graduate within 4 years. 19% grads go on to further study within 1 year. 7% grads pursue arts and sciences degrees. 1% grads pursue business degrees. 4% grads pursue law degrees. 1% grads pursue medical degrees. **Faculty:** Student/faculty ratio 11:1. 174 full-time faculty, 93% hold PhDs. 100% faculty teach undergrads.

ACADEMICS

Degrees: Bachelor's, master's. **Academic Requirements:** Arts/fine arts, humanities, numerical and symbolic reasoning, sciences (biological or physical), social science. **Classes:** Most classes have 10–19 students. Most lab/discussion sections have 10–19 students. **Majors with Highest Enrollment:** Economics, history, political science and government. **Disciplines with Highest Percentage of Degrees Awarded:** Social sciences 30%, history 9%, English 8%, area and ethnic studies 7%, psychology 7%, philosophy and religious studies 6%. **Special Study Options:** 5-year BS/MS in electrical engineering or mechanical engineering with Rensselaer Polytechnic Institute, cross registration, double major, honors program, independent study, internships, student-designed major, study abroad, teacher certification program.

FACILITIES

Housing: Coed dorms, special housing for disabled students, fraternity/sorority housing, community service dorm, quiet dorm, wellness and substance-free, 21+ only, cooking. All dorms are nonsmoking. **Special Academic Facilities/Equipment:** Watkinson Library. **Computers:** 58% of public computers are PCs, 31% of public computers are Macs, 11% of public computers are UNIX, network access in dorm rooms, network access in dorm lounges, online registration, remote student-access to Web through college's connection.

CAMPUS LIFE

Activities: Choral groups, dance, drama/theater, jazz band, literary magazine, music ensembles, musical theater, radio station, student government, student newspaper, student-run film society, television station, yearbook. **Organizations:** 110 registered organizations, 5 honor societies, 5 religious organizations. 7 fraternities (20% men join), 7 sororities (16% women join). **Athletics (Intercollegiate):** *Men:* Baseball, basketball, crew/rowing, cross-country, diving, equestrian sports, fencing, football, golf, ice hockey, lacrosse, riflery, rugby, sailing, soccer, softball, squash, swimming, tennis, track/field (indoor), track/field (outdoor), wrestling. *Women:* Basketball, crew/rowing, cross-country, diving, equestrian sports, fencing, field hockey, ice hockey, lacrosse, riflery, rugby, sailing, soccer, softball, squash, swimming, tennis, track/field (indoor), track/field (outdoor), volleyball.

ADMISSIONS

Freshman Academic Profile: 54% in top 10% of high school class, 83% in top 25% of high school class, 98% in top 50% of high school class. 51% from public high schools. SAT Math middle 50% range 610–690. SAT Critical Reading middle 50% range 600–690. SAT Writing middle 50% range 608–700. ACT middle 50% range 26–29. **Basis for Candidate Selection:** *Very important factors considered include:* Rigor of secondary school record. *Important factors considered include:* Application essay, character/personal qualities, class rank, extracurricular activities, interview, racial/ethnic status, recommendation(s), standardized test scores, talent/ability. *Other factors considered include:* Alumni/ae relation, geographical residence, volunteer work, work experience. **Freshman Admission Requirements:** High school diploma is required, and GED is accepted. *Academic units required:* 4 English, 3 math, 2 science (2 science labs), 2 foreign language, 2 history. **Freshman Admission Statistics:** 5,343 applied, 43% admitted, 27% enrolled. **Transfer Admission Requirements:** High school transcript, college transcript(s), essay or personal statement, standardized test score, statement of good standing from prior institution(s). Minimum college GPA of 3.0 required. Lowest grade transferable C-. **General Admission Information:** Application fee $60. Early decision application deadline 11/15. Regular application deadline 1/1. Regular notification 4/1. Non-fall registration not accepted. Admission may be deferred for a maxiumum of 2 semesters. Credit and/or placement offered for CEEB Advanced Placement tests.

COSTS AND FINANCIAL AID

Annual tuition $35,110. Room and board $9,420. Required fees $1,760. Average book expense $900. **Required Forms and Deadlines:** FAFSA, CSS/Financial Aid PROFILE, noncustodial profile, federal income tax returns. Financial aid filing deadline 3/1. **Notification of Awards:** Applicants will be notified of awards on or about 4/1. **Types of Aid:** *Need-based scholarships/grants:* Pell, SEOG, state scholarships/grants, private scholarships, the school's own gift aid. *Loans:* Direct Subsidized Stafford, Direct Unsubsidized Stafford, Direct PLUS, FFEL Subsidized Stafford, FFEL Unsubsidized Stafford, FFEL PLUS, Federal Perkins, college/university loans from institutional funds. **Student Employment: Financial Aid Statistics:** 36% freshmen, 38% undergrads receive need-based scholarship or grant aid. 28% freshmen, 33% undergrads receive need-based self-help aid. 28% freshmen, 40% undergrads receive any aid. Highest amount earned per year from on-campus jobs $1,800.

See page 1408.

TRINITY COLLEGE OF FLORIDA

2430 Welbilt Boulevard, Trinity, FL 34655
Phone: 727-569-1411 **E-mail:** admissions@trinitycollege.edu
Fax: 727-569-1410 **Website:** www.trinitycollege.edu **ACT Code:** 4876
Financial Aid Phone: 727-569-1413

This private school, affiliated with the Interdenominational Church, was founded in 1932. It has a 40-acre campus.

RATINGS

Admissions Selectivity Rating: 60*   **Fire Safety Rating:** 74   **Green Rating:** 66

STUDENTS AND FACULTY

Enrollment: 181. **Student Body:** 39% female, 61% male, 5% out-of-state, 2% international (5 countries represented). African American 6%, Asian 1%, Caucasian 83%, Hispanic 8%. **Retention and Graduation:** 52% freshmen return for sophomore year. 40% grads go on to further study within 1 year. **Faculty:** Student/faculty ratio 13:1. 6 full-time faculty, 83% hold PhDs. 100% faculty teach undergrads.

ACADEMICS

Degrees: Associate, bachelor's, certificate. **Academic Requirements:** Arts/fine arts, computer literacy, English (including composition), history, humanities, mathematics, philosophy, sciences (biological or physical), social science. **Classes:** Most classes have fewer than 10 students. Most lab/discussion sections have fewer than 10 students. **Majors with Highest Enrollment:** Missions/missionary studies and missiology, pastoral studies/counseling, pre-theology/pre-ministerial studies. **Disciplines with Highest Percentage of Degrees Awarded:** Theology and religious vocations 64%, personal and culinary services 23%, education 8%, business/marketing 5%. **Special Study Options:** Accelerated program, double major, dual enrollment, honors program, independent study, internships, teacher certification program, weekend college.

FACILITIES

Housing: Men's dorms, women's dorms, apartments for single students, special housing for disabled students. **Computers:** 100% of classrooms are wireless, 100% of public computers are PCs, network access in dorm rooms, network access in dorm lounges, remote student-access to Web through college's connection.

CAMPUS LIFE

Activities: Choral groups, drama/theater, student government, yearbook. **Organizations:** 2 religious organizations. **Athletics (Intercollegiate):** *Men:* Basketball. *Women:* Volleyball.

ADMISSIONS

Freshman Academic Profile: SAT Math middle 50% range 345–560. SAT Critical Reading middle 50% range 400–640. ACT middle 50% range 14–20. TOEFL required of all international applicants, minimum paper TOEFL 500, minimum computer TOEFL 173. **Transfer Admission Requirements:** High school transcript, college transcript(s), essay or personal statement, interview. Minimum college GPA of 2.0 required. Lowest grade transferable C. **General Admission Information:** Credit and/or placement offered for CEEB Advanced Placement tests. Regular application deadline 8/2.

COSTS AND FINANCIAL AID

Annual tuition $9,760. Room and board $5,940. Required fees $790. Average book expense $790. **Required Forms and Deadlines:** FAFSA, institution's own financial aid form. Financial aid filing deadline 8/2. **Types of Aid:** *Need-based scholarships/grants:* Pell, SEOG, state scholarships/grants, private scholarships, the school's own gift aid. *Loans:* FFEL Subsidized Stafford, FFEL Unsubsidized Stafford, FFEL PLUS, private loans. **Student Employment:** Federal Work-Study Program available. Institutional employment available. Off-campus job opportunities are fair. **Financial Aid Statistics:** 94% freshmen, 92% undergrads receive need-based scholarship or grant aid. 88% freshmen, 91% undergrads receive need-based self-help aid. 79% freshmen, 73% undergrads receive any aid. Highest amount earned per year from on-campus jobs $9,096.

TRINITY COLLEGE OF VERMONT

208 Colchester Avenue, Burlington, VT 05401
Phone: 802-846-7030 **E-mail:** trinity@hope.trinityvt.edu **CEEB Code:** 3900
Fax: 802-846-7001 **Website:** www.trinityvt.edu **ACT Code:** 4325
Financial Aid Phone: 802-846-7170

This private school was founded in 1925. It has a 19-acre campus.

RATINGS

Admissions Selectivity Rating: 60*   **Fire Safety Rating:** 60*   **Green Rating:** 60*

STUDENTS AND FACULTY

Enrollment: 569. **Student Body:** 92% female, 8% male, 24% out-of-state, 2% international. African American 3%, Asian 1%, Caucasian 42%. **Retention and Graduation:** 60% freshmen return for sophomore year. 42% freshmen graduate within 4 years. 10% grads go on to further study within 1 year. **Faculty:** Student/faculty ratio 10:1. 22 full-time faculty, 77% hold PhDs. 100% faculty teach undergrads.

ACADEMICS

Degrees: Associate, bachelor's, certificate, master's, post-bachelor's certificate, post-master's certificate. **Academic Requirements:** Arts/fine arts, computer literacy, history, humanities, mathematics, philosophy, religious studies, sciences (biological or physical), social science. **Classes:** Most classes have 10–19 students. **Disciplines with Highest Percentage of Degrees Awarded:** Business/marketing 17%, education 17%, psychology 14%, liberal arts/general studies 12%, biological/life sciences 7%, English 7%, mathematics 4%. **Special Study Options:** Cross registration, double major, independent study, internships, liberal arts/career combination, student-designed major, study abroad, teacher certification program, weekend college.

FACILITIES

Housing: Women's dorms, apartments for single students, apartment-style cottages. **Computers:** 95% of public computers are PCs, 5% of public computers are Macs, remote student-access to Web through college's connection.

CAMPUS LIFE

Activities: Drama/theater, student government, student newspaper, yearbook. **Organizations:** 15 registered organizations. **Athletics (Intercollegiate):** *Women:* Basketball, cross-country, equestrian sports, soccer, softball.

ADMISSIONS

Freshman Academic Profile: 89% from public high schools. SAT Math middle 50% range 400–520. SAT Critical Reading middle 50% range 410–540. ACT middle 50% range 15–22. TOEFL required of all international applicants, minimum paper TOEFL 500. **Basis for Candidate Selection:** *Very important factors considered include:* Rigor of secondary school record, standardized test scores. *Important factors considered include:* Interview. *Other factors considered include:* Alumni/ae relation, application essay, character/personal qualities, class rank, extracurricular activities, recommendation(s), talent/ability, volunteer work, work experience. **Freshman Admission Requirements:** High school diploma is required, and GED is accepted. *Academic units recommended:* 4 English, 3 math, 2 science (1 science lab), 2 foreign language, 2 social studies. **Freshman Admission Statistics:** 557 applied, 99% admitted, 14% enrolled. **Transfer Admission Requirements:** College transcript(s). Minimum college GPA of 2.0 required. Lowest grade transferable C-. **General Admission Information:** Application fee $40. Regular notification rolling. Non-fall registration accepted. Admission may be deferred. Common Application accepted. Credit offered for CEEB Advanced Placement tests.

COSTS AND FINANCIAL AID

Annual tuition $13,620. Room & board $6,700. Required fees $500. **Required Forms and Deadlines:** FAFSA, state aid form. **Notification of Awards:** Applicants will be notified of awards on a rolling basis beginning on or about 2/15. **Types of Aid:** *Need-based scholarships/grants:* Pell, SEOG, state scholarships/grants, private scholarships, the school's own gift aid. *Loans:* FFEL Subsidized Stafford, FFEL Unsubsidized Stafford, FFEL PLUS, Federal Perkins, college/university loans from institutional funds, alternative loans. **Student Employment:** Federal Work-Study Program available. Institutional employment available. Off-campus job opportunities are good. **Financial Aid Statistics:** 88% freshmen, 77% undergrads receive need-based scholarship or grant aid. 83% freshmen, 75% undergrads receive need-based self-help aid.

TRINITY INTERNATIONAL UNIVERSITY

2065 Half Day Road, Deerfield, IL 60015
Phone: 847-317-7000 **E-mail:** tcadmissions@tiu.edu **CEEB Code:** 1810
Fax: 847-317-8097 **Website:** www.tiu.edu **ACT Code:** 1150
Financial Aid Phone: 847-317-7033

This private school, affiliated with the Evangelical Free Church of America, was founded in 1897. It has a 111-acre campus.

RATINGS

Admissions Selectivity Rating: 77   **Fire Safety Rating:** 70   **Green Rating:** 62

STUDENTS AND FACULTY

Enrollment: 1,228. **Student Body:** 59% female, 41% male, 36% out-of-state. African American 12%, Asian 2%, Caucasian 60%, Hispanic 4%. **Retention and Graduation:** 75% freshmen return for sophomore year. 59% freshmen graduate within 4 years. **Faculty:** Student/faculty ratio 13:1. 90 full-time faculty, 81% hold PhDs. 54% faculty teach undergrads.

ACADEMICS

Degrees: Bachelor's, doctoral, first professional, master's, post-bachelor's certificate. **Academic Requirements:** Arts/fine arts, Bible, English (including composition), foreign languages, history, humanities, mathematics, philosophy, sciences (biological or physical), social science. **Classes:** Most classes have 10–19 students. Most lab/discussion sections have 10–19 students. **Majors with Highest Enrollment:** Business administration/management, elementary education and teaching, theological studies and religious vocations. **Disciplines with Highest Percentage of Degrees Awarded:** Education 24%, theology and religious vocations 18%, business/marketing 15%, liberal arts/general studies 15%, psychology 8%, health professions and related sciences 5%. **Special Study Options:** Accelerated program, cooperative education program,

cross registration, distance learning, double major, dual enrollment, exchange student program (domestic), graduate courses, honors program, independent study, internships, liberal arts/career combination, REACH (for nontraditional students with previous college credit), student-designed major, study abroad, teacher certification program.

FACILITIES

Housing: Men's dorms, women's dorms, apartments for married students, apartments for single students, special housing for disabled students, special housing for international students. **Computers:** 100% of public computers are PCs, network access in dorm rooms, network access in dorm lounges, online registration, online administrative functions (other than registration), remote student-access to Web through college's connection.

CAMPUS LIFE

Activities: Choral groups, concert band, dance, drama/theater, jazz band, literary magazine, music ensembles, musical theater, opera, pep band, student government, student newspaper, symphony orchestra, yearbook. **Organizations:** 33 registered organizations, 2 honor societies. **Athletics (Intercollegiate):** *Men:* Baseball, basketball, football, soccer. *Women:* Basketball, soccer, softball, volleyball.

ADMISSIONS

Freshman Academic Profile: 22% in top 10% of high school class, 44% in top 25% of high school class, 76% in top 50% of high school class. 56% from public high schools. SAT Math middle 50% range 460–590. SAT Critical Reading middle 50% range 480–630. ACT middle 50% range 20–25. TOEFL required of all international applicants, minimum paper TOEFL 530, minimum computer TOEFL 197. **Basis for Candidate Selection:** *Very important factors considered include:* Academic GPA, rigor of secondary school record, standardized test scores. *Important factors considered include:* Application essay, character/personal qualities, recommendation(s), religious affiliation/commitment. *Other factors considered include:* Class rank, extracurricular activities, level of applicant's interest, talent/ability, volunteer work. **Freshman Admission Requirements:** High school diploma is required, and GED is accepted. *Academic units required:* 3 English, 2 math, 2 science (1 science lab), 2 foreign language, 2 social studies, 3 academic electives. **Freshman Admission Statistics:** 466 applied, 80% admitted, 44% enrolled. **Transfer Admission Requirements:** High school transcript, college transcript(s), essay or personal statement. Minimum college GPA of 2.0 required. Lowest grade transferable C-. **General Admission Information:** Application fee $25. Regular notification is rolling. Non-fall registration accepted. Admission may be deferred for a maximum of 2 years. Credit and/or placement offered for CEEB Advanced Placement tests.

COSTS AND FINANCIAL AID

Annual tuition $21,600. Room and board $7,270. Required fees $390. Average book expense $1,080. **Required Forms and Deadlines:** FAFSA. Financial aid filing deadline 4/1. **Notification of Awards:** Applicants will be notified of awards on a rolling basis beginning on or about 2/15. **Types of Aid:** *Need-based scholarships/grants:* Pell, SEOG, state scholarships/grants, private scholarships, the school's own gift aid. *Loans:* FFEL Subsidized Stafford, FFEL Unsubsidized Stafford, FFEL PLUS, Federal Perkins. **Student Employment:** Federal Work-Study Program available. Institutional employment available. Off-campus job opportunities are excellent. **Financial Aid Statistics:** 74% freshmen, 70% undergrads receive need-based scholarship or grant aid. 67% freshmen, 64% undergrads receive need-based self-help aid. 53 freshmen, 279 undergrads receive athletic scholarships. 79% freshmen, 76% undergrads receive any aid.

TRINITY LUTHERAN COLLEGE

4221 228th Avenue SE, Issaquah, WA 98029
Phone: 425-961-5510 **E-mail:** admission@tlc.edu
Fax: 425-392-0404 **Website:** www.tlc.edu
Financial Aid Phone: 425-961-5514

This private school was founded in 1944.

RATINGS

Admissions Selectivity Rating: 60*   **Fire Safety Rating:** 60*   **Green Rating:** 60*

STUDENTS AND FACULTY

Enrollment: 120. **Student Body:** 55% female, 45% male, 35% out-of-state, 7% international. Asian 3%, Caucasian 85%, Hispanic 2%. **Retention and Graduation:** 78% freshmen return for sophomore year. **Faculty:** 100% faculty teach undergrads.

ACADEMICS

Degrees: Associate, bachelor's, diploma, post-bachelor's certificate. **Academic Requirements:** Arts/fine arts, biblical studies, English (including composition), history, humanities, mathematics, philosophy, sciences (biological or physical), service learning (community service), social science. **Majors with Highest Enrollment:** Bible/biblical studies, music, youth ministry. **Special Study Options:** Double major, independent study, internships, study abroad.

FACILITIES

Housing: Coed dorms, men's dorms, women's dorms, special housing for disabled students, special housing for married students and nontraditional age students. **Computers:** Online administrative functions (other than registration), remote student-access to Web through college's connection.

CAMPUS LIFE

Activities: Choral groups, drama/theater, music ensembles, student government, yearbook. **Athletics (Intercollegiate):** *Men:* Basketball, softball. *Women:* Softball.

ADMISSIONS

Freshman Academic Profile: 33% in top 25% of high school class, 60% in top 50% of high school class. TOEFL required of all international applicants, minimum paper TOEFL 525, minimum computer TOEFL 197. **Basis for Candidate Selection:** *Very important factors considered include:* Character/personal qualities, recommendation(s). *Important factors considered include:* Religious affiliation/commitment, rigor of secondary school record, standardized test scores, volunteer work. *Other factors considered include:* Extracurricular activities, talent/ability, work experience. **Freshman Admission Requirements:** High school diploma is required, and GED is accepted. **Freshman Admission Statistics:** 113 applied, 59% admitted, 30% enrolled. **Transfer Admission Requirements:** College transcript(s). Lowest grade transferable C-. **General Admission Information:** Application fee $30. Regular application deadline 8/15. Regular notification within 1 month of receiving all application materials. Non-fall registration accepted. Admission may be deferred for a maximum of 4 semesters. Common Application not accepted. Credit and/or placement offered for CEEB Advanced Placement tests.

COSTS AND FINANCIAL AID

Annual tuition $13,714. Room and board $6,078. Required fees $450. Average book expense $500. **Required Forms and Deadlines:** FAFSA, institution's own financial aid form. **Notification of Awards:** Applicants will be notified of awards on a rolling basis beginning on or about 1/1. **Types of Aid:** *Need-based scholarships/grants:* Pell, SEOG, private scholarships, the school's own gift aid. *Loans:* FFEL Subsidized Stafford, FFEL PLUS. **Student Employment:** Federal Work-Study Program available. Institutional employment available. Off-campus job opportunities are excellent.

TRINITY UNIVERSITY

One Trinity Place, San Antonio, TX 78212
Phone: 210-999-7207 **E-mail:** admissions@trinity.edu **CEEB Code:** 6831
Fax: 210-999-8164 **Website:** www.trinity.edu **ACT Code:** 4226
Financial Aid Phone: 210-999-8315

This private school was founded in 1869. It has a 117-acre campus.

RATINGS

Admissions Selectivity Rating: 93   **Fire Safety Rating:** 60*   **Green Rating:** 77

STUDENTS AND FACULTY

Enrollment: 2,449. **Student Body:** 54% female, 46% male, 34% out-of-state, 4% international (30 countries represented). African American 3%, Asian 7%, Caucasian 62%, Hispanic 11%, Native American 1%. **Retention and Graduation:** 87% freshmen return for sophomore year. 67% freshmen graduate within 4 years. 52% grads go on to further study within 1 year. 11% grads pursue law degrees. 6% grads pursue medical degrees. **Faculty:** Student/faculty ratio 10:1. 222 full-time faculty, 98% hold PhDs. 100% faculty teach undergrads.

ACADEMICS

Degrees: Bachelor's, master's. **Academic Requirements:** 37-40 hours in 5 areas of understanding, arts/fine arts, computer literacy, English (including composition), foreign languages, humanities, sciences (biological or physical), social science. **Classes:** Most classes have 10–19 students. Most lab/discussion sections have 10–19 students. **Majors with Highest Enrollment:** Business administration/management, communications and media studies, foreign languages/modern languages. **Disciplines with Highest Percentage of Degrees Awarded:** Business/marketing 22%, social sciences 17%, foreign languages and literature 10%, English 8%, communications/journalism 6%. **Special Study Options:** Accelerated program, double major, honors program, independent study, internships, liberal arts/career combination, student-designed major, study abroad, teacher certification program.

FACILITIES

Housing: Coed dorms. **Special Academic Facilities/Equipment:** Steiren Theatre, Richardson Communication Center, Ruth Taylor Arts Complex, Laurie Auditorium. **Computers:** 100% of public computers are PCs, network access in dorm rooms, network access in dorm lounges, online registration, online administrative functions (other than registration), remote student-access to Web through college's connection.

CAMPUS LIFE

Activities: Choral groups, concert band, dance, drama/theater, jazz band, literary magazine, music ensembles, musical theater, opera, pep band, radio station, student government, student newspaper, student-run film society, symphony orchestra, television station, yearbook. **Organizations:** 130 registered organizations, 24 honor societies, 11 religious organization. 8 fraternities (24% men join), 6 sororities (29% women join). **Athletics (Intercollegiate):** *Men:* Baseball, basketball, cross-country, diving, football, golf, soccer, swimming, tennis, track/field (outdoor). *Women:* Basketball, cross-country, diving, golf, soccer, softball, swimming, tennis, track/field (outdoor), volleyball.

ADMISSIONS

Freshman Academic Profile: 46% in top 10% of high school class, 79% in top 25% of high school class, 97% in top 50% of high school class. 65% from public high schools. SAT Math middle 50% range 600–690. SAT Critical Reading middle 50% range 610–690. ACT middle 50% range 27–30. TOEFL required of all international applicants, minimum paper TOEFL 600, minimum computer TOEFL 250. **Basis for Candidate Selection:** *Very important factors considered include:* Academic GPA, character/personal qualities, class rank, rigor of secondary school record, standardized test scores. *Important factors considered include:* Application essay, extracurricular activities, recommendation(s), talent/ability. *Other factors considered include:* Alumni/ae relation, first generation, geographical residence, interview, level of applicant's interest, state residency, volunteer work, work experience. **Freshman Admission Requirements:** High school diploma is required, and GED is accepted. *Academic units required:* 4 English, 3 math, 3 science (2 science labs), 2 foreign language, 3 social studies. *Academic units recommended:* 4 English, 3 math, 3 science (2 science labs), 3 foreign language, 3 social studies, 3 academic electives. **Freshman Admission Statistics:** 3,899 applied, 61% admitted, 28% enrolled. **Transfer Admission Requirements:** High school transcript, college transcript(s), essay or personal statement, standardized test score, statement of good standing from prior institution(s). Minimum college GPA of 3.0 required. Lowest grade transferable C-. **General Admission Information:** Application fee $50. Early decision application deadline 11/1. Regular application deadline 2/1. Regular notification 4/1. Non-fall registration accepted. Admission may be deferred for a maxiumum of 2 semesters. Credit and/or placement offered for CEEB Advanced Placement tests.

COSTS AND FINANCIAL AID

Annual tuition $26,664. Room and board $8,822. Required fees $1,035. Average book expense $950. **Required Forms and Deadlines:** FAFSA. Financial aid filing deadline 5/1. **Notification of Awards:** Applicants will be notified of awards on or about 4/1. **Types of Aid:** *Need-based scholarships/grants:* Pell, SEOG, state scholarships/grants, private scholarships, the school's own gift aid. *Loans:* FFEL Subsidized Stafford, FFEL Unsubsidized Stafford, FFEL PLUS, Federal Perkins, state loans, college/university loans from institutional funds. **Student Employment:** Federal Work-Study Program available. Institutional employment available. Off-campus job opportunities are good. **Financial Aid Statistics:** 43% freshmen, 38% undergrads receive need-based scholarship or grant aid. 34% freshmen, 34% undergrads receive need-based self-help aid. 85% freshmen, 74% undergrads receive any aid.

TRINITY WASHINGTON UNIVERSITY (WASHINGTON, DC)

125 Michigan Avenue, NE, Washington, DC 20017
Phone: 202-884-9400 **E-mail:** admissions@trinitydc.edu **CEEB Code:** 5796
Fax: 202-884-9403 **Website:** www.trinitydc.edu **ACT Code:** 0696
Financial Aid Phone: 202-884-9530

This private school was founded in 1897. It has a 26-acre campus.

RATINGS
Admissions Selectivity Rating: 60*   **Fire Safety Rating:** 60*   **Green Rating:** 60*

STUDENTS AND FACULTY
Enrollment: 962. **Student Body:** 98% female, 2% male, 48% out-of-state, 1% international (42 countries represented). African American 68%, Asian 2%, Caucasian 7%, Hispanic 11%. **Retention and Graduation:** 66% freshmen return for sophomore year. 29% freshmen graduate within 4 years. **Faculty:** Student/faculty ratio 11:1. 61 full-time faculty, 100% hold PhDs. 70% faculty teach undergrads.

ACADEMICS
Degrees: Bachelor's, master's, post-bachelor's certificate. **Academic Requirements:** Arts/fine arts, English (including composition), foreign languages, history, humanities, mathematics, philosophy, sciences (biological or physical), social science. **Classes:** Most classes have 10–19 students. **Majors with Highest Enrollment:** Business administration and management, communications studies/speech communication and rhetoric, social psychology. **Disciplines with Highest Percentage of Degrees Awarded:** Psychology 40%, business/marketing 24%, social sciences 12%, communication technologies 10%, education 5%. **Special Study Options:** Accelerated program, cross registration, distance learning, double major, dual enrollment, honors program, independent study, internships, student-designed major, study abroad, teacher certification program, weekend college.

FACILITIES
Housing: Women's dorms. **Special Academic Facilities/Equipment:** Art gallery, media technology center, writing center, Marilley Computer Classroom. **Computers:** 65% of public computers are PCs, 35% of public computers are Macs, network access in dorm rooms, online registration, remote student-access to Web through college's connection.

CAMPUS LIFE
Activities: Choral groups, dance, drama/theater, literary magazine, student government, student newspaper, student-run film society, yearbook. **Organizations:** 34 registered organizations, 5 honor societies, 2 religious organizations. **Athletics (Intercollegiate):** *Women:* Basketball, field hockey, lacrosse, soccer, softball, swimming, tennis, volleyball.

ADMISSIONS
Freshman Academic Profile: SAT Math middle 50% range 330–480. SAT Critical Reading middle 50% range 360–482. ACT middle 50% range 13–18. TOEFL required of all international applicants, minimum paper TOEFL 550, minimum computer TOEFL 213. **Basis for Candidate Selection:** *Very important factors considered include:* Character/personal qualities, rigor of secondary school record. *Important factors considered include:* Alumni/ae relation, application essay, extracurricular activities, recommendation(s), talent/ability, volunteer work. *Other factors considered include:* Class rank, geographical residence, interview, standardized test scores, work experience. **Freshman Admission Requirements:** High school diploma is required, and GED is accepted. *Academic units required:* 4 English, 3 math, 2 science (1 science lab), 2 foreign language, 3 social studies, 2 history. **Freshman Admission Statistics:** 441 applied, 86% admitted, 39% enrolled. **Transfer Admission Requirements:** College transcript(s), essay or personal statement. Minimum college GPA of 2.5 required. Lowest grade transferable C. **General Admission Information:** Application fee $40. Regular notification within 2 weeks. Non-fall registration accepted. Admission may be deferred for a maxiumum of 2 semesters. Common Application accepted. Credit and/or placement offered for CEEB Advanced Placement tests.

COSTS AND FINANCIAL AID
Annual tuition $17,200. Room & board $7,574. Required fees $160. Average book expense $1,000. **Required Forms and Deadlines:** FAFSA. Financial aid filing deadline 3/1. **Notification of Awards:** Applicants will be notified of awards on a rolling basis beginning on or about 2/1. **Types of Aid:** *Need-based scholarships/grants:* Pell, SEOG, state scholarships/grants, private scholarships, the school's own gift aid. *Loans:* FFEL Subsidized Stafford, FFEL Unsubsidized Stafford, FFEL PLUS, Federal Perkins. **Student Employment:**

Federal Work-Study Program available. Institutional employment available. Off-campus job opportunities are excellent. **Financial Aid Statistics:** 93% freshmen, 86% undergrads receive need-based scholarship or grant aid. 75% freshmen, 74% undergrads receive need-based self-help aid. 97% freshmen, 94% undergrads receive any aid. Highest amount earned per year from on-campus jobs $2,000.

TRINITY WESTERN UNIVERSITY

PO Box 1409, Blaine, WA 98231
Phone: 604-513-2019 **E-mail:** admissions@twu.ca **CEEB Code:** 0876
Fax: 604-513-2064 **Website:** www.twu.ca **ACT Code:** 5242
Financial Aid Phone: 604-513-2061

This private school, affiliated with the Evangelical Free Church of Canada, was founded in 1962. It has a 100-acre campus.

RATINGS
Admissions Selectivity Rating: 60*   **Fire Safety Rating:** 60*   **Green Rating:** 60*

STUDENTS AND FACULTY
Enrollment: 1,968. **Student Body:** 57% female, 43% male. **Retention and Graduation:** 80% freshmen return for sophomore year. 15% grads go on to further study within 1 year. 3% grads pursue law degrees. 3% grads pursue medical degrees. **Faculty:** Student/faculty ratio 18:1. 77 full-time faculty, 90% hold PhDs. 100% faculty teach undergrads.

ACADEMICS
Degrees: Bachelor's, certificate, diploma, doctoral, first professional, master's. **Academic Requirements:** Arts/fine arts, English (including composition), history, interdisciplinary studies, philosophy, physical education, religious studies, sciences (biological or physical), social science. **Disciplines with Highest Percentage of Degrees Awarded:** Liberal arts/general studies 18%, psychology 10%, biological/life sciences 8%, business/marketing 8%, education 8%, communication technologies 6%, health professions and related sciences 6%, social sciences 6%, English 4%, visual and performing arts 4%. **Special Study Options:** Cooperative education program, double major, English as a second language (ESL), honors program, internships, study abroad.

FACILITIES
Housing: Men's dorms, women's dorms, apartments for single students, special housing for disabled students, special housing for international students. **Special Academic Facilities/Equipment:** Museum of Biblical History. **Computers:** 75% of public computers are PCs, 25% of public computers are Macs, network access in dorm rooms, network access in dorm lounges, online administrative functions (other than registration), remote student-access to Web through college's connection.

CAMPUS LIFE
Activities: Choral groups, concert band, dance, drama/theater, jazz band, music ensembles, pep band, student government, student newspaper, yearbook. **Organizations:** 33 registered organizations. **Athletics (Intercollegiate):** *Men:* Basketball, cross-country, ice hockey, rugby, soccer, track/field (outdoor), volleyball. *Women:* Basketball, cross-country, rugby, soccer, track/field (outdoor), volleyball.

ADMISSIONS
Freshman Academic Profile: 80% from public high schools. TOEFL required of all international applicants, minimum paper TOEFL 570. **Basis for Candidate Selection:** *Very important factors considered include:* Recommendation(s), rigor of secondary school record, standardized test scores. *Important factors considered include:* Application essay. *Other factors considered include:* Character/personal qualities, class rank, extracurricular activities, religious affiliation/commitment, talent/ability. **Freshman Admission Requirements:** High school diploma is required, and GED is accepted. *Academic units required:* 4 English, 3 math, 2 science (1 science lab), 2 social studies, 2 academic electives. **Freshman Admission Statistics:** 1,371 applied, 78% admitted, 39% enrolled. **Transfer Admission Requirements:** High school transcript, college transcript(s), essay or personal statement. Minimum college GPA of 2.0 required. Lowest grade transferable D. **General Admission Information:** Application fee $35. Regular application deadline 6/15. Regular notification is rolling. Non-fall registration accepted. Admission may be deferred for a maximum of 3 semesters. Common Application accepted. Credit and/or placement offered for CEEB Advanced Placement tests.

COSTS AND FINANCIAL AID
Annual tuition $10,350. Room & board $5,990. Required fees $120. Average book expense $800. **Required Forms and Deadlines:** Institution's own

financial aid form. Financial aid filing deadline 3/15. **Notification of Awards:** Applicants will be notified of awards on a rolling basis beginning on or about 4/1. **Types of Aid:** *Need-based scholarships/grants:* State scholarships/grants, private scholarships, the school's own gift aid. *Loans:* Direct Subsidized Stafford, Direct Unsubsidized Stafford, Direct PLUS. **Student Employment:** Institutional employment available. Off-campus job opportunities are good. **Financial Aid Statistics:** 1% freshmen, 10% undergrads receive need-based scholarship or grant aid. 19% freshmen, 20% undergrads receive need-based self-help aid. Highest amount earned per year from on-campus jobs $1,000.

TRI-STATE UNIVERSITY

1 University Avenue, Angola, IN 46703
Phone: 260-665-4100 **E-mail:** admit@tristate.edu **CEEB Code:** 1811
Fax: 260-665-4578 **Website:** www.tristate.edu **ACT Code:** 1250
Financial Aid Phone: 260-664-4158

This private school was founded in 1884. It has a 400-acre campus.

RATINGS
Admissions Selectivity Rating: 79   **Fire Safety Rating:** 89   **Green Rating:** 68

STUDENTS AND FACULTY
Enrollment: 1,146. **Student Body:** 31% female, 69% male, 40% out-of-state, 1% international (13 countries represented). African American 3%, Caucasian 80%, Hispanic 1%. **Retention and Graduation:** 62% freshmen return for sophomore year. 25% grads go on to further study within 1 year. 10% grads pursue arts and sciences degrees. 10% grads pursue business degrees. 5% grads pursue law degrees. **Faculty:** Student/faculty ratio 13:1. 69 full-time faculty, 65% hold PhDs. 100% faculty teach undergrads.

ACADEMICS
Degrees: Associate, bachelor's, master's. **Academic Requirements:** Computer literacy, English (including composition), humanities, mathematics, sciences (biological or physical), social science. **Classes:** Most classes have 10–19 students. Most lab/discussion sections have 10–19 students. **Majors with Highest Enrollment:** Civil engineering, criminal justice/safety studies, mechanical engineering. **Disciplines with Highest Percentage of Degrees Awarded:** Engineering 30%, business/marketing 21%, education 18%, security and protective services 9%, engineering technologies 6%. **Special Study Options:** Cooperative education program, distance learning, double major, dual enrollment, honors program, internships, liberal arts/career combination, study abroad, teacher certification program.

FACILITIES
Housing: Coed dorms, apartments for single students, honors housing. **Special Academic Facilities/Equipment:** Lewis Hershey Museum, Wells Gallery of Engravings, Zollner Golf Course. **Computers:** 1% of classrooms are wired, 100% of classrooms are wireless, 100% of public computers are PCs, network access in dorm rooms, network access in dorm lounges, online registration, online administrative functions (other than registration), support for handheld computing, remote student-access to Web through college's connection.

CAMPUS LIFE
Activities: Choral groups, dance, drama/theater, pep band, radio station, student government, student newspaper, yearbook. **Organizations:** 35 registered organizations, 13 honor societies, 3 religious organizations. 8 fraternities (25% men join), 5 sororities (15% women join). **Athletics (Intercollegiate):** *Men:* Baseball, basketball, cross-country, football, golf, lacrosse, soccer, tennis, track/field (indoor), track/field (outdoor), wrestling. *Women:* Basketball, cross-country, golf, lacrosse, soccer, softball, tennis, track/field (indoor), track/field (outdoor), volleyball.

ADMISSIONS
Freshman Academic Profile: 20% in top 10% of high school class, 46% in top 25% of high school class, 80% in top 50% of high school class. 80% from public high schools. SAT Math middle 50% range 490–610. SAT Critical Reading middle 50% range 440–540. ACT middle 50% range 21–26. TOEFL required of all international applicants, minimum paper TOEFL 550, minimum computer TOEFL 217. **Basis for Candidate Selection:** *Very important factors considered include:* Academic GPA, class rank, rigor of secondary school record, standardized test scores. *Important factors considered include:* Extracurricular activities, interview, recommendation(s). *Other factors considered include:* Alumni/ae relation, character/personal qualities, talent/ability, volunteer work, work experience. **Freshman Admission Requirements:** High school diploma is required, and GED is accepted. *Academic units required:* 4 English, 3 math, 3 science (2 science labs), 3 social studies, 2 history, 3 academic electives. **Freshman Admission Statistics:** 1,578 applied, 76%

admitted, 26% enrolled. **Transfer Admission Requirements:** High school transcript, college transcript(s), statement of good standing from prior institution(s). Minimum college GPA of 2.0 required. Lowest grade transferable C. **General Admission Information:** Regular application deadline 8/1. Regular notification Rolling basis. Non-fall registration accepted. Admission may be deferred for a maxiumum of 2 semesters. Credit and/or placement offered for CEEB Advanced Placement tests.

COSTS AND FINANCIAL AID
Annual tuition $23,350. Room and board $6,700. Average book expense $1,200. **Required Forms and Deadlines:** FAFSA. Financial aid filing deadline 3/10. **Notification of Awards:** Applicants will be notified of awards on a rolling basis beginning on or about 2/1. **Types of Aid:** *Need-based scholarships/grants:* Pell, SEOG, state scholarships/grants, private scholarships, the school's own gift aid. *Loans:* FFEL Subsidized Stafford, FFEL Unsubsidized Stafford, FFEL PLUS. **Student Employment:** Federal Work-Study Program available. Institutional employment available. Off-campus job opportunities are good. **Financial Aid Statistics:** 67% freshmen, 42% undergrads receive need-based scholarship or grant aid. 67% freshmen, 70% undergrads receive need-based self-help aid. 90% freshmen, 86% undergrads receive any aid. Highest amount earned per year from on-campus jobs $1,200.

See page 1410.

TROY UNIVERSITY

111 Adams Administration, Troy, AL 36082
Phone: 334-670-3179 **E-mail:** Admit@troy.edu **CEEB Code:** 1738
Fax: 334-670-3733 **Website:** www.troy.edu **ACT Code:** 0048
Financial Aid Phone: 334-670-3186

This public school was founded in 1887. It has a 512-acre campus.

RATINGS
Admissions Selectivity Rating: 81   **Fire Safety Rating:** 60*   **Green Rating:** 60*

STUDENTS AND FACULTY
Enrollment: 19,734. **Student Body:** 55% female, 45% male, 46% out-of-state, 2% international. African American 37%, Asian 1%, Caucasian 51%, Hispanic 4%. **Retention and Graduation:** 64% freshmen return for sophomore year. **Faculty:** 451 full-time faculty, 52% hold PhDs. 100% faculty teach undergrads.

ACADEMICS
Degrees: Associate, bachelor's, master's, post-master's certificate. **Academic Requirements:** Arts/fine arts, computer literacy, English (including composition), history, humanities, mathematics, sciences (biological or physical). **Classes:** Most classes have 10–19 students. Most lab/discussion sections have 20–29 students. **Majors with Highest Enrollment:** Business administration and management; criminal justice/safety studies; liberal arts and sciences, studies, and humanities. **Disciplines with Highest Percentage of Degrees Awarded:** Business/marketing 40%, security and protective services 12%, education 11%, psychology 8%, public administration and social services 3%, health professions and related sciences 3%. **Special Study Options:** Accelerated program, cross-registration, distance learning, double major, dual enrollment, English as a second language (ESL), external degree program, honor program, independent study, internships, study abroad, teacher certification program, weekend college.

FACILITIES
Housing: Coed dorms, men's dorms, women's dorms, apartments for married students, apartments for single students, special housing for international students, fraternity/sorority housing, substance-free housing, honor student housing. **Special Academic Facilities/Equipment:** Art museum, recording studio. **Computers:** 85% of public computers are PCs, 15% of public computers are Macs, network access in dorm rooms, online registration, remote student-access to Web through college's connection.

CAMPUS LIFE
Activities: Choral groups, concert band, dance, drama/theater, jazz band, marching band, music ensembles, musical theater, opera, pep band, radio station, student government, student newspaper, symphony orchestra, television station, yearbook. **Organizations:** 125 registered organizations, 22 honor societies, 7 religious organizations. 12 fraternities (15% men join), 9 sororities (16% women join). **Athletics (Intercollegiate):** *Men:* Baseball, basketball, cheerleading, cross-country, football, golf, rodeo, tennis, track/field (outdoor). *Women:* Basketball, cheerleading, cross-country, golf, rodeo, soccer, softball, tennis, track/field (outdoor), volleyball.

ADMISSIONS

Freshman Academic Profile: 45% in top 25% of high school class, 81% in top 50% of high school class. ACT middle 50% range 17–23. TOEFL required of all international applicants, minimum paper TOEFL 500, minimum computer TOEFL 173. **Basis for Candidate Selection:** *Very important factors considered include:* Academic GPA, rigor of secondary school record, standardized test scores. *Other factors considered include:* Alumni/ae relation, application essay, character/personal qualities, extracurricular activities, interview, recommendation(s), talent/ability. **Freshman Admission Requirements:** High school diploma is required, and GED is accepted. *Academic units required:* 4 English, 4 math, 4 science, 4 social studies. *Academic units recommended:* 2 foreign language. **Freshman Admission Statistics:** 4,902 applied, 74% admitted, 70% enrolled. **Transfer Admission Requirements:** College transcript(s). Minimum college GPA of 2.0 required. **General Admission Information:** Application fee $30. Regular notification rolling basis. Nonfall registration accepted. Admission may be deferred for a maximum of 2 years. Credit and/or placement offered for CEEB Advanced Placement tests.

COSTS AND FINANCIAL AID

Average book expense $890. **Required Forms and Deadlines:** FAFSA, institution's own financial aid form. Financial aid filing deadline 5/1. **Notification of Awards:** Applicants will be notified of awards on a rolling basis beginning on or about 5/1. **Types of Aid:** *Need-based scholarships/grants:* Pell, SEOG, state scholarships/grants, private scholarships, the school's own gift aid. *Loans:* FFEL Subsidized Stafford, FFEL Unsubsidized Stafford, FFEL PLUS, Federal Perkins. **Financial Aid Statistics:** 37% freshmen, 31% undergrads receive need-based scholarship or grant aid. 58% freshmen, 46% undergrads receive need-based self-help aid. 49 freshmen, 168 undergrads receive athletic scholarships. 53% freshmen, 42% undergrads receive any aid. Highest amount earned per year from on-campus jobs $1,652.

TROY UNIVERSITY—DOTHAN

PO Box 8368, Dothan, AL 36304-0368
Phone: 334-983-6556 **E-mail:** ariversjr@troyst.edu
Fax: 334-983-6322 **Website:** www.tsud.edu **ACT Code:** 0015

This public school was founded in 1864. It has a 265-acre campus.

RATINGS

Admissions Selectivity Rating: 70   **Fire Safety Rating:** 60*   **Green Rating:** 60*

STUDENTS AND FACULTY

Enrollment: 1,470. **Student Body:** 68% female, 32% male, 7% out-of-state. African American 22%, Asian 1%, Caucasian 71%, Hispanic 2%, Native American 1%. **Retention and Graduation:** 62% freshmen return for sophomore year. 20% freshmen graduate within 4 years. **Faculty:** Student/faculty ratio 15:1. 57 full-time faculty, 72% hold PhDs. 78% faculty teach undergrads.

ACADEMICS

Degrees: Associate, bachelor's, master's, post-master's certificate. **Academic Requirements:** Arts/fine arts, computer literacy, English (including composition), history, humanities, mathematics, sciences (biological or physical), social science. **Classes:** Most classes have 10–19 students. Most lab/discussion sections have 10–19 students. **Majors with Highest Enrollment:** Accounting, computer and information sciences, elementary education and teaching. **Disciplines with Highest Percentage of Degrees Awarded:** Business/marketing 36%, education 27%, computer and information sciences 9%, psychology 9%, social sciences 6%, biological/life sciences 2%, English 2%. **Special Study Options:** Distance learning, external degree program, independent study, internships, teacher certification program, weekend college.

FACILITIES

Computers: 90% of public computers are PCs, 10% of public computers are Macs, online registration, online administrative functions (other than registration), remote student-access to Web through college's connection.

CAMPUS LIFE

Activities: Literary magazine, student government. **Organizations:** 18 registered organizations, 6 honor societies, 1 religious organization.

ADMISSIONS

Freshman Academic Profile: 98% from public high schools. ACT middle 50% range 20–24. TOEFL required of all international applicants, minimum paper TOEFL 550, minimum computer TOEFL 213. **Basis for Candidate Selection:** *Very important factors considered include:* Rigor of secondary

school record, standardized test scores. *Important factors considered include:* Geographical residence, state residency. *Other factors considered include:* Character/personal qualities. **Freshman Admission Requirements:** High school diploma is required, and GED is accepted. *Academic units required:* 4 English, 4 math, 4 science, 4 social studies, 6 academic electives. **Freshman Admission Statistics:** 176 applied, 66% admitted, 70% enrolled. **Transfer Admission Requirements:** College transcript(s), statement of good standing from prior institution(s). Minimum college GPA of 2.0 required. Lowest grade transferable D. **General Admission Information:** Application fee $20. Regular notification varies depending on type of admission. Non-fall registration accepted. Admission may be deferred for a maxiumum of 2 semesters. Common Application not accepted.

COSTS AND FINANCIAL AID

Annual in-state tuition $3,850. Out-of-state tuition $7,700. Required fees $312. **Required Forms and Deadlines:** FAFSA, institution's own financial aid form. Financial aid filing deadline 3/1. **Notification of Awards:** Applicants will be notified of awards on a rolling basis beginning on or about 2/1. **Types of Aid:** *Need-based scholarships/grants:* Pell, SEOG, state scholarships/grants, private scholarships, the school's own gift aid. *Loans:* FFEL Subsidized Stafford, FFEL Unsubsidized Stafford, FFEL PLUS. **Student Employment:** Federal Work-Study Program available. Off-campus job opportunities are fair. **Financial Aid Statistics:** 34% freshmen, 41% undergrads receive need-based scholarship or grant aid. 56% freshmen, 63% undergrads receive need-based self-help aid.

TROY UNIVERSITY—MONTGOMERY

PO Drawer 4419, Montgomery, AL 36103-4419
Phone: 334-241-9506 **E-mail:** admit@tsum.edu
Fax: 334-241-5448 **Website:** www.tsum.edu
Financial Aid Phone: 334-241-9520

This public school was founded in 1965. It has a 6-acre campus.

RATINGS

Admissions Selectivity Rating: 60*   **Fire Safety Rating:** 60*   **Green Rating:** 60*

STUDENTS AND FACULTY

Enrollment: 2,893. **Student Body:** 67% female, 33% male. African American 52%, Asian 1%, Caucasian 43%, Hispanic 1%. **Faculty:** Student/faculty ratio 47:1. 36 full-time faculty, 78% hold PhDs. 100% faculty teach undergrads.

ACADEMICS

Degrees: Associate, bachelor's, master's, post-master's certificate. **Academic Requirements:** Arts/fine arts, computer literacy, English (including composition), history, humanities, mathematics, philosophy, sciences (biological or physical), social science. **Classes:** Most classes have 10–19 students. **Majors with Highest Enrollment:** Business administration/management, human resources management/personnel administration, liberal arts and sciences/liberal studies. **Disciplines with Highest Percentage of Degrees Awarded:** Business/marketing 59%, psychology 16%, social sciences 8%, computer and information sciences 7%, liberal arts/general studies 6%. **Special Study Options:** Accelerated program, cross registration, distance learning, double major, dual enrollment, exchange student program (domestic), external degree program, honors program, independent study, internships (graduate program only), teacher certification program (graduate program only), weekend college.

FACILITIES

Special Academic Facilities/Equipment: W. A. Gayle Planetarium, Davis Theater, Rosa L. Parks Library & Museum. **Computers:** 100% of public computers are PCs, online registration.

CAMPUS LIFE

Organizations: 7 registered organizations, 2 honor societies.

ADMISSIONS

Basis for Candidate Selection: *Very important factors considered include:* Rigor of secondary school record. *Other factors considered include:* Standardized test scores. **Freshman Admission Requirements:** High school diploma is required, and GED is accepted. *Academic units required:* 3 English. *Academic units recommended:* 4 English. **Freshman Admission Statistics:** 553 applied, 99% admitted, 48% enrolled. **Transfer Admission Requirements:** College transcript(s), statement of good standing from prior institution(s). Lowest grade transferable D. **General Admission Information:** Application fee $20. Non-fall registration accepted. Admission may be deferred for a maximum of 2 semesters. Common Application not accepted.

COSTS AND FINANCIAL AID

Required Forms and Deadlines: FAFSA, institution's own financial aid form. Financial aid filing deadline 5/1. *Types of Aid: Need-based scholarships/grants:* Pell, SEOG, state scholarships/grants, private scholarships. *Loans:* FFEL Subsidized Stafford, FFEL Unsubsidized Stafford, FFEL PLUS. **Student Employment:** Federal Work-Study Program available. Off-campus job opportunities are good. **Financial Aid Statistics:** 44% freshmen, 42% undergrads receive need-based scholarship or grant aid. 38% freshmen, 44% undergrads receive need-based self-help aid.

TRUMAN STATE UNIVERSITY

McClain Hall 205, 100 East Normal Street, Kirksville, MO 63501
Phone: 660-785-4114 **E-mail:** admissions@truman.edu **CEEB Code:** 6483
Fax: 660-785-7456 **Website:** admissions.truman.edu **ACT Code:** 2336 | **Financial Aid Phone:** 660-785-4310

This public school was founded in 1867. It has a 140-acre campus.

RATINGS

Admissions Selectivity Rating: 89　　**Fire Safety Rating:** 77　　**Green Rating:** 79

STUDENTS AND FACULTY

Enrollment: 5,410. **Student Body:** 58% female, 42% male, 22% out-of-state, 3% international (42 countries represented). African American 4%, Asian 2%, Caucasian 85%, Hispanic 2%. **Retention and Graduation:** 85% freshmen return for sophomore year. 38% freshmen graduate within 4 years. 54% grads go on to further study within 1 year. **Faculty:** Student/faculty ratio 16:1. 338 full-time faculty, 85% hold PhDs. 99% faculty teach undergrads.

ACADEMICS

Degrees: Bachelor's, master's. **Academic Requirements:** Arts/fine arts, computer literacy, English (including composition), foreign languages, history, humanities, mathematics, philosophy, sciences (biological or physical), social science. **Classes:** Most classes have 20–29 students. Most lab/discussion sections have fewer than 10 students. **Majors with Highest Enrollment:** Biology/biological sciences, business administration and management, psychology. **Disciplines with Highest Percentage of Degrees Awarded:** Business/marketing 14%, health professions and related sciences 14%, English 10%, biological/life sciences 9%, psychology 9%, social sciences 9%. **Special Study Options:** Double major, dual enrollment, honors program, internships, student-designed major, study abroad, teacher certification program.

FACILITIES

Housing: Coed dorms, women's dorms, apartments for married students, apartments for single students, special housing for disabled students, special housing for international students, sorority housing. **Special Academic Facilities/Equipment:** Art gallery, local history and artifacts museum, human performance lab, greenhouse, observatory, IR and NMR instrumentation. **Computers:** 100% of classrooms are wireless, 88% of public computers are PCs, 12% of public computers are Macs, network access in dorm rooms, network access in dorm lounges, online registration, online administrative functions (other than registration), support for handheld computing, remote student-access to Web through college's connection.

CAMPUS LIFE

Activities: Choral groups, concert band, dance, drama/theater, jazz band, literary magazine, marching band, music ensembles, musical theater, pep band, radio station, student government, student newspaper, symphony orchestra, television station, yearbook. **Organizations:** 230 registered organizations, 19 honor societies, 15 religious organizations. 18 fraternities (31% men join), 11 sororities (22% women join). **Athletics (Intercollegiate):** *Men:* Baseball, basketball, cheerleading, cross-country, football, golf, soccer, swimming, tennis, track/field (indoor), track/field (outdoor), wrestling. *Women:* Basketball, cheerleading, cross-country, golf, soccer, softball, swimming, tennis, track/field (indoor), track/field (outdoor), volleyball. **Environmental Initiatives:** Extensive recycling operation.

ADMISSIONS

Freshman Academic Profile: 51% in top 10% of high school class, 83% in top 25% of high school class, 98% in top 50% of high school class. 80% from public high schools. SAT Math middle 50% range 560–670. SAT Critical Reading middle 50% range 570–690. ACT middle 50% range 25–30. TOEFL required of all international applicants, minimum paper TOEFL 550, minimum computer TOEFL 213. **Basis for Candidate Selection:** *Very important factors considered include:* Academic GPA, class rank, rigor of secondary school record, standardized test scores. *Important factors considered include:* Application essay. *Other factors considered include:* Alumni/ae relation, character/personal qualities, extracurricular activities, first generation, geographical residence, level of applicant's interest, racial/ethnic status, state residency, talent/ability, volunteer work, work experience. **Freshman Admission Requirements:** High school diploma is required, and GED is accepted. *Academic units required:* 4 English, 3 math, 3 science (2 science labs), 2 foreign language, 3 social studies, 1 fine art. *Academic units recommended:* 4 math, 1 fine art. **Freshman Admission Statistics:** 4,337 applied, 81% admitted, 39% enrolled. **Transfer Admission Requirements:** High school transcript, college transcript(s), essay or personal statement, standardized test score. Lowest grade transferable D. **General Admission Information:** Regular application deadline 3/1. Regular notification is rolling. Non-fall registration accepted. Admission may be deferred for a maxiumum of 2 semesters. Credit and/or placement offered for CEEB Advanced Placement tests.

COSTS AND FINANCIAL AID

Annual in-state tuition $5,970. Out-of-state tuition $10,400. Room & board $5,570. Required fees $122. Average book expense $1,000. **Required Forms and Deadlines:** FAFSA, institution's own financial aid form. Financial aid filing deadline 4/1. **Notification of Awards:** Applicants will be notified of awards on a rolling basis beginning on or about 4/1. *Types of Aid: Need-based scholarships/grants:* Pell, SEOG, state scholarships/grants, private scholarships, the school's own gift aid. *Loans:* FFEL Subsidized Stafford, FFEL Unsubsidized Stafford, FFEL PLUS, Federal Perkins, Federal Nursing, state loans, college/university loans from institutional funds, alternative loans. **Student Employment:** Federal Work-Study Program available. Institutional employment available. Off-campus job opportunities are good. **Financial Aid Statistics:** 19% freshmen, 17% undergrads receive need-based scholarship or grant aid. 33% freshmen, 36% undergrads receive need-based self-help aid. 83 freshmen, 306 undergrads receive athletic scholarships. 98% freshmen, 97% undergrads receive any aid. Highest amount earned per year from on-campus jobs $5,399..

See page 1412.

TUFTS UNIVERSITY

Bendetson Hall, Medford, MA 02155
Phone: 617-627-3170 **E-mail:** admissions.inquiry@ase.tufts.edu **CEEB Code:** 3901
Fax: 617-627-3860 **Website:** www.tufts.edu **ACT Code:** 1922
Financial Aid Phone: 617-627-2000

This private school was founded in 1852. It has a 150-acre campus.

RATINGS

Admissions Selectivity Rating: 97　　**Fire Safety Rating:** 96　　**Green Rating:** 94

STUDENTS AND FACULTY

Enrollment: 4,982. **Student Body:** 51% female, 49% male, 75% out-of-state, 6% international (67 countries represented). African American 6%, Asian 13%, Caucasian 58%, Hispanic 6%. **Retention and Graduation:** 95% freshmen return for sophomore year. 87% freshmen graduate within 4 years. 35% grads go on to further study within 1 year. **Faculty:** Student/faculty ratio 7:1. 676 full-time faculty. 100% faculty teach undergrads.

ACADEMICS

Degrees: Bachelor's, doctoral, first professional certificate, first professional, master's, post-bachelor's certificate, post-master's certificate. **Academic Requirements:** Arts/fine arts, English (including composition), foreign languages, humanities, mathematics, sciences (biological or physical), social science. Foundation and distribution requirements for liberal arts. **Classes:** Most classes have 10–19 students. Most lab/discussion sections have 10–19 students. **Majors with Highest Enrollment:** Economics, English language and literature, international relations and affairs. **Disciplines with Highest**

Percentage of Degrees Awarded: Social sciences 33%, engineering 14%, psychology 9%, visual and performing arts 9%, English 7%, biological/life sciences 6%. **Special Study Options:** Cross registration, double major, exchange student program (domestic), honors program, independent study, internships, liberal arts/career combination, student-designed major, study abroad, teacher certification program.

FACILITIES

Housing: Coed dorms, women's dorms, special housing for disabled students, fraternity/sorority housing, cooperative housing, special interest housing. **Special Academic Facilities/Equipment:** Language lab, nutrition institute, research lab for physical electronics, bioelectrical and biochemical labs, computer-aided design (CAD) facility, electro-optics technology and environmental management centers. **Computers:** Network access in dorm rooms, online registration, online administrative functions (other than registration), remote student-access to Web through college's connection.

CAMPUS LIFE

Activities: Choral groups, concert band, dance, drama/theater, jazz band, literary magazine, marching band, music ensembles, musical theater, opera, pep band, radio station, student government, student newspaper, student-run film society, symphony orchestra, television station. **Organizations:** 160 registered organizations, 4 honor societies, 6 religious organizations. 11 fraternities (15% men join), 3 sororities (4% women join). **Athletics (Intercollegiate):** *Men:* Baseball, basketball, crew/rowing, cross-country, diving, football, golf, ice hockey, lacrosse, sailing, soccer, squash, swimming, tennis, track/field (indoor), track/field (outdoor). *Women:* Basketball, cheerleading, crew/rowing, cross-country, diving, fencing, field hockey, golf, lacrosse, sailing, soccer, softball, squash, swimming, tennis, track/field (indoor), track/field (outdoor), volleyball. **Environmental Initiatives:** Reduced green house gas emissions to below 1998 levels. LEED Silver building and comprehensive energy efficiency efforts. Comprehensive recycling and green purchasing and green dining initiatives.

ADMISSIONS

Freshman Academic Profile: 83% in top 10% of high school class, 95% in top 25% of high school class, 99% in top 50% of high school class. 60% from public high schools. SAT Math middle 50% range 670–740. SAT Critical Reading middle 50% range 670–750. SAT Writing middle 50% range 670–740. ACT middle 50% range 30–32. TOEFL required of all international applicants, minimum paper TOEFL 300, minimum computer TOEFL 100. **Basis for Candidate Selection:** *Very important factors considered include:* Rigor of secondary school record. *Important factors considered include:* Academic GPA, application essay, character/personal qualities, class rank, extracurricular activities, recommendation(s), standardized test scores, talent/ability, volunteer work, work experience. *Other factors considered include:* Alumni/ae relation, first generation, geographical residence, interview, racial/ethnic status. **Freshman Admission Requirements:** High school diploma is required, and GED is accepted. *Academic units recommended:* 4 English, 3 math, 2 science, 3 foreign language, 2 history. **Freshman Admission Statistics:** 15,295 applied, 27% admitted, 31% enrolled. **Transfer Admission Requirements:** High school transcript, college transcript(s), essay or personal statement, standardized test score, statement of good standing from prior institution(s). Lowest grade transferable C. **General Admission Information:** Application fee $70. Early decision application deadline 11/1. Regular application deadline 1/1. Regular notification 4/1. Non-fall registration not accepted. Admission may be deferred for a maximum of 2 semesters. Credit and/or placement offered for CEEB Advanced Placement tests.

COSTS AND FINANCIAL AID

Annual tuition $33,906. Room & board $9,770. Required fees $824. Average book expense $800. **Required Forms and Deadlines:** FAFSA, CSS/Financial Aid Profile, Noncustodial PROFILE, Business/Farm Supplement, parent and student federal income tax returns. Financial aid filing deadline 2/15. **Notification of Awards:** Applicants will be notified of awards on or about 4/1. **Types of Aid:** *Need-based scholarships/grants:* Pell, SEOG, state scholarships/grants, private scholarships, the school's own gift aid. *Loans:* FFEL Subsidized Stafford, FFEL Unsubsidized Stafford, FFEL PLUS, Federal Perkins, state loans, college/university loans from institutional funds. **Student Employment:** Federal Work-Study Program available. Institutional employment available. Off-campus job opportunities are good. **Financial Aid Statistics:** 34% freshmen, 35% undergrads receive need-based scholarship or grant aid. 34% freshmen, 35% undergrads receive need-based self-help aid. 38% freshmen, 38% undergrads receive any aid.

TULANE UNIVERSITY

Best 368

6823 St. Charles Avenue, New Orleans, LA 70118
Phone: 504-865-5731 **E-mail:** undergrad.admission@tulane.edu **CEEB Code:** 6832
Fax: 504-862-8715 **Website:** www.tulane.edu **ACT Code:** 1614
Financial Aid Phone: 504-865-5723

This private school was founded in 1834. It has a 110-acre campus.

RATINGS

Admissions Selectivity Rating: 94   **Fire Safety Rating:** 60*   **Green Rating:** 83

STUDENTS AND FACULTY

Enrollment: 6,533. **Student Body:** 52% female, 48% male. **Retention and Graduation:** 60% freshmen graduate within 4 years. **Faculty:** Student/faculty ratio 10:1. 880 full-time faculty, 92% hold PhDs.

ACADEMICS

Degrees: Associate, bachelor's, doctoral, first professional, master's, post-bachelor's certificate. **Academic Requirements:** Arts/fine arts, English (including composition), foreign languages, freshman interdisciplinary seminars, intensive writing, humanities, mathematics, public service, sciences (biological or physical), social science. **Classes:** Most classes have 10–19 students. Most lab/discussion sections have 10–19 students. **Majors with Highest Enrollment:** Business/commerce, engineering, social sciences. **Disciplines with Highest Percentage of Degrees Awarded:** Business/marketing 17%, engineering 7%, psychology 7%, biological/life sciences 5%, foreign languages and literature 5%, natural resources/environmental science 5%, history 5%, communications/journalism 5%. **Special Study Options:** Cross-registration, distance learning, double major, honor program, independent study, internships, student-designed major, study abroad, teacher certification program.

FACILITIES

Housing: Coed dorms, women's dorms, apartments for married students, apartments for single students, special housing for disabled students, special housing for international students. **Special Academic Facilities/Equipment:** Newcomb Art Gallery, Amistad Research Center, Latin American Library, Maxwell Music Library, Hogan Jazz Archives, Louisiana Special Collection, Middle American Research Institute, Manuscripts Department, Koch Herbarium, Tulane Museum of Natural History. **Computers:** 100% of classrooms are wireless, network access in dorm rooms, network access in dorm lounges, online registration, online administrative functions (other than registration), remote student-access to Web through college's connection.

CAMPUS LIFE

Activities: Choral groups, concert band, dance, drama/theater, jazz band, literary magazine, marching band, music ensembles, musical theater, pep band, radio station, student government, student newspaper, student-run film society, symphony orchestra, yearbook. **Organizations:** 250 registered organizations, 43 honor societies, 11 religious organization. 14 fraternities (26% men join), 9 sororities (32% women join). **Athletics (Intercollegiate):** *Men:* Baseball, basketball, football. *Women:* Basketball, cross-country, soccer, track/field (indoor), track/field (outdoor), volleyball. **Environmental Initiatives:** Almost every school within the university offers undergraduates or graduates an environmental major or focus. In addition, the Ecology and Evolutionary Biology and Earth and Environmental Sciences departments have strong programs that address coastal sustainability and global environmental change. Tulane has a number of green building projects on campus, and since Hurricane Katrina many Tulane students, staff and faculty have been engaged in sustainable building, design, and neighborhood planning projects in the larger community.

ADMISSIONS

Freshman Academic Profile: 51% in top 10% of high school class, 74% in top 25% of high school class, 96% in top 50% of high school class. SAT Math middle 50% range 590–680. SAT Critical Reading middle 50% range 600–690. SAT Writing middle 50% range 600–690. ACT middle 50% range 27–31. TOEFL required of all international applicants, minimum paper TOEFL 550, minimum computer TOEFL 213. **Basis for Candidate Selection:** *Very important factors considered include:* Academic GPA, class rank, rigor of secondary school record, standardized test scores. *Important factors considered include:* Application essay, character/personal qualities, recommendation(s). *Other factors considered include:* Alumni/ae relation, extracurricular activities, first generation, interview, talent/ability, volunteer work, work experience. **Freshman Admission Requirements:** High school diploma is required, and GED is accepted. *Academic units recommended:* 4 English, 4 math, 4 science (3 science labs), 3 foreign language, 3 social studies, 3 academic electives. **Freshman Admission Statistics:** 20,756 applied, 38% admitted, 11% enrolled. **Transfer Admission Requirements:** High school transcript, college transcript(s), statement of good standing from prior institution(s). Lowest grade transferable C-. **General Admission Information:** Application fee $55. Early Decision application deadline 11/1. Regular application deadline 1/15. Regular notification 4/1. Nonfall registration accepted. Admission may be deferred for a maximum of 1 year. Credit and/or placement offered for CEEB Advanced Placement tests.

COSTS AND FINANCIAL AID

Annual tuition $28,900. Room & board $7,925. Required fees $2,310. Average book expense $800. **Required Forms and Deadlines:** FAFSA, CSS/Financial Aid PROFILE, Noncustodial PROFILE, Business/Farm Supplement. Financial aid filing deadline 2/1. **Notification of Awards:** Applicants will be notified of awards on a rolling basis beginning on or about 2/1. **Types of Aid:** *Need-based scholarships/grants:* Pell, SEOG, state scholarships/grants, private scholarships, the school's own gift aid. *Loans:* FFEL Subsidized Stafford, FFEL Unsubsidized Stafford, FFEL PLUS, Federal Perkins. **Student Employment:** Federal Work-Study Program available. Institutional employment available. Off-campus job opportunities are good. **Financial Aid Statistics:** 38 freshmen, 161 undergrads receive athletic scholarships. 92% freshmen, 91% undergrads receive any aid. Highest amount earned per year from on-campus jobs $2,800.

See page 1414.

TUSCULUM COLLEGE

PO Box 5051, Greenville, TN 37743
Phone: 423-636-7300 **E-mail:** admissions@tusculum.edu **CEEB Code:** 1812
Fax: 423-638-7166 **Website:** www.tusculum.edu **ACT Code:** 4018
Financial Aid Phone: 800-729-0256

This private school, affiliated with the Presbyterian Church, was founded in 1794. It has a 142-acre campus.

RATINGS
Admissions Selectivity Rating: 73   **Fire Safety Rating:** 60*   **Green Rating:** 60*

STUDENTS AND FACULTY
Enrollment: 2,600. **Student Body:** 60% female, 40% male, 18% out-of-state, 2% international (8 countries represented). African American 11%, Caucasian 83%, Hispanic 2%. **Retention and Graduation:** 62% freshmen return for sophomore year. 26% freshmen graduate within 4 years. 10% grads go on to further study within 1 year. 12% grads pursue arts and sciences degrees. 5% grads pursue business degrees. 1% grads pursue law degrees. 2% grads pursue medical degrees. **Faculty:** Student/faculty ratio 16:1. 75 full-time faculty, 63% hold PhDs. 100% faculty teach undergrads.

ACADEMICS
Degrees: Bachelor's, master's. **Academic Requirements:** Community service, computer literacy, English (including composition), history, humanities, mathematics, sciences (biological or physical), service learning, social science. **Classes:** Most classes have 10–19 students. **Majors with Highest Enrollment:** Biology/biological sciences, business administration and management, elementary education and teaching. **Disciplines with Highest Percentage of Degrees Awarded:** Business/marketing 72%, education 24%. **Special Study Options:** 16-month accelerated evening program for nontraditional students, double major, honors program, independent study, internships, student-designed major, study abroad, teacher certification program.

FACILITIES
Housing: Coed dorms, men's dorms, women's dorms, apartments for single students. **Special Academic Facilities/Equipment:** The Andrew Johnson Presidential Museum and Library, the college archives, The Charles Coffin Collection. **Computers:** 10% of classrooms are wireless, 50% of public computers are PCs, network access in dorm rooms, network access in dorm lounges, online administrative functions (other than registration), remote student-access to Web through college's connection.

CAMPUS LIFE
Activities: Dance, drama/theater, radio station, student government, student newspaper, yearbook. **Organizations:** 12 registered organizations, 1 honor society, 2 religious organizations. 1 fraternity (2% men join), 1 sorority (2% women join). **Athletics (Intercollegiate):** *Men:* Baseball, basketball,

cheerleading, cross-country, football, golf, soccer, tennis. *Women:* Basketball, cheerleading, cross-country, golf, soccer, softball, tennis, volleyball.

ADMISSIONS
Freshman Academic Profile: 16% in top 10% of high school class, 42% in top 25% of high school class, 78% in top 50% of high school class. SAT Math middle 50% range 410–540. SAT Critical Reading middle 50% range 410–540. ACT middle 50% range 18–23. TOEFL required of all international applicants, minimum paper TOEFL 550, minimum computer TOEFL 250. **Basis for Candidate Selection:** *Very important factors considered include:* Rigor of secondary school record, standardized test scores. *Important factors considered include:* Application essay. *Other factors considered include:* Character/personal qualities, class rank, extracurricular activities, interview, recommendation(s), talent/ability, volunteer work. **Freshman Admission Requirements:** High school diploma is required, and GED is accepted. *Academic units required:* 4 English, 3 math, 2 science, 3 social studies. **Freshman Admission Statistics:** 1,456 applied, 81% admitted, 24% enrolled. **Transfer Admission Requirements:** College transcript(s), statement of good standing from prior institution(s). Minimum college GPA of 2.0 required. Lowest grade transferable D. **General Admission Information:** Regular notification is rolling. Non-fall registration accepted. Admission may be deferred for a maxiumum of 2 semesters. Credit offered for CEEB Advanced Placement tests.

COSTS AND FINANCIAL AID
Required Forms and Deadlines: FAFSA. Financial aid filing deadline 2/15. **Notification of Awards:** Applicants will be notified of awards on a rolling basis beginning on or about 3/15. **Types of Aid:** *Need-based scholarships/grants:* Pell, SEOG, state scholarships/grants, private scholarships, the school's own gift aid. *Loans:* FFEL Subsidized Stafford, FFEL Unsubsidized Stafford, FFEL PLUS, Federal Perkins. **Student Employment:** Federal Work-Study Program available. Institutional employment available. Off-campus job opportunities are good. **Financial Aid Statistics:** 60% freshmen, 40% undergrads receive need-based scholarship or grant aid. 62% freshmen, 51% undergrads receive need-based self-help aid. 42 freshmen, 239 undergrads receive athletic scholarships. 90% freshmen, 85% undergrads receive any aid.

TUSKEGEE UNIVERSITY

Best 368

Old Administration Building, Suite 101, Tuskegee, AL 36088
Phone: 334-727-8500 **E-mail:** admi@tuskegee.edu **CEEB Code:** 1813
Fax: 334-727-5750 **Website:** www.tuskegee.edu **ACT Code:** 0050
Financial Aid Phone: 334-727-8500

This private school was founded in 1881. It has a 5,200-acre campus.

RATINGS
Admissions Selectivity Rating: 80   **Fire Safety Rating:** 60*   **Green Rating:** 60*

STUDENTS AND FACULTY
Enrollment: 2,420. **Student Body:** 55% female, 45% male, 59% out-of-state, 1% international (86 countries represented). African American 78%. **Retention and Graduation:** 70% freshmen return for sophomore year. 25% freshmen graduate within 4 years. 23% grads go on to further study within 1 year. 11% grads pursue arts and sciences degrees. 4% grads pursue business degrees. 2% grads pursue law degrees. 3% grads pursue medical degrees. **Faculty:** Student/faculty ratio 12:1. 283 full-time faculty, 77% hold PhDs. 100% faculty teach undergrads.

ACADEMICS
Degrees: Bachelor's, doctoral, first professional, master's. **Academic Requirements:** Arts/fine arts, English (including composition), history, humanities, mathematics, sciences (biological or physical), social science. **Classes:** Most classes have 10–19 students. **Majors with Highest Enrollment:** Electrical engineering, electronics engineering, communications engineering, veterinary medicine (DVM). **Disciplines with Highest Percentage of Degrees Awarded:** Business/marketing 27%, engineering 16%, biological/life sciences 11%, psychology 7%, agriculture 6%, social sciences 6%. **Special Study Options:** Cooperative education program, double major, dual enrollment, honors program, independent study, internships, teacher certification program.

FACILITIES

Housing: Coed dorms, men's dorms, women's dorms, apartments for married students, apartments for single students. **Special Academic Facilities/ Equipment:** Agricultural and natural history museum, electron microscopes, 2 nursery schools. **Computers:** 99% of classrooms are wired, 99% of classrooms are wireless, network access in dorm rooms, online registration, remote student-access to Web through college's connection.

CAMPUS LIFE

Activities: Choral groups, drama/theater, marching band, student government, student newspaper, yearbook. **Organizations:** 36 registered organizations, 22 honor societies, 6 religious organizations. 5 fraternities (6% men join), 6 sororities (5% women join). **Athletics (Intercollegiate):** *Men:* Baseball, basketball, cheerleading, cross-country, diving, fencing, football, golf, gymnastics, riflery, soccer, swimming, tennis, track/field (indoor), track/field (outdoor), volleyball. *Women:* Basketball, cheerleading, cross-country, diving, fencing, golf, gymnastics, riflery, soccer, swimming, tennis, track/field (indoor), track/field (outdoor), volleyball.

ADMISSIONS

Freshman Academic Profile: 20% in top 10% of high school class, 59% in top 25% of high school class, 100% in top 50% of high school class. SAT Math middle 50% range 380–490. SAT Critical Reading middle 50% range 390–500. ACT middle 50% range 17–21. TOEFL required of all international applicants, minimum paper TOEFL 500, minimum computer TOEFL 173. **Basis for Candidate Selection:** *Very important factors considered include:* Academic GPA, class rank, recommendation(s), rigor of secondary school record, standardized test scores, talent/ability. *Important factors considered include:* Alumni/ae relation, character/personal qualities. *Other factors considered include:* Application essay, extracurricular activities, first generation, geographical residence, interview, state residency, volunteer work, work experience. **Freshman Admission Requirements:** High school diploma is required, and GED is accepted. *Academic units required:* 4 English, 3 math, 2 science, 3 social studies, 4 academic electives. **Freshman Admission Statistics:** 1,931 applied, 81% admitted, 45% enrolled. **Transfer Admission Requirements:** College transcript(s). Minimum college GPA of 2.0 required. Lowest grade transferable C. **General Admission Information:** Application fee $25. Regular application deadline 7/15. Regular notification rolling. Non-fall registration accepted. Credit and/or placement offered for CEEB Advanced Placement tests.

COSTS AND FINANCIAL AID

Annual tuition $14,740. Room and board $7,130. Required fees $710. Average book expense $949. **Required Forms and Deadlines:** FAFSA, institution's own financial aid form, CSS/Financial Aid Profile. Financial aid filing deadline 3/31. **Types of Aid:** *Need-based scholarships/grants:* Pell, SEOG, state scholarships/grants, private scholarships, the school's own gift aid, United Negro College Fund, Federal Nursing Scholarships. *Loans:* Direct Subsidized Stafford, Direct Unsubsidized Stafford, Direct PLUS, FFEL Subsidized Stafford, FFEL Unsubsidized Stafford, FFEL PLUS, Federal Perkins, Federal Nursing, state loans, college/university loans from institutional funds. **Financial Aid Statistics:** 66% freshmen, 66% undergrads receive need-based scholarship or grant aid. 51% freshmen, 49% undergrads receive need-based self-help aid. 55 freshmen, 115 undergrads receive athletic scholarships. Highest amount earned per year from on-campus jobs $1,540.

UNION COLLEGE (KY)

310 College Street, Box 5, Barbourville, KY 40906-1499
Phone: 606-546-1657 **E-mail:** enroll@unionky.edu
Fax: 606-546-1667 **Website:** www.unionky.edu **ACT Code:** 1552
Financial Aid Phone: 800-489-8646

This private school, affiliated with the Methodist Church, was founded in 1879. It has a 110-acre campus.

RATINGS

Admissions Selectivity Rating: 60*   **Fire Safety Rating:** 60*   **Green Rating:** 60*

STUDENTS AND FACULTY

Enrollment: 588. **Student Body:** 49% female, 51% male, 4% international (12 countries represented). African American 8%, Caucasian 80%, Hispanic 2%, Native American 1%. **Retention and Graduation:** 57% freshmen return for sophomore year. 22% freshmen graduate within 4 years. **Faculty:** Student/ faculty ratio 10:1. 49 full-time faculty, 69% hold PhDs. 100% faculty teach undergrads.

ACADEMICS

Degrees: Bachelor's, master's. **Academic Requirements:** Arts/fine arts, English (including composition), history, humanities, mathematics, philosophy, sciences (biological or physical), social science. **Classes:** Most classes have 10– 19 students. Most lab/discussion sections have 10–19 students. **Disciplines with Highest Percentage of Degrees Awarded:** Psychology 15%, social sciences 8%. **Special Study Options:** Accelerated program, cooperative education program, double major, dual enrollment, external degree program, independent study, internships, study abroad, teacher certification program.

FACILITIES

Housing: Coed dorms, men's dorms, women's dorms, apartments for married students, apartments for single students. **Special Academic Facilities/ Equipment:** Lincoln Collection. **Computers:** Network access in dorm rooms, network access in dorm lounges, online registration, online administrative functions (other than registration), remote student-access to Web through college's connection.

CAMPUS LIFE

Activities: Choral groups, drama/theater, literary magazine, music ensembles, musical theater, student government, student newspaper. **Organizations:** 33 registered organizations, 6 religious organizations. **Athletics (Intercollegiate):** *Men:* Baseball, basketball, cheerleading, football, golf, soccer, tennis. *Women:* Basketball, cheerleading, golf, soccer, softball, tennis, volleyball.

ADMISSIONS

Freshman Academic Profile: 5% in top 10% of high school class, 23% in top 25% of high school class, 46% in top 50% of high school class. SAT Math middle 50% range 360–550. SAT Critical Reading middle 50% range 360–460. ACT middle 50% range 17–21. TOEFL required of all international applicants, minimum paper TOEFL 550. **Basis for Candidate Selection:** *Very important factors considered include:* Rigor of secondary school record, standardized test scores. *Important factors considered include:* Class rank, extracurricular activities, interview, volunteer work. *Other factors considered include:* Alumni/ ae relation, application essay, character/personal qualities, recommendation(s), talent/ability. **Freshman Admission Requirements:** High school diploma is required, and GED is accepted. *Academic units required:* 4 English, 3 math, 2 science (2 science labs), 1 social studies, 1 history, 8 academic electives. *Academic units recommended:* 2 foreign language. **Freshman Admission Statistics:** 594 applied, 51% admitted, 46% enrolled. **Transfer Admission Requirements:** College transcript(s). Minimum college GPA of 2.0 required. Lowest grade transferable C. **General Admission Information:** Application fee $20. Regular application deadline 9/5. Regular notification is rolling. Non-fall registration accepted. Common Application accepted.

COSTS AND FINANCIAL AID

Annual tuition $15,620. Room and board $5,000. Required fees $400. Average book expense $1,200. **Required Forms and Deadlines:** FAFSA. Financial aid filing deadline 3/15. **Notification of Awards:** Applicants will be notified of awards on or about 3/1. **Types of Aid:** *Need-based scholarships/grants:* Pell, SEOG, state scholarships/grants, private scholarships, the school's own gift aid. *Loans:* FFEL Subsidized Stafford, FFEL Unsubsidized Stafford, FFEL PLUS, Federal Perkins, college/university loans from institutional funds. **Student Employment:** Federal Work-Study Program available. Institutional employment available. Off-campus job opportunities are good. **Financial Aid Statistics:** 85% freshmen, 92% undergrads receive need-based scholarship or grant aid. 80% freshmen, 83% undergrads receive need-based self-help aid. 29 freshmen, 69 undergrads receive athletic scholarships.

UNION COLLEGE (NE)

3800 South Forty-eighth Street, Lincoln, NE 68506-4300
Phone: 402-486-2504 **E-mail:** ucenroll@ucollege.edu
Fax: 402-486-2566 **Website:** www.ucollege.edu **ACT Code:** 2480
Financial Aid Phone: 402-426-2505

This private school, affiliated with the Seventh-Day Adventist Church, was founded in 1891.

RATINGS

Admissions Selectivity Rating: 75   **Fire Safety Rating:** 60*   **Green Rating:** 60*

STUDENTS AND FACULTY

Enrollment: 845. **Student Body:** 56% female, 44% male, 79% out-of-state, 11% international (34 countries represented). African American 2%, Asian 2%, Caucasian 75%, Hispanic 6%, Native American 1%. **Retention and Gradua-**

tion: 69% freshmen return for sophomore year. 21% grads go on to further study within 1 year. 8% grads pursue arts and sciences degrees. 5% grads pursue business degrees. 2% grads pursue law degrees. 6% grads pursue medical degrees. **Faculty:** Student/faculty ratio 13:1. 54 full-time faculty, 54% hold PhDs. 97% faculty teach undergrads.

ACADEMICS

Degrees: Associate, bachelor's, master's. **Academic Requirements:** Arts/fine arts, computer literacy, English (including composition), history, humanities, mathematics, religion, sciences (biological or physical), social science. **Classes:** Most classes have fewer than 10 students. **Majors with Highest Enrollment:** Business administration/management, nursing/registered nurse training (RN, ASN, BSN, MSN), physician assistant. **Disciplines with Highest Percentage of Degrees Awarded:** Health professions and related sciences 26%, business/marketing 12%, visual and performing arts 9%, biological/life sciences 8%. **Special Study Options:** Cross registration, distance learning, double major, dual enrollment, English as a second language (ESL), honors program, independent study, internships, student-designed major, study abroad, teacher certification program.

FACILITIES

Housing: Men's dorms, women's dorms, apartments for married students, apartments for single students. **Computers:** 50% of classrooms are wireless, 90% of public computers are PCs, 5% of public computers are Macs, 5% of public computers are UNIX, network access in dorm rooms, network access in dorm lounges, online administrative functions (other than registration), support for handheld computing, remote student-access to Web through college's connection.

CAMPUS LIFE

Activities: Choral groups, concert band, drama/theater, literary magazine, music ensembles, student government, student newspaper, yearbook. **Organizations:** 1 honor society, 3 religious organizations. **Athletics (Intercollegiate):** *Men:* Basketball, volleyball. *Women:* Basketball, volleyball.

ADMISSIONS

Freshman Academic Profile: 17% in top 10% of high school class, 14% in top 25% of high school class, 57% in top 50% of high school class. 10% from public high schools. ACT middle 50% range 19–25. TOEFL required of all international applicants, minimum paper TOEFL 550, minimum computer TOEFL 213. **Basis for Candidate Selection:** *Very important factors considered include:* Character/personal qualities, recommendation(s), rigor of secondary school record, standardized test scores. *Important factors considered include:* Class rank, extracurricular activities, interview, religious affiliation/commitment. *Other factors considered include:* Alumni/ae relation, application essay, geographical residence, state residency, talent/ability. **Freshman Admission Requirements:** High school diploma is required, and GED is accepted. *Academic units required:* 3 English, 2 math, 2 science (1 science lab), 1 social studies, 1 history, 3 academic electives. *Academic units recommended:* 4 English, 3 math, 3 science, 1 foreign language. **Freshman Admission Statistics:** 635 applied, 43% admitted, 66% enrolled. **Transfer Admission Requirements:** High school transcript, college transcript(s). Minimum college GPA of 2.0 required. Lowest grade transferable C-. **General Admission Information:** Non-fall registration accepted. Common Application accepted. Credit and/or placement offered for CEEB Advanced Placement tests.

COSTS AND FINANCIAL AID

Annual tuition $13,990. Room & board $4,720. Required fees $420. Average book expense $950. **Required Forms and Deadlines:** FAFSA. Financial aid filing deadline 3/15. **Notification of Awards:** Applicants will be notified of awards on a rolling basis beginning on or about 5/1. **Types of Aid:** *Need-based scholarships/grants:* Pell, SEOG, state scholarships/grants, private scholarships, the school's own gift aid. *Loans:* FFEL Subsidized Stafford, FFEL Unsubsidized Stafford, FFEL PLUS, Federal Perkins, Federal Nursing, college/university loans from institutional funds. **Student Employment: Financial Aid Statistics:** 86% freshmen, 87% undergrads receive need-based scholarship or grant aid. 73% freshmen, 77% undergrads receive need-based self-help aid. 100% freshmen, 58% undergrads receive any aid. Highest amount earned per year from on-campus jobs $1,300.

UNION COLLEGE (NY)

Grant Hall, Union College, Schenectady, NY 12308
Phone: 518-388-6112 **E-mail:** admissions@union.edu **CEEB Code:** 2920
Fax: 518-388-6986 **Website:** www.union.edu **ACT Code:** 2970
Financial Aid Phone: 518-388-6123

This private school was founded in 1795. It has a 120-acre campus.

RATINGS

Admissions Selectivity Rating: 95   **Fire Safety Rating:** 83   **Green Rating:** 85

STUDENTS AND FACULTY

Enrollment: 2,161. **Student Body:** 47% female, 53% male, 58% out-of-state, 2% international (20 countries represented). African American 3%, Asian 6%, Caucasian 84%, Hispanic 4%. **Retention and Graduation:** 93% freshmen return for sophomore year. 79% freshmen graduate within 4 years. 33% grads go on to further study within 1 year. 12% grads pursue arts and sciences degrees. 3% grads pursue business degrees. 4% grads pursue law degrees. 6% grads pursue medical degrees. **Faculty:** Student/faculty ratio 11:1. 184 full-time faculty, 95% hold PhDs. 100% faculty teach undergrads.

ACADEMICS

Degrees: Bachelor's. **Academic Requirements:** English (including composition), history, humanities, linguistic and cultural competency, mathematics, sciences (biological or physical), social science. **Classes:** Most classes have 10–19 students. Most lab/discussion sections have 10–19 students. **Majors with Highest Enrollment:** Economics, political science and government, psychology. **Disciplines with Highest Percentage of Degrees Awarded:** Social sciences 29%, engineering 13%, biological/life sciences 10%, psychology 9%, liberal arts/general studies 8%. **Special Study Options:** Accelerated program, cross registration, double major, dual enrollment, honors program, independent study, internships, liberal arts/career combination, student-designed major, study abroad, teacher certification program.

FACILITIES

Housing: Coed dorms, apartments for single students, fraternity/sorority housing, theme housing, Minerva Houses. **Special Academic Facilities/Equipment:** Horticultural garden, theater, Nott Memorial, high technology classroom and laboratory building, multimedia auditorium, collaborative computer classrooms, 20-inch remote-controlled telescope, superconducting nuclear magnetic resonance spectrometer, 2 electron microscopes, tandem pelletron positive ion accelerator. **Computers:** 10% of classrooms are wired, 100% of classrooms are wireless, 76% of public computers are PCs, 24% of public computers are Macs, network access in dorm rooms, network access in dorm lounges, online registration, online administrative functions (other than registration), remote student-access to Web through college's connection.

CAMPUS LIFE

Activities: Choral groups, concert band, dance, drama/theater, jazz band, literary magazine, music ensembles, radio station, student government, student newspaper, student-run film society, symphony orchestra, television station, yearbook. **Organizations:** 100 registered organizations, 14 honor societies, 4 religious organizations. 7 fraternities (26% men join), 3 sororities (33% women join). **Athletics (Intercollegiate):** *Men:* Baseball, basketball, crew/rowing, cross-country, football, ice hockey, lacrosse, soccer, swimming, tennis, track/field (indoor), track/field (outdoor). *Women:* Basketball, crew/rowing, cross-country, field hockey, ice hockey, lacrosse, soccer, softball, swimming, tennis, track/field (indoor), track/field (outdoor), volleyball. **Environmental Initiatives:** Wind power, organic food, recycling.

ADMISSIONS

Freshman Academic Profile: 64% in top 10% of high school class, 84% in top 25% of high school class, 98% in top 50% of high school class. 65% from public high schools. SAT Math middle 50% range 590–680. SAT Critical Reading middle 50% range 560–660. SAT Writing middle 50% range 570–670. ACT middle 50% range 25–29. TOEFL required of all international applicants, minimum paper TOEFL 600, minimum computer TOEFL 250. **Basis for Candidate Selection:** *Very important factors considered include:* Academic GPA, rigor of secondary school record. *Important factors considered include:* Character/personal qualities, class rank, extracurricular activities, recommendation(s), talent/ability. *Other factors considered include:* Alumni/ae relation, application essay, first generation, geographical residence, interview, level of applicant's interest, racial/ethnic status, standardized test scores, state residency, volunteer work, work experience. **Freshman Admission Requirements:** High school diploma is required, and GED is not accepted. *Academic units required:* 4 English, 3 math, 2 science (2 science labs), 2 foreign language, 1 social studies, 1 history. *Academic units recommended:* 4 English, 4 math, 4 science (4 science labs), 4 foreign language, 2 social studies, 2 history. **Freshman Admission Statistics:** 4,373 applied, 43% admitted, 30% enrolled. **Transfer Admission Requirements:** High school transcript, college transcript(s), essay or personal statement, statement of good standing from prior institution(s). Minimum college GPA of 3.0 required. Lowest grade transferable C. **General Admission Information:** Application fee $50. Early decision application deadline 11/15. Regular application deadline 1/15. Regular notification 4/1. Non-fall registration not accepted. Admission may be deferred for a maxiumum of 2 semesters. Credit and/or placement offered for CEEB Advanced Placement tests.

COSTS AND FINANCIAL AID

Comprehensive fee $46,245. Average book expense $450. **Required Forms and Deadlines:** FAFSA, CSS/Financial Aid Profile, state aid form, Business/ Farm Supplement, noncustodial (divorced/separated) parents' statement. Financial aid filing deadline 2/1. **Notification of Awards:** Applicants will be notified of awards on or about 4/1. **Types of Aid:** *Need-based scholarships/ grants:* Pell, SEOG, state scholarships/grants, private scholarships, the school's own gift aid. *Loans:* FFEL Subsidized Stafford, FFEL Unsubsidized Stafford, FFEL PLUS, Federal Perkins, college/university loans from institutional funds. **Financial Aid Statistics:** 60% freshmen, 48% undergrads receive need-based scholarship or grant aid. 45% freshmen, 42% undergrads receive need-based self-help aid. 59% freshmen, 62% undergrads receive any aid. Highest amount earned per year from on-campus jobs $3,500.

See page 1416.

UNION INSTITUTE & UNIVERSITY

440 East McMillan Street, Cincinnati, OH 45206
Phone: 513-861-6400 **E-mail:** admissions@tui.edu
Fax: 513-861-3238 **Website:** www.tui.edu
Financial Aid Phone: 513-861-6400

This private school was founded in 1964.

RATINGS

Admissions Selectivity Rating: 60*   **Fire Safety Rating:** 60*   **Green Rating:** 60*

STUDENTS AND FACULTY

Enrollment: 1,288. **Student Body:** 71% female, 29% male, 23% out-of-state. African American 26%, Asian 1%, Caucasian 51%, Hispanic 8%. **Retention and Graduation:** 79% freshmen return for sophomore year. 18% freshmen graduate within 4 years. 30% grads go on to further study within 1 year. **Faculty:** Student/faculty ratio 15:1. 112 full-time faculty, 91% hold PhDs. 39% faculty teach undergrads.

ACADEMICS

Degrees: Bachelor's, doctoral, master's, post-master's certificate. **Academic Requirements:** Humanities and arts, language and communications, natural sciences and mathematics, social sciences. **Majors with Highest Enrollment:** Criminal justice/safety studies, education, liberal arts and sciences/liberal studies. **Disciplines with Highest Percentage of Degrees Awarded:** Education 18%, liberal arts/general studies 17%, business/marketing 15%, psychology 8%, health professions and related sciences 5%. **Special Study Options:** Distance learning, double major, external degree program, independent study, student-designed major, teacher certification program.

FACILITIES

Computers: 98% of public computers are PCs, 2% of public computers are Macs, remote student-access to Web through college's connection.

ADMISSIONS

Basis for Candidate Selection: *Very important factors considered include:* Application essay, character/personal qualities, interview, recommendation(s). *Important factors considered include:* Talent/ability, volunteer work, work experience. *Other factors considered include:* Extracurricular activities. **Freshman Admission Requirements:** High school diploma is required, and GED is accepted. **Transfer Admission Requirements:** College transcript(s), essay or personal statement, interview. Lowest grade transferable C. **General Admission Information:** Application fee $35. Regular notification varies by

program. Non-fall registration accepted. Admission may be deferred for a maxiumum of 2 semesters. Common Application not accepted. Credit offered for CEEB Advanced Placement tests.

COSTS AND FINANCIAL AID

Annual tuition $3,144. **Required Forms and Deadlines:** FAFSA, institution's own financial aid form. Financial aid filing deadline 8/1. **Notification of Awards:** Applicants will be notified of awards on a rolling basis beginning on or about 5/1. **Types of Aid:** *Need-based scholarships/grants:* Pell, SEOG, state scholarships/grants, private scholarships, the school's own gift aid. *Loans:* FFEL Subsidized Stafford, FFEL Unsubsidized Stafford, FFEL PLUS, Federal Perkins. **Student Employment:** Federal Work-Study Program available. Off-campus job opportunities are good. **Financial Aid Statistics:** 55% freshmen, 38% undergrads receive need-based scholarship or grant aid. 64% freshmen, 77% undergrads receive need-based self-help aid.

UNION UNIVERSITY

1050 Union University Drive, Jackson, TN 38305-3697
Phone: 731-661-5000 **E-mail:** rgrimm@uu.edu **CEEB Code:** 1826
Fax: 731-661-5017 **Website:** www.uu.edu **ACT Code:** 4020
Financial Aid Phone: 731-661-5015

This private school, affiliated with the Southern Baptist Church, was founded in 1823. It has a 290-acre campus.

RATINGS

Admissions Selectivity Rating: 84   **Fire Safety Rating:** 60*   **Green Rating:** 61

STUDENTS AND FACULTY

Enrollment: 1,980. **Student Body:** 59% female, 41% male, 40% out-of-state, 2% international (23 countries represented). African American 10%, Asian 1%, Caucasian 84%, Hispanic 1%. **Retention and Graduation:** 78% freshmen return for sophomore year. 40% grads go on to further study within 1 year. **Faculty:** Student/faculty ratio 12:1. 169 full-time faculty, 81% hold PhDs. 100% faculty teach undergrads.

ACADEMICS

Degrees: Associate, bachelor's, diploma, doctoral, master's, post-master's certificate. **Academic Requirements:** Arts/fine arts, Christian studies, computer literacy, English (including composition), history, humanities, mathematics, sciences (biological or physical), social science. **Classes:** Most classes have fewer than 10 students. Most lab/discussion sections have fewer than 10 students. **Majors with Highest Enrollment:** Christian studies, elementary education and teaching, nursing/registered nurse training (RN, ASN, BSN, MSN). **Disciplines with Highest Percentage of Degrees Awarded:** Health professions and related sciences 27%, business/marketing 21%, education 9%, philosophy and religious studies 7%, psychology 5%, English 5%. **Special Study Options:** Accelerated program, cooperative education program, cross registration, distance learning, double major, dual enrollment, English as a second language (ESL), exchange student program (domestic), honors program, independent study, internships, study abroad, teacher certification program.

FACILITIES

Housing: Men's dorms, women's dorms, apartments for married students, special housing for disabled students. **Special Academic Facilities/ Equipment:** Elementary education lab, 21st-century classroom, TV communications truck, nursing/health assessment labs, health and wellness center, art gallery. **Computers:** 1% of classrooms are wired, 1% of classrooms are wireless, 85% of public computers are PCs, 15% of public computers are Macs, network access in dorm rooms, network access in dorm lounges, online administrative functions (other than registration), remote student-access to Web through college's connection.

CAMPUS LIFE

Activities: Choral groups, concert band, drama/theater, jazz band, literary magazine, music ensembles, pep band, student government, student newspaper, student-run film society, yearbook. **Organizations:** 65 registered organizations, 13 honor societies, 11 religious organization. 3 fraternities (18% men join), 3 sororities (19% women join). **Athletics (Intercollegiate):** *Men:* Baseball, basketball, cheerleading, cross-country, golf, soccer. *Women:* Basketball, cheerleading, cross-country, soccer, softball, volleyball.

ADMISSIONS

Freshman Academic Profile: 33% in top 10% of high school class, 63% in top 25% of high school class, 86% in top 50% of high school class. 73% from public high schools. SAT Math middle 50% range 510–640. SAT Critical Reading

middle 50% range 510–680. ACT middle 50% range 22–28. TOEFL required of all international applicants, minimum paper TOEFL 500, minimum computer TOEFL 173. **Basis for Candidate Selection:** *Very important factors considered include:* Academic GPA, character/personal qualities, level of applicant's interest, rigor of secondary school record. *Important factors considered include:* Class rank, interview, religious affiliation/commitment, standardized test scores, talent/ability. *Other factors considered include:* Alumni/ae relation, application essay, extracurricular activities, first generation, recommendation(s), volunteer work, work experience. **Freshman Admission Requirements:** High school diploma is required, and GED is accepted. *Academic units required:* 4 English, 3 math, 3 science (2 science labs), 1 foreign language, 2 social studies, 1 history, 1 academic elective. *Academic units recommended:* 4 English, 4 math, 4 science, (2 science labs), 2 foreign language, 2 social studies, 2 history, 4 academic electives. **Freshman Admission Statistics:** 1,103 applied, 83% admitted, 47% enrolled. **Transfer Admission Requirements:** College transcript(s), statement of good standing from prior institution(s). Minimum college GPA of 2.3 required. Lowest grade transferable C. **General Admission Information:** Application fee $25. Regular application deadline 8/1. Regular notification is rolling. Non-fall registration accepted. Admission may be deferred for a maxiumum of 2 semesters. Credit offered for CEEB Advanced Placement tests.

COSTS AND FINANCIAL AID

Annual tuition $17,990. Room and board $6,200. Required fees $630. Average book expense $600. **Required Forms and Deadlines:** FAFSA, institution's own financial aid form. Financial aid filing deadline 3/1. **Notification of Awards:** Applicants will be notified of awards on a rolling basis beginning on or about 12/1. **Types of Aid:** *Need-based scholarships/grants:* Pell, SEOG, state scholarships/grants, private scholarships, the school's own gift aid. *Loans:* FFEL Subsidized Stafford, FFEL Unsubsidized Stafford, FFEL PLUS, Federal Perkins. **Student Employment:** Off-campus job opportunities are excellent. **Financial Aid Statistics:** 44 freshmen, 150 undergrads receive athletic scholarships. 68% freshmen, 73% undergrads receive any aid. Highest amount earned per year from on-campus jobs $1,000.

See page 1418.

UNITED STATES AIR FORCE ACADEMY

HQ USAFA/ RRS, 2304 Cadet Drive, Suite 2300, USAF Academy, CO 80840-5025
Phone: 719-333-2520 **E-mail:** rr_webmail@usafa.af.mil
Fax: 719-333-3012 **Website:** www.usafa.af.mil **ACT Code:** 0530

This public school was founded in 1954. It has an 18,000-acre campus.

RATINGS
Admissions Selectivity Rating: 96   **Fire Safety Rating:** 60*   **Green Rating:** 60*

STUDENTS AND FACULTY
Enrollment: 4,524. **Student Body:** 18% female, 82% male, 94% out-of-state, 1% international. African American 4%, Asian 8%, Caucasian 78%, Hispanic 7%, Native American 2%. **Retention and Graduation:** 87% freshmen return for sophomore year. 75% freshmen graduate within 4 years. 5% grads go on to further study within 1 year. 3% grads pursue arts and sciences degrees. 1% grads pursue business degrees. 1% grads pursue medical degrees. **Faculty:** Student/faculty ratio 8:1. 563 full-time faculty, 49% hold PhDs. 100% faculty teach undergrads.

ACADEMICS
Degrees: Bachelor's. **Academic Requirements:** Computer literacy, English (including composition), flight course, foreign languages, history, humanities, mathematics, military arts and sciences, philosophy, physical education courses, sciences (biological or physical), social science. **Classes:** Most classes have 10–19 students. **Majors with Highest Enrollment:** Business administration/management, engineering, social sciences. **Special Study Options:** Academically at-risk program, double major, English as a second language (ESL), exchange student program (domestic), extra instruction program, hospital instruction program, independent study, student-designed major, study abroad, summer programs.

FACILITIES
Housing: Coed dorms. All students are required to live on campus all four

---

years. **Special Academic Facilities/Equipment:** Language learning center, laser and optics research center, USAFA observatory, Dept. of Engineering Mechanics Lab, U.S. Air Force Academy Visitor's Center, planetarium, Air Force Academy cadet chapel, American legion memorial tower, Air Garden, Falcon Stadium, aeronautics laboratory, meterology lab, Arnold Hall Broadway Theatre, ballrooms, historical displays. **Computers:** 100% of classrooms are wired, 100% of classrooms are wireless, 100% of public computers are PCs, network access in dorm rooms, network access in dorm lounges, online registration, online administrative functions (other than registration), remote student-access to Web through college's connection, tuition includes personal computer. Undergraduates are required to own a computer.

CAMPUS LIFE
Activities: Choral groups, dance, drama/theater, marching band, musical theater, pep band, radio station, student government, student newspaper, television station, yearbook. **Organizations:** 110 registered organizations, 2 honor societies. **Athletics (Intercollegiate):** *Men:* Baseball, basketball, cheerleading, cross-country, cycling, diving, fencing, football, golf, gymnastics, ice hockey, lacrosse, martial arts, riflery, soccer, swimming, tennis, track/field (indoor), track/field (outdoor), water polo, wrestling. *Women:* Basketball, cheerleading, cross-country, cycling, diving, fencing, gymnastics, martial arts, riflery, soccer, swimming, tennis, track/field (indoor), track/field (outdoor), volleyball.

ADMISSIONS
Freshman Academic Profile: 50% in top 10% of high school class, 81% in top 25% of high school class, 98% in top 50% of high school class. SAT Math middle 50% range 600–690. SAT Critical Reading middle 50% range 570–650. SAT Writing middle 50% range 550–650. ACT middle 50% range 27–31. **Basis for Candidate Selection:** *Very important factors considered include:* Character/personal qualities, interview, rigor of secondary school record, standardized test scores. *Important factors considered include:* Academic GPA, application essay, class rank, extracurricular activities, talent/ability, volunteer work, work experience. *Other factors considered include:* Alumni/ae relation, racial/ethnic status, recommendation(s). **Freshman Admission Requirements:** High school diploma is required, and GED is not accepted. *Academic units recommended:* 4 English, 4 math, 4 science (4 science labs), 2 foreign language, 3 social studies, 3 history, 1 academic elective, 1 computer. **Freshman Admission Statistics:** 9,296 applied, 19% admitted, 77% enrolled. **Transfer Admission Requirements:** High school transcript, college transcript(s), essay or personal statement, interview, standardized test score. Minimum college GPA of 2.0 required. **General Admission Information:** Regular application deadline 1/31. Regular notification is rolling. Non-fall registration not accepted. Credit and/or placement offered for CEEB Advanced Placement tests.

COSTS AND FINANCIAL AID
Annual in-state tuition $0. Out-of-state tuition $0.

See page 1420.

UNITED STATES COAST GUARD ACADEMY

31 Mohegan Avenue, New London, CT 06320-8103
Phone: 860-444-8503 **CEEB Code:** 5708
Fax: 860-701-6700 **Website:** www.uscga.edu **ACT Code:** 0600

This public school was founded in 1876. It has a 120-acre campus.

RATINGS
Admissions Selectivity Rating: 96   **Fire Safety Rating:** 77   **Green Rating:** 77

STUDENTS AND FACULTY
Enrollment: 996. **Student Body:** 28% female, 72% male, 94% out-of-state, 1% international (7 countries represented). African American 3%, Asian 5%, Caucasian 86%, Hispanic 5%. **Retention and Graduation:** 86% freshmen return for sophomore year. 60% freshmen graduate within 4 years. **Faculty:** Student/faculty ratio 9:1. 97 full-time faculty, 44% hold PhDs. 100% faculty teach undergrads.

ACADEMICS
Degrees: Bachelor's. **Academic Requirements:** Computer literacy, English (including composition), engineering, foreign languages, history, humanities,

mathematics, nautical sciences, philosophy, sciences (biological or physical), social science. **Classes:** Most classes have 10–19 students. Most lab/discussion sections have 10–19 students. **Majors with Highest Enrollment:** Chemical and physical engineering, oceanography, political science and government. **Disciplines with Highest Percentage of Degrees Awarded:** Engineering 36%, social sciences 22%, business/marketing 19%, mathematics 13%, biological/life sciences 10%. **Special Study Options:** Double major, exchange student program (domestic), honors program, independent study, internships.

FACILITIES

Housing: Coed dorms. **Special Academic Facilities/Equipment:** C.G. Museum, library, visitors center. **Computers:** 100% of classrooms are wired, 50% of classrooms are wireless, 100% of public computers are PCs, network access in dorm rooms, network access in dorm lounges, online registration, online administrative functions (other than registration), support for handheld computing, remote student-access to Web through college's connection, tuition includes personal computer. Undergraduates are required to own a computer.

CAMPUS LIFE

Activities: Choral groups, concert band, dance, drama/theater, jazz band, marching band, music ensembles, musical theater, pep band, yearbook. **Organizations:** 2 honor societies, 7 religious organizations. **Athletics (Intercollegiate):** *Men:* Baseball, basketball, crew/rowing, cross-country, diving, football, riflery, sailing, soccer, swimming, tennis, track/field (indoor), track/field (outdoor), wrestling. *Women:* Basketball, cheerleading, crew/rowing, cross-country, diving, riflery, sailing, soccer, softball, swimming, track/field (indoor), track/field (outdoor), volleyball. **Environmental Initiatives:** Federal Electronic Recycling Challenge Participant. RecycleMania.

ADMISSIONS

Freshman Academic Profile: 50% in top 10% of high school class, 90% in top 25% of high school class, 99% in top 50% of high school class. 77% from public high schools. SAT Math middle 50% range 610–680. SAT Critical Reading middle 50% range 570–670. ACT middle 50% range 25–29. TOEFL required of all international applicants, minimum paper TOEFL 560, minimum computer TOEFL 220. **Basis for Candidate Selection:** *Very important factors considered include:* Academic GPA, character/personal qualities, class rank, extracurricular activities, rigor of secondary school record, standardized test scores. *Important factors considered include:* Application essay, recommendation(s), talent/ability. *Other factors considered include:* Alumni/ae relation, interview, level of applicant's interest, volunteer work, work experience. **Freshman Admission Requirements:** High school diploma is required, and GED is accepted. *Academic units required:* 4 English, 4 math, 3 science (3 science labs). **Freshman Admission Statistics:** 1,633 applied, 24% admitted, 70% enrolled. **General Admission Information:** Regular application deadline 3/1. Regular notification is rolling. Non-fall registration not accepted. Placement offered for CEEB Advanced Placement tests.

COSTS AND FINANCIAL AID

Annual in-state tuition $0. Out-of-state tuition $0.

UNITED STATES INTERNATIONAL UNIVERSITY

10455 Pomerado Road, San Diego, CA 92131
Phone: 619-635-4772 **E-mail:** admissions@usiu.edu **CEEB Code:** 4039
Fax: 619-635-4739 **Website:** www.usiu.edu **ACT Code:** 0443
Financial Aid Phone: 858-635-4559

This private school was founded in 1952. It has a 160-acre campus.

RATINGS
Admissions Selectivity Rating: 60*   **Fire Safety Rating:** 60*   **Green Rating:** 60*

STUDENTS AND FACULTY

Enrollment: 400. **Student Body:** 60% out-of-state, 48% international. African American 4%, Asian 5%, Caucasian 23%, Hispanic 15%, Native American 1%. **Retention and Graduation:** 37% freshmen return for sophomore year.

ACADEMICS

Degrees: Associate, bachelor's, doctoral, master's, post-bachelor's certificate, post-master's certificate. **Academic Requirements:** Computer literacy, English (including composition), foreign languages, humanities, mathematics, sciences (biological or physical), social science. **Special Study Options:** English as a second language (ESL), exchange student program (domestic), honors program, internships, study abroad, teacher certification program.

FACILITIES

Housing: Coed dorms, men's dorms, women's dorms, special housing for

---

disabled students. **Computers:** 100% of public computers are PCs, network access in dorm rooms, network access in dorm lounges, online registration, online administrative functions (other than registration), remote student-access to Web through college's connection.

CAMPUS LIFE

Activities: Drama/theater, radio station, student government, student newspaper, television station, yearbook. **Organizations:** 17 registered organizations, 3 honor societies. **Athletics (Intercollegiate):** *Men:* Cross-country, soccer, tennis. *Women:* Cross-country, soccer, tennis, volleyball.

ADMISSIONS

Freshman Academic Profile: SAT Math middle 50% range 430–580. SAT Critical Reading middle 50% range 400–560. ACT middle 50% range 19–23. TOEFL required of all international applicants, minimum paper TOEFL 550, minimum computer TOEFL 213. **Basis for Candidate Selection:** *Very important factors considered include:* Rigor of secondary school record, standardized test scores. *Important factors considered include:* Application essay, recommendation(s). *Other factors considered include:* Character/personal qualities, extracurricular activities, interview, talent/ability, volunteer work. **Freshman Admission Requirements:** *Academic units required:* 4 English, 3 math, 2 science, 2 foreign language, 3 social studies. **Freshman Admission Statistics:** 399 applied, 59% admitted, 13% enrolled. **Transfer Admission Requirements:** High school transcript, college transcript(s), essay or personal statement. Minimum college GPA of 2.5 required. Lowest grade transferable C. **General Admission Information:** Application fee $40. Regular application deadline rolling. Regular notification. Non-fall registration accepted. Common Application accepted. Credit offered for CEEB Advanced Placement tests.

COSTS AND FINANCIAL AID

Comprehensive fee $18,990. Room and board $7,430. Required fees $250. Average book expense $1,224. **Required Forms and Deadlines:** FAFSA, institution's own financial aid form, state aid form, Noncustodial PROFILE. Financial aid filing deadline 3/2. **Notification of Awards:** Applicants will be notified of awards on a rolling basis beginning on or about 3/15. **Types of Aid:** *Need-based scholarships/grants:* Pell, SEOG, state scholarships/grants, private scholarships, the school's own gift aid. *Loans:* FFEL Subsidized Stafford, FFEL Unsubsidized Stafford, FFEL PLUS, Federal Perkins. **Student Employment:** Federal Work-Study Program available. Institutional employment available. Off-campus job opportunities are excellent. **Financial Aid Statistics:** 18% freshmen, 38% undergrads receive need-based scholarship or grant aid. 26% freshmen, 39% undergrads receive need-based self-help aid. Highest amount earned per year from on-campus jobs $3,450.

UNITED STATES MERCHANT
MARINE ACADEMY

Office of Admissions, Kings Point, NY 11024-1699
Phone: 516-773-5391 **E-mail:** admissions@usmma.edu **CEEB Code:** 2923
Fax: 516-773-5390 **Website:** www.usmma.edu **ACT Code:** 2974
Financial Aid Phone: 516-773-5295

This public school was founded in 1943. It has an 82-acre campus.

RATINGS
Admissions Selectivity Rating: 93   **Fire Safety Rating:** 60*   **Green Rating:** 60*

STUDENTS AND FACULTY

Enrollment: 1,007. **Student Body:** 14% female, 86% male, 87% out-of-state, 2% international (3 countries represented). African American 2%, Asian 3%, Caucasian 90%, Hispanic 5%. **Retention and Graduation:** 92% freshmen return for sophomore year. 3% grads go on to further study within 1 year. 1% grads pursue arts and sciences degrees. 2% grads pursue law degrees. **Faculty:** Student/faculty ratio 11:1. 85 full-time faculty.

ACADEMICS

Degrees: Bachelor's, master's. **Academic Requirements:** Computer literacy, English (including composition), history, humanities, mathematics, sciences (biological or physical), sea year. All students must complete at least 300 days aboard ship during their sophomore and junior years. **Classes:** Most classes have 10–19 students. Most lab/discussion sections have 10–19 students. **Majors with Highest Enrollment:** Engineering, naval architecture and marine engineering, transportation and materials moving services. **Disciplines with Highest Percentage of Degrees Awarded:** Engineering 45%. **Special Study Options:** Honors program, internships.

FACILITIES

Housing: Coed dorms. All students required to live on campus in dormitories provided. **Special Academic Facilities/Equipment:** American Merchant Marine Museum. **Computers:** 75% of classrooms are wired, 75% of classrooms are wireless, 100% of public computers are PCs, network access in dorm rooms, network access in dorm lounges, online registration, online administrative functions (other than registration), remote student-access to Web through college's connection, tuition includes personal computer. Undergraduates are required to own a computer.

CAMPUS LIFE

Activities: Choral groups, concert band, drama/theater, marching band, student government, student newspaper, yearbook. **Organizations:** 3 religious organizations. **Athletics (Intercollegiate):** *Men:* Baseball, basketball, crew/rowing, cross-country, diving, football, golf, lacrosse, riflery, sailing, soccer, swimming, tennis, track/field (outdoor), volleyball, water polo, wrestling. *Women:* Basketball, crew/rowing, cross-country, diving, golf, riflery, sailing, softball, swimming, tennis, track/field (outdoor), volleyball.

ADMISSIONS

Freshman Academic Profile: 26% in top 10% of high school class, 64% in top 25% of high school class, 96% in top 50% of high school class. 70% from public high schools. SAT Math middle 50% range 588–669. SAT Critical Reading middle 50% range 540–633. ACT middle 50% range 26–29. TOEFL required of all international applicants, minimum paper TOEFL 550, minimum computer TOEFL 213. **Basis for Candidate Selection:** *Very important factors considered include:* Character/personal qualities, rigor of secondary school record, standardized test scores. *Important factors considered include:* Application essay, class rank, extracurricular activities, geographical residence, recommendation(s), talent/ability. *Other factors considered include:* Interview, racial/ethnic status, state residency, volunteer work, work experience. **Freshman Admission Requirements:** High school diploma is required, and GED is not accepted. *Academic units required:* 4 English, 3 math, 3 science (1 science lab), 8 academic electives. *Academic units recommended:* 4 English, 4 math, 4 science (2 science labs), 2 foreign language, 4 social studies. **Freshman Admission Statistics:** 1,797 applied, 21% admitted, 77% enrolled. **Transfer Admission Requirements:** High school transcript, college transcript(s), essay or personal statement, standardized test score, statement of good standing from prior institution(s). Minimum college GPA of 2.5 required. **General Admission Information:** Early decision application deadline 11/1. Regular application deadline 3/1. Regular notification is rolling. Non-fall registration not accepted. Common Application not accepted.

COSTS AND FINANCIAL AID

Annual in-state tuition $0. Out-of-state tuition $0. Required fees $2,843. **Required Forms and Deadlines:** FAFSA, institution's own financial aid form. Financial aid filing deadline 5/1. **Notification of Awards:** Applicants will be notified of awards on a rolling basis beginning on or about 1/31. **Types of Aid:** *Need-based scholarships/grants:* Pell, private scholarships. *Loans:* FFEL Subsidized Stafford, FFEL Unsubsidized Stafford, FFEL PLUS. **Student Employment:** Off-campus job opportunities are poor. **Financial Aid Statistics:** 15% freshmen, 5% undergrads receive need-based scholarship or grant aid. 15% freshmen, 8% undergrads receive need-based self-help aid.

UNITED STATES MILITARY ACADEMY

646 Swift Road, West Point, NY 10996-1905
Phone: 845-938-4041 **E-mail:** admissions@usma.edu **CEEB Code:** 2924
Fax: 845-938-3021 **Website:** www.usma.edu **ACT Code:** 2976
Financial Aid Phone: 845-938-3516

This public school was founded in 1802. It has a 16,080-acre campus.

STUDENTS AND FACULTY

Enrollment: 4,231. **Student Body:** 15% female, 85% male, 92% out-of-state, 1% international (35 countries represented). African American 6%, Asian 7%, Caucasian 77%, Hispanic 7%. **Retention and Graduation:** 92% freshmen return for sophomore year. 100% grads go on to further study within 1 year. 2% grads pursue medical degrees. **Faculty:** Student/faculty ratio 7:1. 594 full-time faculty, 47% hold PhDs. 100% faculty teach undergrads.

ACADEMICS

Degrees: Bachelor's. **Academic Requirements:** Computer literacy, English (including composition), engineering, foreign languages, geography, history, humanities, information technology, law, mathematics, military science, philosophy, physical education, sciences (biological or physical), social science. **Classes:** Most classes have 10–19 students. Most lab/discussion sections have 10–19 students. **Majors with Highest Enrollment:** Economics, history, political science and government. **Disciplines with Highest Percentage of Degrees Awarded:** Engineering 30%, social sciences 21%, foreign languages and literature 7%, business/marketing 7%, history 7%, computer and information sciences 6%, law/legal studies 5%. **Special Study Options:** Double major, exchange student program (domestic), honors program, independent study, internships, study abroad.

FACILITIES

Housing: Coed dorms. **Special Academic Facilities/Equipment:** West Point Museum, Arvin gymnasium, Michie Stadium, Holleder Center houses Tate, Christl Arena, Shea Stadium outdoor track facility, Gillis Field House, all-weather track, an Astroturf football field, 18-hole golf course, new indoor tennis facility, Eisenhower Hall, 4,500-seat auditorium. **Computers:** 98% of public computers are PCs, 2% of public computers are UNIX, network access in dorm rooms, online registration, online administrative functions (other than registration), support for handheld computing, remote student-access to Web through college's connection. Undergraduates are required to own a computer.

CAMPUS LIFE

Activities: Choral groups, drama/theater, literary magazine, marching band, music ensembles, pep band, radio station, student government, student newspaper, television station, yearbook. **Organizations:** 105 registered organizations, 7 honor societies, 13 religious organizations. **Athletics (Intercollegiate):** *Men:* Baseball, basketball, cross-country, diving, football, golf, gymnastics, ice hockey, lacrosse, riflery, soccer, swimming, tennis, track/field (indoor), track/field (outdoor), wrestling. *Women:* Basketball, cross-country, diving, riflery, soccer, softball, swimming, tennis, track/field (indoor), track/field (outdoor).

ADMISSIONS

Freshman Academic Profile: 48% in top 10% of high school class, 77% in top 25% of high school class, 94% in top 50% of high school class. 86% from public high schools. SAT Math middle 50% range 600–690. SAT Critical Reading middle 50% range 570–670. ACT middle 50% range 21–36. **Basis for Candidate Selection:** *Very important factors considered include:* Academic GPA, application essay, character/personal qualities, class rank, extracurricular activities, recommendation(s), rigor of secondary school record, standardized test scores, talent/ability. *Important factors considered include:* Geographical residence, interview, level of applicant's interest, racial/ethnic status, volunteer work. *Other factors considered include:* Alumni/ae relation, state residency, work experience. **Freshman Admission Requirements:** High school diploma is required, and GED is accepted. *Academic units recommended:* 4 English, 4 math, 4 science (2 science labs), 2 foreign language, 3 social studies, 1 history, 3 academic electives. **Freshman Admission Statistics:** 10,778 applied, 14% admitted, 77% enrolled. **General Admission Information:** Regular application deadline 2/28. Regular notification is rolling. Non-fall registration not accepted. Common Application not accepted. Placement offered for CEEB Advanced Placement tests.

COSTS AND FINANCIAL AID

Annual in-state tuition $0. Out-of-state tuition $0. **Types of Aid:** *Need-based scholarships/grants:* All cadets are on Active Duty as members of the United States Army and receive an annual salary of approximately $10,148. Room and board, medical, and dental care is provided by the U.S. Army. A one-time deposit of $2,900 is required upon admission.

See page 1422.

RATINGS

Admissions Selectivity Rating: 96   **Fire Safety Rating:** 86   **Green Rating:** 60*

UNITED STATES NAVAL ACADEMY

Best 368

117 Decatur Road, Annapolis, MD 21402
Phone: 410-293-4361 **E-mail:** webmail@usna.com **CEEB Code:** 5809
Fax: 410-295-1815 **Website:** www.usna.com **ACT Code:** 1742

This public school was founded in 1845. It has a 330-acre campus.

RATINGS
Admissions Selectivity Rating: 96   **Fire Safety Rating:** 60*   **Green Rating:** 60*

STUDENTS AND FACULTY
Enrollment: 4,479. **Student Body:** 19% female, 81% male, 95% out-of-state, 1% international (25 countries represented). African American 6%, Asian 5%, Caucasian 76%, Hispanic 9%, Native American 2%. **Retention and Graduation:** 96% freshmen return for sophomore year. 87% freshmen graduate within 4 years. 2% grads go on to further study within 1 year. 1% grads pursue medical degrees. **Faculty:** Student/faculty ratio 8:1. 546 full-time faculty, 62% hold PhDs. 100% faculty teach undergrads.

ACADEMICS
Degrees: Bachelor's. **Academic Requirements:** English (including composition), engineering, ethics, history, humanities, leadership, mathematics, military law, naval science, sciences (biological or physical), social science. **Classes:** Most classes have 20–29 students. **Majors with Highest Enrollment:** Economics, political science and government, systems engineering. **Disciplines with Highest Percentage of Degrees Awarded:** Engineering 38%, social sciences 29%, history 9%, physical sciences 8%, English 7%. **Special Study Options:** Double major, exchange student program (domestic), honors program, independent study, Voluntary Graduate Education Program.

FACILITIES
Housing: Coed dorms. All midshipmen live in same dormitory. **Special Academic Facilities/Equipment:** Naval History Museum, Naval Institute, propulsion lab, subsonic and supersonic wind tunnels, flight simulator, subcritical nuclear reactor, 120/380-foot tow tanks, satellite dish, coastal chamber facilities, extensive fleet of small craft (power and sail), oceanographic research vessel. **Computers:** 50% of classrooms are wired, 10% of classrooms are wireless, 97% of public computers are PCs, 2% of public computers are UNIX, network access in dorm rooms, network access in dorm lounges, online registration, online administrative functions (other than registration), support for handheld computing, remote student-access to Web through college's connection, tuition includes personal computer. Undergraduates are required to own a computer.

CAMPUS LIFE
Activities: Choral groups, concert band, drama/theater, jazz band, literary magazine, marching band, musical theater, pep band, radio station, student government, yearbook. **Organizations:** 70 registered organizations, 10 honor societies, 8 religious organizations. **Athletics (Intercollegiate):** *Men:* Baseball, basketball, crew/rowing, cross-country, diving, football, golf, gymnastics, lacrosse, light weight football, riflery, sailing, soccer, squash, swimming, tennis, track/field (indoor), track/field (outdoor), water polo, wrestling. *Women:* Basketball, crew/rowing, cross-country, diving, riflery, sailing, soccer, swimming, track/field (indoor), track/field (outdoor), volleyball.

ADMISSIONS
Freshman Academic Profile: 54% in top 10% of high school class, 81% in top 25% of high school class, 96% in top 50% of high school class. 60% from public high schools. SAT Math middle 50% range 600–690. SAT Critical Reading middle 50% range 560–660. TOEFL required of all international applicants, minimum paper TOEFL 200. **Basis for Candidate Selection:** *Very important factors considered include:* Application essay, character/personal qualities, class rank, extracurricular activities, interview, level of applicant's interest, recommendation(s), rigor of secondary school record, standardized test scores. *Important factors considered include:* Talent/ability. *Other factors considered include:* Alumni/ae relation, first generation, geographical residence, racial/ethnic status, volunteer work, work experience. **Freshman Admission Requirements:** High school diploma or equivalent is not required. *Academic units recommended:* 4 English, 4 math, 2 science (1 science lab), 2 foreign language, 2 history, 1 introductory computer and typing course. **Freshman Admission Statistics:** 10,746 applied, 14% admitted, 81% enrolled. **General Admission Information:** Regular application deadline 1/31. Regular notification is rolling. Non-fall registration not accepted. Credit and/or placement offered for CEEB Advanced Placement tests.

COSTS AND FINANCIAL AID
Annual in-state tuition $0. Out-of-state tuition $0. Average book expense $1,000.

UNITY COLLEGE

PO Box 532, Unity, ME 04988-0532
Phone: 207-948-3131 **E-mail:** admissions@unity.edu **CEEB Code:** 3925
Fax: 207-948-6277 **Website:** www.unity.edu
Financial Aid Phone: 207-948-3131

This private school was founded in 1965. It has a 205-acre campus.

RATINGS
Admissions Selectivity Rating: 70   **Fire Safety Rating:** 60*   **Green Rating:** 99

STUDENTS AND FACULTY
Enrollment: 512. **Student Body:** 31% female, 69% male, 64% out-of-state. Caucasian 98%. **Retention and Graduation:** 67% freshmen return for sophomore year. 13% freshmen graduate within 4 years. 3% grads go on to further study within 1 year. 10% grads pursue arts and sciences degrees. **Faculty:** Student/faculty ratio 14:1. 34 full-time faculty, 62% hold PhDs. 100% faculty teach undergrads.

ACADEMICS
Degrees: Associate, bachelor's. **Academic Requirements:** Arts/fine arts, computer literacy, English (including composition), history, humanities, mathematics, philosophy, sciences (biological or physical), social science. **Special Study Options:** Accelerated program, cooperative education program, double major, dual enrollment, independent study, internships, student-designed major.

FACILITIES
Housing: Coed dorms, 5 residential cottages. **Special Academic Facilities/Equipment:** The Indian Museum, a collection of Indian artifacts. **Computers:** 50% of public computers are PCs, 50% of public computers are Macs, network access in dorm rooms, network access in dorm lounges, remote student-access to Web through college's connection.

CAMPUS LIFE
Activities: Drama/theater, radio station, student government, student newspaper, yearbook. **Organizations:** 27 registered organizations, 1 honor society, 2 religious organizations. **Athletics (Intercollegiate):** *Men:* Basketball, cross-country. *Women:* Cross-country, volleyball. **Environmental Initiatives:** 100% green power. Building retrofits to reduce energy and climate emissions. Only fully carbon neutral new buildings.

ADMISSIONS
Freshman Academic Profile: 3% in top 10% of high school class, 13% in top 25% of high school class, 48% in top 50% of high school class. 98% from public high schools. SAT Math middle 50% range 500–510. SAT Critical Reading middle 50% range 480–500. TOEFL required of all international applicants, minimum paper TOEFL 500. **Basis for Candidate Selection:** *Very important factors considered include:* Application essay, interview, recommendation(s), rigor of secondary school record. *Important factors considered include:* Character/personal qualities, extracurricular activities, talent/ability. *Other factors considered include:* Alumni/ae relation, standardized test scores, volunteer work, work experience. **Freshman Admission Requirements:** High school diploma is required, and GED is accepted. *Academic units required:* 4 English, 2 science. *Academic units recommended:* 4 math, 2 foreign language, 4 social studies. **Freshman Admission Statistics:** 500 applied, 92% admitted, 34% enrolled. **Transfer Admission Requirements:** High school transcript, college transcript(s), essay or personal statement. Minimum college GPA of 2.0 required. Lowest grade transferable C. **General Admission Information:** Application fee $25. Regular notification is rolling. Non-fall registration accepted. Common Application accepted. Credit and/or placement offered for CEEB Advanced Placement tests.

COSTS AND FINANCIAL AID
Annual tuition $12,330. Room & board $5,300. Required fees $560. Average book expense $450. **Required Forms and Deadlines:** FAFSA, institution's own financial aid form. Financial aid filing deadline 3/1. **Notification of Awards:** Applicants will be notified of awards on a rolling basis beginning on or about 3/15. **Types of Aid:** *Need-based scholarships/grants:* Pell, SEOG, state scholarships/grants, private scholarships, the school's own gift aid. *Loans:* FFEL

Subsidized Stafford, FFEL Unsubsidized Stafford, FFEL PLUS. **Student Employment:** Federal Work-Study Program available. Off-campus job opportunities are fair. **Financial Aid Statistics:** 75% freshmen, 67% undergrads receive need-based scholarship or grant aid. 78% freshmen, 74% undergrads receive need-based self-help aid.

UNIVERSITY OF ADVANCING TECHNOLOGY (UAT)

2625 West Baseline Road, Tempe, AZ 85283-1056
Phone: 602-383-8228 **E-mail:** admissions@uat.edu
Fax: 602-383-8222 **Website:** www.uat.edu
Financial Aid Phone: 602-383-8228

This proprietary school was founded in 1983.

RATINGS
Admissions Selectivity Rating: 60*   **Fire Safety Rating:** 60*   **Green Rating:** 60*

STUDENTS AND FACULTY
Enrollment: 259. **Student Body:** 8% female, 92% male, 5% international. African American 12%, Asian 13%, Hispanic 16%, Native American 2%. **Faculty:** Student/faculty ratio 15:1. 100% faculty teach undergrads.

ACADEMICS
Degrees: Associate, bachelor's, diploma, master's. **Academic Requirements:** Computer literacy, English (including composition), history, humanities, mathematics, sciences (biological or physical), social science. **Classes:** Most classes have 20–29 students. **Special Study Options:** Accelerated program, cooperative education program, distance learning, double major, independent study, internships, student-designed major.

FACILITIES
Housing: University-sponsored apartments. **Computers:** 100% of classrooms are wired, 100% of classrooms are wireless, 98% of public computers are PCs, 2% of public computers are Macs, online administrative functions (other than registration), remote student-access to Web through college's connection.

CAMPUS LIFE
Activities: Literary magazine, student government, student-run film society. **Organizations:** 1 religious organization.

ADMISSIONS
Freshman Academic Profile: TOEFL required of all international applicants, minimum paper TOEFL 550, minimum computer TOEFL 213. **Basis for Candidate Selection:** *Very important factors considered include:* Character/personal qualities, interview, level of applicant's interest, talent/ability. *Important factors considered include:* Rigor of secondary school record. *Other factors considered include:* Academic GPA, standardized test scores, volunteer work. **Freshman Admission Requirements:** High school diploma is required, and GED is accepted. **Transfer Admission Requirements:** High school transcript, college transcript(s). Minimum college GPA of 2.0 required. Lowest grade transferable C. **General Admission Information:** Regular notification end of junior high or 18 mon prior to start. Non-fall registration accepted. Admission may be deferred for a maxiumum of 2 semesters. Common Application not accepted.

COSTS AND FINANCIAL AID
Annual tuition $15,400. Average book expense $1,000. **Required Forms and Deadlines:** FAFSA. Financial aid filing deadline 4/6. **Types of Aid:** *Need-based scholarships/grants:* Pell, SEOG, private scholarships, the school's own gift aid. *Loans:* FFEL Subsidized Stafford, FFEL Unsubsidized Stafford, FFEL PLUS.

THE UNIVERSITY OF AKRON

The University of Akron, Akron, OH 44325-2001
Phone: 330-972-7077 **E-mail:** admissions@uakron.edu **CEEB Code:** 1829
Fax: 330-972-7022 **Website:** www.uakron.edu **ACT Code:** 3338
Financial Aid Phone: 800-621-3847

This public school was founded in 1870. It has a 218-acre campus.

RATINGS
Admissions Selectivity Rating: 72   **Fire Safety Rating:** 84   **Green Rating:** 60*

STUDENTS AND FACULTY
Enrollment: 16,932. **Student Body:** 51% female, 49% male, 4% out-of-state. African American 14%, Asian 2%, Caucasian 79%, Hispanic 1%. **Retention and Graduation:** 66% freshmen return for sophomore year. **Faculty:** Student/faculty ratio 18:1. 709 full-time faculty, 84% hold PhDs. 88% faculty teach undergrads.

ACADEMICS
Degrees: Associate, bachelor's, certificate, doctoral, first professional certificate, first professional, master's, post-bachelor's certificate, post-master's certificate. **Academic Requirements:** Arts/fine arts, communication, computer literacy, cultural diversity, English (including composition), foreign languages, history, humanities, mathematics, sciences (biological or physical), social science. **Classes:** Most classes have 10–19 students. Most lab/discussion sections have 10–19 students. **Majors with Highest Enrollment:** Early childhood education and teaching, marketing/marketing management, nursing/registered nurse training (RN, ASN, BSN, MSN). **Disciplines with Highest Percentage of Degrees Awarded:** Business/marketing 20%, education 17%, health professions and related sciences 13%, communications/journalism 8%, engineering 8%. **Special Study Options:** Accelerated program, co-op programs in arts, business, computer science, engineering, family and consumer sciences, humanities, natural science, technologies.distance learning, double major, dual enrollment offered for select graduate level programs, English as a second language (ESL), external degree program, honors program, independent study, internships, student-designed major, study abroad, teacher certification program, weekend college. Undergraduates may also take graduate level courses.

FACILITIES
Housing: Coed dorms, men's dorms, women's dorms, special housing for disabled students, special housing for international students, fraternity/sorority housing, honors student dormitory. **Special Academic Facilities/Equipment:** Performing arts hall, nursery center, language lab, speech and hearing center, nursing learning resource labs, Institute of Polymer Science and Engineering, chemical lab, Institute for Health and Social Policy, Bliss Institute of Applied Politics. **Computers:** 100% of classrooms are wireless, 93% of public computers are PCs, 7% of public computers are Macs, network access in dorm rooms, network access in dorm lounges, online registration, online administrative functions (other than registration), remote student-access to Web through college's connection.

CAMPUS LIFE
Activities: Choral groups, concert band, dance, drama/theater, jazz band, marching band, music ensembles, musical theater, pep band, radio station, student government, student newspaper, symphony orchestra, television station, yearbook. **Organizations:** 225 registered organizations, 22 honor societies, 10 religious organizations. 14 fraternities (2% men join), 8 sororities (2% women join). **Athletics (Intercollegiate):** *Men:* Baseball, basketball, cheerleading, cross-country, football, golf, riflery, soccer, track/field (indoor), track/field (outdoor). *Women:* Basketball, cheerleading, cross-country, diving, riflery, soccer, softball, swimming, tennis, track/field (indoor), track/field (outdoor), volleyball.

ADMISSIONS
Freshman Academic Profile: 12% in top 10% of high school class, 31% in top 25% of high school class, 60% in top 50% of high school class. SAT Math middle 50% range 440–580. SAT Critical Reading middle 50% range 440–560. ACT middle 50% range 18–24. TOEFL required of all international applicants, minimum paper TOEFL 500, minimum computer TOEFL 173. **Basis for Candidate Selection:** *Very important factors considered include:* Academic GPA, class rank, rigor of secondary school record, standardized test scores. **Freshman Admission Requirements:** High school diploma is required, and GED is accepted. *Academic units recommended:* 4 English, 3 math, 3 science, 2 foreign language, 3 social studies. **Freshman Admission Statistics:** 11,181 applied, 79% admitted, 42% enrolled. **Transfer Admission Requirements:** College transcript(s), statement of good standing from prior institution(s). Lowest grade transferable C-. **General Admission Information:** Application

fee $30. Regular application deadline 8/11. Regular notification on a rolling basis within 2 weeks of application. Non-fall registration accepted. Admission may be deferred for a maximum of 2 semesters. Credit offered for CEEB Advanced Placement tests.

COSTS AND FINANCIAL AID

Annual in-state tuition $7,218. Out-of-state tuition $16,467. Room & board $7,640. Required fees $1,164. Average book expense $900. **Required Forms and Deadlines:** FAFSA, institution's own financial aid form. Financial aid filing deadline 2/1. **Notification of Awards:** Applicants will be notified of awards on a rolling basis beginning on or about 4/1. **Types of Aid:** *Need-based scholarships/grants:* Pell, SEOG, state scholarships/grants, the school's own gift aid. *Loans:* FFEL Subsidized Stafford, FFEL Unsubsidized Stafford, FFEL PLUS, Federal Perkins, Federal Nursing, college/university loans from institutional funds. **Student Employment:** Federal Work-Study Program available. Institutional employment available. Off-campus job opportunities are excellent. **Financial Aid Statistics:** 34% freshmen, 35% undergrads receive need-based scholarship or grant aid. 52% freshmen, 54% undergrads receive need-based self-help aid. 65 freshmen, 327 undergrads receive athletic scholarships. 80% freshmen, 85% undergrads receive any aid. Highest amount earned per year from on-campus jobs $5,250.

THE UNIVERSITY OF ALABAMA AT BIRMINGHAM

HUC 260, 1530 Third Avenue South, Birmingham, AL 35294-1150
Phone: 205-934-8221 **E-mail:** undergradadmit@uab.edu **CEEB Code:** 1856
Fax: 205-975-7114 **Website:** http://main.uab.edu **ACT Code:** 0056
Financial Aid Phone: 205-934-8223

This public school was founded in 1969. It has a 265-acre campus.

RATINGS

Admissions Selectivity Rating: 78   Fire Safety Rating: 60*   Green Rating: 60*

STUDENTS AND FACULTY

Enrollment: 10,884. **Student Body:** 61% female, 39% male, 6% out-of-state, 2% international (93 countries represented). African American 31%, Asian 4%, Caucasian 59%, Hispanic 1%. **Retention and Graduation:** 77% freshmen return for sophomore year. **Faculty:** Student/faculty ratio 18:1. 793 full-time faculty, 90% hold PhDs.

ACADEMICS

Degrees: Bachelor's, certificate, doctoral, first professional, master's, post-bachelor's certificate, post-master's certificate. **Academic Requirements:** Arts/fine arts, computer literacy, English (including composition), foreign languages, history, literature, mathematics, philosophy, sciences (biological or physical), social science. **Classes:** Most classes have 20–29 students. Most lab/discussion sections have 20–29 students. **Majors with Highest Enrollment:** Biology/biological sciences, nursing/registered nurse training (RN, ASN, BSN, MSN), psychology. **Disciplines with Highest Percentage of Degrees Awarded:** Business/marketing 20%, health professions and related sciences 19%, psychology 7%, biological/life sciences 6%, education 6%. **Special Study Options:** Cooperative education program, cross registration, distance learning, double major, dual enrollment, honors program, independent study, internships, student-designed major, study abroad, teacher certification program, weekend college.

FACILITIES

Housing: Coed dorms, women's dorms, apartments for married students, apartments for single students. **Special Academic Facilities/Equipment:** Museum of Health Sciences. **Computers:** 90% of classrooms are wireless, network access in dorm rooms, network access in dorm lounges, online registration, online administrative functions (other than registration), remote student-access to Web through college's connection.

CAMPUS LIFE

Activities: Choral groups, concert band, dance, drama/theater, jazz band, literary magazine, marching band, music ensembles, musical theater, opera, pep band, radio station, student government, student newspaper. **Organizations:**

150 registered organizations, 45 honor societies, 9 religious organizations. 6 fraternities (6% men join), 7 sororities (6% women join). **Athletics (Intercollegiate):** *Men:* Baseball, basketball, football, golf, riflery, soccer, tennis. *Women:* Basketball, cross-country, golf, riflery, soccer, softball, synchronized swimming, tennis, track/field (indoor), track/field (outdoor), volleyball.

ADMISSIONS

Freshman Academic Profile: 25% in top 10% of high school class, 49% in top 25% of high school class, 79% in top 50% of high school class. ACT middle 50% range 21–27. TOEFL required of all international applicants, minimum paper TOEFL 500, minimum computer TOEFL 173. **Basis for Candidate Selection:** *Very important factors considered include:* Academic GPA, rigor of secondary school record, standardized test scores. **Freshman Admission Requirements:** High school diploma is required, and GED is accepted. *Academic units required:* 4 English, 3 math, 3 science (2 science labs), 1 foreign language, 3 social studies, 3 academic electives. **Freshman Admission Statistics:** 4,221 applied, 88% admitted, 41% enrolled. **Transfer Admission Requirements:** College transcript(s). Minimum college GPA of 2.0 required. **General Admission Information:** Application fee $30. Regular application deadline 3/1. Regular notification rolling basis beginning preceding fall term. Non-fall registration accepted. Admission may be deferred for a maximum of 2 semesters. Credit offered for CEEB Advanced Placement tests.

COSTS AND FINANCIAL AID

Annual in-state tuition $3,384. Annual out-of-state tuition $8,472. Room and board $7,950. Required fees $824. Average book expense $900. **Required Forms and Deadlines:** FAFSA, institution's own financial aid form. Financial aid filing deadline 4/1. **Notification of Awards:** Applicants will be notified of awards on a rolling basis beginning on or about 4/1. **Types of Aid:** *Need-based scholarships/grants:* Pell, SEOG, state scholarships/grants, private scholarships, the school's own gift aid, United Negro College Fund. *Loans:* Direct Subsidized Stafford, Direct Unsubsidized Stafford, Direct PLUS, Federal Perkins, state loans, college/university loans from institutional funds. **Student Employment:** Federal Work-Study Program available. Institutional employment available. Off-campus job opportunities are excellent. **Financial Aid Statistics:** 27% freshmen, 31% undergrads receive need-based scholarship or grant aid. 43% freshmen, 50% undergrads receive need-based self-help aid. 46 freshmen, 259 undergrads receive athletic scholarships. 46% freshmen, 51% undergrads receive any aid.

See page 1424.

THE UNIVERSITY OF ALABAMA IN HUNTSVILLE

301 Sparkman Drive, Huntsville, AL 35899
Phone: 256-824-6070 **E-mail:** admitme@email.uah.edu **CEEB Code:** 1854
Fax: 256-824-6073 **Website:** www.uah.edu **ACT Code:** 0053
Financial Aid Phone: 256-824-2761

This public school was founded in 1950. It has a 400-acre campus.

RATINGS

Admissions Selectivity Rating: 78   Fire Safety Rating: 88   Green Rating: 60*

STUDENTS AND FACULTY

Enrollment: 5,529. **Student Body:** 49% female, 51% male, 14% out-of-state, 3% international (80 countries represented). African American 15%, Asian 3%, Caucasian 74%, Hispanic 2%, Native American 1%. **Retention and Graduation:** 77% freshmen return for sophomore year. 15% freshmen graduate within 4 years. **Faculty:** Student/faculty ratio 16:1. 287 full-time faculty, 91% hold PhDs. 100% faculty teach undergrads.

ACADEMICS

Degrees: Bachelor's, doctoral, master's, post-bachelor's certificate, post-master's certificate. **Academic Requirements:** Arts/fine arts, computer literacy, English (including composition), history, humanities, mathematics, sciences (biological or physical), social science. **Classes:** Most classes have 20–29 students. Most lab/discussion sections have fewer than 10 students. **Majors with Highest Enrollment:** Biology/biological sciences, mechanical engineering, nursing/registered nurse training (RN, ASN, BSN, MSN). **Disciplines with Highest Percentage of Degrees Awarded:** 3-2 program in engineering, Business/marketing 26%, engineering 24%, health professions and related sciences 15%, visual and performing arts 6%, English 5%. **Special Study Options:** Accelerated program, cooperative education program, cross registration, distance learning, double major, dual enrollment, English as a second language (ESL), honors program, independent study, internships, liberal arts/career combination, study abroad, teacher certification program.

FACILITIES

Housing: Coed dorms, apartments for married students, apartments for single students, special housing for disabled students, fraternity/sorority housing. **Special Academic Facilities/Equipment:** Art museum and galleries, observatory with a solar magnemeter, optics building, centers for applied optics, micro-gravity research, robotics, solar research, space plasma, aeronomic research. **Computers:** 1% of classrooms are wired, 30% of classrooms are wireless, 98% of public computers are PCs, 1% of public computers are Macs, network access in dorm rooms, network access in dorm lounges, online registration, online administrative functions (other than registration), remote student-access to Web through college's connection.

CAMPUS LIFE

Activities: Choral groups, concert band, dance, drama/theater, jazz band, literary magazine, music ensembles, musical theater, opera, pep band, student government, student newspaper, symphony orchestra. **Organizations:** 79 registered organizations, 23 honor societies, 8 religious organizations. 7 fraternities (3% men join), 4 sororities (3% women join). **Athletics (Intercollegiate):** *Men:* Baseball, basketball, cross-country, ice hockey, soccer, tennis, track/field (indoor), track/field (outdoor). *Women:* Basketball, cross-country, soccer, softball, tennis, track/field (indoor), track/field (outdoor), volleyball.

ADMISSIONS

Freshman Academic Profile: 26% in top 10% of high school class, 52% in top 25% of high school class, 78% in top 50% of high school class. 89% from public high schools. SAT Math middle 50% range 500–640. SAT Critical Reading middle 50% range 480–630. ACT middle 50% range 21–27. TOEFL required of all international applicants, minimum paper TOEFL 500, minimum computer TOEFL 173. **Basis for Candidate Selection:** *Very important factors considered include:* Academic GPA, rigor of secondary school record, standardized test scores. **Freshman Admission Requirements:** High school diploma is required, and GED is accepted. *Academic units required:* 4 English, 3 math, 3 science, 4 social studies, 6 academic electives. **Freshman Admission Statistics:** 1,809 applied, 88% admitted, 52% enrolled. **Transfer Admission Requirements:** College transcript(s), statement of good standing from prior institution(s). Minimum college GPA of 2.0 required. Lowest grade transferable D. **General Admission Information:** Application fee $30. Regular application deadline 8/15. Regular notification Students are notified when application is complete. Non-fall registration accepted. Admission may be deferred for a maxiumum of 2 semesters. Credit and/or placement offered for CEEB Advanced Placement tests.

COSTS AND FINANCIAL AID

Comprehensive fee $5,216. Room and board $6,290. Average book expense $942. **Required Forms and Deadlines:** FAFSA. Financial aid filing deadline 4/1. **Notification of Awards:** Applicants will be notified of awards on a rolling basis beginning on or about 4/1. **Types of Aid:** *Need-based scholarships/grants:* Pell, SEOG, state scholarships/grants, private scholarships, the school's own gift aid, Federal Nursing Scholarships. *Loans:* Direct Subsidized Stafford, Direct Unsubsidized Stafford, Direct PLUS. **Financial Aid Statistics:** 36% freshmen, 31% undergrads receive need-based scholarship or grant aid. 34% freshmen, 37% undergrads receive need-based self-help aid. 48 freshmen, 157 undergrads receive athletic scholarships. 85% freshmen, 73% undergrads receive any aid.

UNIVERSITY OF ALABAMA AT TUSCALOOSA

Box 870132, Tuscaloosa, AL 35487-0132
Phone: 205-348-5666 **E-mail:** admissions@ua.edu **CEEB Code:** 1830
Fax: 205-348-9046 **Website:** www.ua.edu **ACT Code:** 0052
Financial Aid Phone: 205-348-6756

This public school was founded in 1831. It has a 1,000-acre campus.

RATINGS

Admissions Selectivity Rating: 86   **Fire Safety Rating:** 75   **Green Rating:** 60*

STUDENTS AND FACULTY

Enrollment: 19,237. **Student Body:** 53% female, 47% male, 24% out-of-state, 1% international (83 countries represented). African American 11%, Caucasian 84%, Hispanic 2%. **Retention and Graduation:** 86% freshmen return for sophomore year. 36% freshmen graduate within 4 years. 30% grads go on to further study within 1 year. 4% grads pursue law degrees. 2% grads pursue medical degrees. **Faculty:** Student/faculty ratio 19:1. 940 full-time faculty, 91% hold PhDs. 71% faculty teach undergrads.

ACADEMICS

Degrees: Bachelor's, doctoral, first professional, master's, post-master's certificate. **Academic Requirements:** Arts/fine arts, computer literacy, English (including composition), foreign languages, history, humanities, mathematics, philosophy, sciences (biological or physical), social science. **Classes:** Most classes have 10–19 students. Most lab/discussion sections have 20–29 students. **Majors with Highest Enrollment:** Biology/biological sciences, finance, nursing/registered nurse training (RN, ASN, BSN, MSN). **Disciplines with Highest Percentage of Degrees Awarded:** Business/marketing 27%, communications/journalism 12%, education 7%, family and consumer sciences 7%, health professions and related sciences 8%. **Special Study Options:** Accelerated program, cooperative education program, cross registration, distance learning, double major, dual enrollment, English as a second language (ESL), exchange student program (domestic), external degree program, honors program, independent study, internships, liberal arts/career combination, student-designed major, study abroad, teacher certification program, weekend college.

FACILITIES

Housing: Coed dorms, men's dorms, women's dorms, apartments for married students, apartments for single students, special housing for disabled students, fraternity/sorority housing, apartments for visiting scholars. **Special Academic Facilities/Equipment:** Art gallery, natural history museum, concert hall, archaeologic site and museum, arboretum, observatory, simulated coal mine, robotics lab, wind tunnel, artificial intelligence lab, jet propulsion engine mini-lab, special collections building. **Computers:** 1% of classrooms are wired, 10% of classrooms are wireless, 80% of public computers are PCs, 15% of public computers are Macs, 5% of public computers are UNIX, network access in dorm rooms, network access in dorm lounges, online registration, online administrative functions (other than registration), support for handheld computing, remote student-access to Web through college's connection.

CAMPUS LIFE

Activities: Choral groups, concert band, dance, drama/theater, jazz band, literary magazine, marching band, music ensembles, musical theater, opera, pep band, radio station, student government, student newspaper, student-run film society, symphony orchestra, television station. **Organizations:** 228 registered organizations, 66 honor societies, 32 religious organizations. 21 fraternities (20% men join), 31 sororities (26% women join). **Athletics (Intercollegiate):** *Men:* Baseball, basketball, cheerleading, cross-country, diving, football, golf, swimming, tennis, track/field (indoor), track/field (outdoor). *Women:* Basketball, cheerleading, crew/rowing, cross-country, diving, golf, gymnastics, soccer, softball, swimming, tennis, track/field (indoor), track/field (outdoor), volleyball.

ADMISSIONS

Freshman Academic Profile: 39% in top 10% of high school class, 54% in top 25% of high school class, 79% in top 50% of high school class. 90% from public high schools. SAT Math middle 50% range 500–620. SAT Critical Reading middle 50% range 490–610. ACT middle 50% range 21–27. TOEFL required of all international applicants, minimum paper TOEFL 500, minimum computer TOEFL 173. **Basis for Candidate Selection:** *Very important factors considered include:* Academic GPA, rigor of secondary school record, standardized test scores. *Important factors considered include:* Class rank. *Other factors considered include:* Alumni/ae relation, application essay, character/personal qualities, extracurricular activities, first generation, interview, recommendation(s), talent/ability, volunteer work, work experience. **Freshman Admission Requirements:** High school diploma is required, and GED is accepted. *Academic units required:* 4 English, 3 math, 3 science (2 science labs), 1 foreign language, 3 social studies, 1 history, 5 academic electives. *Academic units recommended:* 4 English, 3 math, 3 science (2 science labs), 1 foreign language, 3 social studies, 1 history, 5 academic electives. **Freshman Admission Statistics:** 12,513 applied, 70% admitted, 50% enrolled. **Transfer Admission Requirements:** College transcript(s). Minimum college GPA of 2.0 required. Lowest grade transferable D. **General Admission Information:** Application fee $35. Regular notification is rolling. Non-fall registration accepted. Credit and/or placement offered for CEEB Advanced Placement tests.

COSTS AND FINANCIAL AID

Average book expense $950. **Required Forms and Deadlines:** FAFSA. Financial aid filing deadline 3/1. **Notification of Awards:** Applicants will be notified of awards on a rolling basis beginning on or about 4/1. **Types of Aid:** *Need-based scholarships/grants:* Pell, SEOG, state scholarships/grants, private scholarships, the school's own gift aid, Federal Nursing Scholarships. *Loans:* Direct Subsidized Stafford, Direct Unsubsidized Stafford, Direct PLUS, Federal Perkins, college/university loans from institutional funds. **Financial Aid Statistics:** 16% freshmen, 19% undergrads receive need-based scholarship or grant aid. 27% freshmen, 31% undergrads receive need-based self-help aid. 93 freshmen, 386 undergrads receive athletic scholarships. 68% freshmen, 74% undergrads receive any aid.

UNIVERSITY OF ALASKA—ANCHORAGE

3211 Providence Drive, Anchorage, AK 99508-8046
Phone: 907-786-1480 **E-mail:** enroll@uaa.alaska.edu **CEEB Code:** 4896
Fax: 907-786-4888 **Website:** www.alaska.edu **ACT Code:** 0137
Financial Aid Phone: 907-786-1586

This public school was founded in 1954. It has a 384-acre campus.

RATINGS
Admissions Selectivity Rating: 73   **Fire Safety Rating:** 60*   **Green Rating:** 60*

STUDENTS AND FACULTY
Enrollment: 10,064. **Student Body:** 62% female, 38% male, 6% out-of-state, 2% international (35 countries represented). African American 4%, Asian 5%, Caucasian 59%, Hispanic 4%, Native American 8%. **Retention and Graduation:** 67% freshmen return for sophomore year. 6% freshmen graduate within 4 years. **Faculty:** Student/faculty ratio 18:1. 551 full-time faculty, 61% hold PhDs. 94% faculty teach undergrads.

ACADEMICS
Degrees: Associate, bachelor's, certificate, master's, post-bachelor's certificate, post-master's certificate. **Academic Requirements:** Arts/fine arts, computer literacy, English (including composition), history, humanities, mathematics, sciences (biological or physical), social science. These are for baccalaureate degree seeking students only. **Classes:** Most classes have 10–19 students. Most lab/discussion sections have fewer than 10 students. **Disciplines with Highest Percentage of Degrees Awarded:** Business/marketing 21%, health professions and related sciences 18%, psychology 9%, social sciences 7%, history 5%. **Special Study Options:** Accelerated program, Air Force ROTC, cooperative education program, cross registration, distance learning, double major, dual enrollment, English as a second language (ESL), exchange student program (domestic), honors program, independent study, internships, liberal arts/career combination, student-designed major, study abroad, teacher certification program.

FACILITIES
Housing: Coed dorms, apartments for single students, special housing for disabled students, special housing for international students, floors for Alaska natives studying engineering, nursing students, honor students, aviation, psychology. **Special Academic Facilities/Equipment:** Kimura and Student Center Galleries. **Computers:** 80% of public computers are PCs, 20% of public computers are Macs, network access in dorm rooms, network access in dorm lounges, online registration, online administrative functions (other than registration), remote student-access to Web through college's connection.

CAMPUS LIFE
Activities: Choral groups, dance, drama/theater, jazz band, literary magazine,

music ensembles, radio station, student government, student newspaper. **Organizations:** 70 registered organizations, 5 honor societies, 5 religious organizations. 1 fraternity, 2 sororities. **Athletics (Intercollegiate):** *Men:* Basketball, cross-country, ice hockey, skiing (downhill/alpine), skiing (nordic/cross-country). *Women:* Basketball, cross-country, gymnastics, skiing (downhill/alpine), skiing (nordic/cross-country), volleyball.

ADMISSIONS
Freshman Academic Profile: 9% in top 10% of high school class, 28% in top 25% of high school class, 59% in top 50% of high school class. 95% from public high schools. SAT Math middle 50% range 440–570. SAT Critical Reading middle 50% range 440–580. ACT middle 50% range 17–24. TOEFL required of all international applicants, minimum paper TOEFL 450. **Basis for Candidate Selection:** *Very important factors considered include:* Rigor of secondary school record. *Other factors considered include:* Class rank, standardized test scores, talent/ability. **Freshman Admission Requirements:** High school diploma is required, and GED is accepted. *Academic units recommended:* 4 English, 2 math, 3 science, 1 foreign language, 3 social studies, 1 history. **Freshman Admission Statistics:** 2,760 applied, 74% admitted, 76% enrolled. **Transfer Admission Requirements:** College transcript(s), statement of good standing from prior institution(s). Minimum college GPA of 2.0 required. Lowest grade transferable C. **General Admission Information:** Application fee $40. Regular application deadline 7/1. Non-fall registration accepted. Admission may be deferred for a maxiumum of 2 semesters. Common Application not accepted. Credit offered for CEEB Advanced Placement tests.

COSTS AND FINANCIAL AID
Annual in-state tuition $4,020. Annual out-of-state tuition $13,440. Room and board $7,982. Required fees $560. Average book expense $1,022. **Required Forms and Deadlines:** FAFSA. Financial aid filing deadline 4/1. **Notification of Awards:** Applicants will be notified of awards on a rolling basis beginning on or about 3/15. **Types of Aid:** *Need-based scholarships/grants:* Pell, SEOG, state scholarships/grants, private scholarships, the school's own gift aid, Federal Work Study. *Loans:* FFEL Subsidized Stafford, FFEL Unsubsidized Stafford, FFEL PLUS, state loans. **Student Employment:** Federal Work-Study Program available. Institutional employment available. Off-campus job opportunities are good.

UNIVERSITY OF ALASKA—FAIRBANKS

PO Box 757480, Fairbanks, AK 99775-7480
Phone: 907-474-7500 **E-mail:** admissions@uaf.edu **CEEB Code:** 4866
Fax: 907-474-5379 **Website:** www.uaf.edu **ACT Code:** 0064
Financial Aid Phone: 888-474-7256

This public school was founded in 1917. It has a 2,250-acre campus.

RATINGS
Admissions Selectivity Rating: 75   **Fire Safety Rating:** 88   **Green Rating:** 60*

STUDENTS AND FACULTY
Enrollment: 4,684. **Student Body:** 57% female, 43% male, 13% out-of-state, 2% international (56 countries represented). African American 3%, Asian 4%, Caucasian 64%, Hispanic 3%, Native American 19%. **Retention and Graduation:** 74% freshmen return for sophomore year. 10% freshmen graduate within 4 years. **Faculty:** Student/faculty ratio 13:1. 310 full-time faculty.

ACADEMICS
Degrees: Associate, bachelor's, certificate, doctoral, master's. **Academic Requirements:** Arts/fine arts, computer literacy, English (including composition), history, humanities, mathematics, philosophy, sciences (biological or physical), social science. **Classes:** Most classes have 10–19 students. Most lab/discussion sections have 10–19 students. **Majors with Highest Enrollment:** Biology/biological sciences, business administration and management, psychology. **Disciplines with Highest Percentage of Degrees Awarded:** Engineering 12%, business/marketing 10%, biological/life sciences 9%, social sciences 8%, psychology 7%. **Special Study Options:** Accelerated program, cooperative education program, distance learning, double major, dual enrollment, exchange student program (domestic), honors program, independent study, internships, student-designed major, study abroad, teacher certification program.

The Princeton Review's Complete Book of Colleges

FACILITIES

Housing: Coed dorms, apartments for married students, apartments for single students, special housing for disabled students, Alaksa Native cultural housing. **Special Academic Facilities/Equipment:** Museum of Natural/Cultural History of Alaska and the North, Cray Super Computer, extensive telecommunication network, geophysical institute, NASA earth station, Poker Flat Research Range, electron microscope, microprobe. **Computers:** 75% of public computers are PCs, 20% of public computers are Macs, 5% of public computers are UNIX, network access in dorm rooms, network access in dorm lounges, online registration, online administrative functions (other than registration), remote student-access to Web through college's connection.

CAMPUS LIFE

Activities: Choral groups, concert band, dance, drama/theater, jazz band, music ensembles, musical theater, pep band, radio station, student government, student newspaper, student-run film society, symphony orchestra, television station. **Organizations:** 93 registered organizations, 8 honor societies, 9 religious organizations. 1 fraternity, 1 sorority. **Athletics (Intercollegiate):** *Men:* Basketball, cross-country, ice hockey, riflery, skiing (nordic/cross-country). *Women:* Basketball, cross-country, riflery, skiing (nordic/cross-country), swimming, volleyball.

ADMISSIONS

Freshman Academic Profile: 15% in top 10% of high school class, 35% in top 25% of high school class, 64% in top 50% of high school class. SAT Math middle 50% range 450–590. SAT Critical Reading middle 50% range 450–600. ACT middle 50% range 18–25. TOEFL required of all international applicants, minimum paper TOEFL 550, minimum computer TOEFL 213. **Basis for Candidate Selection:** *Very important factors considered include:* Academic GPA, standardized test scores. **Freshman Admission Requirements:** High school diploma is required, and GED is not accepted. *Academic units required:* 4 English, 3 math, 3 science (1 science lab), 3 social studies, 3 academic electives. *Academic units recommended:* 2 foreign language. **Freshman Admission Statistics:** 1,743 applied, 74% admitted, 69% enrolled. **Transfer Admission Requirements:** College transcript(s). Minimum college GPA of 2.0 required. Lowest grade transferable C. **General Admission Information:** Application fee $40. Regular application deadline 8/1. Regular notification rolling. Non-fall registration accepted. Admission may be deferred for a maximum of 1 year. Credit and/or placement offered for CEEB Advanced Placement tests.

COSTS AND FINANCIAL AID

Annual in-state tuition $4,080. Annual out-of-state tuition $13,050. Room and board $6,030. Required fees $738. Average book expense $1,400. **Required Forms and Deadlines:** FAFSA. Financial aid filing deadline 7/1. **Notification of Awards:** Applicants will be notified of awards on or about 3/1. **Types of Aid:** *Need-based scholarships/grants:* Pell, SEOG, private scholarships, the school's own gift aid, Native Alaska non-profit corporations. *Loans:* Direct Subsidized Stafford, Direct Unsubsidized Stafford, Direct PLUS, FFEL Subsidized Stafford, FFEL Unsubsidized Stafford, FFEL PLUS, state loans, college/university loans from institutional funds. **Student Employment:** Federal Work-Study Program available. Institutional employment available. Off-campus job opportunities are good. **Financial Aid Statistics:** 24% freshmen, 26% undergrads receive need-based scholarship or grant aid. 21% freshmen, 28% undergrads receive need-based self-help aid. 18 freshmen, 72 undergrads receive athletic scholarships. 52% freshmen, 55% undergrads receive any aid. Highest amount earned per year from on-campus jobs $13,680.

UNIVERSITY OF ALASKA—SOUTHEAST

11120 Glacier Highway, Juneau, AK 99801-8681
Phone: 907-465-6462 **E-mail:** jngaw@acad1.alaska.edu **CEEB Code:** 4897
Fax: 907-465-6365 **Website:** www.jun.alaska.edu **ACT Code:** 0153
Financial Aid Phone: 907-465-6255

This public school was founded in 1972. It has a 198-acre campus.

RATINGS

Admissions Selectivity Rating: 60*   **Fire Safety Rating:** 60*   **Green Rating:** 60*

STUDENTS AND FACULTY

Student Body: 20% out-of-state.

ACADEMICS

Degrees: Associate, bachelor's, master's. **Special Study Options:** Cooperative education program, co-op programs in business, computer science, humanities, study abroad, graduate level classes for undergrads.

FACILITIES

Housing: Coed dorms, apartments for married students, apartments for single students.

ADMISSIONS

Freshman Academic Profile: 13% in top 10% of high school class, 31% in top 25% of high school class, 64% in top 50% of high school class. 94% from public high schools. TOEFL required of all international applicants, minimum paper TOEFL 500. **Freshman Admission Requirements:** High school diploma is required, and GED is accepted. *Academic units recommended:* 4 English, 2 math, 2 science, 3 social studies. **Transfer Admission Requirements:** Minimum college GPA of 2.0 required. Lowest grade transferable C. **General Admission Information:** Regular application deadline 9/5. Regular notification rolling. Non-fall registration accepted. Common Application not accepted. Credit offered for CEEB Advanced Placement tests.

COSTS AND FINANCIAL AID

Annual in-state tuition $2,168. Out-of-state tuition $6,428. Room & board $7,650. Required fees $134. Average book expense $529. **Required Forms and Deadlines:** FAFSA, institution's own financial aid form, state aid form. **Notification of Awards:** Applicants will be notified of awards on or about 5/1. **Types of Aid:** *Need-based scholarships/grants:* State scholarships/grants. *Loans:* FFEL Subsidized Stafford, FFEL PLUS. **Student Employment:** Federal Work-Study Program available. Institutional employment available. Off-campus job opportunities are good. **Financial Aid Statistics:** Highest amount earned per year from on-campus jobs $1,800.

UNIVERSITY OF ALBERTA

120 Administration Building, Edmonton, Alberta, AB T6G 2M7 Canada
Phone: 780-492-3113 **E-mail:** registrar@ualberta.ca
Fax: 780-492-7172 **Website:** www.ualberta.ca
Financial Aid Phone: 780-492-3483

This public school was founded in 1908.

RATINGS

Admissions Selectivity Rating: 60*   **Fire Safety Rating:** 60*   **Green Rating:** 60*

STUDENTS AND FACULTY

Enrollment: 27,241. **Student Body:** 56% female, 44% male, 12% out-of-province. **Faculty:** Student/faculty ratio 14:1. 1,456 full-time faculty.

ACADEMICS

Degrees: Bachelor's, certificate, diploma, doctoral, first professional, master's. **Academic Requirements:** English (including composition), sciences (biological or physical). **Majors with Highest Enrollment:** Education, psychology. **Disciplines with Highest Percentage of Degrees Awarded:** Education 21%, engineering 10%, business/marketing 8%, health professions and related sciences 5%. **Special Study Options:** Cooperative education program, distance learning, English as a second language (ESL), exchange student program (domestic), honors program, independent study, internships, student-designed major, study abroad, teacher certification program.

FACILITIES

Housing: Coed dorms, apartments for married students, apartments for single students, special housing for disabled students, family accommodations. **Computers:** 90% of public computers are PCs, 10% of public computers are Macs, network access in dorm rooms, online administrative functions (other than registration), remote student-access to Web through college's connection.

CAMPUS LIFE

Activities: Choral groups, concert band, dance, drama/theater, jazz band, music ensembles, radio station, student government, student newspaper, student-run film society. **Organizations:** 250 registered organizations, 9 fraternities, 4 sororities. **Athletics (Intercollegiate):** *Men:* Basketball, cross-country, football, ice hockey, track/field (indoor). *Women:* Basketball, cross-country, field hockey, ice hockey, track/field (indoor).

ADMISSIONS

Freshman Academic Profile: TOEFL required of all international applicants, minimum paper TOEFL 580, minimum computer TOEFL 237. **Basis for Candidate Selection:** *Very important factors considered include:* Rigor of secondary school record. *Important factors considered include:* Standardized test scores, talent/ability. *Other factors considered include:* Interview, racial/ethnic status. **Freshman Admission Requirements:** High school diploma is required, and GED is not accepted. **Freshman Admission Statistics:** 11,005 applied, 47% admitted, 98% enrolled. **Transfer Admission Requirements:**

College transcript(s). **General Admission Information:** Application fee $41. Regular application deadline 5/2. Regular notification Last week of July and first week of August. Non-fall registration accepted. Common Application not accepted.

COSTS AND FINANCIAL AID

Comprehensive fee $2,800. In-province tuition $3,890. Out-of-province tuition $3,890. International tuition $10,000. Room & board $4,500. Required fees $440. Average book expense $1,000. **Student Employment:** Institutional employment available. Off-campus job opportunities are good.

UNIVERSITY OF ARIZONA

Best 368

PO Box 210040, Tucson, AZ 85721-0040
Phone: 520-621-3237 **E-mail:** appinfo@arizona.edu **CEEB Code:** 4832
Fax: 520-621-9799 **Website:** www.arizona.edu **ACT Code:** 0096

This public school was founded in 1885. It has a 378-acre campus.

RATINGS

Admissions Selectivity Rating: 75   **Fire Safety Rating:** 60*   **Green Rating:** 60*

STUDENTS AND FACULTY

Enrollment: 28,013. **Student Body:** 53% female, 47% male, 33% out-of-state, 3% international (124 countries represented). African American 3%, Asian 6%, Caucasian 65%, Hispanic 16%, Native American 2%. **Retention and Graduation:** 79% freshmen return for sophomore year. 31% freshmen graduate within 4 years. 42% grads go on to further study within 1 year. **Faculty:** Student/faculty ratio 18:1. 1,412 full-time faculty, 98% hold PhDs. 78% faculty teach undergrads.

ACADEMICS

Degrees: Bachelor's, doctoral, first professional, master's, post-bachelor's certificate. **Academic Requirements:** Arts/fine arts, English (including composition), foreign languages, humanities, mathematics, sciences (biological or physical), social science. **Classes:** Most classes have 10–19 students. Most lab/discussion sections have 10–19 students. **Majors with Highest Enrollment:** Elementary education and teaching, political science and government, psychology. **Disciplines with Highest Percentage of Degrees Awarded:** Business/marketing 14%, communications/journalism 10%, education 10%, social sciences 10%, biological/life sciences 8%, engineering 8%. **Special Study Options:** Cooperative education program, cross registration, distance learning, double major, dual enrollment, English as a second language (ESL), exchange student program (domestic), honors program, independent study, internships, student-designed major, study abroad, teacher certification program, weekend college.

FACILITIES

Housing: Coed dorms, women's dorms, apartments for single students, special housing for disabled students, special housing for international students, fraternity/sorority housing. **Special Academic Facilities/Equipment:** Art, photography, and natural history museums, tree-ring lab, planetarium, optical sciences center, nuclear reactor. **Computers:** 95% of public computers are PCs, 4% of public computers are Macs, network access in dorm rooms, online registration, online administrative functions (other than registration), remote student-access to Web through college's connection.

CAMPUS LIFE

Activities: Choral groups, concert band, dance, drama/theater, jazz band, literary magazine, marching band, music ensembles, musical theater, opera, pep band, radio station, student government, student newspaper, symphony orchestra, television station, yearbook. **Organizations:** 504 registered organizations, 13 honor societies, 13 religious organizations. 25 fraternities (10% men join), 20 sororities (11% women join). **Athletics (Intercollegiate):** *Men:* Baseball, basketball, cross-country, diving, football, golf, swimming, tennis, track/field (outdoor). *Women:* Basketball, cross-country, diving, golf, gymnastics, soccer, softball, swimming, tennis, track/field (indoor), track/field (outdoor), volleyball.

ADMISSIONS

Freshman Academic Profile: 34% in top 10% of high school class, 62% in top 25% of high school class, 87% in top 50% of high school class. 90% from public

high schools. SAT Math middle 50% range 490–620. SAT Critical Reading middle 50% range 480–600. ACT middle 50% range 21–26. **Basis for Candidate Selection:** *Very important factors considered include:* Academic GPA, rigor of secondary school record. *Other factors considered include:* Application essay, character/personal qualities, class rank, extracurricular activities, first generation, geographical residence, interview, racial/ethnic status, recommendation(s), standardized test scores, state residency, talent/ability, volunteer work. **Freshman Admission Requirements:** High school diploma is required, and GED is accepted. *Academic units required:* 4 English, 4 math, 3 science (3 science labs), 2 foreign language, 1 social studies, 1 history, 1 fine arts. *Academic units recommended:* 4 English, 4 math, 3 science (3 science labs), 2 foreign language, 2 social studies, 1 history, 1 fine arts. **Freshman Admission Statistics:** 16,609 applied, 80% admitted, 45% enrolled. **Transfer Admission Requirements:** College transcript(s). **General Admission Information:** Application fee $50. Regular application deadline 5/1. Regular notification is rolling. Non-fall registration accepted. Credit offered for CEEB Advanced Placement tests.

COSTS AND FINANCIAL AID

Annual in-state tuition $4,824. Annual out-of-state tuition $16,058. Room and board $7,370. Required fees $224. Average book expense $1,000. **Types of Aid:** *Need-based scholarships/grants:* Pell, SEOG, state scholarships/grants, private scholarships, the school's own gift aid, Federal Nursing Scholarships. *Loans:* FFEL Subsidized Stafford, FFEL Unsubsidized Stafford, FFEL PLUS, Federal Perkins, Federal Nursing, college/university loans from institutional funds. **Student Employment:** Federal Work-Study Program available. Institutional employment available. Off-campus job opportunities are good. **Financial Aid Statistics:** 33% freshmen, 34% undergrads receive need-based scholarship or grant aid. 18% freshmen, 26% undergrads receive need-based self-help aid. **Financial Aid Phone:** 520-621-1858.

UNIVERSITY OF ARKANSAS—FAYETTEVILLE

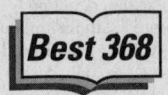

Best 368

232 Silas Hunt Hall, Fayetteville, AR 72701
Phone: 479-575-5346 **E-mail:** uofa@uark.edu **CEEB Code:** 6866
Fax: 479-575-7515 **Website:** www.uark.edu **ACT Code:** 0144

This public school was founded in 1871. It has a 410-acre campus.

RATINGS

Admissions Selectivity Rating: 87   **Fire Safety Rating:** 60*   **Green Rating:** 97

STUDENTS AND FACULTY

Enrollment: 14,350. **Student Body:** 50% female, 50% male, 21% out-of-state, 2% international (103 countries represented). African American 4%, Asian 3%, Caucasian 81%, Hispanic 3%, Native American 2%. **Retention and Graduation:** 83% freshmen return for sophomore year. 30% freshmen graduate within 4 years. **Faculty:** Student/faculty ratio 17:1. 807 full-time faculty, 89% hold PhDs. 96% faculty teach undergrads.

ACADEMICS

Degrees: Bachelor's, doctoral, first professional, master's, post-bachelor's certificate, post-master's certificate. **Academic Requirements:** Arts/fine arts, English (including composition), foreign languages, history, humanities, mathematics, philosophy, sciences (biological or physical), social science. **Classes:** Most classes have 20–29 students. Most lab/discussion sections have 10–19 students. **Majors with Highest Enrollment:** Elementary education and teaching, finance, marketing/marketing management. **Disciplines with Highest Percentage of Degrees Awarded:** Business/marketing 24%, engineering 9%, education 8%, social sciences 6%. **Special Study Options:** Accelerated program, cooperative education program, distance learning, double major, dual enrollment, English as a second language (ESL), honors program, independent study, internships, study abroad, teacher certification program.

FACILITIES

Housing: Coed dorms, men's dorms, women's dorms, apartments for married students, apartments for single students, fraternity/sorority housing, suites with private bedrooms, special interest floors, enhanced learning centers, first-year experience program area.
Special Academic Facilities/Equipment: Public Radio-KUAF, High Density

Electronics Center, Reynolds Center for Enterprise Development, Center for Excellence in Poultry Science, Genesis Small Business Incubation Center, Chemical Hazards Research Center, honors college. **Computers:** 35% of classrooms are wired, 10% of classrooms are wireless, 90% of public computers are PCs, 5% of public computers are Macs, 5% of public computers are UNIX, network access in dorm rooms, network access in dorm lounges, online registration, online administrative functions (other than registration), support for handheld computing, remote student-access to Web through college's connection.

CAMPUS LIFE

Activities: Choral groups, concert band, dance, drama/theater, jazz band, literary magazine, marching band, music ensembles, musical theater, opera, pep band, radio station, student government, student newspaper, student-run film society, symphony orchestra, television station. **Organizations:** 238 registered organizations, 60 honor societies, 20 religious organizations. 15 fraternities (18% men join), 11 sororities (20% women join). **Athletics (Intercollegiate):** *Men:* Baseball, basketball, cheerleading, cross-country, football, golf, tennis, track/field (indoor), track/field (outdoor). *Women:* Basketball, cheerleading, cross-country, diving, golf, gymnastics, soccer, softball, swimming, tennis, track/field (indoor), track/field (outdoor), volleyball.

ADMISSIONS

Freshman Academic Profile: 32% in top 10% of high school class, 61% in top 25% of high school class, 88% in top 50% of high school class. 95% from public high schools. SAT Math middle 50% range 520–650. SAT Critical Reading middle 50% range 510–630. ACT middle 50% range 23–29. TOEFL required of all international applicants, minimum paper TOEFL 550, minimum computer TOEFL 213. **Basis for Candidate Selection:** *Very important factors considered include:* Academic GPA, class rank, rigor of secondary school record, standardized test scores. *Other factors considered include:* Alumni/ae relation, character/personal qualities, extracurricular activities, geographical residence, recommendation(s), state residency, talent/ability, volunteer work, work experience. **Freshman Admission Requirements:** High school diploma is required, and GED is accepted. *Academic units required:* 4 English, 4 math, 3 science (2 science labs), 3 social studies, 2 academic electives. *Academic units recommended:* 2 foreign language. **Freshman Admission Statistics:** 8,443 applied, 68% admitted, 48% enrolled. **Transfer Admission Requirements:** College transcript(s). Minimum college GPA of 2.0 required. Lowest grade transferable C-. **General Admission Information:** Application fee $40. Regular application deadline 8/15. Regular notification is rolling. Non-fall registration accepted. Admission may be deferred for a maxiumum of 2 semesters. Credit and/or placement offered for CEEB Advanced Placement tests.

COSTS AND FINANCIAL AID

Annual in-state tuition $4,772. Annual out-of-state tuition $13,226. Room and board $7,017. Required fees $1,266. Average book expense $966. **Required Forms and Deadlines:** FAFSA. Financial aid filing deadline 3/15. **Notification of Awards:** Applicants will be notified of awards on or about 4/1. **Types of Aid:** *Need-based scholarships/grants:* Pell, SEOG, state scholarships/grants, private scholarships, the school's own gift aid. *Loans:* FFEL Subsidized Stafford, FFEL Unsubsidized Stafford, FFEL PLUS, Federal Perkins, state loans, college/university loans from institutional funds, alternative loans. **Financial Aid Statistics:** 22% freshmen, 24% undergrads receive need-based scholarship or grant aid. 25% freshmen, 31% undergrads receive need-based self-help aid. 98 freshmen, 446 undergrads receive athletic scholarships. 70% freshmen, 64% undergrads receive any aid. Highest amount earned per year from on-campus jobs $3,000. **Financial Aid Phone:** 479-575-3806.

See page 1426.

UNIVERSITY OF ARKANSAS—LITTLE ROCK

2801 South University Avenue, Little Rock, AR 72204
Phone: 501-569-3127 **E-mail:** admissions@ualr.edu **CEEB Code:** 6368
Fax: 501-569-8915 **Website:** www.ualr.edu **ACT Code:** 0132

This public school was founded in 1927. It has a 150-acre campus.

RATINGS
Admissions Selectivity Rating: 60*   **Fire Safety Rating:** 60*   **Green Rating:** 60*

STUDENTS AND FACULTY
Student Body: 2% out-of-state. **Retention and Graduation:** 59% freshmen return for sophomore year. 25% grads go on to further study within 1 year. 20%

grads pursue arts and sciences degrees. 1% grads pursue business degrees. 4% grads pursue law degrees.

ACADEMICS

Degrees: Associate, bachelor's, certificate, doctoral, master's, post-bachelor's certificate. **Academic Requirements:** English (including composition), mathematics.

FACILITIES

Housing: Coed dorms, men's dorms, women's dorms, fraternity/sorority housing. **Special Academic Facilities/Equipment:** Language lab, observatory, planetarium, electron microscope, particle accelerator, nuclear magnetic resonator.

CAMPUS LIFE

Activities: Radio station, student government, student newspaper, television station, yearbook. **Organizations:** 98 registered organizations, 37 honor societies, 16 religious organizations. 5 fraternities (2% men join), 5 sororities (2% women join). **Athletics (Intercollegiate):** *Men:* Basketball, cross-country, diving, soccer, swimming, tennis. *Women:* Basketball, golf, soccer, swimming, tennis, track/field (outdoor), volleyball.

ADMISSIONS

Freshman Academic Profile: TOEFL required of all international applicants, minimum paper TOEFL 525. **Freshman Admission Requirements:** High school diploma is required, and GED is accepted. *Academic units recommended:* 4 English, 3 math, 2 science (2 science labs), 2 foreign language, 1 social studies, 2 history. **Transfer Admission Requirements:** College transcript(s). Minimum college GPA of 2.0 required. Lowest grade transferable C. **General Admission Information:** Early decision application deadline 8/1. Regular application deadline 8/1. Regular notification rolling. Non-fall registration accepted. Common Application not accepted. Credit offered for CEEB Advanced Placement tests.

COSTS AND FINANCIAL AID

Annual in-state tuition $1,131. Out-of-state tuition $2,916. Room & board $2,435. Required fees $138. Average book expense $1,000. **Required Forms and Deadlines:** FAFSA, state aid form. **Types of Aid:** *Need-based scholarships/grants:* State scholarships/grants. *Loans:* FFEL Subsidized Stafford, FFEL PLUS. **Student Employment:** Federal Work-Study Program available. Institutional employment available. Off-campus job opportunities are good. **Financial Aid Phone:** 501-569-3130.

UNIVERSITY OF ARKANSAS—MONTICELLO

UAM PO Box 3600, Monticello, AR 71656
Phone: 870-460-1034 **E-mail:** johnsonj@uamont.edu **CEEB Code:** 6007
Fax: 870-460-1035 **Website:** www.uamont.edu **ACT Code:** 0110

This public school was founded in 1910. It has a 1,600-acre campus.

RATINGS
Admissions Selectivity Rating: 60*   **Fire Safety Rating:** 60*   **Green Rating:** 60*

ACADEMICS
Degrees: Associate, bachelor's, master's. **Special Study Options:** Cooperative education program.

FACILITIES
Housing: Coed dorms, apartments for married students. **Special Academic Facilities/Equipment:** Natural History Museum, language lab, university farm and forest, instructional resource center, planetarium.

CAMPUS LIFE
Activities: Student government, yearbook. **Organizations:** 57 registered organizations, 1 honor society, 1 religious organization. **Athletics (Intercollegiate):** *Men:* Baseball, basketball, football, golf. *Women:* Basketball, cheerleading, cross-country, softball, tennis, track/field (outdoor).

ADMISSIONS
Freshman Academic Profile: 98% from public high schools. TOEFL required of all international applicants, minimum paper TOEFL 500. **Freshman Admission Requirements:** High school diploma is required, and GED is accepted. *Academic units required:* 3 English, 2 math. *Academic units recommended:* 4 English, 4 math, 3 science, 2 foreign language, 4 social studies. **Transfer Admission Requirements:** Minimum college GPA of 2.0 required. Lowest grade transferable C. **General Admission Information:** Regular application deadline 8/16. Regular notification rolling. Non-fall registration accepted. Common Application not accepted. Credit offered for CEEB Advanced Placement tests.

COSTS AND FINANCIAL AID

Annual in-state tuition $2,040. Out-of-state tuition $4,248. Room & board $2,930. Average book expense $600. **Required Forms and Deadlines:** FAFSA. **Types of Aid:** *Need-based scholarships/grants:* State scholarships/grants. *Loans:* FFEL Subsidized Stafford, FFEL PLUS. **Student Employment:** Federal Work-Study Program available. Institutional employment available. Off-campus job opportunities are good. Highest amount earned per year from on-campus jobs $971. **Financial Aid Phone:** 870-460-1050.

UNIVERSITY OF ARKANSAS—PINE BLUFF

1200 North University Drive, Mail Slot 4981, Pine Bluff, AR 71601
Phone: 870-575-8000 **E-mail:** fulton_e@uapb.edu, johnson_f@uapb.edu **CEEB Code:** 6004
Fax: 870-543-8014 **Website:** www.uapb.edu **ACT Code:** 0108
Financial Aid Phone: 501-543-8302

This public school was founded in 1873. It has a 295-acre campus.

RATINGS

Admissions Selectivity Rating: 60*   **Fire Safety Rating:** 60*   **Green Rating:** 60*

STUDENTS AND FACULTY

Enrollment: 2,971. **Student Body:** 55% female, 45% male, 17% out-of-state. African American 96%, Caucasian 3%. **Retention and Graduation:** 64% freshmen return for sophomore year. **Faculty:** Student/faculty ratio 16:1. 168 full-time faculty, 100% hold PhDs.

ACADEMICS

Degrees: Associate, bachelor's, certificate, master's. **Academic Requirements:** Arts/fine arts, English (including composition), foreign languages, history, humanities, mathematics, philosophy, sciences (biological or physical), social science. **Classes:** Most classes have 30–39 students. Most lab/discussion sections have 20–29 students. **Disciplines with Highest Percentage of Degrees Awarded:** Business/marketing 23%, liberal arts/general studies 11%, English 8%, biological/life sciences 7%, agriculture 6%. **Special Study Options:** Cooperative education program, cross registration, distance learning, double major, dual enrollment, honors program, independent study, internships, teacher certification program.

FACILITIES

Housing: Men's dorms, women's dorms. **Special Academic Facilities/Equipment:** Fine arts gallery, child care center, 240-acre farm.

CAMPUS LIFE

Activities: Choral groups, concert band, drama/theater, jazz band, marching band, music ensembles, pep band, radio station, student government, student newspaper, symphony orchestra, television station, yearbook. **Organizations:** 4 honor societies, 5 religious organizations. 4 fraternities, 4 sororities. **Athletics (Intercollegiate):** *Men:* Basketball, cross-country, football, track/field (outdoor), volleyball. *Women:* Basketball, track/field (outdoor), volleyball.

ADMISSIONS

Freshman Academic Profile: SAT Math middle 50% range 350–450. SAT Critical Reading middle 50% range 350–440. ACT middle 50% range 14–18. TOEFL required of all international applicants, minimum paper TOEFL 500. **Basis for Candidate Selection:** *Very important factors considered include:* Standardized test scores. *Important factors considered include:* Rigor of secondary school record. **Freshman Admission Requirements:** High school diploma is required, and GED is accepted. *Academic units required:* 4 English, 3 math, 3 science (2 science labs), 2 foreign language, 3 social studies, 4 academic electives. **Freshman Admission Statistics:** 1,673 applied, 70% admitted, 62% enrolled. **Transfer Admission Requirements:** High school transcript, college transcript(s). Minimum college GPA of 2.0 required. Lowest grade transferable C. **General Admission Information:** Regular notification rolling. Non-fall registration accepted. Common Application accepted.

COSTS AND FINANCIAL AID

Annual in-state tuition $3,300. Annual out-of-state tuition $7,710. Room and board $6,070. Required fees $1,199. Average book expense $1,000. **Notification of Awards:** Applicants will be notified of awards on or about 2/1. **Types of Aid:** *Need-based scholarships/grants:* Pell, SEOG, state scholarships/grants, private scholarships, the school's own gift aid. **Student Employment:** Federal Work-Study Program available. Institutional employment available. Off-campus job opportunities are good. **Financial Aid Statistics:** Highest amount earned per year from on-campus jobs $1,000.

UNIVERSITY OF THE ARTS

320 South Broad Street, Philadelphia, PA 19102
Phone: 215-717-6049 **E-mail:** admissions@uarts.edu **CEEB Code:** 2664
Fax: 215-717-6045 **Website:** www.uarts.edu **ACT Code:** 3664
Financial Aid Phone: 800-616-2787

This private school was founded in 1876. It has an 18-acre campus.

RATINGS

Admissions Selectivity Rating: 79   **Fire Safety Rating:** 60*   **Green Rating:** 60*

STUDENTS AND FACULTY

Enrollment: 2,100. **Student Body:** 54% female, 46% male, 62% out-of-state, 3% international (40 countries represented). African American 11%, Asian 3%, Caucasian 65%, Hispanic 4%. **Retention and Graduation:** 76% freshmen return for sophomore year. 55% freshmen graduate within 4 years. 68% grads go on to further study within 2 semesters. **Faculty:** Student/faculty ratio 9:1. 114 full-time faculty, 49% hold PhDs. 90% faculty teach undergrads.

ACADEMICS

Degrees: Bachelor's, certificate, diploma, master's, post-bachelor's certificate. **Academic Requirements:** Arts/fine arts, computer literacy, English (including composition), history, humanities, mathematics, sciences (biological or physical), social science. **Classes:** Most classes have 10–19 students. **Majors with Highest Enrollment:** Drama and dramatics/theater arts, graphic design, photography. **Disciplines with Highest Percentage of Degrees Awarded:** Visual and performing arts 95%, education 3%, communication technologies 2%. **Special Study Options:** Accelerated program, cross registration, double major, dual enrollment, English as a second language (ESL), exchange student program (domestic), independent study, internships, study abroad, teacher certification program.

FACILITIES

Housing: Coed dorms, apartments for single students. **Special Academic Facilities/Equipment:** Rosenwald-Wolf Gallery, Merriam Theater, arts bank, Borowsky Center for Publication Arts, Gershman Y. **Computers:** 25% of public computers are PCs, 75% of public computers are Macs, network access in dorm rooms, remote student-access to Web through college's connection.

CAMPUS LIFE

Activities: Choral groups, concert band, dance, drama/theater, jazz band, music ensembles, musical theater, radio station, student government. **Organizations:** 5 registered organizations, 1 religious organization.

ADMISSIONS

Freshman Academic Profile: 10% in top 10% of high school class, 32% in top 25% of high school class, 66% in top 50% of high school class. 85% from public high schools. SAT Math middle 50% range 450–570. SAT Critical Reading middle 50% range 470–580. SAT Writing middle 50% range 460–580. ACT middle 50% range 19–26. TOEFL required of all international applicants, minimum paper TOEFL 500, minimum computer TOEFL 173. **Basis for Candidate Selection:** *Very important factors considered include:* Interview, rigor of secondary school record, talent/ability. *Important factors considered include:* Application essay, character/personal qualities, class rank, extracurricular activities, standardized test scores. *Other factors considered include:* Alumni/ae relation, racial/ethnic status, recommendation(s), volunteer work, work experience. **Freshman Admission Requirements:** High school diploma is required, and GED is accepted. *Academic units required:* 4 English. *Academic units recommended:* 3 math, 2 science, 2 foreign language, 2 social studies, 2 history, 2 visual arts, music, dance, drama, or creative writing. **Freshman Admission Statistics:** 2,349 applied, 49% admitted, 49% enrolled. **Transfer Admission Requirements:** High school transcript, college transcript(s), essay or personal statement, standardized test scores. Minimum college GPA of 2.0 required. Lowest grade transferable C. **General Admission Information:** Application fee $60. Regular notification is rolling. Non-fall registration accepted. Admission may be deferred for a maximum of 2 semesters. Credit and/or placement offered for CEEB Advanced Placement tests.

COSTS AND FINANCIAL AID

Annual tuition $23,380. Room & board $7,800. Required fees $950. Average book expense $2,000. **Required Forms and Deadlines:** FAFSA. Financial aid filing deadline 3/1. **Notification of Awards:** Applicants will be notified of awards on or about 3/1. **Types of Aid:** *Need-based scholarships/grants:* Pell, SEOG, state scholarships/grants, private scholarships, the school's own gift aid, merit scholarships. *Loans:* FFEL Subsidized Stafford, FFEL Unsubsidized Stafford, FFEL PLUS, Federal Perkins, alternative loans. **Student Employment:** Federal Work-Study Program available. Institutional employment available. Off-campus job opportunities are excellent. **Financial Aid Statistics:** 43% freshmen, 40% undergrads receive need-based scholarship or grant aid. 65% freshmen, 90% undergrads receive need-based self-help aid. 87% freshmen, 90% undergrads receive any aid. Highest amount earned per year from on-campus jobs $1,200.

See page 1474.

UNIVERSITY OF BALTIMORE

1420 North Charles Street, Baltimore, MD 21201
Phone: 410-837-4777 **E-mail:** admissions@ubmall.ubalt.edu **CEEB Code:** 5810
Fax: 410-837-4793 **Website:** www.ubmall.ubalt.edu
Financial Aid Phone: 410-837-4763

This public school was founded in 1925. It has a 47-acre campus.

RATINGS
Admissions Selectivity Rating: 60*   **Fire Safety Rating:** 60*   **Green Rating:** 66

STUDENTS AND FACULTY
Enrollment: 2,071. **Student Body:** 59% female, 41% male, 1% out-of-state, 8% international. African American 31%, Asian 3%, Caucasian 44%, Hispanic 2%. **Retention and Graduation:** 18% grads go on to further study within 1 year. 10% grads pursue arts and sciences degrees. 9% grads pursue business degrees. 2% grads pursue law degrees. **Faculty:** Student/faculty ratio 14:1. 163 full-time faculty, 87% hold PhDs. 60% faculty teach undergrads.

ACADEMICS
Degrees: Bachelor's, doctoral, first professional, master's, post-bachelor's certificate, post-master's certificate. **Academic Requirements:** Computer literacy, English (including composition), history, humanities, mathematics, social science. **Classes:** Most classes have 20–29 students. Most lab/discussion sections have fewer than 10 students. **Majors with Highest Enrollment:** Business/commerce, criminal justice/police science, health/health care administration/management. **Disciplines with Highest Percentage of Degrees Awarded:** Business/marketing 45%, security and protective services 16%, social sciences 8%, computer and information sciences 7%, health professions and related sciences 6%. **Special Study Options:** Accelerated program, cooperative education program, distance learning, honors program, independent study, internships, student-designed major, study abroad.

FACILITIES
Computers: 100% of classrooms are wired, 100% of public computers are PCs, online registration, online administrative functions (other than registration), remote student-access to Web through college's connection.

CAMPUS LIFE
Activities: Literary magazine, student government, student newspaper. **Organizations:** 26 registered organizations, 10 honor societies, 1 religious organization.

ADMISSIONS
Freshman Academic Profile: SAT Math middle 50% range 460–570. SAT Critical Reading middle 50% range 480–570. SAT Writing middle 50% range 470–550. TOEFL required of all international applicants, minimum paper TOEFL 550, minimum computer TOEFL 275. **Basis for Candidate Selection:** *Important factors considered include:* Academic GPA, rigor of secondary school record. *Other factors considered include:* Alumni/ae relation, application essay, character/personal qualities, class rank, extracurricular activities, first generation, standardized test scores, talent/ability, volunteer work, work experience. **Freshman Admission Requirements:** High school diploma is required, and GED is accepted. *Academic units required:* 4 English, 3 math, 3 science (2 science labs), 3 social studies, 4 academic electives. **Transfer Admission Requirements:** College transcript(s). Minimum college GPA of 2.0 required. Lowest grade transferable C. **General Admission Information:** Application fee $30. Regular notification 4/1. Non-fall registration not accepted. Admission may be deferred for a maxiumum of 2 semesters.

COSTS AND FINANCIAL AID
Types of Aid: *Need-based scholarships/grants:* Pell, SEOG, state scholarships/grants, private scholarships, the school's own gift aid. *Loans:* FFEL Subsidized Stafford, FFEL Unsubsidized Stafford, FFEL PLUS, Federal Perkins. **Financial Aid Statistics:** 73% undergrads receive any aid. Highest amount earned per year from on-campus jobs $4,286.

See page 1428.

UNIVERSITY OF BRIDGEPORT

126 Park Avenue, Bridgeport, CT 06604
Phone: 203-576-4552 **E-mail:** Admit@.bridgeport.edu **CEEB Code:** 3914
Fax: 203-576-4941 **Website:** www.bridgeport.edu **ACT Code:** 0602
Financial Aid Phone: 203-576-4568

This private school was founded in 1927. It has an 86-acre campus.

RATINGS
Admissions Selectivity Rating: 70   **Fire Safety Rating:** 60*   **Green Rating:** 60*

STUDENTS AND FACULTY
Enrollment: 1,694. **Student Body:** 65% female, 35% male, 36% out-of-state, 15% international (81 countries represented). African American 31%, Asian 4%, Caucasian 32%, Hispanic 13%. **Retention and Graduation:** 54% freshmen return for sophomore year. 15% grads go on to further study within 1 year. 10% grads pursue arts and sciences degrees. 10% grads pursue business degrees. 10% grads pursue law degrees. 5% grads pursue medical degrees. **Faculty:** Student/faculty ratio 15:1. 102 full-time faculty, 78% hold PhDs. 85% faculty teach undergrads.

ACADEMICS
Degrees: Associate, bachelor's, doctoral, first professional, master's, post-master's certificate. **Academic Requirements:** Arts/fine arts, English (including composition), history, humanities, mathematics, philosophy, sciences (biological or physical), social science. **Classes:** Most classes have 10–19 students. **Majors with Highest Enrollment:** Business administration/management, computer engineering, dental hygiene/hygienist. **Disciplines with Highest Percentage of Degrees Awarded:** Business/marketing 26%, liberal arts/general studies 25%, visual and performing arts 12%, psychology 10%, health professions and related sciences 10%, public administration and social services 7%. **Special Study Options:** Accelerated program, cooperative education program, cross-registration, distance learning, double major, English as a second language (ESL), honor program, independent study, internships, liberal arts/career combination, student-designed major, study abroad, teacher certification program, weekend college.

FACILITIES
Housing: Coed dorms, men's floors, women's floors. **Computers:** 65% of classrooms are wired, 65% of classrooms are wireless, 90% of public computers are PCs, 10% of public computers are Macs, network access in dorm rooms, network access in dorm lounges, online registration, online administrative functions (other than registration), remote student-access to Web through college's connection.

CAMPUS LIFE
Activities: Choral groups, literary magazine, music ensembles, student government, student newspaper, yearbook. **Organizations:** 30 registered organizations, 11 honor societies, 6 religious organizations. 2 fraternities (2% men join), 4 sororities (2% women join). **Athletics (Intercollegiate):** *Men:* Baseball, basketball, cross-country, soccer. *Women:* Basketball, cross-country, gymnastics, soccer, softball, swimming, volleyball.

ADMISSIONS
Freshman Academic Profile: 1% in top 10% of high school class, 16% in top 25% of high school class, 47% in top 50% of high school class. 89% from public high schools. SAT Math middle 50% range 370–480. SAT Critical Reading middle 50% range 380–480. SAT Writing middle 50% range 380–480. ACT middle 50% range 16–20. TOEFL required of all international applicants, minimum paper TOEFL 500, minimum computer TOEFL 150. **Basis for Candidate Selection:** *Very important factors considered include:* Rigor of secondary school record, standardized test scores. *Important factors considered include:* Academic GPA, application essay, class rank, recommendation(s), talent/ability. *Other factors considered include:* Alumni/ae relation, character/personal qualities, extracurricular activities, interview, level of applicant's interest, volunteer work, work experience. **Freshman Admission Requirements:** High school diploma is required, and GED is accepted. *Academic units required:* 4 English, 3 math, 2 science (2 science labs), 2 social studies, 5 academic electives. *Academic units recommended:* 4 English, 3 math, 2 science (2 science labs), 2 social studies, 5 academic electives. **Freshman Admission Statistics:** 4,007 applied, 64% admitted, 12% enrolled. **Transfer Admission Requirements:** College transcript(s), essay or personal statement. Minimum college GPA of 2.0 required. Lowest grade transferable C-. **General Admission Information:** Application fee $25. Regular notification is rolling. Nonfall registration accepted. Admission may be deferred for a maximum of 1 year. Credit and/or placement offered for CEEB Advanced Placement tests.

COSTS AND FINANCIAL AID

Annual tuition $2,025. Room & board $9,600. Required fees $1,460. Average book expense $1,500. **Required Forms and Deadlines:** FAFSA, institution's own financial aid form, state aid form. Financial aid filing deadline 4/1. **Notification of Awards:** Applicants will be notified of awards on a rolling basis beginning on or about 4/1. **Types of Aid:** *Need-based scholarships/grants:* Pell, SEOG, state scholarships/grants, private scholarships, the school's own gift aid. *Loans:* Direct PLUS, FFEL Subsidized Stafford, FFEL Unsubsidized Stafford, FFEL PLUS, Federal Perkins. **Financial Aid Statistics:** 36% freshmen, 47% undergrads receive need-based scholarship or grant aid. 12% freshmen, 56% undergrads receive need-based self-help aid. Highest amount earned per year from on-campus jobs $2,000.

THE UNIVERSITY OF BRITISH COLUMBIA

Room 2016, 1874 East Mall, Vancouver, BC V6T 1Z1 Canada
Phone: 604-822-3014 **E-mail:** international.reception@ubc.ca
Fax: 604-822-3599 **Website:** www.welcome.ubc.ca
Financial Aid Phone: 604-822-5111

This public school was founded in 1908. It has a 1,000-acre campus.

RATINGS

Admissions Selectivity Rating: 60*   **Fire Safety Rating:** 60*   **Green Rating:** 92

STUDENTS AND FACULTY

Enrollment: 27,192. **Student Body:** 55% female, 45% male. **Retention and Graduation:** 50% grads go on to further study within 1 year. **Faculty:** Student/faculty ratio 15:1.

ACADEMICS

Degrees: Bachelor's, certificate, diploma, doctoral, first professional, master's. **Academic Requirements:** English (including composition), humanities, mathematics, sciences (biological or physical). **Classes:** Most classes have fewer than 10 students. Most lab/discussion sections have 20–29 students. **Majors with Highest Enrollment:** Biological and physical sciences, computer and information sciences, psychology. **Special Study Options:** Cooperative education program, cross-disciplinary first-year options, distance learning, double major, dual enrollment, English as a second language (ESL), exchange student program (domestic), honors program, internships, liberal arts/career combination, student-designed major, study abroad, teacher certification program.

FACILITIES

Housing: Coed dorms, men's dorms, women's dorms, apartments for married students, apartments for single students, special housing for disabled students, fraternity/sorority housing, national theme housing. **Special Academic Facilities/Equipment:** Museum of Anthropology, Barber Learning Centre, Geological Museum, TRIUMF, sub-atomic particle research, botanical gardens, Nitobe Garden, Belkin Art Gallery, Chan Centre for Performing Arts, Chapman Learning Commons, Liu International Studies Centre, St. John's College (Graduate College), Pulp and Paper Centre, Centre for Intergrated Systems Research, Wall Centre for Interdisciplinary Studies **Computers:** Network access in dorm rooms, network access in dorm lounges, online registration, online administrative functions (other than registration), remote student-access to Web through college's connection.

CAMPUS LIFE

Activities: Choral groups, concert band, dance, drama/theater, literary magazine, music ensembles, musical theater, opera, radio station, student government, student newspaper, student-run film society, symphony orchestra. **Organizations:** 250 registered organizations, 1 honor society, 7 religious organizations. 9 fraternities (3% men join), 8 sororities (2% women join). **Athletics (Intercollegiate):** *Men:* Baseball, basketball, crew/rowing, cross-country, field hockey, football, golf, ice hockey, rugby, skiing (downhill/alpine), skiing (nordic/cross-country), soccer, swimming, track/field (outdoor), volleyball. *Women:* Basketball, crew/rowing, cross-country, field hockey, golf, ice hockey, rugby, skiing (downhill/alpine), skiing (nordic/cross-country), soccer, swimming, track/field (outdoor), volleyball. **Environmental initiatives:** UBC has met Kyoto standards. UBC Okanagan heating energy will come from fully sustainable resources by 2009.

ADMISSIONS

Basis for Candidate Selection: *Very important factors considered include:* Academic GPA, rigor of secondary school record. *Important factors considered include:* Standardized test scores. *Other factors considered include:* Application essay, character/personal qualities, extracurricular activities, level of applicant's

interest, recommendation(s), talent/ability, volunteer work, work experience. **Freshman Admission Requirements:** High school diploma is required, and GED is not accepted. *Academic units required:* 4 English, 3 math, 1 academic elective. **Freshman Admission Statistics:** 17,677 applied, 58% admitted, 5% enrolled. **Transfer Admission Requirements:** Statement of good standing from prior institution(s). **General Admission Information:** Application fee $88. Regular application deadline 2/28. Regular notification is rolling. Non-fall registration accepted. Admission may be deferred for a maximum of up to 1 year. Common Application not accepted. Credit and/or placement offered for CEEB Advanced Placement tests.

COSTS AND FINANCIAL AID

Annual in-state tuition $4,257. Annual out-of-state tuition $4,257. Average book expense $1,400. **Student Employment:** Off-campus job opportunities are good.

UNIVERSITY OF CALIFORNIA—BERKELEY

Best 368

Office of Undergraduate Admissions, 110 Sproul Hall #5800, Berkeley, CA 94720-5800
Phone: 510-642-3175 **E-mail:** ouars@uclink4.berkeley.edu **CEEB Code:** 4833
Fax: 510-642-7333 **Website:** www.berkeley.edu **ACT Code:** 0444
Financial Aid Phone: 510-642-6442

This public school was founded in 1868. It has a 1,232-acre campus.

RATINGS

Admissions Selectivity Rating: 97   **Fire Safety Rating:** 76   **Green Rating:** 95

STUDENTS AND FACULTY

Enrollment: 23,863. **Student Body:** 11% out-of-state, 3% international. African American 3%, Asian 41%, Caucasian 32%, Hispanic 11%. **Faculty:** Student/faculty ratio 15:1. 100% faculty teach undergrads.

ACADEMICS

Degrees: Bachelor's, certificate, doctoral, first professional, master's. **Academic Requirements:** American cultures, arts/fine arts, English (including composition), history, international studies, philosophy, sciences (biological or physical), social science. **Majors with Highest Enrollment:** Computer engineering, English language and literature, political science and government. **Special Study Options:** Accelerated program, cross registration, distance learning, double major, dual enrollment, English as a second language (ESL), exchange student program (domestic), honors program, independent study, internships, student-designed major, study abroad, teacher certification program.

FACILITIES

Housing: Coed dorms, men's dorms, women's dorms, apartments for married students, apartments for single students, special housing for disabled students, special housing for international students, fraternity/sorority housing, cooperative housing, theme program housing. **Special Academic Facilities/Equipment:** Lawrence Berkeley National Lab, Pacific Film Archive, earthquake data center, museums of art, anthropology, natural history, paleontology, botanical garden. **Computers:** 80% of public computers are PCs, 40% of public computers are Macs, 10% of public computers are UNIX, network access in dorm rooms, network access in dorm lounges, online registration, online administrative functions (other than registration), remote student-access to Web through college's connection, support for handheld computing.

CAMPUS LIFE

Activities: Choral groups, concert band, dance, drama/theater, jazz band, literary magazine, marching band, music ensembles, musical theater, pep band, radio station, student government, student newspaper, student-run film society, symphony orchestra, television station. **Organizations:** 300 registered organizations, 6 honor societies, 28 religious organizations. 38 fraternities (10% men join), 19 sororities (10% women join). **Athletics (Intercollegiate):** *Men:* Baseball, basketball, crew/rowing, cross-country, diving, football, golf, gymnastics, rugby, sailing, soccer, swimming, tennis, track/field (outdoor), water polo. *Women:* Basketball, crew/rowing, cross-country, diving, field hockey, golf, gymnastics, lacrosse, sailing, soccer, softball, swimming, tennis, track/field (outdoor), volleyball, water polo.

ADMISSIONS

Freshman Academic Profile: 98% in top 10% of high school class, 100% in top 25% of high school class, 100% in top 50% of high school class. 85% from public high schools. SAT Math middle 50% range 620–750. SAT Critical Reading middle 50% range 590–710. SAT Writing middle 50% range 590–710. TOEFL required of all international applicants, minimum paper TOEFL 550, minimum computer TOEFL 213. **Basis for Candidate Selection:** *Very important factors considered include:* Academic GPA, application essay, rigor of secondary school record, state residency. *Important factors considered include:* Character/personal qualities, extracurricular activities, standardized test scores, talent/ability, volunteer work, work experience. *Other factors considered include:* First generation, geographical residence. **Freshman Admission Requirements:** High school diploma is required, and GED is accepted. *Academic units required:* 4 English, 3 math, 2 science (2 science labs), 2 foreign language, 2 social studies, 2 history, 1 academic elective, 1 visual and performing arts. *Academic units recommended:* 4 English, 4 math, 3 science (3 science labs), 3 foreign language, 2 social studies, 2 history, 1 academic elective, 1 visual and performing arts. **Freshman Admission Statistics:** 41,750 applied, 24% admitted, 42% enrolled. **Transfer Admission Requirements:** Essay or personal statement. Minimum college GPA of 2.0 required. Lowest grade transferable D. **General Admission Information:** Application fee $60. Regular application deadline 11/30. Regular notification. Decisions available on website by 3/31. Non-fall registration accepted. Neither credit nor placement offered for CEEB Advanced Placement tests.

COSTS AND FINANCIAL AID

Required Forms and Deadlines: FAFSA, state aid form. Financial aid filing deadline 3/2. **Notification of Awards:** Applicants will be notified of awards on or about 4/15. **Types of Aid:** *Need-based scholarships/grants:* Pell, SEOG, state scholarships/grants, private scholarships, the school's own gift aid. *Loans:* Direct Subsidized Stafford, Direct Unsubsidized Stafford, Direct PLUS, Federal Perkins, college/university loans from institutional funds. **Student Employment:** Federal Work-Study Program available. Institutional employment available. Off-campus job opportunities are excellent. **Financial Aid Statistics:** 44% freshmen, 45% undergrads receive need-based scholarship or grant aid. 40% freshmen, 39% undergrads receive need-based self-help aid. 72 freshmen, 366 undergrads receive athletic scholarships.

UNIVERSITY OF CALIFORNIA—DAVIS

178 Mrak Hall, 1 Shields Avenue, Davis, CA 95616
Phone: 530-752-2971 **E-mail:** undergraduateadmissions@ucdavis.edu **CEEB Code:** 4834
Fax: 530-752-1280 **Website:** www.ucdavis.edu **ACT Code:** 0454
Financial Aid Phone: 530-752-2396

This public school was founded in 1905. It has a 5,200-acre campus.

RATINGS

Admissions Selectivity Rating: 94   **Fire Safety Rating:** 83   **Green Rating:** 96

STUDENTS AND FACULTY

Enrollment: 23,329. **Student Body:** 55% female, 45% male, 2% out-of-state, 2% international (118 countries represented). African American 3%, Asian 41%, Caucasian 36%, Hispanic 11%. **Retention and Graduation:** 90% freshmen return for sophomore year. 43% freshmen graduate within 4 years. 40% grads go on to further study within 1 year. 23% grads pursue arts and sciences degrees. 1% grads pursue business degrees. 4% grads pursue law degrees. 12% grads pursue medical degrees. **Faculty:** Student/faculty ratio 19:1. 1,595 full-time faculty, 98% hold PhDs.

ACADEMICS

Degrees: Bachelor's, doctoral, first professional, master's, post-bachelor's certificate, post-master's certificate. **Academic Requirements:** Arts and humanities (3 courses), English (including composition), science and engineering (3 courses), social/cultural diversity (1 course), social sciences (3 courses). **Classes:** Most classes have 20–29 students. Most lab/discussion sections have 20–29 students. **Majors with Highest Enrollment:** Biology/biological sciences, economics, psychology. **Disciplines with Highest Percentage of Degrees Awarded:** Biological/life sciences 18%, engineering 10%, psychology 8%, agriculture 8%, communications/journalism 6%. **Special**

Study Options: Accelerated program, cross-registration, double major, dual enrollment, English as a second language (ESL), honor program, independent study, internships, student-designed major, study abroad, teacher certification program. Washington, DC, Center.

FACILITIES

Housing: Coed dorms, women's dorms, apartments for married students, apartments for single students, special housing for disabled students, cooperative housing, Academic Theme Program (e.g., Asian Pacific American Theme House, Health Science Community, Rainbow House). **Special Academic Facilities/Equipment:** Art galleries, 150-acre university arboretum, equestrian center, craft center, student experimental farm, nuclear lab, human performance lab, natural reserves, early childhood lab, raptor center, primate research center. **Computers:** Network access in dorm rooms, network access in dorm lounges, online registration, online administrative functions (other than registration), remote student-access to Web through college's connection.

CAMPUS LIFE

Activities: Choral groups, concert band, dance, drama/theater, jazz band, literary magazine, marching band, music ensembles, musical theater, pep band, radio station, student government, student newspaper, student-run film society, symphony orchestra, television station, yearbook. **Organizations:** 364 registered organizations, 1 honor society, 50 religious organizations. 28 fraternities (9% men join), 21 sororities (8% women join). **Athletics (Intercollegiate):** *Men:* Baseball, basketball, cross-country, diving, football, golf, soccer, swimming, tennis, track/field (indoor), track/field (outdoor), water polo, wrestling. *Women:* Basketball, crew/rowing, cross-country, diving, golf, gymnastics, lacrosse, soccer, softball, swimming, tennis, track/field (indoor), track/field (outdoor), volleyball, water polo.

ADMISSIONS

Freshman Academic Profile: 95% in top 10% of high school class, 100% in top 25% of high school class, 100% in top 50% of high school class. 85% from public high schools. SAT Math middle 50% range 540–660. SAT Critical Reading middle 50% range 490–630. SAT Writing middle 50% range 500–630. ACT middle 50% range 20–27. TOEFL required of all international applicants, minimum paper TOEFL 550, minimum computer TOEFL 213. **Basis for Candidate Selection:** *Very important factors considered include:* Academic GPA, rigor of secondary school record, standardized test scores. *Important factors considered include:* Application essay, character/personal qualities, extracurricular activities, first generation, talent/ability. *Other factors considered include:* State residency, volunteer work, work experience. **Freshman Admission Requirements:** High school diploma is required, and GED is accepted. *Academic units required:* 4 English, 3 math, 2 science (2 science labs), 2 foreign language, 2 social studies, 1 academic elective, 1 visual and performing arts. *Academic units recommended:* 4 English, 4 math, 3 science (3 science labs), 3 foreign language, 2 social studies, 1 academic elective, 1 visual and performing arts. **Freshman Admission Statistics:** 32,635 applied, 68% admitted, 25% enrolled. **Transfer Admission Requirements:** High school transcript, college transcript(s), essay or personal statement, statement of good standing from prior institution(s). Lowest grade transferable D-. **General Admission Information:** Application fee $60. Regular application deadline 11/30. Regular notification 3/15. Nonfall registration not accepted. Credit and/or placement offered for CEEB Advanced Placement tests.

COSTS AND FINANCIAL AID

Annual out-of-state tuition $19,620. Room and board $11,533. Required fees $8,124. Average book expense $1,508. **Required Forms and Deadlines:** FAFSA, state aid form. Financial aid filing deadline 3/2. **Notification of Awards:** Applicants will be notified of awards on a rolling basis beginning on or about 3/15. **Types of Aid:** *Need-based scholarships/grants:* Pell, SEOG, state scholarships/grants, private scholarships, the school's own gift aid. *Loans:* Direct Subsidized Stafford, Direct Unsubsidized Stafford, Direct PLUS, Federal Perkins, college/university loans from institutional funds. **Financial Aid Statistics:** 48% freshmen, 44% undergrads receive need-based scholarship or grant aid. 35% freshmen, 35% undergrads receive need-based self-help aid. 46% freshmen, 49% undergrads receive any aid. Highest amount earned per year from on-campus jobs $7,280.

UNIVERSITY OF CALIFORNIA—IRVINE

Office of Admissions & Relations w/Schools, 204 Administration Bldg., Irvine, CA 92697-1075
Phone: 949-824-6703 **E-mail:** admissions@uci.edu **CEEB Code:** 4859
Fax: 949-824-2711 **Website:** www.uci.edu
Financial Aid Phone: 949-824-8262

This public school was founded in 1965. It has a 1,475-acre campus.

RATINGS
Admissions Selectivity Rating: 95   **Fire Safety Rating:** 60*   **Green Rating:** 92

STUDENTS AND FACULTY
Enrollment: 19,930. **Student Body:** 51% female, 49% male, 3% out-of-state, 2% international (102 countries represented). African American 2%, Asian 49%, Caucasian 26%, Hispanic 12%. **Retention and Graduation:** 93% freshmen return for sophomore year. 42% freshmen graduate within 4 years. 30% grads go on to further study within 1 year. **Faculty:** Student/faculty ratio 19:1. 992 full-time faculty, 98% hold PhDs. 100% faculty teach undergrads.

ACADEMICS
Degrees: Bachelor's, doctoral, first professional, master's, post-bachelor's certificate. **Academic Requirements:** Arts/fine arts, computer literacy, English (including composition), foreign languages, history, humanities, mathematics, sciences (biological or physical), social science, writing and multicultural international/global issues. **Classes:** Most classes have 20–29 students. Most lab/discussion sections have 20–29 students. **Majors with Highest Enrollment:** Biology/biological sciences, computer and information sciences, economics. **Disciplines with Highest Percentage of Degrees Awarded:** Social sciences 28%, biological/life sciences 13%, psychology 11%, computer and information sciences 9%, interdisciplinary studies 9%. **Special Study Options:** Distance learning, double major, English as a second language (ESL), honors program, independent study, internships, study abroad, teacher certification program.

FACILITIES
Housing: Coed dorms, women's dorms, apartments for married students, apartments for single students, special housing for disabled students, fraternity/sorority housing, cooperative housing, academic theme houses. **Special Academic Facilities/Equipment:** Museum of systemic biology, freshwater marsh reserve, electron microscope, nuclear reactor, laser institute, research facilities. **Computers:** 55% of classrooms are wireless, 60% of public computers are PCs, 40% of public computers are Macs, network access in dorm rooms, online registration, online administrative functions (other than registration), remote student-access to Web through college's connection.

CAMPUS LIFE
Activities: Choral groups, concert band, dance, drama/theater, jazz band, literary magazine, music ensembles, musical theater, opera, pep band, radio station, student government, student newspaper, student-run film society, symphony orchestra, yearbook. **Organizations:** 378 registered organizations, 21 honor societies, 59 religious organizations. 20 fraternities (9% men join), 20 sororities (9% women join). **Athletics (Intercollegiate):** *Men:* Baseball, basketball, cheerleading, crew/rowing, cross-country, diving, fencing, golf, sailing, soccer, softball, swimming, tennis, track/field (outdoor), volleyball, water polo. *Women:* Basketball, cheerleading, crew/rowing, cross-country, diving, fencing, golf, sailing, soccer, softball, swimming, tennis, track/field (indoor), track/field (outdoor), volleyball, water polo.

ADMISSIONS
Freshman Academic Profile: 96% in top 10% of high school class, 100% in top 25% of high school class, 100% in top 50% of high school class. 84% from public high schools. SAT Math middle 50% range 570–680. SAT Critical Reading middle 50% range 540–630. TOEFL required of all international applicants, minimum paper TOEFL 550, minimum computer TOEFL 213. **Basis for Candidate Selection:** *Very important factors considered include:* Academic GPA, application essay, extracurricular activities, level of applicant's interest, rigor of secondary school record, standardized test scores, talent/ability, volunteer work, work experience. *Important factors considered include:* Character/personal qualities. *Other factors considered include:* Class rank, first generation, state residency. **Freshman Admission Requirements:** High school diploma is required, and GED is accepted. *Academic units required:* 4 English, 3 math, 2 science (2 science labs), 2 foreign language, 2 history, 1 academic elective, 1 visual and performing arts. *Academic units recommended:* 4 English, 4 math, 3 science (3 science labs), 3 foreign language, 2 history, 1 academic elective, 1 visual and performing arts. **Freshman Admission Statistics:** 34,531 applied, 60% admitted, 21% enrolled. **Transfer Admission Requirements:** High school transcript, college transcript(s), essay or personal

statement. Minimum college GPA of 2.0 required. Lowest grade transferable C. **General Admission Information:** Application fee $55. Regular notification 3/31. Non-fall registration not accepted. Common Application not accepted. Credit offered for CEEB Advanced Placement tests.

COSTS AND FINANCIAL AID
Annual in-state tuition $6,141. Out-of-state tuition $24,825. Room & board $9,815. Required fees $653. Average book expense $1,631. **Required Forms and Deadlines:** FAFSA, state aid form. Financial aid filing deadline 3/2. **Notification of Awards:** Applicants will be notified of awards on or about 4/1. **Types of Aid:** *Need-based scholarships/grants:* Pell, SEOG, state scholarships/grants, private scholarships, the school's own gift aid. *Loans:* Direct Subsidized Stafford, Direct Unsubsidized Stafford, Direct PLUS, FFEL Subsidized Stafford, FFEL Unsubsidized Stafford, FFEL PLUS, Federal Perkins, college/university loans from institutional funds, private loans. **Financial Aid Statistics:** 38% freshmen, 41% undergrads receive need-based scholarship or grant aid. 35% freshmen, 35% undergrads receive need-based self-help aid. 39 freshmen, 176 undergrads receive athletic scholarships. Highest amount earned per year from on-campus jobs $8,550.

UNIVERSITY OF CALIFORNIA—LOS ANGELES

Best 368

1147 Murphy Hall, Box 951436, Los Angeles, CA 90095-1436
Phone: 310-825-3101 **E-mail:** ugadm@saonet.ucla.edu **CEEB Code:** 4837
Fax: 310-206-1206 **Website:** www.ucla.edu **ACT Code:** 0448
Financial Aid Phone: 310-206-0400

This public school was founded in 1919. It has a 419-acre campus.

RATINGS
Admissions Selectivity Rating: 98   **Fire Safety Rating:** 86   **Green Rating:** 87

STUDENTS AND FACULTY
Enrollment: 25,432. **Student Body:** 56% female, 44% male, 2% out-of-state, 4% international (132 countries represented). African American 3%, Asian 38%, Caucasian 34%, Hispanic 15%. **Retention and Graduation:** 97% freshmen return for sophomore year. 59% freshmen graduate within 4 years. **Faculty:** Student/faculty ratio 17:1. 1,859 full-time faculty, 98% hold PhDs. 100% faculty teach undergrads.

ACADEMICS
Degrees: Bachelor's, doctoral, first professional, master's. **Academic Requirements:** Arts/fine arts, English (including composition), foreign languages, history, humanities, mathematics, philosophy, sciences (biological or physical), social science. **Classes:** Most classes have 10–19 students. Most lab/discussion sections have 20–29 students. **Majors with Highest Enrollment:** Economics, political science and government, psychology. **Disciplines with Highest Percentage of Degrees Awarded:** Social sciences 27%, psychology 13%, biological/life sciences 11%, engineering 8%, history 7%. **Special Study Options:** Cross registration, distance learning, double major, dual enrollment, English as a second language (ESL), exchange student program (domestic), honors program, independent study, internships, liberal arts/career combination, student-designed major, study abroad, teacher certification program.

FACILITIES
Housing: Coed dorms, apartments for married students, apartments for single students, special housing for disabled students, fraternity/sorority housing, apartments for faculty, apartments for staff, theme housing. **Special Academic Facilities/Equipment:** Art gallery, cultural history museum, sculpture garden, graphic arts center, numerous study centers, research institutes, UCLA Armand Hammer Museum of Art and Cultural Center, Murphy Sculpture Garden, Fowler Museum of Cultural History. **Computers:** 85% of classrooms are wired, 85% of public computers are PCs, 10% of public computers are Macs, 5% of public computers are UNIX, network access in dorm rooms, network access in dorm lounges, online registration, online administrative functions (other than registration), remote student-access to Web through college's connection.

CAMPUS LIFE
Activities: Choral groups, concert band, dance, drama/theater, jazz band, literary magazine, marching band, music ensembles, musical theater, opera, pep band, radio station, student government, student newspaper, student-run film

society, symphony orchestra, television station. **Organizations:** 700 registered organizations, 18 honor societies, 30 religious organizations. 27 fraternities (13% men join), 18 sororities (13% women join). **Athletics (Intercollegiate):** *Men:* Baseball, basketball, cross-country, football, golf, soccer, tennis, track/field (outdoor), volleyball, water polo. *Women:* Basketball, crew/rowing, cross-country, diving, golf, gymnastics, soccer, softball, swimming, tennis, track/field (outdoor), volleyball, water polo.

ADMISSIONS

Freshman Academic Profile: 97% in top 10% of high school class, 100% in top 25% of high school class, 100% in top 50% of high school class. 80% from public high schools. SAT Math middle 50% range 700–760. SAT Critical Reading middle 50% range 660–720. SAT Writing middle 50% range 670–720. ACT middle 50% range 28–31. TOEFL required of all international applicants, minimum paper TOEFL 550, minimum computer TOEFL 220. **Basis for Candidate Selection:** *Very important factors considered include:* Academic GPA, application essay, rigor of secondary school record, standardized test scores. *Important factors considered include:* Character/personal qualities, extracurricular activities, talent/ability, volunteer work, work experience. *Other factors considered include:* First generation, geographical residence. **Freshman Admission Requirements:** High school diploma is required, and GED is accepted. *Academic units required:* 4 English, 3 math, 2 science (2 science labs), 2 foreign language, 2 history, 1 academic elective, 1 visual and performing arts. *Academic units recommended:* 4 English, 4 math, 3 science (3 science labs), 3 foreign language, 2 history, 1 academic elective, 1 visual and performing arts. **Freshman Admission Statistics:** 47,317 applied, 26% admitted, 39% enrolled. **Transfer Admission Requirements:** College transcript(s), essay or personal statement, statement of good standing from prior institution(s). Minimum college GPA of 2.4 required. Lowest grade transferable D. **General Admission Information:** Application fee $60. Regular application deadline 11/30. Regular notification is rolling. Non-fall registration not accepted. Credit and/or placement offered for CEEB Advanced Placement tests.

COSTS AND FINANCIAL AID

Annual out-of-state tuition $19,068. Room and board $12,420. Required fees $7,590. Average book expense $1,515. **Required Forms and Deadlines:** FAFSA. **Notification of Awards:** Applicants will be notified of awards on or about 3/15. **Types of Aid:** *Need-based scholarships/grants:* Pell, SEOG, state scholarships/grants, private scholarships, the school's own gift aid, United Negro College Fund, Federal Nursing Scholarships, National Merit. *Loans:* FFEL Subsidized Stafford, FFEL Unsubsidized Stafford, FFEL PLUS, Federal Perkins, Federal Nursing, state loans, college/university loans from institutional funds. **Student Employment:** Federal Work-Study Program available. Off-campus job opportunities are good. **Financial Aid Statistics:** 52% freshmen, 51% undergrads receive need-based scholarship or grant aid. 37% freshmen, 39% undergrads receive need-based self-help aid. 72 freshmen, 374 undergrads receive athletic scholarships.

See page 1430.

UNIVERSITY OF CALIFORNIA—RIVERSIDE

Best 368

1120 Hinderaker Hall, Riverside, CA 92521
Phone: 951-827-3411 **E-mail:** discover@ucr.edu **CEEB Code:** 4839
Fax: 951-827-6344 **Website:** www.ucr.edu
Financial Aid Phone: 951-827-3878

This public school was founded in 1954. It has a 1,200-acre campus.

RATINGS

Admissions Selectivity Rating: 91   **Fire Safety Rating:** 87   **Green Rating:** 96

STUDENTS AND FACULTY

Enrollment: 14,792. **Student Body:** 52% female, 48% male, 1% out-of-state, 2% international (102 countries represented). African American 7%, Asian 41%, Caucasian 19%, Hispanic 25%. **Retention and Graduation:** 86% freshmen return for sophomore year. 37% freshmen graduate within 4 years. **Faculty:** Student/faculty ratio 18:1. 728 full-time faculty, 98% hold PhDs. 100% faculty teach undergrads.

ACADEMICS

Degrees: Bachelor's, doctoral, master's, post-bachelor's certificate. **Academic Requirements:** English (including composition), ethnic studies, foreign languages, history, humanities, mathematics, sciences (biological or physical), social science. **Classes:** Most classes have 20–29 students. Most lab/discussion sections have 20–29 students. **Majors with Highest Enrollment:** Biology/biological sciences, business administration and management, psychology. **Disciplines with Highest Percentage of Degrees Awarded:** Business/marketing 23%, social sciences 19%, biological/life sciences 12%, psychology 9%, liberal arts/general studies 7%. **Special Study Options:** Accelerated program, cooperative education program, cross registration, double major, dual enrollment, English as a second language (ESL), honors program, independent study, internships, student-designed major, study abroad, teacher certification program.

FACILITIES

Housing: Coed dorms, apartments for married students, apartments for single students, special housing for disabled students, special housing for international students. **Special Academic Facilities/Equipment:** Art gallery, photography museum, botanical gardens, audio-visual resource center/studios, media resource center, statistical consulting center, citrus research center and agricultural experiment station, air pollution research center, center for environmental research and technology, water resources center, geophysics and planetary physics institute, center for bibliographical studies, center for family studies, center for crime and justice studies, natural reserve system. **Computers:** 2% of classrooms are wired, 100% of classrooms are wireless, 80% of public computers are PCs, 4% of public computers are Macs, 16% of public computers are UNIX, network access in dorm rooms, network access in dorm lounges, online registration, online administrative functions (other than registration), support for handheld computing, remote student-access to Web through college's connection.

CAMPUS LIFE

Activities: Choral groups, concert band, dance, drama/theater, jazz band, literary magazine, music ensembles, musical theater, pep band, radio station, student government, student newspaper, student-run film society. **Organizations:** 252 registered organizations, 10 honor societies, 18 religious organizations. 20 fraternities (4% men join), 20 sororities (4% women join). **Athletics (Intercollegiate):** *Men:* Baseball, basketball, cross-country, golf, soccer, tennis, track/field (indoor), track/field (outdoor). *Women:* Basketball, cross-country, golf, soccer, softball, tennis, track/field (indoor), track/field (outdoor), volleyball. **Environmental Initiatives:** Developing a climate neutrality plan. Planning a LEED-Platinum new building for Environmental Health & Safety—not yet approved. Developing a sustainable, native landscape plan for UCR—Palm Desert Campus.

ADMISSIONS

Freshman Academic Profile: 94% in top 10% of high school class, 100% in top 25% of high school class, 100% in top 50% of high school class. 88% from public high schools. SAT Math middle 50% range 470–610. SAT Critical Reading middle 50% range 450–560. SAT Writing middle 50% range 450–560. ACT middle 50% range 18–23. TOEFL required of all international applicants, minimum paper TOEFL 550, minimum computer TOEFL 220. **Basis for Candidate Selection:** *Very important factors considered include:* Academic GPA, first generation, rigor of secondary school record, standardized test scores. *Important factors considered include:* Character/personal qualities. *Other factors considered include:* Application essay, state residency. **Freshman Admission Requirements:** High school diploma is required, and GED is accepted. *Academic units required:* 4 English, 3 math, 2 science (2 science labs), 2 foreign language, 2 history, 1 academic elective, 1 visual and performing arts. *Academic units recommended:* 4 math, 3 science (3 science labs), 3 foreign language. **Freshman Admission Statistics:** 19,982 applied, 83% admitted, 22% enrolled. **Transfer Admission Requirements:** College transcript(s), essay or personal statement, statement of good standing from prior institution(s). Minimum college GPA of 2.4 required. Lowest grade transferable D. **General Admission Information:** Application fee $60. Regular application deadline 11/30. Regular notification is rolling. Non-fall registration not accepted. Credit and/or placement offered for CEEB Advanced Placement tests.

COSTS AND FINANCIAL AID

Annual out-of-state tuition $19,620. Room and board $10,800. Required fees $7,355. Average book expense $1,700. **Required Forms and Deadlines:** FAFSA, state aid form. Financial aid filing deadline 3/2. **Notification of Awards:** Applicants will be notified of awards on a rolling basis beginning on or about 3/1. **Types of Aid:** *Need-based scholarships/grants:* Pell, SEOG, state scholarships/grants, private scholarships, the school's own gift aid, included in state school/grants above. *Loans:* Direct Subsidized Stafford, Direct Unsubsidized Stafford, Direct PLUS, Federal Perkins. **Student Employment:** Federal Work-Study Program available. Institutional employment available. Off-campus job opportunities are excellent. **Financial Aid Statistics:** 55% freshmen, 55% undergrads receive need-based scholarship or grant aid. 51%

freshmen, 47% undergrads receive need-based self-help aid. 30 freshmen, 114 undergrads receive athletic scholarships. 80% freshmen, 70% undergrads receive any aid.

UNIVERSITY OF CALIFORNIA—SAN DIEGO

9500 Gilman Drive, La Jolla, CA 92093-0021
Phone: 858-534-4831 **E-mail:** admissionsinfo@ucsd.edu **CEEB Code:** 4836
Fax: 858-534-5723 **Website:** www.ucsd.edu
Financial Aid Phone: 858-534-4480

This public school was founded in 1959. It has a 1,976-acre campus.

RATINGS
Admissions Selectivity Rating: 96   **Fire Safety Rating:** 60*   **Green Rating:** 60*

STUDENTS AND FACULTY
Enrollment: 20,679. **Student Body:** 52% female, 48% male, 3% out-of-state, 3% international (70 countries represented). African American 1%, Asian 39%, Caucasian 32%, Hispanic 11%. **Retention and Graduation:** 95% freshmen return for sophomore year. 54% freshmen graduate within 4 years. 30% grads go on to further study within 1 year. 35% grads pursue arts and sciences degrees. 8% grads pursue business degrees. 15% grads pursue law degrees. 16% grads pursue medical degrees. **Faculty:** Student/faculty ratio 19:1. 941 full-time faculty, 98% hold PhDs.

ACADEMICS
Degrees: Bachelor's, doctoral, master's. **Academic Requirements:** Arts/fine arts, English (including composition), foreign languages, history, humanities, mathematics, sciences (biological or physical), social science. **Classes:** Most classes have 10–19 students. Most lab/discussion sections have 20–29 students. **Majors with Highest Enrollment:** Economics, microbiology, political science and government. **Disciplines with Highest Percentage of Degrees Awarded:** Social sciences 37%, biological/life sciences 15%, engineering 15%, psychology 8%, communication technologies 6%, computer and information sciences 5%. **Special Study Options:** Accelerated program, cooperative education program, cross registration, double major, English as a second language (ESL), exchange student program (domestic), freshman honors program, honors program, independent study, internships, in-depth academic assignments working in small groups or one-to-one with faculty liberal arts/career combination, research programs, special services for students with learning disabilities, student-designed major, study abroad, summer sessions for credit, teacher certification program.

FACILITIES
Housing: Coed dorms, apartments for married students, apartments for single students, special housing for disabled students, special housing for international students, international house for international students and others interested in international living. **Special Academic Facilities/Equipment:** Art galleries, Center for U.S.-Mexican studies, music recording studio, audiovisual center, Center for Music Experimentation, aquarium, Oceanographic Institute, structural lab, supercomputer, electron microscopes. **Computers:** 40% of public computers are PCs, 45% of public computers are Macs, 15% of public computers are UNIX, network access in dorm rooms, online registration, online administrative functions (other than registration), remote student-access to Web through college's connection.

CAMPUS LIFE
Activities: Choral groups, dance, drama/theater, jazz band, literary magazine, music ensembles, musical theater, opera, pep band, radio station, student government, student newspaper, symphony orchestra, television station, yearbook. **Organizations:** 280 registered organizations, 5 honor societies, 19 fraternities (10% men join), 14 sororities (10% women join). **Athletics (Intercollegiate):** *Men:* Baseball, basketball, crew/rowing, cross-country, diving, fencing, golf, soccer, swimming, tennis, track/field (outdoor), volleyball, water polo. *Women:* Basketball, crew/rowing, cross-country, diving, fencing, soccer, softball, swimming, tennis, track/field (outdoor), volleyball, water polo.

ADMISSIONS
Freshman Academic Profile: 99% in top 10% of high school class, 100% in top 25% of high school class, 100% in top 50% of high school class. SAT Math

middle 50% range 600–700. SAT Critical Reading middle 50% range 540–660. ACT middle 50% range 23–29. TOEFL required of all international applicants, minimum paper TOEFL 550. **Basis for Candidate Selection:** *Very important factors considered include:* Academic GPA, application essay, character/personal qualities, rigor of secondary school record, standardized test scores, state residency, talent/ability, volunteer work. *Important factors considered include:* Extracurricular activities. *Other factors considered include:* Work experience. **Freshman Admission Requirements:** High school diploma is required, and GED is accepted. *Academic units required:* 4 English, 3 math, 2 science labs, 2 foreign language, 2 history, 1 academic elective, 1 visual and performing arts. *Academic units recommended:* 4 English, 4 math, 3 science labs, 3 foreign language, 2 history, 1 academic elective, 1 visual and performing arts. **Freshman Admission Statistics:** 43,586 applied, 49% admitted, 21% enrolled. **Transfer Admission Requirements:** College transcript(s), essay or personal statement, statement of good standing from prior institution(s). Minimum college GPA of 2.4 required. Lowest grade transferable D. **General Admission Information:** Application fee $60. Regular application deadline 11/30. Regular notification is rolling. Non-fall registration accepted. Admission may be deferred for a maxiumum of 2 semesters (limited). Credit and/or placement offered for CEEB Advanced Placement tests.

COSTS AND FINANCIAL AID
Annual out-of-state tuition $19,068. Room and board $10,237. Required fees $7,456. Average book expense $1,487. **Required Forms and Deadlines:** FAFSA, state aid form. Financial aid filing deadline 6/1. **Notification of Awards:** Applicants will be notified of awards on a rolling basis beginning on or about 3/15. **Types of Aid:** *Need-based scholarships/grants:* Pell, SEOG, state scholarships/grants, private scholarships, the school's own gift aid. *Loans:* FFEL Subsidized Stafford, FFEL Unsubsidized Stafford, FFEL PLUS, Federal Perkins, college/university loans from institutional funds, alternative loans. **Financial Aid Statistics:** 51% freshmen, 46% undergrads receive need-based scholarship or grant aid. 46% freshmen, 42% undergrads receive need-based self-help aid. 87% freshmen, 84% undergrads receive any aid.

UNIVERSITY OF CALIFORNIA— SANTA BARBARA

Office of Admissions, 1210 Cheadle Hall, University of California, Santa Barbara, CA 93106-2014
Phone: 805-893-2881 **E-mail:** admissions@sa.ucsb.edu **CEEB Code:** 4835
Fax: 805-893-2676 **Website:** www.ucsb.edu
Financial Aid Phone: 805-893-2432

This public school was founded in 1909. It has a 989-acre campus.

RATINGS
Admissions Selectivity Rating: 95   **Fire Safety Rating:** 88   **Green Rating:** 94

STUDENTS AND FACULTY
Enrollment: 18,210. **Student Body:** 55% female, 45% male, 4% out-of-state, 1% international (112 countries represented). African American 3%, Asian 16%, Caucasian 52%, Hispanic 19%. **Retention and Graduation:** 91% freshmen return for sophomore year. 49% freshmen graduate within 4 years. **Faculty:** Student/faculty ratio 17:1. 917 full-time faculty, 100% hold PhDs.

ACADEMICS
Degrees: Bachelor's, doctoral, master's. **Academic Requirements:** Arts/fine arts, English (including composition), foreign languages, history, humanities, mathematics, philosophy, sciences (biological or physical), social science. **Classes:** Most classes have 10–19 students. Most lab/discussion sections have 20–29 students. **Majors with Highest Enrollment:** Cell/cellular biology and anatomical sciences, economics, psychology. **Disciplines with Highest Percentage of Degrees Awarded:** Social sciences 21%, communication technologies 11%, business/marketing 11%, English 9%, interdisciplinary studies 9%, visual and performing arts 8%, biological/life sciences 7%, psychology 7%. **Special Study Options:** Academic minors, accelerated program, cross registration, distance learning, double major, English as a second language (ESL), exchange student program (domestic), freshman seminars, honors program, independent study, internships, off-campus study in Washington, DC, pre-professional programs and advising, student-designed

major, study abroad, teacher certification program. Undergrads may take grad level classes, undergraduate research.

FACILITIES

Housing: Coed dorms, apartments for married students, apartments for single students, fraternity/sorority housing, cooperative housing. **Special Academic Facilities/Equipment:** Art museum; centers for black studies, Chicano studies, and study of developing nations; institutes for applied behavioral sciences, community/organizational research, marine science, and theoretical physics; Channel Islands field station. **Computers:** 72% of classrooms are wired, network access in dorm rooms, network access in dorm lounges, online registration, online administrative functions (other than registration), remote student-access to Web through college's connection.

CAMPUS LIFE

Activities: Choral groups, concert band, dance, drama/theater, jazz band, literary magazine, music ensembles, musical theater, opera, pep band, radio station, student government, student newspaper, student-run film society, symphony orchestra, television station, yearbook. **Organizations:** 487 registered organizations, 5 honor societies, 37 religious organizations. 18 fraternities (4% men join), 19 sororities (7% women join). **Athletics (Intercollegiate):** *Men:* Baseball, basketball, cross-country, diving, golf, gymnastics, soccer, swimming, tennis, track/field (outdoor), volleyball, water polo. *Women:* Basketball, cross-country, diving, gymnastics, soccer, softball, swimming, tennis, track/field (outdoor), volleyball, water polo.

ADMISSIONS

Freshman Academic Profile: 96% in top 10% of high school class, 98% in top 25% of high school class, 100% in top 50% of high school class. 87% from public high schools. SAT Math middle 50% range 540–660. SAT Critical Reading middle 50% range 530–650. SAT Writing middle 50% range 530–650. ACT middle 50% range 23–29. TOEFL required of all international applicants, minimum paper TOEFL 500, minimum computer TOEFL 173. **Basis for Candidate Selection:** *Very important factors considered include:* Academic GPA, application essay, class rank, standardized test scores. *Important factors considered include:* Character/personal qualities, extracurricular activities, rigor of secondary school record, talent/ability. *Other factors considered include:* First generation, state residency, volunteer work, work experience. **Freshman Admission Requirements:** High school diploma is required, and GED is accepted. *Academic units required:* 4 English, 3 math, 2 science (2 science labs), 2 foreign language, 2 social studies, 2 history, 2 academic electives, 1 visual and performing arts. *Academic units recommended:* 4 math, 3 science (3 science labs), 3 foreign language. **Freshman Admission Statistics:** 39,854 applied, 53% admitted, 19% enrolled. **Transfer Admission Requirements:** High school transcript, college transcript(s), essay or personal statement. Minimum college GPA of 2.4 required. Lowest grade transferable D. **General Admission Information:** Application fee $60. Regular application deadline 11/30. Regular notification 3/15. Non-fall registration accepted. Credit and/or placement offered for CEEB Advanced Placement tests.

COSTS AND FINANCIAL AID

Average book expense $1,505. **Required Forms and Deadlines:** FAFSA. Financial aid filing deadline 5/31. **Notification of Awards:** Applicants will be notified of awards on a rolling basis beginning on or about 3/15. **Types of Aid:** *Need-based scholarships/grants:* Pell, SEOG, state scholarships/grants, private scholarships, the school's own gift aid. Work Study is also available as need-based aid. *Loans:* Direct Subsidized Stafford, Direct Unsubsidized Stafford, Direct PLUS, FFEL PLUS, Federal Perkins, college/university loans from institutional funds. **Financial Aid Statistics:** 40% freshmen, 38% undergrads receive need-based scholarship or grant aid. 33% freshmen, 35% undergrads receive need-based self-help aid. 53 freshmen, 204 undergrads receive athletic scholarships. 64% freshmen, 58% undergrads receive any aid.

UNIVERSITY OF CALIFORNIA—SANTA CRUZ

Office of Admissions, Cook House, 1156 High Street, Santa Cruz, CA 95064
Phone: 831-459-4008 **E-mail:** admissions@ucsc.edu **CEEB Code:** 4860
Fax: 831-459-4452 **Website:** www.ucsc.edu
Financial Aid Phone: 831-459-2963

This public school was founded in 1965. It has a 2,000-acre campus.

RATINGS

Admissions Selectivity Rating: 93   **Fire Safety Rating:** 60*   **Green Rating:** 60*

STUDENTS AND FACULTY

Enrollment: 13,941. **Student Body:** 53% female, 47% male, 3% out-of-state. African American 3%, Asian 19%, Caucasian 52%, Hispanic 15%. **Retention and Graduation:** 89% freshmen return for sophomore year. 48% freshmen graduate within 4 years. **Faculty:** Student/faculty ratio 19:1. 548 full-time faculty. 100% faculty teach undergrads.

ACADEMICS

Degrees: Bachelor's, doctoral, master's, post-bachelor's certificate. **Academic Requirements:** Arts/fine arts, English (including composition), humanities, sciences (biological or physical), senior examination or equivalent body of work, social science, U.S. ethnic minorities/non-Western society course writing-intensive course. **Classes:** Most classes have 20–29 students. Most lab/discussion sections have 20–29 students. **Majors with Highest Enrollment:** Business/managerial economics, classics and classical languages, literatures, and linguistics, psychology. **Disciplines with Highest Percentage of Degrees Awarded:** Social sciences 17%, visual and performing arts 12%, biological/life sciences 10%, business/marketing 10%, psychology 10%. **Special Study Options:** Cooperative education program, cross registration, double major, dual enrollment, English as a second language (ESL), exchange student program (domestic), independent study, internships, student-designed major, study abroad, teacher certification program.

FACILITIES

Housing: Coed dorms, men's dorms, women's dorms, apartments for married students, apartments for single students, special housing for international students, cooperative housing, special interest theme housing, university-sponsored off-campus housing, RV park.
Special Academic Facilities/Equipment: Eloise Pickard Smith Gallery, Mary Porter Sesnon Gallery, center for agroecology, wellness center, Long Marine Laboratory. **Computers:** Network access in dorm rooms, network access in dorm lounges, online registration, online administrative functions (other than registration), remote student-access to Web through college's connection.

CAMPUS LIFE

Activities: Choral groups, dance, drama/theater, jazz band, literary magazine, music ensembles, musical theater, opera, radio station, student government, student newspaper, student-run film society, symphony orchestra, television station. **Organizations:** 129 registered organizations, 2 honor societies, 9 religious organizations. 9 fraternities (1% men join), 11 sororities (1% women join). **Athletics (Intercollegiate):** *Men:* Basketball, diving, soccer, swimming, tennis, volleyball, water polo. *Women:* Basketball, cross-country, diving, golf, soccer, swimming, tennis, volleyball, water polo.

ADMISSIONS

Freshman Academic Profile: 96% in top 10% of high school class, 100% in top 25% of high school class, 100% in top 50% of high school class. 85% from public high schools. SAT Math middle 50% range 520–630. SAT Critical Reading middle 50% range 500–620. SAT Writing middle 50% range 500–620. ACT middle 50% range 21–29. TOEFL required of all international applicants, minimum paper TOEFL 550, minimum computer TOEFL 220. **Basis for Candidate Selection:** *Very important factors considered include:* Academic GPA, application essay, rigor of secondary school record, standardized test scores, state residency. *Important factors considered include:* Character/personal qualities, class rank, extracurricular activities, first generation, geographical residence, talent/ability. *Other factors considered include:* Volunteer work, work experience. **Freshman Admission Requirements:** High school diploma is required, and GED is accepted. *Academic units required:* 4 English, 3 math, 2 science (2 science labs), 2 foreign language, 1 social studies, 1 history, 1 academic elective, 1 visual and performing arts. *Academic units recommended:* 4 English, 4 math, 3 science (3 science labs), 3 foreign language, 1 social studies, 1 history, 1 academic elective, 1 visual and performing art. **Freshman Admission Statistics:** 24,534 applied, 80% admitted, 17% enrolled. **Transfer Admission Requirements:** College transcript(s), essay or personal statement, statement of good standing from prior institution(s). Minimum college GPA of 2.4 required. Lowest grade transferable D. **General Admission Information:** Application fee $60. Regular application deadline 11/30. Regular notification is rolling. Non-fall registration accepted. Neither credit nor placement offered for CEEB Advanced Placement tests.

COSTS AND FINANCIAL AID

Annual out-of-state tuition $20,610. Room and board $12,831. Required fees $9,534. Average book expense $1,356.**Required Forms and Deadlines:** FAFSA. Financial aid filing deadline 6/1. **Notification of Awards:** Applicants will be notified of awards on a rolling basis beginning on or about 4/1. **Types of Aid:** *Need-based scholarships/grants:* Pell, SEOG, state scholarships/grants, private scholarships, the school's own gift aid. *Loans:* Direct Subsidized Stafford, Direct Unsubsidized Stafford, Direct PLUS, Federal Perkins. **Student Employment:** Federal Work-Study Program available. Off-campus job opportunities are excellent. **Financial Aid Statistics:** 42% freshmen, 41% undergrads receive need-based scholarship or grant aid. 41% freshmen, 40% undergrads receive need-based self-help aid.

UNIVERSITY OF CENTRAL ARKANSAS

201 Donaghey Avenue, Bernard Hall, Conway, AR 72035
Phone: 501-450-3128 **E-mail:** admissions@uca.edu **CEEB Code:** 6012
Fax: 501-450-5228 **Website:** www.uca.edu **ACT Code:** 0118
Financial Aid Phone: 501-450-3140

This public school was founded in 1907. It has a 262-acre campus.

RATINGS
Admissions Selectivity Rating: 84   **Fire Safety Rating:** 60*   **Green Rating:** 60*

STUDENTS AND FACULTY
Enrollment: 10,137. **Student Body:** 58% female, 42% male, 6% out-of-state, 2% international (65 countries represented). African American 17%, Asian 2%, Caucasian 71%, Hispanic 2%. **Retention and Graduation:** 70% freshmen return for sophomore year. 20% freshmen graduate within 4 years. **Faculty:** Student/faculty ratio 19:1. 450 full-time faculty, 68% hold PhDs. 100% faculty teach undergrads.

ACADEMICS
Degrees: Associate, bachelor's, certificate, doctoral, master's, post-bachelor's certificate, post-master's certificate. **Academic Requirements:** Arts/fine arts, English (including composition), history, humanities, mathematics, sciences (biological or physical), social science. **Classes:** Most classes have 20–29 students. **Majors with Highest Enrollment:** General studies, health professions and related sciences, nursing/registered nurse training (RN, ASN, BSN, MSN). **Disciplines with Highest Percentage of Degrees Awarded:** Business/marketing 20%, health professions and related sciences 19%, education 11%, family and consumer sciences 8%, English 7%. **Special Study Options:** Accelerated program, cooperative education program, distance learning, double major, dual enrollment, English as a second language (ESL), honors program, independent study, internships, liberal arts/career combination, study abroad, teacher certification program, 5-year professional program in physical and occupational therapy.

FACILITIES
Housing: Coed dorms, men's dorms, women's dorms, apartments for married students, apartments for single students, special housing for disabled students, special housing for international students, fraternity/sorority housing, residential college. **Special Academic Facilities/Equipment:** Greenhouse, Baum Gallery, HPER Center, planetarium, technology plaza, smartboards, H.L. Minton Center for Geospatial Analysis and Research. **Computers:** 100% of classrooms are wireless, 95% of public computers are PCs, 5% of public computers are Macs, network access in dorm rooms, network access in dorm lounges, online registration, online administrative functions (other than registration), remote student-access to Web through college's connection.

CAMPUS LIFE
Activities: Choral groups, concert band, dance, drama/theater, jazz band, literary magazine, marching band, music ensembles, musical theater, opera, radio station, student government, student newspaper, student-run film society, symphony orchestra, television station. **Organizations:** 131 registered organizations, 11 fraternities (10% men join), 9 sororities (10% women join). **Athletics (Intercollegiate):** *Men:* Baseball, basketball, cheerleading, cross-

country, football, golf, soccer, tennis, track/field (indoor). *Women:* Basketball, cheerleading, cross-country, golf, soccer, softball, tennis, track/field (indoor), volleyball.

ADMISSIONS
Freshman Academic Profile: 24% in top 10% of high school class, 50% in top 25% of high school class, 77% in top 50% of high school class. 96% from public high schools. ACT middle 50% range 20–27. TOEFL required of all international applicants, minimum paper TOEFL 500, minimum computer TOEFL 173. **Basis for Candidate Selection:** *Very important factors considered include:* Class rank, standardized test scores. *Other factors considered include:* Character/personal qualities, extracurricular activities, rigor of secondary school record, talent/ability. **Freshman Admission Requirements:** High school diploma is required, and GED is accepted. *Academic units recommended:* 4 English, 4 math, 3 science, 1 social studies, 2 history, 10 academic electives. **Transfer Admission Requirements:** College transcript(s), statement of good standing from prior institution(s). Minimum college GPA of 2.0 required. Lowest grade transferable C. **General Admission Information:** Regular notification is rolling. Non-fall registration accepted. Credit and/or placement offered for CEEB Advanced Placement tests.

COSTS AND FINANCIAL AID
Annual in-state tuition $4,500. Out-of-state tuition $9,000. Room & board $4,320. Required fees $1,164. Average book expense $1,200. **Required Forms and Deadlines:** FAFSA. Financial aid filing deadline 7/1. **Notification of Awards:** Applicants will be notified of awards on a rolling basis beginning on or about 5/4.

UNIVERSITY OF CENTRAL FLORIDA

PO Box 160111, Orlando, FL 32816-0111
Phone: 407-823-3000 **E-mail:** admission@mail.ucf.edu **CEEB Code:** 5233
Fax: 407-823-5625 **Website:** www.ucf.edu **ACT Code:** 0735
Financial Aid Phone: 407-823-2827

This public school was founded in 1963. It has a 1,415-acre campus.

RATINGS
Admissions Selectivity Rating: 89   **Fire Safety Rating:** 84   **Green Rating:** 60*

STUDENTS AND FACULTY
Enrollment: 39,298. **Student Body:** 55% female, 45% male, 5% out-of-state, 1% international (126 countries represented). African American 8%, Asian 5%, Caucasian 68%, Hispanic 13%. **Retention and Graduation:** 82% freshmen return for sophomore year. 30% freshmen graduate within 4 years. **Faculty:** Student/faculty ratio 28:1. 1,202 full-time faculty, 78% hold PhDs. 100% faculty teach undergrads.

ACADEMICS
Degrees: Associate, bachelor's, certificate, doctoral, master's, post-bachelor's certificate. **Academic Requirements:** English (including composition), history, humanities, mathematics, sciences (biological or physical), social science. **Classes:** Most classes have 20–29 students. Most lab/discussion sections have 20–29 students. **Majors with Highest Enrollment:** Management information systems, marketing/marketing management, psychology. **Disciplines with Highest Percentage of Degrees Awarded:** Business/marketing 27%, education 10%, psychology 10%, health professions and related sciences 9%, liberal arts/general studies 6%. **Special Study Options:** Cooperative education program, distance learning, double major, dual enrollment, English as a second language (ESL), honors program, independent study, internships, study abroad, teacher certification program.

FACILITIES
Housing: Coed dorms, men's dorms, women's dorms, apartments for single students, fraternity/sorority housing, living learning communities, honors center. Affiliated student residences available across street from campus with university resident assistants. **Special Academic Facilities/Equipment:** Center for Research and Education in Optics and Lasers, arboretum, observatory, student union, student recreation center. **Computers:** 1% of classrooms are wired, 90% of classrooms are wireless, 90% of public computers are PCs, 5% of public computers are Macs, 5% of public computers are UNIX, network access in dorm rooms, network access in dorm lounges, online registration, online

The Princeton Review's Complete Book of Colleges

administrative functions (other than registration), remote student-access to Web through college's connection, support for handheld computing.

CAMPUS LIFE

Activities: Choral groups, concert band, drama/theater, jazz band, literary magazine, marching band, music ensembles, musical theater, pep band, radio station, student government, student newspaper, student-run film society, symphony orchestra. **Organizations:** 329 registered organizations, 36 honor societies, 22 religious organizations. 24 fraternities (11% men join), 17 sororities (9% women join). **Athletics (Intercollegiate):** *Men:* Baseball, basketball, cheerleading, cross-country, football, golf, soccer, tennis. *Women:* Basketball, cheerleading, crew/rowing, cross-country, golf, soccer, softball, tennis, track/field (indoor), track/field (outdoor), volleyball.

ADMISSIONS

Freshman Academic Profile: 35% in top 10% of high school class, 77% in top 25% of high school class, 93% in top 50% of high school class. SAT Math middle 50% range 540–640. SAT Critical Reading middle 50% range 530–620. SAT Writing middle 50% range 510–600. ACT middle 50% range 23–27. TOEFL required of all international applicants, minimum paper TOEFL 550, minimum computer TOEFL 213. **Basis for Candidate Selection:** *Very important factors considered include:* Academic GPA, rigor of secondary school record, standardized test scores. *Important factors considered include:* Application essay. *Other factors considered include:* Alumni/ae relation, character/personal qualities, class rank, extracurricular activities, geographical residence, interview, level of applicant's interest, recommendation(s), state residency, talent/ability, volunteer work, work experience. **Freshman Admission Requirements:** High school diploma is required, and GED is accepted. *Academic units required:* 4 English, 3 math, 3 science (2 science labs), 2 foreign language, 3 social studies, 4 academic electives. **Freshman Admission Statistics:** 24,345 applied, 52% admitted, 53% enrolled. **Transfer Admission Requirements:** High school transcript, college transcript(s). Minimum college GPA of 2.0 required. Lowest grade transferable D. **General Admission Information:** Application fee $30. Regular application deadline 5/1. Regular notification is rolling. Non-fall registration accepted. Credit offered for CEEB Advanced Placement tests.

COSTS AND FINANCIAL AID

Annual in-state tuition $3,620. Annual out-of-state tuition $17,821. Room and board $8,164. Average book expense $924. **Required Forms and Deadlines:** FAFSA. Financial aid filing deadline 6/30. **Notification of Awards:** Applicants will be notified of awards on a rolling basis beginning on or about 3/15. **Types of Aid:** *Need-based scholarships/grants:* Pell, SEOG, state scholarships/grants, private scholarships, the school's own gift aid, university scholarships and grants. *Loans:* FFEL Subsidized Stafford, FFEL Unsubsidized Stafford, FFEL PLUS, Federal Perkins. **Financial Aid Statistics:** 21% freshmen, 26% undergrads receive need-based scholarship or grant aid. 17% freshmen, 25% undergrads receive need-based self-help aid. 66 freshmen, 283 undergrads receive athletic scholarships. 93% freshmen, 80% undergrads receive any aid.

See page 1432.

UNIVERSITY OF CENTRAL MISSOURI

Office of Admissions, WDE 1400, Warrensburg, MO 64093
Phone: 660-543-4290 **E-mail:** admit@ucmovmb.edu **CEEB Code:** 6090
Fax: 660-543-8517 **Website:** www.ucmo.edu **ACT Code:** 2272
Financial Aid Phone: 660-543-4040

This public school was founded in 1871. It has a 1,561-acre campus.

RATINGS

Admissions Selectivity Rating: 72   **Fire Safety Rating:** 69   **Green Rating:** 60*

STUDENTS AND FACULTY

Enrollment: 8,441. **Student Body:** 56% female, 44% male, 7% out-of-state, 2% international (53 countries represented). African American 5%, Asian 1%, Caucasian 76%, Hispanic 2%. **Retention and Graduation:** 68% freshmen return for sophomore year. 23% freshmen graduate within 4 years. **Faculty:** Student/faculty ratio 19:1. 449 full-time faculty, 73% hold PhDs. 100% faculty teach undergrads.

ACADEMICS

Degrees: Associate, bachelor's, master's, post-bachelor's certificate, post-master's certificate. **Academic Requirements:** Arts/fine arts, computer literacy, English (including composition), history, humanities, integrative studies, mathematics, multicultural education, personal development, sciences (biological or physical), social science, speech. **Classes:** Most classes have 20–29

students. **Majors with Highest Enrollment:** Criminal justice/law enforcement administration, education, marketing/marketing management. **Disciplines with Highest Percentage of Degrees Awarded:** Education 22%, business/marketing 18%, visual and performing arts 8%, engineering technologies 7%, security and protective services 7%, communications/journalism 5%, health professions and related sciences 5%. **Special Study Options:** Accelerated program, cooperative education program, cross registration, distance learning, double major, dual enrollment, English as a second language (ESL), honors program, internships, student-designed major, study abroad, teacher certification program, weekend college.

FACILITIES

Housing: Coed dorms, women's dorms, apartments for married students, apartments for single students, special housing for disabled students, special housing for international students, fraternity/sorority housing, economy suites, town houses. **Special Academic Facilities/Equipment:** Art gallery, Nance Museum & Library of Antiquities, natural history museum, English language center, child development lab, speech and hearing lab, 260-acre farm, Missouri Safety Center, National Police Institute, driving/safety range, center for technology and business research, airport for aviation program, extended campus, Lee's Summit, MO, KCMW-FM, KMOS-TV public broadcasting stations. **Computers:** 1% of classrooms are wireless, 92% of public computers are PCs, 8% of public computers are Macs, network access in dorm rooms, online registration, online administrative functions (other than registration), support for handheld computing, remote student-access to Web through college's connection.

CAMPUS LIFE

Activities: Choral groups, concert band, dance, drama/theater, jazz band, literary magazine, marching band, music ensembles, musical theater, opera, pep band, radio station, student government, student newspaper, student-run film society, symphony orchestra, television station. **Organizations:** 150 registered organizations, 24 honor societies, 14 religious organizations. 9 fraternities (10% men join), 10 sororities (9% women join). **Athletics (Intercollegiate):** *Men:* Baseball, basketball, bowling, cross-country, football, golf, soccer, track/field (outdoor), wrestling. *Women:* Basketball, bowling, cross-country, soccer, softball, track/field (outdoor), volleyball.

ADMISSIONS

Freshman Academic Profile: 12% in top 10% of high school class, 36% in top 25% of high school class, 71% in top 50% of high school class. 90% from public high schools. ACT middle 50% range 20–24. TOEFL required of all international applicants, minimum paper TOEFL 500, minimum computer TOEFL 173. **Basis for Candidate Selection:** *Very important factors considered include:* Class rank, rigor of secondary school record, standardized test scores. *Other factors considered include:* Alumni/ae relation, character/personal qualities, extracurricular activities, recommendation(s), talent/ability. **Freshman Admission Requirements:** High school diploma is required, and GED is accepted. *Academic units required:* 4 English, 3 math, 2 science (1 science lab), 3 social studies, 3 academic electives, 1 arts. *Academic units recommended:* 2 foreign language. **Freshman Admission Statistics:** 3,631 applied, 84% admitted, 52% enrolled. **Transfer Admission Requirements:** College transcript(s). Minimum college GPA of 2.0 required. Lowest grade transferable C. **General Admission Information:** Application fee $30. Regular application deadline 8/18. Regular notification is rolling. Non-fall registration accepted. Admission may be deferred for a maximum of 3 semesters. Credit offered for CEEB Advanced Placement tests.

COSTS AND FINANCIAL AID

Annual in-state tuition $5,835. Out-of-state tuition $11,250. Room & board $5,412. Required fees $420. Average book expense $500. **Required Forms and Deadlines:** FAFSA. Financial aid filing deadline 3/1. **Notification of Awards:** Applicants will be notified of awards on or about 3/1. **Types of Aid:** *Need-based scholarships/grants:* Pell, SEOG, state scholarships/grants, private scholarships, the school's own gift aid. *Loans:* Direct Subsidized Stafford, Direct Unsubsidized Stafford, Direct PLUS, Federal Perkins, state loans. **Financial Aid Statistics:** 27% freshmen, 36% undergrads receive need-based scholarship or grant aid. 43% freshmen, 55% undergrads receive need-based self-help aid. 70 freshmen, 331 undergrads receive athletic scholarships. 51% freshmen, 61% undergrads receive any aid. Highest amount earned per year from on-campus jobs $2,000.

UNIVERSITY OF CENTRAL OKLAHOMA

100 North University Drive, Edmond, OK 73034
Phone: 405-974-2338 **E-mail:** admituco@ucok.edu **CEEB Code:** 6091
Fax: 405-341-4964 **Website:** www.ucok.edu **ACT Code:** 3390
Financial Aid Phone: 405-974-3334

This public school was founded in 1890. It has a 200-acre campus.

RATINGS
Admissions Selectivity Rating: 71   **Fire Safety Rating:** 73   **Green Rating:** 60*

STUDENTS AND FACULTY
Enrollment: 14,246. **Student Body:** 58% female, 42% male, 5% out-of-state, 7% international (76 countries represented). African American 10%, Asian 3%, Caucasian 67%, Hispanic 3%, Native American 6%. **Retention and Graduation:** 61% freshmen return for sophomore year. **Faculty:** Student/faculty ratio 23:1. 416 full-time faculty, 69% hold PhDs. 95% faculty teach undergrads.

ACADEMICS
Degrees: Bachelor's, certificate, master's. **Academic Requirements:** English (including composition), history, humanities, mathematics, sciences (biological or physical). **Classes:** Most classes have 20–29 students. Most lab/discussion sections have 10–19 students. **Majors with Highest Enrollment:** Business administration and management, elementary education and teaching, nursing/registered nurse training (RN, ASN, BSN, MSN). **Disciplines with Highest Percentage of Degrees Awarded:** Business/marketing 30%, education 11%, liberal arts/general studies 11%, communications/journalism 8%, visual and performing arts 5%. **Special Study Options:** Accelerated program, distance learning, double major, dual enrollment, English as a second language (ESL), honors program, independent study, internships, teacher certification program.

FACILITIES
Housing: Coed dorms, men's dorms, women's dorms, apartments for married students, apartments for single students, fraternity/sorority housing. **Special Academic Facilities/Equipment:** Art and history museums, archives. **Computers:** 75% of public computers are PCs, 25% of public computers are Macs, network access in dorm rooms, network access in dorm lounges, online registration, remote student-access to Web through college's connection.

CAMPUS LIFE
Activities: Choral groups, concert band, dance, drama/theater, jazz band, marching band, music ensembles, musical theater, pep band, radio station, student government, student newspaper, symphony orchestra, television station, yearbook. **Organizations:** 150 registered organizations, 27 honor societies, 16 religious organizations. 9 fraternities (5% men join), 10 sororities (3% women join). **Athletics (Intercollegiate):** *Men:* Baseball, basketball, football, golf, wrestling. *Women:* Basketball, cross-country, golf, soccer, softball, tennis, volleyball.

ADMISSIONS
Freshman Academic Profile: 13% in top 10% of high school class, 35% in top 25% of high school class, 72% in top 50% of high school class. 83% from public high schools. ACT middle 50% range 19–24. TOEFL required of all international applicants, minimum paper TOEFL 500, minimum computer TOEFL 173. **Basis for Candidate Selection:** *Very important factors considered include:* Academic GPA, class rank, rigor of secondary school record, standardized test scores. *Other factors considered include:* Extracurricular activities, talent/ability. **Freshman Admission Requirements:** High school diploma is required, and GED is accepted. *Academic units required:* 4 English, 3 math, 2 science (2 science labs), 1 social studies, 2 history, 3 academic electives. *Academic units recommended:* 4 English, 4 math, 3 science (2 science labs), 2 foreign language, 1 social studies, 2 history. **Freshman Admission Statistics:** 4,178 applied, 94% admitted, 54% enrolled. **Transfer Admission Requirements:** College transcript(s), statement of good standing from prior institution(s). Minimum college GPA of 2.0 required. Lowest grade transferable D. **General Admission Information:** Application fee $25. Regular notification is rolling. Non-fall registration accepted. Admission may be deferred for a maximum of 1 semester. Credit and/or placement offered for CEEB Advanced Placement tests.

COSTS AND FINANCIAL AID
Annual in-state tuition $3,027. Out-of-state tuition $8,412. Room & board $4,763. Required fees $512. Average book expense $1,000. **Required Forms and Deadlines:** FAFSA, institution's own financial aid form. Financial aid filing deadline 5/31. **Notification of Awards:** Applicants will be notified of awards on a rolling basis beginning on or about 5/1. **Types of Aid:** *Need-based scholarships/grants:* Pell, SEOG, state scholarships/grants, private scholarships, the school's own gift aid. *Loans:* FFEL Subsidized Stafford, FFEL

Unsubsidized Stafford, FFEL PLUS, Federal Perkins. **Student Employment:** Federal Work-Study Program available. Institutional employment available. Off-campus job opportunities are excellent. **Financial Aid Statistics:** 41% freshmen, 43% undergrads receive need-based scholarship or grant aid. 43% freshmen, 45% undergrads receive need-based self-help aid. 37 freshmen, 228 undergrads receive athletic scholarships. 64% freshmen, 73% undergrads receive any aid. Highest amount earned per year from on-campus jobs $6,958.

UNIVERSITY OF CENTRAL TEXAS

1901 South Clear Creek Drive, PO Box 1416, Killeen, TX 76540-1416
Phone: 245-526-8262 **E-mail:** uct10@vvm.com **CEEB Code:** 6756
Fax: 254-526-8403 **Website:** www.vvm.com/uct **ACT Code:** 4055
Financial Aid Phone: 254-526-8262

This private school was founded in 1973. It has a 10-acre campus.

RATINGS
Admissions Selectivity Rating: 60*   **Fire Safety Rating:** 60*   **Green Rating:** 60*

STUDENTS AND FACULTY
Enrollment: 691. **Student Body:** 58% female, 42% male, 10% out-of-state, 2% international (10 countries represented). African American 18%, Asian 3%, Caucasian 63%, Hispanic 9%, Native American 1%.

ACADEMICS
Degrees: Bachelor's, master's. **Academic Requirements:** Computer literacy, English (including composition), humanities, mathematics, social science. **Special Study Options:** Cooperative education program, teacher certification program.

CAMPUS LIFE
Organizations: 1 honor society.

ADMISSIONS
Freshman Academic Profile: TOEFL required of all international applicants, minimum paper TOEFL 515. **Freshman Admission Requirements:** High school diploma is required, and GED is accepted. **Transfer Admission Requirements:** College transcript(s). Minimum college GPA of 2.0 required. Lowest grade transferable D. **General Admission Information:** Regular application deadline rolling. Regular notification is rolling. Non-fall registration accepted. Common Application accepted.

COSTS AND FINANCIAL AID
Annual tuition $3,144. Room & board $3,449. Required fees $40. Average book expense $800. **Required Forms and Deadlines:** FAFSA, institution's own financial aid form, state aid form. **Types of Aid:** *Need-based scholarships/grants:* Pell, SEOG, state scholarships/grants. *Loans:* FFEL Subsidized Stafford, FFEL Unsubsidized Stafford, FFEL PLUS. **Student Employment:** Federal Work-Study Program available. Off-campus job opportunities are excellent.

UNIVERSITY OF CHARLESTON

2300 MacCorkle Avenue Southeast, Charleston, WV 25304-1099
Phone: 304-357-4750 **E-mail:** admissions@uchaswv.edu **CEEB Code:** 5419
Fax: 304-357-4781 **Website:** www.uchaswv.edu **ACT Code:** 4528
Financial Aid Phone: 304-357-4760

This private school was founded in 1888. It has a 40-acre campus.

RATINGS
Admissions Selectivity Rating: 75   **Fire Safety Rating:** 60*   **Green Rating:** 60*

STUDENTS AND FACULTY
Enrollment: 995. **Student Body:** 67% female, 33% male, 19% out-of-state, 3% international. African American 3%, Caucasian 66%. **Retention and Graduation:** 65% freshmen return for sophomore year. 39% freshmen graduate within 4 years. 14% grads go on to further study within 1 year. 7% grads pursue arts and sciences degrees. 2% grads pursue business degrees. 1% grads pursue law degrees. 3% grads pursue medical degrees. **Faculty:** Student/faculty ratio 12:1. 67 full-time faculty, 36% hold PhDs. 100% faculty teach undergrads.

ACADEMICS

Degrees: Associate, bachelor's, master's. **Academic Requirements:**
Computer literacy, English (including composition), history, humanities,
learning communities, mathematics, sciences (biological or physical), social
science. **Classes:** Most classes have 10–19 students. **Majors with Highest
Enrollment:** Business administration/management, education, nursing/
registered nurse training (RN, ASN, BSN, MSN). **Disciplines with Highest
Percentage of Degrees Awarded:** Health professions and related sciences
34%, business/marketing 16%, biological/life sciences 9%, education 7%, visual
and performing arts 7%, psychology 6%. **Special Study Options:** Accelerated
program, co-op programs in arts, business, health professions, off-campus study
in Washington, DC, political science, double major, dual enrollment,
independent study, internships, student-designed major, study abroad, teacher
certification program.

FACILITIES

Housing: Coed dorms. **Special Academic Facilities/Equipment:**
Frankenberger Art Gallery. **Computers:** 100% of public computers are PCs,
network access in dorm rooms, network access in dorm lounges, online
administrative functions (other than registration), remote student-access to Web
through college's connection.

CAMPUS LIFE

Activities: Choral groups, drama/theater, music ensembles, musical theater,
student government, student newspaper. **Organizations:** 40 registered
organizations, 8 honor societies, 2 religious organizations. 2 fraternities (4%
men join), 3 sororities (4% women join). **Athletics (Intercollegiate):** *Men:*
Baseball, basketball, crew/rowing, cross-country, football, golf, soccer,
swimming, tennis, track/field (indoor), track/field (outdoor). *Women:* Basketball,
cheerleading, crew/rowing, cross-country, soccer, softball, swimming, tennis,
track/field (indoor), track/field (outdoor), volleyball.

ADMISSIONS

Freshman Academic Profile: 21% in top 10% of high school class, 80% in top
50% of high school class. SAT Math middle 50% range 400–560. SAT Critical
Reading middle 50% range 450–570. ACT middle 50% range 19–24. TOEFL
required of all international applicants, minimum paper TOEFL 500. **Basis for
Candidate Selection:** *Very important factors considered include:* Rigor of
secondary school record, standardized test scores. *Important factors considered
include:* Application essay, class rank, interview. *Other factors considered
include:* Alumni/ae relation, character/personal qualities, extracurricular
activities, recommendation(s), talent/ability, volunteer work. **Freshman
Admission Requirements:** High school diploma is required, and GED is
accepted. *Academic units recommended:* 4 English, 3 math, 3 science, 1 foreign
language, 3 social studies, 2 history. **Freshman Admission Statistics:** 939
applied, 75% admitted, 25% enrolled. **Transfer Admission Requirements:**
College transcript(s). Minimum college GPA of 2.0 required. Lowest grade
transferable C. **General Admission Information:** Application fee $25. Early
decision application deadline 12/15. Regular notification is rolling. Non-fall
registration accepted. Admission may be deferred for a maximum of 4
semesters. Common Application accepted. Credit and/or placement offered for
CEEB Advanced Placement tests.

COSTS AND FINANCIAL AID

Annual tuition $16,500. Room & board $6,000. Average book expense $500.
Required Forms and Deadlines: FAFSA. Financial aid filing deadline 3/1.
Notification of Awards: Applicants will be notified of awards on a rolling basis
beginning on or about 3/1. **Types of Aid:** *Need-based scholarships/grants:* Pell,
SEOG, state scholarships/grants, private scholarships, the school's own gift aid.
Loans: FFEL Subsidized Stafford, FFEL Unsubsidized Stafford, FFEL PLUS,
Federal Perkins, Federal Nursing. **Student Employment:** Federal Work-
Study Program available. Institutional employment available. Off-campus job
opportunities are excellent. **Financial Aid Statistics:** 70% freshmen, 70%
undergrads receive need-based scholarship or grant aid. 76% freshmen, 84%
undergrads receive need-based self-help aid. 30 freshmen, 42 undergrads
receive athletic scholarships. Highest amount earned per year from on-campus
jobs $1,000.

UNIVERSITY OF CHICAGO

Best 368

1101 East Fifty-eighth Street, Rosenwald Hall Suite 105, Chicago, IL 60637
Phone: 773-702-8650 **E-mail:** collegeadmissions@uchicago.edu **CEEB Code:** 1832
Fax: 773-702-4199 **Website:** www.uchicago.edu **ACT Code:** 1152
Financial Aid Phone: 773-702-8655

This private school was founded in 1890. It has a 211-acre campus.

RATINGS

Admissions Selectivity Rating: 98   **Fire Safety Rating:** 60*   **Green Rating:** 94

STUDENTS AND FACULTY

Enrollment: 4,790. **Student Body:** 50% female, 50% male, 78% out-of-state,
7% international (59 countries represented). African American 4%, Asian 13%,
Caucasian 48%, Hispanic 8%. **Retention and Graduation:** 98% freshmen
return for sophomore year. 82% freshmen graduate within 4 years. **Faculty:**
Student/faculty ratio 6:1. 1,055 full-time faculty, 100% hold PhDs.

ACADEMICS

Degrees: Bachelor's, doctoral, first professional, master's. **Academic
Requirements:** Arts/fine arts, English (including composition), foreign
languages, history, humanities, mathematics, sciences (biological or physical),
social science. **Classes:** Most classes have 10–19 students. Most lab/discussion
sections have 10–19 students. **Majors with Highest Enrollment:** Biology/
biological sciences, economics, English language and literature. **Disciplines
with Highest Percentage of Degrees Awarded:** Social sciences 37%,
biological/life sciences 10%, foreign languages and literature 7%, mathematics
7%, physical sciences 7%, English 6%. **Special Study Options:** Cross
registration, double major, dual enrollment, English as a second language
(ESL), exchange student program (domestic), independent study, internships,
student-designed major, study abroad.

FACILITIES

Housing: Coed dorms, apartments for married students, special housing for
disabled students, special housing for international students, fraternity/sorority
housing, cooperative housing. **Special Academic Facilities/Equipment:**
Smart Museum, Renaissance Society, Oriental Institute, Business and
Economics Resource Center, D'Angelo Law Library, Echhart Library, John
Crerar Library, Joseph Regenstein Library, Special Collections Research
Center, Social Services Administration Library, Yerkes Obsevatory Library, on-
campus lab school (PreK–12), Argonne National Laboratory, Enrico Fermi
Institute, Court Theater, observatory, 2 telescopes, accelerator laboratory.
Computers: Network access in dorm rooms, network access in dorm lounges,
online registration, remote student-access to Web through college's connection.

CAMPUS LIFE

Activities: Choral groups, concert band, dance, drama/theater, jazz band,
literary magazine, music ensembles, musical theater, pep band, radio station,
student government, student newspaper, student-run film society, symphony
orchestra, yearbook. **Organizations:** 400 registered organizations, 11
fraternities, 4 sororities. **Athletics (Intercollegiate):** *Men:* Baseball, basketball,
cross-country, football, soccer, swimming, tennis, track/field (indoor), track/field
(outdoor), wrestling. *Women:* Basketball, cross-country, soccer, softball,
swimming, tennis, track/field (indoor), track/field (outdoor), volleyball.

ADMISSIONS

Freshman Academic Profile: 80% in top 10% of high school class, 97% in top
25% of high school class, 100% in top 50% of high school class. 63% from
public high schools. SAT Math middle 50% range 660–760. SAT Critical
Reading middle 50% range 670–770. ACT middle 50% range 28–33. TOEFL
required of all international applicants, minimum paper TOEFL 600, minimum
computer TOEFL 250. **Basis for Candidate Selection:** *Very important
factors considered include:* Application essay, character/personal qualities,
recommendation(s), rigor of secondary school record, talent/ability. *Important
factors considered include:* Academic GPA, class rank, extracurricular activities,
volunteer work. *Other factors considered include:* Alumni/ae relation, first
generation, interview, level of applicant's interest, racial/ethnic status,
standardized test scores, work experience. **Freshman Admission Requirements:** High school diploma or equivalent is not required. *Academic units
recommended:* 4 English, 4 math, 4 science, 3 foreign language, 2 social studies,
2 history. **Freshman Admission Statistics:** 9,538 applied, 38% admitted, 34%
enrolled. **Transfer Admission Requirements:** High school transcript, college

transcript(s), essay or personal statement, standardized test score, statement of good standing from prior institution(s). Minimum college GPA of 3.0 required. **General Admission Information:** Application fee $60. Regular application deadline 1/2. Regular notification 4/1. Non-fall registration not accepted. Admission may be deferred for a maximum of 4 semesters. Credit and/or placement offered for CEEB Advanced Placement tests.

COSTS AND FINANCIAL AID
Annual tuition $35,169. Room and board $11,139. Required fees $699. Average book expense $1,050. **Required Forms and Deadlines:** FAFSA, institution's own financial aid form, CSS/Financial Aid Profile, Noncustodial PROFILE, Business/Farm Supplement. Financial aid filing deadline 2/1. **Notification of Awards:** Applicants will be notified of awards on or about 4/15. **Types of Aid:** *Need-based scholarships/grants:* Pell, SEOG, state scholarships/grants, private scholarships, the school's own gift aid. *Loans:* FFEL Subsidized Stafford, FFEL Unsubsidized Stafford, FFEL PLUS, Federal Perkins. **Student Employment: Financial Aid Statistics:** 47% freshmen, 45% undergrads receive need-based scholarship or grant aid. 38% freshmen, 39% undergrads receive need-based self-help aid. 59% freshmen, 56% undergrads receive any aid.

See page 1434.

UNIVERSITY OF CINCINNATI

PO Box 210091, Cincinnati, OH 45221-0091
Phone: 513-556-1100 **E-mail:** admissions@uc.edu **CEEB Code:** 1833
Fax: 513-556-1105 **Website:** www.uc.edu **ACT Code:** 3340
Financial Aid Phone: 513-556-6982

This public school was founded in 1819. It has a 392-acre campus.

RATINGS
Admissions Selectivity Rating: 79   **Fire Safety Rating:** 80   **Green Rating:** 87

STUDENTS AND FACULTY
Enrollment: 19,217. **Student Body:** 51% female, 49% male, 11% out-of-state, 1% international (124 countries represented). African American 12%, Asian 3%, Caucasian 77%, Hispanic 2%. **Retention and Graduation:** 80% freshmen return for sophomore year. 19% freshmen graduate within 4 years. **Faculty:** Student/faculty ratio 14:1. 1,224 full-time faculty, 63% hold PhDs.

ACADEMICS
Degrees: Associate, bachelor's, certificate, doctoral, first professional, master's, post-bachelor's certificate. **Classes:** Most classes have 20–29 students. **Majors with Highest Enrollment:** Communication and rhetoric, communications studies/speech marketing/marketing management, psychology. **Disciplines with Highest Percentage of Degrees Awarded:** Business/marketing 22%, engineering 13%, visual and performing arts 12%, health professions and related sciences 9%, English 8%. **Special Study Options:** Accelerated program, cooperative education program, distance learning, double major, English as a second language (ESL), honors program, independent study, internships, liberal arts/career combination, study abroad, teacher certification program, weekend college.

FACILITIES
Housing: Coed dorms, men's dorms, women's dorms, apartments for married students, apartments for single students, fraternity/sorority housing. **Special Academic Facilities/Equipment:** Art museum, language lab, observatory. **Computers:** 7% of classrooms are wired, 40% of classrooms are wireless, 90% of public computers are PCs, 10% of public computers are Macs, network access in dorm rooms, network access in dorm lounges, online registration, online administrative functions (other than registration), support for handheld computing, remote student-access to Web through college's connection.

CAMPUS LIFE
Activities: Choral groups, concert band, dance, drama/theater, jazz band, marching band, music ensembles, musical theater, opera, pep band, radio station, student government, student newspaper, student-run film society, symphony orchestra, yearbook. **Organizations:** 250 registered organizations, 16 honor societies, 23 religious organizations. 23 fraternities, 10 sororities. **Athletics (Intercollegiate):** *Men:* Baseball, basketball, cheerleading, cross-country, diving, football, golf, soccer, swimming, track/field (outdoor). *Women:*

Basketball, cheerleading, crew/rowing, cross-country, diving, golf, soccer, swimming, tennis, track/field (indoor), track/field (outdoor), volleyball. **Environmental Initiatives:** OH HB 251—Requirement to reduce energy emissions by 25%. ACUPPC—working on carbon footprint; working on implementation plan. All new buildings are required to be LEED Silver; 3 buildings on campus are rated "silver."

ADMISSIONS
Freshman Academic Profile: 21% in top 10% of high school class, 45% in top 25% of high school class, 77% in top 50% of high school class. SAT Math middle 50% range 500–630. SAT Critical Reading middle 50% range 490–610. SAT Writing middle 50% range 470–590. ACT middle 50% range 21–27. Minimum paper TOEFL 515. **Basis for Candidate Selection:** *Very important factors considered include:* Academic GPA, class rank, rigor of secondary school record. *Other factors considered include:* Application essay, extracurricular activities. **Freshman Admission Requirements:** High school diploma is required, and GED is accepted. *Academic units required:* 4 English, 3 math, 2 science, 2 foreign language, 2 social studies, 2 academic electives. *Academic units recommended:* 4 math, 3 science, 1 history. **Freshman Admission Statistics:** 10,741 applied, 76% admitted, 39% enrolled. **Transfer Admission Requirements:** Lowest grade transferable C. **General Admission Information:** Application fee $40. Regular application deadline 9/1. Regular notification is rolling. Non-fall registration accepted. Admission may be deferred for a maximum of 2 semesters. Credit and/or placement offered for CEEB Advanced Placement tests.

COSTS AND FINANCIAL AID
Annual in-state tuition $7,896. Out-of-state tuition $22,419. Room & board $8,286. Required fees $1,503. Average book expense $1,185. **Required Forms and Deadlines:** FAFSA. **Notification of Awards:** Applicants will be notified of awards on a rolling basis beginning on or about 3/10. **Types of Aid:** *Need-based scholarships/grants:* Pell, SEOG, state scholarships/grants, private scholarships, the school's own gift aid, Federal Nursing Scholarships. *Loans:* Direct Subsidized Stafford, Direct Unsubsidized Stafford, Direct PLUS, FFEL Subsidized Stafford, FFEL Unsubsidized Stafford, FFEL PLUS, Federal Perkins, Federal Nursing, state loans, college/university loans from institutional funds. **Student Employment:** Federal Work-Study Program available. Institutional employment available. Off-campus job opportunities are excellent. **Financial Aid Statistics:** 26% freshmen, 24% undergrads receive need-based scholarship or grant aid. 20% freshmen, 18% undergrads receive need-based self-help aid. 41 freshmen, 230 undergrads receive athletic scholarships.

UNIVERSITY COLLEGE OF CAPE BRETON
(CAPE BRETON UNIVERSITY)

PO Box 5300, Sydney, NS B1P 6L2 Canada
Phone: 902-563-1117 **E-mail:** registrar@uccb.ns.ca
Fax: 902-563-1371 **Website:** www.uccb.ns.ca
Financial Aid Phone: 902-563-1420

This public school was founded in 1974. It has a 140-acre campus.

RATINGS
Admissions Selectivity Rating: 60*   **Fire Safety Rating:** 60*   **Green Rating:** 60*

STUDENTS AND FACULTY
Enrollment: 2,682. **Student Body:** 58% female, 42% male. **Retention and Graduation:** 55% freshmen return for sophomore year. 54% freshmen graduate within 4 years. **Faculty:** Student/faculty ratio 15:1. 189 full-time faculty, 41% hold PhDs. 100% faculty teach undergrads.

ACADEMICS
Degrees: Bachelor's, certificate, diploma, master's, post-bachelor's certificate. **Academic Requirements:** Arts/fine arts, computer literacy, English (including composition), humanities, mathematics, philosophy, sciences (biological or physical), social science, communication. **Classes:** Most classes have fewer than 10 students. **Disciplines with Highest Percentage of Degrees Awarded:** Psychology 23%, social sciences 19%, business/marketing 15%, biological/life sciences 8%, natural resources/environmental science 7%. **Special Study Options:** Cooperative education program, distance learning, double major, honors program, independent study, internships, liberal arts/career combination, study abroad.

FACILITIES
Housing: Coed dorms. **Special Academic Facilities/Equipment:** Art gallery, Boardmore Playhouse, CAPR radio. **Computers:** 50% of classrooms are

wireless, 100% of public computers are PCs, network access in dorm rooms, online registration, online administrative functions (other than registration), remote student-access to Web through college's connection.

CAMPUS LIFE

Activities: Drama/theater, literary magazine, radio station, student government, student newspaper, yearbook. **Organizations:** 72 registered organizations, 1 honor society. **Athletics (Intercollegiate):** *Men:* Basketball, soccer. *Women:* Basketball, soccer, volleyball.

ADMISSIONS

Freshman Academic Profile: 80% from public high schools. TOEFL required of all international applicants, minimum paper TOEFL 550, minimum computer TOEFL 213. **Basis for Candidate Selection:** *Important factors considered include:* Rigor of secondary school record. **Freshman Admission Requirements:** High school diploma is required, and GED is not accepted. *Academic units required:* 3 English, 2 math. *Academic units recommended:* 3 math, 6 science, 3 history. **Freshman Admission Statistics:** 1,679 applied, 89% admitted, 85% enrolled. **Transfer Admission Requirements:** College transcript(s). **General Admission Information:** Application fee $20. Regular application deadline 8/1. Regular notification is rolling. Non-fall registration accepted. Admission may be deferred for a maxiumum of 2 semesters. Common Application not accepted.

COSTS AND FINANCIAL AID

Student Employment: Institutional employment available. Off-campus job opportunities are good.

UNIVERSITY COLLEGE OF THE FRASER VALLEY

33844 King Road, Abbotsford, BC V25 7M8 Canada
Phone: 604-854-4501 **E-mail:** reginfo@ucfv.bc.ca
Fax: 604-854-4501 **Website:** www.ucfv.bc.ca
Financial Aid Phone: 604-864-4601

This public school was founded in 1974.

RATINGS
Admissions Selectivity Rating: 60*   **Fire Safety Rating:** 60*   **Green Rating:** 60*

STUDENTS AND FACULTY
Faculty: 100% faculty teach undergrads.

ACADEMICS
Degrees: Associate, bachelor's, certificate, diploma, terminal. **Academic Requirements:** English (including composition), humanities. **Majors with Highest Enrollment:** Business administration/management, criminal justice/law enforcement administration, visual and performing arts. **Disciplines with Highest Percentage of Degrees Awarded:** Social sciences 15%, business/marketing 11%, computer and information sciences 8%, health professions and related sciences 8%, psychology 5%, education 4%. **Special Study Options:** Cooperative education program, distance learning, double major, English as a second language (ESL), student-designed major, study abroad.

FACILITIES
Computers: Online administrative functions (other than registration).

CAMPUS LIFE
Activities: Drama/theater, student government, student newspaper. **Athletics (Intercollegiate):** *Men:* Basketball, soccer. *Women:* Basketball, soccer.

ADMISSIONS
Basis for Candidate Selection: *Important factors considered include:* Rigor of secondary school record. *Other factors considered include:* Interview, talent/ability, volunteer work, work experience. **General Admission Information:** Application fee $15. Regular application deadline 3/31. Regular notification is rolling. Non-fall registration accepted.

COSTS AND FINANCIAL AID
In-province tuition $1,300-$1,640.

UNIVERSITY OF COLORADO—BOULDER

Best 368

552 UCB, Boulder, CO 80309-0552
Phone: 303-492-6301 **CEEB Code:** 4841
Fax: 303-492-7115 **Website:** www.colorado.edu/prospective **ACT Code:** 0532
Financial Aid Phone: 303-492-5091

This public school was founded in 1876. It has a 600-acre campus.

RATINGS
Admissions Selectivity Rating: 82   **Fire Safety Rating:** 86   **Green Rating:** 88

STUDENTS AND FACULTY
Enrollment: 25,495. **Student Body:** 47% female, 53% male, 31% out-of-state, 1% international (115 countries represented). African American 2%, Asian 6%, Caucasian 78%, Hispanic 6%. **Retention and Graduation:** 84% freshmen return for sophomore year. 38% freshmen graduate within 4 years. 38% grads go on to further study within 1 year. 8% grads pursue arts and sciences degrees. 9% grads pursue business degrees. 3% grads pursue law degrees. 5% grads pursue medical degrees. **Faculty:** Student/faculty ratio 16:1. 1,248 full-time faculty, 91% hold PhDs. 88% faculty teach undergrads.

ACADEMICS
Degrees: Bachelor's, doctoral, first professional, master's. **Academic Requirements:** English (including composition), foreign languages, history, humanities, mathematics, sciences (biological or physical), social science, critical thinking, cultural and gender diversity, United States context. **Classes:** Most classes have 10–19 students. Most lab/discussion sections have 20–29 students. **Majors with Highest Enrollment:** English language and literature; physiology; psychology. **Disciplines with Special Study Options:** Accelerated program, cooperative education program, cross-registration, distance learning, double major, dual enrollment, English as a second language (ESL), exchange student program (domestic), honors program, independent study, internships, liberal arts/career combination, student-designed major, study abroad, teacher certification program. Undergraduate research opportunities and concurrent bachelor's/master's programs, small group academic programs include residence hall academic programs, FallFEST, and president's leadership class.

FACILITIES
Housing: Coed dorms, apartments for married students, apartments for single students, special housing for disabled students, fraternity/sorority housing, residential academic programs within specific dorms. **Special Academic Facilities/Equipment:** Art galleries, natural history museum, heritage center, observatory, planetarium and science center, electron microscope, outdoor theater, video interactive foreign language laboratory, mountain research station, centrifuge, a hands-on teaching and learning laboratory for engineering, a multipurpose cultural/athletics/educational events and conference center, concert hall, and an innovative multi-disciplinary IT center. **Computers:** 100% of classrooms are wireless, 53% of public computers are PCs, 45% of public computers are Macs, 2% of public computers are UNIX, network access in dorm rooms, network access in dorm lounges, online registration, online administrative functions (other than registration), remote student-access to Web through college's connection.

CAMPUS LIFE
Activities: Choral groups, concert band, dance, drama/theater, jazz band, literary magazine, marching band, music ensembles, musical theater, opera, pep band, radio station, student government, student newspaper, student-run film society, symphony orchestra, television station, yearbook. **Organizations:** 300 registered organizations, 16 honor societies, 32 religious organizations. 15 fraternities (7% men join), 12 sororities (10% women join). **Athletics (Intercollegiate):** *Men:* Basketball, cross-country, football, golf, skiing (downhill/alpine), skiing (nordic/cross-country), track/field (outdoor). *Women:* Basketball, cross-country, golf, skiing (downhill/alpine), skiing (nordic/cross-country), soccer, tennis, track/field (outdoor), volleyball. **Environmental Initiatives:** Campus commitment to environmental education and research has helped CU—Boulder become one of the nation's top environmental research universities. On Earth Day 1970, students founded the Environmental Center, now the nation's oldest, largest, and most accomplished student-led center of its kind. In 1974, CU-Boulder students founded the nation's first campus recycling program.

ADMISSIONS

Freshman Academic Profile: 23% in top 10% of high school class, 54% in top 25% of high school class, 90% in top 50% of high school class. SAT Math middle 50% range 540–650. SAT Critical Reading middle 50% range 520–630. SAT Writing middle 50% range 1080–1260. ACT middle 50% range 23–28. TOEFL required of all international applicants, minimum paper TOEFL 500, minimum computer TOEFL 173. **Basis for Candidate Selection:** *Very important factors considered include:* Academic GPA, class rank, rigor of secondary school record, standardized test scores. *Important factors considered include:* Application essay, character/personal qualities, first generation, racial/ethnic status, recommendation(s), state residency. *Other factors considered include:* Alumni/ae relation, extracurricular activities, geographical residence, level of applicant's interest, talent/ability, volunteer work, work experience. **Freshman Admission Requirements:** High school diploma is required, and GED is accepted. *Academic units required:* 4 English, 3 math, 3 science (2 science labs), 3 foreign language, 3 social studies, 1 history, 1 geography. **Freshman Admission Statistics:** 18,173 applied, 88% admitted, 36% enrolled. **Transfer Admission Requirements:** High school transcript, college transcript(s). Lowest grade transferable C-. **General Admission Information:** Application fee $50. Regular application deadline 1/15. Regular notification is rolling. Nonfall registration accepted. Admission may be deferred for a maximum of 1 year. Credit and/or placement offered for CEEB Advanced Placement tests.

COSTS AND FINANCIAL AID

Annual in-state tuition $5,418. Annual out-of-state tuition $21,900. Room and board $9,088. Required fees $1,217. Average book expense $1,698. **Required Forms and Deadlines:** FAFSA, tax return required. Financial aid filing deadline 4/1. **Notification of Awards:** Applicants will be notified of awards on a rolling basis beginning on or about 2/1. **Types of Aid:** *Need-based scholarships/grants:* Pell, SEOG, state scholarships/grants, private scholarships, the school's own gift aid. *Loans:* Direct Subsidized Stafford, Direct Unsubsidized Stafford, Direct PLUS, Federal Perkins, college/university loans from institutional funds, private lenders. **Student Employment:** Federal Work-Study Program available. Institutional employment available. Off-campus job opportunities are excellent. **Financial Aid Statistics:** 22% freshmen, 21% undergrads receive need-based scholarship or grant aid. 36% freshmen, 31% undergrads receive need-based self-help aid. 52 freshmen, 243 undergrads receive athletic scholarships. 63% freshmen, 52% undergrads receive any aid. Highest amount earned per year from on-campus jobs $9,000.

UNIVERSITY OF COLORADO AT COLORADO SPRINGS

Admissions Office, PO Box 7150, Colorado Springs, CO 80933-7150
Phone: 719-262-3383 **E-mail:** admrec@uccs.edu **CEEB Code:** 4874
Fax: 719-262-3116 **Website:** www.uccs.edu **ACT Code:** 0535
Financial Aid Phone: 719-262-3460

This public school was founded in 1965. It has a 504-acre campus.

RATINGS

Admissions Selectivity Rating: 79   **Fire Safety Rating:** 60*   **Green Rating:** 60*

STUDENTS AND FACULTY

Enrollment: 6,098. **Student Body:** 60% female, 40% male, 7% out-of-state. African American 4%, Asian 5%, Caucasian 76%, Hispanic 9%. **Retention and Graduation:** 64% freshmen return for sophomore year. 19% freshmen graduate within 4 years. **Faculty:** Student/faculty ratio 18:1. 200 full-time faculty, 100% hold PhDs. 93% faculty teach undergrads.

ACADEMICS

Degrees: Bachelor's, certificate, doctoral, master's, post-bachelor's certificate, post-master's certificate. **Academic Requirements:** Cultural diversity and global awareness, English (including composition), humanities, mathematics, oral communication, quantitative & qualitative reasoning skills, sciences (biological or physical), social science. **Classes:** Most classes have 10–19 students. Most lab/discussion sections have 20–29 students. **Disciplines with Highest Percentage of Degrees Awarded:** Social sciences 17%, business/marketing 16%, health professions and related sciences 12%, communication technologies 11%, psychology 10%. **Special Study Options:** Accelerated program, cooperative education program, cross registration, distance learning, double major, dual enrollment, English as a second language (ESL), exchange student program (domestic), independent study, internships, liberal arts/career combination, student-designed major, study abroad, teacher certification program.

FACILITIES

Housing: Coed dorms, men's dorms, women's dorms, apartments for single students, special housing for disabled students. **Special Academic Facilities/Equipment:** Gallery of contemporary art. **Computers:** Network access in dorm rooms, online registration, remote student-access to Web through college's connection.

CAMPUS LIFE

Activities: Choral groups, dance, drama/theater, jazz band, literary magazine, music ensembles, musical theater, radio station, student government, student newspaper, student-run film society. **Organizations:** 55 registered organizations, 7 religious organizations. 1 sorority. **Athletics (Intercollegiate):** *Men:* Basketball, cross-country, golf, soccer, tennis, track/field (outdoor). *Women:* Basketball, cross-country, softball, tennis, track/field (outdoor), volleyball.

ADMISSIONS

Freshman Academic Profile: 16% in top 10% of high school class, 42% in top 25% of high school class, 78% in top 50% of high school class. SAT Math middle 50% range 470–610. SAT Critical Reading middle 50% range 470–590. SAT Writing middle 50% range 450–560. ACT middle 50% range 20–25. TOEFL required of all international applicants, minimum paper TOEFL 550, minimum computer TOEFL 213. **Basis for Candidate Selection:** *Very important factors considered include:* Academic GPA, class rank, rigor of secondary school record, standardized test scores. *Important factors considered include:* Level of applicant's interest, recommendation(s). *Other factors considered include:* Alumni/ae relation, application essay, character/personal qualities, extracurricular activities, geographical residence, state residency, talent/ability, volunteer work. **Freshman Admission Requirements:** High school diploma is required, and GED is accepted. *Academic units required:* 4 English, 3 math, 3 science (2 science labs), 2 foreign language, 2 social studies, 1 academic elective. *Academic units recommended:* 4 English, 4 math, 3 science (2 science labs), 2 foreign language, 2 social studies, 1 academic elective. **Freshman Admission Statistics:** 3,243 applied, 63% admitted, 37% enrolled. **Transfer Admission Requirements:** High school transcript, college transcript(s). Minimum college GPA of 2.0 required. Lowest grade transferable C. **General Admission Information:** Application fee $50. Regular application deadline 7/1. Regular notification is rolling. Non-fall registration accepted. Admission may be deferred for a maximum of 2 semesters. Neither credit nor placement offered for CEEB Advanced Placement tests.

COSTS AND FINANCIAL AID

Annual in-state tuition $5,490. Out-of-state tuition $22,950. Room & board $7,662. Required fees $1,047. Average book expense $1,296. **Required Forms and Deadlines:** FAFSA. Financial aid filing deadline 4/1. **Notification of Awards:** Applicants will be notified of awards on a rolling basis beginning on or about 4/15. **Types of Aid:** *Need-based scholarships/grants:* Pell, SEOG, state scholarships/grants, private scholarships, the school's own gift aid, Federal Nursing Scholarships. *Loans:* FFEL Subsidized Stafford, FFEL Unsubsidized Stafford, FFEL PLUS, Federal Perkins, college/university loans from institutional funds. **Financial Aid Statistics:** 34% freshmen, 36% undergrads receive need-based scholarship or grant aid. 31% freshmen, 42% undergrads receive need-based self-help aid. 14 freshmen, 68 undergrads receive athletic scholarships.

UNIVERSITY OF COLORADO AT DENVER AND HEALTH SCIENCES CENTER

PO Box 173364, Campus Box 167, Denver, CO 80217
Phone: 303-556-2704 **E-mail:** admissions@cudenver.edu **CEEB Code:** 4875
Fax: 303-556-4838 **Website:** www.uchsc.edu **ACT Code:** 0533
Financial Aid Phone: 303-556-2886

This public school was founded in 1912. It has a 127-acre campus.

RATINGS

Admissions Selectivity Rating: 78   **Fire Safety Rating:** 60*   **Green Rating:** 60*

STUDENTS AND FACULTY

Enrollment: 7,200. **Student Body:** 51% female, 49% male, 5% out-of-state, 2% international (57 countries represented). African American 5%, Asian 11%, Caucasian 70%, Hispanic 12%, Native American 1%. **Retention and Graduation:** 72% freshmen return for sophomore year. 9% grads go on to further study within 1 year. 18% grads pursue arts and sciences degrees. 6% grads pursue business degrees. **Faculty:** Student/faculty ratio 15:1. 625 full-time faculty, 81% hold PhDs. 62% faculty teach undergrads.

ACADEMICS

Degrees: Bachelor's, doctoral, first professional, master's, post-master's certificate. **Academic Requirements:** Arts/fine arts, behavioral science, English (including composition), humanities, mathematics, multicultural diversity, sciences (biological or physical), social science. **Classes:** Most classes have 20–29 students. Most lab/discussion sections have 10–19 students. **Majors with Highest Enrollment:** Biology/biological sciences, Business administration/management, psychology. **Disciplines with Highest Percentage of Degrees Awarded:** Business/marketing 21%, health professions and related sciences 16%, social sciences 14%, psychology 9%, visual and performing arts 8%. **Special Study Options:** Accelerated program, cooperative education program, cross registration, distance learning, double major, English as a second language (ESL), honors program, independent study, internships, student-designed major, study abroad, teacher certification program, weekend college.

FACILITIES

Housing: Coed dorms. **Special Academic Facilities/Equipment:** Emmanual Gallery. **Computers:** 75% of classrooms are wireless, 80% of public computers are PCs, 20% of public computers are Macs, online registration, online administrative functions (other than registration), remote student-access to Web through college's connection.

CAMPUS LIFE

Activities: Choral groups, dance, drama/theater, jazz band, music ensembles, musical theater, student government, student newspaper. **Organizations:** 55 registered organizations, 5 honor societies, 4 religious organizations.

ADMISSIONS

Freshman Academic Profile: 17% in top 10% of high school class, 45% in top 25% of high school class, 78% in top 50% of high school class. SAT Math middle 50% range 490–590. SAT Critical Reading middle 50% range 490–600. ACT middle 50% range 19–25. TOEFL required of all international applicants, minimum paper TOEFL 525, minimum computer TOEFL 197. **Basis for Candidate Selection:** *Very important factors considered include:* Academic GPA, class rank, rigor of secondary school record, standardized test scores. *Important factors considered include:* Application essay, level of applicant's interest, recommendation(s). *Other factors considered include:* Character/personal qualities, extracurricular activities, talent/ability. **Freshman Admission Requirements:** High school diploma is required, and GED is accepted. *Academic units required:* 4 English, 3 math, 3 science, 2 foreign language, 2 social studies, 1 academic elective. *Academic units recommended:* 4 English, 3 math, 3 science (2 science labs), 2 foreign language, 2 social studies, 1 history, 1 academic elective. **Freshman Admission Statistics:** 2,968 applied, 69% admitted, 46% enrolled. **Transfer Admission Requirements:** College transcript(s), statement of good standing from prior institution(s). Minimum college GPA of 2.5 required. Lowest grade transferable C-. **General Admission Information:** Application fee $50. Non-fall registration accepted. Admission may be deferred for a maximum of 1 calendar year. Credit and/or placement offered for CEEB Advanced Placement tests.

COSTS AND FINANCIAL AID

Annual in-state tuition $5,054. Annual out-of-state tuition $17,010. Room and board $9,990. Required fees $878. Average book expense $1,700. **Required Forms and Deadlines:** FAFSA, institution's own financial aid form. Financial aid filing deadline 3/15. **Notification of Awards:** Applicants will be notified of awards on or about 5/1. **Types of Aid:** *Need-based scholarships/grants:* Pell, SEOG, state scholarships/grants, private scholarships, the school's own gift aid, Federal Nursing Scholarships. *Loans:* Direct Subsidized Stafford, Direct Unsubsidized Stafford, Direct PLUS, FFEL Subsidized Stafford, FFEL Unsubsidized Stafford, FFEL PLUS, Federal Perkins, Federal Nursing. **Student Employment:** Federal Work-Study Program available. Off-campus job opportunities are good. **Financial Aid Statistics:** 29% freshmen, 31% undergrads receive need-based scholarship or grant aid. 23% freshmen, 40% undergrads receive need-based self-help aid.

UNIVERSITY OF CONNECTICUT

2131 Hillside Road, Unit 3088, Storrs, CT 06268-3088
Phone: 860-486-3137 **E-mail:** beahusky@uconn.edu **CEEB Code:** 3915
Fax: 860-486-1476 **Website:** www.uconn.edu **ACT Code:** 0604
Financial Aid Phone: 860-486-2819

This public school was founded in 1881. It has a 4,104-acre campus.

RATINGS

Admissions Selectivity Rating: 89   **Fire Safety Rating:** 86   **Green Rating:** 88

STUDENTS AND FACULTY

Enrollment: 16,006. **Student Body:** 51% female, 49% male, 23% out-of-state, (109 countries represented). African American 5%, Asian 7%, Caucasian 70%, Hispanic 5%. **Retention and Graduation:** 93% freshmen return for sophomore year. 53% freshmen graduate within 4 years. 27% grads go on to further study within 1 year. 14% grads pursue arts and sciences degrees. 11% grads pursue business degrees. 6% grads pursue law degrees. 5% grads pursue medical degrees. **Faculty:** Student/faculty ratio 17:1. 987 full-time faculty, 92% hold PhDs. 77% faculty teach undergrads.

ACADEMICS

Degrees: Associate, bachelor's, doctoral, first professional, master's, post-bachelor's certificate, post-master's certificate. **Academic Requirements:** Arts/fine arts, computer literacy, English (including composition), foreign languages, history, humanities, mathematics, sciences (biological or physical), social science. **Classes:** Most classes have 10–19 students. Most lab/discussion sections have 10–19 students. **Majors with Highest Enrollment:** Nursing/registered nurse training (ASN, BSN, MSN, RN); political science and government; psychology. **Disciplines with Highest Percentage of Degrees Awarded:** Social sciences 14%, business/marketing 14%, health professions and related sciences 8%, liberal arts/general studies 8%, psychology 8%, biological/life sciences 7%. **Special Study Options:** Accelerated program, cooperative education program, distance learning, double major, dual enrollment, English as a second language (ESL), exchange student program (domestic), honors program, independent study, internships, liberal arts/career combination, student-designed major, study abroad, teacher certification program, winter inter-session, summer session, urban semester.

FACILITIES

Housing: Coed dorms, men's dorms, women's dorms, apartments for married students, apartments for single students, special housing for disabled students, special housing for international students, fraternity/sorority housing, special interests housing, honors housing, engineering housing, foreign languages housing, substance-free housing, older-student housing, freshman year experience housing. **Special Academic Facilities/Equipment:** Art and natural history museums, child development labs, national undersea research center, arboretum, institute for social inquiry, institute of materials science, electron microscope labs. **Computers:** 72% of public computers are PCs, 26% of public computers are Macs, 2% of public computers are UNIX, network access in dorm rooms, network access in dorm lounges, online registration, online administrative functions (other than registration), remote student-access to Web through college's connection.

CAMPUS LIFE

Activities: Choral groups, concert band, dance, drama/theater, jazz band, literary magazine, marching band, music ensembles, musical theater, opera, pep band, radio station, student government, student newspaper, student-run film society, symphony orchestra, television station, yearbook. **Organizations:** 303 registered organizations, 29 honor societies, 17 religious organizations. 15 fraternities (8% men join), 10 sororities (7% women join). **Athletics (Intercollegiate):** *Men:* Baseball, basketball, cross-country, diving, football, golf, ice hockey, soccer, swimming, tennis, track/field (indoor), track/field (outdoor). *Women:* Basketball, crew/rowing, cross-country, diving, field hockey, ice hockey, lacrosse, soccer, softball, swimming, tennis, track/field (indoor), track/field (outdoor), volleyball. **Environmental Initiatives:** Sustainable Design & Construction Policy: All new construction or renovations costing over $5 million must achieve at least a LEED Silver rating. Biofuels and Fuel Cell Technology. UConn Biofuel Consortion. Connecticut Global Fuel Cell Center. Proposed Compost Facility.

ADMISSIONS

Freshman Academic Profile: 38% in top 10% of high school class, 81% in top 25% of high school class, 98% in top 50% of high school class. 87% from public high schools. SAT Math middle 50% range 560–660. SAT Critical Reading middle 50% range 530–630. SAT Writing middle 50% range 540–640. ACT middle 50% range 23–28. TOEFL required of all international applicants, minimum paper TOEFL 550, minimum computer TOEFL 213. **Basis for Candidate Selection:** *Very important factors considered include:* Academic GPA, class rank, rigor of secondary school record, standardized test scores, talent/ability. *Important factors considered include:* Application essay, character/personal qualities, extracurricular activities, first generation, racial/ethnic status, recommendation(s), volunteer work. *Other factors considered include:* Alumni/ae relation, geographical residence, level of applicant's interest, state residency, work experience. **Freshman Admission Requirements:** High school diploma is required, and GED is accepted. *Academic units required:* 4 English, 3 math, 2 science (2 science labs), 2 foreign language, 2 social studies, 3 academic electives. *Academic units recommended:* 3 foreign language. **Freshman Admission Statistics:** 19,778 applied, 51% admitted, 32% enrolled. **Transfer Admission Requirements:** High school transcript, college transcript(s), essay or personal statement, minimum college GPA of 2.7 required. Lowest grade transferable C. **General Admission Information:** Application fee $70. Regular application deadline 2/1. Regular notification is rolling. Nonfall registration accepted. Admission may be deferred for a maximum of 1 year. Credit and/or placement offered for CEEB Advanced Placement tests.

COSTS AND FINANCIAL AID

Annual in-state tuition $7,200. Annual out-of-state tuition $21,912. Room and board $9,300. Required fees $2,138. Average book expense $800. **Required Forms and Deadlines:** FAFSA. Financial aid filing deadline 3/1. **Notification of Awards:** Applicants will be notified of awards on a rolling basis beginning on or about 3/1. **Types of Aid:** *Need-based scholarships/grants:* Pell, SEOG, state scholarships/grants, private scholarships, the school's own gift aid. *Loans:* FFEL Subsidized Stafford, FFEL Unsubsidized Stafford, FFEL PLUS, Federal Perkins. **Student Employment:** Federal Work-Study Program available. Institutional employment available. Off-campus job opportunities are good. **Financial Aid Statistics:** 38% freshmen, 36% undergrads receive need-based scholarship or grant aid. 36% freshmen, 37% undergrads receive need-based self-help aid. 98 freshmen, 360 undergrads receive athletic scholarships. 48% freshmen, 47% undergrads receive any aid. Highest amount earned per year from on-campus jobs $3,500.

UNIVERSITY OF THE CUMBERLANDS

6178 College Station Drive, Williamsburg, KY 40769
Phone: 606-539-4241 **E-mail:** admiss@ucumberlands.edu **CEEB Code:** 1145
Fax: 606-539-4303 **Website:** www.ucumberlands.edu **ACT Code:** 1510
Financial Aid Phone: 606-539-4220

This private school, affiliated with the Kentucky Baptist Convention Church, was founded in 1888. It has a 50-acre campus.

RATINGS

Admissions Selectivity Rating: 76   **Fire Safety Rating:** 89   **Green Rating:** 60*

STUDENTS AND FACULTY

Enrollment: 1,389. **Student Body:** 53% female, 47% male, 38% out-of-state, 2% international (22 countries represented). African American 5%, Asian 1%, Caucasian 65%, Hispanic 1%. **Retention and Graduation:** 62% freshmen return for sophomore year. 22% freshmen graduate within 4 years. 7% grads go on to further study within 2 semesters. 3% grads pursue arts and sciences degrees. 2% grads pursue business degrees. 1% grads pursue law degrees. 3% grads pursue medical degrees. **Faculty:** Student/faculty ratio 14:1. 85 full-time faculty, 74% hold PhDs. 100% faculty teach undergrads.

ACADEMICS

Degrees: Bachelor's, master's. **Academic Requirements:** Arts/fine arts, computer literacy, English (including composition), history, humanities, mathematics, philosophy, sciences (biological or physical), social science. **Classes:** Most classes have 10–19 students. Most lab/discussion sections have fewer than 10 students. **Majors with Highest Enrollment:** Biology/biological sciences, business administration/management, elementary education and teaching. **Disciplines with Highest Percentage of Degrees Awarded:** Business/marketing 18%, biological/life sciences 9%, health professions and related sciences 8%, communications/journalism 6%, parks and recreation 6%, psychology 6%, security and protective services 5%, visual and performing arts 5%. **Special Study Options:** Accelerated program, cooperative education

program, distance learning, double major, dual enrollment, English as a second language (ESL), honors program, independent study, internships, liberal arts/career combination, student-designed major, study abroad, teacher certification program.

FACILITIES

Housing: Men's dorms, women's dorms. **Special Academic Facilities/Equipment:** Distance learning lab, student art museums. **Computers:** 15% of classrooms are wireless, 95% of public computers are PCs, 5% of public computers are Macs, network access in dorm rooms, network access in dorm lounges, online registration, online administrative functions (other than registration), remote student-access to Web through college's connection.

CAMPUS LIFE

Activities: Choral groups, concert band, dance, drama/theater, jazz band, marching band, music ensembles, musical theater, pep band, radio station, student government, student newspaper, television station. **Organizations:** 45 registered organizations, 11 honor societies, 18 religious organizations. **Athletics (Intercollegiate):** *Men:* Baseball, basketball, cheerleading, cross-country, football, golf, soccer, swimming, tennis, track/field (outdoor), wrestling. *Women:* Basketball, cheerleading, cross-country, golf, soccer, softball, swimming, tennis, track/field (outdoor), volleyball, wrestling.

ADMISSIONS

Freshman Academic Profile: 20% in top 10% of high school class, 44% in top 25% of high school class, 79% in top 50% of high school class. 90% from public high schools. SAT Math middle 50% range 410–570. SAT Critical Reading middle 50% range 410–560. ACT middle 50% range 19–24. TOEFL required of all international applicants, minimum paper TOEFL 550, minimum computer TOEFL 215. **Basis for Candidate Selection:** *Very important factors considered include:* Rigor of secondary school record. *Other factors considered include:* Academic GPA, application essay, character/personal qualities, class rank, extracurricular activities, first generation, interview, level of applicant's interest, recommendation(s), standardized test scores, talent/ability, volunteer work. **Freshman Admission Requirements:** High school diploma is required, and GED is accepted. *Academic units required:* 4 English, 3 math, 2 science, 1 social study. *Academic units recommended:* 4 English, 3 math, 3 science, 1 foreign language, 2 social studies. **Freshman Admission Statistics:** 849 applied, 83% admitted, 50% enrolled. **Transfer Admission Requirements:** College transcript(s), essay or personal statement, statement of good standing from prior institution(s). Minimum college GPA of 2.0 required. Lowest grade transferable C. **General Admission Information:** Application fee $30. Regular notification is rolling. Non-fall registration accepted. Admission may be deferred for a maximum of 1 semester. Credit offered for CEEB Advanced Placement tests.

COSTS AND FINANCIAL AID

Annual tuition $13,298. Room & board $6,626. Required fees $360. Average book expense $1,000. **Required Forms and Deadlines:** FAFSA. Financial aid filing deadline 3/1. **Notification of Awards:** Applicants will be notified of awards on or about 4/1. **Types of Aid:** *Need-based scholarships/grants:* Pell, SEOG, state scholarships/grants, private scholarships, the school's own gift aid. *Loans:* FFEL Subsidized Stafford, FFEL Unsubsidized Stafford, FFEL PLUS, Federal Perkins, college/university loans from institutional funds. **Student Employment:** Federal Work-Study Program available. Institutional employment available. Off-campus job opportunities are fair. **Financial Aid Statistics:** 87% freshmen, 85% undergrads receive need-based scholarship or grant aid. 67% freshmen, 59% undergrads receive need-based self-help aid. 14 freshmen, 39 undergrads receive athletic scholarships. 94% freshmen, 92% undergrads receive any aid. Highest amount earned per year from on-campus jobs $2,400.

See page 1476.

UNIVERSITY OF DALLAS

1845 East Northgate Drive, Irving, TX 75062
Phone: 972-721-5266 **E-mail:** ugadmis@udallas.edu **CEEB Code:** 6868
Fax: 972-721-5017 **Website:** www.udallas.edu **ACT Code:** 4234
Financial Aid Phone: 972-721-5266

This private school, affiliated with the Roman Catholic Church, was founded in 1956. It has a 750-acre campus.

RATINGS
Admissions Selectivity Rating: 86   **Fire Safety Rating:** 93   **Green Rating:** 69

STUDENTS AND FACULTY
Enrollment: 1,137. **Student Body:** 56% female, 44% male, 44% out-of-state, 1% international (12 countries represented). African American 1%, Asian 6%, Caucasian 67%, Hispanic 17%. **Retention and Graduation:** 85% freshmen return for sophomore year. 60% freshmen graduate within 4 years. 40% grads go on to further study within 1 year. 8% grads pursue arts and sciences degrees. 7% grads pursue business degrees. 3% grads pursue law degrees. 7% grads pursue medical degrees. **Faculty:** Student/faculty ratio 11:1. 120 full-time faculty, 90% hold PhDs. 100% faculty teach undergrads.

ACADEMICS
Degrees: Bachelor's, doctoral, master's, post-bachelor's certificate, post-master's certificate. **Academic Requirements:** Arts/fine arts, economics, English (including composition), foreign languages, history, mathematics, philosophy, politics, ciences (biological or physical), theology. **Classes:** Most classes have 20–29 students. Most lab/discussion sections have fewer than 10 students. **Majors with Highest Enrollment:** Biology/biological sciences, Business administration/management, English language and literature. **Disciplines with Highest Percentage of Degrees Awarded:** English 21%, social sciences 12%, biological/life sciences 10%, business/marketing 10%, history 10%, theology and religious vocations 9%, visual and performing arts 7%. **Special Study Options:** Double major, dual enrollment, independent study, internships, liberal arts/career combination, student-designed major, study abroad, teacher certification program.

FACILITIES
Housing: Coed dorms, men's dorms, women's dorms, apartments for single students. **Special Academic Facilities/Equipment:** Art gallery, theater, language science, and computer labs, observatory. **Computers:** 100% of classrooms are wired, 25% of classrooms are wireless, 100% of public computers are PCs, 2% of public computers are Macs, 13% of public computers are UNIX, network access in dorm rooms, network access in dorm lounges, online registration, online administrative functions (other than registration), remote student-access to Web through college's connection.

CAMPUS LIFE
Activities: Choral groups, dance, drama/theater, literary magazine, music ensembles, musical theater, student government, student newspaper, student-run film society, yearbook. **Organizations:** 35 registered organizations, 4 honor societies, 5 religious organizations. **Athletics (Intercollegiate):** *Men:* Baseball, basketball, cross-country, golf, soccer, track/field (outdoor). *Women:* Basketball, cross-country, lacrosse, soccer, softball, track/field (outdoor), volleyball.

ADMISSIONS
Freshman Academic Profile: 41% in top 10% of high school class, 71% in top 25% of high school class, 88% in top 50% of high school class. 45% from public high schools. SAT Math middle 50% range 520–650. SAT Critical Reading middle 50% range 550–680. SAT Writing middle 50% range 530–660. ACT middle 50% range 24–29. TOEFL required of all international applicants, minimum paper TOEFL 550, minimum computer TOEFL 213. **Basis for Candidate Selection:** *Very important factors considered include:* Academic GPA, application essay, character/personal qualities, recommendation(s), rigor of secondary school record, standardized test scores. *Important factors considered include:* Talent/ability. *Other factors considered include:* Alumni/ae relation, class rank, extracurricular activities, first generation, interview, level of applicant's interest, volunteer work, work experience. **Freshman Admission Requirements:** High school diploma is required, and GED is accepted. *Academic units required:* 4 English, 3 math, 3 science, 2 foreign language, 3 social studies, 3 history, 4 academic electives, 2 art/drama. *Academic units recommended:* 4 English, 4 math, 3 science, 3 foreign language, 4 social studies, 4 history, 4 academic electives, 2 art/drama. **Freshman Admission Statistics:** 876 applied, 85% admitted, 42% enrolled. **Transfer Admission Requirements:** College transcript(s), essay or personal statement, statement of good standing from prior institution(s). Minimum college GPA of 2.5 required. Lowest grade transferable C-. **General Admission Information:** Application fee $40. Regular application deadline 8/1. Regular notification is rolling. Non-fall registration accepted. Admission may be deferred for a maxiumum of 2 semesters. Credit and/or placement offered for CEEB Advanced Placement tests.

COSTS AND FINANCIAL AID
Annual tuition $23,250. Room and board $7,885. Required fees $1,520. Average book expense $1,700. **Required Forms and Deadlines:** FAFSA. Financial aid filing deadline 3/1. **Notification of Awards:** Applicants will be notified of awards on a rolling basis beginning on or about 3/15. **Types of Aid:** *Need-based scholarships/grants:* Pell, SEOG, state scholarships/grants, private scholarships, the school's own gift aid. *Loans:* FFEL Subsidized Stafford, FFEL Unsubsidized Stafford, FFEL PLUS, Federal Perkins, state loans. **Financial Aid Statistics:** 62% freshmen, 60% undergrads receive need-based scholarship or grant aid. 50% freshmen, 48% undergrads receive need-based self-help aid. 97% freshmen, 94% undergrads receive any aid. Highest amount earned per year from on-campus jobs $2,000.

See page 1436.

UNIVERSITY OF DAYTON

300 College Park, Dayton, OH 45469-1300
Phone: 937-229-4411 **E-mail:** admission@udayton.edu **CEEB Code:** 1834
Fax: 937-229-4729 **Website:** www.udayton.edu **ACT Code:** 3342
Financial Aid Phone: 800-427-5029

This private school, affiliated with the Roman Catholic Church, was founded in 1850. It has a 259-acre campus.

RATINGS
Admissions Selectivity Rating: 81   **Fire Safety Rating:** 60*   **Green Rating:** 74

STUDENTS AND FACULTY
Enrollment: 7,230. **Student Body:** 50% female, 50% male, 34% out-of-state. African American 4%, Asian 1%, Caucasian 88%, Hispanic 2%. **Retention and Graduation:** 86% freshmen return for sophomore year. 60% freshmen graduate within 4 years. 50% grads go on to further study within 1 year. 12% grads pursue arts and sciences degrees. 3% grads pursue business degrees. 2% grads pursue law degrees. 1% grads pursue medical degrees. **Faculty:** Student/faculty ratio 13:1. 458 full-time faculty, 91% hold PhDs. 81% faculty teach undergrads.

ACADEMICS
Degrees: Bachelor's, doctoral, first professional, master's, post-master's certificate. **Academic Requirements:** Arts/fine arts, English (including composition), history, humanities, mathematics, oral communication competencies, philosophy, sciences (biological or physical), social science. **Classes:** Most classes have 20–29 students. Most lab/discussion sections have 10–19 students. **Majors with Highest Enrollment:** Business administration/management, communication and rhetoric, communications studies/speech, engineering. **Disciplines with Highest Percentage of Degrees Awarded:** Business/marketing 23%, education 13%, communications/journalism 12%, engineering 11%, social sciences 5%. **Special Study Options:** Accelerated program, cooperative education program, cross registration, distance learning courses, double major, dual enrollment, English as a second language (ESL), domestic exchange student program with other Marianist institutions, honors program, independent study, internships, liberal arts/career combination, student-designed major, study abroad, teacher certification program.

FACILITIES
Housing: Coed dorms, men's dorms, women's dorms, apartments for single students, special housing for disabled students, special housing for international students, fraternity/sorority housing, university-owned houses. **Special Academic Facilities/Equipment:** UD Research Institute, Bombeck Family Learning Center, learning teaching center, Davis Center for Portfolio Management, Marian Library, ArtStreet living-learning complex, RecPlex.

College Directory

Computers: 30% of classrooms are wired, 95% of classrooms are wireless, 90% of public computers are PCs, 5% of public computers are Macs, 5% of public computers are UNIX, network access in dorm rooms, network access in dorm lounges, online registration, online administrative functions (other than registration), remote student-access to Web through college's connection, undergraduates are required to own a computer.

CAMPUS LIFE

Activities: Choral groups, concert band, dance, drama/theater, jazz band, literary magazine, marching band, music ensembles, musical theater, opera, pep band, radio station, student government, student newspaper, symphony orchestra, television station, yearbook. **Organizations:** 180 registered organizations, 13 honor societies, 30 religious organizations. 11 fraternities (14% men join), 9 sororities (16% women join). **Athletics (Intercollegiate):** *Men:* Baseball, basketball, cheerleading, cross-country, football, golf, soccer, tennis. *Women:* Basketball, cheerleading, crew/rowing, cross-country, golf, soccer, softball, tennis, track/field (indoor), track/field (outdoor), volleyball. **Environmental Initiatives:** Hiring of an Environmental Sustainability Coordinator on a full-time basis. Installation of CFLs. Recycling of construction and debris materials.

ADMISSIONS

Freshman Academic Profile: 22% in top 10% of high school class, 49% in top 25% of high school class, 80% in top 50% of high school class. 50% from public high schools. SAT Math middle 50% range 530–640. SAT Critical Reading middle 50% range 520–620. ACT middle 50% range 23–28. TOEFL required of all international applicants, minimum paper TOEFL 523, minimum computer TOEFL 193. **Basis for Candidate Selection:** *Very important factors considered include:* Academic GPA, rigor of secondary school record. *Important factors considered include:* Class rank, standardized test scores, talent/ability. *Other factors considered include:* Alumni/ae relation, application essay, character/personal qualities, extracurricular activities, first generation, interview, racial/ethnic status, recommendation(s), volunteer work, work experience. **Freshman Admission Requirements:** High school diploma is required, and GED is accepted. *Academic units required:* 2 units of foreign language are required for admission to the College of Arts & Sciences. *Academic units recommended:* 4 English, 3 math, 2 science, 3 social studies, 4 academic electives. **Freshman Admission Statistics:** 9,045 applied, 79% admitted, 25% enrolled. **Transfer Admission Requirements:** High school transcript, college transcript(s), statement of good standing from prior institution(s). Minimum college GPA of 2.0 required. Lowest grade transferable C. **General Admission Information:** Regular notification is rolling. Non-fall registration accepted. Admission may be deferred for a maximum of 4 semesters. Credit and/or placement offered for CEEB Advanced Placement tests.

COSTS AND FINANCIAL AID

Annual tuition $24,880. **Required Forms and Deadlines:** FAFSA. Financial aid filing deadline 3/31. **Notification of Awards:** Applicants will be notified of awards on or about 3/31. **Types of Aid:** *Need-based scholarships/grants:* Pell, SEOG, state scholarships/grants, private scholarships, the school's own gift aid. *Loans:* FFEL Subsidized Stafford, FFEL Unsubsidized Stafford, FFEL PLUS, Federal Perkins, GATE. **Student Employment:** Federal Work-Study Program available. Institutional employment available. Off-campus job opportunities are good. **Financial Aid Statistics:** 53% freshmen, 58% undergrads receive need-based scholarship or grant aid. 55% freshmen, 66% undergrads receive need-based self-help aid. 21 freshmen, 103 undergrads receive athletic scholarships. 77% freshmen, 82% undergrads receive any aid.

UNIVERSITY OF DELAWARE

Best 368

Admissions Office, 116 Hullihen Hall, Newark, DE 19716-6210
Phone: 302-831-8123 **E-mail:** admissions@udel.edu **CEEB Code:** 5811
Fax: 302-831-6905 **Website:** www.udel.edu **ACT Code:** 0634

This public school was founded in 1743. It has a 1,000-acre campus.

RATINGS

Admissions Selectivity Rating: 93   **Fire Safety Rating:** 93   **Green Rating:** 81

STUDENTS AND FACULTY

Enrollment: 15,211. **Student Body:** 58% female, 42% male, 60% out-of-state. African American 5%, Asian 4%, Caucasian 83%, Hispanic 4%. **Retention and Graduation:** 90% freshmen return for sophomore year. 60% freshmen graduate within 4 years. 17% grads go on to further study within 1 year. 28% grads pursue arts and sciences degrees. 12% grads pursue business degrees. 7% grads pursue law degrees. 8% grads pursue medical degrees. **Faculty:** Student/faculty ratio 12:1. 1,165 full-time faculty, 84% hold PhDs. 95% faculty teach undergrads.

ACADEMICS

Degrees: Associate, bachelor's, doctoral, master's. **Academic Requirements:** 1 course in multicultural, ethnic/gender-related content, English (including composition), foreign languages, humanities, mathematics, sciences (biological or physical), social science. **Classes:** Most classes have 10–19 students. Most lab/discussion sections have 10–19 students. **Majors with Highest Enrollment:** Biology/biological sciences, elementary education and teaching, psychology. **Disciplines with Highest Percentage of Degrees Awarded:** Business/marketing 16%, social sciences 14%, education 12%, health professions and related sciences 6%, family and consumer sciences 6%. **Special Study Options:** Accelerated program, cooperative education program, distance learning, double major, dual enrollment, English as a second language (ESL), honors program, independent study, internships, liberal arts/career combination, student-designed major, study abroad, teacher certification program.

FACILITIES

Housing: Coed dorms, women's dorms, apartments for married students, apartments for single students, special housing for disabled students, fraternity/sorority housing, special-interest communities. **Special Academic Facilities/Equipment:** Lammont du Pont Laboratory, biotechnology center, Fischer Greenhouse Laboratory, 35-acre woodlot harboring numerous wild species of animals and birds, 28 micro-computing sites, art coservation laboratories at Winterthur Museum & Gardens, Bob Carpenter Sports/Convocation Center, livestock arena and working farm, historic costume & textile collection, medical technology laboratories, the mineralogical museum, nursing practice practice laboratories, orthopedic and biomechanical engineering center, Rust & Gold ice skating arenas, textiles, botanical gardens, the university gallery, university laboratory preschool. **Computers:** 79% of public computers are PCs, 11% of public computers are Macs, 10% of public computers are UNIX, network access in dorm rooms, network access in dorm lounges, online registration, online administrative functions (other than registration), support for handheld computing, remote student-access to Web through college's connection.

CAMPUS LIFE

Activities: Choral groups, concert band, dance, drama/theater, jazz band, literary magazine, marching band, music ensembles, musical theater, opera, pep band, radio station, student government, student newspaper, student-run film society, symphony orchestra, television station. **Organizations:** 200 registered organizations, 36 honor societies, 18 religious organizations. 15 fraternities (12% men join), 15 sororities (12% women join). **Athletics (Intercollegiate):** *Men:* Baseball, basketball, cross-country, diving, football, golf, lacrosse, soccer, swimming, tennis, track/field (indoor), track/field (outdoor). *Women:* Basketball, crew/rowing, cross-country, diving, field hockey, lacrosse, soccer, softball, swimming, tennis, track/field (indoor), track/field (outdoor), volleyball. **Environmental Initiatives:** The University of Delaware is at the forefront in research and scholarship on a variety of topics related to sustainability and the environment. Across its seven colleges, through formally established institutes, centers, and agencies. At the University of Delaware environmental initiatives are undertaken across multiple administrative units. The installation of energy monitoring systems and energy efficient lighting systems by the Facilities Department and. The University of Delaware is committed to engaging the campus community, the state, the nation and the world concerning issues of sustainability. UD offers sustainability-related coursework in engineering, history, geography, wildlife, etc.

ADMISSIONS

Freshman Academic Profile: 39% in top 10% of high school class, 80% in top 25% of high school class, 98% in top 50% of high school class. 80% from public high schools. SAT Math middle 50% range 560–660. SAT Critical Reading middle 50% range 540–640. SAT Writing middle 50% range 540–650. ACT middle 50% range 23–28. TOEFL required of all international applicants, minimum paper TOEFL 550, minimum computer TOEFL 213. **Basis for Candidate Selection:** *Very important factors considered include:* Academic GPA, rigor of secondary school record, state residency. *Important factors considered include:* Application essay, character/personal qualities, extracurricular activities, recommendation(s), standardized test scores, talent/ability, volunteer work, work experience. *Other factors considered include:* Alumni/ae relation, class rank, first generation, geographical residence, interview, level of applicant's interest, racial/ethnic status. **Freshman Admission Requirements:** High school diploma is required, and GED is accepted. *Academic units required:* 4 English, 3 math, 3 science (2 science labs), 2 foreign language, 2 social studies, 2 history, 2 academic electives. *Academic units recommended:* 4 English, 4 math, 4 science (3 science labs), 4 foreign language, 2 social studies, 2 history, 2 academic electives. **Freshman Admission Statistics:** 21,930 applied, 47% admitted, 31% enrolled. **Transfer Admission Requirements:** High school transcript, college transcript(s), essay or personal statement, statement of good standing from prior institution(s). Minimum college GPA of 2.5 required. Lowest grade transferable C. **General Admission Information:** Application fee $60. Regular application deadline 1/15. Regular notification 3/15. Non-fall registration accepted. Admission may be deferred for a maxiumum of 2 semesters. Credit offered for CEEB Advanced Placement tests.

COSTS AND FINANCIAL AID

Annual in-state tuition $7,340. Annual out-of-state tuition $18,590. Room and board $7,948. Required fees $810. Average book expense $800. **Required Forms and Deadlines:** FAFSA. Financial aid filing deadline 3/15. **Notification of Awards:** Applicants will be notified of awards on or about 3/15. **Types of Aid:** *Need-based scholarships/grants:* Pell, SEOG, state scholarships/grants, private scholarships, the school's own gift aid. *Loans:* Direct Subsidized Stafford, Direct Unsubsidized Stafford, Direct PLUS, Federal Perkins, Federal Nursing. **Student Employment:** Federal Work-Study Program available. Institutional employment available. **Financial Aid Statistics:** 26% freshmen, 24% undergrads receive need-based scholarship or grant aid. 29% freshmen, 28% undergrads receive need-based self-help aid. 88 freshmen, 402 undergrads receive athletic scholarships. **Financial Aid Phone:** 302-831-8761.

See page 1438.

UNIVERSITY OF DENVER

Office of Admission, 2197 South University Boulevard, Denver, CO 80208
Phone: 303-871-2036 **E-mail:** admission@du.edu **CEEB Code:** 4842
Fax: 303-871-3301 **Website:** www.du.edu **ACT Code:** 0534

This private school was founded in 1864. It has a 125-acre campus.

RATINGS

Admissions Selectivity Rating: 89   **Fire Safety Rating:** 82   **Green Rating:** 60*

STUDENTS AND FACULTY

Enrollment: 5,092. **Student Body:** 55% female, 45% male, 53% out-of-state, 4% international (86 countries represented). African American 2%, Asian 5%, Caucasian 80%, Hispanic 7%, Native American 1%. **Retention and Graduation:** 89% freshmen return for sophomore year. 57% freshmen graduate within 4 years. 17% grads go on to further study within 1 year. **Faculty:** Student/faculty ratio 10:1. 533 full-time faculty, 90% hold PhDs.

ACADEMICS

Degrees: Bachelor's, certificate, doctoral, first professional, master's, post-bachelor's certificate, post-master's certificate. **Academic Requirements:** English (including composition), foreign languages, humanities, mathematics, sciences (biological or physical), social science. **Classes:** Most classes have 10–19 students. Most lab/discussion sections have 10–19 students. **Majors with Highest Enrollment:** Business, communications studies/speech communication and rhetoric; management, marketing and related support services; psychology. **Disciplines with Highest Percentage of Degrees Awarded:** Business/marketing 39%, social sciences 12%, communications/journalism 12%, biological/life sciences 8%, visual and performing arts 8%. **Special Study Options:** Accelerated program, cooperative education program, double major, English as a second language (ESL), honors program, independent study, internships, learning disabilities services, student-designed major, study abroad, teacher certification program, weekend college.

FACILITIES

Housing: Coed dorms, apartments for married students, apartments for single students, fraternity/sorority housing. **Special Academic Facilities/Equipment:** Art gallery, performing arts center, centers for Judaic and Latin American studies, anthropology museum, center for child study, center for gifted and talented children, regional conservation center, high altitude research lab, law enforcement technology center, observatory. **Computers:** 95% of classrooms are wired, 65% of classrooms are wireless, 95% of public computers are PCs, 5% of public computers are Macs, network access in dorm rooms, network access in dorm lounges, online registration, online administrative

functions (other than registration), remote student-access to Web through college's connection, undergraduates are required to own a computer.

CAMPUS LIFE

Activities: Choral groups, concert band, dance, drama/theater, jazz band, literary magazine, music ensembles, musical theater, opera, pep band, radio station, student government, student newspaper, student-run film society, symphony orchestra. **Organizations:** 99 registered organizations, 26 honor societies, 18 religious organizations. 8 fraternities (15% men join), 5 sororities (11% women join). **Athletics (Intercollegiate):** *Men:* Basketball, diving, golf, ice hockey, lacrosse, skiing (downhill/alpine), skiing (nordic/cross-country), soccer, swimming, tennis. *Women:* Basketball, diving, golf, gymnastics, lacrosse, skiing (downhill/alpine), skiing (nordic/cross-country), soccer, swimming, tennis, volleyball.

ADMISSIONS

Freshman Academic Profile: 35% in top 10% of high school class, 67% in top 25% of high school class, 92% in top 50% of high school class. SAT Math middle 50% range 540–640. SAT Critical Reading middle 50% range 530–640. ACT middle 50% range 23–28. TOEFL required of all international applicants, minimum paper TOEFL 525, minimum computer TOEFL 193. **Basis for Candidate Selection:** *Very important factors considered include:* Academic GPA, character/personal qualities, interview, rigor of secondary school record, standardized test scores. *Important factors considered include:* Application essay, extracurricular activities, level of applicant's interest, recommendation(s), talent/ability, volunteer work, work experience. **Freshman Admission Requirements:** High school diploma is required, and GED is accepted. *Academic units recommended:* 4 English, 4 math, 4 science (2 science labs), 3 foreign language, 2 social studies, 2 history. **Freshman Admission Statistics:** 4,656 applied, 73% admitted, 33% enrolled. **Transfer Admission Requirements:** College transcript(s), essay or personal statement, interview, statement of good standing from prior institution(s). Lowest grade transferable C. **General Admission Information:** Application fee $50. Regular application deadline 1/15. Regular notification 3/15. Non-fall registration accepted. Admission may be deferred for a maxiumum of 2 semesters. Credit and/or placement offered for CEEB Advanced Placement tests.

COSTS AND FINANCIAL AID

Required Forms and Deadlines: FAFSA. Financial aid filing deadline 3/1. **Types of Aid:** *Need-based scholarships/grants:* Pell, SEOG, state scholarships/grants, private scholarships, the school's own gift aid. *Loans:* Direct Subsidized Stafford, Direct Unsubsidized Stafford, Direct PLUS, FFEL Subsidized Stafford, FFEL Unsubsidized Stafford, FFEL PLUS, Federal Perkins, college/university loans from institutional funds. **Student Employment:** Federal Work-Study Program available. Institutional employment available. Off-campus job opportunities are excellent. **Financial Aid Statistics:** 44% freshmen, 42% undergrads receive need-based scholarship or grant aid. 39% freshmen, 37% undergrads receive need-based self-help aid. 50 freshmen, 186 undergrads receive athletic scholarships. 85% freshmen, 79% undergrads receive any aid. **Financial Aid Phone:** 303-871-4020.

UNIVERSITY OF DETROIT—MERCY

PO Box 19900, Detroit, MI 48219
Phone: 313-993-1245 **E-mail:** admissions@udmercy.edu **CEEB Code:** 1835
Fax: 313-993-3326 **Website:** www.udmercy.edu **ACT Code:** 2060
Financial Aid Phone: 313-993-1350

This private school, affiliated with the Jesuit order of the Roman Catholic Church, was founded in 1877. It has a 70-acre campus.

RATINGS

Admissions Selectivity Rating: 76   **Fire Safety Rating:** 60*   **Green Rating:** 60*

STUDENTS AND FACULTY

Enrollment: 2,986. **Student Body:** 68% female, 32% male, 4% out-of-state, 3% international. African American 32%, Asian 2%, Caucasian 52%, Hispanic 2%. **Retention and Graduation:** 76% freshmen return for sophomore year. 33% freshmen graduate within 4 years. 20% grads go on to further study within 1 year. 5% grads pursue arts and sciences degrees. 8% grads pursue business degrees. 4% grads pursue law degrees. 3% grads pursue medical degrees. **Faculty:** Student/faculty ratio 15:1. 270 full-time faculty, 85% hold PhDs.

ACADEMICS

Degrees: Associate, bachelor's, certificate, doctoral, first professional certificate, first professional, master's, post-bachelor's certificate, post-master's certificate. **Academic Requirements:** Communications (speech), computer literacy, English (including composition), history, humanities, mathematics, philosophy, sciences (biological or physical), religious studies, social science. **Disciplines with Highest Percentage of Degrees Awarded:** Health professions and related sciences 21%, business/marketing 17%, engineering 13%, education 7%, social sciences 6%. **Special Study Options:** Accelerated program, cooperative education program, double major, dual enrollment, English as a second language (ESL), honors program, independent study, internships, liberal arts/career combination, study abroad, teacher certification program, weekend college.

FACILITIES

Housing: Coed dorms, apartments for married students, fraternity/sorority housing, peace and justice floor, honors floors, WISE (Women in Science & Engineering) floor.

CAMPUS LIFE

Activities: Dance, drama/theater, literary magazine, pep band, radio station, student government, student newspaper. **Organizations:** 55 registered organizations, 1 honor society. 7 fraternities, 3 sororities. **Athletics (Intercollegiate):** *Men:* Baseball, basketball, cheerleading, cross-country, fencing, golf, soccer, track/field (indoor), track/field (outdoor). *Women:* Basketball, cheerleading, cross-country, fencing, soccer, softball, tennis, track/field (indoor), track/field (outdoor).

ADMISSIONS

Freshman Academic Profile: 23% in top 10% of high school class, 53% in top 25% of high school class, 82% in top 50% of high school class. ACT middle 50% range 19-25. **Basis for Candidate Selection:** *Very important factors considered include:* Rigor of secondary school record, standardized test scores. *Other factors considered include:* Alumni/ae relation, application essay, class rank, extracurricular activities, interview, recommendation(s), volunteer work. **Freshman Admission Requirements:** High school diploma is required, and GED is accepted. *Academic units required:* 4 English, 3 math, 2 science (1 science lab), 1 social studies, 1 history. *Academic units recommended:* 2 foreign language, 2 academic electives. **Freshman Admission Statistics:** 2,181 applied, 81% admitted, 27% enrolled. **Transfer Admission Requirements:** College transcript(s). Minimum college GPA of 2.0 required. Lowest grade transferable C. **General Admission Information:** Application fee $25. Regular application deadline 7/1. Regular notification is rolling. Non-fall registration accepted. Common Application not accepted. Credit and/or placement offered for CEEB Advanced Placement tests.

COSTS AND FINANCIAL AID

Annual tuition $20,400. Room & board $7,040. Required fees $570. Average book expense $1,300. **Required Forms and Deadlines:** FAFSA. Financial aid filing deadline 3/1. **Notification of Awards:** Applicants will be notified of awards on or about 3/1. **Types of Aid:** *Need-based scholarships/grants:* Pell, SEOG, state scholarships/grants, private scholarships, the school's own gift aid, Federal Nursing Scholarships. *Loans:* FFEL Subsidized Stafford, FFEL Unsubsidized Stafford, FFEL PLUS, Federal Perkins, Federal Nursing, college/university loans from institutional funds. **Student Employment:** Federal Work-Study Program available. Institutional employment available. Off-campus job opportunities are good. **Financial Aid Statistics:** 66% freshmen, 71% undergrads receive need-based scholarship or grant aid. 59% freshmen, 68% undergrads receive need-based self-help aid. 9 freshmen, 18 undergrads receive athletic scholarships.

UNIVERSITY OF THE DISTRICT OF COLUMBIA

4200 Connecticut Avenue Northwest, Washington, DC 20008
Phone: 202-274-6110 **E-mail:** lflannagan@udc.edu **CEEB Code:** 5929
Fax: 202-274-5552 **Website:** www.udc.edu **ACT Code:** 0695
Financial Aid Phone: 202-274-5060

This public school was founded in 1976. It has a 23-acre campus.

RATINGS

Admissions Selectivity Rating: 60*   **Fire Safety Rating:** 60*   **Green Rating:** 60*

STUDENTS AND FACULTY

Enrollment: 5,300. **Student Body:** 60% female, 40% male, 27% out-of-state. African American 73%, Asian 2%, Caucasian 6%, Hispanic 5%. **Retention and Graduation:** 6% grads go on to further study within 2 semesters. 1% grads pursue arts and sciences degrees. 3% grads pursue business degrees. 1% grads pursue law degrees. 1% grads pursue medical degrees. **Faculty:** Student/faculty ratio 13:1. 215 full-time faculty, 66% hold PhDs. 90% faculty teach undergrads.

ACADEMICS

Degrees: Associate, bachelor's, master's. **Academic Requirements:** Arts/fine arts, computer literacy, English (including composition), foreign languages, literature and advanced writing, mathematics, natural science, personal & community health, philosophy, physical education, sciences (biological or physical), social science, speech. **Classes:** Most classes have 30–39 students. Most lab/discussion sections have 20–29 students. **Disciplines with Highest Percentage of Degrees Awarded:** Business/marketing 41%, education 7%, engineering 7%, social sciences 6%, computer and information sciences 5%, natural resources/environmental science 5%, visual and performing arts 4%. **Special Study Options:** Business, computer science, cooperative education program, English as a second language (ESL), home economics, honors program, independent study, teacher certification program, technologies, weekend college.

FACILITIES

Special Academic Facilities/Equipment: Theater, greenhouse.

CAMPUS LIFE

Activities: Choral groups, concert band, dance, drama/theater, jazz band, literary magazine, music ensembles, opera, pep band, student government, student newspaper, symphony orchestra, television station, yearbook. **Organizations:** 28 registered organizations, 8 honor societies. 3 fraternities (5% men join), 3 sororities (5% women join). **Athletics (Intercollegiate):** *Men:* Basketball, cross-country, soccer, tennis. *Women:* Basketball, tennis, track/field (outdoor), volleyball.

ADMISSIONS

Freshman Academic Profile: 90% from public high schools. TOEFL required of all international applicants, minimum paper TOEFL 550. **Basis for Candidate Selection:** *Very important factors considered include:* Rigor of secondary school record. *Other factors considered include:* Character/personal qualities, extracurricular activities, recommendation(s), state residency, talent/ability. **Freshman Admission Requirements:** High school diploma is required, and GED is accepted. *Academic units required:* 4 English, 2 math, 2 science (2 science labs), 2 foreign language, 2 social studies, 2 history. *Academic units recommended:* 4 English, 2 math, 2 science (2 science labs), 2 foreign language, 2 social studies, 2 history. **Freshman Admission Statistics:** 2,002 applied, 91% admitted, 58% enrolled. **Transfer Admission Requirements:** College transcript(s). Minimum college GPA of 2.0 required. Lowest grade transferable C. **General Admission Information:** Application fee $20. Regular application deadline 6/14. Regular notification rolling. Non-fall registration accepted. Admission may be deferred for a maximum of 1 semester. Placement offered for CEEB Advanced Placement tests.

COSTS AND FINANCIAL AID

Annual in-state tuition $2,160. Out-of-state tuition $4,800. Required fees $510. Average book expense $900. **Required Forms and Deadlines:** FAFSA, institution's own financial aid form. Financial aid filing deadline 5/5. **Notification of Awards:** Applicants will be notified of awards on a rolling basis beginning on or about 5/5. **Types of Aid:** *Need-based scholarships/grants:* Pell, SEOG, state scholarships/grants, private scholarships, the school's own gift aid. *Loans:* FFEL Subsidized Stafford, FFEL Unsubsidized Stafford, FFEL PLUS, Federal Perkins. **Student Employment:** Federal Work-Study Program available. Institutional employment available. Off-campus job opportunities are good. **Financial Aid Statistics:** 55% freshmen, 57% undergrads receive need-based scholarship or grant aid. 10% freshmen, 10% undergrads receive need-based self-help aid. 25 freshmen, 105 undergrads receive athletic scholarships. Highest amount earned per year from on-campus jobs $1,950.

UNIVERSITY OF DUBUQUE

2000 University Avenue, Dubuque, IA 52001-5050
Phone: 319-589-3200 **E-mail:** admssns@dbq.edu **CEEB Code:** 6869
Fax: 319-589-3690 **Website:** www.dbq.edu **ACT Code:** 1358
Financial Aid Phone: 563-589-3396

This private school, affiliated with the Presbyterian Church, was founded in 1852. It has a 56-acre campus.

RATINGS

Admissions Selectivity Rating: 73   **Fire Safety Rating:** 60*   **Green Rating:** 60*

STUDENTS AND FACULTY

Enrollment: 1,234. **Student Body:** 42% female, 58% male, 57% out-of-state. African American 13%, Asian 1%, Caucasian 74%, Hispanic 4%, Native

American 2%. **Retention and Graduation:** 70% freshmen return for sophomore year. 24% freshmen graduate within 4 years. 18% grads go on to further study within 1 year. 10% grads pursue arts and sciences degrees. 5% grads pursue business degrees. 1% grads pursue medical degrees. **Faculty:** Student/faculty ratio 14:1. 72 full-time faculty, 72% hold PhDs. 100% faculty teach undergrads.

ACADEMICS

Degrees: Associate, bachelor's, doctoral, master's. **Academic Requirements:** Computer literacy, English (including composition), foreign languages, history, humanities, mathematics, philosophy, sciences (biological or physical), social science. **Classes:** Most classes have 10–19 students. Most lab/discussion sections have fewer than 10 students. **Majors with Highest Enrollment:** Airline/commercial/professional pilot and flight crew; animation, interactive technology, video graphics and special effects; business administration/management. **Disciplines with Highest Percentage of Degrees Awarded:** Business/marketing 15%, natural resources/environmental science 10%, education 10%, health professions and related sciences 10%, psychology 6%, parks and recreation 5%, philosophy and religious studies 5%, biological/life sciences 3%. **Special Study Options:** Cooperative education program, cross-registration, double major, dual enrollment, independent study, internships, liberal arts/career combination, student-designed major, study abroad, teacher certification program. Undergrads may take grad level classes. Off-campus study: semester-away programs.

FACILITIES

Housing: Coed dorms, apartments for married students, apartments for single students, special housing for disabled students, houses and town houses and suites. **Special Academic Facilities/Equipment:** Art gallery, language labs, electron microscope, gas chromatograph/mass spectrometer, floating science lab on the Mississippi River, computer graphics/interactive media stduios, multimedia project production studio in the new Charles C. Myers Library. **Computers:** 25% of classrooms are wired, 100% of public computers are PCs, network access in dorm rooms, network access in dorm lounges, online registration, online administrative functions (other than registration), remote student-access to Web through college's connection.

CAMPUS LIFE

Activities: Choral groups, dance, drama/theater, jazz band, music ensembles, pep band, student government, student newspaper, student-run film society, yearbook. **Organizations:** 35 registered organizations, 2 honor societies, 3 religious organizations. 5 fraternities (13% men join), 3 sororities (25% women join). **Athletics (Intercollegiate):** *Men:* Baseball, basketball, cross-country, football, golf, soccer, tennis, track/field (indoor), track/field (outdoor), wrestling. *Women:* Basketball, cross-country, golf, soccer, softball, tennis, track/field (indoor), track/field (outdoor), volleyball.

ADMISSIONS

Freshman Academic Profile: 10% in top 10% of high school class, 25% in top 25% of high school class, 65% in top 50% of high school class. 85% from public high schools. SAT Math middle 50% range 410–560. SAT Critical Reading middle 50% range 400–540. ACT middle 50% range 18–23. TOEFL required of all international applicants, minimum paper TOEFL 500, minimum computer TOEFL 275. **Basis for Candidate Selection:** *Very important factors considered include:* Application essay, character/personal qualities, class rank, recommendation(s), rigor of secondary school record, standardized test scores. *Important factors considered include:* Interview. *Other factors considered include:* Alumni/ae relation. **Freshman Admission Requirements:** High school diploma is required, and GED is accepted. *Academic units required:* 4 English, 3 math, 3 science, 3 social studies, 3 academic electives. **Freshman Admission Statistics:** 1,001 applied, 73% admitted, 42% enrolled. **Transfer Admission Requirements:** College transcript(s). Minimum college GPA of 2.0 required. Lowest grade transferable C. **General Admission Information:** Application fee $25. Regular notification is rolling. Nonfall registration accepted. Admission may be deferred for a maximum of 1 year. Credit offered for CEEB Advanced Placement tests.

COSTS AND FINANCIAL AID

Annual tuition $17,960. Room & board $6,200. Required fees $300. Average book expense $750. **Required Forms and Deadlines:** FAFSA. Financial aid filing deadline 4/1. **Notification of Awards:** Applicants will be notified of awards on a rolling basis beginning on or about 3/1. **Types of Aid:** *Need-based scholarships/grants:* Pell, SEOG, state scholarships/grants, private scholarships, the school's own gift aid. *Loans:* FFEL Subsidized Stafford, FFEL Unsubsidized Stafford, FFEL PLUS, Federal Perkins, state loans, college/university loans from institutional funds. **Student Employment:** Federal Work-Study Program available. Institutional employment available. Off-campus job opportunities are excellent. **Financial Aid Statistics:** 89% freshmen, 87% undergrads receive need-based scholarship or grant aid. 80% freshmen, 78% undergrads receive need-based self-help aid. 85% freshmen, 85% undergrads receive any aid. Highest amount earned per year from on-campus jobs $1,500.

UNIVERSITY OF EVANSVILLE

1800 Lincoln Avenue, Evansville, IN 47722
Phone: 812-488-2468 **E-mail:** admission@evansville.edu **CEEB Code:** 1208
Fax: 812-488-4076 **Website:** www.evansville.edu **ACT Code:** 1188
Financial Aid Phone: 812-488-2364

This private school, affiliated with the Methodist Church, was founded in 1854. It has a 75-acre campus.

RATINGS

Admissions Selectivity Rating: 85   **Fire Safety Rating:** 78   **Green Rating:** 76

STUDENTS AND FACULTY

Enrollment: 2,610. **Student Body:** 60% female, 40% male, 39% out-of-state, 6% international (50 countries represented). African American 2%, Asian 1%, Caucasian 72%, Hispanic 1%. **Retention and Graduation:** 78% freshmen return for sophomore year. 21% grads go on to further study within 1 year. **Faculty:** Student/faculty ratio 13:1. 179 full-time faculty, 84% hold PhDs. 100% faculty teach undergrads.

ACADEMICS

Degrees: Associate, bachelor's, first professional, master's. **Academic Requirements:** Arts/fine arts, foreign languages, health and wellness, history, humanities, mathematics, philosophy, sciences (biological or physical), social science. **Classes:** Most classes have 10–19 students. Most lab/discussion sections have 10–19 students. **Majors with Highest Enrollment:** Drama and dramatics/theatre arts, elementary education and teaching, psychology. **Disciplines with Highest Percentage of Degrees Awarded:** Business/marketing 13%, education 13%, health professions and related sciences 12%, visual and performing arts 11%, social sciences 9%. **Special Study Options:** Accelerated program, cooperative education program, double major, dual enrollment, English as a second language (ESL), external degree program, honors program, independent study, internships, student-designed major, study abroad, teacher certification program.

FACILITIES

Housing: Coed dorms, men's dorms, women's dorms, apartments for single students, special housing for international students, fraternity/sorority housing, honors program housing. **Computers:** 5% of classrooms are wired, 100% of classrooms are wireless, 95% of public computers are PCs, 5% of public computers are Macs, network access in dorm rooms, network access in dorm lounges, online registration, online administrative functions (other than registration), remote student-access to Web through college's connection.

CAMPUS LIFE

Activities: Choral groups, concert band, dance, drama/theater, jazz band, literary magazine, music ensembles, musical theater, opera, pep band, radio station, student government, student newspaper, student-run film society, symphony orchestra, yearbook. **Organizations:** 170 registered organizations, 15 honor societies, 11 religious organization. 6 fraternities (24% men join), 5 sororities (21% women join). **Athletics (Intercollegiate):** *Men:* Baseball, basketball, cross-country, diving, golf, soccer, swimming. *Women:* Basketball, cross-country, diving, golf, soccer, softball, swimming, tennis, volleyball. **Environmental Initiatives:** Recycling of paper, plastic, aluminum, cardboard, newspaper, magazines, books, electronic equipment, batteries and ink cartridges. LEED certification of new buildings. Ecology focused classes.

ADMISSIONS

Freshman Academic Profile: 36% in top 10% of high school class, 71% in top 25% of high school class, 93% in top 50% of high school class. SAT Math middle 50% range 510–640. SAT Critical Reading middle 50% range 500–620. SAT Writing middle 50% range 500–600. ACT middle 50% range 22–28. TOEFL required of all international applicants, minimum paper TOEFL 500, minimum computer TOEFL 173. **Basis for Candidate Selection:** *Very important factors considered include:* Academic GPA, rigor of secondary school record, standardized test scores. *Important factors considered include:* Character/personal qualities, class rank, extracurricular activities, interview, recommendation(s), talent/ability, volunteer work. *Other factors considered include:* Alumni/ae relation, work experience. **Freshman Admission Requirements:** High school diploma is required, and GED is accepted. *Academic units required:* 4 English, 3 math, 2 science (2 science labs), 1 social studies, 1 history. *Academic units recommended:* 4 English, 4 math, 3 science (2 science labs), 2 foreign language, 1 social studies, 1 history. **Freshman Admission Statistics:** 2,857 applied, 90% admitted, 25% enrolled. **Transfer Admission Requirements:** High school transcript, college transcript(s), statement of good standing from prior institution(s). Minimum college GPA of 2.0 required. Lowest grade transferable C. **General Admission Information:** Application fee $35. Regular application deadline 2/1. Regular notification 3/1. Non-fall registration accepted. Admission may be deferred for a maxiumum of 2 semesters. Credit and/or placement offered for CEEB Advanced Placement tests.

COSTS AND FINANCIAL AID

Required Forms and Deadlines: FAFSA. Financial aid filing deadline 3/10. **Notification of Awards:** Applicants will be notified of awards on a rolling basis beginning on or about 3/21. **Types of Aid:** *Need-based scholarships/grants:* Pell, SEOG, state scholarships/grants, private scholarships, the school's own gift aid. *Loans:* FFEL Subsidized Stafford, FFEL Unsubsidized Stafford, FFEL PLUS, Federal Perkins, Federal Nursing, college/university loans from institutional funds. **Student Employment:** Federal Work-Study Program available. Institutional employment available. Off-campus job opportunities are good. **Financial Aid Statistics:** 70% freshmen, 69% undergrads receive need-based scholarship or grant aid. 53% freshmen, 49% undergrads receive need-based self-help aid. 15 freshmen, 86 undergrads receive athletic scholarships. 98% freshmen, 96% undergrads receive any aid. Highest amount earned per year from on-campus jobs $1,300.

THE UNIVERSITY OF FINDLAY

1000 North Main Street, Findlay, OH 45840
Phone: 419-424-4732 **E-mail:** admissions@findlay.edu **CEEB Code:** 1223
Fax: 419-434-4898 **Website:** www.findlay.edu/default.htm **ACT Code:** 3272
Financial Aid Phone: 419-424-4791

This private school was founded in 1882. It has a 175-acre campus.

RATINGS
Admissions Selectivity Rating: 81   **Fire Safety Rating:** 60*   **Green Rating:** 60*

STUDENTS AND FACULTY
Enrollment: 3,381. **Student Body:** 57% female, 43% male, 20% out-of-state. African American 4%, Asian 4%, Caucasian 72%, Hispanic 2%. **Retention and Graduation:** 72% freshmen return for sophomore year. 32% freshmen graduate within 4 years. 18% grads go on to further study within 1 year. 3% grads pursue arts and sciences degrees. 3% grads pursue business degrees. 4% grads pursue law degrees. 1% grads pursue medical degrees. **Faculty:** Student/faculty ratio 16:1. 160 full-time faculty, 51% hold PhDs. 90% faculty teach undergrads.

ACADEMICS
Degrees: Associate, bachelor's, doctoral, master's. **Academic Requirements:** Arts/fine arts, computer literacy, English (including composition), foreign languages, humanities, mathematics, philosophy, sciences (biological or physical), social science. **Classes:** Most classes have 10–19 students. **Disciplines with Highest Percentage of Degrees Awarded:** Health professions and related sciences 28%, business/marketing 16%, education 13%, computer and information sciences 6%, engineering 6%, agriculture 5%. **Special Study Options:** 3-1 arrangement with Art Institute Consortium, accelerated program, BS in nursing with Mount Carmel College of Nursing, cooperative education program, distance learning, double major, dual enrollment, English as a second language (ESL), external degree program, honors program, independent study, internships, liberal arts/career combination, student-designed major, study abroad, teacher certification program, weekend college.

FACILITIES
Housing: Men's dorms, women's dorms, apartments for single students, special housing for disabled students, special housing for international students, fraternity/sorority housing, honors house, special interest houses. **Special Academic Facilities/Equipment:** Fine arts pavilion, planetarium, Mazza Gallery (children's book illustrations.) **Computers:** 80% of public computers are PCs, 20% of public computers are Macs, network access in dorm rooms, network access in dorm lounges, online registration, online administrative functions (other than registration), remote student-access to Web through college's connection.

CAMPUS LIFE
Activities: Choral groups, concert band, drama/theater, jazz band, literary magazine, marching band, music ensembles, musical theater, pep band, radio station, student government, student newspaper, student-run film society,

television station, yearbook. **Organizations:** 40 registered organizations, 1 honor society, 1 religious organization. 3 fraternities (2% men join), 2 sororities (2% women join). **Athletics (Intercollegiate):** *Men:* Baseball, basketball, cross-country, diving, equestrian sports, football, golf, ice hockey, soccer, swimming, tennis, track/field (indoor), track/field (outdoor), volleyball, wrestling. *Women:* Basketball, cross-country, diving, equestrian sports, golf, ice hockey, soccer, softball, swimming, tennis, track/field (indoor), track/field (outdoor), volleyball.

ADMISSIONS
Freshman Academic Profile: 26% in top 10% of high school class, 54% in top 25% of high school class, 80% in top 50% of high school class. 92% from public high schools. SAT Math middle 50% range 470–580. SAT Critical Reading middle 50% range 470–580. SAT Writing middle 50% range 460–590. ACT middle 50% range 20–25. TOEFL required of all international applicants, minimum paper TOEFL 500. **Basis for Candidate Selection:** *Very important factors considered include:* Academic GPA, application essay, recommendation(s), rigor of secondary school record, standardized test scores. *Important factors considered include:* Interview. *Other factors considered include:* Alumni/ae relation, character/personal qualities, class rank, extracurricular activities, religious affiliation/commitment, talent/ability, volunteer work. **Freshman Admission Requirements:** High school diploma is required, and GED is accepted. *Academic units recommended:* 4 English, 3 math, 3 science, 2 foreign language, 2 social studies, 1 history, 1 academic elective. **Freshman Admission Statistics:** 2,708 applied, 72% admitted, 37% enrolled. **Transfer Admission Requirements:** College transcript(s). Minimum college GPA of 2.0 required. Lowest grade transferable C. **General Admission Information:** Regular application deadline 7/1. Regular notification is rolling. Non-fall registration accepted. Admission may be deferred for a maximum of 2 semesters. Credit and/or placement offered for CEEB Advanced Placement tests.

COSTS AND FINANCIAL AID
Annual tuition $21,836. Room & board $7,792. Required fees $960. Average book expense $1,000. **Required Forms and Deadlines:** FAFSA. Financial aid filing deadline 8/1. **Notification of Awards:** Applicants will be notified of awards on a rolling basis beginning on or about 3/1. **Types of Aid:** *Need-based scholarships/grants:* Pell, SEOG, state scholarships/grants, private scholarships, the school's own gift aid. *Loans:* Direct Subsidized Stafford, Direct Unsubsidized Stafford, Direct PLUS, Federal Perkins, college/university loans from institutional funds. **Student Employment:** Federal Work-Study Program available. Institutional employment available. Off-campus job opportunities are excellent. **Financial Aid Statistics:** 78% freshmen, 64% undergrads receive need-based scholarship or grant aid. 80% freshmen, 64% undergrads receive need-based self-help aid. 105 freshmen, 300 undergrads receive athletic scholarships. Highest amount earned per year from on-campus jobs $600.

See page 1440.

UNIVERSITY OF FLORIDA

201 Criser Hall, Box 114000, Gainesville, FL 32611-4000
Phone: 352-392-1365 **E-mail:** ourwebrequests@registrar.ufl.edu **CEEB Code:** 5812
Fax: 904-392-3987 **Website:** www.ufl.edu
Financial Aid Phone: 352-392-1275

This public school was founded in 1853. It has a 2,000-acre campus.

RATINGS
Admissions Selectivity Rating: 60*   **Fire Safety Rating:** 72   **Green Rating:** 97

STUDENTS AND FACULTY
Enrollment: 34,534. **Student Body:** 54% female, 46% male, 5% out-of-state. African American 10%, Asian 7%, Caucasian 66%, Hispanic 13%. **Retention and Graduation:** 94% freshmen return for sophomore year. 53% freshmen graduate within 4 years. **Faculty:** Student/faculty ratio 24:1. 2229 full-time faculty, 86% hold PhDs.

ACADEMICS
Degrees: Bachelor's, doctoral, first professional, master's. **Classes:** Most classes have 10–19 students. Most lab/discussion sections have 10–19 students.

Majors with Highest Enrollment: Business administration/management, finance, psychology. **Disciplines with Highest Percentage of Degrees Awarded:** Business/marketing 17%, social sciences 14%, engineering 10%, communications/journalism 8%, health professions and related sciences 7%. **Special Study Options:** Accelerated program, cooperative education program, cross-registration, distance learning, double major, dual enrollment, English as a second language (ESL), exchange student program (domestic), external degree program, honors program, independent study, internships, liberal arts/career combination, student-designed major, study abroad, teacher certification program, weekend college, adult/continuing education, TV-delivered credit-bearing courses, and distance learning courses.

FACILITIES

Housing: Coed dorms, women's dorms, apartments for married students, apartments for single students, special housing for disabled students, special housing for international students, fraternity/sorority housing, honors residential college at Hume Hall, international house at Weaver Hall, "quiet/study" floors, faculty-in-residence program, first-year experience program, wellness floor, no-visitation by opposite sex floor. **Special Academic Facilities/Equipment:** Natural history museum, art museum, art gallery, center for the performing arts, Aeolian Skinner organ, cast-bell carillon, citrus research center, coastal engineering wave tank, 100-kilowatt training and research reactor, academic computing center, microkelvin lab, self-contained intensive care hyperbaric chamber. **Computers:** 60% of public computers are PCs, 10% of public computers are Macs, 30% of public computers are UNIX, network access in dorm rooms, network access in dorm lounges, online registration, online administrative functions (other than registration), remote student-access to Web through college's connection.

CAMPUS LIFE

Activities: Choral groups, concert band, dance, drama/theater, jazz band, literary magazine, marching band, music ensembles, musical theater, pep band, radio station, student government, student newspaper, student-run film society, symphony orchestra, television station, yearbook. **Organizations:** 500 registered organizations, 29 fraternities (14% men join), 18 sororities (12% women join). **Athletics (Intercollegiate):** *Men:* Baseball, basketball, cross-country, diving, football, golf, swimming, tennis, track/field (indoor), track/field (outdoor). *Women:* Basketball, cross-country, diving, golf, gymnastics, soccer, softball, swimming, tennis, track/field (indoor), track/field (outdoor), volleyball. **Environmental Initiatives:** Zero Waste by 2015. Carbon Neutral by 2030. LEED Silver certification for all new construction.

ADMISSIONS

Freshman Academic Profile: SAT Math middle 50% range 580–690. SAT Critical Reading middle 50% range 560–670. ACT middle 50% range 25–29. **Freshman Admission Requirements:** High school diploma is required, and GED is accepted. *Academic units required:* 4 English, 3 math, 3 science, (2 science labs), 2 foreign language, 3 social studies, 3 academic electives. **Freshman Admission Statistics:** 22,093 applied, 48% admitted, 63% enrolled. **Transfer Admission Requirements:** High school transcript, college transcript(s), standardized test score. Minimum college GPA of 2.0 required. **General Admission Information:** Application fee $30. Early decision application deadline 11/1. Regular application deadline 1/17. Regular notification reply dates. Nonfall registration accepted. Credit and/or placement offered for CEEB Advanced Placement tests.

COSTS AND FINANCIAL AID

Annual in-state tuition $3,257. Annual out-of-state tuition $17,841. Room and board $7,020. Average book expense $940. **Required Forms and Deadlines:** FAFSA. Financial aid filing deadline 3/15. **Notification of Awards:** Applicants will be notified of awards on a rolling basis beginning on or about 4/1. **Types of Aid:** *Need-based scholarships/grants:* Pell, SEOG, state scholarships/grants, private scholarships, the school's own gift aid. *Loans:* Direct Subsidized Stafford, Direct Unsubsidized Stafford, Direct PLUS, Federal Perkins, college/university loans from institutional funds. **Student Employment:** Federal Work-Study Program available. Institutional employment available. Off-campus job opportunities are fair. **Financial Aid Statistics:** 21% freshmen, 22% undergrads receive need-based scholarship or grant aid. 14% freshmen, 20% undergrads receive need-based self-help aid. 79 freshmen, 456 undergrads receive athletic scholarships. 97% freshmen, 84% undergrads receive any aid. Highest amount earned per year from on-campus jobs $22,320.

UNIVERSITY OF GEORGIA

Terrell Hall, Athens, GA 30602
Phone: 706-542-8776 **E-mail:** undergrad@admissions.uga.edu **CEEB Code:** 5813
Fax: 706-542-1466 **Website:** www.uga.edu **ACT Code:** 0872
Financial Aid Phone: 706-542-6147

This public school was founded in 1785. It has a 324-acre campus.

RATINGS

Admissions Selectivity Rating: 92   **Fire Safety Rating:** 82   **Green Rating:** 89

STUDENTS AND FACULTY

Enrollment: 25,055. **Student Body:** 57% female, 43% male, 11% out-of-state, (131 countries represented). African American 6%, Asian 6%, Caucasian 83%, Hispanic 2%. **Retention and Graduation:** 94% freshmen return for sophomore year. 46% freshmen graduate within 4 years. 24% grads go on to further study within 1 year. 6% grads pursue arts and sciences degrees. 6% grads pursue business degrees. 14% grads pursue law degrees. 14% grads pursue medical degrees. **Faculty:** Student/faculty ratio 18:1. 1,735 full-time faculty, 94% hold PhDs. 83% faculty teach undergrads.

ACADEMICS

Degrees: Bachelor's, certificate, doctoral, first professional certificate, first professional, master's, post-bachelor's certificate, post-master's certificate. **Academic Requirements:** Arts/fine arts, computer literacy, English (including composition), history, humanities, mathematics, sciences (biological or physical), social science. **Classes:** Most classes have 20–29 students. **Majors with Highest Enrollment:** Art/art studies, biology/biological sciences, psychology. **Disciplines with Highest Percentage of Degrees Awarded:** Business/marketing 20%, social sciences 10%, education 9%, biological/life sciences 8%, family and consumer sciences 7%. **Special Study Options:** Accelerated program, cooperative education program, cross registration, distance learning, double major, dual enrollment, exchange student program (domestic), external degree program, honors program, independent study, internships, liberal arts/career combination, student-designed major, study abroad, teacher certification program.

FACILITIES

Housing: Coed dorms, women's dorms, apartments for married students, apartments for single students, special housing for disabled students, special housing for international students, fraternity/sorority housing, honors and language halls are available. **Special Academic Facilities/Equipment:** Student learning center, Georgia Museum of Art, Georgia Museum of Natural History, Ramsey Student Center for Physical Activities, performing arts center. **Computers:** 30% of classrooms are wired, 60% of classrooms are wireless, 83% of public computers are PCs, 14% of public computers are Macs, 3% of public computers are UNIX, network access in dorm rooms, network access in dorm lounges, online registration, online administrative functions (other than registration), remote student-access to Web through college's connection.

CAMPUS LIFE

Activities: Choral groups, concert band, dance, drama/theater, jazz band, literary magazine, marching band, music ensembles, musical theater, opera, pep band, radio station, student government, student newspaper, student-run film society, symphony orchestra, television station. **Organizations:** 352 registered organizations, 27 honor societies, 20 religious organizations. 25 fraternities (21% men join), 24 sororities (25% women join). **Athletics (Intercollegiate):** *Men:* Baseball, basketball, cross-country, diving, football, golf, swimming, tennis, track/field (outdoor). *Women:* Basketball, cross-country, diving, equestrian sports, golf, gymnastics, soccer, softball, swimming, tennis, track/field (outdoor), volleyball. **Environmental Initiatives:** UGA created the Eugene Odum School of Ecology, the world's first stand-alone school devoted to teaching, research and public service in the areas of ecology and environmental studies. Created the Academy of the Environment. Installed rain gardens, planted native species, installed low-flow toilets and shower heads, reduced water use and are recycling water in research labs and including cisterns in new construction. The result is a 10 percent reduction in water use from a year ago.

ADMISSIONS

Freshman Academic Profile: 48% in top 10% of high school class, 84% in top 25% of high school class, 98% in top 50% of high school class. 81% from public high schools. SAT Math middle 50% range 570–650. SAT Critical Reading

middle 50% range 560–660. SAT Writing middle 50% range 560–640. ACT middle 50% range 25–29. TOEFL required of all international applicants, minimum paper TOEFL 550, minimum computer TOEFL 213. **Basis for Candidate Selection:** *Very important factors considered include:* Academic GPA, rigor of secondary school record. *Important factors considered include:* Standardized test scores. *Other factors considered include:* Application essay, character/personal qualities, extracurricular activities, recommendation(s), talent/ability, volunteer work, work experience. **Freshman Admission Requirements:** High school diploma is required, and GED is accepted. *Academic units required:* 4 English, 4 math, 3 science (2 science labs), 2 foreign language, 3 social studies. *Academic units recommended:* 4 English, 4 math, 3 science (2 science labs), 3 foreign language, 1 social studies, 2 history, 1 academic elective. **Freshman Admission Statistics:** 15,924 applied, 58% admitted, 55% enrolled. **Transfer Admission Requirements:** College transcript(s). Lowest grade transferable D. **General Admission Information:** Application fee $50. Regular application deadline 1/15. Regular notification is rolling. Non-fall registration not accepted. Admission may be deferred for a maximum of 2 semesters. Credit and/or placement offered for CEEB Advanced Placement tests.

COSTS AND FINANCIAL AID

Required Forms and Deadlines: FAFSA. Financial aid filing deadline 3/1. **Notification of Awards:** Applicants will be notified of awards on a rolling basis beginning on or about 5/15. **Types of Aid:** *Need-based scholarships/grants:* Pell, SEOG, state scholarships/grants, private scholarships, the school's own gift aid. *Loans:* Direct Subsidized Stafford, Direct Unsubsidized Stafford, Direct PLUS, Federal Perkins, state loans, college/university loans from institutional funds. **Financial Aid Statistics:** 27% freshmen, 22% undergrads receive need-based scholarship or grant aid. 15% freshmen, 18% undergrads receive need-based self-help aid. 100 freshmen, 392 undergrads receive athletic scholarships. 28% freshmen, 26% undergrads receive any aid.

UNIVERSITY OF GREAT FALLS

1301 20th Street South, Great Falls, MT 59405
Phone: 406-791-5200 **E-mail:** enroll@ugf.edu **CEEB Code:** 4058
Fax: 406-791-5209 **Website:** www.ugf.edu **ACT Code:** 2410
Financial Aid Phone: 406-791-5235

This private school, affiliated with the Roman Catholic Church, was founded in 1932. It has a 44-acre campus.

RATINGS
Admissions Selectivity Rating: 60*   **Fire Safety Rating:** 60*   **Green Rating:** 60*

STUDENTS AND FACULTY
Enrollment: 632. **Student Body:** 69% female, 31% male, 20% out-of-state, 2% international. African American 2%, Asian 2%, Caucasian 80%, Hispanic 5%, Native American 5%. **Retention and Graduation:** 51% freshmen return for sophomore year. **Faculty:** Student/faculty ratio 11:1. 33 full-time faculty, 61% hold PhDs. 100% faculty teach undergrads.

ACADEMICS
Degrees: Associate, bachelor's, master's. **Academic Requirements:** Arts/fine arts, computer literacy, English (including composition), foreign languages, history, humanities, literature, mathematics, philosophy, religion, sciences (biological or physical), social science, speech. **Classes:** Most classes have fewer than 10 students. **Majors with Highest Enrollment:** Criminal justice/safety studies, elementary education and teaching, psychology. **Disciplines with Highest Percentage of Degrees Awarded:** Education 24%, psychology 21%, public administration and social services 9%, security and protective services 7%, computer and information sciences 5%, law/legal studies 5%, business/marketing 5%. **Special Study Options:** Cooperative education program, distance learning, double major, independent study, internships, liberal arts/career combination, teacher certification program.

FACILITIES
Housing: Coed dorms, apartments for married students, apartments for single students. **Special Academic Facilities/Equipment:** Art museum, Dr. Hong Herbarium. **Computers:** 91% of public computers are PCs, 9% of public computers are Macs, network access in dorm rooms, network access in dorm lounges, online registration, remote student-access to Web through college's connection.

CAMPUS LIFE
Activities: Choral groups, concert band, drama/theater, jazz band, music ensembles, pep band, radio station, student government, student newspaper.

Organizations: 10 registered organizations, 2 honor societies, 1 religious organization. **Athletics (Intercollegiate):** *Men:* Basketball, cheerleading, cross-country, wrestling. *Women:* Basketball, cheerleading, cross-country, soccer, softball, volleyball.

ADMISSIONS
Freshman Academic Profile: 87% from public high schools. SAT Math middle 50% range 360–490. SAT Critical Reading middle 50% range 330–430. ACT middle 50% range 18–24. TOEFL required of all international applicants, minimum paper TOEFL 500, minimum computer TOEFL 173. **Basis for Candidate Selection:** *Important factors considered include:* Academic GPA, application essay, character/personal qualities, interview, level of applicant's interest, religious affiliation/commitment, rigor of secondary school record, standardized test scores. *Other factors considered include:* Class rank, extracurricular activities, first generation, racial/ethnic status, recommendation(s), talent/ability, volunteer work, work experience. **Freshman Admission Requirements:** High school diploma is required, and GED is accepted. *Academic units required:* 4 English, 3 math, 3 science (1 science lab), 1 social studies, 3 history, 5 academic electives. *Academic units recommended:* 4 English, 3 math, 3 science (1 science lab), 2 foreign language, 2 social studies, 3 history, 3 academic electives. **Freshman Admission Statistics:** 278 applied, 73% admitted, 59% enrolled. **Transfer Admission Requirements:** College transcript(s), essay or personal statement. Minimum college GPA of 2.0 required. Lowest grade transferable C. **General Admission Information:** Application fee $35. Regular application deadline 8/30. Regular notification is rolling. Non-fall registration accepted. Admission may be deferred for a maximum of 2 semesters. Credit and/or placement offered for CEEB Advanced Placement tests.

COSTS AND FINANCIAL AID
Annual tuition $15,500. Room and board $6,490. Required fees $900. Average book expense $500. **Required Forms and Deadlines:** FAFSA. Financial aid filing deadline 4/1. **Notification of Awards:** Applicants will be notified of awards on a rolling basis beginning on or about 3/1. **Types of Aid:** *Need-based scholarships/grants:* Pell, SEOG, state scholarships/grants, private scholarships, the school's own gift aid. *Loans:* FFEL Subsidized Stafford, FFEL Unsubsidized Stafford, FFEL PLUS, Federal Perkins. **Student Employment:** Federal Work-Study Program available. Institutional employment available. Off-campus job opportunities are fair. **Financial Aid Statistics:** 47% freshmen, 54% undergrads receive need-based scholarship or grant aid. 62% freshmen, 69% undergrads receive need-based self-help aid. 57 freshmen, 177 undergrads receive athletic scholarships. 46% freshmen, 50% undergrads receive any aid. Highest amount earned per year from on-campus jobs $2,000.

UNIVERSITY OF GUELPH

Admission Services, Level 3, University Centre, Guelph, ON N1G 2W1 Canada
Phone: 519-821-2130 **E-mail:** info@registrar.uoguelph.ca
Fax: 519-766-9481 **Website:** www.uoguelph.ca

This public school was founded in 1964. It has a 1,200-acre campus.

RATINGS
Admissions Selectivity Rating: 60*   **Fire Safety Rating:** 60*   **Green Rating:** 60*

STUDENTS AND FACULTY
Enrollment: 13,568. **Student Body:** 64% female, 36% male. **Retention and Graduation:** 91% freshmen return for sophomore year. 43% freshmen graduate within 4 years. **Faculty:** Student/faculty ratio 22:1. 692 full-time faculty.

ACADEMICS
Degrees: Bachelor's, diploma, doctoral, first professional, master's. **Academic Requirements:** Humanities, sciences (biological or physical), social science. **Majors with Highest Enrollment:** Physical sciences. **Disciplines with Highest Percentage of Degrees Awarded:** Biological/life sciences 23%, social sciences 20%, liberal arts/general studies 13%, business/marketing 12%, agriculture 5%. **Special Study Options:** Cooperative education program, distance learning, double major, English as a second language (ESL), external degree program, honors program, independent study, student-designed major, study abroad.

FACILITIES
Housing: Coed dorms, men's dorms, women's dorms, apartments for married students, special housing for disabled students, special housing for international students, themed living/learning centres (arts house, eco house, international house, la maison Francaise). **Special Academic Facilities/Equipment:** Art

The Princeton Review's Complete Book of Colleges

gallery, arboretum. **Computers:** Network access in dorm rooms, online registration, remote student-access to Web through college's connection.

CAMPUS LIFE

Activities: Choral groups, dance, drama/theater, jazz band, music ensembles, musical theater, radio station, student government, student newspaper. **Organizations:** 100 registered organizations. **Athletics (Intercollegiate):** *Men:* Baseball, basketball, cross-country, football, golf, ice hockey, lacrosse, rugby, skiing (nordic/cross-country), soccer, swimming, track/field (indoor), volleyball, wrestling. *Women:* Basketball, cross-country, field hockey, ice hockey, lacrosse, rugby, skiing (nordic/cross-country), soccer, swimming, track/field (indoor), volleyball, wrestling.

ADMISSIONS

Freshman Academic Profile: TOEFL required of all international applicants, minimum paper TOEFL 600, minimum computer TOEFL 600. **Basis for Candidate Selection:** *Very important factors considered include:* Rigor of secondary school record. *Important factors considered include:* Class rank, standardized test scores. *Other factors considered include:* Character/personal qualities, extracurricular activities, recommendation(s), talent/ability, volunteer work, work experience. **Freshman Admission Requirements:** High school diploma is required, and GED is not accepted. *Academic units recommended:* 4 English, 4 math, 4 science, 2 social studies, 2 history. **Freshman Admission Statistics:** 18,222 applied, 78% admitted, 26% enrolled. **Transfer Admission Requirements:** High school transcript, college transcript(s). **General Admission Information:** Application fee $85. Regular application deadline 6/1. Regular notification is rolling. Non-fall registration accepted. Common Application not accepted. Credit and/or placement offered for CEEB Advanced Placement tests.

COSTS AND FINANCIAL AID

Room & board $5,766. Required fees $681. Average book expense $1,000. **Student Employment:** Off-campus job opportunities are good.

UNIVERSITY OF HARTFORD

200 Bloomfield Avenue, West Hartford, CT 06117
Phone: 860-768-4296 **E-mail:** admissions@mail.hartford.edu **CEEB Code:** 3436
Fax: 860-768-4961 **Website:** www.hartford.edu **ACT Code:** 0606
Financial Aid Phone: 800-947-4303

This private school was founded in 1877. It has a 320-acre campus.

RATINGS

Admissions Selectivity Rating: 60* **Fire Safety Rating:** 60* **Green Rating:** 60*

STUDENTS AND FACULTY

Enrollment: 5,318. **Student Body:** 51% female, 49% male, 61% out-of-state, 3% international (65 countries represented). African American 10%, Asian 3%, Caucasian 67%, Hispanic 5%. **Retention and Graduation:** 78% freshmen return for sophomore year. 45% freshmen graduate within 4 years. 22% grads go on to further study within 1 year. 39% grads pursue arts and sciences degrees. 14% grads pursue business degrees. 2% grads pursue law degrees. 2% grads pursue medical degrees. **Faculty:** Student/faculty ratio 13:1. 325 full-time faculty, 72% hold PhDs. 100% faculty teach undergrads.

ACADEMICS

Degrees: Associate, bachelor's, certificate, diploma, doctoral, master's, post-bachelor's certificate, post-master's certificate. **Academic Requirements:** Arts/fine arts, computer literacy, English (including composition), foreign languages, history, humanities, mathematics, philosophy, sciences (biological or physical), social science. **Classes:** Most classes have 10–19 students. Most lab/discussion sections have fewer than 10 students. **Majors with Highest Enrollment:** Architectural engineering technologies/technicians, communications studies/speech communication and rhetoric, psychology. **Disciplines with Highest Percentage of Degrees Awarded:** Visual and performing arts 19%, business/marketing 18%, communications/journalism 10%, health professions and related sciences 10%, education 9%, engineering 6%, engineering technologies 6%. **Special Study Options:** Cooperative education program, cross registration, distance learning, double major, dual enrollment, English as a second language (ESL), exchange student program (domestic), honors program, independent study, internships, liberal arts/career combination, student-designed major, study abroad, teacher certification program.

FACILITIES

Housing: Coed dorms, women's dorms, apartments for single students, special housing for disabled students, honors housing. **Special Academic Facilities/**

Equipment: Museum of Presidential Memorabilia, art gallery, off-campus child care center for student teaching, learning skills and language lab, audiovisual aids center, 8,000-acre environmental center. **Computers:** 100% of classrooms are wireless, 90% of public computers are PCs, 10% of public computers are Macs, network access in dorm rooms, online registration, online administrative functions (other than registration), remote student-access to Web through college's connection.

CAMPUS LIFE

Activities: Choral groups, concert band, dance, drama/theater, jazz band, literary magazine, music ensembles, musical theater, opera, pep band, radio station, student government, student newspaper, symphony orchestra, television station, yearbook. **Organizations:** 93 registered organizations, 22 honor societies, 7 religious organizations. 16 fraternities, 14 sororities **Athletics (Intercollegiate):** *Men:* Baseball, basketball, cross-country, golf, lacrosse, soccer, tennis, track/field (indoor), track/field (outdoor). *Women:* Basketball, cross-country, golf, soccer, softball, tennis, track/field (indoor), track/field (outdoor), volleyball.

ADMISSIONS

Freshman Academic Profile: 76% from public high schools. University of Hartford SAT Math middle 50% range 490–590. SAT Critical Reading middle 50% range 480–580. ACT middle 50% range 21–25. TOEFL required of all international applicants, minimum paper TOEFL 550, minimum computer TOEFL 213. **Basis for Candidate Selection:** *Very important factors considered include:* Rigor of secondary school record. *Important factors considered include:* Class rank, standardized test scores. *Other factors considered include:* Application essay, character/personal qualities, extracurricular activities, interview, recommendation(s), talent/ability. **Freshman Admission Requirements:** High school diploma is required, and GED is accepted. *Academic units required:* 4 English, 2 math, 2 science, 2 social studies, 2 history, 4 academic electives. *Academic units recommended:* 3 math, 3 science, 2 foreign language, 3 social studies. **Freshman Admission Statistics:** 12,065 applied, 66% admitted, 19% enrolled. **Transfer Admission Requirements:** College transcript(s). Minimum college GPA of 2.2 required. Lowest grade transferable C-. **General Admission Information:** Application fee $35. Regular notification is rolling. Non-fall registration accepted. Admission may be deferred for a maxiumum of 2 semesters. Common Application accepted. Credit and/or placement offered for CEEB Advanced Placement tests.

COSTS AND FINANCIAL AID

Annual tuition $24,576. Room & board $9,922. Required fees $1,190. Average book expense $860. **Required Forms and Deadlines:** FAFSA, institution's own financial aid form. Financial aid filing deadline 2/1. **Notification of Awards:** Applicants will be notified of awards on a rolling basis beginning on or about 3/1. **Types of Aid:** *Need-based scholarships/grants:* Pell, SEOG, state scholarships/grants, private scholarships, the school's own gift aid. *Loans:* FFEL Subsidized Stafford, FFEL Unsubsidized Stafford, FFEL PLUS, Federal Perkins. **Financial Aid Statistics:** 64% freshmen, 61% undergrads receive need-based scholarship or grant aid. 59% freshmen, 59% undergrads receive need-based self-help aid. 28 freshmen, 121 undergrads receive athletic scholarships. 97% freshmen, 95% undergrads receive any aid.

See page 1442.

UNIVERSITY OF HAWAII—HILO

200 West Kawili Street, Hilo, HI 96720-4091
Phone: 808-974-7414 **E-mail:** uhhadm@hawaii.edu
Fax: 808-933-0861 **Website:** www.uhh.hawaii.edu **ACT Code:** 0904
Financial Aid Phone: 808-974-7323

This public school was founded in 1970. It has a 225-acre campus.

RATINGS

Admissions Selectivity Rating: 83 **Fire Safety Rating:** 60* **Green Rating:** 60*

STUDENTS AND FACULTY

Enrollment: 3,148. **Student Body:** 60% female, 40% male, 35% out-of-state, 9% international. African American 1%, Asian 40%, Caucasian 36%, Hispanic 2%. **Retention and Graduation:** 66% freshmen return for sophomore year. 11% freshmen graduate within 4 years. **Faculty:** Student/faculty ratio 11:1. 238 full-time faculty, 63% hold PhDs. 100% faculty teach undergrads.

ACADEMICS

Degrees: Bachelor's, certificate, doctoral, first professional, master's, post-bachelor's certificate. **Academic Requirements:** English (including composition), Hawaiian/Asian/Pacific, humanities, mathematics, sciences (biological or physical), social science, world cultures, writing intensive. **Classes:** Most classes have 10–19 students. **Majors with Highest Enrollment:** Business, management, marketing, and related support services, psychology. **Disciplines with Highest Percentage of Degrees Awarded:** Social sciences 17%, psychology 15%, business/marketing 10%, communication technologies 8%, interdisciplinary studies 7%. **Special Study Options:** Cross registration, distance learning, double major, dual enrollment, English as a second language (ESL), exchange student program (domestic), honors program, independent study, internships, student-designed major, study abroad, teacher certification program.

FACILITIES

Housing: Coed dorms, apartments for married students, apartments for single students, special housing for disabled students. **Computers:** 100% of public computers are PCs, online registration, online administrative functions (other than registration), remote student-access to Web through college's connection.

CAMPUS LIFE

Activities: Choral groups, dance, drama/theater, jazz band, literary magazine, music ensembles, radio station, student government, student newspaper. **Organizations:** 43 registered organizations, 4 religious organizations. **Athletics (Intercollegiate):** *Men:* Baseball, basketball, cross-country, golf, tennis. *Women:* Cross-country, softball, tennis, volleyball.

ADMISSIONS

Freshman Academic Profile: 22% in top 10% of high school class, 46% in top 25% of high school class, 82% in top 50% of high school class. SAT Math middle 50% range 440–600. SAT Critical Reading middle 50% range 440–560. ACT middle 50% range 17–24. TOEFL required of all international applicants, minimum paper TOEFL 500, minimum computer TOEFL 173. **Basis for Candidate Selection:** *Very important factors considered include:* Rigor of secondary school record. *Important factors considered include:* Class rank, standardized test scores. *Other factors considered include:* Application essay, extracurricular activities, recommendation(s), talent/ability. **Freshman Admission Requirements:** High school diploma is required, and GED is accepted. *Academic units required:* 4 English, 3 math, 3 science (3 science labs), 7 academic electives. *Academic units recommended:* 4 English, 4 math, 4 science (3 science labs), 2 foreign language, 2 social studies, 2 history. **Freshman Admission Statistics:** 1,612 applied, 51% admitted, 57% enrolled. **Transfer Admission Requirements:** College transcript(s). Minimum college GPA of 2.0 required. Lowest grade transferable C. **General Admission Information:** Application fee $50. Regular application deadline 7/1. Regular notification is rolling. Non-fall registration accepted. Admission may be deferred for a maximum of 1 semester. Credit offered for CEEB Advanced Placement tests.

COSTS AND FINANCIAL AID

Annual in-state tuition $3,000. Out-of-state tuition $9,550. Room & board $6,292. Required fees $148. Average book expense $1,017. **Required Forms and Deadlines:** FAFSA. Financial aid filing deadline 3/1. **Notification of Awards:** Applicants will be notified of awards on or about 4/12. **Types of Aid:** *Need-based scholarships/grants:* Pell, SEOG, state scholarships/grants, private scholarships, the school's own gift aid. *Loans:* FFEL Subsidized Stafford, FFEL Unsubsidized Stafford, FFEL PLUS, Federal Perkins, state loans. **Student Employment:** Federal Work-Study Program available. Institutional employment available. **Financial Aid Statistics:** 35% freshmen, 23% undergrads receive need-based scholarship or grant aid. 30% freshmen, 20% undergrads receive need-based self-help aid. 102 freshmen, 14 undergrads receive athletic scholarships. Highest amount earned per year from on-campus jobs $1,832.

UNIVERSITY OF HAWAII—MANOA

2600 Campus Road, QLCSS Room 001, Honolulu, HI 96822
Phone: 808-956-8975 **E-mail:** ar-info@hawaii.edu **CEEB Code:** 4867
Fax: 808-956-4148 **Website:** www.manoa.hawaii.edu **ACT Code:** 0902
Financial Aid Phone: 808-956-7251

This public school was founded in 1907. It has a 320-acre campus.

RATINGS

Admissions Selectivity Rating: 84   **Fire Safety Rating:** 60*   **Green Rating:** 82

STUDENTS AND FACULTY

Enrollment: 13,542. **Student Body:** 55% female, 45% male, 26% out-of-state, 6% international (78 countries represented). African American 1%, Asian 63%, Caucasian 26%, Hispanic 2%. **Retention and Graduation:** 76% freshmen return for sophomore year. 12% freshmen graduate within 4 years. **Faculty:**

Student/faculty ratio 12:1. 1,180 full-time faculty, 88% hold PhDs. 83% faculty teach undergrads.

ACADEMICS

Degrees: Bachelor's, certificate, doctoral, first professional, master's, post-bachelor's certificate. **Academic Requirements:** Arts/fine arts, English (including composition), foreign languages, humanities, sciences (biological or physical), social science. **Classes:** Most classes have 10–19 students. Most lab/discussion sections have 10–19 students. **Majors with Highest Enrollment:** Art/art studies, biology/biological sciences, psychology. **Disciplines with Highest Percentage of Degrees Awarded:** Business/marketing 23%, social sciences 10%, education 9%, communications/journalism 6%, psychology 6%. **Special Study Options:** Contemporary ethical issues, cooperative education program, distance learning, double major, English as a second language (ESL), exchange student program (domestic), global and multicultural perspectives, Hawaiian/Asian/Pacific studies, honors program, independent study, internships, oral communication, student-designed major, study abroad, symbolic reasoning, teacher certification program.

FACILITIES

Housing: Coed dorms, apartments for married students, apartments for single students, special housing for disabled students. **Special Academic Facilities/Equipment:** UH Art & Commons Galleries, John Young Museum, John F. Kennedy Theatre, Lyon Arboretum, Waikiki Aquarium, Sunset (travel industry) Library, Chuck Gee Technology Learning Center, advanced computing research laboratory, environmental engineering lab, Hawaii Center for Advanced Communications, Coral Reef Science Laboratory, Korean Studies Building, Coconut Island marine biology labs, Wong Audio-Visual Center, speech and hearing and dental hygiene clinics, Hawaiian lo'i (garden), electron microscope and laser laboratories, ship and submersible research fleet, and Maui Super Computer, Jakuan Tea House. **Computers:** 77% of public computers are PCs, 20% of public computers are Macs, 3% of public computers are UNIX, network access in dorm rooms, network access in dorm lounges, online registration, online administrative functions (other than registration), remote student-access to Web through college's connection.

CAMPUS LIFE

Activities: Choral groups, concert band, dance, drama/theater, jazz band, literary magazine, marching band, music ensembles, pep band, radio station, student government, student newspaper, symphony orchestra, television station, yearbook. **Organizations:** 175 registered organizations, 7 honor societies, 23 religious organizations. 2 fraternities, 2 sororities. **Athletics (Intercollegiate):** *Men:* Archery, baseball, basketball, cheerleading, diving, football, golf, sailing, swimming, tennis, volleyball. *Women:* Basketball, cheerleading, cross-country, diving, golf, sailing, soccer, softball, swimming, tennis, track/field (outdoor), volleyball, water polo. **Environmental Initiatives:** Sustainable Saunders Campus Pilot Program. Coconut Island-Hawaii Institute of Marine Biology Lab 21 project. Start Up Kuleana Program Sustainability Volunteer Coordination.

ADMISSIONS

Freshman Academic Profile: 29% in top 10% of high school class, 60% in top 25% of high school class, 91% in top 50% of high school class. 44% from public high schools. SAT Math middle 50% range 510–610. SAT Critical Reading middle 50% range 480–580. SAT Writing middle 50% range 470–570. ACT middle 50% range 21–25. TOEFL required of all international applicants, minimum paper TOEFL 500, minimum computer TOEFL 173. **Basis for Candidate Selection:** *Very important factors considered include:* Academic GPA, rigor of secondary school record, standardized test scores. *Important factors considered include:* State residency. *Other factors considered include:* Application essay, class rank, extracurricular activities, geographical residence, interview, recommendation(s), talent/ability. **Freshman Admission Requirements:** High school diploma is required, and GED is accepted. *Academic units required:* 4 English, 3 math, 3 science (1 science lab), 3 social studies, 4 academic electives. *Academic units recommended:* 2 foreign language. **Freshman Admission Statistics:** 6,167 applied, 68% admitted, 42% enrolled. **Transfer Admission Requirements:** College transcript(s). Minimum college GPA of 2.5 required. Lowest grade transferable D. **General Admission Information:** Application fee $50. Regular application deadline 5/1. Regular notification is rolling. Non-fall registration accepted. Credit and/or placement offered for CEEB Advanced Placement tests.

COSTS AND FINANCIAL AID

Annual in-state tuition $5,952. Annual out-of-state tuition $16,608. Room and board $7,335. Required fees $255. Average book expense $1,179. **Required Forms and Deadlines:** FAFSA. Financial aid filing deadline 3/1. **Notification of Awards:** Applicants will be notified of awards on or about 4/1. **Types of Aid:** *Need-based scholarships/grants:* Pell, SEOG, state scholarships/grants, private scholarships, the school's own gift aid, Federal Nursing Scholarships. *Loans:* FFEL Subsidized Stafford, FFEL Unsubsidized Stafford, FFEL PLUS, Federal Perkins, Federal Nursing, state loans, college/university loans from institutional funds, Nursing Faculty Loan. **Student Employment:** Federal Work-Study Program available. Institutional employment available. Off-campus job opportunities are good. **Financial Aid Statistics:** 27% freshmen, 26% undergrads receive need-based scholarship or grant aid. 20% freshmen, 23% undergrads receive need-based self-help aid. 31 freshmen, 231 undergrads receive athletic scholarships. 44% freshmen, 41% undergrads receive any aid. Highest amount earned per year from on-campus jobs $7,987.

UNIVERSITY OF HAWAII—WEST OAHU

96-129 Ala Ike, Pearl City, HI 96782
Phone: 808-454-4700 **E-mail:** info@uhwo.hawaii.edu
Fax: 808-453-6075 **Website:** www.uhwo.hawaii.edu
Financial Aid Phone: 808-454-4700

This public school was founded in 1976.

RATINGS
Admissions Selectivity Rating: 60*　　**Fire Safety Rating:** 60*　　**Green Rating:** 60*

STUDENTS AND FACULTY
Enrollment: 838. **Student Body:** 68% female, 32% male, 8% out-of-state. African American 2%, Asian 62%, Caucasian 21%, Hispanic 3%. **Faculty:** Student/faculty ratio 13:1. 28 full-time faculty, 93% hold PhDs. 100% faculty teach undergrads.

ACADEMICS
Degrees: Bachelor's, certificate. **Academic Requirements:** English (including composition), history, humanities, mathematics, sciences (biological or physical), social science. **Classes:** Most classes have 20–29 students. **Majors with Highest Enrollment:** Business administration/management, psychology, public administration. **Disciplines with Highest Percentage of Degrees Awarded:** Business/marketing 34%, psychology 21%, security and protective services 17%, social sciences 16%, public administration and social services 7%. **Special Study Options:** Distance learning, double major, independent study, study abroad.

FACILITIES
Computers: 100% of public computers are PCs, online registration, remote student-access to Web through college's connection.

CAMPUS LIFE
Activities: Student government. **Organizations:** 10 registered organizations, 1 honor society.

ADMISSIONS
Freshman Academic Profile: TOEFL required of all international applicants, minimum paper TOEFL 550, minimum computer TOEFL 213. **Basis for Candidate Selection:** *Important factors considered include:* Academic GPA, rigor of secondary school record. *Other factors considered include:* Recommendation(s), standardized test scores. **Freshman Admission Requirements:** High school diploma or equivalent is not required. *Academic units required:* 4 English, 3 math, 3 science, 3 social studies, 5 academic electives, 4 college prep electives. *Academic units recommended:* 4 English, 3 math, 3 science, 3 social studies, 5 academic electives, 4 college prep electives. **Transfer Admission Requirements:** College transcript(s). Lowest grade transferable D. **General Admission Information:** Application fee $50. Regular application deadline 8/1. Regular notification is rolling. Non-fall registration accepted. Admission may be deferred for a maximum of 1 semester.

COSTS AND FINANCIAL AID
Annual in-state tuition $3,216. Out-of-state tuition $10,176. Required fees $10. Average book expense $1,048. **Required Forms and Deadlines:** FAFSA. Financial aid filing deadline 4/1. **Notification of Awards:** Applicants will be notified of awards on a rolling basis beginning on or about 3/1. **Types of Aid:** *Need-based scholarships/grants:* Pell, SEOG, state scholarships/grants, private scholarships. *Loans:* FFEL Subsidized Stafford, FFEL Unsubsidized Stafford. **Student Employment:** Federal Work-Study Program available. Institutional employment available. Off-campus job opportunities are good.

UNIVERSITY OF HOUSTON

Office of Admissions, 122 East Cullen Building, Houston, TX 77204-2023
Phone: 713-743-1010 **E-mail:** admissions@uh.edu **CEEB Code:** 6870
Fax: 713-743-9633 **Website:** www.uh.edu **ACT Code:** 4236
Financial Aid Phone: 713-743-9090

This public school was founded in 1927. It has a 551-acre campus.

RATINGS
Admissions Selectivity Rating: 79　　**Fire Safety Rating:** 60*　　**Green Rating:** 60*

STUDENTS AND FACULTY
Enrollment: 26,243. **Student Body:** 51% female, 49% male, 2% out-of-state, 4% international (140 countries represented). African American 15%, Asian 21%, Caucasian 36%, Hispanic 22%. **Retention and Graduation:** 77% freshmen return for sophomore year. 12% freshmen graduate within 4 years. **Faculty:** Student/faculty ratio 20:1. 1,204 full-time faculty, 81% hold PhDs. 73% faculty teach undergrads.

ACADEMICS
Degrees: Bachelor's, doctoral, first professional, master's. **Academic Requirements:** Arts/fine arts, English (including composition), history, humanities, mathematics, sciences (biological or physical), social science. **Classes:** Most classes have 20–29 students. Most lab/discussion sections have 10–19 students. **Majors with Highest Enrollment:** Business/commerce, engineering, psychology. **Disciplines with Highest Percentage of Degrees Awarded:** Business/marketing 33%, psychology 8%, social sciences 7%, communication technologies 6%, biological/life sciences 6%. **Special Study Options:** Accelerated program, cooperative education program, cross-registration, distance learning, double major, dual enrollment, English as a second language (ESL), exchange student program (domestic), honors program, independent study, internships, study abroad, teacher certification program, weekend college, academic enrichment programs, certification programs, affiliated studies, and continuing education.

FACILITIES
Housing: Coed dorms, apartments for married students, apartments for single students, special housing for disabled students, fraternity/sorority housing, special housing for honors students, upper level and graduate students. Cambridge Oaks & Cullen Oaks. **Special Academic Facilities/Equipment:** Art gallery, language lab, human development lab school, University Hilton (staffed in part by students in college of hotel and restaurant management), opera studio. **Computers:** 100% of classrooms are wired, 92% of classrooms are wireless, 75% of public computers are PCs, 15% of public computers are Macs, 10% of public computers are UNIX, network access in dorm rooms, network access in dorm lounges, online registration, online administrative functions (other than registration), support for handheld computing, remote student-access to Web through college's connection.

CAMPUS LIFE
Activities: Choral groups, concert band, dance, drama/theater, jazz band, literary magazine, marching band, music ensembles, musical theater, opera, pep band, radio station, student government, student newspaper, student-run film society, symphony orchestra, television station, yearbook. **Organizations:** 300 registered organizations, 25 honor societies, 39 religious organizations. 17 fraternities (4% men join), 16 sororities (3% women join). **Athletics (Intercollegiate):** *Men:* Baseball, basketball, cheerleading, cross-country, diving, football, golf, swimming, tennis, track/field (indoor), track/field (outdoor), volleyball, water polo. *Women:* Basketball, cheerleading, cross-country, diving, golf, soccer, softball, swimming, tennis, track/field (indoor), track/field (outdoor), volleyball, water polo.

ADMISSIONS
Freshman Academic Profile: 22% in top 10% of high school class, 53% in top 25% of high school class, 83% in top 50% of high school class. SAT Math middle 50% range 490–610. SAT Critical Reading middle 50% range 460–580. ACT middle 50% range 19–24. TOEFL required of all international applicants, minimum paper TOEFL 550, minimum computer TOEFL 213. **Basis for Candidate Selection:** *Very important factors considered include:* Academic GPA, class rank, rigor of secondary school record, standardized test scores. *Important factors considered include:* Talent/ability. *Other factors considered include:* Alumni/ae relation, application essay, geographical residence, recommendation(s). **Freshman Admission Requirements:** High school diploma is required, and GED is accepted. *Academic units required:* 4 English, 3 math, 2 science, (2 science labs), 2 social studies, 2 history. *Academic units recommended:* 2 foreign language. **Freshman Admission Statistics:** 9,935 applied, 75% admitted, 46% enrolled. **Transfer Admission Requirements:**

College transcript(s). Minimum college GPA of 2.0 required. Lowest grade transferable C-. **General Admission Information:** Application fee $50. Regular application deadline 4/1. Nonfall registration accepted. Admission may be deferred for a maximum of 1 year. Credit and/or placement offered for CEEB Advanced Placement tests.

COSTS AND FINANCIAL AID

Annual in-state tuition $4,260. Out-of-state tuition $12,510. Room & board $6,418. Required fees $2,649. Average book expense $1,050. **Required Forms and Deadlines:** FAFSA. Financial aid filing deadline 4/1. **Notification of Awards:** Applicants will be notified of awards on a rolling basis beginning on or about 5/1. **Types of Aid:** *Need-based scholarships/grants:* Pell, SEOG, state scholarships/grants, private scholarships, the school's own gift aid. *Loans:* FFEL Subsidized Stafford, FFEL Unsubsidized Stafford, FFEL PLUS, Federal Perkins, state loans. **Student Employment:** Federal Work-Study Program available. Institutional employment available. Off-campus job opportunities are good. **Financial Aid Statistics:** 48% freshmen, 44% undergrads receive need-based scholarship or grant aid. 30% freshmen, 36% undergrads receive need-based self-help aid. 55 freshmen, 265 undergrads receive athletic scholarships. 65% freshmen, 62% undergrads receive any aid. Highest amount earned per year from on-campus jobs $2,198.

UNIVERSITY OF HOUSTON—CLEAR LAKE

2700 Bay Area Boulevard, Houston, TX 77058-1098
Phone: 281-283-2521 **E-mail:** admissions@uhcl.edu **CEEB Code:** 6916
Fax: 281-283-2530 **Website:** www.uhcl.edu
Financial Aid Phone: 281-283-2480

This public school was founded in 1974. It has a 524-acre campus.

RATINGS
Admissions Selectivity Rating: 60*   **Fire Safety Rating:** 60*   **Green Rating:** 60*

STUDENTS AND FACULTY
Enrollment: 3,913. **Student Body:** 69% female, 31% male, 1% out-of-state. African American 7%, Asian 6%, Caucasian 69%, Hispanic 17%. **Faculty:** Student/faculty ratio 15:1. 230 full-time faculty, 90% hold PhDs. 70% faculty teach undergrads.

ACADEMICS
Degrees: Bachelor's, master's, post-bachelor's certificate, post-master's certificate. **Classes:** Most classes have 20–29 students. **Majors with Highest Enrollment:** Computer and information sciences, education. **Disciplines with Highest Percentage of Degrees Awarded:** Business/marketing 32%, interdisciplinary studies 19%, psychology 8%, computer and information sciences 5%. **Special Study Options:** Cooperative education program, distance learning, double major, dual enrollment, independent study, internships, student-designed major, study abroad, teacher certification program, weekend college.

FACILITIES
Housing: Privatized housing apartments. **Computers:** 60% of public computers are PCs, 30% of public computers are Macs, 10% of public computers are UNIX, online registration, remote student-access to Web through college's connection.

CAMPUS LIFE
Activities: Literary magazine, student government, student newspaper, student-run film society. **Organizations:** 70 registered organizations, 16 honor societies, 5 religious organizations.

ADMISSIONS
TOEFL required of all international applicants, minimum paper TOEFL 550, minimum computer TOEFL 213. **Transfer Admission Requirements:** College transcript(s), standardized test score, statement of good standing from prior institution(s). Minimum college GPA of 2.0 required. Lowest grade transferable D-. **General Admission Information:** Application fee $35. Regular application deadline 3/28. Non-fall registration accepted. Common Application not accepted.

COSTS AND FINANCIAL AID
Annual in-state tuition $2,010. Out-of-state tuition $10,952. Room $6,456. Required fees $2,643. **Required Forms and Deadlines:** FAFSA, institution's own financial aid form. Financial aid filing deadline 4/1. **Notification of Awards:** Applicants will be notified of awards on a rolling basis beginning on or about 6/1. **Types of Aid:** *Need-based scholarships/grants:* Pell, SEOG, state scholarships/grants, private scholarships, the school's own gift aid. *Loans:* FFEL

Subsidized Stafford, FFEL Unsubsidized Stafford, FFEL PLUS, Federal Perkins, college/university loans from institutional funds. **Student Employment:** Federal Work-Study Program available. Institutional employment available. Off-campus job opportunities are good. **Financial Aid Statistics:** 59% undergrads receive need-based scholarship or grant aid. 82% undergrads receive need-based self-help aid.

See page 1444.

UNIVERSITY OF HOUSTON—DOWNTOWN

Admissions Office, One Main Street, Houston, TX 77002-1001
Phone: 713-221-8522 **E-mail:** uhdadmit@dt.uh.edu
Fax: 713-221-5220 **Website:** www.udh.edu
Financial Aid Phone: 713-221-8041

This public school was founded in 1974.

RATINGS
Admissions Selectivity Rating: 60*   **Fire Safety Rating:** 60*   **Green Rating:** 60*

STUDENTS AND FACULTY
Enrollment: 11,344. **Student Body:** 59% female, 41% male, 1% out-of-state, 3% international (73 countries represented). African American 26%, Asian 10%, Caucasian 23%, Hispanic 38%. **Retention and Graduation:** 52% freshmen return for sophomore year. 2% freshmen graduate within 4 years. **Faculty:** Student/faculty ratio 20:1. 292 full-time faculty, 80% hold PhDs. 100% faculty teach undergrads.

ACADEMICS
Degrees: Bachelor's, master's. **Academic Requirements:** Arts/fine arts, computer literacy, English (including composition), history, humanities, literature, mathematics, political science, sciences (biological or physical), social science, speech. **Classes:** Most classes have 20–29 students. Most lab/discussion sections have 20–29 students. **Majors with Highest Enrollment:** Accounting, criminal justice/safety studies, finance. **Disciplines with Highest Percentage of Degrees Awarded:** Business/marketing 44%, liberal arts/general studies 21%, security and protective services 9%, interdisciplinary studies 6%, psychology 6%, English 4%. **Special Study Options:** Cooperative education program, distance learning, double major, dual enrollment, English as a second language (ESL), honors program, independent study, internships, study abroad, teacher certification program, weekend college.

FACILITIES
Computers: 100% of classrooms are wireless, 50% of public computers are PCs, 50% of public computers are UNIX, online registration, online administrative functions (other than registration).

CAMPUS LIFE
Activities: Drama/theater, jazz band, literary magazine, student government, student newspaper. **Organizations:** 52 registered organizations, 3 honor societies, 2 religious organizations. 4 fraternities, 4 sororities. **Athletics (Intercollegiate):** *Men:* Badminton, basketball, bowling, football, soccer, softball, tennis, volleyball, weight lifting. *Women:* Badminton, basketball, bowling, soccer, softball, tennis, volleyball, weight lifting.

ADMISSIONS
Freshman Academic Profile: TOEFL required of all international applicants, minimum paper TOEFL 550, minimum computer TOEFL 213. **Freshman Admission Requirements:** High school diploma is required, and GED is accepted. *Academic units recommended:* 4 English, 3 math, 3 science, 3 foreign language, 3 social studies, 1 academic elective (economics, fine arts, health education, physical education, speech, and technology). **Freshman Admission Statistics:** 1,957 applied, 99% admitted, 50% enrolled. **Transfer Admission Requirements:** College transcript(s). Lowest grade transferable C. **General Admission Information:** Application fee $35. Regular application deadline 7/1. Regular notification on a rolling basis. Non-fall registration accepted. Admission may be deferred for a maximum of text. Credit offered for CEEB Advanced Placement tests.

COSTS AND FINANCIAL AID
Annual in-state tuition $2,898. Out-of-state tuition $9,498. Required fees $758. Average book expense $1,020. **Required Forms and Deadlines:** FAFSA. Financial aid filing deadline 4/1. **Notification of Awards:** Applicants will be notified of awards on a rolling basis beginning on or about 4/1. **Types of Aid:** *Need-based scholarships/grants:* Pell, SEOG, state scholarships/grants, private scholarships, the school's own gift aid. *Loans:* FFEL Subsidized Stafford, FFEL Unsubsidized Stafford, FFEL PLUS, state loans. **Financial Aid Statistics:**

62% freshmen, 70% undergrads receive need-based scholarship or grant aid. 23% freshmen, 47% undergrads receive need-based self-help aid. 35% freshmen, 77% undergrads receive any aid.

UNIVERSITY OF HOUSTON—VICTORIA

Admissions and Records, UW #104, 3007 North Ben Wilson, Victoria, TX 77901-4450
Phone: 361-570-4110 **E-mail:** admissions@uhv.edu
Fax: 361-570-4114 **Website:** www.uhv.edu
Financial Aid Phone: 316-570-4131

This public school was founded in 1973.

RATINGS
Admissions Selectivity Rating: 60*   **Fire Safety Rating:** 60*   **Green Rating:** 60*

STUDENTS AND FACULTY
Enrollment: 1,299. **Student Body:** 74% female, 26% male, 1% out-of-state. African American 8%, Asian 3%, Caucasian 63%, Hispanic 23%, Native American 1%. **Faculty:** Student/faculty ratio 16:1. 73 full-time faculty, 99% hold PhDs. 90% faculty teach undergrads.

ACADEMICS
Degrees: Bachelor's, master's, post-bachelor's certificate, post-master's certificate. **Academic Requirements:** English (including composition). **Majors with Highest Enrollment:** Business administration/management, education, multi/interdisciplinary studies. **Disciplines with Highest Percentage of Degrees Awarded:** Education 35%, business/marketing 16%, psychology 9%, computer and information sciences 7%. **Special Study Options:** Distance learning, double major, independent study, internships, study abroad, teacher certification program.

FACILITIES
Computers: 100% of public computers are PCs, online registration, online administrative functions (other than registration), remote student-access to Web through college's connection.

CAMPUS LIFE
Activities: Student government, student newspaper.

ADMISSIONS
Freshman Academic Profile: Minimum paper TOEFL 500. **Transfer Admission Requirements:** College transcript(s), standardized test score, statement of good standing from prior institution(s). Minimum college GPA of 2.0 required. Lowest grade transferable C.

COSTS AND FINANCIAL AID
Required Forms and Deadlines: FAFSA, institution's own financial aid form. **Types of Aid:** *Need-based scholarships/grants:* Pell, SEOG, state scholarships/grants, private scholarships, the school's own gift aid. *Loans:* FFEL Subsidized Stafford, FFEL Unsubsidized Stafford, FFEL PLUS, state loans. **Student Employment:** Federal Work-Study Program available. Institutional employment available. Off-campus job opportunities are good. **Financial Aid Statistics:** 34% undergrads receive need-based scholarship or grant aid. 26% undergrads receive need-based self-help aid.

UNIVERSITY OF IDAHO

UI Admissions Office, PO Box 444264, Moscow, ID 83844-4264
Phone: 208-885-6326 **E-mail:** admappl@uidaho.edu **CEEB Code:** 4843
Fax: 208-885-9119 **Website:** www.uihome.uidaho.edu/uihome **ACT Code:** 0928
Financial Aid Phone: 208-885-6312

This public school was founded in 1889. It has a 12,500-acre campus.

RATINGS
Admissions Selectivity Rating: 78   **Fire Safety Rating:** 60*   **Green Rating:** 89

STUDENTS AND FACULTY
Enrollment: 8,636. **Student Body:** 45% female, 55% male, 26% out-of-state, 2% international. African American 1%, Asian 2%, Caucasian 84%, Hispanic 5%, Native American 1%. **Retention and Graduation:** 76% freshmen return for sophomore year. 21% freshmen graduate within 4 years. **Faculty:** Student/faculty ratio 18:1. 548 full-time faculty, 84% hold PhDs. 82% faculty teach undergrads.

ACADEMICS
Degrees: Bachelor's, certificate, doctoral, first professional, master's, post-master's certificate. **Academic Requirements:** Foreign languages, history, mathematics, sciences (biological or physical), social science. **Classes:** Most classes have 20–29 students. Most lab/discussion sections have 10–19 students. **Majors with Highest Enrollment:** Elementary education and teaching, mechanical engineering, psychology. **Disciplines with Highest Percentage of Degrees Awarded:** Business/marketing 14%, education 11%, engineering 11%, communications/journalism 7%, natural resources/environmental science 7%. **Special Study Options:** Accelerated program, cooperative education program, cross registration, distance learning, double major, dual enrollment, English as a second language (ESL), exchange student program (domestic), honors program, independent study, internships, student-designed major, study abroad, teacher certification program.

FACILITIES
Housing: Coed dorms, men's dorms, women's dorms, apartments for married students, apartments for single students, special housing for disabled students, special housing for international students, fraternity/sorority housing, cooperative housing. **Special Academic Facilities/Equipment:** On-campus preschool, experimental forest, electron microscope. **Computers:** 10% of classrooms are wired, 100% of classrooms are wireless, 95% of public computers are PCs, 5% of public computers are Macs, network access in dorm rooms, network access in dorm lounges, online registration, online administrative functions (other than registration), support for handheld computing, remote student-access to Web through college's connection.

CAMPUS LIFE
Activities: Choral groups, concert band, dance, drama/theater, jazz band, literary magazine, marching band, music ensembles, musical theater, opera, pep band, radio station, student government, student newspaper, student-run film society, symphony orchestra, television station. **Organizations:** 186 registered organizations, 13 honor societies, 17 religious organizations. 18 fraternities, 8 sororities. **Athletics (Intercollegiate):** *Men:* Basketball, cross-country, football, golf, track/field (indoor), track/field (outdoor). *Women:* Basketball, cross-country, golf, soccer, swimming, track/field (indoor), track/field (outdoor), volleyball. **Environmental Initiatives:** $35 mil ESCO for energy conservation projects currently underway. Built institutional infrastructure: Hired a Sustainability Coordinator, launched a Sustainability Center, formed committees, task forces, etc. to assess and develop long-term plans for sustainability issues. Converted steam plant to a biomass boiler.

ADMISSIONS
Freshman Academic Profile: 20% in top 10% of high school class, 45% in top 25% of high school class, 77% in top 50% of high school class. 90% from public high schools. SAT Math middle 50% range 480–600. SAT Critical Reading middle 50% range 480–600. SAT Writing middle 50% range 450–570. ACT middle 50% range 20–25. TOEFL required of all international applicants, minimum paper TOEFL 525, minimum computer TOEFL 193. **Basis for Candidate Selection:** *Very important factors considered include:* Rigor of secondary school record, standardized test scores. **Freshman Admission Requirements:** High school diploma is required, and GED is accepted. *Academic units required:* 4 English, 3 math, 3 science (1 science lab), 1 foreign language, 2 social studies, 1 academic elective. **Freshman Admission Statistics:** 4,324 applied, 80% admitted, 47% enrolled. **Transfer Admission Requirements:** College transcript(s). Minimum college GPA of 2.0 required. Lowest grade transferable D. **General Admission Information:** Application fee $40. Regular application deadline 8/1. Regular notification on a rolling basis throughout the year. Non-fall registration accepted. Admission may be deferred for a maximum of 2 years. Credit and/or placement offered for CEEB Advanced Placement tests.

COSTS AND FINANCIAL AID
Annual out-of-state tuition $10,080. Room and board $6,424. Required fees $4,410. Average book expense $1,430. **Required Forms and Deadlines:** FAFSA. Financial aid filing deadline 2/15. **Notification of Awards:** Applicants will be notified of awards on or about 3/30. **Types of Aid:** *Need-based scholarships/grants:* Pell, SEOG, state scholarships/grants, private scholarships, the school's own gift aid. *Loans:* Direct Subsidized Stafford, Direct Unsubsidized Stafford, Direct PLUS, Federal Perkins, college/university loans from institutional funds. **Student Employment:** Off-campus job opportunities are good. **Financial Aid Statistics:** 32% freshmen, 37% undergrads receive need-based scholarship or grant aid. 45% freshmen, 50% undergrads receive need-based self-help aid. 57 freshmen, 278 undergrads receive athletic scholarships. 55% freshmen, 56% undergrads receive any aid.

UNIVERSITY OF ILLINOIS AT CHICAGO

Box 5220, Chicago, IL 60680
Phone: 312-996-4350 **E-mail:** uicadmit@uic.edu **CEEB Code:** 1851
Fax: 312-413-7628 **Website:** www.uic.edu **ACT Code:** 1155
Financial Aid Phone: 312-996-5563

This public school was founded in 1982. It has a 218-acre campus.

RATINGS
Admissions Selectivity Rating: 76   **Fire Safety Rating:** 60*   **Green Rating:** 86

STUDENTS AND FACULTY
Enrollment: 15,828. **Student Body:** 55% female, 45% male, 2% out-of-state, 2% international (87 countries represented). African American 9%, Asian 24%, Caucasian 44%, Hispanic 17%. **Retention and Graduation:** 79% freshmen return for sophomore year. 9% freshmen graduate within 4 years. **Faculty:** Student/faculty ratio 14:1. 1,249 full-time faculty, 88% hold PhDs. 82% faculty teach undergrads.

ACADEMICS
Degrees: Bachelor's, doctoral, first professional certificate, first professional, master's. **Academic Requirements:** English (including composition), humanities, sciences (biological or physical), social science. **Classes:** Most classes have 20–29 students. Most lab/discussion sections have 20–29 students. **Majors with Highest Enrollment:** Information science/studies, psychology. **Disciplines with Highest Percentage of Degrees Awarded:** Business/ marketing 21%, engineering 11%, psychology 11%, health professions and related sciences 9%, biological/life sciences 8%, social sciences 8%, English 6%. **Special Study Options:** Accelerated program, concurrent registration at another campus of the university of Illinois, cooperative education program, distance learning, double major, English as a second language (ESL), exchange student program (domestic), honors program, independent study, internships, student-designed major, study abroad, teacher certification program.

FACILITIES
Housing: Coed dorms, apartments for single students, honors floor, special interest floors, presidential award house. **Special Academic Facilities/ Equipment:** Art galleries, multimedia lecture centers, Jane Addams Hull House museum, James Woodworth prairie preserve, convention/sports/ entertainment center, laboratory facilities. **Computers:** Network access in dorm rooms, network access in dorm lounges, online registration, remote student-access to Web through college's connection.

CAMPUS LIFE
Activities: Choral groups, concert band, dance, drama/theater, jazz band, literary magazine, music ensembles, musical theater, pep band, radio station, student government, student newspaper. **Organizations:** 200 registered organizations, 11 fraternities (3% men join), 13 sororities (3% women join). **Athletics (Intercollegiate):** *Men:* Baseball, basketball, cross-country, diving, gymnastics, soccer, swimming, tennis, track/field (outdoor). *Women:* Basketball, cross-country, diving, gymnastics, softball, swimming, tennis, track/field (outdoor), volleyball. **Environmental Initiatives:** Establishment of Office of Sustainability and appointment of interim associate chancellor for sustainability. Signing up for earth hour—turing out the lights for an hour on March 29, 2009. Formation of a chancellor's committee on sustainability.

ADMISSIONS
Freshman Academic Profile: 24% in top 10% of high school class, 60% in top 25% of high school class, 93% in top 50% of high school class. 79% from public high schools. ACT middle 50% range 21–26. TOEFL required of all interna- tional applicants, minimum paper TOEFL 520, minimum computer TOEFL 190. **Basis for Candidate Selection:** *Very important factors considered include:* Class rank, rigor of secondary school record, standardized test scores. *Other factors considered include:* Application essay, character/personal qualities, racial/ethnic status, recommendation(s), talent/ability, volunteer work, work experience. **Freshman Admission Requirements:** High school diploma is required, and GED is accepted. *Academic units required:* 4 English, 3 math, 3 science (3 science labs), 2 social studies, 1 history, 3 academic electives. *Academic units recommended:* 3 math, 4 foreign language. **Freshman Admission Statistics:** 9,512 applied, 64% admitted, 45% enrolled. **Transfer Admission Requirements:** College transcript(s), statement of good standing from prior institution(s). Minimum college GPA of 2.2 required. Lowest grade transferable D. **General Admission Information:** Application fee $40. Regular application deadline 1/15. Regular notification is rolling. Non-fall registration accepted. Common Application not accepted. Credit and/or placement offered for CEEB Advanced Placement tests.

COSTS AND FINANCIAL AID
Annual in-state tuition $7,424. Annual out-of-state tuition $19,814. Room and board $7,818. Required fees $3,122. Average book expense $1,200. **Required Forms and Deadlines:** FAFSA. Financial aid filing deadline 3/1. **Notification of Awards:** Applicants will be notified of awards on a rolling basis beginning on or about 4/15. **Types of Aid:** *Need-based scholarships/grants:* Pell, SEOG, state scholarships/grants, private scholarships, the school's own gift aid, Federal Nursing Scholarships. *Loans:* Direct Subsidized Stafford, Direct Unsubsidized Stafford, Direct PLUS, Federal Perkins, Federal Nursing, college/university loans from institutional funds. **Student Employment:** Federal Work-Study Program available. Institutional employment available. Off-campus job opportunities are excellent. **Financial Aid Statistics:** 60% freshmen, 57% undergrads receive need-based scholarship or grant aid. 29% freshmen, 37% undergrads receive need-based self-help aid. Highest amount earned per year from on-campus jobs $2,200.

UNIVERSITY OF ILLINOIS AT SPRINGFIELD

One University Plaza, MS UHB 1080, Springfield, IL 62703-5407
Phone: 217-206-4847 **E-mail:** admissions@uis.edu **CEEB Code:** 0834
Fax: 217-206-6620 **Website:** www.uis.edu **ACT Code:** 1137
Financial Aid Phone: 217-206-6724

This public school was founded in 1969. It has a 746-acre campus.

RATINGS
Admissions Selectivity Rating: 60*   **Fire Safety Rating:** 60*   **Green Rating:** 73

STUDENTS AND FACULTY
Enrollment: 2,604. **Student Body:** 58% female, 42% male, 10% out-of-state. African American 10%, Asian 3%, Caucasian 77%, Hispanic 2%. **Retention and Graduation:** 78% freshmen return for sophomore year. **Faculty:** Student/ faculty ratio 12:1. 199 full-time faculty, 91% hold PhDs. 100% faculty teach undergrads.

ACADEMICS
Degrees: Bachelor's, doctoral, master's, post-bachelor's certificate, post- master's certificate. **Academic Requirements:** Arts/fine arts, English (including composition), humanities, life sciences, mathematics, sciences (biological or physical), social science. **Classes:** Most classes have 10–19 students. **Majors with Highest Enrollment:** Business administration/ management, liberal arts and sciences/liberal studies, psychology. **Disciplines with Highest Percentage of Degrees Awarded:** Business/marketing 21%, psychology 13%, liberal arts/general studies 9%, communications/journalism 8%, security and protective services 8%, computer and information sciences 7%. **Special Study Options:** Distance learning, English as a second language (ESL), honors program, independent study, internships, study abroad, teacher certification program.

FACILITIES
Housing: Coed dorms, apartments for married students, apartments for single students, special housing for disabled students, special housing for international students, family housing. **Special Academic Facilities/Equipment:** Norris L. Brookens Library, Sangamon Auditorium, observatory. **Computers:** Network access in dorm rooms, online registration, online administrative functions (other than registration), remote student-access to Web through college's connection.

CAMPUS LIFE
Activities: Choral groups, concert band, dance, drama/theater, jazz band, music ensembles, pep band, student government, student newspaper, student-run film society. **Organizations:** 64 registered organizations, **Athletics (Intercolle- giate):** *Men:* Basketball, soccer, tennis. *Women:* Basketball, cheerleading, softball, tennis, volleyball. **Environmental Initiatives:** Construction of a residence hall with a "green roof." With the support of a grant from the State of Illinois, the university has expanded the recycling program from only academic buildings to include housing. The university has committed 1.95 million dollars to retrofit old single glazed windows in one campus building with double-glazed windows for energy conservation.

ADMISSIONS
Freshman Academic Profile: 95% from public high schools. ACT middle 50% range 19–27. TOEFL required of all international applicants, minimum paper TOEFL 500, minimum computer TOEFL 173. **Basis for Candidate Selection:** *Important factors considered include:* Academic GPA, application essay, class rank, rigor of secondary school record, standardized test scores. *Other factors considered include:* Character/personal qualities, extracurricular activities, first generation, level of applicant's interest, recommendation(s),

volunteer work, work experience. **Freshman Admission Requirements:** High school diploma is required, and GED is accepted. *Academic units required:* 4 English, 3 math, 3 science, 2 foreign language, 3 social studies. **Freshman Admission Statistics:** 1,075 applied, 62% admitted, 37% enrolled. **Transfer Admission Requirements:** College transcript(s). Minimum college GPA of 2.0 required. Lowest grade transferable D-. **General Admission Information:** Application fee $40. Regular notification is rolling. Non-fall registration not accepted. Credit and/or placement offered for CEEB Advanced Placement tests.

COSTS AND FINANCIAL AID

Required Forms and Deadlines: FAFSA. Financial aid filing deadline 4/1. **Notification of Awards:** Applicants will be notified of awards on a rolling basis beginning on or about 1/1. **Types of Aid:** *Need-based scholarships/grants:* Pell, SEOG, state scholarships/grants, private scholarships, the school's own gift aid. *Loans:* Direct Subsidized Stafford, Direct Unsubsidized Stafford, Direct PLUS, Federal Perkins, college/university loans from institutional funds. **Financial Aid Statistics:** 26% freshmen, 42% undergrads receive need-based scholarship or grant aid. 41% freshmen, 48% undergrads receive need-based self-help aid. 3 freshmen, 17 undergrads receive athletic scholarships.

UNIVERSITY OF ILLINOIS AT URBANA-CHAMPAIGN

901 West Illinois Street, Urbana, IL 61801
Phone: 217-333-0302 **E-mail:** ugradadmissions@uiuc.edu **CEEB Code:** 4607
Fax: 217-244-0903 **Website:** www.uiuc.edu **ACT Code:** 1154
Financial Aid Phone: 217-333-0100

This public school was founded in 1867. It has a 4,724-acre campus.

RATINGS

Admissions Selectivity Rating: 89   Fire Safety Rating: 63   Green Rating: 92

STUDENTS AND FACULTY

Enrollment: 30,721. **Student Body:** 47% female, 53% male, 7% out-of-state, 5% international (120 countries represented). African American 7%, Asian 12%, Caucasian 67%, Hispanic 7%. **Retention and Graduation:** 93% freshmen return for sophomore year. 61% freshmen graduate within 4 years. 26% grads go on to further study within 1 year. 4% grads pursue arts and sciences degrees. 2% grads pursue business degrees. 3% grads pursue law degrees. 3% grads pursue medical degrees. **Faculty:** Student/faculty ratio 17:1. 1,988 full-time faculty, 92% hold PhDs. 70% faculty teach undergrads.

ACADEMICS

Degrees: Bachelor's, certificate, doctoral, first professional, master's, post-bachelor's certificate, post-master's certificate. **Academic Requirements:** Cultural studies, English (including composition), foreign languages, history, humanities, mathematics, philosophy, sciences (biological or physical), social science. **Classes:** Most classes have 20–29 students. Most lab/discussion sections have 20–29 students. **Majors with Highest Enrollment:** Cell/cellular and molecular biology, political science and government, psychology. **Disciplines with Highest Percentage of Degrees Awarded:** Business/marketing 15%, engineering 15%, social sciences 10%, English 7%, biological/life sciences 7%, psychology 7%. **Special Study Options:** Accelerated program, cooperative education program, cross registration, distance learning, double major, dual enrollment, English as a second language (ESL), entrepreneurial programs, exchange student program (domestic), honors program, Illinois Leadership Program, independent study, internships, liberal arts/career combination, student-designed major, study abroad, teacher certification program.

FACILITIES

Housing: Coed dorms, men's dorms, women's dorms, apartments for married students, apartments for single students, special housing for disabled students, special housing for international students, fraternity/sorority housing, cooperative housing, living and learning. **Special Academic Facilities/ Equipment:** Art, cultural, and natural history museums; performing arts center; National Center for Supercomputing Applications; Beckman Institute; Siebel Computer Science Center; university library (56 separate libraries and

centers on campus); Japan House and Gardens; assembly hall for large concerts; Allerton Park and Conference Center; arboretum; the Illini Student Union. **Computers:** 16% of classrooms are wired, 65% of classrooms are wireless, 75% of public computers are PCs, 15% of public computers are Macs, 10% of public computers are UNIX, network access in dorm rooms, network access in dorm lounges, online registration, online administrative functions (other than registration), support for handheld computing, remote student-access to Web through college's connection.

CAMPUS LIFE

Activities: Choral groups, concert band, dance, drama/theater, jazz band, literary magazine, marching band, music ensembles, musical theater, opera, pep band, radio station, student government, student newspaper, student-run film society, symphony orchestra, television station. **Organizations:** 1,000 registered organizations, 30 honor societies, 95 religious organizations. 60 fraternities (22% men join), 36 sororities (23% women join). **Athletics (Intercollegiate):** *Men:* Baseball, basketball, cheerleading, cross-country, football, golf, gymnastics, tennis, track/field (outdoor), wrestling. *Women:* Basketball, cheerleading, cross-country, diving, golf, gymnastics, soccer, softball, swimming, tennis, track/field (outdoor), volleyball. **Environmental Initiatives:** $66 million LEED—Gold College of Business building will be dedicated in 2008. We are restructuring our energy accounting system and will now charge units for the energy they use and reward them for using less energy. We are investing $100 million in building retrofits and updates to make our facilities more sustainable, use less energy, and reduce campus sprawl.

ADMISSIONS

Freshman Academic Profile: 55% in top 10% of high school class, 96% in top 25% of high school class, 99% in top 50% of high school class. 75% from public high schools. SAT Math middle 50% range 630–740. SAT Critical Reading middle 50% range 540–670. ACT middle 50% range 26–31. TOEFL required of all international applicants, minimum paper TOEFL 550, minimum computer TOEFL 213. **Basis for Candidate Selection:** *Very important factors considered include:* Academic GPA, application essay, class rank, rigor of secondary school record, standardized test scores. *Important factors considered include:* Character/personal qualities, extracurricular activities, first generation, talent/ability, volunteer work, work experience. *Other factors considered include:* Geographical residence, racial/ethnic status, state residency. **Freshman Admission Requirements:** High school diploma is required, and GED is accepted. *Academic units required:* 4 English, 3 math, 2 science (2 science labs), 2 foreign language, 2 social studies, 2 academic electives. **Freshman Admission Statistics:** 22,367 applied, 65% admitted, 50% enrolled. **Transfer Admission Requirements:** High school transcript, college transcript(s), essay or personal statement. Lowest grade transferable D. **General Admission Information:** Application fee $40. Regular application deadline 1/2. Regular notification 12/15. Non-fall registration not accepted. Admission may be deferred for a maxiumum of 2 semesters. Credit and/or placement offered for CEEB Advanced Placement tests.

COSTS AND FINANCIAL AID

Annual in-state tuition $8,502. Annual out-of-state tuition $21,895. Room and board $8,196. Required fees $2,001. Average book expense $1,200. **Required Forms and Deadlines:** FAFSA. Financial aid filing deadline 3/15. **Notification of Awards:** Applicants will be notified of awards on a rolling basis beginning on or about 3/15. **Types of Aid:** *Need-based scholarships/grants:* Pell, SEOG, state scholarships/grants, private scholarships, the school's own gift aid, United Negro College Fund. *Loans:* Direct Subsidized Stafford, Direct Unsubsidized Stafford, Direct PLUS, Federal Perkins, college/university loans from institutional funds, alternative loans. **Financial Aid Statistics:** 25% freshmen, 26% undergrads receive need-based scholarship or grant aid. 31% freshmen, 32% undergrads receive need-based self-help aid. 57 freshmen, 342 undergrads receive athletic scholarships. 40% freshmen, 38% undergrads receive any aid. Highest amount earned per year from on-campus jobs $13,121.

UNIVERSITY OF THE INCARNATE WORD

4301 Broadway, Box 285, San Antonio, TX 78209-6397
Phone: 210-829-6005 **E-mail:** admis@universe.uiwtx.edu
Fax: 210-829-3921 **Website:** www.uiw.edu **ACT Code:** 4106
Financial Aid Phone: 210-829-6008

This private school, affiliated with the Roman Catholic Church, was founded in 1881. It has a 100-acre campus.

RATINGS

Admissions Selectivity Rating: 76   Fire Safety Rating: 60*   Green Rating: 60*

STUDENTS AND FACULTY

Enrollment: 3,943. **Student Body:** 66% female, 34% male, 3% out-of-state, 4% international. African American 7%, Asian 2%, Caucasian 25%, Hispanic 54%. **Retention and Graduation:** 70% freshmen return for sophomore year. **Faculty:** Student/faculty ratio 14:1. 148 full-time faculty, 67% hold PhDs.

ACADEMICS

Degrees: Associate, bachelor's, doctoral, master's, post-bachelor's certificate, post-master's certificate. **Academic Requirements:** Arts/fine arts, computer literacy, English (including composition), foreign languages, history, humanities, mathematics, philosophy, sciences (biological or physical), social science. **Classes:** Most classes have 10–19 students. Most lab/discussion sections have 20–29 students. **Majors with Highest Enrollment:** Business administration/management, education, nursing/registered nurse training (ASN, BSN, MSN, RN). **Disciplines with Highest Percentage of Degrees Awarded:** Business/marketing 42%, liberal arts/general studies 10%, health professions and related sciences 9%, visual and performing arts 9%, communication technologies 5%, education 5%, psychology 5%, biological/life sciences 3%, social sciences 3%. **Special Study Options:** Accelerated program, cooperative education program, cross registration, distance learning, double major, dual enrollment, English as a second language (ESL), exchange student program (domestic), honors program, independent study, internships, study abroad, teacher certification program.

FACILITIES

Housing: Coed dorms, men's dorms, women's dorms, apartments for single students. **Computers:** 38% of public computers are PCs, 2% of public computers are Macs, network access in dorm rooms, network access in dorm lounges, online registration, online administrative functions (other than registration), remote student-access to Web through college's connection.

CAMPUS LIFE

Activities: Choral groups, concert band, dance, drama/theater, jazz band, literary magazine, music ensembles, musical theater, student government, student newspaper. **Organizations:** 35 registered organizations, 7 honor societies, 1 religious organization. 1 fraternity (2% men join), 3 sororities (2% women join). **Athletics (Intercollegiate):** *Men:* Baseball, basketball, cheerleading, cross-country, golf, soccer, tennis. *Women:* Basketball, cheerleading, cross-country, golf, soccer, softball, swimming, tennis, volleyball.

ADMISSIONS

Freshman Academic Profile: 16% in top 10% of high school class, 40% in top 25% of high school class, 69% in top 50% of high school class. SAT Math middle 50% range 420–520. SAT Critical Reading middle 50% range 430–530. ACT middle 50% range 17–21. TOEFL required of all international applicants, minimum paper TOEFL 550, minimum computer TOEFL 213. **Basis for Candidate Selection:** *Very important factors considered include:* Rigor of secondary school record. *Important factors considered include:* Standardized test scores. *Other factors considered include:* Alumni/ae relation, character/personal qualities, class rank, extracurricular activities, geographical residence, interview, racial/ethnic status, recommendation(s), talent/ability, volunteer work, work experience. **Freshman Admission Requirements:** High school diploma is required, and GED is accepted. *Academic units required:* 4 English, 3 math, 3 science, 2 foreign language, 3 social studies, 1 fine art. *Academic units recommended:* 4 English, 4 math, 3 science, 2 foreign language, 4 social studies, 1 fine art. **Freshman Admission Statistics:** 1,952 applied, 75% admitted, 34% enrolled. **Transfer Admission Requirements:** College transcript(s). Minimum college GPA of 2.5 required. Lowest grade transferable C. **General Admission Information:** Application fee $20. Regular notification is rolling. Non-fall registration accepted. Common Application not accepted. Credit and/or placement offered for CEEB Advanced Placement tests.

COSTS AND FINANCIAL AID

Annual tuition $16,500. Room & board $6,050. Required fees $752. Average book expense $1,000. **Required Forms and Deadlines:** FAFSA. Financial aid filing deadline 4/1. **Notification of Awards:** Applicants will be notified of awards on a rolling basis beginning on or about 2/15. **Types of Aid:** *Need-based scholarships/grants:* Pell, SEOG, state scholarships/grants, private scholarships, the school's own gift aid, United Negro College Fund, Federal Nursing Scholarships. *Loans:* FFEL Subsidized Stafford, FFEL Unsubsidized Stafford, FFEL PLUS, Federal Perkins, Federal Nursing, state loans, private loans. **Student Employment:** Federal Work-Study Program available. Institutional employment available. Off-campus job opportunities are good. **Financial Aid Statistics:** 76% freshmen, 70% undergrads receive need-based scholarship or grant aid. 48% freshmen, 60% undergrads receive need-based self-help aid. 7 freshmen, 75 undergrads receive athletic scholarships. 85% freshmen, 78% undergrads receive any aid.

UNIVERSITY OF INDIANAPOLIS

1400 East Hanna Avenue, Indianapolis, IN 46227-3697
Phone: 317-788-3216 **E-mail:** admissions@uindy.edu **CEEB Code:** 1321
Fax: 317-788-3300 **Website:** www.uindy.edu **ACT Code:** 1204
Financial Aid Phone: 317-788-3217

This private school, affiliated with the Methodist Church, was founded in 1902. It has a 65-acre campus.

RATINGS

Admissions Selectivity Rating: 77   **Fire Safety Rating:** 69   **Green Rating:** 60*

STUDENTS AND FACULTY

Enrollment: 3,306. **Student Body:** 68% female, 32% male, 25% out-of-state, 3% international (47 countries represented). African American 10%, Asian 1%, Caucasian 80%, Hispanic 2%. **Retention and Graduation:** 70% freshmen return for sophomore year. 37% freshmen graduate within 4 years. **Faculty:** Student/faculty ratio 12:1. 177 full-time faculty, 76% hold PhDs. 94% faculty teach undergrads.

ACADEMICS

Degrees: Associate, bachelor's, doctoral, master's. **Academic Requirements:** Arts/fine arts, computer literacy, English (including composition), foreign languages, history, humanities, mathematics, philosophy, sciences (biological or physical), social science, wellness, communication, Judaic-Christian traditions, new student experience. **Classes:** Most classes have 10–19 students. Most lab/discussion sections have 20–29 students. **Majors with Highest Enrollment:** Business administration/management, education, nursing/registered nurse training (ASN, BSN, MSN, RN). **Disciplines with Highest Percentage of Degrees Awarded:** Business/marketing 23%, education 14%, health professions and related sciences 10%, biological/life sciences 7%, psychology 7%, liberal arts/general studies 7%. **Special Study Options:** Accelerated program, cross-registration, double major, dual enrollment, English as a second language (ESL), honors program, independent study, internships, liberal arts/career combination, student-designed major, study abroad, teacher certification program, spring term session (4–4–1).

FACILITIES

Housing: Coed dorms, women's dorms, apartments for married students, apartments for single students. **Special Academic Facilities/Equipment:** Developmental preschool, art gallery, observatory. **Computers:** 60% of public computers are PCs, 40% of public computers are Macs, network access in dorm rooms, network access in dorm lounges, remote student-access to Web through college's connection.

CAMPUS LIFE

Activities: Choral groups, concert band, dance, drama/theater, jazz band, literary magazine, music ensembles, musical theater, opera, pep band, radio station, student government, student newspaper, television station, yearbook. **Organizations:** 53 registered organizations, 14 honor societies, 4 religious organizations. **Athletics (Intercollegiate):** *Men:* Baseball, basketball, cross-country, diving, football, golf, soccer, swimming, tennis, track/field (outdoor), wrestling. *Women:* Basketball, cross-country, diving, golf, soccer, softball, swimming, tennis, track/field (outdoor), volleyball.

ADMISSIONS

Freshman Academic Profile: 23% in top 10% of high school class, 50% in top 25% of high school class, 80% in top 50% of high school class. SAT Math middle 50% range 450–580. SAT Critical Reading middle 50% range 440–560. SAT Writing middle 50% range 420–550. ACT middle 50% range 19–25. TOEFL required of all international applicants, minimum paper TOEFL 500, minimum computer TOEFL 173. **Basis for Candidate Selection:** *Very important factors considered include:* Academic GPA, rigor of secondary school record. *Important factors considered include:* Class rank, standardized test scores. *Other factors considered include:* Extracurricular activities, recommendation(s). **Freshman Admission Requirements:** High school diploma is required, and GED is accepted. *Academic units required:* 4 English, 3 math, 2 science (1 science lab), 1 social studies, 1 history, 3 academic electives. *Academic units recommended:* 4 English, 4 math, 3 science (2 science labs), 2 foreign language, 1 social studies, 1 history, 3 academic electives. **Freshman Admission Statistics:** 3,005 applied, 78% admitted, 32% enrolled. **Transfer Admission Requirements:** High school transcript, college transcript(s), standardized test score, statement of good standing from prior institution(s). Minimum college GPA of 2.0 required. Lowest grade transferable C-. **General Admission Information:** Application fee $20. Regular notification is rolling. Nonfall registration accepted. Credit offered for CEEB Advanced Placement tests.

COSTS AND FINANCIAL AID

Required Forms and Deadlines: FAFSA, institution's own financial aid form. Financial aid filing deadline 3/10. **Notification of Awards:** Applicants will be notified of awards on a rolling basis beginning on or about 3/1. **Types of Aid:** *Need-based scholarships/grants:* Pell, SEOG, state scholarships/grants, private scholarships, the school's own gift aid. *Loans:* FFEL Subsidized Stafford, FFEL Unsubsidized Stafford, FFEL PLUS, Federal Perkins. **Student Employment:** Federal Work-Study Program available. Off-campus job opportunities are good. **Financial Aid Statistics:** 66% freshmen, 63% undergrads receive need-based scholarship or grant aid. 56% freshmen, 56% undergrads receive need-based self-help aid. 62 freshmen, 235 undergrads receive athletic scholarships.

UNIVERSITY OF IOWA

Best 368

107 Calvin Hall, Iowa City, IA 52242
Phone: 319-335-3847 **E-mail:** admissions@uiowa.edu **CEEB Code:** 6681
Fax: 319-333-1535 **Website:** www.uiowa.edu **ACT Code:** 1356
Financial Aid Phone: 319-335-1450

This public school was founded in 1847. It has a 1,900-acre campus.

RATINGS

Admissions Selectivity Rating: 83   **Fire Safety Rating:** 83   **Green Rating:** 75

STUDENTS AND FACULTY

Enrollment: 19,915. **Student Body:** 53% female, 47% male, 37% out-of-state, 1% international (57 countries represented). African American 2%, Asian 3%, Caucasian 80%, Hispanic 2%. **Retention and Graduation:** 84% freshmen return for sophomore year. 40% freshmen graduate within 4 years. **Faculty:** Student/faculty ratio 15:1. 1,584 full-time faculty, 97% hold PhDs. 100% faculty teach undergrads.

ACADEMICS

Degrees: Bachelor's, certificate, doctoral, first professional certificate, first professional, master's, post-master's certificate. **Academic Requirements:** English (including composition), foreign languages, history, humanities, mathematics, sciences (biological or physical), social science. **Classes:** Most classes have 10–19 students. Most lab/discussion sections have 20–29 students. **Majors with Highest Enrollment:** Communications studies/speech communication and rhetoric, English language and literature, psychology. **Disciplines with Highest Percentage of Degrees Awarded:** Business/marketing 18%, social sciences 12%, communications/journalism 11%, psychology 8%, visual and performing arts 8%, English 6%. **Special Study Options:** Accelerated program, cooperative education program, distance learning, double major, dual enrollment, English as a second language (ESL), exchange student program (domestic), external degree program, honors program, independent study, internships, liberal arts/career combination, student-designed major, study abroad, teacher certification program.

FACILITIES

Housing: Coed dorms, apartments for married students, apartments for single students, special housing for disabled students, fraternity/sorority housing, quiet houses available, learning communities for honors, health sciences, performing arts. **Special Academic Facilities/Equipment:** Art and natural history museums, information arcade, newspaper production lab, TV lab, survey research facilities, electron microscope, laser facility, Oakdale Research Park, national advanced driving simulator. **Computers:** 33% of classrooms are wireless, 84% of public computers are PCs, 16% of public computers are Macs, network access in dorm rooms, network access in dorm lounges, online registration, online administrative functions (other than registration), remote student-access to Web through college's connection.

CAMPUS LIFE

Activities: Choral groups, concert band, dance, drama/theater, jazz band, literary magazine, marching band, music ensembles, musical theater, opera, pep band, radio station, student government, student newspaper, student-run film society, symphony orchestra, television station. **Organizations:** 400 registered organizations, 21 honor societies, 16 fraternities (7% men join), 13 sororities (12% women join). **Athletics (Intercollegiate):** *Men:* Baseball, basketball, cheerleading, cross-country, diving, football, golf, gymnastics, swimming, tennis, track/field (indoor), track/field (outdoor), wrestling. *Women:* Basketball,

cheerleading, crew/rowing, cross-country, diving, field hockey, golf, gymnastics, soccer, softball, swimming, tennis, track/field (indoor), track/field (outdoor), volleyball. **Environmental Initiatives:** Iowa has an Energy Conservsation Advisory Council (ECAC) and a Energy Conservation Strategic Plan. Commitment to reduce the UI's reliance on non-renewable energy sources by 2013, unprecendented campus-wide participation, and a direct tie-in with the UI's research and educational missions. Under its contract with the exchange, the UI agreed to cut its carbon emissions by up to 4 percent below an average baseline of 275,769 metric tons over the first four years.

ADMISSIONS

Freshman Academic Profile: 23% in top 10% of high school class, 54% in top 25% of high school class, 93% in top 50% of high school class. 90% from public high schools. SAT Math middle 50% range 550–670. SAT Critical Reading middle 50% range 520–650. ACT middle 50% range 23–27. TOEFL required of all international applicants, minimum paper TOEFL 530, minimum computer TOEFL 197. **Basis for Candidate Selection:** *Very important factors considered include:* Academic GPA, class rank, rigor of secondary school record, standardized test scores. *Other factors considered include:* Character/personal qualities, recommendation(s), state residency, talent/ability. **Freshman Admission Requirements:** High school diploma is required, and GED is accepted. *Academic units required:* 4 English, 3 math, 3 science, 2 foreign language, 3 social studies. *Academic units recommended:* 4 foreign language. **Freshman Admission Statistics:** 14,350 applied, 83% admitted, 36% enrolled. **Transfer Admission Requirements:** High school transcript, college transcript(s). Minimum college GPA of 2.5 required. Lowest grade transferable D. **General Admission Information:** Application fee $40. Regular application deadline 4/1. Regular notification is rolling. Non-fall registration accepted. Credit and/or placement offered for CEEB Advanced Placement tests.

COSTS AND FINANCIAL AID

Annual in-state tuition $5,548. Annual out-of-state tuition $19,662. Room and board $7,673. Required fees $996. Average book expense $1,040. **Required Forms and Deadlines:** FAFSA, institution's own financial aid form. Financial aid filing deadline 1/4. **Notification of Awards:** Applicants will be notified of awards on a rolling basis beginning on or about 3/4. **Types of Aid:** *Need-based scholarships/grants:* Pell, SEOG, state scholarships/grants, private scholarships, the school's own gift aid. *Loans:* Direct Subsidized Stafford, Direct Unsubsidized Stafford, Direct PLUS, Federal Perkins, Federal Nursing, college/university loans from institutional funds. **Student Employment:** **Financial Aid Statistics:** 29% freshmen, 27% undergrads receive need-based scholarship or grant aid. 37% freshmen, 38% undergrads receive need-based self-help aid. 113 freshmen, 462 undergrads receive athletic scholarships. 81% freshmen, 80% undergrads receive any aid. Highest amount earned per year from on-campus jobs $2,500.

UNIVERSITY OF JUDAISM

15600 Mulholland Drive, Bel Air, CA 90077
Phone: 310-476-9777 **E-mail:** Admissions@uj.edu **CEEB Code:** 2741
Fax: 310-471-3657 **Website:** www.uj.edu **ACT Code:** 0462
Financial Aid Phone: 310-440-1252

This private school, affiliated with the Jewish faith, was founded in 1947. It has a 28-acre campus.

RATINGS

Admissions Selectivity Rating: 87   **Fire Safety Rating:** 60*   **Green Rating:** 60*

STUDENTS AND FACULTY

Enrollment: 116. **Student Body:** 56% female, 44% male, 45% out-of-state, 5% international (5 countries represented). African American 3%, Caucasian 77%, Hispanic 9%. **Retention and Graduation:** 86% freshmen return for sophomore year. 82% freshmen graduate within 4 years. **Faculty:** Student/faculty ratio 7:1. 19 full-time faculty, 84% hold PhDs. 25% faculty teach undergrads.

ACADEMICS

Degrees: Bachelor's, master's. **Academic Requirements:** Arts/fine arts, computer literacy, English (including composition), history, humanities; Jewish, Western, and non-Western civilization; mathematics, sciences (biological or physical), social science. **Classes:** Most classes have 10–19 students. **Majors with Highest Enrollment:** Area studies, biological and biomedical sciences, psychology. **Disciplines with Highest Percentage of Degrees Awarded:** Biological/life sciences 10%, psychology 6%, business/marketing 6%, communications/journalism 5%, English 4%, philosophy and religious studies 4%, liberal arts/general studies 2%. **Special Study Options:** Accelerated program, cross-registration, double major, honor program, independent study, internships, student-designed major, study abroad.

FACILITIES

Housing: Coed dorms, apartments for married students, apartments for single students, special housing for disabled students. **Special Academic Facilities/ Equipment: Computers:** 95% of public computers are PCs, 5% of public computers are Macs, network access in dorm rooms, network access in dorm lounges, remote student-access to Web through college's connection.

CAMPUS LIFE

Activities: Choral groups, dance, drama/theater, literary magazine, student government, student newspaper, yearbook. **Organizations:** 20 registered organizations.

ADMISSIONS

Freshman Academic Profile: 21% in top 10% of high school class, 14% in top 25% of high school class, 58% in top 50% of high school class. 70% from public high schools. SAT Math middle 50% range 472–588. SAT Critical Reading middle 50% range 480–675. SAT Writing middle 50% range 453–665. ACT middle 50% range 21–28. TOEFL required of all international applicants, minimum paper TOEFL 550, minimum computer TOEFL 215. **Basis for Candidate Selection:** *Very important factors considered include:* Application essay, character/personal qualities, level of applicant's interest, recommendation(s), volunteer work. *Important factors considered include:* Academic GPA, extracurricular activities, interview, rigor of secondary school record. *Other factors considered include:* Class rank, standardized test scores, talent/ability, work experience. **Freshman Admission Requirements:** High school diploma is required, and GED is accepted. *Academic units recommended:* 4 English, 3 math, 3 science (2 science labs), 2 foreign language, 2 social studies, 2 history. **Freshman Admission Statistics:** 109 applied, 28% admitted, 100% enrolled. **Transfer Admission Requirements:** High school transcript, college transcript(s), essay or personal statement. Lowest grade transferable C. **General Admission Information:** Application fee $35. Early Decision application deadline 12/31. Regular application deadline 7/31. Nonfall registration accepted. Admission may be deferred for a maximum of 1 year. Credit offered for CEEB Advanced Placement tests.

COSTS AND FINANCIAL AID

Annual tuition $20,400. Room & board $11,070. Required fees $900. Average book expense $1,386. **Required Forms and Deadlines:** FAFSA, institution's own financial aid form, state aid form, copy of taxes, copy of all W-2 and 1099 forms. Financial aid filing deadline 3/2. **Types of Aid:** *Need-based scholarships/ grants:* Pell, SEOG, state scholarships/grants, private scholarships, the school's own gift aid. *Loans:* FFEL Subsidized Stafford, FFEL Unsubsidized Stafford, FFEL PLUS. **Student Employment:** Federal Work-Study Program available. Institutional employment available. Off-campus job opportunities are good. **Financial Aid Statistics:** 94% freshmen, 81% undergrads receive need-based scholarship or grant aid. 94% freshmen, 81% undergrads receive need-based self-help aid. Highest amount earned per year from on-campus jobs $1,700.

UNIVERSITY OF KANSAS

Best 368

Office of Admissions and Scholarships, 1502 Iowa Street, Lawrence, KS 66045
Phone: 785-864-3911 **E-mail:** Adm@ku.edu **CEEB Code:** 6871
Fax: 785-864-5017 **Website:** www.ku.edu **ACT Code:** 1470
Financial Aid Phone: 785-864-4700

This public school was founded in 1866. It has a 1,100-acre campus.

RATINGS

Admissions Selectivity Rating: 82   **Fire Safety Rating:** 74   **Green Rating:** 82

STUDENTS AND FACULTY

Enrollment: 20,979. **Student Body:** 50% female, 50% male, 23% out-of-state, 3% international (111 countries represented). African American 4%, Asian 4%, Caucasian 82%, Hispanic 4%, Native American 1%. **Retention and Graduation:** 81% freshmen return for sophomore year. 28% grads go on to further study within 1 year. **Faculty:** Student/faculty ratio 20:1. 1,192 full-time faculty, 96% hold PhDs. 98% faculty teach undergrads.

ACADEMICS

Degrees: Bachelor's, doctoral, first professional, master's, post-master's certificate. **Academic Requirements:** English (including composition), foreign languages, humanities, mathematics, non-Western civilization, oral communication/logic, sciences (biological or physical), social science, Western civilization. **Classes:** Most classes have 20–29 students. Most lab/discussion sections have 10–19 students. **Majors with Highest Enrollment:** Biology/biological sciences, psychology. **Disciplines with Highest Percentage of Degrees Awarded:** Health professions and related sciences 12%, business/marketing 11%, English 9%, communications/journalism 7%, psychology 7%, biological/ life sciences 7%, visual and performing arts 7%, engineering 5%. **Special Study Options:** Accelerated program, cooperative education program, distance learning, double major, dual enrollment, English as a second language (ESL), honor program, independent study, internships, off-campus study (Washington, DC semester), study abroad in more than 60 countries, teacher certification program.

FACILITIES

Housing: Coed dorms, women's dorms, apartments for married students, apartments for single students, fraternity/sorority housing, cooperative housing. **Special Academic Facilities/Equipment:** 12 libraries (including art and architecture, engineering, law, medical, music and dance, rare research materials, special collections, and science), performing arts center, organ recital hall, museums (art, anthropology, classical, entomology).

CAMPUS LIFE

Activities: Choral groups, concert band, dance, drama/theater, jazz band, literary magazine, marching band, music ensembles, musical theater, opera, pep band, radio station, student government, student newspaper, symphony orchestra, television station, yearbook. **Organizations:** 481 registered organizations, 21 honor society, 42 religious organizations. 23 fraternities (13% men join), 16 sororities (16% women join). **Athletics (Intercollegiate):** *Men:* Baseball, basketball, cross-country, football, golf, track/field (indoor), track/field (outdoor). *Women:* Basketball, crew/rowing, cross-country, diving, golf, soccer, softball, swimming, tennis, track/field (indoor), track/field (outdoor), volleyball. **Environmental Initiatives:** Support a comprehensive recycling program that includes fibers, plastics, metals, glass, e-waste and surplus property recovery www.recycle.ku.edu. Established the KU Center for Sustainability in February 2007 with a mission to "facilitate research, learning opportunities, policies, and practices that address environmental, economic, and social responsibility." Conduct research that addresses transportation, the use and development of alternative fuels, melting of ice sheets, and other environmental issues.

ADMISSIONS

Freshman Academic Profile: 28% in top 10% of high school class, 55% in top 25% of high school class, 88% in top 50% of high school class. ACT middle 50% range 22–28. **Basis for Candidate Selection:** *Very important factors considered include:* Academic GPA, class rank, rigor of secondary school record, standardized test scores. **Freshman Admission Requirements:** High school diploma is required, and GED is accepted. *Academic units required:* 4 English, 3 math, 3 science, 3 social studies, 1 computer technology. *Academic units recommended:* 4 English, 4 math, 3 science, 2 foreign language, 3 social studies, 1 computer technology. **Freshman Admission Statistics:** 10,240 applied, 77% admitted, 53% enrolled. **Transfer Admission Requirements:** College transcript(s). Minimum college GPA of 2.5 required. Lowest grade transferable C. **General Admission Information:** Application fee $30. Regular application deadline 4/1. Regular notification is rolling. Nonfall registration accepted. Credit and/or placement offered for CEEB Advanced Placement tests.

COSTS AND FINANCIAL AID

Comprehensive fee $5,844. Room and board $6,144. Required fees $756. Average book expense $750. **Required Forms and Deadlines:** FAFSA. Financial aid filing deadline 3/1. **Notification of Awards:** Applicants will be notified of awards on a rolling basis beginning on or about 4/1. **Types of Aid:** *Need-based scholarships/grants:* Pell, SEOG, state scholarships/grants, private scholarships, the school's own gift aid. *Loans:* Direct Subsidized Stafford, Direct Unsubsidized Stafford, Direct PLUS, Federal Perkins, college/university loans from institutional funds. **Student Employment: Financial Aid Statistics:** 25% freshmen, 26% undergrads receive need-based scholarship or grant aid. 35% freshmen, 33% undergrads receive need-based self-help aid. 83 freshmen, 368 undergrads receive athletic scholarships. 81% freshmen, 61% undergrads receive any aid. Highest amount earned per year from on-campus jobs $4,480.

UNIVERSITY OF KENTUCKY

100 Funkhouser Building, Lexington, KY 40506
Phone: 859-257-2000 **E-mail:** lrasnic@uky.edu **CEEB Code:** 1837
Fax: 859-257-3823 **Website:** www.uky.edu **ACT Code:** 1554
Financial Aid Phone: 859-257-3172

This public school was founded in 1865. It has a 687-acre campus.

RATINGS
Admissions Selectivity Rating: 79 **Fire Safety Rating:** 84 **Green Rating:** 60*

STUDENTS AND FACULTY
Enrollment: 18,960. **Student Body:** 51% female, 49% male, 17% out-of-state. African American 5%, Asian 2%, Caucasian 88%, Hispanic 1%. **Retention and Graduation:** 78% freshmen return for sophomore year. 30% freshmen graduate within 4 years. **Faculty:** Student/faculty ratio 17:1. 1,211 full-time faculty, 89% hold PhDs. 80% faculty teach undergrads.

ACADEMICS
Degrees: Bachelor's, doctoral, first professional, master's. **Academic Requirements:** English (including composition), cross cultural, foreign languages, humanities, inference-logic (with statistics or calculus options) mathematics, oral communication, sciences (biological or physical), social science. **Classes:** Most classes have 20–29 students. Most lab/discussion sections have 20–29 students. **Disciplines with Highest Percentage of Degrees Awarded:** Business/marketing 17%, communications/journalism 11%, education 8%, engineering 7%, agriculture 6%, biological/life sciences 6%, psychology 6%. **Special Study Options:** Accelerated program, cooperative education program, distance learning, double major, English as a second language (ESL), exchange student program (domestic), honor program, independent study, internships, study abroad, teacher certification program, weekend college.

FACILITIES
Housing: Coed dorms, men's dorms, women's dorms, apartments for married students, apartments for single students, special housing for disabled students, special housing for international students, fraternity/sorority housing. **Special Academic Facilities/Equipment:** Anthropology and art museums, center for the humanities, centers for equine research, cancer research, and robotics, pharmacy manufacturing lab. **Computers:** 90% of public computers are PCs, 8% of public computers are Macs, 2% of public computers are UNIX, network access in dorm rooms, online registration, online administrative functions (other than registration), remote student-access to Web through college's connection.

CAMPUS LIFE
Activities: Choral groups, concert band, dance, drama/theater, jazz band, literary magazine, marching band, music ensembles, musical theater, opera, pep band, radio station, student government, student newspaper, symphony orchestra, yearbook. **Organizations:** 348 registered organizations, 28 honor societies, 20 religious organizations. 19 fraternities (15% men join), 16 sororities (19% women join). **Athletics (Intercollegiate):** *Men:* Baseball, basketball, cheerleading, cross-country, diving, football, golf, riflery, soccer, swimming, tennis, track/field (indoor), track/field (outdoor). *Women:* Basketball, cheerleading, cross-country, diving, golf, gymnastics, riflery, soccer, softball, swimming, tennis, track/field (indoor), track/field (outdoor), volleyball.

ADMISSIONS
Freshman Academic Profile: 23% in top 10% of high school class, 50% in top 25% of high school class, 79% in top 50% of high school class. SAT Math middle 50% range 500–630. SAT Critical Reading middle 50% range 490–610. ACT middle 50% range 21–26. TOEFL required of all international applicants, minimum paper TOEFL 527, minimum computer TOEFL 197. **Basis for Candidate Selection:** *Very important factors considered include:* Academic GPA, rigor of secondary school record, standardized test scores. *Other factors considered include:* Alumni/ae relation, application essay, character/personal qualities, class rank, extracurricular activities, first generation, geographical residence, interview, racial/ethnic status, recommendation(s), talent/ability, volunteer work. **Freshman Admission Requirements:** High school diploma is required, and GED is accepted. *Academic units required:* 4 English, 3 math, 3 science, 2 foreign language, 3 social studies, 5 academic electives, 2 fine or performing arts, 1 health (0.5) and physical education (0.5). *Academic units recommended:* 4 English, 4 math, 4 science, 2 foreign language, 3 social studies, 3 academic electives, 2 fine or performing arts, 1 health (0.5) and physical education (0.5). **Freshman Admission Statistics:** 10,024 applied, 81% admitted, 52% enrolled. **Transfer Admission Requirements:** College transcript(s), statement of good standing from prior institution(s). Minimum college GPA of 2.0 required. Lowest grade transferable D. **General Admission Information:** Application fee $40. Regular application deadline 2/15. Regular notification is rolling. Nonfall registration accepted. Admission may be deferred for a maximum of 1 year. Credit and/or placement offered for CEEB Advanced Placement tests.

COSTS AND FINANCIAL AID
Annual in-state tuition $6,302. Out-of-state tuition $14,102. Room & board $7,973. Required fees $794. Average book expense $800. **Required Forms and Deadlines:** FAFSA. Financial aid filing deadline 2/15. **Notification of Awards:** Applicants will be notified of awards on or about 4/1. **Types of Aid:** *Need-based scholarships/grants:* Pell, SEOG, state scholarships/grants, private scholarships, the school's own gift aid. *Loans:* Direct Subsidized Stafford, Direct Unsubsidized Stafford, Direct PLUS, FFEL Subsidized Stafford, FFEL Unsubsidized Stafford, FFEL PLUS, Federal Perkins, state loans, college/university loans from institutional funds. **Student Employment:** Federal Work-Study Program available. **Financial Aid Statistics:** 20% freshmen, 24% undergrads receive need-based scholarship or grant aid. 26% freshmen, 29% undergrads receive need-based self-help aid. 90 freshmen, 357 undergrads receive athletic scholarships. 40% freshmen, 38% undergrads receive any aid.

UNIVERSITY OF KING'S COLLEGE

Registrar's Office, Halifax, NS B3H 2A1 Canada
Phone: 902-422-1271 **E-mail:** Admissions@ukings.ns.ca
Fax: 902-423-3357 **Website:** www.ukings.ca

This public school was founded in 1789. It has a 3-acre campus.

RATINGS
Admissions Selectivity Rating: 60* **Fire Safety Rating:** 60* **Green Rating:** 60*

STUDENTS AND FACULTY
Enrollment: 1,110. **Student Body:** 58% female, 42% male, 51% out-of-state. **Faculty:** Student/faculty ratio 25:1. 45 full-time faculty, 69% hold PhDs. 100% faculty teach undergrads.

ACADEMICS
Degrees: Bachelor's. **Academic Requirements:** Foreign languages, humanities, sciences (biological or physical), writing credit (specified classes in arts and science qualify). **Majors with Highest Enrollment:** English language and literature, history, journalism. **Special Study Options:** Cooperative education program, double major, honor program, internships, study abroad.

FACILITIES
Housing: Coed dorms, men's dorms, women's dorms. **Computers:** Network access in dorm rooms, online registration, online administrative functions (other than registration), remote student-access to Web through college's connection.

CAMPUS LIFE
Activities: Choral groups, dance, drama/theater, literary magazine, radio station, student government, student newspaper, student-run film society, yearbook. **Athletics (Intercollegiate):** *Men:* Basketball, soccer, volleyball. *Women:* Basketball, soccer, volleyball.

ADMISSIONS
Freshman Academic Profile: TOEFL required of all international applicants, minimum paper TOEFL 580. **Basis for Candidate Selection:** *Very important factors considered include:* Rigor of secondary school record, standardized test scores. **Freshman Admission Statistics:** 904 applied, 47% admitted, 73% enrolled. **Transfer Admission Requirements:** College transcript(s). **General Admission Information:** Application fee $38. Regular application deadline 6/1. Regular notification is rolling. Nonfall registration not accepted. Admission may be deferred for a maximum of 1 year.

COSTS AND FINANCIAL AID
In-province tuition $6,840–$7,923. Out-of-province tuition $6,840–$7,923. International tuition $13,290–$14,373. Room & board $7,580. Average book expense $1,000. **Student Employment:** Off-campus job opportunities are good.

UNIVERSITY OF LA VERNE

1950 Third Street, La Verne, CA 91750
Phone: 909-392-2800 **E-mail:** admissions@ulv.edu **CEEB Code:** 4381
Fax: 909-392-2714 **Website:** www.ulv.edu **ACT Code:** 0295
Financial Aid Phone: 909-593-3511

This private school was founded in 1891. It has a 38-acre campus.

RATINGS
Admissions Selectivity Rating: 85   **Fire Safety Rating:** 68   **Green Rating:** 99

STUDENTS AND FACULTY
Enrollment: 1,685. **Student Body:** 64% female, 36% male, 2% out-of-state, 2% international (6 countries represented). African American 8%, Asian 5%, Caucasian 34%, Hispanic 38%. **Retention and Graduation:** 80% freshmen return for sophomore year. 33% freshmen graduate within 4 years. **Faculty:** Student/faculty ratio 12:1. 194 full-time faculty, 79% hold PhDs.

ACADEMICS
Degrees: Associate, bachelor's, certificate, doctoral, first professional, master's, post-bachelor's certificate. **Academic Requirements:** Arts/fine arts, English (including composition), foreign languages, history, humanities, interdisciplinary coursework, mathematics, philosophy, sciences (biological or physical), service learning (community service), social sciences. **Classes:** Most classes have 10–19 students. Most lab/discussion sections have 10–19 students. **Majors with Highest Enrollment:** Business administration/management, liberal arts and sciences/liberal studies, psychology. **Disciplines with Highest Percentage of Degrees Awarded:** Business/marketing 17%, liberal arts/general studies 17%, social sciences 16%, communications/journalism 13%, psychology 11%. **Special Study Options:** Distance learning, double major, English as a second language (ESL), exchange student program (domestic), honors program, independent study, internships, liberal arts/career combination, student-designed major, study abroad, teacher certification program, weekend college.

FACILITIES
Housing: Coed dorms, women's dorms, special housing for disabled students. **Special Academic Facilities/Equipment:** Greenhouse and animal care facility, Montana Field Station–Magpie Ranch, Jeagar Science Specimen Museum, photography and art galleries. **Computers:** 84% of public computers are PCs, 16% of public computers are Macs, network access in dorm rooms, online registration, online administrative functions (other than registration), remote student-access to Web through college's connection.

CAMPUS LIFE
Activities: Choral groups, drama/theater, literary magazine, musical theater, radio station, student government, student newspaper, television station. **Organizations:** 40 registered organizations, 2 honor societies, 1 religious organization. 3 fraternities (6% men join), 6 sororities (15% women join). **Athletics (Intercollegiate):** *Men:* Baseball, basketball, cross-country, diving, football, golf, soccer, swimming, tennis, track/field (outdoor), water polo. *Women:* Basketball, cross-country, diving, soccer, softball, swimming, tennis, track/field (outdoor), volleyball, water polo.

ADMISSIONS
Freshman Academic Profile: 31% in top 10% of high school class, 69% in top 25% of high school class, 90% in top 50% of high school class. SAT Math middle 50% range 440–540. SAT Critical Reading middle 50% range 440–540. SAT Writing middle 50% range 430–530. ACT middle 50% range 17–23. TOEFL required of all international applicants, minimum paper TOEFL 500, minimum computer TOEFL 173. **Basis for Candidate Selection:** *Very important factors considered include:* Academic GPA, application essay, character/personal qualities, recommendation(s), rigor of secondary school record, standardized test scores. *Important factors considered include:* Class rank, extracurricular activities. *Other factors considered include:* Alumni/ae relation, first generation, interview, level of applicant's interest, racial/ethnic status, talent/ability, volunteer work, work experience. **Freshman Admission Requirements:** High school diploma is required, and GED is accepted. *Academic units required:* 4 English, 3 math, 2 science (1 science lab), 2 social studies, 3 history. *Academic units recommended:* 4 English, 4 math, 2 science (2 science labs), 2 foreign language, 2 social studies, 3 history, 2 academic electives. **Freshman Admission Statistics:** 1,606 applied, 60% admitted, 33% enrolled. **Transfer Admission Requirements:** College transcript(s), essay or personal statement. Lowest grade transferable C-. **General Admission Information:** Application fee $50. Regular notification is rolling. Non-fall registration accepted. Admission may be deferred for a maxiumum of 2 semesters. Credit and/or placement offered for CEEB Advanced Placement tests.

COSTS AND FINANCIAL AID
Annual tuition $26,910. Room and board $10,460. Average book expense $1,566. **Required Forms and Deadlines:** FAFSA, state aid form. Financial aid filing deadline 3/2. **Notification of Awards:** Applicants will be notified of awards on a rolling basis beginning on or about 3/2. **Types of Aid:** *Need-based scholarships/grants:* Pell, SEOG, state scholarships/grants, private scholarships, the school's own gift aid. *Loans:* FFEL Subsidized Stafford, FFEL Unsubsidized Stafford, FFEL PLUS, Federal Perkins, college/university loans from institutional funds. **Financial Aid Statistics:** 75% freshmen, 76% undergrads receive need-based scholarship or grant aid. 69% freshmen, 71% undergrads receive need-based self-help aid. 79% freshmen, 80% undergrads receive any aid.

THE UNIVERSITY OF LETHBRIDGE

4401 University Drive, Lethbridge, AB T1K 3M4 Canada
Phone: 403-320-5700 **E-mail:** inquiries@uleth.ca
Fax: 403-329-5159 **Website:** www.uleth.ca **ACT Code:** 5202
Financial Aid Phone: 403-329-2585

This public school was founded in 1967. It has a 568-acre campus.

RATINGS
Admissions Selectivity Rating: 60*   **Fire Safety Rating:** 60*   **Green Rating:** 60*

STUDENTS AND FACULTY
Student Body: 14% out-of-province. **Faculty:** Student/faculty ratio 15:1.

ACADEMICS
Degrees: Bachelor's, certificate, diploma, doctoral, master's, post-bachelor's certificate. **Academic Requirements:** 4 semester courses in each of fine arts and humanities, social sciences, and sciences. **Classes:** Most classes have 20–29 students. Most lab/discussion sections have 10–19 students. **Majors with Highest Enrollment:** Business administration/management, kinesiology and exercise science, psychology. **Disciplines with Highest Percentage of Degrees Awarded:** Business/marketing 40%, education 14%, health professions and related sciences 9%, social sciences 8%, visual and performing arts 7%. **Special Study Options:** Accelerated program, applied studies, cooperative education program, double major, English as a second language (ESL), exchange student program (domestic), honors program, independent study, internships, student-designed major, study abroad, teacher certification program.

FACILITIES
Housing: Coed dorms, apartments for married students, apartments for single students, special housing for disabled students, townhouses for single and married students and students with families. **Special Academic Facilities/Equipment:** Art gallery. **Computers:** Network access in dorm rooms, online registration, online administrative functions (other than registration), remote student-access to Web through college's connection.

CAMPUS LIFE
Activities: Choral groups, dance, drama/theater, jazz band, literary magazine, music ensembles, musical theater, radio station, student government, student newspaper, student-run film society, symphony orchestra. **Organizations:** **Athletics (Intercollegiate):** *Men:* Basketball, ice hockey, soccer, swimming, track/field (outdoor). *Women:* Basketball, ice hockey, rugby, soccer, swimming, track/field (outdoor).

ADMISSIONS
Basis for Candidate Selection: *Very important factors considered include:* Rigor of secondary school record. *Other factors considered include:* Class rank, standardized test scores. **Freshman Admission Statistics:** 2,371 applied, 56% admitted, 77% enrolled. **Transfer Admission Requirements:** College transcript(s). **General Admission Information:** Application fee $60. Regular application deadline 6/1. Non-fall registration accepted. Admission may be deferred for a maximum of 1 semester.

COSTS AND FINANCIAL AID
Annual in-state tuition $4,380. Room and board $4,338. Required fees $1,247. Average book expense $630. **Student Employment:** Institutional employment available. Off-campus job opportunities are good.

UNIVERSITY OF LOUISIANA AT LAFAYETTE

Best 368

P.O. Drawer 41210, Lafayette, LA 70504
Phone: 337-482-6553 **E-mail:** enroll@louisiana.edu **CEEB Code:** 6672
Fax: 337-482-1112 **Website:** www.louisiana.edu **ACT Code:** 1612
Financial Aid Phone: 337-482-6506

This public school was founded in 1898. It has a 1,375-acre campus.

RATINGS
Admissions Selectivity Rating: 74   **Fire Safety Rating:** 87   **Green Rating:** 60*

STUDENTS AND FACULTY
Enrollment: 14,623. **Student Body:** 57% female, 43% male, 4% out-of-state, 1% international (94 countries represented). African American 19%, Asian 2%, Caucasian 72%, Hispanic 2%. **Retention and Graduation:** 73% freshmen return for sophomore year. 14% freshmen graduate within 4 years. **Faculty:** Student/faculty ratio 25:1. 530 full-time faculty, 76% hold PhDs. 100% faculty teach undergrads.

ACADEMICS
Degrees: Bachelor's, doctoral, master's, post-master's certificate. **Academic Requirements:** Arts/fine arts, communication, computer literacy, English (including composition), humanities, mathematics, sciences (biological or physical), social science. **Classes:** Most classes have 20–29 students. **Majors with Highest Enrollment:** Business administration and management, general studies, nursing/registered nurse training (RN, ASN, BSN, MSN). **Disciplines with Highest Percentage of Degrees Awarded:** Business/marketing 24%, liberal arts/general studies 13%, education 12%, health professions and related sciences 10%, engineering 6%. **Special Study Options:** Accelerated program, cooperative education program, cross registration, distance learning, double major, dual enrollment, exchange student program (domestic), honors program, independent study, internships, student-designed major, study abroad, teacher certification program.

FACILITIES
Housing: Men's dorms, women's dorms, apartments for married students, apartments for single students, fraternity/sorority housing. **Special Academic Facilities/Equipment:** Art museum, experimental farm, primate center, CAD/CAM laboratory, marine research facility, on campus restaurant and hotel with instructional facilities, 2 nuclear accelerators, 2 electron microscopes, radio station and television production studio, nursery school laboratory, Louisiana Emersive Technologies Enterprise. **Computers:** Network access in dorm lounges, online registration, online administrative functions (other than registration), remote student-access to Web through college's connection.

CAMPUS LIFE
Activities: Choral groups, concert band, dance, drama/theater, jazz band, literary magazine, marching band, music ensembles, musical theater, opera, radio station, student government, student newspaper, student-run film society, symphony orchestra, yearbook. **Organizations:** 134 registered organizations, 14 honor societies, 8 religious organizations. 10 fraternities (3% men join), 9 sororities (5% women join). **Athletics (Intercollegiate):** *Men:* Baseball, basketball, cheerleading, cross-country, football, golf, tennis, track/field (indoor), track/field (outdoor). *Women:* Basketball, cheerleading, cross-country, soccer, softball, tennis, track/field (indoor), track/field (outdoor), volleyball.

ADMISSIONS
Freshman Academic Profile: 14% in top 10% of high school class, 38% in top 25% of high school class, 72% in top 50% of high school class. 70% from public high schools. ACT middle 50% range 20–24. TOEFL required of all international applicants, minimum paper TOEFL 525, minimum computer TOEFL 195. **Basis for Candidate Selection:** *Very important factors considered include:* Academic GPA, class rank, rigor of secondary school record, standardized test scores. *Other factors considered include:* State residency. **Freshman Admission Requirements:** High school diploma is required, and GED is accepted. *Academic units required:* 4 English, 3 math, 3 science, 2 foreign language, 2 social studies, 1 history, 1 academic elective. **Freshman Admission Statistics:** 7,140 applied, 73% admitted, 56% enrolled. **Transfer Admission Requirements:** College transcript(s). Lowest grade transferable D. **General Admission Information:** Application fee $25. Regular notification rolling basis. Non-fall registration accepted. Admission may be deferred for a

maximum of 1 semester. Credit and/or placement offered for CEEB Advanced Placement tests.

COSTS AND FINANCIAL AID
Annual in-state tuition $3,402. Annual out-of-state tuition $9,582. Room and board $3,820. Average book expense $1,200. **Required Forms and Deadlines:** FAFSA, institution's own financial aid form. Financial aid filing deadline 5/1. **Notification of Awards:** Applicants will be notified of awards on a rolling basis beginning on or about 4/1. **Types of Aid:** *Need-based scholarships/grants:* Pell, SEOG, state scholarships/grants, private scholarships, the school's own gift aid, Federal Nursing Scholarships. *Loans:* FFEL Subsidized Stafford, FFEL Unsubsidized Stafford, FFEL PLUS, Federal Perkins, Federal Nursing. **Student Employment:** Federal Work-Study Program available. Institutional employment available. Off-campus job opportunities are good. **Financial Aid Statistics:** 47% freshmen, 42% undergrads receive need-based scholarship or grant aid. 24% freshmen, 33% undergrads receive need-based self-help aid. 72 freshmen, 308 undergrads receive athletic scholarships. 87% freshmen, 72% undergrads receive any aid.

THE UNIVERSITY OF LOUISIANA AT MONROE

700 University Avenue, Monroe, LA 71209
Phone: 318-342-5252 **E-mail:** hood@ulm.edu **CEEB Code:** 6482
Fax: 318-342-5274 **Website:** www.ulm.edu **ACT Code:** 1598
Financial Aid Phone: 318-342-5320

This public school was founded in 1931. It has a 238-acre campus.

RATINGS
Admissions Selectivity Rating: 60*   **Fire Safety Rating:** 60*   **Green Rating:** 60*

STUDENTS AND FACULTY
Enrollment: 8,542. **Student Body:** 61% female, 39% male, 7% out-of-state, 1% international (47 countries represented). **Retention and Graduation:** 8% freshmen graduate within 4 years. **Faculty:** Student/faculty ratio 17:1. 100% faculty teach undergrads.

ACADEMICS
Degrees: Associate, bachelor's, certificate, doctoral, master's, post-master's certificate. **Academic Requirements:** Arts/fine arts, computer literacy, English (including composition), foreign languages, history, humanities, mathematics, sciences (biological or physical). **Special Study Options:** Accelerated program, cooperative education program, distance learning, English as a second language (ESL), honors program, internships, teacher certification program.

FACILITIES
Housing: Coed dorms, men's dorms, women's dorms, fraternity/sorority housing. **Special Academic Facilities/Equipment:** Agricultural farm lab, soil/plant analysis lab, climatic research center, herbarium, pre-school child lab, educational media center, cancer research center.

CAMPUS LIFE
Activities: Choral groups, concert band, dance, drama/theater, jazz band, literary magazine, marching band, music ensembles, musical theater, pep band, radio station, student government, student newspaper, television station, yearbook. **Organizations:** 128 registered organizations, 22 honor societies, 11 religious organization. 8 fraternities (3% men join), 8 sororities (2% women join).

ADMISSIONS
Freshman Academic Profile: 41% in top 25% of high school class, 74% in top 50% of high school class. ACT middle 50% range 16–22. **Freshman Admission Statistics:** 2,657 applied, 92% admitted, 74% enrolled. **Transfer Admission Requirements:** High school transcript, college transcript(s). **General Admission Information:** Application fee $15. Regular notification is rolling. Non-fall registration accepted. Common Application not accepted.

COSTS AND FINANCIAL AID
Annual in-state tuition $1,644. Out-of-state tuition $2,400. Room & board $3,380. Required fees $282. Average book expense $668. **Required Forms and Deadlines:** FAFSA. **Types of Aid:** *Need-based scholarships/grants:* Pell, private scholarships, the school's own gift aid. **Student Employment:** Federal Work-Study Program available. Off-campus job opportunities are good. **Financial Aid Statistics:** Highest amount earned per year from on-campus jobs $1,000.

UNIVERSITY OF LOUISVILLE

Admissions Office, University of Louisville, Louisville, KY 40292
Phone: 502-852-6531 **E-mail:** admitme@louisville.edu **CEEB Code:** 1838
Fax: 502-852-4776 **Website:** www.louisville.edu **ACT Code:** 1556
Financial Aid Phone: 502-852-5511

This public school was founded in 1798. It has a 170-acre campus.

RATINGS
Admissions Selectivity Rating: 78   **Fire Safety Rating:** 60*   **Green Rating:** 60*

STUDENTS AND FACULTY
Enrollment: 13,893. **Student Body:** 53% female, 47% male, 14% out-of-state, 1% international. African American 11%, Asian 2%, Caucasian 64%, Hispanic 1%. **Retention and Graduation:** 76% freshmen return for sophomore year. 13% freshmen graduate within 4 years. **Faculty:** Student/faculty ratio 17:1. 802 full-time faculty, 89% hold PhDs.

ACADEMICS
Degrees: Associate, bachelor's, certificate, diploma, doctoral, first professional, master's, post-bachelor's certificate, post-master's certificate. **Academic Requirements:** Arts/fine arts, cultural diversity, English (including composition), history, humanities, mathematics, sciences (biological or physical), social science, speech communication. **Classes:** Most classes have 20–29 students. **Disciplines with Highest Percentage of Degrees Awarded:** Business/marketing 22%, social sciences 10%, engineering 9%, psychology 8%, communications/journalism 7%. **Special Study Options:** Cooperative education program, distance learning, double major, dual enrollment, English as a second language (ESL), honors program, independent study, internships, student-designed major, study abroad, teacher certification program.

FACILITIES
Housing: Coed dorms, apartments for married students, apartments for single students, special housing for disabled students, fraternity/sorority housing, suite style rooms. **Special Academic Facilities/Equipment:** Natural history and art museums, planetarium, numerous institutes and centers. **Computers:** 100% of public computers are PCs, network access in dorm rooms, online administrative functions (other than registration), remote student-access to Web through college's connection.

CAMPUS LIFE
Activities: Choral groups, marching band, radio station, student government, student newspaper. **Organizations:** 202 registered organizations, 7 honor societies, 18 religious organizations. 13 fraternities (3% men join), 10 sororities (2% women join). **Athletics (Intercollegiate):** *Men:* Baseball, basketball, cheerleading, cross-country, diving, fencing, football, golf, ice hockey, soccer, softball, swimming, tennis, track/field (outdoor). *Women:* Basketball, cheerleading, crew/rowing, cross-country, diving, fencing, field hockey, golf, soccer, softball, swimming, tennis, track/field (outdoor), volleyball.

ADMISSIONS
Freshman Academic Profile: 22% in top 10% of high school class, 51% in top 25% of high school class, 80% in top 50% of high school class. SAT Math middle 50% range 500–640. SAT Critical Reading middle 50% range 490–610. ACT middle 50% range 21–27. TOEFL required of all international applicants, minimum paper TOEFL 550, minimum computer TOEFL 213. **Basis for Candidate Selection:** *Very important factors considered include:* Rigor of secondary school record, standardized test scores. *Other factors considered include:* Application essay, character/personal qualities, class rank, extracurricular activities, geographical residence, racial/ethnic status, recommendation(s), state residency, talent/ability, volunteer work, work experience. **Freshman Admission Requirements:** High school diploma is required, and GED is accepted. *Academic units required:* 4 English, 3 math, 3 science (1 science lab), 2 foreign language, 3 social studies, 5 academic electives. *Academic units recommended:* 4 math, 4 science. **Freshman Admission Statistics:** 5,712 applied, 79% admitted, 51% enrolled. **Transfer Admission Requirements:** College transcript(s). Minimum college GPA of 2.0 required. Lowest grade transferable D. **General Admission Information:** Application fee $30. Regular application deadline 8/25. Non-fall registration accepted. Admission may be deferred on a case by case basis. Common Application not accepted. Credit and/or placement offered for CEEB Advanced Placement tests.

COSTS AND FINANCIAL AID
Annual in-state tuition $6,940. Annual out-of-state tuition $17,734. Average book expense $800. **Required Forms and Deadlines:** FAFSA. Financial aid filing deadline 3/15. **Notification of Awards:** Applicants will be notified of awards on or about 4/1. **Types of Aid:** *Need-based scholarships/grants:* Pell, SEOG, state scholarships/grants, private scholarships, the school's own gift aid.

Loans: FFEL Subsidized Stafford, FFEL Unsubsidized Stafford, FFEL PLUS, Federal Perkins, Federal Nursing. **Financial Aid Statistics:** 52% freshmen, 43% undergrads receive need-based scholarship or grant aid. 30% freshmen, 35% undergrads receive need-based self-help aid. 62 freshmen, 290 undergrads receive athletic scholarships.

UNIVERSITY OF MAINE

5713 Chadbourne Hall, Orono, ME 04469-5713
Phone: 207-581-1561 **E-mail:** um-admit@maine.edu **CEEB Code:** 3916
Fax: 207-581-1213 **Website:** www.umaine.edu **ACT Code:** 1664
Financial Aid Phone: 207-581-1324

This public school was founded in 1865. It has a 660-acre campus.

RATINGS
Admissions Selectivity Rating: 60*   **Fire Safety Rating:** 60*   **Green Rating:** 60*

STUDENTS AND FACULTY
Enrollment: 8,496. **Student Body:** 50% female, 50% male, 13% out-of-state, 2% international (67 countries represented). Asian 1%, Caucasian 93%, Native American 2%. **Retention and Graduation:** 79% freshmen return for sophomore year. 28% freshmen graduate within 4 years. 25% grads go on to further study within 1 year. **Faculty:** Student/faculty ratio 16:1. 496 full-time faculty, 85% hold PhDs. 83% faculty teach undergrads.

ACADEMICS
Degrees: Bachelor's, doctoral, master's, post-master's certificate. **Academic Requirements:** Arts/fine arts, English (including composition), humanities, mathematics, population & environment: cultural diversity/international perspectives, sciences (biological or physical), social science. **Classes:** Most classes have 10–19 students. Most lab/discussion sections have 10–19 students. **Majors with Highest Enrollment:** Business administration/management, education, engineering. **Disciplines with Highest Percentage of Degrees Awarded:** Education 13%, business/marketing 11%, health professions and related sciences 8%, social sciences 7%, engineering 7%. **Special Study Options:** Accelerated program, cooperative education program, distance learning, double major, English as a second language (ESL), exchange student program (domestic), honors program, independent study, internships, liberal arts/career combination, study abroad, teacher certification program.

FACILITIES
Housing: Coed dorms, apartments for married students, apartments for single students, special housing for disabled students, special housing for international students, fraternity/sorority housing, honor's college housing, graduate student housing, smoke-free. **Special Academic Facilities/Equipment:** Laboratory for Advanced Surface Science and Technology (LASST), Advanced Manufacturing Center, anthropology museum, digital media lab, Folklore and Oral History Museum, art museum, Canadian-American Center, Social Sciences Research Institute, exceptional child research lab, preschool, experimental farms, land/water resources center, Center for Marine Studies, planetarium/observatory, electron microscopes, farm museum, paper-making machine, aquaculture production facility, woodland preserve, botanical garden, arts center, Franco-American Center. **Computers:** 100% of classrooms are wired, 100% of classrooms are wireless, 70% of public computers are PCs, 30% of public computers are Macs, network access in dorm rooms, network access in dorm lounges, online registration, online administrative functions (other than registration), support for handheld computing, remote student-access to Web through college's connection.

CAMPUS LIFE
Activities: Choral groups, concert band, dance, drama/theater, jazz band, marching band, music ensembles, musical theater, opera, pep band, radio station, student government, student newspaper, student-run film society, symphony orchestra, yearbook. **Organizations:** 224 registered organizations, 42 honor societies, 7 religious organizations. 13 fraternities 6 sororities **Athletics (Intercollegiate):** *Men:* Baseball, basketball, cross-country, diving, football, ice hockey, soccer, swimming, track/field (indoor), track/field (outdoor). *Women:* Basketball, cross-country, diving, field hockey, ice hockey, soccer, softball, swimming, track/field (indoor), track/field (outdoor), volleyball.

ADMISSIONS

Freshman Academic Profile: 22% in top 10% of high school class, 52% in top 25% of high school class, 86% in top 50% of high school class. SAT Math middle 50% range 480–600. SAT Critical Reading middle 50% range 480–580. SAT Writing middle 50% range 470–570. ACT middle 50% range 19–25. TOEFL required of all international applicants, minimum paper TOEFL 530, minimum computer TOEFL 197. **Basis for Candidate Selection:** *Very important factors considered include:* Academic GPA, class rank, rigor of secondary school record, standardized test scores. *Important factors considered include:* Application essay, recommendation(s). *Other factors considered include:* Character/personal qualities, extracurricular activities, geographical residence, interview, state residency, talent/ability, volunteer work, work experience. **Freshman Admission Requirements:** High school diploma is required, and GED is accepted. *Academic units required:* 4 English, 3 math, 2 science (2 science labs), 2 foreign language, 2 social studies, 4 academic electives, 1 PE for education majors. *Academic units recommended:* 4 English, 4 math, 4 science (3 science labs), 2 foreign language, 3 social studies, 1 history, 4 academic electives, 1 PE for education majors. **Freshman Admission Statistics:** 5,702 applied, 80% admitted, 39% enrolled. **Transfer Admission Requirements:** High school transcript, college transcript(s), essay or personal statement. Minimum college GPA of 2.0 required. Lowest grade transferable C-. **General Admission Information:** Application fee $40. Regular notification is rolling. Non-fall registration accepted. Admission may be deferred for a maximum of 2 semesters. Common Application accepted. Credit offered for CEEB Advanced Placement tests.

COSTS AND FINANCIAL AID

Annual in-state tuition $6,690. Annual out-of-state tuition $18,960. Room and board $7,484. Required fees $1,790. Average book expense $600. **Required Forms and Deadlines:** FAFSA. Financial aid filing deadline 3/1. **Notification of Awards:** Applicants will be notified of awards on a rolling basis beginning on or about 3/15. **Types of Aid:** *Need-based scholarships/grants:* Pell, SEOG, state scholarships/grants, private scholarships, the school's own gift aid. *Loans:* FFEL Subsidized Stafford, FFEL Unsubsidized Stafford, FFEL PLUS, Federal Perkins, state loans. **Financial Aid Statistics:** 53% freshmen, 49% undergrads receive need-based scholarship or grant aid. 55% freshmen, 56% undergrads receive need-based self-help aid. 16 freshmen, 44 undergrads receive athletic scholarships. 76% freshmen, 61% undergrads receive any aid. Highest amount earned per year from on-campus jobs $4,000.

UNIVERSITY OF MAINE—AUGUSTA

46 University Drive, Augusta, ME 04330
Phone: 207-621-3185 **E-mail:** umaadm@maine.edu **CEEB Code:** 3929
Fax: 207-621-3333 **Website:** www.uma.edu
Financial Aid Phone: 207-621-3455

This public school was founded in 1965. It has a 159-acre campus.

RATINGS

Admissions Selectivity Rating: 60*   **Fire Safety Rating:** 60*   **Green Rating:** 82

STUDENTS AND FACULTY

Enrollment: 4,238. **Student Body:** 75% female, 25% male, 1% out-of-state. Caucasian 96%, Native American 3%. **Retention and Graduation:** 55% freshmen return for sophomore year. **Faculty:** Student/faculty ratio 19:1. 100 full-time faculty, 41% hold PhDs. 100% faculty teach undergrads.

ACADEMICS

Degrees: Associate, bachelor's, certificate, post-bachelor's certificate. **Academic Requirements:** Arts/fine arts, computer literacy, English (including composition), history, humanities, mathematics, sciences (biological or physical), social science. **Classes:** Most classes have 10–19 students. Most lab/discussion sections have 10–19 students. **Majors with Highest Enrollment:** Business administration/management, health services/allied health, social sciences. **Disciplines with Highest Percentage of Degrees Awarded:** Health professions and related sciences 40%, business/marketing 20%, library science 15%, public administration and social services 7%, social sciences 6%. **Special Study Options:** Cross registration, distance learning, double major, dual enrollment, honors program, independent study, internships, liberal arts/career combination, student-designed major, study abroad.

FACILITIES

Special Academic Facilities/Equipment: Jewett Gallery, Katz Library, student center. **Computers:** 100% of classrooms are wireless, 99% of public computers are PCs, 1% of public computers are Macs, online registration,

online administrative functions (other than registration), remote student-access to Web through college's connection.

CAMPUS LIFE

Activities: Drama/theater, jazz band, music ensembles, pep band, student government, student newspaper. **Organizations:** 23 registered organizations, 1 honor society, 1 religious organization. **Athletics (Intercollegiate):** *Men:* Basketball. *Women:* Basketball, soccer. **Environmental Initiatives:** Reduce-Reuse-Recycle program in place since 1990. Energy policy states UMA will purchase at least 15% of its electicity from renewable sources. All new facilities over 5000 sq. ft. and major capital renovations over 50% of building replacement value will seek LEED silver rating or equivalent.

ADMISSIONS

Freshman Academic Profile: 88% from public high schools. TOEFL required of all international applicants, minimum paper TOEFL 500, minimum computer TOEFL 173. **Basis for Candidate Selection:** *Important factors considered include:* Academic GPA, class rank, rigor of secondary school record. *Other factors considered include:* Application essay, character/personal qualities, interview, level of applicant's interest, recommendation(s), standardized test scores, talent/ability, volunteer work, work experience. **Freshman Admission Requirements:** High school diploma is required, and GED is accepted. *Academic units recommended:* 4 English, 2 math, 2 science (2 science labs), 2 social studies, 2 history. **Freshman Admission Statistics:** 1,984 applied, 89% admitted, 60% enrolled. **Transfer Admission Requirements:** College transcript(s). Minimum college GPA of 2.0 required. Lowest grade transferable C-. **General Admission Information:** Application fee $40. Regular application deadline 8/30. Regular notification continuous. Non-fall registration accepted. Admission may be deferred for a maxiumum of 2 semesters. Neither credit nor placement offered for CEEB Advanced Placement tests.

COSTS AND FINANCIAL AID

Required Forms and Deadlines: FAFSA. Financial aid filing deadline 3/1. **Notification of Awards:** Applicants will be notified of awards on a rolling basis beginning on or about 3/15. **Types of Aid:** *Need-based scholarships/grants:* Pell, SEOG, state scholarships/grants, private scholarships, the school's own gift aid. *Loans:* Direct Subsidized Stafford, Direct Unsubsidized Stafford, FFEL Subsidized Stafford, FFEL Unsubsidized Stafford, FFEL PLUS, Federal Perkins, Federal Nursing, state loans. **Student Employment:** Federal Work-Study Program available. Institutional employment available. Off-campus job opportunities are fair. **Financial Aid Statistics:** 73% freshmen, 87% undergrads receive need-based scholarship or grant aid. 59% freshmen, 79% undergrads receive need-based self-help aid. 5 freshmen, 5 undergrads receive athletic scholarships. 86% freshmen, 80% undergrads receive any aid. Highest amount earned per year from on-campus jobs $4,708.

UNIVERSITY OF MAINE—FARMINGTON

246 Main Street, Farmington, ME 04938
Phone: 207-778-7050 **E-mail:** umfadmit@maine.edu **CEEB Code:** 3506
Fax: 207-778-8182 **Website:** www.umf.maine.edu **ACT Code:** 1640
Financial Aid Phone: 207-778-7100

This public school was founded in 1863. It has a 55-acre campus.

RATINGS

Admissions Selectivity Rating: 71   **Fire Safety Rating:** 98   **Green Rating:** 96

STUDENTS AND FACULTY

Enrollment: 2,273. **Student Body:** 66% female, 34% male, 18% out-of-state. Caucasian 97%. **Retention and Graduation:** 76% freshmen return for sophomore year. 20% grads go on to further study within 1 year. 15% grads pursue arts and sciences degrees. 3% grads pursue business degrees. 1% grads pursue law degrees. 1% grads pursue medical degrees. **Faculty:** Student/faculty ratio 15:1. 130 full-time faculty, 93% hold PhDs. 100% faculty teach undergrads.

ACADEMICS

Degrees: Bachelor's, certificate. **Academic Requirements:** Arts/fine arts, English (including composition), humanities, mathematics, physical fitness, sciences (biological or physical), social science. **Classes:** Most classes have 10–19 students. Most lab/discussion sections have 10–19 students. **Majors with Highest Enrollment:** Elementary education and teaching, multi/interdisciplinary studies, psychology. **Disciplines with Highest Percentage of Degrees Awarded:** Education 40%, interdisciplinary studies 11%, health professions and related sciences 11%, psychology 9%, English 8%. **Special Study Options:** Accelerated program, cooperative education program, cross registration, double major, dual enrollment, exchange student program (domestic), honors program, independent study, internships, liberal arts/career combination, nation student exchange, SALT documentary field study in Portland. ME service learning, student-designed major, study abroad, teacher certification program.

FACILITIES

Housing: Coed dorms, women's dorms, special housing for international students, housing for students maintaining a certain GPA, medical rooms, quiet floors, wellness community, international community, independent living environment housing available. **Special Academic Facilities/Equipment:** Art gallery, health and fitness center, computer center, Mantor Library, Alumni Theater, Nordica Auditorium, observatory. **Computers:** 100% of classrooms are wired, 100% of classrooms are wireless, 85% of public computers are PCs, 15% of public computers are Macs, network access in dorm rooms, network access in dorm lounges, online registration, online administrative functions (other than registration), remote student-access to Web through college's connection.

CAMPUS LIFE

Activities: Choral groups, concert band, dance, drama/theater, literary magazine, music ensembles, musical theater, radio station, student government, student newspaper, yearbook. **Organizations:** 52 registered organizations, 3 honor societies, 3 religious organizations. **Athletics (Intercollegiate):** *Men:* Baseball, basketball, cross-country, golf, soccer. *Women:* Basketball, cross-country, field hockey, soccer, softball, volleyball. **Environmental Initiatives:** Construction of LEED certified building. Waste minimization. Environmental education for students and public.

ADMISSIONS

Freshman Academic Profile: 11% in top 10% of high school class, 41% in top 25% of high school class, 80% in top 50% of high school class. 88% from public high schools. SAT Math middle 50% range 430–550. SAT Critical Reading middle 50% range 440–5650. SAT Writing middle 50% range 440–560. TOEFL required of all international applicants, minimum paper TOEFL 550, minimum computer TOEFL 213. **Basis for Candidate Selection:** *Very important factors considered include:* Class rank, extracurricular activities, rigor of secondary school record. *Important factors considered include:* Academic GPA, application essay, character/personal qualities, interview, recommendation(s), talent/ability, volunteer work, work experience. *Other factors considered include:* Alumni/ae relation, first generation, geographical residence, level of applicant's interest, racial/ethnic status, state residency. **Freshman Admission Requirements:** High school diploma is required, and GED is accepted. *Academic units required:* 4 English, 3 math, 2 science (2 science labs), 2 foreign language, 2 social studies. *Academic units recommended:* 4 English, 4 math, 3 science (3 science labs), 3 foreign language, 3 social studies, 2 history, 3 academic electives. **Freshman Admission Statistics:** 1,719 applied, 72% admitted, 44% enrolled. **Transfer Admission Requirements:** High school transcript, college transcript(s), essay or personal statement. Minimum college GPA of 2.0 required. Lowest grade transferable C-. **General Admission Information:** Application fee $40. Regular notification is rolling. Non-fall registration accepted. Admission may be deferred for a maxiumum of 2 semesters. Credit and/or placement offered for CEEB Advanced Placement tests.

COSTS AND FINANCIAL AID

Average book expense $560. **Required Forms and Deadlines:** FAFSA. Financial aid filing deadline 3/1. **Notification of Awards:** Applicants will be notified of awards on or about 3/15. **Types of Aid:** *Need-based scholarships/grants:* Pell, SEOG, state scholarships/grants, private scholarships, the school's own gift aid, Native American scholarships and waivers. *Loans:* Direct Subsidized Stafford, Direct Unsubsidized Stafford, Direct PLUS, FFEL Subsidized Stafford, FFEL Unsubsidized Stafford, FFEL PLUS, Federal Perkins, state loans, Teachers for Maine Loans. **Student Employment:** Federal Work-Study Program available. Institutional employment available. Off-campus job opportunities are fair. **Financial Aid Statistics:** 60% freshmen, 54% undergrads receive need-based scholarship or grant aid. 57% freshmen, 59% undergrads receive need-based self-help aid. 71% freshmen, 67% undergrads receive any aid. Highest amount earned per year from on-campus jobs $1,500.

UNIVERSITY OF MAINE—FORT KENT

23 University Drive, Fort Kent, ME 04743
Phone: 207-834-7500 **E-mail:** umfkadm@maine.maine.edu **CEEB Code:** 3393
Fax: 207-834-7609 **Website:** www.umfk.maine.edu **ACT Code:** 1642
Financial Aid Phone: 207-834-7605

This public school was founded in 1878. It has a 52-acre campus.

RATINGS

Admissions Selectivity Rating: 64   **Fire Safety Rating:** 60*   **Green Rating:** 60*

STUDENTS AND FACULTY

Enrollment: 926. **Student Body:** 64% female, 36% male, 31% out-of-state, 3% international. Caucasian 8%. **Retention and Graduation:** 78% freshmen return for sophomore year. **Faculty:** Student/faculty ratio 18:1. 33 full-time faculty, 70% hold PhDs. 100% faculty teach undergrads.

ACADEMICS

Degrees: Associate, bachelor's. **Academic Requirements:** Arts/fine arts, computer literacy, English (including composition), foreign languages, history, humanities, mathematics, sciences (biological or physical), social science. **Classes:** Most classes have 10–19 students. **Majors with Highest Enrollment:** Business administration/management, elementary education and teaching, nursing/registered nurse training (RN, ASN, BSN, MSN). **Disciplines with Highest Percentage of Degrees Awarded:** Education 48%, business/marketing 12%, psychology 11%, health professions and related sciences 10%, social sciences 6%. **Special Study Options:** Cooperative education program, distance learning, double major, exchange student program (domestic), external degree program, honors program, independent study, internships, student-designed major, study abroad, teacher certification program.

FACILITIES

Housing: Coed dorms. **Computers:** Network access in dorm rooms, network access in dorm lounges, online registration, online administrative functions (other than registration), remote student-access to Web through college's connection.

CAMPUS LIFE

Activities: Choral groups, dance, drama/theater, jazz band, literary magazine, musical theater, radio station, student government, student newspaper. **Organizations:** 25 registered organizations, 3 honor societies, 1 religious organization. 1 sorority (2% women join). **Athletics (Intercollegiate):** *Men:* Basketball, cross-country, golf, skiing (downhill/alpine), soccer. *Women:* Basketball, cheerleading, cross-country, golf, skiing (downhill/alpine), soccer.

ADMISSIONS

Freshman Academic Profile: 11% in top 10% of high school class, 25% in top 25% of high school class, 59% in top 50% of high school class. 96% from public high schools. TOEFL required of all international applicants, minimum paper TOEFL 500. **Basis for Candidate Selection:** *Very important factors considered include:* Rigor of secondary school record. *Important factors considered include:* Application essay. *Other factors considered include:* Character/personal qualities, class rank, extracurricular activities, interview, recommendation(s), standardized test scores, talent/ability, volunteer work, work experience. **Freshman Admission Requirements:** High school diploma is required, and GED is accepted. *Academic units required:* 4 English, 2 math, 2 science (2 science labs), 2 social studies. **Freshman Admission Statistics:** 260 applied, 93% admitted, 54% enrolled. **Transfer Admission Requirements:** College transcript(s). Lowest grade transferable D. **General Admission Information:** Application fee $25. Regular notification start in December. Non-fall registration accepted. Common Application accepted.

COSTS AND FINANCIAL AID

Annual in-state tuition $5,100. Annual out-of-state tuition $12,780. Room and board $6,620. Required fees $653. Average book expense $1,030. **Required Forms and Deadlines:** FAFSA. Financial aid filing deadline 3/15. **Types of Aid:** *Need-based scholarships/grants:* Pell, SEOG, state scholarships/grants, private scholarships, the school's own gift aid. *Loans:* FFEL Subsidized Stafford, FFEL Unsubsidized Stafford, FFEL PLUS, Federal Perkins, state loans. **Student Employment:** Federal Work-Study Program available. Institutional employment available. Off-campus job opportunities are good. **Financial Aid Statistics:** Highest amount earned per year from on-campus jobs $1,000.

See page 1446.

UNIVERSITY OF MAINE AT MACHIAS

Office of Admissions, 90 Brien Avenue, Machias, ME 04654
Phone: 207-255-1318 **E-mail:** ummadmissions@maine.edu **CEEB Code:** 3956
Fax: 207-255-1363 **Website:** www.umm.maine.edu **ACT Code:** 1666
Financial Aid Phone: 207-255-1203

This public school was founded in 1909. It has a 42-acre campus.

RATINGS
Admissions Selectivity Rating: 71   **Fire Safety Rating:** 60*   **Green Rating:** 60*

STUDENTS AND FACULTY
Enrollment: 625. **Student Body:** 67% female, 33% male, 24% out-of-state, 8% international (18 countries represented). African American 1%, Caucasian 85%, Hispanic 2%, Native American 4%. **Retention and Graduation:** 65% freshmen return for sophomore year. 12% freshmen graduate within 4 years. **Faculty:** Student/faculty ratio 15:1. 30 full-time faculty, 73% hold PhDs. 100% faculty teach undergrads.

ACADEMICS
Degrees: Bachelor's. **Academic Requirements:** Arts/fine arts, English (including composition), history, humanities, mathematics, personal wellness, public speaking, sciences (biological or physical), social science. **Classes:** Most classes have 10–19 students. Most lab/discussion sections have 10–19 students. **Majors with Highest Enrollment:** Behavioral sciences, business administration/management, parks, recreation and leisure facilities management. **Disciplines with Highest Percentage of Degrees Awarded:** Interdisciplinary studies 21%, business/marketing 18%, liberal arts/general studies 13%, social sciences 13%, biological/life sciences 10%. **Special Study Options:** Cooperative education program, distance learning, double major, dual enrollment, honors program, independent study, internships, student-designed major, study abroad, teacher certification program.

FACILITIES
Housing: Coed dorms. **Special Academic Facilities/Equipment:** Art gallery. **Computers:** 60% of classrooms are wired, 100% of classrooms are wireless, 95% of public computers are PCs, 5% of public computers are Macs, network access in dorm rooms, network access in dorm lounges, online registration, online administrative functions (other than registration), support for handheld computing, remote student-access to Web through college's connection.

CAMPUS LIFE
Activities: Choral groups, dance, drama/theater, literary magazine, music ensembles, musical theater, pep band, radio station, student government. **Organizations:** 38 registered organizations, 2 religious organizations. 4 fraternities (9% men join), 4 sororities (4% women join). **Athletics (Intercollegiate):** *Men:* Basketball, cross-country, soccer. *Women:* Basketball, cross-country, soccer, volleyball.

ADMISSIONS
Freshman Academic Profile: 15% in top 10% of high school class, 31% in top 25% of high school class, 69% in top 50% of high school class. SAT Math middle 50% range 400–540. SAT Critical Reading middle 50% range 410–540. ACT middle 50% range 19–21. TOEFL required of all international applicants, minimum paper TOEFL 500, minimum computer TOEFL 173. **Basis for Candidate Selection:** *Very important factors considered include:* Application essay, interview, recommendation(s), rigor of secondary school record. *Important factors considered include:* Class rank, extracurricular activities, standardized test scores. *Other factors considered include:* Character/personal qualities, talent/ability, volunteer work, work experience. **Freshman Admission Requirements:** High school diploma is required, and GED is accepted. *Academic units required:* 4 English, 3 math, 2 science (2 science labs), 2 social studies. *Academic units recommended:* 2 foreign language, 3 academic electives. **Freshman Admission Statistics:** 355 applied, 85% admitted, 30% enrolled. **Transfer Admission Requirements:** High school transcript, college transcript(s), statement of good standing from prior institution(s). Minimum college GPA of 2.0 required. Lowest grade transferable C-. **General Admission Information:** Application fee $40. Regular application deadline 8/15. Regular notification rolling. Non-fall registration accepted. Admission may be deferred for a maxiumum of 2 semesters. Common Application accepted. Credit offered for CEEB Advanced Placement tests.

COSTS AND FINANCIAL AID
Annual in-state tuition $4,650. Out-of-state tuition $12,510. Room & board $5,962. Required fees $595. Average book expense $650. **Required Forms and Deadlines:** FAFSA. Financial aid filing deadline 3/1. **Notification of Awards:** Applicants will be notified of awards on a rolling basis beginning on or about 3/1. **Types of Aid:** *Need-based scholarships/grants:* Pell, SEOG, state

scholarships/grants, private scholarships, the school's own gift aid. *Loans:* FFEL Subsidized Stafford, FFEL Unsubsidized Stafford, FFEL PLUS, Federal Perkins. **Financial Aid Statistics:** 79% freshmen, 70% undergrads receive need-based scholarship or grant aid. 66% freshmen, 64% undergrads receive need-based self-help aid. 82% freshmen, 74% undergrads receive any aid. Highest amount earned per year from on-campus jobs $1,200.

UNIVERSITY OF MAINE—PRESQUE ISLE

Office of Admissions, 181 Main Street, Presque Isle, ME 04769
Phone: 207-768-9532 **E-mail:** adventure@umpi.maine.edu **CEEB Code:** 3008
Fax: 207-768-9777 **Website:** www.umpi.maine.edu
Financial Aid Phone: 207-768-9510

This public school was founded in 1903. It has a 150-acre campus.

RATINGS
Admissions Selectivity Rating: 68   **Fire Safety Rating:** 76   **Green Rating:** 60*

STUDENTS AND FACULTY
Enrollment: 1,266. **Student Body:** 64% female, 36% male, 2% out-of-state, 9% international (5 countries represented). Caucasian 71%, Native American 4%. **Retention and Graduation:** 55% freshmen return for sophomore year. **Faculty:** Student/faculty ratio 16:1. 54 full-time faculty, 81% hold PhDs. 100% faculty teach undergrads.

ACADEMICS
Degrees: Associate, bachelor's, certificate. **Academic Requirements:** Arts/fine arts, English (including composition), foreign languages, history, humanities, mathematics, sciences (biological or physical), social science. **Classes:** Most classes have 10–19 students. Most lab/discussion sections have 10–19 students. **Majors with Highest Enrollment:** Elementary education and teaching, liberal arts and sciences/liberal studies, social work. **Disciplines with Highest Percentage of Degrees Awarded:** Liberal arts/general studies 46%, education 17%, business/marketing 9%, public administration and social services 5%, interdisciplinary studies 4%. **Special Study Options:** Accelerated program, cooperative education program, cross registration, distance learning, double major, exchange student program (domestic), honors program, independent study, internships, student-designed major, study abroad, teacher certification program.

FACILITIES
Housing: Coed dorms, apartments for married students. **Special Academic Facilities/Equipment:** Museum and art gallery, Gentile Hall. **Computers:** 100% of classrooms are wired, 100% of classrooms are wireless, 100% of public computers are PCs, network access in dorm rooms, online registration, online administrative functions (other than registration), support for handheld computing, remote student-access to Web through college's connection.

CAMPUS LIFE
Activities: Drama/theater, radio station, student government, student newspaper. **Organizations:** 27 registered organizations, 1 honor society, 1 religious organization. 1 fraternity (1% men join), 1 sorority (1% women join). **Athletics (Intercollegiate):** *Men:* Baseball, basketball, cross-country, golf, skiing (nordic/cross-country), soccer. *Women:* Basketball, cross-country, skiing (nordic/cross-country), soccer, softball, volleyball.

ADMISSIONS
Freshman Academic Profile: 8% in top 10% of high school class, 23% in top 25% of high school class, 51% in top 50% of high school class. SAT Math middle 50% range 390–500. SAT Critical Reading middle 50% range 390–530. TOEFL required of all international applicants, minimum paper TOEFL 550, minimum computer TOEFL 230. **Basis for Candidate Selection:** *Very important factors considered include:* Academic GPA, application essay, class rank, recommendation(s), rigor of secondary school record. *Important factors considered include:* Interview. *Other factors considered include:* Alumni/ae relation, character/personal qualities, extracurricular activities, racial/ethnic status, standardized test scores, state residency, talent/ability, volunteer work, work experience. **Freshman Admission Requirements:** High school diploma is required, and GED is accepted. *Academic units recommended:* 4 English, 3 math, 2 science (2 science labs), 2 foreign language, 3 social studies, 2 academic electives. **Freshman Admission Statistics:** 483 applied, 86% admitted, 51% enrolled. **Transfer Admission Requirements:** High school transcript, college transcript(s), essay or personal statement, statement of good standing from prior institution(s). Minimum college GPA of 2.0 required. Lowest grade transferable C-. **General Admission Information:** Application fee $40. Regular notification within 30 days after receipt of application. Non-fall registration

accepted. Admission may be deferred for a maximum of up to 2 semesters. Common Application accepted. Credit offered for CEEB Advanced Placement tests.

COSTS AND FINANCIAL AID
Annual in-state tuition $4,290. Out-of-state tuition $10,680. Room & board $5,246. Required fees $530. Average book expense $800. **Required Forms and Deadlines:** FAFSA. Financial aid filing deadline 4/1. **Notification of Awards:** Applicants will be notified of awards on a rolling basis beginning on or about 3/1. **Types of Aid:** *Need-based scholarships/grants:* Pell, SEOG, state scholarships/grants, private scholarships, the school's own gift aid. *Loans:* Direct Subsidized Stafford, Direct Unsubsidized Stafford, Direct PLUS, Federal Perkins, state loans, college/university loans from institutional funds. **Financial Aid Statistics:** 66% freshmen, 52% undergrads receive need-based scholarship or grant aid. 50% freshmen, 43% undergrads receive need-based self-help aid. 89% freshmen, 89% undergrads receive any aid.

UNIVERSITY OF MANITOBA

424 University Centre, Winnipeg, MB R3T 2N2 Canada
Phone: 204-474-8808 **E-mail:** admissions@umanitoba.ca
Fax: 204-474-7554 **Website:** www.umanitoba.ca
Financial Aid Phone: 204-474-8197

This public school was founded in 1877. It has a 274-acre campus.

RATINGS
Admissions Selectivity Rating: 60*   **Fire Safety Rating:** 60*   **Green Rating:** 60*

STUDENTS AND FACULTY
Enrollment: 20,534. **Student Body:** 57% female, 43% male, 12% out-of-province. **Faculty:** 1,423 full-time faculty, 94% hold PhDs. 100% faculty teach undergrads.

ACADEMICS
Degrees: Bachelor's, certificate, diploma, doctoral, first professional, master's. **Academic Requirements:** English (including composition), mathematics. **Classes:** Most classes have 20–29 students. **Special Study Options:** Cooperative education program, distance learning, double major, honors program, independent study, internships, teacher certification program, weekend college.

FACILITIES
Housing: Coed dorms. **Special Academic Facilities/Equipment:** Planeterium, zoological museum, archives, art galleries. **Computers:** 57% of public computers are PCs, 9% of public computers are Macs, 33% of public computers are UNIX, network access in dorm lounges, online registration, online administrative functions (other than registration), remote student-access to Web through college's connection.

CAMPUS LIFE
Activities: Choral groups, concert band, drama/theater, jazz band, music ensembles, radio station, student government, student newspaper. **Organizations:** 40 registered organizations, 5 religious organizations. **Athletics (Intercollegiate):** *Men:* Basketball, cross-country, diving, football, golf, gymnastics, ice hockey, swimming, track/field (outdoor), volleyball, wrestling. *Women:* Basketball, cross-country, diving, field hockey, golf, gymnastics, ice hockey, swimming, track/field (outdoor), volleyball, wrestling.

ADMISSIONS
Freshman Academic Profile: TOEFL required of all international applicants, minimum paper TOEFL 550, minimum computer TOEFL 213. **Basis for Candidate Selection:** *Very important factors considered include:* Rigor of secondary school record. **Freshman Admission Requirements:** High school diploma is required, and GED is accepted. *Academic units required:* 4 English, 4 math. *Academic units recommended:* 4 English, 4 math, 4 science (3 science labs). **Freshman Admission Statistics:** 6,810 applied, 85% admitted, 75% enrolled. **Transfer Admission Requirements:** College transcript(s). **General Admission Information:** Application fee $35. Early decision application deadline 12/1. Regular application deadline 7/1. Regular notification is rolling. Non-fall registration accepted. Common Application not accepted. Credit offered for CEEB Advanced Placement tests.

COSTS AND FINANCIAL AID
In-province tuition $3,049–$13,595. Out-of-province tuition $3,049–$13,595. International tuition $5,335–$23,791. Room & board $5,343. Required fees $450. Average book expense $1,200. **Student Employment:** Institutional employment available. Off-campus job opportunities are good.

UNIVERSITY OF MARY

7500 University Drive, Bismarck, ND 58504
Phone: 701-255-7500 **E-mail:** suerood@umary.edu **CEEB Code:** 6428
Fax: 701-255-7687 **Website:** www.umary.edu **ACT Code:** 3201
Financial Aid Phone: 701-255-7500

This private school, affiliated with the Roman Catholic Church, was founded in 1959. It has a 107-acre campus.

RATINGS
Admissions Selectivity Rating: 70   **Fire Safety Rating:** 60*   **Green Rating:** 60*

STUDENTS AND FACULTY
Enrollment: 1,722. **Student Body:** 62% female, 38% male. Caucasian 11%. **Retention and Graduation:** 70% freshmen return for sophomore year. 1% grads pursue arts and sciences degrees. 4% grads pursue business degrees. 2% grads pursue law degrees. **Faculty:** Student/faculty ratio 17:1. 100% faculty teach undergrads.

ACADEMICS
Degrees: Associate, bachelor's, doctoral, master's. **Academic Requirements:** Arts/fine arts, English (including composition), history, humanities, mathematics, philosophy, sciences (biological or physical), social science. **Majors with Highest Enrollment:** Business administration/management, health services/allied health, nursing/registered nurse training (RN, ASN, BSN, MSN). **Special Study Options:** Accelerated program, cooperative education program, distance learning, double major, dual enrollment, external degree program, honors program, independent study, internships, study abroad, teacher certification program.

FACILITIES
Housing: Men's dorms, women's dorms, apartments for single students. **Special Academic Facilities/Equipment:** Art gallery.

CAMPUS LIFE
Activities: Choral groups, concert band, drama/theater, jazz band, literary magazine, music ensembles, musical theater, pep band, radio station, student government, student newspaper, television station, yearbook. **Organizations:** 50 registered organizations, 5 honor societies, 6 religious organizations. **Athletics (Intercollegiate):** *Men:* Baseball, basketball, cross-country, football, golf, soccer, tennis, track/field (indoor), track/field (outdoor), wrestling. *Women:* Basketball, cheerleading, cross-country, golf, soccer, softball, tennis, track/field (indoor), track/field (outdoor), volleyball.

ADMISSIONS
Freshman Academic Profile: 9% in top 10% of high school class, 38% in top 25% of high school class, 71% in top 50% of high school class. ACT middle 50% range 19–24. TOEFL required of all international applicants, minimum paper TOEFL 500. **Basis for Candidate Selection:** *Very important factors considered include:* Standardized test scores. *Important factors considered include:* Class rank, recommendation(s), rigor of secondary school record. *Other factors considered include:* Application essay, character/personal qualities, interview. **Freshman Admission Requirements:** High school diploma is required, and GED is accepted. *Academic units recommended:* 4 English, 2 math, 2 science, 3 social studies. **Freshman Admission Statistics:** 943 applied, 95% admitted, 48% enrolled. **Transfer Admission Requirements:** College transcript(s). Minimum college GPA of 2.0 required. Lowest grade transferable D. **General Admission Information:** Application fee $15. Regular application deadline 8/23. Regular notification is rolling. Non-fall registration accepted. Common Application accepted. Credit and/or placement offered for CEEB Advanced Placement tests.

COSTS AND FINANCIAL AID
Annual tuition $9,200. Room & board $3,540. Required fees $300. Average book expense $610. **Required Forms and Deadlines:** FAFSA. Financial aid filing deadline 5/1. **Types of Aid:** *Need-based scholarships/grants:* Pell, SEOG, state scholarships/grants, private scholarships, the school's own gift aid. *Loans:* FFEL Subsidized Stafford, FFEL Unsubsidized Stafford, FFEL PLUS, Federal Perkins, Federal Nursing. **Student Employment:** Federal Work-Study Program available. Institutional employment available. Off-campus job opportunities are good. **Financial Aid Statistics:** 79% freshmen, 52% undergrads receive need-based scholarship or grant aid. 79% freshmen, 52% undergrads receive need-based self-help aid. Highest amount earned per year from on-campus jobs $1,000.

UNIVERSITY OF MARY HARDIN-BAYLOR

UMHB Box 8004, 900 College Street, Belton, TX 76513
Phone: 254-295-4520 **E-mail:** admissions@umhb.edu **CEEB Code:** 6396
Fax: 254-295-5049 **Website:** www.umhb.edu **ACT Code:** 4128
Financial Aid Phone: 254-295-4517

This private school, affiliated with the Baptist Church, was founded in 1845. It has a 170-acre campus.

RATINGS
Admissions Selectivity Rating: 73   **Fire Safety Rating:** 69   **Green Rating:** 60*

STUDENTS AND FACULTY
Enrollment: 2,575. **Student Body:** 64% female, 36% male, 1% out-of-state. African American 11%, Asian 2%, Caucasian 74%, Hispanic 12%. **Retention and Graduation:** 65% freshmen return for sophomore year. **Faculty:** Student/faculty ratio 13:1. 134 full-time faculty, 69% hold PhDs. 99% faculty teach undergrads.

ACADEMICS
Degrees: Bachelor's, doctoral, master's. **Academic Requirements:** English (including composition), foreign languages, mathematics, physical education, religion, sciences (biological or physical), social science, speech. **Classes:** Most classes have 10–19 students. Most lab/discussion sections have 20–29 students. **Majors with Highest Enrollment:** Elementary education and teaching, nursing/registered nurse training (RN, ASN, BSN, MSN), psychology. **Disciplines with Highest Percentage of Degrees Awarded:** Business/marketing 15%, education 14%, health professions and related sciences 13%, psychology 9%, computer and information sciences 8%. **Special Study Options:** Accelerated program, double major, dual enrollment, English as a second language (ESL), honors program, independent study, internships, study abroad, teacher certification program; tuition exchange program with other participating universities. Undergrads may take grad level classes.

FACILITIES
Housing: Men's dorms, women's dorms, apartments for single students, special housing for disabled students. **Special Academic Facilities/Equipment:** Language lab. **Computers:** 100% of public computers are PCs, network access in dorm rooms, network access in dorm lounges, online administrative functions (other than registration), remote student-access to Web through college's connection.

CAMPUS LIFE
Activities: Choral groups, concert band, drama/theater, jazz band, literary magazine, marching band, music ensembles, musical theater, opera, student government, student newspaper, symphony orchestra, yearbook. **Organizations:** 44 registered organizations, 12 honor societies, 8 religious organizations. **Athletics (Intercollegiate):** *Men:* Baseball, basketball, football, golf, soccer, tennis. *Women:* Basketball, golf, soccer, softball, tennis, volleyball.

ADMISSIONS
Freshman Academic Profile: 19% in top 10% of high school class, 46% in top 25% of high school class, 79% in top 50% of high school class. 92% from public high schools. Math middle 50% range 460–570. SAT Critical Reading middle 50% range 450–560. SAT Writing middle 50% range 440–550. ACT middle 50% range 20–24. **Basis for Candidate Selection:** *Very important factors considered include:* Standardized test scores. *Important factors considered include:* Class rank. *Other factors considered include:* Alumni/ae relation, application essay, character/personal qualities, extracurricular activities, geographical residence, interview, racial/ethnic status, recommendation(s), religious affiliation/commitment, rigor of secondary school record, state residence. **Freshman Admission Requirements:** High school diploma is required, and GED is accepted. *Academic units required:* 4 English, 3 math, 2 social studies. **Freshman Admission Statistics:** 1,261 applied, 75% admitted, 53% enrolled. **Transfer Admission Requirements:** College transcript(s). Minimum college GPA of 2.0 required. Lowest grade transferable C. **General Admission Information:** Application fee $35. Regular notification rolling. Non-fall registration accepted. Credit offered for CEEB Advanced Placement tests.

COSTS AND FINANCIAL AID
Annual tuition $15,750. Room and board $4,700. Required fees $2,010. Average book expense $1,200. **Required Forms and Deadlines:** FAFSA, institution's own financial aid form. Financial aid filing deadline 3/1. **Notification of Awards:** Applicants will be notified of awards on or about 2/1. **Types of Aid:** *Need-based scholarships/grants:* Pell, SEOG, state scholarships/grants, private scholarships, the school's own gift aid, Federal Nursing Scholarships, Federal Work Study, Texas State Work Study, UMHB work duty. *Loans:* FFEL

Subsidized Stafford, FFEL Unsubsidized Stafford, FFEL PLUS, Federal Perkins, state loans, college/university loans from institutional funds. **Financial Aid Statistics:** 39% freshmen, 57% undergrads receive need-based scholarship or grant aid. 19% freshmen, 38% undergrads receive need-based self-help aid. 92% freshmen, 92% undergrads receive any aid. Highest amount earned per year from on-campus jobs $2,300.

UNIVERSITY OF MARY WASHINGTON

1301 College Avenue, Fredericksburg, VA 22401
Phone: 540-654-2000 **E-mail:** admit@umw.edu **CEEB Code:** 5398
Fax: 540-654-1857 **Website:** www.umw.edu **ACT Code:** 4414
Financial Aid Phone: 540-654-2468

This public school was founded in 1908. It has a 176-acre campus.

RATINGS
Admissions Selectivity Rating: 87   **Fire Safety Rating:** 73   **Green Rating:** 83

STUDENTS AND FACULTY
Enrollment: 4,051. **Student Body:** 66% female, 34% male, 28% out-of-state. African American 3%, Asian 4%, Caucasian 73%, Hispanic 3%. **Retention and Graduation:** 84% freshmen return for sophomore year. 71% freshmen graduate within 4 years. 20% grads go on to further study within 1 year. 17% grads pursue arts and sciences degrees. 2% grads pursue business degrees. 2% grads pursue law degrees. **Faculty:** Student/faculty ratio 15:1. 242 full-time faculty, 74% hold PhDs. 94% faculty teach undergrads.

ACADEMICS
Degrees: Bachelor's, certificate, master's, post-bachelor's certificate, post-master's certificate. **Academic Requirements:** Arts/fine arts, computer literacy, English (including composition), foreign languages, history, humanities, mathematics, philosophy, sciences (biological or physical), social science. **Classes:** Most classes have 20–29 students. Most lab/discussion sections have 20–29 students. **Majors with Highest Enrollment:** Business administration and management, English language and literature, psychology. **Disciplines with Highest Percentage of Degrees Awarded:** Social sciences 16%, business/marketing 13%, English 10%, interdisciplinary studies 9%, psychology 8%. **Special Study Options:** Double major, independent study, internships, student-designed major, study abroad, teacher certification program.

FACILITIES
Housing: Coed dorms, men's dorms, women's dorms, apartments for single students, special housing for disabled students, substance-free, service learning. **Special Academic Facilities/Equipment:** Two art galleries, center for historic preservation, language labs, Leidecker Center for Asian Studies, cartography lab. **Computers:** 5% of classrooms are wired, 100% of classrooms are wireless, 75% of public computers are PCs, 15% of public computers are Macs, 10% of public computers are UNIX, network access in dorm rooms, network access in dorm lounges, online registration, online administrative functions (other than registration), support for handheld computing, remote student-access to Web through college's connection.

CAMPUS LIFE
Activities: Choral groups, concert band, dance, drama/theater, jazz band, literary magazine, music ensembles, musical theater, opera, radio station, student government, student newspaper, student-run film society, symphony orchestra, yearbook. **Organizations:** 95 registered organizations, 21 honor societies, 11 religious organizations. **Athletics (Intercollegiate):** *Men:* Baseball, basketball, crew/rowing, cross-country, equestrian sports, lacrosse, soccer, swimming, tennis, track/field (indoor), track/field (outdoor). *Women:* Basketball, crew/rowing, cross-country, equestrian sports, field hockey, lacrosse, soccer, softball, swimming, tennis, track/field (indoor), track/field (outdoor), volleyball. **Environmental Initiatives:** Have partnered with the consulting firm NORESCO to 1) replace energy wasting fixtures throughout campus and 2) educate students about their energy use to encourage shorter showers and turning off electronic equipment when not in use. Received the region's first LEED Certification for a new building at graduate campus.

ADMISSIONS
Freshman Academic Profile: 38% in top 10% of high school class, 74% in top

25% of high school class, 96% in top 50% of high school class. 76% from public high schools. SAT Math middle 50% range 530–630. SAT Critical Reading middle 50% range 560–660. SAT Writing middle 50% range 550–650. ACT middle 50% range 23–27. TOEFL required of all international applicants, minimum paper TOEFL 550, minimum computer TOEFL 230. **Basis for Candidate Selection:** *Very important factors considered include:* Academic GPA, class rank, rigor of secondary school record, standardized test scores. *Important factors considered include:* Application essay, character/personal qualities, extracurricular activities, volunteer work. *Other factors considered include:* Alumni/ae relation, racial/ethnic status, recommendation(s), state residency, talent/ability, work experience. **Freshman Admission Requirements:** High school diploma is required, and GED is accepted. *Academic units required:* 4 English, 3 math, 3 science (3 science labs), 2 social studies, 2 history. *Academic units recommended:* 4 English, 4 math, 4 science (4 science labs), 4 foreign language, 2 social studies, 2 history. **Freshman Admission Statistics:** 4,287 applied, 70% admitted, 31% enrolled. **Transfer Admission Requirements:** High school transcript, college transcript(s), standardized test score, statement of good standing from prior institution(s). Minimum college GPA of 3.0 required. Lowest grade transferable C. **General Admission Information:** Application fee $40. Regular application deadline 2/1. Regular notification 4/1. Non-fall registration accepted. Admission may be deferred for a maximum of 2 semesters. Credit offered for CEEB Advanced Placement tests.

COSTS AND FINANCIAL AID

Annual in-state tuition $6,494. Annual out-of-state tuition $16,968. Room and board $6,606. Average book expense $900. **Required Forms and Deadlines:** FAFSA. Financial aid filing deadline 5/31. **Notification of Awards:** Applicants will be notified of awards on or about 4/15. **Types of Aid:** *Need-based scholarships/grants:* Pell, SEOG, state scholarships/grants, private scholarships, the school's own gift aid. *Loans:* FFEL Subsidized Stafford, FFEL Unsubsidized Stafford, FFEL PLUS, Federal Perkins. **Financial Aid Statistics:** 37% freshmen, 36% undergrads receive need-based scholarship or grant aid. 41% freshmen, 43% undergrads receive need-based self-help aid. 57% freshmen, 59% undergrads receive any aid. Highest amount earned per year from on-campus jobs $1,500.

UNIVERSITY OF MARYLAND— BALTIMORE COUNTY

Best 368

1000 Hilltop Circle, Baltimore, MD 21250
Phone: 410-455-2291 **E-mail:** admissions@umbc.edu **CEEB Code:** 5835
Fax: 410-455-1094 **Website:** www.umbc.edu **ACT Code:** 1751
Financial Aid Phone: 410-455-2387

This public school was founded in 1966. It has a 530-acre campus.

RATINGS

Admissions Selectivity Rating: 85   **Fire Safety Rating:** 85   **Green Rating:** 76

STUDENTS AND FACULTY

Enrollment: 9,274. **Student Body:** 46% female, 54% male, 8% out-of-state, 4% international (90 countries represented). African American 15%, Asian 21%, Caucasian 54%, Hispanic 4%. **Retention and Graduation:** 82% freshmen return for sophomore year. 40% grads go on to further study within 1 year. 34% grads pursue arts and sciences degrees. 5% grads pursue medical degrees. **Faculty:** Student/faculty ratio 17:1. 482 full-time faculty, 88% hold PhDs. 100% faculty teach undergrads.

ACADEMICS

Degrees: Bachelor's, doctoral, master's, post-bachelor's certificate. **Academic Requirements:** Arts/fine arts, English (including composition), foreign languages, humanities, mathematics, sciences (biological or physical), social science. **Classes:** Most classes have 10–19 students. Most lab/discussion sections have 10–19 students. **Majors with Highest Enrollment:** Biology/biological sciences, computer and information sciences, psychology. **Disciplines with Highest Percentage of Degrees Awarded:** Communication technologies 20%, social sciences 17%, psychology 12%, biological/life sciences 12%, visual and performing arts 8%. **Special Study Options:** Cooperative education program, cross registration, distance learning, double major, dual enrollment, English as a second language (ESL), exchange student program

(domestic), honors program, independent study, internships, liberal arts/career combination, student-designed major, study abroad, teacher certification program.

FACILITIES

Housing: Coed dorms, apartments for single students, special housing for disabled students, same sex floors, honors floors, quiet lifestyle, substance-free, living-learning communities: center for women and information technology, emergency health services. **Special Academic Facilities/Equipment:** Albin O. Kuhn Library and Gallery, center for art and visual culture, center for environmental science, center for photonics technology, center on research and teaching in social work, imaging research center, institute for global electronic commerce, joint center for Earth systems technology, laboratory for healthcare informatics, Maryland Institute for Policy Analysis and Research, Shriver Center, Goddard Earth Science and Technology Center. **Computers:** 70% of classrooms are wireless, 85% of public computers are PCs, 15% of public computers are Macs, 85% of public computers are UNIX, network access in dorm rooms, network access in dorm lounges, online registration, online administrative functions (other than registration), support for handheld computing, remote student-access to Web through college's connection.

CAMPUS LIFE

Activities: Choral groups, dance, drama/theater, jazz band, literary magazine, music ensembles, pep band, radio station, student government, student newspaper, student-run film society, symphony orchestra. **Organizations:** 210 registered organizations, 24 honor societies, 22 religious organizations. 11 fraternities, 9 sororities. **Athletics (Intercollegiate):** *Men:* Baseball, basketball, cheerleading, cross-country, diving, lacrosse, soccer, swimming, tennis, track/field (indoor), track/field (outdoor). *Women:* Basketball, cheerleading, cross-country, diving, lacrosse, soccer, softball, swimming, tennis, track/field (indoor), track/field (outdoor), volleyball.

ADMISSIONS

Freshman Academic Profile: 28% in top 10% of high school class, 57% in top 25% of high school class, 87% in top 50% of high school class. 75% from public high schools. SAT Math middle 50% range 560–660. SAT Critical Reading middle 50% range 520–640. SAT Writing middle 50% range 520–630. ACT middle 50% range 22–27. TOEFL required of all international applicants, minimum paper TOEFL 550, minimum computer TOEFL 220. **Basis for Candidate Selection:** *Very important factors considered include:* Academic GPA, rigor of secondary school record, standardized test scores. *Important factors considered include:* Application essay, class rank, recommendation(s). *Other factors considered include:* Character/personal qualities, extracurricular activities, talent/ability, volunteer work. **Freshman Admission Requirements:** High school diploma is required, and GED is accepted. *Academic units required:* 4 English, 3 math, 3 science (2 science labs), 2 foreign language, 2 social studies, 2 history, 4 academic electives. *Academic units recommended:* 4 English, 4 math, 3 science (2 science labs), 2 foreign language, 2 social studies, 2 history, 4 academic electives. **Freshman Admission Statistics:** 5,405 applied, 72% admitted, 37% enrolled. **Transfer Admission Requirements:** College transcript(s). Minimum college GPA of 2.5 required. Lowest grade transferable C. **General Admission Information:** Application fee $50. Regular application deadline 2/1. Regular notification 2/1. Regular decision rolling until 5/1. Non-fall registration accepted. Admission may be deferred for a maxiumum of 2 semesters. Credit and/or placement offered for CEEB Advanced Placement tests.

COSTS AND FINANCIAL AID

Required Forms and Deadlines: FAFSA. Financial aid filing deadline 2/14. **Notification of Awards:** Applicants will be notified of awards on or about 4/1. **Types of Aid:** *Need-based scholarships/grants:* Pell, SEOG, state scholarships/grants, private scholarships, the school's own gift aid. *Loans:* FFEL Subsidized Stafford, FFEL Unsubsidized Stafford, FFEL PLUS, Federal Perkins. **Financial Aid Statistics:** 36% freshmen, 36% undergrads receive need-based scholarship or grant aid. 38% freshmen, 42% undergrads receive need-based self-help aid. 91 freshmen, 358 undergrads receive athletic scholarships. 72% freshmen, 57% undergrads receive any aid.

See page 1448.

UNIVERSITY OF MARYLAND—COLLEGE PARK

Mitchell Building, College Park, MD 20742-5235
Phone: 301-314-9395 **E-mail:** um-admit@uga.umd.edu **CEEB Code:** 5814
Fax: 301-314-9693 **Website:** www.umd.edu **ACT Code:** 1746
Financial Aid Phone: 301-314-9000

This public school was founded in 1856. It has a 1,382-acre campus.

RATINGS

Admissions Selectivity Rating: 94   **Fire Safety Rating:** 83   **Green Rating:** 94

STUDENTS AND FACULTY

Enrollment: 24,590. **Student Body:** 49% female, 51% male, 22% out-of-state, 2% international (142 countries represented). African American 13%, Asian 14%, Caucasian 56%, Hispanic 6%. **Retention and Graduation:** 92% freshmen return for sophomore year. 55% freshmen graduate within 4 years. **Faculty:** Student/faculty ratio 18:1. 1,581 full-time faculty, 93% hold PhDs. 64% faculty teach undergrads.

ACADEMICS

Degrees: Bachelor's, certificate, doctoral, first professional, master's, post-bachelor's certificate, post-master's certificate. **Academic Requirements:** Advanced studies courses outside of one's major, arts/fine arts, English (including composition), diversity course, history, humanities, mathematics, sciences (biological or physical), social science. **Classes:** Most classes have 20–29 students. Most lab/discussion sections have 20–29 students. **Majors with Highest Enrollment:** Criminology, economics, political science and government. **Disciplines with Highest Percentage of Degrees Awarded:** Social sciences 22%, business/marketing 16%, engineering 10%, biological/life sciences 9%, computer and information sciences 5%, education 5%, psychology 5%. **Special Study Options:** Accelerated program, Beyond the Classroom, CIVICUS program, College Park Scholars, cooperative education program, cross registration, distance learning, double major, dual enrollment, English as a second language (ESL), exchange student program (domestic), external degree program, first-year learning communities, gemstone program, global communities, Hinman CEOs, honors program, honors humanities, independent study, internships, Jimenez-Porter Writers House, language house, living learning programs, student-designed major, study abroad, teacher certification program, university honors.

FACILITIES

Housing: Coed dorms, women's dorms, apartments for single students, special housing for disabled students, special housing for international students, fraternity/sorority housing, Gemstone program, College Park Scholars, language house, Beyond the Classroom. **Special Academic Facilities/Equipment:** Aerospace buoyancy lab, art gallery, international piano archives, center for architectural design and research, model nuclear reactor, wind tunnel. **Computers:** 1% of classrooms are wired, 100% of classrooms are wireless, 70% of public computers are PCs, 25% of public computers are Macs, 5% of public computers are UNIX, network access in dorm rooms, network access in dorm lounges, online registration, online administrative functions (other than registration), support for handheld computing, remote student-access to Web through college's connection.

CAMPUS LIFE

Activities: Choral groups, concert band, dance, drama/theater, jazz band, literary magazine, marching band, music ensembles, musical theater, opera, pep band, radio station, student government, student newspaper, student-run film society, symphony orchestra, television station. **Organizations:** 527 registered organizations, 49 honor societies, 49 religious organizations. 31 fraternities, 25 sororities. **Athletics (Intercollegiate):** *Men:* Baseball, basketball, cross-country, diving, football, golf, lacrosse, soccer, swimming, tennis, track/field (indoor), track/field (outdoor), wrestling. *Women:* Basketball, cheerleading, cross-country, diving, field hockey, golf, gymnastics, lacrosse, soccer, softball, swimming, tennis, track/field (indoor), track/field (outdoor), volleyball, water polo. **Environmental Initiatives:** Established an Office of Sustainability. Developing a Climate Action Plan consistant with the American College and University Presidents Climate Committment. Established a LEED-Silver green building requirement for all new construction and major renovations.

ADMISSIONS

Freshman Academic Profile: 50% in top 10% of high school class, 83% in top 25% of high school class, 99% in top 50% of high school class. SAT Math middle 50% range 600–710. SAT Critical Reading middle 50% range 570–680. TOEFL required of all international applicants, minimum paper TOEFL 575, minimum computer TOEFL 232. **Basis for Candidate Selection:** *Very important factors considered include:* Academic GPA, rigor of secondary school record, standardized test scores. *Important factors considered include:* Application essay, class rank, first generation, recommendation(s), state residency, talent/ability. *Other factors considered include:* Alumni/ae relation, character/personal qualities, extracurricular activities, geographical residence, racial/ethnic status, volunteer work, work experience. **Freshman Admission Requirements:** High school diploma is required, and GED is accepted. *Academic units required:* 4 English, 3 math, 3 science (2 science labs), 2 foreign language, 3 social studies. *Academic units recommended:* 4 math. **Freshman Admission Statistics:** 23,546 applied, 44% admitted, 38% enrolled. **Transfer Admission Requirements:** College transcript(s), statement of good standing from prior institution(s). Lowest grade transferable C. **General Admission Information:** Application fee $55. Regular application deadline 1/20. Regular notification 4/1. Non-fall registration accepted. Admission may be deferred for a maxiumum of 2 semesters. Credit and/or placement offered for CEEB Advanced Placement tests.

COSTS AND FINANCIAL AID

Annual in-state tuition $6,566. Out-of-state tuition $20,005. Room & board $8,562. Required fees $1,340. Average book expense $1,002. **Required Forms and Deadlines:** FAFSA. Financial aid filing deadline 2/15. **Notification of Awards:** Applicants will be notified of awards on a rolling basis beginning on or about 4/1. **Types of Aid:** *Need-based scholarships/grants:* Pell, SEOG, state scholarships/grants, private scholarships, the school's own gift aid. *Loans:* FFEL Subsidized Stafford, FFEL Unsubsidized Stafford, FFEL PLUS, Federal Perkins. **Financial Aid Statistics:** 23% freshmen, 26% undergrads receive need-based scholarship or grant aid. 25% freshmen, 28% undergrads receive need-based self-help aid. 119 freshmen, 466 undergrads receive athletic scholarships. 71% freshmen, 60% undergrads receive any aid.

See page 1450.

UNIVERSITY OF MARYLAND—EASTERN SHORE

Office of Admissions, Backbone Road, Princess Anne, MD 21853
Phone: 410-651-6410 **E-mail:** ccmills@mail.umes.edu **CEEB Code:** 5400
Fax: 410-651-7922 **Website:** www.umes.edu **ACT Code:** 1752
Financial Aid Phone: 410-651-6172

This public school was founded in 1886. It has a 620-acre campus.

RATINGS

Admissions Selectivity Rating: 60*   **Fire Safety Rating:** 60*   **Green Rating:** 60*

STUDENTS AND FACULTY

Enrollment: 2,704. **Student Body:** 57% female, 43% male, 26% out-of-state. African American 80%, Asian 1%, Caucasian 14%, Hispanic 1%. **Retention and Graduation:** 76% freshmen return for sophomore year. 19% freshmen graduate within 4 years. 15% grads go on to further study within 1 year. 7% grads pursue arts and sciences degrees. 4% grads pursue business degrees. 2% grads pursue law degrees. 2% grads pursue medical degrees. **Faculty:** Student/faculty ratio 18:1. 133 full-time faculty, 65% hold PhDs.

ACADEMICS

Degrees: Bachelor's, doctoral, master's, terminal. **Academic Requirements:** Arts/fine arts, English (including composition), foreign languages, history, humanities, mathematics, sciences (biological or physical), social science. **Classes:** Most classes have fewer than 10 students. **Disciplines with Highest Percentage of Degrees Awarded:** Business/marketing 20%, biological/life sciences 9%, education 9%, health professions and related sciences 9%, liberal arts/general studies 7%, social sciences 7%, English 6%, natural resources/environmental science 5%. **Special Study Options:** Accelerated program, cooperative education program, cross registration, distance learning, double major, honors program, hotel/restaurant management semester, independent study, internships, NASA program, off-campus study opportunities in marine research, study possible at Wallops Island, VA, teacher certification program.

FACILITIES

Housing: Coed dorms, men's dorms, women's dorms. **Special Academic Facilities/Equipment:** Art museum, performing arts center, college farm, academic center. **Computers:** 94% of public computers are PCs, 3% of public computers are Macs, 3% of public computers are UNIX, network access in dorm rooms.

CAMPUS LIFE
Activities: Choral groups, concert band, dance, drama/theater, jazz band, literary magazine, music ensembles, radio station, student government, student newspaper, student-run film society, symphony orchestra, television station, yearbook. **Organizations:** 60 registered organizations, 4 honor societies, 4 religious organizations. 3 fraternities (5% men join), 2 sororities (5% women join). **Athletics (Intercollegiate):** *Men:* Baseball, basketball, cross-country, tennis, track/field (outdoor). *Women:* Basketball, cheerleading, cross-country, softball, tennis, track/field (outdoor), volleyball.

ADMISSIONS
Freshman Academic Profile: 90% from public high schools. TOEFL required of all international applicants, minimum paper TOEFL 500. **Basis for Candidate Selection:** *Very important factors considered include:* Character/personal qualities, rigor of secondary school record, standardized test scores, talent/ability. *Important factors considered include:* Alumni/ae relation, application essay, class rank, extracurricular activities, interview. *Other factors considered include:* Recommendation(s), volunteer work, work experience. **Freshman Admission Requirements:** High school diploma is required, and GED is accepted. *Academic units required:* 4 English, 3 math, 2 science (2 science labs), 2 foreign language, 3 social studies, 6 academic electives. **Freshman Admission Statistics:** 3,073 applied, 51% admitted, 52% enrolled. **Transfer Admission Requirements:** High school transcript, college transcript(s), essay or personal statement. Minimum college GPA of 2.0 required. Lowest grade transferable C. **General Admission Information:** Application fee $25. Regular application deadline 7/15. Regular notification rolling. Non-fall registration accepted. Common Application accepted. Credit offered for CEEB Advanced Placement tests.

COSTS AND FINANCIAL AID
Annual in-state tuition $3,994. Out-of-state tuition $8,497. Room & board $4,930. Required fees $604. Average book expense $700. **Required Forms and Deadlines:** FAFSA. Financial aid filing deadline 3/1. **Notification of Awards:** Applicants will be notified of awards on or about 4/1. **Types of Aid:** *Need-based scholarships/grants:* Pell, SEOG, state scholarships/grants, private scholarships, the school's own gift aid. *Loans:* Direct Subsidized Stafford, Direct Unsubsidized Stafford, Direct PLUS, Federal Perkins, college/university loans from institutional funds. **Student Employment:** Federal Work-Study Program available. Institutional employment available. Off-campus job opportunities are fair. **Financial Aid Statistics:** Highest amount earned per year from on-campus jobs $1,381.

UNIVERSITY OF MARYLAND— UNIVERSITY COLLEGE

3501 University Boulevard East, Adelphi, MD 20783
Phone: 301-985-7000 **E-mail:** umucinfo@nova.umuc.edu
Fax: 301-985-7364 **Website:** www.umuc.edu
Financial Aid Phone: 301-985-7000

This public school was founded in 1947.

RATINGS
Admissions Selectivity Rating: 60*   **Fire Safety Rating:** 60*   **Green Rating:** 60*

STUDENTS AND FACULTY
Enrollment: 17,527. **Student Body:** 58% female, 42% male, 31% out-of-state. **Faculty:** Student/faculty ratio 24:1. 119 full-time faculty, 66% hold PhDs.

ACADEMICS
Degrees: Associate, bachelor's, certificate, doctoral, master's, post-bachelor's certificate. **Academic Requirements:** Computer literacy, English (including composition), humanities, mathematics, sciences (biological or physical), social science. **Classes:** Most classes have 20–29 students. **Majors with Highest Enrollment:** Business administration/management, information science/studies, multi/interdisciplinary studies. **Disciplines with Highest Percentage of Degrees Awarded:** Interdisciplinary studies 71%, computer and information sciences 12%, business/marketing 9%, psychology 2%, social sciences 2%, communication technologies 1%, law/legal studies 1%. **Special Study Options:** Accelerated program, cooperative education program, cross registration, distance learning, double major, dual enrollment, external degree program, teacher certification program, weekend college.

FACILITIES
Computers: 100% of public computers are PCs, online registration, online administrative functions (other than registration), remote student-access to Web through college's connection.

ADMISSIONS
Freshman Academic Profile: TOEFL required of all international applicants, minimum paper TOEFL 550, minimum computer TOEFL 213. **Freshman Admission Requirements:** High school diploma is required, and GED is accepted. **Freshman Admission Statistics:** 994 applied, 100% admitted, 53% enrolled. **Transfer Admission Requirements:** High school transcript, college transcript(s). Minimum college GPA of 2.0 required. Lowest grade transferable D. **General Admission Information:** Application fee $30. Non-fall registration accepted. Admission may be deferred for a maximum of 2 years. Common Application not accepted. Credit and/or placement offered for CEEB Advanced Placement tests.

COSTS AND FINANCIAL AID
Annual in-state tuition $5,208. Out-of-state tuition $9,576. Required fees $120. Average book expense $1,362. **Required Forms and Deadlines:** FAFSA, institution's own financial aid form. Financial aid filing deadline 6/1. **Notification of Awards:** Applicants will be notified of awards on a rolling basis beginning on or about 5/1. **Types of Aid:** *Need-based scholarships/grants:* Pell, SEOG, state scholarships/grants, private scholarships, the school's own gift aid. *Loans:* Direct Subsidized Stafford, Direct Unsubsidized Stafford, Direct PLUS, Federal Perkins. **Student Employment:** Off-campus job opportunities are good. **Financial Aid Statistics:** 30% freshmen, 34% undergrads receive need-based scholarship or grant aid. 37% freshmen, 46% undergrads receive need-based self-help aid.

UNIVERSITY OF MASSACHUSETTS—AMHERST

University Admissions Center, 37 Mather Drive, Amherst, MA 01003-9291
Phone: 413-545-0222 **E-mail:** mail@admissions.umass.edu **CEEB Code:** 3917
Fax: 413-545-4312 **Website:** www.umass.edu **ACT Code:** 1924
Financial Aid Phone: 413-545-0801

This public school was founded in 1863. It has a 1,463-acre campus.

RATINGS
Admissions Selectivity Rating: 83   **Fire Safety Rating:** 73   **Green Rating:** 82

STUDENTS AND FACULTY
Enrollment: 19,299. **Student Body:** 49% female, 51% male, 18% out-of-state. African American 3%, Asian 6%, Caucasian 60%, Hispanic 3%. **Retention and Graduation:** 83% freshmen return for sophomore year. 48% freshmen graduate within 4 years. 18% grads go on to further study within 1 year. 11% grads pursue arts and sciences degrees. 2% grads pursue business degrees. 1% grads pursue law degrees. 1% grads pursue medical degrees. **Faculty:** Student/faculty ratio 18:1. 1,168 full-time faculty, 93% hold PhDs. 88% faculty teach undergrads.

ACADEMICS
Degrees: Associate, bachelor's, doctoral, master's, post-master's certificate. **Academic Requirements:** Arts/fine arts, English (including composition), foreign languages, history, humanities, mathematics, sciences (biological or physical), social & cultural diversity, social science. **Classes:** Most classes have 20–29 students. Most lab/discussion sections have 20–29 students. **Majors with Highest Enrollment:** Biological and physical sciences, communications studies/speech communication and rhetoric, psychology. **Disciplines with Highest Percentage of Degrees Awarded:** Social sciences 16%, business/marketing 14%, communications/journalism 9%, psychology 8%, biological/life sciences 6%. **Special Study Options:** Accelerated program, cooperative education program, cross registration, distance learning, double major, dual enrollment, English as a second language (ESL), exchange student program (domestic), honors program, independent study, internships, liberal arts/career combination, student-designed major, study abroad, teacher certification program.

FACILITIES
Housing: Coed dorms, women's dorms, apartments for married students,

apartments for single students, special housing for disabled students, special housing for international students, fraternity/sorority housing, special interest. **Special Academic Facilities/Equipment:** Computer science complex, Polymer Research Institute, Herter (Art) Gallery, university art gallery, natural history museum, fine arts center, Mullins Center (sports & entertainment arena). **Computers:** 5% of classrooms are wired, 98% of classrooms are wireless, 80% of public computers are PCs, 20% of public computers are Macs, network access in dorm rooms, online registration, online administrative functions (other than registration), remote student-access to Web through college's connection.

CAMPUS LIFE

Activities: Choral groups, concert band, dance, drama/theater, jazz band, literary magazine, marching band, music ensembles, musical theater, opera, pep band, radio station, student government, student newspaper, student-run film society, symphony orchestra, television station. **Organizations:** 200 registered organizations, 40 honor societies, 12 religious organizations. 20 fraternities (4% men join), 13 sororities (4% women join). **Athletics (Intercollegiate):** *Men:* Baseball, basketball, cross-country, diving, football, ice hockey, lacrosse, skiing (downhill/alpine), soccer, swimming, track/field (indoor), track/field (outdoor). *Women:* Basketball, crew/rowing, cross-country, diving, field hockey, lacrosse, skiing (downhill/alpine), soccer, softball, swimming, tennis, track/field (indoor), track/field (outdoor). University of Massachusetts Amherst **Environmental Initiatives:** Physical Plant Energy Conservation Project and new Central Heating Plant: The campus is close to completing the construction and commissioning of a new combined heat and power facility. The Central Heating Plant will provide all of the campus heating needs and close to 80% of its electrical needs. The campus realized close to a 36% reduction in potable water consumption, or 21 million cubic feet, from FY 04. The Office of Waste Management has historically achieved and maintained significant recycling rates of over 50%. For fiscal years 2006 and 2007 the University realized recycling rates of 56% and 52% respectively.

ADMISSIONS

Freshman Academic Profile: 23% in top 10% of high school class, 58% in top 25% of high school class, 94% in top 50% of high school class. 90% from public high schools. SAT Math middle 50% range 520–630. SAT Critical Reading middle 50% range 510–610. Regular application deadline 1/15. Average book expense $1,000. TOEFL required of all international applicants, minimum paper TOEFL 550, minimum computer TOEFL 213. **Basis for Candidate Selection:** *Very important factors considered include:* Academic GPA, rigor of secondary school record. *Important factors considered include:* Standardized test scores. *Other factors considered include:* Application essay, character/personal qualities, class rank, extracurricular activities, first generation, geographical residence, level of applicant's interest, racial/ethnic status, recommendation(s), state residency, talent/ability, volunteer work. **Freshman Admission Requirements:** High school diploma is required, and GED is accepted. *Academic units required:* 4 English, 3 math, 3 science (2 science labs), 2 foreign language, 2 social studies, 2 academic electives. **Freshman Admission Statistics:** 22,451 applied, 71% admitted, 26% enrolled. **Transfer Admission Requirements:** College transcript(s), essay or personal statement. Minimum college GPA of 2.5 required. Lowest grade transferable C-. **General Admission Information:** Application fee $40. Regular application deadline 1/15. Regular notification is rolling. Non-fall registration accepted. Admission may be deferred for a maxiumum of 2 semesters. Credit and/or placement offered for CEEB Advanced Placement tests.

COSTS AND FINANCIAL AID

Annual in-state tuition $1,714. Out-of-state tuition $9,937. Room & board $6,517. Required fees $7,881. Average book expense $1,000. **Required Forms and Deadlines:** FAFSA. Financial aid filing deadline 3/1. **Notification of Awards:** Applicants will be notified of awards on a rolling basis beginning on or about 4/1. **Types of Aid:** *Need-based scholarships/grants:* Pell, SEOG, state scholarships/grants, private scholarships, the school's own gift aid. *Loans:* Direct Subsidized Stafford, Direct Unsubsidized Stafford, Direct PLUS, Federal Perkins, state loans. **Financial Aid Statistics:** 32% freshmen, 39% undergrads receive need-based scholarship or grant aid. 36% freshmen, 46% undergrads receive need-based self-help aid. 28 freshmen, 186 undergrads receive athletic scholarships. 67% freshmen, 73% undergrads receive any aid.

UNIVERSITY OF MASSACHUSETTS—BOSTON

100 Morrissey Boulevard, Boston, MA 02125-3393
Phone: 617-287-6100 **E-mail:** undergrad@umb.edu **CEEB Code:** 3924
Fax: 617-287-5999 **Website:** www.umb.edu
Financial Aid Phone: 617-287-6300

This public school was founded in 1964. It has a 177-acre campus.

RATINGS

Admissions Selectivity Rating: 60*   **Fire Safety Rating:** 60*   **Green Rating:** 98

STUDENTS AND FACULTY

Enrollment: 8,108. **Student Body:** 58% female, 42% male, 5% out-of-state, 3% international (133 countries represented). African American 16%, Asian 13%, Caucasian 50%, Hispanic 8%. **Retention and Graduation:** 70% freshmen return for sophomore year. 15% freshmen graduate within 4 years. **Faculty:** Student/faculty ratio 15:1. 435 full-time faculty, 95% hold PhDs. 100% faculty teach undergrads.

ACADEMICS

Degrees: Bachelor's, certificate, doctoral, master's, post-bachelor's certificate, post-master's certificate. **Academic Requirements:** Arts/fine arts, computer literacy, English (including composition), foreign languages, history, humanities, mathematics, philosophy, sciences (biological or physical), social science. **Classes:** Most classes have 20–29 students. Most lab/discussion sections have fewer than 10 students. **Majors with Highest Enrollment:** Business/commerce, nursing/registered nurse training (RN, ASN, BSN, MSN), psychology. **Disciplines with Highest Percentage of Degrees Awarded:** Business/marketing 23%, social sciences 17%, psychology 14%, health professions and related sciences 9%, English 7%. **Special Study Options:** Accelerated program, cooperative education program, cross registration, distance learning, double major, dual enrollment, English as a second language (ESL), exchange student program (domestic), honors program, independent study, internships, liberal arts/career combination, student-designed major, study abroad, teacher certification program.

FACILITIES

Housing: University housing referral service. **Special Academic Facilities/Equipment:** Art gallery, tropical greenhouse, observatory, adaptive computer lab. **Computers:** 50% of public computers are PCs, 45% of public computers are Macs, 5% of public computers are UNIX, online registration, online administrative functions (other than registration), support for handheld computing, remote student-access to Web through college's connection.

CAMPUS LIFE

Activities: Choral groups, concert band, dance, drama/theater, jazz band, literary magazine, music ensembles, radio station, student government, student newspaper, student-run film society, symphony orchestra, yearbook. **Organizations:** 74 registered organizations, 1 honor society. **Athletics (Intercollegiate):** *Men:* Baseball, basketball, cross-country, ice hockey, lacrosse, soccer, tennis. *Women:* Basketball, cross-country, ice hockey, soccer, softball, tennis, volleyball. **Environmental Initiatives:** 1. Comprehensive sustainability program, toxics use reduction program, energy conservation and management efforts, master planning. UMB awarded MA Sustainable Campus of the Year in 2004. 2. Signing Tailories and ACUPCC commitments—only public university in Boston to do so. Academic program with environmental focus in both graduate and undergraduate levels—in many colleges within the university.

ADMISSIONS

Freshman Academic Profile: SAT Math middle 50% range 480–580. SAT Critical Reading middle 50% range 460–570. TOEFL required of all international applicants, minimum paper TOEFL 550, minimum computer TOEFL 213. **Basis for Candidate Selection:** *Very important factors considered include:* Academic GPA, character/personal qualities, rigor of secondary school record, standardized test scores. *Important factors considered include:* Application essay, recommendation(s). *Other factors considered include:* Extracurricular activities, first generation, interview, level of applicant's interest, talent/ability, volunteer work, work experience. **Freshman Admission Requirements:** High school diploma is required, and GED is accepted. *Academic units required:* 4 English, 3 math, 3 science (2 science labs), 2 foreign language, 1 social studies, 1 history, 2 academic electives. **Freshman Admission Statistics:** 3,666 applied, 63% admitted, 42% enrolled. **Transfer Admission Requirements:** College transcript(s), essay or personal statement, statement of good standing from prior institution(s). Minimum college GPA of 2.5 required. Lowest grade transferable C-. **General Admission Information:** Application fee $40. Regular application deadline 6/1. Regular notification rolling basis. Non-fall registration accepted. Admission may be deferred for a maximum of 2 semesters. Credit offered for CEEB Advanced Placement tests.

COSTS AND FINANCIAL AID

Annual in-state tuition $1,714. Annual out-of-state tuition $9,758. Required fees $7,397. **Required Forms and Deadlines:** FAFSA. Financial aid filing deadline 3/1. **Notification of Awards:** Applicants will be notified of awards on or about 4/1. **Types of Aid:** *Need-based scholarships/grants:* Pell, SEOG, state scholarships/grants, private scholarships, the school's own gift aid. *Loans:* Direct Subsidized Stafford, Direct Unsubsidized Stafford, Direct PLUS, Federal Perkins. **Financial Aid Statistics:** 66% freshmen, 53% undergrads receive need-based scholarship or grant aid. 67% freshmen, 60% undergrads receive need-based self-help aid.

See page 1452.

UNIVERSITY OF MASSACHUSETTS— DARTMOUTH

285 Old Westport Road, North Dartmouth, MA 02747-2300
Phone: 508-999-8605 **E-mail:** admissions@umassd.edu **CEEB Code:** 3786
Fax: 508-999-8755 **Website:** www.umassd.edu **ACT Code:** 1906
Financial Aid Phone: 508-999-8857

This public school was founded in 1895. It has a 710-acre campus.

RATINGS

Admissions Selectivity Rating: 75   **Fire Safety Rating:** 60*   **Green Rating:** 60*

STUDENTS AND FACULTY

Enrollment: 7,328. **Student Body:** 51% female, 49% male, 4% out-of-state. African American 7%, Asian 3%, Caucasian 80%, Hispanic 2%. **Retention and Graduation:** 28% freshmen graduate within 4 years. **Faculty:** Student/faculty ratio 17:1. 359 full-time faculty, 84% hold PhDs. 99% faculty teach undergrads.

ACADEMICS

Degrees: Bachelor's, certificate, doctoral, master's, post-bachelor's certificate, post-master's certificate. **Academic Requirements:** Arts/fine arts, computer literacy, English (including composition), ethics & social responsibility, global awareness & diversity, humanities, mathematics, oral skills, sciences (biological or physical), social science. **Majors with Highest Enrollment:** Business administration and management, nursing, psychology. **Disciplines with Highest Percentage of Degrees Awarded:** Business/marketing 28%, social sciences 11%, visual and performing arts 11%, health professions and related sciences 9%, psychology 9%. **Special Study Options:** Cooperative education program, cross registration, distance learning, double major, dual enrollment, exchange student program (domestic), honors program, independent study, internships, student-designed major, study abroad, teacher certification program.

FACILITIES

Housing: Coed dorms, apartments for single students, special housing for disabled students, apartments for upperclassmen and graduate students, program dedicated suites. **Special Academic Facilities/Equipment:** Art gallery, language center, center for Jewish culture, Robert F. Kennedy assassination archives, electron microscope, observatory, marine research vessels, advanced manufacturing and technology center, school of marine science and technology. **Computers:** 100% of classrooms are wireless, 56% of public computers are PCs, 42% of public computers are Macs, 2% of public computers are UNIX, network access in dorm rooms, online registration, online administrative functions (other than registration), remote student-access to Web through college's connection.

CAMPUS LIFE

Activities: Choral groups, concert band, dance, drama/theater, jazz band, literary magazine, music ensembles, musical theater, pep band, radio station, student government, student newspaper, symphony orchestra, yearbook. **Organizations:** 109 registered organizations, 8 honor societies, 6 religious organizations. 5 fraternities, 3 sororities. **Athletics (Intercollegiate):** *Men:* Baseball, basketball, cross-country, diving, equestrian sports, football, golf, ice hockey, lacrosse, soccer, swimming, tennis, track/field (indoor), track/field (outdoor). *Women:* Basketball, cheerleading, cross-country, diving, equestrian sports, field hockey, golf, lacrosse, soccer, softball, swimming, tennis, track/field (indoor), track/field (outdoor), volleyball.

ADMISSIONS

Freshman Academic Profile: 10% in top 10% of high school class, 35% in top 25% of high school class, 80% in top 50% of high school class. 90% from public high schools. SAT Math middle 50% range 490–590. SAT Critical Reading

middle 50% range 470–570. ACT middle 50% range 20–24. TOEFL required of all international applicants, minimum paper TOEFL 500, minimum computer TOEFL 173. **Basis for Candidate Selection:** *Very important factors considered include:* Academic GPA, rigor of secondary school record, standardized test scores. *Other factors considered include:* Alumni/ae relation, application essay, character/personal qualities, class rank, extracurricular activities, first generation, recommendation(s), talent/ability, volunteer work, work experience. **Freshman Admission Requirements:** High school diploma is required, and GED is accepted. *Academic units required:* 4 English, 3 math, 3 science (2 science labs), 2 foreign language, 1 social studies, 1 history, 2 academic electives. *Academic units recommended:* 1 additional math and science for some majors. **Freshman Admission Statistics:** 6,972 applied, 67% admitted, 34% enrolled. **Transfer Admission Requirements:** College transcript(s), essay or personal statement. Minimum college GPA of 2.5 required. Lowest grade transferable C-. **General Admission Information:** Application fee $40. Early decision application deadline 11/15. Regular notification is rolling. Non-fall registration accepted. Admission may be deferred for a maximum of 2 semesters. Credit and/or placement offered for CEEB Advanced Placement tests.

COSTS AND FINANCIAL AID

Annual in-state tuition $8,592. Annual out-of-state tuition $18,174. **Required Forms and Deadlines:** FAFSA. Financial aid filing deadline 3/1. **Notification of Awards:** Applicants will be notified of awards on a rolling basis beginning on or about 3/25. **Types of Aid:** *Need-based scholarships/grants:* Pell, SEOG, state scholarships/grants, private scholarships, the school's own gift aid. *Loans:* Direct Subsidized Stafford, Direct Unsubsidized Stafford, Direct PLUS, Federal Perkins, Federal Nursing, state loans. **Student Employment:** Federal Work-Study Program available. Institutional employment available. Off-campus job opportunities are good. **Financial Aid Statistics:** 38% freshmen, 51% undergrads receive need-based scholarship or grant aid. 42% freshmen, 54% undergrads receive need-based self-help aid.

See page 1454.

UNIVERSITY OF MASSACHUSETTS—LOWELL

Office of Undergrad Admissions, Broadway Street Suite 110, Lowell, MA 01854-5104
Phone: 978-934-3931 **E-mail:** admissions@uml.edu **CEEB Code:** 3911
Fax: 978-934-3086 **Website:** www.uml.edu **ACT Code:** 1854
Financial Aid Phone: 978-934-4220

This public school was founded in 1894. It has a 150-acre campus.

RATINGS

Admissions Selectivity Rating: 70   **Fire Safety Rating:** 88   **Green Rating:** 60*

STUDENTS AND FACULTY

Enrollment: 7,419. **Student Body:** 40% female, 60% male, 12% out-of-state, (73 countries represented). African American 1%, Asian 2%, Caucasian 20%, Hispanic 2%. **Retention and Graduation:** 76% freshmen return for sophomore year. 22% freshmen graduate within 4 years. **Faculty:** Student/faculty ratio 14:1. 405 full-time faculty. 100% faculty teach undergrads.

ACADEMICS

Degrees: Associate, bachelor's, doctoral, master's, post-master's certificate. **Academic Requirements:** Arts/fine arts, English (including composition), foreign languages, history, humanities, mathematics, sciences (biological or physical), social science. **Classes:** Most classes have fewer than 10 students. **Majors with Highest Enrollment:** Business administration/management, electrical, electronics and communications engineering, nursing. **Disciplines with Highest Percentage of Degrees Awarded:** Business/marketing 18%, engineering 13%, computer and information sciences 12%, security and protective services 12%, health professions and related sciences 8%, visual and performing arts 7%. **Special Study Options:** Accelerated program, cooperative education program, cross registration, distance learning, double major, dual enrollment, honors program, internships, liberal arts/career combination, study abroad, teacher certification program.

FACILITIES

Housing: Coed dorms, apartments for married students, apartments for single students, special housing for disabled students, cooperative housing. **Special**

Academic Facilities/Equipment: Language lab, media center, audiovisual department, centers for learning, center for field studies, center for performing and visual arts, center for health promotion, research nuclear reactor, multicourt gymnasium, 1/8 mile indoor elevated track, game rooms, a sauna. **Computers:** Network access in dorm rooms, network access in dorm lounges, online registration, online administrative functions (other than registration), remote student-access to Web through college's connection.

CAMPUS LIFE

Activities: Choral groups, concert band, dance, drama/theater, jazz band, literary magazine, marching band, music ensembles, pep band, radio station, student government, student newspaper, student-run film society, symphony orchestra, yearbook. **Organizations:** 100 registered organizations, 16 honor societies, 4 religious organizations. **Athletics (Intercollegiate):** *Men:* Baseball, basketball, crew/rowing, cross-country, golf, ice hockey, soccer, track/field (indoor), track/field (outdoor). *Women:* Basketball, crew/rowing, cross-country, field hockey, soccer, softball, track/field (indoor), track/field (outdoor), volleyball.

ADMISSIONS

Freshman Academic Profile: 13% in top 10% of high school class, 38% in top 25% of high school class, 77% in top 50% of high school class. 98% from public high schools. SAT Math middle 50% range 500–610. SAT Critical Reading middle 50% range 480–570. TOEFL required of all international applicants, minimum paper TOEFL 550, minimum computer TOEFL 213. **Basis for Candidate Selection:** *Very important factors considered include:* Academic GPA, rigor of secondary school record, standardized test scores. *Important factors considered include:* Application essay, first generation, level of applicant's interest, recommendation(s). *Other factors considered include:* Character/personal qualities, class rank, extracurricular activities, interview, talent/ability, volunteer work, work experience. **Freshman Admission Requirements:** High school diploma is required, and GED is accepted. *Academic units required:* 4 English, 3 math, 3 science (2 science labs), 2 foreign language, 2 social studies, 2 academic electives. **Freshman Admission Statistics:** 4,538 applied, 70% admitted, 23% enrolled. **Transfer Admission Requirements:** College transcript(s). Minimum college GPA of 2.0 required. Lowest grade transferable C-. **General Admission Information:** Application fee $60. Regular notification is rolling. Non-fall registration accepted. Admission may be deferred for a maxiumum of 2 semesters. Credit offered for CEEB Advanced Placement tests.

COSTS AND FINANCIAL AID

Annual in-state tuition $1,454. Out-of-state tuition $8,567. Room & board $6,365. Required fees $6,990. Average book expense $600. **Required Forms and Deadlines:** FAFSA. Financial aid filing deadline 3/1. **Notification of Awards:** Applicants will be notified of awards on a rolling basis beginning on or about 3/25. **Types of Aid:** *Need-based scholarships/grants:* Pell, SEOG, state scholarships/grants, private scholarships, the school's own gift aid, Federal Nursing Scholarships. *Loans:* Direct Subsidized Stafford, Direct Unsubsidized Stafford, Direct PLUS, Federal Perkins, state loans. **Student Employment:** Federal Work-Study Program available. Institutional employment available. Off-campus job opportunities are good. **Financial Aid Statistics:** 41% freshmen, 42% undergrads receive need-based scholarship or grant aid. 42% freshmen, 46% undergrads receive need-based self-help aid. 33 freshmen, 148 undergrads receive athletic scholarships. 83% freshmen, 65% undergrads receive any aid. Highest amount earned per year from on-campus jobs $2,710.

See page 1456.

THE UNIVERSITY OF MEMPHIS

229 Administration Building, Memphis, TN 38152
Phone: 901-678-2111 **E-mail:** recruitment@memphis.edu **CEEB Code:** 1459
Fax: 901-678-3053 **Website:** www.memphis.edu **ACT Code:** 3992
Financial Aid Phone: 901-678-2303

This public school was founded in 1912. It has a 1,178-acre campus.

RATINGS

Admissions Selectivity Rating: 60*   **Fire Safety Rating:** 86   **Green Rating:** 94

STUDENTS AND FACULTY

Student Body: 12% out-of-state.

ACADEMICS

Degrees: Bachelor's, certificate, doctoral, master's, terminal. **Academic Requirements:** Arts/fine arts, computer literacy, English (including composi-

tion), foreign languages, history, humanities, mathematics, philosophy, sciences (biological or physical), social science. **Special Study Options:** Distance learning, double major, dual enrollment, English as a second language (ESL), exchange student program (domestic), honors program, independent study, internships, student-designed major, study abroad, teacher certification program.

FACILITIES

Housing: Coed dorms, men's dorms, women's dorms, apartments for married students, apartments for single students, fraternity/sorority housing, townhouses for single students. **Special Academic Facilities/Equipment:** Indian museum and village, music archive, center for study of higher education, center for river studies, center for research on women, center for earthquake research and information, biological field station.

CAMPUS LIFE

Activities: Choral groups, concert band, dance, drama/theater, jazz band, marching band, music ensembles, musical theater, opera, pep band, radio station, student government, student newspaper, student-run film society, symphony orchestra, television station. **Organizations:** 27 honor societies, 12 religious organizations. 11 fraternities (8% men join), 7 sororities (8% women join). **Athletics (Intercollegiate):** *Men:* Baseball, basketball, cheerleading, cross-country, football, golf, riflery, soccer, tennis, track/field (outdoor), volleyball. *Women:* Basketball, cheerleading, golf, soccer, tennis, track/field (outdoor), volleyball.

ADMISSIONS

Freshman Academic Profile: 80% from public high schools. SAT Math middle 50% range 460–580. SAT Critical Reading middle 50% range 460–620. SAT Writing middle 50% range 460–570. ACT middle 50% range 19–25. TOEFL required of all international applicants, minimum paper TOEFL 500. **Freshman Admission Requirements:** High school diploma is required, and GED is accepted. *Academic units required:* 3 math, 2 science, 2 foreign language. *Academic units recommended:* 4 math, 3 science, 2 social studies. **Transfer Admission Requirements:** Minimum college GPA of 2.0 required. Lowest grade transferable C. **General Admission Information:** Regular application deadline 7/1. Regular notification rolling. Non-fall registration accepted. Common Application not accepted. Credit and/or placement offered for CEEB Advanced Placement tests.

COSTS AND FINANCIAL AID

Annual in-state tuition $4,652. Annual out-of-state tuition $15,480. Room and board $5,280. Required fees $1,150. Average book expense $1,000. **Required Forms and Deadlines:** FAFSA, institution's own financial aid form, CSS/Financial Aid PROFILE. Financial aid filing deadline 6/30. **Notification of Awards:** Applicants will be notified of awards on or about 6/1. **Types of Aid:** *Need-based scholarships/grants:* Pell, SEOG, state scholarships/grants, private scholarships, the school's own gift aid, Federal Nursing Scholarships. *Loans:* FFEL Subsidized Stafford, FFEL Unsubsidized Stafford, FFEL PLUS, Federal Perkins, college/university loans from institutional funds. **Student Employment:** Federal Work-Study Program available. Institutional employment available. Off-campus job opportunities are excellent.

UNIVERSITY OF MIAMI

Office of Admission, PO Box 248025, Coral Gables, FL 33124-4616
Phone: 305-284-4323 **E-mail:** admissions@miami.edu **CEEB Code:** 5815
Fax: 305-284-2507 **Website:** www.miami.edu **ACT Code:** 0760
Financial Aid Phone: 305-284-5212

This private school was founded in 1925. It has a 260-acre campus.

RATINGS

Admissions Selectivity Rating: 96   **Fire Safety Rating:** 84   **Green Rating:** 86

STUDENTS AND FACULTY

Enrollment: 9,741. **Student Body:** 59% female, 41% male, 45% out-of-state, 6% international. African American 9%, Asian 6%, Caucasian 52%, Hispanic 24%. **Retention and Graduation:** 87% freshmen return for sophomore year. 53% freshmen graduate within 4 years. 35% grads go on to further study within 1 year. 10% grads pursue medical degrees. **Faculty:** Student/faculty ratio 13:1. 877 full-time faculty, 87% hold PhDs.

ACADEMICS

Degrees: Bachelor's, certificate, doctoral, first professional, master's, post-bachelor's certificate, post-master's certificate. **Academic Requirements:** Arts/fine arts, English (including composition), history, humanities, mathematics, sciences (biological or physical), social science. **Classes:** Most classes have 10–19 students. Most lab/discussion sections have 10–19 students. **Disciplines with Highest Percentage of Degrees Awarded:** Business/marketing 21%, social sciences 13%, visual and performing arts 13%, biological/life sciences 8%, psychology 7%, communication technologies 7%. **Special Study Options:** Accelerated program, distance learning, double major, dual enrollment, English as a second language (ESL), honors program, independent study, internships, learning communities, student-designed major, study abroad, teacher certification program, weekend college.

FACILITIES

Housing: Coed dorms, apartments for single students, special housing for disabled students, fraternity/sorority housing. **Special Academic Facilities/Equipment:** Lowe Art Museum, Gusman Concert Hall, Jerry Herman Ring Theatre, Bill Cosford Cinema, convocation center, wellness center. **Computers:** Network access in dorm rooms, network access in dorm lounges, online registration, online administrative functions (other than registration), remote student-access to Web through college's connection.

CAMPUS LIFE

Activities: Choral groups, concert band, dance, drama/theater, jazz band, literary magazine, marching band, music ensembles, musical theater, opera, pep band, radio station, student government, student newspaper, student-run film society, symphony orchestra, television station. **Organizations:** 217 registered organizations, 55 honor societies, 12 religious organizations. 14 fraternities (13% men join), 10 sororities (13% women join). **Athletics (Intercollegiate):** *Men:* Baseball, basketball, cheerleading, cross-country, football, tennis, track/field (indoor), track/field (outdoor). *Women:* Basketball, cheerleading, crew/rowing, cross-country, diving, golf, soccer, swimming, tennis, track/field (indoor), track/field (outdoor), volleyball. **Environmental Initiatives:** The President signing the ACUPCC and the Talloires Declaration. The University has implemented new building standards for new construction and major renovations to attempt to meet USGBC LEED Silver certification. The University has signed the Panama Pact: a collaboration on a world-class education and research facility addressing present and 22nd century challenges focusing on technologies that are sustainable.

ADMISSIONS

Freshman Academic Profile: 62% in top 10% of high school class, 88% in top 25% of high school class, 98% in top 50% of high school class. SAT Math middle 50% range 600–690. SAT Critical Reading middle 50% range 580–680. SAT Writing middle 50% range 560–650. ACT middle 50% range 27–31. TOEFL required of all international applicants, minimum paper TOEFL 550, minimum computer TOEFL 213. **Basis for Candidate Selection:** *Very important factors considered include:* Application essay, character/personal qualities, class rank, extracurricular activities, recommendation(s), rigor of secondary school record, standardized test scores, talent/ability. *Important factors considered include:* Alumni/ae relation, volunteer work. *Other factors considered include:* Geographical residence, racial/ethnic status, work experience. **Freshman Admission Requirements:** High school diploma is required, and GED is accepted. *Academic units recommended:* 4 English, 4 math, 3 science (2 science labs), 2 foreign language, 3 social studies, 2 history. **Freshman Admission Statistics:** 18,507 applied, 42% admitted, 26% enrolled. **Transfer Admission Requirements:** College transcript(s), statement of good standing from prior institution(s). Lowest grade transferable C. **General Admission Information:** Application fee $65. Early decision application deadline 11/1. Regular application deadline 2/1. Regular notification 4/15. Non-fall registration accepted. Admission may be deferred for a maximum of 2 semesters. Common Application accepted. Credit and/or placement offered for CEEB Advanced Placement tests.

COSTS AND FINANCIAL AID

Annual tuition $30,732. Room & board $9,334. Required fees $556. Average book expense $830. **Required Forms and Deadlines:** FAFSA. Financial aid filing deadline 2/15. **Notification of Awards:** Applicants will be notified of awards on a rolling basis beginning on or about 3/15. **Types of Aid:** *Need-based scholarships/grants:* Pell, SEOG, state scholarships/grants, private scholarships, the school's own gift aid, Federal Nursing Scholarships. *Loans:* FFEL Subsidized Stafford, FFEL Unsubsidized Stafford, FFEL PLUS, Federal Perkins, Federal Nursing, Signature Loan (alternative). **Student Employment:** Federal Work-Study Program available. Institutional employment available. Off-campus job opportunities are excellent. **Financial Aid Statistics:** 55% freshmen, 52% undergrads receive need-based scholarship or grant aid. 41% freshmen, 43% undergrads receive need-based self-help aid. 36 freshmen, 207 undergrads receive athletic scholarships.

UNIVERSITY OF MICHIGAN—ANN ARBOR

Best 368

1220 Student Activities Building, Ann Arbor, MI 48109-1316
Phone: 734-764-7433 **E-mail:** ugadmiss@umich.edu **CEEB Code:** 3129
Fax: 734-936-0740 **Website:** www.umich.edu **ACT Code:** 2062
Financial Aid Phone: 734-763-6600

This public school was founded in 1817. It has a 3,129-acre campus.

RATINGS

Admissions Selectivity Rating: 96   **Fire Safety Rating:** 60*   **Green Rating:** 83

STUDENTS AND FACULTY

Enrollment: 25,422. **Student Body:** 50% female, 50% male, 32% out-of-state, 5% international (117 countries represented). African American 7%, Asian 12%, Caucasian 64%, Hispanic 5%. **Retention and Graduation:** 96% freshmen return for sophomore year. **Faculty:** Student/faculty ratio 15:1. 2,390 full-time faculty, 92% hold PhDs. 72% faculty teach undergrads.

ACADEMICS

Degrees: Bachelor's, doctoral, first professional certificate, first professional, master's, post-bachelor's certificate, post-master's certificate. **Academic Requirements:** Academic requirements vary by program. **Classes:** Most classes have 10–19 students. Most lab/discussion sections have 20–29 students. **Majors with Highest Enrollment:** Economics, English language and literature, mechanical engineering. **Disciplines with Highest Percentage of Degrees Awarded:** Engineering 17%, social sciences 16%, psychology 8%, biological/life sciences 6%, English 6%, business/marketing 6%, visual and performing arts 6%, health professions and related sciences 4%, parks and recreation 4%. **Special Study Options:** Accelerated program, cooperative education program, cross registration, distance learning, double major, dual enrollment, English as a second language (ESL), exchange student program (domestic), honors program, independent study, internships, liberal arts/career combination, student-designed major, study abroad, teacher certificatio program, themed learning communities, weekend college (graduate student only)

FACILITIE

Housing: Coed dorms, women's dorms, apartments for married students apartments for single students, special housing for disabled students, specia housing for international students, fraternity/sorority housing, cooperativ housing, living/learning communities. **Special Academic Facilities /Equipment:** Anthropology, archaeology, art, natural science, paleontology, an zoology museums, audiovisual center, planetarium, electron microscope biology station, geology camp, athletic campus, medical center, nuclear lab botanical garden, herbarium, arboretum. **Computers:** Network access in dor rooms, network access in dorm lounges, online registration, online administrative functions (other than registration), remote student-access to Web throug college's connection

CAMPUS LIF

Activities: Choral groups, concert band, dance, drama/theater, jazz band literary magazine, marching band, music ensembles, musical theater, opera, pe band, radio station, student government, student newspaper, student-run fil society, symphony orchestra, television station. **Organizations:** 100 registere organizations, 21 honor society, 57 religious organizations. 37 fraternities (16 men join), 23 sororities (15% women join). **Athletics (Intercollegiate):** *Men* Baseball, basketball, cross-country, diving, football, golf, gymnastics, ice hockey soccer, swimming, tennis, track/field (indoor), track/field (outdoor), wrestling *Women:* Basketball, crew/rowing, cross-country, diving, field hockey, golf gymnastics, soccer, softball, swimming, tennis, track/field (indoor), track/fiel (outdoor), volleyball, water polo. **Environmental Initiatives:** Recycling an Waste Reduction. Food Waste Compost Program. Green Lights Initiative

ADMISSION

Freshman Academic Profile: 90% in top 10% of high school class, 99% in to 25% of high school class, 100% in top 50% of high school class. 80% fro public high schools. SAT Math middle 50% range 630–730. SAT Critica Reading middle 50% range 590–690. ACT middle 50% range 27–31. TOEF required of all international applicants, minimum paper TOEFL 570, minimu computer TOEFL 230. **Basis for Candidate Selection:** *Very importan factors considered include:* Rigor of secondary school record. *Important factor considered include:* Application essay, character/personal qualities recommendation(s), standardized test scores, state residency, talent/ability. *Other factors considered include:* Alumni/ae relation, class rank, extracurricular activities, geographical residence, level of applicant's interest, volunteer work, work experience. **Freshman Admission Requirements:** High school diploma is required, and GED is accepted. *Academic units required:* 4 English, 3 math, 3 science, 2 foreign language, 3 social studies. *Academic units recommended:* 4 English, 4 math, 4 science (1 science lab), 4 foreign language, 3 social studies, 2 history, 2 academic electives. **Freshman Admission Statistics:** 25,806 applied, 47% admitted, 44% enrolled. **Transfer Admission Requirements:** High school transcript, college transcript(s), essay or personal statement, statement of good standing from prior institution(s). Minimum college GPA of 3.0 required. Lowest grade transferable C. **General Admission Information:** Application fee $40. Regular application deadline 2/1. Regular notification is rolling. Non-fall registration accepted. Admission may be deferred for a maximum of 2 semesters. Credit and/or placement offered for CEEB Advanced Placement tests.

COSTS AND FINANCIAL AID

Annual in-state tuition $10,922. Annual out-of-state tuition $32,211. Room and board $8,190. Required fees $189. Average book expense $1,020. **Required Forms and Deadlines:** FAFSA, CSS/Financial Aid PROFILE, Noncustodial PROFILE, parent and student 1040. Financial aid filing deadline 4/30. **Notification of Awards:** Applicants will be notified of awards on a rolling basis beginning on or about 3/15. **Types of Aid:** *Need-based scholarships/grants:* Pell, SEOG, state scholarships/grants, private scholarships, the school's own gift aid. *Loans:* Direct Subsidized Stafford, Direct Unsubsidized Stafford, Direct PLUS, Federal Perkins, Federal Nursing, state loans, college/university loans from institutional funds, Michigan Loan Program, health professional student loans. **Financial Aid Statistics:** 26% freshmen, 26% undergrads receive need-based scholarship or grant aid. 49% freshmen, 47% undergrads receive need-based self-help aid. 142 freshmen, 480 undergrads receive athletic scholarships.

UNIVERSITY OF MICHIGAN—DEARBORN

4901 Evergreen Road, Dearborn, MI 48128-1491
Phone: 313-593-5100 **E-mail:** admissions@umd.umich.edu **CEEB Code:** 1861
Fax: 313-436-9167 **Website:** www.umd.umich.edu **ACT Code:** 2074
Financial Aid Phone: 313-593-5300

This public school was founded in 1959. It has a 210-acre campus.

RATINGS
Admissions Selectivity Rating: 82   **Fire Safety Rating:** 60*   **Green Rating:** 60*

STUDENTS AND FACULTY
Enrollment: 5,895. **Student Body:** 2% out-of-state, 1% international. African American 7%, Asian 6%, Caucasian 75%. **Retention and Graduation:** 79% freshmen return for sophomore year. 8% freshmen graduate within 4 years. 10% grads go on to further study within 1 year. 10% grads pursue arts and sciences degrees. **Faculty:** Student/faculty ratio 15:1. 259 full-time faculty, 89% hold PhDs.

ACADEMICS
Degrees: Bachelor's, master's, post-bachelor's certificate. **Classes:** Most classes have 20–29 students. Most lab/discussion sections have 10–19 students. **Disciplines with Highest Percentage of Degrees Awarded:** Business/marketing 20%, education 20%, engineering 16%, social sciences 9%, psychology 7%, communication technologies 6%, liberal arts/general studies 6%. **Special Study Options:** Accelerated program, cooperative education program, cross registration, distance learning, double major, dual enrollment, honors program, independent study, internships, liberal arts/career combination, student-designed major, study abroad, teacher certification program.

FACILITIES
Housing: Fraternity/sorority housing. **Special Academic Facilities/Equipment:** Museum at Henry Ford estate, child development center, CAD/CAM robotics lab, environmental study area, Armenian center.

CAMPUS LIFE
Activities: Drama/theater, literary magazine, radio station, student government, student newspaper, student-run film society, television station. **Organizations:** 2 honor societies, 24 religious organizations. 5 fraternities (4% men join), 4 sororities (4% women join). **Athletics (Intercollegiate):** *Men:* Basketball, volleyball. *Women:* basketball, volleyball.

ADMISSIONS
Freshman Academic Profile: 25% in top 10% of high school class, 60% in top 25% of high school class, 94% in top 50% of high school class. 83% from public

high schools. ACT middle 50% range 21–26. TOEFL required of all international applicants, minimum paper TOEFL 550. **Basis for Candidate Selection:** *Very important factors considered include:* Rigor of secondary school record, standardized test scores. *Other factors considered include:* Application essay, class rank, interview, recommendation(s). **Freshman Admission Requirements:** High school diploma is required, and GED is accepted. *Academic units recommended:* 4 English, 4 math, 3 science (1 science lab), 3 foreign language, 3 social studies. **Freshman Admission Statistics:** 2,334 applied, 65% admitted, 47% enrolled. **Transfer Admission Requirements:** High school transcript, college transcript(s). Minimum college GPA of 2.5 required. Lowest grade transferable C. **General Admission Information:** Application fee $30. Regular application deadline rolling Regular notification rolling. Non-fall registration accepted. Common Application not accepted. Credit and/or placement offered for CEEB Advanced Placement tests.

COSTS AND FINANCIAL AID
Comprehensive fee $10,922. Room and board $8,190. Required fees $189. Average book expense $1,020. **Required Forms and Deadlines:** FAFSA. Financial aid filing deadline 4/1. **Notification of Awards:** Applicants will be notified of awards on a rolling basis beginning on or about 5/1. **Types of Aid:** *Need-based scholarships/grants:* Pell, SEOG, state scholarships/grants, private scholarships, the school's own gift aid. *Loans:* Direct Subsidized Stafford, Direct Unsubsidized Stafford, Direct PLUS, Federal Perkins, state loans, college/university loans from institutional funds. **Student Employment:** Federal Work-Study Program available. Institutional employment available. Off-campus job opportunities are good. **Financial Aid Statistics:** 22% freshmen, 24% undergrads receive need-based scholarship or grant aid. 8% freshmen, 22% undergrads receive need-based self-help aid. 12 freshmen, 23 undergrads receive athletic scholarships. Highest amount earned per year from on-campus jobs $1,400.

UNIVERSITY OF MICHIGAN—FLINT

303 East Kearsley Street, 245 UPAV, Flint, MI 48502
Phone: 810-762-3300 **E-mail:** admissions@umflint.edu **CEEB Code:** 1853
Fax: 810-762-3272 **Website:** www.umflint.edu **ACT Code:** 2063
Financial Aid Phone: 810-762-3444

This public school was founded in 1956. It has a 72-acre campus.

RATINGS
Admissions Selectivity Rating: 72   **Fire Safety Rating:** 60*   **Green Rating:** 60*

STUDENTS AND FACULTY
Enrollment: 5,318. **Student Body:** 63% female, 37% male, 3% out-of-state. African American 12%, Asian 1%, Caucasian 76%, Hispanic 2%. **Retention and Graduation:** 70% freshmen return for sophomore year. 11% freshmen graduate within 4 years. **Faculty:** Student/faculty ratio 14:1. 231 full-time faculty, 65% hold PhDs. 100% faculty teach undergrads.

ACADEMICS
Degrees: Bachelor's, doctoral, master's. **Academic Requirements:** Arts/fine arts, English (including composition), foreign languages, history, humanities, mathematics, philosophy, sciences (biological or physical), social science. **Classes:** Most classes have 20–29 students. Most lab/discussion sections have fewer than 10 students. **Majors with Highest Enrollment:** Business administration and management, elementary education and teaching, nursing/registered nurse training (RN, ASN, BSN, MSN). **Disciplines with Highest Percentage of Degrees Awarded:** Education 22%, business/marketing 17%, health professions and related sciences 14%, psychology 6%, biological/life sciences 5%, social sciences 5%. **Special Study Options:** Cooperative education program, distance learning, double major, dual enrollment, honors program, independent study, internships, student-designed major, study abroad, teacher certification program.

FACILITIES
Special Academic Facilities/Equipment: Frances Willson Thompson Library. **Computers:** 100% of classrooms are wireless, 93% of public computers are PCs, 5% of public computers are Macs, 2% of public computers are UNIX, online registration, online administrative functions (other than registration), remote student-access to Web through college's connection.

CAMPUS LIFE

Activities: Choral groups, concert band, dance, drama/theater, jazz band, literary magazine, music ensembles, musical theater, student government, student newspaper, symphony orchestra, television station. **Organizations:** 64 registered organizations, 8 honor societies, 4 religious organizations. 4 fraternities (1% men join), 5 sororities (1% women join).

ADMISSIONS

Freshman Academic Profile: 13% in top 10% of high school class, 38% in top 25% of high school class, 76% in top 50% of high school class. 95% from public high schools. SAT Math middle 50% range 420–583. SAT Critical Reading middle 50% range 428–593. ACT middle 50% range 19–24. TOEFL required of all international applicants, minimum paper TOEFL 550, minimum computer TOEFL 213. **Basis for Candidate Selection:** *Very important factors considered include:* Academic GPA, rigor of secondary school record, standardized test scores. *Important factors considered include:* Extracurricular activities. *Other factors considered include:* Class rank, interview, recommendation(s), talent/ability. **Freshman Admission Requirements:** High school diploma is required, and GED is accepted. *Academic units required:* 4 English, 3 math, 2 science, 3 social studies. *Academic units recommended:* 4 English, 4 math, 4 science (2 science labs), 2 foreign language, 3 social studies, 3 history. **Freshman Admission Statistics:** 1,542 applied, 88% admitted, 39% enrolled. **Transfer Admission Requirements:** High school transcript, college transcript(s). Minimum college GPA of 2.0 required. **General Admission Information:** Application fee $30. Regular notification is rolling. Non-fall registration accepted. Admission may be deferred for a maxiumum of 2 semesters. Credit and/or placement offered for CEEB Advanced Placement tests.

COSTS AND FINANCIAL AID

Comprehensive fee $6,995. Required fees $348. **Required Forms and Deadlines:** FAFSA, institution's own financial aid form, institution's own financial aid form used in spring/summer sessions only. Financial aid filing deadline 3/1. **Notification of Awards:** Applicants will be notified of awards on a rolling basis beginning on or about 3/15. **Types of Aid:** *Need-based scholarships/grants:* Pell, SEOG, state scholarships/grants, private scholarships, the school's own gift aid. *Loans:* Direct Subsidized Stafford, Direct Unsubsidized Stafford, Direct PLUS, Federal Perkins, state loans. **Student Employment:** Off-campus job opportunities are poor. **Financial Aid Statistics:** 30% freshmen, 33% undergrads receive need-based scholarship or grant aid. 32% freshmen, 49% undergrads receive need-based self-help aid. 49% freshmen, 49% undergrads receive any aid.

UNIVERSITY OF MINNESOTA—CROOKSTON

University of Minnesota, Crookston, 2900 University Avenue, Crookston, MN 56716-5001
Phone: 218-281-8560 **E-mail:** nelson@umcrookston.edu
Fax: 218-281-8575 **Website:** www.umcrookston.edu **ACT Code:** 2129
Financial Aid Phone: 218-281-8563

This public school was founded in 1966. It has a 237-acre campus.

RATINGS

Admissions Selectivity Rating: 71   **Fire Safety Rating:** 93   **Green Rating:** 64

STUDENTS AND FACULTY

Enrollment: 1,053. **Student Body:** 44% female, 56% male, 4% international. African American 4%, Asian 2%, Caucasian 81%, Hispanic 2%. **Retention and Graduation:** 70% freshmen return for sophomore year. 20% freshmen graduate within 4 years. 3% grads go on to further study within 1 year. 2% grads pursue business degrees. **Faculty:** Student/faculty ratio 21:1. 53 full-time faculty, 51% hold PhDs. 100% faculty teach undergrads.

ACADEMICS

Degrees: Associate, bachelor's, certificate. **Academic Requirements:** Arts/fine arts, computer literacy, English (including composition), humanities, mathematics, sciences (biological or physical), social science. **Classes:** Most classes have 10–19 students. Most lab/discussion sections have 10–19 students. **Majors with Highest Enrollment:** Business administration/management, information technology, natural resources/conservation. **Disciplines with Highest Percentage of Degrees Awarded:** Business/marketing 34%, agriculture 24%, natural resources/environmental science 15%, engineering 9%, education 6%. **Special Study Options:** Distance learning, double major, dual enrollment, English as a second language (ESL), independent study, internships, study abroad, teacher certification program.

FACILITIES

Housing: Coed dorms, apartments for single students. **Special Academic Facilities/Equipment:** Red River Valley Natural History Area, Northwest Research and Outreach Center, UMC Horse Riding Arena, Valley Technology Park. **Computers:** 90% of classrooms are wired, 95% of classrooms are wireless, 100% of public computers are PCs, network access in dorm rooms, network access in dorm lounges, online registration, online administrative functions (other than registration), remote student-access to Web through college's connection, tuition includes personal computer.

CAMPUS LIFE

Activities: Choral groups, drama/theater, pep band, student government. **Organizations:** 38 registered organizations, 1 honor society, 2 religious organizations. 1 fraternity (3% men join), 1 sorority (2% women join). **Athletics (Intercollegiate):** *Men:* Baseball, basketball, football, golf, ice hockey. *Women:* Basketball, equestrian sports, golf, soccer, softball, tennis, volleyball.

ADMISSIONS

Freshman Academic Profile: 7% in top 10% of high school class, 26% in top 25% of high school class, 63% in top 50% of high school class. SAT Math middle 50% range 405–555. SAT Critical Reading middle 50% range 445–530. ACT middle 50% range 18–23. TOEFL required of all international applicants, minimum paper TOEFL 520, minimum computer TOEFL 190. **Basis for Candidate Selection:** *Very important factors considered include:* Academic GPA, rigor of secondary school record, standardized test scores. *Important factors considered include:* Class rank, talent/ability. *Other factors considered include:* Alumni/ae relation, application essay, character/personal qualities, extracurricular activities, level of applicant's interest, recommendation(s), volunteer work, work experience. **Freshman Admission Requirements:** High school diploma is required, and GED is accepted. *Academic units recommended:* 4 English, 3 math, 3 science, 2 foreign language, 2 social studies. **Freshman Admission Statistics:** 466 applied, 83% admitted, 56% enrolled. **Transfer Admission Requirements:** College transcript(s). Minimum college GPA of 2.0 required. Lowest grade transferable D. **General Admission Information:** Application fee $30. Regular notification within 15 days of completed application. Non-fall registration accepted. Admission may be deferred for a maxiumum of 2 semesters. Credit and/or placement offered for CEEB Advanced Placement tests.

COSTS AND FINANCIAL AID

Comprehensive fee $6,770. Room and board $5,977. Required fees $2,493. Average book expense $800. **Required Forms and Deadlines:** FAFSA. Financial aid filing deadline 2/15. **Notification of Awards:** Applicants will be notified of awards on a rolling basis beginning on or about 3/15. **Types of Aid:** *Need-based scholarships/grants:* Pell, SEOG, state scholarships/grants, the school's own gift aid, Federal Academic Competitiveness Grant and SMART Grant. *Loans:* Direct Subsidized Stafford, Direct Unsubsidized Stafford, Direct PLUS, Federal Perkins, state loans. **Student Employment:** Federal Work-Study Program available. Institutional employment available. Off-campus job opportunities are fair. **Financial Aid Statistics:** 62% freshmen, 58% undergrads receive need-based scholarship or grant aid. 57% freshmen, 61% undergrads receive need-based self-help aid. 67% freshmen, 66% undergrads receive any aid. Highest amount earned per year from on-campus jobs $2,000.

UNIVERSITY OF MINNESOTA—DULUTH

23 Solon Campus Center, 1117 University Drive, Duluth, MN 55812-3000
Phone: 218-726-7171 **E-mail:** umdadmis@d.umn.edu **CEEB Code:** 6873
Fax: 218-726-7040 **Website:** www.d.umn.edu **ACT Code:** 2157
Financial Aid Phone: 800-232-1339

This public school was founded in 1947. It has a 247-acre campus.

RATINGS

Admissions Selectivity Rating: 68   **Fire Safety Rating:** 88   **Green Rating:** 91

STUDENTS AND FACULTY

Enrollment: 9,487. **Student Body:** 48% female, 52% male, 12% out-of-state. **Retention and Graduation:** 76% freshmen return for sophomore year. 20% grads go on to further study within 1 year. **Faculty:** Student/faculty ratio 22:1. 376 full-time faculty. 100% faculty teach undergrads.

ACADEMICS

Degrees: Bachelor's, first professional, master's, post-bachelor's certificate. **Academic Requirements:** Arts/fine arts, computer literacy, cultural diversity and international perspectives, English (including composition), sciences (biological or physical), social science. **Classes:** Most classes have 20–29 students. Most lab/discussion sections have 10–19 students. **Majors with Highest Enrollment:** Business administration/management, elementary education and teaching. **Disciplines with Highest Percentage of Degrees Awarded:** Business/marketing 20%, biological/life sciences 18%, education 12%, social sciences 8%, communications/journalism 6%, communication technologies 6%, engineering 6%, psychology 6%. **Special Study Options:** Accelerated program, cross registration, distance learning, double major, dual enrollment, honors program, independent study, internships, student-designed major, study abroad, teacher certification program.

FACILITIES

Housing: Coed dorms, men's dorms, women's dorms, apartments for single students. **Special Academic Facilities/Equipment:** Art museum, planetarium, music performance hall, theater. **Computers:** Network access in dorm rooms, online registration, remote student-access to Web through college's connection.

CAMPUS LIFE

Activities: Choral groups, concert band, dance, drama/theater, jazz band, music ensembles, musical theater, pep band, radio station, student government, student newspaper. **Organizations:** 150 registered organizations, 10 honor societies, 7 religious organizations. 2 fraternities (1% men join), 2 sororities (1% women join). **Athletics (Intercollegiate):** *Men:* Baseball, basketball, cross-country, football, ice hockey, soccer, track/field (outdoor). *Women:* Basketball, cross-country, ice hockey, soccer, softball, tennis, track/field (outdoor), volleyball. **Environmental Initiatives:** LEED. Stormwater Management Plan. Energy Conservation Projects.

ADMISSIONS

Freshman Academic Profile: 14% in top 10% of high school class, 38% in top 25% of high school class, 89% in top 50% of high school class. 95% from public high schools. ACT middle 50% range 20–25. TOEFL required of all international applicants, minimum paper TOEFL 550, minimum computer TOEFL 213. **Basis for Candidate Selection:** *Very important factors considered include:* Class rank, standardized test scores. *Important factors considered include:* Rigor of secondary school record. *Other factors considered include:* Application essay, racial/ethnic status, recommendation(s), talent/ability. **Freshman Admission Requirements:** High school diploma is required, and GED is accepted. *Academic units required:* 4 English, 3 math, 3 science, 2 foreign language, 2 social studies. **Freshman Admission Statistics:** 7,338 applied, 76% admitted, 42% enrolled. **Transfer Admission Requirements:** High school transcript, college transcript(s). Minimum college GPA of 2.0 required. Lowest grade transferable D. **General Admission Information:** Application fee $35. Regular application deadline 8/1. Regular notification is rolling. Non-fall registration accepted. Admission may be deferred for a maximum of 2 semesters. Credit offered for CEEB Advanced Placement tests.

COSTS AND FINANCIAL AID

Annual in-state tuition $7,700. Annual out-of-state tuition $17,327. Room and board $5,722. Required fees $1,900. Average book expense $1,166. **Required Forms and Deadlines:** FAFSA. Financial aid filing deadline 3/31. **Notification of Awards:** Applicants will be notified of awards on or about 3/1. **Types of Aid:** *Need-based scholarships/grants:* Pell, SEOG, state scholarships/grants, private scholarships, the school's own gift aid. *Loans:* Direct Subsidized Stafford, Direct Unsubsidized Stafford, Direct PLUS, Federal Perkins, state loans, college/university loans from institutional funds. **Student Employment:** Federal Work-Study Program available. Institutional employment available. **Financial Aid Statistics:** 41% freshmen, 37% undergrads receive need-based scholarship or grant aid. 43% freshmen, 45% undergrads receive need-based self-help aid. 33 freshmen, 158 undergrads receive athletic scholarships. 81% undergrads receive any aid.

UNIVERSITY OF MINNESOTA—MORRIS

600 East 4th St, Morris, MN 56267
Phone: 320-589-6035 **E-mail:** admissions@morris.umn.edu **CEEB Code:** 6890
Fax: 320-589-1673 **Website:** www.morris.umn.edu **ACT Code:** 2155
Financial Aid Phone: 800-992-8863

This public school was founded in 1959. It has a 130-acre campus.

RATINGS

Admissions Selectivity Rating: 76   **Fire Safety Rating:** 60*   **Green Rating:** 60*

STUDENTS AND FACULTY

Enrollment: 1,667. **Student Body:** 61% female, 39% male, 13% out-of-state, 1% international (15 countries represented). African American 2%, Asian 3%, Caucasian 74%, Hispanic 1%, Native American 9%. **Retention and Graduation:** 86% freshmen return for sophomore year. 40% freshmen graduate within 4 years. 48% grads go on to further study within 1 year. 30% grads pursue arts and sciences degrees. 3% grads pursue business degrees. 11% grads pursue law degrees. 4% grads pursue medical degrees. **Faculty:** Student/faculty ratio 13:1. 121 full-time faculty, 93% hold PhDs. 100% faculty teach undergrads.

ACADEMICS

Degrees: Bachelor's, certificate. **Academic Requirements:** Arts/fine arts, computer literacy, English (including composition), ethical and civic responsibility, first-year seminar, foreign languages, history, humanities, international perspective, mathematics, sciences (biological or physical), social science. **Classes:** Most classes have 10–19 students. Most lab/discussion sections have 10–19 students. **Majors with Highest Enrollment:** Elementary education and teaching, psychology. **Disciplines with Highest Percentage of Degrees Awarded:** Social sciences 17%, English 11%, biological/life sciences 8%, education 8%, business/marketing 7%, history 7%, public administration and social services 7%, visual and performing arts 6%. **Special Study Options:** Accelerated program, cooperative education program, distance learning, double major, exchange student program (domestic), honors program, independent study, internships, student-designed major, study abroad, teacher certification program.

FACILITIES

Housing: Coed dorms, men's dorms, women's dorms, apartments for single students, special housing for disabled students. **Special Academic Facilities/Equipment:** HFA Art Gallery, conservatory, observatory. **Computers:** 1% of classrooms are wired, 3% of classrooms are wireless, 75% of public computers are PCs, 25% of public computers are Macs, network access in dorm rooms, online registration, online administrative functions (other than registration), remote student-access to Web through college's connection.

CAMPUS LIFE

Activities: Choral groups, concert band, dance, drama/theater, jazz band, literary magazine, music ensembles, musical theater, radio station, student government, student newspaper, symphony orchestra, television station. **Organizations:** 90 registered organizations, 5 honor societies, 12 religious organizations. **Athletics (Intercollegiate):** *Men:* Baseball, basketball, football, golf, tennis, track/field (indoor), track/field (outdoor). *Women:* Basketball, cross-country, diving, golf, soccer, softball, swimming, tennis, track/field (indoor), track/field (outdoor), volleyball.

ADMISSIONS

Freshman Academic Profile: 32% in top 10% of high school class, 60% in top 25% of high school class, 88% in top 50% of high school class. 92% from public high schools. SAT Math middle 50% range 510–650. SAT Critical Reading middle 50% range 520–640. ACT middle 50% range 23–28. TOEFL required of all international applicants, minimum paper TOEFL 550, minimum computer TOEFL 213. **Basis for Candidate Selection:** *Very important factors considered include:* Class rank, rigor of secondary school record, standardized test scores. *Important factors considered include:* Application essay, character/personal qualities, extracurricular activities, recommendation(s), talent/ability, volunteer work, work experience. *Other factors considered include:* Alumni/ae relation, interview, racial/ethnic status. **Freshman Admission Requirements:** High school diploma is required, and GED is accepted. *Academic units required:* 4 English, 3 math, 3 science (2 science labs), 2 foreign language, 4 social studies, 4 history. *Academic units recommended:* 4 math, 4 science, 3 foreign language. **Freshman Admission**

Statistics: 1,067 applied, 84% admitted, 43% enrolled. **Transfer Admission Requirements:** College transcript(s), essay or personal statement, statement of good standing from prior institution(s). Minimum college GPA of 2.5 required. Lowest grade transferable D. **General Admission Information:** Application fee $35. Regular application deadline 3/15. Regular notification is rolling. Non-fall registration accepted. Admission may be deferred for a maximum of 2 semesters. Common Application accepted. Credit and/or placement offered for CEEB Advanced Placement tests.

COSTS AND FINANCIAL AID

Annual in-state tuition $8,720. Out-of-state tuition $8,720. Room & board $6,150. Required fees $1,592. Average book expense $900. **Required Forms and Deadlines:** FAFSA. Financial aid filing deadline 3/1. **Notification of Awards:** Applicants will be notified of awards on a rolling basis beginning on or about 3/15. **Types of Aid:** *Need-based scholarships/grants:* Pell, SEOG, state scholarships/grants, private scholarships, the school's own gift aid. *Loans:* Direct Subsidized Stafford, Direct Unsubsidized Stafford, Direct PLUS, Federal Perkins, state loans. **Student Employment:** Federal Work-Study Program available. Institutional employment available. Off-campus job opportunities are good. **Financial Aid Statistics:** 59% freshmen, 58% undergrads receive need-based scholarship or grant aid. 58% freshmen, 61% undergrads receive need-based self-help aid. 90% freshmen, 87% undergrads receive any aid. Highest amount earned per year from on-campus jobs $2,343.

UNIVERSITY OF MINNESOTA—TWIN CITIES

240 Williamson Hall, 231 Pillsbury Drive SE, Minneapolis, MN 55455-0213
Phone: 612-625-2008 **E-mail:** admissions@tc.umn.edu **CEEB Code:** 6874
Fax: 612-626-1693 **Website:** www.umn.edu **ACT Code:** 2156
Financial Aid Phone: 612-624-1665

This public school was founded in 1851. It has a 2,000-acre campus.

RATINGS
Admissions Selectivity Rating: 89   **Fire Safety Rating:** 60*   **Green Rating:** 91

STUDENTS AND FACULTY
Enrollment: 28,645. **Student Body:** 53% female, 47% male, 27% out-of-state, 2% international. African American 5%, Asian 10%, Caucasian 79%, Hispanic 2%. **Retention and Graduation:** 86% freshmen return for sophomore year. **Faculty:** Student/faculty ratio 15:1. 1,707 full-time faculty, 68% hold PhDs.

ACADEMICS
Degrees: Bachelor's, certificate, diploma, doctoral, first professional certificate, first professional, master's, post-bachelor's certificate, post-master's certificate. **Academic Requirements:** Arts/fine arts, English (including composition), foreign languages, history, humanities, mathematics, sciences (biological or physical), social science. **Classes:** Most classes have 20–29 students. Most lab/discussion sections have 10–19 students. **Disciplines with Highest Percentage of Degrees Awarded:** Social sciences 13%, business/marketing 12%, engineering 9%, English 7%, biological/life sciences 7%, psychology 7%, visual and performing arts 6%. **Special Study Options:** Accelerated program, cooperative education program, cross registration, distance learning, double major, dual enrollment, English as a second language (ESL), exchange student program (domestic), external degree program, honors program, independent study, internships, liberal arts/career combination, student-designed major, study abroad, teacher certification program, minors offered in most majors. Students may register in the College of Continuing Education and take courses in any division for B.A. or B.S. degrees. Programs in foreign service and pre-social work. Phi Beta Kappa. Pass/fail grading option. Qualified undergraduates may take graduate level classes. Pre-professional programs in law, medicine, veterinary science, pharmacy, dentistry, architecture, biology, education, journalism, landscape architecture, management, medical technology, mortuary science, nursing, and occupational/physical therapy.

FACILITIES
Housing: Coed dorms, apartments for married students, apartments for single students, special housing for disabled students, special housing for international students, fraternity/sorority housing, cooperative housing, Honors housing, residential college. **Special Academic Facilities/Equipment:** Frederick R. Weisman Art Museum, Bell Museum of Natural History, Ted Mann Concert Hall, recreational sports center, civil engineering building, basic sciences/

biomedical engineering building, Coffman Memorial Union, West Bank Arts Quarter, Goldstein Gallery, arboretum **Computers:** Network access in dorm rooms, network access in dorm lounges, online registration, online administrative functions (other than registration), remote student-access to Web through college's connection.

CAMPUS LIFE
Activities: Choral groups, concert band, dance, drama/theater, jazz band, literary magazine, marching band, music ensembles, musical theater, opera, pep band, radio station, student government, student newspaper, student-run film society, symphony orchestra, television station. **Organizations:** 600 registered organizations, 10 religious organizations. 22 fraternities, 12 sororities. **Athletics (Intercollegiate):** *Men:* Baseball, basketball, cross-country, diving, football, golf, gymnastics, ice hockey, swimming, tennis, track/field (indoor), track/field (outdoor), wrestling. *Women:* Basketball, cross-country, diving, golf, gymnastics, ice hockey, soccer, softball, swimming, tennis, track/field (indoor), track/field (outdoor), volleyball.

ADMISSIONS
Freshman Academic Profile: 39% in top 10% of high school class, 77% in top 25% of high school class, 97% in top 50% of high school class. SAT Math middle 50% range 580–700. SAT Critical Reading middle 50% range 540–680. SAT Writing middle 50% range 530–660. ACT middle 50% range 24–29. TOEFL required of all international applicants, minimum paper TOEFL 550, minimum computer TOEFL 200. **Basis for Candidate Selection:** *Very important factors considered include:* Academic GPA, class rank, rigor of secondary school record, standardized test scores. *Other factors considered include:* Alumni/ae relation, character/personal qualities, extracurricular activities, first generation, geographical residence, racial/ethnic status, talent/ability, volunteer work, work experience. **Freshman Admission Requirements:** High school diploma is required, and GED is accepted. *Academic units required:* 4 English, 3 math, 3 science, 2 foreign language, 3 social studies, 1 history. **Freshman Admission Statistics:** 24,660 applied, 57% admitted, 38% enrolled. **Transfer Admission Requirements:** College transcript(s). Minimum college GPA of 2.0 required. Lowest grade transferable D. **General Admission Information:** Application fee $45. Non-fall registration accepted. Admission may be deferred for a maximum of 2 semesters. Neither credit nor placement offered for CEEB Advanced Placement tests.

COSTS AND FINANCIAL AID
Annual in-state tuition $9,598. Annual out-of-state tuition $21,228. Room and board $7,240. **Required Forms and Deadlines:** FAFSA, institution's own financial aid form. **Types of Aid:** *Need-based scholarships/grants:* Pell, SEOG, state scholarships/grants, private scholarships, the school's own gift aid, Federal Nursing Scholarships. *Loans:* Direct Subsidized Stafford, Direct Unsubsidized Stafford, Direct PLUS, Federal Perkins, Federal Nursing, state loans, college/university loans from institutional funds. **Financial Aid Statistics:** 37% freshmen, 34% undergrads receive need-based scholarship or grant aid. 42% freshmen, 43% undergrads receive need-based self-help aid.

UNIVERSITY OF MISSISSIPPI

145 Martindale, University, MS 38677
Phone: 662-915-7226 **E-mail:** admissions@olemiss.edu **CEEB Code:** 1840
Fax: 662-915-5869 **Website:** www.olemiss.edu **ACT Code:** 2250
Financial Aid Phone: 800-891-4596

This public school was founded in 1844. It has a 2,500-acre campus.

RATINGS
Admissions Selectivity Rating: 60*   **Fire Safety Rating:** 60*   **Green Rating:** 60*

STUDENTS AND FACULTY
Enrollment: 12,594. **Student Body:** 53% female, 47% male, 33% out-of-state. African American 13%, Asian 1%, Caucasian 82%. **Retention and Graduation:** 80% freshmen return for sophomore year. **Faculty:** Student/faculty ratio 19:1. 647 full-time faculty.

ACADEMICS
Degrees: Bachelor's, certificate, doctoral, first professional, master's. **Academic Requirements:** Arts/fine arts, English (including composition), humanities, mathematics, sciences (biological or physical), social science,

university studies. **Classes:** Most classes have 10–19 students. Most lab/discussion sections have 20–29 students. **Majors with Highest Enrollment:** Accounting, elementary education and teaching, marketing/marketing management. **Disciplines with Highest Percentage of Degrees Awarded:** Business/marketing 29%, education 13%, family and consumer sciences 5%, psychology 5%, English 4%, health professions and related sciences 4%, law/legal studies 4%, mathematics 4%, parks and recreation 4%, visual and performing arts 4%. **Special Study Options:** Accelerated program, cooperative education program, distance learning, double major, English as a second language (ESL), honors program, independent study, internships, study abroad, teacher certification program.

FACILITIES

Housing: Men's dorms, women's dorms, apartments for married students, apartments for single students, special housing for disabled students, special housing for international students, fraternity/sorority housing, graduate/older students. **Special Academic Facilities/Equipment:** Sally McDonnell-Barksdale Honors College, Croft Institute for International Studies, Mississippi Center for Supercomputing Research, art and archaeology museums, Center for Study of Southern Culture, William Faulkner home, Marine Minerals Research Institute, National Center for Physical Acoustics, Biological Field Station, Ford Center for the Performing Arts, William Winter Institutue for Racial Reconciliation, Paris-Yates Chapel, Trent Lott Leadership Institute, Living Blues Archive. **Computers:** Network access in dorm rooms, network access in dorm lounges, online registration, online administrative functions (other than registration), support for handheld computing, remote student-access to Web through college's connection.

CAMPUS LIFE

Activities: Choral groups, concert band, dance, drama/theater, jazz band, literary magazine, marching band, music ensembles, musical theater, pep band, radio station, student government, student newspaper, symphony orchestra, television station, yearbook. **Organizations:** 250 registered organizations, 36 honor societies, 18 religious organizations. 19 fraternities (32% men join), 12 sororities (34% women join). **Athletics (Intercollegiate):** *Men:* Baseball, basketball, cheerleading, cross-country, football, golf, tennis, track/field (indoor), track/field (outdoor). *Women:* Basketball, cheerleading, cross-country, golf, riflery, soccer, softball, tennis, track/field (indoor), track/field (outdoor), volleyball.

ADMISSIONS

Freshman Academic Profile: 47% in top 25% of high school class, 74% in top 50% of high school class. 70% from public high schools. SAT Math middle 50% range 460–590. SAT Critical Reading middle 50% range 460–600. ACT middle 50% range 20–28. TOEFL required of all international applicants, minimum paper TOEFL 550, minimum computer TOEFL 213. **Basis for Candidate Selection:** *Very important factors considered include:* Academic GPA, rigor of secondary school record. *Important factors considered include:* Class rank, standardized test scores. *Other factors considered include:* Alumni/ae relation, state residency, talent/ability. **Freshman Admission Requirements:** High school diploma is required, and GED is accepted. *Academic units required:* 4 English, 3 math, 3 science (3 science labs), 1 foreign language, 1 social studies, 2 history, 1 academic elective. *Academic units recommended:* 4 math, 4 science, 2 foreign language, 2 social studies. **Freshman Admission Statistics:** 7,771 applied, 84% admitted, 40% enrolled. **Transfer Admission Requirements:** College transcript(s). Minimum college GPA of 2.0 required. Lowest grade transferable D. **General Admission Information:** Application fee $25. Regular application deadline 7/20. Regular notification is rolling. Non-fall registration accepted. Credit offered for CEEB Advanced Placement tests.

COSTS AND FINANCIAL AID

Required Forms and Deadlines: FAFSA. Financial aid filing deadline 3/15. **Notification of Awards:** Applicants will be notified of awards on a rolling basis beginning on or about 4/1. **Types of Aid:** *Need-based scholarships/grants:* Pell, SEOG, state scholarships/grants, private scholarships, the school's own gift aid. *Loans:* FFEL Subsidized Stafford, FFEL Unsubsidized Stafford, FFEL PLUS, Federal Perkins, college/university loans from institutional funds. **Student Employment:** Off-campus job opportunities are good. **Financial Aid Statistics:** 21% freshmen, 26% undergrads receive need-based scholarship or grant aid. 20% freshmen, 29% undergrads receive need-based self-help aid. 85 freshmen, 376 undergrads receive athletic scholarships. 72% freshmen, 75% undergrads receive any aid.

UNIVERSITY OF MISSOURI—COLUMBIA

230 Jesse Hall, Columbia, MO 65211
Phone: 573-882-7786 **E-mail:** MU4U@missouri.edu
Fax: 573-882-7887 **Website:** www.missouri.edu **ACT Code:** 2382
Financial Aid Phone: 573-882-7506

This public school was founded in 1839. It has a 1,358-acre campus.

RATINGS

Admissions Selectivity Rating: 77　　**Fire Safety Rating:** 70　　**Green Rating:** 60*

STUDENTS AND FACULTY

Enrollment: 21,258. **Student Body:** 51% female, 49% male, 13% out-of-state, 1% international (118 countries represented). African American 6%, Asian 3%, Caucasian 84%, Hispanic 2%. **Retention and Graduation:** 85% freshmen return for sophomore year. **Faculty:** Student/faculty ratio 18:1. 1,062 full-time faculty, 92% hold PhDs. 100% faculty teach undergrads.

ACADEMICS

Degrees: Bachelor's, doctoral, first professional certificate, first professional, master's, post-master's certificate. **Academic Requirements:** Capstone experience, computer literacy, English (including composition), foreign languages, history, mathematics, sciences (biological or physical), social science. **Classes:** Most classes have 10–19 students. Most lab/discussion sections have 20–29 students. **Majors with Highest Enrollment:** Biological and biomedical sciences, business administration/management, journalism. **Disciplines with Highest Percentage of Degrees Awarded:** Business/marketing 19%, communications/journalism 12%, education 7%, engineering 7%, social sciences 7%, health professions and related sciences 6%. **Special Study Options:** Accelerated program, cooperative education program, cross registration, distance learning, double major, dual enrollment, English as a second language (ESL), evening college, exchange student program (domestic), external degree program, honors program, independent study, internships, MU Direct, student-designed major, study abroad, teacher certification program.

FACILITIES

Housing: Coed dorms, men's dorms, women's dorms, apartments for married students, fraternity/sorority housing, freshamn interest groups. **Special Academic Facilities/Equipment:** Life Sciences Center for Research, TigerPlace, James B. Nutter Family Information Commons, Ellis Library, museum of anthropology, museum of art and archaeology, world's most powerful university research reactor for Nuclear medicine, European Union Center. **Computers:** 1% of classrooms are wired, 80% of classrooms are wireless, 85% of public computers are PCs, 13% of public computers are Macs, 1% of public computers are UNIX, network access in dorm rooms, network access in dorm lounges, online registration, online administrative functions (other than registration), support for handheld computing, remote student-access to Web through college's connection.

CAMPUS LIFE

Activities: Choral groups, concert band, dance, drama/theater, jazz band, literary magazine, marching band, music ensembles, musical theater, opera, pep band, radio station, student government, student newspaper, student-run film society, symphony orchestra, television station. **Organizations:** 518 registered organizations, 26 honor societies, 30 religious organizations. 32 fraternities (17% men join), 18 sororities (24% women join). **Athletics (Intercollegiate):** *Men:* Baseball, basketball, cross-country, diving, football, golf, swimming, track/field (indoor), track/field (outdoor), wrestling. *Women:* Basketball, cross-country, diving, golf, gymnastics, soccer, softball, swimming, tennis, track/field (indoor), track/field (outdoor), volleyball.

ADMISSIONS

Freshman Academic Profile: 27% in top 10% of high school class, 57% in top 25% of high school class, 87% in top 50% of high school class. 81% from public high schools. SAT Math middle 50% range 540–650. SAT Critical Reading middle 50% range 530–650. ACT middle 50% range 23–28. TOEFL required of all international applicants, minimum paper TOEFL 500, minimum computer TOEFL 173. **Basis for Candidate Selection:** *Very important factors considered include:* Academic GPA, class rank, standardized test scores. *Important factors considered include:* Rigor of secondary school record. *Other factors considered include:* Application essay, first generation, level of applicant's interest, racial/ethnic status, recommendation(s), talent/ability, volunteer work, work experience. **Freshman Admission Requirements:** High school diploma is required, and GED is accepted. *Academic units required:* 4 English, 4 math, 3 science (1 science lab), 2 foreign language, 3 social studies, 1 fine art. **Freshman Admission Statistics:** 13,102 applied, 78% admitted, 47% enrolled. **Transfer Admission Requirements:** College transcript(s). Minimum college GPA of 2.5 required. Lowest grade transferable C. **General Admission Information:** Application fee $45. Regular notification is rolling. Non-fall registration accepted. Admission may be deferred for a maximum of 2 semesters. Credit and/or placement offered for CEEB Advanced Placement tests.

COSTS AND FINANCIAL AID

Annual in-state tuition $7,077. Annual out-of-state tuition $17,733. Room and board $7,002. Required fees $1,629. **Required Forms and Deadlines:** FAFSA. Financial aid filing deadline 3/1. **Notification of Awards:** Applicants will be notified of awards on a rolling basis beginning on or about 4/1. **Types of Aid:** *Need-based scholarships/grants:* Pell, SEOG, state scholarships/grants, private scholarships, the school's own gift aid, outside. *Loans:* Direct Subsidized Stafford, Direct Unsubsidized Stafford, Direct PLUS, FFEL PLUS, Federal Perkins, Federal Nursing, state loans, college/university loans from institutional funds, outside or 3rd party. **Financial Aid Statistics:** 39% freshmen, 35% undergrads receive need-based scholarship or grant aid. 34% freshmen, 36% undergrads receive need-based self-help aid. 190 freshmen, 871 undergrads receive athletic scholarships. 82% freshmen, 76% undergrads receive any aid.

UNIVERSITY OF MISSOURI—KANSAS CITY

5100 Rockhill Road, 101 AC, Kansas City, MO 64114
Phone: 816-235-1111 **E-mail:** admit@umkc.edu **CEEB Code:** 6872
Fax: 816-235-5544 **Website:** www.umkc.edu **ACT Code:** 2380
Financial Aid Phone: 816-235-1154

This public school was founded in 1929. It has a 191-acre campus.

RATINGS

Admissions Selectivity Rating: 76   **Fire Safety Rating:** 60*   **Green Rating:** 73

STUDENTS AND FACULTY

Enrollment: 6,512. **Student Body:** 60% female, 40% male, 23% out-of-state, 4% international (81 countries represented). African American 14%, Asian 5%, Caucasian 63%, Hispanic 4%, Native American 1%. **Retention and Graduation:** 73% freshmen return for sophomore year. 11% freshmen graduate within 4 years. **Faculty:** Student/faculty ratio 9:1.

ACADEMICS

Degrees: Bachelor's, doctoral, first professional certificate, first professional, master's, post-master's certificate. **Academic Requirements:** English (including composition), foreign languages, history, humanities, mathematics, sciences (biological or physical). **Majors with Highest Enrollment:** Business administration/management, liberal arts and sciences/liberal studies, psychology. **Disciplines with Highest Percentage of Degrees Awarded:** Liberal arts/general studies 21%, business/marketing 10%, education 8%, social sciences 8%, psychology 7%, computer and information sciences 6%, visual and performing arts 6%. **Special Study Options:** Accelerated program, cooperative education program, double major, dual enrollment, honors program, independent study, internships, study abroad, teacher certification program.

FACILITIES

Housing: Coed dorms, apartments for married students, apartments for single students, fraternity/sorority housing. **Special Academic Facilities/Equipment:** Art gallery, professional theater, geosciences museums, language lab, observatory. **Computers:** 64% of public computers are PCs, 32% of public computers are Macs, 4% of public computers are UNIX, network access in dorm rooms, online registration, online administrative functions (other than registration), remote student-access to Web through college's connection.

CAMPUS LIFE

Activities: Choral groups, concert band, dance, drama/theater, jazz band, music ensembles, opera, student government, student newspaper, symphony orchestra. **Organizations:** 200 registered organizations, 33 honor societies, 13 religious organizations. 6 fraternities (3% men join), 7 sororities (5% women join). **Athletics (Intercollegiate):** *Men:* Basketball, cross-country, golf, riflery, soccer, tennis, track/field (outdoor). *Women:* Basketball, cheerleading, cross-country, golf, riflery, softball, tennis, track/field (outdoor), volleyball. **Environmental Initiatives:** Recycling.

ADMISSIONS

Freshman Academic Profile: 34% in top 10% of high school class, 59% in top 25% of high school class, 84% in top 50% of high school class. SAT Math middle 50% range 560–690. SAT Critical Reading middle 50% range 560–660. ACT middle 50% range 21–28. TOEFL required of all international applicants, minimum paper TOEFL 500. **Basis for Candidate Selection:** *Very important factors considered include:* Class rank, rigor of secondary school record, standardized test scores. *Other factors considered include:* Application essay, character/personal qualities, extracurricular activities, interview, recommendation(s), talent/ability, volunteer work, work experience. **Freshman Admission Requirements:** High school diploma is required, and GED is accepted. *Academic units required:* 4 English, 4 math, 3 science (1 science lab), 2 foreign language, 3 social studies, 1 fine art. *Academic units recommended:* 4 English, 4 math, 3 science (1 science lab), 2 foreign language, 3 social studies, 1 fine arts. **Freshman Admission Statistics:** 1,884 applied, 93% admitted, 44% enrolled. **Transfer Admission Requirements:** College transcript(s). Minimum college GPA of 2.0 required. Lowest grade transferable D. **General Admission Information:** Application fee $35. Non-fall registration accepted. Admission may be deferred for a maximum of 2 semesters. Common Application not accepted. Credit offered for CEEB Advanced Placement tests.

COSTS AND FINANCIAL AID

Annual in-state tuition $4,585. Out-of-state tuition $13,997. Room & board $5,100. Required fees $791. Average book expense $1,068. **Required Forms and Deadlines:** FAFSA. Financial aid filing deadline 3/1. **Notification of Awards:** Applicants will be notified of awards on or about 4/1. **Types of Aid:** *Need-based scholarships/grants:* Pell, SEOG, state scholarships/grants, private scholarships, the school's own gift aid, United Negro College Fund. *Loans:* FFEL Subsidized Stafford, FFEL Unsubsidized Stafford, FFEL PLUS, Federal Perkins, state loans, college/university loans from institutional funds. **Student Employment:** Federal Work-Study Program available. Institutional employment available. Off-campus job opportunities are excellent. **Financial Aid Statistics:** 49% freshmen, 40% undergrads receive need-based scholarship or grant aid. 51% freshmen, 55% undergrads receive need-based self-help aid. 23 freshmen, 151 undergrads receive athletic scholarships. 61% freshmen, 61% undergrads receive any aid. Highest amount earned per year from on-campus jobs $2,930.

UNIVERSITY OF MISSOURI—ST. LOUIS

351 Millenium Student Center, 1 University Boulevard, St. Louis, MO 63121-4400
Phone: 314-516-5451 **E-mail:** admissions@umsl.edu **CEEB Code:** 6889
Fax: 314-516-5310 **Website:** www.umsl.edu **ACT Code:** 2383
Financial Aid Phone: 314-516-5526

This public school was founded in 1963. It has a 475-acre campus.

RATINGS

Admissions Selectivity Rating: 77   **Fire Safety Rating:** 89   **Green Rating:** 71

STUDENTS AND FACULTY

Enrollment: 8,875. **Student Body:** 59% female, 41% male, 6% out-of-state, 2% international (114 countries represented). African American 17%, Asian 3%, Caucasian 66%, Hispanic 2%. **Retention and Graduation:** 70% freshmen return for sophomore year. 15% grads go on to further study within 2 semesters. 36% grads pursue arts and sciences degrees. 17% grads pursue business degrees. 2% grads pursue law degrees. **Faculty:** Student/faculty ratio 17:1. 424 full-time faculty, 77% hold PhDs. 54% faculty teach undergrads.

ACADEMICS

Degrees: Bachelor's, doctoral, first professional, master's, post-bachelor's certificate. **Academic Requirements:** English (including composition), foreign languages, history, humanities, mathematics, sciences (biological or physical), social science. **Classes:** Most classes have 10–19 students. Most lab/discussion sections have 10–19 students. **Majors with Highest Enrollment:** Accounting, business administration/management, nursing/registered nurse training (ASN, BSN, MSN, RN). **Disciplines with Highest Percentage of Degrees Awarded:** Business/marketing 29%, education 13%, social sciences 11%, health professions and related sciences 8%, communications/journalism 7%. **Special Study Options:** Accelerated program, cooperative education program, cross registration, distance learning, double major, dual enrollment, engineering UMSL/Washington University, English as a second language (ESL), exchange student program (domestic), honors program, independent study, internships, optometry 3+4, student-designed major, study abroad, teacher certification program.

FACILITIES

Housing: Coed dorms, women's dorms, apartments for married students, apartments for single students, special housing for disabled students, fraternity/sorority housing, housing for graduate students and students older than 21 in apartments. **Special Academic Facilities/Equipment:** Art galleries, language, writing labs, math labs, Mercantile Library, observatory, radio station. **Computers:** 38% of classrooms are wireless, 80% of public computers are PCs, 10% of public computers are Macs, 10% of public computers are UNIX, network access in dorm rooms, network access in dorm lounges, online registration, online administrative functions (other than registration), support for handheld computing, remote student-access to Web through college's connection.

CAMPUS LIFE

Activities: Choral groups, dance, drama/theater, jazz band, literary magazine, music ensembles, musical theater, opera, pep band, radio station, student government, student newspaper, student-run film society. **Organizations:** 200 registered organizations, 16 honor societies, 9 religious organizations. 3 fraternities (1% men join), 4 sororities (1% women join). **Athletics (Intercollegiate):** *Men:* Baseball, basketball, golf, soccer, tennis. *Women:* Basketball, golf, soccer, softball, tennis, volleyball. **Environmental Initiatives:** Upgrade buildings to include some of the LEED requirements. Energy Conservation and Management. Recycling.

ADMISSIONS

Freshman Academic Profile: 20% in top 10% of high school class, 50% in top 25% of high school class, 85% in top 50% of high school class. 79% from public high schools. SAT Math middle 50% range 520–620. ACT middle 50% range 21–26. TOEFL required of all international applicants, minimum paper TOEFL 500, minimum computer TOEFL 173. **Basis for Candidate Selection:** *Very important factors considered include:* Class rank, rigor of secondary school record, standardized test scores. *Other factors considered include:* Application essay, recommendation(s). **Freshman Admission Requirements:** High school diploma is required, and GED is accepted. *Academic units required:* 4 English, 4 math, 3 science, 2 foreign language, 3 social studies, 1 fine art. **Freshman Admission Statistics:** 2,171 applied, 52% admitted, 46% enrolled. **Transfer Admission Requirements:** College transcript(s). Minimum college GPA of 2.0 required. Lowest grade transferable D. **General Admission Information:** Application fee $35. Regular application deadline 8/18. Regular notification is rolling. Non-fall registration accepted. Credit and/or placement offered for CEEB Advanced Placement tests.

COSTS AND FINANCIAL AID

Average book expense $900. **Required Forms and Deadlines:** FAFSA. Financial aid filing deadline 4/1. **Notification of Awards:** Applicants will be notified of awards on a rolling basis beginning on or about 4/1. **Types of Aid:** *Need-based scholarships/grants:* Pell, SEOG, state scholarships/grants, private scholarships, the school's own gift aid, Federal Nursing Scholarships, Federal ACG and Smart grants. *Loans:* FFEL Subsidized Stafford, FFEL Unsubsidized Stafford, FFEL PLUS, Federal Perkins, Federal Nursing. **Student Employment:** Federal Work-Study Program available. Institutional employment available. Off-campus job opportunities are good. **Financial Aid Statistics:** 46% freshmen, 36% undergrads receive need-based scholarship or grant aid. 43% freshmen, 49% undergrads receive need-based self-help aid. 19 freshmen, 81 undergrads receive athletic scholarships. 76% freshmen, 66% undergrads receive any aid. Highest amount earned per year from on-campus jobs $3,692.

UNIVERSITY OF MOBILE

5437 Parkway Drive, Mobile, AL 36663-0220
Phone: 251-442-2287 **E-mail:** adminfo@mail.umobile.edu **CEEB Code:** 1515
Fax: 251-442-2498 **Website:** www.umobile.edu **ACT Code:** 0029
Financial Aid Phone: 251-442-2252

This private school, affiliated with the Baptist Church, was founded in 1961. It has an 830-acre campus.

RATINGS

Admissions Selectivity Rating: 60*   **Fire Safety Rating:** 60*   **Green Rating:** 60*

STUDENTS AND FACULTY

Enrollment: 1,675. **Student Body:** 71% female, 29% male, 11% out-of-state, 2% international. African American 21%, Caucasian 70%, Native American 2%. **Faculty:** Student/faculty ratio 14:1. 88 full-time faculty, 60% hold PhDs. 100% faculty teach undergrads.

ACADEMICS

Degrees: Associate, bachelor's, master's. **Academic Requirements:** Arts/fine arts, Christian studies, computer literacy, English (including composition), history, HPES, humanities, mathematics, philosophy, sciences (biological or physical), social science. **Classes:** Most classes have 10–19 students. **Majors with Highest Enrollment:** Business administration/management, elementary education and teaching, nursing/registered nurse training (ASN, BSN, MSN, RN). **Disciplines with Highest Percentage of Degrees Awarded:** Education 29%, interdisciplinary studies 21%, business/marketing 8%, health professions and related sciences 8%, social sciences 5%. **Special Study Options:** Accelerated program, cooperative education program, double major, honors program, independent study, internships, liberal arts/career combination, teacher certification program.

FACILITIES

Housing: Men's dorms, women's dorms, special housing for disabled students. **Special Academic Facilities/Equipment:** Art gallery, forest learning center. **Computers:** 95% of public computers are PCs, 5% of public computers are Macs, remote student-access to Web through college's connection.

CAMPUS LIFE

Activities: Choral groups, concert band, dance, drama/theater, jazz band, music ensembles, musical theater, pep band, student government, student newspaper, symphony orchestra, yearbook. **Organizations:** 52 registered organizations, 12 honor societies, 3 religious organizations. **Athletics (Intercollegiate):** *Men:* Baseball, basketball, cheerleading, cross-country, golf, soccer, track/field (indoor), track/field (outdoor). *Women:* Basketball, cheerleading, cross-country, golf, soccer, softball, tennis, track/field (indoor), track/field (outdoor).

ADMISSIONS

Freshman Academic Profile: 76% from public high schools. SAT Math middle 50% range 500–650. SAT Critical Reading middle 50% range 500–700. SAT Writing middle 50% range 450–700. ACT middle 50% range 22–25. TOEFL required of all international applicants, minimum paper TOEFL 550, minimum computer TOEFL 250. **Basis for Candidate Selection:** *Very important factors considered include:* Rigor of secondary school record, standardized test scores. *Other factors considered include:* Class rank, interview, recommendation(s). **Freshman Admission Requirements:** High school diploma is required, and GED is accepted. *Academic units recommended:* 4 English, 3 math, 2 social studies, 3 history. **Freshman Admission Statistics:** 413 applied, 67% admitted, 74% enrolled. **Transfer Admission Requirements:** College transcript(s). Minimum college GPA of 2.0 required. Lowest grade transferable C. **General Admission Information:** Application fee $30. Regular notification is rolling. Non-fall registration accepted. Admission may be deferred for a maximum of 2 semesters. Common Application accepted. Credit offered for CEEB Advanced Placement tests.

COSTS AND FINANCIAL AID

Annual tuition $13,500. Room and board $7,320. Required fees $470. Average book expense $1,000. **Required Forms and Deadlines:** FAFSA, institution's own financial aid form, state aid form. Financial aid filing deadline 3/13. **Notification of Awards:** Applicants will be notified of awards on or about 4/1. **Types of Aid:** *Need-based scholarships/grants:* Pell, SEOG, state scholarships/grants, private scholarships, the school's own gift aid. *Loans:* FFEL Subsidized Stafford, FFEL Unsubsidized Stafford, FFEL PLUS, Federal Perkins. **Student Employment:** Federal Work-Study Program available. Institutional employment available. Off-campus job opportunities are fair. **Financial Aid Statistics:** 83% freshmen, 58% undergrads receive need-based scholarship or grant aid. 84% freshmen, 58% undergrads receive need-based self-help aid. 98% freshmen, 98% undergrads receive any aid. Highest amount earned per year from on-campus jobs $1,545.

THE UNIVERSITY OF MONTANA

Best 368

Lommasson Center 103, Missoula, MT 59812
Phone: 406-243-6266 **E-mail:** admiss@umontana.edu **CEEB Code:** 4489
Fax: 406-243-5711 **Website:** www.umt.edu **ACT Code:** 2422
Financial Aid Phone: 406-243-5373

This public school was founded in 1893. It has a 220-acre campus.

RATINGS

Admissions Selectivity Rating: 74   **Fire Safety Rating:** 81   **Green Rating:** 89

STUDENTS AND FACULTY

Enrollment: 11,371. **Student Body:** 54% female, 46% male, 27% out-of-state, 1% international (60 countries represented). Asian 1%, Caucasian 82%, Hispanic 2%, Native American 4%. **Retention and Graduation:** 70% freshmen return for sophomore year. 20% freshmen graduate within 4 years. 33% grads go on to further study within 1 year. **Faculty:** Student/faculty ratio 19:1. 547 full-time faculty, 80% hold PhDs. 99% faculty teach undergrads.

ACADEMICS

Degrees: Associate, bachelor's, certificate, doctoral, first professional, master's, post-master's certificate. **Academic Requirements:** Arts/fine arts, English (including composition), ethical and human values, foreign languages and symbolic systems, history, historical and cultural studies, humanities, mathematics, sciences (biological or physical), social science. **Classes:** Most classes have 20–29 students. Most lab/discussion sections have 20–29 students. **Majors with Highest Enrollment:** Business administration and management, education, psychology. **Disciplines with Highest Percentage of Degrees Awarded:** Business/marketing 21%, social sciences 14%, communications/journalism 7%, education 7%, natural resources/environmental science 7%, psychology 6%, biological/life sciences 5%, English 5%, history 5%, visual and performing arts 5%. **Special Study Options:** Bachelor of nursing in Missoula in cooperation with Montana State Univeristy-Bozeman Cooperative Education Program, cross registration, distance learning, double major, English as a second language (ESL), exchange student program (domestic), external degree program, honors program, independent study, internships, study abroad, teacher certification program.

FACILITIES

Housing: Coed dorms, men's dorms, women's dorms, apartments for married students, apartments for single students, special housing for disabled students, special housing for international students, fraternity/sorority housing, apartments for students and families. **Special Academic Facilities/Equipment:** Clinical psychology center, environmental studies lab, geology field camp, several biological, biomedical, kinesiology, physiology, forestry-related, and other research labs or centers, art galleries, broadcast media center (public radio and television) and performing arts-radio-television building, practical ethics center, extensive presentation technology equipment and services, and others, biological station, experimental forest, 2-year college of technology (2 locations), Fort Missoula Field Research Center. **Computers:** 5% of classrooms are wired, 20% of classrooms are wireless, 90% of public computers are PCs, 10% of public computers are Macs, network access in dorm rooms, network access in dorm lounges, online registration, online administrative functions (other than registration), remote student-access to Web through college's connection.

CAMPUS LIFE

Activities: Choral groups, concert band, dance, drama/theater, jazz band, literary magazine, marching band, music ensembles, musical theater, opera, pep band, radio station, student government, student newspaper, symphony orchestra, television station. **Organizations:** 150 registered organizations, 5 fraternities (6% men join), 4 sororities (6% women join). **Athletics (Intercollegiate):** *Men:* Basketball, cheerleading, cross-country, football, tennis, track/field (indoor), track/field (outdoor). *Women:* Basketball, cheerleading, cross-country, golf, soccer, tennis, track/field (indoor), track/field (outdoor), volleyball.

ADMISSIONS

Freshman Academic Profile: 16% in top 10% of high school class, 40% in top 25% of high school class, 70% in top 50% of high school class. 44% from public high schools. SAT Math middle 50% range 480–600. SAT Critical Reading middle 50% range 480–600. SAT Writing middle 50% range 470–590. ACT middle 50% range 20–25. TOEFL required of all international applicants, minimum paper TOEFL 500, minimum computer TOEFL 173. **Basis for Candidate Selection:** *Very important factors considered include:* Academic GPA, class rank, rigor of secondary school record, standardized test scores. *Important factors considered include:* Extracurricular activities, talent/ability. *Other factors considered include:* Application essay, recommendation(s). **Freshman Admission Requirements:** High school diploma is required, and GED is accepted. *Academic units required:* 4 English, 3 math, 2 science (2 science labs), 3 social studies, 2 history, 2 academic electives, 2 foreign language, computer science, visual/performing arts, or vocational education. *Academic units recommended:* 2 foreign language. **Freshman Admission Statistics:** 4,855 applied, 96% admitted, 46% enrolled. **Transfer Admission Requirements:** College transcript(s). Minimum college GPA of 2.0 required. Lowest grade transferable D. **General Admission Information:** Application fee $30. Regular notification is rolling. Non-fall registration accepted. Admission may be deferred for a maximum of 2 semesters. Credit and/or placement offered for CEEB Advanced Placement tests.

COSTS AND FINANCIAL AID

Annual in-state tuition $3,883. Out-of-state tuition $13,688. Room & board $5,860. Required fees $1,291. Average book expense $850. **Required Forms and Deadlines:** FAFSA, UM Supplemental Information Sheet. Financial aid

filing deadline 2/15. **Notification of Awards:** Applicants will be notified of awards on a rolling basis beginning on or about 4/1. **Types of Aid:** *Need-based scholarships/grants:* Pell, SEOG, state scholarships/grants, private scholarships, the school's own gift aid. *Loans:* FFEL Subsidized Stafford, FFEL Unsubsidized Stafford, FFEL PLUS, Federal Perkins. **Student Employment:** Federal Work-Study Program available. Institutional employment available. **Financial Aid Statistics:** 34% freshmen, 40% undergrads receive need-based scholarship or grant aid. 43% freshmen, 49% undergrads receive need-based self-help aid. 54 freshmen, 239 undergrads receive athletic scholarships. 82% freshmen, 75% undergrads receive any aid.

UNIVERSITY OF MONTANA— HELENA COLLEGE OF TECHNOLOGY

1115 North Roberts, Helena, MT 59601
Phone: 406-444-6880 **E-mail:** info@umh.umt.edu
Fax: 406-444-6892 **Website:** www.umhelena.edu
Financial Aid Phone: 406-243-5373

This is a public school.

RATINGS

Admissions Selectivity Rating: 60*   **Fire Safety Rating:** 60*   **Green Rating:** 60*

STUDENTS AND FACULTY

Enrollment: 816. **Student Body:** 55% female, 45% male, 1% out-of-state. Caucasian 47%, Hispanic 1%, Native American 3%. **Retention and Graduation:** **Faculty:** Student/faculty ratio 18:1. 34 full-time faculty, 12% hold PhDs.

ACADEMICS

Degrees: Associate, certificate. **Academic Requirements:** English (including composition), mathematics, human relations. **Classes:** Most classes have 10–19 students. **Special Study Options:** Cross registration, distance learning, double major, dual enrollment, independent study, internships.

CAMPUS LIFE

Activities: Student government.

ADMISSIONS

Freshman Admission Requirements: High school diploma is required, and GED is accepted. **Freshman Admission Statistics:** 485 applied, 100% admitted, 27% enrolled. **Transfer Admission Requirements:** College transcript(s), standardized test scores. Minimum college GPA of 2.0 required. Lowest grade transferable C. **General Admission Information:** Application fee $30. Regular notification 4–6 weeks after applying. Non-fall registration accepted. Admission may be deferred for a maximum of two semesters. Common Application not accepted.

COSTS AND FINANCIAL AID

Annual in-state tuition $2,267. Out-of-state tuition $7,581. Required fees $607. Average book expense $1,160.

UNIVERSITY OF MONTANA— MISSOULA COLLEGE OF TECHNOLOGY

909 South Avenue West, Missoula, MT 59801
Phone: 406-243-7882 **E-mail:** kathrynb@selway.umt.edu **CEEB Code:** 4489
Fax: 406-243-7899 **Website:** www.cte.umt.edu **ACT Code:** 2422
Financial Aid Phone: 406-243-5373

This public school was founded in 1893. It has a 220-acre campus.

RATINGS

Admissions Selectivity Rating: 60*   **Fire Safety Rating:** 60*   **Green Rating:** 60*

STUDENTS AND FACULTY

Enrollment: 10,357. **Student Body:** 53% female, 47% male, 31% out-of-state, 3% international. Caucasian 87%, Hispanic 1%, Native American 3%. **Retention and Graduation:** 68% freshmen return for sophomore year. 15% freshmen graduate within 4 years. 42% grads go on to further study within 1 year. 17% grads pursue arts and sciences degrees. 9% grads pursue business degrees. 7% grads pursue law degrees. 9% grads pursue medical degrees. **Faculty:** 100% faculty teach undergrads.

ACADEMICS

Degrees: Associate, bachelor's, certificate, doctoral, first professional, master's. **Academic Requirements:** Computer literacy, English (including composition), mathematics, social science. **Special Study Options:** Combined programs with other institutions, cooperative education program, cross registration, distance learning, double major, dual enrollment, English as a second language (ESL), exchange student program (domestic), honors program, independent study, internships, study abroad, teacher certification program.

FACILITIES

Housing: Coed dorms, men's dorms, women's dorms, apartments for married students, apartments for single students, special housing for disabled students, special housing for international students, fraternity/sorority housing. **Special Academic Facilities/Equipment:** Bureau of Business and Economic Research, clinical psychology center, environmental studies lab, geology field, camp biological research center.

CAMPUS LIFE

Activities: Choral groups, concert band, dance, drama/theater, jazz band, marching band, music ensembles, musical theater, pep band, radio station, student government, student newspaper, symphony orchestra, television station. **Organizations:** 117 registered organizations, 8 honor societies, 15 religious organizations. 7 fraternities (5% men join), 4 sororities (5% women join).

ADMISSIONS

Freshman Academic Profile: TOEFL required of all international applicants, minimum paper TOEFL 500. **Freshman Admission Requirements:** High school diploma is required, and GED is accepted. *Academic units recommended:* 4 English, 3 math, 2 science (1 science lab), 2 foreign language, 3 social studies. **Freshman Admission Statistics:** 852 applied, 85% admitted, 70% enrolled. **Transfer Admission Requirements:** College transcript(s). Minimum college GPA of 2.0 required. Lowest grade transferable D. **General Admission Information:** Application fee $30. Regular notification is rolling. Non-fall registration accepted. Common Application accepted. Credit and/or placement offered for CEEB Advanced Placement tests.

COSTS AND FINANCIAL AID

Annual in-state tuition $2,365. Out-of-state tuition $5,085. Room & board $4,000. **Required Forms and Deadlines:** FAFSA, institution's own financial aid form. Financial aid filing deadline 3/1. **Notification of Awards:** Applicants will be notified of awards on a rolling basis beginning on or about 5/1. **Types of Aid:** *Need-based scholarships/grants:* Pell, SEOG, state scholarships/grants. *Loans:* FFEL Subsidized Stafford, FFEL Unsubsidized Stafford, FFEL PLUS, Federal Perkins. **Student Employment:** Federal Work-Study Program available. Institutional employment available. Off-campus job opportunities are excellent. **Financial Aid Statistics:** 33% freshmen, 35% undergrads receive need-based scholarship or grant aid. 36% freshmen, 40% undergrads receive need-based self-help aid. 39 freshmen, 207 undergrads receive athletic scholarships. Highest amount earned per year from on-campus jobs $1,200.

THE UNIVERSITY OF MONTANA—WESTERN

710 South Atlantic, Dillon, MT 59725
Phone: 406-683-7331 **E-mail:** admissions@umwestern.edu **CEEB Code:** 4945
Fax: 406-683-7493 **Website:** www.umwestern.edu **ACT Code:** 2428
Financial Aid Phone: 406-683-7511

This public school was founded in 1893. It has a 34-acre campus.

RATINGS

Admissions Selectivity Rating: 64 **Fire Safety Rating:** 60* **Green Rating:** 60*

STUDENTS AND FACULTY

Enrollment: 1,159. **Student Body:** 59% female, 41% male, 15% out-of-state. **Retention and Graduation:** 62% freshmen return for sophomore year. 8% freshmen graduate within 4 years. 50% grads go on to further study within 1 year. **Faculty:** Student/faculty ratio 16:1. 50 full-time faculty, 74% hold PhDs. 100% faculty teach undergrads.

ACADEMICS

Degrees: Associate, bachelor's. **Academic Requirements:** Arts/fine arts, computer literacy, English (including composition), history, humanities, mathematics, sciences (biological or physical), social science. **Classes:** Most classes have 10–19 students. **Majors with Highest Enrollment:** Business

---

administration/management, elementary education and teaching, environmental studies. **Disciplines with Highest Percentage of Degrees Awarded:** Education 58%, business/marketing 20%, social sciences 9%, natural resources/environmental science 7%, visual and performing arts 3%. **Special Study Options:** Cooperative education program, distance learning, double major, dual enrollment, honors program, independent study, internships, teacher certification program.

FACILITIES

Housing: Coed dorms, men's dorms, women's dorms, apartments for married students, apartments for single students, special housing for disabled students. **Special Academic Facilities/Equipment:** Art gallery, outdoor education center, learning center. **Computers:** 90% of public computers are PCs, 10% of public computers are Macs, network access in dorm rooms, network access in dorm lounges, online registration, online administrative functions (other than registration), remote student-access to Web through college's connection.

CAMPUS LIFE

Activities: Choral groups, concert band, drama/theater, jazz band, literary magazine, music ensembles, radio station, student government, student newspaper, yearbook. **Organizations:** 25 registered organizations, 2 honor societies, 2 religious organizations. **Athletics (Intercollegiate): Men:** Basketball, cheerleading, football, golf, rodeo. *Women:* Basketball, cheerleading, golf, rodeo, volleyball.

ADMISSIONS

Freshman Academic Profile: 5% in top 10% of high school class, 18% in top 25% of high school class, 49% in top 50% of high school class. 96% from public high schools. SAT Math middle 50% range 430–520. SAT Critical Reading middle 50% range 410–510. ACT middle 50% range 16–22. TOEFL required of all international applicants, minimum paper TOEFL 500, minimum computer TOEFL 173. **Basis for Candidate Selection:** *Very important factors considered include:* Class rank, rigor of secondary school record, standardized test scores. *Other factors considered include:* Alumni/ae relation, extracurricular activities, racial/ethnic status, state residency, talent/ability. **Freshman Admission Requirements:** High school diploma is required, and GED is accepted. *Academic units required:* 4 English, 3 math, 2 science (2 science labs), 3 social studies, 4 academic electives. **Freshman Admission Statistics:** 428 applied, 99% admitted, 57% enrolled. **Transfer Admission Requirements:** College transcript(s). Minimum college GPA of 2.0 required. Lowest grade transferable C. **General Admission Information:** Application fee $30. Regular application deadline 7/1. Regular notification is rolling. Non-fall registration accepted. Admission may be deferred. Common Application accepted. Credit and/or placement offered for CEEB Advanced Placement tests.

COSTS AND FINANCIAL AID

Annual in-state tuition $3,538. Room & board $4,920. Required fees $815. Average book expense $850. **Required Forms and Deadlines:** FAFSA. Financial aid filing deadline 3/1. **Notification of Awards:** Applicants will be notified of awards on or about 5/1. **Types of Aid:** *Need-based scholarships/grants:* Pell, SEOG, state scholarships/grants, the school's own gift aid. *Loans:* FFEL Subsidized Stafford, FFEL Unsubsidized Stafford, FFEL PLUS, Federal Perkins. **Student Employment:** Federal Work-Study Program available. Institutional employment available. Off-campus job opportunities are good. **Financial Aid Statistics:** 65% freshmen, 73% undergrads receive need-based scholarship or grant aid. 65% freshmen, 74% undergrads receive need-based self-help aid. 25 freshmen, 150 undergrads receive athletic scholarships. Highest amount earned per year from on-campus jobs $1,350.

UNIVERSITY OF MONTEVALLO

Station 6030, Montevallo, AL 35115
Phone: 205-665-6030 **E-mail:** admissions@montevallo.edu **CEEB Code:** 1004
Fax: 205-655-6042 **Website:** www.montevallo.edu **ACT Code:** 0004
Financial Aid Phone: 205-665-6050

This public school was founded in 1896. It has a 160-acre campus.

RATINGS

Admissions Selectivity Rating: 60* **Fire Safety Rating:** 66 **Green Rating:** 60*

STUDENTS AND FACULTY

Enrollment: 2,557. **Student Body:** 68% female, 32% male, 3% out-of-state, 2% international. African American 13%, Caucasian 81%, Hispanic 1%. **Retention and Graduation:** 72% freshmen return for sophomore year. 22% freshmen graduate within 4 years. 35% grads go on to further study within 2 semesters. 5% grads pursue arts and sciences degrees. 1% grads pursue business degrees. 1% grads pursue law degrees. 1% grads pursue medical degrees. **Faculty:** Student/faculty ratio 17:1. 140 full-time faculty, 84% hold PhDs. 99% faculty teach undergrads.

ACADEMICS

Degrees: Bachelor's, master's, post-master's certificate. **Academic Requirements:** Arts/fine arts, communication studies (speech), computer literacy, English (including composition), FCS (human behavior & inquiry category), foreign languages, health, history, humanities, kinesiology activities (PE), mathematics, philosophy, psychology, sciences (biological or physical), social science, writing reinforcement. **Classes:** Most classes have 20–29 students. **Majors with Highest Enrollment:** Art/art studies, elementary education and teaching, English language and literature. **Disciplines with Highest Percentage of Degrees Awarded:** Business/marketing 18%, visual and performing arts 12%, English 9%, health professions and related sciences 9%, family and consumer sciences 8%, education 8%, history 7%. **Special Study Options:** Academic remediation, accelerated program, advanced placement credit, cross registration, double major, dual enrollment, exchange student program (domestic), honors program, independent study, internships, learning disabilities services, study abroad, teacher certification program.

FACILITIES

Housing: Coed dorms, men's dorms, women's dorms, apartments for married students, fraternity/sorority housing. **Special Academic Facilities/Equipment:** Art gallery, child development, speech and hearing, traffic safety, undergraduate liberal studies centers, mass communications center with cable TV broadcasting capabilities. **Computers:** 73% of public computers are PCs, 27% of public computers are Macs, network access in dorm rooms, online registration, remote student-access to Web through college's connection.

CAMPUS LIFE

Activities: Choral groups, concert band, dance, drama/theater, jazz band, literary magazine, music ensembles, musical theater, student government, student newspaper, television station, yearbook. **Organizations:** 74 registered organizations, 22 honor societies, 3 religious organizations. 7 fraternities (20% men join), 7 sororities (16% women join). **Athletics (Intercollegiate):** *Men:* Baseball, basketball, cheerleading, golf, tennis. *Women:* Basketball, cheerleading, cross-country, golf, tennis, volleyball. **Environmental Initiatives:** Campus lighting retrofit to energy saving bulbs. Campus-wide retrofit of all toilets, showers and faucets to low use fixtures. An aggressive energy management program.

ADMISSIONS

Freshman Academic Profile: 90% from public high schools. ACT middle 50% range 19–24. TOEFL required of all international applicants, minimum paper TOEFL 525, minimum computer TOEFL 193. **Basis for Candidate Selection:** *Very important factors considered include:* Rigor of secondary school record, standardized test scores. *Other factors considered include:* Alumni/ae relation, character/personal qualities, class rank, extracurricular activities, interview, recommendation(s), talent/ability, work experience. **Freshman Admission Requirements:** High school diploma is required, and GED is accepted. *Academic units required:* 4 English, 2 math, 2 science, 2 social studies, 2 history, 4 academic electives. *Academic units recommended:* 3 math, 3 science, 2 foreign language. **Freshman Admission Statistics:** 1,392 applied, 72% admitted, 47% enrolled. **Transfer Admission Requirements:** College transcript(s). Minimum college GPA of 2.0 required. Lowest grade transferable D. **General Admission Information:** Application fee $25. Regular application deadline 8/1. Regular notification is rolling. Non-fall registration accepted. Admission may be deferred for a maximum of 4 semesters.

COSTS AND FINANCIAL AID

Annual in-state tuition $5,850. Annual out-of-state tuition $11,700. Room and board $4,214. Required fees $230. Average book expense $750. **Required Forms and Deadlines:** FAFSA, institution's own financial aid form. Financial aid filing deadline 4/15. **Notification of Awards:** Applicants will be notified of awards on or about 6/1. **Types of Aid:** *Need-based scholarships/grants:* Pell, SEOG, state scholarships/grants, private scholarships, the school's own gift aid. *Loans:* Direct Subsidized Stafford, Direct Unsubsidized Stafford, Direct PLUS, FFEL PLUS, Federal Perkins. **Student Employment:** Federal Work-Study Program available. Institutional employment available. Off-campus job opportunities are good. **Financial Aid Statistics:** 35% freshmen, 36% undergrads receive need-based scholarship or grant aid. 39% freshmen, 41% undergrads receive need-based self-help aid. 22 freshmen, 75 undergrads receive athletic scholarships. 59% freshmen, 57% undergrads receive any aid. Highest amount earned per year from on-campus jobs $3,100.

UNIVERSITY OF NEBRASKA—KEARNEY

905 West Twenty-fifth Street, Kearney, NE 68849
Phone: 800-532-7639 **E-mail:** admissionsug@unk.edu **CEEB Code:** 6467
Fax: 308-865-8987 **Website:** www.unk.edu **ACT Code:** 2468
Financial Aid Phone: 308-865-8520

This public school was founded in 1903. It has a 235-acre campus.

RATINGS

Admissions Selectivity Rating: 60*   **Fire Safety Rating:** 60*   **Green Rating:** 60*

STUDENTS AND FACULTY

Enrollment: 5,886. **Student Body:** 56% female, 44% male, 6% out-of-state, 3% international. Caucasian 88%, Hispanic 2%.

ACADEMICS

Degrees: Bachelor's, master's. **Academic Requirements:** Arts/fine arts, computers in society, English (including composition), history, humanities, mathematics, personal development (healthful living), personal money management, sciences (biological or physical), social science. **Special Study Options:** Distance learning, double major, English as a second language (ESL), exchange student program (domestic), external degree program, honors program, internships, study abroad, teacher certification program.

FACILITIES

Housing: Coed dorms, men's dorms, women's dorms, apartments for married students, apartments for single students, fraternity/sorority housing. **Special Academic Facilities/Equipment:** Art gallery, language lab, Museum of Nebraska Art.

CAMPUS LIFE

Activities: Choral groups, concert band, dance, drama/theater, jazz band, literary magazine, marching band, music ensembles, musical theater, opera, pep band, radio station, student government, student newspaper, symphony orchestra, television station. **Organizations:** 1 religious organization. 10 fraternities (9% men join), 6 sororities (9% women join). **Athletics (Intercollegiate):** *Men:* Baseball, basketball, cross-country, diving, football, golf, soccer, softball, swimming, tennis, volleyball. *Women:* Basketball, cross-country, diving, football, golf, soccer, softball, swimming, tennis, volleyball.

ADMISSIONS

Freshman Academic Profile: 90% from public high schools. Minimum paper TOEFL 520. **Basis for Candidate Selection:** *Very important factors considered include:* Class rank, rigor of secondary school record, standardized test scores. *Other factors considered include:* Religious affiliation/commitment, talent/ability. **Freshman Admission Requirements:** High school diploma is required, and GED is accepted. *Academic units required:* 4 English, 3 math, 3 science (1 science lab), 2 foreign language, 1 social studies, 1 history, 1 academic elective. **Freshman Admission Statistics:** 2,672 applied. **Transfer Admission Requirements:** High school transcript, college transcript(s). Minimum college GPA of 2.0 required. Lowest grade transferable C. **General Admission Information:** Application fee $25. Regular application deadline 8/1. Regular notification is rolling. Non-fall registration accepted. Common Application accepted. Credit and/or placement offered for CEEB Advanced Placement tests.

COSTS AND FINANCIAL AID

Annual in-state tuition $2,715. Out-of-state tuition $5,550. Room & board $4,156. Required fees $498. Average book expense $700. **Required Forms and Deadlines:** FAFSA, institution's own financial aid form, C. Financial aid filing deadline 3/1. **Notification of Awards:** Applicants will be notified of awards on or about 5/1. **Types of Aid:** *Need-based scholarships/grants:* Pell, SEOG, state scholarships/grants, private scholarships, the school's own gift aid. *Loans:* FFEL Subsidized Stafford, FFEL Unsubsidized Stafford, FFEL PLUS, Federal Perkins. **Student Employment:** Federal Work-Study Program available. Institutional employment available. Off-campus job opportunities are excellent.

UNIVERSITY OF NEBRASKA—LINCOLN

Best 368

1410 Q Street, Lincoln, NE 68588-0256
Phone: 402-472-2023 **E-mail:** admissions@unl.edu **CEEB Code:** 6877
Fax: 402-472-0670 **Website:** www.unl.edu **ACT Code:** 2482
Financial Aid Phone: 402-472-2030

This public school was founded in 1869. It has a 610-acre campus.

RATINGS
Admissions Selectivity Rating: 78   **Fire Safety Rating:** 71   **Green Rating:** 71

STUDENTS AND FACULTY
Enrollment: 17,371. **Student Body:** 46% female, 54% male, 14% out-of-state, 3% international (113 countries represented). African American 2%, Asian 3%, Caucasian 85%, Hispanic 3%. **Retention and Graduation:** 84% freshmen return for sophomore year. 22% freshmen graduate within 4 years. **Faculty:** Student/faculty ratio 19:1. 1,041 full-time faculty, 97% hold PhDs.

ACADEMICS
Degrees: Associate, bachelor's, doctoral, first professional, master's, post-bachelor's certificate, post-master's certificate. **Academic Requirements:** Arts/fine arts, English (including composition), foreign languages, history, humanities, mathematics, race, ethnicity & gender studies, sciences (biological or physical), social science. **Classes:** Most classes have 20–29 students. Most lab/discussion sections have 20–29 students. **Majors with Highest Enrollment:** Biology/biological sciences, business administration/management, psychology. **Disciplines with Highest Percentage of Degrees Awarded:** Business/marketing 22%, engineering 10%, education 9%, communications/journalism 7%, family and consumer sciences 6%. **Special Study Options:** Accelerated program, cooperative education program, cross registration, distance learning, double major, dual enrollment, English as a second language (ESL), exchange student program (domestic), honors program, independent study, internships, liberal arts/career combination, student-designed major, study abroad, teacher certification program.

FACILITIES
Housing: Coed dorms, men's dorms, women's dorms, apartments for married students, apartments for single students, special housing for disabled students, special housing for international students, fraternity/sorority housing, cooperative housing. **Special Academic Facilities/Equipment:** Art gallery, performing arts center, food industries complex, planetarium, center for mass spectrometry, natural science museum, animal science complex, veterinary animal research/diagnosis center. **Computers:** 1% of classrooms are wired, 80% of classrooms are wireless, 85% of public computers are PCs, 15% of public computers are Macs, network access in dorm rooms, network access in dorm lounges, online registration, online administrative functions (other than registration), support for handheld computing, remote student-access to Web through college's connection.

CAMPUS LIFE
Activities: Choral groups, concert band, dance, drama/theater, jazz band, literary magazine, marching band, music ensembles, musical theater, opera, pep band, radio station, student government, student newspaper, student-run film society, symphony orchestra, television station. **Organizations:** 335 registered organizations, 57 honor societies, 25 religious organizations. 27 fraternities (15% men join), 18 sororities (18% women join). **Athletics (Intercollegiate):** *Men:* Baseball, basketball, cross-country, football, golf, gymnastics, rodeo, tennis, track/field (indoor), track/field (outdoor), wrestling. *Women:* Basketball, bowling, cross-country, diving, golf, gymnastics, riflery, rodeo, soccer, softball, swimming, tennis, track/field (indoor), track/field (outdoor), volleyball.

ADMISSIONS
Freshman Academic Profile: 25% in top 10% of high school class, 53% in top 25% of high school class, 83% in top 50% of high school class. SAT Math middle 50% range 530–670. SAT Critical Reading middle 50% range 500–650. ACT middle 50% range 22–28. TOEFL required of all international applicants, minimum paper TOEFL 525, minimum computer TOEFL 193. **Basis for Candidate Selection:** *Very important factors considered include:* Class rank, standardized test scores. *Important factors considered include:* Rigor of secondary school record. *Other factors considered include:* Academic GPA, first generation, recommendation(s), talent/ability. **Freshman Admission Requirements:** High school diploma is required, and GED is accepted.

Academic units required: 4 English, 4 math, 3 science, (1 science lab), 2 foreign language, 3 social studies. *Academic units recommended:* 1 history. **Freshman Admission Statistics:** 7,993 applied, 73% admitted, 66% enrolled. **Transfer Admission Requirements:** High school transcript, college transcript(s). Minimum college GPA of 2.0 required. Lowest grade transferable D. **General Admission Information:** Application fee $45. Regular application deadline 5/1. Regular notification is rolling. Non-fall registration accepted. Neither credit nor placement offered for CEEB Advanced Placement tests.

COSTS AND FINANCIAL AID
Room & board $6,523. Average book expense $950. **Required Forms and Deadlines:** FAFSA. **Notification of Awards:** Applicants will be notified of awards on a rolling basis beginning on or about 4/1. **Types of Aid:** *Need-based scholarships/grants:* Pell, SEOG, state scholarships/grants, private scholarships, the school's own gift aid. *Loans:* Direct Subsidized Stafford, Direct Unsubsidized Stafford, Direct PLUS, FFEL Subsidized Stafford, FFEL Unsubsidized Stafford, FFEL PLUS, Federal Perkins, college/university loans from institutional funds. **Financial Aid Statistics:** 36% freshmen, 34% undergrads receive need-based scholarship or grant aid. 30% freshmen, 34% undergrads receive need-based self-help aid. 49 freshmen, 203 undergrads receive athletic scholarships. 41% freshmen, 41% undergrads receive any aid.

UNIVERSITY OF NEBRASKA MEDICAL CENTER

984230 Nebraska Medical Center, Omaha, NE 68198-4230
Phone: 402-559-6864 **E-mail:** ttonjes@unmc.edu
Fax: 402-559-6796 **Website:** www.unmc.edu
Financial Aid Phone: 402-559-4109

This public school was founded in 1902.

RATINGS
Admissions Selectivity Rating: 60*   **Fire Safety Rating:** 60*   **Green Rating:** 60*

STUDENTS AND FACULTY
Enrollment: 771. **Student Body:** 92% female, 8% male, 10% out-of-state, 1% international. African American 2%, Caucasian 94%, Hispanic 2%. **Faculty:** Student/faculty ratio 15:1. 718 full-time faculty.

ACADEMICS
Degrees: Bachelor's, doctoral, first professional, master's, post-bachelor's certificate, post-master's certificate. **Academic Requirements:** Each program has different requirements. **Majors with Highest Enrollment:** Medicine (MD), nursing/registered nurse training (ASN, BSN, MSN, RN), pharmacy (PHARMD, BS/BPHARM). **Disciplines with Highest Percentage of Degrees Awarded:** Health professions and related sciences 100%. **Special Study Options:** Accelerated program, distance learning, honors program, independent study.

FACILITIES
Computers: 75% of public computers are PCs, remote student-access to Web through college's connection.

CAMPUS LIFE
Activities: Student government

ADMISSIONS
Freshman Academic Profile: TOEFL required of all international applicants, minimum paper TOEFL 551, minimum computer TOEFL 235. **Transfer Admission Requirements:** College transcript(s). Lowest grade transferable C. **General Admission Information:** Non-fall registration not accepted. Common Application not accepted.

COSTS AND FINANCIAL AID
Annual in-state tuition $6,450. Annual out-of-state tuition $18,900. Required fees $310. Average book expense $950. **Required Forms and Deadlines:** FAFSA, institution's own financial aid form. Financial aid filing deadline 3/15. **Notification of Awards:** Applicants will be notified of awards on or about 4/1. **Types of Aid:** *Need-based scholarships/grants:* Pell, SEOG, state scholarships/grants, private scholarships, the school's own gift aid. *Loans:* FFEL Subsidized Stafford, FFEL Unsubsidized Stafford, FFEL PLUS, Federal Perkins, Federal Nursing, state loans. **Student Employment:** Federal Work-Study Program available. Institutional employment available. Off-campus job opportunities are fair. **Financial Aid Statistics:** 88% undergrads receive need-based scholarship or grant aid. 88% undergrads receive need-based self-help aid.

UNIVERSITY OF NEBRASKA—OMAHA

Office of Admissions, 6001 Dodge Street, EAB Room 103, Omaha, NE 68182
Phone: 402-554-2393 **E-mail:** unoadm@unomaha.edu **CEEB Code:** 6420
Fax: 402-554-3472 **Website:** www.unomaha.edu **ACT Code:** 2464
Financial Aid Phone: 402-554-2327

This public school was founded in 1908. It has a 158-acre campus.

RATINGS

Admissions Selectivity Rating: 70 **Fire Safety Rating:** 96 **Green Rating:** 72

STUDENTS AND FACULTY

Enrollment: 10,888. **Student Body:** 52% female, 48% male, 6% out-of-state, 2% international (80 countries represented). African American 6%, Asian 3%, Caucasian 82%, Hispanic 4%. **Retention and Graduation:** 71% freshmen return for sophomore year. 10% freshmen graduate within 4 years. 18% grads go on to further study within 2 semesters. **Faculty:** Student/faculty ratio 17:1. 499 full-time faculty, 84% hold PhDs. 70% faculty teach undergrads.

ACADEMICS

Degrees: Bachelor's, doctoral, master's, post-bachelor's certificate, post-master's certificate. **Academic Requirements:** Arts/fine arts, cultural diversity, English (including composition), history, humanities, mathematics, sciences (biological or physical), social science. **Classes:** Most classes have 20–29 students. Most lab/discussion sections have 20–29 students. **Majors with Highest Enrollment:** Criminal justice/safety studies, elementary education and teaching, marketing/marketing management. **Disciplines with Highest Percentage of Degrees Awarded:** Business/marketing 30%, education 14%, security and protective services 8%, biological/life sciences 7%, communications/journalism 6%. **Special Study Options:** Cooperative education program, cross registration, distance learning, double major, dual enrollment, English as a second language (ESL), exchange student program (domestic), honors program, independent study, internships, student-designed major, study abroad, teacher certification program.

FACILITIES

Housing: Coed dorms, leased apartment dwellings. **Special Academic Facilities/Equipment:** Center for Afghanistan Studies, language lab, physical education facility. **Computers:** 38% of classrooms are wired, 85% of classrooms are wireless, 89% of public computers are PCs, 10% of public computers are Macs, 1% of public computers are UNIX, network access in dorm rooms, network access in dorm lounges, online registration, online administrative functions (other than registration), support for handheld computing, remote student-access to Web through college's connection.

CAMPUS LIFE

Activities: Choral groups, concert band, dance, drama/theater, jazz band, literary magazine, marching band, music ensembles, musical theater, opera, pep band, radio station, student government, student newspaper, student-run film society, symphony orchestra, television station. **Organizations:** 127 registered organizations, 18 honor societies, 14 religious organizations. 4 fraternities (2% men join), 4 sororities (2% women join). **Athletics (Intercollegiate):** *Men:* Baseball, basketball, football, ice hockey, wrestling. *Women:* Basketball, cross-country, diving, golf, soccer, softball, swimming, tennis, volleyball. **Environmental Initiatives:** Examination of Sustainable Operations (with commitment from VC for B & F and FMP Director). Pursuit of single-stream recycling on campus to replace paper-only system. Formation of sustainability Committee.

ADMISSIONS

Freshman Academic Profile: 13% in top 10% of high school class, 35% in top 25% of high school class, 69% in top 50% of high school class. 86% from public high schools. SAT Math middle 50% range 380–440. SAT Critical Reading middle 50% range 390–520. ACT middle 50% range 19–25. TOEFL required of all international applicants, minimum paper TOEFL 500, minimum computer TOEFL 173. **Basis for Candidate Selection:** *Very important factors considered include:* Class rank, rigor of secondary school record, standardized test scores. *Other factors considered include:* Character/personal qualities. **Freshman Admission Requirements:** High school diploma is required, and GED is accepted. *Academic units required:* 4 English, 3 math, 3 science (1 science lab), 2 foreign language, 1 social studies, 2 history, 1 academic elective. **Freshman Admission Statistics:** 3,864 applied, 86% admitted, 52% enrolled. **Transfer Admission Requirements:** College transcript(s), statement of good standing from prior institution(s). Minimum college GPA of 2.0 required. Lowest grade transferable C-. **General Admission Information:** Application fee $45. Regular application deadline 8/1. Regular notification rolling. Non-fall registration accepted. Credit offered for CEEB Advanced Placement tests.

COSTS AND FINANCIAL AID

Annual in-state tuition $4,643. Annual out-of-state tuition $13,680. Room and board $6,810. Required fees $842. Average book expense $800. **Required Forms and Deadlines:** FAFSA. Financial aid filing deadline 3/1. **Notification of Awards:** Applicants will be notified of awards on a rolling basis beginning on or about 4/15. **Types of Aid:** *Need-based scholarships/grants:* Pell, SEOG, state scholarships/grants, private scholarships, the school's own gift aid. *Loans:* FFEL Subsidized Stafford, FFEL Unsubsidized Stafford, FFEL PLUS, Federal Perkins, college/university loans from institutional funds. **Student Employment: Financial Aid Statistics:** 27% freshmen, 34% undergrads receive need-based scholarship or grant aid. 40% freshmen, 35% undergrads receive need-based self-help aid. 70% undergrads receive any aid. Highest amount earned per year from on-campus jobs $9,600.

UNIVERSITY OF NEVADA—LAS VEGAS

4505 Maryland Parkway, Box 451021, Las Vegas, NV 89154-1021
Phone: 702-774-8658 **E-mail:** undergraduate.recruitment@ccmail.nevada.edu
CEEB Code: 4861 **Fax:** 702-774-8008 **Website:** www.unlv.edu **ACT Code:** 2496
Financial Aid Phone: 702-895-3424

This public school was founded in 1957. It has a 337-acre campus.

RATINGS

Admissions Selectivity Rating: 76 **Fire Safety Rating:** 60* **Green Rating:** 60*

STUDENTS AND FACULTY

Enrollment: 20,607. **Student Body:** 56% female, 44% male, 22% out-of-state, 4% international (84 countries represented). African American 8%, Asian 14%, Caucasian 53%, Hispanic 11%. **Retention and Graduation:** 73% freshmen return for sophomore year. 12% freshmen graduate within 4 years. **Faculty:** Student/faculty ratio 20:1. 776 full-time faculty, 90% hold PhDs. 88% faculty teach undergrads.

ACADEMICS

Degrees: Bachelor's, certificate, doctoral, first professional, master's, post-bachelor's certificate, post-master's certificate. **Academic Requirements:** Arts/fine arts, computer literacy, English (including composition), history, humanities, mathematics, sciences (biological or physical), social science. **Classes:** Most classes have 20–29 students. Most lab/discussion sections have 20–29 students. **Majors with Highest Enrollment:** Elementary education and teaching, hospitality administration/management, psychology. **Disciplines with Highest Percentage of Degrees Awarded:** Business/marketing 34%, education 15%, communication technologies 7%, social sciences 7%, psychology 6%. **Special Study Options:** Accelerated program, cooperative education program, cross registration, distance learning, double major, dual enrollment, English as a second language (ESL), exchange student program (domestic), honors program, independent study, internships, student-designed major, study abroad, teacher certification program.

FACILITIES

Housing: Coed dorms. **Special Academic Facilities/Equipment:** Art galleries, national supercomputing center for energy and environment, natural history museum, arboretum, 3 theaters, concert hall, law school, dental school, International Gaming Institute, professional practice school for teachers. **Computers:** 75% of public computers are PCs, 15% of public computers are Macs, 10% of public computers are UNIX, network access in dorm rooms, network access in dorm lounges, online registration, online administrative functions (other than registration), remote student-access to Web through college's connection.

CAMPUS LIFE

Activities: Choral groups, concert band, dance, drama/theater, jazz band, literary magazine, marching band, music ensembles, musical theater, opera, pep band, radio station, student government, student newspaper, student-run film society, symphony orchestra, television station. **Organizations:** 24 honor societies, 14 religious organizations. 8 fraternities (5% men join), 6 sororities (3% women join). **Athletics (Intercollegiate):** *Men:* Baseball, basketball, football, golf, soccer, swimming, tennis. *Women:* Basketball, cross-country, equestrian sports, golf, soccer, softball, swimming, tennis, track/field (outdoor), volleyball.

ADMISSIONS

Freshman Academic Profile: 18% in top 10% of high school class, 47% in top 25% of high school class, 82% in top 50% of high school class. SAT Math middle 50% range 450–580. SAT Critical Reading middle 50% range 440–560. ACT middle 50% range 18–24. TOEFL required of all international applicants, minimum paper TOEFL 500. **Basis for Candidate Selection:** *Very important* *factors considered include:* Rigor of secondary school record, standardized test scores. *Other factors considered include:* Recommendation(s). **Freshman Admission Requirements:** High school diploma is required, and GED is accepted. *Academic units required:* 4 English, 3 math, 3 science (2 science labs), 3 social studies. *Academic units recommended:* 4 English, 3 math, 3 science (2 science labs), 3 social studies. **Freshman Admission Statistics:** 7,042 applied, 81% admitted, 58% enrolled. **Transfer Admission Requirements:** College transcript(s). Minimum college GPA of 2.0 required. Lowest grade transferable D-. **General Admission Information:** Application fee $60. Regular application deadline 4/1. Regular notification is rolling. Non-fall registration accepted. Admission may be deferred for a maximum of 2 semesters. Common Application not accepted. Credit and/or placement offered for CEEB Advanced Placement tests.

COSTS AND FINANCIAL AID

Annual in-state tuition $3,060. Out-of-state tuition $12,527. Room & board $8,326. Required fees $412. Average book expense $850. **Required Forms and Deadlines:** FAFSA, institution's own financial aid form. Financial aid filing deadline 2/1. **Notification of Awards:** Applicants will be notified of awards on a rolling basis beginning on or about 4/1. **Types of Aid:** *Need-based scholarships/grants:* Pell, SEOG, state scholarships/grants, private scholarships, the school's own gift aid. *Loans:* Direct Subsidized Stafford, Direct Unsubsidized Stafford, Direct PLUS, Federal Perkins, state loans, college/university loans from institutional funds. **Student Employment:** Federal Work-Study Program available. Institutional employment available. Off-campus job opportunities are excellent. **Financial Aid Statistics:** 20% freshmen, 24% undergrads receive need-based scholarship or grant aid. 15% freshmen, 20% undergrads receive need-based self-help aid. 123 freshmen, 450 undergrads receive athletic scholarships. Highest amount earned per year from on-campus jobs $3,680.

UNIVERSITY OF NEVADA—RENO

Mail Stop 120, Reno, NV 89557
Phone: 775-784-4700 **E-mail:** asknevada@unr.edu **CEEB Code:** 4844
Fax: 775-784-4283 **Website:** www.unr.edu **ACT Code:** 2497
Financial Aid Phone: 702-784-4666

This public school was founded in 1864. It has a 200-acre campus.

RATINGS

Admissions Selectivity Rating: 60*   **Fire Safety Rating:** 60*   **Green Rating:** 60*

STUDENTS AND FACULTY

Enrollment: 11,605. **Student Body:** 55% female, 45% male, 18% out-of-state, 3% international (56 countries represented). African American 2%, Asian 7%, Caucasian 73%, Hispanic 7%, Native American 1%. **Retention and Graduation:** 76% freshmen return for sophomore year. 15% freshmen graduate within 4 years. **Faculty:** Student/faculty ratio 15:1. 682 full-time faculty, 88% hold PhDs.

ACADEMICS

Degrees: Bachelor's, doctoral, first professional certificate, first professional, master's, post-bachelor's certificate, post-master's certificate. **Academic Requirements:** Arts/fine arts, capstone, diversity, English (including composition), humanities, mathematics, sciences (biological or physical), social science. **Classes:** Most classes have 20–29 students. Most lab/discussion sections have 20–29 students. **Disciplines with Highest Percentage of Degrees Awarded:** Education 16%, business/marketing 12%, engineering 9%, health professions and related sciences 9%, social sciences 8%, psychology 6%, biological/life sciences 6%, psychology. **Special Study Options:** Distance learning, double major, dual enrollment, English as a second language (ESL), exchange student program (domestic), honors program, independent study, internships, study abroad, teacher certification program.

FACILITIES

Housing: Coed dorms, men's dorms, women's dorms, apartments for married students, apartments for single students, special housing for disabled students. **Special Academic Facilities/Equipment:** Audiovisual center, theaters, state historical society, atmospherium/planetarium, seismological lab, research institutes, agricultural experimentation station.

CAMPUS LIFE

Activities: Choral groups, concert band, dance, drama/theater, jazz band, literary magazine, marching band, music ensembles, musical theater, opera, pep band, radio station, student government, student newspaper, yearbook. **Organizations:** 100 registered organizations, 12 honor societies, 6 religious organizations. 11 fraternities (7% men join), 4 sororities (6% women join).

Athletics (Intercollegiate): *Men:* Basketball, cross-country, diving, softball, swimming, tennis, track/field (outdoor), volleyball. *Women:* Basketball, cross-country, diving, soccer, softball, swimming, tennis, track/field (outdoor), volleyball.

ADMISSIONS

Freshman Academic Profile: SAT Math middle 50% range 480–600. SAT Critical Reading middle 50% range 470–590. ACT middle 50% range 20–25. **Basis for Candidate Selection:** *Very important factors considered include:* Rigor of secondary school record. *Other factors considered include:* Standardized test scores. **Freshman Admission Requirements:** High school diploma is required, and GED is not accepted. *Academic units required:* 4 English, 3 math, 3 science (2 science labs), 3 social studies. **Freshman Admission Statistics:** 4,024 applied, 88% admitted, 59% enrolled. **Transfer Admission Requirements:** College transcript(s). Minimum college GPA of 2.0 required. Lowest grade transferable D-. **General Admission Information:** Application fee $60. Regular notification rolling. Non-fall registration accepted. Admission may be deferred for a maximum of 2 semesters. Common Application not accepted. Credit and/or placement offered for CEEB Advanced Placement tests.

COSTS AND FINANCIAL AID

Annual in-state tuition $2,730. Out-of-state tuition $11,404. Required fees $132. Average book expense $1,000. **Required Forms and Deadlines:** FAFSA. Financial aid filing deadline 2/1. **Notification of Awards:** Applicants will be notified of awards on a rolling basis beginning on or about 4/1. **Types of Aid:** *Need-based scholarships/grants:* Pell, SEOG, private scholarships, the school's own gift aid. *Loans:* FFEL Subsidized Stafford, FFEL Unsubsidized Stafford, FFEL PLUS, Federal Perkins, college/university loans from institutional funds. **Student Employment:** Federal Work-Study Program available. Institutional employment available. Off-campus job opportunities are excellent. **Financial Aid Statistics:** 14% freshmen, 17% undergrads receive need-based scholarship or grant aid. 14% freshmen, 20% undergrads receive need-based self-help aid. 67 freshmen, 359 undergrads receive athletic scholarships. Highest amount earned per year from on-campus jobs $3,000.

UNIVERSITY OF NEW ENGLAND

11 Hills Beach Road, Biddeford, ME 04005-9599
Phone: 207-602-2297 **E-mail:** admissions@une.edu **CEEB Code:** 3751
Fax: 207-602-5900 **Website:** www.une.edu **ACT Code:** 3751
Financial Aid Phone: 207-602-2342

This private school was founded in 1831. It has a 550-acre campus.

RATINGS

Admissions Selectivity Rating: 77   **Fire Safety Rating:** 60*   **Green Rating:** 60*

STUDENTS AND FACULTY

Enrollment: 1,698. **Student Body:** 77% female, 23% male, 59% out-of-state. Caucasian 91%. **Retention and Graduation:** 75% freshmen return for sophomore year. 49% freshmen graduate within 4 years. **Faculty:** Student/faculty ratio 11:1. 137 full-time faculty, 85% hold PhDs. 100% faculty teach undergrads.

ACADEMICS

Degrees: Associate, bachelor's, certificate, diploma, first professional, master's, post-bachelor's certificate, post-master's certificate. **Academic Requirements:** Arts/fine arts, citizenship, critical thinking, English (including composition), environmental issues, humanities, mathematics, sciences (biological or physical), social science. **Classes:** Most classes have 20–29 students. Most lab/discussion sections have 10–19 students. **Majors with Highest Enrollment:** Athletic training/trainer, biomedical sciences, marine biology and biological oceanography. **Disciplines with Highest Percentage of Degrees Awarded:** Health professions and related sciences 39%, biological/life sciences 26%, psychology 10%, natural resources/environmental science 7%, education 4%. **Special Study Options:** Advanced standing options for qualified undergraduates in both physician assistant and doctor of osteopathic medicine graduate programs, cross registration, distance learning, double major, English as a second language (ESL), honors program, independent study, internships, student-designed major, study abroad, teacher certification program.

FACILITIES

Housing: Coed dorms, women's dorms. **Special Academic Facilities/Equipment:** Payson Art Gallery, Maine Women Writers Collection, Marine Science Education and Research Center, Marine Animal Rehabilitation Center (MARC), Performance Enhancement and Evaluation Center for Health

Sciences (PEEC), Center for Health Ethics, Law and Policy, Center for Transcultural Health, New England Institute of Cognitive Science and Evolutionary Psychology. **Computers:** 10% of classrooms are wired, 85% of classrooms are wireless, 85% of public computers are PCs, 15% of public computers are Macs, network access in dorm rooms, network access in dorm lounges, online registration, remote student-access to Web through college's connection.

CAMPUS LIFE
Activities: Choral groups, dance, literary magazine, music ensembles, student government, student newspaper, yearbook. **Organizations:** 36 registered organizations, 3 honor societies, 1 religious organization. **Athletics (Intercollegiate):** *Men:* Basketball, cross-country, golf, lacrosse, soccer. *Women:* Basketball, cross-country, field hockey, golf, lacrosse, soccer, softball, swimming, volleyball.

ADMISSIONS
Freshman Academic Profile: 17% in top 10% of high school class, 49% in top 25% of high school class, 86% in top 50% of high school class. SAT Math middle 50% range 470–580. SAT Critical Reading middle 50% range 540–570. TOEFL required of all international applicants, minimum paper TOEFL 550, minimum computer TOEFL 213. **Basis for Candidate Selection:** *Very important factors considered include:* Academic GPA, rigor of secondary school record. *Important factors considered include:* Class rank, interview. *Other factors considered include:* Alumni/ae relation, application essay, character/personal qualities, extracurricular activities, geographical residence, level of applicant's interest, recommendation(s), standardized test scores, talent/ability, volunteer work, work experience. **Freshman Admission Requirements:** High school diploma is required, and GED is accepted. *Academic units required:* 4 English, 3 math, 3 science (2 science labs), 2 social studies, 2 history. *Academic units recommended:* 4 math, 4 science (3 science labs), 2 foreign language, 4 social studies, 4 history, 4 academic electives. **Freshman Admission Statistics:** 2,055 applied, 92% admitted, 25% enrolled. **Transfer Admission Requirements:** College transcript(s). Minimum college GPA of 2.0 required. Lowest grade transferable C-. **General Admission Information:** Application fee $40. Regular notification is rolling. Non-fall registration accepted. Common Application accepted. Credit and/or placement offered for CEEB Advanced Placement tests.

COSTS AND FINANCIAL AID
Annual tuition $22,940. Room & board $9,255. Required fees $850. Average book expense $1,000. **Required Forms and Deadlines:** FAFSA, tax returns, verification worksheet. Financial aid filing deadline 3/1. **Notification of Awards:** Applicants will be notified of awards on a rolling basis beginning on or about 3/15. **Types of Aid:** *Need-based scholarships/grants:* Pell, SEOG, state scholarships/grants, private scholarships, the school's own gift aid. *Loans:* FFEL Subsidized Stafford, FFEL Unsubsidized Stafford, FFEL PLUS, Federal Perkins, Federal Nursing. **Student Employment:** Federal Work-Study Program available. Institutional employment available. Off-campus job opportunities are good. **Financial Aid Statistics:** 83% freshmen, 83% undergrads receive need-based scholarship or grant aid. 72% freshmen, 76% undergrads receive need-based self-help aid. 93% freshmen, 94% undergrads receive any aid. Highest amount earned per year from on-campus jobs $2,000.

See page 1458.

UNIVERSITY OF NEW HAMPSHIRE

4 Garrison Avenue, Durham, NH 03824
Phone: 603-862-1360 **E-mail:** admissions@unh.edu **CEEB Code:** 3918
Fax: 603-862-0077 **Website:** www.unh.edu **ACT Code:** 2524
Financial Aid Phone: 603-862-3600

This public school was founded in 1866. It has a 2,600-acre campus.

RATINGS
Admissions Selectivity Rating: 81   **Fire Safety Rating:** 96   **Green Rating:** 99
STUDENTS AND FACULTY
Enrollment: 11,523. **Student Body:** 57% female, 43% male, 43% out-of-state (26 countries represented). African American 1%, Asian 2%, Caucasian 85%, Hispanic 2%. **Retention and Graduation:** 76% freshmen return for

sophomore year. 55% freshmen graduate within 4 years. **Faculty:** Student/faculty ratio 17:1. 681 full-time faculty, 84% hold PhDs. 89% faculty teach undergrads.

ACADEMICS
Degrees: Associate, bachelor's, doctoral, master's, post-bachelor's certificate, post-master's certificate. **Academic Requirements:** Arts/fine arts, English (including composition), foreign languages, history, humanities, mathematics, philosophy, sciences (biological or physical), social science education requirement—8 components. Intensive writing requirement: students admitted as freshmen or as freshmen transfers must complete 4 writing intensive courses. This must include English composition and 3 additional courses from a prescribed list, 1 of which must be in a student's major and 1 of which must be an upper level course. **Classes:** Most classes have 10–19 students. Most lab/discussion sections have 20–29 students. **Majors with Highest Enrollment:** Business administration and management; English language and literature; psychology. **Disciplines with Highest Percentage of Degrees Awarded:** Social sciences 16%, business/marketing 14%, health professions and related sciences 8%, English 8%, psychology 8%. **Special Study Options:** Cooperative education program, cross-registration, double major, English as a second language (ESL), exchange student program (domestic), honors program, independent study, internships, student-designed major, study abroad, teacher certification program, research/creative projects, learning communities, experiential learning, senior capstone, service learning, work study, honors.

FACILITIES
Housing: Coed dorms, women's dorms, apartments for married students, apartments for single students, special housing for international students, fraternity/sorority housing, 15 special interest minidorms, www.unh.edu/residential-life/sih.html. **Special Academic Facilities/Equipment:** Journalism laboratory, optical observatory, marine research laboratory, experiential learning center, child development center, language lab, art galleries, agricultural and equine facilities, electron microscope, sawmill. **Computers:** 1% of classrooms are wired, 61% of public computers are PCs, 31% of public computers are Macs, 9% of public computers are UNIX, network access in dorm rooms, online registration, online administrative functions (other than registration), remote student-access to Web through college's connection.

CAMPUS LIFE
Activities: Choral groups, concert band, dance, drama/theater, jazz band, literary magazine, marching band, music ensembles, musical theater, pep band, radio station, student government, student newspaper, student-run film society, symphony orchestra, television station, yearbook. **Organizations:** 200 registered organizations, 18 honor societies, 7 religious organizations. 8 fraternities (4% men join), 5 sororities (5% women join). **Athletics (Intercollegiate):** *Men:* Basketball, cross-country, diving, football, ice hockey, skiing (downhill/alpine), skiing (nordic/cross-country), soccer, swimming, tennis, track/field (indoor), track/field (outdoor). *Women:* Basketball, crew/rowing, cross-country, diving, field hockey, gymnastics, ice hockey, lacrosse, skiing (downhill/alpine), skiing (nordic/cross-country), soccer, swimming, tennis, track/field (indoor), track/field (outdoor), volleyball. **Environmental Initiatives:** The UNH University Office of Sustainability (UOS) is the oldest endowed sustainability program in higher education in the U.S. Under its comprehensive Climate Education Initiative and as a key component of its climate action plan and signature to the American College and University Presidents Climate Commitment, in 2008/2009 UNH will become the first university in the U.S. to use landfill gas as its primary energy source. Responding to a need by farmers for scientific research to support organic dairy efforts, UNH is the first land grant university to have an organic dairy farm and education/research center.

ADMISSIONS
Freshman Academic Profile: 20% in top 10% of high school class, 61% in top 25% of high school class, 97% in top 50% of high school class. 75% from public high schools. SAT Math middle 50% range 510–620. SAT Critical Reading middle 50% range 500–610. TOEFL required of all international applicants, minimum paper TOEFL 550, minimum computer TOEFL 213. **Basis for Candidate Selection:** *Very important factors considered include:* Academic GPA, class rank, rigor of secondary school record. *Important factors considered include;* recommendation(s). *Other factors considered include:* Alumni/ae relation, application essay, character/personal qualities, extracurricular activities, first generation, geographical residence, racial/ethnic status, standardized test scores, state residency, talent/ability, volunteer work, work experience. **Freshman Admission Requirements:** High school diploma is required, and GED is accepted. *Academic units required:* 4 English, 3 math, 3 science (3 science labs), 2 foreign language, 3 social studies. *Academic units recommended:* 4 English, 4 math, 3 science (3 science labs), 3 foreign language, 3 social studies, 1 academic elective. **Freshman Admission Statistics:** 13,991 applied, 67% admitted, 33% enrolled. **Transfer Admission Requirements:** High school transcript, college transcript(s), essay or personal statement, standardized test score. Minimum college GPA of 2.8 required. Lowest grade transferable C. **General Admission Information:** Application fee $45. Regular application deadline 2/1. Regular notification 4/15. Nonfall registration

accepted. Admission may be deferred for a maximum of 1 year. Credit and/or placement offered for CEEB Advanced Placement tests.

COSTS AND FINANCIAL AID

Annual in-state tuition $8,810. Annual out-of-state tuition $21,770. Room and board $8,168. Required fees $2,260. Average book expense $1,400. **Required Forms and Deadlines:** FAFSA. Financial aid filing deadline 2/1. **Notification of Awards:** Applicants will be notified of awards on a rolling basis beginning on or about 3/1. **Types of Aid:** *Need-based scholarships/grants:* Pell, SEOG, state scholarships/grants, private scholarships, the school's own gift aid, veterans educational benefits. *Loans:* FFEL Subsidized Stafford, FFEL Unsubsidized Stafford, FFEL PLUS, Federal Perkins, state loans, college/university loans from institutional funds. **Student Employment:** Federal Work-Study Program available. Institutional employment available. Off-campus job opportunities are excellent. **Financial Aid Statistics:** 38% freshmen, 35% undergrads receive need-based scholarship or grant aid. 54% freshmen, 54% undergrads receive need-based self-help aid. 43 freshmen, 189 undergrads receive athletic scholarships. 84% freshmen, 78% undergrads receive any aid. Highest amount earned per year from on-campus jobs $20,540.

UNIVERSITY OF NEW HAMPSHIRE—MANCHESTER

400 Commercial Street, Manchester, NH 03101
Phone: 603-641-4150 **E-mail:** unhm.admissions@unh.edu **CEEB Code:** 2094
Fax: 603-641-4125 **Website:** www.unh.edu/unhm
Financial Aid Phone: 603-629-4114

This public school was founded in 1985.

RATINGS

Admissions Selectivity Rating: 63 **Fire Safety Rating:** 60* **Green Rating:** 60*

STUDENTS AND FACULTY

Enrollment: 704. **Student Body:** 64% female, 36% male, 1% out-of-state. African American 2%, Asian 1%, Caucasian 94%. **Faculty:** Student/faculty ratio 18:1. 23 full-time faculty, 78% hold PhDs. 100% faculty teach undergrads.

ACADEMICS

Degrees: Associate, bachelor's. **Academic Requirements:** Arts/fine arts, English (including composition), foreign culture, foreign languages, history, mathematics, philosophy, sciences (biological or physical), social science. **Classes:** Most classes have 10–19 students. **Disciplines with Highest Percentage of Degrees Awarded:** Health professions and related sciences 27%, psychology 21%, social sciences 18%, communication technologies 16%, English 13%. **Special Study Options:** Cross registration, double major, English as a second language (ESL), exchange student program (domestic), independent study, internships, study abroad, teacher certification program.

FACILITIES

Computers: 67% of public computers are PCs, 15% of public computers are Macs, 18% of public computers are UNIX.

CAMPUS LIFE

Activities: Student government.

ADMISSIONS

Freshman Academic Profile: 3% in top 10% of high school class, 15% in top 25% of high school class, 52% in top 50% of high school class. SAT Math middle 50% range 440–550. SAT Critical Reading middle 50% range 460–550. TOEFL required of all international applicants. **Basis for Candidate Selection:** *Very important factors considered include:* Rigor of secondary school record. *Important factors considered include:* Application essay, class rank, recommendation(s), standardized test scores. *Other factors considered include:* Alumni/ae relation, character/personal qualities, extracurricular activities, interview, racial/ethnic status, state residency, talent/ability, volunteer work, work experience. **Freshman Admission Requirements:** High school diploma is required, and GED is accepted. *Academic units required:* 4 English, 3 math (3 science labs), 2 foreign language, 2 social studies. *Academic units recommended:* 4 math, 4 science lab, 3 foreign language. **Freshman Admission Statistics:** 218 applied, 74% admitted, 66% enrolled. **Transfer Admission Requirements:** High school transcript, college transcript(s), essay or personal statement, statement of good standing from prior institution(s). Minimum college GPA of 2.5 required. Lowest grade transferable C. **General Admission Information:** Application fee $50. Regular application deadline 6/15. Regular notification is rolling. Non-fall registration accepted. Admission may be deferred for a maximum of 2 semesters. Common Application accepted. Credit offered for CEEB Advanced Placement tests.

COSTS AND FINANCIAL AID

Annual in-state tuition $4,630. Out-of-state tuition $12,190. Required fees $54. Average book expense $700. **Required Forms and Deadlines:** FAFSA, Noncustodial PROFILE, Business/Farm Supplement. Financial aid filing deadline 5/1. **Notification of Awards:** Applicants will be notified of awards on or about 4/1. **Types of Aid:** *Need-based scholarships/grants:* Pell, SEOG, state scholarships/grants, private scholarships, the school's own gift aid. *Loans:* FFEL Subsidized Stafford, FFEL Unsubsidized Stafford, FFEL PLUS, Federal Perkins, outside loans. **Student Employment:** Federal Work-Study Program available. Institutional employment available. Off-campus job opportunities are excellent.

UNIVERSITY OF NEW HAVEN

300 Orange Avenue, West Haven, CT 06516
Phone: 203-932-7319 **E-mail:** adminfo@newhaven.edu **CEEB Code:** 3663
Fax: 203-931-6093 **Website:** www.newhaven.edu **ACT Code:** 0576
Financial Aid Phone: 203-932-7315

This private school was founded in 1920. It has a 78-acre campus.

RATINGS

Admissions Selectivity Rating: 76 **Fire Safety Rating:** 60* **Green Rating:** 60*

STUDENTS AND FACULTY

Enrollment: 2,627. **Student Body:** 45% female, 55% male, 38% out-of-state, 4% international. African American 9%, Asian 1%, Caucasian 50%, Hispanic 4%. **Retention and Graduation:** 78% freshmen return for sophomore year. **Faculty:** Student/faculty ratio 10:1. 178 full-time faculty, 90% hold PhDs. 82% faculty teach undergrads.

ACADEMICS

Degrees: Associate, bachelor's, certificate, master's, post-bachelor's certificate. **Academic Requirements:** Arts/fine arts, computer literacy, English (including composition), history, humanities, mathematics, philosophy, sciences (biological or physical), social science. **Classes:** Most classes have 10–19 students. Most lab/discussion sections have 10–19 students. **Majors with Highest Enrollment:** Business administration/management, criminal justice/law enforcement administration, engineering. **Disciplines with Highest Percentage of Degrees Awarded:** Business/marketing 24%, engineering 13%, visual and performing arts 6%, architecture 3%, health professions and related sciences 3%, biological/life sciences 2%, communication technologies 2%, computer and information sciences 2%, English 2%. **Special Study Options:** Accelerated program, cooperative education program, cross registration, double major, dual enrollment, English as a second language (ESL), honors program, independent study, internships, student-designed major, study abroad.

FACILITIES

Housing: Coed dorms, apartments for single students. **Special Academic Facilities/Equipment:** Art gallery, forensic science lab, radio station, TV station, theater, Orchestra New England, music and sound recording studio. **Computers:** 96% of public computers are PCs, 2% of public computers are Macs, 2% of public computers are UNIX, network access in dorm rooms, remote student-access to Web through college's connection.

CAMPUS LIFE

Activities: Choral groups, dance, drama/theater, music ensembles, musical theater, pep band, radio station, student government, student newspaper, television station, yearbook. **Organizations:** 50 registered organizations, 5 honor societies, 1 religious organization. 2 fraternities (3% men join), 3 sororities (3% women join). **Athletics (Intercollegiate):** *Men:* Baseball, basketball, cross-country, golf, lacrosse, soccer, track/field (indoor), track/field (outdoor), volleyball. *Women:* Basketball, cheerleading, cross-country, lacrosse, soccer, softball, tennis, volleyball.

ADMISSIONS

Freshman Academic Profile: 14% in top 10% of high school class, 35% in top 25% of high school class, 67% in top 50% of high school class. 85% from public high schools. SAT Math middle 50% range 450–570. SAT Critical Reading middle 50% range 460–560. TOEFL required of all international applicants, minimum paper TOEFL 520, minimum computer TOEFL 190. **Basis for Candidate Selection:** *Very important factors considered include:* Rigor of secondary school record, standardized test scores. *Important factors considered include:* Application essay, class rank, recommendation(s). *Other factors considered include:* Alumni/ae relation, character/personal qualities, extracurricular activities, interview, talent/ability, volunteer work, work experience. **Freshman Admission Requirements:** High school diploma is required, and GED is accepted. *Academic units required:* 4 English, 3 math, 2 science, 2 history, 3 academic electives. *Academic units recommended:* 2 foreign language, 2 social studies. **Freshman Admission Statistics:** 3,025 applied, 67% admitted, 31% enrolled. **Transfer Admission Requirements:** High school transcript, college transcript(s). Minimum college GPA of 2.5 required. Lowest grade transferable C. **General Admission Information:** Application fee $50. Regular notification is rolling. Non-fall registration accepted. Admission may be deferred for a maximum of 2 semesters. Common Application accepted. Credit and/or placement offered for CEEB Advanced Placement tests.

COSTS AND FINANCIAL AID
Annual tuition $20,130. Room & board $8,040. Required fees $482. Average book expense $750. **Required Forms and Deadlines:** FAFSA, institution's own financial aid form, tax returns. Financial aid filing deadline 3/2. **Notification of Awards:** Applicants will be notified of awards on or about 3/15. **Types of Aid:** *Need-based scholarships/grants:* Pell, SEOG, state scholarships/grants, private scholarships, the school's own gift aid. *Loans:* FFEL Subsidized Stafford, FFEL Unsubsidized Stafford, FFEL PLUS, Federal Perkins. **Student Employment:** Federal Work-Study Program available. Institutional employment available. Off-campus job opportunities are excellent. **Financial Aid Statistics:** 71% freshmen, 68% undergrads receive need-based scholarship or grant aid. 68% freshmen, 67% undergrads receive need-based self-help aid. 14 freshmen, 47 undergrads receive athletic scholarships. Highest amount earned per year from on-campus jobs $900.

UNIVERSITY OF NEW MEXICO

Office of Admissions, PO Box 4895, Albuquerque, NM 87196-4895
Phone: 505-277-2446 **E-mail:** apply@unm.edu **CEEB Code:** 4845
Fax: 505-277-6686 **Website:** www.unm.edu **ACT Code:** 2650
Financial Aid Phone: 505-277-2041

This public school was founded in 1889. It has a 680-acre campus.

RATINGS
Admissions Selectivity Rating: 78   **Fire Safety Rating:** 70   **Green Rating:** 60*

STUDENTS AND FACULTY
Enrollment: 18,330. **Student Body:** 58% female, 42% male, 21% out-of-state. African American 3%, Asian 4%, Caucasian 46%, Hispanic 35%, Native American 6%. **Faculty:** Student/faculty ratio 20:1. 885 full-time faculty, 86% hold PhDs.

ACADEMICS
Degrees: Associate, bachelor's, certificate, doctoral, first professional, master's, post-master's certificate. **Academic Requirements:** Arts/fine arts, English (including composition), foreign languages, humanities, mathematics, sciences (biological or physical), social science. **Classes:** Most classes have 20–29 students. Most lab/discussion sections have 10–19 students. **Majors with Highest Enrollment:** Biology/biological sciences, business administration and management, psychology. **Disciplines with Highest Percentage of Degrees Awarded:** Business/marketing 15%, education 14%, health professions and related sciences 9%, social sciences 8%, psychology 7%, liberal arts/general studies 7%. **Special Study Options:** Accelerated program, cooperative education program, distance learning, double major, dual enrollment, English as a second language (ESL), exchange student program (domestic), honors program, independent study, internships, student-designed major, study abroad, teacher certification program, weekend college.

FACILITIES
Housing: Coed dorms, apartments for married students, apartments for single students, fraternity/sorority housing, special living options include graduate and senior housing, academic floors, scholars wing, and outdoor/wellness units. **Special Academic Facilities/Equipment:** Museums of art, anthropology, geology, and southwestern biology, lithography institute, meteoritics institute, electron and electron scanning microscopes, nuclear reactor, robotics lab, observatory, planetarium, science and technology park. **Computers:** 80% of public computers are PCs, 20% of public computers are Macs, network access in dorm rooms, network access in dorm lounges, online registration, online administrative functions (other than registration), support for handheld computing, remote student-access to Web through college's connection.

CAMPUS LIFE
Activities: Choral groups, concert band, dance, drama/theater, jazz band, literary magazine, marching band, music ensembles, musical theater, opera, pep band, radio station, student government, student newspaper, student-run film society, symphony orchestra, television station. **Organizations:** 363 registered organizations, 20 honor societies, 30 religious organizations. 11 fraternities (3% men join), 11 sororities (3% women join). **Athletics (Intercollegiate):** *Men:* Baseball, basketball, cross-country, football, golf, skiing (downhill/alpine), skiing (nordic/cross-country), soccer, tennis, track/field (indoor), track/field (outdoor). *Women:* Basketball, cross-country, diving, golf, skiing (downhill/alpine), skiing (nordic/cross-country), soccer, softball, swimming, tennis, track/field (indoor), track/field (outdoor), volleyball.

ADMISSIONS
Freshman Academic Profile: 21% in top 10% of high school class, 45% in top 25% of high school class, 79% in top 50% of high school class. SAT Math middle 50% range 470–590. SAT Critical Reading middle 50% range 470–600. ACT middle 50% range 19–25. TOEFL required of all international applicants, minimum paper TOEFL 520, minimum computer TOEFL 190. **Basis for Candidate Selection:** *Very important factors considered include:* Academic GPA, rigor of secondary school record. *Important factors considered include:* Class rank, standardized test scores. *Other factors considered include:* Application essay, character/personal qualities, extracurricular activities, first generation, recommendation(s), volunteer work, work experience. **Freshman Admission Requirements:** High school diploma is required, and GED is accepted. *Academic units required:* 4 English, 3 math, 2 science (1 science lab), 2 foreign language, 1 social studies, 1 history. **Freshman Admission Statistics:** 7,134 applied, 74% admitted, 59% enrolled. **Transfer Admission Requirements:** College transcript(s). Minimum college GPA of 2.0 required. Lowest grade transferable C. **General Admission Information:** Application fee $20. Regular application deadline 6/15. Non-fall registration accepted. Admission may be deferred for a maximum of 2 semesters. Credit and/or placement offered for CEEB Advanced Placement tests.

COSTS AND FINANCIAL AID
Annual in-state tuition $6,094. Annual out-of-state tuition $19,923. **Required Forms and Deadlines:** FAFSA. Financial aid filing deadline 3/1. **Notification of Awards:** Applicants will be notified of awards on a rolling basis beginning on or about 4/15. **Types of Aid:** *Need-based scholarships/grants:* Pell, SEOG, state scholarships/grants, private scholarships, the school's own gift aid, United Negro College Fund, Federal Nursing Scholarships. *Loans:* Direct Subsidized Stafford, Direct Unsubsidized Stafford, Direct PLUS, Federal Perkins, Federal Nursing, state loans, college/university loans from institutional funds.

UNIVERSITY OF NEW ORLEANS

AD 103, Lakefront, New Orleans, LA 70148
Phone: 504-280-6595 **E-mail:** admissions@uno.edu **CEEB Code:** 6379
Fax: 504-280-5522 **Website:** www.uno.edu **ACT Code:** 1591
Financial Aid Phone: 504-280-6603

This public school was founded in 1956. It has a 195-acre campus.

RATINGS
Admissions Selectivity Rating: 74   **Fire Safety Rating:** 60*   **Green Rating:** 60*

STUDENTS AND FACULTY
Enrollment: 9,156. **Student Body:** 54% female, 46% male, 4% out-of-state, 3% international (108 countries represented). African American 21%, Asian 6%, Caucasian 59%, Hispanic 7%. **Retention and Graduation: Faculty:** Student/faculty ratio 17:1. 479 full-time faculty, 65% hold PhDs. 80% faculty teach undergrads.

ACADEMICS
Degrees: Bachelor's, doctoral, master's, post-bachelor's certificate. **Academic Requirements:** Arts/fine arts, computer literacy, English (including composition), foreign languages, history, humanities, mathematics, sciences (biological or physical), social science. **Classes:** Most classes have 10–19 students. **Majors with Highest Enrollment:** Business administration and management, communications studies/speech communication and rhetoric, general studies. **Disciplines with Highest Percentage of Degrees Awarded:** Business/

marketing 39%, liberal arts/general studies 9%, psychology 9%, communications/journalism 7%, education 7%. **Special Study Options:** Cooperative education program, cross-registration, distance learning, double major, dual enrollment, English as a second language (ESL), exchange student program (domestic), honor program, independent study, internships, student-designed major, study abroad, teacher certification program, weekend college.

FACILITIES

Housing: Coed dorms, apartments for married students, apartments for single students, special housing for disabled students. **Special Academic Facilities/ Equipment:** Performing arts center, audiovisual center, TV studio, Eisenhower Leadership Studies Center, child care center, Louisiana collection. **Computers:** 92% of public computers are PCs, 8% of public computers are Macs, network access in dorm rooms, online registration, remote student-access to Web through college's connection.

CAMPUS LIFE

Activities: Choral groups, concert band, dance, drama/theater, jazz band, literary magazine, music ensembles, musical theater, opera, pep band, radio station, student government, student newspaper, student-run film society. **Organizations:** 52 registered organizations, 4 religious organizations. 8 fraternities, 8 sororities (1% women join). **Athletics (Intercollegiate):** *Men:* Baseball, basketball, cheerleading, golf. *Women:* Basketball, cheerleading, swimming, volleyball.

ADMISSIONS

Freshman Academic Profile: 14% in top 10% of high school class, 33% in top 25% of high school class, 66% in top 50% of high school class. 62% from public high schools. SAT Math middle 50% range 480–620. SAT Critical Reading middle 50% range 470–610. SAT Writing middle 50% range 460–590. ACT middle 50% range 20–24. TOEFL required of all international applicants, minimum paper TOEFL 525, minimum computer TOEFL 195. **Basis for Candidate Selection:** *Very important factors considered include:* Academic GPA, class rank, rigor of secondary school record, standardized test scores. *Other factors considered include:* Geographical residence, recommendation(s), state residency. **Freshman Admission Requirements:** High school diploma is required, and GED is accepted. *Academic units required:* 4 English, 3 math, 3 science, 2 foreign language, 1 social studies, 2 history, 1 academic elective, 1 computer literacy or science (0.5 units required). **Freshman Admission Statistics:** 2,522 applied, 77% admitted, 52% enrolled. **Transfer Admission Requirements:** College transcript(s). Minimum college GPA of 2.3 required. Lowest grade transferable D. **General Admission Information:** Application fee $40. Regular application deadline 8/20. Regular notification is rolling. Nonfall registration accepted. Admission may be deferred for a maximum of 1 year. Credit and/or placement offered for CEEB Advanced Placement tests.

COSTS AND FINANCIAL AID

Annual in-state tuition $3,292. Out-of-state tuition $10,336. Room $4,734. Required fees $518. Average book expense $1,250. **Required Forms and Deadlines:** FAFSA, institution's own financial aid form. Financial aid filing deadline 5/15. **Notification of Awards:** Applicants will be notified of awards on a rolling basis beginning on or about 4/20. **Types of Aid:** *Need-based scholarships/grants:* Pell, SEOG, state scholarships/grants, private scholarships, the school's own gift aid. *Loans:* FFEL Subsidized Stafford, FFEL Unsubsidized Stafford, FFEL PLUS, Federal Perkins, college/university loans from institutional funds. **Student Employment: Financial Aid Statistics:** 35% freshmen, 36% undergrads receive need-based scholarship or grant aid. 21% freshmen, 31% undergrads receive need-based self-help aid. 8 freshmen, 89 undergrads receive athletic scholarships. Highest amount earned per year from on-campus jobs $20,780.

UNIVERSITY OF NORTH ALABAMA

UNA Box 5011, Florence, AL 35632-0001
Phone: 256-765-4318 **E-mail:** admissions@una.edu
Fax: 256-765-4329 **Website:** www.una.edu **ACT Code:** 0014
Financial Aid Phone: 256-765-4278

This public school was founded in 1830. It has a 130-acre campus.

RATINGS

Admissions Selectivity Rating: 78   **Fire Safety Rating:** 60*   **Green Rating:** 60*

STUDENTS AND FACULTY

Enrollment: 5,235. **Student Body:** 57% female, 43% male, 19% out-of-state, 9% international (67 countries represented). African American 10%, Caucasian 70%, Hispanic 1%, Native American 1%. **Retention and Graduation:** 68%

freshmen return for sophomore year. **Faculty:** Studd#¥/faculty ratio 21:1. 247 full-time faculty, 63% hold PhDs. 99% faculty teach undergrads.

ACADEMICS

Degrees: Bachelor's, master's, post-master's certificate. **Academic Requirements:** Arts/fine arts, computer literacy, English (including composition), foreign languages, history, humanities, mathematics, sciences (biological or physical), social science. **Classes:** Most classes have fE˜er than 10 students. Most lab/discussion sections have 20–29 students. **Majors with Highest Enrollment:** Business administration/management, nursing/registered nurse training (ASN, BSN, MSN, RN), secondary education and teaching. **Disciplines with Highest Percentage of Degrees Awarded:** Business/marketing 28%, health professions and related sciences 16%, English 8%, education 8%, security and protective services 8%, social sciences 8%, biological/life sciences 5%, computer and information sciences 5%, parks and recreation 3%. **Special Study Options:** Accelerated program, cooperative education program, distance learning, double major, dual enrollment, English as a second language (ESL), honors program, independent study, internships, student-designed major, teacher certification program, weekend college.

FACILITIES

Housing: Coed dorms, men's dorms, women's dorms, apartments for married students, apartments for single students, special housing for international students, fraternity/sorority housing. **Special Academic Facilities/Equipment:** On-campus lab school (N–6), planetarium, observatory, art gallery. **Computers:** 99% of public computers are PCs, 1% of public computers are Macs, network access in dorm rooms, network access in dorm lounges, online registration, remote student-access to Web through college's connection.

CAMPUS LIFE

Activities: Choral groups, concert band, drama/theater, jazz band, literary magazine, marching band, music ensembles, musical theater, pep band, radio station, student government, student newspaper, yearbook. **Organizations:** 98 registered organizations. **Athletics (Intercollegiate):** *Men:* Baseball, basketball, cross-country, football, golf, tennis. *Women:* Basketball, cross-country, soccer, softball, tennis, volleyball.

ADMISSIONS

Freshman Academic Profile: 44% in top 25% of high school class, 76% in top 50% of high school class. 99% from public high schools. ACT middle 50% range 18–24. TOEFL required of all international applicants, minimum paper TOEFL 500, minimum computer TOEFL 173. **Basis for Candidate Selection:** *Very important factors considered include:* Academic GPA, class rank, standardized test scores. *Important factors considered include:* Character/personal qualities, rigor of secondary school record. **Freshman Admission Requirements:** High school diploma is required, and GED is accepted. *Academic units required:* 4 English, 2 math, 2 science, 2 foreign language, 3 social studies. **Freshman Admission Statistics:** 2,227 applied, 84% admitted, 54% enrolled. **Transfer Admission Requirements:** College transcript(s). Minimum college GPA of 2.0 required. Lowest grade transferable C. **General Admission Information:** Application fee $25. Regular notification is rolling. Non-fall registration accepted. Admission may be deferred for a maximum of 1 semester. Credit offered for CEEB Advanced Placement tests.

COSTS AND FINANCIAL AID

Annual in-state tuition $3,768. Out-of-state tuition $7,536. Room & board $4,372. Required fees $883. Average book expense $830. **Required Forms and Deadlines:** FAFSA. Financial aid filing deadline 4/1. **Notification of Awards:** Applicants will be notified of awards on a rolling basis beginning on or about 5/31. **Types of Aid:** *Need-based scholarships/grants:* Pell, SEOG, state scholarships/grants, private scholarships, the school's own gift aid. *Loans:* FFEL Subsidized Stafford, FFEL Unsubsidized Stafford, FFEL PLUS, Federal Perkins. **Financial Aid Statistics:** 28% freshmen, 29% undergrads receive need-based scholarship or grant aid. 26% freshmen, 34% undergrads receive need-based self-help aid. 57 freshmen, 250 undergrads receive athletic scholarships.

THE UNIVERSITY OF NORTH CAROLINA AT ASHEVILLE

CPO #2210, One University Heights, Asheville, NC 28804-8502
Phone: 828-251-6481 **E-mail:** admissions@unca.edu **CEEB Code:** 5013
Fax: 828-251-6482 **Website:** www.unca.edu **ACT Code:** 3064
Financial Aid Phone: 828-251-6535

This public school was founded in 1927. It has a 265-acre campus.

RATINGS

Admissions Selectivity Rating: 84 **Fire Safety Rating:** 82 **Green Rating:** 85

STUDENTS AND FACULTY

Enrollment: 3,220. **Student Body:** 58% female, 42% male, 15% out-of-state. African American 3%, Asian 1%, Caucasian 90%, Hispanic 2%. **Retention and Graduation:** 81% freshmen return for sophomore year. 31% freshmen graduate within 4 years. 21% grads go on to further study within 2 semesters. 18% grads pursue arts and sciences degrees. 1% grads pursue business degrees. 1% grads pursue law degrees. 1% grads pursue medical degrees. **Faculty:** Student/faculty ratio 13:1. 206 full-time faculty, 84% hold PhDs. 100% faculty teach undergrads.

ACADEMICS

Degrees: Bachelor's, master's, post-bachelor's certificate. **Academic Requirements:** Arts/fine arts, computer literacy, English (including composition), foreign languages, health and wellness, humanities, mathematics, sciences (biological or physical), social science. **Classes:** Most classes have 10–19 students. Most lab/discussion sections have 10–19 students. **Majors with Highest Enrollment:** Business administration/management, English language and literature, psychology. **Disciplines with Highest Percentage of Degrees Awarded:** Psychology 15%, visual and performing arts 11%, business/marketing 10%, English 7%, social sciences 7%. **Special Study Options:** Cross registration, distance learning, double major, dual enrollment, exchange student program (domestic), honors program, independent study, internships, liberal arts/career combination, student-designed major, study abroad, teacher certification program.

FACILITIES

Housing: Coed dorms, men's dorms, women's dorms, special housing for disabled students, substance-free dorms, 24 hour quiet dorms. **Special Academic Facilities/Equipment:** Undergraduate research center, Steelcase Teleconference Center, music recording center, Asheville Botanical Gardens, NC Arboretum, environmental quality institute, creative retirement center. **Computers:** 78% of public computers are PCs, 22% of public computers are Macs, network access in dorm rooms, network access in dorm lounges, online registration, online administrative functions (other than registration), remote student-access to Web through college's connection.

CAMPUS LIFE

Activities: Choral groups, concert band, dance, drama/theater, jazz band, literary magazine, music ensembles, musical theater, pep band, radio station, student government, student newspaper. **Organizations:** 80 registered organizations, 14 honor societies, 10 religious organizations. 2 fraternities (3% men join), 2 sororities (2% women join). **Athletics (Intercollegiate):** *Men:* Baseball, basketball, cheerleading, cross-country, soccer, tennis, track/field (outdoor). *Women:* Basketball, cheerleading, cross-country, soccer, tennis, track/field (outdoor), volleyball. **Environmental Initiatives:** New and Planned Campus Construction that incorporates sustainable features. The New Hall classroom building, which opened in January 2006, has an innovative vegetative roof that minimizes rainwater runoff, and geothermal heat pumps for heating and cooling. UNC Asheville is pursuing LEED Silver Certification for new complex. The Steve and Frosene Zeis Science & Multimedia Building, a four-story, 88,500-square-foot building now under construction, will house the biology, chemistry and multimedia arts and sciences departments. The design includes advanced storm water management, low-emitting interior materials, water efficient landscaping, and significant use of natural light throughout the structure.

ADMISSIONS

Freshman Academic Profile: 18% in top 10% of high school class, 56% in top 25% of high school class, 96% in top 50% of high school class. 87% from public high schools. SAT Math middle 50% range 520–620. SAT Critical Reading middle 50% range 540–640. SAT Writing middle 50% range 510–620. ACT middle 50% range 22–26. TOEFL required of all international applicants, minimum paper TOEFL 550, minimum computer TOEFL 213. **Basis for Candidate Selection:** *Very important factors considered include:* Academic GPA, class rank, rigor of secondary school record. *Important factors considered include:* Standardized test scores. *Other factors considered include:* Alumni/ae relation, extracurricular activities, first generation, geographical residence, interview, racial/ethnic status, recommendation(s), state residency, talent/ability, volunteer work, work experience. **Freshman Admission Requirements:** High school diploma is required, and GED is not accepted. *Academic units required:* 4 English, 4 math, 3 science (1 science lab), 2 foreign language, 1 social studies, 1 history. *Academic units recommended:* 4 academic electives. **Freshman Admission Statistics:** 2,654 applied, 71% admitted, 30% enrolled. **Transfer Admission Requirements:** College transcript(s). Lowest grade transferable C. **General Admission Information:** Application fee $50. Regular application deadline 2/15. Regular notification 3/24. Non-fall registration accepted. Admission may be deferred for a maximum of 2 semesters. Credit and/or placement offered for CEEB Advanced Placement tests.

COSTS AND FINANCIAL AID

Annual in-state tuition $2,307. Annual out-of-state tuition $13,297. Room and board $6,230. Required fees $1,857. Average book expense $850. Average book expense $850. **Required Forms and Deadlines:** FAFSA. Financial aid filing deadline 2/15. **Notification of Awards:** Applicants will be notified of awards on a rolling basis beginning on or about 3/15. **Types of Aid:** *Need-based scholarships/grants:* Pell, SEOG, state scholarships/grants, private scholarships, the school's own gift aid. *Loans:* Direct Subsidized Stafford, Direct Unsubsidized Stafford, Direct PLUS, Federal Perkins, state loans, college/university loans from institutional funds. **Financial Aid Statistics:** 34% freshmen, 39% undergrads receive need-based scholarship or grant aid. 22% freshmen, 33% undergrads receive need-based self-help aid. 15 freshmen, 89 undergrads receive athletic scholarships. 62% freshmen, 59% undergrads receive any aid. Highest amount earned per year from on-campus jobs $14,060.

See page 1460.

THE UNIVERSITY OF NORTH CAROLINA AT CHAPEL HILL

Office of Undergrad. Admissions, Jackson Hall 153A - Box #2200, Chapel Hill, NC 27599-2200
Phone: 919-966-3621 **E-mail:** unchelp@admissions.unc.edu **CEEB Code:** 5816
Fax: 919-962-3045 **Website:** www.unc.edu **ACT Code:** 3162
Financial Aid Phone: 919-962-8396

This public school was founded in 1789. It has a 729-acre campus.

RATINGS

Admissions Selectivity Rating: 97 **Fire Safety Rating:** 87 **Green Rating:** 96

STUDENTS AND FACULTY

Enrollment: 16,706. **Student Body:** 59% female, 41% male, 17% out-of-state, 1% international (111 countries represented). African American 11%, Asian 7%, Caucasian 73%, Hispanic 4%. **Retention and Graduation:** 31% grads go on to further study within 2 semesters. 7% grads pursue arts and sciences degrees. 4% grads pursue law degrees. 2% grads pursue medical degrees. **Faculty:** Student/faculty ratio 14:1. 1,490 full-time faculty, 89% hold PhDs.

ACADEMICS

Degrees: Bachelor's, certificate, doctoral, first professional certificate, first professional, master's, post-bachelor's certificate, post-master's certificate. **Academic Requirements:** Arts/fine arts, cultural history, English (including composition), foreign languages, history, humanities, mathematics, philosophy, sciences (biological or physical), social science. **Classes:** Most classes have 10–19 students. Most lab/discussion sections have 10–19 students. **Majors with Highest Enrollment:** Biology/biological sciences, mass communications/media studies, psychology. **Disciplines with Highest Percentage of Degrees Awarded:** Communications/journalism 17%, social sciences 14%, biological/life sciences 10%, business/marketing 9%, psychology 9%, health professions and related sciences 7%. **Special Study Options:** Cross registration, distance learning, double major, dual enrollment, honors program, independent study, internships, student-designed major, study abroad, teacher certification program.

FACILITIES

Housing: Coed dorms, men's dorms, women's dorms, apartments for married students, apartments for single students, special housing for disabled students, special housing for international students, fraternity/sorority housing, substance-free housing. **Special Academic Facilities/Equipment:** Art museum, folklore council, institute of folk music, communications center, Institute of Latin American Studies, Institute of Fisheries Research, Institute of Natural Science, research laboratory of anthropology, planetarium, theater. **Computers:** 10% of classrooms are wired, 80% of classrooms are wireless, 99% of public computers are PCs, network access in dorm rooms, network access in dorm lounges, online registration, online administrative functions (other than registration), support for handheld computing, remote student-access to Web through college's connection. Undergraduates are required to own a computer.

CAMPUS LIFE

Activities: Choral groups, concert band, dance, drama/theater, jazz band, literary magazine, marching band, music ensembles, musical theater, pep band, radio station, student government, student newspaper, student-run film society, symphony orchestra, television station. **Organizations:** 540 registered organizations, 13 honor societies, 46 religious organizations. 34 fraternities 20 sororities **Athletics (Intercollegiate):** *Men:* Baseball, basketball, cross-country, diving, fencing, football, golf, lacrosse, soccer, swimming, tennis, track/field (indoor), track/field (outdoor), wrestling. *Women:* Basketball, crew/rowing, cross-country, diving, fencing, field hockey, golf, gymnastics, lacrosse, soccer, softball, swimming, tennis, track/field (indoor), track/field (outdoor), volleyball. **Environmental Initiatives:** Planning for new campus at Carolina North. Cogeneration Facility with district heating and cooling and thermal storage. Fare Free Transit and Commuter Alternatives Program.

ADMISSIONS

Freshman Academic Profile: 76% in top 10% of high school class, 96% in top 25% of high school class, 99% in top 50% of high school class. 84% from public high schools. SAT Math middle 50% range 610–700. SAT Critical Reading middle 50% range 600–700. SAT Writing middle 50% range 590–690. ACT middle 50% range 25–31. TOEFL required of all international applicants, minimum paper TOEFL 600, minimum computer TOEFL 250. **Basis for Candidate Selection:** *Very important factors considered include:* Academic GPA, application essay, character/personal qualities, class rank, extracurricular activities, recommendation(s), rigor of secondary school record, standardized test scores, state residency, talent/ability. *Important factors considered include:* Alumni/ae relation, first generation, racial/ethnic status, volunteer work, work experience. **Freshman Admission Requirements:** High school diploma is required, and GED is not accepted. *Academic units required:* 4 English, 3 math, 3 science (1 science lab), 2 foreign language, 2 social studies (1 must be U.S. history), 2 academic electives. *Academic units recommended:* 4 English, 4 math, 4 science (1 science lab), 4 foreign language, 3 social studies. **Freshman Admission Statistics:** 19,728 applied, 34% admitted, 57% enrolled. **Transfer Admission Requirements:** High school transcript, college transcript(s), essay or personal statement, statement of good standing from prior institution(s). Minimum college GPA of 2.0 required. Lowest grade transferable C. **General Admission Information:** Application fee $70. Regular application deadline 1/15. Regular notification 1/31, 3/31. Non-fall registration not accepted. Admission may be deferred for a maximum of 2 semesters. Credit and/or placement offered for CEEB Advanced Placement tests.

COSTS AND FINANCIAL AID

Annual in-state tuition $3,705. Annual out-of-state tuition $19,353. Room and board $7,696. Required fees $1,635. Average book expense $1,000. **Required Forms and Deadlines:** FAFSA, CSS/Financial Aid PROFILE. Financial aid filing deadline 3/1. **Notification of Awards:** Applicants will be notified of awards on a rolling basis beginning on or about 3/15. **Types of Aid:** *Need-based scholarships/grants:* Pell, SEOG, state scholarships/grants, private scholarships, the school's own gift aid. *Loans:* FFEL Subsidized Stafford, FFEL Unsubsidized Stafford, FFEL PLUS, Federal Perkins, state loans, college/university loans from institutional funds, alternative loans. **Financial Aid Statistics:** 32% freshmen, 32% undergrads receive need-based scholarship or grant aid. 14% freshmen, 18% undergrads receive need-based self-help aid. 85 freshmen, 365 undergrads receive athletic scholarships. 65% freshmen, 58% undergrads receive any aid.

THE UNIVERSITY OF NORTH CAROLINA AT CHARLOTTE

9201 University City Boulevard, Charlotte, NC 28223-0001
Phone: 704-687-2213 **E-mail:** unccadm@e-mail.uncc.edu **CEEB Code:** 5105
Fax: 704-687-6483 **Website:** www.uncc.edu **ACT Code:** 3163
Financial Aid Phone: 704-687-2461

This public school was founded in 1946. It has a 1,000-acre campus.

RATINGS

Admissions Selectivity Rating: 79   **Fire Safety Rating:** 60*   **Green Rating:** 78

STUDENTS AND FACULTY

Enrollment: 16,885. **Student Body:** 52% female, 48% male, 9% out-of-state, 2% international (89 countries represented). African American 14%, Asian 5%, Caucasian 75%, Hispanic 3%. **Retention and Graduation:** 77% freshmen return for sophomore year. 13% grads go on to further study within 2 semesters. **Faculty:** Student/faculty ratio 14:1. 895 full-time faculty, 86% hold PhDs. 93% faculty teach undergrads.

ACADEMICS

Degrees: Bachelor's, doctoral, master's, post-master's certificate. **Academic Requirements:** Arts/fine arts, computer literacy, English (including composition), foreign languages, history, humanities, mathematics, sciences (biological or physical), social science. **Classes:** Most classes have 20–29 students. Most lab/discussion sections have 10–19 students. **Majors with Highest Enrollment:** Communication studies/speech communication and rhetoric, finance, psyb Ølogy. **Disciplines with Highest Percentage of Degrees Awarded:** Business/marketing 25%, psychology 8%, social sciences 8%, education 7%, engineering 7%, security and protective services 5%. **Special Study Options:** Accelerated program, cooperative education program, cross registration, distance learning, double major, dual enrollment, English as a second language (ESL), honors program, independent study, internships, study abroad, teacher certification program, weekend college, wilderness exploration program.

FACILITIES

Housing: Coed dorms, men's dorms, women's dorms, apartments for single students, special housing for disabled students, special housing for international students, fraternity/sorority housing, limited rooms for students with disabilities. **Special Academic Facilities/Equipment:** Urban studies and community service institute, mock court room, applied research center, language lab, 63-acre ecological reserve, botanical and horticultural complex, tropical rainforest conservatory. **Computers:** 20% of classrooms are wireless; 75% of public computers are PCs, 15% of public computers are Macs, 10% of public computers are UNIX, network access in dorm rooms, online registration, online administrative functions (other than registration), remote student-access to Web through college's connection.

CAMPUS LIFE

Activities: Choral groups, concert band, dance, drama/theater, jazz band, literary magazine, music ensembles, musical theater, opera, pep band, student government, student newspaper, television station, yearbook. **Organizations:** 222 registered organizations, 25 honor societies, 22 religious organizations. 14 fraternities (7% men join), 10 sororities (6% women join). **Athletics (Intercollegiate):** *Men:* Baseball, basketball, cross-country, golf, soccer, tennis, track/field (outdoor). *Women:* Basketball, cross-country, soccer, softball, tennis, track/field (outdoor), volleyball. **Environmental Initiatives:** Recycling. Alternative Fuel Vehicles. Student Green Energy initiative (just starting).

ADMISSIONS

Freshman Academic Profile: 13% in top 10% of high school class, 54% in top 25% of high school class, 90% in top 50% of high school class. SAT Math middle 50% range 480–590. SAT Critical Reading middle 50% range 470–560. SAT Writing middle 50% range 460–550. ACT middle 50% range 19–24. TOEFL required of all international applicants, minimum paper TOEFL 507, minimum computer TOEFL 180. **Basis for Candidate Selection:** *Very important factors considered include:* Academic GPA, rigor of secondary school record, standardized test scores. *Other factors considered include:* Character/personal qualities, extracurricular activities, geographical residence, level of applicant's interest, state residency, talent/ability. **Freshman Admission Requirements:** High school diploma is required, and GED is accepted. *Academic units required:* 4 English, 4 math, 3 science (1 science lab), 2 foreign language, 2 social studies. *Academic units recommended:* 1 foreign language. **Freshman Admission Statistics:** 9,409 applied, 73% admitted, 41% enrolled. **Transfer Admission Requirements:** High school transcript, college transcript(s), statement of good standing from prior institution(s). Minimum college GPA of 2.0 required. Lowest grade transferable C. **General Admission Information:**

Application fee $50. Regular application deadline 7/1. Regular notification is rolling. Non-fall registration accepted. Credit and/or placement offered for CEEB Advanced Placement tests.

COSTS AND FINANCIAL AID
Annual in-state tuition $2,461. Annual out-of-state tuition $12,873. Room and board $6,034. Required fees $1,692. Average book expense $1,200. **Required Forms and Deadlines:** FAFSA. Financial aid filing deadline 4/1. **Notification of Awards:** Applicants will be notified of awards on a rolling basis beginning on or about 3/15. **Types of Aid:** *Need-based scholarships/grants:* Pell, SEOG, state scholarships/grants, private scholarships, the school's own gift aid. *Loans:* FFEL Subsidized Stafford, FFEL Unsubsidized Stafford, FFEL PLUS, Federal Perkins, college/university loans from institutional funds. **Student Employment: Financial Aid Statistics:** 37% freshmen, 37% undergrads receive need-based scholarship or grant aid. 35% freshmen, 38% undergrads receive need-based self-help aid. 33 freshmen, 143 undergrads receive athletic scholarships. 60% freshmen, 54% undergrads receive any aid. Highest amount earned per year from on-campus jobs $2,000.

THE UNIVERSITY OF NORTH CAROLINA AT GREENSBORO

Best 368

1400 Spring Garden Street, Greensboro, NC 27402-6170
Phone: 336-334-5243 **E-mail:** admissions@uncg.edu **CEEB Code:** 5913
Fax: 336-334-4180 **Website:** www.uncg.edu **ACT Code:** 3166
Financial Aid Phone: 336-224-5702

This public school was founded in 1891. It has a 210-acre campus.

RATINGS
Admissions Selectivity Rating: 82   **Fire Safety Rating:** 70   **Green Rating:** 60*

STUDENTS AND FACULTY
Enrollment: 12,757. **Student Body:** 68% female, 32% male, 7% out-of-state. African American 20%, Asian 3%, Caucasian 68%, Hispanic 2%. **Retention and Graduation:** 76% freshmen return for sophomore year. 39% freshmen graduate within 4 years. **Faculty:** Student/faculty ratio 16:1. 750 full-time faculty, 82% hold PhDs. 94% faculty teach undergrads.

ACADEMICS
Degrees: Bachelor's, doctoral, master's, post-bachelor's certificate, post-master's certificate. **Academic Requirements:** Arts/fine arts, English (including composition), foreign languages, history, humanities, mathematics, philosophy, sciences (biological or physical), social science. **Classes:** Most classes have 20–29 students. Most lab/discussion sections have 20–29 students. **Majors with Highest Enrollment:** Biology teacher education, elementary education and teaching, nursing/registered nurse training (ASN, BSN, MSN, RN). **Disciplines with Highest Percentage of Degrees Awarded:** Business/marketing 16%, education 14%, health professions and related sciences 10%, social sciences 8%, visual and performing arts 8%. **Special Study Options:** Accelerated program, cross registration, distance learning, double major, dual enrollment, evening university, honors program, independent study, internships, study abroad, teacher certification program.

FACILITIES
Housing: Coed dorms, women's dorms, apartments for single students, special housing for international students. **Special Academic Facilities/Equipment:** 42-acre recreational site, art gallery, student center, new music building, new science building. **Computers:** 100% of classrooms are wireless, 72% of public computers are PCs, 26% of public computers are Macs, 2% of public computers are UNIX, network access in dorm rooms, network access in dorm lounges, online registration, online administrative functions (other than registration), remote student-access to Web through college's connection.

CAMPUS LIFE
Activities: Choral groups, concert band, dance, drama/theater, jazz band, literary magazine, music ensembles, musical theater, opera, pep band, radio station, student government, student newspaper, student-run film society, symphony orchestra. **Organizations:** 150 registered organizations, 43 honor societies, 12 religious organizations. 6 fraternities, 6 sororities. **Athletics (Intercollegiate):** *Men:* Baseball, basketball, cross-country, golf, soccer, tennis,

wrestling. *Women:* Basketball, cross-country, golf, soccer, softball, tennis, volleyball.

ADMISSIONS
Freshman Academic Profile: 14% in top 10% of high school class, 43% in top 25% of high school class, 86% in top 50% of high school class. 95% from public high schools. SAT Math middle 50% range 470–570. SAT Critical Reading middle 50% range 460–570. SAT Writing middle 50% range 450–550. TOEFL required of all international applicants, minimum paper TOEFL 550, minimum computer TOEFL 213. **Basis for Candidate Selection:** *Very important factors considered include:* Academic GPA, rigor of secondary school record. *Important factors considered include:* Standardized test scores. *Other factors considered include:* Recommendation(s). **Freshman Admission Requirements:** High school diploma is required, and GED is not accepted. *Academic units required:* 4 English, 4 math, 3 science (1 science lab), 2 foreign language, 1 social studies, 1 history. **Freshman Admission Statistics:** 9,905 applied, 49% admitted, 50% enrolled. **Transfer Admission Requirements:** High school transcript, college transcript(s), standardized test score, statement of good standing from prior institution(s). Minimum college GPA of 2.0 required. Lowest grade transferable C-. **General Admission Information:** Application fee $45. Regular application deadline 3/1. Regular notification is rolling. Non-fall registration accepted. Admission may be deferred for a maximum of 1 semester. Credit and/or placement offered for CEEB Advanced Placement tests.

COSTS AND FINANCIAL AID
Annual in-state tuition $2,458. Annual out-of-state tuition $13,726. Room and board $6,151. Required fees $1,571. Average book expense $1,812. **Required Forms and Deadlines:** FAFSA. Financial aid filing deadline 3/1. **Notification of Awards:** Applicants will be notified of awards on a rolling basis beginning on or about 3/15. **Types of Aid:** *Need-based scholarships/grants:* Pell, SEOG, state scholarships/grants, private scholarships, the school's own gift aid. *Loans:* FFEL Subsidized Stafford, FFEL Unsubsidized Stafford, FFEL PLUS, Federal Perkins, college/university loans from institutional funds. **Student Employment:** Federal Work-Study Program available. Institutional employment available. Off-campus job opportunities are good. **Financial Aid Statistics:** 31% freshmen, 31% undergrads receive need-based scholarship or grant aid. 39% freshmen, 43% undergrads receive need-based self-help aid. 41 freshmen, 142 undergrads receive athletic scholarships. 66% freshmen, 62% undergrads receive any aid.

THE UNIVERSITY OF NORTH CAROLINA AT PEMBROKE

One University Drive, PO Box 1510, Pembroke, NC 28372
Phone: 910-521-6262 **E-mail:** admissions@uncp.edu **CEEB Code:** 5534
Fax: 910-521-6497 **Website:** www.uncp.edu **ACT Code:** 3138
Financial Aid Phone: 910-521-6366

This public school was founded in 1887. It has a 126-acre campus.

RATINGS
Admissions Selectivity Rating: 70   **Fire Safety Rating:** 60*   **Green Rating:** 60*

STUDENTS AND FACULTY
Enrollment: 4,710. **Student Body:** 63% female, 37% male, 22% out-of-state, 1% international (21 countries represented). African American 26%, Asian 2%, Caucasian 45%, Hispanic 3%, Native American 21%. **Retention and Graduation:** 68% freshmen return for sophomore year. 21% freshmen graduate within 4 years. **Faculty:** Student/faculty ratio 16:1. 238 full-time faculty, 69% hold PhDs. 99% faculty teach undergrads.

ACADEMICS
Degrees: Bachelor's, master's. **Academic Requirements:** Arts/fine arts, computer literacy, English (including composition), history, humanities, mathematics, philosophy, physical education, sciences (biological or physical), social science. **Classes:** Most classes have 20–29 students. Most lab/discussion sections have 10–19 students. **Majors with Highest Enrollment:** Criminal justice/safety studies, sociology. **Disciplines with Highest Percentage of Degrees Awarded:** Business/marketing 16%, education 13%, social sciences 12%, biological/life sciences 8%, public administration and social services 7%. **Special Study Options:** Accelerated program, cooperative education program, cross registration, distance learning, double major, dual enrollment, English as a second language (ESL), exchange student program (domestic), external degree program, honors program, independent study, internships, study abroad, teacher certification program.

FACILITIES

Housing: Coed dorms, men's dorms, women's dorms, apartments for married students. **Special Academic Facilities/Equipment:** Native American resources center and museum. **Computers:** 100% of public computers are PCs, network access in dorm rooms, network access in dorm lounges, support for handheld computing, remote student-access to Web through college's connection.

CAMPUS LIFE

Activities: Choral groups, concert band, dance, drama/theater, jazz band, literary magazine, marching band, music ensembles, musical theater, pep band, student government, student newspaper, student-run film society, television station, yearbook. **Organizations:** 70 registered organizations, 11 honor societies, 3 religious organizations. 11 fraternities, 10 sororities. **Athletics (Intercollegiate):** *Men:* Baseball, basketball, cheerleading, cross-country, football, soccer, track/field (outdoor), wrestling. *Women:* Basketball, cheerleading, cross-country, soccer, softball, tennis, track/field (outdoor), volleyball.

ADMISSIONS

Freshman Academic Profile: 9% in top 10% of high school class, 29% in top 25% of high school class, 63% in top 50% of high school class. 95% from public high schools. SAT Math middle 50% range 430–530. SAT Critical Reading middle 50% range 420–510. SAT Writing middle 50% range 400–490. ACT middle 50% range 16–20. TOEFL required of all international applicants, minimum paper TOEFL 500. **Basis for Candidate Selection:** *Very important factors considered include:* Academic GPA, class rank, rigor of secondary school record, standardized test scores. *Other factors considered include:* Application essay, character/personal qualities, interview, recommendation(s), talent/ability. **Freshman Admission Requirements:** High school diploma is required, and GED is accepted. *Academic units required:* 4 English, 3 math, 3 science (1 science lab), 2 foreign language, 1 social studies, 1 history. **Freshman Admission Statistics:** 2,511 applied, 84% admitted, 45% enrolled. **Transfer Admission Requirements:** High school transcript, college transcript(s), statement of good standing from prior institution(s). Minimum college GPA of 2.0 required. Lowest grade transferable C. **General Admission Information:** Application fee $40. Regular notification is rolling. Non-fall registration accepted. Admission may be deferred for a maximum of 2 semesters. Credit and/or placement offered for CEEB Advanced Placement tests.

COSTS AND FINANCIAL AID

Annual in-state tuition $2,046. Annual out-of-state tuition $11,769. Room and board $6,190. Required fees $1,589. Average book expense $1,200. **Required Forms and Deadlines:** FAFSA. Financial aid filing deadline 3/15. **Notification of Awards:** Applicants will be notified of awards on a rolling basis beginning on or about 4/15. **Types of Aid:** *Need-based scholarships/grants:* Pell, SEOG, state scholarships/grants, private scholarships, the school's own gift aid. *Loans:* FFEL Subsidized Stafford, FFEL Unsubsidized Stafford, FFEL PLUS, Federal Perkins, college/university loans from institutional funds. **Financial Aid Statistics:** 61% freshmen, 58% undergrads receive need-based scholarship or grant aid. 56% freshmen, 57% undergrads receive need-based self-help aid. 75% freshmen, 72% undergrads receive any aid.

THE UNIVERSITY OF NORTH CAROLINA AT WILMINGTON

601 South College Road, Wilmington, NC 28403-5904
Phone: 910-962-3243 **E-mail:** admissions@uncw.edu **CEEB Code:** 5907
Fax: 910-962-3038 **Website:** www.uncw.edu **ACT Code:** 3174
Financial Aid Phone: 910-962-3177

This public school was founded in 1947. It has a 650-acre campus.

RATINGS

Admissions Selectivity Rating: 87　　**Fire Safety Rating:** 88　　**Green Rating:** 81

STUDENTS AND FACULTY

Enrollment: 10,479. **Student Body:** 58% female, 42% male, 14% out-of-state. African American 5%, Asian 2%, Caucasian 87%, Hispanic 3%. **Retention and Graduation:** 83% freshmen return for sophomore year. 9% grads go on to further study within 2 semesters. 6% grads pursue arts and sciences degrees. 1% grads pursue business degrees. 1% grads pursue law degrees. 1% grads pursue medical degrees. **Faculty:** Student/faculty ratio 18:1. 515 full-time faculty, 86% hold PhDs. 100% faculty teach undergrads.

ACADEMICS

Degrees: Bachelor's, doctoral, master's, post-bachelor's certificate, post-master's certificate. **Academic Requirements:** Arts/fine arts, English (including composition), foreign languages, history, humanities, mathematics, sciences (biological or physical), social science. **Classes:** Most classes have 20–29 students. Most lab/discussion sections have 20–29 students. **Majors with Highest Enrollment:** Communications studies/speech communication and rhetoric, marketing/marketing management, psychology. **Disciplines with Highest Percentage of Degrees Awarded:** Biological/life sciences 7%, business/marketing 25%, education 10%, communications/journalism 7%, English 7%, psychology 7%, visual and performing arts 6%, social sciences 5%, health professions and related sciences 5%. **Special Study Options:** 2+2 engineering program, accelerated program, cooperative education program, cross registration, distance learning, double major, English as a second language (ESL), exchange student program (domestic), honors program, independent study, internships, study abroad, teacher certification program.

FACILITIES

Housing: Coed dorms, women's dorms, apartments for single students, special housing for international students, special housing for honors students. **Special Academic Facilities/Equipment:** Upperman African American Cultural Arts Center, N.C. Teachers Legacy Hall, Ev-Henwood Nature Preserve, center for marine science at Myrtle Grove, Almkuist-Nixon Sports Medicine Building, museum of world cultures, Claude Howell Gallery, UNCW Library Archives and Special Collections. **Computers:** 100% of classrooms are wired, 100% of classrooms are wireless, 94% of public computers are PCs, 6% of public computers are Macs, network access in dorm rooms, network access in dorm lounges, online registration, online administrative functions (other than registration), support for handheld computing, remote student-access to Web through college's connection.

CAMPUS LIFE

Activities: Choral groups, concert band, dance, drama/theater, jazz band, literary magazine, music ensembles, musical theater, opera, pep band, radio station, student government, student newspaper, student-run film society, symphony orchestra, television station. **Organizations:** 172 registered organizations, 8 honor societies, 12 fraternities (7% men join), 12 sororities (8% women join). **Athletics (Intercollegiate):** *Men:* Baseball, basketball, cheerleading, cross-country, diving, golf, soccer, swimming, tennis, track/field (outdoor). *Women:* Basketball, cheerleading, cross-country, diving, golf, soccer, softball, swimming, tennis, track/field (outdoor), volleyball. **Environmental Initiatives:** Bio diesel fuel program. LEED certification for new housing and parking development. Current residence halls going green with students turning in regular lightbulbs for energy efficient ones and conserving water. Dining services—using biopak containers, going trayless, offering free trade coffee, using reusable clean cloths.

ADMISSIONS

Freshman Academic Profile: 22% in top 10% of high school class, 62% in top 25% of high school class, 92% in top 50% of high school class. SAT Math middle 50% range 540–630. SAT Critical Reading middle 50% range 530–610. SAT Writing middle 50% range 510–600. ACT middle 50% range 21–26. TOEFL required of all international applicants, minimum paper TOEFL 550, minimum computer TOEFL 213. **Basis for Candidate Selection:** *Very important factors considered include:* Academic GPA, rigor of secondary school record, standardized test scores, state residency. *Important factors considered include:* Application essay, class rank, recommendation(s). *Other factors considered include:* Alumni/ae relation, character/personal qualities, extracurricular activities, first generation, geographical residence, level of applicant's interest, racial/ethnic status, talent/ability, volunteer work, work experience. **Freshman Admission Requirements:** High school diploma is required, and GED is accepted. *Academic units required:* 4 English, 4 math, 3 science (1 science lab), 2 foreign language, 2 social studies, 1 history, 5 academic electives. **Freshman Admission Statistics:** 8,066 applied, 62% admitted, 39% enrolled. **Transfer Admission Requirements:** High school transcript, college transcript(s). Minimum college GPA of 2.5 required. Lowest grade transferable C. **General Admission Information:** Application fee $45. Regular application deadline 2/1. Regular notification ending date 4/1. Non-fall registration accepted. Admission may be deferred for a maximum of 2 semesters. Credit and/or placement offered for CEEB Advanced Placement tests.

COSTS AND FINANCIAL AID

Annual in-state tuition $2,413. Annual out-of-state tuition $12,376. Room and board $6,998. Required fees $1,985. Average book expense $934. **Required Forms and Deadlines:** FAFSA, institution's own financial aid form. Contact Financial Aid & Veterans Services Office for instructions. **Notification of Awards:** Applicants will be notified of awards on a rolling basis beginning on or about 4/1. **Types of Aid:** *Need-based scholarships/grants:* Pell, SEOG, state scholarships/grants, private scholarships, the school's own gift aid. *Loans:* Direct Subsidized Stafford, Direct Unsubsidized Stafford, Direct PLUS, Federal Perkins, state loans, college/university loans from institutional funds. **Student Employment:** Off-campus job opportunities are good. **Financial Aid Statistics:** 24% freshmen, 30% undergrads receive need-based scholarship or grant aid. 24% freshmen, 31% undergrads receive need-based self-help aid. 38 freshmen, 238 undergrads receive athletic scholarships. 54% freshmen, 58% undergrads receive any aid.

UNIVERSITY OF NORTH DAKOTA

Best 368

205 Twamley Hall, 264 Centennial Drive Stop 8357, Grand Forks, ND 58202-8357
Phone: 800-225-5863 **E-mail:** enrollmentservices@mail.und.nodak.edu **CEEB Code:** 6878
Fax: 701-777-2721 **Website:** www.und.edu **ACT Code:** 3218
Financial Aid Phone: 701-777-3121

This public school was founded in 1883. It has a 550-acre campus.

RATINGS

Admissions Selectivity Rating: 78   **Fire Safety Rating:** 78   **Green Rating:** 82

STUDENTS AND FACULTY

Enrollment: 10,376. **Student Body:** 46% female, 54% male, 49% out-of-state, 2% international (63 countries represented). African American 1%, Asian 1%, Caucasian 91%, Hispanic 1%, Native American 3%. **Retention and Graduation:** 77% freshmen return for sophomore year. 22% freshmen graduate within 4 years. 28% grads go on to further study within 2 semesters. 6% grads pursue arts and sciences degrees. 2% grads pursue business degrees. 2% grads pursue law degrees. 4% grads pursue medical degrees. **Faculty:** Student/faculty ratio 18:1. 631 full-time faculty, 67% hold PhDs. 90% faculty teach undergrads.

ACADEMICS

Degrees: Bachelor's, certificate, diploma, doctoral, first professional, master's, post-master's certificate. **Academic Requirements:** Arts/fine arts, English (including composition), humanities. **Classes:** Most classes have 20–29 students. Most lab/discussion sections have 20–29 students. **Majors with Highest Enrollment:** Airline/commercial/professional pilot and flight crew, nursing/registered nurse training (ASN, BSN, MSN, RN), psychology. **Disciplines with Highest Percentage of Degrees Awarded:** Transportation and materials moving 19%, business/marketing 16%, health professions and related sciences 10%, education 8%, engineering 7%. **Special Study Options:** Accelerated program, cooperative education program, cross registration, distance learning, double major, dual enrollment, English as a second language (ESL), exchange student program (domestic), external degree program, honors program, independent study, internships, liberal arts/career combination,

student-designed major, study abroad, teacher certification program, weekend college.

FACILITIES

Housing: Coed dorms, men's dorms, women's dorms, apartments for married students, apartments for single students, special housing for disabled students, fraternity/sorority housing. **Special Academic Facilities/Equipment:** Hughes Fine Arts Center, Burtness Theatre, North Dakota Museum of Art, Chester Fritz Auditorium, mining/mineral resources research institute/energy research center, remote sensing institute, aviation facilities, meteorology data center, Ralph Engelstad Arena. **Computers:** 100% of classrooms are wired, 20% of classrooms are wireless, 90% of public computers are PCs, 10% of public computers are Macs, network access in dorm rooms, network access in dorm lounges, online registration, online administrative functions (other than registration), remote student-access to Web through college's connection.

CAMPUS LIFE

Activities: Choral groups, concert band, dance, drama/theater, jazz band, literary magazine, marching band, music ensembles, musical theater, opera, pep band, radio station, student government, student newspaper, student-run film society, symphony orchestra, television station. **Organizations:** 230 registered organizations, 42 honor societies, 3 religious organizations. 13 fraternities (9% men join), 7 sororities (7% women join). **Athletics (Intercollegiate):** *Men:* Baseball, basketball, cross-country, diving, football, golf, ice hockey, swimming, track/field (indoor), track/field (outdoor). *Women:* Basketball, cross-country, diving, golf, ice hockey, soccer, softball, swimming, tennis, track/field (indoor), track/field (outdoor), volleyball. **Environmental Initiatives:** Energy ESS. Presidential Committment. Recycling.

ADMISSIONS

Freshman Academic Profile: 16% in top 10% of high school class, 41% in top 25% of high school class, 76% in top 50% of high school class. 92% from public high schools. ACT middle 50% range 20.5–25.5. TOEFL required of all international applicants, minimum paper TOEFL 525, minimum computer TOEFL 195. **Basis for Candidate Selection:** *Very important factors considered include:* Academic GPA, standardized test scores. *Other factors considered include:* Class rank, rigor of secondary school record. **Freshman Admission Requirements:** High school diploma is required, and GED is accepted. *Academic units required:* 4 English, 3 math, 3 science (3 science labs), 3 social studies. *Academic units recommended:* 1 foreign language. **Freshman Admission Statistics:** 3,698 applied, 74% admitted, 70% enrolled. **Transfer Admission Requirements:** College transcript(s). Minimum college GPA of 2.0 required. Lowest grade transferable D. **General Admission Information:** Application fee $35. Regular notification is rolling. Non-fall registration accepted. Admission may be deferred for a maximum of 1 semester. Credit and/or placement offered for CEEB Advanced Placement tests.

COSTS AND FINANCIAL AID

Annual in-state tuition $5,025. Annual out-of-state tuition $13,418. Room and board $5,203. Required fees $1,105. Average book expense $800. **Required Forms and Deadlines:** FAFSA. Financial aid filing deadline 3/15. **Notification of Awards:** Applicants will be notified of awards on or about 5/15. **Types of Aid:** *Need-based scholarships/grants:* Pell, SEOG, state scholarships/grants, private scholarships, the school's own gift aid, Federal Nursing Scholarships. *Loans:* FFEL Subsidized Stafford, FFEL Unsubsidized Stafford, FFEL PLUS, Federal Perkins, Federal Nursing, alternative commercial loans. **Student Employment: Financial Aid Statistics:** 20% freshmen, 24% undergrads receive need-based scholarship or grant aid. 47% freshmen, 49% undergrads receive need-based self-help aid. 68 freshmen, 312 undergrads receive athletic scholarships. 78% freshmen, 76% undergrads receive any aid. Highest amount earned per year from on-campus jobs $3,076.

UNIVERSITY OF NORTH FLORIDA

4567 St. Johns Bluff Road, South, Jacksonville, FL 32224-2645
Phone: 904-620-2624 **E-mail:** admissions@unf.edu **CEEB Code:** 9841
Fax: 904-620-2299 **Website:** www.unf.edu **ACT Code:** 5490
Financial Aid Phone: 904-620-2604

This public school was founded in 1965. It has a 1,300-acre campus.

RATINGS
Admissions Selectivity Rating: 80   **Fire Safety Rating:** 60*   **Green Rating:** 60*

STUDENTS AND FACULTY
Enrollment: 13,821. **Student Body:** 58% female, 42% male, 3% out-of-state, 1% international (106 countries represented). African American 10%, Asian 5%, Caucasian 77%, Hispanic 7%. **Retention and Graduation:** 78% freshmen return for sophomore year. **Faculty:** Student/faculty ratio 23:1. 470 full-time faculty, 94% hold PhDs. 87% faculty teach undergrads.

ACADEMICS
Degrees: Associate, bachelor's, doctoral, master's, post-bachelor's certificate, post-master's certificate. **Academic Requirements:** Arts/fine arts, computer literacy, cultural diversity, English (including composition), foreign languages, history, humanities, mathematics, philosophy, sciences (biological or physical), social science. **Classes:** Most classes have 20–29 students. Most lab/discussion sections have 10–19 students. **Majors with Highest Enrollment:** Business administration and management, nursing/registered nurse training (ASN, BSN, MSN, RN), psychology. **Disciplines with Highest Percentage of Degrees Awarded:** Business/marketing 24%, education 12%, health professions and related sciences 12%, psychology 8%, social sciences 7%, security and protective services 5%, visual and performing arts 5%. **Special Study Options:** Accelerated program, cooperative education program, distanc learning, double major, dual enrollment, English as a second language (ESL), honors program, independent study, internships, learning communities, student-designed major, study abroad, teacher certification program, weekend college.

FACILITIES
Housing: Coed dorms, apartments for married students, apartments for single students, special housing for disabled students, fraternity/sorority housing, suite style housing. **Special Academic Facilities/Equipment:** Art gallery, bird sanctuary, fine arts center. **Computers:** 5% of classrooms are wired, 5% of classrooms are wireless, 84% of public computers are PCs, 15% of public computers are Macs, 1% of public computers are UNIX, network access in dorm rooms, network access in dorm lounges, online registration, online administrative functions (other than registration), remote student-access to Web through college's connection.

CAMPUS LIFE
Activities: Choral groups, concert band, dance, drama/theater, jazz band, literary magazine, music ensembles, pep band, radio station, student government, student newspaper, television station. **Organizations:** 149 registered organizations, 8 honor societies, 14 religious organizations. 8 fraternities (8% men join), 7 sororities (9% women join). **Athletics (Intercollegiate):** *Men:* Baseball, basketball, cheerleading, cross-country, golf, soccer, tennis, track/field (indoor), track/field (outdoor). *Women:* Basketball, cheerleading, cross-country, diving, soccer, softball, swimming, tennis, track/field (indoor), track/field (outdoor), volleyball.

ADMISSIONS
Freshman Academic Profile: 20% in top 10% of high school class, 49% in top 25% of high school class, 83% in top 50% of high school class. SAT Math middle 50% range 510–610. SAT Critical Reading middle 50% range 510–610. ACT middle 50% range 20–23. TOEFL required of all international applicants, minimum paper TOEFL 500, minimum computer TOEFL 213. **Basis for Candidate Selection:** *Very important factors considered include:* Academic GPA, rigor of secondary school record, standardized test scores. *Other factors considered include:* Application essay, class rank, extracurricular activities, level of applicant's interest, recommendation(s), talent/ability, volunteer work, work experience. **Freshman Admission Requirements:** High school diploma is required, and GED is accepted. *Academic units required:* 4 English, 3 math, 3 science (1 science lab), 2 foreign language, 3 social studies, 4 academic electives. **Freshman Admission Statistics:** 8,875 applied, 68% admitted, 42% enrolled. **Transfer Admission Requirements:** College transcript(s).

Minimum college GPA of 2.0 required. Lowest grade transferable D. **General Admission Information:** Application fee $30. Regular application deadline 4/1. Regular notification rolling. Non-fall registration accepted. Admission may be deferred for a maximum of 2 semesters. Credit offered for CEEB Advanced Placement tests.

COSTS AND FINANCIAL AID
Average book expense $800. **Required Forms and Deadlines:** FAFSA, Financial aid transcript for transfer students. Financial aid filing deadline 4/1. **Notification of Awards:** Applicants will be notified of awards on a rolling basis beginning on or about 3/15. **Types of Aid:** *Need-based scholarships/grants:* Pell, SEOG, the school's own gift aid, 2-2 Scholarships jointly sponsored with Florida Community College at Jacksonville. *Loans:* FFEL Subsidized Stafford, FFEL Unsubsidized Stafford, FFEL PLUS, Federal Perkins. **Financial Aid Statistics:** 21% freshmen, 19% undergrads receive need-based scholarship or grant aid. 11% freshmen, 16% undergrads receive need-based self-help aid. 47 freshmen, 177 undergrads receive athletic scholarships. 87% freshmen, 65% undergrads receive any aid. Highest amount earned per year from on-campus jobs $11,800.

UNIVERSITY OF NORTH TEXAS

PO Box 311277, Denton, TX 76203-1277
Phone: 940-565-2681 **E-mail:** undergrad@unt.edu **CEEB Code:** 6481
Fax: 940-565-2408 **Website:** www.unt.edu **ACT Code:** 4136

This public school was founded in 1890. It has an 858-acre campus.

RATINGS
Admissions Selectivity Rating: 75   **Fire Safety Rating:** 84   **Green Rating:** 60*

STUDENTS AND FACULTY
Enrollment: 26,598. **Student Body:** 55% female, 45% male, 3% out-of-state, 2% international (119 countries represented). African American 13%, Asian 5%, Caucasian 66%, Hispanic 12%. **Retention and Graduation:** 76% freshmen return for sophomore year. 18% freshmen graduate within 4 years. **Faculty:** Student/faculty ratio 19:1. 936 full-time faculty, 89% hold PhDs. 83% faculty teach undergrads.

ACADEMICS
Degrees: Bachelor's, doctoral, master's, post-bachelor's certificate. **Academic Requirements:** Arts/fine arts, computer literacy, English (including composition), foreign languages, history, humanities, mathematics, philosophy, sciences (biological or physical), social science. **Classes:** Most classes have 20–29 students. Most lab/discussion sections have 10–19 students. **Majors with Highest Enrollment:** Computer and information sciences, elementary education and teaching, psychology. **Disciplines with Highest Percentage of Degrees Awarded:** Business/marketing 24%, social sciences 15%, education 12%, visual and performing arts 9%, communications/journalism 7%. **Special Study Options:** Accelerated program, cooperative education program, cross registration, distance learning, double major, dual enrollment, English as a second language (ESL), exchange student program (domestic), honors program, independent study, internships, study abroad, teacher certification program, weekend college.

FACILITIES
Housing: Coed dorms, women's dorms, apartments for married students, apartments for single students, special housing for disabled students, fraternity/sorority housing. **Special Academic Facilities/Equipment:** Laser facilities, Sky Theater, Murchison Performing Arts Center. **Computers:** 1% of classrooms are wired, 80% of classrooms are wireless, 92% of public computers are PCs, 7% of public computers are Macs, 1% of public computers are UNIX, network access in dorm rooms, network access in dorm lounges, online registration, online administrative functions (other than registration), remote student-access to Web through college's connection.

CAMPUS LIFE
Activities: Choral groups, concert band, dance, drama/theater, jazz band, literary magazine, marching band, music ensembles, musical theater, opera, radio station, student government, student newspaper, student-run film society, symphony orchestra, television station. **Organizations:** 254 registered organizations, 25 honor societies, 33 religious organizations. 17 fraternities (5% men join), 10 sororities (4% women join). **Athletics (Intercollegiate):** *Men:* Basketball, cross-country, football, golf, track/field (indoor), track/field (outdoor). *Women:* Basketball, cross-country, diving, golf, soccer, softball, swimming, tennis, track/field (indoor), track/field (outdoor), volleyball.

ADMISSIONS

Freshman Academic Profile: 20% in top 10% of high school class, 50% in top 25% of high school class, 89% in top 50% of high school class. 91% from public high schools. SAT Math middle 50% range 510–620. SAT Critical Reading middle 50% range 500–610. ACT middle 50% range 21–26. TOEFL required of all international applicants, minimum paper TOEFL 550, minimum computer TOEFL 213. **Basis for Candidate Selection:** *Very important factors considered include:* Class rank, standardized test scores. *Important factors considered include:* Recommendation(s). *Other factors considered include:* Application essay, character/personal qualities, extracurricular activities, first generation, geographical residence, level of applicant's interest, rigor of secondary school record, talent/ability, volunteer work, work experience. **Freshman Admission Requirements:** High school diploma is required, and GED is accepted. *Academic units required:* 4 English, 4 math, 3 science, 3 foreign language, 2 social studies, 2 history, 2 academic electives. *Academic units recommended:* 4 English, 4 math, 3 science, 3 foreign language, 2 social studies, 2 history, 2 academic electives, health, physical education, computer sciences, fine arts. **Freshman Admission Statistics:** 12,367 applied, 66% admitted, 48% enrolled. **Transfer Admission Requirements:** College transcript(s). Minimum college GPA of 2.0 required. Lowest grade transferable D. **General Admission Information:** Application fee $40. Regular application deadline 8/19. Regular notification is rolling. Non-fall registration accepted. Admission may be deferred for a maximum of 2 semesters. Credit offered for CEEB Advanced Placement tests.

COSTS AND FINANCIAL AID

Annual in-state tuition $4,215. Out-of-state tuition $12,465. Room & board $5,625. Required fees $1,897. Average book expense $1,080. **Required Forms and Deadlines:** FAFSA. Financial aid filing deadline 6/1. **Notification of Awards:** Applicants will be notified of awards on a rolling basis beginning on or about 4/1. **Types of Aid:** *Need-based scholarships/grants:* Pell, SEOG, state scholarships/grants, the school's own gift aid. *Loans:* FFEL Subsidized Stafford, FFEL Unsubsidized Stafford, FFEL PLUS, Federal Perkins, state loans, college/university loans from institutional funds. **Financial Aid Statistics:** 36% freshmen, 34% undergrads receive need-based scholarship or grant aid. 37% freshmen, 40% undergrads receive need-based self-help aid. 31 freshmen, 162 undergrads receive athletic scholarships. 74% freshmen, 63% undergrads receive any aid. Highest amount earned per year from on-campus jobs $8,400. **Financial Aid Phone:** 940-565-3901.

UNIVERSITY NORTHERN BRITISH COLUMBIA

Prince George, BC V2N 4Z9 Canada
Phone: 250-960-6300 **E-mail:** registrar-info@unbc.ca
Fax: 250-960-6330 **Website:** www.unbc.ca
Financial Aid Phone: 250-960-6364

This public school was founded in 1990.

RATINGS

Admissions Selectivity Rating: 60*   **Fire Safety Rating:** 60*   **Green Rating:** 60*

STUDENTS AND FACULTY

Student Body: 8% out-of-province. **Faculty:** Student/faculty ratio 16:1. 144 full-time faculty.

ACADEMICS

Degrees: Bachelor's, certificate, doctoral, master's. **Academic Requirements:** Humanities, sciences (biological or physical). **Majors with Highest Enrollment:** Accounting, computer and information sciences, forest sciences. **Special Study Options:** Accelerated program, cooperative education program, distance learning, double major, exchange student program (domestic), honors program, independent study, study abroad, teacher certification program.

FACILITIES

Housing: Coed dorms. **Computers:** 95% of public computers are PCs, 5% of public computers are Macs, network access in dorm rooms, online registration, online administrative functions (other than registration), remote student-access to Web through college's connection.

CAMPUS LIFE

Activities: Radio station, student government, student newspaper. **Organizations:** 1 honor society, 1 religious organization. 1 sorority. **Athletics (Intercollegiate):** *Men:* Basketball. *Women:* Basketball.

ADMISSIONS

Basis for Candidate Selection: *Very important factors considered include:* Rigor of secondary school record. **Transfer Admission Requirements:** College transcript(s). **General Admission Information:** Application fee $5. Regular application deadline 7/15. Non-fall registration accepted.

COSTS AND FINANCIAL AID

In-province tuition $200–$1,072. Out-of-province tuition $200–$1,072. Room & board $2,450. Required fees $70. Average book expense $500. **Student Employment:** Off-campus job opportunities are excellent.

UNIVERSITY OF NORTHERN COLORADO

UNC Admissions Office, Campus Box 10, Greeley, CO 80639
Phone: 970-351-2881 **E-mail:** admissions.help@unco.edu **CEEB Code:** 4074
Fax: 970-351-2984 **Website:** www.unco.edu **ACT Code:** 5020
Financial Aid Phone: 970-351-2502

This public school was founded in 1890. It has a 236-acre campus.

RATINGS

Admissions Selectivity Rating: 73   **Fire Safety Rating:** 94   **Green Rating:** 74

STUDENTS AND FACULTY

Enrollment: 10,610. **Student Body:** 61% female, 39% male, 9% out-of-state. African American 2%, Asian 3%, Caucasian 59%, Hispanic 6%, Native American 1%. **Retention and Graduation:** 68% freshmen return for sophomore year. 5% grads go on to further study within 2 semesters. 6% grads pursue arts and sciences degrees. 2% grads pursue business degrees. **Faculty:** Student/faculty ratio 24:1. 413 full-time faculty. 100% faculty teach undergrads.

ACADEMICS

Degrees: Bachelor's, doctoral, master's, post-master's certificate. **Academic Requirements:** Arts/fine arts, English (including composition), history, mathematics, sciences (biological or physical), social science. **Classes:** Most classes have 20–29 students. Most lab/discussion sections have 20–29 students. **Majors with Highest Enrollment:** Business administration and management, kinesiology and exercise science, multi/interdisciplinary studies. **Disciplines with Highest Percentage of Degrees Awarded:** Interdisciplinary studies 17%, business/marketing 13%, health professions and related sciences 11%, social sciences 9%, visual and performing arts 8%. **Special Study Options:** Cooperative education program, cross registration, distance learning, double major, English as a second language (ESL), exchange student program (domestic), external degree program, honors program, independent study, internships, student-designed major, study abroad, teacher certification program.

FACILITIES

Housing: Coed dorms, women's dorms, apartments for married students, apartments for single students, special housing for disabled students, fraternity/sorority housing. **Special Academic Facilities/Equipment:** Art museum, music library, James A. Michener Collection. **Computers:** 97% of classrooms are wireless, 75% of public computers are PCs, 22% of public computers are Macs, 3% of public computers are UNIX, network access in dorm rooms, network access in dorm lounges, online registration, online administrative functions (other than registration), remote student-access to Web through college's connection.

CAMPUS LIFE

Activities: Choral groups, concert band, dance, drama/theater, jazz band, literary magazine, marching band, music ensembles, musical theater, opera, pep band, radio station, student government, student newspaper, student-run film society, symphony orchestra. **Organizations:** 137 registered organizations, 9 honor societies, 18 religious organizations. 9 fraternities (6% men join), 8 sororities (2% women join). **Athletics (Intercollegiate):** *Men:* Baseball, basketball, football, golf, tennis, track/field (outdoor), wrestling. *Women:* Basketball, cross-country, diving, golf, soccer, softball, swimming, tennis, track/field (outdoor), volleyball. **Environmental Initiatives:** Performance Contracting. Recycling. Non-Potable Water Usage for Irrigation.

ADMISSIONS

Freshman Academic Profile: 12% in top 10% of high school class, 31% in top 25% of high school class, 67% in top 50% of high school class. 93% from public high schools. SAT Math middle 50% range 460–580. SAT Critical Reading middle 50% range 460–580. SAT Writing middle 50% range 470–585. ACT middle 50% range 20–24. TOEFL required of all international applicants, minimum paper TOEFL 520, minimum computer TOEFL 190. **Basis for**

Candidate Selection: *Very important factors considered include:* Academic GPA, class rank, standardized test scores. *Important factors considered include:* Recommendation(s). *Other factors considered include:* Character/personal qualities, extracurricular activities, interview, racial/ethnic status, rigor of secondary school record, state residency, talent/ability, work experience. **Freshman Admission Requirements:** High school diploma is required, and GED is accepted. *Academic units required:* 3 math. *Academic units recommended:* 4 English, 3 science (1 science lab), 3 social studies. **Freshman Admission Statistics:** 7,581 applied, 80% admitted, 42% enrolled. **Transfer Admission Requirements:** College transcript(s), statement of good standing from prior institution(s). Minimum college GPA of 2.4 required. Lowest grade transferable C. **General Admission Information:** Application fee $40. Regular notification rolling. Non-fall registration accepted. Admission may be deferred for a maximum of 3 semesters. Credit offered for CEEB Advanced Placement tests.

COSTS AND FINANCIAL AID

Annual in-state tuition $3,600. Annual out-of-state tuition $12,180. Room and board $7,342. Required fees $713. Average book expense $1,135. **Required Forms and Deadlines:** FAFSA. Financial aid filing deadline 3/1. **Notification of Awards:** Applicants will be notified of awards on a rolling basis beginning on or about 4/15. **Types of Aid:** *Need-based scholarships/grants:* Pell, SEOG, state scholarships/grants, private scholarships, the school's own gift aid. *Loans:* FFEL Subsidized Stafford, FFEL Unsubsidized Stafford, FFEL PLUS, Federal Perkins, college/university loans from institutional funds. **Student Employment:** Federal Work-Study Program available. Institutional employment available. Off-campus job opportunities are fair. **Financial Aid Statistics:** 20% freshmen, 23% undergrads receive need-based scholarship or grant aid. 37% freshmen, 39% undergrads receive need-based self-help aid. 15 freshmen, 101 undergrads receive athletic scholarships. 80% freshmen, 74% undergrads receive any aid. Highest amount earned per year from on-campus jobs $5,093.

UNIVERSITY OF NORTHERN IOWA

1227 West Twenty-seventh Street, Cedar Falls, IA 50614-0018
Phone: 319-273-2281 **E-mail:** admissions@uni.edu **CEEB Code:** 6307
Fax: 319-273-2885 **Website:** www.uni.edu **ACT Code:** 1322
Financial Aid Phone: 319-273-2701

This public school was founded in 1876. It has a 910-acre campus.

RATINGS

Admissions Selectivity Rating: 72   **Fire Safety Rating:** 70   **Green Rating:** 87

STUDENTS AND FACULTY

Enrollment: 10,453. **Student Body:** 57% female, 43% male, 5% out-of-state, 2% international (73 countries represented). African American 3%, Asian 1%, Caucasian 93%, Hispanic 2%. **Retention and Graduation:** 82% freshmen return for sophomore year. 34% freshmen graduate within 4 years. 12% grads go on to further study within 2 semesters. 9% grads pursue arts and sciences degrees. 1% grads pursue business degrees. 1% grads pursue law degrees. 1% grads pursue medical degrees. **Faculty:** Student/faculty ratio 16:1. 629 full-time faculty, 80% hold PhDs. 90% faculty teach undergrads.

ACADEMICS

Degrees: Bachelor's, doctoral, master's. **Academic Requirements:** Arts/fine arts, capstone experience, English (including composition), foreign languages, history, humanities, mathematics, non-Western cultures, personal wellness, philosophy, sciences (biological or physical), social science. **Classes:** Most classes have 20–29 students. Most lab/discussion sections have 10–19 students. **Majors with Highest Enrollment:** Accounting, business administration and management, elementary education and teaching. **Disciplines with Highest Percentage of Degrees Awarded:** Business/marketing 24%, education 18%, social sciences 7%, visual and performing arts 5%, communications/journalism 5%. **Special Study Options:** 2+2 programs, accelerated program, bachelor's/master's degree programs (BA/MA, BS/MS,BA/MS, BA/MAcc), cooperative education program, distance learning, double major, dual enrollment, English as a second language (ESL), exchange student program (domestic), external degree program, honors program, independent study, internships, liberal arts/career combination, student-designed major, study abroad, teacher certification program, weekend college, combined undergraduate dual degree majors, undergraduate and graduate certificates.

FACILITIES

Housing: Coed dorms, men's dorms, women's dorms, apartments for married students, apartments for single students, fraternity/sorority housing, facilities accessible by persons with disabilities. **Special Academic Facilities/Equipment:** Natural history museum, art gallery, greenhouse and biological preserves, lakeside biology lab and field lab for conservation problems, Tallgrass Prairie Center, educational technology center, on-campus school for student teachers, NASA Regional Teacher Resource Center, speech and hearing clinic, small business development center, Iowa Waste Reduction Center, Center for Applied Research in Metal Casting, satellite video production truck with 3 cameras. **Computers:** 5% of classrooms are wired, 25% of classrooms are wireless, 95% of public computers are PCs, 3% of public computers are Macs, 1% of public computers are UNIX, network access in dorm rooms, network access in dorm lounges, online registration, online administrative functions (other than registration), support for handheld computing, remote student-access to Web through college's connection.

CAMPUS LIFE

Activities: Choral groups, concert band, dance, drama/theater, jazz band, literary magazine, marching band, music ensembles, musical theater, opera, pep band, radio station, student government, student newspaper, symphony orchestra, yearbook. **Organizations:** 184 registered organizations, 19 religious organizations. 8 fraternities (4% men join), 7 sororities (4% women join). **Athletics (Intercollegiate):** *Men:* Archery, baseball, basketball, cross-country, football, golf, track/field (indoor), track/field (outdoor), wrestling. *Women:* Basketball, cross-country, diving, golf, soccer, softball, swimming, tennis, track/field (indoor), track/field (outdoor), volleyball. **Environmental Initiatives:** Currently in the process of hiring a sustainability officer/energy conservation coordinator. Energy Conservation/Sustainability Committee with representatives from faculty, staff, students, and the community. Recycling and Reuse Technology Transfer Center.

ADMISSIONS

Freshman Academic Profile: 18% in top 10% of high school class, 47% in top 25% of high school class, 89% in top 50% of high school class. SAT Math middle 50% range 450.5–630.33. SAT Critical Reading middle 50% range 410–620. ACT middle 50% range 20.97–25.78. TOEFL required of all international applicants, minimum paper TOEFL 550, minimum computer TOEFL 213. **Basis for Candidate Selection:** *Very important factors considered include:* Class rank, rigor of secondary school record, standardized test scores. *Other factors considered include:* Academic GPA, interview, racial/ethnic status, recommendation(s), state residency, talent/ability. **Freshman Admission Requirements:** High school diploma is required, and GED is accepted. *Academic units required:* 4 English, 3 math, 3 science, 3 social studies, 2 academic electives. *Academic units recommended:* 1 science lab, 2 foreign language. **Freshman Admission Statistics:** 4,585 applied, 78% admitted, 49% enrolled. **Transfer Admission Requirements:** College transcript(s). Lowest grade transferable D. **General Admission Information:** Application fee $30. Regular application deadline 8/15. Regular notification is rolling. Non-fall registration accepted. Admission may be deferred indefinitely. Credit and/or placement offered for CEEB Advanced Placement tests.

COSTS AND FINANCIAL AID

Annual in-state tuition $6,246. Annual out-of-state tuition $14,554. Room and board $6,280. Required fees $838. Average book expense $966. **Required Forms and Deadlines:** FAFSA. **Notification of Awards:** Applicants will be notified of awards on a rolling basis beginning on or about 3/1. **Types of Aid:** *Need-based scholarships/grants:* Pell, SEOG, state scholarships/grants, private scholarships, the school's own gift aid. *Loans:* Direct Subsidized Stafford, Direct Unsubsidized Stafford, Direct PLUS, Federal Perkins, state loans, private loans, alternative loans. **Financial Aid Statistics:** 39% freshmen, 34% undergrads receive need-based scholarship or grant aid. 45% freshmen, 50% undergrads receive need-based self-help aid. 69 freshmen, 278 undergrads receive athletic scholarships. 84% freshmen, 84% undergrads receive any aid. Highest amount earned per year from on-campus jobs $4,496.

UNIVERSITY OF NOTRE DAME

220 Main Building, Notre Dame, IN 46556
Phone: 574-631-7505 **E-mail:** admissions@nd.edu **CEEB Code:** 1841
Fax: 574-631-8865 **Website:** www.nd.edu **ACT Code:** 1252
Financial Aid Phone: 574-631-6436

This private school, affiliated with the Roman Catholic Church, was founded in 1842. It has a 1,250-acre campus.

RATINGS

Admissions Selectivity Rating: 98   **Fire Safety Rating:** 92   **Green Rating:** 86

STUDENTS AND FACULTY

Enrollment: 8,346. **Student Body:** 47% female, 53% male, 92% out-of-state, 3% international (98 countries represented). African American 4%, Asian 7%, Caucasian 76%, Hispanic 9%. **Retention and Graduation:** 31% grads go on to further study within 2 semesters. 12% grads pursue arts and sciences degrees. 4% grads pursue business degrees. 7% grads pursue law degrees. 8% grads pursue medical degrees. **Faculty:** 94% faculty teach undergrads.

ACADEMICS

Degrees: Bachelor's, doctoral, first professional, master's. **Academic Requirements:** Arts/fine arts, English (including composition), foreign languages, history, humanities, mathematics, philosophy, physical education, sciences (biological or physical), social science, theology. **Majors with Highest Enrollment:** Business administration/management, engineering, pre-medicine/pre-medical studies. **Disciplines with Highest Percentage of Degrees Awarded:** Business/marketing 21%, social sciences 16%, engineering 8%, health professions and related sciences 7%, foreign languages and literature 6%. **Special Study Options:** Accelerated program, cross registration, distance learning, double major, honors program, independent study, internships, liberal arts/career combination, student-designed major, study abroad, teacher certification program (only available through cross registration with St. Mary's College).

FACILITIES

Housing: Men's dorms, women's dorms. **Special Academic Facilities/Equipment:** Art museum, theater, germ-free research facility, radiation laboratory. **Computers:** 100% of classrooms are wireless, 60% of public computers are PCs, 12% of public computers are Macs, 28% of public computers are UNIX, network access in dorm rooms, network access in dorm lounges, online registration, online administrative functions (other than registration), support for handheld computing, remote student-access to Web through college's connection.

CAMPUS LIFE

Activities: Choral groups, concert band, dance, drama/theater, jazz band, literary magazine, marching band, music ensembles, musical theater, opera, pep band, radio station, student government, student newspaper, student-run film society, symphony orchestra, yearbook. **Organizations:** 260 registered organizations, 10 honor societies, 7 religious organizations. **Athletics (Intercollegiate):** *Men:* Baseball, basketball, cross-country, diving, fencing, football, golf, ice hockey, lacrosse, soccer, swimming, tennis, track/field (outdoor). *Women:* Basketball, crew/rowing, cross-country, diving, fencing, golf, lacrosse, soccer, softball, swimming, tennis, track/field (outdoor), volleyball. **Environmental Initiatives:** Establishment of the Office of Sustainability and the creation of a $2 million green loan fund for capital projects on-campus focused on energy or environmental improvements. Installation of air quality control system upgrades to reduce nitrous oxide (NOx), particulate matter (PM), hydrogren chloride (HCl), and mercury (Hg) emissions at the University's power plant. Selection of the 2008 President's Forum topic, "Charting a Sustainable Energy Future," signals a permanent commitment to sustainability, environmental awareness, and energy concerns.

ADMISSIONS

Freshman Academic Profile: 85% in top 10% of high school class, 97% in top 25% of high school class, 100% in top 50% of high school class. 50% from public high schools. SAT Math middle 50% range 660–760. SAT Critical Reading middle 50% range 640–750. SAT Writing middle 50% range 630–720. ACT middle 50% range 31–34. TOEFL required of all international applicants, minimum paper TOEFL 600, minimum computer TOEFL 250. **Basis for Candidate Selection:** *Very important factors considered include:* Rigor of secondary school record. *Important factors considered include:* Academic GPA, alumni/ae relation, application essay, character/personal qualities, class rank, extracurricular activities, recommendation(s), standardized test scores, talent/ability, volunteer work. *Other factors considered include:* First generation, level of applicant's interest, racial/ethnic status, religious affiliation/commitment, work experience. **Freshman Admission Requirements:** High school diploma is required, and GED is not accepted. *Academic units required:* 4 English, 3 math, 2 science, 2 foreign language, 2 social studies, 3 academic electives. *Academic units recommended:* 4 English, 4 math, 4 science, 4 foreign language, 4 social studies. **Freshman Admission Statistics:** 12,796 applied, 27% admitted, 58% enrolled. **Transfer Admission Requirements:** High school transcript, college transcript(s), essay or personal statement, standardized test score, statement of good standing from prior institution(s). Minimum college GPA of 3.0 required. Lowest grade transferable C. **General Admission Information:** Application fee $50. Regular application deadline 12/31. Regular notification 4/10. Non-fall registration not accepted. Admission may be deferred for a maximum of 2 semesters.

COSTS AND FINANCIAL AID

Annual tuition $34,680. Room and board $9,290. Required fees $507. Average book expense $850. **Required Forms and Deadlines:** FAFSA, CSS/Financial Aid PROFILE, Noncustodial PROFILE, Business/Farm Supplement, signed Federal Income Tax Return & W-2 forms, Student Federal Income Tax Return. Financial aid filing deadline 2/15. **Notification of Awards:** Applicants will be notified of awards on or about 4/1. **Types of Aid:** *Need-based scholarships/grants:* Pell, SEOG, state scholarships/grants, private scholarships, the school's own gift aid, Alumni Club scholarships. *Loans:* FFEL Subsidized Stafford, FFEL Unsubsidized Stafford, FFEL PLUS, Federal Perkins, Privately funded student loan. **Financial Aid Statistics:** 51% freshmen, 46% undergrads receive need-based scholarship or grant aid. 41% freshmen, 41% undergrads receive need-based self-help aid. 76 freshmen, 305 undergrads receive athletic scholarships. Highest amount earned per year from on-campus jobs $6,150.

UNIVERSITY OF OKLAHOMA

1000 Asp Aveune, Norman, OK 73019-4076
Phone: 405-325-2252 **E-mail:** admrec@ou.edu **CEEB Code:** 6879
Fax: 405-325-7124 **Website:** www.ou.edu **ACT Code:** 6879
Financial Aid Phone: 405-325-4521

This public school was founded in 1890. It has a 3,897-acre campus.

RATINGS

Admissions Selectivity Rating: 84   **Fire Safety Rating:** 99   **Green Rating:** 91

STUDENTS AND FACULTY

Enrollment: 20,287. **Student Body:** 51% female, 49% male, 24% out-of-state, 2% international (110 countries represented). African American 5%, Asian 6%, Caucasian 76%, Hispanic 4%, Native American 7%. **Retention and Graduation:** 85% freshmen return for sophomore year. 24% freshmen graduate within 4 years. **Faculty:** Student/faculty ratio 19:1. 1,346 full-time faculty, 83% hold PhDs.

ACADEMICS

Degrees: Bachelor's, certificate, doctoral, first professional certificate, first professional, master's, post-master's certificate. **Academic Requirements:** Arts/fine arts, communication, computer literacy, English (including composition), foreign languages, history, humanities, mathematics, philosophy, sciences (biological or physical), social science. **Classes:** Most classes have 10–19 students. Most lab/discussion sections have 10–19 students. **Majors with Highest Enrollment:** Journalism, nursing/registered nurse training (ASN, BSN, MSN, RN), sociology. **Disciplines with Highest Percentage of Degrees Awarded:** Business/marketing 16%, communications/journalism 11%, social sciences 11%, health professions and related sciences 10%, engineering 8%. **Special Study Options:** Accelerated program, cooperative education program, distance learning, double major, dual enrollment, English as a second language (ESL), external degree program, honors program, independent study, internships, liberal arts/career combination, student-designed major, study abroad, teacher certification program, weekend college.

FACILITIES

Housing: Coed dorms, men's dorms, women's dorms, apartments for married students, apartments for single students, special housing for disabled students, special housing for international students, fraternity/sorority housing, honors house, cultural housing. **Special Academic Facilities/Equipment:** Art and natural history museums, linguistics institute, Institute of Asian Affairs, biological field station, energy center, history of science, Western history collection. **Computers:** 60% of classrooms are wired, 20% of classrooms are wireless, 89% of public computers are PCs, 10% of public computers are Macs, 1% of public computers are UNIX, network access in dorm rooms, network access in dorm lounges, online registration, online administrative functions (other than registration), support for handheld computing, remote student-access to Web through college's connection.

CAMPUS LIFE

Activities: Choral groups, concert band, dance, drama/theater, jazz band, literary magazine, marching band, music ensembles, musical theater, opera, pep band, radio station, student government, student newspaper, student-run film society, symphony orchestra, television station. **Organizations:** 359 registered organizations, 25 honor societies, 31 religious organization. 27 fraternities (18% men join), 22 sororities (24% women join). **Athletics (Intercollegiate):** *Men:* Baseball, basketball, cheerleading, cross-country, football, golf, gymnastics, tennis, track/field (indoor), track/field (outdoor), wrestling. *Women:* Basketball, cheerleading, cross-country, golf, gymnastics, soccer, softball, tennis, track/field (indoor), track/field (outdoor), volleyball. **Environmental Initiatives:** Membership in the Chicago Climate Exchange. Joining with the University Presidents' Campus Climate Challenge. Operation of the Academic Department for Interdisciplinary Perspectives on the Environment.

ADMISSIONS

Freshman Academic Profile: 35% in top 10% of high school class, 68% in top 25% of high school class, 92% in top 50% of high school class. SAT Math middle 50% range 540–660. SAT Critical Reading middle 50% range 510–640. ACT middle 50% range 23–28. TOEFL required of all international applicants, minimum paper TOEFL 550, minimum computer TOEFL 213. **Basis for Candidate Selection:** *Very important factors considered include:* Academic GPA, class rank, rigor of secondary school record, standardized test scores. *Other factors considered include:* Application essay, recommendation(s), state residency. **Freshman Admission Requirements:** High school diploma is required, and GED is accepted. *Academic units required:* 4 English, 3 math, 2 science (2 science labs), 2 social studies, 1 history, 3 academic electives. *Academic units recommended:* 3 foreign language, 1 computer science. **Freshman Admission Statistics:** 7,471 applied, 91% admitted, 49% enrolled. **Transfer Admission Requirements:** College transcript(s). Lowest grade transferable D. **General Admission Information:** Application fee $40. Regular application deadline 4/1. Regular notification when applicants meet admission requirements. Non-fall registration accepted. Credit and/or placement offered for CEEB Advanced Placement tests.

COSTS AND FINANCIAL AID

Annual in-state tuition $2,609. Annual out-of-state tuition $9,900. Room and board $7,058. Required fees $1,925. Average book expense $953. **Required Forms and Deadlines:** FAFSA. Financial aid filing deadline 3/1. **Notification of Awards:** Applicants will be notified of awards on a rolling basis beginning on or about 3/15. **Types of Aid:** *Need-based scholarships/grants:* Pell, SEOG, state scholarships/grants, private scholarships, the school's own gift aid, United Negro College Fund. *Loans:* FFEL Subsidized Stafford, FFEL Unsubsidized Stafford, FFEL PLUS, Federal Perkins, Federal Nursing, college/university loans from institutional funds. **Student Employment:** Federal Work-Study Program available. Institutional employment available. Off-campus job opportunities are excellent. **Financial Aid Statistics:** 11% freshmen, 18% undergrads receive need-based scholarship or grant aid. 38% freshmen, 37% undergrads receive need-based self-help aid. 32 freshmen, 205 undergrads receive athletic scholarships. 78% freshmen, 74% undergrads receive any aid. Highest amount earned per year from on-campus jobs $2,904.

UNIVERSITY OF OREGON

1217 University of Oregon, Eugene, OR 97403-1217
Phone: 541-346-3201 **E-mail:** uoadmit@uoregon.edu **CEEB Code:** 4846
Fax: 541-346-5815 **Website:** www.uoregon.edu
Financial Aid Phone: 800-760-6953

This public school was founded in 1876. It has a 295-acre campus.

RATINGS

Admissions Selectivity Rating: 79 **Fire Safety Rating:** 71 **Green Rating:** 99

STUDENTS AND FACULTY

Enrollment: 16,282. **Student Body:** 53% female, 47% male, 22% out-of-state, 5% international (87 countries represented). African American 2%, Asian 6%, Caucasian 76%, Hispanic 4%, Native American 1%. **Retention and Graduation:** 84% freshmen return for sophomore year. 40% freshmen graduate within 4 years. 22% grads go on to further study within 2 semesters. **Faculty:** Student/faculty ratio 18:1. 789 full-time faculty, 98% hold PhDs. 100% faculty teach undergrads.

ACADEMICS

Degrees: Bachelor's, doctoral, first professional, master's, post-bachelor's certificate. **Academic Requirements:** Computer and information sciences, English (including composition), foreign languages, humanities, mathematics, sciences (biological or physical), social science, bachelor of arts requires proficiency in a foreign language. **Classes:** Most classes have 20–29 students. Most lab/discussion sections have 20–29 students. **Majors with Highest Enrollment:** Business administration/management, journalism, psychology, **Disciplines with Highest Percentage of Degrees Awarded:** Social sciences 22%, business/marketing 12%, communications/journalism 9%, psychology 8%, foreign languages and literature 7%. **Special Study Options:** Distance learning, double major, dual enrollment, English as a second language (ESL), exchange student program (domestic), honors program, independent study, internships, liberal arts/career combination, professional preparation, semester at sea program, student-designed major, study abroad, teacher certification program.

FACILITIES

Housing: Coed dorms, apartments for married students, apartments for single students, special housing for disabled students, fraternity/sorority housing. **Special Academic Facilities/Equipment:** Jordan Schnitzer Museum of Art, museum of natural and cultural history, James Warsaw Sports Marketing Center, Lundquist Center for Entrepreneurship, University of Oregon Many Nations Longhouse, Green Chemistry Laboratory and Alice C. Tyler Instrumentation Center, Future Music Oregon, Pine Mountain Observatory, Oregon Institute of Marine Biology, urban architecture program, BetterBricks Daylighting Laboratory. **Computers:** 5% of classrooms are wired, 95% of classrooms are wireless, 60% of public computers are PCs, 35% of public computers are Macs, 5% of public computers are UNIX, network access in dorm rooms, network access in dorm lounges, online registration, online administrative functions (other than registration), support for handheld computing, remote student-access to Web through college's connection.

CAMPUS LIFE

Activities: Choral groups, concert band, dance, drama/theater, jazz band, literary magazine, marching band, music ensembles, musical theater, opera, pep band, radio station, student government, student newspaper, symphony orchestra. **Organizations:** 250 registered organizations, 22 honor societies, 24 religious organizations. 15 fraternities (7% men join), 8 sororities (8% women join). **Athletics (Intercollegiate):** *Men:* Basketball, cheerleading, cross-country, football, golf, tennis, track/field (outdoor), wrestling. *Women:* Basketball, cheerleading, cross-country, golf, lacrosse, soccer, softball, tennis, track/field (outdoor), volleyball. **Environmental Initiatives:** Signed ACUPCC and currently developing climate action plan. Massive energy efficiency upgrades; lighting retrofits, building upgrades. Free public transportation for all faculty, staff, students; nationally award winning recycling program.

ADMISSIONS

Freshman Academic Profile: 23% in top 10% of high school class, 56% in top 25% of high school class, 89% in top 50% of high school class. 90% from public high schools. SAT Math middle 50% range 496–611. SAT Critical Reading middle 50% range 486–606. TOEFL required of all international applicants, minimum paper TOEFL 500, minimum computer TOEFL 173. **Basis for Candidate Selection:** *Very important factors considered include:* Rigor of secondary school record. *Important factors considered include:* Academic GPA. *Other factors considered include:* Application essay, class rank, extracurricular activities, first generation, geographical residence, interview, racial/ethnic status, recommendation(s), standardized test scores, state residency, talent/ability, volunteer work, work experience. **Freshman Admission Requirements:** High school diploma is required, and GED is accepted. *Academic units required:* 4 English, 3 math, 2 science, 2 foreign language, 3 social studies. *Academic units recommended:* 1 science lab, 2 additional units in required college preparatory areas recommended. **Freshman Admission Statistics:** 10,821 applied, 88% admitted, 36% enrolled. **Transfer Admission Requirements:** College transcript(s). Minimum college GPA of 2.3 required. Lowest grade transferable D. **General Admission Information:** Application fee $50. Regular application deadline 1/15. Regular notification is rolling. Non-fall registration accepted. Credit offered for CEEB Advanced Placement tests.

COSTS AND FINANCIAL AID
Annual in-state tuition $4,494. Annual out-of-state tuition $17,250. Room and board $7,849. Required fees $1,542. Average book expense $1,050. **Required Forms and Deadlines:** FAFSA. Financial aid filing deadline 3/1. **Notification of Awards:** Applicants will be notified of awards on a rolling basis beginning on or about 4/15. **Types of Aid:** *Need-based scholarships/grants:* Pell, SEOG, state scholarships/grants, private scholarships, the school's own gift aid. *Loans:* Direct Subsidized Stafford, Direct Unsubsidized Stafford, Direct PLUS, Federal Perkins, college/university loans from institutional funds. **Financial Aid Statistics:** 16% freshmen, 21% undergrads receive need-based scholarship or grant aid. 29% freshmen, 33% undergrads receive need-based self-help aid. 290 undergrads receive athletic scholarships. 60% freshmen, 60% undergrads receive any aid.

See page 1462.

UNIVERSITY OF THE OZARKS

415 College Avenue, Clarksville, AR 72830
Phone: 479-979-1227 **E-mail:** jdecker@ozarks.edu **CEEB Code:** 6111
Fax: 479-979-1355 **Website:** www.ozarks.edu **ACT Code:** 0120
Financial Aid Phone: 479-979-1221

This private school, affiliated with the Presbyterian Church, was founded in 1834. It has a 56-acre campus.

RATINGS
Admissions Selectivity Rating: 77　　　**Fire Safety Rating:** 70　　　**Green Rating:** 60*

STUDENTS AND FACULTY
Enrollment: 622. **Student Body:** 54% female, 46% male, 30% out-of-state, 16% international (20 countries represented). African American 4%, Asian 1%, Caucasian 63%, Hispanic 4%, Native American 4%. **Retention and Graduation:** 54% freshmen return for sophomore year. 31% freshmen graduate within 4 years. **Faculty:** Student/faculty ratio 13:1. 43 full-time faculty, 84% hold PhDs. 100% faculty teach undergrads.

ACADEMICS
Degrees: Bachelor's. **Academic Requirements:** Computer literacy, English (including composition), humanities, sciences (biological or physical). **Classes:** Most classes have 10–19 students. **Majors with Highest Enrollment:** Broadcast journalism, business administration/management. **Disciplines with Highest Percentage of Degrees Awarded:** Business/marketing 42%, education 12%, liberal arts/general studies 10%, biological/life sciences 8%, mathematics 8%, visual and performing arts 4%. **Special Study Options:** Double major, liberal arts/career combination, study abroad, teacher certification program.

FACILITIES
Housing: Coed dorms, men's dorms, women's dorms, apartments for single students, special housing for disabled students, university owned housing. **Special Academic Facilities/Equipment:** Walton Fine arts Center, Stephens Gallery, Smith-Broyles Science Center, Walker Hall Teacher Education and Communications Center. **Computers:** 100% of public computers are PCs, network access in dorm rooms, remote student-access to Web through college's connection.

CAMPUS LIFE
Activities: Choral groups, drama/theater, literary magazine, music ensembles, radio station, student government, television station, yearbook. **Organizations:**

---

40 registered organizations, 5 honor societies, 6 religious organizations. **Athletics (Intercollegiate):** *Men:* Baseball, basketball, cheerleading, cross-country, soccer, tennis. *Women:* Basketball, cheerleading, cross-country, soccer, softball, tennis.

ADMISSIONS
Freshman Academic Profile: 23% in top 10% of high school class, 44% in top 25% of high school class, 77% in top 50% of high school class. 87% from public high schools. SAT Math middle 50% range 453–590. SAT Critical Reading middle 50% range 423–568. ACT middle 50% range 19–25. TOEFL required of all international applicants, minimum paper TOEFL 500, minimum computer TOEFL 173. **Basis for Candidate Selection:** *Very important factors considered include:* Rigor of secondary school record, standardized test scores. *Important factors considered include:* Class rank, interview. *Other factors considered include:* Alumni/ae relation, application essay, character/personal qualities, extracurricular activities, geographical residence, recommendation(s), talent/ability, volunteer work, work experience. **Freshman Admission Requirements:** High school diploma is required, and GED is accepted. *Academic units required:* 4 English, 4 math, 3 science (2 science labs), 2 foreign language, 1 social study, 2 history. *Academic units recommended:* 4 English, 4 math, 3 science (2 science labs), 2 foreign language, 1 social studies, 2 history. **Freshman Admission Statistics:** 670 applied, 84% admitted, 50% enrolled. **Transfer Admission Requirements:** College transcript(s). Minimum college GPA of 2.0 required. Lowest grade transferable C. **General Admission Information:** Application fee $10. Early decision application deadline 3/15. Regular notification rolling. Non-fall registration accepted. Common Application not accepted. Credit and/or placement offered for CEEB Advanced Placement tests.

COSTS AND FINANCIAL AID
Annual tuition $16,730. Room and board $5,725. Required fees $600. Average book expense $800. **Required Forms and Deadlines:** FAFSA, institution's own financial aid form. Financial aid filing deadline 2/15. **Notification of Awards:** Applicants will be notified of awards on or about 3/15. **Types of Aid:** *Need-based scholarships/grants:* Pell, SEOG, state scholarships/grants, private scholarships, the school's own gift aid. *Loans:* FFEL Subsidized Stafford, FFEL Unsubsidized Stafford, FFEL PLUS, Federal Perkins, college/university loans from institutional funds. **Financial Aid Statistics:** 59% freshmen, 51% undergrads receive need-based scholarship or grant aid. 43% freshmen, 39% undergrads receive need-based self-help aid. Highest amount earned per year from on-campus jobs $1,878.

UNIVERSITY OF THE PACIFIC

Best 368

3601 Pacific Avenue, Stockton, CA 95211
Phone: 209-946-2211 **E-mail:** admissions@pacific.edu **CEEB Code:** 4065
Fax: 209-946-2413 **Website:** www.pacific.edu **ACT Code:** 0240
Financial Aid Phone: 209-946-2421

This private school was founded in 1851. It has a 175-acre campus.

RATINGS
Admissions Selectivity Rating: 88　　　**Fire Safety Rating:** 88　　　**Green Rating:** 60*

STUDENTS AND FACULTY
Enrollment: 3,535. **Student Body:** 56% female, 44% male, 13% out-of-state. **Retention and Graduation:** 83% freshmen return for sophomore year. 45% freshmen graduate within 4 years.

ACADEMICS
Degrees: Bachelor's, doctoral, first professional, master's. **Academic Requirements:** Arts/fine arts, English (including composition), foreign languages, humanities, mathematics, Pacific Seminars, sciences (biological or physical), social science. **Classes:** Most classes have fewer than 10 students. Most lab/discussion sections have 10–19 students. **Majors with Highest Enrollment:** Biology/biological sciences, business administration/management, engineering. **Special Study Options:** Accelerated program, cooperative education program, double major, dual enrollment, English as a second language (ESL), environmental science, ethnic studies, exchange student program (domestic), gender studies, honors program, independent study, internships, liberal arts/career combination, minors, practicum, service learning,

student-designed major, study abroad, teacher certification, thematic minors, undergraduate research.

FACILITIES

Housing: Coed dorms, apartments for married students, apartments for single students, fraternity/sorority housing. **Special Academic Facilities/Equipment:** John Muir Collection, Dave & Iola Brubeck Collection, Brubeck Institute for Jazz Studies, Reynolds Art Gallery. **Computers:** 5% of classrooms are wired, 75% of classrooms are wireless, 90% of public computers are PCs, 9% of public computers are Macs, 1% of public computers are UNIX, network access in dorm rooms, network access in dorm lounges, online registration, online administrative functions (other than registration), remote student-access to Web through college's connection.

CAMPUS LIFE

Activities: Choral groups, concert band, dance, drama/theater, jazz band, literary magazine, music ensembles, musical theater, opera, pep band, radio station, student government, student newspaper, student-run film society, symphony orchestra, yearbook. **Organizations:** 100 registered organizations, 19 honor societies, 7 religious organizations. 8 fraternities (15% men join), 7 sororities (17% women join). **Athletics (Intercollegiate):** *Men:* Baseball, basketball, golf, swimming, tennis, volleyball, water polo. *Women:* Basketball, cross-country, field hockey, soccer, softball, swimming, tennis, volleyball, water polo.

ADMISSIONS

Freshman Academic Profile: 42% in top 10% of high school class, 72% in top 25% of high school class, 93% in top 50% of high school class. 82% from public high schools. SAT Math middle 50% range 543–670. SAT Critical Reading middle 50% range 510–630. SAT Writing middle 50% range 510–630. ACT middle 50% range 23–28. TOEFL required of all international applicants, minimum paper TOEFL 475, minimum computer TOEFL 150. **Basis for Candidate Selection:** *Very important factors considered include:* Rigor of secondary school record. *Important factors considered include:* Academic GPA, application essay, extracurricular activities, first generation, recommendation(s), standardized test scores. *Other factors considered include:* Alumni/ae relation, character/personal qualities, class rank, geographical residence, level of applicant's interest, racial/ethnic status, talent/ability, volunteer work, work experience. **Freshman Admission Requirements:** High school diploma is required, and GED is accepted. *Academic units recommended:* 4 English, 3 math, 2 science lab, 2 foreign language, 3 social studies, 3 academic electives, 1 fine art/performing art. **Freshman Admission Statistics:** 4,976 applied, 69% admitted, 25% enrolled. **Transfer Admission Requirements:** College transcript(s), essay or personal statement. Minimum college GPA of 2.8 required. Lowest grade transferable C. **General Admission Information:** Application fee $60. Regular notification 3/15. Non-fall registration accepted. Admission may be deferred for a maximum of 2 semesters. Credit and/or placement offered for CEEB Advanced Placement tests.

COSTS AND FINANCIAL AID

Annual tuition $28,480. Room and board $9,210. Required fees $500. Average book expense $1,386. **Required Forms and Deadlines:** FAFSA. Financial aid filing deadline 2/15. **Notification of Awards:** Applicants will be notified of awards on a rolling basis beginning on or about 3/15. **Types of Aid:** *Need-based scholarships/grants:* Pell, SEOG, state scholarships/grants, private scholarships, the school's own gift aid. *Loans:* Direct Subsidized Stafford, Direct Unsubsidized Stafford, Direct PLUS, FFEL Subsidized Stafford, FFEL Unsubsidized Stafford, FFEL PLUS, Federal Perkins, Direct Graduate/Professional PLUS Loans. **Financial Aid Statistics:** 63% freshmen, 63% undergrads receive need-based scholarship or grant aid. 59% freshmen, 60% undergrads receive need-based self-help aid. 29 freshmen, 134 undergrads receive athletic scholarships. 65% freshmen, 65% undergrads receive any aid.

UNIVERSITY OF PENNSYLVANIA

1 College Hall, Philadelphia, PA 19104
Phone: 215-898-7507 **E-mail:** info@admissions.ugao.upenn.edu **CEEB Code:** 2926
Fax: 215-898-9670 **Website:** www.upenn.edu **ACT Code:** 3732
Financial Aid Phone: 215-898-1988

This private school was founded in 1740. It has a 269-acre campus.

RATINGS

Admissions Selectivity Rating: 99   **Fire Safety Rating:** 71   **Green Rating:** 93

STUDENTS AND FACULTY

Enrollment: 9,730. **Student Body:** 50% female, 50% male, 80% out-of-state, 11% international (111 countries represented). African American 7%, Asian 17%, Caucasian 47%, Hispanic 6%. **Retention and Graduation:** 98% freshmen return for sophomore year. 87% freshmen graduate within 4 years. 20% grads go on to further study within 2 semesters. 5% grads pursue arts and sciences degrees. 1% grads pursue business degrees. 7% grads pursue law degrees. 5% grads pursue medical degrees. **Faculty:** Student/faculty ratio 7:1. 1078 full-time faculty, 100% hold PhDs. 100% faculty teach undergrads.

ACADEMICS

Degrees: Associate, bachelor's, doctoral, first professional certificate, first professional, master's, post-bachelor's certificate, post-master's certificate. **Academic Requirements:** English (including composition), foreign languages, history, humanities, mathematics, sciences (biological or physical), social science. **Classes:** Most classes have 10–19 students. **Majors with Highest Enrollment:** Business administration and management, finance, nursing/registered nurse training (ASN, BSN, MSN, RN). **Disciplines with Highest Percentage of Degrees Awarded:** Business/marketing 25%, social sciences 19%, engineering 7%, history 7%, health professions and related sciences 5%. **Special Study Options:** Accelerated program, cross registration, distance learning, double major, dual enrollment, English as a second language (ESL), exchange student program (domestic), honors program, independent study, internships, liberal arts/career combination, joint degree programs among schools, preprofessional programs (in predentistry, prelaw, premedicine, and preveterinary studies), student-designed major, study abroad, teacher certification program, Washington semester.

FACILITIES

Housing: Coed dorms, apartments for married students, apartments for single students, special housing for disabled students, fraternity/sorority housing, private off-campus. **Special Academic Facilities/Equipment:** Art gallery, anthropology museum, institute for contemporary art, language lab, large animal research center, primate research center, arboretum, observatory, wind tunnel, electron microscope. **Computers:** 50% of classrooms are wireless, 95% of public computers are PCs, 5% of public computers are Macs, network access in dorm rooms, network access in dorm lounges, online registration, online administrative functions (other than registration), support for handheld computing, remote student-access to Web through college's connection.

CAMPUS LIFE

Activities: Choral groups, concert band, dance, drama/theater, jazz band, literary magazine, marching band, music ensembles, musical theater, opera, pep band, radio station, student government, student newspaper, student-run film society, symphony orchestra, television station. **Organizations:** 365 registered organizations, 9 honor societies, 25 religious organizations. 33 fraternities (30% men join), 12 sororities (26% women join). **Athletics (Intercollegiate):** *Men:* Baseball, basketball, crew/rowing, cross-country, diving, fencing, football, golf, lacrosse, light weight football, soccer, squash, swimming, tennis, track/field (indoor), track/field (outdoor), wrestling. *Women:* Basketball, crew/rowing, cross-country, diving, fencing, field hockey, golf, gymnastics, lacrosse, soccer, softball, squash, swimming, tennis, track/field (indoor), track/field (outdoor), volleyball. **Environmental Initiatives:** 30% (112000 MWH) purchase annually of wind-generated electricity. Ongoing activity of the Environmental Sustainability Advisory Committee. $150,000 annual average investment in upgrading old campus buildings.

ADMISSIONS

Freshman Academic Profile: 94% in top 10% of high school class, 99% in top 25% of high school class, 100% in top 50% of high school class. 52% from public high schools. SAT Math middle 50% range 680–770. SAT Critical

Reading middle 50% range 650–740. SAT Writing middle 50% range 650–740. ACT middle 50% range 29–33. TOEFL required of all international applicants, minimum paper TOEFL 600, minimum computer TOEFL 250. **Basis for Candidate Selection:** *Very important factors considered include:* Academic GPA, character/personal qualities, recommendation(s), rigor of secondary school record, talent/ability. *Important factors considered include:* Application essay, extracurricular activities, first generation, standardized test scores. *Other factors considered include:* Alumni/ae relation, class rank, geographical residence, interview, level of applicant's interest, racial/ethnic status, volunteer work, work experience. **Freshman Admission Requirements:** High school diploma or equivalent is not required. *Academic units recommended:* 4 English, 4 math, 4 science, 4 foreign language, 2 social studies, 2 history. **Freshman Admission Statistics:** 20,483 applied, 18% admitted, 66% enrolled. **Transfer Admission Requirements:** High school transcript, college transcript(s), essay or personal statement, standardized test score, statement of good standing from prior institution(s). Lowest grade transferable C. **General Admission Information:** Application fee $70. Early decision application deadline 11/1. Regular application deadline 1/1. Regular notification 4/1. Non-fall registration not accepted. Admission may be deferred for a maximum of 2 semesters. Credit and/or placement offered for CEEB Advanced Placement tests.

COSTS AND FINANCIAL AID
Annual tuition $30,598. Room and board $10,621. Required fees $3,925. Average book expense $1,043. **Required Forms and Deadlines:** FAFSA, institution's own financial aid form, CSS/Financial Aid PROFILE, Noncustodial PROFILE, Business/Farm Supplement, parents' and students' most recently completed income tax. Financial aid filing deadline 2/1. **Notification of Awards:** Applicants will be notified of awards on or about 4/1. **Types of Aid:** *Need-based scholarships/grants:* Pell, SEOG, state scholarships/grants, private scholarships, the school's own gift aid. *Loans:* FFEL Subsidized Stafford, FFEL Unsubsidized Stafford, FFEL PLUS, Federal Perkins, Federal Nursing, college/university loans from institutional funds, supplemental 3rd party loans guaranteed by institution. **Financial Aid Statistics:** 40% freshmen, 41% undergrads receive need-based scholarship or grant aid. 44% freshmen, 44% undergrads receive need-based self-help aid. 62% freshmen, 55% undergrads receive any aid.

UNIVERSITY OF PHOENIX

Mail Stop AA-K101, 4615 East Elwood Street Phoenix, AZ 85040-1958
Phone: 480-317-6000
Fax: 480-594-1758 **Website:** www.uopxonline.com
Financial Aid Phone: 480-557-1405

This private school was founded in 1976.

RATINGS
Admissions Selectivity Rating: 60*   **Fire Safety Rating:** 60*   **Green Rating:** 60*

STUDENTS AND FACULTY
Enrollment: 112,739. **Student Body:** 64% female, 36% male, 6% international. African American 9%, Asian 2%, Caucasian 33%, Hispanic 4%. **Faculty:** Student/faculty ratio 13:1. 594 full-time faculty, 9% hold PhDs.

ACADEMICS
Degrees: Associate, bachelor's, certificate, doctoral, master's, post-bachelor's certificate, post-master's certificate. **Academic Requirements:** Computer literacy, English (including composition), humanities, mathematics, sciences (biological or physical), social science. **Majors with Highest Enrollment:** Business administration/management, computer and information sciences, management information systems. **Disciplines with Highest Percentage of Degrees Awarded:** Business/marketing 60%, computer and information sciences 20%, health professions and related sciences 15%, interdisciplinary studies 1%. **Special Study Options:** Accelerated program, distance learning, double major, dual enrollment, English as a second language (ESL), independent study, teacher certification program, weekend college.

FACILITIES
Computers: Online registration, online administrative functions (other than registration).

CAMPUS LIFE
Organizations: 2 honor societies.

ADMISSIONS
Freshman Academic Profile: TOEFL required of all international applicants, minimum paper TOEFL 550, minimum computer TOEFL 213. **Basis for**

Candidate Selection: *Important factors considered include:* Level of applicant's interest, work experience. **Freshman Admission Requirements:** High school diploma is required, and GED is accepted. **Freshman Admission Statistics:** 29,452 applied, 100% admitted, 34% enrolled. **Transfer Admission Requirements:** College transcript(s). Lowest grade transferable C-. **General Admission Information:** Application fee $45. Non-fall registration accepted.

COSTS AND FINANCIAL AID
Required Forms and Deadlines: FAFSA, institution's own financial aid form. **Types of Aid:** *Need-based scholarships/grants:* Pell, SEOG. *Loans:* FFEL Subsidized Stafford, FFEL Unsubsidized Stafford, FFEL PLUS, Federal Perkins. **Student Employment:** Institutional employment available.

UNIVERSITY OF PITTSBURGH—BRADFORD

Office of Admissions, Hanley Library, 300 Campus Drive, Bradford, PA 16701
Phone: 814-362-7555 **E-mail:** admissions@upb.pitt.edu **CEEB Code:** 2935
Fax: 814-362-5150 **Website:** www.upb.pitt.edu **ACT Code:** 3731
Financial Aid Phone: 814-362-7550

This public school was founded in 1963. It has a 317-acre campus.

RATINGS
Admissions Selectivity Rating: 71   **Fire Safety Rating:** 80   **Green Rating:** 77

STUDENTS AND FACULTY
Enrollment: 1,269. **Student Body:** 56% female, 44% male, 14% out-of-state. African American 3%, Asian 1%, Caucasian 84%, Hispanic 1%. **Retention and Graduation:** 63% freshmen return for sophomore year. 35% freshmen graduate within 4 years. 20% grads go on to further study within 2 semesters. 9% grads pursue arts and sciences degrees. 1% grads pursue business degrees. 5% grads pursue law degrees. 5% grads pursue medical degrees. **Faculty:** Student/faculty ratio 13:1. 71 full-time faculty, 62% hold PhDs. 100% faculty teach undergrads.

ACADEMICS
Degrees: Associate, bachelor's. **Academic Requirements:** Arts/fine arts, computer literacy, English (including composition), history, humanities, mathematics, philosophy, sciences (biological or physical), social science. **Classes:** Most classes have 10–19 students. Most lab/discussion sections have 10–19 students. **Majors with Highest Enrollment:** Business administration/management, criminal justice/law enforcement administration, nursing/registered nurse training (ASN, BSN, MSN, RN). **Disciplines with Highest Percentage of Degrees Awarded:** Business/marketing 27%, health professions and related sciences 16%, social sciences 14%, security and protective services 10%, English 8%. **Special Study Options:** Cross registration, distance learning, double major, dual enrollment, external degree program, independent study, internships, study abroad, teacher certification program.

FACILITIES
Housing: Apartments for single students, special housing for disabled students. **Computers:** 91% of classrooms are wired, 100% of classrooms are wireless, 87% of public computers are PCs, 13% of public computers are Macs, network access in dorm rooms, online administrative functions (other than registration), remote student-access to Web through college's connection.

CAMPUS LIFE
Activities: Choral groups, dance, drama/theater, literary magazine, radio station, student government, student newspaper. **Organizations:** 50 registered organizations, 9 honor societies, 1 religious organization. 3 fraternities, 3 sororities. **Athletics (Intercollegiate):** *Men:* Baseball, basketball, cross-country, golf, soccer. *Women:* Basketball, cross-country, golf, soccer, softball, volleyball. **Environmental Initiatives:** Development of an Alternative Energy Institute.

ADMISSIONS
Freshman Academic Profile: 9% in top 10% of high school class, 29% in top 25% of high school class, 68% in top 50% of high school class. SAT Math middle 50% range 440–560. SAT Critical Reading middle 50% range 420–530. SAT Writing middle 50% range 430–510. ACT middle 50% range 17–22. TOEFL required of all international applicants, minimum paper TOEFL 550, minimum computer TOEFL 213. **Basis for Candidate Selection:** *Very important factors considered include:* Level of applicant's interest. *Important factors considered include:* Academic GPA, interview, rigor of secondary school record, standardized test scores. *Other factors considered include:* Alumni/ae relation, application essay, character/personal qualities, class rank, extracurricular

activities, recommendation(s), talent/ability, volunteer work, work experience. **Freshman Admission Requirements:** High school diploma is required, and GED is accepted. *Academic units required:* 4 English, 2 math, 1 science (1 science lab), 2 foreign language, 1 history, 5 academic electives. *Academic units recommended:* 4 English, 2 math, 2 science (2 science labs), 2 foreign language, 1 history, 5 academic electives. **Freshman Admission Statistics:** 834 applied, 79% admitted, 51% enrolled. **Transfer Admission Requirements:** College transcript(s), statement of good standing from prior institution(s). Minimum college GPA of 2.0 required. Lowest grade transferable C-. **General Admission Information:** Application fee $35. Regular notification is rolling. Non-fall registration accepted. Admission may be deferred for a maximum of 2 semesters. Credit and/or placement offered for CEEB Advanced Placement tests.

COSTS AND FINANCIAL AID

Annual in-state tuition $10,590. Annual out-of-state tuition $20,170. Room and board $6,850. Required fees $710. Average book expense $1,000. **Required Forms and Deadlines:** FAFSA. Financial aid filing deadline 3/1. **Notification of Awards:** Applicants will be notified of awards on a rolling basis beginning on or about 4/1. **Types of Aid:** *Need-based scholarships/grants:* Pell, SEOG, state scholarships/grants, private scholarships, the school's own gift aid. *Loans:* FFEL Subsidized Stafford, FFEL Unsubsidized Stafford, FFEL PLUS, Federal Perkins. **Student Employment:** Federal Work-Study Program available. Institutional employment available. Off-campus job opportunities are fair. **Financial Aid Statistics:** 58% freshmen, 59% undergrads receive need-based scholarship or grant aid. 68% freshmen, 75% undergrads receive need-based self-help aid. 76% freshmen, 82% undergrads receive any aid. Highest amount earned per year from on-campus jobs $6,864.

UNIVERSITY OF PITTSBURGH—GREENSBURG

150 Finoli Drive, Greensburg, PA 15601
Phone: 724-836-9880 **E-mail:** upgadmit@pitt.edu **CEEB Code:** 2936
Fax: 724-836-7160 **Website:** www.upg.pitt.edu **ACT Code:** 3733
Financial Aid Phone: 724-836-9881

This public school was founded in 1963. It has a 217-acre campus.

RATINGS

Admissions Selectivity Rating: 72   **Fire Safety Rating:** 60*   **Green Rating:** 60*

STUDENTS AND FACULTY

Enrollment: 1,697. **Student Body:** 51% female, 49% male, 1% out-of-state. African American 3%, Asian 2%, Caucasian 93%. **Retention and Graduation:** 71% freshmen return for sophomore year. 50% freshmen graduate within 4 years. 21% grads go on to further study within 2 semesters. 15% grads pursue arts and sciences degrees. 4% grads pursue business degrees. 1% grads pursue law degrees. 1% grads pursue medical degrees. **Faculty:** Student/faculty ratio 19:1. 72 full-time faculty, 88% hold PhDs. 100% faculty teach undergrads.

ACADEMICS

Degrees: Bachelor's, certificate. **Academic Requirements:** Arts/fine arts, computer literacy, English (including composition), foreign languages, history, humanities, mathematics, philosophy, sciences (biological or physical), social science. **Classes:** Most classes have 20–29 students. Most lab/discussion sections have 10–19 students. **Majors with Highest Enrollment:** Criminal justice/law enforcement administration, management information systems, psychology. **Disciplines with Highest Percentage of Degrees Awarded:** Business/marketing 29%, psychology 19%, English 16%, security and protective services 10%, biological/life sciences 8%. **Special Study Options:** Cross registration, double major, dual enrollment, exchange student program (domestic), independent study, internships, liberal arts/career combination, student-designed major, study abroad.

FACILITIES

Housing: Coed dorms. **Computers:** 5% of classrooms are wired, 20% of classrooms are wireless, 99% of public computers are PCs, 1% of public computers are Macs, network access in dorm rooms, online administrative functions (other than registration), remote student-access to Web through college's connection.

CAMPUS LIFE

Activities: Choral groups, dance, drama/theater, literary magazine, musical theater, radio station, student government, student newspaper. **Organizations:** 25 registered organizations, 8 honor societies, 3 religious organizations. **Athletics (Intercollegiate):** *Men:* Baseball, basketball, cross-country, golf, soccer, tennis. *Women:* Basketball, cross-country, golf, soccer, softball, volleyball.

ADMISSIONS

Freshman Academic Profile: 7% in top 10% of high school class, 30% in top 25% of high school class, 77% in top 50% of high school class. 95% from public high schools. SAT Math middle 50% range 480–600. SAT Critical Reading middle 50% range 490–560. SAT Writing middle 50% range 450–510. ACT middle 50% range 20–23. TOEFL required of all international applicants, minimum paper TOEFL 550, minimum computer TOEFL 213. **Basis for Candidate Selection:** *Very important factors considered include:* Academic GPA, rigor of secondary school record. *Important factors considered include:* Class rank, standardized test scores. *Other factors considered include:* Application essay, character/personal qualities, extracurricular activities, interview, level of applicant's interest, recommendation(s), talent/ability, volunteer work. **Freshman Admission Requirements:** High school diploma is required, and GED is accepted. *Academic units required:* 4 English, 2 math, 1 science, 2 social studies, 2 history, 3 academic electives. *Academic units recommended:* 4 English, 4 math, 2 science (2 science labs), 3 foreign language, 2 social studies, 2 history, 1 academic elective. **Freshman Admission Statistics:** 1,156 applied, 80% admitted, 47% enrolled. **Transfer Admission Requirements:** High school transcript, college transcript(s), statement of good standing from prior institution(s). Minimum college GPA of 2.0 required. Lowest grade transferable C. **General Admission Information:** Application fee $45. Regular notification is rolling. Non-fall registration accepted. Admission may be deferred for a maximum of 2 semesters. Credit and/or placement offered for CEEB Advanced Placement tests.

COSTS AND FINANCIAL AID

Annual in-state tuition $9,966. Out-of-state tuition $19,570. Room & board $6,680. Required fees $714. Average book expense $1,000. **Required Forms and Deadlines:** FAFSA, institution's own financial aid form. Financial aid filing deadline 3/1. **Notification of Awards:** Applicants will be notified of awards on a rolling basis beginning on or about 4/1. **Types of Aid:** *Need-based scholarships/grants:* Pell, SEOG, state scholarships/grants, private scholarships, the school's own gift aid, United Negro College Fund. *Loans:* FFEL Subsidized Stafford, FFEL Unsubsidized Stafford, FFEL PLUS, Federal Perkins. **Student Employment:** Federal Work-Study Program available. Institutional employment available. Off-campus job opportunities are excellent. **Financial Aid Statistics:** 53% freshmen, 49% undergrads receive need-based scholarship or grant aid. 79% freshmen, 70% undergrads receive need-based self-help aid. 75% freshmen, 85% undergrads receive any aid. Highest amount earned per year from on-campus jobs $2,400.

UNIVERSITY OF PITTSBURGH—JOHNSTOWN

157 Blackington Hall, 450 Schoolhouse Road, Johnstown, PA 15904
Phone: 814-269-7050 **E-mail:** upjadmit@pitt.edu **CEEB Code:** 2934
Fax: 814-269-7044 **Website:** www.upj.pitt.edu
Financial Aid Phone: 814-269-7045

This public school was founded in 1927. It has a 650-acre campus.

RATINGS

Admissions Selectivity Rating: 71   **Fire Safety Rating:** 60*   **Green Rating:** 60*

STUDENTS AND FACULTY

Enrollment: 3,142. **Student Body:** 48% female, 52% male, 1% out-of-state. African American 2%, Asian 1%, Caucasian 92%. **Retention and Graduation:** 8% grads pursue arts and sciences degrees. 1% grads pursue business degrees. 1% grads pursue law degrees. 2% grads pursue medical degrees. **Faculty:** 100% faculty teach undergrads.

ACADEMICS

Degrees: Associate, bachelor's, certificate. **Academic Requirements:** English (including composition), history, humanities, mathematics, sciences (biological or physical), social science. **Classes:** Most classes have 20–29 students. Most lab/discussion sections have 10–19 students. **Disciplines with Highest Percentage of Degrees Awarded:** Business/marketing 29%, education 17%, engineering 12%, social sciences 9%, communications/journalism 6%. **Special Study Options:** Accelerated program, cooperative education program, cross registration, distance learning, double major, dual enrollment, independent study, internships, liberal arts/career combination, student-designed major, study abroad, teacher certification program.

FACILITIES

Housing: Coed dorms, apartments for single students, town houses, lodges, single-sex residence upon request. **Special Academic Facilities/Equipment:** Art museum, performing arts center, language lab. **Computers:** Network access in dorm rooms, online administrative functions (other than registration), remote student-access to Web through college's connection.

CAMPUS LIFE

Activities: Choral groups, concert band, dance, drama/theater, literary magazine, music ensembles, musical theater, radio station, student government, student newspaper, television station, yearbook. **Organizations:** 70 registered organizations, 11 honor societies, 3 religious organizations. 4 fraternities (6% men join), 3 sororities (5% women join). **Athletics (Intercollegiate):** *Men:* Baseball, basketball, golf, soccer, wrestling. *Women:* Basketball, cheerleading, cross-country, golf, soccer, track/field (outdoor), volleyball.

ADMISSIONS

Freshman Academic Profile: 10% in top 10% of high school class, 31% in top 25% of high school class, 68% in top 50% of high school class. SAT Math middle 50% range 470–560. SAT Critical Reading middle 50% range 450–540. SAT Writing middle 50% range 460–540. ACT middle 50% range 18–22. TOEFL required of all international applicants, minimum paper TOEFL 550, minimum computer TOEFL 213. **Basis for Candidate Selection:** *Very important factors considered include:* Academic GPA, class rank, rigor of secondary school record. *Important factors considered include:* Interview, standardized test scores. *Other factors considered include:* Application essay, character/personal qualities, extracurricular activities, level of applicant's interest, racial/ethnic status, recommendation(s), talent/ability, volunteer work, work experience. **Freshman Admission Requirements:** High school diploma is required, and GED is accepted. *Academic units required:* 4 English, 2 math, 2 science (1 science lab), 2 foreign language, 4 social studies. *Academic units recommended:* 3 math, 2 science lab. **Freshman Admission Statistics:** 2,188 applied, 93% admitted, 40% enrolled. **Transfer Admission Requirements:** High school transcript, college transcript(s), standardized test score. Minimum college GPA of 2.0 required. Lowest grade transferable C. **General Admission Information:** Application fee $45. Regular notification is rolling. Non-fall registration accepted. Admission may be deferred for a maximum of 2 semesters. Credit and/or placement offered for CEEB Advanced Placement tests.

COSTS AND FINANCIAL AID

Required Forms and Deadlines: FAFSA. Financial aid filing deadline 4/1. **Notification of Awards:** Applicants will be notified of awards on a rolling basis beginning on or about 3/15. **Types of Aid:** *Need-based scholarships/grants:* Pell, SEOG, state scholarships/grants, private scholarships, the school's own gift aid, Federal Nursing Scholarships. *Loans:* FFEL Subsidized Stafford, FFEL Unsubsidized Stafford, FFEL PLUS, Federal Perkins. **Student Employment:** Federal Work-Study Program available. Institutional employment available. Off-campus job opportunities are good. **Financial Aid Statistics:** 59% freshmen, 65% undergrads receive need-based scholarship or grant aid. 53% freshmen, 69% undergrads receive need-based self-help aid. 11 freshmen, 66 undergrads receive athletic scholarships. 80% freshmen, 77% undergrads receive any aid.

UNIVERSITY OF PITTSBURGH—
PITTSBURGH CAMPUS

Best 368

4227 Fifth Avenue, First Floor Alumni Hall, Pittsburgh, PA 15260
Phone: 412-624-7488 **E-mail:** oafa@pitt.edu **CEEB Code:** 2927
Fax: 412-648-8815 **Website:** www.pitt.edu **ACT Code:** 3734
Financial Aid Phone: 412-624-7488

This public school was founded in 1787. It has a 132-acre campus.

RATINGS
Admissions Selectivity Rating: 89   **Fire Safety Rating:** 85   **Green Rating:** 78

STUDENTS AND FACULTY
Enrollment: 16,796. **Student Body:** 51% female, 49% male, 15% out-of-state. African American 9%, Asian 4%, Caucasian 81%, Hispanic 1%. **Retention and Graduation:** 89% freshmen return for sophomore year. 52% freshmen graduate within 4 years. 36% grads go on to further study within 2 semesters. 5% grads pursue arts and sciences degrees. 3% grads pursue business degrees. 4% grads pursue law degrees. 4% grads pursue medical degrees. **Faculty:** Student/faculty ratio 16:1. 1,574 full-time faculty, 92% hold PhDs.

ACADEMICS

Degrees: Bachelor's, certificate, doctoral, first professional, master's, post-bachelor's certificate, post-master's certificate. **Academic Requirements:** Arts/fine arts, English (including composition), foreign languages, history, humanities, mathematics, philosophy, sciences (biological or physical), social science. **Classes:** Most classes have 10–19 students. Most lab/discussion sections have 20–29 students. **Majors with Highest Enrollment:** Marketing/marketing management, psychology, speech and rhetorical studies. **Disciplines with Highest Percentage of Degrees Awarded:** Business/marketing 14%, English 12%, health professions and related sciences 11%, social sciences 11%, psychology 10%. **Special Study Options:** Accelerated program, cooperative education program, cross registration, distance learning, double major, dual enrollment, English as a second language (ESL), exchange student program (domestic), external degree program, honors program, independent study, internships, liberal arts/career combination, student-designed major, study abroad, teacher certification program, weekend college.

FACILITIES

Housing: Coed dorms, women's dorms, apartments for single students, fraternity/sorority housing, special living communities (alcohol free, quiet living communities, engineering living learning community, college of business community, undergraduate nursing). **Special Academic Facilities/Equipment:** Stephen Foster Memorial, observatory. **Computers:** 20% of classrooms are wired, 10% of classrooms are wireless, 90% of public computers are PCs, 9% of public computers are Macs, 1% of public computers are UNIX, network access in dorm rooms, online administrative functions (other than registration), support for handheld computing, remote student-access to Web through college's connection.

CAMPUS LIFE

Activities: Choral groups, concert band, dance, drama/theater, jazz band, literary magazine, marching band, music ensembles, pep band, radio station, student government, student newspaper, student-run film society, symphony orchestra, television station, yearbook. **Organizations:** 450 registered organizations, 17 honor societies, 16 fraternities (9% men join), 11 sororities (9% women join). **Athletics (Intercollegiate):** *Men:* Baseball, basketball, cross-country, diving, football, soccer, swimming, track/field (outdoor), wrestling. *Women:* Basketball, cross-country, diving, gymnastics, soccer, softball, swimming, tennis, track/field (outdoor), volleyball. **Environmental Initiatives:** The University recently constructed and is now commissioning a new steam plant which will ultimately house six 100,000 pound per hour national gas fired boilers. The University has incorporated many sustainable design standards into its Professional Design Manual. This manual applies standards to all renovation and construction projects including energy efficient control schemes, energy efficient standard lighting, carpet with a minimum of 25% recycled content, and carpet adhesives containing no volatile organic compounds (VOC's).

ADMISSIONS

Freshman Academic Profile: 43% in top 10% of high school class, 80% in top 25% of high school class, 98% in top 50% of high school class. SAT Math middle 50% range 580–670. SAT Critical Reading middle 50% range 570–670. ACT middle 50% range 24–30. TOEFL required of all international applicants, minimum paper TOEFL 550, minimum computer TOEFL 213. **Basis for Candidate Selection:** *Very important factors considered include:* Academic GPA, rigor of secondary school record. *Important factors considered include:* Class rank, level of applicant's interest, standardized test scores. *Other factors considered include:* Application essay, character/personal qualities, extracurricular activities, first generation, interview, racial/ethnic status, recommendation(s), talent/ability, volunteer work, work experience. **Freshman Admission Requirements:** High school diploma is required, and GED is not accepted. *Academic units required:* 4 English, 3 math, 3 science (3 science labs), 1 foreign language, 1 social studies, 4 academic electives. *Academic units recommended:* 4 math, 4 science, 3 foreign language, 3 social studies, 2 history. **Freshman Admission Statistics:** 18,195 applied, 56% admitted, 34% enrolled. **Transfer Admission Requirements:** College transcript(s). Lowest grade transferable C. **General Admission Information:** Application fee $35. Regular notification is rolling. Non-fall registration accepted. Admission may be deferred for a maximum of 2 semesters. Credit offered for CEEB Advanced Placement tests.

COSTS AND FINANCIAL AID

Annual in-state tuition $11,368. Out-of-state tuition $20,686. Room & board $7,800. Average book expense $1,000. **Required Forms and Deadlines:** FAFSA, institution's own financial aid form. Financial aid filing deadline 3/1. **Notification of Awards:** Applicants will be notified of awards on a rolling basis beginning on or about 3/15. **Types of Aid:** *Need-based scholarships/grants:* Pell, SEOG, state scholarships/grants, private scholarships, the school's own gift aid. *Loans:* FFEL Subsidized Stafford, FFEL Unsubsidized Stafford, FFEL PLUS, Federal Perkins, Federal Nursing, college/university loans from institutional funds. **Student Employment:** Federal Work-Study Program available. Off-campus job opportunities are excellent. **Financial Aid Statistics:** 35% freshmen, 34% undergrads receive need-based scholarship or grant aid. 40% freshmen, 44% undergrads receive need-based self-help aid. 63 freshmen, 358 undergrads receive athletic scholarships.

UNIVERSITY OF PORTLAND

5000 North Willamette Boulevard, Portland, OR 97203-7147
Phone: 503-943-7147 **E-mail:** admissions@up.edu **CEEB Code:** 4847
Fax: 503-943-7315 **Website:** www.up.edu **ACT Code:** 3500
Financial Aid Phone: 503-943-7311

This private school, affiliated with the Roman Catholic Church, was founded in 1901. It has a 130-acre campus.

RATINGS
Admissions Selectivity Rating: 92 **Fire Safety Rating:** 60* **Green Rating:** 88

STUDENTS AND FACULTY
Enrollment: 2,849. **Student Body:** 63% female, 37% male, 58% out-of-state, 1% international (33 countries represented). African American 2%, Asian 10%, Caucasian 75%, Hispanic 4%. **Retention and Graduation:** 86% freshmen return for sophomore year. 58% freshmen graduate within 4 years. 25% grads go on to further study within 1 year. **Faculty:** Student/faculty ratio 12:1. 195 full-time faculty, 89% hold PhDs. 100% faculty teach undergrads.

ACADEMICS
Degrees: Bachelor's, master's, post-master's certificate. **Academic Requirements:** Arts/fine arts, English (including composition), history, mathematics, philosophy, sciences (biological or physical), social science, theology. **Classes:** Most classes have 20–29 students. Most lab/discussion sections have 10–19 students. **Majors with Highest Enrollment:** Business administration/management, engineering, nursing/registered nurse training (RN, ASN, BSN, MSN). **Disciplines with Highest Percentage of Degrees Awarded:** Health professions and related sciences 22%, business/marketing 13%, engineering 11%, biological/life sciences 9%, communications/journalism 9%. **Special Study Options:** Cross-registration, double major, honor program, independent study, internships, liberal arts/career combination, study abroad, teacher certification program.

FACILITIES
Housing: Coed dorms, men's dorms, women's dorms, rental housing. **Special Academic Facilities/Equipment:** Art gallery, observatory. **Computers:** 80% of public computers are PCs, 20% of public computers are Macs, network access in dorm rooms, network access in dorm lounges, online registration, online administrative functions (other than registration), remote student-access to Web through college's connection.

CAMPUS LIFE
Activities: Choral groups, concert band, dance, drama/theater, jazz band, literary magazine, music ensembles, musical theater, pep band, radio station, student government, student newspaper, student-run film society, symphony orchestra, yearbook. **Organizations:** 40 registered organizations, 15 honor societies, 9 religious organizations. **Athletics (Intercollegiate):** *Men:* Baseball, basketball, cross-country, golf, soccer, tennis, track/field (outdoor). *Women:* Basketball, cross-country, golf, soccer, tennis, track/field (outdoor), volleyball.

ADMISSIONS
Freshman Academic Profile: 50% in top 10% of high school class, 81% in top 25% of high school class, 95% in top 50% of high school class. 60% from public high schools. SAT Math middle 50% range 540–640. SAT Critical Reading middle 50% range 530–640. TOEFL required of all international applicants, minimum paper TOEFL 550, minimum computer TOEFL 197. **Basis for Candidate Selection:** *Very important factors considered include:* Academic GPA, rigor of secondary school record, standardized test scores. *Important factors considered include:* Application essay, class rank, extracurricular activities, recommendation(s), talent/ability, volunteer work. *Other factors considered include:* Alumni/ae relation, character/personal qualities, first generation, geographical residence, interview, level of applicant's interest, racial/ethnic status, religious affiliation/commitment, work experience. **Freshman Admission Requirements:** High school diploma is required, and GED is accepted. *Academic units required:* 3 English, 2 math, 2 science, 2 social studies, 2 history, 7 academic electives. *Academic units recommended:* 4 English, 3 math, 2 science, 2 social studies, 2 history, 7 academic electives. **Freshman Admission Statistics:** 6,355 applied, 65% admitted, 18% enrolled. **Transfer Admission Requirements:** College transcript(s), essay or personal statement. Minimum college GPA of 2.5 required. Lowest grade transferable C. **General Admission Information:** Application fee $50. Regular application

deadline 6/1. Regular notification is rolling. Nonfall registration accepted. Admission may be deferred for a maximum of 1 year. Credit and/or placement offered for CEEB Advanced Placement tests.

COSTS AND FINANCIAL AID
Annual tuition $27,500. Room and board $8,300. Required fees $1,354. Average book expense $1,000. **Types of Aid:** *Loans:* College/university loans from institutional funds. **Financial Aid Statistics:** 63% freshmen, 59% undergrads receive any aid. Highest amount earned per year from on-campus jobs $1,300.

UNIVERSITY OF PRINCE EDWARD ISLAND

Office of the Registrar, Charlottetown, PE C1A 4P3 Canada
Phone: 902-566-0439 **E-mail:** registrar@upei.ca
Fax: 902-566-0795 **Website:** www.upei.ca
Financial Aid Phone: 902-566-0358

This public school was founded in 1969. It has a 130-acre campus.

RATINGS
Admissions Selectivity Rating: 60* **Fire Safety Rating:** 60* **Green Rating:** 60*

STUDENTS AND FACULTY
Student Body: 15% out-of-province. **Faculty:** Student/faculty ratio 12:1. 244 full-time faculty.

ACADEMICS
Degrees: Bachelor's, certificate, diploma, doctoral, first professional, master's. **Academic Requirements:** English (including composition). **Classes:** Most classes have 20–29 students. Most lab/discussion sections have fewer than 10 students. **Majors with Highest Enrollment:** Business administration/management, psychology. **Special Study Options:** Accelerated program, cooperative education program, distance learning, double major, English as a second language (ESL), exchange student program (domestic), honors program, internships, study abroad, teacher certification program.

FACILITIES
Housing: Coed dorms, men's dorms, women's dorms, apartments for single students, special housing for disabled students. **Computers:** 5% of classrooms are wireless, 100% of public computers are PCs, network access in dorm rooms, network access in dorm lounges, online registration, online administrative functions (other than registration), support for handheld computing, remote student-access to Web through college's connection.

CAMPUS LIFE
Activities: Choral groups, concert band, drama/theater, music ensembles, radio station, student government, student newspaper, yearbook. **Organizations:** 25 registered organizations, 3 religious organizations. **Athletics (Intercollegiate):** *Men:* Basketball, ice hockey, soccer. *Women:* Basketball, field hockey, ice hockey, rugby, soccer, volleyball.

ADMISSIONS
Freshman Academic Profile: 90% from public high schools. TOEFL required of all international applicants, minimum paper TOEFL 550, minimum computer TOEFL 213. **Basis for Candidate Selection:** *Very important factors considered include:* Academic GPA, rigor of secondary school record. *Important factors considered include:* Class rank, recommendation(s). *Other factors considered include:* Standardized test scores. **Freshman Admission Statistics:** 1,044 applied, 61% admitted, 91% enrolled. **Transfer Admission Requirements:** College transcript(s), statement of good standing from prior institution(s). **General Admission Information:** Application fee $50. Regular application deadline 8/1. Regular notification 8/31. Non-fall registration accepted. Admission may be deferred for a maximum of 1 semester. Neither credit nor placement offered for CEEB Advanced Placement tests.

COSTS AND FINANCIAL AID
Average book expense $500.

UNIVERSITY OF PUGET SOUND

Best 368

1500 North Warner Street, Tacoma, WA 98416-1062
Phone: 253-879-3211 **E-mail:** admission@ups.edu **CEEB Code:** 4067
Fax: 253-879-3993 **Website:** www.ups.edu **ACT Code:** 4450
Financial Aid Phone: 253-879-3214

This private school was founded in 1888. It has a 97-acre campus.

RATINGS
Admissions Selectivity Rating: 90   **Fire Safety Rating:** 75   **Green Rating:** 60*

STUDENTS AND FACULTY
Enrollment: 2,531. **Student Body:** 58% female, 42% male, 69% out-of-state. African American 3%, Asian 9%, Caucasian 75%, Hispanic 3%, Native American 1%. **Retention and Graduation:** 83% freshmen return for sophomore year. 68% freshmen graduate within 4 years. 34% grads go on to further study within 2 semesters. 11% grads pursue arts and sciences degrees. 1% grads pursue business degrees. 3% grads pursue law degrees. 3% grads pursue medical degrees. **Faculty:** Student/faculty ratio 11:1. 223 full-time faculty, 88% hold PhDs. 90% faculty teach undergrads.

ACADEMICS
Degrees: Bachelor's, first professional, master's, post-master's certificate. **Academic Requirements:** Arts/fine arts, English (including composition), Five Approaches to Knowing (fine arts, humanistic, mathematical, natural scientific, social scientific), foreign languages, history, humanities, interdisciplinary connections seminar, mathematics, philosophy, sciences (biological or physical), social science. **Classes:** Most classes have 10–19 students. Most lab/discussion sections have 10–19 students. **Majors with Highest Enrollment:** Business administration/management, English language and literature, psychology, **Disciplines with Highest Percentage of Degrees Awarded:** Social sciences 20%, business/marketing 18%, English 9%, psychology 9%, visual and performing arts 8%. **Special Study Options:** 2 semesters of study in Asia, 3-2 engineering program, business leadership program, cooperative education program, double major, honors program, independent study, internships, student-designed major, study abroad, teacher certification program.

FACILITIES
Housing: Coed dorms, women's dorms, special housing for disabled students, fraternity/sorority housing, small residential houses, theme floors in halls. **Special Academic Facilities/Equipment:** Art gallery, natural history museum, concert hall, transmission and scanning electron microscopes, spectrometers, exercise science lab, observatory, paleomagnetic and x-ray lab, physiology labs, and DNA sequencer. **Computers:** 90% of classrooms are wired, 5% of classrooms are wireless, 90% of public computers are PCs, 5% of public computers are Macs, 5% of public computers are UNIX, network access in dorm rooms, network access in dorm lounges, online registration, online administrative functions (other than registration), support for handheld computing, remote student-access to Web through college's connection.

CAMPUS LIFE
Activities: Choral groups, concert band, dance, drama/theater, jazz band, literary magazine, music ensembles, musical theater, opera, radio station, student government, student newspaper, student-run film society, symphony orchestra, yearbook. **Organizations:** 77 registered organizations, 2 honor societies, 12 religious organizations. 4 fraternities (20% men join), 4 sororities (18% women join). **Athletics (Intercollegiate):** *Men:* Baseball, basketball, crew/rowing, cross-country, football, golf, soccer, swimming, tennis, track/field (indoor), track/field (outdoor). *Women:* Basketball, crew/rowing, cross-country, golf, lacrosse, soccer, softball, swimming, tennis, track/field (indoor), track/field (outdoor), volleyball.

ADMISSIONS
Freshman Academic Profile: 39% in top 10% of high school class, 73% in top 25% of high school class, 98% in top 50% of high school class. 76% from public high schools. SAT Math middle 50% range 570–660. SAT Critical Reading middle 50% range 575–690. SAT Writing middle 50% range 550–660. ACT middle 50% range 25–29. TOEFL required of all international applicants, minimum paper TOEFL 550, minimum computer TOEFL 213. **Basis for Candidate Selection:** *Very important factors considered include:* Academic GPA, rigor of secondary school record, standardized test scores. *Important*

factors considered include: Alumni/ae relation, application essay, character/personal qualities, extracurricular activities, racial/ethnic status, recommendation(s), talent/ability. *Other factors considered include:* Class rank, first generation, interview, level of applicant's interest, volunteer work, work experience. **Freshman Admission Requirements:** High school diploma is required, and GED is accepted. *Academic units recommended:* 4 English, 4 math, 4 science (4 science labs), 3 foreign language, 3 social studies, 3 history, 1 fine/visual/performing art. **Freshman Admission Statistics:** 5,231 applied, 65% admitted, 20% enrolled. **Transfer Admission Requirements:** College transcript(s), essay or personal statement, statement of good standing from prior institution(s). Minimum college GPA of 2.0 required. Lowest grade transferable D. **General Admission Information:** Application fee $40. Early decision application deadline 11/15. Regular application deadline 2/1. Regular notification 4/1. Non-fall registration accepted. Admission may be deferred for a maximum of 2 semesters. Credit and/or placement offered for CEEB Advanced Placement tests.

COSTS AND FINANCIAL AID
Average book expense $800. **Required Forms and Deadlines:** FAFSA. Financial aid filing deadline 2/1. **Notification of Awards:** Applicants will be notified of awards on a rolling basis beginning on or about 3/15. **Types of Aid:** *Need-based scholarships/grants:* Pell, SEOG, state scholarships/grants, private scholarships, the school's own gift aid. *Loans:* FFEL Subsidized Stafford, FFEL Unsubsidized Stafford, FFEL PLUS, Federal Perkins. **Student Employment:** Federal Work-Study Program available. Institutional employment available. Off-campus job opportunities are excellent. **Financial Aid Statistics:** 56% freshmen, 58% undergrads receive need-based scholarship or grant aid. 44% freshmen, 48% undergrads receive need-based self-help aid. 88% freshmen, 90% undergrads receive any aid. Highest amount earned per year from on-campus jobs $2,650.

UNIVERSITY OF REDLANDS

Best 368

1200 East Colton Avenue, Redlands, CA 92373
Phone: 909-335-4074 **E-mail:** admissions@redlands.edu **CEEB Code:** 4848
Fax: 909-335-4089 **Website:** www.redlands.edu **ACT Code:** 464
Financial Aid Phone: 909-748-8047

This private school was founded in 1907. It has a 160-acre campus.

RATINGS
Admissions Selectivity Rating: 88   **Fire Safety Rating:** 77   **Green Rating:** 85

STUDENTS AND FACULTY
Enrollment: 2,310. **Student Body:** 57% female, 43% male, 29% out-of-state, 2% international (16 countries represented). African American 2%, Asian 6%, Caucasian 58%, Hispanic 11%. **Retention and Graduation:** 85% freshmen return for sophomore year. 52% freshmen graduate within 4 years. 25% grads go on to further study within 2 semesters. 6% grads pursue business degrees. 6% grads pursue law degrees. 5% grads pursue medical degrees. **Faculty:** Student/faculty ratio 11:1. 165 full-time faculty, 82% hold PhDs. 100% faculty teach undergrads.

ACADEMICS
Degrees: Associate, bachelor's, certificate, master's, post-bachelor's certificate, post-master's certificate. **Academic Requirements:** Arts/fine arts, computer literacy, English (including composition), foreign languages, history, humanities, mathematics, philosophy, sciences (biological or physical), social science. **Classes:** Most classes have 10–19 students. Most lab/discussion sections have 10–19 students. **Majors with Highest Enrollment:** Business administration/management, liberal arts and sciences studies and humanities, psychology. **Disciplines with Highest Percentage of Degrees Awarded:** Business/marketing 41%, liberal arts/general studies 13%, social sciences 7%, biological/life sciences 6%, psychology 5%, visual and performing arts 5%. **Special Study Options:** Cross registration, double major, dual enrollment, exchange student program (domestic), honors program, independent study, internships, liberal arts/career combination, student-designed major, study abroad, teacher certification program.

FACILITIES
Housing: Coed dorms, men's dorms, women's dorms, apartments for single students, special housing for disabled students, fraternity/sorority housing,

abroad programming, apartments for students with dependent children. **Special Academic Facilities/Equipment:** Art gallery, Far East art collection, Southwest collection, center for communicative disorders, language lab, Helen and Vernon Farquar Anthropology Lab, physics laser photonics lab, Irvine Map Library, geographic information system lab. **Computers:** 25% of classrooms are wired, 11% of classrooms are wireless, 75% of public computers are PCs, 25% of public computers are Macs, network access in dorm rooms, network access in dorm lounges, online registration, online administrative functions (other than registration), remote student-access to Web through college's connection.

CAMPUS LIFE

Activities: Choral groups, concert band, dance, drama/theater, jazz band, literary magazine, music ensembles, musical theater, opera, radio station, student government, student newspaper, student-run film society, symphony orchestra, yearbook. **Organizations:** 105 registered organizations, 8 honor societies, 8 religious organizations. 5 fraternities (5% men join), 5 sororities (8% women join). **Athletics (Intercollegiate):** *Men:* Baseball, basketball, cross-country, diving, football, golf, soccer, swimming, tennis, track/field (outdoor), water polo. *Women:* Basketball, cross-country, diving, golf, lacrosse, soccer, softball, swimming, tennis, track/field (outdoor), volleyball, water polo. **Environmental Initiatives:** Co-Generation facility to provide power to much of the campus. Lewis Hall—a high performance earth-sheltered green building that houses the department of Environmental Studies, the GIS program, and the Resdlands Institute. A planned Art & Theater Center LEED (green) building—about to begin construction.

ADMISSIONS

Freshman Academic Profile: 37% in top 10% of high school class, 67% in top 25% of high school class, 94% in top 50% of high school class. SAT Math middle 50% range 540–620. SAT Critical Reading middle 50% range 520–620. ACT middle 50% range 22–26. TOEFL required of all international applicants, minimum paper TOEFL 550, minimum computer TOEFL 213. **Basis for Candidate Selection:** *Very important factors considered include:* Academic GPA, character/personal qualities, recommendation(s), rigor of secondary school record, talent/ability. *Important factors considered include:* Application essay, standardized test scores. *Other factors considered include:* Alumni/ae relation, extracurricular activities, first generation, geographical residence, interview, racial/ethnic status, volunteer work, work experience. **Freshman Admission Requirements:** High school diploma is required, and GED is accepted. *Academic units required:* 4 English, 3 math, 2 science (1 science lab), 2 foreign language, 2 social studies. *Academic units recommended:* 4 English, 4 math, 3 science, (1 science lab), 3 foreign language, 2 social studies, 1 history. **Freshman Admission Statistics:** 3,480 applied, 65% admitted, 27% enrolled. **Transfer Admission Requirements:** High school transcript, college transcript(s), essay or personal statement. Minimum college GPA of 2.5 required. Lowest grade transferable C. **General Admission Information:** Application fee $45. Regular application deadline 4/1. Regular notification is rolling. Non-fall registration accepted. Admission may be deferred for a maximum of 2 semesters. Credit and/or placement offered for CEEB Advanced Placement tests.

COSTS AND FINANCIAL AID

Annual tuition $28,476. Room & board $9,360. Required fees $300. Average book expense $1,300. **Required Forms and Deadlines:** FAFSA, state aid form, GPA verification form for California residents. Financial aid filing deadline 2/15. **Notification of Awards:** Applicants will be notified of awards on or about 2/28. **Types of Aid:** *Need-based scholarships/grants:* Pell, SEOG, state scholarships/grants, private scholarships, the school's own gift aid. *Loans:* FFEL Subsidized Stafford, FFEL Unsubsidized Stafford, FFEL PLUS, Federal Perkins, college/university loans from institutional funds. **Student Employment:** Federal Work-Study Program available. Off-campus job opportunities are fair. **Financial Aid Statistics:** 65% freshmen, 67% undergrads receive need-based scholarship or grant aid. 60% freshmen, 63% undergrads receive need-based self-help aid. 91% freshmen, 90% undergrads receive any aid. Highest amount earned per year from on-campus jobs $2,000.

UNIVERSITY OF REGINA

3737 Wascana Parkway, Regina, SK S4S 0A2 Canada
Phone: 306-585-4591 **E-mail:** admissions.office@uregina.ca
Fax: 306-585-5203 **Website:** www.uregina.ca
Financial Aid Phone: 306-585-4325

This public school was founded in 1974.

RATINGS

Admissions Selectivity Rating: 60*   **Fire Safety Rating:** 60*   **Green Rating:** 60*

STUDENTS AND FACULTY

Faculty: Student/faculty ratio 26:1.

ACADEMICS

Degrees: Bachelor's, certificate, diploma, doctoral, master's. **Academic Requirements:** English (including composition), humanities, social science. **Majors with Highest Enrollment:** Business administration/management, computer and information sciences, elementary education and teaching. **Special Study Options:** Cooperative education program, double major, English as a second language (ESL), exchange student program (domestic), honors program, independent study, internships, liberal arts/career combination, study abroad, teacher certification program, weekend college.

FACILITIES

Housing: Coed dorms. **Special Academic Facilities/Equipment:** Student-run art gallery. **Computers:** 100% of public computers are PCs, network access in dorm rooms, network access in dorm lounges, online administrative functions (other than registration), remote student-access to Web through college's connection.

CAMPUS LIFE

Activities: Choral groups, concert band, dance, drama/theater, jazz band, literary magazine, music ensembles, student government, student newspaper, student-run film society. **Organizations:** 70 registered organizations. **Athletics (Intercollegiate):** *Men:* Basketball, cross-country, football, ice hockey, swimming, track/field (outdoor), volleyball, wrestling. *Women:* Basketball, cross-country, ice hockey, soccer, swimming, track/field (outdoor), volleyball, wrestling.

ADMISSIONS

Freshman Academic Profile: TOEFL required of all international applicants, minimum paper TOEFL 550, minimum computer TOEFL 213. **Basis for Candidate Selection:** *Very important factors considered include:* Rigor of secondary school record. *Other factors considered include:* Application essay, standardized test scores. **Freshman Admission Requirements:** High school diploma is required, and GED is accepted. *Academic units required:* 2 English. *Academic units recommended:* 2 English, 2 math, 2 science, 1 social studies. **Freshman Admission Statistics:** 3,318 applied, 100% admitted. **Transfer Admission Requirements:** High school transcript, college transcript(s), statement of good standing from prior institution(s). **General Admission Information:** Application fee $60. Regular application deadline 7/1. Non-fall registration accepted. Common Application not accepted.

COSTS AND FINANCIAL AID

In-province tuition $3,300–$4,100. Out-of-province tuition $3,300–$4,100. International tuition $6,600. Room & board $5,000. Required fees $300. Average book expense $1,500.

UNIVERSITY OF RHODE ISLAND

Undergraduate Admissions Office, 14 Upper College Road, Kingston, RI 02881
Phone: 401-874-7000 **E-mail:** uriadmit@etal.uri.edu **CEEB Code:** 3919
Fax: 401-874-5523 **Website:** www.uri.edu **ACT Code:** 3818
Financial Aid Phone: 401-874-7530

This public school was founded in 1892. It has a 1,250-acre campus.

RATINGS

Admissions Selectivity Rating: 78   **Fire Safety Rating:** 80   **Green Rating:** 60*

STUDENTS AND FACULTY

Enrollment: 11,542. **Student Body:** 56% female, 44% male, 39% out-of-state, (53 countries represented). African American 5%, Asian 2%, Caucasian 75%, Hispanic 5%. **Retention and Graduation:** 81% freshmen return for sophomore year. 40% freshmen graduate within 4 years. **Faculty:** Student/faculty ratio 19:1. 674 full-time faculty, 90% hold PhDs. 83% faculty teach undergrads.

ACADEMICS

Degrees: Bachelor's, doctoral, first professional, master's, post-bachelor's certificate. **Academic Requirements:** Arts/fine arts, English (including composition), foreign languages, history, humanities, mathematics, philosophy, sciences (biological or physical), social science. **Classes:** Most classes have 20–29 students. Most lab/discussion sections have 10–19 students. **Majors with Highest Enrollment:** Communications studies/speech communication and rhetoric, nursing/registered nurse training (ASN, BSN, MSN, RN), psychology. **Disciplines with Highest Percentage of Degrees Awarded:** Business/marketing 14%, communications/journalism 11%, education 8%, health professions and related sciences 8%, social sciences 8%. **Special Study Options:** Accelerated program, distance learning, double major, dual enrollment, English as a second language (ESL), exchange student program (domestic), honors program, independent study, internships, study abroad, teacher certification program.

FACILITIES

Housing: Coed dorms, apartments for married students, apartments for single students, special housing for disabled students, fraternity/sorority housing, apartments for undergraduates. **Special Academic Facilities/Equipment:** Center for robotic research, animal science farm, planetarium, Watson House Museum, Narragansett Bay Campus for Marine Sciences, American historic textiles museum, aquaculture center, fisheries and marine technology laboratory, biotechnology center, human performance laboratory. **Computers:** 40% of classrooms are wired, 75% of classrooms are wireless, 75% of public computers are PCs, 25% of public computers are Macs, network access in dorm rooms, network access in dorm lounges, online registration, online administrative functions (other than registration), support for handheld computing, remote student-access to Web through college's connection.

CAMPUS LIFE

Activities: Choral groups, concert band, dance, drama/theater, jazz band, literary magazine, marching band, music ensembles, musical theater, pep band, radio station, student government, student newspaper, television station, yearbook. **Organizations:** 100 registered organizations, 40 honor societies, 5 religious organizations. 11 fraternities (10% men join), 9 sororities (9% women join). **Athletics (Intercollegiate):** *Men:* Baseball, basketball, cross-country, diving, football, golf, soccer, swimming, tennis, track/field (indoor), track/field (outdoor). *Women:* Basketball, crew/rowing, cross-country, diving, field hockey, gymnastics, soccer, softball, swimming, tennis, track/field (indoor), track/field (outdoor), volleyball.

ADMISSIONS

Freshman Academic Profile: 21% in top 10% of high school class, SAT Math middle 50% range 500–600. SAT Critical Reading middle 50% range 490–590. TOEFL required of all international applicants, minimum paper TOEFL 550, minimum computer TOEFL 213. **Basis for Candidate Selection:** *Very important factors considered include:* Rigor of secondary school record. *Important factors considered include:* Academic GPA, application essay, class rank, standardized test scores. *Other factors considered include:* Alumni/ae relation, character/personal qualities, extracurricular activities, first generation, geographical residence, level of applicant's interest, racial/ethnic status, recommendation(s), state residency, talent/ability, volunteer work, work experience. **Freshman Admission Requirements:** High school diploma is required, and GED is accepted. *Academic units required:* 4 English, 3 math, 2 science (1 science lab), 2 foreign language, 2 social studies, 5 academic electives. **Freshman Admission Statistics:** 13,497 applied, 74% admitted, 29% enrolled. **Transfer Admission Requirements:** High school transcript, college transcript(s), essay or personal statement, statement of good standing from prior institution(s). Minimum college GPA of 2.5 required. Lowest grade transferable C. **General Admission Information:** Application fee $50. Regular application deadline 2/1. Regular notification is rolling. Non-fall registration accepted. Credit and/or placement offered for CEEB Advanced Placement tests.

COSTS AND FINANCIAL AID

Annual in-state tuition $6,440. Annual out-of-state tuition $21,294. Room and board $8,732. Required fees $1,744. Average book expense $1,000. **Required Forms and Deadlines:** FAFSA. Financial aid filing deadline 3/1. **Notification of Awards:** Applicants will be notified of awards on a rolling basis beginning on or about 3/31. **Types of Aid:** *Need-based scholarships/grants:* Pell, SEOG, state scholarships/grants, private scholarships, the school's own gift aid. *Loans:* Direct Subsidized Stafford, Direct Unsubsidized Stafford, Direct PLUS, Federal Perkins, Federal Nursing, state loans, college/university loans from institutional funds. **Student Employment:** Federal Work-Study Program available. Institutional employment available. Off-campus job opportunities are good. **Financial Aid Statistics:** 49% freshmen, 53% undergrads receive need-based scholarship or grant aid. 48% freshmen, 48% undergrads receive need-based self-help aid. 7 freshmen, 31 undergrads receive athletic scholarships. 72% freshmen, 63% undergrads receive any aid. Highest amount earned per year from on-campus jobs $2,000.

UNIVERSITY OF RICHMOND

Best 368

28 Westhampton Way, Richmond, VA 23173
Phone: 804-289-8640 **E-mail:** admissions@richmond.edu **CEEB Code:** 5569
Fax: 804-287-6003 **Website:** www.richmond.edu **ACT Code:** 4410
Financial Aid Phone: 804-289-8438

This private school was founded in 1830. It has a 350-acre campus.

RATINGS

Admissions Selectivity Rating: 95   **Fire Safety Rating:** 70   **Green Rating:** 88

STUDENTS AND FACULTY

Enrollment: 2,787. **Student Body:** 51% female, 49% male, 84% out-of-state, 6% international (75 countries represented). African American 6%, Asian 4%, Caucasian 78%, Hispanic 3%. **Retention and Graduation:** 88% freshmen return for sophomore year. 80% freshmen graduate within 4 years. 27% grads go on to further study within 2 semesters. 15% grads pursue arts and sciences degrees. 2% grads pursue business degrees. 5% grads pursue law degrees. 5% grads pursue medical degrees. **Faculty:** Student/faculty ratio 9:1. 274 full-time faculty, 91% hold PhDs. 100% faculty teach undergrads.

ACADEMICS

Degrees: Associate, bachelor's, certificate, diploma, first professional, master's, post-bachelor's certificate. **Academic Requirements:** Arts/fine arts, core class, English (including composition), foreign languages, history, humanities, mathematics, sciences (biological or physical), social science. **Classes:** Most classes have 10–19 students. Most lab/discussion sections have 10–19 students. **Majors with Highest Enrollment:** Business administration/management, English language and literature, political science and government. **Disciplines with Highest Percentage of Degrees Awarded:** Business/marketing 25%, social sciences 20%, English 8%, history 7%, area and ethnic studies 6%, biological/life sciences 6%, foreign languages and literature 6%. **Special Study Options:** Accelerated program, cross registration, distance learning, double major, English as a second language (ESL), exchange student program (domestic), honors program, independent study, internships, student-designed major, study abroad, teacher certification program.

FACILITIES

Housing: Coed dorms, men's dorms, women's dorms, apartments for single students, special housing for disabled students, global house, outdoor house, civic engagement house. **Special Academic Facilities/Equipment:** Art gallery, mineral museum, Virginia Baptist Archives, language lab, neuroscience lab, speech center, music technology lab, Jepson School of Leadership, Center for Civic Engagement. **Computers:** 33% of classrooms are wired, 100% of classrooms are wireless, 86% of public computers are PCs, 14% of public computers are Macs, network access in dorm rooms, network access in dorm lounges, online registration, online administrative functions (other than registration), support for handheld computing, remote student-access to Web through college's connection.

CAMPUS LIFE

Activities: Choral groups, concert band, dance, drama/theater, jazz band, literary magazine, music ensembles, musical theater, pep band, radio station, student government, student newspaper, student-run film society, symphony orchestra. **Organizations:** 220 registered organizations, 22 honor societies, 16 religious organizations. 7 fraternities (31% men join), 8 sororities (44% women join). **Athletics (Intercollegiate):** *Men:* Baseball, basketball, cross-country, football, golf, soccer, tennis, track/field (indoor), track/field (outdoor). *Women:* Basketball, cross-country, diving, field hockey, golf, lacrosse, soccer, swimming, tennis, track/field (indoor), track/field (outdoor).

ADMISSIONS

Freshman Academic Profile: 53% in top 10% of high school class, 84% in top 25% of high school class, 97% in top 50% of high school class. 62% from public high schools. SAT Math middle 50% range 610–690. SAT Critical Reading middle 50% range 590–690. SAT Writing middle 50% range 590–690. ACT middle 50% range 27–31. TOEFL required of all international applicants, minimum paper TOEFL 550, minimum computer TOEFL 213. **Basis for Candidate Selection:** *Very important factors considered include:* Academic GPA, rigor of secondary school record. *Important factors considered include:* Application essay, character/personal qualities, class rank, first generation, standardized test scores, talent/ability. *Other factors considered include:*

Alumni/ae relation, extracurricular activities, geographical residence, racial/ethnic status, recommendation(s), state residency, volunteer work, work experience. **Freshman Admission Requirements:** High school diploma is required, and GED is accepted. *Academic units required:* 4 English, 3 math, 2 science (2 science labs), 2 foreign language, 2 history. *Academic units recommended:* 4 English, 4 math, 4 science (4 science labs), 4 foreign language, 4 history. **Freshman Admission Statistics:** 5,414 applied, 46% admitted, 31% enrolled. **Transfer Admission Requirements:** High school transcript, college transcript(s), essay or personal statement, statement of good standing from prior institution(s). Minimum college GPA of 2.0 required. Lowest grade transferable C. **General Admission Information:** Application fee $50. Early decision application deadline 11/15. Regular application deadline 1/15. Regular notification 4/1. Non-fall registration not accepted. Admission may be deferred for a maximum of 2 semesters. Credit and/or placement offered for CEEB Advanced Placement tests.

COSTS AND FINANCIAL AID

Annual tuition $38,850. Room and board $8,200. Average book expense $1,050. **Required Forms and Deadlines:** FAFSA, institution's own financial aid form. Financial aid filing deadline 2/25. **Notification of Awards:** Applicants will be notified of awards on or about 4/1. **Types of Aid:** *Need-based scholarships/grants:* Pell, SEOG, state scholarships/grants, private scholarships, the school's own gift aid. *Loans:* Direct Subsidized Stafford, Direct Unsubsidized Stafford, Direct PLUS, Federal Perkins. **Student Employment: Financial Aid Statistics:** 41% freshmen, 34% undergrads receive need-based scholarship or grant aid. 36% freshmen, 31% undergrads receive need-based self-help aid. 53 freshmen, 203 undergrads receive athletic scholarships. 65% freshmen, 69% undergrads receive any aid. Highest amount earned per year from on-campus jobs $3,826.

UNIVERSITY OF RIO GRANDE

218 North College Avenue, Admissions, Rio Grande, OH 45774
Phone: 740-245-7206 **E-mail:** mabell@urgrgcc.edu **CEEB Code:** 1663
Fax: 740-245-7260 **Website:** www.urgrgcc.edu **ACT Code:** 3324
Financial Aid Phone: 740-245-7219

This private school was founded in 1876. It has a 68-acre campus.

RATINGS

Admissions Selectivity Rating: 77   **Fire Safety Rating:** 79   **Green Rating:** 60*

STUDENTS AND FACULTY

Enrollment: 1,794. **Student Body:** 61% female, 39% male, 3% out-of-state. African American 3%, Caucasian 89%. **Retention and Graduation:** 58% freshmen return for sophomore year. **Faculty:** Student/faculty ratio 16:1. 92 full-time faculty, 45% hold PhDs. 100% faculty teach undergrads.

ACADEMICS

Degrees: Associate, bachelor's, certificate, master's. **Academic Requirements:** Arts/fine arts, computer literacy, English (including composition), history, humanities, mathematics, philosophy, sciences (biological or physical), social science. **Classes:** Most classes have fewer than 10 students. Most lab/discussion sections have fewer than 10 students. **Majors with Highest Enrollment:** Business/office automation/technology/data entry, elementary education and teaching, nursing/registered nurse training (ASN, BSN, MSN, RN). **Disciplines with Highest Percentage of Degrees Awarded:** Education 29%, history 21%, business/marketing 11%, health professions and related sciences 9%, social sciences 6%. **Special Study Options:** Accelerated program, cooperative education program, distance learning, double major, dual enrollment, English as a second language (ESL), honors program, independent study, internships, liberal arts/career combination, student-designed major, study abroad, teacher certification program.

FACILITIES

Housing: Coed dorms, men's dorms, women's dorms, private housing owned and operated by university available to responsible students. **Special Academic Facilities/Equipment:** Archives of local and college history, art museum, fine woodworking, theater, art annex. **Computers:** 5% of classrooms are wired, 15% of classrooms are wireless, 95% of public computers are PCs, 5% of public computers are Macs, network access in dorm rooms, online registration, online administrative functions (other than registration), support for handheld computing, remote student-access to Web through college's connection.

CAMPUS LIFE

Activities: Choral groups, concert band, dance, drama/theater, jazz band, literary magazine, music ensembles, musical theater, pep band, radio station, student government, student newspaper, television station. **Organizations:** 34

registered organizations, 4 honor societies, 3 religious organizations. 4 fraternities (25% men join), 5 sororities (25% women join). **Athletics (Intercollegiate):** *Men:* Baseball, basketball, cross-country, soccer, track/field (indoor), track/field (outdoor). *Women:* Basketball, cheerleading, cross-country, soccer, softball, track/field (indoor), track/field (outdoor), volleyball.

ADMISSIONS

Freshman Academic Profile: 18% in top 10% of high school class, 36% in top 25% of high school class, 66% in top 50% of high school class. 95% from public high schools. ACT middle 50% range 16–30. TOEFL required of all international applicants, minimum paper TOEFL 400, minimum computer TOEFL 97. **Freshman Admission Requirements:** High school diploma is required, and GED is accepted. *Academic units required:* 4 English, 3 math, 3 science (1 science lab), 3 social studies, 7 academic electives. *Academic units recommended:* 4 English, 3 math, 3 science (2 science labs), 2 foreign language, 2 social studies, 2 history, 9 academic electives. **Freshman Admission Statistics:** 1,626 applied, **Transfer Admission Requirements:** High school transcript, college transcript(s), statement of good standing from prior institution(s). Lowest grade transferable D. **General Admission Information:** Application fee $15. Regular notification rolling. Non-fall registration accepted. Credit and/or placement offered for CEEB Advanced Placement tests.

COSTS AND FINANCIAL AID

Annual tuition $16,600. Room and board $6,840. Required fees $96. Average book expense $1,000. **Required Forms and Deadlines:** FAFSA, institution's own financial aid form. Financial aid filing deadline 3/15. **Notification of Awards:** Applicants will be notified of awards on or about 3/15. **Types of Aid:** *Need-based scholarships/grants:* Pell, state scholarships/grants, private scholarships, the school's own gift aid. *Loans:* Direct Subsidized Stafford, Direct Unsubsidized Stafford, Direct PLUS, FFEL Subsidized Stafford, FFEL PLUS, Federal Perkins, Federal Nursing, college/university loans from institutional funds. **Financial Aid Statistics:** 62% freshmen, 54% undergrads receive need-based scholarship or grant aid. 62% freshmen, 54% undergrads receive need-based self-help aid. 14 freshmen, 31 undergrads receive athletic scholarships.

UNIVERSITY OF ROCHESTER

300 Wilson Boulevard, PO Box 270251, Rochester, NY 14627-0251
Phone: 585-275-3221 **E-mail:** admit@admissions.rochester.edu **CEEB Code:** 2928
Fax: 585-461-4595 **Website:** www.rochester.edu **ACT Code:** 2980
Financial Aid Phone: 716-275-3226

This private school was founded in 1850. It has a 90-acre campus.

RATINGS

Admissions Selectivity Rating: 60*   **Fire Safety Rating:** 60*   **Green Rating:** 75

STUDENTS AND FACULTY

Enrollment: 4,532. **Student Body:** 49% female, 51% male, 4% international. African American 5%, Asian 10%, Caucasian 64%, Hispanic 4%. **Retention and Graduation:** 95% freshmen return for sophomore year. 60% grads go on to further study within 2 semesters. 20% grads pursue arts and sciences degrees. 2% grads pursue business degrees. 10% grads pursue law degrees. 9% grads pursue medical degrees. **Faculty:** 505 full-time faculty, 88% hold PhDs.

ACADEMICS

Degrees: Bachelor's, certificate, doctoral, first professional, master's, post-bachelor's certificate, post-master's certificate. **Academic Requirements:** 1 semester primary writing, 2 semesters upper level writing, humanities, sciences (biological or physical), social science. **Classes:** Most classes have 10–19 students. **Disciplines with Highest Percentage of Degrees Awarded:** Social sciences 22%, psychology 12%, biological/life sciences 10%, visual and performing arts 9%, engineering 8%. **Special Study Options:** Cross registration, double major, dual enrollment, English as a second language (ESL), honors program, independent study, internships, liberal arts/career combination, Quest (1st year courses emphasizing how to learn), Rochester Curriculum (clusters), student-designed major, study abroad, "Take 5" (5th year tuition free to supplement regular requirements), teacher certification program, Washington Semester Program.

FACILITIES

Housing: Coed dorms, men's dorms, women's dorms, apartments for married students, apartments for single students, special housing for disabled students, special housing for international students, fraternity/sorority housing, freshman housing, special interest. **Special Academic Facilities/Equipment:** Art center and gallery, African and African-American studies institute, center for women's studies, visual science and space science centers, Institute of Optics, observatory, laser energetics and nuclear structure research labs, electron microscopes,

Judaic studies center, political economy institute, sign language research center, biomedical ultrasound center, Polish and Central European studies center, electronic imaging systems center, center for future health. **Computers:** Network access in dorm rooms, online administrative functions (other than registration), remote student-access to Web through college's connection.

CAMPUS LIFE

Activities: Choral groups, concert band, dance, drama/theater, jazz band, literary magazine, music ensembles, musical theater, opera, pep band, radio station, student government, student newspaper, student-run film society, symphony orchestra, yearbook. **Organizations:** 170 registered organizations, 6 honor societies, 14 religious organizations. 17 fraternities, 11 sororities. **Athletics (Intercollegiate):** *Men:* Baseball, basketball, cross-country, diving, football, golf, soccer, swimming, tennis, track/field (indoor), track/field (outdoor). *Women:* Basketball, cross-country, diving, field hockey, golf, lacrosse, soccer, softball, swimming, tennis, track/field (indoor), track/field (outdoor), volleyball.

ADMISSIONS

Freshman Academic Profile: 76% in top 10% of high school class, 93% in top 25% of high school class, 98% in top 50% of high school class. SAT Math middle 50% range 630–720. SAT Critical Reading middle 50% range 600–700. ACT middle 50% range 27–31. TOEFL required of all international applicants, minimum paper TOEFL 550. **Basis for Candidate Selection:** *Very important factors considered include:* Character/personal qualities, interview, rigor of secondary school record. *Important factors considered include:* Application essay, class rank, racial/ethnic status, recommendation(s), talent/ability. *Other factors considered include:* Alumni/ae relation, extracurricular activities, standardized test scores, volunteer work, work experience. **Freshman Admission Requirements:** High school diploma is required, and GED is accepted. **Freshman Admission Statistics:** 11,272 applied, 48% admitted, 19% enrolled. **Transfer Admission Requirements:** College transcript(s), essay or personal statement. Lowest grade transferable C. **General Admission Information:** Application fee $50. Early decision application deadline 11/1. Regular application deadline 1/1. Regular notification 4/1. Non-fall registration accepted. Common Application accepted. Credit and/or placement offered for CEEB Advanced Placement tests.

COSTS AND FINANCIAL AID

Annual tuition $30,540. Room & board $9,838. Required fees $757. Average book expense $618. **Required Forms and Deadlines:** FAFSA, CSS/Financial Aid PROFILE, state aid form, Noncustodial PROFILE, Business/Farm Supplement. Financial aid filing deadline 2/1. **Notification of Awards:** Applicants will be notified of awards on or about 4/1. **Types of Aid:** *Need-based scholarships/grants:* Pell, SEOG, state scholarships/grants, the school's own gift aid. *Loans:* Direct Subsidized Stafford, Direct Unsubsidized Stafford, Direct PLUS, Federal Perkins, Federal Nursing, college/university loans from institutional funds. **Student Employment:** Federal Work-Study Program available. Institutional employment available. Off-campus job opportunities are excellent. **Financial Aid Statistics:** 57% freshmen, 56% undergrads receive need-based scholarship or grant aid. 48% freshmen, 47% undergrads receive need-based self-help aid.

See page 1464.

THE UNIVERSITY OF SAINT FRANCIS (IN)

2701 Spring Street, Fort Wayne, IN 46808
Phone: 260-434-3279 **E-mail:** admis@sf.edu **CEEB Code:** 1693
Fax: 260-434-7590 **Website:** www.sf.edu **ACT Code:** 1238
Financial Aid Phone: 260-434-3283

This private school, affiliated with the Roman Catholic Church, was founded in 1890. It has a 70-acre campus.

RATINGS
Admissions Selectivity Rating: 72   **Fire Safety Rating:** 60*   **Green Rating:** 79

STUDENTS AND FACULTY

Enrollment: 1,413. **Student Body:** 66% female, 34% male, 8% out-of-state. African American 7%, Caucasian 70%, Hispanic 2%. **Retention and Graduation:** 71% freshmen return for sophomore year. 27% freshmen graduate within 4 years. 10% grads go on to further study within 1 year. 30% grads pursue arts and sciences degrees. 40% grads pursue business degrees. 8% grads pursue law degrees. 5% grads pursue medical degrees. **Faculty:** Student/faculty ratio 11:1. 106 full-time faculty, 45% hold PhDs.

ACADEMICS

Degrees: Associate, bachelor's, certificate, master's. **Academic Requirements:** Arts/fine arts, computer literacy, English (including composition), history, humanities, mathematics, philosophy, sciences (biological or physical), social science. **Classes:** Most classes have 20–29 students. Most lab/discussion sections have fewer than 10 students. **Disciplines with Highest Percentage of Degrees Awarded:** Education 28%, business/marketing 23%, health professions and related sciences 17%, visual and performing arts 9%, liberal arts/general studies 5%. **Special Study Options:** Double major, dual enrollment, honors program, independent study, internships, student-designed major, study abroad, teacher certification program, weekend college.

FACILITIES

Housing: Coed dorms. **Computers:** 28% of public computers are PCs, 3% of public computers are Macs, network access in dorm rooms, network access in dorm lounges, online registration.

CAMPUS LIFE

Activities: Choral groups, dance, drama/theater, literary magazine, music ensembles, musical theater, pep band, student government, student newspaper, student-run film society. **Organizations:** 30 registered organizations, 1 honor society. **Athletics (Intercollegiate):** *Men:* Baseball, basketball, cheerleading, cross-country, football, golf, soccer, track/field (outdoor). *Women:* Basketball, cheerleading, cross-country, soccer, softball, tennis, track/field (outdoor), volleyball.

ADMISSIONS

Freshman Academic Profile: 12% in top 10% of high school class, 32% in top 25% of high school class, 73% in top 50% of high school class. SAT Math middle 50% range 420–540. SAT Critical Reading middle 50% range 430–530. ACT middle 50% range 17–22. TOEFL required of all international applicants, minimum paper TOEFL 500. **Basis for Candidate Selection:** *Very important factors considered include:* Class rank, rigor of secondary school record, standardized test scores. *Important factors considered include:* Application essay, recommendation(s). *Other factors considered include:* Extracurricular activities, interview, talent/ability. **Freshman Admission Requirements:** High school diploma is required, and GED is accepted. *Academic units recommended:* 4 English, 3 math, 2 science, 2 foreign language, 2 social studies. **Freshman Admission Statistics:** 722 applied, 75% admitted, 51% enrolled. **Transfer Admission Requirements:** High school transcript, college transcript(s). Minimum college GPA of 2.0 required. Lowest grade transferable C. **General Admission Information:** Application fee $20. Regular notification is rolling. Non-fall registration accepted. Common Application not accepted. Credit and/or placement offered for CEEB Advanced Placement tests.

COSTS AND FINANCIAL AID

Comprehensive fee $20,440. Room and board $7,610. Required fees $390. Average book expense $800. **Required Forms and Deadlines:** FAFSA. Financial aid filing deadline 3/1. **Notification of Awards:** Applicants will be notified of awards on a rolling basis beginning on or about 3/1. **Types of Aid:** *Need-based scholarships/grants:* Pell, SEOG, state scholarships/grants, private scholarships, the school's own gift aid. *Loans:* Direct Subsidized Stafford, Direct Unsubsidized Stafford, Direct PLUS, Federal Perkins. **Student Employment:** Federal Work-Study Program available. Institutional employment available. Off-campus job opportunities are excellent. **Financial Aid Statistics:** 84% freshmen, 85% undergrads receive need-based scholarship or grant aid. 77% freshmen, 76% undergrads receive need-based self-help aid. 17 freshmen, 98 undergrads receive athletic scholarships. Highest amount earned per year from on-campus jobs $877.

UNIVERSITY OF SAINT MARY (KS)

4100 South Fourth Street Trafficway, Leavenworth, KS 66048
Phone: 913-758-6118 **E-mail:** admis@hub.smcks.edu **CEEB Code:** 6630
Fax: 913-758-6140 **Website:** www.stmary.edu **ACT Code:** 1455
Financial Aid Phone: 800-752-7043

This private school, affiliated with the Roman Catholic Church, was founded in 1923. It has a 240-acre campus.

RATINGS
Admissions Selectivity Rating: 77   **Fire Safety Rating:** 60*   **Green Rating:** 60*

STUDENTS AND FACULTY

Enrollment: 478. **Student Body:** 56% female, 44% male, 41% out-of-state. African American 12%, Asian 1%, Caucasian 67%, Hispanic 9%. **Retention and Graduation:** 60% freshmen return for sophomore year. 39% freshmen graduate within 4 years. **Faculty:** Student/faculty ratio 11:1. 33 full-time faculty, 61% hold PhDs. 100% faculty teach undergrads.

ACADEMICS

Degrees: Associate, bachelor's, master's. **Academic Requirements:** Arts/fine arts, Common Learning Experiences, English (including composition), foreign languages, history, humanities, lifetime wellness course, mathematics, philosophy, sciences (biological or physical), social science. **Classes:** Most classes have fewer than 10 students. **Majors with Highest Enrollment:** Business administration/management, elementary education and teaching, psychology. **Disciplines with Highest Percentage of Degrees Awarded:** Education 15%, psychology 15%, social sciences 13%, business/marketing 12%, computer and information sciences 8%. **Special Study Options:** Accelerated program, distance learning, double major, dual enrollment, honors program, independent study, internships, semester-away programs, student-designed major, study abroad, teacher certification program.

FACILITIES

Housing: Coed dorms. **Special Academic Facilities/Equipment:** Lincoln Library Collection, art gallery bible collection. **Computers:** Network access in dorm rooms, online registration, online administrative functions (other than registration), remote student-access to Web through college's connection.

CAMPUS LIFE

Activities: Choral groups, concert band, drama/theater, literary magazine, music ensembles, musical theater, pep band, student government. **Organizations:** 22 registered organizations, 2 honor societies, 2 religious organizations. **Athletics (Intercollegiate):** *Men:* Baseball, basketball, football, soccer. *Women:* Basketball, soccer, softball, volleyball.

ADMISSIONS

Freshman Academic Profile: 11% in top 10% of high school class, 36% in top 25% of high school class, 76% in top 50% of high school class. 80% from public high schools. SAT Math middle 50% range 360–510. SAT Critical Reading middle 50% range 400–480. ACT middle 50% range 17–24. TOEFL required of all international applicants, minimum paper TOEFL 500. **Basis for Candidate Selection:** *Very important factors considered include:* Academic GPA, rigor of secondary school record, standardized test scores. *Important factors considered include:* Character/personal qualities, extracurricular activities, interview, talent/ability, volunteer work, work experience. *Other factors considered include:* Alumni/ae relation, class rank, recommendation(s). **Freshman Admission Requirements:** High school diploma is required, and GED is accepted. *Academic units required:* 4 English, 2 math, 2 science, 2 history. *Academic units recommended:* 4 English, 4 math, 4 science (2 science labs), 2 social studies, 4 history, 2 academic electives, 2 computer programming. **Freshman Admission Statistics:** 427 applied, 55% admitted, 36% enrolled. **Transfer Admission Requirements:** College transcript(s). Minimum college GPA of 2.0 required. Lowest grade transferable C. **General Admission Information:** Application fee $25. Regular notification is rolling. Non-fall registration accepted. Admission may be deferred for a maximum of 1 semester. Credit and/or placement offered for CEEB Advanced Placement tests.

COSTS AND FINANCIAL AID

Annual tuition $16,900. Room and board $6,400. Required fees $320. Average book expense $700. **Required Forms and Deadlines:** FAFSA. Financial aid filing deadline 4/1. **Notification of Awards:** Applicants will be notified of awards on a rolling basis beginning on or about 2/1. **Types of Aid:** *Need-based scholarships/grants:* Pell, SEOG, state scholarships/grants, private scholarships, the school's own gift aid. *Loans:* FFEL Subsidized Stafford, FFEL Unsubsidized Stafford, FFEL PLUS, Federal Perkins. **Financial Aid Statistics:** 80% freshmen, 78% undergrads receive need-based scholarship or grant aid. 72% freshmen, 69% undergrads receive need-based self-help aid. 58 freshmen, 200 undergrads receive athletic scholarships. Highest amount earned per year from on-campus jobs $1,500.

UNIVERSITY OF SAINT THOMAS (MN)

2115 Summit Avenue, Mail #32F, St. Paul, MN 55105-1096
Phone: 651-962-6150 **E-mail:** admissions@stthomas.edu **CEEB Code:** 6110
Fax: 651-962-6160 **Website:** www.stthomas.edu **ACT Code:** 2102
Financial Aid Phone: 651-962-6550

This private school, affiliated with the Roman Catholic Church, was founded in 1885. It has a 78-acre campus.

STUDENTS AND FACULTY

Enrollment: 5,682. **Student Body:** 50% female, 50% male, 16% out-of-state. African American 3%, Asian 5%, Caucasian 87%, Hispanic 2%. **Retention and Graduation:** 88% freshmen return for sophomore year. 56% freshmen graduate within 4 years. **Faculty:** 395 full-time faculty.

ACADEMICS

Degrees: Bachelor's, doctoral, first professional, master's, post-bachelor's certificate, post-master's certificate. **Academic Requirements:** Arts/fine arts, computer literacy, English (including composition), faith and Catholic tradition, foreign languages, health and fitness, history, human diversity, humanities, mathematics, philosophy, sciences (biological or physical), social science. **Classes:** Most classes have 20–29 students. Most lab/discussion sections have 10–19 students. **Majors with Highest Enrollment:** Business administration/management. **Disciplines with Highest Percentage of Degrees Awarded:** Business/marketing 40%, social sciences 9%, communications/journalism 7%, biological/life sciences 6%, philosophy and religious studies 6%, psychology 6%. **Special Study Options:** Cross registration, double major, English as a second language (ESL), exchange student program (domestic), honors program, independent study, internships, student-designed major, study abroad, teacher certification program.

FACILITIES

Housing: Men's dorms, women's dorms, apartments for single students, special housing for international students, chemical-free lifestyle, women in science house, first-year experience houses, Catholic women's and Catholic men's communities. **Special Academic Facilities/Equipment:** Seminary. **Computers:** Network access in dorm rooms, network access in dorm lounges, online registration, online administrative functions (other than registration), remote student-access to Web through college's connection.

CAMPUS LIFE

Activities: Choral groups, concert band, dance, drama/theater, jazz band, literary magazine, music ensembles, pep band, radio station, student government, student newspaper, yearbook. **Athletics (Intercollegiate):** *Men:* Baseball, basketball, cross-country, football, golf, ice hockey, soccer, swimming, tennis, track/field (indoor), track/field (outdoor). *Women:* Basketball, cross-country, golf, ice hockey, soccer, softball, swimming, tennis, track/field (indoor), track/field (outdoor), volleyball.

ADMISSIONS

Freshman Academic Profile: 19% in top 10% of high school class, 29% in top 25% of high school class, 40% in top 50% of high school class. SAT Math middle 50% range 520–640. SAT Critical Reading middle 50% range 520–640. ACT middle 50% range 23–27. TOEFL required of all international applicants, minimum paper TOEFL 550, minimum computer TOEFL 213. **Basis for Candidate Selection:** *Very important factors considered include:* Academic GPA, rigor of secondary school record. *Important factors considered include:* Application essay, class rank, standardized test scores. *Other factors considered include:* Alumni/ae relation, character/personal qualities, extracurricular activities, geographical residence, racial/ethnic status, recommendation(s), talent/ability, volunteer work. **Freshman Admission Requirements:** High school diploma is required, and GED is accepted. *Academic units required:* 3 math. *Academic units recommended:* 4 English, 4 math, 2 science, 4 foreign language, 2 social science/history. **Freshman Admission Statistics:** 4,652 applied, 83% admitted, 34% enrolled. **Transfer Admission Requirements:** High school transcript, college transcript(s), essay or personal statement, statement of good standing from prior institution(s). Minimum college GPA of 2.3 required. Lowest grade transferable C-. **General Admission Information:** Regular notification is rolling. Non-fall registration accepted. Admission may be deferred for a maximum of 2 semesters. Credit and/or placement offered for CEEB Advanced Placement tests.

COSTS AND FINANCIAL AID

Required Forms and Deadlines: FAFSA. Financial aid filing deadline 4/1. **Notification of Awards:** Applicants will be notified of awards on a rolling basis beginning on or about 3/1. **Types of Aid:** *Need-based scholarships/grants:* Pell, SEOG, state scholarships/grants, private scholarships, the school's own gift aid. *Loans:* FFEL Subsidized Stafford, FFEL Unsubsidized Stafford, FFEL PLUS, Federal Perkins, state loans, private loans. **Financial Aid Statistics:** 56% freshmen, 53% undergrads receive need-based scholarship or grant aid. 44% freshmen, 45% undergrads receive need-based self-help aid.

RATINGS

Admissions Selectivity Rating: 80 **Fire Safety Rating:** 60* **Green Rating:** 60*

College Directory

UNIVERSITY OF SAN DIEGO

5998 Alcala Park, San Diego, CA 92110-2492
Phone: 619-260-4506 **E-mail:** admissions@sandiego.edu **CEEB Code:** 4849
Fax: 619-260-6836 **Website:** www.sandiego.edu **ACT Code:** 0394
Financial Aid Phone: 619-260-4514

This private school, affiliated with the Roman Catholic Church, was founded in 1949. It has a 180-acre campus.

RATINGS
Admissions Selectivity Rating: 92   **Fire Safety Rating:** 60*   **Green Rating:** 78

STUDENTS AND FACULTY
Enrollment: 4,946. **Student Body:** 60% female, 40% male, 36% out-of-state, 2% international (40 countries represented). African American 2%, Asian 8%, Caucasian 68%, Hispanic 13%. **Retention and Graduation:** 87% freshmen return for sophomore year. 64% freshmen graduate within 4 years. 14% grads go on to further study within 2 semesters. 3% grads pursue arts and sciences degrees. 2% grads pursue business degrees. 5% grads pursue law degrees. 1% grads pursue medical degrees. **Faculty:** Student/faculty ratio 15:1. 363 full-time faculty, 96% hold PhDs. 100% faculty teach undergrads.

ACADEMICS
Degrees: Bachelor's, doctoral, first professional certificate, first professional, master's, post-bachelor's certificate, post-master's certificate. **Academic Requirements:** Arts/fine arts, English (including composition), foreign languages, history, humanities, mathematics, philosophy, religion, sciences (biological or physical), social science. **Classes:** Most classes have 30–39 students. Most lab/discussion sections have 10–19 students. **Majors with Highest Enrollment:** Business administration and management, communications studies/speech communication and rhetoric, psychology. **Disciplines with Highest Percentage of Degrees Awarded:** Business/marketing 34%, social sciences 16%, communications/journalism 10%, psychology 9%, English 5%. **Special Study Options:** Double major, English as a second language (ESL), honors program, independent study, internships, liberal arts/career combination, study abroad, teacher certification program.

FACILITIES
Housing: Coed dorms, men's dorms, women's dorms, apartments for married students, apartments for single students, special housing for disabled students. **Special Academic Facilities/Equipment:** Art gallery, Peace & Justice Institute, child development center, language labs. **Computers:** 15% of classrooms are wireless, 74% of public computers are PCs, 24% of public computers are Macs, 2% of public computers are UNIX, network access in dorm rooms, network access in dorm lounges, online administrative functions (other than registration), support for handheld computing, remote student-access to Web through college's connection.

CAMPUS LIFE
Activities: Choral groups, dance, drama/theater, jazz band, literary magazine, music ensembles, musical theater, pep band, student government, student newspaper, symphony orchestra, television station, yearbook. **Organizations:** 80 registered organizations, 5 honor societies, 3 religious organizations. 4 fraternities (16% men join), 6 sororities (23% women join). **Athletics (Intercollegiate):** *Men:* Baseball, basketball, cheerleading, crew/rowing, cross-country, football, golf, soccer, tennis. *Women:* Basketball, cheerleading, crew/rowing, cross-country, diving, soccer, softball, swimming, tennis, volleyball. **Environmental Initiatives:** Have courses in environmental ethics, justice, economics, history, law, and science across undergraduate and graduate curricula. Recycle 90% of lawn and garden clippings.

ADMISSIONS
Freshman Academic Profile: 43% in top 10% of high school class, 78% in top 25% of high school class, 97% in top 50% of high school class. 56% from public high schools. SAT Math middle 50% range 550–650. SAT Critical Reading middle 50% range 530–630. SAT Writing middle 50% range 540–630. ACT middle 50% range 24–28. TOEFL required of all international applicants, minimum paper TOEFL 550, minimum computer TOEFL 213. **Basis for Candidate Selection:** *Very important factors considered include:* Academic GPA, rigor of secondary school record, standardized test scores. *Important factors considered include:* Application essay, character/personal qualities, class rank, extracurricular activities, talent/ability, volunteer work. *Other factors considered include:* Alumni/ae relation, first generation, racial/ethnic status, recommendation(s), religious affiliation/commitment, work experience. **Freshman Admission Requirements:** High school diploma is required, and GED is accepted. *Academic units required:* 4 English, 3 math, 3 science (2 science labs), 2 foreign language, 3 social studies. *Academic units recommended:* 4 English, 4 math, 4 science (3 science labs), 3 foreign language, 4 social studies. **Freshman Admission Statistics:** 10,048 applied, 46% admitted, 24% enrolled. **Transfer Admission Requirements:** College transcript(s), essay or personal statement. Minimum college GPA of 3.0 required. Lowest grade transferable C. **General Admission Information:** Application fee $55. Regular application deadline 3/1. Regular notification 4/15. Non-fall registration accepted. Admission may be deferred for a maximum of 2 semesters. Credit and/or placement offered for CEEB Advanced Placement tests.

COSTS AND FINANCIAL AID
Annual tuition $34,000. Room and board $11,870. Average book expense $1,566. **Required Forms and Deadlines:** FAFSA. Financial aid filing deadline 2/20. **Notification of Awards:** Applicants will be notified of awards on a rolling basis beginning on or about 3/1. **Types of Aid:** *Need-based scholarships/grants:* Pell, SEOG, state scholarships/grants, private scholarships, the school's own gift aid, Federal Nursing Scholarships. *Loans:* FFEL Subsidized Stafford, FFEL Unsubsidized Stafford, FFEL PLUS, Federal Perkins, college/university loans from institutional funds, non-federal loan programs. **Student Employment:** Federal Work-Study Program available. Institutional employment available. Off-campus job opportunities are good. **Financial Aid Statistics:** 50% freshmen, 45% undergrads receive need-based scholarship or grant aid. 44% freshmen, 44% undergrads receive need-based self-help aid. 23 freshmen, 155 undergrads receive athletic scholarships. 77% freshmen, 68% undergrads receive any aid.

UNIVERSITY OF SAN FRANCISCO

2130 Fulton Street, San Francisco, CA 94117
Phone: 415-422-6563 **E-mail:** admission@usfca.edu **CEEB Code:** 4850
Fax: 415-422-2217 **Website:** www.usfca.edu
Financial Aid Phone: 415-422-6303

This private school, affiliated with the Roman Catholic Church, was founded in 1855. It has a 55-acre campus.

RATINGS
Admissions Selectivity Rating: 85   **Fire Safety Rating:** 60*   **Green Rating:** 82

STUDENTS AND FACULTY
Enrollment: 4,796. **Student Body:** 66% female, 34% male, 24% out-of-state, 7% international (78 countries represented). African American 5%, Asian 24%, Caucasian 38%, Hispanic 14%. **Retention and Graduation:** 84% freshmen return for sophomore year. 44% freshmen graduate within 4 years. 1% grads pursue medical degrees. **Faculty:** Student/faculty ratio 14:1. 354 full-time faculty, 86% hold PhDs. 75% faculty teach undergrads.

ACADEMICS
Degrees: Bachelor's, certificate, doctoral, first professional, master's, post-master's certificate. **Academic Requirements:** Arts/fine arts, cultural diversity, English (including composition), ethics, history, humanities, philosophy, sciences (biological or physical), service learning, social science. **Classes:** Most classes have 10–19 students. Most lab/discussion sections have 10–19 students. **Majors with Highest Enrollment:** Business administration/management, nursing/registered nurse training (ASN, BSN, MSN, RN), psychology. **Disciplines with Highest Percentage of Degrees Awarded:** Business/marketing 29%, social sciences 14%, health professions and related sciences 8%, psychology 8%, communications/journalism 7%. **Special Study Options:** Accelerated program, cross registration, distance learning, double major, English as a second language (ESL), exchange student program (domestic), external degree program, honors program, independent study, internships, liberal arts/career combination, student-designed major, study abroad, teacher certification program.

FACILITIES
Housing: Coed dorms, women's dorms, apartments for single students, converted off campus buildings with flats. **Special Academic Facilities/Equipment:** Rare Book Room, Ricci Institute for Chinese-Western Cultural

The Princeton Review's Complete Book of Colleges

History. **Computers:** 4% of classrooms are wired, 51% of classrooms are wireless, 70% of public computers are PCs, 30% of public computers are Macs, network access in dorm rooms, network access in dorm lounges, online registration, online administrative functions (other than registration), remote student-access to Web through college's connection.

CAMPUS LIFE
Activities: Choral groups, dance, drama/theater, literary magazine, music ensembles, musical theater, pep band, radio station, student government, student newspaper, television station, yearbook. **Organizations:** 60 registered organizations, 14 honor societies, 4 fraternities (1% men join), 4 sororities (1% women join). **Athletics (Intercollegiate):** *Men:* Baseball, basketball, cross-country, golf, riflery, soccer, tennis. *Women:* Basketball, cross-country, golf, riflery, soccer, tennis, volleyball. **Environmental Initiatives:** Sustainability. Placed 5th in National competition in RecycleMania. Currently, USF's co-generation plant produces about half of lower campus' peak energy needs. LEED Goals on new projects Incorporation of "green" building practices in construction, including the renovation of Kalmanovitz Hall (formerly Campion Hall). Installation of Photo voltaic panels. As part of that process, USF is installing new solar panels on top of the Koret Health and Recreation Center, University Center, Cowell Hall, and Kalmanovitz Hall. Together with the solar panels already on Gleeson Library, the panels will produce about 16 percent of lower campus' peak electricity needs.

ADMISSIONS
Freshman Academic Profile: 21% in top 10% of high school class, 59% in top 25% of high school class, 91% in top 50% of high school class. 51% from public high schools. SAT Math middle 50% range 520–620. SAT Critical Reading middle 50% range 510–620. SAT Writing middle 50% range 510–620. ACT middle 50% range 22–27. TOEFL required of all international applicants, minimum paper TOEFL 550, minimum computer TOEFL 213. **Basis for Candidate Selection:** *Very important factors considered include:* Academic GPA, recommendation(s), rigor of secondary school record, standardized test scores. *Important factors considered include:* Application essay, class rank. *Other factors considered include:* Alumni/ae relation, character/personal qualities, extracurricular activities, interview, racial/ethnic status, talent/ability, volunteer work. **Freshman Admission Requirements:** High school diploma is required, and GED is accepted. *Academic units recommended:* 4 English, 3 math, 2 science (2 science labs), 2 foreign language, 3 social studies, 6 academic electives, 2 chemistry and 1 biology or physics is required of nursing and science applicants. **Freshman Admission Statistics:** 7,105 applied, 72% admitted, 21% enrolled. **Transfer Admission Requirements:** College transcript(s), essay or personal statement. Minimum college GPA of 2.5 required. Lowest grade transferable C. **General Admission Information:** Application fee $55. Regular notification within 4 weeks of completed application. Non-fall registration accepted. Admission may be deferred for a maximum of 1 semester. Credit offered for CEEB Advanced Placement tests.

COSTS AND FINANCIAL AID
Annual tuition $30,840. Room and board $10,730. Required fees $340. Average book expense $950. **Required Forms and Deadlines:** FAFSA. Financial aid filing deadline 2/15. **Notification of Awards:** Applicants will be notified of awards on a rolling basis beginning on or about 4/1. **Types of Aid:** *Need-based scholarships/grants:* Pell, SEOG, state scholarships/grants, private scholarships, the school's own gift aid, Federal Nursing Scholarships. *Loans:* Direct Subsidized Stafford, Direct Unsubsidized Stafford, Direct PLUS, FFEL PLUS, Federal Perkins, Federal Nursing, college/university loans from institutional funds. Note: FFEL Loans are for graduate students only. **Student Employment:** Federal Work-Study Program available. Institutional employment available. Off-campus job opportunities are excellent. **Financial Aid Statistics:** 48% freshmen, 47% undergrads receive need-based scholarship or grant aid. 50% freshmen, 50% undergrads receive need-based self-help aid. 30 freshmen, 160 undergrads receive athletic scholarships. Highest amount earned per year from on-campus jobs $2,000.

See page 1466.

1727 West Alabama, Chickasha, OK 73018
Phone: 405-574-1357 **E-mail:** usao-admissions@usao.edu **CEEB Code:** 6544
Fax: 405-574-1220 **Website:** www.usao.edu **ACT Code:** 3418
Financial Aid Phone: 405-574-1240

This public school was founded in 1908. It has a 75-acre campus.

RATINGS
Admissions Selectivity Rating: 78   **Fire Safety Rating:** 82   **Green Rating:** 61

STUDENTS AND FACULTY
Enrollment: 1,195. **Student Body:** 64% female, 36% male, 6% out-of-state, 3% international (14 countries represented). African American 5%, Caucasian 75%, Hispanic 3%, Native American 13%. **Retention and Graduation:** 67% freshmen return for sophomore year. 14% freshmen graduate within 4 years. 35% grads go on to further study within 2 semesters. 15% grads pursue arts and sciences degrees. 8% grads pursue business degrees. 3% grads pursue law degrees. 3% grads pursue medical degrees. **Faculty:** Student/faculty ratio 18:1. 53 full-time faculty, 92% hold PhDs. 100% faculty teach undergrads.

ACADEMICS
Degrees: Bachelor's. **Academic Requirements:** Arts/fine arts, computer literacy, English (including composition), history, humanities, mathematics, philosophy, sciences (biological or physical), social science, interdisciplinary studies. **Classes:** Most classes have fewer than 10 students. Most lab/discussion sections have 20–29 students. **Majors with Highest Enrollment:** Business administration and management, elementary education and teaching, psychology. **Disciplines with Highest Percentage of Degrees Awarded:** Business/marketing 18%, visual and performing arts 18%, education 13%, psychology 10%, communications/journalism 8%. **Special Study Options:** Double major, dual enrollment, independent study, internships, liberal arts/career combination, student-designed major, teacher certification program.

FACILITIES
Housing: Coed dorms, apartments for single students. **Special Academic Facilities/Equipment:** Language labs, speech and hearing clinic, multiple computer labs, herbarium. **Computers:** 100% of classrooms are wireless, 90% of public computers are PCs, 10% of public computers are Macs, network access in dorm rooms, network access in dorm lounges, support for handheld computing, remote student-access to Web through college's connection.

CAMPUS LIFE
Activities: Choral groups, concert band, dance, drama/theater, jazz band, literary magazine, music ensembles, musical theater, pep band, student government, student newspaper, television station. **Organizations:** 24 registered organizations, 7 honor societies, 4 religious organizations. 1 fraternity (2% men join), 1 sorority (1% women join). **Athletics (Intercollegiate):** *Men:* Baseball, basketball, cheerleading, soccer. *Women:* Basketball, cheerleading, soccer, softball.

ADMISSIONS
Freshman Academic Profile: 21% in top 10% of high school class, 49% in top 25% of high school class, 81% in top 50% of high school class. 90% from public high schools. ACT middle 50% range 20–25. TOEFL required of all international applicants, minimum paper TOEFL 500, minimum computer TOEFL 173. **Basis for Candidate Selection:** *Very important factors considered include:* Academic GPA, class rank, standardized test scores. *Important factors considered include:* Talent/ability. *Other factors considered include:* Character/personal qualities, recommendation(s). **Freshman Admission Requirements:** High school diploma is required, and GED is accepted. *Academic units required:* 4 English, 3 math, 2 science (2 science labs), 1 social studies, 2 history, 3 academic electives. *Academic units recommended:* 4 math, 3 science (3 science labs), 2 foreign language, 2 fine arts. **Freshman Admission Statistics:** 628 applied, 65% admitted, 59% enrolled. **Transfer Admission Requirements:** College transcript(s), statement of good standing from prior institution(s). Minimum college GPA of 2.0 required. Lowest grade transferable D. **General Admission Information:** Application fee $15. Regular application deadline 8/31. Regular notification is rolling. Non-fall registration accepted. Credit offered for CEEB Advanced Placement tests.

COSTS AND FINANCIAL AID
Required Forms and Deadlines: FAFSA, institution's own financial aid form. Financial aid filing deadline 3/15. **Notification of Awards:** Applicants will be notified of awards on a rolling basis beginning on or about 3/15. **Types of Aid:** *Need-based scholarships/grants:* Pell, SEOG, state scholarships/grants, private

scholarships, the school's own gift aid. *Loans:* FFEL Subsidized Stafford, FFEL Unsubsidized Stafford, FFEL PLUS, Federal Perkins. **Financial Aid Statistics:** 62% freshmen, 59% undergrads receive need-based scholarship or grant aid. 36% freshmen, 43% undergrads receive need-based self-help aid. 13 freshmen, 57 undergrads receive athletic scholarships. 64% freshmen, 63% undergrads receive any aid.

UNIVERSITY OF THE SCIENCES IN PHILADELPHIA

600 South Forty=third Street, Admission Office, Philadelphia, PA 19104-4495
Phone: 215-596-8810 **E-mail:** admit@usip.edu **CEEB Code:** 2663
Fax: 215-596-8821 **Website:** www.usip.edu **ACT Code:** 3671
Financial Aid Phone: 215-596-8894

This private school was founded in 1821. It has a 35-acre campus.

RATINGS
Admissions Selectivity Rating: 91   **Fire Safety Rating:** 81   **Green Rating:** 60*

STUDENTS AND FACULTY
Enrollment: 2,008. **Student Body:** 59% female, 41% male, 47% out-of-state, 1% international (35 countries represented). African American 34%, Caucasian 49%, Hispanic 2%. **Retention and Graduation:** 85% freshmen return for sophomore year. 13% freshmen graduate within 4 years. **Faculty:** Student/faculty ratio 14:1. 145 full-time faculty, 78% hold PhDs. 95% faculty teach undergrads.

ACADEMICS
Degrees: Bachelor's, doctoral, first professional, master's, post-master's certificate. **Academic Requirements:** Computer literacy, English (including composition), history, humanities, mathematics, sciences (biological or physical), social science. **Classes:** Most classes have fewer than 10 students. Most lab/discussion sections have 10–19 students. **Majors with Highest Enrollment:** Biology/biological sciences, pharmacy (PHarmd, BS/BPharm), physical therapy/therapist. **Disciplines with Highest Percentage of Degrees Awarded:** Health professions and related sciences 44%, biological/life sciences 38%, business/marketing 10%, physical sciences 4%, psychology 4%. **Special Study Options:** Academic remediation, advanced placement credit, cooperative education program, distance learning, double major, English as a second language (ESL), honors program, internships, learning disabilities services, off-campus study, teacher certification program.

FACILITIES
Housing: Coed dorms, fraternity/sorority housing, honor halls in certain dormitories, upper level floor for upper level students. **Special Academic Facilities/Equipment:** Pharmacy museum, electron microscope. **Computers:** 15% of classrooms are wired, 25% of classrooms are wireless, 100% of public computers are PCs, network access in dorm rooms, network access in dorm lounges, online registration, online administrative functions (other than registration), remote student-access to Web through college's connection.

CAMPUS LIFE
Activities: Choral groups, concert band, dance, drama/theater, literary magazine, musical theater, student government, student newspaper, yearbook. **Organizations:** 66 registered organizations, 6 honor societies, 6 religious organizations. 2 fraternities, 2 sororities. **Athletics (Intercollegiate):** *Men:* Baseball, basketball, cross-country, golf, riflery, tennis. *Women:* Basketball, cross-country, golf, riflery, softball, tennis, volleyball.

ADMISSIONS
Freshman Academic Profile: 34% in top 10% of high school class, 75% in top 25% of high school class, 97% in top 50% of high school class. SAT Math middle 50% range 560–660. SAT Critical Reading middle 50% range 530–600. ACT middle 50% range 23–27. TOEFL required of all international applicants, minimum paper TOEFL 550, minimum computer TOEFL 213. **Basis for Candidate Selection:** *Very important factors considered include:* Academic GPA, class rank, rigor of secondary school record, standardized test scores. *Important factors considered include:* Character/personal qualities, level of applicant's interest, talent/ability, volunteer work. *Other factors considered include:* Alumni/ae relation, application essay, extracurricular activities, interview, recommendation(s), work experience. **Freshman Admission Requirements:** High school diploma is required, and GED is accepted. *Academic units required:* 4 English, 3 math, 3 science (3 science labs), 1 social studies, 1 history, 4 academic electives. *Academic units recommended:* 4 math, 4 science. **Freshman Admission Statistics:** 3,240 applied, 52% admitted, 30% enrolled. **Transfer Admission Requirements:** College transcript(s), essay or

personal statement. Lowest grade transferable C. **General Admission Information:** Application fee $45. Regular notification is rolling. Non-fall registration not accepted. Credit offered for CEEB Advanced Placement tests.

COSTS AND FINANCIAL AID
Annual tuition $25,618. Room and board $10,524. Required fees $1,312. Average book expense $1,020. **Required Forms and Deadlines:** FAFSA. Financial aid filing deadline 3/15. **Notification of Awards:** Applicants will be notified of awards on a rolling basis beginning on or about 1/15. **Types of Aid:** *Need-based scholarships/grants:* Pell, SEOG, state scholarships/grants, private scholarships, the school's own gift aid. *Loans:* FFEL Subsidized Stafford, FFEL Unsubsidized Stafford, FFEL PLUS, Federal Perkins, college/university loans from institutional funds. **Financial Aid Statistics:** 76% freshmen, 36% undergrads receive need-based scholarship or grant aid. 70% freshmen, 71% undergrads receive need-based self-help aid. 7 freshmen, 42 undergrads receive athletic scholarships. 100% freshmen, 89% undergrads receive any aid. Highest amount earned per year from on-campus jobs $3,000.

THE UNIVERSITY OF SCRANTON

800 Linden Street, Scranton, PA 18510-4699
Phone: 570-941-7540 **E-mail:** admissions@scranton.edu **CEEB Code:** 2929
Fax: 570-941-5928 **Website:** www.scranton.edu **ACT Code:** 3736
Financial Aid Phone: 570-941-7700

This private school, affiliated with the Jesuit order of the Roman Catholic Church, was founded in 1888. It has a 50-acre campus.

RATINGS
Admissions Selectivity Rating: 86   **Fire Safety Rating:** 73   **Green Rating:** 60*

STUDENTS AND FACULTY
Enrollment: 3,946. **Student Body:** 57% female, 43% male, 51% out-of-state. African American 2%, Asian 2%, Caucasian 82%, Hispanic 5%. **Retention and Graduation:** 89% freshmen return for sophomore year. 75% freshmen graduate within 4 years. 35% grads go on to further study within 1 year. 16% grads pursue arts and sciences degrees. 12% grads pursue business degrees. 2% grads pursue law degrees. 4% grads pursue medical degrees. **Faculty:** Student/faculty ratio 11:1. 253 full-time faculty, 85% hold PhDs. 98% faculty teach undergrads.

ACADEMICS
Degrees: Associate, bachelor's, certificate, doctoral, master's, post-bachelor's certificate, post-master's certificate. **Academic Requirements:** Computer literacy, English (including composition), humanities, mathematics, philosophy, sciences (biological or physical), social science, theology, physical education, cultural diversity, public speaking. **Classes:** Most classes have 10–19 students. Most lab/discussion sections have 10–19 students. **Majors with Highest Enrollment:** Communications studies/speech communication and rhetoric, elementary education and teaching, marketing/marketing management. **Disciplines with Highest Percentage of Degrees Awarded:** Business/marketing 22%, health professions and related sciences 14%, education 13%, social sciences 9%, biological/life sciences 9%. **Special Study Options:** Accelerated program, cross-registration, distance learning, double major, dual enrollment, English as a second language (ESL), exchange student program (domestic), honors program, independent study, internships, study abroad, teacher certification program, baccalaureate/masters degree program.

FACILITIES
Housing: Coed dorms, men's dorms, women's dorms, apartments for single students, theme houses. **Special Academic Facilities/Equipment:** Art gallery, fine arts facility, theater, center for music groups, language lab, microbiology institute, electron microscope, greenhouse. **Computers:** 1% of classrooms are wired, 60% of classrooms are wireless, 94% of public computers are PCs, 5% of public computers are Macs, 1% of public computers are UNIX, network access in dorm rooms, network access in dorm lounges, online registration, online administrative functions (other than registration), support for handheld computing, remote student-access to Web through college's connection.

CAMPUS LIFE

Activities: Choral groups, concert band, dance, drama/theater, jazz band, literary magazine, music ensembles, radio station, student government, student newspaper, television station, yearbook. **Organizations:** 50 registered organizations, 26 honor societies, 14 religious organizations. **Athletics (Intercollegiate):** *Men:* Baseball, basketball, cross-country, golf, ice hockey, lacrosse, soccer, swimming, tennis, wrestling. *Women:* Basketball, cross-country, field hockey, lacrosse, soccer, softball, swimming, tennis, volleyball.

ADMISSIONS

Freshman Academic Profile: 26% in top 10% of high school class, 62% in top 25% of high school class, 90% in top 50% of high school class. 55% from public high schools. SAT Math middle 50% range 520–620. SAT Critical Reading middle 50% range 510–600. TOEFL required of all international applicants, minimum paper TOEFL 500, minimum computer TOEFL 173. **Basis for Candidate Selection:** *Very important factors considered include:* Academic GPA, class rank, rigor of secondary school record, standardized test scores. *Important factors considered include:* Extracurricular activities. *Other factors considered include:* Alumni/ae relation, application essay, character/personal qualities, interview, level of applicant's interest, recommendation(s), talent/ ability, volunteer work, work experience. **Freshman Admission Requirements:** High school diploma is required, and GED is accepted. *Academic units required:* 4 English, 3 math, 1 science, 2 foreign language, 2 social studies, 4 academic electives. *Academic units recommended:* 4 English, 4 math, 2 science, 2 foreign language, 3 social studies, 4 academic electives. **Freshman Admission Statistics:** 6,777 applied, 70% admitted, 21% enrolled. **Transfer Admission Requirements:** High school transcript, college transcript(s). Minimum college GPA of 2.8 required. Lowest grade transferable C. **General Admission Information:** Application fee $40. Regular application deadline 3/1. Regular notification is rolling. Nonfall registration accepted. Admission may be deferred for a maximum of 1 year. Credit and/or placement offered for CEEB Advanced Placement tests.

COSTS AND FINANCIAL AID

Average book expense $1,000. **Required Forms and Deadlines:** FAFSA. Financial aid filing deadline 2/15. **Notification of Awards:** Applicants will be notified of awards on a rolling basis beginning on or about 3/1. **Types of Aid:** *Need-based scholarships/grants:* Pell, SEOG, state scholarships/grants, private scholarships, the school's own gift aid. *Loans:* FFEL Subsidized Stafford, FFEL Unsubsidized Stafford, FFEL PLUS, Federal Perkins, Federal Nursing. **Student Employment:** Federal Work-Study Program available. Institutional employment available. Off-campus job opportunities are good. **Financial Aid Statistics:** 63% freshmen, 62% undergrads receive need-based scholarship or grant aid. 57% freshmen, 57% undergrads receive need-based self-help aid. 82% freshmen, 82% undergrads receive any aid.

See page 1468.

UNIVERSITY OF SIOUX FALLS

1101 West Twenty-second Street, Sioux Falls, SD 57105
Phone: 605-331-6600 **E-mail:** admissions@usiouxfalls.edu **CEEB Code:** 6651
Fax: 605-331-6615 **Website:** www.usiouxfalls.edu **ACT Code:** 3920
Financial Aid Phone: 605-331-6623

This private school, affiliated with the American Baptist Church, was founded in 1883. It has a 26-acre campus.

RATINGS

Admissions Selectivity Rating: 72   **Fire Safety Rating:** 60*   **Green Rating:** 60*

STUDENTS AND FACULTY

Enrollment: 1,186. **Student Body:** 56% female, 44% male, 36% out-of-state. African American 2%, Caucasian 95%. **Retention and Graduation:** 61% freshmen return for sophomore year. 43% freshmen graduate within 4 years. 14% grads go on to further study within 2 semesters. **Faculty:** Student/faculty ratio 18:1. 47 full-time faculty, 72% hold PhDs. 100% faculty teach undergrads.

ACADEMICS

Degrees: Associate, bachelor's, master's, post-master's certificate. **Academic Requirements:** Arts/fine arts, communication, computer literacy, English (including composition), history, humanities, mathematics, religion, sciences (biological or physical), social science, wellness. **Classes:** Most classes have 10–19 students. Most lab/discussion sections have 20–29 students. **Majors with Highest Enrollment:** Business administration/management, teacher education. **Disciplines with Highest Percentage of Degrees Awarded:** Business/marketing 35%, education 16%, social sciences 10%, biological/life

---

sciences 5%, English 4%. **Special Study Options:** Accelerated program, American studies program (Washington, D.C.), cross registration, distance learning, double major, dual enrollment, honors program, independent study, internships, liberal arts/career combination, student-designed major, study abroad, teacher certification program.

FACILITIES

Housing: Coed dorms, men's dorms, women's dorms, apartments for married students, apartments for single students, freshmen/sophomores required to live in college housing unless over 20 years of age or given permission by Director of Residence Life. **Special Academic Facilities/Equipment:** Education curriculum lab, physiology lab, autoclave for research in diagnostic medicine. **Computers:** 85% of public computers are PCs, 15% of public computers are Macs, network access in dorm rooms, network access in dorm lounges, remote student-access to Web through college's connection.

CAMPUS LIFE

Activities: Choral groups, concert band, drama/theater, jazz band, literary magazine, music ensembles, musical theater, radio station, student government, student newspaper, television station. **Organizations:** 8 registered organizations, 2 honor societies, 3 religious organizations. **Athletics (Intercollegiate):** *Men:* Baseball, basketball, cross-country, football, golf, soccer, tennis, track/field (indoor), track/field (outdoor). *Women:* Basketball, cross-country, golf, soccer, softball, tennis, track/field (indoor), track/field (outdoor), volleyball.

ADMISSIONS

Freshman Academic Profile: 16% in top 10% of high school class, 41% in top 25% of high school class, 72% in top 50% of high school class. ACT middle 50% range 19–24. TOEFL required of all international applicants, minimum paper TOEFL 500, minimum computer TOEFL 173. **Basis for Candidate Selection:** *Very important factors considered include:* Class rank, rigor of secondary school record, standardized test scores. *Other factors considered include:* Interview, recommendation(s). **Freshman Admission Requirements:** High school diploma is required, and GED is accepted. *Academic units recommended:* 4 English, 3 math, 2 science, 3 social studies, 3 history, 1 computer. **Freshman Admission Statistics:** 488 applied, 98% admitted, 44% enrolled. **Transfer Admission Requirements:** High school transcript, college transcript(s), statement of good standing from prior institution(s). Minimum college GPA of 2.0 required. Lowest grade transferable C. **General Admission Information:** Application fee $25. Regular notification is rolling. Non-fall registration accepted. Common Application not accepted. Credit and/or placement offered for CEEB Advanced Placement tests.

COSTS AND FINANCIAL AID

Annual tuition $13,900. Room & board $4,000. Required fees $50. Average book expense $700. **Required Forms and Deadlines:** FAFSA. Financial aid filing deadline 3/1. **Notification of Awards:** Applicants will be notified of awards on a rolling basis beginning on or about 3/1. **Types of Aid:** *Need-based scholarships/grants:* Pell, SEOG, private scholarships, the school's own gift aid. *Loans:* Direct Subsidized Stafford, Direct Unsubsidized Stafford, Direct PLUS, FFEL Subsidized Stafford, FFEL Unsubsidized Stafford, FFEL PLUS, Federal Perkins, state loans. **Student Employment:** Federal Work-Study Program available. Off-campus job opportunities are excellent. **Financial Aid Statistics:** 30% freshmen, 32% undergrads receive need-based scholarship or grant aid. 66% freshmen, 67% undergrads receive need-based self-help aid.

THE UNIVERSITY OF THE SOUTH

735 University Avenue, Sewanee, TN 37383-1000
Phone: 931-598-1238 **E-mail:** collegeadmission@sewanee.edu **CEEB Code:** 1842
Fax: 931-538-3248 **Website:** www.sewanee.edu **ACT Code:** 4924
Financial Aid Phone: 800-522-2234

This private school, affiliated with the Episcopal Church, was founded in 1857. It has a 10,000-acre campus.

RATINGS

Admissions Selectivity Rating: 90   **Fire Safety Rating:** 79   **Green Rating:** 88

STUDENTS AND FACULTY

Enrollment: 1,491. **Student Body:** 52% female, 48% male, 78% out-of-state, 2% international (22 countries represented). African American 4%, Asian 2%,

Caucasian 89%, Hispanic 3%. **Retention and Graduation:** 92% freshmen return for sophomore year. 72% freshmen graduate within 4 years. 38% grads go on to further study within 1 year. 24% grads pursue arts and sciences degrees. 4% grads pursue business degrees. 6% grads pursue law degrees. 4% grads pursue medical degrees. **Faculty:** Student/faculty ratio 11:1. 132 full-time faculty, 92% hold PhDs. 100% faculty teach undergrads.

ACADEMICS

Degrees: Bachelor's, doctoral, first professional certificate, first professional, master's, post-bachelor's certificate, post-master's certificate. **Academic Requirements:** Arts/fine arts, English (including composition), foreign languages, history, humanities, mathematics, philosophy, physical education, sciences (biological or physical), social science. **Classes:** Most classes have 10–19 students. Most lab/discussion sections have 10–19 students. **Disciplines with Highest Percentage of Degrees Awarded:** Social sciences 18%, English 15%, history 12%, visual and performing arts 10%, philosophy and religious studies 9%. **Special Study Options:** Double major, independent study, internships, student-designed major, study abroad, teacher certification program.

FACILITIES

Housing: Coed dorms, men's dorms, women's dorms, apartments for married students, special housing for disabled students, fraternity/sorority housing, substance-free housing, language houses. **Special Academic Facilities/Equipment:** Art gallery, observatory, keyboard collection, materials analysis lab with electron microscope. **Computers:** 50% of public computers are PCs, 50% of public computers are Macs, network access in dorm rooms, network access in dorm lounges, online registration, online administrative functions (other than registration), remote student-access to Web through college's connection.

CAMPUS LIFE

Activities: Choral groups, dance, drama/theater, jazz band, literary magazine, music ensembles, musical theater, radio station, student government, student newspaper, student-run film society, symphony orchestra, yearbook. **Organizations:** 110 registered organizations, 9 honor societies, 11 religious organizations. 11 fraternities (70% men join), 6 sororities (68% women join). **Athletics (Intercollegiate):** *Men:* Baseball, basketball, crew/rowing, cross-country, diving, equestrian sports, fencing, football, golf, soccer, swimming, tennis, track/field (outdoor). *Women:* Basketball, cheerleading, crew/rowing, cross-country, diving, equestrian sports, fencing, field hockey, golf, soccer, swimming, tennis, track/field (outdoor), volleyball. Environmental Initiatives: Environmental residents. Current strategic plan initiative for sustainability and environmental programs. Commitment to energy conservation in all building projects including connection to central computer controlled building climate automation system.

ADMISSIONS

Freshman Academic Profile: 42% in top 10% of high school class, 71% in top 25% of high school class, 94% in top 50% of high school class. 52% from public high schools. SAT Math middle 50% range 560–650. SAT Critical Reading middle 50% range 570–680. SAT Writing middle 50% range 580–670. ACT middle 50% range 25–30. TOEFL required of all international applicants, minimum paper TOEFL 550, minimum computer TOEFL 220. **Basis for Candidate Selection:** *Very important factors considered include:* Academic GPA, recommendation(s), rigor of secondary school record. *Important factors considered include:* Application essay, character/personal qualities, extracurricular activities, standardized test scores, volunteer work, work experience. *Other factors considered include:* Alumni/ae relation, class rank, first generation, geographical residence, interview, level of applicant's interest, racial/ethnic status, talent/ability. **Freshman Admission Requirements:** High school diploma is required, and GED is not accepted. *Academic units required:* 4 English, 2 math, 2 science (2 science labs), 2 foreign language, 1 social studies, 1 history. *Academic units recommended:* 4 English, 4 math, 4 science (3 science labs), 4 foreign language, 2 social studies, 2 history. **Freshman Admission Statistics:** 1,932 applied, 71% admitted, 30% enrolled. **Transfer Admission Requirements:** High school transcript, college transcript(s), essay or personal statement, standardized test score, statement of good standing from prior institution(s). Lowest grade transferable C. **General Admission Information:** Application fee $45. Early decision application deadline 11/15. Regular application deadline 2/1. Non-fall registration not accepted. Admission may be deferred for a maximum of 1 year. Credit and/or placement offered for CEEB Advanced Placement tests.

COSTS AND FINANCIAL AID

Annual tuition $30,438. Room and board $8,780. Required fees $222. Average book expense $800. **Required Forms and Deadlines:** FAFSA, institution's own financial aid form, student and/or parent U.S. income tax returns if applicable. Financial aid filing deadline 3/1. **Notification of Awards:** Applicants will be notified of awards on or about 4/1. **Types of Aid:** *Need-based scholarships/grants:* Pell, SEOG, state scholarships/grants, private scholarships, the school's own gift aid. *Loans:* FFEL Subsidized Stafford, FFEL Unsubsidized Stafford, FFEL PLUS, Federal Perkins, state loans, college/university loans from institutional funds, private alternative loans. **Financial**

Aid Statistics: 38% freshmen, 45% undergrads receive need-based scholarship or grant aid. 28% freshmen, 33% undergrads receive need-based self-help aid. Highest amount earned per year from on-campus jobs $1,000.

UNIVERSITY OF SOUTH ALABAMA

Meisler Hall, Room 2500, Mobile, AL 36688-0002
Phone: 334-460-6141 **E-mail:** admiss@jaguar1.usouthal.edu **CEEB Code:** 1880
Fax: 334-460-7023 **Website:** www.usouthal.edu **ACT Code:** 0059
Financial Aid Phone: 251-460-6231

This public school was founded in 1963. It has a 1,215-acre campus.

RATINGS

Admissions Selectivity Rating: 60*   **Fire Safety Rating:** 60*   **Green Rating:** 60*

STUDENTS AND FACULTY

Enrollment: 9,874. **Student Body:** 60% female, 40% male, 16% out-of-state, 5% international (98 countries represented). African American 19%, Asian 3%, Caucasian 68%, Hispanic 2%. **Retention and Graduation:** 72% freshmen return for sophomore year. 16% freshmen graduate within 4 years. **Faculty:** 729 full-time faculty, 76% hold PhDs.

ACADEMICS

Degrees: Bachelor's, certificate, doctoral, first professional, master's, post-bachelor's certificate, post-master's certificate. **Academic Requirements:** Arts/fine arts, computer literacy, English (including composition), history, humanities, mathematics, sciences (biological or physical), social science. **Disciplines with Highest Percentage of Degrees Awarded:** Health professions and related sciences 21%, business/marketing 17%, education 15%, engineering 7%, communications/journalism 6%. **Special Study Options:** Cooperative education program, double major, dual enrollment, English as a second language (ESL), honors program, independent study, internships, student-designed major, study abroad, teacher certification program, weekend college.

FACILITIES

Housing: Men's dorms, women's dorms, apartments for married students, apartments for single students, fraternity/sorority housing. **Special Academic Facilities/Equipment:** Museum/gallery complex, 3 hospitals, center for clinical education in health programs, engineering labs. **Computers:** 10% of classrooms are wireless, 90% of public computers are PCs, 10% of public computers are Macs, network access in dorm rooms, online registration, online administrative functions (other than registration). Undergraduates are required to own a computer.

CAMPUS LIFE

Activities: Concert band, drama/theater, jazz band, literary magazine, music ensembles, musical theater, opera, student government, student newspaper, student-run film society, symphony orchestra, television station. **Organizations:** 185 registered organizations, 2 honor societies, 1 religious organization. 8 fraternities (8% men join), 8 sororities (6% women join). **Athletics (Intercollegiate):** *Men:* Baseball, basketball, cross-country, golf, tennis, track/field (outdoor). *Women:* Basketball, cross-country, golf, soccer, softball, tennis, track/field (outdoor), volleyball.

ADMISSIONS

Freshman Academic Profile: 92% from public high schools. SAT Math middle 50% range 460–610. SAT Critical Reading middle 50% range 440–590. ACT middle 50% range 19–24. Minimum paper TOEFL 500. **Basis for Candidate Selection:** *Very important factors considered include:* Rigor of secondary school record, standardized test scores. **Freshman Admission Requirements:** High school diploma is required, and GED is accepted. *Academic units recommended:* 4 English, 4 math, 2 science, 2 history, 2 academic electives. **Freshman Admission Statistics:** 2,906 applied, 93% admitted, 53% enrolled. **Transfer Admission Requirements:** College transcript(s). Minimum college GPA of 2.0 required. Lowest grade transferable D. **General Admission Information:** Application fee $25. Regular application deadline 9/10. Regular notification rolling. Non-fall registration accepted. Credit and/or placement offered for CEEB Advanced Placement tests.

COSTS AND FINANCIAL AID

Annual in-state tuition $3,810. Out-of-state tuition $7,620. Room & board $4,428. Required fees $692. Average book expense $1,000. **Required Forms and Deadlines:** FAFSA, institution's own financial aid form, state aid form. **Notification of Awards:** Applicants will be notified of awards on a rolling basis beginning on or about 5/15. **Types of Aid:** *Need-based scholarships/grants:* Pell, SEOG, state scholarships/grants, private scholarships, the school's own gift aid. *Loans:* FFEL Subsidized Stafford, FFEL Unsubsidized Stafford, FFEL

PLUS, Federal Perkins, college/university loans from institutional funds. **Financial Aid Statistics:** 70% freshmen, 70% undergrads receive any aid. Highest amount earned per year from on-campus jobs $2,000.

UNIVERSITY OF SOUTH CAROLINA—AIKEN

471 University Parkway, Aiken, SC 29801
Phone: 803-641-3366 **E-mail:** admit@usca.edu **CEEB Code:** 5840
Fax: 803-641-3727 **Website:** www.usca.edu **ACT Code:** 3879
Financial Aid Phone: 803-641-3476

This public school was founded in 1961. It has a 453-acre campus.

RATINGS
Admissions Selectivity Rating: 83   **Fire Safety Rating:** 87   **Green Rating:** 60*

STUDENTS AND FACULTY
Enrollment: 2,910. **Student Body:** 66% female, 34% male, 10% out-of-state, 2% international (24 countries represented). African American 27%, Asian 1%, Caucasian 64%, Hispanic 2%. **Retention and Graduation:** 67% freshmen return for sophomore year. 21% freshmen graduate within 4 years. **Faculty:** Student/faculty ratio 15:1. 148 full-time faculty, 74% hold PhDs. 100% faculty teach undergrads.

ACADEMICS
Degrees: Bachelor's, master's. **Academic Requirements:** Applied speech communication, Arts/fine arts, English (including composition), foreign languages, history, humanities, mathematics, sciences (biological or physical), social science. **Classes:** Most classes have 20–29 students. Most lab/discussion sections have fewer than 10 students. **Majors with Highest Enrollment:** Business administration/management, education, nursing/registered nurse training (ASN, BSN, MSN, RN). **Disciplines with Highest Percentage of Degrees Awarded:** Business/marketing 27%, education 16%, health professions and related sciences 12%, biological/life sciences 9%, social sciences 8%. **Special Study Options:** Accelerated program, cooperative education program, cross registration, distance learning, double major, dual enrollment, exchange student program (domestic), honors program, independent study, internships, study abroad, teacher certification program.

FACILITIES
Housing: Coed dorms, apartments for single students, special housing for disabled students. **Special Academic Facilities/Equipment:** Ruth Patrick Science Education Center, Etherredge Center (fine arts center), wellness center. **Computers:** 100% of classrooms are wireless, 90% of public computers are PCs, 10% of public computers are Macs, network access in dorm rooms, online registration, online administrative functions (other than registration), remote student-access to Web through college's connection.

CAMPUS LIFE
Activities: Choral groups, concert band, dance, drama/theater, jazz band, literary magazine, music ensembles, musical theater, pep band, student government, student newspaper, symphony orchestra, yearbook. **Organizations:** 65 registered organizations, 6 honor societies, 6 religious organizations. 5 fraternities (2% men join), 7 sororities (3% women join). **Athletics (Intercollegiate):** *Men:* Baseball, basketball, golf, soccer, tennis. *Women:* Basketball, cheerleading, cross-country, soccer, softball, tennis, volleyball.

ADMISSIONS
Freshman Academic Profile: 17% in top 10% of high school class, 50% in top 25% of high school class, 84% in top 50% of high school class. SAT Math middle 50% range 450–550. SAT Critical Reading middle 50% range 440–540. SAT Writing middle 50% range 430–540. ACT middle 50% range 18–22. TOEFL required of all international applicants, minimum paper TOEFL 550, minimum computer TOEFL 213. **Basis for Candidate Selection:** *Very important factors considered include:* Rigor of secondary school record, standardized test scores. *Important factors considered include:* Academic GPA, class rank. **Freshman Admission Requirements:** High school diploma is required, and GED is accepted. *Academic units required:* 4 English, 4 math, 3 science (3 science labs), 2 foreign language, 2 social studies, 1 history, 4 academic electives, phyiscal education or ROTC. **Freshman Admission Statistics:** 2,402 applied, 46% admitted, 62% enrolled. **Transfer Admission Requirements:** College transcript(s), statement of good standing from prior institution(s). Minimum college GPA of 2.0 required. Lowest grade transferable C. **General Admission Information:** Application fee $35. Regular application deadline 8/1. Regular notification is rolling. Non-fall registration accepted. Credit and/or placement offered for CEEB Advanced Placement tests.

COSTS AND FINANCIAL AID
Annual in-state tuition $6,806. Annual out-of-state tuition $13,722. Room and board $5,870. Required fees $230. Average book expense $1,105. **Required Forms and Deadlines:** FAFSA. Financial aid filing deadline 3/15. **Notification of Awards:** Applicants will be notified of awards on a rolling basis beginning on or about 4/20. **Types of Aid:** *Need-based scholarships/grants:* Pell, SEOG, state scholarships/grants, private scholarships, the school's own gift aid. *Loans:* FFEL Subsidized Stafford, FFEL Unsubsidized Stafford, FFEL PLUS, Federal Perkins, state loans. **Student Employment:** Federal Work-Study Program available. Institutional employment available. Off-campus job opportunities are fair. **Financial Aid Statistics:** 17% freshmen, 17% undergrads receive need-based scholarship or grant aid. 19% freshmen, 18% undergrads receive need-based self-help aid. 43 freshmen, 163 undergrads receive athletic scholarships.

UNIVERSITY OF SOUTH CAROLINA—BEAUFORT

1 University Boulevard, Bluffton, SC 29909
Phone: 843-208-8000 **E-mail:** webbdh@gwm.sc.edu **CEEB Code:** 5845
Fax: 843-208-8290 **Website:** www.uscb.edu **ACT Code:** 3835
Financial Aid Phone: 843-521-3104

This public school was founded in 1959. It has a 213-acre campus.

RATINGS
Admissions Selectivity Rating: 60*   **Fire Safety Rating:** 60*   **Green Rating:** 60*

STUDENTS AND FACULTY
Enrollment: 1,053. **Student Body:** 64% female, 36% male, 19% out-of-state, 1% international (14 countries represented). African American 17%, Asian 1%, Caucasian 69%, Hispanic 4%, Native American 1%. **Retention and Graduation:** 48% freshmen return for sophomore year. **Faculty:** Student/faculty ratio 15:1. 45 full-time faculty, 76% hold PhDs. 100% faculty teach undergrads.

ACADEMICS
Degrees: Associate, bachelor's. **Academic Requirements:** Arts/fine arts, English (including composition), foreign languages, history, humanities, mathematics, philosophy, sciences (biological or physical), social science. **Majors with Highest Enrollment:** Business administration and management, early childhood education and teaching, social sciences. **Disciplines with Highest Percentage of Degrees Awarded:** Business/marketing 35%, education 21%, liberal arts/general studies 21%, English 10%, social sciences 8%, biological/life sciences 2%. **Special Study Options:** Cooperative education program, cross registration, distance learning, dual enrollment, independent study, internships, study abroad, teacher certification program.

FACILITIES
Housing: Apartments for single students, special housing for disabled students. **Computers:** 30% of public computers are PCs, network access in dorm rooms, network access in dorm lounges, online registration, online administrative functions (other than registration), support for handheld computing.

CAMPUS LIFE
Activities: Drama/theater, literary magazine, musical theater, student government, student newspaper. **Organizations:** 11 registered organizations.

ADMISSIONS
Freshman Academic Profile: TOEFL required of all international applicants, minimum paper TOEFL 550, minimum computer TOEFL 213. **Basis for Candidate Selection:** *Very important factors considered include:* Academic GPA, standardized test scores. *Important factors considered include:* Class rank, rigor of secondary school record. **Freshman Admission Requirements:** High school diploma is required, and GED is accepted. *Academic units required:* 4 English, 3 math, 3 science (3 science labs), 2 foreign language, 2 social studies, 1 history, 4 academic electives, 1 physical education. **Freshman Admission Statistics:** 532 applied, 61% admitted, 72% enrolled. **Transfer Admission Requirements:** College transcript(s). Minimum college GPA of 2.0 required. Lowest grade transferable C-. **General Admission Information:** Application fee $40. Regular notification is rolling. Non-fall registration accepted. Credit offered for CEEB Advanced Placement tests.

COSTS AND FINANCIAL AID
Average book expense $962. **Required Forms and Deadlines:** FAFSA. Financial aid filing deadline 4/15. **Notification of Awards:** Applicants will be notified of awards on a rolling basis beginning on or about 5/31. **Types of Aid:** *Need-based scholarships/grants:* Pell, SEOG, state scholarships/grants, private scholarships, the school's own gift aid. *Loans:* FFEL Subsidized Stafford, FFEL Unsubsidized Stafford, FFEL PLUS, state loans. **Financial Aid Statistics:** 35% freshmen, 65% undergrads receive any aid.

UNIVERSITY OF SOUTH CAROLINA—COLUMBIA

Office of Undergraduate Admissions, University of South Carolina, Columbia, SC 29208
Phone: 803-777-7700 **E-mail:** admissions@sc.edu **CEEB Code:** 5818
Fax: 803-777-0101 **Website:** www.sc.edu **ACT Code:** 3880
Financial Aid Phone: 803-777-8134

This public school was founded in 1801. It has a 372-acre campus.

RATINGS
Admissions Selectivity Rating: 88   **Fire Safety Rating:** 89   **Green Rating:** 85

STUDENTS AND FACULTY
Enrollment: 18,133. **Student Body:** 54% female, 46% male, 11% out-of-state. African American 13%, Asian 3%, Caucasian 71%, Hispanic 2%. **Retention and Graduation:** 86% freshmen return for sophomore year. 40% freshmen graduate within 4 years. **Faculty:** Student/faculty ratio 17:1. 1,231 full-time faculty, 85% hold PhDs. 72% faculty teach undergrads.

ACADEMICS
Degrees: Associate, bachelor's, doctoral, first professional, master's, post-bachelor's certificate, post-master's certificate. **Academic Requirements:** Arts/fine arts, computer literacy, English (including composition), foreign languages, history, humanities, mathematics, philosophy, sciences (biological or physical), social science. **Classes:** Most classes have 20–29 students. Most lab/discussion sections have 20–29 students. **Majors with Highest Enrollment:** Business administration and management, experimental psychology, public relations/image management. **Disciplines with Highest Percentage of Degrees Awarded:** Business/marketing 26%, social sciences 10%, communication technologies 9%, psychology 7%, visual and performing arts 6%. **Special Study Options:** Accelerated program, alternative spring break, cooperative education program, cross registration, distance learning, Dobson Internship Program, double major, dual enrollment, English as a second language (ESL), exchange student program (domestic), external degree program, honors program, independent study, internships, Students Educating and Empowering for Diversity, study abroad, teacher certification program, weekend college.

FACILITIES
Housing: Coed dorms, women's dorms, apartments for married students, apartments for single students, special housing for disabled students, special housing for international students, fraternity/sorority housing, honors housing (undergraduate), wellness. **Special Academic Facilities/Equipment:** Art gallery, movie theater, McKissick Museum, South Caroliniana Library, Melton Observatory, Gibbes Planetarium, Melton Observatory, filtration research engineering demonstration unit, Belser Arboretum, A.C. Moore Gardens. **Computers:** 80% of classrooms are wired, 40% of classrooms are wireless, 90% of public computers are PCs, 5% of public computers are Macs, 5% of public computers are UNIX, network access in dorm rooms, network access in dorm lounges, online registration, online administrative functions (other than registration), support for handheld computing, remote student-access to Web through college's connection.

CAMPUS LIFE
Activities: Choral groups, concert band, dance, drama/theater, jazz band, literary magazine, marching band, music ensembles, musical theater, opera, pep band, radio station, student government, student newspaper, symphony orchestra. **Organizations:** 300 registered organizations, 19 honor societies, 28 religious organizations. 18 fraternities (14% men join), 14 sororities (15% women join). **Athletics (Intercollegiate):** *Men:* Baseball, basketball, diving, football, golf, soccer, swimming, tennis, track/field (outdoor). *Women:* Basketball, cross-country, diving, equestrian sports, golf, soccer, softball, swimming, tennis, track/field (outdoor), volleyball. **Environmental Initiatives:** Purchasing policy for EnergyStar appliances. Public transportation fleet of buses that use biodiesel. Operation of biomass plant producing 4% of energy from renewable sources.

ADMISSIONS
Freshman Academic Profile: 29% in top 10% of high school class, 63% in top 25% of high school class, 93% in top 50% of high school class. SAT Math middle 50% range 540–640. SAT Critical Reading middle 50% range 520–620. ACT middle 50% range 23–28. TOEFL required of all international applicants, minimum paper TOEFL 550, minimum computer TOEFL 210. **Basis for Candidate Selection:** *Very important factors considered include:* Rigor of secondary school record, standardized test scores. *Important factors considered include:* Academic GPA. *Other factors considered include:* Alumni/ae relation, application essay, character/personal qualities, class rank, extracurricular activities, racial/ethnic status, recommendation(s), state residency, talent/ability, volunteer work, work experience. **Freshman Admission Requirements:** High school diploma is required, and GED is accepted. *Academic units required:* 4 English, 3 math, 3 science (3 science labs), 2 foreign language, 2 social studies, 1 history, 4 academic electives, 1 physical education or ROTC. **Freshman Admission Statistics:** 13,946 applied, 63% admitted, 42% enrolled. **Transfer Admission Requirements:** College transcript(s). Minimum college GPA of 2.3 required. Lowest grade transferable C-. **General Admission Information:** Application fee $50. Regular application deadline 12/1. Regular notification is rolling. Non-fall registration accepted. Credit offered for CEEB Advanced Placement tests.

COSTS AND FINANCIAL AID
Annual in-state tuition $7,408. Out-of-state tuition $19,836. Room & board $6,520. Required fees $400. Average book expense $838. **Required Forms and Deadlines:** FAFSA. Financial aid filing deadline 4/1. **Notification of Awards:** Applicants will be notified of awards on or about 4/1. **Types of Aid:** *Need-based scholarships/grants:* Pell, SEOG, state scholarships/grants, private scholarships, the school's own gift aid, United Negro College Fund, Federal Nursing Scholarships, USC Opportunity Grant—Institutional. *Loans:* FFEL Subsidized Stafford, FFEL Unsubsidized Stafford, FFEL PLUS, Federal Perkins, Federal Nursing. **Student Employment:** Federal Work-Study Program available. Off-campus job opportunities are good. **Financial Aid Statistics:** 19% of freshmen, 24% undergrads receive need-based scholarship or grant aid. 34% freshmen, 40% undergrads receive need-based self-help aid. 117 freshmen, 535 undergrads receive athletic scholarships. 95% freshmen, 82% undergrads receive any aid.

UNIVERSITY OF SOUTH CAROLINA—UPSTATE

800 University Way, Spartanburg, SC 29303
Phone: 864-503-5246 **E-mail:** dstewart@uscs.edu **CEEB Code:** 5850
Fax: 864-503-5727 **Website:** www.uscs.edu **ACT Code:** 3889
Financial Aid Phone: 864-503-5340

This public school was founded in 1967. It has a 298-acre campus.

RATINGS
Admissions Selectivity Rating: 79   **Fire Safety Rating:** 60*   **Green Rating:** 60*

STUDENTS AND FACULTY
Enrollment: 4,237. **Student Body:** 65% female, 35% male, 7% out-of-state, 2% international (30 countries represented). African American 26%, Asian 3%, Caucasian 64%, Hispanic 1%. **Retention and Graduation:** 67% freshmen return for sophomore year. 17% freshmen graduate within 4 years. 20% grads go on to further study within 2 semesters. **Faculty:** Student/faculty ratio 17:1. 179 full-time faculty, 79% hold PhDs. 100% faculty teach undergrads.

ACADEMICS
Degrees: Associate, bachelor's, master's. **Academic Requirements:** Arts/fine arts, computer literacy, English (including composition), foreign languages, history, humanities, mathematics, sciences (biological or physical), social science. **Classes:** Most classes have 20–29 students. Most lab/discussion sections have 20–29 students. **Majors with Highest Enrollment:** Business administration/management, education, nursing/registered nurse training (ASN, BSN, MSN, RN). **Disciplines with Highest Percentage of Degrees Awarded:** Education 22%, business/marketing 18%, liberal arts/general studies 17%, health professions and related sciences 11%, psychology 6%. **Special Study Options:** Accelerated program, cross registration, distance learning, double major, exchange student program (domestic), honors program, independent study, internships, student-designed major, study abroad, teacher certification program.

FACILITIES
Housing: Coed dorms, apartments for single students. **Special Academic Facilities/Equipment:** Campus life center, performing arts building with 450 seat theater, arts studies film theater, recital hall, language laboratory, Quality Institute. **Computers:** 10% of public computers are PCs, network access in dorm rooms, online registration, online administrative functions (other than registration), remote student-access to Web through college's connection.

CAMPUS LIFE
Activities: Choral groups, dance, drama/theater, jazz band, literary magazine, music ensembles, musical theater, student government, student newspaper.

Organizations: 61 registered organizations, 5 religious organizations. 2 fraternities (4% men join), 3 sororities (4% women join). **Athletics (Intercollegiate):** *Men:* Baseball, basketball, cross-country, soccer, tennis. *Women:* Basketball, cross-country, soccer, softball, tennis, volleyball.

ADMISSIONS

Freshman Academic Profile: 11% in top 10% of high school class, 37% in top 25% of high school class, 68% in top 50% of high school class. SAT Math middle 50% range 450–540. SAT Critical Reading middle 50% range 440–530. ACT middle 50% range 18–21. TOEFL required of all international applicants, minimum paper TOEFL 500, minimum computer TOEFL 173. **Basis for Candidate Selection:** *Very important factors considered include:* Rigor of secondary school record, standardized test scores. **Freshman Admission Requirements:** High school diploma is required, and GED is accepted. *Academic units required:* 4 English, 3 math, 3 science (2 science labs), 2 foreign language, 2 social studies, 1 history, 4 academic electives, 1 physical education or ROTC. **Freshman Admission Statistics:** 1,904 applied, 49% admitted, 75% enrolled. **Transfer Admission Requirements:** College transcript(s), statement of good standing from prior institution(s). Minimum college GPA of 2.0 required. Lowest grade transferable C. **General Admission Information:** Application fee $35. Regular notification is rolling. Non-fall registration accepted. Admission may be deferred for a maximum of 2 semesters. Common Application not accepted. Credit offered for CEEB Advanced Placement tests.

COSTS AND FINANCIAL AID

Annual in-state tuition $5,310. Out-of-state tuition $10,936. Room & board $4,940. Required fees $226. Average book expense $700. **Required Forms and Deadlines:** FAFSA, Scholarship Application. Financial aid filing deadline 3/1. **Types of Aid:** *Need-based scholarships/grants:* Pell, SEOG, state scholarships/grants, private scholarships, the school's own gift aid. *Non-need-based (college-administered):* Academic merit, athletic state scholarships/grants, ROTC scholarships. *Loans:* FFEL Subsidized Stafford, FFEL Unsubsidized Stafford, FFEL PLUS, Federal Perkins, Federal Nursing, state loans. **Student Employment:** Federal Work-Study Program available. Institutional employment available. Off-campus job opportunities are excellent. **Financial Aid Statistics:** 33% freshmen, 37% undergrads receive need-based scholarship or grant aid. 31% freshmen, 45% undergrads receive need-based self-help aid. 16 freshmen, 87 undergrads receive athletic scholarships.

THE UNIVERSITY OF SOUTH DAKOTA

414 East Clark, Vermillion, SD 57069
Phone: 605-677-5434 **E-mail:** admissions@usd.edu **CEEB Code:** 6881
Fax: 605-677-6323 **Website:** www.usd.edu **ACT Code:** 3928
Financial Aid Phone: 605-677-5446

This public school was founded in 1862. It has a 273-acre campus.

RATINGS

Admissions Selectivity Rating: 74   **Fire Safety Rating:** 91   **Green Rating:** 73

STUDENTS AND FACULTY

Enrollment: 5,751. **Student Body:** 61% female, 39% male, 26% out-of-state. African American 1%, Asian 1%, Caucasian 88%, Native American 2%. **Retention and Graduation:** 71% freshmen return for sophomore year. 23% freshmen graduate within 4 years. 33% grads go on to further study within 1 year. 71% grads pursue arts and sciences degrees. 3% grads pursue business degrees. 7% grads pursue law degrees. 19% grads pursue medical degrees. **Faculty:** Student/faculty ratio 15:1. 287 full-time faculty, 79% hold PhDs. 97% faculty teach undergrads.

ACADEMICS

Degrees: Associate, bachelor's, certificate, doctoral, first professional certificate, first professional, master's, post-bachelor's certificate, post-master's certificate. **Academic Requirements:** Arts/fine arts, computer literacy, English (including composition), humanities, interdisciplinary studies, mathematics, sciences (biological or physical), social science. **Classes:** Most classes have 10–19 students. Most lab/discussion sections have 20–29 students. **Majors with Highest Enrollment:** Business administration/management, psychology. **Disciplines with Highest Percentage of Degrees Awarded:** Business/marketing 18%, psychology 12%, health professions and related

sciences 11%, education 10%, social sciences 8%. **Special Study Options:** Accelerated program, cross registration, distance learning, double major, dual enrollment, English as a second language (ESL), exchange student program (domestic), external degree program, honors program, independent study, internships, liberal arts/career combination, student-designed major, study abroad, teacher certification program.

FACILITIES

Housing: Coed dorms, apartments for married students, apartments for single students, special housing for disabled students, fraternity/sorority housing, apartments for students with dependent children. **Special Academic Facilities/Equipment:** W.H. Over Museum, the National Music Museum, Oscar Howe Art Gallery, Center for Instructional Design and Delivery, Institute of American Indian Studies, Native American Cultural Center, Disaster Mental Health Institute, Neuharth Center for Excellence in Journalism, Missouri Rive Institute. **Computers:** 73% of classrooms are wired, 24% of classrooms are wireless, 87% of public computers are PCs, 10% of public computers are Macs, 3% of public computers are UNIX, network access in dorm rooms, network access in dorm lounges, online registration, online administrative functions (other than registration), support for handheld computing, remote student-access to Web through college's connection.

CAMPUS LIFE

Activities: Choral groups, concert band, dance, drama/theater, jazz band, literary magazine, marching band, music ensembles, musical theater, opera, pep band, radio station, student government, student newspaper, symphony orchestra, television station. **Organizations:** 130 registered organizations, 11 honor societies, 10 religious organizations. 8 fraternities (15% men join), 4 sororities (9% women join). **Athletics (Intercollegiate):** *Men:* Basketball, cross-country, diving, football, golf, swimming, track/field (indoor), track/field (outdoor). *Women:* Basketball, cross-country, diving, golf, soccer, softball, swimming, tennis, track/field (indoor), track/field (outdoor), volleyball.

ADMISSIONS

Freshman Academic Profile: 11% in top 10% of high school class, 32% in top 25% of high school class, 69% in top 50% of high school class. 90% from public high schools. SAT Math middle 50% range 490–590. SAT Critical Reading middle 50% range 420–540. ACT middle 50% range 20–25. TOEFL required of all international applicants, minimum paper TOEFL 550, minimum computer TOEFL 213. **Basis for Candidate Selection:** *Very important factors considered include:* Academic GPA, class rank, rigor of secondary school record, standardized test scores. *Important factors considered include:* Alumni/ae relation. *Other factors considered include:* Application essay, character/personal qualities, extracurricular activities, geographical residence, racial/ethnic status, recommendation(s), state residency, talent/ability, volunteer work, work experience. **Freshman Admission Requirements:** High school diploma is required, and GED is accepted. *Academic units required:* 4 English, 3 math, 3 science (3 science labs), 3 social studies, 1 fine arts. *Academic units recommended:* 4 English, 4 math, 4 science (3 science labs), 2 foreign language, 3 social studies, 1 fine arts. **Freshman Admission Statistics:** 3,044 applied, 86% admitted, 43% enrolled. **Transfer Admission Requirements:** High school transcript, college transcript(s). Minimum college GPA of 2.0 required. Lowest grade transferable D. **General Admission Information:** Application fee $20. Regular notification is rolling. Non-fall registration accepted. Admission may be deferred for a maximum of 1 semester. Credit and/or placement offered for CEEB Advanced Placement tests.

COSTS AND FINANCIAL AID

Annual in-state tuition $2,478. Annual out-of-state tuition $7,872. Room and board $5,174. Required fees $2,915. Average book expense $750. **Required Forms and Deadlines:** FAFSA. Financial aid filing deadline 3/15. **Notification of Awards:** Applicants will be notified of awards on a rolling basis beginning on or about 3/1. **Types of Aid:** *Need-based scholarships/grants:* Pell, SEOG, private scholarships, the school's own gift aid, Federal Nursing Scholarships. *Loans:* FFEL Subsidized Stafford, FFEL Unsubsidized Stafford, FFEL PLUS, Federal Perkins, Federal Nursing, college/university loans from institutional funds. **Financial Aid Statistics:** 23% freshmen, 28% undergrads receive need-based scholarship or grant aid. 52% freshmen, 57% undergrads receive need-based self-help aid. 84 freshmen, 269 undergrads receive athletic scholarships. 93% freshmen, 88% undergrads receive any aid. Highest amount earned per year from on-campus jobs $1,200.

UNIVERSITY OF SOUTH FLORIDA

4202 East Fowler Avenue, SVC-1036, Tampa, FL 33620-9951
Phone: 813-974-3350 **E-mail:** jglassma@admin.usf.edu **CEEB Code:** 5828
Fax: 813-974-9689 **Website:** www.usf.edu **ACT Code:** 0761
Financial Aid Phone: 813-974-4700

This public school was founded in 1956. It has a 1,941-acre campus.

RATINGS
Admissions Selectivity Rating: 87   **Fire Safety Rating:** 60*   **Green Rating:** 60*

STUDENTS AND FACULTY
Enrollment: 33,580. **Student Body:** 59% female, 41% male, 3% out-of-state, 2% international (158 countries represented). African American 12%, Asian 6%, Caucasian 65%, Hispanic 12%. **Retention and Graduation:** 81% freshmen return for sophomore year. 18% grads go on to further study within 2 semesters. **Faculty:** Student/faculty ratio 19:1. 1,660 full-time faculty, 86% hold PhDs. 83% faculty teach undergrads.

ACADEMICS
Degrees: Associate, bachelor's, doctoral, first professional, master's, post-bachelor's certificate. **Academic Requirements:** Arts/fine arts, English (including composition), foreign languages, history, humanities, mathematics, sciences (biological or physical), social science. **Classes:** Most classes have 20–29 students. Most lab/discussion sections have 20–29 students. **Majors with Highest Enrollment:** Curriculum and instruction, marketing/marketing management, social sciences. **Disciplines with Highest Percentage of Degrees Awarded:** Business/marketing 24%, social sciences 16%, education 10%, psychology 9%, English 7%. **Special Study Options:** Accelerated program, cooperative education program, cross registration, distance learning, double major, dual enrollment, exchange student program (domestic), honors program, honors research major, internships, study abroad, teacher certification program, weekend college.

FACILITIES
Housing: Coed dorms, men's dorms, women's dorms, apartments for married students, apartments for single students, special housing for disabled students, special housing for international students, fraternity/sorority housing, cooperative housing. **Special Academic Facilities/Equipment:** Art museum and galleries, planetarium, contemporary art museum, graphic studio, galleries, anthropology museum, fitness center, par course. **Computers:** 10% of classrooms are wired, 85% of classrooms are wireless, 95% of public computers are PCs, 3% of public computers are Macs, 2% of public computers are UNIX, network access in dorm rooms, network access in dorm lounges, online registration, online administrative functions (other than registration), remote student-access to Web through college's connection.

CAMPUS LIFE
Activities: Choral groups, concert band, dance, drama/theater, jazz band, literary magazine, marching band, music ensembles, musical theater, opera, pep band, radio station, student government, student newspaper, student-run film society, symphony orchestra, television station. **Organizations:** 507 registered organizations, 33 honor societies, 42 religious organizations. 16 fraternities (8% men join), 22 sororities (6% women join). **Athletics (Intercollegiate):** *Men:* Baseball, basketball, cheerleading, cross-country, football, golf, soccer, tennis, track/field (indoor), track/field (outdoor). *Women:* Basketball, cheerleading, cross-country, golf, sailing, soccer, softball, tennis, track/field (indoor), track/field (outdoor), volleyball.

ADMISSIONS
Freshman Academic Profile: 27% in top 10% of high school class, 64% in top 25% of high school class, 94% in top 50% of high school class. 95% from public high schools. SAT Math middle 50% range 510–610. SAT Critical Reading middle 50% range 500–600. SAT Writing middle 50% range 470–570. ACT middle 50% range 22–26. TOEFL required of all international applicants, minimum paper TOEFL 550, minimum computer TOEFL 213. **Basis for Candidate Selection:** *Very important factors considered include:* Academic GPA, rigor of secondary school record, standardized test scores. *Important factors considered include:* Class rank, talent/ability. *Other factors considered include:* Application essay, character/personal qualities, extracurricular activities, first generation, geographical residence, recommendation(s), state residency, volunteer work, work experience. **Freshman Admission Requirements:** High

school diploma is required, and GED is accepted. *Academic units required:* 4 English, 3 math, 3 science (2 science labs), 2 foreign language, 3 social studies, 3 academic electives. **Freshman Admission Statistics:** 22,462 applied, 51% admitted, 39% enrolled. **Transfer Admission Requirements:** College transcript(s), statement of good standing from prior institution(s). Minimum college GPA of 2.3 required. Lowest grade transferable D. **General Admission Information:** Application fee $30. Regular application deadline 4/15. Regular notification is rolling. Non-fall registration accepted. Credit and/or placement offered for CEEB Advanced Placement tests.

COSTS AND FINANCIAL AID
Annual in-state tuition $3,383. Annual out-of-state tuition $16,081. Room and board $7,590. Required fees $74. Average book expense $1,300. **Required Forms and Deadlines:** FAFSA. Financial aid filing deadline 3/1. **Notification of Awards:** Applicants will be notified of awards on or about 3/15. **Types of Aid:** *Need-based scholarships/grants:* Pell, SEOG, state scholarships/grants, private scholarships, the school's own gift aid. *Loans:* FFEL Subsidized Stafford, FFEL Unsubsidized Stafford, FFEL PLUS, Federal Perkins, college/university loans from institutional funds. **Financial Aid Statistics:** 20% freshmen, 29% undergrads receive need-based scholarship or grant aid. 13% freshmen, 20% undergrads receive need-based self-help aid. 153 freshmen, 486 undergrads receive athletic scholarships. 68% freshmen, 78% undergrads receive any aid.

See page 1470.

UNIVERSITY OF SOUTHERN CALIFORNIA

Admissions Office: Student Administrative Services, 700 Childs Way, Los Angeles, CA 90089-0911
Phone: 213-740-1111 **E-mail:** admitusc@usc.edu **CEEB Code:** 4852
Fax: 213-740-6364 **Website:** www.usc.edu **ACT Code:** 0470
Financial Aid Phone: 213-740-5445

This private school was founded in 1880. It has a 155-acre campus.

RATINGS
Admissions Selectivity Rating: 98   **Fire Safety Rating:** 96   **Green Rating:** 82

STUDENTS AND FACULTY
Enrollment: 16,449. **Student Body:** 50% female, 50% male, 34% out-of-state, 9% international (138 countries represented). African American 6%, Asian 21%, Caucasian 48%, Hispanic 13%. **Retention and Graduation:** 96% freshmen return for sophomore year. 65% freshmen graduate within 4 years. **Faculty:** Student/faculty ratio 10:1. 1,562 full-time faculty, 90% hold PhDs. 75% faculty teach undergrads.

ACADEMICS
Degrees: Bachelor's, doctoral, first professional certificate, first professional, master's, post-bachelor's certificate, post-master's certificate. **Academic Requirements:** Diversity requirement, English (including composition), foreign languages, humanities, mathematics, sciences (biological or physical), social science. **Classes:** Most classes have 10–19 students. Most lab/discussion sections have 20–29 students. **Majors with Highest Enrollment:** Biology/biological sciences, business administration/management, communications studies/speech communication and rhetoric. **Disciplines with Highest Percentage of Degrees Awarded:** Business/marketing 26%, social sciences 15%, visual and performing arts 13%, communications/journalism 9%, engineering 8%. **Special Study Options:** Cooperative education program, distance learning, double major, English as a second language (ESL), exchange student program (domestic), freshman seminar program, honors program, independent study, internships, learning communities, liberal arts/career combination, student-designed major, study abroad, teacher certification program, thematic option, undergraduate research program, weekend college.

FACILITIES
Housing: Coed dorms, apartments for married students, apartments for single students, special housing for disabled students, special housing for international students, fraternity/sorority housing, special interest floors. **Special Academic Facilities/Equipment:** Art museums, cinema scoring sound stage, media labs, recording studios, exercise physiology lab, many specialized engineering and health laboratories, 652 wireless access points, 280 classrooms outfitted with multiple webcams and microphones. **Computers:** 49% of classrooms are wired,

90% of classrooms are wireless, 80% of public computers are PCs, 15% of public computers are Macs, 5% of public computers are UNIX, network access in dorm rooms, online registration, online administrative functions (other than registration), support for handheld computing, remote student-access to Web through college's connection.

CAMPUS LIFE

Activities: Choral groups, concert band, dance, drama/theater, jazz band, literary magazine, marching band, music ensembles, musical theater, opera, pep band, radio station, student government, student newspaper, student-run film society, symphony orchestra, television station. **Organizations:** 645 registered organizations, 43 honor societies, 79 religious organizations. 30 fraternities (16% men join), 24 sororities (19% women join). **Athletics (Intercollegiate):** *Men:* Baseball, basketball, diving, football, golf, swimming, tennis, track/field (indoor), track/field (outdoor), volleyball, water polo. *Women:* Basketball, crew/rowing, cross-country, diving, golf, soccer, swimming, tennis, track/field (indoor), track/field (outdoor), volleyball, water polo. **Environmental Initiatives:** USC employs a full time Director of Energy Services to manage energy programs including lighting retrofits, equipment upgrades, and a recent retrofit of chillers, cooling towers, and pumps throughout the university. USC counts on the services of a full time Rideshare Coordinator to ensure that transportation programs are available to all members of the University community. The Sustainability Steering Committee's core intent is to help USC maintain its current needs without compromising the ability of future generations to do the same.

ADMISSIONS

Freshman Academic Profile: 86% in top 10% of high school class, 97% in top 25% of high school class, 100% in top 50% of high school class. 55% from public high schools. SAT Math middle 50% range 650–740. SAT Critical Reading middle 50% range 620–720. SAT Writing middle 50% range 640–720. ACT middle 50% range 28–32. **Basis for Candidate Selection:** *Very important factors considered include:* Academic GPA, application essay, recommendation(s), rigor of secondary school record, standardized test scores. *Important factors considered include:* Extracurricular activities, talent/ability. *Other factors considered include:* Alumni/ae relation, character/personal qualities, class rank, first generation, interview, racial/ethnic status, volunteer work, work experience. **Freshman Admission Requirements:** High school diploma is required, and GED is not accepted. *Academic units required:* 4 English, 3 math, 2 science (2 science labs), 2 foreign language, 2 social studies, 3 academic electives. *Academic units recommended:* 4 English, 4 math, 3 science (3 science labs), 3 foreign language, 3 social studies, 3 academic electives. **Freshman Admission Statistics:** 33,979 applied, 25% admitted, 32% enrolled. **Transfer Admission Requirements:** High school transcript, college transcript(s), essay or personal statement. Lowest grade transferable C-. **General Admission Information:** Application fee $65. Regular application deadline 1/10. Regular notification 4/1. Non-fall registration accepted. Credit and/or placement offered for CEEB Advanced Placement tests.

COSTS AND FINANCIAL AID

Annual tuition $35,212. Room and board $10,858. Required fees $598. Average book expense $750. **Required Forms and Deadlines:** FAFSA, CSS/Financial Aid PROFILE, parent and student federal income tax form with all schedules and W-2's, USC non-filing forms for those not required to file. Financial aid filing deadline 1/20. **Notification of Awards:** Applicants will be notified of awards on a rolling basis beginning on or about 3/15. **Types of Aid:** *Need-based scholarships/grants:* Pell, SEOG, state scholarships/grants, private scholarships, the school's own gift aid. *Loans:* FFEL Subsidized Stafford, FFEL Unsubsidized Stafford, FFEL PLUS, Federal Perkins, Credit ready and credit based loans. **Student Employment:** Federal Work-Study Program available. Institutional employment available. Off-campus job opportunities are excellent. **Financial Aid Statistics:** 34% freshmen, 39% undergrads receive need-based scholarship or grant aid. 39% freshmen, 43% undergrads receive need-based self-help aid. 68 freshmen, 351 undergrads receive athletic scholarships. 72% freshmen, 68% undergrads receive any aid.

UNIVERSITY OF SOUTHERN INDIANA

8600 University Boulevard, Evansville, IN 47712
Phone: 812-464-1765 **E-mail:** enroll@usi.edu **CEEB Code:** 1335
Fax: 812-465-7154 **Website:** www.usi.edu **ACT Code:** 1207
Financial Aid Phone: 812-464-1767

This public school was founded in 1965. It has a 330-acre campus.

STUDENTS AND FACULTY

Enrollment: 9,045. **Student Body:** 60% female, 40% male, 9% out-of-state. African American 5%, Caucasian 92%. **Retention and Graduation:** 64% freshmen return for sophomore year. 15% freshmen graduate within 4 years. 16% grads go on to further study within 2 semesters. **Faculty:** Student/faculty ratio 20:1. 299 full-time faculty, 61% hold PhDs. 100% faculty teach undergrads.

ACADEMICS

Degrees: Associate, bachelor's, certificate, master's, post-bachelor's certificate. **Academic Requirements:** Arts/fine arts, computer literacy, English (including composition), history, humanities, mathematics, sciences (biological or physical), social science. **Classes:** Most classes have 20–29 students. Most lab/discussion sections have 20–29 students. **Majors with Highest Enrollment:** Business administration/management, elementary education and teaching, psychology. **Disciplines with Highest Percentage of Degrees Awarded:** Business/marketing 23%, health professions and related sciences 16%, education 14%, communications/journalism 10%, social sciences 7%. **Special Study Options:** Cooperative education program, distance learning, double major, English as a second language (ESL), honors program, independent study, internships, study abroad, teacher certification program.

FACILITIES

Housing: Coed dorms, apartments for married students, apartments for single students, fraternity/sorority housing. **Computers:** 100% of classrooms are wireless, 14% of public computers are PCs, network access in dorm rooms, network access in dorm lounges, online registration, online administrative functions (other than registration), remote student-access to Web through college's connection.

CAMPUS LIFE

Activities: Choral groups, dance, drama/theater, jazz band, literary magazine, pep band, radio station, student government, student newspaper. **Organizations:** 74 registered organizations, 5 honor societies, 8 religious organizations. 4 fraternities (4% men join), 3 sororities (3% women join). **Athletics (Intercollegiate):** *Men:* Baseball, basketball, cross-country, golf, soccer, tennis. *Women:* Basketball, cross-country, golf, soccer, softball, tennis, volleyball. **Environmental Initiatives:** Recycling. Working to implement the requirement of Phase II, Rule 13 of the Federal Clean Water Act which addresses storm water run-off quality within te MS4 area. Business/Engineering Center designed using LEED Critera.

ADMISSIONS

Freshman Academic Profile: 9% in top 10% of high school class, 27% in top 25% of high school class, 61% in top 50% of high school class. SAT Math middle 50% range 420–530. SAT Critical Reading middle 50% range 410–520. SAT Writing middle 50% range 410–510. ACT middle 50% range 17–23. TOEFL required of all international applicants, minimum paper TOEFL 525, minimum computer TOEFL 197. **Basis for Candidate Selection:** *Important factors considered include:* Academic GPA, class rank. *Other factors considered include:* Alumni/ae relation, application essay, character/personal qualities, extracurricular activities, interview, recommendation(s), rigor of secondary school record, standardized test scores, talent/ability, work experience. **Freshman Admission Requirements:** High school diploma is required, and GED is accepted. *Academic units recommended:* 4 English, 4 math, 3 science, 2 foreign language, 2 social studies, 2 history, 2 academic electives. **Freshman Admission Statistics:** 5,145 applied, 83% admitted, 49% enrolled. **Transfer Admission Requirements:** High school transcript, college transcript(s). Minimum college GPA of 2.0 required. Lowest grade transferable C-. **General Admission Information:** Application fee $25. Regular application deadline 8/15. Regular notification is rolling. Non-fall registration accepted. Credit and/or placement offered for CEEB Advanced Placement tests.

COSTS AND FINANCIAL AID

Annual in-state tuition $5,019. Annual out-of-state tuition $11,954. Room and board $6,542. Required fees $200. Average book expense $900. **Required Forms and Deadlines:** FAFSA, institution's own financial aid form. Financial aid filing deadline 3/1. **Notification of Awards:** Applicants will be notified of awards on a rolling basis beginning on or about 4/15. **Types of Aid:** *Need-based scholarships/grants:* Pell, SEOG, state scholarships/grants, private scholarships, the school's own gift aid. *Loans:* FFEL Subsidized Stafford, FFEL Unsubsidized Stafford, FFEL PLUS, Federal Perkins. **Financial Aid Statistics:** 39% freshmen, 34% undergrads receive need-based scholarship or grant aid. 48% freshmen, 46% undergrads receive need-based self-help aid. 30 freshmen, 121 undergrads receive athletic scholarships. 55% freshmen, 52% undergrads receive any aid.

RATINGS

Admissions Selectivity Rating: 70   **Fire Safety Rating:** 60*   **Green Rating:** 74

UNIVERSITY OF SOUTHERN MAINE

37 College Avenue, Gorham, ME 04038
Phone: 207-780-5670 **E-mail:** usmadm@usm.maine.edu **CEEB Code:** 3691
Fax: 207-780-5640 **Website:** www.usm.maine.edu **ACT Code:** 1644
Financial Aid Phone: 207-780-5250

This public school was founded in 1878. It has a 144-acre campus.

RATINGS
Admissions Selectivity Rating: 72   **Fire Safety Rating:** 60*   **Green Rating:** 60*

STUDENTS AND FACULTY
Enrollment: 6,745. **Student Body:** 59% female, 41% male, 4% out-of-state. African American 2%, Asian 1%, Caucasian 95%, Native American 1%. **Retention and Graduation:** 85% freshmen return for sophomore year. **Faculty:** Student/faculty ratio 13:1. 402 full-time faculty, 80% hold PhDs. 90% faculty teach undergrads.

ACADEMICS
Degrees: Associate, bachelor's, certificate, doctoral, first professional, master's, post-master's certificate. **Academic Requirements:** Arts/fine arts, English (including composition), history, humanities, interdisciplinary, mathematics, other times/other cultures, philosophy, sciences (biological or physical), social science. **Classes:** Most classes have 10–19 students. Most lab/discussion sections have fewer than 10 students. **Majors with Highest Enrollment:** Business/commerce, psychology, surgical nurse/nursing. **Disciplines with Highest Percentage of Degrees Awarded:** Health professions and related sciences 18%, social sciences 17%, business/marketing 11%, psychology 6%. **Special Study Options:** Accelerated program, cooperative education program, cross registration, distance learning, double major, English as a second language (ESL), exchange student program (domestic), honors program, independent study, internships, liberal arts/career combination, living/learning scholars program, preengineering program with University of Maine at Orono, student-designed major, study abroad, teacher certification program, weekend college.

FACILITIES
Housing: Coed dorms, apartments for married students, apartments for single students, special housing for disabled students, fraternity/sorority housing, fine arts house, Russell Scholars (living/learning), chemical free floor, 24-hour quiet floor. **Special Academic Facilities/Equipment:** Southworth Planetarium, Osher Map Collection and Smith Center for Cartographic Education, WMPG (radio station), GTV (cable T.V. station), Free Press (campus newspaper), various art galleries on all three campuses. **Computers:** 75% of public computers are PCs, 25% of public computers are Macs, network access in dorm rooms, network access in dorm lounges, online registration, online administrative functions (other than registration), support for handheld computing, remote student-access to Web through college's connection.

CAMPUS LIFE
Activities: Choral groups, concert band, dance, drama/theater, jazz band, literary magazine, music ensembles, musical theater, opera, radio station, student government, student newspaper, symphony orchestra, television station, yearbook. **Organizations:** 100 registered organizations, 2 honor societies, 3 religious organizations. 4 fraternities (2% men join), 4 sororities (2% women join). **Athletics (Intercollegiate):** *Men:* Baseball, basketball, cheerleading, cross-country, golf, ice hockey, lacrosse, soccer, tennis, track/field (indoor), track/field (outdoor), wrestling. *Women:* Basketball, cheerleading, cross-country, field hockey, golf, ice hockey, lacrosse, soccer, softball, tennis, track/field (indoor), track/field (outdoor), volleyball.

ADMISSIONS
Freshman Academic Profile: 9% in top 10% of high school class, 32% in top 25% of high school class, 70% in top 50% of high school class. SAT Math middle 50% range 430–540. SAT Critical Reading middle 50% range 440–550. SAT Writing middle 50% range 440–540. ACT middle 50% range 20–25. TOEFL required of all international applicants, minimum paper TOEFL 550, minimum computer TOEFL 213. **Basis for Candidate Selection:** *Very important factors considered include:* Class rank, rigor of secondary school record, standardized test scores. *Important factors considered include:* Application essay, recommendation(s). *Other factors considered include:* Alumni/ae relation, character/personal qualities, extracurricular activities, geographical residence, interview, racial/ethnic status, state residency, talent/ability, volunteer work, work experience. **Freshman Admission Requirements:** High school diploma is required, and GED is accepted. *Academic units required:* 4 English, 3 math, 2 science (2 science labs), 2 foreign language, 2 social studies, 2 history. *Academic units recommended:* 4 math, 3 science (3 science labs), 3 foreign language, 3 social studies, 3 history. **Freshman Admission Statistics:** 3,642

applied, 78% admitted, 34% enrolled. **Transfer Admission Requirements:** High school transcript, college transcript(s), essay or personal statement. Minimum college GPA of 2.0 required. Lowest grade transferable C-. **General Admission Information:** Application fee $40. Regular application deadline rolling. Regular notification is rolling. Non-fall registration accepted. Admission may be deferred for a maximum of 2 semesters. Credit and/or placement offered for CEEB Advanced Placement tests.

COSTS AND FINANCIAL AID
Annual in-state tuition $5,940. Annual out-of-state tuition $16,410. Room and board $8,038. Required fees $927. Average book expense $900. **Required Forms and Deadlines:** FAFSA. Financial aid filing deadline 2/15. **Notification of Awards:** Applicants will be notified of awards on a rolling basis beginning on or about 3/15. **Types of Aid:** *Need-based scholarships/grants:* Pell, SEOG, state scholarships/grants, private scholarships, the school's own gift aid. *Loans:* FFEL Subsidized Stafford, FFEL Unsubsidized Stafford, FFEL PLUS, Federal Perkins, Federal Nursing, state loans. **Student Employment:** Federal Work-Study Program available. Off-campus job opportunities are excellent. **Financial Aid Statistics:** 70% freshmen, 79% undergrads receive any aid.

UNIVERSITY OF SOUTHERN MISSISSIPPI

118 College Drive #5166, Hattiesburg, MS 39406
Phone: 601-266-5000 **E-mail:** admissions@usm.edu **CEEB Code:** 1479
Fax: 601-266-5148 **Website:** www.usm.edu **ACT Code:** 2218
Financial Aid Phone: 601-266-4774

This public school was founded in 1910. It has a 1,090-acre campus.

RATINGS
Admissions Selectivity Rating: 60*   **Fire Safety Rating:** 60*   **Green Rating:** 85

STUDENTS AND FACULTY
Enrollment: 12,122. **Student Body:** 61% female, 39% male, 11% out-of-state. African American 29%, Asian 1%, Caucasian 65%, Hispanic 1%. **Retention and Graduation:** 73% freshmen return for sophomore year. 24% freshmen graduate within 4 years. 10% grads pursue arts and sciences degrees. 6% grads pursue business degrees. 1% grads pursue law degrees. 1% grads pursue medical degrees. **Faculty:** Student/faculty ratio 17:1. 703 full-time faculty, 78% hold PhDs. 95% faculty teach undergrads.

ACADEMICS
Degrees: Bachelor's, doctoral, master's, post-master's certificate. **Academic Requirements:** Arts/fine arts, English (including composition), history, mathematics, sciences (biological or physical), social science. **Classes:** Most classes have 10–19 students. Most lab/discussion sections have 10–19 students. **Disciplines with Highest Percentage of Degrees Awarded:** Business/marketing 19%, education 13%, health professions and related sciences 11%, psychology 7%, parks and recreation 5%. **Special Study Options:** Accelerated program, cooperative education program, distance learning, double major, dual enrollment, English as a second language (ESL), honors program, independent study, internships, study abroad, teacher certification program.

FACILITIES
Housing: Men's dorms, women's dorms, apartments for married students, special housing for disabled students, fraternity/sorority housing. **Special Academic Facilities/Equipment:** English language institute, human performance and recreation facility, language lab, research institute, speech/hearing clinic, institute of microbiology, polymer science facility. **Computers:** Online registration, remote student-access to Web through college's connection.

CAMPUS LIFE
Activities: Choral groups, concert band, dance, drama/theater, jazz band, literary magazine, marching band, music ensembles, musical theater, opera, pep band, radio station, student government, student newspaper, student-run film society, symphony orchestra, yearbook. **Organizations:** 202 registered organizations, 9 honor societies. 13 fraternities (4% men join), 12 sororities (4% women join). **Athletics (Intercollegiate):** *Men:* Baseball, basketball, cross-country, football, golf, tennis, track/field (outdoor). *Women:* Basketball, cross-country, golf, softball, tennis, track/field (outdoor), volleyball.

ADMISSIONS
Freshman Academic Profile: SAT Math middle 50% range 460–590. SAT Critical Reading middle 50% range 435–590. ACT middle 50% range 19–24. TOEFL required of all international applicants, minimum paper TOEFL 525. **Basis for Candidate Selection:** *Very important factors considered include:* Academic GPA, rigor of secondary school record, standardized test scores.

Important factors considered include: Class rank. *Other factors considered include:* Alumni/ae relation, interview, talent/ability. **Freshman Admission Requirements:** High school diploma is required, and GED is accepted. *Academic units required:* 4 English, 3 math, 3 science (3 science labs), 1 social studies, 2 history, 2 academic electives, 1 semester course in computer applications. *Academic units recommended:* 4 English, 3 math, 3 science (3 science labs), 2 foreign language, 1 social studies, 2 history, 2 academic electives, 1 semester course in computer applications. **Freshman Admission Statistics:** 5,509 applied, 60% admitted, 48% enrolled. **Transfer Admission Requirements:** College transcript(s), statement of good standing from prior institution(s). Minimum college GPA of 2.0 required. Lowest grade transferable C. **General Admission Information:** Regular notification rolling. Non-fall registration accepted. Credit and/or placement offered for CEEB Advanced Placement tests.

COSTS AND FINANCIAL AID

Annual in-state tuition $4,914. Annual out-of-state tuition $11,692. Room and board $5,040. Average book expense $1,000. **Required Forms and Deadlines:** FAFSA, institution's own financial aid form. Financial aid filing deadline 3/15. **Notification of Awards:** Applicants will be notified of awards on a rolling basis beginning on or about 4/1. **Types of Aid:** *Need-based scholarships/grants:* Pell, SEOG, state scholarships/grants, private scholarships, the school's own gift aid. *Loans:* FFEL Subsidized Stafford, FFEL Unsubsidized Stafford, FFEL PLUS, Federal Perkins, Federal Nursing, college/university loans from institutional funds. **Student Employment:** Federal Work-Study Program available. Institutional employment available. Off-campus job opportunities are good. **Financial Aid Statistics:** 57% freshmen, 60% undergrads receive need-based scholarship or grant aid. 45% freshmen, 54% undergrads receive need-based self-help aid. 18 freshmen, 44 undergrads receive athletic scholarships. Highest amount earned per year from on-campus jobs $2,800.

UNIVERSITY OF ST. FRANCIS

500 Wilcox Street, Joliet, IL 60435
Phone: 815-740-3400 **E-mail:** information@stfrancis.edu **CEEB Code:** 1130
Fax: 815-740-5032 **Website:** www.stfrancis.edu **ACT Code:** 1000
Financial Aid Phone: 866-890-8331

This private school, affiliated with the Roman Catholic Church, was founded in 1920. It has a 22-acre campus.

RATINGS

Admissions Selectivity Rating: 76   **Fire Safety Rating:** 90   **Green Rating:** 79

STUDENTS AND FACULTY

Enrollment: 1,265. **Student Body:** 69% female, 31% male, 3% out-of-state, 3% international. African American 9%, Asian 4%, Caucasian 72%, Hispanic 8%. **Retention and Graduation:** 78% freshmen return for sophomore year. 38% freshmen graduate within 4 years. 23% grads go on to further study within 2 semesters. 13% grads pursue arts and sciences degrees. 5% grads pursue business degrees. 3% grads pursue medical degrees. **Faculty:** Student/faculty ratio 13:1. 74 full-time faculty, 62% hold PhDs. 80% faculty teach undergrads.

ACADEMICS

Degrees: Bachelor's, master's, post-bachelor's certificate, post-master's certificate. **Academic Requirements:** Arts/fine arts, computer literacy, English (including composition), history, mathematics, philosophy, religion/theology, sciences (biological or physical), social science. **Classes:** Most classes have 10–19 students. Most lab/discussion sections have 10–19 students. **Majors with Highest Enrollment:** Biology/biological sciences, elementary education and teaching, nursing/registered nurse training (ASN, BSN, MSN, RN). **Disciplines with Highest Percentage of Degrees Awarded:** Health professions and related sciences 24%, education 19%, business/marketing 14%, psychology 6%, parks and recreation 6%. **Special Study Options:** Accelerated program, distance learning, double major, honors program, independent study, internships, student-designed major, study abroad, teacher certification program.

FACILITIES

Housing: Coed dorms, apartments for single students. **Special Academic Facilities/Equipment:** Performing arts center, greenhouse, art gallery. **Computers:** 10% of classrooms are wired, 40% of classrooms are wireless, 95% of public computers are PCs, 5% of public computers are Macs, network access in dorm rooms, network access in dorm lounges, online registration, online administrative functions (other than registration), support for handheld computing, remote student-access to Web through college's connection.

CAMPUS LIFE

Activities: Choral groups, dance, drama/theater, literary magazine, music ensembles, musical theater, radio station, student government, student newspaper, symphony orchestra, television station. **Organizations:** 27 registered organizations, 13 honor societies, 1 religious organization. **Athletics (Intercollegiate): Men:** Baseball, basketball, football, golf, soccer, tennis. *Women:* Basketball, cheerleading, cross-country, golf, soccer, softball, tennis, track/field (indoor), track/field (outdoor), volleyball. **Environmental Initiatives:** Campus-wide recylcing. Energy efficient lighting. Water conservation project (P3) in progress.

ADMISSIONS

Freshman Academic Profile: 16% in top 10% of high school class, 44% in top 25% of high school class, 83% in top 50% of high school class. 74% from public high schools. ACT middle 50% range 20–25. TOEFL required of all international applicants, minimum paper TOEFL 550, minimum computer TOEFL 213. **Basis for Candidate Selection:** *Very important factors considered include:* Academic GPA, class rank, rigor of secondary school record, standardized test scores. *Other factors considered include:* Application essay, character/personal qualities, extracurricular activities, first generation, interview, recommendation(s), talent/ability, volunteer work. **Freshman Admission Requirements:** High school diploma is required, and GED is accepted. *Academic units required:* 4 English, 2 math, 2 science (1 science lab), 2 social studies, 3 academic electives, 3 units from 2 areas in language, computer science, music, or art. *Academic units recommended:* 1 foreign language. **Freshman Admission Statistics:** 850 applied, 71% admitted, 30% enrolled. **Transfer Admission Requirements:** College transcript(s), statement of good standing from prior institution(s). Minimum college GPA of 2.0 required. Lowest grade transferable C. **General Admission Information:** Application fee $30. Regular application deadline 8/1. Regular notification is rolling. Non-fall registration accepted. Admission may be deferred for a maximum of 2 semesters. Credit and/or placement offered for CEEB Advanced Placement tests.

COSTS AND FINANCIAL AID

Annual tuition $20,440. Room and board $7,610. Required fees $390. Average book expense $800. **Required Forms and Deadlines:** FAFSA, institution's own financial aid form. Financial aid filing deadline 3/15. **Notification of Awards:** Applicants will be notified of awards on a rolling basis beginning on or about 2/15. **Types of Aid:** *Need-based scholarships/grants:* Pell, SEOG, state scholarships/grants, private scholarships, the school's own gift aid, Federal Nursing Scholarships. *Loans:* Direct Subsidized Stafford, Direct Unsubsidized Stafford, Direct PLUS, Federal Perkins. **Financial Aid Statistics:** 62% freshmen, 59% undergrads receive need-based scholarship or grant aid. 58% freshmen, 56% undergrads receive need-based self-help aid. 24 freshmen, 51 undergrads receive athletic scholarships. 100% freshmen, 99% undergrads receive any aid. Highest amount earned per year from on-campus jobs $10,271.

UNIVERSITY OF ST. THOMAS (TX)

3800 Montrose Boulevard, Houston, TX 77006-4696
Phone: 713-525-3500 **E-mail:** admissions@stthom.edu **CEEB Code:** 6880
Fax: 713-525-3558 **Website:** www.stthom.edu **ACT Code:** 4238
Financial Aid Phone: 713-942-3465

This private school, affiliated with the Roman Catholic Church, was founded in 1947. It has a 21-acre campus.

RATINGS

Admissions Selectivity Rating: 78   **Fire Safety Rating:** 85   **Green Rating:** 68

STUDENTS AND FACULTY

Enrollment: 1,776. **Student Body:** 61% female, 39% male, 4% out-of-state, 3% international (62 countries represented). African American 6%, Asian 12%, Caucasian 40%, Hispanic 30%. **Retention and Graduation:** 71% freshmen return for sophomore year. 24% freshmen graduate within 4 years. **Faculty:** Student/faculty ratio 14:1. 121 full-time faculty, 88% hold PhDs. 76% faculty teach undergrads.

ACADEMICS

Degrees: Bachelor's, diploma, doctoral, first professional, master's. **Academic Requirements:** Arts/fine arts, English (including composition), foreign languages, history, mathematics, oral communication, philosophy, sciences (biological or physical), social science, theology. **Classes:** Most classes have 10–19 students. Most lab/discussion sections have 10–19 students. **Majors with Highest Enrollment:** Business administration/management, education, international relations and affairs. **Disciplines with Highest Percentage of**

Degrees Awarded: Business/marketing 27%, liberal arts/general studies 16%, social sciences 12%, psychology 7%, biological/life sciences 6%. **Special Study Options:** Cross registration, distance learning, double major, first-year experiences, honors program, independent study, internships, learning communities, senior capstone or culminating academic experiences, service learning, study abroad, teacher certification program, undergraduate research/creative projects.

FACILITIES

Housing: Coed dorms, apartments for single students, houses, living-learning center housing. **Special Academic Facilities/Equipment:** Learning & Writing Center, Chapel of St. Basil. **Computers:** 88% of classrooms are wireless, 66% of public computers are PCs, 2% of public computers are Macs, network access in dorm rooms, network access in dorm lounges, online registration, online administrative functions (other than registration), remote student-access to Web through college's connection.

CAMPUS LIFE

Activities: Choral groups, concert band, drama/theater, jazz band, literary magazine, music ensembles, musical theater, student government, student newspaper. **Organizations:** 80 registered organizations, 26 honor societies, 2 religious organizations.

ADMISSIONS

Freshman Academic Profile: 29% in top 10% of high school class, 58% in top 25% of high school class, 82% in top 50% of high school class. 59% from public high schools. SAT Math middle 50% range 530–630. SAT Critical Reading middle 50% range 510–630. SAT Writing middle 50% range 510–610. ACT middle 50% range 21–27. TOEFL required of all international applicants, minimum paper TOEFL 550, minimum computer TOEFL 213. **Basis for Candidate Selection:** *Very important factors considered include:* Academic GPA, application essay, class rank, rigor of secondary school record, standardized test scores. *Other factors considered include:* Character/personal qualities, extracurricular activities, interview, level of applicant's interest, recommendation(s), talent/ability, volunteer work, work experience. **Freshman Admission Requirements:** High school diploma is required, and GED is accepted. *Academic units required:* 4 English, 3 math, 3 science (2 science labs), 2 foreign language, 2 social studies, 1 history, 3 academic electives. *Academic units recommended:* 4 English, 3 math, 3 science (2 science labs), 2 foreign language, 2 social studies, 1 history, 3 academic electives. **Freshman Admission Statistics:** 807 applied, 92% admitted, 40% enrolled. **Transfer Admission Requirements:** College transcript(s), statement of good standing from prior institution(s). Minimum college GPA of 2.5 required. Lowest grade transferable C. **General Admission Information:** Application fee $35. Regular notification is rolling. Non-fall registration accepted. Admission may be deferred for a maximum of 2 semesters. Common Application accepted. Credit and/or placement offered for CEEB Advanced Placement tests.

COSTS AND FINANCIAL AID

Annual tuition $16,950. Room & board $6,700. Required fees $160. Average book expense $1,000. **Required Forms and Deadlines:** FAFSA. Financial aid filing deadline 3/1. **Notification of Awards:** Applicants will be notified of awards on a rolling basis beginning on or about 3/1. **Types of Aid:** *Need-based scholarships/grants:* Pell, SEOG, state scholarships/grants, the school's own gift aid. *Loans:* FFEL Subsidized Stafford, FFEL Unsubsidized Stafford, FFEL PLUS, Federal Perkins, state loans. **Student Employment:** Federal Work-Study Program available. Off-campus job opportunities are excellent. **Financial Aid Statistics:** 58% freshmen, 54% undergrads receive need-based scholarship or grant aid. 44% freshmen, 48% undergrads receive need-based self-help aid. 85% freshmen, 66% undergrads receive any aid.

UNIVERSITY OF TAMPA

401 West Kennedy Boulevard, Tampa, FL 33606-1490
Phone: 813-253-6211 **E-mail:** admissions@ut.edu **CEEB Code:** 5819
Fax: 813-258-7398 **Website:** www.ut.edu **ACT Code:** 0762
Financial Aid Phone: 813-253-6219

This private school was founded in 1931. It has a 100-acre campus.

RATINGS
Admissions Selectivity Rating: 84   **Fire Safety Rating:** 85   **Green Rating:** 60*

STUDENTS AND FACULTY
Enrollment: 4,711. **Student Body:** 61% female, 39% male, 59% out-of-state, 6% international (101 countries represented). African American 7%, Asian 2%, Caucasian 64%, Hispanic 9%. **Retention and Graduation:** 72% freshmen

return for sophomore year. 44% freshmen graduate within 4 years. 16% grads go on to further study within 2 semesters. 8% grads pursue arts and sciences degrees. 3% grads pursue business degrees. 3% grads pursue law degrees. 2% grads pursue medical degrees. **Faculty:** Student/faculty ratio 15:1. 223 full-time faculty, 90% hold PhDs. 100% faculty teach undergrads.

ACADEMICS

Degrees: Associate, bachelor's, certificate, master's. **Academic Requirements:** Arts/fine arts, computer literacy, English (including composition), humanities, mathematics, sciences (biological or physical), social science. **Classes:** Most classes have 10–19 students. Most lab/discussion sections have 10–19 students. **Majors with Highest Enrollment:** Communications studies/speech communication and rhetoric, management science. **Disciplines with Highest Percentage of Degrees Awarded:** Business/marketing 25%, social sciences 16%, communications/journalism 11%, biological/life sciences 7%, psychology 7%. **Special Study Options:** Double major, dual enrollment, English as a second language (ESL), exchange student program (domestic), honors program, independent study, internships, study abroad, teacher certification program, weekend college.

FACILITIES

Housing: Coed dorms, apartments for single students, special housing for disabled students. **Special Academic Facilities/Equipment:** Victorian art and furniture museum, theaters, studios, music center, language lab, fully equipped research vessel for marine science, H.B. Plant Museum, marine science research center on Tampa Bay. **Computers:** 70% of public computers are PCs, 30% of public computers are Macs, network access in dorm rooms, network access in dorm lounges, online registration, online administrative functions (other than registration), support for handheld computing, remote student-access to Web through college's connection.

CAMPUS LIFE

Activities: Choral groups, concert band, dance, drama/theater, jazz band, literary magazine, music ensembles, musical theater, pep band, radio station, student government, student newspaper, symphony orchestra, television station, yearbook. **Organizations:** 120 registered organizations, 22 honor societies, 5 religious organizations. 8 fraternities (15% men join), 8 sororities (13% women join). **Athletics (Intercollegiate):** *Men:* Baseball, basketball, cross-country, golf, soccer, swimming. *Women:* Basketball, crew/rowing, cross-country, soccer, softball, swimming, tennis, volleyball.

ADMISSIONS

Freshman Academic Profile: 18% in top 10% of high school class, 51% in top 25% of high school class, 84% in top 50% of high school class. 75% from public high schools. SAT Math middle 50% range 490–580. SAT Critical Reading middle 50% range 490–570. SAT Writing middle 50% range 490–570. ACT middle 50% range 21–25. TOEFL required of all international applicants, minimum paper TOEFL 550, minimum computer TOEFL 213. **Basis for Candidate Selection:** *Very important factors considered include:* Academic GPA, standardized test scores. *Important factors considered include:* Application essay, recommendation(s), rigor of secondary school record. *Other factors considered include:* Alumni/ae relation, character/personal qualities, class rank, extracurricular activities, geographical residence, interview, state residency, talent/ability, volunteer work, work experience. **Freshman Admission Requirements:** High school diploma is required, and GED is accepted. *Academic units required:* 4 English, 3 math, 3 science (2 science labs), 2 foreign language, 3 social studies, 3 academic electives. **Freshman Admission Statistics:** 7,558 applied, 56% admitted, 28% enrolled. **Transfer Admission Requirements:** College transcript(s). Minimum college GPA of 2.5 required. Lowest grade transferable C. **General Admission Information:** Application fee $40. Regular application deadline 5/1. Regular notification is rolling. Non-fall registration accepted. Admission may be deferred for a maximum of 1 semester. Credit and/or placement offered for CEEB Advanced Placement tests.

COSTS AND FINANCIAL AID

Annual tuition $18,666. Room & board $7,254. Required fees $962. Average book expense $940. **Required Forms and Deadlines:** FAFSA, state aid form. **Notification of Awards:** Applicants will be notified of awards on a rolling basis beginning on or about 2/1. **Types of Aid:** *Need-based scholarships/grants:* Pell, SEOG, state scholarships/grants, private scholarships, the school's own gift aid. *Loans:* FFEL Subsidized Stafford, FFEL Unsubsidized Stafford, FFEL PLUS, Federal Perkins, college/university loans from institutional funds. **Student Employment:** Off-campus job opportunities are excellent. **Financial Aid Statistics:** 48% freshmen, 50% undergrads receive need-based scholarship or grant aid. 40% freshmen, 43% undergrads receive need-based self-help aid. 8 freshmen, 25 undergrads receive athletic scholarships. 87% freshmen, 88% undergrads receive any aid. Highest amount earned per year from on-campus jobs $2,000.

See page 1472.

THE UNIVERSITY OF TENNESSEE AT CHATTANOOGA

615 McCallie Avenue, 131 Hooper Hall, Chattanooga, TN 37403
Phone: 423-425-4662 **E-mail:** yancy-freeman@utc.edu **CEEB Code:** 1831
Fax: 423-425-4157 **Website:** www.utc.edu **ACT Code:** 4022
Financial Aid Phone: 423-425-4677

This public school was founded in 1886. It has a 120-acre campus.

RATINGS
Admissions Selectivity Rating: 78   **Fire Safety Rating:** 60*   **Green Rating:** 60*

STUDENTS AND FACULTY
Enrollment: 7,381. **Student Body:** 57% female, 43% male, 6% out-of-state. African American 20%, Asian 2%, Caucasian 75%, Hispanic 1%. **Retention and Graduation:** 63% freshmen return for sophomore year. 15% freshmen graduate within 4 years. 29% grads go on to further study within 2 semesters. 12% grads pursue arts and sciences degrees. 4% grads pursue business degrees. 5% grads pursue law degrees. 5% grads pursue medical degrees. **Faculty:** Student/faculty ratio 15:1. 401 full-time faculty, 69% hold PhDs. 90% faculty teach undergrads.

ACADEMICS
Degrees: Bachelor's, doctoral, first professional, master's, post-bachelor's certificate, post-master's certificate. **Academic Requirements:** Arts/fine arts, computer literacy, English (including composition), humanities, mathematics, sciences (biological or physical), social science. **Classes:** Most classes have 20–29 students. Most lab/discussion sections have 20–29 students. **Majors with Highest Enrollment:** Business administration and management, family and consumer sciences/human sciences, psychology. **Disciplines with Highest Percentage of Degrees Awarded:** Business/marketing 24%, family and consumer sciences 11%, psychology 8%, health professions and related sciences 7%, education 7%. **Special Study Options:** Cooperative education program, cross registration, distance learning, double major, dual enrollment, English as a second language (ESL), honors program, independent study, internships, study abroad, teacher certification program.

FACILITIES
Housing: Coed dorms, apartments for single students, fraternity/sorority housing. **Special Academic Facilities/Equipment:** Walker Teaching Resource Center, Jones Observatory, Institute of Archaeology, Odor Research Center, SIM Center. **Computers:** 30% of classrooms are wireless, 95% of public computers are PCs, 5% of public computers are Macs, network access in dorm rooms, online registration, online administrative functions (other than registration), remote student-access to Web through college's connection.

CAMPUS LIFE
Activities: Choral groups, concert band, dance, drama/theater, jazz band, marching band, music ensembles, pep band, radio station, student government, student newspaper, student-run film society, symphony orchestra. **Organizations:** 130 registered organizations, 19 honor societies, 9 religious organizations. 12 fraternities, 7 sororities. **Athletics (Intercollegiate):** *Men:* Basketball, cross-country, football, golf, tennis, track/field (outdoor), wrestling. *Women:* Basketball, cross-country, soccer, softball, tennis, track/field (outdoor), volleyball.

ADMISSIONS
Freshman Academic Profile: 41% in top 25% of high school class, 81% in top 50% of high school class. 75% from public high schools. ACT middle 50% range 19–24. TOEFL required of all international applicants, minimum paper TOEFL 500, minimum computer TOEFL 200. **Basis for Candidate Selection:** *Very important factors considered include:* Academic GPA, rigor of secondary school record, standardized test scores. *Important factors considered include:* Character/personal qualities. *Other factors considered include:* Application essay, extracurricular activities, recommendation(s), talent/ability, volunteer work, work experience. **Freshman Admission Requirements:** High school diploma is required, and GED is accepted. *Academic units required:* 4 English, 3 math, 2 science (2 science labs), 2 foreign language, 2 social studies, 2 history, 2 fine arts. **Freshman Admission Statistics:** 4,524 applied, 83% admitted, 47% enrolled. **Transfer Admission Requirements:** College transcript(s). Minimum college GPA of 1.0 required. Lowest grade transferable D. **General Admission Information:** Application fee $25. Regular notification after processing application. Non-fall registration accepted. Admission may be deferred for a maximum of 1 semester. Credit and/or placement offered for CEEB Advanced Placement tests.

COSTS AND FINANCIAL AID
Annual in-state tuition $4,688. Out-of-state tuition $14,084. Room & board $7,384. Required fees $940. Average book expense $950. **Required Forms and Deadlines:** FAFSA, institution's own financial aid form. Financial aid filing deadline 4/1. **Notification of Awards:** Applicants will be notified of awards on a rolling basis beginning on or about 3/15. **Types of Aid:** *Need-based scholarships/grants:* Pell, SEOG, state scholarships/grants, private scholarships, the school's own gift aid, United Negro College Fund, Federal Nursing Scholarships, Tennessee Lottery Scholarships. *Loans:* FFEL Subsidized Stafford, FFEL Unsubsidized Stafford, FFEL PLUS, Federal Perkins, college/university loans from institutional funds. **Student Employment:** Federal Work-Study Program available. Institutional employment available. Off-campus job opportunities are good. **Financial Aid Statistics:** 50% freshmen, 41% undergrads receive need-based scholarship or grant aid. 47% freshmen, 50% undergrads receive need-based self-help aid. 72 freshmen, 231 undergrads receive athletic scholarships. 50% freshmen, 48% undergrads receive any aid.

THE UNIVERSITY OF TENNESSEE AT KNOXVILLE

320 Student Service Building, Circle Park Drive, Knoxville, TN 37996-0230
Phone: 865-974-2184 **E-mail:** admissions@tennessee.edu **CEEB Code:** 1843
Fax: 865-974-6341 **Website:** www.utk.edu **ACT Code:** 4026
Financial Aid Phone: 865-974-3131

This public school was founded in 1794. It has a 561-acre campus.

RATINGS
Admissions Selectivity Rating: 87   **Fire Safety Rating:** 81   **Green Rating:** 85

STUDENTS AND FACULTY
Enrollment: 20,298. **Student Body:** 51% female, 49% male, 14% out-of-state. African American 9%, Asian 3%, Caucasian 85%, Hispanic 2%. **Retention and Graduation:** 82% freshmen return for sophomore year. 31% freshmen graduate within 4 years. **Faculty:** Student/faculty ratio 15:1. 1,540 full-time faculty, 82% hold PhDs. 74% faculty teach undergrads.

ACADEMICS
Degrees: Bachelor's, doctoral, first professional, master's. **Academic Requirements:** Cultures and civilizations, English (including composition), humanities, mathematics, oral communication, sciences (biological or physical), social science. **Classes:** Most classes have 20–29 students. Most lab/discussion sections have 20–29 students. **Majors with Highest Enrollment:** English language and literature, political science and government, psychology. **Disciplines with Highest Percentage of Degrees Awarded:** Business/marketing 18%, social sciences 13%, psychology 11%, communications/journalism 9%, engineering 7%. **Special Study Options:** Cooperative education program, distance learning, double major, dual enrollment, English as a second language (ESL), exchange student program (domestic), honors program, independent study, internships, liberal arts/career combination, student-designed major, study abroad, teacher certification program.

FACILITIES
Housing: Coed dorms, men's dorms, women's dorms, apartments for married students, apartments for single students, special housing for disabled students, special housing for international students, fraternity/sorority housing, transfer student floor. **Special Academic Facilities/Equipment:** Comprehensive museum of anthropology, archaeology, art, geology, natural history, and medicine, theatre-in-the-round, child development lab, livestock farms, robotics research center, electron microscope, McClung Museum. **Computers:** 100% of classrooms are wireless, 90% of public computers are PCs, 10% of public computers are Macs, network access in dorm rooms, network access in dorm lounges, online registration, online administrative functions (other than registration), support for handheld computing, remote student-access to Web through college's connection.

CAMPUS LIFE
Activities: Choral groups, concert band, dance, drama/theater, jazz band, literary magazine, marching band, music ensembles, musical theater, opera, pep band, radio station, student government, student newspaper, student-run film society, symphony orchestra, television station. **Organizations:** 450 registered organizations, 90 honor societies, 30 religious organizations. 20 fraternities (13%

men join), 18 sororities (19% women join). **Athletics (Intercollegiate):** *Men:* Baseball, basketball, cheerleading, cross-country, diving, football, golf, swimming, tennis, track/field (indoor), track/field (outdoor). *Women:* Basketball, cheerleading, crew/rowing, cross-country, diving, golf, soccer, softball, swimming, tennis, track/field (indoor), track/field (outdoor), volleyball.

ADMISSIONS

Freshman Academic Profile: 42% in top 10% of high school class, 27% in top 25% of high school class, 68% in top 50% of high school class. SAT Math middle 50% range 530–640. SAT Critical Reading middle 50% range 520–630. ACT middle 50% range 23–28. TOEFL required of all international applicants, minimum paper TOEFL 523, minimum computer TOEFL 193. **Basis for Candidate Selection:** *Very important factors considered include:* Academic GPA, rigor of secondary school record, standardized test scores. *Other factors considered include:* Alumni/ae relation, application essay, character/personal qualities, class rank, extracurricular activities, first generation, geographical residence, level of applicant's interest, racial/ethnic status, recommendation(s), state residency, talent/ability. **Freshman Admission Requirements:** High school diploma is required, and GED is accepted. *Academic units required:* 4 English, 3 math, 2 science (1 science lab), 2 foreign language, 1 social studies, 1 history, 1 visual or performing art. **Freshman Admission Statistics:** 12,372 applied, 74% admitted, 46% enrolled. **Transfer Admission Requirements:** High school transcript, college transcript(s), statement of good standing from prior institution(s). Minimum college GPA of 2.0 required. Lowest grade transferable C. **General Admission Information:** Application fee $30. Regular application deadline 2/1. Regular notification January and March. Non-fall registration accepted. Admission may be deferred for a maximum of 1 semester. Credit offered for CEEB Advanced Placement tests.

COSTS AND FINANCIAL AID

Annual in-state tuition $5,376. Annual out-of-state tuition $17,916. Room and board $6,676. Required fees $1,112. Average book expense $1,326. **Required Forms and Deadlines:** FAFSA, Academic College Scholarship Application. Financial aid filing deadline 3/1. **Notification of Awards:** Applicants will be notified of awards on a rolling basis beginning on or about 3/15. **Types of Aid:** *Need-based scholarships/grants:* Pell, SEOG, state scholarships/grants, private scholarships, the school's own gift aid, Federal Nursing Scholarships. *Loans:* FFEL Subsidized Stafford, FFEL Unsubsidized Stafford, FFEL PLUS, Federal Perkins, college/university loans from institutional funds. **Student Employment:** Federal Work-Study Program available. Off-campus job opportunities are good. **Financial Aid Statistics:** 43% freshmen, 35% undergrads receive need-based scholarship or grant aid. 22% freshmen, 28% undergrads receive need-based self-help aid. 33 freshmen, 174 undergrads receive athletic scholarships. 45% freshmen, 43% undergrads receive any aid.

THE UNIVERSITY OF TENNESSEE AT MARTIN

200 Hall-Moody, Administrative Building, Martin, TN 38238
Phone: 731-881-7020 **E-mail:** admitme@utm.edu
Fax: 731-881-7029 **Website:** www.utm.edu **ACT Code:** 4032
Financial Aid Phone: 731-881-7040

This public school was founded in 1900. It has a 930-acre campus.

RATINGS
Admissions Selectivity Rating: 75   **Fire Safety Rating:** 65   **Green Rating:** 84

STUDENTS AND FACULTY
Enrollment: 5,612. **Student Body:** 56% female, 44% male, 5% out-of-state, 2% international (22 countries represented). African American 15%, Caucasian 81%, Hispanic 1%. **Retention and Graduation:** 70% freshmen return for sophomore year. 21% freshmen graduate within 4 years. 22% grads go on to further study within 2 semesters. **Faculty:** Student/faculty ratio 18:1. 252 full-time faculty, 72% hold PhDs. 96% faculty teach undergrads.

ACADEMICS
Degrees: Bachelor's, master's. **Academic Requirements:** Arts/fine arts, English (including composition), humanities, mathematics, sciences (biological or physical), social science. **Classes:** Most classes have 10–19 students. Most lab/discussion sections have 10–19 students. **Majors with Highest Enrollment:** Biology/biological sciences, multi/interdisciplinary studies, nursing/registered nurse training (ASN, BSN, MSN, RN). **Disciplines with Highest Percentage of Degrees Awarded:** Business/marketing 20%, interdisciplinary studies 20%, agriculture 7%, health professions and related sciences 7%, parks

and recreation 5%, engineering 4%. **Special Study Options:** 3-1 programs (in pharmacy, veterinary medicine, dentistry, medicine, optometry, podiatry, chiropractory), accelerated program, cooperative education program, cross registration, distance learning, double major, dual enrollment, English as a second language (ESL), exchange student program (domestic), honors program, independent study, internships, student-designed major, study abroad, teacher certification program.

FACILITIES
Housing: Coed dorms, men's dorms, women's dorms, apartments for married students, apartments for single students, special housing for disabled students, fraternity/sorority housing. **Special Academic Facilities/Equipment:** Paul Meek Library, university museum. **Computers:** 1% of classrooms are wired, 100% of classrooms are wireless, 90% of public computers are PCs, 10% of public computers are Macs, network access in dorm rooms, network access in dorm lounges, online registration, online administrative functions (other than registration), support for handheld computing, remote student-access to Web through college's connection.

CAMPUS LIFE
Activities: Choral groups, concert band, dance, drama/theater, jazz band, literary magazine, marching band, music ensembles, opera, pep band, radio station, student government, student newspaper, television station, yearbook. **Organizations:** 125 registered organizations, 30 honor societies, 5 religious organizations. 11 fraternities (24% men join), 8 sororities (20% women join). **Athletics (Intercollegiate):** *Men:* Baseball, basketball, cheerleading, cross-country, football, golf, riflery, rodeo, tennis. *Women:* Basketball, cheerleading, cross-country, riflery, rodeo, soccer, softball, tennis, volleyball. **Environmental Initiatives:** Recycling all paper, cardboard, cans and plastic bottles. Using carpet made from recycled materials. Retrofit lighting with new, more energy-efficient lamps and ballasts.

ADMISSIONS
Freshman Academic Profile: 20% in top 10% of high school class, 50% in top 25% of high school class, 85% in top 50% of high school class. 90% from public high schools. ACT middle 50% range 19–24. TOEFL required of all international applicants, minimum paper TOEFL 500, minimum computer TOEFL 173. **Basis for Candidate Selection:** *Very important factors considered include:* Academic GPA, rigor of secondary school record, standardized test scores. **Freshman Admission Requirements:** High school diploma is required, and GED is accepted. *Academic units required:* 4 English, 3 math, 2 science (1 science lab), 2 foreign language, 2 history, 1 fine/performing arts. **Freshman Admission Statistics:** 2,773 applied, 82% admitted, 54% enrolled. **Transfer Admission Requirements:** High school transcript, college transcript(s). Minimum college GPA of 2.0 required. Lowest grade transferable D. **General Admission Information:** Application fee $30. Regular application deadline 8/1. Regular notification is rolling. Non-fall registration accepted. Credit and/or placement offered for CEEB Advanced Placement tests.

COSTS AND FINANCIAL AID
Annual in-state tuition $5,005. Annual out-of-state tuition $15,045. Room and board $4,446. **Required Forms and Deadlines:** FAFSA. Financial aid filing deadline 3/1. **Notification of Awards:** Applicants will be notified of awards on or about 4/1. **Types of Aid:** *Need-based scholarships/grants:* Pell, SEOG, state scholarships/grants, private scholarships, the school's own gift aid. *Loans:* FFEL Subsidized Stafford, FFEL Unsubsidized Stafford, FFEL PLUS, Federal Perkins. **Student Employment:** Federal Work-Study Program available. Institutional employment available. Off-campus job opportunities are good. **Financial Aid Statistics:** 41% freshmen, 38% undergrads receive need-based scholarship or grant aid. 30% freshmen, 38% undergrads receive need-based self-help aid. 22 freshmen, 108 undergrads receive athletic scholarships. 91% freshmen, 72% undergrads receive any aid. Highest amount earned per year from on-campus jobs $10,855.

THE UNIVERSITY OF TEXAS AT ARLINGTON

Office of Admissions, PO Box 19111, Arlington, TX 76019-0111
Phone: 817-272-6287 **E-mail:** admissions@uta.edu **CEEB Code:** 6013
Fax: 817-272-3435 **Website:** www.uta.edu **ACT Code:** 4200
Financial Aid Phone: 817-272-3561

This public school was founded in 1895. It has a 394-acre campus.

RATINGS
Admissions Selectivity Rating: 73   **Fire Safety Rating:** 91   **Green Rating:** 60*

STUDENTS AND FACULTY

Enrollment: 19,222. **Student Body:** 53% female, 47% male, 2% out-of-state, 5% international (147 countries represented). African American 14%, Asian 11%, Caucasian 51%, Hispanic 15%. **Retention and Graduation:** 69% freshmen return for sophomore year. 15% freshmen graduate within 4 years. **Faculty:** Student/faculty ratio 22:1. 781 full-time faculty. 100% faculty teach undergrads.

ACADEMICS

Degrees: Bachelor's, doctoral, master's, post-bachelor's certificate, post-master's certificate. **Academic Requirements:** Arts/fine arts, computer literacy, English (including composition), foreign languages, history, mathematics, sciences (biological or physical), social science, liberal arts elective (philosophy, fine arts, etc.). **Classes:** Most classes have 20–29 students. **Majors with Highest Enrollment:** Biology/biological sciences, management information systems, nursing. **Disciplines with Highest Percentage of Degrees Awarded:** Business/marketing 28%, engineering 9%, health professions and related sciences 9%, interdisciplinary studies 9%, biological/life sciences 7%, communications/journalism 6%, architecture 4%, English 4%, social sciences 4%, visual and performing arts 4%. **Special Study Options:** Cooperative education program, cross registration, distance learning, double major, dual enrollment, English as a second language (ESL), honors program, independent study, internships, student-designed major, study abroad, teacher certification program.

FACILITIES

Housing: Coed dorms, men's dorms, women's dorms, apartments for married students, apartments for single students, fraternity/sorority housing, family housing (priority given to students with dependent children). **Special Academic Facilities/Equipment:** Cartographic history library, maps collection, minority cultures collection, Library of Texana and Mexican war, continuing education work force development center, planetarium, automation and robotics research institute, wave scattering research center. **Computers:** 77% of public computers are PCs, 15% of public computers are Macs, 8% of public computers are UNIX, network access in dorm rooms, network access in dorm lounges, online registration, online administrative functions (other than registration), support for handheld computing, remote student-access to Web through college's connection.

CAMPUS LIFE

Activities: Choral groups, concert band, dance, drama/theater, jazz band, literary magazine, marching band, music ensembles, opera, radio station, student government, student newspaper, student-run film society, symphony orchestra. **Organizations:** 459 registered organizations, 30 honor societies, 27 religious organizations. 12 fraternities (4% men join), 13 sororities (3% women join). **Athletics (Intercollegiate):** *Men:* Baseball, basketball, cross-country, golf, tennis, track/field (outdoor). *Women:* Basketball, cross-country, softball, tennis, track/field (outdoor), volleyball.

ADMISSIONS

Freshman Academic Profile: 20% in top 10% of high school class, 60% in top 25% of high school class, 89% in top 50% of high school class. SAT Math middle 50% range 480–590. SAT Critical Reading middle 50% range 460–570. ACT middle 50% range 19–24. TOEFL required of all international applicants, minimum paper TOEFL 550, minimum computer TOEFL 213. **Basis for Candidate Selection:** *Very important factors considered include:* Academic GPA, class rank, standardized test scores. *Important factors considered include:* Rigor of secondary school record. *Other factors considered include:* Application essay, character/personal qualities, extracurricular activities, first generation, interview, level of applicant's interest, recommendation(s), talent/ability, volunteer work, work experience. **Freshman Admission Requirements:** High school diploma is required, and GED is not accepted. *Academic units required:* 4 English, 3 math, 3 science, 2 foreign language, 3 social studies, 5 academic electives, 5 physical education, health, computer proficiency, fine art, music, theater. *Academic units recommended:* 4 English, 4 math, 3 science, 3 foreign language, 4 social studies. **Freshman Admission Statistics:** 5,465 applied, 79% admitted, 49% enrolled. **Transfer Admission Requirements:** High school transcript, college transcript(s), standardized test score. Minimum college GPA of 2.25 required. Lowest grade transferable C. **General Admission Information:** Application fee $35. Regular notification 3-7 days after application file is complete. Non-fall registration accepted. Admission may be deferred for a maximum of 2 semesters. Common Application not accepted. Credit offered for CEEB Advanced Placement tests.

COSTS AND FINANCIAL AID

Annual in-state tuition $3,893. Out-of-state tuition $12,173. Room & board $5,345. Required fees $1,670. Average book expense $800. **Required Forms and Deadlines:** FAFSA. Financial aid filing deadline 5/15. **Notification of Awards:** Applicants will be notified of awards on a rolling basis beginning on or about 4/1. **Types of Aid:** *Need-based scholarships/grants:* Pell, SEOG, state scholarships/grants, private scholarships, the school's own gift aid, United Negro College Fund. *Loans:* FFEL Subsidized Stafford, FFEL Unsubsidized Stafford,

FFEL PLUS, Federal Perkins, state loans, college/university loans from institutional funds. **Student Employment:** Federal Work-Study Program available. Institutional employment available. Off-campus job opportunities are excellent. **Financial Aid Statistics:** 40% freshmen, 37% undergrads receive need-based scholarship or grant aid. 49% freshmen, 45% undergrads receive need-based self-help aid. 45 freshmen, 192 undergrads receive athletic scholarships. 58% freshmen, 51% undergrads receive any aid.

THE UNIVERSITY OF TEXAS AT AUSTIN

Best 368

PO Box 8058, Austin, TX 78713-8058
Phone: 512-475-7440 **E-mail: CEEB Code:** 6882
Fax: 512-475-7475 **Website:** www.utexas.edu **ACT Code:** 4240
Financial Aid Phone: 512-475-6282

This public school was founded in 1883. It has a 350-acre campus.

RATINGS

Admissions Selectivity Rating: 92 **Fire Safety Rating:** 60* **Green Rating:** 60*

STUDENTS AND FACULTY

Enrollment: 36,241. **Student Body:** 52% female, 48% male, 4% out-of-state, 4% international (127 countries represented). African American 4%, Asian 17%, Caucasian 57%, Hispanic 17%. **Retention and Graduation:** 93% freshmen return for sophomore year. 46% freshmen graduate within 4 years. **Faculty:** Student/faculty ratio 18:1. 2,545 full-time faculty. 100% faculty teach undergrads.

ACADEMICS

Degrees: Bachelor's, doctoral, first professional, master's. **Academic Requirements:** Arts/fine arts, English (including composition), foreign languages, history, humanities, mathematics, sciences (biological or physical), social science. **Classes:** Most classes have 10–19 students. Most lab/discussion sections have 10–19 students. **Majors with Highest Enrollment:** Economics, political science and government. **Disciplines with Highest Percentage of Degrees Awarded:** Social sciences 14%, communications/journalism 13%, business/marketing 12%, engineering 11%, biological/life sciences 8%. **Special Study Options:** Accelerated program, cooperative education program, distance learning, double major, dual enrollment, English as a second language (ESL), honors program, independent study, internships, liberal arts/career combination, student-designed major, study abroad, teacher certification program.

FACILITIES

Housing: Coed dorms, men's dorms, women's dorms, apartments for married students, apartments for single students, honors residence, living learning centers (first-time freshmen). **Special Academic Facilities/Equipment:** Blanton Museum of Art, Lyndon Baines Johnson Presidential Library/Museum, performing arts center, Texas Memorial Museum, Harry Ransom Humanities Research Center. **Computers:** Network access in dorm rooms, network access in dorm lounges, online registration, online administrative functions (other than registration), remote student-access to Web through college's connection.

CAMPUS LIFE

Activities: Choral groups, concert band, dance, drama/theater, jazz band, literary magazine, marching band, music ensembles, musical theater, opera, pep band, radio station, student government, student newspaper, student-run film society, symphony orchestra, television station. **Organizations:** 900 registered organizations, 15 honor societies, 95 religious organizations. 26 fraternities (9% men join), 22 sororities (13% women join). **Athletics (Intercollegiate):** *Men:* Baseball, basketball, cross-country, diving, football, golf, swimming, tennis, track/field (outdoor). *Women:* Basketball, crew/rowing, cross-country, diving, golf, soccer, softball, swimming, tennis, track/field (outdoor), volleyball.

ADMISSIONS

Freshman Academic Profile: 73% in top 10% of high school class, 95% in top 25% of high school class, 99% in top 50% of high school class. SAT Math middle 50% range 570–700. SAT Critical Reading middle 50% range 540–670. SAT Writing middle 50% range 540–660. ACT middle 50% range 23–29. TOEFL required of all international applicants, minimum paper TOEFL 550, minimum computer TOEFL 213. **Basis for Candidate Selection:** *Very important factors considered include:* Class rank, rigor of secondary school record. *Important factors considered include:* Application essay, extracurricular activities, standardized test scores, talent/ability, volunteer work, work experience. *Other factors considered include:* Academic GPA, character/personal qualities, first generation, geographical residence, level of applicant's interest, racial/ethnic status, recommendation(s), state residency. **Freshman Admission Requirements:** High school diploma is required, and GED is accepted. *Academic units required:* 4 English, 3 math, 2 science, 2 foreign language, 3 social studies, 2 academic electives. *Academic units recommended:* 4 math, 3 science, 3 foreign language, 1 fine art. **Freshman Admission Statistics:** 23,502 applied, 57% admitted, 56% enrolled. **Transfer Admission Requirements:** College transcript(s), essay or personal statement. Minimum college GPA of 3.0 required. Lowest grade transferable C. **General Admission Information:** Application fee $60. Regular application deadline 2/1. Regular notification is rolling. Non-fall registration accepted. Admission may be deferred for a maximum of 2 semesters. Credit and/or placement offered for CEEB Advanced Placement tests.

COSTS AND FINANCIAL AID

Annual in-state tuition $7,670. Annual out-of-state tuition $24,544. Room and board $8,576. Average book expense $800. **Required Forms and Deadlines:** FAFSA. Financial aid filing deadline 4/1. **Notification of Awards:** Applicants will be notified of awards on a rolling basis beginning on or about 3/15. **Types of Aid:** *Need-based scholarships/grants:* Pell, SEOG, state scholarships/grants, private scholarships, the school's own gift aid, Federal Nursing Scholarships. *Loans:* FFEL Subsidized Stafford, FFEL Unsubsidized Stafford, FFEL PLUS, Federal Perkins, state loans. **Student Employment:** Off-campus job opportunities are fair. **Financial Aid Statistics:** 54% freshmen, 47% undergrads receive need-based scholarship or grant aid. 54% freshmen, 52% undergrads receive need-based self-help aid. 84% freshmen, 74% undergrads receive any aid.

THE UNIVERSITY OF TEXAS AT BROWNSVILLE

80 Fort Brown, Brownsville, TX 78520
Phone: 956-882-8295 **E-mail:** admissions@utb.edu **CEEB Code:** 6825
Fax: 956-882-7810 **Website:** www.utb.edu
Financial Aid Phone: 956-544-8277

This is a public school.

RATINGS
Admissions Selectivity Rating: 60*   **Fire Safety Rating:** 60*   **Green Rating:** 60*

STUDENTS AND FACULTY
Enrollment: 10,683. **Student Body:** 59% female, 41% male, 1% out-of-state, 3% international (20 countries represented). Caucasian 5%, Hispanic 91%. **Retention and Graduation:** 65% freshmen return for sophomore year. **Faculty:** Student/faculty ratio 17:1. 334 full-time faculty, 52% hold PhDs. 89% faculty teach undergrads.

ACADEMICS
Degrees: Associate, bachelor's, certificate, master's. **Academic Requirements:** Arts/fine arts, English (including composition), foreign languages, history, humanities, mathematics, sciences (biological or physical), social science. **Classes:** Most classes have fewer than 10 students. Most lab/discussion sections have 10–19 students. **Majors with Highest Enrollment:** Business administration/management, criminal justice/law enforcement administration, liberal arts and sciences/liberal studies. **Disciplines with Highest Percentage of Degrees Awarded:** Business/marketing 23%, interdisciplinary studies 12%, social sciences 9%, foreign languages and literature 6%, psychology 6%. **Special Study Options:** Cooperative education program, distance learning, double major, dual enrollment, English as a second language (ESL), independent study, internships, teacher certification program.

FACILITIES
Housing: Coed dorms. **Computers:** Network access in dorm rooms, network access in dorm lounges, online registration, online administrative functions (other than registration), remote student-access to Web through college's connection.

CAMPUS LIFE
Activities: Choral groups, dance, jazz band, music ensembles, student government, student newspaper. **Athletics (Intercollegiate):** *Men:* Baseball, golf. *Women:* Golf, volleyball.

ADMISSIONS
Freshman Academic Profile: 95% from public high schools. **Freshman Admission Requirements:** High school diploma or equivalent is not required. **Freshman Admission Statistics:** 2,044 applied, 100% admitted, 76%

enrolled. **Transfer Admission Requirements:** College transcript(s). Minimum college GPA of 2.0 required. Lowest grade transferable D. **General Admission Information:** Regular application deadline 7/1. Non-fall registration accepted. Admission may be deferred for a maximum of 2 semesters. Common Application not accepted. Credit offered for CEEB Advanced Placement tests.

COSTS AND FINANCIAL AID
Annual in-state tuition $1,392. Annual out-of-state tuition $4,728. Room and board $3,100. Required fees $545. **Required Forms and Deadlines:** FAFSA. Financial aid filing deadline 6/1. **Notification of Awards:** Applicants will be notified of awards on or about 5/1. **Types of Aid:** *Need-based scholarships/grants:* Pell, SEOG, state scholarships/grants, private scholarships, the school's own gift aid. *Loans:* FFEL Subsidized Stafford, FFEL Unsubsidized Stafford, FFEL PLUS, college/university loans from institutional funds.

THE UNIVERSITY OF TEXAS AT DALLAS

PO Box 830688, HH 10, Richardson, TX 75083-0688
Phone: 972-883-2270 **E-mail:** interest@utdallas.edu **CEEB Code:** 6897
Fax: 972-883-6803 **Website:** www.utdallas.edu **ACT Code:** 4243
Financial Aid Phone: 972-883-2941

This public school was founded in 1969. It has a 500-acre campus.

RATINGS
Admissions Selectivity Rating: 91   **Fire Safety Rating:** 60*   **Green Rating:** 70

STUDENTS AND FACULTY
Enrollment: 9,193. **Student Body:** 45% female, 55% male, 3% out-of-state, 4% international (103 countries represented). African American 7%, Asian 20%, Caucasian 58%, Hispanic 10%. **Retention and Graduation:** 80% freshmen return for sophomore year. 31% freshmen graduate within 4 years. **Faculty:** Student/faculty ratio 19:1. 484 full-time faculty, 90% hold PhDs. 83% faculty teach undergrads.

ACADEMICS
Degrees: Bachelor's, doctoral, master's, post-bachelor's certificate, post-master's certificate. **Academic Requirements:** Arts/fine arts, computer literacy, English (including composition), history, humanities, mathematics, sciences (biological or physical), social science. **Classes:** Most classes have 10–19 students. Most lab/discussion sections have 20–29 students. **Majors with Highest Enrollment:** Biology/biological sciences; business administration/management; electrical engineering, electronics engineering, communications engineering. **Disciplines with Highest Percentage of Degrees Awarded:** Business/marketing 31%, interdisciplinary studies 16%, social sciences 11%, biological/life sciences 6%, computer and information sciences 8%, engineering 6%, psychology 8%. **Special Study Options:** Accelerated program, cooperative education program, cross registration, distance learning, double major, dual enrollment, honors program, independent study, internships, student-designed major, study abroad, teacher certification program.

FACILITIES
Housing: Apartments for married students, apartments for single students, privately owned and operated on-campus apartments restricted to UTD students. **Special Academic Facilities/Equipment:** McDermott Library Special Collections, History of Aviation Collection, Wineburgh Philatelic Research Library, Louise B. Belsterling Botanical Library. **Computers:** 49% of classrooms are wired, 93% of classrooms are wireless, 83% of public computers are PCs, 17% of public computers are Macs, 1% of public computers are UNIX, network access in dorm rooms, network access in dorm lounges, online registration, remote student-access to Web through college's connection.

CAMPUS LIFE
Activities: Dance, drama/theater, radio station, student government, student newspaper. **Organizations:** 128 registered organizations, 10 honor societies, 15 religious organizations. 7 fraternities (5% men join), 6 sororities (4% women join). **Athletics (Intercollegiate):** *Men:* Baseball, basketball, cross-country, golf, soccer, tennis. *Women:* Basketball, cross-country, golf, soccer, softball, tennis, volleyball.

ADMISSIONS

Freshman Academic Profile: 41% in top 10% of high school class, 74% in top 25% of high school class, 96% in top 50% of high school class. 96% from public high schools. SAT Math middle 50% range 580–690. SAT Critical Reading middle 50% range 540–670. SAT Writing middle 50% range 530–640. ACT middle 50% range 24–29. TOEFL required of all international applicants, minimum paper TOEFL 550, minimum computer TOEFL 215. **Basis for Candidate Selection:** *Very important factors considered include:* Academic GPA, class rank, rigor of secondary school record, standardized test scores. *Important factors considered include:* Application essay, extracurricular activities. *Other factors considered include:* Character/personal qualities, first generation, geographical residence, level of applicant's interest, recommendation(s), state residency, talent/ability, volunteer work, work experience. **Freshman Admission Requirements:** High school diploma is required, and GED is accepted. *Academic units required:* 4 English, 3 math, 3 science (3 science labs), 2 foreign language, 3 social studies, 1 academic elective. *Academic units recommended:* 4 English, 4 math, 3 science (3 science labs), 3 foreign language, 4 social studies, 2 academic electives, 4 health, physical education, computer science, fine art. **Freshman Admission Statistics:** 4,630 applied, 51% admitted, 46% enrolled. **Transfer Admission Requirements:** College transcript(s). Minimum college GPA of 2.5 required. Lowest grade transferable C. **General Admission Information:** Application fee $50. Regular application deadline 7/1. Regular notification as decision is made. Non-fall registration accepted. Admission may be deferred for a maximum of 2 semesters. Credit and/or placement offered for CEEB Advanced Placement tests.

COSTS AND FINANCIAL AID

Annual in-state tuition $8,554. Annual out-of-state tuition $17,854. Room and board $6,671. Average book expense $1,200. **Required Forms and Deadlines:** FAFSA. Financial aid filing deadline 4/12. **Notification of Awards:** Applicants will be notified of awards on a rolling basis beginning on or about 4/15. **Types of Aid:** *Need-based scholarships/grants:* Pell, SEOG, state scholarships/grants, private scholarships, the school's own gift aid. *Loans:* FFEL Subsidized Stafford, FFEL Unsubsidized Stafford, FFEL PLUS, Federal Perkins, state loans, college/university loans from institutional funds. **Student Employment:** Federal Work-Study Program available. Institutional employment available. Off-campus job opportunities are excellent. **Financial Aid Statistics:** 26% freshmen, 34% undergrads receive need-based scholarship or grant aid. 36% freshmen, 39% undergrads receive need-based self-help aid. 80% freshmen, 57% undergrads receive any aid. Highest amount earned per year from on-campus jobs $9,930.

THE UNIVERSITY OF TEXAS AT EL PASO

500 West University Avenue, El Paso, TX 79968-0510
Phone: 915-747-5890 **E-mail:** futureminer@utep.edu **CEEB Code:** 6829
Fax: 915-747-8893 **Website:** www.utep.edu **ACT Code:** 4223
Financial Aid Phone: 915-747-5204

This public school was founded in 1913. It has a 330-acre campus.

RATINGS

Admissions Selectivity Rating: 68   **Fire Safety Rating:** 60*   **Green Rating:** 60*

STUDENTS AND FACULTY

Enrollment: 16,486. **Student Body:** 55% female, 45% male, 3% out-of-state, 9% international (69 countries represented). African American 3%, Asian 1%, Caucasian 9%, Hispanic 76%. **Retention and Graduation:** 68% freshmen return for sophomore year. **Faculty:** Student/faculty ratio 20:1. 678 full-time faculty. 88% faculty teach undergrads.

ACADEMICS

Degrees: Bachelor's, doctoral, master's. **Academic Requirements:** Arts/fine arts, computer literacy, English (including composition), foreign languages, history, humanities, mathematics, sciences (biological or physical), social science, university designated course in core. **Classes:** Most classes have 20–29 students. Most lab/discussion sections have 10–19 students. **Majors with Highest Enrollment:** Criminal justice/safety studies, multi/interdisciplinary studies, psychology. **Disciplines with Highest Percentage of Degrees Awarded:** Business/marketing 19%, interdisciplinary studies 15%, engineering technologies 12%, health professions and related sciences 10%, security and protective services 6%. **Special Study Options:** Accelerated program, cooperative education program, cross registration, distance learning, double major, dual enrollment, English as a second language (ESL), exchange student program (domestic), honors program, independent study, internships, study abroad, teacher certification program, weekend college.

FACILITIES

Housing: Apartments for single students, special housing for disabled students. **Special Academic Facilities/Equipment:** Cross-cultural ethnic study center, natural history and cultural museum, solar pond and solar house, electron microscope, atmospheric and acoustic research lab, seismic observatory. **Computers:** 98% of public computers are PCs, 2% of public computers are Macs, network access in dorm rooms, network access in dorm lounges, online registration, online administrative functions (other than registration), remote student-access to Web through college's connection.

CAMPUS LIFE

Activities: Choral groups, concert band, dance, drama/theater, jazz band, literary magazine, marching band, music ensembles, musical theater, opera, pep band, radio station, student government, student newspaper, student-run film society, symphony orchestra. **Organizations:** 1 honor society, 1 religious organization. 6 fraternities, 4 sororities. **Athletics (Intercollegiate):** *Men:* Basketball, cross-country, football, golf, track/field (indoor), track/field (outdoor). *Women:* Basketball, cross-country, golf, riflery, soccer, softball, tennis, track/field (indoor), track/field (outdoor), volleyball.

ADMISSIONS

Freshman Academic Profile: 18% in top 10% of high school class, 40% in top 25% of high school class, 71% in top 50% of high school class. 94% from public high schools. SAT Math middle 50% range 410–530. ACT middle 50% range 16–21. **Basis for Candidate Selection:** *Very important factors considered include:* Class rank, rigor of secondary school record. *Important factors considered include:* Standardized test scores, state residency. *Other factors considered include:* Academic GPA, alumni/ae relation, character/personal qualities, extracurricular activities, geographical residence, interview, recommendation(s), talent/ability, volunteer work, work experience. **Freshman Admission Requirements:** High school diploma is required, and GED is accepted. *Academic units recommended:* 4 English, 4 math, 3 science, 2 foreign language, 2 social studies, 2 history. **Freshman Admission Statistics:** 5,507 applied, 99% admitted, 45% enrolled. **Transfer Admission Requirements:** College transcript(s). Minimum college GPA of 2.0 required. Lowest grade transferable D. **General Admission Information:** Regular application deadline 7/31. Regular notification when admission file is complete. Non-fall registration accepted. Admission may be deferred for a maximum of 1 semester.

COSTS AND FINANCIAL AID

Annual in-state tuition $4,311. Room and board $4,185. Required fees $1,299. Average book expense $900. **Required Forms and Deadlines:** FAFSA, institution's own financial aid form. Financial aid filing deadline 3/15. **Notification of Awards:** Applicants will be notified of awards on or about 6/30. **Types of Aid:** *Need-based scholarships/grants:* Pell, SEOG, state scholarships/grants, the school's own gift aid, Federal Nursing Scholarships. *Loans:* FFEL Subsidized Stafford, FFEL Unsubsidized Stafford, FFEL PLUS, Federal Perkins, college/university loans from institutional funds. **Student Employment:** Federal Work-Study Program available. Institutional employment available. Off-campus job opportunities are good. **Financial Aid Statistics:** 61% freshmen, 47% undergrads receive need-based scholarship or grant aid. 59% freshmen, 48% undergrads receive need-based self-help aid. 36 freshmen, 168 undergrads receive athletic scholarships. 77% freshmen, 65% undergrads receive any aid.

THE UNIVERSITY OF TEXAS HEALTH SCIENCE CENTER AT HOUSTON

PO Box 20036, Houston, TX 77225
Phone: 713-500-3361 **E-mail:** admissions@uth.tmc.edu
Fax: 713-500-3356 **Website:** www.uth.tmc.edu
Financial Aid Phone: 713-500-3860

This public school was founded in 1972.

RATINGS

Admissions Selectivity Rating: 60*   **Fire Safety Rating:** 60*   **Green Rating:** 60*

STUDENTS AND FACULTY

Student Body: 88% female, 12% male, 2% international. African American 7%, Asian 17%, Caucasian 58%, Hispanic 15%.

ACADEMICS

Degrees: Bachelor's, certificate, doctoral, first professional, master's, post-master's certificate. **Disciplines with Highest Percentage of Degrees Awarded:** Health professions and related sciences 100%.

FACILITIES

Housing: University owns an apartment complex which is located approximately 1.5 miles from campus. **Special Academic Facilities/Equipment:** The student's learning experience takes place in the heart of the Texas Medical Center, among state-of-the-art hospitals and research facilites. **Computers:** Online registration, online administrative functions (other than registration). Undergraduates are required to own a computer.

CAMPUS LIFE

Activities: Student government.

ADMISSIONS

Freshman Academic Profile: TOEFL required of all international applicants, minimum paper TOEFL 565. **Transfer Admission Requirements:** College transcript(s), interview, standardized test score, statement of good standing from prior institution(s). Minimum college GPA of 2.8 required. Lowest grade transferable C. **General Admission Information:** Application fee $30. Regular application deadline 1/1. Non-fall registration not accepted. Common Application not accepted.

COSTS AND FINANCIAL AID

Annual in-state tuition $4,905. Out-of-state tuition $16,571. Required fees $697. Average book expense $2,400. **Required Forms and Deadlines:** FAFSA, institution's own financial aid form. Financial aid filing deadline 3/1. **Types of Aid:** *Need-based scholarships/grants:* Pell, SEOG, state scholarships/grants, the school's own gift aid, Federal Nursing Scholarships, outside Scholarships. *Loans:* FFEL Subsidized Stafford, FFEL Unsubsidized Stafford, FFEL PLUS, Federal Perkins, Federal Nursing, college/university loans from institutional funds, outside loans. **Student Employment:** Off-campus job opportunities are excellent.

UNIVERSITY OF TEXAS MEDICAL BRANCH AT GALVESTON

301 University Boulevard, Galveston, TX 77555-1305
Phone: 409-772-1215 **E-mail:** enrollment.services@utmb.edu **CEEB Code:** 6887
Fax: 409-772-4466 **Website:** www.utmb.edu
Financial Aid Phone: 409-772-4955

This public school was founded in 1891. It has an 85-acre campus.

RATINGS

Admissions Selectivity Rating: 60*   **Fire Safety Rating:** 60*   **Green Rating:** 60*

STUDENTS AND FACULTY

Enrollment: 494. **Student Body:** 78% female, 22% male, 2% out-of-state.

ACADEMICS

Degrees: Bachelor's, doctoral, first professional, master's, post-master's certificate. **Academic Requirements:** Arts/fine arts, computer literacy, English (including composition), history, humanities, mathematics, sciences (biological or physical), social science. **Majors with Highest Enrollment:** Clinical laboratory science/medical technology/technologist, nursing/registered nurse training (ASN, BSN, MSN, RN), occupational therapy/therapist. **Disciplines with Highest Percentage of Degrees Awarded:** Health professions and related sciences 100%. **Special Study Options:** Distance learning, independent study, internships.

FACILITIES

Housing: Coed dorms, apartments for married students, apartments for single students, fraternity/sorority housing. **Special Academic Facilities/Equipment:** Moody Medical Library. **Computers:** Network access in dorm rooms, online registration, online administrative functions (other than registration), remote student-access to Web through college's connection.

CAMPUS LIFE

Activities: Student government, student newspaper, yearbook.

ADMISSIONS

Freshman Academic Profile: TOEFL required of all international applicants, minimum paper TOEFL 550, minimum computer TOEFL 213. **Transfer Admission Requirements:** College transcript(s). Minimum college GPA of 2.0 required. Lowest grade transferable C. **General Admission Information:** Neither credit nor placement offered for CEEB Advanced Placement tests.

COSTS AND FINANCIAL AID

Annual in-state tuition $3,600. Out-of-state tuition $11,850. Room $2,907. Required fees $697. **Required Forms and Deadlines:** FAFSA. **Types of Aid:**

Need-based scholarships/grants: Pell, SEOG, state scholarships/grants, private scholarships, the school's own gift aid. *Loans:* Direct Subsidized Stafford, Direct Unsubsidized Stafford, Direct PLUS, Federal Perkins, Federal Nursing, college/university loans from institutional funds. **Student Employment:** Federal Work-Study Program available. Institutional employment available. Off-campus job opportunities are good. **Financial Aid Statistics:** 63% undergrads receive any aid.

THE UNIVERSITY OF TEXAS—PAN AMERICAN

Admissions and New Student Services, 1201 West University Drive, VC 1.133, Edinburg, TX 78541
Phone: 956-381-2201 **E-mail:** recruitment@utpa.edu
Fax: 956-381-2212 **Website:** www.utpa.edu **ACT Code:** 4142
Financial Aid Phone: 956-381-250

This public school was founded in 1927. It has a 289-acre campus.

RATINGS

Admissions Selectivity Rating: 60*   **Fire Safety Rating:** 60*   **Green Rating:** 70

STUDENTS AND FACULTY

Enrollment: 13,991. **Student Body:** 58% female, 42% male, 1% out-of-state, 5% international (41 countries represented). Asian 1%, Caucasian 4%, Hispanic 90%. **Retention and Graduation:** 73% freshmen return for sophomore year. 10% freshmen graduate within 4 years. **Faculty:** Student/faculty ratio 23:1. 669 full-time faculty.

ACADEMICS

Degrees: Bachelor's, doctoral, master's, post-bachelor's certificate. **Academic Requirements:** Arts/fine arts, computer literacy, English (including composition), foreign languages, history, humanities, mathematics, philosophy, sciences (biological or physical), social science. **Classes:** Most classes have 30–39 students. Most lab/discussion sections have 20–29 students. **Majors with Highest Enrollment:** Business administration/management, multi/interdisciplinary studies, nursing/registered nurse training (RN, ASN, BSN, MSN). **Disciplines with Highest Percentage of Degrees Awarded:** Interdisciplinary studies 18%, business/marketing 16%, health professions and related sciences 10%, biological/life sciences 6%, English 6%. **Special Study Options:** Cooperative education program, distance learning, double major, dual enrollment, English as a second language (ESL), exchange student program (domestic), honors program, independent study, internships, study abroad, teacher certification program, weekend college.

FACILITIES

Housing: Coed dorms, men's dorms, women's dorms, apartments for married students, apartments for single students. **Computers:** 80% of public computers are PCs, 15% of public computers are Macs, 5% of public computers are UNIX, network access in dorm rooms, network access in dorm lounges, online registration, online administrative functions (other than registration), remote student-access to Web through college's connection.

CAMPUS LIFE

Activities: Choral groups, concert band, dance, drama/theater, jazz band, music ensembles, musical theater, student government, student newspaper, symphony orchestra. **Organizations:** 80 registered organizations, 5 honor societies, 7 religious organizations. 4 fraternities (1% men join), 1 sorority (1% women join). **Athletics (Intercollegiate):** *Men:* Baseball, basketball, cross-country, golf, tennis, track/field (outdoor). *Women:* Basketball, cross-country, golf, tennis, track/field (outdoor), volleyball.

ADMISSIONS

Freshman Academic Profile: 17% in top 10% of high school class, 44% in top 25% of high school class, 75% in top 50% of high school class. 99% from public high schools. SAT Math middle 50% range 420–540. SAT Critical Reading middle 50% range 400–510. SAT Writing middle 50% range 410–520. ACT middle 50% range 17–21. TOEFL required of all international applicants, minimum paper TOEFL 500, minimum computer TOEFL 173. **Basis for Candidate Selection:** *Very important factors considered include:* Standardized test scores. *Important factors considered include:* Academic GPA, class rank, rigor of secondary school record. **Freshman Admission Requirements:** High school diploma is required, and GED is accepted. *Academic units required:* 4 English, 3 math, 3 science, 2 foreign language, 4 social studies, 4 academic electives. *Academic units recommended:* 3 academic electives. **Transfer Admission Requirements:** High school transcript, college transcript(s), standardized test score. Minimum college GPA of 2.0 required. **General Admission Information:** Regular application deadline 8/10. Regular notification as received. Non-fall registration accepted. Credit and/or placement offered for CEEB Advanced Placement tests.

COSTS AND FINANCIAL AID
Annual in-state tuition $3,100. Annual out-of-state tuition $9,772. Room and board $4,900. Required fees $799. Average book expense $1,000. **Required Forms and Deadlines:** FAFSA. Financial aid filing deadline 2/28. **Notification of Awards:** Applicants will be notified of awards on a rolling basis beginning on or about 3/1. **Types of Aid:** *Need-based scholarships/grants:* Pell, SEOG, state scholarships/grants, private scholarships, the school's own gift aid. *Loans:* FFEL Subsidized Stafford, FFEL Unsubsidized Stafford, FFEL PLUS, Federal Perkins, college/university loans from institutional funds. **Student Employment: Financial Aid Statistics:** 54% freshmen, 66% undergrads receive need-based scholarship or grant aid. 15% freshmen, 39% undergrads receive need-based self-help aid. Highest amount earned per year from on-campus jobs $1,800.

THE UNIVERSITY OF TEXAS OF THE PERMIAN BASIN

4901 East University Boulevard, Odessa, TX 79762-0001
Phone: 915-552-2605 **E-mail:** admissions@utpb.edu **CEEB Code:** 448
Fax: 915-552-3605 **Website:** www.utpb.edu **ACT Code:** 4225
Financial Aid Phone: 915-552-2620

This public school was founded in 1969. It has a 588-acre campus.

RATINGS
Admissions Selectivity Rating: 68 **Fire Safety Rating:** 60* **Green Rating:** 60*

STUDENTS AND FACULTY
Enrollment: 1,984. **Student Body:** 65% female, 35% male, 2% out-of-state. African American 4%, Caucasian 58%. **Retention and Graduation:** 61% freshmen return for sophomore year. **Faculty:** Student/faculty ratio 18:1. 103 full-time faculty, 84% hold PhDs. 100% faculty teach undergrads.

ACADEMICS
Degrees: Bachelor's, master's. **Academic Requirements:** Computer literacy, English (including composition), history, humanities, mathematics, sciences (biological or physical), Texas Higher Education Coordinating Board Core Curriculum courses. **Classes:** Most classes have 10–19 students. Most lab/discussion sections have 10–19 students. **Majors with Highest Enrollment:** History, humanities/humanistic studies, Spanish language and literature. **Disciplines with Highest Percentage of Degrees Awarded:** Social sciences 22%, business/marketing 16%, liberal arts/general studies 12%, English 8%, foreign languages and literature 8%, psychology 8%, computer and information sciences 7%. **Special Study Options:** Accelerated program, cross registration, distance learning, double major, independent study, internships, teacher certification program.

FACILITIES
Housing: Apartments for married students, apartments for single students, special housing for disabled students. **Special Academic Facilities/Equipment:** Ellen Noel Art Center, applied psychology lab, visual arts studio. **Computers:** 70% of public computers are PCs, 12% of public computers are Macs, 18% of public computers are UNIX, network access in dorm rooms, online registration, online administrative functions (other than registration), remote student-access to Web through college's connection.

CAMPUS LIFE
Activities: Choral groups, dance, drama/theater, literary magazine, pep band, radio station, student government, student newspaper. **Organizations:** 30 registered organizations, 3 honor societies, 3 religious organizations. **Athletics (Intercollegiate):** *Men:* Baseball, basketball, soccer, swimming. *Women:* Basketball, cheerleading, soccer, softball, swimming, volleyball.

ADMISSIONS
Freshman Academic Profile: 21% in top 10% of high school class, 46% in top 25% of high school class, 83% in top 50% of high school class. 99% from public high schools. SAT Math middle 50% range 420–530. SAT Critical Reading middle 50% range 440–530. ACT middle 50% range 18–22. TOEFL required of all international applicants, minimum paper TOEFL 550, minimum computer TOEFL 213. **Basis for Candidate Selection:** *Very important factors considered include:* Class rank, rigor of secondary school record, standardized test scores. *Important factors considered include:* Recommendation(s). **Freshman Admission Requirements:** High school diploma is required, and GED is accepted. *Academic units required:* 4 English,

3 math, 2 science, 2 social studies, 1 history, 6 academic electives. *Academic units recommended:* 1 math, 1 science, 2 foreign language. **Freshman Admission Statistics:** 453 applied, 88% admitted, 57% enrolled. **Transfer Admission Requirements:** College transcript(s). Minimum college GPA of 2.0 required. Lowest grade transferable C. **General Admission Information:** Regular application deadline 8/15. Regular notification rolling, as admission file is completed. Non-fall registration accepted. Admission may be deferred for a maxiumum of 2 semesters. Common Application not accepted. Credit offered for CEEB Advanced Placement tests.

COSTS AND FINANCIAL AID
Required Forms and Deadlines: FAFSA, institution's own financial aid form. Financial aid filing deadline 5/1. **Notification of Awards:** Applicants will be notified of awards on a rolling basis beginning on or about 6/1. **Types of Aid:** *Need-based scholarships/grants:* Pell, SEOG, state scholarships/grants, private scholarships, the school's own gift aid. *Loans:* FFEL Subsidized Stafford, FFEL Unsubsidized Stafford, FFEL PLUS, state loans. **Student Employment:** Federal Work-Study Program available. Institutional employment available. Off-campus job opportunities are good. **Financial Aid Statistics:** 65% freshmen, 65% undergrads receive need-based scholarship or grant aid. 46% freshmen, 61% undergrads receive need-based self-help aid. Highest amount earned per year from on-campus jobs $1,375.

THE UNIVERSITY OF TEXAS AT SAN ANTONIO

6900 North Loop 1604 West, San Antonio, TX 78249-0617
Phone: 210-458-8000 **E-mail:** prospects@utsa.edu **CEEB Code:** 6919
Fax: 210-458-7716 **Website:** www.utsa.edu **ACT Code:** 4239
Financial Aid Phone: 210-458-8000

This public school was founded in 1969. It has a 600-acre campus.

RATINGS
Admissions Selectivity Rating: 63 **Fire Safety Rating:** 60* **Green Rating:** 60*

STUDENTS AND FACULTY
Enrollment: 23,282. **Student Body:** 53% female, 47% male, 4% out-of-state, 2% international (66 countries represented). African American 7%, Asian 5%, Caucasian 39%, Hispanic 46%. **Retention and Graduation:** 58% freshmen return for sophomore year. 6% freshmen graduate within 4 years. **Faculty:** Student/faculty ratio 23:1. 860 full-time faculty, 81% hold PhDs.

ACADEMICS
Degrees: Bachelor's, doctoral, master's. **Academic Requirements:** Arts/fine arts, computer literacy, English (including composition), foreign languages, history, humanities, mathematics, philosophy, sciences (biological or physical), social science. **Classes:** Most classes have 20–29 students. Most lab/discussion sections have 10–19 students. **Majors with Highest Enrollment:** Biology/biological sciences, multi/interdisciplinary studies, psychology. **Disciplines with Highest Percentage of Degrees Awarded:** Business/marketing 29%, interdisciplinary studies 12%, biological/life sciences 9%, psychology 8%, security and protective services 6%. **Special Study Options:** 2+2 Programs with surrounding colleges, distance learning, double major, dual enrollment, English as a second language (ESL), exchange student program (domestic), honors program, independent study, internships, study abroad, teacher certification program.

FACILITIES
Housing: Coed dorms, apartments for married students, apartments for single students, fraternity/sorority housing. **Special Academic Facilities/Equipment:** Art gallery, audiovisual center, Institute of Texan Cultures Museum. **Computers:** 100% of classrooms are wired, 10% of classrooms are wireless, 98% of public computers are PCs, 2% of public computers are Macs, 1% of public computers are UNIX, network access in dorm rooms, online registration, online administrative functions (other than registration), remote student-access to Web through college's connection.

CAMPUS LIFE
Activities: Choral groups, concert band, dance, drama/theater, jazz band, music ensembles, opera, pep band, student government, student newspaper, symphony orchestra, yearbook. **Organizations:** 140 registered organizations, 40 honor societies, 9 religious organizations. 10 fraternities (4% men join), 9 sororities (2% women join). **Athletics (Intercollegiate):** *Men:* Baseball, basketball, cross-country, golf, tennis, track/field (indoor), track/field (outdoor). *Women:* Basketball, cross-country, soccer, softball, tennis, track/field (indoor), track/field (outdoor), volleyball.

ADMISSIONS

Freshman Academic Profile: 9% in top 10% of high school class, 35% in top 25% of high school class, 71% in top 50% of high school class. 94% from public high schools. SAT Math middle 50% range 460–570. SAT Critical Reading middle 50% range 450–560. ACT middle 50% range 18–23. TOEFL required of all international applicants, minimum paper TOEFL 500, minimum computer TOEFL 173. **Basis for Candidate Selection:** *Very important factors considered include:* Class rank, standardized test scores. *Important factors considered include:* Extracurricular activities. *Other factors considered include:* Application essay, character/personal qualities, first generation, recommendation(s), state residency, talent/ability, volunteer work, work experience. **Freshman Admission Requirements:** High school diploma is required, and GED is accepted. *Academic units recommended:* 4 English, 3 math, 3 science, 2 foreign language, 3 social studies, 1 fine art. **Freshman Admission Statistics:** 9,144 applied, 99% admitted, 49% enrolled. **Transfer Admission Requirements:** College transcript(s). Minimum college GPA of 2.0 required. Lowest grade transferable D. **General Admission Information:** Application fee $30. Regular application deadline 7/1. Regular notification is rolling. Non-fall registration accepted. Common Application not accepted. Credit and/or placement offered for CEEB Advanced Placement tests.

COSTS AND FINANCIAL AID

Annual in-state tuition $3,096. Out-of-state tuition $10,656. Room & board $8,151. Required fees $1,368. Average book expense $771. **Required Forms and Deadlines:** FAFSA, institution's own financial aid form. Financial aid filing deadline 3/31. **Notification of Awards:** Applicants will be notified of awards on a rolling basis beginning on or about 4/1. **Types of Aid:** *Need-based scholarships/grants:* Pell, SEOG, state scholarships/grants, private scholarships, the school's own gift aid. *Loans:* FFEL Subsidized Stafford, FFEL Unsubsidized Stafford, FFEL PLUS, Federal Perkins, state loans, college/university loans from institutional funds. **Financial Aid Statistics:** 44% freshmen, 52% undergrads receive need-based scholarship or grant aid. 43% freshmen, 57% undergrads receive need-based self-help aid. 41 freshmen, 191 undergrads receive athletic scholarships. 65% freshmen, 67% undergrads receive any aid.

THE UNIVERSITY OF TEXAS AT TYLER

3900 University Boulevard, Tyler, TX 75799
Phone: 903-566-7202 **E-mail:** admissions@mail.uttyl.edu
Fax: 903-566-7068 **Website:** www.uttyler.edu
Financial Aid Phone: 903-566-7180

This public school was founded in 1971. It has a 204-acre campus.

RATINGS

Admissions Selectivity Rating: 60*   **Fire Safety Rating:** 97   **Green Rating:** 60*

STUDENTS AND FACULTY

Enrollment: 4,700. **Student Body:** 60% female, 40% male, 2% out-of-state. African American 10%, Asian 2%, Caucasian 79%, Hispanic 6%. **Retention and Graduation:** 59% freshmen return for sophomore year. 14% grads go on to further study within 1 year. **Faculty:** Student/faculty ratio 21:1. 234 full-time faculty, 70% hold PhDs.

ACADEMICS

Degrees: Bachelor's, master's. **Academic Requirements:** Arts/fine arts, English (including composition), history, humanities, mathematics, sciences (biological or physical), social science. **Classes:** Most classes have 20–29 students. **Majors with Highest Enrollment:** Business/managerial economics, multi/interdisciplinary studies, nursing/registered nurse training (RN, ASN, BSN, MSN). **Disciplines with Highest Percentage of Degrees Awarded:** Health professions and related sciences 24%, business/marketing 21%, interdisciplinary studies 13%, psychology 6%, English 5%. **Special Study Options:** Cooperative education program, cross registration, distance learning, double major, English as a second language (ESL), exchange student program (domestic), independent study, internships, student-designed major, study abroad, teacher certification program, weekend college.

FACILITIES

Housing: Coed dorms, apartments for married students, apartments for single students. **Computers:** Network access in dorm rooms, network access in dorm lounges, online registration, online administrative functions (other than registration), support for handheld computing, remote student-access to Web through college's connection.

CAMPUS LIFE

Activities: Choral groups, concert band, drama/theater, jazz band, literary magazine, music ensembles, musical theater, opera, pep band, student government, student newspaper, student-run film society. **Organizations:** 60 registered organizations. **Athletics (Intercollegiate):** *Men:* Baseball, basketball, cheerleading, cross-country, golf, soccer, tennis. *Women:* Basketball, cheerleading, cross-country, golf, soccer, tennis, volleyball.

ADMISSIONS

Freshman Academic Profile: SAT Math middle 50% range 480–580. SAT Critical Reading middle 50% range 470–570. ACT middle 50% range 20–25. TOEFL required of all international applicants, minimum paper TOEFL 550, minimum computer TOEFL 213. **Basis for Candidate Selection:** *Very important factors considered include:* Academic GPA, class rank, standardized test scores. *Important factors considered include:* Rigor of secondary school record. *Other factors considered include:* Extracurricular activities, first generation, volunteer work, work experience. **Freshman Admission Requirements:** High school diploma is required, and GED is accepted. *Academic units required:* 4 English, 3 math, 3 science (1 science lab), 2 foreign language, 3 social studies. *Academic units recommended:* 4 math, 3 science labs. **Freshman Admission Statistics:** 1,823 applied, 76% admitted, 46% enrolled. **Transfer Admission Requirements:** College transcript(s). Minimum college GPA of 2.0 required. Lowest grade transferable C. **General Admission Information:** Application fee $25. Regular notification is rolling. Non-fall registration accepted. Admission may be deferred for a maxiumum of 2 semesters.

COSTS AND FINANCIAL AID

Annual in-state tuition $3,304. Out-of-state tuition $9,496. Room & board $5,373. Required fees $742. Average book expense $750. **Required Forms and Deadlines:** FAFSA. Financial aid filing deadline 4/1. **Notification of Awards:** Applicants will be notified of awards on a rolling basis beginning on or about 4/15. **Types of Aid:** *Need-based scholarships/grants:* Pell, SEOG, state scholarships/grants, private scholarships, the school's own gift aid, Texas Grant Program, Teach for Texas Conditional Program. *Loans:* FFEL Subsidized Stafford, FFEL Unsubsidized Stafford, FFEL PLUS, Federal Perkins.

THE UNIVERSITY OF TOLEDO

2801 West Bancroft, Toledo, OH 43606
Phone: 419-530-8700 **E-mail:** enroll@utnet.utoledo.edu **CEEB Code:** 1845
Fax: 419-530-5713 **Website:** www.utoledo.edu **ACT Code:** 3344
Financial Aid Phone: 419-530-8700

This public school was founded in 1872. It has a 400-acre campus.

RATINGS

Admissions Selectivity Rating: 74   **Fire Safety Rating:** 60*   **Green Rating:** 60*

STUDENTS AND FACULTY

Enrollment: 15,288. **Student Body:** 49% female, 51% male, 8% out-of-state, 1% international (108 countries represented). African American 13%, Asian 2%, Caucasian 76%, Hispanic 3%. **Retention and Graduation:** 69% freshmen return for sophomore year. 17% freshmen graduate within 4 years. **Faculty:** Student/faculty ratio 18:1. 813 full-time faculty, 73% hold PhDs.

ACADEMICS

Degrees: Associate, bachelor's, certificate, doctoral, first professional, master's, post-bachelor's certificate, post-master's certificate. **Academic Requirements:** Arts/fine arts, English (including composition), humanities, mathematics, sciences (biological or physical), social science. **Majors with Highest Enrollment:** Education, engineering, marketing/marketing management. **Disciplines with Highest Percentage of Degrees Awarded:** Business/marketing 22%, education 13%, engineering 12%, health professions and related sciences 11%, engineering technologies 5%, interdisciplinary studies 5%. **Special Study Options:** Accelerated program, cooperative education program, cross registration, distance learning, double major, dual enrollment, exchange student program (domestic), honors program, independent study, internships, liberal arts/career combination, student-designed major, study abroad, teacher certification program, weekend college.

FACILITIES

Housing: Coed dorms, men's dorms, women's dorms, special housing for disabled students, special housing for international students, fraternity/sorority housing. **Special Academic Facilities/Equipment:** Language lab, arboretum, planetariums, 2 observatories, electron microscope. **Computers:** 91% of public computers are PCs, 9% of public computers are Macs, network access in dorm rooms, online registration, remote student-access to Web through college's connection.

CAMPUS LIFE
Activities: Choral groups, concert band, dance, drama/theater, jazz band, literary magazine, marching band, music ensembles, musical theater, opera, pep band, radio station, student government, student newspaper, student-run film society, symphony orchestra, television station. **Organizations:** 200 registered organizations. 14 fraternities (5% men join), 13 sororities (5% women join). **Athletics (Intercollegiate):** *Men:* Baseball, basketball, cheerleading, cross-country, diving, football, golf, lacrosse, softball, swimming, tennis, track/field (indoor), track/field (outdoor), volleyball. *Women:* Basketball, cheerleading, cross-country, diving, golf, lacrosse, softball, swimming, tennis, track/field (indoor), track/field (outdoor), volleyball.

ADMISSIONS
Freshman Academic Profile: 16% in top 10% of high school class, 37% in top 25% of high school class, 64% in top 50% of high school class. SAT Math middle 50% range 460–600. SAT Critical Reading middle 50% range 450–570. ACT middle 50% range 19–25. TOEFL required of all international applicants, minimum paper TOEFL 500, minimum computer TOEFL 173. **Basis for Candidate Selection:** *Very important factors considered include:* Rigor of secondary school record, standardized test scores, state residency. **Freshman Admission Requirements:** High school diploma is required, and GED is accepted. *Academic units required:* 4 English, 3 math, 3 science, 3 social studies. *Academic units recommended:* 4 English, 3 math, 3 science (1 science lab), 2 foreign language, 3 social studies, 1 history. **Freshman Admission Statistics:** 8,126 applied, 80% admitted, 49% enrolled. **Transfer Admission Requirements:** College transcript(s), statement of good standing from prior institution(s). Minimum college GPA of 2.0 required. Lowest grade transferable C. **General Admission Information:** Application fee $40. Regular notification is rolling. Non-fall registration accepted. Admission may be deferred for a maximum of 2 semesters. Common Application not accepted. Credit and/or placement offered for CEEB Advanced Placement tests.

COSTS AND FINANCIAL AID
Annual in-state tuition $6,430. Out-of-state tuition $15,242. Room & board $8,213. Required fees $1,091. Average book expense $690. **Required Forms and Deadlines:** FAFSA. Financial aid filing deadline 4/1. **Notification of Awards:** Applicants will be notified of awards on a rolling basis beginning on or about 4/1. **Types of Aid:** *Need-based scholarships/grants:* Pell, SEOG, state scholarships/grants, private scholarships, the school's own gift aid. *Loans:* Direct Subsidized Stafford, Direct Unsubsidized Stafford, Direct PLUS, Federal Perkins, state loans. **Student Employment:** Federal Work-Study Program available. **Financial Aid Statistics:** 38 freshmen, 187 undergrads receive athletic scholarships. 55% undergrads receive any aid.

UNIVERSITY OF TORONTO

315 Bloor Street West, Toronto, ON M5S1A3 Canada
Phone: 416-978-2190 **E-mail:** admissions.help@utoronto.ca **CEEB Code:** 0982
Fax: 416-978-7022 **Website:** www.utoronto.ca
Financial Aid Phone: 416-978-2190

This public school was founded in 1827. It has a 1,767-acre campus.

RATINGS
Admissions Selectivity Rating: 60*   **Fire Safety Rating:** 60*   **Green Rating:** 83

STUDENTS AND FACULTY
Enrollment: 56,819. **Student Body:** 56% female, 44% male, 4% out-of-state, 3% international (160 countries represented). **Retention and Graduation:** 95% freshmen return for sophomore year. 95% grads go on to further study within 1 year. **Faculty:** Student/faculty ratio 26:1. 2,612 full-time faculty.

ACADEMICS
Degrees: Bachelor's, certificate, diploma, doctoral, first professional, master's. **Classes:** Most classes have 10–19 students. **Majors with Highest Enrollment:** General studies, liberal arts and sciences/liberal studies. **Special Study Options:** Cooperative education program, double major, English as a second language (ESL), exchange student program (domestic), honor program, internships, study abroad, teacher certification program.

FACILITIES
Housing: Coed dorms, men's dorms, women's dorms, apartments for married students, cooperative housing. **Computers:** Network access in dorm rooms, network access in dorm lounges, online registration, remote student-access to Web through college's connection.

CAMPUS LIFE
Activities: Choral groups, concert band, dance, drama/theater, jazz band, literary magazine, music ensembles, opera, radio station, student government, student newspaper, student-run film society, symphony orchestra. **Organizations:** 200 registered organizations, 49 religious organizations. **Athletics (Intercollegiate):** *Men:* Badminton, baseball, basketball, crew/rowing, cross-country, curling, fencing, football, golf, ice hockey, lacrosse, mountain biking, rugby, skiing (nordic/cross-country), soccer, squash, swimming, tennis, track/field (indoor), track/field (outdoor), volleyball. *Women:* Badminton, basketball, crew/rowing, cross-country, curling, fencing, field hockey, ice hockey, lacrosse, mountain biking, rugby, skiing (nordic/cross-country), soccer, squash, swimming, tennis, track/field (indoor), track/field (outdoor), volleyball, water polo, wrestling.

ADMISSIONS
Freshman Academic Profile: TOEFL required of all international applicants, minimum paper TOEFL 600, minimum computer TOEFL 250. **Basis for Candidate Selection:** *Very important factors considered include:* Class rank, rigor of secondary school record, standardized test scores. **Freshman Admission Requirements:** High school diploma is required, and GED is accepted. **Freshman Admission Statistics:** 59,115 applied, 67% admitted, 31% enrolled. **Transfer Admission Requirements:** High school transcript, college transcript(s), standardized test score. **General Admission Information:** Application fee $47. Regular application deadline 3/1. Regular notification is rolling. Nonfall registration not accepted. Common Application not accepted.

COSTS AND FINANCIAL AID
Annual in-state tuition $4,570. Annual out-of-state tuition $4,570. Room and board $9,000. Required fees $1,000. Average book expense $1,050.

THE UNIVERSITY OF TULSA

600 South College Avenue, Tulsa, OK 74104
Phone: 918-631-2307 **E-mail:** admission@utulsa.edu **CEEB Code:** 6883
Fax: 918-631-5003 **Website:** www.utulsa.edu **ACT Code:** 3444
Financial Aid Phone: 918-631-2526

This private school, affiliated with the Presbyterian Church, was founded in 1894. It has a 209-acre campus.

RATINGS
Admissions Selectivity Rating: 92   **Fire Safety Rating:** 81   **Green Rating:** 80

STUDENTS AND FACULTY
Enrollment: 2,830. **Student Body:** 50% female, 50% male, 36% out-of-state, 9% international (63 countries represented). African American 7%, Asian 2%, Caucasian 65%, Hispanic 4%, Native American 4%. **Retention and Graduation:** 82% freshmen return for sophomore year. 46% freshmen graduate within 4 years. 38% grads go on to further study within 1 year. 13% grads pursue arts and sciences degrees. 7% grads pursue business degrees. 5% grads pursue law degrees. 4% grads pursue medical degrees. **Faculty:** Student/faculty ratio 11:1. 307 full-time faculty, 96% hold PhDs. 100% faculty teach undergrads.

ACADEMICS
Degrees: Bachelor's, doctoral, first professional certificate, first professional, master's, post-bachelor's certificate. **Academic Requirements:** Arts/fine arts, computer literacy, English (including composition), foreign languages, history, humanities, mathematics, philosophy, sciences (biological or physical), social science. **Classes:** Most classes have 10–19 students. Most lab/discussion sections have 20–29 students. **Majors with Highest Enrollment:** Business administration/management, marketing/marketing management, mechanical engineering. **Disciplines with Highest Percentage of Degrees Awarded:** Business/marketing 24%, engineering 12%, visual and performing arts 8%, biological/life sciences 7%, social sciences 6%, health professions and related sciences 6%. **Special Study Options:** Accelerated program, double major,

English as a second language (ESL), honors program, independent study, internships, liberal arts/career combination, student-designed major, study abroad, teacher certification program.

FACILITIES

Housing: Coed dorms, men's dorms, women's dorms, apartments for married students, apartments for single students, special housing for disabled students, fraternity/sorority housing, honors house. **Special Academic Facilities/Equipment:** Alexandre Hogue Art Gallery, biotechnology institute, center for communicative disorders, charge-coupled camera microscope, Donald W. Reynolds Center, education technology lab, electron microscopes, Kendall Theatre, McFarlin Library Special Collections, multimedia "board-room" style classrooms, ONEOK Multimedia Auditorium, Sadie Adwan Communication Lab, Sidney Born Technical Library, world's largest research flow-loop in petroleum engineering. **Computers:** 95% of classrooms are wireless, 80% of public computers are PCs, 10% of public computers are Macs, 10% of public computers are UNIX, network access in dorm rooms, network access in dorm lounges, online registration, online administrative functions (other than registration), remote student-access to Web through college's connection.

CAMPUS LIFE

Activities: Choral groups, concert band, drama/theater, jazz band, literary magazine, marching band, music ensembles, musical theater, opera, pep band, radio station, student government, student newspaper, symphony orchestra, television station, yearbook. **Organizations:** 245 registered organizations, 40 honor societies, 21 religious organization. 7 fraternities (21% men join), 9 sororities (23% women join). **Athletics (Intercollegiate):** *Men:* Basketball, cheerleading, cross-country, football, golf, soccer, tennis, track/field (indoor), track/field (outdoor). *Women:* Basketball, cheerleading, crew/rowing, cross-country, golf, soccer, softball, tennis, track/field (indoor), track/field (outdoor), volleyball.

ADMISSIONS

Freshman Academic Profile: 59% in top 10% of high school class, 79% in top 25% of high school class, 94% in top 50% of high school class. 78% from public high schools. SAT Math middle 50% range 580–700. SAT Critical Reading middle 50% range 560–700. ACT middle 50% range 24–30. TOEFL required of all international applicants, minimum paper TOEFL 500, minimum computer TOEFL 173. **Basis for Candidate Selection:** *Very important factors considered include:* Academic GPA, class rank, interview, level of applicant's interest, rigor of secondary school record, standardized test scores. *Important factors considered include:* Application essay, character/personal qualities, extracurricular activities, recommendation(s), talent/ability. *Other factors considered include:* Alumni/ae relation, first generation, racial/ethnic status, volunteer work, work experience. **Freshman Admission Requirements:** High school diploma is required, and GED is accepted. *Academic units recommended:* 4 English, 3 math, 3 science (2 science labs), 2 foreign language, 1 social studies, 2 history, 1 academic elective. **Freshman Admission Statistics:** 2,720 applied, 76% admitted, 32% enrolled. **Transfer Admission Requirements:** College transcript(s), essay or personal statement, statement of good standing from prior institution(s). Minimum college GPA of 2.5 required. Lowest grade transferable C. **General Admission Information:** Application fee $35. Regular notification is rolling. Non-fall registration accepted. Admission may be deferred for a maxiumum of 2 semesters. Credit and/or placement offered for CEEB Advanced Placement tests.

COSTS AND FINANCIAL AID

Annual tuition $21,690. Room and board $7,504. Required fees $80. Average book expense $1,200. **Required Forms and Deadlines:** FAFSA, institution's own financial aid form. Financial aid filing deadline 4/1. **Notification of Awards:** Applicants will be notified of awards on a rolling basis beginning on or about 3/1. **Types of Aid:** *Need-based scholarships/grants:* Pell, SEOG, state scholarships/grants, private scholarships, the school's own gift aid. *Loans:* FFEL Subsidized Stafford, FFEL Unsubsidized Stafford, FFEL PLUS, Federal Perkins. **Student Employment:** Federal Work-Study Program available. Institutional employment available. Off-campus job opportunities are good. **Financial Aid Statistics:** 19% freshmen, 24% undergrads receive need-based scholarship or grant aid. 39% freshmen, 40% undergrads receive need-based self-help aid. 73 freshmen, 346 undergrads receive athletic scholarships. 96% freshmen, 90% undergrads receive any aid. Highest amount earned per year from on-campus jobs $4,500.

UNIVERSITY OF UTAH

Best 368

201 South 1460 East, Room 250 S, Salt Lake City, UT 84112
Phone: 801-581-7281 **E-mail:** admissions@sa.utah.edu **CEEB Code:** 4853
Fax: 801-585-7864 **Website:** www.utah.edu
Financial Aid Phone: 801-581-6211

This public school was founded in 1850. It has a 1,534-acre campus.

RATINGS

Admissions Selectivity Rating: 79 **Fire Safety Rating:** 84 **Green Rating:** 89

STUDENTS AND FACULTY

Enrollment: 21,249. **Student Body:** 44% female, 56% male, 16% out-of-state, 2% international (119 countries represented). Asian 5%, Caucasian 81%, Hispanic 5%. **Retention and Graduation:** 77% freshmen return for sophomore year. 21% freshmen graduate within 4 years. **Faculty:** Student/faculty ratio 14:1. 1,214 full-time faculty, 85% hold PhDs. 64% faculty teach undergrads.

ACADEMICS

Degrees: Bachelor's, certificate, doctoral, first professional, master's, post-bachelor's certificate, post-master's certificate. **Academic Requirements:** Arts/fine arts, English (including composition), history, humanities, mathematics, sciences (biological or physical), social science. **Classes:** Most classes have 20–29 students. Most lab/discussion sections have 10–19 students. **Majors with Highest Enrollment:** Economics, mass communications/media studies, political science and government. **Disciplines with Highest Percentage of Degrees Awarded:** Social sciences 20%, business/marketing 14%, engineering 7%, visual and performing arts 7%, health professions and related sciences 6%, psychology 5%. **Special Study Options:** Accelerated program, cooperative education program, distance learning, double major, English as a second language (ESL), exchange student program (domestic), honors program, independent study, internships, student-designed major, study abroad, teacher certification program.

FACILITIES

Housing: Men's dorms, women's dorms, apartments for married students, apartments for single students, special housing for disabled students, fraternity/sorority housing, theme houses, limited visitation, 24-hour quiet. **Special Academic Facilities/Equipment:** Museums of natural history and fine arts, government institute, environmental biological research facilities, human genetics lab. **Computers:** 5% of classrooms are wired, 75% of classrooms are wireless, 75% of public computers are PCs, 25% of public computers are Macs, network access in dorm rooms, network access in dorm lounges, online registration, online administrative functions (other than registration), support for handheld computing, remote student-access to Web through college's connection.

CAMPUS LIFE

Activities: Choral groups, concert band, dance, drama/theater, jazz band, literary magazine, marching band, music ensembles, musical theater, opera, pep band, radio station, student government, student newspaper, student-run film society, symphony orchestra, television station. **Organizations:** 286 registered organizations, 4 honor societies, 19 religious organizations. 8 fraternities (1% men join), 7 sororities (1% women join). **Athletics (Intercollegiate):** *Men:* Baseball, basketball, cheerleading, diving, football, golf, skiing (downhill/alpine), skiing (nordic/cross-country), swimming, tennis. *Women:* Basketball, cheerleading, cross-country, diving, gymnastics, skiing (downhill/alpine), skiing (nordic/cross-country), soccer, softball, swimming, tennis, track/field (indoor), track/field (outdoor), volleyball. **Environmental Initiatives:** Free public transportation (Ed-Pass) for all students, staff and faculty; gas-electric hybrid, biodiesel, and natural gas-powered campus vehicles. Offset more than 10% of our electricity consumption with windpower purchases; new co-generation plant under construction will cut outside energy purchases by another 10%, ongoing building retrofits for lighting, HVAC, and other efficiency gains. Campus as a sustainability learning lab for courses; numerous on-campus "green" groups; environmental service opportunities with Bennion Community Service Center, student internships available through the Office of Sustainability, and also the greater community through Environmental Studies and Master's in Science and Technology programs.

ADMISSIONS

Freshman Academic Profile: 23% in top 10% of high school class, 50% in top 25% of high school class, 82% in top 50% of high school class. 93% from public high schools. SAT Math middle 50% range 490–630. SAT Critical Reading middle 50% range 490–630. ACT middle 50% range 21–27. TOEFL required of all international applicants, minimum paper TOEFL 500, minimum computer TOEFL 173. **Basis for Candidate Selection:** *Very important factors considered include:* Academic GPA, rigor of secondary school record, standardized test scores. *Important factors considered include:* Talent/ability. *Other factors considered include:* Class rank, extracurricular activities, interview, racial/ethnic status, recommendation(s). **Freshman Admission Requirements:** High school diploma is required, and GED is accepted. *Academic units required:* 4 English, 2 math, 3 science (2 science labs), 2 foreign language, 1 history, 4 academic electives. **Freshman Admission Statistics:** 6,770 applied, 84% admitted, 42% enrolled. **Transfer Admission Requirements:** College transcript(s). Minimum college GPA of 2.6 required. Lowest grade transferable D-. **General Admission Information:** Application fee $35. Regular application deadline 4/1. Regular notification rolling basis, within 2 weeks of file completion. Non-fall registration accepted. Credit and/or placement offered for CEEB Advanced Placement tests.

COSTS AND FINANCIAL AID

Annual in-state tuition $4,320. Annual out-of-state tuition $14,944. Room and board $5,778. Required fees $717. Average book expense $1,080. **Required Forms and Deadlines:** FAFSA, institution's own financial aid form. Financial aid filing deadline 3/15. **Notification of Awards:** Applicants will be notified of awards on a rolling basis beginning on or about 4/15. **Types of Aid:** *Need-based scholarships/grants:* Pell, SEOG, state scholarships/grants, private scholarships, the school's own gift aid. *Loans:* FFEL Subsidized Stafford, FFEL Unsubsidized Stafford, FFEL PLUS, Federal Perkins, Federal Nursing, college/university loans from institutional funds, private alternative loans. **Student Employment:** Federal Work-Study Program available. Institutional employment available. Off-campus job opportunities are excellent. **Financial Aid Statistics:** 22% freshmen, 28% undergrads receive need-based scholarship or grant aid. 19% freshmen, 28% undergrads receive need-based self-help aid. 1 freshman, 6 undergrads receive athletic scholarships. 29% freshmen, 38% undergrads receive any aid. Highest amount earned per year from on-campus jobs $8,800.

UNIVERSITY OF VERMONT

Admissions Office, 194 South Prospect Street, Burlington, VT 05401-3596
Phone: 802-656-3370 **E-mail:** admissions@uvm.edu **CEEB Code:** 3920
Fax: 802-656-8611 **Website:** www.uvm.edu **ACT Code:** 4322
Financial Aid Phone: 802-656-5700

This public school was founded in 1791. It has a 460-acre campus.

RATINGS

Admissions Selectivity Rating: 83   **Fire Safety Rating:** 78   **Green Rating:** 96

STUDENTS AND FACULTY

Enrollment: 9,040. **Student Body:** 55% female, 45% male, 64% out-of-state. African American 1%, Asian 2%, Caucasian 93%, Hispanic 2%. **Retention and Graduation:** 84% freshmen return for sophomore year. 52% freshmen graduate within 4 years. 26% grads go on to further study within 2 semesters. 8% grads pursue arts and sciences degrees. 1% grads pursue business degrees. 3% grads pursue law degrees. 3% grads pursue medical degrees. **Faculty:** Student/faculty ratio 15:1. 569 full-time faculty, 86% hold PhDs. 86% faculty teach undergrads.

ACADEMICS

Degrees: Bachelor's, certificate, doctoral, first professional, master's, post-bachelor's certificate, post-master's certificate. **Academic Requirements:** Arts/fine arts, English (including composition), humanities, mathematics, race and cultural awareness, sciences (biological or physical), social science. **Classes:** Most classes have 10–19 students. Most lab/discussion sections have 10–19 students. **Majors with Highest Enrollment:** Business administration/management, English language and literature, psychology. **Disciplines with Highest Percentage of Degrees Awarded:** Social sciences 18%, business/marketing 11%, education 8%, natural resources/environmental science 7%,

health professions and related sciences 7%, English 7%. **Special Study Options:** Cooperative education program, distance learning, double major, dual enrollment, exchange student program (domestic), honors program, independent study, internships, liberal arts/career combination, student-designed major, study abroad, teacher certification program. Evening university option in several programs.

FACILITIES

Housing: Coed dorms, apartments for married students, apartments for single students, fraternity/sorority housing. **Special Academic Facilities/Equipment:** Art/ethnography museum, chemistry/physics library, medical library, on-campus preschool, government research and world affairs centers, agricultural experiment station, horse farm, multinuclear magnetic resonance spectrometers, mass spectrometer. **Computers:** 10% of classrooms are wired, 31% of classrooms are wireless, 76% of public computers are PCs, 19% of public computers are Macs, 5% of public computers are UNIX, network access in dorm rooms, network access in dorm lounges, online registration, online administrative functions (other than registration), remote student-access to Web through college's connection.

CAMPUS LIFE

Activities: Choral groups, concert band, dance, drama/theater, jazz band, literary magazine, music ensembles, musical theater, pep band, radio station, student government, student newspaper, student-run film society, television station. **Organizations:** 133 registered organizations, 30 honor societies, 8 religious organizations. 9 fraternities (7% men join), 5 sororities (5% women join). **Athletics (Intercollegiate):** *Men:* Baseball, basketball, cross-country, ice hockey, lacrosse, skiing (downhill/alpine), skiing (nordic/cross-country), soccer, track/field (indoor), track/field (outdoor). *Women:* Basketball, cross-country, diving, field hockey, ice hockey, lacrosse, skiing (downhill/alpine), skiing (nordic/cross-country), soccer, softball, swimming, track/field (indoor), track/field (outdoor). **Environmental Initiatives:** Office of Sustainability supports commission, forum, grants, and connects with teaching and research. Eco-Reps Program provides peer education in residence halls and supports campus events. LEED Silver minimum; energy efficiency investments have yielded millions of dollars in avoided costs.

ADMISSIONS

Freshman Academic Profile: 23% in top 10% of high school class, 62% in top 25% of high school class, 95% in top 50% of high school class. 70% from public high schools. SAT Math middle 50% range 540–640. SAT Critical Reading middle 50% range 540–630. SAT Writing middle 50% range 530–630. ACT middle 50% range 23–28. TOEFL required of all international applicants, minimum paper TOEFL 550, minimum computer TOEFL 213. **Basis for Candidate Selection:** *Very important factors considered include:* Rigor of secondary school record. *Important factors considered include:* Academic GPA, application essay, character/personal qualities, class rank, standardized test scores, state residency. *Other factors considered include:* Alumni/ae relation, extracurricular activities, first generation, geographical residence, interview, level of applicant's interest, racial/ethnic status, recommendation(s), talent/ability, volunteer work, work experience. **Freshman Admission Requirements:** High school diploma is required, and GED is accepted. *Academic units required:* 4 English, 3 math, 2 science (1 science lab), 2 foreign language, 3 social studies. **Freshman Admission Statistics:** 17,731 applied, 65% admitted, 19% enrolled. **Transfer Admission Requirements:** High school transcript, college transcript(s), essay or personal statement. Minimum college GPA of 2.5 required. Lowest grade transferable C. **General Admission Information:** Application fee $45. Regular application deadline 1/15. Regular notification 3/31. Non-fall registration accepted. Admission may be deferred for a maximum of 2 semesters. Credit and/or placement offered for CEEB Advanced Placement tests.

COSTS AND FINANCIAL AID

Annual in-state tuition $10,422. Annual out-of-state tuition $26,306. Room and board $8,024. Required fees $1,632. Average book expense $936. **Required Forms and Deadlines:** FAFSA. Financial aid filing deadline 2/10. **Notification of Awards:** Applicants will be notified of awards on a rolling basis beginning on or about 3/15. **Types of Aid:** *Need-based scholarships/grants:* Pell, SEOG, state scholarships/grants, private scholarships, the school's own gift aid, Federal Nursing Scholarships. *Loans:* FFEL Subsidized Stafford, FFEL Unsubsidized Stafford, FFEL PLUS, Federal Perkins, Federal Nursing, college/university loans from institutional funds. **Financial Aid Statistics:** 48% freshmen, 48% undergrads receive need-based scholarship or grant aid. 45% freshmen, 46% undergrads receive need-based self-help aid. 36 freshmen, 112 undergrads receive athletic scholarships. 85% freshmen, 72% undergrads receive any aid.

UNIVERSITY OF VICTORIA

PO Box 3025, STN CSC, Victoria, BC V8W 3P2 Canada
Phone: 250-472-4935 **E-mail:** admit@uvic.ca
Fax: 250-721-6225 **Website:** www.uvic.ca
Financial Aid Phone: 250-721-8423

This private school was founded in 1963. It has a 380-acre campus.

RATINGS
Admissions Selectivity Rating: 60*   **Fire Safety Rating:** 60*   **Green Rating:** 60*

STUDENTS AND FACULTY
Enrollment: 14,812. **Student Body:** 59% female, 41% male. **Faculty:** 623 full-time faculty.

ACADEMICS
Degrees: Bachelor's, certificate, diploma, doctoral, master's, post-bachelor's certificate. **Academic Requirements:** English (including composition). **Disciplines with Highest Percentage of Degrees Awarded:** Social sciences 33%, biological/life sciences 24%, health professions and related sciences 13%, education 9%, business/marketing 8%. **Special Study Options:** Cooperative education program, distance learning, double major, dual enrollment, English as a second language (ESL), exchange student program (domestic), honors program, independent study, internships, study abroad, teacher certification program.

FACILITIES
Housing: Coed dorms, apartments for married students, apartments for single students, town houses. **Special Academic Facilities/Equipment:** Maltwood Museum. **Computers:** Network access in dorm rooms, online registration, online administrative functions (other than registration).

CAMPUS LIFE
Activities: Drama/theater, music ensembles, musical theater, radio station, student government, student newspaper, symphony orchestra. **Athletics (Intercollegiate):** *Men:* Basketball, crew/rowing, cross-country, field hockey, golf, rugby, soccer, swimming, volleyball. *Women:* Basketball, crew/rowing, cross-country, field hockey, golf, rugby, soccer, swimming, volleyball.

ADMISSIONS
Freshman Academic Profile: TOEFL required of all international applicants, minimum paper TOEFL 575, minimum computer TOEFL 233. **Basis for Candidate Selection:** *Very important factors considered include:* Rigor of secondary school record. *Other factors considered include:* Racial/ethnic status, recommendation(s), standardized test scores. **Freshman Admission Requirements:** High school diploma is required, and GED is accepted. *Academic units required:* 4 English, 4 math, 3 science, 2 foreign language, 2 social studies. **Freshman Admission Statistics:** 7,044 applied, 62% admitted, 51% enrolled. **Transfer Admission Requirements:** College transcript(s), statement of good standing from prior institution(s). **General Admission Information:** Application fee $70. Early decision application deadline 2/28. Regular application deadline 2/28. Regular notification is rolling. Non-fall registration accepted. Common Application not accepted. Credit and/or placement offered for CEEB Advanced Placement tests.

COSTS AND FINANCIAL AID
In-province tuition $1,435. Out-of-province tuition $1,435. International tuition $4,472. Room & board $3,811. Required fees $181. **Student Employment:** Off-campus job opportunities are good.

UNIVERSITY OF THE VIRGIN ISLANDS

2 John Brewers Bay, St. Thomas, VI 00802-9990
Phone: 340-693-1150 **E-mail:** admissions@uvi.edu **CEEB Code:** 0879
Fax: 340-693-1220 **Website:** www.uvi.edu
Financial Aid Phone: 340-693-109

This public school was founded in 1962.

RATINGS
Admissions Selectivity Rating: 60*   **Fire Safety Rating:** 60*   **Green Rating:** 60*

STUDENTS AND FACULTY
Enrollment: 1,972. **Student Body:** 80% female, 20% male, 36% out-of-state, 7% international. African American 71%, Caucasian 2%, Hispanic 3%. **Faculty:** Student/faculty ratio 14:1. 99 full-time faculty, 68% hold PhDs.

ACADEMICS
Degrees: Associate, bachelor's, master's. **Academic Requirements:** Computer literacy, English (including composition), foreign languages, history, humanities, mathematics, sciences (biological or physical), social science. **Disciplines with Highest Percentage of Degrees Awarded:** Business/marketing 37%, education 17%, biological/life sciences 13%, foreign languages and literature 10%, psychology 6%, social sciences 6%. **Special Study Options:** Cooperative education program, distance learning, dual enrollment, exchange student program (domestic), independent study, internships, teacher certification program.

FACILITIES
Housing: Men's dorms, women's dorms. **Computers:** 100% of public computers are PCs, network access in dorm rooms, online administrative functions (other than registration), remote student-access to Web through college's connection.

CAMPUS LIFE
Activities: Choral groups, concert band, dance, drama/theater, jazz band, music ensembles, student government, student newspaper, yearbook. **Organizations:** 27 registered organizations, 2 honor societies, 2 religious organizations. 1 fraternity, 3 sororities. **Athletics (Intercollegiate):** *Men:* Basketball, soccer, swimming, tennis, volleyball. *Women:* Basketball, swimming, tennis, volleyball.

ADMISSIONS
Freshman Academic Profile: SAT Math middle 50% range 330–450. SAT Critical Reading middle 50% range 360–470. **Basis for Candidate Selection:** *Very important factors considered include:* Rigor of secondary school record. *Other factors considered include:* Standardized test scores, state residency. **Freshman Admission Requirements:** High school diploma is required, and GED is accepted. *Academic units recommended:* 4 English, 2 math, 2 science, 1 foreign language, 2 social studies. **Freshman Admission Statistics:** 854 applied, 73% admitted, 45% enrolled. **Transfer Admission Requirements:** High school transcript, college transcript(s), statement of good standing from prior institution(s). Minimum college GPA of 2.0 required. Lowest grade transferable C. **General Admission Information:** Application fee $20. Regular application deadline 4/30. Non-fall registration accepted. Common Application not accepted.

COSTS AND FINANCIAL AID
Annual in-state tuition $1,500. Out-of-state tuition $4,500. Room & board $2,715. Required fees $133. Average book expense $400. **Types of Aid:** *Need-based scholarships/grants:* Pell.

UNIVERSITY OF VIRGINIA

Office of Admission, PO Box 400160, Charlottesville, VA 22906
Phone: 434-982-3200 **E-mail:** undergradadmission@virginia.edu **CEEB Code:** 5820
Fax: 434-924-3587 **Website:** www.virginia.edu **ACT Code:** 4412
Financial Aid Phone: 434-982-6000

This public school was founded in 1819. It has a 1,160-acre campus.

RATINGS
Admissions Selectivity Rating: 97   **Fire Safety Rating:** 63   **Green Rating:** 92

STUDENTS AND FACULTY
Enrollment: 13,440. **Student Body:** 55% female, 45% male, 28% out-of-state, 5% international (119 countries represented). African American 8%, Asian 11%, Caucasian 65%, Hispanic 4%. **Retention and Graduation:** 97% freshmen return for sophomore year. 83% freshmen graduate within 4 years. 26% grads go on to further study within 2 semesters. 13% grads pursue arts and sciences degrees. **Faculty:** Student/faculty ratio 15:1. 1,217 full-time faculty, 91% hold PhDs.

ACADEMICS
Degrees: Bachelor's, doctoral, first professional, master's, post-master's certificate. **Academic Requirements:** English (including composition), foreign

languages, history, humanities, mathematics, non-Western perspectives, sciences (biological or physical), social science. **Classes:** Most classes have 10–19 students. Most lab/discussion sections have 10–19 students. **Majors with Highest Enrollment:** Business administration/management, economics, psychology. **Disciplines with Highest Percentage of Degrees Awarded:** Social sciences 22%, engineering 9%, psychology 9%, business/marketing 8%, history 7%, English 6%, liberal arts/general studies 6%. **Special Study Options:** Accelerated program, cooperative education program, double major, English as a second language (ESL), exchange student program (domestic), honors program, independent study, internships, January term, liberal arts/career combination, semester at sea, student-designed major, study abroad, teacher certification program.

FACILITIES

Housing: Coed dorms, apartments for married students, apartments for single students, special housing for international students, fraternity/sorority housing, French, German, Spanish and Russian houses, 3 residential colleges. **Special Academic Facilities/Equipment:** 14 libraries, art museum, Center for Studies in Political Economy, Bureau of Public Administration, experimental farm, biological station, labs, observatory/planetarium, nuclear information center, media center (multimedia editing). **Computers:** 1% of classrooms are wired, 85% of classrooms are wireless, network access in dorm rooms, network access in dorm lounges, online registration, online administrative functions (other than registration), support for handheld computing, remote student-access to Web through college's connection.

CAMPUS LIFE

Activities: Choral groups, concert band, dance, drama/theater, jazz band, literary magazine, marching band, music ensembles, musical theater, opera, pep band, radio station, student government, student newspaper, student-run film society, symphony orchestra, television station. **Organizations:** 562 registered organizations, 3 honor societies, 42 religious organizations. 31 fraternities (30% men join), 16 sororities (30% women join). **Athletics (Intercollegiate):** *Men:* Baseball, basketball, cross-country, diving, football, golf, lacrosse, soccer, swimming, tennis, track/field (indoor), track/field (outdoor), wrestling. *Women:* Basketball, crew/rowing, cross-country, diving, field hockey, golf, lacrosse, soccer, softball, swimming, tennis, track/field (indoor), track/field (outdoor), volleyball. **Environmental Initiatives:** 2006 Sustainability Assessment. Ongoing Energy/Water, Recycling and Storm Water Management conservation programs. 2007 LEED certification requirement for all new construction and renovation.

ADMISSIONS

Admssions Selectivity Rating: 97 (out of 100). **Freshman Academic Profile:** 88% in top 10% of high school class, 97% in top 25% of high school class, 100% in top 50% of high school class. 74% from public high schools. SAT Math middle 50% range 610–720. SAT Critical Reading middle 50% range 590–700. SAT Writing middle 50% range 600–710. TOEFL required of all international applicants, minimum paper TOEFL 600, minimum computer TOEFL 250. **Basis for Candidate Selection:** *Very important factors considered include:* Academic GPA, alumni/ae relation, class rank, first generation, racial/ethnic status, recommendation(s), rigor of secondary school record, state residency. *Important factors considered include:* Application essay, character/personal qualities, extracurricular activities, standardized test scores, talent/ability. *Other factors considered include:* Geographical residence, volunteer work, work experience. **Freshman Admission Requirements:** High school diploma is required, and GED is accepted. *Academic units required:* 4 English, 4 math, 2 science, 2 foreign language, 1 social studies. *Academic units recommended:* 5 math, 4 science, 5 foreign language, 4 social studies. **Freshman Admission Statistics:** 16,086 applied, 37% admitted, 51% enrolled. **Transfer Admission Requirements:** High school transcript, college transcript(s), essay or personal statement, statement of good standing from prior institution(s). Minimum college GPA of 2.0 required. Lowest grade transferable C. **General Admission Information:** Application fee $60. Regular application deadline 1/2. Regular notification 4/1. Non-fall registration not accepted. Admission may be deferred for a maximum of 2 semesters. Credit and/or placement offered for CEEB Advanced Placement tests.

COSTS AND FINANCIAL AID

Required Forms and Deadlines: FAFSA, institution's own financial aid form. Financial aid filing deadline 3/1. **Notification of Awards:** Applicants will be notified of awards on or about 4/5. **Types of Aid:** *Need-based scholarships/grants:* Pell, SEOG, state scholarships/grants, private scholarships, the school's own gift aid. *Loans:* Direct Subsidized Stafford, Direct Unsubsidized Stafford, Direct PLUS, Federal Perkins, Federal Nursing, college/university loans from institutional funds. **Financial Aid Statistics:** 20% freshmen, 19% undergrads receive need-based scholarship or grant aid. 16% freshmen, 17% undergrads receive need-based self-help aid. 115 freshmen, 415 undergrads receive athletic scholarships. 51% freshmen, 45% undergrads receive any aid.

UNIVERSITY OF VIRGINIA'S COLLEGE AT WISE

1 College Avenue, Wise, VA 24293
Phone: 276-328-0102 **E-mail:** admissions@uvawise.edu **CEEB Code:** 5124
Fax: 276-328-0251 **Website:** www.uvawise.edu **ACT Code:** 4343
Financial Aid Phone: 540-328-0193

This public school was founded in 1954. It has a 367-acre campus.

RATINGS

Admissions Selectivity Rating: 77   **Fire Safety Rating:** 60*   **Green Rating:** 60*

STUDENTS AND FACULTY

Enrollment: 1,505. **Student Body:** 54% female, 46% male, 6% out-of-state. African American 5%, Asian 1%, Caucasian 92%, Hispanic 1%. **Retention and Graduation:** 73% freshmen return for sophomore year. 33% freshmen graduate within 4 years. 14% grads go on to further study within 2 semesters. 7% grads pursue arts and sciences degrees. 4% grads pursue business degrees. 6% grads pursue law degrees. 1% grads pursue medical degrees. **Faculty:** Student/faculty ratio 15:1. 65 full-time faculty, 80% hold PhDs. 100% faculty teach undergrads.

ACADEMICS

Degrees: Bachelor's. **Academic Requirements:** Arts/fine arts, computer literacy, English (including composition), foreign languages, history, humanities, literature, mathematics, physical education, sciences (biological or physical), social science. **Classes:** Most classes have 20–29 students. Most lab/discussion sections have 10–19 students. **Disciplines with Highest Percentage of Degrees Awarded:** Business/marketing 29%, social sciences 25%, psychology 14%, English 8%, biological/life sciences 7%. **Special Study Options:** Accelerated program, cooperative education program, distance learning, double major, dual enrollment, honors program, independent study, internships, student-designed major, study abroad, teacher certification program.

FACILITIES

Housing: Coed dorms, men's dorms, women's dorms, apartments for single students, special housing for disabled students. **Computers:** 80% of public computers are PCs, 20% of public computers are Macs, network access in dorm rooms, online administrative functions (other than registration), remote student-access to Web through college's connection.

CAMPUS LIFE

Activities: Choral groups, concert band, dance, drama/theater, literary magazine, music ensembles, musical theater, pep band, radio station, student government, student newspaper, television station, yearbook. **Organizations:** 40 registered organizations, 3 honor societies, 3 religious organizations. 3 fraternities (13% men join), 2 sororities (8% women join). **Athletics (Intercollegiate):** *Men:* Baseball, basketball, cross-country, football, golf, tennis, track/field (outdoor). *Women:* Basketball, cross-country, softball, tennis, track/field (outdoor), volleyball.

ADMISSIONS

Freshman Academic Profile: 24% in top 10% of high school class, 50% in top 25% of high school class, 82% in top 50% of high school class. 99% from public high schools. SAT Math middle 50% range 430–550. SAT Critical Reading middle 50% range 440–550. ACT middle 50% range 17–22. TOEFL required of all international applicants, minimum paper TOEFL 550. **Basis for Candidate Selection:** *Very important factors considered include:* Rigor of secondary school record. *Important factors considered include:* Class rank, standardized test scores, talent/ability. *Other factors considered include:* Application essay, character/personal qualities, extracurricular activities, interview, racial/ethnic status, recommendation(s), volunteer work, work experience. **Freshman Admission Requirements:** High school diploma is required, and GED is accepted. *Academic units required:* 4 English, 3 math, 2 science (2 science labs), 2 foreign language, 2 history. **Freshman Admission Statistics:** 987 applied, 78% admitted, 46% enrolled. **Transfer Admission Requirements:** College transcript(s). Minimum college GPA of 2.3 required. Lowest grade transferable C-. **General Admission Information:** Application fee $25. Regular application deadline 8/1. Regular notification is rolling. Non-fall registration accepted. Admission may be deferred for a maximum of 2 semesters. Common Application not accepted. Credit and/or placement offered for CEEB Advanced Placement tests.

COSTS AND FINANCIAL AID

Annual in-state tuition $1,885. Out-of-state tuition $8,379. Room & board $4,696. Required fees $1,445. Average book expense $638. **Required Forms and Deadlines:** FAFSA. Financial aid filing deadline 4/1. **Notification of Awards:** Applicants will be notified of awards on a rolling basis beginning on or about 4/1. **Types of Aid:** *Need-based scholarships/grants:* Pell, SEOG, state scholarships/grants, private scholarships, the school's own gift aid. *Loans:* FFEL Subsidized Stafford, FFEL Unsubsidized Stafford, FFEL PLUS, Federal Perkins, state loans, college/university loans from institutional funds. **Student Employment:** Federal Work-Study Program available. Institutional employment available. Off-campus job opportunities are fair. **Financial Aid Statistics:** 60% freshmen, 63% undergrads receive need-based scholarship or grant aid. 43% freshmen, 51% undergrads receive need-based self-help aid. 36 freshmen, 115 undergrads receive athletic scholarships. Highest amount earned per year from on-campus jobs $900.

UNIVERSITY OF WASHINGTON

Best 368

UW Box 355852, Seattle, WA 98195
Phone: 206-543-9686 **E-mail: CEEB Code:** 4854
Fax: 206-685-3655 **Website:** www.washington.edu **ACT Code:** 4484
Financial Aid Phone: 206-543-6101

This public school was founded in 1861. It has a 680-acre campus.

RATINGS
Admissions Selectivity Rating: 94   **Fire Safety Rating:** 93   **Green Rating:** 99

STUDENTS AND FACULTY
Enrollment: 26,002. **Student Body:** 52% female, 48% male, 14% out-of-state, 4% international (98 countries represented). African American 3%, Asian 28%, Caucasian 53%, Hispanic 5%, Native American 1%. **Retention and Graduation:** 93% freshmen return for sophomore year. 48% freshmen graduate within 4 years. **Faculty:** Student/faculty ratio 11:1. 2,941 full-time faculty, 93% hold PhDs.

ACADEMICS
Degrees: Bachelor's, doctoral, first professional, master's. **Academic Requirements:** English (including composition), foreign languages, humanities, mathematics, sciences (biological or physical), social science. **Classes:** Most classes have 20–29 students. Most lab/discussion sections have 20–29 students. **Majors with Highest Enrollment:** Economics; political science and government; psychology. **Disciplines with Highest Percentage of Degrees Awarded:** Business/marketing 11%, biological/life sciences 9%, engineering 9%, psychology 6%, English 5%, communications/journalism 5%, visual and performing arts 5%, area and ethnic studies 4%, foreign languages and literature 4%, health professions and related sciences 4%, history 4%. **Special Study Options:** Cooperative education program, distance learning, double major, English as a second language (ESL), exchange student program (domestic), honor program, independent study, internships, student-designed major, study abroad, teacher certification program, Friday harbor labs.

FACILITIES
Housing: Coed dorms, apartments for married students, apartments for single students, special housing for disabled students, special housing for international students, fraternity/sorority housing, cooperative housing. **Special Academic Facilities/Equipment:** Multiple art galleries, an anthropology and natural history museum, arboretum, closed-circuit TV studio. **Computers:** Network access in dorm rooms, network access in dorm lounges, online registration, online administrative functions (other than registration), support for handheld computing, remote student-access to Web through college's connection.

CAMPUS LIFE
Activities: Choral groups, concert band, dance, drama/theater, jazz band, literary magazine, marching band, music ensembles, musical theater, opera, pep band, radio station, student government, student newspaper, symphony orchestra, television station, yearbook. **Organizations:** 550 registered organizations, 4 honor societies, 16 religious organizations. 27 fraternities 16 sororities **Athletics (Intercollegiate):** *Men:* Baseball, basketball, crew/rowing, cross-country, football, golf, soccer, swimming, tennis, track/field (outdoor). *Women:* Basketball, crew/rowing, cross-country, golf, gymnastics, soccer, softball, swimming, tennis, track/field (outdoor), volleyball.

ADMISSIONS
Freshman Academic Profile: 84% in top 10% of high school class, 96% in top 25% of high school class, 100% in top 50% of high school class. SAT Math middle 50% range 560–670. SAT Critical Reading middle 50% range 530–650. SAT Writing middle 50% range 520–630. ACT middle 50% range 23–29.

TOEFL required of all international applicants, minimum paper TOEFL 537, minimum computer TOEFL 207. **Basis for Candidate Selection:** *Very important factors considered include:* Academic GPA, application essay, rigor of secondary school record. *Important factors considered include:* Character/personal qualities, extracurricular activities, first generation, standardized test scores, talent/ability, volunteer work, work experience. *Other factors considered include:* State residency. **Freshman Admission Requirements:** High school diploma or equivalent is not required. *Academic units required:* 4 English, 3 math, 2 science (1 science lab), 2 foreign language, 3 social studies. *Academic units recommended:* 4 English, 4 math, 3 science (3 science labs), 3 foreign language, 4 social studies, 1 history, 1 fine arts. **Freshman Admission Statistics:** 16,571 applied, 68% admitted, 48% enrolled. **Transfer Admission Requirements:** High school transcript, college transcript(s), essay or personal statement. Minimum college GPA of 2.5 required. Lowest grade transferable D-. **General Admission Information:** Application fee $50. Regular application deadline 1/15. Regular notification is rolling. Nonfall registration accepted. Credit and/or placement offered for CEEB Advanced Placement tests.

COSTS AND FINANCIAL AID
Annual in-state tuition $5,985. Out-of-state tuition $17,592. Room & board $8,001. Required fees $507. Average book expense $945. **Required Forms and Deadlines:** FAFSA. Financial aid filing deadline 2/28. **Notification of Awards:** Applicants will be notified of awards on or about 3/31. **Types of Aid:** *Need-based scholarships/grants:* Pell, SEOG, state scholarships/grants, private scholarships, the school's own gift aid. *Loans:* Direct Subsidized Stafford, Direct Unsubsidized Stafford, Direct PLUS, Federal Perkins, Federal Nursing, college/university loans from institutional funds. **Student Employment:** Federal Work-Study Program available. Institutional employment available. Off-campus job opportunities are excellent. **Financial Aid Statistics:** 20% freshmen, 26% undergrads receive need-based scholarship or grant aid. 26% freshmen, 30% undergrads receive need-based self-help aid. 80 freshmen, 400 undergrads receive athletic scholarships. 50% freshmen, 50% undergrads receive any aid.

UNIVERSITY OF WATERLOO

200 University Avenue West, Waterloo, ON N2L 3G1 Canada
Phone: 519-888-4567, ext. 3777 **E-mail:** watquest@uwaterloo.ca
Fax: 519-746-2882 **Website:** www.findoutmore.uwaterloo.ca
Financial Aid Phone: 519-888-4567

This public school was founded in 1957. It has a 900-acre campus.

RATINGS
Admissions Selectivity Rating: 60*   **Fire Safety Rating:** 60*   **Green Rating:** 60*

STUDENTS AND FACULTY
Student Body: 2% out-of-province. **Retention and Graduation:** 98% freshmen return for sophomore year. **Faculty:** Student/faculty ratio 15:1. 769 full-time faculty. 100% faculty teach undergrads.

ACADEMICS
Degrees: Bachelor's, certificate, diploma, doctoral, first professional, master's. **Academic Requirements:** Varies by program. **Majors with Highest Enrollment:** Computer and information sciences, kinesiology and exercise science, mathematics. **Disciplines with Highest Percentage of Degrees Awarded:** Engineering 24%, computer and information sciences 9%, social sciences 9%, health professions and related sciences 8%, mathematics 8%, natural resources/environmental science 6%. **Special Study Options:** Accelerated program, cooperative education program, cross registration, distance learning, double major, exchange student program (domestic), external degree program, honors program, independent study, internships, liberal arts/career combination, student-designed major, study abroad.

FACILITIES
Housing: Coed dorms, men's dorms, women's dorms, apartments for single students. **Special Academic Facilities/Equipment:** State-of-the-art high-tech computer, engineering and science labs, optometry and applied health studies clincs and labs, art galleries, theatres, games, earth sciences/biology, historic and optometry museums, art and architecture studios, multimedia-link rooms, observatory, greenhouse. **Computers:** 80% of public computers are PCs, 10% of public computers are Macs, 10% of public computers are UNIX, network access in dorm rooms, network access in dorm lounges, online registration, online administrative functions (other than registration), remote student-access to Web through college's connection.

934

CAMPUS LIFE

Activities: Choral groups, dance, drama/theater, literary magazine, music ensembles, radio station, student government, student newspaper, student-run film society, yearbook. **Organizations:** 80 registered organizations, 1 fraternity (1% men join), 1 sorority (1% women join). **Athletics (Intercollegiate):** *Men:* Baseball, basketball, cross-country, football, golf, ice hockey, rugby, skiing (nordic/cross-country), soccer, squash, swimming, tennis, track/field (indoor), track/field (outdoor), volleyball. *Women:* Basketball, cross-country, field hockey, ice hockey, rugby, skiing (nordic/cross-country), soccer, swimming, tennis, track/field (indoor), track/field (outdoor), volleyball.

ADMISSIONS

Freshman Academic Profile: 80% in top 10% of high school class. TOEFL required of all international applicants, minimum paper TOEFL 600, minimum computer TOEFL 250. **Basis for Candidate Selection:** *Very important factors considered include:* Rigor of secondary school record. *Other factors considered include:* Application essay, class rank, extracurricular activities, interview, recommendation(s), standardized test scores, talent/ability, volunteer work, work experience. **Freshman Admission Requirements:** High school diploma is required, and GED is not accepted. **Freshman Admission Statistics:** 23,557 applied, 61% admitted, 33% enrolled. **Transfer Admission Requirements:** High school transcript. **General Admission Information:** Application fee $95. Regular application deadline 5/1. Regular notification is rolling. Non-fall registration accepted. Common Application not accepted.

COSTS AND FINANCIAL AID

In-province tuition $4,030–$6,086. Out-of-province tuition $12,666–$21,650. Room & board $5,950. Average book expense $800. **Student Employment:** Institutional employment available. Off-campus job opportunities are good. **Financial Aid Statistics:** 47% undergrads receive need-based scholarship or grant aid. 47% undergrads receive need-based self-help aid.

UNIVERSITY OF WEST ALABAMA

Station 4, Livingston, AL 35470
Phone: 888-636-8800 **E-mail:** admissions@umamail.westal.edu **CEEB Code:** 1737
Fax: 205-652-3522 **Website:** www.uwa.edu **ACT Code:** 0024
Financial Aid Phone: 205-652-3576

This public school was founded in 1835. It has a 600-acre campus.

RATINGS

Admissions Selectivity Rating: 60*   **Fire Safety Rating:** 60*   **Green Rating:** 60*

STUDENTS AND FACULTY

Enrollment: 1,813. **Student Body:** 56% female, 44% male, 20% out-of-state. African American 47%, Caucasian 51%. **Retention and Graduation:** 15% grads go on to further study within 2 semesters. 12% grads pursue arts and sciences degrees. 1% grads pursue business degrees. 1% grads pursue law degrees. 1% grads pursue medical degrees. **Faculty:** Student/faculty ratio 19:1. 93 full-time faculty, 68% hold PhDs. 100% faculty teach undergrads.

ACADEMICS

Degrees: Associate, bachelor's, master's. **Academic Requirements:** Arts/fine arts, computer literacy, English (including composition), foreign languages, history, humanities, mathematics, philosophy, sciences (biological or physical). **Disciplines with Highest Percentage of Degrees Awarded:** Education 32%, business/marketing 22%, biological/life sciences 9%, engineering technologies 8%, social sciences 8%, psychology 5%, history 5%. **Special Study Options:** Cooperative education program, distance learning, double major, exchange student program (domestic), honors program, internships, teacher certification program.

FACILITIES

Housing: Coed dorms, men's dorms, women's dorms, apartments for married students, apartments for single students, special housing for disabled students, fraternity/sorority housing. **Computers:** Network access in dorm rooms, network access in dorm lounges, online administrative functions (other than registration), remote student-access to Web through college's connection.

CAMPUS LIFE

Activities: Choral groups, concert band, dance, drama/theater, literary magazine, marching band, music ensembles, musical theater, pep band, radio station, student government, student newspaper, television station, yearbook. **Organizations:** 30 registered organizations, 8 honor societies, 5 religious organizations. 7 fraternities (20% men join), 6 sororities (15% women join). **Athletics (Intercollegiate):** *Men:* Baseball, basketball, cheerleading, cross-

country, football, rodeo. *Women:* Basketball, cheerleading, cross-country, rodeo, softball, volleyball.

ADMISSIONS

Freshman Academic Profile: 88% from public high schools. ACT middle 50% range 15–22. TOEFL required of all international applicants, minimum paper TOEFL 500. **Basis for Candidate Selection:** *Very important factors considered include:* Rigor of secondary school record, standardized test scores. **Freshman Admission Requirements:** High school diploma is required, and GED is accepted. *Academic units required:* 3 English, 3 math, 3 science, 3 social studies, 3 academic electives. **Freshman Admission Statistics:** 899 applied, 75% admitted, 52% enrolled. **Transfer Admission Requirements:** College transcript(s), statement of good standing from prior institution(s). Minimum college GPA of 2.0 required. Lowest grade transferable C. **General Admission Information:** Application fee $20. Regular notification rolling. Non-fall registration accepted. Admission may be deferred for a maximum of 2 semesters. Credit and/or placement offered for CEEB Advanced Placement tests.

COSTS AND FINANCIAL AID

Annual in-state tuition $3,838. Out-of-state tuition $7,676. Room & board $3,438. Required fees $976. Average book expense $900. **Required Forms and Deadlines:** FAFSA. Financial aid filing deadline 4/1. **Notification of Awards:** Applicants will be notified of awards on a rolling basis beginning on or about 6/1. **Types of Aid:** *Need-based scholarships/grants:* Pell, SEOG, state scholarships/grants, private scholarships, the school's own gift aid. *Loans:* FFEL Subsidized Stafford, FFEL Unsubsidized Stafford, FFEL PLUS, Federal Perkins, college/university loans from institutional funds. **Student Employment:** Federal Work-Study Program available. Off-campus job opportunities are good. **Financial Aid Statistics:** 40% undergrads receive need-based scholarship or grant aid. 48% undergrads receive need-based self-help aid. Highest amount earned per year from on-campus jobs $1,317.

UNIVERSITY OF WEST FLORIDA

11000 University Parkway, Pensacola, FL 32514-5750
Phone: 850-474-2230 **E-mail:** admissions@uwf.edu **CEEB Code:** 5833
Fax: 850-474-3360 **Website:** www.uwf.edu **ACT Code:** 0771
Financial Aid Phone: 850-474-2400

This public school was founded in 1963. It has a 1,600-acre campus.

RATINGS

Admissions Selectivity Rating: 87   **Fire Safety Rating:** 85   **Green Rating:** 73

STUDENTS AND FACULTY

Enrollment: 7,887. **Student Body:** 60% female, 40% male, 13% out-of-state. African American 10%, Asian 5%, Caucasian 76%, Hispanic 5%. **Retention and Graduation:** 75% freshmen return for sophomore year. **Faculty:** Student/faculty ratio 18:1. 343 full-time faculty, 85% hold PhDs.

ACADEMICS

Degrees: Associate, bachelor's, doctoral, master's, post-master's certificate. **Academic Requirements:** English (including composition), mathematics. **Classes:** Most classes have 20–29 students. Most lab/discussion sections have 20–29 students. **Majors with Highest Enrollment:** Elementary education and teaching, mass communications/media studies, psychology. **Disciplines with Highest Percentage of Degrees Awarded:** Business/marketing 20%, education 12%, communication technologies 10%, psychology 7%, security and protective services 7%, social sciences 7%, computer and information sciences 6%. **Special Study Options:** Cooperative education program, distance learning, dual enrollment, exchange student program (domestic), honors program, independent study, internships, learning disability services, study abroad, teacher certification program.

FACILITIES

Housing: Coed dorms, apartments for single students, fraternity/sorority housing, special dorm rooms for disabled students. **Special Academic Facilities/Equipment:** Archaeology museum; instructional media center; biology, chemistry, physics, and psychology labs, property on the Gulf of Mexico for marine and ecology research. **Computers:** 85% of classrooms are wireless, 80% of public computers are PCs, 5% of public computers are Macs, 5% of public computers are UNIX, network access in dorm rooms, online registration, online administrative functions (other than registration), support for handheld computing, remote student-access to Web through college's connection.

CAMPUS LIFE

Activities: Choral groups, concert band, dance, drama/theater, jazz band, music ensembles, musical theater, radio station, student government, student newspaper, symphony orchestra, television station. **Organizations:** 134 registered organizations, 10 honor societies, 13 religious organizations. 10 fraternities (5% men join), 8 sororities (5% women join). **Athletics (Intercollegiate): Men:** Baseball, basketball, cross-country, golf, soccer, tennis. **Women:** Basketball, cross-country, golf, soccer, softball, tennis, volleyball. **Environmental Initiatives:** All new buildings must be at least LEED Silver Certified. Energy Consumption Program. Environmentally Friendly/Green Purchasing Initiative.

ADMISSIONS

Freshman Academic Profile: 40% in top 10% of high school class, 84% in top 25% of high school class, 99% in top 50% of high school class. 90% from public high schools. SAT Math middle 50% range 490–600. SAT Critical Reading middle 50% range 500–600. ACT middle 50% range 21–26. TOEFL required of all international applicants, minimum paper TOEFL 525, minimum computer TOEFL 213. **Basis for Candidate Selection:** *Very important factors considered include:* Academic GPA, level of applicant's interest, rigor of secondary school record, standardized test scores, state residency. *Other factors considered include:* Alumni/ae relation, application essay, character/personal qualities, class rank, extracurricular activities, first generation, geographical residence, recommendation(s), talent/ability, volunteer work, work experience. **Freshman Admission Requirements:** High school diploma is required, and GED is accepted. *Academic units required:* 4 English, 3 math, 3 science (2 science labs), 2 foreign language, 3 social studies, 4 academic electives. **Freshman Admission Statistics:** 3,072 applied, 72% admitted, 44% enrolled. **Transfer Admission Requirements:** College transcript(s). Minimum college GPA of 2.0 required. Lowest grade transferable D. **General Admission Information:** Application fee $30. Regular application deadline 6/30. Regular notification is rolling. Non-fall registration accepted. Admission may be deferred for a maximum of 2 semesters. Credit offered for CEEB Advanced Placement tests.

COSTS AND FINANCIAL AID

Annual in-state tuition $2,211. Out-of-state tuition $14,778. Room & board $6,600. Required fees $1,100. Average book expense $1,000. **Required Forms and Deadlines:** FAFSA, institution's own financial aid form. **Notification of Awards:** Applicants will be notified of awards on a rolling basis beginning on or about 2/1. **Types of Aid:** *Need-based scholarships/grants:* Pell, SEOG, state scholarships/grants, private scholarships, the school's own gift aid. *Loans:* Direct Subsidized Stafford, Direct Unsubsidized Stafford, Direct PLUS, Federal Perkins, college/university loans from institutional funds.

UNIVERSITY OF WEST GEORGIA

1601 Maple Street, Carrollton, GA 30118
Phone: 678-839-4000 **E-mail:** admiss@westga.edu **CEEB Code:** 5900
Fax: 678-839-4747 **Website:** www.westga.edu **ACT Code:** 0878
Financial Aid Phone: 678-839-6421

This public school was founded in 1906. It has a 395-acre campus.

RATINGS

Admissions Selectivity Rating: 60*   **Fire Safety Rating:** 80   **Green Rating:** 60*

STUDENTS AND FACULTY

Enrollment: 8,475. **Student Body:** 60% female, 40% male, 3% out-of-state, 1% international (32 countries represented). African American 24%, Asian 1%, Caucasian 69%, Hispanic 2%. **Retention and Graduation:** 71% freshmen return for sophomore year. 11% freshmen graduate within 4 years. **Faculty:** Student/faculty ratio 18:1. 395 full-time faculty, 79% hold PhDs. 98% faculty teach undergrads.

ACADEMICS

Degrees: Bachelor's, doctoral, master's, post-master's certificate. **Academic Requirements:** Arts/fine arts, computer literacy, English (including composition), foreign languages, history, humanities, mathematics, sciences (biological or physical), social science. **Classes:** Most classes have 20–29 students. Most lab/discussion sections have 20–29 students. **Majors with Highest Enrollment:** Biology/biological sciences, elementary education and teaching, nursing/registered nurse training (ASN, BSN, MSN, RN). **Disciplines with Highest Percentage of Degrees Awarded:** Business/marketing 28%, education 21%, social sciences 9%, health professions and related sciences 7%, psychology 5%. **Special Study Options:** Accelerated program, cooperative education program, distance learning, double major, dual enrollment, external degree program, honors program, independent study, internships, study abroad, teacher certification program.

FACILITIES

Housing: Coed dorms, men's dorms, women's dorms, special housing for disabled students, special housing for international students, fraternity/sorority housing, cooperative housing. **Special Academic Facilities/Equipment:** Archaelolgical laboratory, art gallery, electron microscope, observatory, preschool, performing arts center, TV studio. **Computers:** 1% of classrooms are wired, 85% of public computers are PCs, 15% of public computers are Macs, network access in dorm rooms, online registration, online administrative functions (other than registration), support for handheld computing, remote student-access to Web through college's connection.

CAMPUS LIFE

Activities: Choral groups, concert band, dance, drama/theater, jazz band, literary magazine, marching band, music ensembles, musical theater, opera, pep band, radio station, student government, student newspaper, television station. **Organizations:** 55 registered organizations, 23 honor societies, 10 religious organizations. 13 fraternities (3% men join), 8 sororities (2% women join). **Athletics (Intercollegiate): Men:** Baseball, basketball, cheerleading, cross-country, football, golf. **Women:** Basketball, cheerleading, cross-country, golf, soccer, softball, volleyball.

ADMISSIONS

Freshman Academic Profile: 96% from public high schools. SAT Math middle 50% range 450–540. SAT Critical Reading middle 50% range 460–550. SAT Writing middle 50% range 440–530. ACT middle 50% range 18–22. TOEFL required of all international applicants, minimum paper TOEFL 523, minimum computer TOEFL 193. **Basis for Candidate Selection:** *Very important factors considered include:* Academic GPA, standardized test scores. *Important factors considered include:* Rigor of secondary school record. **Freshman Admission Requirements:** High school diploma is required, and GED is not accepted. *Academic units required:* 4 English, 4 math, 3 science (2 science labs), 2 foreign language, 1 social studies, 2 history. **Freshman Admission Statistics:** 5,696 applied, 52% admitted, 69% enrolled. **Transfer Admission Requirements:** College transcript(s). Minimum college GPA of 2.0 required. Lowest grade transferable C. **General Admission Information:** Application fee $20. Regular application deadline 6/1. Regular notification is rolling. Non-fall registration accepted. Credit and/or placement offered for CEEB Advanced Placement tests.

COSTS AND FINANCIAL AID

Annual in-state tuition $5,791. Annual out-of-state tuition $20,200. Room and board $6,676. Required fees $837. Average book expense $758. **Required Forms and Deadlines:** FAFSA. Financial aid filing deadline 7/1. **Notification of Awards:** Applicants will be notified of awards on or about 3/1. **Types of Aid:** *Need-based scholarships/grants:* Pell, SEOG, state scholarships/grants, private scholarships, the school's own gift aid. *Loans:* Direct Subsidized Stafford, Direct Unsubsidized Stafford, Direct PLUS, Federal Perkins, state loans. **Student Employment:** Federal Work-Study Program available. Institutional employment available. **Financial Aid Statistics:** 47% freshmen, 39% undergrads receive need-based scholarship or grant aid. 39% freshmen, 39% undergrads receive need-based self-help aid. 18 freshmen, 92 undergrads receive athletic scholarships. 53% freshmen, 80% undergrads receive any aid. Highest amount earned per year from on-campus jobs $5,150.

UNIVERSITY OF WEST LOS ANGELES

1155 West Arbor Vitae Street, Inglewood, CA 90301
Phone: 310-342-5254 **E-mail:** lfreeman@uwla.edu
Fax: 310-342-5295 **Website:** www.uwla.edu
Financial Aid Phone: 310-342-5257

This private school was founded in 1966. It has a 4-acre campus.

RATINGS

Admissions Selectivity Rating: 60*   **Fire Safety Rating:** 60*   **Green Rating:** 60*

STUDENTS AND FACULTY

Enrollment: 31. **Student Body:** 74% female, 26% male. **Faculty:** Student/faculty ratio 30:1. 10 full-time faculty, 100% hold PhDs.

ACADEMICS

Degrees: Bachelor's, certificate, first professional certificate. **Academic Requirements:** English (including composition). **Classes:** Most classes have 10–19 students. **Special Study Options:** independent study, internships, extension, evening, weekend courses.

FACILITIES

Housing: No on-campus housing.

CAMPUS LIFE

Activities: Student newspaper.

ADMISSIONS

Freshman Admission Requirements: High school diploma or equivalent is not required. **Transfer Admission Requirements:** College transcript(s), essay or personal statement. Minimum college GPA of 2.0 required. Lowest grade transferable C. **General Admission Information:** Application fee $55. Non-fall registration not accepted. Admission may be deferred for a maximum of 1 semester. Common Application not accepted.

COSTS AND FINANCIAL AID

Annual tuition $235. Required fees $120. Average book expense $175. **Types of Aid:** *Need-based scholarships/grants:* Pell, SEOG, private scholarships. *Loans:* Direct Subsidized Stafford, Direct Unsubsidized Stafford, Direct PLUS, FFEL Subsidized Stafford, FFEL Unsubsidized Stafford, FFEL PLUS. **Student Employment:** Off-campus job opportunities are fair.

THE UNIVERSITY OF WESTERN ONTARIO

Stevenson-Lawson Building Rm. 165, London, ON N6A5B8 Canada
Phone: 519-661-2100 **E-mail:** reg-admissions@uwo.ca
Fax: 519-661-3710 **Website:** www.uwo.ca
Financial Aid Phone: 519-661-2100

This public school was founded in 1878. It has a 1,050-acre campus.

RATINGS

Admissions Selectivity Rating: 60*   **Fire Safety Rating:** 60*   **Green Rating:** 60*

STUDENTS AND FACULTY

Enrollment: 28,513. **Student Body:** 59% female, 41% male, 6% out-of-province. **Retention and Graduation:** 95% freshmen return for sophomore year. **Faculty:** Student/faculty ratio 12:1. 1,165 full-time faculty.

ACADEMICS

Degrees: Bachelor's, certificate, diploma, doctoral, master's. **Academic Requirements:** Arts/fine arts, humanities, sciences (biological or physical), social science. **Majors with Highest Enrollment:** Biology/biological sciences, digital communications and media/multimedia, medicine. **Special Study Options:** Accelerated program, cooperative education program, cross registration, distance learning, double major, dual enrollment, English as a second language (ESL), exchange student program (domestic), honors program, independent study, internships, liberal arts/career combination, student-designed major, study abroad, teacher certification program.

FACILITIES

Housing: Coed dorms, men's dorms, women's dorms, apartments for married students, apartments for single students, special housing for disabled students, special housing for international students. **Special Academic Facilities/Equipment:** McIntosh Gallery, Hume Cronyn Memorial Observatory. **Computers:** 50% of public computers are PCs, 50% of public computers are UNIX, network access in dorm rooms, network access in dorm lounges, online registration, online administrative functions (other than registration), support for handheld computing, remote student-access to Web through college's connection.

CAMPUS LIFE

Activities: Choral groups, concert band, dance, drama/theater, jazz band, marching band, music ensembles, musical theater, opera, pep band, radio station, student government, student newspaper, student-run film society, symphony orchestra, television station. **Organizations:** 171 registered organizations, **Athletics (Intercollegiate):** *Men:* Badminton, baseball, basketball, crew/rowing, cross-country, curling, fencing, football, golf, ice hockey, rugby, skiing (nordic/cross-country), soccer, squash, swimming, tennis, track/field (outdoor), volleyball, water polo, wrestling. *Women:* Badminton, basketball, crew/rowing, cross-country, curling, fencing, field hockey, golf, ice hockey, lacrosse, rugby, skiing (nordic/cross-country), soccer, squash, swimming, tennis, track/field (outdoor), volleyball, wrestling.

ADMISSIONS

Freshman Academic Profile: TOEFL required of all international applicants, minimum paper TOEFL 550. **Basis for Candidate Selection:** *Very important factors considered include:* Academic GPA, rigor of secondary school record, standardized test scores. *Other factors considered include:* Class rank,

extracurricular activities, first generation, recommendation(s), talent/ability, volunteer work. **Freshman Admission Requirements:** High school diploma is required, and GED is not accepted. *Academic units required:* 4 English. **Freshman Admission Statistics:** 28,679 applied, 59% admitted, 26% enrolled. **Transfer Admission Requirements:** College transcript(s). **General Admission Information:** Application fee $105. Regular application deadline 6/1. Regular notification is rolling. Non-fall registration not accepted. Admission may be deferred for a maximum of 2 semesters. Common Application not accepted. Credit offered for CEEB Advanced Placement tests.

COSTS AND FINANCIAL AID

Room & board $6,582. Required fees $863. Average book expense $1,200. **Financial Aid Statistics:** 6 undergrads receive athletic scholarships. 68% freshmen, 40% undergrads receive any aid.

UNIVERSITY OF WINDSOR

Office of the Registrar, 401 Sunset Avenue, Windsor, ON N9B3P4 Canada
Phone: 519-253-3000 **E-mail:** liaison@uwindsor.ca
Fax: 519-971-3653 **Website:** www.uwindsor.ca
Financial Aid Phone: 519-253-3000

This public school was founded in 1857. It has a 13-acre campus.

RATINGS

Admissions Selectivity Rating: 60*   **Fire Safety Rating:** 60*   **Green Rating:** 81

STUDENTS AND FACULTY

Enrollment: 16,670. **Student Body:** 51% female, 49% male. **Faculty:** Student/faculty ratio 24:1. 520 full-time faculty, 84% hold PhDs. 100% faculty teach undergrads.

ACADEMICS

Degrees: Bachelor's, certificate, doctoral, first professional, master's. **Academic Requirements:** Arts/fine arts, humanities, sciences (biological or physical), social science. **Majors with Highest Enrollment:** Business administration/management, engineering, social sciences, **Disciplines with Highest Percentage of Degrees Awarded:** Education 20%, liberal arts/general studies 20%, business/marketing 12%, social sciences 12%, psychology 6%, law/legal studies 5%, engineering 5%. **Special Study Options:** Cooperative education program, distance learning, double major, exchange student program (domestic), honors program, independent study, internships, MBA for managers and professionals (on weekends), study abroad, teacher certification program.

FACILITIES

Housing: Coed dorms, apartments for married students, apartments for single students, special housing for disabled students, special housing for international students, fraternity/sorority housing, cooperative housing, off campus housing lists. **Special Academic Facilities/Equipment:** C.A.R.E. (Centre for Automotive Research & Education), GLIER (Great Lakes Institute for Environemntal Research), Jackman Dramatic Art Centre. **Computers:** 1% of classrooms are wired, 100% of classrooms are wireless, 75% of public computers are PCs, 4% of public computers are Macs, 21% of public computers are UNIX, network access in dorm rooms, network access in dorm lounges, online registration, online administrative functions (other than registration), support for handheld computing, remote student-access to Web through college's connection.

CAMPUS LIFE

Activities: Choral groups, dance, drama/theater, jazz band, literary magazine, music ensembles, musical theater, radio station, student government, student newspaper, student-run film society. **Organizations:** 166 registered organizations, 1 honor society, 10 religious organizations. 3 fraternities (1% men join), 3 sororities (1% women join). **Athletics (Intercollegiate):** *Men:* Basketball, cross-country, curling, football, golf, ice hockey, rugby, soccer, track/field (indoor), track/field (outdoor), volleyball. *Women:* Basketball, cross-country, curling, golf, ice hockey, soccer, track/field (indoor), track/field (outdoor), volleyball. **Environmental Initiatives:** LEEDS Certified Buildings—Medical School. $90 Million Engineering facility forthcoming. Consistent internationally recognized research from The Great Lakes Institute for Environmental Research and many other areas on-campus.

ADMISSIONS

Required Forms and Deadlines: Financial aid filing deadline 1/31. **Freshman Academic Profile:** TOEFL required of all international applicants, minimum paper TOEFL 560, minimum computer TOEFL 220. **Basis for**

Candidate Selection: *Very important factors considered include:* Academic GPA, rigor of secondary school record. *Other factors considered include:* Extracurricular activities, geographical residence, interview, recommendation(s), standardized test scores, volunteer work. **Freshman Admission Statistics:** 9,899 applied, 87% admitted, 41% enrolled. **Transfer Admission Requirements:** College transcript(s). **General Admission Information:** Application fee $60. Regular notification 4/1. Non-fall registration accepted.

COSTS AND FINANCIAL AID

In-province tuition $4,948–$5,936. Out-of-province tuition $4,948–$5,936. International tuition $11,807–$14,799. Room & board $7,544. Required fees $150. Average book expense $800.

UNIVERSITY OF WISCONSIN—EAU CLAIRE

105 Garfield Avenue, Eau Claire, WI 54701
Phone: 715-836-5415 **E-mail:** admissions@uwec.edu **CEEB Code:** 1913
Fax: 715-836-2409 **Website:** www.uwec.edu **ACT Code:** 4670
Financial Aid Phone: 715-836-3373

This public school was founded in 1916. It has a 333-acre campus.

RATINGS
Admissions Selectivity Rating: 80   **Fire Safety Rating:** 71   **Green Rating:** 70

STUDENTS AND FACULTY
Enrollment: 9,901. **Student Body:** 59% female, 41% male, 21% out-of-state. Asian 2%, Caucasian 68%. **Retention and Graduation:** 82% freshmen return for sophomore year. 19% freshmen graduate within 4 years. 9% grads go on to further study within 2 semesters. **Faculty:** Student/faculty ratio 19:1. 412 full-time faculty, 84% hold PhDs. 100% faculty teach undergrads.

ACADEMICS
Degrees: Associate, bachelor's, master's, post-bachelor's certificate, post-master's certificate. **Academic Requirements:** Arts/fine arts, computer literacy, English (including composition), foreign languages, history, humanities, mathematics, philosophy, sciences (biological or physical), social science. **Classes:** Most classes have 20–29 students. Most lab/discussion sections have 20–29 students. **Majors with Highest Enrollment:** Business administration/management, elementary education and teaching, marketing/marketing management. **Disciplines with Highest Percentage of Degrees Awarded:** Business/marketing 23%, health professions and related sciences 11%, education 9%, communications/journalism 9%, social sciences 7%, security and protective services 6%. **Special Study Options:** Accelerated program, cooperative education program, distance learning, double major, dual enrollment, English as a second language (ESL), exchange student program (domestic), honors program, independent study, internships, program with University of Wisconsin-Stout in early childhood education, study abroad, teacher certification program.

FACILITIES
Housing: Coed dorms, men's dorms, women's dorms, apartments for single students. **Special Academic Facilities/Equipment:** Art gallery, human development center, bird museum, field station, planetarium. **Computers:** 5% of classrooms are wired, 98% of classrooms are wireless, 80% of public computers are PCs, 20% of public computers are Macs, network access in dorm rooms, network access in dorm lounges, online registration, online administrative functions (other than registration), support for handheld computing, remote student-access to Web through college's connection.

CAMPUS LIFE
Activities: Choral groups, concert band, dance, drama/theater, jazz band, literary magazine, marching band, music ensembles, musical theater, opera, pep band, radio station, student government, student newspaper, student-run film society, symphony orchestra, television station. **Organizations:** 219 registered organizations, 34 honor societies, 16 religious organizations. 4 fraternities 4 sororities. **Athletics (Intercollegiate):** *Men:* Basketball, cross-country, diving, football, golf, ice hockey, swimming, tennis, track/field (outdoor), wrestling. *Women:* Basketball, cross-country, diving, golf, gymnastics, ice hockey, soccer, softball, swimming, tennis, track/field (outdoor), volleyball. **Environmental Initiatives:** Strategic Planning committee is developing plan to become "climate neutral" campus. Annual completion and updating of an inventory of all the campus's greenhouse gas emissions.

ADMISSIONS

Freshman Academic Profile: 17% in top 10% of high school class, 54% in top 25% of high school class, 97% in top 50% of high school class. 93% from public high schools. SAT Math middle 50% range 550–680. SAT Critical Reading middle 50% range 530–680. SAT Writing middle 50% range 530–630. ACT middle 50% range 22–26. TOEFL required of all international applicants, minimum paper TOEFL 525, minimum computer TOEFL 197. **Basis for Candidate Selection:** *Very important factors considered include:* Class rank, rigor of secondary school record. *Important factors considered include:* Standardized test scores. *Other factors considered include:* Academic GPA, alumni/ae relation, application essay, character/personal qualities, extracurricular activities, first generation, interview, level of applicant's interest, racial/ethnic status, recommendation(s), talent/ability, volunteer work, work experience. **Freshman Admission Requirements:** High school diploma is required, and GED is accepted. *Academic units required:* 4 English, 3 math, 3 science, 2 foreign language, 3 social studies, 2 academic electives. **Freshman Admission Statistics:** 7,351 applied, 69% admitted, 40% enrolled. **Transfer Admission Requirements:** High school transcript, college transcript(s), standardized test score, statement of good standing from prior institution(s). Minimum college GPA of 2.0 required. Lowest grade transferable D-. **General Admission Information:** Application fee $35. Regular notification is rolling. Non-fall registration accepted. Credit and/or placement offered for CEEB Advanced Placement tests.

COSTS AND FINANCIAL AID
Annual in-state tuition $5,845. Annual out-of-state tuition $13,418. Room and board $5,150. Average book expense $460. **Required Forms and Deadlines:** FAFSA. Financial aid filing deadline 4/15. **Notification of Awards:** Applicants will be notified of awards on a rolling basis beginning on or about 4/15. **Types of Aid:** *Need-based scholarships/grants:* Pell, SEOG, state scholarships/grants, private scholarships, the school's own gift aid, Federal Nursing Scholarships. *Loans:* Direct Subsidized Stafford, Direct Unsubsidized Stafford, Direct PLUS, Federal Perkins, state loans, college/university loans from institutional funds. **Student Employment:** Federal Work-Study Program available. Institutional employment available. Off-campus job opportunities are good. **Financial Aid Statistics:** 24% freshmen, 24% undergrads receive need-based scholarship or grant aid. 37% freshmen, 39% undergrads receive need-based self-help aid. 69% freshmen, 67% undergrads receive any aid. Highest amount earned per year from on-campus jobs $12,602.

UNIVERSITY OF WISCONSIN—GREEN BAY

2420 Nicolet Drive, Green Bay, WI 53411-7001
Phone: 920-465-2111 **E-mail:** uwgb@uwgb.edu **CEEB Code:** 1859
Fax: 920-465-5754 **Website:** www.uwgb.edu **ACT Code:** 4688
Financial Aid Phone: 920-465-2075

This public school was founded in 1965. It has a 700-acre campus.

RATINGS
Admissions Selectivity Rating: 60*   **Fire Safety Rating:** 60*   **Green Rating:** 79

STUDENTS AND FACULTY
Enrollment: 5,378. **Student Body:** 66% female, 34% male, 5% out-of-state. Asian 3%, Caucasian 91%, Hispanic 1%, Native American 2%. **Retention and Graduation:** 77% freshmen return for sophomore year. 23% freshmen graduate within 4 years. 15% grads go on to further study within 2 semesters. 10% grads pursue arts and sciences degrees. 3% grads pursue business degrees. 1% grads pursue law degrees. 1% grads pursue medical degrees. **Faculty:** Student/faculty ratio 24:1. 177 full-time faculty, 86% hold PhDs. 99% faculty teach undergrads.

ACADEMICS
Degrees: Associate, bachelor's, master's, post-bachelor's certificate. **Academic Requirements:** Arts/fine arts, English (including composition), ethnic studies, humanities, mathematics, sciences (biological or physical), social science, world culture studies. **Classes:** Most classes have 20–29 students. Most lab/discussion sections have 20–29 students. **Majors with Highest Enrollment:** Biological and biomedical sciences, business administration/management, psychology. **Disciplines with Highest Percentage of Degrees Awarded:** Business/marketing 20%, psychology 17%, education 11%, biological/life sciences 10%, social sciences 7%. **Special Study Options:** Cross registration, distance learning, double major, exchange student program (domestic), external degree program, independent study, internships, liberal arts/career combination, student-designed major, study abroad, teacher certification program.

FACILITIES

Housing: Coed dorms, apartments for single students, suites with private bedrooms. **Special Academic Facilities/Equipment:** 290-acre arboretum, herbarium, regional performing arts center. **Computers:** 25% of classrooms are wired, 5% of classrooms are wireless, 94% of public computers are PCs, 5% of public computers are Macs, 1% of public computers are UNIX, network access in dorm rooms, network access in dorm lounges, online registration, online administrative functions (other than registration), remote student-access to Web through college's connection.

CAMPUS LIFE

Activities: Choral groups, dance, drama/theater, jazz band, literary magazine, music ensembles, pep band, radio station, student government, student newspaper, television station. **Organizations:** 100 registered organizations, 7 honor societies, 5 religious organizations. 2 fraternities (1% men join), 2 sororities (1% women join). **Athletics (Intercollegiate):** *Men:* Basketball, cheerleading, cross-country, diving, golf, skiing (nordic/cross-country), soccer, swimming, tennis. *Women:* Basketball, cheerleading, cross-country, diving, skiing (nordic/cross-country), soccer, softball, swimming, tennis, volleyball. **Environmental Initiatives:** Building integrated photovoltaics in Mary Ann Cofrin Hall. Historically strong academic programs in environmental science and environmental policy and planning at both bachelor's and master's level. Campus design connects buildings with energy efficient underground tunnels.

ADMISSIONS

Freshman Academic Profile: 90% from public high schools. ACT middle 50% range 20–25. **Basis for Candidate Selection:** *Very important factors considered include:* Academic GPA, extracurricular activities, rigor of secondary school record, standardized test scores, talent/ability. *Important factors considered include:* Volunteer work, work experience. *Other factors considered include:* Application essay, character/personal qualities, interview, level of applicant's interest, racial/ethnic status, recommendation(s), state residency. **Freshman Admission Requirements:** High school diploma is required, and GED is accepted. *Academic units required:* 4 English, 3 math, 3 science (1 science lab), 3 social studies, 4 academic electives. *Academic units recommended:* 4 English, 3 math, 3 science (1 science lab), 2 foreign language, 3 social studies, 4 academic electives. **Freshman Admission Statistics:** 3,500 applied, 70% admitted, 42% enrolled. **Transfer Admission Requirements:** College transcript(s). Minimum college GPA of 2.0 required. Lowest grade transferable D. **General Admission Information:** Application fee $35. Regular notification is rolling. Non-fall registration accepted. Admission may be deferred for a maximum of 2 semesters. Credit and/or placement offered for CEEB Advanced Placement tests.

COSTS AND FINANCIAL AID

Average book expense $800. **Required Forms and Deadlines:** FAFSA. Financial aid filing deadline 4/15. **Notification of Awards:** Applicants will be notified of awards on a rolling basis beginning on or about 11/1. **Types of Aid:** *Need-based scholarships/grants:* Pell, SEOG, state scholarships/grants, private scholarships, the school's own gift aid. *Loans:* FFEL Subsidized Stafford, FFEL Unsubsidized Stafford, FFEL PLUS, Federal Perkins. **Student Employment:** Federal Work-Study Program available. Institutional employment available. Off-campus job opportunities are good. **Financial Aid Statistics:** 35% freshmen, 33% undergrads receive need-based scholarship or grant aid. 40% freshmen, 41% undergrads receive need-based self-help aid. 16 freshmen, 72 undergrads receive athletic scholarships. 56% freshmen, 56% undergrads receive any aid.

UNIVERSITY OF WISCONSIN—LA CROSSE

1725 State Street, LaCrosse, WI 54601-3742
Phone: 608-785-8939 **E-mail:** admissions@uwlax.edu **CEEB Code:** 1914
Fax: 608-785-8940 **Website:** www.uwlax.edu **ACT Code:** 4672
Financial Aid Phone: 608-785-8604

This public school was founded in 1909. It has a 120-acre campus.

RATINGS

Admissions Selectivity Rating: 81   **Fire Safety Rating:** 60*   **Green Rating:** 60*

STUDENTS AND FACULTY

Enrollment: 8,097. **Student Body:** 59% female, 41% male, 15% out-of-state. Asian 3%, Caucasian 92%, Hispanic 1%. **Retention and Graduation:** 86% freshmen return for sophomore year. 25% freshmen graduate within 4 years. 21% grads go on to further study within 2 semesters. **Faculty:** Student/faculty ratio 24:1. 343 full-time faculty, 76% hold PhDs. 100% faculty teach undergrads.

ACADEMICS

Degrees: Associate, bachelor's, doctoral, master's. **Academic Requirements:** Arts/fine arts, computer literacy, English (including composition), health/wellness, history, humanities, mathematics, sciences (biological or physical), social science. **Classes:** Most classes have 20–29 students. Most lab/discussion sections have 20–29 students. **Majors with Highest Enrollment:** Elementary education and teaching, kinesiology and exercise science, marketing/marketing management. **Disciplines with Highest Percentage of Degrees Awarded:** Business/marketing 20%, parks and recreation 13%, social sciences 11%, biological/life sciences 10%, education 9%. **Special Study Options:** Cooperative education program, cross registration, distance learning, double major, dual enrollment, English as a second language (ESL), honors program, independent study, internships, study abroad, teacher certification program.

FACILITIES

Housing: Coed dorms, women's dorms, special housing for disabled students, special housing for international students, fraternity/sorority housing, substance free, first-year experience. **Special Academic Facilities/Equipment:** Greenhouse, planetarium, health science center, Mississippi Valley Archaeology Center, river studies center, business development center, La Crosse Exercise & Health Program. **Computers:** 95% of public computers are PCs, 5% of public computers are Macs, network access in dorm rooms, online registration, online administrative functions (other than registration), support for handheld computing, remote student-access to Web through college's connection.

CAMPUS LIFE

Activities: Choral groups, concert band, dance, drama/theater, jazz band, literary magazine, marching band, music ensembles, musical theater, pep band, radio station, student government, student newspaper, symphony orchestra, television station. **Organizations:** 140 registered organizations, 13 honor societies, 10 religious organizations. 4 fraternities, 2 sororities. **Athletics (Intercollegiate):** *Men:* Baseball, basketball, cross-country, diving, football, swimming, tennis, track/field (indoor), track/field (outdoor), wrestling. *Women:* Basketball, cross-country, diving, gymnastics, soccer, softball, swimming, tennis, track/field (indoor), track/field (outdoor), volleyball.

ADMISSIONS

Freshman Academic Profile: 26% in top 10% of high school class, 71% in top 25% of high school class, 76% in top 50% of high school class. SAT Math middle 50% range 500–580. SAT Critical Reading middle 50% range 500–600. ACT middle 50% range 23–26. TOEFL required of all international applicants, minimum paper TOEFL 550, minimum computer TOEFL 213. **Basis for Candidate Selection:** *Very important factors considered include:* Academic GPA, class rank, rigor of secondary school record, standardized test scores. *Important factors considered include:* Application essay. *Other factors considered include:* Alumni/ae relation, character/personal qualities, extracurricular activities, first generation, geographical residence, interview, level of applicant's interest, racial/ethnic status, recommendation(s), state residency, talent/ability, volunteer work, work experience. **Freshman Admission Requirements:** High school diploma is required, and GED is accepted. *Academic units required:* 4 English, 3 math, 3 science (2 science labs), 3 social studies, 4 academic electives. *Academic units recommended:* 4 English, 4 math, 4 science (2 science labs), 3 foreign language, 4 social studies, 2 academic electives. **Freshman Admission Statistics:** 6,836 applied, 64% admitted, 40% enrolled. **Transfer Admission Requirements:** High school transcript, college transcript(s), statement of good standing from prior institution(s). Minimum college GPA of 2.5 required. Lowest grade transferable D. **General Admission Information:** Application fee $35. Regular notification is rolling. Non-fall registration accepted. Credit and/or placement offered for CEEB Advanced Placement tests.

COSTS AND FINANCIAL AID

Annual in-state tuition $4,876. Annual out-of-state tuition $12,448. Room and board $5,130. Average book expense $300. **Required Forms and Deadlines:** FAFSA, institution's own financial aid form. Financial aid filing deadline 3/15. **Notification of Awards:** Applicants will be notified of awards on a rolling basis beginning on or about 3/10. **Types of Aid:** *Need-based scholarships/grants:* Pell, SEOG, state scholarships/grants, private scholarships, the school's own gift aid. *Loans:* FFEL Subsidized Stafford, FFEL Unsubsidized Stafford, FFEL PLUS, Federal Perkins, state loans, college/university loans from institutional funds. **Financial Aid Statistics:** 16% freshmen, 17% undergrads receive need-based scholarship or grant aid. 34% freshmen, 37% undergrads receive need-based self-help aid. 65% freshmen, 72% undergrads receive any aid. Highest amount earned per year from on-campus jobs $7,020.

UNIVERSITY OF WISCONSIN—MADISON

Armory & Gymnasium, 716 Langdon Street, Madison, WI 53706-1481
Phone: 608-262-3961 **E-mail:** onwisconsin@admissions.wisc.edu **CEEB Code:** 1846
Fax: 608-262-7706 **Website:** www.wisc.edu **ACT Code:** 4656
Financial Aid Phone: 608-262-3060

This public school was founded in 1848. It has a 933-acre campus.

RATINGS
Admissions Selectivity Rating: 94　　　**Fire Safety Rating:** 60*　　　**Green Rating:** 60*

STUDENTS AND FACULTY
Enrollment: 28,462. **Student Body:** 53% female, 47% male, 31% out-of-state, 4% international (110 countries represented). African American 3%, Asian 6%, Caucasian 85%, Hispanic 3%. **Retention and Graduation:** 93% freshmen return for sophomore year. 46% freshmen graduate within 4 years. **Faculty:** Student/faculty ratio 13:1. 2,379 full-time faculty, 92% hold PhDs.

ACADEMICS
Degrees: Bachelor's, doctoral, first professional certificate, first professional, master's, post-master's certificate. **Academic Requirements:** English (including composition), ethnic studies, foreign languages, humanities, mathematics, sciences (biological or physical), social science. **Classes:** Most classes have 10–19 students. Most lab/discussion sections have 10–19 students. **Majors with Highest Enrollment:** Biology/biological sciences, English language and literature, political science and government. **Disciplines with Highest Percentage of Degrees Awarded:** Social sciences 14%, biological/life sciences 11%, engineering 10%, business/marketing 9%, communications/journalism 6%. **Special Study Options:** Accelerated program, cooperative education program, distance learning, double major, dual enrollment, English as a second language (ESL), honors program, independent study, internships, liberal arts/career combination, student-designed major, study abroad, teacher certification program.

FACILITIES
Housing: Coed dorms, men's dorms, women's dorms, apartments for married students, apartments for single students, special housing for international students, fraternity/sorority housing, cooperative housing, residential learning communities. **Special Academic Facilities/Equipment:** Art, physics, and geology museums; nuclear reactor; biotron; electron microscopes; observatory. **Computers:** 5% of classrooms are wired, 60% of classrooms are wireless, 70% of public computers are PCs, 20% of public computers are Macs, 5% of public computers are UNIX, network access in dorm rooms, network access in dorm lounges, online registration, online administrative functions (other than registration), support for handheld computing, remote student-access to Web through college's connection.

CAMPUS LIFE
Activities: Choral groups, concert band, dance, drama/theater, jazz band, literary magazine, marching band, music ensembles, musical theater, opera, pep band, radio station, student government, student newspaper, student-run film society, symphony orchestra, television station. **Organizations:** 617 registered organizations, 27 honor societies. 26 fraternities (9% men join), 11 sororities (8% women join). **Athletics (Intercollegiate):** *Men:* Basketball, cheerleading, crew/rowing, cross-country, football, golf, ice hockey, soccer, swimming, tennis, track/field (outdoor), wrestling. *Women:* Basketball, cheerleading, crew/rowing, cross-country, golf, ice hockey, soccer, softball, swimming, tennis, track/field (outdoor), volleyball.

ADMISSIONS
Freshman Academic Profile: 58% in top 10% of high school class, 93% in top 25% of high school class, 100% in top 50% of high school class. SAT Math middle 50% range 620–710. SAT Critical Reading middle 50% range 550–670. SAT Writing middle 50% range 560–670. ACT middle 50% range 26–30. TOEFL required of all international applicants, minimum paper TOEFL 550, minimum computer TOEFL 213. **Basis for Candidate Selection:** *Very important factors considered include:* Academic GPA, class rank, rigor of secondary school record. *Important factors considered include:* Application essay, standardized test scores, state residency. *Other factors considered include:* Alumni/ae relation, character/personal qualities, extracurricular activities, first generation, interview, level of applicant's interest, racial/ethnic status, recommendation(s), talent/ability, volunteer work, work experience. **Freshman**

Admission Requirements: High school diploma is required, and GED is accepted. *Academic units required:* 4 English, 3 math, 3 science, 2 foreign language, 3 social studies, 2 academic electives. *Academic units recommended:* 4 English, 4 math, 4 science, 4 foreign language, 4 social studies, 2 academic electives. **Freshman Admission Statistics:** 22,816 applied, 58% admitted, 42% enrolled. **Transfer Admission Requirements:** High school transcript, college transcript(s), essay or personal statement, standardized test score. Lowest grade transferable D. **General Admission Information:** Application fee $35. Regular application deadline 2/1. Regular notification is rolling. Non-fall registration accepted. Admission may be deferred for a maximum of 2 semesters. Credit and/or placement offered for CEEB Advanced Placement tests.

COSTS AND FINANCIAL AID
Required Forms and Deadlines: FAFSA, institution's own financial aid form. **Notification of Awards:** Applicants will be notified of awards on a rolling basis beginning on or about 4/1. **Types of Aid:** *Need-based scholarships/grants:* Pell, SEOG, state scholarships/grants, private scholarships, the school's own gift aid. *Loans:* FFEL Subsidized Stafford, FFEL Unsubsidized Stafford, FFEL PLUS, Federal Perkins, Federal Nursing, state loans. **Financial Aid Statistics:** 17% freshmen, 20% undergrads receive need-based scholarship or grant aid. 23% freshmen, 27% undergrads receive need-based self-help aid. 93 freshmen, 432 undergrads receive athletic scholarships.

UNIVERSITY OF WISCONSIN—MILWAUKEE

PO Box 749, Milwaukee, WI 53201
Phone: 414-229-2222 **E-mail:** uwmlook@uwm.edu **CEEB Code:** 1473
Fax: 414-229-6940 **Website:** www.uwm.edu **ACT Code:** 4658
Financial Aid Phone: 414-229-4541

This public school was founded in 1956. It has a 93-acre campus.

RATINGS
Admissions Selectivity Rating: 72　　　**Fire Safety Rating:** 60*　　　**Green Rating:** 86

STUDENTS AND FACULTY
Enrollment: 22,066. **Student Body:** 52% female, 48% male, 2% out-of-state. African American 7%, Asian 5%, Caucasian 83%, Hispanic 4%. **Retention and Graduation:** 70% freshmen return for sophomore year.

ACADEMICS
Degrees: Bachelor's, certificate, doctoral, master's, post-bachelor's certificate, post-master's certificate. **Academic Requirements:** Arts/fine arts, cultural diversity, English (including composition), foreign languages, history, humanities, mathematics, sciences (biological or physical), social science. **Classes:** Most classes have 20–29 students. Most lab/discussion sections have 20–29 students. **Disciplines with Highest Percentage of Degrees Awarded:** Business/marketing 22%, communications/journalism 9%, education 9%, health professions and related sciences 9%, visual and performing arts 8%, social sciences 7%. **Special Study Options:** Accelerated program, cooperative education program, cross registration, distance learning, double major, dual enrollment, English as a second language (ESL), external degree program, honors program, independent study, internships, liberal arts/career combination, student-designed major, study abroad, teacher certification program.

FACILITIES
Housing: Coed dorms, apartments for single students, special housing for disabled students. **Special Academic Facilities/Equipment:** Art and geology museums, childhood education center, foreign language resource center, Great Lakes research facility, environmental studies field station, planetarium.

CAMPUS LIFE
Activities: Choral groups, concert band, dance, drama/theater, jazz band, literary magazine, marching band, music ensembles, musical theater, pep band, radio station, student government, student newspaper, student-run film society, symphony orchestra. **Organizations:** 250 registered organizations, 1 honor society, 4 religious organizations. 8 fraternities, 4 sororities. **Athletics (Intercollegiate):** *Men:* Baseball, basketball, cross-country, diving, soccer, swimming, track/field (outdoor). *Women:* Basketball, cross-country, soccer, swimming, tennis, track/field (outdoor), volleyball.

ADMISSIONS
Freshman Academic Profile: 7% in top 10% of high school class, 26% in top 25% of high school class, 67% in top 50% of high school class. SAT Math middle 50% range 500–630. SAT Critical Reading middle 50% range 470–610. SAT Writing middle 50% range 460–600. ACT middle 50% range 19–25. TOEFL required of all international applicants, minimum paper TOEFL 500. **Basis for**

Candidate Selection: *Very important factors considered include:* Academic GPA, class rank, rigor of secondary school record, standardized test scores. *Other factors considered include:* Application essay, character/personal qualities, extracurricular activities, first generation, geographical residence, interview, level of applicant's interest, racial/ethnic status, recommendation(s), state residency, talent/ability, volunteer work, work experience. **Freshman Admission Requirements:** High school diploma is required, and GED is accepted. *Academic units required:* 4 English, 3 math, 3 science (1 science lab), 3 social studies, 2 academic electives, 2 from computer science, fine arts, or other appropriate courses. *Academic units recommended:* 4 English, 3 math, 3 science (1 science lab), 2 foreign language, 3 social studies, 2 academic electives, 2 from computer science, fine arts, or other appropriate courses. **Freshman Admission Statistics:** 11,525 applied, 78% admitted, 45% enrolled. **Transfer Admission Requirements:** High school transcript, college transcript(s). Minimum college GPA of 2.0 required. Lowest grade transferable D-. **General Admission Information:** Application fee $35. Regular application deadline 7/1. Regular notification is rolling. Non-fall registration accepted. Admission may be deferred for a maximum of 1 semester. Credit offered for CEEB Advanced Placement tests.

COSTS AND FINANCIAL AID

Annual in-state tuition $5,868. Out-of-state tuition $15,470. Room and board $5,314. Required fees $758. Average book expense $800. **Required Forms and Deadlines:** FAFSA. Financial aid filing deadline 3/1. **Types of Aid:** *Need-based scholarships/grants:* Pell, SEOG, state scholarships/grants, private scholarships, the school's own gift aid, Federal Nursing Scholarships. *Loans:* FFEL Subsidized Stafford, FFEL Unsubsidized Stafford, FFEL PLUS, Federal Perkins, Federal Nursing, alternative loans. **Student Employment:** Federal Work-Study Program available. Institutional employment available. Off-campus job opportunities are good. **Financial Aid Statistics:** 20% freshmen, 23% undergrads receive need-based scholarship or grant aid. 44% freshmen, 45% undergrads receive need-based self-help aid. 2 freshmen, 85 undergrads receive athletic scholarships.

UNIVERSITY OF WISCONSIN—OSHKOSH

Dempsey Hall 135, 800 Algoma Boulevard, Oshkosh, WI 54901
Phone: 920-424-0202 **E-mail:** oshadmuw@uwosh.edu **CEEB Code:** 1916
Fax: 920-424-1098 **Website:** www.uwosh.edu **ACT Code:** 4674
Financial Aid Phone: 920-424-4025

This public school was founded in 1871. It has a 192-acre campus.

RATINGS

Admissions Selectivity Rating: 73　　**Fire Safety Rating:** 60*　　**Green Rating:** 87

STUDENTS AND FACULTY

Enrollment: 9,598. **Student Body:** 59% female, 41% male, 2% out-of-state. African American 1%, Asian 3%, Caucasian 92%, Hispanic 2%, Native American 1%. **Retention and Graduation:** 76% freshmen return for sophomore year. 15% freshmen graduate within 4 years. **Faculty:** Student/faculty ratio 22:1. 373 full-time faculty, 84% hold PhDs. 99% faculty teach undergrads.

ACADEMICS

Degrees: Associate, bachelor's, certificate, master's. **Academic Requirements:** Arts/fine arts, English (including composition), history, humanities, mathematics, non-Western culture, physical education, sciences (biological or physical), social science, speech. **Classes:** Most classes have 20–29 students. Most lab/discussion sections have 20–29 students. **Majors with Highest Enrollment:** Business administration/management, elementary education and teaching, nursing/registered nurse training (ASN, BSN, MSN, RN). **Disciplines with Highest Percentage of Degrees Awarded:** Business/marketing 22%, health professions and related sciences 13%, education 10%, communications/journalism 8%, social sciences 8%, public administration and social services 6%. **Special Study Options:** Accelerated program, cooperative education program, distance learning, double major, English as a second language (ESL), exchange student program (domestic), external degree program, honors program, independent study, internships, student-designed major, study abroad, teacher certification program, weekend college.

FACILITIES

Housing: Coed dorms. **Special Academic Facilities/Equipment:** Art gallery, ceramics lab, electron microscope. **Computers:** Network access in dorm rooms, network access in dorm lounges, online registration.

CAMPUS LIFE

Activities: Choral groups, drama/theater, literary magazine, music ensembles,

---

musical theater, radio station, student government, student newspaper, student-run film society, television station. **Organizations:** 175 registered organizations, 15 honor societies, 6 religious organizations. 8 fraternities (4% men join), 5 sororities (5% women join). **Athletics (Intercollegiate):** *Men:* Baseball, basketball, cross-country, diving, football, riflery, soccer, swimming, tennis, track/field (indoor), track/field (outdoor), wrestling. *Women:* Basketball, cross-country, diving, golf, gymnastics, riflery, soccer, softball, swimming, tennis, track/field (indoor), track/field (outdoor), volleyball. **Environmental Initiatives:** The recent development of a comprehensive campus sustainability plan that covers the four areas of operations, teaching, research, and outreach. The leadership of the campus in the purchase of alternative energy. The campus was the first major educational institution in the state of Wisconsin to purchase alternative energy, and continues to be a leader in this area. This May the campus will conduct a faculty college on intergrating sustainability across the urriculum based on the AASHE model.

ADMISSIONS

Freshman Academic Profile: 11% in top 10% of high school class, 39% in top 25% of high school class, 89% in top 50% of high school class. ACT middle 50% range 20–24. TOEFL required of all international applicants, minimum paper TOEFL 525, minimum computer TOEFL 197. **Basis for Candidate Selection:** *Very important factors considered include:* Rigor of secondary school record. *Important factors considered include:* Class rank, standardized test scores. *Other factors considered include:* Academic GPA, application essay, character/personal qualities, extracurricular activities, first generation, level of applicant's interest, racial/ethnic status, recommendation(s), talent/ability, volunteer work, work experience. **Freshman Admission Requirements:** High school diploma is required, and GED is accepted. *Academic units required:* 4 English, 3 math, 3 science (2 science labs), 3 social studies, 1 history, 4 academic electives. *Academic units recommended:* 4 math, 4 science (4 science labs). **Freshman Admission Statistics:** 4,827 applied, 80% admitted, 46% enrolled. **Transfer Admission Requirements:** College transcript(s). Minimum college GPA of 2.0 required. Lowest grade transferable D. **General Admission Information:** Application fee $35. Regular application deadline 8/1. Regular notification is rolling. Non-fall registration accepted. Credit offered for CEEB Advanced Placement tests.

COSTS AND FINANCIAL AID

Annual in-state tuition $5,693. Annual out-of-state tuition $13,266. Room and board $5,746. Average book expense $800. **Required Forms and Deadlines:** FAFSA. Financial aid filing deadline 3/15. **Notification of Awards:** Applicants will be notified of awards on or about 4/1. **Types of Aid:** *Need-based scholarships/grants:* Pell, SEOG, state scholarships/grants, private scholarships, the school's own gift aid, Federal Nursing Scholarships. *Loans:* FFEL Subsidized Stafford, FFEL Unsubsidized Stafford, FFEL PLUS, Federal Perkins, Federal Nursing, state loans, college/university loans from institutional funds. **Student Employment:** Federal Work-Study Program available. Institutional employment available. **Financial Aid Statistics:** 29% freshmen, 45% undergrads receive need-based scholarship or grant aid. 51% freshmen, 53% undergrads receive need-based self-help aid.

UNIVERSITY OF WISCONSIN—PARKSIDE

Box 2000, Kenosha, WI 53141-2000
Phone: 262-595-2355 **E-mail:** matthew.jensen@uwp.edu **CEEB Code:** 1860
Fax: 262-595-2008 **Website:** www.uwp.edu **ACT Code:** 4690
Financial Aid Phone: 262-595-2574

This public school was founded in 1968. It has a 700-acre campus.

RATINGS

Admissions Selectivity Rating: 62　　**Fire Safety Rating:** 60*　　**Green Rating:** 60*

STUDENTS AND FACULTY

Enrollment: 4,590. **Student Body:** 57% female, 43% male, 7% out-of-state, 1% international (28 countries represented). African American 8%, Asian 3%, Caucasian 69%, Hispanic 6%. **Retention and Graduation:** 65% freshmen return for sophomore year. 9% freshmen graduate within 4 years. **Faculty:** Student/faculty ratio 18:1. 181 full-time faculty, 74% hold PhDs. 100% faculty teach undergrads.

ACADEMICS

Degrees: Bachelor's, certificate, master's. **Academic Requirements:** Arts/fine arts, English (including composition), ethnic diversity, foreign languages, humanities, mathematics, sciences (biological or physical), social science. **Classes:** Most classes have fewer than 10 students. Most lab/discussion sections have 20–29 students. **Majors with Highest Enrollment:** Business administration/management, criminal justice/law enforcement administration, sociology. **Disciplines with Highest Percentage of Degrees Awarded:** Business/marketing 21%, social sciences 14%, security and protective services 11%, communications/journalism 9%, visual and performing arts 8%. **Special Study Options:** Accelerated program, cooperative nursing program with University of Wisconsin—Milwaukee, distance learning, double enrollment, exchange student program (domestic), honors program, independent study, internships, liberal arts/career combination, study abroad, teacher certification program, weekend college.

FACILITIES

Housing: Coed dorms, apartments for single students, special housing for disabled students, special housing for international students. **Special Academic Facilities/Equipment:** Language lab, electron microscope. **Computers:** 80% of public computers are PCs, 15% of public computers are Macs, 5% of public computers are UNIX, network access in dorm rooms, network access in dorm lounges, online registration, online administrative functions (other than registration), support for handheld computing, remote student-access to Web through college's connection.

CAMPUS LIFE

Activities: Choral groups, concert band, dance, drama/theater, jazz band, literary magazine, music ensembles, musical theater, pep band, radio station, student government, student newspaper, symphony orchestra. **Organizations:** 48 registered organizations, 5 honor societies, 1 religious organization. 3 fraternities (1% men join), 3 sororities (1% women join). **Athletics (Intercollegiate):** *Men:* Baseball, basketball, cross-country, golf, soccer, track/field (indoor), track/field (outdoor), wrestling. *Women:* Basketball, cross-country, soccer, softball, track/field (indoor), track/field (outdoor), volleyball.

ADMISSIONS

Freshman Academic Profile: 5% in top 10% of high school class, 23% in top 25% of high school class, 56% in top 50% of high school class. 92% from public high schools. ACT middle 50% range 18–22. TOEFL required of all international applicants, minimum paper TOEFL 525, minimum computer TOEFL 197. **Basis for Candidate Selection:** *Very important factors considered include:* Academic GPA, class rank, rigor of secondary school record, standardized test scores. *Other factors considered include:* Alumni/ae relation, application essay, character/personal qualities, extracurricular activities, first generation, interview, level of applicant's interest, racial/ethnic status, recommendation(s), talent/ability, volunteer work, work experience. **Freshman Admission Requirements:** High school diploma is required, and GED is accepted. *Academic units required:* 4 English, 3 math, 3 science, 3 social studies, 4 academic electives. *Academic units recommended:* 4 English, 4 math, 4 science (2 science labs), 2 foreign language, 3 social studies, 1 history, 4 academic electives. **Freshman Admission Statistics:** 1,868 applied, 92% admitted, 51% enrolled. **Transfer Admission Requirements:** High school transcript, college transcript(s), statement of good standing from prior institution(s). Minimum college GPA of 2.0 required. Lowest grade transferable D-. **General Admission Information:** Application fee $35. Regular application deadline 8/1. Regular notification is rolling. Non-fall registration accepted. Admission may be deferred for a maximum of 2 semesters. Common Application not accepted. Credit and/or placement offered for CEEB Advanced Placement tests.

COSTS AND FINANCIAL AID

Annual in-state tuition $4,277. Out-of-state tuition $14,323. Room & board $5,550. Required fees $720. Average book expense $784. **Required Forms and Deadlines:** FAFSA. Financial aid filing deadline 3/15. **Notification of Awards:** Applicants will be notified of awards on a rolling basis beginning on or about 4/1. **Types of Aid:** *Need-based scholarships/grants:* Pell, SEOG, state scholarships/grants, private scholarships, the school's own gift aid, Federal Nursing Scholarships. *Loans:* FFEL Subsidized Stafford, FFEL Unsubsidized Stafford, FFEL PLUS, Federal Perkins, state loans. **Student Employment:** Federal Work-Study Program available. Institutional employment available. Off-campus job opportunities are excellent. **Financial Aid Statistics:** 46% freshmen, 47% undergrads receive need-based scholarship or grant aid. 44% freshmen, 37% undergrads receive need-based self-help aid.

UNIVERSITY OF WISCONSIN—PLATTEVILLE

1 University Plaza, Platteville, WI 53818
Phone: 608-342-1125 **E-mail:** admit@uwplatt.edu **CEEB Code:** 1917
Fax: 608-342-1122 **Website:** www.uwplatt.edu **ACT Code:** 4676
Financial Aid Phone: 608-342-1836

This public school was founded in 1866. It has an 820-acre campus.

RATINGS

Admissions Selectivity Rating: 66   **Fire Safety Rating:** 65   **Green Rating:** 60*

STUDENTS AND FACULTY

Enrollment: 5,631. **Student Body:** 38% female, 62% male, 10% out-of-state. Asian 1%, Caucasian 95%. **Retention and Graduation:** 76% freshmen return for sophomore year. **Faculty:** Student/faculty ratio 20:1. 249 full-time faculty, 83% hold PhDs. 100% faculty teach undergrads.

ACADEMICS

Degrees: Associate, bachelor's, certificate, diploma, master's. **Academic Requirements:** Arts/fine arts, English (including composition), foreign languages, history, humanities, mathematics, sciences (biological or physical), social science. **Classes:** Most classes have fewer than 10 students. Most lab/discussion sections have 10–19 students. **Majors with Highest Enrollment:** Business administration and management, criminal justice/safety studies, mechanical engineering. **Disciplines with Highest Percentage of Degrees Awarded:** Engineering 24%, business/marketing 13%, education 12%, security and protective services 9%, agriculture 8%. **Special Study Options:** Cooperative education program, distance learning, double major, dual enrollment, English as a second language (ESL), exchange student program (domestic), external degree program, honors program, independent study, internships, liberal arts/career combination, student-designed major, study abroad, teacher certification program.

FACILITIES

Housing: Coed dorms, men's dorms, women's dorms, fraternity/sorority housing. **Special Academic Facilities/Equipment:** Electron microscope, Nohr Art Gallery, the Wisconsin Room. **Computers:** 25% of classrooms are wired, 50% of classrooms are wireless, 90% of public computers are PCs, 10% of public computers are Macs, network access in dorm rooms, network access in dorm lounges, online registration, online administrative functions (other than registration), support for handheld computing, remote student-access to Web through college's connection.

CAMPUS LIFE

Activities: Choral groups, concert band, drama/theater, jazz band, literary magazine, marching band, music ensembles, musical theater, pep band, radio station, student government, student newspaper, symphony orchestra, television station. **Organizations:** 180 registered organizations, 15 honor societies, 9 religious organizations. 9 fraternities (3% men join), 5 sororities (2% women join). **Athletics (Intercollegiate):** *Men:* Baseball, basketball, cross-country, football, soccer, track/field (indoor), track/field (outdoor), wrestling. *Women:* Basketball, cross-country, golf, soccer, softball, track/field (indoor), track/field (outdoor), volleyball.

ADMISSIONS

Freshman Academic Profile: 12% in top 10% of high school class, 35% in top 25% of high school class, 77% in top 50% of high school class. 94% from public high schools. ACT middle 50% range 20–25. TOEFL required of all international applicants, minimum paper TOEFL 550. **Basis for Candidate Selection:** *Very important factors considered include:* Class rank, rigor of secondary school record, standardized test scores. *Important factors considered include:* Geographical residence, state residency. *Other factors considered include:* Academic GPA, extracurricular activities, interview, recommendation(s), talent/ability. **Freshman Admission Requirements:** High school diploma is required, and GED is accepted. *Academic units required:* 4 English, 3 math, 3 science (2 science labs), 3 social studies, 4 academic electives. *Academic units recommended:* 3 math. **Freshman Admission Statistics:** 3,075 applied, 85% admitted, 46% enrolled. **Transfer Admission Requirements:** College transcript(s), statement of good standing from prior institution(s). Minimum college GPA of 2.0 required. Lowest grade transferable D. **General Admission Information:** Application fee $35. Regular notification is rolling. Non-fall registration accepted. Admission may be deferred for a maximum of 1 semester. Common Application not accepted. Credit offered for CEEB Advanced Placement tests.

COSTS AND FINANCIAL AID

Annual in-state tuition $4,277. Annual out-of-state tuition $14,323. Room and board $4,654. Required fees $848. Average book expense $320. **Required**

Forms and Deadlines: FAFSA. Financial aid filing deadline 1/3. **Notification of Awards:** Applicants will be notified of awards on or about 6/2. **Types of Aid:** *Need-based scholarships/grants:* state scholarships/grants. *Loans:* FFEL Subsidized Stafford, FFEL Unsubsidized Stafford, FFEL PLUS, Federal Perkins.

UNIVERSITY OF WISCONSIN—RIVER FALLS

410 South Third Street, 112 South Hall, River Falls, WI 54022
Phone: 715-425-3500 **E-mail:** admit@uwrf.edu **CEEB Code:** 1918
Fax: 715-425-0676 **Website:** www.uwrf.edu **ACT Code:** 4678
Financial Aid Phone: 715-425-3141

This public school was founded in 1874. It has a 225-acre campus.

RATINGS
Admissions Selectivity Rating: 60*   **Fire Safety Rating:** 60*   **Green Rating:** 60*

STUDENTS AND FACULTY
Enrollment: 5,216. **Student Body:** 60% female, 40% male, 42% out-of-state. **Retention and Graduation:** 25% freshmen graduate within 4 years. 17% grads go on to further study within 2 semesters. **Faculty:** Student/faculty ratio 18:1. 235 full-time faculty. 85% faculty teach undergrads.

ACADEMICS
Degrees: Bachelor's, master's, post-bachelor's certificate, post-master's certificate. **Academic Requirements:** Arts/fine arts, English (including composition), humanities, mathematics, sciences (biological or physical), social science. **Classes:** Most classes have 20–29 students. Most lab/discussion sections have 10–19 students. **Majors with Highest Enrollment:** Animal sciences, biological and physical sciences, business administration/management. **Disciplines with Highest Percentage of Degrees Awarded:** Business/marketing 24%, education 16%, agriculture 13%, biological/life sciences 9%, social sciences 9%. **Special Study Options:** Accelerated program, cooperative education program, distance learning, double major, dual enrollment, exchange student program (domestic), honors program, independent study, internships, student-designed major, study abroad, teacher certification program.

FACILITIES
Housing: Coed dorms, women's dorms, apartments for single students, fraternity/sorority housing. **Special Academic Facilities/Equipment:** Local history museum, 20-inch reflecting telescope, observatory, electron microscope, greenhouse, lab farms, educational technology center. **Computers:** 90% of public computers are PCs, 10% of public computers are Macs, network access in dorm rooms, network access in dorm lounges, online registration, online administrative functions (other than registration), remote student-access to Web through college's connection.

CAMPUS LIFE
Activities: Choral groups, concert band, dance, drama/theater, jazz band, literary magazine, music ensembles, musical theater, pep band, radio station, student government, student newspaper, symphony orchestra, television station. **Organizations:** 120 registered organizations, 9 honor societies, 12 religious organizations. 5 fraternities (2% men join), 4 sororities (2% women join). **Athletics (Intercollegiate):** *Men:* Basketball, cross-country, football, ice hockey, swimming, track/field (indoor), track/field (outdoor). *Women:* Basketball, cross-country, golf, ice hockey, soccer, softball, swimming, tennis, track/field (indoor), track/field (outdoor), volleyball.

ADMISSIONS
Freshman Academic Profile: 95% from public high schools. ACT middle 50% range 18–24. TOEFL required of all international applicants, minimum paper TOEFL 500, minimum computer TOEFL 180. **Basis for Candidate Selection:** *Very important factors considered include:* Class rank, rigor of secondary school record, standardized test scores. *Other factors considered include:* Academic GPA, recommendation(s). **Freshman Admission Requirements:** High school diploma is required, and GED is accepted. *Academic units required:* 4 English, 3 math, 3 science, 3 social studies, 4 academic electives. *Academic units recommended:* 2 foreign language. **Freshman Admission Statistics:** 3,183 applied, 81% admitted, 50% enrolled. **Transfer Admission Requirements:** College transcript(s), statement of good standing from prior institution(s). Minimum college GPA of 2.6 required. Lowest grade transferable D. **General Admission Information:** Application fee $35. Regular notification is rolling. Non-fall registration accepted. Admission may be deferred for a maximum of 2 semesters. Credit and/or placement offered for CEEB Advanced Placement tests.

COSTS AND FINANCIAL AID
Annual in-state tuition $5,728. Out-of-state tuition $13,202. Room & board $4,586. Average book expense $300. **Required Forms and Deadlines:** FAFSA, institution's own financial aid form. Financial aid filing deadline 3/15. **Notification of Awards:** Applicants will be notified of awards on a rolling basis beginning on or about 4/1. **Types of Aid:** *Need-based scholarships/grants:* Pell, SEOG, state scholarships/grants, private scholarships, the school's own gift aid. *Loans:* FFEL Subsidized Stafford, FFEL Unsubsidized Stafford, FFEL PLUS, Federal Perkins. **Student Employment:** Federal Work-Study Program available. Institutional employment available. Off-campus job opportunities are good. **Financial Aid Statistics:** 30% freshmen, 38% undergrads receive need-based scholarship or grant aid. 37% freshmen, 49% undergrads receive need-based self-help aid.

UNIVERSITY OF WISCONSIN—STEVENS POINT

Student Services Center, Stevens Point, WI 54481
Phone: 715-346-2441 **E-mail:** admiss@uwsp.edu **CEEB Code:** 1919
Fax: 715-346-3957 **Website:** www.uwsp.edu **ACT Code:** 4680
Financial Aid Phone: 715-346-4771

This public school was founded in 1894. It has a 335-acre campus.

RATINGS
Admissions Selectivity Rating: 75   **Fire Safety Rating:** 67   **Green Rating:** 92

STUDENTS AND FACULTY
Enrollment: 8,589. **Student Body:** 53% female, 47% male, 6% out-of-state, 2% international (31 countries represented). Asian 2%, Caucasian 92%, Hispanic 1%. **Retention and Graduation:** 78% freshmen return for sophomore year. 22% freshmen graduate within 4 years. 11% grads go on to further study within 2 semesters. **Faculty:** Student/faculty ratio 22:1. 355 full-time faculty, 86% hold PhDs. 100% faculty teach undergrads.

ACADEMICS
Degrees: Associate, bachelor's, certificate, doctoral, master's. **Academic Requirements:** English (including composition), history, humanities, mathematics, sciences (biological or physical), social science. **Classes:** Most classes have 20–29 students. Most lab/discussion sections have 20–29 students. **Majors with Highest Enrollment:** Biological and physical sciences, business administration/management, elementary education and teaching. **Disciplines with Highest Percentage of Degrees Awarded:** Natural resources/environmental science 12%, social sciences 10%, visual and performing arts 10%, business/marketing 9%, biological/life sciences 8%, education 8%, communications/journalism 7%. **Special Study Options:** Accelerated program, distance learning, double major, dual enrollment, English as a second language (ESL), independent study, internships, student-designed major, study abroad, teacher certification program.

FACILITIES
Housing: Coed dorms, men's dorms, women's dorms, alcohol-free house, eco hall, international program hall, language house, quiet floors, nontraditional hall, wellness emphasis program. **Special Academic Facilities/Equipment:** Art galleries, costume and goblet collections, museum of natural history, early childhood study institute, communicative disorders center, map center, observatory, planetarium, Foucault pendulum, nature preserve, environmental station, groundwater center, herbarium, aviary, wellness institute. **Computers:** 89% of public computers are PCs, 11% of public computers are Macs, network access in dorm rooms, online registration, online administrative functions (other than registration), support for handheld computing, remote student-access to Web through college's connection.

EXTRACURRICULAR
Activities: Choral groups, concert band, dance, drama/theater, jazz band, literary magazine, music ensembles, musical theater, opera, pep band, radio station, student government, student newspaper, student-run film society, symphony orchestra, television station. **Organizations:** 185 registered organizations, 12 honor societies, 9 religious organizations. 4 fraternities (1% men join), 3 sororities (1% women join). **Athletics (Intercollegiate):** *Men:* Baseball, basketball, cross-country, diving, football, ice hockey, swimming, track/field (outdoor), wrestling. *Women:* Basketball, cross-country, diving, golf, ice hockey, soccer, softball, swimming, tennis, track/field (outdoor), volleyball.

ADMISSIONS
Freshman Academic Profile: 15% in top 10% of high school class, 46% in top 25% of high school class, 92% in top 50% of high school class. ACT middle 50% range 20–25. TOEFL required of all international applicants, minimum paper

TOEFL 523, minimum computer TOEFL 193. **Basis for Candidate Selection:** *Very important factors considered include:* Academic GPA, class rank, rigor of secondary school record, standardized test scores. *Important factors considered include:* Application essay, recommendation(s). *Other factors considered include:* Character/personal qualities, extracurricular activities, first generation, level of applicant's interest, racial/ethnic status, talent/ability, volunteer work, work experience. **Freshman Admission Requirements:** High school diploma is required, and GED is accepted. *Academic units required:* 4 English, 3 math, 3 science, 3 social studies, 4 academic electives. *Academic units recommended:* 2 foreign language. **Freshman Admission Statistics:** 4,832 applied, 79% admitted, 43% enrolled. **Transfer Admission Requirements:** High school transcript, college transcript(s), statement of good standing from prior institution(s). Lowest grade transferable D. **General Admission Information:** Application fee $35. Regular application deadline rolling. Regular notification rolling. Non-fall registration accepted. Credit and/or placement offered for CEEB Advanced Placement tests.

COSTS AND FINANCIAL AID
Annual in-state tuition $4,277. Out-of-state tuition $14,324. Room & board $4,322. Required fees $785. Average book expense $450. **Required Forms and Deadlines:** FAFSA. Financial aid filing deadline 6/15. **Notification of Awards:** Applicants will be notified of awards on a rolling basis beginning on or about 5/1. **Types of Aid:** *Need-based scholarships/grants:* Pell, SEOG, state scholarships/grants, private scholarships, the school's own gift aid. *Loans:* FFEL Subsidized Stafford, FFEL Unsubsidized Stafford, FFEL PLUS, Federal Perkins. **Financial Aid Statistics:** 20% freshmen, 25% undergrads receive need-based scholarship or grant aid. 39% freshmen, 44% undergrads receive need-based self-help aid. 78% freshmen, 79% undergrads receive any aid.

UNIVERSITY OF WISCONSIN—STOUT

Admissions UW–Stout, Menomonie, WI 54751
Phone: 715-232-1411 **E-mail:** admissions@uwstout.edu **CEEB Code:** 1740
Fax: 715-232-1667 **Website:** www.uwstout.edu **ACT Code:** 4652
Financial Aid Phone: 715-232-1363

This public school was founded in 1891. It has a 110-acre campus.

RATINGS
Admissions Selectivity Rating: 71   **Fire Safety Rating:** 60*   **Green Rating:** 60*

STUDENTS AND FACULTY
Enrollment: 7,383. **Student Body:** 49% female, 51% male, 31% out-of-state, 1% international (28 countries represented). African American 1%, Asian 2%, Caucasian 93%. **Retention and Graduation:** 72% freshmen return for sophomore year. 15% freshmen graduate within 4 years. 9% grads go on to further study within 2 semesters. **Faculty:** Student/faculty ratio 19:1. 327 full-time faculty, 73% hold PhDs. 100% faculty teach undergrads.

ACADEMICS
Degrees: Bachelor's, certificate, master's, post-master's certificate. **Academic Requirements:** Arts/fine arts, English (including composition), history, humanities, mathematics, philosophy, sciences (biological or physical), social science. **Classes:** Most classes have 20–29 students. Most lab/discussion sections have 20–29 students. **Majors with Highest Enrollment:** Business administration/management, design and applied arts, hospitality administration/management. **Disciplines with Highest Percentage of Degrees Awarded:** Business/marketing 40%, personal and culinary services 14%, foreign languages and literature 11%, visual and performing arts 9%, engineering 7%. **Special Study Options:** Accelerated program, cooperative education program, cross registration, distance learning, double major, dual enrollment, exchange student program (domestic), external degree program, honors program, independent study, internships, study abroad, teacher certification program.

FACILITIES
Housing: Coed dorms, apartments for single students, special housing for disabled students, freshmen housing, smoke-free housing, upperclass/graduate housing, alcohol-free housing. **Special Academic Facilities/Equipment:** Specialized labs for degree programs throughout the campus, Furlong Art Gallery. **Computers:** 5% of classrooms are wired, 60% of classrooms are wireless, 80% of public computers are PCs, 15% of public computers are Macs, 5% of public computers are UNIX, network access in dorm rooms, network access in dorm lounges, online registration, online administrative functions (other than registration), remote student-access to Web through college's connection, tuition includes personal computer. Undergraduates are required to own a computer.

CAMPUS LIFE
Activities: Choral groups, concert band, dance, drama/theater, jazz band, literary magazine, marching band, music ensembles, musical theater, pep band, radio station, student government, student newspaper, student-run film society. **Organizations:** 120 registered organizations, 1 honor society, 12 religious organizations. 5 fraternities (2% men join), 3 sororities (3% women join). **Athletics (Intercollegiate):** *Men:* Baseball, basketball, cross-country, football, ice hockey, track/field (outdoor). *Women:* Basketball, cross-country, gymnastics, soccer, softball, tennis, track/field (outdoor), volleyball.

ADMISSIONS
Freshman Academic Profile: 6% in top 10% of high school class, 27% in top 25% of high school class, 77% in top 50% of high school class. ACT middle 50% range 19–23. TOEFL required of all international applicants, minimum paper TOEFL 500, minimum computer TOEFL 173. **Basis for Candidate Selection:** *Very important factors considered include:* Class rank, standardized test scores. *Other factors considered include:* Academic GPA, alumni/ae relation, application essay, character/personal qualities, extracurricular activities, first generation, interview, level of applicant's interest, racial/ethnic status, recommendation(s), rigor of secondary school record, talent/ability. **Freshman Admission Requirements:** High school diploma is required, and GED is accepted. *Academic units required:* 4 English, 3 math, 3 science, 3 social studies, 4 academic electives. *Academic units recommended:* 2 foreign language. **Freshman Admission Statistics:** 3,920 applied, 78% admitted, 49% enrolled. **Transfer Admission Requirements:** College transcript(s), statement of good standing from prior institution(s). Minimum college GPA of 2.5 required. Lowest grade transferable D. **General Admission Information:** Application fee $35. Regular notification is rolling. Non-fall registration accepted. Credit offered for CEEB Advanced Placement tests.

COSTS AND FINANCIAL AID
Annual in-state tuition $5,367. Annual out-of-state tuition $13,113. Room and board $4,994. Required fees $1,905. Average book expense $334. **Required Forms and Deadlines:** FAFSA. Financial aid filing deadline 3/15. **Notification of Awards:** Applicants will be notified of awards on a rolling basis beginning on or about 4/1. **Types of Aid:** *Need-based scholarships/grants:* Pell, SEOG, state scholarships/grants, private scholarships, the school's own gift aid, BIA, GearUp. *Loans:* FFEL Subsidized Stafford, FFEL Unsubsidized Stafford, FFEL PLUS, Federal Perkins, alternative educational loans. **Student Employment:** Federal Work-Study Program available. Institutional employment available. Off-campus job opportunities are good. **Financial Aid Statistics:** 22% freshmen, 22% undergrads receive need-based scholarship or grant aid. 50% freshmen, 49% undergrads receive need-based self-help aid. 71% freshmen, 74% undergrads receive any aid. Highest amount earned per year from on-campus jobs $948.

UNIVERSITY OF WISCONSIN—SUPERIOR

Belknap & Catlin, PO Box 2000, Superior, WI 54880-4500
Phone: 715-394-8230 **E-mail:** admissions@uwsuper.edu **CEEB Code:** 1920
Fax: 715-394-8407 **Website:** www.uwsuper.edu **ACT Code:** 4682
Financial Aid Phone: 715-394-8200

This public school was founded in 1893. It has a 230-acre campus.

RATINGS
Admissions Selectivity Rating: 71   **Fire Safety Rating:** 61   **Green Rating:** 66

STUDENTS AND FACULTY
Enrollment: 2,508. **Student Body:** 57% female, 43% male, 43% out-of-state, 5% international (30 countries represented). African American 1%, Asian 1%, Caucasian 88%, Native American 3%. **Retention and Graduation:** 69% freshmen return for sophomore year. 13% grads go on to further study within 2 semesters. 2% grads pursue arts and sciences degrees. 2% grads pursue business degrees. 1% grads pursue law degrees. 1% grads pursue medical degrees. **Faculty:** Student/faculty ratio 18:1. 112 full-time faculty, 79% hold PhDs. 100% faculty teach undergrads.

ACADEMICS
Degrees: Associate, bachelor's, certificate, master's, post-master's certificate. **Academic Requirements:** Arts/fine arts, communicating arts, computer literacy, English (including composition), history, human performance/health, humanities, mathematics, philosophy, sciences (biological or physical), social science. **Classes:** Most classes have 20–29 students. Most lab/discussion sections have 10–19 students. **Majors with Highest Enrollment:** Biology/biological sciences, business administration and management, elementary

education and teaching. **Disciplines with Highest Percentage of Degrees Awarded:** Business/marketing 23%, education 14%, social sciences 11%, interdisciplinary studies 9%, communications/journalism 8%. **Special Study Options:** Cooperative education program, cross registration, distance learning, double major, dual enrollment, English as a second language (ESL), exchange student program (domestic), external degree program, independent study, internships, liberal arts/career combination, student-designed major, study abroad, teacher certification program.

FACILITIES

Housing: Coed dorms, women's dorms, special housing for disabled students, residence hall rooms for married couples. **Special Academic Facilities/ Equipment:** TV, radio, and film facilities, observatory, greenhouse, 2 art galleries, recital hall, 4 theaters, modern health and wellness center. **Computers:** 45% of classrooms are wireless, 98% of public computers are PCs, 2% of public computers are Macs, network access in dorm rooms, network access in dorm lounges, online registration, online administrative functions (other than registration), support for handheld computing, remote student-access to Web through college's connection.

CAMPUS LIFE

Activities: Choral groups, concert band, dance, drama/theater, jazz band, music ensembles, musical theater, pep band, radio station, student government, student newspaper, symphony orchestra, television station. **Organizations:** 70 registered organizations, 1 honor society, 5 religious organizations. 1 sorority. **Athletics (Intercollegiate):** *Men:* Baseball, basketball, cross-country, ice hockey, soccer, track/field (outdoor). *Women:* Basketball, cross-country, golf, ice hockey, soccer, softball, track/field (outdoor), volleyball. **Environmental Initiatives:** LEED certification for new buildings that are now in the planning/construction process. Establishing a Sustainability Council that will guide the implementation of environmental commitment. A new student group— SWARM-Superior.

ADMISSIONS

Freshman Academic Profile: 11% in top 10% of high school class, 39% in top 25% of high school class, 83% in top 50% of high school class. 95% from public high schools. SAT Math middle 50% range 355–570. SAT Critical Reading middle 50% range 415–620. ACT middle 50% range 20–24. TOEFL required of all international applicants, minimum paper TOEFL 525, minimum computer TOEFL 195. **Basis for Candidate Selection:** *Very important factors considered include:* Class rank, rigor of secondary school record, standardized test scores. *Other factors considered include:* Application essay, character/personal qualities, interview, level of applicant's interest, racial/ethnic status, recommendation(s), talent/ability, volunteer work, work experience. **Freshman Admission Requirements:** High school diploma is required, and GED is accepted. *Academic units required:* 4 English, 3 math, 3 science, 3 social studies, 4 academic electives. *Academic units recommended:* 2 foreign language. **Freshman Admission Statistics:** 902 applied, 73% admitted, 48% enrolled. **Transfer Admission Requirements:** College transcript(s). Minimum college GPA of 2.0 required. Lowest grade transferable D. **General Admission Information:** Application fee $35. Regular notification is rolling. Non-fall registration accepted. Admission may be deferred for a maximum of 2 semesters. Credit offered for CEEB Advanced Placement tests.

COSTS AND FINANCIAL AID

Annual in-state tuition $4,969. Annual out-of-state tuition $12,542. Room and board $4,720. Required fees $938. Average book expense $860. **Required Forms and Deadlines:** FAFSA. Financial aid filing deadline 4/15. **Notification of Awards:** Applicants will be notified of awards on a rolling basis beginning on or about 3/15. **Types of Aid:** *Need-based scholarships/grants:* Pell, SEOG, state scholarships/grants, private scholarships, the school's own gift aid. *Loans:* Direct Subsidized Stafford, Direct Unsubsidized Stafford, Direct PLUS, Federal Perkins, state loans, college/university loans from institutional funds. **Financial Aid Statistics:** 26% freshmen, 33% undergrads receive need-based scholarship or grant aid. 49% freshmen, 53% undergrads receive need-based self-help aid. 72% freshmen, 73% undergrads receive any aid. Highest amount earned per year from on-campus jobs $11,000.

UNIVERSITY OF WISCONSIN—WHITEWATER

800 West Main Street, Baker Hall, Whitewater, WI 53190-1791
Phone: 262-472-1440 **E-mail:** uwwadmit@uww.edu **CEEB Code:** 1921
Fax: 262-472-1515 **Website:** www.uww.edu **ACT Code:** 4684
Financial Aid Phone: 262-472-1130

This public school was founded in 1868. It has a 385-acre campus.

RATINGS

Admissions Selectivity Rating: 66   **Fire Safety Rating:** 75   **Green Rating:** 60*

STUDENTS AND FACULTY

Enrollment: 4,822. **Student Body:** 50% female, 50% male, 4% out-of-state. African American 8%, Asian 4%, Caucasian 84%, Hispanic 4%. **Retention and Graduation:** 74% freshmen return for sophomore year. 21% freshmen graduate within 4 years. **Faculty:** Student/faculty ratio 22:1. 392 full-time faculty, 85% hold PhDs. 100% faculty teach undergrads.

ACADEMICS

Degrees: Associate, bachelor's, master's. **Academic Requirements:** Arts/fine arts, English (including composition), history, humanities, mathematics, sciences (biological or physical), social science. **Classes:** Most classes have 30–39 students. **Majors with Highest Enrollment:** Elementary education and teaching, journalism, physical education, teaching and coaching. **Disciplines with Highest Percentage of Degrees Awarded:** Business/marketing 29%, education 16%, social sciences 10%, computer and information sciences 5%, public administration and social services 5%, visual and performing arts 5%, psychology 4%. **Special Study Options:** Accelerated program, cooperative education program, cross registration, distance learning, double major, dual enrollment, English as a second language (ESL), exchange student program (domestic), external degree program, honors program, independent study, internships, liberal arts/career combination, student-designed major, study abroad, teacher certification program, weekend college.

FACILITIES

Housing: Coed dorms, women's dorms, special housing for disabled students, special housing for international students. **Special Academic Facilities/ Equipment:** Two electron microscopes, state of the art theater/auditorium. **Computers:** 80% of public computers are PCs, 19% of public computers are Macs, 1% of public computers are UNIX, network access in dorm rooms, network access in dorm lounges, online registration, online administrative functions (other than registration), remote student-access to Web through college's connection.

CAMPUS LIFE

Activities: Choral groups, concert band, dance, drama/theater, jazz band, literary magazine, marching band, music ensembles, musical theater, opera, radio station, student government, student newspaper, symphony orchestra, television station. **Organizations:** 130 registered organizations, 4 honor societies, 8 religious organizations. 9 fraternities, 8 sororities. **Athletics (Intercollegiate):** *Men:* Baseball, basketball, cross-country, diving, football, soccer, swimming, tennis, track/field (indoor), track/field (outdoor), wrestling. *Women:* Basketball, bowling, cross-country, diving, golf, gymnastics, soccer, softball, swimming, tennis, track/field (indoor), track/field (outdoor), volleyball.

ADMISSIONS

Freshman Academic Profile: 9% in top 10% of high school class, 32% in top 25% of high school class, 77% in top 50% of high school class. 90% from public high schools. SAT Math middle 50% range 480–600. SAT Writing middle 50% range 470–610. ACT middle 50% range 20–24. TOEFL required of all international applicants, minimum paper TOEFL 500, minimum computer TOEFL 214. **Basis for Candidate Selection:** *Very important factors considered include:* Class rank, rigor of secondary school record, standardized test scores. *Other factors considered include:* Academic GPA, application essay, character/personal qualities, extracurricular activities, first generation, geographical residence, interview, level of applicant's interest, racial/ethnic status, recommendation(s), state residency, talent/ability, volunteer work. **Freshman Admission Requirements:** High school diploma is required, and GED is accepted. *Academic units required:* 4 English, 3 math, 3 science (1 science lab), 3 social studies, 4 academic electives. *Academic units recommended:* 4 math, 4 science, 2 foreign language, 4 social studies. **Freshman Admission Statistics:** 5,570 applied, 76% admitted, 43% enrolled. **Transfer Admission Requirements:** High school transcript, college transcript(s). Minimum college GPA of 2.0 required. Lowest grade transferable D. **General Admission Information:** Application fee $35. Regular notification is rolling. Non-fall registration accepted. Admission may be deferred for a maximum of 3 terms or 2 semesters. Credit offered for CEEB Advanced Placement tests.

COSTS AND FINANCIAL AID

Annual in-state tuition $5,568. Out-of-state tuition $13,042. Room & board $4,322. Required fees $710. Average book expense $170. **Required Forms and Deadlines:** FAFSA. Financial aid filing deadline 3/15. **Notification of Awards:** Applicants will be notified of awards on a rolling basis beginning on or about 4/1. **Types of Aid:** *Need-based scholarships/grants:* Pell, SEOG, state scholarships/grants, private scholarships, the school's own gift aid. *Loans:* Direct Subsidized Stafford, Direct Unsubsidized Stafford, Direct PLUS, Federal Perkins, college/university loans from institutional funds, alternative loans. **Financial Aid Statistics:** 20% freshmen, 21% undergrads receive need-based scholarship or grant aid. 45% freshmen, 39% undergrads receive need-based self-help aid. 52% freshmen, 42% undergrads receive any aid. Highest amount earned per year from on-campus jobs $3,000.

UNIVERSITY OF WYOMING

Best 368

Dept 3435, 1000 East University Avenue, Laramie, WY 82071
Phone: 307-766-5160 **E-mail:** Why-Wyo@uwyo.edu **CEEB Code:** 4855
Fax: 307-766-4042 **Website:** www.uwyo.edu **ACT Code:** 5006
Financial Aid Phone: 307-766-2118

This public school was founded in 1886. It has a 785-acre campus.

RATINGS
Admissions Selectivity Rating: 88   **Fire Safety Rating:** 60*   **Green Rating:** 88

STUDENTS AND FACULTY

Enrollment: 9,111. **Student Body:** 52% female, 48% male, 27% out-of-state. 2% international (69 countries represented). African American 1%, Asian 1%, Caucasian 84%, Hispanic 3%, Native American 1%. **Retention and Graduation:** 74% freshmen return for sophomore year. **Faculty:** Student/faculty ratio 15:1. 666 full-time faculty, 86% hold PhDs. 97% faculty teach undergrads.

ACADEMICS

Degrees: Bachelor's, certificate, doctoral, first professional, master's, post-master's certificate. **Academic Requirements:** Arts/fine arts, Diversity in the U.S., English (including composition), humanities, Information Literacy, Intellectual Community, mathematics, oral communication, physical education, sciences (biological or physical), social science, U.S. and WY Constitutions. **Classes:** Most classes have 20–29 students. Most lab/discussion sections have 20–29 students. **Majors with Highest Enrollment:** Business administration and management, elementary education and teaching, psychology. **Disciplines with Highest Percentage of Degrees Awarded:** Business/marketing 17%, education 16%, engineering 9%, health professions and related sciences 7%, biological/life sciences 6%. **Special Study Options:** Accelerated program, distance learning, double major, dual enrollment, English as a second language (ESL), exchange student program (domestic), external degree program, honor program, independent study, internships, student-designed major, study abroad, teacher certification program.

FACILITIES

Housing: Coed dorms, apartments for married students, apartments for single students, special housing for disabled students, fraternity/sorority housing, floor-specific living plans in residence halls, Health Sciences Living House. **Special Academic Facilities/Equipment:** Art gallery, geology museum, American Heritage Center, Rocky Mountain Herbarium, mycological herbarium, art museum, planetarium, environmental biology lab, anthropology museum, on-site elementary school, state veterinary lab, infrared telescope. **Computers:** 87% of public computers are PCs, network access in dorm rooms, network access in dorm lounges, online registration, online administrative functions (other than registration), support for handheld computing, remote student-access to Web through college's connection.

CAMPUS LIFE

Activities: Choral groups, concert band, dance, drama/theater, jazz band, literary magazine, marching band, music ensembles, musical theater, opera, pep band, radio station, student government, student newspaper, symphony orchestra, television station. **Organizations:** 195 registered organizations, 15 honor societies, 16 religious organizations. 8 fraternities, 3 sororities. **Athletics (Intercollegiate):** *Men:* Basketball, cheerleading, cross-country, diving, football, golf, swimming, track/field (outdoor), wrestling. *Women:* Basketball,

cheerleading, cross-country, diving, golf, soccer, swimming, tennis, track/field (outdoor), volleyball. **Environmental Initiatives:** Campus Sustainability Committee. College of Business Sustainable Business Program. Presidents Climate Commitment.

ADMISSIONS

Freshman Academic Profile: SAT Math middle 50% range 500–630. SAT Critical Reading middle 50% range 480–610. ACT middle 50% range 21–26. TOEFL required of all international applicants, minimum paper TOEFL 525, minimum computer TOEFL 197. **Basis for Candidate Selection:** *Very important factors considered include:* Academic GPA, rigor of secondary school record, standardized test scores. *Important factors considered include:* Level of applicant's interest. *Other factors considered include:* Application essay, character/personal qualities, extracurricular activities, interview, recommendation(s), state residency, talent/ability. **Freshman Admission Requirements:** High school diploma is required, and GED is accepted. *Academic units required:* 4 English, 3 math, 3 science (3 science labs), 3 cultural context electives, 3 behavioral or social sciences, 3 visual or performing arts, 3 humanities or earth/space sciences. *Academic units recommended:* 4 English, 4 math, 4 science (3 science labs), 2 foreign language, 3 cultural context electives, 3 behavioral or social sciences, 3 visual or performing arts, 3 humanities or earth/space sciences. **Freshman Admission Statistics: Transfer Admission Requirements:** College transcript(s). Minimum college GPA of 2.0 required. Lowest grade transferable D. **General Admission Information:** Application fee $40. Regular application deadline 8/10. Regular notification is rolling: within 2 weeks of receipt of required materials. Nonfall registration accepted. Admission may be deferred for a maximum of 1 year. Credit and/or placement offered for CEEB Advanced Placement tests.

COSTS AND FINANCIAL AID

Annual in-state tuition. $2,820 Out-of-state tuition $9,660. Room & board $7,274. Required fees $734. Average book expense $1,200. **Required Forms and Deadlines:** FAFSA. Financial aid filing deadline 3/1. **Notification of Awards:** Applicants will be notified of awards on or about 3/15. **Types of Aid:** *Need-based scholarships/grants:* Pell, SEOG, state scholarships/grants, private scholarships, the school's own gift aid. *Loans:* FFEL Subsidized Stafford, FFEL Unsubsidized Stafford, FFEL PLUS, Federal Perkins. **Student Employment:** Federal Work-Study Program available. Institutional employment available. Off-campus job opportunities are good. **Financial Aid Statistics:** 35% freshmen, 27% undergrads receive need-based scholarship or grant aid. 48% freshmen, 38% undergrads receive need-based self-help aid. 855 freshmen, 3,063 undergrads receive athletic scholarships. 92% freshmen, 75% undergrads receive any aid. Highest amount earned per year from on-campus jobs $46.

See page 1478.

UPPER IOWA UNIVERSITY

Parker Fox Hall Box 1859, Fayette, IA 52142-1859
Phone: 800-553-4150 **E-mail:** admission@uiu.edu
Fax: 319-425-5277 **Website:** www.uiu.edu
Financial Aid Phone: 319-425-5274

This private school was founded in 1857. It has an 80-acre campus.

RATINGS
Admissions Selectivity Rating: 64   **Fire Safety Rating:** 60*   **Green Rating:** 60*

STUDENTS AND FACULTY

Enrollment: 5,138. **Student Body:** 59% female, 41% male, 40% out-of-state. African American 13%, Asian 2%, Caucasian 77%, Hispanic 3%. **Retention and Graduation:** 62% freshmen return for sophomore year. 8% grads go on to further study within 2 semesters. 4% grads pursue arts and sciences degrees. 2% grads pursue business degrees. 1% grads pursue law degrees. 1% grads pursue medical degrees. **Faculty:** Student/faculty ratio 16:1. 37 full-time faculty, 27% hold PhDs.

ACADEMICS

Degrees: Associate, bachelor's, certificate, master's. **Academic Requirements:** Arts/fine arts, computer literacy, English (including composition), history, humanities, mathematics, sciences (biological or physical), social science. **Classes:** Most classes have 10–19 students. Most lab/discussion sections have 10–19 students. **Disciplines with Highest Percentage of Degrees Awarded:** Business/marketing 50%, public administration and social services 15%, social sciences 13%, psychology 10%, education 9%. **Special Study Options:** Accelerated program, distance learning, double major, dual enrollment, external degree program, independent study, internships, student-designed major, teacher certification program.

FACILITIES

Housing: Coed dorms, men's dorms, women's dorms. **Computers:** Remote student-access to Web through college's connection.

CAMPUS LIFE

Activities: Choral groups, student government, student newspaper. **Organizations:** 40 registered organizations, 1 honor society, 1 religious organization. 6 fraternities (30% men join), 6 sororities (30% women join). **Athletics (Intercollegiate): Men:** Baseball, basketball, cheerleading, cross-country, football, golf, soccer, softball, tennis, track/field (outdoor), wrestling. **Women:** Basketball, cheerleading, cross-country, golf, soccer, softball, tennis, track/field (outdoor), volleyball.

ADMISSIONS

Freshman Academic Profile: 5% in top 10% of high school class, 18% in top 25% of high school class, 74% in top 50% of high school class. TOEFL required of all international applicants, minimum paper TOEFL 550. **Basis for Candidate Selection:** *Very important factors considered include:* Level of applicant's interest, rigor of secondary school record, standardized test scores. *Important factors considered include:* Academic GPA, character/personal qualities, class rank. *Other factors considered include:* Alumni/ae relation, application essay, extracurricular activities, interview, recommendation(s), talent/ability, volunteer work, work experience. **Freshman Admission Requirements:** High school diploma is required, and GED is accepted. *Academic units recommended:* 4 English, 3 math, 3 science (1 science lab), 2 social studies, 1 history. **Freshman Admission Statistics:** 1,024 applied, 67% admitted, 25% enrolled. **Transfer Admission Requirements:** High school transcript, college transcript(s). Minimum college GPA of 2.0 required. Lowest grade transferable D. **General Admission Information:** Application fee $15. Regular notification is rolling. Non-fall registration accepted. Admission may be deferred for a maximum of 4 semesters. Credit and/or placement offered for CEEB Advanced Placement tests.

COSTS AND FINANCIAL AID

Annual tuition $18,778. Room & board $5,665. Average book expense $1,160. **Required Forms and Deadlines:** FAFSA. Financial aid filing deadline 6/1. **Types of Aid:** *Need-based scholarships/grants:* Pell, SEOG, state scholarships/grants, private scholarships, the school's own gift aid. *Loans:* FFEL Subsidized Stafford, FFEL Unsubsidized Stafford, FFEL PLUS, Federal Perkins. **Student Employment:** Federal Work-Study Program available. Off-campus job opportunities are fair. **Financial Aid Statistics:** 35% undergrads receive need-based scholarship or grant aid. 40% undergrads receive need-based self-help aid. Highest amount earned per year from on-campus jobs $675.

URBANA UNIVERSITY

579 College Way, Urbana, OH 43078-2091
Phone: 937-484-1356 **E-mail:** admiss@urbana.edu
Fax: 937-484-1389 **Website:** www.urbana.edu **ACT Code:** 3346
Financial Aid Phone: 937-484-1355

This private school was founded in 1850. It has a 128-acre campus.

RATINGS

Admissions Selectivity Rating: 66   **Fire Safety Rating:** 60*   **Green Rating:** 60*

STUDENTS AND FACULTY

Enrollment: 1,221. **Student Body:** 55% female, 45% male, 4% out-of-state. **Faculty:** 100% faculty teach undergrads.

ACADEMICS

Degrees: Associate, bachelor's, master's, post-bachelor's certificate. **Academic Requirements:** Arts/fine arts, computer literacy, English (including composition), history, humanities, mathematics, philosophy, sciences (biological or physical), social science. **Special Study Options:** Accelerated program, cooperative education program, cross registration, honors program, independent study, internships, teacher certification program.

FACILITIES

Housing: Men's dorms, women's dorms, apartments for single students. **Special Academic Facilities/Equipment:** Johnny Appleseed Museum, Barclay Hall, Bailey Hall, Lewis and Jean Moore Math/Science Center. **Computers:** 100% of public computers are PCs.

CAMPUS LIFE

Activities: Choral groups, drama/theater, pep band, student government, student newspaper. **Organizations:** 37 honor societies, 11 religious organization. **Athletics (Intercollegiate): Men:** Baseball, basketball, football, golf, soccer. **Women:** Basketball, cheerleading, soccer, softball, volleyball.

ADMISSIONS

Freshman Academic Profile: 8% in top 10% of high school class, 23% in top 25% of high school class, 35% in top 50% of high school class. ACT middle 50% range 17–21. TOEFL required of all international applicants, minimum paper TOEFL 500. **Basis for Candidate Selection:** *Very important factors considered include:* Rigor of secondary school record, standardized test scores. *Important factors considered include:* Application essay, extracurricular activities. *Other factors considered include:* Alumni/ae relation, character/personal qualities, class rank, interview, racial/ethnic status, recommendation(s), talent/ability, volunteer work, work experience. **Freshman Admission Requirements:** High school diploma is required, and GED is accepted. *Academic units required:* 4 English, 2 math, 2 science, 2 social studies. *Academic units recommended:* 2 academic electives. **Freshman Admission Statistics:** 520 applied, 57% admitted, 62% enrolled. **Transfer Admission Requirements:** High school transcript, college transcript(s), essay or personal statement. Minimum college GPA of 2.0 required. Lowest grade transferable C. **General Admission Information:** Application fee $25. Regular notification as admissions files are completed. Non-fall registration accepted. Admission may be deferred for a maximum of 1 semester. Common Application not accepted.

COSTS AND FINANCIAL AID

Annual tuition $11,862. Room & board $5,000. Required fees $200. Average book expense $500. **Required Forms and Deadlines:** FAFSA, institution's own financial aid form. **Types of Aid:** *Need-based scholarships/grants:* Pell, SEOG, state scholarships/grants, private scholarships, the school's own gift aid, Phi Theta Kappa Scholarship. *Loans:* Direct Subsidized Stafford, Direct Unsubsidized Stafford, Direct PLUS, Federal Perkins. **Student Employment:** Federal Work-Study Program available. Institutional employment available. Off-campus job opportunities are good. **Financial Aid Statistics:** Highest amount earned per year from on-campus jobs $1,000.

URSINUS COLLEGE

Ursinus College, Admissions Office, Collegeville, PA 19426
Phone: 610-409-3200 **E-mail:** admissions@ursinus.edu **CEEB Code:** 2931
Fax: 610-409-3662 **Website:** www.ursinus.edu **ACT Code:** 3738
Financial Aid Phone: 610-409-3600

This private school was founded in 1869. It has a 170-acre campus.

RATINGS

Admissions Selectivity Rating: 89   **Fire Safety Rating:** 89   **Green Rating:** 91

STUDENTS AND FACULTY

Enrollment: 1,565. **Student Body:** 52% female, 48% male, 38% out-of-state, 1% international (24 countries represented). African American 7%, Asian 4%, Caucasian 75%, Hispanic 3%. **Retention and Graduation:** 92% freshmen return for sophomore year. 76% freshmen graduate within 4 years. 34% grads go on to further study within 2 semesters. 16% grads pursue arts and sciences degrees. 2% grads pursue business degrees. 3% grads pursue law degrees. 10% grads pursue medical degrees. **Faculty:** Student/faculty ratio 12:1. 120 full-time faculty, 92% hold PhDs. 100% faculty teach undergrads.

ACADEMICS

Degrees: Bachelor's. **Academic Requirements:** Arts/fine arts, Common Intellectual Experience, diversity (within U.S. and abroad), foreign languages, humanities, mathematics, sciences (biological or physical), social science. **Classes:** Most classes have fewer than 10 students. Most lab/discussion sections have 10–19 students. **Majors with Highest Enrollment:** Biology/biological sciences, economics, psychology. **Disciplines with Highest Percentage of Degrees Awarded:** Social sciences 26%, biological/life sciences 14%, psychology 13%, parks and recreation 9%, English 8%. **Special Study Options:** Double major, dual enrollment, exchange student program (domestic), honors program, Howard University semester, independent study, internships, student-designed major, study abroad, teacher certification program.

FACILITIES

Housing: Coed dorms, men's dorms, women's dorms, special housing for international students, cluster of 25 restored Victorian-era houses, theme houses (Musser International, unity, wellness, language, biology). **Special**

Academic Facilities/Equipment: The Kaleidoscope (performing arts center), new field house, new 143-bed dormitory, Berman Museum of Art, 6 new telescopes, scanning electron microscope, Bruker 300 MHz NMR, Perkin Elmer Spectrum 1000 FTIR, LKB isothermal calorimeter, an assortment of spectrometers, an HPLC, recently-renovated Pfahler Hall of Science. **Computers:** 100% of classrooms are wired, 20% of classrooms are wireless, 99% of public computers are PCs, 1% of public computers are Macs, network access in dorm rooms, network access in dorm lounges, online registration, online administrative functions (other than registration), remote student-access to Web through college's connection, tuition includes personal computer. Undergraduates are required to own a computer.

CAMPUS LIFE

Activities: Choral groups, concert band, dance, drama/theater, jazz band, literary magazine, music ensembles, musical theater, pep band, radio station, student government, student newspaper, student-run film society, television station, yearbook. **Organizations:** 88 registered organizations, 27 honor societies, 4 religious organizations. 7 fraternities (17% men join), 7 sororities (28% women join). **Athletics (Intercollegiate):** *Men:* Baseball, basketball, cross-country, football, golf, lacrosse, soccer, swimming, tennis, track/field (indoor), track/field (outdoor), wrestling. *Women:* Basketball, cross-country, field hockey, golf, gymnastics, lacrosse, soccer, softball, swimming, tennis, track/field (indoor), track/field (outdoor), volleyball. **Environmental Initiatives:** Establishment of an Environmental Studies Program that requires public service of its students, who in turn develop problem solving skills in sustainability and conservation through course and extracurricular work. Active participation in Focus the Nation, including four days of programming in 2008. Energy efficiency study and implementation: Ursinus College has established an independent, annual budget to fund energy efficiency initiatives.

ADMISSIONS

Freshman Academic Profile: 47% in top 10% of high school class, 75% in top 25% of high school class, 93% in top 50% of high school class. 61% from public high schools. SAT Math middle 50% range 560–660. SAT Critical Reading middle 50% range 550–660. SAT Writing middle 50% range 550–660. ACT middle 50% range 22–29. TOEFL required of all international applicants, minimum paper TOEFL 500, minimum computer TOEFL 173. **Basis for Candidate Selection:** *Very important factors considered include:* Class rank, extracurricular activities, rigor of secondary school record. *Important factors considered include:* Academic GPA, alumni/ae relation, application essay, racial/ethnic status, recommendation(s), standardized test scores, talent/ability, volunteer work, work experience. *Other factors considered include:* Character/personal qualities, first generation, geographical residence, interview, level of applicant's interest. **Freshman Admission Requirements:** High school diploma is required, and GED is not accepted. *Academic units required:* 4 English, 3 math, 1 science (1 science lab), 2 foreign language, 1 social studies, 5 academic electives. *Academic units recommended:* 4 math, 3 science, 4 foreign language, 3 social studies. **Freshman Admission Statistics:** 4,408 applied, 47% admitted, 20% enrolled. **Transfer Admission Requirements:** High school transcript, college transcript(s), essay or personal statement. Minimum college GPA of 3.0 required. Lowest grade transferable C. **General Admission Information:** Application fee $50. Early decision application deadline 1/15. Regular application deadline 2/15. Regular notification 4/15. Non-fall registration accepted. Admission may be deferred for a maximum of 2 semesters. Credit and/or placement offered for CEEB Advanced Placement tests.

COSTS AND FINANCIAL AID

Annual tuition $36,750. Room and board $8,800. Required fees $160. Average book expense $1,000. **Required Forms and Deadlines:** FAFSA, institution's own financial aid form, CSS/Financial Aid PROFILE. Financial aid filing deadline 2/15. **Notification of Awards:** Applicants will be notified of awards on or about 3/15. **Types of Aid:** *Need-based scholarships/grants:* Pell, SEOG, state scholarships/grants, private scholarships, the school's own gift aid. *Loans:* FFEL Subsidized Stafford, FFEL Unsubsidized Stafford, FFEL PLUS, Federal Perkins, college/university loans from institutional funds, Ursinus Gate First Marblehead Loans. **Student Employment:** Federal Work-Study Program available. Institutional employment available. Off-campus job opportunities are excellent. **Financial Aid Statistics:** 78% freshmen, 80% undergrads receive need-based scholarship or grant aid. 78% freshmen, 80% undergrads receive need-based self-help aid. 78% freshmen, 80% undergrads receive any aid. Highest amount earned per year from on-campus jobs $1,200.

See page 1480.

URSULINE COLLEGE

2550 Lander Road, Pepper Pike, OH 44124-4398
Phone: 440-449-4203 **E-mail:** admission@ursuline.edu **CEEB Code:** 1848
Fax: 440-684-6138 **Website:** www.ursuline.edu
Financial Aid Phone: 440-646-8309

This private school, affiliated with the Roman Catholic Church, was founded in 1871. It has a 110-acre campus.

RATINGS

Admissions Selectivity Rating: 73   **Fire Safety Rating:** 84   **Green Rating:** 63

STUDENTS AND FACULTY

Enrollment: 1,159. **Student Body:** 93% female, 7% male, 5% out-of-state. African American 26%, Asian 1%, Caucasian 68%, Hispanic 2%. **Retention and Graduation:** 74% freshmen return for sophomore year. 27% freshmen graduate within 4 years. **Faculty:** Student/faculty ratio 10:1. 72 full-time faculty, 65% hold PhDs. 80% faculty teach undergrads.

ACADEMICS

Degrees: Bachelor's, certificate, master's, post-bachelor's certificate, post-master's certificate. **Academic Requirements:** Arts/fine arts, humanities, mathematics, philosophy, religious studies, sciences (biological or physical), social science, Ursuline studies. **Classes:** Most classes have 10–19 students. Most lab/discussion sections have 10–19 students. **Majors with Highest Enrollment:** Early childhood education and teaching, nursing/registered nurse training (ASN, BSN, MSN, RN), psychology. **Disciplines with Highest Percentage of Degrees Awarded:** Health professions and related sciences 37%, business/marketing 22%, education 10%, visual and performing arts 6%, interdisciplinary studies 4%. **Special Study Options:** Accelerated program, cooperative education program, cross registration, distance learning, double major, independent study, internships, teacher certification program.

FACILITIES

Housing: Coed dorms, women's dorms. **Special Academic Facilities/ Equipment:** Fritsche Gallery (art), fitness center, swimming pool. **Computers:** 100% of classrooms are wired, 25% of classrooms are wireless, 97% of public computers are PCs, 3% of public computers are Macs, network access in dorm rooms, network access in dorm lounges, remote student-access to Web through college's connection.

CAMPUS LIFE

Activities: Choral groups, drama/theater, literary magazine, student government. **Organizations:** 21 registered organizations, 4 honor societies. **Athletics (Intercollegiate):** *Women:* Basketball, cross-country, golf, soccer, softball, tennis, track/field (outdoor), volleyball.

ADMISSIONS

Freshman Academic Profile: 27% in top 10% of high school class, 44% in top 25% of high school class, 82% in top 50% of high school class. 76% from public high schools. SAT Math middle 50% range 450–550. SAT Critical Reading middle 50% range 44–560. ACT middle 50% range 19–23. TOEFL required of all international applicants, minimum paper TOEFL 500, minimum computer TOEFL 173. **Basis for Candidate Selection:** *Very important factors considered include:* Academic GPA, standardized test scores. *Important factors considered include:* Application essay, recommendation(s). *Other factors considered include:* Alumni/ae relation, class rank, interview, rigor of secondary school record. **Freshman Admission Requirements:** High school diploma is required, and GED is accepted. *Academic units recommended:* 4 English, 3 math, 3 science (2 science labs), 2 foreign language, 3 social studies, 2 fine/performing arts, 1 physical education/health. **Freshman Admission Statistics:** 302 applied, 92% admitted, 45% enrolled. **Transfer Admission Requirements:** College transcript(s), essay or personal statement. Minimum college GPA of 2.5 required. Lowest grade transferable C. **General Admission Information:** Application fee $25. Regular notification within 3 weeks of completed application. Non-fall registration accepted. Admission may be deferred for a maximum of 2 semesters. Credit and/or placement offered for CEEB Advanced Placement tests.

COSTS AND FINANCIAL AID

Average book expense $1,000. **Required Forms and Deadlines:** FAFSA. Financial aid filing deadline 3/1. **Notification of Awards:** Applicants will be notified of awards on a rolling basis beginning on or about 4/1. **Types of Aid:** *Need-based scholarships/grants:* Pell, SEOG, state scholarships/grants, private scholarships, the school's own gift aid. *Loans:* FFEL Subsidized Stafford, FFEL Unsubsidized Stafford, FFEL PLUS, Federal Perkins, college/university loans from institutional funds. **Financial Aid Statistics:** 90% freshmen, 89%

freshmen, 80% undergrads receive need-based self-help aid. 27 freshmen, 77 undergrads receive athletic scholarships. 90% freshmen, 70% undergrads receive any aid.

UTAH STATE UNIVERSITY

0160 Old Main Hill, Logan, UT 84322-0160
Phone: 435-797-1079 **E-mail:** admit@cc.usu.edu
Fax: 435-797-3708 **Website:** www.usu.edu **ACT Code:** 4276
Financial Aid Phone: 435-797-0173

This public school was founded in 1888. It has a 400-acre campus.

RATINGS
Admissions Selectivity Rating: 72   **Fire Safety Rating:** 60*   **Green Rating:** 60*

STUDENTS AND FACULTY
Enrollment: 12,572. **Student Body:** 48% female, 52% male, 27% out-of-state, 3% international (76 countries represented). Asian 1%, Caucasian 89%, Hispanic 2%. **Retention and Graduation:** 23% grads go on to further study within 2 semesters. 1% grads pursue medical degrees. **Faculty:** Student/faculty ratio 17:1. 692 full-time faculty. 95% faculty teach undergrads.

ACADEMICS
Degrees: Associate, bachelor's, certificate, doctoral, master's, post-bachelor's certificate, post-master's certificate. **Academic Requirements:** American Institutions, arts/fine arts, computer literacy, English (including composition), history, humanities, interdisiplinary courses, mathematics, sciences (biological or physical), social science. **Classes:** Most classes have 20–29 students. Most lab/discussion sections have 10–19 students. **Majors with Highest Enrollment:** Accounting, information science/studies, marketing/marketing management. **Disciplines with Highest Percentage of Degrees Awarded:** Business/marketing 16%, education 13%, engineering 8%, family and consumer sciences 8%, social sciences 7%, visual and performing arts 6%. **Special Study Options:** Accelerated program, cooperative education program, cross registration, distance learning, double major, dual enrollment, English as a second language (ESL), exchange student program (domestic), honors program, independent study, internships, liberal arts/career combination, student-designed major, study abroad, teacher certification program, weekend college.

FACILITIES
Housing: Coed dorms, men's dorms, women's dorms, apartments for married students, apartments for single students, special housing for disabled students, special housing for international students, fraternity/sorority housing, mobile home park. **Special Academic Facilities/Equipment:** Art gallery, agricultural and engineering experiment station, water research lab, wildlife and fishery research unit, on-campus school, intermountain herbarium, electron microscope, space dynamics lab. **Computers:** 8% of classrooms are wired, 25% of classrooms are wireless, 90% of public computers are PCs, 10% of public computers are Macs, network access in dorm rooms, network access in dorm lounges, online registration, online administrative functions (other than registration), remote student-access to Web through college's connection.

CAMPUS LIFE
Activities: Choral groups, concert band, drama/theater, jazz band, marching band, music ensembles, musical theater, opera, pep band, student government, student newspaper, symphony orchestra. **Organizations:** 281 registered organizations, 32 honor societies, 8 religious organizations. 5 fraternities (2% men join), 3 sororities (2% women join). **Athletics (Intercollegiate):** *Men:* Basketball, cross-country, football, golf, tennis, track/field (indoor), track/field (outdoor). *Women:* Basketball, cross-country, gymnastics, soccer, softball, tennis, track/field (indoor), track/field (outdoor), volleyball.

ADMISSIONS
Freshman Academic Profile: 25% in top 10% of high school class, 51% in top 25% of high school class, 81% in top 50% of high school class. SAT Math middle 50% range 490–620. SAT Critical Reading middle 50% range 470–600. ACT middle 50% range 20–27. TOEFL required of all international applicants, minimum paper TOEFL 500, minimum computer TOEFL 173. **Basis for Candidate Selection:** *Very important factors considered include:* Academic GPA, standardized test scores. *Important factors considered include:* Rigor of secondary school record. *Other factors considered include:* Class rank, recommendation(s). **Freshman Admission Requirements:** High school diploma is required, and GED is accepted. *Academic units required:* 4 English, 3 math, 3 science (1 science lab), 1 history, 4 academic electives. *Academic units recommended:* 2 foreign language. **Freshman Admission Statistics:** 5,209 applied, 97% admitted, 51% enrolled. **Transfer Admission Requirements:** College transcript(s). Minimum college GPA of 2.2 required. Lowest grade transferable D. **General Admission Information:** Application fee $40. Regular notification when accepted. Non-fall registration accepted. Credit and/or placement offered for CEEB Advanced Placement tests.

COSTS AND FINANCIAL AID
Required Forms and Deadlines: FAFSA, institution's own financial aid form. **Notification of Awards:** Applicants will be notified of awards on a rolling basis beginning on or about 4/1. **Types of Aid:** *Need-based scholarships/grants:* Pell, SEOG, state scholarships/grants, private scholarships, the school's own gift aid. *Loans:* FFEL Subsidized Stafford, FFEL Unsubsidized Stafford, FFEL PLUS, Federal Perkins, college/university loans from institutional funds. **Financial Aid Statistics:** 22% freshmen, 36% undergrads receive need-based scholarship or grant aid. 18% freshmen, 27% undergrads receive need-based self-help aid. 56 freshmen, 279 undergrads receive athletic scholarships. 61% freshmen, 59% undergrads receive any aid. Highest amount earned per year from on-campus jobs $15,600.

UTICA COLLEGE

1600 Burrstone Road, Utica, NY 13502-4892
Phone: 315-792-3006 **E-mail:** admiss@utica.edu **CEEB Code:** 2932
Fax: 315-792-3003 **Website:** www.utica.edu **ACT Code:** 2932
Financial Aid Phone: 315-792-3179

This private school was founded in 1946. It has a 128-acre campus.

RATINGS
Admissions Selectivity Rating: 72   **Fire Safety Rating:** 79   **Green Rating:** 60*

STUDENTS AND FACULTY
Enrollment: 2,339. **Student Body:** 60% female, 40% male, 16% out-of-state, 1% international (22 countries represented). African American 10%, Asian 2%, Caucasian 64%, Hispanic 3%. **Retention and Graduation:** 66% freshmen return for sophomore year. 31% freshmen graduate within 4 years. 36% grads go on to further study within 2 semesters. 1% grads pursue law degrees. 2% grads pursue medical degrees. **Faculty:** Student/faculty ratio 17:1. 123 full-time faculty. 86% hold PhDs. 100% faculty teach undergrads.

ACADEMICS
Degrees: Bachelor's, first professional, master's, post-bachelor's certificate. **Academic Requirements:** Arts/fine arts, English (including composition), foreign languages, history, humanities, mathematics, philosophy, sciences (biological or physical), social science. **Classes:** Most classes have 10–19 students. Most lab/discussion sections have 10–19 students. **Majors with Highest Enrollment:** Business administration/management, corrections and criminal justice, health services/allied health. **Disciplines with Highest Percentage of Degrees Awarded:** Health professions and related sciences 18%, security and protective services 18%, psychology 15%, business/marketing 15%, communications/journalism 9%, biological/life sciences 6%. **Special Study Options:** Accelerated program, BS health studies/MS OT weekend program, cooperative education program, cross registration, distance learning, double major, dual enrollment, ECI online program for undergraduate transfer students, exchange student program (domestic), honors program, independent study, internships, liberal arts/career combination, study abroad, teacher certification program, weekend college.

FACILITIES
Housing: Coed dorms, apartments for single students, special housing for disabled students, women's floors men's floors. **Special Academic Facilities/Equipment:** Edith Langley Barrett Art Gallery. **Computers:** 100% of classrooms are wireless, 90% of public computers are PCs, 10% of public computers are Macs, network access in dorm rooms, online administrative functions (other than registration), remote student-access to Web through college's connection.

CAMPUS LIFE
Activities: Choral groups, concert band, dance, drama/theater, literary magazine, radio station, student government, student newspaper, student-run film society, yearbook. **Organizations:** 80 registered organizations, 8 honor societies, 4 religious organizations. 5 fraternities (1% men join), 4 sororities (1%

women join). **Athletics (Intercollegiate):** *Men:* Baseball, basketball, cross-country, diving, football, golf, ice hockey, lacrosse, soccer, swimming, tennis. *Women:* Basketball, cross-country, diving, field hockey, ice hockey, lacrosse, soccer, softball, swimming, tennis, volleyball, water polo.

ADMISSIONS

Freshman Academic Profile: 10% in top 10% of high school class, 30% in top 25% of high school class, 65% in top 50% of high school class. SAT Math middle 50% range 430–540. SAT Critical Reading middle 50% range 420–520. SAT Writing middle 50% range 410–510. ACT middle 50% range 18–23. TOEFL required of all international applicants, minimum paper TOEFL 525, minimum computer TOEFL 195. **Basis for Candidate Selection:** *Very important factors considered include:* Academic GPA, rigor of secondary school record. *Important factors considered include:* Application essay, character/personal qualities, extracurricular activities, interview, recommendation(s), talent/ability, volunteer work, work experience. *Other factors considered include:* Alumni/ae relation, class rank, first generation, level of applicant's interest, standardized test scores. **Freshman Admission Requirements:** High school diploma is required, and GED is accepted. *Academic units required:* 4 English, 3 math, 3 science, 2 foreign language, 3 social studies, 1 academic elective. **Freshman Admission Statistics:** 2,335 applied, 77% admitted, 27% enrolled. **Transfer Admission Requirements:** College transcript(s), essay or personal statement. Minimum college GPA of 2.5 required. Lowest grade transferable C. **General Admission Information:** Application fee $40. Regular notification is rolling. Non-fall registration accepted. Admission may be deferred for a maximum of 2 semesters. Credit and/or placement offered for CEEB Advanced Placement tests.

COSTS AND FINANCIAL AID

Annual tuition $22,030. Room & board $9,056. Required fees $310. Average book expense $850. **Required Forms and Deadlines:** FAFSA, state aid form. Financial aid filing deadline 2/15. **Notification of Awards:** Applicants will be notified of awards on a rolling basis beginning on or about 2/1. **Types of Aid:** *Need-based scholarships/grants:* Pell, SEOG, state scholarships/grants, private scholarships, the school's own gift aid, Federal Nursing Scholarships. *Loans:* Direct Subsidized Stafford, Direct Unsubsidized Stafford, Direct PLUS, Federal Perkins, alternative loans. **Financial Aid Statistics:** 91% freshmen, 91% undergrads receive need-based scholarship or grant aid. 89% freshmen, 87% undergrads receive need-based self-help aid. 96% freshmen, 90% undergrads receive any aid. Highest amount earned per year from on-campus jobs $6,141.

VALDOSTA STATE UNIVERSITY

1500 North Patterson Street, Valdosta, GA 31698
Phone: 229-333-5791 **E-mail:** admissions@valdosta.edu **CEEB Code:** 5855
Fax: 229-333-5482 **Website:** www.valdosta.edu **ACT Code:** 0874
Financial Aid Phone: 229-333-5935

This public school was founded in 1906. It has a 178-acre campus.

RATINGS
Admissions Selectivity Rating: 60*   **Fire Safety Rating:** 81   **Green Rating:** 60*

STUDENTS AND FACULTY
Enrollment: 9,401. **Student Body:** 59% female, 41% male, 6% out-of-state, 2% international. African American 23%, Asian 1%, Caucasian 71%, Hispanic 2%. **Retention and Graduation:** 74% freshmen return for sophomore year. 18% freshmen graduate within 4 years. **Faculty:** 438 full-time faculty.

ACADEMICS
Degrees: Associate, bachelor's, doctoral, master's, post-master's certificate. **Academic Requirements:** English (including composition), history, humanities, mathematics, perspectives, sciences (biological or physical), social science. **Classes:** Most classes have 20–29 students. Most lab/discussion sections have 20–29 students. **Majors with Highest Enrollment:** Biology/biological sciences, early childhood education and teaching, nursing/registered nurse training (ASN, BSN, MSN, RN). **Disciplines with Highest Percentage of Degrees Awarded:** Education 24%, business/marketing 19%, health professions and related sciences 9%, English 7%, social sciences 6%. **Special Study Options:** Cooperative education program, distance learning, double major, dual enrollment, English as a second language (ESL), external degree program, honors program, independent study, internships, study abroad, teacher certification program, weekend college.

FACILITIES
Housing: Coed dorms, men's dorms, women's dorms, apartments for married students, apartments for single students, special housing for disabled students,

special housing for international students, wellness floors and honors floors. **Special Academic Facilities/Equipment:** Planetarium, herbarium, art gallery, VSU Archives. **Computers:** 98% of public computers are PCs, 1% of public computers are Macs, 1% of public computers are UNIX, network access in dorm rooms, network access in dorm lounges, online registration, online administrative functions (other than registration), remote student-access to Web through college's connection.

CAMPUS LIFE

Activities: Choral groups, concert band, dance, drama/theater, jazz band, literary magazine, marching band, music ensembles, pep band, radio station, student government, student newspaper, symphony orchestra, television station. **Organizations:** 140 registered organizations, 22 honor societies, 11 religious organizations. 12 fraternities, 10 sororities. **Athletics (Intercollegiate):** *Men:* Baseball, basketball, cross-country, football, golf, tennis. *Women:* Basketball, cheerleading, cross-country, softball, tennis, volleyball.

ADMISSIONS

Freshman Academic Profile: SAT Math middle 50% range 470–560. SAT Critical Reading middle 50% range 480–560. ACT middle 50% range 20–23. TOEFL required of all international applicants, minimum paper TOEFL 523, minimum computer TOEFL 193. **Basis for Candidate Selection:** *Very important factors considered include:* Standardized test scores. *Important factors considered include:* Academic GPA, class rank, rigor of secondary school record. **Freshman Admission Requirements:** High school diploma is required, and GED is not accepted. *Academic units required:* 4 English, 4 math, 3 science (2 science labs), 2 foreign language, 3 social studies. **Freshman Admission Statistics:** 6,281 applied, 61% admitted, 52% enrolled. **Transfer Admission Requirements:** College transcript(s). Minimum college GPA of 2.0 required. Lowest grade transferable D. **General Admission Information:** Application fee $40. Regular application deadline 7/1. Regular notification is rolling. Non-fall registration accepted. Admission may be deferred for a maximum of 4 semesters. Credit and/or placement offered for CEEB Advanced Placement tests.

COSTS AND FINANCIAL AID

Annual in-state tuition $2,536. Out-of-state tuition $10,144. Room & board $5,680. Required fees $930. Average book expense $1,000. **Required Forms and Deadlines:** FAFSA. Financial aid filing deadline 5/1. **Notification of Awards:** Applicants will be notified of awards on a rolling basis beginning on or about 5/15. **Types of Aid:** *Need-based scholarships/grants:* Pell, SEOG, state scholarships/grants, private scholarships, the school's own gift aid, LEAP, ACG, SMART Grant. *Loans:* Direct Subsidized Stafford, Direct Unsubsidized Stafford, Direct PLUS, FFEL Subsidized Stafford, FFEL Unsubsidized Stafford, FFEL PLUS. **Student Employment:** Federal Work-Study Program available. Institutional employment available. Off-campus job opportunities are good. **Financial Aid Statistics:** 47% freshmen, 47% undergrads receive need-based scholarship or grant aid. 45% freshmen, 53% undergrads receive need-based self-help aid. 32 freshmen, 214 undergrads receive athletic scholarships. 99% freshmen, 90% undergrads receive any aid. Highest amount earned per year from on-campus jobs $4,000.

VALLEY CITY STATE UNIVERSITY

101 College Street Southwest, Valley City, ND 58072
Phone: 701-845-7101 **E-mail:** enrollment.services@vcsu.edu
Fax: 701-845-7299 **Website:** www.vcsu.edu **ACT Code:** 3216
Financial Aid Phone: 701-845-7412

This public school was founded in 1890. It has a 55-acre campus.

RATINGS
Admissions Selectivity Rating: 70   **Fire Safety Rating:** 60*   **Green Rating:** 60*

STUDENTS AND FACULTY
Enrollment: 1,013. **Student Body:** 53% female, 47% male, 28% out-of-state, 5% international (7 countries represented). African American 2%, Caucasian 89%, Native American 2%. **Retention and Graduation:** 64% freshmen return for sophomore year. **Faculty:** Student/faculty ratio 18:1. 55 full-time faculty, 36% hold PhDs. 100% faculty teach undergrads.

ACADEMICS
Degrees: Bachelor's, master's. **Academic Requirements:** Arts/fine arts, computer literacy, English (including composition), history, humanities, mathematics, physical education (fitness/wellness), sciences (biological or physical), social science. **Majors with Highest Enrollment:** Computer and information sciences and support services, elementary education and teaching.

Disciplines with Highest Percentage of Degrees Awarded: Education 51%, business/marketing 24%, computer and information sciences 9%, biological/life sciences 3%, interdisciplinary studies 3%, psychology 3%, English 2%, visual and performing arts 2%. **Special Study Options:** Accelerated program, cooperative education program, distance learning, double major, dual enrollment, internships, liberal arts/career combination, student-designed major, teacher certification program.

FACILITIES

Housing: Coed dorms, men's dorms, women's dorms, apartments for married students, special housing for disabled students, fraternity/sorority housing, apartments for students with dependant children. **Special Academic Facilities/Equipment:** Planetarium. **Computers:** Network access in dorm rooms, network access in dorm lounges, online registration, online administrative functions (other than registration), remote student-access to Web through college's connection.

CAMPUS LIFE

Activities: Choral groups, concert band, drama/theater, jazz band, music ensembles, musical theater, pep band, student government, student newspaper, yearbook. **Organizations:** 16 registered organizations, 5 honor societies, 3 religious organizations. 1 fraternity (1% men join), 1 sorority (1% women join). **Athletics (Intercollegiate):** *Men:* Baseball, basketball, football. *Women:* Basketball, cheerleading, softball, volleyball.

ADMISSIONS

Freshman Academic Profile: 6% in top 10% of high school class, 22% in top 25% of high school class, 54% in top 50% of high school class. 98% from public high schools. SAT Math middle 50% range 450–570. SAT Critical Reading middle 50% range 450–580. ACT middle 50% range 18–23. TOEFL required of all international applicants, minimum paper TOEFL 525, minimum computer TOEFL 195. **Basis for Candidate Selection:** *Very important factors considered include:* Rigor of secondary school record. *Other factors considered include:* Class rank, standardized test scores. **Freshman Admission Requirements:** High school diploma is required, and GED is accepted. *Academic units required:* 4 English, 3 math, 3 science (3 science labs), 3 social studies. *Academic units recommended:* 2 foreign language. **Freshman Admission Statistics:** 256 applied, 94% admitted, 73% enrolled. **Transfer Admission Requirements:** College transcript(s), statement of good standing from prior institution(s). Minimum college GPA of 2.0 required. Lowest grade transferable D. **General Admission Information:** Application fee $35. Regular notification As applications arrive. Non-fall registration accepted. Common Application accepted. Neither credit nor placement offered for CEEB Advanced Placement tests.

COSTS AND FINANCIAL AID

Annual in-state tuition $3,536. Out-of-state tuition $9,761. Room & board $4,694. Required fees $1,504. Average book expense $700. **Required Forms and Deadlines:** FAFSA. Financial aid filing deadline 3/15. **Notification of Awards:** Applicants will be notified of awards on a rolling basis beginning on or about 1/15. **Types of Aid:** *Need-based scholarships/grants:* Pell, SEOG, state scholarships/grants. *Loans:* FFEL Subsidized Stafford, FFEL Unsubsidized Stafford, FFEL PLUS, Federal Perkins. **Financial Aid Statistics:** 36% freshmen, 33% undergrads receive need-based scholarship or grant aid. 62% freshmen, 54% undergrads receive need-based self-help aid. 10 freshmen, 43 undergrads receive athletic scholarships. 93% freshmen, 86% undergrads receive any aid.

VALPARAISO UNIVERSITY

Office of Admission, Kretzmann Hall, 1700 Chapel Drive, Valparaiso, IN 46383
Phone: 219-464-5011 **E-mail:** undergrad.admissions@valpo.edu **CEEB Code:** 1874
Fax: 219-464-6898 **Website:** www.valpo.edu **ACT Code:** 1256
Financial Aid Phone: 219-464-5015

This private school, affiliated with the Lutheran Church, was founded in 1859. It has a 310-acre campus.

RATINGS

Admissions Selectivity Rating: 85   **Fire Safety Rating:** 63   **Green Rating:** 80

STUDENTS AND FACULTY

Enrollment: 2,904. **Student Body:** 52% female, 48% male, 64% out-of-state, 2% international (49 countries represented). African American 4%, Asian 2%, Caucasian 85%, Hispanic 3%. **Retention and Graduation:** 81% freshmen return for sophomore year. 64% freshmen graduate within 4 years. 27% grads go on to further study within 2 semesters. 18% grads pursue arts and sciences degrees. 1% grads pursue business degrees. 3% grads pursue law degrees. 2% grads pursue medical degrees. **Faculty:** Student/faculty ratio 12:1. 254 full-time faculty, 88% hold PhDs. 100% faculty teach undergrads.

ACADEMICS

Degrees: Associate, bachelor's, certificate, first professional, master's, post-bachelor's certificate, post-master's certificate. **Academic Requirements:** Arts/fine arts, diversity, English (including composition), foreign languages, history, mathematics, philosophy, sciences (biological or physical), social science, theology. **Classes:** Most classes have 10–19 students. Most lab/discussion sections have 10–19 students. **Majors with Highest Enrollment:** Atmospheric sciences and meteorology, nursing/registered nurse training (ASN, BSN, MSN, RN), psychology. **Disciplines with Highest Percentage of Degrees Awarded:** Business/marketing 15%, education 11%, social sciences 9%, engineering 8%, health professions and related sciences 7%. **Special Study Options:** Accelerated program, cooperative education program, cross registration, distance learning, double major, English as a second language (ESL), exchange student program (domestic), honors program, independent study, internships, liberal arts/career combination, student-designed major, study abroad, teacher certification program.

FACILITIES

Housing: Coed dorms, women's dorms, apartments for single students, fraternity/sorority housing, residence hall for German language students. **Special Academic Facilities/Equipment:** Art museum, galleries, language lab, planetarium, electron microscope, observatory, TV studio, weather station, virtual nursing learning center, VisBox, non-linear video editing, Christopher Center for Learning and Information Resources, doppler radar facility. **Computers:** 10% of classrooms are wired, 45% of classrooms are wireless, 85% of public computers are PCs, 10% of public computers are Macs, 5% of public computers are UNIX, network access in dorm rooms, network access in dorm lounges, online registration, online administrative functions (other than registration), support for handheld computing, remote student-access to Web through college's connection.

CAMPUS LIFE

Activities: Choral groups, concert band, dance, drama/theater, jazz band, literary magazine, music ensembles, musical theater, pep band, radio station, student government, student newspaper, student-run film society, symphony orchestra, yearbook. **Organizations:** 83 registered organizations, 33 honor societies, 10 religious organizations. 9 fraternities (26% men join), 6 sororities (20% women join). **Athletics (Intercollegiate):** *Men:* Baseball, basketball, cross-country, diving, football, soccer, swimming, tennis, track/field (indoor), track/field (outdoor). *Women:* Basketball, cross-country, diving, soccer, softball, swimming, tennis, track/field (indoor), track/field (outdoor), volleyball. **Environmental Initiatives:** New construction and renovation projects in compliance with LEED standards. High level of energy conservation and management. Elimination of cooling towers. Biodegradable water treatment chemicals. Ground tires in asphalt mix. Ground tires in new artificial turf eliminating lawn mowing and chemicals. Mulch from chipped yard waste. Storm water detention on-campus, now adding bioswales. Smaller service vehicles. Fewer service vehicles. Electric service vehicles. In the process of developing fry oil as a biofuel.

ADMISSIONS

Freshman Academic Profile: 35% in top 10% of high school class, 67% in top 25% of high school class, 93% in top 50% of high school class. 80% from public high schools. SAT Math middle 50% range 500–640. SAT Critical Reading middle 50% range 490–610. SAT Writing middle 50% range 480–610. ACT middle 50% range 22–28. TOEFL required of all international applicants, minimum paper TOEFL 550, minimum computer TOEFL 213. **Basis for Candidate Selection:** *Very important factors considered include:* Academic GPA, rigor of secondary school record. *Important factors considered include:* Class rank, extracurricular activities, standardized test scores, talent/ability. *Other factors considered include:* Alumni/ae relation, application essay, character/personal qualities, first generation, interview, level of applicant's interest, racial/ethnic status, recommendation(s), religious affiliation/commitment, volunteer work. **Freshman Admission Requirements:** High school diploma is required, and GED is accepted. *Academic units required:* 4 English, 3 math, 2 science (2 science labs), 3 social studies, 3 academic electives. *Academic units recommended:* 4 English, 4 math, 3 science (3 science labs), 2 foreign language, 3 social studies, 3 academic electives. **Freshman Admission Statistics:** 3,785 applied, 89% admitted, 23% enrolled. **Transfer Admission Requirements:** College transcript(s), essay or personal statement, statement of good standing from prior institution(s). Minimum college GPA of

2.0 required. Lowest grade transferable C-. **General Admission Information:** Application fee $30. Regular application deadline 8/15. Regular notification is rolling. Non-fall registration accepted. Admission may be deferred for a maximum of 2 semesters. Credit and/or placement offered for CEEB Advanced Placement tests.

COSTS AND FINANCIAL AID

Annual tuition $24,360. Room and board $7,150. Required fees $840. Average book expense $1,200. **Required Forms and Deadlines:** FAFSA. Financial aid filing deadline 3/1. **Notification of Awards:** Applicants will be notified of awards on a rolling basis beginning on or about 3/1. **Types of Aid:** *Need-based scholarships/grants:* Pell, SEOG, state scholarships/grants, private scholarships, the school's own gift aid. *Loans:* Direct Subsidized Stafford, Direct Unsubsidized Stafford, Direct PLUS, Federal Perkins, college/university loans from institutional funds. **Student Employment:** Federal Work-Study Program available. Institutional employment available. Off-campus job opportunities are good. **Financial Aid Statistics:** 71% freshmen, 67% undergrads receive need-based scholarship or grant aid. 54% freshmen, 55% undergrads receive need-based self-help aid. 22 freshmen, 86 undergrads receive athletic scholarships. 98% freshmen, 95% undergrads receive any aid. Highest amount earned per year from on-campus jobs $7,430.

VANDERBILT UNIVERSITY

2305 West End Avenue, Nashville, TN 37203
Phone: 615-322-2561 **E-mail:** admissions@vanderbilt.edu **CEEB Code:** 1871
Fax: 615-343-7765 **Website:** www.vanderbilt.edu **ACT Code:** 4036
Financial Aid Phone: 800-288-0204

This private school was founded in 1873. It has a 323-acre campus.

RATINGS
Admissions Selectivity Rating: 98   **Fire Safety Rating:** 60*   **Green Rating:** 79

STUDENTS AND FACULTY
Enrollment: 6,330. **Student Body:** 52% female, 48% male, 83% out-of-state, 2% international (52 countries represented). African American 8%, Asian 6%, Caucasian 67%, Hispanic 5%. **Retention and Graduation:** 96% freshmen return for sophomore year. 83% freshmen graduate within 4 years. 32% grads go on to further study within 1 year. 20% grads pursue arts and sciences degrees. 1% grads pursue business degrees. 7% grads pursue law degrees. 4% grads pursue medical degrees. **Faculty:** Student/faculty ratio 9:1. 818 full-time faculty.

ACADEMICS
Degrees: Bachelor's, doctoral, first professional, master's. **Academic Requirements:** English (including composition), foreign languages, humanities, mathematics, sciences (biological or physical), social science. **Classes:** Most classes have 10–19 students. Most lab/discussion sections have 10–19 students. **Majors with Highest Enrollment:** Engineering science, psychology, sociology. **Disciplines with Highest Percentage of Degrees Awarded:** Engineering 15%, psychology 7%, foreign languages and literature 7%, English 6%, mathematics 4%, history 4%. **Special Study Options:** Accelerated program, cooperative education program, cross-registration, distance learning, double major, dual enrollment, English as a second language (ESL), honor program, independent study, internships, student-designed major, study abroad, teacher certification program.

FACILITIES
Housing: Coed dorms, men's dorms, women's dorms, apartments for married students, apartments for single students, special housing for disabled students, special housing for international students. **Special Academic Facilities/Equipment:** Art galleries, center for research on education and human development, multimedia classrooms, teaching center, observatories, free-electron laser, electron microscope. **Computers:** 65% of public computers are PCs, 35% of public computers are Macs, network access in dorm rooms, network access in dorm lounges, online registration, online administrative functions (other than registration), support for handheld computing, remote student-access to Web through college's connection.

CAMPUS LIFE
Activities: Choral groups, concert band, dance, drama/theater, jazz band, literary magazine, marching band, music ensembles, musical theater, opera, pep band, radio station, student government, student newspaper, student-run film society, symphony orchestra, yearbook. **Organizations:** 329 registered organizations, 20 honor societies, 18 religious organizations. 19 fraternities (34% men join), 12 sororities (50% women join). **Athletics (Intercollegiate):** *Men:* Baseball, basketball, cross-country, football, golf, tennis. *Women:* Basketball, cross-country, golf, lacrosse, soccer, tennis, track/field (outdoor). **Environmental Initiatives:** LEED certification—Vanderbilt was the first university in TN to have any LEED certified buildings. Currently have two LEED-Silver certified residence halls and have applied for several more of new or extensively renovated buildings. Are also a designated "Best Workplaces for Commuters" by the EPA and DOT. Vanderbilt has significantly expanded solid waste recycling programs this past year by hiring a full-time recycling coordinator to direct the activities of 1.5 recycling technicians and a number of part-time students. VU has had a robust e-wast/computer recycling program in place sice 2000 and has recently expanded to include batteries, CFLs, and pallets. Large event recycling is planned for implementation in 2008.

ADMISSIONS
Freshman Academic Profile: 79% in top 10% of high school class, 95% in top 25% of high school class, 99% in top 50% of high school class. 60% from public high schools. SAT Math middle 50% range 650–740. SAT Critical Reading middle 50% range 630–720. SAT Writing middle 50% range 630–710. ACT middle 50% range 28–32. TOEFL required of all international applicants, minimum paper TOEFL 570. **Basis for Candidate Selection:** *Very important factors considered include:* Academic GPA, class rank, extracurricular activities, rigor of secondary school record, standardized test scores. *Important factors considered include:* Application essay, recommendation(s). *Other factors considered include:* Character/personal qualities, first generation, interview, racial/ethnic status, talent/ability, volunteer work, work experience. **Freshman Admission Requirements:** High school diploma is required, and GED is not accepted. *Academic units required:* 4 English, 3 math, 2 science (2 science labs), 2 foreign language, 2 social studies. *Academic units recommended:* 4 English, 4 math, 4 science (4 science labs), 4 foreign language, 4 social studies. **Freshman Admission Statistics:** 12,189 applied, 34% admitted, 39% enrolled. **Transfer Admission Requirements:** High school transcript, college transcript(s), essay or personal statement, standardized test score, statement of good standing from prior institution(s). Lowest grade transferable C. **General Admission Information:** Application fee $50. Early Decision application deadline 11/1. Regular application deadline 1/3. Regular notification 4/1. Nonfall registration not accepted. Admission may be deferred for a maximum of 1 year. Credit and/or placement offered for CEEB Advanced Placement tests.

COSTS AND FINANCIAL AID
Annual tuition $34,414. Average book expense $1,140. **Required Forms and Deadlines:** FAFSA, CSS/Financial Aid PROFILE, Noncustodial PROFILE. Financial aid filing deadline 2/1. **Notification of Awards:** Applicants will be notified of awards on or about 4/1. **Types of Aid:** *Need-based scholarships/grants:* Pell, SEOG, state scholarships/grants, private scholarships, the school's own gift aid. *Loans:* FFEL Subsidized Stafford, FFEL Unsubsidized Stafford, FFEL PLUS, Federal Perkins, Federal Nursing , college/university loans from institutional funds, Undergrad Education Loan. **Student Employment:** Federal Work-Study Program available. Institutional employment available. **Financial Aid Statistics:** 42% freshmen, 38% undergrads receive need-based scholarship or grant aid. 26% freshmen, 26% undergrads receive need-based self-help aid. 32 freshmen, 224 undergrads receive athletic scholarships.

See page 1482.

VANDERCOOK COLLEGE OF MUSIC

3140 South Federal Street, Chicago, IL 60616-3886
Phone: 312-225-6288 **E-mail:** admissions@vandercook.edu **CEEB Code:** 1872
Fax: 312-225-5211 **Website:** www.vandercook.edu **ACT Code:** 1156
Financial Aid Phone: 312-225-6288

This private school was founded in 1909. It has a 1-acre campus.

RATINGS
Admissions Selectivity Rating: 60*   **Fire Safety Rating:** 60*   **Green Rating:** 60*

STUDENTS AND FACULTY
Enrollment: 93. **Student Body:** 48% female, 52% male, 34% out-of-state, 2% international (2 countries represented). African American 15%, Asian 2%,

Caucasian 71%, Hispanic 9%. **Retention and Graduation:** 39% freshmen graduate within 4 years.

ACADEMICS

Degrees: Bachelor's, master's. **Academic Requirements:** Arts/fine arts, computer literacy, education, English (including composition), history, humanities, mathematics, sciences (biological or physical). **Disciplines with Highest Percentage of Degrees Awarded:** Education 100%. **Special Study Options:** Independent study, teacher certification program.

FACILITIES

Housing: Coed dorms, men's dorms, women's dorms, fraternity/sorority housing. **Computers:** 5% of public computers are PCs, 95% of public computers are Macs, remote student-access to Web through college's connection.

CAMPUS LIFE

Activities: Choral groups, concert band, jazz band, music ensembles, musical theater, student newspaper. **Organizations:** 5 registered organizations. 1 fraternity.

ADMISSIONS

Freshman Academic Profile: SAT Math middle 50% range 350–590. SAT Critical Reading middle 50% range 440–670. ACT middle 50% range 16–22. TOEFL required of all international applicants, minimum paper TOEFL 500, minimum computer TOEFL 173. **Basis for Candidate Selection:** *Very important factors considered include:* Interview, talent/ability. *Important factors considered include:* Application essay, extracurricular activities, rigor of secondary school record. *Other factors considered include:* Alumni/ae relation, character/personal qualities, class rank, recommendation(s), standardized test scores, volunteer work, work experience. **Freshman Admission Requirements:** High school diploma is required, and GED is accepted. *Academic units required:* 3 English, 2 math, 2 science, 2 foreign language, 3 social studies, 3 academic electives. **Freshman Admission Statistics:** 43 applied, 91% admitted, 72% enrolled. **Transfer Admission Requirements:** High school transcript, college transcript(s), essay or personal statement, interview, standardized test score. Minimum college GPA of 2.5 required. Lowest grade transferable C. **General Admission Information:** Application fee $35. Regular application deadline 5/1. Non-fall registration accepted. Admission may be deferred on a case by case basis. Common Application not accepted. Credit offered for CEEB Advanced Placement tests.

COSTS AND FINANCIAL AID

Annual tuition $15,130. Room & board $6,900. Required fees $630. Average book expense $1,200. **Required Forms and Deadlines:** FAFSA. **Types of Aid:** *Need-based scholarships/grants:* state scholarships/grants. *Loans:* FFEL Subsidized Stafford, FFEL PLUS.

VANGUARD UNIVERSITY OF
SOUTHERN CALIFORNIA

55 Fair Drive, Costa Mesa, CA 92626
Phone: 714-556-3610 **E-mail:** admissions@vanguard.edu **CEEB Code:** 4701
Fax: 714-966-5471 **Website:** www.vanguard.edu **ACT Code:** 0432
Financial Aid Phone: 714-556-3610

This private school, affiliated with the Assemblies of God Church, was founded in 1920. It has a 38-acre campus.

RATINGS

Admissions Selectivity Rating: 77   **Fire Safety Rating:** 60*   **Green Rating:** 60*

STUDENTS AND FACULTY

Enrollment: 1,847. **Student Body:** 63% female, 37% male, 14% out-of-state. African American 3%, Asian 4%, Caucasian 66%, Hispanic 17%, Native American 1%. **Retention and Graduation:** 76% freshmen return for sophomore year. 37% freshmen graduate within 4 years. **Faculty:** Student/faculty ratio 16:1. 66 full-time faculty, 77% hold PhDs. 100% faculty teach undergrads.

ACADEMICS

Degrees: Bachelor's, master's. **Academic Requirements:** Arts/fine arts, English (including composition), history, mathematics, multicultural, religion, sciences (biological or physical), social science. **Classes:** Most classes have 10–19 students. Most lab/discussion sections have fewer than 10 students. **Majors with Highest Enrollment:** Business administration/management, education, psychology. **Disciplines with Highest Percentage of Degrees Awarded:**

Business/marketing 32%, psychology 16%, social sciences 11%, liberal arts/general studies 7%, theology and religious vocations 7%, visual and performing arts 5%. **Special Study Options:** Accelerated program, cooperative education program, cross registration, double major, dual enrollment, external degree program, independent study, internships, study abroad, teacher certification program.

FACILITIES

Housing: Men's dorms, women's dorms, 1 coed dorm, apartments for married students, apartments for single students, special housing for disabled students. **Special Academic Facilities/Equipment:** Lyceum Theater, computer lab, communications lab. **Computers:** 1% of classrooms are wired, 100% of classrooms are wireless, 90% of public computers are PCs, 10% of public computers are Macs, network access in dorm rooms, network access in dorm lounges, online registration, online administrative functions (other than registration), remote student-access to Web through college's connection.

CAMPUS LIFE

Activities: Choral groups, concert band, dance, drama/theater, jazz band, music ensembles, musical theater, opera, pep band, student government, student newspaper, symphony orchestra, yearbook. **Organizations:** 50 registered organizations, 5 honor societies, 25 religious organizations. **Athletics (Intercollegiate):** *Men:* Baseball, basketball, cross-country, soccer, tennis, track/field (indoor), track/field (outdoor). *Women:* Basketball, cross-country, soccer, softball, tennis, track/field (indoor), track/field (outdoor), volleyball.

ADMISSIONS

Freshman Academic Profile: 22% in top 10% of high school class, 49% in top 25% of high school class, 78% in top 50% of high school class. 73% from public high schools. SAT Math middle 50% range 430–560. SAT Critical Reading middle 50% range 450–570. ACT middle 50% range 19–24. TOEFL required of all international applicants, minimum paper TOEFL 550, minimum computer TOEFL 213. **Basis for Candidate Selection:** *Very important factors considered include:* Academic GPA, application essay, character/personal qualities, recommendation(s), rigor of secondary school record. *Important factors considered include:* Religious affiliation/commitment, standardized test scores. *Other factors considered include:* Extracurricular activities, interview, level of applicant's interest, talent/ability, volunteer work, work experience. **Freshman Admission Requirements:** High school diploma is required, and GED is accepted. *Academic units recommended:* 4 English, 2 math, 2 science, 3 social studies. **Freshman Admission Statistics:** 899 applied, 83% admitted, 53% enrolled. **Transfer Admission Requirements:** College transcript(s), essay or personal statement. Minimum college GPA of 2.0 required. Lowest grade transferable C-. **General Admission Information:** Application fee $45. Regular notification is rolling. Non-fall registration accepted. Credit offered for CEEB Advanced Placement tests.

COSTS AND FINANCIAL AID

Annual tuition $22,466. Room and board $7,270. Required fees $520. Average book expense $1,314. **Required Forms and Deadlines:** FAFSA, state aid form. Financial aid filing deadline 3/2. **Notification of Awards:** Applicants will be notified of awards on a rolling basis beginning on or about 4/1. **Types of Aid:** *Need-based scholarships/grants:* Pell, SEOG, state scholarships/grants, private scholarships, the school's own gift aid. *Loans:* FFEL Subsidized Stafford, FFEL Unsubsidized Stafford, FFEL PLUS, Federal Perkins. **Student Employment:** Federal Work-Study Program available. Institutional employment available. Off-campus job opportunities are excellent. **Financial Aid Statistics:** 54% freshmen, 58% undergrads receive need-based scholarship or grant aid. 54% freshmen, 79% undergrads receive need-based self-help aid. 10 freshmen, 23 undergrads receive athletic scholarships. 94% freshmen, 99% undergrads receive any aid. Highest amount earned per year from on-campus jobs $6,000.

VASSAR COLLEGE

124 Raymond Avenue, Poughkeepsie, NY 12604
Phone: 845-437-7300 **E-mail:** admissions@vassar.edu **CEEB Code:** 2956
Fax: 845-437-7063 **Website:** www.vassar.edu **ACT Code:** 2982
Financial Aid Phone: 845-437-5320

This private school was founded in 1861. It has a 1,000-acre campus.

RATINGS
Admissions Selectivity Rating: 97   **Fire Safety Rating:** 81   **Green Rating:** 60*

STUDENTS AND FACULTY
Enrollment: 2,379. **Student Body:** 60% female, 40% male, 73% out-of-state, 5% international (43 countries represented). African American 5%, Asian 9%, Caucasian 75%, Hispanic 6%. **Retention and Graduation:** 95% freshmen return for sophomore year. 85% freshmen graduate within 4 years. 20% grads go on to further study within 2 semesters. 11% grads pursue arts and sciences degrees. 1% grads pursue business degrees. 2% grads pursue law degrees. 3% grads pursue medical degrees. **Faculty:** Student/faculty ratio 8:1. 281 full-time faculty, 91% hold PhDs. 100% faculty teach undergrads.

ACADEMICS
Degrees: Bachelor's, master's. **Academic Requirements:** 1 communication course, 1 quantitative course, foreign languages, language proficiency. **Classes:** Most classes have 10–19 students. Most lab/discussion sections have 10–19 students. **Majors with Highest Enrollment:** English language and literature, political science and government, psychology. **Disciplines with Highest Percentage of Degrees Awarded:** Social sciences 23%, visual and performing arts 17%, English 11%, psychology 8%, interdisciplinary studies 6%, foreign languages and literature 6%. **Special Study Options:** Cooperative education program, cross registration, double major, exchange student program (domestic), independent study, internships, liberal arts/career combination, student-designed major, study abroad, teacher certification program.

FACILITIES
Housing: Coed dorms, women's dorms, apartments for married students, apartments for single students, special housing for disabled students, special housing for international students, cooperative housing. **Special Academic Facilities/Equipment:** Art center, theaters, nursery school, environmental field station, geology museum, electron microscope, observatory, Skinner Music Hall, fitness center. **Computers:** 98% of classrooms are wired, 100% of classrooms are wireless, 20% of public computers are PCs, 80% of public computers are Macs, 2% of public computers are UNIX, network access in dorm rooms, network access in dorm lounges, online registration, online administrative functions (other than registration), remote student-access to Web through college's connection.

CAMPUS LIFE
Activities: Choral groups, concert band, dance, drama/theater, jazz band, literary magazine, music ensembles, musical theater, opera, radio station, student government, student newspaper, student-run film society, symphony orchestra, television station, yearbook. **Organizations:** 105 registered organizations, 2 honor societies, 11 religious organizations. **Athletics (Intercollegiate):** *Men:* Baseball, basketball, crew/rowing, cross-country, diving, fencing, lacrosse, soccer, squash, swimming, tennis, volleyball. *Women:* Basketball, crew/rowing, cross-country, diving, fencing, field hockey, golf, lacrosse, soccer, squash, swimming, tennis, volleyball.

ADMISSIONS
Freshman Academic Profile: 67% in top 10% of high school class, 93% in top 25% of high school class, 100% in top 50% of high school class. 65% from public high schools. SAT Math middle 50% range 640–710. SAT Critical Reading middle 50% range 660–750. SAT Writing middle 50% range 650–740. ACT middle 50% range 29–32. TOEFL required of all international applicants, minimum paper TOEFL 600, minimum computer TOEFL 250. **Basis for Candidate Selection:** *Very important factors considered include:* Rigor of secondary school record. *Important factors considered include:* Academic GPA, application essay, character/personal qualities, class rank, extracurricular activities, recommendation(s), standardized test scores. *Other factors considered include:* Alumni/ae relation, first generation, geographical residence, interview, level of applicant's interest, racial/ethnic status, talent/ability, volunteer work, work experience. **Freshman Admission Requirements:** High school diploma is required, and GED is accepted. *Academic units required:* 4 English, 4 math, 4 science (3 science labs), 3 foreign language, 2 social studies, 1 history, 4 academic electives. *Academic units recommended:* 4 English, 4 math, 4 science (3 science labs), 4 foreign language, 4 social studies, 2 history. **Freshman Admission Statistics:** 6,075 applied, 30% admitted, 37% enrolled. **Transfer Admission Requirements:** High school transcript, college transcript(s), essay or personal statement, standardized test score, statement of good standing from prior institution(s). Minimum college GPA of 3.3 required. Lowest grade transferable C. **General Admission Information:** Application fee $60. Early decision application deadline 11/15. Regular application deadline 1/1. Regular notification 4/1. Non-fall registration not accepted. Admission may be deferred for a maximum of 2 semesters. Credit and/or placement offered for CEEB Advanced Placement tests.

COSTS AND FINANCIAL AID
Annual tuition $37,570. Room and board $8,570. Required fees $545. Average book expense $860. **Required Forms and Deadlines:** FAFSA, institution's own financial aid form, CSS/Financial Aid PROFILE, state aid form, Noncustodial PROFILE, Business/Farm Supplement. Financial aid filing deadline 2/1. **Notification of Awards:** Applicants will be notified of awards on or about 3/30. **Types of Aid:** *Need-based scholarships/grants:* Pell, SEOG, state scholarships/grants, private scholarships, the school's own gift aid. *Loans:* Federal Perkins, loans for non-citizens with need. **Student Employment:** Federal Work-Study Program available. Institutional employment available. Off-campus job opportunities are fair. **Financial Aid Statistics:** 48% freshmen, 45% undergrads receive need-based scholarship or grant aid. 48% freshmen, 46% undergrads receive need-based self-help aid. 55% freshmen, 55% undergrads receive any aid. Highest amount earned per year from on-campus jobs $4,560.

VAUGHN COLLEGE OF AERONAUTICS AND TECHNOLOGY

86-01 Twenty-third Avenue, Flushing, NY 11369
Phone: 718-429-6600 **E-mail:** admitme@vaughn.edu **CEEB Code:** 2001
Fax: 718-779-2231 **Website:** www.vaughn.edu
Financial Aid Phone: 718-429-6600

This private school was founded in 1932. It has a 6-acre campus.

RATINGS
Admissions Selectivity Rating: 60*   **Fire Safety Rating:** 60*   **Green Rating:** 62

STUDENTS AND FACULTY
Enrollment: 1,076. **Student Body:** 13% female, 87% male, 1% out-of-state, 3% international. African American 20%, Asian 13%, Caucasian 19%, Hispanic 34%. **Retention and Graduation:** 76% freshmen return for sophomore year. 8% freshmen graduate within 4 years. 5% grads pursue business degrees. **Faculty:** Student/faculty ratio 11:1. 41 full-time faculty, 24% hold PhDs.

ACADEMICS
Degrees: Associate, bachelor's, certificate. **Academic Requirements:** Computer literacy, English (including composition), mathematics, sciences (biological or physical). **Classes:** Most classes have 10–19 students. Most lab/discussion sections have 10–19 students. **Majors with Highest Enrollment:** Airframe mechanics and aircraft maintenance technology/technician, business administration/management, electrical/electronics equipment installation and repair. **Special Study Options:** Cooperative education program, distance learning, double major, internships.

FACILITIES
Housing: Coed dorms, assistance provided to find housing. **Computers:** 99% of public computers are PCs, 1% of public computers are Macs.

CAMPUS LIFE
Activities: Student government, student newspaper. **Organizations:** 5 registered organizations. **Athletics (Intercollegiate):** *Men:* Basketball, softball, volleyball. *Women:* Basketball, softball, volleyball.

ADMISSIONS
Freshman Academic Profile: SAT Math middle 50% range 490–590. SAT Critical Reading middle 50% range 470–560. TOEFL required of all international applicants, minimum paper TOEFL 560, minimum computer TOEFL 200. **Basis for Candidate Selection:** *Very important factors considered include:* Rigor of secondary school record, standardized test scores. *Other factors considered include:* Academic GPA, application essay, character/personal qualities, extracurricular activities, first generation, interview, level of

applicant's interest, recommendation(s), talent/ability, volunteer work, work experience. **Freshman Admission Requirements:** High school diploma is required, and GED is accepted. *Academic units required:* 4 English, 3 math, 3 science (3 science labs), 2 foreign language, 2 social studies, 1 history. *Academic units recommended:* 4 English, 3 math, 3 science (3 science labs), 3 foreign language, 3 social studies, 1 history, 3 academic electives. **Freshman Admission Statistics:** 137 applied, 42% admitted, 28% enrolled. **Transfer Admission Requirements:** College transcript(s). Minimum college GPA of 2.0 required. Lowest grade transferable C. **General Admission Information:** Application fee $40. Regular notification is rolling. Non-fall registration accepted. Admission may be deferred for a maximum of 2 semesters. Neither credit nor placement offered for CEEB Advanced Placement tests.

COSTS AND FINANCIAL AID

Annual tuition $7,400. Room & board $10,000. Required fees $280. Average book expense $1,500. **Required Forms and Deadlines:** FAFSA, state aid form. Financial aid filing deadline 1/15. **Notification of Awards:** Applicants will be notified of awards on a rolling basis beginning on or about 4/15. **Types of Aid:** *Need-based scholarships/grants:* Pell, SEOG, state scholarships/grants, private scholarships, the school's own gift aid. *Loans:* FFEL Subsidized Stafford, FFEL Unsubsidized Stafford, FFEL PLUS. **Student Employment:** Federal Work-Study Program available. Institutional employment available. **Financial Aid Statistics:** 77% freshmen, 79% undergrads receive need-based scholarship or grant aid. 77% freshmen, 79% undergrads receive need-based self-help aid. .

See page 1484.

VILLA JULIE COLLEGE

1525 Greenspring Valley Road, Stevenson, MD 21153
Phone: 410-486-7001 **E-mail:** admissions@mail.vjc.edu
Fax: 443-352-4440 **Website:** www.vjc.edu
Financial Aid Phone: 443-334-2559

This private school was founded in 1947. It has a 150-acre campus.

RATINGS

Admissions Selectivity Rating: 78   **Fire Safety Rating:** 60*   **Green Rating:** 60*

STUDENTS AND FACULTY

Enrollment: 2,886. **Student Body:** 71% female, 29% male, 5% out-of-state. African American 14%, Asian 3%, Caucasian 72%, Hispanic 1%. **Retention and Graduation:** 82% freshmen return for sophomore year. 52% freshmen graduate within 4 years. 5% grads go on to further study within 2 semesters. 2% grads pursue arts and sciences degrees. 2% grads pursue business degrees. 1% grads pursue law degrees. **Faculty:** Student/faculty ratio 14:1. 105 full-time faculty, 70% hold PhDs. 99% faculty teach undergrads.

ACADEMICS

Degrees: Bachelor's, master's. **Academic Requirements:** Arts/fine arts, computer literacy, English (including composition), history, humanities, mathematics, philosophy, sciences (biological or physical), social science. **Classes:** Most classes have 10–19 students. **Majors with Highest Enrollment:** Business administration and management, legal assistant/paralegal, nursing/registered nurse training (ASN, BSN, MSN, RN). **Disciplines with Highest Percentage of Degrees Awarded:** Business/marketing 26%, health professions and related sciences 22%, education 12%, visual and performing arts 11%, interdisciplinary studies 6%. **Special Study Options:** Accelerated program, cooperative education program, cross registration, distance learning, double major, dual enrollment, honors program, independent study, internships, liberal arts/career combination, student-designed major, study abroad, teacher certification program, weekend college.

FACILITIES

Housing: Apartments for single students, suite style (2 bedrooms share 1 bath). **Special Academic Facilities/Equipment:** Art gallery, theater. **Computers:** 95% of classrooms are wired, 80% of public computers are PCs, 19% of public computers are Macs, 1% of public computers are UNIX, network access in dorm rooms, network access in dorm lounges, online registration, online administrative functions (other than registration), remote student-access to Web through college's connection.

CAMPUS LIFE

Activities: Choral groups, dance, drama/theater, jazz band, literary magazine, music ensembles, pep band, student government, student newspaper, symphony orchestra. **Organizations:** 30 registered organizations, 7 honor societies, 4 religious organizations. 1 sorority (2% women join). **Athletics**

(Intercollegiate): *Men:* Baseball, basketball, cheerleading, cross-country, golf, lacrosse, soccer, tennis, track/field (indoor), volleyball. *Women:* Basketball, cheerleading, cross-country, field hockey, lacrosse, soccer, softball, tennis, track/field (indoor), volleyball.

ADMISSIONS

Freshman Academic Profile: 22% in top 10% of high school class, 50% in top 25% of high school class, 81% in top 50% of high school class. 75% from public high schools. SAT Math middle 50% range 430–550. SAT Critical Reading middle 50% range 450–550. SAT Writing middle 50% range 450–550. ACT middle 50% range 17.5–23.25. TOEFL required of all international applicants, minimum paper TOEFL 550, minimum computer TOEFL 213. **Basis for Candidate Selection:** *Very important factors considered include:* Academic GPA, rigor of secondary school record. *Important factors considered include:* Application essay, extracurricular activities, standardized test scores, talent/ability. *Other factors considered include:* Alumni/ae relation, character/personal qualities, class rank, interview, recommendation(s), volunteer work. **Freshman Admission Requirements:** High school diploma is required, and GED is accepted. *Academic units required:* 4 English, 3 math, 3 science (2 science labs), 2 social studies, 1 history, 4 academic electives. *Academic units recommended:* 4 English, 3 math, 3 science (2 science labs), 2 foreign language, 2 social studies, 1 history, 4 academic electives. **Freshman Admission Statistics:** 2,574 applied, 73% admitted, 34% enrolled. **Transfer Admission Requirements:** College transcript(s), statement of good standing from prior institution(s). Minimum college GPA of 2.5 required. Lowest grade transferable C. **General Admission Information:** Application fee $25. Regular notification is rolling. Non-fall registration accepted. Admission may be deferred for a maximum of 2 semesters. Credit and/or placement offered for CEEB Advanced Placement tests.

COSTS AND FINANCIAL AID

Required Forms and Deadlines: FAFSA. Financial aid filing deadline 2/15. **Notification of Awards:** Applicants will be notified of awards on a rolling basis beginning on or about 3/15. **Types of Aid:** *Need-based scholarships/grants:* Pell, SEOG, state scholarships/grants, private scholarships, the school's own gift aid. *Loans:* FFEL Subsidized Stafford, FFEL Unsubsidized Stafford, FFEL PLUS, Federal Perkins. **Student Employment:** Off-campus job opportunities are excellent. **Financial Aid Statistics:** 59% freshmen, 53% undergrads receive need-based scholarship or grant aid. 37% freshmen, 37% undergrads receive need-based self-help aid. .

VILLA MARIA COLLEGE OF BUFFALO

240 Pine Ridge Road, Buffalo, NY 14225
Phone: 716-961-1805 **E-mail:** admissions@villa.edu
Fax: 716-896-0705 **Website:** www.villa.edu **ACT Code:** 2983
Financial Aid Phone: 716-961-1850

This private school, affiliated with the Roman Catholic Church, was founded in 1960. It has a 9-acre campus.

RATINGS

Admissions Selectivity Rating: 61   **Fire Safety Rating:** 60*   **Green Rating:** 60*

STUDENTS AND FACULTY

Enrollment: 505. **Student Body:** 70% female, 30% male. African American 26%, Caucasian 69%, Hispanic 3%. **Retention and Graduation:** 69% freshmen return for sophomore year. **Faculty:** Student/faculty ratio 10:1. 29 full-time faculty, 31% hold PhDs. 100% faculty teach undergrads.

ACADEMICS

Degrees: Associate, bachelor's. **Academic Requirements:** Arts/fine arts, computer literacy, English (including composition), foreign languages, history, mathematics, philosophy, sciences (biological or physical), social science. **Classes:** Most classes have fewer than 10 students. Most lab/discussion sections have 10–19 students. **Majors with Highest Enrollment:** Business administration/management, interior design, music management and merchandising. **Special Study Options:** Cooperative education program, cross registration, double major, dual enrollment, internships, liberal arts/career combination, study abroad, evening modules for adult students.

FACILITIES

Special Academic Facilities/Equipment: Art gallery, music building, recording studio, student center. **Computers:** 80% of classrooms are wired, 10% of classrooms are wireless, 60% of public computers are PCs, 40% of public computers are Macs, online administrative functions (other than registration), remote student-access to Web through college's connection.

CAMPUS LIFE

Activities: Choral groups, jazz band, literary magazine, music ensembles, student government, student newspaper. **Organizations:** 10 registered organizations, 1 honor society, 1 religious organization.

ADMISSIONS

Freshman Academic Profile: 2% in top 10% of high school class, 10% in top 25% of high school class, 32% in top 50% of high school class. 85% from public high schools. SAT Math middle 50% range 410–490. SAT Critical Reading middle 50% range 380–520. TOEFL required of all international applicants, minimum paper TOEFL 450, minimum computer TOEFL 133. **Basis for Candidate Selection:** *Very important factors considered include:* Interview. *Important factors considered include:* Rigor of secondary school record. *Other factors considered include:* Academic GPA, alumni/ae relation, application essay, character/personal qualities, class rank, extracurricular activities, level of applicant's interest, recommendation(s), standardized test scores, talent/ability, volunteer work, work experience. **Freshman Admission Requirements:** High school diploma is required, and GED is accepted. *Academic units required:* 4 English, 1 math, 1 science, 2 social studies. *Academic units recommended:* 4 English, 2 math, 2 science, 4 social studies. **Freshman Admission Statistics:** 491 applied, 77% admitted, 40% enrolled. **Transfer Admission Requirements:** College transcript(s), interview. Lowest grade transferable C. **General Admission Information:** Regular notification rolling. Non-fall registration accepted. Admission may be deferred for a maximum of 2 semesters.

COSTS AND FINANCIAL AID

Annual tuition $13,500. Required fees $490. **Required Forms and Deadlines:** FAFSA. Financial aid filing deadline 4/1. **Notification of Awards:** Applicants will be notified of awards on a rolling basis beginning on or about 5/1. **Types of Aid:** *Need-based scholarships/grants:* Pell, SEOG, state scholarships/grants, private scholarships, the school's own gift aid. **Student Employment:** Off-campus job opportunities are fair. **Financial Aid Statistics:** 74% freshmen, 54% undergrads receive need-based scholarship or grant aid. 21% freshmen, 17% undergrads receive need-based self-help aid. 93% freshmen, 70% undergrads receive any aid. .

VILLANOVA UNIVERSITY

Best 368

800 Lancaster Avenue, Villanova, PA 19085-1672
Phone: 610-519-4000 **E-mail:** gotovu@villanova.edu **CEEB Code:** 2959
Fax: 610-519-6450 **Website:** www.villanova.edu **ACT Code:** 3744
Financial Aid Phone: 610-519-4010

This private school, affiliated with the Roman Catholic Church, was founded in 1842. It has a 254-acre campus. ⚬

RATINGS

Admissions Selectivity Rating: 95　　**Fire Safety Rating:** 89　　**Green Rating:** 81

STUDENTS AND FACULTY

Enrollment: 6,877. **Student Body:** 51% female, 49% male, 67% out-of-state, 2% international (32 countries represented). African American 4%, Asian 7%, Caucasian 79%, Hispanic 6%. **Retention and Graduation:** 95% freshmen return for sophomore year. 82% freshmen graduate within 4 years. 28% grads go on to further study within 2 semesters. 10% grads pursue arts and sciences degrees. 2% grads pursue business degrees. 6% grads pursue law degrees. 3% grads pursue medical degrees. **Faculty:** Student/faculty ratio 12:1. 549 full-time faculty, 89% hold PhDs. 100% faculty teach undergrads.

ACADEMICS

Degrees: Associate, bachelor's, doctoral, first professional, master's, post-bachelor's certificate, post-master's certificate. **Academic Requirements:** Computer literacy, English (including composition), foreign languages, history, humanities, mathematics, philosophy, sciences (biological or physical), social science. **Classes:** Most classes have 10–19 students. Most lab/discussion sections have 10–19 students. **Majors with Highest Enrollment:** Biological and physical sciences, finance, nursing/registered nurse training (ASN, BSN, MSN, RN). **Disciplines with Highest Percentage of Degrees Awarded:** Business/marketing 33%, social sciences 11%, engineering 11%, health professions and related sciences 11%, communications/journalism 9%, English

5%, biological/life sciences 5%. **Special Study Options:** Accelerated program, cooperative education program, cross registration, distance learning, double major, dual enrollment, English as a second language (ESL), exchange student program (domestic), honors program, independent study, internships, study abroad, teacher certification program.

FACILITIES

Housing: Coed dorms, men's dorms, women's dorms, apartments for single students, special housing for disabled students. **Special Academic Facilities/Equipment:** Augustinian Historical Museum, two observatories, art gallery, center for instructional technologies, math-learning resource center, writing center. **Computers:** 23% of classrooms are wired, 100% of classrooms are wireless, 92% of public computers are PCs, 3% of public computers are Macs, 5% of public computers are UNIX, network access in dorm rooms, network access in dorm lounges, online registration, online administrative functions (other than registration), support for handheld computing, remote student-access to Web through college's connection, tuition includes personal computer. Undergraduates are required to own a computer.

CAMPUS LIFE

Activities: Choral groups, dance, drama/theater, jazz band, literary magazine, music ensembles, musical theater, pep band, radio station, student government, student newspaper, student-run film society, television station, yearbook. **Organizations:** 300 registered organizations, 31 honor society, 23 religious organizations. 9 fraternities (11% men join), 9 sororities (31% women join). **Athletics (Intercollegiate):** *Men:* Baseball, basketball, cheerleading, cross-country, diving, football, golf, lacrosse, soccer, swimming, tennis, track/field (indoor), track/field (outdoor), volleyball. *Women:* Basketball, cheerleading, crew/rowing, cross-country, diving, field hockey, lacrosse, soccer, softball, swimming, tennis, track/field (indoor), track/field (outdoor), volleyball, water polo. **Environmental Initiatives:** Signed of the ACUPCC President's Climate Commitment. Designing and building the University's two newest buildings to achieve LEED Certification. Composting initiative in dining halls.

ADMISSIONS

Freshman Academic Profile: 51% in top 10% of high school class, 88% in top 25% of high school class, 97% in top 50% of high school class. 55% from public high schools. SAT Math middle 50% range 610–700. SAT Critical Reading middle 50% range 580–680. SAT Writing middle 50% range 590–680. ACT middle 50% range 27–31. TOEFL required of all international applicants, minimum paper TOEFL 550, minimum computer TOEFL 213. **Basis for Candidate Selection:** *Very important factors considered include:* Academic GPA, class rank, rigor of secondary school record, standardized test scores. *Important factors considered include:* Application essay, character/personal qualities, extracurricular activities, recommendation(s), talent/ability, volunteer work, work experience. *Other factors considered include:* Alumni/ae relation, first generation, geographical residence, level of applicant's interest, racial/ethnic status, state residency. **Freshman Admission Requirements:** High school diploma is required, and GED is accepted. *Academic units required:* 4 English, 4 math, 4 science (2 science labs), 2 foreign language, 2 academic electives. *Academic units recommended:* 4 English, 4 math, 4 science (3 science labs), 4 foreign language, 2 academic electives. **Freshman Admission Statistics:** 12,913 applied, 43% admitted, 30% enrolled. **Transfer Admission Requirements:** High school transcript, college transcript(s), essay or personal statement, standardized test score, statement of good standing from prior institution(s). Lowest grade transferable C. **General Admission Information:** Application fee $70. Regular application deadline 1/7. Regular notification 4/1. Non-fall registration not accepted. Admission may be deferred for a maximum of 2 semesters. Credit and/or placement offered for CEEB Advanced Placement tests.

COSTS AND FINANCIAL AID

Annual tuition $31,643. Room and board $9,810. Required fees $300. Average book expense $950. **Required Forms and Deadlines:** FAFSA, institution's own financial aid form. Financial aid filing deadline 2/7. **Notification of Awards:** Applicants will be notified of awards on or about 4/1. **Types of Aid:** *Need-based scholarships/grants:* Pell, SEOG, state scholarships/grants, private scholarships, the school's own gift aid. *Loans:* FFEL Subsidized Stafford, FFEL Unsubsidized Stafford, FFEL PLUS, Federal Perkins, Federal Nursing. **Student Employment:** Federal Work-Study Program available. Institutional employment available. Off-campus job opportunities are excellent. **Financial Aid Statistics:** 44% freshmen, 39% undergrads receive need-based scholarship or grant aid. 46% freshmen, 40% undergrads receive need-based self-help aid. 40 freshmen, 170 undergrads receive athletic scholarships. 68% freshmen, 63% undergrads receive any aid. Highest amount earned per year from on-campus jobs $24,250. .

VIRGINIA COMMONWEALTH UNIVERSITY

821 West Franklin Street, PO Box 842526, Richmond, VA 23284
Phone: 804-828-1222 **E-mail:** upgrad@vcu.edu **CEEB Code:** 5570
Fax: 804-828-1899 **Website:** www.vcu.edu
Financial Aid Phone: 804-828-6669

This public school was founded in 1838. It has a 141-acre campus.

RATINGS
Admissions Selectivity Rating: 77 **Fire Safety Rating:** 82 **Green Rating:** 60*

STUDENTS AND FACULTY
Enrollment: 19,497. **Student Body:** 59% female, 41% male, 7% out-of-state, 3% international (107 countries represented). African American 20%, Asian 10%, Caucasian 57%, Hispanic 4%. **Retention and Graduation:** 82% freshmen return for sophomore year. **Faculty:** Student/faculty ratio 18:1. 1,787 full-time faculty, 78% hold PhDs.

ACADEMICS
Degrees: Bachelor's, certificate, doctoral, first professional certificate, first professional, master's, post-bachelor's certificate, post-master's certificate. **Academic Requirements:** Arts/fine arts, computer literacy, English (including composition), history, humanities, mathematics, philosophy, sciences (biological or physical), social science. **Classes:** Most classes have 10–19 students. Most lab/discussion sections have 10–19 students. **Majors with Highest Enrollment:** Biology/biological sciences, mass communications/media studies, psychology. **Disciplines with Highest Percentage of Degrees Awarded:** Visual and performing arts 17%, business/marketing 15%, psychology 10%, health professions and related sciences 10%, security and protective services 7%. **Special Study Options:** Accelerated program, distance learning, double major, dual enrollment, English as a second language (ESL), honors program, independent study, internships, student-designed major, study abroad, teacher certification program.

FACILITIES
Housing: Coed dorms, apartments for single students, special housing for disabled students, special housing for international students. **Special Academic Facilities/Equipment:** Anderson Gallery, student art gallery, Larrick Student Center, Shafer Court dining facilities, student commons, Siegel Center, Cabell Library, biotech research buildings, Tompkins McCaw Library, VCU bookstores. **Computers:** 1% of classrooms are wired, 2% of classrooms are wireless, 90% of public computers are PCs, 8% of public computers are Macs, 2% of public computers are UNIX, network access in dorm rooms, network access in dorm lounges, online registration, online administrative functions (other than registration), remote student-access to Web through college's connection.undergraduates are required to own a computer.

CAMPUS LIFE
Activities: Choral groups, concert band, dance, drama/theater, jazz band, literary magazine, marching band, music ensembles, opera, pep band, radio station, student government, student newspaper, symphony orchestra, yearbook. **Organizations:** 226 registered organizations, 87 honor societies, 24 religious organizations. 10 fraternities (3% men join), 10 sororities (3% women join). **Athletics (Intercollegiate):** *Men:* Baseball, basketball, cheerleading, cross-country, golf, soccer, tennis, track/field (outdoor). *Women:* Basketball, cheerleading, cross-country, field hockey, soccer, tennis, track/field (outdoor), volleyball.

ADMISSIONS
Freshman Academic Profile: 15% in top 10% of high school class, 42% in top 25% of high school class, 83% in top 50% of high school class. SAT Math middle 50% range 480–580. SAT Critical Reading middle 50% range 480–590. SAT Writing middle 50% range 460–570. ACT middle 50% range 19–24. TOEFL required of all international applicants, minimum paper TOEFL 550, minimum computer TOEFL 213. **Basis for Candidate Selection:** *Very important factors considered include:* Academic GPA, rigor of secondary school record. *Important factors considered include:* Standardized test scores, talent/ability. *Other factors considered include:* Application essay, class rank, extracurricular activities, first generation, interview, recommendation(s), volunteer work, work experience. **Freshman Admission Requirements:** High school diploma is required, and GED is accepted. *Academic units required:* 4 English, 3 math, 2 science (1 science lab), 2 foreign language, 1 social studies, 2 history, 5 academic electives. *Academic units recommended:* 4 English, 4 math, 4 science (1 science lab), 3 foreign language, 1 social studies, 3 history, 4 academic electives. **Freshman Admission Statistics:** 13,155 applied, 66% admitted, 41% enrolled. **Transfer Admission Requirements:** College transcript(s). Minimum college GPA of 2.2 required. Lowest grade transferable C. **General**

Admission Information: Application fee $30. Regular notification is rolling. Non-fall registration accepted. Admission may be deferred for a maximum of 2 semesters. Credit offered for CEEB Advanced Placement tests.

COSTS AND FINANCIAL AID
Required Forms and Deadlines: FAFSA. Financial aid filing deadline 3/1. **Notification of Awards:** Applicants will be notified of awards on or about 3/15. **Types of Aid:** *Need-based scholarships/grants:* Pell, SEOG, state scholarships/grants, private scholarships, the school's own gift aid, Federal Nursing Scholarships. *Loans:* Direct Subsidized Stafford, Direct Unsubsidized Stafford, Direct PLUS, Federal Perkins, Federal Nursing, college/university loans from institutional funds. **Student Employment:** Federal Work-Study Program available. Institutional employment available. Off-campus job opportunities are good. **Financial Aid Statistics:** 32% freshmen, 32% undergrads receive need-based scholarship or grant aid. 33% freshmen, 38% undergrads receive need-based self-help aid. 28 freshmen, 165 undergrads receive athletic scholarships. 68% freshmen, 61% undergrads receive any aid. .

VIRGINIA INTERMONT COLLEGE

1013 Moore Street, Bristol, VA 24201-4298
Phone: 276-466-7856 **E-mail:** viadmit@vic.edu **CEEB Code:** 5857
Fax: 276-466-7855 **Website:** www.vic.edu **ACT Code:** 4416
Financial Aid Phone: 276-466-7872

This private school, affiliated with the Baptist Church, was founded in 1884. It has a 27-acre campus.

RATINGS
Admissions Selectivity Rating: 76 **Fire Safety Rating:** 80 **Green Rating:** 60*

STUDENTS AND FACULTY
Enrollment: 885. **Student Body:** 69% female, 31% male, 68% out-of-state, 8% international. African American 7%, Caucasian 78%, Hispanic 2%. **Retention and Graduation:** 74% freshmen return for sophomore year. 10% grads go on to further study within 2 semesters. 3% grads pursue arts and sciences degrees. 2% grads pursue business degrees. 1% grads pursue law degrees. 1% grads pursue medical degrees. **Faculty:** Student/faculty ratio 12:1. 44 full-time faculty, 61% hold PhDs. 100% faculty teach undergrads.

ACADEMICS
Degrees: Associate, bachelor's. **Academic Requirements:** Arts/fine arts, computer literacy, English (including composition), history, humanities, mathematics, philosophy, physical education, sciences (biological or physical), social science. **Classes:** Most classes have fewer than 10 students. Most lab/discussion sections have fewer than 10 students. **Majors with Highest Enrollment:** Business administration/management, equestrian/equine studies, photography. **Disciplines with Highest Percentage of Degrees Awarded:** Visual and performing arts 12%, agriculture 7%, social sciences 5%, computer and information sciences 4%, education 4%. **Special Study Options:** Accelerated program, cross registration, distance learning, double major, English as a second language (ESL), honors program, independent study, internships, study abroad, teacher certification program.

FACILITIES
Housing: Coed dorms, men's dorms, women's dorms, apartments for married students, apartments for single students, special housing for disabled students. **Special Academic Facilities/Equipment:** Museum/gallery, 129-acre riding center for equestrian program, fine arts center. **Computers:** 75% of classrooms are wired, 50% of classrooms are wireless, 85% of public computers are PCs, 15% of public computers are Macs, network access in dorm rooms, network access in dorm lounges, online registration, online administrative functions (other than registration), remote student-access to Web through college's connection.

CAMPUS LIFE
Activities: Choral groups, dance, drama/theater, musical theater, student government, yearbook. **Organizations:** 26 registered organizations, 4 honor societies, 2 religious organizations. **Athletics (Intercollegiate):** *Men:* Baseball, basketball, cross-country, equestrian sports, golf, soccer, tennis, track/field (indoor), track/field (outdoor). *Women:* Basketball, cheerleading, cross-country, equestrian sports, soccer, softball, tennis, track/field (indoor), track/field (outdoor), volleyball.

ADMISSIONS
Freshman Academic Profile: 8% in top 10% of high school class, 20% in top 25% of high school class, 58% in top 50% of high school class. 85% from public high schools. SAT Math middle 50% range 410–540. SAT Critical Reading

middle 50% range 410–530. ACT middle 50% range 17–25. TOEFL required of all international applicants, minimum paper TOEFL 500, minimum computer TOEFL 173. **Basis for Candidate Selection:** *Very important factors considered include:* Academic GPA, rigor of secondary school record, standardized test scores. *Other factors considered include:* Alumni/ae relation, application essay, character/personal qualities, class rank, extracurricular activities, first generation, interview, level of applicant's interest, recommendation(s), talent/ability, work experience. **Freshman Admission Requirements:** High school diploma is required, and GED is accepted. *Academic units required:* 4 English, 2 math, 1 science (1 science lab), 2 social studies, 6 academic electives. **Freshman Admission Statistics:** 624 applied, 55% admitted, 44% enrolled. **Transfer Admission Requirements:** College transcript(s), essay or personal statement, statement of good standing from prior institution(s). Minimum college GPA of 2.0 required. Lowest grade transferable C. **General Admission Information:** Application fee $25. Regular notification rolling. Non-fall registration accepted. Admission may be deferred for a maximum of 2 semesters. Credit and/or placement offered for CEEB Advanced Placement tests.

COSTS AND FINANCIAL AID

Annual tuition $16,895. Room & board $6,095. Required fees $950. Average book expense $900. **Required Forms and Deadlines:** FAFSA, state aid form. Financial aid filing deadline 3/1. **Notification of Awards:** Applicants will be notified of awards on a rolling basis beginning on or about 2/15. **Types of Aid:** *Need-based scholarships/grants:* Pell, SEOG, state scholarships/grants, private scholarships, the school's own gift aid. *Loans:* FFEL Subsidized Stafford, FFEL Unsubsidized Stafford, FFEL PLUS, Federal Perkins. **Student Employment:** Federal Work-Study Program available. Off-campus job opportunities are good. **Financial Aid Statistics:** 65% freshmen, 73% undergrads receive need-based scholarship or grant aid. 50% freshmen, 67% undergrads receive need-based self-help aid. 25 freshmen, 94 undergrads receive athletic scholarships. 65% freshmen, 73% undergrads receive any aid. Highest amount earned per year from on-campus jobs $1,500. .

VIRGINIA MILITARY INSTITUTE

VMI Office of Admissions, Lexington, VA 24450-0304
Phone: 540-464-7211 **E-mail:** admissions@mail.vmi.edu **CEEB Code:** 5858
Fax: 540-464-7746 **Website:** www.vmi.edu **ACT Code:** 4418
Financial Aid Phone: 540-464-7208

This public school was founded in 1839. It has a 140-acre campus.

RATINGS
Admissions Selectivity Rating: 82　　　**Fire Safety Rating:** 60*　　　**Green Rating:** 60*

STUDENTS AND FACULTY
Enrollment: 1,377. **Student Body:** 8% female, 92% male, 43% out-of-state, 2% international (9 countries represented). African American 4%, Asian 3%, Caucasian 87%, Hispanic 3%. **Retention and Graduation:** 76% freshmen return for sophomore year. 16% grads go on to further study within 2 semesters. 11% grads pursue arts and sciences degrees. 2% grads pursue law degrees. 2% grads pursue medical degrees. **Faculty:** Student/faculty ratio 11:1. 114 full-time faculty, 97% hold PhDs. 100% faculty teach undergrads.

ACADEMICS
Degrees: Bachelor's. **Academic Requirements:** English (including composition), foreign languages, history, mathematics, physical education, ROTC, sciences (biological or physical). **Classes:** Most classes have 10–19 students. **Majors with Highest Enrollment:** Business/managerial economics, history, mechanical engineering. **Disciplines with Highest Percentage of Degrees Awarded:** Engineering 25%, social sciences 24%, history 19%, psychology 13%, biological/life sciences 7%. **Special Study Options:** Accelerated program, double major, exchange student program (domestic), honors program, independent study, internships, study abroad, summer transition program, teacher certification program.

FACILITIES
Housing: Barracks (3–5 students/room). **Special Academic Facilities/ Equipment:** VMI Museum, George C. Marshall Museum. **Computers:** 100% of classrooms are wireless, 100% of public computers are PCs, network access in dorm rooms, network access in dorm lounges, online registration, online administrative functions (other than registration), remote student-access to Web through college's connection.

CAMPUS LIFE
Activities: Choral groups, concert band, drama/theater, jazz band, literary magazine, marching band, music ensembles, musical theater, pep band, student government, student newspaper, yearbook. **Organizations:** 50 registered organizations, 11 honor societies, 3 religious organizations. **Athletics (Intercollegiate):** *Men:* Baseball, basketball, cross-country, football, golf, lacrosse, riflery, soccer, swimming, track/field (indoor), track/field (outdoor), wrestling. *Women:* Cross-country, riflery, soccer, swimming, track/field (indoor), track/field (outdoor).

ADMISSIONS
Freshman Academic Profile: 12% in top 10% of high school class, 42% in top 25% of high school class, 82% in top 50% of high school class. 84% from public high schools. SAT Math middle 50% range 520–620. SAT Critical Reading middle 50% range 510–610. SAT Writing middle 50% range 480–580. ACT middle 50% range 21–25. TOEFL required of all international applicants, minimum paper TOEFL 500, minimum computer TOEFL 173. **Basis for Candidate Selection:** *Very important factors considered include:* Character/ personal qualities, class rank, rigor of secondary school record, standardized test scores. *Important factors considered include:* Extracurricular activities, interview, racial/ethnic status, state residency, volunteer work. *Other factors considered include:* Alumni/ae relation, geographical residence, recommendation(s), talent/ability. **Freshman Admission Requirements:** High school diploma is required, and GED is not accepted. *Academic units required:* 4 English, 3 math, 3 science (3 science labs), 3 foreign language. *Academic units recommended:* 4 math, 4 foreign language. **Freshman Admission Statistics:** 1,534 applied, 57% admitted, 47% enrolled. **Transfer Admission Requirements:** High school transcript, college transcript(s), standardized test score. Minimum college GPA of 2.0 required. Lowest grade transferable C. **General Admission Information:** Application fee $35. Early decision application deadline 11/15. Regular application deadline 2/15. Regular notification is rolling. Non-fall registration not accepted. Credit and/or placement offered for CEEB Advanced Placement tests.

COSTS AND FINANCIAL AID
Annual in-state tuition $5,062. Annual out-of-state tuition $20,906. **Required Forms and Deadlines:** FAFSA, institution's own financial aid form. Financial aid filing deadline 3/1. **Notification of Awards:** Applicants will be notified of awards on a rolling basis beginning on or about 3/15. **Types of Aid:** *Need-based scholarships/grants:* Pell, SEOG, state scholarships/grants, private scholarships, the school's own gift aid. *Loans:* Direct Subsidized Stafford, Direct Unsubsidized Stafford, Direct PLUS, Federal Perkins. **Financial Aid Statistics:** 37% freshmen, 33% undergrads receive need-based scholarship or grant aid. 21% freshmen, 24% undergrads receive need-based self-help aid. 40 freshmen, 121 undergrads receive athletic scholarships. 73% freshmen, 80% undergrads receive any aid. Highest amount earned per year from on-campus jobs $825. .

VIRGINIA POLYTECHNIC AND STATE UNIVERSITY (VIRGINIA TECH)

Best 368

Undergraduate Admissions, 201 Burruss Hall, Blacksburg, VA 24061
Phone: 540-231-6267 **E-mail:** vtadmiss@vt.edu **CEEB Code:** 5859
Fax: 540-231-3242 **Website:** www.vt.edu **ACT Code:** 4420
Financial Aid Phone: 540-231-5179

This public school was founded in 1872. It has a 2,600-acre campus.

RATINGS
Admissions Selectivity Rating: 89　　　**Fire Safety Rating:** 82　　　**Green Rating:** 90

STUDENTS AND FACULTY
Enrollment: 21,912. **Student Body:** 42% female, 58% male, 25% out-of-state, 2% international (65 countries represented). African American 4%, Asian 7%, Caucasian 72%, Hispanic 2%. **Retention and Graduation:** 89% freshmen return for sophomore year. 52% freshmen graduate within 4 years. 22% grads go on to further study within 2 semesters. 33% grads pursue arts and sciences degrees. 6% grads pursue business degrees. 7% grads pursue law degrees. 16% grads pursue medical degrees. **Faculty:** Student/faculty ratio 16:1. 1,340 full-time faculty, 90% hold PhDs. 75% faculty teach undergrads.

ACADEMICS
Degrees: Associate, bachelor's, doctoral, first professional, master's, post-master's certificate. **Academic Requirements:** Arts/fine arts, English

The Princeton Review's Complete Book of Colleges

(including composition), foreign languages, history, humanities, mathematics, sciences (biological or physical), social science. **Classes:** Most classes have 20–29 students. Most lab/discussion sections have 20–29 students. **Majors with Highest Enrollment:** Biology/biological sciences, communications studies/speech communication and rhetoric, engineering. **Disciplines with Highest Percentage of Degrees Awarded:** Business/marketing 22%, engineering 21%, family and consumer sciences 9%, social sciences 7%, biological/life sciences 6%. **Special Study Options:** Accelerated program, cooperative education program, distance learning, double major, English as a second language (ESL), exchange student program (domestic), honors program, independent study, internships, student-designed major, study abroad, teacher certification program.

FACILITIES

Housing: Coed dorms, men's dorms, women's dorms, special housing for disabled students, special housing for international students, fraternity/sorority housing, housing for corps of cadets, housing for athletes, "The World" (cross cultural environment). **Special Academic Facilities/Equipment:** Art gallery, digital music facilities, multimedia labs, Black Cultural Center, television studio, anaerobic lab, CAD-CAM labs, observatory, wind tunnel, farms, Math Emporium, the CAVE (virtual reality learning facility). **Computers:** Network access in dorm rooms, online registration, online administrative functions (other than registration), remote student-access to Web through college's connection. Undergraduates are required to own a computer.

CAMPUS LIFE

Activities: Choral groups, concert band, dance, drama/theater, jazz band, literary magazine, marching band, music ensembles, musical theater, pep band, radio station, student government, student newspaper, symphony orchestra, television station, yearbook. **Organizations:** 600 registered organizations, 35 honor societies, 26 religious organizations. 31 fraternities (13% men join), 12 sororities (19% women join). **Athletics (Intercollegiate):** *Men:* Baseball, basketball, cheerleading, cross-country, diving, football, golf, soccer, swimming, tennis, track/field (indoor), track/field (outdoor), wrestling. *Women:* Basketball, cheerleading, cross-country, diving, lacrosse, soccer, softball, swimming, tennis, track/field (indoor), track/field (outdoor), volleyball. **Environmental Initiatives:** Energy efficiency and conservation. Major power plant equipment enhancements and upgrades to the infrastructure distribution system have resulted in significant energy efficiencies and reductions in fuel consumption. The university has an outstanding recycling program and is an active participant in RecycleMania.

ADMISSIONS

Freshman Academic Profile: 38% in top 10% of high school class, 81% in top 25% of high school class, 98% in top 50% of high school class. 95% from public high schools. SAT Math middle 50% range 570–670. SAT Critical Reading middle 50% range 530–630. SAT Writing middle 50% range 530–630. TOEFL required of all international applicants, minimum paper TOEFL 550, minimum computer TOEFL 207. **Basis for Candidate Selection:** *Very important factors considered include:* Academic GPA, rigor of secondary school record, standardized test scores. *Other factors considered include:* Alumni/ae relation, character/personal qualities, extracurricular activities, first generation, geographical residence, racial/ethnic status, recommendation(s), state residency, talent/ability, volunteer work, work experience. **Freshman Admission Requirements:** High school diploma is required, and GED is accepted. *Academic units required:* 4 English, 3 math, 2 science (2 science labs), 1 social studies, 1 history, 4 academic electives. *Academic units recommended:* 4 math, 3 science, 3 foreign language. **Freshman Admission Statistics:** 19,046 applied, 66% admitted, 40% enrolled. **Transfer Admission Requirements:** College transcript(s), statement of good standing from prior institution(s). Minimum college GPA of 3.0 required. Lowest grade transferable C. **General Admission Information:** Application fee $50. Early decision application deadline 11/1. Regular application deadline 1/15. Regular notification 4/1. Non-fall registration accepted. Admission may be deferred for a maximum of 2 semesters. Credit and/or placement offered for CEEB Advanced Placement tests.

COSTS AND FINANCIAL AID

Average book expense $1,067. **Required Forms and Deadlines:** FAFSA, General Scholarship. Financial aid filing deadline 3/11. **Notification of Awards:** Applicants will be notified of awards on a rolling basis beginning on or about 3/30. **Types of Aid:** *Need-based scholarships/grants:* Pell, SEOG, state scholarships/grants, private scholarships, the school's own gift aid, cadet scholarships/grants. *Loans:* Direct Subsidized Stafford, Direct Unsubsidized Stafford, Direct PLUS, Federal Perkins, college/university loans from institutional funds. **Student Employment:** Federal Work-Study Program available. Off-campus job opportunities are excellent. **Financial Aid Statistics:** 28% freshmen, 25% undergrads receive need-based scholarship or grant aid. 28% freshmen, 29% undergrads receive need-based self-help aid. 102 freshmen, 403 undergrads receive athletic scholarships. 36% freshmen, 34% undergrads receive any aid. Highest amount earned per year from on-campus jobs $1,500. .

VIRGINIA STATE UNIVERSITY

1 Hayden Street, PO Box 9018, Petersburg, VA 23806
Phone: 804-524-5902 **E-mail:** admiss@vsu.edu **CEEB Code:** 5860
Fax: 804-524-5055 **Website:** www.vsu.edu **ACT Code:** 4424
Financial Aid Phone: 804-524-5990

This public school was founded in 1882. It has a 246-acre campus.

RATINGS

Admissions Selectivity Rating: 69   **Fire Safety Rating:** 60*   **Green Rating:** 60*

STUDENTS AND FACULTY

Enrollment: 4,278. **Student Body:** 61% female, 39% male, 32% out-of-state. African American 96%, Caucasian 2%, Hispanic 1%. **Retention and Graduation:** 72% freshmen return for sophomore year. 18% freshmen graduate within 4 years. **Faculty:** Student/faculty ratio 17:1. 226 full-time faculty, 81% hold PhDs. 100% faculty teach undergrads.

ACADEMICS

Degrees: Associate, bachelor's, doctoral, master's, post-master's certificate. **Academic Requirements:** Arts/fine arts, English (including composition), foreign languages, history, humanities, mathematics, sciences (biological or physical), social science. **Classes:** Most classes have 20–29 students. Most lab/discussion sections have 20–29 students. **Majors with Highest Enrollment:** Liberal arts and sciences/liberal studies, physical education teaching and coaching, sociology. **Disciplines with Highest Percentage of Degrees Awarded:** Business/marketing 15%, education 11%, liberal arts/general studies 10%, interdisciplinary studies 8%, security and protective services 7%, social sciences 7%. **Special Study Options:** Cooperative education program, double major, dual enrollment, exchange student program (domestic), honors program, independent study, internships, teacher certification program.

FACILITIES

Housing: Coed dorms, men's dorms, women's dorms, apartments for single students, honors coeducational residence facility. **Computers:** 100% of public computers are PCs, network access in dorm rooms, network access in dorm lounges, online administrative functions (other than registration), remote student-access to Web through college's connection.

CAMPUS LIFE

Activities: Choral groups, concert band, dance, drama/theater, jazz band, literary magazine, marching band, music ensembles, radio station, student government, student newspaper, television station, yearbook. **Organizations:** 70 registered organizations, 6 honor societies, 4 religious organizations. 5 fraternities (5% men join), 4 sororities (5% women join). **Athletics (Intercollegiate):** *Men:* Baseball, basketball, cheerleading, cross-country, football, golf, tennis, track/field (indoor), track/field (outdoor). *Women:* Basketball, bowling, cheerleading, cross-country, golf, softball, tennis, track/field (indoor), track/field (outdoor), volleyball.

ADMISSIONS

Freshman Academic Profile: 4% in top 10% of high school class, 19% in top 25% of high school class, 59% in top 50% of high school class. SAT Math middle 50% range 400–480. SAT Critical Reading middle 50% range 410–480. TOEFL required of all international applicants, minimum paper TOEFL 500, minimum computer TOEFL 173. **Basis for Candidate Selection:** *Very important factors considered include:* Application essay, recommendation(s), rigor of secondary school record, standardized test scores. *Other factors considered include:* Alumni/ae relation, character/personal qualities, extracurricular activities, geographical residence, state residency, talent/ability, volunteer work, work experience. **Freshman Admission Requirements:** High school diploma is required, and GED is accepted. *Academic units required:* 4 English, 3 math, 2 science (1 science lab), 2 social studies. *Academic units recommended:* 2 foreign language. **Freshman Admission Statistics:** 4,000 applied, 79% admitted, 35% enrolled. **Transfer Admission Requirements:** College transcript(s), essay or personal statement, statement of good standing from prior institution(s). Minimum college GPA of 2.0 required. Lowest grade transferable C. **General Admission Information:** Application fee $25. Regular application deadline 5/1. Regular notification is rolling. Non-fall registration accepted. Common Application accepted. Credit offered for CEEB Advanced Placement tests.

COSTS AND FINANCIAL AID

Annual in-state tuition $3,186. Annual out-of-state tuition $10,838. Room and board $7,340. Required fees $2,469. Average book expense $900. **Required Forms and Deadlines:** FAFSA, institution's own financial aid form. Financial aid filing deadline 5/1. **Notification of Awards:** Applicants will be notified of awards on a rolling basis beginning on or about 5/1. **Types of Aid:** *Need-based* scholarships/grants: Pell, SEOG, state scholarships/grants, private scholarships, the school's own gift aid. Loans: Direct Subsidized Stafford, Direct Unsubsidized Stafford, Direct PLUS, FFEL PLUS, Federal Perkins, college/university loans from institutional funds. Student Employment: Federal Work-Study Program available. Institutional employment available. .

VIRGINIA WESLEYAN COLLEGE

1584 Wesleyan Drive, Norfolk/Virginia Beach, VA 23502-5599
Phone: 757-455-3208 **E-mail:** admissions@vwc.edu **CEEB Code:** 5867
Fax: 757-461-5238 **Website:** www.vwc.edu **ACT Code:** 4429
Financial Aid Phone: 757-455-3345

This private school, affiliated with the Methodist Church, was founded in 1961. It has a 300-acre campus.

RATINGS
Admissions Selectivity Rating: 71   **Fire Safety Rating:** 68   **Green Rating:** 60*

STUDENTS AND FACULTY
Enrollment: 1,347. **Student Body:** 63% female, 37% male, 23% out-of-state. African American 16%, Asian 2%, Caucasian 75%, Hispanic 4%. **Retention and Graduation:** 64% freshmen return for sophomore year. 34% freshmen graduate within 4 years. 20% grads go on to further study within 2 semesters. 12% grads pursue arts and sciences degrees. 3% grads pursue business degrees. 2% grads pursue law degrees. 2% grads pursue medical degrees. **Faculty:** Student/faculty ratio 10:1. 88 full-time faculty, 82% hold PhDs. 100% faculty teach undergrads.

ACADEMICS
Degrees: Bachelor's. **Academic Requirements:** Arts/fine arts, English (including composition), foreign languages, freshmen seminar, history, humanities, mathematics, sciences (biological or physical), senior integrative experience, social science. **Classes:** Most classes have 10–19 students. Most lab/discussion sections have 10–19 students. **Majors with Highest Enrollment:** Business, management, marketing, and related support services, communications, journalism and related fields, social sciences. **Disciplines with Highest Percentage of Degrees Awarded:** Business/marketing 21%, social sciences 19%, law/legal studies 10%, communications/journalism 9%, education 8%. **Special Study Options:** Accelerated program, cross registration, distance learning, double major, exchange student program (domestic), externships, honors program, independent study, internships, liberal arts/career combination, PORTfolio, student-designed major, study abroad, teacher certification program.

FACILITIES
Housing: Coed dorms, women's dorms, apartments for single students, special housing for disabled students, special housing for international students, fraternity/sorority housing, town houses, honors and scholars hall, wellness hall (substance free). **Special Academic Facilities/Equipment:** Greenhouse, language lab, teleconferencing facility, social science lab, radio station, TV studio, Barclay Sheaks Art Gallery, computerized classrooms, Internet access all classrooms, 24-hour computer lab, Lambuth M. Clarke Hall with state-of-the-art teaching technologies, 3 academic villages combining residences and campus offices and services. **Computers:** 100% of classrooms are wireless, 100% of public computers are PCs, network access in dorm rooms, network access in dorm lounges, online administrative functions (other than registration), remote student-access to Web through college's connection.

CAMPUS LIFE
Activities: Choral groups, dance, drama/theater, literary magazine, music ensembles, musical theater, radio station, student government, student newspaper, yearbook. **Organizations:** 60 registered organizations, 17 honor societies, 2 religious organizations. 2 fraternities (5% men join), 3 sororities (6% women join). **Athletics (Intercollegiate): Men:** Baseball, basketball, cross-country, golf, lacrosse, soccer, tennis, track/field (indoor), track/field (outdoor). *Women:* Basketball, cheerleading, cross-country, field hockey, lacrosse, soccer, softball, tennis, track/field (indoor), track/field (outdoor), volleyball.

ADMISSIONS
Freshman Academic Profile: 10% in top 10% of high school class, 30% in top 25% of high school class, 65% in top 50% of high school class. 65% from public high schools. SAT Math middle 50% range 430–540. SAT Critical Reading middle 50% range 440–530. ACT middle 50% range 17–21. TOEFL required of all international applicants, minimum paper TOEFL 550, minimum computer TOEFL 213. **Basis for Candidate Selection:** *Very important*

factors considered include: Academic GPA, level of applicant's interest, rigor of secondary school record. *Important factors considered include:* Application essay, extracurricular activities, recommendation(s), standardized test scores. *Other factors considered include:* Alumni/ae relation, character/personal qualities, class rank, interview, talent/ability, volunteer work, work experience. **Freshman Admission Requirements:** High school diploma is required, and GED is accepted. *Academic units required:* 4 English, 3 math, 2 science (2 science labs), 2 foreign language, 1 history. *Academic units recommended:* 4 English, 3 math, 3 science (3 science labs), 3 foreign language, 2 social studies, 1 history. **Freshman Admission Statistics:** 1,342 applied, 84% admitted, 33% enrolled. **Transfer Admission Requirements:** College transcript(s), essay or personal statement, statement of good standing from prior institution(s). Minimum college GPA of 2.5 required. Lowest grade transferable C. **General Admission Information:** Application fee $40. Regular notification is rolling. Non-fall registration accepted. Credit and/or placement offered for CEEB Advanced Placement tests.

COSTS AND FINANCIAL AID
Annual tuition $24,355. Room and board $6,900. Required fees $160. Average book expense $1,000. **Required Forms and Deadlines:** FAFSA, state aid form. Financial aid filing deadline 5/1. **Notification of Awards:** Applicants will be notified of awards on a rolling basis beginning on or about 2/1. **Types of Aid:** *Need-based scholarships/grants:* Pell, SEOG, state scholarships/grants, private scholarships, the school's own gift aid, United Negro College Fund. *Loans:* FFEL Subsidized Stafford, FFEL Unsubsidized Stafford, FFEL PLUS, Federal Perkins, alternative loans. **Financial Aid Statistics:** 27% freshmen, 26% undergrads receive need-based scholarship or grant aid. 61% freshmen, 57% undergrads receive need-based self-help aid. 64% freshmen, 60% undergrads receive any aid. Highest amount earned per year from on-campus jobs $1,200.

VITERBO UNIVERSITY

900 Viterbo Drive, La Crosse, WI 54601
Phone: 608-796-3010 **E-mail:** admission@viterbo.edu **CEEB Code:** 1878
Fax: 608-796-3020 **Website:** www.viterbo.edu **ACT Code:** 4662
Financial Aid Phone: 608-496-3900

This private school, affiliated with the Roman Catholic Church, was founded in 1890. It has a 25-acre campus.

RATINGS
Admissions Selectivity Rating: 72   **Fire Safety Rating:** 61   **Green Rating:** 60*

STUDENTS AND FACULTY
Enrollment: 1,881. **Student Body:** 73% female, 27% male, 19% out-of-state, 1% international (15 countries represented). African American 1%, Asian 2%, Caucasian 92%, Hispanic 2%. **Retention and Graduation:** 76% freshmen return for sophomore year. 30% freshmen graduate within 4 years. 7% grads go on to further study within 2 semesters. 4% grads pursue arts and sciences degrees. 1% grads pursue law degrees. 2% grads pursue medical degrees. **Faculty:** Student/faculty ratio 13:1. 110 full-time faculty, 56% hold PhDs. 100% faculty teach undergrads.

ACADEMICS
Degrees: Associate, bachelor's, master's, post-bachelor's certificate. **Academic Requirements:** Arts/fine arts, English (including composition), foreign language (for BA), history, humanities, mathematics, philosophy, religious studies, sciences (biological or physical), social science. **Classes:** Most classes have 10–19 students. Most lab/discussion sections have 10–19 students. **Majors with Highest Enrollment:** Business administration and management, elementary education and teaching, nursing/registered nurse training (ASN, BSN, MSN, RN). **Disciplines with Highest Percentage of Degrees Awarded:** Health professions and related sciences 34%, business/marketing 17%, education 11%, visual and performing arts 7%, interdisciplinary studies 6%. **Special Study Options:** Accelerated program, cross registration, distance learning, double major, dual enrollment, honors program, independent study, internships, liberal arts/career combination, student-designed major, study abroad, teacher certification program, weekend college (master's level programs).

FACILITIES
Housing: Coed dorms, apartments for single students, theme floors in dorms, university-owned theme houses. **Special Academic Facilities/Equipment:** Fine arts center, center for ethics, science and technology with distance education labs and video conferencing, nursing center with labs and simulated equipment, new recreation and education center co-sponsored by Viterbo

University and the Boys and Girls Club. **Computers:** 90% of classrooms are wireless, 95% of public computers are PCs, 5% of public computers are Macs, network access in dorm rooms, network access in dorm lounges, online registration, online administrative functions (other than registration), remote student-access to Web through college's connection.

CAMPUS LIFE

Activities: Choral groups, dance, drama/theater, literary magazine, music ensembles, musical theater, opera, pep band, student government, student newspaper. **Organizations:** 22 registered organizations, 2 honor societies, 2 religious organizations. **Athletics (Intercollegiate):** *Men:* Baseball, basketball, golf, soccer. *Women:* Basketball, golf, soccer, softball, volleyball.

ADMISSIONS

Freshman Academic Profile: 11% in top 10% of high school class, 38% in top 25% of high school class, 75% in top 50% of high school class. 97% from public high schools. ACT middle 50% range 20–24. TOEFL required of all international applicants, minimum paper TOEFL 550, minimum computer TOEFL 213. **Basis for Candidate Selection:** *Very important factors considered include:* Academic GPA, character/personal qualities, level of applicant's interest, rigor of secondary school record, standardized test scores. *Important factors considered include:* Class rank, interview, talent/ability. *Other factors considered include:* Alumni/ae relation, application essay, extracurricular activities, first generation, recommendation(s), volunteer work. **Freshman Admission Requirements:** High school diploma is required, and GED is accepted. *Academic units required:* 3 English, 2 math, 2 science, 2 social studies, 5 academic electives. *Academic units recommended:* 4 English, 2 math, 2 science (2 science labs), 2 foreign language, 2 social studies, 5 academic electives. **Freshman Admission Statistics:** 1,107 applied, 89% admitted, 32% enrolled. **Transfer Admission Requirements:** High school transcript, college transcript(s), statement of good standing from prior institution(s). Minimum college GPA of 2.0 required. Lowest grade transferable C-. **General Admission Information:** Application fee $25. Regular notification within 2 weeks of complete submission. Non-fall registration accepted. Admission may be deferred for a maximum of 4 semesters. Credit offered for CEEB Advanced Placement tests.

COSTS AND FINANCIAL AID

Annual tuition $18,170. Room & board $6,140. Required fees $420. Average book expense $800. **Required Forms and Deadlines:** FAFSA, institution's own financial aid form. Financial aid filing deadline 3/15. **Notification of Awards:** Applicants will be notified of awards on a rolling basis beginning on or about 4/1. **Types of Aid:** *Need-based scholarships/grants:* Pell, SEOG, state scholarships/grants, private scholarships, the school's own gift aid. *Loans:* FFEL Subsidized Stafford, FFEL Unsubsidized Stafford, FFEL PLUS, Federal Perkins, Federal Nursing, state loans. **Student Employment:** Federal Work-Study Program available. Institutional employment available. Off-campus job opportunities are good. **Financial Aid Statistics:** 95% freshmen, 79% undergrads receive need-based scholarship or grant aid. 91% freshmen, 76% undergrads receive need-based self-help aid. 1 freshmen, 13 undergrads receive athletic scholarships. 98% freshmen, 89% undergrads receive any aid. Highest amount earned per year from on-campus jobs $2,500.

VOORHEES COLLEGE

PO Box 678, Denmark, SC 29042
Phone: 803-703-7111 **E-mail:** white@voorhees.edu **CEEB Code:** 5863
Fax: 803-793-1117 **Website:** www.voorhees.edu **ACT Code:** 3882
Financial Aid Phone: 803-703-7109

This private school, affiliated with the Episcopal Church, was founded in 1897. It has a 350-acre campus.

RATINGS

Admissions Selectivity Rating: 73   **Fire Safety Rating:** 60*   **Green Rating:** 60*

STUDENTS AND FACULTY

Enrollment: 738. **Student Body:** 64% female, 36% male, 30% out-of-state, 1% international. African American 98%, Caucasian 1%. **Retention and Graduation:** 70% freshmen return for sophomore year. 100% freshmen graduate within 4 years. 25% grads go on to further study within 2 semesters. 17% grads pursue arts and sciences degrees. 5% grads pursue business degrees. 2% grads pursue law degrees. 4% grads pursue medical degrees. **Faculty:** Student/faculty ratio 20:1. 43 full-time faculty, 44% hold PhDs. 100% faculty teach undergrads.

ACADEMICS

Degrees: Bachelor's. **Academic Requirements:** Arts/fine arts, computer

literacy, English (including composition), foreign languages, history, humanities, mathematics, philosophy, sciences (biological or physical), social science. **Disciplines with Highest Percentage of Degrees Awarded:** Social sciences 13%, business/marketing 12%, law/legal studies 8%, biological/life sciences 7%. **Special Study Options:** Cooperative education program, honors program, internships, weekend college.

FACILITIES

Housing: Men's dorms, women's dorms, fraternity/sorority housing, faculty and staff apartments, housing for single mothers. **Computers:** 91% of public computers are PCs, 8% of public computers are Macs, 1% of public computers are UNIX, network access in dorm lounges, online administrative functions (other than registration), remote student-access to Web through college's connection.

CAMPUS LIFE

Activities: Choral groups, drama/theater, literary magazine, pep band, radio station, student government, student newspaper, yearbook. **Organizations:** 33 registered organizations, 2 honor societies, 3 religious organizations. 4 fraternities (30% men join), 4 sororities (22% women join). **Athletics (Intercollegiate):** *Men:* Baseball, basketball, cheerleading, cross-country. *Women:* Basketball, cheerleading, cross-country, softball, volleyball.

ADMISSIONS

Freshman Academic Profile: 1% in top 10% of high school class, 44% in top 25% of high school class, 50% in top 50% of high school class. 95% from public high schools. SAT Math middle 50% range 390–410. SAT Critical Reading middle 50% range 300–400. ACT middle 50% range 11–18. TOEFL required of all international applicants, minimum paper TOEFL 500. **Basis for Candidate Selection:** *Very important factors considered include:* Class rank, rigor of secondary school record, standardized test scores. *Important factors considered include:* Alumni/ae relation, character/personal qualities, recommendation(s), talent/ability. *Other factors considered include:* Extracurricular activities. **Freshman Admission Requirements:** High school diploma is required, and GED is accepted. *Academic units required:* 4 English, 3 math, 2 science, 2 foreign language, 1 social studies, 1 history, 7 academic electives. *Academic units recommended:* 4 English, 3 math, 3 science, 2 foreign language, 1 social studies, 1 history, 7 academic electives. **Freshman Admission Statistics:** 3,511 applied, 37% admitted, 19% enrolled. **Transfer Admission Requirements:** College transcript(s), statement of good standing from prior institution(s). Minimum college GPA of 2.0 required. Lowest grade transferable C. **General Admission Information:** Application fee $25. Regular notification is rolling. Non-fall registration accepted. Admission may be deferred for a maximum of 4 semesters. Common Application accepted. Credit offered for CEEB Advanced Placement tests.

COSTS AND FINANCIAL AID

Annual tuition $6,460. Room & board $3,516. Required fees $170. Average book expense $2,500. **Required Forms and Deadlines:** FAFSA, institution's own financial aid form. Financial aid filing deadline 4/15. **Notification of Awards:** Applicants will be notified of awards on or about 5/1. **Types of Aid:** *Need-based scholarships/grants:* Pell, SEOG, state scholarships/grants, private scholarships, the school's own gift aid, United Negro College Fund. *Loans:* FFEL Subsidized Stafford, FFEL Unsubsidized Stafford, FFEL PLUS, Federal Perkins. **Student Employment:** Federal Work-Study Program available. Institutional employment available. Off-campus job opportunities are poor. **Financial Aid Statistics:** 88% freshmen, 85% undergrads receive need-based scholarship or grant aid. 85% freshmen, 88% undergrads receive need-based self-help aid.

WABASH COLLEGE

PO Box 352, 301 West Wabash Avenue, Crawfordsville, IN 47933
Phone: 765-361-6225 **E-mail:** admissions@wabash.edu **CEEB Code:** 1895
Fax: 765-361-6437 **Website:** www.wabash.edu **ACT Code:** 1260
Financial Aid Phone: 765-361-6370

This private school was founded in 1832. It has a 60-acre campus.

RATINGS

Admissions Selectivity Rating: 89   **Fire Safety Rating:** 81   **Green Rating:** 71

STUDENTS AND FACULTY

Enrollment: 874. **Student Body:** 100% male, 26% out-of-state, 5% international (25 countries represented). African American 5%, Asian 2%, Caucasian 80%, Hispanic 5%. **Retention and Graduation:** 87% freshmen return for sophomore year. 69% freshmen graduate within 4 years. 37% grads go on to further study within 2 semesters. 20% grads pursue arts and sciences degrees. 9% grads pursue law degrees. 8% grads pursue medical degrees. **Faculty:** Student/faculty ratio 10:1. 85 full-time faculty, 98% hold PhDs. 100% faculty teach undergrads.

ACADEMICS

Degrees: Bachelor's. **Academic Requirements:** Arts/fine arts, cultures and traditions course, English (including composition), foreign languages, freshman tutorial, history, humanities, mathematics, philosophy, sciences (biological or physical), social science. **Classes:** Most classes have 10–19 students. Most lab/discussion sections have 10–19 students. **Majors with Highest Enrollment:** English language and literature, history, psychology. **Disciplines with Highest Percentage of Degrees Awarded:** Social sciences 14%, history 14%, psychology 13%, English 12%, philosophy and religious studies 11%, biological/life sciences 10%, foreign languages and literature 10%. **Special Study Options:** Double major, independent study, internships, student designed majors, minors, or areas of concentration, study abroad, teacher certification program.

FACILITIES

Housing: Men's dorms, apartments for single students, fraternity/sorority housing, college-owned houses and apartments. **Special Academic Facilities/Equipment:** Malcolm X Institute of Black Studies, 2 art galleries, language lab, electron microscope, atomic absorption, nuclear and infrared spectrometers, Beowulf supercomputer, Center of Inquiry in the Liberal Arts, Wabash Center for Teaching & Learning in Theology & Religion, Ramsey Archival Center. **Computers:** 100% of classrooms are wired, 95% of classrooms are wireless, 93% of public computers are PCs, 7% of public computers are Macs, network access in dorm rooms, network access in dorm lounges, online administrative functions (other than registration), support for handheld computing, remote student-access to Web through college's connection.

CAMPUS LIFE

Activities: Choral groups, concert band, drama/theater, jazz band, literary magazine, music ensembles, musical theater, pep band, radio station, student government, student newspaper, student-run film society, symphony orchestra, yearbook. **Organizations:** 52 registered organizations, 6 honor societies, 5 religious organizations. 10 fraternities (54% men join). **Athletics (Intercollegiate):** *Men:* Baseball, basketball, cross-country, diving, football, golf, soccer, swimming, tennis, track/field (indoor), track/field (outdoor), wrestling. **Environmental Initiatives:** Campus-wide recycling. New, state-of-the-art, energy efficient boilers. Green Bikes.

ADMISSIONS

Freshman Academic Profile: 39% in top 10% of high school class, 73% in top 25% of high school class, 96% in top 50% of high school class. 93% from public high schools. SAT Math middle 50% range 540–660. SAT Critical Reading middle 50% range 520–630. SAT Writing middle 50% range 500–610. ACT middle 50% range 21–27. TOEFL required of all international applicants, minimum paper TOEFL 550, minimum computer TOEFL 213. **Basis for Candidate Selection:** *Very important factors considered include:* Academic GPA, class rank, rigor of secondary school record. *Important factors considered include:* Character/personal qualities, extracurricular activities, interview, recommendation(s), standardized test scores, talent/ability. *Other factors considered include:* Alumni/ae relation, application essay, first generation, geographical residence, level of applicant's interest, racial/ethnic status, volunteer work, work experience. **Freshman Admission Requirements:** High school diploma is required, and GED is accepted. *Academic units recommended:* 4 English, 4 math, 2 science (2 science labs), 2 foreign language, 2 social studies, 2 history. **Freshman Admission Statistics:** 1,319 applied, 51% admitted, 40% enrolled. **Transfer Admission Requirements:** High school transcript, college transcript(s), standardized test score, statement of good standing from prior institution(s). Minimum college GPA of 2.0 required. Lowest grade transferable C. **General Admission Information:** Application fee $30. Early decision application deadline 11/15. Regular notification is rolling. Non-fall registration not accepted. Admission may be deferred for a maximum of 2 semesters. Credit and/or placement offered for CEEB Advanced Placement tests.

COSTS AND FINANCIAL AID

Annual tuition $25,900. Room and board $7,200. Required fees $450. Average book expense $800. **Required Forms and Deadlines:** FAFSA, CSS/Financial Aid PROFILE, Noncustodial PROFILE, Federal tax returns and W-2 statements. Financial aid filing deadline 3/1. **Notification of Awards:** Applicants will be notified of awards on or about 3/31. **Types of Aid:** *Need-based scholarships/grants:* Pell, state scholarships/grants, private scholarships, the school's own gift aid. *Loans:* FFEL Subsidized Stafford, FFEL

Unsubsidized Stafford, FFEL PLUS, college/university loans from institutional funds. **Student Employment:** Institutional employment available. Off-campus job opportunities are good. **Financial Aid Statistics:** 81% freshmen, 70% undergrads receive need-based scholarship or grant aid. 63% freshmen, 57% undergrads receive need-based self-help aid. 93% freshmen, 88% undergrads receive any aid. Highest amount earned per year from on-campus jobs $2,000.

WAGNER COLLEGE

1 Campus Road, Staten Island, NY 10301-4495
Phone: 718-390-3411 **E-mail:** adm@wagner.edu **CEEB Code:** 2966
Fax: 718-390-3105 **Website:** www.wagner.edu **ACT Code:** 2984
Financial Aid Phone: 718-390-3183

This private school, affiliated with the Lutheran Church, was founded in 1883. It has a 110-acre campus.

RATINGS

Admissions Selectivity Rating: 88   **Fire Safety Rating:** 85   **Green Rating:** 60*

STUDENTS AND FACULTY

Enrollment: 1,941. **Student Body:** 64% female, 36% male, 59% out-of-state. African American 5%, Asian 2%, Caucasian 78%, Hispanic 5%. **Retention and Graduation:** 82% freshmen return for sophomore year. 59% freshmen graduate within 4 years. **Faculty:** Student/faculty ratio 13:1. 98 full-time faculty, 91% hold PhDs. 100% faculty teach undergrads.

ACADEMICS

Degrees: Bachelor's, master's, post-master's certificate. **Academic Requirements:** Arts/fine arts, computer literacy, English (including composition), history, humanities, learning community, mathematics, sciences (biological or physical), social science. **Classes:** Most classes have 10–19 students. Most lab/discussion sections have fewer than 10 students. **Majors with Highest Enrollment:** Biology/biological sciences, business administration/management, psychology. **Disciplines with Highest Percentage of Degrees Awarded:** Business/marketing 23%, visual and performing arts 19%, health professions and related sciences 17%, psychology 11%, social sciences 11%. **Special Study Options:** Double major, exchange student program (domestic), honors program, independent study, internships, learning community, study abroad, teacher certification program.

FACILITIES

Housing: Coed dorms, apartments for single students, fraternity/sorority housing. **Special Academic Facilities/Equipment:** Art gallery, early childhood center, nursing resource center, planetarium, 2 electron microscopes, solar energy project. **Computers:** 16% of classrooms are wireless, 75% of public computers are PCs, 8% of public computers are Macs, 17% of public computers are UNIX, network access in dorm rooms, online administrative functions (other than registration), remote student-access to Web through college's connection.

CAMPUS LIFE

Activities: Choral groups, dance, drama/theater, jazz band, literary magazine, music ensembles, musical theater, pep band, radio station, student government, student newspaper, yearbook. **Organizations:** 66 registered organizations, 11 honor societies, 4 religious organizations. 5 fraternities (8% men join), 4 sororities (11% women join). **Athletics (Intercollegiate):** *Men:* Baseball, basketball, cross-country, football, golf, lacrosse, tennis, track/field (indoor), track/field (outdoor), wrestling. *Women:* Basketball, cross-country, golf, lacrosse, soccer, softball, swimming, tennis, track/field (indoor), track/field (outdoor), volleyball, water polo.

ADMISSIONS

Freshman Academic Profile: 18% in top 10% of high school class, 66% in top 25% of high school class, 92% in top 50% of high school class. SAT Math middle 50% range 540–650. SAT Critical Reading middle 50% range 530–640. SAT Writing middle 50% range 530–640. ACT middle 50% range 24–28. TOEFL required of all international applicants, minimum paper TOEFL 550, minimum computer TOEFL 217. **Basis for Candidate Selection:** *Very important factors considered include:* Academic GPA, class rank, rigor of secondary school record, standardized test scores. *Important factors considered include:* Application essay, extracurricular activities, interview, recommendation(s).

Other factors considered include: Character/personal qualities, level of applicant's interest, talent/ability, volunteer work, work experience. **Freshman Admission Requirements:** High school diploma is required, and GED is accepted. *Academic units required:* 4 English, 3 math, 2 science (1 science lab), 2 foreign language, 1 social studies, 3 history, 6 academic electives. **Freshman Admission Statistics:** 2,862 applied, 59% admitted, 31% enrolled. **Transfer Admission Requirements:** College transcript(s), essay or personal statement, statement of good standing from prior institution(s). Minimum college GPA of 3.0 required. Lowest grade transferable C. **General Admission Information:** Application fee $50. Early decision application deadline 1/1. Regular application deadline 3/1. Regular notification 3/1. Non-fall registration accepted. Admission may be deferred for a maximum of 2 semesters. Credit offered for CEEB Advanced Placement tests.

COSTS AND FINANCIAL AID
Annual tuition $29,400. Room and board $8,900. Average book expense $725. **Required Forms and Deadlines:** FAFSA, institution's own financial aid form. Financial aid filing deadline 2/15. **Notification of Awards:** Applicants will be notified of awards on or about 3/1. **Types of Aid:** *Need-based scholarships/ grants:* Pell, SEOG, state scholarships/grants, private scholarships, the school's own gift aid. *Loans:* FFEL Subsidized Stafford, FFEL Unsubsidized Stafford, FFEL PLUS, Federal Perkins, Federal Nursing. **Financial Aid Statistics:** 69% freshmen, 52% undergrads receive need-based scholarship or grant aid. 44% freshmen, 40% undergrads receive need-based self-help aid. 22 freshmen, 130 undergrads receive athletic scholarships. 95% freshmen, 89% undergrads receive any aid. Highest amount earned per year from on-campus jobs $1,000.

WAKE FOREST UNIVERSITY

Box 7305, Reynolda Station, Winston-Salem, NC 27109
Phone: 336-758-5201 **E-mail:** admissions@wfu.edu **CEEB Code:** 5885
Fax: 336-758-4324 **Website:** www.wfu.edu **ACT Code:** 3168
Financial Aid Phone: 336-758-5154

This private school was founded in 1834. It has a 340-acre campus.

RATINGS
Admissions Selectivity Rating: 95   **Fire Safety Rating:** 90   **Green Rating:** 76

STUDENTS AND FACULTY
Enrollment: 4,313. **Student Body:** 51% female, 49% male, 74% out-of-state, 1% international. African American 6%, Asian 5%, Caucasian 84%, Hispanic 2%. **Retention and Graduation:** 93% freshmen return for sophomore year. 79% freshmen graduate within 4 years. 31% grads go on to further study within 1 year. 15% grads pursue arts and sciences degrees. 1% grads pursue business degrees. 7% grads pursue law degrees. 5% grads pursue medical degrees. **Faculty:** Student/faculty ratio 10:1. 466 full-time faculty, 89% hold PhDs. 100% faculty teach undergrads.

ACADEMICS
Degrees: Bachelor's, doctoral, first professional, master's. **Academic Requirements:** Arts/fine arts, English (including composition), foreign languages, health and exercise science, history, mathematics, philosophy, sciences (biological or physical), social science. **Classes:** Most classes have 10–19 students. Most lab/discussion sections have 10–19 students. **Majors with Highest Enrollment:** Business administration/management, communications studies/speech communication and rhetoric, political science and government. **Disciplines with Highest Percentage of Degrees Awarded:** Business/ marketing 18%, communications/journalism 9%, psychology 7%, history 7%, foreign languages and literature 7%, biological/life sciences 6%. **Special Study Options:** Cross-registration, double major, dual enrollment, honor program, independent study, internships, study abroad, teacher certification program.

FACILITIES
Housing: Coed dorms, apartments for single students, special housing for disabled students, fraternity/sorority housing, theme housing, substance-free housing, off-campus foreign language houses. **Special Academic Facilities/ Equipment:** Museum of Anthropology; Charlotte and Philip Hanes Art Gallery; Scales Fine Arts Center; Reynolda House, Museum of American Art; Laser and Electron Microscope Labs. **Computers:** 10% of classrooms are wired, 100% of classrooms are wireless, 90% of public computers are PCs, 10%

of public computers are UNIX, network access in dorm rooms, network access in dorm lounges, online registration, online administrative functions (other than registration), support for handheld computing, remote student-access to Web through college's connection, tuition includes personal computer. Undergraduates are required to own a computer.

CAMPUS LIFE
Activities: Choral groups, concert band, dance, drama/theater, literary magazine, marching band, music ensembles, pep band, radio station, student government, student newspaper, student-run film society, symphony orchestra, television station, yearbook. **Organizations:** 155 registered organizations, 15 honor societies, 16 religious organizations. 14 fraternities (34% men join), 9 sororities (50% women join). **Athletics (Intercollegiate):** *Men:* Baseball, basketball, cheerleading, cross-country, football, golf, soccer, tennis, track/field (indoor), track/field (outdoor). *Women:* Basketball, cheerleading, cross-country, field hockey, golf, soccer, tennis, track/field (indoor), track/field (outdoor), volleyball.

ADMISSIONS
Freshman Academic Profile: 62% in top 10% of high school class, 88% in top 25% of high school class, 98% in top 50% of high school class. 65% from public high schools. SAT Math middle 50% range 630–710. SAT Critical Reading middle 50% range 610–690. TOEFL required of all international applicants, minimum paper TOEFL 600, minimum computer TOEFL 250. **Basis for Candidate Selection:** *Very important factors considered include:* Academic GPA, application essay, character/personal qualities, class rank, rigor of secondary school record, standardized test scores. *Important factors considered include:* Extracurricular activities, recommendation(s), talent/ability. *Other factors considered include:* Alumni/ae relation, first generation, geographical residence, interview, level of applicant's interest, racial/ethnic status, religious affiliation/commitment, state residency, volunteer work. **Freshman Admission Requirements:** High school diploma is required, and GED is accepted. *Academic units required:* 4 English, 3 math, 1 science, 2 foreign language, 2 social studies. *Academic units recommended:* 4 English, 4 math, 4 science, 4 foreign language, 4 social studies. **Freshman Admission Statistics:** 7,341 applied, 43% admitted, 36% enrolled. **Transfer Admission Requirements:** High school transcript, college transcript(s), essay or personal statement, standardized test score, statement of good standing from prior institution(s). Minimum college GPA of 2.0 required. Lowest grade transferable C. **General Admission Information:** Application fee $50. Early Decision application deadline 11/15. Regular application deadline 1/15. Regular notification 4/1. Nonfall registration accepted. Admission may be deferred for a maximum of 1 year. Credit and/or placement offered for CEEB Advanced Placement tests.

COSTS AND FINANCIAL AID
Annual tuition $34,230. Room & board $9,500. Required fees $100. Average book expense $850. **Required Forms and Deadlines:** FAFSA, CSS/Financial Aid PROFILE, state aid form, Noncustodial PROFILE. Financial aid filing deadline 3/1. **Notification of Awards:** Applicants will be notified of awards on or about 4/1. **Types of Aid:** *Need-based scholarships/grants:* Pell, SEOG, state scholarships/grants, private scholarships, the school's own gift aid. *Loans:* FFEL Subsidized Stafford, FFEL Unsubsidized Stafford, FFEL PLUS, Federal Perkins, state loans, college/university loans from institutional funds, private alternative loans. **Financial Aid Statistics:** 36% freshmen, 34% undergrads receive need-based scholarship or grant aid. 28% freshmen, 29% undergrads receive need-based self-help aid. 74 freshmen, 276 undergrads receive athletic scholarships.

WALDORF COLLEGE

106 South Sixth Street Forest City, IA 50436
Phone: 641-585-8112 **E-mail:** admissions@waldorf.edu
Fax: 641-585-8125 **Website:** www.waldorf.edu **ACT Code:** 1895
Financial Aid Phone: 641-585-8120

This private school, affiliated with the Lutheran Church, was founded in 1903. It has a 40-acre campus.

RATINGS
Admissions Selectivity Rating: 60*   **Fire Safety Rating:** 60*   **Green Rating:** 60*

STUDENTS AND FACULTY
Enrollment: 573. **Student Body:** 53% female, 47% male, 6% international. **Faculty:** Student/faculty ratio 15:1. 64 full-time faculty, 25% hold PhDs. 100% faculty teach undergrads.

ACADEMICS

Degrees: Associate, bachelor's. **Academic Requirements:** Arts/fine arts, computer literacy, English (including composition), history, humanities, mathematics, sciences (biological or physical), social science. **Classes:** Most classes have 10–19 students. Most lab/discussion sections have fewer than 10 students. **Majors with Highest Enrollment:** Business, management, marketing, and related support services, communications, computer and information sciences and support services, journalism and related fields. **Disciplines with Highest Percentage of Degrees Awarded:** Business/marketing 35%, communication technologies 18%, education 16%, computer and information sciences 12%, social sciences 8%. **Special Study Options:** Accelerated program, cooperative education program, double major, English as a second language (ESL), honors program, internships, student-designed major, study abroad, teacher certification program.

FACILITIES

Housing: Coed dorms, men's dorms, women's dorms, special housing for disabled students. **Computers:** Network access in dorm rooms, network access in dorm lounges, online administrative functions (other than registration), remote student-access to Web through college's connection.

CAMPUS LIFE

Activities: Choral groups, concert band, dance, drama/theater, jazz band, music ensembles, musical theater, radio station, student government, student newspaper, television station, yearbook. **Athletics (Intercollegiate):** *Men:* Baseball, basketball, football, golf, soccer, wrestling. *Women:* Basketball, cheerleading, golf, soccer, softball, volleyball.

ADMISSIONS

Freshman Academic Profile: 95% from public high schools. TOEFL required of all international applicants, minimum paper TOEFL 500, minimum computer TOEFL 173. **Basis for Candidate Selection:** *Very important factors considered include:* Recommendation(s), rigor of secondary school record, standardized test scores. *Important factors considered include:* Extracurricular activities, talent/ability. *Other factors considered include:* Alumni/ae relation, character/personal qualities, class rank, interview, racial/ethnic status, religious affiliation/commitment. **Freshman Admission Requirements:** High school diploma is required, and GED is accepted. *Academic units recommended:* 4 English, 3 math, 3 science, 2 foreign language, 4 history. **Freshman Admission Statistics:** 584 applied, 67% admitted, 50% enrolled. **Transfer Admission Requirements:** High school transcript, college transcript(s), standardized test score, statement of good standing from prior institution(s). Minimum college GPA of 2.0 required. Lowest grade transferable C-. **General Admission Information:** Regular notification is rolling. Non-fall registration not accepted. Admission may be deferred for a maximum of 2 semesters.

COSTS AND FINANCIAL AID

Annual tuition $14,599. Room & board $5,670. Required fees $662. Average book expense $350. **Required Forms and Deadlines:** FAFSA. Financial aid filing deadline 3/4. **Notification of Awards:** Applicants will be notified of awards on or about 3/4. **Types of Aid:** *Need-based scholarships/grants:* Pell, SEOG, state scholarships/grants, private scholarships, the school's own gift aid. *Loans:* Direct Subsidized Stafford, Direct Unsubsidized Stafford, Direct PLUS, Federal Perkins, state loans. **Financial Aid Statistics:** 79% freshmen, 81% undergrads receive need-based scholarship or grant aid. 68% freshmen, 73% undergrads receive need-based self-help aid. 28 freshmen, 55 undergrads receive athletic scholarships.

WALLA WALLA UNIVERSITY

Office of Admissions, 204 South College Avenue, College Place, WA 99324-1198
Phone: 509-527-2327 **E-mail:** info@wwc.edu **CEEB Code:** 4940
Fax: 509-527-2397 **Website:** www.wwc.edu **ACT Code:** 4486
Financial Aid Phone: 509-527-2815

This private school, affiliated with the Seventh-Day Adventist Church, was founded in 1892. It has a 77-acre campus.

RATINGS

Admissions Selectivity Rating: 73   **Fire Safety Rating:** 60*   **Green Rating:** 60*

STUDENTS AND FACULTY

Enrollment: 457. **Student Body:** 47% female, 53% male, 60% out-of-state, 4% international (30 countries represented). **Retention and Graduation:** 71% freshmen return for sophomore year. 18% freshmen graduate within 4 years. **Faculty:** Student/faculty ratio 13:1. 114 full-time faculty, 70% hold PhDs. 100% faculty teach undergrads.

ACADEMICS

Degrees: Associate, bachelor's, master's. **Academic Requirements:** Arts/fine arts, English (including composition), history, humanities, mathematics, religion, sciences (biological or physical), social science. **Classes:** Most lab/discussion sections have fewer than 10 students. **Majors with Highest Enrollment:** Business administration/management, engineering, social work. **Disciplines with Highest Percentage of Degrees Awarded:** Health professions and related sciences 17%, business/marketing 16%, engineering 12%, education 11%, visual and performing arts 7%. **Special Study Options:** Cross registration, distance learning, double major, honors program, independent study, internships, liberal arts/career combination, study abroad, teacher certification program.

FACILITIES

Housing: Men's dorms, women's dorms, apartments for married students, apartments for single students, special housing for disabled students. **Special Academic Facilities/Equipment:** Marine station on the Rosario Strait of the Puget Sound. **Computers:** 90% of public computers are PCs, 10% of public computers are Macs, network access in dorm rooms, online registration, remote student-access to Web through college's connection.

CAMPUS LIFE

Activities: Choral groups, concert band, drama/theater, literary magazine, music ensembles, radio station, student government, student newspaper, symphony orchestra, television station, yearbook. **Organizations:** 33 registered organizations, 7 honor societies, 6 religious organizations. **Athletics (Intercollegiate):** *Men:* Basketball, golf, soccer, volleyball. *Women:* Basketball, softball, volleyball.

ADMISSIONS

Freshman Academic Profile: 13% in top 10% of high school class, 33% in top 25% of high school class, 62% in top 50% of high school class. 9% from public high schools. ACT middle 50% range 19.7–25.7. TOEFL required of all international applicants, minimum paper TOEFL 550, minimum computer TOEFL 213. **Basis for Candidate Selection:** *Very important factors considered include:* Academic GPA, recommendation(s), rigor of secondary school record. *Important factors considered include:* Character/personal qualities, level of applicant's interest. *Other factors considered include:* Class rank, extracurricular activities, standardized test scores, talent/ability. **Freshman Admission Requirements:** High school diploma is required, and GED is accepted. *Academic units required:* 4 English, 3 math, 2 science (2 science labs), 2 history, *Academic units recommended:* 4 English, 4 math, 3 science (2 science labs), 2 foreign language, 1 social studies, 2 history. **Freshman Admission Statistics:** 824 applied, 94% admitted, 42% enrolled. **Transfer Admission Requirements:** College transcript(s). Minimum college GPA of 2.0 required. Lowest grade transferable D-. **General Admission Information:** Application fee $40. Regular notification is rolling. Non-fall registration accepted. Admission may be deferred for a maximum of 2 semesters. Credit and/or placement offered for CEEB Advanced Placement tests.

COSTS AND FINANCIAL AID

Annual tuition $21,735. Room and board $5,055. Required fees $210. Average book expense $1,014. **Required Forms and Deadlines:** FAFSA, institution's own financial aid form. **Notification of Awards:** Applicants will be notified of awards on a rolling basis beginning on or about 3/15. **Types of Aid:** *Need-based scholarships/grants:* Pell, SEOG, state scholarships/grants, private scholarships, the school's own gift aid. *Loans:* FFEL Subsidized Stafford, FFEL Unsubsidized Stafford, FFEL PLUS, Federal Perkins, Federal Nursing, college/university loans from institutional funds. **Student Employment:** Federal Work-Study Program available. Institutional employment available. Off-campus job opportunities are good. **Financial Aid Statistics:** 55% freshmen, 54% undergrads receive need-based scholarship or grant aid. 62% freshmen, 62% undergrads receive need-based self-help aid. 84% freshmen, 83% undergrads receive any aid.

WALSH COLLEGE OF ACCOUNTANCY AND BUSINESS ADMINISTRATION

3838 Livernois Road, PO Box 7006, Troy, MI 48007-7006
Phone: 248-689-8282 **E-mail:** admissions@walshcollege.edu
Fax: 248-689-0938 **Website:** www.walshcollege.edu
Financial Aid Phone: 248-689-8282

This private school was founded in 1922. It has a 20-acre campus.

RATINGS
Admissions Selectivity Rating: 60*   **Fire Safety Rating:** 60*   **Green Rating:** 60*

STUDENTS AND FACULTY
Enrollment: 939. **Student Body:** 57% female, 43% male, 8% international. African American 5%, Asian 3%, Caucasian 62%, Hispanic 1%. **Faculty:** Student/faculty ratio 28:1. 16 full-time faculty, 50% hold PhDs.

ACADEMICS
Degrees: Bachelor's, master's, post-bachelor's certificate, post-master's certificate. **Academic Requirements:** Computer literacy, English (including composition), mathematics. **Classes:** Most classes have 20–29 students. **Disciplines with Highest Percentage of Degrees Awarded:** Business/marketing 100%. **Special Study Options:** Distance learning, double major, dual enrollment, independent study, internships.

FACILITIES
Computers: 100% of public computers are PCs, online registration, online administrative functions (other than registration), remote student-access to Web through college's connection.

CAMPUS LIFE
Activities: Student government. **Organizations:** 6 registered organizations, 1 honor society.

ADMISSIONS
Transfer Admission Requirements: College transcript(s). Minimum college GPA of 2.0 required. Lowest grade transferable C. **General Admission Information:** Application fee $25.

COSTS AND FINANCIAL AID
Annual tuition $7,500. Required fees $320. **Required Forms and Deadlines:** FAFSA. Financial aid filing deadline 3/23. **Types of Aid:** *Need-based scholarships/grants:* Pell, SEOG, state scholarships/grants, the school's own gift aid. *Loans:* FFEL Subsidized Stafford, FFEL Unsubsidized Stafford, state loans.

WALSH UNIVERSITY

Walsh University, 2020 East Maple Street North Canton, OH 44720-3396
Phone: 800-362-9846 **E-mail:** admissions@walsh.edu **CEEB Code:** 1926
Fax: 330-490-7165 **Website:** http://walsh.edu **ACT Code:** 3349
Financial Aid Phone: 330-490-7146

This private school, affiliated with the Roman Catholic Church, was founded in 1958. It has a 134-acre campus.

RATINGS
Admissions Selectivity Rating: 75   **Fire Safety Rating:** 95   **Green Rating:** 71

STUDENTS AND FACULTY
Enrollment: 2,078. **Student Body:** 64% female, 36% male, 2% out-of-state, 1% international (15 countries represented). African American 6%, Caucasian 81%. **Retention and Graduation:** 77% freshmen return for sophomore year. 37% freshmen graduate within 4 years. 22% grads go on to further study within 2 semesters. 10% grads pursue arts and sciences degrees. 4% grads pursue business degrees. 2% grads pursue law degrees. 3% grads pursue medical degrees. **Faculty:** Student/faculty ratio 15:1. 92 full-time faculty, 82% hold PhDs. 75% faculty teach undergrads.

ACADEMICS
Degrees: Associate, bachelor's, master's. **Academic Requirements:** Arts/fine arts, English (including composition), foreign languages, history, humanities, mathematics, philosophy, sciences (biological or physical), social science, theology. **Classes:** Most classes have 10–19 students. Most lab/discussion sections have 20–29 students. **Majors with Highest Enrollment:** Biological and physical sciences, business administration/management, nursing/registered nurse training (ASN, BSN, MSN, RN). **Disciplines**

with Highest Percentage of Degrees Awarded: Business/marketing 37%, education 21%, health professions and related sciences 11%, communications/journalism 9%, communication technologies 9%, biological/life sciences 6%. **Special Study Options:** Accelerated program, combined bachelor's/master's degree programs, cooperative education program, cross registration, double major, dual enrollment, English as a second language (ESL), exchange student program (domestic), external degree program, honors program, independent study, internships, liberal arts/career combination, study abroad, teacher certification program.

FACILITIES
Housing: Coed dorms, apartments for single students, special housing for disabled students. **Special Academic Facilities/Equipment:** Bioinformatics lab, Hoover Museum, human cadaver lab (prosection for undergrad), gathering garden for education activities with schoolchildren, religious education center. **Computers:** 3% of classrooms are wired, 14% of classrooms are wireless, 100% of public computers are PCs, network access in dorm rooms, network access in dorm lounges, online registration, online administrative functions (other than registration), remote student-access to Web through college's connection.

CAMPUS LIFE
Activities: Choral groups, dance, drama/theater, literary magazine, music ensembles, pep band, radio station, student government, student newspaper, yearbook. **Organizations:** 30 registered organizations, 4 honor societies, 3 religious organizations. **Athletics (Intercollegiate):** *Men:* Baseball, basketball, cheerleading, cross-country, football, golf, soccer, tennis, track/field (indoor), track/field (outdoor). *Women:* Basketball, cheerleading, cross-country, golf, soccer, softball, synchronized swimming, tennis, track/field (indoor), track/field (outdoor), volleyball. **Environmental Initiatives:** HVAC & electrical managament system. recycling program for paper, plastic, and aluminum. ink cartridge recycle system.

ADMISSIONS
Freshman Academic Profile: 15% in top 10% of high school class, 44% in top 25% of high school class, 78% in top 50% of high school class. 78% from public high schools. SAT Math middle 50% range 470–580. SAT Critical Reading middle 50% range 450–560. ACT middle 50% range 19–25. TOEFL required of all international applicants, minimum paper TOEFL 500, minimum computer TOEFL 173. **Basis for Candidate Selection:** *Very important factors considered include:* Academic GPA, rigor of secondary school record, standardized test scores. *Important factors considered include:* Application essay, character/personal qualities, class rank, recommendation(s), volunteer work. *Other factors considered include:* Extracurricular activities, interview. **Freshman Admission Requirements:** High school diploma is required, and GED is accepted. *Academic units recommended:* 4 English, 3 math, 3 science, 2 foreign language, 3 social studies, 1 academic elective. **Freshman Admission Statistics:** 1,357 applied, 80% admitted, 44% enrolled. **Transfer Admission Requirements:** High school transcript, college transcript(s). Minimum college GPA of 2.0 required. Lowest grade transferable C. **General Admission Information:** Application fee $25. Regular application deadline 8/15. Regular notification is rolling. Non-fall registration accepted. Admission may be deferred for a maximum of 2 semesters. Credit offered for CEEB Advanced Placement tests.

COSTS AND FINANCIAL AID
Annual tuition $19,390. Room and board $7,760. Required fees $660. Average book expense $1,000. **Required Forms and Deadlines:** FAFSA, institution's own financial aid form. Financial aid filing deadline 8/15. **Notification of Awards:** Applicants will be notified of awards on a rolling basis beginning on or about 3/15. **Types of Aid:** *Need-based scholarships/grants:* Pell, SEOG, state scholarships/grants, private scholarships, the school's own gift aid. *Loans:* FFEL Subsidized Stafford, FFEL Unsubsidized Stafford, FFEL PLUS, Federal Perkins, state loans. **Financial Aid Statistics:** 71% freshmen, 72% undergrads receive need-based scholarship or grant aid. 72% freshmen, 66% undergrads receive need-based self-help aid. 81 freshmen, 345 undergrads receive athletic scholarships. 96% freshmen, 84% undergrads receive any aid. Highest amount earned per year from on-campus jobs $3,002.

WARNER PACIFIC COLLEGE

Office of Admissions, 2219 Southeast Sixty-eighth, Portland, OR 97215
Phone: 503-517-1020 **E-mail:** admiss@warnerpacific.edu **CEEB Code:** 4595
Fax: 503-517-1352 **Website:** www.warnerpacific.edu
Financial Aid Phone: 503-517-1017

This private school, affiliated with the Church of God, was founded in 1937. It has a 15-acre campus.

RATINGS
Admissions Selectivity Rating: 60*   **Fire Safety Rating:** 60*   **Green Rating:** 60*

STUDENTS AND FACULTY

Enrollment: 644. **Student Body:** 65% female, 35% male. **Faculty:** Student/faculty ratio 14:1. 35 full-time faculty.

ACADEMICS

Degrees: Associate, bachelor's, certificate, master's. **Academic Requirements:** Arts/fine arts, English (including composition), humanities, mathematics, religion, sciences (biological or physical), social science. **Special Study Options:** Adult degree program, cooperative education program, double major, internships, student-designed major, study abroad, teacher certification program, weekend college.

FACILITIES

Housing: Coed dorms, men's dorms, women's dorms, apartments for married students, apartments for single students. **Special Academic Facilities/Equipment:** Early learning center, electron microscopes. **Computers:** 95% of public computers are PCs, 5% of public computers are Macs, network access in dorm rooms, network access in dorm lounges, remote student-access to Web through college's connection.

CAMPUS LIFE

Activities: Choral groups, dance, drama/theater, jazz band, music ensembles, musical theater, student government, student newspaper, yearbook. **Organizations:** 20 registered organizations, 2 religious organizations. **Athletics (Intercollegiate):** *Men:* Basketball, cross-country, soccer. *Women:* Basketball, cross-country, volleyball.

ADMISSIONS

Freshman Academic Profile: 78% from public high schools. TOEFL required of all international applicants, minimum paper TOEFL 525, minimum computer TOEFL 195. **Freshman Admission Requirements:** High school diploma is required, and GED is accepted. *Academic units recommended:* 4 English, 2 math, 2 science (2 science labs), 3 social studies. **Freshman Admission Statistics:** 1,242 applied. **Transfer Admission Requirements:** College transcript(s), essay or personal statement. Minimum college GPA of 2.5 required. Lowest grade transferable D. **General Admission Information:** Application fee $50. Early decision application deadline 6/1. Regular notification rolling. Non-fall registration accepted. Admission may be deferred for a maximum of 2 semesters. Credit offered for CEEB Advanced Placement tests.

COSTS AND FINANCIAL AID

Average book expense $500. **Required Forms and Deadlines:** FAFSA. Financial aid filing deadline 3/1. **Notification of Awards:** Applicants will be notified of awards on a rolling basis beginning on or about 3/1. **Types of Aid:** *Need-based scholarships/grants:* Pell, SEOG, state scholarships/grants, private scholarships, the school's own gift aid. *Loans:* FFEL Subsidized Stafford, FFEL Unsubsidized Stafford, FFEL PLUS, Federal Perkins. **Financial Aid Statistics:** 88% freshmen, 83% undergrads receive need-based scholarship or grant aid. 80% freshmen, 76% undergrads receive need-based self-help aid. 2 freshmen, 14 undergrads receive athletic scholarships. 97% freshmen, 96% undergrads receive any aid. Highest amount earned per year from on-campus jobs $4,000.

WARNER SOUTHERN COLLEGE

13985 Highway 27, Lake Wales, FL 33859
Phone: 863-638-7212 **E-mail:** admissions@warner.edu **CEEB Code:** 5883
Fax: 863-638-7290 **Website:** www.warner.edu **ACT Code:** 0777
Financial Aid Phone: 863-638-7203

This private school, affiliated with the Church of God, was founded in 1968. It has a 320-acre campus.

RATINGS

Admissions Selectivity Rating: 74   **Fire Safety Rating:** 60*   **Green Rating:** 60*

STUDENTS AND FACULTY

Enrollment: 937. **Student Body:** 58% female, 42% male, 1% international (17 countries represented). African American 17%, Caucasian 56%, Hispanic 8%. **Retention and Graduation:** 26% freshmen graduate within 4 years. **Faculty:** Student/faculty ratio 13:1. 34 full-time faculty, 59% hold PhDs. 100% faculty teach undergrads.

ACADEMICS

Degrees: Associate, bachelor's, certificate, master's. **Academic Requirements:** Arts/fine arts, Bible & theology courses, computer literacy, English (including composition), history, humanities, mathematics, philosophy, sciences (biological or physical), social science. **Classes:** Most classes have 10–19 students. Most lab/discussion sections have fewer than 10 students. **Majors with Highest Enrollment:** Business administration/management, education, pastoral studies/

counseling. **Disciplines with Highest Percentage of Degrees Awarded:** Business/marketing 74%, education 9%, philosophy and religious studies 5%, public administration and social services 4%, communication technologies 2%, parks and recreation 2%, psychology 2%. **Special Study Options:** Accelerated program, distance learning, double major, dual enrollment, English as a second language (ESL), independent study, internships, study abroad, teacher certification program.

FACILITIES

Housing: Men's dorms, women's dorms. **Computers:** 20% of classrooms are wireless, 85% of public computers are PCs, 15% of public computers are Macs, network access in dorm rooms, network access in dorm lounges, remote student-access to Web through college's connection.

CAMPUS LIFE

Activities: Choral groups, music ensembles, student government, student newspaper. **Organizations:** 2 registered organizations, 6 honor societies, 1 religious organization. 2 fraternities, 2 sororities. **Athletics (Intercollegiate):** *Men:* Baseball, basketball, cheerleading, cross-country, golf, soccer, tennis, track/field (indoor), track/field (outdoor). *Women:* Basketball, cheerleading, cross-country, golf, soccer, softball, tennis, track/field (indoor), track/field (outdoor), volleyball.

ADMISSIONS

Freshman Academic Profile: 11% in top 10% of high school class, 23% in top 25% of high school class, 66% in top 50% of high school class. 90% from public high schools. SAT Math middle 50% range 351–613. SAT Critical Reading middle 50% range 342–580. ACT middle 50% range 15–24. TOEFL required of all international applicants, minimum paper TOEFL 500, minimum computer TOEFL 173. **Basis for Candidate Selection:** *Important factors considered include:* Academic GPA, class rank, level of applicant's interest, recommendation(s), standardized test scores. *Other factors considered include:* Alumni/ae relation, application essay, character/personal qualities, extracurricular activities, interview, rigor of secondary school record, talent/ability, volunteer work. **Freshman Admission Requirements:** High school diploma is required, and GED is accepted. *Academic units recommended:* 4 English, 3 math, 2 science, 1 social studies, 1 history, 2 academic electives. **Freshman Admission Statistics:** 363 applied, 66% admitted, 47% enrolled. **Transfer Admission Requirements:** College transcript(s), essay or personal statement, statement of good standing from prior institution(s). Minimum college GPA of 2.0 required. Lowest grade transferable D. **General Admission Information:** Application fee $20. Regular notification is rolling. Non-fall registration accepted. Neither credit nor placement offered for CEEB Advanced Placement tests.

COSTS AND FINANCIAL AID

Annual tuition $13,600. Room & board $5,730. Required fees $150. Average book expense $1,000. **Required Forms and Deadlines:** FAFSA, state aid form, verification form. Financial aid filing deadline 5/1. **Notification of Awards:** Applicants will be notified of awards on a rolling basis beginning on or about 1/15. **Types of Aid:** *Need-based scholarships/grants:* Pell, SEOG, state scholarships/grants, private scholarships, the school's own gift aid. *Loans:* FFEL Subsidized Stafford, FFEL Unsubsidized Stafford, FFEL PLUS, Federal Perkins, alternative loans. **Student Employment:** Federal Work-Study Program available. Institutional employment available. Off-campus job opportunities are good. **Financial Aid Statistics:** 56% freshmen, 45% undergrads receive need-based scholarship or grant aid. 58% freshmen, 61% undergrads receive need-based self-help aid. 65 freshmen, 259 undergrads receive athletic scholarships. 100% freshmen, 93% undergrads receive any aid. Highest amount earned per year from on-campus jobs $1,200.

WARREN WILSON COLLEGE

Best 368

PO Box 9000, Asheville, NC 28815-9000
Phone: 828-771-2073 **E-mail:** admit@warren-wilson.edu **CEEB Code:** 5886
Fax: 828-298-1440 **Website:** www.warren-wilson.edu **ACT Code:** 3170
Financial Aid Phone: 828-771-2082

This private school, affiliated with the Presbyterian Church, was founded in 1894. It has a 1,100-acre campus.

RATINGS

Admissions Selectivity Rating: 84   **Fire Safety Rating:** 60*   **Green Rating:** 95

STUDENTS AND FACULTY

Enrollment: 838. **Student Body:** 60% female, 40% male, 82% out-of-state, 3% international (12 countries represented). Caucasian 93%, Hispanic 1%. **Retention and Graduation:** 69% freshmen return for sophomore year. 32% freshmen graduate within 4 years. 30% grads go on to further study within 2 semesters. 30% grads pursue arts and sciences degrees. 1% grads pursue business degrees. **Faculty:** Student/faculty ratio 12:1. 57 full-time faculty, 93% hold PhDs. 100% faculty teach undergrads.

ACADEMICS

Degrees: Bachelor's, master's. **Academic Requirements:** Arts/fine arts, English (including composition), history, humanities, mathematics, philosophy, sciences (biological or physical), social science. **Classes:** Most classes have 10–19 students. **Majors with Highest Enrollment:** Elementary education and teaching, environmental science, psychology. **Disciplines with Highest Percentage of Degrees Awarded:** Natural resources/environmental science 17%, interdisciplinary studies 14%, social sciences 14%, education 9%, history 8%, psychology 8%, biological/life sciences 5%, philosophy and religious studies 5%, public administration and social services 5%. **Special Study Options:** Cross registration, double major, dual enrollment, English as a second language (ESL), exchange student program (domestic), honors program, independent study, internships, liberal arts/career combination, student-designed major, study abroad.

FACILITIES

Housing: Coed dorms, men's dorms, women's dorms, apartments for married students, apartments for single students, cooperative housing. **Special Academic Facilities/Equipment:** 300-acre farm, 700-acre forest, archaeological dig on campus, organic garden. **Computers:** 100% of public computers are PCs, network access in dorm rooms, network access in dorm lounges, remote student-access to Web through college's connection.

CAMPUS LIFE

Activities: Choral groups, dance, drama/theater, jazz band, literary magazine, music ensembles, musical theater, student government, student newspaper, yearbook. **Organizations:** 25 registered organizations, 5 religious organizations. **Athletics (Intercollegiate):** *Men:* Basketball, cross-country, diving, kayaking, mountain biking, soccer, swimming, ultimate frisbee. *Women:* Basketball, cross-country, diving, kayaking, mountain biking, soccer, swimming, Ultimate Frisbee.

ADMISSIONS

Freshman Academic Profile: 13% in top 10% of high school class, 35% in top 25% of high school class, 79% in top 50% of high school class. 71% from public high schools. SAT Math middle 50% range 510–620. SAT Critical Reading middle 50% range 550–670. SAT Writing middle 50% range 530–630. ACT middle 50% range 22–27. TOEFL required of all international applicants, minimum paper TOEFL 550. **Basis for Candidate Selection:** *Very important factors considered include:* Application essay, character/personal qualities, interview, rigor of secondary school record, standardized test scores, volunteer work, work experience. *Important factors considered include:* Class rank, recommendation(s). *Other factors considered include:* Alumni/ae relation, extracurricular activities, state residency, talent/ability. **Freshman Admission Requirements:** High school diploma is required, and GED is accepted. *Academic units required:* 4 English, 3 math, 2 science (2 science labs), 3 history. *Academic units recommended:* 2 foreign language. **Freshman Admission Statistics:** 840 applied, 74% admitted, 36% enrolled. **Transfer Admission Requirements:** High school transcript, college transcript(s), standardized test score. Minimum college GPA of 3.0 required. Lowest grade transferable C. **General Admission Information:** Early decision application deadline 11/15. Regular application deadline 3/15. Regular notification Notification begins 2/1. Non-fall registration accepted. Credit and/or placement offered for CEEB Advanced Placement tests.

COSTS AND FINANCIAL AID

Annual tuition $21,384. Room and board $6,700. Required fees $300. Average book expense $870. **Required Forms and Deadlines:** FAFSA, institution's own financial aid form. Financial aid filing deadline 4/2. **Notification of Awards:** Applicants will be notified of awards on a rolling basis beginning on or about 3/2. **Types of Aid:** *Need-based scholarships/grants:* Pell, SEOG, state scholarships/grants, private scholarships, the school's own gift aid. *Loans:* FFEL Subsidized Stafford, FFEL Unsubsidized Stafford, FFEL PLUS, Federal Perkins, college/university loans from institutional funds. **Financial Aid Statistics:** 45% freshmen, 43% undergrads receive need-based scholarship or grant aid. 49% freshmen, 50% undergrads receive need-based self-help aid. Highest amount earned per year from on-campus jobs $2,472.

WARTBURG COLLEGE

100 Wartburg Boulevard, PO Box 1003, Waverly, IA 50677-0903
Phone: 319-352-8264 **E-mail:** admissions@wartburg.edu **CEEB Code:** 6926
Fax: 319-352-8579 **Website:** www.wartburg.edu **ACT Code:** 1364

This private school, affiliated with the Lutheran Church, was founded in 1852. It has a 118-acre campus.

RATINGS

Admissions Selectivity Rating: 82   **Fire Safety Rating:** 69   **Green Rating:** 72

STUDENTS AND FACULTY

Enrollment: 1,727. **Student Body:** 53% female, 47% male, 24% out-of-state, 5% international (37 countries represented). African American 3%, Asian 2%, Caucasian 85%, Hispanic 1%. **Retention and Graduation:** 73% freshmen return for sophomore year. 57% freshmen graduate within 4 years. 20% grads go on to further study within 2 semesters. 3% grads pursue arts and sciences degrees. 1% grads pursue business degrees. 2% grads pursue law degrees. 5% grads pursue medical degrees. **Faculty:** Student/faculty ratio 12:1. 107 full-time faculty, 78% hold PhDs. 100% faculty teach undergrads.

ACADEMICS

Degrees: Bachelor's. **Academic Requirements:** Diversity, English (including composition), faith and reflection, foreign languages, health and wellness, humanities, interdisciplinary study, mathematics, oral communication, philosophy, sciences (biological or physical), social science. **Classes:** Most classes have 10–19 students. Most lab/discussion sections have 20–29 students. **Majors with Highest Enrollment:** Biology/biological sciences, business, management, marketing, and related support services, public relations/image management. **Disciplines with Highest Percentage of Degrees Awarded:** Education 17%, business/marketing 15%, communication technologies 13%, biological/life sciences 9%, social sciences 5%. **Special Study Options:** Accelerated program, double major, dual enrollment, Hispanic cultural immersion (Colorado), honors program, independent study, internships, liberal arts/career combination, Navajo Nation (Arizona), student-designed major, study abroad, teacher certification program, Wartburg West program (Colorado).

FACILITIES

Housing: Coed dorms, men's dorms, women's dorms, suite-style living. **Special Academic Facilities/Equipment:** International museum, art gallery, fine arts center, Institute for Leadership Education, planetarium, prairie preserve, state-of-the-art library, Center for Community Engagement. **Computers:** 100% of classrooms are wired, 1% of classrooms are wireless, 73% of public computers are PCs, 23% of public computers are Macs, 4% of public computers are UNIX, network access in dorm rooms, network access in dorm lounges, online registration, online administrative functions (other than registration), remote student-access to Web through college's connection.

CAMPUS LIFE

Activities: Choral groups, concert band, dance, drama/theater, jazz band, literary magazine, music ensembles, musical theater, opera, pep band, radio station, student government, student newspaper, student-run film society, symphony orchestra, television station, yearbook. **Organizations:** 68 registered organizations, 12 honor societies, 9 religious organizations. **Athletics (Intercollegiate):** *Men:* Baseball, basketball, cross-country, football, golf, soccer, tennis, track/field (indoor), track/field (outdoor), wrestling. *Women:* Basketball, cross-country, golf, soccer, softball, tennis, track/field (indoor), track/field (outdoor), volleyball. **Environmental Initiatives:** LEED requirements for new Sports and Wellness Center. Partnership with Waverly Light and Power on wind generation to offset carbon-based energy in new Sports and Wellness Center.

ADMISSIONS

Freshman Academic Profile: 36% in top 10% of high school class, 63% in top 25% of high school class, 86% in top 50% of high school class. SAT Math middle 50% range 510–630. SAT Critical Reading middle 50% range 480–610. SAT Writing middle 50% range 510–640. ACT middle 50% range 21–26. TOEFL required of all international applicants, minimum paper TOEFL 480, minimum computer TOEFL 157. **Basis for Candidate Selection:** *Very important factors considered include:* Academic GPA, class rank, recommendation(s), rigor of secondary school record, standardized test scores. *Important factors considered include:* Character/personal qualities, interview. *Other factors considered include:* Extracurricular activities, level of applicant's interest, racial/ethnic status, talent/ability, volunteer work, work experience. **Freshman Admission Requirements:** High school diploma is required, and GED is accepted. *Academic units recommended:* 4 English, 3 math, 3 science, 2 foreign language, 2 social studies, 1 computer. **Freshman Admission Statistics:** 1,719 applied, 85% admitted, 35% enrolled. **Transfer Admission Requirements:** High school transcript, college transcript(s), standardized test score, statement of good standing from prior institution(s). Minimum college GPA of 2.0 required. Lowest grade transferable C-. **General Admission Information:** Application fee $20. Regular notification is rolling. Non-fall registration accepted. Admission may be deferred for a maximum of 2 semesters. Credit and/or placement offered for CEEB Advanced Placement tests.

COSTS AND FINANCIAL AID

Annual tuition $23,600. Room and board $6,985. Required fees $700. Average book expense $900. **Required Forms and Deadlines:** FAFSA. Financial aid filing deadline 3/1. **Notification of Awards:** Applicants will be notified of awards on a rolling basis beginning on or about 3/21. **Types of Aid:** *Need-based scholarships/grants:* Pell, SEOG, state scholarships/grants, private scholarships, the school's own gift aid. *Loans:* FFEL Subsidized Stafford, FFEL Unsubsidized Stafford, FFEL PLUS, Federal Perkins. **Student Employment:** Federal Work-Study Program available. Institutional employment available. Off-campus job opportunities are good. **Financial Aid Statistics:** 77% freshmen, 78% undergrads receive need-based scholarship or grant aid. 64% freshmen, 68% undergrads receive need-based self-help aid. 90% freshmen, 85% undergrads receive any aid. Highest amount earned per year from on-campus jobs $4,500. **Financial Aid Phone:** 319-352-8262.

WASHBURN UNIVERSITY

1700 Southwest College Avenue, Topeka, KS 66621
Phone: 785-231-1030 **E-mail:** zzdpadm@washburn.edu **CEEB Code:** 6928
Fax: 785-296-7933 **Website:** www.washburn.edu **ACT Code:** 1474
Financial Aid Phone: 785-231-1151

This public school was founded in 1865. It has a 160-acre campus.

RATINGS
Admissions Selectivity Rating: 70   **Fire Safety Rating:** 60*   **Green Rating:** 60*

STUDENTS AND FACULTY

Enrollment: 5,098. **Student Body:** 62% female, 38% male, 4% out-of-state, (45 countries represented). African American 6%, Asian 2%, Caucasian 67%, Hispanic 4%, Native American 1%. **Retention and Graduation:** 67% freshmen return for sophomore year. 27% freshmen graduate within 4 years. **Faculty:** Student/faculty ratio 15:1. 227 full-time faculty, 88% hold PhDs. 100% faculty teach undergrads.

ACADEMICS

Degrees: Associate, bachelor's, certificate, first professional certificate, first professional, master's, post-bachelor's certificate. **Academic Requirements:** Arts/fine arts, English (including composition), foreign languages, humanities, mathematics, physical education, sciences (biological or physical), social science. **Classes:** Most classes have 10–19 students. Most lab/discussion sections have fewer than 10 students. **Majors with Highest Enrollment:** Business administration/management, criminal justice/law enforcement administration, nursing/registered nurse training (ASN, BSN, MSN, RN). **Disciplines with Highest Percentage of Degrees Awarded:** Business/marketing 19%, health professions and related sciences 14%, education 8%, communication technologies 7%, social sciences 7%, computer and information sciences 6%. **Special Study Options:** Cooperative education program, cross registration, distance learning, double major, English as a second language (ESL), honors program, independent study, internships, student-designed major, study abroad, teacher certification program.

FACILITIES

Housing: Coed dorms, fraternity/sorority housing, off-campus referral service. **Special Academic Facilities/Equipment:** Mulvane Art Museum, White Concert Hall, university theater, observatory, planetarium, language lab, mediated classrooms, living learning center. **Computers:** 20% of public computers are PCs, 10% of public computers are Macs, 70% of public computers are UNIX, network access in dorm rooms, network access in dorm lounges, online registration, online administrative functions (other than registration), remote student-access to Web through college's connection.

CAMPUS LIFE

Activities: Choral groups, concert band, drama/theater, jazz band, literary magazine, marching band, music ensembles, musical theater, pep band, student government, student newspaper, television station, yearbook. **Organizations:** 71 registered organizations, 8 honor societies, 4 religious organizations. 4 fraternities (7% men join), 4 sororities (6% women join). **Athletics (Intercollegiate):** *Men:* Baseball, basketball, cheerleading, football, golf, tennis. *Women:* Basketball, cheerleading, softball, tennis, volleyball.

ADMISSIONS

Freshman Academic Profile: 20% in top 10% of high school class, 32% in top 25% of high school class, 65% in top 50% of high school class. 99% from public high schools. ACT middle 50% range 19–25. TOEFL required of all international applicants, minimum paper TOEFL 520, minimum computer TOEFL 193. **Basis for Candidate Selection:** *Other factors considered include:* Alumni/ae relation, character/personal qualities, class rank, extracurricular activities, rigor of secondary school record, standardized test scores, talent/ability, volunteer work, work experience. **Freshman Admission Requirements:** High school diploma is required, and GED is accepted. *Academic units recommended:* 4 English, 4 math, 4 science, 3 foreign language, 2 social studies, 2 history, 1 computer tech. **Freshman Admission Statistics:** 1,238 applied, 100% admitted, 60% enrolled. **Transfer Admission Requirements:** College transcript(s), statement of good standing from prior institution(s). Minimum college GPA of 2.0 required. Lowest grade transferable D. **General Admission Information:** Application fee $20. Regular notification is rolling. Non-fall registration accepted. Common Application not accepted. Credit offered for CEEB Advanced Placement tests.

COSTS AND FINANCIAL AID

Annual in-state tuition $3,300. Out-of-state tuition $7,440. Room & board $4,300. Required fees $56. Average book expense $690. **Required Forms and Deadlines:** FAFSA, institution's own financial aid form. Financial aid filing deadline 3/1. **Notification of Awards:** Applicants will be notified of awards on a rolling basis beginning on or about 1/1. **Types of Aid:** *Need-based scholarships/grants:* Pell, SEOG, state scholarships/grants, private scholarships, the school's own gift aid. *Loans:* FFEL Subsidized Stafford, FFEL Unsubsidized Stafford, FFEL PLUS, Federal Perkins. **Student Employment:** Federal Work-Study Program available. Institutional employment available. Off-campus job opportunities are excellent. **Financial Aid Statistics:** 28% freshmen, 38% undergrads receive need-based scholarship or grant aid. 38% freshmen, 59% undergrads receive need-based self-help aid. 51 freshmen, 169 undergrads receive athletic scholarships. Highest amount earned per year from on-campus jobs $1,600.

WASHINGTON & JEFFERSON COLLEGE

Best 368

60 South Lincoln Street, Washington, PA 15301
Phone: 724-223-6025 **E-mail:** admission@washjeff.edu **CEEB Code:** 2967
Fax: 724-223-6534 **Website:** www.washjeff.edu **ACT Code:** 3746
Financial Aid Phone: 724-223-6019

This private school was founded in 1781. It has a 60-acre campus.

RATINGS
Admissions Selectivity Rating: 92   **Fire Safety Rating:** 85   **Green Rating:** 85

STUDENTS AND FACULTY

Enrollment: 1,505. **Student Body:** 46% female, 54% male, 25% out-of-state. African American 3%, Asian 1%, Caucasian 88%, Hispanic 1%. **Retention and Graduation:** 86% freshmen return for sophomore year. 64% freshmen graduate within 4 years. 35% grads go on to further study within 2 semesters. 21% grads pursue arts and sciences degrees. 1% grads pursue business degrees. 6% grads pursue law degrees. 8% grads pursue medical degrees. **Faculty:** Student/faculty ratio 12:1. 104 full-time faculty, 89% hold PhDs. 100% faculty teach undergrads.

ACADEMICS

Degrees: Associate, bachelor's. **Academic Requirements:** Arts/fine arts, computer literacy, English (including composition), foreign languages, humanities, mathematics, sciences (biological or physical), social science. **Classes:** Most classes have 10–19 students. Most lab/discussion sections have 10–19 students. **Majors with Highest Enrollment:** Biology/biological sciences, business administration/management, English language and literature. **Disciplines with Highest Percentage of Degrees Awarded:** Business/marketing 29%, English 13%, psychology 12%, social sciences 11%, biological/life sciences 10%. **Special Study Options:** Accelerated program, advanced placement credit, double major, dual enrollment, honors program, independent study, internships, student-designed major, study abroad, teacher certification program.

FACILITIES

Housing: Coed dorms, men's dorms, women's dorms, special housing for disabled students, special housing for international students, fraternity/sorority housing, on-campus suites. **Special Academic Facilities/Equipment:** Atomic absorption unit, spectrometers, isolator lab, X-ray diffraction unit, neuropsychology lab, refrigerated centrifuge, global learning unit, Olin Exhibit Gallery, language lab. **Computers:** 100% of classrooms are wired, 50% of classrooms are wireless, 95% of public computers are PCs, 5% of public computers are Macs, network access in dorm rooms, network access in dorm lounges, online registration, online administrative functions (other than registration), support for handheld computing, remote student-access to Web through college's connection.

CAMPUS LIFE

Activities: Choral groups, concert band, dance, drama/theater, jazz band, literary magazine, music ensembles, musical theater, pep band, radio station, student government, student newspaper, student-run film society, yearbook. **Organizations:** 85 registered organizations, 19 honor societies, 4 religious organizations. 6 fraternities (32% men join), 4 sororities (42% women join). **Athletics (Intercollegiate):** *Men:* Baseball, basketball, cheerleading, cross-country, diving, football, golf, lacrosse, soccer, swimming, tennis, track/field (indoor), track/field (outdoor), water polo, wrestling. *Women:* Basketball, cheerleading, cross-country, diving, field hockey, golf, lacrosse, soccer, softball, swimming, tennis, track/field (indoor), track/field (outdoor), volleyball, water polo. **Environmental Initiatives:** President's Climate Commitment. Silver LEED Certification for new Science building. Food service sustainability initiatives.

ADMISSIONS

Freshman Academic Profile: 30% in top 10% of high school class, 65% in top 25% of high school class, 94% in top 50% of high school class. 80% from public high schools. SAT Math middle 50% range 530–640. SAT Critical Reading middle 50% range 520–620. ACT middle 50% range 23–27. TOEFL required of all international applicants, minimum paper TOEFL 500, minimum computer TOEFL 267. **Basis for Candidate Selection:** *Very important factors considered include:* Academic GPA, application essay, class rank, interview, recommendation(s), rigor of secondary school record. *Important factors considered include:* Character/personal qualities, extracurricular activities, standardized test scores. *Other factors considered include:* Alumni/ae relation, geographical residence, level of applicant's interest, racial/ethnic status, state residency, talent/ability, volunteer work. **Freshman Admission Requirements:** High school diploma is required, and GED is accepted. *Academic units required:* 3 English, 3 math, 1 science, 2 foreign language, 6 academic electives. **Freshman Admission Statistics:** 5,591 applied, 36% admitted, 22% enrolled. **Transfer Admission Requirements:** High school transcript, college transcript(s), essay or personal statement, standardized test score, statement of good standing from prior institution(s). Lowest grade transferable C. **General Admission Information:** Application fee $25. Early decision application deadline 12/1. Regular application deadline 3/1. Regular notification is rolling. Non-fall registration accepted. Admission may be deferred for a maximum of 2 semesters. Credit and/or placement offered for CEEB Advanced Placement tests.

COSTS AND FINANCIAL AID

Average book expense $800. **Required Forms and Deadlines:** FAFSA. Financial aid filing deadline 2/15. **Notification of Awards:** Applicants will be notified of awards on a rolling basis beginning on or about 3/1. **Types of Aid:** *Need-based scholarships/grants:* Pell, SEOG, state scholarships/grants, private scholarships, the school's own gift aid, ACG and SMART Grants. *Loans:* FFEL Subsidized Stafford, FFEL Unsubsidized Stafford, FFEL PLUS, Federal Perkins, college/university loans from institutional funds. **Financial Aid Statistics:** 67% freshmen, 62% undergrads receive need-based scholarship or grant aid. 69% freshmen, 63% undergrads receive need-based self-help aid. 99% freshmen, 96% undergrads receive any aid. Highest amount earned per year from on-campus jobs $2,400.

WASHINGTON AND LEE UNIVERSITY

Letcher Avenue, Lexington, VA 24450-0303
Phone: 540-458-8710 **E-mail:** admissions@wlu.edu **CEEB Code:** 5887
Fax: 540-458-8062 **Website:** www2.wlu.edu **ACT Code:** 4430
Financial Aid Phone: 540-463-8715

This private school was founded in 1749. It has a 322-acre campus.

RATINGS

Admissions Selectivity Rating: 98   **Fire Safety Rating:** 60*   **Green Rating:** 60*

STUDENTS AND FACULTY

Enrollment: 1,747. **Student Body:** 49% female, 51% male, 85% out-of-state, 4% international (47 countries represented). African American 4%, Asian 3%, Caucasian 86%, Hispanic 1%. **Retention and Graduation:** 94% freshmen return for sophomore year. 84% freshmen graduate within 4 years. 24% grads go on to further study within 2 semesters. 6% grads pursue arts and sciences degrees. 1% grads pursue business degrees. 9% grads pursue law degrees. 5% grads pursue medical degrees. **Faculty:** Student/faculty ratio 10:1. 215 full-time faculty, 94% hold PhDs. 100% faculty teach undergrads.

ACADEMICS

Degrees: Bachelor's, first professional, master's. **Academic Requirements:** Computer literacy, English (including composition), foreign languages, humanities, mathematics, physical education (including swim test), sciences (biological or physical), social science. **Classes:** Most classes have 10–19 students. Most lab/discussion sections have fewer than 10 students. **Majors with Highest Enrollment:** Business administration/management, economics, history. **Disciplines with Highest Percentage of Degrees Awarded:** Business/marketing 26%, social sciences 20%, communications/journalism 8%, English 5%, foreign languages and literature 5%. **Special Study Options:** Double major, exchange student program (domestic), honors program, independent study, internships, liberal arts/career combination, student-designed major, study abroad, teacher certification program.

FACILITIES

Housing: Coed dorms, apartments for single students, special housing for international students, fraternity/sorority housing, outing club house, Spanish house, Chavis house. **Special Academic Facilities/Equipment:** History and porcelain museums, performing arts center, communications labs, nuclear science lab, scanning electron microscope. **Computers:** 91% of public computers are PCs, 7% of public computers are Macs, 2% of public computers are UNIX, network access in dorm rooms, network access in dorm lounges, online registration, online administrative functions (other than registration), remote student-access to Web through college's connection.

CAMPUS LIFE

Activities: Choral groups, dance, drama/theater, jazz band, literary magazine, music ensembles, radio station, student government, student newspaper, student-run film society, symphony orchestra, television station, yearbook. **Organizations:** 90 registered organizations, 5 honor societies, 11 religious organizations. 14 fraternities (83% men join), 5 sororities (74% women join). **Athletics (Intercollegiate):** *Men:* Baseball, basketball, cross-country, equestrian sports, football, golf, lacrosse, soccer, swimming, tennis, track/field (indoor), track/field (outdoor), wrestling. *Women:* Basketball, cheerleading, cross-country, equestrian sports, field hockey, lacrosse, soccer, swimming, tennis, track/field (indoor), track/field (outdoor), volleyball.

ADMISSIONS

Freshman Academic Profile: 81% in top 10% of high school class, 98% in top 25% of high school class, 100% in top 50% of high school class. SAT Math middle 50% range 650–730. SAT Critical Reading middle 50% range 660–730. ACT middle 50% range 28–31. TOEFL required of all international applicants. **Basis for Candidate Selection:** *Very important factors considered include:* Character/personal qualities, class rank, extracurricular activities, rigor of secondary school record, standardized test scores. *Important factors considered include:* Interview, recommendation(s). *Other factors considered include:* Alumni/ae relation, application essay, geographical residence, racial/ethnic status, state residency, talent/ability, volunteer work, work experience. **Freshman Admission Requirements:** *Academic units required:* 4 English, 3 math, 1 science (1 science lab), 3 foreign language, 1 social studies, 1 history, 4 academic electives. *Academic units recommended:* 4 math, 3 science, 4 foreign language, 2 history. **Freshman Admission Statistics:** 4,215 applied, 27% admitted, 39% enrolled. **Transfer Admission Requirements:** High school transcript, college transcript(s), essay or personal statement, standardized test score, statement of good standing from prior institution(s). Minimum college GPA of 2.0 required. Lowest grade transferable C. **General Admission Information:** Application fee $50. Early decision application deadline 11/15.

Regular application deadline 1/15. Regular notification 4/1. Non-fall registration not accepted. Admission may be deferred for a maximum of 2 semesters. Credit and/or placement offered for CEEB Advanced Placement tests.

COSTS AND FINANCIAL AID

Annual tuition $27,960. Room & board $7,225. Required fees $675. Average book expense $1,500. **Required Forms and Deadlines:** FAFSA, CSS/Financial Aid PROFILE, Noncustodial PROFILE, Business/Farm Supplement. Financial aid filing deadline 2/9. **Notification of Awards:** Applicants will be notified of awards on or about 4/6. **Types of Aid:** *Need-based scholarships/grants:* Pell, SEOG, state scholarships/grants, private scholarships, the school's own gift aid. *Loans:* FFEL Subsidized Stafford, FFEL Unsubsidized Stafford, FFEL PLUS, Federal Perkins, college/university loans from institutional funds. **Student Employment:** Federal Work-Study Program available. Institutional employment available. Off-campus job opportunities are fair. **Financial Aid Statistics:** 31% freshmen, 27% undergrads receive need-based scholarship or grant aid. 13% freshmen, 14% undergrads receive need-based self-help aid.

WASHINGTON BIBLE COLLEGE

6511 Princess Garden Parkway, Lanham, MD 20706-3599
Phone: 301-552-1400 **E-mail:** admissions@bible.edu
Fax: 301-552-2775 **Website:** www.bible.edu **ACT Code:** 1462
Financial Aid Phone: 301-552-1400

This private school was founded in 1938. It has a 63-acre campus.

RATINGS
Admissions Selectivity Rating: 60*   **Fire Safety Rating:** 60*   **Green Rating:** 60*

STUDENTS AND FACULTY
Enrollment: 352. **Student Body:** 42% female, 58% male. **Retention and Graduation:** 10% freshmen graduate within 4 years. **Faculty:** 70% faculty teach undergrads.

ACADEMICS
Degrees: Associate, bachelor's, certificate. **Academic Requirements:** Bible theology. **Special Study Options:** English as a second language (ESL), independent study, internships.

FACILITIES
Housing: Men's dorms, women's dorms, apartments for married students. **Computers:** 100% of public computers are PCs, remote student-access to Web through college's connection.

CAMPUS LIFE
Activities: Choral groups, music ensembles, student government, yearbook. **Organizations:** 1 honor society, **Athletics (Intercollegiate):** *Men:* Basketball, soccer. *Women:* Basketball, cheerleading, volleyball.

ADMISSIONS
Freshman Academic Profile: TOEFL required of all international applicants, minimum paper TOEFL 550. **Basis for Candidate Selection:** *Very important factors considered include:* Application essay, recommendation(s), religious affiliation/commitment. *Important factors considered include:* Character/personal qualities, class rank, rigor of secondary school record, standardized test scores. *Other factors considered include:* Alumni/ae relation, extracurricular activities, interview, talent/ability, volunteer work. **Freshman Admission Requirements:** High school diploma is required, and GED is accepted. *Academic units recommended:* 4 English, 2 math, 2 science, 2 social studies, 5 academic electives. **Freshman Admission Statistics:** 56 applied, 29% admitted, 262% enrolled. **Transfer Admission Requirements:** College transcript(s), essay or personal statement, statement of good standing from prior institution(s). Minimum college GPA of 2.0 required. Lowest grade transferable C. **General Admission Information:** Application fee $25. Regular application deadline 8/4. Non-fall registration accepted. Common Application not accepted.

COSTS AND FINANCIAL AID
Annual tuition $10,140. Room & board $4,180. Required fees $100. Average book expense $300. **Required Forms and Deadlines:** FAFSA, institution's own financial aid form. Financial aid filing deadline 6/1. **Notification of Awards:** Applicants will be notified of awards on a rolling basis beginning on or about 1/30. **Types of Aid:** *Need-based scholarships/grants:* Pell, SEOG, state scholarships/grants, private scholarships, the school's own gift aid. *Loans:* FFEL Subsidized Stafford, FFEL Unsubsidized Stafford, FFEL PLUS. **Student Employment:** Federal Work-Study Program available. Institutional employment available. Off-campus job opportunities are excellent. **Financial Aid**

Statistics: 20% freshmen, 13% undergrads receive need-based scholarship or grant aid. 32% freshmen, 66% undergrads receive need-based self-help aid. Highest amount earned per year from on-campus jobs $3,000.

WASHINGTON COLLEGE

300 Washington Avenue, Chestertown, MD 21620
Phone: 410-778-7700 **E-mail:** adm.off@washcoll.edu **CEEB Code:** 5888
Fax: 410-778-7287 **Website:** www.washcoll.edu **ACT Code:** 1754
Financial Aid Phone: 410-778-7214

This private school was founded in 1782. It has a 144-acre campus.

RATINGS
Admissions Selectivity Rating: 88   **Fire Safety Rating:** 97   **Green Rating:** 60*

STUDENTS AND FACULTY
Enrollment: 1,259. **Student Body:** 60% female, 40% male, 50% out-of-state, 3% international (34 countries represented). African American 4%, Asian 1%, Caucasian 85%. **Retention and Graduation:** 87% freshmen return for sophomore year. 68% freshmen graduate within 4 years. 50% grads go on to further study within 2 semesters. 12% grads pursue arts and sciences degrees. 8% grads pursue business degrees. 4% grads pursue law degrees. 3% grads pursue medical degrees. **Faculty:** Student/faculty ratio 12:1. 91 full-time faculty, 88% hold PhDs. 100% faculty teach undergrads.

ACADEMICS
Degrees: Bachelor's, master's. **Academic Requirements:** Arts/fine arts, English (including composition), foreign languages, humanities, intensive writing course, mathematics, sciences (biological or physical), social science. **Classes:** Most classes have 10–19 students. Most lab/discussion sections have 10–19 students. **Majors with Highest Enrollment:** Business administration/management, English language and literature, psychology. **Disciplines with Highest Percentage of Degrees Awarded:** Social sciences 24%, psychology 12%, business/marketing 10%, English 9%, liberal arts/general studies 8%. **Special Study Options:** Double major, English as a second language (ESL), exchange student program (domestic), independent study, internships, liberal arts/career combination, student-designed major, study abroad, teacher certification program.

FACILITIES
Housing: Coed dorms, men's dorms, women's dorms, special housing for disabled students, special housing for international students, fraternity/sorority housing. **Special Academic Facilities/Equipment:** Language lab, computer classroom, C.V. Starr Center for the Study of the American Experience, the Center for the Environment and Society, O'Neil Literary House. **Computers:** 15% of classrooms are wired, 100% of classrooms are wireless, 50% of public computers are PCs, 25% of public computers are Macs, 25% of public computers are UNIX, network access in dorm rooms, network access in dorm lounges, online administrative functions (other than registration), support for handheld computing, remote student-access to Web through college's connection.

CAMPUS LIFE
Activities: Choral groups, concert band, dance, drama/theater, jazz band, literary magazine, music ensembles, student government, student newspaper, student-run film society, symphony orchestra, yearbook. **Organizations:** 50 registered organizations, 13 honor societies. 3 fraternities (20% men join), 3 sororities (20% women join). **Athletics (Intercollegiate):** *Men:* Baseball, basketball, crew/rowing, lacrosse, sailing, soccer, swimming, tennis. *Women:* Basketball, crew/rowing, field hockey, lacrosse, sailing, soccer, softball, swimming, tennis, volleyball.

ADMISSIONS
Freshman Academic Profile: 29% in top 10% of high school class, 61% in top 25% of high school class, 89% in top 50% of high school class. 67% from public high schools. SAT Math middle 50% range 520–610. SAT Critical Reading middle 50% range 520–630. SAT Writing middle 50% range 520–610. ACT middle 50% range 21–27. **Basis for Candidate Selection:** *Very important factors considered include:* Academic GPA, interview, rigor of secondary school record. *Important factors considered include:* Class rank, level of applicant's

interest, standardized test scores. *Other factors considered include:* Alumni/ae relation, application essay, character/personal qualities, extracurricular activities, first generation, geographical residence, racial/ethnic status, recommendation(s), state residency, talent/ability, volunteer work, work experience. **Freshman Admission Requirements:** High school diploma is required, and GED is accepted. *Academic units required:* 4 English, 3 math, 3 science (2 science labs), 2 foreign language, 2 social studies. *Academic units recommended:* 4 English, 4 math, 4 science (3 science labs), 4 foreign language, 4 social studies. **Freshman Admission Statistics:** 2,134 applied, 60% admitted, 25% enrolled. **Transfer Admission Requirements:** High school transcript, college transcript(s), essay or personal statement, statement of good standing from prior institution(s). Minimum college GPA of 2.5 required. Lowest grade transferable C-. **General Admission Information:** Application fee $45. Early decision application deadline 11/1. Regular application deadline 3/1. Regular notification is rolling. Non-fall registration accepted. Admission may be deferred for a maximum of 2 semesters. Credit and/or placement offered for CEEB Advanced Placement tests.

COSTS AND FINANCIAL AID

Annual tuition $31,570. Room and board $6,790. Required fees $590. Average book expense $1,200. **Required Forms and Deadlines:** FAFSA, institution's own financial aid form. Financial aid filing deadline 2/15. **Notification of Awards:** Applicants will be notified of awards on a rolling basis beginning on or about 3/15. **Types of Aid:** *Need-based scholarships/grants:* Pell, SEOG, state scholarships/grants, private scholarships, the school's own gift aid. *Loans:* FFEL Subsidized Stafford, FFEL Unsubsidized Stafford, FFEL PLUS, Federal Perkins, college/university loans from institutional funds. **Student Employment:** Federal Work-Study Program available. Institutional employment available. Off-campus job opportunities are good. **Financial Aid Statistics:** 36% freshmen, 43% undergrads receive need-based scholarship or grant aid. 27% freshmen, 32% undergrads receive need-based self-help aid. 79% freshmen, 85% undergrads receive any aid. Highest amount earned per year from on-campus jobs $2,000.

WASHINGTON STATE UNIVERSITY

Best 368

PO Box 641067, Pullman, WA 99164-1067
Phone: 509-335-5586 **E-mail:** admiss2@wsu.edu **CEEB Code:** 4705
Fax: 509-335-4902 **Website:** www.wsu.edu **ACT Code:** 4482
Financial Aid Phone: 509-335-9711

This public school was founded in 1890. It has a 1,875-acre campus.

RATINGS

Admissions Selectivity Rating: 83   **Fire Safety Rating:** 82   **Green Rating:** 96

STUDENTS AND FACULTY

Enrollment: 18,995. **Student Body:** 52% female, 48% male, 8% out-of-state, 2% international (82 countries represented). African American 3%, Asian 6%, Caucasian 76%, Hispanic 4%, Native American 1%. **Retention and Graduation:** 82% freshmen return for sophomore year. 33% freshmen graduate within 4 years. **Faculty:** Student/faculty ratio 14:1. 1,087 full-time faculty, 91% hold PhDs. 84% faculty teach undergrads.

ACADEMICS

Degrees: Bachelor's, doctoral, first professional, master's, post-bachelor's certificate, post-master's certificate. **Academic Requirements:** Arts/fine arts, English (including composition), foreign languages, history, humanities, mathematics, sciences (biological or physical), social science. **Classes:** Most classes have 20-29 students. **Majors with Highest Enrollment:** Education, mass communications/media studies, nursing/registered nurse training (ASN, BSN, MSN, RN). **Disciplines with Highest Percentage of Degrees Awarded:** Business/marketing 19%, social sciences 14%, health professions and related sciences 7%, education 6%, engineering 6%. **Special Study Options:** Accelerated program, cross registration, distance learning, double major, dual enrollment, English as a second language (ESL), exchange student program (domestic), honors program, independent study, internships, liberal arts/career combination, student-designed major, study abroad, teacher certification program.

FACILITIES

Housing: Coed dorms, men's dorms, women's dorms, apartments for married students, apartments for single students, special housing for international students, fraternity/sorority housing, single undergrad freshmen under age 20 required to live on campus. **Special Academic Facilities/Equipment:** Art, natural history, and anthropology museums and special collections, performing arts center, mycological herbarium, energy research center, primate research center, observatory and planetarium, electron microscopy center, nuclear radiation center, state-of-the-art Center for Undergraduate Education building, recording studio. **Computers:** 100% of classrooms are wired, 70% of classrooms are wireless, 91% of public computers are PCs, 8% of public computers are Macs, 1% of public computers are UNIX, network access in dorm rooms, network access in dorm lounges, online registration, online administrative functions (other than registration), support for handheld computing, remote student-access to Web through college's connection.

CAMPUS LIFE

Activities: Choral groups, dance, drama/theater, jazz band, literary magazine, marching band, music ensembles, opera, pep band, radio station, student government, student newspaper, student-run film society, symphony orchestra, television station, yearbook. **Organizations:** 330 registered organizations, 23 honor societies, 25 religious organizations. 23 fraternities (15% men join), 16 sororities (18% women join). **Athletics (Intercollegiate):** *Men:* Baseball, basketball, cross-country, football, golf, track/field (outdoor). *Women:* Basketball, crew/rowing, cross-country, golf, soccer, swimming, tennis, track/field (outdoor), volleyball. **Environmental Initiatives:** RecycleMania. President's Climate Commitment: Executive policy establishing a sustainability initiative.

ADMISSIONS

Freshman Academic Profile: 38% in top 10% of high school class, 62% in top 25% of high school class, 91% in top 50% of high school class. 88% from public high schools. SAT Math middle 50% range 510-610. SAT Critical Reading middle 50% range 490-600. TOEFL required of all international applicants, minimum paper TOEFL 520, minimum computer TOEFL 190. **Basis for Candidate Selection:** *Very important factors considered include:* Academic GPA, standardized test scores. *Important factors considered include:* Application essay, recommendation(s), rigor of secondary school record. *Other factors considered include:* Extracurricular activities. **Freshman Admission Requirements:** High school diploma is required, and GED is accepted. *Academic units required:* 4 English, 3 math, 2 science (1 science lab), 2 foreign language, 2 social studies, 1 history, 1 academic elective. *Academic units recommended:* 4 English, 4 math, 2 science (1 science lab), 2 foreign language, 2 social studies, 1 history, 1 academic elective. **Freshman Admission Statistics:** 9,314 applied, 77% admitted, 40% enrolled. **Transfer Admission Requirements:** College transcript(s). Minimum college GPA of 2.5 required. Lowest grade transferable D. **General Admission Information:** Application fee $50. Regular notification is rolling. Non-fall registration accepted. Credit offered for CEEB Advanced Placement tests.

COSTS AND FINANCIAL AID

Annual in-state tuition $5,812. Annual out-of-state tuition $16,126. Room and board $7,316. Required fees $1,054. Average book expense $912. **Required Forms and Deadlines:** FAFSA. Financial aid filing deadline 3/1. **Notification of Awards:** Applicants will be notified of awards on a rolling basis beginning on or about 4/15. **Types of Aid:** *Need-based scholarships/grants:* Pell, SEOG, state scholarships/grants, private scholarships, the school's own gift aid, United Negro College Fund, Federal Nursing Scholarships. *Loans:* FFEL Subsidized Stafford, FFEL Unsubsidized Stafford, FFEL PLUS, Federal Perkins, Federal Nursing. **Financial Aid Statistics:** 22% freshmen, 32% undergrads receive need-based scholarship or grant aid. 38% freshmen, 43% undergrads receive need-based self-help aid. 78 freshmen, 353 undergrads receive athletic scholarships. 73% freshmen, 67% undergrads receive any aid. Highest amount earned per year from on-campus jobs $3,585.

WASHINGTON UNIVERSITY IN ST. LOUIS

Best 368

Campus Box 1089, One Brookings Drive, St. Louis, MO 63130-4899
Phone: 314-935-6000 **E-mail:** admissions@wustl.edu **CEEB Code:** 6929
Fax: 314-935-4290 **Website:** www.wustl.edu **ACT Code:** 2386
Financial Aid Phone: 888-547-6670

This private school was founded in 1853. It has a 169-acre campus.

RATINGS
Admissions Selectivity Rating: 99   **Fire Safety Rating:** 87   **Green Rating:** 60*

STUDENTS AND FACULTY
Enrollment: 6,601. **Student Body:** 50% female, 50% male, 89% out-of-state, 4% international (106 countries represented). African American 9%, Asian 12%, Caucasian 63%, Hispanic 3%. **Retention and Graduation:** 97% freshmen return for sophomore year. 33% grads go on to further study within 2 semesters. **Faculty:** Student/faculty ratio 7:1. 859 full-time faculty, 98% hold PhDs. 92% faculty teach undergrads.

ACADEMICS
Degrees: Bachelor's, certificate, doctoral, first professional, master's, post-bachelor's certificate. **Academic Requirements:** English (including composition), varies by school. **Classes:** Most classes have fewer than 10 students. Most lab/discussion sections have 10–19 students. **Majors with Highest Enrollment:** Biology/biological sciences, finance, psychology. **Disciplines with Highest Percentage of Degrees Awarded:** Social sciences 17%, engineering 14%, business/marketing 12%, psychology 11%, biological/life sciences 8%. **Special Study Options:** Accelerated program, cooperative education program, cross registration, double major, dual enrollment, English as a second language (ESL), exchange student program (domestic), independent study, internships, liberal arts/career combination, student-designed major, study abroad, teacher certification program. The University Scholars Program at Washington University gives selected students the opportunity to be admitted to undergraduate study and a graduate program at the same time.

FACILITIES
Housing: Coed dorms, apartments for married students, apartments for single students, fraternity/sorority housing, cooperative housing, special interest suites, upper-class housing, single sex floors in coed buildings, on-campus transfer-specific housing. **Special Academic Facilities/Equipment:** Art gallery, business/economics experimental lab, botanical garden, NASA planetary imaging facility, TAP reactor system, triple monochromator, computer automated radioactive particle tracking and gamma ray computed tomography, observatory, EADS learning center, Student Enterprise Zone, Edison Theatre, lab science building, outdoor Tyson Research Center. **Computers:** Network access in dorm rooms, network access in dorm lounges, online registration, online administrative functions (other than registration), remote student-access to Web through college's connection.

CAMPUS LIFE
Activities: Choral groups, concert band, dance, drama/theater, jazz band, literary magazine, music ensembles, musical theater, opera, pep band, radio station, student government, student newspaper, student-run film society, symphony orchestra, television station, yearbook. **Organizations:** 200 registered organizations, 18 honor societies, 18 religious organizations. 12 fraternities (25% men join), 6 sororities (25% women join). **Athletics (Intercollegiate):** *Men:* Baseball, basketball, cross-country, diving, football, soccer, swimming, tennis, track/field (indoor), track/field (outdoor). *Women:* Basketball, cross-country, diving, soccer, softball, swimming, tennis, track/field (indoor), track/field (outdoor), volleyball.

ADMISSIONS
Freshman Academic Profile: 95% in top 10% of high school class, 100% in top 25% of high school class, 100% in top 50% of high school class. 66% from public high schools. SAT Math middle 50% range 690–780. SAT Critical Reading middle 50% range 680–750. ACT middle 50% range 30–33. TOEFL required of all international applicants, minimum paper TOEFL 550, minimum computer TOEFL 213. **Basis for Candidate Selection:** *Very important factors considered include:* Academic GPA, application essay, character/personal qualities, class rank, extracurricular activities, recommendation(s), rigor of secondary school record, standardized test scores, talent/ability, volunteer work, work experience. *Other factors considered include:* Alumni/ae relation, first

generation, interview, level of applicant's interest, racial/ethnic status. **Freshman Admission Requirements:** High school diploma is required, and GED is accepted. *Academic units recommended:* 4 English, 4 math, 4 science (4 science labs), 2 foreign language, 4 social studies, 4 history. **Freshman Admission Statistics:** 22,251 applied, 21% admitted, 32% enrolled. **Transfer Admission Requirements:** College transcript(s), essay or personal statement, statement of good standing from prior institution(s). Lowest grade transferable C. **General Admission Information:** Application fee $55. Early decision application deadline 11/15. Regular application deadline 1/15. Regular notification 4/1. Non-fall registration not accepted. Admission may be deferred for a maximum of 4 semesters. Credit and/or placement offered for CEEB Advanced Placement tests.

COSTS AND FINANCIAL AID
Annual tuition $36,200. Room and board $11,636. Required fees $1,048. Average book expense $1,220. **Required Forms and Deadlines:** FAFSA, CSS/Financial Aid PROFILE, Noncustodial PROFILE, student and parent 1040 tax return or signed waiver if there is no tax return. Financial aid filing deadline 2/15. **Notification of Awards:** Applicants will be notified of awards on or about 4/1. **Types of Aid:** *Need-based scholarships/grants:* Pell, SEOG, state scholarships/grants, private scholarships, the school's own gift aid, United Negro College Fund, Academic Competitiveness Grant, SMART Grant. *Loans:* FFEL Subsidized Stafford, FFEL Unsubsidized Stafford, FFEL PLUS, Federal Perkins, state loans, college/university loans from institutional funds. **Student Employment:** Federal Work-Study Program available. Institutional employment available. Off-campus job opportunities are excellent. **Financial Aid Statistics:** 39% freshmen, 42% undergrads receive need-based scholarship or grant aid. 32% freshmen, 32% undergrads receive need-based self-help aid. 40% freshmen, 42% undergrads receive any aid. Highest amount earned per year from on-campus jobs $2,000.

WAYLAND BAPTIST UNIVERSITY

1900 West 7th Street, CMB 712, Plainview, TX 79072
Phone: 806-291-3500 **E-mail:** admityou@wbu.edu
Fax: 806-291-1960 **Website:** www.wbu.edu **ACT Code:** 4246
Financial Aid Phone: 806-291-3520

This private school, affiliated with the Southern Baptist Church, was founded in 1908. It has an 80-acre campus.

RATINGS
Admissions Selectivity Rating: 74   **Fire Safety Rating:** 84   **Green Rating:** 60*

STUDENTS AND FACULTY
Enrollment: 883. **Student Body:** 55% female, 45% male, 13% out-of-state, 2% international (18 countries represented). African American 3%, Caucasian 63%, Hispanic 25%. **Retention and Graduation:** 69% freshmen return for sophomore year. 12% freshmen graduate within 4 years. **Faculty:** Student/faculty ratio 12:1. 66 full-time faculty, 71% hold PhDs. 100% faculty teach undergrads.

ACADEMICS
Degrees: Associate, bachelor's, master's. **Academic Requirements:** Arts/fine arts, computer literacy, English (including composition), foreign languages, history, humanities, mathematics, sciences (biological or physical), social science. **Classes:** Most classes have 10–19 students. **Majors with Highest Enrollment:** Business administration/management, Christian studies, elementary education and teaching. **Disciplines with Highest Percentage of Degrees Awarded:** Education 28%, business/marketing 16%, philosophy and religious studies 9%, biological/life sciences 7%, security and protective services 6%. **Special Study Options:** Accelerated program, distance learning, double major, dual enrollment, external degree program, honors program, internships, teacher certification program.

FACILITIES
Housing: Men's dorms, women's dorms, apartments for married students. **Special Academic Facilities/Equipment:** Llano Estacado Museum. **Computers:** 100% of public computers are PCs, network access in dorm rooms, remote student-access to Web through college's connection.

CAMPUS LIFE
Activities: Choral groups, concert band, drama/theater, marching band, music ensembles, musical theater, pep band, radio station, student government, student newspaper, television station, yearbook. **Organizations:** 29 registered organizations, 3 honor societies, 7 religious organizations. **Athletics (Intercollegiate):** *Men:* Baseball, basketball, cheerleading, cross-country, golf, track/field

(indoor), track/field (outdoor). *Women:* Basketball, cheerleading, cross-country, soccer, track/field (indoor), track/field (outdoor), volleyball.

ADMISSIONS

Freshman Academic Profile: 19% in top 10% of high school class, 45% in top 25% of high school class, 76% in top 50% of high school class. SAT Math middle 50% range 450–590. SAT Critical Reading middle 50% range 410–570. SAT Writing middle 50% range 430–590. ACT middle 50% range 18–24. TOEFL required of all international applicants, minimum paper TOEFL 500, minimum computer TOEFL 173. **Basis for Candidate Selection:** *Very important factors considered include:* Class rank, standardized test scores. *Important factors considered include:* Rigor of secondary school record. **Freshman Admission Requirements:** High school diploma is required, and GED is accepted. *Academic units required:* 3 English, 2 math, 2 science, 2 history. *Academic units recommended:* 3 math, 3 science. **Freshman Admission Statistics:** 356 applied, 98% admitted, 61% enrolled. **Transfer Admission Requirements:** College transcript(s), statement of good standing from prior institution(s). Minimum college GPA of 2.0 required. Lowest grade transferable D. **General Admission Information:** Application fee $35. Non-fall registration accepted. Credit offered for CEEB Advanced Placement tests.

COSTS AND FINANCIAL AID

Annual tuition $10,200. Room & board $3,986. Required fees $600. Average book expense $1,000. **Required Forms and Deadlines:** FAFSA, institution's own financial aid form, tax returns/verification worksheet. Financial aid filing deadline 5/1. **Notification of Awards:** Applicants will be notified of awards on a rolling basis beginning on or about 2/15. **Types of Aid:** *Need-based scholarships/grants:* Pell, SEOG, state scholarships/grants, private scholarships, the school's own gift aid. *Loans:* FFEL Subsidized Stafford, FFEL Unsubsidized Stafford, FFEL PLUS, Federal Perkins, state loans. **Financial Aid Statistics:** 73% freshmen, 73% undergrads receive need-based scholarship or grant aid. 50% freshmen, 59% undergrads receive need-based self-help aid. 86 undergrads receive athletic scholarships.

WAYNE STATE COLLEGE

1111 Main Street, Wayne, NE 68787
Phone: 402-375-7234 **E-mail:** admit1@wsc.edu **CEEB Code:** 6469
Fax: 402-375-7204 **Website:** www.wsc.edu **ACT Code:** 2472
Financial Aid Phone: 402-375-7230

This public school was founded in 1909. It has a 128-acre campus.

RATINGS

Admissions Selectivity Rating: 69   **Fire Safety Rating:** 60*   **Green Rating:** 60*

STUDENTS AND FACULTY

Enrollment: 2,748. **Student Body:** 56% female, 44% male, 14% out-of-state. African American 3%, Caucasian 88%, Hispanic 2%, Native American 1%. **Retention and Graduation:** 70% freshmen return for sophomore year. **Faculty:** Student/faculty ratio 18:1. 129 full-time faculty, 78% hold PhDs. 89% faculty teach undergrads.

ACADEMICS

Degrees: Bachelor's, master's, post-master's certificate. **Academic Requirements:** Arts/fine arts, computer literacy, English (including composition), health and physical education, history, humanities, mathematics, philosophy, sciences (biological or physical), social science, technology and society. **Classes:** Most classes have 20–29 students. Most lab/discussion sections have 10–19 students. **Majors with Highest Enrollment:** Biology/biological sciences, business administration and management, elementary education and teaching. **Disciplines with Highest Percentage of Degrees Awarded:** Education 25%, business/marketing 23%, psychology 7%, security and protective services 7%, computer and information sciences 5%. **Special Study Options:** Cooperative education program, distance learning, double major, dual enrollment, honors program, independent study, internships, learning communities, student-designed major, study abroad, teacher certification program.

FACILITIES

Housing: Coed dorms. **Special Academic Facilities/Equipment:** Art gallery, fine arts center, planetarium, recreation center, telecommunications network. **Computers:** 25% of classrooms are wired, 85% of classrooms are wireless, 92% of public computers are PCs, 3% of public computers are Macs, 5% of public computers are UNIX, network access in dorm rooms, network access in dorm lounges, online registration, online administrative functions (other than

through college's connection.

CAMPUS LIFE

Activities: Choral groups, concert band, dance, drama/theater, jazz band, literary magazine, marching band, music ensembles, musical theater, pep band, radio station, student government, student newspaper, television station. **Organizations:** 95 registered organizations, 19 honor societies, 7 religious organizations. 1 fraternity, 3 sororities. **Athletics (Intercollegiate):** *Men:* Baseball, basketball, cross-country, football, golf, track/field (indoor), track/field (outdoor). *Women:* Basketball, cross-country, golf, soccer, softball, track/field (indoor), track/field (outdoor), volleyball. **Environmental Initiatives:** Recycling Program. Gray Water Project.

ADMISSIONS

Freshman Academic Profile: 11% in top 10% of high school class, 29% in top 25% of high school class, 58% in top 50% of high school class. ACT middle 50% range 18–24. TOEFL required of all international applicants, minimum paper TOEFL 550, minimum computer TOEFL 213. **Freshman Admission Requirements:** High school diploma is required, and GED is accepted. *Academic units recommended:* 4 English, 3 math, 2 science, 3 social studies. **Freshman Admission Statistics:** 1,224 applied, 100% admitted, 50% enrolled. **Transfer Admission Requirements:** College transcript(s), statement of good standing from prior institution(s). Minimum college GPA of 2.0 required. Lowest grade transferable C-. **General Admission Information:** Application fee $30. Regular application deadline 8/25. Regular notification is rolling. Non-fall registration accepted. Admission may be deferred for a maximum of 1 semester. Credit and/or placement offered for CEEB Advanced Placement tests.

COSTS AND FINANCIAL AID

Annual in-state tuition $3,075. Out-of-state tuition $6,150. Room & board $4,470. Required fees $938. Average book expense $900. **Required Forms and Deadlines:** FAFSA. Financial aid filing deadline 5/1. **Notification of Awards:** Applicants will be notified of awards on a rolling basis beginning on or about 3/15. **Types of Aid:** *Need-based scholarships/grants:* Pell, SEOG, state scholarships/grants, private scholarships, the school's own gift aid. *Loans:* FFEL Subsidized Stafford, FFEL Unsubsidized Stafford, FFEL PLUS, Federal Perkins. **Student Employment:** Federal Work-Study Program available. Institutional employment available. Off-campus job opportunities are fair. **Financial Aid Statistics:** 41% freshmen, 42% undergrads receive need-based scholarship or grant aid. 51% freshmen, 52% undergrads receive need-based self-help aid. 34 freshmen, 103 undergrads receive athletic scholarships.

WAYNE STATE UNIVERSITY

42 West Warren, "The Welcome Center," Detroit, MI 48202
Phone: 313-577-3577 **E-mail:** admissions@wayne.edu **CEEB Code:** 1898
Fax: 313-577-7536 **Website:** www.wayne.edu **ACT Code:** 2064
Financial Aid Phone: 313-577-3378

This public school was founded in 1868. It has a 219-acre campus.

RATINGS

Admissions Selectivity Rating: 60*   **Fire Safety Rating:** 60*   **Green Rating:** 60*

STUDENTS AND FACULTY

Enrollment: 19,113. **Student Body:** 59% female, 41% male, 1% out-of-state, 4% international (90 countries represented). African American 32%, Asian 5%, Caucasian 47%, Hispanic 3%. **Retention and Graduation:** 76% freshmen return for sophomore year. **Faculty:** Student/faculty ratio 17:1. 1,001 full-time faculty, 61% hold PhDs.

ACADEMICS

Degrees: Bachelor's, doctoral, first professional, master's, post-bachelor's certificate, post-master's certificate. **Academic Requirements:** Arts/fine arts, computer literacy, English (including composition), foreign culture, foreign languages, history, humanities, mathematics, oral communication, philosophy, sciences (biological or physical), social science. **Majors with Highest Enrollment:** Elementary education and teaching, nursing/registered nurse training (ASN, BSN, MSN, RN), psychology. **Disciplines with Highest Percentage of Degrees Awarded:** Business/marketing 16%, education 16%, health professions and related sciences 12%, engineering 8%, psychology 6%, social sciences 6%, visual and performing arts 6%, biological/life sciences 5%. **Special Study Options:** Accelerated program, cooperative education program, cross registration, distance learning, double major, dual enrollment, English as a second language (ESL), external degree program, honors program, indepen-

certification program, weekend college.

FACILITIES

Housing: Coed dorms, apartments for married students, apartments for single students, special housing for disabled students, fraternity/sorority housing. **Special Academic Facilities/Equipment:** Detroit Institute of Arts, Detroit Historical Museum, Detroit Science Museum, Charles H. Wright Museum of African American History. **Computers:** 76% of public computers are PCs, 15% of public computers are Macs, network access in dorm rooms, network access in dorm lounges, online registration, online administrative functions (other than registration), remote student-access to Web through college's connection.

CAMPUS LIFE

Activities: Choral groups, concert band, dance, drama/theater, jazz band, literary magazine, music ensembles, musical theater, opera, pep band, student government, student newspaper, student-run film society, symphony orchestra, yearbook. **Organizations:** 166 registered organizations, 4 honor societies, 12 religious organizations. 7 fraternities (2% men join), 8 sororities (2% women join). **Athletics (Intercollegiate):** *Men:* Baseball, basketball, cross-country, diving, fencing, football, golf, ice hockey, swimming, tennis. *Women:* Basketball, cross-country, diving, fencing, ice hockey, softball, swimming, tennis, volleyball.

ADMISSIONS

Freshman Academic Profile: ACT middle 50% range 16–24. TOEFL required of all international applicants, minimum paper TOEFL 550, minimum computer TOEFL 213. **Basis for Candidate Selection:** *Very important factors considered include:* Rigor of secondary school record, standardized test scores. *Other factors considered include:* Class rank, extracurricular activities. **Freshman Admission Requirements:** High school diploma is required, and GED is accepted. *Academic units recommended:* 4 English, 4 math, 3 science, 2 foreign language, 3 social studies, 2 academic electives. **Freshman Admission Statistics:** 9,680 applied, 63% admitted, 51% enrolled. **Transfer Admission Requirements:** College transcript(s). Minimum college GPA of 2.0 required. Lowest grade transferable C. **General Admission Information:** Application fee $30. Regular application deadline 8/1. Regular notification all year. Non-fall registration accepted. Admission may be deferred for a maximum of 2 semesters. Common Application not accepted. Credit and/or placement offered for CEEB Advanced Placement tests.

COSTS AND FINANCIAL AID

Annual in-state tuition $4,773. Out-of-state tuition $10,941. Room & board $6,700. Required fees $626. **Required Forms and Deadlines:** FAFSA. Financial aid filing deadline 3/1. **Notification of Awards:** Applicants will be notified of awards on a rolling basis beginning on or about 4/1. **Types of Aid:** *Need-based scholarships/grants:* Pell, SEOG, state scholarships/grants, private scholarships, the school's own gift aid. *Loans:* FFEL Subsidized Stafford, FFEL Unsubsidized Stafford, FFEL PLUS, Federal Perkins, Federal Nursing, state loans, college/university loans from institutional funds. **Student Employment:** Institutional employment available. Off-campus job opportunities are fair. **Financial Aid Statistics:** 43% freshmen, 40% undergrads receive need-based scholarship or grant aid. 31% freshmen, 41% undergrads receive need-based self-help aid. 75 freshmen, 315 undergrads receive athletic scholarships.

WAYNESBURG COLLEGE

51 West College Street, Waynesburg, PA 15370
Phone: 724-852-3248 **E-mail:** admissions@waynesburg.edu **CEEB Code:** 2969
Fax: 724-627-8124 **Website:** www.waynesburg.edu **ACT Code:** 3748
Financial Aid Phone: 724-852-3208

This private school, affiliated with the Presbyterian Church, was founded in 1849. It has a 30-acre campus.

RATINGS

Admissions Selectivity Rating: 60*   **Fire Safety Rating:** 94   **Green Rating:** 60*

STUDENTS AND FACULTY

Enrollment: 1,542. **Student Body:** 59% female, 41% male, 12% out-of-state. African American 4%, Caucasian 91%. **Retention and Graduation:** 74% freshmen return for sophomore year. 45% freshmen graduate within 4 years. 7% grads go on to further study within 2 semesters. 9% grads pursue arts and sciences degrees. 8% grads pursue business degrees. 2% grads pursue law degrees. 1% grads pursue medical degrees. **Faculty:** Student/faculty ratio 13:1. 63 full-time faculty, 62% hold PhDs. 100% faculty teach undergrads.

ACADEMICS

Degrees: Associate, bachelor's, master's. **Academic Requirements:** Arts/fine

arts, computer literacy, English (including composition), history, humanities, life skills, mathematics, philosophy, religion, sciences (biological or physical), service learning, social science. **Classes:** Most classes have 10–19 students. Most lab/discussion sections have 10–19 students. **Majors with Highest Enrollment:** Business, management, marketing, and related support services; communications, journalism and related fields; nursing/registered nurse training (ASN, BSN, MSN, RN). **Disciplines with Highest Percentage of Degrees Awarded:** Health professions and related sciences 37%, business/marketing 20%, public administration and social services 10%, communications/journalism 7%, education 6%. **Special Study Options:** Accelerated program, cooperative education program, distance learning, double major, dual enrollment, English as a second language (ESL), honors program, independent study, internships, liberal arts/career combination, student-designed major, study abroad, teacher certification program.

FACILITIES

Housing: Coed dorms, men's dorms, women's dorms. **Special Academic Facilities/Equipment:** Geology, biology, archaeology, and ceramics museum, arboretum, 174-acre farm. **Computers:** 10% of classrooms are wired, 90% of classrooms are wireless, 85% of public computers are PCs, 15% of public computers are Macs, network access in dorm rooms, network access in dorm lounges, online registration, online administrative functions (other than registration), support for handheld computing, remote student-access to Web through college's connection.

CAMPUS LIFE

Activities: Choral groups, concert band, dance, drama/theater, literary magazine, marching band, music ensembles, musical theater, radio station, student government, student newspaper, television station, yearbook. **Organizations:** 30 registered organizations, 16 honor societies, 7 religious organizations. **Athletics (Intercollegiate):** *Men:* Baseball, basketball, cross-country, football, golf, soccer, tennis, track/field (outdoor), wrestling. *Women:* Basketball, cross-country, golf, soccer, softball, tennis, track/field (outdoor), volleyball.

ADMISSIONS

Freshman Academic Profile: 19% in top 10% of high school class, 42% in top 25% of high school class, 72% in top 50% of high school class. TOEFL required of all international applicants, minimum paper TOEFL 550, minimum computer TOEFL 213. **Basis for Candidate Selection:** *Very important factors considered include:* Academic GPA, class rank, interview, rigor of secondary school record, standardized test scores. *Other factors considered include:* Application essay, character/personal qualities, extracurricular activities, recommendation(s), work experience. **Freshman Admission Requirements:** High school diploma is required, and GED is accepted. *Academic units required:* 4 English, 3 math, 2 science, 2 social studies, 5 academic electives. *Academic units recommended:* 2 foreign language. **Freshman Admission Statistics:** 1,680 applied, 67% admitted, 29% enrolled. **Transfer Admission Requirements:** High school transcript, college transcript(s), statement of good standing from prior institution(s). Minimum college GPA of 2.5 required. Lowest grade transferable C. **General Admission Information:** Application fee $20. Regular notification rolling. Non-fall registration accepted. Credit offered for CEEB Advanced Placement tests.

COSTS AND FINANCIAL AID

Annual tuition $16,080. Room and board $6,700. Required fees $340. Average book expense $1,100. **Required Forms and Deadlines:** FAFSA. Financial aid filing deadline 3/15. **Notification of Awards:** Applicants will be notified of awards on a rolling basis beginning on or about 2/15. **Types of Aid:** *Need-based scholarships/grants:* Pell, SEOG, state scholarships/grants, private scholarships, the school's own gift aid. *Loans:* FFEL Subsidized Stafford, FFEL Unsubsidized Stafford, FFEL PLUS, Federal Perkins, Federal Nursing, private alternative loans. **Student Employment:** Federal Work-Study Program available. Institutional employment available. Off-campus job opportunities are good. **Financial Aid Statistics:** 41% freshmen, 64% undergrads receive need-based scholarship or grant aid. 36% freshmen, 58% undergrads receive need-based self-help aid. 87% freshmen, 84% undergrads receive any aid. Highest amount earned per year from on-campus jobs $2,000.

WEBB INSTITUTE

298 Crescent Beach Road, Glen Cove, NY 11542
Phone: 516-674-9838 **E-mail:** admissions@Webb-institute.edu **CEEB Code:** 2970
Fax: 516-674-9838 **Website:** www.webb-institute.edu
Financial Aid Phone: 516-671-2213

This private school was founded in 1889. It has a 26-acre campus.

RATINGS
Admissions Selectivity Rating: 98   **Fire Safety Rating:** 65   **Green Rating:** 60*

STUDENTS AND FACULTY
Enrollment: 87. **Student Body:** 20% female, 80% male, 76% out-of-state. Asian 1%, Caucasian 95%, Hispanic 2%. **Retention and Graduation:** 82% freshmen return for sophomore year. 75% freshmen graduate within 4 years. 25% grads go on to further study within 2 semesters. **Faculty:** Student/faculty ratio 8:1. 10 full-time faculty, 60% hold PhDs. 100% faculty teach undergrads.

ACADEMICS
Degrees: Bachelor's. **Academic Requirements:** Computer literacy, engineering, English (including composition), history, humanities, mathematics, philosophy, sciences (biological or physical), social science. **Classes:** Most classes have 20–29 students. **Disciplines with Highest Percentage of Degrees Awarded:** Engineering 100%. **Special Study Options:** Double major, independent study, internships.

FACILITIES
Housing: Coed dorms, men's dorms, women's dorms. **Special Academic Facilities/Equipment:** Towing tank for model testing, marine engineering lab. **Computers:** 100% of classrooms are wireless, 100% of public computers are PCs, network access in dorm rooms, network access in dorm lounges, online administrative functions (other than registration), remote student-access to Web through college's connection.

CAMPUS LIFE
Activities: Choral groups, drama/theater, student government, symphony orchestra, yearbook. **Organizations:** 2 registered organizations. **Athletics (Intercollegiate):** *Men:* Basketball, cross-country, sailing, soccer, tennis, volleyball. *Women:* Basketball, cross-country, sailing, soccer, tennis, volleyball.

ADMISSIONS
Freshman Academic Profile: 69% in top 10% of high school class, 100% in top 25% of high school class, 80% from public high schools. SAT Math middle 50% range 680–740. SAT Critical Reading middle 50% range 620–700. SAT Writing middle 50% range 600–710. **Basis for Candidate Selection:** *Very important factors considered include:* Academic GPA, character/personal qualities, class rank, interview, rigor of secondary school record, standardized test scores. *Important factors considered include:* Extracurricular activities, level of applicant's interest, recommendation(s). *Other factors considered include:* Talent/ability, volunteer work, work experience. **Freshman Admission Requirements:** High school diploma is required, and GED is not accepted. *Academic units required:* 4 English, 4 math, 2 science (2 science labs), 2 social studies, 4 academic electives. **Freshman Admission Statistics:** 90 applied, 34% admitted, 77% enrolled. **Transfer Admission Requirements:** High school transcript, college transcript(s), interview, standardized test score. Minimum college GPA of 3.5 required. **General Admission Information:** Application fee $25. Early decision application deadline 10/15. Regular application deadline 2/15. Regular notification 3/15–4/30. Non-fall registration not accepted. Neither credit nor placement offered for CEEB Advanced Placement tests.

COSTS AND FINANCIAL AID
Room & board $9,500. Average book expense $750. **Required Forms and Deadlines:** FAFSA. Financial aid filing deadline 7/1. **Notification of Awards:** Applicants will be notified of awards on or about 8/1. **Types of Aid:** *Need-based scholarships/grants:* Pell, state scholarships/grants, private scholarships, the school's own gift aid. *Loans:* FFEL Subsidized Stafford, FFEL Unsubsidized Stafford, FFEL PLUS. **Student Employment:** Off-campus job opportunities

WEBBER INTERNATIONAL UNIVERSITY

PO Box 96, Babson Park, FL 33827
Phone: 863-638-2910 **E-mail:** admissions@webber.edu **CEEB Code:** 5893
Fax: 863-638-1591 **Website:** www.webber.edu **ACT Code:** 0773
Financial Aid Phone: 863-638-2930

This private school was founded in 1927. It has a 110-acre campus.

RATINGS
Admissions Selectivity Rating: 71   **Fire Safety Rating:** 83   **Green Rating:** 60*

STUDENTS AND FACULTY
Enrollment: 558. **Student Body:** 42% female, 58% male, 9% out-of-state, 16% international (36 countries represented). African American 23%, Caucasian 52%, Hispanic 8%. **Retention and Graduation:** 50% freshmen return for sophomore year. 34% freshmen graduate within 4 years. 20% grads go on to further study within 2 semesters. 18% grads pursue business degrees. 2% grads pursue law degrees. **Faculty:** Student/faculty ratio 18:1. 20 full-time faculty, 65% hold PhDs. 98% faculty teach undergrads.

ACADEMICS
Degrees: Associate, bachelor's, master's. **Academic Requirements:** Business core, computer literacy, English (including composition), humanities, mathematics, sciences (biological or physical), social science. **Classes:** Most classes have 20–29 students. **Majors with Highest Enrollment:** Business administration and management, business administration/management, parks, recreation and leisure facilities management. **Special Study Options:** Cooperative education program, cross registration, double major, dual enrollment, external degree program, internships, study abroad, weekend college.

FACILITIES
Housing: Men's dorms, women's dorms. **Computers:** 100% of public computers are PCs, network access in dorm rooms, online administrative functions (other than registration), remote student-access to Web through college's connection.

CAMPUS LIFE
Activities: Student government, student newspaper. **Organizations:** 6 registered organizations. **Athletics (Intercollegiate):** *Men:* Baseball, basketball, cheerleading, cross-country, football, golf, soccer, tennis, track/field (outdoor). *Women:* Basketball, cheerleading, cross-country, golf, soccer, softball, tennis, track/field (outdoor), volleyball.

ADMISSIONS
Freshman Academic Profile: 5% in top 10% of high school class, 26% in top 25% of high school class, 60% in top 50% of high school class. 76% from public high schools. SAT Math middle 50% range 420–515. SAT Critical Reading middle 50% range 375–495. ACT middle 50% range 16–19. TOEFL required of all international applicants, minimum paper TOEFL 500, minimum computer TOEFL 173. **Basis for Candidate Selection:** *Very important factors considered include:* Academic GPA, standardized test scores. *Important factors considered include:* Rigor of secondary school record. *Other factors considered include:* Alumni/ae relation, application essay, character/personal qualities, class rank, interview, recommendation(s). **Freshman Admission Requirements:** High school diploma is required, and GED is accepted. *Academic units required:* 4 English, 2 math, 1 science, 2 social studies. *Academic units recommended:* 3 math, 3 science, 1 foreign language, 2 history, 4 academic electives. **Freshman Admission Statistics:** 393 applied, 54% admitted, 69% enrolled. **Transfer Admission Requirements:** College transcript(s), statement of good standing from prior institution(s). Minimum college GPA of 2.0 required. Lowest grade transferable C. **General Admission Information:** Application fee $35. Regular application deadline 8/1. Regular notification is rolling. Non-fall registration accepted. Admission may be deferred for a maximum of 1 semester. Credit offered for CEEB Advanced Placement tests.

COSTS AND FINANCIAL AID
Annual tuition $16,760. Room and board $5,960. Average book expense $700. **Required Forms and Deadlines:** FAFSA, state aid form. Financial aid filing deadline 8/1. **Notification of Awards:** Applicants will be notified of awards on a rolling basis beginning on or about 4/1. **Types of Aid:** *Need-based scholarships/grants:* Pell, SEOG, state scholarships/grants, private scholarships, the school's own gift aid. *Loans:* FFEL Subsidized Stafford, FFEL Unsubsidized Stafford, FFEL PLUS, Federal Perkins. **Financial Aid Statistics:** 55%

freshmen, 8% undergrads receive need-based self-help aid. 55 freshmen, 165 undergrads receive athletic scholarships. 100% freshmen, 97% undergrads receive any aid. Highest amount earned per year from on-campus jobs $1,300.

See page 1486.

See page 1486.

WEBER STATE UNIVERSITY

1137 University Circle, Ogden, UT 84408-1137
Phone: 801-626-6744 **E-mail:** admissions@Weber.edu **CEEB Code:** 4941
Fax: 801-626-6747 **Website:** www.weber.edu **ACT Code:** 4282
Financial Aid Phone: 801-626-6586

This public school was founded in 1889. It has a 526-acre campus.

RATINGS
Admissions Selectivity Rating: 71   **Fire Safety Rating:** 60*   **Green Rating:** 76

STUDENTS AND FACULTY
Enrollment: 17,849. **Student Body:** 51% female, 49% male, 6% out-of-state. African American 1%, Asian 2%, Caucasian 63%, Hispanic 4%. **Retention and Graduation:** 71% freshmen return for sophomore year. 14% freshmen graduate within 4 years. **Faculty:** Student/faculty ratio 22:1. 460 full-time faculty, 85% hold PhDs. 98% faculty teach undergrads.

ACADEMICS
Degrees: Associate, bachelor's, certificate, master's, post-bachelor's certificate. **Academic Requirements:** Arts/fine arts, computer literacy, English (including composition), history, humanities, mathematics, sciences (biological or physical), social science. **Classes:** Most classes have 10–19 students. Most lab/discussion sections have 10–19 students. **Majors with Highest Enrollment:** Accounting, elementary education and teaching, liberal arts and sciences/liberal studies. **Disciplines with Highest Percentage of Degrees Awarded:** Business/marketing 21%, health professions and related sciences 15%, education 14%, security and protective services 7%, computer and information sciences 6%. **Special Study Options:** Accelerated program, cooperative education program, distance learning, double major, dual enrollment, English as a second language (ESL), exchange student program (domestic), external degree program, first-year experience, honors program, independent study, internships, student-designed major, study abroad, teacher certification program.

FACILITIES
Housing: Men's dorms, women's dorms, apartments for married students, apartments for single students, special housing for disabled students. **Special Academic Facilities/Equipment:** Art gallery, language lab, TV studio, communication arts/technologies facilities, natural science museum, herbarium, planetarium, aerospace technology equipment for developing satellite projects, dental hygiene clinic. **Computers:** network access in dorm rooms, network access in dorm lounges, online registration, online administrative functions (other than registration), remote student-access to Web through college's connection.

CAMPUS LIFE
Activities: Choral groups, concert band, dance, drama/theater, jazz band, literary magazine, marching band, music ensembles, musical theater, opera, pep band, radio station, student government, student newspaper, student-run film society, symphony orchestra, television station. **Organizations:** 100 registered organizations, 1 honor society, 1 religious organization. 1 fraternity (1% men join); 1 sorority (1% women join). **Athletics (Intercollegiate):** *Men:* Basketball, cheerleading, cross-country, football, golf, tennis, track/field (indoor), track/field (outdoor). *Women:* Basketball, cheerleading, cross-country, golf, soccer, tennis, track/field (indoor), track/field (outdoor), volleyball.

ADMISSIONS
Freshman Academic Profile: 52% in top 25% of high school class, 86% in top 50% of high school class. 99% from public high schools. ACT middle 50% range 19–24. **Basis for Candidate Selection:** *Important factors considered include:* Rigor of secondary school record, standardized test scores. *Other factors considered include:* Character/personal qualities, extracurricular activities, interview. **Freshman Admission Requirements:** High school diploma is required, and GED is accepted. *Academic units recommended:* 4 English, 2 math, 2 science, 2 foreign language, 1 history, 4 academic electives. **Freshman Admission Statistics:** 4,380 applied, 100% admitted, 56% enrolled. **Transfer Admission Requirements:** College transcript(s). Minimum college GPA of 2.0 required. Lowest grade transferable C. **General Admission Information:** Application fee $45. Regular application deadline 8/22. Regular notification ongoing. Non-fall registration accepted. Admission may be deferred for a

maximum of 2 semesters. Placement offered for CEEB Advanced Placement tests.

COSTS AND FINANCIAL AID
Annual in-state tuition $2,990. Annual out-of-state tuition $10,459. Room and board $6,634. Required fees $675. Average book expense $1,200. **Required Forms and Deadlines:** FAFSA, institution's own financial aid form. Financial aid filing deadline 3/1. **Notification of Awards:** Applicants will be notified of awards on a rolling basis beginning on or about 3/15. **Types of Aid:** *Need-based scholarships/grants:* Pell, SEOG, state scholarships/grants, private scholarships, the school's own gift aid. *Loans:* FFEL Subsidized Stafford, FFEL Unsubsidized Stafford, FFEL PLUS, Federal Perkins, short-term tuition loan. **Student Employment:** Federal Work-Study Program available. Institutional employment available. **Financial Aid Statistics:** 25% freshmen, 33% undergrads receive need-based scholarship or grant aid. 17% freshmen, 28% undergrads receive need-based self-help aid. 244 undergrads receive athletic scholarships. 50% freshmen, 56% undergrads receive any aid.

WEBSTER UNIVERSITY

470 East Lockwood Avenue, St. Louis, MO 63119-3194
Phone: 314-968-6991 **E-mail:** admit@webster.edu **CEEB Code:** 6933
Fax: 314-968-7115 **Website:** www.webster.edu **ACT Code:** 2388
Financial Aid Phone: 314-968-6992

This private school was founded in 1915. It has a 47-acre campus.

RATINGS
Admissions Selectivity Rating: 85   **Fire Safety Rating:** 89   **Green Rating:** 60*

STUDENTS AND FACULTY
Enrollment: 3,434. **Student Body:** 59% female, 41% male, 28% out-of-state. 3% international (59 countries represented). African American 12%, Asian 1%, Caucasian 75%, Hispanic 2%. **Retention and Graduation:** 78% freshmen return for sophomore year. 41% freshmen graduate within 4 years. 20% grads go on to further study within 2 semesters. **Faculty:** Student/faculty ratio 13:1. 168 full-time faculty, 78% hold PhDs. 100% faculty teach undergrads.

ACADEMICS
Degrees: Bachelor's, certificate, doctoral, master's, post-bachelor's certificate, post-master's certificate. **Academic Requirements:** Arts/fine arts, critical thinking and values, English (including composition), history, humanities, mathematics, sciences (biological or physical), social science. **Classes:** Most classes have 10–19 students. **Majors with Highest Enrollment:** Business administration/management, communications studies/speech communication and rhetoric, visual and performing arts. **Disciplines with Highest Percentage of Degrees Awarded:** Business/marketing 35%, communications/journalism 14%, visual and performing arts 11%, computer and information sciences 7%, social sciences 7%, psychology 6%. **Special Study Options:** Accelerated program, certificate programs, combination bachelor's/master's, cooperative education program, cross registration, distance learning, double major, dual enrollment, English as a second language (ESL), independent study, internships, student-designed major, student leadership development program, study abroad, teacher certification program, undergraduate degree completion programs at extended campus locations both domestic and abroad.

FACILITIES
Housing: Coed dorms, apartments for married students, apartments for single students, special housing for international students. **Special Academic Facilities/Equipment:** Loretto-Hilton Center for Performing Arts (houses St. Louis Repertory Company, Opera Theatre of St. Louis, and Webster Symphony). **Computers:** 67% of public computers are PCs, 33% of public computers are Macs, network access in dorm rooms, network access in dorm lounges, online registration, online administrative functions (other than registration), remote student-access to Web through college's connection.

CAMPUS LIFE
Activities: Choral groups, dance, drama/theater, jazz band, literary magazine, music ensembles, musical theater, opera, radio station, student government, student newspaper, student-run film society, symphony orchestra, television station, yearbook. **Organizations:** 61 registered organizations, 1 honor society, 2 religious organizations. **Athletics (Intercollegiate):** *Men:* Baseball, basketball, golf, soccer, swimming, tennis. *Women:* Basketball, cross-country, soccer, softball, swimming, tennis, volleyball. **Environmental Initiatives:** Recycling program.

ADMISSIONS

Freshman Academic Profile: 24% in top 10% of high school class, 52% in top 25% of high school class, 81% in top 50% of high school class. 70% from public high schools. SAT Math middle 50% range 500–610. SAT Critical Reading middle 50% range 530–650. ACT middle 50% range 21–28. TOEFL required of all international applicants, minimum paper TOEFL 490, minimum computer TOEFL 163. **Basis for Candidate Selection:** *Very important factors considered include:* Academic GPA, standardized test scores, talent/ability. *Important factors considered include:* Application essay, character/personal qualities, class rank, level of applicant's interest, racial/ethnic status, recommendation(s), rigor of secondary school record. *Other factors considered include:* Extracurricular activities, geographical residence, interview, volunteer work. **Freshman Admission Requirements:** High school diploma is required, and GED is accepted. *Academic units recommended:* 4 English, 3 math, 3 science (2 science labs), 2 foreign language, 3 social studies, 4 academic electives, 1 fine arts. **Freshman Admission Statistics:** 1,319 applied, 57% admitted, 58% enrolled. **Transfer Admission Requirements:** College transcript(s), essay or personal statement. Minimum college GPA of 2.5 required. Lowest grade transferable C. **General Admission Information:** Application fee $25. Regular application deadline 6/1. Regular notification is rolling. Non-fall registration accepted. Admission may be deferred for a maximum of 2 semesters. Credit offered for CEEB Advanced Placement tests.

COSTS AND FINANCIAL AID

Annual tuition $19,330. Room and board $8,220. Average book expense $800. **Required Forms and Deadlines:** FAFSA, institution's own financial aid form. Financial aid filing deadline 4/1. **Notification of Awards:** Applicants will be notified of awards on a rolling basis beginning on or about 2/1. **Types of Aid:** *Need-based scholarships/grants:* Pell, SEOG, state scholarships/grants, private scholarships, the school's own gift aid. *Loans:* FFEL Subsidized Stafford, FFEL Unsubsidized Stafford, FFEL PLUS, Federal Perkins. **Student Employment:** Federal Work-Study Program available. Institutional employment available. Off-campus job opportunities are good. **Financial Aid Statistics:** 56% freshmen, 57% undergrads receive need-based scholarship or grant aid. 57% freshmen, 61% undergrads receive need-based self-help aid. 91% freshmen, 82% undergrads receive any aid.

WELLESLEY COLLEGE

Best 368

Board of Admission, 106 Central Street, Wellesley, MA 02481-8203
Phone: 781-283-2270 **E-mail:** admission@wellesley.edu **CEEB Code:** 3957
Fax: 781-283-3678 **Website:** www.wellesley.edu **ACT Code:** 1926
Financial Aid Phone: 781-283-2360

This private school was founded in 1870. It has a 500-acre campus.

RATINGS

Admissions Selectivity Rating: 97   **Fire Safety Rating:** 86   **Green Rating:** 87

STUDENTS AND FACULTY

Enrollment: 2,215. **Student Body:** 100% female, 88% out-of-state, 8% international (79 countries represented). African American 6%, Asian 26%, Caucasian 47%, Hispanic 7%. **Retention and Graduation:** 95% freshmen return for sophomore year. 88% freshmen graduate within 4 years. 22% grads go on to further study within 2 semesters. 32% grads pursue arts and sciences degrees. 5% grads pursue business degrees. 10% grads pursue law degrees. 20% grads pursue medical degrees. **Faculty:** Student/faculty ratio 9:1. 225 full-time faculty, 99% hold PhDs. 100% faculty teach undergrads.

ACADEMICS

Degrees: Bachelor's. **Academic Requirements:** Arts/fine arts, English (including composition), foreign languages, history, humanities, mathematics, philosophy, sciences (biological or physical), social science, writing program. **Classes:** Most classes have 10–19 students. Most lab/discussion sections have 10–19 students. **Majors with Highest Enrollment:** Economics, English language and literature, psychology. **Disciplines with Highest Percentage of Degrees Awarded:** Social sciences 27%, area and ethnic studies 10%, foreign

student program (domestic), honors program, independent study, internships, student-designed major, study abroad, teacher certification program.

FACILITIES

Housing: Coed dorms, women's dorms, apartments for single students, special housing for disabled students, cooperative housing. **Special Academic Facilities/Equipment:** Clapp Library, Davis Museum and Cultural Center, Harambee House, Houghton Memorial Chapel, Hunnewell Arboretum, Alexandra Botanic Gardens, Ferguson Greenhouse, Jewett Art Museum, Keohane Sports Center, Knapp Media and Technology Center, Knapp Social Science Center, Lake Waban, Pforzheimer Learning and Teaching Center, Ruth Nagel Jones Theatre, science center including NMR spectrometers, Slater International Center, Wang Campus Center, Wellesley Centers for Women, Whitin Observatory including 3 telescopes. **Computers:** 13% of classrooms are wired, 5% of classrooms are wireless, 50% of public computers are PCs, 49% of public computers are Macs, 1% of public computers are UNIX, network access in dorm rooms, network access in dorm lounges, online registration, online administrative functions (other than registration), remote student-access to Web through college's connection.

CAMPUS LIFE

Activities: Choral groups, dance, drama/theater, jazz band, literary magazine, music ensembles, radio station, student government, student newspaper, student-run film society, yearbook. **Organizations:** 160 registered organizations, 7 honor societies, 30 religious organizations. **Athletics (Intercollegiate):** *Women:* Basketball, crew/rowing, cross-country, diving, fencing, field hockey, golf, lacrosse, soccer, softball, swimming, tennis, track/field (indoor), track/field (outdoor), volleyball. **Environmental Initiatives:** The College has made a large difference in improving the landscape by turning two significant brown field sites into green fields. Have greatly increased the recycling program over the past several years. Wellesley College is now focusing on reduction in consumption of materials while maintaining a strong recycling program. Have significantly reduced electrical consumption. In this effort, WC is implementing additional practices and equipment to further reduce electrical use. Since 2003 have reduced electrical consumption by 11.5% even though a new, highly programmed, 50,000 square foot building was brought on line during that period.

ADMISSIONS

Freshman Academic Profile: 85% in top 10% of high school class, 98% in top 25% of high school class, 100% in top 50% of high school class. 64% from public high schools. SAT Math middle 50% range 640–730. SAT Critical Reading middle 50% range 660–750. SAT Writing middle 50% range 660–730. ACT middle 50% range 29–32. **Basis for Candidate Selection:** *Very important factors considered include:* Academic GPA, application essay, character/personal qualities, recommendation(s), rigor of secondary school record, standardized test scores. *Important factors considered include:* Class rank, extracurricular activities. *Other factors considered include:* Alumni/ae relation, first generation, geographical residence, interview, level of applicant's interest, racial/ethnic status, state residency, talent/ability, volunteer work, work experience. **Freshman Admission Requirements:** High school diploma or equivalent is not required. *Academic units recommended:* 4 English, 4 math, 3 science (2 science labs), 4 foreign language, 4 social studies, 4 history. **Freshman Admission Statistics:** 3,974 applied, 36% admitted, 41% enrolled. **Transfer Admission Requirements:** High school transcript, college transcript(s), essay or personal statement, interview, standardized test score, statement of good standing from prior institution(s). **General Admission Information:** Application fee $50. Early decision application deadline 11/1. Regular application deadline 1/15. Regular notification 4/1. Non-fall registration not accepted. Admission may be deferred for a maximum of 2 semesters. Credit and/or placement offered for CEEB Advanced Placement tests.

COSTS AND FINANCIAL AID

Annual tuition $32,384. Room & board $10,216. Required fees $688. Average book expense $800. **Required Forms and Deadlines:** FAFSA, institution's own financial aid form, CSS/Financial Aid PROFILE, Business/Farm Supplement, Parents' and student's tax returns and W-2's, CSS Non-custodial Parent Form. Financial aid filing deadline 1/22. **Notification of Awards:** Applicants will be notified of awards on or about 4/1. **Types of Aid:** *Need-based scholarships/grants:* Pell, SEOG, state scholarships/grants, the school's own gift aid. *Loans:* FFEL Subsidized Stafford, FFEL Unsubsidized Stafford, FFEL PLUS, Federal Perkins, state loans, college/university loans from institutional funds. **Student Employment:** Federal Work-Study Program available. Off-campus job opportunities are excellent. **Financial Aid Statistics:** 53% freshmen, 58% undergrads receive need-based scholarship or grant aid. 47% freshmen, 54% undergrads receive need-based self-help aid. 56% freshmen, 60% undergrads receive any aid.

WELLS COLLEGE

Best 368

Route 90, Aurora, NY 13026
Phone: 315-364-3264 **E-mail:** admissions@wells.edu **CEEB Code:** 2971
Fax: 315-364-3227 **Website:** www.wells.edu **ACT Code:** 2971
Financial Aid Phone: 315-364-3289

This private school was founded in 1868. It has a 365-acre campus.

RATINGS
Admissions Selectivity Rating: 85   **Fire Safety Rating:** 84   **Green Rating:** 81

STUDENTS AND FACULTY
Enrollment: 469. **Student Body:** 84% female, 16% male, 32% out-of-state, 2% international (8 countries represented). African American 6%, Asian 2%, Caucasian 65%, Hispanic 4%. **Retention and Graduation:** 72% freshmen return for sophomore year. 47% freshmen graduate within 4 years. 25% grads go on to further study within 2 semesters. 18% grads pursue arts and sciences degrees. 1% grads pursue business degrees. 4% grads pursue law degrees. 2% grads pursue medical degrees. **Faculty:** Student/faculty ratio 8:1. 49 full-time faculty, 94% hold PhDs. 100% faculty teach undergrads.

ACADEMICS
Degrees: Bachelor's. **Academic Requirements:** Arts/fine arts, computer literacy, English (including composition), first-year seminar multi/interdisciplinary course, foreign languages, history, humanities, mathematics, philosophy, physical education, sciences (biological or physical), senior seminar, social science. **Classes:** Most classes have 10–19 students. **Majors with Highest Enrollment:** English language and literature, psychology, visual and performing arts. **Disciplines with Highest Percentage of Degrees Awarded:** Social sciences 19%, psychology 18%, English 13%, biological/life sciences 9%, visual and performing arts 9%, foreign languages and literature 6%. **Special Study Options:** Accelerated program, cross registration, double major, English as a second language (ESL), independent study, internships, student-designed major, study abroad, teacher certification program.

FACILITIES
Housing: Coed dorms, women's dorms, off campus college affiliated housing. **Special Academic Facilities/Equipment:** 2 greenhouses, environmentally regulated animal room, the college theatre (Phillips Auditorium), recital hall, electronic music studio, 15 pianos, a Dowd harpsichord, an early instrument collection, a sculpture and ceramics studio, dark rooms, painting and drawing studio, Book Arts Center, lithography presses, an extensive art library, art gallery, general and specialized clusters for the social sciences, foreign languages, and natural and mathematical sciences. **Computers:** 100% of classrooms are wired, 1% of classrooms are wireless, 85% of public computers are PCs, 15% of public computers are Macs, network access in dorm rooms, network access in dorm lounges, remote student-access to Web through college's connection.

CAMPUS LIFE
Activities: Choral groups, dance, drama/theater, literary magazine, music ensembles, student government, student newspaper, yearbook. **Organizations:** 35 registered organizations, 2 honor societies, 2 religious organizations. **Athletics (Intercollegiate):** *Men:* Cross-country, soccer, swimming. *Women:* Cross-country, field hockey, lacrosse, soccer, softball, swimming, tennis.

ADMISSIONS
Freshman Academic Profile: 26% in top 10% of high school class, 61% in top 25% of high school class, 93% in top 50% of high school class. 97% from public high schools. SAT Math middle 50% range 490–590. SAT Critical Reading middle 50% range 510–640. ACT middle 50% range 23–27. TOEFL required of all international applicants, minimum paper TOEFL 550, minimum computer TOEFL 213. **Basis for Candidate Selection:** *Very important factors considered include:* Academic GPA, extracurricular activities, recommendation(s), rigor of secondary school record, standardized test scores. *Important factors considered include:* Application essay, interview. *Other factors considered include:* Alumni/ae relation, character/personal qualities, class rank, level of applicant's interest, talent/ability, volunteer work, work experience. **Freshman Admission Requirements:** High school diploma is required, and GED is accepted. *Academic units required:* 4 English, 3 math, 2 science (2

science labs), 1 social studies, 3 history, 2 academic electives. *Academic units recommended:* 4 math, 3 science (3 science labs), 2 foreign language, 2 social studies, 2 history, 3 academic electives, 2 music, art, computer science. **Freshman Admission Statistics:** 1,075 applied, 71% admitted, 23% enrolled. **Transfer Admission Requirements:** High school transcript, college transcript(s), essay or personal statement, standardized test score, statement of good standing from prior institution(s). Minimum college GPA of 2.0 required. Lowest grade transferable C-. **General Admission Information:** Application fee $40. Early decision application deadline 12/15. Regular application deadline 3/1. Regular notification 4/1. Non-fall registration not accepted. Admission may be deferred for a maximum of 2 semesters. Credit and/or placement offered for CEEB Advanced Placement tests.

COSTS AND FINANCIAL AID
Annual tuition $17,580. Room and board $8,420. Required fees $1,900. Average book expense $800. **Required Forms and Deadlines:** FAFSA, CSS/Financial Aid PROFILE for early decision applicants only. Financial aid filing deadline 2/15. **Notification of Awards:** Applicants will be notified of awards on a rolling basis beginning on or about 3/1. **Types of Aid:** *Need-based scholarships/grants:* Pell, SEOG, state scholarships/grants, private scholarships, the school's own gift aid. *Loans:* FFEL Subsidized Stafford, FFEL Unsubsidized Stafford, FFEL PLUS, Federal Perkins. **Student Employment:** Federal Work-Study Program available. Institutional employment available. Off-campus job opportunities are fair. **Financial Aid Statistics:** 83% freshmen, 76% undergrads receive need-based scholarship or grant aid. 80% freshmen, 75% undergrads receive need-based self-help aid. 90% freshmen, 89% undergrads receive any aid. Highest amount earned per year from on-campus jobs $1,400.

See page 1488.

WENTWORTH INSTITUTE OF TECHNOLOGY

550 Huntington Avenue, Admissions Office, Boston, MA 02115-5998
Phone: 617-989-4000 **E-mail:** admissions@wit.edu **CEEB Code:** 3958
Fax: 617-989-4010 **Website:** www.wit.edu
Financial Aid Phone: 617-989-4020

This private school was founded in 1904. It has a 35-acre campus.

RATINGS
Admissions Selectivity Rating: 60*   **Fire Safety Rating:** 60*   **Green Rating:** 60*

STUDENTS AND FACULTY
Enrollment: 3,585. **Student Body:** 19% female, 81% male, 40% out-of-state, 3% international (50 countries represented). African American 4%, Asian 5%, Caucasian 77%, Hispanic 3%. **Retention and Graduation:** 79% freshmen return for sophomore year. **Faculty:** Student/faculty ratio 24:1. 146 full-time faculty, 40% hold PhDs. 100% faculty teach undergrads.

ACADEMICS
Degrees: Associate, bachelor's, certificate, post-bachelor's certificate. **Academic Requirements:** Computer literacy, co-op program, English (including composition), mathematics, sciences (biological or physical), social science. **Classes:** Most classes have 20–29 students. Most lab/discussion sections have 10–19 students. **Majors with Highest Enrollment:** Architecture (BArch, BA/BA, MArch, MA/MS, PhD), computer and information sciences, engineering technology. **Disciplines with Highest Percentage of Degrees Awarded:** Engineering technologies 49%, business/marketing 20%, computer and information sciences 12%, architecture 8%, visual and performing arts 7%. **Special Study Options:** Cooperative education program, cross registration, honors program, independent study, student-designed major, study abroad, weekend college.

FACILITIES
Housing: Coed dorms, apartments for single students. **Computers:** 80% of public computers are PCs, 15% of public computers are Macs, 5% of public computers are UNIX, network access in dorm rooms, network access in dorm lounges, online registration, online administrative functions (other than registration), remote student-access to Web through college's connection, tuition includes personal computer.

CAMPUS LIFE
Activities: Choral groups, drama/theater, literary magazine, music ensembles, musical theater, radio station, student government, student newspaper, student-run film society, yearbook. **Organizations:** 50 registered organizations, 2 honor societies. **Athletics (Intercollegiate):** *Men:* Baseball, basketball, golf, ice hockey, lacrosse, riflery, soccer, tennis, volleyball. *Women:* Basketball, golf, riflery, soccer, softball, tennis, volleyball.

ADMISSIONS

Freshman Academic Profile: SAT Math middle 50% range 560–600. SAT Critical Reading middle 50% range 470–510. ACT middle 50% range 21–25. TOEFL required of all international applicants, minimum paper TOEFL 525, minimum computer TOEFL 197. **Basis for Candidate Selection:** *Very important factors considered include:* Rigor of secondary school record. *Important factors considered include:* Application essay, recommendation(s), standardized test scores. *Other factors considered include:* Academic GPA, extracurricular activities, interview, level of applicant's interest, volunteer work, work experience. **Freshman Admission Requirements:** High school diploma is required, and GED is accepted. *Academic units required:* 4 English, 3 math, 1 science (1 science lab). *Academic units recommended:* 4 math, 3 science (2 science labs). **Freshman Admission Statistics:** 2,326 applied, 77% admitted, 44% enrolled. **Transfer Admission Requirements:** High school transcript, college transcript(s), essay or personal statement. Minimum college GPA of 2.0 required. Lowest grade transferable C. **General Admission Information:** Application fee $30. Regular notification is rolling. Non-fall registration accepted. Admission may be deferred for a maximum of 2 semesters. Credit and/or placement offered for CEEB Advanced Placement tests.

COSTS AND FINANCIAL AID

Annual tuition $19,300. Average book expense $1,000. **Required Forms and Deadlines:** FAFSA. Financial aid filing deadline 3/1. **Notification of Awards:** Applicants will be notified of awards on a rolling basis beginning on or about 3/15. **Types of Aid:** *Need-based scholarships/grants:* Pell, SEOG, state scholarships/grants, the school's own gift aid. *Loans:* Direct Subsidized Stafford, Direct Unsubsidized Stafford, Direct PLUS, Federal Perkins, state loans. **Student Employment:** Federal Work-Study Program available. Institutional employment available. Off-campus job opportunities are good. **Financial Aid Statistics:** 17% freshmen, 11% undergrads receive need-based scholarship or grant aid. 57% freshmen, 47% undergrads receive need-based self-help aid. 78% freshmen, 78% undergrads receive any aid.

WESLEY COLLEGE (DE)

120 North State Street, Dover, DE 19901-3875
Phone: 302-736-2400 **E-mail:** admissions@wesley.edu **CEEB Code:** 1433
Fax: 302-736-2382 **Website:** www.wesley.edu **ACT Code:** 0636
Financial Aid Phone: 302-736-2338

This private school, affiliated with the Methodist Church, was founded in 1873. It has a 40-acre campus.

RATINGS

Admissions Selectivity Rating: 79   **Fire Safety Rating:** 60*   **Green Rating:** 60*

STUDENTS AND FACULTY

Enrollment: 1,605. **Student Body:** 52% female, 48% male, 63% out-of-state. African American 22%, Asian 2%, Caucasian 72%, Hispanic 3%. **Retention and Graduation:** 82% freshmen return for sophomore year. 34% freshmen graduate within 4 years. 30% grads go on to further study within 2 semesters. 2% grads pursue arts and sciences degrees. 10% grads pursue business degrees. 1% grads pursue law degrees. **Faculty:** Student/faculty ratio 19:1. 66 full-time faculty, 79% hold PhDs. 100% faculty teach undergrads.

ACADEMICS

Degrees: Associate, bachelor's, certificate, master's, post-bachelor's certificate. **Academic Requirements:** Arts/fine arts, English (including composition), humanities, mathematics, philosophy, sciences (biological or physical), social science. **Classes:** Most classes have 10–19 students. Most lab/discussion sections have fewer than 10 students. **Majors with Highest Enrollment:** Business administration/management, mass communications/media studies, psychology. **Disciplines with Highest Percentage of Degrees Awarded:** Business/marketing 30%, education 16%, psychology 16%, social sciences 8%, communication technologies 7%, parks and recreation 6%. **Special Study Options:** Double major, honors program, independent study, internships, liberal arts/career combination, teacher certification program.

FACILITIES

Housing: Coed dorms, men's dorms, women's dorms, apartments for single students. **Computers:** 100% of public computers are PCs, 11% of public computers are Macs, network access in dorm rooms, online registration, online administrative functions (other than registration), remote student-access to Web through college's connection.

---

tions: 30 registered organizations, 2 honor societies, 2 religious organizations. 3 fraternities (1% men join), 3 sororities (5% women join). **Athletics (Intercollegiate):** *Men:* Baseball, basketball, cheerleading, cross-country, football, golf, lacrosse, soccer, tennis. *Women:* Basketball, cheerleading, cross-country, field hockey, golf, lacrosse, soccer, softball, tennis.

ADMISSIONS

Freshman Academic Profile: 24% in top 10% of high school class, 56% in top 25% of high school class, 78% in top 50% of high school class. 80% from public high schools. SAT Math middle 50% range 400–500. SAT Critical Reading middle 50% range 499–490. SAT Writing middle 50% range 390–490. TOEFL required of all international applicants, minimum paper TOEFL 550, minimum computer TOEFL 250. **Basis for Candidate Selection:** *Very important factors considered include:* Academic GPA. *Important factors considered include:* Class rank, rigor of secondary school record, standardized test scores. *Other factors considered include:* Alumni/ae relation, application essay, character/personal qualities, extracurricular activities, interview, level of applicant's interest, recommendation(s), talent/ability, volunteer work, work experience. **Freshman Admission Requirements:** High school diploma is required, and GED is accepted. *Academic units recommended:* 4 English, 4 math, 4 science (2 science labs), 2 foreign language, 2 social studies, 2 academic electives. **Freshman Admission Statistics:** 2,633 applied, 76% admitted, 25% enrolled. **Transfer Admission Requirements:** High school transcript, college transcript(s). Minimum college GPA of 2.0 required. Lowest grade transferable C. **General Admission Information:** Application fee $25. Regular notification 4 weeks. Non-fall registration accepted. Admission may be deferred for a maximum of 2 semesters. Credit and/or placement offered for CEEB Advanced Placement tests.

COSTS AND FINANCIAL AID

Annual tuition $16,750. Room & board $7,800. Required fees $829. Average book expense $1,000. **Required Forms and Deadlines:** FAFSA, institution's own financial aid form. Financial aid filing deadline 4/15. **Notification of Awards:** Applicants will be notified of awards on a rolling basis beginning on or about 1/1. **Types of Aid:** *Need-based scholarships/grants:* Pell, SEOG, state scholarships/grants, private scholarships. *Loans:* Direct PLUS, FFEL Subsidized Stafford, FFEL Unsubsidized Stafford, FFEL PLUS, Federal Perkins. **Financial Aid Statistics:** 60% freshmen, 75% undergrads receive need-based scholarship or grant aid. 77% freshmen, 86% undergrads receive need-based self-help aid. 95% freshmen, 95% undergrads receive any aid. Highest amount earned per year from on-campus jobs $2,550.

WESLEY COLLEGE (MS)

PO Box 1070, Florence, MS 39073
Phone: 800-748-9972 **E-mail:** wccadmit@aol.com
Fax: 601-845-2266 **Website:** www.wesleycollege.com **ACT Code:** 2253
Financial Aid Phone: 601-845-2265

This private school was founded in 1944. It has a 40-acre campus.

RATINGS

Admissions Selectivity Rating: 60*   **Fire Safety Rating:** 60*   **Green Rating:** 60*

STUDENTS AND FACULTY

Enrollment: 74. **Student Body:** 39% female, 61% male, 5% international (4 countries represented). African American 15%, Asian 1%, Caucasian 74%. **Faculty:** 100% faculty teach undergrads.

ACADEMICS

Degrees: Bachelor's, certificate. **Academic Requirements:** Arts/fine arts, English (including composition), history, mathematics, sciences (biological or physical), social science, theology and Bible courses.

FACILITIES

Housing: Men's dorms, women's dorms, apartments for married students, apartments for single students.

CAMPUS LIFE

Activities: Choral groups, drama/theater, music ensembles, student government, student newspaper, yearbook.

ADMISSIONS

Freshman Academic Profile: TOEFL required of all international applicants, minimum paper TOEFL 550. **Freshman Admission Requirements:** High school diploma is required, and GED is accepted. Transfer admission

Lowest grade transferable C. **General Admission Information:** Application fee $20. Regular application deadline rolling. Regular notification. Non-fall registration accepted. Common Application not accepted.

COSTS AND FINANCIAL AID

Annual tuition $3,500. Room & board $2,150. Required fees $150. Average book expense $200. **Required Forms and Deadlines:** FAFSA. **Types of Aid:** *Loans:* Direct Subsidized Stafford, Direct Unsubsidized Stafford. **Student Employment:** Federal Work-Study Program available. Off-campus job opportunities are excellent. **Financial Aid Statistics:** 100% freshmen, 100% undergrads receive need-based scholarship or grant aid. 89% freshmen, 100% undergrads receive need-based self-help aid.

WESLEYAN COLLEGE

4760 Forsyth Road, Macon, GA 31210-4462
Phone: 478-477-1110 **E-mail:** admissions@wesleyancollege.edu **CEEB Code:** 5895
Fax: 478-757-4030 **Website:** www.wesleyancollege.edu **ACT Code:** 0876
Financial Aid Phone: 478-757-5205

This private school, affiliated with the Methodist Church, was founded in 1836. It has a 200-acre campus.

RATINGS

Admissions Selectivity Rating: 88   **Fire Safety Rating:** 60*   **Green Rating:** 83

STUDENTS AND FACULTY

Enrollment: 561. **Student Body:** 100% female, 8% out-of-state, 14% international (24 countries represented). African American 30%, Asian 2%, Caucasian 48%, Hispanic 3%. **Retention and Graduation:** 64% freshmen return for sophomore year. 43% freshmen graduate within 4 years. 26% grads go on to further study within 2 semesters. 6% grads pursue arts and sciences degrees. 5% grads pursue business degrees. 2% grads pursue law degrees. 3% grads pursue medical degrees. **Faculty:** Student/faculty ratio 8:1. 49 full-time faculty, 82% hold PhDs. 100% faculty teach undergrads.

ACADEMICS

Degrees: Bachelor's, master's. **Academic Requirements:** Arts/fine arts, English (including composition), first-year seminar course, foreign languages, humanities, mathematics, sciences (biological or physical), social science. **Classes:** Most classes have 10–19 students. Most lab/discussion sections have fewer than 10 students. **Majors with Highest Enrollment:** Business/managerial operations; communications, journalism, and related fields; psychology. **Disciplines with Highest Percentage of Degrees Awarded:** Business/marketing 29%, communication technologies 12%, psychology 11%, biological/life sciences 10%, visual and performing arts 10%, social sciences 8%. **Special Study Options:** Accelerated program, cross registration, double major, dual degree engineering (3/2), dual enrollment, English as a second language (ESL), exchange student program (domestic), honors program, independent study, internships, student-designed major, study abroad, teacher certification program, weekend college.

FACILITIES

Housing: Women's dorms, apartments for single students. Students are required to live on campus unless married or living with family in the local area. **Special Academic Facilities/Equipment:** Art and history museums, special collection of Georgiana and Americana, on-campus equestrian center. **Computers:** 5% of classrooms are wired, 1% of classrooms are wireless, 95% of public computers are PCs, 5% of public computers are Macs, network access in dorm rooms, online registration, online administrative functions (other than registration), remote student-access to Web through college's connection. Undergraduates are required to own a computer.

CAMPUS LIFE

Activities: Choral groups, dance, drama/theater, literary magazine, music ensembles, student government, student newspaper, yearbook. **Organizations:** 40 registered organizations, 10 honor societies, 5 religious organizations. **Athletics (Intercollegiate):** *Women:* Basketball, equestrian sports, soccer, softball, tennis, volleyball. **Environmental Initiatives:** We are currently renovating a main teaching building to achieve LEED Silver Certification. Have established an Energy Star purchasing policy in accordance with the President's Climate Commitment. Have begun a campus-wide recycling program.

ADMISSIONS

Freshman Academic Profile: 34% in top 10% of high school class, 57% in top 25% of high school class, 85% in top 50% of high school class. 81% from public high schools. SAT Math middle 50% range 480–580. SAT Critical Reading middle 50% range 490–640. ACT middle 50% range 19–25. TOEFL required of all international applicants, minimum paper TOEFL 550, minimum computer TOEFL 213. **Basis for Candidate Selection:** *Very important factors considered include:* Rigor of secondary school record. *Important factors considered include:* Application essay, character/personal qualities, class rank, extracurricular activities, recommendation(s), standardized test scores, talent/ability, volunteer work. *Other factors considered include:* Alumni/ae relation, interview, work experience. **Freshman Admission Requirements:** High school diploma is required, and GED is accepted. *Academic units required:* 4 English, 3 math, 3 science (2 science labs), 2 foreign language, 3 social studies. *Academic units recommended:* 4 English, 4 math, 4 science (3 science labs), 4 foreign language, 4 social studies, 2 academic electives. **Freshman Admission Statistics:** 483 applied, 55% admitted, 42% enrolled. **Transfer Admission Requirements:** College transcript(s), statement of good standing from prior institution(s). Minimum college GPA of 2.0 required. Lowest grade transferable C. **General Admission Information:** Application fee $30. Early decision application deadline 11/15. Regular application deadline 8/1. Regular notification is rolling. Non-fall registration not accepted. Admission may be deferred for a maximum of 2 semesters. Common Application accepted. Credit and/or placement offered for CEEB Advanced Placement tests.

COSTS AND FINANCIAL AID

Annual tuition $16,500. Room and board $7,600. Average book expense $900. **Required Forms and Deadlines:** FAFSA, institution's own financial aid form, state aid form. Financial aid filing deadline 6/30. **Notification of Awards:** Applicants will be notified of awards on a rolling basis beginning on or about 3/1. **Types of Aid:** *Need-based scholarships/grants:* Pell, SEOG, state scholarships/grants, private scholarships, the school's own gift aid. *Loans:* FFEL Subsidized Stafford, FFEL Unsubsidized Stafford, FFEL PLUS, Federal Perkins, college/university loans from institutional funds, CitiAssist, Wells FARGO, Collegiate Loans, key alternative loans. **Student Employment:** Federal Work-Study Program available. Off-campus job opportunities are good. **Financial Aid Statistics:** 43% freshmen, 44% undergrads receive need-based scholarship or grant aid. 30% freshmen, 34% undergrads receive need-based self-help aid. 96% freshmen, 91% undergrads receive any aid. Highest amount earned per year from on-campus jobs $1,224.

WESLEYAN UNIVERSITY

The Stewart M. Reid House, 70 Wyllys Avenue, Middletown, CT 06459-0265
Phone: 860-685-3000 **E-mail:** admiss@wesleyan.edu **CEEB Code:** 3959
Fax: 860-685-3001 **Website:** www.wesleyan.edu **ACT Code:** 0614
Financial Aid Phone: 860-685-2800

This private school was founded in 1831. It has a 240-acre campus.

RATINGS

Admissions Selectivity Rating: 97   **Fire Safety Rating:** 86   **Green Rating:** 92

STUDENTS AND FACULTY

Enrollment: 2,805. **Student Body:** 50% female, 50% male, 92% out-of-state, 6% international (48 countries represented). African American 7%, Asian 11%, Caucasian 60%, Hispanic 8%. **Retention and Graduation:** 95% freshmen return for sophomore year. 84% freshmen graduate within 4 years. **Faculty:** Student/faculty ratio 9:1. 333 full-time faculty, 92% hold PhDs. 100% faculty teach undergrads.

ACADEMICS

Degrees: Bachelor's, doctoral, master's, post-master's certificate. **Classes:** Most classes have 10–19 students. Most lab/discussion sections have 10–19 students. **Majors with Highest Enrollment:** English language and literature, political science and government, psychology. **Disciplines with Highest Percentage of Degrees Awarded:** Social sciences 24%, visual and performing arts 14%, psychology 13%, area and ethnic studies 12%, English 12%. **Special Study Options:** Cross registration, double major, dual enrollment, exchange student program (domestic), honors program, independent study, internships, student-designed major, study abroad.

FACILITIES

Housing: Coed dorms, apartments for married students, apartments for single students, special housing for disabled students, fraternity/sorority housing, cooperative housing, 17 residence halls, 25 program houses, 122 woodframe houses. **Special Academic Facilities/Equipment:** Art center, art galleries, Center for Afro-American Studies, East Asian Studies Center, Cinema Archives, concert hall, Public Affairs Center, language lab, electron microscope, observatory, nuclear magnetic resonance spectrometers. **Computers:** 8% of classrooms are wired, 100% of classrooms are wireless, 70% of public computers are PCs, 25% of public computers are Macs, 5% of public computers are UNIX, network access in dorm rooms, network access in dorm lounges, online registration, online administrative functions (other than registration), remote student-access to Web through college's connection.

CAMPUS LIFE

Activities: Choral groups, concert band, dance, drama/theater, jazz band, literary magazine, music ensembles, musical theater, pep band, radio station, student government, student newspaper, student-run film society, symphony orchestra, yearbook. **Organizations:** 220 registered organizations, 2 honor societies, 10 religious organizations. 9 fraternities (2% men join), 4 sororities (1% women join). **Athletics (Intercollegiate):** *Men:* Baseball, basketball, crew/rowing, cross-country, diving, football, golf, ice hockey, lacrosse, soccer, squash, swimming, tennis, track/field (indoor), track/field (outdoor), wrestling. *Women:* Basketball, crew/rowing, cross-country, diving, field hockey, ice hockey, lacrosse, soccer, softball, squash, swimming, tennis, track/field (indoor), track/field (outdoor), volleyball. **Environmental Initiatives:** Education of campus community on Wesleyan's Carbon footprint and the steps required to meet the 2010, 2020 and 2050 goals towards carbon neutrality. Reduction of GHG to 1990 levels by 2010. Campus community commitment to climate change and education of personal impact on global climate change starting with your home and office.

ADMISSIONS

Freshman Academic Profile: 68% in top 10% of high school class, 91% in top 25% of high school class, 100% in top 50% of high school class. 57% from public high schools. SAT Math middle 50% range 650–740. SAT Critical Reading middle 50% range 650–750. SAT Writing middle 50% range 650–740. ACT middle 50% range 27–32. TOEFL required of all international applicants, minimum paper TOEFL 600, minimum computer TOEFL 250. **Basis for Candidate Selection:** *Very important factors considered include:* Rigor of secondary school record. *Important factors considered include:* Academic GPA, application essay, character/personal qualities, class rank, first generation, racial/ethnic status, recommendation(s), standardized test scores, talent/ability. *Other factors considered include:* Alumni/ae relation, extracurricular activities, geographical residence, interview, volunteer work, work experience. **Freshman Admission Requirements:** High school diploma or equivalent is not required. *Academic units required:* 4 English, 3 math, 3 science, 3 foreign language, 3 social studies. *Academic units recommended:* 4 English, 4 math, 4 science (3 science labs), 4 foreign language, 4 social studies. **Freshman Admission Statistics:** 7,242 applied, 28% admitted, 36% enrolled. **Transfer Admission Requirements:** High school transcript, college transcript(s), essay or personal statement, standardized test score, statement of good standing from prior institution(s). Lowest grade transferable C-. **General Admission Information:** Application fee $55. Early decision application deadline 11/15. Regular application deadline 1/1. Regular notification 4/1. Non-fall registration not accepted. Admission may be deferred for a maximum of 2 semesters. Credit and/or placement offered for CEEB Advanced Placement tests.

COSTS AND FINANCIAL AID

Required Forms and Deadlines: FAFSA, institution's own financial aid form, CSS/Financial Aid PROFILE, state aid form, Business/Farm Supplement, Non-custodial (Divorced/Separated) Parents statement. Financial aid filing deadline 2/15. **Notification of Awards:** Applicants will be notified of awards on or about 4/1. **Types of Aid:** *Need-based scholarships/grants:* Pell, SEOG, state scholarships/grants, private scholarships, the school's own gift aid. *Loans:* FFEL Subsidized Stafford, FFEL Unsubsidized Stafford, FFEL PLUS, Federal Perkins, college/university loans from institutional funds. **Financial Aid Statistics:** 41% freshmen, 45% undergrads receive need-based scholarship or grant aid. 44% freshmen, 48% undergrads receive need-based self-help aid. 39% freshmen, 43% undergrads receive any aid.

WEST CHESTER UNIVERSITY OF PENNSYLVANIA

Messikomer Hall, 100 West Rosedale Avenue, West Chester, PA 19383
Phone: 610-436-3411 **E-mail:** ugadmiss@wcupa.edu **CEEB Code:** 3328
Fax: 610-436-2907 **Website:** www.wcupa.edu
Financial Aid Phone: 610-436-2627

This public school was founded in 1871. It has a 388-acre campus.

RATINGS

Admissions Selectivity Rating: 85　　　**Fire Safety Rating:** 60*　　　**Green Rating:** 79

STUDENTS AND FACULTY

Enrollment: 10,458. **Student Body:** 61% female, 39% male, 12% out-of-state. African American 9%, Asian 2%, Caucasian 86%, Hispanic 3%. **Retention and Graduation:** 85% freshmen return for sophomore year. 31% freshmen graduate within 4 years. **Faculty:** Student/faculty ratio 13:1. 570 full-time faculty. 75% hold PhDs. 100% faculty teach undergrads.

ACADEMICS

Degrees: Bachelor's, certificate, master's, post-bachelor's certificate, post-master's certificate. **Academic Requirements:** Arts/fine arts, computer literacy, English (including composition), foreign languages, history, humanities, mathematics, sciences (biological or physical), social science. **Classes:** Most classes have 20–29 students. Most lab/discussion sections have 20–29 students. **Majors with Highest Enrollment:** Elementary education and teaching, health and physical education, psychology. **Disciplines with Highest Percentage of Degrees Awarded:** Education 16%, business/marketing 15%, health professions and related sciences 10%, liberal arts/general studies 10%, English 9%. **Special Study Options:** Cooperative education program, distance learning, double major, dual enrollment, English as a second language (ESL), exchange student program (domestic), honors program, independent study, internships, liberal arts/career combination, student-designed major, study abroad, teacher certification program.

FACILITIES

Housing: Coed dorms, men's dorms, women's dorms, apartments for single students, special housing for disabled students, special housing for international students, fraternity/sorority housing. **Special Academic Facilities/Equipment:** McKinney Gallery, Long Gallery, Mitchell Gallery, Emile K. Asplundh Concert Hall, Swope Auditorium, EO Bull Main Stage, Sykes Theater, Frances Harvey Green Library, music library, Darlington Herbarium, geology museum, speech and hearing clinic, Philips Autograph Library, Farrell Stadium, Hollinger Fieldhouse, Schmucker Science Center, Materials Research Center, WCU Planetarium, WCU Observatory, Center for GIS and Spatial Analysis, Robert B. Gordon Natural Area for Environmental Studies. **Computers:** 40% of classrooms are wireless, 95% of public computers are PCs, 5% of public computers are Macs, network access in dorm rooms, network access in dorm lounges, online registration, online administrative functions (other than registration), support for handheld computing, remote student-access to Web through college's connection.

CAMPUS LIFE

Activities: Choral groups, concert band, dance, drama/theater, jazz band, literary magazine, marching band, music ensembles, musical theater, radio station, student government, student newspaper, yearbook. **Organizations:** 215 registered organizations, 27 honor societies, 17 religious organizations. 10 fraternities, 13 sororities. **Athletics (Intercollegiate):** *Men:* Baseball, basketball, cross-country, diving, football, golf, soccer, swimming, tennis, track/field (outdoor). *Women:* Basketball, cross-country, diving, field hockey, golf, gymnastics, lacrosse, rugby, soccer, softball, swimming, tennis, track/field (outdoor), volleyball. **Environmental Initiatives:** LEED certification sought for new buildings on campus. Geothermal heating and cooling used for new residence halls, renovations, and buildings. University vehicle fleet includes some that use compressed natural gas.

ADMISSIONS

Freshman Academic Profile: 9% in top 10% of high school class, 66% in top 25% of high school class, 79% in top 50% of high school class. SAT Math middle 50% range 490–580. SAT Critical Reading middle 50% range 480–570. SAT Writing middle 50% range 480–570. TOEFL required of all international applicants, minimum paper TOEFL 550, minimum computer TOEFL 213. **Basis for Candidate Selection:** *Very important factors considered include:*

ethnic status, talent/ability, volunteer work, work experience. **Freshman Admission Requirements:** High school diploma is required, and GED is accepted. *Academic units required:* 4 English, 3 math, 2 science (1 science lab), 2 social studies, 4 history, 1 academic elective. *Academic units recommended:* 4 English, 4 math, 3 science (2 science labs), 2 foreign language, 2 social studies, 4 history, 2 academic electives. **Freshman Admission Statistics:** 11,669 applied, 46% admitted, 71% enrolled. **Transfer Admission Requirements:** College transcript(s), essay or personal statement. Minimum college GPA of 2.0 required. Lowest grade transferable C. **General Admission Information:** Application fee $35. Non-fall registration accepted. Credit and/or placement offered for CEEB Advanced Placement tests.

COSTS AND FINANCIAL AID

Annual in-state tuition $5,177. Annual out-of-state tuition $12,944. Room and board $6,590. Required fees $1,341. Average book expense $1,200. **Required Forms and Deadlines:** FAFSA. **Types of Aid:** *Need-based scholarships/grants:* Pell, state scholarships/grants, private scholarships, the school's own gift aid, United Negro College Fund, Federal Nursing Scholarships. *Loans:* Direct Subsidized Stafford, Direct Unsubsidized Stafford, Federal Perkins, Federal Nursing. **Student Employment:** Federal Work-Study Program available. Off-campus job opportunities are good. **Financial Aid Statistics:** 13% freshmen, 15% undergrads receive need-based scholarship or grant aid. 55% freshmen, 56% undergrads receive any aid.

WEST LIBERTY STATE COLLEGE

PO Box 295, West Liberty, WV 26074
Phone: 304-336-8076 **E-mail:** wladmsn1@wlsc.edu **CEEB Code:** 5901
Fax: 304-336-8403 **Website:** www.wlsc.edu **ACT Code:** 4534
Financial Aid Phone: 304-336-8016

This public school was founded in 1837. It has a 290-acre campus.

RATINGS

Admissions Selectivity Rating: 67   Fire Safety Rating: 60*   Green Rating: 60*

STUDENTS AND FACULTY

Enrollment: 2,305. **Student Body:** 55% female, 45% male, 28% out-of-state. African American 3%, Caucasian 95%. **Retention and Graduation:** 43% grads go on to further study within 2 semesters. 6% grads pursue arts and sciences degrees. 1% grads pursue business degrees. 1% grads pursue law degrees. 1% grads pursue medical degrees. **Faculty:** Student/faculty ratio 18:1. 98 full-time faculty, 45% hold PhDs. 100% faculty teach undergrads.

ACADEMICS

Degrees: Associate, bachelor's. **Academic Requirements:** Arts/fine arts, computer literacy, English (including composition), history, humanities, mathematics, philosophy, sciences (biological or physical), social science. **Classes:** Most classes have 10–19 students. Most lab/discussion sections have 10–19 students. **Majors with Highest Enrollment:** Business administration/management, criminal justice/safety studies, elementary education and teaching. **Disciplines with Highest Percentage of Degrees Awarded:** Education 25%, business/marketing 23%, health professions and related sciences 10%, liberal arts/general studies 9%, communication technologies 4%, psychology 4%. **Special Study Options:** Accelerated program, double major, external degree program, honors program, independent study, internships, student-designed major, teacher certification program.

FACILITIES

Housing: Coed dorms, men's dorms, women's dorms, apartments for married students, honors dorm. **Special Academic Facilities/Equipment:** Book museums, language lab, clinical lab sciences, dental hygiene labs. **Computers:** 85% of public computers are PCs, 15% of public computers are Macs, network access in dorm rooms, remote student-access to Web through college's connection.

CAMPUS LIFE

Activities: Choral groups, concert band, drama/theater, jazz band, literary magazine, marching band, music ensembles, musical theater, pep band, radio station, student government, student newspaper, television station. **Organizations:** 50 registered organizations, 10 honor societies, 4 religious organizations. 5 fraternities, 4 sororities. **Athletics (Intercollegiate):** *Men:* Baseball, basketball, cheerleading, cross-country, football, golf, swimming, tennis, track/field (outdoor), wrestling. *Women:* Basketball, cheerleading, cross-country, golf, softball, swimming, tennis, track/field (outdoor), volleyball.

ADMISSIONS

Freshman Academic Profile: 5% in top 10% of high school class, 32% in top 25% of high school class, 58% in top 50% of high school class. 88% from public high schools. SAT Math middle 50% range 390–490. SAT Critical Reading middle 50% range 400–500. ACT middle 50% range 17–22. TOEFL required of all international applicants, minimum paper TOEFL 500, minimum computer TOEFL 173. **Basis for Candidate Selection:** *Very important factors considered include:* Rigor of secondary school record, standardized test scores. **Freshman Admission Requirements:** High school diploma is required, and GED is accepted. *Academic units required:* 4 English, 2 math, 2 science (2 science labs), 2 social studies, 1 history. *Academic units recommended:* 2 foreign language. **Freshman Admission Statistics:** 1,202 applied, 98% admitted, 38% enrolled. **Transfer Admission Requirements:** College transcript(s). Minimum college GPA of 2.0 required. Lowest grade transferable D. **General Admission Information:** Regular notification is rolling. Non-fall registration accepted. Common Application not accepted. Credit offered for CEEB Advanced Placement tests.

COSTS AND FINANCIAL AID

Annual in-state tuition $3,138. Out-of-state tuition $7,790. Room & board $4,730. Average book expense $800. **Required Forms and Deadlines:** FAFSA. Financial aid filing deadline 3/1. **Notification of Awards:** Applicants will be notified of awards on a rolling basis beginning on or about 2/15. **Types of Aid:** *Need-based scholarships/grants:* Pell, SEOG, state scholarships/grants, private scholarships, the school's own gift aid. *Loans:* Direct Subsidized Stafford, Direct Unsubsidized Stafford, Direct PLUS, Federal Perkins, Federal Nursing. **Student Employment:** Off-campus job opportunities are good. **Financial Aid Statistics:** 46% freshmen, 44% undergrads receive need-based scholarship or grant aid. 40% freshmen, 58% undergrads receive need-based self-help aid.

WEST SUBURBAN COLLEGE OF NURSING

3 Erie Court, Oak Park, IL 60302
Phone: 708-763-6530 **E-mail:** admission@wscn.edu
Fax: 708-763-1531 **Website:** www.wscn.edu
Financial Aid Phone: 708-763-1426

This private school was founded in 1982.

RATINGS

Admissions Selectivity Rating: 60*   Fire Safety Rating: 60*   Green Rating: 60*

STUDENTS AND FACULTY

Enrollment: 124. **Student Body:** 91% female, 9% male. African American 22%, Asian 21%, Caucasian 30%, Hispanic 10%. **Faculty:** 11 full-time faculty, 27% hold PhDs. 100% faculty teach undergrads.

ACADEMICS

Degrees: Bachelor's. **Academic Requirements:** Arts/fine arts, computer literacy, English (including composition), history, humanities, mathematics, sciences (biological or physical), social science. **Classes:** Most classes have 10–19 students. Most lab/discussion sections have fewer than 10 students. **Disciplines with Highest Percentage of Degrees Awarded:** Health professions and related sciences 100%. **Special Study Options:** Accelerated program.

FACILITIES

Computers: 100% of classrooms are wired, 100% of public computers are PCs, online registration, online administrative functions (other than registration), remote student-access to Web through college's connection.

CAMPUS LIFE

Activities: Student government. **Organizations:** 2 registered organizations.

ADMISSIONS

Freshman Admission Requirements: High school diploma is required, and GED is accepted. **Transfer Admission Requirements:** College transcript(s), essay or personal statement, standardized test score, Lowest grade transferable C. **General Admission Information:** Regular application deadline varies.

COSTS AND FINANCIAL AID

Annual tuition $18,100. Required fees $350. Average book expense $1,500. **Types of Aid:** *Need-based scholarships/grants:* Pell, SEOG, state scholarships/grants, private scholarships, the school's own gift aid, Federal Nursing Scholarships. *Loans:* FFEL Subsidized Stafford, FFEL Unsubsidized Stafford, FFEL PLUS, college/university loans from institutional funds. **Student Employment:** Federal Work-Study Program available. Institutional employment available. Off-campus job opportunities are good. **Financial Aid Statistics:** 95% undergrads receive any aid.

WEST TEXAS A&M UNIVERSITY

PO Box 60907, Canyon, TX 79016-0001
Phone: 806-651-2020 **E-mail:** admissions@mail.wtamu.edu **CEEB Code:** 3665
Fax: 806-651-5268 **Website:** www.wtamu.edu **ACT Code:** 4250
Financial Aid Phone: 806-651-2055

This public school was founded in 1910. It has a 135-acre campus.

RATINGS
Admissions Selectivity Rating: 71   **Fire Safety Rating:** 68   **Green Rating:** 60*

STUDENTS AND FACULTY
Enrollment: 5,804. **Student Body:** 57% female, 43% male, 10% out-of-state, 1% international (37 countries represented). African American 4%, Asian 2%, Caucasian 75%, Hispanic 17%, Native American 1%. **Retention and Graduation:** 63% freshmen return for sophomore year. 14% freshmen graduate within 4 years. **Faculty:** Student/faculty ratio 24:1. 239 full-time faculty, 71% hold PhDs. 95% faculty teach undergrads.

ACADEMICS
Degrees: Bachelor's, diploma, doctoral, master's. **Academic Requirements:** Arts/fine arts, English (including composition), history, humanities, mathematics, sciences (biological or physical), social science, lifetime fitness BA degree requires foreign languages. **Classes:** Most classes have 10–19 students. Most lab/discussion sections have 10–19 students. **Majors with Highest Enrollment:** Business administration/management; multi/interdisciplinary studies; nursing/registered nurse training (ASN, BSN, MSN, RN). **Disciplines with Highest Percentage of Degrees Awarded:** Business/marketing 18%, interdisciplinary studies 18%, liberal arts/general studies 13%, health professions and related sciences 7%, agriculture 5%, biological/life sciences 5%. **Special Study Options:** Cooperative education program, distance learning, double major, English as a second language (ESL), honors program, independent study, internships, liberal arts/career combination, study abroad, teacher certification program.

FACILITIES
Housing: Coed dorms, men's dorms, women's dorms, special housing for disabled students, fraternity/sorority housing, honors program. **Special Academic Facilities/Equipment:** Regional history museum, research center, Panhandle Plains Historical Museum, Killgore Research Center. **Computers:** 1% of classrooms are wired, 95% of classrooms are wireless, 75% of public computers are PCs, 25% of public computers are Macs, network access in dorm rooms, network access in dorm lounges, online registration, online administrative functions (other than registration), support for handheld computing, remote student-access to Web through college's connection.

CAMPUS LIFE
Activities: Choral groups, concert band, dance, drama/theater, jazz band, literary magazine, marching band, music ensembles, musical theater, opera, radio station, student government, student newspaper, symphony orchestra. **Organizations:** 110 registered organizations, 15 honor societies, 13 religious organizations. 5 fraternities (4% men join), 5 sororities (4% women join). **Athletics (Intercollegiate):** *Men:* Baseball, basketball, cross-country, football, golf, soccer. *Women:* Basketball, cheerleading, cross-country, equestrian sports, golf, soccer, softball, volleyball.

ADMISSIONS
Freshman Academic Profile: 15% in top 10% of high school class, 49% in top 25% of high school class, 86% in top 50% of high school class. 96% from public high schools. SAT Math middle 50% range 420–520. SAT Critical Reading middle 50% range 460–600. SAT Writing middle 50% range 440–530. ACT middle 50% range 18–23. TOEFL required of all international applicants, minimum paper TOEFL 525, minimum computer TOEFL 197. **Basis for Candidate Selection:** *Very important factors considered include:* Class rank, standardized test scores. *Important factors considered include:* Academic GPA, rigor of secondary school record. **Freshman Admission Requirements:** High school diploma is required, and GED is accepted. *Academic units required:* 4 English, 3 math, 3 science, *Academic units recommended:* 2 foreign language, 3 social studies. **Freshman Admission Statistics:** 2,224 applied, 73% admitted, 82% enrolled. **Transfer Admission Requirements:** College transcript(s). Minimum college GPA of 2.0 required. Lowest grade transferable C. **General Admission Information:** Application fee $25. Regular notification is rolling

Nonfall registration accepted. Admission may be deferred for a maximum of 1 year. Credit offered for CEEB Advanced Placement tests.

COSTS AND FINANCIAL AID
Average book expense $900. **Required Forms and Deadlines:** FAFSA. **Types of Aid:** *Need-based scholarships/grants:* Pell, SEOG, state scholarships/grants, private scholarships, the school's own gift aid. *Loans:* FFEL Subsidized Stafford, FFEL Unsubsidized Stafford, FFEL PLUS, Federal Perkins, state loans. **Financial Aid Statistics:** 37% freshmen, 40% undergrads receive need-based scholarship or grant aid. 30% freshmen, 40% undergrads receive need-based self-help aid. 46 freshmen, 211 undergrads receive athletic scholarships. 52% freshmen, 53% undergrads receive any aid. Highest amount earned per year from on-campus jobs $5,850.

WEST VIRGINIA STATE UNIVERSITY

106 Ferrell Hall, Institute, WV 25112
Phone: 304-766-3033 **E-mail:** admissions@wvstateu.edu **CEEB Code:** 5903
Fax: 304-766-5182 **Website:** www.wvstateu.edu **ACT Code:** 4538
Financial Aid Phone: 304-766-3131

This public school was founded in 1891. It has a 95-acre campus.

RATINGS
Admissions Selectivity Rating: 60*   **Fire Safety Rating:** 60*   **Green Rating:** 60*

STUDENTS AND FACULTY
Enrollment: 3,455. **Student Body:** 59% female, 41% male, 8% out-of-state. African American 15%, Asian 1%, Caucasian 81%, Hispanic 1%. **Retention and Graduation:** 6% grads go on to further study within 2 semesters. 3% grads pursue arts and sciences degrees. 1% grads pursue business degrees. 1% grads pursue law degrees. 1% grads pursue medical degrees. **Faculty:** 100% faculty teach undergrads.

ACADEMICS
Degrees: Bachelor's, master's. **Majors with Highest Enrollment:** Business administration and management, elementary education and teaching, general studies. **Special Study Options:** Cooperative education program, off-campus study in Washington, DC.

FACILITIES
Housing: Coed dorms, men's dorms, women's dorms, apartments for married students. **Special Academic Facilities/Equipment:** On-campus day-care center, art gallery, ROTC Hall of Fame, Sports Hall of Fame.

CAMPUS LIFE
Activities: Choral groups, concert band, jazz band, literary magazine, marching band, music ensembles, radio station, student government, student newspaper, television station, yearbook. **Organizations:** 4 honor societies, 2 religious organizations. 6 fraternities, 3 sororities. **Athletics (Intercollegiate):** *Men:* Baseball, basketball, cross-country, football, softball, tennis, track/field (outdoor), volleyball. *Women:* Basketball, cross-country, softball, tennis, track/field (outdoor), volleyball.

ADMISSIONS
Freshman Academic Profile: 99% from public high schools. **Freshman Admission Requirements:** High school diploma is required, and GED is accepted. *Academic units required:* 4 English, 2 math, 2 science, 2 foreign language, 3 social studies, 1 history. **Transfer Admission Requirements:** College transcript(s). Minimum college GPA of 2.0 required. Lowest grade transferable D. **General Admission Information:** Regular application deadline 8/22. Regular notification rolling. Non-fall registration accepted. Common Application accepted. Credit and/or placement offered for CEEB Advanced Placement tests.

COSTS AND FINANCIAL AID
Annual in-state tuition $2,116. Out-of-state tuition $5,150. Room & board $3,550. Required fees $125. Average book expense $500. **Required Forms and Deadlines:** FAFSA, institution's own financial aid form. **Types of Aid:** *Need-based scholarships/grants: Loans:* FFEL Subsidized Stafford, FFEL PLUS. **Financial Aid Statistics:** Highest amount earned per year from on-campus jobs $1,300.

WEST VIRGINIA UNIVERSITY

Admissions Office, PO Box 6009, Morgantown, WV 26506-6009
Phone: 304-293-2121 **E-mail:** go2wvu@mail.wvu.edu **CEEB Code:** 5904
Fax: 304-293-3080 **Website:** www.wvu.edu **ACT Code:** 4540
Financial Aid Phone: 304-293-5242

This public school was founded in 1867. It has a 913-acre campus.

RATINGS
Admissions Selectivity Rating: 76   **Fire Safety Rating:** 86   **Green Rating:** 87

STUDENTS AND FACULTY
Enrollment: 20,590. **Student Body:** 46% female, 54% male, 43% out-of-state, 2% international (91 countries represented). African American 3%, Asian 2%, Caucasian 90%, Hispanic 2%. **Retention and Graduation:** 81% freshmen return for sophomore year. **Faculty:** Student/faculty ratio 23:1. 811 full-time faculty, 81% hold PhDs.

ACADEMICS
Degrees: Bachelor's, doctoral, first professional, master's. **Academic Requirements:** Computer science (recommended), English (including composition), fine arts (recommended), humanities, keyboarding (recommended), mathematics, sciences (biological or physical), social science. **Classes:** Most classes have 20–29 students. Most lab/discussion sections have 20–29 students. **Majors with Highest Enrollment:** Business administration/management, engineering, health professions and related sciences. **Disciplines with Highest Percentage of Degrees Awarded:** Business/marketing 12%, communications/journalism 10%, engineering 10%, liberal arts/general studies 9%, social sciences 8%. **Special Study Options:** Accelerated program, distance learning, double major, English as a second language (ESL), exchange student program (domestic), external degree program, honors program, independent study, internships, student-designed major, study abroad, teacher certification program, weekend college.

FACILITIES
Housing: Coed dorms, men's dorms, women's dorms, apartments for married students, apartments for single students, special housing for disabled students, special housing for international students, fraternity/sorority housing, special interest floors. **Special Academic Facilities/Equipment:** Art galleries, creative arts center, arboretum, herbarium, planetarium, concurrent engineering research center, discovery lab (for inventors), Appalachian hardwood center, small business development center, pharmacy museum, coal and energy museum, center for economic research, fluidization center, center for software development. **Computers:** 20% of classrooms are wired, 30% of classrooms are wireless, 90% of public computers are PCs, 3% of public computers are Macs, 7% of public computers are UNIX, network access in dorm rooms, network access in dorm lounges, online registration, online administrative functions (other than registration), support for handheld computing, remote student-access to Web through college's connection.

CAMPUS LIFE
Activities: Choral groups, concert band, dance, drama/theater, jazz band, literary magazine, marching band, music ensembles, musical theater, pep band, radio station, student government, student newspaper, symphony orchestra, television station, yearbook. **Organizations:** 300 registered organizations, 22 honor societies, 19 religious organizations. 13 fraternities (12% men join), 10 sororities (13% women join). **Athletics (Intercollegiate):** *Men:* Baseball, basketball, diving, football, riflery, soccer, swimming, wrestling. *Women:* Basketball, crew/rowing, cross-country, diving, gymnastics, riflery, soccer, swimming, tennis, track/field (indoor), track/field (outdoor), volleyball.

ADMISSIONS
Freshman Academic Profile: 17% in top 10% of high school class, 40% in top 25% of high school class, 73% in top 50% of high school class. SAT Math middle 50% range 490–590. SAT Critical Reading middle 50% range 470–560. ACT middle 50% range 21–26. TOEFL required of all international applicants, minimum paper TOEFL 550, minimum computer TOEFL 173. **Basis for Candidate Selection:** *Very important factors considered include:* Academic GPA, standardized test scores. *Important factors considered include:* Level of applicant's interest, state residency. *Other factors considered include:* Extracurricular activities, recommendation(s), volunteer work. **Freshman**

Admission Requirements: High school diploma is required, and GED is accepted. *Academic units required:* 4 English, 3 math, 3 science (2 science labs), 3 social studies. *Academic units recommended:* 2 foreign language. **Freshman Admission Statistics:** 12,047 applied, 92% admitted, 44% enrolled. **Transfer Admission Requirements:** College transcript(s). Minimum college GPA of 2.0 required. Lowest grade transferable D. **General Admission Information:** Application fee $25. Regular application deadline 8/1. Regular notification is rolling. Non-fall registration accepted. Admission may be deferred for a maximum of 2 semesters. Credit and/or placement offered for CEEB Advanced Placement tests.

COSTS AND FINANCIAL AID
Annual in-state tuition $4,476. Out-of-state tuition $13,840. Room & board $6,630. Average book expense $900. **Required Forms and Deadlines:** FAFSA, state aid form. Financial aid filing deadline 3/1. **Notification of Awards:** Applicants will be notified of awards on a rolling basis beginning on or about 3/15. **Types of Aid:** *Need-based scholarships/grants:* Pell, SEOG, state scholarships/grants, private scholarships, the school's own gift aid. *Loans:* Direct Subsidized Stafford, Direct Unsubsidized Stafford, Direct PLUS, Federal Perkins, college/university loans from institutional funds. **Financial Aid Statistics:** 34% freshmen, 37% undergrads receive need-based scholarship or grant aid. 33% freshmen, 43% undergrads receive need-based self-help aid. 72 freshmen, 353 undergrads receive athletic scholarships. 69% freshmen, 86% undergrads receive any aid. Highest amount earned per year from on-campus jobs $2,500.

WEST VIRGINIA UNIVERSITY INSTITUTE OF TECHNOLOGY

Box 10 Old Main, Montgomery, WV 25136
Phone: 304-442-3167 **E-mail:** admissions@wvutech.edu **CEEB Code:** 3825
Fax: 304-442-3097 **Website:** www.wvutech.edu **ACT Code:** 4536
Financial Aid Phone: 304-442-3228

This public school was founded in 1895. It has a 200-acre campus.

RATINGS
Admissions Selectivity Rating: 72   **Fire Safety Rating:** 60*   **Green Rating:** 60*

STUDENTS AND FACULTY
Enrollment: 2,001. **Student Body:** 39% female, 61% male, 6% out-of-state, 4% international. African American 8%, Caucasian 87%. **Retention and Graduation:** 62% freshmen return for sophomore year. 14% freshmen graduate within 4 years. **Faculty:** Student/faculty ratio 16:1. 119 full-time faculty, 47% hold PhDs.

ACADEMICS
Degrees: Associate, bachelor's, certificate, master's. **Academic Requirements:** Computer literacy, English (including composition), humanities, mathematics, sciences (biological or physical), social science. **Classes:** Most classes have 10–19 students. Most lab/discussion sections have 20–29 students. **Disciplines with Highest Percentage of Degrees Awarded:** Engineering 23%, interdisciplinary studies 13%, health professions and related sciences 12%, business/marketing 8%, biological/life sciences 4%. **Special Study Options:** Cooperative education program, distance learning, double major, dual enrollment, internships, student-designed major.

FACILITIES
Housing: Coed dorms, men's dorms, women's dorms, fraternity/sorority housing. **Computers:** 85% of public computers are PCs, 85% of public computers are Macs, network access in dorm rooms, network access in dorm lounges, online administrative functions (other than registration), remote student-access to Web through college's connection.

CAMPUS LIFE
Activities: Choral groups, concert band, drama/theater, jazz band, marching band, music ensembles, pep band, student government, student newspaper. **Organizations:** 52 registered organizations, 9 honor societies, 2 religious organizations. 5 fraternities (11% men join), 2 sororities (9% women join). **Athletics (Intercollegiate):** *Men:* Baseball, basketball, football, golf, tennis. *Women:* Basketball, cheerleading, soccer, softball, tennis, volleyball.

ADMISSIONS
Freshman Academic Profile: 20% in top 10% of high school class, 21% in top 25% of high school class, 43% in top 50% of high school class. 95% from public high schools. SAT Math middle 50% range 430–560. SAT Critical Reading

middle 50% range 420–550. SAT Writing middle 50% range 430–550. ACT middle 50% range 20–26. TOEFL required of all international applicants, minimum paper TOEFL 500, minimum computer TOEFL 173. **Basis for Candidate Selection:** *Very important factors considered include:* Rigor of secondary school record, standardized test scores. *Other factors considered include:* Alumni/ae relation, character/personal qualities, class rank, extracurricular activities, interview, recommendation(s), state residency, talent/ability, volunteer work. **Freshman Admission Requirements:** High school diploma is required, and GED is accepted. *Academic units required:* 4 English, 2 math, 2 science (2 science labs), 3 social studies. *Academic units recommended:* 4 English, 3 math, 2 science (2 science labs), 2 foreign language, 3 social studies. **Freshman Admission Statistics:** 1,191 applied, 74% admitted, 47% enrolled. **Transfer Admission Requirements:** College transcript(s). Minimum college GPA of 1.7 required. Lowest grade transferable D. **General Admission Information:** Regular notification is rolling. Non-fall registration accepted. Admission may be deferred for a maximum of 1 semester. Common Application accepted. Credit offered for CEEB Advanced Placement tests.

COSTS AND FINANCIAL AID
Annual tuition $22,030. Room and board $6,470. Required fees $850. Average book expense $1,000. **Required Forms and Deadlines:** FAFSA, institution's own financial aid form. Financial aid filing deadline 2/3. **Notification of Awards:** Applicants will be notified of awards on a rolling basis beginning on or about 3/3. **Types of Aid:** *Need-based scholarships/grants:* Pell, SEOG, state scholarships/grants, private scholarships, the school's own gift aid. *Loans:* Direct Subsidized Stafford, Direct Unsubsidized Stafford, Direct PLUS, FFEL Subsidized Stafford, FFEL Unsubsidized Stafford, FFEL PLUS, Federal Perkins. **Student Employment:** Federal Work-Study Program available. Off-campus job opportunities are fair. **Financial Aid Statistics:** 47% freshmen, 43% undergrads receive need-based scholarship or grant aid. 35% freshmen, 38% undergrads receive need-based self-help aid. 10 freshmen, 99 undergrads receive athletic scholarships. Highest amount earned per year from on-campus jobs $1,250.

WEST VIRGINIA WESLEYAN COLLEGE

59 College Avenue, Buckhannon, WV 26201
Phone: 304-473-8510 **E-mail:** admission@wvwc.edu **CEEB Code:** 5905
Fax: 304-473-8108 **Website:** www.wvwc.edu **ACT Code:** 4544
Financial Aid Phone: 304-473-8080

This private school, affiliated with the Methodist Church, was founded in 1890. It has a 100-acre campus.

RATINGS
Admissions Selectivity Rating: 77 **Fire Safety Rating:** 60* **Green Rating:** 60*

STUDENTS AND FACULTY
Enrollment: 1,153. **Student Body:** 54% female, 46% male, 47% out-of-state, 3% international (12 countries represented). African American 5%, Caucasian 73%, Hispanic 2%. **Retention and Graduation:** 70% freshmen return for sophomore year. 41% freshmen graduate within 4 years. **Faculty:** Student/faculty ratio 13:1. 72 full-time faculty, 81% hold PhDs. 100% faculty teach undergrads.

ACADEMICS
Degrees: Bachelor's, master's. **Academic Requirements:** Arts/fine arts, computer literacy, English (including composition), history, humanities, mathematics, philosophy, sciences (biological or physical), social science. **Classes:** Most classes have 10–19 students. Most lab/discussion sections have 10–19 students. **Disciplines with Highest Percentage of Degrees Awarded:** Business/marketing 20%, education 14%, social sciences 13%, health professions and related sciences 6%, parks and recreation 6%, biological/life sciences 5%, computer and information sciences 5%, psychology 5%, visual and performing arts 5%. **Special Study Options:** Double major, English as a second language (ESL), exchange student program (domestic), honors program, independent study, internships, liberal arts/career combination, student-designed major, study abroad, teacher certification program.

FACILITIES
Housing: Coed dorms, men's dorms, women's dorms, apartments for single students, fraternity/sorority housing. **Computers:** 100% of public computers are PCs, network access in dorm rooms, online registration, remote student-access to Web through college's connection. Undergraduates are required to own a computer.

CAMPUS LIFE
Activities: Choral groups, concert band, dance, drama/theater, jazz band, literary magazine, music ensembles, musical theater, radio station, student government, student newspaper, yearbook. **Organizations:** 75 registered organizations, 31 honor societies, 6 religious organizations. 6 fraternities (25% men join), 5 sororities (25% women join). **Athletics (Intercollegiate):** *Men:* Baseball, basketball, cross-country, football, golf, soccer, softball, swimming, tennis, track/field (outdoor). *Women:* Basketball, cross-country, golf, soccer, swimming, tennis, track/field (outdoor), volleyball.

ADMISSIONS
Freshman Academic Profile: 24% in top 10% of high school class, 51% in top 25% of high school class, 77% in top 50% of high school class. SAT Math middle 50% range 435–560. SAT Critical Reading middle 50% range 440–560. SAT Writing middle 50% range 430–550. ACT middle 50% range 20–26. TOEFL required of all international applicants, minimum paper TOEFL 500, minimum computer TOEFL 200. **Basis for Candidate Selection:** *Very important factors considered include:* Rigor of secondary school record. *Important factors considered include:* Academic GPA, alumni/ae relation, character/personal qualities, class rank, extracurricular activities, first generation, interview, level of applicant's interest, standardized test scores, talent/ability, volunteer work. *Other factors considered include:* Application essay, geographical residence, recommendation(s), religious affiliation/commitment, state residency, work experience. **Freshman Admission Requirements:** High school diploma is required, and GED is accepted. *Academic units recommended:* 4 English, 3 math, 3 science (3 science labs), 2 foreign language, 3 social studies. **Freshman Admission Statistics:** 1,065 applied, 96% admitted, 29% enrolled. **Transfer Admission Requirements:** High school transcript, college transcript(s), statement of good standing from prior institution(s). Minimum college GPA of 2.5 required. Lowest grade transferable C-. **General Admission Information:** Application fee $35. Regular notification is rolling. Non-fall registration accepted. Admission may be deferred for a maximum of 2 semesters. Credit offered for CEEB Advanced Placement tests.

COSTS AND FINANCIAL AID
Annual tuition $20,250. Room & board $5,550. Required fees $1,080. Average book expense $1,000. **Required Forms and Deadlines:** FAFSA. Financial aid filing deadline 2/15. **Notification of Awards:** Applicants will be notified of awards on a rolling basis beginning on or about 3/1. **Types of Aid:** *Need-based scholarships/grants:* Pell, SEOG, state scholarships/grants, private scholarships, the school's own gift aid, ACG and SMART Grants. *Loans:* FFEL Subsidized Stafford, FFEL Unsubsidized Stafford, FFEL PLUS, Federal Perkins, college/university loans from institutional funds. **Student Employment:** Federal Work-Study Program available. Institutional employment available. Off-campus job opportunities are fair. **Financial Aid Statistics:** 76% freshmen, 75% undergrads receive need-based scholarship or grant aid. 76% freshmen, 75% undergrads receive need-based self-help aid. 20 freshmen, 75 undergrads receive athletic scholarships. Highest amount earned per year from on-campus jobs $1,000.

WESTERN CAROLINA UNIVERSITY

242 HFR Administration, Cullowhee, NC 28723
Phone: 828-227-7317 **E-mail:** admiss@e-mail.wcu.edu **CEEB Code:** 5897
Fax: 828-227-7319 **Website:** www.wcu.edu **ACT Code:** 3172
Financial Aid Phone: 828-227-7290

This public school was founded in 1889. It has a 589-acre campus.

RATINGS
Admissions Selectivity Rating: 72 **Fire Safety Rating:** 82 **Green Rating:** 80

STUDENTS AND FACULTY
Enrollment: 7,051. **Student Body:** 52% female, 48% male, 4% out-of-state, (43 countries represented). African American 6%, Caucasian 87%, Hispanic 1%, Native American 1%. **Retention and Graduation:** 72% freshmen return for sophomore year. 23% freshmen graduate within 4 years. **Faculty:** Student/faculty ratio 14:1. 457 full-time faculty, 73% hold PhDs. 95% faculty teach undergrads.

ACADEMICS
Degrees: Bachelor's, doctoral, master's, post-master's certificate. **Academic Requirements:** Arts/fine arts, computer literacy, English (including composition), history, humanities, mathematics, oral communications, sciences

students. **Majors with Highest Enrollment:** Criminal justice/safety studies, elementary education and teaching, nursing/registered nurse training (ASN, BSN, MSN, RN). **Disciplines with Highest Percentage of Degrees Awarded:** Education 23%, business/marketing 20%, health professions and related sciences 12%, security and protective services 6%, engineering technologies 5%, communications/journalism 5%. **Special Study Options:** Accelerated program, cooperative education program, distance learning, double major, dual enrollment, English as a second language (ESL), exchange student program (domestic), honors program, independent study, internships, student-designed major, study abroad, teacher certification program.

FACILITIES

Housing: Coed dorms, men's dorms, women's dorms, apartments for married students, special housing for disabled students, special housing for international students, fraternity/sorority housing. **Special Academic Facilities/Equipment:** Two art galleries, Mountain Resource Center, Mountain Heritage Center, reading center, State Center for the Advancement of Teaching, speech/hearing center, high technology workplace development building, CATA Lab (high technology computer lab), fine and performing arts center. **Computers:** 10% of classrooms are wired, 50% of classrooms are wireless, 76% of public computers are PCs, 23% of public computers are Macs, 1% of public computers are UNIX, network access in dorm rooms, network access in dorm lounges, online registration, online administrative functions (other than registration), remote student-access to Web through college's connection. Undergraduates are required to own a computer.

CAMPUS LIFE

Activities: Choral groups, concert band, dance, drama/theater, jazz band, literary magazine, marching band, music ensembles, musical theater, pep band, radio station, student government, student newspaper, student-run film society, television station, yearbook. **Organizations:** 91 registered organizations, 22 honor societies, 5 religious organizations. 11 fraternities (9% men join), 9 sororities (8% women join). **Athletics (Intercollegiate):** *Men:* Baseball, basketball, cheerleading, cross-country, football, golf, track/field (outdoor). *Women:* Basketball, cheerleading, cross-country, golf, soccer, tennis, track/field (outdoor), volleyball. **Environmental Initiatives:** Participating in STARS. Developing and improving WCU WHEE Save—Energy Conservation Initiative & WHEE Recycling—recycling program. Itron—Energy Management Software; Bill Analyst, Meter Data Analyst & Advanced forecasting. Reduce & track greenhouse gas emissions. Use ENERGY STAR National Energy Rating System.

ADMISSIONS

Freshman Academic Profile: 8% in top 10% of high school class, 28% in top 25% of high school class, 62% in top 50% of high school class. 95% from public high schools. SAT Math middle 50% range 470–560. SAT Critical Reading middle 50% range 450–550. SAT Writing middle 50% range 430–530. ACT middle 50% range 18–23. TOEFL required of all international applicants, minimum paper TOEFL 550, minimum computer TOEFL 213. **Basis for Candidate Selection:** *Very important factors considered include:* Rigor of secondary school record, standardized test scores. *Important factors considered include:* Character/personal qualities, class rank, extracurricular activities, level of applicant's interest, talent/ability, volunteer work, work experience. *Other factors considered include:* Application essay, interview, recommendation(s), state residency. **Freshman Admission Requirements:** High school diploma is required, and GED is accepted. *Academic units required:* 4 English, 3 math, 3 science (3 science labs), 2 foreign language, 2 social studies, 1 history, 5 academic electives. *Academic units recommended:* 4 English, 3 math, 3 science (3 science labs), 2 foreign language, 2 social studies, 1 history, 7 academic electives. **Freshman Admission Statistics:** 4,830 applied, 77% admitted, 42% enrolled. **Transfer Admission Requirements:** High school transcript, college transcript(s), standardized test score, statement of good standing from prior institution(s). Minimum college GPA of 2.0 required. Lowest grade transferable C. **General Admission Information:** Application fee $40. Early decision application deadline 10/15. Regular application deadline 4/1. Regular notification is rolling. Non-fall registration accepted. Credit and/or placement offered for CEEB Advanced Placement tests.

COSTS AND FINANCIAL AID

Annual in-state tuition $2,078. Annual out-of-state tuition $11,611. Room and board $5,626. Required fees $2,337. Average book expense $605. **Required Forms and Deadlines:** FAFSA, institution's own financial aid form. Financial aid filing deadline 3/31. **Notification of Awards:** Applicants will be notified of awards on or about 4/1. **Types of Aid:** *Need-based scholarships/grants:* Pell, SEOG, state scholarships/grants, private scholarships, the school's own gift aid. *Loans:* Direct Subsidized Stafford, Direct Unsubsidized Stafford, Direct PLUS, Federal Perkins. **Student Employment:** Federal Work-Study Program available. Institutional employment available. Off-campus job opportunities are fair. **Financial Aid Statistics:** 47% freshmen, 48% undergrads receive any aid. Highest amount earned per year from on-campus jobs $5,220.

WESTERN CONNECTICUT STATE UNIVERSITY

Undergraduate Admissions Office, 181 White Street, Danbury, CT 06810-6855
Phone: 203-837-9000 **E-mail:** admissions@wcsu.edu **CEEB Code:** 3350
Website: ACT Code: 0558
Financial Aid Phone: 203-837-8580

This public school was founded in 1903. It has a 400-acre campus.

RATINGS

Admissions Selectivity Rating: 75　　　**Fire Safety Rating:** 85　　　**Green Rating:** 73

STUDENTS AND FACULTY

Enrollment: 4,480. **Student Body:** 54% female, 46% male, 9% out-of-state. African American 6%, Asian 4%, Caucasian 82%, Hispanic 7%. **Retention and Graduation:** 71% freshmen return for sophomore year. 14% freshmen graduate within 4 years. 23% grads go on to further study within 2 semesters. 10% grads pursue arts and sciences degrees. 3% grads pursue business degrees. 2% grads pursue law degrees. 1% grads pursue medical degrees. **Faculty:** Student/faculty ratio 15:1. 197 full-time faculty, 78% hold PhDs. 100% faculty teach undergrads.

ACADEMICS

Degrees: Associate, bachelor's, doctoral, master's. **Academic Requirements:** English (including composition), humanities, mathematics, sciences (biological or physical), social science. **Classes:** Most classes have 20–29 students. **Majors with Highest Enrollment:** Criminal justice/police science, elementary education and teaching, nursing/registered nurse training (ASN, BSN, MSN, RN). **Disciplines with Highest Percentage of Degrees Awarded:** Business/marketing 29%, education 13%, social sciences 10%, communication technologies 8%. **Special Study Options:** Accelerated program, cooperative education program, cross registration, distance learning, double major, dual enrollment, English as a second language (ESL), honors program, independent study, internships, student-designed major, study abroad, teacher certification program.

FACILITIES

Housing: Coed dorms, women's dorms, apartments for single students, On campus housing assigned on a first-come basis. **Special Academic Facilities/Equipment:** Language lab, observatory, electron microscope, nature preserve, computer-enhanced classrooms, business library, Jane Goodall Institute. **Computers:** 22% of classrooms are wired, 20% of classrooms are wireless, 94% of public computers are PCs, 15% of public computers are Macs, 1% of public computers are UNIX, network access in dorm rooms, online registration, online administrative functions (other than registration), support for handheld computing, remote student-access to Web through college's connection.

CAMPUS LIFE

Activities: Choral groups, concert band, dance, drama/theater, jazz band, literary magazine, music ensembles, musical theater, opera, pep band, radio station, student government, student newspaper, symphony orchestra, yearbook. **Organizations:** 40 registered organizations, 8 honor societies, 3 religious organizations. 3 fraternities, 3 sororities. **Athletics (Intercollegiate):** *Men:* Baseball, basketball, football, soccer, tennis. *Women:* Basketball, lacrosse, soccer, softball, swimming, tennis, volleyball. **Environmental Initiatives:** Think Green: Go Blue recycling efforts (with distribution campus wide of an instruction brochure). Building Automation. Controls monitoring.

ADMISSIONS

Freshman Academic Profile: 4% in top 10% of high school class, 24% in top 25% of high school class, 62% in top 50% of high school class. 91% from public high schools. SAT Math middle 50% range 440–530. SAT Critical Reading middle 50% range 430–540. SAT Writing middle 50% range 430–530. TOEFL required of all international applicants, minimum paper TOEFL 550, minimum computer TOEFL 213. **Basis for Candidate Selection:** *Very important factors considered include:* Rigor of secondary school record, standardized test scores, talent/ability. *Important factors considered include:* Class rank, extracurricular activities. *Other factors considered include:* Alumni/ae relation, application essay, interview, racial/ethnic status, recommendation(s), state residency, volunteer work, work experience. **Freshman Admission Requirements:** High school diploma is required, and GED is accepted. *Academic units required:* 4 English, 3 math, 2 science (2 science labs), 2 foreign language, 1 social studies, 1 history. *Academic units recommended:* 3 foreign language. **Freshman Admission Statistics:** 3,469 applied, 58% admitted, 39% enrolled. **Transfer Admission Requirements:** College transcript(s). Minimum college GPA of 2.0 required. Lowest grade transferable C-. **General Admission Information:** Application fee $40. Regular notification is rolling. Non-fall registration accepted. Admission may be deferred for a maximum of 2 semesters. Common Application accepted. Credit offered for CEEB Advanced Placement tests.

COSTS AND FINANCIAL AID

Annual in-state tuition $3,034. Out-of-state tuition $9,820. Room & board $7,193. Required fees $2,766. Average book expense $1,000. **Required Forms and Deadlines:** FAFSA, institution's own financial aid form. Financial aid filing deadline 4/15. **Notification of Awards:** Applicants will be notified of awards on a rolling basis beginning on or about 3/15. **Types of Aid:** *Need-based scholarships/grants:* Pell, SEOG, state scholarships/grants, private scholarships, the school's own gift aid. *Loans:* FFEL Subsidized Stafford, FFEL Unsubsidized Stafford, FFEL PLUS, Federal Perkins. **Financial Aid Statistics:** 36% freshmen, 34% undergrads receive need-based scholarship or grant aid. 34% freshmen, 32% undergrads receive need-based self-help aid. Highest amount earned per year from on-campus jobs $2,273.

WESTERN ILLINOIS UNIVERSITY

1 University Circle, 115 Sherman Hall, Macomb, IL 61455-1390
Phone: 309-298-3157 **E-mail:** wiuadm@wiu.edu **CEEB Code:** 1900
Fax: 309-298-3111 **Website:** www.wiu.edu **ACT Code:** 1158
Financial Aid Phone: 309-298-2446

This public school was founded in 1899. It has a 1,050-acre campus.

RATINGS

Admissions Selectivity Rating: 67   **Fire Safety Rating:** 70   **Green Rating:** 82

STUDENTS AND FACULTY

Enrollment: 11,327. **Student Body:** 48% female, 52% male, 7% out-of-state, 1% international (52 countries represented). African American 7%, Asian 1%, Caucasian 81%, Hispanic 4%. **Retention and Graduation:** 73% freshmen return for sophomore year. 32% freshmen graduate within 4 years. 21% grads go on to further study within 2 semesters. 14% grads pursue arts and sciences degrees. 6% grads pursue business degrees. 1% grads pursue law degrees. 1% grads pursue medical degrees. **Faculty:** Student/faculty ratio 16:1. 656 full-time faculty, 69% hold PhDs. 97% faculty teach undergrads.

ACADEMICS

Degrees: Bachelor's, doctoral, master's, post-bachelor's certificate, post-master's certificate. **Academic Requirements:** English (including composition), human well-being, humanities, mathematics, multicultural studies, public speaking, sciences (biological or physical), social science. **Classes:** Most classes have 20–29 students. Most lab/discussion sections have fewer than 10 students. **Majors with Highest Enrollment:** Business administration and management, criminal justice/law enforcement administration, elementary education and teaching. **Disciplines with Highest Percentage of Degrees Awarded:** Business/marketing 15%, security and protective services 13%, education 10%, liberal arts/general studies 10%, communications/journalism 8%. **Special Study Options:** Distance learning, double major, dual enrollment, English as a second language (ESL), external degree program, honors program, independent study, internships, student-designed major, study abroad, teacher certification program, weekend college.

FACILITIES

Housing: Coed dorms, men's dorms, women's dorms, apartments for married students, special housing for international students, fraternity/sorority housing. **Special Academic Facilities/Equipment:** Art gallery, electron microscope. **Computers:** 20% of classrooms are wireless, 75% of public computers are PCs, 20% of public computers are Macs, 5% of public computers are UNIX, network access in dorm rooms, network access in dorm lounges, online registration, online administrative functions (other than registration), remote student-access to Web through college's connection.

CAMPUS LIFE

Activities: Choral groups, concert band, dance, drama/theater, jazz band, marching band, music ensembles, musical theater, pep band, radio station, student government, student newspaper, symphony orchestra, television station, yearbook. **Organizations:** 195 registered organizations, 25 honor societies, 12 religious organizations. 14 fraternities (9% men join), 11 sororities (8% women join). **Athletics (Intercollegiate):** *Men:* Baseball, basketball, cross-country, diving, football, golf, soccer, swimming, tennis, track/field (indoor), track/field (outdoor). *Women:* Basketball, cheerleading, cross-country, diving, golf, soccer, softball, swimming, tennis, track/field (indoor), track/field (outdoor), volleyball. **Environmental Initiatives:** In the last year Western has received two Illinois

upgrades. Western students have been involved in campus beautification through the Litter Patrol, the Adopt-a-Street Program and the We Care Program to keep the campus and community clean and attractive.

ADMISSIONS

Freshman Academic Profile: 7% in top 10% of high school class, 23% in top 25% of high school class, 59% in top 50% of high school class. ACT middle 50% range 18–23. TOEFL required of all international applicants, minimum paper TOEFL 550, minimum computer TOEFL 213. **Basis for Candidate Selection:** *Very important factors considered include:* Academic GPA, class rank, rigor of secondary school record, standardized test scores. **Freshman Admission Requirements:** High school diploma is required, and GED is accepted. *Academic units recommended:* 4 English, 3 math, 3 science, 3 social studies. **Freshman Admission Statistics:** 7,620 applied, 70% admitted, 36% enrolled. **Transfer Admission Requirements:** College transcript(s). Minimum college GPA of 2.0 required. Lowest grade transferable D. **General Admission Information:** Application fee $30. Regular application deadline 5/15. Regular notification within 24-48 hours after receiving application. Non-fall registration accepted. Credit offered for CEEB Advanced Placement tests.

COSTS AND FINANCIAL AID

Required Forms and Deadlines: FAFSA. Financial aid filing deadline 2/15. **Notification of Awards:** Applicants will be notified of awards on a rolling basis beginning on or about 1/15. **Types of Aid:** *Need-based scholarships/grants:* Pell, SEOG, state scholarships/grants, private scholarships, the school's own gift aid. *Loans:* FFEL Subsidized Stafford, FFEL Unsubsidized Stafford, FFEL PLUS, Federal Perkins, college/university loans from institutional funds. **Financial Aid Statistics:** 36% freshmen, 38% undergrads receive need-based scholarship or grant aid. 46% freshmen, 48% undergrads receive need-based self-help aid. 69 freshmen, 312 undergrads receive athletic scholarships. 76% freshmen, 75% undergrads receive any aid. Highest amount earned per year from on-campus jobs $4,500.

WESTERN KENTUCKY UNIVERSITY

Potter Hall 117, 1906 College Heights Boulevard, Bowling Green, KY 42101-1020
Phone: 270-745-2551 **E-mail:** admission@wku.edu **CEEB Code:** 1901
Fax: 270-745-6133 **Website:** www.wku.edu **ACT Code:** 1562
Financial Aid Phone: 270-745-2755

This public school was founded in 1906. It has a 200-acre campus.

RATINGS

Admissions Selectivity Rating: 72   **Fire Safety Rating:** 86   **Green Rating:** 60*

STUDENTS AND FACULTY

Enrollment: 15,415. **Student Body:** 58% female, 42% male, 17% out-of-state, 2% international (55 countries represented). African American 9%, Caucasian 84%, Hispanic 1%. **Retention and Graduation:** 72% freshmen return for sophomore year. 30% freshmen graduate within 4 years. **Faculty:** Student/faculty ratio 18:1. 726 full-time faculty, 71% hold PhDs. 93% faculty teach undergrads.

ACADEMICS

Degrees: Associate, bachelor's, certificate, doctoral, master's, post-bachelor's certificate, post-master's certificate. **Academic Requirements:** Arts/fine arts, English (including composition), foreign languages, history, humanities, mathematics, sciences (biological or physical), social science. **Classes:** Most classes have 20–29 students. Most lab/discussion sections have 10–19 students. **Majors with Highest Enrollment:** Business administration and management, elementary education and teaching, nursing/registered nurse training (ASN, BSN, MSN, RN). **Disciplines with Highest Percentage of Degrees Awarded:** Education 18%, business/marketing 15%, social sciences 11%, communications/journalism 10%, liberal arts/general studies 8%. **Special Study Options:** Cooperative education program, distance learning, double major, dual enrollment, English as a second language (ESL), exchange student program (domestic), external degree program, honors program, independent study, internships, learning communities/block scheduling, student-designed major, study abroad, teacher certification program.

FACILITIES

Housing: Coed dorms, men's dorms, women's dorms, special housing for disabled students, special housing for international students, fraternity/sorority housing, learning communities, themed living options, honors. **Special Academic Facilities/Equipment:** Kentucky Museum, university farm, Hardin Planetarium, public computers are Macs, network access in dorm rooms, online registration, online administrative functions (other than registration), support for handheld computing, remote student-access to Web through college's connection.

CAMPUS LIFE

Activities: Choral groups, concert band, dance, drama/theater, jazz band, literary magazine, marching band, music ensembles, musical theater, opera, pep band, radio station, student government, student newspaper, student-run film society, symphony orchestra, television station. **Organizations:** 251 registered organizations, 36 honor societies, 28 religious organizations. 16 fraternities (8% men join), 12 sororities (7% women join). **Athletics (Intercollegiate):** *Men:* Baseball, basketball, cross-country, diving, football, golf, riflery, soccer, swimming, tennis, track/field (outdoor). *Women:* Basketball, cross-country, diving, golf, riflery, softball, swimming, tennis, track/field (outdoor), volleyball.

ADMISSIONS

Freshman Academic Profile: 17% in top 10% of high school class, 39% in top 25% of high school class, 69% in top 50% of high school class. SAT Math middle 50% range 450–560. SAT Critical Reading middle 50% range 440–550. ACT middle 50% range 18–24. TOEFL required of all international applicants, minimum paper TOEFL 525, minimum computer TOEFL 197. **Basis for Candidate Selection:** *Very important factors considered include:* Academic GPA, standardized test scores. **Freshman Admission Requirements:** High school diploma is required, and GED is accepted. *Academic units required:* 4 English, 3 math, 3 science (1 science lab), 2 foreign language, 3 social studies, 1.5 health and physical education, 1.5 history, 1.5 performing arts. **Freshman Admission Statistics:** 6,954 applied, 91% admitted, 51% enrolled. **Transfer Admission Requirements:** College transcript(s), statement of good standing from prior institution(s). Minimum college GPA of 2.0 required. Lowest grade transferable D°. **General Admission Information:** Application fee $35. Regular application deadline 8/1. Non-fall registration accepted. Credit and/or placement offered for CEEB Advanced Placement tests.

COSTS AND FINANCIAL AID

Annual in-state tuition $5,952. Out-of-state tuition $14,440. Room & board $5,348. Average book expense $800. **Required Forms and Deadlines:** FAFSA. Financial aid filing deadline 4/1. **Notification of Awards:** Applicants will be notified of awards on a rolling basis beginning on or about 3/1. **Types of Aid:** *Need-based scholarships/grants:* Pell, SEOG, state scholarships/grants, private scholarships, the school's own gift aid, United Negro College Fund. *Loans:* FFEL Subsidized Stafford, FFEL Unsubsidized Stafford, FFEL PLUS, Federal Perkins, alternative private loans. **Financial Aid Statistics:** 35% freshmen, 35% undergrads receive need-based scholarship or grant aid. 33% freshmen, 38% undergrads receive need-based self-help aid. 67 freshmen, 365 undergrads receive athletic scholarships. 53% freshmen, 54% undergrads receive any aid.

WESTERN MICHIGAN UNIVERSITY

1903 West Michigan Avenue, Kalamazoo, MI 49008-5211
Phone: 269-387-2000 **E-mail:** ask-wmu@umich.edu **CEEB Code:** 1902
Fax: 269-387-2096 **Website:** www.umich.edu **ACT Code:** 2066
Financial Aid Phone: 269-387-6000

This public school was founded in 1903. It has a 1,200-acre campus.

RATINGS

Admissions Selectivity Rating: 71   **Fire Safety Rating:** 66   **Green Rating:** 78

STUDENTS AND FACULTY

Enrollment: 19,966. **Student Body:** 51% female, 49% male, 6% out-of-state, 2% international (84 countries represented). African American 6%, Asian 2%, Caucasian 87%, Hispanic 2%. **Retention and Graduation:** 74% freshmen return for sophomore year. 20% freshmen graduate within 4 years. **Faculty:** Student/faculty ratio 19:1. 924 full-time faculty, 8% hold PhDs.

ACADEMICS

Degrees: Bachelor's, doctoral, master's, post-bachelor's certificate. **Academic Requirements:** Arts/fine arts, computer literacy, English (including composition), foreign languages, humanities, mathematics, sciences (biological or physical), social science. **Classes:** Most classes have 20–29 students. Most lab/discussion sections have 20–29 students. **Majors with Highest Enrollment:** Communications, journalism, and related fields; education; marketing/marketing management. **Disciplines with Highest Percentage of Degrees Awarded:** Business/marketing 24%, education 22%, communications/journalism 6%, engineering 6%, health professions and related sciences 5%.

Special Study Options: Accelerated program, cooperative education program, cross-registration, distance learning, double major, dual enrollment, English as a second language (ESL), exchange student program (domestic), honors program, independent study, internships, student-designed major, study abroad, teacher certification program, weekend college.

FACILITIES

Housing: Coed dorms, men's dorms, women's dorms, apartments for married students, apartments for single students, special housing for disabled students, special housing for international students, fraternity/sorority housing, each hall has a special thematic concept that is developed through programming and student involvment. Examples are: health and wellness, community service, honors, arts and athletics, first year initiative, upper class students, diversity. **Special Academic Facilities/Equipment:** Pilot plant for manufacturing and printing of paper and for fiber recovery, behavior research and development center, nuclear accelerator, center for electron microscopy, particle accelerator lab, library department of special collections: Cistercian and monastic studies collections, medieval studies collections, Carol Ann Haenicke American Women's Poetry Collection, 19th and 20th century literature and history collection, book arts collections: paper and fine printing. **Computers:** 100% of classrooms are wired, 100% of classrooms are wireless, 70% of public computers are PCs, 25% of public computers are Macs, 5% of public computers are UNIX, network access in dorm rooms, network access in dorm lounges, online registration, online administrative functions (other than registration), remote student-access to Web through college's connection.

CAMPUS LIFE

Activities: Choral groups, concert band, dance, drama/theater, jazz band, literary magazine, marching band, music ensembles, musical theater, opera, pep band, radio station, student government, student newspaper, student-run film society, symphony orchestra. **Organizations:** 275 registered organizations, 18 honor societies, 24 religious organizations. 19 fraternities (4% men join), 13 sororities (6% women join). **Athletics (Intercollegiate):** *Men:* Baseball, basketball, football, ice hockey, soccer, tennis. *Women:* Basketball, cross-country, golf, gymnastics, soccer, softball, tennis, track/field (indoor), track/field (outdoor), volleyball. **Environmental Initiatives:** Energy comsumption. Recycling/waste reduction. Alternative fuels.

ADMISSIONS

Freshman Academic Profile: 12% in top 10% of high school class, 33% in top 25% of high school class, 69% in top 50% of high school class. ACT middle 50% range 20–25. TOEFL required of all international applicants, minimum paper TOEFL 550, minimum computer TOEFL 215. **Basis for Candidate Selection:** *Very important factors considered include:* Academic GPA, rigor of secondary school record. *Important factors considered include:* Alumni/ae relation, standardized test scores, talent/ability. *Other factors considered include:* Application essay, character/personal qualities, extracurricular activities, interview, recommendation(s), volunteer work, work experience. **Freshman Admission Requirements:** High school diploma is required, and GED is accepted. *Academic units required:* 4 English, 3 math, 2 science (1 science lab), 2 social studies, 1 history, 2 academic electives, *Academic units recommended:* 4 math, 2 foreign language. **Freshman Admission Statistics:** 11,830 applied, 86% admitted, 35% enrolled. **Transfer Admission Requirements:** College transcript(s). Minimum college GPA of 2.0 required. Lowest grade transferable C. **General Admission Information:** Application fee $35. Regular application deadline 8/1. Regular notification is rolling. Nonfall registration accepted. Admission may be deferred for a maximum of 1 semester. Credit and/or placement offered for CEEB Advanced Placement tests.

COSTS AND FINANCIAL AID

Forms and Deadlines: FAFSA. Financial aid filing deadline 3/15. **Notification of Awards:** Applicants will be notified of awards on a rolling basis beginning on or about 3/15. **Types of Aid:** *Need-based scholarships/grants:* Pell, SEOG, state scholarships/grants, private scholarships, the school's own gift aid, Federal Nursing Scholarships. *Loans:* Direct Subsidized Stafford, Direct Unsubsidized Stafford, Direct PLUS, Federal Perkins, Alternative Loans. **Financial Aid Statistics:** 17% freshmen, 22% undergrads receive need-based scholarship or grant aid. 45% freshmen, 44% undergrads receive need-based self-help aid. 90 freshmen, 530 undergrads receive athletic scholarships. 70% freshmen, 69% undergrads receive any aid. Highest amount earned per year from on-campus jobs $3,475.

See page 1490.

WESTERN NEW ENGLAND COLLEGE

Admissions Office, 1215 Wilbraham Road, Springfield, MA 01119
Phone: 413-782-1321 **E-mail:** ugradmis@wnec.edu **CEEB Code:** 3962
Fax: 413-782-1777 **Website:** www.wnec.edu **ACT Code:** 1930
Financial Aid Phone: 413-796-2080

This private school was founded in 1919. It has a 215-acre campus.

RATINGS
Admissions Selectivity Rating: 76   **Fire Safety Rating:** 60*   **Green Rating:** 60*

STUDENTS AND FACULTY
Enrollment: 2,804. **Student Body:** 38% female, 62% male, 60% out-of-state. African American 3%, Asian 2%, Caucasian 87%, Hispanic 3%. **Retention and Graduation:** 73% freshmen return for sophomore year. 50% freshmen graduate within 4 years. **Faculty:** Student/faculty ratio 15:1. 169 full-time faculty, 91% hold PhDs. 100% faculty teach undergrads.

ACADEMICS
Degrees: Associate, bachelor's, certificate, first professional, master's. **Academic Requirements:** Arts/fine arts, computer literacy, English (including composition), history, humanities, mathematics, philosophy, sciences (biological or physical), social science. **Classes:** Most classes have 20–29 students. Most lab/discussion sections have 10–19 students. **Majors with Highest Enrollment:** Business administration/management, criminal justice/safety studies, psychology. **Disciplines with Highest Percentage of Degrees Awarded:** Business/marketing 33%, security and protective services 30%, engineering 9%, psychology 8%, social sciences 5%. **Special Study Options:** 3+3 law program with Western New England School of Law, 5 year BSBS/MBA, 6 year BSBE/Law, cross registration, distance learning, double major, dual enrollment, honors program, independent study, internships, liberal arts/career combination, student-designed major, study abroad, teacher certification program, Washington semester program.

FACILITIES
Housing: Coed dorms, apartments for single students, special housing for disabled students. **Special Academic Facilities/Equipment:** Art gallery, math, writing, science centers. **Computers:** Network access in dorm rooms, network access in dorm lounges, online registration, online administrative functions (other than registration), remote student-access to Web through college's connection.

CAMPUS LIFE
Activities: Choral groups, concert band, dance, drama/theater, jazz band, literary magazine, music ensembles, pep band, radio station, student government, student newspaper, yearbook. **Organizations:** 60 registered organizations, 8 honor societies. **Athletics (Intercollegiate):** *Men:* Baseball, basketball, cross-country, football, golf, ice hockey, lacrosse, soccer, tennis, wrestling. *Women:* Basketball, cross-country, field hockey, lacrosse, soccer, softball, swimming, tennis, volleyball.

ADMISSIONS
Freshman Academic Profile: 11% in top 10% of high school class, 33% in top 25% of high school class, 73% in top 50% of high school class. SAT Math middle 50% range 485–590. SAT Critical Reading middle 50% range 470–560. ACT middle 50% range 20–24. TOEFL required of all international applicants, minimum paper TOEFL 500, minimum computer TOEFL 173. **Basis for Candidate Selection:** *Very important factors considered include:* Academic GPA, recommendation(s), standardized test scores. *Other factors considered include:* Alumni/ae relation, application essay, character/personal qualities, class rank, extracurricular activities, interview, racial/ethnic status, rigor of secondary school record, talent/ability, volunteer work, work experience. **Freshman Admission Requirements:** High school diploma is required, and GED is accepted. *Academic units required:* 4 English, 2 math, 1 science (1 science lab), 1 social studies, 1 history. *Academic units recommended:* 4 English, 4 math, 2 science (2 science labs), 2 foreign language, 2 social studies, 2 history. **Freshman Admission Statistics:** 4,534 applied, 73% admitted, 22% enrolled. **Transfer Admission Requirements:** High school transcript, college transcript(s). Minimum college GPA of 2.3 required. Lowest grade transferable C-. **General Admission Information:** Application fee $50. Regular notification is rolling. Non-fall registration accepted. Admission may be deferred for a maximum of 2 semesters. Credit and/or placement offered for CEEB Advanced Placement tests.

COSTS AND FINANCIAL AID
Required Forms and Deadlines: FAFSA, student and parent 1040, W-2s. Financial aid filing deadline 4/15. Notification...

notified of awards on a rolling basis beginning on or about 3/15. **Types of Aid:** *Need-based scholarships/grants:* Pell, SEOG, state scholarships/grants, private scholarships, the school's own gift aid. *Loans:* Direct Subsidized Stafford, Direct Unsubsidized Stafford, Direct PLUS, FFEL PLUS, Federal Perkins, state loans, private loan programs. **Financial Aid Statistics:** 75% freshmen, 70% undergrads receive need-based scholarship or grant aid. 65% freshmen, 64% undergrads receive need-based self-help aid. 90% freshmen, 90% undergrads receive any aid.

See page 1492.

WESTERN OREGON UNIVERSITY

345 North Monmouth Avenue, Monmouth, OR 97361
Phone: 503-838-8211 **E-mail:** wolfgram@wou.edu **CEEB Code:** 4585
Fax: 503-838-8067 **Website:** www.wou.edu **ACT Code:** 3480
Financial Aid Phone: 503-838-8684

This public school was founded in 1856. It has a 157-acre campus.

RATINGS
Admissions Selectivity Rating: 71   **Fire Safety Rating:** 90   **Green Rating:** 73

STUDENTS AND FACULTY
Enrollment: 4,103. **Student Body:** 59% female, 41% male, 9% out-of-state, 2% international (19 countries represented). African American 2%, Asian 3%, Caucasian 78%, Hispanic 6%, Native American 2%. **Retention and Graduation:** 65% freshmen return for sophomore year. 21% freshmen graduate within 4 years. **Faculty:** 174 full-time faculty, 84% hold PhDs. 100% faculty teach undergrads.

ACADEMICS
Degrees: Associate, bachelor's, master's, post-bachelor's certificate. **Academic Requirements:** Arts/fine arts, computer literacy, English (including composition), humanities, mathematics, sciences (biological or physical), social science. **Classes:** Most classes have 10–19 students. Most lab/discussion sections have 20–29 students. **Majors with Highest Enrollment:** Business administration/management, social sciences, teacher education. **Disciplines with Highest Percentage of Degrees Awarded:** Education 25%, social sciences 16%, business/marketing 15%, psychology 9%, security and protective services 8%. **Special Study Options:** Distance learning, double major, dual enrollment, English as a second language (ESL), honors program, independent study, internships, study abroad, teacher certification program.

FACILITIES
Housing: Coed dorms, apartments for married students, apartments for single students, special housing for disabled students. **Special Academic Facilities/Equipment:** Jensen Arctic Museum. **Computers:** 70% of public computers are PCs, 30% of public computers are Macs, network access in dorm rooms, network access in dorm lounges, online registration, online administrative functions (other than registration), remote student-access to Web through college's connection.

CAMPUS LIFE
Activities: Choral groups, concert band, dance, drama/theater, jazz band, literary magazine, music ensembles, musical theater, pep band, student government, student newspaper, symphony orchestra, television station. **Organizations:** 50 registered organizations, 4 honor societies, 6 religious organizations. **Athletics (Intercollegiate):** *Men:* Baseball, basketball, cheerleading, cross-country, football, track/field (outdoor). *Women:* Basketball, cheerleading, cross-country, soccer, softball, track/field (outdoor), volleyball. **Environmental Initiatives:** Recyling.

ADMISSIONS
Freshman Academic Profile: 13% in top 10% of high school class, 36% in top 25% of high school class, 73% in top 50% of high school class. 95% from public high schools. SAT Math middle 50% range 430–530. SAT Critical Reading middle 50% range 420–530. SAT Writing middle 50% range 400–510. ACT middle 50% range 17–23. TOEFL required of all international applicants, minimum paper TOEFL 500, minimum computer TOEFL 180. **Basis for Candidate Selection:** *Very important factors considered include:* Academic GPA, rigor of secondary school record. *Important factors considered include:* Class rank, standardized test scores. *Other factors considered include:* Character/personal qualities, extracurricular activities, first generation, volunteer work. **Freshman Admission Requirements:** High school diploma is required, and GED is accepted. *Academic units required:* 4 English, 3 math...

88% admitted, 47% enrolled. **Transfer Admission Requirements:** College transcript(s), statement of good standing from prior institution(s). Minimum college GPA of 2.0 required. Lowest grade transferable D-. **General Admission Information:** Application fee $50. Non-fall registration accepted. Credit and/or placement offered for CEEB Advanced Placement tests.

COSTS AND FINANCIAL AID

Annual in-state tuition $4,725. Annual out-of-state tuition $15,075. Room and board $7,380. Required fees $1,257. Average book expense $1,125. **Required Forms and Deadlines:** FAFSA. Financial aid filing deadline 3/1. **Notification of Awards:** Applicants will be notified of awards on a rolling basis beginning on or about 3/20. **Types of Aid:** *Need-based scholarships/grants:* Pell, SEOG, state scholarships/grants, private scholarships, the school's own gift aid. *Loans:* Direct Subsidized Stafford, Direct Unsubsidized Stafford, Direct PLUS, Federal Perkins, college/university loans from institutional funds. **Financial Aid Statistics:** 56% freshmen, 53% undergrads receive need-based scholarship or grant aid. 61% freshmen, 67% undergrads receive need-based self-help aid. 20 freshmen, 77 undergrads receive athletic scholarships.

WESTERN STATE COLLEGE OF COLORADO

600 North Adams Street Gunnison, CO 81231
Phone: 970-943-2119 **E-mail:** discover@western.edu **CEEB Code:** 4946
Fax: 970-943-2212 **Website:** www.western.edu **ACT Code:** 0536
Financial Aid Phone: 970-943-3085

This public school was founded in 1911. It has a 228-acre campus.

RATINGS
Admissions Selectivity Rating: 70   Fire Safety Rating: 76   Green Rating: 60*

STUDENTS AND FACULTY
Enrollment: 2,152. **Student Body:** 40% female, 60% male, 25% out-of-state. African American 1%, Caucasian 85%, Hispanic 5%. **Retention and Graduation:** 61% freshmen return for sophomore year. 13% freshmen graduate within 4 years. 15% grads go on to further study within 2 semesters. **Faculty:** Student/faculty ratio 20:1. 109 full-time faculty, 76% hold PhDs. 100% faculty teach undergrads.

ACADEMICS
Degrees: Bachelor's. **Academic Requirements:** Arts/fine arts, English (including composition), history, humanities, mathematics, sciences (biological or physical), social science. **Classes:** Most classes have 20–29 students. Most lab/discussion sections have 10–19 students. **Majors with Highest Enrollment:** Business/commerce, parks, recreation and leisure studies. **Disciplines with Highest Percentage of Degrees Awarded:** Business/marketing 31%, parks and recreation 14%, social sciences 13%, visual and performing arts 10%, psychology 8%. **Special Study Options:** Cooperative education program, distance learning, double major, dual enrollment, exchange student program (domestic), honors program, independent study, internships, liberal arts/career combination, study abroad, teacher certification program.

FACILITIES
Housing: Coed dorms, men's dorms, women's dorms, apartments for married students, apartments for single students, fraternity/sorority housing, theme housing (honors, art, wilderness/outdoor activities). **Special Academic Facilities/Equipment:** Botanical garden, dinosaur museum, archaeological site. **Computers:** 92% of public computers are PCs, 8% of public computers are Macs, network access in dorm rooms, network access in dorm lounges, online registration, online administrative functions (other than registration), remote student-access to Web through college's connection.

CAMPUS LIFE
Activities: Choral groups, concert band, drama/theater, jazz band, literary magazine, music ensembles, pep band, radio station, student government, student newspaper, symphony orchestra, television station. **Organizations:** 60 registered organizations, 1 honor society, 5 religious organizations. 1 fraternity, 1 sorority. **Athletics (Intercollegiate):** *Men:* Basketball, cross-country, football, skiing (downhill/alpine), skiing (nordic/cross-country), track/field (indoor), track/field (outdoor), wrestling. *Women:* Basketball, cross-country, skiing (downhill/alpine), skiing (nordic/cross-country), track/field (indoor), track/field (outdoor), volleyball.

ADMISSIONS
Freshman Academic Profile: 5% in top 10% of high school class, 21% in top 25% of high school class, 52% in top 50% of high school class. SAT Math middle 50% range 460–550. SAT Critical Reading middle 50% range 440–550. ACT middle 50% range 18–23. TOEFL required of all international applicants,

minimum paper TOEFL 550, minimum computer TOEFL 213. **Basis for Candidate Selection:** *Very important factors considered include:* Class rank, rigor of secondary school record, standardized test scores. *Important factors considered include:* Character/personal qualities, extracurricular activities, talent/ability. *Other factors considered include:* Alumni/ae relation, application essay, interview, recommendation(s). **Freshman Admission Requirements:** High school diploma is required, and GED is accepted. *Academic units required:* 4 English, 3 math, 2 science (2 science labs), 2 social studies, 2 history, 3 academic electives. *Academic units recommended:* 4 English, 4 math, 3 science, 2 foreign language, 3 social studies, 3 history. **Freshman Admission Statistics:** 1,586 applied, 85% admitted, 36% enrolled. **Transfer Admission Requirements:** College transcript(s). Minimum college GPA of 2.0 required. Lowest grade transferable C. **General Admission Information:** Application fee $40. Regular application deadline 8/1. Regular notification is rolling. Non-fall registration accepted. Admission may be deferred for a maximum of 2 semesters. Common Application accepted. Credit and/or placement offered for CEEB Advanced Placement tests.

COSTS AND FINANCIAL AID
Annual in-state tuition $1,980. Out-of-state tuition $9,966. Average book expense $950. **Required Forms and Deadlines:** FAFSA. Financial aid filing deadline 4/15. **Notification of Awards:** Applicants will be notified of awards on or about 4/1. **Types of Aid:** *Need-based scholarships/grants:* Pell, SEOG, state scholarships/grants, private scholarships, the school's own gift aid. *Loans:* FFEL Subsidized Stafford, FFEL Unsubsidized Stafford, FFEL PLUS, Federal Perkins. **Student Employment:** Federal Work-Study Program available. Institutional employment available. Off-campus job opportunities are good. **Financial Aid Statistics:** 30% freshmen, 26% undergrads receive need-based scholarship or grant aid. 46% freshmen, 28% undergrads receive need-based self-help aid. 50 freshmen, 150 undergrads receive athletic scholarships. 75% freshmen, 65% undergrads receive any aid. Highest amount earned per year from on-campus jobs $1,500.

WESTERN WASHINGTON UNIVERSITY

Mail Stop 9009, Bellingham, WA 98225-9009
Phone: 360-650-3440 **E-mail:** admit@cc.wwu.edu **CEEB Code:** 4947
Fax: 360-650-7369 **Website:** www.wwu.edu **ACT Code:** 4490
Financial Aid Phone: 360-650-3470

This public school was founded in 1893. It has a 300-acre campus.

RATINGS
Admissions Selectivity Rating: 85   Fire Safety Rating: 62   Green Rating: 93

STUDENTS AND FACULTY
Enrollment: 12,711. **Student Body:** 55% female, 45% male. African American 2%, Asian 8%, Caucasian 78%, Hispanic 3%, Native American 2%. **Retention and Graduation:** 86% freshmen return for sophomore year. 29% freshmen graduate within 4 years. **Faculty:** Student/faculty ratio 19:1. 485 full-time faculty, 83% hold PhDs. 99% faculty teach undergrads.

ACADEMICS
Degrees: Bachelor's, master's, post-bachelor's certificate. **Academic Requirements:** Comparative, gender, and multicultural studies, English (including composition), humanities, mathematics, sciences (biological or physical), social science. **Classes:** Most classes have fewer than 10 students. Most lab/discussion sections have 20–29 students. **Majors with Highest Enrollment:** Accounting, general studies, psychology. **Disciplines with Highest Percentage of Degrees Awarded:** Business/marketing 15%, social sciences 13%, English 7%, psychology 7%, visual and performing arts 6%, liberal arts/general studies 5%, parks and recreation 5%, foreign languages and literature 5%. **Special Study Options:** Distance learning, double major, English as a second language (ESL), exchange student program (domestic), honors program, independent study, internships, student-designed major, study abroad, teacher certification program.

FACILITIES
Housing: Coed dorms, apartments for married students, apartments for single students, special housing for disabled students, wellness floors, multicultural floors available. **Special Academic Facilities/Equipment:** Outdoor art museum, planetarium, electronic music studio, air pollution lab, motor vehicle research lab, marine lab, wind tunnel, electron microscope, neutron generator lab. **Computers:** 100% of classrooms are wired, 50% of classrooms are wireless, 95% of public computers are PCs, 4% of public computers are Macs, network access in dorm rooms, network access in dorm lounges, online registration,

online administrative functions (other than registration), support for handheld computing, remote student-access to Web through college's connection.

CAMPUS LIFE

Activities: Dance, drama/theater, jazz band, literary magazine, music ensembles, musical theater, opera, radio station, student government, student newspaper, symphony orchestra, television station. **Organizations:** 150 registered organizations, 4 honor societies, 18 religious organizations. **Athletics (Intercollegiate):** *Men:* Basketball, cheerleading, crew/rowing, cross-country, football, golf, soccer, track/field (indoor), track/field (outdoor). *Women:* Basketball, cheerleading, crew/rowing, cross-country, golf, soccer, softball, track/field (indoor), track/field (outdoor), volleyball.

ADMISSIONS

Freshman Academic Profile: 25% in top 10% of high school class, 61% in top 25% of high school class, 93% in top 50% of high school class. 90% from public high schools. SAT Math middle 50% range 500–610. SAT Critical Reading middle 50% range 490–610. SAT Writing middle 50% range 480–590. ACT middle 50% range 21–26. TOEFL required of all international applicants, minimum paper TOEFL 550, minimum computer TOEFL 213. **Basis for Candidate Selection:** *Very important factors considered include:* Rigor of secondary school record. *Important factors considered include:* Academic GPA, application essay, class rank, standardized test scores, state residency, volunteer work, work experience. *Other factors considered include:* Character/personal qualities, extracurricular activities, geographical residence, level of applicant's interest, recommendation(s), talent/ability. **Freshman Admission Requirements:** High school diploma is required, and GED is accepted. *Academic units required:* 4 English, 3 math, 2 science (1 science lab), 2 foreign language, 3 social studies. **Freshman Admission Statistics:** 8,034 applied, 74% admitted, 41% enrolled. **Transfer Admission Requirements:** College transcript(s), statement of good standing from prior institution(s). Minimum college GPA of 2.0 required. Lowest grade transferable D-. **General Admission Information:** Application fee $50. Regular application deadline 3/1. Regular notification is rolling. Non-fall registration accepted. Admission may be deferred for a maximum of 2 semesters. Credit and/or placement offered for CEEB Advanced Placement tests.

COSTS AND FINANCIAL AID

Required Forms and Deadlines: FAFSA. Financial aid filing deadline 2/15. **Notification of Awards:** Applicants will be notified of awards on a rolling basis beginning on or about 3/20. **Types of Aid:** *Need-based scholarships/grants:* Pell, SEOG, state scholarships/grants, private scholarships, the school's own gift aid. *Loans:* Direct Subsidized Stafford, Direct Unsubsidized Stafford, Direct PLUS, FFEL PLUS, Federal Perkins, state loans, college/university loans from institutional funds, private loans. **Financial Aid Statistics:** 29% freshmen, 29% undergrads receive need-based scholarship or grant aid. 27% freshmen, 30% undergrads receive need-based self-help aid. 28 freshmen, 128 undergrads receive athletic scholarships. 67% freshmen, 57% undergrads receive any aid. Highest amount earned per year from on-campus jobs $16,413.

WESTFIELD STATE COLLEGE

Westfield State, Westfield, MA 01086
Phone: 413-572-5218 **E-mail:** admission@wsc.ma.edu **CEEB Code:** 3523
Fax: 413-572-0520 **Website:** www.wsc.ma.edu **ACT Code:** 1912
Financial Aid Phone: 413-572-5407

This public school was founded in 1838. It has a 227-acre campus.

RATINGS
Admissions Selectivity Rating: 60*   **Fire Safety Rating:** 60*   **Green Rating:** 60*

STUDENTS AND FACULTY
Enrollment: 4,078. **Student Body:** 56% female, 44% male, 7% out-of-state. African American 3%, Caucasian 83%, Hispanic 3%. **Retention and Graduation:** 76% freshmen return for sophomore year. 38% freshmen graduate within 4 years. 12% grads pursue arts and sciences degrees. 5% grads pursue business degrees. 1% grads pursue law degrees. **Faculty:** Student/faculty ratio 18:1. 168 full-time faculty, 87% hold PhDs. 100% faculty teach undergrads.

ACADEMICS
Degrees: Bachelor's, master's, post-bachelor's certificate, post-master's certificate. **Academic Requirements:** American history or government, arts/fine arts, diversity, English (including composition), literature or philosophy, mathematics, sciences (biological or physical), social science. **Classes:** Most

Disciplines with Highest Percentage of Degrees Awarded: Liberal arts/general studies 14%, education 12%, business/marketing 11%, psychology 10%, communication technologies 9%. **Special Study Options:** Cooperative education program, cross registration, distance learning, double major, dual enrollment, exchange student program (domestic), honors program, independent study, internships, student-designed major, study abroad, teacher certification program.

FACILITIES
Housing: Coed dorms, apartments for single students, special housing for disabled students, living/learning unit (honors/academic intensive), quiet living section, all women section, designated smoking section (other housing smoke free). **Special Academic Facilities/Equipment:** Art gallery, language lab, electron microscope.

CAMPUS LIFE
Activities: Choral groups, concert band, drama/theater, jazz band, literary magazine, music ensembles, musical theater, pep band, radio station, student government, student newspaper, television station, yearbook. **Athletics (Intercollegiate):** *Men:* Baseball, basketball, cross-country, football, golf, soccer, track/field (outdoor). *Women:* Basketball, cheerleading, cross-country, field hockey, soccer, softball, swimming, volleyball.

ADMISSIONS
Freshman Academic Profile: SAT Math middle 50% range 460–560. SAT Critical Reading middle 50% range 460–560. TOEFL required of all international applicants, minimum paper TOEFL 550. **Basis for Candidate Selection:** *Very important factors considered include:* Rigor of secondary school record, standardized test scores. *Important factors considered include:* Extracurricular activities, talent/ability. *Other factors considered include:* Application essay, character/personal qualities, racial/ethnic status, recommendation(s), volunteer work, work experience. **Freshman Admission Requirements:** High school diploma is required, and GED is accepted. *Academic units required:* 4 English, 3 math, 3 science (2 science labs), 2 foreign language, 1 social studies, 1 history, 2 academic electives. **Freshman Admission Statistics:** 3,566 applied, 67% admitted, 36% enrolled. **Transfer Admission Requirements:** College transcript(s). Minimum college GPA of 2.0 required. Lowest grade transferable C-. **General Admission Information:** Application fee $25. Regular application deadline 3/1. Regular notification between 1/1 and 4/15. Non-fall registration accepted. Admission may be deferred for a maximum of 1 semester. Common Application not accepted. Credit and/or placement offered for CEEB Advanced Placement tests.

COSTS AND FINANCIAL AID
Annual in-state tuition $970. Out-of-state tuition $7,050. Room & board $5,742. Required fees $3,887. Average book expense $800. **Required Forms and Deadlines:** FAFSA. Financial aid filing deadline 3/1. **Notification of Awards:** Applicants will be notified of awards on or about 4/15. **Types of Aid:** *Need-based scholarships/grants:* Pell, SEOG, state scholarships/grants, private scholarships, the school's own gift aid. *Loans:* FFEL Subsidized Stafford, FFEL Unsubsidized Stafford, FFEL PLUS, Federal Perkins, state loans. **Student Employment:** Federal Work-Study Program available. Off-campus job opportunities are good. **Financial Aid Statistics:** 40% freshmen, 32% undergrads receive need-based scholarship or grant aid. 47% freshmen, 38% undergrads receive need-based self-help aid. Highest amount earned per year from on-campus jobs $1,000.

WESTMINSTER CHOIR COLLEGE OF RIDER UNIVERSITY

101 Walnut Lane, Princeton, NJ 08540-3899
Phone: 800-962-4647 **CEEB Code:** 2758
Fax: 609-921-8829 **Website:** www.rider.edu **ACT Code:** 2590
Financial Aid Phone: 609-921-7100

This private school was founded in 1926. It has a 23-acre campus.

RATINGS
Admissions Selectivity Rating: 60*   **Fire Safety Rating:** 60*   **Green Rating:** 60*

STUDENTS AND FACULTY
Enrollment: 328. **Student Body:** 64% female, 36% male, 56% out-of-state. 4% international. African American 7%, Asian 2%, Caucasian 75%, Hispanic 4%. **Retention and Graduation:** 79% freshmen return for sophomore year.

teacher education, music theory and composition, voice and opera. **Disciplines with Highest Percentage of Degrees Awarded:** Visual and performing arts 31%.

FACILITIES
Housing: Coed dorms.

CAMPUS LIFE
Activities: Choral groups, concert band, dance, jazz band, music ensembles, opera. **Organizations:** 8 registered organizations, 4 honor societies.

ADMISSIONS
Freshman Academic Profile: SAT Math middle 50% range 490–610. SAT Critical Reading middle 50% range 490–620. TOEFL required of all international applicants, minimum paper TOEFL 563, minimum computer TOEFL 202. **Basis for Candidate Selection:** *Very important factors considered include:* Academic GPA, application essay, recommendation(s), rigor of secondary school record, standardized test scores. *Important factors considered include:* Level of applicant's interest. *Other factors considered include:* Alumni/ae relation, character/personal qualities, class rank, extracurricular activities, geographical residence, interview, state residency, talent/ability, volunteer work, work experience. **Freshman Admission Requirements:** High school diploma is required, and GED is accepted. *Academic units required:* 4 English, 3 math. *Academic units recommended:* 4 math, 4 science (2 science labs), 2 foreign language, 2 social studies, 2 history. **Freshman Admission Statistics:** 206 applied, 76% admitted, 56% enrolled. **General Admission Information:** Application fee $45. Regular application deadline rolling.

COSTS AND FINANCIAL AID
Annual tuition $22,910. Room & board $9,200. Required fees $560. Average book expense $1,000.

WESTMINSTER COLLEGE

1840 South 1300 East, Salt Lake City, UT 84105
Phone: 801-832-2200 **E-mail:** admission@westminstercollege.edu **CEEB Code:** 4948
Fax: 801-832-3101 **Website:** www.westminstercollege.edu **ACT Code:** 4284
Financial Aid Phone: 801-832-2500

This private school was founded in 1875. It has a 27-acre campus.

RATINGS
Admissions Selectivity Rating: 82   **Fire Safety Rating:** 98   **Green Rating:** 76

STUDENTS AND FACULTY
Enrollment: 1,929. **Student Body:** 58% female, 42% male, 14% out-of-state, 1% international (41 countries represented). Asian 3%, Caucasian 78%, Hispanic 5%. **Retention and Graduation:** 79% freshmen return for sophomore year. 39% freshmen graduate within 4 years. 27% grads go on to further study within 2 semesters. **Faculty:** Student/faculty ratio 11:1. 119 full-time faculty, 67% hold PhDs. 100% faculty teach undergrads.

ACADEMICS
Degrees: Bachelor's, master's, post-bachelor's certificate. **Academic Requirements:** Arts/fine arts, computer literacy, English (including composition), foreign languages, history, humanities, mathematics, philosophy, public speaking, sciences (biological or physical), social science. **Classes:** Most classes have 10–19 students. Most lab/discussion sections have fewer than 10 students. **Majors with Highest Enrollment:** Business administration/management, education, nursing/registered nurse training (ASN, BSN, MSN, RN). **Disciplines with Highest Percentage of Degrees Awarded:** Business/marketing 35%, health professions and related sciences 14%, psychology 9%, communications/journalism 6%, education 6%, biological/life sciences 4%, transportation and materials moving 4%. **Special Study Options:** Accelerated program, cooperative education program, double major, dual enrollment, honors program, independent study, internships, liberal arts/career combination, student-designed major, study abroad, teacher certification program, weekend college.

FACILITIES
Housing: Coed dorms, men's dorms, women's dorms, apartments for single

students. **Special Academic Facilities/Equipment:** Emma Ecceles Jones Conservatory, Gore School of Business, Giovale Library, Dick Science Building, climbing wall, Converse Hall, Dolores Dore Eccles Health, wellness, athletic center. **Computers:** 10% of classrooms are wired, 44% of classrooms are wireless, 97% of public computers are PCs, 2% of public computers are Macs, 1% of public computers are UNIX, network access in dorm rooms, network access in dorm lounges, online registration, online administrative functions (other than registration), support for handheld computing, remote student-access to Web through college's connection.

CAMPUS LIFE
Activities: Choral groups, dance, drama/theater, jazz band, literary magazine, music ensembles, musical theater, student government, student newspaper, student-run film society, symphony orchestra. **Organizations:** 38 registered organizations, 5 honor societies, 4 religious organizations. **Athletics (Intercollegiate):** *Men:* Basketball, cross-country, golf, soccer. *Women:* Basketball, cross-country, golf, volleyball. **Environmental Initiatives:** Blue Sky Visionary and EPA Green Power Partner, with 11% of campus electricity derived from renwable sources. First campus in Utah with onsite solar electricity generation (8kW). American College & University Presidents' Climate Commitment charter signatory.

ADMISSIONS
Freshman Academic Profile: 27% in top 10% of high school class, 53% in top 25% of high school class, 84% in top 50% of high school class. 83% from public high schools. SAT Math middle 50% range 480–610. SAT Critical Reading middle 50% range 490–632.5. ACT middle 50% range 21–27. TOEFL required of all international applicants, minimum paper TOEFL 550, minimum computer TOEFL 213. **Basis for Candidate Selection:** *Very important factors considered include:* Academic GPA, rigor of secondary school record. *Important factors considered include:* Application essay, class rank, interview, standardized test scores. *Other factors considered include:* Alumni/ae relation, character/personal qualities, extracurricular activities, geographical residence, recommendation(s), talent/ability. **Freshman Admission Requirements:** High school diploma is required, and GED is accepted. *Academic units required:* 4 English, 2 math, 3 science, 2 foreign language, 2 social studies, 1 history, 2 academic electives. *Academic units recommended:* 4 English, 3 math, 3 science, 3 foreign language, 2 social studies, 1 history, 3 academic electives. **Freshman Admission Statistics:** 1,182 applied, 79% admitted, 40% enrolled. **Transfer Admission Requirements:** High school transcript, college transcript(s), essay or personal statement. Minimum college GPA of 2.5 required. Lowest grade transferable C-. **General Admission Information:** Application fee $40. Regular notification is rolling. Non-fall registration accepted. Admission may be deferred for a maximum of 2 semesters. Credit and/or placement offered for CEEB Advanced Placement tests.

COSTS AND FINANCIAL AID
Annual tuition $21,984. Room and board $6,354. Required fees $390. Average book expense $1,000. **Required Forms and Deadlines:** FAFSA. Financial aid filing deadline 4/15. **Notification of Awards:** Applicants will be notified of awards on or about 3/15. **Types of Aid:** *Need-based scholarships/grants:* Pell, SEOG, state scholarships/grants, private scholarships, the school's own gift aid, United Negro College Fund. *Loans:* FFEL Subsidized Stafford, FFEL Unsubsidized Stafford, FFEL PLUS, Federal Perkins. **Student Employment:** Federal Work-Study Program available. Institutional employment available. Off-campus job opportunities are excellent. **Financial Aid Statistics:** 61% freshmen, 65% undergrads receive need-based scholarship or grant aid. 55% freshmen, 63% undergrads receive need-based self-help aid. 8 freshmen, 13 undergrads receive athletic scholarships. 83% freshmen, 85% undergrads receive any aid. Highest amount earned per year from on-campus jobs $3,200.

See page 1494.

WESTMINSTER COLLEGE (MO)

501 Westminster Avenue, Fulton, MO 65251-1299
Phone: 573-592-5251 **E-mail:** admissions@westminster-mo.edu **CEEB Code:** 6937
Fax: 573-592-5255 **Website:** www.westminster-mo.edu/index.html **ACT Code:** 2392
Financial Aid Phone: 800-475-3361

This private school, affiliated with the Presbyterian Church, was founded in 1851. It has a 65-acre campus.

RATINGS
Admissions Selectivity Rating: 78   **Fire Safety Rating:** 73   **Green Rating:** 60*

STUDENTS AND FACULTY

Enrollment: 936. **Student Body:** 43% female, 57% male, 26% out-of-state, 11% international (47 countries represented). African American 4%, Asian 1%, Caucasian 78%, Hispanic 2%, Native American 2%. **Retention and Graduation:** 80% freshmen return for sophomore year. 51% freshmen graduate within 4 years. 30% grads go on to further study within 2 semesters. 10% grads pursue arts and sciences degrees. 6% grads pursue business degrees. 4% grads pursue law degrees. 3% grads pursue medical degrees. **Faculty:** Student/faculty ratio 13:1. 58 full-time faculty, 69% hold PhDs. 100% faculty teach undergrads.

ACADEMICS

Degrees: Bachelor's. **Academic Requirements:** Arts/fine arts, English (including composition), foreign languages, history, humanities, mathematics, non-western culture, philosophy, sciences (biological or physical), social science. **Classes:** Most classes have 10–19 students. **Majors with Highest Enrollment:** Biology/biological sciences, business administration/management, political science and government. **Disciplines with Highest Percentage of Degrees Awarded:** Business/marketing 31%, education 14%, social sciences 14%, biological/life sciences 10%, English 6%, communications/journalism 3%, computer and information sciences 3%, history 3%, natural resources/environmental science 3%. **Special Study Options:** Cooperative education program, cross registration, double major, dual enrollment, exchange student program (domestic), honors program, independent study, internships, liberal arts/career combination, student-designed major, study abroad, teacher certification program, urban studies program (Chicago). Other off-campus study opportunities supported through Office of International Programs.

FACILITIES

Housing: Coed dorms, men's dorms, women's dorms, apartments for single students, fraternity/sorority housing, theme houses. **Special Academic Facilities/Equipment:** Winston Churchill Memorial Museum, Coulter Science Center, language lab, NMR spectrometer, laser equipment. **Computers:** 100% of classrooms are wireless, 95% of public computers are PCs, 5% of public computers are Macs, network access in dorm rooms, network access in dorm lounges, online registration, online administrative functions (other than registration), support for handheld computing, remote student-access to Web through college's connection.

CAMPUS LIFE

Activities: Choral groups, drama/theater, jazz band, literary magazine, music ensembles, musical theater, student government, student newspaper, yearbook. **Organizations:** 49 registered organizations, 15 honor societies, 2 religious organizations. 6 fraternities (53% men join), 2 sororities (32% women join). **Athletics (Intercollegiate):** *Men:* Baseball, basketball, cheerleading, football, golf, soccer, tennis. *Women:* Basketball, cheerleading, golf, soccer, softball, tennis, volleyball.

ADMISSIONS

Freshman Academic Profile: 17% in top 10% of high school class, 49% in top 25% of high school class, 82% in top 50% of high school class. 70% from public high schools. SAT Math middle 50% range 500–620. SAT Critical Reading middle 50% range 480–610. SAT Writing middle 50% range 470–610. ACT middle 50% range 23–28. TOEFL required of all international applicants, minimum paper TOEFL 550, minimum computer TOEFL 213. **Basis for Candidate Selection:** *Very important factors considered include:* Character/personal qualities, rigor of secondary school record, standardized test scores. *Important factors considered include:* Class rank, extracurricular activities, recommendation(s), volunteer work. *Other factors considered include:* Alumni/ae relation, application essay, interview, talent/ability, work experience. **Freshman Admission Requirements:** High school diploma is required, and GED is accepted. *Academic units required:* 4 English, 3 math, 2 science (2 science labs). *Academic units recommended:* 2 foreign language, 2 social studies, 2 academic electives. **Freshman Admission Statistics:** 1,074 applied, 79% admitted, 33% enrolled. **Transfer Admission Requirements:** College transcript(s). Minimum college GPA of 2.0 required. Lowest grade transferable C. **General Admission Information:** Regular notification is rolling. Non-fall registration accepted. Admission may be deferred for a maximum of 2 semesters. Credit and/or placement offered for CEEB Advanced Placement tests.

COSTS AND FINANCIAL AID

Annual tuition $15,650. Room and board $6,720. Required fees $600. Average book expense $800. **Required Forms and Deadlines:** FAFSA. Financial aid filing deadline 2/15. **Notification of Awards:** Applicants will be notified of awards on a rolling basis beginning on or about 2/28. **Types of Aid:** *Need-based scholarships/grants:* Pell, SEOG, state scholarships/grants, private scholarships, the school's own gift aid. *Loans:* FFEL Subsidized Stafford, FFEL Unsubsidized Stafford, FFEL PLUS, Federal Perkins. **Financial Aid**

Statistics: 53% freshmen, 55% undergrads receive need-based scholarship or grant aid. 39% freshmen, 44% undergrads receive need-based self-help aid. 98% freshmen, 98% undergrads receive any aid. Highest amount earned per year from on-campus jobs $2,500.

WESTMINSTER COLLEGE (PA)

319 South Market Street, New Wilmington, PA 16172
Phone: 724-946-7100 **E-mail:** admis@westminster.edu **CEEB Code:** 2975
Fax: 724-946-7171 **Website:** www.westminster.edu **ACT Code:** 2975
Financial Aid Phone: 724-946-7102

This private school, affiliated with the Presbyterian Church, was founded in 1852. It has a 350-acre campus.

RATINGS

Admissions Selectivity Rating: 79   **Fire Safety Rating:** 98   **Green Rating:** 60*

STUDENTS AND FACULTY

Enrollment: 1,387. **Student Body:** 64% female, 36% male, 21% out-of-state. African American 3%, Caucasian 80%. **Retention and Graduation:** 83 freshmen return for sophomore year. 65% freshmen graduate within 4 years 21% grads go on to further study within 2 semesters. 2% grads pursue busines degrees. 3% grads pursue law degrees. 3% grads pursue medical degrees **Faculty:** Student/faculty ratio 12:1. 100 full-time faculty, 83% hold PhDs. 100 faculty teach undergrads

ACADEMICS

Degrees: Bachelor's, master's. **Academic Requirements:** Arts/fine arts, computer literacy, English (including composition), foreign languages, history, humanities, intellectual perspectives, inquiry, mathematics, philosophy, sciences (biological or physical), social science, speech, writing. **Classes:** Most classes have 10–19 students. Most lab/discussion sections have 10–19 students. **Majors with Highest Enrollment:** Biology/biological sciences, business administration/management, education. **Disciplines with Highest Percentage of Degrees Awarded:** Education 21%, business/marketing 16%, social sciences 13%, communication technologies 8%, biological/life sciences 7%. **Special Study Options:** Double major, exchange student program (domestic), honors program, independent study, internships, liberal arts/career combination, student-designed major, study abroad, teacher certification program.

FACILITIES

Housing: Men's dorms, women's dorms, special housing for disabled students, fraternity/sorority housing, townhouses for upperclass men and women. **Special Academic Facilities/Equipment:** On-campus preschool, Moeller pipe organs, planetarium, observatory, electron microscopes, X-ray diffractor, spectrometer. **Computers:** 2% of classrooms are wired, 100% of public computers are PCs, network access in dorm rooms, online administrative functions (other than registration), remote student-access to Web through college's connection.

CAMPUS LIFE

Activities: Choral groups, concert band, dance, drama/theater, jazz band, literary magazine, marching band, music ensembles, musical theater, pep band, radio station, student government, student newspaper, television station, yearbook. **Organizations:** 60 registered organizations, 21 honor societies, 3 religious organizations. 5 fraternities (33% men join), 5 sororities (34% women join). **Athletics (Intercollegiate):** *Men:* Baseball, basketball, cheerleading, cross-country, football, golf, soccer, swimming, tennis, track/field (indoor), track/field (outdoor). *Women:* Basketball, cheerleading, cross-country, golf, soccer, softball, swimming, tennis, track/field (indoor), track/field (outdoor), volleyball.

ADMISSIONS

Freshman Academic Profile: 20% in top 10% of high school class, 55% in top 25% of high school class, 87% in top 50% of high school class. 90% from public high schools. SAT Math middle 50% range 480–590. SAT Critical Reading middle 50% range 480–592. ACT middle 50% range 20–25. TOEFL required of all international applicants, minimum paper TOEFL 550, minimum computer TOEFL 213. **Basis for Candidate Selection:** *Very important*

factors considered include: Interview, rigor of secondary school record, standardized test scores. *Important factors considered include:* Application essay, character/personal qualities, class rank, recommendation(s). *Other factors considered include:* Alumni/ae relation, extracurricular activities, racial/ethnic status, talent/ability, volunteer work, work experience. **Freshman Admission Requirements:** High school diploma is required, and GED is accepted. *Academic units required:* 4 English, 3 math, 2 science (2 science labs), 2 foreign language, 2 social studies, 1 history, 3 academic electives. **Freshman Admission Statistics:** 1,302 applied, 77% admitted, 36% enrolled. **Transfer Admission Requirements:** High school transcript, college transcript(s), essay or personal statement, interview, standardized test score. Minimum college GPA of 2.5 required. Lowest grade transferable C. **General Admission Information:** Application fee $35. Early decision application deadline 11/15. Regular application deadline 4/15. Regular notification is rolling. Non-fall registration not accepted. Admission may be deferred for a maximum of 2 semesters. Common Application not accepted. Credit and/or placement offered for CEEB Advanced Placement tests.

COSTS AND FINANCIAL AID

Annual tuition $25,530. Room and board $7,660. Required fees $1,000. Average book expense $900. **Required Forms and Deadlines:** FAFSA, institution's own financial aid form. Financial aid filing deadline 5/1. **Notification of Awards:** Applicants will be notified of awards on a rolling basis beginning on or about 11/1. **Types of Aid:** *Need-based scholarships/grants:* Pell, SEOG, state scholarships/grants, private scholarships, the school's own gift aid. *Loans:* FFEL Subsidized Stafford, FFEL Unsubsidized Stafford, FFEL PLUS, Federal Perkins, resource loans. **Financial Aid Statistics:** 81% freshmen, 79% undergrads receive need-based scholarship or grant aid. 68% freshmen, 65% undergrads receive need-based self-help aid. Highest amount earned per year from on-campus jobs $1,300.

WESTMONT COLLEGE

955 La Paz Road, Santa Barbara, CA 93108
Phone: 805-565-6200 **E-mail:** admissions@westmont.edu **CEEB Code:** 4950
Fax: 805-565-6234 **Website:** www.westmont.edu **ACT Code:** 0478
Financial Aid Phone: 888-963-4624

This private school, affiliated with the Christian (nondenominational) Church, was founded in 1937. It has a 133-acre campus.

RATINGS

Admissions Selectivity Rating: 90   **Fire Safety Rating:** 60*   **Green Rating:** 60*

STUDENTS AND FACULTY

Enrollment: 1,319. **Student Body:** 60% female, 40% male, 35% out-of-state. African American 2%, Asian 7%, Caucasian 73%, Hispanic 10%, Native American 3%. **Retention and Graduation:** 89% freshmen return for sophomore year. 67% freshmen graduate within 4 years. **Faculty:** Student/faculty ratio 12:1. 90 full-time faculty, 89% hold PhDs. 100% faculty teach undergrads.

ACADEMICS

Degrees: Bachelor's, post-bachelor's certificate. **Academic Requirements:** Arts/fine arts, English (including composition), foreign languages, history, humanities, mathematics, philosophy, physical education, religious studies, sciences (biological or physical), social science. **Classes:** Most classes have 10–19 students. Most lab/discussion sections have 10–19 students. **Majors with Highest Enrollment:** Cell/cellular and molecular biology, communications studies/speech communication and rhetoric, English/language arts teacher education. **Disciplines with Highest Percentage of Degrees Awarded:** Social sciences 24%, biological/life sciences 11%, English 10%, communications/journalism 9%, parks and recreation 8%. **Special Study Options:** Accelerated program, double major, exchange student program (domestic), honors program, independent study, internships, student-designed major, study abroad, teacher certification program.

FACILITIES

Housing: Coed dorms (segregated floors and/or suites), apartments for single students. **Special Academic Facilities/Equipment:** Reynolds Art Gallery, Carroll Observatory, Mericos Whittier Science facility includes state of the art technical equipment such as ultracentrifuge, Fouriertransform NMR spectrometer, Voskuyl Library, Ellen Porter Hall of Fine, physiology lab, fitness center. **Computers:** 15% of public computers are PCs, 8% of public computers are Macs, 2% of public computers are UNIX, network access in dorm rooms, online administrative functions (other than registration), remote student-access

to Web through college's connection.

CAMPUS LIFE

Activities: Choral groups, dance, drama/theater, jazz band, literary magazine, music ensembles, musical theater, radio station, student government, student newspaper, student-run film society, yearbook. **Organizations:** 50 registered organizations, 7 honor societies, 40 religious organizations. **Athletics (Intercollegiate):** *Men:* Baseball, basketball, cross-country, soccer, tennis, track/field (outdoor). *Women:* Basketball, cross-country, soccer, tennis, track/field (outdoor), volleyball.

ADMISSIONS

Freshman Academic Profile: 44% in top 10% of high school class, 76% in top 25% of high school class, 94% in top 50% of high school class. 84% from public high schools. SAT Math middle 50% range 540–660. SAT Critical Reading middle 50% range 540–650. SAT Writing middle 50% range 540–650. ACT middle 50% range 24–28. TOEFL required of all international applicants, minimum paper TOEFL 560, minimum computer TOEFL 220. **Basis for Candidate Selection:** *Very important factors considered include:* Academic GPA, character/personal qualities, religious affiliation/commitment, standardized test scores. *Important factors considered include:* Application essay, extracurricular activities, interview, racial/ethnic status, recommendation(s), rigor of secondary school record, talent/ability. *Other factors considered include:* Alumni/ae relation, class rank, first generation, geographical residence, level of applicant's interest, state residency, volunteer work, work experience. **Freshman Admission Requirements:** High school diploma is required, and GED is accepted. *Academic units required:* 4 English, 3 math, 3 science (2 science labs), 2 foreign language, 2 social studies, 4 academic electives. **Freshman Admission Statistics:** 1,807 applied, 65% admitted, 28% enrolled. **Transfer Admission Requirements:** High school transcript, college transcript(s), essay or personal statement, statement of good standing from prior institution(s). Lowest grade transferable C-. **General Admission Information:** Application fee $50. Regular notification is rolling. Non-fall registration accepted. Credit and/or placement offered for CEEB Advanced Placement tests.

COSTS AND FINANCIAL AID

Annual tuition $30,422. Room and board $9,622. Required fees $790. Average book expense $1,386. **Required Forms and Deadlines:** FAFSA, Cal Grant GPA Verification Form (if student is a California resident). Financial aid filing deadline 3/2. **Notification of Awards:** Applicants will be notified of awards on a rolling basis beginning on or about 4/1. **Types of Aid:** *Need-based scholarships/grants:* Pell, SEOG, state scholarships/grants, private scholarships, the school's own gift aid. *Loans:* FFEL Subsidized Stafford, FFEL Unsubsidized Stafford, FFEL PLUS, Federal Perkins, college/university loans from institutional funds, work-study. **Student Employment:** Federal Work-Study Program available. Institutional employment available. **Financial Aid Statistics:** 57% freshmen, 53% undergrads receive need-based scholarship or grant aid. 51% freshmen, 46% undergrads receive need-based self-help aid. 11 freshmen, 51 undergrads receive athletic scholarships. 85% undergrads receive any aid.

WESTWOOD COLLEGE OF AVIATION TECHNOLOGY

Office of Admissions, Inglewood, CA 90301
Phone: 310-337-4444
Fax: 310-337-1176 **Website:** www.redstoneaviation.com
Financial Aid Phone: 310-337-4444

This proprietary school was founded in 1936. It has a 4-acre campus.

RATINGS

Admissions Selectivity Rating: 60*   **Fire Safety Rating:** 60*   **Green Rating:** 60*

STUDENTS AND FACULTY

Enrollment: 277. **Student Body:** 6% female, 94% male. **Faculty:** 100% faculty teach undergrads.

ACADEMICS

Degrees: Associate, bachelor's. **Academic Requirements:** Airframe & powerplant, arts/fine arts, computer literacy, English (including composition), history, humanities, mathematics, philosophy, sciences (biological or physical).

FACILITIES

Computers: 100% of public computers are PCs.

ADMISSIONS

Freshman Academic Profile: TOEFL required of all international applicants, minimum paper TOEFL 500. **Basis for Candidate Selection:** *Important factors considered include:* Interview, standardized test scores, talent/ability, work experience. *Other factors considered include:* Character/personal qualities, class rank, recommendation(s), rigor of secondary school record, volunteer work. **Freshman Admission Requirements:** High school diploma is required, and GED is accepted. **Freshman Admission Statistics:** 48 applied, 92% admitted, 75% enrolled. **Transfer Admission Requirements:** College transcript(s), interview. **General Admission Information:** Application fee $75. Regular application deadline 9/17. Regular notification is rolling. Non-fall registration accepted. Common Application not accepted. Neither credit nor placement offered for CEEB Advanced Placement tests.

COSTS AND FINANCIAL AID

Annual tuition $8,750. Required fees $75. Average book expense $1,400. **Types of Aid:** *Need-based scholarships/grants:* Pell, SEOG. *Loans:* FFEL Subsidized Stafford, FFEL Unsubsidized Stafford, FFEL PLUS, Federal Perkins. **Student Employment:** Off-campus job opportunities are excellent.

WESTWOOD COLLEGE OF TECHNOLOGY

7350 North Broadway, Denver, CO 80221
Phone: 303-426-7000 **E-mail:** bsimms@westwood.edu
Fax: 303-426-1832 **Website:** www.westwood.edu

This proprietary school was founded in 1953. It has a 7-acre campus.

RATINGS
Admissions Selectivity Rating: 60*   **Fire Safety Rating:** 60*   **Green Rating:** 60*

STUDENTS AND FACULTY

Enrollment: 1,363. **Student Body:** 29% female, 71% male, 27% out-of-state. African American 4%, Asian 3%, Caucasian 59%, Hispanic 18%, Native American 3%. **Faculty:** Student/faculty ratio 14:1. 44 full-time faculty, 7% hold PhDs. 100% faculty teach undergrads.

ACADEMICS

Degrees: Associate, bachelor's, diploma. **Academic Requirements:** Computer literacy, English (including composition), mathematics, social science. **Classes:** Most classes have 10–19 students. **Majors with Highest Enrollment:** Computer programming/programmer, computer systems networking and telecommunications, graphic design. **Disciplines with Highest Percentage of Degrees Awarded:** Computer and information sciences 43%, communication technologies 21%, visual and performing arts 21%, engineering 15%. **Special Study Options:** Accelerated program, cooperative education program, distance learning, independent study, internships, liberal arts/career combination.

FACILITIES

Housing: Apartments for single students. **Computers:** 90% of public computers are PCs, 8% of public computers are Macs, 2% of public computers are UNIX.

CAMPUS LIFE

Organizations: 1 honor society.

ADMISSIONS

Freshman Academic Profile: TOEFL required of all international applicants, minimum paper TOEFL 475, minimum computer TOEFL 153. **Basis for Candidate Selection:** *Very important factors considered include:* Character/personal qualities, interview, standardized test scores, talent/ability. *Other factors considered include:* Application essay. **Freshman Admission Requirements:** High school diploma is required, and GED is accepted. **Transfer Admission Requirements:** High school transcript, college transcript(s), interview, standardized test score. Minimum college GPA of 2.0 required. Lowest grade transferable C. **General Admission Information:** Application fee $25. Non-fall registration accepted. Common Application not accepted. Credit and/or placement offered for CEEB Advanced Placement tests.

COSTS AND FINANCIAL AID

Required fees $100. Average book expense $1,500. **Required Forms and Deadlines:** FAFSA, institution's own financial aid form, state aid form. **Notification of Awards:** Applicants will be notified of awards on a rolling basis beginning on or about 1/1. **Types of Aid:** *Need-based scholarships/grants:* Pell, SEOG, state scholarships/grants, private scholarships, the school's own gift aid.

Loans: FFEL Subsidized Stafford, FFEL Unsubsidized Stafford, FFEL PLUS, Federal Perkins, college/university loans from institutional funds. **Student Employment:** Federal Work-Study Program available. Institutional employment available. Off-campus job opportunities are good. **Financial Aid Statistics:** 42% freshmen, 25% undergrads receive need-based scholarship or grant aid. 90% freshmen, 90% undergrads receive need-based self-help aid.

WHEATON COLLEGE (IL)

Best 368

501 College Avenue, Wheaton, IL 60187
Phone: 630-752-5005 **E-mail:** admissions@wheaton.edu **CEEB Code:** 1905
Fax: 630-752-5285 **Website:** www.wheaton.edu **ACT Code:** 1160
Financial Aid Phone: 630-752-5021

This private school, affiliated with the Christian non-denominational Church, was founded in 1860. It has an 80-acre campus.

RATINGS
Admissions Selectivity Rating: 95   **Fire Safety Rating:** 87   **Green Rating:** 83

STUDENTS AND FACULTY

Enrollment: 2,350. **Student Body:** 51% female, 49% male, 79% out-of-state, 1% international (18 countries represented). African American 2%, Asian 7%, Caucasian 85%, Hispanic 3%. **Retention and Graduation:** 94% freshmen return for sophomore year. 78% freshmen graduate within 4 years. 28% grads go on to further study within 2 semesters. 17% grads pursue arts and sciences degrees. 1% grads pursue business degrees. 2% grads pursue law degrees. 7% grads pursue medical degrees. **Faculty:** Student/faculty ratio 12:1. 193 full-time faculty, 94% hold PhDs. 90% faculty teach undergrads.

ACADEMICS

Degrees: Bachelor's, doctoral, master's, post-bachelor's certificate. **Academic Requirements:** Arts/fine arts, biblical studies, English (including composition), foreign languages, history, humanities, mathematics, philosophy, sciences (biological or physical), social science. **Classes:** Most classes have 10–19 students. Most lab/discussion sections have 10–19 students. **Majors with Highest Enrollment:** Business/managerial economics, English language and literature, psychology. **Disciplines with Highest Percentage of Degrees Awarded:** Social sciences 18%, theology and religious vocations 10%, business/marketing 8%, English 8%, visual and performing arts 7%. **Special Study Options:** Cross registration, double major, exchange student program (domestic), independent study, internships, liberal arts/career combination, student-designed major, study abroad, teacher certification program.

FACILITIES

Housing: Men's dorms, women's dorms, apartments for married students, apartments for single students, cooperative housing, housing for disabled provided as needed. **Special Academic Facilities/Equipment:** World Evangelism Museum, language lab, observatory, collection of works/papers of seven British authors, Billy Graham Center Museum. **Computers:** 100% of classrooms are wired, 5% of classrooms are wireless, 95% of public computers are PCs, 5% of public computers are Macs, network access in dorm rooms, network access in dorm lounges, online registration, online administrative functions (other than registration), remote student-access to Web through college's connection. **Environmental Initiatives:** Environmental Studies Major. LEED Certifications. Recycling.

CAMPUS LIFE

Activities: Choral groups, concert band, drama/theater, jazz band, literary magazine, music ensembles, musical theater, pep band, radio station, student government, student newspaper, symphony orchestra, television station, yearbook. **Organizations:** 75 registered organizations, 13 honor societies, 11 religious organization. **Athletics (Intercollegiate):** *Men:* Baseball, basketball, cross-country, football, golf, soccer, swimming, tennis, track/field (indoor), track/field (outdoor), wrestling. *Women:* Basketball, cross-country, golf, soccer, softball, swimming, tennis, track/field (indoor), track/field (outdoor), volleyball, water polo.

ADMISSIONS

Freshman Academic Profile:

middle 50% range 630–720. SAT Writing middle 50% range 610–710. ACT middle 50% range 27–31. TOEFL required of all international applicants, minimum paper TOEFL 550, minimum computer TOEFL 213. **Basis for Candidate Selection:** *Very important factors considered include:* Academic GPA, application essay, character/personal qualities, recommendation(s), rigor of secondary school record, standardized test scores. *Important factors considered include:* Interview, level of applicant's interest, talent/ability. *Other factors considered include:* Alumni/ae relation, class rank, extracurricular activities, first generation, geographical residence, racial/ethnic status, religious affiliation/commitment, state residency, volunteer work. **Freshman Admission Requirements:** High school diploma is required, and GED is accepted. *Academic units recommended:* 4 English, 4 math, 4 science, 3 foreign language, 4 social studies. **Freshman Admission Statistics:** 2,115 applied, 56% admitted, 49% enrolled. **Transfer Admission Requirements:** High school transcript, college transcript(s), essay or personal statement. Minimum college GPA of 3.0 required. Lowest grade transferable C-. **General Admission Information:** Application fee $50. Regular application deadline 1/10. Regular notification 4/1. Non-fall registration accepted. Credit and/or placement offered for CEEB Advanced Placement tests.

COSTS AND FINANCIAL AID

Annual tuition $23,730. Room and board $7,252. Average book expense $768. **Required Forms and Deadlines:** FAFSA, institution's own financial aid form. Financial aid filing deadline 2/15. **Notification of Awards:** Applicants will be notified of awards on a rolling basis beginning on or about 3/1. **Types of Aid:** *Need-based scholarships/grants:* Pell, SEOG, state scholarships/grants, the school's own gift aid. *Loans:* FFEL Subsidized Stafford, FFEL Unsubsidized Stafford, FFEL PLUS, Federal Perkins, college/university loans from institutional funds, alternative loans. **Student Employment:** Federal Work-Study Program available. Institutional employment available. Off-campus job opportunities are excellent. **Financial Aid Statistics:** 39% freshmen, 40% undergrads receive need-based scholarship or grant aid. 44% freshmen, 46% undergrads receive need-based self-help aid. 69% freshmen, 68% undergrads receive any aid. Highest amount earned per year from on-campus jobs $5,889.

See page 1496.

WHEATON COLLEGE (MA)

Best 368

Office of Admission, Norton, MA 02766
Phone: 508-286-8251 **E-mail:** admission@wheatoncollege.edu **CEEB Code:** 3963
Fax: 508-286-8271 **Website:** www.wheatoncollege.edu **ACT Code:** 1932
Financial Aid Phone: 508-286-8232

This private school was founded in 1834. It has a 385-acre campus.

RATINGS

Admissions Selectivity Rating: 93　　**Fire Safety Rating:** 83　　**Green Rating:** 86

STUDENTS AND FACULTY

Enrollment: 1,550. **Student Body:** 62% female, 38% male, 67% out-of-state, 2% international (34 countries represented). African American 4%, Asian 3%, Caucasian 79%, Hispanic 3%. **Retention and Graduation:** 86% freshmen return for sophomore year. 74% freshmen graduate within 4 years. 29% grads go on to further study within 2 semesters. 17% grads pursue arts and sciences degrees. 2% grads pursue business degrees. 7% grads pursue law degrees. 3% grads pursue medical degrees. **Faculty:** Student/faculty ratio 12:1. 119 full-time faculty, 97% hold PhDs. 100% faculty teach undergrads.

ACADEMICS

Degrees: Bachelor's. **Academic Requirements:** Arts/fine arts, English (including composition), foreign languages, history, humanities, mathematics, sciences (biological or physical), social science. **Classes:** Most classes have 10–19 students. Most lab/discussion sections have 10–19 students. **Majors with Highest Enrollment:** Economics, English language and literature, psychology. **Disciplines with Highest Percentage of Degrees Awarded:** Social sciences 27%, English 12%, area and ethnic studies 11%, psychology 11%, visual and performing arts 11%, biological/life sciences 7%, history 5%, physical sciences 5%. **Special Study Options:** Accelerated program, cross registration, double major, dual enrollment, exchange student program (domestic), honors program, independent study, internships, liberal arts/career combination, student-designed major, study abroad, teacher certification program.

FACILITIES

Housing: Coed dorms, men's dorms, women's dorms, special housing for disabled students, special housing for international students, special interest houses. **Special Academic Facilities/Equipment:** Art gallery, language lab, photography darkrooms, dance studio, on-campus nursery school, media center, observatory. **Computers:** 5% of classrooms are wired, 5% of classrooms are wireless, 51% of public computers are PCs, 49% of public computers are Macs, network access in dorm rooms, network access in dorm lounges, online registration, online administrative functions (other than registration), remote student-access to Web through college's connection.

CAMPUS LIFE

Activities: Choral groups, dance, drama/theater, jazz band, literary magazine, music ensembles, musical theater, pep band, radio station, student government, student newspaper, student-run film society, symphony orchestra, yearbook. **Organizations:** 65 registered organizations, 8 honor societies, 3 religious organizations. **Athletics (Intercollegiate):** *Men:* Baseball, basketball, cross-country, diving, lacrosse, soccer, swimming, tennis, track/field (indoor), track/field (outdoor). *Women:* Basketball, cross-country, diving, field hockey, lacrosse, soccer, softball, swimming, synchronized swimming, tennis, track/field (indoor), track/field (outdoor), volleyball. **Environmental Initiatives:** Recycling. Energy conservation. Education.

ADMISSIONS

Freshman Academic Profile: 53% in top 10% of high school class, 83% in top 25% of high school class, 99% in top 50% of high school class. 63% from public high schools. SAT Math middle 50% range 560–650. SAT Critical Reading middle 50% range 580–670. ACT middle 50% range 25–28. TOEFL required of all international applicants, minimum paper TOEFL 550, minimum computer TOEFL 213. **Basis for Candidate Selection:** *Very important factors considered include:* Academic GPA, application essay, character/personal qualities, extracurricular activities, first generation, rigor of secondary school record, talent/ability. *Important factors considered include:* Alumni/ae relation, class rank, interview, recommendation(s), volunteer work, work experience. *Other factors considered include:* Geographical residence, level of applicant's interest, racial/ethnic status, standardized test scores, state residency. **Freshman Admission Requirements:** High school diploma is required, and GED is accepted. *Academic units recommended:* 4 English, 4 math, 3 science (2 science labs), 4 foreign language, 3 social studies, 2 history. **Freshman Admission Statistics:** 3,614 applied, 41% admitted, 28% enrolled. **Transfer Admission Requirements:** high school transcript, College transcript(s), essay or personal statement, statement of good standing from prior institution(s). Minimum college GPA of 3.0 required. Lowest grade transferable C. **General Admission Information:** Application fee $55. Early decision application deadline 11/1. Regular application deadline 1/15. Regular notification 4/1. Non-fall registration accepted. Admission may be deferred for a maximum of 2 semesters. Credit and/or placement offered for CEEB Advanced Placement tests.

COSTS AND FINANCIAL AID

Annual tuition $36,430. Room and board $8,640. Required fees $260. Average book expense $940. **Required Forms and Deadlines:** FAFSA, CSS/Financial Aid PROFILE, Noncustodial PROFILE, Business/Farm Supplement, parent and student federal tax returns and W2's. Financial aid filing deadline 2/1. **Notification of Awards:** Applicants will be notified of awards on or about 4/1. **Types of Aid:** *Need-based scholarships/grants:* Pell, SEOG, state scholarships/grants, private scholarships, the school's own gift aid. *Loans:* FFEL Subsidized Stafford, FFEL Unsubsidized Stafford, FFEL PLUS, Federal Perkins, state loans. **Financial Aid Statistics:** 52% freshmen, 48% undergrads receive need-based scholarship or grant aid. 53% freshmen, 49% undergrads receive need-based self-help aid. 63% freshmen, 62% undergrads receive any aid. Highest amount earned per year from on-campus jobs $1,800.

WHEELING JESUIT UNIVERSITY

316 Washington Avenue, Wheeling, WV 26003
Phone: 304-243-2359 **E-mail:** admiss@wju.edu **CEEB Code:** 5906
Fax: 304-243-2397 **Website:** www.wju.edu **ACT Code:** 4546
Financial Aid Phone: 304-243- 2304

This private school, affiliated with the Roman Catholic Church, was founded in 1954. It has a 70-acre campus.

RATINGS

Admissions Selectivity Rating: 81　　**Fire Safety Rating:** 79　　**Green Rating:** 60*

STUDENTS AND FACULTY

Enrollment: 1,135. **Student Body:** 62% female, 38% male, 63% out-of-state, 2% international (12 countries represented). African American 2%, Asian 1%, Caucasian 83%, Hispanic 2%. **Retention and Graduation:** 72% freshmen return for sophomore year. 45% freshmen graduate within 4 years. 32% grads go on to further study within 2 semesters. 17% grads pursue arts and sciences degrees. 8% grads pursue business degrees. 3% grads pursue law degrees. 4% grads pursue medical degrees. **Faculty:** 75 full-time faculty, 72% hold PhDs.

ACADEMICS

Degrees: Bachelor's, doctoral, master's. **Academic Requirements:** Arts/fine arts, English (including composition), foreign languages, history, humanities, mathematics, philosophy, sciences (biological or physical), social science, theology/religion. **Classes:** Most classes have 20–29 students. Most lab/discussion sections have 10–19 students. **Disciplines with Highest Percentage of Degrees Awarded:** Business/marketing 33%, health professions and related sciences 18%, liberal arts/general studies 8%, biological/life sciences 6%, psychology 6%, security and protective services 5%. **Special Study Options:** Accelerated program, distance learning, double major, dual enrollment, English as a second language (ESL), exchange student program (domestic), honors program, independent study, internships, liberal arts/career combination, off-campus study in Washington, DC, student-designed major, study abroad, teacher certification program.

FACILITIES

Housing: Coed dorms, men's dorms, women's dorms, apartments for married students. **Special Academic Facilities/Equipment:** Center for Educational Technologies (NASA).

CAMPUS LIFE

Activities: Choral groups, dance, drama/theater, literary magazine, pep band, student government, student newspaper, television station, yearbook. **Organizations:** 30 registered organizations, 9 honor societies, 6 religious organizations. **Athletics (Intercollegiate):** *Men:* Baseball, basketball, cross-country, golf, lacrosse, soccer, swimming, track/field (indoor), track/field (outdoor). *Women:* Basketball, cross-country, golf, soccer, softball, swimming, track/field (indoor), track/field (outdoor), volleyball.

ADMISSIONS

Freshman Academic Profile: 22% in top 10% of high school class, 49% in top 25% of high school class, 78% in top 50% of high school class. 62% from public high schools. SAT Math middle 50% range 450–570. SAT Critical Reading middle 50% range 460–540. ACT middle 50% range 20–25. TOEFL required of all international applicants, minimum paper TOEFL 550, minimum computer TOEFL 213. **Basis for Candidate Selection:** *Very important factors considered include:* Academic GPA, rigor of secondary school record, standardized test scores. *Important factors considered include:* Application essay, character/personal qualities, interview. *Other factors considered include:* Alumni/ae relation, class rank, extracurricular activities, level of applicant's interest, recommendation(s), talent/ability, volunteer work, work experience. **Freshman Admission Requirements:** High school diploma is required, and GED is accepted. *Academic units required:* 4 English, 2 math, 1 science (1 science lab), 2 social studies, 2 history, 6 academic electives. *Academic units recommended:* 2 foreign language. **Freshman Admission Statistics:** 1,173 applied, 72% admitted, 33% enrolled. **Transfer Admission Requirements:** College transcript(s). Minimum college GPA of 2.3 required. Lowest grade transferable C. **General Admission Information:** Application fee $25. Regular notification is rolling. Non-fall registration accepted. Admission may be deferred for a maximum of 1 semester. Credit and/or placement offered for CEEB Advanced Placement tests.

COSTS AND FINANCIAL AID

Annual tuition $23,590. Room and board $8,640. Required fees $800. Average book expense $900. **Required Forms and Deadlines:** FAFSA. Financial aid filing deadline 2/15. **Notification of Awards:** Applicants will be notified of awards on a rolling basis beginning on or about 3/15. **Types of Aid:** *Need-based scholarships/grants:* Pell, SEOG, state scholarships/grants, private scholarships, the school's own gift aid. *Loans:* Direct Subsidized Stafford, Direct Unsubsidized Stafford, Direct PLUS, Federal Perkins, Federal Nursing, private alternative loans. **Financial Aid Statistics:** 65% freshmen, 63% undergrads receive need-based scholarship or grant aid. 60% freshmen, 63% undergrads receive need-based self-help aid. 13 freshmen, 43 undergrads receive athletic scholarships. 99% freshmen, 90% undergrads receive any aid. Highest amount earned per year from on-campus jobs $1,500.

WHEELOCK COLLEGE

200 The Riverway, Boston, MA 02215
Phone: 617-879-2206 **E-mail:** undergrad@wheelock.edu **CEEB Code:** 3964
Fax: 617-879-2449 **Website:** www.wheelock.edu **ACT Code:** 1934
Financial Aid Phone: 617-879-2206

This private school was founded in 1888. It has a 6-acre campus.

RATINGS

Admissions Selectivity Rating: 74   **Fire Safety Rating:** 88   **Green Rating:** 60*

STUDENTS AND FACULTY

Enrollment: 717. **Student Body:** 96% female, 4% male, 48% out-of-state. African American 9%, Asian 2%, Caucasian 76%, Hispanic 5%. **Retention and Graduation:** 84% freshmen return for sophomore year. 25% grads go on to further study within 2 semesters. 12% grads pursue arts and sciences degrees. 1% grads pursue law degrees. **Faculty:** Student/faculty ratio 11:1. 58 full-time faculty, 83% hold PhDs.

ACADEMICS

Degrees: Bachelor's, master's, post-bachelor's certificate, post-master's certificate. **Academic Requirements:** Arts/fine arts, computer literacy, English (including composition), history, human growth and development, humanities, mathematics, sciences (biological or physical), social science. **Majors with Highest Enrollment:** Elementary education and teaching, human development, family studies and related services, social work. **Special Study Options:** Cross registration, double major, independent study, internships, liberal arts/career combination, study abroad, teacher certification program.

FACILITIES

Housing: Coed dorms, men's dorms, women's dorms, wellness floor, first-year floors. **Special Academic Facilities/Equipment:** Art studio, resource center with fully equipped workshop for creating and developing original curriculum tools. **Computers:** 50% of public computers are PCs, 50% of public computers are Macs, network access in dorm rooms, network access in dorm lounges, remote student-access to Web through college's connection.

CAMPUS LIFE

Activities: Choral groups, dance, drama/theater, music ensembles, musical theater, student government, symphony orchestra. **Organizations:** 20 registered organizations, 1 honor society, 1 religious organization. **Athletics (Intercollegiate):** *Men:* Basketball, tennis. *Women:* Basketball, diving, field hockey, soccer, softball, swimming.

ADMISSIONS

Freshman Academic Profile: 8% in top 10% of high school class, 35% in top 25% of high school class, 70% in top 50% of high school class. 85% from public high schools. SAT Math middle 50% range 420–530. SAT Critical Reading middle 50% range 440–530. SAT Writing middle 50% range 440–530. ACT middle 50% range 18–21. TOEFL required of all international applicants, minimum paper TOEFL 500, minimum computer TOEFL 173. **Basis for Candidate Selection:** *Very important factors considered include:* Academic GPA, application essay, rigor of secondary school record. *Important factors considered include:* Character/personal qualities, class rank, extracurricular activities, recommendation(s), volunteer work. *Other factors considered include:* Alumni/ae relation, interview, standardized test scores, talent/ability, work experience. **Freshman Admission Requirements:** High school diploma is required, and GED is accepted. *Academic units required:* 4 English, 3 math, 2 science (1 science lab), 2 social studies. **Freshman Admission Statistics:** 793 applied, 74% admitted, 31% enrolled. **Transfer Admission Requirements:** High school transcript, college transcript(s), essay or personal statement. Minimum college GPA of 2.0 required. Lowest grade transferable C. **General Admission Information:** Application fee $30. Regular application deadline 3/1. Regular notification is rolling. Non-fall registration accepted. Admission may be deferred for a maximum of 2 semesters. Credit offered for CEEB Advanced Placement tests.

COSTS AND FINANCIAL AID

Annual tuition $25,400. Room and board $10,400. Required fees $680. Average book expense $880. **Required Forms and Deadlines:** FAFSA. Financial aid filing deadline 5/1. **Notification of Awards:** Applicants will be notified of awards on a rolling basis beginning on or about 3/5. **Types of Aid:** *Need-based scholarships/grants:* Pell, SEOG, state scholarships/grants, the school's own gift aid, merit scholarships are available for all freshmen applicants with a 3.0 GPA

Student Employment: Federal Work-Study Program available. Institutional employment available. Off-campus job opportunities are good. **Financial Aid Statistics:** 80% freshmen, 81% undergrads receive need-based scholarship or grant aid. 80% freshmen, 86% undergrads receive need-based self-help aid. 85% freshmen, 81% undergrads receive any aid. Highest amount earned per year from on-campus jobs $2,000.

See page 1498.

WHITMAN COLLEGE

345 Boyer Avenue, Walla Walla, WA 99362
Phone: 509-527-5176 **E-mail:** admission@whitman.edu **CEEB Code:** 4951
Fax: 509-527-4967 **Website:** www.whitman.edu **ACT Code:** 4492
Financial Aid Phone: 509-527-5178

This private school was founded in 1883. It has a 117-acre campus.

RATINGS
Admissions Selectivity Rating: 95   **Fire Safety Rating:** 60*   **Green Rating:** 91

STUDENTS AND FACULTY
Enrollment: 1,421. **Student Body:** 54% female, 46% male, 59% out-of-state, 3% international (32 countries represented). African American 2%, Asian 10%, Caucasian 64%, Hispanic 5%, Native American 1%. **Retention and Graduation:** 93% freshmen return for sophomore year. 80% freshmen graduate within 4 years. **Faculty:** Student/faculty ratio 10:1. 119 full-time faculty, 97% hold PhDs. 100% faculty teach undergrads.

ACADEMICS
Degrees: Bachelor's. **Academic Requirements:** Arts/fine arts, English (including composition), humanities, sciences (biological or physical), social science, writing intensive first year seminar. **Classes:** Most classes have 10–19 students. Most lab/discussion sections have 10–19 students. **Majors with Highest Enrollment:** English language and literature, political science and government, psychology. **Disciplines with Highest Percentage of Degrees Awarded:** Social sciences 24%, biological/life sciences 12%, physical sciences 9%, visual and performing arts 9%, English 8%, history 8%, philosophy and religious studies 7%, psychology 7%. **Special Study Options:** Accelerated program, cooperative education program, cross registration, double major, dual enrollment, exchange student program (domestic), honors program, independent study, liberal arts/career combination, student-designed major, study abroad, undergraduate research conference.

FACILITIES
Housing: Coed dorms, women's dorms, apartments for single students, special housing for international students, fraternity/sorority housing, interest houses. **Special Academic Facilities/Equipment:** Art gallery, Asian art collection, anthropology museum, planetarium, outdoor observatory, 2 electron microscopes, outdoor sculpture walk, technology/video-conferencing center, indoor and outdoor rock-climbing walls, organic garden. **Computers:** 6% of classrooms are wired, 95% of classrooms are wireless, 70% of public computers are PCs, 26% of public computers are Macs, 4% of public computers are UNIX, network access in dorm rooms, network access in dorm lounges, online registration, online administrative functions (other than registration), support for handheld computing, remote student-access to Web through college's connection.

CAMPUS LIFE
Activities: Choral groups, concert band, dance, drama/theater, jazz band, literary magazine, music ensembles, musical theater, radio station, student government, student newspaper, student-run film society, symphony orchestra. **Organizations:** 60 registered organizations, 3 honor societies. 4 fraternities (41% men join), 3 sororities (31% women join). **Athletics (Intercollegiate):** *Men:* Baseball, basketball, cross-country, golf, skiing (downhill/alpine), skiing (nordic/cross-country), soccer, softball, swimming, tennis. *Women:* Basketball, cross-country, golf, skiing (downhill/alpine), skiing (nordic/cross-country), soccer, softball, swimming, tennis, volleyball.

ADMISSIONS
Freshman Academic Profile: 58% in top 10% of high school class, 89% in top 25% of high school class, 98% in top 50% of high school class. 75% from public high schools. SAT Math middle 50% range 620–700. SAT Critical Reading middle

50% range 620–730. SAT Writing middle 50% range 610–700. ACT middle 50% range 27–32. TOEFL required of all international applicants, minimum paper TOEFL 560, minimum computer TOEFL 220. **Basis for Candidate Selection:** *Very important factors considered include:* Application essay, character/personal qualities, rigor of secondary school record. *Important factors considered include:* Academic GPA, interview, racial/ethnic status, recommendation(s), standardized test scores, talent/ability. *Other factors considered include:* Alumni/ae relation, class rank, extracurricular activities, first generation, geographical residence, level of applicant's interest, state residency, volunteer work, work experience. **Freshman Admission Requirements:** High school diploma is required, and GED is accepted. *Academic units recommended:* 4 English, 4 math, 3 science (3 science labs), 2 foreign language, 2 social studies, 2 history, 1 art. **Freshman Admission Statistics:** 2,740 applied, 47% admitted, 28% enrolled. **Transfer Admission Requirements:** High school transcript, college transcript(s), essay or personal statement, statement of good standing from prior institution(s). Lowest grade transferable C-. **General Admission Information:** Application fee $45. Early decision application deadline 11/15. Regular application deadline 1/15. Regular notification 4/1. Non-fall registration accepted. Admission may be deferred for a maximum of 2 semesters. Credit and/or placement offered for CEEB Advanced Placement tests.

COSTS AND FINANCIAL AID
Annual tuition $32,670. Room and board $8,310. Required fees $310. Average book expense $1,400. **Required Forms and Deadlines:** FAFSA, CSS/Financial Aid PROFILE. Financial aid filing deadline 2/1. **Notification of Awards:** Applicants will be notified of awards on a rolling basis beginning on or about 12/20. **Types of Aid:** *Need-based scholarships/grants:* Pell, SEOG, state scholarships/grants, private scholarships, the school's own gift aid. *Loans:* FFEL Subsidized Stafford, FFEL Unsubsidized Stafford, FFEL PLUS, Federal Perkins, state loans, alternative student loans. **Student Employment:** Federal Work-Study Program available. Institutional employment available. **Financial Aid Statistics:** 51% freshmen, 46% undergrads receive need-based scholarship or grant aid. 47% freshmen, 43% undergrads receive need-based self-help aid. 81% freshmen, 86% undergrads receive any aid.

See page 1500.

WHITTIER COLLEGE

13406 Philadelphia Street, PO Box 634, Whittier, CA 90608
Phone: 562-907-4238 **E-mail:** admission@whittier.edu **CEEB Code:** 4952
Fax: 562-907-4870 **Website:** www.whittier.edu **ACT Code:** 0480
Financial Aid Phone: 562-907-4285

This private school was founded in 1887. It has a 75-acre campus.

RATINGS
Admissions Selectivity Rating: 84   **Fire Safety Rating:** 83   **Green Rating:** 83

STUDENTS AND FACULTY
Enrollment: 1,313. **Student Body:** 54% female, 46% male, 30% out-of-state, 2% international (21 countries represented). African American 4%, Asian 8%, Caucasian 47%, Hispanic 27%, Native American 1%. **Retention and Graduation:** 72% freshmen return for sophomore year. 55% freshmen graduate within 4 years. 18% grads go on to further study within 2 semesters. 7% grads pursue arts and sciences degrees. 3% grads pursue business degrees. 2% grads pursue law degrees. 1% grads pursue medical degrees. **Faculty:** Student/faculty ratio 13:1. 87 full-time faculty, 100% hold PhDs. 100% faculty teach undergrads.

ACADEMICS
Degrees: Bachelor's, first professional, master's. **Academic Requirements:** Arts/fine arts, English (including composition), history, humanities, mathematics, philosophy, sciences (biological or physical), social science. **Classes:** Most classes have 10–19 students. Most lab/discussion sections have fewer than 10 students. **Majors with Highest Enrollment:** Business administration/management, child development, English language and literature. **Disciplines with Highest Percentage of Degrees Awarded:** Social sciences 27%, business/marketing 14%, psychology 9%, biological/life sciences 8%, parks and recreation 8%, English 7%, family and consumer sciences 7%. **Special Study Options:** Double major, independent study, internships, liberal arts/career

combination, student-designed major, study abroad, teacher certification program.

FACILITIES

Housing: Coed dorms, women's dorms, substance-free residence halls, multicultural residence hall, honors floor, living and learning community, special interest housing. **Special Academic Facilities/Equipment:** Performing arts center, on-campus pre-school/ elementary school, image processing lab, state-of-the-art nightclub. **Computers:** 93% of classrooms are wireless, 86% of public computers are PCs, 14% of public computers are Macs, network access in dorm rooms, network access in dorm lounges, online registration, online administrative functions (other than registration), remote student-access to Web through college's connection.

CAMPUS LIFE

Activities: Choral groups, dance, drama/theater, jazz band, literary magazine, music ensembles, musical theater, radio station, student government, student newspaper, yearbook. **Organizations:** 68 registered organizations, 14 honor societies, 2 religious organizations. 3 fraternities (8% men join), 5 sororities (18% women join). **Athletics (Intercollegiate):** *Men:* Baseball, basketball, cross-country, diving, football, golf, lacrosse, soccer, swimming, tennis, track/field (outdoor), water polo. *Women:* Basketball, cross-country, diving, lacrosse, soccer, softball, swimming, tennis, track/field (outdoor), volleyball, water polo. **Environmental Initiatives:** Climate Commitment signatory. EnergyStar purchasing policy. Waste minimization program.

ADMISSIONS

Freshman Academic Profile: 27% in top 10% of high school class, 57% in top 25% of high school class, 88% in top 50% of high school class. SAT Math middle 50% range 480–602. SAT Critical Reading middle 50% range 480–600. SAT Writing middle 50% range 480–590. ACT middle 50% range 20–27. TOEFL required of all international applicants, minimum paper TOEFL 550, minimum computer TOEFL 230. **Basis for Candidate Selection:** *Very important factors considered include:* Application essay, rigor of secondary school record. *Important factors considered include:* Academic GPA, character/personal qualities, extracurricular activities, interview, recommendation(s), standardized test scores, talent/ability, volunteer work. *Other factors considered include:* Alumni/ae relation, class rank, first generation, geographical residence, racial/ethnic status, state residency, work experience. **Freshman Admission Requirements:** High school diploma is required, and GED is accepted. *Academic units required:* 3 English, 2 math, 1 science (1 science lab), 2 foreign language, 1 social studies. *Academic units recommended:* 4 English, 3 math, 2 science, 3 foreign language, 2 social studies. **Freshman Admission Statistics:** 3,089 applied, 58% admitted, 19% enrolled. **Transfer Admission Requirements:** High school transcript, college transcript(s), essay or personal statement, Lowest grade transferable C-. **General Admission Information:** Application fee $50. Regular notification is rolling. Non-fall registration accepted. Admission may be deferred for a maximum of 2 semesters. Credit and/or placement offered for CEEB Advanced Placement tests.

COSTS AND FINANCIAL AID

Annual tuition $31,950. Room and board $9,050. Required fees $520. Average book expense $1,566. **Required Forms and Deadlines:** FAFSA, CSS/Financial Aid PROFILE. Financial aid filing deadline 6/30. **Notification of Awards:** Applicants will be notified of awards on a rolling basis beginning on or about 2/15. **Types of Aid:** *Need-based scholarships/grants:* Pell, SEOG, state scholarships/grants, private scholarships, the school's own gift aid. *Loans:* Direct PLUS, FFEL Subsidized Stafford, FFEL Unsubsidized Stafford, FFEL PLUS, Federal Perkins, alternative financing loans. **Student Employment:** Federal Work-Study Program available. Off-campus job opportunities are good. **Financial Aid Statistics:** 54% freshmen, 55% undergrads receive need-based scholarship or grant aid. 59% freshmen, 64% undergrads receive need-based self-help aid. 92% freshmen, 89% undergrads receive any aid. Highest amount earned per year from on-campus jobs $1,250.

WHITWORTH COLLEGE

300 West Hawthorne Road, Spokane, WA 99251
Phone: 509-777-4786 **E-mail:** admission@whitworth.edu **CEEB Code:** 4953
Fax: 509-777-3758 **Website:** www.whitworth.edu **ACT Code:** 4494
Financial Aid Phone: 509-777-4306

This private school, affiliated with the Presbyterian Church, was founded in 1890. It has a 200-acre campus.

STUDENTS AND FACULTY

Enrollment: 2,233. **Student Body:** 61% female, 39% male, 37% out-of-state. African American 3%, Asian 4%, Caucasian 86%, Hispanic 2%, Native American 1%. **Retention and Graduation:** 89% freshmen return for sophomore year. 59% freshmen graduate within 4 years. 50% grads go on to further study within 2 semesters. **Faculty:** Student/faculty ratio 12:1. 123 full-time faculty, 74% hold PhDs. 100% faculty teach undergrads.

ACADEMICS

Degrees: Bachelor's, master's. **Academic Requirements:** Arts/fine arts, English (including composition), foreign languages, history, humanities, mathematics, philosophy, sciences (biological or physical), social science. **Classes:** Most classes have 10–19 students. Most lab/discussion sections have 10–19 students. **Majors with Highest Enrollment:** Business administration/management, elementary education and teaching, English language and literature. **Disciplines with Highest Percentage of Degrees Awarded:** Business/marketing 18%, education 8%, social sciences 8%, visual and performing arts 8%, psychology 7%, health professions and related sciences 6%, liberal arts/general studies 6%. **Special Study Options:** Cooperative education program, cross registration, double major, dual enrollment, English as a second language (ESL), exchange student program (domestic), honors program, independent study, internships, liberal arts/career combination, student-designed major, study abroad, teacher certification program.

FACILITIES

Housing: Coed dorms, men's dorms, women's dorms, theme houses. **Special Academic Facilities/Equipment:** Language laboratory, art gallery, computer labs. **Computers:** 100% of classrooms are wired, 100% of classrooms are wireless, 90% of public computers are PCs, 10% of public computers are Macs, network access in dorm rooms, network access in dorm lounges, online registration, online administrative functions (other than registration), support for handheld computing, remote student-access to Web through college's connection.

CAMPUS LIFE

Activities: Choral groups, concert band, dance, drama/theater, jazz band, music ensembles, musical theater, pep band, radio station, student government, student newspaper, symphony orchestra, yearbook. **Organizations:** 50 registered organizations, 5 honor societies. **Athletics (Intercollegiate):** *Men:* Baseball, basketball, cheerleading, cross-country, football, golf, soccer, swimming, tennis, track/field (outdoor). *Women:* Basketball, cheerleading, cross-country, golf, soccer, softball, swimming, tennis, track/field (outdoor), volleyball.

ADMISSIONS

Freshman Academic Profile: 41% in top 10% of high school class, 74% in top 25% of high school class, 92% in top 50% of high school class. 87% from public high schools. SAT Math middle 50% range 540–650. SAT Critical Reading middle 50% range 540–660. SAT Writing middle 50% range 530–640. ACT middle 50% range 23–28. TOEFL required of all international applicants, minimum paper TOEFL 550, minimum computer TOEFL 250. **Basis for Candidate Selection:** *Very important factors considered include:* Application essay, class rank, recommendation(s), rigor of secondary school record, standardized test scores. *Important factors considered include:* Alumni/ae relation, character/personal qualities, extracurricular activities, geographical residence, interview, talent/ability. *Other factors considered include:* Racial/ethnic status, religious affiliation/commitment, volunteer work. **Freshman Admission Requirements:** High school diploma is required, and GED is accepted. *Academic units recommended:* 4 English, 3 math, 3 science (2 science labs), 2 foreign language, 3 social studies, 3 history. **Freshman Admission Statistics:** 2,686 applied, 63% admitted, 28% enrolled. **Transfer Admission Requirements:** High school transcript, college transcript(s), essay or personal statement, standardized test score, statement of good standing from prior institution(s). Minimum college GPA of 2.5 required. Lowest grade transferable C-. **General Admission Information:** Regular application deadline 3/1. Regular notification is rolling. Non-fall registration accepted. Admission may be deferred for a maximum of 1 year. Credit offered for CEEB Advanced Placement tests.

COSTS AND FINANCIAL AID

Annual tuition $23,850. Room & board $7,030. Required fees $304. Average book expense $792. **Required Forms and Deadlines:** FAFSA. Financial aid filing deadline 3/1. **Notification of Awards:** Applicants will be notified of awards on a rolling basis beginning on or about 4/1. **Types of Aid:** *Need-based scholarships/grants:* Pell, SEOG, state scholarships/grants, private scholarships, the school's own gift aid. *Loans:* Direct Subsidized Stafford, Direct Unsubsidized Stafford, Direct PLUS, Federal Perkins, college/university loans from institutional funds. **Financial Aid Statistics:** 67% freshmen, 67% undergrads receive need-based scholarship or grant aid. 52% freshmen, 55% undergrads...

WICHITA STATE UNIVERSITY

1845 Fairmount, Wichita, KS 67260
Phone: 316-978-3085 **E-mail:** admissions@wichita.edu **CEEB Code:** 6884
Fax: 316-978-3174 **Website:** www.wichita.edu **ACT Code:** 1472
Financial Aid Phone: 800-522-2978

This public school was founded in 1895. It has a 330-acre campus.

RATINGS
Admissions Selectivity Rating: 75   **Fire Safety Rating:** 60*   **Green Rating:** 60*

STUDENTS AND FACULTY
Enrollment: 10,037. **Student Body:** 57% female, 43% male, 3% out-of-state, 5% international (81 countries represented). African American 7%, Asian 6%, Caucasian 68%, Hispanic 5%, Native American 1%. **Retention and Graduation:** 70% freshmen return for sophomore year. 14% freshmen graduate within 4 years. **Faculty:** Student/faculty ratio 17:1. 480 full-time faculty, 80% hold PhDs. 95% faculty teach undergrads.

ACADEMICS
Degrees: Associate, bachelor's, certificate, diploma, doctoral, master's, post-bachelor's certificate, post-master's certificate. **Academic Requirements:** Arts/fine arts, computer literacy, English (including composition), foreign languages, history, humanities, mathematics, philosophy, sciences (biological or physical), social science. **Classes:** Most classes have 20–29 students. Most lab/discussion sections have 10–19 students. **Majors with Highest Enrollment:** Business administration/management, nursing science (MS, PhD), psychology. **Disciplines with Highest Percentage of Degrees Awarded:** Business/marketing 21%, health professions and related sciences 11%, education 9%, engineering 7%, social sciences 7%, psychology 6%, security and protective services 6%, visual and performing arts 6%. **Special Study Options:** Accelerated program, cooperative education program, cross registration, distance learning, double major, dual enrollment, English as a second language (ESL), exchange student program (domestic), honors program, independent study, internships, student-designed major, study abroad, teacher certification program, weekend college.

FACILITIES
Housing: Coed dorms, apartments for married students, apartments for single students, fraternity/sorority housing. **Special Academic Facilities/Equipment:** Art museum, performance hall, media resource center, observatory, national institute of aviation research, supersonic wind tunnels, 24-hour study room in library. **Computers:** 69% of public computers are PCs, 19% of public computers are Macs, 12% of public computers are UNIX, network access in dorm rooms, online registration, online administrative functions (other than registration), remote student-access to Web through college's connection.

CAMPUS LIFE
Activities: Choral groups, concert band, dance, drama/theater, jazz band, literary magazine, music ensembles, musical theater, opera, pep band, radio station, student government, student newspaper, student-run film society, symphony orchestra, television station. **Organizations:** 158 registered organizations, 12 honor societies, 12 religious organizations. 7 fraternities (7% men join), 9 sororities (4% women join). **Athletics (Intercollegiate):** *Men:* Baseball, basketball, cheerleading, cross-country, golf, lacrosse, rugby, swimming, tennis, track/field (outdoor). *Women:* Basketball, cheerleading, cross-country, golf, lacrosse, softball, swimming, tennis, track/field (outdoor), volleyball. **Environmental Initiatives:** State's Facility Conservation Improvement Program.

ADMISSIONS
Freshman Academic Profile: 17% in top 10% of high school class, 42% in top 25% of high school class, 74% in top 50% of high school class. SAT Math middle 50% range 485–620. SAT Critical Reading middle 50% range 480–585. ACT middle 50% range 21–26. TOEFL required of all international applicants, minimum paper TOEFL 530, minimum computer TOEFL 197. **Basis for Candidate Selection:** *Very important factors considered include:* Class rank, rigor of secondary school record, standardized test scores. **Freshman Admission Requirements:** High school diploma is required, and GED is accepted. *Academic units recommended:* 4 English, 3 math, 3 science, 2 foreign language, 3 social studies, 1 computer proficiency. **Freshman Admission Statistics:** 2,781 applied, 82% admitted, 55% enrolled. **Transfer Admission Requirements:** Minimum college GPA of 2.0 required. Lowest grade transferable C. **General Admission Information:** Application fee $30. Regular notification rolling. Non-fall registration accepted. Admission may be deferred for a maximum of 4 semesters. Credit and/or placement offered for CEEB Advanced Placement tests.

COSTS AND FINANCIAL AID
Annual in-state tuition $3,912. Annual out-of-state tuition $11,259. Room and board $5,580. Required fees $892. Average book expense $900. **Required Forms and Deadlines:** FAFSA, state aid form, WSU scholarship application. Financial aid filing deadline 3/15. **Notification of Awards:** Applicants will be notified of awards on a rolling basis beginning on or about 4/1. **Types of Aid:** *Need-based scholarships/grants:* Pell, SEOG, state scholarships/grants, private scholarships, the school's own gift aid, Bureau of Indian Affairs grants/scholarships. *Loans:* FFEL Subsidized Stafford, FFEL Unsubsidized Stafford, FFEL PLUS, Federal Perkins, college/university loans from institutional funds, various alternative loan programs. **Student Employment:** Federal Work-Study Program available. Institutional employment available. Off-campus job opportunities are excellent. **Financial Aid Statistics:** 30% freshmen, 33% undergrads receive need-based scholarship or grant aid. 34% freshmen, 44% undergrads receive need-based self-help aid. 56 freshmen, 202 undergrads receive athletic scholarships. 66% freshmen, 61% undergrads receive any aid.

WIDENER UNIVERSITY

One University Place, Chester, PA 19013
Phone: 610-499-4126 **E-mail:** admissions.office@widener.edu **CEEB Code:** 2642
Fax: 610-499-4676 **Website:** www.widener.edu **ACT Code:** 3652
Financial Aid Phone: 610-499-4174

This private school was founded in 1821. It has a 110-acre campus.

RATINGS
Admissions Selectivity Rating: 75   **Fire Safety Rating:** 60*   **Green Rating:** 60*

STUDENTS AND FACULTY
Enrollment: 3,050. **Student Body:** 57% female, 43% male, 36% out-of-state. African American 15%, Asian 2%, Caucasian 71%, Hispanic 3%. **Retention and Graduation:** 71% freshmen return for sophomore year. 41% freshmen graduate within 4 years. 20% grads go on to further study within 2 semesters. **Faculty:** Student/faculty ratio 12:1. 319 full-time faculty, 91% hold PhDs. 70% faculty teach undergrads.

ACADEMICS
Degrees: Associate, bachelor's, certificate, doctoral, first professional, master's. **Academic Requirements:** Computer literacy, English (including composition), humanities, mathematics, sciences (biological or physical), social science. **Classes:** Most classes have 10–19 students. Most lab/discussion sections have fewer than 10 students. **Majors with Highest Enrollment:** Business administration/management, civil engineering, nursing/registered nurse training (ASN, BSN, MSN, RN). **Disciplines with Highest Percentage of Degrees Awarded:** Business/marketing 28%, health professions and related sciences 19%, engineering 10%, education 8%, psychology 7%. **Special Study Options:** Accelerated program, cooperative education program, distance learning, double major, English as a second language (ESL), honors program, independent study, internships, liberal arts/career combination, student-designed major, study abroad, teacher certification program, weekend college.

FACILITIES
Housing: Coed dorms, men's dorms, women's dorms, apartments for single students, fraternity/sorority housing, cooperative housing, wellness housing, special interest. **Special Academic Facilities/Equipment:** Art gallery, restaurant lab, child development center education lab, recording studio, commercial graphics lab, physical therapy lab, science labs, engineering labs, nursing labs, multimedia classrooms, media center. **Computers:** 35% of classrooms are wired, 25% of classrooms are wireless, 95% of public computers are PCs, 5% of public computers are Macs, network access in dorm rooms, network access in dorm lounges, online registration, online administrative functions (other than registration), remote student-access to Web through college's connection.

CAMPUS LIFE
Activities: Choral groups, concert band, dance, drama/theater, jazz band, literary magazine, music ensembles, pep band, radio station, student government, student newspaper, student-run film society, television station, yearbook. **Organizations:** 80 registered organizations, 29 honor societies, 3 religious organizations. 7 fraternities (12% men join), 3 sororities (11% women join). **Athletics (Intercollegiate):** *Men:* Baseball, basketball, cross-country, football, golf, lacrosse, soccer, swimming, tennis, track/field (indoor), track/field (outdoor). *Women:* Basketball, cheerleading, cross-country, field hockey, lacrosse, soccer, softball, swimming, tennis, track/field (indoor), track/field (outdoor), volleyball.

ADMISSIONS

Freshman Academic Profile: 12% in top 10% of high school class, 32% in top 25% of high school class, 67% in top 50% of high school class. 55% from public high schools. SAT Math middle 50% range 460–560. SAT Critical Reading middle 50% range 440–530. TOEFL required of all international applicants, minimum paper TOEFL 500, minimum computer TOEFL 173. **Basis for Candidate Selection:** *Very important factors considered include:* Academic GPA, class rank, rigor of secondary school record, standardized test scores. *Other factors considered include:* Alumni/ae relation, application essay, character/personal qualities, extracurricular activities, interview, level of applicant's interest, recommendation(s), talent/ability, volunteer work. **Freshman Admission Requirements:** High school diploma is required, and GED is accepted. *Academic units required:* 4 English, 3 math, 3 science, 2 foreign language, 3 social studies, 3 academic electives. *Academic units recommended:* 4 English, 4 math, 4 science (2 science labs), 2 foreign language, 4 social studies, 3 academic electives. **Freshman Admission Statistics:** 4,160 applied, 69% admitted, 26% enrolled. **Transfer Admission Requirements:** College transcript(s). Minimum college GPA of 2.0 required. Lowest grade transferable C. **General Admission Information:** Application fee $35. Regular notification is rolling. Non-fall registration accepted. Admission may be deferred for a maximum of 2 semesters. Credit offered for CEEB Advanced Placement tests.

COSTS AND FINANCIAL AID

Annual tuition $28,180. Room and board $10,240. Required fees $450. Average book expense $990. **Required Forms and Deadlines:** FAFSA. Financial aid filing deadline 2/15. **Notification of Awards:** Applicants will be notified of awards on a rolling basis beginning on or about 3/15. **Types of Aid:** *Need-based scholarships/grants:* Pell, SEOG, state scholarships/grants, private scholarships, the school's own gift aid, Federal Nursing Scholarships. *Loans:* FFEL Subsidized Stafford, FFEL Unsubsidized Stafford, FFEL PLUS, Federal Perkins. **Financial Aid Statistics:** 68% freshmen, 65% undergrads receive need-based scholarship or grant aid. 71% freshmen, 69% undergrads receive need-based self-help aid.

WILBERFORCE UNIVERSITY

1055 North Bickett Road, PO Box 1001, Wilberforce, OH 45384
Phone: 800-367-8568 **E-mail:** kchristm@shorter.wilberforce **CEEB Code:** 1906
Fax: 937-376-4751 **Website:** www.wilberforce.edu **ACT Code:** 3360
Financial Aid Phone: 800-367-8565

This private school was founded in 1856. It has a 125-acre campus.

RATINGS

Admissions Selectivity Rating: 60*   **Fire Safety Rating:** 60*   **Green Rating:** 60*

STUDENTS AND FACULTY

Enrollment: 1,180. **Student Body:** 60% female, 40% male, 39% out-of-state. African American 90%, Caucasian 5%. **Faculty:** Student/faculty ratio 17:1. 49 full-time faculty.

ACADEMICS

Degrees: Bachelor's. **Special Study Options:** Accelerated program, cooperative education program, cross registration, distance learning, double major, external degree program, honors program, independent study, internships, liberal arts/career combination, student-designed major, study abroad.

FACILITIES

Housing: Coed dorms, men's dorms, women's dorms, apartments for married students. **Special Academic Facilities/Equipment:** African Methodist Church Archives.

CAMPUS LIFE

Activities: Choral groups, concert band, dance, jazz band, literary magazine, music ensembles, radio station, student government, student newspaper, yearbook. **Organizations:** 4 religious organizations. 4 fraternities, 4 sororities.

ADMISSIONS

Freshman Academic Profile: 24% in top 10% of high school class, 54% in top 25% of high school class, 85% in top 50% of high school class. Minimum paper TOEFL 500. **Freshman Admission Requirements:** High school diploma is required, and GED is accepted. *Academic units required:* 4 English, 2 math, 2 science, 2 social studies, 5 academic electives. **Freshman Admission**

Lowest grade transferable C. **General Admission Information:** Application fee $20. Regular application deadline 6/1. Regular notification rolling. Non-fall registration accepted. Common Application accepted. Credit and/or placement offered for CEEB Advanced Placement tests.

COSTS AND FINANCIAL AID

Annual tuition $9,720. Room & board $5,320. Required fees $1,060. Average book expense $1,000. **Required Forms and Deadlines:** FAFSA, institution's own financial aid form, state aid form. **Types of Aid:** *Need-based scholarships/grants:* United Negro College Fund. *Loans:* FFEL Subsidized Stafford, FFEL PLUS. **Student Employment:** Federal Work-Study Program available. Off-campus job opportunities are good. **Financial Aid Statistics:** Highest amount earned per year from on-campus jobs $2,000.

WILEY COLLEGE

711 Wiley Avenue, Marshall, TX 75670
Phone: 903-927-3311 **E-mail:** admissions@wileynrts.wileyc.edu **CEEB Code:** 6940
Fax: 903-938-8100 **Website:** www.wileyc.edu
Financial Aid Phone: 903-927-3217

This private school was founded in 1873. It has a 63-acre campus.

RATINGS

Admissions Selectivity Rating: 60*   **Fire Safety Rating:** 60*   **Green Rating:** 60*

STUDENTS AND FACULTY

Student Body: 38% out-of-state. **Retention and Graduation:** 11% freshmen return for sophomore year. 11% grads go on to further study within 2 semesters. 10% grads pursue arts and sciences degrees. 1% grads pursue medical degrees.

ACADEMICS

Degrees: Associate, bachelor's.

FACILITIES

Housing: Coed dorms.

CAMPUS LIFE

Activities: Radio station, student government, student newspaper, yearbook. **Organizations:** 12 registered organizations, 5 honor societies, 5 religious organizations. 4 fraternities (50% men join), 3 sororities (60% women join).

ADMISSIONS

Freshman Academic Profile: 99% from public high schools. Minimum paper TOEFL 400. **Freshman Admission Requirements:** High school diploma is required, and GED is accepted. *Academic units recommended:* 3 English, 3 math, 2 science, 1 foreign language, 2 social studies, 1 history. **Transfer Admission Requirements:** Minimum college GPA of 2.0 required. Lowest grade transferable C. **General Admission Information:** Regular application deadline 8/10. Regular notification rolling. Non-fall registration accepted. Common Application accepted.

COSTS AND FINANCIAL AID

Annual tuition $4,080. Room & board $3,230. Required fees $596. Average book expense $256. **Required Forms and Deadlines:** FAFSA. **Types of Aid:** *Need-based scholarships/grants:* State scholarships/grants, United Negro College Fund. *Loans:* FFEL Subsidized Stafford, FFEL PLUS. **Student Employment:** Federal Work-Study Program available. Off-campus job opportunities are good.

WILKES UNIVERSITY

84 West South Street, Wilkes-Barre, PA 18766
Phone: 570-408-4400 **E-mail:** admissions@wilkes.edu **CEEB Code:** 2977
Fax: 570-408-4904 **Website:** www.wilkes.edu **ACT Code:** 3756
Financial Aid Phone: 570-408-4345

This private school was founded in 1933. It has a 27-acre campus.

RATINGS

Admissions Selectivity Rating: 74   **Fire Safety Rating:** 60*   **Green Rating:** 72

STUDENTS AND FACULTY

Enrollment: 2,186. **Student Body:** 52% female, 48% male, 20% out-of-state. African American 3%, Asian 3%, Caucasian 91%, Hispanic 2%. **Retention and Graduation:** 74% freshmen return for sophomore year. 42% freshmen graduate within 4 years. **Faculty:** Student/faculty ratio 15:1. 133 full-time faculty, 86% hold PhDs. 100% faculty teach undergrads.

ACADEMICS

Degrees: Bachelor's, first professional, master's. **Academic Requirements:** Arts/fine arts, computer literacy, English (including composition), humanities, interdisciplinary courses, mathematics, oral presenting, sciences (biological or physical), social science, writing intensive. **Classes:** Most classes have 20–29 students. Most lab/discussion sections have 10–19 students. **Majors with Highest Enrollment:** Biology/biological sciences, business administration and management, nursing/registered nurse training (ASN, BSN, MSN, RN). **Disciplines with Highest Percentage of Degrees Awarded:** Liberal arts/general studies 15%, business/marketing 14%, biological/life sciences 9%, health professions and related sciences 9%, education 7%, psychology 7%. **Special Study Options:** Cooperative education program, cross registration, distance learning, double major, dual enrollment, English as a second language (ESL), honors program, independent study, internships, student-designed major, study abroad, teacher certification program, weekend college.

FACILITIES

Housing: Coed dorms, men's dorms, women's dorms, apartments for single students. **Special Academic Facilities/Equipment:** Art gallery, performing arts center, electron microscope, television studio. **Computers:** 1% of classrooms are wired, 90% of classrooms are wireless, 75% of public computers are PCs, 20% of public computers are Macs, 5% of public computers are UNIX, network access in dorm rooms, network access in dorm lounges, online registration, online administrative functions (other than registration), support for handheld computing, remote student-access to Web through college's connection.

CAMPUS LIFE

Activities: Choral groups, dance, drama/theater, jazz band, literary magazine, music ensembles, musical theater, pep band, radio station, student government, student newspaper, television station, yearbook. **Organizations:** 65 registered organizations, 12 honor societies. **Athletics (Intercollegiate):** *Men:* Baseball, basketball, football, golf, soccer, tennis, wrestling. *Women:* Basketball, field hockey, lacrosse, soccer, softball, tennis, volleyball.

ADMISSIONS

Freshman Academic Profile: 20% in top 10% of high school class, 48% in top 25% of high school class, 87% in top 50% of high school class. SAT Math middle 50% range 470–600. SAT Critical Reading middle 50% range 460–560. SAT Writing middle 50% range 440–560. TOEFL required of all international applicants, minimum paper TOEFL 500, minimum computer TOEFL 183. **Basis for Candidate Selection:** *Very important factors considered include:* Class rank, rigor of secondary school record. *Important factors considered include:* Academic GPA, character/personal qualities, extracurricular activities, standardized test scores. *Other factors considered include:* Alumni/ae relation, interview, recommendation(s), talent/ability, volunteer work, work experience. **Freshman Admission Requirements:** High school diploma is required, and GED is accepted. *Academic units required:* 2 introduction to computing. *Academic units recommended:* 4 English, 3 math, 3 science (2 science labs), 2 foreign language, 3 social studies, 3 history, 1 introduction to computing. **Freshman Admission Statistics:** 2,988 applied, 73% admitted, 27% enrolled. **Transfer Admission Requirements:** College transcript(s), statement of good standing from prior institution(s). Minimum college GPA of 2.0 required. Lowest grade transferable C. **General Admission Information:** Application fee $40. Regular notification is rolling. Non-fall registration accepted. Admission may be deferred for a maximum of 2 semesters. Credit and/or placement offered for CEEB Advanced Placement tests.

COSTS AND FINANCIAL AID

Annual tuition $22,820. Room and board $10,310. Required fees $1,260. Average book expense $1,050. **Required Forms and Deadlines:** FAFSA, institution's own financial aid form. Financial aid filing deadline 3/1. **Notification of Awards:** Applicants will be notified of awards on a rolling basis beginning on or about 3/1. **Types of Aid:** *Need-based scholarships/grants:* Pell, SEOG, state scholarships/grants, private scholarships, the school's own gift aid. *Loans:* FFEL Subsidized Stafford, FFEL Unsubsidized Stafford, FFEL PLUS, Federal Perkins, Federal Nursing, state loans, college/university loans from institutional funds. **Student Employment:** Federal Work-Study Program available. Institutional employment available. Off-campus job opportunities are good. **Financial Aid Statistics:** 84% freshmen, 78% undergrads receive need-based scholarship or grant aid. 80% freshmen, 75% undergrads receive need-based self-help aid. 96% freshmen, 98% undergrads receive any aid.

See page 1502.

WILLAMETTE UNIVERSITY

900 State Street, Salem, OR 97301
Phone: 503-370-6303 **E-mail:** libarts@willamette.edu **CEEB Code:** 4954
Fax: 503-375-5363 **Website:** www.willamette.edu **ACT Code:** 3504
Financial Aid Phone: 503-370-6273

This private school, affiliated with the Methodist Church, was founded in 1842. It has a 72-acre campus.

RATINGS

Admissions Selectivity Rating: 90   **Fire Safety Rating:** 81   **Green Rating:** 88

STUDENTS AND FACULTY

Enrollment: 1,961. **Student Body:** 56% female, 44% male, 67% out-of-state. African American 2%, Asian 7%, Caucasian 59%, Hispanic 5%. **Retention and Graduation:** 88% freshmen return for sophomore year. 71% freshmen graduate within 4 years. 35% grads go on to further study within 2 semesters. 15% grads pursue arts and sciences degrees. 5% grads pursue business degrees. 10% grads pursue law degrees. 5% grads pursue medical degrees. **Faculty:** Student/faculty ratio 10:1. 184 full-time faculty. 100% faculty teach undergrads.

ACADEMICS

Degrees: Bachelor's, first professional certificate, first professional, master's. **Academic Requirements:** Arts/fine arts, English (including composition), foreign languages, history, humanities, mathematics, quantitative and analytical reasoning, sciences (biological or physical), social science, world views, writing-centered courses. **Classes:** Most classes have 10–19 students. Most lab/discussion sections have 10–19 students. **Majors with Highest Enrollment:** Biology/biological sciences, economics, political science and government. **Disciplines with Highest Percentage of Degrees Awarded:** Social sciences 18%, biological/life sciences 12%, foreign languages and literature 10%, history 10%, visual and performing arts 9%. **Special Study Options:** Accelerated program, cooperative education program, double major, dual enrollment, exchange student program (domestic), independent study, internships, student-designed major, study abroad, teacher certification program.

FACILITIES

Housing: Coed dorms, apartments for single students, fraternity/sorority housing, themed housing options (substance-free residence, environmental residence, intensive study residence). **Special Academic Facilities/Equipment:** Hallie Ford Art Museum, U.S. Senator Mark Hatfield's collected papers, herbarium, Japanese and botanical gardens. **Computers:** 90% of classrooms are wireless, 80% of public computers are PCs, 17% of public computers are Macs, 3% of public computers are UNIX, network access in dorm rooms, network access in dorm lounges, online registration, online administrative functions (other than registration), remote student-access to Web through college's connection.

CAMPUS LIFE

Activities: Choral groups, concert band, dance, drama/theater, jazz band, literary magazine, music ensembles, musical theater, opera, pep band, radio station, student government, student newspaper, symphony orchestra, yearbook. **Organizations:** 107 registered organizations, 7 honor societies, 5 religious organizations. 3 fraternities (27% men join), 3 sororities (29% women join). **Athletics (Intercollegiate):** *Men:* Baseball, basketball, crew/rowing, cross-country, football, golf, soccer, swimming, tennis, track/field (outdoor). *Women:* Basketball, crew/rowing, cross-country, golf, soccer, softball, swimming, tennis, track/field (outdoor), volleyball. **Environmental Initiatives:** Kaneko Commons Residential Hall New Construction Achieved LEED Gold status in 2007. FLEX CAR program initiated, purchase of Green Power, energy star appliances, and more. Development and approval of a sustainability law certificate program in the University Law School (2007), and planning for a sustainable MBA tract in the MBA program and sustainability concentration in the undergraduate curriculum (2008).

ADMISSIONS

Freshman Academic Profile: 47% in top 10% of high school class, 77% in top 25% of high school class, 98% in top 50% of high school class. 80% from public high schools. SAT Math middle 50% range 550–660. SAT Critical Reading middle 50% range 570–690. SAT Writing middle 50% range 550–660. ACT middle 50% range 25–29. TOEFL required of all international applicants,

minimum paper TOEFL 550, minimum computer TOEFL 213. **Basis for Candidate Selection:** *Very important factors considered include:* Academic GPA, class rank, recommendation(s), rigor of secondary school record, standardized test scores. *Important factors considered include:* Application essay, character/personal qualities, extracurricular activities, interview, talent/ability. *Other factors considered include:* Alumni/ae relation, first generation, geographical residence, racial/ethnic status, volunteer work, work experience. **Freshman Admission Requirements:** High school diploma is required, and GED is accepted. *Academic units recommended:* 4 English, 4 math, 3 science (3 science labs), 3 foreign language, 1 social studies, 2 history. **Freshman Admission Statistics:** 2,968 applied, 75% admitted, 21% enrolled. **Transfer Admission Requirements:** High school transcript, college transcript(s), essay or personal statement. Minimum college GPA of 2.0 required. Lowest grade transferable C. **General Admission Information:** Application fee $50. Regular application deadline 2/1. Regular notification 4/1. Non-fall registration accepted. Admission may be deferred for a maximum of 2 semesters. Credit and/or placement offered for CEEB Advanced Placement tests.

COSTS AND FINANCIAL AID

Annual tuition $28,416. Room & board $7,000. Required fees $170. Average book expense $800. **Required Forms and Deadlines:** FAFSA, CSS/Financial Aid PROFILE, PROFILE only required for early action applicants (to be filed by 12/1). Financial aid filing deadline 2/1. **Notification of Awards:** Applicants will be notified of awards on or about 4/1. **Types of Aid:** *Need-based scholarships/grants:* Pell, SEOG, state scholarships/grants, private scholarships, the school's own gift aid. *Loans:* FFEL Subsidized Stafford, FFEL Unsubsidized Stafford, FFEL PLUS, Federal Perkins, state loans, private loans. **Student Employment:** Federal Work-Study Program available. Institutional employment available. Off-campus job opportunities are fair. **Financial Aid Statistics:** 66% freshmen, 62% undergrads receive need-based scholarship or grant aid. 57% freshmen, 56% undergrads receive need-based self-help aid. 94% freshmen, 94% undergrads receive any aid. Highest amount earned per year from on-campus jobs $2,000.

WILLIAM CAREY COLLEGE

498 Tuscan Avenue, Hattiesburg, MS 39401-5499
Phone: 601-318-6103 **E-mail:** admissions@wmcarey.edu **CEEB Code:** 1907
Fax: 601-318-6765 **Website:** www.wmcarey.edu **ACT Code:** 2254
Financial Aid Phone: 601-318-6153

This private school, affiliated with the Baptist Church, was founded in 1906. It has a 64-acre campus.

RATINGS

Admissions Selectivity Rating: 60*   **Fire Safety Rating:** 60*   **Green Rating:** 60*

STUDENTS AND FACULTY

Enrollment: 1,239. **Student Body:** 61% female, 39% male, 22% out-of-state, 2% international (10 countries represented). **Retention and Graduation:** 69% freshmen return for sophomore year. 27% freshmen graduate within 4 years. **Faculty:** Student/faculty ratio 15:1. 96 full-time faculty, 65% hold PhDs. 100% faculty teach undergrads.

ACADEMICS

Degrees: Bachelor's, master's. **Academic Requirements:** Arts/fine arts, computer literacy, English (including composition), foreign languages, history, humanities, mathematics, philosophy, religion, sciences (biological or physical), social science. **Classes:** Most classes have 10–19 students. **Majors with Highest Enrollment:** Business administration/management, elementary education and teaching, nursing/registered nurse training (ASN, BSN, MSN, RN). **Disciplines with Highest Percentage of Degrees Awarded:** Education 20%, health professions and related sciences 20%, liberal arts/general studies 17%, psychology 12%, business/marketing 7%, visual and performing arts 7%, biological/life sciences 3%, parks and recreation 3%. **Special Study Options:** Affiliation with Gulf Coast Research Lab, Ocean Springs, Mississippi; cooperative education program; distance learning; double major; dual enrollment; honors program; independent study; internships; study abroad; teacher certification program.

FACILITIES

Housing: Coed dorms, men's dorms, women's dorms, apartments for married students, apartments for single students, special housing for disabled students. **Special Academic Facilities/Equipment:** Historic Tatum Court, Lucille Parker Gallery. **Computers:** 84% of publi...

CAMPUS LIFE

Activities: Choral groups, concert band, drama/theater, jazz band, literary magazine, music ensembles, musical theater, pep band, student government, student newspaper, yearbook. **Organizations:** 26 registered organizations, 7 honor societies, 1 religious organization. 1 fraternity, 2 sororities (5% women join). **Athletics (Intercollegiate):** *Men:* Baseball, basketball, cheerleading, golf, soccer. *Women:* Basketball, cheerleading, golf, soccer, softball.

ADMISSIONS

Freshman Academic Profile: 90% from public high schools. SAT Math middle 50% range 430–540. SAT Critical Reading middle 50% range 370–540. ACT middle 50% range 18–23. TOEFL required of all international applicants, minimum paper TOEFL 525, minimum computer TOEFL 195. **Basis for Candidate Selection:** *Very important factors considered include:* Class rank, rigor of secondary school record, standardized test scores. *Important factors considered include:* Alumni/ae relation, character/personal qualities, extracurricular activities, talent/ability. *Other factors considered include:* Recommendation(s), volunteer work. **Freshman Admission Requirements:** High school diploma is required, and GED is accepted. *Academic units recommended:* 4 English, 3 math, 3 science, 2 social studies. **Freshman Admission Statistics:** 232 applied, 59% admitted, 93% enrolled. **Transfer Admission Requirements:** College transcript(s). Minimum college GPA of 2.0 required. Lowest grade transferable D. **General Admission Information:** Application fee $20. Regular application deadline 7/15. Regular notification rolling. Non-fall registration accepted. Common Application not accepted. Credit offered for CEEB Advanced Placement tests.

COSTS AND FINANCIAL AID

Annual tuition $7,350. Room & board $3,150. Required fees $315. Average book expense $1,350. **Required Forms and Deadlines:** FAFSA. Financial aid filing deadline 4/1. **Notification of Awards:** Applicants will be notified of awards on a rolling basis beginning on or about 2/1. **Types of Aid:** *Need-based scholarships/grants:* Pell, SEOG, state scholarships/grants, private scholarships, the school's own gift aid. *Loans:* FFEL Subsidized Stafford, FFEL Unsubsidized Stafford, FFEL PLUS, Federal Perkins, college/university loans from institutional funds. **Student Employment:** Federal Work-Study Program available. Off-campus job opportunities are excellent. **Financial Aid Statistics:** 93% undergrads receive need-based scholarship or grant aid. 90% undergrads receive need-based self-help aid. 10 undergrads receive athletic scholarships. Highest amount earned per year from on-campus jobs $1,000.

WILLIAM JEWELL COLLEGE

500 College Hill, Liberty, MO 64068
Phone: 816-781-7700 **E-mail:** admission@william.jewell.edu **CEEB Code:** 6941
Fax: 816-415-5040 **Website:** www.jewell.edu **ACT Code:** 2394
Financial Aid Phone: 800-753-7009

This private school, affiliated with the Historically Baptist Church, was founded in 1849. It has a 200-acre campus.

RATINGS

Admissions Selectivity Rating: 87   **Fire Safety Rating:** 79   **Green Rating:** 65

STUDENTS AND FACULTY

Enrollment: 1,404. **Student Body:** 62% female, 38% male, 20% out-of-state. African American 5%, Caucasian 88%, Hispanic 3%, Native American 1%. **Retention and Graduation:** 76% freshmen return for sophomore year. 51% freshmen graduate within 4 years. **Faculty:** Student/faculty ratio 12:1. 77 full-time faculty, 87% hold PhDs. 100% faculty teach undergrads.

ACADEMICS

Degrees: Bachelor's, certificate. **Academic Requirements:** Humanities, intermediate foreign language or cross-cultural course, introductory literature-based course, mathematical reasoning, natural sciences, religious studies, senior capstone, social sciences, written and oral communication. **Classes:** Most classes have fewer than 10 students. Most lab/discussion sections have 10–19 students. **Majors with Highest Enrollment:** B...

psychology 10%, social sciences 6%, communications/journalism 5%, English 5%, history 5%, interdisciplinary studies 5%, visual and performing arts 5%. **Special Study Options:** Accelerated program, double major, dual enrollment, honors program, independent study, internships, liberal arts/career combination, student-designed major, study abroad, teacher certification program.

FACILITIES

Housing: Coed dorms, men's dorms, women's dorms, special housing for disabled students, special housing for international students, fraternity/sorority housing, off-campus housing utilized like residence halls. **Special Academic Facilities/Equipment:** Radio station, art gallery, observatory, language and computer labs, teleconferencing center. **Computers:** 8% of classrooms are wired, 33% of classrooms are wireless, 80% of public computers are PCs, 20% of public computers are Macs, network access in dorm rooms, network access in dorm lounges, online registration, online administrative functions (other than registration), remote student-access to Web through college's connection.

CAMPUS LIFE

Activities: Choral groups, concert band, dance, drama/theater, jazz band, literary magazine, music ensembles, musical theater, pep band, radio station, student government, student newspaper, symphony orchestra. **Organizations:** 51 registered organizations, 13 honor societies, 3 religious organizations. 3 fraternities (29% men join), 4 sororities (31% women join). **Athletics (Intercollegiate):** *Men:* Baseball, basketball, cheerleading, cross-country, football, golf, soccer, tennis, track/field (indoor), track/field (outdoor). *Women:* Basketball, cheerleading, cross-country, golf, soccer, softball, tennis, track/field (indoor), track/field (outdoor), volleyball.

ADMISSIONS

Freshman Academic Profile: 38% in top 10% of high school class, 66% in top 25% of high school class, 96% in top 50% of high school class. 90% from public high schools. SAT Math middle 50% range 500–650. SAT Critical Reading middle 50% range 530–650. ACT middle 50% range 22–28. TOEFL required of all international applicants, minimum paper TOEFL 550, minimum computer TOEFL 213. **Basis for Candidate Selection:** *Very important factors considered include:* Rigor of secondary school record. *Important factors considered include:* Academic GPA, application essay, character/personal qualities, class rank, extracurricular activities, first generation, level of applicant's interest, recommendation(s), standardized test scores, talent/ability. *Other factors considered include:* Alumni/ae relation, interview, racial/ethnic status, volunteer work, work experience. **Freshman Admission Requirements:** High school diploma is required, and GED is accepted. *Academic units required:* 4 English, 3 math, 3 science (1 science lab), 2 foreign language, 3 social studies. *Academic units recommended:* 4 English, 4 math, 3 science (1 science lab), 3 foreign language, 3 social studies, 2 academic electives. **Freshman Admission Statistics:** 1,312 applied, 63% admitted, 30% enrolled. **Transfer Admission Requirements:** College transcript(s), statement of good standing from prior institution(s). Minimum college GPA of 2.5 required. Lowest grade transferable C-. **General Admission Information:** Application fee $25. Regular application deadline 8/15. Regular notification is rolling. Non-fall registration accepted. Admission may be deferred for a maximum of 2 semesters, pending approval. Credit and/or placement offered for CEEB Advanced Placement tests.

COSTS AND FINANCIAL AID

Annual tuition $23,000. Room and board $6,130. Required fees $300. Average book expense $1,000. **Required Forms and Deadlines:** FAFSA. Financial aid filing deadline 3/1. **Notification of Awards:** Applicants will be notified of awards on a rolling basis beginning on or about 2/15. **Types of Aid:** *Need-based scholarships/grants:* Pell, SEOG, state scholarships/grants, the school's own gift aid. *Loans:* FFEL Subsidized Stafford, FFEL Unsubsidized Stafford, FFEL PLUS, Federal Perkins, Federal Nursing, non-federal alternative loans (non-college). **Student Employment:** Off-campus job opportunities are excellent. **Financial Aid Statistics:** 71% freshmen, 64% undergrads receive need-based scholarship or grant aid. 50% freshmen, 48% undergrads receive need-based self-help aid. 33 freshmen, 136 undergrads receive athletic scholarships. 99% freshmen, 96% undergrads receive any aid. Highest amount earned per year from on-campus jobs $1,500.

See page 1504.

WILLIAM PATERSON UNIVERSITY

Admissions Hall, 300 Pompton Road, Wayne, NJ 07470
Phone: 973-720-2125 **E-mail:** admissions@wpunj.edu **CEEB Code:** 2518
Fax: 973-720-2910 **Website:** ww2.wpunj.edu **ACT Code:** 2584
Financial Aid Phone: 973-720-2202

This public school was founded in 1855. It has a 370-acre campus.

RATINGS
Admissions Selectivity Rating: 70   **Fire Safety Rating:** 97   **Green Rating:** 86

STUDENTS AND FACULTY
Enrollment: 8,754. **Student Body:** 57% female, 43% male, 1% out-of-state, (61 countries represented). African American 14%, Asian 6%, Caucasian 57%, Hispanic 17%. **Retention and Graduation:** 77% freshmen return for sophomore year. 16% freshmen graduate within 4 years. 27% grads go on to further study within 1 year. 18% grads pursue arts and sciences degrees. 15% grads pursue business degrees. **Faculty:** Student/faculty ratio 16:1. 366 full-time faculty, 89% hold PhDs. 100% faculty teach undergrads.

ACADEMICS
Degrees: Bachelor's, master's, post-bachelor's certificate, post-master's certificate. **Academic Requirements:** Arts/fine arts, English (including composition), foreign languages, history, humanities, mathematics, philosophy, sciences (biological or physical), social science, students must also take a course in health or movement science, 1 course in racism and/or sexism, and a course in some aspect of non-Western culture. **Classes:** Most classes have 20–29 students. **Majors with Highest Enrollment:** Business administration/management, communications studies/speech communication and rhetoric, psychology. **Disciplines with Highest Percentage of Degrees Awarded:** Business/marketing 19%, social sciences 14%, communications/journalism 14%, psychology 10%, English 9%. **Special Study Options:** Accelerated program, cross-registration, distance learning, double major, dual enrollment, English as a second language (ESL), exchange student program (domestic), honors program, independent study, internships, study abroad, teacher certification program, cluster courses (a program that provides opportunities for students and faculty to study and learn together in courses grouped in interdisciplinary clusters of 3. 3 faculty members teach these courses that meet together once every week to help students see the interdisciplinary connections), university honors program (honors major tracks are available, and "honors" general education courses are offered), international exchange program.

FACILITIES
Housing: Coed dorms, apartments for single students, special housing for disabled students, a floor for women is available in one of the residence halls, apartment style housing is available in groups of single students who are 21 or older or are 20 with 58 or more credits. Academic interest housing is available; for example, 1 floor of a residence hall is reserved for nursing, biology, and community health students with a 2.5 GPA or better. Other floors combine majors; all must have 2.5 GPA or over. One residence hall is reserved for students who are 21 or older. **Special Academic Facilities/Equipment:** Art galleries; collection of NJ state documents; collection of William Paterson's private papers; interactive television classroom; neurobiology facility; e-trading, campus network with ATM technology; center for computer art and animation; state-of-the-art electron microscopy facility; teleconference center with uplink and downlink capabilities; 44,000 square foot, state-of-the-art studio art facility; center for electro-acoustic music (CEM); E-Trade financial learning center, a real-time simulated trading and financial educational facility; Russ Berrie Institute for professional sales including real-time sales laboratory. **Computers:** 100% of classrooms are wired, 35% of classrooms are wireless, 94% of public computers are PCs, 5% of public computers are Macs, 1% of public computers are UNIX, network access in dorm rooms, network access in dorm lounges, online registration, online administrative functions (other than registration), remote student-access to Web through college's connection.

CAMPUS LIFE
Activities: Choral groups, concert band, dance, drama/theater, jazz band, literary magazine, music ensembles, radio station, student government, student newspaper, student-run film society, television station, yearbook. **Organizations:** 61 registered organizations, 21 honor societies, 4 religious organizations. 8 fraternities, 11 sororities. **Athletics (Intercollegiate):** *Men:* Baseball, basketball, cross-country, football, soccer, swimming, track/field (indoor), track/field (outdoor). *Women:* Basketball, cheerleading, cross-country, field hockey, soccer, softball, swimming, track/field (indoor), track/field (outdoor), volleyball.

ADMISSIONS
Freshman Academic Profile: 12% in top 10% of high school class, 30% in top 25% of high school class, 68% in top 50% of high school class. 86% from public

high schools. SAT Math middle 50% range 440–540. SAT Critical Reading middle 50% range 440–530. TOEFL required of all international applicants, minimum paper TOEFL 550, minimum computer TOEFL 213. **Basis for Candidate Selection:** *Very important factors considered include:* Class rank, rigor of secondary school record, standardized test scores. *Important factors considered include:* Academic GPA, level of applicant's interest. *Other factors considered include:* Alumni/ae relation, application essay, character/personal qualities, extracurricular activities, geographical residence, interview, recommendation(s), talent/ability, volunteer work. **Freshman Admission Requirements:** High school diploma is required, and GED is accepted. *Academic units required:* 4 English, 3 math, 2 science, (2 science labs), 2 social studies, 5 additional college preparatory courses (in advanced math, literature, foreign language and social science) are also required. **Freshman Admission Statistics:** 5,110 applied, 75% admitted, 36% enrolled. **Transfer Admission Requirements:** College transcript(s). Minimum college GPA of 2.0 required. Lowest grade transferable C. **General Admission Information:** Application fee $50. Regular application deadline 5/1. Regular notification is rolling. Nonfall registration accepted. Admission may be deferred for a maximum of 1 semester. Credit and/or placement offered for CEEB Advanced Placement tests.

COSTS AND FINANCIAL AID
Annual in-state tuition $9,422. Out-of-state tuition $15,370. Room & board $9,380. **Required Forms and Deadlines:** FAFSA. Financial aid filing deadline 4/1. **Notification of Awards:** Applicants will be notified of awards on a rolling basis beginning on or about 3/1. **Types of Aid:** *Need-based scholarships/grants:* Pell, SEOG, state scholarships/grants, the school's own gift aid. *Loans:* FFEL Subsidized Stafford, FFEL Unsubsidized Stafford, FFEL PLUS, Federal Perkins. **Student Employment:** Federal Work-Study Program available. Institutional employment available. Off-campus job opportunities are good. **Financial Aid Statistics:** 82% freshmen, 83% undergrads receive any aid. Highest amount earned per year from on-campus jobs $3,200.

See page 1506.

WILLIAM PENN UNIVERSITY

201 Trueblood Avenue, Oskaloosa, IA 52577
Phone: 641-673-1012 **E-mail:** admissions@wmpenn.edu **CEEB Code:** 6943
Fax: 641-673-2113 **Website:** www.wmpenn.edu **ACT Code:** 1372
Financial Aid Phone: 641-673-1060

This private school, affiliated with the Society of Friends, was founded in 1873. It has a 53-acre campus.

RATINGS
Admissions Selectivity Rating: 66   **Fire Safety Rating:** 60*   **Green Rating:** 60*

STUDENTS AND FACULTY
Enrollment: 1,462. **Student Body:** 48% female, 52% male, 28% out-of-state, 1% international. African American 8%, Caucasian 89%, Hispanic 3%. **Faculty:** Student/faculty ratio 14:1. 35 full-time faculty, 49% hold PhDs. 100% faculty teach undergrads.

ACADEMICS
Degrees: Associate, bachelor's. **Academic Requirements:** Arts/fine arts, computer literacy, English (including composition), history, humanities, leadership, mathematics, philosophy, religion, sciences (biological or physical), social science, wellness and fitness. **Classes:** Most classes have fewer than 10 students. **Majors with Highest Enrollment:** Business administration/management, education, psychology. **Disciplines with Highest Percentage of Degrees Awarded:** Business/marketing 70%, education 7%, psychology 5%, social sciences 4%, communication technologies 3%. **Special Study Options:** College for working adults, cooperative education program, double major, English as a second language (ESL), independent study, internships, study abroad, teacher certification program.

FACILITIES
Housing: Coed dorms, women's dorms, apartments for married students, apartments for single students. **Special Academic Facilities/Equipment:** Foyer Gallery, Mid-East art and artifact collection. **Computers:** 71% of public computers are PCs, 29% of public computers are Macs, network access in dorm rooms, network access in dorm lounges, remote student-access to Web through college's connection.

CAMPUS LIFE
Activities: Choral groups, drama/theater, jazz band, literary magazine, music ensembles, musical theater, radio station, student government, student newspaper, yearbook. **Organizations:** 34 registered organizations, 3 honor

societies, 4 religious organizations. 3 fraternities (5% men join), 3 sororities (5% women join). **Athletics (Intercollegiate):** *Men:* Baseball, basketball, cheerleading, cross-country, football, golf, soccer, track/field (outdoor), wrestling. *Women:* Basketball, cheerleading, cross-country, soccer, softball, track/field (outdoor), volleyball.

ADMISSIONS
Freshman Academic Profile: 7% in top 10% of high school class, 25% in top 25% of high school class, 60% in top 50% of high school class. 97% from public high schools. TOEFL required of all international applicants, minimum paper TOEFL 500, minimum computer TOEFL 173. **Basis for Candidate Selection:** *Very important factors considered include:* Rigor of secondary school record. *Important factors considered include:* Character/personal qualities, class rank, standardized test scores. *Other factors considered include:* Alumni/ae relation, application essay, extracurricular activities, interview, recommendation(s), talent/ability, volunteer work, work experience. **Freshman Admission Requirements:** High school diploma is required, and GED is accepted. *Academic units recommended:* 3 English, 2 math, 2 science, 2 foreign language, 2 social studies, 2 history, 2 academic electives. **Freshman Admission Statistics:** 781 applied, 62% admitted, 48% enrolled. **Transfer Admission Requirements:** College transcript(s). Minimum college GPA of 2.0 required. Lowest grade transferable D. **General Admission Information:** Application fee $20. Regular notification is rolling. Non-fall registration accepted. Common Application not accepted. Credit offered for CEEB Advanced Placement tests.

COSTS AND FINANCIAL AID
Annual tuition $11,924. Room & board $4,140. Required fees $356. Average book expense $675. **Required Forms and Deadlines:** FAFSA. Financial aid filing deadline 7/1. **Notification of Awards:** Applicants will be notified of awards on a rolling basis beginning on or about 1/1. **Types of Aid:** *Need-based scholarships/grants:* Pell, SEOG, state scholarships/grants, private scholarships, the school's own gift aid. *Loans:* FFEL Subsidized Stafford, FFEL Unsubsidized Stafford, FFEL PLUS, Federal Perkins. **Student Employment:** Federal Work-Study Program available. Institutional employment available. Off-campus job opportunities are excellent.

WILLIAM TYNDALE COLLEGE

35700 West Twelve Mile Road, Farmington Hills, MI 48331-3147
Phone: 800-483-0707 **E-mail:** admissions@williamtyndale.edu **CEEB Code:** 1167
Fax: 248-553-5963 **Website:** www.williamtyndale.edu **ACT Code:** 2252
Financial Aid Phone: 800-483-0707

This private school, affiliated with the Christian Church, was founded in 1945. It has a 28-acre campus.

RATINGS
Admissions Selectivity Rating: 85   **Fire Safety Rating:** 60*   **Green Rating:** 60*

STUDENTS AND FACULTY
Enrollment: 278. **Student Body:** 45% female, 55% male, 7% out-of-state, 3% international (6 countries represented). African American 31%, Asian 1%, Caucasian 63%, Native American 1%. **Retention and Graduation:** 66% freshmen return for sophomore year. 21% freshmen graduate within 4 years. **Faculty:** Student/faculty ratio 8:1. 4 full-time faculty, 50% hold PhDs. 100% faculty teach undergrads.

ACADEMICS
Degrees: Associate, bachelor's, certificate. **Academic Requirements:** Arts/fine arts, Christian thought, computer literacy, English (including composition), foreign languages, history, humanities, mathematics, philosophy, sciences (biological or physical), social science. **Classes:** Most classes have fewer than 10 students. **Majors with Highest Enrollment:** Business administration/management, counseling psychology, religion/religious studies. **Disciplines with Highest Percentage of Degrees Awarded:** Business/marketing 58%, psychology 11%, English 6%, computer and information sciences 6%, social sciences 2%, law/legal studies 1%, visual and performing arts 1%. **Special Study Options:** Accelerated program, distance learning, double major, dual enrollment, independent study, internships.

FACILITIES
Housing: Coed dorms.

CAMPUS LIFE
Activities: Choral groups, drama/theater, music ensembles, student ment, student newspaper. **Organizations:** 2 registered organization societies.

ADMISSIONS

Freshman Academic Profile: 20% in top 10% of high school class, 60% in top 25% of high school class, 40% in top 50% of high school class. 76% from public high schools. ACT middle 50% range 23–24. TOEFL required of all international applicants, minimum paper TOEFL 500, minimum computer TOEFL 173. **Basis for Candidate Selection:** *Very important factors considered include:* Rigor of secondary school record, standardized test scores. *Other factors considered include:* Application essay, character/personal qualities, interview, recommendation(s), religious affiliation/commitment. **Freshman Admission Requirements:** High school diploma is required, and GED is accepted. *Academic units recommended:* 4 English, 3 math, 3 science, 2 foreign language, 2 social studies, 2 history. **Freshman Admission Statistics:** 40 applied, 50% admitted, 80% enrolled. **Transfer Admission Requirements:** High school transcript, college transcript(s), statement of good standing from prior institution(s). Minimum college GPA of 2.0 required. Lowest grade transferable C. **General Admission Information:** Regular notification rolling. Non-fall registration accepted. Admission may be deferred for a maximum of 2 semesters. Common Application accepted. Credit and/or placement offered for CEEB Advanced Placement tests.

COSTS AND FINANCIAL AID

Annual tuition $8,550. Room & board $3,520. Required fees $100. Average book expense $1,328. **Required Forms and Deadlines:** FAFSA, institution's own financial aid form. Financial aid filing deadline 2/15. **Notification of Awards:** Applicants will be notified of awards on or about 3/15. **Types of Aid:** *Need-based scholarships/grants:* Pell, SEOG, state scholarships/grants, private scholarships, the school's own gift aid. *Loans:* FFEL Subsidized Stafford, FFEL Unsubsidized Stafford, FFEL PLUS. **Student Employment:** Federal Work-Study Program available. Institutional employment available. Off-campus job opportunities are good. **Financial Aid Statistics:** 71% freshmen, 18% undergrads receive need-based scholarship or grant aid. 53% freshmen, 30% undergrads receive need-based self-help aid. 60% freshmen, 60% undergrads receive any aid. Highest amount earned per year from on-campus jobs $1,500.

WILLIAM WOODS UNIVERSITY

One University Avenue, Fulton, MO 65251
Phone: 573-592-4221 **E-mail:** admissions@williamwoods.edu
Fax: 573-592-1146 **Website:** www.williamwoods.edu **ACT Code:** 2396
Financial Aid Phone: 573-592-4236

This private school, affiliated with the Disciples of Christ Church, was founded in 1870. It has a 170-acre campus.

RATINGS

Admissions Selectivity Rating: 77   **Fire Safety Rating:** 77   **Green Rating:** 60*

STUDENTS AND FACULTY

Enrollment: 1,118. **Student Body:** 75% female, 25% male, 19% out-of-state, 4% international. African American 3%, Caucasian 87%, Hispanic 2%. **Retention and Graduation:** 76% freshmen return for sophomore year. 39% freshmen graduate within 4 years. **Faculty:** Student/faculty ratio 13:1. 50 full-time faculty. 100% faculty teach undergrads.

ACADEMICS

Degrees: Associate, bachelor's, master's, post-master's certificate. **Academic Requirements:** Arts/fine arts, communications, diversity, English (including composition), history, humanities, mathematics, sciences (biological or physical), social science. **Classes:** Most classes have fewer than 10 students. Most lab/discussion sections have fewer than 10 students. **Majors with Highest Enrollment:** Animal sciences, business administration/management, education. **Disciplines with Highest Percentage of Degrees Awarded:** Business/marketing 45%, computer and information sciences 12%, agriculture 11%, education 8%, visual and performing arts 6%. **Special Study Options:** Accelerated program, cross registration, double major, dual enrollment, honors program, Hollywood semester, independent study, internships, liberal arts/career combination, student-designed major, study abroad, teacher certification program.

FACILITIES

Housing: Coed dorms, men's dorms, women's dorms, apartments for single students, special housing for disabled students, special housing for international students, fraternity/sorority housing. **Special Academic Facilities/Equipment:** Weitzman Court Room, Mildred Cox Gallery, Gladys Woods Kemper Center for the Arts, ASL interpreting lab, equestrian facilities. **Computers:** 5% of classrooms are wired, 5% of classrooms are wireless, 100% of public computers are PCs, network access in dorm rooms, online administrative

functions (other than registration), remote student-access to Web through college's connection.

CAMPUS LIFE

Activities: Choral groups, dance, drama/theater, literary magazine, musical theater, radio station, student government, student newspaper. **Organizations:** 42 registered organizations, 3 honor societies, 1 religious organization. 2 fraternities (22% men join), 4 sororities (29% women join). **Athletics (Intercollegiate):** *Men:* Baseball, golf, soccer. *Women:* Basketball, golf, soccer, softball, volleyball.

ADMISSIONS

Freshman Academic Profile: 15% in top 10% of high school class, 40% in top 25% of high school class, 77% in top 50% of high school class. SAT Math middle 50% range 420–570. SAT Critical Reading middle 50% range 455–575. ACT middle 50% range 19–25. TOEFL required of all international applicants, minimum paper TOEFL 550. **Basis for Candidate Selection:** *Very important factors considered include:* Academic GPA, class rank, rigor of secondary school record. *Important factors considered include:* Extracurricular activities, recommendation(s), standardized test scores. *Other factors considered include:* Character/personal qualities, interview. **Freshman Admission Requirements:** High school diploma is required, and GED is accepted. *Academic units required:* 3 English, 3 math. *Academic units recommended:* 4 English, 3 math, 3 science, 1 foreign language, 3 social studies, 2 history, 4 academic electives. **Freshman Admission Statistics:** 792 applied, 68% admitted, 43% enrolled. **Transfer Admission Requirements:** College transcript(s), statement of good standing from prior institution(s). Minimum college GPA of 2.5 required. Lowest grade transferable C. **General Admission Information:** Application fee $25. Regular notification is rolling. Non-fall registration accepted. Common Application not accepted. Credit and/or placement offered for CEEB Advanced Placement tests.

COSTS AND FINANCIAL AID

Annual tuition $14,700. Room & board $5,900. Required fees $420. Average book expense $1,000. **Required Forms and Deadlines:** FAFSA, institution's own financial aid form. Financial aid filing deadline 3/1. **Notification of Awards:** Applicants will be notified of awards on a rolling basis beginning on or about 3/15. **Types of Aid:** *Need-based scholarships/grants:* Pell, SEOG, state scholarships/grants, private scholarships, the school's own gift aid. *Loans:* FFEL Subsidized Stafford, FFEL Unsubsidized Stafford, FFEL PLUS, Federal Perkins, college/university loans from institutional funds. **Student Employment:** Federal Work-Study Program available. Institutional employment available. Off-campus job opportunities are good. **Financial Aid Statistics:** 56% freshmen, 61% undergrads receive need-based scholarship or grant aid. 42% freshmen, 49% undergrads receive need-based self-help aid. 5 freshmen, 26 undergrads receive athletic scholarships. 100% freshmen, 95% undergrads receive any aid. Highest amount earned per year from on-campus jobs $800.

WILLIAMS BAPTIST COLLEGE

PO Box 3665, Walnut Ridge, AR 72476
Phone: 870-886-6741 **E-mail:** admissions@wbcoll.edu
Fax: 870-886-3924 **Website:** www.wbcoll.edu **ACT Code:** 0140
Financial Aid Phone: 800-722-4434

This private school was founded in 1941. It has a 180-acre campus.

RATINGS

Admissions Selectivity Rating: 60*   **Fire Safety Rating:** 60*   **Green Rating:** 60*

STUDENTS AND FACULTY

Enrollment: 504. **Student Body:** 53% female, 47% male, 4% international. African American 2%, Caucasian 91%. **Retention and Graduation:** 69% freshmen return for sophomore year. 16% freshmen graduate within 4 years. **Faculty:** 100% faculty teach undergrads.

ACADEMICS

Degrees: Associate, bachelor's. **Academic Requirements:** Arts/fine arts, English (including composition), history, humanities, mathematics, sciences (biological or physical), social science. **Special Study Options:** Cooperative education program, double major, independent study, internships, teacher certification program.

FACILITIES

Housing: Men's dorms, women's dorms, apartments for married students, apartments for single students. **Computers:** 100% of public computers are PCs, online registration, online administrative functions (other than registration), remote student-access to Web through college's connection.

CAMPUS LIFE

Activities: Choral groups, drama/theater, student government. **Organizations:** 29 registered organizations, 6 honor societies, 5 religious organizations. 2 fraternities, 2 sororities. **Athletics (Intercollegiate):** *Men:* Baseball, basketball, cross-country, golf, soccer. *Women:* Basketball, cross-country, softball, volleyball.

ADMISSIONS

Freshman Academic Profile: 62% from public high schools. TOEFL required of all international applicants, minimum paper TOEFL 500. **Basis for Candidate Selection:** *Very important factors considered include:* Standardized test scores. *Important factors considered include:* Class rank, interview, rigor of secondary school record. *Other factors considered include:* Application essay, character/personal qualities, extracurricular activities, recommendation(s), talent/ability, volunteer work. **Freshman Admission Requirements:** High school diploma is required, and GED is accepted. *Academic units recommended:* 4 English, 3 math, 2 science, 2 foreign language, 3 history. **Freshman Admission Statistics:** 385 applied, 78% admitted, 49% enrolled. **Transfer Admission Requirements:** College transcript(s). Minimum college GPA of 2.0 required. **General Admission Information:** Application fee $20. Regular application deadline 9/3. Regular notification is rolling. Non-fall registration accepted. Common Application not accepted.

COSTS AND FINANCIAL AID

Annual tuition $6,000. Room & board $3,200. Required fees $270. Average book expense $850. **Required Forms and Deadlines:** FAFSA. Financial aid filing deadline 5/1. **Notification of Awards:** Applicants will be notified of awards on a rolling basis beginning on or about 4/1. **Types of Aid:** *Need-based scholarships/grants:* Pell, SEOG, state scholarships/grants, private scholarships, the school's own gift aid. *Loans:* Direct Subsidized Stafford, Direct Unsubsidized Stafford, Direct PLUS, college/university loans from institutional funds. **Student Employment:** Federal Work-Study Program available. Institutional employment available. Off-campus job opportunities are good. **Financial Aid Statistics:** 67% freshmen, 72% undergrads receive need-based scholarship or grant aid. 53% freshmen, 63% undergrads receive need-based self-help aid. 36 freshmen, 79 undergrads receive athletic scholarships. Highest amount earned per year from on-campus jobs $1,142.

WILLIAMS COLLEGE

33 Stetson Court, Williamstown, MA 01267
Phone: 413-597-2211 **E-mail:** admission@williams.edu **CEEB Code:** 3965
Fax: 413-597-4052 **Website:** www.williams.edu **ACT Code:** 1936
Financial Aid Phone: 413-597-4181

This private school was founded in 1793. It has a 450-acre campus.

RATINGS

Admissions Selectivity Rating: 99   **Fire Safety Rating:** 60*   **Green Rating:** 60*

STUDENTS AND FACULTY

Enrollment: 1,965. **Student Body:** 51% female, 49% male, 83% out-of-state, 6% international (65 countries represented). African American 10%, Asian 11%, Caucasian 64%, Hispanic 9%. **Retention and Graduation:** 97% freshmen return for sophomore year. 91% freshmen graduate within 4 years. **Faculty:** Student/faculty ratio 7:1. 268 full-time faculty, 99% hold PhDs. 100% faculty teach undergrads.

ACADEMICS

Degrees: Bachelor's, master's. **Academic Requirements:** Arts and humanities, intensive writing, math, peoples and culture, quantitative/formal reasoning, sciences (biological or physical), social science, social studies. **Classes:** Most classes have 10–19 students. Most lab/discussion sections have 10–19 students. **Majors with Highest Enrollment:** Art/art studies, economics, political science and government. **Disciplines with Highest Percentage of Degrees Awarded:** Social sciences 29%, visual and performing arts 11%, biological/life sciences 10%, history 9%, English 8%, physical sciences 8%, psychology 8%. **Special Study Options:** Double major, independent study, internships, student-designed major, study abroad.

FACILITIES

Housing: Coed dorms, cooperative housing. **Special Academic Facilities/ Equipment:** Hopkins Observatory, Williams College Museum of Art, Adams Memorial Theatre, Chapin Rare Books Library, Spencer Studio Art Building. **Computers:** 10% of classrooms are wired, 24% of classrooms are wireless, 56% of public computers are PCs, 44% of public computers are Macs, network access in dorm rooms, network access in dorm lounges, online registration, online administrative functions (other than registration), support for handheld computing, remote student-access to Web through college's connection.

CAMPUS LIFE

Activities: Choral groups, dance, drama/theater, literary magazine, music ensembles, radio station, student government, student newspaper, yearbook. **Organizations:** 110 registered organizations, 3 honor societies, 13 religious organizations. **Athletics (Intercollegiate):** *Men:* Baseball, basketball, crew/ rowing, cross-country, diving, football, golf, ice hockey, lacrosse, skiing (downhill/alpine), skiing (nordic/cross-country), soccer, squash, swimming, tennis, track/field (indoor), track/field (outdoor), wrestling. *Women:* Basketball, crew/rowing, cross-country, diving, field hockey, ice hockey, lacrosse, skiing (downhill/alpine), skiing (nordic/cross-country), soccer, softball, squash, swimming, tennis, track/field (indoor), track/field (outdoor), volleyball.

ADMISSIONS

Freshman Academic Profile: 90% in top 10% of high school class, 95% in top 25% of high school class, 100% in top 50% of high school class. 59% from public high schools. SAT Math middle 50% range 670–760. SAT Critical Reading middle 50% range 670–760. ACT middle 50% range 29–33. **Basis for Candidate Selection:** *Very important factors considered include:* Academic GPA, application essay, recommendation(s), rigor of secondary school record, standardized test scores. *Important factors considered include:* Class rank, extracurricular activities, talent/ability. *Other factors considered include:* Alumni/ae relation, character/personal qualities, first generation, geographical residence, racial/ethnic status, volunteer work, work experience. **Freshman Admission Requirements:** *Academic units recommended:* 4 English, 4 math, 3 science (3 science labs), 4 foreign language, 3 social studies. **Freshman Admission Statistics:** 5,999 applied, 19% admitted, 47% enrolled. **Transfer Admission Requirements:** High school transcript, college transcript(s), essay or personal statement, standardized test score, statement of good standing from prior institution(s). Minimum college GPA of 3.5 required. Lowest grade transferable C-. **General Admission Information:** Application fee $60. Early decision application deadline 11/10. Regular application deadline 1/1. Regular notification 4/1. Non-fall registration not accepted. Placement offered for CEEB Advanced Placement tests.

COSTS AND FINANCIAL AID

Annual tuition $35,438. Room and board $9,470. Required fees $232. Average book expense $800. **Required Forms and Deadlines:** FAFSA, CSS/Financial Aid PROFILE, Noncustodial PROFILE, Business/Farm Supplement, Parent and student federal taxes and W-2s. Financial aid filing deadline 2/1. **Notification of Awards:** Applicants will be notified of awards on or about 4/1. **Types of Aid:** *Need-based scholarships/grants:* Pell, SEOG, state scholarships/grants, private scholarships, the school's own gift aid. *Loans:* Direct Subsidized Stafford, Direct Unsubsidized Stafford, Direct PLUS, Federal Perkins, college/ university loans from institutional funds. **Student Employment:** Federal Work-Study Program available. Institutional employment available. **Financial Aid Statistics:** 46% freshmen, 43% undergrads receive need-based scholarship or grant aid. 46% freshmen, 43% undergrads receive need-based self-help aid. 47% freshmen, 44% undergrads receive any aid.

WILLISTON STATE COLLEGE

PO Box 1326, Williston, ND 58802-1326
Phone: 701-774-4210 **E-mail:** Lacey.Madison@wsc.nodak.edu
Fax: 701-774-4211 **Website:** www.wsc.nodak.edu
Financial Aid Phone: 701-774-4244

This public school was founded in 1961. It has an 80-acre campus.

RATINGS

Admissions Selectivity Rating: 60*   **Fire Safety Rating:** 60*   **Green Rating:** 60*

STUDENTS AND FACULTY

Enrollment: 937. **Student Body:** 71% female, 29% male, 19% out-of-state, 2% international (2 countries represented). African American 1%, Caucasian 91%, Hispanic 1%, Native American 4%. **Faculty:** Student/faculty ratio 12:1. 38

full-time faculty. 100% faculty teach undergrads.

ACADEMICS

Degrees: Associate, certificate, diploma. **Academic Requirements:** Computer literacy, English (including composition), humanities, mathematics, sciences (biological or physical). **Special Study Options:** Cooperative education program, distance learning, dual enrollment, external degree program, independent study, internships, liberal arts/career combination.

FACILITIES

Housing: Coed dorms, men's dorms, women's dorms, special housing for disabled students, athletic housing units married/family housing units. **Computers:** Network access in dorm rooms, network access in dorm lounges.

CAMPUS LIFE

Activities: Choral groups, drama/theater, literary magazine, pep band, student government. **Organizations:** 18 registered organizations, 1 honor society, 1 religious organization. **Athletics (Intercollegiate): Men:** Baseball, basketball, golf. **Women:** Basketball, golf, volleyball.

ADMISSIONS

Freshman Academic Profile: ACT middle 50% range 16–22. TOEFL required of all international applicants, minimum paper TOEFL 330, minimum computer TOEFL 195. **Freshman Admission Requirements:** High school diploma is required, and GED is accepted. *Academic units recommended:* 4 English, 3 math, 3 science (3 science labs), 1 foreign language, 3 social studies. **Freshman Admission Statistics:** 191 applied, 91% admitted, 100% enrolled. **Transfer Admission Requirements:** College transcript(s), statement of good standing from prior institution(s). Lowest grade transferable D. **General Admission Information:** Application fee $35. Regular notification is rolling. Non-fall registration accepted. Common Application accepted. Credit and/or placement offered for CEEB Advanced Placement tests.

COSTS AND FINANCIAL AID

Required Forms and Deadlines: FAFSA. Financial aid filing deadline 3/15. **Notification of Awards:** Applicants will be notified of awards on or about 5/15. **Types of Aid:** *Need-based scholarships/grants:* Pell, SEOG, state scholarships/grants, private scholarships, the school's own gift aid. *Loans:* FFEL Subsidized Stafford, FFEL Unsubsidized Stafford, FFEL PLUS, Federal Perkins. **Student Employment:** Federal Work-Study Program available. Institutional employment available. Off-campus job opportunities are good.

WILMINGTON COLLEGE (DE)

320 Dupont Highway, New Castle, DE 19720
Phone: 302-328-9401 **E-mail:** mlee@wilmcoll.edu **CEEB Code:** 5925
Fax: 302-328-5902 **Website:** www.wilmcoll.edu **ACT Code:** 0635
Financial Aid Phone: 302-328-9437

This private school was founded in 1967. It has a 15-acre campus.

RATINGS
Admissions Selectivity Rating: 60*   **Fire Safety Rating:** 60*   **Green Rating:** 60*

STUDENTS AND FACULTY
Enrollment: 4,399. **Student Body:** 3% out-of-state. African American 14%, Caucasian 64%, Hispanic 2%. **Retention and Graduation:** 87% freshmen return for sophomore year. 50% grads go on to further study within 2 semesters. 9% grads pursue arts and sciences degrees. 80% grads pursue business degrees. 10% grads pursue law degrees. 1% grads pursue medical degrees. **Faculty:** Student/faculty ratio 18:1. 100% faculty teach undergrads.

ACADEMICS
Degrees: Associate, bachelor's, certificate, doctoral, master's, post-master's certificate. **Academic Requirements:** Arts/fine arts, computer literacy, English (including composition), humanities, mathematics, sciences (biological or physical), social science. **Majors with Highest Enrollment:** Business administration/management, education. **Special Study Options:** Accelerated program, cooperative education program, distance learning, double major, independent study, internships, teacher certification program, weekend college.

FACILITIES
Housing: All housing is off campus.

CAMPUS LIFE
Activities: Student government. **Organizations:** 1 honor society. **Athletics (Intercollegiate): Men:** Baseball, basketball, cross-country, soccer. **Women:**

Basketball, softball.

ADMISSIONS
Freshman Academic Profile: 70% from public high schools. TOEFL required of all international applicants, minimum paper TOEFL 500. **Basis for Candidate Selection:** *Important factors considered include:* Recommendation(s), rigor of secondary school record. **Freshman Admission Requirements:** High school diploma is required, and GED is accepted. **Transfer Admission Requirements:** College transcript(s). Minimum college GPA of 2.0 required. Lowest grade transferable C. **General Admission Information:** Application fee $25. Regular notification rolling. Non-fall registration accepted. Admission may be deferred for a maximum of 2 semesters. Common Application not accepted. Credit offered for CEEB Advanced Placement tests.

COSTS AND FINANCIAL AID
Annual tuition $6,060. Required fees $50. Average book expense $500. **Required Forms and Deadlines:** FAFSA. **Student Employment:** Federal Work-Study Program available. Off-campus job opportunities are excellent. **Financial Aid Statistics:** Highest amount earned per year from on-campus jobs $1,000.

WILMINGTON COLLEGE (OH)

Pyle Center Box 1325, 251 Ludovic Street, Wilmington, OH 45177
Phone: 937-382-6661 **E-mail:** admission@wilmington.edu **CEEB Code:** 1909
Fax: 937-383-8542 **Website:** www.wilmington.edu **ACT Code:** 3362
Financial Aid Phone: 800-341-9318

This private school, affiliated with the Society of Friends, was founded in 1870. It has a 65-acre campus.

RATINGS
Admissions Selectivity Rating: 60*   **Fire Safety Rating:** 60*   **Green Rating:** 60*

STUDENTS AND FACULTY
Enrollment: 1,723. **Student Body:** 54% female, 46% male, 4% out-of-state. **Retention and Graduation:** 73% freshmen return for sophomore year. **Faculty:** Student/faculty ratio 14:1. 71 full-time faculty, 69% hold PhDs. 100% faculty teach undergrads.

ACADEMICS
Degrees: Bachelor's, master's. **Academic Requirements:** Arts/fine arts, computer literacy, English (including composition), history, humanities, mathematics, sciences (biological or physical), social science. **Classes:** Most classes have 10–19 students. Most lab/discussion sections have 10–19 students. **Disciplines with Highest Percentage of Degrees Awarded:** Business/marketing 31%, education 22%, social sciences 6%, agriculture 6%, communications/journalism 6%. **Special Study Options:** Accelerated program, cross registration, double major, dual enrollment, honors program, independent study, internships, liberal arts/career combination, student-designed major, study abroad, teacher certification program, weekend college.

FACILITIES
Housing: Coed dorms, women's dorms, apartments for single students, fraternity/sorority housing. **Special Academic Facilities/Equipment:** Hiroshima-Nagasaki memorial collection and peace resource center, education lab, language lab, 3 farms, observatory, electron microscope. **Computers:** Network access in dorm rooms.

CAMPUS LIFE
Activities: Choral groups, concert band, drama/theater, literary magazine, music ensembles, musical theater, student government, student newspaper, yearbook. **Organizations:** 48 registered organizations, 3 honor societies, 3 religious organizations. 6 fraternities (7% men join), 5 sororities (11% women join). **Athletics (Intercollegiate): Men:** Baseball, basketball, cheerleading, cross-country, football, golf, soccer, swimming, tennis, track/field (outdoor), wrestling. **Women:** Basketball, cheerleading, cross-country, golf, soccer, softball, swimming, tennis, track/field (outdoor), volleyball.

ADMISSIONS
Freshman Academic Profile: SAT Math middle 50% range 450–550. SAT Critical Reading middle 50% range 420–510. ACT middle 50% range 18–23. TOEFL required of all international applicants, minimum paper TOEFL 500, minimum computer TOEFL 173. **Basis for Candidate Selection:** *Very important factors considered include:* Academic GPA. *Important factors considered include:* Alumni/ae relation, character/personal qualities, class rank,

rigor of secondary school record, standardized test scores, talent/ability. *Other factors considered include:* Extracurricular activities, interview, level of applicant's interest, recommendation(s), volunteer work. **Freshman Admission Requirements:** High school diploma is required, and GED is accepted. *Academic units required:* 4 English, 2 math, 2 science (2 science labs), 2 social studies. *Academic units recommended:* 2 foreign language. **Freshman Admission Statistics:** 1,409 applied, 98% admitted, 28% enrolled. **Transfer Admission Requirements:** College transcript(s), statement of good standing from prior institution(s). Minimum college GPA of 2.0 required. Lowest grade transferable C-. **General Admission Information:** Regular notification rolling. Non-fall registration accepted. Admission may be deferred for a maximum of 2 semesters. Common Application accepted. Credit and/or placement offered for CEEB Advanced Placement tests.

COSTS AND FINANCIAL AID

Student Employment: Federal Work-Study Program available. Institutional employment available. Off-campus job opportunities are excellent.

WILSON COLLEGE

1015 Philadelphia Avenue, Chambersburg, PA 17201
Phone: 717-262-2002 **E-mail:** admissions@wilson.edu **CEEB Code:** 2979
Fax: 717-262-2546 **Website:** www.wilson.edu **ACT Code:** 3758
Financial Aid Phone: 717-262-2016

This private school, affiliated with the Presbyterian Church, was founded in 1869. It has a 300-acre campus.

RATINGS
Admissions Selectivity Rating: 80   **Fire Safety Rating:** 67   **Green Rating:** 82

STUDENTS AND FACULTY
Enrollment: 533. **Student Body:** 96% female, 4% male, 26% out-of-state, 7% international (10 countries represented). African American 5%, Caucasian 82%, Hispanic 3%. **Retention and Graduation:** 74% freshmen return for sophomore year. 30% grads go on to further study within 2 semesters. 6% grads pursue arts and sciences degrees. 8% grads pursue business degrees. 9% grads pursue law degrees. 8% grads pursue medical degrees. **Faculty:** Student/faculty ratio 10:1. 38 full-time faculty, 82% hold PhDs. 100% faculty teach undergrads.

ACADEMICS
Degrees: Associate, bachelor's, master's. **Academic Requirements:** Arts/fine arts, computer literacy, English (including composition), foreign languages, humanities, mathematics, sciences (biological or physical), social science. **Classes:** Most classes have 10–19 students. Most lab/discussion sections have 10–19 students. **Majors with Highest Enrollment:** Business administration/management, elementary education and teaching, veterinary/animal health technology/technician and veterinary assistant. **Disciplines with Highest Percentage of Degrees Awarded:** Health professions and related sciences 33%, agriculture 11%, education 8%, interdisciplinary studies 7%, business/marketing 7%, social sciences 6%. **Special Study Options:** Cooperative education program, cross registration, double major, English as a second language (ESL), honors program, independent study, internships, student-designed major, study abroad, teacher certification program.

FACILITIES
Housing: Women's dorms, single residence hall room guaranteed for juniors and seniors, housing for mothers (maxiumum of 2 children). **Special Academic Facilities/Equipment:** Art gallery, natural history museum, electron microscope, NMR spectrometer. **Computers:** 100% of public computers are PCs, network access in dorm rooms, network access in dorm lounges, online registration, online administrative functions (other than registration), remote student-access to Web through college's connection.

CAMPUS LIFE
Activities: Choral groups, dance, drama/theater, literary magazine, music ensembles, radio station, student government, student newspaper, yearbook. **Organizations:** 23 registered organizations, 1 honor society, 1 religious organization. **Athletics (Intercollegiate):** *Women:* Basketball, equestrian sports, field hockey, gymnastics, soccer, softball, tennis, volleyball. **Environmental Initiatives:** Organic farm. Alternative Energy Production. Environmental Sustainability mission statement of college.

ADMISSIONS
Freshman Academic Profile: 12% in top 10% of high school class, 44% in top 25% of high school class, 70% in top 50% of high school class. 88% from public high schools. SAT Math middle 50% range 440–550. SAT Critical Reading middle 50% range 460–560. ACT middle 50% range 20–25. TOEFL required

of all international applicants, minimum paper TOEFL 500, minimum computer TOEFL 173. **Basis for Candidate Selection:** *Very important factors considered include:* Rigor of secondary school record. *Important factors considered include:* Character/personal qualities, class rank, recommendation(s). *Other factors considered include:* Alumni/ae relation, application essay, extracurricular activities, interview, standardized test scores, talent/ability, volunteer work, work experience. **Freshman Admission Requirements:** High school diploma is required, and GED is accepted. *Academic units required:* 4 English, 3 math, 2 science (2 science labs), 2 foreign language, 4 social studies. **Freshman Admission Statistics:** 307 applied, 51% admitted, 49% enrolled. **Transfer Admission Requirements:** High school transcript, college transcript(s), essay or personal statement. Minimum college GPA of 2.0 required. Lowest grade transferable C. **General Admission Information:** Application fee $35. Regular application deadline 8/1. Regular notification is rolling. Non-fall registration accepted. Admission may be deferred for a maximum of 2 semesters. Credit and/or placement offered for CEEB Advanced Placement tests.

COSTS AND FINANCIAL AID
Annual tuition $21,333. Room & board $7,916. Required fees $500. Average book expense $800. **Required Forms and Deadlines:** FAFSA, institution's own financial aid form, state aid form. Financial aid filing deadline 4/30. **Notification of Awards:** Applicants will be notified of awards on a rolling basis beginning on or about 2/15. **Types of Aid:** *Need-based scholarships/grants:* Pell, SEOG, state scholarships/grants, private scholarships, the school's own gift aid. *Loans:* FFEL Subsidized Stafford, FFEL Unsubsidized Stafford, FFEL PLUS, Federal Perkins, college/university loans from institutional funds. **Financial Aid Statistics:** 76% freshmen, 72% undergrads receive need-based scholarship or grant aid. 65% freshmen, 67% undergrads receive need-based self-help aid. 92% freshmen, 77% undergrads receive any aid. Highest amount earned per year from on-campus jobs $1,340.

See page 1508.

WINGATE UNIVERSITY

Campus Box 3059, Wingate, NC 28174
Phone: 704-233-8200 **E-mail:** admit@wingate.edu **CEEB Code:** 5908
Fax: 704-233-8110 **Website:** www.wingate.edu **ACT Code:** 3176
Financial Aid Phone: 704-233-8209

This private school, affiliated with the Baptist Church, was founded in 1896. It has a 390-acre campus.

RATINGS
Admissions Selectivity Rating: 80   **Fire Safety Rating:** 76   **Green Rating:** 60*

STUDENTS AND FACULTY
Enrollment: 1,378. **Student Body:** 53% female, 47% male, 37% out-of-state, 2% international (10 countries represented). African American 11%, Asian 1%, Caucasian 80%, Hispanic 2%. **Retention and Graduation:** 90% freshmen return for sophomore year. 38% freshmen graduate within 4 years. 20% grads go on to further study within 2 semesters. 9% grads pursue arts and sciences degrees. 8% grads pursue business degrees. 2% grads pursue law degrees. 1% grads pursue medical degrees. **Faculty:** Student/faculty ratio 14:1. 105 full-time faculty, 94% hold PhDs. 100% faculty teach undergrads.

ACADEMICS
Degrees: Bachelor's, first professional, master's. **Academic Requirements:** Arts/fine arts, computer literacy, English (including composition), foreign languages, history, humanities, intensive writing, mathematics, religion, sciences (biological or physical), social science. **Classes:** Most classes have 20–29 students. Most lab/discussion sections have 10–19 students. **Majors with Highest Enrollment:** Biology/biological sciences, business administration/management, sports and fitness administration/management. **Disciplines with Highest Percentage of Degrees Awarded:** Business/marketing 24%, communications/journalism 13%, education 11%, parks and recreation 10%, biological/life sciences 8%. **Special Study Options:** Cross registration, double major, dual enrollment, honors program, independent study, internships, study abroad, teacher certification program.

FACILITIES
Housing: Men's dorms, women's dorms, apartments for single students. **Special Academic Facilities/Equipment:** Douglas Helms Art Gallery, outdoor recreation lab, Batte Fine Arts Center. **Computers:** 1% of classrooms

are wireless, 100% of public computers are PCs, network access in dorm rooms, online administrative functions (other than registration), remote student-access to Web through college's connection.

CAMPUS LIFE

Activities: Choral groups, drama/theater, jazz band, literary magazine, music ensembles, musical theater, student government, student newspaper, television station, yearbook. **Organizations:** 45 registered organizations, 10 honor societies, 8 religious organizations. 4 fraternities (7% men join), 4 sororities (11% women join). **Athletics (Intercollegiate):** *Men:* Baseball, basketball, cheerleading, cross-country, football, golf, lacrosse, soccer, swimming, tennis. *Women:* Basketball, cheerleading, cross-country, golf, soccer, softball, swimming, tennis, volleyball.

ADMISSIONS

Freshman Academic Profile: 19% in top 10% of high school class, 41% in top 25% of high school class, 72% in top 50% of high school class. 85% from public high schools. SAT Math middle 50% range 450–570. SAT Critical Reading middle 50% range 440–540. ACT middle 50% range 18–24. TOEFL required of all international applicants, minimum paper TOEFL 550, minimum computer TOEFL 213. **Basis for Candidate Selection:** *Very important factors considered include:* Class rank, rigor of secondary school record. *Important factors considered include:* Academic GPA, recommendation(s), standardized test scores. *Other factors considered include:* Character/personal qualities, extracurricular activities, talent/ability. **Freshman Admission Requirements:** High school diploma is required, and GED is accepted. *Academic units recommended:* 4 English, 3 math, 2 science (1 science lab), 2 foreign language, 2 social studies. **Freshman Admission Statistics:** 3,437 applied, 50% admitted, 22% enrolled. **Transfer Admission Requirements:** High school transcript, college transcript(s), statement of good standing from prior institution(s). Minimum college GPA of 2.0 required. Lowest grade transferable C. **General Admission Information:** Application fee $30. Regular notification is rolling. Non-fall registration accepted. Admission may be deferred for a maximum of 2 semesters. Credit and/or placement offered for CEEB Advanced Placement tests.

COSTS AND FINANCIAL AID

Annual tuition $16,000. Room & board $6,750. Required fees $1,050. Average book expense $1,000. **Required Forms and Deadlines:** FAFSA. Financial aid filing deadline 5/1. **Notification of Awards:** Applicants will be notified of awards on or about 3/1. **Types of Aid:** *Need-based scholarships/grants:* Pell, SEOG, state scholarships/grants, private scholarships, the school's own gift aid. *Loans:* Direct Subsidized Stafford, Direct Unsubsidized Stafford, Direct PLUS, FFEL Subsidized Stafford, FFEL Unsubsidized Stafford, FFEL PLUS. **Student Employment:** Federal Work-Study Program available. Institutional employment available. Off-campus job opportunities are good. **Financial Aid Statistics:** 56% freshmen, 51% undergrads receive need-based scholarship or grant aid. 40% freshmen, 45% undergrads receive need-based self-help aid. 36 freshmen, 112 undergrads receive athletic scholarships. 97% freshmen, 96% undergrads receive any aid. Highest amount earned per year from on-campus jobs $1,200.

WINONA STATE UNIVERSITY

Office of Admissions, Winona State University, Winona, MN 55987
Phone: 507-457-5100 **E-mail:** admissions@winona.edu **CEEB Code:** 6680
Fax: 507-457-5620 **Website:** www.winona.edu **ACT Code:** 2162
Financial Aid Phone: 507-457-5090

This public school was founded in 1858. It has a 40-acre campus.

RATINGS
Admissions Selectivity Rating: 69   **Fire Safety Rating:** 60*   **Green Rating:** 87

STUDENTS AND FACULTY

Enrollment: 7,608. **Student Body:** 62% female, 38% male, 36% out-of-state, 4% international (53 countries represented). African American 1%, Asian 2%, Caucasian 85%. **Retention and Graduation:** 71% freshmen return for sophomore year. 26% freshmen graduate within 4 years. 15% grads go on to further study within 2 semesters. 10% grads pursue arts and sciences degrees. 6% grads pursue business degrees. 1% grads pursue law degrees. 1% grads pursue medical degrees. **Faculty:** Student/faculty ratio 24:1. 322 full-time faculty, 89% hold PhDs. 95% faculty teach undergrads.

ACADEMICS

Degrees: Associate, bachelor's, master's, post-bachelor's certificate, post-

master's certificate. **Academic Requirements:** Arts/fine arts, English (including composition), history, humanities, mathematics, sciences (biological or physical), social science. **Classes:** Most classes have 20–29 students. **Majors with Highest Enrollment:** Business administration/management, elementary education and teaching, nursing/registered nurse training (ASN, BSN, MSN, RN). **Disciplines with Highest Percentage of Degrees Awarded:** Business/marketing 21%, education 21%, health professions and related sciences 12%, social sciences 6%, communications/journalism 5%, public administration and social services 5%, biological/life sciences 4%, English 4%, psychology 4%. **Special Study Options:** Accelerated program, cross registration, distance learning, double major, dual enrollment, external degree program, independent study, internships, student-designed major, study abroad, teacher certification program.

FACILITIES

Housing: Coed dorms, men's dorms, women's dorms, apartments for single students, special housing for disabled students. **Computers:** 100% of classrooms are wired, 100% of classrooms are wireless, 90% of public computers are PCs, 10% of public computers are Macs, network access in dorm rooms, network access in dorm lounges, online registration, online administrative functions (other than registration), remote student-access to Web through college's connection. Undergraduates are required to own a computer.

CAMPUS LIFE

Activities: Choral groups, concert band, dance, drama/theater, jazz band, literary magazine, music ensembles, musical theater, pep band, radio station, student government, student newspaper, student-run film society, symphony orchestra, television station. **Organizations:** 204 registered organizations, 20 honor societies, 10 religious organizations. 2 fraternities, 3 sororities. **Athletics (Intercollegiate):** *Men:* Baseball, basketball, cross-country, football, golf, tennis. *Women:* Basketball, cross-country, field hockey, golf, gymnastics, soccer, softball, tennis, track/field (indoor), track/field (outdoor), volleyball.

ADMISSIONS

Freshman Academic Profile: 13% in top 10% of high school class, 28% in top 25% of high school class, 42% in top 50% of high school class. 68% from public high schools. ACT middle 50% range 21–24. TOEFL required of all international applicants, minimum paper TOEFL 550, minimum computer TOEFL 270. **Basis for Candidate Selection:** *Very important factors considered include:* Class rank, rigor of secondary school record, standardized test scores. *Other factors considered include:* Recommendation(s). **Freshman Admission Requirements:** High school diploma is required, and GED is accepted. *Academic units required:* 4 English, 3 math, 3 science (3 science labs), 2 foreign language, 2 social studies, 1 history, 1 academic elective. **Freshman Admission Statistics:** 5,359 applied, 79% admitted, 41% enrolled. **Transfer Admission Requirements:** College transcript(s). Minimum college GPA of 2.4 required. Lowest grade transferable D. **General Admission Information:** Application fee $20. Regular application deadline rolling. Regular notification is rolling. Non-fall registration accepted. Admission may be deferred for a maximum of 2 semesters. Credit and/or placement offered for CEEB Advanced Placement tests.

COSTS AND FINANCIAL AID

Annual in-state tuition $5,600. Annual out-of-state tuition $10,080. Room and board $6,490. Required fees $1,720. Average book expense $1,120. **Required Forms and Deadlines:** FAFSA. **Notification of Awards:** Applicants will be notified of awards on or about 5/1. **Types of Aid:** *Need-based scholarships/grants:* Pell, SEOG, state scholarships/grants, private scholarships, the school's own gift aid. *Loans:* FFEL Subsidized Stafford, FFEL Unsubsidized Stafford, FFEL PLUS, Federal Perkins, state loans, college/university loans from institutional funds. **Financial Aid Statistics:** Highest amount earned per year from on-campus jobs $1,800.

WINSTON-SALEM STATE UNIVERSITY

601 Martin Luther King Jr. Drive, Winston-Salem, NC 27110
Phone: 336-750-2070 **E-mail:** admissions@wssu1.adp.wssu.edu **CEEB Code:** 5909
Fax: 336-750-2079 **Website:** www.wssu.edu **ACT Code:** 3178
Financial Aid Phone: 910-750-3280

This public school was founded in 1892. It has a 94-acre campus.

RATINGS
Admissions Selectivity Rating: 61   **Fire Safety Rating:** 60*   **Green Rating:** 60*

STUDENTS AND FACULTY

Enrollment: 2,776. **Student Body:** 67% female, 33% male, 6% out-of-state. African American 83%, Caucasian 19%. **Retention and Graduation:** 72% freshmen return for sophomore year. 13% freshmen graduate within 4 years. **Faculty:** 100% faculty teach undergrads.

ACADEMICS

Degrees: Bachelor's. **Academic Requirements:** Arts/fine arts, computer literacy, English (including composition), history, humanities, mathematics, sciences (biological or physical), social science. **Special Study Options:** Cooperative education program, double major, dual enrollment, exchange student program (domestic), honors program, independent study, internships, liberal arts/career combination, study abroad, teacher certification program.

FACILITIES

Housing: Coed dorms, men's dorms, women's dorms. **Special Academic Facilities/Equipment:** Art gallery.

CAMPUS LIFE

Activities: Choral groups, jazz band, marching band, music ensembles, radio station, student government, student newspaper, yearbook.

ADMISSIONS

Freshman Academic Profile: 1% in top 10% of high school class, 13% in top 25% of high school class, 31% in top 50% of high school class. **Basis for Candidate Selection:** *Very important factors considered include:* Class rank, rigor of secondary school record, standardized test scores. *Other factors considered include:* Alumni/ae relation, character/personal qualities, extracurricular activities, interview, talent/ability. **Freshman Admission Statistics:** 1,353 applied, 80% admitted, 46% enrolled. **Transfer Admission Requirements:** College transcript(s). Minimum college GPA of 2.0 required. Lowest grade transferable C. **General Admission Information:** Application fee $20. Regular application deadline rolling. Regular notification. Non-fall registration accepted. Common Application not accepted.

COSTS AND FINANCIAL AID

Annual in-state tuition $1,575. Out-of-state tuition $7,868. **Required Forms and Deadlines:** FAFSA. Financial aid filing deadline 4/1. **Notification of Awards:** Applicants will be notified of awards on or about 5/15. **Types of Aid:** *Need-based scholarships/grants:* Pell, SEOG, state scholarships/grants, private scholarships, the school's own gift aid, Federal Nursing Scholarships. *Loans:* FFEL Subsidized Stafford, FFEL Unsubsidized Stafford, FFEL PLUS, Federal Perkins, state loans, college/university loans from institutional funds. **Student Employment:** Federal Work-Study Program available. Institutional employment available. Off-campus job opportunities are good. **Financial Aid Statistics:** Highest amount earned per year from on-campus jobs $800.

WINTHROP UNIVERSITY

701 Oakland Avenue, Rock Hill, SC 29733
Phone: 803-323-2137 **E-mail:** admissions@winthrop.edu **CEEB Code:** 5910
Fax: 803-323-2137 **Website:** www.winthrop.edu **ACT Code:** 3884
Financial Aid Phone: 803-323-2189

This public school was founded in 1886. It has a 418-acre campus.

RATINGS

Admissions Selectivity Rating: 78   **Fire Safety Rating:** 60*   **Green Rating:** 77

STUDENTS AND FACULTY

Enrollment: 4,900. **Student Body:** 69% female, 31% male, 13% out-of-state, 2% international (51 countries represented). African American 28%, Asian 1%, Caucasian 67%, Hispanic 1%. **Retention and Graduation:** 76% freshmen return for sophomore year. 32% freshmen graduate within 4 years. 11% grads go on to further study within 2 semesters. 20% grads pursue arts and sciences degrees. 25% grads pursue business degrees. 3% grads pursue law degrees. 5% grads pursue medical degrees. **Faculty:** Student/faculty ratio 15:1. 273 full-time faculty, 81% hold PhDs. 98% faculty teach undergrads.

ACADEMICS

Degrees: Bachelor's, master's, post-bachelor's certificate. **Academic Requirements:** Computer literacy, English (including composition), foreign languages, history, humanities, mathematics, sciences (biological or physical), social science. **Classes:** Most classes have 20–29 students. Most lab/discussion sections have 10–19 students. **Majors with Highest Enrollment:** Business administration/management, design and visual communications, psychology. **Disciplines with Highest Percentage of Degrees Awarded:** Education 19%, business/marketing 18%, visual and performing arts 15%, history 12%,

psychology 6%. **Special Study Options:** Cooperative education program, cross registration, distance learning, double major, exchange student program (domestic), honors program, independent study, internships, study abroad, teacher certification program.

FACILITIES

Housing: Coed dorms, men's dorms, women's dorms, apartments for married students, apartments for single students, fraternity/sorority housing. **Special Academic Facilities/Equipment:** Art gallery, on-campus nursery and kindergarten. **Computers:** 80% of public computers are PCs, 16% of public computers are Macs, 4% of public computers are UNIX, network access in dorm rooms, network access in dorm lounges, online registration, online administrative functions (other than registration), remote student-access to Web through college's connection.

CAMPUS LIFE

Activities: Choral groups, concert band, dance, drama/theater, jazz band, literary magazine, music ensembles, opera, pep band, radio station, student government, student newspaper, yearbook. **Organizations:** 145 registered organizations, 21 honor society, 16 religious organizations. 7 fraternities (12% men join), 8 sororities (14% women join). **Athletics (Intercollegiate):** *Men:* Baseball, basketball, cross-country, golf, soccer, tennis, track/field (outdoor). *Women:* Basketball, cross-country, golf, soccer, softball, tennis, track/field (outdoor), volleyball. **Environmental Initiatives:** Very strong recycling program. Commitment to have all new buildings be green certified. Outstanding record of reducing energy use by upgrading historic buildings through things like new windows.

ADMISSIONS

Freshman Academic Profile: 18% in top 10% of high school class, 43% in top 25% of high school class, 87% in top 50% of high school class. SAT Math middle 50% range 480–570. SAT Critical Reading middle 50% range 470–570. ACT middle 50% range 20–24. TOEFL required of all international applicants, minimum paper TOEFL 520, minimum computer TOEFL 190. **Basis for Candidate Selection:** *Very important factors considered include:* Rigor of secondary school record. *Important factors considered include:* Academic GPA, standardized test scores. *Other factors considered include:* Application essay, recommendation(s), talent/ability. **Freshman Admission Requirements:** High school diploma is required, and GED is accepted. *Academic units required:* 4 English, 3 math, 3 science (3 science labs), 2 foreign language, 2 social studies, 1 history, 4 academic electives, 1 physical education or ROTC. **Freshman Admission Statistics:** 5,328 applied, 70% admitted, 32% enrolled. **Transfer Admission Requirements:** College transcript(s), statement of good standing from prior institution(s). Minimum college GPA of 2.0 required. Lowest grade transferable C. **General Admission Information:** Application fee $40. Regular application deadline 5/1. Regular notification is rolling. Non-fall registration accepted. Admission may be deferred for a maximum of 1 semester. Credit offered for CEEB Advanced Placement tests.

COSTS AND FINANCIAL AID

Average book expense $950. **Required Forms and Deadlines:** FAFSA. Financial aid filing deadline 3/1. **Notification of Awards:** Applicants will be notified of awards on a rolling basis beginning on or about 3/15. **Types of Aid:** *Need-based scholarships/grants:* Pell, SEOG, state scholarships/grants, private scholarships, the school's own gift aid. *Loans:* Direct Subsidized Stafford, Direct Unsubsidized Stafford, FFEL PLUS, Federal Perkins. **Financial Aid Statistics:** 59% freshmen, 48% undergrads receive need-based scholarship or grant aid. 41% freshmen, 47% undergrads receive need-based self-help aid. 47 freshmen, 151 undergrads receive athletic scholarships. 95% freshmen, 65% undergrads receive any aid. Highest amount earned per year from on-campus jobs $1,200.

WISCONSIN LUTHERAN COLLEGE

8800 West Bluemound Road, Milwaukee, WI 53226
Phone: 414-443-8811 **E-mail:** admissions@wlc.edu **CEEB Code:** 1513
Fax: 414-443-8514 **Website:** www.wlc.edu **ACT Code:** 4699
Financial Aid Phone: 414-443-8856

This private school, affiliated with the Lutheran Church, was founded in 1973. It has a 21-acre campus.

RATINGS

Admissions Selectivity Rating: 79   **Fire Safety Rating:** 60*   **Green Rating:** 60*

STUDENTS AND FACULTY

Enrollment: 687. **Student Body:** 60% female, 40% male, 19% out-of-state,

1% international (10 countries represented). African American 1%, Caucasian 95%, Hispanic 1%. **Retention and Graduation:** 80% freshmen return for sophomore year. 47% freshmen graduate within 4 years. **Faculty:** Student/faculty ratio 11:1. 47 full-time faculty, 64% hold PhDs. 100% faculty teach undergrads.

ACADEMICS

Degrees: Bachelor's. **Academic Requirements:** Arts/fine arts, English (including composition), foreign languages, history, humanities, mathematics, sciences (biological or physical), social science, theology. **Classes:** Most classes have 10–19 students. Most lab/discussion sections have fewer than 10 students. **Majors with Highest Enrollment:** Communications studies/speech communication and rhetoric, psychology. **Disciplines with Highest Percentage of Degrees Awarded:** Communication technologies 20%, biological/life sciences 12%, visual and performing arts 12%, business/marketing 11%, education 11%, psychology 11%, English 8%, social sciences 4%. **Special Study Options:** Double major, dual enrollment, independent study, internships, student-designed major, study abroad, teacher certification program.

FACILITIES

Housing: Men's dorms, women's dorms, apartments for single students. **Special Academic Facilities/Equipment:** Center for Arts and Performance. **Computers:** 90% of public computers are PCs, 10% of public computers are Macs, network access in dorm rooms, network access in dorm lounges, remote student-access to Web through college's connection.

CAMPUS LIFE

Activities: Choral groups, concert band, dance, drama/theater, jazz band, music ensembles, pep band, student government, student newspaper, yearbook. **Organizations:** 31 registered organizations. **Athletics (Intercollegiate):** *Men:* Baseball, basketball, cross-country, football, golf, soccer, track/field (outdoor). *Women:* Basketball, cross-country, golf, soccer, softball, tennis, track/field (outdoor), volleyball.

ADMISSIONS

Freshman Academic Profile: 23% in top 10% of high school class, 53% in top 25% of high school class, 83% in top 50% of high school class. 41% from public high schools. ACT middle 50% range 22–27. TOEFL required of all international applicants, minimum paper TOEFL 550, minimum computer TOEFL 213. **Basis for Candidate Selection:** *Very important factors considered include:* Rigor of secondary school record, standardized test scores. *Important factors considered include:* Character/personal qualities, class rank, extracurricular activities, interview, recommendation(s), religious affiliation/commitment. *Other factors considered include:* Application essay, geographical residence, racial/ethnic status, state residency, talent/ability, volunteer work. **Freshman Admission Requirements:** High school diploma is required, and GED is accepted. *Academic units required:* 4 English, 3 math, 2 science (1 science lab), 2 foreign language, 2 history, 3 academic electives. *Academic units recommended:* 4 English, 4 math, 3 science (2 science labs), 4 foreign language, 2 history, 3 academic electives. **Freshman Admission Statistics:** 531 applied, 84% admitted, 47% enrolled. **Transfer Admission Requirements:** College transcript(s), statement of good standing from prior institution(s). Minimum college GPA of 2.5 required. **General Admission Information:** Application fee $20. Regular notification is rolling. Non-fall registration accepted. Common Application accepted. Credit and/or placement offered for CEEB Advanced Placement tests.

COSTS AND FINANCIAL AID

Required fees $130. Average book expense $700. **Required Forms and Deadlines:** FAFSA, institution's own financial aid form, Business/Farm Supplement. Financial aid filing deadline 3/1. **Notification of Awards:** Applicants will be notified of awards on a rolling basis beginning on or about 3/15. **Types of Aid:** *Need-based scholarships/grants:* Pell, SEOG, state scholarships/grants, private scholarships, the school's own gift aid. *Loans:* FFEL Subsidized Stafford, FFEL Unsubsidized Stafford, FFEL PLUS, state loans, private alternative loans. **Student Employment:** Federal Work-Study Program available. Institutional employment available. Off-campus job opportunities are excellent. **Financial Aid Statistics:** 77% freshmen, 75% undergrads receive need-based scholarship or grant aid. 69% freshmen, 67% undergrads receive

need-based self-help aid. 100% freshmen, 98% undergrads receive any aid. Highest amount earned per year from on-campus jobs $2,600.

WITTENBERG UNIVERSITY

Best 368

PO Box 720, Springfield, OH 45501
Phone: 800-677-7558 **E-mail:** admission@wittenberg.edu **CEEB Code:** 1922
Fax: 937-327-6379 **Website:** www.wittenberg.edu **ACT Code:** 3364
Financial Aid Phone: 937-327-7321

This private school, affiliated with the Lutheran Church, was founded in 1845. It has a 71-acre campus.

RATINGS

Admissions Selectivity Rating: 79   **Fire Safety Rating:** 97   **Green Rating:** 70

STUDENTS AND FACULTY

Enrollment: 1,873. **Student Body:** 56% female, 44% male, 25% out-of-state, 2% international (23 countries represented). African American 6%, Caucasian 83%, Hispanic 1%. **Retention and Graduation:** 82% freshmen return for sophomore year. 26% grads go on to further study within 2 semesters. 62% grads pursue arts and sciences degrees. 8% grads pursue business degrees. 8% grads pursue law degrees. 23% grads pursue medical degrees. **Faculty:** Student/faculty ratio 12:1. 142 full-time faculty, 89% hold PhDs. 100% faculty teach undergrads.

ACADEMICS

Degrees: Bachelor's, master's. **Academic Requirements:** Arts/fine arts, computer literacy, English (including composition), foreign languages, history, humanities, mathematics, philosophy, sciences (biological or physical), social science. **Classes:** Most classes have 10–19 students. Most lab/discussion sections have 10–19 students. **Majors with Highest Enrollment:** Biological and physical sciences, business/commerce, teacher education. **Disciplines with Highest Percentage of Degrees Awarded:** Social sciences 14%, business/marketing 12%, education 12%, biological/life sciences 9%, English 8%, communications/journalism 7%, psychology 7%. **Special Study Options:** Cross registration, double major, dual enrollment, honors program, independent study, internships, liberal arts/career combination, student-designed major, study abroad, teacher certification program, weekend college.

FACILITIES

Housing: Coed dorms, men's dorms, women's dorms, apartments for married students, apartments for single students, special housing for international students, fraternity/sorority housing, university owned houses around campus. **Special Academic Facilities/Equipment:** Language lab, electron microscope, observatory. **Computers:** 100% of classrooms are wired, 3% of classrooms are wireless, 95% of public computers are PCs, 5% of public computers are Macs, network access in dorm rooms, network access in dorm lounges, online registration, online administrative functions (other than registration), remote student-access to Web through college's connection.

CAMPUS LIFE

Activities: Choral groups, concert band, dance, drama/theater, jazz band, literary magazine, music ensembles, musical theater, opera, pep band, radio station, student government, student newspaper, student-run film society, symphony orchestra, yearbook. **Organizations:** 130 registered organizations, 6 honor societies, 10 religious organizations. 6 fraternities (8% men join), 6 sororities (18% women join). **Athletics (Intercollegiate):** *Men:* Baseball, basketball, cheerleading, cross-country, diving, football, golf, lacrosse, soccer, swimming, tennis, track/field (indoor), track/field (outdoor). *Women:* Basketball, cheerleading, cross-country, diving, field hockey, golf, lacrosse, soccer, softball, swimming, tennis, track/field (indoor), track/field (outdoor), volleyball. **Environmental Initiatives:** Campus-wide recycling. Minimization of packaging materials on received goods. Recycling of building materials.

ADMISSIONS

Freshman Academic Profile: 32% in top 10% of high school class, 62% in top 25% of high school class, 86% in top 50% of high school class. SAT Math middle 50% range 500–559. SAT Critical Reading middle 50% range 490–610. ACT middle 50% range 22–27. TOEFL required of all international applicants, minimum paper TOEFL 550, minimum computer TOEFL 213. **Basis for Candidate Selection:** *Very important factors considered include:* Application essay, class rank, interview, recommendation(s), rigor of secondary school record, standardized test scores. *Important factors considered include:* Character/personal qualities, extracurricular activities, talent/ability, volunteer work. *Other factors considered include:* Alumni/ae relation, work experience. **Freshman Admission Requirements:** High school diploma is required, and GED is not accepted. *Academic units required:* 4 English, 3 math, 3 science (2 science labs), 2 foreign language, 2 history. *Academic units recommended:* 4 English, 4 math, 4 science (2 science labs), 3 foreign language, 3 history. **Freshman Admission Statistics:** 2,392 applied, 82% admitted, 29% enrolled. **Transfer Admission Requirements:** College transcript(s). Minimum college GPA of 2.0 required. Lowest grade transferable C. **General Admission Information:** Application fee $40. Early decision application deadline 11/15. Regular notification is rolling. Non-fall registration accepted. Admission may be deferred for a maximum of 2 semesters. Credit and/or placement offered for CEEB Advanced Placement tests.

COSTS AND FINANCIAL AID

Annual tuition $32,936. Room and board $8,314. Required fees $300. Average book expense $800. **Required Forms and Deadlines:** FAFSA. Financial aid filing deadline 3/15. **Notification of Awards:** Applicants will be notified of awards on a rolling basis beginning on or about 3/1. **Types of Aid:** *Need-based scholarships/grants:* Pell, SEOG, state scholarships/grants, private scholarships, the school's own gift aid. *Loans:* FFEL Subsidized Stafford, FFEL Unsubsidized Stafford, FFEL PLUS, Federal Perkins, college/university loans from institutional funds. **Financial Aid Statistics:** 71% freshmen, 73% undergrads receive need-based scholarship or grant aid. 69% freshmen, 69% undergrads receive need-based self-help aid. 99% freshmen, 99% undergrads receive any aid. Highest amount earned per year from on-campus jobs $3,985.

WOFFORD COLLEGE

Best 368

429 North Church Street, Spartanburg, SC 29303-3663
Phone: 864-597-4130 **E-mail:** admission@wofford.edu **CEEB Code:** 5912
Fax: 864-597-4147 **Website:** www.wofford.edu **ACT Code:** 3886
Financial Aid Phone: 864-597-4160

This private school, affiliated with the Methodist Church, was founded in 1854. It has a 200-acre campus.

RATINGS

Admissions Selectivity Rating: 91   **Fire Safety Rating:** 60*   **Green Rating:** 60*

STUDENTS AND FACULTY

Enrollment: 1,234. **Student Body:** 48% female, 52% male, 38% out-of-state. African American 6%, Asian 2%, Caucasian 88%, Hispanic 1%. **Retention and Graduation:** 90% freshmen return for sophomore year. 72% freshmen graduate within 4 years. 35% grads go on to further study within 2 semesters. 14% grads pursue business degrees. 9% grads pursue law degrees. 8% grads pursue medical degrees. **Faculty:** Student/faculty ratio 11:1. 98 full-time faculty, 92% hold PhDs. 100% faculty teach undergrads.

ACADEMICS

Degrees: Bachelor's. **Academic Requirements:** Arts/fine arts, computer literacy, English (including composition), foreign languages, history, humanities, mathematics, philosophy, sciences (biological or physical), social science. **Classes:** Most classes have 10–19 students. **Majors with Highest Enrollment:** Biology/biological sciences, business/managerial economics, political science and government. **Disciplines with Highest Percentage of Degrees Awarded:** Business/marketing 24%, biological/life sciences 17%, social sciences 11%, foreign languages and literature 8%, history 7%. **Special Study Options:** Accelerated program, Bonner Scholars, Community of Scholars, creative writing concentration, cross registration, double major, dual enrollment, independent study, internships, learning communities, Milliken Research Corporation Summer Challenge, Presidential International Scholar Program, student-designed major, study abroad, success initiative, teacher certification program.

FACILITIES

Housing: Coed dorms, apartments for single students, fraternity/sorority housing, separate floors for each gender. **Special Academic Facilities/ Equipment:** Arboretum, art gallery, Franklin W. Olin Building (teaching technology center), Milliken Science Center. **Computers:** 2% of classrooms are wired, 20% of classrooms are wireless, 85% of public computers are PCs, 15% of public computers are Macs, network access in dorm rooms, network access in dorm lounges, online registration, online administrative functions (other than registration), remote student-access to Web through college's connection.

CAMPUS LIFE

Activities: Choral groups, concert band, drama/theater, literary magazine, music ensembles, pep band, student government, student newspaper, yearbook. **Organizations:** 91 registered organizations, 10 honor societies, 8 religious organizations. 8 fraternities (50% men join), 4 sororities (61% women join). **Athletics (Intercollegiate):** *Men:* Baseball, basketball, cross-country, football, golf, riflery, soccer, tennis, track/field (indoor), track/field (outdoor). *Women:* Basketball, cross-country, golf, riflery, soccer, tennis, track/field (indoor), track/field (outdoor), volleyball.

ADMISSIONS

Freshman Academic Profile: 61% in top 10% of high school class, 83% in top 25% of high school class, 98% in top 50% of high school class. 64% from public high schools. SAT Math middle 50% range 570–680. SAT Critical Reading middle 50% range 560–680. SAT Writing middle 50% range 560–660. ACT middle 50% range 22–27. TOEFL required of all international applicants, minimum paper TOEFL 550, minimum computer TOEFL 213. **Basis for Candidate Selection:** *Very important factors considered include:* Academic GPA, rigor of secondary school record. *Important factors considered include:* Application essay, character/personal qualities, class rank, extracurricular activities, standardized test scores, talent/ability. *Other factors considered include:* Alumni/ae relation, first generation, geographical residence, racial/ethnic status, recommendation(s), volunteer work, work experience. **Freshman Admission Requirements:** High school diploma is required, and GED is accepted. *Academic units recommended:* 4 English, 4 math, 3 science labs, 3 foreign language, 2 social studies, 1 history, 3 academic electives. **Freshman Admission Statistics:** 2,089 applied, 57% admitted, 31% enrolled. **Transfer Admission Requirements:** High school transcript, college transcript(s), essay or personal statement, standardized test score, statement of good standing from prior institution(s). Minimum college GPA of 2.5 required. Lowest grade transferable C. **General Admission Information:** Application fee $40. Early decision application deadline 11/15. Regular application deadline 2/1. Regular notification 3/15. Non-fall registration accepted. Admission may be deferred for a maximum of 2 semesters. Credit and/or placement offered for CEEB Advanced Placement tests.

COSTS AND FINANCIAL AID

Annual tuition $27,830. Room and board $7,705. Average book expense $907. **Required Forms and Deadlines:** FAFSA. Financial aid filing deadline 3/15. **Notification of Awards:** Applicants will be notified of awards on or about 3/31. **Types of Aid:** *Need-based scholarships/grants:* Pell, SEOG, state scholarships/grants, private scholarships, the school's own gift aid. *Loans:* FFEL Subsidized Stafford, FFEL Unsubsidized Stafford, FFEL PLUS, Federal Perkins, state loans. **Financial Aid Statistics:** 53% freshmen, 52% undergrads receive need-based scholarship or grant aid. 22% freshmen, 26% undergrads receive need-based self-help aid. 33 freshmen, 99 undergrads receive athletic scholarships. 95% freshmen, 90% undergrads receive any aid. Highest amount earned per year from on-campus jobs $750.

WOODBURY UNIVERSITY

7500 Glenoaks Boulevard, Burbank, CA 91510-7846
Phone: 818-767-0888 **E-mail:** admissions@woodbury.edu **CEEB Code:** 4955
Fax: 818-767-7520 **Website:** www.woodbury.edu **ACT Code:** 0481
Financial Aid Phone: 818-767-0888

This private school was founded in 1884. It has a 22-acre campus.

RATINGS

Admissions Selectivity Rating: 73   **Fire Safety Rating:** 78   **Green Rating:** 60*

STUDENTS AND FACULTY

Enrollment: 1,278. **Student Body:** 57% female, 43% male, 10% out-of-state, 6% international (39 countries represented). African American 6%, Asian 11%, Caucasian 42%, Hispanic 34%. **Retention and Graduation:** 76% freshmen return for sophomore year. **Faculty:** Student/faculty ratio 12:1. 45 full-time faculty, 82% hold PhDs. 100% faculty teach undergrads.

ACADEMICS

Degrees: Bachelor's, master's. **Academic Requirements:** Arts/fine arts, computer literacy, English (including composition), history, humanities, mathematics, philosophy, sciences (biological or physical), social science. All undergraduate students are required to complete internships or related work experience. **Classes:** Most classes have 10–19 students. **Majors with Highest Enrollment:** Architecture (BArch, BA/BS, MArch, MA/MS, Phd), business administration and management, organizational behavior studies. **Disciplines with Highest Percentage of Degrees Awarded:** Business/marketing 43%, architecture 25%, visual and performing arts 19%, psychology 6%, computer and information sciences 3%. **Special Study Options:** Accelerated program, double major, independent study, internships, liberal arts/career combination, student-designed major, study abroad, weekend college.

FACILITIES

Housing: Coed dorms, off-campus overflow apartments. **Special Academic Facilities/Equipment:** Art gallery, architecture gallery. **Computers:** 70% of public computers are PCs, 30% of public computers are Macs, online registration, online administrative functions (other than registration), remote student-access to Web through college's connection.undergraduates are required to own a computer.

CAMPUS LIFE

Activities: Literary magazine, student government, student newspaper, yearbook. **Organizations:** 20 registered organizations, 3 honor societies, 1 religious organization. 2 fraternities (1% men join), 2 sororities (1% women join).

ADMISSIONS

Freshman Academic Profile: 5% in top 10% of high school class, 45% in top 25% of high school class, 92% in top 50% of high school class. 75% from public high schools. SAT Math middle 50% range 420–550. SAT Critical Reading middle 50% range 410–530. SAT Writing middle 50% range 410–530. TOEFL required of all international applicants, minimum paper TOEFL 500, minimum computer TOEFL 173. **Basis for Candidate Selection:** *Very important factors considered include:* Rigor of secondary school record, standardized test scores. *Important factors considered include:* Level of applicant's interest, recommendation(s). *Other factors considered include:* Alumni/ae relation, application essay, class rank, extracurricular activities, first generation, interview, volunteer work, work experience. **Freshman Admission Requirements:** High school diploma is required, and GED is accepted. *Academic units recommended:* 4 English, 3 math, 3 science (2 science labs), 2 foreign language, 3 social studies, 2 history. **Freshman Admission Statistics:** 410 applied, 77% admitted, 46% enrolled. **Transfer Admission Requirements:** College transcript(s). Minimum college GPA of 2.5 required. Lowest grade transferable C. **General Admission Information:** Application fee $35. Regular notification is rolling. Non-fall registration accepted. Admission may be deferred for a maximum of 4 semesters. Credit offered for CEEB Advanced Placement tests.

COSTS AND FINANCIAL AID

Annual tuition $24,858. Room and board $8,510. Required fees $340. Average book expense $1,386. **Required Forms and Deadlines:** FAFSA, institution's own financial aid form. Financial aid filing deadline 4/2. **Notification of Awards:** Applicants will be notified of awards on or about 3/15. **Types of Aid:** *Need-based scholarships/grants:* Pell, SEOG, state scholarships/grants, private scholarships, the school's own gift aid. *Loans:* FFEL Subsidized Stafford, FFEL Unsubsidized Stafford, FFEL PLUS, Federal Perkins, college/university loans from institutional funds, alternative private loans. **Student Employment:** Federal Work-Study Program available. Institutional employment available. Off-campus job opportunities are poor. **Financial Aid Statistics:** 70% freshmen, 79% undergrads receive need-based scholarship or grant aid. 57% freshmen, 74% undergrads receive need-based self-help aid.

WORCESTER POLYTECHNIC INSTITUTE

Best 368

100 Institute Road, Admissions Office, Bartlett Center, Worcester, MA 01609
Phone: 508-831-5286 **E-mail:** admissions@wpi.edu **CEEB Code:** 3969
Fax: 508-831-5875 **Website:** www.wpi.edu **ACT Code:** 1942
Financial Aid Phone: 508-831-5469

This private school was founded in 1865. It has an 80-acre campus.

RATINGS

Admissions Selectivity Rating: 93 **Fire Safety Rating:** 84 **Green Rating:** 60*

STUDENTS AND FACULTY

Enrollment: 2,857. **Student Body:** 26% female, 74% male, 50% out-of-state,

---

7% international (81 countries represented). African American 2%, Asian 6%, Caucasian 79%, Hispanic 4%. **Retention and Graduation:** 90% freshmen return for sophomore year. 64% freshmen graduate within 4 years. 21% grads go on to further study within 2 semesters. 3% grads pursue law degrees. 5% grads pursue medical degrees. **Faculty:** Student/faculty ratio 13:1. 240 full-time faculty, 95% hold PhDs. 100% faculty teach undergrads.

ACADEMICS

Degrees: Bachelor's, doctoral, master's, post-bachelor's certificate, post-master's certificate. **Academic Requirements:** Humanities, mathematics, sciences (biological or physical), social science. **Classes:** Most classes have fewer than 10 students. Most lab/discussion sections have 20–29 students. **Majors with Highest Enrollment:** Computer science, electrical, electronics and communications engineering, mechanical engineering. **Disciplines with Highest Percentage of Degrees Awarded:** Engineering 64%, computer and information sciences 14%, biological/life sciences 9%, business/marketing 4%, physical sciences 3%. **Special Study Options:** Accelerated program, cooperative education program, cross registration, degree-required projects at off-campus locations (international and domestic), double major, dual enrollment, English as a second language (ESL), exchange student program (domestic), honors program, independent study, liberal arts/career combination, student-designed major, study abroad, teacher certification program.

FACILITIES

Housing: Coed dorms, apartments for single students, special housing for disabled students, special housing for international students, fraternity/sorority housing, 4 coed residential houses/special interest housing. **Special Academic Facilities/Equipment:** Several off-campus project centers, TV studio, robotics lab, CAD-CAM lab, laser labs, electron microscopes, wind tunnel, manufacturing engineering applications center, VLSI design lab, nuclear reactor. **Computers:** 17% of classrooms are wired, 83% of classrooms are wireless, 97% of public computers are PCs, 1% of public computers are Macs, 2% of public computers are UNIX, network access in dorm rooms, network access in dorm lounges, online registration, online administrative functions (other than registration), support for handheld computing, remote student-access to Web through college's connection.

CAMPUS LIFE

Activities: Choral groups, concert band, dance, drama/theater, jazz band, literary magazine, marching band, music ensembles, musical theater, pep band, radio station, student government, student newspaper, student-run film society, symphony orchestra, yearbook. **Organizations:** 200 registered organizations, 15 honor societies, 4 religious organizations. 11 fraternities (29% men join), 3 sororities (31% women join). **Athletics (Intercollegiate):** *Men:* Baseball, basketball, crew/rowing, cross-country, diving, football, soccer, swimming, track/field (indoor), track/field (outdoor), wrestling. *Women:* Basketball, crew/rowing, cross-country, diving, field hockey, soccer, softball, swimming, track/field (indoor), track/field (outdoor), volleyball.

ADMISSIONS

Freshman Academic Profile: 53% in top 10% of high school class, 83% in top 25% of high school class, 99% in top 50% of high school class. 66% from public high schools. SAT Math middle 50% range 640–720. SAT Critical Reading middle 50% range 560–670. SAT Writing middle 50% range 550–640. ACT middle 50% range 25–30. TOEFL required of all international applicants, minimum paper TOEFL 550, minimum computer TOEFL 213. **Basis for Candidate Selection:** *Very important factors considered include:* Academic GPA, rigor of secondary school record. *Important factors considered include:* Application essay, character/personal qualities, class rank, extracurricular activities, recommendation(s), standardized test scores. *Other factors considered include:* Alumni/ae relation, geographical residence, interview, level of applicant's interest, racial/ethnic status, talent/ability, volunteer work, work experience. **Freshman Admission Requirements:** High school diploma is required, and GED is accepted. *Academic units required:* 4 English, 4 math, 2 science (2 science labs). *Academic units recommended:* 4 science, 2 foreign language, 2 social studies, 1 history. **Freshman Admission Statistics:** 4,931 applied, 67% admitted, 24% enrolled. **Transfer Admission Requirements:** College transcript(s), essay or personal statement, statement of good standing from prior institution(s). Minimum college GPA of 3.0 required. Lowest grade transferable C. **General Admission Information:** Application fee $60. Regular application deadline 2/1. Regular notification 4/1. Non-fall registration accepted. Admission may be deferred for a maximum of 2 semesters. Credit and/or placement offered for CEEB Advanced Placement tests.

COSTS AND FINANCIAL AID

Comprehensive fee $45,240. Average book expense $1,000. **Required Forms and Deadlines:** FAFSA, CSS/Financial Aid PROFILE, Noncustodial PROFILE, parents' and student's federal tax return. Financial aid filing deadline 2/1. **Notification of Awards:** Applicants will be notified of awards on or about 4/1. **Types of Aid:** *Need-based scholarships/grants:* Pell, SEOG, state scholarships/grants, private scholarships, the school's own gift aid. *Loans:* FFEL Subsidized Stafford, FFEL Unsubsidized Stafford, FFEL PLUS, Federal Perkins, state loans, college/university loans from institutional funds. **Financial**

Aid Statistics: 76% freshmen, 67% undergrads receive need-based scholarship or grant aid. 51% freshmen, 54% undergrads receive need-based self-help aid. 98% freshmen, 93% undergrads receive any aid.

See page 1510.

WORCESTER STATE COLLEGE

486 Chandler Street, Department of Admissions, Worcester, MA 01602-2597
Phone: 508-929-8040 **E-mail:** admissions@worcester.edu **CEEB Code:** 3524
Fax: 508-929-8183 **Website:** www.worcester.edu **ACT Code:** 1914
Financial Aid Phone: 508-929-8058

This public school was founded in 1874. It has a 58-acre campus.

RATINGS

Admissions Selectivity Rating: 60*   **Fire Safety Rating:** 90   **Green Rating:** 79

STUDENTS AND FACULTY

Enrollment: 3,982. **Student Body:** 59% female, 41% male, 3% out-of-state, 2% international (26 countries represented). African American 4%, Asian 3%, Caucasian 78%, Hispanic 4%. **Retention and Graduation:** 74% freshmen return for sophomore year. 16% grads go on to further study within 2 semesters. **Faculty:** Student/faculty ratio 17:1. 173 full-time faculty, 74% hold PhDs. 86% faculty teach undergrads.

ACADEMICS

Degrees: Bachelor's, master's, post-bachelor's certificate, post-master's certificate. **Academic Requirements:** Arts/fine arts, English (including composition), history, humanities, mathematics, sciences (biological or physical), social science. **Classes:** Most classes have 10–19 students. Most lab/discussion sections have 20–29 students. **Majors with Highest Enrollment:** Business administration and management, nursing/registered nurse training (ASN, BSN, MSN, RN), psychology. **Disciplines with Highest Percentage of Degrees Awarded:** Business/marketing 24%, health professions and related sciences 15%, psychology 14%, social sciences 11%, communications/journalism 7%. **Special Study Options:** Cooperative education program, cross registration, distance learning, double major, dual enrollment, English as a second language (ESL), exchange student program (domestic), evening college program for chemistry, honors program, independent study, internships, liberal arts/career combination, study abroad, teacher certification program.

FACILITIES

Housing: Coed dorms, men's dorms, women's dorms, special housing for disabled students. **Special Academic Facilities/Equipment:** Art studio. **Computers:** 95% of public computers are PCs, 5% of public computers are UNIX, network access in dorm rooms, network access in dorm lounges, online registration, online administrative functions (other than registration), remote student-access to Web through college's connection.undergraduates are required to own a computer.

CAMPUS LIFE

Activities: Choral groups, concert band, dance, drama/theater, jazz band, music ensembles, radio station, student government, student newspaper, television station, yearbook. **Organizations:** 40 registered organizations, 18 honor societies, 1 religious organization. **Athletics (Intercollegiate):** *Men:* Baseball, basketball, crew/rowing, cross-country, football, golf, ice hockey, soccer, tennis, track/field (outdoor), volleyball. *Women:* Basketball, cheerleading, cross-country, field hockey, lacrosse, soccer, softball, tennis, track/field (outdoor), volleyball. **Environmental Initiatives:** 100 KW photovoltaic installation (solar panels). Single stream recycling process. Presidents climate commitment.

ADMISSIONS

Freshman Academic Profile: SAT Math middle 50% range 460–560. SAT Critical Reading middle 50% range 450–540. ACT middle 50% range 20–24. TOEFL required of all international applicants, minimum paper TOEFL 550, minimum computer TOEFL 213. **Basis for Candidate Selection:** *Very important factors considered include:* Rigor of secondary school record, standardized test scores. *Other factors considered include:* Application essay, extracurricular activities, interview, recommendation(s), talent/ability. **Freshman Admission Requirements:** High school diploma is required, and GED is accepted. *Academic units required:* 4 English, 3 math, 3 science (2 science labs), 2 foreign language, 1 social studies, 1 history, 2 academic electives. **Freshman Admission Statistics:** 3,364 applied, 56% admitted, 36% enrolled. **Transfer Admission Requirements:** High school transcript, college transcript(s). Minimum college GPA of 2.5 required. Lowest grade transferable C-. **General Admission Information:** Application fee $20. Regular application deadline 6/1. Regular notification is rolling. Non-fall registration accepted. Admission may be deferred for a maximum of 2 semesters. Credit and/or placement offered for CEEB Advanced Placement tests.

COSTS AND FINANCIAL AID

Annual in-state tuition $970. Out-of-state tuition $7,050. Room & board $7,738. Required fees $4,569. Average book expense $984. **Required Forms and Deadlines:** FAFSA, institution's own financial aid form. Financial aid filing deadline 3/1. **Notification of Awards:** Applicants will be notified of awards on a rolling basis beginning on or about 3/1. **Types of Aid:** *Need-based scholarships/grants:* Pell, SEOG, state scholarships/grants, private scholarships, the school's own gift aid. *Loans:* FFEL Subsidized Stafford, FFEL Unsubsidized Stafford, FFEL PLUS, Federal Perkins, state loans. **Student Employment:** Federal Work-Study Program available. Institutional employment available. Off-campus job opportunities are good. **Financial Aid Statistics:** 48% freshmen, 38% undergrads receive need-based scholarship or grant aid. 53% freshmen, 44% undergrads receive need-based self-help aid. 55% freshmen, 48% undergrads receive any aid.

WRIGHT STATE UNIVERSITY

3640 Colonel Glenn Highway, Dayton, OH 45435
Phone: 937-775-5700 **E-mail:** admissions@wright.edu **CEEB Code:** 1179
Fax: 937-775-5795 **Website:** www.wright.edu **ACT Code:** 3295
Financial Aid Phone: 937-775-572

This public school was founded in 1964. It has a 557-acre campus.

RATINGS

Admissions Selectivity Rating: 73   **Fire Safety Rating:** 95   **Green Rating:** 60*

STUDENTS AND FACULTY

Enrollment: 11,770. **Student Body:** 56% female, 44% male, 4% out-of-state, 1% international (67 countries represented). African American 13%, Asian 2%, Caucasian 76%, Hispanic 1%. **Retention and Graduation:** 69% freshmen return for sophomore year. 19% freshmen graduate within 4 years. **Faculty:** Student/faculty ratio 19:1. 731 full-time faculty. 87% faculty teach undergrads.

ACADEMICS

Degrees: Associate, bachelor's, certificate, doctoral, first professional, master's, post-master's certificate. **Academic Requirements:** Arts/fine arts, English (including composition), history, humanities, mathematics, sciences (biological or physical), social science. **Classes:** Most classes have 20–29 students. Most lab/discussion sections have 10–19 students. **Majors with Highest Enrollment:** Elementary education and teaching, nursing/registered nurse training (ASN, BSN, MSN, RN), psychology. **Disciplines with Highest Percentage of Degrees Awarded:** Business/marketing 26%, education 14%, health professions and related sciences 11%, social sciences 9%, psychology 7%. **Special Study Options:** Cooperative education program, cross registration, distance learning, double major, English as a second language (ESL), honors program, independent study, internships, student-designed major, study abroad, teacher certification program.

FACILITIES

Housing: Coed dorms, apartments for married students, apartments for single students, special housing for disabled students, honors dorm. **Special Academic Facilities/Equipment:** Art gallery. **Computers:** Network access in dorm rooms, network access in dorm lounges, online registration, online administrative functions (other than registration), remote student-access to Web through college's connection.

CAMPUS LIFE

Activities: Choral groups, concert band, dance, drama/theater, jazz band, literary magazine, music ensembles, musical theater, opera, pep band, radio station, student government, student newspaper, symphony orchestra, television station. **Organizations:** 145 registered organizations, 9 honor societies, 14 religious organizations. 11 fraternities (2% men join), 7 sororities (2% women join). **Athletics (Intercollegiate):** *Men:* Baseball, basketball, cheerleading, cross-country, diving, golf, soccer, swimming, tennis. *Women:* Basketball, cheerleading, cross-country, diving, soccer, softball, swimming, tennis, track/field (outdoor), volleyball.

ADMISSIONS

Freshman Academic Profile: 15% in top 10% of high school class, 36% in top 25% of high school class, 67% in top 50% of high school class. 85% from public high schools. SAT Math middle 50% range 430–570. SAT Critical Reading middle 50% range 440–550. ACT middle 50% range 18–24. TOEFL required of all international applicants, minimum paper TOEFL 500, minimum computer TOEFL 173. **Basis for Candidate Selection:** *Very important*

factors considered include: Rigor of secondary school record, standardized test scores. *Important factors considered include:* Academic GPA, class rank. *Other factors considered include:* Recommendation(s), state residency. **Freshman Admission Requirements:** High school diploma is required, and GED is accepted. *Academic units required:* 4 English, 3 math, 3 science (3 science labs), 2 foreign language, 3 social studies. **Freshman Admission Statistics:** 5,495 applied, 79% admitted, 51% enrolled. **Transfer Admission Requirements:** College transcript(s). Minimum college GPA of 2.0 required. Lowest grade transferable C. **General Admission Information:** Application fee $30. Regular notification is rolling. Non-fall registration accepted. Admission may be deferred for a maximum of 4 quarters. Credit and/or placement offered for CEEB Advanced Placement tests.

COSTS AND FINANCIAL AID

Annual in-state tuition $7,278. Out-of-state tuition $14,004. Room & board $7,180. Average book expense $1,500. **Required Forms and Deadlines:** FAFSA. Financial aid filing deadline 2/15. **Notification of Awards:** Applicants will be notified of awards on or about 2/15. **Types of Aid:** *Need-based scholarships/grants:* Pell, SEOG, state scholarships/grants, private scholarships, the school's own gift aid, United Negro College Fund, Federal Nursing Scholarships. *Loans:* FFEL Subsidized Stafford, FFEL Unsubsidized Stafford, FFEL PLUS, Federal Perkins, Federal Nursing, state loans, college/university loans from institutional funds. **Student Employment: Financial Aid Statistics:** 37% freshmen, 43% undergrads receive need-based scholarship or grant aid. 74% freshmen, 61% undergrads receive need-based self-help aid. 58 freshmen, 198 undergrads receive athletic scholarships. 60% freshmen, 63% undergrads receive any aid.

XAVIER UNIVERSITY (OH)

3800 Victory Parkway, Cincinnati, OH 45207-5311
Phone: 513-745-3301 **E-mail:** xuadmit@xavier.edu **CEEB Code:** 1965
Fax: 513-745-4319 **Website:** www.xavier.edu **ACT Code:** 3366
Financial Aid Phone: 513-745-3142

This private school, affiliated with the Jesuit order of the Roman Catholic Church, was founded in 1831. It has a 140-acre campus.

RATINGS
Admissions Selectivity Rating: 87   **Fire Safety Rating:** 68   **Green Rating:** 73

STUDENTS AND FACULTY
Enrollment: 3,770. **Student Body:** 57% female, 43% male, 40% out-of-state, 1% international (50 countries represented). African American 11%, Asian 2%, Caucasian 80%, Hispanic 3%. **Retention and Graduation:** 88% freshmen return the sophomore year. 28% grads go on to further study within 2 semesters. 12% grads pursue arts and sciences degrees. 4% grads pursue business degrees. 2% grads pursue law degrees. 6% grads pursue medical degrees. **Faculty:** Student/faculty ratio 13:1. 300 full-time faculty, 80% hold PhDs. 97% faculty teach undergrads.

ACADEMICS
Degrees: Associate, bachelor's, certificate, doctoral, master's, post-bachelor's certificate, post-master's certificate. **Academic Requirements:** Arts/fine arts, cultural diversity, English (including composition), ethics/religion and society, foreign languages, history, mathematics, philosophy, sciences (biological or physical), social science, theology. **Classes:** Most classes have 20–29 students. Most lab/discussion sections have 10–19 students. **Majors with Highest Enrollment:** Education, liberal arts and sciences/liberal studies, marketing/marketing management. **Disciplines with Highest Percentage of Degrees Awarded:** Business/marketing 24%, liberal arts/general studies 17%, communications/journalism 8%, education 8%, health professions and related sciences 6%. **Special Study Options:** Cooperative education program, cross registration, double major, dual enrollment, English as a second language (ESL), honors program, independent study, internships, service learning semester, study abroad, teacher certification program, weekend college.

FACILITIES
Housing: Coed dorms, apartments for single students, theme housing. **Special Academic Facilities/Equipment:** Student-run art gallery, Montessori lab

school. **Computers:** 2% of classrooms are wired, 100% of classrooms are wireless, 85% of public computers are PCs, 15% of public computers are Macs, network access in dorm rooms, network access in dorm lounges, online registration, online administrative functions (other than registration), remote student-access to Web through college's connection.

CAMPUS LIFE
Activities: Choral groups, concert band, dance, drama/theater, jazz band, literary magazine, music ensembles, musical theater, opera, pep band, radio station, student government, student newspaper, student-run film society, television station. **Organizations:** 102 registered organizations, 8 honor societies, 4 religious organizations. **Athletics (Intercollegiate):** *Men:* Baseball, basketball, cross-country, golf, soccer, swimming, tennis, track/field (indoor), track/field (outdoor). *Women:* Basketball, cross-country, golf, soccer, swimming, tennis, track/field (indoor), track/field (outdoor), volleyball. **Environmental Initiatives:** New construction will be required to be LEED Silver.

ADMISSIONS
Freshman Academic Profile: 33% in top 10% of high school class, 63% in top 25% of high school class, 90% in top 50% of high school class. 46% from public high schools. SAT Math middle 50% range 540–640. SAT Critical Reading middle 50% range 530–640. SAT Writing middle 50% range 510–620. ACT middle 50% range 23–29. TOEFL required of all international applicants, minimum paper TOEFL 530, minimum computer TOEFL 197. **Basis for Candidate Selection:** *Very important factors considered include:* Rigor of secondary school record. *Important factors considered include:* Academic GPA, application essay, character/personal qualities, class rank, recommendation(s), standardized test scores. *Other factors considered include:* Alumni/ae relation, extracurricular activities, first generation, level of applicant's interest, talent/ability, volunteer work, work experience. **Freshman Admission Requirements:** High school diploma is required, and GED is accepted. *Academic units recommended:* 4 English, 3 math, 3 science, 2 foreign language, 3 social studies, 5 academic electives, 1 health/physical education. **Freshman Admission Statistics:** 5,500 applied, 72% admitted, 21% enrolled. **Transfer Admission Requirements:** High school transcript, college transcript(s), statement of good standing from prior institution(s). Minimum college GPA of 2.0 required. Lowest grade transferable C. **General Admission Information:** Application fee $35. Regular application deadline 2/1. Regular notification 1/15 and 3/15. Non-fall registration accepted. Admission may be deferred for a maximum of 2 semesters. Credit and/or placement offered for CEEB Advanced Placement tests.

COSTS AND FINANCIAL AID
Average book expense $900. **Required Forms and Deadlines:** FAFSA. Financial aid filing deadline 2/15. **Notification of Awards:** Applicants will be notified of awards on a rolling basis beginning on or about 2/15. **Types of Aid:** *Need-based scholarships/grants:* Pell, SEOG, state scholarships/grants, private scholarships, the school's own gift aid. *Loans:* FFEL Subsidized Stafford, FFEL Unsubsidized Stafford, FFEL PLUS, Federal Perkins. **Student Employment:** Federal Work-Study Program available. Institutional employment available. Off-campus job opportunities are excellent. **Financial Aid Statistics:** 56% freshmen, 52% undergrads receive need-based scholarship or grant aid. 44% freshmen, 41% undergrads receive need-based self-help aid. 37 freshmen, 153 undergrads receive athletic scholarships. 96% freshmen, 96% undergrads receive any aid. Highest amount earned per year from on-campus jobs $7,350.

XAVIER UNIVERSITY OF LOUISIANA

One Drexel Drive, Box 132, New Orleans, LA 70125-1098
Phone: 504-520-7388 **E-mail:** apply@xula.edu **CEEB Code:** 6975
Fax: 504-520-7941 **Website:** www.xula.edu **ACT Code:** 1618
Financial Aid Phone: 504-520-7517

This private school, affiliated with the Roman Catholic Church, was founded in 1915. It has a 29-acre campus.

RATINGS
Admissions Selectivity Rating: 76   **Fire Safety Rating:** 60*   **Green Rating:** 60*

STUDENTS AND FACULTY

Enrollment: 3,290. **Student Body:** 75% female, 25% male, 55% out-of-state, 2% international (8 countries represented). African American 82%, Asian 5%, Caucasian 2%. **Retention and Graduation:** 79% freshmen return for sophomore year. 38% freshmen graduate within 4 years. 46% grads go on to further study within 2 semesters. 14% grads pursue arts and sciences degrees. 2% grads pursue business degrees. 2% grads pursue law degrees. 17% grads pursue medical degrees. **Faculty:** Student/faculty ratio 16:1. 241 full-time faculty, 90% hold PhDs. 98% faculty teach undergrads.

ACADEMICS

Degrees: Bachelor's, first professional, master's, post-master's certificate. **Academic Requirements:** African American studies, arts/fine arts, computer literacy, English (including composition), foreign languages, history, humanities, mathematics, philosophy, sciences (biological or physical), social science. **Classes:** Most classes have 20–29 students. Most lab/discussion sections have 20–29 students. **Majors with Highest Enrollment:** Pre-pharmacy studies, psychology. **Disciplines with Highest Percentage of Degrees Awarded:** Biological/life sciences 40%, psychology 13%, social sciences 9%, business/marketing 8%, communication technologies 6%. **Special Study Options:** Accelerated program, cross registration, double major, exchange student program (domestic), honors program, independent study, internships, study abroad, teacher certification program.

FACILITIES

Housing: Coed dorms, men's dorms, women's dorms. **Computers:** 95% of public computers are PCs, 5% of public computers are Macs, network access in dorm rooms, network access in dorm lounges, online registration, online administrative functions (other than registration), remote student-access to Web through college's connection.

CAMPUS LIFE

Activities: Choral groups, concert band, dance, jazz band, literary magazine, music ensembles, opera, student government, student newspaper, symphony orchestra, television station, yearbook. **Organizations:** 88 registered organizations, 8 honor societies, 1 religious organization. 4 fraternities (1% men join), 4 sororities (3% women join). **Athletics (Intercollegiate):** *Men:* Basketball, cross-country, tennis, track/field (indoor), track/field (outdoor). *Women:* Basketball, cross-country, tennis, track/field (indoor), track/field (outdoor), volleyball.

ADMISSIONS

Freshman Academic Profile: 30% in top 10% of high school class, 55% in top 25% of high school class, 83% in top 50% of high school class. 81% from public high schools. SAT Math middle 50% range 400–550. SAT Critical Reading middle 50% range 400–520. SAT Writing middle 50% range 410–510. ACT middle 50% range 18–23. TOEFL required of all international applicants, minimum paper TOEFL 550. **Basis for Candidate Selection:** *Very important factors considered include:* Recommendation(s), rigor of secondary school record, standardized test scores. *Important factors considered include:* Class rank. *Other factors considered include:* Alumni/ae relation, application essay, character/personal qualities, extracurricular activities, interview, racial/ethnic status, talent/ability, volunteer work, work experience. **Freshman Admission Requirements:** High school diploma is required, and GED is accepted. *Academic units required:* 4 English, 2 math, 1 science, 1 social studies, 8 academic electives. *Academic units recommended:* 4 math, 3 science, 1 foreign language, 2 social studies, 1 history. **Freshman Admission Statistics:** 4,248 applied, 83% admitted, 28% enrolled. **Transfer Admission Requirements:** College transcript(s). Lowest grade transferable C. **General Admission Information:** Application fee $25. Regular application deadline 7/1. Regular notification 4/15. Non-fall registration accepted. Common Application accepted. Credit and/or placement offered for CEEB Advanced Placement tests.

COSTS AND FINANCIAL AID

Annual tuition $13,700. Room and board $6,975. Required fees $1,000. Average book expense $1,200. **Required Forms and Deadlines:** FAFSA. Financial aid filing deadline 1/1. **Notification of Awards:** Applicants will be notified of awards on a rolling basis beginning on or about 4/1. **Types of Aid:** *Need-based scholarships/grants:* Pell, SEOG, state scholarships/grants, private scholarships, the school's own gift aid, United Negro College Fund. *Loans:* Direct Subsidized Stafford, Direct Unsubsidized Stafford, Direct PLUS, FFEL Subsidized Stafford, FFEL Unsubsidized Stafford, FFEL PLUS, Federal Perkins. **Student Employment:** Federal Work-Study Program available. Institutional employment available. Off-campus job opportunities are good. **Financial Aid Statistics:** 44% undergrads receive need-based self-help aid. 15 freshmen, 72 undergrads receive athletic scholarships. 79% freshmen, 84% undergrads receive any aid. Highest amount earned per year from on-campus jobs $1,000.

YALE UNIVERSITY

PO Box 208234, New Haven, CT 06520-8234
Phone: 203-432-9300 **E-mail:** undergraduate.admissions@yale.edu **CEEB Code:** 3987
Fax: 203-432-9392 **Website:** www.yale.edu **ACT Code:** 0618
Financial Aid Phone: 203-432-2700

This private school was founded in 1701. It has a 310-acre campus.

RATINGS

Admissions Selectivity Rating: 99   **Fire Safety Rating:** 60*   **Green Rating:** 99

STUDENTS AND FACULTY

Enrollment: 5,303. **Student Body:** 49% female, 51% male, 93% out-of-state, 8% international (108 countries represented). African American 8%, Asian 13%, Caucasian 50%, Hispanic 8%. **Retention and Graduation:** 99% freshmen return for sophomore year. 27% grads go on to further study within 2 semesters. 9% grads pursue arts and sciences degrees. 6% grads pursue law degrees. 8% grads pursue medical degrees. **Faculty:** 1,121 full-time faculty, 90% hold PhDs.

ACADEMICS

Degrees: Bachelor's, doctoral, first professional, master's, post-master's certificate. **Academic Requirements:** English (including composition), foreign languages, humanities, sciences (biological or physical), social science. **Classes:** Most classes have 10–19 students. **Majors with Highest Enrollment:** Economics, history, political science and government. **Disciplines with Highest Percentage of Degrees Awarded:** Social sciences 26%, history 14%, biological/life sciences 9%, English 9%, interdisciplinary studies 8%, psychology 6%, visual and performing arts 6%. **Special Study Options:** Accelerated program, distance learning, double major, English as a second language (ESL), honors program, independent study, internships, liberal arts/career combination, student-designed major, study abroad, teacher certification program.

FACILITIES

Housing: Coed dorms, special housing for disabled students, residential colleges. **Special Academic Facilities/Equipment:** Art and history museums, observatory, electron microscopes, nuclear accelerators, center for international and areas studies, child study center, Marsh Botanical Gardens, center for parallel supercomputing. **Computers:** Network access in dorm rooms, online registration, online administrative functions (other than registration), remote student-access to Web through college's connection.

CAMPUS LIFE

Activities: Choral groups, concert band, dance, drama/theater, jazz band, literary magazine, marching band, music ensembles, musical theater, opera, pep band, radio station, student government, student newspaper, student-run film society, symphony orchestra, television station. **Organizations:** 200 registered organizations. **Athletics (Intercollegiate):** *Men:* Baseball, basketball, crew/rowing, cross-country, diving, fencing, football, golf, ice hockey, lacrosse, sailing, soccer, squash, swimming, tennis, track/field (indoor), track/field (outdoor). *Women:* Basketball, crew/rowing, cross-country, diving, fencing, field hockey, golf, gymnastics, ice hockey, lacrosse, sailing, soccer, softball, squash, swimming, tennis, track/field (indoor), track/field (outdoor), volleyball.

ADMISSIONS

Freshman Academic Profile: 95% in top 10% of high school class. 55% from public high schools. SAT Math middle 50% range 690–790. SAT Critical Reading middle 50% range 700–780. ACT middle 50% range 31–34. TOEFL required of all international applicants, minimum paper TOEFL 600, minimum computer TOEFL 250. **Basis for Candidate Selection:** *Very important factors considered include:* Academic GPA, application essay, character/personal qualities, class rank, extracurricular activities, recommendation(s), rigor of secondary school record, standardized test scores, talent/ability. *Other factors considered include:* Alumni/ae relation, first generation, geographical residence, interview, level of applicant's interest, racial/ethnic status, state residency, volunteer work, work experience. **Freshman Admission Statistics:** 21,101 applied, 9% admitted, 70% enrolled. **Transfer Admission Requirements:** High school transcript, college transcript(s), essay or personal statement, standardized test score, statement of good standing from prior institution(s). Lowest grade transferable C. **General Admission Information:** Application fee $75. Regular application deadline 12/31. Regular notification 4/1. Non-fall registration not accepted. Admission may be deferred for a maximum of 2 semesters. Placement offered for CEEB Advanced Placement tests.

COSTS AND FINANCIAL AID

Annual tuition $34,530. Room and board $10,470. Average book expense $2,700. **Required Forms and Deadlines:** FAFSA, CSS/Financial Aid PROFILE, Noncustodial PROFILE, Business/Farm Supplement, parent tax returns. Financial aid filing deadline 3/1. **Notification of Awards:** Applicants will be notified of awards on or about 4/1. **Types of Aid:** *Need-based scholarships/grants:* Pell, SEOG, state scholarships/grants, private scholarships, the school's own gift aid, United Negro College Fund. *Loans:* FFEL Subsidized Stafford, FFEL Unsubsidized Stafford, FFEL PLUS, Federal Perkins, state loans, college/university loans from institutional funds. **Financial Aid Statistics:** 42% freshmen, 41% undergrads receive need-based scholarship or grant aid. 44% freshmen, 42% undergrads receive need-based self-help aid.

YESHIVA UNIVERSITY

500 West 185th Street, New York, NY 10033-3299
Phone: 212-960-5277 **E-mail:** yuadmit@yu.edu **CEEB Code:** 2990
Fax: 212-960-0086 **Website:** www.yu.edu **ACT Code:** 2992
Financial Aid Phone: 212-960-5269

This private school was founded in 1886. It has a 12-acre campus.

RATINGS
Admissions Selectivity Rating: 60*   **Fire Safety Rating:** 60*   **Green Rating:** 60*

STUDENTS AND FACULTY

Enrollment: 1,970. **Student Body:** 55% out-of-state, 4% international (53 countries represented). Caucasian 100%. **Retention and Graduation:** 85% freshmen return for sophomore year. **Faculty:** 100% faculty teach undergrads.

ACADEMICS

Degrees: Bachelor's, doctoral, master's. **Majors with Highest Enrollment:** Jewish/Judaic studies, political science and government, psychology. **Special Study Options:** Honors program, study abroad.

FACILITIES

Housing: Men's dorms, women's dorms, apartments for married students, apartments for single students. **Special Academic Facilities/Equipment:** Archives and rare book collection; Museum of Jewish Art, Architecture, History, and Culture.

CAMPUS LIFE

Activities: Choral groups, drama/theater, music ensembles, radio station, student government, student newspaper, yearbook. **Athletics (Intercollegiate):** *Men:* Basketball, fencing, tennis, volleyball. *Women:* Basketball, tennis.

ADMISSIONS

Freshman Academic Profile: TOEFL required of all international applicants, minimum paper TOEFL 500. **Freshman Admission Requirements:** High school diploma is required, and GED is accepted. *Academic units required:* 4 English, 2 math, 2 science, 2 foreign language, 2 history, 4 academic electives. **Freshman Admission Statistics:** 1,768 applied, 78% admitted, 68% enrolled. **Transfer Admission Requirements:** Minimum college GPA of 3.0 required. Lowest grade transferable C. **General Admission Information:** Application fee $40. Regular application deadline 2/15. Regular notification rolling. Non-fall registration accepted. Common Application not accepted. Credit and/or placement offered for CEEB Advanced Placement tests.

COSTS AND FINANCIAL AID

Annual tuition $19,065. Room & board $6,426. Required fees $445. Average book expense $800. **Required Forms and Deadlines:** FAFSA, institution's own financial aid form, CSS/Financial Aid PROFILE, state aid form, Noncustodial PROFILE, Business/Farm Supplement. Financial aid filing deadline 3/15. **Types of Aid:** *Need-based scholarships/grants:* Pell, SEOG, state scholarships/grants, private scholarships, the school's own gift aid. *Loans:* FFEL Subsidized Stafford, FFEL Unsubsidized Stafford, FFEL PLUS, Federal Perkins, college/university loans from institutional funds. **Student Employment:** Federal Work-Study Program available. Institutional employment

available. Off-campus job opportunities are good. **Financial Aid Statistics:** 41% freshmen, 40% undergrads receive need-based scholarship or grant aid. 35% freshmen, 32% undergrads receive need-based self-help aid. Highest amount earned per year from on-campus jobs $500.

YORK COLLEGE OF PENNSYLVANIA

Country Club Road, York, PA 17405-7199
Phone: 717-849-1600 **E-mail:** admissions@ycp.edu **CEEB Code:** 2991
Fax: 717-849-1607 **Website:** www.ycp.edu **ACT Code:** 3762
Financial Aid Phone: 717-849-1682

This private school was founded in 1787. It has a 125-acre campus.

RATINGS
Admissions Selectivity Rating: 79   **Fire Safety Rating:** 92   **Green Rating:** 60*

STUDENTS AND FACULTY

Enrollment: 5,367. **Student Body:** 57% female, 43% male, 39% out-of-state. African American 1%, Asian 1%, Caucasian 69%, Hispanic 1%. **Retention and Graduation:** 80% freshmen return for sophomore year. 41% freshmen graduate within 4 years. 25% grads go on to further study within 2 semesters. 7% grads pursue arts and sciences degrees. 14% grads pursue business degrees. 2% grads pursue law degrees. 2% grads pursue medical degrees. **Faculty:** Student/faculty ratio 15:1. 145 full-time faculty, 83% hold PhDs. 100% faculty teach undergrads.

ACADEMICS

Degrees: Associate, bachelor's, master's. **Academic Requirements:** Arts/fine arts, computer literacy, English (including composition), history, humanities, mathematics, sciences (biological or physical), social science. **Classes:** Most classes have 20–29 students. Most lab/discussion sections have 10–19 students. **Majors with Highest Enrollment:** Business administration/management, criminal justice/law enforcement administration, nursing/registered nurse training (ASN, BSN, MSN, RN). **Disciplines with Highest Percentage of Degrees Awarded:** Business/marketing 18%, health professions and related sciences 15%, education 12%, communications/journalism 10%, social sciences 10%, security and protective services 7%. **Special Study Options:** Cooperative education program, distance learning, double major, dual enrollment, honors program, independent study, internships, liberal arts/career combination, student-designed major, study abroad, teacher certification program.

FACILITIES

Housing: Coed dorms, men's dorms, women's dorms, apartments for single students, minidorms featuring units of 10 students, suites, sponsored houses and apartments. **Special Academic Facilities/Equipment:** Museum, telecommunications center, science and foreign language labs. **Computers:** 20% of classrooms are wired, 15% of classrooms are wireless, 95% of public computers are PCs, 5% of public computers are Macs, 100% of public computers are UNIX, network access in dorm rooms, network access in dorm lounges, online registration, online administrative functions (other than registration), remote student-access to Web through college's connection.

CAMPUS LIFE

Activities: Choral groups, concert band, drama/theater, jazz band, literary magazine, music ensembles, musical theater, radio station, student government, student newspaper, symphony orchestra, television station, yearbook. **Organizations:** 80 registered organizations, 7 honor societies, 4 religious organizations. 10 fraternities (8% men join), 7 sororities (7% women join). **Athletics (Intercollegiate):** *Men:* Baseball, basketball, cheerleading, cross-country, golf, lacrosse, soccer, swimming, tennis, track/field (outdoor), wrestling. *Women:* Basketball, cheerleading, cross-country, field hockey, lacrosse, soccer, softball, swimming, tennis, track/field (outdoor), volleyball.

ADMISSIONS

Freshman Academic Profile: 18% in top 10% of high school class, 28% in top 25% of high school class, 65% in top 50% of high school class. 80% from public high schools. SAT Math middle 50% range 500–600. SAT Critical Reading middle 50% range 490–580. SAT Writing middle 50% range 480–570. ACT middle 50% range 19–24. TOEFL required of all international applicants, minimum paper TOEFL 530, minimum computer TOEFL 200. **Basis for Candidate Selection:** *Very important factors considered include:* Rigor of secondary school record. *Important factors considered include:* Character/personal qualities, class rank, standardized test scores. *Other factors considered include:* Alumni/ae relation, application essay, extracurricular activities, interview, recommendation(s), talent/ability, volunteer work, work experience.

Freshman Admission Requirements: High school diploma is required, and GED is accepted. *Academic units required:* 4 English, 3 math, 3 science, 2 foreign language, 3 social studies. *Academic units recommended:* 4 math. **Freshman Admission Statistics:** 4,856 applied, 66% admitted, 35% enrolled. **Transfer Admission Requirements:** College transcript(s). Minimum college GPA of 2.0 required. Lowest grade transferable C. **General Admission Information:** Application fee $30. Regular notification is rolling. Non-fall registration accepted. Credit and/or placement offered for CEEB Advanced Placement tests.

COSTS AND FINANCIAL AID

Annual tuition $11,500. Room and board $7,410. Required fees $1,250. Average book expense $1,000. **Required Forms and Deadlines:** FAFSA. **Notification of Awards:** Applicants will be notified of awards on a rolling basis beginning on or about 2/15. **Types of Aid:** *Need-based scholarships/grants:* Pell, SEOG, state scholarships/grants, private scholarships, the school's own gift aid. *Loans:* Direct Subsidized Stafford, Direct Unsubsidized Stafford, Direct PLUS, FFEL Subsidized Stafford, FFEL Unsubsidized Stafford, FFEL PLUS, Federal Perkins, Federal Nursing, state loans, college/university loans from institutional funds. **Student Employment:** Federal Work-Study Program available. Institutional employment available. Off-campus job opportunities are good. **Financial Aid Statistics:** 38% freshmen, 35% undergrads receive need-based scholarship or grant aid. 48% freshmen, 47% undergrads receive need-based self-help aid. 85% freshmen, 74% undergrads receive any aid. Highest amount earned per year from on-campus jobs $1,200.

YORK UNIVERSITY

N300 Student Services Centre, Toronto, ON M3J 1P3 Canada
Phone: 416-736-5000 **E-mail:** intlenq@yorku.ca **CEEB Code:** 894
Fax: 416-736-5536 **Website:** www.yorku.ca
Financial Aid Phone: 416-872-9675

This public school was founded in 1959. It has a 550-acre campus.

RATINGS

Admissions Selectivity Rating: 60*   **Fire Safety Rating:** 60*   **Green Rating:** 60*

STUDENTS AND FACULTY

Enrollment: 45,895. **Student Body:** 62% female, 38% male, 3% out-of-province. **Faculty:** Student/faculty ratio 17:1. 1,415 full-time faculty, 100% hold PhDs. 100% faculty teach undergrads.

ACADEMICS

Degrees: Bachelor's, certificate, diploma, doctoral, first professional, master's, post-bachelor's certificate. **Academic Requirements:** Humanities, sciences (biological or physical), social science. **Majors with Highest Enrollment:** Business/commerce, psychology, visual and performing arts. **Disciplines with Highest Percentage of Degrees Awarded:** Liberal arts/general studies 30%, psychology 13%, education 12%, business/marketing 9%, English 5%, visual and performing arts 5%. **Special Study Options:** Accelerated program, distance learning, double major, English as a second language (ESL), exchange student program (domestic), honors program, independent study, internships, student-designed major, study abroad, teacher certification program.

FACILITIES

Housing: Coed dorms, apartments for married students, special housing for disabled students, cooperative housing, some women-only or men-only floors. **Special Academic Facilities/Equipment:** 5 museums, observatory with 2 telescopes, robotics laboratory, 2 art galleries, 6 student-run art exhibition spaces, 3 theatres, 2 cinemas, 1 screening room, wide-variety professional standard film and video production facilities. **Computers:** 80% of public computers are PCs, 10% of public computers are Macs, 10% of public computers are UNIX, network access in dorm rooms, online registration, online administrative functions (other than registration), remote student-access to Web through college's connection.

CAMPUS LIFE

Activities: Choral groups, concert band, dance, drama/theater, jazz band, literary magazine, music ensembles, musical theater, radio station, student government, student newspaper, student-run film society, symphony orchestra, yearbook. **Organizations:** 259 registered organizations, 35 religious organizations. **Athletics (Intercollegiate):** *Men:* Badminton, basketball, cross-country, fencing, football, ice hockey, soccer, swimming, tennis, track/field (outdoor), volleyball, water polo. *Women:* Badminton, basketball, cross-country, fencing, field hockey, ice hockey, soccer, swimming, tennis, track/field (outdoor), volleyball, water polo.

ADMISSIONS

Freshman Academic Profile: TOEFL required of all international applicants, minimum paper TOEFL 560, minimum computer TOEFL 220. **Basis for Candidate Selection:** *Very important factors considered include:* Academic GPA, rigor of secondary school record. *Important factors considered include:* Standardized test scores. *Other factors considered include:* Class rank, interview. **Freshman Admission Requirements:** High school diploma is required, and GED is not accepted. **Transfer Admission Requirements:** College transcript(s). **General Admission Information:** Application fee $60. Regular application deadline 2/1. Regular notification is rolling. Non-fall registration accepted. Admission may be deferred for a maximum of 2 semesters. Common Application not accepted. Credit offered for CEEB Advanced Placement tests.

COSTS AND FINANCIAL AID

Annual in-state tuition $4,544. Annual out-of-state tuition $4,544. Room and board $5,154. Required fees $125. Average book expense $1,000. **Student Employment:** Institutional employment available. Off-campus job opportunities are good.

YOUNGSTOWN STATE UNIVERSITY

One University Plaza, Youngstown, OH 44555
Phone: 330-941-2000 **E-mail:** enroll@ysu.edu **CEEB Code:** 1975
Fax: 330-941-3674 **Website:** www.ysu.edu **ACT Code:** 3368
Financial Aid Phone: 330-941-3505

This public school was founded in 1908. It has a 200-acre campus.

RATINGS

Admissions Selectivity Rating: 71   **Fire Safety Rating:** 90   **Green Rating:** 77

STUDENTS AND FACULTY

Enrollment: 11,712. **Student Body:** 54% female, 46% male, 9% out-of-state. African American 13%, Caucasian 75%, Hispanic 2%. **Retention and Graduation:** 73% freshmen return for sophomore year. 13% freshmen graduate within 4 years. **Faculty:** Student/faculty ratio 18:1. 426 full-time faculty, 84% hold PhDs.

ACADEMICS

Degrees: Associate, bachelor's, certificate, diploma, doctoral, master's, post-bachelor's certificate. **Academic Requirements:** Arts/fine arts, English (including composition), health, humanities, mathematics, physical education, sciences (biological or physical), social science. **Classes:** Most classes have 20–29 students. Most lab/discussion sections have fewer than 10 students. **Majors with Highest Enrollment:** Business administration/management, elementary education and teaching, nursing/registered nurse training (ASN, BSN, MSN, RN). **Disciplines with Highest Percentage of Degrees Awarded:** Education 22%, business/marketing 17%, health professions and related sciences 10%, engineering 6%, security and protective services 6%. **Special Study Options:** Accelerated program, cooperative education program, cross registration, distance learning, double major, English as a second language (ESL), exchange student program (domestic), honors program, internships, off campus study with Lorain Country Community College, student-designed major, study abroad, teacher certification program, weekend college.

FACILITIES

Housing: Coed dorms, women's dorms, apartments for single students, fraternity/sorority housing, honors housing. **Special Academic Facilities/Equipment:** Art museum, human services development center, engineering services center, planetarium, center for urban studies, industrial development center. **Computers:** 15% of classrooms are wireless, 100% of public computers are PCs, 10% of public computers are Macs, 1% of public computers are UNIX, network access in dorm rooms, network access in dorm lounges, online registration, online administrative functions (other than registration), remote student-access to Web through college's connection.

CAMPUS LIFE

Activities: Choral groups, concert band, dance, drama/theater, jazz band, literary magazine, marching band, music ensembles, musical theater, opera, pep band, radio station, student government, student newspaper, student-run film society, symphony orchestra, yearbook. **Organizations:** 151 registered organizations, 36 honor societies, 12 religious organizations. 9 fraternities (3% men join), 6 sororities (1% women join). **Athletics (Intercollegiate):** *Men:* Baseball, basketball, cross-country, football, golf, tennis, track/field (outdoor). *Women:* Basketball, cross-country, golf, soccer, softball, swimming, tennis, track/field (outdoor), volleyball.

ADMISSIONS

Freshman Academic Profile: 9% in top 10% of high school class, 25% in top 25% of high school class, 54% in top 50% of high school class. SAT Math middle 50% range 410–550. SAT Critical Reading middle 50% range 400–550. ACT middle 50% range 17–23. TOEFL required of all international applicants, minimum paper TOEFL 500, minimum computer TOEFL 173. **Basis for Candidate Selection:** *Important factors considered include:* Class rank, rigor of secondary school record, standardized test scores. **Freshman Admission Requirements:** High school diploma is required, and GED is accepted. *Academic units recommended:* 4 English, 3 math, 3 science (1 science lab), 2 foreign language, 3 social studies, 1 fine and performing art. **Freshman Admission Statistics:** 4,219 applied, 78% admitted, 70% enrolled. **Transfer Admission Requirements:** High school transcript, college transcript(s), minimum college GPA of 2.0 required. Lowest grade transferable D. **General Admission Information:** Application fee $30. Regular application deadline 8/15. Non-fall registration accepted. Admission may be deferred for a maximum of 2 semesters. Credit and/or placement offered for CEEB Advanced Placement tests.

COSTS AND FINANCIAL AID

Annual in-state tuition $6,492. Annual out-of-state tuition $12,165. Room and board $6,740. Required fees $229. Average book expense $1,057. **Required Forms and Deadlines:** FAFSA, institution's own financial aid form. Financial aid filing deadline 2/15. **Notification of Awards:** Applicants will be notified of awards on a rolling basis beginning on or about 5/30. **Types of Aid:** *Need-based scholarships/grants:* Pell, SEOG, state scholarships/grants, private scholarships, the school's own gift aid. *Loans:* FFEL Subsidized Stafford, FFEL Unsubsidized Stafford, FFEL PLUS, Federal Perkins, state loans. **Financial Aid Statistics:** 87% freshmen, 83% undergrads receive any aid.

ONLINE SCHOOLS

ALASKA PACIFIC UNIVERSITY

4101 University Drive, Anchorage, AK, 99508
Contact: Esther Beth Sullivan, Director of Distance Education
Contact Phone: 907-564-8355 **Contact E-mail:** rana@alaskapacific.edu
Website: http://rana.alaskapacific.edu

GENERAL INFORMATION
School type: Private.
Alaska Pacific University offers both online and on-campus degree programs. Institution is accredited by Northwest Commission on Colleges and Universities. Online programs follow the same semester calendar as on-campus programs. All or most programs can be completed entirely online. Students can transfer from online to on-campus programs and from on-campus to online programs. There is no difference between physical diplomas awarded by online programs and those awarded by on-campus programs.

ALLEN COLLEGE

1825 Logan Avenue, Waterloo, IA, 50704
Contact: Molly Quinn, Recruiter
Contact Phone: 319-226-2000 **Contact E-mail:** Quinnme@ihs.org
Website: www.allencollege.edu

GENERAL INFORMATION
School type: Private.
Allen College offers both online and on-campus degree programs. Institution is accredited by NCA-HLC. Online programs follow the same semester calendar as on-campus programs. All or most programs can be completed entirely online. Students can transfer from online to on-campus programs and from on-campus to online programs. There is no difference between physical diplomas awarded by online programs and those awarded by on-campus programs.

AMERICAN MILITARY UNIVERSITY

111 West Congress Street, Charles Town, WV, 25414
Contact: Terry Grant, Director of Admissions
Contact Phone: 877-468-6268 **Contact E-mail:** info@apus.edu
Website: www.amu.apus.edu

GENERAL INFORMATION
School type: Private.
American Military University offers only online degree programs. Institution is accredited by the Higher Learning Commission, North Central Association, and the Distance Education and Training Council. All degrees can be completed entirely online.

AMERICAN PUBLIC UNIVERSITY SYSTEM

111 West Congress Street, Charles Town, WV, 25414
Contact: Office of Admissions
Contact Phone: 877-468-6268 **Contact E-mail:** info@apus.edu
Website: www.apus.edu

GENERAL INFORMATION
School type: Proprietary.
American Public University System offers only online degree programs. Institution is accredited by North Central Association of Colleges and Schools. All degrees can be completed entirely online.

AMERICAN SENTINEL UNIVERSITY

2101 Magnolia Avenue, Suite 200, Birmingham, AL, 35205
Contact: Natalie Nixon, Director of Admissions
Contact Phone: 205-458-4181 **Contact E-mail:** natalie.nixon@americansentinel.edu
Website: www.americansentinel.edu

GENERAL INFORMATION
School type: Private.
American Sentinel University offers only online degree programs. Institution is accredited by DETC—Distance Education and Training Council. All degrees can be completed entirely online.

ARKANSAS TECH UNIVERSITY

Doc Bryan Student Center, Arkansas Tech University, Russellville, AR, 72801
Contact: Shauna Donnell, Director/Assistant VP of Enrollment Management
Contact Phone: 800-582-6953 **Contact E-mail:** tech.enroll@atu.edu
Website: http://admissions.atu.edu

GENERAL INFORMATION
School type: Public.
Arkansas Tech University offers both online and on-campus degree programs. Institution is accredited by NCA/HLC. Online programs follow the same semester calendar as on-campus programs. All or most programs can be completed entirely online. Students can transfer from online to on-campus programs and from on-campus to online programs. There is no difference between physical diplomas awarded by online programs and those awarded by on-campus programs.

AUBURN MONTGOMERY

PO Box 244023, Montgomery, AL, 36124-4023
Contact: Jeffrey Barksdale, Director, Clinical Laboratory Sciences
Contact Phone: 334-244-3606 **Contact E-mail:** jbarksdale@mail.aum.edu
Website: www.aum.edu

GENERAL INFORMATION
School type: Public.
Auburn Montgomery offers both online and on-campus degree programs. Institution is accredited by SACS. Online programs follow the same semester calendar as on-campus programs. All or most programs can be completed entirely online. Students cannot transfer from online to on-campus programs, nor from on-campus to online programs. There is no difference between physical diplomas awarded by online programs and those awarded by on-campus programs.

BAKER COLLEGE ONLINE

1116 West Bristol Road, Flint, MI, 48507
Contact: Chuck Gurden, Vice President for Admissions
Contact Phone: 810-766-4390 **Contact E-mail:** chuck@baker.edu
Website: www.bakercollegeonline.com

GENERAL INFORMATION
School type: Private.
Baker College Online offers both online and on-campus degree programs. Institution is accredited by Higher Learning Comission. Online programs follow the same semester calendar as on-campus programs. All or most programs can be completed entirely online. Students can transfer from online to on-campus programs and from on-campus to online programs. There is no difference between physical diplomas awarded by online programs and those awarded by on-campus programs.

BALL STATE UNIVERSITY

School of Extended Education, Carmichael Hall, Room 200, Muncie, IN, 47306
Contact: Diane Watters, Director of Marketing
Contact Phone: 800-872-0369 **Contact E-mail:** distance@bsu.edu
Website: www.bsu.edu/distance

GENERAL INFORMATION
School type: Public.
Ball State University offers both online and on-campus degree programs. Institution is accredited by North Central Association of Colleges and Schools. Online programs calendar differs from on-campus programs in that, at the undergraduate level, the complete programs that we offer online are facilitated through the Independent Learning Program. These courses have open enrollment periods. All or most programs can be completed entirely online. Students can transfer from online to on-campus programs and from on-campus to online programs. There is no difference between physical diplomas awarded by online programs and those awarded by on-campus programs.

BAPTIST COLLEGE OF FLORIDA

5400 College Drive, Graceville, FL, 32440
Contact: David Coggins, Director of Distance Learning
Contact Phone: 850-263-3261, ext. 482
Contact E-mail: jdcoggins@baptistcollege.edu
Website: www.baptistcollege.edu

GENERAL INFORMATION
School type: Private.
Baptist College of Florida offers both online and on-campus degree programs. Institution is accredited by Southern Association of Colleges and Schools. Online programs follow the same semester calendar as on-campus programs. Most programs cannot be completed entirely online. General Education not offered online. Students can transfer from online to on-campus programs and from on-campus to online programs. There is no difference between physical diplomas awarded by online programs and those awarded by on-campus programs.

BERKELEY COLLEGE

44 Rifle Camp Road, West Paterson, NJ, 7424
Contact: Susan Mandra, Director of Online Admissions
Contact Phone: 800-446-5400 **Contact E-mail:** online@berkeleycollege.edu
Website: www.berkeleycollege.edu/Online/INDEX.HTM

GENERAL INFORMATION
School type: Proprietary.
Berkeley College offers both online and on-campus degree programs. Institution is accredited by Middle States Commission on Higher Education. Online programs follow the same semester calendar as on-campus programs. All or most programs can be completed entirely online. Students can transfer from online to on-campus programs and from on-campus to online programs. There is no difference between physical diplomas awarded by online programs and those awarded by on-campus programs.

BRENAU UNIVERSITY THE WOMEN'S COLLEGE

Brenau University, 500 Washington Street Southeast, Gainesville, GA, 30501
Contact: Dr. Heather Gibbons, Associate VP for IT and Online Studies
Contact Phone: 770-718-5328 **Contact E-mail:** hgibbons@brenau.edu
Website: http://online.brenau.edu

GENERAL INFORMATION
School type: Private.
Brenau University offers both online and on-campus degree programs. Institution is accredited by Commission on Colleges of the Southern Association of Colleges and Schools (SACS). The online programs calendar differs from on-campus programs in that the Brenau University schedule is semester based. Courses in the Online College are typically offered in one of two 7-week sessions per semester (two 6-week sessions in the summer semester). Some courses will last for 14 weeks. All or most programs can be completed entirely online. Students can transfer from online to on-campus programs and from on-campus to online programs. There is no difference between physical diplomas awarded by online programs and those awarded by on-campus programs.

BUENA VISTA UNIVERSITY

610 West Fourth Street, Storm Lake, IA, 50588
Contact: Laura Harris, Online Student Services Coordinator
Contact Phone: 877-288-0423 **Contact E-mail:** harrisl@bvu.edu
Website: www.bvuonline.org

GENERAL INFORMATION
School type: Private.
Buena Vista University offers both online and on-campus degree programs. Institution is accredited by NCA. Online programs calendar differs from on-campus programs in that there are 8-week terms (2 terms equals 1 semester). Most programs cannot be completed entirely online. Degree completion only. Students can transfer from online to on-campus programs and from on-campus to online programs. There is no difference between physical diplomas awarded by online programs and those awarded by on-campus programs.

CAL STATE UNIVERSITY, SAN BERNARDINO

5500 University Parkway, PL-254, San Bernardino, CA, 92407
Contact: Dr. James Monaghan, Director
Contact Phone: 909-537-7439 **Contact E-mail:** odl@csusb.edu
Website: http://odl.csusb.edu

GENERAL INFORMATION
School type: Public.
Cal State University, San Bernardino offers both online and on-campus degree programs. Institution is accredited by WASC. Online programs follow the same semester calendar as on-campus programs. All or most programs can be completed entirely online. Students can transfer from online to on-campus programs and from on-campus to online programs. There is no difference between physical diplomas awarded by online programs and those awarded by on-campus programs.

CALIFORNIA UNIVERSITY OF PENNSYLVANIA

250 University Avenue, Box 105, California, PA, 15419
Contact: Millie Rodriguez, Director, Office of Web-Based Programs
Contact Phone: 724-983-5958 **Contact E-mail:** calugo@cup.edu
Website: www.cup.edu/go

GENERAL INFORMATION
School type: Public.
California University of Pennsylvania offers both online and on-campus degree programs. Institution is accredited by Commission on Higher Education of the Middle States Association of Colleges and Secondary Schools. Online programs follow the same semester calendar as on-campus programs. All or most programs can be completed entirely online. Students can transfer from online to on-campus programs and from on-campus to online programs. There is no difference between physical diplomas awarded by online programs and those awarded by on-campus programs.

CALIFORNIA UNIVERSITY OF PENNSYLVANIA

250 University Avenue, Box 105, California, PA, 15419
Contact: Millie Rodriguez, Director Office of Web-Based Programs
Contact Phone: 724-983-5958 **Contact E-mail:** calugo@cup.edu
Website: www.cup.edu/go

GENERAL INFORMATION
School type: Public.
California University of Pennsylvania offers both online and on-campus degree programs. Institution is accredited by Commission on Higher Education of the Middle States Association of Colleges and Secondary Schools. Online programs follow the same semester calendar as on-campus programs. All or most programs can be completed entirely online. Students can transfer from online to on-campus programs and from on-campus to online programs. There is no difference between physical diplomas awarded by online programs and those awarded by on-campus programs.

CAMPBELLSVILLE UNIVERSITY

Campbellsville University, One University Drive, Campbellsville, KY, 42718
Contact: Ms. Karla Deaton, Coordinator of Extended Programs
Contact Phone: 270-789-5078 **Contact E-mail:** krdeaton@campbellsville.edu
Website: www.campbellsville.edu

GENERAL INFORMATION
School type: Private.
Campbellsville University offers both online and on-campus degree programs. Institution is accredited by Southern Association of Colleges. Online programs follow the same semester calendar as on-campus programs. All or most programs can be completed entirely online. Students can transfer from online to on-campus programs and from on-campus to online programs. There is no difference between physical diplomas awarded by online programs and those awarded by on-campus programs.

CENTER FOR EXTENDED LEARNING

Bemidji State University, 1500 Birchmont Drive Northeast #4, Bemidji, MN, 56601
Contact: Center for Extended Learning
Contact Phone: 218-755-2068 **Contact E-mail:** cel@bemidjistate.edu
Website: http://distance.bemidjistate.edu

GENERAL INFORMATION
School type: Public.
Center for Extended Learning offers only online degree programs. Institution is accredited by Higher Learning Commission—NCA. All degrees can be completed entirely online.

CENTRAL MICHIGAN UNIVERSITY

Off Campus Programs, Central Michigan Universtiy, Mount Pleasant, MI, 48859
Contact: Kendra Brown, Associate Director, Student Services
Contact Phone: 800-688-4268 **Contact E-mail:** help-ddl@cmich.edu
Website: www.cel.cmich.edu/ecampus

GENERAL INFORMATION
School type: Public.
Central Michigan University offers both online and on-campus degree programs. Institution is accredited by North Central Association of Colleges and Schools. Online programs calendar differs from on-campus programs in that it offers 8-week compressed terms (5 total). Most programs cannot be completed entirely online. Additional online courses are being developed. Students can transfer from online to on-campus programs and from on-campus to online programs. There is no difference between physical diplomas awarded by online programs and those awarded by on-campus programs.

CHARTER OAK STATE COLLEGE

55 Paul Manafort Drive, New Britain, CT, 6053
Contact: Lori Pendleton, Director of Admissions
Contact Phone: 860-832-3800 **Contact E-mail:** info@charteroak.edu
Website: www.charteroak.edu/Prospective/Admissions

GENERAL INFORMATION
School type: Public.
Charter Oak State College offers only online degree programs. Institution is accredited by New England Association of Schools and Colleges. All degrees can be completed entirely online.

CHATHAM COLLEGE

Woodland Road, Pittsburgh, PA 15232
Contact: Jenna Godfrey, Program Coordinator, Enrollment Services
Contact Phone: Contact E-mail: sce@chathame.du
Website: http://chathamonline.info

GENERAL INFORMATION
School type: Private.
Chatham College offers both online and on-campus degree programs. Institution is accredited by Middle States. Online programs calendar differs from on-campus programs in that two 7-week sessions are offered each fall and spring; there is one 7-week summer session. All or most programs can be completed entirely online. Students cannot transfer from online to on-campus programs, nor from on-campus to online programs. There is no difference between physical diplomas awarded by online programs and those awarded by on-campus programs.

CLARION UNIVERSITY OF PENNSYLVANIA

Extended Programs, 840 Wood Street, Clarion, PA, 16214
Contact: Lynne M. Lander Fleisher, Associate Director
Contact Phone: 814-393-2774 **Contact E-mail:** lfleisher@clarion.edu
Website: www.clarion.edu/academic/distance/index.shtml

GENERAL INFORMATION

School type: Public.
Clarion University of Pennsylvania offers both online and on-campus degree programs. The Institution is accredited by the Pennsylvania Department of Education and the Middle States Commission. Online programs follow the same semester calendar as on-campus programs. All or most programs can be completed entirely online. Students can transfer from online to on-campus programs and from on-campus to online programs. There is no difference between physical diplomas awarded by online programs and those awarded by on-campus programs.

COLORADO STATE UNIVERSITY

Spruce Hall, 1040 Campus Delivery, Fort Collins, CO, 80523-1040
Contact: Frances Betts, Assistant to Program Director
Contact Phone: 970-491-0675 **Contact E-mail:** frances.betts@colostate.edu
Website: www.learn.colostate.edu

GENERAL INFORMATION

School type: Public.
Colorado State University offers both online and on-campus degree programs. Institution is accredited by North Central Association of Colleges and Schools. Online programs follow the same semester calendar as on-campus programs. Most programs cannot be completed entirely online. The final 2 years of the degree completion is entirely online. Students can transfer from online to on-campus programs and from on-campus to online programs. There is no difference between physical diplomas awarded by online programs and those awarded by on-campus programs.

COLLEGE OF MOUNT SAINT JOSEPH

5701 Delhi Road, Cincinnati, OH, 45233-1670
Contact: Peggy Minnich, Director of Admission
Contact Phone: 513-244-4814 **Contact E-mail:** admissions@mail.msj.edu
Website: www.msj.edu/admission/apply/online/index.asp

GENERAL INFORMATION

School type: Private.
College of Mount Saint Joseph offers both online and on-campus degree programs. Institution is accredited by North Central Association of Colleges and Schools. Online programs follow the same semester calendar as on-campus programs. All or most programs can be completed entirely online. Students can transfer from online to on-campus programs and from on-campus to online programs. There is no difference between physical diplomas awarded by online programs and those awarded by on-campus programs.

COLUMBIA COLLEGE

1001 Rogers Street, Columbia, MO, 65201
Contact: Cindy Dunn, Prospect Coordinator
Contact Phone: 800-231-2391, ext. 7246 **Contact E-mail:** onlinecampus@ccis.edu
Website: www.ccis.edu/online

GENERAL INFORMATION

School type: Private.
Columbia College offers both online and on-campus degree programs. Institution is accredited by North Central Association (HLC). Online programs calendar differs from on-campus programs calendar in that the online program is offered five times annually, in 8-week sessions. All or most programs can be completed entirely online. Students can transfer from online to on-campus programs and from on-campus to online programs. There is no difference between physical diplomas awarded by online programs and those awarded by on-campus programs.

COLLEGE OF THE SOUTHWEST

6610 Lovington Highway, Hobbs, NM, 88240
Contact: Kerrie Mitchell, Coordinator of Financial Aid and Admission
Contact Phone: 505-392-6563 **Contact E-mail:** kmitchell@csw.edu
Website: www.csw.edu

GENERAL INFORMATION

School type: Private.
College of the Southwest offers both online and on-campus degree programs. Institution is accredited by The Higher Learning Commission of the North Central Association of Colleges and Schools. Online programs follow the same semester calendar as on-campus programs. All or most programs can be completed entirely online. Students can transfer from online to on-campus programs and from on-campus to online programs. There is no difference between physical diplomas awarded by online programs and those awarded by on-campus programs.

CONCORDIA UNIVERSITY, NEBRASKA

800 North Columbia Ave, Seward, NE, 68434
Contact: Dr. Nancy Elwell, Director, Department of Lifelong Learning
Contact Phone: 800-535-5494, ext. 7337 **Contact E-mail:** nancy.elwell@cune.edu
Website: www.cune.edu/dll

GENERAL INFORMATION

School type: Private.
Concordia University, Nebraska offers both online and on-campus degree programs. Institution is accredited. Online programs calendar differs from on-campus programs in that Semester I takes places from January through June and Semester II from July through December. Most programs cannot be completed entirely online. Additional hours can be earned in a variety of ways. Students can transfer from online to on-campus programs and from on-campus to online programs. There is no difference between physical diplomas awarded by online programs and those awarded by on-campus programs.

CONCORDIA UNIVERSITY—ST. PAUL

Concordia University, 275 Syndicate Street North, St. Paul, MN, 55104-5494
Contact: Kim Craig, Director of Graduate & Cohort Admission
Contact Phone: 800-333-4705 **Contact E-mail:** admission@csp.edu
Website: www.csp.edu

GENERAL INFORMATION
School type: Private.
Concordia University—St. Paul offers both online and on-campus degree programs. Institution is accredited by Higher Learning Commission of the NCA. Online programs follow the same semester calendar as on-campus programs. All or most programs can be completed entirely online. Students can transfer from online to on-campus programs and from on-campus to online programs. There is no difference between physical diplomas awarded by online programs and those awarded by on-campus programs.

CORNERSTONE UNIVERSITY

Professional and Graduate Studies, 1001 East Beltline Northeast, Grand Rapids, MI, 49525
Contact: Laurie Wittbrodt, Enrollment Manager
Contact Phone: 800-947-2382 **Contact E-mail:**
Website: http://pgs.cornerstone.edu

GENERAL INFORMATION
School type: Private.
Cornerstone University offers both online and on-campus degree programs. Institution is accredited by North Central. Online programs calendar differs from on-campus programs in that the program begins when 14 or more students have registered for it. Most programs cannot be completed entirely online. Students must attend 5 residency days. Students can transfer from online to on-campus programs and from on-campus to online programs. There is no difference between physical diplomas awarded by online programs and those awarded by on-campus programs.

CROWN COLLEGE

8700 College View Drive, St. Bonifacius, MN, 55375
Contact: Maria Kolb, Enrollment Coordinator
Contact Phone: 866-276-9665 **Contact E-mail:** cconline@crown.edu
Website: http://crown.edu

GENERAL INFORMATION
School type: Private.
Crown College offers only online degree programs. Institution is accredited by NCA and ABHE. All degrees can be completed entirely online.

CULVER-STOCKTON COLLEGE

One College Hill, Canton, MO, 63435
Contact: Dr. Chelona Edgerly, Director of Extended Programs
Contact Phone: 573-288-6468 **Contact E-mail:** cedgerly@culver.edu
Website: www.culver.edu/connectedcampus

GENERAL INFORMATION
School type: Private.
Culver-Stockton College offers both online and on-campus degree programs. Institution is accredited. Online programs calendar differs from on-campus programs in that it offers 8-week continuous sessions. All or most programs can be completed entirely online. Students can transfer from online to on-campus programs and from on-campus to online programs. There is no difference between physical diplomas awarded by online programs and those awarded by on-campus programs.

DALLAS BAPTIST UNIVERSITY

3000 Mountain Creek Parkway, Dallas, TX, 75211-9211
Contact: Julie Smith, Online Student Coordinator
Contact Phone: 214-333-6893 **Contact E-mail:** online@dbu.edu
Website: http://online.ebu.edu.

GENERAL INFORMATION
School type: Private.
Dallas Baptist University offers both online and on-campus degree programs. Institution is accredited by SACS. Online programs follow the same semester calendar as on-campus programs. All or most programs can be completed entirely online. Students can transfer from online to on-campus programs and from on-campus to online programs. There is no difference between physical diplomas awarded by online programs and those awarded by on-campus programs.

DEPAUL UNIVERSITY

25 East Jackson Boulevard, Suite 200, Chicago, IL, 60604
Contact: School for New Learning Advising Center
Contact Phone: 866-SNL-FORU **Contact E-mail:** snladvising@depaul.edu
Website: www.snlonline.net

GENERAL INFORMATION
School type: Private.
DePaul University offers both online and on-campus degree programs. Institution is accredited by North Central Association. Online programs follow the same semester calendar as on-campus programs. All or most programs can be completed entirely online. Students can transfer from online to on-campus programs and from on-campus to online programs. There is no difference between physical diplomas awarded by online programs and those awarded by on-campus programs.

DEVRY UNIVERSITY

DeVry University Online, One Tower Lane, Oakbrook Terrace, IL, 60181
Contact Phone: 800-773-3879
Website: www.devry.edu/online

GENERAL INFORMATION
School type: Proprietary.
DeVry University offers both online and on-campus degree programs. Institution is accredited by The Higher Learning Commission of the North Central Association. Online programs follow the same semester calendar as on-campus programs. All or most programs can be completed entirely online. Students can transfer from online to on-campus programs and from on-campus to online programs. There is no difference between physical diplomas awarded by online programs and those awarded by on-campus programs.

DICKINSON STATE UNIVERSITY

291 Campus Drive, Dickinson, ND, 58601
Contact: Anthony Willer, Online Coordinator
Contact Phone: 701-483-2166 **Contact E-mail:** Anthony.Willer@dsu.nodak.edu
Website: www.dsu.nodak.edu/online.asp

GENERAL INFORMATION

School type: Public.
Dickinson State University offers both online and on-campus degree programs. Institution is accredited by Accredidation by the Higher Learning Commission. Online programs follow the same semester calendar as on-campus programs. All or most programs can be completed entirely online. Students can transfer from online to on-campus programs and from on-campus to online programs. There is no difference between physical diplomas awarded by online programs and those awarded by on-campus programs.

DRURY UNIVERSITY

900 North Benton Avenue, Springfield, MO, 65802
Contact: Teresa Montgomery, Academic Advisor
Contact Phone: 417-873-7502 **Contact E-mail:** tmontgom@drury.edu
Website: www.drury.edu/online

GENERAL INFORMATION

School type: Private.
Drury University offers both online and on-campus degree programs. Institution is accredited by Higher Learning Commission. Online programs follow the same semester calendar as on-campus programs. All or most programs can be completed entirely online. Students can transfer from online to on-campus programs and from on-campus to online programs. There is no difference between physical diplomas awarded by online programs and those awarded by on-campus programs.

DUQUESNE UNIVERSITY

222 Rockwell Hall, 600 Forbes Avenue, Pittsburgh, PA, 15282
Contact: Ruth Newberry, Director, Education Technology
Contact Phone: 412-396-1813 **Contact E-mail:** newberryr@duq.edu
Website: www.duq.edu

GENERAL INFORMATION

School type: Private.
Duquesne University offers both online and on-campus degree programs. Institution is accredited by Middle States Association of Colleges and Schools. Online programs calendar differs from on-campus programs: Fall Term1 is September–November; Fall Term2 is November—January; Spring Term3 is January—March; Spring Term4 is March—May; and Summer Term5 June—July. All or most programs can be completed entirely online. Students can transfer from online to on-campus programs and from on-campus to online programs. There is no difference between physical diplomas awarded by online programs and those awarded by on-campus programs.

EAST TENNESSEE STATE UNIVERSITY

Box 70659, East Tennessee State University, Johnson City, TN, 37614
Contact: Amy Johnson, Coordinator, Online Student Success
Contact Phone: 423-439-4223 **Contact E-mail:** johnsoad@etsu.edu
Website: www.etsu.edu

GENERAL INFORMATION

School type: Public.
East Tennessee State University offers both online and on-campus degree programs. Institution is accredited by SACS. Online programs follow the same semester calendar as on-campus programs. All or most programs can be completed entirely online. Students can transfer from online to on-campus programs and from on-campus to online programs. There is no difference between physical diplomas awarded by online programs and those awarded by on-campus programs.

EASTERN MICHIGAN UNIVERSITY

101 Boone Hall, Eastern Michigan University, Ypsilanti, MI, 48197
Contact: Jody Cebina, Assistant Director, Distance Education
Contact Phone: 734-487-1081 **Contact E-mail:** distance.education@emich.edu
Website: www.emuonline.edu

GENERAL INFORMATION

School type: Public.
Eastern Michigan University offers both online and on-campus degree programs. Institution is accredited by North Central Association. Online programs follow the same semester calendar as on-campus programs. All or most programs can be completed entirely online. Students can transfer from online to on-campus programs.

EASTERN OREGON UNIVERSITY

One University Boulevard, La Grande, OR, 97850
Contact: Division of Distance Education
Contact Phone: 541-962-3378 **Contact E-mail:** dde@eou.edu
Website: www.eou.edu

GENERAL INFORMATION

School type: Public.
Eastern Oregon University offers both online and on-campus degree programs. Institution is accredited by NWCCU. Online programs follow the same semester calendar as on-campus programs. All or most programs can be completed entirely online. Students can transfer from online to on-campus programs and from on-campus to online programs. There is no difference between physical diplomas awarded by online programs and those awarded by on-campus programs.

EMPIRE STATE COLLEGE

One Union Avenue, Saratoga Springs, NY, 12866-4391
Contact: Student Information Center
Contact Phone: 518-587-2100, ext. 2285
Website: www.esc.edu

GENERAL INFORMATION

School type: Public.
Empire State College offers both online and on-campus degree programs. Institution is accredited by Middle States Association of Colleges and Schools. Online programs follow the same semester calendar as on-campus programs. All or most programs can be completed entirely online. Students can transfer from online to on-campus programs and from on-campus to online programs. There is no difference between physical diplomas awarded by online programs and those awarded by on-campus programs.

EMPORIA STATE UNIVERSITY

Campus Box 4052, 1200 Commercial, Emporia, KS, 66801
Contact: Brad Goebel, Director, Lifelong Learning
Contact Phone: 620-341-5385 **Contact E-mail:** tgoebel@emporia.edu
Website: www.emporia.edu/lifelong

GENERAL INFORMATION
School type: Public.
Emporia State University offers both online and on-campus degree programs. Institution is accredited by HLC. Online programs follow the same semester calendar as on-campus programs. All or most programs can be completed entirely online. Students can transfer from online to on-campus programs and from on-campus to online programs. There is no difference between physical diplomas awarded by online programs and those awarded by on-campus programs.

FLORIDA STATE UNIVERSITY

Contact: Karen Bickley, Assistant Director of Academic Programs
Contact Phone: 877-FLSTATE **Contact E-mail:** inquiries@campus.fsu.edu
Website: http://learningforlife.fsu.edu/online/index.cfm

GENERAL INFORMATION
School type: Public.
Florida State University offers both online and on-campus degree programs. Institution is accredited by SACS. Online programs follow the same semester calendar as on-campus programs. All or most programs can be completed entirely online. Students can transfer from online to on-campus programs and from on-campus to online programs. There is no difference between physical diplomas awarded by online programs and those awarded by on-campus programs.

FORT HAYS STATE UNIVERSITY

600 Park Street, Hays, KS, 67601
Contact: Virtual College
Contact Phone: 800-628-3478 **Contact E-mail:** vcollege@fhsu.edu
Website: www.fhsu.edu/virtualcollege

GENERAL INFORMATION
School type: Public.
Fort Hays State University offers both online and on-campus degree programs. Institution is accredited by Higher Learning Commission of North Central Association of Colleges and Schools. Online programs follow the same semester calendar as on-campus programs. All or most programs can be completed entirely online. Students can transfer from online to on-campus programs and from on-campus to online programs. There is no difference between physical diplomas awarded by online programs and those awarded by on-campus programs.

GEORGIA SOUTHERN UNIVERSITY

PO Box 8018, Statesboro, Ga, 30460
Contact: Ms. Pam Deal, Director, Emerging Technology Center
Contact Phone: 912-681-0882 **Contact E-mail:** etc@georgiasouthern.edu
Website: http://academics.georgiasouthern.edu/etc

GENERAL INFORMATION
School type: Public.
Georgia Southern University offers both online and on-campus degree programs. Institution is accredited by Southern Association of Colleges and Schools. Online programs follow the same semester calendar as on-campus programs. All or most programs can be completed entirely online. Students can transfer from online to on-campus programs and from on-campus to online programs. There is no difference between physical diplomas awarded by online programs and those awarded by on-campus programs.

GRANTHAM UNIVERSITY

7200 Northwest Eighty-sixth Street, Kansas City, MO, 64153
Contact: Admissions Department
Contact Phone: 800-955-2527 **Contact E-mail:** admissions@grantham.edu
Website: www.grantham.edu

GENERAL INFORMATION
School type: Proprietary.
Grantham University offers only online degree programs. Institution is accredited by Distance Education and Training Council. All degrees can be completed entirely online.

HAMPTON UNIVERSITY

PO Box 6162, Hampton, VA, 23668
Contact: Drusilla Pair, Distance Education Coordinator
Contact Phone: 757-727-5773 **Contact E-mail:** continuinged@hamptonu.edu
Website: www.hamptonu.edu/academics/continuing_ed/distance_learning

GENERAL INFORMATION
School type: Private.
Hampton University offers both online and on-campus degree programs. Institution is accredited by Southern Association of Colleges and Schools. Online programs follow the same semester calendar as on-campus programs. All or most programs can be completed entirely online. Students can transfer from online to on-campus programs and from on-campus to online programs. There is no difference between physical diplomas awarded by online programs and those awarded by on-campus programs.

HOPE INTERNATIONAL UNIVERSITY

2500 East Nutwood Avenue, Fullerton, CA, 92831-3199
Contact: Office of Graduate Admissions
Contact Phone: 714-879-3901, ext. 2634 **Contact E-mail:**
Website: www.hiu.edu

GENERAL INFORMATION
School type: Private.
Institution is accredited by The Western Association of Schools and Colleges (WASC) and Association for Biblical Higher Education (ABHE). Online programs follow the same semester calendar as on-campus programs. All or most programs can be completed entirely online. Students can transfer from online to on-campus programs and from on-campus to online programs. There is no difference between physical diplomas awarded by online programs and those awarded by on-campus programs.

INDIANA WESLEYAN UNIVERSITY

College of Adult and Professional Studies, 1900 West Fiftieth Street, Marion, IN, 46953
Contact: Dennis Zuber, Executive Director of Online Admissions
Contact Phone: 765-677-1043 **Contact E-mail:** dennis.zuber@indwes.edu
Website: http://caps.indwes.edu/onlineDegrees

GENERAL INFORMATION
School type: Private.
Indiana Wesleyan University offers both online and on-campus degree programs. Institution is accredited by Higher Learning Commission of the NCA. Online programs calendar differs from on-campus programs in that a one-course-at-a-time cohort model is used. All or most programs can be completed entirely online. Students can transfer from online to on-campus programs and from on-campus to online programs. There is no difference between physical diplomas awarded by online programs and those awarded by on-campus programs.

INDIANA UNIVERSITY—
SCHOOL OF CONTINUING STUDIES

Owen Hall 205, 790 East Kirkwood Avenue, Bloomington, IN, 47405-7101
Contact: Learner Services, Customer Services
Contact Phone: 800-855-2292 **Contact E-mail:** scs@indiana.edu
Website: http://scs.indiana.edu

GENERAL INFORMATION
School type: Public.
Indiana University—School of Continuing Studies offers both online and on-campus degree programs. Institution is accredited by North Central Association of Colleges and Schools, Higher Learning Commisssion. Online programs calendar differs from on-campus programs in that students have the option to enroll in a course that follows a regular semester, one full year from the date they register for a course. All or most programs can be completed entirely online. Students can transfer from online to on-campus programs and from on-campus to online programs. There is no difference between physical diplomas awarded by online programs and those awarded by on-campus programs.

JONES INTERNATIONAL UNIVERSITY

9697 East Mineral Avenue, Centennial, CO, 80112
Contact: Jones International University, Admissions Counselor
Contact Phone: 800-811-5663 **Contact E-mail:** info@international.edu
Website: www.jiu.edu

GENERAL INFORMATION
School type: Proprietary.
Jones International University offers only online degree programs. Institution is accredited by The Higher Learning Commission; a member of the North Central Association. All degrees can be completed entirely online.

KANSAS STATE UNIVERSITY

131 College Court Building, Manhattan, KS, 66506
Contact: Division of Continuing Education
Contact Phone: 800-432-8222 **Contact E-mail:** registerdce@ksu.edu
Website: www.dce.k-state.edu/dce/distance/current/index.html

GENERAL INFORMATION
School type: Public.
Kansas State University offers both online and on-campus degree programs. Institution is accredited by Higher Learning Commissions of the North Central Association of Colleges and Schools. Online programs calendar differs from on-campus programs in that classes start at various times throughout the semester. Most programs cannot be completed entirely online. Students can transfer from online to on-campus programs and from on-campus to online programs. There is no difference between physical diplomas awarded by online programs and those awarded by on-campus programs.

LAKE REGION STATE COLLEGE

1801 College Drive North, Devils Lake, ND, 58301
Contact: Daniel Driessen, Director of Continuing Education
Contact Phone: 701-662-1510 **Contact E-mail:** daniel.driessen@lrsc.nodak.edu
Website: www.lrsc.nodak.edu

GENERAL INFORMATION
School type: Public.
Lake Region State College offers both online and on-campus degree programs. Institution is accredited by LRSC is accredited by the Higher Learning Commission of the North Central Association of Colleges and Secondary Schools. Online programs follow the same semester calendar as on-campus programs. All or most programs can be completed entirely online. Students can transfer from online to on-campus programs and from on-campus to online programs. There is no difference between physical diplomas awarded by online programs and those awarded by on-campus programs.

LAKELAND COLLEGE

Lakeland College, PO Box 359, Sheboygan, WI, 53082
Contact: Charles Grubisic, Online Counselor
Contact Phone: 800-569-2166 **Contact E-mail:** lconline@lakeland.edu
Website: www.lakeland.edu

GENERAL INFORMATION
School type: Private.
Lakeland College offers both online and on-campus degree programs. Institution is accredited by The Higher Learning Commission of the North Central Association. Online programs follow the same semester calendar as on-campus programs. All or most programs can be completed entirely online. Students can transfer from online to on-campus programs and from on-campus to online programs. There is no difference between physical diplomas awarded by online programs and those awarded by on-campus programs.

LANDER UNIVERSITY

320 Stanley, Greenwood, SC, 29649-2099
Contact: Jonathan T. Reece, Director of Admissions
Contact Phone: 864-388-8307 or 888-4LANDER **Contact E-mail:** admissions@lander,edu
Website: www.lander.edu/admissions

GENERAL INFORMATION
School type: Public.
Lander University offers both online and on-campus degree programs. Institution is accredited by SACS. Online programs follow the same semester calendar as on-campus programs. All or most programs can be completed entirely online. Students cannot transfer from online to on-campus programs, but can transfer from on-campus to online programs. There is no difference between physical diplomas awarded by online programs and those awarded by on-campus programs.

LIBERTY UNIVERSITY

Distance Learning Program, 1971 University Boulevard, Lynchburg, VA, 24502
Contact: Admissions
Contact Phone: 800-424-9595 **Contact E-mail:** dlpadmissions@liberty.edu
Website: www.liberty.edu/dlp

GENERAL INFORMATION
School type: Private.
Liberty University offers both online and on-campus degree programs. Institution is regionally accredited by the Southern Association of Colleges and Schools (SACS). Online programs calendar differs from on-campus programs in that most online courses are 8 weeks long, while a select few are 16 weeks long. All or most programs can be completed entirely online. Students can transfer from online to on-campus programs and from on-campus to online programs. There is no difference between physical diplomas awarded by online programs and those awarded by on-campus programs.

LIFE PACIFIC COLLEGE

1100 West Covina Boulevard, San Dimas, CA, 91773
Contact: Frank Markow, Director of Degree Completion
Contact Phone: 909-599-5433 **Contact E-mail:** fmarkow@lifepacific.edu
Website: www.lifepacific.edu/dcp

GENERAL INFORMATION
School type: Private.
Life Pacific College offers both online and on-campus degree programs. Institution is accredited by WASC and ABHE. Online programs calendar differs from on-campus programs in that degree completion is in 5-week blocks throughout the year. All or most programs can be completed entirely online. Students can transfer from online to on-campus programs and from on-campus to online programs. There is no difference between physical diplomas awarded by online programs and those awarded by on-campus programs.

LIMESTONE COLLEGE

Limestone College Extended Campus, 1115 College Drive, Gaffney, SC, 29340-3799
Contact: Iuliana Watson, Internet Academic Advisor/WebCT Trainer
Contact Phone: 864-488-4539 **Contact E-mail:** iwatson@limestone.edu
Website: www.limestonevirtualcampus.net

GENERAL INFORMATION
School type: Private.
Limestone College offers both online and on-campus degree programs. Institution is accredited by Southern Association of Colleges and Schools. Online programs calendar differs from on-campus programs in that online programs adhere to the following schedule: spring semester, January–June, three 8-week terms; fall semester, July–December, three 8-week terms. All or most programs can be completed entirely online. Students can transfer from online to on-campus programs and from on-campus to online programs. There is no difference between physical diplomas awarded by online programs and those awarded by on-campus programs.

LINFIELD COLLEGE

Unit 456, 900 Southeast Baker Street, McMinnville, OR, 97140
Contact Phone: 800-452-4176 **Contact E-mail:** dce@linfield.edu
Website: www.linfield.edu/dce/index.php

GENERAL INFORMATION
School type: Private.
Linfield College offers both online and on-campus degree programs. Institution is accredited by NWCCU (regional) and CCNE (nursing); other professional accreditations are not applicable to online programs (music, athletic training). Online programs follow the same semester calendar as on-campus programs. All or most programs can be completed entirely online. Students can transfer from online to on-campus programs and from on-campus to online programs. There is no difference between physical diplomas awarded by online programs and those awarded by on-campus programs.

MALONE COLLEGE

Malone College, 515 Twenty-fifth Street Northwest, Canton, OH, 44709-3897
Contact: Joyce E. Thompson, Director of Enrollment for Continuing Studies
Contact Phone: 330-471-8246 **Contact E-mail:** jthompson@malone.edu
Website: www.malone.edu/online

GENERAL INFORMATION
School type: Private.
Malone College offers both online and on-campus degree programs. Institution is accredited by Higher Learning Commission-North Central Association. Online programs calendar differs from on-campus programs in that online program is in trimesters. All or most programs can be completed entirely online. Students can transfer from online to on-campus programs and from on-campus to online programs. There is no difference between physical diplomas awarded by online programs and those awarded by on-campus programs.

MANSFIELD UNIVERSITY OF PENNSYLVANIA

Alumni Hall, Mansfield, PA, 16933
Contact: Judi Brayer, Assistant Director of Enrollment Services
Contact Phone: 570-662-4818 **Contact E-mail:** jbrayer@mansfield.edu
Website: www.mansfield.edu

GENERAL INFORMATION

School type: Public.
Mansfield University offers both online and on-campus degree programs. Institution is accredited by Middle States Association of Colleges and Secondary Schools. Online programs follow the same semester calendar as on-campus programs. Most programs cannot be completed entirely online. Not all general education courses are available online. You may transfer these from other institutions. Students can transfer from online to on-campus programs and from on-campus to online programs. There is no difference between physical diplomas awarded by online programs and those awarded by on-campus programs.

MARLBORO COLLEGE GRADUATE CENTER

28 Vernon Street, Brattleboro, VT, 5301
Contact: Bethany Catron, Associate Director of Admissions
Contact Phone: 802-258-9209 **Contact E-mail:** bcatron@gradcenter.marlboro.edu
Website: http://gradcenter.marlboro.edu

GENERAL INFORMATION

School type: Private.
Marlboro College Graduate Center offers both online and on-campus degree programs. Institution is accredited by NEASC. Online programs calendar differs from on-campus programs in that online programs operate on a trimester basis. Most programs cannot be completed entirely online. The Bachelor's Completion Program requires 60 credits. Students cannot transfer from online to on-campus programs but can transfer from on-campus to online programs. There is no difference between physical diplomas awarded by online programs and those awarded by on-campus programs.

MARSHALL UNIVERSITY

One John Marshall Drive, Huntinton, WV, 25755-2050
Contact: Richard McCray, Director, RBA Bachelor's Program
Contact Phone: 800-906-4723 **Contact E-mail:** mccray@marshall.edu
Website: www.marshall.edu/rba

GENERAL INFORMATION

School type: Public.
Marshall University offers both online and on-campus degree programs. Institution is accredited by North Central Association Commission on Accreditation. Online programs follow the same semester calendar as on-campus programs. All or most programs can be completed entirely online. Students can transfer from online to on-campus programs and from on-campus to online programs. There is no difference between physical diplomas awarded by online programs and those awarded by on-campus programs.

MASSACHUSETTS COLLEGE OF PHARMACY AND HEALTH SCIENCES

179 Longwood Avenue, Boston, MA, 2115
Contact: Jennifer Mercado, Admission Counselor
Contact Phone: 617-732-2850 **Contact E-mail:** admissions@mcphs.edu
Website: www.mcphs.edu/admission

GENERAL INFORMATION

School type: Private.
Massachusetts College of Pharmacy and Health Sciences offers both online and on-campus degree programs. Institution is accredited by New England Association of Schools and Colleges. Online programs follow the same semester calendar as on-campus programs. Most programs cannot be completed entirely online. MCPHS offers an online option of the Bachelor of Science in Dental Hygiene completion program. Students enter the program having already completed prerequisite courses. Students can transfer from online to on-campus programs, but not from on-campus to online programs. There is no difference between physical diplomas awarded by online programs and those awarded by on-campus programs.

MAYVILLE STATE UNIVERSITY

330 Third Street Northeast, Mayville, ND, 58257
Contact: Robert Bertsch, Director of Office of Worldwide Learning
Contact Phone: 701-788-4631 **Contact E-mail:** r_bertsch@mayvillestate.edu
Website: www.mayvillestate.edu/worldwide_learning/index.cfm

GENERAL INFORMATION

School type: Public.
Mayville State University offers both online and on-campus degree programs. Institution is accredited by Higher Education Learning Commission. Online programs follow the same semester calendar as on-campus programs. All or most programs can be completed entirely online. Students can transfer from online to on-campus programs and from on-campus to online programs. There is no difference between physical diplomas awarded by online programs and those awarded by on-campus programs.

MIDWESTERN STATE UNIVERSITY

3410 Taft Boulevard, Wichita Falls, TX, 76308
Contact: Pamela Morgan, Director of Extended Education
Contact Phone: 940-397-4785 **Contact E-mail:** pamela.morgan@mwsu.edu
Website: http://web.mwsu.edu

GENERAL INFORMATION

School type: Public.
Midwestern State University offers both online and on-campus degree programs. Institution is accredited by Southern Association of Colleges and Schools. Online programs follow the same semester calendar as on-campus programs. All or most programs can be completed entirely online. Students can transfer from online to on-campus programs and from on-campus to online programs. There is no difference between physical diplomas awarded by online programs and those awarded by on-campus programs.

MONROE COLLEGE

Monroe College Way, Bronx, NY, 10468
Contact: Martin Cintron, Director of On Line Admissions
Contact Phone: 718 933-6700 **Contact E-mail:** mcintron@monroecollege.edu
Website: http://monroecollege.edu

GENERAL INFORMATION
School type: Proprietary.
Monroe College offers both online and on-campus degree programs. Institution is accredited by Middle States Commission on Higher Education. NYS Board of Regents. Online programs follow the same semester calendar as on-campus programs. All or most programs can be completed entirely online. Students can transfer from online to on-campus programs and from on-campus to online programs. There is no difference between physical diplomas awarded by online programs and those awarded by on-campus programs.

MOUNTAIN STATE UNIVERSITY

609 South Kanawha Street, PO Box 9003, Beckley, WV, 25802-9003
Contact: Tammy Murphy, Lead Enrollment Coordinator—Online
Contact Phone: 304-929-1702 **Contact E-mail:** tmurphy@mountainstate.edu
Website: www.mountainstate.edu/prospective/programs/extended_Distance/online

GENERAL INFORMATION
School type: Private.
Mountain State University offers both online and on-campus degree programs. Institution is accredited by The Higher Learning Commission of the North Central Association of Colleges and Schools. Online programs calendar differs from on-campus programs in that cohorts offer various calendars. All or most programs can be completed entirely online. Students can transfer from online to on-campus programs and from on-campus to online programs. There is no difference between physical diplomas awarded by online programs and those awarded by on-campus programs.

MURRAY STATE UNIVERSITY

303 Sparks Hall, Murray, KY 42071, KY, 42071
Contact: Crystal Riley, Coordinator, Distance Learning
Contact Phone: 270-809-2159 **Contact E-mail:** crystal.riley@murraystate.edu
Website: http://ceao.murraystate.edu

GENERAL INFORMATION
Murray State University offers both online and on-campus degree programs. Institution is accredited. Online programs follow the same semester calendar as on-campus programs. Most programs cannot be completed entirely online. Our programs are Degree Completion Programs. Students can transfer from online to on-campus programs and from on-campus to online programs. There is no difference between physical diplomas awarded by online programs and those awarded by on-campus programs.

NEW ENGLAND COLLEGE

7 Main Street, Henniker, NH, 3242
Contact: Jennifer Le Duc, Director of Admission GPP
Contact Phone: 603-428-2297 **Contact E-mail:** jleduc@nec.edu
Website: www.nec.edu

GENERAL INFORMATION
School type: Private.
New England College offers both online and on-campus degree programs. Institution is accredited by NEASC. Online programs calendar differs from on-campus programs in that it operates on a 7-week-term basis. All or most programs can be completed entirely online. Students can transfer from online to on-campus programs and from on-campus to online programs. There is no difference between physical diplomas awarded by online programs and those awarded by on-campus programs.

NEW JERSEY INSTITUTE OF TECHNOLOGY

University Heights, Newark, NJ 07102
Contact: Gale Spak
Contact Phone: 973-596-3063 **Contact E-mail:** gale.spak.njit.edu, elearning@njit.edu
Website: www.njit.edu

GENERAL INFORMATION
School type: Public.
New Jersey Institute of technology offers both online and on-campus degree programs. Institution is accredited by Middle States, ABET, NAAB, and AACSB. Online programs follow the same semester calendar as on-campus programs. All or most programs can be completed entirely online. Students can transfer from online to on-campus programs and from on-campus to online programs. There is no difference between physical diplomas awarded by online programs and those awarded by on-campus programs.

NORTHERN ARIZONA UNIVERSITY

Box 4117, Flagstaff, AZ, 86011
Contact: NAU—Office of Distance Learning
Contact Phone: 800-426-8315 **Contact E-mail:** distance.programs@nau.edu
Website: www.distance.nau.edu/?MAINNAU

GENERAL INFORMATION
School type: Public.
Northern Arizona University offers both online and on-campus degree programs. Institution is accredited by North Central Association of Colleges and Schools. Online programs follow the same semester calendar as on-campus programs. All or most programs can be completed entirely online. Students can transfer from online to on-campus programs and from on-campus to online programs. There is no difference between physical diplomas awarded by online programs and those awarded by on-campus programs.

NORTHWEST MISSOURI STATE UNIVERSITY

800 University Drive, Maryville, MO, 64468
Contact: Admissions, Office of Admissions
Contact Phone: 800-633-1175 **Contact E-mail:** admissions@nwmissouri.edu
Website: www.nwmissouri.edu

GENERAL INFORMATION
School type: Public.
Northwest Missouri State University offers both online and on-campus degree programs. Institution is accredited by North Central. Online programs follow the same semester calendar as on-campus programs. All or most programs can be completed entirely online. Students can transfer from online to on-campus programs and from on-campus to online programs. There is no difference between physical diplomas awarded by online programs and those awarded by on-campus programs.

NORTHWESTERN STATE UNIVERSITY

100 South Hall, Northwestern State University, Natchitoches, LA, 71497
Contact: Misty Lacour, Assistant Director of University Recruiting
Contact Phone: 800-327-1903 **Contact E-mail:** lacourm@nsula.edu
Website: www.nsula.edu/enrollmentservices/recruiting

GENERAL INFORMATION
School type: Public.
Northwestern State University offers both online and on-campus degree programs. Institution is accredited by SACS. Online programs follow the same semester calendar as on-campus programs. All or most programs can be completed entirely online. Students can transfer from online to on-campus programs and from on-campus to online programs. There is no difference between physical diplomas awarded by online programs and those awarded by on-campus programs.

NORTHWOOD UNIVERSITY

4000 Whiting Drive, Midland, MI, 48640
Contact: Amy Thomas, Program Center Assistant
Contact Phone: 800-445-5873 **Contact E-mail:** athomas@northwood.edu
Website: www.northwood.edu/adults/onlinedegrees

GENERAL INFORMATION
School type: Private.
Northwood University offers both online and on-campus degree programs. Institution is accredited through the Higher Learning Commission and is a member of the North Central Association. Online programs calendar differs from on-campus programs in that the online program offers 4 terms, each of which are 12 weeks in length, with the exception of the summer term, which is 6 weeks. The traditional program operates on three 10-week terms per year plus a summer session. Most programs cannot be completed entirely online. All courses may be completed online with the exception of one 3-day seminar which must be taken on campus. Students can transfer from online to on-campus programs and from on-campus to online programs. There is no difference between physical diplomas awarded by online programs and those awarded by on-campus programs.

NOVA SOUTHEASTERN UNIVERSITY

3301 College Avenue, Fort Lauderdale, FL, 33314
Contact Phone: 800-338-4723 ext 8000 **Contact E-mail:** admissions@nova.edu
Website: www.undergrad.nova.edu

GENERAL INFORMATION
School type: Private.
Nova Southeastern University offers both online and on-campus degree programs. Institution is accredited by Southern Association of Colleges and Schools. Online programs follow the same semester calendar as on-campus programs. All or most programs can be completed entirely online. Students can transfer from online to on-campus programs and from on-campus to online programs. There is no difference between physical diplomas awarded by online programs and those awarded by on-campus programs.

OLD DOMINION UNIVERSITY

425 Gornto Center, Norfolk, VA, 23529
Contact: Lisa Hall, Director of Transfer Services
Contact Phone: 757-683-6493 **Contact E-mail:** lhall@odu.edu
Website: http://dl.odu.edu

GENERAL INFORMATION
School type: Public.
Old Dominion University offers both online and on-campus degree programs. Institution is accredited. Online programs follow the same semester calendar as on-campus programs. Most programs cannot be completed entirely online. Degree completion programs are available and provide the last 2 years of content. Students can transfer from online to on-campus programs and from on-campus to online programs. There is no difference between physical diplomas awarded by online programs and those awarded by on-campus programs.

OREGON STATE UNIVERSITY

4943 The Valley Library, Oregon State University, Corvallis, OR, 97331
Contact: William McCaughan, Dean, OSU Extended Campus
Contact Phone: 800-235-6559 **Contact E-mail:** ecampus@oregonstate.edu
Website: http://ecampus.oregonstate.edu

GENERAL INFORMATION
School type: Public.
Oregon State University offers both online and on-campus degree programs. Institution is accredited by NASC. Online programs follow the same semester calendar as on-campus programs. Most programs cannot be completed entirely online. Some lower-division courses may be completed at a community college or other institution. Students can transfer from online to on-campus programs and from on-campus to online programs. There is no difference between physical diplomas awarded by online programs and those awarded by on-campus programs.

PACE UNIVERSITY

One Pace Plaza, E201A, New York, NY, 10038
Contact: Christine Moloughney, Coordinator of Online Support Services
Contact Phone: 212-346-1471 **Contact E-mail:** online@pace.edu
Website: http://online.pace.edu

GENERAL INFORMATION
School type: Private.
Pace University offers both online and on-campus degree programs. Institution is accredited by Middle States Commission on Higher Education. Online programs calendar differs from on-campus programs in that on-campus fall and spring terms are 15 weeks and summer sessions are 6 weeks, while online-degree fall, spring, and summer terms are 12 weeks each. All or most programs can be completed entirely online. Students can transfer from online to on-campus programs and from on-campus to online programs. There is no difference between physical diplomas awarded by online programs and those awarded by on-campus programs.

PARK UNIVERSITY

College for Distance Learning, Park University, 8700 Northwest River Park Drive, Parkville, MO, 64152
Contact: Online Student Support Administrator
Contact Phone: 877-505-1059 **Contact E-mail:** megan.doyle@park.edu
Website: www.park.edu

GENERAL INFORMATION
School type: Private.
Park University offers both online and on-campus degree programs. Institution is accredited by North Central Association of Colleges and Schools. Online programs follow the same semester calendar as on-campus programs. All or most programs can be completed entirely online. Students can transfer from online to on-campus programs and from on-campus to online programs. There is no difference between physical diplomas awarded by online programs and those awarded by on-campus programs.

PENN FOSTER COLLEGE

14624 North Scottsdale Road, Suite 310, Scottsdale, AZ, 85254
Contact: Administrative Office
Contact Phone: 888-427-1000 **Contact E-mail:** info@pennfoster.edu
Website: www.pennfostercollege.edu

GENERAL INFORMATION
School type: Proprietary.
Penn Foster College offers only online degree programs. Institution is accredited by Distance Education and Training Council. All degrees can be completed entirely online.

PENNSYLVANIA STATE UNIVERSITY

128 Outreach Building, University Park, PA, 16802
Contact: Pennsylvania State University—World Campus
Contact Phone: 814-865-5403 **Contact E-mail:** psuwd@psu.edu
Website: www.worldcampus.psu.edu

GENERAL INFORMATION
School type: Public.
Pennsylvania State University offers both online and on-campus degree programs. Institution is accredited by Middle States. Online programs follow the same semester calendar as on-campus programs. All or most programs can be completed entirely online. Students can transfer from online to on-campus programs and from on-campus to online programs. There is no difference between physical diplomas awarded by online programs and those awarded by on-campus programs.

REGENT UNIVERSITY

1000 Regent University, Virginia Beach, VA, 23662
Contact: Kenneth Baker, Director of Admissions
Contact Phone: 800-210-0060 **Contact E-mail:** RegentUndergrad@regent.edu
Website: www.regent.edu/acad/undergrad

GENERAL INFORMATION
School type: Private.
Regent University offers both online and on-campus degree programs. Institution is accredited by the Commission on Colleges of the Southern Association of Colleges and Schools (SACS). Online programs follow the same semester calendar as on-campus programs. All or most programs can be completed entirely online. Students can transfer from online to on-campus programs and from on-campus to online programs. There is no difference between physical diplomas awarded by online programs and those awarded by on-campus programs.

ROBERTS WESLEYAN COLLEGE

Roberts Wesleyan College, 2301 Westside Drive, Rochester, NY, 14624
Contact: Matt Maher, Admissions Coordinator
Contact Phone: 585-594-6904 **Contact E-mail:** om@roberts.edu
Website: www.roberts.edu/om

GENERAL INFORMATION
School type: Private.
Roberts Wesleyan College offers both online and on-campus degree programs. Institution is accredited by Middle States. All or most programs can be completed entirely online. Students can transfer from online to on-campus programs and from on-campus to online programs. There is no difference between physical diplomas awarded by online programs and those awarded by on-campus programs.

ROCHESTER INSTITUTE OF TECHNOLOGY

58 Lomb Memorial Drive, Rochester, NY, 14623
Contact: Kandice King, Online Learning Marketing Coordinator
Contact Phone: 866-260-3950 **Contact E-mail:** distance@rit.edu
Website: www.rit.edu/online

GENERAL INFORMATION

School type: Private.
Rochester Institute of Technology offers both online and on-campus degree programs. Institution is accredited by Middle States. Online programs follow the same semester calendar as on-campus programs. All or most programs can be completed entirely online. Students can transfer from online to on-campus programs and from on-campus to online programs. There is no difference between physical diplomas awarded by online programs and those awarded by on-campus programs.

SACRED HEART UNIVERSITY

5151 Park Avenue, Fairfield, CT, 6825
Contact: Alma Haluch, Coordinator of Student Services-Nursing
Contact Phone: 203-371-7715 **Contact E-mail:** halucha@sacredheart.edu
Website: http://nursing.sacredheart.edu

GENERAL INFORMATION

School type: Private.
Sacred Heart University offers both online and on-campus degree programs. Institution is accredited by Commission on Collegiate Nursing Education. Online programs follow the same semester calendar as on-campus programs. All or most programs can be completed entirely online. Students can transfer from online to on-campus programs and from on-campus to online programs. There is no difference between physical diplomas awarded by online programs and those awarded by on-campus programs.

SAVANNAH COLLEGE OF ART AND DESIGN

PO Box 2072, Savannah, GA, 31402-2072
Contact: Ginger Hansen, Executive Director of Recruitment
Contact Phone: 912-525-5100 **Contact E-mail:** admission@scad.edu
Website: www.scad.edu

GENERAL INFORMATION

School type: Private.
Savannah College of Art and Design offers both online and on-campus degree programs. Institution is accredited by Southern Association of Colleges and Schools. Online programs follow the same semester calendar as on-campus programs. All or most programs can be completed entirely online. Students can transfer from online to on-campus programs and from on-campus to online programs. There is no difference between physical diplomas awarded by online programs and those awarded by on-campus programs.

SOUTHEAST MISSOURI STATE UNIVERSITY

One University Plaza, Cape Girardeau, MO, 63701
Contact: Heather Jones, Online Academic Advisor
Contact Phone: 573-651-2889 **Contact E-mail:** southeastonline@semo.edu
Website: http://online.semo.edu

GENERAL INFORMATION

School type: Public.
Southeast Missouri State University offers both online and on-campus degree programs. Institution is accredited by North Central Associaiton of Colleges and Schools. Online programs follow the same semester calendar as on-campus programs. All or most programs can be completed entirely online. Students can transfer from online to on-campus programs and from on-campus to online programs. There is no difference between physical diplomas awarded by online programs and those awarded by on-campus programs.

SOUTHEASTERN LOUISIANA UNIVERSITY

SLU 10752, Hammond, LA, 70402
Contact: Richard Beaugh, Director of Admissions
Contact Phone: 800-222-7358 **Contact E-mail:** admissions@selu.edu
Website: www.selu.edu/admin/admissions

GENERAL INFORMATION

School type: Public.
Southeastern Louisiana University offers both online and on-campus degree programs. Institution is accredited by Southern Association of Colleges and Schools (SACS). Online programs follow the same semester calendar as on-campus programs. All or most programs can be completed entirely online. Students can transfer from online to on-campus programs and from on-campus to online programs. There is no difference between physical diplomas awarded by online programs and those awarded by on-campus programs.

SOUTHERN NEW HAMPSHIRE UNIVERSITY

2500 North River Road, Manchester, NH, 3106
Contact: Admissions Counselor
Contact Phone: 866-860-0449 **Contact E-mail:** online@snhu.edu
Website: www.snhu.edu/online

GENERAL INFORMATION

School type: Private.
Southern New Hampshire University offers both online and on-campus degree programs. Institution is accredited by NEASC. Online programs follow the same semester calendar as on-campus programs. All or most programs can be completed entirely online. Students can transfer from online to on-campus programs and from on-campus to online programs. There is no difference between physical diplomas awarded by online programs and those awarded by on-campus programs.

SOUTHERN POLYTECHNIC STATE UNIVERSITY

1100 South Marietta Parkway, Marietta, GA, 30060-2896
Contact: Dawn Ramsey, Dean—Extended University
Contact Phone: 678-915-4287 **Contact E-mail:** dramsey@spsu.edu
Website: http://dl.spsu.edu

GENERAL INFORMATION
School type: Public.
Southern Polytechnic State University offers both online and on-campus degree programs. Institution is accredited by SACS. Online programs follow the same semester calendar as on-campus programs. All or most programs can be completed entirely online. Students can transfer from online to on-campus programs and from on-campus to online programs. There is no difference between physical diplomas awarded by online programs and those awarded by on-campus programs.

SOUTHWESTERN COLLEGE

2040 South Rock Road, Wichita, KS, 67207
Contact: Kelley Krahn, Online Program Representative
Contact Phone: 888-684-5335, ext. 124 **Contact E-mail:** Kelley.Krahn@sckans.edu
Website: www.sckans.edu/ps

GENERAL INFORMATION
School type: Private.
Southwestern College offers both online and on-campus degree programs. Institution is accredited by Higher Learning Commission North Central Division. Online programs calendar differs from on-campus programs in that it offers eight 6-week sessions per year. All or most programs can be completed entirely online. Students can transfer from online to on-campus programs and from on-campus to online programs. There is no difference between physical diplomas awarded by online programs and those awarded by on-campus programs.

ST. JOHN'S UNIVERSITY

8000 Utopia Parkway, Queens, NY, 11439
Contact: Antonio Lodato, Assistant Dean
Contact Phone: 718-990-5974 **Contact E-mail:** lodatoa@stjohns.edu
Website: www.stjohns.edu/distancelearning

GENERAL INFORMATION
School type: Private.
St. John's University offers both online and on-campus degree programs. Institution is accredited by Middle States. Online programs follow the same semester calendar as on-campus programs. All or most programs can be completed entirely online. Students can transfer from online to on-campus programs and from on-campus to online programs. There is no difference between physical diplomas awarded by online programs and those awarded by on-campus programs.

STATE UNIVERSITY OF NEW YORK—ALFRED STATE COLLEGE, COLLEGE OF TECHNOLOGY

10 Upper College Drive, Alfred, NY, 14802
Contact: Admissions Office **Contact Phone:** 800-4-ALFRED (Option 1)
Contact E-mail: admissions@alfredstate.edu **Website:** http://alfredstate.edu

GENERAL INFORMATION
School type: Public.
SUNY Alfred State College offers both online and on-campus degree programs. Institution is accredited by Middle States Assoc (MSCHE). Online programs follow the same semester calendar as on-campus programs. All or most programs can be completed entirely online. Students can transfer from online to on-campus programs, and from on-campus to online programs.

STEPHENS COLLEGE

1200 East Broadway, Box 2083, Columbia, MO, 65215
Contact: Mellodie Wilson, Associate Director, GCS
Contact Phone: 800-388-7579 **Contact E-mail:** online@stephens.edu
Website: www.stephens.edu/gcs

GENERAL INFORMATION
School type: Private.
Stephens College offers both online and on-campus degree programs. Institution is accredited by NCA/HLC. Online programs follow the same semester calendar as on-campus programs. Most programs cannot be completed entirely online. Students can transfer from online to on-campus programs but not from on-campus to online programs. There is no difference between physical diplomas awarded by online programs and those awarded by on-campus programs.

TAYLOR UNIVERSITY—FORT WAYNE

1025 West Rudisill Boulevard, Fort Wayne, IN, 46807
Contact: Kevin Mahaffy, Director, CLL
Contact Phone: 800-845-3149 **Contact E-mail:** cllinfo@taylor.edu
Website: http://cll.taylor.edu

GENERAL INFORMATION
School type: Private.
Taylor University—Fort Wayne offers both online and on-campus degree programs. Institution is accredited by NCA. Online programs follow the same semester calendar as on-campus programs. All or most programs can be completed entirely online. Students can transfer from online to on-campus programs and from on-campus to online programs. There is no difference between physical diplomas awarded by online programs and those awarded by on-campus programs.

TENNESSEE TECHNOLOGICAL UNIVERSITY

PO Box 5073, Henderson Hall Room 3, Cookeville, TN, 38505
Contact: Jane Sipes, RODP Campus Administrator
Contact Phone: 931-372-6098 **Contact E-mail:** jsipes@tntech.edu
Website: www.tntech.edu

GENERAL INFORMATION
School type: Public.
Tennessee Technological University offers both online and on-campus degree programs. Institution is accredited by SACS Commission on Colleges. Online programs follow the same semester calendar as on-campus programs. All or most programs can be completed entirely online. Students can transfer from online to on-campus programs and from on-campus to online programs. There is no difference between physical diplomas awarded by online programs and those awarded by on-campus programs.

TEXAS STATE UNIVERSITY—SAN MARCOS

302 Academic Services Building—North, 601 University Drive, San Marcos, TX, 78666-4616
Contact: James Andrews, Director of Correspondence and Extension
Contact Phone: 512-245-2322 **Contact E-mail:** corrstudy@txstate.edu
Website: www.studyanywhere.txstate.edu/home

GENERAL INFORMATION
School type: Public.
Texas State University—San Marcos offers both online and on-campus degree programs. Institution is accredited by Southern Association of Colleges and Schools. Online programs follow the same semester calendar as on-campus programs. All or most programs can be completed entirely online. Students can transfer from online to on-campus programs and from on-campus to online programs. There is no difference between physical diplomas awarded by online programs and those awarded by on-campus programs.

TEXAS TECH UNIVERSITY

Box 42191, Lubbock, TX, 79409-2191
Contact: Michele Moskos, Marketing Director
Contact Phone: 806-742-7200, ext. 276 **Contact E-mail:** michele.moskos@ttu.edu
Website: www.de.ttu.edu

GENERAL INFORMATION
School type: Public.
Texas Tech University offers both online and on-campus degree programs. Institution is accredited by Southern Association of Colleges and Schools (SACS). Online programs calendar differs from on-campus programs depending on the program. Most programs follow the same calendar as on campus progras, but Texas Tech University does offer self-paced, independent study programs. Students can transfer from online to on-campus programs and from on-campus to online programs. There is no difference between physical diplomas awarded by online programs and those awarded by on-campus programs.

THOMAS EDISON STATE COLLEGE

101 West State Street, Trenton, NJ, 8608
Contact: Ms. Renee San Giacomo, Director of Admissions
Contact Phone: 888-442-8372 **Contact E-mail:** admissions@tesc.edu
Website: www.tesc.edu

GENERAL INFORMATION
School type: Public.
Thomas Edison State College offers only online degree programs. Institution is accredited by Thomas Edison State College and by the Middle States Association of Colleges and Schools. The RN-BSN degree program is accredited by the New Jersey Board of Nursing and the National League for Nursing Accrediting Commission. All degrees can be completed entirely online.

TOURO UNIVERSITY INTERNATIONAL

5665 Plaza Drive, Cypress, CA, 90630
Contact: Wei Ren, Registrar
Contact Phone: 714-816-0366 **Contact E-mail:** registration@tourou.edu
Website: www.tourou.edu

GENERAL INFORMATION
School type: Private.
Touro University International offers only online degree programs. Institution is accredited. All degrees can be completed entirely online.

TROY UNIVERSITY

Southeastern Region, 501 Manchester Expressway, Columbus, GA, 31904
Contact: David White, Director of eCampus
Contact Phone: 706-653-9653 **Contact E-mail:** whited@troy.edu
Website: www.troy.edu

GENERAL INFORMATION
School type: Public.
Troy University offers both online and on-campus degree programs. Institution is accredited by SACS. Online programs follow the same semester calendar as on-campus programs. All or most programs can be completed entirely online. Students can transfer from online to on-campus programs and from on-campus to online programs. There is no difference between physical diplomas awarded by online programs and those awarded by on-campus programs.

UNION INSTITUTE & UNIVERSITY

36 College Street, Montpelier, VT, 5602
Contact: Rick Zand, Director of Admissions
Contact Phone: 800-486-3116 **Contact E-mail:** rick.zand@tui.edu
Website: www.tui.edu

GENERAL INFORMATION
School type: Private.
Union Institute & University offers both online and on-campus degree programs. Institution is accredited by The Higher Learning Commission of the North Central Association of Colleges and Schools. Online programs follow the same semester calendar as on-campus programs. All or most programs can be completed entirely online. Students can transfer from online to on-campus programs and from on-campus to online programs. There is no difference between physical diplomas awarded by online programs and those awarded by on-campus programs.

UNIVERSITY OF BRIDGEPORT

126 Park Avenue, Bridgeport, CT, 6604
Contact: Michael J. Giampaoli, Dean, School of Continuing and Professional Studies
Contact Phone: 203-476-4168 **Contact E-mail:** gmichael@beidgeport.edu
Website: www.bridgeport.edu

GENERAL INFORMATION
School type: Private.
University of Bridgeport offers both online and on-campus degree programs. Institution is accredited by NEASC and CTDHE. Online programs follow the same semester calendar as on-campus programs. Most programs cannot be completed entirely online. Dental Hygiene is a degree completion program. Students can transfer from online to on-campus programs and from on-campus to online programs. There is no difference between physical diplomas awarded by online programs and those awarded by on-campus programs.

UNIVERSITY OF CENTRAL FLORIDA

3100 Technology Parkway, Suite 234, Orlando, FL, 32826
Contact: Lori Allison, Program Coordinator
Contact Phone: 407-823-4910 **Contact E-mail:** lallison@mail.ucf.edu
Website: http://online.ucf.edu

GENERAL INFORMATION
School type: Public.
Institution is accredited by SACS. Online programs follow the same semester calendar as on-campus programs. Most programs cannot be completed entirely online. Online baccalaureate programs are degree completion programs, offering upper division study only. Students can transfer from online to on-campus programs and from on-campus to online programs. There is no difference between physical diplomas awarded by online programs and those awarded by on-campus programs.

UNIVERSITY OF CINCINNATI

PO Box 210635, Cincinnati, OH, 45221-0635
Contact: Melody Clark, Academic Director, Distance Learning
Contact Phone: 513-556-9154 **Contact E-mail:** melody.clark@uc.edu
Website: www.uc.edu/distance

GENERAL INFORMATION
School type: Public.
University of Cincinnati offers both online and on-campus degree programs. Institution is accredited by North Central Association of Colleges and Schools and The Higher Learning Commission. Online programs calendar differs from on-campus programs—varies by program. Many follow a 5-week schedule within the quarter calendar. All or most programs can be completed entirely online. There is no difference between physical diplomas awarded by online programs and those awarded by on-campus programs.

UNIVERSITY OF COLORADO AT DENVER AND HEALTH SCIENCE CENTER

PO Box 173364, Campus Box 105, Denver, CO, 80217-3364
Contact: CU Online
Contact Phone: 303-556-6505 **Contact E-mail:** inquiry@cuonline.edu
Website: www.cuonline.edu

GENERAL INFORMATION
School type: Public.
University of Colorado at Denver and Health Science Center offers both online and on-campus degree programs. Institution is accredited by Higher Learning Commission. Online programs follow the same semester calendar as on-campus programs. All or most programs can be completed entirely online. Students can transfer from online to on-campus programs and from on-campus to online programs. There is no difference between physical diplomas awarded by online programs and those awarded by on-campus programs.

UNIVERSITY OF FLORIDA

201 Criser Hall, Gainesville, FL 32611
Contact: Varies by degree program
Website: www.distancelearning.ufl.edu

GENERAL INFORMATION
School type: Public.
University of Florida offers both online and on-campus degree programs. Institution is accredited by Southern Association of Colleges and Schools Commission on Colleges. Online programs follow the same semester calendar as on-campus programs. All or most programs can be completed entirely online. Students can transfer from online to on-campus programs and from on-campus to online programs. There is no difference between physical diplomas awarded by online programs and those awarded by on-campus programs.

UNIVERSITY OF GREAT FALLS

1301 Twentieth Street South, Great Falls, MT, 59405
Contact: Jim Gretch, Director of Distance Learning
Contact Phone: 406-791-5320 **Contact E-mail:** jgretch@ugf.edu
Website: www.ugf.edu/DistanceLearning/Index.aspx

GENERAL INFORMATION
School type: Private.
University of Great Falls offers both online and on-campus degree programs. Institution is accredited by Northwest Commission on Colleges and Universities. Online programs follow the same semester calendar as on-campus programs. All or most programs can be completed entirely online. Students can transfer from online to on-campus programs and from on-campus to online programs. There is no difference between physical diplomas awarded by online programs and those awarded by on-campus programs.

UNIVERSITY OF HOUSTON—DOWNTOWN

University of Houston–Downtown, One Main Street, Houston, TX, 77002
Contact: Gail S.M. Evans, Executive Director of Distance Education
Contact Phone: 713-221-2735 **Contact E-mail:** evansg@uhd.edu
Website: www.uhd.edu/academic/distance.htm

GENERAL INFORMATION
School type: Public.
University of Houston—Downtown offers both online and on-campus degree programs. Institution is accredited by SACS, AACSB, and ABET. Online programs follow the same semester calendar as on-campus programs. Most programs cannot be completed entirely online. We offer the upper division courses to complete the degree; students take the lower division courses from community colleges. Students can transfer from online to on-campus programs and from on-campus to online programs. There is no difference between physical diplomas awarded by online programs and those awarded by on-campus programs.

UNIVERSITY OF ILLINOIS AT SPRINGFIELD

University of Illinois at Springfield, University Plaza, MS UHB 3013, Springfield, IL, 62703
Contact: Holly McCracken, Director of Online Programs
Contact Phone: 217-206-7421 **Contact E-mail:** mccracken.holly@uis.edu
Website: www.uis.edu

GENERAL INFORMATION
School type: Public.
University of Illinois at Springfield offers both online and on-campus degree programs. Institution is accredited by Higher Learning Commission. Online programs follow the same semester calendar as on-campus programs. All or most programs can be completed entirely online. Students can transfer from online to on-campus programs and from on-campus to online programs. There is no difference between physical diplomas awarded by online programs and those awarded by on-campus programs.

UNIVERSITY OF LA VERNE

1950 Third Street, La Verne, CA, 91711
Contact: Cheryl DeVroom, Marketing Assistant
Contact Phone: 800-695-4858, ext. 5202 **Contact E-mail:** cdevroom@ulv.edu
Website: www.ulv.edu/ulvonline

GENERAL INFORMATION
School type: Private.
University of La Verne offers both online and on-campus degree programs. Institution is accredited by WASC. Online programs calendar differs from on-campus programs: Fall 2006 (October 2–December 17); Winter 2007 (January 8–March 18), Spring 2007 (March 19–May 27), Summer I (June 4–August 12), Summer II (August 20–September 30). Most programs cannot be completed entirely online. Completing all General Education requirements may require the student to take the course locally at a community college or at the University of La Verne—Central Campus. Students cannot transfer from online to on-campus programs, nor from on-campus to online programs.

UNIVERSITY OF MAINE AT AUGUSTA

46 University Drive, Augusta, ME, 4330
Contact: Kelly Thibodeau, Admissions Associate
Contact Phone: 207-621-3465 **Contact E-mail:** kellynt@maine.edu
Website: www.uma.maine.edu

GENERAL INFORMATION
School type: Public.
University of Maine at Augusta offers both online and on-campus degree programs. Institution is accredited by NEASC. Online programs follow the same semester calendar as on-campus programs. All or most programs can be completed entirely online. Students can transfer from online to on-campus programs and from on-campus to online programs. There is no difference between physical diplomas awarded by online programs and those awarded by on-campus programs.

UNIVERSITY OF MARYLAND—UNIVERSITY COLLEGE

3501 University Boulevard East, Adelphi, MD, 20783
Contact: Ms. Jessica Sadaka, Director of Admissions
Contact Phone: 301-985-7000 **Contact E-mail:** umucinfo@umuc.edu
Website: www.umuc.edu/students/admissions.shtml

GENERAL INFORMATION
School type: Public.
University of Maryland—University College offers both online and on-campus degree programs. Institution is accredited by Middle States Association. Online programs follow the same semester calendar as on-campus programs. All or most programs can be completed entirely online. Students can transfer from online to on-campus programs and from on-campus to online programs. There is no difference between physical diplomas awarded by online programs and those awarded by on-campus programs.

UNIVERSITY OF MASSACHUSETTS—AMHERST

100 Venture Way, Suite 201, Hadley, MA, 01035-9430
Contact: Bill McClure, Director, Continuing and Professional Education
Contact Phone: 413-545-3351 **Contact E-mail:** academicprorams@contined.umass.edu
Website: www.umassonline.net

GENERAL INFORMATION
School type: Public.
University of Massachusetts Amherst offers both online and on-campus degree programs. Institution is accredited by New England Association of Schools and Colleges. Online programs follow the same semester calendar as on-campus programs. All or most programs can be completed entirely online. Students can transfer from online to on-campus programs and from on-campus to online programs. There is no difference between physical diplomas awarded by online programs and those awarded by on-campus programs.

UNIVERSITY OF MASSACHUSETTS—BOSTON

100 Morrissey Boulevard, Boston, MA, 02125
Contact: Katharine Galaitsis, Director of Online Education
Contact Phone: 617-287-7918 **Contact E-mail:** Katharine.Galaitsis@umb.edu
Website: http://ccde.umb.edu/dl

GENERAL INFORMATION
School type: Public.
University of Massachusetts—Boston offers both online and on-campus degree programs. Institution is accredited by New England Association of Schools and Colleges. Online programs follow the same semester calendar as on-campus programs. Most programs cannot be completed entirely online. Students can enroll in a 2-year program from RN to BS in Nursing and a completer program requiring 30 credits from UMB. Students cannot transfer from online to on-campus programs but can transfer from on-campus to online programs. There is no difference between physical diplomas awarded by online programs and those awarded by on-campus programs.

UNIVERSITY OF MASSACHUSETTS—LOWELL

One University Avenue, Southwick 202, Lowell, MA, 1854
Contact: Continuing Education Faculty and Student Support Center
Contact Phone: 978-934-2474 **Contact E-mail:** Continuinged@uml.edu
Website: http://Continuinged.uml.edu/online

GENERAL INFORMATION
School type: Public.
University of Massachusetts—Lowell offers both online and on-campus degree programs. Institution is accredited by NEASC. Online programs follow the same semester calendar as on-campus programs. All or most programs can be completed entirely online. Students can transfer from online to on-campus programs and from on-campus to online programs. There is no difference between physical diplomas awarded by online programs and those awarded by on-campus programs.

UNIVERSITY OF MICHIGAN—FLINT

237 French Hall, 303 East Kearsley, Flint, MI, 48502-1950
Contact: Theresa Stevens, Academic Online Programs
Contact Phone: 810-762-3200 **Contact E-mail:** tmsteven@umflint.edu
Website: http://oel.umflint.edu

GENERAL INFORMATION
School type: Public.
University of Michigan—Flint offers both online and on-campus degree programs. Institution is accredited by NCA. Online programs follow the same semester calendar as on-campus programs. All or most programs can be completed entirely online. Students can transfer from online to on-campus programs and from on-campus to online programs. There is no difference between physical diplomas awarded by online programs and those awarded by on-campus programs.

UNIVERSITY OF MINNESOTA—CROOKSTON

208C Selvig Hall, 2900 University Avenue, Crookston, MN, 56716-5001
Contact: Michelle Christopherson, Director
Contact Phone: 218-281-8679 **Contact E-mail:** mchristo@umcrookston.edu
Website: www.umcrookston.edu/online

GENERAL INFORMATION
School type: Public.
University of Minnesota—Crookston offers both online and on-campus degree programs. Institution is accredited by Higher Learning Commission of the North Central Association of Colleges and Schools. Online programs follow the same semester calendar as on-campus programs. All or most programs can be completed entirely online. Students can transfer from online to on-campus programs and from on-campus to online programs. There is no difference between physical diplomas awarded by online programs and those awarded by on-campus programs.

UNIVERSITY OF MISSOURI—COLUMBIA

102 Whitten Hall, Columbia, MO, 65211
Contact: MU Direct
Contact Phone: 573-882-3598 or 800-545-2604 **Contact E-mail:** MUdirect@missouri.edu
Website: http://mudirect.missouri.edu

GENERAL INFORMATION
School type: Public.
University of Missouri—Columbia offers both online and on-campus degree programs. Institution is accredited by North Central Association. Online programs calendar differs from on-campus programs in that one of the four online programs do not follow the same semester calendar as on-campus programs, while the remaining 3 do. Most programs cannot be completed entirely online. Bachelor Completion Programs: Students enter as transfer students. Students can transfer from online to on-campus programs and from on-campus to online programs. There is no difference between physical diplomas awarded by online programs and those awarded by on-campus programs.

THE UNIVERSITY OF MONTANA

Continuing Education, The University of Montana, Missoula, MT, 59812
Contact: Program Director, UMOnline **Contact Phone:** 406-243-4999 **Contact E-mail:** UMOnline@umontana.edu
Website: http://UMOnline.umt.edu

GENERAL INFORMATION
School type: Public.
The University of Montana offers both online and on-campus degree programs. Institution is accredited by Northwest Commission on Colleges and Universities (NWCCU). Online programs follow the same semester calendar as on-campus programs. Students can transfer from online to on-campus programs and from on-campus to online programs. There is no difference between physical diplomas awarded by online programs and those awarded by on-campus programs.

UNIVERSITY OF NEBRASKA—LINCOLN

900 North Twenty-second Street, Lincoln, NE, 68588-8805
Contact: Nancy Aden, Director, Distance Education Services
Contact Phone: 402-472-5515
Website: www.admissions.unl.edu/apply

GENERAL INFORMATION
School type: Public.
University of Nebraska—Lincoln offers both online and on-campus degree programs. Institution is accredited by NCA. Online programs follow the same semester calendar as on-campus programs. All or most programs can be completed entirely online. Students can transfer from online to on-campus programs and from on-campus to online programs. There is no difference between physical diplomas awarded by online programs and those awarded by on-campus programs.

THE UNIVERSITY OF NORTH CAROLINA AT CHAPEL HILL

School of Nursing, CB #7460, University of North Carolina at Chapel Hill, Chapel Hill, NC, 27599-7460
Contact: Carolyn James, RN-BSN Admissions Specialist
Contact Phone: 919-966-3654 **Contact E-mail:** cfjames@e-mail.unc.edu
Website: http://nursing.unc.edu

GENERAL INFORMATION
School type: Public.
University of North Carolina at Chapel Hill offers both online and on-campus degree programs. Institution is accredited by Southern Association of Colleges and Schools. Online programs follow the same semester calendar as on-campus programs. All or most programs can be completed entirely online. Students cannot transfer from online to on-campus programs, nor from on-campus to online programs. There is no difference between physical diplomas awarded by online programs and those awarded by on-campus programs.

THE UNIVERSITY OF NORTH CAROLINA AT CHARLOTTE

Distance Education, 9201 University City Boulevard, Charlotte, NC, 28223
Contact: Mary Faye Englebert, Associate Director, Distance Education
Contact Phone: 704-687-3008 or 877-583-2966 **Contact E-mail:** distanceed@uncc.edu
Website: www.distanceed.uncc.edu

GENERAL INFORMATION
School type: Public.
The University of North Carolina at Charlotte offers both online and on-campus degree programs. Institution is accredited by Southern Association (COC). Online programs follow the same semester calendar as on-campus programs. All or most programs can be completed entirely online. Students can transfer from online to on-campus programs and from on-campus to online programs. There is no difference between physical diplomas awarded by online programs and those awarded by on-campus programs.

THE UNIVERSITY OF NORTH CAROLINA AT WILMINGTON

University of North Carolina at Wilmington, 601 South College Road, Wilmington, NC, 28403-5978
Contact: Cecil L. Willis, Assistant VC, Academic Affairs
Contact Phone: 910-962-3548 **Contact E-mail:** willis@uncw.edu
Website: www.uncw.edu

GENERAL INFORMATION
School type: Public.
University of North Carolina at Wilmington offers both online and on-campus degree programs. Institution is accredited. Online programs follow the same semester calendar as on-campus programs. All or most programs can be completed entirely online. Students can transfer from online to on-campus programs and from on-campus to online programs. There is no difference between physical diplomas awarded by online programs and those awarded by on-campus programs.

UNIVERSITY OF NORTH DAKOTA

Gustafson Hall Room 205, 3264 Campus Road Stop 9021, Grand Forks, ND, 58202-9021
Contact: Heidi Flaten, Distance Degree Program Coordinator
Contact Phone: 877-450-1842 **Contact E-mail:** distancedegreeprograms@mail.und.edu
Website: www.conted.und.edu/ddp

GENERAL INFORMATION
School type: Public.
University of North Dakota offers both online and on-campus degree programs. Institution is accredited by North Central Association. Online programs follow the same semester calendar as on-campus programs. All or most programs can be completed entirely online. Students can transfer from online to on-campus programs and from on-campus to online programs. There is no difference between physical diplomas awarded by online programs and those awarded by on-campus programs.

UNIVERSITY OF NORTH TEXAS

PO Box 310889, Denton, TX, 76203
Contact: Dr. Arlita Harris, Senior Marketing Specialist
Contact Phone: 940-565-2942 **Contact E-mail:** arlita@unt.edu
Website: www.untecampus.com

GENERAL INFORMATION
School type: Public.
University of North Texas offers both online and on-campus degree programs. Institution is accredited by Southern Association of Colleges and Schools. Online programs follow the same semester calendar as on-campus programs. All or most programs can be completed entirely online. Students can transfer from online to on-campus programs and from on-campus to online programs. There is no difference between physical diplomas awarded by online programs and those awarded by on-campus programs.

UNIVERSITY OF OKLAHOMA

College of Liberal Studies, 1610 Asp Avenue, Suite 108, Norman, OK, 73072-6405
Contact: Clint Hardesty, Recruitment Coordinator
Contact Phone: 405-325-1061/800-522-4389 **Contact E-mail:** clinth@ou.edu
Website: www.ou.edu/cls

GENERAL INFORMATION
School type: Public.
University of Oklahoma offers both online and on-campus degree programs. Institution is accredited by Higher Learning Commission of the North Central Association of Colleges and Schools. Online programs follow the same semester calendar as on-campus programs. All or most programs can be completed entirely online. Students can transfer from online to on-campus programs and from on-campus to online programs. There is no difference between physical diplomas awarded by online programs and those awarded by on-campus programs.

UNIVERSITY OF PHOENIX ONLINE

CF-A101, 3157 East Elwood Street, Phoenix, AZ, 85034-7209
Contact: Enrollment Counselor
Contact Phone: 602-387-7000
Website: www.uopxonline.com

GENERAL INFORMATION
School type: Proprietary.
University of Phoenix Online offers only online degree programs. Institution is accredited by Higher Learning Commission of the North Central Association. All degrees can be completed entirely online.

UNIVERSITY OF SAINT MARY (KS)

University of Saint Mary, 4100 South Fourth Street, Leavenworth, KS, 66048
Contact: Rick Hite, Director of the Online Program
Contact Phone: 913-758-4345 **Contact E-mail:** HiteR@stmary.edy
Website: www.stmary.edu

GENERAL INFORMATION
School type: Private.
University of Saint Mary offers both online and on-campus degree programs. Institution is accredited by NCATE and The Higher Learning Commission. Online programs follow the same semester calendar as on-campus programs. All or most programs can be completed entirely online. Students cannot transfer from online to on-campus programs, nor from on-campus to online programs. There is no difference between physical diplomas awarded by online programs and those awarded by on-campus programs.

UNIVERSITY OF SOUTH ALABAMA

University of South Alabama, SSB2500, Mobile, AL, 36688
Contact: Melissa Haab, Director, Admissions
Contact Phone: 251-460-6141 **Contact E-mail:** admiss@usouthal.edu
Website: http://usouthal.edu

GENERAL INFORMATION
School type: Public.
University of South Alabama offers only online degree programs. Institution is accredited by Southern Association of Colleges. All degrees can be completed entirely online.

THE UNIVERSITY OF SOUTH DAKOTA

414 East Clark Street, Vermillion, SD, 57069
Contact: Gary Girard, Program Manager
Contact Phone: 800-233-7937 **Contact E-mail:** ceinfo@usd.edu
Website: www.usd.edu/ce

GENERAL INFORMATION
School type: Public.
The University of South Dakota offers both online and on-campus degree programs. Institution is accredited by North Central Association of Colleges and School. Online programs follow the same semester calendar as on-campus programs. All or most programs can be completed entirely online. Students can transfer from online to on-campus programs and from on-campus to online programs. There is no difference between physical diplomas awarded by online programs and those awarded by on-campus programs.

UNIVERSITY OF ST. FRANCIS

University of St. Francis, 500 Wilcox Street, Joliet, IL, 60435
Contact: Sandee Sloka, Director, Graduate/Degree Completion Admissions
Contact Phone: 800-735-7500 **Contact E-mail:** ssloka@stfrancis.edu
Website: www.stfrancis.edu/admissions/index.htm

GENERAL INFORMATION
School type: Private.
University of St. Francis offers both online and on-campus degree programs. Institution is accredited by Higher Learning Commission of the North Central Association of Schools and Colleges. Online programs follow the same semester calendar as on-campus programs. All or most programs can be completed entirely online. Students can transfer from online to on-campus programs and from on-campus to online programs. There is no difference between physical diplomas awarded by online programs and those awarded by on-campus programs.

THE UNIVERSITY OF TENNESSEE AT MARTIN

The University of Tennessee at Martin, Online University Studies, Martin, TN, 38238
Contact: Dr. Tommy Cates, Director
Contact Phone: 731-881-7589 **Contact E-mail:** utonline.utm.edu
Website: www.utm.edu/onlinestudies.php

GENERAL INFORMATION
School type: Public.
The University of Tennessee at Martin offers both online and on-campus degree programs. Institution is accredited by Southern Association of Colleges and Schools. Online programs follow the same semester calendar as on-campus programs. Most programs cannot be completed entirely online. Degree Completion Program Students can transfer from online to on-campus programs and from on-campus to online programs. There is no difference between physical diplomas awarded by online programs and those awarded by on-campus programs.

UNIVERSITY OF WEST FLORIDA

11000 University Parkway, Building 77 Room 138, Pensacola, FL, 32514
Contact: Sharon Cobb, Office Administrator
Contact Phone: 850-473-7468 **Contact E-mail:** online@uwf.edu
Website: http://onlinecampus.uwf.edu

GENERAL INFORMATION
School type: Public.
University of West Florida offers both online and on-campus degree programs. Institution is accredited by SACS and others. Online programs follow the same semester calendar as on-campus programs. Most programs cannot be completed entirely online. AA/AS students can transfer from online to on-campus programs and from on-campus to online programs. There is no difference between physical diplomas awarded by online programs and those awarded by on-campus programs.

UNIVERSITY OF WESTERN ONTARIO

University of Western Ontario, Stevenson-Lawson Building, Room 170, London, ON, N6A 5B8
Contact: Debbie Sims, Distance Studies **Contact Phone:** 519-661-3982
Contact E-mail: dist.studies@uwo.ca
Website: www.registrar.uwo.ca/distance

GENERAL INFORMATION
School type: Public.
University of Western Ontario offers both online and on-campus degree programs. Institution is accredited by the Association of Universities and Colleges of Canada. Online programs follow the same semester calendar as on-campus programs. All or most programs can be completed entirely online. Students can transfer from online to on-campus programs and from on-campus to online programs. There is no difference between physical diplomas awarded by online programs and those awarded by on-campus programs.

UNIVERSITY OF WISCONSIN—GREEN BAY

2420 Nicolet Drive, Green Bay, WI, 54311
Contact: Jan Thornton, Associate Provost, Outreach and Adult Access
Contact Phone: 920-465-2641 **Contact E-mail:** thorntoj@uwgb.edu
Website: www.uwgb.edu/adult

GENERAL INFORMATION
School type: Public.
University of Wisconsin—Green Bay offers both online and on-campus degree programs. Institution is accredited by Higher Learning Commission of the North Central Association. Online programs follow the same semester calendar as on-campus programs. Students can transfer from online to on-campus programs and from on-campus to online programs. There is no difference between physical diplomas awarded by online programs and those awarded by on-campus programs.

UNIVERSITY OF WISCONSIN—STOUT

140B Voc Rehab Building, Menomonie, WI, 54751
Contact: Doug Stevens, Outreach Program Manager
Contact Phone: 715-232-2693 **Contact E-mail:** stevensdo@uwstout.edu
Website: www.uwstout.edu/de

GENERAL INFORMATION
School type: Public.
University of Wisconsin—Stout offers both online and on-campus degree programs. Institution is accredited by The Higher Learning Commission of the North Central Association of Colleges and Schools. Online programs follow the same semester calendar as on-campus programs. Most programs cannot be completed entirely online, as they are degree completion programs. Students can transfer from online to on-campus programs and from on-campus to online programs.

UNIVERSITY OF WYOMING

Dept 3274, 1000 East University Avenue, Laramie, WY, 82071
Contact: Outreach Credit Programs, Online UW
Contact Phone: 800-448-7801 **Contact E-mail:** outreach@uwyo.edu
Website: http://outreach.uwyo.edu

GENERAL INFORMATION
School type: Public.
University of Wyoming offers both online and on-campus degree programs. Institution is accredited by HLC. Online programs follow the same semester calendar as on-campus programs. All or most programs can be completed entirely online. Students can transfer from online to on-campus programs and from on-campus to online programs. There is no difference between physical diplomas awarded by online programs and those awarded by on-campus programs.

UPPER IOWA UNIVERSITY

1101 Fifth Street, West Des Moines, IA, 50265
Contact: Becky Godwin, Lead Online Recruiter/Academic Advisor
Contact Phone: 515-225-3192 **Contact E-mail:** godwinr@uiu.edu
Website: www.uiu.edu

GENERAL INFORMATION
School type: Private.
Upper Iowa University offers both online and on-campus degree programs. Institution is accredited by Higher Learning Commission-North Central Association. Online programs follow the same semester calendar as on-campus programs. All or most programs can be completed entirely online. Students can transfer from online to on-campus programs and from on-campus to online programs. There is no difference between physical diplomas awarded by online programs and those awarded by on-campus programs.

UTAH STATE UNIVERSITY

5000 Old Main Hill, Logan, ut, 84321
Contact: Dr. Edie Loo, Director of Online Education
Contact Phone: 435-797-2137 or 800-233-2137 **Contact E-mail:** distance.info@usu.edu
Website: http://campuses.usu.edu

GENERAL INFORMATION
School type: Public.
Utah State University offers both online and on-campus degree programs. Institution is accredited by North West Association of Schools and Colleges. Online programs follow the same semester calendar as on-campus programs. All or most programs can be completed entirely online. Students can transfer from online to on-campus programs and from on-campus to online programs. There is no difference between physical diplomas awarded by online programs and those awarded by on-campus programs.

UTICA COLLEGE

1600 Burrstone Road, Utica, NY, 13502
Contact: Graduate and Extended Studies
Contact Phone: 315-792-3001 **Contact E-mail:** sneun@utica.edu
Website: www.onlineuticacollege.com

GENERAL INFORMATION
School type: Private.
Utica College offers both online and on-campus degree programs. Institution is accredited by Middle States Commission on Higher Education. Online programs follow the same semester calendar as on-campus programs. All or most programs can be completed entirely online. Students can transfer from online to on-campus programs and from on-campus to online programs. There is no difference between physical diplomas awarded by online programs and those awarded by on-campus programs.

VITERBO UNIVERSITY

Viterbo Univesity, 900 Viterbo Drive, La Crosse, WI, 54601
Contact: Darcie Mueller, Assistant Director and Outreach Coordinator
Contact Phone: 608-796-3370 **Contact E-mail:** dlmueller@viterbo.edu
Website: www.viterbo.edu/sal.aspx?id=13136

GENERAL INFORMATION
School type: Private.
Viterbo University offers both online and on-campus degree programs. Institution is accredited by NCA/HLC. Online programs follow the same semester calendar as on-campus programs. All or most programs can be completed entirely online. Students can transfer from online to on-campus programs and from on-campus to online programs. There is no difference between physical diplomas awarded by online programs and those awarded by on-campus programs.

WALDEN UNIVERSITY

1001 Fleet Street, Fourth Floor, Baltimore, MD, 21202
Contact: Walden University Admission Office
Contact Phone: 866-492-5336
Website: www.waldenu.edu

GENERAL INFORMATION
School type: Proprietary.
Walden University offers only online degree programs. Institution is accredited by The Higher Learning Commission, North Central Association. All degrees can be completed entirely online.

WASHINGTON STATE UNIVERSITY

PO Box 645220, Pullman, WA, 99164-5220
Contact: Lenore Chambers, Call Center Staff
Contact Phone: 800-222-4978 **Contact E-mail:** distance@wsu.edu
Website: www.distance.wsu.edu

GENERAL INFORMATION
School type: Public.
Washington State University offers both online and on-campus degree programs. Institution is accredited by Northwest Commission on Colleges and Universities. Online programs follow the same semester calendar as on-campus programs. All or most programs can be completed entirely online. Students can transfer from online to on-campus programs and from on-campus to online programs. There is no difference between physical diplomas awarded by online programs and those awarded by on-campus programs.

WESTERN GOVERNORS UNIVERSITY

4001 South 700 East, Salt Lake City, UT, 84107
Contact: Enrollment Department
Contact Phone: 866-225-5948 **Contact E-mail:** info@wgu.edu
Website: www.wgu.edu

GENERAL INFORMATION
School type: Private.
Western Governors University offers only online degree programs. Institution is accredited by Northwest Commission on Colleges and Universities. All degrees can be completed entirely online.

WESTERN ILLINOIS UNIVERSITY

6 Horrabin Hall, One University Circle, Macomb, IL, 61455
Contact: Richard Carter, Director, BOT/BA Degree Program
Contact Phone: 309-298-1929 **Contact E-mail:** r-carter@wiu.edu
Website: www.wiu.edu/BOTdegree

GENERAL INFORMATION
School type: Public.
Western Illinois University offers both online and on-campus degree programs. Institution is accredited by North Central Association. Online programs follow the same semester calendar as on-campus programs. Most programs cannot be completed entirely online. Students can transfer from online to on-campus programs and from on-campus to online programs. There is no difference between physical diplomas awarded by online programs and those awarded by on-campus programs.

WRIGHT STATE UNIVERSITY

160 University Hall, Wright State University, Dayton, OH, 45435
Contact: Kathy Skarzynski RN, MS, Outreach Coordinator—RN to BSN Program
Contact Phone: 937-775-2591 **Contact E-mail:** kathy.skarzynski@wright.edu
Website: www.wright.edu/nursing/prog_info/rn_bsn.html

GENERAL INFORMATION
School type: Public.
Wright State University offers both online and on-campus degree programs. Institution is accredited by North Central Associates of Colleges and Schools; Ohio Board of Nursing; Commission on Collegiate Nursing Education. Online programs follow the same semester calendar as on-campus programs. Students can transfer from online to on-campus programs and from on-campus to online programs. There is no difference between physical diplomas awarded by online programs and those awarded by on-campus programs.

YORK UNIVERSITY

Bennett Centre for Student Services, York University, 99 Ian MacDonald Boulevard,
Toronto, ON, M3J 1P3
Contact: Office of Admissions
Contact Phone: 416-736-5825 **Contact E-mail:** intlenq@yorku.ca
Website: www.yorku.ca/futurestudents

GENERAL INFORMATION

School type: Public.
York University offers both online and on-campus degree programs. Institution is accredited by Association of Universities and Colleges of Canada. Online programs follow the same semester calendar as on-campus programs. All or most programs can be completed entirely online. Students can transfer from online to on-campus programs and from on-campus to online programs. There is no difference between physical diplomas awarded by online programs and those awarded by on-campus programs.

SCHOOL SAYS . . .

In this section you'll find hundreds of colleges with extended listings describing admissions, curriculum, internships, and much more. This is your chance to get in-depth information on colleges that interest you. The Princeton Review charges each school a small fee to be listed, and the editorial responsibility is solely that of the college.

ADELPHI UNIVERSITY

AT A GLANCE

Adelphi University, chartered in 1896, was the first institution of higher education for the liberal arts and sciences on Long Island. Through its schools and programs—the College of Arts and Sciences, the Derner Institute of Advanced Psychological Studies, the Honors College, the Ruth S. Ammon School of Education, University College, and the Schools of Business, Nursing, and Social Work—the coeducational university offers undergraduate and graduate degrees as well as professional and educational programs for adults. Adelphi University currently enrolls more than 5,100 undergraduate students from 36 states and 47 foreign countries. With its main campus in Garden City and centers in Manhattan, Hauppauge, and Poughkeepsie, the university maintains a commitment to liberal studies in tandem with rigorous professional preparation and active citizenship.

LOCATION AND ENVIRONMENT

Could there be a better location for a college campus than ours? Nestled in beautiful suburban Garden City, New York, Adelphi's home is in the heart of Long Island. Shops, banks, and restaurants are within walking distance, and legendary beaches, museums, entertainment venues, and premiere shopping destinations are a short car-ride away. A short walk and 45-minute train ride takes you into New York City, the financial and cultural center of the world.

OFF-CAMPUS OPPORTUNITIES

Our students take full advantage of the benefits of our location. Learning outside the classroom is truly a part of the Adelphi experience, in formal internships, field placements, and clinical training as well as the informal interaction of our students with the riches of Long Island and metropolitan New York. In virtually every major, Adelphi students have access to world-class resources—museums, theaters and galleries, health care and research facilities, corporate headquarters, and government facilities on Long Island and New York City.

MAJORS AND DEGREES OFFERED

Programs of study: accounting, African American and ethnic studies, anthropology/forensic anthropology, art° (art history, fine arts [ceramics, painting, photography, printmaking, sculpture], graphic design, art education°, Asian studies, biochemistry, biology, chemistry, communications, communication sciences and disorders, computer and management information systems, computer science, criminal justice, dance°°, economics, education studies (Childhood Education [STEP], Adolescence Education [STEP]), English, Environmental Studies, Exercise Physiology, Finance, Foreign language studies, French, gender studies, history, interdisciplinary studies, international studies, journalism, Latin American studies, management (finance, marketing, human resource management, management information systems), mathematics, music°°, nursing, performing arts°° (acting, design tech), philosophy, physical education, physical education/health education, physics, political science, psychology, public service, social work, sociology, Spanish, sport management.

° Art portfolio required

°° Audition required

Students who declare an undecided major must declare a major by their fifth semester, or after the completion of 60 credits of course work.

ACADEMIC PROGRAMS

Five-year bachelor's and master's programs: Scholars Teacher Education Program (STEP), childhood education, adolescence education, social work. Pre-Professional Opportunities: pre-dental, pre-engineering, pre-law, pre-medicine, pre-optometry, pre-physical therapy/allied health.

CAMPUS FACILITIES AND EQUIPMENT

While you're changing and growing, we are, too. That's because we're building your future even as we're building ours. The new Performing Arts Center, opening in 2008, will showcase our prestigious programs in acting, design/technical theater, music, and dance together under one roof. The new center will feature a 500-seat music performance hall, dance recital rooms, music practice rooms, temperature-controlled instrument storage rooms, and a Black Box theater. Also opening in 2008, the Recreation and Sports Center will become the new home of Adelphi's successful athletics programs. The center's 3-story, 3-court gym, which converts into a 2,200-seat arena for basketball games and other events, will accommodate recreational and intercollegiate athletes and health and physical education students, and can host NCAA tournaments and championships. Other recent and planned additions to the Adelphi campus include a new Alice Brown Early Learning Center, a learning lab for students in education, psychology, and health care programs, which will provide age-appropriate classrooms plus indoor and outdoor space for children ages 1.5 to 5; a new residence hall, scheduled to open in 2009, which will join our 6 current halls that are home to more than 1,200 students; and the new Adele and Herbert J. Klappercenter for Fine Arts, dedicated in November 2007, which features ceramics, sculpture, printmaking, and painting studios, and exhibition space.

TUITION, ROOM, BOARD, AND FEES

Tuition and fees for 2007-2208 is $23,000; a typical double room is $6,700; the basic meal plan is $2,200; and the average financial aid package was $14,900 per full-time student in 2006-2007.

FINANCIAL AID

Financing your education may be one of biggest decisions you and your family will make together. Scholarships, loans, and grants can sometimes be a deciding factor in which college you choose to attend. Since this is one of the most important investments you will make, Adelphi's Office of Student Financial Services is dedicated to providing sound financial guidance and ready to help you explore the full range of financial alternatives available to you. We are committed to making private higher education affordable and to providing you with the best value for your tuition dollar. That's one reason why the prestigious Fiske Guide to Colleges named Adelphi a "Best Buy" in higher education in both its 2007 and 2008 editions. Adelphi is one of only 26 private universities nationwide and the only private university on Long Island to earn a "Best Buy" distinction.

STUDENT ORGANIZATIONS AND ACTIVITIES

Take part in or watch your classmates in our thriving cultural arts programs, including plays, art exhibits, concerts, and lectures. Attend a sporting event with friends, or check out the comprehensive sports and fitness services available, including intramural athletics and group classes in Pilates and yoga. With more than 80 student organizations, including community service, academic, cultural, and religious clubs, student-run media, 7 Greek-letter social sororities and fraternities, and 20 academic honor societies, there's something for everyone.

ADMISSIONS PROCESS

If you can see yourself at Adelphi, we encourage you to apply. To be considered for admission, you must graduate from a recognized 4-year high school or academy and complete 16 units of college preparatory course work or an equivalent preparation. Your co-curricular activities, interests, and your personal interview are important to us as well.

ALBERTUS MAGNUS COLLEGE

AT A GLANCE

Albertus Magnus College, a four-year, private, liberal arts college located in the heart of vibrant southern Connecticut, has chosen its small size on purpose. Founded in 1925 by the Dominican Sisters of St. Mary's of the Springs, Albertus Magnus College educates men and women to become leaders in all areas of their lives.

Faculty members at Albertus Come from leading universities and are one of the College's greatest assets. Ninety percent of the 75 full- and part-time faculty members hold a Ph.D. or the equivalent. The student-staff ratio of 13:1 means that they want to get to know students on an individual basis, and they are readily accessible for academic and personal counseling. The College believes that training in the liberal arts is excellent preparation for life and offers the groundwork for a multitude of professions.

The 500 students who attend the traditional undergraduate program at Albertus come from various parts of the United States, Europe, Africa, Asia, and South and Central America. The highest percentages of students come from the regional New England states. About 60 percent of the students live on campus in housing that has been converted from large former estate homes. The housing program fosters a strong sense of community spirit, and students often plan informal gatherings and other social events in their residence halls. The Campus Center is a hub of student activities such as comedians, live music, contests, and other unique celebrations.

Being an active part of the Albertus Community is an important part of stepping into your future. After all, the numerous extracurricular activities offered at Albertus are essential to an education committed to engaging your mind, body, and spirit.

LOCATION AND ENVIRONMENT

The 50 acre campus is located in a residential neighborhood of New Haven's historic north end. Boasting several turn-of-the-century mansions sprawled over rolling green lawns; the Albertus campus is located in an idyllic New England setting. New Haven is a multicultural city with a population of more than 130,000 people. Both New York City and Boston are easily accessible by train, and for the outdoor enthusiast, there are numerous beaches and hiking trails in the immediate vicinity.

OFF-CAMPUS OPPORTUNITIES

Practica and Internships

Practica and internships are required for many majors and recommended for all students. The College gives academic credit for work done outside the classroom that is related to the student's primary field of study. For more information please visit www.albertus.edu.

Study Abroad

Students may spend a semester or full academic year studying abroad in approved American college-sponsored programs. Credits received in these programs are transferable to Albertus. All students are encouraged to take advantage of opportunities for foreign study and travel. Language majors in particular find residence in a country where the language they study is spoken rewarding. Study abroad is arranged through the Department Chair and is generally recommended for a student's junior year.

MAJORS AND DEGREES OFFERED

The most popular majors at Albertus include business, communications, criminal justice, education, psychology and sociology. However, there are over 30 areas of study including accounting, art (history and studio), art therapy, biology, business administration, chemistry, child development and mental health, communications, creative writing, criminal justice, education (grades 4–12), English, finance, general studies, graphic design, history, humanities, human services, industrial and organizational psychology, international business, computer information systems, marketing, mathematics, performance communications, philosophy/religion, photography, physical sciences, political science, pre-law, pre-medicine, psychology, Spanish, sports communications, social science, social work, sociology, urban studies, and visual arts.

STUDENT ORGANIZATIONS AND ACTIVITIES

The Student Government Association is the governing body for all student organizations, publications and clubs. It also operates the House of Bollstadt, the College's pub, which features entertainment such as comedians, hypnotists, theme nights, billiards, ping pong, music and television. Students plan major events and activities on campus that include semi-formals, drive-in movies, midnight study breaks, and performances.

Albertus has an active non-residential student population that takes full advantage of all student activites and athletic opportunities. A Commuter representative is elected each year to the Student Government Association to address concerns and issues of specific importance to commuters.

The Common Ground is our new cyber lounge where students can check their email, work on their homework, and enjoy a cup of coffee or tea. It is a popular setting for students to relax in between classes or after a long day.

Other current clubs include:

Art Club

Breakwater the student literary magazine

Business Club

Campus Ministry

Dance Team

English Club

History Society

Multicultural Student Union

Psychology Club

Outspoken—Gay/Straight Alliance

Residence Hall Association

Science Club

ADMISSIONS PROCESS

Albertus Magnus College welcomes applications from students of all ages, all nationalities, and all ethnic, racial, and religious groups.

The College operates on a rolling admission system. Students are encouraged to contact the Office of Admission for an information packet and application. Students may also visit our website to apply online or download a copy of our application.

Freshmen

Students who either plan to graduate from fully accredited high schools, have received a GED, or have been home schooled with a diploma from an accredited high school.

Transfer

Students who have studied at other accredited institutions. Normally, a cumulative average of 2.0 on a grade scale of 4.0 is required of students transferring from fully accredited institutions. We accept transfer credits from classes in which a grade of C or better was earned. How those credits will transfer into a specific degree program will be determined in an individual session with a representative from the Office of the Registrar.

International

Students who are not United States citizens are encouraged to consider continuing their education at Albertus Magnus College. The small classes and personal attention are a good fit for students who are adjusting culturally to this country. Please note that Albertus Magnus College is unable to offer financial aid or scholarships to international students.

The following items are required of every applicant to Albertus:

1. A completed application form.

2. An official high school transcript.

3. Official ACT or SAT I Scores.

4. At least one letter of recommendation from a guidance counselor, teacher or college advisor who is familiar with the applicant's academic ability and potential.

5. A non-refundable application fee of thirty-five dollars ($35).

6. An essay of your choice is also strongly recommended.

7. An official college or university transcript for transfer students.

The information required above will be used by the Office of Admission in deciding on the merits of applicants. Special consideration may be given to selected candidates whose preparation varies from the recommended pattern, but whose record gives evidence of genuine intellectual ability and interest.

FINANCIAL AID

Albertus Magnus College seeks to make it possible for every student accepted for admission to attend the College. Financial assistance is available in the form of scholarships, grants, loans, and employment.

Albertus uses the Free Application for Federal Student Aid (FAFSA) to determine the demonstrated need of each applicant for assistance. We encourage students to complete the FAFSA online at www.fafsa.ed.gov. The Albertus Magnus College school code is 001374.

Students who are accepted for admission and complete their FAFSA prior to February 28 are given first priority for awarding funds.

Each year Albertus Magnus College awards a variety of schoalrships. All scholarships awarded from the Office of Admission require the application to the College be submitted and complete by March 15. Students are eligible to recieve only one scholarship from the College, and must be graduating from a regionally accredited institution.

Please visit www.albertus.edu for more detailed information about scholarships and Financial Aid.

Tuition for full-time students during the 2007–2008 academic year is $20,166 ($10,083 per semester). Part-time students (individuals taking fewer than 12 credits a semester) are charged $840 per credit. Room and board totals $8907.

Fees total $908 for the 2007–2008 school year.

700 Prospect Street

Phone: 800-578-9160

New Haven, CT, 06511

Fax: 203-773-5248

Website: www.albertus.edu

ALVERNIA COLLEGE

AT A GLANCE

Alvernia is a private Franciscan college rooted in the Catholic and liberal arts traditions. We stress the development of the whole person academically, emotionally, and spiritually. The roots that became Alvernia were planted in 1926 when the Bernardine Sisters of the Third Order of Saint Francis established a teachers' seminar for the education of the Sisters. Thirty-2 years later, in 1958, the institution expanded into a 4-year liberal arts college. The student population in 1958 included only 23 freshmen and 8 sophomores, and has expanded to its current enrollment of more than 2,800 male and female students, including a growing graduate program. The mission statements of the Bernadine Congregation and Alvernia College are based on the 5 core values of the Franciscan tradition: service, humility, peacemaking, contemplation, and collegiality. We honor our core Catholic traditions while respecting and welcoming students, faculty, and staff of many religious backgrounds. We foster moral leadership and service to others in the interest of peace and justice locally and globally. We prepare our graduates to achieve their personal dreams and professional success, and to be engaged citizens and lifelong learners. Alvernia has been honored by the Templeton Foundation as one of the top 100 character-building colleges in the nation and a model of excellence in education.

Since 1967, the Middle States Association of Colleges and Schools has granted Alvernia accreditation. The Education program for elementary and secondary teachers is approved by the Pennsylvania Department of Education. The Occupational Therapy program is fully accredited by the American Occupational Therapy Association. The bachelor of science in nursing has approval by the Pennsylvania State Board of Nursing and is accredited by the Commission on Collegiate Nursing Education. The athletic training program is accredited by the Commission on Accreditation of Allied Health Education Programs in cooperation with the Joint Review Committee on Educational Programs in Athletic Training. The social work program is accredited by the Council on Social Work Education. The Addiction Studies Program is certified by the Pennsylvania Certification Board. The business department is accredited by the Association of Collegiate Business Schools and Programs.

LOCATION AND ENVIRONMENT

Located on a beautiful campus on the outskirts of Reading, Pennsylvania, Alvernia offers a setting conducive to learning. The school is set in a tree-lined suburban neighborhood 3 miles from the center of Reading (population 81,000) in the scenic Blue Mountain area of Eastern Pennsylvania. Reading offers a mix of cultural and entertainment destinations, such as the GoggleWorks Center for the Arts, the Reading Public Museum, outlet shopping, minor league sports, and concerts at the Sovereign Center. Students also find opportunities for community involvement, internships, and field work experience at many local businesses, agencies, and organizations.

The 55-acre campus, overlooking Angelica Park and set on the Schuylkill River along the majestic Appalachian Mountain Trail, gives students access to a wide range of outdoor activities, including hiking, boating, camping, and skiing. In addition, Alvernia is just a few hours by train or car to Philadelphia, New York, Washington, DC, and Baltimore. The Pocono Mountains and the New Jersey and Delaware shores are also close by.

OFF-CAMPUS OPPORTUNITIES

The Washington Center experience is a popular way students expand their educational opportunities beyond the classroom. Earning college credit while spending a semester in Washington, DC, students serve as interns in a congressional office, government agency, major corporation, newspaper, or news network, or an agency devoted to legal affairs, international relations, or business and economics. Others intern with nonprofit groups dealing with the environment, women's issues, the arts, education, science, or labor relations.

Study abroad is increasingly popular. In recent years, Alvernia students have studied in Great Britain, Germany, Spain, and on a Semester-at-Sea program.

Some majors require that students earn practical experience working hands-on in their field of interest. These practical opportunities help students make career choices and establish important professional contacts.

MAJORS AND DEGREES OFFERED

Alvernia offers more than 50 Academic Programs of study. Bachelor's degrees are awarded in the following majors: accounting, addiction studies, athletic training, biochemistry, biology (including a medical technology emphasis), business management, chemistry (including a medical technology emphasis), communications, computer information systems, criminal justice administration, education (concentrations in early childhood/elementary, secondary, and special), English, forensic science, general science, history, human resource management, liberal studies, marketing, mathematics, nursing, philosophy, political science, psychology, social work, sport management, and theology. Pre-professional programs are available in dentistry, law, medicine, and veterinary studies. Alvernia also offers minors and certificate programs.

Master's degrees are awarded in occupational therapy, business administration, community counseling, education, and liberal studies. A PhD program in leadership is also available.

ACADEMIC PROGRAMS

Alvernia offers both a traditional course schedule and a flexible year-round program for working adults. To earn a bachelor's degree, students must complete a minimum of 123 credits, with 54 credits in the liberal arts, 40 in the major, and 30 in electives. Requirements vary by program.

Logical and critical thinking, accurate comprehension, and effective communication are at the heart of Alvernia's academic program. Students' personal development is also highly valued, and the college promotes integrity in academic pursuits, social responsibility, and moral values.

The Genesis Program at Alvernia provides academic advisement for students who have not declared a major. It is an incredible opportunity to dedicate the first few semesters of college to pure exploration of potential fields of study. Through careful examination and counseling, students gain exposure to the opportunities available at Alvernia.

Qualified students participate in the Alvernia's Honors Program. The Honors Program assists students of outstanding intellectual promise and high motivation who are interested in pursuing future graduate or professional studies or who prefer a more challenging program at the undergraduate level. The program recognizes and encourages students to achieve academic excellence, often letting them work at their own pace, and facilitates a stimulating exchange of ideas and information between their varied interests and different disciplines. The Honors Program includes co-curricular activities, provides service opportunities, intellectual and social support, and injects significant additional depth in the student's academic program. Honors courses are team-taught by faculty from diverse areas and involve student-led discussions. Students and faculty wishing to do research or explore topics not offered in established courses can arrange independent studies under the direction of a faculty member and often present their work at a departmental seminar.

CAMPUS FACILITIES AND EQUIPMENT

Alvernia's newest building, the O'Pake Science Center, a $9.3 million state-of-the-art facility, opened in 2006. The O'Pake Science Center added 31,582 square feet of classroom, laboratory, and faculty office space to Alvernia's campus. Each of 2 floors is equipped with 5 laboratory/classrooms, all of which have smart capability, or Internet access, to bring resources, research, and data from other schools and laboratories into Alvernia's classrooms.

The center of campus academic life is the Franco Library and Learning Center, a beautiful facility that provides a quiet place to study. This facility supports the curriculum of the college with a growing collection of information resources, including books, periodicals, non-print materials, CD-ROM programs, the Internet, and online resources. Students enjoy access to a number of interlibrary loan services.

The Student Center includes student organization meeting rooms, seminar rooms, dining facilities, informal gathering areas, the bookstore, and student development offices. Student services offered at Alvernia include a campus ministry and career, counseling, and health services.

On-campus housing includes traditional residence halls, apartments, suites, and town houses. The newest residence hall was completed in the fall of 2005. Residence hall facilities are equipped with laundry, cable TV, and phones with voice mail. Computer hookup is also available.

Alvernia's campus is fully networked. Students have access to the college's academic information network and the Internet from their residence hall rooms as well as from other campus locations, including classrooms, the library, and labs. All students may hook up personal computers through our secure system. Network access and Alvernia e-mail accounts are available to all students.

TUITION, ROOM, BOARD, AND FEES

For the 2008-2009 academic year, tuition is $22,800, and room and board is $8,660 (an approximate cost based on the highest priced residence hall and a 19-meal plan).

FINANCIAL AID

Ninety-nine percent of students attending Alvernia receive some form of financial aid. Alvernia offers financial aid to students whose personal and family resources are unable to meet the full cost of their Alvernia education. Each year we offer more than $3 million in assistance. Aid usually comes in the form of scholarships, grants, loans, and work-study arrangements. Freshmen who have an outstanding GPA and SAT scores may be eligible for one of the following 3 merit-based scholarships: the Presidential Scholarship ($12,000), the Trustee's Scholarship ($10,000), and the Veronica Founder's Scholarship ($6,000). Students must be enrolled full-time or part-time to be considered for assistance. Applicants interested in financial aid should submit the FAFSA by mid-February. Continuing Education students must be accepted in a degree program and complete a matriculation form to be eligible for financial aid.

STUDENT ORGANIZATIONS AND ACTIVITIES

Alvernia encourages students to take advantage of learning opportunities outside of the classroom by participating in any of our more than 50 student clubs, organizations, and service programs. Learning in college takes place by being involved in curricular programs as well as extracurricular activities. Campus organizations offer opportunities to suit the interests of all students, to meet new people, to learn various skills, and to develop leadership abilities.

Athletics are an integral part of the educational mission at Alvernia College. Students may participate in intercollegiate, intramural, and club-level athletic programs. Intercollegiate teams compete at the NCAA Division III level. Continuing a proud athletic tradition, Alvernia has accepted an invitation to compete in the Middle Atlantic States Athletic Conference (MAC), a highly competitive conference, beginning in 2008-2009, and is also a member of the Eastern Collegiate Athletic Conference.

The Office of Student Activities works with the college's many student organizations to provide a calendar of social, cultural, and other co-curricular activities. The Student Government Association provides an opportunity for leadership through the exercise of personal and group responsibility. All students complete approved community service hours as part of Alvernia's commitment to fostering a reverence for the dignity of all life. Our commitment to peace and justice, and a devotion to the service of others, is especially focused on the materially and spiritually disadvantaged of the local and global community.

ADMISSIONS PROCESS

Our warm Alvernia attitude extends to the ease of applying for admission. Many factors are considered for admission, including academic performance, standardized test scores, class rank, extracurricular activities, and community involvement. Application and admission notification is on a rolling basis; however, applicants are encouraged to submit the admission application as early as possible. In addition to their transcripts and SAT or ACT scores, nursing applicants must also submit 2 letters of reference.

Alvernia accepts and/or offers special programs for accelerated high school students, non-traditional students (older than 24), transfer students, students with disabilities, and international students.

The best way to get to know Alvernia is through a campus visit and tour. Applicants and those considering the school are strongly encouraged to come for an individual campus visit. We will personalize the campus visit to match each student's unique interests. Alvernia also hosts information sessions and open houses throughout the year. They allow prospective freshmen or transfers to meet current students, talk to admissions and financial aid counselors, and meet faculty and coaches. Overnight and shadow visits are also available. We invite you to discover Alvernia.

AMERICAN INTERNATIONAL COLLEGE

Choosing a college is a big decision, and at American International we'll help you reach your dream. We're here for you every step of the way . . . you won't go it alone!

AT A GLANCE

American International College is a 4-year private coeducational institution. Founded in 1885, AIC is located in Springfield, Massachusetts—a city of 160,000 people in the Connecticut River Valley. We offer a variety of undergraduate and graduate programs, with courses held in the fall and spring semesters, as well as intersession and summer sessions. The student body consists of 1,389 full-time undergraduate students from 30 states and 46 countries, 121 part time undergraduate students, and 992 graduate students.

LOCATION AND ENVIRONMENT

The American International Campus is located in the geographic center of the City of Springfield, Massachusetts. Springfield is a typical moderate-sized American city of nearly 160,000 people, currently transforming itself from a manufacturing to a service center with a global outreach. It is the hub of a metropolitan statistical area of more than 500,000 people.

OFF-CAMPUS OPPORTUNITIES

The campus is fewer than 2 miles from Springfield's tourist and entertainment center, including the National Basketball Hall of Fame. To the east, the campus is fewer than 3 miles from the city's premiere shopping mall. All locations are accessible by an efficient and timely public transportation system operated by the Pioneer Valley Transit Authority. The city is proud of its professional theater, the symphony orchestra, and its art and natural science museums. The MassMutual Center complex offers a varied venue of concerts, shows, and sporting events.

MAJORS AND DEGREES OFFERED

Arts, education, and sciences: American studies, human services (minor), biomedical science, interdepartmental science, biochemistry, international studies, bio-education, liberal studies, biology, mathematics, cell and molecular biology, middle/school education, chemistry, political science, coaching (certificate), psychology, communication, public administration, criminal justice, secondary education, early childhood education, social studies, ecology/environmental science, sociology, elementary education, special education, English, zoology, history, human biology. Business administration: accounting, economics/finance, international business, management, marketing, sports and recreation management. Health sciences: nursing, occupational science, undergrad PT (program). Continuing and extended studies: accounting, business studies, general business, gerontology, human resource management, human services, human services administration, liberal studies, management, management and technology, marketing, social sciences. Graduate majors/programs: clinical psychology, early childhood education, educational psychology (MA and DEEP), elementary education, forensic psychology, human resource development, middle/secondary education, reading, school adjustment counselor, school administration, school guidance counselor, special education, teaching. Accounting and taxation: business administration (MBA), nonprofit management, public administration (MPA), organizational development. Nursing: occupational therapy, physical therapy.

ACADEMIC PROGRAMS

The Office of Career Services promotes, coordinates, and provides services to assist students with career guidance and job search strategies. The staff provides not only general information and support, but also individual career counseling to assist in exploring and setting career goals. In addition, there are available resources to assist with career selection and employment outlook and trends in occupational fields. Students looking for internships and jobs, whether full-time, part-time, or summer employment, can find assistance.

The Eugene A. Dexter Student Counseling Center, located on the 2nd floor of Mallary Hall, provides confidential assistance to students with personal problems as well as to those in need of academic and vocational counseling. Students may obtain help in evaluating their interests, choosing a major, and in improving personal study habits.

The ESL program provides non-native English-speaking students an opportunity to improve their English language skills in preparation for successful matriculation in the college program to which they are admitted. The goals of the program are to help students integrate linguistically, academically, and socially into the college community and to assist the student in the successful completion of graduation requirements.

The International Student Office provides both necessary immigration information and programs for international students at American International College.

The Academic Resource Center offers something for all students on campus. Some of the services include helping students learn to manage their time more effectively, read more efficiently, take notes and tests more easily, and write papers more effectively. In addition to enhancing these basic study skills, the Academic Resource Center provides free tutoring for selected courses, aids students in choosing a major, and serves as a general liaison to other campus resources.

The college has been a pioneer in the field of ensuring full participation and equal educational opportunity for students with disabilities. The college is committed to making reasonable academic, social, and physical accommodations for students with disabilities. These accommodations may include, but are not limited to, oral and/or extended-time exams, taped textbooks, adjustments of nonessential program requirements, note-taking assistance, readers, pass/fail options, physical accessibility. These accommodations are provided at no charge to the student.

The American International College Core Education (ACE) Program is a federally funded program designed to assist with the personal growth and professional development of qualified students. The ACE staff works closely with students to help them to adjust to college life, explore educational opportunities, develop study skills, get involved in campus activities, clarify career plans and prepare for life after graduation.

The American International College Writing Center is a student-operated service agency that provides academic writing support to all students in both the day and evening divisions. Trained tutors work with students at all stages of the writing process, from initial brainstorming to final revision, with the goal of teaching students how to prepare, write, and revise quality compositions.

CAMPUS FACILITIES AND EQUIPMENT

The James J. Shea Sr. Memorial Library serves the college as an active learning environment to support undergraduate instruction, graduate research, and independent study. It also houses the Media Center, the Education Resource Center, the Communication Center, the Oral History Center, and the College Archives.

Computer terminals in the library provide patrons with access to the Internet, as well as 30 databases and the online catalog. Patrons who have access to the Internet from their homes or dorm rooms can access our databases and online catalog from their own computers. Through the availability of a wireless network, some areas of the library allow patrons using laptops with appropriate hardware to access the Internet.

The Schwartz Campus Center houses the offices of the Student Government, the radio station, the student newspaper, the yearbook, and Model Congress.

The Karen Sprague Cultural Arts Center and The Esther B. Griswold Theatre for the Performing Arts: the West Wing is devoted to the visual and literary arts, with studios and galleries, as well as classroom, conference, and seminar facilities. The 500-seat Esther B. Griswold Theatre for the Performing Arts has a proscenium stage with flying space and quality acoustics to permit the presentation of professional musical and dramatic productions.

The college network and the Internet are accessed in each of the 4 computer labs in the Academic Computer Center. There are printers and scanners in each lab. Computer labs are available to the general student population as posted during the semester.

TUITION, ROOM, BOARD, AND FEES

Undergraduate: tuition, $22,500; room $5,080; board $4,662. Graduate: tuition: $11,120.

FINANCIAL AID

All applicants for need-based financial aid (including AIC Grants, Stafford Loans, Perkins Loans, and Federal Work-Study) must file a FAFSA. If they are notified, based on the results of the FAFSA, that they have been selected for verification then they are required to file a signed copy of their parents' most recent U.S. Internal Revenue Service Form 1040 or 1040A, including all schedules and W-2 forms, for income verification purposes. Students also must verify their income by filing a signed copy of their own 1040, 1040A, or 1040EZ with all schedules and W-2 forms. Alternate forms or income verification should be obtained from the Financial Aid Office for those who do not file tax returns. For new students there is no application deadline, but early application is advised, since funds are limited. Upperclassmen must have all application materials, including the processor's analysis of the FAFSA, in the Financial Aid Office on or before May 1. Financial aid programs are available to Continuing Education students who register for at least 6 credits. Programs may include Pell Grants, State Grants, and Stafford Loans.

STUDENT ORGANIZATIONS AND ACTIVITIES

AIC currently offers 25 active clubs and organizations on campus, as well as several honor societies. AIC creates an environment that makes it very easy for students to get involved, as well as create new clubs or organizations on campus. The college also conducts a broad recreational program, providing non-varsity students opportunities to engage in basketball, softball, flag football, soccer, volleyball, dodgeball, as well as many other sports. The recreation department also sponsors special events such as ski trips and extramural tournaments against other regional institutions. Students have the opportunity to spend a semester studying on the Dingle Peninsula of Ireland. AIC also offers a similar in Salerno, Italy.

ADMISSIONS PROCESS

The undergraduate admissions process at American International College is designed with the prospective student in mind. The application is conveniently found within the Undergraduate View Book, which you may receive upon request from the Office of Admissions. Students may also apply online. To access the online application, go to www.aic.edu and click on Admissions.

American International College employs a policy of rolling admissions, that is, an application is processed upon receipt and a decision about acceptance is made and immediately communicated to the applicant. Rolling admissions provides both the applicant and the college with a degree of flexibility that eliminates the need to set a specific deadline date for application. However, candidates for admission are encouraged to apply early in the academic year (October, November, December) and may expect an admission decision soon after the necessary credentials have been received. Acceptance to the college is contingent upon the successful completion of high school or its equivalent. A final transcript documenting graduation is required.

Students with academic records satisfactory to American International College are admitted from other colleges in September and January. A transfer student must submit official transcripts of all work undertaken at all institutions attended after high school graduation, whether or not advanced credit is desired. Students transferring from other accredited colleges are not required to take the SAT.

AMERICAN UNIVERSITY

AT A GLANCE

Founded in 1893, American University's 84-acre campus is located in the residential "Embassy Row" neighborhood in the northwest quadrant of Washington, D.C. Nestled among embassies and ambassadorial residences, AU's campus offers a safe, suburban environment with easy access via the Metrorail subway system to Washington's countless cultural destinations.

A global center of government, Washington, D.C. stands unmatched in academic, professional and cultural resources. Building on the strength of our location, AU's faculty include scholars, journalists, artists, diplomats, authors and scientists in 70 programs across five undergraduate schools. Combining a liberal arts core curriculum with in-depth professional programs, academics at AU provide the necessary balance between theoretical study and hands-on experience. Our nationally recognized Career Center, ranked 13th in the country by The Princeton Review, will work with you to enhance this experience with access to unique internship and career opportunities available only in Washington, D.C. Combine this with our diverse national and international student body and our nationally recognized study abroad program, and American University can open up a world of possibilities.

LOCATION AND ENVIRONMENT

On campus, almost all first-year students and some 75 percent of all undergraduate students live in one of seven recently renovated residence halls, all with laundry and cooking facilities on each floor. Dining options include AU's Terrace Dining Room, Subway, Chick-fil-A, McDonalds and many others. AU's completely wireless campus means that you can take your laptop, PDA or smart phone and work from anywhere. With NCAA Division I Patriot League championship teams, club and intramural sports and a state-of-the-art fitness center, staying active is easy. The over 180 clubs and organizations on AU's campus ensure that you can connect with a group that shares your interests and ideals.

OFF-CAMPUS OPPORTUNITIES

Going to school in Washington, D.C. opens up a world of possibilities. You have access to internship and career opportunities found no where else in the world. You can visit monuments and sights with national and international significance. With scores of libraries, museums and theatres, culture and knowledge is only ever a few minutes away. Add to that the city's world-renowned restaurants and entertainment venues, and it's clear you'll never be at a loss for something to do. The free shuttle service connecting AU's campus to the Tenleytown/AU Metro station ensures that all of Washington, D.C. is easily and safely accessible.

STUDENT BODY

AU students have more than 180 undergraduate organizations to choose from. Learn more about clubs and organizations ranging from social and political activity groups to religious and media organizations to student government and performing groups.

One of AU's largest student organizations, the award-winning, student-run Kennedy Political Union brings a diverse group of speakers to AU students. Past speakers include former president Bill Clinton, the Dalai Lama, Madeleine Albright, Rev. Jesse Jackson and Norman Mineta. AU's commencement ceremony offers another opportunity to hear prominent speakers each year.

In addition, the Student Union Board brings concerts and comedians to campus on a regular basis and welcomes volunteer help with production tasks. Previous performers include Jon Stewart, Chris Rock, Green Day and Weezer.

The Student Confederation represents the interests of undergraduate students at American University. Its objectives are met by sponsoring clubs and organizations that meet the diversified needs of the undergraduate student body and by standing as the voice of the undergraduate student body.

The AU Ambassador Program works with the admissions office to recruit prospective freshman and transfer students to American University. Ambassadors share experiences with prospective students during AU Preview Days and Freshman Day, conduct daily tours and day visits, participate in online chats and respond to student e-mails. International students can become an AU Ambassador or participate in the similar AU Diplomat program.

ACADEMICS

College of Arts and Sciences

The College of Arts and Sciences offers some 50 majors and almost 70 minors in the arts, education, humanities, sciences and social sciences as well as premedical and prelaw programs. This liberal arts curriculum is designed not only to impart knowledge, but to build the intellectual skills necessary to be successful in any field.

KOGOD SCHOOL OF BUSINESS

The Kogod School of Business offers a Bachelor of Science in Business Administration (BSBA) with the option to specialize in one of several business disciplines: Accounting, Finance, Information Systems and Technology (IST), International Business, International Finance, International Management, International Marketing, Management, Marketing and Real Estate. The school also recently introduced a Bachelor of Science in Business Administration and Language and Culture Studies for those students whose passion for language rivals their passion for business.

SCHOOL OF COMMUNICATION

The School of Communication offers four majors: Communication Studies (BA), Print/Broadcast Journalism (BA), Public Communication (BA) and Visual Media (BA). Interdisciplinary degrees in Communication, Legal Institutions, Economics and Government (CLEG); multimedia design and development and foreign language and communication media are also available.

SCHOOL OF INTERNATIONAL SERVICE

The School of International Service (SIS) offers a major in International Studies (BA) and interdisciplinary degrees in Language and Area Studies (BA). SIS majors combine idealism and pragmatism with a strong sense of community. The school's distinguished faculty is noted for its academic diversity and professional experience in the United States and abroad.

SCHOOL OF PUBLIC AFFAIRS

The School of Public Affairs (SPA) offers majors in Justice (BA), Law and Society (BA) and Political Science (BA). The school also offers the interdisciplinary CLEG major, consisting of Communication, Legal Institutions, Economics and Government (BA). There is one consistent theme in these programs: academic study combined with practical experience and a focus on internships and opportunities to participate in special programs. You will work and study with others involved in campus organizations, student government, neighborhood outreach projects and political campaigns.

UNIVERSITY HONORS PROGRAM

The University Honors Program invites the top 15 percent of admitted freshmen and selected transfers to participate each year. The program is characterized by small seminars, individual attention from faculty, unique access to the resources of Washington, D.C., individualized Honors advising, preparation and support for national scholarship competitions, an opportunity to live on an Honors floor in a residence hall and the special atmosphere of a community of committed faculty and students.

DEGREES OFFERED AT AMERICAN UNIVERSITY

Certificate, Associate, Bachelor's, Postbachelor's certificate, Master's, Doctoral, First-Professional and Combined Bachelors/Masters Degrees

You may earn both a bachelor's and a master's degree in a planned program of study that begins during your junior or senior year. Each AU school or college has its own specific requirements for admission to a combined degree program.

Undergraduate Majors:

American Studies (BA); Anthropology (BA); Art History (BA); Audio Production (BS); Audio Technology (BS); Biochemistry (BS); Biology (BS); Business Administration (BSBA); Business Administration and Language and Cultural Studies (BS); Chemistry (BS); Communication Studies (BA); Journalism (BA); Public Communication (BA); Visual Media (BA); Computer Science (BS); Economics (BA, BS); Elementary Education (BA); Environmental Studies (BA); Fine Arts (BFA); Foreign Language and Communication Media (BA); French Studies (BA); German Studies (BA); Graphic Design (BA); Health Promotion (BS); History (BA); Interdisciplinary Studies (BA, BS); Communication, Legal Institutions, Economics and Government (BA); International Studies (BA); Jewish Studies (BA); Justice (BA); Language and Area Studies:; French/Europe (BA); German/Europe (BA); Russian/Area Studies (BA); Spanish/Latin America (BA); Law and Society (BA); Liberal Studies (BA); Literature (BA); Marine Science (BS); Mathematics (BS); Mathematics, Applied (BS); Multimedia (BA); Music (BA); Musical Theatre (BA); Theatre (BA); Philosophy (BA); Physics (BS); Political Science (BA); Psychology (BA); Russian Studies (BA); Secondary Education (secondary major only); Sociology (BA); Spanish Studies (BA); Statistics (BS); Studio Art (BA)

Women's and Gender Studies (BA)

FACILITIES AND EQUIPMENT

AU students have access to a 50,000-watt broadcast center, a state-of-the-art language resource center, multimedia design and development labs, science and computer science laboratories and well-equipped buildings for art and performing arts.

The Katzen Arts Center provides academic space for AU students studying the arts: music, dance, theatre, music theatre, arts management, studio art, sculpture, art history, multimedia and graphic design. The center also has a 30,000 square-foot museum that features art and performance installations by local, national and internationally known artists. The Greenberg Theatre hosts quality theatre, music and dance performances by the AU arts programs and professional companies for the AU and Washington, D.C. communities.

Computing resources are delivered via a fiber optic network as well as a wireless network. Wireless access for laptop computers and other devices is available everywhere on campus. A HelpDesk for assistance is available via telephone, Web and e-mail.

The Bender Library and Learning Resources Center serves campus information needs with over one million volumes and close to 50,000 sound recordings, videos and other media materials. Its electronic collections include nearly 15,000 electronic journals in all subjects. The library is part of the eight-member Washington Research Library Consortium with a shared online catalog.

Students enjoy our state-of-the-arts fitness center, sports center with indoor and outdoor tracks, soccer and intramural fields and an Olympic-size pool. Reeves Field, which is used as a soccer and lacrosse competition site, is recognized as one of the finest fields in the nation.

Our Kay Spiritual Life Center is an interdenominational religious center for over 30 faiths. The center also sponsors a monthly Table Talk series, alternative Spring Break service opportunities and an Interfaith Council.

ADMISSIONS

We encourage applicants to set up an AU Prospective Student Portal in order to apply online, check application status, register for events and interviews, change contact information and apply for financial aid (the AU IFAA) online.

We accept the following applications from U.S. and international freshman and transfer applicants:

• Mail-in Undergraduate Application (Requires a $45 nonrefundable application fee)

• AU Online Undergraduate Application (No application fee)

• Common Application (No application fee for online form. Fees apply for per form)

U.S. Freshman Admissions Application Deadlines:

• Fall Semester Early Decision: November 15

• Fall Semester Regular Decision: January 15

• Spring Semester: December 1

• Summer Semester: April 1

U.S. Transfer Student Admission Application Deadlines:

• Fall Semester: March 1 to be considered for scholarships/financial aid

• Fall Semester: July 1

• Spring Semester: November 1

• Summer Semester: April 1

International Freshman Admission Application Deadlines:

• Fall Semester Early Decision Freshmen: November 15

• Fall Semester Regular Decision: January 15

• Spring Semester: September 1

International Transfer Admission Application Deadlines:

• Fall Semester: May 1

• Spring Semester: September 1

ANNA MARIA COLLEGE

AT A GLANCE

Anna Maria College, a coeducational Catholic institution of higher education founded in 1946 by the Sisters of St. Anne, is dedicated to the liberal arts and professional studies. At Anna Maria College, students build the strong foundation they need to live meaningful lives and pursue productive careers. Liberal arts courses sharpen students' critical thinking skills, leading to lifelong personal and professional growth. In fulfillment of the college's Catholic mission, the faculty and staff integrate the importance of personal values, social responsibility, and spiritual growth into their teaching. Through internships, field experiences, and work, students apply what they've learned in the classroom to the real world. In the process, they discover that learning never ends and that fulfilling their potential is a lifelong journey.

LOCATION AND ENVIRONMENT

Located in Paxton, Massachusetts, on a 180-acre campus, the Anna Maria College campus offers students a New England setting just minutes from Worcester, Massachusetts, New England's third largest city and home to 13 other colleges and universities. The picturesque town of Paxton offers students the best of both worlds: a relaxed setting in which to live and study, and close proximity to a vibrant college town. Anna Maria College was recently ranked first by the APBnews.com and CAP Index, Inc. among the nearly 1,500 4-year colleges for the campus neighborhood with the lowest risk of violent crime.

OFF-CAMPUS OPPORTUNITIES

Off-campus social and cultural life centers around the city of Worcester. Anna Maria College students, along with the thousands of nearby college students, take advantage of social, cultural, and recreational events at venues, including the DCU Center, the Palladium, the Worcester Art Museum, Worcester Center for Crafts, and Mechanics Hall, to name a few. The city of Worcester also boasts many restaurants and shops. Boston, Hartford, and Providence are within an hour's drive. Daily train service to Boston is available from Worcester.

MAJORS AND DEGREES OFFERED

Whether you want to be a business professional, nurse or health care professional, public safety officer, social worker, or teacher, you have the potential to make a positive contribution to your career and community. With a core curriculum designed to build a strong liberal arts foundation emphasizing moral and spiritual values, critical thinking, and an appreciation for the diversity of human culture, all of the majors offered at Anna Maria help prepare you to do just that.

Four-year undergraduate majors at Anna Maria College lead to bachelor of arts, bachelor of music, or bachelor of science degrees. Some majors offer a 2-year associate degree option.

The Fifth-Year Option provides students with the opportunity to plan undergraduate studies in a way that allows them to begin graduate work in their senior year. Students add 2 graduate courses to their senior course work and these 2 courses are placed on the master's transcript. Fifth-Year options include: business, counseling psychology, criminal justice, justice administration education, emergency management, fire science, occupational and environmental health and safety, pastoral ministry, and visual art.

ACADEMIC PROGRAMS

The cornerstone of Anna Maria College's Academic Programs is the core curriculum, which integrates the college's Catholic character with its commitment to liberal arts education. Rather than seeing a college education as simply fulfilling a series of unrelated requirements, Anna Maria sees it as building an interdisciplinary foundation so strong that it will sustain students for life.

There are 5 divisions within the academic departments. Division I is humanities and international studies; Division II is business, law, and public policy; Division III is human development and human services; Division IV is environmental, natural, and technological sciences; and, Division V is fine arts. Though each division has a particular focus, the program's ultimate goal is to illuminate the commonalities between each area of study. Students are encouraged to look outside their major discipline to find similarities of methodology, history, or theory in different materials. As a result, students receive a broad-based and interdisciplinary liberal arts foundation, which complements the professional preparation in their major field.

Anna Maria College is one of 13 colleges within the Colleges of Worcester Consortium, Inc., which collectively enrolls more than 30,000. The benefits of affiliation with 12 nearby colleges and universities include cross-registration, joint degree programs, collaborative career services, and sharing of recreational and research facilities.

CAMPUS FACILITIES AND EQUIPMENT

Much of student life on campus centers around the Bishop Flanagan Campus Center, which houses the dining room, post office, bookstore, and The Hub, which offers a lounge, several televisions, pool tables and air hockey. Other outstanding facilities include the Mondor-Eagan Library; Miriam Hall, complete with a recital space; and the Zecco Performing Arts Center, a state-of-the-art facility that seats 350. Approximately 50 percent of the college's students live on campus in one of 3 residence facilities. Anna Maria College's focus on technology translates into exceptional resources, including computer laboratories in the library, science center, residence halls, and art center, as well as Internet access in every dorm room. The Fuller Activities Center houses a fully equipped fitness facility for aerobics and weight training. Exercise equipment includes treadmills, exercycles, and stair climbers, along with free weights and a complete universal machine.

TUITION, ROOM, BOARD, AND FEES

Expenses for the 2007- 2008 academic year include tuition, $22,360; fees, $2,257; and room and board, $8,915. Tuition for music majors is $25,504.

FINANCIAL AID

Anna Maria College is dedicated to keeping a college education affordable. The college offers merit-based scholarships to students who excel inside and outside the classroom. The generous financial aid packages include a combination of grants, loans, and work-study, with a majority of the money coming from grants. Ninety-four percent of the 2007-2008 freshman class received institutional aid in the form of grants.

STUDENT ORGANIZATIONS AND ACTIVITIES

For its more than 677 full-time undergraduates, Anna Maria College offers a multitude of opportunities in a caring, close knit environment. Student can participate in any of the colleges 10 Division III athletic teams, intramurals, internships, and clubs and organizations. The majority of Anna Maria College students take part in co-curricular life. The college's small size lets students take a very active role immediately. Through more than a dozen clubs and organizations, students will develop leadership skills and experience that will translate into the real world. Students are encouraged to get involved in any capacity they can, whether through Student Government, Class Boards, or any one of several clubs. These transferable skills, learned by all students who are involved in activities on campus will assist in their transition into post graduate life. Beginning in the fall of 2008, Anna Maria students will have the opportunity to join men's and women's tennis and lacrosse teams and in the fall of 2009, the college will launch its first football team.

ADMISSIONS PROCESSES

The Admission Office reviews each application individually and weighs high school curriculum and grades, SAT I or ACT scores, recommendations from teachers and guidance counselors, the applicant's essay, and extracurricular activities, including work experience and a1-year. Applications for admission are reviewed on a rolling basis but the priority deadline is March 1. The Office of Admission strongly encourages tours of the campus, attending open houses and Accepted Student Day. Students can schedule any or all of these by calling 800-344-4586, ext. 360. The college seeks candidates who are capable of benefiting from a career-oriented liberal arts education in the Catholic tradition, offered in a small community environment.

AQUINAS COLLEGE

AT A GLANCE

Aquinas College, located in Grand Rapids, Michigan, is a Catholic, coeducational, liberal arts college with an enrollment of just over 2,500 students. The College enjoys all the advantages of its location in the second largest city in Michigan, and students seize the opportunities offered in one of the fastest growing cities in

America. Internships abound, providing hands-on learning experiences for any major. Participating organizations range from Miramax Films for communication internships to Ernst and Young for accounting internships.

At Aquinas we have laid the groundwork for the future. By pushing a few keys on a campus computer, you can open the doors to hundreds of libraries and databases all over the world without ever leaving campus. Our newest high-tech learning center is a model for classrooms of the future that provides network plug-ins every few feet. Our core curriculum was designed to give students the critical foundation needed to be successful in an ever-changing world. Faculty bring to the classroom portfolios of academic scholarship and real world experience.

Of course, not all learning takes place in the classroom. Students travel overseas to countries such as France, Spain, Ireland, Japan, Germany, and Costa Rica. They are also involved in the many and varied service learning opportunities taking place in locations such as Oaxaca, Mexico; El Salvador; and Appalachia. Students at Aquinas believe in giving back to the community in which they live. Professors at Aquinas believe who you are is just as important as what you choose to do. Scholarship awards are available to students who not only excel academically but who also are leaders, volunteers, activists, and athletes. A private education can be more affordable than you think.

LOCATION AND ENVIRONMENT

Aquinas College's campus buildings run the gamut from early-nineteenth-century structures to more modern facilities, but all intermingle nicely to create a charming atmosphere that some call the most beautiful small school in the state. The 107-acre campus is peppered with inviting natural beauties: small ponds, full-grown trees, winding wooded paths, and bubbling creeks. This peaceful campus is set on the edge of Grand Rapids, western Michigan's center of economic, educational, and cultural life and growth. This is a big city with a small-town feel that has amenities to fulfill anyone's interests, including restaurants, entertainment venues, recreational access, and sports stadiums. Other popular points of interest include festivals, special events, and arts attractions. With nearly half a million residents, Grand Rapids is Michigan's second largest city and just a three-hour drive from the state's largest city of Detroit and the Midwest's biggest city, Chicago.

OFF-CAMPUS OPPORTUNITIES

Aquinas students have the opportunity to participate in many off-campus programs both in the United States and abroad. The Dominican College Campus Interchange Program allows students to study at any of the following cooperating institutions: Barry University in Miami, Florida; Dominican College in San Rafael, California; and St. Thomas Aquinas College in Spark Hill, New York. Another option for students who want to remain in the United States is the semester in Montana, where students live and study on a Native American reservation. Aquinas has a study center in Tully Cross, Ireland, where two Aquinas faculty members accompany 25 students for a study abroad program worth a full semester of credit. This program introduces students to life in a rural Irish community and allows them to experience traveling abroad.

Students are involved in service learning opportunities from as near as the inner city of Chicago to as far away as El Salvador, and Costa Rica.

The College also offers study abroad opportunities in France, Spain, Germany, and Japan.

Aquinas students are also encouraged to take advantage of a variety of internship programs. Opportunities are available in business, government agencies, local hospitals, accounting firms, social service agencies, art and cultural venues, and other organizations.

MAJORS AND DEGREES OFFERED

Aquinas College offers the following undergraduate degrees: Bachelor of Arts, Bachelor of Fine Arts, Bachelor Arts in General Education, Bachelor of Music Education, Bachelor of Science, Bachelor of Science in Business Administration, and Bachelor of Science in International Business.

The College offers majors/programs of study in the following: accounting, accounting/business administration, art, art/business administration, art history, biology, business administration, business administration/communication arts, business administration/sports management, chemistry, communication, community leadership, computer information systems, conductive education, drawing, economics, education, English, environmental science, environmental studies, foreign language, French, geography, German, health, history, international studies, Japanese, journalism/publications, Latin, learning disabilities, mathematics, medical technology, music, nursing organizational communication, painting, philosophy, photography, physical education and recreation, physics, political science, pre-engineering, printmaking, psychology, sculpture, social science, sociology, Spanish, studio art, sustainable business, theatre, urban studies, and women's studies.

Pre-professional courses are available in dentistry, law, and medicine. A Bachelor of Science in Nursing is offered in collaboration with University of Detroit Mercy and St. Mary's Mercy Medical Center.

Associate's degrees are also available, including the Associate of Arts and the Associate of Science.

ACADEMIC PROGRAMS

The academic program at Aquinas College follows a unique structure outside of the major/minor course study. This structure maintains certain requirements for each of the four years. Each course exposes students to a broad philosophical theory meant to provide all graduates with an understanding of the human condition. Our core curriculum and liberal arts distribution plan ensure academic competencies that are critical to our ever-changing world.

Freshmen are required to take an integrated skills course called Inquiry and Expression. The thematic content of this course is American Pluralism: The Individual in a Diverse America. This semester-long course emphasizes writing and reading critically, oral communication skills, critical thinking, library/electronic research methods, computer utilization, and basic quantitative reasoning. Sophomores take a year-long Humanities course. The junior-year requirement consists of completing the three-hour course Religious Dimensions of Human Existence, with a choice of emphasis in Scripture, Catholic/Christian Thought, or Contemporary Religious Experience.

All students are required to demonstrate proficiency in a foreign language through the "102" level. The general education plan covers Business/Economics, Psychology/Sociology, Communication/Political Science/Geography, Natural World, Artistic and Creative Studies, Mathematics, Technology, History and Philosophy.

During the freshman year students begin a career/professional development component, which lasts throughout the four years. Topics include assessment of students' strengths, skills, and interests; development of goals and a learning plan and setting a direction; focus on individual wellness, personal finances, and leadership/team skills; awareness of careers, professions, and graduate study; information on making and maintaining a professional portfolio and resume; participating in a professional/career mentor program; career fairs and networking; and experiential learning (choices include co-op, internship, service learning, service trips, and study abroad).

The College follows a two-semester calendar with a summer session. Aquinas also accepts credit through CLEP and Advanced Placement.

CAMPUS FACILITIES AND EQUIPMENT

Students will find centrally located PC-based labs having over 100 Pentium computers with additional PC's in such areas as residence halls, and the Cook Carriage House. The lab technology works in a network environment to allow access to standard applications such as Windows 2000, the Microsoft Office 97 Suite, Internet access using Netscape 4.04, and Pegasus e-mail, as well as over 85 discipline specific applications; printing to high quality laser printers; and access to multi-media technology.

The Woodhouse Library provides students access to audiovisual materials, circulation and course reserve materials, reference services, a public access catalog, and interlibrary loan services (free access to 27 million books and documents from libraries across the country). On-line indexes, databases, catalog and serials.

The Jarecki Center for Advanced Learning and three new student housing apartment buildings opened in the fall of 1999. Other facilities include a student center, the Cook Carriage House, and the modern Art and Music Center, which includes a darkroom, a 200-seat auditorium, an art gallery, and a sculpture studio. The seven million dollar Circle Theatre is scheduled to open summer of 2003. Future plans for a new library and fieldhouse expansion are in the works.

TUITION, ROOM, BOARD AND FEES

The 2003-2004 tuition is $16,400; room and board is $5,494. Other expenses, including books, travel, and personal supplies, average $2,000.

FINANCIAL AID

Aquinas College awards both merit-based and traditional need-based financial assistance to qualified students who complete the FAFSA. More than 90 percent of entering freshmen receive some form of financial assistance. The College administers the traditional grant and loan programs, including Federal Stafford Student Loans and Federal PLUS Loans. As recognition for achievement in academics, leadership, and service, some students are awarded the Spectrum Scholarship. Students who display outstanding athletic ability are eligible for athletic grants. The College participates in the Facts Payment Plan, which allows students to pay College tuition and fees over a period of time. Part-time employment is available to all students.

STUDENT ORGANIZATIONS AND ACTIVITIES

Aquinas College encourages all students to participate in the more than 40 extra-curricular organizations that are available, ranging from intramural teams and academic clubs to performing arts activities, student-run publications, and service groups. One such group of note is Insignis, in which students of exceptional academic record participate in social activities in the form of lectures, receptions, and cultural outings based on intellectual interests.

The Student Senate is the governing body of the Aquinas students, which votes on issues that are brought before the College's Academic Assembly. The Senate brings many academic, social, recreational, and cultural activities to campus.

An on-campus coffeehouse, the "Moose," offers select coffees, a juice bar, and light snacks. Students and faculty congregate in the Moose to relax or carry on discussions that have continued long after class has ended.

Weekly, students are treated to live entertainment on campus ranging from eclectic acoustic performers to comedians. A spring theatre festival is also a popular event.

Five time all sports trophy recipients in the Wolverine Hoosier Athletic Conference, Aquinas fields athletic competition for students interested in Baseball, men and women's basketball, cheerleading, men and women's cross country, men and women's golf, men and women's track, men and women's soccer, softball; man and women's tennis, and volleyball.

ADMISSIONS PROCESS

The Aquinas College admissions committee admits students on the basis of several factors, including the following: academic preparation, scholarship, character, high school transcript, SAT or ACT score, curriculum, and extracurricular activities. Transfer students must have a minimum 2.0 grade point average on a 4.0 scale. Each application is reviewed on a case-by-case basis so that all factors can be considered in the final decision.

Applicants must remit a $25 application fee. Letters of recommendation are encouraged but not required. Freshman and transfer students are accepted on a rolling basis. Applications submitted via the Internet do not require an application fee. Submit at www.aquinas.edu.

ARCADIA UNIVERSITY

AT A GLANCE

Arcadia University is a coeducational, private university serving more than 3,500 undergraduate and graduate students. Founded in 1853, Arcadia is a comprehensive university offering more than 80 undergraduate and graduate programs of study in a personalized setting. Arcadia offers a wide variety of undergraduate majors, each leading to a bachelor of arts, bachelor of fine arts, or bachelor of science degree.

The Arcadia promise affirms that each student will receive an educational experience that is global, integrative, and personal. The university offers an excellent combination of strengths—the diversity and academic options typical to a larger university in the context of a close-knit and supportive small college environment. Arcadia's faculty, 89 percent of whom hold a doctorate or terminal degree in their field, strives to meet the individual needs of students. Arcadia's commitment to personal attention is at the core of students' educational experiences with an average class size of 16 and a 13:1 student to faculty ratio. *U.S. News & World Report* ranks Arcadia among the top universities in the north, and among the top schools nationally for international study. Arcadia's highly regarded Center for Education Abroad offers more than 70 study abroad programs around the world.

The campus in Glenside, Pennsylvania, offers students the best of all worlds. Located just 25 minutes north of Center City, Philadelphia, Arcadia resides on a beautiful campus. The campus, on the grounds of a former private estate, is distinguished by historic buildings, including Grey Towers Castle, a national historic landmark. With more than two-thirds of all full-time undergraduate students residing on campus, Arcadia offers a wide variety of activities, including Division III athletics and more than 40 clubs and organizations.

LOCATION AND ENVIRONMENT

Arcadia University is located on 81 acres in Glenside, just outside of Philadelphia. While the immediate area is suburban, Philadelphia is a quick trip away, giving students all the advantages of proximity to a major city, while living in a beautiful college campus setting. The centerpiece of campus is Grey Towers Castle, a National Historic Landmark. In addition to Arcadia's historic buildings, the campus offers modern facilities with wireless access, smart classrooms, and a recently expanded and upgraded library.

In addition to the wide variety of resources in lively Philadelphia, the metropolitan areas of New York City and Washington, DC, are only a few hours from campus and easily accessible via train and air.

OFF-CAMPUS OPPORTUNITIES

Arcadia's Center for Education Abroad, top-ranked in the nation by *U.S. News & World Report*, is one of the largest campus-based international study programs in the United States. Students have the opportunity to study overseas for a summer, semester, or full-year for approximately the same cost as remaining on the Glenside campus.

Arcadia offers 2 distinct opportunities for students to study abroad during their first year of college. The unique First Year Study Abroad Experience sends 90 selected freshmen for either their first or second semester to England, Scotland, or Ireland to study abroad. The university's London/Scotland/Spain Preview program enables all first-year students in good academic standing to spend their freshman spring break in London, Edinburgh, or Toledo and Madrid. The Scotland and Spain Previews include credit-bearing mini-courses.

Arcadia offers many other opportunities to study for periods from a few days to an entire year in another part of the United States or overseas. The curriculum provides many pathways to study away from the Glenside campus while staying on track to complete their degrees in 4 years.

MAJORS AND DEGREES OFFERED

Bachelor of arts degrees: accounting, art (studio art, pre-art therapy), art history, biology, business administration, chemistry, communications, computer science, computing technology, criminal justice, education (elementary, elementary and early childhood), English, health administration, history, interdisciplinary science, international business and culture, international studies, management information systems, mathematics, philosophy, political science, psychobiology, psychology, scientific illustration, sociology, Spanish, and theater arts and English. Students may also participate in a special program to complete the bachelor of arts in education and a master of education in special education over the course of 5 years.

Bachelor of science degrees: accounting, business administration, chemistry, chemistry and business, computer science, management information systems, and mathematics.

Bachelor of fine arts degrees: acting, studio arts with concentrations offered in ceramics, graphic design, interior design, metals and jewelry, painting, photography, and printmaking. Arcadia also offers a certification program in art education in conjunction with the BFA program.

The university offers a number of professionally oriented programs that are designed to complement undergraduate majors. These programs facilitate the pursuit of graduate study and/or professional certifications at Arcadia or at another institution. These programs include: pre-dental, pre-medical, pre-veterinary medicine, and a pre-law minor. Arcadia offers a 4+2 1/2 year program leading to a bachelor's degree and doctorate of physical therapy, and 4+2 year programs leading to bachelor's degrees and master's degrees in forensic science, international peace and conflict resolution and physician assistant studies.

Arcadia also offers a dual-degree (3-2) program in engineering with Columbia University and an accelerated program for the bachelor of arts/doctor of optometry degree (3-4) with Pennsylvania College of Optometry. Arcadia also works in partnership with Jefferson University to offer a 2-2 program for a bachelor of science degree in nursing.

ACADEMIC PROGRAMS

The Academic Programs at Arcadia University take a personalized approach to education. An Arcadia education emphasizes critical thinking and collaborative learning and promotes each student's unique intellectual and personal growth. Close interaction with faculty, including the ability to be a part of research both in the United States and abroad, further allows students to apply their classroom learning in real-world settings.

Arcadia University operates on a 2-semester academic calendar. Between the 2 semesters, from May to early August, the school offers summer sessions. It is typical for students to take 4 courses each semester for a total of 128 semester hours upon graduation. Students have the option of taking a limited number of courses on a pass-fail basis.

CAMPUS FACILITIES AND EQUIPMENT

Arcadia University's Landman Library, named for Arcadia's eighteenth president, Dr. Bette E. Landman, furthers the university's global mission by offering students and faculty increased technology and access to resources both on campus and around the globe.

The university's "technology smart" classroom building, Brubaker Hall, provides students with an integrated system of instructional technology, including video conferencing and computer access to the campus network and the Internet via wireless and cable connections. Brubaker is also home to the university's master of medical science physician assistant (PA), community health, and undergraduate business/health administration and economics programs. The latest facility, Brubaker 2, which includes a student café, is will be operational for the fall of 2008.

Arcadia's Kuch Recreation and Athletic Center features the Alumni Gymnasium, which seats 1,500 and includes basketball and volleyball courts. The Lenox Pool is a 6-lane wave-resistant swimming pool with adjacent Jacuzzi. The Kuch Center also includes the Kuch Hospitality Suite, an indoor track that overlooks the Alumni Gymnasium, an aerobics/dance studio, fitness center, locker rooms, saunas, first aid/training rooms, and the University Bookstore. The Kuch Center will be expanded and upgraded as part of the next campus development project.

All students have access to Internet services, including Web access, Telnet, ftp, and e-mail. Every room in the residence halls is hooked up to the campus computer network and students have access to computer labs around campus. Additionally, wireless network access points are available in all buildings on campus. Computer purchasing plans are available through an educational partnership with Dell.

TUITION, ROOM, BOARD, AND FEES

For 2008-2009, undergraduate tuition is $29,340 and room and board is $10,280. Student fees total $360 per year. Part-time undergraduate courses will cost $490 per credit.

FINANCIAL AID

Arcadia believes that a qualified student should not have to choose their college based on financial factors alone. With this philosophy in mind, Arcadia University will help qualified students find the financial assistance they need to attend Arcadia. On average, 98 percent of students at Arcadia receive financial aid, and more than 97 percent receive grants and scholarships.

Arcadia offers financial aid in the form of grants, loans, and on-campus employment, as well as merit-based scholarships. The university determines financial need through the Free Application for Federal Student Aid (FAFSA) and the Arcadia University Financial Aid Application. In addition, the school awards a number of scholarships to students who have displayed exemplary academic or extracurricular achievement. Distinguished Scholarships recognizing academic achievement range from $13,500 to $18,000 per year. Arcadia University Achievement Awards, recognizing extracurricular involvement, leadership, and community service, range from $1,000 to $13,000 per year (higher level award amounts of $6,500-$13,000 also reflect academic achievements/standardized test scores). A limited number of full-tuition Landman Scholarships are also awarded based on exemplary academic performance. Transfer students receive separate consideration for Distinguished Scholarships ranging from $5,000-$15,000 and for Achievement Awards ranging from $1,000-$6,000 annually. All awards are renewable for 4 years provided student is a full-time undergraduate in good academic standing.

Arcadia offers a unique online financial aid calculator tailored for high school juniors and seniors and prospective transfer students. The calculator allows students to estimate their eligibility for federal, state, and Arcadia University financial aid (including merit scholarships). A student can get financial aid information in as little as 5 minutes, even before applying for admission, by visiting www.arcadia.edu/calculator.

STUDENT ORGANIZATIONS AND ACTIVITIES

With more than 40 clubs and organizations at Arcadia, it's easy to get involved in campus life. Arcadia's student organizations provide students with opportunities to meet others who have similar interests and to develop leadership, organizational, and management skills. Participation develops networks of people and enriches the university experience. Options include student government, religious and cultural organizations, musical, academic and media-related groups, community service organizations, and athletics.

Arcadia is a member of the National Collegiate Athletic Association (NCAA) Division III and Middle Atlantic States Collegiate Athletic Corporation (MASCAC), the largest Division III Conference holding NCAA membership. Student-athletes compete in 14 intercollegiate sports. Men's sports include baseball, basketball, golf, soccer, swimming, and tennis. Women's sports include basketball, field hockey, lacrosse, soccer, softball, swimming, tennis, and volleyball. Club sports include a very strong equestrian team that competes in both English and Western Intercollegiate Horse Show Association (IHSA) shows.

ADMISSIONS PROCESS

Prospective students are evaluated on the basis of their academic preparation, intellectual achievement, and potential for success. The admissions staff evaluates each application individually. The most important factors in an admissions decision are the student's academic transcript, including the quality of their secondary school program, GPA, and class rank. Arcadia also looks closely at standardized test scores, recommendations, and the student's involvement in extracurricular or community activities.

Prospective freshmen must submit a secondary school transcript, official scores from the SAT or ACT, a personal essay, and recommendations from a high school teacher and guidance counselor. Students are strongly encouraged to follow a strong high school program of at least 19 academic units. Though not required, it is recommended that students visit the campus and schedule an admissions interview before applying. Students applying for transfer admission may apply for the fall or spring semester, and must submit college transcripts from each school they have attended. Transfer students with fewer than 30 college credits are also required to submit their high school transcript.

THE ART INSTITUTE OF ATLANTA

Atlanta offers a wonderful mix of Southern hospitality with high-tech sophistication and economic opportunity. The Art Institute of Atlanta offers city sophistication, suburban convenience, and natural beauty, just as Atlanta does.

AT A GLANCE

Since 1949, the Art Institute of Atlanta has been committed to educating students for career success. From typing to media arts and animation, from speedwriting to designing for the Web, from fashion merchandising to the culinary arts, the Art Institute has long been on the forefront of providing educational opportunities in leading-edge career skills. Excellence in both education and job placement has distinguished the college in its more than 50-year history, reflecting the Art Institute's market responsiveness, entrepreneurial spirit, and commitment to student success. Founded as Massey Business College, with diploma programs in basic business and secretarial skills, the school added liberal arts, fashion, and interior design during the next 2 decades. After becoming the Art Institute of Atlanta in 1975, the college shifted its focus to a creative applied arts curriculum. Accreditation by the Commission on Colleges of the Southern Association of Colleges and Schools soon followed. The culinary arts program was added in 1991. The program is professionally accredited by the American Culinary Federation (ACF) for the associate in arts degree in culinary arts and the bachelor of science degree in culinary arts management. The college also holds professional accreditation with the Council for Interior Design Accreditation (formerly FIDER) for the bachelor of fine arts degree in interior design.

LOCATION AND ENVIRONMENT

The Art Institute of Atlanta is housed primarily in a 5-story, 115,000-square-foot building in a beautifully landscaped office park about 15 minutes north of city center. Each of the 5 floors offers the industry-related technology required for a career-focused, hands-on education.

OFF-CAMPUS OPPORTUNITIES

Built by pioneering entrepreneurs of transportation and business, Atlanta has always been a city of vision. After General Sherman's army burned and pillaged the city during the Civil War, Atlantans took the mythical phoenix as their symbol and rose from the ashes to build what renowned nineteenth-century Atlanta journalist Henry Grady called "a brave and beautiful city." Atlanta is more than its internationally known, fictional portrait in *Gone with the Wind*. The city's reality includes being the birthplace of Martin Luther King Jr., part of its long tradition of tolerance and diversity. Atlanta, like the Art Institute, welcomes people from all over the United States and all over the world, especially since the 1996 Centennial Olympic Games.

MAJORS AND DEGREES OFFERED

The Art Institute of Atlanta offers a bachelor of science in culinary management, and food & beverage management; bachelor of arts in advertising, audio production, fashion and retail management, and visual and game programming; bachelor of fine arts degrees in game art and design, graphic design, interior design, illustration and design, media art and animation, interactive media design, digital media production, visual effects & motion graphics, and photographic imaging, and associate in arts degrees in graphic design, photographic imaging, video production, interactive media design, culinary arts, and wine, spirits & beverage management. Program offerings are designed to stay current with the needs of a rapidly changing business environment.

ACADEMIC PROGRAMS

The most valuable experience that an Art Institutes education may provide is one that turns the entire world into an exciting and dynamic classroom. The Art Institutes Study Abroad Consortium is dedicated to giving our students the chance not only to deepen their knowledge in their chosen career field but also to broaden their world view by adding a global perspective that will help them compete in today's increasingly global economy.

The career services department offers the following services for Art Institute of Atlanta graduates: instruction in critical job search skills, resume writing, interviewing, and networking; individual job-search assistance for full-time employment in the student's field of interest; Access to career services resources at other Art Institutes locations across the United States; participation in quarterly Portfolio Shows where employers can meet new graduates and view their work; participation in career days and job fairs that give students and employers an opportunity to interact.

CAMPUS FACILITIES AND EQUIPMENT

At the Art Institute, you'll find professional equipment and resources along with experienced faculty. This is preparation for the real thing. Facilities and equipment include a library with nearly 39,000 volumes and 6,100 non-print items, research computers, and access via Galileo to college and university libraries throughout the area, as well as national research databases; multi-camera video studio with digital and nonlinear video editing suites featuring AVID Xpress, AVID Xpress DV, and Final Cut Pro; digital audio lab suites complete with ProTools, Digi 001 hardware, 12- and 16-channel mixers, sound recording booth, and studio monitors; computer labs with both Mac and PC platforms (programs include Adobe Illustrator, Adobe InDesign, Adobe Photoshop, Adobe Premiere, Quark

XPress, Corel Painter, Maya, Peak, Java Development Kit, AutoCad, Dreamweaver, Flash, Character Studio, Toon Boom, Sound Forge, Director, DVD Studio Pro, Eye-One Match, SoundEdit, Final Cut Pro, and more); professional photography studios and darkroom facilities, including 2 Dicomed digital capture systems, PowerMac computer stations with color-calibrated monitors, and an Epson 10000 printer; 5 teaching kitchens and a dining lab open to the public.

TUITION, ROOM, BOARD, AND FEES

Your actual program length may vary depending on your program, transfer credits, and other factors, and your total program tuition may vary from that listed below. Tuition is charged on a quarter-by-quarter basis. Students are not obligated beyond the quarter they are currently attending. Tuition for repeat courses is charged on a per credit basis.

Current per credit hour charge is $435; 12-credit hours per quarter: $5,220; academic year cost: $15,660; 16-credit hours per quarter: $6,960; academic year cost: $20,880.

Estimated cost of supplies and textbooks averages from $100 to $250 per month, depending on program. Please note that such costs may not fall evenly across all months. Some programs require purchase of additional equipment in addition to the starting kit.

The starting kit includes basic equipment, first-quarter texts and materials required for each program, and a Supply Store credit for additional items. A list of the components of the starting kit is provided to each enrolled student. Starting kit prices may change without notice.

FINANCIAL AID

The Art Institute of Atlanta understands the significant financial commitment a college education requires. The student financial services staff works one-on-one with students and their families to develop a personal financial plan, based on each individual's particular financial needs, which allows students to reach their educational and career goals. The college's financial aid officers guide families through the process of assessing educational costs, applying for financial aid programs, completing financial aid paperwork (including the Free Application for Federal Student Aid or FAFSA), and developing a payment plan.

STUDENT ORGANIZATIONS AND ACTIVITIES

Student and professional organizations are an excellent way for you to grow personally and professionally, as well as to get involved in the decision-making process at the college. These organizations are excellent forums for asking questions, making suggestions, and interacting with other students, faculty, and staff.

Membership in field-related societies and groups gives students the opportunity to network with industry professionals, take part in educational programs, and get involved in community outreach projects. The Student Association provides a responsive forum for students to express their interests and concerns.

Students are encouraged to get involved with student and professional organizations.

ADMISSIONS PROCESS

Students attending college for the first time and pursuing their first associate or bachelor's degree or diploma program must complete the following in order to begin the enrollment process:

Personal interview: Students are required to meet with an assistant director of admissions. A telephone interview can fulfill this requirement under certain circumstances. The purpose of the interview is to explore the student's background and interests and how they relate to the Art Institute's programs, to assist the student in identifying the appropriate area of study consistent with his or her background and interests, and to provide information concerning the curriculum and support services at the Art Institute.

Application for admission, including essay and enrollment agreement. High school transcript or General Educational Development (GED) test scores: Transcripts must show grades for all years of high school attended and date of graduation. An applicant still in high school will be considered for early acceptance contingent upon proof of graduation. Transcripts should be mailed or faxed directly to the college. Before a student may begin studies at the Art Institute of Atlanta, he or she must have received a diploma from a regionally accredited high school or a state-approved home school program, demonstrating satisfactory completion of state high school equivalency requirements, or earned a General Educational Development (GED). A certificate of attendance or completion is not acceptable. Official report of COMPASS test scores. SAT, ACT, or ASSET test scores can be used in place of the COMPASS test. If the applicant has not taken any of these tests prior to application, the COMPASS test may be taken free of charge at the Art Institute of Atlanta. When taking the SAT or ACT, please use code number 5429 to have scores reported directly to the college. A U.S. $50 nonrefundable application fee and a U.S. $100 refundable tuition deposit. A portfolio of the student's artwork is not required for admission, but is required for high school seniors entering the annual scholarship competition. Work experience in the food service or hospitality industry is not required for culinary arts applicants. Readmission students, transfer students, those with a college degree, and international students have slightly different requirements.

*Refundable up to 90 days before class start date.

ASSUMPTION COLLEGE

AT A GLANCE

In 1904, Augustinians of the Assumption founded Assumption College, a Catholic institution that offers high-caliber programs in the liberal arts, the sciences, and professional studies in the rich Catholic intellectual tradition.

Located in Worcester, Massachusetts, New England's second largest city, the college's 185-acre campus features exciting new additions to its excellent academic and housing facilities, including a new state-of-the-art science center, information technology center, air-conditioned suite-style residence halls, an extensive library, and a world-class recreational center.

Within a lively spiritual and intellectual environment, Assumption College provides a traditional liberal education while teaching the modern skills and ideas necessary to succeed professionally. Assumption confers 35 majors and offers 12 special Academic Programs. Students are encouraged to enroll in honors classes or work with faculty on individual research projects. With an impressive student-faculty ratio of just 12:1, Assumption's academic atmosphere is close-knit and community-oriented. Ninety-seven percent of graduates are employed or in graduate school within 6 months of graduation.

There are more than 2,150 undergraduate students at Assumption College, and more than 600 graduate and continuing education students. Ninety percent of undergraduates choose to live on campus in one of 14 residence halls. On-campus housing is guaranteed all 4 years.

LOCATION AND ENVIRONMENT

Assumption College's beautiful 185-acre campus is located in a suburban neighborhood in Worcester, Massachusetts. Worcester County is home to 13 colleges. A lively collegiate environment, Worcester provides students with many academic opportunities, including a rich selection of internship opportunities, community volunteerism, and service learning placements. Worcester is culturally rich, boasting the world-class Worcester Art Museum, Tuckerman Hall, and the new Hanover Theatre, as well as a renowned annual music festival and symphony orchestra, and the Ecotarium, a museum of science and nature. There are many outdoor and recreational activities in Worcester and its environs. Worcester is also home to minor league baseball's Worcester Tornadoes and the AHL Worcester Sharks. Boston and Providence are only 45 minutes away.

OFF-CAMPUS OPPORTUNITIES

Assumption College is a member of the Colleges of Worcester Consortium, an association of the 13 higher learning institutions in the Worcester metropolitan area. Through the Consortium, Assumption students can register for courses at the other 12 colleges, as well as participate in social and cultural events with the 30,000 students who attend the other colleges and universities in metro Worcester.

Assumption College undergraduates can choose to spend a semester or year abroad. In recent years, Assumption College students have studied at schools throughout the world—from France and England, to the Netherlands, the Czech Republic, and Australia. Many students augment their education and hone professional skills through national and international internships. Assumption students have worked in diverse organizations around the globe, from the Department of Commerce, Central America Bureau, and the Department of State (NAFTA Agreement), to Smith Barney, Fidelity, Dean Witter Reynolds, ABC News, and the Alliance Francaise in Paris.

MAJORS AND DEGREES OFFERED

Assumption College offers majors in accounting, biology, biology with concentration in biotechnology and molecular biology, chemistry, classics, computer science, economics, economics with a business concentration, economics with international concentration, education concentration (with appropriate major), English, English with concentration in writing and mass communications, environmental science, foreign languages, French, French with concentration in francophone culture and civilization, global studies, global studies with business concentration, history, human services and rehabilitation studies, international business, Italian studies, Latin American studies, management, marketing, mathematics, music, organizational communication, philosophy, political science, psychology, sociology, sociology with concentration in criminology or social policy, Spanish, Spanish with concentration in Hispanic culture and civilization, theology, and visual arts.

In addition, the college offers special programs, including community service learning, finance, Fortin and Gonthier Foundations of Western Civilization, gerontology studies, joint 7-year programs in physical therapy, podiatry, and optometry, medical technology, peace and conflict studies, pre-medical/pre-dental and pre-law, and women's studies.

ACADEMIC PROGRAMS

Assumption College is committed to the pursuit of truth through a strong liberal arts education in the rich Catholic, intellectual tradition.

Assumption College teaches not just how to ask questions, but also how to find answers. In the classroom, faculty encourages a hands-on approach to learning through group projects, writing assignments, and tasks that urges students to think about materials, not just memorize them. Classes are generally discussions, not lectures.

Assumption College follows a 2-semester academic calendar, beginning in late August and ending in May. An online intersession is also available in early January. There are 2 summer programs run by the Center for Continuing and Career Education and the Graduate School.

In addition to major requirements, Assumption College requires all students to complete a course in English composition and a writing emphasis course, 2 courses in philosophy, 2 courses in theology, and 3 courses in 2 of the following 3 areas: mathematics, laboratory science, or foreign language. Students must complete additional courses in literature, humanities, and history. Three courses in social science, and 1 course in either art, music, or theater are also required. In order to graduate, students must have 120 semester credits, with 9 to 12 in the upper division of the major.

Assumption students have the option of participating in Army and Air Force ROTC programs through a nearby university.

CAMPUS FACILITIES AND EQUIPMENT

Assumption College has recently completed a 5-year, $60 million physical plant expansion program including:

The Richard and Janet Testa Science Center is an $18-million facility, housing the Department of Natural Sciences. The Testa Center features 5 multi-use classrooms with state-of-the-art technology; 10 teaching laboratories; 7 laboratories dedicated for faculty and student research; 2 conference rooms; a greenhouse and inviting, spacious lounge areas.

A Multi-Sport Stadium with an in-filled synthetic turf field was completed in the fall of 2005. This 1,200-seat, lighted stadium serves 6 intercollegiate teams (field hockey, football, men's and women's lacrosse, and men's and women's soccer), as well as an extensive outdoor intramural program.

The Information Technology Center contains administrative offices, computer labs, and classrooms used for collaborative projects, multimedia, foreign language work and access to leading-edge systems. The facility offers wired and wireless high-speed networking for both laptop and desktop users. The facility also houses the support staff and core of ResNet, which provides high-speed networking in every living space on campus. The college is an active participant in Internet 2.

Although not part of the recent expansion, another key academic facility, the Emmanuel d'Alzon Library, offers a seating capacity of 350 in a variety of arrangements conducive to study, research, and relaxation. In addition to its collection of 200,000 volumes, the library subscribes to 1,125 journal titles that support the concentrations of study offered at the college. Access to other resources is available through access to local, regional and national library networks and the Web. Four new residence halls were constructed in recent years. West Hall, our newest modern and fully equipped facility is home to 130 students in 32 2-bedroom, 1-bathroom suites, each housing 4 students.

TUITION, ROOM, BOARD, AND FEES

Tuition for the 2007-2008 school year is $27,320, plus $9,492 room and board.

FINANCIAL AID

Assumption College offers need-based financial aid, as well as merit-based assistance. The college's commitment to academic excellence and student leadership is reflected in our merit-based scholarship program. All students who apply for admission are considered for merit scholarships ranging from $2,500 to $20,000 annually. To qualify for need-based financial aid, students should submit the Free Application for Federal Student Aid (FAFSA) by February 1. This past year, Assumption awarded more than $23 million in financial assistance to students.

STUDENT ORGANIZATIONS AND ACTIVITIES

The student body at Assumption includes more than 2,150 undergraduates representing 25 states and 8 foreign countries. Ninety percent of the student body resides on campus; housing is guaranteed all 4 years.

Student Activities at Assumption College seeks to complement the educational process that begins in the classroom by coordinating many of the social, athletic, recreational and cultural activities that are offered on- and off-campus.

Assumption offers a wide range of varsity, club and intramural sports. The Assumption Greyhounds sponsor 23 sports for men and women at the intercollegiate level. Men's sports include: baseball, basketball, cross country, football, golf, hockey, lacrosse, soccer, tennis, and track & field (indoor and outdoor). Women's

sports include: basketball, cross country, field hockey, lacrosse, rowing, soccer, softball, swimming, tennis, track & field (indoor and outdoor), and volleyball. The college is a charter member of the Northeast-10 Conference and competes as an NCAA Division II institution.

The Department of Student Activities is responsible for student leadership development, first-year student orientation, campus programming and the Hagan Campus Center. Through the Student Government Association (SGA), the Campus Activities Board (CAB), and the many student clubs and organizations, Assumption College offers a wide range of co-curricular events. This includes many large-scale events, such as Family Weekend, Siblings Weekend, Welcome Week, Midnight Madness, and the Spring Concert. Other more frequent events include comedians, coffeehouses, films, lectures, off-campus trips, and many special events.

Student Activities also offers many opportunities for leadership experiences. A variety of student leadership positions are offered each year to students who are interested in getting involved outside of the classroom and looking to enhance their classroom learning. Students seek out various roles, from student government president to general organization members, to give back to the student body and to the Assumption College community.

ADMISSIONS PROCESS

Assumption College admits men and women who demonstrate an active intellect and self-motivation from applicants who have compiled a solid academic record and completed all prescribed high school requirements.

Assumption College encourages prospective students to schedule a campus visit prior to applying for admission. During the summer months, high school students are encouraged to attend group information sessions, tours, and interviews Monday through Friday. In the fall semester, prospective students may attend group information sessions on Saturdays, or schedule a campus visit during the week by appointment.

To apply, students are required to submit an online or paper application (the Common Application is accepted), a $50 application fee, official high school transcripts, scores from the SAT I or ACT, and a letter of recommendation. Applications, including all supporting documents and recommendations, must be received in the Office of Admissions by February 15. Students who want to be considered for Early Action must apply by November 15.

For more information, please contact:

Assumption College

Office of Admissions

500 Salisbury Street

Worcester, MA 01609

Telephone: 866-477-7776 (toll free) or 508-767-7285

Website: www.assumption.edu

E-mail: admiss@assumption.edu

ARGOSY UNIVERSITY

Argosy University is a leading institution offering a variety of degree programs that focus on the human side of success alongside professional competence.

AT A GLANCE

To succeed in today's competitive workforce, you need a solid foundation of knowledge and the power to put it to work. And that's exactly what an Argosy University education offers.

For students looking for a more personal approach to education, Argosy University may just be the answer. All graduate and undergraduate programs (and there are 48 nationwide, across 18 campuses and 11 states) emphasize interpersonal skills as well as academic learning. And all are taught by practicing professionals who bring top-level, real-world experience—and clear-eyed realism—into the classroom. So students graduate with both a solid foundation of knowledge, and the power to put it to work. To accommodate busy working adults, many programs at Argosy University are structured flexibly: with both campus and online learning, and evening, weekend, and daytime classes. There's also a wide range of financial aid options for students who qualify.

Argosy University is committed to creating a supportive learning environment and providing our students with a wealth of opportunities and resources. Our focus on personal development coupled with a curriculum that includes relevant, real-world skills is designed to provide our students with a high quality education.

LOCATION AND ENVIRONMENT

Atlanta Campus: College of Psychology and Behavioral Sciences; College of Business; College of Education

980 Hammond Drive, Suite 100

Atlanta, GA 30328

770-671-1200 or 888-671-4777

Chicago Campus: College of Psychology and Behavioral Sciences; College of Business; College of Education

350 North Orleans Street

Chicago, IL 60654

312-777-7600 or 800-626-4123

Dallas Campus: College of Psychology and Behavioral Sciences; College of Business; College of Education

8080 Park Lane, Suite 400A

Dallas, TX 75231

214-890-9900 or 866-954-9900

Denver Campus: College of Psychology and Behavioral Sciences; College of Business; College of Education

1200 Lincoln Street

Denver, CO 80203

303-248-2700 or 866-431-5981

Hawaii Campus: College of Psychology and Behavioral Sciences; College of Business; College of Education

400 ASB Tower, 1001 Bishop Street

Honolulu, HI 96813

808-536-5555 or 888-323-2777

Inland Empire: College of Psychology and Behavioral Sciences; College of Business; College of Education

636 East Brier Drive, Suite 235

San Bernardino, CA 92408

909-915-3800 or 866-217-9075

Nashville Campus: College of Psychology and Behavioral Sciences; College of Business; College of Education

100 Centerview Drive, Suite 225

Franklin, TN 37214

615-525-2800 or 866-833-6598

Orange County Campus: College of Psychology and Behavioral Sciences; College of Business; College of Education

3501 West Sunflower Avenue, Suite 110

Santa Ana, CA 92704

714-338-6200 or 800-716-9598

Phoenix Campus: College of Psychology and Behavioral Sciences; College of Business; College of Education

2233 West Dunlap Avenue

Phoenix, AZ 85021

602-216-2600 or 866-216-2777

San Diego: College of Psychology and Behavioral Sciences; College of Business; College of Education

7650 Mission Valley Road

San Diego, CA 92108

858-598-1900 or 866-505-0333

San Francisco Bay Area Campus: College of Psychology and Behavioral Sciences; College of Business; College of Education

999-A Canal Boulevard

Point Richmond, CA 94804

510-215-0277 or 866-215-2777

Santa Monica: College of Psychology and Behavioral Sciences; College of Business; College of Education

2950 Thirty-first Street

Santa Monica, CA 90405

310-866-4000 or 866-505-0332

Sarasota Campus: College of Psychology and Behavioral Sciences; College of Business; College of Education

5250 Seventeenth Street

Sarasota, FL 34235

941-379-0404 or 800-331-5995

Schaumburg Campus: College of Psychology and Behavioral Sciences; College of Business; College of Education

1000 North Plaza Drive, Suite 100

Schaumburg, IL 60173

847-969-4900 or 866-290-2777

Seattle Campus: College of Psychology and Behavioral Sciences; College of Business; College of Education

2601-A Elliott Avenue

Seattle, WA 98121

206-283-4500 or 888-283-2777

Tampa Campus: College of Psychology and Behavioral Sciences; College of Business; College of Education

Parkside at Tampa Bay Park

4401 North Himes Avenue, Suite 150

Tampa, FL 33614

813-393-5290 or 800-850-6488

Twin Cities Campus: College of Psychology and Behavioral Sciences; College of Business; College of Education; College of Health Sciences

1515 Central Parkway

Eagan, MN 55121

651-846-2882 or 888-844-2004

Washington, DC, Campus: College of Psychology and Behavioral Sciences; College of Business; College of Education

1550 Wilson Boulevard, Suite 600

Arlington, VA 22209

703-526-5800 or 866-703-2777

MAJORS AND DEGREES OFFERED

Argosy University offers doctoral, master's, and bachelor's degrees in 4 major disciplines through our College of Psychology and Behavioral Sciences, College of Education, College of Business, and College of Health Sciences. Our College of Health Sciences also offers associate's degree programs.

Associate's: dental hygiene, diagnostic medical sonography, histotechnology, medical assisting,

medical laboratory technology, radiation therapy, radiologic technology, and veterinary technology.

Bachelor's: business, psychology.

Master's: business, education, health service, counseling, and psychology

Doctoral: business, education, counseling, and psychology.

ACADEMIC PROGRAMS

A degree is an important part of professional success. Argosy University is accredited by the Higher Learning Commission and is a member of the North Central Association (NCA), 30 North LaSalle Street, Suite 2400, Chicago, IL 60602, 312-263-0456, NCAHLC.org.

The Committee on Accreditation of the American Psychological Association (APA) (750 First Street N.E., Washington, DC 20002-4242, 1-202-336-5979) has granted accreditation to the doctor of psychology in clinical psychology programs at the following Argosy University campuses: Atlanta, Chicago, Hawaii, Phoenix, San Francisco Bay Area, Schaumburg, Tampa, Twin Cities, and Washington, DC.

The Council for Accreditation of Counseling and Related Educational Programs (CACREP), a specialized accrediting body recognized by the Council for Higher Education Accreditation (CHEA), has granted accreditation to the Mental Health Counseling (MA degree) program at Argosy University, Sarasota Campus. Council for Accreditation of Counseling and Related Educational Programs, 599 Stevenson Avenue, Alexandria, VA 22304, 703-823-9800, www.cacrep.org.

The Council for Accreditation of Counseling and Related Educational Programs (CACREP), a specialized accrediting body recognized by the Council for Higher Education Accreditation (CHEA), has granted accreditation to the Community Counseling (MA degree) program at Argosy University, Schaumburg Campus. Council for Accreditation of Counseling and Related Educational Programs, 599 Stevenson Avenue, Alexandria, VA 22304, 703-823-9800, www.cacrep.org.

The Associate of Applied Science in Diagnostic Medical Sonography Degree Program is accredited by the Commission on Accreditation of Allied Health Education Programs (1361 Park Street, Clearwater, FL 33756, 1-727-210-2350) on recommendation of the Joint Review Committee on Education in Diagnostic Medical Sonography (2025 Woodlane Drive, Saint Paul, MN 55125, 651-731-1582).

The Commission on Accreditation of Allied Health Education Programs has awarded initial accreditation to the Echocardiography concentration upon the recommendation of the Joint Review Committee on Education in Diagnostic Medical Sonography (JRC-DMS). The initial accreditation status will expire on 9/30/08.

The Associate of Applied Science in Histotechnology Degree Program is accredited by the National Accrediting Agency for Clinical Laboratory Sciences (8410 West Bryn Mawr, Suite 670, Chicago, IL 60631, 1-773-714-8880).

The Associate of Applied Science in Medical Assisting Degree Program is accredited by the Commission on Accreditation of Allied Health Education Programs (www.caahep.org) upon the recommendation of the Curriculum Review Board of the American Association of Medical Assistants Endowment (AAMAE) (1361 Park Street, Clearwater, FL 33756, 1-727-210-2350).

The Associate of Applied Science in Radiologic Technology Degree Program is accredited by the Joint Review Committee on Education in Radiologic Technology (20 North Wacker Drive, Suite 2850, Chicago, IL 60606, 1-312-704-5300).

The Associate of Applied Science in Veterinary Technology Degree Program is accredited through the American Veterinary Medical Association (AVMA) Committee on Veterinary Technician Education and Activities (CVTEA) (1931 North Meacham Road, Suite 100, Schaumburg, IL 60173, 1-847-925-8070).

The Associate of Science in Dental Hygiene Degree Program is accredited by the Commission on Dental Accreditation. The Commission is a specialized accrediting body recognized by United States Department of Education. The Commission on Dental Accreditation can be contacted at 1-312-440-4653 or at 211 East Chicago Avenue, Chicago, IL 60611.

The Associate of Science in Medical Laboratory Technology Degree Program is accredited by the National Accrediting Agency for Clinical Laboratory Sciences (8410 West Bryn Mawr, Suite 670, Chicago, IL 60631, 1-773-714-8880).

The Associate of Science in Radiation Therapy Degree Program is accredited by the Joint Review Committee on Education in Radiologic Technology (20 North Wacker Drive, Suite 2850, Chicago, IL 60606-3182, 1-312-704-5300).

FINANCIAL AID

Different types of financial aid are available to students who qualify—from federal aid programs and merit-based awards to loans and a work-study program. We work individually with students to guide you through the application process. Our financial aid experts can help determine the types of aid you are eligible to receive. In many cases, payments can be deferred until after graduation. For more information, please contact the Director of Admissions at the campus of your choice or visit www.argosyu.edu.

ADMISSIONS PROCESS

Each program of study carries specific admission requirements. A personal contact in our Admissions Department can answer questions, arrange a campus tour, and help you through the admission process. To determine the admission requirements for the program you wish to enter, contact the Office of Admissions at the campus of your choice or visit www.argosy.edu/pr.

AURORA UNIVERSITY

AT A GLANCE

An institution that describes itself as "an inclusive community dedicated to the transformative power of learning," Aurora University offers an education that will literally change the lives of students. Student learning begins in the classroom, but is rapidly taken out into the real world for testing and validation. Whether students are engaged in service learning projects or completing an internship or clinical experience, reflection upon the knowledge gained is emphasized. Many of the majors offered at AU are in pre-professional fields such as education, social work, or nursing. In addition, traditional college majors are among the 40 Academic Programs offered.

Founded in 1893, Aurora University is accredited at the bachelor's, master's, and doctoral degree levels and offers major fields based in a liberal arts foundation. Located in an attractive residential neighborhood on the southwest side of Aurora, Illinois—the state's second largest city with a population of 170,000—the 30-acre campus is located only minutes from the Illinois Research and Development Corridor, home to dozens of nationally and internationally based businesses and industries. Besides the campus in Aurora, undergraduate and graduate degree programs are offered at the George Williams College campus near Lake Geneva, Wisconsin.

The university offers the range of programs characteristic of a university as well as the benefits of the personal attention more frequently associated with a small college. Students who are undecided about a major will discover the right field of study through the general education program. Highly motivated students with a high school GPA of 3.0 or above and an ACT of 25 or higher can apply for the AU Honors Program. At the heart of the program is the opportunity to participate in advanced course work, innovative seminars, and special events.

The campus centers on "the Quad"—a grassy area at the center of the campus. Surrounding the Quad, housing is offered to undergraduates. The newest academic building completed in 2006 is the Institute for Collaboration, which houses the College of Education as well as classrooms for AU students and 200 elementary students from the West Aurora School District. Total university enrollment is almost 4,000, including 2,000 undergraduates. More than 95 percent of students receive financial aid with more than $10.5 million in scholarships awarded in 2006-2007.

LOCATION AND ENVIRONMENT

Located on the southwest side of Aurora, Illinois, the state's second largest city, Aurora University is nestled in a residential area just minutes from the prestigious high -tech corridor that stretches along I-88 across the northern part of the state. The university is housed on a 30-acre campus with a blend of historic and new academic, administrative, and residential buildings. The newest building is the Institute for Collaboration, which opened in 2006 and houses the College of Education as well as classrooms and faculty offices. The university's George Williams College campus and conference center sits 70 miles to the north, along the banks of Geneva Lake in Wisconsin.

The campus is welcoming with faculty members who are passionate about their subject matter and have devoted their professional lives to students. There are no packed lecture halls with teaching assistants. Rather classes are small, 23 students on average, and faculty knows students by name. The first-year program recognizes the unique needs of first-year students and guides them through the transition from high school to college.

Campus organizations abound with more than 60 musical, literary, religious, social, and service groups to consider. Students can develop their leadership skills or make lifelong friends through student government or academic societies. Studies show that students who are involved in activities outside of the classroom are more satisfied with their college experience.

Athletics are an important tradition at Aurora University. About one-third of traditional AU students participate in intercollegiate athletics. Students have a choice of 18 intercollegiate NCAA Division III sports for men and women. In recent years, Spartan teams have compiled an amazing 47 conference titles. Twelve intramural sports allow students to compete in round robin tournaments with fellow students.

OFF-CAMPUS OPPORTUNITIES

Getting involved in activities on campus is a great way to meet new people and learn skills that will be helpful in life after college. With more than 60 clubs and organizations and division III intercollegiate athletics, it is easy to find other students with similar interests. There are academic and professional clubs, fine arts, and cultural opportunities, and many ways to develop leadership skills.

MAJORS AND DEGREES OFFERED

Bachelor of arts and/or sciences (check catalog for specifics): accounting, actuarial science, art, athletic training, biology, business and commerce, business administration, coaching and youth sport development, communication, computer science, criminal justice, elementary education, English, finance, health science (allied health program, pre-dentistry, pre-medicine, pre-veterinary medicine), history, management information technology, marketing, mathematics, museum studies (minor only), music (minor only), nursing (BSN), organizational management, physical education (fitness and health promotion, K-12 teaching certification), political science, pre-law (supplemental major), psychology, recreation administration (commercial and public recreation management, outdoor leadership, professional golf management), religion, secondary education (supplemental major), social work (BSW), sociology, Spanish, special education, theater, YMCA senior director certificate (supplemental major).

ACADEMIC PROGRAMS

Bachelor of arts, bachelor of science, bachelor of science in nursing, bachelor of science in social work, master of science in social work, master of business administration, master of science in recreation administration, master of arts in teaching, master of arts in educational leadership, master of arts in special education, master of arts in teaching with certification, master of science in mathematics, master of arts in reading instruction, ESL/bilingual endorsement, doctor of education.

CAMPUS FACILITIES AND EQUIPMENT

Aurora University's 30-acre campus is home to 23 instructional, recreational, administrative, and residential buildings. Some are historic, while others are new. But all surround the Quad—a grassy area at the center of the campus. The newest building completed in 2006 is the Institute for Collaboration, which houses the College of Education as well as classrooms for AU students and faculty offices. New performance venues include the 500-seat Crimi Auditorium and 200-seat Perry Theatre in the Aurora Foundation Center for Community Enrichment. The Schingoethe Museum of Native American Culture welcomes student groups, the general public, and scholars. Just 70 miles to the north sits the university's George Williams College campus and conference center on the banks of Geneva Lake in Wisconsin.

TUITION, ROOM, BOARD, AND FEES

2008-2009 Tuition:

Full-time, $17,400 per year

Part-time, $530 per semester hour

Room and Board, $7,540 per year

Activity Fee, $50 per year

Lab Fees, $36 per course

Parking Permit, $25 per year

School Says . . .

FINANCIAL AID

Scholarships, many of which are endowed by generous donors to the university, and some grants are awarded to full-time undergraduate students based on high school academic record and ACT score. Awards are renewable for up to 4 years for students who maintain the required renewable GPA for each scholarship level. Merit awards for 2006-2007 academic year ranged from $2,000 to $10,000 per year.

Need-based financial aid is based on information received from the Free Application for Federal Student Aid (FAFSA). Need-based financial aid includes grants, loans, and student employment. Grants include the Federal Pell Grant, Federal Supplemental Educational Opportunity Grants (SEOG), State of Illinois MAP Grants, and Aurora University Grants. Loans that are available include the Federal Perkins Loans, Federal Stafford Loans (both subsidized and unsubsidized), Federal Undergraduate PLUS Loans, alternative loans and Aurora University Student Loans (AUSL). Federal Work Study (FWS) and on-campus employment are available.

In order to be considered for scholarships or financial aid, students must first apply and be approved for admission. The FAFSA makes it possible to be considered for all need-based federal and state funding. Students are urged to complete the FAFSA on the Web at www.fafsa.ed.gov.

STUDENT ORGANIZATIONS AND ACTIVITIES

Accounting Club, Aurora University Arts United, Aurora University Student Association, Activities Programming Board, Accounting Club, American Criminal Justice Association, AU Communication Club, Black Student Association, Cheerleading and Dance Team, Circle K International, Club Fit, Colleges Against Cancer, Delta Mu Delta (business club), Drama/Theater Club, Fellowship of Christian Athletes, Feminist Society, Fitness and Health Promotion, Future Attorneys of Aurora, Future Educators of Aurora University, Future Leaders of the World, Games Club, GLOBAL, History Club, Inter Varsity Christian Fellowship, Kappa Delta (International Honor Society), Kappa Delta Pi (International Honor Society in Education), Lambda Pi Eta (National Honorary Society for Speech Communication), Latin American Student Organization, Management Information Technology Club, Model United Nations, Native American Club, Omicron Delta Kappa (National Leadership Honor Society), Organized Action Council, Orgs Council, Paladins (Karate Club), Phi Alpha (Social Work Honor Society), Phi Alpha Theta (National History Honors Society), Phi Eta Sigma (Freshman Honor Society), Photography Club, Physical Educators Club, Political Science Club, Pre-Law Club, Psi Chi (National Honor Society in Psychology), Psychology Club, Science Club, Sigma Tau Delta (English Association), Social Worker Association, Spartan Athletic Training Students Organization, Spartan Physical Educators Club, Spartan Pride, Spartan Student Newspaper, Straight Edge, Student Accounting Society, Student Athlete Advisory Committee, Students for Wellness, Student Nurses Association, Student Rec-Majors Club, Students for Wellness, Third City Epic, Ultimate Frisbee Club, University Chorale.

ADMISSIONS PROCESS

Aurora University welcomes applications early in the senior year of high school. To apply for admission, apply online at www.aurora.edu or call 630-844-5533 or 800-742-5281 to request a paper application. Submit the completed AU application along with official transcripts from your high school or college and official ACT or SAT scores. Admission is determined on a rolling basis. The application deadline is May 1 for fall admission. Once admitted, a $100 tuition deposit is required to hold a space in the class. Students planning to live on campus must submit a housing contract and a $100 housing deposit. Both deposits are refundable until May 1.

BABSON COLLEGE

AT A GLANCE

This small New England school, the nation's top ranked small business college, enrolls about 440 students each year into its freshman class, keeping the student population around 1,750. Set in beautiful Wellesley, Massachusetts, Babson's 370 acre residential campus is alive with intellectual, cultural, athletic, and social activities. Babson College offers a strong business curriculum with a liberal arts foundation. Students are immersed in an enriching environment that fosters leadership, teamwork, creativity, communication, and diversity. About 20 percent of undergraduates are international students who represent 60 countries; students of color comprise more than 20 percent; and more than 40 percent of the Babson undergraduates are women.

Babson is accredited by the New England Association of Schools and Colleges, the International Association for Management Education, and AACSB International - the Association to Advance Collegiate Schools of Business.

LOCATION AND ENVIRONMENT

This 370-acre suburban campus is located in Wellesley, Massachusetts (population 26,650). This is the ideal charming New England town, a classic setting for a college environment. A mere 14 miles outside of Boston, students here are sure to experience the best of both worlds: the quaintness of small town life bordering the cultural and social excitement of the big city. Although Boston is accessible by means of public transportation, approximately half of all students have cars.

MAJORS AND DEGREES OFFERED

Students are required to take 50 percent liberal arts courses and 50 percent business courses. Babson offers unique programs including First-Year Seminar, Foundations in Management and Entrepreneurship, field-based learning programs, independent study, and an honors program. All students start and operate their own businesses with money loaned by Babson during their freshman year as part of Foundations in Management and Entrepreneurship. Students also have the opportunity to work as consultants to nonprofit organizations as part of the Management Consulting Field Experience. All students are encouraged to self-design their course of study. Rarely do students' goals exactly parallel a pre-designed major. This unique opportunity allows students to cultivate their own course of study to best prepare them to meet their immediate career goals upon graduation. Although all students will graduate Babson College with a Bachelors Degree in Business Administration, most courses of study incorporate one or more of the following fields: accounting, economics, entrepreneurship, finance, international business, investment banking, management, management information systems, marketing and quantitative methods. In addition, students may choose to plan their course of study around one of twenty-four optional concentrations in both business and liberal arts disciplines.

ACADEMIC PROGRAMS

Babson College operates on the semester system and has one winter session and one six-week-long summer session.

Students are required to take 50 percent liberal arts courses and 50 percent business courses. Babson offers unique programs including First-Year Seminar, Foundations in Management and Entrepreneurship, field-based learning programs, independent study, and an honors program. All students start and operate their own businesses with money loaned by Babson during their freshman year as part of Foundations in Management and Entrepreneurship. Students also have the opportunity to work as consultants to nonprofit organizations as part of the Management Consulting Field Experience.

All students are encouraged to self-design their course of study. Rarely do students' goals exactly parallel a pre-designed major. This unique opportunity allows students to cultivate their own course of study to best prepare them to meet their immediate career goals upon graduation. Although all students will graduate Babson College with a Bachelor's Degree in Business Administration, most courses of study incorporate one or more of the following fields: accounting, economics, entrepreneurship, finance, international business, investment banking, management, management information systems, marketing and quantitative methods. In addition, students may choose to plan their course of study around one of twenty-four optional concentrations in both business and liberal arts disciplines.

CAMPUS FACILITIES AND EQUIPMENT

Technology is essential to the world of business, and is therefore a vital part of a Babson education. Babson has made many investments in technology, much of the campus is wireless and the college provides the latest in computer lab technology, and has established a well-staffed campus technology support center for student use. Included in tuition is a leased IBM ThinkPad laptop—a computer widely used in the business world. After their sophomore year, Babson students return their ThinkPads and receive brand new ones, which are then returned at the end of their senior year. When students graduate, they have the option to purchase a new IBM ThinkPad at Babson's discounted rate. Babson provides microcomputer accounts for student use complete with Internet access and email. The schools computer network can be accessed from the residence halls, library, computer center, and student center. The library houses a selection of the best business and liberal arts books, newspapers, journals, CD-ROMs, audiocassettes, videocassettes, and videodiscs. It also holds the Sir Isaac Newton Collection, archives, and a museum. The school is a member of a library consortium, which allows students to borrow books from other libraries.

TUITION, ROOM, BOARD AND FEES

The tentative tuition for the 2008-09 academic year is approximately $36,096, room and board is approximately $12,020.

These rates are pending board approval in February, 2008.

FINANCIAL AID

Babson is committed to educating students from diverse backgrounds, and we will do all we can to make it financially possible for you to attend Babson. In 2007-2008, Babson is awarding $18.5 million from its own funds to undergraduate students. Federal and state grants, loans, and work-study are awarded based on financial need. Students who wish to apply for financial aid should submit the CSS/Financial Aid PROFILE and FAFSA by February 15.

Parents loans are available through the Massachusetts Educational Finance Authority (MEFA) and the Federal PLUS program. A tuition payment plan is available through AMS.

STUDENT ORGANIZATIONS AND ACTIVITIES

Babson offers students an extensive variety of student activities. These extracurriculars include 22 NCAA Division III (11 men's and 11 women's) intercollegiate athletic teams. Intramural sports are also popular student activities. A variety of student-run clubs, organizations, and publishing opportunities are available across every interest spectrum. Some of these activities include: Choral Groups, Concert Band, Dance, Theater, Literary Magazine, Jazz Band, Music Ensembles, Radio Station, Student Government, Student Newspaper, and the Yearbook. The school also has four fraternities and three sororities. Approximately 10 percent of students are involved in Greek life.

ADMISSIONS PROCESS

Babson College bases its acceptance of students on both academic and nonacademic factors. The academic factors that are very important include high school record, recommendations, standardized test scores, and essays. The nonacademic factors that are important include extracurricular activities, shown leadership, character/personal qualities, volunteer work, and work experience. Graduation from secondary school is required for admission; the GED is accepted. The most competitive students have taken approximately 5 solid academic courses per year at the highest available level (Honors, Advanced Placement or International Baccalaureate). The SAT I or ACT with writing is required for admission. The TOEFL is required for students who are nonnative speakers of English. The nonrefundable application fee is $65. The application fee may be waived in cases of financial need. Please contact your school guidance office for more details on fee waivers. Babson offers several application programs. Students may apply Early Decision (binding process), Early Action or Regular Decision. The deadline for Early Decision and Early Action is November 15. The Regular Decision Deadline is January 15. Transfer students may apply for September entrance by April 1 and for January entrance by November 1.

BAKER UNIVERSITY

The first university in Kansas, Baker is regarded as a top private school in the Midwest, serving nearly 4,000 students through 4 schools, including more than 900 undergraduates at the College of Arts and Sciences in Baldwin City.

AT A GLANCE

Founded in 1858 and affiliated with the United Methodist Church, Baker is an affordable liberal arts college where students have been academically challenged in a supportive environment for 150 years. With a 12:1 student-faculty ratio, undergraduates receive personal attention from their approachable professors. Alumni include 4 Rhodes Scholars and a Pulitzer Prize winner. The College of Arts and Sciences at the campus in Baldwin City, Kansas, is for students pursuing undergraduate degrees in more than 40-plus areas of study. The School of Professional and Graduate Studies serves working adults in the Kansas City area, Topeka, and Wichita. The School of Nursing, operated in partnership with Stormont-Vail HealthCare in Topeka, offers a Bachelor of Science in nursing degree. Baker's academic reputation is strong, having been ranked in the *U.S. News & World Report* as a top school in the Midwest and for its value in *Money* magazine and *Barron's Best Buys in College Education*. The School of Education serves undergraduates at the campus in Baldwin City and graduate students in Overland Park, Kansas, Topeka, Kansas, Wichita, Kansas, and Lee's Summit, Mo.

LOCATION AND ENVIRONMENT

Located in the heart of Baldwin City in northeast Kansas, Baker University is just 40 minutes southwest of Kansas City and 15 minutes south of Lawrence. The Baldwin City community of 3,500 residents enjoys a rich history and a vibrant arts community.

Nearly every building on the campus has been renovated in the past 20 years, including a $6 million renovation of Collins Library. Three buildings are listed on the National Historic Register. For more than a decade the Clarice L. Osborne Chapel has served as a spiritual haven for more than 100 students during weekly worship services. In the mid-1990s, the chapel was moved to campus stone-by-stone from its original site in England.

A $6.3 million living and learning center is being constructed on the north edge of campus. The 51,000-square-foot facility is on schedule to be completed in August 2008. In addition to housing nearly 200 students, the state-of-the art residence hall will include 2 classrooms and a computer lobby.

All classes are within walking distance from residence halls.

OFF-CAMPUS OPPORTUNITIES

Long known for their involvement in the fine arts, Baker University annually hosts the Artist and Lecture Series, where musicians and other entertainers perform throughout the year at Rice Auditorium on the Baldwin City campus. Baker students also take pride in operating the Art Affair gallery in downtown Baldwin and showcasing their artwork at Holt-Russell Gallery on campus. For 50 years, Baldwin City has been host to the popular Maple Leaf Festival, which attracts 40,000 visitors to enjoy crafts, food, and live music.

Nearby Kansas City and Lawrence are popular destinations for evening and weekend entertainment. Kansas City offers professional sporting events, theater, and live music venues. The new Sprint Center in Downtown Kansas City attracts some of the biggest names in entertainment.

For students preferring the outdoors, lakes, and biking trails within driving distance of Baldwin City provide plenty of recreational options.

MAJORS AND DEGREES OFFERED

The College of Arts and Sciences provides BA, BME, and BS degrees in 40-plus areas of study. Majors include the following: accounting, art education, art history, studio art, biology, wildlife biology, molecular bioscience, business, economics, international business, chemistry, computer science, elementary and secondary education, engineering, English, exercise science, forestry, French, German, history, international studies, mass communication, mathematics, middle level mathematics education, music and music education, philosophy, physical education, physics, political science, psychology, and religion.

The School of Nursing in Topeka is highly regarded throughout the region for its strong clinical component and personalized approach to nursing. Students study for 2 years at CAS, then study and perform clinical work for 2 years at the Stormont-Vail HealthCare campus. It offers the BSN and BSN completion degree programs.

The School of Education offers the BA, BS, MAEd, MASL, and EdD degree programs. Baker is the first private university in Kansas to offer a doctorate.

ACADEMIC PROGRAMS

The Career Development Center and faculty help students receive meaningful job experiences through large and small businesses before they enter the workforce. The internships often result in first jobs for many Baker students.

During 3 weeks in January, students enroll in one unique class or travel opportunity. Recent interterm courses included scuba diving, exploring business in China, a concert tour in Ireland and England, taxidermy, and constructing a home for Habitat for Humanity.

Students have many opportunities to help others through community service. They assist Baldwin City and area residents with yard cleanup, volunteer at shelters and kitchens, and conduct fund-raisers for worthy causes.

Baker encourages its students to study abroad. The most popular destination is Harlaxton College in England, where students live and study in an English manor and where 4-day weekends are saved for travel. Baker's study-abroad coordinator can locate opportunities in virtually every part of the world.

CAMPUS FACILITIES AND EQUIPMENT

Individual computers and computer labs for student use are located in the recently renovated Collins Library. A portion of the library is open 24 hours a day for late-night and early-morning studiers. A new living and learning center, scheduled to open in August 2008, will have a computer lobby.

Baker University's football, baseball, softball, and track facilities have been upgraded in recent years and are considered among the finest in the Heart of America Athletic Conference. A new artificial surface and 8-lane track was installed at Liston Stadium in 2006.

TUITION, ROOM, BOARD, AND FEES

Baker offers students a quality private education at an affordable price. Tuition for 2007–2008 is $18,750. Room and board is $6,150.

FINANCIAL AID

More than 90 percent of Baker students receive financial aid of scholarships and grants that total thousands of dollars. The average financial aid package is worth more than $18,000. Scholarships include the prestigious full-ride Harter, the Presidential Scholarship, University Scholarship, and Academic Scholarship. Students also receive assistance through participation awards and campus work programs. Baker's financial aid programs at the College of Arts and Sciences are designed to help stretch your college dollars. Students find that Baker's outstanding quality and reasonable cost add up to a quality education value.

In order to begin the financial aid process, students must complete the Free Application for Federal Student Aid (FAFSA), available from Baker University or high school guidance offices. This federal form determines a student's eligibility for state and federal funds by analyzing income and asset data. Some form of need analysis is required for all applicants, and all recipients of Baker-funded aid must be enrolled full-time. Follow these steps to apply for scholarships, grants, and loans at Baker: Baker University's policy is to provide financial assistance to as many students as possible. Early action on the student's part is very important. It is strongly recommended that the student complete the combined Application for Admission and Financial Aid by March 1 to be granted priority consideration for funds. The FAFSA must be submitted by March 1 to receive consideration for all funds. Applications will be accepted until funds are exhausted. Not all categories of aid will be available for spring semester incoming applicants.

STUDENT ORGANIZATIONS AND ACTIVITIES

Half of the student body is a member of a Baker's 10 Greek organizations—5 fraternities and 5 sororities. The Greeks take their philanthropic roles seriously, taking leadership roles in their house, and being active in the community.

Baker students are actively involved in more than 40 activity groups and organizations. Music groups are popular with 3 choirs, 2 bands, 1 orchestra, and 8 chamber ensembles.

Forty-five percent of Baker students participate in intercollegiate athletics. Baker is a member of the National Association of Intercollegiate Athletics and is in the Heart of America Athletic Conference. Baker offers 9 men's and 9 women's athletic programs.

ADMISSIONS PROCESS

Admission to Baker University is selective. Freshmen applicants must meet 2 of the following 3 criteria to be admitted: an ACT composite of 18 or above; a high school GPA of at least 2.75 and a high school class ranking of 50 percent or above. Transfer students must have a 2.3 cumulative college GPA.

BARNARD COLLEGE

AT A GLANCE

Founded in 1889, Barnard College was one of the first colleges to offer young women the chance to earn a college degree. Today, Barnard College is still committed to the education of more than 2,360 undergraduate women from more than 40 countries and 48 states. Barnard College partnered with Columbia University in 1900 under an agreement unique in the world of higher education. As an independent college for women, Barnard continues to maintain its own Board of Trustees, campus, curriculum, faculty, staff, and admissions process. Barnard also operates from its own endowment, while Columbia University confers degrees to Barnard students. The fully residential campus features countless, independent resources and facilities; students at Barnard also have academic and extracurricular access to the Columbia campus across the street, including cross-registration for courses. The small, personal, and close-knit character of Barnard is augmented by the resources of a large research university.

Barnard is located in Manhattan in the quiet neighborhood of Morningside Heights. The school stretches from 116th Street to 120th Street on Broadway, and the 4-acre campus has everything its students need. A full gymnasium is located on the first floor of Barnard Hall, which faces the college's main entrance. Brooks, Reid, Hewitt, and Sulzberger Halls make up the residence life complex situated at the southern end of campus. Off-campus housing options include opportunities for coeducational living. The heart of student life will be the exciting NEXUS Student Center, opening in fall 2009, where students will have access to many amenities to augment academic life.

LOCATION AND ENVIRONMENT

Barnard is situated in New York City, an urban location that offers students endless cultural, academic, and professional opportunities. Barnard incorporates New York as an extension of the classroom, and students make use of its resources for study and exploration. The Office of Career Development, for example, lists a selection of more than 2,500 student internships throughout the whole of New York City. Institutions neighboring the Barnard campus include the Manhattan School of Music, Teachers College, Bank Street College of Education, Union Theological Seminary, and the Jewish Theological Seminary.

OFF-CAMPUS OPPORTUNITIES

There are numerous opportunities for Barnard students to explore academics beyond the Barnard gates. Barnard students have full access to Columbia resources and often take graduate or professional-level courses with instructor permission. The Jewish Theological Seminary offers credit for courses Barnard students take there, and Juilliard and the Manhattan School of Music allow qualified Barnard musicians to take lessons at their institutions.

Barnard students also explore academics beyond both New York and the United States through more than 300 study-abroad programs in 70 different countries including Argentina, China, Egypt, Greece, Kenya, Russia, and Tibet. Reid Hall, a Barnard-Columbia facility in Paris, offers programs for both semesters and full years. The Inter-collegiate Center for Classical Studies offers classics students the opportunity to study in Rome. Institutions offering study-abroad programs in England alone include Somerville College in Oxford; Newnham College in Cambridge; and University College, London School of Economics, King's College, or Queen Mary College at the University of London. Atlanta's Spelman College and Washington, DC's Howard University offer domestic exchange programs.

MAJORS AND DEGREES OFFERED

Barnard offers the bachelor of arts degree, and students choose from more than 50 majors, including African studies, American studies, ancient studies, anthropology, architecture, art history, Asian and Middle Eastern cultures, biochemistry, biological studies, chemistry, classics (Greek and Latin), comparative literature, computer science, dance, economics, education, English, environmental science, film studies, foreign area studies, French, German, history, human rights studies, Italian, Jewish studies, mathematics, Medieval and Renaissance studies, music, neuroscience and behavior, philosophy, physics and astronomy, political science, psychology, religion, Slavic studies, sociology, Spanish and Latin American cultures, statistics, theater, urban studies, and women's studies.

There are also opportunities for double and joint degrees, which students earn from both Barnard and other schools within the Columbia University system. One option is the 5-year AB/MIA program where students earn their masters from Columbia's School of International Affairs. Another 5-year option gives students the chance to earn an AB/MPA after studying in Columbia's public affairs and administration program. Barnard also has the option of nominating, in conjunction with the Columbia University School of Law, juniors with outstanding records to enter the Law School under the Accelerated Program in Interdisciplinary Legal Education (AILE) after only 3 years of undergraduate work as well as candidates for Columbia's School of Oral and Dental Surgery. Science and engineering students can earn both AB and BS degrees in a 5-year (3-2) program with Columbia's Fu Foundation School of Engineering and Applied Science; there, students specialize in various engineering fields, including aerospace, civil, and electrical. Music students can apply and audition for the Juilliard School's 5-year (3-2) program; they spend 3 years earning their AB from Barnard, then 2 years at Juilliard earning their MM degree. Finally, students have the chance to earn simultaneously an AB from Barnard and a BA from the nearby Jewish Theological Seminary's List College.

ACADEMIC PROGRAMS

A Barnard education seeks to provide women with the tools and techniques needed to think critically and act effectively in the world today. Barnard requires students to complete 122 points of course work (including First-year English, First-year Seminar, and 2 semesters of physical education) for the AB degree. Barnard believes that a successful liberal arts education revolves around central ways of knowing the world. This philosophy forms the basis of the general education requirements within the Nine Ways of Knowing curriculum: reason and value, social analysis, cultures in comparison, language, laboratory science, historical studies, literature, visual and performing arts, and quantitative reasoning. To allow for flexibility within this framework, a student chooses among the designated courses that fulfill each of the 8 requirement areas. Thus, each student will shape her own academic program by electing a combination of wide-ranging introductory courses and more specialized upper-level courses.

The college has a long-standing commitment to prepare students sufficiently in a subject so that they may undertake a semester or yearlong project, usually during the senior year, on a topic related to their major. Students are encouraged to explore internships in their field, thereby acquiring information and experience that complement what is learned through formal study. A student may major in 2 fields by satisfying all the major requirements prescribed by each department.

CAMPUS FACILITIES AND EQUIPMENT

Milbank Hall, a nationally registered historic landmark, contains offices, classrooms, a cutting-edge greenhouse, and the Minor Latham Playhouse. The 14-story Altschul Hall houses state-of-the-art science research facilities and equipment, along with classrooms, offices, and laboratories. Students will gather in the NEXUS Student Center, starting in 2009, for recreational facilities including a cafeteria, the Java City Café, multiple lounges, music practice rooms, and offices for College Activities and Multicultural Affairs, along with more than 80 student organizations. NEXUS will also house art and architecture studios and will have a blackbox theater as well as a green roof. Finally, Wollman Library offers 3 floors of study space and maintains 204,900 volumes housed in open stacks.

TUITION, ROOM, BOARD, AND FEES

$33,776 is the total for 2007-2008 tuition and fees at Barnard, and room and board are an additional $11,786.

FINANCIAL AID

Financial aid at Barnard is strictly need-based. A student's need is determined using criteria established by both the federal government and Barnard's Financial Aid office. The financial aid awarded by Barnard should supplement a family's own financial resources, while Barnard covers 100 percent of the remaining need. Financial aid awards typically consist of grants, work study jobs, and student loans. Students who are awarded Barnard College grants should expect grants throughout their 4 years at Barnard, providing the students' families maintain their level of need and the students maintain their academic standing. More than 55 percent of first-year students receive some form of financial aid. Need plays no role in the Barnard admissions process; Barnard admission is need-blind, and students are evaluated solely on merit.

STUDENT ORGANIZATIONS AND ACTIVITIES

The Barnard College community offers numerous activities and opportunities to an active student body. Using a holistic, student-centered approach in advising, programming, and community development, the College Activities Office strives to engage each student and promote active and involved citizenship through leadership development, multicultural education, and a social justice foundation. All Barnard students are eligible to be members of the elected Student Government Association and more than 80 student-run organizations, including Asian American Alliance, Barnard Bulletin, Gospel Choir, Community Impact, Late Nite Theatre, Model United Nations, Mujeres, McIntosh Activities Council, Orchesis Dance Troupe, Russian Cultural Association, Students Against Silence, and Women's International Business Council. Barnard and Columbia students take part in organizations and activities on both campuses, and Barnard women take leadership roles in many of the 270 Columbia-sponsored clubs. Women's intercollegiate, intramural, and club athletics are also popular. Barnard's varsity athletes compete in the NCAA Division I and the Ivy League through the Barnard/Columbia Athletic Consortium. The 15 intercollegiate teams include archery, basketball, crew, cross-country, fencing, field hockey, golf, indoor and outdoor track and field, lacrosse, soccer, softball, swimming and diving, tennis, and volleyball. Intramural and club sports include cycling, equestrian, ice hockey, martial arts, rugby, and sailing.

ADMISSIONS PROCESS

High school transcripts, letters of recommendation, standardized test scores, and personal attributes and achievements all play a role in Barnard's highly selection admissions process. The college seeks women with strong academic records who exhibit the capacity and desire to grow intellectually and personally. While there is not a set group of criteria that an applicant must match, the student must have completed a college preparatory program or its equivalent, with a recommended 4 years of English, 3 or more years of math, 3 or more years of a foreign language, 3 or more years of laboratory science, and 3 or more years of history. Every applicant is evaluated on both the qualities that she personally espouses and her potential for success at Barnard. Applicants must submit the following test scores: either the ACT with writing, or the SAT Reasoning Test (with writing) and 2 SAT Subject Tests. Students for whom English is not their primary language of instruction or who have been in the United States for fewer than 4 years must submit results from the TOEFL exam. Interviews are recommended but are not required for admission.

BARRY UNIVERSITY

AT A GLANCE

Barry University is an independent, Catholic university that provides an affordable, high-quality education, a caring environment, and a religious dimension and encourages a commitment to community service. The University was founded in 1940 by the Dominican Sisters of Adrian, Michigan. Barry is recognized as a "College of Distinction" for its engaging campus community, excellence in teaching, and successful alumni. Barry graduates have the second highest earnings of all 28 institutions of the Independent Colleges and Universities of Florida. The Spanish-style main campus is five miles from the ocean in sunny, suburban Miami Shores, Florida. Programs are offered at 48 additional sites from Tallahassee to Homestead. Students come from all compass points, age groups, ethnicities, and faiths, representing 49 states and more than 80 countries. Of the more than 8,500 students enrolled, approximately 4,000 are full-time undergraduates and approximately 3,500 are graduate and continuing education students. At Barry, you can choose from more than 50 undergraduate majors, more than 50 graduate degree programs, and accelerated bachelor's degrees for working adults. Classes are small, so you receive personal attention from distinguished faculty and advisors. The student-to-faculty ratio is 14 to 1. You gain hands-on professional experience before graduation through internships, service learning, and research projects.

ACADEMIC PROGRAMS

Barry University offers a personalized educational experience that will encourage you to think critically, expand your skills, and find answers. With more than 50 traditional undergraduate programs, accelerated bachelor's programs designed specifically for working adults, and more than 50 graduate programs, Barry offers superb opportunities for study, networking, community service, and professional growth. Barry University is a coeducational, international, Catholic university that is focused on quality academics, hands-on experience, and your success. Barry's Honors Program challenges students with a stimulating, rigorous curriculum designed to develop critical thinking, communication, and leadership skills. The Center for Advanced Learning supports students with learning disabilities through tutoring, counseling, testing and classroom accommodations, and advocacy with faculty.

CAMPUS FACILITIES AND EQUIPMENT

At Barry, you will find the facilities you need to enhance and support your studies. The Monsignor William Barry Library houses over 950,000 items of print and non-print materials, 2,500 periodicals, including over 700 journals in electronic full text, and 6,900 audiovisual items. The Southeast Florida Library Information Network provides access to more than 12 million items and 30,000 periodical titles. The library is also a member of the Florida Library Information Network and the Southeastern Library Network. The Division of Information Technology's main computer lab is available to all students and faculty and provides access to various application packages, various operating systems, e-mail, and the Internet. The lab is equipped with more than 80 Windows-based computers, scanners, and laser and color printers. The lab is open weekdays, evenings, and weekends to accommodate students' schedules. The Science Building houses classroom labs, research labs, and lecture rooms. A wide range of general and specialized equipment in the biomedical sciences is available. In 2008, the building will also have a state-of-the-art aquarium system for teaching and research purposes. The Health and Sports Center has a fully-equipped human performance laboratory, athletic training room, and biomechanics lab. In addition, there is a complete weight training facility and an outdoor sports and recreation center. The David Brinkley Television Studio houses the latest broadcast and production equipment, including a Grass Valley switcher, a nonlinear digital editor, and a 16-position Yamaha audio board.

TUITION, ROOM, BOARD AND FEES

Your Barry education is a valuable investment in your future. When considering a private education, costs may be a factor, but they need not be the determining factor. Your Barry education can be quite affordable. All students are assessed tuition and fees on a semester basis. Please be aware that all rates given are subject to change without notice.

Full-time tuition for the 2007-08 school year is $24,500. Room and board averages an additional $7,900. Students may incur other expenses for books, supplies, laboratory fees, and transportation.

FINANCIAL AID

Barry University has a generous scholarship program, with awards up to $15,500. These awards are based upon your cumulative GPA and standard test scores.

More than 80 percent of our student body receives some form of financial assistance. Barry also participates in the full array of federal and state financial aid programs. The only way to know if you are eligible for financial aid is to submit the Free Application for Federal Student Aid (FAFSA). We encourage you to apply as soon as possible. You may complete and mail the paper FAFSA, or you may complete the electronic FAFSA by logging onto the Department of Education's secure Web Site at www.fafsa.ed.gov.

STUDENT ORGANIZATIONS AND ACTIVITIES

Barry has more than 55 registered student clubs and organizations, 19 national honor societies, three sororities and three fraternities, as well as intramural sports including basketball, golf, sand volleyball, soccer, softball, and tennis. Some of the wellness activities include body sculpting, kickboxing, salsa, tai chi, and yoga. Barry also has an active athletic department. Barry's 12 NCAA Division II teams (Sunshine State Conference) include men's baseball, basketball, golf, soccer, and tennis, and women's basketball, golf, rowing, soccer, softball, tennis, and volleyball. Barry has won seven national championships - one in men's golf, three in women's soccer, and three in volleyball. In addition, Barry has crowned 90 All-Americans and 60 Scholar All-Americans, and has sent numerous teams and individuals to postseason playoffs and national championship competitions. Barry's Student Government Association (SGA), which is responsible for overseeing the 55 student organizations on campus, has been recognized for its excellence by Florida Leader magazine. Students also run the Campus Activities Board, which is responsible for planning and coordinating campus-wide events, including barbecues, lectures, dances, concerts, sailing trips, and casino nights.

ADMISSIONS PROCESS

Barry University accepts applications on a rolling basis. Applicants who have never attended a college or university and applicants who are coming to Barry with less than 12 hours of transferable college credits are considered first-year applicants. First-year applicants are required to complete and submit the online undergraduate application at www.barry.edu (or receive a copy of the paper application by contacting the Office of Admissions), submit the nonrefundable application fee ($20/online application, $30/paper application), and submit official transcripts from all secondary and post-secondary institutions. In addition, Barry University requires that applicants submit official SAT or ACT scores. The Barry University codes are 5053 (SAT I) and 0718 (ACT). Barry recommends that prospective students apply well in advance. Applications can be accepted as early as after the junior year in high school.

A completed application can be submitted online or to:

Barry University, Office of Admissions

11300 NE Second Avenue

Miami Shores, FL 33161-6695

Phone: 305-899-3100 or 800-695-2279

Fax: 305-899-2971

E-mail: admissions@mail.barry.edu

Web site: www.barry.edu

BECKER COLLEGE

Since 1784, we've integrated marketplace demands with our enriched programs; we deliver first-quality education and discover unique, high-demand career niches that distinguish us—and our students—apart from the rest.

AT A GLANCE

Founded in 1784, Becker College remains on the cutting edge and is still a hotspot. Becker's private, high-tech campuses are entirely wireless and full-time students are provided with laptops to ensure they receive the maximum benefits of information technology.

Outstanding professors have unique field experience and interweave their classes with an invaluable perspective to further complement instruction. Carefully crafted curricula provide a contemporary and meaningful context, and the student-faculty ratio of 18:1 ensures that students get the individual attention and recognition they deserve. Students have every opportunity and are encouraged to gain hands-on experience; invaluable field experience and unparalleled education render recent Becker graduates highly desired professionals.

LOCATION AND ENVIRONMENT

Located right in the heart of Massachusetts on 2 convenient campuses only 6 miles apart, the 2 campuses offer a choice of living environments to appeal to all; the Worcester campus provides an urban setting and the Leicester campus offers a peaceful, bucolic setting.

Becker's 2 beautiful campuses provide a robust residential life. On the Worcester campus, historic homes have been restored and serve as residence halls. In Leicester, students may choose to live in restored apartment-style homes or contemporary residence halls. Either campus offers all-female, all-male, co-ed, over 21, and all-freshman facilities. Each campus has its own dining hall, library (the combined libraries approach 73,000 volumes), and fitness facility.

OFF-CAMPUS OPPORTUNITIES

Located on 2 convenient campuses, Becker is located less than an hour from Boston and 3 hours from New York City. Becker is located 70 miles away or less from 3 major international airports.

MAJORS AND DEGREES OFFERED

Becker is proud to offer more than 25 bachelor's degree programs of study that are distinctly innovative and exceptional 2- and 4-year degree programs which fully prepare students to achieve their professional career goals. Becker actively enriches its programs by uniting marketplace demands with your passions. Major programs range from Nursing, to Equine Management, to Video Game Design to Criminal Justice.

Associate degree programs: animal care, nursing (RN), veterinary technology.

Bachelor degree programs: applied behavior analysis, applied behavior analysis (honors), computer game design, computer game development and programming, computer information systems, criminal justice, early childhood education, elementary education, equine management, equine studies major, exercise science, financial accounting, forensics / crime scene processing, graphic design, hospitality and tourism, human resources, interior design, laboratory animal management, legal studies, liberal arts, management, marketing, nursing, pre-veterinary concentration, psychology, psychology (honors), sports management, veterinary science.

ACADEMIC PROGRAMS

Rich, hands-on experiences are invaluable when students can simultaneously gain the perspectives and absorb the insights of our knowledgeable faculty as they pursue their goals. Many of these lessons are so powerful that students rely on them throughout their careers. At Becker, we deliver a dynamic combination of hands-on experience and an outstanding staff and curriculum to ensure that students have the best foundation there is.

In addition to our core curriculum programs, Becker provides students with numerous opportunities to participate in guided observations and to complete internships or practical experiences in rural, suburban, and inner-city settings. Our childhood education and psychology programs provide these opportunities. Our flexible nursing bachelor of science program enables students to continue working as registered nurses while they attend classes and accelerate their careers. To support the animal care programs, students have access to our in-house laboratories and clinic; field trips to area research facilities additionally supplement the hands-on experience in the classroom and laboratory. Students also are encouraged to work part-time in a bio-technical research setting to enhance learned technical skills. Additionally, Becker's accelerated degree programs in business are designed so that students can continue to work while they earn their degrees.

We know that hands-on experience and education work synergistically to provide an unbeatable foundation and train students to become high-demand professionals. We deliver a dynamic combination of hands-on experience and an outstanding staff and curriculum to support students' goals. Students can exchange their experiences from the workplace and gain invaluable perspectives and insights of our knowledgeable faculty as they accrue career experience and earn the degrees they need to accelerate their careers and become one of the best in their field.

CAMPUS FACILITIES AND EQUIPMENT

A variety of housing options are available for those students who choose to live on campus. Students may select to live on either campus through the admissions office. The Worcester campus offers housing in refurbished historic homes, and the Leicester campus offers both historic homes and contemporary residence halls. Both campuses offer all-female, all-male, co-ed, over 21, and all-freshman living spaces. Each campus has its own dining hall, library (the combined libraries approach 73,000 volumes), and fitness facility.

All students in the equine studies programs are involved in the daily maintenance and care of the horses in our own equestrian facility, and all students involved in the animal care and veterinary technician programs have access to the state-of-the-art on-campus veterinary clinic which houses a kennel, laboratory animal rooms, dog training and grooming rooms in addition to clinical facilities.

TUITION, ROOM, BOARD, AND FEES

The current tuition for the year 2007-2008 is $23,600. Room and Board for the year is $9,300.

FINANCIAL AID

Financial aid is available for all eligible students through federal, state, and Becker College programs. Currently, nearly 100 percent of all Becker students who apply for aid receive some form of financial assistance.

STUDENT ORGANIZATIONS AND ACTIVITIES

Opportunities for extracurricular involvement are pervasive and all students are encouraged to participate in numerous activities to enrich learning and enhance personal development. There are several organizations on campus, including ALANA-Multicultural Club, Animal Health Club, Gay Straight Alliance, Black Student Union, Community Service Club, Photography Club, Fitness Club, Music Club, Nursing Club, Residence Life Club, Ski/Snowboard Club, Student Activities Committee, Student Alumni Society , Student Government Association, the student newspaper (the *Becker Journal*), Travel Club, and the Yearbook Club.

Athletically, Becker College competes nationally at the NCAA Division III level and offers soccer, football, equestrian, tennis, golf, cross-country, basketball, ice hockey, volleyball, baseball, softball, and lacrosse at the Division III level.

ADMISSIONS PROCESS

For more information, or to apply online, please visit www.becker.edu. For additional questions, please call us at 877-523-2537, or e-mail us at admissions@becker.edu.

Becker College

61 Sever Street

Worcester, MA 01609

BELMONT UNIVERSITY

AT A GLANCE

Belmont is a private, coeducational, comprehensive university. It is the largest Christian university in Tennessee and among the fastest growing in the nation. We offer undergraduate degrees in more than 75 major areas of study through our 7 undergraduate colleges and schools: Arts & Sciences, Business Administration, Mike Curb College of Entertainment and Music Business, Gordon E. Inman College of Health Sciences & School of Nursing, Religion, University College, and Visual & Performing Arts. In addition, master's degrees are available in Accountancy, business administration, education, English, music, nursing, occupational therapy, and sport administration. Doctoral degrees are offered in occupational therapy, physical therapy, and pharmacy. Belmont is home to about 4,800 undergraduate and graduate students. The student body includes representatives from almost every state and more than 25 different countries.

LOCATION AND ENVIRONMENT

Belmont University occupies a 65-acre campus in southeast Nashville. With more than 500,000 residents, Nashville is a cultural, educational, health care, commercial, and financial center in the mid-South. Practical educational opportunities, offered through diverse curriculums, provide students with the hands-on experience they need in preparation for a meaningful career. The city's location, halfway between the northern and southern boundaries of the United States, with 3 intersecting interstate highways and an international airport, makes it accessible to students from across the country.

OFF-CAMPUS OPPORTUNITIES

Several programs at Belmont have agreements with area organizations to provide students practical training. Nursing students gain clinical experience at various local medical centers including Vanderbilt Medical Center, Baptist Hospital, Centennial Medical Center, St. Thomas Hospital, and Summit Hospital. Education students gain classroom experience in Metro-Davidson County Schools. Music business students gain real-world experience through internships in the Nashville music industry as well as in the Los Angeles, California, and New York; New York markets through the Belmont West and Belmont East programs of study and internships.

Through a wide variety of international study programs, Belmont offers students the opportunity to broaden and deepen their education while earning credit hours toward their degrees. These programs, which range in duration from 2 weeks to a year, are available in Australia, the Bahamas, China, Costa Rica, England, France, Germany, Ireland, Italy, Mexico, New Zealand, Nicaragua, Russia, Scotland, South Africa, and Spain.

A unique Washington Center Intern Program that places Belmont students in individualized internships in the Washington, DC, area is also available.

MAJORS AND DEGREES OFFERED

Belmont University is accredited by the Commission on Colleges of the Southern Association of Colleges and Schools to award baccalaureate, master's, and doctoral degrees. Belmont grants 7 undergraduate degrees: the bachelor of arts, the bachelor of business administration, the bachelor of fine arts, the bachelor of music, the bachelor of science, the bachelor of science in nursing, and the bachelor of social work.

College of Arts and Sciences

School of Education: early childhood education, exercise science and health promotion, health, middle school education, physical education, secondary education.

School of Humanities: classics, English, French, German, Spanish, philosophy.

School of Sciences: applied discrete mathematics, biochemistry and molecular biology, biology, chemistry, computer science, engineering physics, environmental studies, mathematics, medical imaging technology, medical physics, medical technology, neuroscience, pharmaceutical studies, physics, psychology, science and engineering management, Web programming and development.

School of Social Sciences: audio and video production, communication studies, European studies, history, international politics, journalism, mass communication, organizational and corporate communication, political economy, political science, politics and public law, public relations, sociology.

College of Business Administration: accounting, business administration, economics, entrepreneurship, finance, information systems management, international business, international economics, management, marketing.

Mike Curb College of Entertainment and Music Business: audio engineering technology, entertainment industry studies, music business, songwriting.

Gordon E. Inman College of Health Sciences & Nursing: nursing, social work.

College of Visual and Performing Arts

Department of Art: art education, design communications, studio art.

School of Music: church music, commercial music, music composition, musical theater, music education, music with an outside minor, music theory, music performance, piano pedagogy.

Department of Theatre and Dance: theater and drama.

School of Religion: biblical languages, biblical studies, Christian ethics, Christian leadership, religion and the arts, religious studies.

ACADEMIC PROGRAMS

Uniquely positioned to provide the best of liberal arts and professional education, Belmont University offers celebrated professional programs structured to provide an academically well-rounded education. Belmont University operates on a 2-semester schedule with classes beginning in late August and ending in early May. Two summer sessions are also offered. The academic program is arranged by school: the College of Arts and Sciences, the College of Business Administration, the Mike Curb College of Entertainment and Music Business, the Gordon E. Inman College of Health Sciences & School of Nursing, the College of Visual and Performing Arts, University College, and the School of Religion.

In addition to the degrees offered through the schools, Belmont University offers an honors program, which was created to provide an enrichment opportunity for students who have potential for superior academic performance and who seek added challenge and breadth to their studies. Students enrolled in the honors program are led in designing and working through a flexible, individual curriculum by a private tutor who is an honors faculty member.

The university's advancements in undergraduate research are credited to a faculty committed to helping students practice their disciplines. The annual Belmont Undergraduate Research Symposium puts Belmont at the forefront of this national movement by providing a public forum for in-depth research at the undergraduate level.

CAMPUS FACILITIES AND EQUIPMENT

Belmont offers a quiet, secluded environment for study. Classes are held in 11 academic buildings, with the library and other multifunction facilities located in proximity to those classrooms. The renovated and expanded Lila D. Bunch Library includes a microcomputer center and has 162,000 volumes. Located next to the library is the newly constructed Leu Center for the Visual Arts, featuring state-of-the-art studios with natural lighting and spacious work areas and the 3,000-square-foot Leu Art Gallery. The Sam A. Wilson School of Music Building houses classrooms, a resource room, seminar rooms, studio/offices, music practice rooms, a piano lab, and a music technology lab. The Jack C. Massey Business Center, encompassing 115,000 square feet, provides classrooms, office space, study lounges, seminar and conference rooms, and a convenience store. A state-of-the-art learning center includes 5 computer labs. In addition, Massey Business Center houses the 9,000-square-foot Center for Music Business, which provides classrooms, an academic resource center, 2 state-of-the-art recording studios and control rooms, 4 isolation booths, a MIDI pre-postproduction room, and an engineering repair shop.

The Beaman Student Life Center is located on the southern end of Belmont's campus, which includes a fitness center with strength training and cardiovascular equipment, an aerobics area for a wide variety of classes, 2 racquetball/squash courts, an intramural/recreational gym, a rock climbing wall, dance studio, and locker rooms. Cardiovascular equipment is also stationed on the balcony level around the center's atrium overlooking Belmont's campus.

In addition to the health and wellness facilities, the center features a convenience store and game room, as well as ample gathering spaces and comfortable seating areas for students to study, relax, and interact with fellow classmates. There are also several rooms and spaces for student activities and club meetings. Wireless connection to the internet is available throughout the building.

The Curb Event Center affirms Belmont University's status as one of the strongest comprehensive universities in the South. It is the most visible sign of Belmont's commitment to students, the local community, and NCAA Division I athletics. The state-of-the-art facility represents the fulfillment of a decade of dreams about a center that can accommodate events of all types for up to 5,000 people, including special convocations, Commencements, concerts, and major speakers. The center also features superior acoustics and equipment for the recording of live concerts. And of course, the Curb Event Center is also the home court of the Belmont Bruins. In October 2008, the center will host 1 of the 3 national presidential debates.

TUITION, ROOM, BOARD, AND FEES

The total cost of attending Belmont is only 80 percent of the national average for a private college. For a full-time student living on campus the total cost for the 2007-2008 academic year is approximately $27,700, which includes tuition, fees, books, room and board, and meal plan. The total cost for a full-time student living off campus is approximately $18,780.

FINANCIAL AID

The financial aid program at Belmont combines merit-based assistance with need-based assistance to make the university education affordable. Institutional merit awards range from full-tuition Presidential Scholarships to various levels of partial merit awards. Athletic and performance scholarships are also available. Belmont also administers traditional state and federal programs, including the Federal Pell Grant, Federal Stafford Student Loan, Federal Perkins Loan, Federal PLUS Loan, and Tennessee Student Assistance Grants and Scholarships. Campus employment is available. Parents may arrange monthly tuition payments through an outside vendor. To apply for assistance, the student must complete the Free Application for Federal Student Aid (FAFSA). FAFSA Code: 003479

STUDENT ORGANIZATIONS AND ACTIVITIES

All told, more than 80 clubs and organizations are active on Belmont's campus, including academic clubs, honor societies, professional fraternities, special interest and Christian organizations, student government, publications, social fraternities and sororities, music and drama groups, and debate and forensics teams.

The Belmont Bruins compete at the NCAA Division I level in the Atlantic Sun Conference in men's and women's basketball, tennis, cross country, track, soccer, and golf; men's baseball; and women's softball and volleyball. An extensive intramural sports program is also available.

ADMISSIONS PROCESS

Belmont admissions officers consider applications based on the total picture that a student's credentials present. High school students will be considered competitive for admission if they present a rigorous course of college-preparatory, academic studies. Students should have an above-average academic and cumulative grade point average and rank in the top half of their graduating class. Any college-level work is also expected to be at the above-average level. A strong correlation between high school grades and entrance examination scores is expected. The personal supplemental information, resume of activities, and recommendations are also strongly considered as indicators of success at Belmont. Additional requirements such as portfolios or auditions are considered in conjunction with the academic credentials for those programs that require them. Each application is considered on an individual basis. No 2 applicants will present the same credentials or the same fit with the university. Our desire is to work with each student to determine the likelihood of that student to enroll in, graduate from, and use the benefits of the Belmont educational experience.

Further information and application materials may be obtained by contacting:

Office of Admissions

Belmont University

1900 Belmont Boulevard

Nashville, TN 37212

Telephone: 615-460-6785

800-56ENROL (toll free)

Fax: 615-460-5434

E-mail: buadmission@mail.belmont.edu

Website: www.belmont.edu

CEEB Code: 1058

ACT Code: 3946

BELOIT COLLEGE

AT A GLANCE

Beloit College is a four-year, independent, national college of liberal arts and sciences where the focus is great teaching grounded in rigorous study that encourages independent research, fieldwork, and collaboration with peers and professors.

The college is a dynamic and uncommonly diverse community where cliques, stereotypes, and exclusivity are left behind and the flexible curriculum is interdisciplinary, experiential, and global in scope. Beloit is a residential college whose 1,300 students come from nearly every state and over 40 countries. With an incredible breath of opportunities, modern facilities, an award winning faculty, and creative, motivated students, Beloit has been named to the Business 50, International 50, and Science 50 (only 21 colleges, including Beloit, appear on all three lists). Founded in 1846 to serve a frontier society, Beloit is Wisconsin's first college.

LOCATION AND ENVIRONMENT

Beloit's 40-acre campus is located on the Wisconsin-Illinois state line 90 miles northwest of Chicago, 50 miles south of Madison, and 70 miles southwest of Milwaukee in a small city about which noted anthropologist Margaret Mead said "[This is] American Society in a microcosm." Students take advantage of the varied resources offered by the three major metropolitan areas, as well as those offered by the city itself. Beloit's hospital, clinics, industry, and various civic and service organizations provide numerous internship, job shadowing, enrichment, and community outreach opportunities. The academic buildings of Beloit cluster around lawns dotted with ancient Indian burial mounds, while across the campus residence halls form a community of their own. A 25-acre athletic field and recently renovated Strong Memorial Stadium are located a few blocks east of the main campus.

OFF-CAMPUS OPPORTUNITIES

Over half of Beloit graduates study off campus in international and domestic programs. International: Beloit students have studied in over 30 countries worldwide, including Australia, Brazil, Cameroon, China, Costa Rica, Czech Republic, Denmark, Ecuador, England, France, Germany, Greece, Hong Kong, Hungary, India, Indonesia, Ireland, Israel, Italy, Jamaica, Japan, Morocco, Nepal, Netherlands, Poland, Russia, Scotland, Senegal, South Africa, Tahiti, Tanzania, Thailand, Turkey, and Zimbabwe. Domestic: Oak Ridge National Laboratory, Wilderness Field Station, Marine Biological Laboratory, Urban Studies, Newberry Library, and the Washington Semester. Students arrange internship, field term, and summer employment opportunities through the Office of Field and Career Services.

MAJORS AND DEGREES OFFERED

Beloit is an undergraduate college that confers the bachelor of arts and bachelor of science degrees. There are more than 50 fields of study in 19 departments.

Majors: anthropology, art history, art (studio), biochemistry, biology (cellular and molecular; ecology, evolution, and behavioral; environmental; integrative and medical; mathematical), business administration, chemistry (applied, environmental), classical civilization, classical philology, comparative literature, computer science, East Asian languages and cultures, economics, economics & management, education and youth studies, English (creative writing, literary studies, and rhetoric and discourse), environmental studies, French, geology (environmental), German, health and society, history, interdisciplinary studies, international relations, mathematics, modern languages and literatures, music, philosophy, physics, political science, psychology, religious studies, Russian, science for elementary teaching, sociology, Spanish, theatre arts (acting, communications, dance, design, directing, stage management, theatre history), women's and gender studies.

Education certification (BA, BS): Children & schools (grades 1-8), Adolescents & schools (grades 9-12), Art (birth-21), Drama (grades 1-12), Foreign language (grades 1-12), and coaching. Minors: African studies, American studies, ancient Mediterranean studies, anthropology, Asian studies, biology and society, chemistry, computer science, computational visualization & modeling, English, environmental studies, European studies, geology, health & society, history, integra-

tive biology, interdisciplinary studies, journalism, Latin American & Caribbean studies, legal studies, mathematics, medieval studies, museum studies, music, peace & justice studies, performing arts, philosophy, philosophy and religious studies, physics, political science, religious studies, Russian studies, women's and gender studies.

Pre-professional programs: Special engineering programs; forestry and environmental management program; pre-law; and medical professions programs.

ACADEMIC PROGRAMS

Beloit students learn by doing; the college provides international study opportunities to its students, ranging from technical/production work with the Guthrie Theatre in Minneapolis to archaeological excavations in Lubeck, Germany. There are a variety of programs that supplement the academic curriculum. First-Year Initiatives links each student with an experienced professor and a group of peers in an interdisciplinary seminar to investigate the nature of learning. The Sophomore-Year Program offers students multiple experiences to explore diverse topics, possible majors, and to develop a comprehensive academic plan. The Center for Language Studies offers intensive summer language instruction in Chinese, Japanese, Portuguese, Russian, and Arabic. The International Education Program is dedicated to getting Beloit students abroad and nearly half of all students do. The anthropology field training program takes students to excavation sites from Colorado to Chile, and geology field expeditions include trips to Iceland, New Zealand, and Scotland. Further experiential opportunities exist through Beloit's memberships in the Keck Consortium in Geology, and the Pew Midstates Science and Mathematics Consortium. Each spring students present their own research at the Student Symposium and the fall International Symposium Day is a forum for research that students have conducted abroad. Beloit students sit on the editorial board of the acclaimed Beloit Fiction Journal. The Lois Wilson Mackey '45 Chair of Creative Writing brings a well-known writer to campus to conduct a semester writing workshop, including Billy Collins, Bei Dao, Amy Hempel, Denise Levertov, Peter Matthiessen, William Least-Heat Moon, and Robert Stone. Funding for entrepreneurial or academic projects by first-year students is provided through the Venture Grant program. The Center for Entrepreneurship in Liberal Education at Beloit (CELEB) serves as an incubator for student ventures in a variety of fields, with special emphasis on entrepreneurship in the fine arts.

CAMPUS FACILITIES AND EQUIPMENT

Student organizations have offices in the Jeffris-Wood Campus Center, Pearsons Hall, along with the radio station (WBCR), snack bar, coffee house, game room, mail center, and an all-night study lounge. The Beloit College bookstore, Turtle Creek, features 10,000 square feet of books, supplies, and clothing, and is located just two blocks from campus in downtown Beloit.

Beloit's sports and recreation facilities reflect that 70 percent of the students participate in club, intramural, and varsity athletics. The $6 million Sports Center includes the Flood Arena, with three collegiate basketball/volleyball courts; the Marvin Field House, with indoor facilities for soccer, tennis, track, golf, baseball, and softball; a fitness center; dance studio; handball and racquetball courts; and a six-lane swimming pool. The 25-acre Hancock Field complex offers the 3,500-seat Strong Stadium for football and soccer; softball, lacrosse, and baseball fields, and six all-weather surface tennis courts.

The Colonel Robert H. Morse Library and the Richard Black Information Center also house the Cullister International Center and the Kohler Science Library. Holdings include over a quarter million books, periodicals, and government documents. There is an extensive listening and viewing area designed for the individual use of audio/video materials, and computers with Internet access to virtually any college's or university's library in the world are available students. Beloit has access to a statewide interlibrary loan system, and students may use the University of Wisconsin-Madison library.

The Logan Museum of Anthropology is home to the largest archaeological and ethnographic collection owned by any U.S. college. The Logan's $4.5- million renovation gained national recognition. Its collections of French Paleolithic, pre-Columbian ceramic, and North American Indian work are worldclass. The Wright

Museum of Art has extensive collections in American, Asian, and European arts. Both facilities are operated by Beloit students under the supervision of faculty and staff. The College's museum studies program is one of just three in the nation offered to undergraduates.

The Beloit College campus has been transformed by the new LEED-certified, environmentally sustainable Center for the Sciences. The innovative design of classroom and laboratory spaces facilitate new approaches to teaching and learning, such as studio format and inquiry-based courses that integrate class, laboratory, and collaborative group work. The building encourages interdisciplinary learning, critical for today's science students to take a leadership role in 21st century science. Special facilities include a visualization lab with GIS/ArcView and GeoWall, a 1,900 square foot greenhouse with three climate zones, an herbarium, a rooftop small-telescope astronomy area and garden. Major scientific equipment includes a scanning electron microscope with EDS elemental analysis system, a nuclear magnetic resonance spectrometer, circular dichroism fluorescence spectrophotometer, digital polarized light microscope systems, a remote 22-inch telescope, and more. Off-campus facilities include Chamberlin Springs, 50 acres of oak and hickory woods and wildlife northwest of the city; the Smith Limnology Lab, a small boat launch and aquatic station on the Rock River; and the Newark Road Prairie, a 32.5 acre virgin prairie with more than 300 species of flowering plants.

World Affairs Center Language Lab: The language lab includes 18 student stations, each equipped with a multimedia PC and tape deck, and an instructor station. There is an enclosed area for viewing foreign videotapes and foreign language TV programs and newscasts taken from the lab's satellite antenna.

The Laura Aldrich Neese Performing Arts Theatre features a large thrust stage theater built to Equity standards, a black box theater with flexible staging, a scenic design studio, computerized lighting equipment, complete costume shop, make-up rooms, dressing rooms, and a greenroom. The Neese complex also houses a television studio with full production facilities and equipment. The wired campus network is accessible from every campus building and wireless access is available throughout the academic side of campus. Beloit College has over 50 buildings connected via a fiber-optic network. Wireless access points are located throughout the academic side of campus for students, faculty, and staff.

TUITION, ROOM, BOARD AND FEES

Costs for the 2008-2009 academic year are as follows:

Tuition and fees: $31,540

Room: $3,282

Board: $3,414

Total: $38,236

FINANCIAL AID

Approximately three-quarters of students receive Financial Aid in the form of merit scholarships, grants, loans, and campus employment. Students may qualify for Financial Aid on the basis of financial need, scholastic ability and achievement, and personal qualities. The Early Action Plan is strongly advised for students who wish to be considered for merit scholarships.

STUDENT ORGANIZATIONS AND ACTIVITIES

Beloit students are eclectic, defy definition, and place a premium on individual expression. The range of their extracurricular activities reflects a spectrum of their interests and involvement. Beloit students serve on college governance committees, establish their own organizations, oversee the weekly Cafe Series, and have their own radio and cable TV shows, for example. The college has over 100 different clubs and activities, and each year a variety of performers and lecturers chosen by a student-faculty committee come to enrich Beloit's programming. As an NCAA Division III school, Beloit offers numerous varsity and club sports. Men's varsity sports include baseball, basketball, cross country, football, golf, soccer, swimming, tennis, and track. Women's varsity sports include basketball, cross country, golf, soccer, softball, swimming, tennis, track, and volleyball. Intramural and club sports include basketball, fencing, flag football, floor hockey, indoor soccer, lacrosse, martial arts, racquetball, rowing, Frisbee golf, Ultimate Frisbee, volleyball, walleyball, water polo, rock climbing, scuba, ski/snowboarding, and triathlon.

ADMISSIONS PROCESS

Beloit's non-binding Early Action deadline is December 1 with notification by January 15. The Regular Decision application deadline is January 15, with notification beginning in March. Admitted students have until May 1 to reply to Beloit. A complete application includes the Common Application & Supplement (available at www.beloit.edu/apply), personal essay, secondary school report, high school transcript, SAT or ACT test scores, TOEFL or IELTS scores for international students, and a teacher recommendation. Interviews are not required but are recommended.

BENTLEY COLLEGE

AT A GLANCE

Bentley is a national leader in business education. Centered on education and research in business and related professions, Bentley blends the breadth and technological strength of a university with the values and student focus of a small college. A Bentley education combines an unparalleled array of business courses with hands-on technology experience and a strong foundation in the liberal arts. The result is that students gain expertise for a competitive edge in today's economy and broad-based skills essential for success in all areas of life.

LOCATION AND ENVIRONMENT

Bentley is situated on 163 acres in Waltham, Massachusetts. The suburban setting represents the best of New England college campuses and creates an inviting atmosphere for study and socializing. Bentley's location, just minutes west of Boston, puts the city's many resources within easy reach. Boston is the country's ultimate college town, with the proverbial "something for everyone." Options range from theater to art exhibits, dance clubs to alternative rock concerts, and championship sports to championship shopping. Getting to the city is easy. The free Bentley shuttle makes regular trips to Harvard Square in Cambridge, which is a great location and just a quick subway ride from the heart of Boston.

The 4,250 students that attend Bentley live and learn in a multicultural environment that reflects and prepares them for a diverse working world. Students come from approximately 40 states and 70 countries. All students explore the topic of diversity and embrace the vitality that a varied student body adds to the college experience. Supporting this commitment are offices such as the Multicultural Center, Spiritual Life Center, International Services, and the Women's Center.

OFF-CAMPUS OPPORTUNITIES

Hands-on experience is emphasized across the Bentley curriculum. Internships, group consulting projects, study abroad, service-learning assignments, and other opportunities allow students to apply classroom theory in the workplace and community.

Each year, through Bentley's nationally recognized Service-Learning Center hundreds of students build valuable skills in business, communication, and teamwork while assisting nonprofit and community-based organizations both locally and internationally. Study abroad programs allow Bentley students to gain valuable insight into different countries and cultures. There are a range of study abroad options, including one week, one semester, or full academic year opportunities to take students to places such as Australia, Italy, France, China, Brazil, Spain, and more.

Internships in the United States and abroad enable students to fine-tune skills, explore interests, and make valuable connections. About 94 percent of students complete at least 1 internship during their Bentley career; many internships lead to job offers before graduation.

Other CCS resources include an on-campus recruiting program involving some 500 national and international companies, an online job-listing service available to Bentley students and alumni, an online database of student and alumni resumes, career fairs, and workshops on topics such as effective resume writing, interviewing, and job-search strategies. Thanks to these and other unique programs, more than 90 percent of Bentley students find employment or enroll in graduate school within 6 months of graduation.

MAJORS AND DEGREES OFFERED

Bentley offers a strong curriculum, focusing on business, technology, and the liberal arts that provides students with many options for shaping an academic program that fits their skills, interests, and career goals. Bachelor of science (BS) degree programs enable students to gain in-depth knowledge and skills in specific business disciplines. BS degrees are offered in accountancy, computer information systems, corporate finance and accounting, economics-finance, finance, information design and corporate communication, information systems audit and control, management, managerial economics, marketing, and mathematical sciences.

Bentley offers bachelor of arts (BA) degree programs, with majors in media and culture (English), history, international studies, liberal arts, and philosophy. In addition, students can choose from a number of minors and concentration programs that offer them the opportunity to develop expertise in an area outside their chosen major. The Bentley Five Year program allows students to earn a bachelor's degree and a master's degree in only 5 years, rather than the usual 6. Bentley has 2 doctoral programs: accountancy and business.

Bentley also offers students the opportunity to pursue a double major in business and liberal studies, so students can graduate from college prepared to work expansively, live meaningfully, and stand out to future employers. This optional double major allows students to combine courses that fulfill general education requirements with related electives to pursue one of several concentrations. Students take the same number of courses, but add another credential to their degree.

ACADEMIC PROGRAMS

At Bentley, students benefit from a unique integration of business and the liberal arts. As the largest business school in New England, Bentley offers remarkable depth in business topics. In addition, there is a strong commitment to the liberal arts which allows students to build skills in critical thinking, decision making, communication, and other areas essential to becoming a well-rounded, contributing member of the community. Ethics and social responsibility are key themes woven into both business and liberal arts offerings and are supported by Bentley's internationally renowned Center for Business Ethics and nationally ranked Service-Learning Center.

Over the course of 4 years, Bentley students develop a solid understanding of the latest technologies and the ways that businesses use them to stay competitive. The focus on information technology begins early, as all Bentley freshmen receive a laptop that is fully loaded and network ready. With computer ports and wireless coverage all over campus in classrooms, residence hall rooms, dining halls, and the library students have incredibly fast and convenient access to the Internet, the Bentley network, and many other information sources. This commitment to high-tech learning is supported by an array of academic resources, including classrooms equipped with multimedia technology, student computer laboratories, and a Virtual Lab that offers online access to specialized software from anywhere on campus.

CAMPUS FACILITIES AND EQUIPMENT

Pride in facilities is a constant at Bentley. The campus continues to develop and has seen a number of construction projects in recent years, including a renovated athletic center, an updated library, and expanded athletic fields.

Unique to Bentley are 6 state-of-the-art, high-tech labs, including the financial Trading Room, Center for Marketing Technology, Accounting Center for Electronic Learning and Business Measurement, Center for Languages and International Collaboration, Media Arts Lab, and Design and Usability Center. The Trading Room, the largest in higher education, combines state-of-the-art technology and real-time data to offer firsthand exposure to financial concepts. In simulated trading sessions, students build investment portfolios and analyze financial risk. Trading Room resources include Bloomberg, DataStream, FactSet, WONDA, and Thomson One Analytics.

TUITION, ROOM, BOARD, AND FEES

Tuition for resident and nonresident students for the 2007-08 academic year is $31,450. Room and board (double room, meal plan) costs are $10,940. Additional expenses include books, supplies, laptop computer, and personal and travel expenses.

FINANCIAL AID

Bentley administers about $70 million in undergraduate financial assistance every year to ensure that all academically qualified students have access to educational choices regardless of financial resources. Assistance comprises scholarships, grants, loans, employment, and payment plans. Currently, 70 percent of Bentley undergraduates receive some form of financial assistance.

STUDENT ORGANIZATIONS AND ACTIVITIES

Bentley offers students many avenues for getting involved, making friends, and having fun. The wide range of on-campus activities includes athletic events, music and theater programs, lectures on topical issues, as well as more than 100 clubs and student organizations. Students can choose from academically oriented groups, the creative and performing arts, student government, campus newspapers and the radio station, fraternity and sorority life, and much more.

Bentley fields 23 varsity sports teams, which compete at the NCAA Division I and II levels. The college is a member of the Northeast-10 Conference and the Division I Atlantic Hockey League. Many teams regularly qualify for post-season competition, and individual athletes routinely earn honors. Recreational athletes at Bentley take part in an ever-growing list of intramural sports and activities that include dance and fitness training, street hockey, ultimate Frisbee, and flag football, along with traditional sports such as soccer, softball, volleyball, and basketball.

ADMISSIONS PROCESS

Students applying for admission to Bentley are encouraged to complete a competitive college-preparatory program. Recommendations include 4 years of English, 4 years of mathematics (preferably algebra I and II, geometry, and precalculus or its equivalent), and 3 to 4 years each of history, laboratory science, and foreign language.

Along with the application, students must submit a secondary school transcript, letters of recommendation from a teacher and a counselor, and official scores of either the SAT or ACT, including the ACT Writing Test. The college has special applications for international students and transfer students. Applicants who are nonnative speakers of English must also have official scores of the Test of English as a Foreign Language (TOEFL) forwarded to the Office of Undergraduate Admission.

Bentley College accepts the Common Application. The application deadline for students planning to enter in September is January 15. For students planning to begin study in January, the deadline is November 15. Candidates for the fall semester are notified by April 1; spring semester candidates are notified on a rolling basis.

The Early Decision program is designed for academic achievers for whom Bentley is their first choice. Students who are admitted through this binding program agree to withdraw any applications submitted to other colleges. The Early Decision application deadline is November 15.

The Early Action program is designed for students who are seriously considering Bentley, but are not prepared to commit through the Early Decision program. This program provides students with an earlier admission decision, but gives them the ability to consider other options. The application deadline is November 15.

For more information, students should contact:

Office of Undergraduate Admission

Bentley College

175 Forest Street

Waltham, Massachusetts 02452-4705

United States

Phone: 781-891-2244 or 800-523-2354 (toll free)

Fax: 781-891-3414

E-mail: ugadmission@bentley.edu

Website: www.bentley.edu

BLOOMFIELD COLLEGE

Bloomfield College students come from a rich mixture of backgrounds and experiences. Reflecting the contemporary world, they learn together, share interests, build friendships to last a lifetime, and graduate fully prepared for careers and continued education.

AT A GLANCE

Bloomfield College, founded in 1868, is an affordable 4-year independent college historically related to the Presbyterian Church (USA). The college awards bachelor of arts and bachelor of science degrees. The curriculum is designed to provide students with a liberal arts education as well as specialized career training. More than 55 nationalities are represented on campus, reflecting the college's commitment to its distinctive mission: to prepare students to attain academic, personal, and professional excellence in a multicultural and global society. Bloomfield College ranked sixth in campus diversity among Northern Comprehensive Colleges according to *U.S. News & World Report's* 2004 higher education rankings. Its unique mission means that the college pays particular attention to fostering the attitudes and skills one needs to thrive in a global world.

Programs of study are rooted in the liberal arts and assist students in obtaining the skills, knowledge, and values they need to become empowered, active individuals engaged in renewing themselves, their relationships, their workplaces, and their communities. In joining Bloomfield College, each person assumes a personal responsibility to strive to achieve academic excellence, to take full advantage of the resources offered, and to contribute to the quality of the college community.

Bloomfield College enrolls approximately 2,300 students per semester, about two-thirds of whom are full-time.

LOCATION AND ENVIRONMENT

Located 12 miles west of New York City, Bloomfield College students can take advantage of the educational, social, and cultural experiences offered in Manhattan and the region. The college's 12-acre campus reflects the area's history and architecture. The Robert V. Van Fossan Theatre is a 300-seat, state-of-the-art facility housed in Westminster Hall, a Romanesque, sandstone edifice also known for its magnificent stained glass windows. Seibert Hall, the oldest of the 28 buildings on the campus, was built in 1810. The college's high tech, high touch, library provides material in both print and digital format as well as offers computer labs and laptop workstations. The newly renovated Talbott Hall is the new technology hub and media center of the college. The lower level houses classrooms featuring laptop and desktop computers, a conference room, a general computer lab, and a café lounge. A Web-based radio station, which is part of the college's communications program, occupies the lower mezzanine level.

ACADEMIC PROGRAMS

Bloomfield College offers major programs in the following disciplinary areas:

Bachelor of arts (BA): creative arts and technology, education, English, history, philosophy, political science, psychology, religion, sociology.

Bachelor of science (BS): allied health technologies, accounting, applied mathematics, biology, business administration, chemistry, clinical laboratory science, computer information systems, network engineering, nursing and pre-medical studies.

Bloomfield College is accredited by the Middle States Association of Colleges and Schools.

FINANCIAL AID

Bloomfield College recognizes that many families need assistance in meeting the costs of their education. Students who have documented financial need are encouraged to seek advice and assistance through the Office of Enrollment Management and Admission.

STUDENT ORGANIZATIONS AND ACTIVITIES

With more than 30 organizations to choose from, there are many extracurricular programs for students to

enrich their educational experience. Students can meet friends through joining social clubs, organizations,

fraternities, sororities, workshops, and study groups. In addition to an active student government, student activities include a full program of intercollegiate and intramural athletics for men and women.

Bloomfield College was elected to full membership in NCAA Division in 2002. Bloomfield's athletic teams compete in men's and women's basketball, cross country and soccer, women's softball and volleyball, and men's baseball and tennis as part of the Central Atlantic Collegiate Conference (CACC).

Bloomfield is also a member of the Eastern College Athletic Conference (ECAC) and the New Jersey Association of Intercollegiate Athletics for Women (NJAIAW).

Students may also participate in intramural sports programs such as basketball, volleyball, and indoor soccer.

ADMISSIONS PROCESS

In order to apply, applicants must submit the following information: admission application, with a $40 application fee; official secondary school and/or university transcripts in English; an essay in English containing autobiographical information; 2 letters of recommendation; TOEFL scores (minimum of 500 PBT and 173 CBT); health form; financial support evidence.

BOSTON UNIVERSITY

AT A GLANCE

Located along Boston's Charles River, Boston University is a coeducational, private, independent university with a stimulating learning environment. The university is a well-known and respected research institution dedicated to cultivating innovation and ingenuity. Boston University boasts a faculty of world-renowned authorities who are committed to undergraduate education. Most freshman and sophomore level classes have 27 students or fewer. Boston University's 10 undergraduate colleges and schools together offer more than 250 major and minor programs of study. Students have a wide variety of programs from which to choose, including biochemistry, broadcast journalism, business, computer engineering, elementary education, international relations, physical therapy, psychology, and theater. Boston University's student body is one of the most geographically diverse in the nation; it includes students from nearly 100 foreign countries as well as from all 50 U.S. states. More than 400 campus organizations invite students to participate, including community service groups, intramural sports teams, performing arts groups, and student government, as well as academic, cultural, and professional clubs.

LOCATION AND ENVIRONMENT

Boston provides an environment rich in intellectual and cultural stimuli; no other city in the world can compete with Boston's remarkable concentration of higher education facilities. Boston attractions include numerous museums, Major League baseball at Fenway Park, the Boston Symphony Orchestra, and a thriving theater district. The city has an atmosphere of excitement abetted by its many college students, who make up 20 percent of Boston's population during the academic year. Boston is the quintessential college town. The city of Boston provides many opportunities for internship and research positions. The Boston University Undergraduate Research Opportunities Program (UROP) helps students locate research positions both within and beyond the university; the university's Career Center works to provide students with internships in any number of fields.

OFF-CAMPUS OPPORTUNITIES

Boston University also has one of the world's most extensive study abroad programs, offering opportunities for students to work and study all over the world. Among the university's study abroad offerings are language and liberal arts programs; programs that combine studies with an internship; fieldwork programs for students wishing to pursue academic or scientific research; and summer programs. Study abroad programs are available in Argentina, Australia, China, Denmark, Ecuador, England, France, Germany, Guatemala, Ireland, Israel, Italy, Japan, Mexico, New Zealand, Niger, Peru, Senegal, Spain, Switzerland, and Turkey. Students in the College of Communication may also spend a semester in Washington, DC, or Los Angeles as part of their curriculum.

MAJORS AND DEGREES OFFERED

The university awards the BA, BS, BSBA, BSEd, BAS, BLS, BAA, MusB, and BFA undergraduate degrees. Ten of Boston University's 16 colleges and schools have undergraduate study programs. The listing below shows the wide variety of study options available to undergraduates.

College of Arts and Sciences students may pursue degrees in American studies, Ancient Greek, Ancient Greek and Latin, anthropology, anthropology/religion, archaeology, art history, astronomy, astronomy/ physics, biochemistry, biochemistry/molecular biology, biology, biology with a specialization in ecology and conservation, biology with a specialization in marine science, biology with a specialization in neuroscience, chemistry, chemistry: teaching, classical civilization, classics/philosophy, classics/religion, computer science, earth sciences, East Asian studies, economics, economics/mathematics, English, environmental analysis and policy, environmental earth sciences, environmental science, French/continental European literatures, French language and literature, geography with specialization in human geography, geography with specialization in physical geography, geophysics and planetary sciences, German/continental European literatures, German language and literature, Hispanic/continental European literatures, Hispanic language and literatures, history, independent concentration, international relations, Italian/continental European literatures, Italian studies, Japanese language and literature, Latin, Latin American studies, linguistics, mathematics, mathematics/computer science, mathematics/philosophy, Modern Greek studies, music (nonperformance), philosophy, philosophy/anthropology, philosophy/physics, philosophy/political science, philosophy/psychology, philosophy/religion, physics, planetary and space sciences, political science, psychology, religion, Russian/continental European literatures, Russian/East European studies, Russian language and literature, and sociology. Special curricula are also available, including a dual-degree program, 7-year programs in liberal arts and dentistry and liberal arts and medicine, the modular medical integrated curriculum, and a variety of combined BA/MA degree programs. Pre-medical, pre-veterinary, and pre-dental studies are supported through the College of Arts and Sciences with nearly any major.

Through the College of Communication, students can pursue concentrations in advertising, film, television, journalism (including broadcast journalism, magazine journalism, news-editorial print journalism, and photojournalism), mass communication, and public relations.

At the College of Engineering, students may choose from programs in biomedical, computer systems, electrical, interdisciplinary, mechanical, mechanical with specialization in aerospace, and mechanical with specialization in manufacturing engineering. Students may also pursue the Engineering/Medical Integrated Curriculum to begin medical school courses in their junior year.

The School of Education allows students to pursue bilingual education, deaf studies, early childhood education, elementary education, English education, history and social science education, mathematics education, modern foreign languages education, science education, and special education.

The School of Hospitality Administration's intense curriculum trains students in the management of hotels, restaurants, food and beverage service, travel and tourism, and entertainment.

The School of Management allows students to pursue concentrations in accounting, entrepreneurship, finance, general management, international management, law, management information systems, marketing, operations and technology management, and organizational behavior.

At the College of Fine Arts, students may pursue studies in the School of Music (music education, musicology, performance, and theory and composition), the School of Theater (acting, theater arts, design, management, production), and the School of Visual Arts (art education, graphic design, painting, and sculpture).

At the Sargent College of Health and Rehabilitation Sciences, students may pursue concentrations in athletic training; health science; human physiology; nutrition; and speech, language, and hearing sciences. Also available are a 5-year combined BS/MS degree program in occupational therapy and 6-year combined BS/DPT programs in physical therapy and athletic training/physical therapy (AD/DPT).

The College of General Studies offers a 2-year, liberal arts-based program centered on a core curriculum and rigorous team teaching. The program allows students to advance to the university's specific schools and colleges in their junior year.

The Metropolitan College Science and Engineering Program is a 5-semester program aimed at students requiring further preparation for the study of sciences or engineering.

ACADEMIC PROGRAMS

Boston University is committed to providing well-rounded instruction, merging the fundamentals of a liberal arts program with preparation for the professional job market. Additionally, honors programs in both the College of Arts and Sciences and the School of Management are offered to outstanding freshmen and sophomores.

CAMPUS FACILITIES AND EQUIPMENT

Boston University's academic and athletic facilities are some of the best in the country. The Life Sciences and Engineering building includes 41 laboratories for faculty-led research, while the $80 million, 235,000 square-foot Photonics Center houses state-of-the-art laboratories devoted to developing new light-based technologies. The School of Management has 4,000 data connections throughout the school, providing Internet access from every classroom seat and from hallway kiosks. The Student Village, Boston University's most ambitious building project in 50 years, is the centerpiece of campus life, providing students with superior recreation, athletics, living, dining, and outdoor spaces. In addition to 2 high-rise residences and a Track and Tennis Center, the Village includes the ultramodern Fitness and Recreation Center and the state-of-the-art Agganis Arena, offering space for university sporting events as well as concerts and family shows.

TUITION, ROOM, BOARD, AND FEES

Tuition for the 2007-2008 academic year was $34,930; standard room and board was $10,950. Additional, mandatory fees equaled $488. Allowances for the cost of books, supplies, travel, and other incidental expenses brought the total cost of attendance for a resident student to $48,900. Costs for the 2008-2009 academic year have not yet been announced.

FINANCIAL AID

The Office of Financial Assistance offers comprehensive services to help students and their families finance the cost of a Boston University education. The university offers a wide variety of financial assistance programs and provides resources to help students and their families become as well informed about payment strategies and financing options as possible. Merit awards, need-based grants, loans, student employment, and a payment plan are all offered.

Because Boston University believes scholars should be encouraged and recognized for their efforts and abilities, the university is committed to offering a variety of scholarships to selected freshmen. University need-based grants are offered based on several factors, including calculated financial need, academic achievement, and the availability of funds for a student's program of study. While every effort is made to assist students with limited resources, the university does not have sufficient funds to offer a grant award to every admitted student who has calculated financial need. Those who present the strongest academic credentials are most likely to be offered grant or scholarship aid.

STUDENT ORGANIZATIONS AND ACTIVITIES

Boston University students excel every day, participating in academic clubs, cultural or religious organizations, cutting-edge research, community service groups, and professional internships. A separate student government exists at each school and college to manage student affairs, and the Student Union, the governing body that presides over all of the university's student governments, includes members who represent all branches of the university.

ADMISSIONS PROCESS

The Board of Admissions judges each prospective student individually. The board's main focus centers on the merits of a student's high school record, but required standardized test scores (SAT and SAT Subject Tests or ACT), personality and integrity, interests, teacher and counselor references, and other relevant qualities are also considered carefully. All candidates must have graduated from high school or earned an equivalency diploma to be considered. For admission to the College of Fine Arts, students must either audition or submit a portfolio. A few select programs require interviews.

Students should consult the Boston University website at www.bu.edu/admissions for additional information. Boston University also considers students with transferable credit from other institutions for admission. Boston University considers applicants for September or January admission, depending on the program of interest.

Transfer students cannot be admitted to the Accelerated Liberal Arts Medical or Dental Programs, the College of General Studies, or the Metropolitan College Science and Engineering Program. Transfer students also may not apply for January admission to the College of Fine Arts School of Theater. Boston University does not allow transfer students to apply as "undeclared" to any school or college.

Boston University offers early decision (which is binding on the applicant), early admission, and deferred admission options. All applications for early decision must be submitted by November 1 and applications for regular admission must be submitted by January 1. Accelerated program and select scholarship applications must be submitted by December 1.

Transfer students seeking September admission must submit application forms by April 1.

Boston University accepts qualified applicants regardless of age, color, disability, national origin, race, religion, or gender to all of its activities and programs.

BREVARD COLLEGE

AT A GLANCE

Brevard College offers a range of distinctive baccalaureate degree programs on a beautiful residential campus in Brevard, North Carolina.

With close to forty majors and minors and a deeply dedicated faculty, Brevard College offers an engaging education for just about everyone, whether a student is leaning toward a more traditional degree or would like to do something that is a little out-of-the-box. Brevard offers everything from business and organizational leadership and religion studies to a wilderness leadership and experiential education program that shows students how to turn mountain climbing and kayaking into a career. The College's music and fine arts program remains one of the finest in the region.

Brevard offers an education that is supportive, flexible, and challenging. Every Brevard College student takes part in a one-semester course called the First-Year Forum (FYF). FYF allows students to learn about traditions, service opportunities, academic resources, and clubs and gives students a chance to meet weekly with a faculty mentor and other first-year students. Brevard's unique orientation program is ranked as one of the best freshman-year experience programs in the country by U.S. News & World Report.

The College's low 10:1 student-faculty ratio allows professors to design their classes based on student interest and to forge bonds with students that last the entire four years, if not a lifetime. Brevard also offers an honors program for students seeking greater challenges in the classroom as well as a Learning Enrichment Center that provides one-on-one academic support and weekly tutoring sessions.

Brevard has an active student government association and approximately twenty student-run clubs and organizations, including Omicron Delta Kappa, the national leadership honor society; Campus Crusade for Christ, a nondenominational fellowship group; and the Outing Club, which sponsors the Banff Mountain World Tour, an outdoor adventure film festival, each year. Service to others is a big part of the Brevard College experience; in fact, every student club and organization is involved in volunteer work in the surrounding forests or at local schools, churches, and hospitals.

The residence halls are the center of student life at Brevard College. Most have all of the amenities of home: high-speed Internet access, free washers and dryers, and kitchens. All are located near the recently updated Myers Dining Hall and the new food court, which is housed within the student commons. The Annabel Jones women's residence hall recently completed a $1.9-million renovation. In addition to an updated heating and cooling system, residents enjoy new windows, carpets, and furniture as well as modern bathrooms, a fitness room and ballet practice room, and new student lounge and vending areas. The College completed a renovation of its Beam freshmen residence hall in 2005.

Recognized as a "Champion of Character Institution" by the National Association of Intercollegiate Athletics (NAIA), the Brevard Tornadoes is one of the best varsity sports teams in the region. More than half of the College's 16 varsity teams have placed in the top twenty in the NAIA. The College will add both football and cycling teams to its list of varsity sports in 2006.

The College boasts a state-of-the-art tennis facility, which is one of the finest in the Southeast. It also recently opened its new Reuter Family Fitness Center. Located within the Jenkins Campus Activity Center of the Boshamer Gym, the Center includes two completely renovated wellness areas stocked with new cardiovascular, free-weight and other fitness equipment.

Students enjoy a variety of intramural sports, including basketball, beach volleyball, bowling, flag football, floor hockey, softball, Ultimate Frisbee, volleyball, and other sport-of-the-month activities.

LOCATION AND ENVIRONMENT

Brevard College is located in the beautiful Blue Ridge Mountains of western North Carolina, next to the 157,000-acre Pisgah National Forest and right in the middle of a vibrant region known for its arts, music, and culture. Once students arrive on campus, they are surrounded by the forests and rivers of the Blue Ridge Mountains. Nearby Pisgah National Forest offers hiking and mountain-biking trails, white water, pristine trout waters, and some of the most challenging rock-climbing sites east of the Rockies. In fact, Outside magazine calls Brevard one of the forty Best College Towns in the United States. The College is less than 30 minutes from the Asheville airport (45 minutes from Asheville); 2 hours from Charlotte, North Carolina; and 3 hours from Atlanta, Georgia.

MAJORS AND DEGREES OFFERED

At Brevard, students can explore many fields of study, including majors in art, business and organizational leadership, ecology, English/interdisciplinary studies, environmental science, environmental studies, exercise science, health science studies, history, integrated studies, mathematics, music, psychology, religion studies, theater studies, and wilderness leadership and experiential education. Minors are available in art, biology, chemistry, coaching, ecology, English, environmental art and design, environmental science, environmental studies, fitness leadership, geology, history, information technology, management and organizational leadership, mathematics, music, natural history, personal fitness, prelaw, psychology, religion, sports and event management, theater, and wilderness leadership and experiential education. Preprofessional programs are offered in dentistry, law, medicine, nursing, and veterinary science. Brevard College also offers programs that will enable students to earn teacher licensure in elementary (grades K-6), art and music (grades K-12), and math and science (grades 9-12). A program in criminal justice is currently being developed.

ACADEMIC PROGRAMS

Brevard College education is partially characterized by its distinctive, sometimes individually designed, combination of the newly revised general education program and a strong academic major program. Neither the general education program nor a major can fully define a Brevard College education. Brevard College uses a semester calendar and offers Bachelor of Arts degrees. In addition to traditional disciplines, Brevard incorporates the surrounding natural resources into course work, taking students to study in the Pisgah National Forest, the Davidson and French Broad River ecosystems, the Great Smoky Mountain National Park, and the Cradle of Forestry in America. A special, selective academic program called "Voice of the Rivers" blends wilderness leadership skills with environmental studies. The College also offers strong programs in music and art, in which students benefit from on- and off-campus performance and exhibition opportunities at the Porter Center for Performing Arts at Brevard College, the Brevard Music Center, and the Asheville Art Museum. Other opportunities for students include internships, study-abroad programs, and the honor societies Alpha Chi, Beta Beta Beta, and Omicron Delta Kappa. Brevard College incorporates community service into the academic curriculum through a variety of service-oriented classes.

CAMPUS FACILITIES AND EQUIPMENT

Brevard College's 120-acre campus reflects the beauty of its mountain setting, the balance of tradition, and the energy of change. Major buildings on campus include the McLarty-Goodson Building for the humanities and social sciences, the Moore Science Building, the Porter Center for Performing Arts, the Dunham Music Building, the Sims Art Center, and the Beam Administration Building.

The College's new Moore Science Building annex offers additional classroom spaces, including an ecology/environmental studies lab and a state-of-the-art chemistry/biochemistry laboratory. The expansion was necessitated by the growth of the College's programs in ecology, environmental studies, and the sciences.

Brevard's Lyday Natural Science Lab, an outdoor laboratory on the banks of the French Broad River, supports eighteen field research courses and provides boat access for College field trips.

The Porter Center, which houses a 700-seat auditorium, a magnificent 3,500-pipe organ, and an experimental black box theater, offers students their first chance to stage their own theater and music productions and to perform with nationally recognized artists. The Porter Center is a world-class performance hall, hosting the finest in jazz, classical, bluegrass, opera, and pop from Herbie Hancock to Doc Watson to Harry Belafonte to the Moscow Chamber Orchestra.

The Sims Art Building is the home of the College's Spiers Gallery, which hosts exhibitions by visiting artists, students, faculty members, and community artists throughout the year.

The James A. Jones Library provides access to diverse information resources, including more than 55,000 volumes, 40,000 eBooks, 300 print subscriptions, access to 15,000 electronic journals, and 3,800 audiovisual materials, such as compact discs and videos. Internet access is available to eighty databases containing indexes, abstracts, and thousands of full-text resources, including NC LIVE, a gateway to North Carolina's electronic information. The library also offers wireless Internet access to students.

The College recently opened its new Academic Enrichment Center, which offers students specialized academic support from faculty, professional staff, community volunteers, and student mentors. As the central academic resource and support center on campus, the Center provides space for individual and group study; one-on-one academic counseling; trained tutors in a variety of subjects; and other special out-of-class study or examination needs. The AEC also houses the College's writing and math labs as well as the Office for Students with Special Needs and Disabilities (OSSND), the Office for Career and Service Learning, the Brevard Common Experience Program (including the Freshman Year Program), and the Honors Program.

The College also maintains several state-of-the-art computer labs on campus. The College also has several specialty labs, including a Macintosh-based lab for graphic design and a Macintosh-based music lab.

TUITION, ROOM, BOARD AND FEES

The College makes every effort to offer high-quality educational programs while keeping costs as reasonable as possible. At Brevard College, students are able to obtain an education for less than the actual cost of instruction and other student services. The difference, which averages about 35 percent of the total cost, is provided through the support of earnings on endowment investments and gifts from friends of the College.

For 2005-06, tuition is $15,620 and room and board cost $5980. For North Carolina residents, total costs are reduced by the North Carolina Legislative Tuition Grant, which was at the rate of $1800 for the 2004-05 academic year.

FINANCIAL AID

Brevard is ranked among the top comprehensive colleges in the South, and we're a great value, too. In fact, we've barely raised tuition during a time when college costs everywhere are skyrocketing. What's more, close to 94% of Brevard students receive financial aid in the form of merit- and need-based grants, scholarships, and work-study programs. For more information on admissions and how to apply for financial aid, go to www. brevard.edu/admissions.

STUDENT ORGANIZATIONS AND ACTIVITIES

Brevard College makes a special commitment to experiential learning opportunities through the Student Government Association (SGA). SGA seeks broad representation from students so they can work together to make a difference in academic and campus life. This organization gives students invaluable experience in leadership and governance. SGA leaders meet regularly with the administration, faculty members, and trustees and are actively engaged in the shared governance of the institution, holding places on all campus committees.

ADMISSIONS PROCESS

Brevard College seeks to admit students who distinguish themselves by their talents, creativity, adventurous spirit, motivation, and concern for others. At Brevard, students have every opportunity to take advantage of educational programs, small classes, and caring faculty members in order to realize their potential as students and as leaders among their peers. The College is interested in enrolling students who give proof of academic curiosity, creativity, and community concern and actively seeks those who add diversity to the student body, welcoming students of any race, national origin, religious belief, gender, or physical ability. The College seeks students who display a willingness to exhibit personal initiative and leadership and are likely to contribute their energies to the campus community.

An admissions staff of energetic and caring people invites all interested students to visit and learn about Brevard's special community. The application process is candidate-oriented; the admissions staff serves as the applicant's advocate.

When the applicant's file is complete, it is reviewed by an Admissions Counselor and/or Committee. The Admissions Counselor notifies the candidate of the decision. Decisions are made on a rolling basis, every week. A completed applicant file comprises a completed application; a nonrefundable $30 application fee; official transcript(s) showing all high school work, grades, and test scores; and official SAT or ACT scores. Transfer applicants must also include transcripts of all college work attempted. International students for whom English is a second language must also submit Test of English as a Foreign Language (TOEFL) scores.

For students wishing to be considered for degree programs in music or studio art, an audition with a Brevard College music faculty member or submission of a ten-slide portfolio of the student's artwork is required. For freshmen who have not successfully completed at least a semester of collegiate work, the high school transcript should show successful completion of college preparatory work, including 4 units of English, 3 units of mathematics, and courses in social studies, laboratory sciences, foreign language, and the arts. The program at Brevard College requires completion of core requirements that include studies in the above fields.

Specific guidelines for freshman, transfer, and international students can be found on the admissions Web site at http://www.brevard.edu/admissions.

Application and Information

For more information, students should contact:

Office of Admissions

Brevard College

400 North Broad Street

Brevard, North Carolina 28712

United States

Telephone: 800-527-9090 (toll-free)

E-mail: admissions@brevard.edu

World Wide Web: http://www.brevard.edu

BRIDGEWATER STATE COLLEGE

AT A GLANCE

In 1840 Bridgewater State College opened its doors to a freshman class of just 21 students. Since then, the college has been steadily growing in size and prestige, and today, it is a comprehensive, liberal arts school with a total enrollment of nearly 10,000 students. Academic programs at Bridgewater State College are augmented by the school's lively and social atmosphere. Every year, students benefit from a wide variety of cultural and recreational programs on campus, such as lectures, guest speakers, movie screenings, concerts, and art exhibits. In addition to programs and entertainment, students participate in over 100 extracurricular clubs and organizations, many of which operate from the Rondileau Campus Center, the hub of student life. Bridgewater State College is a member of the NCAA Division III, competing in men's baseball, basketball, cross-country, football, soccer, swimming, tennis, track and field, and wrestling and women's basketball, cross-country, field hockey, lacrosse, soccer, softball, swimming, tennis, track and field, and volleyball. There is also an active club sports program, including the popular men's lacrosse club, as well as ultimate Frisbee, karate, cheerleading, men's ice hockey, and men's and women's rugby. The Adrian Tinsley Center, which opened in Fall 2003, is a focal point for fitness and sports activities for all students.

Situated on 255 picturesque acres in Bridgewater, Massachusetts, the college campus contains 8 student residence halls and 20 classroom and administrative buildings. A friendly and informal academic atmosphere, the college is a true community with shared interests and goals. The college offers all major student support services, such as career counseling academic counseling, and personal counseling, disability services, health services, and housing assistance.

There are 24 graduate programs leading to master's degrees or to certificates of Advanced Graduate Studies.

LOCATION AND ENVIRONMENT

The location in the heart of southeastern Massachusetts, midway between Boston and Cape Cod, makes a BSC a key educational hub that serves the area's 51 cities and towns and more than a million nearby residents with a wide range of programs and services.

Bridgewater State College is only 30 miles from the world-class city of Boston and 25 miles from the historic Cape Cod seashore. A town of over 20,000 people, Bridgewater offers ample social and recreational opportunities in the immediate vicinity. In addition to the town's many resources, there is daily train service to Boston from the MBTA Commuter Rail station on campus.

OFF-CAMPUS OPPORTUNITIES

While at Bridgewater State College, students are encouraged to take courses or spend a semester at other colleges and universities. The College Academic Program Sharing (CAPS) allows full-time students to take courses at any other Massachusetts state school. The college is also a part of the Southeastern Association for Cooperation of Higher Education in Massachusetts (SACHEM), which allows the college's students to take classes at any other member institutions, which include Bristol Community, Cape Cod Community, Dean, Massasoit Community, Stonehill, and Wheaton colleges, Massachusetts Maritime Academy, and the University of Massachusetts at Dartmouth. Bridgewater recently joined National Student Exchange Program, which affords students the opportunity to study at other national public colleges and universities.

In addition to course work, students can earn academic credit for off-campus internships. Internships give students the opportunity to learn valuable real-world skills while pursuing their degree. Faculty is available to help students locate internships in their field of study. In recent years, Bridgewater students have participated in internships in many different aspects of business, education, and government.

MAJORS AND DEGREES OFFERED

Bridgewater State College awards the Bachelor of Arts, Bachelor of Science, and Bachelor of Science in Education degrees.

Undergraduate students may choose to major in the following subject areas: anthropology, art, aviation science (aviation management and flight training), biology, business, chemistry, communication arts and sciences (dance education, speech communication, speech education, theater arts, and theater education), computer science, criminal justice, early childhood education, earth sciences, economics, elementary education, English, geography, history, management science (accounting, energy and environmental resources management, finance, general management, global management, information systems management, marketing and transportation), mathematics, music, philosophy, physical education, physics, political science, psychology, social work, sociology, Spanish, and special education (communication disorders).

ACADEMIC PROGRAMS

Bridgewater State College offers 30 major fields in a variety of disciplines. In addition to providing an in-depth understanding in the major field, the college aims to educate students in a broad range of liberal arts, sciences, and professional fields through general education courses. To earn an undergraduate degree, students must satisfactorily complete at least 120 units, of which 30–36 semester hours must be completed in the major area. In addition, students in every subject area must fulfill the core requirements in the general education courses. Accomplished students have the opportunity to enroll in Honor's Programs through the college or through their major department. All incoming students receive individual academic counseling through the Academic Achievement Center. Bridgewater State College operates on a traditional two-semester academic calendar, and operates two optional summer sessions.

CAMPUS FACILITIES AND EQUIPMENT

Named after the celebrated Massachusetts congressman, the John Joseph Moakley Center for Technological Applications offers cutting-edge technological resources. The center is home to four high-tech classrooms, the largest public computer lab on campus, a TV studio and control room, teleconferencing facilities, and a spacious lecture hall with a large, computer-based, display screen. In addition, the building is wired to a campus wide voice and video network. The four-story Clement C. Maxwell Library houses an extensive collection—28,5956 books, serial backfiles and other paper materials, as well as 3,949 microforms, 10,923 audiovisual materials, and 4,470 e-books. In addition to these excellent resources, the school has a first rate astronomy observatory, a Zeiss electron microscope, radio and television production facilities, a modern electronic learning lab, the Burnell Campus Laboratory School, a Human Performance Laboratory, Teacher Technology Center, Tinsley Athletic Center and the East Campus Commons.

TUITION, ROOM, BOARD, AND FEES

Tuition for the 2006–2007 academic year was $910 for in-state residents and $7,050 for out-of-state residents. Mandatory student fees total $4,878.00 annually. Books and supplies generally cost about $800 per year. Resident students pay an additional $3,776 for room, plus $2,620 for board, annually.

FINANCIAL AID

Seventy-five percent of Bridgewater students receive financial aid.

Bridgewater State College offers many forms of financial aid, including Federal Pell Grants, Federal Supplemental Educational Opportunity Grants, Federal Perkins Loans, Federal Stafford Student Loans, HELP loans, alumni scholarships, and Federal Work-Study awards.

Prospective students may request an informative brochure from the Office of Financial Aid, which covers forms of aid, application procedures, and qualification guidelines. Applicants can request a brochure by mail from or via telephone from the Financial Aid Office at 508-531-1341. Students applying for aid for the fall semester must submit the Free Application for Federal Student Aid (FAFSA) by March 1.

STUDENT ORGANIZATIONS AND ACTIVITIES

Bridgewater State College takes pride in the fact that there are many opportunities to complement classroom learning, expand personal interests or explore new horizons. Whatever your interest—recreational, athletic, social, cultural, or political—there is a student club on campus or an organization within the community to meet your needs. At Bridgewater you will find a diversity of ideas and concerns represented, and your co-curricular options are endless.

Accounting and Finance Club: To provide ongoing opportunities to expand members' knowledge and expertise within the disciplines of accounting and finance.

Adventure Role Playing Club

Afro-American Society

Alpha Eta Rho

Marketing Association

Anime Club

Armed Forces Club

Athletic Training Club

Aware

Biology Club

BSC Jazz Band

BSC Marching Band

BSC Stompers

Bridgewater State College History Club (BSCHC)

Bridgewater Video and Film Association (BVFA)

Broadcasting Club

Cape Verdean Student Association

Chemistry Club

Christian Fellowship

Circle K

Club de Español

The Comment

Commuter Association

Crimson Ambassadors Dance Company

Earth Science and Geography Club

Ensemble Theater

Feminists at Bridgewater (FAB)

Fraternities and Sororities

International and Exchange Club

La Sociedad Latina

Men Integrated in Brotherhood (MIB)

Model United Nations Club

Order of Omega

Outdoor Adventure Club

Philosophy Club

Physics Club

Political Science Club: Promotes the study and discussion of politics.

Program Committee

Public Relations Society: Cultivates a favorite relationship between students and public relations practitioners.

R.E.A.P.S.

Residence Hall Association

Student Government Association

The College Radio Station

The Yearbook

ADMISSIONS PROCESS

Bridgewater State College seeks students of strong intellectual capacity, who have demonstrated motivation, character, and sound academic preparation. Applicants are considered for admission without regard for race, religion, national origin, sex, age, color, ethnic origin, or handicap. The most important factors in an admissions decision are the student's high school course work, SAT or ACT scores, and personal qualifications. Students may submit a personal essay along with their application materials. Admissions interviews and recommendations are not required. Transfer students are required to submit a transcript from all previous work at an accredited college or university.

Accomplished high school students may apply through the Early Admission program as soon as they have finished their third year of secondary school. The school also offers an Early Action program.

Qualified international students are invited to apply to the college. International students should submit all application materials at least 9 months previous to the desired enrollment date. In addition, international students must submit official Test of English as a Foreign Language (TOEFL) scores.

Prospective freshman must submit application materials before February 15. Applications for on-campus housing must also be submitted before February 15. Transfer students who wish to enter in the spring semester must apply before November 15. Transfer students who wish to enter in the fall semester must apply by April 1.

Early Action applicants should take the SAT or ACT at the end of their junior year. Students applying through the Early Action program must submit all application materials by November 15. All Early Action applicants will be notified of their admissions by December 15.

To request an application form or more information about Bridgewater State College, please contact: Director of Admissions, Bridgewater State College, Bridgewater, MA 02325 Telephone: 508-531-1237 Fax: 508-531-1746 E-mail: admission@bridgew.edu World Wide Web: www.bridgew.edu

BRYANT UNIVERSITY

AT A GLANCE

Founded in 1863, Bryant is a four-year, private university in New England that offers undergraduate and graduate degrees and helps students build knowledge, develop character, and achieve success – as they define it.

Continuing a 145-year tradition, a Bryant education empowers students to realize their personal best in life and their chosen careers. Bryant is the choice for individuals seeking the best integration of business and liberal arts, utilizing state-of-the-art technology. Our cross-disciplinary approach provides a well-rounded education that teaches students the creative problem-solving and communication skills they need to successfully compete in a complex, global environment.

Bryant's 3,268 full-time undergraduate students represent 32 states and 34 countries. They enjoy all the advantages of small classes and close relationships among students, faculty, and administrators. In this environment, students come to understand the interactions among various academic disciplines and their practical applications.

LOCATION AND ENVIRONMENT

Bryant University is situated on a beautiful 420-acre campus in Smithfield, Rhode Island. The campus is only 15 minutes away from R.I.'s state capital, Providence; 45 minutes from Boston; and three hours from New York City. Students can enjoy an array of activities on and off campus, excellent restaurants, and sports events.

Students are able to take advantage of internship and employment opportunities at many small and large businesses, Fortune 1000 companies, and nonprofit organizations within driving distance of Bryant.

All undergraduates, including freshmen, may have a car on campus. Additional transportation is available from a train station in Providence, and airports are located in nearby Warwick, R.I., and Boston.

OFF-CAMPUS OPPORTUNITIES

The Amica Center for Career Education offers students opportunities to expand their learning beyond the classroom. Through relationships with more than 350 companies, the Amica Career Center helps students get practical internships at organizations such as Walt Disney World, Fidelity Investments, PricewaterhouseCoopers, the New England Patriots, Textron, several local media outlets, and a variety of nonprofit organizations. The Amica Center for Career Education recently was ranked #9 in the nation for its career and job placement services in the 2008 edition of *The Princeton Review's* "Best 366 Colleges."

Qualifying students may participate in Bryant's Study Abroad Program, where they can choose to study in one of 43 partner countries. The University also offers a Sophomore International Experience where students spend two weeks overseas learning about other cultures and how businesses operate globally.

MAJORS AND DEGREES OFFERED

Bryant's College of Arts and Sciences offers Bachelor of Arts degrees in Applied Economics; Applied Psychology; Communication; Global Studies; History; Literary and Cultural Studies; Politics and Law; and Sociology; and Bachelor of Science degrees in Actuarial Mathematics and Applied Mathematics and Statistics. The College of Business offers a Bachelor of Science in Business Administration with concentrations in accounting, computer information systems, finance, financial services, management, and marketing; a Bachelor of Science in Information Technology; and a Bachelor of Science in International Business with concentrations in computer information systems, finance, management, and marketing. Students can pursue one of 27 minors in business and liberal arts. To view additional areas of study, go to http://www.bryant.edu/areasofstudy.

Bryant's Graduate School of Business offers a Master of Business Administration (M.B.A.); a Master of Science in Taxation (M.S.T.); and a Master of Professional Accountancy (M.P.Ac.).

ACADEMIC PROGRAMS

Bryant's rigorous Academic Programs are accredited by the New England Association of Schools and Colleges (NEASC). The University's College of Business is accredited by AACSB International – The Association to Advance Collegiate Schools of Business, a distinction earned by only 10 percent of universities worldwide.

Students pursuing a four-year baccalaureate degree must complete a core curriculum that integrates business, liberal arts, and technology. The Honors Program allows motivated students to stretch their intellectual limits each semester.

Bryant's faculty are dedicated to helping students develop to their full potential. Ninety-eight percent of full-time faculty hold Ph.D.s or have earned the highest degree in their field of expertise. They continuously engage in research, publishing, consulting, community service, and practical experience. With a 16:1 student-to-faculty ratio each student can develop relationships with faculty for guidance and support.

CAMPUS FACILITIES AND EQUIPMENT

Bryant's modern campus is anchored by the Unistructure, the center of academic and social activity. The Bryant Center houses the bookstore, student organizations, a dining hall, and a food court. The Koffler Building and Communications Complex feature several computer labs, a state-of-the-art digital television studio and editing suites, as well as Bryant's student-run radio station.

The George E. Bello Center for Information and Technology has thousands of wired and wireless data ports and banks of high-speed computers. The C. V. Starr Financial Markets Center receives real-time data transferred by live feeds through Reuters 3000®, the leading information service for finance professionals. The Bello Center also houses The Douglas and Judith Krupp Library. It holds more than 150,000 items and thousands of reference databases and online resources, making it one of the most comprehensive business library collections in the region.

Students can balance their academic pursuits with their overall well-being by utilizing the Elizabeth and Malcolm Chace Wellness and Athletic Center. This impressive facility features a fully-equipped fitness center, a six-lane swimming pool, circuit-training equipment and free weights, and a group exercise room. The University has a variety of athletic fields and the 4,000-seat Bulldog Stadium.

Bryant is home to the John H. Chafee Center for International Business, which houses the World Trade Center Rhode Island, the Rhode Island Export Assistance Center, and the U.S.-China Institute. These organizations offer students hands-on experience in a variety of international endeavors.

TUITION, ROOM, BOARD AND FEES

For 2008, the estimated tuition is $30,571. As part of their tuition, freshmen receive new Thinkpad® laptop computers fully loaded with software and network-ready for Bryant's wireless campus. Prior to their junior year, students exchange this laptop for a new model, which they keep upon graduation.

Estimated residence hall room and board fees are $11,251. Approximately 87 percent of students live on campus. There are several housing arrangements, including the first-year complex, suite-style residence halls, Suite Village for upperclassmen, and the townhouse apartments for seniors. In addition, two floors of Hall 6 are reserved for select students majoring in international business.

Tuition and fees are subject to change.

FINANCIAL AID

More than $63 million in Financial Aid was processed for Bryant students last year, and the majority of freshmen receive Financial Aid through a combination of scholarships, loans, grants, and part-time jobs. Bryant also participates in the Army ROTC Scholarship Program.

Students interested in applying for need-based grants, work-study, and education loans must file a Free Application for Federal Student Aid (FAFSA). The FAFSA can be obtained online at http://www.fafsa.ed.gov, in high school guidance offices, or through the Bryant University Financial Aid Office. The FAFSA can be submitted as early as January 1; February 1 is the deadline.

FOR FINANCIAL AID INFORMATION, PLEASE

telephone: 401-232-6020 or 800-248-4036 (toll-free)

fax: 401-232-6319

e-mail: finaid@bryant.edu

Web site: http://admission.bryant.edu

STUDENT ORGANIZATIONS AND ACTIVITIES

Bryant's has close to 80 student clubs and organizations that benefit many social causes, provide recreational enjoyment, promote intellectual exploration, and offer opportunities to develop new talents and passions. Organizations include the Student Programming Board, the Multicultural Student Union, the Arts & Culture Club, the Marketing Association, the Student Senate, and Big Brothers Big Sisters. In addition, Bryant students benefit from special events and prestigious guest speakers and performers, such as acclaimed filmmaker Ken Burns, renowned former CEO of General Electric Jack Welch, and legendary jazz musician Duke Robillard.

Bryant has 22 varsity sports teams that have begun transitioning to Division I. The transition is a four-year process, but Bryant begins playing a Division I schedule in the 2008-2009 academic year, with full Division I membership officially beginning in the fall of 2012. Bryant also offers many club and intramural sports programs.

ADMISSION PROCESS

Bryant University seeks students who are motivated learners and have a history of academic achievement.

Minimum entrance requirements include: four years each of English and preparatory mathematics, including a year beyond Algebra II (with a preference for pre-calculus or calculus in the senior year); and two years each of history or social science, laboratory science, and foreign language. Remaining secondary course work should be in foreign language, mathematics, science, and social studies. Entering students may receive credit through the Advanced Placement (AP) Program or the College-Level Examination Program (CLEP) administered by the College Board. Credit is also awarded for International Baccalaureate (IB) Higher Level exams.

SAT I or ACT scores must be submitted. The Admission Committee considers recommendations from the secondary school's guidance office and faculty concerning character and personal qualifications not shown in the academic record. Interviews, though not required, may be scheduled in advance of a campus visit.

Applications must be submitted to the Office of Admission with a nonrefundable fee of $50 by November 15 (early decision) or February 1 (regular decision). It is the responsibility of the applicant to request that the secondary school guidance office send a copy of the student's school record directly to Bryant and to have SAT I or ACT scores sent to the University. International applicants must also submit TOEFL scores and a completed Certification of Finances form.

For more information, contact:

Director of Admission

Bryant University

1150 Douglas Pike

Smithfield, RI 02917-1285

(401) 232-6100

(800) 622-7001

admission@bryant.edu

CABRINI COLLEGE

AT A GLANCE

Cabrini College is a small private Catholic college located in the Main Line suburb of Radnor, approximately 20 minutes west of Philadelphia. Presently, there are 1,675 full-time undergraduate students and more than 1000 reside on-campus. The top majors at Cabrini are as follows: education (early childhood, elementary, special education, and secondary education), English, communication, business, biology/pre-med, graphic design, and psychology. The college operates on a rolling admissions basis. There is a 2-week turnaround time once a prospective student has submitted the application, application fee, official copy of their high school transcript, and an official copy of their SAT or ACT scores. (Essays and letters of recommendation are not required but are encouraged.) Merit-based scholarships are awarded to students whose SAT/ACT and GPA meet the necessary criteria. The average SAT score for an incoming Cabrini student is a combined Math and Verbal score of 1000 and the average GPA is a 3.0. The average class size at Cabrini is 18 with a student/teacher ratio of 16:1. A location such as Cabrini's is ideal for internships and co-ops. A Division III school, Cabrini students are able to participate in sports while maintaining excellent grades. Cabrini College has earned more Pennsylvania Athletic Conference (PAC) championships than any other school in the PAC. From men's lacrosse to women's tennis, Cabrini athletes are accomplishing extraordinary goals.

There are 3 traditional residence halls: Woodcrest (all-female freshman), Xavier (co-ed freshmen), and East Residence (co-ed freshmen and sophomores). There are 7 residential-style houses (typically for sophomore and juniors). West Residence, a suite-style complex for juniors and seniors, opened in fall 2006. There is also the apartment-style complex for juniors and seniors. Housing is not guaranteed for 4 years.

LOCATION AND ENVIRONMENT

Cabrini College is located 20 minutes west of Philadelphia, in the Main Line suburb of Radnor. Surrounded by trees and mansions, the college is just minutes from the King of Prussia Mall. Buildings on the 112-acre campus are close together, which makes the walk to and from classes and residence halls relatively short. Cabrini is located only a few hours from New York, Washington DC, and Harrisburg.

OFF-CAMPUS OPPORTUNITIES

With the King of Prussia Mall located just 5 minutes from campus, there are ample job opportunities for students, and on the other side of the college is the quaint little town of Wayne, complete with a movie theater, restaurants, and shops. Internship opportunities are readily available with easy access to companies such as Vanguard, Unisys, Wyeth, Merck, ING, KPMG, CHOP, ABC, NBC, and numerous other places where Cabrini students gain valuable hands-on experience.

MAJORS AND DEGREES OFFERED

Cabrini students can earn a bachelor of arts, bachelor of science, bachelor of science in education, or a bachelor of science in social work by majoring in any one of the programs offered at Cabrini. The college also has 3 graduate programs as well as an advanced degree program.

ACADEMIC PROGRAMS

The benefit of a liberal arts education is that Cabrini offers various majors and minors so students can find the right one for them.

Business: accounting, business administration, finance, human resources management, marketing.

Education: early childhood education, educational studies, elementary education, secondary education certification, special education.

History and political science: American studies, history, political science.

Information science and technology: computer information science, information systems.

Other: communication, criminology, English, exercise science and health promotion, graphic design, individualized major, liberal arts, mathematics, philosophy, psychology, religious studies, social work, sociology.

Romance languages and literatures: French, Italian, Spanish.

Science (non-degree granting): pre-nursing, pre-occupational therapy, pre-pharmacy, pre-physical therapy.

CAMPUS FACILITIES AND EQUIPMENT

In fall 2006, West Residence Hall, a suite-style complex for upperclassmen, joined 9 other housing facilities for resident students. Founders Hall is where the Marketplace is located (the campus dining hall) as well as several of the student classrooms. The Communications Wing of Founders Hall is where the College Radio Station and TV studio are located. In fall 2005, the Center for Science, Education, and Technology (SET) opened. This building has state-of-the-art science labs and research tools for students as well as a lecture hall. The Center for Teaching and Learning provides individualized support for students in math, writing and specific subjects. Grace Hall is where the Admissions Office, Registrar's Office, Career Services Office, and faculty offices are located. In fall 2006, the new artificial turf field opened with seating for 700 fans and lights for night games. The field is located beside the Dixon Center, which houses the pool, squash courts, basketball courts, workout gym, and exercise science lab. The Widener Center is home to 2 eating establishments—Jazzman's Cafe and Sandella's. Also located in the Widener Center is the Bookstore and Student Activities Office. The turn-of-the-century Mansion is the centerpiece of the campus. It houses several college offices, including the President's Office, the Business Office, and Public Safety. The campus Chapel holds Mass several times a week for the campus community.

STUDENT ORGANIZATIONS AND ACTIVITIES

There are various organizations and activities for Cabrini students.

Students also are encouraged to start their own club or organization. All Student Organizations must register through the Office of Student Activities (OSA) in order to be recognized by the college. Below is a list of all student organizations that are currently active on campus. To learn more about any of the organizations, contact OSA at 610-902-8410 or via e-mail at studentactivities@cabrini.edu.

Accounting Association, AIGA Graphic Design Organization, Alpha Kappa Delta International Sociology Honor Society, A.I.R.E. Student Ambassadors Mentors (ASAM), Baseball Club, Beta Zeta Sigma, Zeta Chapter, Black Student Union, CAEYC Educational Associates, Campus Activities and Programming Board (CAP Board), CAV Sound, Cavaliers for Life, Cheerleading Squad, Chapter for the Society of Human Resources Management, College Republicans, Commuter Club, Council for Exceptional Children (CEC), Dance Team, Debate Society, Delta Epsilon Sigma National Scholastic Honor Society, Film Society, Finance Association, French Club, Habitat for Humanity, History/Political Science Club, Honors Council, International Club, Kappa Delta Pi, International Honor Society in Education (Sigma Rho Chapter), Math Club, National Science Teachers Association (NSTA) Cabrini College Chapter, Pennsylvania State Education Association (PSEA), Philosophy Club, Psi Chi—Psychology Honors Club, Psychology Club, Religious Studies Club, Residence Hall Association (RHA), Roller Hockey Team, Roots & Shoots, Science Club, Sigma Zeta, Beta Zeta Chapter—National Science & Mathematics Honor Society, Ski and Outdoor Club, Sociology / Criminal Justice Club, Student Athletic Advisory Committee (SAAC), Student Government Association (SGA), Up Til Dawn - Benefiting St Jude Children's Research Hospital.

A Division III school, Cabrini provides the following sports teams for its students. Men's: basketball, cross country, golf, lacrosse, soccer, swimming, tennis, track & field. Women's: basketball, cross-country, field hockey, lacrosse, soccer, softball, swimming, tennis, track & field, volleyball.

ADMISSIONS PROCESS

The admissions process is rolling admissions, which means that students can enroll until the class is full. To be considered for admission, students must submit the following: application, application fee, official high school transcript, and an official copy of the SAT or ACT scores. Essays and letters of recommendation are not required but are encouraged. Students whose files are complete will hear back from an admissions representative within 2 weeks. Merit scholarships are awarded based on SAT/ACT scores and the high school GPA.

CALDWELL COLLEGE

AT A GLANCE

Caldwell College is a Catholic, coeducational, 4-year liberal arts institution with a proud 800-year Dominican tradition of rigorous scholarship, committed teaching, and ethical values. Caldwell College's most popular programs include undergraduate degrees in business, education, and psychology. Caldwell College has undergraduate and graduate degrees, as well as certificate programs. Caldwell College's Website makes information about the college easily available at www.caldwell.edu.

Caldwell College supports work-based internship and cooperative education opportunities. These programs allow students to integrate work experience with classroom learning. Approximately 40 percent of the students who participate in internship and cooperative education programs are offered full-time positions upon graduation.

Caldwell College enrolls 2,313 full-time, part-time, and graduate students each year. Fully qualified faculty members, a 13:1 student-faculty ratio and 80 percent of classes having 20 students or fewer provide students with close, personal attention.

Approximately 91 percent of full-time students are from New Jersey. In addition, the college's rich cultural diversity draws individuals from 19 states and from more than 22 other countries. The cultural mix of full-time, part-time, and graduate students includes white, 64 percent; African American, 13 percent; Hispanic, 11 percent; Asian American, 3 percent; international, 5 percent, with approximately 4 percent not reported.

Forty-six percent of full-time students live on campus. Single, double, triple, and suite options are available. All students, including incoming freshmen, can have automobiles on campus. A full program of student activities involves both residents and commuters in campus life.

LOCATION AND ENVIRONMENT

Located on a beautiful, secure 70-acre campus, 20 miles west of New York City, students share in numerous educational, cultural, and social experiences while still enjoying a comfortable atmosphere of campus life. The center of Caldwell, with a variety of shops and restaurants, is within walking distance.

Area attractions include theaters, museums, parks, ski resorts, malls, the New Jersey Performing Arts Center, the Meadowlands sports complex, and the New Jersey shore. Many corporate headquarters are readily accessible from Caldwell and provide a variety of internship opportunities.

The college is convenient to major highways, including Routes 280, 80, and 287; the Garden State Parkway; and the New Jersey Turnpike. All can be reached by public transportation.

MAJORS AND DEGREES OFFERED

Caldwell College offers various programs of study in the liberal arts and sciences leading to bachelor of arts (BA), bachelor of science (BS), or bachelor of fine arts (BFA) degrees. There are 2 undergraduate certificate programs in computer forensics and networking and security. Degree programs have been designed to provide students with a well-rounded general education in order to prepare them for careers in the professional or business world and to enable them to gain admission to professional or graduate schools.

The BA degree is offered in art, biology, chemistry, communication arts, criminal justice, elementary and secondary education, English, French, history, individualized major, mathematics, music, political science, psychology, social studies, sociology, Spanish, and theology.

The BS degree is offered in accounting, business administration, computer information systems, international business, management, marketing, and medical technology.

The BFA degree is offered in art.

The Education Department offers teacher certification programs in elementary education (pre-school through grade 8) and K-12 in the subject areas of art, biology, English, French, mathematics, music, social studies, and Spanish.

Additionally, Caldwell College offers 20 graduate degree programs, 9 graduate certificate programs, as well as education certification in 21 disciplines.

CAMPUS FACILITIES AND EQUIPMENT

Dominican Hall, a new state-of-the-art apartment-style residence hall opened in fall 2007. The new facility houses approximately 200 students. It meets the demands of an increased resident student enrollment.

A new roadway entrance from Bloomfield Avenue was completed during the summer of 2006. The new entrance provides students, visitors, faculty, and staff with convenient, direct access to the campus.

The 60,000 square foot George R. Newman Student Activities and Recreation Center houses a large gym with 2 practice basketball courts, which can be used simultaneously and a game court with retractable seating for 1,800 spectators. A running/walking track circles the perimeter of the gym above the basketball courts. In addition, the Newman Center has meeting and activity rooms, a game room, student activities offices, a fitness center, aerobics room, locker rooms, athletic offices, and the campus store.

Campus facilities also include a library, 4 classroom and administrative buildings, and a theater.

Jennings Library contains 148,250 volumes and subscribes to 440 periodicals. Through 54 comprehensive and specialized online databases, more than 2,500 journals are available in full-text format for access either in the library, or remotely through students' home computers. There is also complete interlibrary loan service available through various consortia.

Computer laboratories, which include up-to-date personal computers, installed with current software, multimedia equipment, also provide free scanning and laser printing. Other computer labs dedicated to specific areas of study include art, lab, communication lab, education lab, ESL lab, foreign language lab, math lab, music lab, physics lab, and writing lab.

There are 2 technology-rich classrooms, the Academic Computer Classroom and the Business Computer Classroom, and 15 technology-enhanced classrooms equipped with digital audio, video, and computer equipment. All offices, classrooms, and labs are connected to the campus network and the Internet. Resident students also have Internet access from their rooms.

Caldwell possesses psychology labs equipped with computers and specialized state-of-the-art hardware and software to allow students to conduct psychological studies related to their class work, as well as allowing opportunities for independent student and faculty psychological research. The room provides a camera and media equipment to allow the development of counseling skills and role-playing by students and to allow practice in the observation and data collection of behavior.

The art department contains a gallery studio highlighting professional and student work.

A curriculum laboratory has texts for K-12, visual aids, films, and other resources.

A broadcast studio affords hands-on experience in working with television and radio production equipment. Separate radio and television facilities let students perform and produce news and entertainment shows. These programs are done for training in communication arts classes and as part of the extracurricular Caldwell Communications Network (CCN), which broadcasts live to the dormitories. The facilities include a nonlinear videotape editing systems, a modern radio console, and a complete television production studio.

TUITION, ROOM, BOARD, AND FEES

For the 2007-2008 academic year, full-time tuition and fees are $21,400 and campus room and board is $8,500. Tuition rate for part-time adult students is $529 per credit. Tuition rate for part-time traditional undergraduate students is $599 per credit. Tuition rate for graduate students is $656 per credit.

FINANCIAL AID

Approximately 90 percent of current students receive financial aid. Caldwell provides generous financial assistance to students who have distinguished themselves through academics, art or music, athletics, or outstanding service to their school or community, as well as for students who demonstrate financial need. Our undergraduate financial aid recipients receive, on average, a combination of scholarships, grants, loans and work opportunities of $17,500 per year, including almost $13,000 in grants.

The Federal Financial Aid Program sources include the Federal Pell Grant, Federal Stafford Student Loan, Federal Work-Study, and Federal Supplemental Educational Opportunity Grant programs. Caldwell College offers scholarships for academic and athletic excellence. In addition, special interest and privately sponsored scholarships, tuition grants, and campus employment are available. New Jersey offers tuition aid grants for state residents.

The New Jersey Educational Opportunity Fund (EOF) makes it possible for all students to pursue higher education, especially the educationally and economically disadvantaged, for which college might otherwise be an unrealistic goal. All financial aid applicants must file the Free Application for Federal Student Aid (FAFSA). The priority-filing deadline is April 15.

STUDENT ORGANIZATIONS AND ACTIVITIES

The Caldwell College community provides its students with numerous activities. There are more than 25 clubs and organizations, including Student Government Association, Campus Ministry, Student Activities Club, Residence Council BACCHUS, yearbook, Criminal Justice Club, and many more.

Activities on campus include casino nights, game shows, recreational sports, comedians, hypnotists, guest speakers, sports games, and many other on- and off-campus activities.

Some upcoming events include Backpack to Briefcase Day where more than 80 employers come to meet current students. Also, a student-run fund-raiser for St. Jude's Children's Research Hospital, "Up till Dawn Extravaganza;" the winter break service week at Nazareth Farm in West Virginia; and the alternative spring break volunteering with the Christian Appalachian Program in Kentucky show how willing students are to give their time for worthy causes outside the classroom.

For more information and up to date activities visit us at www.caldwell.edu/student_services/clubs.aspx.

ADMISSIONS PROCESS

The Office of Admissions reviews each applicant's file using many tools including high school record, courses selected, academic rigor of curriculum, class rank, high school performance, SAT I and/or ACT scores, letters of recommendation, essay, and counselor evaluation to determine the student's ability to succeed at Caldwell College.

A student must complete at least 16 high school academic units, including 4 units of English, 2 units of foreign language, 2 units of college preparatory mathematics, 2 units of science (at least 1 of which must be laboratory science), and 1 unit of history. Caldwell College does not discriminate against applicants on the basis of race, color, creed, age, national or ethnic origin, or handicap.

Applications are accepted throughout the school year based on a rolling admissions policy; however, applicants are encouraged to apply early. A nonrefundable $40 fee must accompany each application. Applicants are notified by mail of the action taken on the application after the transcripts, test scores, essay, and letter(s) of recommendation have been received and evaluated by the Office of Admissions.

For further information, students should contact:

Office of Admissions

Caldwell College

9 Ryerson Avenue

Caldwell, New Jersey 07006-6195

Telephone: 973-618-3500 or 888-864-9516 (toll free outside New Jersey)

Fax: 973-618-3600

E-mail: admissions@caldwell.edu

Website: www.caldwell.edu

CALIFORNIA COLLEGE OF THE ARTS

AT A GLANCE

CCA empowers students to make the only art that matters: art that makes a difference. Founded in 1907, it is the largest nonprofit, regionally accredited, independent school of art and design in the western United States. Noted for the interdisciplinary nature of its programs, CCA offers studies in 20 undergraduate and 8 graduate majors in the areas of fine arts, architecture, design, and writing. The college has world-class facilities at its 2 campuses in Oakland and San Francisco. More than 400 highly regarded artists and scholars instruct a population of approximately 1,300 undergraduate and 300 graduate students. The average class size is 18.

Students gain hands-on gallery experience through a variety of campus exhibition spaces. On the Oakland campus, undergraduate students organize exhibitions of their work at the Irwin Student Center gallery, the Isabelle Percy West Gallery, the North/South Galleries, and the campus café. On the San Francisco campus, undergraduates participate in exhibitions and departmental reviews in the Tecoah and Thomas Bruce Galleries. Exhibitions change weekly.

The CCA Wattis Institute for Contemporary Arts, housed on the college's San Francisco campus, presents international exhibitions. Artist talks and other events take place on both campuses almost every day. And the Center for Art and Public Life puts students into direct contact with the diverse communities of the Bay Area.

CCA's intimate residential communities are a vibrant part of campus life. Students have a variety of affordable housing options that foster community spirit and create opportunities to develop friendships. Throughout the year, the residential life staff hosts social and educational programs ranging from movie nights and barbecues to museum trips and professional lectures. Campus housing is guaranteed for first-year students and entering international students. College housing is accessible to both the Oakland and San Francisco campuses via the college shuttle and public transportation. The First-Year Community, located on the Oakland campus, provides leadership opportunities, theme halls, and many ways for first-year students to meet new people and connect to the college and the art community.

Students are encouraged to join existing clubs and organizations or to form new ones. Clubs and activities range in focus from community building and politics to physical fitness. Students may also choose to get involved in student government. The Student Council sponsors a range of activities throughout the year, including all-college dinners, films, receptions, and shuttles to San Francisco galleries.

Our students are active in many pre-professional groups that are affiliated with corresponding Bay Area professional chapters: American Institute of Architecture Students (AIAS), American Institute of Graphic Arts (AIGA), Industrial Designers Society of America (IDSA), and International Interior Design Association (IIDA).

CCA alumni have been at the forefront of nearly every major art movement of the past century. Noted alumni include the painters Nathan Oliveira and Raymond Saunders; the ceramicists Robert Arneson, Viola Frey, and Peter Voulkos; the filmmaker Wayne Wang; the conceptual artists David Ireland and Dennis Oppenheim; and the designers Lucille Tenazas and Michael Vanderbyl.

And our students do not wait for graduation to begin making their mark. Architecture undergraduate Jessica Kmetovic was a finalist in the World Trade Center competition while she was completing her degree. Media Arts undergrad Juan Leguizamon was one of 10 student filmmakers chosen by Adobe to participate in its Reel Ideas Studio at the 2007 Cannes Film Festival. The November 2007 issue of *Surface* magazine featured student thesis projects from various design schools, and CCA had more student work selected than any other school. CCA students have participated in Yahoo!'s Annual University Design Expo, shown their films at the Venice Biennale, won the VH1 / IFILM Show Us Your Junk competition, and presented their product designs at the Milan Furniture Fair, the International Contemporary Furniture Fair, and the International Home and Housewares Show.

ACADEMIC PROGRAMS

CCA students develop their individual voices and styles as part of a dynamic conversation that engages global currents of thought and practice. Their work is informed by a multidisciplinary context in which crossing boundaries is encouraged and celebrated.

The First Year Program emphasizes skill building, experimentation, and critical thinking in a year of cross-disciplinary study. Through a combination of core studios and academic courses, the program orients students to the rigor of building a creative practice while introducing them to foundation skills that apply to all programs at the college.

CCA's faculty, a diverse group of artists, architects, and designers, support students in their explorations while challenging them to take risks, clarify and deepen their processes of inquiry, and refine their techniques. The faculty also advise students, helping them select a major and design a path of study. Students officially choose from one of 20 majors in their second year.

The college has an international exchange program with schools in Belgium, Denmark, England, France, Germany, Israel, Italy, Japan, Mexico, the Netherlands, Scotland, Spain, Sweden, and Switzerland. Financial aid is available for study abroad. The college also offers its own summer study-abroad courses in El Salvador, England, France, Ireland, Italy, Mexico, Peru, Switzerland, and other countries.

Most of the design and architecture programs require an internship, and all of CCA's programs encourage them. Internships allow students to gain valuable work experience, make contacts, and refine their portfolios while they are still in school. Often they lead directly to employment opportunities after college.

CAMPUS FACILITIES AND EQUIPMENT

CCA offers outstanding facilities for making art at both its San Francisco and Oakland campuses. Studios and technology resources are usually accessible 16 to 24 hours daily.

Students have access to a wide range of digital technologies. There are media centers (with equipment available for checkout) and computer labs on both campuses. Wireless access is available on both campuses in studio spaces, classrooms, cafés, libraries, and open spaces. The computer labs are generally available to all students when they are not being used for classes. There are currently 13 dedicated labs on the 2 campuses: 6 classroom labs, 2 open labs, a Windows PC lab, a 4-D lab, a photography lab, a textiles lab, and a rapid prototyping lab for 3-D printing devices. With the exception of the PC lab, which has Windows machines, the labs are equipped with Macintosh OS X computers. The labs offer a diverse and complete range of software for print and Web graphics, audio/video editing, and 3-D modeling and animation. Available hardware includes slide and flatbed scanning devices, audio/video decks, graphics tablets, CD/DVD burners, large-format color printers, a laser cutter, a 3-D prototyping machine, and more.

CCA's libraries hold more than 60,000 books, periodicals, and audiovisual titles as well as an extensive visual resources collection.

The Oakland campus houses most of CCA's fine arts studios and first-year studios as well as classrooms, galleries, an auditorium, a library, a café, and administrative offices. Treadwell Ceramic Arts Center has numerous gas and electric kilns, a large car kiln, a glaze lab, 3 work areas devoted to jewelry making and metallurgy, professional jeweler's benches with flexible shafts, and a wide range of tools. Sculpture facilities include the Barclay Simpson Sculpture Studio (which houses one of the largest working college foundries), a metal fabrication studio, a plaster room, and a woodshop. The glass facility has a 2-bench hot shop with a glass furnace and equipment for casting, fusing, and coldworking. Our textiles facilities are equipped with a computer lab and a T1 computerized loom, a weaving studio, and a large-scale printing studio. The Oakland campus also offers painting and drawing studios. The Blattner Print Studio has lithography presses, a 40 by 60 American French Tool etching press and other etching presses, relief presses, a polymer plate maker, approximately 100 litho stones, a silk-screening and papermaking complex, and a letterpress lab. The Blattner Print Studio also features a 2-floor photography center with 2 large black-and-white darkrooms, 12 individual darkrooms for color printing, a 42-inch RA4 color processor, high-end Macs, a mural darkroom for both black-and-white and color printing, an alternative-processes lab, a dedicated lighting studio, and more. A film and video facility includes a computer lab, numerous editing and sound suites, a streaming radio station and screening room, and a dedicated first-year studio facility with a computer lab, a fully equipped woodshop, and a dedicated 4-D computer lab and classroom.

The San Francisco campus houses the architecture and design programs, selected fine-arts programs, and graduate studies. There are several large design studios, including shared open studios and dedicated studios for each program; fashion facilities for cutting, draping, and sewing; painting and drawing rooms; media-ready seminar rooms; shops for model making, woodworking, and furniture production; multiple computer labs; a rapid prototyping studio; individual graduate studios for fine-arts students; and additional graduate studios for students in curatorial practice, design, film, and writing. The college recently opened an expanded, dynamic Graduate Center, which features fine-arts studios, seminar rooms, and film and media facilities. CCA also recently acquired a new building for its writing program. The New Materials Resource Center on this campus contains thousands of material samples.

ADMISSIONS PROCESS

Applications are reviewed on an individualized basis, taking into account academic achievements, creative abilities, individual achievements and activities, a personal essay, recommendations, and a portfolio. Undergraduate applicants must have a high school diploma or the equivalent. First-year applicants should follow a college preparatory program in high school, including courses in studio art and art history whenever possible.

CCA is strongly committed to making its arts education accessible and affordable. More than 76 percent of our students receive CCA scholarship assistance. The college uses more than $12 million of its own funds each year to provide scholarships for our most promising students. Applicants are also eligible for numerous grants and work-study options. In all, 80 percent of CCA students receive some kind of financial assistance from various aid programs, totaling more than $32 million per year.

There are 2 priority deadlines for fall undergraduate admissions: February 1 and March 1. Those interested in applying for CCA merit scholarships should submit their applications by February 1. The priority deadline for all other undergraduate applicants is March 1. The priority deadline for spring undergraduate applicants is October 1. Students who meet the admissions priority deadlines receive first consideration for admission, housing, and financial aid. Admissions decisions are made on a rolling basis; applications are reviewed in the order they are received. There is a nonrefundable application fee of $50. It is possible to register for courses as a nondegree student (on a space-available basis).

Students are encouraged to apply online at www.cca.edu/admissions. To request a catalog or for more information please contact

Office of Enrollment Services

California College of the Arts

1111 Eighth Street

San Francisco CA 94107

Phone: 800-447-1ART

Web: www.cca.edu

E-mail: enroll@cca.edu

CALIFORNIA UNIVERSITY OF PENNSYLVANIA

AT A GLANCE

California University of Pennsylvania, a member of the Pennsylvania State System of Higher Education, is a comprehensive regional institution of higher education with more than 150 years of educational excellence and intellectual rigor. To achieve its mission to build character and careers, the university focuses on student achievement and success, institutional excellence, and community service.

The university boasts a distinguished faculty who challenge and mentor students to help them attain their full potential. An Honor's Program, which includes an honor's residence hall, provides an opportunity for an enhanced educational experience for the most academically talented students.

The university is a member of the American Association of State Colleges and Universities and the American Association of Colleges of Teacher Education. It is fully accredited by the Commission on Higher Education of the Middle States Association of Colleges and Schools and the National Council for Accreditation of Teacher Education. Many programs are accredited by their specific agencies or affiliated organizations.

LOCATION AND ENVIRONMENT

California University of Pennsylvania is located in the Borough of California, a community of approximately 6,000 residents, less than an hour's drive south of Pittsburgh.

The main campus consists of 34 buildings situated on 90 beautifully maintained acres. The 98-acre George H. Roadman University Park, located one mile from campus, includes a variety of sport and recreational opportunities.

OFF-CAMPUS OPPORTUNITIES

In the southwestern corner of Pennsylvania, the university is a short drive from camping, hiking, fishing, hunting, white-water rafting, canoeing, and skiing. Students have easy access to the Pittsburgh metropolitan area, located only 35 miles north of the campus. Within less than an hour's drive, students can enjoy a long list of cultural, social, and recreational activities. The university sponsors student outings to a variety of these events.

MAJORS AND DEGREES OFFERED

California University of Pennsylvania awards the following undergraduate degrees: Bachelor of Arts, Bachelor of Fine Arts, Bachelor of Science, Bachelor of Science in Education, Bachelor of Science in Athletic Training, Bachelor of Science in Nursing, Bachelor of Science in Sports Management, Associate of Applied Science, Associate of Science, and Associate of Arts.

The university requires a minimum of 120 semester credits, including satisfactory completion of all required credits, for graduation. Students in all curricula must complete a minimum of 30 credits of the last 60 credits at California University of Pennsylvania. Students may choose from more than 80 4-year degree options and concentrations, from accounting to fisheries and wildlife biology.

ACADEMIC PROGRAMS

The College of Education and Human Services carries on the university's long traditional of excellence in teacher education and offers a variety of other programs as well. Students can also choose from other programs in the college including athletic training, gerontology, physical therapist assistant, sport management studies and professional golf management. Also available is a BSEd in communication disorders, a pre-professional degree that prepares students for future graduate training before employment as a speech-language pathologist, and social work, which provides career opportunities in a variety of human service settings.

Departments in the College of Liberal Arts offer a diverse array of major and minor programs of study. A broad general education course of study, based on the liberal arts, encourages students to explore a variety of course offerings and to become aware of the ways many different disciplines understand and view the world. The liberal arts are concerned with human values and social issues. They depend on the ability to think analytically, to understand other cultures and their history, as well as our own, and to appreciate artistic responses to our world.

The Eberly College of Science and Technology offers associate's and bachelor's degree programs designed to prepare students to meet present and future requirements of specific professions and/or to undertake further study in graduate and professional schools. Each curriculum in the Eberly College includes both general and professional education components. General education component ensures students receive a well-rounded education, while the professional component includes the necessary technical, scientific business and/or support courses to provide the basis for advanced study in a professional area or employment in a chosen field.

CAMPUS FACILITIES AND EQUIPMENT

Residence Life

California University offers a variety of residence life options for students—designed to fit freshman through graduate students—including six new suite-style residence halls on the lower campus and a garden-style apartment complex on the upper campus at Jefferson@California. All housing is air-conditioned and furnished. Most students on the lower campus share a bathroom with only one other person; many apartments at Jefferson@California have private baths for each suitemate.

Students who live on the lower campus must purchase a food service plan, but Jefferson@California apartments have fully equipped kitchens, so a meal plan is optional. All student rooms have free Internet, cable, and phone access.

Manderino Library

The Louis L. Manderino Library offers a collection of more than 250,000 print titles and 400,000 print volumes, 3,200 audiovisual materials, 15,000 government documents, 3,500 Pennsylvania documents, 325 print periodical and standing order subscriptions, and online access to more than 6,000 e-books and 16,000 full-text journals. PILOT, the library's online public access catalog, is a user-friendly resource that can be used to locate books and other resources in the library's collection and is accessible by anyone on the Internet. Manderino also offers public-access computers, wireless Internet connectivity on all floors, and 20 wireless laptop computers that students can borrow for use in the library.

Other Services

Registered students have a VMS and Windows computer account for their use. Computer labs are available in many departments, all residence halls, and in special locations such as the Student Access Center Computer Lab in the Natali Student Center and the Instructional Computing Facility in Noss Hall.

Career Services assists students in developing, evaluating, and effectively implementing career plans. An Internship Center offers students an opportunity to acquire college-level knowledge and skills outside a traditional classroom setting through affiliations with community organizations, governmental agencies, or private businesses.

TUITION, ROOM, BOARD, AND FEES

Tuition

California University is a member of the Pennsylvania State System of Higher Education, and the Board of Governors of the State System sets its tuition. Tuition is usually set in July for the academic year that begins in August.

California University tuition, per semester for the 2006-2007 academic year, is $2,519 for full-time undergraduate students who are Pennsylvania residents; non-Pennsylvania residents who are full-time undergraduate students pay $3,779. This cost is for students who are taking 12 to 18 credits, additional student credit hours are charged at $210 for in-state students and $315 for non-Pennsylvania residents. International full-time undergraduate students (12 to 18 credits) pay $6,299 per semester and $525 for each additional student credit hour.

Fees

Full-time Pennsylvania resident students pay $62.50 technology fee; full-time nonresidents pay $94. All full-time students pay per semester a university service fee of $85, a Student Association fee of $210, and a Student Union Building fee of $81, Student Center Operations and Maintenance fee of $84, and academic support fee of $251.90.

Room and Board

Rooms in the new lower campus residence halls range from $2,494 to $3,638 per semester. Meal plans per semester range from $1,188 to $1,439 per semester for on-campus residents. Off-campus students may purchase meal plans that range from $580 to $1,439.

FINANCIAL AID

There are several types of financial available. Grants and scholarships are considered "gift aid" because they generally do not have to be repaid. Loans and employment are considered "self-help aid" because loans have to be repaid, and by working, students earn money for educational expenses. Loans are by far the largest source of financial aid for the majority of students and families. Most grants, some loans (Subsidized Stafford and the Perkins Loan), and Federal Work-Study are need-based financial aid programs. The Unsubsidized Stafford and the Parent Loan for Undergraduate Students (PLUS) are considered non-need-based. Scholarships can be based upon merit, financial need, or both.

Approximately 78 percent of all students attending California University receive some type of financial aid that helps students and families meet educational expenses that cannot be met through their own resources. The results of the Free Application for Federal Student Aid (FAFSA) along with the cost of education will determine whether a student has financial need. To receive financial aid, students must complete the FAFSA or Renewal FAFSA. FAFSA can be obtained from high school guidance counselors, public libraries, or the financial aid office of a college or university—including the Financial Aid Office at California University.

STUDENT ORGANIZATIONS AND ACTIVITIES

A large array of active clubs and student organizations are offered through academic departments and the Student Association, Inc. These groups provide social, educational, community service, and leadership opportunities for students. Their range is as varied as the interests of the students.

ADMISSIONS PROCESS

To be considered for admission as a degree-seeking student at California University, applicants must submit the following:

1. Completed application form.

2. Application fee.

3. Official high school transcript that includes class rank if applicable (or GED certificate and scores).

4. Scholastic Aptitude Test (SAT) or American College Test (ACT) scores (may be waived for applicants who have been out of high school for a least 2 years or who have an associate's, RN or baccalaureate degree).

5. Transfer students must submit official transcripts from all colleges and universities attended.

Students can apply and pay their application fee online by visiting www.cup.edu. All applications are individually evaluated. As soon as applications are complete, decisions are reached and applicants notified. This process usually takes less than 2 weeks.

Admission standards have been established by the university to select those students who will be most likely to succeed.

1. Academics. An applicant must be a graduate of an approved or accredited secondary school or have an equivalent preparation as determined by any state's Department of Education.

2. Assessment and Ability Standards. An ability to do work in higher education should be evident from an assessment examination such as the SAT. In certain circumstances, other kinds of evidence may be used to determine the ability to do such work.

3 . Character and Personality. Applicants must be able to demonstrate that they possess the personality traits, interests, attitudes, and personal characteristics necessary for higher education. Recommendation letters are also welcome.

4. Admission to Special Curricula. A student seeking admission to a special curriculum may be required to complete additional requirements or have earned specific credentials.

The Admissions Office considers as many variables as possible in making admission decisions: class rank, cumulative grade point average, type of curriculum completed in relation to proposed major, guidance counselor or other recommendations, on-campus interview, standardized test scores, activities, and maturity. Each of these variables contributes to the overall assessment of applicants.

CASTLETON STATE COLLEGE

AT A GLANCE

Founded in 1787, Castleton State College is the eighteenth oldest higher-learning institute in the United States and the oldest in the state of Vermont. The historic village of Castleton in western Vermont is home to the college's 165-acre campus. Of the 1,750 undergraduates who attend Castleton full-time, nearly 1,100 hail from the state of Vermont. Other students come to Castleton from Vermont's New England neighbors and the Mid-Atlantic states.

Castleton State College is dedicated to providing an education that embraces the principles of liberal arts and the fundamentals of career preparation. Among the innovative aspects of Castleton's curriculum is a program called Soundings, in which first-year students must attend a series of events in order to earn their academic credits. The Soundings events range from theater and dance to debates and speeches by renowned leaders. Freshman also enroll in First-Year Seminar, a normal general education course with an additional component designed to teach them the skills they'll need to thrive in a collegiate environment.

Castleton's 7 residence halls house a total of 900 students. Three new residence houses opened in the fall of 2006. Every room in the residence halls includes 2 (or more) Internet connections, which guarantees that all students with computers will have access to e-mail and the Web. Students can use these connections at no charge. Phone lines and television cable outlets are connected to each room. On-campus students enjoy meals at the Huden Dining Hall. Students who live off-campus find housing in the village of Castleton, as well as nearby Fair Haven and Rutland. All students may bring automobiles to campus.

The science center was enlarged and renovated in 2007. Currently Castleton is implementing a $25.7 million series of projects to enlarge and renovate the Campus Center and the gymnasium, while improving athletic fields and building a 1,500-seat stadium. Football begins in the fall of 2009.

The array of student activities at Castleton is wide. With more than 40 student groups to choose from, Castleton's undergrads are involved in club sports, the student newspaper, the campus radio station, the outing club, rugby, and dozens of other recreations. Other clubs focus on majors or prospective careers. And yet others strive to service the college or surrounding communities. Men can choose from 8 varsity sports: baseball, basketball, cross-country, golf, ice hockey, lacrosse, skiing, soccer, and tennis. Women choose from 10: basketball, cross-country, field hockey, ice hockey, lacrosse, skiing, soccer, softball, tennis, and volleyball. A large portion of Castleton's undergrads participate in intramural or recreational sports. And skiing, snowboarding, and other snow sports are favorite pastimes all around.

LOCATION AND ENVIRONMENT

Castleton's campus is located in western Vermont. Rutland, one of Vermont's largest cities, is 12 miles east. Albany, Boston, Burlington, Hartford, Montreal, and New York City can all be reached by car or via the public transportation options in Rutland. Outdoor enthusiasts regularly take advantage of the college's proximity to the ski slopes at Pico, Killington, Okemo, and Bromley Mountain. Lake Bomoseen and the Green Mountains also offer excellent outdoor recreation, not to mention pristine environments for living as well as learning.

OFF-CAMPUS OPPORTUNITIES

Castleton offers great opportunities in community service, internships, and service-learning through the Stafford Center for the Support and Study of the Community.

Two annual Career Fairs allow all students to make job contacts and begin networking.

Off-campus employment is available in nearby Rutland and at Killington, the largest ski area in the East.

MAJORS AND DEGREES OFFERED

Bachelor degrees: art, athletic training, biology, business administration (accounting, management, marketing), communication (digital media, journalism, mass media, public relations), computer information systems, criminal justice, environmental science, exercise science, geology, health science, history, literature, mathematics (statistics), multidisciplinary studies, music, natural science, philosophy, physical education (teaching licensure, sports administration), psychology (developmental, forensic), social sciences, social studies, social work, sociology (criminology), Spanish language and literature, sports medicine (athletic training, exercise science), theater arts.

Associate degrees: business, chemistry, communication, computer programming, criminal justice, general studies, nursing.

Education licensure programs: elementary education, secondary education, special education.

Graduate programs: master of arts in education (curriculum and instruction), education leadership, language arts and reading, special education, certificate of advanced graduate study.

ACADEMIC PROGRAMS

Castleton's Academic Programs allow students to build a firm foundation in liberal arts at the same time that they prepare for particular careers. By graduation, all 4-year undergraduates must fulfill a core curriculum of 42 liberal arts credits. Many students use their freshman year to explore various academic opportunities and majors. Students who arrive at Castleton with specific career paths in mind may opt to begin work in the chosen major immediately. By the end of sophomore year, each 4-year student must declare an academic major.

Typically, each student takes 5 courses per semester. Fall and spring semester are 15 weeks long; courses are also offered in 3 4-week blocks during the summer. Castleton employs traditional methods of grading, including pass/fail options. While internships and fieldwork can strengthen many academic degrees, they are required for students in the following programs: communication, criminal justice, education, and social work.

Two-year students already enrolled at Castleton may transfer to 4-year tracks if they are pursuing degrees in business, communications, computer information systems, criminal justice, or general studies. Castleton will recognize as many as 64 credits (or the amount needed to earn the associate's degree) from students who arrive at the college with a 2-year degree from another accredited institution.

First-year students who earn a GPA of 3.5 or higher will be inducted into Castleton's chapter of the national freshman honor society, Phi Eta Sigma. Similarly, the Castleton Chapter of Alpha Chi acknowledges the academic achievements of outstanding juniors and seniors. Education, psychology, Spanish, and theater arts majors are eligible for discipline-related honors societies as well. The Dean's List consists of students who achieve at least a 3.5 GPA; the President's List of Outstanding Students recognizes undergraduates who achieve a 4.0.

CAMPUS FACILITIES AND EQUIPMENT

Castleton's Calvin Coolidge Library contains more than half a million books, microforms, periodicals, non-print media sources, and online and CD databases. The library's electronic system is both networked and up-to-date, and can be accessed via the Web. Established inter-library relationships allow students to choose from expanded offerings. The audiovisual media center, which operates in cooperation with the library, offers a variety of instructional and practical services in areas such as film production and slide transparency.

In the college's Stafford Academic Center, students can enjoy the benefits of a state-of-the-art multimedia lecture room, the Computing Center, and distance-learning facilities. The education, mathematics, and nursing departments are housed in Stafford as well.

In addition to providing well-equipped laboratories and computer facilities, Castleton's science center, which was renovated and expanded in summer of 2007, boasts labs for faculty and student research, an observatory, a greenhouse, and a state-of-the-art auditorium with seating for 120.

The Fine Arts Center is the home of the newly renovated 500-seat Casella Theater, as well television studios and work spaces for students studying art, drama, dance, and music.

Glenbrook Gymnasium provides students with an expansive indoor activity area, a pool, a new state-of-the-art fitness center, an athletic training room, and the Human Performance Center.

In total, computer labs around campus offer more than 225 computers for students to use.

TUITION, ROOM, BOARD, AND FEES

For the 2007-2008 academic year, Vermont residents paid $7,056 for tuition and non-residents paid $15,240. Room and Board was $7,220. Fees for new students were $195, and fees for continuing students was $188. The grand total for residents was $14,659, and the grand total for non-residents was $22,843.

FINANCIAL AID

Eighty-four percent of Castleton's full-time undergrads are recipients of college, state, federal, or other financial aid, including grants, scholarships, work-study programs, and loans. To be eligible for financial aid, students must submit the Free Application for Federal Student Aid (FAFSA) form preferably by April 1 of the academic year prior to enrollment. After February 15, aid is first-come, first-served. Financial aid is offered on a need basis.

The Castleton Honors Program provides the majority of scholarships. The amount of funding can vary from $1,000 to $5,000 a year. To be eligible to apply, incoming students must meet the following criteria: graduate in the top 20 percent of their high school class; or score at least a total of 1100 on the SAT (Critical Reading and Math only) or graduate with a GPA of 3.3 or higher. Transfer students must have a GPA of at least 3.0 to be eligible. Students interested in music or Spanish programs may apply for program-specific scholarships.

STUDENT ORGANIZATIONS AND ACTIVITIES

The Student Association serves as the primary body of student government on campus. Each student who is enrolled in at least 8 credit hours is considered a member of the association. The association's elected representatives are granted membership in many college committees as well. Beyond the Student Association, students develop skills in leadership and decision-making through participation in student organizations.

ADMISSIONS PROCESS

Applicants are assessed according to their prior achievement in high school classrooms and on standardized tests. Additionally, recommendations are strongly considered. Applicants will be admitted to Castleton based on their demonstrated capacity to excel in a post-secondary education atmosphere.

Application forms can be obtained via the college website listed below. Incoming students may enroll in either the fall or spring semester. Applications are considered on a rolling basis. Applicants will receive notification from the admissions office after their folders have been completed.

To learn more about Castleton State College or to set up a visit, please contact:

Director of Admissions Maurice Ouimet

Castleton State College

Castleton, VT 05735

Telephone: 802-468-1213

800-639-8521 (toll free)

Fax: 802-468-1476

E-mail: info@castleton.edu

Website: www.castleton.edu

CATAWBA COLLEGE

Catawba College, a private, liberal arts institution, is committed to "providing students an education rich in personal attention that blends the knowledge and competencies of liberal studies with career preparation."

AT A GLANCE

Catawba College in Salisbury, North Carolina, is not just a beautiful campus or the ideal location with a great faculty to student ratio. We know that you've made a promise to yourself—a promise to strive, to achieve, and to become what you want to be. And that's why we're here—to help you realize your full potential and keep that promise to yourself. At Catawba, "Our Purpose" is "Your Promise." Established in 1851, Catawba College is the sixth oldest college in North Carolina. It is a private, coeducational college, affiliated with the United Church of Christ, which has deliberately chosen to remain a 4-year institution rooted in the liberal arts tradition. Its purpose is to enrich the educational experiences of students and to prepare these students for productive and meaningful lives of purpose following their graduation.

Catawba's enrollment stands at 1,300 students with a little more than 950 of them enrolled in the traditional day program; more than two-thirds of these students live on campus. The institution has students from 27 different states and several different countries enrolled.

Catawba's seal bears 4 words: scholarship, character, culture, and service, and the college strives to develop these attributes in its students. Students are encouraged to broaden their cultural perspectives, to strengthen their character, to become responsible citizens with a carefully crafted sense of community, and to enrich human life through their knowledge and personal talents.

A strong sense of community is fostered at Catawba. Caring and engaged faculty challenge and support new students making the academic transition from high school to college. With the average class including only 15 to 20 students, faculty can offer personal attention and get to know the strengths, weaknesses, and dreams of students.

LOCATION AND ENVIRONMENT

Catawba's campus is located in the historic Piedmont City of Salisbury and consists of 35 buildings on 276 acres. It is a beautiful blend of neo-gothic architecture set on a shaded hillside adjacent to its own ecological preserve. Centrally located, it is only 2 hours away from the Appalachian Mountains of western North Carolina and 4 hours away from some of the best beaches on the Atlantic Coast.

Catawba is halfway between Charlotte, a major metropolitan city with its own international airport (only 30 minutes away to the south down Interstate 85) and the Winston-Salem/Greensboro area, approximately 45 minutes to the north.

OFF-CAMPUS OPPORTUNITIES

With a population of 30,000 residents, the city of Salisbury offers a place of tremendous promise for Catawba students. Filled with numerous historic districts and a vibrant downtown, Catawba students find a welcoming home-away-from-home with numerous culture, social, and athletic events. Located just off I-85, Catawba is less than an hour away from Charlotte—home of Lowe's Motor Speedway, the Carolina Panthers (NFL), the Charlotte Bobcats (NBA), large-scale malls, and an outdoor amphitheater that presents numerous concerts and events.

MAJORS AND DEGREES OFFERED

Catawba offers a variety of different majors and 3 undergraduate degrees, including bachelor of arts, bachelor of fine arts, and bachelor of science, along with a graduate degree, master of education. While course work is demanding, Catawba also effectively prepares students to both ponder the meaning of vocation within a liberal arts context and to ultimately pursue careers or graduate studies.

Students can major in more than 40 different Academic Programs, including: athletic training; biology; business administration (concentrations in accounting, economics, general management, information systems, marketing); chemistry; communication arts; education (elementary K-6; middle school 6-9 with specializations in language arts, mathematics, science, social studies; licensure in secondary subjects, 9-12: biology, chemistry, comprehensive science, comprehensive social studies, English, mathematics; or special subjects, K-12: music, physical education); English (concentrations in literature or writing); environmental education, environmental science; environmental studies; French; history; mathematics; medical technology; music (concentrations in music business, music education, music performance, sacred music); musical theater; physical education; political science (emphasis in American political experience, international relations, public administration, pre-law); pre-health (dentistry, medicine, veterinary medicine); pre-ministerial; pre-pharmacy; psychology; recreation; religion and philosophy (concentrations in Christian education; outdoor ministries); sociology; Spanish; sports management; sustainable business and community development; theater arts; theater arts administration; or therapeutic recreation.

ACADEMIC PROGRAMS

All students have faculty advisors to guide them through academic advising and registration. In addition, the college provides an Academic Resource Center that aids students with tutoring and disability services, and a Center for Career and Service Learning, which guides students through career choices and internship opportunities.

All freshmen at Catawba enroll in a yearlong First-Year Experience designed to help them make the academic transition to college-level study. Through an integrated set of programs, students are introduced to the interconnectedness of liberal and professional education.

The college offers a strong honors program, challenging able students with opportunities to participate in research and study with engaging faculty. Honors courses may feature travel components, with recent Catawba's honors students traveling to Ireland, Costa Rica, Italy, Jamaica, and England.

Beyond the Honors Program, the college offers opportunities for students to travel abroad, most notably through the Center for International Studies. A popular program is the Semester Abroad in Harlaxton, England, where students can participate in one of the nation's oldest and most highly regarded foreign study programs. Harlaxton College combines intensive study of British culture and history with a broad selection of elective courses and ample opportunity for additional travel within Britain and on the European continent.

Other opportunities include a summer language program in Costa Rica, as well as travel excursions associated with classes (for example, Britain, Ireland, France, Italy, Estonia, Japan, and China, most recently). Students can also arrange independent foreign study through the center.

Catawba's Academy for Teaching answers the ongoing need for excellent teachers by equipping its participants with twenty-first-century teaching skills and offering extensive field experiences through travel within the state of North Carolina, and community leadership development and service learning. The academy selects students to become Teaching Scholars who demonstrate leadership, community involvement, and a commitment to teaching.

Catawba's Lilly Center strives to promote thought-provoking journeys of self-exploration by helping students discover and use their gifts in ways that serve others and by encouraging students to consider how they can make a real difference in today's world through the Christian ministry.

CAMPUS FACILITIES AND EQUIPMENT

In 2007, construction of 5 new residence halls on campus was completed. These new halls feature apartment-style and suite-style housing for upper-class students. All residence halls are air-conditioned and co-ed. Catawba requires all full-time students (enrolled for 12 or more semester hours), who are not 23 years of age and who do not room and board at the home of their parents, guardians, or spouses to live in one of the college's residence halls.

In addition to new residence halls, the Corriher-Linn-Black Library underwent a substantial renovation, and provides study rooms, wireless connectivity, and a large reading room and information commons, with numerous computer workstations as well. The Cannon Student Center has also been renovated, with expanded dining facilities, meeting areas, and a renovated bookstore and student affairs offices.

Catawba's Center for the Environment features a 21,000 square foot building constructed of recycled and recyclable materials and sustainably grown wood, with an environmentally friendly geoexchange system to heat and cool the facility. Adjacent to the center is a 189-acre ecological preserve that provides students and faculty with numerous opportunities for research and study; the college also has a 300-acre wildlife refuge that allows for students to learn more about wildlife management and land conservation.

TUITION, ROOM, BOARD, AND FEES

Tuition and general fees for 2008-09 is estimated to be $22,290 with room and board totaling $7,700.

FINANCIAL AID

Committed to making a private liberal arts education affordable to its students, Catawba offers generous, competitive scholarships and financial aid packages. In fact, more than 95 percent of all Catawba students receive financial assistance.

The most prestigious scholarship is Catawba's First Family Scholarships, which are by invitation only and range from full tuition to $14,500 for first-time incoming freshmen. Two competitions are typically held each year (one in the fall and one in the spring); students must first be accepted by Catawba in order to be invited. Students competing for this scholarship are required to have a 3.5 high school GPA and a combined 1150 score on their SAT Critical Reading and Math sections (or a 25 on the ACT).

Once you have applied for admissions, our Office of Financial Aid will forward information to you, including a Free Application for Federal Student Aid (FAFSA). You are expected to complete the FAFSA and submit it to the federal processor as soon as possible after January 1 of the year you intend to enter college. Once you have been accepted to Catawba College and we have received the valid results of your FAFSA, the Office of Financial Aid will process your financial aid package.

Other Catawba scholarships include the Presidential Scholarships, which range from $5,500 to $8,000; Trustee Scholarships, which range from $4,000 to $7,000; athletic grants in aid; talent/performance scholarships; and other scholarship opportunities.

STUDENT ORGANIZATIONS AND ACTIVITIES

If athletics and extracurricular activities are important to you, Catawba has plenty to offer. There are 18 NCAA Division II athletic teams and more than 40 student clubs and organizations to join. Men's teams include baseball, basketball, cross country, football, golf, lacrosse, soccer, swimming, and tennis; women's teams include basketball, cross country, field hockey, golf, soccer, softball, swimming, tennis, and volleyball.

From national honor societies to academic-related clubs and service-oriented societies, campus life is vibrant and active on the Catawba campus. Wigwam Productions, the student programming board, offers a variety of week and weekend activities for students, including the spring festival Catawbapalooza.

ADMISSIONS PROCESS

For students applying as a first-time freshman, each applicant must submit a completed application for admission; either an official copy of the student's high school transcript (a notarized English translation is required when records are in another language), a General Education Development (GED) certificate or a certified Adult High School Diploma; an official copy of scores on either the SAT or ACT; a completed essay from a question on the application; a letter of recommendation (required from a teacher in a core class: math, science, history, etc.); and a nonrefundable $25 processing fee for U.S. citizens or international candidates.

For students applying as a transfer, each applicant must submit a completed application for admission; an official college transcript from every institution of higher learning that you have attended; an official copy of your high school transcript, a General Education Development (GED) certificate or a certified Adult High School Diploma; a completed essay following guidelines provided on the application for admission; and a nonrefundable $25 (USD) processing fee. Applicants must submit their complete material to Catawba College by August 1 for the fall semester and no later than 2 weeks prior to the Spring semester.

CENTRAL CONNECTICUT STATE UNIVERSITY

AT A GLANCE

Selected as one of the "Great Colleges for the Real World" and honored as a "Leadership Institution" by the Association of American Colleges & Universities, Central Connecticut State University (CCSU) is a comprehensive public university dedicated to learning in the liberal arts and sciences and to education for the professions. Made up of 5 schools—Arts & Sciences, Business, Education & Professional Studies, Engineering & Technology, and Graduate Studies—CCSU offers full- and part-time undergraduate programs in more than 100 areas of study.

CCSU's innovative undergraduate curriculum inspires student learning in a wide range of fields, while extensive internship and co-op opportunities help students prepare for rewarding careers. The university's Division I athletics teams provide exciting opportunities to play or watch.

LOCATION AND ENVIRONMENT

CCSU is located in suburban New Britain, conveniently located in the center of Connecticut, approximately 2 hours from Boston and New York. The campus has been recently renovated. The university is surrounded by a pleasant neighborhood, with shopping and dining facilities nearby.

OFF-CAMPUS OPPORTUNITIES

CCSU's Office of Career Services and Cooperative Education coordinates a comprehensive Co-op Education Program as well as internships at local and area corporations, agencies, and government offices. Annual career fairs bring some 200 area and regional businesses to campus. CCSU Co-op students annually earn $4 million, and more than 65 percent are offered full-time career starting jobs with their co-op employers.

The School of Education has many connections to area schools, including several Professional Development Schools, which provide CCSU students nearly unique opportunities to perfect their teaching skills in a full range of elementary and secondary classrooms.

The School of Engineering & Technology offers a wide array of internship opportunities in area manufacturing and technology businesses.

The George R. Muirhead Center for International Education offers students a rich variety of study-abroad opportunities.

And the university and the New Britain Museum of American Art (an internationally acclaimed museum) have a partnership allowing students and faculty to visit the museum free.

MAJORS AND DEGREES OFFERED

CCSU is accredited by the New England Association of Schools and Colleges (NEASC). The university operates on a 2-semester calendar and offers 4 summer sessions plus 1 winter session. Undergraduate programs include: accounting, anthropology, art (art history), athletic training, biochemistry, biology (ecology, biodiversity, evolutionary, environmental science, general), biomolecular sciences, chemistry, civil engineering technology, communication (broadcast journalism, media studies, organizational communications, promotion/public relations), computer engineering technology, computer science, construction management, criminology, design (graphic/information), earth sciences, economics (general, operations research), education (elementary, K-12, secondary, special education), electronics technology, engineering technology, English, entrepreneurship, exercise science, finance, French, geography (environmental, general regional, planning, geographic information science, tourism), German, history, hospitality and tourism, industrial technology (electro-mechanical technology, environmental and occupational safety, graphics technology, manufacturing, networking technology, technology management), interdisciplinary science (environmental interpretation, physical sciences), international business, international studies, Italian, management (entrepreneurship, human resource), management information systems, manufacturing engineering technology, marketing, mathematics (actuarial; statistics), mechanical engineering, mechanical engineering technology, music, nursing (BSN only), philosophy, physical education (exercise science and health promotion), physics, political science (general, public administration), psychology, social work, sociology, Spanish, technology education, theater. Degrees: BA, BFA (theater), BS, BSN, teacher certification (elementary, secondary, K-12).

ACADEMIC PROGRAMS

CCSU also offers a number of interdisciplinary programs as well as independently designed majors. The honors program, a challenging interdisciplinary program of study for academically qualified students, offers half- and full-tuition merit scholarships and a variety of other benefits and resources, including a new honors lab.

The academic excellence of CCSU's innovative undergraduate education was nationally recognized when the Association of American Colleges & Universities selected CCSU as a "Leadership Institution," one of only 16 in the nation and the only one in Connecticut. Together with such other prestigious institutions as Colgate University, Duke University, and the University of Michigan, CCSU stands as a national example of quality undergraduate education. Central Connecticut State University is fast realizing its aspiration to become the best public comprehensive university in the region.

CAMPUS FACILITIES AND EQUIPMENT

CCSU offers an attractive campus with new and renovated buildings adding to the classic collegiate style of its historical architecture. Most of the academic buildings feature technologically state-of-the-art "smart classrooms" and seminar rooms, and the entire campus offers wireless access. The recently renovated and expanded Student Center provides lounges, dining services, conference and game rooms, information services, and a range of other support services. Three theaters offer space for plays, symphonies, and guest lectures. The S. T. Chen Art Gallery hosts shows by student, faculty, and visiting artists. The Microcomputer Lab features 230 computers plus printers and scanners for student use. A cutting-edge media center offers space and equipment for video, audio, and computer work. Campus-based TV and radio stations provide exciting entertainment as well as opportunities to learn about the professions. The Elihu Burritt Library provides access to more than 2 million books through an online catalog, a wide array of electronic databases and online resources, and special collections ranging from the unparalleled collection of Polish American materials to the Equity Archive. The university also offers many new athletic facilities, including an Olympic-sized swimming pool, modern exercise equipment, a state-of-the-art fitness center, a weight-training room, and an athletic training center. In the Kaiser Annex students can walk, jog, and play tennis or a pickup basketball game. CCSU recently opened new football, soccer, softball, and baseball fields to complement its basketball and volleyball arena. The residence halls and most classrooms are fully networked. Approximately 20 percent of the students live on campus in 8 residence halls.

TUITION, ROOM, BOARD, AND FEES

Expenses for the 2007-08 academic year include tuition (in-state: $6,735; out-of-state: $15,454), room and board ($7,000 [approx.]). Expenses for books, transportation, fees, and other expenses range from $5000 (in residence) to $6000 (off-campus residence).

FINANCIAL AID

Annually, 52 percent of CCSU full-time students receive some form of financial aid. CCSU's Office of Financial Aid works with students to help them meet educational expenses from their first year until graduation. To apply for financial aid students must complete the FAFSA form. For more information, call 860-832-2200, e-mail FinancialAid3@ccsu.edu, or visit us on the Web at www.ccsu.edu/finaid.

STUDENT ORGANIZATIONS AND ACTIVITIES

There are 120 student clubs and organizations, which cover a broad spectrum of interests.

Academic: Anthropology Club, Investment Club. Athletic: Crew Club, Flying Club. Cultural: the Art Club, the jazz band, and other musical organizations. Ethnic: Black Student Union, Latin American Students Organization, and the Muslim Student Association. Religious: Hillel, the Newman Club. Honors organizations: Delta Mu Delta, Lambda Delta, and Kappa Delta Pi. On-campus entertainment is wide and varied, including, most recently, Devils Den@ 10, student-run entertainment on Thursday evenings.

ADMISSIONS PROCESS

CCSU is a learning community of students with a broad range of abilities, interests, and backgrounds. We value excellence and achievement in academic scholarship, community involvement, and extracurricular activities. Our admissions process evaluates the readiness of applicants to succeed based on past demonstrations of academic and personal successes. The preferred deadlines for best consideration are June 1 (for fall semester) and December 1 (for spring). First-year applicants are considered on the basis of performance in college preparatory classes, rank in class, SAT or ACT test scores, recommendations, and community and extracurricular involvement and leadership. A personal essay is required. For some applicants an interview with a representative of the Office of Recruitment & Admissions may be necessary. If the applicant ranks in the top 20 percent of his/her class, is an A-B student, and has SAT scores of 1100 or higher, the student should consider finding out about CCSU's honors program by calling 860-832-2938 for details. CCSU accepts most Advanced Placement (AP) courses for college credit, provided the minimum CCSU required score is achieved. Check with Admissions for the required scores.

Admission criteria include graduation from an accredited secondary school. High school work should include college preparatory courses in: English (4 years), mathematics (covering algebra I, geometry, and algebra II), science (2 years, including 1-year lab science), social sciences (2 to 3 years, including U.S. history). Course work in foreign language is recommended (at least 3 consecutive years of the same foreign language). Students whose preparation does not follow this pattern may still qualify for admission if, in the judgment of the Director of Recruitment and Admissions, there is strong evidence that they have the potential to complete a degree program or if they meet other established criteria as authorized by the university president under authority delegated by the Board of Trustees of the Connecticut State University System. Applicants who are not graduates of a secondary school should submit their secondary school transcript up to the time of withdrawal and a copy of their high school equivalency diploma and scores. Students interested in enrolling part-time on a non-degree basis should contact Continuing Education at 860-832-2255. The most important thing for the applicant to remember is to provide as much information as possible—achievements, awards, and examples of leadership—when applying.

Students are encouraged to apply online at www.ccsu.edu. For paper applications, please provide the Office of Recruitment & Admissions with completed application for undergraduate admission, official high school transcript, SAT or ACT test scores, recommendations, and essay, and a nonrefundable application fee of $50. All correspondence should be sent to the Office of Recruitment and Admissions, CCSU, PO Box 4010, 1615 Stanley Street, New Britain, CT 06050-4010.

Tours and information sessions may be arranged by calling 860-832-2289 or via e-mail at: admissions@ccsu.edu.

CHAMINADE UNIVERSITY OF HONOLULU

AT A GLANCE

Chaminade University of Honolulu is a small, comprehensive university, accredited by the Accrediting Commission for Senior Colleges and Universities of the Western Association of Schools and Colleges. It is located on a hillside in suburban Honolulu, 2 miles from Waikiki beach. Chaminade University was established in 1955 by the Society of Mary (Marianists) and named after Father William Joseph Chaminade, a French Catholic priest who founded the society in 1817. The university encourages learning through cooperation, caring, and mutual respect while offering individualized attention to promote personal and intellectual growth.

Chaminade currently offers 3 bachelors degrees in 23 undergraduate majors, 7 graduate degree programs, and several professional certificate programs. At any one time, 2,500 to 2,800 students are enrolled in daytime and evening classes. Approximately 1,200 are full-time undergraduates, 1,000 are part-time undergraduates enrolled in the evening program, and 600 are graduate students. Approximately 50 percent of the full-time undergraduate students are from Hawaii, 30 percent from the mainland, 15 percent from the Pacific Islands, and 5 percent are from other countries. The student body consists of students from 41 states and 30 countries.

With the continued increase in the student body, Chaminade now has a wide range of academic, professional, religious, and service clubs. The diversity of its students is reflected in the roster of clubs. Students may join clubs with a professional and academic focus, such as the Hogan Entrepreneurial Program and ROTC.

Chaminade recognizes the value of a well-rounded education and works to provide its students with academic, athletic, and club programs that balance diversity and participation in order to develop the whole person. Chaminade University is anchored and invigorated by the founding traditions of faith, education, reasoning, and social responsibility.

LOCATION AND ENVIRONMENT

Chaminade University is located on a hillside of Honolulu, approximately 2 miles from Waikiki, with splendid views of Diamond Head, Waikiki, and downtown Honolulu. Honolulu is a multicultural community, enriched by a great diversity of ethnic traditions.

The collegiate experience is much more than class, work in labs, and academic research. The Chaminade experience is also rich with opportunities for the personal development of each student. Charged with facilitating and providing opportunities for such growth, the Student Affairs division is committed to enhancing the quality of student life at Chaminade. The division provides programs in career planning, recreational sports, intercollegiate sports, and personal counseling.

Chaminade University has 3 residence halls for first-year students on campus and 3 off-campus residence halls for upper-class students. Single, 2-, 3-, 4-, and 5-person furnished suites and apartments are available. Dining services are provided at 2 on-campus locations. The Courtyard at Henry Hall provides breakfast entrees, hot entrees for lunch, and hot entrees for dinner, as well as snacks. The Silversword Café, located in Tredtin Hall, has a program designed more for the traditional residential dining program and is open for service 7 days a week for lunch, brunch on weekends, and dinner.

The Office of Student Activities and Leadership offers opportunities that will connect and involve students in university life through a broad range of co-curricular and extracurricular events, activities and programs.

Clubs and Organizations offer all students a chance to pursue interests and extend their activities beyond the classroom.

The Recreational and Intramural Sports program is designed to provide an opportunity for enjoyable, organized recreational activities. Diverse programming is geared to promote healthy lifestyles through fitness, social engagement, skill development, and competition. Past recreational classes and intramural sports include Muay Thai Kickboxing, Self-Defense, Wellness and Nutrition, Latin Dancing, Hip-Hop Dancing, basketball, volleyball, billiards, softball, soccer, surfing, X-Box/Playstation, and many others.

Chaminade University competes at the NCAA Division II level. The institution is a member of the Pacific West Conference. Intercollegiate sports include men's basketball, cross-country, golf, and soccer; women's basketball, cross-country, soccer, softball, tennis, and volleyball.

OFF-CAMPUS OPPORTUNITIES

Chaminade University students have the opportunity to study for a semester or 2 at either of the other Marianist universities in the United States: the University of Dayton in Ohio or St. Mary's University in San Antonio, Texas. Chaminade students may also study for 1 semester at Bay Path College in Longmeadow, Massachusetts.

In addition, Chaminade offers study abroad programs in 10 different countries to students through an agreement with the University of Hawaii—Manoa. Students can choose from either summer or semester programs.

MAJORS AND DEGREES OFFERED

Chaminade University offers 23 undergraduate major programs and 7 graduate degree programs.

The bachelor of arts (BA) degree is offered in biology, business administration, communication, English, historical and political studies, humanities, international studies, marketing, psychology, religious study, social studies.

Bachelor of fine arts (BFA) offered in interior design.

Bachelor of science (BS) offered in accounting, behavioral sciences, biology, computer information systems, computer science, criminology and criminal justice, elementary education, environmental studies, forensic sciences.

Master's degrees are offered in the following disciplines: business administration (MBA), counseling psychology (MSCP), criminal justice administration (MSCJA), education (MEd), forensic sciences (MSFS), pastoral leadership (MAPL), pastoral theology (MPT).

ACADEMIC PROGRAMS

The core curriculum at Chaminade is in the liberal arts tradition as such an education provides students with the basis for personal growth and is the foundation for many careers and jobs. Baccalaureate students must complete at least 120 semester hours of credit. Detailed 4-year plans are available for each major through the Office of Admissions or the Office of Academic Advising and Retention.

Chaminade students in almost all fields of study are required to complete internships where they apply their academic experience to on-the-job-practice for academic credit. Many of these internships lead, after graduation, to the students' first full-time employment.

TUITION, ROOM, BOARD, AND FEES

For the 2008-09 academic year, tuition is $16,000. Room costs range from $3,710 to $7,880. Dining costs range from $3,700 to $5,000 depending on the student's choice of meal plan.

FINANCIAL AID

Chaminade University financial aid is provided through a combination of federal, institutional, and private donor-based sources, and comes in 3 forms: grants and scholarships (gift aid), work-study programs that provide students the opportunity to earn money while being employed in campus jobs, loans provided at low interest rates and reasonable repayment terms. Awards are determined by the student's enrollment status, level of financial need, and fund availability; 93.7 percent of student body receives some form of financial aid.

ADMISSIONS PROCESS

Chaminade University welcomes applications from all students who have the ability, motivation, and preparation to benefit from the various programs offered. All applicants should have earned a high school diploma or equivalent. Adequate preparation typically includes: English, 4 years; social studies, 3 years; mathematics, 3 years; science, 2 years; college preparatory electives, 4 years.

The Admissions Office operates on a rolling admission basis; the following dates are recommended to ensure adequate time for receipt and processing of all admissions documents: May 1 for fall, and December 1 for spring.

First-time college students who have or will be completing high school are required to send the completed application form with a $50 application fee to the Admissions Office. Online applications are also accepted and free of charge. Online applications are listed on our website at www.chaminade.edu; request that an official high school transcript be submitted to the Admissions Office. Also, arrange to complete either the SAT or ACT and have the official results sent to the Admissions Office.

Transfer students from 2- or 4-year colleges may transfer at any time. No minimum number of units is required for transfer. Applicants who have completed high school and are attending college or have attended college and earned more than 24 semester hours of college credit are required to submit a completed application form accompanied by a $50 application fee. Online applications are also accepted free of charge. A complete official transcript of the applicant's university or college record and a list of courses in progress will be required. If transfer students have earned fewer than 24 semester hours of college credits, high school transcripts and official SAT/ACT scores are also required.

CHAPMAN UNIVERSITY

AT A GLANCE

Originally organized in 1861 as Hesperian College, Chapman University has steadily evolved from a small traditional church-related liberal arts school, into a vibrant midsize and nationally recognized university with renowned programs in areas such as film and television production, business and economics, theatre, dance, music, and teacher education.

Set in suburban and historic "Old Towne Orange", California, Chapman's beautiful tree-lined campus features a blending of historic and contemporary structures, tranquil gardens, world-class recreational facilities, and "smart" classrooms. With wireless technology throughout the campus, Chapman was recently named one of the top 50 "Best Wired" campuses by Yahoo!

Chapman's academic preparation and wide breadth of excellence is evidenced by the University's accomplished alumni, who include Loretta Sanchez ('88), member of Congress; David Bonior ('85), member of Congress and former house minority whip; Jose Gomez ('75) member of the Panamanian National Assembly; television and film producers John Copeland ('73), Jon Garcia ('90) and John David Currey ('98); cinematographer Gene Jackson ('70); television sports analyst, Steve Lavin ('88); Tony Award nominee and Broadway star of Showboat, Michel Bell ('68); Indy car racing star, Jaques Lazier ('93); former major league baseball stars Tim Flannery ('80), Marty Castillo ('80), Gary Lucas ('76) and Randy Jones ('72); and George L. Argyros ('65), philanthropist and former U.S. Ambassador to Spain.

LOCATION AND ENVIRONMENT

Chapman University is located in Orange County's beautiful south coast, famous for its ideal climate, cultural and recreational opportunities, and varied natural resources. With the San Diego and Los Angeles metropolitan areas in close proximity, students can attend concerts, see professional sports, or go to world famous theme parks like Disneyland and Knott's Berry Farm. There are outdoor activities throughout the year, with Pacific beaches only 10 miles from campus and winter ski resorts only 90-minutes away. Add to these benefits an average year-round temperature of 71° F, and it's no surprise that Places Rated Almanac recently named Orange County, California "the #1 place to live in North America."

On campus, Chapman students take part in the dynamic student activities program. There are over 70 student run clubs, including community service organizations, eleven national fraternities and sororities, 20 NCAA D-III intercollegiate athletic programs, an active intramural sports program, and music, art, and theatre productions.

Though Chapman students are predominantly from California, the student body is diverse, with students hailing from 40 states and 34 foreign countries. Chapman students have distinguished themselves in a variety of forums. In the preceding five years, Chapman students have been recognized as Truman Scholars, Coro Fellows, USA Today All-USA College Academic Team members, NCAA All-Americans, and NCAA Academic All-Americans.

OFF-CAMPUS OPPORTUNITIES

Chapman's Career Development Center provides a variety of services to students, graduates, and former students. These include: internship opportunities, an on-campus recruiting program, full-time job postings and computer-networked job listings, individual career counseling and career assessment, a career resource library, job search and resume writing skills development, interview coaching, and an Alumni Mentor Program. The center will assist teachers in establishing a self-managed educational placement file.

Chapman students are encouraged to participate in study abroad programs in many academic fields in almost every part of the world. Students studying abroad through Chapman-approved programs are enrolled in a full course of study at the host institution, but receive academic credit from Chapman. The study abroad program directly supports Chapman's emphasis on encouraging students to recognize and develop their roles as global citizens in an increasingly interdependent world.

MAJORS AND DEGREES OFFERED

Chapman University confers degrees in the following field of study:

Accounting

Art

Athletic training

Biological Sciences

Business administration

Chemistry

Communications

Computer information systems

Computer science

Dance

Economics

English

Film Production

Film Studies

French

History

Leadership and organizational studies

Liberal studies (teaching)

Mathematics

Music

Peace studies

Philosophy

Political science

Psychology

Psychobiology

Public relations and advertising

Religious Studies

Screenwriting

Sociology

Spanish

Television and Broadcast Journalism

Theatre

ACADEMIC PROGRAMS

Chapman University strives to provide every student with a comprehensive, liberal arts-based course of study which will result in producing an engaging, articulate and communicative world citizen with specific skills to offer. A unique aspect of the Chapman curriculum is the assignment of an *InsideTrack* life success coach to each freshman in an effort to motivate, inspire, and help sharpen time management and organizational skills. Academic departments are divided into the Wilkinson College of Letters and Sciences; the Argyros School of Business and Economics (AACSB); the School of Education (CTC); the Dodge College of Film and Media Arts (CILECT); the College of Performing Arts (NASM); the School of Law (ABA); and University College, the off-campus program for working adults. Chapman is also home to the APTA-accredited graduate program in Physical Therapy. The A. Gary Anderson Center for Economic Research is recognized throughout the world for its excellence in economic forecasting. Chapman was recently named a "Character-Building College" by the Templeton Foundation.

CAMPUS FACILITIES AND EQUIPMENT

Chapman's park-like and ivy-covered, tree-lined campus is set in beautiful and historic Old Towne Orange and features a blending of fully refurbished historic structures with state-of-the-art internet and satellite connected learning environments. The Leatherby Libraries house eight individual libraries, each specific to one of the University's areas of study, as well as a holocaust library and museum. The 90,000 square foot Argyros Forum includes the primary campus dining area, conference and classroom facilities, and associated students offices. Bertea Hall, Oliphant Hall, and Moulton Center are home to the renowned College of Performing Arts (Theatre, Dance, and the NASM-accredited Conservatory of Music which includes a complete music library, classrooms, recital halls (5), concert hall, and practice rooms, 250-seat Waltmar Theatre, and Guggenheim Art Gallery. Memorial Hall (executive offices and Chapman Auditorium), Roosevelt Hall (faculty offices), Wilkinson Hall (Economic Science Institute), Reeves Hall (School of Education and classrooms), and Smith Hall (Psychology faculty offices and classrooms) are all buildings listed on the National Register of Historic Places. Although designated as historic, each of these structures has been fully refurbished internally and externally to provide both a historic and contemporary learning environment. The Lastinger Athletics Complex includes a 3,000-seat indoor arena, 3,500-seat outdoor stadium, 500-seat swim stadium, four championship tennis courts, and training and fitness facilities for the campus and surrounding community. Beckman Hall for business and technology houses the mathematics and computer sciences programs, as well as the AACSB-accredited Argyros School of Business and Economics. The Hashinger Science Center features laboratories for nuclear science, radiation, crystallography, genetics, food science, and physical therapy. Wilkinson Hall and Chapman's Economic Science Institute is home to 2002 Nobel Economics laureate, Vernon Smith and his team of scholars. Five residence halls and six on-campus apartment buildings are conveniently located on the edge of the campus with a new residence hall and conference center currently under construction. Marion Knott Studios houses the University's renowned Dodge College of Film and Media Arts including the undergraduate school of film and television, the graduate Conservatory of Motion Pictures, and the think tank-style Institute for the Study of Media and the Public Interest. Knott Studios also includes two 18,000-square foot sound stages, pre and post-production facilities, computer and digital editing labs, and 500-seat cinema. Kennedy Hall is home to Chapman's ABA-accredited School of Law, and Liberty Plaza which includes a reflection pond and replica Lincoln chair featuring a memorial to President Ronald Reagan facing a 5-ton section of the Berlin Wall brought to campus in 2000.

TUITION, ROOM, BOARD AND FEES

Undergraduate tuition (annual, 12–18 semester credits) room, board, and fees for the 2007–2008 academic are as follows:

Annual tuition: $31,700

Accident/Sickness plan: 368

Associated students fee: 120

Wellness Center fee: 210

Total tuition/fees: $32,398

Average room/board cost for academic year 2007–2008:

Room: $6,740

Telecommunications fee: 260

Activity fee: 40

Board plan: 3,576

Total room/board (average)$10,616

FINANCIAL AID

Almost 90% of 2007 freshman received some form of need based aid, merit, or talent scholarship. Awards are made through a combination of grants, scholarships, loans, and work-study programs. Awards may be renewed throughout a student's term of study. A student's financial needs are usually met through a combination of internal assets and federal and state funding. Chapman awards merit scholarships, regardless of financial need, to all eligible admitted new students using a standardized test score/ entering grade point average-driven formula. Chapman also offers talent scholarships in areas such as art, music, dance, theatre, writing, film and television, and science awarded regardless of financial need. Audition, submission of portfolio, or supplemental application materials will be required to be considered for talent awards.

STUDENT ORGANIZATIONS AND ACTIVITIES

Programs and services offered include over 70 clubs and organizations, career development, community outreach, multicultural programs, student health and counseling, international student services, PEER and health education, and new student orientation. Six national fraternities, and five national sororities are active and all include special programming directed toward stewardship and community service activities.

A complete and comprehensive offering of intramural sports and activities involve the entire campus community to create an involving, electric, and outdoor-oriented environment.

Intercollegiate athletics are a big part of undergraduate life at Chapman and almost 20 percent of students compete in varsity sports. Chapman is an independent in the NCAA Division III, often qualifying for championships. Last year, 4 students were named NCAA All-American and 14 were honored as Academic All-Americans. Chapman competes in men's baseball, basketball, water polo, crew, cross-country, football, golf, lacrosse, soccer, softball, tennis, and women's basketball, crew, cross country, soccer, swimming, tennis, track and field, volleyball, and water polo.

ADMISSIONS PROCESS

Chapman University seeks accomplished students who will thrive in a challenging academic environment. Admission to Chapman is selective. In 2007, 47% of the applicant pool was offered admission to the University. Prospective students are evaluated on the strength of their secondary school course work and GPA, and SAT I or ACT scores. Interested students are encouraged to visit the campus, schedule a campus tour, and participate in an information session hosted by an admission officer. Arrangements can be made by contacting the Office of Admission. Chapman offers a non-binding Early Action deadline for freshman applicants. To apply in the Early Action period, students must submit the applica-

CHATHAM COLLEGE UNIVERSITY

AT A GLANCE

For more than 137 years Chatham College University has prepared its students as leaders and innovators. Social consciousness, awareness, and understanding of the environment, interest in public service, a strong grounding in the sciences and liberal arts, and the ability to communicate effectively are characteristics that Chatham students share. The university houses 3 distinctive colleges: Chatham College for Women houses academic and co-curricular programs for undergraduate women and embodies the traditions and rituals of one of the nation's oldest colleges for women. The College for Graduate Studies offers women and men both master's and doctoral programs. The College for Continuing and Professional Studies provides online and hybrid undergraduate and graduate degree programs for women and men, certificate programs, and community programming.

Chatham's undergraduate curriculum, combined with the Senior Tutorial, an original research project guided one-on-one with a Chatham professor, provides an excellent foundation to continue to graduate and professional schools. Chatham offers strong preparation for law school, medical school, and science-based graduate programs as well as the college's own graduate degree programs. The Five-Year Master's Program enables all undergraduate students to apply to one of the college's graduate programs during sophomore or junior year, allowing them to earn both a bachelor's and master's degree in as few as 5 years. Student's personal, professional, and leadership skills are developed to their fullest potential through internships, study abroad, service-learning and leadership training opportunities, and personal development seminars. All first-year students receive HP tablet computers, which are integrated into course work, with access to a wireless campus network. The Chatham environment features a student-teacher ratio of 10:1, which ensures greater interaction between students and faculty. Ninety percent of all faculty members hold terminal degrees.

LOCATION AND ENVIRONMENT

Chatham College University is home to nearly 1,600 900 undergraduate and graduate students on 39 park-like acres only 6 miles from downtown Pittsburgh. Students at Chatham College immerse themselves in academics, co-curricular activities, and the multicultural events that Pittsburgh offers—from music and theater to sports and recreation. Chatham's learning environment promotes intellectual growth and early exposure to the professional world through experiential and service learning. At Chatham, students are not numbers—from professors to alumni and fellow students, the Chatham community stresses the individual. The college's mission is based on a desire to increase self-awareness, encourage social responsibility, enhance cultural awareness, develop leadership ability, establish a lifestyle of wellness, and make connections with others as students endeavor to serve in the societies of today and lead in the world of tomorrow.

OFF-CAMPUS OPPORTUNITIES

The college's undergraduate and graduate students have easy access to Pittsburgh's dynamic career, cultural, and entertainment opportunities. Students may cross-register with any of 8 other colleges and universities, including Carnegie Mellon University and the University of Pittsburgh. Extracurricular learning and service are also important components to a Chatham education. Most students complete at least 2 internships or career-related experiences in their fields. Chatham Abroad, a multi-week travel experience with classmates and faculty, has taken students to Belize, Gal Galapagos Islands, Morocco, Egypt, Italy, Spain, France, Ireland, England, Russia, Norway, Iceland, Greece, and Haiti.

MAJORS AND DEGREES OFFERED

Chatham College University offers the following majors, leading to a bachelor of arts or bachelor of science degree: accounting, art (electronic media, photography, studio arts), art history, arts management, biochemistry, biology, business economics, chemistry, cultural studies, economics, education, engineering, English, environmental studies, exercise science, film and digital video-making, forensics, French, global policy studies, history, interior architecture, international business, management, marketing, mathematics, music, physics, political science, policy studies (global and public), professional communication (broadcast journalism, print journalism, professional writing, public relations), psychology, public policy studies, social work, Spanish, theater, visual arts (emerging media, photography, studio arts), and women's studies. Students may choose a traditional major, an interdisciplinary major, a double major, or a self-designed major. Pre-professional programs are offered in education with teaching certification, law, medicine and health professions, physical therapy, and veterinary medicine. There is also a joint-degree engineering program with Carnegie Mellon University in Pittsburgh. Post-baccalaureate certificate programs are available in accounting, children's and adolescent writing, education for gifted and talented children, English as a second language, instructional technology, landscape studies, nonfiction writing, pre-med, school counseling, and special education. Teacher certification is available through the education program in early childhood, elementary, environmental, school counseling, special education, and secondary education.

Chatham's coeducational graduate program includes the following degrees: accounting, biology (MA and MS), business administration (MBA), counseling psychology, creative writing (MFA), film and digital technology (MFA), interior architecture (first- and post-professional), landscape architecture, landscape studies, leadership and organizational transformation, nursing (master's degree and post-professional doctorate), occupational therapy (master's degree and post-professional doctorate), physical therapy (doctorate and post-professional transitional doctorate), physician assistant studies, teaching.

The Chatham College Five-Year Master's Program allows undergraduates to apply to one of the college's graduate programs during junior year, enabling them to earn both a bachelor's and master's degree in as few as 5 years. The program includes the following degrees: accounting, biology, master of arts in landscape studies, master of arts in leadership and organizational transformation, master of arts in teaching, master of business administration, master of fine arts in film and digital technology, master of fine arts in creative writing, master of occupational therapy, master of physician assistant studies, master of science in counseling psychology, master of arts in landscape studies, master of arts in leadership and organizational transformation, master of arts in teaching, master of business administration, master of fine arts in film and digital technology, master of fine arts in writing, master of occupational therapy, master of physician assistant studies, master of science in counseling psychology.

Chatham also offers a Five-Year Master's Program with the H. John Heinz III School of Public Policy at Carnegie Mellon University. Students may apply during junior year to one of the following Heinz School programs: master of science in public policy and management, master of science in health care policy and management, master of information systems management, and master of arts management. Once accepted, students take courses at both Chatham and the Heinz School during senior year and then earn a bachelor's degree from Chatham College and a master's degree from Carnegie Mellon.

ACADEMIC PROGRAMS

Chatham's general education curriculum includes 6 required interdisciplinary courses plus analytical reasoning, an international or intercultural experience, and wellness courses. Graduation requirements include general education courses, a major, and the Senior Tutorial. The college's 4-4-1 academic calendar consists of fall and spring terms, plus a 3-week "Maymester." Maymester programs include study abroad, concentrated study, experimental projects, travel and field experiences, internships, interdisciplinary study, and student exchanges with other colleges, among other programs. The First-Year Student Sequence introduces students to the Chatham community and its culture and provides opportunities to learn about the resources of the urban environment and study issues of concern to women. These courses provide students with the analytical and communication skills essential for successful college performance. The PACE (Programs for Academic Advising, Career Development, and Educational Enrichment) Center offers students a comprehensive approach to academic and career planning as well as an academic support network designed to maximize each student's academic success at the college. PACE coordinates student internships, placement, workshops, recruitment, and mentor programs.

CAMPUS FACILITIES AND EQUIPMENT

The Jennie King Mellon Library contains more than 87,962 volumes and 700 subscriptions to online and print periodicals. The library offers individual study areas, special seminar rooms and a 24/7 study room. Through consortium memberships, the JKM Library provides access to print materials from hundreds of academic libraries nationwide. The Science Laboratory Complex houses state-of-the-art science laboratories and individual laboratory units. The college's new Broadcast Studio contains sophisticated audio and video editing technology, Macintosh G-5iMac computers, and a multi-functional studio. With completion of the new Athletic and Fitness Center, the college converted its old gymnasium into the new Art and Design Center, which features fine and applied art studios, a computer lab, classroom, and gallery and student exhibition space. On-campus housing includes 3 former mansions, a traditional residence hall, and apartment buildings. All rooms are wired to the campus network. Residency is required for first-years and sophomores (unless students commute from home).

There are more than 30 clubs ranging from academic to volunteer and community service to arts and outdoor activities. Chatham Student Government coordinates student involvement in the affairs of the college, gives voice to student concerns, maintains student participation on College Chatham College for Women committees, and oversees various student boards and organizations. Chatham is an NCAA Division III school with 9 varsity teams: basketball, cross country, ice hockey, soccer, softball, swimming, tennis, volleyball, and water polo. Chatham has the first women's ice hockey team in the region. Intramural sports and recreational activities are also available. Other events on campus, including music recitals, theater, concerts, gallery exhibits, movie screenings, and more, happen almost every night of the week.

TUITION, ROOM, BOARD, AND FEES

For 2007-08, full-time tuition was $25,215 per year and room and board fees were approximately $7,891. A 1-time deposit of $100 for tuition and $100 for on-campus housing is paid by newly admitted students and is applied to first-semester charges. Students currently pay a $600-per-year technology fee.

FINANCIAL AID

Financial aid is awarded on the basis of an individual's financial need, as determined through the Free Application for Federal Student Aid. The awards combine grants, loans, and employment. The priority financial aid deadline is May 1. Sources of financial aid include Chatham grants and loans, state grants, Federal Pell Grants, Federal Supplemental Educational Opportunity Grants, federally funded student loans, and jobs provided under the Federal Work-Study Program. Chatham Merit scholarships for entering students are awarded on the basis of high academic achievement and an on-campus interview without regard to need. Scholarships begin at approximately $4,000 and are awarded based upon the students match with Chatham's mission, as well as the academic merits accompanying the student's application for admission. Minna Kaufmann Ruud Scholarships are available for students with exceptional ability in vocal music, based on an on-campus audition.

ADMISSIONS PROCESS

The prospective student must demonstrate academic strength, motivation, an enthusiasm for learning, and potential for growth. Evaluation of students is made on the basis of the student's academic record, recommendations, involvement in activities, essay, and other submitted material. The college seeks to enroll students representing a variety of cultural, geographical, racial, religious, and socio-economic backgrounds and with diverse talents in both academic and creative areas. The admissions requirements now include a Standardized Test-Optional Policy. Applicants may self-select whether to submit their standardized test scores (SAT or ACT). In lieu of SAT/ACT scores, applicants may instead submit a graded writing sample and resume or list of curricular and co-curricular activities, as well as a portfolio or special project/activity. These materials, which are reviewed by Chatham faculty, may be applied toward Chatham's scholarship review process. It is strongly recommended that candidates arrange to visit the school for a personal appointment, a tour of the campus with a student guide, observation of one or more classes, and conversations with faculty members, staff members, and students. Early entrance is available for well qualified and mature students who wish to begin college at the close of their junior year in high school; early entrance candidates are required to come to the college for interviews. Chatham also welcomes the opportunity to discuss future educational plans with transfer candidates, including junior college and community college graduates, in good academic standing. Chatham grants college course credit for grades of 4 or 5 on the Advanced Placement examinations of the College Board. Certain prerequisites in course offerings may be fulfilled by attaining scores of 3, 4, or 5. Candidates for admission must file an application with the Admissions Office, together with a nonrefundable processing fee in the amount of $35. Students may also take advantage of the college's free online application on the Website. Applications are accepted on a rolling basis.

CLEMSON UNIVERSITY

AT A GLANCE

Clemson University, one of the country's top public universities, combines the best of small-college teaching with big-time science, engineering, and technology. With nearly half of the classes at Clemson having fewer than 20 students, Clemson professors get to know their students and explore innovative ways of teaching. It is one reason Clemson's retention and graduation rates rank among the highest in the country among public schools. It is why Clemson continues to attract some of the country's best students who seek intellectual challenge.

Clemson provides educational and enrichment opportunities to create leaders, thinkers, and entrepreneurs solving real-world problems through research, outreach, and public service.

The university's 17,000 students can select from 70 undergraduate and 100 graduate degree programs offered by 5 colleges: Agriculture, Forestry and Life Sciences; Architecture, Arts and Humanities; Business and Behavioral Science; Engineering and Science; and Health, Education, and Human Development.

Clemson is well known for its prominent athletic programs and for the spirit of its fans. Another important aspect of Clemson is its dedication to improving the world through public service, which is why the university encourages faculty to engage their classes through service learning. Recently, Clemson was recognized by The Princeton Review as one of a few select American universities as a Campus with a Conscience for its work in community service.

With its college town, lakefront setting against a backdrop of mountains and forests, Clemson is characterized by a strong sense of community, a commitment to service, and a love of winning in academics, in athletics, and in life.

LOCATION AND ENVIRONMENT

Clemson is spread out on a 1,400-acre campus along the shores of Lake Hartwell; it s located in the middle of the I-85 corridor between Atlanta, Georgia, and Charlotte, North Carolina. The Blue Ridge Mountains are well within sight, and the climate is as warm as the welcome you'll receive when you make a visit to campus.

OFF-CAMPUS OPPORTUNITIES

Clemson undergraduates can obtain professional work experience at hundreds of different organizations through the university's Cooperative Education program. This voluntary program allows students to alternate periods of academic study with periods of related work at organizations ranging from small consulting firms to Fortune 500 companies.

When you take advantage of Clemson s international study abroad programs, you can study almost anywhere in the world. From France to Malta, Fiji to the Galapagos Islands, chances are there's a program of study for you. In many cases, studying abroad costs the same as studying at Clemson. In fact, many scholarships and financial aid plans will cover costs.

When you want to make a difference, Clemson's Community Service Office provides plenty of opportunities. You can join a student service organization, find ongoing service projects, participate in 1-time service events either on campus or in the community, or explore national and international service opportunities. If you want to help people who need your help, learn more about yourself, develop relationships, or you just want to have fun this is a great way to do it.

Extracurricular activities are a vital part of any student's life. If you re a dancer, a musician, want to build houses for Habitat for Humanity, or join a fraternity or sorority, you can find your niche at Clemson. There are more than 300 student clubs and organizations to try.

MAJORS AND DEGREES OFFERED

Clemson offers more than 70 undergraduate and 100 graduate degree programs through 5 academic colleges: Agriculture, Forestry and Life Sciences; Architecture, Arts and Humanities; Business and Behavioral Science; Engineering and Science; and Health, Education, and Human Development.

To find out what majors are available go to: www.clemson.edu/admission/academicprograms.html

ACADEMIC PROGRAMS

The step from high school to college can be enormous. The standards are different, the work more demanding, and the personal freedoms much greater. For students who are making the transition from high school to college, Clemson has developed Student Success Programs to help meet the academic challenges.

The Academic Success Center offers free tutoring and supplemental instruction to all students. Supplemental instruction allows students enrolled in specific courses to work with student leaders who have already successfully completed the course and who have been trained to lead study sessions. Student leaders work with the professor of the course, attend class, and do homework with their assigned students. They also host study sessions 3 times a week where they review course content and teach learning and study strategies.

The First Year Experience (FYE) is a comprehensive program for all first-year students who live on campus. The program assists freshmen in making the transition from the high school and home environment to the Clemson University community. In addition to FTE, there are other programs in place to help first-year students, including the Freshman Web Portal, which offers online information for new students, and the Freshman Mentoring Program, which provides upperclassmen as peer mentors.

Living and Learning Communities offer the chance for students to live and work with others who have similar interests and goals. There are living options for students interested in business, engineering, science, civics and service, honors courses, and professional golf management. There is also a living community for international students. The Living and Learning Communities are designed to help students be more successful by offering on-site advising and academic support, common course assignments, guest speakers, service opportunities, and a variety of social activities.

Calhoun Honors College offers honors courses and the opportunity to be actively involved in research. Students in the Calhoun Honors College enjoy priority registration and special library privileges. Many also live in honors housing. The New York Times is delivered to honors students each day in keeping with Clemson's mission of encouraging students to be responsible and informed citizens.

Communication Across the Curriculum is a program designed to help all students, whether they are studying engineering, biology, history, or architecture, become strong communicators. Clemson's mission is not to train students on just the technical aspects of their chosen profession, but rather to prepare students to become leaders in their fields. To do that, it is vital that students become good communicators and adept in the latest communication technology so they can sell their ideas and inspire those they will lead. Clemson's Communication Across the Curriculum program is regarded as one of the best in the country.

Creative Inquiry includes carefully planned research projects that teach by allowing students to apply classroom learning to real-life situations. Led by a special task force of representatives from all academic colleges, these projects include hands-on research opportunities, require several semesters of dedication, and give students and teachers a whole new world of learning environments. In fact, many students find that they have the freedom to travel around the state, the country, and even abroad to gather and share information. Projects are integrated in almost every major with the goal of building students' capabilities to find, analyze, and evaluate information.

Freshman Reading is designed to enrich the intellectual environment of Clemson students, to encourage them to look at things from different perspectives and to be open to new ideas. The summer before their freshman year, students receive a copy of the year's selected book. They read the book and write a paper before arriving on campus in the fall. During orientation, students come to Littlejohn Coliseum to hear the author speak and break into small groups to discuss what they've read and heard.

CAMPUS FACILITIES AND EQUIPMENT

Clemson University's modern laboratories and classrooms are well equipped for instruction, research, and lectures. The academic buildings, student housing, service facilities, and equipment are valued at $350 million. Beyond the main campus, stretching into Oconee, Pickens, and Anderson Counties are 24,000 acres devoted to its Agricultural Experiment Station research and 4-H Club activities.

Michelin Career Center is designed to help launch the promising careers of Clemson graduates, the and offers resume critiques, campus interviewing, career fairs, experiential education and internship programs, workshops, and much more. The Princeton Review ranked Clemson's Michelin Career Center fourth in the nation among college and university career/job placement services.

Located within a 10- to 15-minute walk to class, Clemson's 24 residence halls and 5-apartment complexes offer a vast selection of living arrangements.

Fike is a renovated 200,000 square foot recreation center that features a fitness atrium complete with a suspended running track that overlooks the indoor courts, indoor swimming facilities, fitness studios, racquetball courts, state-of-the-art cardio equipment, weights, locker rooms, and even a climbing wall. If you are into staying in shape, Fike is the place to be.

The Hendrix Center is the hub of campus activity and is located a step away from most housing. Here you can find people taking a yoga class outside, or enjoying a meal at the food court. It is home to the university bookstore and offers plenty of quiet places to stop and study. It has a movie theater, ice cream parlor, and much more.

Redfern Health Center provides Medical Services, Counseling and Psychological Services, and health-related programs like Alcohol and Drug Education and is one of the nation's few on-campus accredited health centers.

TUITION, ROOM, BOARD, AND FEES

For the 2007-2008 academic year, annual resident fees for full-time students were:

Tuition and fees: $10,370

Room and board (approximate): $6,170

Books and supplies (approximate): $924

Total: $17,464

Annual nonresident fees for full-time students were:

Tuition and fees: $22,300

Room and board (approximate): $6,170

Books and supplies (approximate): $924

Total: $29,394

All freshmen are required to own a laptop computer.

FINANCIAL AID

Academic scholarships are available at Clemson, and they are awarded based on academic merit. Financial aid is usually given on the basis of need to supplement the amount you and your parents can contribute to your college expenses. Clemson offers financial aid in the form of: grants, scholarships, loans, and part-time employment.

STUDENT ORGANIZATIONS AND ACTIVITIES

At Clemson, "school spirit" is a color—solid orange—and it's hard to miss on fall Saturdays in Death Valley when more than 80,000 fans cheer on the Clemson Tigers. Take a walk through campus on any night, and you'll see the campus alive with students playing intramural sports, going to concerts, attending Greek mixers, or gathering to meet with any of Clemson's 300 student organizations.

ADMISSIONS PROCESS

More than 90 percent of Clemson applicants visit www.clemson.edu/admission to quickly and easily submit their applications online. Application fees may be processed online using a credit card or an electronic check. Freshman applicants should arrange to have their high school transcripts sent directly from their high schools and SAT or ACT scores sent directly from the testing service.

Students applying for admission must take the new versions of the SAT or ACT that require a writing test.

COLLEGE OF THE ATLANTIC

AT A GLANCE

The first college to reach the Carbon Net Zero goal, COA's focus on sustainability and social justice stretches from course offerings to administrative practices.

LOCATION AND ENVIRONMENT

COA is located on 35 acres along the shore of Frenchman Bay. The town of Bar Harbor is a short walk from campus and Acadia National Park is in the school's backyard. The college also owns off-shore island research stations and an 80 acre organic farm.

OFF-CAMPUS OPPORTUNITIES

The school offers courses that take students to Mexico, Guatemala, Europe, the Caribbean and Canada.

MAJORS AND DEGREES OFFERED

All students create self-designed majors, allowing interdisciplinary study of how humans interact with the environment. Each student graduates with a BA in Human Ecology.

ACADEMIC PROGRAMS

Marine Studies; International Studies; Conservation and Field Biology; Educational Studies; Environmental Policy and Planning; Arts and Design; Literature and Writing.

CAMPUS FACILITIES AND EQUIPMENT

Just over half of the students live on campus, with Davis Student Village being named the "greenest" dorm in New England. Deering Common Campus Center has a student organization meeting space, a cafe, dance space, game and TV room, a meditation room, and health offices. Student performance space is in Gates Center. Meals for students, faculty and staff are served in Blair Dining Hall, also known as Take-A-Break.

TUITION, ROOM, BOARD AND FEES

For the 2008-2009 school year, Tuition is $31,470. Room is $5,400 and board is $3,090.

FINANCIAL AID

Close to 85% of COA students receive Financial Aid based on a combination of financial need and merit. Students must fill out the FAFSA and COA's own Financial Aid application.

STUDENT ORGANIZATIONS AND ACTIVITIES

Sustain US Club

Soccer

Cricket

Ultimate Frisbee

Amnesty International

Student Activities

Governance

Water Polo

THE COLLEGE OF NEW JERSEY

AT A GLANCE

The College of New Jersey (TCNJ) has created a culture of constant questioning. In small classes, students and faculty members collaborate in a rewarding process. They seek to understand fundamental principles, apply key concepts, reveal new problems, and pursue lines of inquiry to gain a fluency of thought in their disciplines. This transformative process is at the core of the educational experience at the college.

Many students extend their classroom work by participating in research with faculty members or studying abroad. Often, professors and students coauthor papers published in academic journals. The mentor relationship helps students discuss career options and land pertinent fellowships, internships, and summer research positions.

TCNJ admits a class each year full of ambitious students, eager to build on their earlier education and plunge into new topics. The most successful admits are prepared to steer their own academic pursuits toward post-graduation goals of graduate school, professional training, or satisfying careers.

Prestigious graduate schools, including the University of Pennsylvania, Georgetown Law School, Maxwell School at Syracuse University, NYU Law School, and Harvard, Yale, and Northwestern Universities, routinely welcome TCNJ alumni into their ranks. Eighty-five percent of TCNJ students who apply to medical school are accepted.

Many top corporations recruit TCNJ graduates, providing avenues into rewarding jobs directly after graduation. Other barometers of student success include the 99 percent pass rate of education majors taking the state teacher preparation test and the 85 percent 3-year pass rate for nursing students going for their license. The variety of learning opportunities at the college prepare students to prosper in any arena after leaving the campus.

LOCATION AND ENVIRONMENT

Neoclassical Georgian Colonial architecture, meticulous landscaping, and thoughtful design merge to more than meet the evolving needs of TCNJ students. Students enjoy a campus with 289 acres of trees, lakes, and open spaces within the suburban setting of Ewing Township, New Jersey. Two out of three undergraduate students live in campus residence halls. The residence halls vary in configuration from the freshman towers to suites and townhouse arrangements for upperclass students. An on-campus 600-bed apartment complex is set to open in Fall 2007. The college ensures that on-campus housing is available to all students in their first 2 years.

More that 150 student organizations flourish at the college. Anyone can find an intramural sports team, Greek organization, cultural club, or academic group to suit his or her interests. Many students make friends and enjoy their leisure time participating in one of these groups. In addition, the College Union Board organizes events, including concerts, performances, and comedy nights. The college's highly successful Division III teams also provide an opportunity to socialize and cheer on fellow classmates. Nearby cities, such as Trenton, Philadelphia, and New York, allow for abundant entertainment, employment, and social options. Many courses incorporate field trips to New York City or Washington, DC.

OFF-CAMPUS OPPORTUNITIES

TCNJ administers an extensive international study program, featuring exchange programs in locations as diverse as London and the University of Santiago. Some students choose to attend one of the 131 available institution in the U.S., while others venture to one of the 33 countries offering full-year or semester-long programs.

Student internships, both on and off campus, expose students to career options as they gain professional skills. With the college's location in the center of corporate activity close to New York and Philadelphia, many internships are available—some with pay and some for credit.

Faculty members lend their advice and help students locate and procure appropriate opportunities including fellowships, research positions, and internships. Students may also use resources at the Office of Career Services to find positions in New York, Philadelphia, or any of the corporations, government agencies, or research organizations closer to campus.

MAJORS AND DEGREES OFFERED

The College of New Jersey hosts seven schools: Art, Media, and Music; Business; Culture and Society; Education; Engineering; Nursing; and Science. The college offers programs leading to the Bachelor of Arts, Bachelor of Fine Arts, Bachelor of Music, Bachelor of Science, and Bachelor of Science in Nursing.

TCNJ grants degrees in the following majors: accountancy, art°, art history, digital arts, fine arts, graphic design, interactive multimedia, biology°, business administration (specializations: finance, general business, information systems management, international business, management, marketing), chemistry°, communication studies, computer science, economics, early childhood education°, education of the deaf and hard of hearing°, elementary education°, health and physical education°, special education for the developmentally handicapped°, engineering (biomedical engineering, computer engineering, electrical engineering, mechanical engineering, and engineering science), English° (options: liberal arts, journalism, professional writing), history°, international studies, law and justice, mathematics° (option: statistics), music°, nursing, philosophy, physics° (options: scientific computer programming and earth science), political science, psychology, sociology (option: pre-social work), Spanish°, technology education°, and women's and gender studies.

°Programs in which students may prepare for teacher certification

Students may also choose to complete a minor in one of the previously mentioned fields or another subject area, such as African American studies, classical studies, comparative literature, religion, public administration, French, Italian, and Spanish.

Joint degrees are also available at TCNJ. In conjunction with UMDNJ, students can pursue a 7-year combined BS/MD degree. A 7-year combined BS/OD degree program is also available through the State University of New York College of Optometry. There is also a 4.5 combined BS/MA degree in law and justice with Rutgers University. Students can study for 5 years to receive their dual certification in the education of the deaf and hard of hearing and elementary education/master of arts in teaching.

ACADEMIC PROGRAMS

A Liberal Learning Curriculum ensures that all students are grounded in the beliefs and values of civic responsibility and intellectual and scholarly growth and that they receive a well-rounded education in the liberal arts.

In 2004, the college completed a transformation of its curriculum requiring fewer, more in-depth courses. All courses have been transformed and contain a significant out of class requirement and will provide for even more student and faculty interaction.

The small classes enable dialog between students, and every class at TCNJ is taught by a professor, not a graduate student. The college shapes its curricula and educational experiences around the concept of the accomplished and engaged learner.

The required First-Year Seminar, the cornerstone of the new Liberal Learning program, introduces students to the habits of mind and the methodologies of research; its seminar format of no more than 15 students reinforces the message that students are not to be passive recipients of knowledge but rather active contributors to their own learning. Requirements are grouped as diversity and community engagement goals, proficiencies, and depth requirements that can be self-designed or designated interdisciplinary concentrations.

Top students may enroll in TCNJ's Honor's Program, designed to provide a core curriculum with additional challenges and opportunities for individualized work. Most honor's classes take an interdisciplinary approach to the history of civilizations, its accomplishments, and its problems. Independent study arrangements fall easily within the parameters of the Honor's Program, as well.

CAMPUS FACILITIES AND EQUIPMENT

Learning, like everything else, is contextual: the surroundings in which students learn and the tools they use influence their experience. Not surprisingly, the college supports its educational aspirations with careful attention to the quality of its facilities. In the first decade of the twenty-first century, more than $250 million in ongoing and new facilities construction is ensuring that TCNJ students continue to have an environment that not only meets their academic, athletic, social, and living needs but extends their reach—resulting in higher scholarship, better health and fitness, closer community, and greater comfort.

TUITION, ROOM, BOARD, AND FEES

Because TCNJ is a public institution, costs are lower than most equivalent private institutions. The tuition and fees for undergraduates in the 2005–2006 academic year are as follows:

In-state tuition and fees: $10,000

Out-of-state tuition and fees: $12,000

Room and board (all students): $8,000

FINANCIAL AID

Close to 50 percent of full-time undergraduates benefit from financial aid, which can come in the form of merit-based scholarships, work-study programs, loans, or government or institutional grants. All students seeking financial aid must submit the Free Application for Federal Student Aid (FAFSA) form or renewal FAFSA to apply. The Title IV FAFSA Code for the college is 002642.

Students may compete for the college's merit scholarships, which are funded by the state government as well as private donors. These awards are offered to those applicants with top SAT scores and class rankings; there is no separate application process for scholarships. Over the last 6 years, TCNJ has given scholarships totaling more than $12 million.

STUDENT ORGANIZATIONS AND ACTIVITIES

Classroom learning at TCNJ is complemented by an extensive and acclaimed Leadership Development Program. Life outside the classroom is not something our students do on the side. It's an extension of the learning experience. At every turn from the first year on, students blur the boundary between living and learning, closing the gap between "student" and "life."

For fun or experience, student can participate in any of the more than 150 TCNJ clubs, catering to interests as diverse as theater, professional training, writing, fraternities and sororities, and athletics. TCNJ teams play in the NCAA Division III, as nonscholarship student-athlete s. The men field teams in 11 sports, while the women compete in 10. The college holds the record for championship and runner-up titles since Division III was started in 1979.

For those looking for something a little less competitive, intramural sports, including flag football, volleyball, softball, floor hockey, and basketball, have thriving coed leagues of their own. Intramural teams play in state, regional, and national tournaments. The college was proud to send its top-ten flag football team to the recent championship in New Orleans.

TCNJ students administer both the Student Finance Board and College Union Board. They organize popular student events, bringing people to the campus such as Tonic, Jim Breuer, and John Leguizamo.

ADMISSIONS PROCESS

The admissions committee at TCNJ accepts a class of motivated, ambitious, and highly talented students. Most successful applicants have taken 16 college-preparatory units in high school. They also show impressive class ranks and SAT scores. Most students admitted into the class fall within the top 10 percent of their graduating class. The committee also considers extracurricular involvement, individual pursuits, and community participation. Students applying to the art, music, and health and exercise science departments are evaluated on additional criteria specific to their intended course of study.

Those applying for September admission must have their applications submitted by February 15. TCNJ offers an Early Decision program to those who know the college is their first choice: Applications received by November 15 will receive a response by December 30. A small number of students begin classes in January, and they must apply by November 1. For further information, please contact:

Office of Admissions

The College of New Jersey

PO Box 7718

Ewing, NJ 08628-0718

Telephone: 800-624-0967

E-mail: admiss@vm.tcnj.edu

COLORADO STATE UNIVERSITY

AT A GLANCE

As one of the nation's top research universities, Colorado State is grounded in a rich tradition of scholarship, innovation, and public service. Regardless of which field you choose to pursue, you'll have every opportunity to take your studies to the highest level.

But CSU is more than just a place where you can explore your interests wherever they take you. It's also a community in every sense of the word, and that means you'll develop connections that will literally change your life. Our Living Learning Communities will unite you with people who share your interests. Our faculty will open the door to incredible research and internship experiences. And our career advising and support services will give you the tools you need to excel in your chosen field.

Colorado State's 8 colleges encompass the major areas of human knowledge, with more than 150 programs of study in the sciences, arts, humanities, and professions. From internationally known programs in veterinary medicine and chemistry to our highly ranked business college, you'll work with professors who know their fields inside and out.

But the faculty at Colorado State are more than just experts who make significant contributions to our understanding of the world. They're also some of the most talented and personable instructors you'll ever meet. Whether they're leading a spirited class discussion or making themselves available outside office hours, your professors will give you the kind of attention you might not expect at a university of 25,000 students.

"The professors here aren't just academically gifted—they really know how to relate to students," says Jake Blumberg, a senior technical journalism major. "There's not a communication gap, and they expect us to act like adults. If I could list the best friends I've had, some of them would be professors. I feel that makes the education here so much more varied and purposeful."

At Colorado State, you'll discover that an exceptional education isn't simply about amassing knowledge. It's about using what you've learned to change lives for the better—and if you choose to pursue your education here, you'll join forces with students, faculty, and alumni who are making an impact on a global scale.

LOCATION AND ENVIRONMENT

With 300 days of sun per year and the Rockies at our doorstep, it's no wonder Money Magazine singled out Fort Collins as the "Best Place to Live in America" in 2006 among cities with a population of more than 50,000. Whether you're into winter sports, water sports, or extreme sports, Northern Colorado is a great place to play. And whether you like biking, catching live music, or sampling a wide assortment of restaurants in Old Town, Fort Collins is a great place to enjoy life. But Fort Collins is more than just a recreational and social hot spot. It's also a community where the lives of students and citizens blend seamlessly to form bonds that aren't easily broken. Colorado State has been the focal point of the city since the university was founded in 1870, and countless alumni remain here long after they've graduated. Whether you're taking advantage of internship and service opportunities throughout Fort Collins or inviting people of all ages to campus events, you'll be part of a community that values what you have to offer.

ACADEMIC PROGRAMS

With more than 150 undergraduate programs of study, Colorado State gives you the flexibility to design a course of study that meets your personal and professional goals. The All-University Core Curriculum (AUCC) is the centerpiece of Colorado State's integrated learning experience and provides all students with a well-rounded education. Typically, students meet the AUCC requirements in their freshman and sophomore years and devote their junior and senior years to specialization in their major field.

MAJORS AND DEGREES OFFERED

You're required to complete a minimum of 120 credit hours for graduation. Many of our students choose to pursue a minor, an interdisciplinary studies program, or a double major. Here's a look at the majors we offer in 8 colleges:

The College of Agricultural Sciences offers bachelor of science degrees in agricultural business, agricultural economics, agricultural education, animal science, equine science, horticulture, landscape architecture, landscape horticulture, and soil and crop sciences.

The College of Applied Human Sciences offers bachelor of science degrees in apparel and merchandising, construction management, family and consumer sciences, health and exercise science, human development and family studies, interior design, nutrition and food science, and restaurant and resort management. The college also offers bachelor of arts degrees in social work.

The College of Business offers bachelor of science degrees in business administration, with concentrations in accounting, finance, information systems, marketing, real estate, and organization and innovation management.

The College of Engineering offers bachelor of science degrees in civil, computer, electrical, environmental, mechanical, and chemical and biological engineering, as well as engineering science.

The College of Liberal Arts offers bachelor of arts degrees in anthropology, art, economics, English, history, liberal arts, music, performing arts, philosophy, political science, sociology, speech communication, technical journalism, and languages, literatures, and cultures. The college also offers bachelor of fine arts and bachelor of music degrees in art and music.

The Warner College of Natural Resources offers bachelor of science degrees in forestry, geology, natural resource recreation and tourism, natural resources management, rangeland ecology, watershed science, and fish, wildlife, and conservation biology.

The College of Natural Sciences offers bachelor of science degrees in applied computing technology, biochemistry, biological science, chemistry, computer science, mathematics, natural sciences, physics, psychology, and zoology.

The College of Veterinary Medicine and Biomedical Sciences offers bachelor of science degrees in biomedical sciences, environmental health, and microbiology.

In addition, teacher licensure is available in early childhood education; at the secondary level in biology, biology/natural resources, chemistry, English, French, general science, geology, German, mathematics, physics, social studies, Spanish, and speech; and in grades K-12 in art and music. Vocational secondary education licensure is available in agricultural education, business education, consumer and family studies, marketing education, and trade and industrial education.

CSU also offers pre-professional programs in dentistry, law, medicine (chiropractic, optometry, osteopathy, physical therapy, physician assistant studies, and podiatry), nursing, occupational therapy, pharmacy, and veterinary medicine.

If you'd like to pursue a particularly challenging course of study, the university's honors program is an outstanding option. If you're accepted into the program, you can sign up for small, seminar-style courses that fulfill many of the university's graduation requirements. The classes touch on a variety of disciplines, but all of them challenge you to communicate with the utmost precision.

If you're interested in immersing yourself in another culture, the Office of International Programs coordinates a variety of study abroad programs that allow you to pursue your studies almost anywhere in the world. These programs range from 2-week seminars to semester and yearlong periods of study in any major.

CAMPUS FACILITIES AND EQUIPMENT

Our students come from 50 states and 86 countries, so you can count on a diversity of opinion at Colorado State. You also can count on students who treat you with respect and appreciate what you bring to the table—narrow-mindedness and superficiality simply aren't part of the campus scene.

If you enter the university as a freshman, you'll live in one of our 11 residence halls. You'll have easy access to recreation and study areas and a wide variety of activities, including educational programs, social gatherings, and recreational events. Several floors within the residence halls are designated for either academic or leisure interests, giving you a chance to live with students who share your interests. Our 13 Living Learning Communities include honors, leadership, engineering, and pre-veterinary medicine.

When it's time to focus on your studies, the William E. Morgan Library is a comfortable place to work on individual or group projects. The library features a coffee cart, vending machines, couches, and an unmatched view of the foothills. And with more than 330 desktop computers available for general use, you'll always have the technological resources you need.

Looking at the bigger picture, Colorado State is made up of 4 campuses covering about 4,900 acres. The main campus is situated in the center of Fort Collins and includes nearly 100 academic and administrative buildings. South of the main campus is the Veterinary Teaching Hospital, one of the nation's top facilities for teaching and research in the clinical sciences. The agricultural campuses support instruction and research in agronomy and animal science, including the nationally recognized Equine Teaching and Research Center. The Foothills Campus, located 2 miles west of the main campus, is home to many of the university's research projects. Pingree Park (elev.: 9,000 feet) is used primarily for summer educational and research programs in forestry and natural resources.

There's no doubt about it: A Colorado State education will empower you and unite you with people who understand that one person really can make a difference. Our students and alumni are teaming up with nonprofit organizations, scientists, and engineers worldwide to transform their knowledge into a force for the greater good.

So go ahead and combat diseases at one of the most sophisticated labs in the nation. Develop a business plan and watch your company take off. Design a 2-stroke engine that will improve air quality in Tibet. No matter what you do at CSU, you'll build a foundation for a future of unlimited possibilities.

TUITION, ROOM, BOARD, AND FEES

For the 2007-2008 school year, full-time tuition and fees for undergraduates are $5,418 for Colorado residents and $18,858 for non-residents. The average cost for room and board in on-campus housing is $7,092, based on standard residence hall rates. For books and classroom supplies, expenses are estimated at $990.

FINANCIAL AID

A variety of financial aid programs are available at Colorado State, including grants, scholarships, work-study, loans, and student employment. CSU focuses its dollars primarily on need-based aid, but we also award merit-based scholarships to selected outstanding students. About two-thirds of our students receive some type of financial assistance.

STUDENT ORGANIZATIONS AND ACTIVITIES

Once you settle in, you'll have a chance to participate in more than 300 clubs and organizations, including student government, honor societies, sororities and fraternities, athletic and recreation clubs, cultural and religious organizations, advocacy offices, and major-oriented or professionally oriented clubs. Many students participate in intramural sports and sport clubs, which feature nationally recognized teams in polo, soccer, lacrosse, hockey, rugby, and other sports. Men's and women's intercollegiate athletic teams are part of the Mountain West Conference at the NCAA Division I level. If you enjoy community service, you should check out the Office of Student Leadership, Involvement and Community Engagement. You can choose from one-day special events, yearlong service work, community-based research projects, and other volunteer opportunities.

ADMISSIONS PROCESS

Colorado State chooses candidates for admission based on course rigor, GPA, test scores, evidence of leadership and service, and individual potential. Colorado State is a selective university, so applications are carefully and individually reviewed. In fall 2007, the middle 50 percent of entering freshmen had a GPA range of 3.2 to 3.8, an ACT composite score of 22 to 26, and an SAT I Verbal and Math combined score between 1020 and 1220.

If you're interested in visiting campus, we offer student-led tours and admissions/financial aid presentations every weekday. For more details, go to http://admissions.colostate.edu/visit.

For additional admissions information and application forms, contact:

Office of Admissions

1062 Campus Delivery

Colorado State University

Fort Collins, Colorado 80523-1062

Telephone: 970-491-6909

Website: admissions.colostate.edu

School Says . . .

COLORADO TECHNICAL UNIVERSITY

Colorado Tech Online takes career-focused education to a new level of technological sophistication.

AT A GLANCE

Colorado Tech Online is dedicated to helping motivated professionals retain their competitive edge, strive for new plateaus of career satisfaction, or add real-world credentials to their academic accomplishments. On our amazing Virtual Campus, you can scale the new face of modern education and earn a career-focused degree completely online, no matter where you work, live, or travel.

LOCATION AND ENVIRONMENT

Colorado Technical University is a multi-campus institution of higher learning that has been educating students since 1965. At all of our campuses, we are committed to providing a learning environment that is progressive, supportive, and equipped to help students prepare for the demanding and fiercely competitive working world.

Our campuses include Colorado Tech Online, CTU Colorado Springs, CTU Denver, CTU North Kansas City, CTU Pueblo, and CTU Sioux Falls.

MAJORS AND DEGREES OFFERED

Colorado Tech Online offers bachelor's degree programs in business administration, information technology, criminal justice, and accounting, as well as master's degree programs in business administration and management. We remain committed to addressing real-world issues with flexible online learning programs that accommodate the many and varying needs of a diverse student population.

CAMPUS FACILITIES AND EQUIPMENT

Colorado Tech Online offers an amazing academic experience from any Internet-connected computer. Our industry-current course delivery system provides a rich, dynamic, interactive experience. Courses are fully Web-based and not simply an e-mail exchange, and you'll have multiple opportunities to interact with instructors and classmates.

FINANCIAL AID

We realize that how you pay for your education is an important decision. At Colorado Tech Online, we are committed to helping students develop financial plans to achieve their educational goals. Colorado Tech Online provides all students with a dedicated financial aid advisor who will personally walk them through every step of the financial aid process.

ADMISSIONS PROCESS

Colorado Tech Online makes it easy and fast for you to apply, enroll and register for classes at our university. Just complete these 4 steps to apply for admission to Colorado Tech Online, and you'll be on your way to taking your career to new heights.

Start by submitting an application for admission. Then, conduct a personal telephone interview with one of our admissions advisors. Next, you'll be asked to submit appropriate, official school documentation. Finally, let's make sure your proficiency in English is sufficient for you to succeed at Colorado Tech Online.

COLUMBIA COLLEGE CHICAGO (IL)

AT A GLANCE

Columbia College Chicago is the nation's largest and most diverse private arts college. Columbia takes a pragmatic approach to education in the visual, performing, media, and communication arts that encourages students to fully explore their chosen program of study. Columbia is centrally located in Chicago's South Loop, near Chicago's major theaters, museums, concert halls, restaurants, clubs, parks, galleries, recreational facilities, and Lake Michigan. Our campus sits at the heart of the city's major corporations, ad agencies, television and radio stations, public relations firms, production houses, recording facilities, design studios, and dance companies.

The foundation of a Columbia education features intimate class settings (average class size: fewer than 20 students) that ensure close interaction with a faculty of working professionals, plentiful internship opportunities with major employers in Chicago and national marketplaces, outstanding facilities that encourage learning by doing, and a required core of liberal arts classes that provide the broad and enriching underpinnings of our students' courses of study.

MAJORS AND DEGREES OFFERED

Columbia offers the BA, BFA, BM, MA, MFA, MAT, and MAM.

The faculty at Columbia College Chicago are actively engaged in the subjects they teach and are uniquely qualified to share their expertise in the classroom. As scholars and working professionals who are accomplished in their fields, Columbia's faculty bring insight on industry-current aesthetics, techniques, and viewpoints to the classroom. Students at Columbia learn from Pulitzer-prize-winning journalists, Emmy-award-winning producers, and nationally recognized artists; in short, faculty who do what they teach. In turn, students are inspired to work hard, get their hands dirty, take risks, and push themselves and their ideas to the fullest. Together, these ingredients combine to create an extraordinary academic environment that transcends the traditional collegiate classroom experience.

Columbia College's Portfolio Center helps graduating students present their body of work in the most professional way, by refining and selecting appropriate pieces and samples for inclusion in their professional portfolios. The Portfolio Center connects students to the larger professional world through workshops, presentations, and networking opportunities.

Academic and social assistance include: Conaway Achievement Project (services for students with disabilities), Comprehensive Academic and Career Advising Center, Bridge Program, Mentorship Programs, ESL, Portfolio Center, Student Counseling Services, off-campus study, and immersion experience on site at the CBS studio lot in Los Angeles. Students can also elect to participate in affiliated study abroad programs. The most common destinations are England, Mexico, Russia, Czech Republic, and Italy. High School Summer Institute is an opportunity for motivated high school juniors and seniors to experience college life and earn academic credit.

ACADEMIC PROGRAMS

The School of Fine and Performing Arts

Art and design: art and design (BA), art history (BA), advertising art direction (BFA), fashion design (BFA), fine art (BFA), graphic design (BFA), illustration (BFA), interior architecture (BFA), product design (BFA).

Arts, entertainment, and media management: fashion/retail management (BA), media management (BA), music business management (BA), performing arts management (BA), arts entrepreneurship, small business management (BA), visual arts management (BA), sports management (BA).

Dance: dance (BA), dancemaking (BA), dance studies (BA), choreography (BFA), teaching (BFA).

Fiction writing: fiction writing (BA, BFA), playwriting (BA, BFA).

Music: composition (BA; BMus), Contemporary urban and popular music (BA), instrumental performance (BA), vocal performance (BA), vocal jazz (BA).

Photography: photography (BA, BFA).

Theater: acting (BA, BFA), directing (BA, BFA), musical theater performance (BA, BFA), theater (BA), technical theater (BA), theater design (BA, BFA).

The School of Media Arts

Audio arts and acoustics: acoustics (BA), audio arts and acoustics (BA), audio for visual media (BA), audio design and production (BA), sound contracting (BA), sound reinforcement (BA).

Film and video: alternative forms (BA), animation (computer/BA), animation (traditional/BA), audio for visual media (BA), cinematography (BA), critical studies (BA), directing (BA), documentary (BA), editing (BA), film/video (BA), post-production (BA), producing (BA), screenwriting (BA).

Interactive arts & media: game design (BA), interactive arts & media (BA).

Journalism: broadcast journalism (BA), magazine writing/editing (BA), news reporting and writing (BA), reporting on health, science and the environment (BA).

Marketing communication: advertising (BA), marketing (BA), public relations (BA).

Television: interactive television (BA), post-production/effects (BA), production/directing (BA), writing/producing (BA).

The School of Liberal Arts and Sciences: American Sign Language-English Interpretation: ASL-English (BA).

Cultural studies (BA/offered through the liberal education department).

Early childhood education: early childhood education (BA), teacher certification (BA).

Poetry (BA).

Creative nonfiction (BA/offered through the English department).

CAMPUS FACILITIES AND EQUIPMENT

Columbia College Chicago's campus is made up of 23 buildings located primarily in the historic South Loop neighborhood of downtown Chicago. Advanced facilities for radio, television, art, computer graphics, photography, interactive multimedia, fashion design, and film are state-of-the-industry and include professionally equipped color and black-and-white darkrooms, digital imaging computer facilities, photography and film stages, film and video editing suites, and studios for painting, drawing, and 3-D design. The campus also includes the Museum of Contemporary Photography, one of only a few such facilities in the United States, and the Audio Technology Center, a recording production and research facility. The centers for dance, music, and theater are separate but conveniently located and are designed for their specific performance needs, including individual and group rehearsal and specialized performance spaces.

The college's 258,000-volume library and instructional service center provides comprehensive information and study facilities. Reading/study rooms and special audiovisual equipment are available for use in individual projects and research. As a member of a statewide online computer catalog and resource-sharing network, Columbia's library provides students with access to the resources of 45 academic institutions in Illinois, effectively creating an information base of several million volumes. The library also houses special collections, such as the George S. Lurie Memorial Collection of books and resource materials on art, photography, and film; the Black Music Resource Center of books and sound recordings; the Screenwriters' Collection of film and television manuscripts; the History of Photography microfilm collection of books and periodicals; and a nonprint collection of 100,000 slides and more than 7,300 videotapes and films. The latest addition to the library is the Albert P. Weisman Center for the Study of Contemporary Issues in Chicago Journalism. The center includes a print and audiovisual collection and a learning center that explores the development of Chicago's political and social history.

TUITION, ROOM, BOARD, AND FEES

Costs and financial aid for 2008-2009 academic year

Undergraduate in-state tuition (academic year): $17,950

Undergraduate out-of-state tuition (academic year): $17,950

Room and board (academic year): $8,000-$12,000

STUDENT ORGANIZATIONS AND ACTIVITIES

When they aren't showing at campus galleries, publishing in award-winning magazines, or free-styling at poetry slams, Columbia students take an active role in Chicago's arts community. The influence of Columbia's young talent can be felt in theaters, bookstores, and radio stations throughout the city. And every spring, students return the favor by inviting Chicago to their doorstep for Manifest, the city's largest student arts exhibition.

ADMISSIONS PROCESS

Columbia seeks to admit a culturally, economically, and educationally diverse student body. You can't do, can't learn, can't excel at what you want to do in the arts and communications fields without exposure to a widely diverse range of students, faculty, and staff to challenge your thinking, to inspire your growth, and to move your art form forward.

Columbia College Chicago will review your admission materials with an eye toward the big picture, the whole person. We want to learn as much as we can about your academic and creative achievements (and challenges), your aspirations, and your goals.

We will consider your full potential—as well as your experience and education. We won't look only at who you are now and where you've been; we will look at who you will be.

Columbia makes admissions decisions on a rolling basis, notifying students of their admission decision within 3 to 4 weeks of completing their application file.

COLUMBIA UNIVERSITY SCHOOL OF GENERAL STUDIES

AT A GLANCE

The School of General Studies of Columbia University is the finest liberal arts college in the country, dedicated specifically to students with nontraditional backgrounds seeking a traditional education at an Ivy League university. Most students at the School of General Studies (GS) have, for personal or professional reasons, interrupted their education, never attended college, or are only able to attend part-time. GS is unique among colleges of its type because its students are fully integrated into the Columbia undergraduate curriculum: They take the same courses, with the same faculty, and earn the same degree as all other Columbia undergraduates.

General Studies students come from varied backgrounds and all walks of life. They have the option to study either full- or part- time. Many work full-time while pursuing a degree, and many have family responsibilities; others attend classes full-time, experiencing Columbia's more traditional college life. In the classroom the diversity and varied personal experience of the student body promotes discussion and debate, fostering an environment of academic rigor and intellectual development. The school has approximately 1,200 undergraduate degree candidates and close to 400 post-baccalaureate pre-medical students. The average age of a GS student is 29. Approximately half of GS students attend classes full-time. Between 80 and 85 percent of the school's students continue on to graduate and professional study after graduation. The acceptance rate for General Studies post-baccalaureate pre-medical students applying to U.S. medical schools is more than 90 percent.

In addition to its bachelor's degree program, the School of General Studies offers combined undergraduate/graduate degree programs with Columbia's Schools of Social Work, International and Public Affairs, Law, Business, Dental Medicine, Teachers College, and the College of Physicians and Surgeons.

LOCATION AND ENVIRONMENT

Columbia University is located in Morningside Heights, on the Upper West Side of Manhattan. The university's neighbors include the Union Theological Seminary, the Jewish Theological Seminary, the Manhattan School of Music, St. Luke's Hospital, Women's Hospital, Riverside Church, and the Cathedral of St. John the Divine. The diversity of intellectual and social activities offered by these institutions is one of Columbia's great assets as a university; another is New York City itself, which offers students at Columbia a rich and almost boundless variety of social, cultural, and recreational opportunities that are themselves an education.

OFF-CAMPUS OPPORTUNITIES

Columbia students may enhance their academic experiences through various study-abroad programs around the world. For example, students may spend a term at the Reid Hall Program in the Montparnasse district of Paris, the Berlin Consortium for German Studies, Kyoto Consortium for Japanese Studies, or the Language Program in Beijing, China. Additionally, students may apply to participate in one of the Columbia approved study abroad programs located in countries all over the world.

MAJORS AND DEGREES OFFERED

The School of General Studies grants the BA and BS degrees and offers the following majors: African studies; African American studies; American studies; ancient studies; anthropology; applied mathematics; archaeology; architecture; art history; art history/visual arts; Asian American studies; astronomy; biochemistry; biology; chemistry; classical studies; classics; comparative literature and society; computer science; dance; drama and theater arts; earth and environmental sciences; East Asian languages and cultures; ecology, evolution, and environmental biology; economics; economics/mathematics; economics/operations research; economics/philosophy; economics/political science; economics/statistics; English and comparative literature; environmental biology; evolutionary biology of the human species; film studies; French; French and Francophone studies; German literature and cultural history; Hispanic studies; history; human rights; Italian cultural studies; Italian literature; Latino studies; literature/writing; mathematics; mathematics/statistics; Middle East and Asian languages and cultures; music; neuroscience and behavior; philosophy; physics; political science; psychology; religion; Slavic languages; sociology; Spanish; Spanish and Portuguese; statistics; urban studies; visual arts; and women's and gender studies. Individually designed majors are also available. In addition, the school offers 2 undergraduate dual-degree programs: one in conjunction with Columbia's School of Engineering and Applied Science and the other in conjunction with the Jewish Theological Seminary.

ACADEMIC PROGRAMS

The School of General Studies offers a traditional liberal arts education designed to provide students with the broad knowledge and intellectual skills that foster continued education and growth in the years after college, as well as providing a sound foundation for positions of responsibility in the professional world. Requirements for the bachelor's degree comprise 3 elements: 1) core requirements, intended to develop in students the ability to write and communicate clearly; to understand the modes of thought that characterize the humanities, social sciences, and sciences; to gain familiarity with central cultural ideas through literature, fine arts, and music; and to acquire a working proficiency in a foreign language; (2) major requirements, designed to give students sustained and coherent exposure to a particular discipline in an area of strong intellectual interest; and (3) elective courses, in which students pursue particular interests and skills for their own personal growth or for their relationship to future professional or personal objectives. Students are required to complete a minimum of 124 credits for the bachelor's degree; 60 of these may be in transfer credit, but at least 64 credits (including the last 30 credits) must be completed at Columbia. In addition to the usual graduation honors (cum laude, magna cum laude, and summa cum laude), honors programs for superior students are available in a majority of the university's departments.

CAMPUS FACILITIES AND EQUIPMENT

The Columbia University libraries constitute the nation's sixth-largest academic library system, with a collection of more than 8.6 million volumes, more than 5 million microform pieces, and 26 million manuscript items in 850 separate collections. Of the 25 libraries in the system, 5 are designated Distinctive Collections because of their unusual depth and nationally recognized excellence. All library divisions are available to General Studies students. The university's Computer Center is one of the largest and most powerful university installations in the world and has remote units and terminals in several parts of the campus to enhance its accessibility. The Fairchild Life Science Building houses research facilities, laboratories, electron microscopes, and a vast amount of biochemical equipment used for teaching and research. The university's physics building has been the scene of many important developments in the recent history of physics, including the invention of the laser and the first U.S. demonstration of nuclear fission.

TUITION, ROOM, BOARD, AND FEES

For the 2007-2008 academic year, tuition was $1,146 per credit, room and board costs were $13,034, fees were approximately $1,600, and books and supplies were $2,000.

FINANCIAL AID

The School of General Studies awards financial aid based upon need and academic ability. Approximately 70 percent of General Studies degree candidates receive some form of financial aid, including Federal Pell Grants, New York State TAP Grants, Federal Stafford and unsubsidized Stafford Loans, Federal Perkins Loans, General Studies Scholarships, and Federal Work-Study Program awards. Priority application deadlines for new students are June 1 for the fall semester and October 15 for the spring semester.

STUDENT ORGANIZATIONS AND ACTIVITIES

One student of the school represents General Studies students in the University Senate, a decision-making body made up of students, faculty, and administrative staff members from each division of the university. In addition, 2 General Studies students sit as voting members on the Committee on Instruction, which oversees the curriculum of the school. The General Studies Student Council elects officers each year and sponsors activities for students. The Observer, the school's student-run magazine, is published several times each year. The Premedical Association (PMA) sponsors events related to the medical school admissions process.

Additionally, students are eligible to participate in any of the more than 250 student organizations on campus.

ADMISSIONS PROCESS

The admission policy of the school is geared to the maturity and varied backgrounds of its students. Aptitude and motivation are considered along with past academic performance, standardized test scores, and employment history. The school's admission decisions are based on a careful review of each application and reflect the Admissions Committee's considered judgment of the applicant's maturity, academic potential, and present ability to undertake course work at Columbia.

Admission requirements include a completed application form; a 1,500- to 2,000-word autobiographical statement describing the applicant's past educational history and work experience, present situation, and future plans; 2 letters of recommendation from academic or professional evaluators; an official high school transcript; official transcripts from all colleges and universities attended; official SAT or ACT scores (applicants may also take the General Studies Admissions Examination); and a nonrefundable application fee of $65.

Students from outside the United States may apply to the School of General Studies to start or complete a baccalaureate degree. In addition to the materials described above, international applicants must submit official TOEFL scores.

Application deadlines are March 1 for early action (non-binding), June 1 for the fall semester, and October 15 for the spring semester. Applicants from countries outside the U.S. are urged to apply by August 15 for the spring semester and April 1 for the fall semester. Applications are reviewed as they are completed, and applicants are notified of decisions shortly thereafter.

For more information, students should contact:

OFFICE OF ADMISSIONS AND FINANCIAL AID

School of General Studies

408 Lewisohn Hall

2970 Broadway

Columbia University, Mail Code 4101

New York, New York 10027

United States

Phone: 212-854-2772

E-mail: gsdegree@columbia.edu

Website: www.gs.columbia.edu

CONCORDIA UNIVERSITY—PORTLAND

Founded in 1905, Concordia University is a Christian, liberal arts university open to students of any faith. We respect diversity, promote spirited dialogue, and integrate faith into every aspect of learning, service, and life.

AT A GLANCE

Think what you can do. Students of any faith can benefit from Concordia's Lutheran approach to higher education. This is a place of challenge and support, where assumptions are tested and encouragement is given, where individual beliefs encounter the ideas of others and become stronger for the contest. Spirited intellectual inquiry and opportunities for community service strengthen our students' commitment to faith, justice, compassion, and moral integrity. The relationships that are formed in the process go beyond the superficial to become lifelong.

LOCATION AND ENVIRONMENT

Centrally located on 14 acres in Northeast Portland, the Concordia campus hums with life. You and your friends can take in movies, go to dances, enjoy live music, or just kick back. Take part in residence hall tournaments and competitive sports. Attend community seminars about current topics. Get involved in the semi-annual service project or one of many community and volunteer opportunities on or around campus.

Living on the Concordia University campus is a great opportunity to make friends and experience college life at its best. Our 4 residence halls have got you covered—every room comes pre-loaded with a micro-fridge, free local phone service, free in-room high-speed Internet access (e-mail account included), and optional cable. In addition, we provide beds, desks, closets, dressers, bookshelves, and a community lounge, with cable television in every hall. Laundry facilities are on-site and the dining hall is just steps away. Concordia University offers a mix of traditional residence halls and apartments that have full kitchens, unfurnished living areas, and furnished bedrooms.

OFF-CAMPUS OPPORTUNITIES

Portland is full of action: NBA basketball, pro hockey, soccer, lacrosse, art galleries, museums, live theater, the symphony, open-air markets, and home-grown coffee shops on every corner. Just an hour to the west, the beautiful Oregon Coast offers miles of pristine beaches. Travel an hour in the other direction and you'll find hiking, fishing, boating, and wind surfing in the scenic Columbia Gorge. Or hit the slopes for snowboarding at Mt. Hood, less than 60 miles away.

MAJORS AND DEGREES OFFERED

Whatever your chosen field of study, you will find that Concordia's Lutheran approach to higher education is liberating, inclusive, and purposeful.

Concordia University has 4 colleges—College of Education; College of Health and Human Services; College of Theology, Arts, and Sciences; and School of Management.

Programs include: business administration, biology, chemistry, Christian education, education, English, health care administration, health and fitness management, history, honors, humanities, interdisciplinary studies, music, nursing, physical therapy, Phi Theta Kappa, professional church work, psychology, social sciences, theology, social work.

Concordia also offers master's degrees in education, business administration, and teaching.

CAMPUS FACILITIES AND EQUIPMENT

In fall of 2009, Concordia will open a new 74,000 square foot Library & Learning Center that will house the library, a coffee shop, classrooms, technology resources, and more. In addition to the university's main academic buildings, Centennial Hall and Luther Hall, Concordia has many other mixed-use spaces on campus. The Fine Arts Building houses a stage, 6 practice studios for music students, and a classroom. Concordia's gymnasium, home to the Cavalier teams, is 33,500 square feet and houses a weight room and cardio equipment for student use in addition to classroom space. Just outside of the gym, are the university's tennis courts, where students can spend some free time hitting the ball, or take a class to learn the sport. In June of 2008, the university will open a world-class Throw Center, where Cavalier athletes, Olympic hopefuls, and area youth will train in the javelin, hammer, discus, and shot put. In 2010, the university will open a new athletics complex that will serve the university's soccer and baseball teams in addition to the entire campus community and its surrounding neighborhood.

TUITION, ROOM, BOARD, AND FEES

Tuition: $21,800

Average fees: $300

Room & board: $6,400

Books & supplies: $800

Transportation: $600

Personal expenses: $1,600

Total: $31,500

FINANCIAL AID

Concordia provides financial assistance to more than 97 percent of our students and the average gift aid for freshmen is more than $10,000. In addition to federal aid, there are student loans and work-study opportunities.

Merit scholarship: Based on cumulative GPA, these scholarships can be awarded regardless of need. They are renewable all 4 years, based on maintaining a certain GPA. Merit scholarships range from $4,000 to $13,500.

Leadership scholarship: This scholarship is geared toward students active in school, church, and community who are planning to be involved in activities at Concordia University. Recipients can receive up to a $1,000 renewable scholarship.

Talent scholarships: Talent scholarships are available in the following areas: choir, handbells, men's and women's basketball, soccer, golf, track & field, cross country, men's baseball, and women's softball and volleyball.

Lutheran scholarship: The following are available: Professional Church Workers (PCW) in a LCMS church, $1,500/year; Sylwester LCMS PCW Family Scholarship (student has a parent who is a PCW), $1,000/year; Lutheran Family Pastor Scholarship (Non-LCMS), $1,000/year; Lutheran High School Graduate, $1,000/year.

Phi Theta Kappa: This scholarship is reserved for transfer students who are active members of Phi Theta Kappa and meet a minimum GPA requirement. These awards start at $6,000.

STUDENT ORGANIZATIONS AND ACTIVITIES

Whether you want to join a touring choir, publish a first-rate literary journal, act for peace and justice, or sharpen your 3-on-3 basketball skills, Concordia University offers plenty of fun and enriching activities to enjoy outside the classroom. There are a variety of clubs and organizations, which include the Accounting Club, Associated Students of Concordia University, Christian Life Ministries, the *Concordia Chronicles* (campus newspaper, Concordia Nerd Alliance, Concordia Teacher Corps, Concordia Theatre Club C3-Concordia Collage Club, CU Film Club, CU Crew (Spirit/Booster Club), Epsilon Pi Delta (Professional Church Workers), Fellowship of Christian Athletes, Hawaiian Club, Health & Sciences Club, HOPE (Helping Other People Every Day), Independent International Mission Club, Intramural Athletics, Music Ensembles, One Voice, Peace Club, Psychology Club, SIFE (Students in Free Enterprise), SIGMA Tau Delta (English Honors Society), Social Work Club, Yoga Club.

Concordia University athletics is recognized as one of the top programs in the National Association of Intercollegiate Athletics (NAIA). The Cavaliers regularly appear in national competitions and enjoy a tradition of leadership in the Cascade Collegiate Conference. Concordia athletic programs create powerful experiences of individual and team success so that students who excel in athletics can apply that experience to excelling in life. We offer baseball (men), basketball (men and women), cross country (men and women), golf (men and women), soccer (men and women), softball (women), track and field (men and women), volleyball (women).

For more information about Concordia's student activities, visit www.cuportland.edu/campuslife.

ADMISSIONS PROCESS

Incoming freshman students are high school graduates and college transfer students with fewer than 12 semester hours or 18 quarter hours of transferable credits. Concordia University has a rolling admission process; however, applications submitted by the following dates are given priority:

Fall semester: May 1

Spring semester: December 1

Summer semester: March 1

The only exception to these deadlines is the Nursing Program; freshman nursing applications are due to the university no later than February 1.

Freshmen may apply online free or may download the print application and submit it with the $40 application fee.

CONNECTICUT COLLEGE

One of the nation's premiere liberal arts colleges, Connecticut College is a small, highly selective, residential, private institution drawing national and international students.

AT A GLANCE

Chartered in 1911, Connecticut College was founded in the spirit of political and social equality, self-determination, and shared governance. The college actively seeks out students who are not only smart and intellectually curious, but who also bring a wide range of life experiences and perspectives that enable this spirit to endure within the college community. The college's near century-old Honor Code defines campus life and is observed by all students, faculty, and staff. Intellectually and academically, the Honor Code inspires students to challenge themselves and their peers to see the world from diverse perspectives, to remain receptive to new ideas and experiences, and, by instilling a sense of mutual respect, to consider how their actions and education may ultimately better the common good. The college offers more than 50 majors and minors and participates in the NCAA Division III New England Small College Athletic Conference (NESCAC). The college is nationally known for career and internship placement and has been called a "college with a conscience," as one of the top schools sending students to Teach for America or the Peace Corp. Enrollment at the college for 2007-2008 is 1,857. In 2007, 5 Connecticut College students were awarded Fulbright scholarships.

LOCATION AND ENVIRONMENT

Connecticut College is located 2 hours from Boston and 2.5 hours from New York City, in historic New London, Connecticut, a small city (pop. 28,000) founded in 1646. The college's 750-acre campus, which is maintained as an arboretum, features a centralized series of granite and limestone buildings adjacent to wooded trails. At the heart of the campus, the Green sweeps down to offer commanding views of Long Island Sound. The college's athletic and fitness center is located along the Thames River.

OFF-CAMPUS OPPORTUNITIES

The college is located convenient to shopping and to the New London transportation center, which features train, bus, and ferry service to points along the eastern seaboard. New London is a diverse community home to numerous restaurants and cafes, galleries, historic sites, and Pfizer's Global Research and Development Center. The college operates a free shuttle service for students to area locations, although students are permitted to have cars on campus. The college's career and volunteer offices work closely with students to arrange for volunteer or internship opportunities. Many students volunteer in local schools or after-school programs and may, in conjunction with course work, receive certification for elementary or secondary education.

MAJORS AND DEGREES OFFERED

Connecticut College offers more than 50 majors and minors, including self-designed study, as part of a liberal arts curriculum designed for intellectual breadth, critical thinking, and acquisition of the fundamental skills and habits of a mind conducive to lifelong inquiry. Courses lead toward a bachelor of arts degree. Students complete general education requirements to ensure broad engagement with the range of disciplines that constitute the liberal arts. Connecticut College students launch their inquiry across disciplines and geographic boundaries and consider the campus and course catalog open to them in this pursuit. The college, for example, offers free music lessons to all students. Through a course of study, students in a variety of majors may become certified for elementary, secondary, music, or private school education, or receive a certificate demonstrating experience in museum studies. The most popular majors at the college are economics, government, English, psychology, international relations, and biological sciences. The college's dance program is internationally reputed, as is its theater program, which offers students the opportunity to study at the Eugene O'Neill Theater Center in Waterford, Connecticut, and/or the Eugene O'Neill Moscow Art Theater in Russia.

ACADEMIC PROGRAMS

Students benefit from small classes that foster discussion and lead to personalized relationships with professors who serve as teacher-scholars. Professors frequently spark the interest that will inspire a student for their lifetime. The faculty to student ratio is 1 to 9. Average class size is 19. First-year students enroll in a seminar course (in which maximum enrollment is 16). Ninety percent of full-time faculty member have a PhD or other terminal degree.

More than half of all students study away in a variety of domestic or international programs. Study away is a crucial component of a Connecticut College education, as it complements and informs a liberal arts curriculum (students who choose to study away do so primarily through the college's affiliation with institutions in more than 40 countries). The college also maintains domestic affiliations, including those with the Williams-Mystic Seaport Program, the Martine Biological Laboratory Ecosystems Center at Woods Hole, and the Twelve College Exchange. In addition, students study away through Connecticut College's Study Away-Teach Away (SATA) program, in which a group of 10 to 15 students and 1 or 2 professors travel overseas and affiliate with a foreign university. SATA programs have been conducted in the Czech Republic, Peru, Egypt, Ghana, Greece, India, Italy, Mexico, Morocco, South Africa, Spain, Tanzania, and Vietnam.

To ensure that students consider the practical application of their study, the college provides each student with $3,000 to fund an internship or a research project between their junior and senior year. About 80 percent of all students attend a series of seminars and work in conjunction with professors and career services to become eligible for the funding. Recent internships have been conducted with such organizations as the Field Museum of Chicago, J. P. Morgan in Hong Kong, Azafady in Madagascar, Vera Wang, New Line Cinema, and CBS Sports.

To illustrate how several areas of study may be fused to best equip a student to understand and resolve complex issues, the college operates a series of interdisciplinary centers. The Centers are certificate-granting programs within the college that serve as an intellectual commons to bring together professors, students, and outside experts. There are 5 centers, each with their own focus: the Toor Cummings Center for International Studies and the Liberal Arts, the Ammerman Center for Arts and Technology, the Holleran Center for Community Action and Public Policy, the Goodwin-Niering Center for Conservation Biology and Environmental Studies, and the Center for the Comparative Study of Race and Ethnicity. Students combine their course work with an integrated project and a paid overseas or domestic internship organized through the center to receive a certificate from their chosen center.

CAMPUS FACILITIES AND EQUIPMENT

Connecticut College occupies 750 acres (all of which is included in the Connecticut College arboretum) on a hill overlooking the Thames River and Long Island Sound. The arboretum's diverse acreage includes the landscaped grounds of the campus as well as the surrounding plant collections and natural areas. The resources of the arboretum support the college's mission of preparing the next generation of citizen leaders to craft a sustainable relationship with the natural world. The symbiosis of the environmental studies major and the Goodwin-Niering Center provides an outstanding model of an ethically and environmentally sound community and places the college in a singular environment that offers a quality of life unique among liberal arts institutions.

Located at the center of the campus, the Charles E. Shain Library consists of more than 600,000 books and bound periodicals, 150,000 media and computing materials, and 2,700 subscriptions to periodicals. The collection is augmented through a consortium with Trinity College and Wesleyan University that provides fast access to more than 2.2 million items.

Other key buildings, include Hale Laboratory; the Frank Loomis Palmer Auditorium; the F. W. Olin Science Center; Dayton Arena; the College Athletic Center; the Lyn and David Silfen Track and Field; and Cummings Arts Center, which includes the Greer Music Library.

In 2007, the college completed $9 million in renovations and will perform $50 million in renovation and construction over the next 10 years. The college announced in 2007 that it will build a new $8 million fitness center overlooking the Thames River. The center will more than triple the amount of exercise and wellness space at the college. Construction is expected to begin in the fall of 2008 and be completed by the fall of 2009.

TUITION, ROOM, BOARD, AND FEES

Tuition, fees, room, and board cost $46,675 in 2007-2008. Housing is guaranteed for all students for 4 years. Ninety-nine percent of students live on campus. There is no Greek system.

FINANCIAL AID

Connecticut College offers need-based financial aid and meets 100 percent of demonstrated need. In 2007, the college awarded $17.8 million in institutional grants. The average aid award was $30,311. In 2006, Connecticut College began eliminating loans and replacing them with grants for students with particular family incomes and expected family contributions. The funding will provide institutional grants to offset loans and reduce them by 50 percent for newly enrolled freshmen beginning in fall 2008.

In addition, the National Science Foundation in 2007 awarded Connecticut College more than $1 million in 4 separate grants. A National Science Foundation S-STEM grant of $513,900 will support under-represented students graduating from Connecticut College with a degree and research experience in chemistry, physics, environmental science, neuroscience, and laboratory-based biological sciences.

STUDENT ORGANIZATIONS AND ACTIVITIES

As a small, residential liberal arts college, Connecticut College encourages students to pursue many interests outside the classroom, with the Crozier-Williams Student Center serving as the main hub for extracurricular activity as the site of club offices, WCNI-FM radio station, the weekly *College Voice* newspaper, and forums for live music, debate, dance, and poetry. Galleries, cafes, and performance spaces are found throughout campus, along with the Tansill Theater, a blackbox theater frequently home to student written productions. Students participate in dozens of clubs and organizations, including the Pegotty Investment Club, the Connecticut College Asian/Asian American Student Association, Students Taking Action Now: Darfur (STAND), Hillel, the Multifaith Student Council, and Habitat for Humanity. Students compete in a range of varsity, club, and intramural sports. The campus LGBTQ Center hosts events focused on issues of sexuality and gender, while Unity House is the campus multicultural center and works with the Dean of Multicultural Affairs to host events focused on issues of race.

ADMISSIONS PROCESS

Connecticut College is one of the nation's most highly selective colleges. In 2006-2007, 34.5 percent of applicants were offered a place in the class of 2011. The college requires the Common Application and Supplement to the Common Application. An interview is recommended but not required. The college does not require the SAT Reasoning Test. An applicant is required to submit either the ACT or scores of 2 SAT Subject Tests. The college expects applicants will have taken the most appropriately rigorous courses available.

Application deadlines: Early Decision I, November 15 for all ED1 application materials; Early Decision II and Regular Decision, December 15 for the Supplement to the Common Application, January 1 for all other application materials. Financial Aid application dates: ED I, November 15; ED II, January 15; Regular Decision, February 1.

CONVERSE COLLEGE

AT A GLANCE

A Converse education serves as a solid foundation for graduate school placements in some of the nation's most renowned programs, launches incredible careers, and develops engaged, adaptable, ethical, and globally aware citizens who effect positive change in the world.

Converse prepares students for advanced study. Ninety percent of Converse applicants are accepted to medical school on their first attempt and have been consistently accepted for the last 20 years. One hundred percent of Converse applicants are accepted to veterinary school and have been consistently accepted for the past 5 years. One hundred percent of Converse applicants are accepted into pharmacy school programs and have been consistently accepted for the past 30 years. Eighty-five percent of Converse applicants are accepted into law schools on their first attempt. One hundred percent of Converse education majors pass their Praxis II certification exam. Ninety-five percent of survey respondents either have a job or a graduate school placement upon graduation from Converse.

Converse scores among nation's top colleges in 2007 National Survey of Student Engagement (NSSE).

Results of the 2007 NSSE, the most comprehensive assessment of effective practices in higher education, demonstrate that a Converse College education prepares young women for the dynamic demands of the professions, workplaces, and communities that await them in the twenty-first century. In fact, Converse students evaluated their overall educational experience as excellent at nearly twice the rate of students at other NSSE institutions. Converse exceeded the national average in all 5 benchmarks of excellence: level of academic challenge, active and collaborative learning, student-faculty interaction, enriching educational experiences, and supportive campus environment.

Converse scored in the top 10 percent of colleges in the nation for providing enriching educational experiences. Compared with the national average, Converse freshmen are twice as likely to ask questions or contribute to class discussions; twice as many Converse students discuss their career plans with faculty; more than twice as many Converse students study abroad; nearly twice as many students study a foreign language; twice as many Converse freshmen interact with faculty on activities other than course work; twice as many Converse students receive regular feedback from faculty on academic performance.

Converse also received high scores on encouraging students to take advantage of cultural and social opportunities: twice as many Converse seniors say they often attend music and theater performances, art exhibits, athletic events, guest lectures, etc.; twice as many Converse freshmen discuss ideas from classes with others outside of class at nearly twice the national average; 66 percent of Converse students say they often have serious conversations with students of a different race or ethnicity of their own.

LOCATION AND ENVIRONMENT

Converse is located in the heart of downtown Spartanburg, South Carolina, a college town with 6 colleges that collaboratively offer social and academic events for the city's 14,000 college students.

The Upstate region is commonly dubbed as South Carolina's melting pot, blending diversity with Southern hospitality. Spartanburg offers a culturally rich community with beautiful scenery, historically significant sites, and a plentiful supply of arts events.

More than 100 international firms—including German automaker BMW—make Spartanburg an international and cultural center. The city offers a multitude of internship and job placement opportunities, and local and regional companies visit the campus each year to recruit Converse graduates.

The Blue Ridge Parkway, Great Smoky Mountains, Asheville, Atlanta, Charleston, Charlotte, and Myrtle Beach are all within a short drive. Greenville-Spartanburg International Airport, located 20 minutes west of the city, is served by 6 major airlines.

OFF-CAMPUS OPPORTUNITIES

Converse students can travel the world in their educational pursuits with full-year and semester-long study-abroad programs that promote research at colleges and universities in Australia, England, France, Iceland, Spain, and many other countries. Fifty percent of our undergraduates have participated in study-travel.

Through the college's Office of Career Services, students can gain real world experience through high powered internships with organizations like NASA, Entertainment Tonight, Merrill Lynch, the National Endowment for the Arts, and the Oak Ridge National Laboratory. Converse guarantees each student an internship and 70 percent of our students complete at least 1 internship during their time here. Many students complete 2 or more internships.

Converse students who conduct independent and collaborative research are often invited to present their findings at national and regional professional conferences and frequently have their work published in major scholarly journals.

ACADEMIC PROGRAMS

The Nisbet Honors Program provides academically gifted students with opportunities to learn in specially designed honors seminars, conduct independent research with faculty mentors, meet nationally known visiting scholars, and gather socially to discuss intellectually challenging topics.

The college's academic calendar includes a 4-week January term designed to encourage students to participate in study/travel, internships, interdisciplinary courses, and other learning opportunities both inside and outside the classroom. January term also provides faculty with opportunities for innovative course design and collaborative teaching.

MAJORS AND DEGREES OFFERED

Converse offers bachelor of arts, bachelor of science, bachelor of fine arts, and bachelor of music degrees. Students can tailor their course of study through the individualized major program, in which they design an interdisciplinary degree program linking academic interests from at least 3 disciplines. Most Converse graduates earn their degrees within 4 years, and 55 percent double major.

The College of Arts and Sciences offers majors in accounting, art (art education, art history, art therapy, interior design, and studio art), biology, business, business administration (economics, finance, human resource management, international business, and marketing), chemistry, biochemistry, computer science, creative and professional writing, education (comprehensive special education, deaf and hard of hearing/interpreting, early childhood, educable mentally handicapped, elementary, emotionally handicapped, learning disabilities, and secondary), engineering, English, foreign language (French, German, and Spanish), history, mathematics, modern languages, politics, psychology, religion, and theater. Pre-professional programs include dentistry, law, medicine, ministry, nursing, pharmacy, arts management, publication and media, and Army ROTC. Converse also offers a 3+2 dual-degree engineering program in conjunction with Clemson University.

Converse is the only women's college in the country to be named a Steinway School. Music majors include composition, music business, music education, music history, music therapy, performance, piano pedagogy, and theory. The Petrie School of Music's bachelor of music therapy degree program combines the fields of music, education, and psychology with on-site clinical work.

CAMPUS FACILITIES AND EQUIPMENT

The 70-acre campus includes 7 residence halls (each with a community advisor and resident counselor), 6 academic buildings, a student center and an athletic complex.

Located in the heart of the Converse campus, Montgomery Student Center is the hub for all student life activities. It houses the Daniels Center, the wireless hotspot Sneakers cyber caf and Loafers—a game room with plasma screen televisions office space for student government organizations, a fitness center, the offices of Campus Life and Career Services, the college bookstore, the Gibbs Chapel, and the campus post office.

Phifer Science Hall is a 36,000-square-foot facility specifically designed for instruction in the natural sciences. Dynamic teaching methods and the latest technology are integrated into science instruction via smart classrooms and laboratories. Science majors are provided space for upper-level research and advanced learning opportunities. Converse has also recently added a new physics lab, as well as a DNA sequencer and DNA analysis software.

Blackman Hall is home to the Petrie School of Music, and houses more than 30 practice rooms, 75 Steinway pianos, soundproof classrooms, faculty teaching studios, an electronic piano lab, and a music media lab with Macintosh computers. Daniel Recital Hall, a 340-seat auditorium cited in Chamber Music America as an exemplary performance facility, is also located in Blackman Hall.

The Physical Activity Complex houses courts for basketball and volleyball, a fully equipped fitness training room, locker rooms, coaches' offices, a regulation-sized soccer field, and tennis courts.

The Milliken Fine Arts Building is equipped with painting and drawing studios, a CAD and interior design lab, darkrooms, ceramic kiln and sculpture yards, and a historic preservation studio. A permanent collection of more than 100 prints, photographs, and other works by such artists as Joan Mir , Salvador Dali, Helmut Newton, and Andy Warhol is on display in the facility, enhancing the student experience of art. Milliken Gallery is filled with works by a wide variety of professional and student artists throughout the year.

The fully automated Mickel Library is a powerful resource for Converse students. With 150,000 books, subscriptions to more than 4,500 periodicals, 18,000 electronic journals, and an interlibrary loan system, virtually any publication is at students' fingertips. The Gwathmey Music Library is one of the largest music libraries in the Southeast.

TUITION, ROOM, BOARD, AND FEES

For 2008-2009, tuition will be $24,500 and room and board will be $7,550.

FINANCIAL AID

More than 90 percent of Converse students receive some form of financial assistance through scholarships, federal student assistance programs, loans, and work-study programs. Converse awards $7 million each year in scholarships for academics, music, visual arts, theater, the natural sciences and math, athletics, and leadership. These merit-based awards do not require the FAFSA, and are renewable for 3 additional years. Scholarships and grant awards range up to the full comprehensive fee. A scholarship calculator is available on the Converse Website.

South Carolina residents may also qualify for South Carolina state scholarships and/or grants, such as Palmetto Fellows, the Life and Hope Scholarships, and the Tuition Grant program. The Free Application for Federal Student Aid (FAFSA) must be submitted by students who wish to be considered for need-based loans and grants.

STUDENT ORGANIZATIONS AND ACTIVITIES

Converse is all about women, and leadership opportunities on campus abound with more than 60 student organizations. The Converse Student Government Association (SGA) is the second oldest in the Southeast. In addition, a big sister/little sister mentor program begins in the freshman year and often creates life-long friendships. Student can take advantage of concerts, cultural events, and sporting events on campus as well as the numerous opportunities to have fun and meet people in a metropolitan area of 250,000 people.

ADMISSIONS PROCESS

Priority deadline for freshmen admission: April 1

Priority deadline for freshmen scholarships: February 1

Priority deadline for transfer scholarships: April 1

Candidate reply deadline for enrollment deposit: May 1 (freshmen only)

Sixteen units of high school academic work are recommended. Admissions criteria in addition to high school transcripts, SAT or ACT scores include a personal essay, the teacher or guidance counselor recommendation, extracurricular activities, and demonstrated exceptional talent. Converse participates in the Advanced Placement program administered by the College Entrance Examination Board, and accepts credits earned through dual enrollment or through participation in the International Baccalaureate program.

Transfer students are accepted each academic term from accredited institutions. Scholarships are available to transfer students.

To begin the application process, students must send a completed application for admission, an official transcript of at least 6 semesters of secondary school, official SAT or ACT scores (for freshmen), a teacher or counselor recommendation form, and a graded writing sample. Admissions information and an online application are available from the Converse Website.

Send inquiries to:

Office of Admissions

Converse College

580 East Main Street

Spartanburg, South Carolina 29302

United States

Telephone: 864-596-9040 or 800-766-1125 (toll free)

E-mail: admissions@converse.edu

Website: www.converse.edu

CORCORAN COLLEGE OF ART AND DESIGN

AT A GLANCE

The Corcoran College of Art + Design is dedicated to providing an excellent education in the visual arts and to promoting the value of the visual arts in the human experience. Through degree programs, continuing education, and community outreach, the College prepares students to become productive artists and designers. In pursuit of its philosophy, the College is inextricably linked to the Corcoran Museum of Art. The symbiotic partnership between the College and the Museum benefits both institutions by presenting unique educational opportunities and creating a vibrant community of artists, scholars, designers, museum professionals, and educators. As the only museum-school in Washington, and the only accredited art college in the District of Columbia, the Corcoran plays a distinct role in the artistic life of the nation's Capital.

There is a long tradition of partnership between art schools and museums; a logical relationship when one considers the extraordinary opportunity shared by students and faculty in a museum environment. Surrounded by great art and frequently by the contemporary masters whose work is regularly exhibited, the atmosphere of a museum art school is charged by the excitement of direct contact with the world of art. The Corcoran College of Art and Design is special, for it remains one of America's very few examples of a "pure" museum art school by maintaining its original relationship to one of Washington's greatest museums.

LOCATION AND ENVIRONMENT

Washington is a city of monuments, set off by the classical architecture of government buildings, parks, trees, and greenery, all enhanced by a climate of long, balmy fall and spring seasons. With 16 major colleges and universities in the metropolitan area, there exists a feeling of a giant "campus" in which restaurants, coffee shops, movie theaters, and nightspots are intermingled with bookstores, clothing boutiques, and academic facilities. A short walk from the Corcoran brings us to the world famous Mall, ringed by museums, galleries, and the country's most distinguished monuments. Not only is the mall the physical center of our nation's cultural history, it is one of the world's largest playgrounds: an ideal spot for jogging, biking, picnicking, kite-flying, or a simple morning stroll. Within a mile, there exist numerous beacons of quality and innovation in the performing arts, such as the Kennedy Center, Ford's Theater, and the National Theater. Washington remains the center of world power as well as a cultural and intellectual capital.

OFF-CAMPUS OPPORTUNITIES

Student life at the Corcoran is closely linked to the life of the Washington, D.C. community. The city becomes an extended campus and offers limitless opportunities for cultural, social, artistic, academic, and professional growth. With numerous internships and jobs for college students available in the metropolitan area, this community is a magnet for young people from across the country and the world.

Corcoran is a member of the Association of Independent Colleges of Art and Design (AICAD), a consortium of 35 art colleges from across the country (www.aicad.org). AICAD's mobility program allows students from any of the member schools to spend a semester at another AICAD college of their choice. Students in good standing who have met the academic requirements may apply for mobility for the fall semester of their junior year. Enrollment is based on space availability at the host institution.

The Corcoran is actively pursuing partnerships with colleges in other countries where students may study abroad for short periods of time. Current affiliations include The University of Georgia Studies Abroad Program in Cortona, Italy; the Studio Art Centers International (SACI) in Florence, Italy; and the Canberra School of Art, The Australian National University, in Canberra, Australia.

The Corcoran is a member of the Washington Consortium, a group of DC colleges and universities who have joined together to provide a broad range of opportunities and resources to its students. Corcoran students may take classes at many of the area schools to extend their already rich curricular offerings.

In addition, opportunities are available through the Corcoran Museum to travel across the country and abroad as well as to nonaffiliated institutions through study programs that vary by year.

MAJORS AND DEGREES OFFERED

Whether your goal is to become a fine artist, a photographer, a designer, or an art educator, the Corcoran College of Art + Design will help you navigate a path for your future by immersing you in a professional educational experience with extraordinary cultural resources in the world's most important capital city.

The Corcoran is an innovative leader in visual arts education. Our renowned faculty includes some of the most active, cutting-edge artists, designers and photographers in the country. The College emphasizes a conservatory approach to education, which means classes are small, professors are accessible, and classmates know one another.

The College offers the Bachelor of Fine Arts degree in the following majors: art education, fine art, graphic design, digital media design, interior design, photojournalism, and photography. Studio art courses comprise 65 percent of the BFA degree requirements, with the remaining degree credits earned in academic disciplines such as art history, writing, and humanities. Graduate degrees are offered in art education, decorative arts, exhibition design, and interior design.

ACADEMIC PROGRAMS

In the first year of study, students follow a unified and structured Foundation Program developing essential visual and technical skills in a wide variety of media. A distinctive aspect of the Corcoran's Foundation program is team-teaching in several studio courses, encouraging maximum participation, interchange, and dialogue between students and faculty. Students are exposed to multiple points of view to promote independent thinking, expand perceptual phenomena, and build an artistic vocabulary.

Students select a major in the second year choosing between fine art, graphic design, interior design, teaching (art education), photojournalism, and photography. Sophomore studio courses are designed to bridge the ongoing development of technical skills and the increasing personal knowledge of artistic expression. Conceptual abilities are also challenged by academic requirements in art history and humanities.

In the junior and senior year, the focus shifts towards one's personal vision, individual initiative, and professional development. Internships, individual projects, directed studies, and advanced academic and studio electives hone each student's specific career goals. The degree studies culminate in formal exhibitions of senior thesis projects in a formal gallery of the Corcoran Museum of Art.

CAMPUS FACILITIES AND EQUIPMENT

The Corcoran College of Art and Design' downtown campus is located a block from the White House in the heart of Washington, D.C. The Georgetown campus is home to interior design, graphic design, and foundations courses. Georgetown houses our state-of-the-art computer laboratories of the Corcoran Computer Graphics Institute. Student services, the library, tutoring resource center, classrooms, and faculty offices are housed at our downtown campus. All students will have the opportunity to take classes at both of our campuses.

The Corcoran library provides students with access to a collection of over 20,000 volumes; 45,000 slides; and a large periodical and artists' book collection. Resource equipment includes televisions, video cassette recorder, video camera, slide equipment, typewriter, copier, and a variety of computer equipment for word processing, scanning, printing, and Internet access.

The College is within easy walking distance of several desirable Washington neighborhoods. Corcoran Housing is conveniently located between the downtown and Georgetown campuses. DC Suites at the Pennsylvania House provides fully furnished studios and one-bedroom apartments for undergraduate and graduate students. Fully secured, and with laundry, gym, and parking facilities, the housing provides a good option for students to partake in traditional college life.

Starting fall 2011, the Corcoran will expand to a new building in Southwest Washington, the historic Randall School building. The building will incorporate approximately 100,000 square feet of college art and will serve as the Corcoran's third College campus. It will be the home of undergraduate classroom and studio space for many of the equipment-intensive subject areas, such as sculpture and ceramics, as well as student exhibition space. Classes will continue to be taught at both the Seventeenth Street (Gallery) and Georgetown sites.

TUITION, ROOM, BOARD AND FEES

Tuition for the 2007–2008 academic year is $25,890 for all full-time students taking 12 to 18 credits per semester. Room and board is $10,795 and required fees are $200. Expenses for books and art supplies are estimated at $2,500 annually but will vary with personal preference.

The Corcoran participates in many federal and state loan and grant programs. Our merit scholarship program awards a wide range of awards to students based on academic and artistic achievement.

FINANCIAL AID

Admission to Corcoran is need-blind, and we are committed to assisting students with their educational expenses throughout their undergraduate careers. Over 70 percent of our students receive some form of financial aid, including need- and merit-based scholarships. Corcoran participates in all of the major financial aid programs offered by the U.S. Department of Education and provides institutional funds to supplement federal or state financial aid. We provide a payment plan through Academic Management Services as well as information about other options for our students to meet their educational expenses.

The Corcoran College of Art and Design is committed to helping students meet their educational expenses and encourages potentially eligible students to apply for financial aid as soon after January 1 as possible. Application for financial aid must be made each year. While there is no deadline for application, priority consideration is given to new and continuing students who apply by March 1.

Given the complex nature of the financial aid system, assumptions about eligibility should not be made prior to a consultation and careful review with the Director of Financial Aid 202-639-1851.

STUDENT ORGANIZATIONS AND ACTIVITIES

The staff of the Office of Student Affairs helps students to take advantage of this unique city-campus and career life as a student-artist. Career services, medical insurance, housing, international student services, a job bank, special need services, and personal/professional counseling are available. In addition, Student Services sponsors a wide variety of educational, career, cultural, and social events and activities throughout the year, including the Student Activities Programming Board, the publication of an online student newsletter, and student-sponsored art shows and sales. As museum members from the outset, students are able to take advantage of numerous special opportunities in the arts offered by the Corcoran Museum of Art.

ADMISSIONS PROCESS

The Corcoran College of Art and Design enrolls approximately 350 full-time students in the four-year BFA program. Students from more than 20 countries and 25 states attend the Corcoran, contributing to the cultural, ethnic, and artistic diversity of the College community. We seek applications from candidates who are committed to the professional study of the visual arts and demonstrate artistic, as well as intellectual talent. As a rolling admission institution, we review applications year-round for programs beginning in the fall or spring semesters.

The Admissions Committee prioritizes their review of applications beginning with the candidate's academic record (high school and college/university); a portfolio of artwork; personal attributes (interview, recommendations, essays, extracurricular activities); and official results of standardized tests such as the SAT I, ACT, or the TOEFL. All applicants are encouraged to contact our office to arrange for a campus tour, personal interview, and portfolio review. Portfolios may be submitted on slides, CD, or DVD. Candidates may also meet with our representatives for interviews and portfolio reviews during National Portfolio Days, which are held nationally (www.npda.org), or by appointment as we travel across the country for high school visits and college fairs.

CORNELL COLLEGE

AT A GLANCE

A national liberal arts college with a distinctive One-Course-At-A-Time (block) academic calendar, Cornell College offers one extraordinary opportunity after another, in the classroom, on campus, and in the world.

Cornell's extraordinary opportunities in the classroom are grounded in the college's commitment to the liberal arts. Faculty members serve as mentors as well as teachers and work closely with students to nurture intellectual growth and creativity. Students are challenged to seek new ideas, delve into complex issues, achieve new levels of understanding, and present ideas clearly.

Extraordinary opportunities on the campus help Cornell students develop their capacity to lead and serve. As a residential college of 1,200 students, Cornell offers students the opportunity to develop the full array of their skills in living and learning experiences outside the classroom. In activities that include athletics, intramurals, student government, student activities, the arts, and spiritual life, students grow physically, socially, and emotionally. They learn important lessons about the responsibilities of living in a community, of caring for self and others.

Extraordinary opportunities in the world are possible because One-Course-At-A-Time allows classes to be mobile. Faculty and student are free to study away from campus, in whatever venues best suit the subject. In addition, international study prepares Cornell students for living, leading, and serving in a world of intense and regular global interaction. Cornell is committed to enabling as many students as possible to spend some time engaged in academic work outside of the United States, producing graduates who can contribute to positive change in a global society.

A diverse student body from 45 states and 16 countries is enrolled at Cornell, which is situated atop a hill overlooking the Cedar River valley. Centered on a pedestrian mall, the campus covers 129 acres and has more than 40 buildings.

Ninety-five percent of Cornell graduates complete their degree programs in four years or less, half with a double major. Two-thirds earn an advanced degree at many of the nation's finest universities.

LOCATION AND ENVIRONMENT

Cornell College is located in Mount Vernon, Iowa. Cornell students believe the college's location provides the best of both worlds—a classically beautiful campus in a small college town minutes from Cedar Rapids and Iowa City. These two metropolitan areas contain three additional colleges and universities and 350,000 people. Cornell is 15 minutes from Cedar Rapids (airport, movies, and malls) and 20 minutes from Iowa City, the home of the University of Iowa. Cornell students can find great hiking and camping in some of Iowa's lovely river bluff state parks, including the nearby Palisades Kepler.

The State of Iowa is aptly nicknamed the Heartland, since it actually is the regional center of the United States. A number of Midwestern metropolitan areas such as Chicago, St. Louis, the Twin Cities, Kansas City, and Milwaukee lie within a half-day's drive. Block breaks of almost five days open the way to more ambitious adventures within a day's drive: Michigan's Upper Peninsula; Minnesota's gorgeous Lake Superior North Shore; the ski resorts of Colorado; and the Missouri-Arkansas Ozarks, to name just a few.

OFF-CAMPUS OPPORTUNITIES

Student internship experiences can be central to understanding the realities, demands, and rewards of the workplace. Internships arranged within Cornell's One-Course-At-A-Time academic calendar have a clear advantage in opportunity and placement over those arranged within a semester system. Students are able to become immersed in the experience every day for an entire month and, as a result, can be assigned engaging and meaningful projects as part of their internship. In addition to internships in the local region, the competitive Alumni Fellows program provides distinctive internship experiences with a stipend, enabling Cornell students to pursue their career interests across the nation and around the world.

Through Cornell courses abroad and college-affiliated off-campus programs, students may study and travel in other countries and become acquainted with other cultures. Cornell students may elect to have a study-abroad experience for one or two terms, a semester, or a full academic year.

MAJORS AND DEGREES OFFERED

Cornell College awards the Bachelor of Arts, Bachelor of Music, Bachelor of Philosophy, and Bachelor of Special Studies degrees. Majors are offered in art, biochemistry and molecular biology, biology, chemistry, classical studies, computer science, economics and business, elementary and secondary education, English, environmental studies, French, geology, German, history, international business, international relations, Latin American studies, mathematics, medieval and Renaissance studies, music education (general, instrumental, and vocal), music performance, philosophy, physical education, physics, politics, psychology, religion, Russian, Russian studies, sociology, sociology and anthropology, Spanish, theater, theater and speech, and women's studies. Pre-law and premedicine programs are available, as are programs to prepare for graduate study in social work/human services and theology. Students may design their own interdisciplinary majors.

Combined-degree programs include a 3-2 program in forestry and environmental management offered in cooperation with Duke University, 3-2 programs in engineering and a 3-4 program in architecture with Washington University in St. Louis.

ACADEMIC PROGRAMS

To increase the focus and flexibility of a Cornell education, the college's academic calendar incorporates the One-Course-At-A-Time schedule. Cornell divides the traditional September–May academic year into nine 3 1/2-week terms. During each term, students concentrate on one course chosen from the more than 60 offered and take one final examination. Students take eight terms per year, which leaves a ninth term free for internships, off-campus programs, independent study, rest and relaxation, or another course.

The college's emphasis on One-Course-At-A-Time enhances the learning experience for students, allowing them increased contact with faculty members, no interference from competing courses, and greater efficiency of study. It also provides timely feedback to students about their progress. In addition, the pressure of having to prepare for several courses and examinations at the same time is eliminated.

Another liberalizing feature of One-Course-At-A-Time is the possibility of having classes meet for periods longer or shorter than the typical 50-minute period. Professors may opt to divide the day into a series of short meetings, with work assignments given and completed from one session to the next. Laboratories are not necessarily limited to one afternoon. Faculty members are also able to take students on daylong field trips or teach their courses off campus, either in the United States or abroad.

Cornell's student/faculty ratio of 13:1 enables its exceptional faculty to provide students with highly personalized attention. Classes are capped at no more than 25 students. Students choose from more than 40 majors or create individualized majors; and two-thirds graduate with double majors or a major plus a minor. Internships and study abroad programs are also common pursuits, as OCAAT provides a powerful and flexible structure for off-campus study.

CAMPUS FACILITIES AND EQUIPMENT

Cornell's entire campus has been designated a National Historic District, and its carefully restored nineteenth-century academic architecture is combined with contemporary facilities. King Chapel is the historic landmark of the campus, has a 130-foot clock tower, and a main auditorium accommodating up to 1,600 and featuring a Moller organ with 3,800 pipes.

Cole Library includes more than 120,000 volumes, an extensive serials collection, and a suite of online databases to provide information to support Cornell's curriculum. It also houses the Teaching and Learning Center, featuring the Academic Media Studio, Quantitative Reasoning Studio, and Writing Studio. Students may also take advantage of the Humanities Lab located in College Hall.

Law Hall Technology Center offers among other resources a statistics classroom and psychology research and observation rooms. In addition, the campus is fully wired, with numerous "smart" classrooms and internet access in every residence hall room. Wireless access is available in key campus locations.

Facilities and equipment in West Science Center include a Cadaver Lab, renovated greenhouse, computerized and hydrogen-alpha solar telescopes, NMR spectrometer, HPLC, cell culture, X-ray diffraction machine, wet chemistry lab, alpha spectrometer, radon extraction/detection unit, electronic beam luminoscope, virtual physics instrumentation, and Fourier transform real-time spectrum analyzer. Norton Geology Center houses a Geographic Information Systems Lab, rock and fossil preparation laboratory, and the Anderson Geology Museum.

The college recently completed over a 16 million-dollar enhancement of its fine arts facilities, fully renovating Armstrong Hall and McWethy Hall and adding the state-of-the-art 265-seat Kimmell Theatre in Youngker Hall.

Athletic facilities include historic Ash Park (football) Stadium with an eight-lane all-weather track as well as soccer, baseball, softball, and intramural fields. The Richard and Norma Small Multi-Sport Center equipped with a 2,000-seat gymnasium for basketball, wrestling, and volleyball; the Meyer Strength Training Facility; fitness training room; six-lane, 200-meter indoor track; batting cages and hitting nets; racquetball courts; and multipurpose courts for basketball, volleyball, and tennis.

The Commons is where students dine, socialize, buy books, and pick up their mail. They also gather for activity on the Orange Carpet, a traditional meeting place where the carpet is, well, bright orange. The building also contains the Roe Howard Fitness Center; Ratt Coffeehouse; classrooms, conference and activities rooms; offices for student government, volunteer services, KRNL-FM, The Cornellian student newspaper and Royal Purple yearbook.

Cornell has ten residence halls and offers many room options from Living and Learning Communities to singles, doubles, triples, suites, and apartments.

TUITION, ROOM, BOARD AND FEES

The comprehensive cost for 2006–2007 is $31,460, including tuition, fees, and room and board.

FINANCIAL AID

Cornell College has been identified as one of the nation's "best value" undergraduate institutions by The Princeton Review in the 2006 edition of its book, America's Best Value Colleges. Cornell is committed to making higher education financially accessible to qualified students. Need-based financial assistance is determined by the FAFSA, which should be completed no later than March 1. An early financial aid evaluation is available from the college upon request.

Cornell's competitive scholarship program includes academic scholarships ranging from $10,000 to $20,000 per year. Performance arts, Methodist, and Academic and Community Enrichment (ACE) scholarships are also offered.

STUDENT ORGANIZATIONS AND ACTIVITIES

Cornell students are known for their independence, social consciousness, and sense of adventure, whether it's in the classroom or in the myriad activities they pursue. Cornell is a place where you'll develop lifelong friendships and be given the opportunity to explore new interests amid a diverse campus community that values individual and cultural differences. Approximately 90 percent of students reside on campus, contributing to a strong sense of community.

Students participate actively in the governance of the college, serving on faculty-student committees, the Student Senate, the Residence Hall Council, and the Performing Arts and Activities Council. There are more than 100 clubs, organizations, and special interest groups on campus. A strong ethic of service is rooted in the fact that Cornell students are cause-oriented and globally aware. Student-athletes compete in 19 sports in the Iowa Intercollegiate Athletic Conference, regarded as one of the nation's finest NCAA Division III conferences.

ADMISSIONS PROCESS

Admission to Cornell is selective. Applicants are judged on their high school records, test scores, interests, and achievements in such co-curricular activities as debate, student government, music, theater, athletics, and school publications as well as through personal recommendations and, in some cases, interviews. These are not exclusive criteria. Motivation, energy, and persistence are basic to Cornell. Students with the desire to succeed at Cornell and an enthusiasm for learning may apply with confidence, knowing that these are important factors in the admission decision.

Cornell College offers several application plans: Early Decision (November 1 deadline); Early Action (December 1 deadline); and Regular Decision (March 1 deadline). Students may also apply online at http://applyweb.com/apply/cornia/menu.html. Cornell also accepts The Common Application consortium, www.commonapp.org.

COTTEY COLLEGE

AT A GLANCE

Cottey College, a 2-year, independent, liberal arts college, educates women to be contributing members of a global society through a challenging curriculum and a dynamic campus experience. In our diverse and supportive environment, women develop their potential for personal and professional lives of intellectual engagement and thoughtful action as learners, leaders, and citizens.

Cottey was founded in 1884 by Virginia Alice Cottey who believed that women deserved the same educational opportunities as men. Virginia Alice and her sisters pooled their $3,000 life savings to establish their school. On September 8, 1884, Vernon Seminary, as it was called then, opened with 28 students in a 2-story red brick schoolhouse.

Virginia Alice was intimately invested in the success of her school. Because of her personal interest and involvement, the locals refused to call the school Vernon Seminary. It was the "Cottey sisters' school," or Cottey College. In 1887, the school was chartered by the State of Missouri as Cottey College and produced its first collegiate graduate, Olive Gatewood.

When Virginia Alice joined the PEO Sisterhood in 1926, she realized how similar the goals of the 2 organizations were. In 1927, she gave her college to the Sisterhood, which made it the only nonsectarian college owned and supported by women. The PEO Sisterhood, a philanthropic education organization of almost 250,000 members, is dedicated to providing excellent educational opportunities for women. Today Cottey's campus comprises 14 buildings on 11 city blocks and a 33-acre wooded recreation area with a lodge. The residential student capacity of 350 students typically represents 40 states and 10 to 14 international countries annually. The campus and the times may have changed, but the principles of a Cottey education have not. Cottey still emphasizes high academic standards with unique opportunities for personal growth through residential, cultural, and intellectual experiences.

LOCATION AND ENVIRONMENT

Cottey is located in Nevada, Missouri, a town of approximately 9,000 residents. The local climate offers pleasant falls, mild winters, and colorful springs as campus community gardens burst into bloom. Nevada has become the hub for recreational, educational, and medical amenities for the area.

Of course there are also beautiful city parks, roller skating, and bowling facilities, a 6-screen movie theater, active community theater and choir group, a newly redesigned water park/swimming pool, and an excellent YMCA facility.

To learn more about Nevada and Vernon County, we encourage you to visit the official site of the Nevada/Vernon County Chamber of Commerce, www.visitnevadamo.com/, and the official City of Nevada site, www.nevadamo.org/index.htm.

Nevada is a great place to call home during your 2 years at Cottey.

OFF-CAMPUS OPPORTUNITIES

More than 35 clubs and organizations at Cottey represent our students' interests in academics, culture, recreation, social concerns, religion, and volunteerism. With all these groups, there are plenty of leadership positions that need to be filled each year. Cottey is a veritable leadership lab where young women like you can gain valuable leadership experiences that will help shape your future, your education, and your career path. You'll also be a part of helping to shape student life at Cottey, while developing leadership skills and self-confidence in new areas.

Many students also become involved in the programs at Cottey's Helen and George Washburn Center for Women's Leadership, which was established to build girl's and women's lives through enrichment, education, and leadership development. The CWL not only brings in special guest lecturers and notable speakers, but Cottey students can also get leadership certification through the LEO (Leadership, Experiences, Opportunity) program, which provides student leaders with an opportunity to document and receive recognition for their experiences inside and outside the classroom and further develop leadership skills. The LEO program offers 4 levels of certification. Approximately 60 students participate in the LEO program annually. Participation in LEO enables students to discover their own leadership style. LEO allows students to connect with women leaders both on campus and in the community. In LEO, students focus on the leadership aspects of the activities they are already doing. The Center for Women's Leadership hosts special events for LEO students, including dinners, guest speakers, and trips to cultural events. Throughout the year students participate in a variety of enrichment events and workshops to reach their LEO goals. Cottey offers a credit course on leadership team taught by Cottey's president and other faculty members.

This year, Cottey students participated in a 1-hour credit service learning course, which involved a trip to Guatemala.

"Being a leader, being a woman in a man's world does not mean you need to be a man or act like one. You should use your skills and the talents you have as a woman to lead others."

—Stephanie Mosbrucker, participant in the Presidential Leadership Program

MAJORS AND DEGREES OFFERED

Associate in arts, associate in science.

ACADEMIC PROGRAMS

Academic departments: anthropology & sociology, art, biology, business and economics, chemistry, computer science, dance, education, English, foreign languages, history & political science, international relations, journalism, mass communication, mathematics, music, philosophy & religion, physical education, physics & astronomy, psychology, theater/speech.

Learning opportunities: leadership, learning communities, internships.

CAMPUS FACILITIES AND EQUIPMENT

The campus occupies 14 buildings on 11 city blocks, and a 33-acre wooded recreational area with lodge.

TUITION, ROOM, BOARD, AND FEES

For 2008-09, total cost at Cottey is $19,360. This includes:

Tuition: $13,200

Room and board:° $5,400

Student activity fee: $300

Technology fee: $150

Telephone fee: $130

Student Health Service fee: $180

° For PEO and Reeves residents. Students living in Robertson Hall add $500 to annual cost. Also, there is an additional $600 charge for single rooms in any residence hall

Families may elect pay the balance remaining after financial aid in full each semester or make monthly payments with a 1 percent monthly interest charge.

Fall semester payment due dates: August 15, September 15, October 15

Spring semester payment due dates: December 15, January 15 , February 15

FINANCIAL AID

The financial aid staff is committed to helping students and their families understand and navigate the financial aid process. We know you are concerned about financing a college education. The good news is that Cottey has been able to remain affordable due to our strong financial foundation, endowment, and the continued financial support of the PEO Sisterhood, a philanthropic educational organization dedicated solely to furthering education for women. A Cottey degree is a smart investment.

We offer a comprehensive program of financial assistance options, including scholarships, grants, student employment, and loans.

More than $4.5 million in financial aid was awarded to our students in 2007-08. Typically, 97 percent of Cottey students receive some kind of financial aid. The average financial aid package for the 2007-08 academic year was almost $14,800.

STUDENT ORGANIZATIONS AND ACTIVITIES

The coordinator of campus activities and calendar works with student organization officers and sponsors, other college faculty and staff, and numerous agents and performers to schedule and promote activities events on campus. The coordinator also organizes student developmental programming, provides support to student organizations and sponsors, conducts leadership training, and coordinates individual and series ticket sales.

Campus clubs and organizations: AIDS Activists Coming Together (AACT), Alpha Mu Gamma, Anime,

Associated Cottey College Artists (ACCA), BACCHUS (Boosting Alcohol Consciousness Concerning the Health of University Students), Class Organizations: Senior Class and Freshman Class, Cottey Big Sisters,

Cottey College Handbell Choir, Cottey Computer Club (CCC), Cottey Diversity Corps, Cottey Intramural Association (CIA), Delta Psi Omega (national honorary dramatics fraternity), Explorer's Club (participates in such activities as camping, cookouts, canoeing, rock climbing, etc.), Feminist Majority Foundation, Golden Key (Cottey's honorary service organization), International Friendship Circle (IFC), Intersociety,

InterVarsity Christian Fellowship, Japanese Club, Mu Sigma Epsilon (campus honorary music society),

Phi Beta Lambda (collegiate level association of student members preparing for a career in business), Phi Theta Kappa (Epsilon Chapter) (national scholastic honorary society for 2-year colleges), Prayer Shawl Ministry, Pride Alliance (GLBTS), Psi Beta (national honor society in psychology and sociology), Residence Hall Organizations (PEO Hall, Reeves Hall, and Robertson Hall), *Retrospect* (Cottey's annual yearbook), Rotaract (affiliated with Rotary International), Sigma Kappa Delta, (the national honor society for English), societies (Alphan, Delphian, Emerson, and Magnoperian), the *Spectrum* (Cottey's student newspaper), Student Activities Committee (SAC), Students Against a Vanishing Environment (SAVE), Student Government Association.

CURRY COLLEGE

AT A GLANCE

Founded in 1879, Curry College is a private, 4-year, liberal arts-based institution located on a wooded 137-acre campus in Milton, Massachusetts, just 7 miles from downtown Boston. Accredited by the New England Association of Schools and Colleges (NEASC), Curry College currently offers 20 undergraduate majors, as well as 3 graduate programs. The college serves a combined enrollment of approximately 4,000 students, consisting of more than 2,000 traditional students from more than 40 states and 32 countries; 1,600 continuing education students; and 400 graduate students. More than 1,400 of its students reside on the Curry campus. Under the leadership of President Kenneth K. Quigley, there's a culture of excellence that exists at Curry College as it continues to rise to a place of prominence and great promise among New England's finest colleges. As we enter our 129th year, we invite you to meet the people of Curry on the Web or at an upcoming campus event to truly experience excellence in action.

LOCATION AND ENVIRONMENT

The wooded, 137-acre Milton campus is one of the most attractive small college campuses in New England. Right on campus, you'll have at your fingertips the resources to help you excel academically, socially, and physically, and find endless sources of entertainment, action, and challenge. Unlike other isolated suburban or rural campuses, Curry is just a stone's throw away from Boston, one of the most exciting cities in the world. Only 7 miles from downtown Boston, Curry can offer its students an exceptional advantage through access to Boston's cultural and educational institutions. A hub of not only intellectual but also social activity, Boston is known as the ultimate college town and is famous for its history and tradition as well as its legendary sports teams. The opportunity for internships and entertainment in this New England capital is a significant part of the Curry experience.

Curry's location has yet another advantage: it is less than 2 miles from the scenic Blue Hills, a natural reservation that offers skiing, hiking, horseback riding, and a range of resources for environmental education and recreation. The Milton campus is a beautiful retreat in the woods, with the excitement of the city waiting right outside. Back on campus, students also enjoy the comfort Curry's tight-knit, friendly community and the security services provided by the Department of Public Safety, which administers a highly professional system for the enforcement of rules and regulations designed to promote the general safety and security of people and properties on the campus. Curry College is home to a caring and committed community where visitors are always welcome. We invite you to visit our interactive campus map online to learn about our campus facilities and to consider visiting Curry in person. We hope to see you on campus soon.

MAJORS AND DEGREES OFFERED

At Curry, we recognize the potential in all of our students. We take a personalized approach to education that allows you to build on your dreams while you simultaneously explore new ideas and uncover talents, strengths, and abilities you never thought you had. A Curry education will lead you to a level of excellence that will touch all facets of your life. You can select from 20 majors and 65-plus minors and concentrations ranging from biology to theater. Challenge yourself with the Curry Honors Program as well as support through the Program for Advancement of Learning. You can choose from a wide array of extracurricular activities ranging from 13 NCAA Division III athletic teams to an outstanding theater program. The Curry College experience is as unique as you are and the opportunities are endless. At Curry, you can achieve excellence in the classroom—and beyond.

OFF-CAMPUS OPPORTUNITIES

As an alumnus/alumna of Curry College, you are always welcome to use the Office of Career Services. We recognize that you have different challenges than current students, whether it's undertaking a career change, dealing with job loss, or brushing up on your job search skills. You have free access to individual career counseling, including skills/interests assessments, career exploration, and job search planning; assistance in selecting and applying to graduate school; resume and cover letter reviews; online and print resources; and job postings.

CAMPUS FACILITIES AND EQUIPMENT

The Gertrude M. Webb Learning Center is a unique, Tudor-style building with several thousand square feet of space dedicated to PAL students. The architecture of the learning center is based in the earlier part of this century and features majestic touches, including cathedral ceilings and ornate fireplaces. The Kennedy Academic Center, located on South Campus, houses many of Curry's classrooms as well as PC and MAC computer labs. The John S. Hafer Academic Building, erected in 1965, is located on the Academic Quadrangle on North Campus and houses many of Curry's classrooms. The Hafer Building is also a popular location on campus for hosting cultural activities and guest speakers. In 2001, our state-of-the art television studio, the Hirsh Communication Center, complete with full TV production facilities, was added to the facility. In August 2006, the college's newest facility, the Academic and Performance Center, opened to the college community. The new 3-story, 30,000 square foot building has 8 classrooms, including an amphitheater-style lecture hall and a stock trading classroom, faculty office suites, a student lounge, conference and breakout meeting rooms, and a 2-story atrium with a smart-café offering quick and healthy eating options. In addition, the building includes a 229-seat multi-purpose auditorium, the first dedicated performance space for Curry College students. Construction has also begun on a new 83,000 square foot Student Center that will include a fitness center, expanded dining hall, a sports café, a game room, and so much more.

TUITION, ROOM, BOARD, AND FEES

The total cost for resident students is based on 14 meals per week and a multiple occupancy room. The plan, including 17 meals per week, would increase the cost by $490. The 10 meals per week plan would decrease the total cost by $1,080. A single-occupancy room would increase the total cost by $1,630. Additional fees may apply.

FINANCIAL AID

Recognizing that meeting the total cost of a higher education today can be challenging for students and families, Curry College provides a variety of financing options and participates in federal and state financial aid programs. The Student Financial Services staff is committed to helping you create a financial plan that will allow you to reach your enrollment goals. In order to be considered for need-based financial aid, students must complete a FAFSA annually. You can fill out a FAFSA online at www.fafsa.ed.gov or use the paper application. If you would like us to mail you a paper FAFSA application, please contact our office and we will be happy to mail one to you. FAFSA forms are also available at any high school. Financial aid comes in 3 forms: grants and scholarships, loans, and student employment. Curry College provides students with millions of dollars in financial aid each year. The college uses its own endowment funds; gifts from friends, foundations, and corporations; alumni; parents; and other donors to be able to provide this funding to our students. We believe in the potential of every Curry College student and realize that financing a student's education can be a difficult task for a family. Curry also receives substantial funding from the various state and federal financial aid programs.

STUDENT ORGANIZATIONS AND ACTIVITIES

College is a time for making lifelong connections—with new people, new interests, and passions—a time of endless possibilities. It's a time to go beyond life as you know it now and do the things you've always dreamed of doing. At Curry College, you'll instantly become part of a unique, upbeat community with all the resources to help you excel academically, socially, and physically. Whether you're a resident student or commuter student, we'll help you find your niche. Right on campus you'll find countless sources of entertainment, action, and challenge. You can unwind at the Colonel's Corner snack bar over a game of pool, meet friends at a movie night, take a turn behind the mic, or just listen at a coffeehouse or comedy night. Work out in the weight room or exercise your voice in the *Currier Times* newspaper or campus chorale. Join one of the many student clubs and organizations or volunteer for community service projects.

Life as a Curry student extends beyond the campus, too. You can hike or ski in the nearby Blue Hills Reservation, and will have easy access to big city excitement and resources just 7 miles away in downtown Boston. The staff in the offices of Student Affairs—Student Activities, Residence Life, Public Safety, Health and Counseling, and the Chaplaincy—are all committed to helping you develop your personal goals and establish relationships within the Curry College community. We encourage your involvement and leadership in all aspects of college life.

ADMISSIONS PROCESS

As you explore enrollment at Curry College, the Office of Admission encourages you to visit the campus. To be considered for admission to Curry College, we require you to submit the following: a completed application with a nonrefundable fee of $40, an official high school transcript, results of the SAT or ACT, a letter of recommendation from a guidance counselor or high school teacher, and a college essay.

D'YOUVILLE COLLEGE

AT A GLANCE

Focused on professional studies and the liberal arts, D'Youville College is a private institution with a co-ed student body of more than 3,000. Founded in 1908, D'Youville has a proud history: The college was the first in western New York to grant undergraduate degrees to female students. Today, D'Youville offers degrees in more than 35 different undergraduate and graduate programs. The college's holistic approach to education, as well as the 14:1 student-faculty ratio, encourages personal development alongside of academic pursuits.

D'Youville hosts one of the nation's biggest 4-year, private nursing programs. The multiple-option Nursing Degree Program allows students to choose between BSN, BSN/MS (5 years), and RN to BSN courses of study. Students can also undertake a 5-year program resulting in a combined bachelor's/master's (BS/MS) degree in the areas of accounting, education, information technology, occupational therapy, international business, physician assistant, and dietetics. Those seeking master's degrees may apply in elementary, secondary, special education, community health nursing, occupational therapy, international business, and health services administration. There is also a 7-year bachlor's and doctorate of chiropractic and 6-year bachelor's and doctorate of physical therapy. Upon graduating from D'Youville, 96 percent of students either secure jobs in their chosen field or go on to graduate school.

The college's location by the Niagara River and Lake Erie provides breathtaking vistas, enjoyed by students living in Marguerite Hall. The Koessler Administration Building houses the president's offices as well as the offices of admissions, financial aid, student accounts, and registrar. The Learning Center and Kavinoky Theatre also share that building. When it's time to relax, students head to the Student Center, outfitted with a gymnasium, swimming pool, weight-training room, dance studio, general recreation center, and dining facilities.

Campus life thrives thanks to student organizations, including social groups, academic clubs, and the college newspaper. For athletes of any persuasion, the ski club, intramural teams, and NCAA Division III intercollegiate sports (baseball, basketball, volleyball, golf, cross-country, crew, soccer, and softball) provide athletic activities.

LOCATION AND ENVIRONMENT

Located in Buffalo, the D'Youville campus enjoys a residential setting. The downtown shopping center, the Kleinhans Music Hall, the Albright-Knox Art Gallery, 2 museums, and several theaters are all nearby. Toronto, a mere 90 miles away, offers additional metropolitan attractions, and Niagara Falls can be reached in just 25 minutes. Skiers can make it to Holiday Valley in about an hour. Buffalo can be reached via the New York State Thruway, Amtrak, Greyhound and Trailways bus lines, and most major airlines.

D'Youville connects itself to the community by forging relationships with local schools, hospitals, and social groups. Buffalo is home to more than 60,000 college students in all.

Specific departments affiliate with the appropriate area organizations. For instance, the nursing program works with 13 local hospitals and public health agencies. Nearby elementary, junior high, and secondary schools, as well as special education centers, are available for student teaching assignments for those in the education program. D'Youville students pursuing degrees in occupational therapy, physical therapy, and the physician assistant program can get hands-on experience at clinics across the country.

MAJORS AND DEGREES OFFERED

D'Youville students can pursue the degrees of bachelor of arts (BA), bachelor of science (BS), bachelor of science in nursing (BSN), 5-year 2-degree BS+MS programs, and combined BS+DC or BS +DPT programs. They choose from majors that include bachelor degrees in accounting, biology, biology, chemistry, interdisciplinary studies (education), English, exercise and sports studies, global studies, health services, history, information technology, mathematics, management, nursing, philosophy, pre-professional, science (pre-medical, pre-dental, pre-veterinary, pre-pharmacy, pre-law), psychology, sociology. For the BS+MS programs, achieved over 5 years, these include accounting, dietetics, international business, nursing, occupational therapy, physician assistant, informational technology (BS) + international business (MS), and education.

Additionally, there is a 6-year, BS+ DPT, physical therapy program and a 7-year, BS + DC, chiropractic program.

We are now offering a doctoral degree, EdD, in health policy and health education physical therapy, and chiropractic.

ACADEMIC PROGRAMS

Students select a major based on their interests and career goals. Any area of study provides a solid background for post-college pursuits. In order to graduate, students must fulfill the requirements of their department, complete the core requirements, pass a total of 120 credit hours, and maintain a minimum grade point average of 2.0. The core requirements cover humanities, 24 hours; social science, 12 hours; science, 7 hours; mathematics/computer science, 6 hours; and electives, 9 hours. Most students take 5 or 6 classes, approximately 16 credit hours, each semester. Internships can complement classroom experiences in any course of study.

Students who are undecided regarding their major can benefit from participation in the Career Discovery Program. Over the course of 2 years, students explore career options through classes and internships.

The academic year is divided into 2 15-week semesters. Students complete the final exams for the first semester prior to winter break. Summer programs, lasting 8 weeks, are also available for certain classes.

In order to better prepare for D'Youville courses, students can find assistance at the College Learning Center. For help in a specific subject, the Tutor Bank provides trained peer tutors.

CAMPUS FACILITIES AND EQUIPMENT

Living on campus is a great way to make the most of your college years. A D'Youville education extends further than the classroom, and being a campus resident is a major part of that education. Living on campus, students often make friendships that last a lifetime. Close proximity to the labs and library makes it easier to use free moments for study. Living on campus also puts you closer to campus events.

Marguerite Hall, a 12-story co-ed residence hall, is home to up to 308 students. Each floor in Marguerite houses approximately 28 students. Students can select from several options, including single-gender floors, co-ed floors, intensive study floors, and an over-21 floor. Based on availability, students may select a single, double, or triple room. Singles are not available for freshmen.

The new Student Apartment Complex has 4 fully furnished bedroom apartments with cooking facilities. These are available to upperclassmen.

Twenty-four-hour security coverage is provided in the residence halls. All visitors must sign in and be accompanied by their student host. Limited campus parking is available to residence students.

Computer and Network Services (CANS) provides the infrastructure and technical support necessary for many services on campus including e-mail, Web access, file and print sharing, and application support for distance learning, the library, and administrative offices. We take pride in being a wired campus, providing high-speed network access in our offices, classrooms, and dorms. Dial-up and VPN access is also provided on a limited basis, and technical support is available free of charge to the college community.

TUITION, ROOM, BOARD, AND FEES

In 2008-2009, tuition totaled $18,800 annually, and another $7,600 to $9,300 is charged for room and board. A mandatory college fee is assessed according to the number of credit hours a student enrolls in. There is a $40 Student Association fee, which defrays the costs of concerts, yearbooks, guest lectures, and other activities. Additionally, there is a $25 orientation fee and $20 liability insurance fee.

FINANCIAL AID

Financial aid is intended to ensure that D'Youville is financially accessible to students of all backgrounds. The allocations of grants, loans, and work-study opportunities are determined by review of the Free Application for Federal Student Aid.

Ninety percent of D'Youville freshmen receive financial aid. This includes nearly $2,000,000 in grants and scholarships. Grants include Federal Pell Grants and Supplemental Education Opportunity Grants, New York State Tuition Assistance Program, and Aid for Part-Time Study. Federal Work-Study programs, federally insured loans, and flexible payment plans are also available.

All applicants are reviewed for academic scholarships at the time of acceptance. Notifications of awards are made upon acceptance. Awards include Presidential Honors Scholarships, Academic Initiative Scholarships, Achievement Scholarships, and Transfer Achievement Scholarships. These scholarships are based on academic performance and could be worth up to $58,600.

All continuing students may apply for thousands of dollars from endowed and restricted scholarships.

Canadian students receive a 20 percent tuition waiver unless the student receives a RN nursing waiver. All undergraduate Canadian students are eligible for academic scholarships.

Nursing students in the BSN completion program for RNs receive a 50 percent tuition-only waiver.

D'Youville is a member of the Council of Independent Colleges Tuition Exchange Program and the Tuition Exchange Program, Inc. Both are tuition remission program.

STUDENT ORGANIZATIONS AND ACTIVITIES

Student representatives elected to the Student Association (SA) work with the administration and faculty to make decisions regarding the college's academic, social, and moral life. The SA is made up of the executive council and student senate, and any D'Youville attendees can run for a position or participate in any of the 17 related academic and social organizations.

Extracurricular activities are an important part of college life and at D'Youville we want your academic experience to be safe, successful, and fun. Several key services and programs will help you meet your goals and enjoy your time outside of the classroom.

Our intercollegiate program is a Division III member of the National Collegiate Athletic Association, competing in the Eastern College Athletic Conference. A variety of recreational activities are available as well as a fitness center, swimming pool, and game room.

Students can also join academic, cultural, and recreational clubs, serve on campus wide committees, contribute to student publications, perform in the arts, attend special events, and take advantage of many volunteer opportunities.

As a new student, you will be invited to attend an orientation program for freshmen, families, transfers, certificate, or graduate students. Here you'll learn about program requirements, course selection with an academic advisor, registration, and information seminars.

The D'Youville Freshman Experience (DFX) is designed to help make your first year exciting, fun, and challenging. At orientation, you'll be assigned a college mentor and registered for the FOCUS Freshmen Seminar. There are also activities and leadership opportunities (D'Youville Leads) as well as a Peer Mentor Program coordinated through the Leadership Development Institute.

ADMISSIONS PROCESS

Admission to D'Youville College is moderately competitive. Our selection process identifies those qualified men and women who will benefit most from the programs the college offers. In making admissions decisions, we consider grades, class rank, standardized test scores, recommendations, and any additional information you can provide.

To apply you'll need to submit a completed application along with a $25 processing fee, official high school transcripts, or, if you're a transfer student, official transcripts from colleges previously attended. You must also submit SAT I or ACT scores and letters of recommendation. Review the admission requirements for the major of your choice on our website.

Applications are reviewed on a rolling basis for all programs except the physicians assistant program. You can expect to receive an admissions decision within 3 weeks of the time we receive all the necessary forms, test scores, and transcripts. The sooner you complete your application, the sooner you'll receive a decision.

Admission to D'Youville College is granted without regard to age, race, gender, national origin, religious affiliation, or disability.

DAEMEN COLLEGE

AT A GLANCE

Located in the beautiful suburbs north of Buffalo, New York, Daemen College is a private college offering strong liberal arts majors, exceptional professional degrees, and widely acclaimed graduate programs. Daemen is distinguished by a low student-faculty ratio and consistently small class sizes, which encourage students to interact with professors and grow as individuals. Daemen students have their education enriched by challenging opportunities that engage them in learning experiences through international education programs, collaborative research with faculty, clinical and field experiences, internships for credit, and service learning positions. Daemen students embrace an academically challenging atmosphere where they are encouraged to develop a strong repertoire of knowledge and skills. A recent survey of Daemen students conducted as part of the nationally prominent National Survey of Student Engagement concluded that Daemen students find the institution's intellectual and creative work challenging. Daemen College meets the individual goals and needs of each student, preparing them for leadership and professional life in a global economy.

LOCATION AND ENVIRONMENT

Daemen's beautiful 39-acre campus is located in Amherst, New York, a safe, peaceful suburb of Buffalo. Money Magazine has reported Amherst, New York, as one of America's safest cities. Due to its proximity to Buffalo (New York State's second largest city), Daemen's campus is close to many major rail, plane, and motor routes. While the campus setting is tranquil and residential, Buffalo is a vibrant cultural city, bustling with world-class entertainment, such as the Philharmonic Orchestra, the Albright-Knox Art Gallery, and the Studio Arena Theater. The greater Buffalo area is rich with sports and recreational activities all year-round, whether it be skiing and swimming, or watching our professional sports teams. The surrounding Niagara Frontier boasts numerous historic and scenic locations. For example, Niagara Falls is only 30 minutes away and the attractive, international city of Toronto is just 2 hours by car. On campus, the numerous trees and open green spaces create a lovely environment to work and study, and complement the nearby urban environment.

OFF-CAMPUS OPPORTUNITIES

Daemen's Office of Career Development and Cooperative Education Center provides students and graduates with a wide variety of services specially geared to the vocational and self-development needs of the college community before and after graduation. The center helps students find an internship or a co-op position so that they can gain real-world experience in their area of interest. Students often express how lucky they are to have the chance to experience what careers in their fields are really like. An added bonus, internship employers frequently offer Daemen interns full-time positions. Employers run the gamut and include business, the sports industry, the arts, industry, government, health-related entities, nonprofits, educational institutions, and cultural organizations. The opportunities are local, national, or international, including excellent opportunities with the Washington Internship Institute.

Daemen believes in learning through service. While at Daemen virtually all undergraduate students engage in various service-learning activities. Students from every major and class level participate as individuals or groups in short-term and long-term projects or assignments that benefit the local, national, or global communities. Students work with environmental organizations, refugee groups, build environment agencies, tax credits for the poor programs, residents of nursing homes, hospitals and clinics, tutoring children, mentoring in city schools, and service activities in various cities throughout the city and the world, just to name a few of the hundreds of possibilities.

MAJORS AND DEGREES OFFERED

Daemen College offers BA, BFA, and BS programs in the following subject areas: accounting, art; applied design/printmaking, drawing/illustration, graphic design, painting/sculpture, visual arts education, biology; adolescence education, environmental studies, biochemistry; pre-professional, business administration; human resource management, international business, management information systems, marketing, sport management, weekend business, education; childhood education, early childhood education/special education, childhood education/

special education, English; adolescence education, communications/public relations, French; adolescence education, health care studies, history and government; adolescence education, environmental studies, mathematics; adolescence education, natural sciences; environmental studies, forensic science, health science, individualized studies, nursing, physical therapy, physician assistant, political science, psychology; human services, religious studies, social work, Spanish; adolescence education, Interdisciplinary studies; environmental studies, health care studies, individualized study, and pre-professional programs; pre-dentistry, pre-law, pre-medicine, and pre-veterinary. Graduate programs include MS programs in accounting; professional accountancy, education; adolescence education, childhood education, special education, executive leadership and change, global business, nursing; adult nurse practitioner, nursing education, nursing executive leadership, palliative care nursing, physician assistant, and a doctorate program in physical therapy.

ACADEMIC PROGRAMS

Daemen College is committed to complementing the depth of study in a major field with a well-rounded academic understanding in the liberal arts. The college's new core curriculum ensures that every student graduates with the following 7 core competencies: critical thinking and creative problem solving; oral, written and visual communication; information and multimedia technologies; civic responsibility; contextual understanding; affective judgment; and moral and ethical discernment. This innovative core curriculum competes with those of Ivy League Institutions and prepares the student in a holistic manner, which not only makes them more marketable upon graduation, but also instructs them on alternative ways of approaching education and learning.

Classes at Daemen are taught by professors, not teaching assistants. Daemen provides students with small classes and a caring and committed faculty, allowing for a personalized educational experience. Academics at Daemen will challenge

you to test your knowledge, raise your expectations, and think critically and creatively. Daemen's core competencies, honors program, academic exchanges, global programs, and undergraduate research are just a few examples of what makes the college challenging and distinctive.

Daemen students are well prepared for professional success. The vast majority of them obtain a position of choice or admission to graduate study in less than a year after graduation. They are leaders in their communities, with a strong dedication to the improvement of the communities in which they live.

Daemen graduates are informed citizens, prepared to play productive roles in local and global communities both as effective participants and leaders. They make reasoned ethical choices and consider connections between values and behavior. They can effectively access, evaluate, and apply relevant and valid information using a variety of information resources. They have the writing and speaking skills necessary for effective communication.

Daemen College graduates are well prepared to pursue advanced study in graduate or professional school.

CAMPUS FACILITIES AND EQUIPMENT

Modern apartment-style residence halls provide separate housing for male and female students, in addition to our existing 5-story residence hall for freshmen. All residence halls have kitchens, laundry facilities, lounges, and in-room phone/Internet connections. Full-service meals are served in the main dining hall, with an a la carte selection in the snack bar. The recreation room and Cyber Café are popular spots for socializing and relaxing during the day or evening. Marian Library supports the curriculum of the college, provides academic enrichment, and makes recreational reading available. The library is fully automated, with free access to bibliographic database research on the Internet. The Academic Computing Center maintains servers for remote access, electronic mail, the Web, and other Internet services. Internet accounts are available without charge to all Daemen students.

New in 2008-2009 is the Center for Information, Research, and Community programs that will transform the campus, both aesthetically and academically. The center will be a technological showcase that will be the hub of academic research, as well as the academic and social heart of the campus. The facility itself will be viewed as a complex ecological system, and will be utilized as an on going research and educational project for the Environmental Studies Program at Daemen. The center will impact the college's entire undergraduate and graduate student population and will provide informational, technical, and research support to the faculty.

TUITION, ROOM, BOARD, AND FEES

Tuition for the 2007-2008 academic year is $18,750, with additional room and board fees of $8,610 (varies according to meal plan and residence facility).

FINANCIAL AID

Learning to navigate the financial aid system can be a daunting task. That's why Daemen has trained professionals on hand to assist you every step of the way. Their Admissions Staff and Financial Aid Officers are available to assist you and your family with the financial aid application process, and to ensure that you understand the necessary paperwork and deadlines required in order for you to receive the best financial aid package available.

Daemen College believes that every eligible student should have the opportunity to pursue a college education, regardless of their financial situation. With this philosophy in mind, Daemen College offers merit-based and need-based financial assistance, as well as aid based on a combination of financial need and academic achievement. More than 90 percent of current Daemen students receive some form of financial assistance through the New York State Tuition Assistance Program, the college's scholarships and grants, work-study awards, or loans. In addition to the college's own scholarships, Daemen College participates in all federal and state programs.

STUDENT ORGANIZATIONS AND ACTIVITIES

Student activities provide for the development of the whole person outside of the classroom. The Student Activities director on campus helps students participate in recognized organizations, form new ones, and plan events. All students are encouraged to join in extracurricular activities. With more than 50 student organizations the possibilities for involvement at Daemen are limitless. Whether your interests are in art or skiing, there is bound to be something that grabs your interest and introduces you to students who share similar passions. Daemen knows that there's more to being a student than just sitting in a classroom or studying at the library. Daemen believes that now is the time to discover exactly who you are; cultivating your hidden talents, taking new risks, and challenging yourself to grow are all part of the Daemen experience. Daemen encourages all of their students to become actively engaged in the campus community.

Daemen athletic teams have won 6 American Mideast Conference North titles in the past 3 years. Daemen offers 5 varsity sports (4 men's: basketball, cross country, soccer, golf; 4 women's: basketball, cross country, volleyball, soccer). Club sports: cheerleading, indoor soccer, volleyball, lacrosse, rugby, and ice hockey. More casual athletes take part in intramural sports and keep fit in the exercise and weight rooms. Our student athletes work hard to achieve success on the field and in the classroom.

ADMISSIONS PROCESS

The Admissions committee weighs each student's overall academic record, the extracurricular profile, the High School counselor recommendation and the standardized test score. Students admitted last year had an average GPA of 90 percent. We consider this along with the academic rigor throughout the past 4 years in high school to be the single best predicator of academic success. We encourage an on campus interview and any other information a prospective student wishes to provide.

Daemen has a rolling admissions policy. However, due to program and residence-hall capacity limits, we highly encourage you to send your deposit before May 1 to secure your spot.

The best way to get to know Daemen is in person. On your visit, we'll take you on a campus tour, arrange for you to meet professors and current students, and plan a one-on-one meeting with an Admissions Counselor. To schedule your appointment, contact the Office of Admissions at 800-462-7652 or register inline at www.daemen.edu/admissions. You may make an individual visit anytime, attend our Fall and Spring Open Houses, or join us for many of our other special admissions events. We hope to see you on campus soon.

DAVIDSON COLLEGE

AT A GLANCE

With a dedication to undergraduate teaching and learning, Davidson is consistently recognized as one of the country's most outstanding private liberal arts colleges. Its 1,700 students are selected not only for their academic promise but also for their character, curiosity, initiative, and enthusiasm for learning. In and out of class, Davidson students inspire and challenge each other, respecting and learning from their differences. Through a broad education across academic disciplines, Davidson encourages students to engage in an academic exploration that leads to a lifelong appreciation of learning.

The Davidson Honor Code serves as the foundation of the campus community. Take-home tests are common, students self-schedule their exams, and library stacks are open.

LOCATION AND ENVIRONMENT

Located in the town of Davidson, 19 miles from Charlotte, North Carolina, Davidson students enjoy the freedom and safety of living in a classic college town and access to one of America's fastest growing cities. Davidson students are an active part of the local community, frequenting coffee shops and restaurants and volunteering at area schools, community centers, and retirement homes. In Charlotte, the country's second largest banking center, students explore internships with businesses, hospitals, and law firms, and enjoy access to cultural, arts, and sporting events.

OFF-CAMPUS OPPORTUNITIES

Approximately 70 percent of the student body takes advantage of Davidson's extensive study abroad options, studying literature in England and Germany, art history in Italy and France, culture in India and Ghana, and environmental issues in Kenya, Australia, and the Virgin Islands. Many students may also choose to study abroad or in the states on programs from other institutions.

MAJORS AND DEGREES OFFERED

Majors: anthropology, art, biology, chemistry, classics, economics, English, French, German, history, interdisciplinary studies, mathematics, music, philosophy, physics, political science, psychology, religion, sociology, Spanish, and theater.

Concentrations: applied mathematics, Asian studies, computer science, education, ethnic studies, film and media studies, gender studies, genomics, international studies, medical humanities, neuroscience, southern studies.

ACADEMIC PROGRAMS

Davidson encourages students to foster a lifelong appreciation of learning. At Davidson, you will be engaged in exploring the life of the mind. This exploration begins in the classroom, but you will be challenged and directed in learning well beyond the bounds of the campus. Davidson's curriculum is dedicated to allowing students to explore their interests while at the same time challenging students to discover new interests, strengths, and talents. Davidson's core curriculum requires that each student take courses across all disciplines: humanities, social sciences, fine arts, science, and mathematics.

Students can choose from among 21 majors, 12 minors, and 12 concentrations. In addition, students have the option of designing their own majors through the Center for Interdisciplinary Studies. Davidson offers pre-professional programs in medicine, dentistry, law, education, and engineering. Davidson incorporates a level of faculty-student collaborative research that is remarkable at an undergraduate college. Students perform research in world-class facilities, present papers at professional conferences, and publish in academic journals.

CAMPUS FACILITIES AND EQUIPMENT

Davidson's signature academic hall, the 1921 Chambers Building, was fully refurbished in fall 2004. The social and co-curricular centerpiece of Davidson's lush, well-tended campus is the Knobloch Campus Center, housing the Alvarez College Union and a 650-seat, state-of-the-art performance space, Duke Family Performance Hall. Sloan Music Building was completed in 2002, including a concert hall and studio-quality rehearsal and recording spaces, as well as a comprehensive music library. The renovation of Duke Residence Hall, which houses the Dean Rusk Program for International Studies, was completed in 2007. Comprehensive campus connectivity includes wireless connections and public workstations. E. H. Little Library houses more than 500,000 volumes, all listed in the online catalog, plus access to more than 5,000 journals and databases online. An official depository for U.S. government documents for more than 100 years, the library has electronic reserves, wireless network, an electronic classroom, and extensive interlibrary loan capabilities.

TUITION, ROOM, BOARD, AND FEES

Thanks to careful financial management, Davidson is able to keep its costs moderate in comparison to other institutions of similar quality and national stature. Tuition and fees pay only about 55 percent of the actual cost of educating each Davidson student, and the college makes up the difference.

Costs for the 2008-2009 academic year are:

Tuition and fees: $33,479

Room: $5,001

Meals: $4,470

Total: $42,950

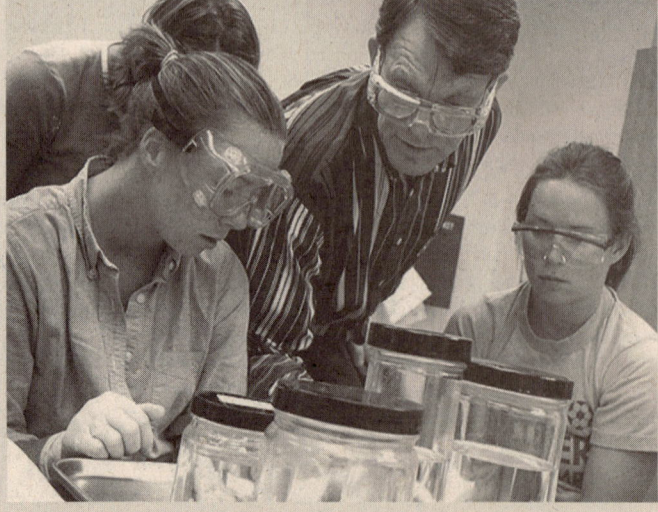

FINANCIAL AID

Through a strong commitment to providing financial assistance to help those who need it, Davidson enables students of many backgrounds and circumstances to attend, giving all students the benefits of a diverse learning community. All admission decisions are made without regard to financial need, with the exception of international students.

At Davidson, financial aid packages do not include student loans; 100 percent of demonstrated need is met with a combination of grants and on-campus student employment. Approximately one-third of each entering class receives some form of need-based financial aid. To apply for financial aid, applicants must complete the CSS/Financial Aid PROFILE Application and the Free Application for Federal Student Aid (FAFSA). These forms should be completed online. Financial aid is normally renewable for 4 years provided the student makes satisfactory progress toward a degree and family financial circumstances do not change appreciably.

In addition to need-based aid programs, Davidson awards merit-based scholarships that recognize the academic promise, special talents, and personal qualities of students without regard to their financial circumstances. Approximately 20 percent of first-year students are offered merit awards.

STUDENT ORGANIZATIONS AND ACTIVITIES

Approximately 85 percent of students participate in intramural or club sports; Davidson also enrolls scholar-athletes to play 11 different NCAA Division I sports for men and 10 for women.

Davidson students are involved in a myriad of activities that reflect a diversity of interests and talents. By participating in more than 200 campus organizations, students influence college policy, organize campus events, and promote social causes and multicultural interests.

Knobloch Campus Center opened in spring 2001, and has quickly become the focal point of campus social and cultural life. Inside Knobloch, Alvarez College Union houses a café and grill, a convenience store, the campus bookstore, a full-service U.S. Post Office, a fitness center, and venues for concerts, lectures, and socials. Alvarez is also home to student government offices; the Davidsonian and Libertas publications; the Career Services office; and Davidson Outdoors, which sponsors excursions throughout the year to sites like the Florida Everglades and the Rio Grande. Knobloch also houses the acclaimed Duke Family Performance Hall, which opened in winter 2002 and has recently hosted an annual 2-week residency and performances by the Royal Shakespeare Company.

Seven national fraternities, 1 historically black sorority, and 4 women's eating houses are located on Patterson Court. Houses have both dining and social facilities, and serve as places where members can gather. In addition to sponsoring social events open to the entire campus community, members are actively involved in a variety of community service projects. More than 800 students each year get involved in community outreach programs in Davidson and the greater Charlotte community.

ADMISSIONS PROCESS

In selecting a first-year class, Davidson seeks students who will contribute to the life of the college both inside and outside the classroom. Thus, the Office of Admission reviews each application with great care, looking at the high school academic record (rigor and grades), application essays, personal activities and achievements, recommendations, and test scores. The rigor of the student's high school curriculum is of prime importance, and Davidson encourages students to take advantage of the most challenging curriculum available in their high schools. Three-quarters of Davidson students graduated in the top tenth of their high school classes. The middle 50 percent of those accepted had SAT scores of 660-750 (Critical Reading), 660-740 (Math), and 650-740 (Writing). Of those students who submitted ACT scores, the middle 50 percent scored between 30 and 34.

DENISON UNIVERSITY

AT A GLANCE

You'll feel a sense of momentum and vitality as you arrive at Denison University's picturesque campus in Granville, Ohio. A highly selective, independent, residential college of liberal arts and sciences for men and women, Denison was founded in 1831. It is steeped in tradition and focused on the success of its approximately 2,100 students who can select from 48 courses of study and 12 pre-professional programs. Denison has an alumni body of 28,000 and an endowment of $642 million that places it among the top colleges and universities in the United States. United States Senator Richard Lugar and ESPN and ABC Sports President George Bodenheimer are among its well-known alumni. Denison is situated atop a ridge overlooking Granville, a quaint, New England-like village with shopping, restaurants, and services conveniently located adjacent to campus. Denison's continuing enhancement of its hillside campus includes the award-winning Campus Common project (2003) of Samson Talbot Hall of Biological Science and Burton D. Morgan Center for student, faculty, and alumni activities; 8 apartment-style residence halls (2005) to accommodate interested seniors; and the current $13-million restoration of historic Cleveland Hall, scheduled for completion in 2009. The student body is geographically and ethnically diverse, representing 46 states and territories and 22 countries, with nearly 18 percent being multicultural. The 201 members of the faculty are both teachers and scholars and thrive on the stimulation provided by their students through joint research and lively discussions in small classes, all of which are taught by professors, not teaching assistants. Typically, more than 125 students do research with faculty as Summer Scholars. In 2007, 77 percent of Denison graduating seniors were accepted into medical school; 86 percent were accepted into law school—both numbers well above national averages. Each year, approximately 10 percent of Denison students may opt for off-campus study in 85 selective programs abroad and in the United States. The university offers 3-2 programs in engineering, forestry, medical technology, natural resources management, and occupational therapy. The unique Denison Internship Program allows students to select from more than 300 internship offerings each summer. Denison is a founding member of the North Coast Athletic Conference and offers a broad-based program of 23 varsity sports for men and women. The university has won 94 conference championships since 1984, and 8 consecutive All-Sports Championships. Denison athletes rank third among more than 400 NCAA Division III colleges throughout the country in Postgraduate Scholarship winners and are regularly honored as All-Americans and Academic All-Americans.

LOCATION AND ENVIRONMENT

The 900-acre Denison campus overlooks the village of Granville. Founded in 1805 by settlers from Massachusetts, Granville bears a marked resemblance to a New England village and has several fine restaurants and shopping facilities. Columbus, the state capital with a population of 1.5 million, is 27 miles to the west and is served by numerous national airlines. The university is a cultural and recreational center for the local community, and the Denison Community Association encourages student participation in community service activities, providing more than 18,000 hours of volunteer fieldwork each year.

OFF-CAMPUS OPPORTUNITIES

As part of Denison's effort to cultivate intellectual responsibility and develop the capacity for their students' civic engagement and sense of responsibility, Denison students are given the opportunity to explore off-campus study in Asia and Oceania, Latin America and the Caribbean, Africa, eastern and western Europe, and portions of Scandinavia, the Middle East, and North America. Each year, about one-half of the graduating class has taken part in these 150 selective programs from around the world.

MAJORS AND DEGREES OFFERED

Denison offers 3 undergraduate degrees: bachelor of arts, bachelor of science, and bachelor of fine arts. The college offers 48 academic majors and concentrations and 12 pre-professional programs. Denison's majors include: art history; art studio; athletic training; biochemistry; biology; black studies; chemistry; cinema; communication; computer science; dance; East Asian studies; economics; educational studies; English literature; English writing; environmental studies; French; geosciences; German; history; international studies; Latin; mathematics; music; philosophy; philosophy, politics and economics; physics; political science; psychology; religion; sociology/anthropology; Spanish; theater; and women's studies. Departmental, interdepartmental, and individually designed majors, as well as concentrations within the departments, are available within the degree programs. Pre-professional preparation is available in business, dentistry, engineering, environmental management, forestry, law, medicine, natural resources, nursing, occupational therapy, veterinary science, and medical technology. Denison offers 3-2 programs in engineering with Rensselaer Polytechnic Institute, Washington University, Case Western Reserve University, and Columbia University; in forestry and environmental studies with Duke University; in natural resources management with the University of Michigan; in medical technology with Rochester General Hospital; and in occupational therapy with Washington University.

DENISON

ACADEMIC PROGRAMS

Denison expects its students to profit from exposure to a broad liberal arts education and to achieve proficiency in a major field. Degree requirements include successful completion of approximately 35 courses (127 semester hours) with a 2.0 or better average, both overall and in the major and minor fields; fulfillment of all general education requirements; achievement of passing scores on comprehensive examinations if required in the major; and fulfillment of minimum residence requirements. About one-third of a student's course work (13 courses) must be chosen from core course offerings in the humanities, sciences, social sciences, and fine arts. Another one-third is taken in the major field of study, and the remainder is fulfilled in electives. Denison offers opportunities for directed study and independent study. Students may receive advanced placement or credit through College Board's Advanced Placement (AP) tests, "A" Level or International Baccalaureate (IB) examinations. Credit is usually given for an AP score of 4 or 5. Denison's academic calendar consists of 2 semesters and an optional Denison Internship Program that includes internships and travel seminars. The academic year begins in late August and ends in early May.

CAMPUS FACILITIES AND EQUIPMENT

The beautiful wooded campus successfully combines historical and modern facilities and has 14 buildings that are listed on the National Register of Historic Places. Prominent among the 8 academic and administrative buildings on the Academic Quadrangle is the Denison University library, housed in the William Howard Doane Library/Seeley G. Mudd Learning Center. As a member of the Five Colleges of Ohio consortium and OhioLink, the library offers access through a combined state-of-the-art online catalog to collections of 45.3 million volumes. Access to computing resources, the campus network, the Internet, and the research-rich Internet2 is available. A network outlet is also provided to every student living in a residence hall, and wireless networking covers the majority of the campus. The Denison Mulberry Intermedia eXperience (MIX) lab is a digital media teaching facility and public computing lab for the university's fine arts departments. The Chemistry Center contains well-equipped laboratories and a 292-seat circular auditorium. Features of the F. W. Olin Science Hall include a 42-seat planetarium with a Zeiss Skymaster projector, a laser spectrometer, and computer-based learning centers. The Fine Arts Center comprises 6 buildings with classrooms and performance facilities for art, music, theater and cinema, and dance. The 550-acre Biological Reserve is a natural laboratory for bio-ecologists and the Polly Anderson Field Station provides laboratory and study spaces for students. The 81,500-square-foot Mitchell Recreation and Athletic Center features international squash courts, a regulation indoor track, tennis courts, aerobics and classrooms, and state-of-the-art strength and fitness rooms.

TUITION, ROOM, BOARD, AND FEES

Annual charges for the 2008-2009 academic year are as follows: tuition, $34,410; room and board, $8,830; and student fees, $890, for a total annual cost of $44,130.

FINANCIAL AID

The financial aid decision is entirely separate from the admission decision. In 2007-2008 academic year, $34,017,000 in Denison grants and merit-based scholarships was awarded to 95 percent of the students. Financial aid packages based on need are composed of grants, loans, and employment on campus. Applicants for both federal and Denison grant aid must complete a Free Application for Federal Student Aid (FAFSA) as early as possible after January 1 and request that the information be sent to Denison. In addition to the institutional need-based grants, Denison offers nearly 2,000 merit-based scholarships ranging from $8,000 to full tuition. Among these is the Paschal Carter Scholarship that approximates full tuition and is awarded to as many as 30 applicants who earn National Merit Finalist status. Recipients also receive a $3,000 fellowship to do research, travel abroad, or internships while enrolled at Denison. Alumni Awards that recognize academic achievement, leadership, and talent range from $8,000 to $13,000. For more information, students should write to Denison's Office of Financial Aid and ask for the financial aid brochure.

STUDENT ORGANIZATIONS AND ACTIVITIES

The Denison Campus Governance Association (DCGA) with its annual budget of approximately 700,000, supports 100 campus organizations, providing the students with opportunities to participate in athletics, write for several publications, volunteer in the local community, learn about various cultures, and hear nationally recognized speakers. Denison students are active volunteers and contribute more than 18,000 hours each year through the Denison Community Association in areas such as adult literacy, the AIDS task force, Habitat for Humanity, homelessness and hunger, and Hope for Autism. Thirty-five percent of the students are members of the 7 sororities and 7 fraternities; 26 percent play varsity sports, 35 percent play club sports, and 73 percent participate in intramural sports.

ADMISSIONS PROCESS

The quality of the academic performance, rigor of courses selected and grade point average are the

most important factors considered by the Admissions Committee. Submission of the results of the SAT I or the ACT is optional. SAT II Subject Tests are also not required although these scores may be provided as additional information in support of the application for admission. International applicants must submit the results of the TOEFL or the results of the SAT I. The application essay, as well as written statements from the college advisor and an academic teacher, provide a greater understanding of personal characteristics and motivation. Important also is the quality, rather than the quantity, of extracurricular accomplishments, whether school, community, job-related, or life experience. Independent of the admission process and solely for the purpose of the college's research, students who have taken the standardized tests must submit the official results of these tests upon matriculation. An interview is strongly encouraged but not required. Denison University admits students of any race, color, religion, age, personal handicap, sex, sexual orientation, veteran status, and national or ethnic origin.

All students requesting admissions information will receive the Viewbook. Denison is an exclusive Common Application college. The Common Application (www.commonapp.org) may be submitted any time between September 1 and January 15 of the senior year. Denison University has a 3-part application. Completing Part I will begin the application process and enable Denison to start the file. Part I may be completed online at www.denison.edu/admissions/apppart1.html. Part II requires the student to fill out the Common Application and Part III requires the applicant to complete Denison's Supplement. Denison will waive the $40 application fee for students who apply online at www.commonapp.org (Part II and Part III can be completed there).

School Says . . .

DESALES UNIVERSITY

DeSales University is a medium-sized Catholic liberal arts university for men and women administered by the Oblates of St. Francis de Sales.

AT A GLANCE

Founded in 1964, DeSales University is a Catholic liberal arts university that offers courses in a wide range of disciplines. DeSales provides personal attention, small class size, and a feeling of community. The university uses a holistic approach to help students develop a sense of self, enabling every student to reach their personal and academic potential. This student-centered philosophy is conveyed by an enthusiastic, accessible faculty.

LOCATION AND ENVIRONMENT

DeSales University's suburban campus is located 15 minutes south of Bethlehem and Allentown, Pennsylvania, and only 1 hour from Philadelphia, 90 minutes from Scranton and Wilkes-Barre, Pennsylvania, less than 2 hours from New York City, and 3 hours from Baltimore. The campus is 450 acres with more than 16 major buildings.

OFF-CAMPUS OPPORTUNITIES

Allentown and Bethlehem are a short 15-minute drive from campus and offer many dining, shopping, and outdoor activities, including the Promenade Shops at Saucon Valley, just minutes from campus. The Lehigh Valley, aka College Valley, boasts beautiful hiking and biking trails, historic sites, museums, cultural festivals, and Dorney Park and Wildwater Kingdom. Skiing at nearby Blue Mountain and other Pocono resorts is just a short drive away. The Poconos also offer white-water rafting trips down the Lehigh and Delaware Rivers.

MAJORS AND DEGREES OFFERED

DeSales University offers 36 bachelor's degrees, including 10 pre-professional programs, and 6 graduate programs through the departments of business, humanities, math and computer science, social science, performing arts, natural science, nursing and health, and theology and philosophy. Our newest majors include digital art, marriage and family studies, international business, and special education.

ACADEMIC PROGRAMS

DeSales University defines global competence as using an open, inquisitive mind to understand the norms and expectations of other cultures, and using this acquired knowledge to communicate and to work effectively outside of one's usual environment in the promotion of human solidarity. DeSales University presents opportunities for students to enlarge their world view, from activities and concerts to short- and long-term study abroad programs.

The university's cultural affairs committee offers a diverse series of weekly performances that bring cultural liveliness to campus. Flamenco dancing, a Cuban percussion group, and a Japanese tea ceremony are recent examples of our Wednesday in the Commons series.

Study abroad programs through DeSales present the opportunity for our students to live and work in this vibrantly interdependent world and range from semester-long study to short stay-travel of 10 days. Our students have spent semesters in England, Australia, Italy, Latin America, among others. More important, DeSales is employing a new model of intensive hands on engagement through short-stay co-curricular trips of students, faculty, and staff. Trips to Ireland, Germany, Peru, and South Africa for short-stay intensive travel have been combined with academic courses, the activities of student organizations such as SIFE or PACE, or out of season competition for our athletic teams.

Freshman students are asked to participate in the Character U program, a self assessment program based on the Golden Counsels of St. Francis de Sales. Each month, university programming addresses one of these Golden Counsels or traits, including patience, trust and cooperation, and perseverance.

The university's Academic Resource Center can offer assistance in reading comprehension, study skills, time management, and effective writing techniques. Additionally they can help find a tutor if you need it or provide you with the opportunity to become a peer tutor.

CAMPUS FACILITIES AND EQUIPMENT

Trexler Library has a collection of more than 500,000 items and there are electronic databases of newspapers, journal articles, and the *Oxford Dictionary of National Biography*. There are computer and multimedia labs and a staff who will help with any research topic. Trexler Library has wireless access both with personal laptops or laptops that can be borrowed to use in the building. The library's resources can be accessed from anywhere on campus. There is online access to databases and full text journal articles. Students can also instant message a librarian with a question.

The DeSales University Center is one of the newest additions to the campus and features many menu choices—especially for healthy eaters—in a food court setting. The University Center also has wireless laptop capability so you can eat and surf, as well as panoramic views of campus.

The Priscilla Payne Hurd Science Center, a 37,500 square foot facility, is equipped with up-to-date computers, labs, and medical equipment. The Hurd Science Center also features a sterile molecular/cell biology suite, complete with a freezer room, bench room, support room, dark room, and instrument room. An ecology/environmental lab with a growing chamber, an analytical/physical chemistry/inorganic laboratory, and a bioinformatics/physics lab also inhabit the 2-story building.

TUITION, ROOM, BOARD, AND FEES

Tuition and fees (2007-08): $23,000

Room and board: $8,750

Student and technology fee: $800

Total: $32,550

FINANCIAL AID

Nine out of 10 DeSales University students receive financial aid in the form of grants, scholarships, work study, and loans. About 85 percent of the students receive grants directly from DeSales University, and funds are also available from federal and state programs to those who qualify. The amount of aid received and the composition of an aid package will depend on financial need and on academic achievement and potential.

Academic scholarships are also available through DeSales University. All applicants for admission are automatically considered for each of the scholarships offered by the university.

STUDENT ORGANIZATIONS AND ACTIVITIES

DeSales University has more than 31 campus organizations, including the Student Activities crew, which helps plan student events, bus trips, and on-campus performances. Recent renovations to the McShea Student Center include the Dog Pound, a student activities lounge open to students for entertainment and socializing, and Café McShea, an internet café with late night hours. Both new areas are just the beginning of increased special events such as independent movie nights, comedians, music acts, and expanded space for programs sponsored by various student organizations.

DeSales University has 16 intercollegiate varsity sports teams and all are members of the NCAA Division III, Middle Atlantic States Collegiate Athletic Corporation (MAC) Freedom Conference, and the Eastern College Athletic Conference (ECAC). The university's men's sports are baseball, basketball, cross-country, golf, lacrosse, soccer, tennis, and track and field. Women's sports are basketball, cross-country, field hockey, soccer, softball, tennis, track & field, and volleyball. The university also has 6 club sports: cheerleading, cycling, disc golf, equestrian, ice hockey, and men's volleyball. There are 30 intramural sports for all seasons, or students can visit the state-of-the-art Billera Hall fitness center, which offers aerobic, Nautilus, and free-weight training.

ADMISSIONS PROCESS

To Apply for Admission you need to: complete a DeSales University application and submit it with a nonrefundable $30 fee to our Admissions Office; have your high school guidance department send your official high school transcript to our Admissions Office; have your standardized test scores (SAT or ACT) sent to our Admissions Office (our code number for SAT scores is 2021); have a guidance counselor and teacher complete the recommendation forms and send to our Admissions Office.

DEVRY UNIVERSITY

AT A GLANCE

Since its founding in 1931, DeVry has grown to become one of the largest accredited degree-granting higher education systems in North America, with more than 57,000 students currently enrolled at its 89 locations in 26 states and Canada, as well as through DeVry University Online. DeVry University is one of the first schools to help its graduates step straight out of the classroom and into a specific career in their field of study—and for more than 75 years, hundreds of thousands of DeVry grads have done just that.

We Major in Careers.™ Over the decades, DeVry University has remained uniquely committed to the single goal of setting up its graduates for successful careers straight out of school. System-wide between October 2006 and June 2007, 93 percent of DeVry University† graduates in the active job market were employed in their field of study within 6 months of graduation at an average salary of $43,000. And this level of success holds up over time. Since 1975, 90 percent of DeVry's 227,000 undergraduate students in the active job market were employed in career-related positions within 6 months of graduation—a statistic that outshines most traditional universities.

The DeVry classroom experience: Once underway, DeVry University students learn from faculty who are experienced professionals themselves, many of them still active in business. Present and former students speak positively of their instructors' supportive attitude and willingness to help outside the classroom. When in session, class sizes are small to allow a maximum of individual instruction. Classes include not just theory but also practical lab experience, helping DeVry graduates hit the ground running in the workplace.

LOCATION AND ENVIRONMENT

DeVry locations, class schedules, and online instruction. To give every student maximum access to a DeVry education, DeVry University offers a flexible mix of day, night, and online classes that accommodates virtually any student's schedule. DeVry students can also opt for concentrated programs that let them complete a bachelor's degree in just 3 years, or an associate degree in fewer than 2 years. DeVry maintains more than 89 locations throughout North America, including Arizona, California, Colorado, Florida, Georgia, Illinois, Indiana, Kentucky, Maryland, Michigan, Minnesota, Missouri, Nevada, New Jersey, New York†, North Carolina, Ohio, Oklahoma, Oregon, Pennsylvania, Tennessee, Texas, Utah, Virginia, Washington, Wisconsin, Alberta, Canada†

MAJORS AND DEGREES OFFERED

DeVry University provides high-quality, career-oriented undergraduate and graduate degree programs in technology, business, and management. Students access these programs through its North American locations and through DeVry University Online to meet the needs of a diverse and geographically dispersed student population.

Master's degree programs and certificates: educational technology (MSET), electrical engineering (MSEE), educational technology (certificate).

Through Keller Graduate School of Management: master of business administration, master of accounting and financial management, master of human resource management, master of project management, master of public administration, master of information systems management, master of network and communications management.

Bachelor's degree programs: business administration with emphasis in: accounting, business information systems, finance, health services management, hospitality management, human resource management, operations management, project management, sales and marketing, security management, small business management and entrepreneurship, technical communication, biomedical engineering technology, computer engineering technology, computer information systems, business/management, computer forensics, database management, information systems security, systems analysis and integration, Web development and administration, electronics engineering technology, game and simulation programming, network & communications management, technical management, criminal justice, health information management.

Associate degree programs: accounting, electronics and computer technology, health information technology, network systems administration, Web graphic design.

FINANCIAL AID

Everything about a DeVry University education is designed to turn even the most uncertain freshman entrant into a savvy, career-ready graduate. Before enrollment, each student has access to a DeVry career consultant who helps guide the enrollee's career choice, so even the first courses start to propel the student immediately toward the chosen field. At the same time, financial aid for qualified students is thoroughly explored. DeVry University acts on its belief that no student should be deprived of a DeVry education because of money. This commitment has made DeVry University one of the nation's leading issuers of college financial assistance, specifically including aid to minority students.

ADMISSIONS PROCESS

Contact us to find out more about DeVry University or to discover which DeVry programs might be right for you. Call us, visit DeVry.com, or stop by any DeVry location.

Telephone: TFN: 866-DEVRY-81 (1-866-338-7981)

Our Administrative Offices are open 9 a.m. to 5 p.m., central time, Monday through Friday.

Website: www.DeVryStories.com/Review

Learn more about a DeVry education or chat live with one of our consultants.

†DeVry University operates as DeVry Institute of Technology in New York and Calgary.

DRAKE UNIVERSITY

AT A GLANCE

Drake University provides a thriving intellectual environment offering more than 70 majors, covering subjects from the liberal arts to professional and pre-professional programs. The university employs professors who demonstrate a dedication to students along with academic prowess. Students benefit from the low 14:1 student-faculty ratio, and they never take classes from graduate students or teaching assistants. Drake enrolls a heterogeneous group of 5,200 students, from 48 U.S. states and approximately 60 foreign countries. Drake prides itself on alumni success, noting that more than 93 percent of Drake graduates embark on careers or start graduate programs during their first 6 months out of school.

Drake grants master's degrees in: accounting, business administration, communication leadership, education, financial management, and public administration. Students may also pursue their doctor of pharmacy, doctor of jurisprudence, and doctor of education degrees. Joint degrees are also available in MBA/JD, MPA/JD, MBA/PharmD, MPA/PharmD, and PharmD/JD.

LOCATION AND ENVIRONMENT

Students take advantage of Drake's location in Des Moines, Iowa, the state capital and a thriving business center. Internships are available in fields such as government, banking, insurance, publishing, nonprofit organizations, and health care, and nearly three-quarters of students participate in at least 1internship during their 4 years at the university.

OFF-CAMPUS OPPORTUNITIES

Many students take advantage of overseas studies options offered by the Center for International Programs and Services. Through the Center s work with international institutions and consortia, semester- and year-long programs are offered in more than 60 countries.

MAJORS AND DEGREES OFFERED

Those studying in the College of Arts and Sciences receive a classic liberal arts education, preparing them for futures in science, mathematics, politics, or the arts. Students may earn their bachelor of arts and bachelor of science degrees in the following areas: anthropology and sociology; astronomy; biochemistry, cell and molecular biology; biology; chemistry; computer science; English; environmental policy; environmental science; history; international relations; law, politics, and society; mathematics; mathematics education (secondary); neuroscience; philosophy; physics; politics; psychology; religion; rhetoric and communication studies; sociology; study of culture and society; and writing. Some students design their own majors, while others opt for open enrollment and do not immediately declare a major. The university also administers pre-professional study in dentistry, engineering, law, medicine, and veterinary medicine. Concentrations are available in anthropology, geography, Latin American studies, and women's studies, and most fields that offer majors.

Students who attend the School of Fine Arts pursue their bachelor of arts, bachelor of fine arts, bachelor of music, and bachelor of music education degrees. The available fields include art, music, and theater arts with a dual focus on teaching excellence and artistic creativity. Holding accreditation from by the National Association of Schools of Art and Design, Drake's Department of Art and Design offers instruction in art history, graphic design, and studio art (drawing, painting, printmaking, and sculpture). Students in the Department of Music select from degrees in applied music (instrumental, piano or vocal music performance) and music education. Other alternatives exist, such as a bachelor of arts degree with a music major, a bachelor of music degree with elective studies in business, and a bachelor of music with a jazz studies concentration. Those who wish to study theater, acting, directing, theater design, musical theater, and theater education enroll in the Department of Theatre Arts.

Students enrolled in Drake University's College of Business and Public Administration complete their undergraduate degree of Bachelor of science in business administration in 4 years. Available majors include accounting, actuarial science, economics, entrepreneurship, finance, general business, information systems, information technology, international business, management, and marketing. A human resource management concentration, insurance concentration, and law and business concentration are also available. The college allows interdisciplinary majors, combinations of majors, and open business (undeclared) status. The college is accreditation by the AACSB—the International Association for to Advance Collegiate Schools of Business.

First-year students admitted directly to the PharmD program in the College of Pharmacy and Health Sciences complete a 2-year pre-pharmacy program then begin a 4-year PharmD program. A health sciences major with 3 tracks—clinical and applied, health sciences management, and pharmaceutical sciences—is also available. The college is accredited by the American Council on Pharmaceutical Education and belongs to the American Association of Colleges of Pharmacy.

Students who wish to pursue bachelor of arts majors in advertising (management and creative tracks), electronic media (broadcast news and radio/television), magazines, news/Internet, and public relations study in the School of Journalism and Mass Communication. The school allows an open enrolled (undeclared) option and holds accreditation from the Accrediting Council on Education in Journalism and Mass Communication.

In addition, the College of Arts and Sciences, the College of Business and Public Administration, and the School of Journalism offer combined 3+3 programs with the Drake Law School. Students in this program can obtain their undergraduate degrees in 3 years in one of the aforementioned colleges or schools, then pursue a law degree for the next 3 years at the law school.

Programs at the School of Education lead to degrees in elementary or secondary education. Students may earn a bachelor of science or bachelor of arts degree that is tailored to prepare graduates for employment in elementary or secondary schools. Other options include adding middle school and coaching endorsements to teaching credentials. Drake University has belonged to the American Association of Colleges for Teacher Education since the association's founding.

ACADEMIC PROGRAMS

From their first classes on the Drake campus, students have the chance to learn in an individualized, challenging, and supportive environment. Research opportunities abound; students work closely with their professors and often publish their findings. With more than 160 student-run organizations on campus, there is an outlet for every allow students to investigate career paths and network with professionals in their field.

Students benefit from a combination of liberal arts training and professional preparation. Through the Drake Curriculum, all students take interactive classes that develop their critical thinking and expressive skills. Students also receive personalized academic advising. At the end of their 4 years, students undertake the Senior Capstone, which is a research project, thesis, or other major work that shows the concepts and skills the student has acquired at Drake. Drake's Honors Program is open to top students who wish to undertake a rigorous, interdisciplinary course of study.

CAMPUS FACILITIES AND EQUIPMENT

Students have access to the Cowles Library and its more than more than 550,000 books and journals, 94,000 federal and state government documents, 777,000 microform records, 80 electronic databases, and approximately 16,000 scholarly online journals. The collections also include DVDs and music CDs, as well as a digital repository of scholarship and historical material unique to Drake. Many classes utilize the resources in specialized collections in the Law School, College of Pharmacy and Health Sciences, Center for Teacher Education, and School of Fine Arts. Between the Dwight D. Opperman Hall and Law Library, there are 320,000 volumes, along with computer labs and study facilities. The Studio Theater, the Monroe Recital Hall, and the Hall of the Performing Arts are housed in the Harmon Fine Arts Center. Another performance hall, the Sheslow Auditorium with a capacity of 755 seats, is located in Old Main. The Bell Center offers a gym, pool, aerobic dance room, fitness room, basketball, volleyball, and badminton courts. Additional athletic facilities are available in the Knapp Center, such as racquetball, volleyball and basketball courts, a jogging track, and a weight room. More than 7,000 people can congregate in Knapp for major events. Basketball courts and a track are available at the Fieldhouse, while the Tennis Center provides 6 indoor and 6 outdoor tennis courts.

TUITION, ROOM, BOARD, AND FEES

Tuition and fees total $23,692 in 2007-2008. Room and board cost $6,920 annually.

FINANCIAL AID

Approximately 98 percent of full-time students at Drake have their education financed to some degree with the help of financial aid. In the 2006-2007 school year, a typical financial aid package totaled $18,860. More than 5,000 awards, worth $50 million, are given annually, in the form of need- or merit-based grants and scholarships.

STUDENT ORGANIZATIONS AND ACTIVITIES

With more than 160 organizations operating on campus, students can always find activities that suit their interests. Elected student representatives run the Student Senate Students also hold seats on some committees in the Faculty Senate. The Student Activities Board is charged with putting on special events, including cultural celebrations, social functions, guest speakers, and concerts. Drake also maintains the Residence Hall Association, composed of students who manage the logistics and activities surrounding residential life.

ADMISSIONS PROCESS

While admission is selective, Drake University considers the full record of each candidate for admission. Since the university prefers students with varied talents and interests, there is no single and inflexible set of admission standards applied to all candidates for admission. The admission process involves a comprehensive review of a student's academic background (courses and grades), standardized test scores (ACT or SAT), personal essay, recommendations, and activities both in high school and the community. Drake University does not discriminate on the basis of age, sex, sexual orientation, race, religion, color, national or ethnic origin, or disability.

A complete application file for first-year admission contains the following items: a completed application form, the $25 nonrefundable application fee (the fee is waived for those who apply online), the High School Report and Counselor Recommendation Form, an official high school transcript, and ACT or SAT scores. While it is not mandatory, applicants are strongly encouraged to write a personal essay as well. Students applying to transfer to Drake are required to submit official transcripts for all previous college-level course work.

Application for admission to undergraduate degree programs, except pre-pharmacy, may be made for any fall, spring, or summer term. Beginning October 1, students are notified of the admission decision within 4 to 6 weeks of the date that all materials are received. March 1 is the priority deadline for consideration for admission and merit- and need-based financial aid. Freshman applicants to the pre-pharmacy program in the College of Pharmacy and Health Sciences must the December 1 deadline. Transfer students are only admitted to the professional PharmD program.

Candidates should contact:

Drake University

Office of Admission

2507 University Avenue

Des Moines, IA 50311

800-44-DRAKE, x3181

515-271-3181 (locally and outside the U.S.)

Fax: 515-271-2831

www.choose.drake.edu

admission@drake.edu

ELMHURST COLLEGE

AT A GLANCE

A private liberal arts college in the heart of metropolitan Chicago, Elmhurst College ranks in the top tier of its category, according to *U.S. News & World Report*. With a student-faculty ratio of only 13:1, Elmhurst offers a personal approach where every student counts. All classes at Elmhurst are taught by professors, not teaching assistants, and about 85 percent of the college's 127 full-time faculty hold the highest degree in their field.

The college is located in Elmhurst, Illinois, a quiet suburb that ranks number 1 in a Chicago magazine survey of the best places to live. Downtown Chicago is a 30-minute train ride away, offering a wealth of professional, cultural, and recreational opportunities.

Students come to Elmhurst from many states and countries, and from nearly every religious, racial, and ethnic background. The student body is made up of nearly 3,000 undergraduates and about 300 graduate students.

LOCATION AND ENVIRONMENT

Elmhurst College is located 16 miles west of downtown Chicago in the quiet suburb of Elmhurst, a community of 43,000 that has been called the quintessential Chicago suburb. Within walking distance from campus are 2 art museums, a library, an 8-screen movie house, lots of great restaurants, and more.

The college is just a short train ride from downtown Chicago, where students enjoy unlimited access to world-class cultural and professional opportunities—from internships to sporting events to concerts of all kinds.

Elmhurst's campus looks like a college ought to look, with big trees, broad lawns, and 24 classy red-brick buildings. The campus is a 38-acre arboretum with 650 varieties of trees and plants.

OFF-CAMPUS OPPORTUNITIES

Elmhurst offers international education experiences in many countries, including Spain, the Netherlands, Poland, Bulgaria, and England. Students can go abroad for a semester, a year, or a month during the college's distinctive January term.

Other Off-Campus Opportunities include a wealth of internship and job-shadowing experiences. One student recently shadowed a renowned neurosurgeon in San Francisco, for example; another worked on staff at the Mayo Clinic in Rochester, Minnesota. A third traveled to New York to participate in a high-level discussion of medical ethics.

MAJORS AND DEGREES OFFERED

Elmhurst offers 54 majors, ranging from accounting to exercise science to jazz studies. Students may complete a double major, add a minor, or create their own interdisciplinary major. The Honors Program provides extra opportunities for students who are especially talented, curious, and motivated. We also offer a range of pre-professional programs leading to graduate study in health care, law, and more. Nine graduate programs lead to the master's degree.

ACADEMIC PROGRAMS

Elmhurst is a private, 4-year college in the liberal arts tradition. The curriculum combines liberal learning and professional preparation to prepare students for lives of meaningful work and personal fulfillment.

Academic Programs at Elmhurst are characterized by their real-world connections and demonstrated responsiveness to student needs. Students conduct research and defend their results. They analyze data, think critically, solve problems collaboratively, study and write across the disciplines, and learn to formulate new ideas and to convey them with maximum impact.

All classes at Elmhurst are taught by professors, not teaching assistants, and about 85 percent of the college's 127 full-time faculty hold the highest degree in their field. With a student-faculty ratio of only 13:1, faculty members get to know their students as individuals.

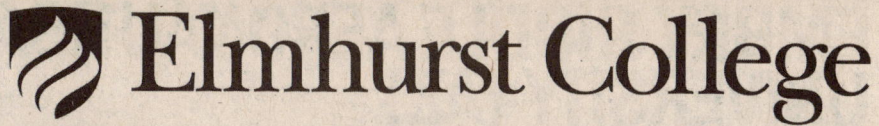

Elmhurst College

CAMPUS FACILITIES AND EQUIPMENT

Elmhurst's facilities include a newly renovated student center and an excellent library and computer center. At the Speech-Language-Hearing Clinic, student clinicians practice their skills and treat patients. Old Main, built in 1879, is on the National Register of Historic Places. The Tyrrell Fitness Center offers more than 6,000 square feet of weight training and physical fitness equipment. Facilities are open throughout the day and evening and are readily accessible to all students.

TUITION, ROOM, BOARD, AND FEES

Full-time tuition for 2007-2008 is $24,600; room (double occupancy) is $4,200; standard meal plan is $2,924. For more details, see our Tuition & Fees pages at www.elmhurst.edu.

FINANCIAL AID

Elmhurst provides financial aid to about 85 percent of full-time students. Financial aid programs include scholarships (based on academic merit), and grants, loans, and student employment (based on financial need). More than 600 students work on campus. The college makes admission decisions independently from any consideration of financial need.

STUDENT ORGANIZATIONS AND ACTIVITIES

Students come to Elmhurst from many states and countries, and from nearly every religious, racial, and ethnic background. The student body is made up of nearly 3,000 undergraduates and about 300 graduate students.

Life at Elmhurst is active and creative. Students get involved in more than 100 activities, from theater to intramurals to the Mock Trial Team. The student newspaper wins awards; the radio station has been on the air since 1947. The campus regularly hosts performances, art exhibits, and an array of excellent guest speakers.

Elmhurst's 18 varsity sports teams compete in the CCIW, one of the top conferences in NCAA Division III athletics. We're big enough to offer a wide choice of sports, but small enough that you can really contribute to your team's success. In the past decade, Bluejay teams have won conference championships in 5 sports. And they compete in first-rate facilities.

ADMISSIONS PROCESS

Rolling admission begins on October 1 and continues until all spaces are filled.

To apply complete the application for admission. It's available online at www.elmhurst.edu or by mail from the Elmhurst Admission Office. Next, submit your high school transcript, your ACT or SAT scores, and a recommendation from a teacher or counselor. (An essay and a campus interview are recommended but not required.) If you're applying as a transfer student, also submit an official transcript from all colleges or universities you've attended.

EMBRY RIDDLE AERONAUTICAL UNIVERSITY (AZ)

AT A GLANCE

Embry-Riddle Aeronautical University's Prescott, Arizona campus is recognized and respected worldwide as a center for cutting-edge instruction and training for tomorrow's leaders. For the last 30 years, the Prescott campus has developed a reputation based on its leadership role in aviation and aerospace education as well as its commitment to strong academic preparation and a solid learning environment.

Embry-Riddle is a private, independent, 4-year university and is accredited by the Commission on Colleges of the Southern Association of Colleges and Schools. The campus offers 12 undergraduate degree programs, all with a special emphasis on aviation, aerospace, and related fields of global influence. The co-ed student population of 1,700 undergraduates comes from all 50 states and 30 different countries. The average class size is 21 students, with an overall student-faculty ratio of 14:1. Faculty members bring both teaching and industry backgrounds to the classroom; most have extensive practical experience in their field along with outstanding academic credentials.

Guided by its worldwide network of alumni, Embry-Riddle's reputation has grown steadily in the aviation, aerospace, and business communities. Within 1 year of graduation, 96 percent of Embry-Riddle graduates from all campuses are either employed or have decided to continue their education.

LOCATION AND ENVIRONMENT

Just like its people, the university's location is warm and friendly. Prescott, a mile-high city on the Colorado Plateau, is home to the world's largest stand of ponderosa pine trees. The campus is about 100 miles northwest of Phoenix, 260 miles southeast of Las Vegas, and 375 miles east of Los Angeles. Prescott's climate reflects seasonable weather that is excellent for flying, with daytime averages of 80°F in the summer and 45°F in the winter. The local mountains exhibit the spirit of the rugged West, with students enjoying snow skiing, hiking, mountain biking, rock climbing, and tours of the Grand Canyon.

Known as a vacation getaway, Prescott offers shopping, entertainment, health, and recreational options in a friendly small-town atmosphere. For a taste of big city life, Phoenix is a 1.5 hour drive. The campus is situated on 539 acres, but campus life is centered in a 1-mile walking radius. The Flight Training Center is located nearby at the Prescott Municipal Airport.

MAJORS AND DEGREES OFFERED

The undergraduate academic preparation provides a strong foundation for all students, whether or not they choose a career in aviation. Each major is a combination of general education, specialized focus, and applied technology.

The bachelor of science in aeronautical science, the professional pilot program, emphasizes hands-on training and prepares students for a career in the aviation industry with airlines, corporate and commercial aviation, or the military. Flight courses lead to certification as an instrument-rated multi-engine commercial pilot.

The bachelor of science in aeronautics provides an opportunity to acquire a broad-based education in aviation-specific courses and related instruction in business, computer science, economics, humanities, communication, social science, mathematics physical science, and other non-aviation-related fields.

The bachelor of science in applied meteorology provides a practical understanding of the physics and dynamics of the atmosphere and prepares graduates for a range of meteorologist positions in government or industry. With a focus on climatology and its applications, this program offers areas of concentration in flight, meteorology for aviation operations, military meteorology, and research.

The bachelor of science in aerospace engineering allows students to focus on the design of either aircraft or spacecraft. The program's focus is primarily on the engineering of mission-oriented vehicles for atmospheric or space flight.

The bachelor of science in computer engineering degree gives a broad background in computer hardware design, including embedded control systems, real-time systems, software engineering, and telecommunication systems.

The bachelor of science degree in electrical engineering is a systems-oriented program of study that includes analog and digital circuits, communication systems, computers, control systems, electromagnetic fields, energy sources and systems, and electronic materials and devices related to aerospace and avionics.

The bachelor of science in mechanical engineering focuses on the design of propulsion or robotic systems, such as autonomous ground, air, or space vehicles. Courses cover robotics, controls, vibration and acoustics, machine design, and numerical modeling.

The bachelor of science in global security and intelligence studies (GSIS) program is designed to prepare security and intelligence professionals to become problem-solvers with expertise in such issues as terrorism and asymmetrical warfare, transportation security (especially aviation and aerospace), threats to manufacturing facilities and corporate offices, as well as threats to computer systems and telecommunications infrastructure.

The bachelor of science in aviation environmental science program offers a multidisciplinary education with areas of concentration in applied environmental science and environmental management. Graduates have the knowledge and technical skills needed to tackle the unique environmental and safety problems found in the aviation and aerospace industry, such as noise abatement, wildlife habitat, and hazardous materials.

The bachelor of science degree in aviation business administration integrates in-depth study of aviation, transportation, and government interface with a strong business foundation. Specialized aviation-related studies include management, finance, flight operations, and airport management.

The bachelor of science in space physics prepares students to excel in a wide range of careers and scientific pursuits, from solving problems associated with prolonged space missions to unraveling the mysteries of the universe. Areas of concentration include astrophysics, particle physics and cosmology, exotic propulsion, and remote sensing.

The bachelor of science in aerospace studies is a unique interdisciplinary degree with unlimited potential. Aerospace Studies allows students to customize their undergraduate curriculum to match their specific career goals and interests by choosing 3 minor areas of study to create their own major.

ACADEMIC PROGRAMS

Along with their major, students may opt to select a minor from many fields, such as air traffic control, Asian Studies, aviation safety, or helicopter flight; or they may work toward an Aircraft Dispatcher Certificate. Army and Air Force Reserve Officer Training Corps (ROTC) courses are also available to all Embry-Riddle students and may lead to a position as a commissioned officer.

Education at Embry-Riddle goes far beyond the classroom. Through participation in internships and cooperative education (co-op) arrangements, students in all fields of study gain valuable work experience with companies such as Continental Airlines, Delta Air Lines, the Federal Aviation Administration (FAA), Honeywell, Gulfstream Aerospace Corporation, Lockheed Martin, NASA, Northwest Airlines, the Naval Air Systems Command, the CIA, and Raytheon.

Study abroad programs provide a variety of international study options. A Foreign Language Institute at the Prescott campus offers summer immersion in either Arabic or Chinese.

Opportunities for undergraduate research abound, including FAA-supported research exploring wildlife management at airports and NSF-funded research in both astrophysics and emerging threats to aviation facilities.

CAMPUS FACILITIES AND EQUIPMENT

Tucked into the rolling hillsides, the campus blends nature with the layout of its buildings. The new Hazy Library and Learning Center is under final construction and scheduled to open in 2008; a brand new dining hall just opened in January 2008. An interfaith chapel is also under construction and will open in 2008 as well.

The Robertson Aviation Safety Center houses the nation's only university level accident investigation laboratory. This outdoor facility features an in-the-field investigation lab for studying wreckage sites of actual aircraft accidents.

Classroom buildings house specialized labs, including an airway science lab, a particle physics lab, exotic propulsion lab, optics lab, and remote sensing lab. There is also a campus observatory housing a CCD (charged coupled device) debris telescope.

The Academic Complex has 2 computer design labs for engineering students and a weather center. Rooftop weather instrumentation includes state-of-the-art weather observing equipment, a weather radar, and a weather balloon launching facility.

The Aerospace Experimentation and Fabrication Building (AXFAB) offers leading edge resources to students. Labs include a fabrication suite with a machine shop, materials science and testing labs, structures lab, structural dynamics lab, and a space systems lab. Within its labs, students will utilize the 2-axis electromagnetic shaker to simulate the vibration environment of a space launch, vacuum chambers to simulate space environment, and 2 stereo-lithography 3-D printers to bring their own designs to life.

Students are able to test their designs in 4 wind tunnels—3 subsonic and 1 supersonic, located in the Tracy Doryland Wind Tunnel Building. Additional equipment includes a water tunnel for flow visualization and a micro-turbojet used in a rockets and turbine engines course.

The 22,000-square-foot King Engineering and Technology Center houses a computer science classroom, the Computer-Aided Engineering Lab, and the UNIX Lab, which provide students with the latest in computer technologies. This center also houses the Linear Lab, Electrical Engineering Senior Design Lab, Electronics Power Lab, Honeywell Control, System Integration Lab, and the Machine Vision Lab. This particular lab specializes in applied research and development leading to the advancement of robust solutions for machine vision, machine perception, and robotics applications.

College of Engineering labs and equipment at the Prescott Campus are easily accessible and used exclusively by undergraduate students. Numerous hands-on lab and design experiences provide students the opportunity to use their knowledge, test their analyses, and work in a team environment.

Two miles from campus, the Embry-Riddle Flight Training Center occupies several buildings at the Prescott Municipal Airport. Currently, the Prescott fleet includes Cessna 172s, Piper Seminoles, an American Champion Decathlon for extreme attitude recovery, a Cessna 182-RG and 2 Cessna 150s for the flight team. New DA42 Diamond Twin Stars will be added to the fleet this summer. All aircraft are ADS-b equipped and the Cessnas and Diamonds are equipped with Garmin G1000 navigation systems. Also at the flight line are flight-training devices (FTDs), including 3 Cessna 172s and 2 Seminole Level 6 FTDs, all with 220-degree visual display, 2 Frasca 141 FTDs, 1 Frasca 142 FTD, and an Airbus A320 simulator.

Athletic facilities on campus include an activities hub with indoor volleyball and basketball courts, a fitness center, a training room with a whirlpool, a multi-purpose gym, and a matted room for wrestling, aerobics, and martial arts. Other facilities include a softball field, intercollegiate soccer field, tennis courts, sand volleyball courts, a 25 yard swimming pool, racquetball courts, a running track, and a multi-sport recreation field.

STUDENT ORGANIZATIONS AND ACTIVITIES

There are more than 75 student clubs and organizations, including professional associations, fraternities and sororities, specialty clubs, and intramural sports. The National Association of Intercollegiate Athletics (NAIA) men's soccer and wrestling teams and the NAIA women's soccer and volleyball teams compete both regionally and nationally. The Golden Eagles intercollegiate precision flight team has consistently ranked among the top in the country in the Safety and Flight Evaluation Conference (SAFECON) competitions and has captured the national championship title 6 times.

TUITION, ROOM, BOARD, AND FEES

The 2008-2009 academic year tuition for all programs is $13,210 per semester for full-time students. Flight fees are charged in addition to tuition on a pay as you proceed basis. On-campus housing accommodations range from $2,175 to $2,350 per semester, depending on the residence hall; the required meal plan for freshmen is $1,675 per semester. Fees include parking, student government, technology, and health services, totaling $805. Students also need to account for the cost of books, transportation, and personal expenses.

FINANCIAL AID

Students and their families find many sources of aid available to assist with paying the costs of a private university. Embry-Riddle participates in all national and state assistance programs. The completion of the Department of Education's Free Application for Federal Student Aid (FAFSA) form is necessary for students to receive consideration for these funds. In addition, Embry-Riddle provides assistance in the form of academic scholarships, need-based grants, on campus jobs, veterans' educational benefits, and ROTC incentives.

ADMISSIONS PROCESS

Each student receives individual consideration for admission, which is based on a variety of factors and circumstances. Completion of the Embry-Riddle application for admission begins this process; students also need to submit official transcripts, score reports for either the SAT or ACT, as well as 2 letters of recommendation. Acceptance notification takes place throughout the year.

EMMANUEL COLLEGE

AT A GLANCE

Emmanuel College is a co-ed, residential, Catholic liberal arts and sciences college located on 17 acres in the middle of the excitement, resources, and culture of the city of Boston. Emmanuel's neighbors include a world-class medical center, 2 major art museums, and Fenway Park. With a strong liberal arts and sciences core curriculum, our proud tradition since 1919, Emmanuel has more than 1,700 undergraduate students from 24 countries and 32 states. A new Academic Science Center, opening in 2009, will advance Emmanuel's education mission, as it reflects the college's goal of building distinctive Academic Programs in the liberal arts and sciences through leveraging its unique location in the Longwood Medical Area.

LOCATION AND ENVIRONMENT

Our campus is alive with energy of teaching and learning, exploration, and research. Our grassy quad is framed by classic brick buildings and contemporary architecture, flowering bushes, simple benches and peaceful stone statuary. We sit on 17 acres in the midst of the excitement, resources and culture of Boston. Our neighbors are the world-class surgeons of the Longwood Medical area, the Monets and Gauguins of the Museum of Fine Arts, and 250,000 college students at institutions across the city.

OFF-CAMPUS OPPORTUNITIES

Emmanuel's neighbors include a world-class medical center, 2 major art museums, and Fenway Park. Emmanuel College's unique location allows student and faculty the opportunities to explore real-world experiences through internships, research, and strategic partnerships within the Longwood Medical area and the city of Boston, our extended classroom. We also believe in the transforming power of education through service learning, travel, and opportunities abroad. You can choose to spend a summer, a semester or a year at one of many universities, Emmanuel students have studied around the world, including management in China, education in Australia, art in Italy, and political and economic development in Central America.

Our 5 neighboring colleges, Massachusetts College of Art and Design, Massachusetts College of Pharmacy and Health Sciences, Simmons College, Wentworth Institute of Technology, and Wheelock College, join as the Colleges of the Fenway, where we share resources so that you can take a highly specialized course we may not offer, find an unusual library book, or play in our shared orchestra.

MAJORS AND DEGREES OFFERED

We offer opportunities in the pursuit of learning, teaching, exploration, and research in more than 25 areas of study. We take these studies to new levels from art, education, English, and history to biology, psychology, global studies, and chemistry. We encourage the pursuit of an individualized major by tailoring a course of study from our offerings.

Students may pursue majors in American studies, art (art therapy, graphic design and technology, studio art), biochemistry, biology, biostatistics, chemistry, education (elementary and secondary), English (communication, literature, and writing and literature), environmental science, forensic science, global studies, history, management, mathematics, neuroscience, political science, psychology (counseling and health, developmental, and general/ experimental), sociology, Spanish, individualized major.

Students may also minor in applied ethics, Catholic studies, economics, information technology, Latin American studies, organizational leadership, performance arts, philosophy, religious studies, speech/ theater arts, and women studies.

ACADEMIC PROGRAMS

All first-year students are required to take a first-year seminar of his or her choice in the fall or spring semester. This innovative program is designed to build a strong academic foundation for the rest of your college career.

Each year, highly motivated students are invited to participate in our honors program. First-year students are eligible to take part in the Emmanuel Honors Colloquium, an intense, bi-monthly discussion of books and other texts with faculty.

The Carolyn A. Lynch Institute is dedicated to preparing teachers in mathematics, science, and technology for urban elementary and secondary levels. The Carolyn A. Lynch Institute awards scholarships to talented undergraduates with a commitment to this goal.

To help students continue to succeed beyond our campus, our pre-health and pre-law advisory committee helps you tailor your academic program toward your goals and will guide you through the application process.

From workshops to individual peer tutoring, the Academic Research Center offers specially designed programs to help any students in any major meet her or his academic goals.

LEADERS: This is a unique program that recognizes that learning takes place outside of the classroom. The program fosters confidence, leadership skills, and inner strength by focusing on leadership, ethics, activities, dedication to service, exploration, relationships, and spirituality.

CAMPUS FACILITIES AND EQUIPMENT

The Jean Yawkey Center for Community Leadership is dedicated to developing service opportunities and leadership skills for our students while building bridges between this community and the young people of the city of Boston through after-school and summer programs.

Emmanuel College is the only college in the country to boast a 12-story 300,000 square-foot private research facility right on campus that is doing research in fields of cancer treatment, Alzheimer's disease, and obesity. It is owned by Merck & Co., the global research-driven pharmaceutical company, on land they lease from the college. In return, Emmanuel has access and opportunity to a world few undergraduates get to see.

With more than 80 different co-curricular clubs, activities, and organizations on campus, this is a community alive with a string sense of mission, a vibrant, confident faith, and a joyful spirit. Emmanuel students are changes to act, to lead, and to give generously to others; community service is a hallmark of the Emmanuel experience.

Emmanuel's NCAA Division III athletics programs give every recruit a chance to make his or her mark. Emmanuel offers 14 varsity teams. Our strong intramural sports program keeps everyone in the game. Our athletic program focuses on the development of the whole person. At Emanuel, everyone who wants to play, gets to play.

FINANCIAL AID

At Emmanuel, financial assistance programs include a combination of scholarships, institutional grants, federal and state grants, federal loans, and part-time employment. Merit scholarships are based on a combination of your high school GPA and SAT/ACT test results, or other factors, including leadership and community service, or recommendations from an alumna or a current faculty or a staff member of the college.

TUITION, ROOM, BOARD, AND FEES

Emmanuel College is committed to providing students with a quality education at an affordable cost. And we offer billing options and payment plans to ensure that you're able to pay for college in the way most convenient for you.

2007-2008 Tuition and Fees

Tuition: $26,100

Room and board: $11,200 (double occupancy)

Fees: $525

Health insurance: $1,375 (Emmanuel plan 2007-2008)

Total: $ 37,825 (plus own health insurance), $39,200 (including Emmanuel insurance)

ADMISSIONS PROCESS

For more information or to apply for admission, please visit www.emmanuel.edu. We require an Emmanuel College application or the Common Application, available online, an essay, a secondary school transcript that includes first semester grades, 2 letters of recommendation, and the SAT or ACT test. Students whose native language is not English should submit the TOEFL.

Everyone is unique at Emmanuel, where "there are students that are very religious, not at all religious, very into sports, not at all into sports, those that love art, music and theater, and those that don't care about such things. There is a good balance of types here. Everyone can find a group that they get along well with." Different types of students "all tend to hang out with others like them, but people intermingle as well." Most students "are involved with at least 1 organization or sports team" and "get their work done on the weekdays but party on the weekends." The student body is largely drawn "from the New England suburbs or the city of Boston itself." Emmanuel has a roughly 3:1 female to male ratio, but with total enrollment increasing "at an incredible rate," students hope this will balance out soon.

EMORY AND HENRY COLLEGE

AT A GLANCE

Founded in 1836, Emory & Henry is the oldest college in Southwest Virginia. It is one of the few Southern colleges to have operated more than 170 years under the same name and with the same affiliation: the United Methodist Church. The campus and surrounding village is home to students as well as professors, administrators, and retired college employees. It is an academic environment that underscores the broad dedication within the community to each student's enlightenment and success.

LOCATION AND ENVIRONMENT

Emory & Henry is located in Emory, Virginia, which is approximately 25 miles north of Bristol, a city that offers large shopping areas, movies, and restaurants. The area surrounding Emory is known for its scenic beauty, recreational opportunities, and talented craftsmen. Within an hour's drive are slopes for snow skiing, lakes for waterskiing, the Appalachian Trail for hiking, and locations for horseback riding, canoeing, and many other sports. The historic town of Abingdon, Virginia, which lies just 7 miles south of Emory, is the home of the renowned Barter Theatre, the oldest professional theater in the United States. Abingdon's downtown district includes shopping areas, movie theaters, restaurants, and museums. The city also hosts the annual Virginia Highlands Festival, bringing together musicians, artists, and craftsmen for exhibitions and competition.

OFF-CAMPUS OPPORTUNITIES

The Appalachian Center for Community Service is available for students committed to community service and integrates service learning into many classes. The King Health and Physical Education Center includes a new fitness center and enhances the college athletics program. Varsity sports for men are baseball, basketball, cross-country, football, golf, soccer, and tennis; women compete in basketball, cross-country, soccer, softball, swimming, tennis, and volleyball. Several sports are played on a club basis. A large percentage of E&H students engage in community projects that often involve policy research and advocacy aimed at benefiting the region. An aggressive internship program provides on-the-job opportunities for students in most of the college's programs, providing academic credit for off-campus work in community agencies and businesses. Many students have completed internships in the surrounding communities, while others have opted for internships outside the region, including several in Washington, DC, in positions related to the Congress or the federal government. Emory & Henry students participate in a wide variety of study-abroad programs. From Rome to Beijing and from Eastern Europe to East Asia, Emory and Henry students experience cultures and people in a way that enriches their perspective on their studies, their lives, and their futures. Emory and Henry helps students prepare for these experiences through language study and with courses offered through a comprehensive international studies program and an international studies and business program. The college has exchange agreements with colleges and universities in Asia, Europe, and Central and South America. Students who desire other types of travel/study are assisted by faculty and staff members in locating suitable programs.

MAJORS AND DEGREES OFFERED

Emory & Henry College offers programs of study in art, athletic training, biology, business administration, chemistry, computer information management, economics, education (early childhood through high school, including many subject-area options), English, environmental studies, geography, history, international studies (East Asia, European community, or Middle Eastern and Islamic studies), languages, mass communications, mathematics, music, philosophy, physical education, physics, political science, psychology, public policy and community service; religion, sociology, and anthropology, and theater (in association with the Barter Theatre, the state theater of Virginia). Pre-professional preparation in dentistry, law, medicine, and veterinary medicine may be completed within several of the programs. The bachelor of arts degree is awarded in all programs of study and the bachelor of science degree in selected areas. Individualized programs of study may be developed in consultation with a faculty advisor.

ACADEMIC PROGRAMS

Emory & Henry offers a liberal arts program with an emphasis on writing, reasoning, value inquiry, and knowledge of global concerns, as well as a broad introduction to liberal arts subjects. All students complete a core curriculum, which includes a year-long, interdisciplinary Western tradition course and a writing course for all first-year students. Sophomores complete an ambitious Great Books program, and upperclass students take courses related to value inquiry and global studies. Along with the core curriculum, each student completes a major and a minor or a combined program referred to as an area of concentration. Students also have the opportunity to choose elective courses and to participate in international exchange programs. Undergraduate programs of study include art, athletic training, biology, business administration, chemistry, computer information management, economics, education, English, geography, history, languages, mass communications, mathematics, music, philosophy, physical education, physics, political science, psychology, religion, sociology and anthropology, and theater. Special and interdisciplinary programs of study offered are environmental studies, international studies, pre-engineering, pre-law, pre-medicine, and public policy and community service. Emory & Henry operates on a semester calendar from late August to mid-December and from mid-January to mid-May. A summer session runs from late May to early July. First-year students typically carry a 4-course load of 13 to 14 credit hours per semester, including the year-long course on Western tradition. Upperclass students carrying a full load complete 5 courses (14 to 15 credit hours) each semester. Thirty-eight courses are required for graduation. Classes meet on Monday-Wednesday-Friday or Tuesday-Thursday schedules. One important feature of the Emory and Henry curriculum is its orientation toward helping students make a smooth transition from high school to college. The Powell Resource Center provides academic support, advising, career services, and personal counseling. The Writing Center helps students in every department to use writing for effective communication.

CAMPUS FACILITIES AND EQUIPMENT

McGlothlin-Street Hall is a 70,000-square-foot academic center that houses the departments of biology, business, chemistry, education, environmental studies, geography, international studies, and psychology; a 104-seat auditorium; and a tiered 60-seat auditorium. Classrooms and laboratories in McGlothlin-Street Hall are equipped with the most current technological equipment, including Internet access and interactive TV. Miller-Fulton Hall contains computerized classrooms used for instruction in such fields as accounting and computer science. Another computerized classroom in Byars Hall is used for instruction in writing, desktop publishing, and related fields. Science departments located in Miller-Fulton and McGlothlin-Street Halls feature a variety of equipment, such as a microcomputer-based laboratory for physics students, computerized chromatography for chemistry students, a DNA sequencer in the biology department, and biofeedback equipment. Art students have access to studios, an exhibition area, and printing equipment, and music students make use of practice rooms and a recital hall. In 2006, the construction on 2 new student residence halls was completed. The residence halls, which are located in Emory a few blocks from the main campus, enhance the Emory and Henry academic village where professors, students, and administrators live, work, and learn together. Built in 1889 the newly renovated Byars Hall houses 3 stories of classrooms, seminar rooms choir and ensemble rehearsal halls, a digital art lab, a dark room, 2 large art studios, practice rooms for instrumental music, and a theater support room. Wiley Hall, which was built in 1929, houses numerous administrative offices as well as some faculty offices and classroom space. The combined cost of the renovations would run close to $10 million. The library collection consists of more than 350,000 items, including books, periodicals, government documents, audio and videotapes, compact discs, DVDs, and electronic databases. The library contains a group of computers reserved for library research, an open computer lab, and a computer classroom.

Students at Emory & Henry are encouraged to take part in campus decision making. They have voting representatives on nearly every faculty committee and on the Board of Trustees. The central body in campus government is the Student Senate, which brings together representatives of the student body, faculty, and administration. Students have opportunities for involvement in a variety of campus activities: service clubs, Christian fellowship, fraternities, sororities, sports clubs, honor groups, and multicultural groups. Student staffs produce a yearbook, an online magazine, and a literary magazine; others operate an educational FM radio station. Musically talented students have opportunities to participate in a choral program and a pep band. The prestigious Concert Choir has toured throughout the United States and in parts of Europe. The Barter Theatre, a professional theater in nearby Abingdon, works with Emory and Henry College to provide a theater education program that integrates college-level drama study with the benefits of experience on a professional stage.

TUITION, ROOM, BOARD, AND FEES

For 2007-08, resident students pay a comprehensive fee of $29,990, which includes tuition, room, and board.

FINANCIAL AID

Our Financial Aid Office works to ensure students receive an Emory and Henry education with a minimal amount of debt. Compared with other private colleges, our annual out-of-pocket expenses are among the lowest in Virginia. The average award to our incoming first-year students, including only grants and scholarships, is $17,746. Approximately 98 percent of all students receive financial aid. Virginia residents may qualify for the Tuition Assistance Grant (TAG), currently a $3,200 value. In recent years, the rate of alumni giving has ranged between 40 and 50 percent. This percentage of giving says volumes about the high degree of satisfaction Emory & Henry graduates have with their education. This level of giving also has translated into tremendous support for scholarships that are offered to Emory & Henry students. To determine your eligibility for these awards, visit www.ehc.edu, and click on Scholarship Calculator.

ADMISSIONS PROCESS

Emory & Henry College utilizes a rolling admissions process. In most instances, admissions decisions are made within 2 weeks of receipt of a completed application. Admission to Emory & Henry is determined on the basis of both academic achievement and personal qualifications. An applicant's secondary school preparation must include the following: 4 years of English, 3 years of mathematics (algebra I, algebra II, and geometry), 2 years of laboratory sciences, 2 years of a single foreign language, and 2 years of history and social studies. It is strongly recommended that 1 year of study in the fine arts be included. Strong emphasis is also placed on involvement and leadership in extracurricular and community activities. For financial aid, please submit a completed Free Application for Federal Student Aid (FAFSA) as soon as possible after January 1. Indicate that you want results sent to Emory & Henry College, code 003709. Virginia residents need to submit the Virginia Tuition Assistance Grant (VTAG) application by July 31.

EMORY UNIVERSITY

AT A GLANCE

Emory University is internationally recognized for its outstanding liberal arts college, highly ranked professional schools, and comprehensive health care system. Emory College, the 4-year undergraduate division of Emory University, offers a broad and rigorous liberal arts curriculum with more than 70 majors and 55 minors to choose from. With only 5,500 undergraduates, Emory provides the resources and facilities you'd expect from a major research university but the small classes and faculty attention of a smaller liberal arts college. Take a look at all Emory has to offer; you'll see why Emory students feel inspired to do more with what they learn here.

LOCATION AND ENVIRONMENT

One of Emory's most compelling features is its proximity to the vibrant city of Atlanta. Located only 15 minutes from downtown, Emory's campus is situated on 635 acres of property in the historic residential neighborhood of Druid Hills. As home to more than 700 of the country's Fortune 1000 companies, Atlanta has become a cultural, technological, and financial hub of both the Southeast and the nation. In fact, with one of the largest college student populations nationwide and endless cultural, intellectual, and social opportunities, Atlanta ranks as one of the best college towns in the United States.

OFF-CAMPUS OPPORTUNITIES

At Emory, students enjoy a balance of rigorous academics, real-world experience, and an exciting social life that are all enhanced by the campus' close proximity to Atlanta. Recently voted one of the nation's most livable cities, you'll find there's more to this Southern city than warm weather. Eclectic restaurants and independent shops surround campus, and a quick subway ride takes you to the Atlanta's sports facilities, concerts, and arts venues. Nearly 90 percent of Emory students supplement their studies with internships or research at places like the Centers for Disease Control, the Yerkes Primate Center, the Carter Center, CNN, Home Depot, and many other companies and organizations with offices in Atlanta. Volunteerism is a major component of a student's experience; on any given day Emory students can be found engaged in numerous service projects around campus and throughout the city of Atlanta.

MAJORS AND DEGREES OFFERED

From small classroom settings to lectures given by prominent scholars to opportunities for study abroad, Emory provides a rich environment for learning. Expert faculty members who emphasize teaching choose Emory for the opportunity to work with intelligent and ambitious students. The curriculum is grounded in the liberal arts, providing a challenging, broad-based education that emphasizes critical thinking and connecting ideas. With more than 75 majors, 55 minors, 9 pre-professional programs, 10 4-year combined bachelor/master degrees, and 2 dual degree programs with Georgia Tech in engineering, your options are limitless.

ACADEMIC PROGRAMS

Undergraduate programs in humanities, sciences, business, and nursing allow Emory students to explore their interests and talents in the classroom and in the field. Our 7 to one student-faculty ratio guarantees meaningful interaction between professors and students; 90 percent of classes have fewer than 40 students and 90 percent of classes are taught by full-time faculty members. Unique seminar-style classes are required for all first-year students.

Moreover, at Emory you won't just find students getting an education. Emory students are twice as likely to do research outside of the classroom as their peers. While studying environmental science, why not help build a greener building as part of the LEED initiative? Instead of simply reading about ancient history, why not help preserve mummies at the Carlos Museum on campus? How about transferring the class discussion during a political science seminar into an internship at a think tank or at the Georgia State Capitol? Take a look at the resources for learning at Emory and think about what you could do with them. You might discover the desire to choreograph modern dance or to develop an AIDS vaccine. Regardless of what you choose to tackle first, Emory will give you the tools to transform the world.

In 2007, Emory celebrated many exciting faculty appointments and new acquisitions for the extensive archive collections, including: His Holiness the XIV Dalai Lama was named Presidential Distinguished Professor at Emory University, the first university appointment accepted by the 1989 Nobel Peace Laureate and leader of the Tibetan exile community. Also joining the Emory faculty in 2007 was Sir Salman Rushdie, one of the world's most celebrated contemporary authors. Rushdie's 5 year appointment in the English Department as Distinguished Writer in Residence is his first extended relationship with a university and he will also place his archive at Emory's Woodruff Library. And in December 2007, Alice Walker, Pulitzer Prize-winner and internationally known Georgia-born novelist and poet, announced her plans to place her archive with Emory University.

CAMPUS FACILITIES AND EQUIPMENT

Emory is a dynamic place that is constantly in a state of growth and improvement. In congruence with the university's commitment to the environment, Emory is a national leader in the construction of green buildings, which meet certification standards set by Leadership in Energy and Environmental Design (LEED). Recent projects include a 2-building initiative to expand facilities for physical science and mathematical research; the creation of a pedestrian-friendly campus with more walking paths and common gathering areas; an apartment-style living complex for upper-class students; a multimedia library addition; renovation of the Cox Hall Food Court, a 10 building LEED certified Freshman Residence Hall Complex, a new psychology building, and a new performing arts center.

Thanks to numerous benefactors over the years, Emory is able to consistently improve student resources ranging from facilities and communications to faculty and staff. With wired classrooms and satellite conferencing, Emory is on the cutting edge of teaching technology. Computer labs and Ethernet ports are available throughout campus, as well as wireless access points in the library, residence halls, and the Quad. Students often use our computer labs for group work, so our Cox Computing Center is a sleek, high-tech space designed specifically for collaborative activity. Students who wish to integrate technology into academic work may do so at the Center for Interactive Teaching, where they can access resources including digital video systems, presentation design, Web design, and audio and video editing.

TUITION, ROOM, BOARD, AND FEES

Undergraduate Expenses 2007-2008

Tuition: $33,900

Fees: $436

Room: $6,284

Board: $3,936

Estimated books and supplies: $1,000

Estimated travel and incidentals: $600

Total: $46,956

FINANCIAL AID

We understand that paying for a college education is a big investment. The undergraduate admission process at Emory is need-blind, and we are committed to meeting 100 percent of each student's demonstrated need. We offer both need-based and merit-based financial assistance that can make an Emory education affordable for all families. Additionally, Emory Advantage reduces debt burden for families with annual incomes less than $100,000 who demonstrate a need for financial aid. We're committed to opening our doors to all qualified students who want a world-class education and to use their talents to impact the world. www.emory.edu/FINANCIAL_AID/.

STUDENT ORGANIZATIONS AND ACTIVITIES

Emory students are highly involved in extracurricular activities, dedicating 6 to 10 hours per week to more than 220 clubs, teams, and organizations. Whether it's Jazz Ensemble, intramural sports, the *Emory Wheel* (student newspaper), Concert Choir, or Outdoor Emory, there's an organization for you. Furthermore, 80 percent of our students share their passion for service and enthusiasm for Emory by volunteering on-campus and throughout the local community.

ADMISSIONS PROCESS

Emory's Admission Committee closely assesses high school course work and grades. Within the context of the curriculum available at your high school, we determine if a student has taken the most rigorous courses possible. We also consider your extracurricular involvement, paying close attention to your commitment and leadership in after-school activities. SAT I and ACT (with writing) scores are important but not as important as the rigor of the course work and grades earned. The middle 50th percent range for successful applicants is 640-730 for the SAT Critical Reading, 660-740 for SAT Math, and 640-730 for the SAT Writing. The middle 50th percent range for the ACT (with writing) Composite is 29-33. Ninety percent of Emory's freshman class came from the top 10 percent of their graduating high school class with an average GPA of 3.8.

FELICIAN COLLEGE

AT A GLANCE

Felician College is a liberal arts, coeducational, Catholic Franciscan college located in northern New Jersey. Founded in 1942 by the Franciscan Sisters, Felician College currently enrolls 2,200 students in more than 40 undergraduate and graduate programs in the arts and sciences, business and management sciences, health sciences, and teacher education. Felician College's NCAA Division II athletic teams compete in basketball, soccer, baseball, softball, cross country, and women's volleyball. Cheerleading and dance teams root the athletes on and show off their own skills in competitions throughout the year.

With a mission to provide a values-oriented education based in the liberal arts, Felician College prepares students for meaningful lives and careers in today's competitive marketplace. Day, evening, and weekend programs are offered to meet the needs of Felician's diverse student body, and students may take course work through semester or accelerated trimester formats. Two summer sessions are also available each year for non-matriculated students.

Felician College is accredited by the Middle States Association of Colleges and Schools and carries program accreditation from the National League for Nursing Accrediting Commission, the National Accrediting Agency for Clinical Laboratory Sciences, the International Assembly for Collegiate Business Education, and the Teacher Education Accrediting Council.

On the graduate level, Felician College offers a master of business administration, master of science in nursing (MSN), a master of arts in religious education, and master of arts in education and educational leadership. Additionally, Felician offers joint programs in the health sciences terminating on the Doctoral or master's level in audiology, podiatric medicine chiropractic studies, physician assistant studies, physical therapy, optometry, and occupational therapy collaboration with several universities including the University of Medicine and Dentistry of New Jersey (UMDNJ).

LOCATION AND ENVIRONMENT

Felician College is located on 2 beautifully landscaped campuses in Lodi and Rutherford, New Jersey. Both campuses, set in suburban towns, are a 30-minute bus or train ride from New York City and a few miles from the New Jersey Meadowlands sports complex. With classes offered on both campuses, free shuttle buses transport students between the campuses, which are located just a few miles apart.

The college houses an impressive library collection with more than 120,000 books, professional journals, periodicals, microforms, CD-ROMs, and PCs for online learning. A curriculum library serves as a resource center for the teacher education programs.

MAJORS AND DEGREES OFFERED

Felician College offers programs of study in the arts and sciences, business and management sciences, health sciences, and teacher education.

Departmental majors for a bachelor of arts degree include art with a concentration in fine art, graphic art, or new media, biology, business administration with concentrations in accounting, marketing/management, communications with concentrations in journalism, theater arts, and video production, computer science with a concentration in computer security and information assurance, criminal justice, English, history, humanities, mathematics, natural sciences, including general science, mathematical sciences, philosophy, psychology, religious studies, social sciences, including international education and foreign language, political science, and sociology.

Bachelor of arts degree programs in early childhood education, elementary education, elementary education with specialization, teachers of students with disabilities, and mathematics education K-12 enable students to seek New Jersey certification.

The health sciences division offers a generic bachelor of science in nursing degree program for high school graduates and an upper division bachelor of science in nursing degree program for registered nurses. Students who complete the 4-year generic nursing degree program are eligible to take the examination for licensure as a Registered Nurse (RN) given by the New Jersey Board of Nursing. A bachelor's degree in clinical laboratory science is also available in conjunction with UMDNJ School of Health Related Professions. For this degree, a stu-

dent may concentrate in cytotechnology, medical technology, or toxicology. Also offered in conjunction with UMDNJ is a bachelor of science program in allied-health technology. Students may study medical sonography, nuclear medicine technology, respiratory care, or vascular technology.

With a students first philosophy, Felician College provides a number of services designed to meet a variety of needs. Housed on campus are the Center for Learning, a nursing skills laboratory, and a child care center. To help students plan for their futures, a career services center coordinates field experiences, career seminars, internships, and job placements. The honors program provides an opportunity for students with strong academic records to conduct scholarly research and develop leadership skills through service learning.

ACADEMIC PROGRAMS

A candidate for the BA in liberal arts is required to complete an organized program of study comprising 120 semester hours distributed among prescribed and elective courses. Four interdisciplinary courses are required in the Core Curriculum focusing on the College Mission. In addition, students must complete 46 to 48 credits of general education courses beyond the 12-credit core. Each baccalaureate degree student in arts and sciences is required to prepare a written and oral senior research project. A minimum of 45 credit hours must be earned at the college. A student who pursues an AA degree is required to complete 64 to 68 credits in an approved program of study.

A candidate for the BA in elementary or special education is required to complete a program of 126 to 130 semester hours, including credits in general education, professional education, and a major in the arts and sciences. Field experience begins in the freshman year and students participate in a practicum in the junior year. Students conduct supervised teaching during the senior year in a public elementary school. The education programs are approved by the National Association of State Directors of Teacher Education and Certification (NASDTEC).

Clinical experiences in the medical laboratory techniques begin during the first semester, continue throughout each semester, and include a summer internship.

TUITION, ROOM, BOARD, AND FEES

The cost of undergraduate tuition for 2008-2009 is $22,200 per year for full-time students. The annual cost of room and board is $9,350 per year.

FINANCIAL AID

Felician College participates in federal, state, and institutional aid programs for financial assistance. Financial aid is available to qualified students through grants, loans, and work-study. A number of academic scholarships are awarded annually ranging from $4,500 to full tuition for 4 years based on merit or need. A tuition payment plan is also available. More than half the students attending Felician College receive financial aid.

STUDENT ORGANIZATIONS AND ACTIVITIES

Felician College offers a competitive athletic program. The college is a member of the National Collegiate Athletic Association (NCAA) Division II. The Golden Falcons athletic teams compete in men's baseball, soccer, basketball, cross-country, as well as women's softball, soccer, basketball, volleyball, cross-country. The athletic department also sponsors cheerleading and dance teams as well as numerous intramural sports activities.

With residence halls on the Rutherford campus, students may elect to reside in one of the spacious suites in Elliot Hall or Milton Court, which accommodate up to 600 students. The campuses offer comfortable student lounge areas, meeting rooms, dining halls, a gymnasium, a fitness center, and a campus green for outdoor recreation. With student events and activities dotting the calendar throughout the year, campus life bounds with energy. There are more than 23 clubs and organizations on campus to meet the special interests of the students. At orientation, new students are introduced to college life through a broad program that begins with pre-admission interviews followed by an orientation day and ongoing orientation sessions. A special theme, chosen by students, sets the tone for the year's orientation program.

ADMISSIONS PROCESS

Applicants for admission are considered for the fall semester (late August/early September) and the spring semester (January) on a rolling basis. Students are informed of an admission decision within approximately 4 weeks of the completion of their file. A completed file includes a transcript from an accredited high school (with date of graduation) or a high school equivalency certificate, satisfactory SAT I or ACT scores, a 500-word personal statement and a physician's certificate of health.

Students are eligible to transfer to Felician. Transcripts of previous college work from recognized junior or 4-year colleges are required and an evaluation will be made upon receipt of official college transcripts—students are eligible to transfer up to 90 credits. Admission requirements may be adjusted for adults on the basis of maturity and experience. Felician College offers credit for acceptable scores on the College Board Advanced Placement tests and College-Level Examination Program (CLEP) tests.

Open Houses and tours of all facilities are available through the Office of Admission. For more information on admissions, contact:

Felician College Lodi Campus

262 S. Main Street

Lodi, NJ 07644

Telephone: 201-559-6131

Website: www.felician.edu

FIVE TOWNS COLLEGE

AT A GLANCE

Nestled in the rolling hills of Long Island's North Shore, Five Towns College offers students the opportunity to study in a suburban environment that is within easy access of New York City. Founded in 1972 by a group of educators and community leaders who wished to provide students with an alternative to the large university atmosphere, Five Towns College is a nonsectarian, coeducational institution that places its emphasis on the student as an individual. Many students are drawn to Five Towns College because of its strong programs in music and music-related fields. Five Towns College is an institution of higher learning that offers 2-year, 4-year, and master and doctoral degree programs.

From as far away as England and Japan and from as close as Long Island and New York City, the 1,000 full-time students who attend the college reflect a rich cultural diversity. The college's enrollment is currently 60 percent men and 40 percent women; there is a minority population of approximately 30 percent. The college's music programs are contemporary in nature although classical musicians are also part of this creative community.

Coeducational living accommodations are available on campus. Each Residence hall contains single- and double-occupancy rooms equipped with private bathrooms, broadband Internet access, cable television, and other amenities.

The college serves the cause of business, education, and the performing arts with emphasis on jazz/commercial music. The most popular programs are audio recording technology, broadcasting, journalism, music performance, music business, music and elementary education, theater, and film/video production.

The college seeks to foster, in those who participate in its intimate community, a noble commitment to ethical, intellectual, and social values, and seeks to encourage and stimulate the pursuit of lifelong learning. It encourages its students to respect the differences of others as well as to develop their own unique talents to the fullest. To ensure that students place such high demands upon themselves, the college seeks out for its faculty, men and women who are committed to excellence in teaching, guidance, and scholarship.

Five Towns College, in its recruitment and retention of individuals for membership in our college community, remains open to all qualified persons.

LOCATION AND ENVIRONMENT

The college's serene 40-acre campus, located in the wooded countryside of Dix Hills in the town of Huntington, New York, provides students with a park-like refuge where they can pursue their studies. Just off campus is Long Island's bustling Route 110 corridor, the home of numerous national and multinational corporations. New York City, with everything from Lincoln Center to Broadway is just a train ride away and provides students with some of the best cultural advantages in the world. Closer to campus, the many communities of Long Island abound with the cultural and recreational opportunities. The college is located within the historic town of Huntington, which is home to the Cinema Arts Center, InterMedia Arts Center, Hecksher Museum, Vanderbilt Museum, numerous restaurants, coffeehouses, and quaint shops. The nearby shores of Jones Beach State Park and the Fire Island National Seashore are world-renowned for their white, sandy beaches.

OFF-CAMPUS OPPORTUNITIES

Off-campus internship opportunities are available for all Five Towns College students who have fulfilled the necessary prerequisites, including a cumulative GPA of at least 3.0, with a 2.5 in their major. In recent semesters, students have obtained valuable field experience interning for major corporations such as MTV, Atlantic Records, Polygram Records, CBS Records, EMI Records, MCA Records, Cablevision, Channel 12 News, the Power Station, SONY Records, Pyramid Recording Studios, and many others.

MAJORS AND DEGREES OFFERED

Associate in arts (AA) in liberal arts, teaching assistant, literature.

Associate in science (AS) in business administration.

Associate in applied science (AAS) in business management, accounting, audio recording technology, business management, computer business applications, music business.

Associate in applied science (AAS) in jazz/commercial music, music performance.

Bachelor of music (MusB) in jazz/commercial music, music performance, composition/songwriting, musical theater, audio recording technology, music business.

Bachelor of music (MusB) in music education.

Bachelor of professional studies (BPS) in business management, audio recording technology, music business.

Bachelor of fine arts (BFA) in theater arts.

Bachelor of fine arts (BFA) in film/video.

Bachelor of science (BS) in childhood education.

Bachelor of science (BS) in mass communication, broadcasting, journalism.

Master of music (MusM) in jazz/commercial music concentrations: music performance, composition/arranging, music history, music technology.

Master of music (MusM) in music education.

Master of education (MSEd) in childhood education

Doctor of musical arts (DMA) in music performance, composition and arranging, music education, music history, literature.

ACADEMIC PROGRAMS

The comprehensive program in jazz/commercial music provides both a common core of technical studies and a foundation for specialized courses in the student's major are of concentration.

The audio recording technology includes the study of the theory of sound, recording electronics, engineering procedures, music production techniques, and audio/video post production in a sequence of courses designed to develop practical and technical skills.

The composition/songwriting concentration provides intensive instruction in harmony, orchestration, counterpoint, MIDI, songwriting, keyboard techniques, form and analysis, commercial arranging, and composition.

In the music business concentration, the course work includes the technical, legal, production, management, and merchandising and licensing aspects of the music business.

The musical theatre/vocal concentration includes course work in music, movement, acting, voice, general education, and musical theater production.

The performance concentration provides a foundation of specialized courses such as music history, harmony, counterpoint, improvisation, ensemble performance, and private instruction.

The music education program leads to New York State provisional certification in grades K-12.

The business management program is designed for students planning to pursue careers as business management/marketing executives with firms in the area of record and music production, broadcasting, concert promotion, radio, television, theater, and communications.

The childhood education program fulfills the New York State Education Department requirements for the Initial Certificate in Childhood Education (1-6).

The film/video program is designed to provide the knowledge and technical expertise required to succeed in the wide range of career paths this interesting and expanding field has to offer; including cinematography, motion picture editing, and multi-camera television production.

The broadcasting students explore the technical, legal, programming, and marketing issues that guide mass media companies. In the Journalism concentration, students explore a variety of different journalistic styles, including news, script, feature, magazine, editorial, and review writing.

The theatre arts program is designed for students interested in a career in the performing arts field as an actor, entertainer, director, stage managers, lighting or sound technician, or any other related aspect of the dynamic and rapidly expanding entertainment industry.

CAMPUS FACILITIES AND EQUIPMENT

The Five Towns College campus is equipped with the latest information technology and a wide variety of facilities that support the college's instructional program, student services, and extracurricular activities.

These state-of-the-art facilities include 3 audio recording studios, a film/television studio, piano lab, MIDI lab hosted by Apple G5 iMACs, computer graphics/video editing lab hosted by Apple G5 PowerMacs, PC lab, as well as the college library, learning center, music rooms and music studios, new space and studio theatres, Upbeat Café, performing arts center, and the college bookstore.

Five Towns College is licensed by the Federal Communication Commission to operate commercial radio station WFTU (1570 AM). The main broadcast studio is located on the college campus at Dix Hills. The radio station is also streamed on the Web.

The college library has more than 35,000 print and non-print materials. These includes nearly 30,000 books and print items, 500 periodical subscriptions, and approximately 5,000 records, 2,500 videos and DVD's, and more than 2,000 CD's. Through its membership in the Long Island Library Resource Council (LILRC), students have access to other libraries around the country.

Multi-strand Fiber optic cabling is the college's backbone for its Local Area Network (LAN). A 50Mbps Ethernet hand off provides access to the Web. All students have access to this network and are provided with an e-mail account.

TUITION, ROOM, BOARD, AND FEES

For the 2007-2008 academic year, the tuition at Five Towns College was $17,400. Miscellaneous fees are approximately $600, and books are about $1,000. Private instruction fees for music students are $675 per semester. For information regarding on-campus room and board charges, contact the Five Towns College Admissions Office.

FINANCIAL AID

Although Five Towns College is a modestly priced private institution, we recognize that tuition and fees is beyond the reach of many students. Five Towns College responds to the needs of these students with a comprehensive financial aid program.

Approximately 72 percent of all FTC students receive some financial assistance. The Financial Aid Office administers several million dollars of student aid monies every year. FTC students are eligible to participate in all Title IV Student Financial Assistance programs, including Pell, FSEOG, FCWS, and the Direct Student Loan Program. New York State Residents may also participate in the Tuition Assistance Program (TAP). Five Towns College also administers approximately $2,000,000 in grants and scholarships to eligible students.

For applications and specific program requirements for each Financial Aid Program, students should contact the Five Towns College Financial Aid Office at 631-424-7000 x 2164 as early as possible.

ADMISSIONS PROCESS

Five Towns College seeks students who are generally able to benefit from the programs of study available at the college and who will enrich the lives of their fellow students by actively participating in the academic process and debate. Although all applicants are considered, the college encourages applications from students who have attained a minimum high school grade point average of 80 percent, and SAT-1 scores of approximately 980 (old version) or 1350 (new version). Prospective students must submit a completed application and an official high school transcript. Transfer students must also submit official transcripts of all college-level work attempted. International students must present a TOEFL score of at least 520 or its equivalent. The Admissions Office will consider the entirety of a candidate's application before rendering a decision on admissions. Students submitting GED scores of at least 2500 are also invited to apply for admission. Students may be admitted for deferred entrance or advanced standing. The college does accept students on an early admissions basis, although early decision is available.

Admission into the bachelor of music program is contingent upon passing an audition demonstrating skill in performance on a major instrument or vocally. Applicants for a bachelor of fine arts program are also auditioned. An interview may be required. Students are accepted on a rolling admission basis and are notified shortly after all required documents have been filed with the admissions office. New students may begin their studies at the start of either the fall semester or the spring semester. There is an application fee of $35.

For further information, students should contact:

Five Towns College

Director of Admissions

305 North Service Road

Dix Hills, NY 11746-5871

Telephone: 631-424-7000, ext. 2110

Website: www.fivetowns.edu

FLORIDA ATLANTIC UNIVERSITY

AT A GLANCE

Florida Atlantic University is a public research university with multiple campuses along the southeast Florida coast serving a uniquely diverse community. It promotes academic and personal development, discovery, and lifelong learning. FAU fulfills its mission through excellence and innovation in teaching, outstanding research and creative activities, public engagement, and distinctive scientific and cultural alliances, all within an environment that fosters inclusiveness. Florida Atlantic University was established by the Florida State Legislature in 1961 as the fifth university in the state system. When it originally opened in 1964, FAU was the first university in the country to offer only upper-division and graduate-level work, on the theory that freshmen and sophomores could be served by the community college system. Located in rapidly growing Southeast Florida, the university responded to the need to provide increased access to educational opportunities by opening its doors to freshmen in 1984. Today, with its developed system of distributed campuses, where the same high-quality education is offered at 7 different locations, Florida Atlantic University serves as a model for urban, regional universities of the future. It offers a comprehensive array of undergraduate and graduate programs, and enrolls students who reflect the rich cultural diversity of the region. FAU has Eminent Scholar Chairs in multiple disciplines and is the home of nationally recognized research centers. The university's burgeoning Research Park is facilitating exciting new research and learning initiatives by bringing high-tech industries into close collaboration with FAU's faculty and students. In recognition of the university's research funding and doctoral programs, the Florida Board of Regents has designated FAU as one of the states public research universities. Florida Atlantic University is a member of the Southern Association of Colleges and Schools, the National Association of State Universities and Land-Grant Colleges, and the Council of Graduate Schools in the United States.

LOCATION AND ENVIRONMENT

The university's campus locations along the Florida Gold and Treasure coasts, which boast a temperate climate and beautiful beaches, innovative industry, and unique cultural opportunities, provide a stimulating environment for its outstanding scholars and researchers. FAUs main campus in Boca Raton is on an 850-acre site located only 3 miles from the Atlantic Ocean. The campus is conveniently located halfway between Palm Beach and Fort Lauderdale and offers a broad range of Academic Programs, activities, and services. Students attending FAU—Boca Raton have some honored guests: burrowing owls. In fact, the Audubon Society has named the site a burrowing owl sanctuary and FAU varsity athletic teams are known as the Owls in their honor. Our campuses throughout South Florida can be conveniently reached from Interstate 95 or from the Florida Turnpike.

MAJORS AND DEGREES OFFERED

Florida Atlantic University prepares its undergraduate students to be productive and thoughtful citizens by offering a broad liberal education coupled with the development of competency in fields of special interest. FAU encourages students to think creatively and critically and provides intellectual tools needed for lifelong learning. A variety of curricular and extracurricular opportunities enables students to appreciate the rich diversity that characterizes their region and world.

Florida Atlantic University's 9 colleges include the College of Architecture, Urban and Public Affairs, Dorothy F. Schmidt College of Arts and Letters, Barry Kaye College of Business, Charles E. Schmidt College of Biomedical Science, College of Education, College of Engineering, College of Nursing, Charles E. Schmidt College of Science, and the Harriet L. Wilkes Honors College in Jupiter; which is the first public honors institution to be built from the ground up in the United States. Through these colleges, FAU offers 78 bachelors degrees, 76 masters programs, 19 doctoral degrees, and 3 specialist programs.

Through its partnerships with other educational institutions, local businesses, industries, and civic and cultural organizations, FAU enhances the economic, human, and cultural development of the surrounding communities and beyond.

Students at Florida Atlantic University may participate in a work-study program that coincides their classroom learning with hands-on experience. Many local businesses and government laboratories participate in the program each year. Students who wish to study overseas can become involved in FAU international programs in various locations from China to Germany.

FAU has developed a new program in medical sciences offered in cooperation with the University of Miami School of Medicine. Students in this program take their first 2 years of medical school at FAU and complete their clinical studies at the University of Miami.

ACADEMIC PROGRAMS

Florida Atlantic University's colleges include the College of Architecture, Urban and Public Affairs, the Dorothy F. Schmidt College of Arts and Letters, the Barry Kaye College of Business, Charles E. Schmidt College of Biomedical Science, College of Education, College of Engineering, Christine E. Lynn College of Nursing, and the Charles E. Schmidt College of Science. These colleges offer 125 different academic degree programs. In 1999, FAU opened a new residential Honors College, which provides a unique and challenging 4-year curriculum for the brightest students from Florida and beyond. In addition, the university is home to one of the largest lifelong learning and continuing education programs in the nation.

TUITION, ROOM, BOARD, AND FEES

Undergraduate tuition is $116.23 per semester credit for Florida residents and $547.69 per semester credit for non-Florida residents. Graduate tuition is $255.97 per semester credit for Florida residents and $914.37 for non-Florida residents. In addition, students living on campus should expect to pay an average of $8,960 for room and board; books and supplies cost approximately $766.

FINANCIAL AID

FAU distributes close to $60 million in financial aid annually, based on the policies of the College Scholarship Service of the College Board. Based on individual applications, students may receive a combination of scholarships, grants, loans, and work-study opportunities. Aid packages may be adjusted over the course of a student's academic career, but assistance can be earned from the first year of attendance all the way through graduate study.

Students seeking need-based aid must submit the Free Application for Federal Student Aid (FAFSA). It is recommended that students planning on fall admission turn in their FAFSA forms by the previous January, though the deadline for priority applications is March 1. Typically, the application procedure takes 6 to 8 weeks. Students are notified about their financial aid packages after they are informed of their acceptance to the university.

Merit-based scholarships are also available for outstanding students. Funding is reserved for top performers in academics, athletics, and the arts. For further information, please refer to the FAU catalog under Financial Assistance.

STUDENT ORGANIZATIONS AND ACTIVITIES

By joining one of FAUs 150 student clubs and organizations, students have the opportunity to make new acquaintances outside of the classroom. Getting involved on campus helps students develop leadership, management, and interpersonal skills while contributing to the FAU community. Students are welcome to participate in academic organizations, honor societies, spiritual/religious organizations, personal interest clubs, diversity association organizations, service organizations, sports clubs, and Greek life.

ADMISSIONS PROCESS

Admission to the university is limited to applicants who have graduated from regionally accredited high schools or who hold a General Equivalency Degree (GED). Evaluation is based on the academic course grade point average combined with acceptable results on the SAT or the ACT. Candidates for admission should have 18 academic high school units, including 4 units of English, 3 units of mathematics, 3 units of natural science, 3 units of social science, 2 units of 1 foreign language in sequence, and 3 academic electives. Score reports will be accepted directly from the testing agency or from the student's official high school transcript. FAUs SAT school code number is 5229. FAUs ACT school code number is 0729. Applicants who have completed the GED (General Educational Development) should request official high school transcripts (if applicable) and an official GED score report from the Florida Department of Education. The Florida Department of Education GED Division can be reached at 1-877-352-4331. Admission for freshman students requires an application for admission, a nonrefundable $30 application fee, official transcripts from an accredited high school, and the results of the SAT or ACT administrations. All admitted freshmen must confirm their intention to enroll and secure their place with the freshman class by submitting a required $200 admissions tuition deposit. Please contact the Undergraduate Admissions office for details or visit our website. Admission into FAU as a transfer with fewer than 60 transferable credits requires students to be in good academic standing at their previous regionally accredited colleges or universities a minimum 2.5 GPA. Please submit an application for admission, a nonrefundable $30 application fee, official transcripts from high school and previously attended colleges, and the results of the SAT or ACT administrations. For students with 60 or more transferable credits, please submit an application for admission, a nonrefundable $30 application fee, and official transcripts from each previously attended college. Please note that meeting the minimum admission requirements does not guarantee admission into the university. For application deadlines or further information, please contact:

Office of Undergraduate Admissions

Florida Atlantic University

777 Glades Road Boca Raton, FL 33431

Telephone: 1-800-299-4FAU (toll free)

Website: www.fau.edu.

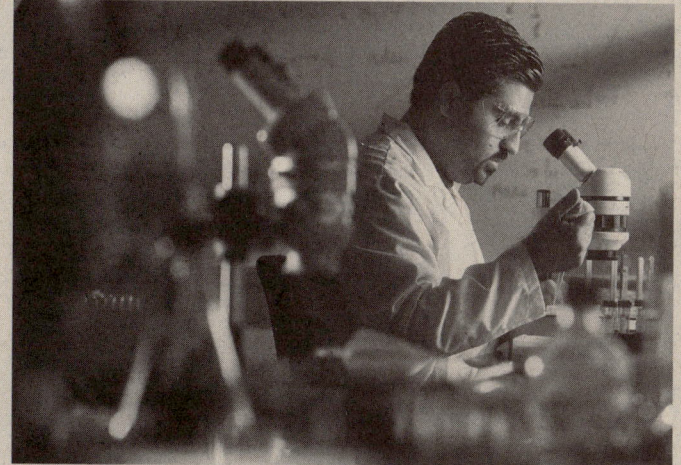

FORDHAM UNIVERSITY

AT A GLANCE

Fordham is a world-renowned Jesuit, Catholic university with 2 campuses in New York City. In our programs and policies, we draw on the 450-year history of the Jesuits, a distinguished, intellectual, and spiritual community within the Catholic Church. We offer numerous academic challenges and expect excellence; we care for the whole person; we ask the members of our community to be men and women for others—to put their education in service to the common good.

LOCATION AND ENVIRONMENT

Fordham's Rose Hill campus is located in the Bronx, one of New York's most diverse, multifaceted boroughs; only a 20-minute ride from Grand Central Station. The quintessential college campus is spread across 85 green, leafy acres, with several athletic fields and distinguished Gothic buildings.

Fordham's Lincoln Center campus is located in midtown Manhattan, in one of the nation's premier cultural destinations. Situated on 8 landscaped acres, the campus is adjacent to the Lincoln Center for the Performing Arts and a few blocks from Central Park, Columbus Circle, and the headquarters of major media corporations.

OFF-CAMPUS OPPORTUNITIES

New York is the nation's biggest college town, with more than 600,000 students enrolled in dozens of college and universities. The Manhattan location of Fordham's Lincoln Center campus is home to the biggest, the best, and the most of everything: the Metropolitan Museum of Art and the United Nations, Wall Street and SoHo, Broadway and Chinatown, Harlem and Times Square. Students can take advantage of the city's efficient public transportation system and find ways of volunteering, performing, interning—to join an exceptionally inclusive local community. The Rose Hill campus is in the heart of the Borough of Parks, the home of the Yankees, the origin of a million immigrant success stories: the Bronx. It's home to the country's largest metropolitan zoo—the Bronx Zoo; and one of the country's premier urban gardens and plant research facilities—the New York Botanical Garden.

MAJORS AND DEGREES OFFERED

The undeniable strength of Fordham's academic program is the unbreakable link between its widely regarded core curriculum and 56 outstanding major areas of study offered within Fordham College at Rose Hill, Fordham College at Lincoln Center, and the College of Business Administration. Many students choose to major in widely recognized departments, such as biology, communications, English, or psychology, while others pursue smaller programs unique to the liberal arts colleges—classical languages, philosophy, or theology.

Fordham offers a variety of degrees and programs within its 3 traditional undergraduate colleges. Among a full slate of programs in the humanities, social sciences, and physical and natural sciences, Fordham College at Rose Hill offers several unique programs. Special programs include a new 4-year bachelor of science in engineering physics, and an interdisciplinary concentration in American Catholic studies, sponsored by the university's Francis and Ann Curran Center for American Catholic Studies.

In the College of Business Administration (CBA), business students can select among 7 degree programs and 2 dual degree programs. The Global Learning Opportunities and Business Experiences (GLOBE) Program within CBA combines course work in history, literature, and language, as well as global business courses, study abroad experiences, and/or an international internship.

The theater program at Fordham College at Lincoln Center offers a comprehensive BA grounded in hands-on experience. Theater majors work with award-winning faculty and stellar guest artists in small classes and ambitious main stage productions. In addition to the rich mix of majors and courses, Fordham offers an innovative 4-year BFA program in dance, conducted in partnership with the Ailey School of the Alvin Ailey American Dance Theater. The Fordham Law School and our graduate schools in business administration, religion, arts and sciences, education, and social services, provide additional opportunities for advanced education.

ACADEMIC PROGRAMS

The university offers numerous programs and services to expand the minds and hearts of students. Academic advising at Fordham puts into practice the Jesuit ideal of cura personalis, the care of the whole person.

The Service-Learning Program allows students to integrate serious scholarship with civic action.

The 3-3 Law Program allows qualified students to transfer to Fordham's top-ranked School of Law after 3 years of undergraduate study.

The Pre-Medical and Pre-Health Professions Advising Program claims a proud history of guiding students into the country's finest medical schools; boasting a 90 percent acceptance rate for a recent graduating class.

Fordham's extensive relationships with firms and organizations provide 2,600 internship opportunities every year.

The university offers access to yearlong, semester-long and summer study abroad programs in more than 50 countries, on 6 continents including the London School of Economics and La Sorbonne in Paris.

The Manresa Program is a living-learning opportunity for freshmen, who live and study together in the newly renovated Tierney Hall, engage with faculty in interactive seminars and participate in activities that nurture the development of the whole person.

The university's honors programs are intentionally small, unabashedly intense and deeply supportive of exceptional academic ability.

CAMPUS FACILITIES AND EQUIPMENT

Our athletic facilities include fitness centers and sports fields; the Vince T. Lombardi Memorial Center for intramurals, swimming, water polo, and track; and the Walsh Athletic Training Center, a 3,200-square-foot varsity weight training and conditioning facility.

Our award-winning public radio station, WFUV 90.7 FM, pulls in about 300,000 listeners each week. Students are active in all operations of the station, now in its sixtieth year.

Fordham's libraries house more than 2.2 million volumes and offer access to extensive library archives and special collections. The William D. Walsh Family Library at Rose Hill is also home to the Fordham Museum of Greek, Etruscan and Roman Art.

Fordham's biological field station, the Calder Center, is set on 113-forested acres in Armonk, New York.

Fordham's 12,000-square-foot Visual Arts Complex at the Lincoln Center campus includes drawing studios; a computer imaging lab; film and video editing screening facilities; an architectural workspace; and 2 galleries.

Fordham is home to the oldest Catholic university press in America, Fordham University Press, with 500 titles in print and one million dollars in sales every year.

Fordham offers essential labs and equipment for students studying in a range of fields including chemistry, biology, and languages. Students in communications and media studies take advantage of the Edward Walsh Digital Media lab and a fully equipped multimedia lab and AVID editing equipment. And our undergraduates benefit from a university-wide network of more than 200 technology-enabled classrooms.

TUITION, ROOM, BOARD, AND FEES

Tuition and fees for the academic year 2007-2008: $32,857; room and board: $12,285 for double occupancy, including meal plan. For more information, visit www.fordham.edu/tuition.

FINANCIAL AID

As a Jesuit University, Fordham is committed to providing an outstanding education to qualified students. We try our best to support students and families who don't have the resources to pay our full tuition. Fordham also claims a long tradition of welcoming and supporting first-generation college students. More than 80 percent of our students typically receive some form of financial aid including both need-based and merit-based aid.

Fall freshman applicants should file FAFSA ad CSS Profile forms by February 1. Spring freshman applicants should file by November 1.

STUDENT ORGANIZATIONS AND ACTIVITIES

Fordham students run 135 clubs and organizations—award-winning newspapers and celebrated musical groups, ambitious academic societies, and vibrant cultural groups. A few examples: Mimes and Mummers is one of the nation's oldest collegiate theatrical troupes. Our top-ranked Fordham Debate Society is the eighth oldest collegiate debate society in the United States. Fordham claims a proud history of intercollegiate athletic competition. We support 22 NCAA Division I teams; cheerleading; 7 club teams, including our league champion ice hockey team; a spirited intramural program; and many recreational programs.

ADMISSIONS PROCESS

Admission to Fordham is highly selective. We consider our applicants' academic records, standardized test scores, letters of recommendation, co-curricular activities, and admission essays—not in isolation, but as parts of a unified whole. This information helps to convey what applicants might do at Fordham, how Fordham might help them and how they might contribute to the community. Applicants can complete and deliver an application online or through the mail. You can apply in one of 2 ways: Regular Decision or Early Action. Freshman applicants should complete 4 years of high school English, 3 to 4 years of science, 3 to 4 years of math, 3 to 4 years of social studies, and 2 to 3 years of a foreign language. Students who want to pursue a math, science, or pre-medical curriculum should have at least 4 years of math and 1 each of physics and chemistry. Business students should have 4 years of college preparatory mathematics. Most successful candidates will have maintained an A/A- average.

FROSTBURG STATE UNIVERSITY

At Frostburg State University, students thrive in our diverse learning community, reaping the benefits of an environment that focuses on their needs—academically, socially, economically, and personally.

AT A GLANCE

At Frostburg, you'll receive an engaging classroom and education experiences (real-world opportunities and internships are available in almost every major); a multicultural student body; small class sizes (17:1 student-faculty ratio) for individual attention; a variety of blended and online courses; professors who are focused on teaching; new facilities (including our new $33 million science center) and the latest technology; wireless and fiber optics networks (and a 24/7 student computer lab); nationally accredited programs in education, business, social work, and recreation, which means FSU has been recognized by national and international professionals (which will look great on your resume); study abroad opportunities to locations on almost every continent (sorry, Antarctica).

LOCATION AND ENVIRONMENT

At Frostburg, we help you in your educational journey by offering strong and nationally recognized, Academic Programs with real-world opportunities in and out of the classroom; medium-size campus (about 4,500 students so you won't get lost); faculty who will see you as a person, not just a number or seat-filler; a wide range of co-curricular clubs and organizations and many social and sports activities; an open and friendly campus located in one of the most beautiful parts of the country (some even call it breath-taking); and, of course, we have snow. After all, we are located in the beautiful, but sometimes chilly, mountainside of Western Maryland.

OFF-CAMPUS OPPORTUNITIES

Frostburg's historic Main Street district is within walking distance from campus and features stores, pubs, cafes, pizza shops, convenience stores, and restaurants to suit most tastes and budgets. A great aspect of going to Frostburg is its location in the great outdoors. Within minutes from campus, you can downhill and cross-country ski, snowboard, whitewater raft, kayak, sail, swim at Deep Creek Lake (41 minutes); camp, swim, and boat at Rocky Gap State Park (15 minutes); bike on the C&O Canal Towpath (10 minutes); hike the Great Allegheny Passage Trail (2 minutes); watch the views from Dan's Rock (go at sunrise and prepare to be amazed… 15 minutes); mountain bike, horseback ride, picnic, fish, golf, and countless other opportunities for exploration await you in every direction.

MAJORS AND DEGREES OFFERED

Bachelor's degree programs: accounting (combined BS/MBA option), art & design (teaching certification option), athletic training, biology (pre-health professions option; concentrations in biotechnology & environmental science; teaching certification option), business administration (concentrations in finance, general management, human resource management, integrated business, marketing, small business/entrepreneurship), chemistry (track in traditional chemistry; concentrations in professional chemistry and biochemistry; teaching certification option), communication studies, computer science (concentration in information systems and networks), earth science (concentration in environmental science; teaching certification option), economics (concentrations in business economics, public policy economics, quantitative economics), early childhood/elementary education, elementary education, education: K-12 programs (teaching certification), secondary programs (teaching certification), secondary/adult generic special education (teaching certification), engineering - dual-degree program, engineering-collaborative programs (general education program for electrical & mechanical engineering majors), electrical engineering collaborative program, mechanical engineering collaborative program, English (concentrations in literature, creative writing, professional writing; teaching certification option), environmental analysis & planning, ethnobotany, exercise & sports science, foreign languages & literature (concentrations in French & Spanish; teaching certification option), geography (concentrations in mapping sciences, global systems analysis), health & physical education (major with teaching certification), health science administration (collaborative program), history (concentrations in international history, history of the Americas), information technology management (collaborative program), international studies (concentrations in international business, international politics, international economics, international development), interpretive biology and natural history, law, bachelor/juris doctor program (dual-degree program), law and society (concentrations in criminal justice, legal studies), liberal studies, mass communications, mathematics (teaching certification option), music (concentrations in vocal performance, music management; teaching certification option; track in instrumental performance), philosophy, physics (tracks in traditional physics, engineering physics; teaching certification option), applied physics (bachelor's/master's collaborative program; dual-degree program), political science , psychology (certificate in child and family psychology), recreation and parks management (concentrations in adventure sports, community program delivery, hospitality, management & tourism, therapeutic recreation), social science (teaching certification option), social work, sociology (tracks in general sociology, applied social research; option in data analysis), theater (tracks in acting, directing, production/design, general theater), urban and regional planning, wildlife & fisheries.

Master's degree programs: master of arts in teaching, master of business administration, master of education, master of science in applied computer science, biological sciences, master of science in counseling psychology, master of science in park & recreation resource management, professional master of engineering.

ACADEMIC PROGRAMS

In addition to regional accreditation, several individual FSU programs and colleges have also earned accreditation. This includes the College of Business (AACSB), Athletic Training Education (CAATE), Education (NCATE), Recreation and Parks Management (NRPA/AALR Council on Accreditation), Psychology (MPAC), and the Social Work (Council on Social Work Education).

Learning Communities have been set up for all freshmen to study 3 to 5 special themed courses with the same small group of students. This allows you to interact with a core of your peers with similar interests. Many find support with in their communities and establish lifelong friendship with their fellow students and professors.

The FSU Honors Program is set up for promising and motivated students (3.5 high school GPA or minimum 1800 SAT score) to receive research stipends, special courses, and housing options.

Sometimes you have to close your textbook. Our professors value out-of-classroom experiences. Interested in biology? Step outside and delve in the natural plant and wildlife surrounding our campus. Want to study history? The Frostburg area is rich with heritage of early America. Does teaching interest you? Experiences in real-life classrooms (with real kids!) are offered as soon as you enroll in the education professions major. Is business more your speed? Professional development workshops allow students to merge their number and people skills to make a well-rounded and marketable businessperson.

CAMPUS FACILITIES AND EQUIPMENT

Our classroom buildings include Compton Science Center, a fine arts center, a performing arts center, and the Cordts Physical Education Center. The Appalachian Laboratory of the USM Center for Environmental Studies also provides research facilities for FSU students and faculty, and the new Allegany Business Center at Frostburg State University will bring increased opportunities to students.

The Lewis J. Ort Library provides a wealth of research and reference materials for student and community use. The library services include more than one-half million print volumes in the collection, with more than 4,000 onsite reference titles; Web access to library holdings from other University System of Maryland and Affiliated Institutions' (USMAI) libraries (a consortium of 30 academic libraries); U.S. government documents, including electronic repository and Maryland Government documents and maps; and a periodical collection with more than 700 print subscriptions and 22,000 Web-access titles.

TUITION, ROOM, BOARD, AND FEES

Full-time tuition for Maryland State residents for the 2007-2008 school year is $5,000; tuition for students residing in contiguous counties in Pennsylvania, Virginia, and West Virginia is $10,920. All other out-of-state tuition is $14,612.

Mandatory fees (such as technology, athletics, activities, etc.) are $1,500 per year per student. Room fees range from $3,420 to $4,178 per year; board fees range from $2,654 to $3,406 per year. Meal plans can be used at various venues throughout the campus. Other fees may apply based on academic program or specialized activities.

FINANCIAL AID

In addition to institutional and private scholarships, a number of state and federal programs are available to reduce the cost of attending Frostburg. The FSU Financial Aid Office works closely with each student to help him or her meet their educational requirements

STUDENT ORGANIZATIONS AND ACTIVITIES

Frostburg offers so much for you to explore in terms of programming, your time out of class will be time packed.

Whatever your interests are, we bet you can find like-minded students and a club at Frostburg.

Several large organizations exist, like Student Government Association, Black Student Alliance, and University Programming Council. There are nearly 20 academic clubs for a variety of majors and smaller organizations with specific interests like creative writing and poetry, snowboarding, fashion, and even grappling (Google it).

Chances are you'll find something for you in FSU's list of 90-plus clubs and organizations. And if we don't have a specific club of interest, we encourage you to start your own. (Who knows? You may want to create a club for poetic fashion enthusiasts who grapple while snowboarding!)

Several nationally recognized Greek fraternities and sororities have FSU chapters at FSU. These organizations are a good way to experience brotherhood/sisterhood on campus and beyond, as well as enhance your networking, leadership, and service skills.

FSU has also been recognized around the country for its community service programs. Student volunteers have given almost 50,000 hours of service in one year by assisting elderly or tutoring/mentoring area youth. FSU students have also traveled over their Spring Break to in-need locations, as well strong participation in national movements like Hunger and Homeless Week, Special Olympics, Make a Difference Day, V-Day, and Relay for Life.

ADMISSIONS PROCESS

Frostburg State University operates on a rolling admission basis, though we may have to close admissions when no further space for students is available. Applicants from high school should apply in the fall or early winter of the senior year. Beginning on September 15, the admissions office will start accepting applications for the fall semester of the following year.

Admission for the spring semester is granted on a space-available basis. Applications will be considered if received no later than December 1 for the subsequent spring semester. The university does accept applications from first-year students who would like to begin in the spring semester.

Freshmen applicants must complete the FSU Online Application, which includes an essay (gobobcats.frostburg.edu) and submit with a $30 nonrefundable application fee (mail or provide credit card information). The Request for Academic Record should be given to the guidance counselor or other appropriate official at your high school. SAT scores are required for most freshman applicants.

Transfer applicants must also complete the entire FSU Online Application and submit with a $30 nonrefundable application fee, along with official transcripts from each institution of higher education attended. If currently enrolled, an official transcript of the final grades must be submitted. If the applicant has less than 24 transferable credits, the student must also submit an official high school transcript and SAT scores.

GEORGIA COLLEGE & STATE UNIVERSITY

AT A GLANCE

As the state's designated public liberal arts university, Georgia College & State University is committed to combining the educational experiences typical of esteemed private liberal arts colleges with the affordability of public higher education. The faculty is dedicated to challenging students and fostering excellence in the classroom and beyond. GCSU seeks to endow its graduates with a passion for achievement, a lifelong curiosity, and exuberance for learning.

GCSU was chartered in 1889 as Georgia Normal and Industrial College. The institution had several name changes over the years and became coeducational in 1967. In August of 1996, the Board of Regents approved a new name, Georgia College & State University, and a change of mission that designated the university to serve the entire state of Georgia as the public liberal arts university.

Recent national recognition of Georgia College involves its selection as the only public school in Georgia to be included in *Colleges of Distinction*; being cited as one of the "100 Best Values in Public Colleges" by Kiplinger *Personal Finance* magazine; and being named in the annual report on "America's 100 Best College Buys."

LOCATION AND ENVIRONMENT

Milledgeville is approximately 100 miles southeast of Atlanta, and 30 miles northeast of Macon. The town, which is the former capital of Georgia, has a population of more than 20,000 and is a center of history and culture featuring beautiful homes and historic buildings. Located on the fall line in a setting of rolling hills and recreational lakes, Milledgeville's natural beauty is among its most appealing assets.

The university is an integral part Milledgeville's downtown environment and it enhances the town with its architectural blending of majestic buildings of red brick and white Corinthian columns. Georgia's Old Governor's Mansion, one of the finest examples of Greek revival architecture in the United States, is the founding building of the university. "West Campus," made up of the athletic complex and the Village at West Campus apartment community, is located on a 546-acre site one mile away from the main campus.

OFF-CAMPUS OPPORTUNITIES

Service Learning allows students to apply classroom knowledge to the benefit of others under the auspices of nonprofit agencies with the particular experience tailored to a specific class or major. Participation in community service allows students to gain important experience in implementation of various projects and tasks, reveals a sense of commitment and responsibility, and offers wide-ranging leadership opportunities. Participation in Study Abroad Programs provides experience and understanding of the global context of the society in which we live. Cross-cultural experiences help students appreciate and respect cultural diversity and develop an important sense of the role Americans play around the world. Internships offer paid and unpaid practical work experience directly related to a student's major. Not only do internships enhance skills and knowledge first gained in the classroom, but such experiences also provide important networking advantages for students preparing to graduate and seeking career opportunities. Participation in undergraduate research resulting in presentations or publication, such as in GCSU's own Corinthian, indicates a student's commitment to critical thinking, development of analytical skills, self-motivation, and thirst for knowledge.

MAJORS AND DEGREES OFFERED

The School of Liberal Arts and Sciences provides Academic Programs in the fine and applied arts; the humanities; the behavioral and social sciences; the physical, biological, and mathematical sciences; and various professional fields. Students may choose from more than 50 different degree programs at the undergraduate and graduate levels. There are a variety of opportunities for students to participate in internships, field placements, research projects, and study abroad.

The John H. Lounsbury School of Education offers teacher education programs that are accredited by the National Council for the Accreditation of Teacher Education (NCATE) and is the recipient of the 2007 Wisniewski Award for "singularly significant contributions to the theory and practice of teacher education." Most of the undergraduate initial certification programs at GCSU are nationally recognized by Specialty Program Areas. Early Childhood, Middle Grades, and Special Education-Interrelated make up the undergraduate degrees. Initial certification for Secondary Education is offered at the master's level. Music Education and Health Education are located in their respective departments in the School of Liberal Arts (Music) and School of Health Sciences (Kinesiology).

The student who enrolls in the J. Whitney Bunting School of Business is first provided with educational opportunities in the broad areas of arts and humanities, natural sciences, and the social sciences. During the junior and senior years, there is an opportunity for in-depth understanding of the entire field of business, as well as for the selection of a major and/or minor field of study that is consistent with the individual's career objectives. The J. Whitney Bunting School of Business is nationally accredited by and is a member of AACSB International, the Association to Advance Collegiate Schools of Business. The following degrees are offered: BS, BBA, MBA, MMIS, and MAcc.

The mission of the School of Health Sciences is to provide undergraduate and graduate programs in disciplines that emphasize health education, promotion, maintenance, and restoration. By engaging in the university's liberal arts experience, School of Health Sciences graduates attain intellectual integrity, appreciation of diversity, and commitment to the best for self, family, society, and the world. Students emerge with a world view that promotes leadership, initiative, accountability, stewardship, ethical respect for self and others, and the ability to effect change in a dynamic society.

ACADEMIC PROGRAMS

The Center for Student Success has a strong commitment to the retention of GCSU students through the First-Year Experience programs, each of which seek to establish a solid base of academic success skills. Focus is directed to academic advisement at GCSU that is a faculty-based system that assures each student contact with a faculty member who can guide a student's course selection and assist in career preparation.

Our Residential Learning Communities bridge the gap between learning inside and outside of the classroom. Incoming students have the ability to apply to one of 7 living-learning communities based upon their interests. Activities are designed to provide participants with experiences beneficial to their personal development while at GCSU.

The Coverdell Institute promotes the GCSU leadership education and experiential programs. The institute is one of many contributors to enhancing the quality of leadership among GCSU students. The Coverdell Institute fosters civic engagement and democratic leadership skills among GCSU students by promoting Senator Paul Coverdell's legacy values of liberty, learning, and leadership and serving the public good. The Coverdell Archives serve as a center for scholarship and a resource for educational exhibits to be enjoyed by those who visit the campus.

The Georgia College Honors and Scholars Program is an integrated program of learning that presents challenging opportunities for students with proven academic strength. The program promotes student interaction with faculty through small group discussion, supervised projects, internships, interdisciplinary studies, and service learning. Through capstone experiences such as a senior thesis, a creative project, or an internship, the Honors and Scholars Program extends study into the student's academic major.

CAMPUS FACILITIES AND EQUIPMENT

Approximately 150 million dollars of construction has transformed the GCSU campus in the last 10 years. New campus venues include the Wellness Depot (a student fitness facility created from an 1853 train station), a new student activities center (adapted from a former Methodist church), renovated bookstore, expanded dining facilities, and a complete replacement of all campus housing—creating on-campus suites and off-campus apartments.

One of the most impressive additions to campus is the renovation and expansion of the Library and Information Technology Center. Now one of the largest library complexes in Georgia, the GCSU Library and Information Technology Center houses close to 200,000 volumes and holds subscriptions to more than 23,000 serials. The library also possesses several special collections, including the Flannery O'Connor Collection, the GCSU Horology Collection, and Senator Paul Coverdell's Papers. The library is a selective depository of United States government documents.

GCSU infuses a strong emphasis on technology into its liberal arts environment. The comprehensive wireless system frees faculty and students to surf the Web from virtually anywhere on campus. GCSU has also received national acclaim for its innovative partnership and programs utilizing Apple Computer products and creative uses of Apple's iPod to enhance learning environments.

TUITION, ROOM, BOARD, AND FEES

For the 2007-2008 year, freshman tuition and fees for a full-time Georgia resident equal $2,533 per semester. Full-time out-of-state freshman tuition and fees total $8,844 per semester. Current housing and meal plan rates vary and can be reviewed at the GCSU website.

FINANCIAL AID

Through financial aid programs, GCSU makes every effort to assure that no qualified student will be denied the opportunity to attend school because of lack of funds.

Financial aid awards at Georgia College are based on scholastic ability, financial need, contribution to the campus community, or a combination thereof. Students may receive aid in the form of scholarships, grants, loans, or work opportunities. All students are encouraged to apply by using the Free Application for Federal Student Aid (FAFSA). First consideration will be given to any student whose file is complete by March 1. Students must have a complete file by July 1 to guarantee aid will be available at the beginning of the fall term.

STUDENT ORGANIZATIONS AND ACTIVITIES

Georgia College students may participate in a variety of activities that are coordinated or organized through the Office of Student Activities. Such activities include concerts, drama productions, comedians, intramurals, movies, and more. More than 100 registered student organizations include club sports, special interest groups, academic organizations, honor societies, student media, student government, and Greek organizations, to name a few. The Intramural Program provides team as well as individual sports. The university offers a number of indoor and outdoor campus facilities for student use as well.

ADMISSIONS PROCESS

The successful freshman applicant will demonstrate his or her potential for success by completing a rigorous college preparatory curriculum with a competitive grade point average, show strong SAT or ACT score results, and provide a well-developed personal essay. The middle 50 percent of the fall 2007 entering freshmen class had SAT Critical Reading and Mathematics sub-scores ranging from 1060 to 1180, and high school academic grade point averages ranging from 3.06 to 3.60. These numbers are provided only as guidelines.

Admissions decisions are based on the total student portfolio and demonstrated potential for contribution to the university and probability for success in the unique environment of GCSU.

Freshmen applicants must submit to the Office of Admissions, Campus Box 23, Milledgeville, GA 31061, the following documents for admission consideration, no later than April 1 (November 1 for Early Action): application for admission; application fee; official high school transcript; official SAT and/or ACT score report, including writing sample(s) (GCSU school codes are 5252 (SAT) and 0828 (ACT)); official transcripts from all colleges attended, if any; personal essay; while not mandatory, a resume of activities and a teacher recommendation letter are encouraged.

GONZAGA UNIVERSITY

AT A GLANCE

Gonzaga University, founded in 1887, is an independent, comprehensive university with a distinguished background in the Catholic, Jesuit, and humanistic tradition. Gonzaga emphasizes the moral and ethical implications of learning, living, and working in today's global society. Through the university core curriculum, each student develops a strong liberal arts foundation, which many alumni cite as a most valuable asset. In addition, students specialize in any of more than 75 Academic Programs and majors. Gonzaga enrolls approximately 4,300 undergraduates and 2,200 graduate and law students.

Gonzaga's 110-acre campus combines the old and new: College Hall, the original administration building, and DeSmet Residence Hall with the modern architectural structures of Foley Library, Jundt Art Center and Museum, and the Rosauer Center for Education. The campus is characterized by sprawling green lawns and majestic evergreen trees. Towering above the campus are the stately spires of St. Aloysius Church, the well-recognized landmark featured in the university logo.

Gonzaga encompasses 5 undergraduate schools: Arts and Sciences, Business Administration, Education, Engineering and Applied Science, and Professional Studies. The university offers the BA, BBA, BE, BEd, BGS, BS, BSCE, BSCpE, BSCS, BSGE, BSEE, BSME, and BSN degrees.

Gonzaga offers several unique options for students. The honors program provides a rigorous liberal arts curriculum for intellectually curious students who thrive in a competitive academic environment. Business leaders mentor the Hogan Entrepreneurial Leadership Program students, and internships are an integral part of the program. The award-winning Gonzaga Alumni Mentor Program (GAMP) connects current students and recent graduates with alumni in their professional areas of interest. Students in the Comprehensive Leadership Program take a leadership certificate curriculum that may be combined with any major, and they participate in valuable, interactive leadership experiences. The Army ROTC unit prepares select women and men as leaders in service for their communities and their country. Gonzaga's nationally ranked debate team includes all skill levels. The Mock Trial Team competes nationally and involves students majoring in many different areas of study. Internships, research with faculty, and community service learning enhance class time while providing students firsthand experience.

LOCATION AND ENVIRONMENT

As the hub of the Inland Northwest, Spokane plays a vital role in shaping the university's character. While offering urban advantages such as museum exhibits, shopping, symphony, Broadway, and ballet performances, Spokane still maintains an intimate, friendly, and community atmosphere. Used for running and cycling, part of the 61-mile Centennial Trail, runs through campus and to Coeur d' Alene, Idaho. Within a short distance of campus, students snow and water ski, hike, cycle, rock climb, swim, camp, and golf. With an average rainfall of only 16.7 inches per year, outdoor activities are easily accessible.

The 23 residence halls on campus, both single-sex and co-ed, house 40 to 361 students each. Freshmen and sophomores are required to live on campus. The ZagNet network provides students round-the-clock electronic access to e-mail, Internet, campus Intranet, and library holdings, all directly from residence hall rooms. Resident Directors and Assistants, along with a Resident Chaplain, provide a fun, secure, and nurturing environment.

OFF-CAMPUS OPPORTUNITIES

Recognizing the importance of an international perspective for learning, Gonzaga offers study-abroad programs in Australia, Benin, British West Indies, China, Costa Rica, Ecuador, El Salvador, England, France, Italy, Japan, Mexico, the Netherlands, Spain, and Zambia. Gonzaga's campus in Florence, Italy, is the most popular option.

MAJORS AND DEGREES OFFERED

Gonzaga offers the following areas of study in the 5 undergraduate schools. The School of Arts and Sciences offers applied communication studies, art, biology, broadcast and electronic media studies, chemistry (with a biochemistry option), classical civilizations, criminal justice, economics, English, French, history, integrated studies, international studies (including international relations and Asian, European, and Latin American studies), Italian studies, journalism, literary studies, mathematics, mathematics/computer science, music (including emphases in composition, literature, liturgical, and performance and a jazz minor), music education, philosophy, physics, political science, psychology, public relations, religious studies, sociology, Spanish, and theater arts. Additionally, the School offers concentrations in Catholic studies, environmental studies, and women's studies and minors only in advertising, dance, and Italian. Students interested in the following areas take tracks of classes respectively in pre-dentistry, pre-law, pre-medicine, pre-physical therapy, and pre-veterinary studies. The School of Business Administration offers majors in accounting or business administration (with concentrations in economics, entrepreneurship (through the Hogan Program), finance, human resource management, individualized study, international business, law and public policy, management information systems, marketing, and operations and supply chain management). As well as granting teacher certification on both the elementary and secondary levels, the School of Education offers degrees in physical education, special education, and sports management. The School of Engineering and Applied Science offers computer science and civil, computer, electrical, and mechanical engineering degrees, as well as a general engineering degree and a 5-year BSGE/MBA option. Also, The School of Professional Studies offers exercise science, general studies, and nursing degrees. Advanced degrees in accounting, business, education, law, leadership studies, nursing, philosophy, and religious studies are also offered.

ACADEMIC PROGRAMS

The core curriculum (a basic set of courses in thought and expression, philosophy, religious studies, mathematics, and English literature) is at the foundation of every student's academic experience at Gonzaga. In keeping with the Jesuit ethos of the university, all students share a framework of 31 credits: a trio block of thought and expression courses including English composition, critical thinking, and speech communication; 3 additional courses in philosophy; 3 religious studies courses; and 1 course each in math and English literature. Various schools in the university add courses that complement the core such as modern/classical language requirements, history and science classes, additional math courses, etc. Often, classes at Gonzaga require oral presentations or use of the written and discussion-based communication skills emphasized in the core curriculum.

CAMPUS FACILITIES AND EQUIPMENT

The Foley Library contains more than 800,000 volumes and microform titles, with 2 special collections of material especially rich in the areas of philosophy and classical civilization, as well as the nation's most extensive collection of works concerning the famous Jesuit poet Gerard Manley Hopkins. The historic College Hall houses Russell Theatre, a 24-hour computer lab, a Florentine-style university chapel, and numerous classrooms and faculty offices.

Students are able to produce sophisticated multimedia presentations and research hundreds of libraries across the country from their own residence hall rooms or from one of the 10 labs on campus. The Communications Building offers an arts lab for the *Bulletin* (the weekly student-published newspaper), KAGU, the university's radio station, and GUTV, a state-of-the-art TV production station where students learn all aspects of broadcast and electronic media studies. The Herak Center for Engineering offers state-of-the-art CAD/CAM, electronic, digital, microwave, and calibration labs, and the PACCAR Center for Applied Science, scheduled to open in the summer of 2008, will add more classroom space, a robotics lab, a computer science lab with a high-speed cluster computer array, and the rapidly growing Electric Utility Transmission & Distribution program.

The Martin Athletic Centre boasts a 13,000 square feet state-of-the-art fitness center, and next door, the 6,000-seat McCarthey Athletic Center houses the men's and women's basketball games as well as concerts and events throughout the year. Opened in 2007, Washington Trust Field at Patterson Baseball Complex hosts the Gonzaga baseball program.

TUITION, ROOM, BOARD, AND FEES

Tuition for the 2007-2008 academic year is $26,120; room and board is estimated at $7,520. Including tuition, room and board, books, fees, transportation, and living expenses, Gonzaga estimates $38,000 as the total cost of attendance for the 2007-2008 year.

FINANCIAL AID

More than 95 percent of students receive financial aid. The average package for 2006-07 was $20,280 awarded in the form of grants, scholarships, loans, and campus employment. A number of merit-based, merit/need-based, athletic, music, debate, and other program scholarships are awarded to students each year. Students should file the Free Application for Federal Student Aid (FAFSA) by the priority date of February 1. Gonzaga is committed to working with students and families to finance their investment in a quality education.

STUDENT ORGANIZATIONS AND ACTIVITIES

GU students enjoy a wide variety of activities on and off campus. The Gonzaga Student Body Association (GSBA) oversees more than 75 academic, social, and cultural clubs and provides the structure of student government. Some of the most popular clubs include the Outdoors Club, THIRST (a non-denominational worship group), GUTS (an improvisational comedy team), and the Hawaii Pacific Islanders Club. GSBA organizes service and conservation projects, dances, and countless other activities to channel and challenge the talents and passions of motivated men and women who seek to make a difference.

As the leading provider of service hours in the entire city of Spokane, Gonzaga University encourages students to volunteer their services at any of the area non-profit organizations. University Ministry, the Gonzaga Student Body Association, Unity House and the Office of Intercultural Relations, and the Center for Community Action and Service Learning (CCASL) provide organized projects through which students become involved in the greater Spokane community.

Division I, West Coast Conference sports include baseball (men), basketball, crew, cross-country/track, golf, soccer, tennis, and volleyball (women). Approximately 85 percent of students participate in intramural and club sports such as ultimate Frisbee and rugby. Russell Theatre hosts main-stage plays (including musicals), dance recitals, GUTS, and numerous one-acts and student directed scenes. Gonzaga's musical groups include a nationally recognized university choir, a chorale, the GU symphony, the jazz band, the Gregorian Schola, the Big Bing Theory, and numerous other ensembles. GU's students also host programs on Gonzaga's TV and radio stations. Additionally, many students participate in University Ministry events, such as retreats, the annual Pilgrimage hike, THIRST, Masses, and interdenominational and/or interfaith services.

ADMISSIONS PROCESS

The university seeks diligent, inquisitive applicants with diverse backgrounds who will benefit from the rigorous Jesuit instruction at Gonzaga as well as enhance the university environment. A Common Application (www.commonapp.org) and the Gonzaga supplement, SAT I (Writing Section not used universally) or ACT scores (Writing section not required), a teacher recommendation, a counselor report, an activities list or resume, and an essay are required.

Transfer students and students with any college credit must submit official transcripts from all colleges. Transfer students must also complete a transfer student clearance report.

International students must also submit official transcripts from all colleges attended. Additionally, international students must submit official results of their TOEFL examination. The Non-binding Early Action application deadline for freshmen is November 15 (postmarked). The main advantages of the Early Action Program are early communication of admission and potential scholarship notice (by January 15). The Regular Decision application date is February 1 (postmarked). Students applying Regular Decision by this date will receive an admission decision in the middle of March. After February 1, applications will be accepted only if space is available.

GOUCHER COLLEGE

AT A GLANCE

Goucher is an independent, coeducational liberal arts college located on 287 wooded acres just north of Baltimore City. Since its founding in 1885, the college has been firmly committed to providing an excellent liberal arts and sciences education. To that end, Goucher offers a wide variety of majors and encourages its 1,472 undergraduate students from 43 states and 7 foreign countries to create individualized, interdisciplinary programs of study. We believe that international awareness is a requirement for anybody who wants to lead a satisfying and successful life in the global community of today - and we offer a wide range of opportunities to help our students develop that awareness. In 2006, Goucher College became the first college in the nation to require all of its undergraduates to study abroad at least once before graduation. Beginning with the class of 2010 (the incoming first-year class of 2006), Goucher will give each student a voucher of at least $1,200 to help cover travel expenses. Study abroad options have grown significantly in recent years, with more than two dozen programs on six continents. Nearby Baltimore and Washington, D.C. are also rich resources for internships, field work, and other hands-on learning. Goucher was one of the first colleges in the country to recognize the importance of integrating real-world experience into a liberal arts education: the internship program has been in continuous operation for over 75 years. Students can intern during the school year, over the summer, or during a break, in the U.S. or abroad. Undergraduates are also required to participate in one internship or community service project to test and enhance their classroom learning through real, firsthand experience in the field. Close interaction with faculty is another cornerstone of a Goucher education, as is Goucher's strong belief in the importance of staying connected to the world outside campus through community action, intercultural awareness, and international exploration.

LOCATION AND ENVIRONMENT

Located on a 287-acre wooded campus nestled in a sprawling northern suburb of Baltimore, Goucher is eight miles from Baltimore city. Immediately surrounding the campus is a lively business and residential community with a wide variety of shopping, dining, and entertainment opportunities. From campus, students can easily walk to a movie complex, one of the area's largest and most popular malls, shops, churches, and a choice of restaurants and night spots. Downtown Baltimore is accessible by bus, and Washington, D.C. is 45 minutes by train.

OFF-CAMPUS OPPORTUNITIES

An off campus experience is an essential component of a Goucher education: students take part in internships, study abroad or do independent study and research to complete their off campus requirement. Nearby Baltimore and Washington, D.C., are rich resources for internships, field work, and other hands-on learning. Goucher was one of the first colleges in the country to recognize the importance of integrating real-world experience into a liberal arts education: the internship program has been in continuous operation for over 75 years. Students can intern during the school year, over the summer or during a break, in the U.S. or abroad. Study abroad options have grown significantly in recent years, with more than a dozen programs on four continents. Goucher is a member of the "International 50," a select group of colleges whose graduates have made special contributions to the international arena.

MAJORS AND DEGREES OFFERED

Goucher offers majors in 18 departments and five interdisciplinary areas, and gives students the option to design their own majors. Goucher students may create double, combination, or individualized majors or majors with minors. A 3+2 engineering program with Johns Hopkins University is also offered. Areas of study and concentration include: American Studies, Art, Arts Administration, Biological Sciences, Chemistry, Cognitive Studies, Communication, Computer Science, Dance, Economics, Education, English, Historic Preservation, History, International Relations, International and Intercultural Studies (British, European, Latin American, and Russian), Management, Mathematics, Modern Languages (French, German, Russian, and Spanish), Music, Peace Studies, Philosophy, Physics, Politics and Public Policy, Pre-law Studies, Pre-medical Studies, Psychology, Religion, Sociology-Anthropology, Special Education, Theater, and Women's Studies.

ACADEMIC PROGRAMS

Goucher's core curriculum exposes students to both the diversity of human thought and the connections among the disciplines. Students will choose a sequence of two courses from each of four Goucher divisions: arts, humanities, natural sciences and mathematics, and social sciences. Proficient writing is expected of all Goucher students, and is measured twice during each student's college career: on a general college level and in a student's major area of study. Competence in a language other than one's own is an integral part of the liberal arts. All students are required to complete the intermediate level of a foreign language. A computer proficiency requirement in the major area of study is also required. A series of seminars taught by faculty from across the disciplines and organized around a common theme, is taught to all freshmen and is called "frontiers." Each class is small like a senior seminar and emphasizes student participation. The Goucher degree requires 120 semester hours of credit, with the departmental major consisting of at least 30 credits. In addition, a 5-credit off campus experience, either as an internship, independent study, or study abroad, is required. The academic calendar follows the semester system.

CAMPUS FACILITIES AND EQUIPMENT

Goucher's campus is home to impressive facilities in technology, the sciences, and the arts. Goucher was one of the first colleges in the nation to offer computer courses as part of the undergraduate curriculum and to require computer literacy of all graduates. The college's network of computer resources includes several computer labs, the Thormann International Technology and Media Center, NationsBank Technology Learning Center, and the Advanced Technology Laboratory. The campus is fully wired, from classrooms to residence halls, for electronic telecommunications, providing access to the Internet and cable television, as well as to internal campus networks. Students in the sciences benefit from the well-equipped laboratories, extensive faculty and student research space, observatory, greenhouse, nuclear magnetic resonance spectrometer, and specimen preparation rooms in the Hoffberger Science Building. There are superb theater and studio arts facilities in the Meyerhoff Arts Center, as well as practice and performance space in the 1,000 seat Kraushaar Auditorium, Dunnock Theatre, and Todd Dance Studio. The Julia Rogers Library, open 94 hours a week, includes a collection of 287,000 volumes and 1,100 periodical subscriptions, along with extensive audiovisual materials and computerized reference tools. The Sports and Recreation Center features a large gymnasium, racquetball and squash courts, a training room, a weight room, classrooms, and a multi-purpose room used for aerobic dancing. Other facilities include a swimming pool, tennis courts, five playing fields, indoor and outdoor equestrian riding rings, trails and space for students to board their horses, and five miles of hiking, riding, and jogging trails. The College's five fieldstone residence halls are divided into houses, with 40 to 50 students each. A substance-free residence option has become a popular choice for students. A popular focal point for student life is in the Gopher Hole, a non-alcoholic pub on campus that often features local entertainment and is a popular gathering place. The newly-renovated Pearlstone Student Center includes a cafe, lounge, bookstore, student offices, post office, game room, and commuter lounge.

TUITION, ROOM, BOARD AND FEES

Tuition for the 2007-2008 academic year is $31,082 for two semesters. For two semesters, the cost for room and board is $9,478. Books and Supplies average $800.

FINANCIAL AID

Goucher will work with families to develop financing strategies, trying to assist as many qualified students as possible. The need-based financial aid offered is based on the principle that it is the responsibility of the parents to help pay for the education of their children to the extent that they are able. This commitment may require a significant financial effort on the part of all family members. Over 75 percent of the student body receives some form of need- or merit-based assistance. In recent years, the average award totaled more than $17,000. Goucher participates in the Federal Work-Study Program and helps students benefit from Federal Supplemental Educational Opportunity Grants, Federal Perkins Loans, Federal Stafford Student Loans, Federal Pell Grants, and college loans. Through a competitive merit award program, known as the Global Citizen Scholars Program, Goucher typically awards many merit-based scholarships each year to incoming freshmen. Based chiefly on academic and leadership performance, these awards are designed to reward and encourage the brightest, most talented applicants and range from $5,000 per year to $12,500 per year. Fine and performing arts single-year scholarships are awarded at a $5,000 level. Approximately 10 full tuition scholarships are awarded annually to Dean's Scholars.

STUDENT ORGANIZATIONS AND ACTIVITIES

Students looking for more ways to be involved on campus, more opportunities to get to know other Goucher community members, or for an avenue to express their interests may choose to join one of more of over 50 student clubs or organizations. The activities fall into the following general categories: academic/departmental, recreational, performing and visual arts, publications, special interest, governance, and student mentors. Examples of clubs include: Amnesty International, a Career Development Board, Goucher Chamber Symphony, Hillel, International Club, UMOJA-The African Alliance, Community Auxiliary for Service (CAUSE), and Seekers, a Christian Fellowship group. The Student Government Association (SGA) regulates and enforces social policies and the honor code. A yearbook, newspaper, and literary magazine are among the student publications.

ADMISSIONS PROCESS

The Admissions Committee seeks applications from students who have the ability to succeed academically at Goucher College and who, as individuals, feel they can contribute positively to the college's diverse community of scholars. Chosen from over 2,750 applicants, the most successful students bring with them a commitment to their academic development, along with a wide variety of talents, interests and extracurricular activity. The applicants' personal qualities are weighed along with academic potential. Consequently, secondary school transcripts and recommendations are critically important. Test scores are but one measurement in this context. No one is accepted or rejected solely on the basis of test results. The SAT mid 50 percent range is 570-670 on the verbal portion and 540-640 on the math portion. An application essay is required. Applicants are encouraged to apply as early in the fall as possible. The Early Action application deadline, which is nonbinding, is December 1; these candidates are notified by January 30. The Regular Decision closing deadline is February 1, with notification by April 1. Candidate reply date is May 1. Applications from transfer students filed by May 1 are given priority. Those filed after that date are considered on a rolling admissions basis.

GRAND VALLEY STATE UNIVERSITY

AT A GLANCE

Founded in 1960, Grand Valley State University is a public institution devoted to providing students with the highest quality undergraduate and graduate education. The main campus in Allendale, Michigan is located approximately 15 miles east of Lake Michigan and 12 miles west of Grand Rapids, the location of Grand Valley's Robert C. Pew Campus.

We offer more than 200 areas of study, including 69 undergraduate majors and 26 graduate programs. Grand Valley is dedicated to building a liberal education for each student emphasizing critical thinking, creative problem solving, and cultural understanding. Students benefit from small class sizes (average 27 students), and personalized instruction from first-rate faculty who are dedicated to teaching. Students collaborate with professors on advanced research projects, gaining knowledge and skills more commonly associated with graduate-level study.

Grand Valley has been named one of the "100 Best College Buys in the United States" for 12 consecutive years. With enrollment of more than 23,000 students, Grand Valley has campuses in Allendale, Grand Rapids, and Holland, and centers in Muskegon and Traverse City.

The academic excellence, first-rate faculty, great return on investment, outstanding locations, and state-of-the-art facilities make Grand Valley a great place to live, learn, and study.

LOCATION AND ENVIRONMENT

Grand Valley's main campus in Allendale is located between downtown Grand Rapids (Michigan's second largest city) and Lake Michigan. Grand Valley's 1,275-acre campus features wooded ravines penetrating a high bluff overlooking the Grand River.

The Pew Grand Rapids campus includes a number of learning and living facilities. The Cook-DeVos Center for Health Sciences has made Grand Valley a catalyst for unique health care partnerships and joint research ventures that put students in the heart of unique learning experiences in Grand Rapids' Health Hill. The latest addition to the Grand Rapids campus is the new John C. Kennedy Hall of Engineering containing state-of-the-art laboratories and classrooms. In addition, the L.V. Eberhard Center, Fred M. Keller Engineering Laboratories, Meijer Public Broadcast Center, and Richard M. DeVos Center put students closer to employment, internships, and community outreach programs.

OFF-CAMPUS OPPORTUNITIES

Some of the most important learning at Grand Valley happens outside the classroom. Our office of Career Services has teamed up with hundreds of businesses and organizations to offer student internships in nearly every field. Each year, more than 5,100 students participate, gaining valuable experience while often laying the groundwork for employment after graduation.

Grand Valley offers many ways for students to explore the diversity and complexity of the world around them. In addition to the many classes on foreign languages and cultures, students in every major have opportunities to study in another country. The Barbara H. Padnos International Center sponsors summer, semester, and yearlong study abroad programs through partnerships with worldwide universities.

MAJORS AND DEGREES OFFERED

Grand Valley offers undergraduate programs in these fields: accounting, advertising and public relations, anthropology, art and design, art history, athletic training, behavioral science, biology, biomedical sciences, biopsychology, broadcasting, business, cell and molecular biology, chemistry, classics, clinical laboratory science, communications, computer science, criminal justice, dance, earth science, economics, education, engineering, English language and literature, exercise science, film and video, finance, French, geochemistry, geography, geology, German, health communication, health professions, history, hospitality and tourism management, information systems, integrated science, international business, international relations, journalism, legal studies, liberal studies, management, marketing, mathematics, medical imaging/radiation sciences, music, music education, natural resource management, nursing, occupational safety and health management, philosophy, photography, physical education, physics, political science, pre-law, pre-dental, pre-medical, pre-veterinarian, psychology, psychology special education, public administration, Russian studies, social studies group, social work, sociology, Spanish, statistics, theater, therapeutic recreation, and writing.

Graduate degrees are offered in these fields: accounting, biology, biomedical sciences, biostatistics, business administration, communications, computer information systems, criminal justice, education, engineering, English language and literature, health administration, health sciences, leadership, medical and bioinformatics, nursing, nursing/business, occupational therapy, physical therapy, physician assistant studies, professional science masters, public administration, social work, and taxation.

ACADEMIC PROGRAMS

Grand Valley offers more than 200 areas of study, including 69 undergraduate degree and 26 graduate degree programs. The Academic Programs are built around our liberal education curriculum. Our liberal education focus emphasizes critical thinking, creative problem solving, and cultural understanding.

CAMPUS FACILITIES AND EQUIPMENT

The James H. Zumberge Library houses more than 708,000 volumes, 70,892 electronic journals, and other materials necessary to effectively support instructional programs at Grand Valley.

The Performing Arts Center houses classrooms, practice rooms, teaching studios for the performing arts, a music technology lab, and 2 dance studios. Located in this building is the 490-seat Louis Armstrong Theatre for presentations of plays, operas, and concerts. The art gallery is also located in this building.

The Alexander Calder Fine Arts Center houses facilities for graphic design, painting, print making, art education, drawing, ceramics, and 2 computer graphics labs.

The fieldhouse/recreation complex includes playing fields, baseball and softball diamonds, tennis courts, and the Lubbers Stadium for football and track. The fieldhouse includes a multi-purpose arena for a variety of events, including basketball, volleyball, track, and cultural events. The arena has a seating capacity for up to 5,900 for concerts and 4,200 for center court athletic events. The complex includes a 26.5-foot-high rock-climbing center within the gymnastics room. New in fall 2008 is the Movement Sciences and Indoor Recreation Facility containing a six-lane indoor track and 100-yard indoor sport turf field.

The Meadows is a championship 18-hole public golf course on the western edge of the main campus in Allendale. Located on the course are a clubhouse and a learning center. The clubhouse includes a restaurant and pro shop. The learning center is staffed by PGA and LPGA golf professionals and includes a short game area and 2 practice holes.

The Richard M. DeVos Center on the 37-acre Pew campus in downtown Grand Rapids has 22 classrooms, 6 computer labs, a student project area, and a 242,000 volume library with a computer-operated robotic retrieval system and New York-style reading room. The Eberhard Center has 43 classrooms and labs, a tutoring center, high-technology teleconference and conference facilities, and 2 interactive television rooms. The new Kennedy Hall for Engineering and the Keller Engineering Laboratories are located adjacent to the Eberhard Center. The buildings contain state-of-the-art laboratories and classrooms for instruction and research in electronics, instrumentation and controls, manufacturing processes and control, materials, vibrations, and fluid and thermal systems.

The Cook-DeVos Center for Health Sciences is also located on the Pew Grand Rapids Campus. It was strategically built in the "West Michigan Life Sciences Corridor" to place health science students near the hospitals and other medical facilities in Grand Rapids.

Grand Valley also has a regional campus in Holland, and centers in Muskegon and Traverse City. The Meijer Campus in Holland has 16 classrooms and labs. Muskegon is home to the regional center on the campus of Muskegon Community College, the Lake Michigan Center, located on the south shore of Muskegon Lake, home to the Robert B. Annis Water Resources Institute, and the nearby Michigan Alternative and Renewable Energy Center, a multidisciplinary research and education facility involving alternative and renewable energy technology and innovation. The Traverse City Regional Center is a part of Northwestern Michigan College's University Center.

TUITION, ROOM, BOARD, AND FEES

For the 2006-2007 academic year, estimated expenses are:

Michigan residents

Tuition and fees: $7,240

Room and board: $6,880

Books/supplies: $900

Non-Michigan residents

Tuition and fees: $12,510

Room and board: $6,880

Books/supplies: $900

FINANCIAL AID

In 2006-2007, 76 percent of Grand Valley's full-time dependent students received an average financial aid award of $8,129. The 3 basic types of financial aid are merit-based programs, need-based programs, and student employment. Merit-based programs include the Awards of Distinction level for the Presidential and Faculty Scholarships, the Awards of Excellence, Urban Schools Scholarship, and the Early Awareness Scholarship. The application for admission is also the application for these scholarships and must be submitted by December 31 for eligibility. Other merit-based awards include departmental scholarships, athletic, and performing arts scholarships. Merit-based scholarships are also available for community college transfer students. Need-based loans, grants, college work-study, and other aid programs are provided for students who demonstrate financial need. To be considered, students should complete the Free Application for Federal Student Aid by March 1 for the fall semester.

STUDENT ORGANIZATIONS AND ACTIVITIES

Grand Valley has nearly 300 clubs, societies, groups, and organizations to make it simple to connect with other students who share common interests, academic goals, hobbies, ethnic backgrounds, and religious beliefs.

Volunteer GVSU coordinated more than 150,000 hours of volunteer time by the Grand Valley community last year. Fraternities and sororities offer students social and service opportunities. Campus ministry activities include alternative spring breaks, group study opportunities, and many club programs. Concerts and lectures are scheduled regularly and provide learning and entertainment experiences. Diversity is celebrated through activities coordinated by Student Life and the Office of Multicultural Affairs. Opportunities for musical and theater performance abound.

The Grand Valley Recreation Center is open for all students, faculty and staff. It includes weight training circuits, cardiovascular machines, an elevated indoor running track, 5 basketball/volleyball courts, and a climbing wall.

Grand Valley is a member of NCAA Division II in athletics and is a member of the Great Lakes Intercollegiate Athletic Conference. Additionally, Grand Valley is a member of the Midwest Intercollegiate Football Conference. Grand Valley participates in 19 collegiate sports, which include baseball (M), basketball (M, W), cross country (M, W), football (M), golf (M, W), soccer (W), softball (W), swimming and diving (M, W), tennis (M, W), track (M, W), and volleyball (W). Grand Valley won the Director's Cup for being the top NCAA Division II athletic program in the nation from 2004-2007. Laker teams and individuals have competed for and won recent national championships in a variety of women's and men's sports.

Our on-campus residential housing is among the newest and most contemporary in Michigan. Housing is available on both the Allendale Campus and the Pew Grand Rapids Campus. More than 5,500 students live on campus putting them just steps away from classes, professors, campus dining, and extracurricular activities. New freshman students who wish to guarantee a space are encouraged to apply for housing by March 1 of their senior year in high school. Housing options include traditional-style residence halls, suite-style, and apartment-style living centers. Upper-class students may choose from different apartment complexes on campus. New for fall 2008 is our state-of-the-art honors housing building.

ADMISSIONS PROCESS

A complete application for admission for freshman will include: a signed application, official high school transcripts, scores from ACT or SAT, and nonrefundable $30 application fee (check or money order payable to Grand Valley State University). Although not required, letters of recommendation from teachers or counselors and personal essays may be included.

Admission to Grand Valley State University is based on a combination of factors including: a college preparatory curriculum consisting of 4 years of English, including one composition, 3 years of mathematics, including 2 years of algebra, 3 years of social studies, 3 years of science, including 2 years of laboratory science. A fourth year of math, additional science, computer science, and 2 years of a single foreign language are strongly recommended.

A transfer applicant will be evaluated based on previous course work at the college level. High school performance will also be considered for those who have earned fewer than 30 semester credit hours of college level course work. Transfer students are normally admitted based upon the completion of 30 semester credit hours and a cumulative grade point average of 2.5 or higher. A signed application, official transcripts from each post-secondary institution attended, and nonrefundable $30 application fee (check or money order payable to Grand Valley State University). Applicants with less than 30 semester credit hours must also furnish official high school transcripts.

GRANTHAM UNIVERSITY

Grantham University's online degree programs are designed for busy working adults. There are no required login times, so students can complete their course work when it fits their schedule.

AT A GLANCE

Established in 1951, Grantham University is a private institution that specializes in online education for the working adult student. Its mission is to provide accessible, affordable and academically challenging online courses and degree programs that prepare its graduates for careers in business, engineering technology, computer science, criminal justice, information technology, and other professional fields.

For more than 57 years, Grantham University has contributed to the formal education of thousands of working adults. Students from each of the 50 states and in many countries around the world have discovered the benefits and convenience of the Grantham distance education model. Grantham University's degree programs are 100 percent online and are designed to meet the needs of busy working adult students. There are no required login times, so students can complete their course work at times and places that fit their busy schedule.

Grantham offers undergraduate degrees in Criminal justice, business administration, general studies, business management, computer science, and engineering, as well as graduate degree programs in business, project management, information management, and information technology.

Grantham University offers a military scholarship and discount program for active duty, reserve, guard, veterans, and military family members, as well as scholarships for law enforcement professionals.

Grantham's faculty, administration, and advisors are comprised of educators, business executives, industry professionals, entrepreneurs, and retired military officers. Among them are Dr. Herbert I. London, founder, endowed chair, and former Dean of Students at New York University's Gallatin School of Individualized Study; John Ashford, an advisor to Fortune 100 companies as chairman and CEO of The Hawthorn Group; David E. Baker, Brig. Gen. (USAF, Ret.), a decorated fighter pilot and senior vice president for the Stanford Washington Research Group; and Rear Admiral Karen Harmeyer, former Chief Staff Officer, Navy Surgeon General, OPNAV 093R.

Grantham University is accredited by the Accrediting Commission of the Distance Education and Training Council, 1601 Eighteenth Street, N.W., Washington, DC 20009 (www.detc.org).

MAJORS AND DEGREES OFFERED

Associate and bachelor's degree programs: business administration, business management, criminal justice, computer science, computer engineering technology, electronics engineering technology, general studies, and interdisciplinary studies.

Master's degree programs: master of business administration with specialties in project management and information management and master of science in information technology with specialties in information management technology and information management-project management

Non-degree related course topics offered: accounting, business administration, business law, chemistry, computer engineering technology, computer programming, computer networks & telecommunications, economics, English, electronics engineering technology, finance, government, history, management, mathematics, marketing, physics, psychology, technical writing, Web design, sociology.

ACADEMIC PROGRAMS

Students are given 8 weeks to complete each course; however, students may accelerate course completion based on study habits and time devoted to the material.

Students must complete a minimum of 61 credit hours for an associate degree, of which 25 percent of the credit hours must be completed with Grantham. The bachelor's programs require a minimum of 121 credit hours, of which 25 percent of the credit hours must be completed with Grantham. The master's degree programs require 36 credit hours, of which 27 credit hours must be completed with Grantham.

Grantham University makes every effort to apply college credit for military training and previous course work whenever possible. CLEP tests and DSST exams, along with military and work-related training courses, may be eligible for transfer credit.

CAMPUS FACILITIES AND EQUIPMENT

Grantham University's degree programs are offered through distance education, or e-learning formats. None of the programs requires on-campus, or in-classroom attendance. Grantham students are not required to log onto the Internet on specific days or at specific times. Grantham students enjoy self-paced, self-directed methods of study and course completion. This unique method of learning is advantageous for those students with full-time jobs, or who have family or other commitments that do not allow them to participate in a regular classroom environment. Other students who are attracted to the Grantham's distance education model are those who travel extensively or find that the nearest college or university may be hundreds of miles away. Grantham University also attracts thousands of military students who appreciate the benefit of being able to complete classes from almost anywhere in the world. These military students never have to worry about frequent deployments or transfers because they can take their course work with them and complete it when and where it is convenient.

TUITION, ROOM, BOARD, AND FEES

Grantham University's tuition rate for full-time enrollments is $265 per credit hour. Required textbooks and software are covered by a Textbook and Technology Grant. Shipping is included for APO/FPO and North American delivery addresses.

Tuition for students enrolling in individual courses is $265 per credit hour. Required textbooks and software are covered by a Textbook and Technology Grant. Shipping is included for APO/FPO and North American delivery addresses.

Grantham does not charge an application fee. Grantham University offers its students financing options through the SLM Financial Corporation, a Sallie Mae company, and Education One, a Chase company. Prospective students who require financing for tuition and fees may contact Grantham's Admissions Department for more information about applying for these student loans: admissions@grantham.edu.

ADMISSIONS PROCESS

Students wishing to apply to Grantham must have earned a high school diploma, GED, or equivalent. Applicants with high school or previous education in a foreign country, who do not reside in the United States, the United Kingdom or Canada, must demonstrate English language proficiency. A minimum score of 500 on the Test of English as a Foreign Language (TOEFL) is required for admission.

Applications are accepted on a rolling basis. Students interested in applying can visit www.grantham.edu/admissions/admission_forms.php to download an application.

Prospective students with questions should e-mail: admissions@grantham.edu or call 800-955-2527 to speak with an Admissions Representative.

HAMLINE UNIVERSITY

AT A GLANCE

Founded in 1854 as Minnesota's first university, Hamline today is a nationally ranked liberal arts university with a College of Liberal Arts, School of Law, and Graduate Schools of Management, Education, and Liberal Studies. Hamline is affiliated with the United Methodist Church. Hamline is one of only 276 colleges and universities nationwide to have a chapter of Phi Beta Kappa, the nation's oldest and most prestigious undergraduate honor society.

The College of Liberal Arts offers bachelor of arts degrees in 37 major areas of study. Post-baccalaureate, certificate, and licensure programs are also available. It is ranked ninth out of 142 Midwest comprehensive universities by *U.S. News & World Report* magazine. Student-faculty ratio is 14:1. It belongs to the NCAA Division III Minnesota Intercollegiate Athletic Conference and offers 19 teams for men and women. The enrollment for 2007-2008 was as follows: 1,986 undergraduate degree-seeking students from 30 states and 31 countries, including 14 percent students of color and 3 percent international students. Twenty-two percent of students come from the top 10 percent of their high school classes; 50 percent come from the top 25 percent. More than 80 percent of first-year students received scholarships and/or need-based financial assistance. The average first-year student award for 2006-2007 was $25,932. For more information about Hamline, please visit our website at www.hamline.edu/cla/admission

LOCATION AND ENVIRONMENT

The Hamline campus is located in a quiet, residential area midway between the downtowns of Minneapolis and St. Paul, so you will get the best of both worlds: the safety and security of our small community and the excitement and opportunities of the cities. Shopping, dining, entertainment, and sporting event options abound in the Hamline-Midway neighborhood surrounding campus. The neighborhood is home to an estimated 700 businesses and in recent years has had the highest increase in residential property values in Minnesota.

The Twin Cities offer easy access to internships and employment through large corporations, nonprofit organizations, entrepreneurial companies, and state and local government offices that include U.S. Bancorp, General Mills, 3M, Best Buy, Medtronic, and Northwest Airlines. There are 19 Fortune 500 companies based in the Twin Cities.

For directions and more information about Hamline, please visit www.hamline.edu/hamline_info/locations/locations.html

MAJORS AND DEGREES OFFERED

American law and legal studies, anthropology, art, art history, biochemistry, biology, chemistry, communication studies, criminal justice, East Asian studies, economics, education (see pre-professional and certificate programs), English, environmental studies, exercise and sports science, French, German, global studies, history, international management, Latin American studies, legal studies, management, mathematics, music, philosophy, physical education, physics, political science, psychology, religion, social justice, social studies, sociology, Spanish, theater arts, urban studies, women's studies.

ACADEMIC PROGRAMS

Dual degree cooperative programs: law: 3/3 BA/JD with Hamline University School of Law; engineering: 3/2 and 4/2 with University of Minnesota, and 3/2 with Washington University, St. Louis.

Pre-professional programs: dentistry, engineering, law, medicine, occupational therapy, physical therapy, veterinary medicine.

Certificate programs: conflict studies, education (elementary, secondary, K-12), forensic sciences, international journalism, paralegal.

CAMPUS FACILITIES AND EQUIPMENT

The Hamline campus in St. Paul covers 45 attractive acres with a combination of new and old buildings set with gardens and restful areas. The central symbolic landmark of Hamline's 37-building campus is Old Main, built in 1884 and listed in the National Register of Historic Places.

New in 2004, the innovative Klas Center combines a new sports stadium with a community and learning facility, including casual dining, an outdoor plaza, classroom and conference space, and a third-level ballroom with panoramic views of the fields and Old Main Mall.

Hamline's art collection is extraordinary for a small university. Art exhibitions are on campus frequently. The 288-seat Simley Theatre is one of the best-equipped college stages in Minnesota. Our facilities include a large scene shop with equipment for both steel and wood construction, the costume shop stores hundreds of period costumes used in performances and our control booth houses state of the art lighting equipment. A Studio Theatre in Drew Hall serves as the production base for a regular series of student directed one-acts and original works. Sundin Music Hall is a 315-seat concert hall featuring a German Steinway grand piano and perfect acoustics. Concerts at Sundin Hall attract people from all over the region.

New to campus in 1998, the Lloyd W.D. Walker Fieldhouse is one of the highest quality physical activity facilities in the state. It contains: 3 courts for basketball, tennis, volleyball; gymnastics training center; strength and fitness training center; jogging track; sports medicine training center; and 3 racquetball courts. A swimming pool and Hutton Arena are located in an adjacent complex.

TUITION, ROOM, BOARD, AND FEES

For 2007-2008

Tuition: $26,060

Room/board/phone: $7,392

Student fees: $554

Books/supplies/miscellaneous: $1,200

Total: $35,206

FINANCIAL AID

During the 2006-2007 academic year, more than 80 percent of Hamline students received scholarships and/or need-based financial assistance in the form of grants, low interest loans, and work opportunities amounting to nearly $8.5 million. The average first-year student award was $25,932.

Hamline's federal school code is 002354.

For more information about scholarships at Hamline, check out our website at www.hamline.edu/cla/admission/first_year/scholarships.html

For more information about financial aid at Hamline, check out our website at

www.hamline.edu/cla/admission/main_pages/financial_aid.html

STUDENT ORGANIZATIONS AND ACTIVITIES

Student activities and leadership development features Jump into the Action, which provides major services, coordinates new student orientation programs, serves as a resource and support for all student organizations, advises student government, assists with weekend programming activities, commuter student services, provides leadership development programs and workshops, coordinates and assists with a variety of social, cultural, and educational programs and events, offers students the chance to connect in the community through the Office of Service Learning and Volunteerism (OSLV), recognizes outstanding student leaders, manages student center front desk operation, and coordinates summer conferences.

ADMISSIONS PROCESS

First-year applicants: To complete your application for admission to Hamline University, you need to complete the application form, including the personal statement and list of activities. You can apply online at www.hamline.edu/cla/admission/first_year/applyonline.html. Submit an official high school transcript, including a list of senior courses (this should be sent directly from your school). Have your ACT or SAT scores sent to us (these may be listed on your transcript). Hamline's ACT code is 2114 and our SAT Code is 6265. We encourage you to have your counselor and one academic teacher provide us written recommendations describing your academic and leadership record and potential.

Hamline has a holistic admission process. We look carefully at your high school transcript (grades 9-12). Course selection, grades, weighted/unweighted cumulative GPA, weighted/unweighted class rank (if available), ACT or SAT scores, activity list, and recommendations are all important factors considered in our review process. Additionally, your senior year courses and performance are important.

Because we review files in a holistic manner we do not have a minimum ACT or SAT score or minimum GPA. All factors are important. Specifically, your college prep courses (English, math, social, science, language) and grades are the best predictors for college success. We look for consistency, improvement, and rigor of courses (AP, IB, accelerated, PSEO, CIS, etc). You may provide a supporting statement to help us better understand your application file.

All transfer students must submit the following: completed online application and personal statement submitted before admission plan deadline. You may now complete the personal statement separately at www.hamline.edu/cla/admission/forms/personal_statement.html. Letters of recommendation are encouraged. Transfer Students must have completed either a high school diploma or equivalent, and have enrolled in a post-secondary institution. Students who have pursued PSEO (Post-secondary Enrollment Options) as high school students without having graduated high school—are not transfers students. Please review the application materials for first-year students. Transfer applicants who have completed less than one year of full-time college course work (32 semester credits or 48 quarter credits) need to submit the following: ACT or SAT results sent to Hamline from the testing agency or your high school (Institutional code for ACT is 2114, for SAT 6265); official high school transcripts sent to Hamline directly from your high school. In addition to the above, additional materials may be requested by the Office of Undergraduate Admission.

To be considered for admission to Hamline, the applicant must be eligible to return to the institution from which he or she wishes to transfer, or have graduated from that institution. Applicants must have earned an overall grade point average of C (2.0) in all college courses completed. Enrolling students are generally expected to have a 2.5 grade point average. Students with 2.0 to 2.5 grade point averages may be considered for admission.

Students who have earned less than 16 semester credits or the equivalent, must also submit a copy of their official high school transcripts with their admission materials. We reserve the right to request high school transcripts for any transfer applicant.

Admission to Hamline University is selective. The International Admission Committee admits students who have achieved academic success in mathematics, sciences, social sciences, and languages. The committee selects new students through a review of academic documentation. International applicants should: complete the entire international student application online at www.hamline.edu/cla/admission/forms/international/application.html. Send us official or certified copies of your academic records from all secondary schools and colleges or universities that you have attended. If your academic records are not in English, you must have them translated into English by a certified public translator.

Have an official copy of your language proficiency exam sent to Hamline University. You must have achieved a TOEFL score of 550 or above (written exam) or 213 or above (computer-based exam) or 79-80 or above (Internet-based exam) or you must have achieved an IELTS score of 7.0 or above. You may also submit an SAT or ACT exam in place of a TOEFL or IELTS. For more information about these exams, see www.ets.org/toefl, www.ielts.org, www.collegeboarstudent-facultyom (SAT) or www.act.org (ACT). The language proficiency exam score must be sent to us directly from the test agency (TOEFL, IELTS, College Board, ACT). Hamline's TOEFL and SAT code is 6265, the ACT code is 2114.

Provide evidence of financial support. You must submit documentary evidence of the amount of financial support that will be available to you. This information must be provided through bank statements and affidavits of support. Write a personal statement; this is part of the application form. We encourage you to provide any information you think the admission committee should consider when reviewing your application.

All supporting application materials should be sent to:

Office of Undergraduate Admission

Hamline University MS-C1930

1536 Hewitt Avenue

Saint Paul, MN 55104-1284

USA

Hamline University does not discriminate on the basis of race, color, national origin, ancestry, sex, disability, religion, age, sexual orientation, or veteran status in its education or employment programs or activities.

HAVERFORD COLLEGE

AT A GLANCE

Haverford is a coeducational, residential liberal arts college located 8 miles west of center city Philadelphia. Haverford was founded in 1833 by members of the Religious Society of Friends (Quakers). While the College is no longer formally affiliated with any religious body, the values of academic strength, intellectual freedom, individual worth, and tolerance upon which it was founded remain central to its character.

Haverford's 1,200 students represent a wide variety of interests, backgrounds, and talents. They come from public and independent schools from all 50 States, DC, Puerto Rico, and more than 30 countries around the world.

Extensive cooperation with nearby Bryn Mawr College adds an important dimension to the resources available at Haverford. Educational opportunities are further enhanced by cooperation with Swarthmore College and the University of Pennsylvania.

Although students choose Haverford because of its academic excellence, a strong sense of community participation informs the Haverford College experience both inside the classroom and out. Haverford is well known for its emphasis on self-governance, and students work together through the arts and cultural activities, service programs, athletic programs, and day-to-day campus life.

The Honor Code, affirmed by the student body each year, embodies the philosophy of conduct within the College. Students are expected to maintain a strong sense of individual responsibility as well as intellectual integrity, honesty, and genuine concern for others.

Haverford College offers an atmosphere of intellectual and personal challenge, excitement, and growth in a close-knit community that is dedicated to encouraging humane values during the undergraduate years and for a lifetime.

LOCATION AND ENVIRONMENT

Originally landscaped by the English gardener William Carvill, the park-like, 204-acre campus includes more than 400 species of trees and shrubs, a nature walk, and a duck pond. The varied architectural styles of campus buildings, representing more than 150 years of architectural evolution, give the campus a unique character and charm. Just 8 miles away from Haverford are the cultural and educational resources of Philadelphia. Frequent train service to and from the city add to campus resources and enhance student opportunities.

OFF-CAMPUS OPPORTUNITIES

In addition to course offerings at Swarthmore, Bryn Mawr and the University of Pennsylvania, there are numerous opportunities for internships and volunteer service in the surrounding communities and in Philadelphia. If students want to go farther afield they may participate in one of the 50 study abroad programs supported by Haverford. Domestic study away programs include exchanges with Claremont McKenna, Spellman, and Fiske Colleges.

MAJORS AND DEGREES OFFERED

Haverford College offers the Bachelor of Arts Degree in the following areas:

In the Natural Sciences: astronomy, biology, chemistry, computer science, geology, mathematics, physics.

In the Social Sciences: anthropology, archaeology, East Asian studies, economics, growth and structure of cities, history, political science, psychology, sociology.

In the Humanities: Chinese, classics, comparative literature, English, fine arts, French, German, history of art, Italian, Japanese, music, philosophy, religion, Russian, Spanish.

Science majors have the option of choosing a Bachelor of Science.

ACADEMIC PROGRAMS

Haverford offers the following Academic Programs in addition to majors and minors as Concentrations: Africana and African studies, biochemistry and biophysics, creative writing, dance, education, environmental studies, gender and sexuality studies, Hebrew and Judaic studies, Hispanic and Hispanic American studies, international economic relations, Latin American and Iberian studies, mathematical economics, neural and behavioral sciences, peace and conflict studies, 3/2 liberal arts and engineering, and theater studies.

Students may pursue pre-medical, pre-law or pre-business intentions through any major; special advising is offered in these areas.

CAMPUS FACILITIES AND EQUIPMENT

A listing of facilities and equipment would fill several pages. Please visit Haverford's website at www.haverford.edu for a campus tour and an overview of the College's facilities. The newest facilities are the Koshland Integrated Natural Sciences Center, completed in 2002, with state of the art laboratories, computer workrooms, faculty offices and classrooms, and, completed in Fallfall 2005, the Gardner Integrated Athletic Center, a 100,000 square foot athletic complex serving the entire College community.

TUITION, ROOM, BOARD AND FEES

For the 2006-2007 School Year, tuition for Haverford College is as follows: For Tuition, the cost is $33,3947,175, for Room and Board $10,3901,450. In addition, there is an activity Fee of $316350, and an orientation Fee of $170 180 (new students only)

FINANCIAL AID

Haverford has always sought to enroll the most qualified students regardless of their financial circumstances. To that end, the admission staff admits students without regard to their financial need. An application for Financial Aid will have no bearing on admission decisions for all US citizens and permanent residents.

Financial Aid decisions are made solely according to a need-based allocation formula developed by the College. In other words, Haverford does not offer any Financial Aid on the basis of academic, musical, athletic, or any other evaluation of merit. For many years, Haverford has provided aid to all admitted students who were judged eligible according to the College's formula and procedures. We do, however, have limitations on the amount of funds we can commit to students without US citizenship or permanent residency status. Beginning with the Class of 2012, Haverford will no longer include loans as part of a student's Financial Aid package, replacing this form of aid with College grant funds.

Applicants are required to fill and submit the FAFSA and the PROFILE application if they want to be considered for Financial Aid. Regular Decision candidates must register for the PROFILE by January 1 of the senior year of high school and submit by January 31. The FAFSA should be mailed to the federal government with Haverford's Federal Code (003274) by January 31. Early Decision candidates are held to different deadlines; please visit http://www.haverford.edu/admindepthome/Finaid/A.overview.html for further details.

STUDENT ORGANIZATIONS AND ACTIVITIES

There are more than 100 150 student organizations on campus. Musicians, athletes, writers, actors, rock climbers, gourmet cooks, feminists, political activists . . . everyone finds ways to pursue their extracurricular passions at Haverford. There are 10 11 varsity sports for women and 11 for women, including the only varsity cricket team in the nation. In addition, the students support a host of club sports and intramural teams.

ADMISSIONS PROCESS

The Admission Process at Haverford is conducted as a comprehensive review, treating each application personally and individually and with extraordinary care and attention to detail. We aim to provide you with the opportunity to convey the broadest sense possible of who you are, what you have achieved during your secondary school experience, and how you will both contribute to and grow from a Haverford education.

Our primary consideration in the evaluation process is academic excellence. Haverford is interested in students who demonstrate ability and interest in achieving at the highest levels of scholarship and service; who will engage deeply and substantively with the community; and who are intent on growing deeply both intellectually and personally. To this end, we consider:

• Secondary school transcript

• Standardized tests

• Teacher and counselor recommendations

• Quality of writing as demonstrated in your essays, testing, and recommendations

• Potential for contribution to the campus community

• Interview

Students may begin their studies in the fall semester only. The College uses the Common Application, along with a Supplement, both of which can be obtained and submitted on-line or by mail. All applications should be accompanied by a non-refundable $60 application fee payable to Haverford College. Decisions are announced before April 10. Students are required to submit all forms and supporting documents included in the application. In addition, they must also have their official SAT or ACT scores and two SAT II test scores sent to Haverford.

HAWAII PACIFIC UNIVERSITY

AT A GLANCE

Hawaii Pacific University (HPU) is a private, nonprofit, nonsectarian university founded in 1965. HPU offers more than 50 undergraduate programs as well as 12 graduate programs. HPU prides itself on maintaining strong Academic Programs, small class sizes, individual attention to students, and a diverse faculty and student population. HPU is accredited by the Western Association of Schools and Colleges, the National League for Nursing Accrediting Commission, and the Council on Social Work Education, to name a few.

HPU is the largest private university in Hawaii, with 8,200 students from every state in the United States and more than 100 countries. The diversity of the student body stimulates learning about other cultures firsthand, both inside and outside of the classroom. There is no majority population at HPU. Students are encouraged to examine the values, customs, traditions, and principles of others to gain a clearer understanding of their own perspectives. HPU students develop friendships with students from throughout the United States and the world and form important connections for success in the global economy of the twenty-first century.

HPU has NCAA Division II intercollegiate sports. Men's athletic programs include baseball, basketball, cross-country, golf, soccer, and tennis. Women's athletics include basketball, cross-country, soccer, softball, tennis, and volleyball.

The housing office at HPU offers many services and living options for students. Residence halls with cafeteria service are available on the windward Hawaii Loa campus, while off-campus apartments are available in the Honolulu and Waikiki areas for those seeking more independent living arrangements.

HPU faculty members are renowned for the personal interest they take in each of their students. HPU is proud to offer more than 500 full-time and part-time faculty members with outstanding academic and business credentials from around the world, ensuring that HPU students can easily access a world's worth of knowledge and experiences. A vast majority of HPU faculty members hold the highest degrees in their fields. The student-faculty ratio is 18:1, and the average class size is less than 25.

LOCATION AND ENVIRONMENT

HPU combines the best of all possible worlds, operating 3 campuses as one. Each of the campuses has its own distinct qualities and all the campuses are linked by a free shuttle.

The main campus, located in downtown Honolulu, provides a fast-paced, exciting urban environment in the heart of the business community. The downtown campus comprises 6 buildings in the center of Honolulu's business district. HPU's newest facility is the Frear Center, which houses state-of-the-art classrooms, a communication lab, a robotics lab, and a high-tech information systems classroom. HPU's Meader Library provides a multitude of general and specialized resources, including a business reference collection, a National Endowment for the Humanities (NEH) collection, and many online databases and journals. The circulating book collections support communications, computer studies, education, literature, social sciences, and other curriculum areas. Ample study areas, group study rooms, computer work stations, and wireless Internet are also available. The Tutoring and Testing Center provides free tutoring in all core subjects. The Learning Assistance Center is the home of language labs and an audiotape and audiovisual library as well as the multimedia lab with the latest in interactive computer and CD-ROM technology. The recently expanded computer lab has more than 420 IBM-compatible PCs.

Eight miles away, the 135-acre windward Hawaii Loa campus, which is set in the lush foothills of the Ko'olau mountains, is the home to the School of Nursing, the Marine Science program, and a variety of course offerings. The Hawaii Loa campus has residence halls, dining commons, the Educational Technology Center, a student center, and outdoor recreational facilities including a soccer field, tennis courts, a softball field, and an exercise room.

Academic life on the Hawaii Loa campus revolves around the Amos N. Starr and Juliette Montague Cooke Academic Center (AC). The AC houses classrooms, Organic Chemistry, Nuclear Magnetic Resonance, and regular laboratories, faculty and staff offices, a theater, an art gallery, and the Atherton Library, which includes circulating and reference book collections in the areas of art, history, marine science, nursing, and Hawaii and the Pacific. Additionally, the library provides access to electronic books (e-books), databases, study rooms, and wireless Internet. Computers are also available for library research, e-mail, and word processing. The Academic Computer Center provides access to IBM computers. The third campus, Oceanic Institute, is a major research center specializing in marine biology, marine aquaculture, biotechnology, and ocean resource management. It is located on a 56-acre site at Makapuu Point on the windward coast of Oahu, Hawaii. Learning, internship, and research opportunities for graduates and undergraduates abound in this hands-on learning environment.

MAJORS AND DEGREES OFFERED

Hawaii Pacific University offers programs that lead to the undergraduate degrees of bachelor of arts (BA), bachelor of science (BS), bachelor of science in business administration (BSBA), bachelor of science in nursing (BSN), and bachelor of social work (BSW).

Undergraduate majors include the BA in anthropology, applied sociology (concentrations in business or government service, criminal justice, and family and gender studies), communication, East-West classical studies, economics, English, environmental studies, history, human resource development, human services (general and concentrations in nonprofit management, recreation management, and substance abuse counseling), international relations, international studies (concentrations in American, Asian, comparative, European, and Pacific studies), journalism (general and concentrations in broadcast, design, photojournalism, and print), justice administration, multimedia (concentrations in media studies, video production, and Web design), political science, psychology, social science, and teaching English as a second language. The BS is available in advertising/public relations, biochemistry, biology, computer science, diplomacy and military studies, environmental science, marine biology, mathematics (concentrations in 3-2 engineering, applied math, math education and pure math), nursing, oceanography, pre-chiropractic, pre-medical studies, pre-occupational therapy, and pre-physical therapy. The BSBA is available in accounting, business economics, computer information systems, entrepreneurial studies, finance, general business, human resource management, international business, management, marketing, public administration, and travel industry management. As mentioned, the Bachelor of Science in Nursing (BSN.) and Bachelor of Social Work (BSW.) are also available. Dual degrees, double majors, and minors are also offered.

In addition to the undergraduate programs, HPU offers 12 graduate programs. The master of arts (MA) is offered in communications, diplomacy and military studies, global leadership and sustainable development, human resource management, organizational change, and teaching English as a second language. The master of business administration (MBA) is available in accounting, e-business, economics, finance, human resource management, information systems, international business, management, marketing, and travel industry management. The master of education in secondary education (MEd), the master of science in information systems (MSIS), the master of science in marine science (MSMS), the master of science in nursing (MSN), as well as the master of social work (MSW) are also offered.

OFF-CAMPUS OPPORTUNITIES

As part of its emphasis on international education and global citizenship, Hawaii Pacific University offers study abroad opportunities that complement and enhance students' academic experience. Study abroad opportunities are available in Australia, Austria, Brazil, France, Germany, Great Britain, Japan, Korea, Mexico, Norway, Spain, Sweden, Taiwan, and Thailand. HPU undergraduates and graduates who have completed at least 1 semester of studies at HPU and intend to complete a degree at HPU are eligible to apply.

HPU's academic and co-curricular programs are intertwined with the world of work. The university's Career Services Center offers a comprehensive cooperative education / internship program in which a student may enroll throughout his or her course of study. This program enables students to gain significant experience in a career-related position as well as earn academic credit and a salary. HPU students have done co-ops and internships at some of the world's best known companies and organizations, including American Express Financial Advisors; Deloitte & Touche, LLP; FBI; Hilton Hotels; Microsoft; Oceanic Institute; Polo Ralph Lauren; and Walt Disney World. The staff at the Career Services Center continues to work with students after graduation, assisting with everything from resume writing to job interview preparation.

TUITION, ROOM, BOARD, AND FEES

For the 2008-09 academic year, tuition is $13,900 for most majors while books, supplies, and health insurance cost approximately $2,300. Tuition for marine science majors is $15,192, and tuition for junior- or senior-year nursing majors is $18,500. The cost to live in on-campus residence halls or off-campus apartments is comparable; room and board are $10,560 for a double occupancy room. There is an additional $500 refundable security deposit required for residence halls and off-campus apartments.

FINANCIAL AID

HPU participates in most forms of federal financial aid including student grant and loan programs, as well as loans for parents of dependent students. More than 60 percent of the university's students benefit from federal financial aid programs, or a wide range of institutional scholarships. Students should complete the Free Application for Federal Student Aid (FAFSA) to be considered for federal aid programs. While aid can be awarded throughout the academic year, students should complete the application prior to the March 1 priority deadline to be considered for all available funding. Visit www.hpu.edu/financialaid for current Financial Aid and Scholarship information.

STUDENT ORGANIZATIONS AND ACTIVITIES

A variety of on-campus activities and events are organized for students by the Student Life Office, including Movie on the Mall, Music on the Mall, intramural sports tournaments, and recreational activities. Annual events include Club Carnival, Welcome Week, Da Freakshow, Halloween Hoopla, and Pacific Bowl. HPU students can join one of the more than 70 student clubs; run for office in the Associated Students of Hawaii Pacific University (ASHPU), the university's governing body; participate in Army or Air Force ROTC; write for the student newspaper, *Kalamalama*; edit the school's literary journal, *Hawaii Pacific Review*; or join HPU's stage and pep band or International Choral program.

ADMISSIONS PROCESS

Hawaii Pacific University seeks students who are motivated and show academic promise. The Admissions Office requires that applicants complete and forward the admission application and their high school transcripts. Transfer students should also submit college transcripts. SAT and/or ACT scores should be submitted if these scores are not posted in their transcripts. First-time freshmen are expected to have a minimum GPA of 2.5 (on a 4.0 scale) in college-preparatory courses. HPU recommends that students complete 4 years of English, 4 years of history or social science, 3 years of math, and 2 years of science. Transfer students with 24 or more post-secondary credits are required to have a GPA of 2.0 or above. For students with less than 24 credits, a combination of college and high school GPA is used.

The Marine Science and Environmental Science Programs require a GPA of 3.0 or above and 3 years of science, including biology, chemistry (physics is recommended), as well as mathematics through trigonometry (calculus is recommended). Transfer students must demonstrate ability in science and math at the college level. Students not meeting the above criteria are encouraged to enroll at HPU without declaring a major to demonstrate the ability to do college-level work in science and math.

Candidates are notified of admission decisions on a rolling basis, usually within 2 weeks of receipt of application materials. Early entrance and deferred entrance are available.

For further information and for application materials, students should contact:

Office of Admissions

Hawaii Pacific University

1164 Bishop Street, Suite 200

Honolulu, Hawaii 96813

Phone: 808-544-0238 / 866-CALL-HPU (toll free in U.S. and Canada)

Fax: 808-544-1136

E-mail: admissions@hpu.edu

Website: www.hpu.edu

HILLSDALE COLLEGE

AT A GLANCE

Hillsdale College has remained private, non-sectarian, coeducational, and focused on the traditional liberal arts since its founding in 1844. Hillsdale has preserved its unalloyed dedication to the Judeo-Christian and Greco-Roman tradition by remaining independent of any state or federal funding. Widespread private support from a national leadership audience provides for competitive financial aid and scholarship programs, as well as numerous faculty chairs and state-of-the-art facilities.

The small undergraduate population of 1,300 is roughly half women and half men. Students arrive from 48 states and 10 countries other than the United States, though just more than a third of attendees are Michigan residents. The class of 2007 entered Hillsdale with an average high school GPA of 3.72 along with strong SAT or ACT scores falling near the 90th percentile nationwide. High student satisfaction levels are shown in the fact that 90 percent of the freshman class returns for their second year. Most students (70 percent) complete their degree in 4 years, and 74 percent are finished after 5 years. Students live in single-sex dormitories staffed by a resident director and upperclassmen. All first-year students who are not commuting must live on campus.

Students may choose from 33 different majors, culminating in either a bachelor of arts or bachelor of science degree. Study abroad programs in England, France, Spain, and Germany are available and encouraged. Representative campus activities include NCAA Division II athletics, intramurals, Greek life, theater and music groups, student publications (including a weekly newspaper, yearbook, and literary magazine), and student government.

Convinced that it is the best preparation for meeting the challenges of modern life, Hillsdale maintains its defense of the traditional liberal arts curriculum. The college's refusal to accept state or federal funding allows for the preservation of an authentic liberal arts education that is dedicated to stimulating students' intellectual curiosity, to encouraging the critical, well-disciplined mind, and to fostering personal growth through academic challenge and civic responsibility.

LOCATION AND ENVIRONMENT

Hillsdale College, set amid the idyllic setting of south-central Michigan, is conveniently reached by the Ohio or Indiana Turnpikes. The college's hometown of Hillsdale is a county seat and home to 10,000 people and plenty of businesses, churches, and places to eat. Students can easily travel to cities including Detroit, Chicago, Cleveland, Toledo, and Indianapolis. Hillsdale's location offers the beauty and experience of all 4 seasons.

OFF-CAMPUS OPPORTUNITIES

Students often compliment their classroom studies with internship experiences. Two popular programs are the Washington-Hillsdale Intern Program (WHIP), which places students at the ERI National Journalism Center or in congressional and government offices in Washington DC. The National Sales Internship Program provides paid sales and business internships with national placements.

Many students also elect to study abroad. They may take advantage of Hillsdale's affiliation with Keble College of Oxford University and attend as associate members. Other students travel to Spain, France, or Germany. The college works with students to design a course of study that will allow them to advance their Hillsdale degree work while studying overseas and experiencing a different culture.

MAJORS AND DEGREES OFFERED

Students can pursue their bachelor of arts or bachelor of science degree in accounting, art, biology, chemistry, classical studies, computational mathematics, economics, education, (elementary, secondary and early childhood), English, Finance, French, German, history, Marketing, mathematics, music, philosophy, physical education, physics, political science, psychology, religion, sociology, Spanish, speech and theater. The following majors incorporate interdisciplinary work: American studies, Christian studies, comparative literature, sociology and social thought, European studies, international business, and political economy. The college also grants pre-professional degrees in dentistry, engineering, forestry, law, medicine, nursing, optometry, osteopathy, pharmacy, physical therapy, theology, and veterinary medicine.

ACADEMIC PROGRAMS

The academic year runs on 2 semesters, one from late August to mid-December and the other from mid-January to mid-May. Students may also attend 2 different 3-week sessions during the summer.

All students complete core requirements in the humanities, natural sciences, and social sciences, ensuring a well-rounded education. First-year students will complete a year of history, English and science as well as a semester studying the U.S. Constitution. Majors must be selected by the end of students' second year. A minimum of 124 credits are necessary for graduation. These credits must include the course requirements for a particular major. The BA course of study focuses on language skills, foreign language proficiency, literature, the arts, and social sciences. Students working on their BS concentrate on math, natural science, and social science.

Top students may enroll in the honors program. During their first 2 years, they work together in honors classes; in their junior and senior years, participants undertake advanced colloquia.

During their 4 years at Hillsdale, students are also required to attend 2 weeklong seminars run by the Center for Constructive Alternatives (CCA). Guest speakers facilitate the seminars, addressing topics as diverse as politics, religion, or culture. The goal is to connect classroom learning with real-world applications and issues. Students can choose from 4 seminars offered each year.

CAMPUS FACILITIES AND EQUIPMENT

Students utilize the classrooms, research facilities, language laboratories, and special laboratory facilities for experimental psychology in Lane and Kendall Halls. Most of the facilities for the study of biology, chemistry, mathematics, and physics are housed in the brand-new Herbert Henry Dow Science Building and the Strosacker Science Center. Many departments sponsor their own libraries and research facilities. The college's IBM AS400 computer and Microsoft SQL server support 4 computer labs as well as numerous terminal and printer stations located throughout the campus. The 30 megabyte bandwidth allows all the dorms and two-thirds of the campus wireless access to the internet. Students do most of their word processing in the new Grewcock Student Union or in the Knorr Student Center. Students head to the Mossey Library for more than 300,000 books, 61,000 microforms, 1,600 periodicals, videocassette and videodisc players, record and tape players, and a large collection of recordings, audiotapes, and videotapes. The inter-library loan program ensures access to a plethora of materials, accessible through the computerized system that contains 20 million bibliographical records (books, periodicals, and microfilm).

The college runs the Mary Randall Preschool, facility called "a model for the nation," which offers students in the fields of childhood education and psychology hands-on experience observing and working with nursery school children. The Hillsdale Academy, founded in 1990, teaches K-12 students as part of the college's Teacher Education Program.

Students head to the George Roche Health Education and Sports Complex for the swimming pool, 6-lane indoor track, basketball, volleyball, tennis, and racquetball courts. The college also has a Pro Grass football field in its 7,000-person capacity stadium. Runners enjoy the all-weather, 8-lane Olympic-quality Mondo track around the football field. Students may also utilize the baseball and softball diamonds and 10 lighted tennis courts. Those involved in the performing arts benefit from the Sage Center for the Arts. Since 1992, this facility has provided art studios, galleries, music rehearsal and recital halls, theater rehearsal rooms, costume and set design shops, and a stage that includes a hydraulic orchestra pit/thrust-stage option. Since 2002, Howard Music Hall has provided a state of the art facility to support a 150 member choir and a full orchestra. The recently dedicated 53,000 square-foot, 2-story Grewcock Student Union is a warm and inviting hub of student activity and provides students with formal and café dining, TV lounges, conference rooms, wireless technology, game rooms, fireplace, outdoor patios, and houses the college's bookstore.

TUITION, ROOM, BOARD, AND FEES

For the 2007-2008 academic year, tuition costs $18,600. An additional $3,740 is paid for room and $3,600 for board. Student fees total $490.

FINANCIAL AID

Hillsdale does not participate in state or federal financial aid programs. Nonetheless, institutional aid is available. Merit-based academic scholarships typically go to students from the top 10 percent of their high school class who also earn standardized test scores in the top 8 percent nationally. There is not a separate scholarship application so students must complete their admission application by January 1. Top student-athletes receive athletic scholarships. Fine arts scholarships are also available. Students seeking need-based aid must submit the Confidential Family Financial Statement (CFFS) which is available on Hillsdale's website. Students may also compete for grants sponsored by Hillsdale. Work-study programs may also be arranged.

STUDENT ORGANIZATIONS AND ACTIVITIES

Hillsdale College fields teams in the Great Lakes Intercollegiate Athletic Conference of the NCAA's Division II. Men participate in baseball, basketball, cross-country, football and indoor and outdoor track. The women compete in basketball, cross-country, softball, swimming, indoor and outdoor track, and volleyball. Hillsdale College is proud of the academic awards granted to many of the school's student-athletes. Aside from varsity competition, students organize intramural leagues and club sports, including hockey, soccer, basketball, football, ultimate Frisbee and skiing.

Students get involved in a variety of extracurricular activities, joining organizations such as fraternities, sororities, InterVarsity Christian Fellowship, College Republicans, Catholic Society, and Charis. Other clubs and groups focus on community service, academics, philanthropy, or social activities. Students interested in the performing arts can join the drama troupe, dance ensemble, jazz band, pep band, wind ensemble, concert choir, chorale, and/or the college community orchestra. Debate and forensics teams are also popular.

Eighteen students are elected by their peers to serve on the Student Federation, which makes decisions on behalf of the student body. The Student Federation allocates funds, organizes events, and responds to student needs and opinions. Additional social events are thrown each month by the Activities Board. The Men's Council and Women's Council work with the administration to function as legislative and judicial bodies. Participation in these organizations allows students to hone their leadership skills, which are applicable at Hillsdale and in the workforce.

ADMISSIONS PROCESS

The admissions committee looks for students who are prepared to get the most out of college life and share their talents with the Hillsdale community. Successful applicants demonstrate intellectual curiosity, motivation, and social awareness. Students should present strong grades, test scores, class rank, extracurricular involvement, leadership experience, and volunteerism. Other factors include strength of curriculum, interviews, application essay, and recommendations from high school counselors or teachers. Admissions decisions are based on a combination of all of these criteria.

Transfer students need to send in the following materials: the application form, high school transcripts, ACT or SAT scores, transcripts from all previously attended colleges, and a transfer form from the dean of students of the last college attended.

Hillsdale offers 3 application plans. The Early Decision deadline is 11/15 with notification 12/01. The Early Action deadline is 1/01 with a 1/25 notification and the Regular Decision deadline is 2/15 with a 4/01 notification. Applicants can submit their application free online or via paper with a $35 application fee. Two academic letters of recommendation, ACT/SAT scores, a high school transcript and 2 essay questions are required to complete the application. Hillsdale College has adhered to its non-discriminatory admissions policy—"to furnish all persons who wish, irrespective of nation, color, or sex, a literary and scientific education"—since long before the government passed non-discrimination laws.

To make a request or submit records or forms, please use the following contact information:

Office of Admissions

Hillsdale College

33 E. College Street

Hillsdale, MI 49242-1298

Telephone: 517-607-2327

Fax: 517-607-2223

E-mail: admissions@hillsdale.edu

Website: www.hillsdale.edu

HIRAM COLLEGE

AT A GLANCE

Founded in 1850, Hiram College is a highly respected, nationally ranked, private liberal arts college of 1,239 students. Students here are diverse—men and women come from 23 different countries to attend Hiram, and minorities represent 11 percent of the population. Class sizes at Hiram are small. Almost all have fewer than 25 students, and the average size is 15. Professors know their students' names, their academic strengths, and their interests. Hiram's close-knit, residential learning environment blends academic challenge, mentoring from faculty, and a vibrant campus atmosphere to create a distinctive undergraduate experience.

LOCATION AND ENVIRONMENT

Hiram's safe, picturesque campus is located in the Western Reserve region of Northeast Ohio. The college, which is tucked away amid lush, rolling countryside, is part of a historic village that contains restored century homes and public gardens. Students find that life on the Hiram campus is rather self-contained, and for the most part, they like it that way. Almost everyone lives in college housing, and students are guaranteed a spot in Hiram's residence halls for all 4 years they are enrolled. Students are immersed in a comfortable, supportive academic community where they are encouraged to focus on their studies and college life. According to one student, the village of Hiram "is one of the safest places on earth. Where else can you take a walk at 3:00 A.M. and never have to worry?" On the weekends, there's always something happening on campus. The most popular activities are student directed—such as music and theater performances, poetry readings, parties organized by social clubs, and intramural and varsity sports. The college also regularly hosts performances by area musicians and comedians, and hosts campus wide screenings of popular films every other weekend.

When the urge to get off campus strikes, students find that Cleveland is just a short drive away. Hiram students regularly take advantage of the area's cultural and recreational opportunities. The college plans excursions to performances by the world-renowned Cleveland Orchestra (an area foundation provides Hiram students with free tickets) and professional sporting events. Professors, as well, frequently make use of resources in cities surrounding the Hiram campus for their courses. For example, classes will make excursions to the Cleveland Museum of Art, the Natural History Museum, and other cultural destinations.

OFF-CAMPUS OPPORTUNITIES

At Hiram, off-campus study opportunities are incorporated into the academic curriculum. Each academic term, several courses are offered that incorporate overseas study programs into the course work. Small groups of students will travel alongside their Hiram professors to countries such as Italy, England, France, Vietnam, Bhutan, China, Russia, and others, expanding their understanding of the world while earning college credit.

In addition to international travel experiences, Hiram students are strongly encouraged to participate in at least one internship during their undergraduate years. Students work closely with their faculty advisor and the Career Center and Academic Services to coordinate off-campus internships with organizations in fields that are of interest to the student.

MAJORS AND DEGREES OFFERED

Hiram College awards the Bachelor of Arts (BA) degree for undergraduate studies. The major areas of study include accounting and financial management, art, biochemistry, biology, 3-year accelerated biomedical humanities, biomedical humanities, chemistry, communication, computer science, economics and management, education, English, English with a creative writing emphasis, environmental studies, French, history, mathematics, music, neuroscience, philosophy, physics, political science, psychology, religious studies, sociology, Spanish, and theater arts. A Bachelor of Science in nursing will be offered in 2007. Minors are available in all major areas of study, plus exercise and sport science, gender studies, international studies, photography, urban studies, and writing. Pre-professional programs offer preparation for study in a wide variety of fields, including accountancy, seminary, optometry, dentistry, engineering, law, business, medicine, physical therapy, and veterinary medicine.

Hiram also offers the Master of Arts in Interdisciplinary Studies (MAIS) degree. This selective, 2-year graduate degree program is designed as an alternative to highly specialized graduate programs with a strict vocational focus. Through close faculty advising, students in Hiram's MAIS program design an individualized course of study that emphasizes interdisciplinary learning and student-directed areas of concentration.

CAMPUS FACILITIES AND EQUIPMENT

In 2005, Hiram opened a new 140,000-square-foot sports, recreation, and fitness center. Other distinctive facilities include a state-of-the-art science facility, a 390-acre scientific field station for biological research, an observatory, a writing center, and recently renovated residence halls. The computer facilities include wireless networks, several computer laboratories and classrooms, and cart-based computer projection systems. Students have 24-hour access to the Hiram network from their residence hall rooms, and each room is wired for cable television.

TUITION, ROOM, BOARD, AND FEES

For the 2007–2008 academic year, costs will be as follows:

Tuition: $24,215

Fee: $670

Average Room: $3,990

Board: $3,990

Hiram College has a tuition guarantee, which eliminates annual increases to tuition and fees. The rate of tuition and fees during a student's first year will remain the same through the student's fourth year.

FINANCIAL AID

Ninety-three percent of all Hiram students receive Financial Aid. The average Financial Aid award exceeds $21,200.

STUDENT ORGANIZATIONS AND ACTIVITIES

Hiram has more than 80 active student organizations. In addition, Hiram has 14 varsity sports and competes in one of the tougher Division III conferences in the country, the North Coast Athletic Conference.

ADMISSIONS PROCESS

Hiram's Admission Committee prizes students who combine solid academic credentials with an open mind, a sense of adventure, and a creative flair. Your record should show a strong college preparatory program in high school, including a minimum of 17 academic units in the humanities, mathematics, natural sciences, and foreign language. Consideration is given to students who have not taken the recommended program but who demonstrate that they can be successful at Hiram. Your application must include a secondary school report, the results of the SAT or ACT, recommendations (including one from a teacher), and an essay. International students must submit TOEFL scores. A personal interview with a member of the Admission Staff is highly recommended for all applicants. For more information about applying to Hiram, consult our website at http://admission.hiram.edu.

HOFSTRA UNIVERSITY

AT A GLANCE

Hofstra University is building its reputation as a center of academic excellence. With an outstanding faculty, advanced technological resources, and state-of-the-art facilities, Hofstra is recognized, both nationally and internationally, as a university on the rise. The university's plans to host the final 2008 presidential debate and to establish New York's newest medical school on the Hofstra campus indicate that Hofstra University's reputation has gained momentum and that the university's programs and offerings have grown.

While it plays an increasingly prominent national role, Hofstra continues to focus primarily on its students. Undergraduate class size is small, averaging just 22 students, and the student-to-faculty ratio is 14-to-1, providing an environment that fosters interaction, critical thinking and analysis.

Hofstra's distinctive, 240-acre campus is located just 25 miles east of New York City--and all its cultural and internship opportunities. The Hofstra campus is energized, with an increasingly accomplished student body that is engaged in the community and eager to take advantage of all Hofstra has to offer.

LOCATION AND ENVIRONMENT

Something is always in bloom on the Hofstra campus. A recognized arboretum, the campus is home to both ivy-covered classroom buildings and sleek, modern buildings. The New Academic Building, an architecturally distinct structure that houses a theater, a music rehearsal space, faculty offices, and seminar rooms, is the newest building on campus.

With New York City just a short ride by train or car, students take advantage of the theaters, museums, concerts, and professional sports as well as the internship opportunities the city offers. Broadway shows, the Metropolitan Museum of Art, Madison Square Garden, Chinatown and Little Italy, and Wall Street all are within easy reach.

Students can also explore Long Island, which offers world-class beaches and parks; the Hamptons; sport fishing and boating; Nassau Coliseum, home of the New York Islanders; and conveniently located shopping malls.

OFF-CAMPUS OPPORTUNITIES

Hofstra extends learning beyond the classroom through an active internship program and many study abroad opportunities. The internship program takes advantage of the proximity of New York City, allowing students to gain on-the-job experience in areas such as finance, business, media, advertising, and entertainment. Through study abroad programs in Europe, Asia, South America, and elsewhere, students can explore the world while earning college credits.

MAJORS AND DEGREES OFFERED

Hofstra offers degrees in 145 undergraduate programs of study: African studies, American studies, anthropology, applied physics, art history, Asian studies, biochemistry, biology, business, accounting, business education, entrepreneurship, finance, information technology, international business, legal studies in business, management, marketing, chemistry, Chinese, Chinese studies, classics, communication, audio/radio, audio/video/film, broadcast journalism, film studies/production, mass media studies, print journalism, public relations, speech communication & rhetorical studies, video/television, video/television & business, video/television & film, community health, comparative literature and languages, computer science, computer science & mathematics, dance, drama, economics, business economics, mathematical business economics, mathematical economics, education, art education, athletic training, biology education, business education, chemistry education, community health, early childhood and childhood education, earth science education, elementary education, English education, exercise specialist, fine arts education, foreign language education French, foreign language education German, foreign language education Italian, foreign language education Russian, foreign language education Spanish, health education, math education, music education, physical education, physics education, secondary education, social studies, engineering, electrical engineering, electrical engineering computer engineering, engineering science biomedical, engineering science civil, engineering science environmental, engineering science production & manufacturing, industrial engineering, mechanical engineering, English, English (creative writing & literature), English (English & American literature), English (publishing studies & literature), environmental resources, fine arts, fine arts ceramics, fine arts design, fine arts painting, fine arts photography, fine arts sculpture jewelry, fine arts education, foreign language education, forensic science, French, Geography, geology, German, Hebrew, History, Ibero-American studies, interdisciplinary studies, Italian, Jewish studies, labor studies, Latin, Latin American & Caribbean studies, liberal arts, linguistics, mathematics, mathematical business economics, mathematical economics, mathematics actuarial science, mathematics applied math, mathematics chemistry, mathematics computer science, mathematics engineering, mathematics, mathematics physics, mathematics education, mechanical engineering, music, music concentration in history/literature, music concentration in jazz & commercial music, music concentration in music merchandising, music concentration in performance, music concentration in theory & composition, music education, new college, creative arts, humanities, natural sciences, social sciences, philosophy, physician assistant studies, physics, political science, professional studies, psychology, religion, Russian, school health education, science education, social studies education, sociology, Spanish, speech-language-hearing sciences, theater arts, theater arts performance sequence, theater arts production sequence, university without walls, women's studies.

ACADEMIC PROGRAMS

Hofstra University is composed of Hofstra College of Liberal Arts and Sciences, the Frank G. Zarb School of Business, School of Communication, School of Education and Allied Human Services, School of Law, Honors College, New College, and School for University Studies. Honors College is a program for high-achieving students; New College (a division of Hofstra College of Liberal Arts and Sciences) offers individualized programs of study and innovative block scheduling; and School for University Studies was developed for students with academic challenges.

Within these schools are many innovative programs designed to meet the needs of our diverse student body. These include Legal Education Accelerated Program (LEAP), a program that allows students to earn both a BA and JD in 6 years; and First-Year Connections, an academic and social program that helps first-year students connect to all the resources and opportunities available at the university.

CAMPUS FACILITIES AND EQUIPMENT

The Hofstra campus contains 112 buildings, including state-of-the-art teaching facilities, 37 residence halls, and libraries containing 1.2 million print volumes and providing 24/7 electronic access to more than 50,000 journals and electronic books. C. V. Starr Hall, home to the Zarb School of Business, features the Martin B. Greenberg Trading Room, one of the most advanced academic trading rooms in the nation. The School of Communication's Dempster Hall contains one of the largest noncommercial broadcast facilities in the Northeast as well as a cutting-edge converged newsroom and multimedia classroom. In addition, there are 6 theaters, including a new black box theater, and an accredited museum.

Recreational and athletic facilities include an Olympic-sized swimming pool, a recreational center, an indoor sports and entertainment arena, and well-maintained athletic fields.

There are 18 eateries, a post office, a salon, and a full-service bank.

TUITION, ROOM, BOARD, AND FEES

The annual cost of tuition and fees at Hofstra University for 2007-2008 for a full-time undergraduate student is $26,730. The average housing and meal plan is $9,616. Books and supplies cost approximately $1,000; personal expenses and transportation generally amount to $2,640. For the full tuition and fees schedule, visit hofstra.edu/tuition.

FINANCIAL AID

A college degree has always been the surest way to success. To help you achieve your education goals, Hofstra University offers several financial aid options. Hofstra awarded more than $55 million in financial assistance in 2007-2008, and 81 percent of all Hofstra students received some type of financial aid. For more detailed information, visit hofstra.edu/FinancialAid.

STUDENT ORGANIZATIONS AND ACTIVITIES

Hofstra has a dynamic campus life, with more than 150 student clubs and organizations, including about 30 fraternities and sororities; 18 varsity sports; and more than 500 cultural events each year. Students can choose from organizations as diverse as the Geology Club, Danceworks, and the Hofstra Organization of Latin Americans.

Hofstra's Division I athletic program includes baseball, football, wrestling, softball, volleyball, field hockey, and men's and women's basketball, lacrosse, cross-country, golf, soccer, and tennis. Students who are not Division I athletes can join the student section "Lion's Den" or participate with more than 25 percent of our students in numerous intramural sports.

Students can also attend debates, lectures, and readings by the many scholars, business leaders, writers, and celebrities who visit campus each year. Some great events include the annual "Great Writers, Great Readings" series, the Center for Civic Engagement's Day of Dialogue, and the Distinguished Faculty Lectures.

ADMISSIONS PROCESS

Hofstra University seeks to enroll talented first-year and transfer students from diverse backgrounds and locations, with varied interests. Applications are accepted for fall and spring admission.

The Admission Committee reviews each application individually to assess academic achievement, curricular rigor, leadership potential, depth of extracurricular activities, standardized test scores and overall interest in attending Hofstra University. The application process provides an opportunity for the applicant to share information that may not be apparent on a transcript or through a test score.

Questions about the application process should be directed to the Admission Office in Bernon Hall:

In writing:

100 Hofstra University

Hempstead, New York 11549-1000

By telephone: 516-463-6700 or 1-800-HOFSTRA, ext. 610

By e-mail: Admitme@Hofstra.edu

For more information, visit our Website: hofstra.edu/admission

HUSSON COLLEGE

AT A GLANCE

Since Husson opened its doors in 1898, it has continued to focus on providing a solid education in professional careers. The College is proud of its strong traditions but continues to move forward in meeting the needs of its students and community. Husson has been located on the same 170-acre campus since 1968, just a mile from downtown Bangor. Our campus is a visual mosaic of classic brick buildings, walking paths, sports fields, forests and rolling lawns. The College's enrollment is approximately 2,200 students, of which 1,800 are undergraduate. Husson athletic teams compete at the NCAA Division III level. Athletic opportunities include football, baseball, field hockey, golf, basketball, soccer, softball, volleyball and swimming. Most of the athletic facilities are new, having been built within the last few years. Our new soccer pitch, and softball field (dedicated in 2005) join the 135,000-square-foot artificial turf sports complex that houses the baseball, football and field hockey teams. In addition to athletics, Husson has numerous student clubs and organizations. Husson offers opportunities to grow, have fun and experience something new. There are also various professional clubs for students to join that relate directly to their major. The College also sponsors guest lecturers, concerts, films and a number of other activities. Residential life is an important aspect of undergraduate education at Husson. The campus has three residence halls, each with a personality all their own. Another important part of campus life is the food at the dining hall. Husson is proud that the National Association of College and University Food Services has cited the Husson Dining Service as among the best in the nation for its strong efforts to cater to the dietary needs of a diverse campus community. Husson is accredited by the New England Association of Schools and Colleges, Inc., the Commission on Collegiate Nursing Education, the International Assembly for Collegiate Business Education, the Commission on Accreditation in Physical Therapy Education, the Accreditation Council for Occupational Therapy Education, and is approved by the Maine State Board of Education.

LOCATION AND ENVIRONMENT

Located on the shores of the Penobscot River and only 40 miles from the famous Bar Harbor and beautiful Acadia National Park. Mount Katahdin, Baxter State Park, and Moosehead Lake, as well a number of noted ski resorts, are all within close proximity to campus. Maine is also home to the great shopping of Freeport, including L.L. Bean. If you're looking for a place to fully experience all four seasons, this is it. Bangor is a city of about 33,000 residents, with 140,000 in the metropolitan area, and is located within a day's drive to Quebec City, Boston, New York, or Montreal.

OFF-CAMPUS OPPORTUNITIES

The Bangor area offers numerous opportunities typical to a city environment, including museums, art exhibits, music festivals, theatre, films, and sports. The beautiful surrounding area offers opportunities to ski, snowboard, hike, go whitewater rafting, and mountain biking.

MAJORS AND DEGREES OFFERED

Husson confers the Doctor of Physical Therapy (D.P.T.), the Master of Science (M.S.), the Bachelor of Science (B.S.), and the Associate of Science (A.S.) degrees. The Pharm.D. program is currently under development. Associate of Science degrees: Accounting, Business Administration, Business Studies, Information Systems, Criminal Justice, and Paralegal Studies. Bachelor of Science degrees: Accounting, Accounting/Computer Information Systems, Business Administration (with concentrations in Financial Management, General, Hospitality Management, International Business, Management, Marketing, Small/Family Business Management and Sports Management), Business and Technology, Computer Information Systems, Elementary Education, Physical Education, Secondary Education, Health Care Studies, Nursing, Biology, Chemistry, Criminal Justice, Criminal Justice/Psychology, English, Paralegal Studies, Psychology, and Science and Humanities. Master of Science degree programs: Students can earn both their Bachelor of Science degree and Master of Science degree within 5 years including a B.S. Accounting/M.S. in Business, B.S. Business Administration/M.S. in Business (with concentrations in Financial Management, International Business, Management and Marketing), a B.S. Computer Information Systems/M.S. in Business. From the School of Health: M.S. in Nursing or a Post-Master's Certificate with a focus on Family and Community Nurse Practitioner or Advanced Practice Psychiatric Nursing. Students may also earn an M.S. in Occupational Therapy, an M.S. in Occupational Therapy/B.S. in Psychology, a Doctor of Physical Therapy (DPT), or a Doctor of Physical Therapy/B.S. in Kinesiology. The School of Science and Humanities: M.S. in Criminal Justice Administration and The M.S. in Counseling Psychology. The School of Education: M.S. in School Counseling. A one-year Undeclared program is also available for students wishing to explore academic fields before committing to a particular program.

ACADEMIC PROGRAMS

Husson offers associate, bachelor's, master's and a doctoral degree through the Schools of Business, Health, Education, and Science and Humanities. Students may pursue degrees in the following fields of study: accounting, business administration (with concentrations in management, marketing, finance, general, international business, sports management, hospitality management, and small/family business management), computer information systems, paralegal studies, health care studies, chemistry, nursing, physical therapy, occupational therapy, elementary education, secondary education (with concentrations in English, physical science, and life science), physical education, criminal justice, psychology, biology, science and humanities, and a one-year undeclared major. There are approximately 1,800 undergraduate students and 400 graduate students at Husson's Bangor campus. Incoming undergraduates usually have a combined score at least 940 on the SAT or a composite score of 22 on the ACT. Incoming students usually have a secondary school GPA of 3.06 or better, and most were ranked in the top fifty percent of their high school class. The College's job placement rate is 95 percent. Undergraduates in all fields of study must take the College's core curriculum and participate in an experiential learning program.

CAMPUS FACILITIES AND EQUIPMENT

The campus features two interconnected academic buildings, three residence halls, an architecturally unique dining commons, and a gymnasium, sports complex and fitness center. Cutting-edge laboratory spaces (including the Dahl Anatomy Lab) give Husson students a competitive edge. Quickly joining the landscape is the Meeting House, future home of the School of Science and Humanities, Alumni Offices and The Gracie Theater. Looking deeper, you will find a campus center with a glorious granite fireplace, the brand-new Furman Student Center designed with entertainment in mind, a performance area, chapel, computer labs, a coffee shop and a number of other areas to unwind, study or just hang out. Husson athletes are able to take advantage of some of the best athletic facilities within their conference. A new FieldTurf soccer pitch and up-dated softball complex were recently completed for the 2007-2008 seasons, joining an impressive outdoor multi-use FieldTurf sports complex. With NCAA Division III sports, plenty of intramural sports, a state-of-the-art fitness center and a fitness consultant, there are plenty of ways for students to stay active and healthy. Also on campus is the Center for Family Business, the New England School of Communications and the Bangor Theological Seminary.

TUITION, ROOM, BOARD AND FEES

For the 2007-2008 academic year, undergraduate base tuition is $11,970 plus $6,500 in room and board fees. The comprehensive fee is an additional $280 annually, plus a $75 graduation fee. The cost of living is lower than in most parts of the United States; however, students should expect to spend some additional money on books, supplies, and personal expenses.

FINANCIAL AID

Husson aims to help every student cover the cost of their education through a proper financial aid package. Currently, almost 90 percent of Husson students receive some form of financial assistance. The financial package awarded to each student is based on the need demonstrated through the Free Application for Federal Student Aid (FAFSA). Students may receive financial aid from Federal Pell Grants, Federal Supplemental Educational Opportunity Grants, Federal Perkins Loans, and Federal Work-Study programs. In addition, Husson awards a number of merit-based scholarships based on a student's success academically or in leadership to the community. Many students also cover the cost of their education through part-time, off campus jobs.

STUDENT ORGANIZATIONS AND ACTIVITIES

Student involvement is encouraged on the Husson campus. Student Senate members and other student representatives serve on a variety of the College's administrative committees including the Undergraduate Student Conduct Board, and the president of the Student Senate sits on the College Board of Trustees as a voting member.

ADMISSIONS PROCESS

Husson believes that everyone who wants to enhance their life and career through higher education should have the opportunity to attend college. The College reviews every applicant individually. Freshman applicants are evaluated on the basis of their high school curriculum, GPA, class rank, recommendations from high school counselor, and scores on the SAT or ACT. Students may be accepted on a conditional basis if their secondary school transcripts are average but they have also submitted a positive recommendation from their high school counselor or other official, and demonstrate potential for success. Students applying for admission to some majors may need to fulfill specific academic requirements prior to submitting their application. Along with their completed application for admission, students must submit a $25 application fee. Once these materials have been submitted, students should forward their official transcripts to the Admissions Office as soon as possible. The College welcomes transfer applications. All transfer students must submit both high school and college transcripts. Successful transfer students must be in good academic standing at the previous college attended and must have maintained a GPA of 2.0 or better. Husson admits students on a rolling basis and applications are reviewed as soon as all required materials have been submitted. Students may apply for admission for the fall or spring semester, except for those applying to the physical or occupational therapy programs, which only begin in September. Physical Therapy applicants must apply by March 15 and are accepted on a rolling basis until the program is full. Husson encourages prospective students to visit the campus and experience student life through a tour or open house.

To request more information or application materials, please contact:

Director of Admissions

Husson One College Circle

Bangor, ME 04401

Telephone: 207-941-7100 800-448-7766

Fax: 207-941-7935

E-mail: admit@husson.edu

World Wide Web: www.husson.edu

ILLINOIS INSTITUTE OF TECHNOLOGY

AT A GLANCE

A private, independent, PhD-granting, coeducational research university founded in 1890, Illinois Institute of Technology (IIT) offers today's students a superb education in engineering, business, architecture, the sciences, psychology, and the humanities, in an environment geared toward the undergraduate student. IIT's mission is to advance knowledge through research and scholarship, to cultivate invention improving the human condition, and to educate students from throughout the world for a life of professional achievement, service to society and individual fulfillment. Through committed faculty members, close personal attention, and its signature inter-professional programs, Illinois Institute of Technology provides a challenging academic program focused on the integration of education and the professional world.

Our students come to us from 50 states and more than 90 countries: 69 percent men/31 percent women, 14 percent international, 42 percent in top 10 percent of high school class; 2,576 undergraduate students; 3,714 graduate; and 1,119 law students make up the entire student body of IIT, including the Stuart School of Business, Chicago-Kent College of Law, and the Institute of Design.

OFF-CAMPUS OPPORTUNITIES

Over the past 6 years, IIT alumni in all fields have enjoyed a 92 percent placement rate in the workplace and in graduate and professional school programs within 6 months of graduation. The 8:1 student-faculty ratio invites direct mentoring by faculty who are groundbreaking leaders in their respective fields. Combining the resources of a top research university with the small classes and personal attention of a liberal arts college, IIT allows students to deepen their knowledge and gain a better sense of their place in the world. And since that world continually faces unanticipated challenges as new advances and technologies emerge in every field, IIT offers an education that gives students the power to navigate complex ideas, demystify technology for others, and take on important problems as they arise. Much of the learning here happens through collaboration with faculty members who offer insightful and relevant perspectives—whether by incorporating the latest materials in design projects or exploring questions posed by their own research in the lab. IIT has established the Office of Undergraduate Research in order to enhance existing programs at IIT and provide new opportunities for mentored collaborative research experiences for undergraduates.

Reality-based education IIT's Interprofessional Projects (IPRO) program isn't found at any other college or university. Students on an IPRO team take on real challenges facing today's corporations, nonprofits, entrepreneurs, government organizations, and faculty and student researchers. IPRO instructors don't lecture, they coach. Students work as an integral part of a team to research, brainstorm, analyze, experiment, build, demonstrate—whatever it takes to create a solution and advance the project to the next level. Undergraduates develop teamwork, problem-solving, decision-making, project-management, communication, and leadership skills—while enjoying work within a team and building experience and career credentials. IPROs (and their cousins, EnPROs, based on new venture ideas that may even be your own) have proven so worthwhile that every student takes part in at least 2 of the semester-long projects while at IIT.

The addition of the University Technology Park at IIT (UTP), an incubator for technology companies located on the Main Campus, and the university's access to more than 29 research facilities, amplifies student's access to outstanding research and professional opportunities. IIT has a rich history with Chicago's professional world, giving students the ability to create relationships and connections with countless multinational businesses and organizations in the city.

MAJORS AND DEGREES OFFERED

Undergraduate majors are aerospace engineering, applied mathematics, architectural engineering, architecture, biochemistry, biology, biomedical engineering, business administration, business administration and applied science, chemical engineering, chemistry, civil engineering, computer engineering, computer science, electrical engineering, humanities, journalism of technology, science and business, materials science and engineering, molecular biochemistry and biophysics, physics. IIT has more than 54 minors including artificial intelligence, energy/environment/economics, organizational psychology, polymer science and engineering. Specializations include cell and tissue engineering, finance, and marketing. Dual Admission Programs offered are BS/D.O. (osteopathic medicine), BS/JD (law), BS/MBA (business), BS/PharmD (pharmacy). Special programs are also available in math and science education, pre-law, pre-medicine, and pre-optometry.

CAMPUS FACILITIES AND EQUIPMENT

The internationally famous 120-acre main campus is based on a master plan developed by the late Ludwig Mies van der Rohe, one of the most influential architects of the century, who served for 20 years as director of IIT's College of Architecture. IIT is located in the heart of Chicago, Illinois, just 10 minutes from the Loop. Students are able to experience one of the greatest cultural cities in the world. More than 70 percent of IIT undergraduates live on campus in 13 residence halls, 6 fraternity houses and 2 sorority houses. The newest student residence, State Street Village was featured in *Time* magazine. It has balconies with sweeping views of the Chicago skyline and lounges and multimedia entertainment centers.

TUITION, ROOM, BOARD, AND FEES

The Office of Financial Aid works hard to bring the cost of an IIT education within reach of anyone with the talent and desire to be here. Annual tuition for 2007-08 was $24,962. Other expenses were $8,618-11,540 for room and board (depending on selections) and $794 for fees. Ninety-seven percent of IIT students receive financial aid. Every student is evaluated for significant merit-based scholarships upon admission. Our highest undergraduate academic honor, the Camras Scholars Program, challenges the top 1 percent of our applicant pool to apply and interview with a faculty member for a place as a Camras Scholar. Chosen Camras Scholars are awarded full-tuition scholarships for 4 years (5 years for Architecture majors). Special deadlines apply. ROTC and athletic scholarships are also available to qualified students. Students applying for need-based aid must submit the Free Application for Federal Student Aid (FAFSA).

STUDENT ORGANIZATIONS AND ACTIVITIES

Students are encouraged to participate in many social, cultural, and athletic opportunities. Student activities include the campus newspaper, the WIIT radio station, special interest clubs, theater and music groups, intramural and varsity athletics, fraternities and sororities, honor and professional societies, student government, residence hall organizations, and the student-run Union Board. IIT has more than 100 student organizations on campus such as rock climbing, club intramural athletics, and enjoy events such as Chicago's famous theater and improv performances, Taste of IIT, Homecoming Week and International Festival and Pumpkin launch. Counseling, job placement, and student health services are included in the various campus services. The library has access to more than 22 million volumes. Recreational activities include weekly movies, intramural sports, a swimming pool, a recreation center, and discount tickets to area events.

In the athletic arena, IIT student athletes challenge themselves both physically and mentally. In the classroom, they are committed to the highest standard of academic excellence. They compete on a national stage in basketball, cross-country, soccer, swimming and diving, men's baseball, and women's volleyball. Our athletes have earned All-American and All-Conference Honors in the National Association Intercollegiate Athletics (NAIA) Division I.

ADMISSIONS PROCESS

In our application review process, each student is considered on an individual and holistic basis by the Admissions Committee. Our counselors and faculty evaluate not only academic standing, but also extracurricular, social, and community-based activities and leadership. We want to know a student's future goals—whether specific or broad. Overall, we seek to enroll students whose diverse intellectual and professional interests will enable them to make full use of the resources available to them at IIT. We may be just the right school for students who share our goals of innovation and integrity as part of their academic and professional interests. IIT admits the majority of its students on a rolling basis. Special application deadlines do apply for the College of Architecture, special programs, and some scholarships (see admission.iit.edu for details). We start accepting applications in July of 2007 and will continue to accept them beyond the academic year.

Contact us

Office of Undergraduate Admission

10 West Thirty-third Street, Perlstein hall Room 101

Chicago, Illinois 60616

Telephone: 312-567-3025 or 800-448-2329 (toll free)

E-mail: admission@iit.edu

Website: http://admission.iit.edu

Illinois Institute of Technology is accredited by the Higher Learning Commission of the North Central Association of Colleges and Schools. www.ncahigherlearningcommission.org/

It is the intention of Illinois Institute of Technology to act in accordance with all regulations of the federal, state, and local governments with respect to providing equality of opportunity in employment and in education, insofar as those regulations may pertain to IIT. IIT prohibits and will act to eliminate discrimination on the basis of race, color, religion, national origin, gender, sexual orientation, age, disability, or veteran status. Illinois Institute of Technology provides individuals with disabilities reasonable accommodations to participate in university activities, programs and services. Individuals with disabilities requiring an accommodation to participate in an activity, program or service should call the activity, program, or service director. disabilities@iit.edu

IONA COLLEGE

AT A GLANCE

Founded by the Christian Brothers in 1940, Iona is one of the only colleges in the region to hold several prestigious national accreditations in business (AACSB), social work (CSWE), teacher education (NCATE), computer science (ABET), and journalism and mass communication (ACEJMC). Iona's marriage and family therapy program is a candidate for COAMFTE accreditation. A medium-sized college with a student-teacher ratio of 13:1, Iona has approximately 3,500 undergraduate students and 4,500 total students. There are 5 residence halls on the college's picturesque 35-acre campus in New Rochelle, NY; an additional non-residential campus houses the Rockland Graduate Center in Pearl River, NY, which offers master's degrees to students in Rockland and neighboring Westchester, Bergen, Orange, and Westchester counties. Students are encouraged to integrate the spiritual, intellectual, emotional, and physical dimensions of their lives, immersed in a community where ethical decisions and service to others are primary considerations. Iona College is a diverse community of learners and scholars dedicated to academic excellence in the tradition of the Christian Brothers and American Catholic Higher Education. The college is currently listed in *U.S. News & World Report*'s "Top Tier" in "America's Best Colleges 2008," the Princeton Review's *Best Northeastern Colleges* and *Best 290 Business Schools* 2008 editions, as well as *BusinessWeek*'s "Best 140 National Undergraduate Business Schools 2008."

LOCATION AND ENVIRONMENT

Iona is located just 20 minutes north of Manhattan. Its proximity to New York City provides students with exceptional cultural, educational, internships, and career opportunities. Recruiters from top Fortune 500 companies participate in Iona's Internship/Career Expo every year, and students have held internships at some of the best-known corporations in New York City and the surrounding area.

MAJORS AND DEGREES OFFERED

Iona College offers more than 40 majors including accounting, biochemistry, biology (general, pre-professional), business administration, chemistry, computer science, criminal justice, economics, education (childhood, adolescence), English, environmental science, finance, foreign languages (French, Italian, Spanish), history, information systems, interdisciplinary studies, science, international business, international studies, management, marketing, mass communication (advertising, journalism, public relations, TV/video), mathematics and applied mathematics, medical technology, philosophy, physics, political science, psychology, religious studies, social work, sociology, speech communication studies, and speech/language pathology and audiology. Five-year combined bachelor's and master's degree programs are offered in computer science, English, history, and psychology. Minors are available in many of the above programs, as well as film studies, fine and performing arts, peace and justice studies, pre-law, sports and entertainment studies, women's studies, and writing. A number of programs offer a business minor.

ACADEMIC PROGRAMS

The college offers BA, BS, BPS, and BBA degrees to undergraduate students. The BA, BS, and BPS degrees require a total of 120 credits for completion; for BBA degrees, a total of 126 credits are required. An honors program, with special courses, seminars, mentoring, advising, and Off-Campus Opportunities, is available to top students. Iona also offers master's degrees, certificates, and post-master's certificates in a variety of programs: communication, computer technology, counseling (substance abuse, mental health, marriage and family therapy, and pastoral), criminal justice, education, educational technology, English, finance, health services administration, history, Italian, journalism, psychology, public relations, Spanish, and telecommunications. Iona's Hagan School of Business offers an AACSB-accredited MBA program and certificates. Part-time and adult students returning to college can pursue a bachelor's degree through the Professional Studies Program.

CAMPUS FACILITIES AND EQUIPMENT

The college has undertaken an ambitious $83 million building campaign which has transformed the campus. The new Hynes Athletics Center provides students with access to cardio machines and free weights, an aerobic/dance studio and classes, a pool, a rowing tank and more. New residence halls, arts center, and a student union offer students impressive facilities for classes and extracurricular activities. With its radio station, extensive room for clubs, comfortable lounges, bookstore, a food court and café, the Robert V. LaPenta Student Union is the living room of the campus. In fall 2007, groundbreaking took place for a library expansion and renovation that will provide a multimedia seminar room and group study facilities equipped for students to collaborate on podcasts and digital projects-all while enjoying a Starbucks from the library's café (1 of 2 outlets on campus). The library has already installed 52 dual-boot iMacs, which can run both Microsoft Windows and the latest Mac OS, making Iona one of a handful of colleges to invest in the cutting-edge technology.

The Office of Student Development hosts hundreds of on and off-campus events throughout the year, and students can participate in more than 60 student-run organizations. Iona College encourages students to broaden their educational experience through study abroad; it sponsors summer, semester, and intersession programs in Australia, England, France, Ireland, Italy, and Spain. Campus Ministries provides multiple opportunities for students to engage in service and ministry projects, while Iona in Mission offers students the chance to travel to aid the disadvantaged in the United States and abroad. The college has a vibrant athletics program with more than 400 student-athletes in Iona's 22 NCAA Division I teams in the Metro Atlantic Athletic Conference. Recently both the men's and women's cross-country teams won MAAC Championships: the sixteenth consecutive championship for the men's team, and the third straight for the women's team. The men's team placed second at the NCAA championship.

TUITION, ROOM, BOARD, AND FEES

Undergraduate tuition for the 2008-09 academic year is $26,206. Room and board is an additional $11,100.

ADMISSIONS PROCESS

Admission decisions at Iona are based on a wide range of criteria. Most important is an applicant's academic record, including the level of curriculum and grades earned. Also considered are SAT I or ACT scores, grade trends, a writing sample, activities and recommendations. For the class entering in September of 2007, the average grade point average was an 89 percent or 3.4; the middle 50 percent on the SAT ranged from 1080 to 1300. Slightly more than 6,000 applications were submitted and about 3,550 (59 percent) of the applications were accepted and offered admission. Campus visits are available on most weekdays that school is in session and on selected Saturdays; appointments are recommended. To schedule a visit, please contact our Campus Visit Center at 914-633-2622 or e-mail eenglish@iona.edu.

ITHACA COLLEGE

AT A GLANCE

Coeducational and nonsectarian, Ithaca is a nationally recognized college of 6,400 students. As a comprehensive institution, Ithaca offers an excellent foundation in the liberal arts as well as strong professional programs at the undergraduate level. Moreover, all of our degree programs are supplemented by independent and interdisciplinary studies, dual majors, minors, and elective courses in other academic fields. Nearly every state and 67 countries are represented in the student population; 2,800 men and 3,400 women are currently enrolled. Some 400 of those students are enrolled in graduate programs. Founded in 1892 as the Ithaca Conservatory of Music, the school eventually grew into a private college offering Academic Programs in several professional fields. At mid-century the institutions curricula in liberal arts were unified, and the large and diversified School of Humanities and Sciences now forms the core of the Ithaca educational experience. In the 1960s the college moved from downtown Ithaca to its current home on South Hill. Here, the college's 750 acres command a majestic vista of the city of Ithaca and Cayuga Lake.

LOCATION AND ENVIRONMENT

Ithaca is located in the center of upstate New York's Finger Lakes region; approximately 97,000 people live in the surrounding county. Major air and bus lines serve the city, which is 60 miles south of Syracuse, 60 miles north of Binghamton, and an hour's flight from New York City.

OFF-CAMPUS OPPORTUNITIES

You'll have access to extensive opportunities for internships in business, communications, music, athletic training, speech-language pathology, health policy studies, community health education, humanities, natural sciences, and more. If you attend the School of Communications, you might apply to spend a semester at our communications program in Los Angeles. Ready access to internships and industry experts make this program a fast-paced working and learning experience. Any student may apply to our internship-focused program in Washington, DC.

Study abroad is also popular. Programs are available at the college's own London Center or through our study centers and exchange programs in Singapore, Sweden, Spain, the Czech Republic, Japan, and elsewhere. There are also opportunities for study at some 50 affiliated programs throughout the world.

MAJORS AND DEGREES OFFERED

Ithaca College offers more than 2,000 courses and more than 100 degree programs and confers the bachelor of arts, bachelor of science, bachelor of fine arts, bachelor of music, master of business administration, master of science, master of music, and doctor of physical therapy degrees.

ACADEMIC PROGRAMS

Whether you know exactly what you want to do after graduation or need to explore your options, Ithaca has a program to suit you. In our 5 schools—Business, Communications, Health Sciences and Human Performance, Humanities and Sciences, and Music—and the Division of Interdisciplinary and International Studies, we combine the breadth of a university with the intimate feel of a college.

First-year students from all areas of the college can also choose from among several special seminar-style classes that combine rigorous study with transition-to-college topics.

Students in our School of Music are part of one of the nations most highly regarded music programs. From your first year at Ithaca, you'll be learning with the best and performing on a regular basis in our modern recital halls.

Our AACSB-accredited School of Business offers a wide range of courses covering the world of business. From our new business school building to the real-time stock ticker in our trading room, you'll have the tools at your fingertips to shape a successful start to your career.

Other options include our 5-year program in occupational therapy and 6-year program in physical therapy, each leading to professional certification; our 4 + 1 MBA program; New York State teacher certification programs in more than a dozen fields; and joint agreements with other schools that provide opportunities to study engineering or optometry.

Our Exploratory Program allows you to sample classes from all of the schools before deciding on a major. And if your interests are not encapsulated by a single major, you can turn to our planned studies program, which affords the opportunity to craft your own major across several programs.

No matter what you choose, all of our programs are imbued with an intensive, hands-on approach to education. Close contact with advisers and frequent opportunities to take learning beyond the classroom are Ithaca's hallmarks. That approach pays off; surveys show that 97 percent of our alumni find employment and/or attend graduate school within a year of graduation.

CAMPUS FACILITIES AND EQUIPMENT

Campus life is sparked by some 150 student organizations, 25 intercollegiate sports teams, and hundreds of lectures, films, and other events each year. Our NCAA Division III teams enjoy frequent success: they hold 15 national titles in football (3), women's soccer (2), women's crew (2), wrestling (3), baseball (2), field hockey, softball, and gymnastics. Music and theater performances by students are frequent, and national acts visit campus often; recently Less Than Jake, Mae, Something Corporate, and the Roots performed here.

ADMISSIONS PROCESS

Admission to Ithaca College is based on high school record, personal recommendations, SAT or ACT scores, and, for some programs, audition or portfolio. Admission is selective and competitive; individual talents and circumstances are always given serious consideration by the admission committee. Typically, some 13,100 men and women apply for 1,630 places in the freshman class; applicants are notified of their status as soon as possible after all admission materials are received. We advise you to submit your application early in your senior year of high school and no later than February 1. Ithaca College also accepts the Common Application; contact the Office of Admission or your high school guidance office for more information. Applicants will receive a decision no later than April 15. Students offered admission are asked to respond by May 1, the candidate reply date established by the College Board.

Transfer applicants generally follow the same admission procedures as freshmen. Applications for fall admission should be submitted by March 1; applications for spring admission should be submitted by November 1.

JOHNS HOPKINS UNIVERSITY

AT A GLANCE

Ever since its founding in 1876, Johns Hopkins has made the undergraduate experience all about exploration and discovery. We believe in learning through independent inquiry—for anyone in any major. Our students work in every discipline and with every subject imaginable, from *Beowulf* to bioengineering. And they do it all with the resources of Baltimore and Washington, D.C., at their fingertips, from the comfort of an active and close-knit campus community. You'll have the opportunity to make your own discoveries and the guidance you need to get there: in groups; through faculty mentorships; and through internships, study abroad, and the cultural connections of one of the most exciting cities around.

ACADEMIC PROGRAMS

Classes are small here, and the resources are big. That means you get to know your professors and classmates the way you would at a small liberal arts college, but you have all the opportunities of a major research institution with a global reach—right at your fingertips, as an undergraduate. Many students complete independent projects with professors, mentors, and teams. Lots more take advantage of study abroad, internships, semesters in Washington, D.C., and advanced graduate study. Johns Hopkins has schools, centers, and affiliates all over the Baltimore/Washington, D.C., area—often linked by free shuttle bus—and across the country and around the world. Cross registration, independent projects, and internships are all encouraged options. Two awards—the Provost's Undergraduate Research Awards, worth up to $3,000, and the Woodrow Wilson Undergraduate Research Fellowships, worth up to $10,000—give participants the chance to complete projects of their own choosing under the guidance of a faculty mentor. Instead of a rigid core of compulsory courses, Johns Hopkins leaves you free to concentrate on what you love, or to explore more broadly. Academic and faculty advisers, career advisers, and pre-professional advisers help you chart the waters.

CAMPUS FACILITIES AND EQUIPMENT

The Mattin Center offers space for student groups and artistic endeavors. The center features a theater, cafe, art studios, darkrooms, music practice rooms, dance studio, the Digital Media Center, multipurpose rooms, and meeting spaces. An Arts Certificate program offers a certificate in five areas: dance, digital media, fine/visual arts, music, and theater. The Ralph S. O'Connor Recreation Center, open for use by all students, houses basketball and volleyball courts, a rock-climbing wall, a weight room, and fitness training and aerobics areas, as well as access to the Athletic Center's swimming facilities. Popular fitness classes include yoga, pilates, kickboxing, step aerobics, spinning, West African dance, sports conditioning, and, believe it or not, Ballet for Jocks. Charles Commons, a two-building residential complex opened for the 2006-2007 school year, features suites with single rooms, kitchenettes, and in many cases, living rooms. The complex is also home to a number of student amenities and common areas.

TUITION, ROOM, BOARD AND FEES

Tuition: $35,900

Room and Board: $11,092°

Matriculation Fee: $500 (onetime fee only)

Books and Supplies: $1,000 (estimated)

Personal Expenses: $1,000 (estimated)

°In a typical room with a 19-meal plan

STUDENT ORGANIZATIONS AND ACTIVITIES

There are at least 350 student groups and organizations on campus. All Johns Hopkins student groups are governed and managed by students, and there is literally something for everybody, from theater and performing arts groups, to political, special interest, and cultural groups, to publications, student government, and religious groups. Published since 1896, the *News-Letter* is one of the oldest student papers in the country, and it's where Pulitzer Prize-winning journalist Russell Baker got his start. In 120 years of competition, the men's lacrosse team has won 44 national championships, including the 2005 and 2007 NCAA Division I National Championship, and twice represented the United States in the Olympic Games. For the past eight years, the women's team has also competed in Division I. Outside of lacrosse, one out of six Johns Hopkins students participates in Division III or club athletics, and more than half participate in the popular intramural program.

ADMISSIONS PROCESS

Each year we review more than 14,800 applications, from which we must select a freshman class of around 1,200. Also each year, transfer students from other colleges and universities apply for entrance during their sophomore or junior years. Each application we receive represents an individual, and the Admissions Committee considers each one individually. High school students should inquire by the fall term of senior year and complete and submit applications by January 1 (by November 1 for Early Decision). The application booklet and its online version include detailed information about the application process. To apply, complete Part I of the application and submit it as soon as possible, but no later than the deadline, with your $70 nonrefundable application fee. This will open your application file. Supporting materials may be received at any time up until the application deadline.

please note this important policy: Students wishing to enroll in the biomedical engineering (BME) major must indicate BME as their first-choice major on their application. Students are admitted specifically into the BME major, based on evaluation of credentials and space available. Students can be admitted to the university without acceptance to the BME major. No separate application is required. Notification of acceptance into the BME major is given at the time of decision notification. A limited number of transfer majors for matriculated students may be available through the Biomedical Engineering Department at the close of each academic year. Early Decision applicants who are admitted to Johns Hopkins but who are not admitted to the biomedical engineering (BME) major at that time will be allowed to apply to and consider offers of admission from other institutions. The commitment to matriculate at Johns Hopkins if accepted is null and void in this circumstance.

STANDARDIZED TEST REQUIREMENTS

Freshman: SAT Reasoning Test or the ACT with Writing Test are required. For those submitting SAT scores, Johns Hopkins recommends submitting SAT Subject Test scores, and if submitted, requests results from three tests.

Transfer: SAT Reasoning Test scores are optional; SAT Subject Tests are not required. International: The TOEFL is required of applicants whose native language is not English and who attend a non-English-speaking high school. If you attend an English-language school but do not speak English at home, you should take the TOEFL. If your native language is not English and you attend high school in the U.S., you must take the TOEFL if you have been here for fewer than five years. Applicants should score a minimum of 600 (written test) or 250 (computer test). Applicants taking the Internet-based TOEFL (iBT) should have minimum sub-scores of 26 (Reading), 26 (Listening), 22 (Writing), and 25 (Speaking). A Critical Reading SAT score of 670 or higher may be substituted for the TOEFL.

JOHNSON & WALES UNIVERSITY AT PROVIDENCE

AT A GLANCE

Founded in Providence in 1914, Johnson & Wales University (JWU) is a private, career-oriented institution. The university's 16,561 students attend classes at campuses in Providence, Rhode Island; North Miami, Florida; Denver, Colorado; and Charlotte, North Carolina. Most are recent graduates of high school business, college-preparatory, and vocational/technical programs, representing 50 states and 89 countries. The university's 467 full-time and 218 part-time undergraduate faculty members (all campuses) are oriented toward instruction rather than research. Many are chosen for their professional experience in business, culinary arts, hospitality services, or technology. The student-faculty ratio university wide is 31:1. The academic focus of the university is on degree programs in business, culinary arts, hospitality, and technology. M.BA programs include global business leadership (with a concentration in accounting, financial management, international trade, organizational leadership, or marketing) and hospitality & tourism global business leadership (with concentrations in finance and marketing). MA programs in teaching include business, food service, and Special Ed. The university also offers a doctoral program in educational leadership. The university maintains 24 residence halls throughout its 4 campuses. Student services include academic counseling and testing, a tutorial center, and health services. The university's Career Development Office provides extensive career planning and placement services. Within 60 days of graduation, 98 percent of JWU students from the 50 states have jobs in their chosen career field. Johnson & Wales is accredited by the New England Association of Schools and Colleges. The hospitality programs in Providence are accredited by the Accreditation Commission for Programs in Hospitality Administration.

LOCATION AND ENVIRONMENT

The location of each of the university's campuses enables students to take advantage of a variety of internship and part-time work activities. The urban setting of the Providence, Rhode Island, campus provides students proximity to the city's many cultural and recreational facilities. In North Miami, Florida, the campus is a short trip from the sun and fun of Fort Lauderdale and the culture and diversity of Miami. Denver, Colorado, offers students great opportunities as *Fortune* magazine's "second best city in America to work and live." The Charlotte, North Carolina campus is located in a vibrant urban setting that combines commercial and residential life. More than 300 Fortune 500 companies have offices in Charlotte, which is known as the second largest financial center in the United States.

OFF-CAMPUS OPPORTUNITIES

Many of our majors offer internships at university-owned facilities to expand learning beyond the classroom. The hotel and restaurant management programs feature an internship at the Johnson & Wales Inn, Radisson Airport Hotel, Bay Harbor Inn and Suites, or the DoubleTree Hotel; all are full-service hotel complexes owned and/or operated by the university. For all majors optional selective career co-ops are available throughout the United States and worldwide, such as Marriott International; Hyatt Regency Hotels; Food Network; Foxwoods Resort and Casino; and Putnam Investments. Most internships and co-ops are one term in duration and carry 13.5 quarter hours of credit. Study abroad programs are also offered.

MAJORS AND DEGREES OFFERED

The degree programs described below are for the 2007-2008 academic year and are subject to change. Students may pursue concentrations related to their program of study to further tailor their degrees to their specific interests and career goals. They also have the opportunity to take concentrations through the School of Arts & Sciences.

Johnson & Wales University's Providence campus offers degree programs in accounting, advertising and marketing communications, baking and pastry arts, business administration, business/information systems analysis, computer graphics and new media, criminal justice, culinary arts, culinary arts and food service management, culinary nutrition, electronics engineering, engineering design and configuration management, entrepreneurship, equine business management, equine business management/riding, fashion merchandising and retail marketing, financial services management, food marketing, food service entrepreneurship, hotel and lodging management, international business, international hotel and tourism management, management, marketing, network engineering, pastry arts and food service management, restaurant, food and beverage management, software engineering, sports/entertainment/event management, technology services management, travel, tourism and hospitality management, Web management and Internet commerce, and website development.

In its Continuing Education division, JWU's Providence Campus offers associate and bachelor degrees in business, culinary arts, hospitality, and technology. The North Miami, Florida, campus offers degree programs in baking and pastry arts, business administration, criminal justice, culinary arts, culinary arts and food service management, fashion merchandising and retail marketing, hotel and lodging management, management, marketing, pastry arts and food service management, restaurant, food and beverage management, sports/entertainment/event management, and travel, tourism and hospitality management.

The Denver, Colorado, campus offers degree programs in advertising and marketing communications, baking and pastry arts, business administration, criminal justice, culinary arts, culinary arts and food service management, culinary nutrition, entrepreneurship, fashion merchandising and retail marketing, hotel and lodging management, international business, management, marketing, pastry arts and food service management, restaurant, food and beverage management, and sports/entertainment/event management. The Charlotte, North Carolina, campus offers degree programs in accounting, baking and pastry arts, business administration, culinary arts, culinary arts and food service management, fashion merchandising and retail marketing, hotel and lodging management, international hotel and tourism management, management, marketing, pastry arts and food service management, restaurant, food and beverage management, and sports/entertainment/event management.

ACADEMIC PROGRAMS

Johnson & Wales University offers its programs within an academic structure of 3 11-week terms. The university's "upside-down" curriculum provides immediate focus in the student's chosen major. Many programs include laboratory studies as well as formal internship requirements. Special advanced placement programs are featured for high school seniors with exceptional skills in culinary arts or baking and pastry arts. In addition, the university awards credit for certain courses based on the successful completion of Challenge, CLEP or Portfolio Assessments. All degree candidates must successfully complete the required number of courses and/or quarter credit hours, as prescribed in the various curricula, with a minimum average of 2.0.

CAMPUS FACILITIES AND EQUIPMENT

The facilities of the Providence Campus are located throughout the intimate state of Rhode Island and in nearby Massachusetts. The downtown Providence Campus is home to the university's College of Business, Hospitality College, and School of Technology. The Harborside Campus, located nearby in Providence, houses the university's College of Culinary Arts. This campus has 5 student residence halls as well as classrooms and laboratories, production kitchens, bakeshops, dining rooms, a storeroom, and meat-cutting facilities.

This campus is also home to the Alan Shawn Feinstein Graduate School and the School of Education. Other facilities at this campus include the University Recreation and Athletic Center and a dining center. In Florida, the campus is located in the heart of North Miami, between Miami and Ft. Lauderdale. Facilities include classrooms, production/demonstration kitchens, a bakeshop, residence halls, and a conference center. The Denver Campus, located in the Park Hill neighborhood, combines stately turn-of-the-century buildings and newer student centers in a quiet park landscape. The campus has computers in every classroom and laboratory. The Charlotte Campus is located in the heart of Gateway Village in Uptown Charlotte. The academic center is home to a 200-seat auditorium with a production kitchen; top-of-the-line culinary laboratories, classrooms, seminar rooms, and computer labs. A 750-bed student residence center with dining facilities is located within walking distance of the academic building.

TUITION, ROOM, BOARD, AND FEES

Tuition at all campuses for 2007-08 is $20,478. Basic room and board plans range from $7,650 to $9,600. Each student is also charged a general fee of $984, and there is an orientation fee of $255 for new students. Books and supplies are estimated at $700-$900 per year, depending upon the program. Room and board fees may vary at each campus.

FINANCIAL AID

Johnson & Wales students are eligible to apply for a variety of financial aid programs, including federal programs, university-based student scholarship programs and state-supported grants and scholarships. In the past, approximately 90 percent of the university's entering students have received some sort of financial assistance. Students must submit the Free Application for Federal Student Aid (FAFSA) to the Federal Student Aid Processor after January 1 to be considered for financial aid. Early application is strongly suggested for full consideration.

STUDENT ORGANIZATIONS AND ACTIVITIES

Students are involved in a variety of extracurricular activities. Nearly 20 percent of the university's population are members of National Student Organizations such BPA, DECA, FBLA, FCCLA, FFA, SkillsUSA, and TSA. The Student Activities Office and fraternities and sororities are among the many groups that schedule social functions throughout the academic year. Sports and fitness programs include aerobics, baseball, basketball, sailing, soccer, tennis, golf, wrestling, ice hockey, and volleyball.

ADMISSIONS PROCESS

Johnson & Wales University seeks students who are career-focused and who have a true desire to succeed. Academic qualifications are important, but an applicant's motivation and interest in doing well are given special consideration. Graduation from high school or equivalent credentials are required for admission. It is recommended that students applying for admission into the culinary arts and baking & pastry arts programs have some prior education or experience in food service. Although no tests are required for most programs, all applicants are encouraged to submit scores from the SAT or ACT. Students who wish to apply for the Honors Program must have either a score of at least 500 math and 500 critical reading on the SAT or a score of 21 math and 21 verbal on the ACT. High school juniors may apply for early admission under the Early Enrollment Program (EEP). Transfer students are required to submit official high school and college transcripts and to have a minimum GPA of 2.0 for most programs. Credits to be transferred from other institutions are evaluated on the basis of their equivalent at Johnson & Wales. Johnson & Wales does not require an application fee. After submitting the application, the student is responsible for requesting that appropriate transcripts be forwarded to the Admissions Office of the university. While there is no deadline, students are advised to apply as early as possible before the intended date of enrollment to ensure full consideration of their application. Applications are accepted for terms beginning in September, December, and March and for the summer sessions. Inquiries and applications should be addressed to: Kenneth DiSaia, Vice President of Enrollment Management, Johnson & Wales University, 8 Abbott Park Place, Providence, Rhode Island 02903. Telephone: 401-598-1000 1-800-DIAL-JWU (toll free) Fax: 401-598-4901 E-mail: jwu@admissions.jwu.edu.

JONES INTERNATIONAL UNIVERSITY

AT A GLANCE

Jones International University is the pioneer in online learning. Founded in 1993 by Glenn R. Jones, JIU was the first university to exist entirely online, and, in 1999, became the first fully online institution in the U.S. to be granted regional accreditation by the Higher Learning Commission and a member of the North Central Association. JIU continues to set the bar in delivering engaging, relevant Academic Programs to working adults who are motivated to advance their careers and transform their lives.

JIU's primary goal is to provide its students with quality educations and arm them with the practical skills, strategies, and confidence to become total professionals. Whether you choose its School of Education or its School of Business, JIU offers busy professionals the most flexible and convenient way to earn a top-level graduate or undergraduate degree.

LOCATION AND ENVIRONMENT

JIU is the first university to exist entirely online. Everything you need to earn a quality graduate or undergraduate degree is online and accessible 24 hours a day, 7 days a week. All you need is a computer, Internet access, any standard web browser, and a desire to learn.

OFF-CAMPUS OPPORTUNITIES

This is an online university program.

MAJORS AND DEGREES OFFERED

JIU programs were designed with your professional advancement in mind. Content experts from leading universities around the globe design our courses, and experienced educators and industry leaders facilitate them. JIU programs can equip you with the knowledge and skills you'll need to maximize your potential.

JIU's School of Business offers the following degree programs:

Master of Business Administration

Master of Arts in Business Communication

Bachelor of Business Administration

Bachelor of Arts in Business Communication

In addition, we also offer an array of Business Administration certificate programs.

JIU's School of Education offers several Master of Education content—rich, project-based degree programs to fully prepare teachers, administrators, and instructors to lead and inspire their students in any academic setting.

ACADEMIC PROGRAMS

Whether you are an educator seeking the academic credentials and knowledge to lead in your learning community or are a motivated professional who wants to reach your potential in the business world, JIU can get you to where you want to go.

Leading business and education professionals from around the globe have tapped into the Internet's extraordinary power for business, technical, and managerial support. JIU brings superior-quality online learning to the next level with a comprehensive selection of graduate, undergraduate and certificate programs. Our School of Business targets individuals seeking training in business administration and business communication so they may excel in today's fast-paced, competitive, and global marketplace. JIU's programs are professionally oriented and authentically based, so what you learn here may be applied directly to your work situation.

JIU's Master of Education programs are designed not only to advance our students' professional development in an exceptional way but to foster a sense of community and purpose in their careers that will last a lifetime. Our School of Education's project-based learning model will empower students to learn in ways that are personally and professionally meaningful. Our students explore theory and its application to the solutions of important education challenges, giving them everything they need to make a difference.

CAMPUS FACILITIES AND EQUIPMENT

Jones e-global library®

Access to information and a library of resources is an essential key to a stellar education. But who says libraries need walls? Through our renowned Jones e-global library, JIU students have 24-hour-a-day online access to the resources you need to find the information they want. As the first fully online university in the U.S. to be accredited, JIU developed its library to serve as the ultimate full-service resource center on the Web. That is why Jones e-global library is used by many of the top universities and organizations. As a JIU student, you will have full, unfettered access to this comprehensive online library, enriching your educational experience to the fullest.

The JIU library is composed of several elements, all geared to serve the needs of time-constrained adult learners, including

- 28 electronic databases that will provide you with full-text articles, citations, and abstracts
- 31,000 electronic books covering business and economics, computers, technology and engineering, humanities, life and physical sciences, and social and behavioral science
- Federated searching through eglobalSearch that will allow you to search quickly across a variety of databases and catalogs using a single web interface
- Nearly 100 research guides outlining the broad range of research resources available
- 7,000 evaluated content-rich websites
- 325 federal government sites that lead to more than 150,000 documents
- 775 government agency sites
- Tutorials that will help you conduct research more effectively
- 24/7 live-chat reference assistance from on-call librarians to help you locate reference and research information
- No-cost document delivery of up to five articles, two books, and two dissertations per course

Jones e-global library has a staff of librarians that offer one-on-one training in the use of the library. To arrange for an appointment, contact Manual Santos (msantos@international.edu or 303-784-8256). In addition to 24/7 live-chat reference, we offer phone and e-mail reference Monday–Friday, 8:00 A.M.–5:00 P.M. with a minimum 24-hour turnaround.

TUITION, ROOM, BOARD, AND FEES

The course tuition for JIU varies depending on the program you are enrolled in. Here are the 2007 JIU Tuition rates:

For 3-credit courses for admitted MBA and MABC students, the cost is U.S. $2,100.

For 3-credit courses for admitted MEd students, the cost is U.S. $1,500.

In addition, there are other fees that the student is responsible for. These include a Technology Fee of $ 65 per course and an application fee of U.S. $50.

FINANCIAL AID

JIU makes every effort to make education an achievable goal for each student. As a result, we've aligned with various organization and agencies in order to offer Financial Aid to our students. Here is a listing of help available to students.

Federal Student Aid—Most JIU students who are U.S. citizens or eligible noncitizens admitted to a JIU degree program and attending at least half time may be eligible to receive student loan assistance across the years of their Academic Programs.

SLM Financial Loan—Available to individuals who are U.S. citizens, U.S. national, or permanent residents who have demonstrated credit-worthiness. This program has fast approval processing and high acceptance rates. Funds are disbursed to you via JIU.

Key Bank Career Loan—This is specifically designed for graduate and undergraduate students attending school on a part-time to full-time basis, including weekend, evening, distance learning, and continuing-education programs. Low interest rates, no application fee, quick credit decision when you apply online, and electronic signature are available.

Corporate Tuition Assistance: Your company may offer tuition assistance.

VA Benefits: Veterans, active servicepersons, reservists, and dependents and survivors of veterans of U.S. Armed Forces may qualify for financial assistance.

Military Tuition Assistance: JIU offers a special tuition scholarship program for military personnel. If you are a U.S. serviceperson, you may also qualify for the Military Tuition Assistance program.

Scholarship Search: JIU recommends two online sources of scholarship information for students.

STUDENT ORGANIZATIONS AND ACTIVITIES

There's no better way to understand what it is like to attend JIU than to talk to a current student. Several JIU students have volunteered to speak with you about their experiences attending an online university, what it is like to go back to school, class demands on their time, etc. If you would like to speak with a JIU student, contact Career Development Services Coordinator Kim DeCoste via kdecoste@international.edu or by calling 800-811-5663, ext. 8458 (U.S. or Canada only).

ADMISSIONS PROCESS

The admission requirements vary based on the degree. To learn more about the Admissions Process, call a JIU Enrollment Counselor at 800-811-5663.

KEAN UNIVERSITY

AT A GLANCE

Founded in 1855, Kean University has grown to become one of New Jersey's largest institutions of higher learning. In 1958, Kean moved from Newark to Union and currently occupies more than 150 acres in Union and Hillside townships. Kean was granted university status on September 26, 1997. While maintaining its significant role in the training of teachers, Kean has become a comprehensive institution offering more than 50 undergraduate and 30 graduate degree programs serving more than 13,000 students. With its 4 undergraduate colleges, the School of Visual and Performing Arts, and the Nathan Weiss Graduate College, Kean's Academic Programs cover an exceptional range of disciplines.

Kean is a metropolitan, comprehensive, interactive, teaching university. A campus dedicated to the pursuit of excellence in higher education, Kean University supports a student-centered learning environment that nurtures the development of the whole student for rewarding careers, lifelong learning, and fulfilling lives in a global society. It maintains a commitment to excellence and equity in enrollment, instruction and administration. Kean is accredited by all major accrediting organizations. Many majors have accreditation in their field.

LOCATION AND ENVIRONMENT

Kean University is in a great location—metropolitan Union County. The campus is a short distance from Newark Liberty International Airport, NJ Transit trains, and major highways. Just 10 miles outside of New York City, the campus is conveniently reached by road, sea, or air.

OFF-CAMPUS OPPORTUNITIES

Students may enroll in Kean University's study-abroad programs at schools located around the world and lasting for a semester or less. Course credit is available in these programs, or students may choose to travel simply for personal development. Students also have the opportunity to learn in nontraditional settings through service projects or by enrolling in distance learning programs.

MAJORS AND DEGREES OFFERED

Kean University grants bachelor degrees in nearly 50 majors and more than 70 options and collateral programs.

Students can pursue bachelor of arts degrees in art history, biology, chemistry, communications, early childhood education, earth science, economics, elementary education, English, fine arts, foreign languages (Spanish), history, mathematics, music, music education, philosophy and religion, physical education, political science, psychology, public administration, recreation administration, sociology, special education, speech and hearing, and theater. The university has recently added bachelor of arts programs in industrial education, visual communication, interior design, finance, studio art, marketing, graphic communications, criminal justice administration, speech, and theater arts.

Bachelor of science degrees can be earned in accounting, computer science, health information management, industrial technology, management science, medical technology, occupational therapy, and psychology/psychiatric rehabilitation. Students may also work toward their bachelor of fine arts, bachelor of social work, and bachelor of science in nursing (for RNs only) degrees.

Undergraduates may undertake the dual MS program in physical therapy and the physician's assistant program. Both programs are available through an alliance with the University of Medicine and Dentistry of New Jersey (UMDNJ). Undergraduates may also undertake a dual BA/MS program in occupational therapy which is available through the Nathan Weiss Graduate College.

Kean now offers an exciting opportunity for students dedicated to pursuing a career in medicine. Kean University, Drexel University College of Medicine and St. Peter's University Hospital have formed a partnership offering a 4 + 4 Bachelor of Science/Medical Degree (BS/MD) Scholars Program to highly qualified undergraduate students. Preference will be given to candidates primarily from the northeast and central regions of New Jersey who are inclined toward careers in family medicine, general internal medicine and general pediatrics. Students must meet all requirements of this joint program during their bachelor's degree in order to remain in the program, and then proceed to medical school at Drexel University College of Medicine upon graduation from Kean University.

ACADEMIC PROGRAMS

To complete a degree, students must complete the general education requirements, totaling 52 units. Eighteen of these credits are earned in the humanities-based core curriculum. The remaining 34 are distributed between departments to lay a broad liberal arts background on which to base later, specialized study. Each department specifies major requirements, with a minimum of 30 units, and students also take elective courses.

Most departments can arrange internships for juniors and seniors. Some subject areas also provide course options that students can complete from off-campus locations. Two semesters make up the academic year, along with 2 summer sessions.

CAMPUS FACILITIES AND EQUIPMENT

Kean University's Nancy Thompson Library provides resources including 270,000 volumes (including rare books), 11,164 serial subscriptions, CD-ROMs, online databases, and 14,200 bound periodicals and microfilms. Resources are located using the online catalog, VOYAGER, or CD-ROM databases. To access books not available at Kean, students can utilize the inter-library loan system. For a small fee, students may use the journal document delivery service. Non-print materials, such as multi-media items and media services, are located in the Instructional Resource Center (IRC).

Kean University hosts laboratory facilities such as the Reading Institute, the Institute of Child Study, and the Clinic in Learning Disabilities. Other research tools include the electron microscope and meteorological station. In addition, the extensive statewide computer network is always available.

TUITION, ROOM, BOARD, AND FEES

Tuition and fees for full-time undergraduates with New Jersey residency for Fall semester 2007 was $4,252.50. Out-of-state students paid $6,322.50 in the fall 2007 semester. (These figures may be adjusted for the fall 2008 semester.) In addition to tuition and fees, indirect costs for books and supplies will vary but usually average $1,119 per year. Personal expenses average $1,399 per year, and transportation expenses range from $912 (on campus) and $1,820 (off-campus) per year. Room and board expenses for students living away from home average $11,456 (on and off campus) per year, while the average room and board expenses for students living at home (with parents or relatives) is $2,239 per year.

FINANCIAL AID

Kean University remains one of the most affordable universities in the nation. We recognize that financial aid is an integral part of the financial planning process for our students and their families. The university is committed to assisting students with financial aid programs and services to supplement the resources of the family. The goal of our financial aid programs is to keep the university affordable for all students, regardless of financial need, by offering a wide variety of grant, loan, scholarship, work, alternative loans, and installment payment programs.

Financial aid, which may be Federal Perkins Loans, Federal Pell Grants, Federal Supplemental Educational Opportunity Grants, Federal Work Study Program Awards, or Federal Direct Loans, is awarded to about 50 percent of full-time undergraduates. The state of New Jersey offers Garden State Scholarships, Educational Opportunity Fund awards, and Tuition Aid Grants. To be considered, applicants must submit the Free Application for Federal Student Aid (FAFSA) to the university no later than March 15.

STUDENT ORGANIZATIONS AND ACTIVITIES

There are 130 different clubs and organizations on the Kean University campus. These range from fraternities and sororities, religious clubs, cultural organizations, and departmental clubs.

ADMISSIONS PROCESS

The admissions committee evaluates students' apparent capacity to succeed at Kean. Decisions are not based on age, sex, race, color, creed, or national origin. High school transcripts should display a minimum cumulative GPA of 2.8 and a minimum of 16 academic units completed. Applications must include letters of recommendation from a guidance counselor, teacher, employer, etc., and an essay is required. Students may enter Kean with advanced standing considering CLEP scores or substantial life experience.

Most transfer students must have a 2.0 GPA for admission. Certain departments, such as physical therapy, demand a higher GPA.

Those applying to enter their freshman year must submit their application by May 31 for fall admission and December 1 for spring admission. Kean employs a rolling admissions system. International students must also submit their application and all supporting documentation by May 31 for fall admission and November 1 for spring admission. Complete application packets include the following items: the Kean University application, a $50.00 nonrefundable application fee, official high school transcripts, and official SAT I results. For those wishing to visit the campus, the information session and campus tours are Fridays at 10 a.m. from mid-September through mid-May, and Thursdays at 10 a.m. from May 15 through mid-August. For other times, please contact the Office to arrange an appointment.

For additional information and application forms, students should refer to the Kean University Web site or contact:

Kean University

Office of Undergraduate Admissions

1000 Morris Avenue

Union, NJ 07083

Telephone: 908-737-7100

Fax: 908-737-7105

E-mail: admitme@kean.edu

Website: www.kean.edu

KENDALL COLLEGE OF ART & DESIGN OF FERRIS STATE UNIVERSITY

AT A GLANCE

Kendall College of Art and Design of Ferris State University, founded in 1928, offers an art and design education to a select group of students who are serious about refining their talent and seek in-depth preparation for careers in art and design. The faculty consists of working artists, designers, and scholars dedicated to providing students with the necessary tools to explore and pursue their own creative journey. Faculty members continually weigh changing methods and technology, striving to provide students with meaningful, real world experiences while maintaining a solid and proven art and design education. Kendall provides a personalized approach to education that not only helps students learn the principles of visual thinking but also provides the skills necessary to achieve career success. Kendall offers a BFA degrees in art education, digital media (with concentrations in 2-D animation, 3-D animation, illustration, interactive design and motion graphic design), fine art (with concentrations in drawing, painting, photography, printmaking, sculpture/functional art), furniture design, graphic design, illustration, industrial design, interior design, metals/jewelry design, painting, photography, and sculpture/functional art. A BS degree is offered in art history. Kendall also offers a MFA degree with concentrations in drawing, painting, photography, and printmaking. The college's individual programs are based on a strong foundation program that includes intense classical training while also allowing freedom and variety. A wide range of special lectures, exhibits, and seminars by noted artists and designers enhance the academic environment.

LOCATION AND ENVIRONMENT

Kendall College of Art and Design of Ferris State University is located in Grand Rapids, Michigan, right in the center of things. Kendall lives at the heart of the city's vibrant cultural district, in the heart of downtown. Surrounded by art galleries, coffee houses and funky eateries, sports arenas, concert halls, festival venues, and riverside walks. Grand Rapids is friendly, like a small town, with the cultural opportunities of a big city. The Grand River flows through the city out to Lake Michigan's fabulous sandy beaches, where you'll find getaway towns like Saugatuck and Grand Haven, a short drive, but a world away.

MAJORS AND DEGREES OFFERED

BS in art history. BFA program offering the following programs: art education, digital media, fine art, furniture design, graphic design, illustration, industrial design, interior design, metals/jewelry design, painting, photography, sculpture/functional art.

MFA program offering concentrations in: drawing, painting, photography, printmaking, masters of art education (MAE).

CAMPUS FACILITIES AND EQUIPMENT

Working Spaces for Working Artists. When you're a visual artist, where your work matters. Kendall offers extraordinary places for artists and designers to work and learn. Studios are lofty and open, bright and comfortable. Labs and workshops are well-resourced with the tools of both modern and traditional processes. Each program has its own home base of classrooms, workshops, studios, resource rooms, and exhibit spaces, with all the specialized technology and tools to support your studies. Collectively, our students have access to great spaces to gather, study, contemplate, or caffeinate. There's no trudging around campus to get from one space to another. All our facilities are housed in 2 large urban buildings. A 3-story central atrium provides dramatic exhibition spaces and ideal gathering places for Kendall students and faculty. In terms of housing (check our artful living spaces) the brilliantly rehabbed 5 Lyon Building, just a block from campus. Exposed brick walls, contemporary furnishings, affordable living, and great skyline views are just the highlights. Choose your own roommates or opt for roommate placement. See kcad.edu/admissions/housing for a virtual tour.

FINANCIAL AID

In order to be considered for financial aid, you must first be admitted to Kendall College of Art and Design of Ferris State University. You must also complete a Free Application for Federal Student Aid, (FAFSA) and have your results released to Ferris State University, with a Title IV code number of 002260. Students are encouraged to complete the FAFSA online. An electronic signature (PIN number) makes the process even faster and more convenient. Visit www.fafsa.ed.gov to obtain a PIN number and complete the FAFSA. Students applying for financial aid at Kendall/Ferris will receive priority consideration if all forms are received by March 1 for the following school year. All files completed after that date will be considered for financial aid based on availability of funds. For more detailed information on these financial aid types, please visit the Kendall website at www.kcad.edu. We encourage you to apply for scholarship opportunities utilizing resources from the Internet. There are several reputable national database search engines that will search for scholarship opportunities at no charge. For a complete list of these search engines and links, please visit the Kendall website at www.kcad.edu.

STUDENT ORGANIZATIONS AND ACTIVITIES

AIGA (American Institute of Graphic Arts), Animators and Comic Book Club, ASID/IIDA (Association of Student Interior Designers), Collective Pressure (Printmaking Club), Fashion Club (Bodies of Art Association), Freshman Class Club, Furniture Club, Gay Straight Alliance, Illustration Club, Kendall Christian Fellowship, Kendall Gamers Bureau, Kendall Green Council, Metals/Jewelry Design Club, MAEA Student Chapter (Art Education), Painting Club, Philanthropy Club, Photography Student Association.

ADMISSIONS PROCESS

An incoming freshman student is required to submit/complete the following: completed admissions application form; submit $30 application fee; have official high school transcripts released to Kendall; release official ACT or SAT test scores to Kendall (ACT or SAT tests are required); have official college transcripts released to Kendall if any college credits earned; statement of purpose; present and complete a portfolio review (not required if majoring in art history, interior design, or furniture design). An incoming transfer student is required to submit/complete the following: completed admissions application form; submit $30 application fee; have official high school transcripts released to Kendall; release official ACT or SAT test scores to Kendall, if student has been out of high school for fewer than 2 years; have official college transcripts released to Kendall, from all colleges previously attended; statement of purpose; present and complete a portfolio review (not required if majoring in art history, interior design or furniture design)

KETTERING UNIVERSITY

AT A GLANCE

Kettering University (formerly GMI Engineering and Management Institute) has taken college education and put a spin on it. Billed as "America's premiere co-op university" this college, based in Flint, Michigan, has more than 700 corporate partners, corporations, and agencies that employ Kettering's co-op students throughout 800 locations in North America, Europe, and Asia.

The philosophy of this fully accredited school is that college students work while they earn their college education, and in essence, Kettering's corporate partners "grow their own" engineers, scientists, and managers. The program is 4.5 years long, with students' time split evenly between classroom training (in processes, products, corporate culture, and technology, with an emphasis in engineering, the sciences, and business) and paid, full-time professional co-op work experience off-site.

The Kettering's corporate partners represent major industries that include leaders in business innovation and manufacturing technology. The list of current co-op companies reads like an honor roll of America's top corporations, representing automotive, aerospace, medical, chemical, computer, plastics, and delivery systems industries, just to name a few. Graduates have the skills and experience to succeed in key executive leadership positions, as many have done. Year after year, nearly 100 percent of Kettering graduates have a full-time job offer or are accepted into a top graduate program by the time they receive their diploma.

LOCATION AND ENVIRONMENT

Flint is located in east-central Michigan, just 60 miles west of Lake Huron and the Canadian boarder, and 60 miles north of Detroit. Flint is a small city that has approximately 155,000 residents and has a metropolitan area of 450,000. The College Cultural Center Complex is located just 1.5 miles from campus is the College Cultural Center Complex, which and houses a museum, a performing arts auditorium, a planetarium, and the Flint Public Library. The proximity to outdoor activities, city culture, and Flint's own distinctive resources provides students with access to a wide range of activities and opportunities.

OFF-CAMPUS OPPORTUNITIES

More than half of a Kettering student's time is spent off campus, fulfilling professional co-op work requirements outside the Flint area. On average, students spend 11 academic semesters working for their co-op employer and 9 academic semesters in the classroom. The 700 corporate partners, corporations, and agencies that employ Kettering students are located throughout North America, Europe , and Asia, although approximately 70 percent of students work for a corporation located in their hometown, which allows them to live at home during the work experience portion of their education. On average, students earn between $40,000 and $65,000 over the entire professional co-op program.

MAJORS AND DEGREES OFFERED

The 4.5four and a half year professional cooperative education program allows students to earn designated bachelor of science degrees in: computer engineering, electrical engineering (specialties in electronics, communication systems, control systems, and power systems), industrial engineering (specialties in computer systems integration, human factors & work design, quality assurance & reliability, production control systems, and manufacturing systems design), mechanical engineering (specialties in bioengineering, applications, automotive power train, automotive body & chassis, mechanical systems design, design for durability, and plastic product design).

A designated bachelor of science degree in: business management (concentrations in accounting/finance, information systems, manufacturing management, marketing, materials management).

A designated bachelor of science degree in: applied mathematics (minors in applied & computational mathematics, applied statistics), applied physics (concentrations in acoustics, applied optics, and materials science), computer science, environmental chemistry, engineering physics, business administration (BSBA), and a designated bachelor of art in business administration (BBA).

Minors are available in applied chemistry, applied mathematics, applied optics, computer science, liberal arts, and management. Kettering University offers master of science degree programs in engineering, engineering management, manufacturing management, manufacturing operations, and operations management and an accredited MBA program.

ACADEMIC PROGRAMS

The unique structure of the Kettering program allows students to fulfill the academic requirements of 160 credit hours throughout a 4.5four and a half year period. This is completed more than 9 academic semesters and up to 11 co-op work semesters. Many students also complete a capstone thesis project on behalf of their co-op employer during their senior year for credit toward the 160 required hours. The academic year consists of 2 11-week academic terms on-campus in Flint and 2 12-week academic terms working for the corporate employer; students alternate their time between Flint and the employer's site. On average, a freshman student who spends 24 weeks during the academic year working for the professional co-op employer earns $11,000.

CAMPUS FACILITIES AND EQUIPMENT

Kettering University opened its new $42 million Mechanical Engineering & Chemistry Center in spring 2003. This state-of-the-art facility is loaded with hands-on learning laboratories such as automotive labs with several unique test cells and the most advanced chemistry labs around. Engineering and chemistry facilities of this caliber are usually found only in graduate-level programs labs.

The Academic Building houses more classrooms, laboratories, and department offices. More than 100,000 square feet of this facility is dedicated to more labs, which are stocked with equipment to demonstrate and experiment with methods in the engineering industry, from basic machining to emerging technologies.

The entire campus, including residence hall rooms, campus apartments, and labs, is networked, providing each student with 24-hour access to computer resources and the Internet.

The library contains more than 94,118,000 volumes, more than 390540 periodicals, and various online services. Special facilities include a microfilm area, database search services, record and tape listening- and videotape viewing-facilities, and a special collection of SAE, SME, and ASME technical papers.

TUITION, ROOM, BOARD, AND FEES

Tuition for the 2007-2008 academic year: $25,248

Room 1 rate: $3,708

Board, including 19 meals per week: $3,708

Technology fee: $200/term

Student activity fee: $18,693/term

Residence hall activity fee: $2412/term

Orientation fee (1-time only): $150

FINANCIAL AID

Kettering University offers all the traditional need- and merit-based financial aid, including a generous merit scholarship program. All Kettering students also benefit from the substantial co-op salaries that they earn throughout their years enrolled in school. The average range of salaries over the entire period is from $40,000 to $65,000. About 70 percent of students are able to live at home during their work experience terms, and are then able to contribute more of their salaries to their educational expenses. Many students win scholarships from agencies and organizations from their local communities. The primary purpose of Kettering's financial aid program is to supplement students' financial need after co-op earnings and parents' contributions. Aid is given as grants, scholarships, loans, and work-study awards. Students who wish to apply for financial aid should complete the FAFSA.

STUDENT ORGANIZATIONS AND ACTIVITIES

Kettering students enjoy the activities and participate in the organizations that make college exciting and unique. College is a place to get to know people, and to make contacts you'll students will have throughout your their professional lives. Students can make these vital connections at Kettering University by participating in one of the 75 more than 50 clubs and organizations represented on campus. Whatever your their social or professional interests, you'll find there are opportunities to work together with other students who share those interests, planning and organizing activities, and perfecting essential leadership and teamwork skills.

Outside of class, you'll students will find plenty of ways to enjoy your their free time at Kettering. To name just a few opportunities... The following list represents just a few of Kettering's many clubs and organizations:

Firebirds (autocross club),Student Government ,International Club, Aquaneers (scuba diving club) Campus Crusade for Christ, Christians In Action (CIA),Cycling Club , Bulldog Band, Outdoors Club, SADD, Tech Sailors, Hockey Club Karate Club Black Unity Congress, Political Awareness Club (PAC) ,Intramural Sports (including basketball, cross country, golf, soccer, swimming, tennis, and volleyball), and Swing Club.

Kettering also has one of the largest student chapters of the Society of Automotive Engineers (SAE), and Delta Epsilon Chi Chapter (college version of DECA) annually wins top awards in state and national competitions. Students compete in an intense intramural athletic program and are involved in clubs and professional organizations. More than approximately a third half of Kettering students join the 14 national fraternities and 6 sororities that are represented on campus. The school's active student government produces programs to develop peers' leadership skills, self-confidence, interpersonal relations, and organizational operations. Because enrolled students represent approximately 48 states and 18 countries, they have a lot to share with and learn from one another.

ADMISSIONS PROCESS

Admission to Kettering University is competitive and based on scholastic achievement and extracurricular interests, activities, and achievements. Applicants are required to have completed the following courses (1 credit represents 2 semesters or 1 year of study): 2 credits algebra, 1 credit geometry, 0.5 credit trigonometry, 2 credits laboratory science (1 of these credits must be from physics or chemistry, and both are strongly recommended), and 3 credits English. A minimum of 16 credits is required, but 20 credits are strongly encouraged. Applicants must submit SAT I or ACT scores. Most Kettering University students rank at or near the top 10 percent of their high school class.

Although applications are accepted all yearlong, prospective students are encouraged to file their application early in their senior year. Early application significantly improves students' chances for early co-op employment. Kettering University also accepts transfer students. Admission decisions for transfer applicants are based on college records for those who have completed at least 30 credits. The Application fee is $35. Interested students can apply on line free at www.admissions.kettering.edu.

KEYSTONE COLLEGE

AT A GLANCE

Keystone College is a small, private, liberal arts college located in Northeastern Pennsylvania. Our nearly 140-year tradition has been to personalize an education for each of our students. We put our promise to our students in writing. We pledge to students in good academic, financial, and social standing that within 6 months after graduating from Keystone and fulfilling the requirements of the Career Development Center, you will have received at least one job offer, or where appropriate, be accepted into a transfer or graduate program. In the event this does not occur, we will provide you with additional courses and career counseling at no additional charge. We offer you a nationally recognized First-Year Experience seminar to enable you to acquire the skills necessary for academic, personal, and career success, and a portfolio/resume designed to give you a competitive edge in the job market, as well as a Real World Experience that explores the world of work. Our Bridge and a Capstone Experience combines knowledge acquired in both the classroom and the real world, and our Pre-Major program offers academic and career counseling to assist undecided students who need to make an informed decision about a major. We guarantee on-campus housing to our resident students for as long they remain full-time students.

LOCATION AND ENVIRONMENT

Keystone College is located in northeastern Pennsylvania, just 20 minutes outside of the small city of Scranton. The college truly provides the best of both worlds for students; a safe, quiet campus ideal for learning, yet within easy distance to everything from hiking, mountain biking, skiing, movies, shopping, pubs, concerts, museums, and the main cities on the East Coast (NYC and Philadelphia).

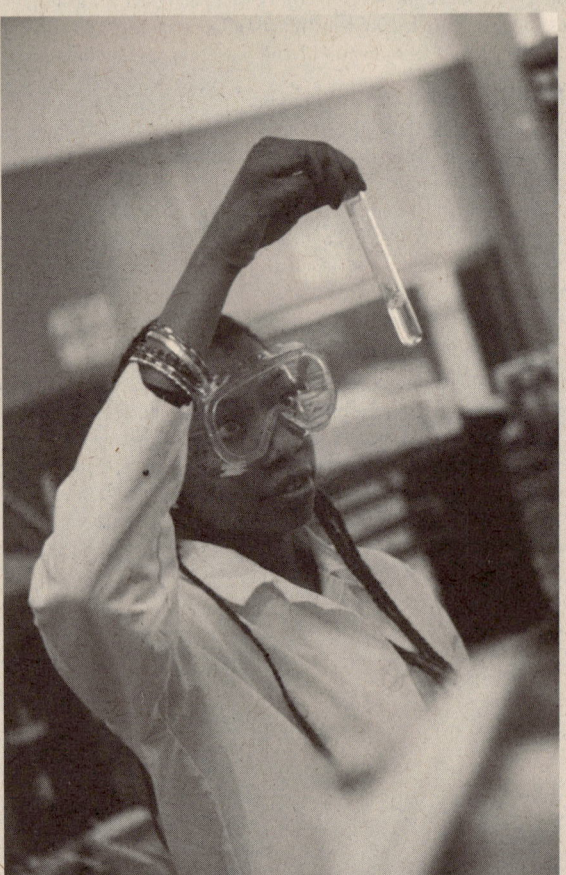

OFF-CAMPUS OPPORTUNITIES

Downhill skiing: Elk Mountain Ski Resort and Sno Mountain (formerly Montage) as well as a host of other ski areas in the Pocono Mountains of Pennsylvania. Other: Steamtown Mall, Viewmont Mall, Cinemark Movie Theatre, the Crossings Shopping Outlets, Northeastern Pennsylvania Philharmonic, Everhart Museum, home of the New York Yankees farm team, home of the Pittsburgh Penguins Ice Hockey development team, Wachovia Arena for concerts, Ford Pavilion for concerts.

MAJORS AND DEGREES OFFERED

Bachelor of arts, bachelor of science, associate in arts, associate in fine arts, associate in science, associate in applied science, post-baccalaureate certificates in education, certificate programs.

ACADEMIC PROGRAMS

Accounting, business, information technology, communications, liberal studies, early childhood education, elementary education, teaching: child and society, teaching: art education, teaching: math education, teaching: social studies education, environmental resource management, environmental studies, forest/resource management, wildlife biology, landscape architecture, fine arts, visual arts, health sciences, culinary arts, hotel and restaurant management, sport and recreation management, biology, pre-med tracks, forensic biology, environmental biology, criminal justice, pre-law advising track, organizational leadership, social sciences, undecided.

Minors: accounting, art, biology, business, chemistry, communications, criminal justice, criminal justice investigation, environmental science, forensic biology, finance, homeland security, human resource management, information technology, leadership, mathematics, political science, psychology, sociology, sport and recreation management, theater.

CAMPUS FACILITIES AND EQUIPMENT

State-of-the art Smart Classrooms, the Chef's Table restaurant (student-run), WKCV-FM radio station, Oppenheim Children's Center, Cupillari Astronomical Observatory, Riparian Hiking Trails, delayed harvest trout stream, Student Success Center, wireless campus, Willary Water Resource Center, U.S. Mid-Atlantic Urban Forestry Center, Countryside Conservancy, GPS/GIS classes, state-of-the-art forensic science and DNA laboratory equipment.

TUITION, ROOM, BOARD, AND FEES

For the 2008-2009 Academic Year:

Tuition & fees: $17,805/year

Room & board: $8,580/year

Cost per credit: $375

FINANCIAL AID

Students need only submit the FAFSA form in order to determine eligibility for aid at Keystone College. Merit scholarships are awarded to students based on academic and leadership activities during high school; these scholarships range from $5,000 to full tuition and are renewable each year. Students are notified of scholarship awards at the point of acceptance.

Keystone also participates in the new ACG and Smart Grant program. Students should ensure that their guidance office submits a final transcript to Keystone in order to determine eligibility.

STUDENT ORGANIZATIONS AND ACTIVITIES

ACT 101, Art Society, Campus Activities Board, Campus Prayer and Bible Study Club, Career Exploration Club, Commuter Council, Criminal Justice Club, Forensic Science Club, Honors Program, Intercollegiate Leadership, Inter-Hall Council, Junior Professional Chefs of NEPA, Keystone Players, Keystone Service Club, Keystone Steppers Mofyah Club, Multicultural Affairs Student Organization (MCASA), Nokomian Student Yearbook, Opposing Prejudice Ending Negativity (OPEN), Phi Theta Kappa National Honors Fraternity, Prevention Activities Committee, SIFE (Students in Free Enterprise), Snow Team, Sport Management and Recreation Team (SMART), Student Senate, the *Key* student newspaper, the *Plume* student literary magazine, TOPS club, WKCV radio.

ADMISSIONS PROCESS

Students submit application for Admission (online or paper, Common Application accepted), official high school transcript, official college transcripts from all schools attended, SAT or ACT scores, 1 teacher evaluation, personal essay, TOEFL or the equivalent for students whose primary language is not English, any other documents that you feel would be helpful to the admissions committee. Art students must have a portfolio interview. International students must submit a certification of finances.

Keystone College practices a rolling admissions process; however students should adhere to the following final deadlines for application submission. For students entering in the fall semester: freshmen: July 1; transfers: August 1; international students: June 1. For students entering in the spring semester: freshmen: December 15; transfers: December 15; international students: November 1. Students are notified of the admissions decision generally within 2 weeks of the college receiving the completed application.

KING COLLEGE

AT A GLANCE

Located in Bristol, Tennessee, King College is a private, comprehensive college founded in the Presbyterian tradition. Founded in 1867, King offers more than 80 majors, minors, concentrations, and pre-professional programs.

LOCATION AND ENVIRONMENT

Nestled in the foothills of the Smoky Mountains, King College is located in Bristol, Tennessee, next to its twin city of Bristol, Virginia. The main campus of King College sits on 135 wooded acres and its buildings feature Georgian-style architecture that provides a quiet, beautiful learning environment that's just 2 minutes away from bustling downtown Bristol.

OFF-CAMPUS OPPORTUNITIES

Bristol is part of the Tri-Cities metropolitan area and has a combined total population of nearly 450,000. Bristol is known as the "Birthplace of Country Music." It's also home of the Bristol Motor Speedway, which attracts thousands of people to the area each year for NASCAR races on the world's fastest half-mile track.

In addition to auto racing, you'll find plenty of entertainment, dining, and shopping options in the area. You might explore the winding paths and breathtaking scenery of Bristol Caverns, shop the specialty stores and coffeehouses along State Street, or absorb some culture at the Paramount Center of the Arts, Theater Bristol, and Viking Hall Civic Center—entertainment venues that offer everything from rock concerts to ballet. Outdoor enthusiasts will enjoy plentiful opportunities for hiking, biking, whitewater rafting, skiing, and other activities only short distance from campus.

MAJORS AND DEGREES OFFERED

King College offers bachelor degree programs in more than 80 majors, minors, pre-professional degrees, and concentrations in fields such as business, computer science, nursing, law, medical and health sciences, education, humanities, and pharmaceutical science.

Bachelor and master's degrees are also offered in business administration, nursing, education, and chemistry through King's Graduate and Professional Studies program.

ACADEMIC PROGRAMS

King College is structured on a university model with 5 schools and offers students a choice of more than 80 majors, minors, concentrations, and pre-professional programs that prepare them for "hot" career fields like forensic science, neuroscience, nursing, online media and marketing, technical and professional communication, and biobusiness.

First-year students at King will participate in an integrated and innovative program called The Quest, which incorporates readings, discussions, and even a class trip to Washington, DC, to open their minds to new knowledge.

At King we believe students should broaden their knowledge of other cultures by experiencing them, rather than just reading about them in a book. That's why our students have plentiful opportunities to see the world through a wide range of domestic and international travel programs extending from China to Ireland, which available as early as your first semester.

If intellectual challenge is especially important to you, you'll want to be a part of the Jack E. Snider Center for Honors. As a member of the honors program, you'll engage in special opportunities that include meeting with faculty members and outside guests who demonstrate a passionate commitment to students, examining ideas from a variety of academic disciplines during the honors seminar (often over coffee and dessert), participating in selected courses that stimulate thinking and allow for creative response, and much more. Students with a 3.0 GPA or higher and who have scored at least a 28 ACT or 1260 SAT are invited to participate in the program. For more information about the Jack E. Snider Center for Honors, contact the Office of Admissions at 1-800-362-0014 or admissions@king.edu.

TUITION, ROOM, BOARD, AND FEES

King College's full-time charges for the 2008-2009 academic year total $27,482, which includes $19,426 in tuition, a $1,156 comprehensive fee, $3,450 for room, and $3,450 for board. Tuition costs are the same for both in-state and out-of-state students. For more information visit www.king.edu/admissions/costs/index.asp.

FINANCIAL AID

If you're committed to attending King College, we're committed to helping you finance your education. Each year, we award more than $19 million in financial aid to 98 percent of our students with an average annual award of $15,229.71. We'll work with you and your family to make King a reality for you, too.

Based on guidelines established by the United States Congress, the information you provide on the Free Application for Federal Student Aid (FAFSA) will determine the amount your family is expected to contribute toward the cost of your education. The financial aid you are then eligible for is determined by the following formula: College cost - family contribution = financial need. The family contribution remains the same regardless of the cost of the college.

At King College, we try to meet most of your financial need with various sources of financial aid, including scholarships, grants, and loans. Work opportunities are usually available on campus as well to assist students who wish to work. For more information about the financial aid available at King, visit www.king.edu/admissions/costs/FinancialAid/index.asp.

STUDENT ORGANIZATIONS AND ACTIVITIES

When you ask our students what it's like to experience King College, they're sure to tell you about hanging out with friends on the campus oval or in the dorms. They'll also tell you about all the great opportunities to get involved at King. From performing and visual arts, to activities with the Student Life and Activities Committee at King (better known as SLACK) to athletics and intramural athletics, our students always have something to do. And because of our size, students have more chances to get involved in key positions on boards, committees, and teams. Whether you're exploring your spirituality through service opportunities, plugging into one of the most advanced computer networks of any college in the region, or competing on one of our newly renovated athletic fields, you'll find lots of reasons to experience King. For more information about the activities and organizations available at King, we invite you to visit www.king.edu/experienceking.

ADMISSIONS PROCESS

King College uses a rolling admissions process, and admissions decisions are usually made within a few weeks of receiving a student's completed application. The application fee is waived for students who apply online, and students are encouraged to visit www.king.edu/apply to submit their application.

King College requires that high school graduates who are seeking admission as first-time freshmen must have satisfactorily completed at least 16 academic units at high school level. Course work should include the following minimum requirements: 4 units of English; 2 units of algebra (algebra I and II) and one unit of geometry; 2 units of a foreign language; 2 units of history and social studies; one unit of natural sciences; and 4 other academic electives. Students should also have a 2.6 grade-point average on a 4.0 scale and an ACT score of 19 or SAT score of 890. Students who do not meet these requirements may be conditionally accepted with permission from the Admissions Committee.

If you've participated in the Advanced Placement Program of the College Entrance Examination Board, and you've achieved a grade of 3, you will receive advance placement in the appropriate subject areas without college credit. If you scored a 4 or 5, you'll be granted college credit.

If you've participated in the College Level Examination Program (CLEP) of the College Entrance Examination Board, you may receive college credit for corresponding courses taught at King College. Contact the registrar for additional information.

Students enrolled in the college are granted exemption from basic courses when their level of preparation enables then to progress to more advanced courses. This is particularly true in foreign languages, mathematics, and English. Interested students should inquire of the of the appropriate academic division chairperson for more information.

Most freshmen and transfer students will be asked to complete tests used for placement into appropriate course.

King College recognizes the International Baccalaureate Diploma. King will grant a maximum of 8 semester hours of credit for scores of 5, 6, and 7 on each of the IB Higher Level examinations. The amount of credit awarded will be decided by the Registrar in conference with the Dean of Faculty. The maximum number of credit hours awarded for IB is 30.

KING'S COLLEGE (PA)

AT A GLANCE

King's is a liberal arts Catholic college that offers growth and personal development in a supportive environment. Founded in 1946 by the Congregation of Holy Cross from the University of Notre Dame, we're a small urban campus in Wilkes-Barre, Pennsylvania.

Small classes and labs allow for meaningful interaction with professors. Our average class size is 18 students, average lab size is 13 students, and the student/faculty ratio. 16:1. This personal attention translates into better graduation rates than at institutions with larger classroom environments.

At King's we offer 35 Majors in Business, Humanities, Social Sciences, Education, Sciences and Allied Health programs, 7 Pre-professional programs and 8 Special Concentrations. With our 50 clubs and activities and 19 NCAA Division III athletic programs for men and women there is plenty to do outside the classroom.

King's consistently ranks high in the top college national review issues of several major publications.

—For 13 straight years, King's has been ranked in the top tier of U.S. News & World Report's list of Best Colleges in the United States.

—Barron's Best Buys in College Education selected King's among the nation's top 10% of colleges for its sixth consecutive edition.

—The American Association of Colleges and Universities' Greater Expectations Initiative named King's as one of only 16 "Leadership Institutions" nationwide for visionary innovations in undergraduate education.

—The John Templeton Foundation Honor Roll for Character-Building Colleges recognizes King's in its select group of 100 colleges nationwide.

In addition to King's ranking in national publications, many of our individual academic programs are accredited by several highly respected organizations.

—AACSB International—The Association to Advance Collegiate Schools of Business for the William G. McGowan School of Business, one of only 42 undergraduate schools of business in the country to be accredited.

—Pre-candidate, the National Council for the Accreditation of Teacher Education.

—The Commission on Accreditation of Healthcare Management Education.

—The Accreditation Review Commission on Education for Physician Assistants.

—A ten-year re-accreditation from the Middle States Commission on Higher Education.

Our accomplishments and national reputation add value to your degree because employers know that as a King's graduate you challenged yourself…and succeeded.

LOCATION AND ENVIRONMENT

King's College is ideally situated in northeastern Pennsylvania within driving distance to New York and Philadelphia, Washington, D.C. and East Coast attractions. Our campus is close to the Pocono Mountains, offering skiing, snowboarding, kayaking and biking trails. The local area features Triple A baseball, the Wilkes-Barre/Scranton Penguins ice hockey team and a several venues for concerts.

Our atmosphere is friendly and inviting, with a strong sense of community. Our campus is walkable and accessible, yet you will find impressive facilities, equal to those at much larger institutions. Classes average 18 students—allowing for personal interaction with professors, which often translates into better graduation rates than at institutions with larger classroom environments.

OFF-CAMPUS OPPORTUNITIES

The Pocono Mountain resorts offer skiing, skating, and snowboarding during the winter.

Visit nearby Kirby Park and state parks for hiking and biking trails minutes from campus, or kayak and mountain bike nearby.

Visit the Lackawanna County Stadium for New York Yankees Triple A baseball.

The Wachovia Arena has both Pittsburgh Penguins minor league hockey and Pioneers arena football.

For the concert connection, it's the Wachovia Arena and the Montage Performing Arts Center. The Kirby Center for the Performing Arts is just two blocks from campus!

Venture out to the shopping malls, cineplexes, coffeehouses, restaurants, malls, specialty shops, cultural events, ethnic celebrations and festivals.

MAJORS AND DEGREES OFFERED

Accounting; Business Administration; Finance; Human Resource Management; International Business; Marketing; Humanities and; Social Sciences; Computers and Information Systems; Criminal Justice; Economics; English/Literature; English/Writing; Environmental Studies; French; History; Mass Communications; Philosophy; Political Science; Psychology; Sociology; Spanish; Theatre; Theology; Education; Early Childhood; Elementary; Secondary Certification; Special Education°; Sciences; Biology; Chemistry; Computer Science; Environmental Science; General Science; Mathematics; Neuroscience; Allied Health; Athletic Training Education; Clinical Laboratory Science/Medical Technology; Physician Assistant; (Five-year Master's); 7 Pre-Professional Programs; 11 Special Concentrations

Campus Facilities and Equipment

We offer a state-of-the-art sports medicine clinic for our athletic training program. New science labs and equipment enable hands-on research. We have a radio station on-campus and offer audio and video editing equipment, along with desktop publishing equipment featuring LCD screens for those interested in communications or media.

The School of Business is completely wireless, offering students the ability to log in anywhere. The D. Leonard Corgan Library offers an amazing collection of books, periodicals and catalogs to provide students with the informational resources they need to enhance your skills.

Residence halls offer a variety of living arrangements from single rooms to apartments. There are 24-hour computer labs in several residence halls and lest you think we're all work and no fun, each lounge features cable television (and many students). These facilities are all secure, accessible either by student ID card or by the desk attendant on staff 24-hours a day. King's takes pride in our campus security efforts and can assure you that safety is a top priority here.

ATHLETICS FACILITIES

The 33-acre Robert L. Betzler Fields is one of the finest facilities in the MAC for football, field hockey, baseball, softball, soccer, and lacrosse.

The 13,000 square-foot John J. Dorish Field House features locker rooms, an equipment room, and an outdoor weight training facility.

The William S. Scandlon Physical Education Center has a state-of-the-art sports medicine clinic, an Olympic-sized swimming pool, handball and racquetball courts, wrestling room, new locker rooms, and the Robert McGrane Basketball Arena with a seating capacity of 3,200. Outdoor basketball courts are adjacent to the Center.

"The Mines," King's fitness center, is one of the finest weight training facilities at the small-college level. The 5,000 square-foot facility offers aerobic exercise machines and over 13,000-pounds of free weights. The College also features a completely outfitted wellness facility in Alumni Hall.

The tennis teams play on the newly-surfaced courts at Kirby Park, one of the top facilities in the MAC. (The Kingston Indoor Tennis Center is utilized during the winter.)

The golf team plays at the Wyoming Valley Country Club, a par 72, 6,391-yard course that is only 10 minutes from campus.

Tuition, Room, Board and Fees

When determining the cost of a college education, one should also take into consideration the value. U.S. News & World Report has ranked King's among America's best colleges for twelve straight years and Barrons consistently considers us one of the best buys in college education.

Approximately 95% of all full-time students attending King's College receive financial assistance, with the average scholarship being $9,600. We encourage every student to apply for financial aid no matter what their family circumstances are. Only after you have applied and been considered for all available assistance will you have a true idea of what your costs will be.

King's offers deferred payment plans, which allows families to make monthly payments on the balance of tuition, fees, room and board less any financial aid received.

FINANCIAL AID

Applicants for financial aid will be considered for all need-based programs which include private, state and federal grants (gifts), loans and work study programs. King's even has financial aid programs specific to transfer students, so all applicants should take the time to review their options.

KING'S COLLEGE GRANTS

King's Grant-In-Aid; Sibling Grant; Transfer Student Awards

FEDERAL

Federal Pell Grant; Federal Supplemental Education Opportunity Grant (SEOG)

STATE

PHEAA State Grant; New Economy Technology Scholarship (NETS)

ACT 101

For additional information on PHEAA programs, go to www.pheaa.org.

STUDENT LOANS

Federal Perkins Loan; Federal Stafford Loan Program; Subsidized Stafford Loan; Unsubsidized Stafford Loan; Additional Unsubsidized Stafford; Graduate Plus Loan

PARENT

Federal Parent Plus Loan

FEDERAL WORK STUDY

Federal campus-based work program allows students to earn money through employment to help pay for educational costs. Average annual amount is $1,200. FAFSA must be filed each year by May 1 to be considered.

The Office of financial aid is here to educate you about the various financial aid programs available and to answer your questions. We'll make the application process as simple and painless as possible because our goal is have you join us at King's. Contact us at 1-888-Kings-PA or finaid@kings.edu.

STUDENT ORGANIZATIONS AND ACTIVITIES

King's recognizes that involvement in student clubs and organizations is an important part of your educational experience. There are a large number of organizations to support your academic, social, and special interests, providing opportunities for leadership, recreation, and the development of special abilities and skills. King's offers the opportunity to participate in a club in the following general areas:

ACADEMIC

Business Related Organizations; Health Related Organizations; Arts & Sciences Organizations

INTERNATIONAL

Foreign Languages Club ; Multicultural/International Club

MEDIA & PUBLISHING

Media Club ; The Crown (student newspaper) ; Regis (yearbook) ; WRKC (radio station)

MUSIC / ARTS

Campion Society; King's Players; Monarch Dancers; Music Ensembles at King's; SCOP (fine arts magazine)

SERVICE

Blood Council ; Circle K Club ; Emergency Response Team (ERT) ; Knights of Columbus ; Sigma Kappa Sigma (EKE-men) ; Sigma Kappa Tau (EKT-women)

SPECIAL INTEREST

Commuter Life Association ; Debate Team ; Monarch Ambassadors ; Residence Hall Council

ROTC

Ski and Snowboard Club ; Track and Field

ADMISSIONS PROCESS

APPLYING TO KING'S FOR FRESHMAN

The Office of Admission offers two methods for candidates to apply for admission: The SAT/ACT Traditional Choice and the Standardized Test Option/ Essay Choice. Applicants are required to state their preference prior to the application review and the decision is non-reversible.

SAT/ACT Traditional Choice:

—Completed application

—Official high school transcripts

—SAT I or ACT scores

—Guidance counselor recommendation

—Essay

—$30 Application fee

Standardized Test Option/Essay Choice:

—Completed application

—Official high school transcripts

—Official graded writing sample from either junior or senior year submitted and notarized by the high school guidance office

—Guidance counselor recommendation

—Essay

—$30 Application fee

—General Guidelines

While each application for admission is reviewed individually, here are some general guidelines:

The most important criteria in the admission decision are a student's four-year academic record, GPA, strength of curriculum and overall rank in class. Recommendations, the personal statement, co-curricular activities, leadership and community service help to complete your profile. March 1 is the preferred application deadline for first-year students. Applications may be submitted after September 1 and are reviewed on a rolling admission basis. Decisions are released in mid-October. Once we have received your application materials, we will notify you with a decision in two to three weeks. Students choosing the standardized test option are required to notify the Office of Admission on the application. A students' decision is non-reversible and must be made prior to application review.

APPLYING FOR TRANSFER STUDENTS

Transferring to King's could not be easier, especially if you're transferring from LCCC. King's offers generous financial assistance packages so don't let cost be a deterrent.

Individual interviews and campus tours may be scheduled Monday through Friday throughout the year. Group information sessions and campus tours are offered on Saturdays during the academic year.

LABORATORY INSTITUTE OF MERCHANDISING

AT A GLANCE

The Laboratory Institute of Merchandising (LIM) is the College for the Business of Fashion. LIM is located in New York City, the world's undisputed fashion capital. The campus includes 4 locations in Midtown Manhattan, all within walking distance of each other.

LIM is accredited by the Commission on Higher Education of the Middle States Association of Colleges and Schools.

The LIM curriculum stresses both professional and academic preparation, a combination that makes their students highly successful. Students at LIM receive highly individualized attention as they study the fashion industry. The student body consists of approximately 1,120 students; this small size means that students have near-universal access to instructors, staff, and administrators, including the president.

The LIM curriculum requires students to complete a core set of courses in fashion, business, and the liberal arts, and also emphasizes the importance of hands-on experience. This unique approach opens numerous options to graduates, whom the college prepares for work in management, marketing, and merchandising in both the traditional fashion world and fashion-related businesses.

The Office of Career Services is one of LIM's chief assets. Each student receives extensive career counseling throughout their time at the college, beginning their first fall semester. This counseling helps direct him or her to a position within his/her field of study. LIM is extremely proud of its placement record: more than 90 percent of its graduates are employed in their fields of study within 6 months of graduation, a remarkable feat within the highly competitive fashion industry.

LIM housing is currently located at the de Hirsch Résidence at the 92nd Street Y, the New Yorker Residence in midtown Manhattan, and the Clark Residence in Brooklyn Heights. Single and double rooms are available to students on a first come, first served basis.

LIM welcomes all who are interested to its Open House program. This program invites students and their families to tour the college with current students, learn about career opportunities in the fashion industry, explore Academic Programs and financing options, meet with faculty and administrators, and enjoy a complimentary lunch. Visiting students may also sit for a personal interview, which is a required part of the application process. LIM has many other opportunities to tour the college, including information sessions on Wednesdays and Fridays and Transfer Nights.

LIM's student body is diverse, but they have one thing in common: a passion for fashion. As of fall 2007, approximately 1,120 students were enrolled at LIM; 79 percent of the student body is from the Tri-State area. 32 percent of students live in LIM housing; 94 percent of students are female; 80 percent of students receive some form of financial aid.

LOCATION AND ENVIRONMENT

LIM students benefit from an amazing location in the heart of New York City. World-famous works of architecture, such as St. Patrick's Cathedral, Central Park, the Museum of Modern Art, the Garment District, and Rockefeller Center are all a short walk away from the college. The fashion universe literally waits just beyond LIM's front door.

New York City is the center of many fashion and fashion-related industries, including cosmetics, textiles, visual merchandising, styling, and fashion publishing. The college's location and prestige guarantee that students will interact with many principals in these areas. Additionally, the curriculum frequently incorporates New York City's numerous resources, including people and places. For example a student taking LIM's fashion magazines course would visit showrooms and magazines, meet designers, and enjoy other similar experiences. No city can offer the breadth of experiences and fashion-related opportunities that New York offers.

ACADEMIC PROGRAMS

Students learn in a variety of settings at LIM. Classroom instruction is supplemented by field work performed under the supervision of industry professionals. The entire curriculum is aimed at preparing students for entry-level executive positions throughout the fashion industry.

LIM offers 4 majors: fashion merchandising, visual merchandising, marketing, and management. Students can earn the bachelor of business administration (BBA) degree in these fields or a bachelor of professional studies (BPS) in fashion merchandising. An associate degree is also offered in fashion merchandising. Qualified students may apply for a 1-year associate degree (through the ACCESS program).

LIM is also very proud to have added 8 minors to its academic offerings. The current list of minors includes: fashion merchandising, visual merchandising, styling, event planning, cosmetics, fashion publishing, entrepreneurship, international marketing, and retailing.

The curriculum includes frequent field trips to various centers of the fashion industry as well as guest lectures given by leaders of the fashion industry.

All students receive extensive work experience as part of their LIM education; it is LIM's internship program that helps students become truly prepared for their successful careers within the industry. During the freshman and sophomore years, student complete five-week internships called Work Projects I & II. Work Project I highlights the retail experience, while Work Project II allows students to branch into other fields, including management, publishing, cosmetics, advertising and public relations, and fashion forecasting. Both Work Projects dovetail with the Academic Programs the students pursued during the fall semesters. The third and final internship is the semester-long Senior Co-op; a required four-day-a-week placement in a field related to the student's chosen area of specialization. Co-ops may take students to fashion magazines, public relations firms, buying offices, or other essential areas of the fashion industry. The Senior Co-op serves as an ideal culminating experience and perfect transition into the business world, preparing undergraduates for the challenge and excitement of their next steps.

LIM operates on a 2-semester calendar and students may enter in either semester.

The college also offers a summer and Saturday programs that are open to high school students. Fashion lab courses, which include fashion magazines, fashion show production, fashion photography, trend spotting, buying, and fashion and celebrity styling, combine traditional course work with hands-on activities. These classes are a great way for high school students to jump into the world of fashion.

CAMPUS FACILITIES AND EQUIPMENT

LIM is situated in 4 buildings in Midtown Manhattan, on Forty-fifth, Fifty-third, and Fifty-fourth Streets, and on Fifth Avenue. All facilities house a blend of classrooms, administrative offices, computer labs, studios, and student lounges.

LIM's Adrian G. Marcuse Library contains 11,500 volumes pertaining to the liberal arts, fashion merchandising and related fields, as well as 130 professional and academic journals. The library also offers Internet access and access to an extensive array of online databases worldwide.

Personal computers are available for use throughout the college. The student/computer ratio is 4:1. LIM also offers wireless internet throughout all 4 of its locations.

The Math and Writing Centers offer peer tutoring and special programs to supplement and reinforce classroom learning and further develop students' skills in those areas.

TUITION, ROOM, BOARD, AND FEES

Tuition for the 2008-2009 academic year will be $19,300 and mandatory fees will be $525. On average, students spend an additional $1,000 per year on books and supplies. All other expenses, such as room and board, vary according to individual circumstances. Commuters normally spend $750 to $2,000 for transportation, depending on commuting distance. LIM room and board is approximately $15,000 for a student in a double room. Students should also budget about $2,000 per year for personal expenses.

FINANCIAL AID

LIM wants every student it admits to be able to attend the college and works hard to make its education affordable to all. Admissions decisions are made independently of financial aid considerations. Approximately 76 percent of our undergraduates receive financial assistance in some form: grants, scholarships, loans, and work-study are made available to students who qualify.

Students should submit the Free Application for Federal Student Aid (FAFSA) by April 1 to receive priority consideration for financial assistance. Aid in all forms is available on a need basis. Merit scholarships are awarded to those with high academic achievement and other significant talents, regardless of financial need.

LIM offers merit scholarships to both incoming freshmen and transfer students. The college gives these awards to candidates who demonstrate exceptional academic ability in high school or college. It is recommended that freshmen applicants submit a completed admissions application by March 1 to receive priority consideration for merit scholarships. Transfer applicants should submit completed applications by May 1 to receive priority merit consideration. Recipients remain eligible for their scholarships for their entire tenure at LIM by maintaining a GPA of at least 3.0.

Please consult our website to learn about other need and non-need based scholarships. You can also contact the Office of Student Financial Services for more details.

STUDENT ORGANIZATIONS AND ACTIVITIES

The Mission of Student Life is to provide a supportive social environment and a wealth of cultural opportunities that cultivates personal and academic growth.

LIM student clubs and activities are a fun and informal way to get involved and interact with fellow students and faculty. Club advisors are experienced in the field and can help you connect with key people in the industry. You can meet friends, build a resume, and make the most of your college experience by joining a student club.

Co-curricular organizations include the Student Council, the Fashion Club, the Styling Club, SIFE, and various other clubs formed by students to serve special needs and interests. Students produce the annual yearbook (called *Limlight*), produce the annual fashion show, and organize cultural and social activities. Eligible students may be nominated for Sigma Beta Delta, the national honor society. Other activities include the Explore New York program, the annual ski trip, and the Multicultural Festival.

Each year, LIM students participate in several different volunteer activities including the Revlon Run/Walk for Women's Cancers and the Annual LIM Blood Drive.

Fashion is a notably international industry, and LIM recognizes and appreciates that through its Off-Campus Opportunities, all offered for academic credit. For students who are interested in seeing the broad scope of European fashion, there is a short-term study abroad each January. This tour highlights European fashion capitols as well as figures and companies in each of the locations (which are determined on an annual basis).

A second opportunity is a summer study-abroad in Paris, France. This 2-week program allows students the opportunity to get their feet wet in one of the industry's oldest and most prestigious world capitals.

The final opportunity gives students the chance to study abroad for a full semester during their junior year at Westminster University in England. The Westminster Exchange program is ideal for students who are looking for a more long-term immersion program and includes an internship as part of its experience.

ADMISSIONS PROCESS

LIM has a rolling admissions policy. All students are required to submit the LIM application for admission, an essay, a $40 fee, SAT or ACT scores, 2 letters of recommendation, and official high school transcripts from all high schools attended. Applicants are also required to have a personal interview on campus. LIM strongly suggests all applicants submit an activity sheet.

Transfer students must also submit official transcripts from all colleges attended. SAT/ACT scores are not required for transfer students with more than 30 credits or who are over 25. International students must also submit TOEFL scores of 550 or higher.

To be considered for Early Action Admission, applicants must complete all the requirements and submit the Early Action Applicant Form (obtained from the LIM website) on or before November 15.

LAKE ERIE COLLEGE

AT A GLANCE

Lake Erie College, founded in 1856, is an independent, coeducational institution located in the city of Painesville in Northeastern Ohio. Instruction is provided at the baccalaureate and master's degree levels to academically qualified individuals. Programs of study, founded in the liberal arts, are offered in the following areas: education, equine studies, fine arts, languages & communication, management studies, social sciences, and science & math. Lake Erie College accommodates both residential and commuting students of various ages on a full-time and part-time basis. Local, national, and international students benefit from the college's traditional emphasis on intercultural programs.

Intercollegiate sports play an important role in student life. Athletic Teams compete at the NCAA Division II level. Men compete in baseball, basketball, cross-country, football, golf, lacrosse , soccer, and track & field. Women compete in basketball, cross-country, soccer, softball, volleyball, lacrosse, and track & field. The college also sponsors an intercollegiate equestrian team.

Lake Erie College invites students to feel at home in one of 4 residence halls. Each spacious room is equipped with high-speed Internet access, individual phone lines, cable access, and furniture (desks, beds, and chairs). The college's residence halls have laundry facilities, community lounges, and kitchen areas. Upperclassmen have the opportunity to experience apartment-style living in a college-owned complex, Founders Court adjacent to campus. Since many students bring their cars to campus, convenient parking is available near each residence hall.

LOCATION AND ENVIRONMENT

Lake Erie College is located on 57 acres of naturally wooded land in Painesville, Ohio. Painesville is an attractive community in Northeast Ohio, which is 28 miles east of Cleveland and 3 miles south of Lake Erie. The Cleveland Museum of Art; Playhouse Square; Lake Metro Parks; Holden Arboretum; professional baseball, football, and basketball teams; theaters; comedy clubs; and other recreational attractions are located nearby. The area is served by 2 national highways: U.S. 90 and 20, and state routes 2 and 44.

OFF-CAMPUS OPPORTUNITIES

Through the college's Academic Program Abroad, students live and study at one of many foreign colleges or universities while earning Lake Erie College credits. This affords students the opportunity to study within the special educational experience that is part of living in another country, speaking another language, and learning another culture. Academic experiences abroad range in duration from 1 semester to an entire year, depending upon individual schedules. Following the fourth semester of full-time study, students may have the opportunity to participate in a shorter study trip abroad.

MAJORS AND DEGREES OFFERED

At the undergraduate level, Lake Erie College offers the bachelor of arts, bachelor of science, and bachelor of fine arts degrees. Majors are available in accounting, arts management, biology, business administration, chemistry, communications, criminal justice, dance, early childhood education, middle childhood education, secondary/young adult education, English, entrepreneurship, environmental science, equine facilities management, equestrian teacher/trainer, fine arts (multidisciplinary), fine arts (with concentrations in art, dance, music, and theater), forensic psychology, international business, legal studies, management, marketing, mathematics, modern foreign language (French, German, Italian, and Spanish), music, psychology, pre-professional studies (dentistry, law, medicine, pharmacy and veterinary science), social sciences (history, sociology), sports management and therapeutic horsemanship. Students may also pursue an individualized academic major.

ACADEMIC PROGRAMS

The philosophy of Lake Erie College is that the well-being and enrichment of society are dependent upon the abilities of individuals to think both creatively and critically, to make reasoned and informed decisions, and to assume responsibility for their personal actions and continuing education.

Education at Lake Erie College promotes the knowledge and understanding of various cultures and the growth of personal and social responsibilities associated with the acquisition of knowledge and the mastery of skills. The liberal arts and career-oriented disciplines the college offers are not mutually exclusive bodies of knowledge, and the best education is one that promotes the integration of both types of disciplines. The process of education is as vital as the subject matter communicated. It is through intercultural awareness, directed practice in discerning relationships among disciplines, and making informed judgments that a person becomes educated and acquires the flexibility necessary to meet the rapidly changing demands of the marketplace and the world.

28 semester hours are required to earn a bachelor's degree.

CAMPUS FACILITIES AND EQUIPMENT

The scenic Lake Erie College campus provides the ideal setting to pursue an academic career; it reflects the college's commitment to provide a high-quality education in a personalized environment. The focal point of the campus is College Hall, completed in 1859. College Hall is a center for classroom and student administrative activities.

The Arthur S. Holden Center houses a telecommunications center, a computer center, computerized classrooms, conference rooms, and faculty offices. In the Holden Center, students will also find the bookstore, Storm Café, a cafeteria student life offices, student government offices, Lake Erie College security, and student mailboxes. Since its dedication in 1997, this facility has been Lake Erie College's premier student center.

The Fine Arts Building houses the 200-seat C. K. Rickel Theatre, the B. K. Smith Gallery, art studios, the dance studio, photography laboratories, faculty offices, and classrooms. The Austin Hall of Science includes laboratories, classrooms, and offices and will be completely renovated in 2009 to include added laboratory spaces, SMART classrooms and improved study area for students. The new Athletic, Recreation, and Wellness Center, completed in August 2004, includes 2 full-size gymnasiums, an indoor track, a complete fitness center, multiple locker rooms, an athletic training room, classrooms, team conference room, and coaches' offices. Adjacent to the center is Jack Slattery Field, with fields for soccer and softball. Kilcawley Hall houses the President's Office, the Institutional Advancement Office, Human Resources and College Relations.

The Lincoln Library/Learning Resource Center maintains a collection of more than 90,000 books and subscribes to more than 750 periodicals. Audiovisual services, educational media and media production centers, 2 computerized indexes, and 2 computer laboratories are also located in the library.

The 85-acre George M. Humphrey Equestrian Center is located just 5 miles from the campus. Served daily by the college van, the equestrian center includes an indoor arena of 100 feet by 225 feet, with seating for 1,000 spectators, and an indoor warm-up area of 75 feet by 130 feet. The Clarence T. Reinberger Equestrian Work Center has an additional indoor ring of 80 feet by 96 feet. Other facilities include the Equine Stud Farm Laboratory and breeding facilities as well as stabling for 100 horses. The equestrian center also features outdoor riding rings with all weather footing and a hunt field with several cross-country obstacles.

TUITION, ROOM, BOARD, AND FEES

Tuition per year for 2008-09 is $23,950 for full-time students (12-18 credit hours) and $655 per credit hour for part-time students. The room charges per year are $3,860 based on double-occupancy. Residential students may choose from 3 meal plans, with the fourteen-meal per week plan equaling $3,540 per year. Yearly fees (student activity, library, and computer) are $1,120 for full-time students and $47 per credit hour for part-time students. At the established sites, the fees for the Academic Program Abroad are comparable to a semester's costs on the Lake Erie campus.

FINANCIAL AID

Lake Erie College offers a number of competitive scholarship programs that are not based on need. Most incoming freshman students receive a renewable scholarship ranging from $3000 to $14,000 per academic year based on cumulative high school grade point average, standardized test score, letters of recommendation and essay.

Five Presidential Honors Scholarships, which cover 90 percent tuition, are awarded to incoming students ranking in the top 5 percent of their graduating high school class and achieving a minimum ACT score of 27 or minimum SAT score of 1800 (minimum combination of the 3 section scores). The award is competitive, with an essay required after the initial GPA and ACT/SAT test score requirements are met. The essay, admissions application, and transcripts are reviewed by a selection committee, and 5 winners are selected. Recipients of the scholarship must live on campus, maintain at least a 3.5 GPA, and take part in the Honors Scholars Program.

Other forms of financial aid, all based on need, include scholarships, grants (federal, state, local, and College), loans (federal and state), and work-study programs; the priority date for need-based aid is March 1. Approximately 98 percent of full-time undergraduate students receive financial aid. Estimates of the expected family contribution are available from the Office of Financial Aid. To apply for aid, students must submit a Free Application for Federal Student Aid (FAFSA), Form 1040, and other documents required by Lake Erie. The deadline for priority consideration is March 1.

The Lake Erie College faculty members are well qualified, capable, and eager to teach. Eighty-five percent of the faculty members hold doctoral or terminal degrees in their field. Many bring firsthand experiences in their disciplines to the classroom. They remain active in their respective academic disciplines and are able to provide students with information on current research, new trends, and career opportunities. The average class size is 15, and the student-faculty ratio is 13:1.

STUDENT ORGANIZATIONS AND ACTIVITIES

Students at Lake Erie College play an important role in decision making in many aspects of campus life. Students retain membership on most faculty and administrative committees. The Student Government Association provides a means for students to govern their nonacademic lives and to maintain channels of communication with the faculty and administration.

ADMISSIONS PROCESS

A composite evaluation is made of each applicant, with special attention given to high school credentials. A college-preparatory background is highly recommended and should include 4 units of English, 3 units of mathematics, 3 units of science, 3 units of social studies, and 6 additional units from other academic areas; 2 units of foreign language are advised. ACT and/or SAT scores are required. Lake Erie College welcomes students of all races and backgrounds.

Lake Erie College operates with a rolling admission policy; however, it is recommended that students complete their application and financial aid processes by May 1 in order to maximize their academic and financial aid opportunities. Applicants are notified of the admission decision within 2 weeks of receipt of all materials.

For further information, students may contact:

Office of Admissions

Lake Erie College

391 West Washington Street

Painesville, Ohio 44077

United States

Phone: 440-375-7050

800-916-0904 (toll free)

E-mail: admissions@lec.edu

Website: www.lec.edu

School Says . . .

LAKE FOREST COLLEGE

AT A GLANCE

Founded in 1857, Lake Forest College is a national liberal arts institution located 30 miles north of Chicago along Lake Michigan. The college is situated on a beautiful wooded 107-acre campus within walking distance to the train to downtown Chicago, historic Lake Forest, and the beaches of Lake Michigan.

The college enrolls 1,400 full-time undergraduates from 47 states and 65 countries. Fifteen percent of Lake Forest students are members of a racial or ethnic minority, and 13 percent are international students. International students and members of minority groups make up 25 percent of the Lake Forest student body. Approximately 80 percent of students live on campus in co-ed and single-sex residence facilities.

The college has a distinguished faculty of excellent teachers and accomplished scholars. Professors have won national teaching awards and routinely lecture and consult throughout the U.S. and abroad. More than 30 percent have published books in their discipline. Faculty members, not graduate students, teach all classes and serve as advisors and mentors.

The college's proximity to Chicago offers student unique experiential learning opportunities, and professors regularly use the city's resources to complement course work. Lake Forest encourages study, internship, and research opportunities in the Chicago area, the U.S., and abroad.

LOCATION AND ENVIRONMENT

Located in Lake Forest, Illinois just 30 miles north of Chicago along the shores of Lake Michigan, the 107-acre residential campus is a safe academic home in a beautiful wooded suburban setting.

The college is only 25 miles from O'Hare International Airport is also served by Midway Airport, Mitchell International Airport in Milwaukee, and Metra commuter railroad.

The campus is surrounded by lush wooded neighborhoods, ravines, natural prairies, the beautiful beaches along Lake Michigan, and an extensive network of bike and running trails. Nearby Chicago boasts nearly 70 world-class museums, more than 200 theaters, 7 major league sports teams, and one of the nation's top opera companies. Chicago is known for its cleanliness, abundant green space, good transportation system, and friendly people.

OFF-CAMPUS OPPORTUNITIES

Lake Forest provides a variety of opportunities for off-campus study, both domestic and international. Semester-long options in the U.S. include the Chicago Arts Program, The Oak Ridge Science Semester in Tennessee, The Chicago Urban Studies Program, the Chicago Program in Business and Society, the Newberry Library Program in the Humanities, and the Washington Semester Program at American University. International programs are offered in students earn credit in off-campus programs across the country and in Beijing, Botswana, Czech Republic, Chile, Costa Rica, England, France, Italy, Greece, Turkey, India, Italy, Japan, France, Great Britain, Russia, and Tanzania. The Off-Campus Program director works with students to facilitate participation in other approved off-campus study programs.

The college offers internship programs in Paris, France and Santiago, Chile, and locally. Internship opportunities are plentiful in the Chicago area and students have interned at places such as the Art Institute of Chicago, Chicago Blackhawks, Chicago Board of Trade, Chicago Council on Foreign Relations, Edelman Public Relations Worldwide, Morgan Stanley, NBC Chicago, Second City, and the John G. Shedd Aquarium, among others.

MAJORS AND DEGREES OFFERED

The academic calendar of Lake Forest College is based on 2 15-week semesters, beginning in August and January. Students normally take 4 course credits per semester (the equivalent of 16 semester hours).

There are no teaching assistants at the college. Courses are taught in small classroom settings by professors who are experts in their fields and who also serve students as one-on-one advisors.

A Lake Forest graduate will have studied a broad range of ideas; developed real competence in writing, speaking, and quantitative skills; and gained significant experience in humanities, natural sciences and mathematics, and social sciences while completing requirements for a major in an academic department or interdisciplinary program. The college's General Education Curriculum, advising system, and major requirements are designed to support these educational ideals.

Lake Forest graduates receive awards the bachelor of arts (BA) degree in both traditional academic departments and interdisciplinary programs., and students can choose from more than 500 classes in 20 academic disciplines and 7 interdisciplinary majors. Areas of study include: African American studies, American studies, anthropology, area studies, studio art, art history, Asian studies, biology, business, chemistry, classical studies, communication, computer science, economics, education (elementary and secondary), engineering (dual degree), English (literature and writing), environmental studies, modern foreign languages and literatures (Arabic, Chinese, French, German, Italian, Japanese, Russian, and Spanish), history, international relations, Latin American studies, mathematics, metropolitan studies, music, philosophy, physics, politics, psychology, religion, sociology, theater, and women's and gender studies. Lake Forest also offers pre-professional programs in: law, medicine, dentistry, and veterinary medicine.

ACADEMIC PROGRAMS

The First-Year Studies Program (FIYS). First-year studies classes are small in size (12-14 students) to encourage interaction and discussion. The FIYS professors also serve as the students' primary academic advisors and help them navigate the college's academic offerings during their first year. With more than 20 topics to choose from, first-year studies courses cover a wide range of academic interests from music, art, and politics to neuroscience, terrorism and religion, many with a focus on Chicago or directly utilizing the resources available there. Chicago plays an integral role in the FIYS program. Students travel to Chicago with their class during orientation week, providing a first-hand introduction to how the educational, cultural, and social resources of this city will impact their course work and experiences during their 4 years at Lake Forest.

The Richter Apprentice Scholars Program. This program provides students, early in their academic careers, with the opportunity to conduct independent, individual research with Lake Forest faculty. In the summer after their first year, each student in the Richter Program is employed for a ten-week period and does independent research one-on-one with a faculty member. Students are selected through their applications to the program during the admissions process.

The Independent Scholar Program. This program allows students to develop an academic major of their own, working closely with a faculty advisor, culminating in a thesis or a creative project. Recent topics include: sports management, ancient Mediterranean civilizations, graphic design, business theory, medieval studies, lighting design for the theater, metaphysics, and feminist theory.

CAMPUS FACILITIES AND EQUIPMENT

Lake Forest College recently opened the Donnelley and Lee Library, a twenty-first century library and information technology center having recently undergone an $18 million expansion and renovation. The facility project that incorporates the latest learning and technological innovations while providing a comfortable environment for collaboration and study. Features of the new library include: a cyber café; wireless network; 24-hour computing labs; numerous study spaces and workstations; a production and rhetoric room; speech and Video Production room for video recording presentations; and "smart" classrooms, and a café.

The Mohr Student Center is a student-centered social space that is the hub of social activity on campus. It features pool tables and other games, stage and performance space, large-screen TVs, lounges, deli/snack bar, and an outdoor terrace with seating.

Lake Forest is one of the only national liberal arts colleges whose students regularly engage a major city. Chicago provides a hands-on resource for student learning through research, internships, study, and fun. At the Center for Chicago Programs, students can plan visits to the city and professors can get help incorporating Chicago resources into their classrooms. The center also brings well-known Chicagoans to the college for lectures and performances.

The Dixon Science Research Center is designed for student-faculty research and contains 13 laboratories with state-of-the-art equipment including a nuclear magnetic resonance spectrometer, a solid-state gamma-ray spectrometer, a multi-imaging phosphorimager, digital-storage oscilloscopes, and fluorescence microscopes.

TUITION, ROOM, BOARD, AND FEES

Tuition: $30,600

Room: $3,700

Board: $3,626

Fees: $464

FINANCIAL AID

Lake Forest College provides an affordable, high-quality education through maintaining a strong commitment to supporting each student's demonstrated financial need. Financial assistance is available to all who qualify and submit all admission, financial aid, and scholarship applications by the deadlines.

The college offers academic scholarships ranging from $16,000 to full tuition and talent scholarships ranging from $1,000 to $5,000 in recognition of academic achievement or recognized dedication in the fine arts, foreign languages, leadership, music, sciences (including math and computers), theater, or writing.

STUDENT ORGANIZATIONS AND ACTIVITIES

Lake Forest College is a place to study, work, and live. Students hail from 47 states and 65 countries so there is an eclectic mix of activities and opportunities outside the classroom.

Student organizations include student government, international interest groups, Greek Life, academic honor societies, community service, publications and media, music and performance, spiritual and religious groups, and many others.

They have a voice in how the college is run and are actively involved in governance committees such as the College Council and have representation on the Board of Trustees. Student writers and performers can showcase their talents on stage with the Garrick Players, by hosting a show on "WMXM," the college's FM radio station, or through the student newspaper, literary magazines, chorus and instrumental ensembles. Academic honor societies enjoy active student participation as do the community service groups and many special-interest clubs. The college provides and maintains a comprehensive intramural and intercollegiate athletic program. There are 3 national fraternities and 5 national sororities, all housed within the residence halls. All students have equal opportunity to take advantage of the richness of the college's programs.

Lake Forest College competes in the NCAA Division III fielding 8 women's and 8 men's intercollegiate varsity teams. Women's teams include basketball, cross-country, handball, ice hockey, soccer, softball, swimming and diving, tennis, and volleyball. Men's teams include basketball, cross-country, football, handball, ice hockey, soccer, swimming and diving, and tennis. The college also offers an extensive roster of intramural and club sports.

The college's Center for Chicago Programs facilitates engagement with the resources of Chicago, which often complements programs for student organizations as well as provides students with information on cultural and social activities happening downtown. The train to Chicago is a short walk from campus and students enjoy traveling to the city for fun and entertainment. The college shuttle provides service 7 days a week to popular shopping areas and destinations around campus.

ADMISSIONS PROCESS

The criteria used for selection include assessment of a student's program of study, academic achievement, aptitude, intellectual curiosity, qualities of character and personality, and activities.

Standardized test scores (ACT/SAT) are optional, except for international or home-schooled candidates, and those applying for some academic scholarships. A personal interview is required for students who do not submit scores.

LANDMARK COLLEGE

AT A GLANCE

Our Integrated Approach

While many colleges offer special programs for students with learning difficulties, Landmark College is one of the only accredited colleges in the U.S. designed exclusively for students with dyslexia, attention deficit hyperactivity disorder (ADHD), or other specific learning disabilities.

Why does Landmark's approach succeed? Because we teach the skills and strategies necessary for success in college and the workforce. At Landmark, you learn how to learn, and this knowledge helps you become more confident and independent.

All of this is achieved through an integrated approach to learning. Landmark College strongly believes that bright students who learn differently can also learn to achieve and thrive.

Students at Landmark get far more personal, directed assistance than at other colleges. Each student receives individualized attention from classroom instructors—in courses tailored to meet your individual learning style. We have courses for skills development, college credit, and Associate Degree Programs for individuals who have average-to-superior intellectual potential. Our experienced advisors meet frequently with you to review and guide your progress. All instructors are trained professional educators, not teaching assistants or peer tutors.

Growth and Discovery

Your time at Landmark College is a time of exploration and learning. A time for you to discover your own personal strengths and abilities. A time for you to grow into your full potential.

It's also a time to make friends, discover talents, and explore interests. The college offers you a wide variety of sports and social activities, both on our beautiful wooded campus and in the surrounding community.

In addition to athletics, activities, and all the off-campus resources of beautiful New England, an important aspect of student life at Landmark College is life in the residence halls. If you choose to live on campus, along with social and educational programs, you'll develop a strong sense of community. There's a true commitment to learning—inside and outside of the classroom. Student development professionals also live in each residence hall.

LOCATION AND ENVIRONMENT

Landmark College is located in southeastern Vermont. In summer and spring, you can hike, run, mountain bike, and swim. In winter students find an atmosphere perfect for snowboarding, cross-country and downhill skiing, and winter camping. For those who prefer something more urban, Boston is 2 and a half hours away by car and New York City is only 4 and a half hours away.

OFF-CAMPUS OPPORTUNITIES

Students enjoy exploring the diverse social and cultural offerings in the local Vermont towns of Putney and Brattleboro, and Massachusetts' Northampton. These areas all have bustling downtowns with shops, restaurants, and entertainment. Brattleboro has a vibrant arts community with galleries, music, and theater. Northampton is home to Smith College and a thriving crafts scene.

Larger cities like Boston, Montreal, and New York are close enough for day and weekend trips.

At Landmark College, interactive learning abroad is a reality. Every year, our students have the opportunity to study at locations around the world. January experiences in Costa Rica, as well as summer semesters in England, Ireland, Greece, India, Italy, and Spain enable our students to experience other cultures. While expanding their horizons, they are engaged in rigorous college course work, taught by our own professional faculty members.

MAJORS AND DEGREES OFFERED

AA Business Studies

AA General Studies

ACADEMIC PROGRAMS

Your path through Landmark College can be one of many. Our programs offer you many opportunities to develop the academic skills and strategies that match your abilities.

We offer associate's degrees in general and business studies. Our other programs include study abroad, a college skills summer session, a high school summer session, and a summer transition to college session for recent high school graduates.

CAMPUS FACILITIES AND EQUIPMENT

The campus includes several multipurpose classroom buildings, five traditional residence halls, two apartment and condominium-style residential buildings, and a fine arts building housing two theaters.

The campus library houses a growing print, audiovisual, and digital materials collection as well as specialized areas for research, instruction, LD research, and media production. Other campus facilities include the Academic Support Center, a Women's Resource Center, the Click Sports Center and the Strauch Family Student Center.

TUITION, ROOM, BOARD, AND FEES

The comprehensive fees listed below include the cost of taking classes and living at Landmark College. They include all courses, residence hall, and meal plan.

Fees for the 2005–2006 Academic Year (30 weeks):

Tuition: $37,000

Room Fee: $3,400

Board Fee: $3,400

Damage Deposit: $300

Health Insurance: $450 (International Students: $644)

Total: $44,550

FINANCIAL AID

By researching, applying to, and choosing Landmark College, you've decided on your educational path. Now you need to get the funding to pursue your goal.

The Financial Aid Office is here to help you navigate the financial obstacles that you may encounter along the way. While you look for outside sources to help make your Landmark College education a reality, we work from the inside. We'll provide information and guidance on applying for federal grants and loans as well as other sources.

Every family is encouraged to apply for financial assistance through Landmark College. Determining how best to finance a college education can create a lot of questions and concerns. All families are eligible for some form of assistance.

In addition to primary resources of family income and savings, students may be eligible for federal grants, loans, or Landmark College scholarships. Landmark College's tuition and fees can also lead to tax advantages for qualified students and families.

The Financial Aid Office is here to assist with this process and answer all of your questions.

Cathy Mullins

Director of Financial Aid

Office Telephone: 802-387-6736

Fax: 802-387-6868

E-mail: cmullins@landmark.edu

STUDENT ORGANIZATIONS AND ACTIVITIES

When you come to Landmark College, you have the chance to learn about yourself in more ways than you would expect. We believe that there's more to education than just what you find in textbooks and classrooms. We offer you growth in all areas of your life—body, mind, and spirit.

The Division of Student Life contributes to your educational experience by providing numerous opportunities, programs, and services, so you can get involved. These are designed to enhance your intellectual, social, ethical, physical, and cultural development. You'll discover current favorites and learn to enjoy new activities. We'll help you build the self-esteem you need to push your horizons as far as you can go.

At Landmark College, you'll find people who understand where you're coming from—whether they're fellow students or the faculty members and staff. You'll relax in an atmosphere where we all recognize your capabilities. We want you to strive for success at everything you try. Why? Because we know you can do it.

We endeavor to work with you and for you. We'll encourage you to become involved in the campus community, and to take advantage of the leadership role you can play here and in the world. The friendships, experiences, and connections that you will make at Landmark College will create an exciting environment where you will live and learn. Our goal is to provide the widest possible spectrum of activities, and to offer something that will appeal to every student.

Clubs and weekly activities range from jazz band, poetry readings, fencing, Business Management Club, Women's Resources, Multicultural Club, on-campus movies, spiritual life, chorus, to the community garden project. Dances, clubs, and athletic events at the school featuring our Pep Band and mascot "Jerry Jaws" are only a small part of the on-campus events.

Activities at Landmark College take advantage of Vermont's natural beauty, as well as providing opportunities to visit sites further afield. Trips to Fenway Park in Boston to see the Red Sox or to Montreal to experience French-Canadian culture are part of the yearly program.

The student-run Campus Activities Board is a subcommittee of our Student Government Association, and is responsible for scheduling the wide range of activities provided by the college.

ADMISSIONS PROCESS

Our Admissions Process is as straightforward as we can make it. Here is a brief overview (full details are in the application package or visit our website: www.landmark.edu).

What We Consider

We are looking for students who meet two essential criteria:

- Average to superior intellectual potential, *and*
- Diagnosis of dyslexia, ADHD, or other specific learning disability

The Steps We Follow

The Admissions Process has three steps:

1. You complete the application and personal statement (preferably in your own handwriting) and submit these to the Admissions Office with the application fee.

2. You ensure that all required records and recommendations get to us in time for consideration by the Admissions Committee.

3. Our Admissions Committee reviews your completed application package and determines whether to:

- Request further documentation
- Invite you for an interview
- Decline your application
- Admit you directly to a degree program

LAWRENCE TECHNOLOGICAL UNIVERSITY

AT A GLANCE

Lawrence Technological University is a private, fully accredited university focused on providing superior education through cutting-edge technology, small class sizes, and innovative programs. All undergraduate students receive training and experience in leadership as part of their curriculum. The university enrolls nearly 5,000 students in more than 60 undergraduate, master's, and doctoral programs in Colleges of Architecture and Design, Arts and Sciences, Engineering, and Management.

Founded in 1932 by brothers Russell and E. George Lawrence on the grounds of Henry Ford's first moving assembly line, Lawrence Tech has traditionally provided students a high-quality, affordable education with an emphasis on theory and practice. The university, including the graduate programs in business, architecture, and engineering, is accredited by the Higher Learning Commission and is a member of the North Central Association of Colleges and schools. Lawrence Tech was in the top tier category of Best University-Masters-Midwest in the *U.S. News & World Report*'s 2008 America's Best Colleges rankings.

Lawrence Tech's student-faculty ratio is 13:1. Approximately 74 percent of the undergraduate classes have 19 or fewer students, and fewer than 1 percent of the classes have more than 50. Approximately 600 students live in university housing. Women make up 24 percent of the student body, and 25 states and 25 nations are represented on campus.

LOCATION AND ENVIRONMENT

The university is located in Southfield, a suburb of more than 78,000 people. Lawrence Tech's campus is conveniently close to major freeways and about a 30-minute drive north of downtown Detroit. Southeastern Michigan offers a rich variety of recreational and cultural activities, with public transportation making most areas accessible to students. Research, manufacturing, scientific, and business enterprises also are located nearby, aiding students who work full- or part-time while attending classes as well as those working in co-op and internship programs.

OFF-CAMPUS OPPORTUNITIES

Lawrence Tech chemistry, computer science, engineering, and technology students may participate in co-op programs, alternating semesters of classes and work. Internships also are available.

The university also offers programs at Education Centers in southeastern and northern Michigan as well as international programs in Canada, China, Germany, India, Mexico, and Taiwan.

The Detroit Studio gives students the opportunity to explore community-based architectural, urban design, and community development projects. Architecture students regularly build homes for Habitat for Humanity. The Paris Summer Study-Abroad Program is open to junior and senior architecture students. The Global Engineering Program arranges for Lawrence Tech engineering students to work and study abroad.

MAJORS AND DEGREES OFFERED

Lawrence Tech offers more than 60 undergraduate, master's, and doctoral programs in Colleges of Architecture and Design, Arts and Sciences, Engineering, and Management. Most programs are available during the day or evening; some are offered on weekends and online. Dual majors and customized degree programs combining either associate and bachelor's programs or bachelor's and master's programs also are available. Pre-professional preparation includes predental, pre-law, and pre-medical programs. Lawrence Tech offers an undergraduate honors program for highly motivated and qualified students. A scholars program is also available, designed to ease the transition from high school to college by providing support services, including course previews, tutoring and mentoring, and social activities.

Bachelor's degrees in architecture and design are offered in architecture, imaging (concentrations in digital arts and digital design), interior architecture, and transportation design. Lawrence Tech enrolls more architectural students than any other school in Michigan, and its program is among the top 10 largest in the nation.

Lawrence Tech's arts and sciences bachelor's degrees include chemical biology, chemistry, computer science, English and communication arts, environmental chemistry, humanities, information technology, mathematics, mathematics and computer science, media communication, molecular and cell biology, physics, physics and computer science, and psychology.

Management degrees offered are business management (with optional concentrations in industrial management and technology management), construction management, and information technology. Advanced degrees in management also are available.

Engineering bachelor's degrees are available in biomedical engineering, civil engineering, computer engineering, construction management, electrical engineering (concentrations in computer engineering, electronics engineering, and energy engineering), engineering technology, industrial operations engineering, and mechanical engineering (concentrations in automotive engineering, manufacturing, mechanical system design, and thermal system design).

Minors are available in aeronautical engineering, business management, chemistry, computer science, economics, energy engineering, English, general sciences, history, mathematics, philosophy, physics, psychology, Spanish, and technical and professional communication.

Associate degrees are offered in chemical technology, communications engineering technology, construction engineering technology, general studies, manufacturing engineering technology, mechanical engineering technology, and radio and television broadcasting.

Certificates can be earned in aeronautical engineering, energy engineering, entrepreneurial strategy, entrepreneurship, industrial/organizational psychology, leadership and change management, and technical and professional communication.

ACADEMIC PROGRAMS

The university is involved in a number of innovative applied research partnerships with industry and government that offer students, even as undergraduates, remarkable hands-on experiences solving real-world problems.

The U.S. Department of Energy selected Lawrence Tech to be one of 20 university teams from the United States, Canada, and Europe to compete in the 2007 Solar Decathlon, which challenges students to design, build, and operate highly efficient, completely solar homes. Lawrence Tech was the only university in Michigan chosen to compete.

Lawrence Tech is the recipient of a grant from the State of Michigan for the development and implementation of materials and practices that are expected to double the lifespan of bridges using box-beam construction.

In another project, Lawrence Tech students are educational partners with the regional utility and assess the operation of the first and largest hydrogen technology park of its type in the world, a pilot project developed with support from the U.S. Department of Energy.

Student engineering teams design, build, and race Baja and Formula-style vehicles. Each year students also compete in bridge building and assembling, designing zero energy homes, and in airplane design, robotics, and concrete canoe competitions. The Lear Entrepreneurial Center teaches engineering students how to create, promote, and bring to market products and services.

Co-op, part-time work, internships, student projects, and participation in professional organizations provide opportunities to network with industry leaders.

CAMPUS FACILITIES AND EQUIPMENT

Lawrence Tech is Michigan's first wireless laptop computer campus and is ranked among the nation's top 50 "unwired" universities. All undergraduates are provided high-end laptops that are customized with the software students need for their academic specialty. Other computers, workstations, terminals, and microcomputers are located in campus labs.

Lawrence Tech has 2 co-ed residence halls, featuring one- and 2-bedroom apartment-style suites that accommodate 2 to 4 students. Single rooms also are available. All utilities, wireless Internet access, basic cable television service, and individual telephone lines and voice-mail are included in the housing cost.

The library houses a broad selection of print and electronic resources and is part of a nationwide network of more than 6,000 libraries. Lawrence Tech also is surrounded by numerous outstanding municipal and research libraries, many with reciprocal borrowing privileges.

Facilities include architectural and design studios; senior project lab and studio space; fabrication labs; a wind tunnel; wood, metal, and model shops; chemistry and biology labs; an anechoic chamber for sound studies; a structural testing center; alternative energy, mechanical, and electrical labs; thermal dynamics lab; graphics lab; and the DENSO Instructional Technology Lab. Lawrence Tech also owns a nearby Frank Lloyd Wright-designed home that is used as a study center.

The A. Alfred Taubman Student Services Center consolidates all student support services—from admissions through career services—into a convenient one-stop center. This innovative 42,000-square-foot center also utilizes many energy-efficient and environmentally-friendly features and technologies, serving as a living laboratory. The Center for Innovative Materials Research is a state-of-the-art laboratory for the research, development, and testing of materials for defense and infrastructure applications.

The Automotive Engineering Institute provides students opportunities to conduct sponsored research on a unique 4 by 4 vehicle chassis dynamometer, which measures many areas of vehicle performance.

TUITION, ROOM, BOARD, AND FEES

Tuition for all undergrads includes a high-powered laptop computer. The 2007-08 tuition for students majoring in arts and sciences and management is $629 per credit hour for freshmen and $653 per credit hour for sophomores. The tuition for juniors and seniors majoring in arts and sciences and management is $682 per credit hour. In architecture and design and engineering, tuition for freshmen and sophomores is $682 per credit hour; for juniors and seniors, it is $704 per credit hour. A normal course load is 12-17 credit hours per semester. The undergraduate registration fee is $115 each semester. International students on temporary visas must have sufficient funds to pay for an entire year of tuition, room and board, and books at the time of first registration. Additional fees for specific labs and studio courses vary.

Room costs vary by residence hall and occupancy rate (single, double, or multiple), but average $5,292 per year. Average board is $2,580, with a variety of meal plans available.

FINANCIAL AID

Approximately 70 percent of students receive some form of financial assistance, and the university awards nearly $32 million in scholarships, grants, loans, and work-study funds each academic year. The average annual financial aid package is $14,636. Many privately funded scholarships are awarded to qualified students, based on need and/or scholastic performance. Part-time employment is available at the university on a first-come, first-served basis for full-time students. Student loans are also available from a variety of sources – state, federal, and private. Prospective students are urged to contact the Office of Financial Aid for information on deadlines and requirements for eligibility (ltu.edu/financial_aid).

STUDENT ORGANIZATIONS AND ACTIVITIES

More than 50 student clubs and organizations, including fraternities, sororities, honor societies, and student chapters of professional groups, are active on campus and sponsor a variety of activities during the year. The Student Government sponsors and supports a variety of campus activities.

Recreational facilities include the Don Ridler Field House, which features a fitness track, a gymnasium, racquetball courts, a game room, saunas, and a weight and conditioning room. Intramural and club sports teams in hockey, volleyball, flag football, basketball, indoor soccer, softball, racquetball, billiards, tennis, curling, and table tennis are active throughout the academic year. The Lawrence Tech Blue Devils ice hockey team competes in the North Region of the American College Hockey Association.

ADMISSIONS PROCESS

A high school diploma or the equivalent is required of all students applying to baccalaureate or associate degree programs. Most baccalaureate applicants must have a minimum 2.5 overall GPA in academic subjects; architecture students must have a minimum 2.75 overall GPA. Applicants to associate degree programs are required to have a minimum 2.0 average in 4 academic areas (English, mathematics, social science, and natural science) combined. ACT or SAT results are required of all entering freshmen. An essay and a letter of recommendation from a mentor or high school teacher or counselor are required. Lawrence Tech's ACT code is 2020 and SAT is 1399. Required high school courses vary with the curriculum, and Lawrence Tech offers a number of basic studies courses designed to augment incoming students' backgrounds if deficiencies exist.

Programs start in August and January. An optional summer semester begins in May. Entry in the fall semester is advised but not required. Students must submit transcripts from all schools attended, along with a nonrefundable $30 application fee. To obtain a university catalog and an application form, students should contact:

Office of Admissions

Lawrence Technological University

21000 West Ten Mile Road

Southfield, MI 48075-1058

Telephone: 800-CALL-LTU

E-mail: admissions@ltu.edu

Website: http://ltu.edu

School Says . . .

LAWRENCE UNIVERSITY

AT A GLANCE

Lawrence University is an internationally recognized undergraduate institution consisting of a college of liberal arts and sciences and a conservatory of music. Our 1,400 students come from nearly every state and more than 50 countries to enjoy our unique blend of academic and extracurricular offerings. International students make up 11 percent of our student population, making us one of the nation's most internationally diverse colleges. While many colleges promise an abundance of great opportunities to study one-on-one with their professors, few (if any) can deliver on that promise like Lawrence University. By the time they graduate, nearly 90 percent of our students will have had at least one course—tutorial, independent study, studio classes, honors projects—where they were able to study individually under the direct guidance of a professor.

LOCATION AND ENVIRONMENT

Lawrence is proud to make its home in Appleton, a city of 70,000 people, located on the banks of the historic Fox River in northeast Wisconsin. The metropolitan area (pop.: 250,000) is not only one of the safest metro areas in the United States, but also frequently cited in national publications as one of the country's best places to live and work. Our 84-acre campus, adjacent to Appleton's thriving downtown, overlooks the northward-flowing Fox River. Appleton offers the cultural and commercial advantages (and airport) of a larger urban area with the recreational opportunities and convenience of a Midwestern town.

ACADEMIC PROGRAMS

Lawrence offers a number of meaningful differences that set it apart from other colleges: freshman studies, a nationally-renowned seminar that draws material from across the university's academic departments to develop your ability to think critically, argue civilly, and write confidently; individualized study, which gives students the flexibility and freedom to explore and combine their multiple interests; the honor code, which ensures academic integrity, promotes mutual trust and respect, and values cooperation and collaboration over competition in all aspects of campus life; and a world-class conservatory of music.

CAMPUS FACILITIES AND EQUIPMENT

Seeley G. Mudd Library, one of the top libraries among liberal arts colleges, has, among its hundreds of thousands of books, government documents, and periodical subscriptions, more than 20,000 recordings and videos along with thousands of musical scores. In addition to the online catalog, the library can access national computerized bibliographic databases. Science facilities include 23 general laboratories for student use; 25 special laboratories for research, including a laser physics lab; a graphics and computational physics lab; 4 environmentally controlled rooms; animal rooms for psychology and biology; a greenhouse; multiple electron microscopes; a variety of spectroscopic instruments (nuclear magnetic resonance, infrared, UV-visible, atomic absorbance); and an X-ray diffractometer. The Music-Drama Center and the Shattuck Hall of Music house private practice studios, classrooms, a recital hall, large and small ensemble rehearsal halls, a digital recording studio, performance facilities for the theater department, and WLFM, Lawrence's Internet-based radio station. Lawrence has 2 theaters: Stansbury, with a proscenium stage, seats 500 people; Cloak is an experimental theater, adaptable to arena or thrust-stage productions. The Memorial Chapel seats 1,250 people and is the primary venue for convocations, performances by Lawrence's large ensembles, and other public events and concerts. The Wriston Art Center offers a first-rate facility for the studio art and art history programs. It includes an outdoor amphitheater, 3 galleries, 2- and 3-dimensional art studios, and houses the university's outstanding permanent collection. The Buchanan Kiewit Recreation Center offers an indoor track; swimming pool; weight/exercise room; dance room; racquetball courts; gymnasium; and saunas. Alexander Gymnasium, Whiting Field, and the Banta Bowl (a 5,300-seat football stadium) house 23 varsity (NCAA Division III) and 4 club sports teams.

Lawrence offers the kind of 24-7 social life that only a fully residential community can. (Housing is required and guaranteed.) Nearly all of our students live on campus in one of our 7 residence halls or theme houses, apartments and small residences. Every day on campus, you will find countless concerts, recitals, theater performances, intercollegiate athletic competitions, poetry slams, artist exhibitions and lectures. More than 80 student clubs and organizations provide a wide variety of activities, ranging from performances by major music ensembles and an international film series to the annual Trivia Weekend (the longest-running and most notorious trivia contest in the country), crew on the Fox River, and winter camping along Lake Michigan.

TUITION, ROOM, BOARD, AND FEES

Tuition and fees $32,264; room and board: $6,957.

ADMISSIONS PROCESS

Whether you apply to our college of liberal arts and sciences or our conservatory of music (or both, as a double-degree candidate), the admission staff will consider the strength of your curriculum, academic performance (grades and rank, if applicable), recommendations, extracurricular activities, and standardized test results (if you choose to submit them; Lawrence does not require ACT or SAT results for admission). Additionally, music candidates are judged on musicianship, performance potential, recommendations of teachers, and general academic ability. To that end, all music applicants must perform an audition—either on campus, at one of our regional sites, or on a high-quality digital recording—as well as submit a music resume and music teacher's recommendation. Roughly half of Lawrence's students graduated in the top 10 percent of their high school class. A personal interview is not required, but a campus visit is strongly recommended. Lawrence accepts the Common Application. One early decision plan (deadline November 15, notification December 1) as well as a nonbinding early action application plan (deadline December 1, notification January 15) and a regular decision plan (deadline January 15, notification April 1) are available for high school seniors. International students should apply under the regular decision plan. Lawrence also encourages applications from transfer students.

LEWIS & CLARK COLLEGE

AT A GLANCE

On a stunning campus in one of the most exciting and progressive cities anywhere, the next generation of global thinkers gathers to discard conventional thinking, civic complacency, and outmoded preconceptions. Leaders, visionaries, and problem-solvers, we come together to explore new ways of knowing through classic liberal learning and innovative collaboration.

At Lewis & Clark College in Portland, Oregon, we welcome all who are alive to inquiry, open to diversity, and eager to shape the new global century. Through our undergraduate programs in the arts, humanities, and sciences, and through our graduate and professional studies in education, counseling, and law, we undertake original research, interdisciplinary studies, and community service. We push beyond what is known in order to discover something new every day.

Reflecting the college's national and global reach, approximately 81 percent of Lewis & Clark's 1,900 undergraduate students come from outside Oregon, representing nearly every state and 51 countries.

LOCATION AND ENVIRONMENT

Founded in 1867, Lewis & Clark College moved to its present location in Portland's southwest hills in 1942. The 137-acre campus sits on a wooded hilltop just 6 miles from Portland's exciting downtown, offering stunning views of snow-covered Mount Hood.

Portland is a very livable city with an excellent public transportation system that includes buses, light-rail, and the Portland Street Car. In addition, a free College shuttle runs frequently into the heart of the city and back to campus. The scenic Willamette River bisects Metropolitan Portland, which is home to approximately 2 million people. There are endless things to do in Portland: Park space occupying 10,477 acres of parks, 33 music groups, 35 theater and dance companies, 90 galleries and museums, and more than 1,000 restaurants. The city also offers professional baseball, hockey, lacrosse, and the NBA's Portland Trailblazers basketball team.

Just 50 miles east of campus is Mount Hood and its 10-month-a-year skiing and snow-boarding. The rugged Oregon coastline is just 90 miles to the west. Throughout the state lie innumerable hiking, climbing, and backpacking opportunities.

OFF-CAMPUS OPPORTUNITIES

Overseas and off-campus study programs have been a big part of Lewis & Clark for more than 40 years. Each year, about 300 students participate in 2 dozen programs abroad and in selected areas of the United States. During the next few years, programs will be offered in Australia, Chile, China, Cuba, Dominican Republic, Ecuador, England, France, Germany, Ghana, Greece, India, Ireland, Italy, Japan, Kenya/Tanzania, New York, New Zealand, Russia, Scotland, Senegal, Spain, and Washington, DC.

Whether their off-campus study is domestic or abroad, students earn credit (equivalent to a full semester or year) for their academic work. Depending on the specific program content, it is possible to earn General Education and/or major credit during these programs. Typically, more than 50 percent of students participate in one of these programs prior to graduating from Lewis & Clark. Students can use Lewis & Clark's financial aid and scholarships for assistance in these programs.

MAJORS AND DEGREES OFFERED

The college offers one degree: the bachelor of arts. Students have a wide selection of majors from which to choose: art, biochemistry and molecular biology, biology, chemistry, communication, computer science and mathematics, East Asian studies, economics (international, management, public policy, and theory), English, environmental studies, foreign languages, French, German, Hispanic studies, history, international affairs, mathematics, music, philosophy, physics, political science, psychology, religious studies, sociology/anthropology, and theater. Students may also design their own major, pursue a double major, or select from 25 minors. Pre-professional programs are available in dentistry, education, law, and medicine. Dual degree programs in engineering (3-2 or 4-2) are available in conjunction with Columbia University in New York, Washington University in St. Louis, the University of Southern California in Los Angeles, and the OGI School of Science & Engineering in Beaverton, Oregon. A dual degree, 4-1 B.A/ M.A.T program is available in conjunction with Lewis & Clark's Graduate School of Education and Counseling.

ACADEMIC PROGRAMS

A liberal arts education at Lewis & Clark connects classical learning with fresh inquiry and exciting research that pushes the frontiers of knowledge. Lewis & Clark considers the following elements essential to a liberal arts education: mastery of the fundamental techniques of intellectual inquiry: effective writing and speaking, active reading, and critical and imaginative thinking; exposure to the major assumptions, knowledge, and approaches in the fine arts, humanities, natural sciences and social sciences; critical understanding of important contemporary and historical issues; awareness of international and cross-cultural issues and gender relations; application of theory and knowledge to the search for informed, thoughtful and responsible solutions to important human problems.

The curriculum combines structure and freedom. Depth and breadth of subject matter are highly valued, but equally important are creativity and critical thinking. There are many opportunities for students to take their learning to a higher level, such as honors projects within academic departments, independent research, and internships.

Two 15-week semesters make up the academic year, and each semester students normally take 4 4-semester-hour courses, and one or more activity courses. The average student course load is 16 credits per semester. The requirement for graduation is 128 semester hours—approximately 8 classes each year.

CAMPUS FACILITIES AND EQUIPMENT

Located on Palatine Hill on a former estate, the Lewis & Clark campus offers students a campus of unmatched physical beauty, along with academic and residential buildings designed to support a rigorous academic environment and strong sense of community.

The academic buildings include: the Aubrey R. Watzek library, which is open 24 hours on weekdays during the school year and houses more than 710,000 items including books, documents, audiovisual materials, microforms, and periodicals. Through the Summit catalog, access to approximately 27 million items from 33 member institutions in the Pacific Northwest. Also houses the most extensive collection of printed materials known to exist on the Lewis and Clark Expedition. Evans Music Center, which includes a 410-seat recital hall equipped with an orchestra pit and stage elevator, 22 practice rooms, 43 pianos, 2 harpsichords, 4 pipe organs including an 85-rank Casavant pipe organ, a Baroque organ, Javanese gamelan, and an electronic music studio with CD production capability; Fir Acres Theatre, which houses a 225-seat Main Stage performance/teaching theater and a black-box experimental theater (also used as dance studio) along with a scene shop, costume room, green room and design lab; the Olin Center (physics and

The Princeton Review's Complete Book of Colleges

chemistry), the Biology-Psychology building, and BoDine (mathematical sciences), which all house well-equipped classrooms and extensive laboratory spaces for our natural sciences. Among our notable science facilities are a scanning electron microscope, a molecular modeling lab, a gas chromatograph/mass spectrometer, a high-pressure liquid chromatograph, 300 MHz FTNRM spectrometer, inert spectrophotometers, infrared spectrometers, observatory with Newtonian and solar telescopes, computer-enhanced optical microscope, a solid-state physics lab with variable temperature cryostat and superconducting magnet, a lab for studying the biomechanics of animal locomotion, an astrophysics lab and a lab for studying parallel computing. Nearby Tryon Creek State Park and the Columbia River Gorge are frequently used as laboratories for field courses in biology and geology.

Among other academic buildings are the Fields Center, which includes studio facilities for drawing, painting, sculpture, ceramics, computer graphics, graphic design, and photography; the Miller Center and Howard Hall (opened in 2005), are home to the humanities and social sciences with state-of-the-art classrooms, small auditoriums, and the Keck Interactive Language Lab.

Our computer facilities include several labs in academic buildings available for student use. More than 130 Mac, IBM, and compatible computers are available for students, along with peripherals such as color scanners, color printers, digital cameras and digital-video editing equipment. All residence halls have direct Internet access, and parts of the campus also have wireless network capability. We have recently increased our bandwidth to 150 Mbps (Megabits per second).

TUITION, ROOM, BOARD, AND FEES

In 2007-08, tuition and fees were $31,840 and room and board were $8,380. Students have several meal plan options. Books and miscellaneous expenses were approximately $1,900.

FINANCIAL AID

During the 2007-08 academic year approximately 75 percent of Lewis & Clark students received some form of financial assistance. Individual aid packages ranged from $1,000 to $40,554. Institutional, state, and federal resources including grants, loans and work-study may be part of an aid package. Eligibility for need-based funds is based primarily on an analysis of the income and asset information submitted on the Free Application for Federal Student Aid (FAFSA) and the College Board's CSS/Financial Aid PROFILE. Household size and the number of students in college (excluding parents) are also considered in the analysis. Students must submit the FAFSA and PROFILE by March 1 in order to get priority consideration for financial aid.

STUDENT ORGANIZATIONS AND ACTIVITIES

With more than 40 student organizations, there's never a lack of things to do at Lewis & Clark. Cultural events include lectures, symposia, art exhibits, plays, musical events, and dance performances. Athletics play a big role on campus, where 19 varsity teams, 8 club teams, and numerous intramural sports keep students physically active. Nature-lovers will enjoy the College Outdoors Program, which offers activities such as hiking, backpacking, rafting, skiing, and kayaking in the wilderness of the Pacific Northwest. There are also plenty of opportunities for volunteering in and around the Portland area.

Lewis & Clark is committed to residential education, to creating a community dedicated to the exploration of ideas, values, beliefs and backgrounds, to the discovery of lifelong friendships; and to collaboration, both formal and informal, with peers, faculty, and staff. There is no Greek system at Lewis & Clark.

About 67 percent of undergraduates live on campus in residence halls; most of our residential space is co-ed. Along with personal living space (usually shared by 2 to 4 students) are several community venues within the residence halls, including coffee houses, convenience stores, art centers, outdoor basketball courts, recreation and fitness centers, lounges, and game rooms.

ADMISSIONS PROCESS

Commitment to academic excellence and personal and intellectual growth is imperative for successful Lewis & Clark applicants. Lewis & Clark is very selective, and every part of the application matters: academic records, essays, involvement in activities at school and in the community, leadership, and the strength of recommendations. Students are encouraged to visit our campus. Interviews are available but not required. The best-prepared applicants will have had 4 years of English, 4 years of mathematics, 3 to 4 years of history or social sciences, 3 years of laboratory sciences, 2 to 3 years of a foreign language, and one year of fine arts. Required credentials include: an essay; an official transcript including senior grades from first semester; a counselor recommendation; and one academic teacher recommendation. Lewis & Clark requires the SAT or ACT, except if the student is applying via the Portfolio Path (see www.lclark.edu for details). Students apply using either the online or paper version of the Common Application. The $50 application fee is waived for students applying online. Keep in mind these deadlines: First-year applicants - November 1 for non-binding Early Action (notification, January 15) and February 1 for Regular Decision (notification, April 1). Transfer applicants are reviewed on a rolling basis.

School Says . . .

LIMESTONE COLLEGE

AT A GLANCE

Founded in 1845, Limestone is a fully accredited, private, coeducational liberal arts college. The college maintains a small student body and a well-qualified faculty in order to create an atmosphere in which each student develops intellectually, physically, and socially. The college endeavors to help students prepare for a satisfying, useful life through effective communication skills, responsible decision-making abilities, meaningful leisure-time activities, and lifelong aspirations. In addition to its programs on campus, Limestone offers several of its academic majors in an accelerated format called the Extended Campus.

Extracurricular activities play a vital part in the development of all students at Limestone College. Among these activities are intercollegiate athletics in baseball, basketball, cross-country, golf, lacrosse, soccer, softball, swimming, tennis, volleyball, and wrestling. Music and theater programs are also available.

The 115-acre Limestone campus is well laid out for pleasant college living. The classrooms, library, laboratories, auditorium, bookstore, post office, and administrative offices are housed in buildings that border the central and circular drives, making each easily accessible to the others. The back campus has a plaza of 4 dormitories, and a dining hall is located nearby. The Timken LYFE Center is a physical education complex that houses the gymnasium, and an AAU-size swimming pool. The Limestone Physical Education Center houses the athletic training education program, a fitness center, and a wrestling practice area. The college also has 8-lighted tennis courts, a baseball field, a softball field, a soccer/lacrosse field, and several practice fields.

LOCATION AND ENVIRONMENT

Limestone College is located in the Piedmont region of South Carolina in the city of Gaffney. Rich in culture and tradition, Gaffney, a city of 25,000 people, is a beautiful place, picturesque with its historic homes and large trees. Gaffney has numerous restaurants, grocery stores and discount shopping such as Prime Outlets, an outlet shopping mall with more than 80 stores.

Whereas the distractions associated with a large city are absent from daily life, the cultural programs and services offered in Charlotte, North Carolina, and Spartanburg/Greenville, South Carolina, are all within a 50-mile radius of the campus. Interstate 85 connects all to Gaffney.

MAJORS AND DEGREES OFFERED

Limestone College offers the bachelor of arts, bachelor of science, and bachelor of social work degrees with majors in art (concentrations in studio art, and graphic design), athletic training, biology, business administration (concentrations in accounting, computer science programming, computer science software applications, e-business, economics, general business, management, and marketing), chemistry, computer science (concentrations in computer and information systems security, internet management, information technology, and programming), criminal justice, elementary education, English, history, liberal studies, mathematics, music, physical education (concentrations in athletic training and fitness/wellness), pre-professional programs, psychology, social work, sports management, and theater. Majors approved for South Carolina teacher certification are elementary education, English education, mathematics education, music education, physical education, and secondary education.

The associate of arts degree is offered with majors in business administration, computer science, and liberal studies.

ACADEMIC PROGRAMS

The course of study leading to the BA, BS, BSW, or AA degree consists of 4 elements: requirements in communication and quantitative skills; a general liberal arts program, involving 5 different subject groups; courses in the major; and appropriate electives. The baccalaureate degree programs require the completion of a minimum of 123 semester hours. The associate degree programs require the completion of a minimum of 62 semester hours. Advanced placement and credit are given for scores of 3 or higher on the Advanced Placement examinations of the College Board.

An honors program involving special courses, seminars, and lectures is available for exceptional students. Admission to this program is contingent upon outstanding high school grades and scores on the SAT I of the College Board, the completion of a special application, and an interview. Almost 10 percent of all Limestone students are enrolled in this rigorous academic program.

A Program for Alternative Learning Styles (PALS) is available for qualified students with certified learning disabilities.

The Developmental Studies Program recognizes that some students have special needs in such areas as reading, writing, and mathematics. For this reason, a number of courses are offered to help students improve his/her basic skills.

CAMPUS FACILITIES AND EQUIPMENT

The Career Services Center staff provides direction in defining career goals and directing academic preparation toward those goals. The A. J. Eastwood Library houses more than 112,000 volumes. The library is accessible online at www.limestone.edu/lib.html. The Carroll Fine Arts Building houses a music technology lab, practice rooms, classrooms, and a formal recital hall. The computer labs at Limestone offer a wide array of the latest data processing and data communication technology. The Dobson Student Center houses the Academic Success Center, Health Center, and the Mail Center. It also has a game room, sitting areas with television and vending machines. Fullerton Auditorium, an acoustically excellent hall, with a seating capacity of 975, serves for drama and musical productions, and is one of the finest such facilities in the state of South Carolina.

The Academic Success Center offers tutorial services in all academic subjects, as well as specially trained tutors for writing and math.

Athletic teams consist of men's baseball, basketball, cross country, golf, lacrosse, soccer, swimming,

tennis, track & field, and wrestling, and women's basketball, cross country, golf, lacrosse, soccer, softball, swimming, tennis, track & field, and volleyball.

Athletic Facilities include the Saints Game Field, the Bob Prevatte Baseball Field, the Emmie Evans Rector Tennis, Pavilion, the softball field, 4 practice fields, the Timken Lyfe Center and the Limestone Physical Education Center. A registered nurse is available in the health center for all non-emergency situations. The school mail center offers convenience for students to receive letters and care packages from home and to mail packages from campus.

Residence halls are equipped with laundry facilities and vending machines. Each room provides a phone, cable, and Internet access.

The Sib Collins Counseling Center provides services to students struggling with academic, social, and psychological issues.

TUITION, ROOM, BOARD, AND FEES

The direct cost for a student at Limestone College for the 2008-09 school year is $23,700; the tuition is 17,300, and room and board costs are $6,400.

FINANCIAL AID

Limestone College, one of the least costly private colleges in South Carolina, endeavors to meet the financial need of any qualified student through scholarships, grants, loans, work-study opportunities, or a combination of these. Limestone offers merit scholarships to students with outstanding academic, leadership, or athletic abilities as well as to those who have exceptional talents in such areas as art, music, and theater.

More than 90 percent of Limestone College day students receive some type of financial aid. Because institutional financial aid is limited, students are urged to submit their applications for admission and financial aid as early as possible.

STUDENT ORGANIZATIONS AND ACTIVITIES

Alpha Chi Honor Society, Alpha Phi Sigma, Art League, Chi Alpha Sigma, Criminal Justice Student Org., Limestone College Research Group, Limestone College Outdoor Recreation and Education Club, Music Educators National Conf., Phi Alpha Theta, Student Organization of Social Workers, Students in Free Enterprise, Royal Flush Step Team, the *Calciid Annual,* the *Candelabra Literary Magazine,* Student Alumni Leadership Council, Student Government Association, brass ensemble, community chorus, gospel choir, jazz ensemble, Joyful Saints, saxophone quartet, show choir, wind ensemble, Baptist Student Union, Christian Education and Leadership Program, Fellowship of Christian Athletes, basketball, bowling, spades, table tennis, tennis, volleyball, Alcohol Awareness Week, Campus Cookouts, Christian Mission Trips, Christmas Luminaries, Comedians, Diversity Awareness Week, Earth Day Celebration, exam breaks, faculty/student athletic games, family weekend, hypnotist, homecoming activities, live bands, mid-term madness events, spirit week, theme dinners.

ADMISSIONS PROCESS

Limestone College does not discriminate on the basis of race, color, creed, national origin, financial need, or physical handicap. Each candidate for admission is evaluated as an individual. The college recommends that applicants have the following high school preparation: English, 4 units; social science, 3 units; mathematics, 3 units; and science, 2 units.

Applicants must submit an official transcript of the secondary school record, scores on the SAT I, and a nonrefundable $25 application fee. The application fee is waived if the student applies online at www.limestone.edu. Transfer applications are encouraged.

Completed application forms for admission and for financial aid should be sent to the Office of Admissions at Limestone College. It is recommended that applications be submitted by May 1. Any admission applications received after that date are considered on a space-available basis. The college practices a rolling admissions policy. As soon as the application, high school transcript, and test scores have been received, the applicant is notified of his or her status. Upon acceptance, a student is required to submit a $100 tuition deposit.

LOUISIANA STATE UNIVERSITY

AT A GLANCE

You know the questions that come with choosing a college. With so many decisions to make, so many options to consider, why not simplify things? Have it *all* at Louisiana State University.

LSU is home to a beautiful campus that showcases opportunities that can only be found at a comprehensive university. At LSU, you will find degree programs that are right for you as well as a friendly, supportive community. Students have so much to do on campus that you will forget how it feels to be bored. All you will know is that at LSU, you are getting a great education and having a great time.

You've worked hard to make it this far, and you deserve to have it all. You deserve LSU.

LOCATION AND ENVIRONMENT

LSU is located near the banks of the Mississippi River in Baton Rouge, the capital of Louisiana. Baton Rouge is a hotbed of financial, political, creative, and industrial activity. As an LSU student, you will find all the resources you need, plus the down-home friendliness you want. Because Baton Rouge is a medium-sized city, students have greater access to professionals in your field, which can help you reach your professional goals.

MAJORS AND DEGREES OFFERED

Majors and Concentrations at LSU

College of Agriculture

°Agricultural Business (BS)

- Animal, Dairy, and Poultry Sciences (BS)
- Environmental Management Systems (BS)
- Family, Child, and Consumer Sciences (BS)
- Food Science and Technology (BS)
- Forestry (Forest Management) (BSF)
- Human Resource Education and Workforce Development (BS)
- Natural Resource Ecology and Management (BS)
- Nutritional Sciences (BS)
- Plant and Soil Systems (BS)
- Textiles, Apparel, and Merchandising (BS)

College of Art and Design

- Architecture (BArch)
- Interior Design (BID)
- Landscape Architecture (BLA)
- Studio Art (BFA)

College of Arts and Sciences

- Anthropology (BA)
- Communication Disorders (BA)
- Communication Studies (BA)
- Economics (BA)
- English (BA)
- French (BA)
- General Studies (BGS)
- Geography (BA and BS)
- German (BA)
- History (BA)
- International Studies (BA)
- Latin (BA)
- Liberal Arts (BA)

- Mathematics (BS)
- Philosophy (BA)
- Political Science (BA)
- Psychology (BA and BS)
- Sociology (BA)
- Spanish (BA)
- Women's and Gender Studies (BA)

College of Basic Sciences

- Biochemistry (BS)
- Biological Sciences (BS)
- Chemistry (BS)
- Computer Science (BS)
- Geology (BSGeol)
- Microbiology (BS)
- Physics (BS)

E. J. Ourso College of Business

- Accounting (BS)
- Economics (BS)
- Finance (BS)
- General Business Administration (BS)
- Information Systems and Decision Sciences (BS)
- International Trade and Finance (BS)
- Management (BS)
- Marketing (BS)

College of Education

- Early Childhood Education: PK—3 Teacher Certification (BS)
- Elementary Grades Education (BS)
- Kinesiology (BS)
- Secondary Education (BS)

College of Engineering

- Biological Engineering (BSBE)
- Chemical Engineering (BSCheE)
- Civil Engineering (BSCE)
- Computer Engineering (BSEE)
- Construction Management (BSCM)
- Electrical Engineering (BSEE)
- Environmental Engineering (BSEnvE)
- Industrial Engineering (BSIE)
- Mechanical Engineering (BSME)
- Petroleum Engineering (BSPE)

Manship School of Mass Communication

- Mass Communication (BAMC)

College of Music and Dramatic Arts

- Music (BA)
- Music (BM)
- Music Education (BMEd)
- Theater (BA)

Pre-professional Programs (Nondegree)

- Allied Health Programs
- The final 2 to 3 years of these pre-professional programs are offered by the LSU Health Sciences Center and/or other medical schools. These are nondegree programs. If you do not see your area of interest listed above, contact a representative at the Office of Recruiting Services (225-578-6652 or recruiting@lsu.edu) or a counselor at the University College Center for Freshman Year (225-578-6822 or ucinfo@lsu.edu).

ACADEMIC PROGRAMS

Fore more information about academic programs, please contact the Office of Recruiting Services at 225-578-6652 or online at www.lsu.edu/recruiting.

TUITION, ROOM, BOARD, AND FEES

Estimated Yearly Expenses

Tuition and Fees for Louisiana Residents .... $4,617 per year

Tuition and Fees for Non-Louisiana Residents .... $12,917 per year

On-Campus Housing (Per Person) .... $3,700–$4,480 per year

Campus Dining (Cost varies with plans) .... $800–$2,788 per year

(must purchase plan for first year if you reside on campus)

Books and Supplies .... $900 per year

Tuition, fees, campus housing rental rates, and costs for dining plans may change without advance notice. Refer to www.lsu.edu/students/expenses for the most accurate information.

FINANCIAL AID

Scholarship programs are highly competitive and are awarded primarily on the basis of ACT/SAT scores and high school grade-point average.

The LSU Application for Undergraduate Admissions includes the application for scholarships.

The priority date for full consideration is November 15.

Application, and application fee ($40)

Official high school transcript

Standardized test scores

All required information must be submitted by November 15 to ensure full consideration.

Scholarships are awarded in the form of cash awards, full tuition, and nonresident fee exemptions, room and board scholarships, and employment opportunities to students meeting certain academic qualifications.

Some senior colleges and academic departments award scholarships. For more information, please contact the college or department you are interested in.

Financial Aid

3 categories: Grants, loans, and work-study

Help students cover school expenses; including tuition and fees, room and board, books, and supplies.

Apply by completing the FAFSA (Free Application for Federal Student Aid). Available January 1 each year.

www.fafsa.ed.gov

For more information on student aid and for a complete list of scholarships:

www.lsu.edu/financialaid

225-578-3103

financialaid@lsu.edu

STUDENT ORGANIZATIONS AND ACTIVITIES

LSU has a very spirited and involved student body from across the United States and the world. All students are encourage to become involved in the environment of the university—either through campus organizations, academic/cultural events, or athletic events. The university has over 350 registered student organizations on campus. Students are encouraged to make their college experience complete by joining a student organization that suits their needs.

For more information, please visit www.lsu.edu/csli or call 225-578-5160.

ADMISSIONS PROCESS

Minimum expectations for consideration for admission are 3.0 academic GPA° on 18 units of college-preparatory high school courses (see courses below) as outlined in the LSU Core and a 1030 SAT (Critical Reading and Math)/22 Composite ACT.

Freshman applicants are required to submit at least one writing assessment portion of the ACT and/or SAT. All test scores must be submitted officially from ACT and/or College Board (SAT).

Students must be eligible to enroll in university-level English and mathematics courses, as evidenced by a minimum SAT Critical Reading score of 450 (ACT English sub score of 18) and a minimum SAT Math score of 440 (ACT Math sub score of 18). Preference for admission to LSU will be given to those students whose credentials indicate the greatest promise of academic success and the greatest potential for contributing to the diverse missions of the university.

Admission decisions are based on both the strength of the applicant pool and the needs and capacity of the university. As an advisory, the fall entering class of 2006 had an average ACT of 25.2/1150 SAT, and over 75 percent had a high school GPA of at least 3.25/4.0.

College Preparatory Course Work for Admission to LSU: # Units High School Courses:

- Four English composition and literature: English I, II, III, and IV.
- Three Mathematics (4 units are strongly recommended.): One unit of Algebra I, 1 unit of Algebra II, and one additional unit consisting of courses such as geometry, trigonometry, advanced mathematics I or II, pre-calculus, calculus, Algebra III, probability and statistics, discrete mathematics, applied math III, integrated math III.
- Three natural sciences: One unit of biology, 1 unit of chemistry, and 1 unit of physics.
- Three social studies: One unit in American history; 1 unit in world history, world geography, or history of western civilization; and 1 unit consisting of civics, free enterprise, economics, or American government.
- Two foreign language: Two units in a single language.
- One math/science elective: One unit of math or natural science, such as geometry, trigonometry, advanced mathematics I or II, pre-calculus, calculus, Algebra III, probability and statistics, discrete mathematics, applied math III, integrated math III, earth science, environmental science, physical science, biology II, chemistry II, physics II, or physics for technology. LSU will accept, as 1 unit of the requirement, 2 units of agriscience for 1 unit of natural science.
- One-half unit in computer studies, or substitute one-half unit from any of the above.
- One and one-half additional courses: Two-and-one-half units from the categories above and/or certain courses in the visual and performing arts. Two units may be from advanced course work in the arts—e.g., fine arts survey, Art III, Art IV, advanced band, applied music, advanced chorus, Dance III, jazz ensemble, Music Theory II, advanced orchestra, wind ensemble, or Studio Piano III. LSU will accept, as 1 unit of this requirement, 2 units of basic performance courses in music, dance, theater, or studio art.

LOYOLA UNIVERSITY—CHICAGO

AT A GLANCE

Consistently ranked a top national university and best value by U.S. News and World Report, Loyola University Chicago is the largest Jesuit Catholic university in the United States, enrolling 15,545 students from 50 states and 82 countries, and offering 72 undergraduate majors, 77 graduate, 36 doctoral and three professional programs: law, medicine and nursing. Loyola prepares people to lead extraordinary lives by building upon its Jesuit tradition with: an innovative Core Curriculum, which equips students with lifelong skills for success; and a strong commitment to develop the whole person.

Committed to preparing people to lead extraordinary lives, Loyola University Chicago is the largest Jesuit Catholic university in the U.S., with 15,545 students. Loyola has three campuses in the Chicago area, and one in Rome, Italy.

LOCATION AND ENVIRONMENT

Loyola gives students the best of campus and city life with diverse living and learning opportunities in world-class Chicago. Located off North Michigan Avenue, Chicago's Magnificent Mile, Loyola's dynamic Water Tower Campus is home to the Schools of Business Administration, Communication, Continuing and Professional Studies, Education, Law and Social Work, and connects students to myriad internship, job and service opportunities. Loyola's Lake Shore Campus, home to the College of Arts and Sciences, the Graduate School and the Marcella Niehoff School of Nursing, is located on the picturesque shores of Lake Michigan and offers students a traditional residential campus. The Stritch School of Medicine is housed at the Loyola University Medical Center Campus in west suburban Maywood, Illinois. Students may also study abroad at Loyola's fourth campus, the John Felice Rome Center in Italy; or they may attend The Beijing Center for Chinese Studies or choose from one of 60 other study abroad programs in 29 countries.

MAJORS AND DEGREES OFFERED

Loyola students may choose from 72 undergraduate majors and 72 minors. Undergraduate degrees offered include the Bachelor of Arts (B.A.), B.A. Classics, Bachelor of Science (B.S.), Bachelor of Business Administration (B.B.A.), Bachelor of Science in Education (B.S.Ed.), Bachelor of Science in Nursing (B.S.N.) and the Bachelor of Social Work (B.S.W.) degrees.

The College of Arts and Sciences offers undergraduate majors in anthropology, biochemistry, bioinformatics, biology, Black world studies, chemistry, classical civilization, communications networks and security, computer science, criminal justice, ecology, economics, English, environmental sciences (chemistry), environmental studies, fine arts, forensic science, French, Greek (ancient), history, human services, information technology, international film and media studies, international studies, Italian, Latin, mathematics, mathematics and computer science, molecular biology, music, philosophy, philosophy: social justice, physics, physics and computer science, physics and engineering, political science, psychology, religious studies, sociology, sociology and anthropology, software development, Spanish, statistical science, theater, theology, theoretical physics and applied mathematics, and women's studies and gender studies (as a second major only).

The School of Business Administration offers majors in accounting, economics, entrepreneurship, finance, human resource management, information systems, international business, management, marketing, operations management and sport management.

The School of Communication offers majors in advertising and public relations, communication studies and journalism.

The School of Education offers majors in bilingual/bicultural education, elementary education, mathematics education, science education and special education, along with an expanded secondary education dual-degree program.

The Marcella Niehoff School of Nursing offers the Bachelor of Science in Nursing, a health systems management major and an accelerated B.S.N. program, which is available to students who have already completed a baccalaureate degree.

The School of Social Work offers an undergraduate major in social work and a combined bachelor's and master's degree in social work, which may be completed in five years.

ACADEMIC PROGRAMS

Loyola's Core Curriculum sets goals for undergraduate education that focus on the skills, values and knowledge that prepare students for the realities of living and working in today's world. The Core gives students who have not yet selected an academic major the opportunity to explore many courses while earning college credit before deciding on a field of study.

Exceptionally well-qualified students may apply to the Interdisciplinary Honors Program.

Other special academic opportunities include pre-professional programs for law and health professions; 18 five-year (bachelor's/master's) degree programs; 19 interdisciplinary programs; six-year early admission to Loyola's School of Law; early assurance to Loyola's Stritch School of Medicine; and the Loyola/Midwestern University Dual-Acceptance Pharmacy Program.

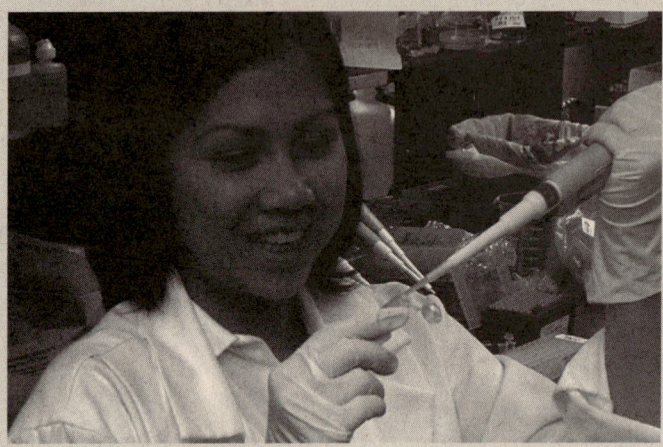

CAMPUS FACILITIES AND EQUIPMENT

The Information Commons, opened in Spring 2008, is a new four-story lakeside research facility that provides: individual and group study space for students; state-of-the-art technology with 222 computers; wireless Internet connections and a lakefront cafe. Loyola's Michael R. and Marilyn C. Quinlan Life Sciences Education and Research Center provides numerous opportunities for undergraduates to engage in the latest scientific research alongside their professors in modern labs for biology, bioinformatics, chemistry, ecology and other life sciences. The Loyola University Museum of Art (LUMA) showcases permanent and rotating exhibitions of professional and student work. The Sullivan Center for Student Services consolidates a dozen student services offices into one convenient location.

Recently opened residence halls include: seven-story Regis Hall, located at the Lake Shore Campus; and the 25-story Baumhart Hall and Terry Student Center at the Water Tower Campus, in the heart of Chicago's Magnificent Mile, which provides upper-class student housing and a fitness center, study lounge, food court, outdoor terrace and wireless access.

For more information about campus facilities, visit: www.luc.edu/undergrad/new.shtml#new2.

Tuition, Room, Board and Fees

Tuition for 2008-2009 entering students (per year): $28,700

Room and board (per year): Room and board cost is dependent on students' selection of residence hall and meal plan (average is $10,380).

Tuition part-time (per credit hour): $580

FINANCIAL AID

Loyola strives to meet the financial need of as many students as possible, offering more than $180 million in aid each year from numerous sources, including more than $45 million in Loyola-funded scholarships. Ninety-one percent of Loyola freshmen receive some form of aid, including university-funded scholarships and grants, federal and state grants, work-study and loans. Students are encouraged to file the Free Application for Federal Student Aid (FAFSA) by February 15 in order to meet Loyola's March 1 priority processing date.

In addition to the many scholarships awarded with admission, students may also explore more than 75 types of additional scholarships. For more information, visit: www.luc.edu/finaid/scholarships.

STUDENT ORGANIZATIONS AND ACTIVITIES

Loyola offers students the chance to develop leadership and social skills by participating in any of its more than 154 academic, athletic, cultural, hobby, media, political, social and spiritual student organizations.

ADMISSION PROCESS

Students seeking admission to Loyola are evaluated on their overall academic record, including ACT or SAT scores. The freshman class entering in Fall 2007 had middle 50% ACT score ranges between 23 and 28, middle 50% range on the SAT Verbal between 540 and 640, middle 50% range on the SAT Math between 520 and 640, and an average GPA of 3.54. Most Loyola students rank in the upper quarter of their graduating class, but consideration is given to students in the upper half.

Transfer students with 20 credit hours or more are evaluated on the basis of their college work only. The minimum acceptable GPA varies from 2.0 2.5, depending upon academic interest. Candidates must also be in good standing at the last college attended.

Loyola notifies applicants three to four weeks after the application, supporting credentials, secondary school counselor recommendation and $25 application fee are received. The application fee is waived for students who apply online.

Prospective students are encouraged to visit campus by arranging individual appointments and campus tours up to two weeks in advance. To arrange a visit, please view our online scheduler at: www.luc.edu/undergrad/schedule.shtml.

To obtain an application, get more information or arrange a visit, contact:

Undergraduate Admission Office

Loyola University Chicago

820 North Michigan Avenue

Chicago, IL 60611

Telephone: 312.915.6500 or 800.262.2373 (toll-free)

E-mail: admission@luc.edu

Website: www.luc.edu/undergrad

LOYOLA UNIVERSITY—NEW ORLEANS

AT A GLANCE

Loyola's unique combination of quality faculty and Academic Programs; an ideal size that fosters a positive learning environment and individual attention; and the centuries-old Jesuit tradition of educating the whole person distinguishes us from other institutions. Loyola provides big school experiences with small school relationships.

We consistently rank among the top regional colleges and universities in the South and one of the top 60 in the United States. Our students have been awarded British Marshall, Fulbright, Goldwater, Mellon, Mitchell, and Rhodes scholarships, and have been included as *USA Today's* top students.

Loyola is part of the Jesuit educational network, one of the largest systems in American higher education. This rich history and Jesuit influence dates back to the early eighteenth century when the Jesuits first arrived among the earliest settlers in New Orleans and Louisiana. The Jesuits are renowned for liberal arts; a value-centered education of the whole person; and a commitment to lifelong learning, social justice, and service.

Now more than ever, our students are offered an education like no other in the United States. They will become actively engaged in the creation of a strong future of both a city and a region. The opportunities for community service and other completely unique experiences cannot be duplicated at any national institution of higher learning.

Accredited by the AACSB and recognized by *U.S. News & World Report* as one of the "Best Business Programs" in the country, the College of Business is equally proud of its consistent wins at the American Marketing Association competitions.

Within the College of Social Sciences, the School of Mass Communication houses award-winning programs in public relations, journalism, and advertising. This includes the Loyola Bateman team which won the 2005 national competition sponsored by the Public Relations Student Society of America (PRSSA), the 2006 Pacemaker Award-winning *Maroon* student newspaper, and the advertising team.

The Loyola College of Law offers the Early Admission Program to Loyola students interested in attending law school. This program allows qualified Loyola undergraduates the opportunity to matriculate to the College of Law after their junior year.

LOCATION AND ENVIRONMENT

Located in New Orleans, Louisiana, our campuses sit conveniently on the route of the famous St. Charles Avenue streetcar in one of the most prestigious neighborhoods. We are directly across from Audubon Zoo and Audubon Park, home to a premier 18-hole public golf course and a walking, running and cycling trail. We are approximately a 20-minute drive away from downtown and the French Quarter.

OFF-CAMPUS OPPORTUNITIES

All venues for New Orleans jazz and for world-class cuisine are close at hand. Additionally, New Orleans offers a wide variety of educational and cultural attractions including the Aquarium of the Americas, the New Orleans Museum of Art, the National World War II Museum, and the historic French Quarter. New Orleans is home to New Orleans Saints football and New Orleans Hornets basketball, the annual Jazz and Heritage Festival, the Tennessee Williams Literary Festival, French Quarter Festival, Satchmo Summerfest, and the annual Mardi Gras celebration.

MAJORS AND DEGREES OFFERED

Loyola University New Orleans has 4 undergraduate colleges with 60 Academic Programs as well as a College of Law.

The Joseph A. Butt, S.J., College of Business is fully accredited through the AACSB and offers the bachelor of accountancy and the bachelor of business administration. Undergraduate majors include accounting, international business, management, economics, finance, marketing, and music industry studies. The college offers the master of business administration and the master of business administration/juris doctorate. The College of Business has a renowned history of preparing men and women to become the effective and socially responsible business and community leaders of tomorrow.

The college of Humanities and Natural Sciences serves as the anchor for all undergraduate study. Students in the College of Humanities and Natural Sciences have distinguished themselves in scholarship, research, and service. In recent years, students have been awarded prestigious Rhodes, British Marshall, Mellon, and Fulbright scholarships. The college confers the following degrees: bachelor of arts and bachelor of science. The majors include the following: biology, biology/pre-med, chemistry, chemistry/pre-med, chemistry/forensic science, English (literature or writing), history, mathematics, classical studies, French, Spanish, philosophy, physics, psychology, psychology/pre-med, religious studies/Christianity, and religious studies/world religions.

The College of Music and Fine Arts provides students with an opportunity to pursue both a strong foundation in the liberal arts and professional training in the performing and fine arts. The following undergraduate degrees are offered: bachelor of music, bachelor of arts in music, bachelor of music education, bachelor of music therapy, bachelor of arts and bachelor of fine Arts. The majors include the following: jazz studies, music industry studies (performance track), music industry studies (non-performance track), music education, music therapy, music with elective studies, instrumental/voice performance, theater arts, theater arts/communications, theater arts with a minor in business administration, visual arts, and graphic arts.

The College of Social Sciences houses the departments of counseling, criminal justice, sociology, and political science, and the School of Mass Communication and the School of Nursing. The college offers a bachelor of arts and a bachelor of criminal justice and bachelor of science in nursing (bachelor's degree for registered nurses returning to school) on the undergraduate level; on the graduate level it offers the master of criminal justice and master of science degrees in community counseling and nursing. The College of Law awards the juris doctorate.

ACADEMIC PROGRAMS

Loyola offers 60 programs of undergraduate study. Some of the most popular majors include communications, international business, pre-medicine, psychology, music, and political science. Once enrolled at Loyola, students are introduced to the common curriculum, designed to give them a well-rounded preparation in the liberal arts and sciences. Writing, literature, and mathematics requirements combine with philosophy, history, religious studies, and other courses to afford students the perspective, skills, and knowledge that can enable them to form their convictions, beliefs, and commitments in an atmosphere of study and reflection.

CAMPUS FACILITIES AND EQUIPMENT

Resources at Loyola include 17 computer labs with program specific software, e-mail and Ethernet connections throughout campus and in each residence hall room. There are up-to-date audio recording studios for music students, broadcast newsrooms and graphics labs for communications students, and a computer-aided software engineering instruction center for mathematics students.

Loyola's J. Edgar and Louise S. Monroe Library was recently recognized by Princeton Review's *The 361 Best Colleges* ranking sixth in the "Best College Library" category for 2007-2008. The library was also honored with the 2003 Excellence in Academic Libraries Award sponsored by the Association of College and Resource Libraries (ACRL).

The Loyola Recreational Sports Complex is open to all students and offers the following: 6-lane, Olympic-style swimming pool, whirlpool, elevated jogging track, indoor tennis courts, free weight and fitness rooms, racquetball courts, courts for basketball and volleyball, and aerobics and multi-purpose rooms.

TUITION, ROOM, BOARD, AND FEES

The 2007-2008 annual costs are as follows:

Tuition: $25,632

Fees: $1,086 resident, $1,026 commuter

Room: $5,428

Board: $3,600

FINANCIAL AID

Loyola offers need-based and non-need-based aid. To apply for need-based aid, students must file the FAFSA. In addition, Loyola offers both academic and talent-based scholarships to qualified students which typically range from $2,000 to $20,000 per year. About 84 percent of students enrolled receive some type of need-based aid. More than 450 academic and talent-based scholarships may be given each year for a typical freshman class size of 850. For best consideration for admission and scholarship, students should submit an application for admission by December 1 of their senior year.

STUDENT ORGANIZATIONS AND ACTIVITIES

Students can choose from more than 120 on-campus organizations. These include academic and professional societies, social and honorary fraternities and sororities, service organizations, special interest groups, sports clubs, and media organizations.

The Loyola Wolfpack intercollegiate athletic program competes in the NAIA Division I as a member of the Gulf Coast Athletic Conference (GCAC). Loyola has intercollegiate men's and women's basketball, cross-country, and track (distance); women's volleyball; and men's baseball. Students can participate in a host of intramural recreational sports or club sports, such as rugby, dance team, and lacrosse.

ADMISSIONS PROCESS

As a selective institution, Loyola considers all of the credentials presented in the admissions process. These credentials include the following: official high school transcript, ACT or SAT (writing scores required), counselor or teacher evaluation, essay and resume of activities including leadership roles and extracurricular activities. Admission decisions are made on a rolling basis. The priority deadline is December 1 of the senior year. Meeting this deadline promises the student best consideration for admission and scholarship.

LYNN UNIVERSITY

AT A GLANCE

Located on the southeast Florida coast near Miami and Palm Beach, Lynn University is in an area more commonly known as paradise. Our nearly 2,500 students come from more than 90 countries and almost every state, making Lynn one of the most international private universities in the southeast.

OFF-CAMPUS OPPORTUNITIES

The curriculum emphasizes study abroad opportunities that culminate with trips during the January term or school breaks. Lynn's career center helps you find internships and jobs with top companies and government organizations around the country and the world.

ACADEMIC PROGRAMS

Lynn University faculty members love teaching and challenge you to become active, intentional, and purposeful learners. We welcome students who have varying levels of academic abilities and learning styles and a strong desire to excel. Classes average 15 students. The innovative curriculum gives you a broad-based liberal arts background that stresses critical thinking and real-life applications. You'll develop technological, scientific, and quantitative literacy, as well as cross-cultural communication, sensitivity, and understanding of how to deal with change.

In addition to colleges of arts and sciences, business, communication, education and hospitality, Lynn has a school of aeronautics and conservatory of music.

CAMPUS FACILITIES AND EQUIPMENT

Classrooms have SMART boards and the entire campus is wireless. Besides 5 dormitories, a student center and library, the campus even includes 2 pools, athletic and fitness facilities and 220-seat concert hall, with a performing arts center scheduled to open in 2010.

TUITION, ROOM, BOARD, AND FEES

Tuition for 2008-09 is $27,800. Room and board varies depending on meal plan chosen.

ADMISSIONS PROCESS

Lynn has rolling admissions with a priority deadline of March 1. Lynn accepts the Common Application, or you can apply online at www.lynn.edu. Lynn University's school code for the SAT is 5437; the school code for the ACT is 0706.

MANCHESTER COLLEGE

AT A GLANCE

Manchester College is the perfect environment to study, explore new interests, make lifelong friends, and play hard. Often, faculty and staff join in, dashing out to the mall for a game of ultimate Frisbee, or inviting students into their homes for meals or discussions, or just sharing lunch. Students from all backgrounds come together, sharing their faith, their cultures, their interests, and their laughter. An international consciousness is enhanced by students from at least 23 countries. A rich multitude of faiths is represented and religious tolerance is embraced. Petersime Chapel sits at the center of campus, the home for many faith-based spirituality groups and gatherings. The campus also offers an Islamic center.

LOCATION AND ENVIRONMENT

A picturesque and vibrant downtown North Manchester is within walking distance, where students and visitors will find a major pharmacy, restaurants and sandwich shops, a florist, and other shops. The town of about 5,000 also has a supermarket and the usual fast-food chains. In a Victorian setting, the town feels comfortably like home.

When it is city life you crave, Fort Wayne, a vibrant city of more than 200,000 and the second-largest city in the state is just 35 miles away. There, students enjoy a world of cultural, recreational, interesting activities, as well as an international airport. Of course, Indianapolis and Chicago are only a couple of hours away.

ACADEMIC PROGRAMS

At Manchester College, we think a college education should help students learn to think deeply and critically across a wide range of fields to prepare them for the career they want. Manchester's foundation in the liberal arts prepares graduates for a lifetime of learning opportunities. With more than 55 areas of study, students can tailor their educations to their own needs and interests.

Bright students who are highly motivated may qualify for Fast Forward, combining online study with classroom schedules to complete a bachelor's degree in every major in 3 years.

A January session nestled between the fall and spring semesters lets students focus on specialty course work, take a class abroad with a full-time faculty member, participate in research and internships, or do pre-medical service in Nicaragua.

Manchester's honors program continues to increase in popularity, as do its applications for Fulbright scholarships. With 23 at last count, the college leads all colleges and universities in the state in Fulbrights per enrollment.

CAMPUS FACILITIES AND EQUIPMENT

Manchester College is a residential campus; about 85 percent of students live in the 5 residence halls. Some of the halls are co-ed, some are separated by floors or walls. One residence hall is women-only, by choice of its residents. Students will find computer labs in their residence halls and across campus, including wireless connections.

Meals and a coffee shop are in the new College Union, a hugely popular gathering spot for study, chat, partying, and browsing the campus store.

TUITION, ROOM, BOARD, AND FEES

2008-2009 Tuition and Fees

Tuition and fees: $22,720

Room and board: $8,100

Total direct costs: $30,820

Students also will have costs associated with books, travel, and personal expenses.

FINANCIAL AID

Manchester College students receive financial aid based on their high school academic records and family financial need. Merit-based aid is available based on academic ability; special abilities and interest in service, languages, the arts, and nonprofit management; and leadership and academic ability for students of color. Manchester has hundreds of scholarships that can be used with private and government grants and loans.

ADMISSIONS PROCESS

There is no application fee when applying to Manchester College online. You may apply upon completion of your junior year of high school; applications are considered on a rolling basis.

After completing the student portion of the application, please ask your guidance counselor to complete and send the High School Report and the Guidance Counselor Reference Form the Manchester College Office of Admissions.

Transfer students must submit a high school report and a Transfer Student Information Form (TSI). If you have been out of school more than 5 years, request at least one letter of reference from someone who can evaluate your potential for academic success in college.

MARLBORO COLLEGE

AT A GLANCE

Marlboro College is a liberal arts college unlike any other in the country. Known for the rigor of its academic program, the philosophy at Marlboro is that of self-governance and students who value learning for its own sake. The curriculum combines wide exploration in many courses within the first 2 years with more focused research and independent study in the second 2 years, culminating in a major body of work known as the Plan of Concentration. Marlboro College also offers numerous opportunities to study abroad through the World Studies Program and a variety of faculty-led trips to locations such as Cambodia, Cuba, Chile, and Vietnam.

LOCATION AND ENVIRONMENT

Nestled in the foothills of southern Vermont, Marlboro College offers the benefits of living in the country, with more urban areas nearby. The campus itself is situated on the side of Potash Hill in the town of Marlboro, Vermont. Most of the 350-acre campus is deliberately preserved as natural forest with trails and streams running through the property. Our location serves to both inspire and inform the unique nature of our undergraduate experience.

With the location of Brattleboro, a town of 12,000, just 10 miles away and Northampton, Massachusetts, 45 minutes away, Marlboro students have access to many resources, activities, and cultural life in central New England. Vans run from the college into Brattleboro multiple times a day and trips to Northeastern cities such as Boston, New York, and Montreal occur several weekends each semester.

OFF-CAMPUS OPPORTUNITIES

The World Studies Program (WSP) is an especially popular aspect of Marlboro's curriculum. Formed in 1984, the World Studies Program integrates the best traditions of liberal arts learning and international studies with a 6- to 8-month working internship in a foreign culture. Students use their experiences abroad in their Plan of Concentration work. Students in the WSP design and carry out their internships in numerous fields, including photojournalism, business, education, relief work, development, anthropology, and scientific research, to name just a few. Graduates of the program have been accepted to many prestigious graduate schools, and more than two-thirds of the program's graduates now work or study in international fields. The World Studies Program operates in conjunction with the School for International Training in Brattleboro, Vermont, about 15 miles away from Marlboro's campus.

MAJORS AND DEGREES OFFERED

Marlboro College provides a liberal arts education where students are able to work independently and at the same time closely with their teachers to achieve their academic goals. The college offers more than 30 degree fields in the arts, the humanities, the natural sciences and the social sciences. In developing their own courses of study, students are encouraged, though not required, to draw from more than one area and design an interdisciplinary Plan of Concentration. Degrees offered include bachelor of arts, bachelor of science and, through the world studies program, bachelor of arts or science in international studies.

American studies, anthropology, art history, Asian studies, astronomy, biochemistry, biology, ceramics, chemistry, classics, computer science, cultural history, dance, economics, environmental studies, film/video studies, foreign languages, history, literature, mathematics, music, painting, philosophy, photography, physics, political science, psychology, religion, sociology, theater, visual arts, world studies program, writing.

ACADEMIC PROGRAMS

The first 2 years at Marlboro are designed to give students the opportunity to study broadly in many different courses and areas. With the approval of their faculty advisor, students choose their own course schedules incorporating course work from all 4 areas of the curriculum: arts, humanities, sciences, and social sciences. In addition to this broad exploration of liberal arts courses, students must also pass the Clear Writing Requirement within the first 3 semesters. When a student moves from the sophomore to the junior year, it is referred to as going "on Plan."

The Plan of Concentration is what sets Marlboro's curriculum apart from other colleges and is Marlboro's alternative to traditional majors. Plans are often interdisciplinary and self-designed with faculty sponsors. In the junior year, Plan students spend time strengthening their knowledge in the particular areas of study on which they are focusing. In the senior year, students complete a great deal of independent study and research. Throughout the whole process of working on their Plan, students benefit from the close academic sponsorship they receive from faculty members. Ultimately, outside examiners from beyond the college are also included in the assessment of a student's "Plan of Concentration".

CAMPUS FACILITIES AND EQUIPMENT

Many of the campus buildings were originally farmhouses and barns renovated by the first students who attended Marlboro. These include Dalrymple Hall, which is the main classroom building; the dining hall; the admissions building; the health center; and Mather Hall, the administrative building. Over many years the college added more buildings, including residence halls, student cabins and cottages, the Whittemore Theater, the Rice-Aron Library, and a post-and-beam campus center, which the students and faculty built through a joint effort. Recently the college has winterized its auditorium and built an art gallery, an art studio, a photography darkroom, an integrated science lab, a DNA lab, and a new residence hall. The Serkin Center for the Performing Arts is an outstanding new facility providing performance and rehearsal space, in support of all performing arts programs. In 2007-08, a new Total Health Center will be under construction.

TUITION, ROOM, BOARD, AND FEES

For the 2007-2008 academic year, the fees are as follows:

Tuition: $29,700

Fees: $980

Room: $4,880

Board: $3,980

Total: $39,540

FINANCIAL AID

Students should not refrain from applying to Marlboro College because of perceived inability to meet costs. Marlboro College is committed to helping every student who qualifies for financial aid assemble the resources necessary to attend. More than 80 percent of all Marlboro students receive financial aid. Applicants should contact the Financial Aid Office directly to request a financial aid packet, which includes step-by-step instructions. The deadline for completing the Free Application for Federal Student Aid (FAFSA) is March 1. After that date, the college cannot promise a full financial aid package. The financial aid office can be reached at 802-258-9312 or finaid@marlboro.edu.

STUDENT ORGANIZATIONS AND ACTIVITIES

One particularly unique feature of Marlboro College is the college-wide Town Meeting held every 3 weeks during each semester. On these Wednesday afternoons, the whole college community, including students, faculty, and staff, gathers after lunch to discuss and debate any variety of college issues. Town Meeting's all-inclusive nature distinguishes it from more traditional student body governments.

Marlboro College is not the type of college that has a football team, unless you count a pick-up game of tag football. Instead, one of the most heavily used student activities is the Outdoor Program, OP for short. The OP offers a variety of activities from weeklong orientation trips for new students to weekend mini trips, to winter- and spring-break trips in tropical climates. Some of the popular activities have been rock climbing, hiking, rafting, kayaking, camping, yoga, intramural soccer, and ultimate Frisbee.

Marlboro College has no fraternities or sororities. Students enjoy a wide range of social, artistic, and cultural activities. A sampling of student activities in one semester would include performances by rock, folk, jazz, and ethnic bands; dances; lectures; poetry readings; recitals; plays; and concerts. Annual events that are considered traditions are Convocation, Fall and Spring Rites, Cabaret, Broomball Tournament, Community Dinners, Baccalaureate, and Commencement.

ADMISSIONS PROCESS

Marlboro College seeks students with intellectual promise, a high degree of motivation, self-discipline, creativity, social concern, and the ability and desire to contribute to the college community. The admissions committee—composed of students, admissions counselors and faculty members—assesses student preparedness and academic potential in the unique context of each applicant's personal experience without the confines of G.P.A or standardized test score minimums.

Students may apply to Marlboro under 3 different application plans.

Early Decision: Deadline-December 1; Notification-December 15.

Early Action: Deadline-February 1; Notification-February 15.

Regular Admission: Priority Deadline-March 1; Notification-April 1.

Please note that if you are applying for financial aid it is important to file the FAFSA no later than March 1.

In order to be considered for admission, please submit the following: a completed Common Application and Marlboro College Supplement with the "Why Marlboro?" personal statement, the $50 nonrefundable application fee, all high school and college transcript(s), SAT or ACT scores, academic writing sample, and 2 letters of recommendation (teacher and general).

MARQUETTE UNIVERSITY

Your world. Your talents. Your beliefs. Your passion. Your dreams. Discover Marquette University: a place where you'll find not just what you want to do, but who you want to become.

AT A GLANCE

Marquette is a Catholic, Jesuit university located in the heart of Milwaukee, Wisconsin. Our 12,000 undergraduate and graduate students come from all 50 states and 80 countries to create a vibrant, diverse, residential learning experience. They learn from professors who believe that there is such a thing as a student-centered university that conducts world-class research.

Our rigorous Academic Programs in 100 undergraduate majors are recognized for challenging students to grow intellectually, socially, and spiritually. You will take a demanding core curriculum grounded in the humanities, social sciences, and natural sciences. This liberal arts core, coupled with your academic major, will provide you with the balance of knowledge you'll need to succeed as a professional and as a person.

You will have instant access to top-notch professors who win international awards and grants, publish influential works, and conduct cutting-edge research. And you won't just hear about that research: You'll have the chance to jump into the lab and get your hands dirty. Working side by side with faculty mentors, you'll advance your field while getting unrivaled experience.

You will have a diverse experience. As one of approximately 8,000 undergraduates, you will meet students who look, think and act very much like you, and more who don't. More than 90 percent of freshmen live on campus, so you're sure to find your niche in the Marquette family.

Although the university recently celebrated its 125th anniversary, its tradition is more than 450 years old. As a Catholic and Jesuit university, Marquette University embraces service to others and the pursuit of knowledge for students of all religious backgrounds.

We'll ask you tough questions: "What do you believe in?" "What do you stand for?" "Why?" You will be challenged to lead a thoughtful and reflective life.

You will join a student population that is so active in the community it has been recognized by the Princeton Review's *Colleges with a Conscience: 81 Great Schools with Outstanding Community Involvement. U.S. News & World Report* also singled out Marquette as one of the best examples of service learning.

Marquette encourages students to find God in all things. Through retreats, religious services, prayers, and conversations within the university community, Marquette fosters an environment that nurtures spiritual growth for students of all faiths.

LOCATION AND ENVIRONMENT

With a metro population of more than 1.5 million, Milwaukee has all the bonuses you'd expect from a big city (like the arts, major-league sports, fantastic restaurants and shopping) with fewer of the hassles. And right at the heart of that city is Marquette University's approximately 80-acre campus, giving you easy access to all the city has to offer, including internships, service opportunities, and social activities. Your education at Marquette will extend from the classrooms on campus to the larger, more expansive classroom that is the city of Milwaukee. It's a place where you can connect what you're learning with what you can do with it.

OFF-CAMPUS OPPORTUNITIES

Your education doesn't need to be limited to Milwaukee. Each year, many Marquette students grab their passports, pack their bags, and head off to distant lands to study for a few weeks, a semester or an entire year. The experience is life changing. Marquette offers study-abroad and exchange program opportunities on every continent but Antarctica; and even if you want to go there, we can probably arrange something for you.

If you prefer to stay in the States, Marquette University's Les Aspin Center for Government is one of the top legislative internship programs in Washington, DC. For a semester or a summer, you can live, learn, and work on Capitol Hill. Take an active role in the legislative process while you work as an intern or aide in the House of Representatives, the Senate, and various federal agencies. You'll also take special courses and meet with government officials and dignitaries. And you'll be able to get well-connected in a city where connections are everything.

MAJORS AND DEGREES OFFERED

Marquette University is classified by the Carnegie Foundation as a research university with high research activity, offering a wide variety of bachelor's, master's, doctoral, and professional degrees. Marquette offers rigorous Academic Programs in 100 undergraduate majors and excellent advanced education in 36 master's degree programs, 16 doctoral programs, 10 certificates, and 8 joint master's programs. Marquette is also home to the state's only School of Dentistry and a Law School with a reputation as a forum for public policy debate.

U.S. News & World Report ranks Marquette 81st among the nation's top 100 universities in the 2007 edition of *America's Best Colleges* and highlights the programs in dispute resolution, biomedical engineering and education. *BusinessWeek* ranks the College of Business Administration among the top 50 undergraduate business schools in the nation.

ACADEMIC PROGRAMS

At the heart of whichever academic program you choose at Marquette, you'll take courses in 8 knowledge areas designed to teach you how to examine, engage, and evaluate the world: rhetoric, mathematical reasoning, individual and social behavior, diverse cultures, literature, history of cultures and societies, science and nature, human nature and ethics, and theology. These courses will teach you how to understand and to be understood, to act responsibly and to think for yourself. These courses make up the core of your studies, and they add considerable value to your major, whether you're studying philosophy or electrical engineering (or both).

Marquette University is a direct-entry university, allowing you to begin studying your major right away. Because you can deepen your interest, knowledge and expertise early, you begin practicing what you've learned through internships both in and beyond Milwaukee. If you are undecided about a major, your adviser at Marquette can help you find the right fit for your passions and abilities.

CAMPUS FACILITIES AND EQUIPMENT

More than 90 percent of Marquette's freshmen and sophomores live on campus in 8 residence halls. While some juniors and seniors live in the residence halls, most live off-campus in university-owned or independent apartments and houses. The high concentration of residential students lends Marquette a vitality not often found in urban universities. A new library and information commons provides students a place to study individually or in groups. The only thing wired about the library is the coffee shop; students have wireless access throughout the building. When students aren't doing their research, you might find them at one of the 2 (always busy) recreation centers.

TUITION, ROOM, BOARD, AND FEES

For the 2008-2009 academic year, full-time tuition will be $27,720. Room and board averages about $9,200 (rates vary by location and meal plan).

FINANCIAL AID

We recognize that Marquette University is a great place—we also know that private school tuition can be rather expensive. That's why Marquette University offers a variety of partial to full-tuition, merit-based scholarships. To apply for need-based financial aid, Marquette requests that you file only the Free Application for Federal Student Aid (FAFSA). Financial need that is demonstrated on this form determines our ability to award federal, state, and university-funded grants and loans, as well as some forms of student employment.

STUDENT ORGANIZATIONS AND ACTIVITIES

With about 230 student organizations vying for your time, you won't be bored at Marquette. And because most of our students spend their weekends on campus, there's plenty to do here and around the city. Our students don't hesitate to get out into the community, and 90 percent of undergraduates participate in service through a wide range of programs, student organizations, service-learning classes, and one-day projects. Sports fans will want to note that Marquette belongs to the NCAA Division I Big East Conference. If you're more into club and recreational sports, we offer 22 co-ed, men's, or women's clubs.

ADMISSIONS PROCESS

For all of its Academic Programs, Marquette University has a priority admission deadline of December 1 (postmark date). Applications postmarked after December 1 will be considered on a space-available basis for admission and scholarship. Admission decisions are based on a thorough review of course selection, academic performance (grade point average), class rank (when applicable), ACT and/or SAT, recommendations, your essay, and extracurricular activities. Visit Marquette's website at www.marquette.edu/explore for more information about deadlines and requirements.

School Says . . .

MARYMOUNT UNIVERSITY

AT A GLANCE

Marymount is a comprehensive Catholic university offering undergraduate, graduate, and certificate programs through 4 schools: Arts and Sciences, Business Administration, Education and Human Services, and Health Professions. The university is located in Arlington, Virginia, just across the Potomac River from the nation's capital.

The university's undergraduate programs combine a strong liberal arts foundation with solid career preparation. Small classes and professors who take a personal interest in student success provide a supportive academic environment. The selective honors program draws on all facets of the curriculum to offer highly motivated students extra opportunities for academic enrichment.

Marymount students enjoy the benefits of the many educational and cultural resources of Washington, DC. Distinguished speakers of national and international stature are frequent visitors to campus; recent Marymount guests have included Nobel Laureate Desmond Tutu, General Colin L. Powell (USA, retired), and fashion designer Michael Kors. Required internships provide invaluable hands-on experience in exciting locations in and around Washington, DC, including Capitol Hill, the National Institutes of Health, the Smithsonian museums, and international businesses. Study abroad programs offer students the chance to live, study, and complete an internship in another country.

Marymount's vibrant campus offers something for everyone: athletics, student government, Campus Ministry, volunteer service programs, and more than 30 clubs address diverse interests and provide opportunities for involvement. An NCAA Division III school, Marymount fields men's and women's basketball, cross-country, lacrosse, soccer, and swimming, plus men's golf and women's volleyball.

As a Catholic university, Marymount is a community where people of all faiths and cultures are welcome. The student body represents more than 40 states and 70 countries, bringing a wide array of experiences and perspectives that enrich the learning experience.

Visit Marymount and see for yourself all that the university has to offer! A student ambassador will give you a campus tour and answer questions about everything from academics and the social scene to cafeteria food. An admissions counselor will provide details on the admissions process, financial aid and scholarship opportunities, and academic requirements. You can also arrange to talk with faculty or coaches.

To learn more about Marymount University, call 800-548-7638; e-mail admissions@marymount.edu, or visit us online at www.marymount.edu.

LOCATION AND ENVIRONMENT

Marymount's Main Campus and Ballston Center are located in Arlington, Virginia, just minutes from Washington, DC. The public Metrorail system connects the university with the entire metropolitan Washington area. The university also maintains a free shuttle service that connects the Main Campus, Ballston Center, and Ballston MU-Metro station. Students have easy access to national landmarks, cultural sites, restaurants, and shopping. Marymount's Reston Center opened in spring 2007 and is located in western Fairfax County. The Reston Center is an adult education center that offers programs in business, education, and nursing.

OFF-CAMPUS OPPORTUNITIES

University faculty and students take full advantage of the resources in and around the nation's capital. Popular internship sites include Congressional offices, the Smithsonian museums, the White House, major media outlets, international businesses, and prestigious health care institutions. Students also have access to incredible research facilities, including the Library of Congress and the National Institutes of Health. During your Marymount years, you'll have the opportunity to fully experience Washington, DC, and many of the activities are free! Sit in on a Congressional hearing, attend the National Christmas Tree Lighting, enjoy "Screen on the Green" on the National Mall in summer, or view the latest exhibit at the National Gallery of Art. Culture, history, world-class museums, shopping, restaurants, theater, and music are all just across the Potomac River from Marymount.

MAJORS AND DEGREES OFFERED

The university offers a strong liberal arts education combined with solid career preparation. The following is a listing of Marymount's undergraduate majors and degree programs:

Art (BA): art management, pre-art therapy; biology (BS): general biology, molecular and cellular biology, pre-medicine; business administration (BBA, BBA/MBA): accounting, business law and paralegal studies, finance, general business, international business, management, marketing; communications (BA); criminal justice (BA); criminal justice (BS): forensic science; economics in society (BA); English (BA): dramatic arts, literature, writing; fashion design (BA); fashion merchandising (BA); graphic design (BA); health sciences (BS, BS/MS): health promotion, pre-physical therapy; history (BA); information technology (BS): computer science, forensic computing, information systems; interior design (BA); liberal studies (BA); Mathematics (BS); nursing (BSN); philosophy (BA); politics (BA); psychology (BA); sociology (BA); theology and religious studies (BA).

Pre-professional studies: pre-law, pre-medicine, pre-physical therapy.

Teaching licensure programs (art education, English as a second language, learning disabilities, secondary education, mathematics).

ACADEMIC PROGRAMS

Undergraduates can choose from such diverse fields as business, education, the arts and sciences, psychology, technology, and the health professions.

All Marymount undergraduate students complete an internship in their major. Other academic initiatives include Study Abroad programs and original undergraduate research conducted under the direction of faculty advisors. The university's selective honors program offers highly motivated students extra opportunities for academic enrichment. Benefits include substantial scholarship support, one-one-faculty mentoring, and special seminar and field-trip opportunities.

Marymount is dedicated to educating the whole person   to helping students develop every aspect of their potential. The college years are years of transformation. They are a time to explore interests and to grow in knowledge and understanding. The university's emphasis on ethics across the curriculum and throughout campus life helps students further develop critical thinking and ethical decision-making skills.

CAMPUS FACILITIES AND EQUIPMENT

Marymount University has 2 locations in Arlington, Virginia—the Main Campus and the Ballston Center. Marymount's Reston Center located in western Fairfax County focuses on meeting the educational needs of adult learners. The Main Campus consists of the Main House, academic buildings, residence halls, the Emerson G. Reinsch Library, and the Lee University Center. The Main House with its stately white columns is the signature symbol of Marymount University. This beautiful Georgian structure is where Marymount hosts programs honoring outstanding students and faculty, special alumni events, and receptions for distinguished friends and visitors. The Lee University Center serves as the hub of campus life. The Center is home to the Verizon Sports Arena and also houses Bernie's Café, the bookstore, pool, recreational gym, fitness center, and meeting rooms and lounges.

Academic facilities on the Main Campus include computer labs and wireless access areas, science labs, and studios for fine and graphic arts, fashion design, and interior design. The Reinsch Library provides print, electronic, and audiovisual material to supplement Marymount's curriculum as well as computers, video viewing stations, and study rooms. The Barry Art Gallery is also located in the Reinsch Library and features a variety of exhibitions throughout the year.

Marymount's Ballston Center, located in the Ballston professional district, is home to Marymount's School of Business Administration and the Department of Physical Therapy. It is just minutes from the Main Campus and students travel to and from both locations on free Marymount shuttles. The Ballston Center houses classrooms, seminar rooms, computer labs, physical therapy labs, the Truland Auditorium, the Electronic Learning Center, and the recently opened Verizon Information Security Lab. This state-of-the-art lab provides students with hands-on experience to prepare them for current and future cybersecurity challenges.

The Reston Center, an adult education center located in northern Virginia's thriving business and technology region, has 8 classrooms, including 2 executive conference/seminar rooms, a computer lab, student lounge, and administrative offices.

TUITION, ROOM, BOARD, AND FEES

The undergraduate tuition for 2008-09 is $21,300 per academic year; room and board is $9,190 per academic year for double occupancy there is an additional fee of $1,750 per academic year for single occupancy, subject to availability. Other mandatory fees include a one-time new student fee of $175 (first college freshmen); a student activity fee of $60 per academic year; and a technology fee of $168 per academic year.

FINANCIAL AID

Marymount has an extensive scholarship and grant program and participates in all federal and state aid programs. To be considered for aid, students must file the Free Application for Federal Student Aid (FAFSA) with the College Scholarship Service. There are 3 categories of scholarships offered by Marymount University: Academic/Service Scholarships, awarded on the basis of academic and/or service performance; Need-based Scholarships; and Other Scholarships which have variable eligibility criteria. All scholarships are designed for full-time, first-degree, or transfer undergraduates and can be applied to undergraduate tuition only, unless otherwise specified. In fall 2007, 77 percent of full-time degree-seeking undergraduates received financial assistance.

STUDENT ORGANIZATIONS AND ACTIVITIES

Athletics, student government, volunteer opportunities, and lots of campus activities mean there's always plenty to do at Marymount. More than 30 clubs and organizations are active on campus. An NCAA Division III institution, Marymount fields men's and women's teams in basketball, lacrosse, soccer, swimming, and cross country, as well as women's volleyball and men's golf. Intramural sports are also popular, including extreme Frisbee!

The Activities Programming Board, composed of Marymount students and staff, plans and implements ongoing events such as comedy nights, movies, theme parties, dances, music concerts, coffee houses, and trips to off-campus events. Major annual events that Marymount students plan, participate in, and enjoy include SpringFest, a week-long celebration of the arts; HalloweenFest, a trick-or-treat extravaganza for disadvantaged children; and the Special Olympics Basketball Tournament, a community outreach program organized and staffed by Marymount volunteers.

ADMISSIONS PROCESS

The Admissions team reviews the strength of an applicant's academic record, national test scores, breadth of academic preparation, and letters of recommendation. Applicants to the freshman class are considered if a student's high school grade point average in academic courses is 2.5 or better on a 4.0 scale; the combined SAT score is within 100 points of the national average or better; and the student's academic preparation, recommendations, and character indicate that he or she is qualified to undertake Marymount programs. It is recommended that students have at least 4 years of English; 3 years of a foreign language, mathematics, and the social sciences; and 2 years of science. A campus interview is not required but is strongly recommended. It gives students a chance to see if Marymount would be a good fit. The university holds Campus Visit Days in the fall and spring. Visitors are welcome at any time, and appointments with Admissions staff may be made in advance.

High school students seeking admission are advised to apply early during their senior year. They should submit an application (which can be completed online), a nonrefundable fee of $40, a high school transcript, SAT or ACT scores, evidence of expected graduation from an accredited high school, and a recommendation from a high school counselor or an appropriate school official. Those who have attended another college or university must also submit transcripts of college-level study and a recommendation from the Dean of Students at the previous institution. The university has a rolling admission policy and notifies applicants soon after the application process is completed and a decision on admission has been made.

MASSACHUSETTS COLLEGE OF PHARMACY AND HEALTH SCIENCES

AT A GLANCE

Exciting health care careers start at Massachusetts College of Pharmacy and Health Sciences (MCPHS).

We know making a commitment to attend a specialized college isn't an easy one, but it will be a rewarding one. At MCPHS we'll provide you with the education needed to succeed in an exciting and fulfilling career in health care. Our graduates have gone on to become outstanding leaders in their respective fields.

At MCPHS, we embrace a core set of values that reflect a strong commitment to preparing competent, caring, ethical health care professionals for tomorrow's health care world. When you attend MCPHS, you'll gain access to renowned health care institutions, and educators and peers who share the same interests and goals. Plus, we offer a close-knit academic community with a world of resources at our doorstep. Visit www.mcphs.edu to find out more about the benefits of being an MCPHS student.

Founded in 1823, Massachusetts College of Pharmacy and Health Sciences is a private, coeducational college offering graduate, professional, and undergraduate degrees in the health sciences. With campuses in Boston and Worcester, Massachusetts and Manchester, New Hampshire, the college enrolls approximately 2,900 students, who are drawn from 40 states and 34 foreign countries, and employs over 300 faculty and staff. Professional or undergraduate degrees are offered in Pharmacy, Nursing, Physician Assistant Studies, Dental Hygiene, Radiologic Sciences, Health Psychology, Chemistry, and Premedical and Health Studies. Graduate programs are offered in Drug Regulatory Affairs and Health Policy, Drug Discovery and Development, Pharmaceutical Sciences, Medicinal Chemistry, and Pharmacology.

MCPHS is the oldest institution of higher education in the City of Boston; its pharmacy program is the second oldest in the United States and the largest in the world.

LOCATION AND ENVIRONMENT

Student Life

Enjoy the exciting life of a college student in Boston, Worcester, or Manchester! All three campuses are conveniently located near numerous recreational, cultural, and nightlife activities—making our campuses a hub for academic and social opportunities.

Access to Renowned Medical Centers

Our three campuses are affiliated with renowned hospitals, research centers, and medical centers. From Brigham and Woman's Hospital in Boston to St. Vincent's Hospital in Worcester to Concord Hospital in Concord, New Hampshire, our students benefit from hands-on experiences that prepare them for rewarding careers in health care.

MAJORS AND DEGREES OFFERED

Alphabetical Listing of Programs by Degree Level:

BS in Chemistry

BS in Dental Hygiene

The Accelerated 33-Month Bachelor of Science in Dental Hygiene Curriculum

Postbaccalaureate Certificate in Dental Hygiene

The On-Campus Bachelor of Science in Dental Hygiene Degree Completion Program

The Online Bachelor of Science in Dental Hygiene Degree Completion Program

BS in Environmental Science

BS in Health Psychology

BS in Health Sciences

BS in Nursing

BS in Pharmaceutical Marketing and Management

BS in Pharmaceutical Sciences

BS in Premedical and Health Studies

BS in Premedical and Health Studies/Doctor of Optometry (Dual-Degree Program)

BS in Premedical and Health Studies/Doctorate in Osteopathic Medicine (professional pathway)

BS in Radiologic Sciences

Postbaccalaureate Bachelor of Science Degree in Radiologic Sciences

Master's Programs:

MS in Drug Discovery and Development

MS in Drug Regulatory Affairs and Health Policy

MS in Pharmacy Systems Administration

MPAS in Physician Assistant Studies—Boston Campus

MPAS in Physician Assistant Studies—Manchester Campus

MRAS in Radiologist Assistant Studies

Master's and PhD Programs:

MS, PhD in Analytical Medicinal Chemistry

MS, PhD in Organic/ Medicinal Chemistry

MS, PhD in Pharmaceutics/Industrial Pharmacy

MS, PhD in Pharmacology

Doctor of Pharmacy—Boston

Doctor of Pharmacy—Worcester

Doctor of Pharmacy—Manchester Satellite

Nontraditional PharmD Pathway

Certificate and Postbaccalaureate Programs:

Certificate Program in Medical Imaging

Postbaccalaureate Certificate Program in Dental Hygiene

Postbaccalaureate Certificate Program in Magnetic Resonance Imaging (MRI)

Professional Experience Program

Residencies

CAMPUS FACILITIES AND EQUIPMENT

The faculty and staff at MCPHS campuses are leaders in their fields and are actively involved in the latest research and professional community services. They utilize cutting-edge technology and research, giving students a competitive advantage in their specialized fields. In addition, with the low student to faculty ratio at MCPHS, students have the opportunity to work closely with faculty and clinical experts at renowned health care institutions such as Brigham and Women's Hospital, St. Vincent's Hospital, and New England Medical Center.

MCPHS students truly benefit from hands-on learning at the college's state-of-the-art facilities. The college recently completed major renovations at their Worcester and Boston campuses, including academic living and learning centers, topnotch new clinics, laboratories, and classrooms for students in dental hygiene, nursing, physician assistant studies, and radiologic sciences. In addition, a new library and laboratories for pharmacy opened last year.

TUITION, ROOM, BOARD, AND FEES

Visit www.mcphs.edu/financial/index.html for up-to-date Financial Aid information.

STUDENT ORGANIZATIONS AND ACTIVITIES

MCPHS offers a number of organizations, activities and fraternities for students. Please visit www.mcphs.edu/studentLife/studentActivities/clubOrg.html for more details.

ADMISSIONS PROCESS

If you are interested in learning more about MCPHS, we recommend that you visit the campus and attend one of our information sessions, open houses, off-campus events, or other special events. In addition, you can preview our campus visitation schedule, or find out about our daily information sessions, campus tours, or individual appointments by viewing our Visiting MCPHS page and/or Upcoming Events page at www.mcphs.edu.

Mailing Instructions

Send your paper application and other documents to the appropriate address below:

Boston Campus

Massachusetts College of Pharmacy & Health Sciences

Office of Admission

179 Longwood Avenue

Boston, MA 02115

Tel: 617-732-2850

Fax: 617-732-2118

Worcester Campus (Including the Manchester Satellite PharmD program)

Massachusetts College of Pharmacy & Health Sciences

Office of Admission

19 Foster Street

Worcester, MA 01608

Tel: 508-890-8855

Fax: 508-890-7987

Manchester Campus (Manchester Physician Assistant program only)

Massachusetts College of Pharmacy & Health Sciences

Office of Admission

1260 Elm Street

Manchester, NH 03101

Tel: 603-314-1701

Fax: 603-314-0213

MCGILL UNIVERSITY

AT A GLANCE

Founded in 1821 with a bequest by Montreal merchant James McGill, McGill University has earned an international reputation for scholarly achievement and scientific discovery. The only Canadian university ranked in the top 25 universities in the world by the *Times Higher Education Supplement* for 3 years running, McGill was also picked as the top medical-doctoral school in the country by *Maclean's* magazine in 2007.

Innovative research programs and cutting-edge facilities attract internationally respected faculty and the best students, who have the highest average entering grade of any university in Canada. With a reputation built on teaching and research excellence, McGill offers its 33,000 students unparalleled opportunities to enrich their educational experience through hands-on research opportunities, international exchanges, internships, field-study, and study-abroad programs.

McGill's 21 faculties and professional schools offer degrees in more than 300 fields of study. McGill offers a full range of bachelor's, master's, and doctoral programs as well as professional degrees in law, dentistry, business, and medicine. The world-renowned Faculty of Medicine has 4 affiliated teaching hospitals and graduates more than 1,000 health care professionals each year. With almost 20 percent of its students coming from 150 countries around the globe, McGill has the most internationally diverse student body of any medical-doctoral university in Canada. The ability to balance academic excellence with extracurricular activities is another hallmark of students at McGill. In addition to a rich athletic tradition that includes many Olympians, thousands of McGill students participate in the hundreds of clubs, associations and community groups that enrich Montreal and contribute to a vibrant campus life.

Our website, www.mcgill.ca, provides an excellent introduction to McGill, including descriptions of Academic Programs and links to major publications, resources and events. An Open House for prospective students is held annually, and our Welcome Centre arranges walking tours and the student-for-a-day program, information about accommodation close to campus and much more in the way of support for prospective students and their families. For information on applying to McGill University, go to www.mcgill.ca/applying .

LOCATION AND ENVIRONMENT

Lively and sophisticated, yet safe and affordable, the bilingual and multicultural city of Montreal boasts 4 universities and one of the highest number of university students per capita in North America. McGill's main campus, a mosaic of heritage and modern buildings laid out around an oasis of green space, is set in the heart of Montreal's vibrant downtown core. A short drive west of downtown, the Macdonald campus occupies 650 hectares of woods and waterfront property, providing unique opportunities for fieldwork and research activities.

CAMPUS FACILITIES AND EQUIPMENT

McGill has 13 branch libraries and special collections housing more than 6 million volumes, about a million e-books, more than 40,000 electronic journals and hundreds of databases for different disciplines. The McLennan-Redpath Library Building complex includes provisions of high-tech, high-touch computer labs, group study rooms available to students on demand, a variety of individual study spaces, an innovative e-classroom, and informal discussion areas.

Advanced high-speed data networks, both wired and wireless, are available to students, staff and faculty on both campuses.

TUITION, ROOM, BOARD, AND FEES

All dollar figures quoted are in Canadian funds. Costs are approximate, subject to change and based on a normal course load (30 credits) for the full academic year (fall and winter terms) in 2007-2008.

Students from the province of Quebec (off-campus/on-campus)

Quebec tuition fees: $1,700/$1,700

Ancillary fees: $1,200-$1,600/$1,200-$1,600

Books and supplies: $1,000/$1,000

Lodging (8 months): $4,400/$8,800-$11,800

Food (8 months): $2,400/-included above

Other expenses: $2,000/$2,000

Total: Quebec Students: $12,700-$13,100/14,700-$18,100

Students from other parts of Canada (Off-campus/On-campus)

Canadian tuition fees: $5,100/$5,100

Ancillary fees: $1,200-$1,600/$1,200-$1,600

Books and supplies: $1,000/$1,000

Lodging (8 months): $4,400/$8,800-$11,800

Food (8 months): $2,400/-included above

Other expenses: $2,000/$2,000

Total: Canadian Students: $16,100-$16,500/$18,100-$21,500

U.S. and International students (Off-campus/On-campus)

International tuition fees: $14,000-$15,400/$14,000-$15,400

Ancillary fees: $1,200-$1,600/$1,200-$1,600

Mandatory health insurance (single coverage): $700/$700

Immigration fees: $250/$250

Books and supplies: $1,000/$1,000

Lodging (8 months): $4,400/$8,800-$11,800

Food (8 months): $2,400/-included above

Other expenses: $2,000/$2,000

Total: International Students: $25,950-$27,750/$30,350-$32,150

FINANCIAL AID

McGill University has an extensive program of entrance awards to recognize and honor academic excellence. These awards are available to students entering any full-time undergraduate degree program and entering university for the first time. Entrance scholarships range in value from $3,000 to $10,000 per annum, both renewable and 1-year awards. Additional information on scholarships can be found online at www.mcgill.ca/studentaid/scholarships.

STUDENT ORGANIZATIONS AND ACTIVITIES

In addition to a rich athletic tradition that includes many Olympians, thousands of McGill students participate in the hundreds of clubs, associations and community groups that enrich Montreal and contribute to a vibrant campus life. As well, students have the opportunity to participate in University governance, including McGill's Senate and Board of Governors, through the Students' Society of McGill University, the Post-Graduate Students' Society, and other organizations.

ADMISSIONS PROCESS

Prospective students are evaluated on the strength of their entire academic dossier. Academic performance over the past 3 years, the level of programs taken, class rank, and standardized test scores (if applicable) are all given the proper consideration. Applicants should have at least a B+ average or the equivalent, depending on where they have completed their studies. McGill University is very selective. For transfer applicants, the university/college record is reviewed in addition to the above criteria. First-year applicants who wish to enroll in September must meet the following deadlines: January 15 for international and U.S. institution first-year and transfer applicants and non-Canadian/nonpermanent resident transfer applicants from Canadian institutions; February 1 for first-year applicants from Canadian provinces other than Quebec; March 1 for first-year applicants from Quebec CEGEPs; May 1 for exchange and Canadian/permanent resident transfer applicants from Canadian institutions and non-Canadian/nonpermanent resident special and visiting applicants; and July 1 for Canadian/permanent resident special and visiting applicants. Confirmation of deadlines is available at www.mcgill.ca/applying. Depending on space availability, January admission is occasionally open to non-Quebec applicants. Refer to McGill's website for program availability and deadlines.

School Says . . .

MERCYHURST COLLEGE

AT A GLANCE

When you drive through the Mercyhurst Gates, the Tudor-Gothic stateliness of Old Main forms an immediate impression of collegiality and tradition. Mercyhurst College is a fully accredited, 4-year, Catholic liberal arts institution for men and women. The 60-acre main campus is located in southeastern Erie, Pennsylvania, overlooking the city and Lake Erie. Mercyhurst North East (its second campus), is located just 20 minutes away in the heart of the largest Concord grape region in the world. Both campuses are located in suburban settings, their matured and modern facilities are masterfully blended into unified architectural settings that are as collegiate-looking as they come.

A Mercyhurst education combines a rich sense of tradition with a progressive approach to the complexities of modern life. Ever since Mother Borgia Egan and the Sisters of Mercy established Mercyhurst College in 1926, it has consistently sought to teach, to build, and to act with that sense of excellence and style that characterizes quality in human society. It has developed a sense of community on its campus, where teachers and learners reinforce one another in the learning process. The college is consistently ranked among the best regional liberal arts colleges in the North, and for each of the past 5 years applications for admission have set record numbers. Alumni of Mercyhurst College are found in every major profession and in every state in the nation.

LOCATION AND ENVIRONMENT

The Mercyhurst campus is situated at a beautiful site overlooking Lake Erie. One block from the city limits, the college enjoys the advantages of a suburban setting only minutes from downtown. A medium-sized city with a metropolitan population of 280,000, Erie boasts many of the amenities normally associated with larger cities: a professional symphony orchestra, several theater companies, an art museum, a children's museum and a first-rate history center, to name just a few. Located on the southern shore of Lake Erie, the city also offers a complete range of recreational activities including fishing, boating and sunbathing. The beautiful Presque Isle State Park is home to some of the best beaches on the Great Lakes, where breathtaking sunsets and a variety of wildlife can be seen year-round.

CAMPUS FACILITIES AND EQUIPMENT

At Mercyhurst, all freshmen and sophomores (that are not designated as commuter students) are required to live in on campus housing. Traditional residence halls and suites are available to freshmen, while apartments and town houses are reserved for upperclassmen. A large majority of students live in campus housing for all 4 years of their undergraduate career. The Residence Life program supports all students living on campus by working to create an environment which enhances student growth socially, culturally, physically, and emotionally while fostering academic success. The Residence Life staff, consisting of Assistant Directors and Residence Assistants, helps students plan social, cultural, and educational events in their living areas.

All students at Mercyhurst have access to a variety of facilities that enhance their academic experience. The Sr. Carolyn Herrmann Student Union houses a variety of organizations and the Laker Inn, a newly refurbished food service facility featuring a variety of dining options. The bookstore features comfortable seating areas, a coffee bar, and offers a large selection of trade books, periodicals, textbooks, and college merchandise. There are numerous computer labs throughout campus as well as wireless internet access. During the academic year the Hammermill Library is open from 8am until 2am (Mondays through Thursdays), providing students with ample study space. The library also features Café Diem and print and copy stations.

The college's athletic facilities include the Mercyhurst Athletic Center (MAC), the Mercyhurst Ice Center (MIC), the Student Fitness and Recreation Center, Tullio Field, and several additional playing fields. The Mercyhurst Athletic Center houses a gymnasium complex, contains crew tanks, and a newly renovated and enlarged athletic training facility. The Mercyhurst Ice Center includes an ice rink, 4 locker rooms, and seating for 1200. The Student Fitness and Recreation Center contains a large physical fitness center, and 2 all-purpose floors for basketball and volleyball. Improvements to the college playing fields include installing Astroturf to the football stadium and Pro Grass to the baseball and soccer fields. The Fitness Center was tripled in size to 12,000 square feet and features state-of-the-art equipment, and special rooms for aerobics, martial arts programs, and spinning bikes.

ACADEMIC PROGRAMS

Mercyhurst places a great value on the role of the liberal arts as part of the preparation for any career or life objective. Every Mercyhurst student must complete a core of liberal studies courses as part of the degree requirement. The core curriculum is designed to be completed throughout a student's academic career so that skills such as critical thinking, effective communication, global awareness and moral understanding can be built gradually. Students at Mercyhurst attain skills vital to their major as well as an understanding of the interdisciplinary character of knowledge.

Some students know early on what they want to major in at college, while for many others the decision does not come that easily. Mercyhurst offers 50 undergraduate majors and 67 concentrations in a wide variety of subjects. From Business Management to Criminal Justice, Elementary Education to Chemistry, there are majors for all types of students. Mercyhurst also offers several unique majors such as Intelligence Studies, Forensics Science, Archaeology, Dance, and Sportsmedicine. For a full listing of majors please visit: www.mercyhurst.edu/academics/programs/index.php. At Mercyhurst, you can choose a single major, a double major, a major and a minor, or if nothing seems to quite match your particular interest, our faculty will help you design a special contract major.

Adult students can find the guidance and commitment they are searching for at the Catherine McAuley Adult Education Center, including a streamlined admission and registration process, advising during convenient times, access to tutors, life and career counseling, and an informative newsletter. Mercyhurst also offers graduate programs in administration of justice, special education, organizational leadership, applied forensic & biological anthropology, and applied intelligence studies.

FINANCIAL AID

Mercyhurst College, rated as one of *U.S. News & World Report's* "Best Value" schools, is dedicated to making a college education affordable to students from all socioeconomic backgrounds. By using institutional, federal and state aid, Mercyhurst has traditionally awarded aid to more than 95 percent of our incoming freshmen.

Merit-Based Programs The Egan Scholarship is the primary, merit-based scholarship awarded by Mercyhurst College. Ranging from $10,000 to $12,000, the Egan Scholarship goes to deserving students based on students received at least a 1070 (critical reading and math) SAT or a 23 composite ACT, and a GPA of at least a 3.0 or higher.

Talent-Based Scholarships Mercyhurst College is home to a nationally renowned ballet program, historically strong music and art programs, and 25 NCAA scholarship athletic teams. Talent-based scholarships are available in these areas, determined by the various department heads and coaches who will be directly involved with the student.

Need-Based Opportunities To determine your eligibility for need-based financial aid and/or student loans, you must submit the Free Application for Federal Student Aid (FAFSA). The FAFSA will be available at your high school's guidance office or online at www.fafsa.ed.gov after January 1. Be sure to list Mercyhurst College (Title IV School Code #003297) as your school of choice.

The FAFSA will help Mercyhurst College determine the type of Federal, State and Institutional grants and loans for which you may be eligible.

For more detailed information about Mercyhurst financial aid, please visit http://merit.mercyhurst.edu

STUDENT ORGANIZATIONS AND ACTIVITIES

Mercyhurst College is committed to the growth and development of the individual student not only in academic work but also in growth as a human being living in a community. There are more than 100 different organizations on campus offering a variety of opportunities for students to become involved outside of the classroom. In particular, the Student Activities Council (SAC) is the primary student programming organization whose function is to provide activities that will enrich the college community both socially and culturally. All students are encouraged to participate in SAC sponsored activities, which are generally held on Friday and Saturday evenings throughout the academic year. At Mercyhurst, students have a voice through Mercyhurst Student Government (MSG). This group of student elected officers and members acts as a liaison between students and the administration. All students are welcome to attend MSG's weekly meetings every Monday evening.

All students at Mercyhurst are encouraged to find ways to experience our global community both on campus and abroad. The Office of International Relations and Services/Study Abroad recruits students from overseas and assists domestic students with their desires to study abroad. Currently, there are more than 200 international students representing more than 30 countries at Mercyhurst. Acting in part as ambassadors of their countries, these students bring their customs and cultures to campus. For students wishing to travel, there are a wide variety of study abroad programs to choose from. Mercyhurst students are encouraged to use one that best suits their needs. However, as the college is determined to provide our students with the best options, the study abroad office maintains close relationships with 6 unique and diverse programs. All of these programs are well-established and internationally recognized.

ADMISSIONS PROCESS

Mercyhurst operates on a rolling admission cycle. Students generally begin applying in September of their senior year in high school. Beginning in early November, notification will be given to prospective students who:

Apply online for free (https://apply.mercyhurst.edu) or complete Mercyhurst's traditional paper application (requires $30 processing fee). Submit an official copy of all high school transcripts, as well as official copies of SAT and/or ACT scores. Provide Letters of reference (recommended but not required). Complete any audition requirements of the dance and music departments.

Please visit the Mercyhurst website at admissions.mercyhurst.edu for more information on applying.

If you have any additional questions about the application process, please send us an e-mail at admissions@mercyhurst.edu or call us at 1-800-825-1926 ext. 2202 to speak with an admissions representative.

MEREDITH COLLEGE

AT A GLANCE

Meredith was chartered in 1891. Today Meredith is an independent private women's college—one of the largest in the United States. Meredith offers a comprehensive education with an emphasis on an innovative liberal arts curriculum.

At the undergraduate level, Meredith offers more than 50 programs of study. Each major is grounded in a new general education curriculum that emphasizes interdisciplinary study, experiential learning and global awareness. The Meredith academic experience is enhanced by a series of initiatives that offer a bold vision for the future. The Meredith Technology Initiative provides every full-time undergraduate student with a laptop and enhances the use of technology across the curriculum. The Science and Mathematics Initiative features extensive new facilities and programs. The Undergraduate Research Program encourages student-faculty research in every discipline. The Service Learning and Leadership Initiatives expand our longtime commitment to community service and stewardship.

Meredith also offers numerous opportunities for graduate and professional study and lifelong learning. Through the John E. Weems Graduate School, Meredith offers coeducational graduate programs in business, music, nutrition, and education. The Professional Studies Program provides non-credit continuing education to business and health care professionals, teachers, human resource managers, and paralegals. The Community Outreach Program features a wide variety of non-credit programs for men, women, and children.

The Meredith community is diverse, spirited and culturally engaged. Campus life is shaped by more than 2,100 students from 30 states and 16 foreign countries. Students advance their leadership skills by participating in more than 100 clubs and organizations, playing NCAA Division III sports, producing campuswide events, taking leadership roles in the community, and joining in college traditions.

LOCATION AND ENVIRONMENT

Meredith College is located in Raleigh, North Carolina's, capital city. Meredith students are part of the more than 108,000 college students who reside in the Research Triangle Park area, the country's premiere research and development hub.

OFF-CAMPUS OPPORTUNITIES

Study abroad options include a summer program in Italy, Switzerland, and England, plus a variety of semester and yearlong travel opportunities throughout the world. Semester programs at the United Nations in New York City or in Washington, DC, are also available.

MAJORS AND DEGREES OFFERED

Meredith offers more than 50 majors and concentrations. Each program allows students to pursue intensive study, conduct independent research, and work closely with talented, committed professors.

Accounting; American civilization; art (art education, graphic design, studio art); biology (environmental science, health science, molecular biology); business administration; chemistry (engineering dual degree program between Meredith and NCSU, College of Engineering); child development; communication (interpersonal communication, mass communication, computer information systems); computer science; dance (performance and choreography, private studio teaching); economics; English; environmental studies; exercise and sports science (health and wellness); family and consumer sciences; fashion design merchandising and design (design, merchandising); food and nutrition; French; history; interior design; international studies; mathematics (engineering dual degree program between Meredith and NCSU, College of Engineering); music (keyboard, instrument or composition, musical theatre, music performance, piano pedagogy, voice); political science; international relations (law and justice); psychology; public history; religion; social work; sociology; Spanish; theatre (musical theatre, theatre performance); women's studies.

ACADEMIC PROGRAMS

In 2001, Meredith became the first women's college to adopt a campus-wide laptop program as part of the Meredith Technology Initiative. Full-time students receive a ThinkPad loaded with professional and educational software to use on Meredith's wireless campus environment.

Honors and Teaching Fellows programs are offered. Meredith is one of 5 private colleges participating in the N.C. Teaching Fellows program.

Internships and cooperative education are available in all areas of study.

The Cooperating Raleigh Colleges consortium allows students to take courses at other Raleigh colleges and universities. Meredith offers a dual degree program with NC State University's College of Engineering.

The Undergraduate Research Program supports student-faculty partnerships in the pursuit of research and creative activity in all fields. College funds support these projects and underwrite travel costs for students presenting their work at conferences.

CAMPUS FACILITIES AND EQUIPMENT

Meredith's 225-acre campus includes a 1,200-seat amphitheater on a lake, 7 residence halls, a music library, art galleries, a research greenhouse, music practice rooms, auditoriums, a theater, concert halls, a student center, computer labs, a child care lab, a learning center, an autism lab, an astronomy observation deck, an indoor swimming pool, a fitness center, a dance studio, lighted tennis courts, a putting green, a soccer field, and 2 miles of greenway connecting our campus to the community.

Carlyle Campbell Library has more than 186,100 volumes, 15,626 microforms and 669 newspaper and journal subscriptions. With more than 80,000 square feet of space, the new science and mathematics building includes unique classroom settings, specialized labs, and a telescope observatory deck.

TUITION, ROOM, BOARD, AND FEES

Tuition for full-time undergraduate students in 2007-2008 is $22,400, with room and board at $6,300, for a total of $28,700. Cost for part-time students is $585 per credit hour. Tuition for graduate students in 2007-2008 is $385 per credit hour and $520 per credit hour for MBA students.

FINANCIAL AID

Financial aid programs are available for students with demonstrated need. These grant programs, which do not need to be repaid, include Federal Pell Grants that range from $400 to $4,310; Federal Supplemental Educational Opportunity Grants that range from $100 to $4,000; Meredith College grants; and the North Carolina Legislative Tuition Grant that is available to full-time students who are legal residents of the state, currently about $1,900.

To apply, complete the Free Application for Federal Student Aid (FAFSA). You do not have to wait until you are formally accepted by Meredith to apply.

The Office of Financial Assistance uses the FAFSA form to determine a student's eligibility for grants, loans, scholarships and work-study opportunities. The FAFSA is available online at www.fafsa.ed.gov. Printed copies are available from the Office of Financial Assistance or from a high school guidance counselor. FAFSA forms should be sent directly to the Federal Student Aid Programs by March 1 each year. Meredith College's FAFSA code is 002945. Students must apply for financial aid annually.

STUDENT ORGANIZATIONS AND ACTIVITIES

Meredith sponsors a Presidential Lecture Series, juried student exhibitions, an active concert schedule, visiting artists and exhibitions featuring professional artists.

Students participate in 4 theater and dance performance troupes, 3 choral groups and 4 musical ensembles.

Meredith students advance their leadership skills in programs such as the Emerging Leader Seminar Series, Leadership Enrichment Series Organization, Officer and Advisor Training, Peer Leadership Consultant Program, Sloan Family Leadership Program, Sophie Lanneau Women's Leadership Development Program and the LeaderShape Institute.

Meredith athletes compete in 6 NCAA Division III sports as a member of the USA South Athletic Conference: basketball, soccer, volleyball, tennis, softball, and cross-country.

Meredith's Aqua Angels are a synchronized swimming group, performing twice per academic year.

ADMISSIONS PROCESS

Freshman Applicants: Meredith expects applicants to have taken a challenging academic program, including honors, advanced placement or international baccalaureate level work. Applicants should present a solid grade report with at least a C average in English, foreign language, mathematics, history and natural sciences, and have successfully completed standardized tests including the SAT or ACT. In recent years, the middle 50 percent of enrolling students at Meredith scored between 950 and 1150 on the SAT (Math and Verbal) and 19 and 24 on the ACT. Recommendations from a school official and teacher are also requested.

We offer 2 freshman admission programs: Early Decision and Regular Decision. Early Decision is designed for students who are ready to withdraw applications to other schools and enroll at Meredith. Regular Decision candidates should apply during fall and early winter of their senior year. Decisions begin on a rolling basis in early November. Applicants are invited to come for a visit and experience life as a Meredith student. Schedule a visit online, or call 1-800-MEREDITH or e-mail requests to admissions@meredith.edu.

MERRIMACK COLLEGE

AT A GLANCE

Located on a beautiful 220-acre campus, 25 miles north of Boston in the suburban towns of North Andover and Andover, Massachusetts, Merrimack College is a 4-year coeducational institution that delivers a superior Catholic education in the Augustinian tradition. The 2,000 undergraduate students come from 28 states and 17 countries; approximately 80 percent live on campus. The college offers a comprehensive undergraduate curriculum emphasizing the liberal arts, business and international commerce, science, and award winning programs in civil, electrical, and computer engineering. In the Augustinian tradition, Merrimack's community is committed to scholarship and service to others, and provides students myriad opportunities to develop intellectually, spiritually, socially, and ethically.

LOCATION AND ENVIRONMENT

The suburban towns of North Andover and Andover, Massachusetts, are rich in historical and cultural heritage. On our beautifully maintained campus you'll find birch-lined walkways and traditional red-brick buildings alongside our newly renovated and modern facilities, the oldest usable iron bridge in America, and the Collegiate Church of Christ the Teacher, the spiritual center of our community.

The college's Sakowich Campus Center creatively mixes both social and athletic functions and provides a true crossroads for all members of the college community. Additionally, the beautiful Rogers Center for the Arts includes a theater, orchestra pit, art gallery, and state-of-the-art acoustics, lighting, and sound systems.

The college's Gregor Mendel Center for Science, Engineering and Technology includes laboratories, computer facilities, and an astronomy dome and telescope. Because of Merrimack's extraordinary location, students may choose internship/cooperative education placements in Boston, New England, and beyond.

OFF-CAMPUS OPPORTUNITIES

The Cooperative Education program provides our students with paid work experiences and is available to all students regardless of their degree program. It is an opportunity to strengthen your degree program and work experience in the field you intend to pursue upon graduating. The Stevens Service Learning Center provides students the opportunity to learn and develop through active participation in organized service at volunteer community sites while enrolled in traditional course work. While pursuing a full course load, students may immerse themselves in the history and culture of another country and study abroad for a year, semester, or the summer.

MAJORS AND DEGREES OFFERED

Merrimack College awards the BA and BS degrees through both day and evening programs within the Division of Continuing Education. In addition, numerous certificate programs are also offered including financial planning, project management, oracle, and human resource management.

Bachelor of arts degree programs in the liberal arts include communication studies, criminology, digital media arts, economics, English, fine arts, French, history, romance languages, philosophy, political science, psychology, religious studies, self-designed major, sociology, and Spanish. Teacher certification is available for elementary, middle, secondary and moderate disabilities education. In addition a 5 year bachelor/master's in elementary education is available.

Students in the sciences or engineering may attain the bachelor of arts degree in biology and mathematics and the Bachelor of Science degree in biochemistry, biotechnology, civil engineering, computer science, electrical engineering, environmental science, health science, information technology, physics and sports medicine. The bachelor of science degree is also offered in business administration, including a new concentration in sports management.

Merrimack College also awards a master of education (MEd) in elementary education. The MEd program offers both standard and advanced provisional certification for elementary teachers.

ACADEMIC PROGRAMS

Merrimack offers 38 academic majors in the liberal arts, business, engineering and the sciences. The college's contemporary academic approach of fusing liberal arts with professional education and offering a richer 4 course- 4 credit curriculum means students become engaged and ready to make critical, moral and informed decisions of thought, communication and action in their own lives and in service to others. Merrimack graduates are able to demonstrate the knowledge, skills, competencies, and values needed to achieve their personal and professional goals.

Students may combine majors, double major, or participate in interdepartmental majors. The college participates in the Northeast Consortium for Study Abroad, allowing students to pursue Academic Programs in many overseas sites in Europe, South America, Africa, and Australia. Students may also participate in cross registration programs through the NECCUM consortium or the American University, Washington, DC, semester.

Students learn by doing at Merrimack-not only in the classroom and the laboratory, but also in the field and in the real world. With intensive, hands-on experiences such as internships, study abroad or volunteer opportunities to complement class work, students make deeper connections to their studies, gain invaluable real-world experience, build their resumes, and boost confidence as they learn to think on their feet and learn by doing.

Merrimack offers students the opportunity to gain relevant work experience and explore career choices while attending college through our Cooperative Education program or through a variety of departmental internships. The college is also home to the Center for the Study of Jewish-Christian Relations, the Center for Augustinian Study and Legacy, and Study Group English programs.

CAMPUS FACILITIES AND EQUIPMENT

The Rogers Center for the Arts enhances the performing arts offerings through numerous cultural programs. The Sakowich Campus Center offers a creative mix of athletic space, student lounges, and a completely renovated dining services area, a new food court, and a Cyber-cafe. The McQuade Library, a wireless facility, has more than 116,000 volumes, 1,100 periodicals, a computerized catalog, and access to numerous electronic databases ranging from online to CDs. It also houses a Media Center with a TV Studio, the Information Technology Center, Math and Writing Centers, a 180-seat auditorium, and an art gallery.

Merrimack College Information Technology Center houses a Digital Equipment Corporation VMS cluster alongside several Digital graphic workstations. The Technology Center supports several Computer labs fitted with Windows, Macintosh, microcomputers, and Digital Equipment workstations. The S. Peter Volpe Physical Athletic Center houses basketball courts in a 1,700 seat gymnasium, a 3,600 seat hockey arena, and a fitness center. The Center is adjacent to outdoor facilities that include tennis courts and baseball, football, soccer, softball, practice, and intramural athletic fields including a new turf field for student use.

Our approximately 1,600 resident students have many options, including singles, doubles, suites, town houses, and apartments.

TUITION, ROOM, BOARD, AND FEES

For the academic year 2008-2009

Tuition: $29,300

Room and board: $10,000

Fees: $500

Total: $39,800

FINANCIAL AID

The financial aid staff is dedicated to making the application process as simple as possible. We work closely with families to put together a financial aid package that makes the best use of all available resources. Complete the Free Application for Federal Student Aid (FAFSA) beginning January 1; mail it no later than FEBRUARY 1, the financial aid deadline. You will be notified of your financial aid award beginning March 15.

STUDENT ORGANIZATIONS AND ACTIVITIES

At Merrimack College, you will live and learn on a campus filled with energy, involvement, and fun. You will have the opportunity to participate in traditional events like Welcome Week, Winter Weekend, and the Christmas Celebration of Light and Hope. Our community is active year round. Student Government association coordinates a varied program of social and cultural events for the college community.

Clubs and organizations: Accounting and Finance Society, Alpha Chi Epsilon, American Marketing Association (AMA) American Society of Civil Engineers (ASCE), Amnesty International, Ash Hall Council, Benzene Ring (Chemistry Club), Biology Club, Brothers and Sisters United (BSU), Class Council 2006, Class Council 2007, Class Council 2008, Class Council 2009, Commuter Council, CO-OP Council, English Club, IEEE (Engineering Club), International Students Union, InterFraternity Council IEC), Jazz Band, Math Club, Merrimack College Concert Choir, Merrimackian (Yearbook), Monican Hall Council, Merrimack Out Reach Experience (MORE), Political Science Society, On-Stagers (Dramatic society), Orientation Committee, Outing Club, Panhellenic Council, Phi Kappa Theta, Program Board, Psi Chi (Psychology Honors Society), Psychology Club, Republicans Club, Right Choice Peer Educators, Sigma Phi Omega, Ski Club, Student Government, Student Newspaper, Tau Kappa Epsilon, Theta Phi Alpha, Xi Lambda Psi.

Men's varsity: baseball, basketball, cross country, football, hockey, lacrosse, soccer, tennis. Women's varsity: basketball, cross country, field hockey, lacrosse, soccer, softball, tennis, volleyball. In addition, numerous intramural sports are offered for all students including softball, hockey, basketball, soccer, baseball, and more.

ADMISSIONS PROCESS

The Admission Committee places primary emphasis on the secondary school record (courses completed, grades earned and class rank), the student essay and a teacher or guidance counselor recommendation. Test results from SAT or ACT are optional. Applicants must have earned the following high school units: 4 years of college preparatory English, 2 years of social studies, 3 years of mathematics (including algebra II) 2 years of a foreign language, 2 years of science and 5 electives. Applicants for the sciences or engineering programs, however, are expected to have at least 4 years of mathematics, and 3 years of science, including physics for engineering, but need have only 3 electives.

Merrimack College offers Early Action admission to properly qualified applicants. Merrimack also gives credit and advanced placement for scores of 3 or better on the Advanced Placement examinations sponsored by the College Board. Transfer applicants for the fall or spring semester should be in good academic standing at the institution last attended, not be on academic or disciplinary probation, and have a quality point average of at least a 2.5 on the Merrimack College scale. International applicants must also submit the results of the test of English as a Foreign Language (TOEFL) and the Certificate of Finance.

MESSIAH COLLEGE

AT A GLANCE

Messiah College is an independent, liberal arts and sciences college committed to providing a rigorous education in the context of the Christian tradition. The college aims to develop each student's intellect, character, and faith, preparing them for successful lives in the church and in society. There are more than 2,800 students at Messiah College, hailing from 37 U.S. states and 23 foreign countries. Collectively, students represent more than 50 religious denominations and 6.5 percent of students are ethnic minorities and 2.1 percent are international. Messiah has a distinctive residential atmosphere and a strong sense of community; More than 80 percent of undergraduates live on campus.

LOCATION AND ENVIRONMENT

Messiah College is situated on 471 beautiful acres, just 12 miles southwest of Harrisburg, Pennsylvania. In addition to the numerous internship and service opportunities available in the city of Harrisburg, the college is just 2 hours from the major urban centers of Philadelphia, Baltimore, and Washington, DC. There are many recreational and outdoor activities in the immediate vicinity, including the Yellow Breeches Creek, which runs right through the campus, and the Susquehanna River. The college also operates a satellite campus in Philadelphia, Pennsylvania in conjunction with Temple University.

ACADEMIC PROGRAMS

Messiah students must complete 126 units to graduate. In addition to courses required by their major field, all students must complete a set of required courses in writing, the arts and sciences, language and culture, Christian faith, and physical education. Students fill the remaining required units through elective courses. The college operates on a 2 semester academic calendar, with a January Term between the fall and spring terms. During January term, students take one intensive, month-long course of study. Qualified students are also encouraged to participate in the Honors Program, to design an individual major or an independent study program, or participate in service learning programs and internships.

CAMPUS FACILITIES AND EQUIPMENT

Messiahs top-notch academic facilities includes Murray Library, a research library with more than 295,000 volumes; the Jordan Science Center and the Oakes Museum of Natural History which contains a large collection of North American and African animals; Frey Hall, an engineering, mathematics, and business building; Climenhaga, a fine arts center; Sollenberger, a sports center with indoor track, natatorium and exercise area and Boyer Hall, a new academic facility which opened Fall 2003. Academic facilities are modern and up to date, all completed within the last 25 years. Students have access to more than 400 computers in several labs located in various academic and residence hall facilities, all of which are connected to the campus network. In addition to public computing resources, every student room has a direct hookup to the campus network and the internet. In addition, wireless connections to the campus network are available in all major campus buildings, all academic halls, and residence halls. The college offers 8 traditional residence halls and 4 apartment-style residences on campus, all offering carpeting, air conditioning, cable television, Internet and telephone services.

TUITION, ROOM, BOARD, AND FEES

For the 2007-2008 academic year:

Tuition: $23,710

Room and board: $7,340

Fees: $710

STUDENT ORGANIZATIONS AND ACTIVITIES

A lively campus community, Messiah students participate in more than 75 groups and organizations, including theater groups, a campus newspaper, and a student-produced radio station. More than 35 percent of undergraduates participate in student government elections. Messiah College maintains one of the overall most successful athletics programs in the nation, competing in the NCAA Division III. Messiah competes in men's baseball, basketball, cross-country, golf, lacrosse, soccer, tennis, track and field, and wrestling, as well as women's basketball, cross-country, field hockey, lacrosse, soccer, softball, swimming, tennis, track and field, and volleyball. Messiah does not have any fraternities or sororities, at either the national or local level. The college operates a number of campus safety services for students, such as an after hours transport and escort service, 24-hour emergency telephone alarm devices, day and night professional security patrol, and student security patrols. In addition, all entrances to the residence halls are electronically operated.

ADMISSIONS PROCESS

Messiah seeks students with demonstrated academic promise, who wish to share in the college's ardent commitment to Christ. Messiah encourages transfer, home school, international, and minority students to apply. The college provides 2 methods for candidates to apply for admission: the Standard Choice and the Write Choice. Both options require the submission of the application form, high school transcript, application essay, and one Christian Life recommendation form. In addition, the following materials or activities are required to complete an application for admission: Standard Choice - Applicant must submit the New SAT or ACT score results. Write Choice - Applicant must be in the top 20 percent class ranking, participate in an admissions interview, and submit an additional graded writing sample. The Admissions Office seeks to admit those candidates who have exhibited scholastic competence and excellence as well as those who are most likely to succeed, benefit from, and contribute to the Messiah College community. Decision Options - Messiah College operates on a rolling admission basis. On occasion, the Admissions Office may require an interview to clarify academic or personal issues pertaining to a candidate's application for admission. The application for admission must be completed and received prior to the admission interview. Appointments can be made Monday through Friday, 8:00 a.m. to 5:00 p.m. by contacting the Visit Coordinator at 1-800-233-4220 or e-mail: admiss@messiah.edu (2 weeks notice is suggested).

MOLLOY COLLEGE

AT A GLANCE

At Molloy College, students gain that "I will" attitude they need to make a difference in our fast-paced, ever changing world. Located in Rockville Centre, New York, Molloy offers students a rich and multidimensional educational experience. Our faculty is accomplished, yet approachable, leading small classes where students are encouraged to think critically and explore creatively. Through our Global-Learning Program, students study abroad, traveling to such exotic and enriching destinations as India, Thailand, Spain, Italy, Belgium, and even Australia.

Molloy's campus provides for abundant opportunities to explore new interests, pursue career goals, and enrich our community. Whether it's participating in a music ensemble, writing for a campus publication, or serving as a student government representative, with more than 40 clubs and honor societies, Molloy has something for each and every student. For those who choose to combine athletic with scholastic success, Molloy offers a number of winning programs. Students participate competitively in the East Coast Conference (ECC) and in the NCAA Division II. Students have exciting opportunities to "fast track" their careers. With dual bachelor's/master's degree program offerings in accounting, business management, criminal justice, and education, Molloy students can complete a dual degree in 5 years. Students are encouraged to make a difference in local communities and many become involved in Molloy-sponsored service projects such as BoxTown, a simulation program that educates students about homelessness.

The college also provides forums welcoming regional, national, and international leaders such as Secretary of State Gen. Colin Powell, the late Prime Minister of Pakistan Benazir Bhutto, and editor of *Newsweek International* Fareed Zakaria.

Molloy College has built a rich, dynamic, and diverse educational environment over the past 50 years. It is within this welcoming yet challenging environment that Molloy College students develop that all-important confidence, that strong, "I will" attitude that enables them to succeed in their careers, and more important, to make a difference in our world.

LOCATION AND ENVIRONMENT

Molloy College is located on the South Shore of Long Island in Rockville Centre. Our proximity to New York City allows for our students to benefit from the cultural and social opportunities that Manhattan has to offer - and it's just a short train ride away from our 30-acre campus. Molloy College also offers off campus locations for study at the Suffolk Center in East Farmingdale, just off of the Rt. 110 corridor. In addition, the college offers courses at area hospitals and schools, all designed to provide convenience for our graduate and continuing education students.

OFF-CAMPUS OPPORTUNITIES

You can stay local, but still go far, with the Global-Learning Program available at Molloy College. At Molloy you can study what you want, where you want, for as long as you want.

Molloy College also offers students the opportunity to combine job experience and classroom exposure through its internship program. At Molloy, students are encouraged to participate in internships so that they can gain first-hand knowledge and experience in their future career path.

MAJORS AND DEGREES OFFERED

Molloy College offers the AA degree in liberal arts; the AAS degree in cardiovascular technology, nuclear medicine technology and respiratory care; and the BA or BS degree in accounting, art, biology, business management, communications, computer science, computer information systems, criminal justice, education, English, earth and environmental studies, health service leadership, history, interdisciplinary studies, mathematics, music, music therapy, nursing, philosophy, political science, psychology, sociology, Spanish, speech language pathology/audiology, theater arts and theology; and the BSW in Social Work; and the BFA in art and music. Teacher certification programs are available in childhood (1-6), adolescence (7-12), and special education. Master's degree programs are available in accounting, business, criminal justice, education, music therapy, nursing, and personal financial planning.

Students interested in pre-dental, pre-law, pre-medical, or pre-veterinary programs are offered special advisement.

ACADEMIC PROGRAMS

A minimum of 128 credit hours is required for a baccalaureate degree; these courses include a strong liberal arts general education curriculum for every major field of study. Students may choose a double major, and many minors are available. Molloy has a 4-1-4 academic calendar.

Students may earn CLEP and CPE credit, and advanced placement credit is granted for a score of 3 or better on the AP exam. Qualified full-time students may participate in the Army ROTC program at Hofstra University or St. John's University on a cross enrolled basis. Molloy students may also elect Air Force ROTC on a cross enrolled basis with New York Institute of Technology.

CAMPUS FACILITIES AND EQUIPMENT

Today, a school's computer facilities are very important to students. They want access to computers, the Internet, e-mail, and good software; this is certainly something that Molloy College provides. Molloy is a wireless campus and our computer labs house more than 325 PCs. Also, many departments have their own computer labs with state-of-the-art equipment.

The James E. Tobin Library is the center of academic research on the Molloy College campus. The library houses 110,000 volumes, as well as 685 journals and periodicals in its collection. Online access to information is very important. The library subscribes to more than 40 subscription databases, including but not limited to EBSCO's Academic Search Premier, ProQuest Direct and Sage's Nursing and Health Sciences database giving students and faculty access to thousands of full-text resources. Also in the library is a "smart" classroom used by the librarians for library instruction classes.

The media center houses an extensive collection of DVD's and videos as well as state of the art digital equipment. There is a faculty development / instructional technology lab in the Media Center. The library is a wireless facility.

The Wilbur Arts Center features numerous art and music studios, a cable television studio, and the Lucille B. Hays Theatre. The school also has 6 science labs, a language lab, the education resource center, 2 nursing labs, and a behavioral sciences research facility.

TUITION, ROOM, BOARD, AND FEES

Full-time undergraduate tuition is $ 17,640. In addition, there is approximately $900 in required fees. Students can expect to spend about $900 on books and supplies, and approximately $2,200 in miscellaneous expenses.

FINANCIAL AID

Financial aid, which is based on academic achievement and financial need, is awarded to more than 85 percent of the student body. Aid is awarded in the form of scholarships, grants, loans, and Federal Work-Study Program employment. Non-need scholarships and grants are also available. Students are required to complete the FAFSA. Students who graduate from high school with a 95 percent average and a minimum combined score of 1280 on the SAT I are considered for the Molloy Scholars' Program, which awards full tuition scholarships. Partial scholarships are available through the following: Dominican Scholarships, Fine and Performing Arts Scholarships, and Community Service Awards, and other funded scholarships. The Transfer Scholarship Program awards partial tuition scholarships to students transferring into Molloy College with at least a 3.0 cumulative GPA. Athletic grants (Division II only) are awarded to full-time students who show superior athletic ability in baseball, basketball, cross-country, equestrian, lacrosse, soccer, softball, tennis, or volleyball.

STUDENT ORGANIZATIONS AND ACTIVITIES

Molloy students are involved in a highly active life outside the classroom, something that the college administration supports and encourages. Whether you are an athlete, an aspiring journalist, someone with a strong opinion, or just someone with a desire to expand your horizons, you will find a group to join here. Such organizations provide students with the opportunity to interact with fellow students as leaders, as part of a team, or in a social environment.

Student-run publications include the yearbook, a literary magazine, and the school newspaper. Molloy College sponsors 12 varsity sports, which include baseball, men's and women's basketball, men's and women's cross country, men's and women's lacrosse, men's and women's soccer, softball, women's tennis and women's volleyball. The college is a member of the East Coast Conference (ECC), the Eastern Collegiate Athletic Conference (ECAC) and the NCAA. In addition, they sponsor a club dance team and a co-ed club equestrian team. The equestrian team is part of the Intercollegiate Horse Show Association.

The student government is elected from the Molloy Student Association, made up of every member of the student body. Members of the Molloy Student Government provide their classmates with a leadership that keeps extracurricular activities alive, productive, and practical.

ADMISSIONS PROCESS

Molloy College's admissions committee recommends that applicants meet the following admission qualifications: graduation from a 4-year public or private high school or equivalent (GED test) with a minimum of 20.5 units, including 4 in English, 4 in social studies, 3 in a foreign language, 3 in mathematics, and 3 in science. Nursing applicants must have completed biology and chemistry courses. Mathematics applicants must have taken 4 units of math and 2 of science (including chemistry or physics). Biology applicants must have credits in biology, chemistry, and physics and 4 units in math. Art applicants must submit a portfolio; music and theater arts students must audition. The committee selects candidates based on the following: high school record, SAT I or ACT scores, class rank, and the school's recommendation. Personality and character are considered in admissions decisions, as are talent or ability in a non-curricular field, as well as alumni relationships.

A select group of freshmen are invited to participate in the Molloy College Honors Program. This program offers challenging course work and encourages reflection and personal growth. Honors students are provided with several special participation incentives such as a laptop computer, and priority registration.

The St. Thomas Aquinas Program, which includes both HEOP and the Albertus Magnus Program, may be an option for students not normally eligible for admission.

Early admission is available. Molloy admits students on a rolling basis and students are advised of the admission decision within a few weeks of completion of the application filing process.

Prospective students should submit the following to the admissions office to be considered for enrollment: a completed application for admission, a nonrefundable $30 application fee, an official high school transcript or GED score report, official SAT I or ACT score, and official college transcripts (transfer students only).

MONROE COLLEGE

AT A GLANCE

At Monroe College, students obtain knowledge and competencies in their chosen field of study in preparation for a career or further education. Monroe College, a leading provider of higher education in business, technology, and professional studies, offers associate, baccalaureate, and graduate programs. The curriculum blends general education and theory with sophisticated practical application, utilizing state-of-the art technology.

As a teaching-oriented institution of higher learning, Monroe emphasizes instructional excellence and is committed to sustaining faculty who are caring, dedicated, and knowledgeable in their fields.

Monroe maintains two vibrant campuses in and close to New York City. The main campus is located on Fordham Road in the center of the Bronx. The branch campus is located along Main Street in New Rochelle. Both are a 30-minute train ride from Manhattan's famed Grand Central Station.

Recognizing the worth of each individual, Monroe offers a diverse experience to traditional and nontraditional students that engenders respect for individual differences. Monroe provides academic and administrative support services essential to helping students surmount academic, personal, social, or economic barriers. A student's success is our entire focus.

LOCATION AND ENVIRONMENT

Monroe is very much a part of New York City and we like to think of the city as part of our extended campus. Our campuses' proximity to Manhattan offers students tremendous cultural, academic, and professional resources.

Our Bronx campus in the Fordham section of the Bronx is easily accessed by public bus and a variety of subway lines.

Our New Rochelle campus in downtown New Rochelle in the heart of Westchester County, provides a variety of living accommodations. Stroll by the college on Main Street or pop into the ice rink, arcade, and IMAX theater at the entertainment complex across the street.

OFF-CAMPUS OPPORTUNITIES

Cooperative Education is conducted by Monroe College in cooperation with businesses, industries, government agencies, and nonprofit organizations. The program integrates on-campus study with off-campus work experience. Employment is usually directly related to the student's academic area. In addition to gaining valuable experience, co-op students also receive three academic credits at the end of their internship.

MAJORS AND DEGREES OFFERED

Bachelor's Degree Programs

Monroe College awards Bachelor of Science (BS) degrees in Criminal Justice and Bachelor of Business Administration (BBA) degrees in Accounting, Business Management, Computer Information Systems, General Business, Health Services Administration, and Hospitality Management. For specific information regarding application or transfer requirements, please see the Office of Bachelor's Degree Programs at the Bronx or New Rochelle campus.

The college currently offers an online degree program in Business Management (BBA) and Criminal Justice (BS) and a variety of courses in other majors which are taught in an online format as well as "Blended Learning" (a combination of online and on-site sessions).

Associate Degree Programs

The college awards the Associate in Science (AS) in Criminal Justice and Associate in Applied Science (AAS) degrees in Accounting, Business Administration, Business Technologies, Computer Information Systems, Culinary Arts, Hospitality Management, Medical Administration and Medical Assisting.

The college currently offers online degree programs in Business Administration (AAS) and Criminal Justice (AS) and a variety of courses in other majors which are taught in an online format as well as "Blended Learning" (a combination of online and onsite sessions).

ACADEMIC PROGRAMS

All of our programs are developed with input from professionals that are currently working in the field. This insures that your education will be relevant once you begin your career. Whatever field you choose, you can be sure that your Monroe education will be academically rigorous. That's because many of our professors are from the top of their professions. They know how to blend theory with practical insights so that the material comes to life in the classroom setting.

CAMPUS FACILITIES AND EQUIPMENT

Monroe College's Learning Resource Centers provide unlimited academic support. There the students receive tutorial assistance, catch up on schoolwork, or view instructional videos. The centers at both campuses are open 6 days a week from early morning to late evening.

The Thomas P. Schmitzer Library at the Bronx campus and the Library at the New Rochelle campus have vast resources for students. Both libraries are open over 60 hours a week, and are equipped with direct Internet access and CD-ROM databases for research. Volumes of encyclopedias and research materials line the walls, and students can locate everything from recent best sellers to the latest marketing trends with the help of expert staff.

Monroe College Culinary Arts classes are taught in the new Culinary Arts Center on the New Rochelle campus, perhaps the most state-of-the-art culinary instructional facility in Metropolitan New York. In addition to four new kitchen/labs, the center's design includes large windows and custom-designed electric lighting.

TUITION, ROOM, BOARD, AND FEES

Undergraduate Tuition for 2006–2007 Academic Year

Full-time Tuition per semester (up to 18 credits): $4800

Part-time Tuition per course (1–3 classes): $1,200

Full-time Administrative Fee (3–6 classes): $300

Part-time Administrative Fee (1–2 classes): $150

Housing and Meal Plan Fees for 2006–2007 Academic Year

Housing (single): $3,250 per semester

Housing (double): $2,550 per semester

Housing (triple): $2,400 per semester

Housing (quad): $1,725

Meal Plan: $625

Fees for 2006–2007 Academic Year

Application Fee: $ 35

Housing Application Fee: $150

Administrative Fee (1–2 Classes): $150 per semester

Administrative Fee (3–6 Classes): $300 per semester

FINANCIAL AID

Need-based Financial Aid for eligible students can include both grants, which are not paid back, and loans, which must be paid back after completing a degree or leaving the college. Both New York State and the federal government offer need-based aid, which is calculated according to a family's ability to pay for school.

Merit scholarships are available to students based on SAT and class rankings, as well as a variety of scholarships for some of our degree programs. High school students who graduate and immediately enroll at Monroe may be eligible for one of the following:

New York Metro Grant—awarded to students who graduate from a New York City High School who plan on attending school while living at home. This award can be up to $1,800 annually.

Early Incentive Grant—awarded to any student who is accepted by March 1. This award can be up to $900 annually.

STUDENT ORGANIZATIONS AND ACTIVITIES

Monroe College fields varsity athletic teams in men's and women's basketball, men's soccer, softball, baseball, and women's volleyball. Intramural athletics are available to students at the New Rochelle campus.

In addition to sponsoring a wide variety of extracurricular activities, the Office of Student Services also oversees a number of student clubs and organizations that give Monroe students the opportunity to explore their interests further.

Students in Free Enterprise (SIFE)

Monroe College is proud to be the home of the 2005 national championship SIFE team. SIFE is dedicated to building and promoting local and international businesses and organizations that contribute to the community.

International Student Union (ISU)

The focus of the ISU is to provide international students with a social group to help with acculturation issues. The ISU sponsors field trips, sightseeing activities, tourist venues, and guest speakers every semester. Additionally, the ISU puts together a yearly Multicultural Fair where students exhibit art, music, photographs, ethnic foods and clothes of their countries to the college community. Membership is open to all students at the college. Meetings take place at the New Rochelle campus.

STAND.COM

This student group is committed to utilizing the tools and knowledge gained in the classrooms of Monroe, and putting it to greater community use. Currently, STAND.COM is working with world renowned Habitat for Humanity, building a home for a family in Westchester. Additional activities include voter registration drives, field trips, guest speakers, social events, and additional community projects.

Hospitality Management Club

Open to students of this major. This club promotes experiential learning while incorporating skills learned during the semester. The club establishes connections to future employers in the field of hospitality. Activities include fieldtrips and guest speaker events.

Health Information Technology Club

Open to students of this major. The HIT Club visits local and regional hospitals, and area health care facilities. The club utilizes the visits and guest speakers to stay abreast of the most recent technological advances used in the health care field.

Computer Information Systems Club

Open to students of this major and the Business Technology major. The club conducts workshops, provides guest speakers, and schedules visits to technological fairs to keep up with the latest changes in this ever-evolving field.

Creative Campus

Monroe's literary journal presents poetry, essays, and short stories from Monroe students. The journal is published every semester by the English Department at the college.

Chess Club

Monroe's Chess Club enables students to learn and compete in this challenging and thought-provoking ancient game. The club meets once a week at the Bronx or New Rochelle campus.

ADMISSIONS PROCESS

Applicants may apply online at www.monroecollege.edu, by mail, or in person at the Admissions Offices at either the Bronx or New Rochelle campuses. Admissions is conducted on a rolling basis. Your admissions package will include an application, essay and $35 admissions fee, as well as SAT scores, a high school diploma, and transcript from your high school if you are applying for a scholarship. Once your admissions package is complete, we require an interview with an admissions counselor.

If you have any questions about admissions, please contact us at 800-55-MONROE.

NAROPA UNIVERSITY

AT A GLANCE

Accredited by the Higher Learning Commission of the North Central Association of Colleges and Schools, Naropa University is a private, nonprofit, nonsectarian liberal arts institution whose mission is contemplative education. This learning approach integrates the best of Eastern and Western educational traditions, enabling students to integrate academic knowledge with self-knowledge through contemplative practice. Founded in 1974 by Chögyam TrunGPA, Rinpoche, a lineage holder in the Tibetan Buddhist tradition, the university offers BA and BFA degrees through its 4-year undergraduate program as well as MA, MDiv, and MFA degrees through its graduate school.

LOCATION AND ENVIRONMENT

Naropa University is located in Boulder, Colorado, at the base of the Rocky Mountain foothills and 25 miles northwest of Denver. Boulder has earned a reputation for great quality of life with a dynamic arts community. Hiking, skiing and snowboarding enthusiasts have ample opportunity to pursue their sport and recreation activities. Boulder has extensive bike paths, and public transportation provides a frequent and comprehensive bus schedule throughout the day.

Naropa has 3 Boulder campuses, 2 of which serve undergraduate programs. The Arapahoe Campus is home to undergraduate advising, administration, a performing arts center, a meditation hall, the Allen Ginsberg Library, a computer lab, student lounges, the bookstore, classrooms for most undergraduate courses and the Naropa Café. The Nalanda Campus, 3.5 miles from the Arapahoe Campus, is home to performing and visual arts programs.

OFF-CAMPUS OPPORTUNITIES

Naropa University students may study abroad during their sophomore and junior years and the fall semester of their senior year. Studying and living overseas with Naropa fosters intercultural competence and critical thinking and lays the ground for compassionate engagement with the world. A study abroad program is offered in Prague, Czech Republic.

The Community Studies Center provides opportunities for students and faculty to develop skills for participating in the public life of their communities. Through its emphasis on applied, experiential projects, community-based learning offers innovative tools to forward the knowledge of academic and artistic disciplines, augment student learning and educate a citizenry to perform the public work of a democracy. AmeriCorps scholarship funds are provided for Naropa students involved in community work.

MAJORS AND DEGREES OFFERED

Upon completion of 30 semester credits, a student may declare a major. A total of 120 semester credits is required to earn an undergraduate degree.

Contemplative Psychology integrates Western psychology and Eastern approaches to healing mind and body, through concentrations include in Somatic psychology; psychology of health and healing; transpersonal and humanistic psychology; and psychological science.

Early Childhood Education nurtures the genuine and compassionate nature of teachers and applies methods drawn from traditions such as Waldorf, Montessori, Shambhala and Reggio EmiliaBuddhist traditions. The major offers apprentice-style internships with master teachers from these traditions.

Environmental Studies empowers students to develop skills and the interdisciplinary understanding needed to skillfully address complex environmental issues. Courses emphasize field science, sacred ecology, sustainability, horticulture, environmental history and justice, and learning community emphasizes experiential learning, natural science, personal growth, and an awakened relationship between self and world.

Interdisciplinary Studies invites students to design a focus of study major within by selecting courses from 2 or 3 disciplines at Naropa. Recent examples of senior work include "Documentary Poetics" and "Shambhala Path of Hip-Hop Warriorship."

Music offers gives students fundamental training in musicianship that includes performance, harmonic analysis, ear training, aural and rhythmic acuity, music theory, improvisation, composition, history and multicultural perspectives. Grounded in the practice of improvisation, creativity extends to composition, recording, and innovative uses of music technology.

Peace Studies focuses on the study of peace and explores the causes of violence and war through 4 related areas of inquiry: history and politics of social change; theory and practice of peacemaking; the arts in peacemaking; and engaged learning.

Religious Studies explores religion in a variety of ways, with an emphasis upon the statement of historical traditions in contemporary life. Significance is placed on the role of contemplative practice in the world's great religions, especially Buddhism. the role of contemplative practice in the world's great religions, especially Buddhism, and places special emphasis on the expression of historical traditions in contemporary life.

Traditional Eastern Arts is the only degree program of its kind in the country that combines using the practice of sitting meditation and an in-depth study of the philosophy, history and culture of a body-mind awareness discipline. Concentrations are offered in T'ai-chi Ch'uan, Aikido and Yoga Teacher Training.

Visual Arts blends traditional and contemporary visual arts study with contemplative practice and offers studio courses in several painting mediums and calligraphic forms, sculpture, pottery and photography. Courses in drawing, the history of visual art, meditation and studio practice, and studio foundations and portfolio preparation form the major's foundation.

Writing and literature offers intensive training in the practice and study of writing through small writing workshops, literary studies courses, contemplative practice and exposure to a range of contemporary writing through the Summer Writing Program.

The BFA in performance training curriculum is interdisciplinary, combining physical acting, contemporary dance and extended vocal techniques drawn from world traditions complemented by elements of the visual arts and music.

offers rigorous technical training, an emphasis on student-centered creative process and a contemplative approach to performance and performance studies.

A BA program in Peace Studies is pending approval by the North Central Association of Colleges and Schools.

ACADEMIC PROGRAMS

Through core courses students are introduced to the values, modes of inquiry and essential skills of contemplative education at Naropa University. Grounded in Naropa's mission, courses strike a living balance between scholarship, contemplative practice, artistic expression and civic engagement. This multidimensional approach to teaching and learning is unique to Naropa, reflecting its singular goal to bridge the gap between knowledge and wisdom.

CAMPUS FACILITIES AND EQUIPMENT

Residential living at Naropa University combines housing, education and community to create an inspired college experience. Naropa housing, which is required for entering undergraduate students ages 21 and younger who arrive with fewer than 30 credits, Naropa housing incorporates co-curricular programming, peer development, community activities and resident advisors to create a living-learning environment.

There are 2 computer labs at Naropa: the main lab in the Administration Building basement on the Arapahoe Campus and a smaller lab on the Paramita Campus. The main lab has 72 Windows 2000 PCs, 5 Windows XP PCs and 3 Macs, while there are 12 Windows 2000 PCs and 2 Macs in the Paramita lab. Both labs have laser printers and scanners. All computers are set up for Internet access and word processing. Both labs have lab assistants who can help students with hardware and software. The The Nalanda Campus reading room also has 4 Windows XP PCs. Wireless Hot Spots are located at all campuses for notebook users with Windows 2000 or XP and a new Linksys wireless card.

TUITION, ROOM, BOARD, AND FEES

Full-time undergraduate tuition for 2007-08 was $971,320,738 per semester year plus a $387 bus pass fee. Part-time undergraduates were charged $63,073 per credit plus a $250 per semester registration fee and a $37 per semester bus pass fee. It costs an average of $1,300 per month to live in Boulder. This estimate includes room and board, transportation, books, and miscellaneous expenses.

FINANCIAL AID

Naropa University offers institutional grants and scholarships, as well as all types of federal student aid. Some financial aid for international students is also available. Approximately 70 percent of Naropa's degree-seeking students receive financial assistance in the form of loans, student employment, scholarships and grants.

STUDENT ORGANIZATIONS AND ACTIVITIES

Naropa students are encouraged to participate in university governance by taking part in university committees. Town Hall meetings bring together students, faculty and staff to discuss issues of shared concern.

Some student groups active in the last year include: Amnesty International; A TONO (Latina/o student group); Bombay Gin (literary journal); El Centro de la Gente Committee (multicultural center activities); Chanoyu Club (tea ceremonies); Dharma Artists Collective; International Student Group; GLLGBTQIA Group; International Student Group; Ma Paya Pang Paraan (martial arts); Naropa Freestyle Hip-Hop Group; Naropa Soccer Team; Naropa 12 Step Group; Peak Oil Discussion Group; ROOT (outdoor group); Students of Color Group; Tendrel (Naropa's diversity journal)

ADMISSIONS PROCESS

A completed application for admission includes a $50 application fee; 3 essays; 2 letters of recommendation; official high school transcripts for first-time freshman and freshman transfer applicants (0 to 30 credits); and official college transcripts for every university attended. Many departments also require supplemental application materials and a phone or in-person interview.

Prospective students are encouraged to visit. The Admissions Office hosts a preview weekend each semester, and guided campus tours are available throughout the year.

The suggested deadline for receiving completed applications for the fall semester is January 15 and for the spring semester is October 15. Applications received after the suggested deadline are reviewed on a space-available basis. For additional information, please contact:

Admissions Office

Naropa University

2130 Arapahoe Avenue

Boulder, Colorado 80302-6697

Telephone: 303-546-3572; 800-772-6951 (toll free)

Fax: 303-546-3583

E-mail: admissions@naropa.edu

Website: www.naropa.edu

NAZARETH COLLEGE OF ROCHESTER

AT A GLANCE

Founded in 1924, Nazareth College is a coeducational college with undergraduate and graduate studies in the liberal arts and sciences and professional programs in health and human services, education, and management. The college is located on 150 scenic acres near Rochester, New York, and currently enrolls approximately 2,000 undergraduate and 800 graduate students. Nazareth has a strong commitment to experience-based learning and civic engagement. In the past decade, Nazareth has produced 18 Fulbright recipients and 2 Pickering Foreign Affairs Fellowships.

More than 40 majors and minors are available, with internship opportunities to provide students with participatory experience in their field of study. Nazareth competes in Division III of the NCAA. Its intercollegiate teams include men's and women's basketball, cross-country, equestrian, golf, lacrosse, soccer, swimming, diving, tennis, volleyball, track and field; and women's field hockey and softball.

LOCATION AND ENVIRONMENT

The Nazareth campus is a short walk from the village of Pittsford, which offers a selection of restaurants and specialty shops, as well as bike trails and boat rides along the Erie Canal. The campus is 7 miles from Rochester, the third largest city in the state of New York. Rich in culture and entertainment, the city serves as world headquarters for 2 major corporations: Eastman Kodak and Bausch and Lomb. A major Xerox facility is also located in Rochester. The city offers a broad array of museums, annual festivals, shopping malls, tourist attractions, professional sporting events, and ski resorts. Two museums of international import—the George Eastman House/International Museum of Film and Photography, and Strong National Museum of Play—make their homes in Rochester.

OFF-CAMPUS OPPORTUNITIES

Nazareth students are able to gain valuable work-related experience off campus no matter what their program of study. Student teaching assignments, clinical work with our therapy-related programs, social work placements, and internships are just a few of the opportunities available. The school offers internships in conjunction with all undergraduate majors.

Nazareth students have access to study abroad programs across 5 continents. In addition to well-known destinations such as France, Italy, Spain, and Germany, students travel to South America, Asia, Africa, Australia, and the Middle East. Programs include traditional academic semesters abroad, as well as those that address special study in archeology, business, and other topics of interest. The college has institutional relationships with many highly regarded institutions across the globe, allowing students a myriad of choices.

MAJORS AND DEGREES OFFERED

Nazareth offers Bachelor of arts, bachelor of music, and bachelor of science degrees in the following areas: accounting, American studies, anthropology, art (studio), art education, art history, biochemistry, biology, business administration, business education, chemistry, communication sciences and disorders (speech pathology), communication and rhetoric, economics, English, environmental science, French, German, history, information technology, international studies, Italian, literature and language, management science, mathematics, music, music/business, music education, music history, music performance, music theater, music theory, music therapy, nursing, peace and justice studies, philosophy, physical therapy (6-year DPT program) political science, psychology, religious studies, social science, social work, sociology, Spanish, and theater arts. Nazareth offers pre-professional programs in dentistry, law, medicine, and veterinary science. Students may combine education certification with their declared major to earn certification in elementary, middle and special education (grades 1-9), or secondary education (grades 7-12). Nazareth offers certification in art, music, speech and hearing for grades K-12. Most majors are also available as academic minors. Students may pursue interdisciplinary minors in gerontology, multicultural studies, and women's studies.

CAMPUS FACILITIES AND EQUIPMENT

The college's 150-acre campus features more than 20 buildings of contemporary and Gothic design. The Otto A. Shults Community Center houses a full gymnasium, a 25-meter swimming pool, fitness center, the student union, college radio station, and student personnel offices. Classrooms—including many smart rooms—are located in Smyth Hall, the Arts Center, Carroll Hall, and Golisano Academic Center. Computer labs are found throughout campus, and a campus Wi-Fi system is installed in all major academic buildings. The Golisano Academic Center houses faculty and administrative offices, a full service dining facility, and multi-faith chapel. Roughly 63 percent of the full-time student body lives on campus. Nazareth's 10 residence halls include both co-ed and single-sex options. Singles, doubles, suites and apartments are all available. Construction on a four-story, environmentally friendly residence hall, to be complete in Fall 08, is currently underway. Foreign language majors have the option of rooming at the La Maison Française. The Casa Hispana and Casa Italiana, as well as a German Cultural Center, serve as social, academic, and cultural centers for students wishing to immerse themselves in Spanish, Italian, and German language and customs.

TUITION, ROOM, BOARD, AND FEES

Estimated costs for 2008-2009 academic year are $33,850 ($23,050 for tuition; $9,900 for room and board; $1050 for college fees). Books, transportation, and personal expenses are not included in this estimate. Fees may change at any time. For the most current information, contact the Admissions Office.

FINANCIAL AID

Nazareth provides its students with more than $15 million in grant and scholarship assistance; the school is committed to making a Nazareth education possible for every applicant it admits. Financial need is the primary consideration in the granting of most awards, but the school also offers an assortment of merit-based awards for those demonstrating excellence in academics, the arts, music and drama. Those seeking aid must submit a completed Free Application for Federal Student Aid (FAFSA); the form must reach federal processors between January 1 and February 15. Those seeking early decision must submit the CSS Profile by November 15.

STUDENT ORGANIZATIONS AND ACTIVITIES

Nazareth offers a wealth of co-curricular choices for students of all interests and backgrounds. Campus clubs and organizations include Amnesty International, Art Club, Asian Club, Association of Student Social Workers, Campus Ministry Council, Cultural Affairs/CALEB, Dance Team, Economics Club, Environmental Club, French Club, German Club, Gleaner (the student newspaper), History Club, i Club, Italian Club, Inter-ethnic Nazareth Coalition, Lambda Association, Math Club, Music Therapy Club, Nazareth Commuter Association, Nazareth Speech, Hearing, and Language Association, Peer Health Educators, Physical Therapy Club, Pre-Med Club, Residence Hall Association, Science Club, *Sigilium* (yearbook), Spanish Club, Student Activities Council, Theater League, *Verity* (literary magazine), WNAZ (radio station) and Wilderness Club. The student political voice is heard through the Undergraduate Association.

ADMISSIONS PROCESS

A complete application to Nazareth includes and application form, an original essay or graded writing sample, a letter of recommendation from a teacher or guidance counselor, an official transcript of high school academic achievement, a nonrefundable $40 application fee, and Standardized Test scores, if the student decides he/she would like those scores to be used in the admissions process (Nazareth is a Standardized Test Option College). Early Decision, Early Action and Regular Decision applications are welcome. The deadline for Early Decision applications is November 15; applicants are notified starting December 15th; the due date for enrollment deposit is February 1. Those applying for Early Action must submit their application by December 15; notification for Early Action applicants begins January 15; students have until May 1to make a decision about attending Nazareth. Those applying for Regular Decision are encouraged to file before the final deadline of February 15. Regular Decision applicants receive notification of the college's decision starting on March 1. Admitted applicants must make a final decision on whether they will attend Nazareth by May 1. The school recommends that the applicants complete a college-preparatory curriculum including English, Mathematics, Social Studies, Science and Foreign Language. Academic achievement is the primary consideration in admissions decisions, but the Admissions Committee also considers special talent in drama, music and art; it also looks at students' co-curricular activities. A personal interview is recommended in order to familiarize you with the campus and all that it has to offer. An interview is not, however, a required part of the application. You can plan a visit or ask for more information by contacting: Office of Admissions, Nazareth College, 4245 East Avenue, Rochester, NY 14618; Telephone: 585-389-2860; Toll Free Line: 800-462-3944; E-mail: admissions@naz.edu; Website: www.naz.edu.

NEUMONT UNIVERSITY

AT A GLANCE

Neumont University is educating the most sought-after software developers. Founded in 2003, Neumont University offers accelerated 24-month Bachelor of Science in Computer Science (BSCS) degrees and Master of Science in Computer Science (MSCS) degrees in one and two-year formats. Neumont University is accredited by the Accrediting Council for Independent Colleges and Schools (ACICS). Some of the careers in software development include software engineer, systems architect, web development, systems analyst, data modeler, and programmer/analyst. www.neumont.edu.

LOCATION AND ENVIRONMENT

The Neumont campus is a 48,000 square foot marble, glass and steel facility inside a high-end commercial and corporate park, nestled against the west bank of the Jordan River Parkway. The Neumont University Campus is located at 10701 South River Front Parkway in South Jordan, Utah.

OFF-CAMPUS OPPORTUNITIES

Located south of Salt Lake City, Neumont University is minutes away from a major metropolitan area, world-class skiing and snowboarding, and miles of open trails. Student housing options are within walking distance of dozens of shops and restaurants and are serviced by the Utah Transit Authority bus lines and Neumont-run shuttles. This makes getting to and from campus very simple.

Students live in fully furnished apartments with a complete package of amenities including wireless internet, a washer and dryer, tennis courts, pools, and weight rooms. Students room with like-minded peers, who are driven by a desire to learn in a stimulating technology-driven environment.

MAJORS AND DEGREES OFFERED

Bachelor of Science in Computer Science

The Neumont University Bachelor of Science in Computer Science (BSCS) distinguishes itself with an integrated, project-based curriculum that focuses on the skills most valued by today's employers. Graduates of this innovative program are motivated software developers who are well-equipped for success in the corporate world. BSCS projects and coursework (including general education requirements) are designed to provide students with a strong foundation in relevant technical skills and standards, a unique understanding of the business environment, and the ability to work and communicate in a software development team.

PROJECT COURSES

Neumont believes the key to a useful and applicable degree in CS is team-based, hands-on experience with real software projects. In support of this, students spend the majority of their time working in teams on pertinent, real-world software development projects.

Upon completing the instructional and project hours, the Neumont University graduate has a B.S. degree in Computer Science and a portfolio of project work.

Master of Science in Computer Science

This program was developed utilizing the strengths of Neumont's renowned Bachelor of Science in Computer Science program and prepares graduates for leadership roles in organizations seeking to utilize leading-edge technologies that lie on the boundary of research and commercial application. The MCSC curriculum emphasizes information modeling, model-driven development and business rules through Advanced Computing Seminars, Lectures, Labs, and Research Projects.

Advanced Computing Seminars

Students develop the analytical and communication skills needed to understand advanced topics in computing and effectively communicate those concepts through papers and presentations.

Lectures and Labs

Students explore cutting-edge computing applications with one major theme, the successful application of technology in a business environment.

Research Projects

Students research, review and analyze the current state-of-the-art and develop proposals that extend the relevant body of knowledge.

ACADEMIC PROGRAMS

Career Services

Neumont also offers an extensive Career Services Center for all students. The Neumont University Career Services assists students in networking, preparing for, and finding careers when they graduate from the university.

Each quarter, Neumont University hosts a Career Fair where students and employers are come together to network, explore career opportunities, and interview. Prior to the fair, students are offered Resume and Interview Skills Workshops and may request interviews with specific employers coming to the fair. Additionally, employers are given a book of student resumes and can request interviews with specific students who have the skills they are seeking.

CAMPUS FACILITIES AND EQUIPMENT

The campus features standard lecture rooms, project rooms, cafeteria, bookstore, student commons and enterprise-level wireless internet connections. Each student is issued a high-end laptop, when they start the program, to use throughout their education at Neumont.

Tuition, Room, Board, and Fees

Tuition is charged per quarter based on the full-time rate for the academic year in effect at the time of enrollment. An academic year is equivalent to three quarters. This rate will remain in effect throughout the student's first academic year. The academic year rate in effect at the time the student moves into subsequent academic years will determine the rate charged during those terms.

The minimum full-time course load is 12 credits per quarter. If a student falls below a full-time load, a per unit charge will be assessed in place of the quarterly charge described above.

Textbook costs per quarter are dependent upon the classes for which the student is registered and the textbooks purchased. Textbooks are sold through the bookstore in accordance with official University policies. At the time of issuance, textbooks become the responsibility of the student.

There are no tuition differences for out-of-state students.

Technology fees and a library fee (outlined below) are assessed each quarter.

Non-refundable application fee $35. Required of all applicants

Enrollment fee $100. Required of all first time students

Tuition $9,000 Per quarter

Per unit charge (applies to part-time students only) $495. Per unit, assessed in place of the quarterly charge, only when the student is carrying less than 12 units per term

Technology fees $50 Per quarter

Computer Fee $350 Per quarter

Library fee $25 Per quarter

Security deposit on computer hardware issued to student $3000 Refundable under terms of Laptop Usage Policy. See the student handbook for more details.

Re-entry fee $50. Non-refundable fee required of all applicants for re-enrollment after withdrawal has occurred

Graduation fee $100

Transcript fee $10. Students are provided one official transcript upon graduation without charge, subsequent transcript requests will incur this fee

Duplicate diploma $25

Returned check penalty $25. Per item

ROOM AND BOARD FEES

Non-refundable application fee $75

Refundable housing deposit $275

Sterling Village – Shared Room $425. Per Month

Hunter Pointe – Shared Room $400. Per Month

Hunter Point – Private Room $275. Per Month

FINANCIAL AID

Neumont University participates in the Federal Student Financial Aid programs (Title IV Funding). Students interested in attending Neumont University will have the opportunity to complete a Free Application for Federal Financial Aid as well as an in-house Neumont University Financial Aid application in order to determine Title IV eligibility. Although Title IV eligibility will not cover all expenses incurred from program costs, it will aid in covering some of those costs.

By completing and submitting the Federal application to the Financial Aid Office, Neumont University is able to provide all incoming students with the best Financial Aid package possible including Pell Grant and Title IV loans. The Department of Education requires that students complete this form as well as additional documentation in order to determine eligibility.

Neumont offers Financial Aid for those who qualify. For questions regarding Financial Aid please email financial.aid@Neumont.edu or visit http://neumont.edu/future-students/financial-aid-scholarships.html.

STUDENT ORGANIZATIONS AND ACTIVITIES

Neumont student life isn't about frat parties and football games. Neumont is a one-of-a-kind opportunity for immersion into the culture and challenges of the technology industry. Students work hard and they play hard too. Intramural basketball, coding competitions, and gaming tournaments take place throughout the year. Some of the student organizations included:

• Robotics and Science

• Rhythm-based Game Lovers Association

• Unified Student Government

• Neumont chapter of the Society of Women Engineers

• Soccer Club

• LDSSA (LDS Student Association)

• Athletic Club

ADMISSIONS PROCESS

As part of the Admissions Process, we evaluate the whole student and their potential to succeed in our rigorous program.

Applicants are evaluated on a variety of factors including: GPA, SAT or ACT scores, essays, community service, extracurricular activities, work experience, academic potential, technical knowledge and level of motivation.

Prospective students can complete an application for admissions at: www.neumont.edu/apply.

Transfer Students

Neumont University may award transfer credits for courses that meet our evaluation criteria from any institution accredited by an agency recognized by the U.S. Department of Education. Courses taken at a foreign institution will be accepted for transfer on the basis of the report of a credential evaluation service.

For courses to be considered for transfer credit, a student must submit official transcripts and course descriptions from the time period when the courses were taken.

Credit will be accepted only for courses in which a grade of "C" or higher was earned. The number of credits awarded for a course will not exceed the number of credits offered for the related Neumont University course.

THE NEW SCHOOL

AT A GLANCE

Located in Greenwich Village, in the heart of New York City, The New School is the ultimate urban university. Founded nearly a century ago as a bastion of intellectual and artistic freedom, The New School today offers some of the nation's most highly regarded programs in design, liberal arts, the performing arts, and social and political thought.

Artists, scholars, and students from all 50 states and around the world attend The New School to earn bachelor's, master's, or doctoral degrees, complete certifi-

cate programs, or take continuing education classes. The 9,000 matriculated students and 15,000 continuing education students who study on campus or online from anywhere in the world (www.newschool.edu/online) enjoy the benefits of small class sizes, superior resources, and a renowned working faculty who practice what they teach. Find out more about The New School at **www.newschool.edu**.

For undergraduates, The New School offers four colleges in the arts and the humanities: Parsons The New School for Design, Eugene Lang College The New School for Liberal Arts, Mannes College The New School for Music, and The New School for Jazz and Contemporary Music. (In addition, The New School for General Studies offers a liberal arts bachelor's program designed specifically for adults. Find out more at www.newschool.edu/adultba.)

PARSONS THE NEW SCHOOL FOR DESIGN
www.newschool.edu/parsons

One of the largest and most prestigious degree-granting colleges of art and design in the nation, Parsons The New School for Design has been a leader in the field of art

and design since its founding in 1896. Its intensive programs and distinguished faculty embrace innovation, pioneer new uses of technology, and instill in students a global perspective on design. Parsons' more than 15 undergraduate programs are supplemented by interdisciplinary collaboration, international study opportunities, and professional internships with top designers and artists.

EUGENE LANG COLLEGE THE NEW SCHOOL FOR LIBERAL ARTS
www.newschool.edu/lang

Eugene Lang College The New School for Liberal Arts combines the advantages of a small, intimate liberal arts college with the resources of a major university. Lang attracts top students who value individualized attention and the opportunity to be challenged in small seminar-style classes. Committed leaders, scholars, and newsmakers teach these students in an interdisciplinary context. Rather than taking required courses in a single academic discipline, students map out an individual path through Lang's more than 10 areas of study.

MANNES COLLEGE THE NEW SCHOOL FOR MUSIC
www.newschool.edu/mannes

Mannes College The New School for Music is a preeminent conservatory of classical music that provides a professional trajectory for serious undergraduate students. The Mannes community is made up of students and a faculty of professional musicians from every corner of the world. Here, aspiring artists learn and play music with scholars, composers, conductors, and performing artists from some of the world's renowned orchestras, ensembles, and opera companies. The school produces more than 400 concerts each year at its two concert halls and venues throughout the New York metropolitan area, most of which feature Mannes students. With only 300 college students, Mannes offers an intimate, supportive atmosphere that allows for close and constructive relationships among students, faculty, and administrators.

THE NEW SCHOOL FOR JAZZ AND CONTEMPORARY MUSIC
www.newschool.edu/jazz

The New School for Jazz and Contemporary Music offers an innovative course of study in which a passionately engaged faculty of professional artists, drawn from New York City's renowned jazz community, guides serious and talented students toward high standards of achievement and the development of an individual creative voice. Since its inception in 1986, the program has been distinguished by a curriculum based on the time-honored tradition of artist as mentor, a focus on small-group performance, and faculty members who have played a major role in the history and evolution of jazz, blues, pop, and new genres. The ultimate proof of the program's success can be heard in the musical voices of a generation of New School Jazz alumni, represented at the highest artistic levels in every musical genre.

LOCATION AND ENVIRONMENT

The New School's New York City location offers access to hundreds of world-class cultural events and venues, including museums, concerts, theaters, restaurants, parks, and the streets themselves. From the main campus in Greenwich Village to Mannes' home on the Upper West Side, New School students live and learn in one of the most vibrant, diverse, and exciting cities in the world.

MAJORS AND DEGREES OFFERED
PARSONS THE NEW SCHOOL FOR DESIGN
www.newschool.edu/parsons

Parsons offers undergraduate programs in Architectural Design, Art and Design Studies, Communication Design, Design and Management, Design and Technology, Fashion Design, Fashion Marketing, Fashion Studies, Fine Arts, Foundation, Graphic Design, Illustration, Integrated Design, Interior Design, Photography, Product Design, and Environmental Studies°. Degrees offered are BFA, BBA, BS, AAS, and a joint BA/BFA degree with Eugene Lang College (described below).

EUGENE LANG COLLEGE THE NEW SCHOOL FOR LIBERAL ARTS
www.newschool.edu/lang

Eugene Lang College offers a BA in Liberal Arts in the following areas of study: The Arts (with tracks in arts in context, theater, dance, music, and visual arts); Education Studies; History; Literature; Religious Studies; Science, Technology, and Society; Social Inquiry; Urban Studies; and Writing. Lang College also offers BA degrees in Culture and Media, Philosophy, Psychology, and Environmental Studies°, and dual BA/BFA degrees with Parsons and The New School for Jazz and Contemporary Music (described below).

Lang students can accelerate their progress toward a master's degree by combining undergraduate work with graduate study at one of The New School's graduate schools. Dual bachelor's/master's degree programs offered at Lang include Media Studies and International Affairs (with The New School); Anthropology, Economics, Liberal Studies, Philosophy, Political Science, Psychology, and

Sociology (with The New School for Social Research); and Urban Policy Analysis and Management, Health Services Management and Policy, Organizational Change Management, and Nonprofit Management (with Milano The New School of Management and Urban Policy).

MANNES COLLEGE THE NEW SCHOOL FOR MUSIC
www.newschool.edu/mannes

Students major in either performance or music in a variety of concentrations (including Orchestral Instruments, Piano, Harpsichord, Voice, Classical Guitar, Orchestral Conducting, Choral Conducting, Composition, and Theory) and can earn a BM, BS, or undergraduate diploma.

THE NEW SCHOOL FOR JAZZ AND CONTEMPORARY MUSIC
www.newschool.edu/jazz

New School Jazz offers concentrations in voice, instrumentals, composition, and liberal studies. Students can earn a BFA or joint BA/BFA degree with Eugene Lang College (as described below).

BA/BFA DUAL-DEGREE PROGRAM
www.newschool.edu/babfa

The BA/BFA program at The New School is a five-year dual-degree program through which students can earn a liberal arts bachelor of arts degree from Eugene Lang College The New School for Liberal Arts and a bachelor of fine arts degree from either Parsons The New School for Design or The New School for Jazz and Contemporary Music. The BA/BFA program allows students to explore two areas of interest throughout their studies— with classes and studios located conveniently on one campus.

ACADEMIC PROGRAMS

See the degree section above and visit each school's website for more information on specific programs.

ENVIRONMENTAL STUDIES
www.newschool.edu/environmentalstudies

Beginning in fall 2008, pending approval from the New York State Department of Education, The New School will offer two new programs of study focusing on the environment, a Bachelor of Arts and Bachelor of Science in Environmental Studies.

Both degree programs will allow students to focus their work on one of two areas of concentration within the degree programs. For the bachelor of arts degree offered at Eugene Lang College, students can concentrate in urban ecosystems or policy. Students working toward a bachelor of science degree at Parsons can choose to concentrate in Urban Ecosystem Design or Sustainable Design.

Located in the heart of one of the world's largest and most complex urban ecosystems, this innovative program will make the New York City region its focus and laboratory.

OFF-CAMPUS OPPORTUNITIES

The New School believes that students learn both in and out of the classroom. The university offers students access to a wide array of internships, apprenticeships with top designers, and performance opportunities in venues from downtown clubs to Lincoln Center, enabling students to shape their education and take advantage of all the city has to offer.

PARSONS THE NEW SCHOOL FOR DESIGN
www.newschool.edu/parsons

In 1920, Parsons School of Design, as it was then known, became the first American school of art and design to found a campus abroad. Today, the school offers its students the opportunity to expand their horizons by studying at art and design schools around the world. During their junior year, bachelor's degree students may enroll for one or two semesters in another school in the United States or abroad. Several departments assist students in securing noncredit internships that provide valuable work experience and professional contacts. Companies and institutions that have offered New School students internships include Marc Jacobs, Polo—Ralph Lauren, HBO, MTV, *The New York Times*, *Rolling Stone* magazine, Marvel Comics, and the Museum of Modern Art.

EUGENE LANG COLLEGE THE NEW SCHOOL FOR LIBERAL ARTS
www.newschool.edu/lang

Many Lang students spend a semester, academic year, or summer abroad taking courses, working as interns, and pursuing volunteer projects. Lang offers foreign study options both through the school (in-house) and through other institutions. Experiential courses at Lang draw on the intellectual and cultural richness of New York City. Many of these courses provide students with tickets to cultural and artistic sites and events around the city. Offerings might include Arts in NYC, Lang at the Guggenheim, Lang at Judson Church, Lang at the Public, and Seeing Performance.

Internships and community activism are an essential part of the undergraduate program in liberal arts at Lang. Student interns receive professional guidance, gain hands-on experience, develop confidence, and establish an expansive network of contacts. Students can pursue internships for academic credit in a variety of fields, including publishing, politics, health care, the arts, radio, television, music, online media, nonprofit administration, and environmental activism.

Recently, Lang students have won coveted spots at MTV, HBO, Beth Israel Hospital, *The Village Voice*, Sony Entertainment, Gay Men's Health Crisis, Miramax Films, and the ACLU.

MANNES COLLEGE THE NEW SCHOOL FOR MUSIC
www.newschool.edu/mannes

A distinct advantage of studying music in New York, a center of the international music scene, is the opportunity to gain professional-level experience at major performance venues. Mannes students have recently performed at Carnegie Hall, Lincoln Center, Symphony Space, the Morgan Library, and other prominent venues throughout the city.

THE NEW SCHOOL FOR JAZZ AND CONTEMPORARY MUSIC
www.newschool.edu/jazz

More than 150 concerts are presented in the jazz program's performance space every year. Jazz students also play at venues outside the school, including the jazz club Sweet Rhythm, where students perform weekly, and appearances at festivals and music conferences worldwide. Students also gain valuable professional experience through performances at special events, including private parties and corporate functions, arranged by the jazz program's Gig Office.

—Continued on next page

FACILITIES AND EQUIPMENT

New School students have access to excellent resources, including a vast library consortium that houses approximately three million volumes and fully equipped performance spaces, practice rooms, and design studios. Each school's unique facilities are described on its website.

Over the past several years, The New School has invested more than $30 million in a number of fully equipped labs. The Knowledge Union consists of state-of-the-art technology spread over four floors; the 600 networked workstations include all relevant platforms. Servers support work that ranges from traditional print output to online projects using webcasting and secure transaction technology. Specialty work—whether audio or video production, MIDI, recording, or physical computing installation—takes place in private studios across the campus.

Portable production equipment, including digital still, video, and audio, is readily available. Digital projectors, surround sound, and active whiteboards feed into equipment racks that allow for media presentations of all kinds. The University Computing Center, on the third and fourth floors of Alvin Johnson/J.M. Kaplan Hall, is a hub of technologies. Computers and hands-on classrooms support multimedia, Web design, and desktop publishing as well as word processing and research.

TUITION, ROOM AND BOARD, AND FEES

The cost of attending The New School varies from program to program and sometimes from student to student. For information on tuition for each program of study and on-campus housing fees, visit www.newschool.edu/tuition.

FINANCIAL AID

Many students enrolled in degree programs at The New School take advantage of financial aid. U.S. citizens or eligible noncitizens must complete the Free Application for Federal Student Aid (FAFSA); degree-seeking undergraduate international students interested in grants or scholarships from The New School should complete the Undergraduate International Student Scholarship Application. Students attending Mannes College The New School for Music and The New School for Jazz and Contemporary Music are not required to fill out this form. For forms and more information, visit **www.newschool.edu/financialaid.html.**

FULL-TIME AND PART-TIME FACULTY

The New School prides itself on its low student-to-faculty ratio. Thanks to its strong academic programs and dedication to the arts, the school attracts leading professionals in their fields; it is not unusual to find a prominent or award-winning musician, scholar, artist, or designer at the front of the class. See each school's website for more information.

STUDENT ORGANIZATIONS AND ACTIVITIES

Students at The New School play an active role in the life of the university. From informal clubs to student unions, art shows to film festivals, there are hundreds of opportunities for students to get involved outside the classroom. The university recognizes more than 25 student organizations, including Buddhism for Global Peace; Out, Proud Environment at The New School (OPEN); Women of Color; Sketch Comedy Group; The New School Philosophy Club; and Project Africa.

ADMISSIONS PROCESSES AND REQUIREMENTS

The New School seeks talented and dedicated undergraduates who demand serious study in a nontraditional setting. Additional information about the admissions requirements for each school can be found on its website.

PARSONS THE NEW SCHOOL FOR DESIGN
www.newschool.edu/parsons

Parsons seeks serious, responsible, and highly motivated applicants. Each applicant is reviewed with a focus on experience, achievements, and potential for artistic growth. While Parsons recognizes the benefits of strong artistic preparation, some applicants are admitted on the basis of their academic strengths more than their visual material. For BFA applicants, a large part of the Admissions Committee's decision is based on portfolio evaluations and the Parsons Challenge as well as academic achievement. For BBA applicants, academic achievement is weighted heavily along with the Parsons Challenge. The AAS program is best suited to students who have some college experience, are clear about their interests within the world of design, and are prepared for rapid immersion in a professional course of study.

All applicants must submit a completed application, a nonrefundable $50 application fee, and original copies of official high school and/or college transcripts. Bachelor's applicants must also submit SAT or ACT scores if they are residents of the United States or TOEFL scores if they are international students (minimum of 580 on the paper-based exam or 237 on the computerized exam). All applicants must submit the multipart Parsons Challenge exercise. A portfolio is required of all BFA applicants except those applying to study design and management. The portfolio must consist of eight to 12 pieces of work, including but not limited to, drawings, paintings, photographs, digital media, or design. A personal interview is recommended for all applicants.

The admission and financial aid deadline for the fall semester is February 1, and the deadline for spring admission is October 15. The Admissions Committee reviews applications and sends students its decision a few weeks after all materials are received.

Admissions Office
Albert List Academic Center
Parsons The New School for Design
65 Fifth Avenue
New York, NY 10011
212.229.8989
Email: parsadm@newschool.edu

EUGENE LANG COLLEGE THE NEW SCHOOL FOR LIBERAL ARTS
www.newschool.edu/lang

Eugene Lang College encourages students of diverse racial, ethnic, religious, and political backgrounds to apply. The Admissions Committee looks for students who demonstrate an ability to make the best use of college-level resources and contribute to the Lang community. Qualities the college looks for include the ability to question, seriousness of purpose, and the capacity for progressive liberal arts study.

The Admissions Committee takes the whole student into account when making admissions decisions. A student's personal convictions and creative work, as discussed in the personal essay and required interview, are weighed along with scholastic achievement, as represented by transcripts, recommendations, and SAT or ACT scores. Most successful candidates have completed a college-preparatory course load in high school. Applicants are encouraged to take a tour and sit in on a seminar. The early decision application option is strongly recommended for applicants who know that Lang is their first choice.

High school juniors who display a high level of achievement may apply for early entrance, turning in two teacher recommendations with their application materials. Transfer students with a minimum of one year of college work behind them may apply and enroll in upper-level seminars upon acceptance. Those applying internationally follow regular application procedures. Non-native English speakers should submit their TOEFL scores. Students attending other institutions can come to Lang and participate in an internship through the New York Connections program.

Certain programs have special application requirements. Students wishing to enter the five-year dual-degree BA/BFA Jazz Studies program with Jazz and Contemporary Music must audition. Fine arts applicants to the five-year joint BA/BFA program with Parsons The New School for Design must submit a portfolio and a home exercise.

All categories of admitted applicants may begin their studies at Lang in the fall (September) or spring (January) semester. A $50 application fee is required. Waivers may be issued under the College Board's Fee Waiver Service. All required materials must be submitted by the following deadlines: November 15 for spring semester or for fall semester Early Decision; February 1 for freshman general admission and freshman early entrants (April 1 notification). May 15 is the deadline for transfers and visiting students.

Office of Admissions
Eugene Lang College The New School for Liberal Arts
65 West 11th Street
New York, NY 10011
212.229.5665
Email: lang@newschool.edu
www.newschool.edu/lang

MANNES COLLEGE THE NEW SCHOOL FOR MUSIC

www.newschool.edu/mannes

The Mannes College admissions process is designed to obtain a complete picture of an applicant. In reviewing applications, the Admissions Committee considers performance ability and potential, musical skills, English language aptitude (for applicants whose first language is not English), musical and academic background, and recommendation letters. Applicants must audition in person. In order for an applicant to be considered for an audition and entrance examination appointment within a given audition period, his or her application must be postmarked by the stated deadline. December 1 is the deadline for the main audition period (March 2–9), April 1 is the deadline for the late audition period (May 20–21), and November 1 is the deadline for spring semester entrance.

Most Mannes courses run the entire academic year, so students enroll in September. Undergraduate students transferring from other colleges may enter at the start of the second semester in January, subject to the approval of the Admissions Committee.

Applicants for the piano, violin, cello, flute, and voice concentrations must submit a prescreening recording in order to qualify for an in-person audition. Recordings must be postmarked by the application deadline stated above.

Office of Admissions
Mannes College The New School for Music
150 West 85th Street
New York, NY 10024
800.292.3040 or 212.580.0210 x4862
Email: mannesadmissions@newschool.edu
www.newschool.edu/mannes

THE NEW SCHOOL FOR JAZZ AND CONTEMPORARY MUSIC

www.newschool.edu/jazz

Students applying for the fall semester should submit their applications by January 1. Applicants for the spring (January) semester should apply by September 15. Live auditions are held in February and March. If you would like to schedule a live audition for the citywide audition week in March, you must submit your application by December 15. Applying early allows applicants to take full advantage of financial aid, scholarship, and live audition opportunities at the school. Late applications are due by March 15 for the fall semester and November 1 for the spring semester.

A performance audition is required of all students applying to The New School for Jazz and Contemporary Music. A prescreen tape or CD is required for all applicants on drums, guitar, and voice. The tape or CD must be received within one week of submission of an online application. Vocalists who pass the prescreen must audition live at The New School for Jazz and Contemporary Music; drummers and guitarists may audition live or online or submit an audition tape or CD.

A complete application includes a completed and signed application form (online applicants sign electronically), a nonrefundable application fee of $100 (online credit card payment, check, or money order), a personal statement, a live or recorded audition (prescreen tape or CD for drummers, guitarists, and vocalists); official high school or secondary school transcript or school records; and a letter of recommendation from a teacher, counselor, or professional who is able to comment on your qualifications for study at The New School for Jazz and Contemporary Music. The school will accept one additional recommendation if the applicant chooses to submit one.

Office of Admissions
The New School for Jazz and Contemporary Music
79 Fifth Avenue, 5th floor
New York, NY 10003
212.229.5896 x4589
Email: jazzadm@newschool.edu
www.newschool.edu/jazz

The eight schools that make up the university are The New School for General Studies; The New School for Social Research; Parsons The New School for Design; Eugene Lang College The New School for Liberal Arts; Mannes College The New School for Music; The New School for Drama; and The New School for Jazz and Contemporary Music.

For a list of graduate program offerings at The New School, visit **www.newschool.edu/graduateprograms**.

www.newschool.edu/jazz

THE NEW SCHOOL

°Pending New York State approval

NEW YORK UNIVERSITY

AT A GLANCE

Located in Greenwich Village, New York University (NYU) is unlike any other U.S. institution of higher education in the United States. When you enter NYU, you become part of a close-knit community that combines the nurturing atmosphere of a small- to medium-sized college with the myriad offerings and research opportunities of a global, urban university. The energy and resources of New York City serve as an extension of our campus, providing unique opportunities for research, internships, and job placement. On campus, NYU's intellectual climate is fostered by a faculty of world-famous scholars, researchers, and artists who teach both undergraduate and graduate courses. Students have the opportunity to work on individual projects with these outstanding professors. NYU students come from every state and nearly 130 countries. They enroll in one of 8 schools or colleges and choose from 2,500 courses in 160 majors.

LOCATION AND ENVIRONMENT

New York City is the integral backdrop to NYU's undergraduate experience. Undergraduate study takes place at the university's Washington Square campus in the heart of Greenwich Village. One of the city's most creative communities, the Village is a historic neighborhood that has attracted generations of writers, musicians, artists, and intellectuals. Rather than building walls to separate the campus from the community, NYU embraces the city as an essential element of academic life.

Because NYU is located in New York City, a world center of finance, media, and the arts, internships, part-time jobs and research experiences complement course work with practical experience. The city offers students the best in theater, dance, music, film, libraries, museums, and galleries. NYU undergraduates can be found presenting academic papers at annual undergraduate conferences; entering their student films and winning prizes at film festivals; working on scientific research projects in innovative laboratories; interning on Wall Street; and completing field work in some of the world's best hospitals and schools.

OFF-CAMPUS OPPORTUNITIES

In addition to working part time and interning, students find many other ways to incorporate the city—and the world—into their studies. They perform in jazz ensembles at the Blue Note, the top jazz venue in Greenwich Village. They shoot their student films on the streets of New York.

Beyond our New York City campus, NYU offers 8 study abroad sites—in Berlin, Buenos Aires, Florence, Ghana, London, Madrid, Paris, Prague, and Shanghai. Studying abroad is considered an integral element of the NYU academic experience, and our programs stand out for their world-renowned faculty; bright, enthusiastic students; fully staffed sites; and academic centers that enable you to take advantage of the best each city has to offer.

MAJORS AND DEGREES OFFERED

At NYU, students enroll directly into one of the university's undergraduate schools, colleges, or programs, each of which has earned national recognition: College of Arts and Science, General Studies Program, Leonard N. Stern School of Business, Steinhardt School of Culture, Education, and Human Development, Tisch School of the Arts, Gallatin School of Individualized Study, Silver School of Social Work, Preston Robert Tisch Center for Hospitality, Tourism, and Sports Management, and College of Nursing.

Among the 160 undergraduate majors offered by the university are: Africana Studies, Anthropology, Biochemistry, Economics, Dance, Education, Engineering, Film and Television, Finance, Hotel and Tourism Management, Marketing, Metropolitan Studies, Neural Science, Sociology, Theatre, Recorded Music, and many more.

ACADEMIC PROGRAMS

At NYU, students enroll directly into one of the university's undergraduate schools, colleges, or programs. The College of Arts and Science offers an extensive curriculum in liberal arts and science, including pre-professional programs in law, medicine, and dentistry. The General Studies Program is a 2-year liberal arts program under the aegis of the College of Arts and Science, and enrollment is offered to a select group of students, who upon successful completion of the program then enroll as juniors in the undergraduate school or college to which they originally applied. The Leonard N. Stern School of Business ranks among the top 10 nationally, and combines a liberal arts core with an outstanding business curriculum. The Steinhardt School of Culture, Education, and Human Development is focused on the human service professions, including education, health, communications, and the arts. The Tisch School of the Arts combines a liberal arts education with conservatory training. The Gallatin School of Individualized Study allows highly motivated students to design their own curriculum. The Silver School of Social Work combines a liberal arts education with a firm grounding in social work. The Preston Robert Tisch Center for Hospitality, Tourism, and Sports Management offers programs in hotel and tourism management and sports management and leisure studies. The College of Nursing offers strong liberal arts combined with nursing science.

All students, regardless of their major, receive a firm foundation in the liberal arts. NYU faculty members are among country's leading intellectuals, including world-famous scholars and researchers who have received Nobel, Crafoord, and Pulitzer Prizes; MacArthur, Guggenheim, and Fulbright Fellowships; and Oscar and Emmy Awards. Faculty members teach both graduate and undergraduate courses, making it possible for undergraduate students to become directly involved in research projects with internationally known scholars.

CAMPUS FACILITIES AND EQUIPMENT

NYU offers an exceptional range of facilities and student services and an enormously varied program of clubs and activities, residence halls, meal plans, and dining locations. Academic facilities include 8 libraries and centers and institutes renowned for their research in applied mathematics, physics, neural science, and fine arts. Foreign language and cultural centers offer a wide variety of lectures, films, and concerts. In addition, students have access to our award-winning NYU Wasserman Center for Career Development, advanced computer and multimedia resources, and specialized offices that address almost every student need—from medical attention to discount theater tickets. The Kimmel Center for Student Life houses dining facilities, student lounges, computers, space for student clubs, and the Skirball Center for the Performing Arts, the largest performance space in lower Manhattan.

TUITION, ROOM, BOARD, AND FEES

2008-2009 Costs°

Tuition and fees for 2008-2009 are $$37,372; average room and board (includes up to 14 meals a week) is $12,810.

°Tisch School of the Arts and Leonard N. Stern School of Business rates vary.

FINANCIAL AID

We believe that you should be able to choose a college that offers the best range of educational opportunities. In order to make this choice possible, we attempt to aid students who are in need of financial assistance.

A high percentage of students entering NYU receive some form of financial aid. Scholarships and grants are based on financial need, academic merit, or both. Low-interest education loans are available for both students and parents. Part-time employment, on and off campus, is another source of funding.

NYU also offers or participates in a variety of payment plans. They range from interest-free prepayment plans to extensive loan programs that allow families to finance the cost of a college education over many years.

There are many sources of financial aid at NYU, and all students are invited to apply for financial aid or one of NYU's financing plans. At NYU, 74 percent of all full-time undergraduates receive some form of financial aid.

A financial aid package might include any combination of scholarships or grants, loans, or work-study programs. Students who wish to be considered for aid must submit the Free Application for Federal Student Aid (FAFSA). The FAFSA's submission deadline is February 15 for the fall semester and November 1 for the spring semester.

STUDENT ORGANIZATIONS AND ACTIVITIES

With more than 400 student clubs, NCAA Division III, intramural and club athletics, and numerous community service activities, NYU students participate in ways that match their varied interests.

Student-run clubs are as varied as the NYU student body. Whether their interests lie in a foreign language, politics, ballroom dancing, writing for the Washington Square News or working at NYU's own radio station, students are sure to find something to suit their tastes.

Two gyms—Coles Sports and Recreation Center and the Palladium Athletic Facility— provide the setting for intramurals, recreation classes, and 24 intercollegiate teams. NYU also has a partnership with the Chelsea Piers Sports and Entertainment Complex, which includes facilities for golf, ice and roller skating, indoor soccer, and sand volleyball.

Many NYU students volunteer their time through the NYU Office of Community Service. They offer their knowledge and experience to more than 60 nonprofit organizations throughout New York City, delivering meals to the needy, tutoring children, and offering crisis intervention and counseling services to people in need.

ADMISSIONS PROCESS

Admission to the undergraduate colleges of New York University is highly selective. The admission process involves a comprehensive review of the applicant's academic background, standardized test scores, extracurricular activities, an essay, and letters of recommendation. Several programs also require the applicant to audition or submit creative materials. The Admissions Committee pays particular attention to the number of honors, AP, and IB courses the applicant has completed in high school. We carefully consider the applicant's level of involvement in school and/or community activities, his or her special talents, alumni affiliation, socioeconomic background, geographic location, and race or ethnicity.

Applicants must submit scores from either the SAT Reasoning Test or the ACT examination (with Writing Test). Scores from the TOEFL examination are also required if English is not the applicant's native language. The Admissions Committee requires applicants (except those applying to the Tisch School of the Arts and the art and music program in the Steinhardt School of Culture, Education, and Human Development) to submit scores from 2 SAT II Subject Tests.

The admissions staff also visits high schools and hosts receptions throughout the country. Please check with your college counselor or the Admissions Web site at admissions.nyu.edu for dates and times.

A campus tour or an appointment for an information session can be arranged by calling 212-998-4524 or online at http://events.embark.com/event/nyu/on_campus/.

NIAGARA UNIVERSITY

AT A GLANCE

Founded in 1856 by the Vincentian fathers and brothers, Niagara University (NU) is a private, Catholic, comprehensive, co-educational institution. Located minutes from the scenic Niagara Falls, Niagara University's suburban campus is a blend of historic ivy-covered structures and elegant modern buildings. There are more than 2,900 undergraduates and about 914 graduate students at Niagara. NU is comprised of four academic divisions: the College of Arts and Sciences, College of Education, College of Business Administration, and the College of Hospitality & Tourism Management. While at NU, students have access to a range of important support services that help them develop academically and chose a major. In fact, incoming students who have not decided on a field of study may enroll in the Academic Exploration Program (AEP). In addition, select students have the opportunity to participate in the honors program, a special academic program designed to stimulate and challenge accomplished students.

The Middle States Association of Colleges and Schools accredits Niagara University. NU also holds the other accreditations and memberships. Its programs in education are accredited by National Council for Accreditation of Teacher Education. Its business programs are accredited the Association to Advance Collegiate Schools of Business (AASCB International). Its social work program is accredited by the Council on Social Work Education and the department of chemistry has the approval of the American Chemical Society. The Commission for Programs in Hospitality Administration accredits NU's Hospitality & Tourism Management curriculum. NU's faculty is dedicated to teaching and takes an active interest in their students' academic and personal growth. With a student-faculty ratio of just 14:1 and an average class size of about 25, students have ample opportunity for personal interaction with their professors.

LOCATION AND ENVIRONMENT

Niagara University's suburban campus is located outside the quaint village of Lewiston. It is also s within minutes of Niagara Falls. The campus is about 20 minutes from Buffalo, N.Y. and 90 minutes from Toronto, Canada. This area boasts a wide variety of resources and attractions, including the famous Niagara Falls. In addition, the Canadian border and the vibrant cities of Toronto and Buffalo are easily accessible from NU. The campus community is an ideal size, combining a strong community spirit with a friendly campus setting.

Residence life at NU is a creative, social, and educational. Student rooms have comfortable furniture and hookups for telephone, cable television, and computers. Commuting students and resident students discover that the University offers a wide range of programs and activities designed to help new students become a part of the NU community and the surrounding area.

OFF-CAMPUS OPPORTUNITIES

Off-campus and other learning opportunities abound at Niagara University. Students may choose to participate in programs such as: the study abroad program, various internships, cooperative education and /or cross registering at other colleges through the Western New York Consortium.

In keeping with the spirit of St. Vincent de Paul, many Niagara students volunteer off campus through the Niagara University Community Action Program and the Learn & Serve program. Learn & Serve grants students academic credit for volunteer work. These programs are designed to help students utilize their time and talents in service to the less fortunate.

MAJORS AND DEGREES OFFERED

Niagara University (NU) offers over 50 academic programs and majors within the four academic divisions. The University confers Bachelor of Arts, Bachelor of Science, Bachelor of Business Administration, Bachelor of Fine Arts, Associate in Arts, Associate in Science, Associate in Applied Science, Master of Arts, Master of Science, Master of Science in Education, and Master of Business Administration Degrees.

ACADEMIC PROGRAMS

Through the College of Arts and Sciences, students can pursue a Bachelor of Arts in the following areas of study: chemistry, with concentration in chemistry or environmental studies; communications studies; English; French; history; international studies; liberal arts; life sciences; mathematics; philosophy; political science with concentration in political science or environmental studies; psychology; religious studies; social sciences; sociology; and Spanish. NU also offers the Bachelor of Fine Arts degree in theatre studies and the Associate in Arts in general studies. NU offers the Bachelor of Science in biochemistry with a concentration in biochemistry or bioinformatics; biology with concentration in biology, biotechnology, or environmental studies; chemistry with concentration in chemistry, computational chemistry, or environmental studies; computer and information sciences; criminology and criminal justice; mathematics; and social work. The College of Arts and Sciences also offers a five-year B.S./M.S. program in criminal justice. Niagara University also offers several pre-professional partnerships with other universities. In conjunction with the State University of New York at Buffalo, NU offers a 3+4 partnership in dentistry and pharmacy. In conjunction with The Lake Erie College of Osteopathic Medicine, NU also offers a 3+4 partnership in medicine and a 2+3 program in pharmacy. Qualified students are eligible to apply for early assurance at the State University of New York at Buffalo.

For students who do not wish to declare a major, the University offers the Academic Exploration Program to help them explore fields and hone their individual interests.

Through the College of Business Administration, students can pursue a Bachelor of Business Administration, accounting, or a Bachelor of Science degree in commerce, with concentrations in economics & finance, general business, human resources, international business, management, marketing, or supply chain management. The College of Business Administration also offers a five-year B.B.A./M.B.A. degree in accounting. Students in this division can also pursue an Associate in Applied Science degree in business.

The College of Education offers Bachelor's degree programs for the New York State initial certification in early childhood and childhood (birth-grade 6), childhood (grades 1–6), childhood and middle childhood (grades 1–9), adolescence (grades 7–12), special education & childhood (grades 1–6) special education and adolescence

(grades 7–12) and TESOL—Teaching English to Speakers of Other Languages (grades K–12). Education majors must choose an academic concentration in English, mathematics, social studies, French, Spanish, biology, chemistry, or business. Education students who choose a concentration in business education can only pursue certification for grades 5–12.

Students in the College of Hospitality & Tourism Management may receive a Bachelor of Science in hotel & restaurant management with concentrations in hotel & restaurant planning and control, foodservice management, restaurant entrepreneurship; sport management with a concentration in sports operations; tourism and recreation management with concentrations in special events & conference management and tourism destination management.

NU also offers pre-professional programs in pre-dental, pre-legal, pre-medical, pre-pharmacy, pre-veterinary; and Army-ROTC.

Campus Facilities and Equipment

Niagara University is committed to providing students facilities that will enhance their academic, social, cultural, athletic, recreational, and moral development. Below is a sampling of some of these facilities.

The Kiernan Center, NU's fitness and recreation facility, provides a multipurpose gym, a swimming pool and diving pool, an indoor track and racquetball courts, free-weight and Nautilus rooms, and aerobics rooms. In addition, there are several outdoor athletic fields, basketball and tennis courts.

NU also offers student services such as academic and personal counseling, orientation, academic planning and career planning services. The University's library has an extensive collection which exceeds 273,000 hard volumes, 21,000 periodicals, composed of print and electronic subscriptions and 24,140 units of microfilm. The library is affiliated with the On-line Computer Library Center (OCLC) network.

The Academic Complex, which open in the fall of 2007, is a state-of-the-art facility which houses the College of Business Administration and the College of Education. Dunleavy Hall houses the television production centers and a computerized lecture room. The University's other first-rate facilities include the Leary Theatre, the Computer Center, St. Vincent's Hall, the Castellani Art Museum, the student apartments, and the Dwyer Ice Complex, which houses a dual rink ice hockey facility.

TUITION, ROOM, BOARD AND FEES

Fees for the 2007–2008 academic year included: tuition $21,400; room and board $9,300; and student fees $900.

FINANCIAL AID

Over 98 percent of the incoming freshmen at NU receive financial assistance. NU offers a merit-based scholarship and grant program, as well as athletic, transfer, service, and talent scholarships. Niagara encourages students of all financial backgrounds to apply to the University.

STUDENT ORGANIZATIONS AND ACTIVITIES

NU has an active, diverse, and social campus culture, with more than 80 student-operated clubs and organizations. Ranging from academic and cultural groups to social and athletic clubs, NU has an activity to suit every taste. Niagara is a member of the NCAA Division I and competes in men's and women's basketball, cross-country, ice hockey, swimming and diving, tennis, and soccer, men's baseball and golf, and women's volleyball and softball. There is also an active intramural and recreational athletic program.

Students seeking off-campus activities need go no further than the Campus Activities Office. This office coordinates many off-campus excursions to local attractions, professional sports competitions, theatre events, and trips to Toronto. Campus Activities also provides local transportation by means of the NU Cruiser. The NU Cruiser transports students to a central area with a bank, grocery store, outlet mall and eateries.

ADMISSIONS PROCESS

Niagara University encourages all men and women whose aptitude and demonstrated academic achievement in high school or college give evidence of their ability to successfully complete the various university programs to apply for admission. Consistent with our Catholic mission, Niagara University welcomes all students, regardless of age, race, creed, color, national origin, sexual orientation, military status, sex, disability, predisposing genetic characteristics, or marital status.

To apply for admission, freshmen students must complete an admissions application; submit a $30.00 application fee and their official high school transcript including official scores from the SAT or ACT. It is anticipated that all students who apply for admissions will complete and will receive their high school diploma prior to the first day of classes at N.U. Although not required, NU recommends that prospective students schedule an admissions interview and a tour of campus.

Transfer students may apply to enter any of the three semesters - fall, spring, or summer. Transfer students must complete an admissions application, submit a $30.00 application fee, an official high school transcript, official transcript(s) from any college/university previously/presently attending, and, if appropriate, a list of courses being pursued at the time of the application. The dean of each academic division evaluates transfer credit.

Students who complete a strong high school curriculum in three years can apply for early admission. New York State residents who come from an economically and educationally disadvantaged background may apply through the Higher Educational Opportunity Program (HEOP).

International students should refer to our web-site at www.niagara.edu/admissions/intl.htm for complete application information.

NICHOLS COLLEGE

AT A GLANCE

We take our commitment to help you thrive very seriously. It's ingrained in our culture and the inspiration for everything we do.

The best way to show you the value of a Nichols degree is to share some statistics from our Class of 2006. In just 6 months after Graduation:

- 96% were fully employed in their major area of study,
- the average starting salary of $40,000, and
- 83% of those starting salaries were over $30,000.

1 out of 10 Nichols graduates is a CEO, corporate president or business owner. That's what we mean by success!

LOCATION AND ENVIRONMENT

Nichols College is situated across more than 200 acres of rolling hills in Dudley, Mass.

Nichols is located twenty minutes south of Worcester in central Massachusetts. We are also within an hour's drive of Boston, Springfield, Hartford, and Providence.

You'll love your Nichols home away from home!

Please schedule a campus visit because there's no substitute for seeing it in person.

You can walk to your classrooms, Lombard Dining Hall, Daniels Auditorium, the Library, and the Athletic Center in less than 10 minutes.

If you want to go into surrounding towns for fun or a late-night pizza or sub, it's a short car ride. Major highways to Worcester, Boston, Providence, or Hartford are easily accessible.

In addition, you will find that all of our facilities, dorm rooms, classrooms, and Library are access ready for the Internet.

OFF-CAMPUS OPPORTUNITIES

The greater Worcester area is an active, vibrant and energetic community. Downtown Worcester is in the midst of a dynamic revitalization effort as over $1 billion is being invested in new development projects including CitySquare, the Hanover Theatre for the Performing Arts and the Blackstone Canal District Initiative.

Whether it's catching the latest concert at the DCU Center, sampling the restaurants on Shrewsbury Street, or watching the Worcester Tornadoes (Can-Am League baseball), Worcester Sharks (American Hockey League), or New England Surge (Continental Indoor Football League) in thrilling sports action, Worcester is the place to be for fun and exciting attractions.

MAJORS AND DEGREES OFFERED

There are two undergraduate degrees offered:

- Bachelor of Science in Business Administration (B.S.B.A.)
- Bachelor of Arts (B.A.)

B.S.B.A.

Business students must complete 121 credit hours.

The Business Core curriculum of 37 credits offers a firm grounding in key areas of business including accounting, computer information systems, finance, management and marketing.

In addition, students complete 18-27 credits in their area of specialization.

B.S.B.A. Specializations: Accounting, Arts & Entertainment Management, Business Communication, Criminal Justice Management, Economics, Finance, General Business, Human Resource Management, International Business, Legal Studies, Management, Management Information Systems, Marketing, Sport Management

B.A.

Liberal Arts students must complete 120 credit hours. The Liberal Arts core of 12 credit hours includes selected studies in the humanities and world culture. In addition, students complete 30 credits in their major.

B.A. Majors: Economics, English, History, Mathematics, Psychology

EDUCATOR PREPARATION

Nichols College Educator Preparation Program courses prepare you to teach business, history, English or mathematics in middle or secondary schools.

GRADUATE OPTIONS
Traditional MBA

- MBA with an emphasis in Sport Management
- MBA with an emphasis in Security Management
- Master of Organizational Leadership

ACADEMIC PROGRAMS

Professional Development Seminar

Our four-year Professional Development Seminar (PDS) program helps you develop career skills that set you apart.

In the program's 3rd and 4th years, you will increasingly focus on career decision making, refining interview skills, and developing a presentation portfolio of your accomplishments.

Students in particular find the mock interview process helpful. They also enjoy the "Etiquette Dinner" for seniors, and our fashion shows depicting the "do's and don'ts" of professional dress.

Internship Program

An internship lets you test drive a career, develop a work portfolio, and make a network of professional contacts for future employment opportunities.

At Nichols, four business specializations require internships, and our students have been placed in top-tier venues, from Madison Square Garden to Abbott Labs.

Career Services

Our Career Services Office is renowned throughout New England. In fact, prominent corporations participate in our Annual Career Fair, one of the largest in central Massachusetts.

Career Services has a host of job opportunities and our staff will help you keep your resume current, develop a strong cover letter, and create a complete list of references.

Honors Program

Our undergraduate students have the opportunity to be recognized for outstanding academic achievement. To be eligible, a student must maintain a GPA of 3.2 or higher and have earned a minimum of 29 credit hours. Participating students complete additional study requirements to earn an extra fourth credit in 300-level or 400-level courses. After achieving a B+ or higher grade in each of the three courses, students are qualified to apply for entrance into a senior-year Honors Scholar Seminar.

Student may select honor courses from across the curriculum in business communications, economics, English, environmental science, history, human resource management, management, and political science.

CAMPUS FACILITIES AND EQUIPMENT

The Athletics Center opened its doors in 2000. It features an indoor climbing wall, squash courts, raquet ball courts, a conference room, administrative offices, a weight room, a fitness room, and four locker rooms.

Once known as the Bison Bowl, Nichols College now plays all of its home football, field hockey and lacrosse games on the new Michael J. Vendetti Multi-Purpose Field. The men's and women's soccer teams also play some of their home contests on the field. The field includes an eight-lane rubberized quarter-mile track surrounding a turf field surface. To facilitate media coverage, there is a new press box with online capabilities and Musco lighting to light the field for night contests.

TUITION, ROOM, BOARD, AND FEES

Tuition: 25,400

Room: 4,800

Board: 4,160

Fees: 300

Total: 34,660

FINANCIAL AID

Nichols awards merit-based and need-based scholarships and grants. You can supplement your Nichols awards with federal and state grants and/or loans.

At Nichols College, the average full-time student receives in excess of $24,000 in Financial Aid from all sources!

High-need students may receive up to $35,000 in Financial Aid. We also have numerous financing plans to fit nearly every budget.

STUDENT ORGANIZATIONS AND ACTIVITIES

90% of our student body participates in an on-campus group.

Nichols can provide you with the living and learning experience that you deserve.

All you have to do is get connected, and we make sure that's easy and fun to do during your Orientation program.

Academic Honor Societies, Delta Mu Delta, Mu Kappa Tau, Omicron Delta Epsilon, Phi Alpha Theta, Zeta Alpha Phi, Athletic Honor Societies, The Student Athlete Advisory Council (SAAC), Elbridge Boyden Society, Student Government and Service Organizations, Campus Activities Board (CAB), Campus Ministry Association, The Student Government Association (SGA), Student Publications and Communications Media, The College Yearbook, The College Literary Magazine, WNRC Radio Station

Club Sports: Paintball Club, Racquetball Club, Men's Ice Hockey Club, Women's Ice Hockey Club, Men's Rugby Club, Women's Volleyball Club

General Interest: Accounting Club, Commuter Club, Criminal Justice Management Club, Economics/Finance Club, History Club, Human Resource Club, Management Club, Marketing Club, MIS Club, Psychology Club, Sport Management Club, Umoja

NCAA Division III Athletics: Nichols competes in The Commonwealth Coast Conference, New England Football Conference, ECAC Northeast Hockey League, and the ECAC Women's East Hockey League.

Men's Teams

- Baseball
- Basketball
- Football
- Golf
- Ice Hockey
- Lacrosse
- Soccer
- Tennis

Women's Teams

- Basketball
- Field Hockey
- Ice Hockey
- Lacrosse
- Soccer
- Softball
- Tennis

ADMISSIONS PROCESS

Nichols College regards each prospective student as an individual, considering each application as it is submitted throughout the academic year. The Admissions Process is a joint partnership between the applicant and the College. We want to ensure each admitted student is the "right fit", both for the student and for Nichols. Admission candidacy requires that every applicant is either a high school graduate or has earned a high school equivalency diploma (GED). Our typical applicants' credentials vary greatly and many factors go into the admissions decision. We look at the areas of strength and weakness in each candidate and assess the student's ability to succeed at Nichols. Our typical admitted student has a GPA above 2.4, an average SAT score of 1,400 (combined verbal, math and essay scores), and a strong desire to succeed.

Proficiency in certain academic areas is a basic requirement for entrance to the College. Successful candidates for admission will follow a college preparatory course of study prior to applying to Nichols. We encourage students to challenge themselves with a rigorous secondary school curriculum. Though there is no specific schedule of courses required, an ideal four-year program includes the following coursework:

English - 4 units , Social Science - 2 units, Laboratory Science - 2 units, Academic Electives - 5 units, Foreign Language - 2 units and College Preparatory Mathematics - 3 units (Recommended courses include: Algebra I, Geometry, Algebra II, and Advanced Mathematics.

NORTH PARK UNIVERSITY

AT A GLANCE

Founded in 1891 by the Evangelical Covenant Church, North Park University is located on Chicago's north side and enrolls more than 3,250 students from around the country and the world. At North Park, excellence implies not only a deep tradition in the liberal arts and the Christian faith, but also a spirit of innovation, reaching out to serve and to learn from the dynamic community around us. Cultural study centers enrich the life of the campus and connect the campus to the diverse people of Chicago whose roots extend around the globe. Graduate and special undergraduate programs bring adult, working professionals to the campus on evenings and weekends, enhancing the university's resources in the liberal arts as well as in specialized areas such as business, the health sciences, and education. North Park is a Christian university, committed to relating Christian faith to the aims of higher education. North Park welcomes students who recognize that education always implies values who desire an education rooted in the values and perspectives of the Christian tradition. In North Park's classrooms, students find a full-time faculty of accomplished Christian teachers and scholars, and on our campus, a community of faith. We are looking for men and women who long to grow in knowledge and faith, and who seek a sense of vocation through leadership and servant-hood in a global society.

The North Park student body is diverse from multiple perspectives. Students come from about 40 states and 25 other countries. Less than 60 percent are from Illinois. The male/female ratio is about the national average. 27 percent of students come from the sponsoring denomination, the Evangelical Covenant Church. Another 30 percent from various Protestant traditions, 14 percent Roman Catholic, 1 percent Orthodox, 18 percent indicate other, and 10 percent no response. Racial and ethnic diversity data shows 59 percent of students are Caucasian, 9 percent African American, 9 percent Hispanic/Latino, 7 percent Asian/Pacific Islander, 11 percent unknown, and 4 percent non-resident alien.

LOCATION AND ENVIRONMENT

North Park University is located on a beautiful park-like campus in one of the North Side neighborhoods of Chicago. Public transportation provides the necessary link to internships, jobs and entertainment. A student can easily and successfully attend North Park without having a car! O'Hare and Midway Airports provide consistently inexpensive travel options compared with many destinations.

OFF-CAMPUS OPPORTUNITIES

As students become familiar with Chicago and established in their studies, many find internships & employment opportunities in their junior and senior years at one of the many businesses or non-profit organizations in the city. The North Park professional staff will set up internships and help students search for jobtertainment and sports opportunities are too numerous to mention as are the range of restaurants offered by the city. Students are engaged in significant volunteer service throughout the neighborhood and city through North Parks Urban Outreach program.

MAJORS AND DEGREES OFFERED

Advertising (BA, BS), Africana studies (BA), art (BA), athletic training (BS), biblical and theological studies (BA), biology (BA, BS), business and economics (BA, BS), chemistry (BA, BS), clinical laboratory science (BS), communication arts (BA), computer science (BS), education (BA), English (BA), exercise science (BA, BS), French (BA), French studies (BA), global studies (BA), history (BA), information systems (BA, BS), mathematics (BA, BS), music (BA, BM), nursing (BSN), philosophy (BA), physical education (BA, BS), physics (BA, BS), politics and government (BA), psychology (BA), Scandinavian studies (BA), sociology (BA), Spanish (BA), youth ministry (BA).

ACADEMIC PROGRAMS

North Park offers a Liberal Arts education with a broad array of traditional liberal arts majors as well as programs that offer professional and pre-professional preparation. The core curriculum takes about one-third of the 120 hours required for graduation. Students select a major with the option of a minor or a double major. BS degrees have more required hours for degree completion, allowing less time for electives. 87 percent of the faculty hold the PhD or the highest degree in their field of expertise. Average class size is 18, with less than 2 percent of classes containing more than 50 students. The student to faculty ratio is 11:1.

Pre-professional programs include pre-med, pre-law, occupational therapy, physical therapy, and a 3/2 engineering program. North Park offers certificates in Nonprofit Leadership Studies, Conflict Transformation, and Music Theater.

CAMPUS FACILITIES AND EQUIPMENT

North Park occupies more than 30 acres at the intersection of Foster and Kedzie Avenues in Chicago. Four residence halls are supplemented by a wide array of apartments and house more than 1,100 students. Classroom learning takes place in Carlson Tower and Magnuson Center, with additional classrooms scattered throughout another 7 buildings. Brandel Library, opened in 2000, houses a collection of 225,000 volumes and 1,000 periodicals. Helwig Recreation Center, opened in 2006, provides state-of-the-art indoor training and recreation facilities for the whole student body. Parking is more than adequate and is available in 3 main lots and numerous smaller lots. The inner campus is a beautiful green space with brick-lined sidewalks and abundant grass, trees and plantings.

TUITION, ROOM, BOARD, AND FEES

2008/2009 Tuition and Fees Tuition $17,600 Room/Board $8,130 (20 meal plan)

FINANCIAL AID

Average percent of need met: 74 percent Average financial aid package: $9,875 Average need-based loan: $2,331 Average need-based scholarship or grant award: $7,186 Average non-need based aid: $3,070 Average indebtedness at graduation: $19,300

STUDENT ORGANIZATIONS AND ACTIVITIES

North Park students enjoy a full range of campus activities, including an active University Ministries Program, inter-collegiate athletics, intramural sports, student organizations, and easy access to the vast resources of Chicago. Alcohol is not permitted on campus and all facilities are smoke-free environments. Most, but not all, students come from the Christian faith tradition, which is reflected in the life and culture of the campus. While North Park students have fun and enjoy life, it is not a party school.

ADMISSIONS PROCESS

North Park reviews applications as they are completed and makes decisions on a rolling basis, usually within a week of all materials being received. The application priority deadline is April 1. To be considered, students must submit an application, including essay or writing sample, SAT or ACT scores, high school and/or college transcripts, an academic reference and a personal reference. Students are encouraged to schedule a campus visit, including an interview with an admission counselor.

NORTHEASTERN UNIVERSITY

AT A GLANCE

Northeastern University is a private, research university, offering a comprehensive range of undergraduate and graduate programs leading to degrees from bachelor through doctorate. Students benefit from a unique combination of experiential learning opportunities, anchored by our signature cooperative education program, which enable them to link course work in liberal arts and professional students with a variety of practical experiences, including global experiences, undergraduate research and civic engagement opportunities.

LOCATION AND ENVIRONMENT

Northeastern's main campus is located in the heart of Boston's Avenue of the Arts, between the Museum of Fine Arts and Symphony Hall. Also in close proximity is Fenway Park, home of the World Champion Boston Red Sox, and the Fens, part of famous landscape designer Frederick Law Olmstead's Emerald Necklace park system. Northeastern is nestled among 4 historic and vibrant neighborhoods: the South End, Mission Hill, Roxbury and the Fenway. Through the university's many interactions with the city of Boston, students and faculty alike benefit from the resource-rich and diverse urban environment.

Northeastern's residential campus, situated on 67 acres, consists of 40 academic and administrative building and 35 residence facilities. Freshman who enter in the fall are guaranteed housing for their first 3 years. Freshman housing includes 10 co-ed residence halls or special theme housing with other students who share similar interests. Upperclassman can choose from new apartment complexes, many of which offer spectacular views of Boston. Honors students who are admitted into the Program can choose to live in the newest residence hall, West Village F. Residential life staff enrich the lively community with organized social activities, including move nights, ice cream socials, trips to museums and more. In total, more than 7,400 students are housed in university owned or leased residence facilities. The university recently opened West Village F which is the new home for the John D. O'Bryant African-American Institute, 8 new classrooms including a new 275 seat auditorium, and 229 new beds for Honors program students. Residence halls have a port-per-pillow and some newer halls are wireless. Two dining halls and more than 100 Husky vendors give students ample opportunity for variety. Students will find an array of food choices on-campus, including brick-oven pizza, stir-fry, salads and more. One dining hall features a kitchen where guest chefs teach students how to create tasty dishes with relative ease.

OFF-CAMPUS OPPORTUNITIES

Ask students what they enjoy most about being at Northeastern, and one common response is "Boston." It's easy to see why: Boston is the ultimate college town. The city is a hub of cultural, educational and social activity, yet it's small enough to navigate on foot. More than 300,000 college students from around the country and the world call Boston home, and the city is alive with their energy. The Office for Off Campus Student Services is a resource for students who choose to live off campus in the surrounding neighborhoods.

MAJORS AND DEGREES OFFERED

Northeastern offers bachelor of arts and bachelor of science degrees in more than 70 areas of study including:

College of Arts and Sciences: majors are offered in African American studies (including cultural studies, historical studies, and social/behavioral studies), American Sign Language_ English interpreting, anthropology, applied physics, art (in collaboration with the School of the Museum of Fine Arts), behavioral neuroscience, biochemistry, biology (including marine biology), biomedical physics, chemistry, communication studies (including organizational communication, radio and television, and speech and rhetoric), economics, English, environmental geology, environmental studies, geology, graphic design, history, human services, independent studies, international affairs, journalism, linguistics, mathematics, multimedia studies (including animation, graphic design, media arts and design, music technology, and photography), music (including music technology, music industry, music literature, and music literature and performance), philosophy, physics, political science (including international relations and comparative politics, law and legal issues, and public administration), psychology, sociology, and theater (including performance, production, and theater generalist).

Bouvé College of Health Sciences: majors are offered in athletic training, health science, nursing, pharmacy, physical therapy, and speech-language pathology and audiology.

College of Business Administration: the bachelor of science is offered in business administration and in international business with majors in accounting, entrepreneurship and small business management, finance and insurance, human resources management, international business, management, management information systems, marketing, and supply chain management.

College of Computer Science: the bachelor of science or bachelor of arts is offered in computer science and a Bachelor of Science is offered in information science.

College of Criminal Justice: the bachelor of science is offered in criminal justice.

College of Engineering: majors are offered in chemical engineering, civil and environmental engineering, computer engineering, electrical engineering, general engineering, industrial engineering, and mechanical engineering.

ACADEMIC PROGRAMS

Northeastern offers a wide variety of curricula through 6 undergraduate colleges, 8 graduate and professional schools, 2 part-time undergraduate divisions, and numerous continuing- and special-education programs and institutes. Many dual degrees and minor/concentration options, such as information science and business, computer science and cognitive psychology, biology and geology, or political science and international affairs, enable students to balance their studies with programs in the liberal arts and sciences.

CAMPUS FACILITIES AND EQUIPMENT

The campus environment is enriched by all the conveniences students need to complement their busy lifestyles. The state-of-the-art Marino Center offers fitness equipment, basketball courts, a climbing wall, free weights and more. Nineteen varsity teams compete in national and international arenas, and almost 40 intramural and club teams offer less demanding competition. In addition to the campus bookstore, students have access to a travel agency, hair salon, overnight mail facility, dry cleaner, grocery store, ATM machines, and more.

Campus highlights include the full-service Curry Student Center, Matthews Arena, Snell Library, the Egan Research Center, the Behrakis Health Sciences Center, and the West Village residence community.

The university provides a broad range of academic and administrative computer resources available to students, faculty, and staff. Accessible 24 hours a day, 7 days a week, the InfoCommons offers an e-bar, Computer Help Desk, training, and more than 200 computers for general use. Internet access is available in Northeastern-owned residence halls through ResNet. The myNEU portal allows students to access many administrative and academic functions online, including e-mail, class schedules, co-op information, student payroll, financial services, and more.

TUITION, ROOM, BOARD, AND FEES

For 2007-08, annual tuition for undergraduates is $31,500. Standard room and board rates are $11,010. Tuition and other costs depend on your pattern of attendance. Northeastern's five-year programs usually include 3 terms of co-op, during which you do not pay tuition. If you choose to live in campus housing while on co-op, you will be responsible for room and board charges.

FINANCIAL AID

Financial need, academic promise, and the availability of university funds determine how much aid a student receives. Supplemental loans and external scholarships may provide additional financial support. The Office of Student Financial Services prides itself on offering expert advice, friendly service, and personalized support. Regardless of your family income, consider applying for financial aid. Northeastern offers more than $70 million in grant and scholarship assistance, participates in all federal aid programs and offers an array of alternative financing and payment plans. About 83 percent of all freshmen received some type of aid. The deadline for all forms of financial aid is February 15.

Northeastern has established several competitive scholarship programs to reward outstanding academic achievement. To be considered for one or more of these prestigious awards, students must apply for undergraduate admission to Northeastern no later than January 15. Only fall freshman applicants may be considered for most of these scholarships. For more information on scholarships, visit www.financialaid.neu.edu/grants/northeastern/need-based_grant.php.

STUDENT ORGANIZATIONS AND ACTIVITIES

Students have access to more than 240 clubs and organizations and an extensive network of advisement and counseling services. More than 5,000 students participate in student organizations. Programs and services sponsored by the African American Institute, the Latino/a Student Cultural Center, the International Student Office, and many other organizations enrich Northeastern's social life and cultural fabric. In athletics, Northeastern competes in NCAA Division I and maintains varsity teams in 9 men's and 10 women's sports.

ADMISSIONS PROCESS

Admission to Northeastern is selective and competitive. Building a talented and diverse incoming class is the primary goal of the Admissions Committee. The applicant's academic record is the most important aspect of the admissions application. We give special consideration to applicants who have chosen to challenge themselves in honors, Advanced Placement, International Baccalaureate, and college-level courses. In addition to the applicant's academic record, we also consider the extent to which students have contributed to their school and greater community in a meaningful way. Personal qualities such as leadership ability, creative and innovative thinking, and resiliency are important to us.

Last year, more than 35,000 applications were received for 2,800 spots in the class. November 15 is the deadline for the Early Action admission program. Students who have carefully explored their college options and have decided that Northeastern is where they want to enroll may choose to apply under the Early Action program. The deadline for the regular admission program is January 15.

To apply, students should submit the completed application and application fee along with official high school record(s), including senior-year first-quarter and mid-term grades; a recommendation from a guidance counselor; a recommendation from a teacher; and the results of the College Board SAT (Northeastern's College Board code is 3667) or the American College Testing Program. Students may enter the university with advanced credit earned on the basis of Advanced Placement (AP) examinations, the College-Level Examination Program (CLEP), the International Baccalaureate (IB) program, and successful completion of accredited college-level courses.

Northeastern does accept transfer students in the fall and spring semesters. Transfer students should include a list of past and anticipated courses and their individual credit values, by term, and submit it with the Northeastern application.

For more information, contact: Office of Undergraduate Admissions Northeastern University 150 Richards Hall 360 Huntington Avenue Boston, MA 02115 Telephone: 617-373-2200 Fax: 617-373-8780 E-mail: admissions@neu.edu Website: www.northeastern.edu/admissions

NORTHWOOD UNIVERSITY

Developing the future leaders of a global, free-enterprise society. Northwood University is for those who wish to achieve a successful career in business and entrepreneurship. Discover the leader in you.

AT A GLANCE

Founded in 1959 by Dr. Arthur E. Turner and Dr. R. Gary Stauffer—and based on the free-enterprise concept—Northwood University students learn the business strategies and principles necessary for success in today's competitive global market, while acquiring ethical leadership skills through a curriculum that goes beyond textbook learning.

A Code of Ethics is embodied by the entire Northwood community–students, faculty and staff. A Northwood education is also driven by 12 outcomes which emphasize an understanding of the American tradition of freedom and the essential value of free-enterprise. An understanding of the value of creativity and appreciation for the arts is also stressed.

The Northwood Idea. We are a special purpose institution guided by a business philosophy. We call this The Northwood Idea: We focus on education for a life of contribution in the private sector. We specialize, in that we develop and build all our curriculums around the principles of the market economy. We believe that competitive, productive effort can overcome obstacles, solve problems and achieve goals. We believe that political and economic freedom are of paramount importance in releasing creativity and productivity. We believe that sacrifice—savings—is a necessary prerequisite to progress. Consumption of everything produced, with no investment for the future, is the most certain blueprint for the decline of society. We can affect the total productivity and quality of the lives we live. We believe that equality of opportunity based on contribution and inequality of reward using the same criteria are not only appropriate, but the necessary conditions to provide important incentives which act as the driving forces of much of our societal action. We believe that freedom from conformity releases the juices of creativity and our differences become strengths of our association, not hindrances to our existence. We believe in the freedom to fail. We believe that in a competitive system. We practice a healthy skepticism of large and powerful government because we think history has clearly demonstrated that such structures move rapidly from being of the people toward being over the people, and freedom is lost in the balance. Overall, we favor a society based on the unchanging values of individual choice, individual effort and individual responsibility. We endorse free enterprise and the competitive market for ideas and things as a way to insure that. We also believe that an understanding and appreciation of the arts and humanities is a primary source of human enrichment in the lives of productive human beings. Finally, we believe that education is never something that one person can do to another. It is, rather, something 2 people do together.

The university is accredited through the Higher Learning Commission and is a member of the North Central Association, the accrediting body for Northwood's geographical area. Northwood is a private, nonsectarian, residential, coeducational, not-for-profit university.

Outcomes. A university education is more than the courses offered and the experiences made available. It is the architecture of those elements designed to create defined results. As a learning community, we focus our efforts to the accomplishment of 12 outcomes which become characteristics our graduates share. Our students understand the tradition of freedom; have a broad practical understanding of their chosen field; are familiar with the ideas driving enterprise leaders; communicate effectively in speech and writing; understand complex global issues; have a constant attraction to new ideas; can explain their personal values; understand the aesthetic, creative, and spiritual elements of life; are effective self-evaluators; are action oriented; are skilled at detecting and solving problems; seek lifelong education.

LOCATION AND ENVIRONMENT

Northwood University offers 3 residential campuses, adult degree programs nation-wide, and the DeVos Graduate School of Management. The campuses are points of pride at Northwood and boast, stunning architecture–in the buildings and in the landscapes,

West Palm Beach, Florida: Located on 90 acres of land with several small lakes, this pristine, residential campus is situated in the heart of business and industry.

Midland, Michigan: Located on 434 beautifully wooded acres along the banks of the Tittabawassee River, this residential campus is located 135 miles north of Detroit and is most famous as the international world headquarters of The Dow Chemical Company.

Cedar Hill, Texas: Made up of rugged, cedar-covered hills and valleys this residential campus includes the highest point in the Dallas/Fort Worth Metroplex.

Adult Degree Programs and DeVos Graduate School of Management: Located worldwide. Visit www.northwood.edu for a complete list of locations and programs.

Northwood also partners with more than 150 universities world-wide. It was one of the first universities to teach capitalism in communist China, with locations in Jilin and the southern Yangtze area.

OFF-CAMPUS OPPORTUNITIES

We believe in promoting and leveraging the global, diverse and multi-cultural nature of enterprise. Our local and international presence next to hubs of entrepreneurial activity and successful businesses is proof of this.

Northwood students regularly participate in industry events that broaden their educational experience. Some of which include:

Specialty Equipment Market Association Convention: The premier automotive specialty products trade event in the world that is not open to the public. It draws the industry's brightest minds and hottest products to one place, the Las Vegas Convention Center.

National Automobile Dealers Association Exposition: More than 600 exhibits are on display for 4 days and include aftermarket exhibits, seminars, discussion groups, and networking opportunities.

Outstanding Business Leader Awards: Acquaints college students with the lives and achievements of present-day business leaders. Each awardee is selected on the basis of personal achievements which typify the unique philosophy of Northwood University.

MAGIC Show: The fashion industry converges on Las Vegas as thousands of retailers come to the Marketplace to access more than 3,600 manufacturers showcasing more than 5,000 brands and private label resources.

Distinguished Women Event: recognize the enormous contribution women make to communities, businesses, volunteer agencies, and public and private sector services world-wide.

Mock Trial: Students with an interest in law are responsible for the development of a case to be tried in a court of law—including opening statement, introduction of testimony, physical, and demonstrative evidence, direct and cross examination of witnesses, closing arguments, etc. Students will participate in competitions both on and off campus.

The campus locations also offer vast social opportunities.

MAJORS AND DEGREES OFFERED

Northwood University's traditional programs offer students the opportunity to earn a single, double, or triple major in 4 years or less in 17 different business specialties. Students start classes in their major day one of year one. Every student, regardless of major, takes a business core which includes accounting, management, business law, marketing, and economics. Northwood offers bachelor of business administration degrees, exclusively.

Single majors: accounting, management.

Double majors combined with a major in management: advertising & marketing, automotive aftermarket management, automotive marketing management, banking & finance, computer information management, economics, entertainment/sport & promotion mgmt., entrepreneurship, fashion marketing management, hotel/restaurant/resort management, international business, management information systems, marketing.

Triple majors combined with a major in management: automotive marketing/banking & finance, banking & finance/economics.

For a complete list of programs offered at each campus, visit www.northwood.edu. A student may also choose to continue their education at the DeVos Graduate School of Management.

ACADEMIC PROGRAMS

Northwood University provides students with the opportunity to apply what they're learning in the classroom to real world situations. Auto shows, fashion shows, concerts, hospitality and culinary events, and more, are all organized and produced solely by students. These events are produced as businesses; profits are expected.

Omniquest: A provocative and challenging book is selected each term. The theme of the book is adopted for discussion and analysis during that term on all campuses and within all programs, simultaneously. We want students to be more diverse in their reading than just textbooks.

Dual Enrollment and AP Credit: Accepted providing scores and courses correspond with Northwood requirements.

Honors Program, Internships, and multiple Study Abroad opportunities are available to current students. Tutoring services are also available as needed. The faculty at Northwood are experienced business professionals who bring real world scenarios to the classroom.

Engagement and community service are expected of Northwood University students. Upon graduation, 2 transcripts are issued, a traditional one and then an EXCEL transcript. The EXCEL transcript documents all volunteer hours and extended, beyond the classroom learning activities, from freshmen year through senior.

CAMPUS FACILITIES AND EQUIPMENT

Classrooms with advanced technological capabilities, wireless access, athletic fields, student activities centers, libraries and dormitories can be found at all 3 residential campuses. Each campus also hosts buildings of either historic or architectural significance.

The best way to learn about what a campus has to offer is to schedule a campus visit. Call to arrange your personalized visit or visit www.northwood.edu for more information. Tour the campus, speak to current students, sit in on a class, and maybe even enjoy a trip to our cafeteria!

TUITION, ROOM, BOARD, AND FEES

Visit www.northwood.edu to learn more about the tuition, room, board and fees for each campus.

FINANCIAL AID

Generous academic, business club, private donor, and athletic scholarships are available. Students are required to file the Free Application for Federal Student Aid (FAFSA). School Code: 004072. Any private school a student is considering must be listed first on the FAFSA to be eligible for the maximum amount of aid.

STUDENT ORGANIZATIONS AND ACTIVITIES

There are many students groups, fraternal organizations, athletic opportunities, and service organizations available at each campus and students are encouraged to participate to enhance the collegiate experience. Visit www.northwood.edu for more information.

ADMISSIONS PROCESS

Apply online to Northwood University free at www.northwood.edu.

The following must be provided with or immediately following application submission: high school/college transcript(s); ACT/SAT scores; personal documentation requiring special consideration, if applicable.

Once you have applied and provided the supporting documents, your application will be evaluated by the Dean of Admissions. Many factors are considered in determining a student's acceptance to Northwood University, and all aspects of a student's formal and informal education are considered. The Admissions staff is committed to providing personal attention to guide you through the admissions process, and encourages you to contact them to answer questions or address concerns that you may have about a Northwood business education.

NOTRE DAME COLLEGE

AT A GLANCE

Notre Dame College is an affordable, private, liberal arts college located in a quiet suburban neighborhood just east of Cleveland.

Notre Dame offers students quality Academic Programs with over 30 majors including our nationally accredited Education major, a Bachelor of Science in Nursing, Intelligence Analysis and Research and Criminal Justice.

Notre Dame's athletic department has 18 scholarship athletic teams including a new men's swimming and diving team beginning in 2008. All of these teams all compete in the American Mideast Conference of the NAIA.

CAMPUS FACILITIES AND EQUIPMENT

Students with documented learning differences can enroll in our Academic Support Center to receive comprehensive support services, including tutoring, academic advising and access to a large array of adaptive equipment.

The Career Services Center provides students with a variety of services to assist with career planning including résumé writing, interview skills development and locating co-ops and internships.

TUITION, ROOM, BOARD AND FEES

Notre Dame College offers merit, need and athletic scholarships to all full-time undergraduate students. To be eligible, students must complete the Free Application for Federal Student Aid (FAFSA).

FINANCIAL AID

Notre Dame believes that all qualified students should have the opportunity to attend college and provides need and merit-based aid to our students.

ADMISSIONS PROCESS

Notre Dame College admits students who demonstrate potential for success in rigorous academic work. A free application is available online at www.NotreDameCollege.edu.

The College has a fair and generous policy on the transfer of academic credit earned within the preceding five years at a regionally accredited college or university.

Telephone: 877-NDC-OHIO ext. 5355 Fax: 216-373-5278

Email: admissions@ndc.edu

Web: www.NotreDameCollege.edu

Oberlin College

LOCATION AND ENVIRONMENT

Oberlin College is located in the center of Oberlin, Ohio, a town of 8,000 residents, about a 35-minute drive from Cleveland. Oberlin is an idyllic residential town, which is made lively and exciting by the presence of the college. Cultural events dominate the social scene, with over 400 concerts and recitals, 40+ theater and dance productions and 200 films annually. Though there are a multitude of bicycles in Oberlin, everything a student needs is within walking distance of campus.

OFF-CAMPUS OPPORTUNITIES

Oberlin offers an extensive study away program, including several programs sponsored by Oberlin, programs sponsored by the Great Lakes College Association, and a large variety of programs from other sources. Oberlin's Career Services office helps students to find a variety of summer internships, and research opportunities can be found through the Career Services office and also through academic departments. Oberlin's Center for Service and Learning helps coordinate a multitude of community service opportunities.

MAJORS AND DEGREES OFFERED

The College of Arts and Sciences and the Conservatory of Music are both on the same campus. The College offers a Bachelor of Arts; the Conservatory offers a Bachelor of Music and some Master of Music degrees as well. Oberlin also offers a unique five-year "Double Degree" program in which a student attends both the College and the Conservatory and graduates with both the BA and BMus degrees.

ACADEMIC PROGRAMS

In addition to traditional academic offerings, Oberlin offers a winter term, in which students complete independent and often self-designed projects, either on or off campus. Projects include, but are not limited to: research projects, internships, reading projects, arts projects, and community service. Oberlin is also home to the Experimental College, a series of classes in a huge variety of traditional and nontraditional subjects. Experimental College classes are taught by all members of the Oberlin community, including students.

CAMPUS FACILITIES AND EQUIPMENT

Oberlin's five libraries contain more than 1.75 million items, including 1.1 million catalogued volumes, which makes Oberlin's library one of the two largest small-college libraries in the nation. The Allen Memorial Art Museum is considered one of the top college and university art museums in the United States.

The Conservatory of Music contains more than 150 practice rooms, and houses 177 Steinway grand pianos. There are also two concert halls at the conservatory, music studios, and extensive dance and drama performance space as well.

Oberlin's Irving E. Houck Computing Center provides a multitude of Macintosh and IBM-compatible computers in several locations on campus. All dorms are wired for connection to the mainframe and the Internet. Many areas of the campus provide wireless access. Oberlin's top-notch athletic facilities include the Jesse Philips Physical Education Center, the John W. Heisman Club Field House, 22 practice and playing fields, indoor and outdoor tracks and tennis courts, a 3,000-seat football stadium, a cross-country course, two pools, a Nautilus center and weight room, basketball and volleyball courts, racquetball and squash courts, a training room, and much more.

TUITION, ROOM, BOARD AND FEES

Tuition for the 2007-2008 academic year is $6,064. Room and board fees total $9,280. The student activity fee is $218. Costs for the College of Arts and Sciences and the Conservatory of Music are the same.

FINANCIAL AID

Oberlin meets the full evaluated need of all admitted students. In 2007-2008, approximately 66 percent of students received need-based aid. The average package was about $24,495, of which $19,035 or so was grant money. Oberlin requires Financial Aid applicants to complete both the FAFSA and the PROFILE.

STUDENT ORGANIZATIONS AND ACTIVITIES

Students on Oberlin's campus are presented with a rich diversity of extracurricular options. There are almost 120 student clubs and organizations funded through the Student Union. Over 400 concerts and recitals are presented annually by students, along with almost 100 theater, musical theater, and opera performances. A large number of visiting artists perform at Oberlin, as do many lecturers and speakers. Oberlin also sponsors an excellent film series, and there are numerous campus parties, dorm and co-op picnics, and special events sponsored by the Student Union.

ADMISSIONS PROCESS

Admission to both the College of Arts and Sciences and the Conservatory of Music is highly selective. In the Arts and Sciences class entering in 2007, the middle 50 percent of enrolled students scored between 650 and 750 on the Critical Reading portion of the SAT I and between 650 and 710 on the Math section. The median unweighted GPA was 3.60 and the middle 50 percent had unweighted GPAs between 3.4 and 3.8 in rigorous high school curriculums. The Conservatory seeks talented music students who have demonstrated records of achievement, potential for further growth and development, the ability to meet Oberlin's demanding standards, and the dedication required to become professional musicians. The most important factor in admission to the Conservatory is the performance audition, or in the case of certain programs, the compositions, tapes, and supporting materials submitted.

OBERLIN COLLEGE

ACADEMICS

In addition to the traditional academic offerings listed above, Oberlin offers a winter term, in which students complete independent and often self-designed projects, either on or off campus. Projects include, but are not limited to, research projects, internships, reading projects, arts projects, and community service. Oberlin is also home to the Experimental College, a series of classes in a huge variety of traditional and nontraditional subjects. Experimental College classes are taught by all members of the Oberlin community, including students.

ADMISSIONS

Admission to both the College of Arts and Sciences and the Conservatory of Music is highly selective. In the Arts and Sciences class entering in 2007, the middle 50 percent of enrolled students scored between 650 and 750 on the Critical Reading portion of the SAT I and between 650 and 710 on the Math section. The median unweighted GPA was 3.60 and the middle 50 percent had unweighted GPAs between 3.4 and 3.8 in rigorous high school curriculums. The Conservatory seeks talented music students who have demonstrated records of achievement, potential for further growth and development, the ability to meet Oberlin's demanding standards, and the dedication required to become professional musicians. The most important factor in admission to the Conservatory is the performance audition, or in the case of certain programs, the compositions, tapes, and supporting materials submitted.

CAMPUS FACILITIES AND EQUIPMENT

Oberlin's five libraries contain more than 1.75 million items, including 1.1 million catalogued volumes, which makes Oberlin's library one of the two largest small-college libraries in the nation. The Allen Memorial Art Museum is considered one of the top college and university art museums in the United States.

The Conservatory of Music contains more than 150 practice rooms, and houses 177 Steinway grand pianos. There are also two concert halls at the conservatory, music studios, and extensive dance and drama performance space as well.

Oberlin's Irving E. Houck Computing Center provides a multitude of Macintosh and IBM-compatible computers in several locations on campus. All dorms are wired for connection to the mainframe and the Internet. Many areas of the campus provide wireless access. Oberlin's top-notch athletic facilities include the Jesse Philips Physical Education Center, the John W. Heisman Club Field House, 22 practice and playing fields, indoor and outdoor tracks and tennis courts, a 3,000-seat football stadium, a cross-country course, two pools, a Nautilus center and weight room, basketball and volleyball courts, racquetball and squash courts, a training room, and much more.

CAMPUS LIFE

Students on Oberlin's campus are presented with a rich diversity of extracurricular options. There are almost 120 student clubs and organizations funded through the Student Union. Over 400 concerts and recitals are presented annually by students, along with almost 100 theater, musical theater, and opera performances. A large number of visiting artists perform at Oberlin, as do many lecturers and speakers. Oberlin also sponsors an excellent film series, and there are numerous campus parties, dorm and co-op picnics, and special events sponsored by the Student Union.

LOCATION AND ENVIRONMENT

Oberlin College is located in the center of Oberlin, Ohio, a town of 8,000 residents, about a 35-minute drive from Cleveland. Oberlin is an idyllic residential town, which is made lively and exciting by the presence of the College. Cultural events dominate the social scene with over 400 concerts and recitals, 40+ theater and dance productions and 200 films annually. Though there are a multitude of bicycles in Oberlin, everything a student needs is within walking distance of campus.

MAJORS AND DEGREES

The College of Arts and Sciences and the Conservatory of Music are both on the same campus. The College offers a Bachelor of Arts; the Conservatory offers a Bachelor of Music and some Master of Music degrees as well. Oberlin also offers a unique five-year "Double Degree" program in which a student attends both the College and the Conservatory and graduates with both the BA and BMus degrees.

OFF-CAMPUS OPPORTUNITIES

Oberlin offers an extensive study away program, including several programs sponsored by Oberlin, programs sponsored by the Great Lakes College Association, and a large variety of programs from other sources. Oberlin's Career services office helps students to find a variety of summer internships, and research opportunities can be found through the Career Services office and also through academic departments. Oberlin's Center for Service and Learning helps coordinate a multitude of community service opportunities.

TUITION AND AID

Oberlin meets the full evaluated need of all admitted students. In 2007-2008, approximately 66 percent of students received need-based aid. The average package was about $24,495, of which $19,035 or so was grant money. Oberlin requires financial aid applicants to complete both the FAFSA and the PROFILE.

Tuition And Fees

Tuition for the 2007–2008 academic year is $6,064. Room and board fees total $9,280. The student activity fee is $218. Costs for the College of Arts and Sciences and the Conservatory of Music are the same.

OHIO NORTHERN UNIVERSITY

AT A GLANCE

Discover Your True North. On the journey to True North there are choices, opportunities and outcomes. Discover a vibrant intellectual experience, committed guidance and lifelong support. Find it at Ohio Northern University. Founded in 1871, Ohio Northern is a competitive, private, coeducational university affiliated with the United Methodist church. ONU has long been distinguished as an outstanding university that graduates professionals who are successful in their careers. With four distinct undergraduate colleges (Arts & Sciences, Business Administration, Engineering, and Pharmacy) and the College of Law, Ohio Northern offers 3,600 students a diverse setting for professional learning in a liberal arts environment. From the start of their first year on campus, students discover the personal attention given from faculty and staff a prominent characteristic of Ohio Northern. ONU appeals to students who want to get more out of their education than simply a degree. Classroom participation is not only encouraged, but also expected. The professors at Northern are highly qualified and accessible, with over 80% having terminal degrees in their respective fields. They create a can-do environment where students can customize their areas of interest with mentorship and inspiration from faculty who champion their success. Topnotch academics and teaching + talented students = quality education and reputation. At Ohio Northern, students experience many different opportunities, grow as individuals, and develop as well-trained professionals in their chosen field. There are endless possibilities at Ohio Northern. Come see for yourself!

TUITION, ROOM, BOARD AND FEES

Tuition, room and board, and the technology fee for the 2008-2009 year total $38,655 for the College of Arts and Sciences and Business Administration, $40,740 for the College of Engineering and $42,450 for the College of Pharmacy. The average students spend $900 per year on books and fees.

STUDENT ORGANIZATIONS AND ACTIVITIES

Excitement, creativity, and tradition are the cornerstone of campus life at Ohio Northern. Students of all backgrounds come together to form a common bond in and outside of the classroom. With over 150 clubs and organizations to get involved in, including 21 varsity sports, there are new friends and experiences awaiting you! You'll make new friendships and memories, have leadership opportunities, participate in meaningful activities and have fun! Our top-notch intercollegiate sports teams involve just about everyone in the campus community. Ohio Northern participates in the Ohio Athletic Conference and in NCAA Division III. Athletics include 11 men's sports and 10 women's sports. During the 2006-2007 season, ONU's women won OAC titles in volleyball, cross country, swimming, golf and softball and had upper division finishes in all 10 sports. It was also a strong year for the ONU men's teams, as they received OAC championships in soccer, swimming and tennis and had upper division finishes in nine of the 11 sports. Thus far in the 2007-2008 season, ONU athletics have continued this tradition with OAC championship teams in volleyball and women's soccer. ONU's football and men's soccer teams also placed among the national rankings. Visit www.onusports.com! ONU offers ecumenical and interfaith opportunities for spiritual growth and development. Active religious life programs include many groups such as Habitat for Humanity, Northern Christian Fellowship, Fellowship of Christian Athletes, Chapel Band and Choir, and the Newman Club. The culture of ONU is one of respect, friendship, and community. Greek life is an active part of campus life at ONU where approximately 20 percent of ONU's student body are members of the six national fraternities and four national sororities. Service and philanthropy are core values of the Greek organizations. In addition, members are also involved in other student organizations on campus, adding a unique mixture of diversity to their chapters. The arts are the most exciting and rapidly expanding programs at Ohio Northern University. Monthly exhibitions of student artwork, ten theatrical productions and upwards of forty instrumental and voice performances annually by the respective departments allow a myriad of opportunities for any and all majors within the University. Multicultural students contribute to the diversity and richness of the ONU student body. The Office of Multicultural Development (OMD) encourages students to take an active role in all University activities and seeks to develop an identity for multicultural students. A variety of programs are hosted each year including regular cultural celebrations that feature speakers, performers, music, films, dinners, exhibits and workshops. There are many student organizations students can be a part of including: Asian American Student Union, The Black Student Union, The Indian Student Association, The Latino Student Union, The Muslim Student Union, Men of Distinction, Sister Circle, The Gospel Ensemble, Open Doors, World Student Organization, and Vision Builders.

ADMISSIONS PROCESS

Applicants should provide high school transcripts reflecting completion of 16 units of high school credit including the following: College of Arts and Sciences: 12 academic units as follows; 4 in English, 2 in mathematics and 6 in history, socials studies, language, and/or natural science. College of Business Administration: 13 academic units as follows; 4 in English, 3 in mathematics (including algebra and geometry), and 6 in history, social studies, language, and/or natural sciences. College of Engineering: 16 academic units as follows; 4 in English, 4 in mathematics (including 2 units in algebra, geometry, and trigonometry), 2 in science (including physics and preferably chemistry), and 6 in history, social studies, language, and/or natural sciences. College of Pharmacy: 18 academic units as follows; 4 in English, 4 in mathematics (algebra I and II, plane geometry, trigonometry and pre-calculus and/or calculus), 4 in science (including biology, chemistry, and physics), and 6 in history, social studies, language, and/or natural sciences. Applicants to the College of Pharmacy are also encouraged to send the following supplementary materials: Two letters of recommendation (at least one from a high school science or math teacher), a letter of why the applicant wants to pursue pharmacy, and a resume. The applicant is also highly encouraged to make a visit to campus. All of these materials are due to campus no later than November 1 of the senior year. All applicants must submit standardized test scores (ACT or SAT I). The writing portion is not required but recommended. For top scholarship consideration, all applicants must apply and be accepted by December 1 of the senior year. The Colleges of Arts and Sciences, Business, and Engineering are on rolling admissions.

OLD DOMINION UNIVERSITY

AT A GLANCE

Old Dominion University is a young and vital institution leading Virginia into the twenty-first century by embracing new technology and providing the educational environment of the future. The university offers a wide range of programs of study in engineering, science, health sciences, business and public administration, education, and arts and letters. Old Dominion University offers 68 undergraduate programs, 60 master's degrees, 35 doctoral, and two educational specialists' degrees. Physical therapy, engineering management, coastal physical oceanography, and nuclear physics have gained national ranking. In the university's dynamic 75 -year history, it has produced numerous award-winning faculty, Rhodes and Truman scholars, and a USA Today Academic All-American.

Founded in 1930 as a division of the College of William and Mary, Old Dominion is one of the 101 public universities with the Carnegie Foundation's Doctoral / Research Universities - Extensive distinction. Proud of its past, Old Dominion constantly looks to the future and prides itself on expanding research and teaching programs. Over 17,000 undergraduate students and 6,000 graduate students are enrolled at Old Dominion University. The University is accredited by the Southern Association of Colleges and Schools.

LOCATION AND ENVIRONMENT

Old Dominion University is located in Norfolk, Virginia, the city Money magazine ranked as the best large city in the South. A few miles north of downtown Norfolk, the campus is less than an hour from historic Williamsburg, Yorktown, and Jamestown, and about 20 minutes from the Virginia Beach oceanfront. Norfolk affords tremendous opportunities for students to enjoy festivals, professional sports, world-class theater, and numerous business and industry employers for co-op, internships, and post-graduate employment. The local climate has been rated as one of the best in the nation by the National Weather Service, allowing for year-round outdoor activities. Washington, D.C., and the Blue Ridge Mountains are only a few hours away. Located near the world's largest naval base, Old Dominion University maintains a close relationship with the military and offers excellent opportunities for Navy ROTC and Army ROTC students.

The 188 acres of the Old Dominion University campus stretch from the Elizabeth River to the Lafayette River. The University offers a small-college look and feel, with tree-lined walkways, a mix of old and new buildings, and colorful gardens and ponds. One of the most exciting developments on the campus today is the University Village, with its impressive centerpiece, the Ted Constant Convocation Center, which hosts everything from basketball games to concerts and commencements. The University Village will be the home of athletics, academics, and living and social activities for the campus in the near future. This will add to the world-class campus environment which features a newly renovated and nationally respected library, and new facilities including oceanography and physics building, a performing arts center, a renovated university center and student union, athletic fields and recreational facilities, new student housing, golf course, hotel, research park, and a new stadium for football, which will begin in fall 2009!

OFF-CAMPUS OPPORTUNITIES

Some off-campus opportunities you will enjoy at Old Dominion University are: Old Dominion guarantees an internship for every student in their field of study. ODU students can use Hampton Roads Transit public transportation system for free. Old Dominion is less than three miles from downtown Norfolk, conveniently close to shopping, restaurants, and jobs. Norfolk is the epicenter of the greater Hampton Roads region, and is close to the cities of Virginia Beach, Chesapeake, Portsmouth, Suffolk, Newport News, Williamsburg, and Hampton. The Old Dominion Study Abroad Program allows students to spend a semester of study at one of numerous overseas locations.

MAJORS AND DEGREES OFFERED

Old Dominion enrolls about 16,000 undergraduates and 6,000 graduate students, who are from all fifty states and U.S. territories as well as 110 countries. Old Dominion University offers 68 undergraduate programs, 60 master's degrees, 35 doctoral, and two educational specialists' degrees. Old Dominion University is accredited by the Commission on Colleges of the Southern Association of Colleges and Schools.

ACADEMIC PROGRAMS

The university offers a wide range of programs of study in engineering, science, health sciences, business and public administration, education, and arts and letters. Physical therapy, engineering management, coastal physical oceanography, and nuclear physics have achieved national ranking. In the university's dynamic 75-year history, it has produced numerous award-winning faculty, Rhodes and Truman scholars, and a USA Today Academic All-American.

CAMPUS FACILITIES AND EQUIPMENT

Some of Old Dominion's facility features include: At least 1 computer lab in each academic building Testing Center Writing Center Women's Center Bookstore A Wireless network throughout the campus and the dorms Food facilities: Starbucks, Quiznos, Asian Express, Grille Works, Chick-fil-a, Pizza Hut, and Taco Bell in addition to regular cafeteria facilities in Webb University Center. Nautilus/Weight/Conditioning rooms all free for use by presenting a valid student ID card. The University Village offers The Boar's Nest (Delicatessen and club at night), La Herradura Mexican Restaurant, Harvey Ts Natural Market, Borjo Coffee House, Perfectly Frank, Tropical Smoothie, Zeros, the University Village Fitness Center, Sabrina's Signature Salon, Data Tech Central and Surf & Adventure (clothing company). Marriott's Springhill Suites offers on-campus hotel accommodations. The University Bookstore is also located in the Village.

TUITION, ROOM, BOARD AND FEES

Tuition and fees for average full-time undergraduates in 2006-07 were $5,910 for in-state students and $16,470 for out-of-state students. Room and board were $6,640. In addition, there is a fee of approximately $800 for books and supplies, and $158 in required fees.

FINANCIAL AID

Old Dominion University participates in all federal and state financial aid programs. In fact, nearly 55 percent of Old Dominion students receive financial aid in the form of grants, loans, work-study, and academic merit based scholarships. Students often find it easy to attain part-time employment on campus or in the local area. Old Dominion offers more than $6.5 million in scholarships. All incoming freshmen who submit their applications and credentials by the December 1 early action deadline and transfer students who submit their applications and credentials by March 15 are automatically considered for merit-based scholarships. To be considered for endowed scholarships, students need to complete the Free Application for Student Financial Assistance (FASFA) and submit the form to the Department of Education by February 15 for priority consideration. Students should also complete the section of the admissions application for additional financial assistance. The university does not require a supplemental scholarship application. Annually, Old Dominion is one of the first institutions in Virginia to award financial aid to prospective students.

STUDENT ORGANIZATIONS AND ACTIVITIES

The students at Old Dominion share a special sense of excitement derived in part from the rich tapestry of backgrounds, cultures and ages represented here. The 1,400 international students and the 200 student organizations reflect the diversity that exists on campus. The Office of Student Activities and Leadership (OSAL) sponsors a wide variety of programs which complement academic excellence, offer a supportive environment, and engage students in exciting learning experiences. Old Dominion University has 18 varsity sports and affiliated with NCAA Division I. Women's teams are Basketball, Soccer, Field Hockey, Swimming and Diving, Lacrosse, Tennis, Golf, Sailing, and Rowing. Men's teams include Basketball, Soccer, Football (2009), Wrestling, Baseball, Tennis, Golf, Swimming and Diving. Old Dominion teams have won 18 national championships and 4 individual titles.

ADMISSIONS PROCESS

Old Dominion University is a selective university that reviews applications on an individual basis. Each application is read and reviewed by the admissions staff. While academic performance is a vital factor in the decision-making process, Old Dominion also takes into account any athletic, student organization, or community service involvement. The average freshman admitted to Old Dominion ranks in the top third of his or her graduating class; earned a minimum of 16 high school academic units in English, math, science, foreign language, and social studies; and is actively involved in school and/or community-based clubs, organizations, and athletics. Approximately 50 percent of the transfer students have earned an associate degree or have completed 60 semester hours at another institution prior to enrolling at Old Dominion.

OTTERBEIN COLLEGE

AT A GLANCE

Otterbein College combines an award-winning liberal arts core curriculum with experiential learning and pre-professional training in the restored village suburb of Westerville, near Columbus, Ohio. Our lovely, wooded 140 acre campus includes state of the art academic classrooms, athletic and recreation centers, radio and television studios, art classrooms and exhibit space, and equine facility. Our innovative faculty ignites student passion for learning. Small class sizes and a student faculty ratio of 12/1 lead to individual attention and supportive relationships, encouraging our 3,100 students to reach their full potential. We offer 56 academic majors, 41 minors plus over 100 student organizations.

Otterbein lays claim to many "firsts" or "near firsts." Among these are being the first to admit women without restrictions on what they could study, one of the first to admit students of color, the first to include women faculty and among the first to offer a program balancing classical liberal arts, service learning and practical career training. Currently, Otterbein was one of three schools to receive Presidential Awards for General Community Service in the second annual 2007 President's Higher Education Community Service Honor Roll. During the 2007-08 school year, 83 service-learning courses enrolled over 1,300 students.

We don't impose specific values on students, we challenge them to define their values and live "the examined life." We view a comprehensive liberal arts education as one that expands the soul and mind and provides a consistent influence over a lifetime.

LOCATION AND ENVIRONMENT

Otterbein is set apart by its superb location in the heart of Westerville, a restored village suburb at the edge of the 15th largest city in the nation, Columbus, Ohio: A charming, comfortable setting for study yet with enormous opportunities for internships, cultural events, shopping and dining and exciting social venues right next door.

Hot spots on campus: The Otterbean Cafe, the campus coffee house, is a popular gathering spot for socializing and group discussions. The Clements Recreation Center is a popular fitness destination. The Campus Center houses the main dining hall and Quiznos. Theme houses where groups of students with a common interest can live and host events are also gathering places.

OFF-CAMPUS OPPORTUNITIES

Hot spots off campus: In Westerville, popular coffee houses include Heavenly Cup and Starbucks. Two popular Westerville restaurants include Classic Pizza and The Old Bag of Nails Pub. Two malls are located within 15 minutes on either side of campus: Easton Town Center and Polaris Fashion Place are extremely popular with students. Gallery Hops in the Short North Gallery district, concerts at Nationwide Arena, Germain Amphitheatre and PromoWest Pavillion are frequented by students. Longstreet Dance Club and Nyohs are also popular dance destinations. For Outdoor recreation, the Columbus area MetroParks system affords miles of tree-lined jogging and bike paths. The Columbus Zoo—made famous by Jack Hanna's appearances on Letterman—is one of the country's best.

MAJORS AND DEGREES OFFERED

Accounting: BA, BS; Accounting, Public: BA, BS; Actuarial Science: BS; Allied Health: BS; Art: BA; Athletic Training: BA, BS; Biochemistry: BA, BS; Broadcasting: BA; Business Administration: BA, BS; Chemistry: BA, BS; Computer Science: BA, BS; Economics: BA, BS; Education/Early Childhood & Middle Childhood: BSE (Students planning to teach at the secondary level seek BA or BS degrees in their subject area); English: BA; Environmental Science: BA. BS; Equine Business and Facility Management: BA, BS; Equine Health Technology: BA, BS; Equine Science Preveterinary and Pregraduate Studies: BA, BS; French: BA; Health Education: BA; Health Promotion and Fitness: BA; History: BA; Individualized: BA, BS; International Studies: BA; Journalism: BA; Life Science: BA, BS; Mathematics: BA, BS; Molecular Biology: BA, BA; Music: BA; Music Performance: BM ; Music and Business: BA; Music Education:BME; Musical Theatre: BFA; Nursing: BSN; Organizational Communication: BA; Philosophy: BA; Physical Education: BA; Physics: BA, BS; Political Science: BA; Psychology: BA, BS; Public Relations: BA; Religion: BA; Sociology: BA; Spanish: BA; Speech Communication: BA; Sport Management: BA; Theatre: BA, BFA

ACADEMIC PROGRAMS

Special Minors: Art History; Arts Administration; Black Studies; Dance; German; Japanese; Language and Culture of the Deaf Community; Legal Studies; Sound Production (open to BA music majors only); Women's Studies

Special Programs:

Dual degree engineering (3+2) guaranteed progress into engineering at Case Western University, Cleveland or Washington University, St. Louis.

Pre-professional Studies: Pre-Dentistry; Pre-Law; Pre-Medicine; Pre-Physical Therapy; Pre-Veterinary Medicine

CAMPUS FACILITIES AND EQUIPMENT

Otterbein's 140-acre campus includes 50 buildings. The historic Towers Hall was constructed in 1872. The college completed interior renovation of Towers Hall designed to update the facilities and technology and still recapture the essence of the time period in which Towers was built. The Edwin L. and Mary Louise Roush Hall, dedicated June 1993, is the first general purpose academic facility built on the Otterbein campus since Towers and houses the business, education and graduate programs. Cowan Hall houses facilities for Otterbein's renowned theatre program, including an extensive scene shop, and underwent major renovation in 2004 and 2005 to improve the acoustics, scene shop, lobby and The Fritsche Theatre.

The Department of Art's new facility was renovated with the special needs of artists in mind. The new Miller Gallery is also located in this building, with state-of-the-art lighting for optimal exhibition viewing. The other half of the same building is the new home to the Department of Communication, housing brand new television and radio stations, as well as a writing lab for the student run newspaper, the Tan and Cardinal. Otterbein also runs The Frank Museum of Art, a renovated church near campus that has rotating exhibitions from the college's collection. The Battelle Fine Arts Center is home for programs in music and dance. Schear-McFadden Science Building has science and nursing laboratories, classrooms, and the Weitkamp Planetarium/Observatory; in June 2007, construction began on a $20 million expansion to these science facilities and to purchase new equipment for the programs. The project will add 30,000 square feet to the existing facility creating 96,000 total square feet. After completion, the facility will have up-to-date and well-equipped science laboratories, technology based classrooms and dedicated research space. Other facilities on campus include the Courtright Memorial Library and the Campus Center.

Athletic facilities include The Frank and Vida Clements Recreation and Fitness Center, opened in the fall of 2002, a $9.5 million center providing facilities for athletic training, sports management, and health and fitness programs with a 75,000 square-foot field house, a high-tech cardiovascular fitness area for all students, fully-equipped training and rehabilitation center, coaching offices, classrooms and a student lounge area. The Clements is connected to the Rike Center which houses men's and women's varsity locker rooms, a newly renovated weight room and basketball, handball and racquetball courts. In fall 2005, the Cardinals football program moved into its new home in Memorial Stadium, a $3.2 million grandstand built on the same site of the original Memorial Stadium, both of which were dedicated to student and alumni veterans. Additional outdoor sports facilities include tennis courts, and separate fields for softball, baseball and soccer.

TUITION, ROOM, BOARD AND FEES

2008-2009 school year

Tuition: 26,319

Room: 3,570

Board: 3,891

FINANCIAL AID

95% of our students receive financial assistance, including over $19 million in scholarships and grants.

Students applying for need-based Financial Aid must complete the FAFSA form with a priority deadline of April 1.

Otterbein offers the following scholarships:

President's Scholar Awards $12,500

Otterbein Scholar Awards $8,000

Otterbein Scholar Awards $6,000

Otterbein Transfer Scholar Awards $2,500

National Merit Finalist $2000

International Baccalaureate Scholarships $1,000 to 7,000

Endowed Scholarships $800 - 1500

Ammons-Thomas Awards $500 - 6000

Community Service Awards $1500

Talent Awards $500 - 8000

Legacy Awards $1000

Premier Departmental Scholar Awards $1000

STUDENT ORGANIZATIONS AND ACTIVITIES

Academic Interest Groups: Accounting Club; Actuarial Club of Otterbein College; American Chemical Society Student Affiliate; Association for Computing Machinery; Ohio Collegiate Music Education Association; Otterbein College Assoc. of Animal Health; Care Professionals; Otterbein College Middle Level Assoc.; Otterbein Club of Athletic Training Students; Otterbein Nursing Students Association; Pre-Law Club; Public Relations Student Society of America; (PRSSA); Sociology Club; Sports Management Club; Student Education Association (OSEA); Teacher Education Committee

Governance: Academic Council; Administrative Council; Affirmative Action Committee; Appeals Council; Constitution Review Committee; Cultural Affairs Committee; Curriculum Committee; Distinction Committee; Faculty Council; Governance, Bylaws and Communication; Committee; Judicial Council; Otterbein College Senate; Personnel Committee; Retention Committee; Student Life Committee; Student Media Board; Student Trustee; Traffic Council; United Greek Governing Board

Honoraries: Alpha Epsilon Delta, pre-medicine; Alpha Lambda Delta, freshmen women's academic; Delta Omicron, music; Mortar Board; Order of Omega, Greek leadership; Phi Alpha Theta (History); Phi Eta Sigma, freshmen men's academic; Phi Sigma Iota, foreign language; Pi Kappa Delta, forensics/speech; Psi Chi, psychology; Sigma Zeta, science; Torch and Key, scholarship

Media: Aegis, humanities journal; Ottervine, Otterbein Campus news publication; Quiz and Quill, student literary magazine; Sibyl Yearbook; Student Media Board; Tan & Cardinal, weekly student newspaper; WOBN-FM and WOCC-TV3

Religious Life: Campus Crusade for Christ/Athletes in Action; Otterbein Christian Fellowship; Religious Life Council

Greek Fraternity: Interfraternity Council (IFC); United Greek Governing Board; Alpha Phi Alpha; Alpha Sigma Phi (Phoenix); Eta Phi Mu; Lambda Gamma Epsilon (Kings); Pi Beta Sigma (Pi Sig); Pi Kappa Phi (Country Club); Sigma Delta Phi (Sphinx); Zeta Phi (Rats); Omega Psi Phi

Greek Sorority: Panhellenic Council; United Greek Governing Board; Alpha Kappa Alpha; Delta Sigma Theta; Epsilon Kappa Tau (EKT); Kappa Phi Omega (Kappa Phi); Sigma Alpha Tau (Owls); Tau Delta (Deltas); Tau Epsilon Mu (TEM); Theta Nu; Zeta Phi Beta

Special Interest Groups: African American Student Union (AASU); Asian Student Interest Association (ASIA); Campus Green Party; Campus Programming Board (CPB); Commuter Association; Emerging Leaders; Free Thinkers Club; Freezone; International students Association (ISA); Host & Tour; Model United Nations Club; Orientation Leaders; Otterbein College Crew Club; Otterbein College Democrats; Otterbein Equestrian Team; Otterbein Film Club; Otterbein Peace Coalition; Otterbein Young Republicans; Outdoor Adventure Club; Sisters United; Student Athletic Advisory Committee; Volleyball Club; Women's Forum

Sports: Baseball (M); Basketball (M/W); Cross Country (M/W); Equestrian Team (M/W); Football (M); Golf (M/W); Indoor Track (M/W); Outdoor Track (M/W); Soccer (M/W); Softball (M/W); Tennis (M/W); Volleyball (W); Intramurals available in basketball, softball,; football, and volleyball; Cheerleading

Musical Groups and Theater: Big Band; Camerata; Cap and Dagger; Cardinal Dance Team; Cardinal Marching Band; Chamber Ensembles; Concert Band; Concert Choir; Gospel Choir; Jazz Ensemble; Men's Glee Club; Opera Theatre; Opus One (vocal jazz ensemble); Otterbein Vocal Ensemble; Pep Band; Percussion Ensemble; String Ensemble; Westerville Symphony; Wind Ensemble; Women's Chorale

Service Groups:

Community Service T.E.A.M.; Habitat for Humanity; Leadership in Volunteer Experience (LIVE); M.O.S.T. (Mentoring Organizational Students Today); Rotaract

ADMISSIONS PROCESS

Otterbein College seeks to admit students who are best qualified to benefit from the educational offerings of the college and to contribute to the campus community. Each applicant's credentials are reviewed individually; admission decisions are based on academic performance, standardized test scores, and the potential for future growth and success. Special talents and participation in extracurricular and community activities will also be considered. Preference is given to applicants who have successfully completed a college preparatory curriculum. Students are admitted without regard to gender, race, sexual orientation, creed, color, national origin or handicap.

Application process:

Otterbein admits students on a rolling basis beginning in mid-October with a recommended deadline of March 1. After that, students will be admitted on a space-available basis; some programs may be closed by then.

A completed application file includes:

1. Application—either paper with $25 fee or on-line with fee waived

(www.otterbein.edu)

2. Official copy of high school transcript

3. Official record of ACT or SAT scores. Test scores will be accepted if reported on an official transcript.

PENNSYLVANIA COLLEGE OF TECHNOLOGY

AT A GLANCE

Penn College is a special mission affiliate of Penn State, committed to applied technology education. Located in Williamsport, it is the second largest campus in the Penn State system, enrolling more than 6,500 students.

Bachelor—and associate—degree and certificate majors represent more than 100 career fields related to:

- business and computer technologies
- construction and design technologies
- health sciences
- hospitality
- industrial and engineering technologies
- integrated studies
- natural resources management
- transportation technology

LOCATION AND ENVIRONMENT

The main campus is located in Williamsport (Northcentral Pennsylvania) – no more than a four-hour drive from major cities including Philadelphia, New York, Pittsburgh, and Washington, D.C.

Air service is provided at the Williamsport Regional Airport.

In addition to the main campus, the College operates an aviation facility at the regional airport and nearby centers for the earth sciences and advanced automotive technologies.

OFF-CAMPUS OPPORTUNITIES

Students benefit from internships, work-based, and other experiences outside of the classroom. For many, these experiences are the first step toward a full-time job after graduation. "Whether it be pursuing a master's degree or working in industry, I have not only a foot in the door at that company … I have a good understanding of what happens throughout the industry," said Scott Jacobs, Manufacturing Engineering Technology. "The internship, by far, was one of the most important things I've ever done," he added.

While working on a Culinary Arts Technology degree, Rachel Hall studied abroad in Italy and worked with students and chefs from around the world during a summer internship at Gaylord Opryland Resort and Convention Center in Nashville. "Penn College gives students great opportunities to expand their education through the Visiting Chef Series, Study Abroad programs, and getting internships," Hall declares.

MAJORS AND DEGREES OFFERED

Bachelor of Science:

Accounting

Applied Health Studies

Applied Human Services

Automotive Technology Management

Aviation Maintenance Technology

Building Automation Technology

Business Administration (Banking & Finance, Human Resource Management, Management, Management Information Systems, Marketing, Small Business & Entrepreneurship)

Civil Engineering Technology

Computer-Aided Product Design

Construction Management

Culinary Arts and Systems

Dental Hygiene (Health Policy & Administration, Special Population Care)

Electronics and Computer Engineering Technology

Graphic Communications Management

Graphic Design

HVAC Technology

Information Technology (Information Technology Security Specialist, Network Specialist, Web & Applications Development)

Legal Assistant/Paralegal Studies

Manufacturing Engineering Technology

Nursing

Physician Assistant

Plastics and Polymer Engineering Technology

Residential Construction Technology and Management

Technology Management

Welding and Fabrication Engineering Technology

Associate of Applied Arts:

Advertising Art

Mass Media Communication

Associate of Arts:

General Studies

Studio Arts

Associate of Applied Science:

Accounting

Architectural Technology

Automated Manufacturing Technology

Automotive Service Sales and Marketing

Automotive Technology (Ford ASSET & Honda)

Aviation Technology

Baking and Pastry Arts

Building Construction Technology

Building Construction Technology: Masonry

Business Management

Civil Engineering Technology

Collision Repair Technology

Computer-Aided Drafting Technology

Culinary Arts Technology

Dental Hygiene

Diesel Technology

Diesel Technology: Mack

Early Childhood Education

Electric Power Generation Technology

Electrical Technology

Electromechanical Maintenance Technology

Electronics and Computer Engineering Technology (Cisco® Systems, Communications & Fiber Optics, Electronics & Computer Engineering, Nanofabrication Technology, Robotics & Automation)

Emergency Medical Services

Forest Technology

Graphic Communications Technology

Health Arts

Health Arts: Practical Nursing

Health Information Technology

HVAC Technology

Heavy Construction Equipment Technology (Caterpillar Equipment, Operator, Technician)

Hospitality Management

Human Services

Individual Studies

Information Technology (Cisco® Technology, Network Technology, Technical Support Technology, Web & Applications Technology)

Landscape/Nursery Technology: Turfgrass Management

Legal Assistant/Paralegal

Nursing

Occupational Therapy Assistant

Office Information Technology (Medical Office Information, Specialized Office Information)

Ornamental Horticulture (Horticulture Retail Management, Landscape Technology, Plant Production)

Physical Fitness Specialist

Plastics and Polymer Technology

Radiography

Surgical Technology

Surveying Technology

Toolmaking Technology

Welding Technology

Certificates:

Automotive Service Technician

Aviation Maintenance Technician

Collision Repair Technician

Construction Carpentry

Diesel Technician

Electrical Occupations

Health Information Coding Specialist

Machinist General

Nurse/Health Care Paralegal Studies

Paramedic Technician

Plumbing

Practical Nursing

Welding

ACADEMIC PROGRAMS

Classrooms and laboratories offer extensive "hands-on" experiences that prepare graduates for success in the workplace. Applied technology in each major gives students the opportunity to learn the most current advances in their fields of study. To ensure an ever-present connection to the workforce, business, and industry, advisers provide guidance on matters of curriculum, facilities, and equipment.

Small classes (1:19 faculty-to-student ratio)—and no graduate assistants teaching classes—mean students have access to faculty. "The interactions and the relationships that the students build with the faculty here is just unbelievable," says

Jennifer Fritz, Physician Assistant. She goes on to say that the bonds she has with her instructors have "done a world of good for my education."

For those who need alternatives beyond the traditional, on-campus programs of study, Penn College also offers a variety of courses and bachelor-degree completion programs via distance learning. Bachelor's degrees that can be completed through distance learning include: Applied Health Studies, Automotive Technology Management, Dental Hygiene, Nursing, and Technology Management.

Taking courses online made it possible for Crista Dailey, Technology Management, to earn her degree while working full time and raising a family. She says that "it provided me with the flexibility I needed to complete my education."

Bachelor-degree, associate-degree, and certificate majors combine hands-on experience with theory and management education. Among the majors with the most students enrolled in Fall 2007 were Information Technology, Business Administration, Nursing, Building Construction, Automotive Technology, and Residential Construction Technology and Management.

For those who are undecided or have specific career goals not addressed in other programs, Penn College offers associate-degree General Studies and Individual Studies majors. For those undecided about a career or college major, counseling and career services are available.

FINANCIAL AID

Four out of five Penn College students receive some form of Financial Aid. Regardless of family income, students are encouraged to apply for Financial Aid, including grants, loans, scholarships, and work-study options. For the most current information, visit www.pct.edu/finaid/.

In 2007-08, Pennsylvania residents attending Penn College paid approximately $19,720 per year and out-of-state residents, approximately $22,600 per year. These estimated costs are based upon tuition and fees for an average 15 credits per semester, plus estimated expenses for housing, meals, books, and supplies. For the most current information, visit www.pct.edu/finaid/cost.htm.

STUDENT ORGANIZATIONS AND ACTIVITIES

In addition to clubs and organizations—many of which are affiliated with national and professional organizations—Penn College offers 15 intercollegiate athletic teams and various intramural sport activities.

Matthew Grimminger, Heavy Construction Equipment, explains that getting involved outside of classes is very important. He says, "It's real important to me to be involved with your friends and getting out to play some sports … It lets you relax and relieves stress so you can keep up with the school work and enjoy it both at the same time."

ADMISSIONS PROCESS

Application deadline for fall is July 1. Submit application and $50 application fee online at www.pct.edu/princeton or contact the Admissions Office for an application.

Applicants for bachelor-degree majors must submit SAT/ACT test scores in addition to high school transcripts to be considered for admission.

Applicants must satisfactorily complete placement testing and satisfy other major-specific admission criteria in order to be offered acceptance into a major program of study.

Information on all Penn College majors, as well as details on admissions and enrollment, is offered online at www.pct.edu/princeton.

Pennsylvania College of Technology

One College Avenue

Williamsport, PA 17701

(800) 367-9222 or (570) 327-4761

Fax: 570.321.5551

admissions@pct.edu

www.pct.edu/princeton

PITZER COLLEGE

AT A GLANCE

Pitzer is a comprehensive liberal arts college founded in 1963 as the sixth member of The Claremont Colleges and ranks as the fifth most diverse private co-ed national liberal arts college. Our emphasis on interdisciplinary learning, intercultural understanding, and social responsibility distinguishes us from most other American colleges and universities. Interdisciplinary learning encourages you to explore how different academic fields intersect and draw on each other's wisdom and ideas; intercultural understanding enables you to see issues and events from cultural perspectives different from your own; and social responsibility shows you how to transform knowledge into action as you strive to make the world a better place to live for yourself and future generations.

What's more, Pitzer requires fewer general education courses than most other colleges, so you get to take more of the courses that appeal to your individual interests. You can also choose among a range of courses that connect classroom learning to real-world experience, whether it's working inside a labor union, assisting with a faculty member's research, advising a neighboring city about economic development, or helping underprivileged children prepare for a future that includes college. Such experiences help you grasp the deeper implications of your actions and how your education at Pitzer prepares you to make a difference in society.

Pitzer offers an intimate academic and social community alongside access to the resources of a larger university through membership in The Claremont Colleges, and students are allowed to cross-register at the other Claremont Colleges. This opportunity greatly enhances the range of courses available to students. The total enrollment of all the colleges is about 6,000 students.

In addition, Pitzer has completed phase one of a three-phase residence hall construction project in which we expect to become, upon its completion, the only college in the nation to have all Gold LEED certified buildings by the U.S. Green Building Council.

LOCATION AND ENVIRONMENT

We are located in the city of Claremont (population 35,000) at the base of the San Gabriel Mountains, about 35 miles east of Los Angeles and 78 miles west of Palm Springs. Pitzer is a short distance from rock climbing at Joshua Tree National Park; the Getty, Norton Simon, and other LA County museums; beaches of Southern California; and skiing at Mt. Baldy and Big Bear. Claremont's quaint village, a short walk from campus, has a wide variety of restaurants, galleries, and shops.

OFF-CAMPUS OPPORTUNITIES

More than 60 percent of our students participate in study abroad programs with an emphasis on community involvement at sites throughout the world. Pitzer administers its own language and culture programs and exchanges in Argentina, Australia, Botswana, Bulgaria, Canada, China, Costa Rica, Denmark, Ecuador, England, Finland, France, Germany, Ghana, Ireland, Italy, Japan, Korea, Latvia, Mexico, Morocco, Nepal, South Africa, Spain, Thailand, and Turkey. Students in all majors can arrange a semester of study abroad but those who prefer not to take a full semester away from Pitzer may participate in Pitzer summer programs in Costa Rica and Japan.

MAJORS AND DEGREES OFFERED

Pitzer grants the bachelor of arts degree in 44 fields of study: American studies; anthropology; art; Asian American studies; Asian studies; biology; biology/chemistry; Black studies; chemistry; Chicano studies; classics; dance; economics; English and world literature; environmental science; environmental studies; European studies; French; gender and feminist studies; history; human biology; international and intercultural studies; Latin American and Caribbean studies; linguistics; mathematical economics; mathematics; media studies; molecular biology; music; neuroscience; organismal biology and ecology; organizational studies; philosophy; physics; political economy; political studies; psychology; religious studies; science and management; science, technology, and society; sociology; Spanish; theater; and third-world studies. There is also the opportunity to create one's own major.

ACADEMIC PROGRAMS

To earn the bachelor of arts degree, students are required to complete 32 courses, about one-third of which are in the field of major. Pitzer co-sponsors a science program with Claremont McKenna and Scripps Colleges. The Keck Science Center has state-of-the-art laboratories for teaching and research and a large biological field station. Pitzer joins Western University of Health Sciences in nearby Pomona to offer a seven-year program culminating in the BA and the Doctor of Osteopathic Medicine degrees.

CAMPUS FACILITIES AND EQUIPMENT

Pitzer provides a variety of special resources and facilities. These facilities include the arboretum (featuring ecologically and sustainable landscapes); computer centers (one laboratory features Macintosh computers, another features PC-compatible computers); the Gold Student Center (housing a fitness room for aerobics and weight training, simulated rock climbing, martial arts and yoga classes, a recreational room, a snack bar, a swimming pool, a video production studio); the W. M. Keck Science Center (housing biology, chemistry, and physics labs); the psychology lab; and the writing lab.

In addition, Pitzer shares a variety of facilities with the other Claremont Colleges: Honnold/Mudd Library, Rancho Santa Ana Botanic Garden, Bernard Biological Field Station, Chicano/Latino Student Affairs Center, Office of Black Student Affairs, Asian American Resource Center, Baxter Student Health Services, Monsour Counseling and Psychological Services, McAlister Center for Religious Activities, campus security, and Huntley Bookstore.

TUITION, ROOM, BOARD AND FEES

Costs for the 2007-2008 academic year are as follows:

Tuition: $32,704

Room: $6,456

Board: $3,756

Fees: $3,208

Books and personal expenses: $2,000 (estimated)

Travel expenses will vary.

Costs are subject to change for the 2008-2009 academic year.

FINANCIAL AID

Pitzer's Financial Aid program supports the goals of the admission program: to enroll a student body of quality and diversity. Financial Aid is based on financial need. Approximately 45 percent of the students receive Financial Aid in the form of grants, loans, and work study. To apply for aid, you must complete and submit the CSS PROFILE Form and the Free Application for Federal Student Aid (FAFSA) by February 1. California residents must apply for a CAL Grant by March 2.

STUDENT ORGANIZATIONS AND ACTIVITIES

The spirit of involvement extends well beyond the classroom, and is the essence of a Pitzer education. Opportunities abound within the college to participate in more than 50 student organizations, intramural sports, community service programs, and social activities, as well as the 150 clubs and organizations available consortium-wide. Students participate in all college committees and play a key part in the governance of the college. Pitzer joins Pomona College to field NCAA Division III teams in baseball, basketball, cross-country, football, golf, soccer, softball, swimming and diving, tennis, track and field, volleyball, and water polo. In addition, there are numerous club sports to participate in, including cycling, lacrosse, badminton, fencing and rugby.

ADMISSIONS PROCESS

Pitzer College strives to attract a diverse student body with demonstrated academic ability, maturity, and independence. Each applicant is evaluated on an individual basis. Your application should show the ways in which you feel you will profit from and contribute to Pitzer College. Pitzer expects that students seeking admission would have selected a rigorous academic program in high school. Your senior year is very important and should include a variety of solid academic courses.

Early Decision: If Pitzer is clearly your first choice, we invite you to use this option. This application deadline is November 15.

Regular Admission: First-year applicants seeking regular admission should have their admission applications submitted by January 1.

Pitzer's admission policy for first-year students provides applicants with greater flexibility in presenting application materials that accurately reflect their diverse academic abilities and potentials.

Pitzer exempts students graduating in the top 10 percent of their class, or those who have an unweighted cumulative GPA of 3.50 or higher in academic subjects, from having to submit any standardized tests. Applicants not falling into either one of those categories will be required to submit at least one of the following options:

(a) ACT scores, or (b) SAT scores, or (c) Two or more Advanced Placement test scores of at least 4: one must be in English or English language, and one must be in mathematics or a natural science, or (d) Two International Baccalaureate exam scores: one must be in English 1A and one must be in the Mathematics Methods (Standard Level), or a higher level course in mathematics, or (e) Two exams: one recent junior or senior year graded, analytical writing sample from a humanities or social science course, and one recent graded exam from an advanced mathematics course (Algebra 2 or above). The samples must include the student's name, the teacher's comments, grades, and the assignment.

Pitzer College adheres to the May 1 National Candidate's Reply Date Agreement.

POINT LOMA NAZARENE UNIVERSITY

LOCATION AND ENVIRONMENT

PLNU is located on the coast of San Diego - literally. We have beach access from our campus, but we are also very centrally located. PLNU's campus is five minutes from the airport, ten minutes from downtown San Diego, thirty minutes from the border, an hour from Orange County and two hours from Los Angeles.

OFF-CAMPUS OPPORTUNITIES

Students have many opportunities to take advantage of what is available off campus. Through PLNU-sponsored study-abroad programs and affiliations with other accredited programs, almost 11 percent of our current undergraduate population (compared to one percent nationally) and 30 percent of our recent graduates have studied abroad, traveling to countries such as Brazil, New Zealand, Italy, Egypt, Israel, France and South Africa. Students are also encouraged to be a part of internships, whether your major is Business or Fashion Merchandising. In past internships, students have worked with the Birch Aquarium, NBC 7/39 San Diego, the San Diego Mayor's Office, Naval Ocean System Center and the San Diego Padres. With more than sixty different majors and concentrations, students have a variety of options available to them at PLNU.

Part of the experience of college is living, studying and breathing the same air as your classmates. You will likely make some of the best friends you will ever have, create a ton of memories and learn a lot about people in the process. At Point Loma, we understand that this is an important part of university life, and we do everything we can to help make it happen. We asked current students to tell us their favorite places to go in San Diego. Here are their answers:

Miguel's Cocina

Petco Park Downtown San Diego

The beach

The park on Shelter Island

Pat and Oscars Seaport Village

Qualcomm Stadium

Fashion Valley Mall

In-N-Out Burger

Balboa Park

Santana's

The Gaslamp District

La Jolla

The Farmers Market

The Living Room Horton Plaza

Adalbertos

Yogurt Mill

Kobeys Swap Meet

Coronado

Little Italy

Konos

Hodad's Burgers

MAJORS AND DEGREES OFFERED

Point Loma Nazarene University's graduate and undergraduate programs have a long tradition of academic excellence. Our faculty includes nationally-recognized experts and industry leaders in a variety of disciplines. The faculty at Point Loma takes seriously the university's mission to "teach, shape and send" its students. By emphasizing critical thinking, practical knowledge, and real world experience, classes at Point Loma prepare students to be dynamic leaders and difference-makers in many fields and places. PLNU offers more than 60 specific areas of study and is accredited by the Western Association of Schools and Colleges (WASC).

ACADEMIC PROGRAMS

Our largest majors are Business, Liberal Studies (Education), Nursing, Psychology and Communication. PLNU is also one of the few Christian schools to offer an accredited Dietetics program, an accredited Athletic Training program, a Fashion Merchandising program and a Women's Studies program. For more information, please visit http://www.pointloma.edu/academics.

CAMPUS FACILITIES AND EQUIPMENT

Point Loma is constantly striving to better our Campus Facilities and Equipment for our students. Our music and athletic training facilities are state of the art. Just within the past three years, PLNU has finished construction on a new Student Financial Services building, new residence halls, the new Fermanian School of Business, and is nearing completion on the new School of Theology and Christian Ministry. Our sciences have recently benefited from an NSF grant that allowed for the purchase of brand new lab equipment. Every area of PLNU is kept up to date to ensure easy informational access on campus.

TUITION, ROOM, BOARD AND FEES

For the 2008-2009 Academic year: Tuition (12-17 units): 24,580 per year. General Fee: $540 per year. Room and Board (based on shared room, mid-priced meal plan): $8,170 per year. Total: $16,645 per semester; $33,290 per year.

STUDENT ORGANIZATIONS AND ACTIVITIES

You have a wide variety of skills, desires, experience, and passion - and PLNU has a wide variety of places to put all of that to use for the Kingdom of God. Maybe you are compelled to see the way that God's people worship in another country... or to get to know families in need... or to play the bass in a worship band... or to lead your hall's Bible study... or to visit those in prison. PLNU, a university dedicated to the practical call of Jesus to love God and love others, invites you to explore those interests here. We are committed to opening up as many doors as possible for you to serve. There are many opportunities for students to become involved in Clubs and Organizations at Point Loma. Most of these fall under the direction of ASB (Associated Student Body). PLNU and the ASB Board of Directors encourages you to participate in the wide range of opportunities that we provide. For more information, please visit www.pointloma.edu/campuslife.

FAQ

Besides clubs and ministry groups, what else can I get involved in at the university?

There is no shortage of opportunities for you to get involved outside the classroom. Here is just a sampling of some of the opportunities (review the Student Handbook for more options): Outdoor Leadership and Recreation Mission Trips/ LoveWorks Chapel Covenant and Discipleship Groups Worship Ministries Time-Out Team Barnabas Intramural Sports Peer Educator

What are the lifestyle expectations for PLNU students?

In signing a covenant with Point Loma Nazarene University as part of your application process, you agreed to follow institutional policies as outlined in the Student Handbook and in the university catalog. In turn, the university community is committed to helping you achieve your goals. PLNU is committed to fostering a healthy environment. As a part of that commitment, all members of the community are expected to abstain from all alcohol, tobacco, and illegal drug use on and off campus.

Will I have access to the Internet?

Students can research and communicate using the campus wireless network and from computer labs, library, or residence hall rooms. Each student is given a network and an e-mail account. For more information, please visit www.pointloma.edu/campuslife.

ADMISSIONS PROCESS

Early Action deadline: 15 November

Notification: 19 December

General Admissions and Transfer Student deadline: 15 February

Notification: 1st week of April

To apply online, request a paper application or download an application, please visit www.pointloma.edu/apply. We would love to have you visit our campus! For campus tours, interviews, class or chapel visits, or more information about special one-day or overnight Preview Day events, please visit www.pointloma.edu/visit. Admissions questions? Please visit www.pointloma.edu/admissions.

POINT PARK UNIVERSITY

LOCATION AND ENVIRONMENT

Point Park University is an independent, four-year coeducational institution located in the heart of downtown Pittsburgh, one of America's most dynamic cities. Its central location means that students are just minutes away from internship opportunities, entertainment and sports venues. Point Park's growing, yet compact campus includes the University Center, housing the Point Park University library; the new television studio and cinema and digital arts classrooms and labs; Academic Hall, with classrooms, laboratories, a newsroom, computer center and administrative offices; Lawrence Hall, a 21-story building with dance studios, classrooms, student lounges, recreation center, cafeteria, administrative offices and dormitory rooms; and Thayer Hall, home of the Point Park Children's School and additional dormitory rooms. The Playhouse of Point Park University is a multi-theater complex which serves as the educational arm for the University's Conservatory of Performing Arts.

The University's expansion includes a newly-opened dance studio building adjacent to Lawrence Hall and, in addition to its existing dorms, two downtown buildings just two blocks from campus featuring suite housing for students. Cultural attractions including the Pittsburgh Symphony, the Three Rivers Arts Festival, the Three Rivers Regatta, and sporting events featuring the Pittsburgh Steelers, Pittsburgh Pirates and Pittsburgh Penguins, are within walking distance of campus.

OFF-CAMPUS OPPORTUNITIES

Point Park University encourages students to enrich their educational experience through course work overseas. Trips to Europe at affordable rates are arranged, occasionally by Point Park University faculty, for university credit.

Students may take classes at Regent's College in London, Wells College in Paris and The American University in Rome. At Regent's, which is located in the heart of London, courses are taught American-style by British instructors, and credits may be transferred to Point Park. At Wells, courses are available in all forms of dance, and most fine and studio arts, including photography and music. The American University offers a board selection of courses in the arts and sciences and business courses, with some fine and studio arts courses available, including photography.

Fees at Regent's and at Point Park are approximately the same; students who register for courses at Regent's are fully eligible for state and federal Financial Aid. For further information, please contact Elaine Luther via email at eluther@pointpark.edu or by phone at (412) 392-3947.

MAJORS AND DEGREES OFFERED

Since its founding, Point Park has been known for providing its students with an education that combines the liberal arts with career education. While some of the programs of study are those traditionally found in the liberal arts and sciences, others reflect the cultural, business and industrial needs of the community. Emphasizing career preparation within a broad educational context, these programs enhance the prospects of graduates seeking professional positions in today's highly competitive job market.

Point Park offers bachelor's and associate's degrees in a number of majors, including accounting, applied history, arts management, behavioral sciences, biological sciences, business management, children's theater, criminal justice, dance, digital and cinema arts, education (early childhood, elementary and secondary), engineering technology (civil, electrical and mechanical), English, environmental protection science, human resources management, information technology, intelligence and national security, journalism and mass communications, political science, psychology, public administration, sport, arts & entertainment management and theater arts.

The University has earned national distinction in a number of fields, including dance, theater, journalism and mass communication, and sport, arts and entertainment management.

The University also awards eight graduate degrees: the master of arts degree in curriculum and instruction; the master of arts degree in educational administration; the master of arts degree in journalism and mass communication; the master of arts degree in organizational leadership, the master of fine arts in theater arts; the master of business administration degree; the master of science in criminal justice; and the master of science degree in engineering management.

Learning is an interactive process at Point Park where the average class size is between 15-20 students. All courses are taught by experienced, full-time faculty, augmented by working practitioners who bring a practical knowledge of the workplace into the classroom.

CAMPUS FACILITIES AND EQUIPMENT

The Point Park University facilities include the library, whose collections include 125,000 volumes, over 650 DVDs, musical CDs, and videos, subscriptions to 274 print periodicals and newspapers, 34 periodicals and newspapers on microfilm, and access to over 17,000 serial titles through online databases.

University facilities include engineering technology, science and computer labs, a television studio, black and white and color photo labs, the Program for Academic Success, dance studios, and a radio station. Performing arts majors gain practical experience at the landmark Playhouse of Point Park University.

In recent years the University has embarked upon a major renovation of its facilities, including new science labs, state-of-the-art color television studios and digital film editing suites. It has also upgraded classrooms, the residence halls, dining facilities, and the overall physical plant. The addition of F. Tracy Henderson Alumni Park and the Academic Hall Atrium has brightened the campus while providing students with more places for study and relaxation.

A major renovation project was completed in 2005 when the Lawrence Hall façade and lobby were restored to their former glory. The 21-story Lawrence Hall, which houses classrooms, offices, dorms, the recreation center and other University facilities, was opened in 1928 as a health club, later becoming a hotel. This first phase of the Lawrence Hall renovation included creating a street level bookstore, restoring a series of Gothic arched window openings, and updating the building's infrastructure and building connectivity with the dance studio complex.

Point Park University is an institution that utilizes green principles as it renovates. The University's new dance studio complex, which connects to Lawrence Hall, opened in August, 2007. One of the distinguishing characteristics of this project is that the new dance studio reflects an environmentally friendly design.

The dance studio complex is located in the footprint of three buildings on the Boulevard of the Allies next to Lawrence Hall. The 14,400 square foot space features cushioned, non-slip floor, glare-free lighting and the latest audio and visual equipment, in addition to a 60' x 60' performance area with a master control room, dressing room, and sound isolated lighting and editing equipment, so performances can be taped and broadcast.

One of the most exciting aspects of college life for many students is the opportunity to live on campus. The University's residence halls have been filled to capacity (600) during the past few years. To provide additional housing, the University entered into an agreement with a developer converting several former Wood Street office buildings into suites and apartments. Opened in the fall of 2006, Pioneer Suites and Conestoga Suites house approximately 120 more Point Park students and are located just a block from campus.

The residence halls at Point Park mean easy access to classes, dance studios, student lounges, the library, the recreation center, and the excitement of downtown Pittsburgh. More than 30 percent of full-time students reside in campus housing, which, in addition to the Conestoga and Pioneer Hall suites, includes the 10-story Thayer Hall and the 21-story Lawrence Hall. Contact the Residence Life Office at (412) 392-3824 with any questions.

The Recreation Center is open year-round and offers fitness training, intramural sports activities, and informal recreation. It is staffed by a recreation professional and student personnel who are available for individual and group programming. All activities sponsored at the Recreation Center are coed and free to participants.

Point Park is continually seeking ways to empower the region by partnering with various community organizations. Partnerships include the Guest Artists-in-Residence Program with the Pittsburgh High School for Creative and Performing Arts, which brings distinguished artists in dance and theatre to work with students at both institutions. As part of its popular Summer in the City program, the Point Park has partnered with Radio City to become the only university in the nation to host the Rockette Summer Intensive program.

The University's Gerald E. McGinnis Distinguished Lectureship Series, which is open to the public, brings in high-profile speakers who will enrich the campus life of Point Park as well as that of the general community

TUITION, ROOM, BOARD AND FEES

For the 2007-08 academic years, undergraduate tuition is $18, 460. Tuition for Conservatory students is $21,420.

Room and board are $8,440 and student fees cost about $530.

FINANCIAL AID

We understand that choosing a college can be a complex decision. We believe that you should have the opportunity to select the college that best suits your needs and interests, regardless of your financial situation. Point Park University has made a commitment to offering outstanding academic and co-curricular programs while keeping tuition and fees affordable for students and their families. We want you to know that nearly all our students receive financial assistance. Last year more than $60 million in Financial Aid was awarded to our students. Our Office of Financial Aid coordinates a variety of both merit and need-based financial assistance programs to make it possible for full-time students to take advantage of the educational opportunities at Point Parks. Scholarships, awards, grants, loans, and employment are available from several federal, state and institutional sources. Please contact the Office of Admissions at (412) 392-3430 or 800-321-0129 to receive an informational brochure about financing your Point Park education.

Financial Aid awards for full-time students at Point Park University are determined on the basis of academic achievement, community service, artistic or athletic talent, and financial need. Financial need is the difference between what it would cost for you to attend Point Park University and how much you and your family can reasonably be expected to contribute to those expenses. Point Park University develops a Financial Aid budget that takes into consideration direct costs (tuition, fees, room and board) and indirect costs (books and supplies, travel, and personal expenses). Your expected family contribution is determined through a standard called federal needs analysis methodology, which measures a family's ability to pay for higher education. The FAFSA is the form used to collect data needed to perform needs analysis. To determine a student's Financial Aid eligibility, the university subtracts the student's expected family contribution from his or her budget and awards funds available through federal, state, and institutional aid programs.

POLYTECHNIC UNIVERSITY—BROOKLYN

AT A GLANCE

Polytechnic University, the nation's second oldest private engineering university, was founded in 1854 in Brooklyn, New York. Today, it is the New York metropolitan area's preeminent resource in science and technology education and research. A private, co-educational institution, Polytechnic has a distinguished history in electrical engineering, polymer chemistry and aerospace and microwave engineering. Currently, it is a leader in telecommunications, information science and technology management. The University is also known for its outstanding research centers as well as its outreach programs to encourage math and science education in New York elementary and high schools. In addition to its main campus at MetroTech Center in Brooklyn, Polytechnic offers programs at sites throughout the region, including Long Island, Manhattan and Westchester. Additionally, the University offers several programs in Israel.

LOCATION AND ENVIRONMENT

There is simply no way to separate the Polytechnic experience from New York City. Our location enriches your college and residence life by connecting you to the world's greatest metropolis and everything it has to offer.

Polytechnic is located in the heart of downtown Brooklyn in the middle of MetroTech Center, a 16-acre, $1-billion academic/professional park, situated at the foot of the famous Brooklyn Bridge, just across from the tip of Manhattan. Our campus is your gateway to such places as Wall Street, Broadway, the South Street Seaport on one side of the river, and the Brooklyn Museum and Prospect Park on the other.

OFF-CAMPUS OPPORTUNITIES

Great careers start with great preparation. That's one of the main advantages of studying at Polytechnic University. Internships, co-op experiences and research opportunities prepare our students to be more than narrowly trained specialists. They become global thinkers who draw upon broad professional knowledge and work well in teams. That's why our graduates excel not only as engineers, but also as doctors, attorneys, scientists and business people.

Polytechnic's Career Services Office will help you prepare for success. Our professional staff members offer assistance in areas such as business etiquette, resume writing and interviewing. They also provide a variety of valuable services, including recruiting fairs, internships, resume banks for employers and co-op experiences. Our Cooperative Education Program allows you to gain "real-world" perspectives by combining classroom study with paid professional experience earning $12 to $15 an hour in widely recognized companies.

MAJORS AND DEGREES OFFERED

Our technology-focused degree programs, whether engineering, computer science, management or liberal studies, are designed to get you into the top-paying jobs quickly. A unique core curriculum will ensure that your education is well-rounded. And our faculty will challenge your mind and intellect, helping you grow as a person.

Each degree program at Polytechnic is designed to give specific preparation in a particular field of specialty, while providing a general education strong enough to provide a pathway into virtually any career.

ENGINEERING

Civil Engineering

Construction Management

Computer Engineering

Electrical Engineering

Mechanical Engineering

- Aerospace Engineering

CHEMICAL & BIOLOGICAL SCIENCES & ENGINEERING

Biomolecular Science (Pre-Med)

- Pre-Med early assurance program

Chemical & Biological Engineering

Chemistry

COMPUTER AND INFORMATION SCIENCE

Computer Science

MANAGEMENT

Business & Technology Management

ARTS & SCIENCES

Liberal Studies

- Digital Media Studies

- Education

- History of Technology & Science

- International/Global Studies

- Literature

- Philosophy

Mathematics

Pre-Law

Psychology

Technical & Professional Communication

ACADEMIC PROGRAMS

Polytechnic students receive a rigorous education in engineering, the sciences, liberal arts, and management. An innovative core curriculum introduces students to engineering in the freshman year and emphasizes projects requiring a multi-disciplinary approach. Polytechnic's graduate division has a strong international reputation.

The engineering doctoral program has been rated in the nation's top ten by the American Society of Engineering Education, based on a study by the Conference Board of Associated Research Councils, and Poly is among the nation's most successful institutions in producing science and engineering graduates who go on to earn Ph.D. degrees.

CAMPUS FACILITIES AND EQUIPMENT

Polytechnic University has outstanding resources to aid you in your study and research. Most recently, a $100-million upgrade to the MetroTech campus is reflected in a newly constructed academic building, a modern residence hall, a new athletic facility, new labs, and a state-of-the-art computing infrastructure.

Wireless networking is available on campus, allowing students to connect to the University network and the Internet from virtually anywhere. New computer labs feature high-end workstations for research, 3D modeling and dynamic simulation.

The Bern Dibner Library of Science and Technology offers you an education without limits. It has more than 190,000 titles; 200,000 volumes; numerous serials; online databases; CD-ROM learning tools; and multimedia resources. The library is also a member of the Online Computer Library Center, which maintains an international database with over 4,000 participating libraries.

"Centers of excellence" provide the latest tools and technologies for research and study in various fields, including telecommunications, supercomputing, wireless, polymers, construction management, imaging, biocatalysis and others.

TUITION, ROOM, BOARD AND FEES

2001-2002 EXPENSES

All charges below are computed on an annual basis. Education related costs - housing, board, etc. are estimated.

Tuition — $24,800

University Fees — $970

Room and Board — $8,000

Books & Supplies— $750

Personal Expense — $2,450

FINANCIAL AID

We are committed to providing an affordable education.

Because it's one of the most important decisions of their lives, we make an extra effort to secure the best financial aid package for the students we accept. That's why we prepared this section of our Web site. You'll find the most up-to-date information on financing your Polytechnic education. Many people don't realize the many ways there are to afford this valuable degree through grants, loans, scholarships, and work.

ADMISSIONS PROCESS

All qualified applicants to Polytechnic will need:

SAT I or ACT scores

Four years of science (including chemistry and physics)

Four years of mathematics (algebra through pre-calculus)

POST UNIVERSITY

AT A GLANCE

Founded in 1890, the mission of Post University is to provide our students with the knowledge, personal skills, and experiences required to become leaders in tomorrow's careers. We prepare Each Student, Every Day to be confident, competent, and competitive participants in a global marketplace. NCAA division II athletics, coupled with a curriculum focus on career and self-awareness, as well as interdisciplinary leadership core classes, provide a lively, challenging and fun environment to help graduates transition into the world of advanced studies, and eventually work. At Post, students learn how to think and they experience how education impacts the world of work. Approximately two thirds of Post University's students live on campus in one of the six residence halls. Over 70% of undergraduates participate in activities including student government, campus activities team, clubs and organizations, intramural sports or NCAA division II athletics. Students also enjoy the nearby cultural and social activities in Waterbury and West Hartford, as well as trips to New York City and Boston. Post students participate in a year-round schedule of intercollegiate and intramural athletic activities. The Post University Eagles are members of the National Collegiate Athletic Association (NCAA) Division II and the Central Atlantic Collegiate Conference (CACC). Men's intercollegiate sports teams include baseball, basketball, cross-country, golf, soccer, and tennis. Women's athletic teams include basketball, cross-country, soccer, softball, tennis, and volleyball. The University also sponsors an active, coeducational equestrian team. Intramural sports are diverse, ranging from softball and volleyball to basketball and flag football. Students enjoy the facilities of the Drubner Conference and Fitness Center, including a gymnasium, a swimming pool, tennis and racquetball courts, a fitness club, and weight-training rooms. The Drubner Conference and Fitness Center also houses the campus bookstore.

LOCATION AND ENVIRONMENT

Post University is located midway between New York City and Boston. Post University occupies a 58-acre hilltop residential campus in the suburbs of Waterbury, Connecticut. Post's campus and surrounding community offer a safe, scenic, friendly, and convenient residence. Whether students want to visit museums, shops or the shores of Connecticut, they are in close proximity to a wide variety of cultural and recreational attractions.

ACADEMIC PROGRAMS

For the bachelor's degree, students must complete a minimum of 120 credit hours. To receive an associate's degree from Post, students must complete a minimum of 60 credit hours. All programs offer opportunities for internships and cooperative education. For students seeking additional academic challenges, the Post University Honors Program offers the opportunity to pursue independent research and special projects under the guidance of a faculty member. The University has a two-semester calendar.

TUITION, ROOM, BOARD AND FEES

For 2008-09, full-time resident students pay a comprehensive fee of $32,525, covering tuition, room, and board. For commuting students, the comprehensive fee is $23,525 per year. Equine and laboratory fees, the $40 application fee, and an estimated $500 per year for books and supplies are not included in this basic comprehensive fee.

STUDENT ORGANIZATIONS AND ACTIVITIES

Students play active roles in the day-to-day functioning of Post University. The student's official voice at the University is the Student Government Association (SGA), which expresses recommendations pertaining to student life, oversees the operations of each active student group, and decides on funding for each group. The Student Activities Committee participates in the scheduling and programming of campus events. A large percentage of Post University's standing committees include student representatives.

ADMISSIONS PROCESS

Post University welcomes applicants who are motivated to succeed academically and in life. Admission to Post University is based upon an evaluation of the candidate's qualifications and the recommendation of an admissions representative. All decisions are made without regard to race, creed, color, religion, national origin, handicap, or sexual orientation. Criteria for admission are objective as well as subjective. The applicant's academic experience, standardized test scores, personal qualities, recommendations, and individual characteristics are considered. Post has a rolling admissions policy. The Admissions Committee makes a decision with respect to a candidate's admission to the University as soon as the candidate's file is complete. The minimum requirements to make an admissions decision are official high school transcripts, standardized test scores, and the recommendation of an admissions representative, which is gained through an admissions interview. International students are required to earn a minimum score of 500 on the paper-based version or 173 on the computer-based version of the TOEFL and adhere to the above requirements. Campus visit appointments may be scheduled Monday through Friday, from 10 a.m. to 4 p.m. and on select Saturday's from 10 a.m. to 2 p.m. Post periodically offers Group Information Sessions, on-site and off-site Open Houses. To schedule a campus visit, students should call the Office of Admission at 800-345-2562 (toll-free) or send an e-mail message to admissions@post.edu. Transfer candidates must have a minimum GPA of 2.0 and must file transcripts from all other colleges and universities attended. Grades of C or higher may receive transfer credits. The maximum number of transfer credits allowed for bachelor's candidates is 90; the maximum for associate candidates is 30. To apply, students should submit the application form, the nonrefundable $40 application fee, a recommendation, SAT or ACT scores, and the applicable transcripts. A file must be completed before an admissions decision is made. Post employs a system of rolling admissions. However, each student should attempt to file the application packet as soon as possible. This gives the Admissions Committee the opportunity to carefully review the application and grants the student a chance to begin preparation for life at college. Online applications are available through the University's Web site. For additional information, students should contact:

Office of Admission

Post University

800 Country Club Road

P.O. Box 2540

Waterbury, Connecticut 06723-2540

United States

Phone: 203-596-4520 800-345-2562 (toll-free)

Fax: 203-756-5810

E-mail: admissions@post.edu

Web site: http://www.post.edu

PRESBYTERIAN COLLEGE

AT A GLANCE

By providing a challenging and supportive environment focused on academics, ethics, and social involvement, Presbyterian College develops perceptive students into inquisitive scholars and values-based leaders. Founded in 1880, PC is a fully accredited, private, residential, baccalaureate institution affiliated with the Presbyterian Church (USA). The College provides a liberal arts education within a community of faith, learning, and intellectual freedom. As a nationally-ranked college, Presbyterian College sustains a Christian heritage of integrity and service, not only by striving for academic excellence, but also by a comprehensive honor code, wide-ranging opportunities for volunteer service, and close attention to the needs of each student. The compelling purpose of Presbyterian College is to develop the mental, physical, moral, and spiritual capacities of each student in preparation for a lifetime of personal and vocational fulfillment and responsible contribution to the global community.

Peterson's Competitive Colleges, The Fiske Guide to Colleges, and Barron's Best Buys in College Education consistently recognize PC as an outstanding institution. U. S. News lists PC as one of 360 "Best Values" among national liberal arts colleges, and Washington Monthly listed PC as the top liberal arts college in the nation in 2007. Six PC professors have been recognized as SC CASE Professors of the Year.

The Russell Program helps PC students recognize the influence and responsibilities of modern communications media. Recent on-campus speakers have included newspaper columnist David Broder, author/journalist Bill Moyers, media critic Jean Kilbourne, former White House Press Secretary DeeDee Myers, television anchor Soledad O'Brien, and gifted economist/author Ben Stein. Our Cultural Enrichment Program brings outstanding speakers and performers to campus each year. Some recent performers have included the Chinese Golden Dragon Acrobats, the Boston Brass, and tenor Rodrick Dixon.

Study abroad opportunities for students abound. PC's collaborative partnership with Ghuizou University in China expands the global awareness of students and faculty through academic and cultural exchanges. PC also has a cooperative program with the University of Havana in Cuba. Our Washington Semester program allows students to participate in an academically challenging internship in the DC area as part of their coursework for the fall term. The PC-at-Oxford program is a joint venture with Corpus Christi College at Oxford University.

Students at PC have unique opportunities to interact with faculty through freshman seminar courses, research, internships, independent study, and capstone experiences. A living-learning approach to residence life offers faculty and students opportunities within the residence halls for small study groups. Personal attention and interaction between faculty and students is a hallmark at PC. Our faculty are very student-centered and truly care about our students as individuals.

LOCATION AND ENVIRONMENT

Presbyterian College is located in Clinton, South Carolina. There is easy access to Greenville (40 miles north), Columbia (70 miles southeast), Charleston (160 miles southeast), the South Carolina beaches (about 3 hours away), the mountains (2 hours north), Charlotte (two hours northeast), and Atlanta (two and half hours west). The college town community of Clinton is very supportive of PC and its students.

MAJORS AND DEGREES OFFERED

Presbyterian College offers the Bachelor of Arts and the Bachelor of Science degrees. The College offers 30 majors: art, biology, business/accounting, business/management, business/economics, chemistry, computer science, economics, early childhood education, English, Fine Arts (art, drama/speech, and music), French, German, mathematics, medical physics, middle school education, modern foreign languages, music, music education, philosophy, physics, political science, psychology, religion, religion - Christian education, sacred music, sociology, Spanish, and theatre arts.

Minor concentration areas include Africana studies, arts administration, athletic coaching, Christian youth work, interdisciplinary studies, international studies, Latin American studies, media studies - business, media studies - journalism, physical education, secondary education, and women's studies.

Presbyterian College has a long history and strong reputation of pre-professional programs: pre-dental, pre-law, pre-medical, pre-pharmacy, pre-physical therapy, pre-theology, pre-veterinary medicine, pre-nursing, teaching certification and Army ROTC. In addition, PC offers two dual-degree programs: Engineering/physics dual degree with Vanderbilt University, Clemson University, and Auburn University; Environmental Science/Forestry dual degree with Duke University.

ACADEMIC PROGRAMS

The College strives to develop in students the capacity of understanding, the intellectual curiosity, and the strength of character necessary for leadership. Small classes give increased personal attention and greater opportunity for self-expression on the part of all students. Leading professors in all departments teach all level classes; thus, the benefit of their wide knowledge and experience can be shared with freshmen and upperclassmen.

All entering freshmen must take freshman seminar courses which emphasize critical thinking, communication, and small group experiences. These courses offer new students the opportunity to interact with faculty and fellow students in a unique manner. All students must fulfill an intercultural education requirement by either studying abroad, completing coursework that provides an intercultural perspective, or completing a practicum experience that focuses on enhancing learning through internship opportunities. There are general education requirements for all students which include courses in English composition and literature, fine arts, history, mathematics, natural sciences, physical education, religion, foreign languages, and social sciences. Study abroad is encouraged and opportunities abound in many different countries. The Carol International House and the Senior Hall provide living learning opportunities in intercultural programming.

The Presbyterian College faculty is comprised of 84 full-time professors and instructors, 94 percent of whom have their doctorate or other terminal degree, and 30 part-time faculty. With one professor for every thirteen students, the PC faculty provides close personal attention in a rigorous liberal arts curriculum. Their training comes from over 100 colleges and universities including Harvard, Princeton, and Cornell. PC faculty have been selected as Fulbright Scholars and Fulbright-Hayes recipients in recent years.

In recent years, PC students have received 55 academic honors and grants, including a Rhodes Scholarship, Fulbright Scholar, Rotary International Scholarships, Hansard Scholarships, Jacob Javits Scholarships, Pew Fellowships, and a National Science Foundation Fellowship.

CAMPUS FACILITIES AND EQUIPMENT

Presbyterian College's 240-acre campus includes 29 major buildings situated within the corporate limits of Clinton. Columned halls featuring Jeffersonian-style Georgian architecture sit on grassy, oak-shaded plazas, blending new structures with those listed in the National Registry of Historic Places. The dedication of Lassiter Hall in spring, 2008, marked the opening of a state-of-the-art science facility housing the department of biology.

TUITION, ROOM, BOARD AND FEES

In 2007-2008, tuition at Presbyterian College was reported to cost $24,030; required fees totaled $2,290, and it is estimated that students spent $2,786 on books, supplies, transportation, and other miscellaneous expenses. Room and board is $7,610.

FINANCIAL AID

The Financial Aid office uses the Free Application for Federal Student Aid (FAFSA) as its primary application for institutional, state and federal aid programs. Approximately 95% of our student body receives some form of Financial Aid, including academic scholarships, athletic scholarships, grants, endowed scholarships, loans, work study, private grants and scholarships, federal and state aid. PC offers competitive scholarships in recognition for outstanding academic merit, leadership, musical talent, talent in the theater arts, church leadership, and multicultural student leadership. Music scholarships are available to non-music majors interested in participating in the various music programs. Army ROTC scholarships are also available.

STUDENT ORGANIZATIONS AND ACTIVITIES

Presbyterian College offers a plethora of Student Organizations and Activities. Our honorary clubs include Alpha Psi Omega, Beta Beta Beta, Delta Omicron, Omicron Delta Kappa, Order of Omega, Phi Sigma Theta, Phi Sigma Alpha, Pi Gamma Mu, Psi Chi, Sigma Kappa Alpha, Sigma Pi Sigma, Sigma Tau Delta. Leadership clubs and organizations include Inter-Fraternity Council, Honor Council, Leadership PC, Pan-Hellenic Council, President's Council, Residence Hall Association, Student Alumni Council, Student Government Association, Student Union Board, Wysor Rangers. There are academic clubs in virtually every discipline. We also offer several student publications and on-campus student-fun radio station. There are many religious clubs and many, varied fine arts groups and choirs.

We also have a very strong athletic program transitioning to Division I (FCS), offering opportunities in men's varsity teams in football, basketball, tennis, cross country, golf, soccer, lacrosse, and baseball and women's varsity teams in basketball, golf, tennis, soccer, volleyball, softball, cross country, and lacrosse. Intramural sports provide every student with the opportunity to participate in a varied program conducted throughout the year. Activities include football, soccer, basketball, tennis, swimming, racquetball, billiards, softball, volleyball, ping pong, indoor soccer, sports trivia, and a road race. There are also co-educational opportunities in aerobics, snow skiing, and whitewater rafting.

A 31-acre tract adjacent to the eastern end of the campus has been developed as a comprehensive intramural complex.

ADMISSIONS PROCESS

The Presbyterian College campus is home to students who have demonstrated high levels of achievement in academic, leadership, and community service. The majority of incoming freshmen rank in the top quarter of their high school classes and have participated in activities ranging from athletics to music to volunteer services to student government.

Presbyterian College admits students based on their academic and personal qualifications. Admission decisions are made after careful review of the application, essay, high school transcript, class rank, scores from the Scholastic Assessment Test (SAT) or the American College Testing program (ACT), and the recommendation of a high school official. An interview is preferred, and interested students are urged to visit the campus. The College does not discriminate against applicants or students on the basis of race, religion, sex, handicap, or national or ethnic origin. PC adheres to the National Association for College Admissions Counseling's Statements of Principles of Good Practice and the Statement of Students' Rights and Responsibilities.

The College recommends applicants take the highest level coursework offered in their high school, including at least four units of college preparatory English, four units of math (including Algebra I, Algebra II, geometry, and pre-calculus/calculus), and three or more units each of a foreign language, laboratory science, history, and social science. An early decision plan is available for prospective students who have decided that Presbyterian College is their college choice. Applicants interested in Early Decision must have completed the application process by November 1st of their senior year. If offered an acceptance, the early decision students must submit a $400 non-refundable deposit by January 15th and must withdraw any applications filed with other institutions. The Early Action option requires that the application process be completed by Nov. 15th (also deadline to be considered for Quattlebaum, PC USA, Founders, and music scholarships, as well as the Chinese language program) and offers decision notification by Dec. 15th. The Regular Decision deadline is February 1st with a March 15th notification date.

The College welcomes transfer student applicants from regionally accredited four-year institutions or junior colleges provided they have a minimum overall 2.50 grade point average in college work completed and, at the time of registration at PC, they are eligible to re-enroll in the institution last attended or, in the case of junior colleges, they have graduated.

PRINCETON UNIVERSITY

AT A GLANCE

Princeton combines the strengths of a major research university with the qualities of an outstanding liberal arts college. Princeton prepares its 4,850 undergraduates for lives of leadership and service.

Chartered in 1746, Princeton is the fourth-oldest college in the nation. It is a private, non-sectarian university that seeks to fulfill its informal motto, which was first expressed by its 13th president, Woodrow Wilson: "Princeton in the nation's service and in the service of all nations."

LOCATION AND ENVIRONMENT

Princeton is a residential campus set on 500 park-like acres located in the small town of Princeton in central New Jersey. Known for its beauty and architectural variety, the campus is home to historic landmarks such as Nassau Hall, which was built in 1756 and played an important role during the American Revolution.

Princeton students enjoy easy rail connections to New York City and Philadelphia. Nearby attractions include the Jersey Shore, the Delaware River, and numerous parks, cultural venues, and commercial hubs. For arts lovers, the McCarter Theatre is a campus treasure within easy walking distance.

MAJORS AND DEGREES OFFERED

Princeton undergraduates pursue either the bachelor of arts (A.B.) or the bachelor of science in engineering (B.S.E.) degree. Students in the A.B. degree program choose a concentration (major) in one of 29 departments in the arts, humanities, social sciences, and natural sciences, including undergraduate programs in the Woodrow Wilson School of Public and International Affairs and the School of Architecture. The B.S.E. degree is granted by the School of Engineering and Applied Science, which has six engineering departments.

Princeton offers doctoral programs in a range of subjects in the humanities, natural sciences, social sciences, School of Architecture, School of Engineering and Applied Science, and Woodrow Wilson School of Public and International Affairs.

Students also are encouraged to enroll in certificate programs, which offer diverse fields of study along with the major. For example, a student may wish to concentrate in ecology and evolutionary biology while pursuing a certificate in musical performance.

ACADEMIC PROGRAMS

Undergraduates benefit from small class sizes and one-on-one advising with faculty, particularly while doing independent work such as the junior paper and senior thesis. The university's 850 faculty members are leaders in their disciplines, and it is not uncommon for students to learn from a Nobel laureate, Pulitzer Prize winner, or MacArthur fellow. During their freshman year, students are introduced to many of Princeton's finest faculty through the freshman seminars program, which offers small discussion-focused classes on a variety of topics. One such freshman seminar may study the chemistry of chocolate; another may explore the ideas and arguments of "great books."

From the outset, students are encouraged to bring a multidisciplinary approach to their studies, pulling together what they discover in different classes and through their own research. This approach may be informal, based on a student's particular avenue of study, or it may be more formally structured, such as with the integrated science curriculum that combines the study of physics, mathematics, computer science, and molecular biology.

A global perspective to learning also is emphasized across the curriculum, with special learning opportunities from entities such as the Study Abroad Program and the Princeton Institute for International and Regional Studies.

Academic support services include academic advising centered in the residential colleges (for A.B. students) and in the engineering school (for B.S.E. students); the McGraw Center, which offers workshops and individual consultations with students as they evolve as scholars; and the Writing Program, which strengthens students' writing skills through a required seminar. Ongoing tutoring sessions also are available at the program's Writing Center.

CAMPUS FACILITIES AND EQUIPMENT

Throughout their undergraduate careers, Princeton students are supported by a range of first-rate academic resources, such as libraries, laboratories, and even an art museum. The largest library on campus is Firestone Library, which has more than 70 miles of shelving and a vast range of electronic resources. A new science library, designed by renowned architect Frank Gehry, is slated to open in fall 2008. Over the past year, new initiatives in African American studies and neuroscience have resulted in expanded facilities. Numerous venues for the arts as well as a range of athletic facilities also are available.

TUITION, ROOM, BOARD AND FEES

Estimated cost of attendance for 2008-09:

Tuition: $34,290

Room charge: $6,205

Board rate: $5,200

Books and personal expenses: $3,495

Total: $49,190

FINANCIAL AID

Princeton offers one of the strongest need-based Financial Aid programs in the country, ensuring that it is affordable for a diverse group of qualified students. There is no income cutoff on Princeton's aid application; any family who feels they may need help paying for a Princeton education is welcome to apply for aid.

Since 2001, when Princeton initiated its landmark no-loan Financial Aid program, the university has been a leader in changing the face of Financial Aid policy. Central to the program is Princeton's groundbreaking "no-loan" policy; the university offers every aid recipient a Financial Aid package that replaces loans with grant aid that students do not pay back.

If admitted, applicants can be confident that their financial need as determined by Princeton's aid office will be met. Today, more than half of each entering class benefits from Princeton's Financial Aid program. As a result, Princeton has been able to enroll growing numbers of students from low- and middle-income backgrounds. The average grant award for the Class of 2011 was $31,187.

STUDENT ORGANIZATIONS AND ACTIVITIES

Princeton is a residential campus that provides a close-knit living environment for its undergraduates. Through its six residential colleges, students pursue a host of recreational and academic activities. The residential colleges also are home base for academic advising for students, who learn about all that the university has to offer from faculty and staff advisers, peer mentors, and fellow students.

With more than 200 student organizations, as well as an extensive calendar of cultural and athletic events, students find numerous ways to get involved. The Frist Campus Center serves as the hub of campus life, and is home to the Women's Center, the Davis International Center, the LGBT Center, the Pace Center for civic engagement, and the Undergraduate Student Government, among others.

For many students, social life at Princeton includes becoming a member of an eating club. The 10 historic eating clubs are open to juniors and seniors and are run independently of the university. Fraternities and sororities are not recognized as official student organizations on campus.

Princeton is an NCAA Division I school. The university offers 38 varsity sports and nearly 40 club teams. Each year more than 1,000 students participate in intercollegiate varsity and junior varsity sports. In any given year, more than half of Princeton's varsity athletic teams compete in national championships.

ADMISSIONS PROCESS

Princeton's Admission Process goes beyond simply looking for academically accomplished students. For each freshman class, Princeton brings together a varied mix of high-achieving, intellectually gifted students from diverse backgrounds to create an exceptional learning community. Princeton cares about what students have accomplished in and out of the classroom. The process is highly selective. In recent years, the university has offered admission to only about 10 percent of applicants.

In preparing the application to Princeton, students are asked to describe their talents, academic accomplishments, and personal achievements. A transcript and recommendations also are required. To be considered for admission to Princeton, students must submit the results of the SAT Reasoning Test or ACT (with Writing, where offered). In addition, all applicants must submit the results of three different SAT Subject Tests. The university accepts both online and paper applications. Princeton does not offer a transfer Admission Process.

QUINNIPIAC UNIVERSITY

AT A GLANCE

Quinnipiac University, founded in 1929, is a private, co-educational, non-sectarian institution of higher education. It is primarily a residential campus in a uniquely attractive New England setting. Quinnipiac's mission is to provide a supportive and stimulating environment for the intellectual and personal growth of undergraduate, graduate, and law students.

The university offers broadly based undergraduate programs together with graduate programs in selected professional fields. At the undergraduate level, through integrated liberal arts and professional curricula, programs in the Schools of Business, Communications, Health Sciences, the College of Liberal Arts and the Division of Education prepare students for career entry or advanced studies. Graduate programs are designed to provide professional qualifications for success in business, education, health sciences, communications, and law.

An education at Quinnipiac embodies the university's commitment to three important values: excellence in education, a sensitivity to students, and a spirit of community. The entire university shares a service orientation toward students and their needs. Its collegial atmosphere fosters a strong sense of community, identity, and purpose among faculty, staff, and students.

LOCATION AND ENVIRONMENT

Hamden, Connecticut is located 8 miles north of New Haven and 20 miles south of Hartford, and is midway between Boston and New York City. Quinnipiac offers a suburban environment with 500 acres on two sites. The Mount Carmel campus is adjacent to Sleeping Giant State Park, with 1,700 acres of hills and trails for hiking and walking. A picturesque setting and quiet surroundings provide an enjoyable campus experience. A campus shuttle system provides free and easy access to theater, shopping, museums, sports, recreation, and a variety of dining and entertainment options in Hamden and New Haven. The nearby York Hill campus is home to the TD Banknorth Sports Center with 3500 seat twin arenas for ice hockey (ECAC) and basketball (NEC). New residence halls to accommodate 2000 students, plus a student center are currently under construction on the York Hill site.

Students from over 24 states and 10 countries study at Quinnipiac. Ninety-five percent of all freshmen choose to live on campus, and housing is guaranteed to incoming freshmen for three years. Housing options include traditional residence halls, suites, and suites with full kitchens. Housing will be available for seniors on a space available basis as the new residence hall construction begins to phase in, beginning fall, 2009. Seniors may also choose to move off campus to a variety of apartments/condos in the area.

Driving time to Quinnipiac from Boston or New York City is about two hours. Metro-North railroad from Grand Central Terminal in New York City and Amtrak Northeast Corridor trains also arrive in New Haven. The campus is a 10-minute taxi ride (students can take the campus shuttle) from the station. Bradley Airport (BDL), just north of Hartford is the nearest international airport, about 40 minutes from campus. Students can also arrive at John F. Kennedy, Newark, or LaGuardia airports in the New York area and travel via Connecticut Limousine to New Haven.

OFF-CAMPUS OPPORTUNITIES

All programs at Quinnipiac offer an excellent combination of classroom learning with internships or clinical affiliations. Students in the health sciences are placed in clinical affiliations as part of their course work. Students in business, communications, and liberal arts have nearby corporations, health care agencies, or media outlets available for internships.

Career Services, offered by each of the academic schools, can provide excellent assistance in resume writing and job placement. A survey of recent graduates shows that 90 percent were either employed or in graduate school within six months of graduation. Each year about half of students in internships are offered permanent jobs as a result of their work.

Students in all majors can also take advantage of study abroad opportunities either during the summer months or during the academic year. Program sites include: Ireland, Australia; Austria; Czech Republic; England; France; Spain; Italy; Netherlands; Russia; South Africa; Spain and Independent Programs, and affiliates such as AIFS, API, Australearn, and Semester at Sea. Tuition is paid to Quinnipiac University so that you receive resident credit, and you pay housing and board plus any other fees to the host program. Study abroad is an experience of a lifetime allowing you to live a different country for a period of time while earning credits at your home institution. Any student in any major can apply to study abroad with at least a 3.0 GPA.

Students can also become involved in a variety of organizations, clubs, greek life, student government, campus publications, and media outlets. Over 75 campus clubs and organizations, community service, an extensive recreation and intramural program, and Division I athletics in 21 sports give students the chance to be active and involved throughout the year.

MAJORS AND DEGREES OFFERED

Undergraduate students can choose from more than 50 majors through the College of Liberal Arts and the Schools of Business, Communications and Health Sciences. Freshmen entry-level master degree programs are available in education (5 year BA/MAT), occupational therapy (5 year BS/MOT) and physician assistant (6 year BS/MHS). Physical Therapy is a 6 1/2 year freshmen entry-level doctorate program (BS/DPT).

Graduate students specialize in law, accounting, business, health management, computer information systems, journalism, interactive communications, education, and health science programs for physician assistant, pathologist's assistant, medical and laboratory sciences, molecular and cell biology, forensic nursing, and nurse practitioner. The College of Professional Studies offers online graduate degrees in organizational leadership.

ACADEMIC PROGRAMS

Undergraduate Programs in the School of Business include: accounting, advertising, biomedical marketing, information systems management (dual majors available with math and other business areas), economics, entrepreneurship, finance, international business, management and marketing.

The School of Health Sciences programs include: athletic training/sports medicine, biochemistry, biology, biomedical science, chemistry, diagnostic imaging, health/science studies, microbiology/molecular biology, nursing, occupational therapy (a 5-year freshmen entry-level Master's program), physician assistant (6-year freshmen entry-level Master's program), physical therapy (a 6 1/2 year freshmen entry-level doctorate) and veterinary technology.

The pre-med program is designed to provide the undergraduate student interested in a career as a health professional the appropriate background necessary to meet the entrance requirements of a variety of different medical schools.

The College of Liberal Arts programs include: English, computer science, criminal justice, gerontology, history, independent major, interactive digital design, legal studies, mathematics, political science, psychology (human services, industrial psychology), social services, sociology, Spanish and theater.

Within the School of Communications, the programs include: media production, media arts, journalism, and public relations. The Ed McMahon Center for Communications provides a state of the art facility with a fully digital high-definition production studio, a news technology center and editing suites.

For those interested in teaching, completion of an undergraduate major in an area in the liberal arts or natural sciences, combined with junior and senior year courses in education, ending with a fifth year full-time graduate education program, culminates in the Master of Arts in Teaching degree.

CAMPUS FACILITIES AND EQUIPMENT

Quinnipiac is among the top 20 wired campuses in the country, and this is reflected in its academic facilities and programs. All incoming students must purchase a University recommended laptop computer (currently DELL) for use in the classroom and in the residence halls.

Academic life focuses on the Bernhard Library, a state of the art building. Automated library systems and over 100 personal computer workstations and 600 data ports are located throughout the library.

In the School of Communications, the Ed McMahon Center for Mass Communications handles the electronic demands of multi-media production and journalism, with a state-of-the-art fully-digital high-definition production studio.

The AACSB accredited School of Business provides case method classrooms, a high-tech Financial Technology Center 'trading room' and small team study rooms for project work.

In the health sciences, in addition to well-equipped laboratories for life and physical sciences, there are suites for diagnostic imaging, clinical spaces and equipment for physical and occupational therapy, a nursing arts laboratory with an examining room and two critical care rooms that duplicate their hospital counterparts.

TUITION, ROOM, BOARD AND FEES

Tuition and Fees for 2007-08 are $28,7200, with $11,200 for room and board.

FINANCIAL AID

The Quinnipiac University Financial Aid Office works with all applicants to assure that they receive the maximum state and federal aid for which they are eligible. The University offers merit-based scholarships to incoming freshmen in the fall semester (admission application deadline February 1st) for which no financial need is required. There is no additional application necessary for scholarship consideration and students are notified by the admissions office.

If you have any questions, please feel free to call the Office of Financial Aid at (203) 582-8750 or (800) 462-1944. Or you can e-mail us at: finaid@quinnipiac.edu. Quinnipiac University's FAFSA ID code is 001402.

STUDENT ORGANIZATIONS AND ACTIVITIES

Quinnipiac University has more than 70 clubs and organizations: including student government, newspaper, yearbook, radio station, service organizations, community activities, religious fellowships (Hillel, Christian Fellowship, Branches), diversity awareness (Black Student Union, Latino Cultural Society, Asian and Pacific Islander Association), dance and drama productions, and Greek life, along with numerous recreation activities, providing a balanced college experience. An active Intramural program has team competition in more than 20 sports.

Quinnipiac Bobcats: The Division I athletics program in 21 sports includes Men: basketball, baseball, cross country and track (indoor and outdoor), lacrosse, ice hockey, golf, tennis, and soccer. Women: Basketball, softball, cross country and track (indoor and outdoor), field hockey, ice hockey, lacrosse, soccer, tennis, and volleyball. Quinnipiac competes in the NEC (Northeast Conference) and the ECAC for Men's and Women's Ice Hockey.

The athletic facilities include a multi-purpose gymnasium, locker rooms, training rooms, steam room, and a 24,000-square-foot, fully-equipped recreation and fitness center, with a suspended indoor track, outdoor lighted tennis, and racquetball courts, plus the TD Banknorth Sports Center with twin 3500 seat arenas for ice hockey and basketball.

ADMISSIONS PROCESS

High school students should begin applying for admissions early in their senior year. A completed application consists of the application form, official high school transcript, SAT I test scores (QU SAT code—3712) or ACT scores (QU ACT code—0582) senior year, first-quarter grades, essay, and one letter of recommendation. The admissions office begins reviewing folders as soon as they are complete, and begins notifying students of their decisions in early January. Students applying for the physical therapy, nursing and physician assistant programs should apply by November 1st. We recommend February 1st as the deadline for all other applicants.

All programs subscribe to the nationally recognized candidate reply date of May 1. Any students placed on a waitlist who responds that they are interested in being considered if spaces are available will be notified as soon after May 1 as possible if there is room in the incoming class. In general, Quinnipiac admits about 40% of their applicants.

Transfer students who have or will receive an associate's degree prior to entrance do not need to provide high school transcripts and SAT results. We must receive transcripts of all courses taken at other colleges. The physician assistant program is not available to transfer students.

For questions, please call us at 800-462-1944; 203-582-8600 or email: admissions@quinnipiac.edu or check our website at: http://www.quinnipiac.edu.

RADFORD UNIVERSITY

AT A GLANCE

Students come to Radford University for the small class sizes, residential community, dedicated professors, and academic excellence. Since its founding in 1910, the University has grown to encompass the following Colleges: College of Business and Economics, the College of Education and Human Development, the College of Humanities and Behavioral Sciences, the College of Science and Technology, the Waldron College of Health and Human Services, the College of Visual and Performing Arts, and the College of Graduate and Extended Studies. Currently, 87 percent of the approximately 9,200 students attending the University are pursuing one of the 106 undergraduate degrees. The 38 graduate programs grant the MS, MA, MBA, MFA, MSN, MSW, or EdS degrees.

More than one third of students, including all freshmen, live on campus in one of the fifteen residence halls, all configured as two-room suites. A variety of learning/residential communities are available to suit the interests and needs of students. Upperclass students who choose to live off-campus typically rent an apartment within walking distance of the University. The student body is composed of students from many parts of Virginia in addition to 45 other states and 47 foreign countries. The University offers students ample opportunity to participate in overseas study programs. Radford organizes activities including guest speakers, theater performances, concerts, film screenings, Greek events, student publications, radio and television stations, and intramural sports competition. People congregate in the new Hurlburt Student Center to utilize the lounges, recreation facilities, study rooms, and meeting areas. Starbucks, Chik-Fil-A, Tsunami Sushi and other dining options are also available in the student center. Dalton Hall houses a food court, which includes Sbarro Pizzeria, Au Bon Pain, Wendy's and Freshens Frozen Yogurt. The campus bookstore, post office and a newly renovated dining hall are also found in Dalton. The $10.8-million Dedmon Center is home to the University's 19 NCAA Division I athletic teams; it also provides students with comprehensive sports and fitness facilities.

LOCATION AND ENVIRONMENT

The University's hometown of Radford, Virginia, about half an hour outside of Roanoke in the western half of the state, is set amid the scenic Blue Ridge Mountains. The town's population of 16,200 supports a variety of restaurants and shops. Students who enjoy the outdoors take advantage of the campus's proximity to The Blue Ridge Parkway, the Appalachian Trail, New River, and Claytor Lake. Available activities include skiing, hiking, canoeing, biking, and camping. The campus is convenient to I-81 for motorists and close to the Roanoke airport for those arriving by plane.

MAJORS AND DEGREES OFFERED

At Radford, students may work toward their BA, BS, BFA, BM, BBA, BSN or BSW degree. For undergraduates, the following majors are offered: accounting; anthropology; art; biology; chemistry; communication; communication sciences and disorders; computer science and technology; criminal justice; dance; economics; English; exercise sport and health education; fashion; finance; foods and nutrition; foreign languages; geography; geology; history; information science and systems; interdisciplinary studies (education); interior design; management; marketing; mathematics and statistics; media studies; medical technology; music; music therapy; nursing; philosophy and religious studies; physical science; political science; psychology; recreation, parks, and tourism; social science; social work; sociology; and theater.

ACADEMIC PROGRAMS

Radford requires 120 units of credit to complete an undergraduate degree. Fifty of these units are earned in general education classes. The Highlander Scholars Program administers honors courses for top students. The University assists students in adjusting to college life with specially designed new-student programs, including the University 100 class and Success Starts Here. The LARC (Learning Assistance Resource Center) provides tutoring and mentoring programs for student support. During Quest, the orientation that takes place over the summer, incoming freshmen meet with advisors, sign up for classes, and meet their classmates. Radford offers the Army ROTC program to students pursuing a career in the military. The academic calendar is made up of fall (August to December) and spring (January to May) semesters.

CAMPUS FACILITIES AND EQUIPMENT

All academic buildings, all residence halls, common areas in student service buildings, such as the student center and dining halls, and even some green spaces are locations where students and faculty are able to use mobile computing. In other words, our learning community has anytime, anywhere wireless access.

More than 500,000 books and periodicals are available to students in the McConnell Library. When researching, students utilize these volumes as well as film, microfilm, records, compact audio discs, and tapes. The catalog can be searched on the computer. The University participates in interlibrary loans to supplement the on-campus collection.

The recent addition of Waldron Hall, now hosts the Waldron College of Health and Human Services, renowned for its high-tech learning facilities. Students in the Schools of Nursing, Social Work, and Allied Health attend Waldron to study communication sciences and disorders; foods and nutrition; and recreation, parks, and tourism. Students gain practical experience working alongside of faculty members at the on-site clinic, which offers medical and psychological treatment to patients without health care. The newly rennovated, Peters Hall is home to the College of Education and Human Development. With smart board technology, a state of the art Teaching Resource Center, dance studios and an indoor climbing wall, this building is not only conducive to learning, but an enjoyable place for students to spend their free time as well.

TUITION, ROOM, BOARD AND FEES

In the 2007-2008 school year, in-state undergraduates paid $6,176 for tuition and fees. Out-of-state students paid $14,510. An additional $6,398 was charged for room and board. In addition, students spend roughly $800 on books and supplies.

FINANCIAL AID

Students may receive need- or merit-based Financial Aid awards in the form of loans, work-study programs, private or government grants, or department-based fellowships. Some scholarships are given for outstanding demonstrations of leadership, character, or academic work. Those applying for Financial Aid must turn in the Free Application for Federal Student Aid (FAFSA) to Federal Student Aid Programs by the March 1 deadline. Transfer students are also required to submit the Financial Aid Transcript form, showing their former colleges or universities, whether or not they received Financial Aid.

In order to qualify for the Radford University Foundation's scholarship competition, students must ensure that their first-year applications arrive at the Office of Admissions and become complete (including official high school transcript and standardized test scores) by December 15. Those applicants with top high-school records can become finalists through essay competition. Full scholarships, which include the equivalent of in-state tuition and fees, room and board, and a book stipend, are available. Partial scholarships, which cover the cost of living on campus are also available.

STUDENT ORGANIZATIONS AND ACTIVITIES

All Radford undergraduates are part of the Student Government Association, and elected representatives voice student opinions as part of the following committees: the executive council, cabinet, senate, house of representatives, off-campus student council, graduate student council, class representatives council, black student affairs council, international student affairs council, and diversity promotions council.

RU has over 250 clubs and organizations available for students, including the Radford Redcoats, equestrian team; RU Outdoors; Ultimate Frisbee; social sororities and fraternities; academic, service, sport and religious organizations are all popular options for students to get involved in.

ADMISSIONS PROCESS

The Admissions Committee at RU evaluates each applicant's academic record, looking for signs of scholastic and personal potential. Factors include high school course selection, GPA, class rank, SAT I or ACT scores, and extracurricular pursuits. It is recommended that students take the following classes in high school: 4 units of English, 4 units of college-preparatory mathematics, 3-4 units of foreign language, 4 units of lab science, and 4 units of social science (including American history). Applicants intending to pursue a degree in nursing should have both biology and chemistry on their transcripts. The University does not discriminate on the basis of race, sex, handicap, age, veteran status, national origin, religious or political affiliation, or sexual preference.

Students must submit all of the following materials in their completed application: the application form, the nonrefundable application fee, an official high school transcript, and official SAT I or ACT scores. Transfer applicants are required to send the application form along with official transcripts from their previously attended accredited college or university. For fall admission the early action deadline is December 15 and the regular decision deadline is February 1 for new freshmen. The priority deadline for new transfer applicants is June 1. Applications that arrive later than the deadlines listed will be evaluated as space is available.

Campus visits can be arranged between 8 a.m. and 5 p.m., Monday through Friday. Prospective students may also attend a campus tour at 10 a.m., noon, and 2 p.m. on Monday and Friday, 10 a.m. and 2 p.m. on Tuesday, Wednesday, and Thursday, and at 10 a.m., 11 a.m., and noon on Saturday during the school year

REED COLLEGE

AT A GLANCE

Serious. Quirky. Rigorous. Laid back. Classical. Liberal. College guides grapple to define the Reed College experience, but they all tend to agree on two points: Reed is one of the most distinctive colleges in the nation and it is not for everyone. Reed attracts serious students—and often brings out the best in them. Usually engaged, often engrossed, and occasionally engulfed in a demanding, exhilarating educational adventure, "Reedies" thrive on a mix of classical study, critical analysis, and guided inquiry that rewards creativity, independence, and reflection. Classes are small, faculty make themselves accessible, and students adhere to an honor principle both in and out of the classroom.

Reed recruits nationally, with California and the Pacific Northwest well represented and 5 percent international students. A recent survey of graduating seniors at 52 liberal arts colleges found Reed students one and a half times more likely to be satisfied with their education than the national average and twice as likely to say they would choose Reed again. Reed ranks first among U.S. liberal arts colleges in percentage of graduates going on to earn doctoral degrees and third among all institutions of higher education. The breadth, depth, and rigor of the curriculum provide great preparation for many endeavors. Many Reed alumni found or lead companies and organizations, earn medical or law degrees, write books or create works of art, or work to make life on the planet better for all.

LOCATION AND ENVIRONMENT

Talk about the best of both worlds! Located in a quiet residential neighborhood on a 100-acre campus of verdant lawns, winding paths, statuesque trees, a wooded wetland, and a spring-fed lake frequented by migratory birds and other wildlife, Reed is a short bicycle or bus ride from the energy and excitement of downtown Portland, which is widely cited as the nation's most livable urban center. Portland boasts a wealth of diverse cultural, entertainment, shopping, and dining opportunities in an environment characterized by a combination of youthful exuberance and West Coast reserve. The Oregon Coast is an hour to the west and Mt. Hood an hour to the east (but reserve early to be sure of securing weekend accommodations at Reed's own ski cabin).

On the campus itself, century-old brick Tudor Gothic buildings are interspersed with newer traditionally designed and remodeled facilities. The library, classrooms, and laboratories resonate with the history of decades of inquiry and discovery, supported with modern technology. Extensive facility expansion and renovation financed by a $112-million development campaign has increased the overall square footage of Reed's buildings by almost 30 percent and added seven acres of contiguous property to the northwest corner of the campus.

OFF-CAMPUS OPPORTUNITIES

Reed undergraduates may participate in a number of domestic exchange and study abroad opportunities. Domestic exchange programs are run in conjunction with Howard University in Washington, DC; Sarah Lawrence College in New York; and Sea Semester, based in Woods Hole, Massachusetts. Study abroad programs are established at universities around the world. Reed encourages students to pursue independent study off campus and must be developed with the assistance of appropriate Reed faculty members, the Director for Off-Campus Studies, and the Registrar.

MAJORS AND DEGREES OFFERED

Reed confers the Bachelor of Arts degree in a wide selection of fields, both in traditional academic departments and in interdisciplinary combinations. Undergraduates are encouraged to design interdisciplinary majors; such majors must be planned with the approval of faculty advisers from each department involved.

Reed offers a number of 3-2 (dual degree) programs; these allow undergraduates to earn a 3-year bachelor's degree from Reed, then earn a professional degree from a cooperating institution in two additional years.

ACADEMIC PROGRAMS

The curriculum at Reed is both demanding and wide-ranging. Through required studies, Reed students receive a solid grounding in the liberal arts and sciences. All freshmen must complete "Hum 110," a survey of Greek and Roman scholars from Homer to St. Augustine. Distribution requirements set a substantial portion of a student's curriculum for the first 2 years at Reed. Freshmen and sophomores must complete two courses in each of the four major divisions of the college. No specific courses are required; students are free to pursue their interests within the strictures of the requirements.

Reed juniors must pass a comprehensive exam in their major, to allow faculty members the chance to determine the student's readiness for his or her senior thesis project. The required senior thesis is the capstone experience of a Reed education. Every senior must produce an original independent research project over the course of the final year.

Reed strongly believes that learning should be undertaken for its own sake, not for the sake of letter grades. Accordingly, students do not receive grade reports unless they wish to. A student's transcript does include letter grades for all courses taken, but students can better gauge their progress through professors' written evaluations of their work and one-on-one meetings with faculty. Most prefer this system, which greatly eases competition among students and thus allows them to focus entirely on the content of their academic work.

CAMPUS FACILITIES AND EQUIPMENT

Facilities and Equipment

The Reed College campus was established on a tract of land known in 1910 as Crystal Springs Farm; it was a part of the Ladd Estate, which was formed in the 1870s from original land claims. The social center of the college is the Gray Campus Center. It includes a commons building, student union, kitchen, dining room, private meeting rooms, student activities offices, bookstore, and mail services. The Gray Campus Center includes the 6,000-square-foot Kaul Auditorium, which is designed for multimedia presentations, musical performances, lectures, meetings, dinners, and special events. In a park-like setting near the heart of the city, the rolling lawns and open spaces of Reed's 100-acre campus include some of the largest and finest specimen trees in the Portland area. At the center of the campus is the canyon, a beautiful wooded upland surrounding a spring-fed lake and emergent marsh. A walking trail around the lake provides numerous opportunities to observe migratory birds and other woodland wildlife. The college recently built a fish passageway that creates a link from the upper Reed Lake area to the Crystal Springs stream below. Three new residence halls have been built since 1997. Steele East and Steele West were completed in the fall of 1997, and Bragdon Hall was completed in January 1998. Steele features outstanding views of the west hills and downtown Portland. Bragdon Hall takes full advantage of the view overlooking Reed Lake and the canyon interior. In 2003, Reed opened the Educational technology Center (ETC) for computer-assisted learning as well as a new library wing.

TUITION, ROOM, BOARD, AND FEES

Tuition (and fees) for the 2005–2006 academic year is $32,360. A $230 student body fee is added. Room and board is an additional $8,516, bringing the yearly total cost to $41,106.

FINANCIAL AID

Reed provides financial assistance to roughly 55 percent its undergraduates. The college maintains a need-based assistance program that allows students of all economic backgrounds to attend the college; it further guarantees that full need will be met for all continuing students who maintain good academic standing and who meet all other requirements of the aid process (such as application deadlines). The college makes every effort to meet the need of all admitted incoming students but cannot guarantee that it will do so. Each year, approximately half of all first-year and transfer students receive aid packages equaling their demonstrated need. The college budgeted approximately $13 million for grant aid in 2005–2006; individual awards ranged from $1,000 to $40,000. For the 2005–2006 academic year, the average financial aid package, including grants, loans, and work opportunities, was approximately $28,205. The college is the primary source of grant money for its students. Reed also administers federal grants and a number of other awards. Students may take Perkins Loans and other federally subsidized loans; campus employment and work-study programs also figure into many aid packages.

STUDENT ORGANIZATIONS AND ACTIVITIES

Reed shuns exclusive organizations and activities, so the college has no Greek organizations and no NCAA or NAIA athletic teams (more about sports below). All campus organizations are student-created and student-run. The student activity fund of approximately $85,000 is administered by the Student Senate. Student organizations must lobby the Student Senate for funding annually, after which the Senate oversees a vote in which the entire student body decides what organizations should be funded. Thus, the number and nature of campus organizations at Reed changes every year to meet current student interests. Reed may not compete at the NCAA or NAIA level, but most students participate in sports on an informal basis. Intramural sports and club sports proliferate in basketball, fencing, rugby, sailing, soccer, and Ultimate Frisbee. A three-semester physical education requirement demonstrates that the school recognizes the importance of physical fitness and the salutary effects of exercise.

ADMISSIONS PROCESS

Reed seeks students who demonstrate a commitment to learning and to the ideals embodied by a liberal arts education. Freshman and transfer applications are welcome. The Admissions Committee attempts to determine which candidates will benefit most from a Reed education as well as who is most likely to succeed at Reed. The ideal incoming class is diverse in its range of talents, interests, backgrounds, and perspectives, yet constituted of students who share a common passion for academic inquiry. The Admissions Committee places most emphasis on an applicant's record of previous academic accomplishment. A rigorous secondary school curriculum that includes honor's and advanced courses affords the applicant a great advantage; such a program typically includes 4 years of English, at least 3 years of a foreign or classical language, 3 to 4 years of mathematics, 3 to 4 years of science, and 3 to 4 years of history or social studies. Because secondary school curricula vary widely in quality and content, the school sets no fixed requirements in this area. With rare exceptions, incoming students have obtained a secondary school diploma prior to enrollment. The Admissions Committee sets no "cutoff points" for high school grades, college grades (for transfer students), or standardized test scores.

Reed seeks candidates who demonstrate excellence of character, particularly in areas of motivation, intellectual curiosity, individual responsibility, and social consciousness. These qualities often help the chances of admission for candidates whose academic records might not otherwise meet Reed's standards. The Admission Committee recognizes the importance of creating a diverse community in which individual differences contribute to the vitality of the campus. The school strongly recommends a personal interview, especially for Early Decision candidates, but an interview is not required. Early Decision applications should arrive at Reed by November 15 (Option 1) or January 2 (Option 2). Early Decision at Reed is binding: students who are accepted under Early Decision are expected to matriculate. The deadline for regular freshman admission applications is January 15. Transfer candidates should apply no later than March 1.

REGIS UNIVERSITY

AT A GLANCE

Since its inception in 1877, Regis University has achieved a reputation for outstanding teaching and groundbreaking programs. The Jesuit tradition stands as the cornerstone of the university, placing an emphasis on top academics alongside of community service. Every student that graduates from Regis leaves with the scholastic, social, spiritual, and physical background then need to serve them in the real world. All undergraduates complete the core curriculum, covering a broad range of study in literature, writing, speech communications, natural science, math, philosophy, religious studies, fine arts, and the social sciences. Annual seminars amplify this foundation by providing practical applications of classroom learning and exploring the question of "How Ought We To Live." First-year students participate in the Freshman Seminar to get oriented at Regis and work with the faculty member who will be their advisor. Because of the Regis Graduation Guarantee, students can be confident that they will be able to complete their degrees in 4 years; otherwise, the university pays for the additional tuition, pending eligibility. Regis offers a work-study program that guarantees qualified students a job that pays up to $2,400 a year. The university was acknowledged by the latest *U.S. News & World Report* ratings as one of the "Tier One Western Colleges and Universities."

LOCATION AND ENVIRONMENT

Regis sits just outside of Denver, Colorado, enjoying 90 acres of Rocky Mountain scenery. The campus is located amid a quiet, residential neighborhood, but nearby Denver offers all the opportunities of a major city. The "Mile High City" provides major-league sporting events as well as access to internship opportunities and government positions. Winter sports enthusiasts appreciate the proximity to the ski slopes of Keystone, Breckenridge, and Copper Mountains. The climate is excellent, and the area's thriving population of 2 million enjoys the 300 days of sunshine annually.

OFF-CAMPUS OPPORTUNITIES

Whether students want to explore the outdoors or take advantage of Denver resources, they have access to it all at Regis. The local professional sports teams, the Denver Broncos, the Denver Nuggets, the Colorado Rockies, the Colorado Rapids, and the Colorado Avalanche, draw a loyal fan base. Denver is a highly educated city, with the second highest number of college graduates per capita. The city offers attractions including the lower downtown historic district (LoDo), the zoo, the Museum of Natural History, the Denver Botanic Gardens, the Denver Art Museum, the U.S. Mint and the State Capitol, and Red Rocks Amphitheater. Those interested in theater attend the Denver Center for the Performing Arts, which puts on at least 10 Broadway show each season. At the altitude of one mile, Denver offers a dry, sunny Rocky Mountain. Even in the middle of winter, the temperature can climb into the 60s due to the chinook. There are endless chances for skiing, snowboarding, mountain biking, climbing, rafting, and hiking.

MAJORS AND DEGREES OFFERED

Undergraduates choose from more than 70 degree programs at Regis College. In addition, interested students may design an interdisciplinary individual major.

ACADEMIC PROGRAMS

Regis adheres to the Jesuit philosophy of offering a value-centered, top-notch liberal arts education that incorporates both community service and career training at the same time. Every student gets their liberal arts foundation from the core curriculum, which teaches critical-thinking skills and the basic philosophical and religious tenets. Students wrestle with spiritual concepts and consider questions regarding human life. The classes encourage open-mindedness and show a multiplicity of perspectives.

Students must complete the required 128 semester hours to earn their bachelor's degree. Qualified applicants may enroll in the university's Honor's Program. A wide array of courses are available during the Summer School Program as well. Outside of the classroom, Regis organizes community service projects, internships, and opportunities for study overseas.

CAMPUS FACILITIES AND EQUIPMENT

Regis has kept up to date with the rapidly changing computer technology, allowing students to utilize these powerful learning and research tools. Computer clusters are available around the clock, and all dormitories have computer labs with internet access. Each Regis student has an individual e-mail account.

Students conduct research in the four libraries' collection of more than 280,000 volumes, 2,100 periodical subscriptions, 600 CD-ROMs, 110,000 microforms, and an 85,000-slide art history collection. It is easy to locate materials using the CARL online catalog, which also connects top 140 databases and document delivery services. In the newly renovated main library, every study station has a network port, making the facility one of the most wired in the country.

The Coors Life Directions Center provides facilities for the Offices of Career Services and Personal Counseling in addition to the Fitness Program and Health Center.

TUITION, ROOM, BOARD, AND FEES

In the 2005–2006 school year, students paid $23,700 in tuition and feels. It is $8,190 for the standard room and board package.

FINANCIAL AID

The Financial Aid Program strives to meet the needs of qualified students who wish to attend Regis. Nine out of ten full-time students benefit from financial awards, totaling $14 million annually. A financial aid package typically includes some or all of the following: scholarships, grants, loans, and work-study income. Qualified first-year students can obtain campus jobs that pay up to $2,400 annually. Many federal and state-funded scholarships are available to Regis admits. Students seeking financial aid must submit the Free Application for Federal Student Aid (FAFSA) or Renewal Application as close to January 1 as they can. Early application is encouraged since financial aid is allotted on a first-come, first-served basis.

STUDENT ORGANIZATIONS AND ACTIVITIES

Out of Regis's wide variety of student organizations, students can find groups for any social, recreational, academic, or athletic interest. The popular intramural athletic program organizes leagues for basketball, billiards, bowling, flag football, floor hockey, softball, swim club, ski team, ultimate Frisbee, and volleyball. Club teams participate in men's rugby, ice hockey, spirit team, and lacrosse. Regis fields NCAA Division II teams in men's baseball, basketball, cross-country, golf, and soccer and women's and basketball, cross-country, lacrosse, soccer, softball, and volleyball. Community service programs are organized by the Center for Service-Learning. Past opportunities have included spring service trips to Mexico, the Romero House project, the Cascade Mentoring project, service-learning courses, all-campus service days, tutoring at-risk students, and assisting at shelters. Students enrolled in the Regis Leadership Program attend seminars, work at internships, volunteer for charities, and go on a retreat over the course of their 4 years. Leaderships skills are developed in positions in student government, residence halls, orientation committees, and peer counseling groups.

ADMISSIONS PROCESS

Applicants to Regis College are evaluated on the basis of the following: high school transcripts, ACT or SAT scores, personal attributes, and leadership skills. The college adheres to a nondiscrimination policy and grants equal opportunity to all applicants. To be admitted as freshmen, students should have a high school diploma or the equivalent, and a total of 15 secondary academic units is strongly encouraged. Regis also requires letters of recommendation from teachers or counselors.

Regis suggests that students turn in their applications as early in the senior year as possible. Typically, applicants can expect a decision from the Office of Admissions within 8 weeks of receiving the complete application package. Any requests for information or application forms should be sent to the Regis College Office of Admissions.

RENSSELAER POLYTECHNIC INSTITUTE

AT A GLANCE

Rensselaer Polytechnic Institute, founded in 1824, is the nation's oldest technological university. The Institute offers bachelor's, master's, and doctoral degrees in engineering, the sciences, information technology, architecture, business, and the humanities and social sciences. Rensselaer faculty are known for pre-eminence in research conducted in a wide range of fields, with particular emphasis in biotechnology, nanotechnology, information technology, and the media arts and technology. Prominent graduates include Ed Zander '68, the chairman of Motorola, Texas Instruments founder J. Erik Jonsson '22, and Nobel Laureate Ivar Giaever '64.

LOCATION AND ENVIRONMENT

Rensselaer is located in the northeastern United States in the heart of New York's Capital Region. The region, which includes the cities of Albany, Schenectady, and Troy and their suburbs, has a combined population of approximately 870,000 and is an important business, government, industrial, and academic hub. There are more than 40,000 college students at fourteen colleges and universities in the immediate area. Overlooking the city of Troy and the historic Hudson River, Rensselaer's 275-acre campus blends recently constructed facilities with a cluster of classical-style, ivy-covered brick buildings dating from the turn of the century. A program of extensive renovation has equipped the campus with ultramodern teaching facilities while preserving the traditional elegance of its historic buildings. Rensselaer retains the quiet and natural beauty of a park like setting while offering many conveniences of an urban campus. Students enjoy easy ac-

cess to Boston (3 hours away), New York City (2 hours away), and Montreal (4 hours away). The Adirondacks, the Berkshires, and the Catskills, all within an hour of Troy, offer hundreds of areas for camping, hiking, and skiing. Many student clubs take full advantage of these natural resources.

OFF-CAMPUS OPPORTUNITIES

Rensselaer has study-abroad programs in Australia, China, Denmark, England, France, Germany, India, Italy, Japan, Spain, Switzerland, and Turkey. Cooperative programs with 15 two- and four-year area institutions allow Rensselaer students to take courses for credit at no additional cost. More than 200 Rensselaer students use this cross-registration program each year. Rensselaer has transfer agreements with more than ninety institutions, including the 107 campuses of the California community college system.

ACADEMIC PROGRAMS

While each of Rensselaer's schools has its own sequence requirements, the following minimums apply to all students: 124 credit hours and a 1.8 quality point average in all courses; 24 credit hours in physical, life, and engineering sciences; 24 in humanities and social sciences; 30 in a selected discipline; and 24 in electives. Students are strongly encouraged to learn outside of the classroom through independent projects, study abroad, cooperative education, internships, and partnering with faculty members on specific research projects. The Undergraduate Research Program offers hands-on experience to students in hundreds of areas where a full-time undergraduate may participate for credit or pay during the academic year or the summer. Co-op assignments give students the opportunity to add practical experience to their academic study. Air Force, Army, and Naval/Marine ROTC programs are available on an elective basis. Computing is integrated into the curriculum at Rensselaer, and all incoming undergraduates are required to have a laptop computer. Rensselaer's Mobile Computing Program provides students with the latest computing technology choices. Students may bring their own laptops to the campus, but they must comply with Rensselaer's computing requirements.

TUITION, ROOM, BOARD AND FEES

Tuition for 2008-09 is $36,950. Fees are $1040. Room and board costs average $10,730. Books and miscellaneous personal expenses are $1815. A required laptop, offered through Rensselaer, costs $2000. All incoming undergraduate students are required to have a laptop computer that meets Rensselaer's specifications.

FINANCIAL AID

Nearly all freshmen who have financial need are offered assistance under a comprehensive program of scholarships, loans, and part-time employment that provides annual assistance ranging from $100 up to full tuition, room, and board. Available federal funds include student loans, Federal Work-Study Program awards, and ROTC scholarships.

ADMISSIONS PROCESS

All applications are reviewed individually by the admissions committee. It is important to note that some differences in preparation and academic background may be considered. The applicants who are best suited for Rensselaer will have completed four years of English, four years of mathematics through pre-calculus, three years of science, and two years of social studies and/or history. In addition, the admissions committee pays particular attention to candidates who demonstrate qualities and talents that will contribute to the richness of the Rensselaer community. Students must submit official scores for the SAT (critical reading, math, and writing); the ACT, which must include the optional writing component, may be substituted for the SAT. Applicants for accelerated programs must also submit scores for SAT Subject Tests in a math and a science; ACT scores, which must include the optional writing component, may be submitted in lieu of SAT and SAT Subject Tests. Portfolios are part of the application process for some students. Electronic arts applicants are required to submit a creative portfolio by November 1 (early decision I), January 1 (early decision II), or January 15 (regular admission). Architecture applicants should submit a creative portfolio by November 1 (early decision I), January 1 (early decision II), or January 15 (regular admission). Students with unusually strong academic profiles may be reviewed without the portfolio. Students expressing interest in product design and innovation who have completed design projects should submit a portfolio or documentation describing program-related work. International applicants' official transcripts must be translated into English, and the international financial statement should be completed and mailed with the application. International applicants who do not achieve a minimum SAT verbal score of 580 must take the TOEFL. Rensselaer expects a TOEFL score of at least 230 on the computer-based test (CBT), 88 on the Internet-based test (iBT), or 580 on the paper-based test (PBT). The early decision application deadlines are November 1 for early decision I, January 1 for early decision II, and the regular admission application deadline for September admission is January 15 of the student's senior year. Rensselaer admits qualified students without regard to race, color, sexual orientation, national or ethnic origin, religion, gender, age, or disability.

RICHARD STOCKTON COLLEGE OF NEW JERSEY

AT A GLANCE

The Richard Stockton College of New Jersey is a selective, medium-sized, highly-ranked, public liberal arts college offering programs in the arts and humanities, business, professional studies, and social, behavioral and natural sciences. Founded in 1969, the College was named for Richard Stockton, one of the New Jersey signers of the Declaration of Independence.

Stockton enrolls more than 7,000 students from New Jersey and the surrounding Mid-Atlantic States, providing distinctive traditional educational programs and alternative educational experiences that extend learning beyond the classroom. Internships are required for most majors with direct opportunities through the Washington, D.C. Internship Program, study abroad, Semester at Sea, and independent study with the One-on-One Connect mentor/scholar program. Special off-campus facilities include a library research center, educational and technology training center, marine science field station, and environmental field station. In addition, a regional medical center, a rehabilitation center, and an observatory are located on campus. Stockton students make use of a campus-wide wireless network to access online resources such as WebMail, WebCT, WebBoard, Loki, Library Online, distance education and electronic conferencing. All residence rooms provide Internet access and students have access to the Stockton network from home.

In addition to traditionally strong programs in the arts, sciences, business, education and humanities, Stockton offers in-demand and unique programs such as Computational Science, Tourism and Hospitality Management, Homeland Security and Physical Therapy. Students receive the kind of one-on-one attention usually found at smaller, private colleges, only in a mid-sized diverse public setting. With small class sizes and no teaching assistants, Stockton boasts a Pulitzer Prize winner, a Guggenheim Fellow, two Fulbright scholars and many recognized experts in their respective fields on staff to assist students in achieving their educational goals.

Essential to the Stockton experience is preparation for graduate, professional and medical schools. The undergraduate curriculum emulates aspects of graduate-level education. A very high percentage of students are successful in moving directly into a graduate experience on Stockton's campus or at other highly-respected institutions. Stockton also prepares students to move into successful careers upon graduation with the ability to apply concepts and ideas learned through the many real-world experiences gained as part of a Stockton education.

LOCATION AND ENVIRONMENT

The Richard Stockton College of New Jersey is located on a stunning 1,600-acre campus in Pomona, New Jersey, nestled in the Pinelands National Reserve, 12-miles from Atlantic City, with easy access to Philadelphia and New York City. The environmentally-friendly campus has a rural park-like setting yet is close to a variety of cultural and recreational activities with nearby opportunity for shopping and dining. A full schedule of concerts, art exhibitions, lectures, recreation and sports on campus is complemented by the nearby Jersey Shore resort destinations. Within a 15-minute drive students will find fishing, boating, swimming and cultural attractions, as well as Atlantic City.

OFF-CAMPUS OPPORTUNITIES

Off-campus educational experiences for credit are a key feature of most degree programs at Stockton. Internships, research projects, and field studies extend the principles and methods learned beyond the classroom. Study abroad, Semester at Sea, and four-year independent study with the One-on-One Connect mentor/scholar program are also available. The Washington, D.C., Internship Program gives students the opportunity to gain professional working experience. Stockton sends more students to the program than any other college or university outside the Washington, D.C. area.

ADVANCED PRE-PROFESSIONAL DEGREE OPTION:

Seven-year dual degree with the University of Medicine and Dentistry of New Jersey (Robert Wood Johnson Medical School, New Jersey Medical School, School of Osteopathic Medicine, New Jersey Dental School); Pennsylvania College of Podiatric Medicine; New York College of Podiatric Medicine; New York State College of Optometry; Rutgers School of Pharmacy.

Cornell University; veterinary medicine.

Five-year, "3+2" Engineering with New Jersey Institute of Technology; Rutgers University

Dual degree, Doctor of Pharmacy, with the Ernest Mario School of Pharmacy at Rutgers University.

Doctorate of Physical Therapy; The Richard Stockton College of New Jersey. (Bacharach Institute for Rehabilitation and AtlantiCare Regional Medical Center located on campus.)

4+1 BA/MA; Criminal Justice at The Richard Stockton College of New Jersey

4+1 BS/MS; Computational Science at The Richard Stockton College of New Jersey

4+1 BS/MBA; Business Administration at The Richard Stockton College of New Jersey

4+1 BA or BS/Certificate; Paralegal Studies at The Richard Stockton College of New Jersey

MAJORS AND DEGREES OFFERED

Bachelor of Arts/Bachelor of Science; Arts, Studies in Applied Physics, Biochemistry/Molecular Biology, Biology; Business Studies (Accounting, Finance, Hospitality & Tourism Management, International Business, Management, Marketing); Chemistry; Communication; Computational Science; Computer Science and Information Systems; Criminal Justice (Forensic Science); Economics; Education; Engineering dual-degree; Environmental Studies; Geology; Historical Studies; Languages & Cultural Studies; Liberal Studies; Literature; Marine Science; Mathematics; Nursing; Philosophy and Religion; Physics; Political Science; Psychology; Public Health; Sociology & Anthropology; Social Work; Speech Pathology & Audiology

PRE-PROFESSIONAL STUDIES

Pre-Dentistry; Pre-Law; Pre-Medical; Pre-Occupational Therapy; Pre-Optometry; Pre-Pharmacy; Pre-Physical Therapy; Pre-Podiatry; Pre-Veterinary

ACADEMIC PROGRAMS

The Stockton study plan combines solid academic preparation with a self-directed approach. Students have many options for engaging in independent study and faculty-guided research projects. The curricular framework is flexible in that students have special opportunities to influence what and how they learn by participating in the major decisions that shape their academic lives; choose a traditional path of study, or one which is tailor suited to their individual needs.

Special Academic Options: credit for Advanced Placement, accelerated degree programs, dual-degree programs, distance learning, self-designed majors, summer session, adult/continuing education programs, internships, graduate courses open to undergrads.

Academic Year:

Two fifteen-week semesters

Eight summer terms

Graduation requirements: 128 credit hours; internships for some majors; senior project for honors program students.

Preceptorial advising days are set aside each semester for student/ faculty advisor sessions.

CAMPUS FACILITIES AND EQUIPMENT

Art gallery

Astronomical observatory

Campus Cable TV network

Campus-wide wireless network, computer labs, WebMail, WebCT, WebBoard, Library Online, Loki

Carnegie Library Research Center, Atlantic City

Electronic conferencing network

Environmental science field stations; on-campus outdoor research lab

Holocaust Resource Center

Marine science laboratory, field station and marina

On-campus child care facilities

Performing Arts Center

Radio station WLFR-fm

Southern branch of New Jersey Network (NJN)

Southern Regional Institute and Educational Technology Training Center, Mays Landing

Library: The Richard Stockton College of New Jersey Library contains more that 683,000 volumes, including books, reference materials, periodicals, newspapers, microforms, computer software, archival materials and government documents as well as a full-text of over 11,000 electronic journals.

Housing: Stockton provides on-campus housing in traditional residence halls and apartment-style living. All facilities are fully furnished and air-conditioned with cable TV, phone and Internet provided.

TUITION, ROOM, BOARD AND FEES

Undergraduate Students

2007-2008 costs based on tuition $199/credit in-State, $352/credit out-of-State and fees $105/credit. Totals below for 32 credits/year, double occupancy residence room and 180 meal block plan.

	In-State Resident	Out-of-State Resident
Tuition & Fees	$9,697	$14,597
Room & Board	$8,993	$ 8,993
Books (apx.)	$1,200	$ 1,200
TOTAL	$19,890/year	$24,790/year

Graduate Students 2007-2008 costs

	In-State Resident	Out-of-State Resident
Tuition	$439/credit	$663/credit
Fees	$105/credit	$105/credit
TOTAL	$544/credit	$768/credit

FINANCIAL AID

Financial Aid is available in the form of scholarships, grants, loans and work-study. Need-based aid is awarded according to family need. Merit-based aid is awarded to recognize academic excellence with Stockton offering aggressive and generous scholarships to academically talented students.

STUDENT ORGANIZATIONS AND ACTIVITIES

Co-curricular activities are an extremely important aspect of the college experience providing countless opportunities for students to develop leadership, social, and recreational skills outside the formal academic setting. Stockton offers over 100 clubs and organizations and 21 sororities and fraternities. Participation in activities can be documented through Stockton's student development program, ULTRA (Undergraduate Learning, Training and Awareness), culminating in a Co-curricular Transcript issued to students.

STOCKTON ATHLETICS

At the intercollegiate level, Stockton fields NCAA Division III sports teams in men's baseball, basketball, lacrosse, and soccer; women's basketball, crew, field hockey, soccer, softball, tennis and volleyball; and men's and women's cross-country and track and field. Stockton participates in the New Jersey Athletic Conference (NJAC) and the Eastern College Athletic Conference (ECAC), two of the most competitive Division III conferences in the nation. The College boasts a new sports center with fitness facilities, a glass-enclosed indoor swimming pool, racquetball courts, weight rooms and outdoor recreational facilities. In addition, students, faculty and staff members join together in an extensive intramural and club sport program.

ADMISSIONS PROCESS

Admission to Stockton is competitive, but we encourage students from all backgrounds to apply. Every application received is evaluated on the basis of both demonstrated proficiency and potential for success on the college level.

Stockton operates on rolling admissions with deadlines. This means students may apply for admission to the fall or spring term and receive an admissions decision when their application files are completed. For most freshman majors, the deadline for fall admission is May 1. Check our website for special program deadlines. Transfer student deadline for fall admission is June 1. Spring admission deadline for all students is December 1.

Application fee: $50. Enrollment deposit: $100. Housing deposit: $200.

Freshman Application Requirements: application, essay, official high school transcript, SAT or ACT scores, TOEFL for international students. Suggested: letters of recommendation.

Transfer Student Application Requirements: official transcripts from ALL colleges attended. Transfer students with fewer than 16 transferable credits at the date of application must provide official high school transcripts or high school equivalency certificate (GED), equivalency test scores, and SAT or ACT scores. Transfers with 16 or more transfer credits who have not attained an associate's degree at the date of application must provide a copy of the high school diploma or GED, equivalency test scores and transcripts from years attended.

Students graduating from a New Jersey county/community college with an AA/AS degree in a Stockton-approved transfer program may be granted up to a maximum of 64 credits upon notification of acceptance. An associate in applied science (AAS) degree is not generally transferable and is evaluated on a course-by-course basis.

For more information, contact:

The Richard Stockton College of New Jersey

Office of Enrollment Management

PO Box 195

Pomona, NJ 08240-0195

Telephone: 609-652-4261

Toll free: 866-RSC-2885

Fax: 609-748-5541

Email: admissions@stockton.edu

Website: www.stockton.edu

RIPON COLLEGE

AT A GLANCE

Together with the other members of our tightly-knit learning community, at Ripon you'll learn more deeply, live more fully, and achieve more success. You'll be surprised to discover that here you have more opportunities to be involved, to lead, to speak out, to make a difference, to explore new interests than you would at a college 10 times our size. Through collaborative learning, group living, teamwork, and networking, you'll tap into the power of a community where we all work together to ensure your success at Ripon and beyond.

LOCATION AND ENVIRONMENT

All of the best residential liberal arts colleges strive to be true learning communities like Ripon. We succeed better than most because our enrollment of 1,000 students is perfect for fostering connections inside and outside the classroom. Our students flourish in this environment of mutual respect, where shared values are elevated and diverse ideas are valued. If you are seeking academic challenge and want to benefit from an environment of personal attention and support then you should take a closer look at Ripon.

In classes that average 20 students, your professors are able to know you, your strengths, and your capabilities extraordinarily well. They'll tailor your course work to make sure you're always challenged to perform at the top of your game. Yet they're always ready to provide extra support when you need it. Faculty collaborate with you on research projects, suggest independent study topics, and connect you with internships and other active learning experiences.

OFF-CAMPUS OPPORTUNITIES

U.S. or abroad? Three weeks, one semester, two semesters? We offer you more than 40 different programs to choose from, each one officially sanctioned by and affiliated with Ripon. Although most programs are connected with a major or minor program, all are open to every Ripon student, regardless of major.

U.S. Programs: Chicago Urban Studies Semester; Fisk University-Ripon Exchange Program; Newberry Seminar in the Humanities; Oak Ridge Science Semester; Washington Semester; Woods Hole Marine Biology.

International Programs: Budapest Semester; Central European Studies Program in the Czech Republic; Cost Rica; Cross-Cultural Study Center in Seville, Spain; Florence Program; France and Spain; Bonn, Germany Program; Global Studies Program in Turkey; India Studies; Japan Study; London and Florence Program in the Arts; Madrid Program; Montpellier, France; Paris, France; Ripon and York St. John Exchange; Russia Program; Sea Semester at Woods Hole; Swansea Program; Tanzania; Toledo, Spain; University of Wales in Bangor; Sea Education Association (marine biology abroad).

MAJORS AND DEGREES OFFERED

Majors include anthropology, art, art history, biology, business administration, chemistry, chemistry/biology, communication, computer science, economics, educational studies, English, environmental sciences, exercise science, foreign languages, French, German, global studies, history, Latin American area studies, mathematics, music, philosophy, physics, politics and government, psychobiology, psychology, religion, sociology/anthropology, Spanish, theater.

Pre-professional programs include dentistry, journalism, law and government, library and information science, medicine, ministry, optometry, physical therapy, veterinary medicine.

Dual-degree programs include engineering, forestry, allied health sciences/medical technology, and social welfare.

Certification programs include education certification, early childhood, elementary, elementary/middle school, secondary, secondary/middle, music K-12, and physical education K-12.

Programs are also available in leadership studies, women's studies, Army ROTC, and sports medicine/athletic training.

ACADEMIC PROGRAMS

Ripon's liberal arts curriculum is designed to introduce you to a wide variety of disciplines. About 40 percent of our students complete double or triple majors, while some create special self-designed majors. Excellent communications skills written and oral as well as critical-thinking and problem-solving skills, are the hallmark of a Ripon education, no matter what your major. In addition, our leadership studies program and our newly established ethical leadership program provide a strong foundation for leadership skills.

A Ripon education will take you anywhere! You could study psychology and play basketball at Ripon, and then become a five-time Grammy winner like jazz singer Al Jarreau (1962). You could guide the space shuttle into orbit like Jeff Bantle (1980), a chief flight director with NASA, or become an international opera star like Gail Dobish (1976). Perhaps you'll set records in medical science like neonatologist Dr. John Muraskas (1978), who is on record for saving the world's smallest premature baby, or cover world events, like Richard Threlkeld (1959), former

Moscow correspondent for CBS News. Or perhaps you'll end up in Donald Trump's inner circle like Ashley Cooper (1982), a senior manager of Trump National Golf Club who has served as an advisor to The Donald on "The Apprentice."

CAMPUS FACILITIES AND EQUIPMENT

Located on 250 tree-lined, rolling acres adjacent to downtown Ripon, the campus looks and feels like a college should. Ripon's 25 first-rate buildings are a striking combination of historic (10 campus structures listed on the national register of historic buildings) and modern architecture. Constant improvements, like a new apartment-style residence hall, a multimillion dollar renovation of one of our main classroom buildings, upgrades to the student union, the campus bookstore, our dining facilities, and numerous student activity spaces maintain Ripon's ability to meet the needs of today and tomorrow.

Technology services include high-speed Internet and e-mail, telephone, and video communication. Intranet and Internet services are accessible from systems located throughout the college. Our campus wide network provides access from every room, and several wireless "hot-spots" in key areas let you access the world without tying you down.

Our science labs contain a variety of high-tech instruments, including a 300-Mhz FTNMR Spectrometer, spectrophotometers, an X-ray diffraction instrument, chromatographs, a spectrofluorimeter, modern electroanalytical instrumentation, a HeliumCadmium Laser Lab, transmission and scanning electron microscopes, a super-speed refrigerated centrifuge, a Zeiss universal microscope with digitizing tablet and two Nikon diaphot inverted microscopes. Ripon also houses a small planetarium classroom, but since research is not limited to the lab, Ripon's Ceresco Prairie Conservancy provides the ultimate outdoor classroom_a 130-acre area natural prairie ecosystem where students can not only study science but also become involved in service learning through prairie restoration.

The library staff provides friendly, efficient circulation, reference, instruction, and interlibrary loan services that aid in research. The library also houses the college archives, a computer lab, and more than a dozen online databases. Library holdings include 164,000 volumes, 800 current periodicals, and microfilms.

The C.J. Rodman Center for the Arts is home to a theater with a state-of-the-art computerized lighting system, a recital hall with one of only 50 existing Bedient organs, an art gallery, and a sculpture garden.

The J.M. Storzer Center includes an Olympic-size pool, a first-class gymnasium, tennis and racquetball courts, a dance studio, training facilities, and a weight room. Our outdoor playing fields and courts are the best in their class. In addition, a large, modern exercise facility was recently added in the main student residence area.

TUITION, ROOM, BOARD AND FEES

Ripon is one of just 81 colleges and universities in the country recognized as a Best Value by the Princeton Review in the 2007 edition of America's Best Value Colleges, which noted, "Best of all, Ripon strives to provide aid in a form that reduces your long-term debt." Nearly 100 percent of Ripon students receive some form of merit-based scholarship and/or need-based grants and loans.

Tuition is $23,970, room and board is $6,770, and fees are $275, for a total cost of $31,015.

FINANCIAL AID

We recognize and reward your success in high school with Ripon's institutionally funded scholarships, based not only on academic merit, but also on special achievements in other areas such as the creative arts. Our scholarships range from $1,000 to full tuition. Ripon participates in all federal and state need-based Financial Aid programs. Our Financial Aid counselors will work individually with you and your family to investigate every possible financial resource for which you are eligible.

STUDENT ORGANIZATIONS AND ACTIVITIES

The list of student clubs and organizations is ever-changing, reflecting our students' ever-changing interests. A recent addition is FUERZA Alliance, designed to educate students about Latino cultures and to provide services to the Spanish-speaking community of Ripon.

Every day at Ripon is packed with a host of activities that include: Concerts we have eight vocal and instrumental groups that perform regularly on campus, as well as many individual student and faculty recitals. The Caestecker Fine Arts Series and the Chamber Music at Ripon Series annually bring national performers to campus. The Ethical Leadership Program sponsors an annual ethics conference which included nationally-known personalities Tim Russert, Miles Brand, and Bud Selig. The Theatre Department sponsors two major productions annually, plus a series of student-directed one-acts. Our most recent Ripon Film Festival (an annual showcase for independent films from around the country) included the premiere of a feature-length horror film written, directed by, and starring a Ripon student.

Ripon's NCAA Division III Intercollegiate Teams compete in the Midwest Conference:

Men's varsity sports: baseball, basketball, cross-country, cycling, football, golf, soccer, swimming and diving, tennis, and indoor and outdoor track and field.

Women's varsity sports: basketball, cross-country, cycling, golf, soccer, softball, swimming and diving, tennis, indoor and outdoor track and field.

ADMISSIONS PROCESS

Ripon enrolls students who will contribute to and benefit from the academic and residential programs we provide. Ripon does not discriminate on the basis of gender, sexual orientation, race, color, age, religion, national and ethnic origin, or disability in the administration of its educational policies, admission practices, scholarship and loan programs, athletic, and other college-administered programs.

The faculty committee on academic standards establishes the criteria for admission. The school considers a variety of factors, including secondary school record, standardized test scores (SAT or ACT), recommendations, a written essay, and extracurricular or community service activities. Ripon's Admission Process reflects the personal attention students can expect to receive during their college careers, and applicants are encouraged to provide any additional information that they consider helpful.

For more information contact:

Admission Office

Ripon College

300 Seward Street

PO Box 248

Ripon, WI 54971

Telephone: 800-947-4766

E-mail: adminfo@ripon.edu

ROBERT MORRIS COLLEGE (IL)

AT A GLANCE

Robert Morris College is an independent, not-for-profit, multi-campus institution offering associate, baccalaureate, and graduate degree programs that focus on integrating theory, concepts, and applications. Robert Morris College prepares students to be practitioners in their chosen fields, socially responsible to their communities, and foundations for their families. Robert Morris College is accredited by the Higher Learning Commission and is a member of the North Central Association, 30 North LaSalle Street, Suite 2400, Chicago, Illinois 60602, (312) 263-0456.

With over a 90-year history of excellence, Robert Morris College offers professional, career-focused education in a collegiate setting to diverse communities. Through the teaching and learning process, students achieve intellectual, personal and cultural growth. Robert Morris College is dedicated to providing opportunities for academically capable students from diverse backgrounds the competencies necessary for entry into and advancement within career fields.

Robert Morris College is a member of the National Association of Intercollegiate Athletics (NAIA) and the Chicagoland Collegiate Athletic Conference (CCAC), Division II. The College offers men's and women's basketball, cross-country, soccer, and hockey, as well as women's volleyball, women's lacrosse, and softball.

LOCATION AND ENVIRONMENT

Chicago Campus, 401 S. State Street, Chicago, IL 60605

Located across the street from the renowned Harold Washington Public Library in the heart of the city's bustling cultural and financial districts. Minutes away from museums, the lakefront, sports arenas, theaters, and all forms of public transportation.

Housing is available for out-of-state students attending RMC's Chicago Campus. The 320 North Michigan housing option is centrally located in Chicago, just steps away from theaters, concert halls, retailers, restaurants, and art galleries as well as Chicago's beautiful Lake Michigan, famous skyline, and expansive parks. 320 North Michigan is sure to provide students with an exciting residential environment in a stimulating urban setting.

DuPage Campus, 905 Meridian Lake Drive, Aurora, IL 60504

50,000 square feet in a new modern building in Meridian Lakes Business Park in Aurora. This is in a community that is accessible, convenient, in a great location and close to the Metra. Enjoy what the City of Aurora has to offer: great history, the Fox Valley mall, outstanding golf courses and many restaurants.

Lake County Campus, 1507 Waukegan Road, Waukegan, IL 60085

Located in the northern Chicago suburb of Waukegan. New, modern facilities with a unique, open-space design. Featuring hi-tech computer labs and an expanded library.

Bensenville Campus, 1000 Tower Lane, Bensenville, IL 60106

Surrounding areas has an ever increasing demand for qualified employees in business and computer technology. Convenience commuter campus with easy access to expressways.

Orland Park Campus, 82 Orland Square, Orland Park, IL 60462

Recently named one of the most livable cities in the country. Near golf courses, parks, trails, and the Orland Square Mall. Beautiful two-building campus features over 65,000 square feet, including student lounge, outdoor atrium and a newly completed Technology Center.

Peoria Campus, 211 Fulton Street, Peoria, IL 61602

Strengthens RMC's commitment to serving central Illinois. Located in a modern office building in the heart of Peoria's business district. Offering the latest technological facilities in education.

Springfield Campus, 3101 Montvale Drive, Springfield, IL 62704

Ideally situated in Abraham Lincoln's hometown and the Illinois state capital. Offers plenty of opportunities for historic, cultural and recreational activities as well as access to a thriving business district.

OFF-CAMPUS OPPORTUNITIES

Housing is available for out-of-state students attending RMC's Chicago Campus. The 320 North Michigan housing option is centrally located in Chicago, just steps away from theaters, concert halls, retailers, restaurants, and art galleries as well as Chicago's beautiful Lake Michigan, famous skyline, and expansive parks. 320 North Michigan is sure to provide students with an exciting residential environment in a stimulating urban setting.

Majors and Degrees Offered

Our career-focused degrees are designed to prepare you for the most in-demand jobs in the fastest growing industries. Our caring faculty members many of whom are active professionals in their fields will give you all the support you need to succeed. And you can complete your bachelor's degree in as little as three years or a graduate degree in as little as 18 months.

ACADEMIC PROGRAMS

Bachelor's Degrees

Bachelor of Business Administration Degree

Bachelor of Applied Science Degree in Computer Studies

Bachelor of Applied Science Degree in Graphic Design

Associate Degrees

Accounting

Business Administration/Honors

Computer Aided Drafting and Design (CADD)

Culinary Arts

Fitness & Exercise

Graphic Arts

Interior Space Planning & Design

Paralegal

Nursing

Medical Assisting

Computer Networking

Surgical Technology

TUITION, ROOM, BOARD AND FEES

Can I afford RMC?

Definitely. Robert Morris College is an affordable investment in your future. In fact, once you're admitted to the College, you may be eligible to apply for a variety of financial aid programs to help you pay for the cost of your education. In 2005-2006, RMC awarded more than $18 million in scholarships to our students.

Financial Aid

There are many ways to finance an education. At Robert Morris College, we look for them all. An admissions representative will help you complete the financial aid forms and explore the many scholarship opportunities available. When your forms have been processed, you will also learn what grants and loans may be available, as well as how a part-time job can help. We know how important getting a degree can be for your future — how spending some money today can lead to a great salary tomorrow. At Robert Morris College, you have many options. Let us show you.

Student Organizations and Activities

College should be more than time spent in a classroom. At Robert Morris College there are plenty of opportunities to experience growth beyond the classroom and have fun. Student life at our seven campuses helps to create a community of students. You can join one of our many clubs or student organizations from the accounting club to the soccer club. Share your interests, network, learn about future careers and bond with other students. Participate in your favorite sport or root for one of our many sports teams. Work out at the fitness center or just relax and enjoy a cup of coffee at the café. Enjoy the college experience and be a part of a dynamic campus community.

ADMISSIONS PROCESS

We'll base our admission decision on a review of your academic record and professional experience. Throughout the process, we'll consider you as an individual. In order to do that, we'll need the information listed below, though these requirements may change if you're an adult, transfer, returning, international student, or have been home-schooled.

GENERAL ADMISSION REQUIREMENTS

High school records or GED transcript

Examination results (one of):

American College Testing (ACT)

Scholastic Aptitude Test (SAT/SATII)

You may also be required to take a placement exam through Robert Morris College, Applied Education Skills Assessment Advanced Placement (AESA)

Adult Students

If you are 23 years or older, you probably possess enough personal and professional experiences to demonstrate your ability to be successful in college, so we'll consider your employment history in addition to the general admission requirements.

Transfer Students

If you've earned 12 semester hours (18 quarter hours) or more of coursework at another regionally accredited institution of higher learning, you qualify as a transfer student. In making admission decisions for transfer students, the following materials are required:

High school record

It's also possible that your community college has a special arrangement with Robert Morris College to apply most or all of the credit you've already earned toward your RMC degree. Visit the Transfer Students page for more details.

International Students

No matter how you say it, we know you will feel welcome at Robert Morris College, where we help your dreams become a reality. The following information will assist you in applying for a student visa to our college. Please note that all documents must be submitted at the same time.

Home-Schooled Students

If you were home-schooled, you must submit a transcript of classes, curriculum documentation and state certification. In addition, you must take a nationally standardized examination to demonstrate an achievement level acceptable to the College.

ROBERT MORRIS UNIVERSITY

AT A GLANCE

Robert Morris University, founded in 1921, is one of the leading universities in the Pittsburgh region and among the largest private institutions of higher learning in Pennsylvania. More than 5,000 full- and part-time undergraduate and graduate students from 32 states and 31 countries are enrolled at RMU.

The 230-acre campus in Moon Township is located 15 minutes from Pittsburgh International Airport and 17 miles from downtown. The Center for Adult and Continuing Education is located in the heart of the city, among the nation's seventh largest concentration of Fortune 500 corporate headquarters. The 32-acre Island Sports Center on Neville Island provides state-of-the-art athletic facilities for the university and the community.

RMU built its reputation by offering strong academic programs in traditional business fields such as accounting, finance, marketing and management. To prepare students for success in a changing and competitive workforce, the university has created programs in communications, information systems, engineering, mathematics, science, education, social sciences and nursing in the past decade. The university now offers 30 bachelor's degree programs and 18 master's and doctoral degree programs.

RMU is a teaching-centered institution, featuring small classes taught by faculty members. The student/faculty ratio is 16:1, and the average class size is 24.

More than 60 clubs and organizations help students develop leadership skills, network professionally and meet new friends. Student activities include varsity, club and intramural sports, sororities, fraternities and student government. The 23 varsity athletic programs are affiliated with NCAA Division I.

For more information, visit www.rmu.edu.

LOCATION AND ENVIRONMENT

Robert Morris University is ideally situated on 230 rolling acres in suburban Moon Township, Pennsylvania. RMU's campus continues to blossom and grow: A new on-campus football stadium opened in 2005, and a new apartment-style residence hall opened in 2006.

OFF-CAMPUS OPPORTUNITIES

City or country, quiet or excitement, our location puts it all within reach. Pittsburgh is compact, cultured, safe, neighborly, historic, and very affordable. Activities abound: professional sports, concerts, cultural events, nightlife, museums, amusement parks, bike trails and more. And with 28 colleges and universities in the region, you'll find plenty of fun and people to share in the excitement.

MAJORS AND DEGREES OFFERED

Robert Morris University offers traditional bachelor's degree programs in the following fields of study. Many degrees offer several concentrations (listed in parentheses) to enable students to tailor their degree to meet their specific career interests.

Accounting, Actuarial Science, Applied Mathematics (Secondary Teacher Certification), Applied Psychology, Business Education (Secondary Teacher Certification), Communication (Advertising, Applied Journalism, Communication Studies, Corporate Communication, Public Relations, Secondary Teacher Certification, Theater), Competitive Intelligence Systems, Computer Information Systems (Health Care Systems, Network Administration, Office Information Systems, Security, Software Development, Web Development), Economics, Elementary Education (English/Communications, Mathematics, Science, Social Studies, Technology), Engineering (Logistics, Software), English (English Studies, English Literature, Secondary Teacher Certification), Environmental Science (Premedicine), Finance, Hospitality and Tourism Management, Information Sciences (Health Care Systems, Network Administration, Office Information Systems, Security, Software Development), Management, Manufacturing Engineering, Marketing, Media Arts (Graphic Design, TV/Video Production, Web Design), Nursing (RN Completion, Second Degree, Traditional), Social Science (Secondary Teacher Certification), Sport Management.

ACADEMIC PROGRAMS

Other programs open to qualified undergraduate students include:

The Patriot Scholars International Honor's Program, in which students take honor's-level courses and complete at least one semester of international travel and study.

The Cooperative Education Program, in which students alternate semesters of academic study with up to four semesters of paid employment in their career field to gain extensive work experience and earn up to $35,000 (open to students majoring in accounting, computer information systems, management/international business, and manufacturing engineering only).

Study Abroad, which offers opportunities for international study in countries including Australia, England, France, Ireland, Italy, Japan, Mexico, Switzerland and Turkey.

CAMPUS FACILITIES AND EQUIPMENT

We believe your education is too important to leave to chance. It's not enough that you hear or read the material; you need to live it. Experiment and make mistakes. Learn to self-critique and self-correct. Practice the ways of mastery. At RMU, you'll be surrounded by technology, whether you're an aspiring engineer, designer, nurse, or news anchor. Our state-of-the-art facilities include new science and nursing laboratories equipped with the latest technology, an industry-grade engineering laboratory, a cutting-edge design studio and the region's second-largest television studio.

TUITION, ROOM, BOARD, AND FEES

Robert Morris University has one of the lowest tuition rates among all private universities in Pennsylvania. The annual tuition for first-time undergraduates in 2006–2007 was $16,290, based on a 24- to 36-credit, two-semester schedule. Additional tuition charges apply for certain majors. Room and board fees are $8,410 annually, based on double occupancy and a full meal plan.

FINANCIAL AID

More than 90 percent of full-time undergraduate students receive some sort of financial aid, including grants, loans, scholarships and work-study jobs.

STUDENT ORGANIZATIONS AND ACTIVITIES

Getting involved on campus and in the community is part of the total educational experience at Robert Morris University. A wide range of activities and experiences is available to you at RMU. Students are encouraged to get involved in existing activities and/or establish new organizations. The more than 60 existing student organizations include academic/professional organizations, student government, honor societies, service and philanthropic organizations, special interest organizations and activities, fraternities and sororities, club, intramural and varsity sports. The university sponsors 23 NCAA Division I intercollegiate athletics teams: basketball (M/W), crew (W), cross country (M/W), field hockey (W), football (M), golf (M/W), ice hockey (M/W), lacrosse (M/W), soccer (M/W), softball (W), tennis (M/W), indoor and outdoor track and field (M/W), and volleyball (W).

ADMISSIONS PROCESS

Robert Morris University has a rolling admissions process. Students are considered for acceptance as soon as all application materials are received and evaluated. Applications, official transcripts, official test scores and letters of recommendation should be sent directly to: Office of Admissions, Robert Morris University, 6001 University Boulevard, Moon Township, PA 15108. Apply for free on the RMU website at www.rmu.edu.

ROCHESTER INSTITUTE OF TECHNOLOGY

AT A GLANCE

RIT is one of the world's leading career-oriented, technological universities. At RIT, some of the world's most talented, ambitious, and creative students find a remarkable array of Academic Programs; diverse, talented and accessible faculty; an unusual emphasis on experiential learning; and a vibrant, connected community that is home to students from more than 95 countries. RIT's eight colleges offer more than 90 undergraduate programs in areas such as engineering, computing, information technology, engineering technology, business, hospitality, art, design, science, psychology, public policy, game design and development and biomedical sciences. Regardless of background or academic interest, students find that RIT offers a stimulating environment for intellectual and personal growth.

LOCATION AND ENVIRONMENT

RIT's 1,300-acre campus is located in the suburbs, about six miles from downtown Rochester, NY. More than 6,800 diverse, creative, ambitious students live on campus in residence halls or apartments, and the self-contained, suburban location gives the campus a safe, residential atmosphere.

OFF-CAMPUS OPPORTUNITIES

Rochester provides a perfect setting—it's large enough to provide the dining, shopping, and night life opportunities found in a bigger city, yet small and friendly enough to be inviting and accessible. In fact, Rochester was ranked 10th best among large cities in the Northeast in a recent Money magazine Best Places to Live in America survey. The greater Rochester area is home to more than 1 million people, making it the third-largest metropolitan area in New York State. Rochester's reputation as an active and inventive community is supported by extensive cultural and intellectual opportunities.

MAJORS AND DEGREES OFFERED

Few universities provide RIT's variety of career-oriented programs. Our eight colleges offer 92 bachelor's degree programs in art and design, business, engineering, science and mathematics, criminal justice, photography, film, environmental studies, hospitality and service management, computer science, information technology, bioinformatics urban studies, advertising and public relations and many more.

ACADEMIC PROGRAMS

Regardless of background or academic interest, students find that RIT offers a stimulating environment for intellectual and personal growth. RIT's eight colleges offer more than 90 undergraduate programs in areas such as engineering, computing, information technology, engineering technology, business, hospitality, art, design, science, psychology, public policy, game design and development and biomedical sciences. Students looking to distinguish themselves from the crowd may want to consider one of the more than 80 minors available at RIT. Students can also complete a master's degree in five years through one of the university's accelerated BS/MS or BS/MBA programs. Other academic enrichments include study abroad, undergraduate research, internships, cooperative education, and double majors.

CAMPUS FACILITIES AND EQUIPMENT

The campus is filled with the latest equipment, software, laboratories, and conveniences to give students the tools they need to excel. RIT offers academic facilities that are rarely matched on other university campuses, and students use the latest technology to solve problems creatively. RIT plays leadership role in academic computing and gives students maximum access to research and information resources via two OC3 connections to the Internet, 20,000 network connections, and an eight-million-foot fiber-optic backbone. RIT is one of a select group of universities with access to the Internet 2 research network.

STUDENT ORGANIZATIONS AND ACTIVITIES

Clubs and Organizations exist to bring students of similar interest together and provide them with opportunities to become effective leaders. These groups enhance the quality of student life by fostering social interaction, leadership development, school spirit and an affinity to RIT. Clubs and Organizations promote activities, diversity, service and learning outside of the classroom. Currently there are approximately 160 active clubs, 10 Major Student Organizations, and 29 Greek Organizations on campus.

ADMISSIONS PROCESS

RIT seeks a diverse and multicultural student body. Entering students come from a variety of geographic, social, cultural, economic, and ethnic backgrounds. Admission to RIT is competitive, but the Admission Process is a personal one. The university is interested in learning about students' interests, abilities, and goals in order to provide the best information and guidance as they select the college that is right for them. Students applying for freshman admission for the fall quarter (September) may apply through an Early Decision Plan or Regular Decision Plan. The Early Decision Plan is designed for students who consider RIT their first-choice college and wish to make an early commitment regarding admission. Early Decision requires that candidates file their applications and supporting documents by December 1 in order to receive admission notification by January 15. Freshmen who choose not to apply for Early Decision are considered under our Regular Decision Plan. Regular Decision applicants who have provided all required application materials by February 1 will receive admission notification by March 15. Applications received after February 1 will be reviewed on a space-available basis, with notification letters mailed four to six weeks after the application is complete. Students interested in being considered for merit-based (academic and extracurricular) scholarships or the RIT Honors program must apply by February 1. All applications for transfer admission are reviewed as they are received, and notification letters are mailed four to six weeks after the application is complete. Factors considered in our admission decisions include, but are not limited to, past high school and/or college performance (particularly in required academic subjects), admission test scores, competitiveness of high school or previous college, and academic program selected. Recommendations from those familiar with your academic performance and interviews with admissions counselors are often influential. Students applying to RIT choose a specific academic program as part of the Admission Process. This is important because there are a variety of Academic Programs, and admission requirements may differ from one program to another. For example, a student applying for admission to our computer science program would present a strong academic record with particular strength in mathematics, while a student applying for a fine art or design major would need to show artistic talent through a required portfolio.

ROCKFORD COLLEGE

AT A GLANCE

At Rockford College, our vision is to be Jane Addams' college in the 21st century. By that, we signal an aspiration to live, learn and work in a contemporary way that honors the principles of Jane Addams, our distinguished 1881 graduate and 1931 Nobel Peace Prize winner.

The core component of Rockford College's vision is civic engagement. This supports our mission to prepare students for & participation in a modern and changing global society. Because of this, we have been named by The Princeton Review as a "College with a Conscience."

Like everything else about Rockford College, our Academic Programs are "hands-on." And with fewer than 20 students per class, you'll have significant one-on-one contact with your professors. Our professors have been known to rearrange entire days just to work individually with a student. They also host informal group discussions, where your thoughts and opinions on everything from modern medicine to conflict in the Middle East are encouraged, and even insisted upon.

Students at Rockford College don't hesitate to volunteer their time and talents. They teach adults to read, spend spring break building a house for an underprivileged family, volunteer in a soup kitchen and just recently they built a shelter in Thailand.

Whether it be in a classroom, on an athletic team, in our theater, as a volunteer for a community service project or through experiences studying abroad, your time at Rockford College will change your world.

LOCATION AND ENVIRONMENT

Rockford is a metro area of 375,000 people and scores of restaurants, theatres, clubs, coffeehouses, museums, gardens and galleries. Rockford also has pro sports, CBA basketball, UHL hockey, NISL soccer, minor league baseball and football, and so many fairways that Golf Digest calls this the country's best mid-sized city for golf.

We're just 90 minutes away from Chicago, Madison and Milwaukee. That means triple the job, internship and entertainment opportunities.

OFF-CAMPUS OPPORTUNITIES

A traditional study abroad choice for Rockford College students is Regent's College in central London. Students who've been there say it's a great place to begin getting to know the larger world. You can spend a semester at Regent's for about the same tuition, room and board you'd pay at Rockford College.

If you want a more challenging destination than Regent's, take your pick. Rockford College offers study abroad opportunities on just about every continent on earth. If you prefer a trip in the United States, Rockford College participates in the Washington and United Nations semesters.

MAJORS AND DEGREES OFFERED

Rockford College offers undergraduate degrees in Accounting, Anthropology and Sociology (concentrations in Criminal Justice and Social Work), Art (concentrations in studio arts such as Ceramics, Drawing, Painting, Photography, Printmaking and Sculpture), Art History, Biochemistry, Biology, Business Administration (Management Track and Marketing Track), Chemistry, Classics, Computer Science (Management Information Systems), Economics (Finance Track, International Economics Track, Public Policy Track), Elementary Education, English, French (Literature and Culture Track, International Studies Track), History, Humanities, International Studies, Latin, Mathematics, Music, Musical Theatre Performance, Nursing (Basic BSN Track, BSN Completion Track), Philosophy, Physical Education (Sports Management, Teaching Track), Political Science, Psychology, Romance Languages, Science and Mathematics, Social Sciences, Spanish (Literature Track, Language and Culture Track, International Studies Track), Special Education and Theatre Arts.

In addition, Rockford offers meticulously designed pre-professional programs for those interested in health professions: (Pre-Dentistry, Pre-Medicine, Pre-Pharmacy, Pre-Veterinary Medicine), Pre-Law and Pre-Social Work.

Rockford College students may also minor in any of the following areas: Ancient and Medieval Studies, Classical Civilization, Coaching, Communications, Greek, Human Development, Peace and Conflict Studies, Physics, Religious Studies and Secondary Education (6-12).

ACADEMIC PROGRAMS

Our academic program is designed to help you think first, deeply and broadly. Then act as if you can change the world.

At Rockford College we believe in a 'practical' education. What's the difference between training (for a job or a profession) and education? An education is for a lifetime. We offer the academic tools needed to change your life and your world.

The liberal arts curriculum requires both broad-based learning and concentration in a major area. To graduate, students must complete a minimum of 124 credit hours. Rockford College operates on a two-semester calendar and also offers summer courses. The college admits academically strong students to its Honors Program in Liberal Arts, whose extensive core curriculum and thorough distribution requirements place particular emphasis on the humanities. Students must apply separately for admission to the Honors Program. All students may participate in the Forum Series, which focuses on great ideas, significant scholars and influential artists. Rockford hosts a chapter of Phi Beta Kappa as well as other scholastic honor societies.

CAMPUS FACILITIES AND EQUIPMENT

Once you pass through our gates, the first thing you will see will be our 1,000 seat Sam Greeley Field. Next, you will come to The Jane Addams International Peace Garden.

Rockford College students can enjoy Internet access in every room, nice-sized rooms (singles and doubles), lounges with big screen televisions and plenty of activist friends from all over the world.

Thanks to our campus-wide high-speed wireless network, Rockford folks can surf the Internet from just about any place on campus—indoors or out. The 130 acres of wooded rolling hills surrounding our campus are home to not just students, but also to wildlife. Our dining room offers food for everyone, including fresh baked breads, homemade soups, a deli and a salad bar, ethnic favorites and, of course, desserts. If you're visiting as a prospective student, lunch is on us!

Rockford's major academic buildings include the Howard Colman Library (170,000 bound volumes, over 800 periodical subscriptions). Starr Science Building is home to the science departments. The facility includes biology and psychology teaching and research laboratories, physics laboratories, chemistry laboratories (teaching and research) with a well-equipped instrumentation lab and nursing laboratories.

Clark Arts Center is home to the fine and performing arts programs. The facility includes 570-seat Maddox Theatre equipped with high-tech lighting and sound equipment; an experimental theater; sculpture garden; art studios, including those for ceramics, lithography and printmaking; an art gallery; a darkroom and performance and practice space for music and dance.

Seaver Physical Education Building houses a pool, a basketball court, a fitness center, a training room, a free-weight room, locker rooms and classrooms.

Students can receive free tutoring at the Rockford Learning Center in the Starr Science Building. A writing center, classrooms and faculty offices are located in Scarborough Hall.

TUITION, ROOM, BOARD AND FEES

Tuition for the 2008-2009 academic year is $23,500. A double occupancy room costs $3,850 per year. Board plans start at $2,730 per year. Students should expect to spend about $900 per year on books and $2,000 on additional expenses (transportation, discretionary spending, and other expenses).

FINANCIAL AID

Rockford College awards Financial Aid on the basis of financial need and academic achievement. We want to help you; then you'll be able to help others.

Students must enroll for a minimum of 6 credit hours per semester to be eligible for aid. Rockford uses the Free Application for Federal Student Aid (FAFSA) to determine need and to award need-based aid, which includes college grants and loans and state and federal aid programs. Students are encouraged to submit aid applications by March 15th. Students remain eligible for Rockford aid when they study at Regent's College in London.

Rockford College offers several scholarships to incoming students. The Presidential Scholarship reaches up to $20,000 and is awarded each fall to new first-year and new transfer students who attend full time. The qualifications for this scholarship are, for first-year students: ACT of 27/SAT equivalent or higher and a 3.5 GPA or higher. Transfer students must have a 3.5 or higher college GPA and completed 30 or more college credits. Presidential Scholars must live on campus and participate in campus life. The deadline to apply for the Presidential Scholarship is January 31. The Trustee Scholarship ranges up to $15,000 and is awarded each fall to new first-year and new transfer students who attend full time. The qualifications for this scholarship are, for first-year students: ACT of 25/SAT equivalent or higher and a 3.35 GPA. Transfer students must have a 3.35 or higher college GPA and completed 12 or more college credits. Trustee Scholars must participate in campus life. The deadline to apply for the Trustee Scholarship is January 31. The Dean's, Regent's and Merit awards reach up to $9,400 and are awarded to all new full-time students based upon academic achievement and co-curricular activity involvement.

STUDENT ORGANIZATIONS AND ACTIVITIES

Named by the Princeton Review as a 'College with a Conscience,' Rockford College offers more than enough opportunities to get involved inside and outside the campus community. Make your voice heard in student government, prepare a dish for the International Food Fair or display your leadership skills in more than a dozen academic clubs and organizations. It's your right (and responsibility) to be as active as you possibly can be.

Start with the Jane Addams Center for Civic Engagement. The Center is a one-stop-shop for information on volunteer and service-related activities. Wash windows for a good cause, collect diapers for young mothers or show the world you're a drama queen—by helping local kids put on a play. You can do as little or as much as you'd like.

What about athletics? Rockford is a Division III college, and we compete regionally and nationally with three goals in mind: to play well, achieve academically and serve others. Last year, seven players earned All-Conference honors and many more than that volunteered to work in soup kitchens and tutor grade school kids.

ADMISSIONS PROCESS

The Office of Admission considers each application individually with the goal of assessing candidates' potential for academic success at the college. The school looks primarily at an applicant's record of academic and personal achievement, including class rank, GPA, quality of high school curriculum and standardized test scores (ACT or SAT I). Applicants must demonstrate at least a 2.65 high school GPA, placement in the top half of their class and minimum standardized test scores of 19 for the ACT (with no subscore below 17) or a combined 910 on the SAT I. All application files must include official transcripts and standardized test score reports. Students may submit applications any time after the completion of their junior year in high school. Transfer students are assessed based on their college coursework (once they have completed at least 12 hours of college-level study) and must provide transcripts from all colleges and universities they have attended. Transfer students must show a minimum college GPA of 2.3.

An international admissions representative handles all applications from international students. Applicants must earn a minimum TOEFL score of 550 written or 213 on the computer based test.

Rockford College admits applicants on a rolling basis; however, there is a fall application deadline of

August 15.

To receive additional information, please contact:

Office of Admission

Blanche Walker Burpee Center

Rockford College

5050 East State Street

Rockford, IL 61108-2393

Telephone: 815-226-4050 or 800-892-2984 (toll free in the U.S. and Canada)

Fax: 815-226-2822

E-mail: RCAdmissions@rockford.edu

Website: www.rockford.edu

ROCKY MOUNTAIN COLLEGE OF ART AND DESIGN

AT A GLANCE

As one of the top art and design schools in the nation, RMCAD attracts students from around the country and around the world.

RMCAD is regionally accredited by the Higher Learning Commission of the North Central Association of Colleges and Schools and nationally accredited by the National Association of Schools of Art and Design (NASAD). The Interior Design program is accredited by the Council for Interior Design Accreditation.

RMCAD offers a BFA degree in the following areas: Animation (2D or 3D), Art Education, Illustration, Interior Design, Painting & Drawing, Photography/Video Art, Sculpture and Graphic Design + Interactive Media.

Students are admitted on a rolling or continuous basis up until approximately 2 weeks before the start of each semester. For a listing of our current admissions requirements and other information about the College, visit www.rmcad.edu or contact the Admissions Office at 800.888.ARTS or admissions@rmcad.edu.

LOCATION AND ENVIRONMENT

Is there a lot to do at RMCAD? The answer is simple - yes! Many new RMCAD students jump right into the mix of activities - everything from barbeques on the Quad to field trips to local galleries. Other RMCAD students spend their free time engrossed in their artwork. Most students strike a happy balance of both.

MAJORS AND DEGREES OFFERED

ANIMATION (2D or 3D)

Rocky Mountain College of Art + Design's animation program merges the arts of writing, storytelling, design, illustration, sculpture, theatre, photography and film-making with the technology of computers. The professional animators within the department teach students about the history of animation, current developments in animation and the future of animation. Since the field of animation is ever-changing, the departmental faculty continues to develop their own skills while helping to develop and nurture future generations of artists and animators.

ART EDUCATION

At RMCAD, art education is approached as a visual language. Students who earn a Bachelor of Fine Arts in Art Education are well prepared to motivate and inspire others to creatively think about and make art. The mission of the department is simple - to give talented artists the skills necessary to be articulate and sensible art educators. Through rigorous coursework, classroom projects and class interaction, the program teaches artists how to accurately communicate ideas, experiences and events while emphasizing vision, creativity, innovation, leadership, conceptual thinking, and technical expertise.

One unique aspect of RMCAD's Art Education program is that students must choose painting, illustration or sculpture as an area of specialization. By developing their skills both as artists and as teachers, RMCAD graduates are able to merge both kinds of expertise as they begin to teach elementary and secondary school students.

FINE ARTS (Photo/Video, Painting & Drawing, Sculpture)

Students in RMCAD's Fine Arts department can customize their course of study to fit their specific interests and career goals. Regardless of the specific set of courses they choose, all students in the Fine Arts program are challenged to expand their definition of art and develop the critical thinking skills that will help them be successful creating artwork in the context of the current art world. By studying the human form, drawing, and basic design concepts, students develop their visual and technical skills and leave RMCAD prepared to be important and successful members of the world-wide arts community.

GRAPHIC DESIGN + INTERACTIVE MEDIA

RMCAD's Graphic Design + Interactive Media program combines theory and practice to inspire students and help them discover their own individual design expression, while at the same time preparing them for today's new business environment. With the development of new technologies and interactive media, the global marketplace is changing the role of the contemporary designer. RMCAD recognizes and embraces this enormous potential by combining these technologies with a classical grounding in drawing, sociology, photography, theory, and form. This gives students a solid base for creating new ideas while maintaining a strong emphasis on process and content.

ILLUSTRATION

The RMCAD program provides advanced professional skills in representational drawing, painting, visual communication and business. These are the critical elements for success in the commercial field. No other college or university in the western states offers a full illustration program such as ours. Our student work is seen regularly in the Society of Illustrators Student Competition in New York City, where our program has been endorsed by the jury's stringent selection process. Furthermore, RMCAD's Illustration Department faculty is working artists, all experts in their field with many years of significant professional practice.

INTERIOR DESIGN

Rocky Mountain College of Art + Design's Interior Design program prepares students to be successful design professionals who are qualified to enhance the function and quality of interior environments. In accordance with the accreditation requirements of the Council for Interior Design Accreditation (CIDA), the curriculum is focused on the development of interior spaces for the purpose of improving the quality of life, increasing productivity, and protecting the health, safety, and welfare of the public.

ACADEMIC PROGRAMS

FOUNDATION STUDIES

Each RMCAD student, regardless of major, is required to take approximately 21 credit hours of foundation coursework during their freshman and sophomore years. Students transferring to RMCAD who have studied basic art concepts at another school may receive credit for all or some of these credits.

In Foundation Studies classes you'll get to build upon the skills you already have and experiment with everything that RMCAD offers. You'll expand your two-dimensional skills such as drawing, composition, and color theory and sharpen your three dimensional skills through sculpture, wood-shop projects, and structural design. Creative problem solving, computer skills and digital image making round out the Foundations curriculum.

LIBERAL STUDIES

At RMCAD we believe the liberal arts are the essential human context within which all art is made. Artists and designers who understand the essential ideas of civilization — the civilizations of history and of the times in which we live now — will have much to say in their chosen fields and in their own work.

CAMPUS FACILITIES AND EQUIPMENT

After experiencing many years of growth at a location on the eastern side of the city, RMCAD moved in 2003 to its current location in Lakewood, a west-central suburb of Denver.

RMCAD's 23-acre wooded campus combines modern approaches to learning in a historical setting. Our unique campus contains 13 buildings, all but two of which are on the National Historic Register.

TUITION, ROOM, BOARD AND FEES

Starting with the 2008-2009 academic year, RMCAD's tuition rate is $11,496 per semester for full time enrollment (12 - 18 credit hours), which includes all fees. Students are advised to budget $600 - $800 per term for books and supplies.

There is no housing requirement for new students, but students are encouraged to live at The Regency (www.regencystudenthousing.com). Current room and board rates are available on The Regency website or by calling 303.447.1950.

FINANCIAL AID

RMCAD awards Federal and state Financial Aid to students who qualify through the Free Application for Federal Student Aid (FAFSA). New students can also apply for a talent scholarship.

ADMISSIONS PROCESS

Rocky Mountain College of Art + Design selectively admits students who have a desire to explore new possibilities, work hard to realize their personal best, and who are eager to produce original, innovative works. Although a variety of evaluation criteria are necessary for a sound admission decision, evidence of potential in the college's fine and applied art disciplines is the primary consideration in the Admissions Process.

RMCAD has a continuous enrollment process. Applications are reviewed for any up-coming semester upon receipt of all admissions materials. In order to provide optimal service, it is recommended students wait no longer than 1 month before the start of any term to begin the Admission Process. RMCAD accepts application paperwork, admits and accepts students and/or awards Financial Aid after the priority dates.

Applicants are notified in writing of their acceptance as soon as the application requirements have been filled, with most decisions made within two weeks from the date all documents are received. Students with transfer credits from accredited colleges will receive a credit evaluation prior to scheduling. All admission decisions are binding. An appeal will be heard only if a student is able to introduce new information or material that has not already been reviewed in making the original decision. Acceptance alone does not secure enrollment in the College. Accepted students are required to sign an Intent to Enroll agreement and remit a non-refundable deposit of $150 in order to secure their place in the incoming class and be scheduled into classes. The $150 deposit will be applied toward the first semester tuition bill.

Application Process for Domestic (U.S.) Students

1. Application for Admission—Submit a completed Application for Admission and $50 application fee. You may also apply online via our website at www.rmcad.edu

2. Transcripts—Official or unofficial high school transcripts or GED test scores should be sent directly to the Admissions Department. Transfer students must submit official transcripts from each college attended. Credit may not be awarded at a later date from colleges not listed on the application. Applicants who do not possess a cumulative grade point average of 2.0 or higher may be admitted with a provisional status.

3. Interview—An interview with an Admissions Counselor, either in person or by telephone, is required. Through the personal interview, applicants will gain a better understanding of the visual arts education at Rocky Mountain College of Art + Design. To arrange an interview time, please contact the Admissions Office.

4. Portfolio—We require both advanced students with extensive artistic training, as well as eager students who have had limited exposure to artistic training, to produce a portfolio. Students seeking admission to the Interior Design program do not need to submit a portfolio. Digital portfolio submissions are preferred, although photographs or slides are acceptable. Original work, except for sketchbooks, will not be accepted unless you receive special permission from your Admissions Counselor. You may also submit one sketchbook as evidence of your conceptual development. Time-based media such as video or computer animation on a CD-ROM or floppy disk may also be presented for consideration.

5. Standardized Test Scores—You must take the SAT or ACT examination and have your test score sent to RMCAD either at the time you take the test, or a copy of your score can be included when you provide your transcripts. This requirement applies to first-time freshmen students only, not transfer students, returning students or students with a prior degree. Your score will be used for the purpose of academic counseling and placement, but it is not a factor in the admission decision.

6. Personal Statement—All students must submit a personal statement, no longer than 1 page in length, which provides insight to your goals, interests, educational and artistic aspirations. Please send this with your Application for Admission form.

SAINT ANSELM COLLEGE

AT A GLANCE

As a four-year Catholic liberal arts college in the Benedictine tradition, Saint Anselm College seeks to provide an educational experience that promotes your intellectual, spiritual, and personal growth. Saint Anselm College encourages you not only to challenge yourself academically, but also to lead a life that is both creative and generous.

Because democracy depends on active participation of citizens, Saint Anselm College is committed to graduating men and women who view themselves as citizens of their communities and of the world.

LOCATION AND ENVIRONMENT

Nestled in its breathtaking New Hampshire surroundings, the Saint Anselm campus melds traditional and contemporary architecture to create a beautiful academic environment. Students from 21 countries and 28 states attend the College. Roughly 88 percent of Saint Anselm's students enjoy on-campus housing in apartments, dormitories, suites, and townhouses.

Situated on the outer edge of Manchester, New Hampshire's largest city, Saint Anselm College provides the advantages of a chiefly residential neighborhood in a suburban locale. Manchester has a great deal to offer, including a variety of movie theaters, restaurants, and shopping malls. Furthermore, public transportation runs hourly between Manchester and the campus. Southern New Hampshire provides a perfect atmosphere for students desiring a dynamic college lifestyle. The exciting city of Boston, the majestic mountains, and Hampton Beach on the Atlantic Ocean are all within an hour's drive from campus.

OFF-CAMPUS OPPORTUNITIES

The majority of departments throughout Saint Anselm College offer internship positions to students who wish to apply their classroom knowledge to a real-life work experience. Students normally acquire internship positions as juniors or seniors. Internships are offered in Boston, in and around Manchester, New York City, or in Washington, DC.

Saint Anselm encourages students to consider spending a year, semester, or summer studying in another country (usually during the junior year). Studying abroad presents an invaluable opportunity to gain a more informed perspective on your world, your country, and yourself.

In recent years, students have studied marine biology on Australia's Great Barrier Reef, art history in the museums of Florence, finance in London, language in Spain and France, and political history in Ireland.

Students' experiences studying abroad often remain the most memorable times of their college careers. In addition to the obvious cultural benefits gained from living abroad, students often make intellectual and personal gains as well. Experience studying abroad is a desirable qualification on your r sum.

In lieu of participating in study abroad during the academic year, students can sign up for faculty-led programs which include travel to such destinations as France, Greece, Italy, and Spain during the summer.

For more information about studying abroad, contact the Office of Academic Advisement at (603) 641-7465.

MAJORS AND DEGREES OFFERED

At Saint Anselm College, students may pursue the Bachelor of Arts degree in accounting, biochemistry, biology, business, chemistry, classics, computer science, computer science with business, computer science with mathematics, criminal justice, economics, English, environmental science, financial economics, fine arts, French, history, international business, international relations, liberal studies in the great books, mathematics, mathematics with economics, natural science, philosophy, physics, politics, psychology, sociology, Spanish, and theology. A program that leads to the Bachelor of Science in Nursing (BSN) degree is also offered at the College.

Saint Anselm students may pursue pre-professional programs in dentistry, education (secondary), law, medicine, and theology.

A 3-2 engineering program is offered in partnership with the University of Notre Dame, University of Massachusetts-Lowell, Catholic University of America, and Manhattan College.

ACADEMIC PROGRAMS

Students at Saint Anselm College are provided with an outstanding liberal arts education. Students normally take between 10 and 15 courses directly related to their major; the remainder of the 40 courses needed in order to graduate consist of liberal arts core curriculum and a variety of electives. Students in the Honors Program take additional courses in order to earn their Honors Degree.

As freshmen and sophomores, all students take part in Saint Anselm's humanities program, which is a nationally recognized program. This rigorous program known as "Portraits of Human Greatness" focuses on a series of group seminars and lectures that explore various facets of western civilization.

Saint Anselm College is also home to the New Hampshire Institute of Politics (NHIOP). The NHIOP is a place where students of all majors interact with world leaders, members of Congress, scholars, journalists, public policy makers, public officials, and innovators of all types. All Saint Anselm College students will have courses held at the NHIOP.

Saint Anselm takes part in the College Board's Advanced Placement program. Students who earn a score of 3 or greater on the AP examinations may gain credit and advanced placement in the related course of study. Students who have taken examinations through the College-Level Examination Program may be awarded credit and advanced placement if they earn satisfactory scores.

CAMPUS FACILITIES AND EQUIPMENT

Saint Anselm College has over 41 different campus facilities. The John Maurus Carr Activities Center is a versatile recreational area that includes a complete fitness center as well as racquetball courts. The Davison Hall dining area, open all day long, provides a spacious and pleasant atmosphere in which students enjoy spending time.. Additional facilities include the Academic Resource Center, the Cushing Student Center (where students will find career and academic counseling services), health services, the Multicultural Center, Stoutenburgh Gymnasium (where varsity games are played), Sullivan Ice Arena, and The New Hampshire Institute of Politics—home of the 1st in the nation Presidential Primary.

Saint Anselm residential housing accommodates more than 1,800 students in various living arrangements, from traditional residence halls to suites, townhouses, and apartments. More than 88 percent of students choose to live on campus and enjoy a balance of academic study, rest and relaxation, and social life.

Housing is guaranteed for all four years to students who enter as freshmen. Each residence hall has a staff of student resident assistants (RAs) and a residence director (RD) who assist students and are responsible for maintaining the College's residence hall regulations.

TUITION, ROOM, BOARD AND FEES

The 2007-2008 school year tuition is $26,960, and room and board costs are $10,200.

FINANCIAL AID

Saint Anselm provides students with financial aid opportunities through both private and federal aid programs. The College provides financial aid to offset the reasonable monetary investment that the student and family are expected to contribute. 86 percent of the College's undergraduates receive some degree of financial aid. Saint Anselm's financial aid opportunities include grants, loans, scholarships, and employment positions. Merit awards (Presidential Scholarships) are awarded to outstanding students. Two forms are required in applying for aid; the student must submit the CSS/Financial Aid PROFILE and the Free Application for Federal Student Aid (FAFSA) by March 15.

STUDENT ORGANIZATIONS AND ACTIVITIES

Student government helps to create an atmosphere of camaraderie and unity on campus. Saint Anselm's student government consists of three branches: Campus Activities Board, the Class Councils, and the Student Senate. The student government's primary goal is to ensure that all students have as many educational opportunities open to them as possible. Student government coordinates academic, cultural, and social, functions, all of which are essential to a broad liberal arts education.

There are over 80 organizations catering to a wide variety of interests. Among these are the Abbey Players (theater group), choral groups, the debate group, an economics club, a jazz band, a local Knights of Columbus chapter, a music society, an outing club, a pre-law society, a pre-med society, and a volunteer center.

Saint Anselm offers men's intercollegiate sports in baseball, basketball, cross-country, football, golf, ice hockey, lacrosse, skiing, soccer, and tennis and offers women's sports in basketball, cross-country, field hockey, ice hockey, lacrosse, skiing, soccer, softball, tennis, and volleyball. Intramural sports at the College include basketball, ice hockey, indoor and outdoor soccer, racquetball, softball, tennis, and volleyball. There are men's and women's club sports in Alpine, cycling, rugby, ski and snowboard, swimming, and track. Thee is also a cheerleading club for women, and a volleyball club for men.

ADMISSIONS PROCESS

In reviewing applicants to the freshman class, the admissions committee considers each prospective student individually and carefully. The committee assesses each applicant's secondary school performance, SAT I or ACT scores, recommendation letters, and the written essay included in the application for admission. Of highest priority is the applicant's secondary school transcript, with a specific focus on both the rigor of course study and the marks received. Saint Anselm invites transfer and international students to apply.

Saint Anselm College has the following admission deadlines:

Early Decision, December 1st

Nursing Majors, January 15th

International Citizens, February 1st

Priority Filing for Regular Decision, March 1st

It is highly suggested that all students visit the Saint Anselm College campus for a tour, information session and/or interview.

For more information, students should contact:

Office of Admission

Saint Anselm College

100 Saint Anselm Drive

Manchester, NH 03102-1310

Telephone: 603-641-7500 or 888-426-7356 (toll-free)

Fax: 603-641-7550

Email: admission@anselm.edu

World Wide Web: www.anselm.edu

SAINT EDWARD'S UNIVERSITY

AT A GLANCE

Located in Austin, Texas —a diverse and thriving city—St. Edward's University provides an ideal combination of highly qualified teachers, individual attention and a community focused on service. St. Edward's is a private, Catholic, liberal arts university with about 5,220 students. Undergraduates come from 37 states, 37 countries, and a variety of faiths and walks of life. Thirty-one percent are Hispanic, 3 percent are African American, 3 percent are Asian/Pacific Islander, and 3 percent are international students. The university also has 900-plus graduate students pursuing degrees in six programs, including Business Administration and Human Services.

St. Edward's was founded by the Congregation of Holy Cross in 1885. This Catholic heritage endures today through the Holy Cross ideals of thinking critically, acting ethically, appreciating diversity, striving for social justice and developing the courage to take risks. Professors at St. Edward's guide students through hands-on research and projects to solve problems creatively.

LOCATION AND ENVIRONMENT

Austin, the capital of Texas, is a regional center for politics, education and culture. The city lies in the Texas Hill Country along the Colorado River. With the fourth-largest population in the state, Austin offers unlimited opportunities to enjoy the arts and recreation, including galleries, museums and theaters that highlight the city's vibrant artistic community. National and local music acts find the spotlight at more than 100 venues, including those along Sixth Street, the most popular stretch of nightspots in town. Dubbed the "Live Music Capital of the World," Austin hosts the world-renowned South by Southwest music and film festival each spring. With a diverse population made up of approximately 40 percent minorities, Austin also offers a variety of city events, such as Mardi Gras, the Pecan Street Festival, the Bob Marley Fest, and more.

Outdoor enthusiasts take advantage of 300 days of sunshine, more than 200 parks, and three major lakes. They also find a wealth of opportunity for boating, canoeing rowing, tubing, swimming, wind surfing, water skiing, cycling, mountain biking, hiking, rock climbing, frisbee golf, camping and more. And after working up an appetite, it's nice to know that Austin has the highest per capita restaurant population in the state—higher than Houston, Dallas or San Antonio. It's not surprising that Austin has been named the country's coolest, best-read, most computer-literate and most fit city, as well as the third best place to live in the United States.

MAJORS AND DEGREES OFFERED

St. Edward's offers bachelor's degrees through five schools. Students in the School of Behavioral and Social Sciences can earn undergraduate degrees in:

- Criminal Justice
- Criminology
- Environmental Science and Policy
- Forensic Science
- Global Studies
- History
- Latin American Studies
- Political Science
- Psychology
- Social Work
- Sociology

School of Management and Business students can earn degrees in:

- Accounting
- Accounting Information Technology
- Business Administration
- Digital Media
- Economics
- Entrepreneurship
- Finance
- International Business
- Management
- Marketing

Degrees through the School of Natural Sciences are available in:

- Biochemistry
- Bioinformatics
- Biology
- Chemistry
- Computer Information Science
- Computer Science
- Environmental Chemistry
- Forensic Chemistry
- Mathematics

The School of Humanities offers degrees in:

- Art
- Communication
- English Literature
- English Writing and Rhetoric
- Graphic Design
- Liberal Studies
- Philosophy
- Photocommunications
- Religious Studies
- Spanish
- Theater Arts

The School of Education also prepares students to teach in early childhood, elementary, middle school or secondary settings. Certification subject areas include art, kinesiology, English/language arts, bilingual education, biology, chemistry, history, mathematics, social studies, Spanish and theater. Students may also pursue certification in secondary religious education for Catholic schools.

Students who have not chosen a major participate in the innovative Academic Exploration Program, designed to familiarize students with their own strengths and interests as well as the university's Academic Programs.

In addition, St. Edward's offers pre-professional programs in Dentistry, Engineering, Law, Medicine and Physical Therapy. Six master's programs are also available:

- Master of Arts in Counseling
- Master of Arts in Human Services
- Master of Business Administration
- Master of Liberal Arts
- Master of Science in Computer Information Systems
- Master of Science in Organizational Leadership and Ethics

ACADEMIC PROGRAMS

Each student completes an intensive, 57-credit-hour general education program that covers three areas: foundational skills (college math, computational skills, English writing, foreign language and oral communication); cultural foundations (a six-course cluster including American Dilemmas, Literature and Human Experience, and Contemporary World Issues); and foundation for values and decision (a five-course cluster that includes Ethics and Science in Perspective). A course called Capstone—focusing on oral and written examination, analysis, and problem solving of a controversial topic—is the culmination of the gen-ed program.

A vital aspect of the St. Edward's experience is a focus on career exploration, preparation (through workshops and advising), and experience (through internships). Graduate school guidance is also available. Nearly all of the majors at St. Edward's include opportunities for internships or research. Because opportunities are so prevalent, interested students can participate in more than one internship or research experience. And adventurous students can learn about the university's study abroad and work abroad opportunities by contacting the Office of International Education.

Students must complete 120 credit hours to graduate. St. Edward's operates on a two-semester basis. Day and evening class are available during the summer.

CAMPUS FACILITIES AND EQUIPMENT

A range of academic, recreational, and service-oriented facilities are part of the university's 198-acre hilltop campus. One of the crowning architectural features of this hilltop campus is Main Building, a 100-year-old edifice that has been designated a Texas Historic Landmark.

With a collage of modern and historic buildings, the St. Edward's campus reflects a legacy of progress. Other campus buildings include five residential halls, including Dujarié Hall, which opened in 2005, and various student apartments for upperclassmen. Also on campus are academic building Trustee Hall, Scarborough-Phillips Library, the Mary Moody Northen Theatre, the Recreation and Convocation Center, and the Robert and Pearle Ragsdale Center. Inside the Ragsdale Center is the Meadows Coffeehouse, the South Congress Market cafeteria, the Jones Auditorium, the Mabee Ballrooms, the Student Life Office, a computing center, and study rooms. At the RCC students can take advantage of a fitness center, an indoor pool, and basketball, volleyball, and racquetball/handball courts. Unless living at their parents' home, freshmen must stay in residence halls. Sophomores may also choose on-campus housing. On-campus residence halls include communal kitchens, laundry rooms, and computer facilities. Internet access is provided for each room, and a computer helpline and resident technology assistant provide assistance with technical problems.

The small classes that are held in university classrooms signify a dedication to individual attention. Moody Hall is the site of many class meetings. Academic Planning and Support, the Office of Career Planning, the Office of International Education, and the Counseling and Consultation Center are also found in Moody Hall. The Fine Arts Center includes studios and professional-grade labs for photo processing. In addition, the 65,000-square-foot John Brooks Williams Natural Sciences Center-North Building opened in Fall 2006 and features state-of-the-art classrooms and laboratories.

TUITION, ROOM, BOARD AND FEES

Tuition for the 2008-2009 academic year is $22,150. Room and board costs range from $5,855 to $8,509, with variations according to selection of residence hall and meal plan. Freshmen who received grants were awarded an average of $10,965 in assistance, not including loans and campus jobs, and 89 percent of freshmen received some form of aid. Annually, St. Edward's awards more than $14 million in financial assistance.

FINANCIAL AID

St. Edward's University is dedicated to making education affordable for its students and their families. Financial assistance at St. Edward's is provided through federal, state, and university sources and includes grants, scholar awards, loans, and work-study. As part of the Admission Process, each student is automatically reviewed for academic scholar awards. These scholarships are distributed on the basis of merit. Students awarded academic scholarships are granted between $5,000 and $11,000 annually for all four years. To be considered, students must rank within the top 25 percent of their graduating high-school classes and earn SAT critical reading plus math scores of at least 1100 or ACT scores of at least 24.

Other considerations include participation in extracurricular activities and strength of the admissions essay. Interested students should submit their applications for admission by Feb. 1 for scholar award consideration and the best financial assistance package.

All applicants are encouraged to file the Free Application for Federal Student Aid, or FAFSA. March 1 is the priority deadline to complete the FAFSA for students who plan to start in the fall semester. Families not applying for Financial Aid should inquire about payment options through the Office of Student Financial Services.

STUDENT ORGANIZATIONS AND ACTIVITIES

While classes are small and personal, St. Edward's offers a large variety of student organizations—more than 70 in all. Students at the university share extracurricular interests in academic and professional pursuits, in cultural and community service activities, in social and special interest topics. The student body is encouraged to be vocal, and the Student Government Association—consisting of elected members of the student body and representatives from constituencies around campus—is the primary vehicle for the student voice. The Association holds general meetings every two weeks to organize and implement campus activities. The president of the Association is in regular attendance at the meetings of the Board of Trustees.

Aspiring writers often contribute to the university's student-run newspaper, creative journal, and academic journal. Students taking part in the University Programming Board and the Residence Hall Association coordinate campus-wide events. St. Edward's hosts popular comedians, independent film screenings, poetry readings, and well-known local bands. The university's volunteer fair provides service-oriented students with an incredible number of possibilities to get involved in the surrounding community.

As an NCAA Division II member, St. Edward's offers plenty of opportunities for its athletes. Men's teams include baseball, basketball, cross country, golf, soccer, and tennis. Women have teams in basketball, cross country, soccer, softball, tennis and volleyball. On the club level, soccer and lacrosse are available. And let's not forget a range of intramural sports.

ADMISSIONS PROCESS

All applicants to St. Edward's are reviewed individually and evaluated according to demonstrations of academic accomplishment, challenging curriculum, extracurricular participation, and results on standardized tests. Candidates for admission should have finished among the top half of their high-school class and earned a minimum score of 500 on both the critical reading and math sections of the SAT or a composite score of 21 on the ACT. Students are required to submit the results of the applicable writing test.

The University accepts applications on a rolling basis. A student will be notified of admissions decisions four weeks after the Office of Admission has received the student's completed file. A file is not complete until each of the following has been submitted: the application form, the nonrefundable application fee, results from the SAT or ACT test, and official transcripts from high school. Students are encouraged to submit personal statements and recommendation letters, though they are not mandatory. For more specific information on the policies and procedures of admission, visit the University web site at www.gotostedwards.com.

For additional information, please contact:

Office of Admission

St. Edward's University

3001 South Congress Avenue

Austin, TX 78704-6489

Telephone: 512-448-8500 or 800-555-0164 (toll free)

Fax: 512-464-8877

E-mail: seu.admit@ stedwards.edu

Web: www.gotostedwards.com

SAINT JOHN'S UNIVERSITY

AT A GLANCE

One of America's leading Catholic universities, St. John's University offers world-class academics, high-tech resources, dynamic study abroad programs and friendly residential campuses in exciting New York City.

Founded in 1870 by the Vincentian Fathers, St. John's has five campuses: a 105-acre residential campus in Queens, NY; a 16.5-acre residential campus on Staten Island, New York; a ten-story campus in Manhattan's financial district; a 175-acre location in Oakdale, NY; and a Graduate Center in Rome, Italy.

St. John's is chartered by the State Education Department of New York and accredited by the Middle States Association of Colleges and Schools. Its varied Academic Programs are accredited by such leading organizations as AACSB International - the Association to Advance Collegiate Schools of Business; the American Council on Pharmaceutical Education; the American Library Association; and the American Bar Association.

LOCATION AND ENVIRONMENT

St. John's park-like Queens Campus is in a quiet residential area near to the Grand Central Parkway. The Staten Island campus is a few miles from the Verrazano-Narrows Bridge. Each campus is a short drive to the unsurpassed attractions of Manhattan, including the Museum Mile, Greenwich Village and Times Square.

The Manhattan campus is located in the heart of the Financial District, near Wall Street, TriBeCa and City Hall.

St. John's Oakdale location is on the South Shore of Suffolk County. The Rome Graduate Center is located at the Pontificio Oratorio San Pietro, off Via Aurelia on Via Santa Maria Mediatrice.

MAJORS AND DEGREES OFFERED

St. John's students may choose from over 100 Academic Programs in five undergraduate colleges. At the Queens campus, St. John's College of Liberal Arts and Sciences confers the Bachelor of Arts in anthropology, economics, English, environmental studies (social science), French, government and politics, history, Italian, mathematics, philosophy, psychology, public administration and public service, sociology, Spanish, speech (general and public address), speech pathology and audiology, and theology.

The Bachelor of Science is offered in biology, chemistry, environmental studies (ecology), mathematical physics, mathematics, physical science, and physics.

St. John's confers the Bachelor of Fine Arts in fine arts, creative photography, graphic design, and illustration.

Also available is a BA/MA program in English, government and politics, history, mathematics, sociology, Spanish, and theology. Other accelerated degree programs include five-year BS/MS programs in biology and chemistry; a BA/JD or BS/JD degree combining any undergraduate degree with a law degree from St. John's School of Law; a BS/OD degree combining an undergraduate biology degree with a Doctor of Optometry degree from the State University of new York College of Optometry; a BS/DPM degree combining an undergraduate biology degree with a Doctor of Podiatric Medicine Degree from the New York College of Podiatric Medicine; and a BS/MS degree combining an undergraduate biology degree with Master of Science in Biomedical Engineering from Polytechnic University.

A pre-MBA program is available to students pursuing the bachelor's degree at St. John's College.

Students also may pursue a BA in Asian studies and a five-year BA/MA in East Asian studies through the Institute of Asian Studies.

The Peter J. Tobin College of Business confers the BS in accounting, actuarial science, economics, finance, management, management information systems, marketing and risk management. Business students may also pursue a five-year BS/MS in accounting.

The School of Education offers a number of programs, including those leading to the Bachelor of Science degree in education (BSEd) both in childhood education grades 1-6 and childhood education/special education grades 1-6; the school also offers a BS/MS degree in childhood education/special education. Also offered is the BSEd in adolescent education, with concentrations in English grades 7-12; biology 7-12; mathematics grades 7-12; physical science 7-12; social studies grades 7-12; and Spanish grades 7-12.

The College of Pharmacy and Allied Health Professions confers the Doctor of Pharmacy (PharmD, six years) and the Bachelor of Science in medical technology, pathologist assistant, physician assistant and toxicology.

The College of Professional Studies offers programs leading to the BS degree in administrative studies, advertising communication, communication arts, computer science, criminal justice, funeral service administration, health services administration, hospitality management, homeland and corporate security, human services, information technology, journalism, legal studies, public relations, sport management, telecommunications, and television and film production. The College also offers five-year BS/MA programs in communication arts/government and politics; communication arts/sociology; criminal justice/government and politics; criminal justice/sociology; health-care administration/government and politics; health-care administration/sociology; journalism/government and politics; and paralegal studies/sociology.

Undergraduates in any field may pursue a combined BA/JD or BS/JD degree program.

The College of Professional Studies also offers an AA degree in liberal arts and AS degrees in business (accounting option), criminal justice, information technology, legal studies, telecommunications and television and film. The College offers certificates programs in business administration, computer science, health services administration, legal studies, sport management, and telecommunications. Evening and weekend options are available for most programs.

At the Staten Island campus, St. John's College of Liberal Arts and Sciences confers the BA or BS degree in computer science, English, government and politics, history, mathematics, philosophy, psychology, social studies, sociology, speech language pathology and theology. A five-year BA/MA program in government and politics is available, as are BA/JD or BS/JD degrees combining any undergraduate degree with a law degree from St. John's School of Law.

The Peter J. Tobin College of Business at Staten Island confers the BS in accounting, actuarial science, finance, management, marketing, and risk management and insurance. The school also offers a five-year BS/MS in accounting.

The School of Education at Staten Island offers the BSEd degree in childhood education grades 1-6, and childhood education/special education grades 1-6, and a BS/MS degree in childhood education/special education. Also available is the BS degree in adolescent education with concentrations in English, mathematics, and social studies.

The College of Professional Studies on the Staten Island campus offers a number of degree and certificate programs: the BS in administrative studies, communication arts, criminal justice, funeral service administration, health-care administration, hospitality management, paralegal studies, real estate management, safety and forensic science, funeral service administration, hospitality management, legal studies, sport management, telecommunications and television and film. Also offered is a combined BA/JD or BS/JD program, as well as AA and AS degrees in business, criminal justice, liberal arts, legal studies, telecommunications and television and film.

The Staten Island campus offers pre-professional programs in dentistry, engineering, law, medicine, osteopathy, social work, veterinary medicine, and other health-related fields.

ACADEMIC PROGRAMS

Students in St. John's College of Liberal Arts and Sciences must complete at least 126 semester hours to graduate with a BA or BS; 144 semester hours are required for the BFA. The various degrees awarded at the School of Education and Human Services require students to complete between 126 and 139 semester hours.

Students in the College of Professional Studies must complete 126 or 127 semester hours for the BS and BA degree. The Tobin College of Business generally requires 130 to 134 semester hours to graduate. For the six-year pharmacy program at the College of Pharmacy and Allied Health Professions, students complete a minimum of 201 semester hours. The physician assistant program requires the completion of 134 semester hours; the toxicology or pathologist assistant program requires 133 semester hours to complete, and 132 semester hours are required for the medical technology program.

Associate degrees are awarded to students completing 60 to 63 semester hours.

All undergraduates must complete core curriculum requirements, major requirements, and distribution requirements covering their choice of electives.

CAMPUS FACILITIES AND EQUIPMENT

The St. John's University Libraries comprise three major research libraries on two campuses. Their collections total more than 1.7 million volumes of books, periodicals, microfilm, microfiche, and audiovisual materials.

The Queens campus is home to the Main Library and the Law School Library. St. Augustine Hall houses the Main Library, including a selective depository for United States government documents. The Main Library also comprises the Governor Hugh L. Carey Collection, the William M. Fischer Lawn Tennis Library, the Asian Collection, the Health Education Resource Center, an instructional materials center containing pre-K through grade 12 curriculum materials, and a media center.

At Staten Island, the Loretto Memorial Library includes a collection of literary masterpieces, a record collection of music and poetry readings, a language laboratory, and an audiovisual department.

Both campuses feature state-of-the-art computer laboratories, with approximately 400 microcomputers available for student use. There are more than 100 high-tech classrooms and advanced laboratories for research in biology, chemistry, physics, pharmacy, and allied health majors. The Queens campus also has a language laboratory.

On the Queens campus, a magnificent "residential village" and new residential townhouses offer students the best in on-campus living, including wireless connectivity, 24-hour security, club space, and a spacious dining hall. On Staten Island, students can choose comfortable, apartment-style residences adjacent to campus.

TUITION, ROOM, BOARD AND FEES

Full-time tuition (12-18 credits a semester) is $26,200 per academic year. Tuition can vary according to program and class year. All students must pay annual fees of $500. Average room and board is $11,050.

Students may wish to consider our Fixed Rate Tuition Option, which guarantees a single tuition rate for the full four years of undergraduate study.

FINANCIAL AID

During 2006-2007 academic year, approximately 95% of St. John's students received in excess of $338 million in financial assistance through scholarships, loans, grants and work-study programs.

STUDENT ORGANIZATIONS AND ACTIVITIES

More than 180 student clubs and academic organizations are available to St. John's students. Clubs and organizations are funded through St. John's active Student Government, which serves as a liaison between students and the faculty and administration.

The Student Government provides motivated students with the opportunity to assume leadership roles within the University community. Students also can leadership experience through the Residence Hall Association.

ADMISSIONS PROCESS

The Office of Admission considers an applicant's record of academic achievement, performance on appropriate standardized tests, letters of recommendations, and other indications of academic promise and personal motivation.

To be admitted, students must earn a minimum of 16 academic units at an accredited high school or receive an appropriate score on the GED test. Units of high-school study should include 4 English; 2 mathematics (elementary algebra, plane geometry, or 10th-year mathematics); 2 foreign language; 1 history; 1 science; and 6 electives, (a minimum of 3 in academic subjects). Requirements can vary from program to program.

Applicants must submit an official high school transcript, official standardized test scores (SAT I or ACT), and a signed, completed application for admission. St. John's welcomes transfer students, who constitute a large portion of the undergraduate student body. Transfer applicants should forward all academic records—high school and college—to the Office of Admission. Applications may arrive any time, with the exception of pharmacy degree candidates, whose applications are due by February 1. The Office of Admission conducts on-campus interviews.

For further information, contact:

St. John's University Office of Admissions at 1 (877) 404-0105, select option 2 or visit us at www.stjohns.edu/learnmore/01314.stj.

SAINT LAWRENCE UNIVERSITY

AT A GLANCE

St. Lawrence University is a private, independent, non-denominational, university that seeks to provide a stimulating and rigorous liberal arts education to undergraduate students chosen for their intellectual potential and seriousness of purpose. Chartered in 1856, it is New York State's oldest continuously coeducational college or university. St. Lawrence's 2,100 students arrive from 41 states and 24 countries. The school is situated in Canton, New York (pop. 6,500), midway between the Adirondacks Mountains and Ottawa, Canada's national capital. The University provides unmatched access to social and cultural opportunities, international government, and outdoor recreation.

LOCATION AND ENVIRONMENT

St. Lawrence University provides a distinctive learning environment, offering 35 majors, 35 minors, 14 interdepartmental programs, and 3 graduate programs in education. Its First-Year Program is nationally recognized. St. Lawrence offers international study programs in 14 nations; it also belongs to the International Student Exchange Program. The University offers three off-campus programs within the United States, including a semester program in the Adirondack wilderness. St. Lawrence is currently undergoing an educational renaissance; bold academic initiatives are underway to maximize the learning potential of each and every student. A major facilities upgrade, fueled by a $130 million capital campaign, is providing expanded resources to undergraduates.

OFF-CAMPUS OPPORTUNITIES

St. Lawrence University offers international programs in 14 countries: Australia, Austria, Canada, China, Costa Rica, Denmark, England, France, India, Italy, Japan, Kenya, Spain, and Trinidad and Tobago; students can also direct-enroll in foreign universities in more than 35 additional countries through the International Student Exchange Program (ISEP).

The University also offers three off-campus study programs within the United States. These are located at: American University, Washington, D.C.; Fisk University, Nashville, Tennessee; and the Adirondack Semester, near Tupper Lake, New York.

MAJORS AND DEGREES OFFERED:

Students may major in: African studies, anthropology, Asian studies, biochemistry, biology, biology/physics, Canadian studies, chemistry, computer science, conservation biology, economics, economics/mathematics, English, environmental studies, fine arts, French, geology, geology/physics, German, global studies, government, history, mathematics, mathematics/computer science, multi-field (self-designed), multi-language, music, neuroscience, performance & communication arts, philosophy, physics, psychology, religious studies, sociology, and Spanish.

Students may pursue an optional minor in: African studies, anthropology, applied statistics, Asian studies, biology, Canadian studies, Caribbean and Latin American studies, chemistry, computer science, cultural encounters, economics, education, European studies, film studies, fine arts, French, gender studies, geology, German, global studies, government, history, literature (English), mathematics, multi-field, music, outdoor studies, philosophy, physics, psychology, religious studies, sociology, speech and theatre, Spanish, sports studies and exercise science, US cultural and ethnic studies and writing (English).

ACADEMIC PROGRAMS

The University confers the Bachelor of Arts and Bachelor of Science degrees; it also awards graduate degrees in education.

35 majors are available, as is the option to declare a double major.

The University offers 35 optional minors.

Qualified students may pursue five-year programs in business administration (this program leads to the MBA) and engineering, combining coursework at St. Lawrence with work at other institutions.

Specialized advising is available for postgraduate work in dentistry, law, medicine, and veterinary medicine.

The St. Lawrence distribution requirements involve coursework in six areas.

All students are expected to demonstrate writing competence before graduating.

The University provides extensive opportunities for honors projects and independent work.

CAMPUS FACILITIES AND EQUIPMENT

The University's two libraries, the Owen D. Young Library and Launders Science Library, contain more than half a million volumes, electronic resources, and ample space for reading and research. "ODY" completed thorough renovations in summer 1999 to provide more group study space and greater electronic access to resources.

Students also enjoy an arts center with recital hall, two theaters, and an art gallery as well as a 7,000-piece art collection. It has undergone recent significant renovations and additional renovation plans are underway.

St. Lawrence's science complex—including the new Johnson Hall of Science—is connected to the science library and computing center.

A 15,000-square-foot Student Center opened spring 2004, and new student townhouse-style residences for seniors opened fall 2003.

Recreational facilities include cross-country ski and running trails; a 133-station fitness center; a three-story clombing wall; indoor and outdoor tennis courts; and two gymnasium/fieldhouse complexes, one with a 9-lane/400-meter track and five tennis/basketball courts and the other with a 200-meter track, three tennis courts, and nine squash courts. Facilities also include a pool, ice arena, equestrian center, golf course, indoor golf facility, a new boathouse, astroturf field, baseball, soccer and softball fields.

Tuition, Room, Board and Fees

For the 2007-2008 academic year, the comprehensive fee (including tuition, fees, and typical room and board) is $44,660.

Typically, annual personal costs and book expenditures cost an additional $1,450.

FINANCIAL AID

St. Lawrence University offers merit scholarships as well as need-based financial assistance.

The school grants aid in some form to more than 84 percent of its students. Aid packages typically consist of grants, student loans, and campus jobs.

Aid applicants must submit the Free Application for Federal Student Aid (FAFSA) between January 1 and February 1, and request that results be sent to St. Lawrence. Applicants must also submit the St. Lawrence financial aid application or the CSS PROFILE form.

STUDENT ORGANIZATIONS AND ACTIVITIES

Undergraduates commence their studies with the First-Year Program, which places approximately 30 first-year students in communities that live and learn together.

Once they achieve upper-class status, students may choose to live in traditional residence halls, interest-based theme suites, theme cottages, Greek houses, or senior townhouses.

St. Lawrence provides a full range of services to students, including comprehensive career planning as well as graduate and professional school guidance

Students seeking co-curricular activities can choose from nearly 100 organizations, including everything from student government to interest groups to arts and culture.

St. Lawrence boasts 32 intercollegiate teams including NCAA Division I teams in men's and women's ice hockey. All other teams compete in the NCAA's Division III. Club sports are also available, as is participation in a broad range of popular intramural sports.

The University is home to numerous recreational facilities, including: a 133-station fitness center; a three-story climbing wall; cross-country ski and running trails; and indoor and outdoor tennis courts. Students enjoy access to two gymnasium/fieldhouse complexes; one has a 9-lane/400-meter track as well as five basketball/tennis courts, while the other has a 200-meter track, nine squash courts, and three tennis courts. Other facilities include an astroturf field; baseball, softball, and soccer fields; an equestrian center; a golf course; an indoor golf facility; an ice arena; a new boathouse; and a pool.

ADMISSIONS PROCESS

St. Lawrence seeks undergraduates with the capacity to manage a demanding academic regimen successfully. In addition, the ideal student contributes substantially to the quality of community life. The University strives to enroll students who represent the broadest possible range of economic, ethnic, geographic, and social backgrounds. The admissions committee values academic achievement, but ability in athletics, community service, or the creative arts is also considered a strong indicator of a student's capacity to benefit from his or her time at St. Lawrence. The University is test optional; students may choose whether they would like the results of their SAT Reasoning Test and/or ACT used during the evaluation process. Students are strongly encouraged to plan a campus visit; interviews may be scheduled to occur on campus. In certain areas, off-campus interviews are also an option.

The University makes no requirement of applicants' high school curricula; however, successful applicants generally demonstrate extensive preparation in the humanities, mathematics, the natural sciences, and the social sciences. Advanced Placement, IB and honors work are looked upon favorably, as they demonstrate the applicants intellectual curiosity and maturity. These are qualities that are highly sought by the admission committee.

St. Lawrence uses the Common Application exclusively and students are free to use any version of the Common Application. An application supplement is required and is available on-line or from the Admissions Office. The application processing fee is $60. Applicants pursuing regular decision should submit all materials by February 1; they will be notified by late March. Students whose first choice is St. Lawrence may apply for Early Decision: the deadlines for Early Decision applications are November 15 and January 15. Early decision applicants are notified approximately one month after the deadline. Applicants for transfer to St. Lawrence should submit all application materials by November 1 for the spring semester or March 1 for the fall semester.

To request an application or for more information, students should contact:

OFFICE OF ADMISSIONS AND FINANCIAL AID

St. Lawrence University

Canton, NY 13617

Telephone: 315-229-5261

800-285-1856 (toll free)

admissions@stlawu.edu

www.stlawu.edu

AOL AIM Screen Name: SLUAdmissions

SAINT LOUIS UNIVERSITY

AT A GLANCE

Saint Louis University is a Jesuit, Catholic university ranked among the top research institutions in the nation.

Founded in 1818, SLU is the first institution of higher education west of the Mississippi River and the second oldest Jesuit university in the United States.

Today, Saint Louis University fosters the intellectual and character development of more than 12,000 students on campuses in St. Louis, Missouri, and Madrid, Spain.

Our urban, residential campus in St. Louis has undergone more than $840 million in construction, renovations and beautification since 1987. The campus now includes the new $82 million Edward A. Doisy Research Center and $81 million Chaifetz Arena, a new on-campus multipurpose arena.

With more than 85 undergraduate majors and more than 50 graduate and professional programs, including highly ranked programs in business, law and engineering, students are sure to find the one that's right for them. Students also can take advantage of special opportunities such as direct-entry nursing and health sciences programs, early admission to the University's medical and law schools and study-abroad programs.

While academics are very important, a Saint Louis University education extends far beyond the classroom.

The University offers students something rare in higher education: the opportunity to study at a place where academic achievement and scientific advancement unite with community commitment and Jesuit values. Here, 99 percent of faculty members hold a Ph.D. or the highest degree in their field. And SLU students get to do more than just sit in class; they collaborate with premier scholars and researchers and conduct research that will change the face of their disciplines—and the lives of others.

SLU students come from all 50 states and more than 80 foreign countries. Six months after graduation, 94 percent of our graduates are either working or in graduate or professional school. SLU alumni have written books and movies, created comic book characters, become mayors of major cities, presidents of countries, helped put a man on the moon and even worked with Mother Theresa. They're also highly successful doctors, lawyers, physical therapists, engineers and social workers.

Learn more about SLU at www.slu.edu.

LOCATION AND ENVIRONMENT

At Saint Louis University, in St. Louis you'll be in the center of the county, right in the middle of it all. Our urban campus in midtown St. Louis has undergone more than $840 million in construction, renovations and beautification since 1987 and now stretches across more than 230 acres of flowers, fountains and lush greenery. Visitors say it's the "nicest city campus in the country." We invite you to check out our Web site, or better yet plan a visit and come see for yourself.

SLU's neighborhood, Midtown St. Louis, offers access to affordable living as well as the excitement of the Grand Center Arts district. Art. Theatre. Dance. From Powell Symphony Hall and the historic Fox Theatre to the St. Louis Black Repertory Company and the Contemporary Art Museum—it's all here, within walking distance of SLU.

Minutes away, you can play in Forest Park, one of the largest urban parks in the country, surpassing New York's Central Park. The site of the 1904 World's Fair, Forest Park today is home to the world-class St. Louis Art Museum, the St. Louis Zoo and lots of opportunities for recreation. Window-shop in the U. City Loop, the place for the fun, the funky and the unusual. Or head downtown and catch a game of one of St. Louis' three professional sports teams—the St. Louis Rams, the St. Louis Cardinals and the St. Louis Blues.

St. Louis is a big city—2.7 million people live in the greater St. Louis area—with small-town charm.

Home to the Gateway Arch, eight Fortune 500 companies and countless cultural, historic and sporting attractions, St. Louis is a great place to learn, live and make a difference.

But that's not all SLU has to offer. The University expanded internationally in 1969 by establishing a campus in Madrid, Spain. The first freestanding campus operated by an American university in Europe, the Madrid campus has been recognized by Spain's higher education authority as an official foreign university, the first United States institution ever so recognized.

OFF-CAMPUS OPPORTUNITIES

Midtown St. Louis offers access to affordable living as well as the excitement of the Grand Center Arts district. Art. Theatre. Dance. From Powell Symphony Hall and the historic Fox Theatre to the St. Louis Black Repertory Company and the Contemporary Art Museum—it's all here, within walking distance of SLU.

Minutes away, you can play in Forest Park, the site of the 1904 World's Fair and now home to the world-class St. Louis Art Museum, the St. Louis Zoo and lots of opportunities for recreation. Window-shop at the U. City Loop, the place for the fun, the funky and the unusual. Or head downtown and catch a game of one of St. Louis' three professional sports teams—the St. Louis Rams, the St. Louis Cardinals and the St. Louis Blues.

St. Louis is a big city—2.7 million people live in the greater St. Louis area—with small-town charm. The small-town feel coupled with the amenities of a large city helped St. Louis achieve its ranking as one of the best cities for young professionals.

Home to the Gateway Arch, eight Fortune 500 companies and a variety of cultural, historic and sporting attractions, St. Louis is a great place to learn, live and make a difference.

MAJORS AND DEGREES OFFERED

Saint Louis University offers more than 85 programs of study, with undergraduate degrees in the following areas:

Doisy College of Health Sciences

Athletic Training °; Clinical Laboratory Science; Cytotechnology; Health Administration; Health Information Management ; Investigative and Medical Sciences; Nuclear Medicine Technology; Nutrition and Dietetics (Culinary Emphasis); Occupational Science and Occupational Therapy °; Physical Therapy °; Radiation Therapy; Still Deciding (Health Sciences)

School of Nursing

Nursing

College of Arts and Sciences

American Studies; Art History; Biochemistry; Biology; Chemistry; Classical Humanities; Communication; Communication Sciences and Disorders; Computer Science; Criminal Justice; Economics (B.A.); English; Environmental Science; French; Geology; Geophysics; German; Greek and Latin Languages and Literature; History; International Studies; Mathematics; Meteorology; Music; Philosophy; Physics (B.A.); Political Science; Psychology; Russian; Sociology; Spanish; Still Deciding; Studio Art; Theater; Theological Studies; Women's Studies

John Cook School of Business

Business Administration (Areas of Emphasis): Accounting; Economics (B.S.); Entrepreneurship; Finance; Human Resource Management; International Business; Leadership and Change Management; Management Information Systems; Marketing; Still Deciding (Business)

Parks College of Engineering

Aviation and Technology; Aerospace Engineering; Aircraft Maintenance Management; Biomedical Engineering; Electrical Engineering (Areas of Emphasis: Computer Engineering; Bioelectronics; Flight Science); Mechanical Engineering; Physics (B.S.); Still Deciding (Engineering)

College of Education and Public Service

Education (Areas of Emphasis: Early Childhood; Elementary; Middle School; Secondary); Special Education (Areas of Emphasis: Behavior Disorders; Early Childhood; Learning Disabilities; Mental Handicaps); Urban Affairs; Still Deciding

School of Social Work

Social Work; Still Deciding

College of Philosophy and Letters

Philosophy °°

KEY

° A five-year, direct-entry master's degree program.

   Students are strongly encouraged to apply by December 1 for the Flight Science program.

° Physical Therapy is a direct-entry doctoral program. Students must apply by December 1 for consideration. NOTE: Admission decisions for the Physical Therapy program will be released in February 2009.

°° For students who are entering the Catholic priesthood only.

" For students who are "Still Deciding" but have not yet narrowed their interests to a particular college or school at the University.

Students who are "Still Deciding" but have narrowed their interests to either the College of Arts and Sciences, Doisy College of Health Sciences, John Cook School of Business, College of Education and Public Service or Parks College of Engineering, Aviation and Technology should choose the "Still Deciding" program that corresponds with the appropriate college or school.

ACADEMIC PROGRAMS

Saint Louis University offers more than 85 undergraduate programs of study and more than 50 graduate and professional programs. For more information, please visit www.slu.edu.

CAMPUS FACILITIES AND EQUIPMENT

Under the leadership of University President Lawrence Biondi, S.J., Saint Louis University has fueled a renaissance of midtown St. Louis. Saint Louis University improvements and expansions have totaled approximately $840 million since 1987. The University now stretches across more than 230 acres of flowers, fountains and lush greenery. Visitors often say it's the "nicest city campus in the country."

Saint Louis University recently unveiled the two most significant building projects in its history. The new $82 million Edward A. Doisy Research Center offers SLU's world-class researchers a world-class facility. The $81 million Chaifetz Arena is the new home for Billiken men's and women's basketball, volleyball and also will host concerts, family shows, sporting events, trade shows and other events. The arena complex consists of a 10,600-seat arena, athletics practice facility and offices and support facilities for all Division I sports and the athletic department.

Recent campus additions also include a new 40,000-foot expansion to the award-winning Simon Recreation Center, the 60,000-square-foot John and Lucy Cook Hall expansion of the John Cook School of Business and an expanded and renovated Busch Student Center. The SLU Laclede Park Recreational Complex includes three lakes, walking paths, a picnic area, waterfall, softball field and recreation fields. The campus is also home to the historic Cupples House, a fully restored mansion built in 1890, as well as several unique art galleries and St. Francis Xavier College Church, an outstanding example of English Gothic architecture.

TUITION, ROOM, BOARD AND FEES

Annual tuition for full-time undergraduate students is $30,330. Room and board amounts to approximately $8,760 per student (depending on specific residence hall and board plan). Fees average $300 per year.

FINANCIAL AID

Saint Louis University takes its Jesuit mission seriously. SLU is committed to serving others, in part, by providing financial access to a remarkable education.

In 2006-2007, 97 percent of first-time freshmen were awarded Financial Aid assistance. More than $249 million in total Financial Aid was awarded to students at Saint Louis University during the last fiscal year.

Saint Louis University scholarship programs are awarded based on academic merit, talents, service, leadership and financial need. In addition to SLU Financial Aid programs, the state of Missouri and the federal government also provide assistance.

Please contact our office of Scholarship and Financial Aid at 314-977-2350, 800-SLU-FOR-U or finaid@slu.edu.

STUDENT ORGANIZATIONS AND ACTIVITIES

Our students have interests and ideas enough to support more than 170 clubs, honor societies and service organizations; 16 NCAA Division I teams; intramural sports; and community service efforts that engage the SLU community in nearly 780,000 volunteer hours in a typical year.

Talent and commitment matter at Saint Louis University, and high levels of energy and dedication exist in everything our students pursue: academic societies, athletics, performing arts and media groups, student government, cultural and political organizations, and fraternities and sororities. Students come out in force to support Billiken sports, and the Simon Recreation Center is popular with both serious and more casual athletes. Co-curricular life extends throughout the campus with numerous lectures, films, festivals, concerts and plays.

ADMISSIONS PROCESS

For information on the Admission Process at Saint Louis University, or to schedule a campus visit, call the Office of Undergraduate Admission at 800-SLU-FOR-U, e-mail admitme@slu.edu, or visit www.slu.edu/x5186.xml.

SAINT MARY'S COLLEGE OF CALIFORNIA

AT A GLANCE

Saint Mary's College of California was founded in 1863, and is one of the oldest colleges in the Western United States. The school has been directed since 1868 by the Christian Brothers, the largest Catholic order dedicated exclusively to teaching. The founder of the order, Saint John Baptist de La Salle, is the patron saint of teachers.

Saint Mary's is a Division I college. We are a liberal arts college influenced by our rich Catholic and Lasallian traditions. We encourage an appreciation of all faiths, a respect for the dignity of human life, a willingness to explore the mystery of existence, and an understanding of the whole person—mind and body, soul and spirit. Our Lasallian traditions emphasize the power of teaching to transform the individual and a commitment to social justice and to one's community.

LOCATION AND ENVIRONMENT

Our 420-acre campus is set among rolling hills and marked by a stately chapel, villa-style architecture, quiet courtyards, and fragrant pines. The College is 20 miles east of San Francisco and is surrounded by natural treasures, from redwood forests to the Pacific coastline, from spectacular mountain ranges to alpine lakes.

OFF-CAMPUS OPPORTUNITIES

Nestled in the quaint, scenic town of Moraga, Saint Mary's overlooks the San Francisco Bay Area. Framed by the Pacific Ocean, the Golden Gate Strait, and the San Francisco Bay, the College is a short drive to San Francisco, Berkeley, and Oakland. All three of these communities offer a wealth of cultural and academic opportunities for the Saint Mary's student.

San Francisco features high-end boutiques, world-class culture, sprawling parks and bustling ethnic neighborhoods. It is also a hub of worldwide commerce, communications, and technology—and a great source of internships and career opportunities for Saint Mary's students.

Berkeley and Oakland are even closer to Saint Mary's than San Francisco. Berkeley is brash, brainy, and inventive. A small city stocked with tiny cafés, vast bookstores, and a serious commitment to social activism. Oakland is a mid-sized port city with major parks and museums, a strikingly renovated downtown, and civic festivals in every season.

The Bay Area also boasts a wealth of natural resources, including Mt. Diablo, the 2,000-acre Redwood Regional Park, Yosemite National Park, Lake Tahoe, the Mendocino coast, and the Pacific beaches.

MAJORS AND DEGREES OFFERED

Our academic program includes advanced study in 30 major fields—in the arts and humanities, the sciences and social sciences, education and business. Our labs and classes are small—averaging around 20 students—and student centered, enabling intense discussions, lively debates, and a strong sense that ideas matter. Many of our nearly 200 full-time professors are internationally renowned for their research and scholarship, all are skilled teachers and dedicated mentors, and virtually all possess the highest degree available in their field of study. The college offers 4-year undergraduate degrees in the School of Liberal Arts, the School of Science, and the School of Economics and Business Administration. Available majors are listed by school here.

The School of Liberal Arts offers undergraduate degrees in Anthropology, Art and Art History, Classics, Communication, English and Drama, Environmental Studies, French, Greek, History, Integral Program, International Area Studies, Kinesiology, Latin, Liberal and Civic Studies, Performing Arts: Music, Dance, and Theatre, Philosophy, Politics, Religious Studies, Sociology, Spanish, and Women's Studies.

The School of Science offers undergraduate degrees in Biochemistry, Biology, Chemistry, Computer Science, Engineering (3+2 Program), Environmental Science, Health Science, Mathematics, Physics, Pre-dental, Pre-medical, Pre-nursing (first year students only), Pre-physical therapy, Pre-veterinary, and Psychology.

The School of Economics and Business Administration offers undergraduate degrees in Accounting, Business Administration, and Economics (B.A. or B.S.).

ACADEMIC PROGRAMS

Saint Mary's rigorous core curriculum includes the Collegiate Seminar, a series of discussion-based classes examining the world's great ideas. Faculty members participate as equal partners, contributing to the discussions of the meaning and relevance of the major works of Western civilization.

The January Term program allows students to pursue a single specialized topic in depth. This month-long session gives Saint Mary's a 4-1-4 academic calendar, two four-month long terms and one four-week January Term. January Term features highly specialized courses on and off campus, exchanges with other 4-1-4 colleges, and independent study projects.

Saint Mary's sponsors semester-abroad programs at universities in Spain and South Africa, Mexico and Italy—plus the Centre for Medieval and Renaissance Studies in Oxford, England. Many of our students also participate in programs in less-traveled parts of the world: China, the Czech Republic, Ghana, Korea, Russia, and Vietnam.

The Integral Program is a college within the College, a learning community dedicated to the Great Books—foundational texts in math, music, literature, philosophy, theology, and science. Senior faculty—called tutors—approach each class as a conversation, a series of questions and possible answers, arguments, proofs, dialogues, and debates. Each seminar class relates to the others; each year builds upon the last.

CAMPUS FACILITIES AND EQUIPMENT

Saint Mary's facilities include the Saint Mary's Library, featuring a collection of more than 200,000 volumes, more than 10,000 print and electronic periodicals, and over 50 research databases. The Library's membership in Link+, a consortium of 31 academic and public libraries, allows students to access more than 12 million additional volumes and items. The Library also houses a collection of over 5,000 items about John Baptist de La Salle, the Lasallian community, and French religious and spiritual thought in the 16th, 17th, and 18th centuries.

The College offers a number of academic and non-academic support services. The Office of Academic Support and Achievement Programs offers guidance and support for students throughout their Saint Mary's experience. Services include workshops, tutorials, study skills and support programs for first-year and sophomore students, assistance for students with disabilities, and a peer mentoring program. Our Offices of Asian Pacific American, Black, and Hispanic/Latino Student Programs offer culturally specific academic support, career guidance, and skills training. The College's Counseling Center offers individual sessions, support groups, group counseling, and alcohol and drug intervention. The Women's Resource Center sponsors campus-wide lectures and symposia, empowerment workshops, and specialized programming for classes, residence halls, and student organizations.

The Student Health and Wellness Center is staffed by trained physicians, nurses, and educators, and it provides the primary medical services for common minor illnesses and injuries. All services and most medications are offered at no cost to the student.

SAINT MARY'S COLLEGE OF MARYLAND

TUITION, ROOM, BOARD, AND FEES
Expenses for 2008-2009

Tuition: Full-time (7 to 9.5 courses per year) $33,100

Room and Board:

Room—Double $6,570

Board—Carte Blanche, per year $5,110

Miscellaneous Fees:

Registration Fee $30

Tuition Commitment Deposit $300

Room Reservation Deposit $350

Orientation Fee $250

Student Activity Fee $300

Medical Insurance Fee $646

FINANCIAL AID

Over 70% of Saint Mary's students receive Financial Aid, and the average aid package is over $23,000. All applicants for Financial Aid should fill out a Free Application for Federal Student Aid (FAFSA) and include Saint Mary's College of California (Code 001302) on the form. California residents should also submit the GPA Verification Form to the State Commission by March 2nd to be considered for a Cal Grant. The deadline for priority Financial Aid consideration is February 15.

Financial Aid packages typically consist of scholarships, grants, and student loans. The College offers a number of academic scholarships, consideration for which is automatic with the student's application. All scholarships are renewable for up to four years. They are listed here.

Presidential Scholars Scholarships

Competitive scholarship of $8,000 annually. To be eligible to compete, first-year students must be admitted with a GPA of at least 3.8 and an ACT composite score of at least 31 or a combined math and critical reading score of at least 1350 on the SAT Reasoning Test. Recipients also qualify for and receive the $12,000 Freshman Honors at Entrance Scholarships for a total of $20,000.

Freshman Honors at Entrance Scholarship

$12,000 annually. Qualifications: all first-year students admitted with a GPA of at least 3.7 and an ACT composite score of at least 27 or a combined math and critical reading score of at least 1200 on the SAT Reasoning Test.

Transfer Honors at Entrance Scholarship

$8,000 annually. Qualifications: transfer students entering with 30 or more transfer academic semester units or the equivalent and a 3.5 college GPA.

Lasallian Leadership Scholarship

$8,000 annually. Qualifications: first-year students from a Christian Brothers high school with a GPA of at least 3.3.

International Honors Scholarship

$8,000 annually. Qualifications: A minimum academic score of 3.30 GPA or equivalent, and a minimum TOEFL score of 80-IBT or 213-CBT or equivalent. This scholarship is offered to new incoming bachelor degree-seeking students only.

STUDENT ORGANIZATIONS AND ACTIVITIES

Saint Mary's offers a rich student life. There are 15 cultural clubs, 15 service and politics clubs, and 25 arts and media clubs. Service activities are spearheaded by the Catholic Institute for Lasallian Social Action (CILSA), a national model for campus-based service programs. CILSA is a clearinghouse for service opportunities and an incubator for projects dedicated to social justice and the common good.

The College features a recreational program staffed and run *by* students *for* students. Club teams play in fierce interleague competition, and the men's rugby team has been ranked in the top ten teams in the nation for the past six years. Our campus-based intramural leagues offer friendly, spirited matches in competitive and non-competitive divisions in a wide variety of sports. Athletics facilities on campus include the Tim Korth Tennis Center, the Louis Guisto Baseball Field, the Sil Garaventa Sr. Soccer Field, Cottrell Field (softball), Saint Mary's Stadium (lacrosse), McKeon Pavillion (basketball and volleyball) and Madigan Gymnasium (recreational sports). We also maintain the Pat Vincent Memorial Field (rugby, intramural competition), a swimming pool, and outdoor basketball and volleyball courts. The Brother Albert Rahill Athletic Center includes aerobics and dance studios. The Power Plant is our fully stocked exercise and weightlifting center.

ADMISSIONS PROCESS

There is a $55 USD non-refundable application fee for all applicants. Saint Mary's College accepts applications for the Fall Semester, January Term and Spring Semester. The deadlines for applications are as follows:

Students who have all required application materials in by the Priority Deadline will hear back from the Admissions Committee by the second week of January. If accepted, these students are not required to enroll early or to pay an early deposit. Students who have all required application materials in by the Regular Deadline should expect a response within 4 to 6 weeks.

Applicants are required to submit:

- *a completed application*
- *essay / personal statement*
- *official scores from SAT 1 or ACT (freshmen and international students only)*
- *official scores from TOEFL, IELTS or other English proficiency exam result (international students only)*
- *one academic letter of recommendation from a counselor or teacher (freshmen and international students only; highly encouraged for transfers, but not required)*
- *official high school transcript (transfer students should also submit official college transcripts)*
- *Certificate of Finances Form (international students only)*
- *$55 USD application fee*

You may apply online or download an application at www.smcadmit.com/application. Application materials should be sent to:

Saint Mary's College Office of Admissions

P.O. Box 4800

Moraga, CA 94575-4800

Please call (800) 800-4SMC or 925-631-4224 if you have questions or need assistance during the application process. You may also email us at: smcadmit@stmarys-ca.edu.

SAINT MARY'S COLLEGE OF MARYLAND

AT A GLANCE

St. Mary's College of Maryland is designated the Honors College of the State of Maryland in recognition of the quality of our students, faculty and curriculum. St. Mary's offers an undergraduate, liberal arts education and small-college experience like those found at exceptional private colleges. Home to approximately 1900 students, the campus is located on the St. Mary's River in the heart of the Chesapeake region, about 70 miles outside of Washington D.C.

The school shares the hallmarks of private institutions: an outstanding faculty, talented students, high academic standards, a challenging curriculum, small classes, a sense of community, and a spirit of intellectual inquiry. By combining the virtues of public and private education, St. Mary's provides a unique alternative for students and their families. The special identity underpins the College's success and its reputation for excellence.

In 1992, the Maryland legislature designated this public, coeducational institution the state's honors college. Over 97% of the faculty holds the Ph.D. or other terminal degree and eleven of the current faculty have received Fulbright Awards. Although professors are exceptionally active in research and writing, the faculty's primary interest and central concern is teaching. The College is home to the Zeta Chapter of Phi Beta Kappa.

Small classes, dedicated teachers, and an informal atmosphere encourage faculty and students to share in the intellectual life of the College, both in and out of the classroom. Professors serve as academic advisers, work with students in extracurricular programs, involve students in research, and mentor them in individualized projects.

More than 50% of St. Mary's graduates continue on to graduate school. St. Mary's alumni have distinguished themselves in every academic field and creative pursuit. When the State of Maryland surveys graduates of its public colleges and universities, St. Mary's alumni consistently report higher levels of satisfaction with their education than do alumni of other institutions.

Students describe their classmates as "open," "down-to-earth," "laid-back," and write that the only attribute "typical" of a Seahawk is uniqueness. In the cafeteria, "you can witness a girl wearing Abercrombie & Fitch sitting with a farm girl, a goth, a hippie, and they are all hysterically laughing." Another thing you'll notice in the cafeteria: SMCM has a "large vegan/vegetarian population." Students are "on the whole more likely to be liberal," and at SMCM, "closed-minded behavior is usually not taken well by most students." Students are so trusting of each other that "no one locks any doors on campus . . . Knocking is just not a St. Mary's thing to do!" If undergrads could shake a magic wand, they'd like to see SMCM become more "ethnically diverse." "The school is made up of mostly white, higher-income-level kids," says a senior. That said, everyone is "accepted and accepting."

LOCATION AND ENVIRONMENT

St. Mary's College of Maryland is located on a horseshoe bend of the St. Mary's River just upstream from the confluence of the Potomac River and the Chesapeake Bay. In 1634, the first English settlers arrived here by boat and founded the fourth oldest permanent English colony in North America. By the Act of Toleration adopted by the colonists, St. Mary's City became an early site of religious freedom in the New World, and toleration remains an abiding precept of life at the College, where diversity of thought and expression are highly valued.

OFF-CAMPUS OPPORTUNITIES

Located about 20 minutes from the College is Solomons Island, a quiet waterfront fishing village offering museums and attractions, shopping, waterfront dining, sailing and other water sports. Historic Leonardtown, located 20 minutes from St. Mary's, boasts one of the state's few preserved town squares. Maryland's state capitol, Annapolis, is located 70 miles from the College. The Nation's Capitol, Washington, D.C., is 75 miles from the College and the harbor city of Baltimore is approximately 120 miles from campus.

MAJORS AND DEGREES OFFERED

Anthropology

Art and Art History

Asian Studies

Biochemistry

Biology

Chemistry

Computer Science

Economics

Educational Studies

English

History

Human Studies

International Languages and Cultures

Mathematics

Music

Natural Science

Philosophy

Physics

Political Science

Psychology

Public Policy

Religious Studies

Sociology

Student Designed Major

Theater, Film and Media Studies

ACADEMIC PROGRAMS

St. Mary's offers a wide and diverse variety of majors and minors and a Master of Arts in Teaching (M.A.T.) for certification in early childhood, elementary and secondary education.

St. Mary's also provides students the opportunity to explore cross-disciplinary studies in African and African Diaspora Studies, Asian Studies, Environmental Studies, Museum Studies, Neurosciences, and Women, Gender and Sexuality Studies. Cross-disciplinary studies can increase intellectual community across disciplines, encourage cohesion in the choice of electives, and promote combinations of methods and materials that challenge the boundaries of knowledge.

Many St. Mary's students consider careers in professional fields such as medicine, the law, and business. Our pre-professional programs work with interested students throughout their four years by providing academic advice, career exploration, and help applying to profession programs. These include Pre-Dentistry, Pre-Engineering (3-2 program with the University of Maryland at College Park), Pre-Law, Pre-Medicine, Pre-Nursing (3-2 program with Johns Hopkins University), Pre-Optometry, Pre-Pharmacy, and Pre-Veterinary Science.

The Paul H. Nitze Scholars Program is designed for highly motivated students with exceptional academic potential and a proven record of leadership and service. Students accepted into this program have more flexibility in curricular choices than other students. As a small cohort of peers, Nitze Scholars meet some of the components of the general education curriculum through a series of thematically organized interdisciplinary courses with special components such as a study-tour abroad and collaborative activities on campus.

In compliance with St. Mary's College's position as Maryland's public honors college, the St. Mary's Project (SMP) is the capstone of study at the College. The project is an eight-credit, independent, sustained endeavor of research or creative expression that is supervised by a faculty mentor and presented in a public forum.

St. Mary's College of Maryland offers semester and year-long international exchange programs, study tours, and international internship opportunities. Participation in our signature programs at Oxford in England, Alba in Italy, Shanghai in China, or The Gambia in West Africa is at about the same cost as attending St. Mary's.

St. Mary's operates on a two-semester academic calendar. Students customarily complete four courses, or 16 credits, each semester and must complete 128 credits for graduation. Students do not need to declare a major until the end of their sophomore year.

CAMPUS FACILITIES AND EQUIPMENT

A unique aspect of St. Mary's culture is the influence of the river. Our campus is located on 319 acres and sits on a horseshoe bend of the St. Mary's River just upstream from the confluence of the Potomac River and Chesapeake Bay. You just can't help being affected. It is no wonder we have earned 12 National Sailing Championships. You don't have to be an expert, the waterfront is open to recreational and novice sailors alike. With our unique location, students also swim, kayak, windsurf, row and are drawn to environmental research. Once you see the campus you'll know you have arrived at a college like no other.

Living at college should be a pleasurable experience. Almost 90% of our students live on campus all four years, contributing a wonderful and safe learning and living environment. Our students enjoy the options of residence halls, suites, apartments and townhouses, and find living on campus an essential part of their college experience.

When our students are not in the classroom, they are busy doing independent research, traveling abroad, interning, and volunteering in the community. They unwind by enjoying the waterfront recreation, watching movies in Cole Cinema, partaking in our 90 clubs and organizations, and competing in intramural and varsity athletics. Our facilities are state-of-the-art and the abundant opportunities provide students a wonderful balance of work and play.

TUITION, ROOM, BOARD AND FEES

Basic educational fees for 2007-2008

Tuition and Fees

$12,604 per year (Maryland Resident)

$23,454 per year (Out-of-State Resident)

Room

$5,315

Board

$3,925

FINANCIAL AID

St. Mary's College believes that qualified students should have an opportunity for a college education. The primary responsibility for paying for the cost of education is the family's. However, as a public institution, St. Mary's College recognizes that students and their families are not always able to fund the full cost of a college education. For this, the school offers a variety of programs designed to assist in meeting college expenses. These programs include scholarships, grants, loans, work opportunities, and a tuition payment plan. In the end, the goal is to ensure that qualified applicants have the opportunity to obtain a liberal arts education at St. Mary's.

To be considered for Need-Based Aid, including federal, state and college grants, loan, and employment programs, students must fill out the Free Application for Federal Student Aid (FAFSA). In order to be considered for Merit-Based Aid from St. Mary's, students need only to apply to the College. Every accepted student is automatically reviewed by the Scholarship Review Committee with consideration in the areas of academic record, standardized test scores, strength of curriculum, essay, recommendations, and co-curricular resume.

ADMISSIONS PROCESS

St. Mary's College is a selective institution. We admit students with records of high academic achievements, personal abilities, and accomplishments of superior quality. High school or college grades, the quality of course selection, standardized test scores, and letters of recommendation provide evidence of academic accomplishment and potential. These measures are supplemented by the required application essay and resume of co-curricular activities. Individual involvement outside the classroom and in the community also is given attention. Activities that have resulted in honors and awards, or other recognition of special talents, should be listed on the application.

At St. Mary's, we are proud to be a public honors college and are looking for students who are ready to be challenged. We accept applications from first-year and transfer students for the fall and spring semesters. Our Early Decision Deadlines are November 1 and December 1. When students apply under the Early Decision option, they are indicating to us that St. Mary's is their top choice and will attend if admitted. Notification of a decision is approximately one month past the Early Decision deadline. Regular Decision applicants must apply by January 1 and notification will be no later than April 1. Fall transfer applicants must apply March 1 and Spring transfer students must apply by November 1. For details, visit www.smcm.edu.

Prospective students are strongly encouraged to come to campus for an interview with an admissions counselor and tour. These visits should be scheduled in advance by calling 800-492-7181.

SAINT PETER'S COLLEGE

AT A GLANCE

Saint Peter's College is a Jesuit, Catholic, coeducational, liberal arts college that seeks to develop the whole person in preparation for a lifetime of learning, leadership, and service in a diverse and global society.

Sitting on 18 acres in Jersey City, the College is 12 minutes by train from New York City and seconds from "The Gold Coast," the rejuvenated Jersey City waterfront district that is home to some of the nation's most respected financial, insurance and real estate companies including Goldman, Sachs and Co., American Express, Morgan Stanley, Dean Witter, Merrill Lynch, Lehman Brothers, and Deutsche Bank. The College has a branch campus for adults in Englewood Cliffs; courses are also offered at various corporate sites and at a location right within the Jersey City waterfront.

The total enrollment at Saint Peter's College in Fall 2007 was 3,081. This figure includes 2,366 full-time, day undergraduate students of the Jersey City Campus and 715 graduate students. In 1993, the College opened a new, traditional-style dormitory, Whelan Hall; and in 1994 another student residence, Saint Peter Hall, the former Jesuit residence, was opened. A total of 795 students, about 35 percent of the full-time day session students now reside on campus. Saint Peter's College students, born in at least 58 different countries, reflect the increasing diversity of our nation. Approximately 29 percent of Jersey City Day Session full-time undergraduate students identify themselves as Hispanic; 23 percent are African American; 10 percent are Asian. Saint Peter's College students come from 25 states. New Jersey is home for 80 percent of Jersey City Day Session full-time undergraduates; 16 percent come from other states and 4 percent from foreign countries.

LOCATION AND ENVIRONMENT

The main campus of Saint Peter's College, the Jersey City campus, covers approximately 18 acres, and is divided by Kennedy Boulevard in the heart of Jersey City. Jaroschak Field, for athletic and recreational activities, is located about a mile away. Much of the College's personality comes from its location in Jersey City, where, for nearly 125 years, some of the best teachers in the nation have educated the children of long-established families along with those of recent arrivals. Within the past decade, Jersey City, located directly across the Hudson River from lower Manhattan, has developed its waterfront area into an impressive hub for business and finance.

In 1975, Saint Peter's established a branch campus at Englewood Cliffs in Bergen County. The campus, located on the Palisades about 15 miles up the Hudson River from Jersey City, enrolls primarily working adults from nearby corporate parks and medical centers who are pursuing undergraduate and graduate degrees through evening and weekend study.

OFF-CAMPUS OPPORTUNITIES

Supervised, off-campus cooperative education opportunities and internships are available in all fields. Students in SPC's nationally ranked Cooperative Education Program may earn a maximum of 9 academic credits and up to $10,000. Sixty percent of Saint Peter's undergraduates take advantage of the unique and exciting opportunities afforded by the College's proximity to the nation's business, financial, and media capital, New York City. They work, earning college credit and a salary, with firms such as Lehman Brothers, Atlantic Records, Jane Magazine, Morgan Stanley, WKTU, Panasonic, Unilever, ABC, Walgreens, Merrill Lynch, the National Basketball Association, MLB Productions, Madison Square Garden, Hackensack University Medical Center, and the NJ Sports and Exposition Authority.

Up to 15 credits are awarded through the Washington Center Program in Washington, D.C., which provides experience working in the nation's capital in a wide range of internship positions. Study abroad is arranged through the International Student Exchange Program, which conducts programs at more than 60 universities in Europe, Asia, Africa, and Latin America.

MAJORS AND DEGREES OFFERED

As befits a school founded in the classic Jesuit liberal arts tradition, Saint Peter's has a rich and varied range of academic offerings. Undergraduate programs include Accountancy, American Studies, Art History, Biology, Biological Chemistry, Biotechnology, Business Law°, Business Management, Chemistry, Classical Civilization, Classical Languages & Literatures, Communications, Computer Science (CIS/MIS, and an E-Commerce concentration available), Criminal Justice, Economics and Finance Elementary & Secondary Education (leads to New Jersey State Teaching Certification), English Literature, Finance°, Fine Arts, Graphic Arts, History, Interdisciplinary Studies, International and Intercultural Studies°, International Business and Trade, Journalism°, Latin American Studies, Marketing Management, Mathematical Economics, Mathematics, Modern Languages and Literatures, Music°, Natural Sciences, Nursing, Philosophy, Physics, Political Science, Psychology, Social Justice°, Sociology, Spanish, Theater Arts°, Theology, Urban Studies, Visual Arts and Women's Studies°. °Minor program only. Five-year bachelor's degree programs in cytotechnology, medical technology, and toxicology are offered in affiliation with the University of Medicine and Dentistry of New Jersey. Pre-Professional programs in accountancy, dentistry, pre-law, and pre-medicine are also offered.

ACADEMIC PROGRAMS

Saint Peter's Academic Programs are designed to offer students a wide breadth of knowledge along with providing the skills necessary to be successful in their chosen field. The College's academic departments offer 40 major programs, an Honors Program, individualized majors, and opportunities to earn credit for internships, service learning and other off-campus learning experiences

Undergraduate day courses are offered on a semester calendar, evening and Saturday courses on a trimester basis. Day and evening summer sessions are available on both campuses. A four-year honors program provides academically talented students an opportunity to do extensive scholarly research and participate in small seminars that emphasize class discussion. Selected students are invited to join this program and, upon successful completion, are awarded degrees in cursu honorum. The College recognizes the Advanced Placement (AP) program and generally offers credit for scores of 3 or better.

All students complete a core curriculum requirement consisting of at least 60 credits, distributed as follows: 3 credits each of composition and fine arts; 6 credits each of literature, a modern language, history, social sciences, philosophy, and theology; 6 to 8 credits of mathematics; 9 credits of natural science; and a 3 credit values course. The remainder of the academic program is devoted to the major field of specialization. Students must earn 120 credits to graduate.

Students may pursue a double major by completing requirements for two separate majors or may design a composite major in consultation with the appropriate academic dean. Minors are available in 29 areas of concentration.

CAMPUS FACILITIES AND EQUIPMENT

The Edward and Theresa O'Toole Library contains more than 50,000 sq. ft. of space. Students benefit from interlibrary loan arrangements as well as access to the New Jersey state-supported university library system. Students may obtain referral cards to other metropolitan area libraries and have access to the research collections of the New York Public Library and the Science, Industry, and Business Library, both located in midtown Manhattan, minutes from the campus. The library at the branch campus at Englewood Cliffs offers an additional 25,000 volumes.

Saint Peter's was one of the first colleges in the nation to adopt a wireless Ethernet throughout the campus. Students are offered individual e-mail accounts and Internet connectivity through the campus local area network (LAN). All offices, classrooms, and meeting spaces are connected to the Internet and the networked library resources.

The College operates 14 labs in the academic buildings on campus. In addition to general purpose computer labs distributed throughout the academic buildings, each residential hall has a mini-lab open 24 hours a day, 7 days a week. Saint Peter's also has several specialized computer labs to support learning in specific academic areas. The Fine Arts department operates a networked Graphic Arts lab with Apple and PC computer stations. The Modern Language department has its own computerized language lab and the Psychology department has a dedicated computer instruction lab.

Saint Peter's extends its commitment to integrating state of the art technology with high quality instruction beyond the use of computers. Gannon Hall, the science building, recently underwent an $8 million renovation and now offers sophisticated laboratory support to the College's course offerings in the natural sciences. The College has also implemented smart classroom technologies in all of its facilities, combining fully networked computer systems with powerful multimedia capabilities.

The Yanitelli Recreational Life Center is a modern multi-million dollar facility offering five indoor tennis courts, a state-of-the-art fitness center with strength training and cardiovascular equipment, an Olympic-sized swimming pool, free weight room, racquetball, squash, indoor track, and three regulation basketball courts. The Center is home to the College's extensive intramural program as well as its 17 Division I athletic teams.

TUITION, ROOM, BOARD AND FEES

Undergraduate tuition for the 2007-2008 school year is a flat rate of $23,426 for 12-18 credits per semester. Annual tuition and fees are $24,251. Annual room and board is $9,750. Annual tuition for graduate students is $19,848 (24 credits at $827 per credit).

FINANCIAL AID

In 2006-07, 89% of full-time students received financial assistance and the average aid award was just over $20,000. Saint Peter's College admits students regardless of financial status. The only form required is the Free Application for Federal Student Aid (FAFSA). It is recommended that students file the FAFSA by March 15 for fullest consideration of all federal, state (including EOF), and institutional sources available. All applications for admission are reviewed for academic scholarships, athletic scholarships, and need-based grants. Students should call the Office of Student Financial Aid (201-761-6073) for more information.

STUDENT ORGANIZATIONS AND ACTIVITIES

Academic life at Saint Peter's College is enriched by many programs and services that complement classroom instruction. The Counseling Center assists students with their social, psychological, and academic adjustment to college. At the Career Development Center, students can receive assistance in career planning and help in the search for meaningful jobs. The Cooperative Education Program gives participants a chance to earn money and college credit for practical work experience. Students can also take advantage of a center for information and assistance in applying for admission to graduate, law, or medical schools. The Campus Ministry Office offers religious services, seminars, and counseling. Students can also make use of the Office of Community Service and Service Learning. The Office of Campus Activities sponsors annual events on campus featuring popular entertainment, guest lecturers, and social events, both on and off campus. New York City, just a short distance away, offers countless cultural opportunities.

Each year over 1,000 men and women participate in an extensive intramural program. On the varsity level, Saint Peter's competes in basketball, baseball, bowling, cross-country, football, golf, swimming, soccer, softball, track, and volleyball. Saint Peter's is a member of the Metro Atlantic Athletic Conference.

ADMISSIONS PROCESS

Saint Peter's College requires students to have the following academic units:

- four years of English
- three years of college prep math
- two years of history
- two years of a foreign language
- two years of science, with at least on year of lab science
- at least three additional units in any combination of the
- subject areas listed above.

To satisfy admissions requirements, the complete admissions file must include:

- a completed application
- an official high school transcript
- official ACT or SAT scores
- two letters of recommendation
- personal statement/essay

Notification of the admission decision is made on a rolling basis once the admission file is complete. Students are awarded an academic scholarship based on the academic index comprised of GPA and SAT scores. Scholarships range from $5,000 to full tuition, room and fees.

SAVANNAH COLLEGE OF ART AND DESIGN

AT A GLANCE

The Savannah College of Art and Design exists to prepare talented students for professional careers, emphasizing learning through individual attention in a positively oriented university environment.. The goal of the college is to nurture and cultivate the unique qualities of each student through an interesting curriculum, in an inspiring environment, under the leadership of involved professors. SCAD features locations in Atlanta and Savannah, Ga., and in Lacoste, France, and offers online programs through SCAD-eLearning. SCAD is a private, nonprofit institution accredited by the Commission on Colleges of the Southern Association of Colleges and Schools (1866 Southern Lane, Decatur, Georgia 30033-4097; telephone number 404.679.4501) to award bachelors and master's degrees. The college offers Bachelor of Arts, Bachelor of Fine Arts, Master of Architecture, Master of Arts, Master of Arts in Teaching, Master of Fine Arts and Master of Urban Design degrees, as well as undergraduate and graduate certificates. The five-year professional M.Arch. degree is accredited by the National Architectural Accrediting Board. For more information about the college, visit www.scad.edu.

To see when SCAD will be in your area, visit www.scad.edu/admission/yourarea.

E-mail may be sent to admission@scad.edu.

Savannah, Lacoste and SCAD-eLearning inquiries may be directed to 800.869.7223 or 912.525.5100; Atlanta inquiries may be directed to 877.722.3285 or 404.253.2700.

LOCATION AND ENVIRONMENT

Whether in fast-paced Atlanta, sultry Savannah, quaint Lacoste, or online via SCAD-eLearning, all Savannah College of Art and Design students are offered many opportunities to enrich their learning experience through both formal and informal student life programming. Residence halls, dining rooms, fitness centers, and online chat rooms become gathering places for organized and casual interactions.

MAJORS AND DEGREES OFFERED

Degree programs include advertising design, animation, architectural history, architecture, art history, arts administration, broadcast design and motion graphics, cinema studies, commercial photography, design management, digital photography, documentary photography, dramatic writing, fashion, fibers, film and television, furniture design, graphic design, historic preservation, illustration, illustration design, industrial design, interactive design and game development, interior design, metals and jewelry, painting, performing arts, photography, printmaking, production design, professional writing, sculpture, sequential art, sound design, teaching, urban design and visual effects. Most degree programs have corresponding undergraduate minors. Additional minors are offered in accessory design, British-American studies, business management and entrepreneurship, ceramic arts, creative writing, cultural landscape, dance, decorative arts, drawing, electronic design, exhibition design, interaction design, marine design, museum studies, music performance, new media art, portrait arts, storyboarding and technical direction.

ACADEMIC PROGRAMS

Undergraduate programs embrace a wide range of major areas and are designed to challenge students to perform at a high level, preparing them for careers in the visual and performing arts, design, the building arts, and the history of art and architecture. Bachelor of Arts Degree The bachelor of arts degree program is a four-year course of study requiring 180 quarter credit hours and incorporating a fine arts foundation studies curriculum, general education curriculum, area of concentration curriculum and electives. The majority of the Bachelor of Arts curriculum consists of fine arts, humanities, general education and liberal arts courses. An area of study concentration complements the coursework. Bachelor of Fine Arts Degree The bachelor of fine arts degree program is a four-year course of study requiring 180 quarter credit hours and incorporating a fine arts foundation studies curriculum, general education curriculum, major program curriculum and electives. Graduate programs at the Savannah College of Art and Design are designed for dedicated, self-motivated students who are committed to the pursuit of excellence in the visual and performing arts, design, the building arts, and the history of art and architecture. Graduate degrees may prepare individuals to hold leadership positions in art and design, to enter a variety of professional disciplines, to teach, or to accomplish other personal and professional goals. The graduate experience culminates in a thesis or final project demonstrating a mature and resolved body of work and/or research.

TUITION, ROOM, BOARD AND AID

The Savannah College of Art and Design Financial Aid office exists to process federal, state and alternative loan aid available to students.

STUDENT ORGANIZATIONS AND ACTIVITIES

Student athletics, fitness and recreation programs help develop a well-rounded student by encouraging physical fitness and recreational activities and events that support community through social interaction, team building and promoting college spirit. These programs include intercollegiate and intramural sports, free-sport activities and personal challenges, wellness activities, outings and fitness centers.

ADMISSIONS PROCESS

Students may apply online at the College's Web site (http://www.scad.edu). Undergraduate application requirements include SAT or ACT scores, official transcripts from the last high school or college attended, a minimum of three recommendations, a statement of purpose, a completed application form, and a non-refundable application fee of $25 for online applicants and $50 for applications submitted via mail. Portfolio/auditions and interviews are encouraged but are not required for undergraduate admission. Homeschooled, transient, and non-degree-seeking applicants are welcome. A minimum SAT math score of 540 or ACT math score of 23 is required for regular acceptance into the professional architecture program. Transfer students may receive a maximum of 90 quarter hours toward a B.F.A. degree. All students must complete in residence the final 45 hours of any degree earned at the College. As a general rule, applications for fall quarter should be completed no later than March 1 in order for admission decisions to be rendered by April 1. Scholarships for fall quarter are awarded by May 1 and students are requested to indicate their acceptance of admission and of institutional scholarship offers by June 1 through payment of a one-time matriculation fee. This same time frame applies with corresponding dates for students entering winter, spring or summer quarters. Applications received less than one month prior to the intended entry date are considered only on a space available basis.

SCHOOL OF THE ART INSTITUTE OF CHICAGO

AT A GLANCE

Since 1866, the School of the Art Institute of Chicago (SAIC) has been providing a leading global vision for the education of artists, designers and others who shape contemporary practice. SAIC fosters the conceptual and technical education of artists, designers and scholars in a highly professional, studio-oriented and academically rigorous environment. SAIC encourages excellence, critical inquiry, and experimentation. In 2002, SAIC was recognized as "the most influential art school in the nation" in a poll of national art critics conducted by Columbia University. SAIC's Master of Fine Arts program has been consistently ranked as number one by U.S. News and World Report. 2,200 undergraduate and 600 graduate students work in an environment that facilitates the exchange of ideas, resource sharing and the refinement of technical abilities and conceptual concerns. SAIC students have access to a wide variety of unique resources, beginning with the premiere collection of the Art Institute of Chicago and its Ryerson Library and Burnham Library of Architecture, the largest art and architecture research libraries in the country. The Gene Siskel Film Center, located in the same building as our 162 North State Street residence, presents significant programs of world cinema and video presentations by an international array of film and video artists. The Video Data Bank houses more than 1,800 titles and is the leading resource in the United States for videotapes by and about contemporary artists. The Poetry Center brings renowned poets and writers to Chicago to share their work with the public. SAIC is accredited by the North Central Association of Colleges and Schools and the National Association of Schools of Art and Design.

ACADEMIC PROGRAMS

Completion of 132 hours is required for the B.A., B.F.A. and B.I.A. degrees, approximately two thirds being in studio areas and one third in academic course work. All entering students who have completed fewer than 15 credit hours of college-level studio art must enroll in the First Year Experience, an intense, interdisciplinary studio concentration that emphasizes simultaneous development of technical skills and conceptual thinking. After the first-year English requirements are completed, students take liberal arts courses in the humanities, natural science and mathematics and social sciences. Students are also required to complete an art history requirement. Our credit/no-credit grading system encourages students to investigate, develop or resolve a creative problem or theme by exploring new approaches or different media, and to develop the self-motivation and discipline necessary for life as a practicing artist, designer and scholar in the 21st century. Students are required to complete 6 semester hours of off-campus study.

TUITION, ROOM, BOARD AND FEES

Tuition for the 2007-08 academic year is $30,750 for full-time undergraduate students or $1025 per credit hour. For 2007-08, student housing costs $8900 per academic year for a double room.

STUDENT ORGANIZATIONS AND ACTIVITIES

SAIC builds a strong sense of community on campus with special activities and programs. The Visiting Artist Program hosts approximately 50 public presentations by artists each year in lectures, symposia, performances and screenings. It showcases artists working in all media including sound, video, performance, poetry, painting, and independent film, in addition to curators, critics, and art historians. The Student Union Galleries (SUGs) program provides a professional student exhibition space that is operated by students. Students are involved in every facet of the gallery's operation—from administration and program design to the selection of exhibitions, curating, advertising, installation and de-installation. Student Government represents all students enrolled at SAIC and provides funds for the nearly 35 student groups on campus, as well as planning events such as a Welcome Back to School Party, Monthly Morning Coffees, Open Forums, barbecues, Holiday Art Sale, and a Materials Event. Students may also participate in SAIC's award-winning newspaper, "F Newsmagazine," or Free Radio SAIC, a student-run Internet radio station airing approximately 40 hours of original programming per week.

ADMISSIONS PROCESS

To be considered for the undergraduate program, applicants are required to submit the admissions application; a nonrefundable application fee of $65 for domestic students and a fee of $85 for international students; a portfolio usually consisting of ten to fifteen examples of recent work, a minimum of five minutes of time-based work, or an alternative portfolio submission that demonstrates the applicant's creative intent; a statement of purpose; transcript(s) from high school(s) or an official copy of the high school equivalency certificate; transcripts from any college previously attended; one letter of recommendation. Domestic applicants must submit either scores from the SAT or the ACT test. Any transfer applicant who has successfully completed SAIC English requirements and/or other Liberal Arts coursework at another accredited college may be exempt from standardized test requirements for admission. All international undergraduate students who are not U.S. citizens, permanent residents or are not native English speakers are required to take either the TOEFL or IELTS. Prospective students may apply to SAIC through the Immediate Decision Option (IDO) or the traditional admission procedure. IDO Days allow prospective students who have submitted all their application materials an opportunity to receive an admissions decision by the end of the IDO day while on the SAIC campus. All students are required to submit their applications electronically by applying online at http://www.saic.edu/ugapp. Students are admitted on a rolling basis and are informed of the committee's decision by mail. Students must be admitted to SAIC by February 15 for the fall semester and November 15 for the spring semester to be considered for merit scholarship. Application deadline for first-time freshmen is June 30. Transfer students have no application deadline. Admissions Office School of the Art Institute of Chicago 36 South Wabash Chicago, Illinois 60603

SCHOOL OF THE MUSEUM OF FINE ARTS

AT A GLANCE

The School of the Museum of Fine Arts, Boston (SMFA), or Museum School, is a division of the Museum of Fine Arts, Boston (MFA), and affiliated with Tufts University. In partnership with Tufts, the School offers the following degree programs: the Bachelor of Fine Arts, the Bachelor of Fine Arts Plus Master of Arts in Teaching in Art Education, the five-year Combined-Degree program (BA/BFA or BS/BFA), the Master of Fine Arts, and the Master of Arts in Teaching in Art Education. All students in degree programs are fully enrolled at the School of the Museum of Fine Arts and Tufts University, and graduate with a Tufts degree. The School also offers the Studio Program and the one-year Post-Baccalaureate Certificate Program.

As in an artists' colony, the Museum School's focus is on creative investigation, risk-taking, and the exploration of an individual vision. A truly interdisciplinary institution, the School does not have a mandatory foundations program, nor does it have majors. Students are given the freedom to design a program of study that best suits their needs and goals. This freedom comes with strong support and guidance from faculty advisers.

LOCATION AND ENVIRONMENT

Boston is home to many educational and cultural institutions. The Museum School is an active part of the cultural scene, presenting a dynamic schedule of exhibitions, lectures, and panel discussions throughout the year. A variety of social events and activities are also available, including frequent trips to New York City. An extensive public transportation system includes subways, buses, and commuter trains.

The Museum School campus features several buildings with classrooms, studios, state-of-the-art equipment, a library, computer labs, a professional development center, and a wealth of exhibition spaces. A limited amount of residential housing is available in the Artists' Residence Hall, which features apartment-style living and common studio areas. Many students choose to live in nearby off-campus apartments, and our Student Affairs Office can help find the right location and the right roommate.

MAJORS AND DEGREES OFFERED

BACHELOR OF FINE ARTS

Combining studio work with academic studies, the Bachelor of Fine Arts (BFA) is designed for students who wish to complete an art-focused bachelor's degree. BFA students are enrolled at both the Museum School and Tufts University, and graduate with a BFA degree from Tufts.

BACHELOR OF FINE ARTS PLUS MASTER OF ARTS IN TEACHING IN ART EDUCATION

Bachelor of Fine Arts students who want to become art teachers have the option to pursue a Master of Arts in Teaching (MAT) in Art Education through the new BFA Plus MAT in Art Education Program—and it takes only an additional 12 months to complete. The MAT in Art Education provides students with eligibility to apply for a Massachusetts teaching license of Visual Art for grades PK-8 or 5-12.

THE COMBINED DEGREE PROGRAM

As a student in the Combined-Degree Program, you will pursue your artistic vision while exploring an academic field of your choice. Students in this program are enrolled at both the Museum School and Tufts University and graduate with both an academic degree (the Bachelor of Arts or the Bachelor of Science) and a fine arts degree (the Bachelor of Fine Arts) from Tufts.

THE STUDIO PROGRAM

One of the nation's oldest programs of its kind, the Studio is an intensive, all-elective program—an ideal choice for motivated students both young and old who want to shape their own creative direction. As a Studio student, you may concentrate within one discipline or construct your own interdisciplinary practice.

THE POST-BACCALAUREATE CERTIFICATE PROGRAM

The Post-Baccalaureate Certificate Program offers an intensive year of studio art study and practice, closely advised and supported by SMFA faculty.

MASTER OF FINE ARTS

Both rigorous and highly selective, the Master of Fine Arts (MFA) Program will prepare you for a career as a working artist or a teacher at the college level. MFA students are enrolled at both the SMFA and Tufts University, and graduate in two or three years with an MFA degree from Tufts.

MASTER OF ARTS IN TEACHING

The Master of Arts in Teaching (MAT) in Art Education Program prepares the artist to teach in elementary, middle, and high schools with a critical focus on both contemporary visual culture and traditional arts. The resources of Tufts University and the Museum School combine to enhance your understanding of urban and multicultural education and to develop your capacity as a reflective studio artist.

TUITION, ROOM, BOARD AND FEES

The total cost of attendance includes tuition, fees, books and supplies, personal expenses, and a living allowance. Personal expenses, room and board, and transportation costs vary according to the individual. Below is an average budget for a nine-month period based on 2007-2008 charges (subject to change).

Full-time tuition: Studio = $26,950 BFA = $26,950 plus academics ($2,140 per 4.0 credit course)

Comprehensive Fee: $1,020

(includes general, material, technology, and student activity fee)

Orientation Fee: $125

Graduation Fee: $100

Room and Board: $13,575

Transportation: $1,245

Books and Supplies: $1,500

Personal: $1,600

FINANCIAL AID

We understand that figuring out how to pay for school is a vital part of planning for your education. Our advice is to begin the process of applying for Financial Aid as early as possible, before you receive your acceptance to the School. You and your family are welcome to meet individually with a member of the Financial Aid Office to discuss financial resources that are available from the School, the federal government, state programs, and other institutions and organizations. Various private educational loans are also available and are a potential source of funding for international students. Understanding the Financial Aid application process is critical. In addition to our staff, please make use of our Web site's information and resources.

STUDENT ORGANIZATIONS AND ACTIVITIES

The Student Affairs staff works with students, faculty, and staff to create a vital artists' community. Many of the programs, groups, and activities are driven by student interest. We encourage you to become involved with student-curated exhibitions, school committees, and student events and student interest groups such as SBInc. (student government), New York City bus trips, Animation Festival, Drawing Marathon, Open Studios, annual Student Sidewalk Sale, Thanksgiving Pot Luck, World AIDS Day events, yoga, and dodgeball, just to name a few.

The Artist's Resource Center provides access to the arts and cultural communities, the world of education, and the spheres of business through special courses and civic engagement in the arts. It also offers opportunities to partner, to intern, and to be employed in many arts related fields, integrating those experiences into your studio arts curriculum. These are tangible and comprehensive opportunities ensuring long-term relationships for students of the Museum School.

ADMISSIONS PROCESS

We highly recommend visiting the School for a personal interview, a portfolio review, and a tour. This visit can take place before you apply or at any time during the application process. If you are unable to visit, we encourage you to meet with one of our Admissions representatives at a Portfolio Day, an off-site interview, a college fair, or on a scheduled class visit. Should you discover that we are not coming to your school, ask your art teacher to call us and see if we can arrange to visit.

We recommend that you show your original artwork during your interview, on a Portfolio Day, or on a day that we visit your school. This will help you prepare a stronger portfolio that you can later submit for review as part of your application. We make no stipulations about the composition of your portfolio. Your portfolio may take any shape or form. Technical ability may or may not be considered more important than the creative and artistic efforts evident in your portfolio. Showing your portfolio does not automatically mean that your portfolio has been accepted. You are still required to submit a portfolio for the Admissions Committee to review, especially if you would like to be considered for a merit scholarship.

The following materials are required for application: an application for admission; $70 application fee; official high school transcript or General Equivalency Diploma (GED), unless applicant has a college degree; a portfolio and inventory of your portfolio; an essay; SAT, ACT, or AP scores; two letters of recommendation; proof of immunization or waiver; and list of extracurricular activities (optional). Combined-Degree applicants only must submit a separate application to Tufts. For SMFA application materials, visit www.smfa.edu. To obtain a Tufts application, visit www.tufts.edu.

SCHOOL OF VISUAL ARTS

AT A GLANCE

The School of Visual Arts, in the heart of New York City, offers students the opportunity to become involved in one of America's largest and most vibrant cities. The energy, spirit, and desire to be the best that characterizes New York is embodied in SVA's renowned faculty of more than 700 working professionals, who challenge and inspire their students.

LOCATION AND ENVIRONMENT

The official SVA campus is placed near the city's photography, art, and advertising centers. SVA life is New York City life. Students come here to be immersed in real-world experience, not the insulated experience of other schools. They get a whole other chunk of learning from this, which eases the transition from student to working adult.

OFF-CAMPUS OPPORTUNITIES

SVA students have the opportunity of participating in art programs abroad during the summer semester. SVA offers Painting in Barcelona; Painting in Florence; Digital Photo in Florence; and Cinema in Toulouse. Third-year students in film and video, fine arts, graphic design, illustration, interior design, and photography have the opportunity to study abroad for one semester at an AIAS (Association of Independent Art Schools) affiliate in Europe.

The college also has an Internship for Credit Program, which allows qualified juniors and seniors to work part-time for studio credit.

MAJORS AND DEGREES OFFERED

Bachelor of Fine Arts degrees are offered in advertising; animation; cartooning; computer art; graphic design; illustration; interior design; film and video; fine arts; photography; and visual and critical studies.

Master of Fine Arts degrees are offered in art criticism and writing; computer art; design; fine arts; illustration as visual essay; and photography and related media.

A Master of Professional Studies degree is offered in art therapy and digital photography.

A Master of Arts in Teaching degree is offered in art education.

SVA also offers workshops, continuing education classes, studio residencies, international student programs, summer programs abroad, and a precollege program for high school students.

CAMPUS FACILITIES AND EQUIPMENT

The Film, Video, and Animation departments have two fully equipped animation studios, a Stop Motion Control Studio, a 16-35mm Master Oxberry stand, five digital pencil test facilities, a Motion Control Pencil test stand, a motion control table, and a Digital Compositing Ink and Paint System.

Film offers students 60 Bolex cameras, 15 Arriflex S camera packages, and 10 Arriflex BL camera packages. Thesis students reserve Arriflex SR camera packages along with a variety of support accessories. The department also houses a large inventory of lighting and grip equipment. Sound equipment consists of Sony D-10 Pro II DAT recorders, 10 Nagra recorders, Fostex digital time code recorders, a sound transfer facility, and a large collection of microphones and mixers. Film editing facilities include 19 flatbed steenbeck suites.

The film library houses more than 1,500 titles from a variety of film, video, DVD, laser, and tape formats. A 90-seat film theater is available for cinema studies classes to screen films and to provide students a forum for screening their work.

Video offers students VX1000 digital video cameras, PD-100 and EZ-1 digital video cameras, and more than 40 combination Hi-8 cameras.

Post-production facilities include a state-of-the-art AVID center housing 10 Meridian nonlinear workstations, a Pro Tools work facility complete with 24 mix workstations, dub rooms, a telecine room, 9 offline rooms, and a Beta online/AVID studio. A nonlinear facility houses two FinalCut Pro workstations, one Excel, and three AVIDS.

In the Fine Arts Department, there are studios with slop sinks and storage closets for foundation, second and third year drawing and painting workshops. Fourth-year students have their own 24-hour studio spaces.

Printmaking studios are equipped for etching, lithography, silkscreen, papermaking, woodcut/lino and mono print. The litho room has five lithography presses and a graining sink, etching has four etching presses, rosin box and hot plates and silkscreen has an exposure unit and screen darkroom and reclaiming facilities. There is a complete plate-making darkroom containing a flip top Nu Arc exposing unit for making photo lithography and etching plates, a developing sink and plate cutter. In addition to traditional hand-drawn separations, students can create digital color separations in the printmaking output facilities.

The Sculpture Center has facilities for welding, woodworking, stone carving, ceramics, performance and video art. The wood shop has a table saw, a sliding compound miter saw, panel saw, table sander, four band saws, and two drill presses. In the metal shop are three MIG welders, two ARC welders, one TIG welder, two plasma cutters, a horizontal and vertical band saw, a sand blaster, and OXY-ACE torches. Stone facilities have air hammers and stone chisels. The ceramic studio has two electric kilns that fire up to cone 7, a clay extruder, six potters wheels, and a slab roller. In addition to these facilities there is a tool room stocked with power hand tools and safety equipment. The Sculpture Center also has a performance area, live model area and a slide room for presentations. There are two window vitrines on Seventeenth Street to provide a public venue for student work. The video computer lab has seven digital video cameras, three video projectors and a post-production facility consisting of three G3 iMacs, G4 iMacs and two G4s with Photoshop, Illustrator, Flash, Final Cut Pro and DVD pro software which allows for professional editing and special effects. The center also manages an audiovisual facility with slide, and video projectors, VCRs, DVDs, monitors and audio equipment.

Graphic design and advertising students use the Digital Imaging Center, which houses 140 Power Macintosh G4 computers with CD/DVD burners. Peripheral drives include Floppy Drives, Zip Drives, and Compact Flash/Smart Media Card Readers. There are 16 high-definition flatbed scanners, a Polaroid film recorder, a Polaroid slide scanner, as well as nine high-quality laser printers, including two HP color printers and three Fuji dye-sub printers.

The Broadcast Media room has SONY DV decks, JVC S-VHS VCRs, and SONY NTSC monitors. Students have access to Nikon digital cameras and Sony DV video cameras.

Software includes Adobe Photoshop, Adobe Illustrator, Adobe InDesign, Adobe Premiere, Adobe After Effects, Quark Xpress, Macromedia Director, Macromedia Dreamweaver, Macromedia Flash, Apple Final Cut Pro, and Discreet Cleaner.

The Digital Imaging Center's Studio has 22 drafting tables for drawing, cutting, and mounting artwork for presentations, and also provides the students with color copiers, high quality Fiery color printing, and large format printing.

In the Computer Art Department, there are 21 SGI, 21 Intergraph, 21 Boxx, and more than 200 Apple Macintosh computers in 15 instructional labs and DV editing facilities. The department features the latest software applications, including Alias Wavefront Maya, SoftImage, Discreet Logic Flint, 3D Studio Max, Adobe AfterEffects, Adobe Photoshop, Macromedia Director, and Quark XPress.

The Photography Department black and white darkrooms are equipped with 54 Omega D5 condenser enlargers capable of working with any film format from Minox through 4x5. We also house nine black and white film processing workstations. The color labs are equipped with 28 Omega D5 Dichroic enlargers and two 30-inch Kreonite Promate RA4 processors. The color print viewing area is equipped with GTI 5000K viewing booths. Systems for working with negatives up to 8 by 10 inches are available for both black and white and color. The digital labs have 48 G4 Macintosh workstations with flat-screen monitors, flat-bed and multiformat film scanners, Smart Card readers, Epson inkjet printers, film recorders, and CD/DVD burners. All of these workstations are networked together and provide Internet access for students.

The seven shooting studios are included in the department's computer network, and each studio is set up with an iMac equipped with a CD burner, Zip 250, and a Smart Card reader to allow students to download and save digital images. Digital cameras available for student use, including over two dozen assorted Nikon Coolpix, as well as 18 Canon D30 camera kits. Students have access to a wide range of studio equipment, including Profoto strobes, Vivitar, Quantum, and Lumidyne portable flashes; Lowel quartz lights; Ari quartz lights; and an assortment of lighting accessories. SVA provides large- and medium-format cameras for the students to use. Our stock includes the entire Mamiya line of cameras as well as lenses, Haselblad cameras and lenses, Toyo 4x5 View Cameras and Field Cameras, 8x10 Toyo's, and view camera lenses from 65 mm through 500 mm.

Interior Design students have a personal 3x5 fully equipped drafting station and unlimited use of computers. AutoCAD, Form Z, Render-Zone, and 3D Studio Viz software are in a 3D AutoCAD lab for exclusive use by interior design students. Output options include a large-format Hewlett Packard Designjet ColorPro CAD and a Hewlett-Packard Designjet 1055CM plotter.

TUITION, ROOM, BOARD, AND FEES

Expenses For 2007–2008

Application fee: $50 ($80 for international applicants)

Tuition: $23,520 per year

Departmental fees: $200 to $1,200 per semester depending on major

Estimated supplies: $1,050 to $3,150

Housing charges: range from $8,500 to $11,600 per year

FINANCIAL AID

Currently, 74 percent of SVA students receive some form of financial aid. Merit scholarships are also available through the Office of Admissions. A payment plan is available.

STUDENT ORGANIZATIONS AND ACTIVITIES

The Office of Student Activities provides a diverse range of programming designed to enrich the SVA student's experience. Students are offered the opportunity to tap into a multitude of social, cultural, educational, and recreational activities. Students are encouraged to take advantage of all New York City has to offer.

The Visual Arts Student Association (VASA), the student government, represents the students' point of view at SVA. Participating in VASA gives students the opportunity to develop leadership skills by coordinating events and activities. VASA funds and supports a number of clubs and activities that are organized by students.

ADMISSIONS PROCESS

Undergraduate Application Deadlines

Deadline for freshman and transfers: rolling

Deadline for Early Decision: December 1, 2007

Deadline for applying to the Silas H. Rhodes Scholarship Program: February 1, 2008 for first-time freshman applicants and March 1, 2008 for transfer applicants

Requirements:

- Application for Undergraduate Admission
- A nonrefundable $50 application fee ($80 for international applicants)
- Official transcripts from all high schools and colleges attended
- Results of the SAT or ACT
- Statement of intent
- Portfolio
- Interview (optional)
- Demonstration of English proficiency (required of all applicants whose primary language is not English)
- Copy of the front of Alien Registration card (for permanent residents/alien residents only)

SCRIPPS COLLEGE

AT A GLANCE

From its founding in 1926 as one of the few institutions in the West dedicated to educating women for professional careers as well as personal growth, Scripps College has championed the qualities of mind and spirit described by its founder, newspaper entrepreneur and philanthropist Ellen Browning Scripps. Scripps remains a women's college because it believes that having women at the core of its concerns provides the best environment for intellectually ambitious women to learn from a distinguished teaching faculty and from each other.

Scripps emphasizes a challenging Core Curriculum based on interdisciplinary humanistic studies, combined with rigorous training in the disciplines, as the best possible foundation for any goals a woman may pursue. This central feature of a Scripps education consists of a closely integrated sequence of three interdisciplinary courses that focus on our ideas about the world and the methods we use to generate these ideas. Scripps women learn to see the connections not only among academic subjects, but also among the major areas of their own lives, so that alumnae often remark that Scripps "prepared me for life." Above all, Scripps gives women an intensive, challenging education that will help them to lead, in the words of its founder, "lives filled with confidence, courage, and hope."

LOCATION AND ENVIRONMENT

Scripps is listed on the National Register of Historic Places. Located in Claremont, California, a college town with a population of 36,500, Scripps is 35 miles west of Los Angeles. Within driving distance are mountains, beaches, and deserts, all of which can be enjoyed in the beautiful southern California climate. Part of the Claremont Consortium, Scripps shares facilities and resources with Claremont McKenna, Harvey Mudd, Pitzer, and Pomona Colleges.

OFF-CAMPUS OPPORTUNITIES

Scripps students can take courses at any Claremont College, so they have over 2,500 classes to choose from each semester. More than half of the student body participates in study abroad programs in any of 36 countries. Career Planning and Resources, among other services, offers students a wide range of internship opportunities. Students may pursue a joint Scripps/Claremont Graduate University combined degree program that results in a B.A. and master's degree in five years. The seven master's degree programs offered are in American politics, business administration, economics, international studies, philosophy, public policy and religion. Engineering students have the opportunity to participate in a 3-2 program, through which students spend three years on the Scripps campus and two years at an engineering campus (choices include Boston University, Columbia University, Harvey Mudd College, Rensselaer Polytechnic Institute, USC, and Washington University in St. Louis) and graduate with a combined B.A./B.S. degree.

MAJORS AND DEGREES OFFERED

The following majors are available at Scripps or through cross-registration at other Claremont Colleges: accounting; American Studies; anthropology; art history; Asian studies; Asian American studies; biology; biology-chemistry; Black studies; chemistry; Chicana/o Studies; Chinese; Classics; computer science; dance; economics; engineering; English; environment, economics and politics; environmental science; environmental studies; European studies; French studies; gender and women's studies; geology; German studies; Hispanic studies; history; human biology; humanities: interdisciplinary studies in culture; Italian;; Japanese; Jewish studies; Latin American Studies; legal studies; linguistics; management engineering; mathematics; media studies; molecular biology; music; neuroscience; organismal biology; organizational studies; philosophy; physics; politics and international relations; psychology; religious studies; Russian; science and management; science, technology, and society; sociology; studio art; and theatre.

ACADEMIC PROGRAMS

At least 32 courses are required for the Bachelor of Arts degree at Scripps. Included in these courses are the Core Curriculum requirements, breadth requirements (in fine arts, foreign language(s), letters, mathematics, natural sciences, social sciences, and writing), coursework for the chosen major, and elective courses or courses for a minor. Students also complete one course each that fulfills a requirement of race and ethnic studies and gender and women's studies. More than half of Scripps students dual or double major. Students may elect to pursue an honors program in their chosen major. All students complete a senior thesis or, in the case of music, dance, studio art, or theater, a senior performance or project.

There are two semesters to each academic year at Scripps, and the year runs from early September to mid-May.

CAMPUS FACILITIES AND EQUIPMENT

The center of community life at Scripps is the Malott Commons. Here, students have most of their meals (in a choice of four dining areas), pick up their mail, and meet friends at the student-run Motley Coffeehouse for a cappuccino or for live music. It is also home to Career Planning and Resources, Seal Court, the Student Activities and Residential Life Office and lounge, and the student store. The Malott Commons hosts a myriad of cultural, educational, and social events such as speakers, open mic events, literary readings, and meetings.

With 2,000,000 volumes, the library system is the third largest private academic library in California. Scripps' science facilities are jointly shared with Claremont McKenna and Pitzer Colleges, offering faculty and facility resources no small college alone could sustain. The European Union Center of California and the Humanities Institute are both special education and research facilities housed on the Scripps campus.

In late 2008, the new Sallie Tiernan Field House will be completed, offering students a 24,000-square-foot, state-of-the art recreational and athletic facility with an aerobics studio, cardio machine room, weight room, and other spaces for fitness and health education. The Field House is located next to Scripps' 25-meter swimming pool.

TUITION, ROOM, BOARD AND FEES

Costs for the 2007-2008 academic year:

Tuition and fees: $35,850

Room and board: $10,800

Total: $46,650

FINANCIAL AID

Scripps seeks out the very best students and offers admission without regard to ability to pay. Financial Aid is awarded to approximately 60 percent of students, and this aid can include grants, scholarships, loans, and part-time student employment. Financial need determines the type and amount of awards. High-achieving students are also eligible for academic scholarships through the James E. Scripps and New Generation Scholarship Programs. The deadline for academic scholarship applications is November 1.

Mandatory Financial Aid forms: FAFSA and CSS/PROFILE

Priority filing date: February 1

Financial Aid inquiries should be directed to David Levy, Director of Financial Aid, at 909-621-8275.

STUDENT ORGANIZATIONS AND ACTIVITIES

Over 200 clubs and organizations are available at the Claremont Colleges. Students can also choose from a variety of five-college and Scripps campus events, 10 NCAA Division III sports teams, intramural and club sports teams. Scripps' intercollegiate sports teams are composed of students from Claremont McKenna, Harvey Mudd, and Scripps Colleges (CMS). In addition, the five-time national championship titleholders, the Claremont Colleges Ballroom Dance Company (CCBDC), is a 5-college organization with some 80 student participants who host frequent performances, workshops and dance activities.

ADMISSIONS PROCESS

The desired Scripps applicant is involved, intellectually curious, and interested in exploring an intensive liberal arts curriculum. High academic achievement is expected, as is personal success. Scripps also highly regards leadership, motivation, honesty, and creativity.

Every part of a student's application is important to the Admission Committee. The quality of a student's academic work is key, and a recommended course of study includes five academic subjects in each year of high school, for a total of 4 years of English, 4 years of mathematics, 3 years of social studies, 3 years of laboratory science (biology, chemistry, or physics), and either 3 years of a foreign language or 2 years each of two different languages. Honors, Advanced Placement, or International Baccalaureate courses are highly regarded by the Committee. Applicants are encouraged to take the SAT II: Subject Tests and to schedule an interview. Also required are an essay and a graded writing assignment from the junior or senior year of high school. Art or music supplements are welcomed. Scripps College is an exclusive user of the Common Application, which must be submitted online.

SAT scores for class entering fall of 2007:

> Middle 50 percent critical reading: 650-740

> Middle 50 percent math: 630-700

Average Weighted GPA for class entering fall of 2007: 3.9

Early Decision Application Deadlines: November 1, January 1

Academic Scholarship Application Deadline: November 1

Regular Decision Application Deadline: January 1

SEATTLE UNIVERSITY

AT A GLANCE

Seattle University, founded in 1891, is one of 28 Jesuit colleges and universities in the United States. The undergraduate student body numbers 4,253 and includes representatives from 55 states and territories and 76 nations. Seattle University provides an ideal environment for motivated students interested in self-reliance, awareness of different cultures, social justice, and the fulfillment that comes from making a difference. Our location in the center of one of the nation's most diverse and progressive cities attracts a student body, faculty, and staff rich in diversity. Our urban setting promotes the development of leadership skills and independence and provides the opportunity for students to apply what they learn through internships, clinical experiences, and volunteer work.

The student life program includes over 80 extracurricular clubs and organizations. Three residence halls and an on-campus apartment complex house 1,700 students, and undergraduate housing is available all four years. Approximately 89% of the freshmen and sophomores live on campus. The Connolly Athletic Center serves as the major facility for varsity and intramural athletics and recreation. It features two swimming pools, two gymnasiums, and saunas. A 6-acre complex provides fields for outdoor sports.

Seattle University is accredited by the Northwest Commission on Colleges and Universities, the Accreditation Board for Engineering and Technology, AACSB International-Association to Advance Collegiate Schools of Business, the American Chemical Society, the Commission on Accreditation of Allied Health Education Programs, the National Association of Schools of Public Affairs and Administration, the National Council for Accreditation of Teacher Education, Association of Theological Schools, the Commission on Collegiate Nursing Education, Council on Social Work Education, and the American Bar Association.

LOCATION AND ENVIRONMENT

Seattle University is located in a port city of unsurpassed natural beauty. As the Pacific Northwest's largest city (and the 14th largest metropolitan area in the United States), Seattle is a scenic and cultural center in a setting that includes breathtaking mountain views of the Cascades to the east and the Olympics to the west. In addition to being situated along Puget Sound, Seattle also contains Lakes Union and Washington.

The campus is located in the center of the city. Seattle's sights and sounds, rich ethnic diversity, celebrated restaurants, first-run entertainment, major-league athletics, theater, opera, and ballet enhance campus life.

OFF-CAMPUS OPPORTUNITIES

Seattle University offers three international study programs- programs for French in France, Latin American Studies in Mexico, Chinese in China, and three reciprocal exchange programs with the University of Graz in Austria, Sophia University in Japan, and Taejon University in Korea. Additional study abroad programs in other nations, in conjunction with other colleges' overseas programs, are also offered.

Seattle University is affiliated with the Council for International Educational Exchange, a consortium of colleges and universities which sponsor a variety of Academic Programs around the world.

MAJORS AND DEGREES OFFERED

Seattle University offers the following undergraduate degrees: Bachelor of Arts, Bachelor of Science, Bachelor of Science in Nursing, Bachelor of Social Work, Bachelor of Criminal Justice, and the Bachelor of Arts in Business Administration. The University offers 53 majors and 31 minors in five academic units: The Albers School of Business and Economics; The College of Arts and Sciences; The College of Nursing; The College of Science and Engineering; and The Matteo Ricci College.

Undergraduate Programs include accounting; art history; Asian studies, biochemistry; biology; business administration; business economics; chemistry; clinical laboratory science; communication; computer engineering, computer science; criminal justice; cultural anthropology; diagnostic ultrasound; e-commerce, environmental science; environmental studies; economics; electronic commerce; engineering (civil, computer, electrical, environmental, and mechanical); English/creative writing; exercise science; finance; fine, applied, and performing arts; French; general science; German; history; humanities; humanities for teaching; international business; international studies; journalism; liberal studies; management; marketing; mathematics; military science/ROTC; music; nursing; philosophy; physics; political science; pre-law; pre-medical/pre-dental; psychology; public affairs; sociology; Spanish; theology/religious studies; and women's studies.

ACADEMIC PROGRAMS

Students at Seattle University take a program of liberal studies called the core curriculum. The university core curriculum has several distinguishing characteristics: it provides an integrated freshman year; gives order and sequence to student learning; provides experience in the methods and content of the range of liberal arts, sciences, philosophy, and theology; calls for active learning in all classes, for practice in writing and thinking, and for an awareness of values; fosters a global perspective and a sense of social and personal responsibility. Our academic offerings provide leadership opportunities and enable graduates to serve society through a demanding liberal arts and social sciences foundation. In the Jesuit educational tradition we teach students how to think, not what to think.

Seattle University offers two honors program options for students seeking the greatest possible challenge. The University Honors Program is a small select two year long learning community. It is humanities focused, and its fully integrated curriculum examines the most significant texts and ideas of Western culture. The Core Honors Program involves seminar sections of nine required courses in English, history, philosophy, social science, and theology/religious studies. This option is particularly suited to students in profession oriented majors where participation in University Honors is less feasible due to specific major requirements and scheduling conflicts. Admission is competitive and requires a separate application.

CAMPUS FACILITIES AND EQUIPMENT

The University is located on 58 acres in the First Hill neighborhood in the center of Seattle. There are 28 buildings recently enhanced by additions, renovations, and new construction. Total assets is valued at $497.2 million and the endowment is $214.8 million.

TUITION, ROOM, BOARD AND FEES

For the 2008-2009 academic year, full-time tuition is $28,260; room and meals are $8,340. The estimate for books, supplies, fees and personal expenses is an additional $3,495. Travel costs vary among students. Costs are subject to change. Seattle University operates on a quarter calendar with fall term beginning in late September.

FINANCIAL AID

Approximately 87 percent of new freshmen receive an average Financial Aid award of $20,360 per year. These awards usually include scholarships, grants, loans, and Federal Work-Study. Last year, Seattle University awarded more than $72.3 million in aid to undergraduates - nearly $30.6 million of that came from the university's own funds. Students are required to apply for Financial Aid by February 1, as awards are made early each spring for the following fall quarter. Applications that are received after this deadline will be evaluated in the order received for any remaining aid. Students must submit the Free Application for Federal Student Aid (FAFSA) and be accepted for admission to be considered for financial assistance. There are a number of scholarships for freshmen that are awarded on the basis of academic achievement, extracurricular involvement, and community service. Transfer scholarships are also available.

STUDENT ORGANIZATIONS AND ACTIVITIES

All undergraduates belong to the Associated Students of Seattle University (ASSU), the central student organization on campus, which is organized around an elected president, an executive vice president, and an activities vice president. Additionally, a 12-member representative council oversees every facet of the student body and is responsible for policy making, a diverse activities program, and the communication of student needs to the administration and faculty.

ADMISSIONS PROCESS

Seattle University is committed to qualitative decision making based upon evaluations of students as a whole. Decisions are based primarily upon individual course selection, performance, and trends. The expected academic program comprises 16 units of coursework, including 4 years of English, 3 years of social studies or history, 2 years of a foreign language, 3 years of college-preparatory mathematics, and 2 units of lab science (3 are preferred). Laboratory physics and chemistry, as well as 4 units of college-preparatory mathematics are required for engineering; we require laboratory chemistry and biology for admission to the nursing program. Also required for all programs are offical scores from either the ACT or the SAT I. The middle 50 percent of enrolling freshmen have secondary school averages of 3.3-3.8 (on a 4.0 scale).

Essays or personal statements are required for admission and are carefully considered during application review. College credit is awarded to those who have successfully earned minimum scores on Advanced Placement or International Baccalaureate examinations.

Applications and information can be obtained by contacting the Admissions Office. Secondary school students who have completed at least six semesters are encouraged to complete the application process by February 1 of their senior year. Transfer students must submit official transcripts from all post-secondary institutions attended, regardless of whether course work was completed. The recommended Financial Aid/admission deadline for transfers is March 1. Applications are accepted after these dates but Financial Aid funds may no longer be available.

Campus visits can be scheduled Monday through Friday and many Saturdays. Guests can attend a class, meet with faculty, participate in a campus tour, and speak individually with representatives from admissions. Students can apply directly or online via our website, www.seattleu.edu. Seattle University is a member of The Common Application and the Universal College Application.

SETON HALL UNIVERSITY

AT A GLANCE

Seton Hall University was founded in 1856 and has been dedicated to supporting the vision of its founder, Bishop James Roosevelt Bayley, as providing "a home for the mind, the heart, and the spirit."

FOR THE MIND: We offer more than 60 majors and concentrations taught by 860 full-time faculty, in six undergraduate schools with practical, real-world emphasis. FOR THE HEART: We offer a compassionate, diverse and collaborative environment that focuses on academic and ethical development. FOR THE SPIRIT: Our faith and spiritual commitments inspire faculty to educate students to become servant leaders in their personal and professional lives, and in society.

Seton Hall's campus spans 58 acres, and is home to 5,300 undergraduate students, with 82 percent of its freshmen living on campus. While Seton Hall certainly enjoys a big reputation, our campus community is actually close-knit and inclusive. Students receive personal attention with an average class ranging from 25 to 30 students and a student to faculty ratio of 14:1. Students, faculty and staff come from around the world, representing all 50 states and 67 countries, creating a diverse yet unified campus environment.

LOCATION AND ENVIRONMENT

Seton Hall provides students with the best of both worlds. Nestled in the charming Village of South Orange, New Jersey, our campus is only 14 miles from one of the world's most exciting cities. So while you're close to the action, fun and excitement of New York City, you are still able to live your day-to-day life in a more relaxed atmosphere.

South Orange remains a suburban residential area. Our campus is located just a few minutes away from the Village center where you will find clothing stores, grocery stores, ice cream and coffee shops, restaurants, hair stylists and a movie/performing arts theater.

"Everything is at my fingertips, everything is here."

Andrea Granda

Biology

Jersey City, New Jersey

Once in town, it's easy to hop on a train and arrive in the heart of midtown Manhattan in just 30 minutes. Known as the capital of finance, fashion, art and entertainment, the Big Apple offers the best of everything. From there, visit the neighborhood and destination of your choice to enjoy world-renowned restaurants, popular night spots and concert venues featuring bands and comedians, unforgettable sightseeing, Tony Award-winning plays and musicals, and unbeatable shopping.

"I love our proximity to New York. Our location just sweetened the deal for me."

Matt Steele

Political Science/Classical Studies/History

Cincinnati, Ohio

Consider all the international companies and organizations based in the New York/New Jersey Metropolitan area. Seton Hall's prime location puts you at the center of endless opportunities where students can take advantage of internships with museums, nonprofit and government agencies, law and accounting firms, television and print media…the list goes on and on.

MAJORS AND DEGREES OFFERED

Seton Hall University is committed to academic excellence. During their first two years, undergraduate students are exposed to a world of ideas from great scholars, and concepts that open their mind to new perspectives, history and achievements of many cultures. This approach helps many of our students choose their majors and minors, while giving them plenty of time to focus on these areas in their third and fourth years.

And if you're worried that you will be just one of many students vying for your professors' time, you can relax. At Seton Hall, you are more than just a number. Most classes average 25 students and fewer than 4 percent of courses are taught by teaching assistants. Our low student-to-faculty ratio of 14:1 ensures that you get the personal attention you need.

"I give the highest importance to my contact with students—they are the school's most important asset."

Ambassador S. Azmat Hassan

Senior Faculty Associate

Whitehead School of Diplomacy and International Relations

We offer core courses in broad range of disciplines within our six undergraduate schools and colleges:

- College of Arts and Sciences—offering an impressive 33 majors and 34 minors in fields ranging from English, art and music to physics, biology and health professions.

- College of Education and Human Services—with 95 percent of our students passing the national teaching exam in 2006-2007, it's not surprising that education graduates have a nearly 100 percent job placement rating. Furthermore, the College of Education and Human Services is accredited by the National Council for Accreditation of Teacher Education.

- College of Nursing—the oldest and largest nursing school in New Jersey, educates more than one-third of New Jersey's nurses. Students are working toward degrees in the BSN, MSN and MA programs the school offers. The College of Nursing is accredited by the New Jersey State Board of Nursing and the National League for Nursing and there is not a hospital in the state of New Jersey that does not employee a Seton Hall University nursing graduate.

- Immaculate Conception Seminary School of Theology—offers programs for seminarians studying for Catholic priesthood as well a BA degree in Catholic Theology. Founded in 1861, it is the major seminary of the Catholic Archdiocese of Newark.

- Stillman School of Business—ranked in the top 10 of undergraduate business programs at Catholic Colleges and is accredited by the Association to Advance Collegiate School of Business (AACSB). The school offers programs in accounting, economics, finance, management information systems, management, marketing and sports management.

- Whitehead School of Diplomacy and International Relations—the newest school on campus, is the first professional school of international affairs to be established after the Cold War. Among our faculty are six current and former ambassadors and U.N. officials. The school also has an exclusive alliance with the United Nations Association of the USA.

"We are constantly exposed to new opportunities, new ways of thinking. Through the Hall's experiential programs, possibilities I otherwise never would have considered have been placed before me."

Christen Walker-James

Religious Studies

New York, New York

The Princeton Review's Complete Book of Colleges

Choosing Seton Hall is just the start of your academic journey. Our rigorous programs, dedicated faculty and small classes will support you as you learn, grow and prepare to become a responsible leader in a global society.

CAMPUS FACILITIES AND EQUIPMENT

At Seton Hall, there is a major emphasis on the use of state-of-the-art technology and available facilities to aid in the overall development and college experience for all students, including:

- Our award-winning Mobile Computing Program provides all incoming, full-time freshman a brand new, fully loaded laptop. Two years later, you'll trade it for a newer model with a faster processor and the latest software. And when you graduate in four years, you can keep it.

- Seton Hall's Recreation Center serves the recreational and fitness needs of the Seton Hall community. Here students can work out on cardio machines, go for a swim in our Olympic sized pool, run on the indoor track or tear-up the six indoor basketball courts. The brand new fitness center features a free-weight center, new cardiovascular equipment, plasma screen televisions and wireless headsets to listen to the TVs.

- The Walsh library is a state-of-the-art research facility complete with a computerized card catalog, 10 CD-ROM data search and retrieval stations, 200 computer terminals for undergraduates, four electronic multimedia facilities and approximately one million holdings.

- The University Center houses most of Seton Hall's cultural, social and recreational activities. The University Center is the hub of student activity, and includes the Galleon Dining Room/food court, the Pirate's Cove (lounge and coffee house), Theatre-in-the-Round, a study lounge and the student government office.

- The University offers students such services as aptitude testing, career counseling, career services, health services, personal counseling and special services.

TUITION, ROOM, BOARD AND FEES

Seton Hall offers a flat-tuition rate for students taking between 12-18 credit hours. The 2007-2008 flat-tuition rate is $27,850, including the Mobile Computing Program fee. Room and Board fees range depending on meal plans; however, an average cost is $9,710. An example of tuition, fees, and room & board for an incoming freshman of the 2007-2008 academic year, based on 31 credits, would be $37,860 for the year.

FINANCIAL AID

Financing a college education is a major family investment. That's why Seton Hall University is committed to providing you with the resources you need to make your dreams a reality. Here at Seton Hall, 90 percent of our students receive some form of Financial Aid and 2/3 of entering freshmen receive scholarships or grants directly from the University.

At Seton Hall, all that is required to begin the process of applying for need-based Financial Aid is the completion and submission of the Free Application for Federal Student Aid (FAFSA) form. Merit-based aid does not require a FAFSA but it is strongly encouraged, as these scholarships rarely pay the entire cost of attendance. Most scholarships do not require a separate application.

STUDENT ORGANIZATIONS AND ACTIVITIES

Your experiences at Seton Hall extend way beyond the classroom. As a student, you're always learning—whether you're joining a Greek organization, spinning discs at our award-winning radio station, WSOU, touring as a member of our Madrigal Choir or serving as a member of our Student Government Association. From student media to sports to professional societies to religious organizations, our 100-plus clubs and organizations offers something for everyone.

Athletics is a big part of life at Seton Hall and there is almost nothing more thrilling than Pirate Athletics. With 17 men's and women's varsity athletic teams competing in the BIG EAST Conference, Seton Hall gives you the opportunity to see college athletics at its most competitive level. In addition to varsity athletics, you can join a club sport or gather a team to play one of 18 different intramural sports, with about 70 percent of the student population participating.

ADMISSIONS PROCESS

In selecting new students, Seton Hall University takes into account secondary school performance records, SAT 1 or ACT scores, and guidance counselor and teacher evaluations. Applicants must have graduated from an accredited secondary school or have received satisfactory marks on the GED test. The University requires that applicants complete 16 high school credits: four in English, two in foreign language (consecutively), one in laboratory science, three in mathematics, two in social studies, and four in accepted academic electives.

Applicants requesting a transfer to the University must have at least a 2.5 GPA (some Academic Programs may require a higher GPA) and must have performed satisfactorily at the previous school attended. Credit is generally awarded for grades of C or better in university-level curriculum taken at recognized institutions; students may transfer up to 100 credit hours to apply toward a bachelor's program at Seton Hall. The deadlines for transfer students to apply to the University are June 1 for the fall semester and December 1 for the spring semester.

Freshman applicants must provide high school transcript, SAT I or ACT scores, and complete either a print or online application. Applicants must also submit a teacher evaluation, counselor report and a personal essay. They may also wish to take part in a personal interview.

Admission to the University is granted on a rolling basis, however, Seton Hall's early action deadline is November 15. Students applying non-binding early action will receive an admission decision on or before December 30. Seton Hall's preferred deadline for regular admission is March 1.

For more information, contact the Office of Undergraduate Admission:

Website: www.shu.edu

Telephone: 1-800-THE-HALL

E-mail: thehall@shu.edu

SHENANDOAH UNIVERSITY

AT A GLANCE

Admission to Shenandoah University is selective, but we want you to consider this: It's not about where you get in; it's about where you fit in. Students who fit in at Shenandoah value the size advantage, the academic programs, the opportunity to be involved, and the university's location.

Shenandoah enrolls 3,000 students. The average class size is 14 students and the student/faculty ratio is 10:1.

SU offers more than 80 academic programs. Athletic training, physical therapy, and pharmacy are very popular these programs combine undergraduate and graduate studies in a way that allow students to earn a master's or doctoral degree in five to six years. Environmental studies, kinesiology, psychology, political science, sociology, history, foreign languages, biology, chemistry, teacher education, and mass communications are popular liberal arts majors.

The School of Business allows students to personalize their studies with an emphasis in accounting, finance, marketing, management, computer technology, and international business.

Students in the nursing program can major in nursing or respiratory care.

The Shenandoah Conservatory enjoys a national reputation. Great facilities and abundant performance opportunities benefit every conservatory student. Arts management, music performance, music education, theater, musical theater, and dance are popular majors.

SU offers more than 50 clubs and organizations, with student government, the university newspaper, academic fraternities and sororities, and the campus television station being the most popular. Student athletes fit in at SU and participate in one or more of the 16 NCAA Division III athletic teams fielded by the university. Students can live on campus or join other students in nearby apartments and rental houses.

The surrounding city of Winchester is a safe community with shopping malls, boutiques, movie theaters, restaurants, and coffee shops. Road trips to the metropolitan areas of Washington, DC; Baltimore, MD; and Richmond, VA are popular.

FINANCIAL AID
Federal Work Study is available.

ADMISSIONS PROCESS
Average SAT: 1066

Average Verbal: 534

Average Math: 532

Average ACT: 23

Average GPA: 3.4

SIENA COLLEGE

AT A GLANCE

Siena develops leaders capable of extraordinary achievement. Students realize their potential through a blending of the liberal arts and professional studies that combines challenging academics with real-world experiences. Committed to the development of the whole person, Siena, a Franciscan and Catholic college, advances the intellectual, spiritual, religious, and ethical growth of its students. Siena offers 28 degree programs and 46 minors and certificates. These academic areas can be blended in many combinations to prepare you for the career of your choice. By combining these programs, Siena College graduates are prepared to enter graduate or professional school or their professions.

Our students benefit from engaging classroom experiences, taught by qualified faculty (93% of whom hold the highest degree in their field), in small settings designed to develop meaningful mentorship for our students. The student to faculty ratio is 14:1, class sizes average 21 students and science labs have no more than 19 students! Siena students engage in independent study and research projects with faculty. Over one-third of Siena faculty work along side Siena students doing original research.

Our 166 acre suburban campus is located in Loudonville, two miles north of Albany, New York, the state capital. The Capital Region is home to over 60,000 college students and offers more than you can imagine. Outings can include shopping or a movie at Crossgates Mall or Colonie Center, cheering on the Siena Saints or Bon Jovi at the Times Union Center or skiing at one of the five mountains within a one hour drive of campus. Students enjoy significant internship and employment opportunities in the Capital Region too.

LOCATION AND ENVIRONMENT

Siena College, a residential campus in a suburban setting, is located minutes from New York's Capital, Albany. The Capital Region economy is vibrant due to significant career opportunities in the following industries: technology, research and development, health care, education, financial services, government and communications. This diverse economic foundation provides Siena students many internships opportunities. Albany is also home to the Times Union Center, a premier concert and athletic venue, and the home of our Division I basketball team, the Siena Saints!

OFF-CAMPUS OPPORTUNITIES

Students can go to the Times Union Center, a premier concert and athletic venue, and the home of our Division I basketball team, the Siena Saints! Other off-campus options include three shopping malls, numerous restaurants, grocery stores, and mountains to go skiing/ hiking. With all of these options students won't be bored!

MAJORS AND DEGREES OFFERED

Siena College offers 28 degree programs and 46 minors and certificates. These academic areas can be blended in many combinations to prepare you for the career of your choice. For more information on specific majors please see www.siena.edu/academics

ACADEMIC PROGRAMS

School of Liberal Arts

American Studies

Classics

Creative Arts

Economics

English

French

History

Philosophy

Political Science

Psychology

Religious Studies

Social Work

Sociology

Spanish

School of Business

Accounting

Economics

Finance

Marketing and Management

School of Science

Biochemistry

Biology

Chemistry

Computational Science

Computer Science

3-2 Engineering

Environmental Studies

Mathematics

Physics

CAMPUS FACILITIES AND EQUIPMENT

Located on a 166 acre campus, the campus has undergone extensive building and renovation in the past few years. Recent additions to campus include the Standish Library, Morrell Science Center, Hickey Financial Technology Center, Business Marketing Research Lab, Sarazen Student Union and Serra Dining Hall.

The Morrell Science Center enhances both learning and research. The modern expanded labs are equipped with the latest technologies, modern lighting and HVAC systems. The Sarazen Student Union is a place to learn, relax, get involved, buy books, or grab a bite to eat. It is the hub of student activity at Siena. The Hickey Financial Technology Center is home to the William Raub Market Trading Room. The trading room provides our students with the ability to trade stocks, bonds, currency and commodities in a virtual environment. The Business Marketing Research Lab allows students to apply their analytical, computer, and research skills to real problems in marketing and related business areas.

TUITION, ROOM, BOARD AND FEES

Cost: $31,385 (Tuition, Room, Board and Fees for 2007-2008)

FINANCIAL AID

Siena College is founded on a clear set of values: to assist students in realizing their potential for extraordinary achievement and to assure its quality undergraduate liberal arts education is accessible to those who seek it. 86% of Siena Students receive Financial Aid. For more information, please visit www.siena.edu/financialaid

STUDENT ORGANIZATIONS AND ACTIVITIES

21st Century Leadership Society

Asian Students Association

Siena Mentoring Program

Best Buddies

Biology Club

Black and Latino Student Union

Campus Action

Cheerleading Squad

Chemistry Club

Colleges Against Cancer

Comic Book Club

Computer Science Club

Dance Team

Delta Sigma Pi

Dog Pound

English Society

Education Club

Equestrian Team

Financial Management Association

Habitat for Humanity

History Club

Hockey (Men)

Gaelic Society

Gaming Club

Gay Straight Alliance

Habitat for Humanity

History Club

Karate Club

Model United Nations

Moot Court / Mock Trial

Musical Appreciation Program

Muslim Students Association

Outing Club

Pendragon

Philosophy Club

Physics Club

Political Science Society

Pre-Law Society

Promethean - Student Newspaper.

Psychology Club

Republican Club

Rotaract

Men's Rugby

Women's Rugby Club

SCTV (Siena College Television)

SC Productions

Siena College Democrats

Siena Greens

Ski Club

Social Work Club

Stage III Theatre

Students in Free Enterprise

Table Tennis Club

Volleyball Club

Volunteer Ministries Board

Yearbook

ADMISSIONS PROCESS

Siena's Admissions Committee looks for the following when examining prospective students' applications:

A SOLID ACADEMIC CURRICULUM including:

Four years of high school English

Four years of high school History/ Social Science

Four years of high school Mathematics through trigonometry

Three to four years of high school Science

Three years of high school Foreign Language

AN ACADEMIC AVERAGE of 87 or higher (solid B to B+).

EVIDENCE OF ACTIVITY showing the student's enthusiasm for extra-curricular engagement and involvement within his or her community.

A PERSONAL ESSAY that is interesting and well-written. This can consist of a graded essay assignment from their junior or senior year.

STANDARDIZED TEST SCORES, our Critical Reading and Math combined score average is an 1153 for accepted students. The ACT composite score average is 24 for accepted students. Students may submit ACT test scores in place of SAT Reasoning scores. Siena requires applicants to submit SAT writing scores and ACT writing sub-scores during the 2007-2008 Admissions cycle.

SOLID LETTER OF RECOMMENDATION from the high school counselor/college advisor. Any additional letters of recommendation that a student wishes to have evaluated are welcome.

The Admissions Committee also encourages students interested in Siena College to visit the campus for a program, tour or interview. Students who feel comfortable on campus and connected to its community are well positioned to succeed, to be happy with themselves and their place at the College, and to graduate in four years.

SIMMONS COLLEGE

AT A GLANCE

In 1899, decades before women in America gained the right to vote, Simmons College was founded on a revolutionary idea, that women should be able to earn independent livelihoods and lead meaningful lives. Simmons College was the result. Today, Simmons provides a strong liberal arts education for undergraduate women that is integrated with professional career preparation, interdisciplinary study, and global perspectives. Simmons also encompasses the many benefits of a small university, including renowned coeducational graduate programs and the world's only M.B.A. designed specifically for women.

Simmons's interdisciplinary approach offers great advantages: a broad education and view of the world; personalized plans of study; and a chance to develop a range of professional skills and strengths needed for graduate school and an increasingly competitive job market. Every student explores a variety of subjects while gaining an in-depth theoretical and practical understanding of her major. First-year core courses emphasize critical thinking and writing skills, while integrating two or more subjects, ranging from bioethics and Buddhist studies to computational linguistics and visual communication.

Students fulfill their independent learning requirement through internships, fieldwork, and research projects. In doing so, they develop skills, confidence, and a network of professional contacts. Many spend one or more semesters interning for businesses and organizations, ranging from Boston Public Schools and The Boston Globe to the Museum of Fine Arts, Smash Advertising, and the World Affairs Council. Simmons's Longwood Medical Area partnerships provide exceptional clinical opportunities at Boston's world-renowned hospitals. On campus, students conduct research in state-of-the-art labs, in areas such as materials science, gene splicing, and computer modeling. Moreover, professors frequently invite undergraduates to collaborate on professional research projects, articles, and presentations.

Acquiring a global outlook is integral at Simmons, including an understanding of languages, cultures, and international politics. Programs such as Africana studies, East Asian studies, international relations, and modern languages offer a direct route to cross-cultural immersion. Simmons encourages students to spend an entire semester or year abroad, and also offers short-term courses that allow students to explore topics such as journalism in South Africa, music in Austria, or history and civilization in Japan. Students also participate in local and international service learning projects, ranging from education initiatives in Boston to health care in Nicaragua.

Above all, Simmons offers a learning experience that is highly collaborative and much more personal than that of large universities. A 12:1 student/teacher ratio ensures that each student receives individual attention. The Simmons faculty includes noted researchers, authors, and experts in their respective fields, yet professors passionately uphold their primary obligation to teach. Students say the small classes, intellectual focus, and welcoming environment contribute to their confidence and success.

There is not one "type" of Simmons student, but there are some common qualities. Simmons women are extremely motivated and open-minded. They are serious about their personal and professional goals, and they are determined to make a difference in the world.

Approximately 80 percent of Simmons's 2,072 undergraduates live in college housing, two blocks from the main campus. The "quintessential New England" residence campus features nine residence halls and a private, landscaped quad, as well as Bartol Dining Hall, the state-of-the-art Holmes Sports Center, a student-run cafe, and the campus health center. From campus, it's a short stroll to nearby shops, cafes, clubs, museums, movie theaters, parks, and public transportation. Students say they love the fact that they can easily access the city's rich social and cultural resources, and then come home to a safe, friendly campus.

LOCATION AND ENVIRONMENT

According to students, Simmons offers the best of both words, an intimate college environment in the heart of a vibrant city. The historic, tree-lined Simmons campus is located in Boston's eclectic Fenway neighborhood, which is alive with music and fine arts, medical care and research, action and activism, and the re-

sounding cheers of baseball fans at legendary Fenway Park. Considered by many to be the best "college town" in the nation, Boston has more than 50 colleges and universities and approximately 300,000 students. Compact, historic, charming, and clean, the city is easy to get around on foot or via the public transportation system.

OFF-CAMPUS OPPORTUNITIES

Simmons is a member of the Colleges of the Fenway consortium, which allows students to cross-register with neighboring colleges, including Emmanuel College, Massachusetts College of Art, Massachusetts College of Pharmacy and Allied Health Sciences, Wentworth Institute of Technology, and Wheelock College. A domestic exchange program allows juniors to spend a semester at Mills College, Spelman College, or Fisk University. Students interested in international study may elect to spend one semester or one year at an approved university exchange, or participate in intensive study abroad programs during the spring semester. Qualified students, usually juniors, also may apply for the Washington Semester at American University in Washington, D.C. Other opportunities include Success Connection, a mentoring program that matches select seniors with highly successful Simmons alumnae, and the Barbara Lee Internship Fellows program, which places students in Massachusetts legislators' offices and policy advocacy groups for one semester.

MAJORS AND DEGREES OFFERED

Simmons offers more than 40 majors and programs. In 2007, the top five majors were nursing, communications, psychology, sociology, and English. The OPEN program (Option for Personalized Educational Needs) allows students to custom design majors. A number of integrated degrees and accelerated programs allow students to go directly from an undergraduate program to earning a graduate degree in areas such as education, liberal arts, health care, physical therapy, and science information technology. Simmons offers a dual-degree undergraduate/

The Princeton Review's Complete Book of Colleges

graduate degree program in chemistry/pharmacy in collaboration with Massachusetts College of Pharmacy and Allied Health Sciences, as well as individually designed preprofessional programs for dentistry, law, medicine, and veterinary medicine. Simmons students typically declare a major by the end of their sophomore year, and nearly a third of Simmons students choose to double major. Visit www.simmons.edu/academics/undergraduate for a complete list of majors and Academic Programs.

ACADEMIC PROGRAMS

Simmons offers a strong liberal arts education integrated with professional preparation, interdisciplinary study, and global perspectives. A minimum of 128 semester hours is required for graduation. Students must demonstrate competence in math and foreign language, complete a core curriculum in the liberal arts and sciences (40 semester hours), complete the courses required for the selected major/s (20 to 40 semester hours for each major depending on the program), fulfill an independent learning requirement (8 to 16 semester hours), and round out their program with appropriate electives.

Students may select interdepartmental programs, declare double majors, or participate in an undergraduate-to-graduate degree program. In addition, the OPEN program allows students to design their own program of study, combining courses from several fields. Other special academic opportunities include Simmons's outstanding honors, service learning, and study-abroad programs. The Dorothea Lynde Dix Scholars option is available for women who are 24 years or older, or who hold a previous bachelor's degree.

CAMPUS FACILITIES AND EQUIPMENT

The beautiful Simmons campus offers an attractive, practical mix of historic and modern architecture, including state-of-the-art facilities and conveniences. The Main College Building houses a dining area and coffee bar, lecture halls and classrooms, administrative and faculty offices, the bookstore, the Student Activities Center, art studios, music practice rooms, and the Trustman Art Gallery.

Park Science Center offers technologically advanced learning environments, including faculty and student research facilities, fully equipped science laboratories, environmental rooms, observation rooms for psychological testing, and food science kitchens.

One Palace Road, the new state-of-the-art home for Simmons' s School of Social Work and Graduate School of Library and Information Science, features electronic classrooms and also houses the centers for academic support, counseling, career education and resources, media, and technology. Simmons just completed a major renovation and expansion of Beatley Library, which offers a number of high tech services, including a wireless network, laptop loans, sophisticated online library service, technology-equipped group study rooms, and more. Construction is almost complete on a new state-of-the-art "green" building that will house the School of Management.

TUITION, ROOM, BOARD AND FEES

Tuition and fees for the 2007-2008 academic year are as follows:

Undergraduate tuition and fees: $27,468

Room and board: $11,138

Total: $38,606

Graduate tuition costs vary by program.

FINANCIAL AID

Approximately 82 percent of Simmons students receive Financial Aid. Scholarships, grants, loans, and federal work-study are determined by the Free Application for Federal Student Aid (FAFSA). Simmons also awards academic merit scholarships, ranging from $1,500 for Federal Student Aid (FAFSA).

STUDENT ORGANIZATIONS AND ACTIVITIES

Simmons has more than 50 student organizations and academic liaisons, including eight NCAA Division III varsity teams, honor societies, cultural organizations, volunteer programs, a literary magazine, and more.

ADMISSIONS PROCESS

Although there isn't one "type" of Simmons student, there are common qualities. Simmons women are intellectually motivated and open-minded. They are serious about their personal and professional goals, and they are determined to make a difference in the world. With this in mind, the Simmons admission team reviews applications to see not only what applicants have accomplished, but also who they are and what kind of person they hope to become.

The admission team also evaluates high school performance, SAT I or ACT scores, recommendations, and the application essay. If English is not the applicant's first language, TOEFL or IELTS scores are required. Additional English language proficiency exams are accepted on a case by case basis.

Simmons welcomes applications from prospective freshmen, transfer students, international students, and students who are beyond the traditional college age.

Although not required, an interview is highly recommended. This gives admission officers better perspective about an applicant's abilities, interests, and personality, and at the same time, allows the applicant to evaluate Simmons and decide if it's the right place for her.

Students may apply online or submit a print application. The Common Application, Universal Application or a Simmons College Application are all welcome. Applications should be submitted along with the $35 fee and all supporting credentials. Simmons waives the application fee for students who use an online application. For freshman the early action deadline is December 1 and is a nonbinding deadline; the regular decision deadline is February 1. Transfer students are evaluated on a continual basis; the preferred filing date for fall enrollment is April 1. All students applying for the semester beginning in January should apply by November 15.

Simmons encourages prospective students and their families to attend an admission event or request an individual visit. They are welcome to tour the campus, sit in on a class, talk to current students, or speak with a professor, department chair, or program director.

For further information, contact:

Office of Undergraduate Admission

Simmons College

300 The Fenway

Boston, MA 02115

Telephone: 800-345-8468 (toll free)

Fax: 617-521-3190

E-mail: ugadm@simmons.edu

Website: http://www.simmons.edu

SKIDMORE COLLEGE

AT A GLANCE

Skidmore College is an independent, coeducational liberal arts college located in Saratoga Springs, N.Y. With a student body of 2,200 and a faculty of 200 dedicated teacher-scholars, the college offers a wide array of academic majors in the liberal arts as well as in career-specific fields such as business, social work, education, and the fine and performing arts. Skidmore's history underscores a nimble spirit and adaptability to changing student needs that is still apparent. Founded in 1903 as a school for women, it was chartered as a four-year degree-granting college in 1922. As it grew and evolved, the college made the bold decision in the 1960s to build an entirely new campus. In the 1970s, Skidmore began admitting men, was chartered by Phi Beta Kappa, and launched its highly regarded University Without Walls, a nonresidential program for adult students. A program for the Master of Arts degree in liberal studies was added in 1993. Skidmore's academic program is designed to promote creative thinking across the disciplines. Skidmore believes that creative thought matters and the curriculum emphasizes strong foundations in the liberal arts and interdisciplinary study, and builds upon the colleges founding principle of linking theoretical and applied learning. It is not unusual for students to design cross-disciplinary double majors such as art history and business, or education and Spanish, and the curriculums flexibility allows for self-determined majors as well. The beautiful 650-acre campus has been upgraded and enhanced in the past decade with key renovations to the library, science center, athletic facilities, student center, and technology infrastructure. The spectacular Tang Teaching Museum and Art Gallery, opened in 2000, enriches the campus scene with experimental programming closely allied with the college's interdisciplinary focus. Co-curricular life on campus offers many options. The colleges 100 student clubs and organizations run the gamut and include student government, a cappella singing groups, The Skidmore News (student newspaper), WSPN Radio, comedy and cabaret troupes, and a number of cultural awareness groups. Skidmore athletes compete at the NCAA Division III level, and the college fields 19 intercollegiate teams. The riding and women's tennis teams have won national championships in recent years. Students are very active in the intramural sports program and enjoy abundant opportunities for personal fitness and recreation, both on campus and in the nearby Adirondack Mountains.

CAMPUS FACILITIES AND EQUIPMENT

Scribner Library, housing approximately 325,000 volumes, has been designated a depository for United States government documents. Students have access to 40 libraries in the region through the Colleges membership in an area council. Skidmore also participates in the Lockheed/Dialog system for information search and retrieval. Dana Science Center has laboratories and sophisticated equipment for the biology, chemistry, physics, and geoscience departments including two electron microscopes and a confocal scanning microscope. The Filene Music Building contains a large recital hall, practice and listening rooms, and a music library. Other special facilities include a language laboratory in Bolton Hall; the Art Building (open 24 hours), with studio space, numerous kilns, and ceramics, weaving, and jewelry-making studios; the Skidmore Theatre; and dance studios. Students have access to a computer center served by a cluster of nine SunSPARC-2 workstations. In 2000 2001, Skidmore opened an $11 million art museum at the center of its campus. September 2006 saw two major additions to the campus. The Northwoods Apartments opened with 380 single room units across ten new buildings. All are geothermally heated and cooled. A brand new dining hall also opened. The new facility offers extensive vegetarian options, fresh made pasta, locally grown organic items and a broad range of daily choices. A new music building with a 700 seat auditorium will be added in the next two years.

SKIDMORE
C O L L E G E

STUDENT ORGANIZATIONS AND ACTIVITIES

Skidmore students participate in all aspects of academic and social life on campus. They play a major role in governing the College through the Student Government Association (SGA) and numerous major College committees on which students serve as members. The SGA is authorized by the Board of Trustees; it is committed to the goals of responsible behavior and democratic self-government. The SGA concerns itself with a broad range of issues including educational policy, freshman orientation, SGA elections, social events, student publications, and student organizations and clubs. Elected faculty members and students serve side-by-side on three panels: the Academic Integrity Board, the All-College Council, and the Social Integrity Board.

ADMISSIONS PROCESS

Those seeking admission to Skidmore's freshman class should complete a secondary school curriculum that includes at least 16 credits in college-preparatory courses. The Admissions Committee is also pleased to consider applications from qualified high school juniors who plan to accelerate and enter college early. Applicants typically have completed 4 years of English, 4 years of a foreign language, 4 years of mathematics, 3 years of social studies, and 3 years of laboratory science. Applicants must provide a secondary school transcript, standardized test scores (SAT I with writing or ACT with writing), letters of recommendation from two teachers of academic subjects, and a report from their guidance counselor. Skidmore recommends that applicants submit scores for three SAT II Subject Tests. The school also strongly recommends a campus visit and interview. Through its participation in the Higher Education Opportunity Program (HEOP), Skidmore enrolls capable, energetic, and ambitious New Yorkers who, because of their academic and financial situations, would not otherwise gain admission to the College under traditional requirements. An applicant for admission registers by completing the Common Application and returning it with a $60 fee. All information should be postmarked by January 15. Applications from early decision candidates should be submitted by November 15 for the Round I early decision plan or by January 15 for the Round II early decision plan. Transfer candidates are urged to apply by April 1 for the next fall term and by November 15 for the next spring term.

SOUTH DAKOTA STATE UNIVERSITY

AT A GLANCE

South Dakota State University is located in Brookings, South Dakota. This small but lively town of nearly 19,000 people is just miles from the Minnesota border and less than an hour's drive to the state's largest city, Sioux Falls. SDSU has an enrollment of over 10,000 students making it the largest university in the state. You'll find a diverse campus experience here, with over 200 majors and minors and unique opportunities for "hands-on" learning in every field of study.

In addition to academics, SDSU has hundreds of activities to participate in, including academic and sports clubs, intramurals, theater, music, art, student government, student publications, multi-cultural events and more. All of this in addition to a beautiful campus, motivated professors and a safe, friendly atmosphere makes South Dakota State University a great place to get a quality education.

LOCATION AND ENVIRONMENT

South Dakota State University is located in Brookings, South Dakota. This small but lively town of nearly 19,000 people is just miles from the Minnesota border and less than an hour's drive to the state's largest city, Sioux Falls. SDSU has an enrollment of over 10,000 students making it the largest university in the state.

MAJORS AND DEGREES OFFERED

Degrees are offered through eight colleges: Agriculture and Biological Sciences, Arts and Science, Education and Counseling, Engineering, Family and Consumer Sciences, General Studies and Outreach Programs, Nursing, and Pharmacy, as well as the Graduate School. Additionally, the Honors College, operating within the existing university structure, provides highly motivated students with the opportunity to pursue a challenging honors course study as they work toward a degree in any major.

More than 200 majors, minors and options are available with more than 6,000 course offerings. Master's degrees are offered in more than thirty areas, and doctorates are available in eight fields. The University also offers degree programs through USDSU in Sioux Falls. Evening, DDN, Internet, off-campus courses and classes through the Cooperative Extension Service Learning Centers are available through the Outreach Programs Office.

ACADEMIC PROGRAMS

Undergraduate Programs

Associate degree programs in General Studies and General Agriculture.

Baccalaureate programs in the agricultural sciences, education, engineering and technology, family and consumer sciences, humanities and liberal arts, nursing, performing and visual arts, pharmaceutical sciences, physical and biological sciences, and social sciences.

Graduate Programs

Masters degrees in arts and sciences, agricultural and biological sciences, family and consumer sciences, education and counseling, engineering and technology, and nursing.

Doctor of Philosophy Degrees in Agriculture and Engineering, and the Computational, Physical, Biological, and Social Sciences; and Nursing.

Professional programs - the Doctor of Pharmacy (Pharm D).

CAMPUS FACILITIES AND EQUIPMENT

SDSU is home to the South Dakota Art Museum, the first fully accredited museum in the state to be recognized by the American Association of Museums. SDAM's collections include early masterpieces of Sioux Indian Tribal art, the famed Harvey Dunn paintings of pioneer life, and an extensive collection of Oscar Howe and Paul Goble's American Indian art. The exclusive Vera Way Marghab Linen Collection, the world's largest complete collection, features nearly 3,000 pieces of the exquisite, handstitched linen.

In only two years of operation, the Performing Arts Center's acoustics, its many uses, its flexibility, the number of events it hosts, and the high-caliber performances witnessed by audiences have given the facility a well-deserved reputation. The Performing Arts Center with its state-of-the-art Concert Hall with room for 1,000 and its 280-seat Studio Theatre, has become a bragging right not only of SDSU and Brookings, but, arguably, of the entire region.

The State Agricultural Heritage Museum transformed the former Stock Judging Pavilion into a home for exhibits that record and preserve the agrarian heritage of South Dakota. Visitors come from all fifty states and forty-five foreign countries.

Hilton M. Briggs Library, the state's largest, was opened in 1977. Briggs Library is a founding member of the South Dakota Library Network (SDLN), which provides electronic access to the holdings of forty academic, public, school, and special libraries in South Dakota. The SDLN Online Catalog provides bibliographic access to a database of approximately 2.5 million volumes available at the cooperating libraries. Through the network, library users have access to holdings from all ten of the State libraries, including official documents and more than one million other holdings at Briggs.

The seventy-acre McCrory Gardens and South Dakota Arboretum provide a beautiful setting for area residents and tourists to enjoy a stroll through the radiant colors and fragrances of one of the most beautiful small ornamental gardens in the nation. The South Dakota Arboretum's purpose is to test woody plants needed to protect agricultural fields and livestock from the region's harsh environment, to provide hardy trees to shade our towns and cities, and to test ornamental shrubs for both durability and beauty. Both the arboretum and gardens are managed by the SDSU Horticulture, Forestry, Landscape and Parks Department.

TUITION, ROOM, BOARD AND FEES

SD Residents

Tuition—16 credit semester $1,264

General Activity Fee—$22 per credit / 16 credit semester $352

University Support Fee—$67 per credit / 16 credit semester $1,072

Books—Estimate, per semester $350

Residence Hall Rent (double occupancy)— $1,120

Average Meal Plan per semester—$1,000

TOTAL SEMESTER COST—$5,158

TOTAL YEARLY COST—$10,316

Non-Residents & Children of Alumni

Tuition—16 credit semester $1,904

General Activity Fee—$22 per credit / 16 credit semester $352

University Support Fee—$67 per credit / 16 credit semester $1,072

Books—Estimate, per semester $350

Residence Hall Rent (double occupancy)— $1,120

Average Meal Plan per semester—$1,000

TOTAL SEMESTER COST—$5,758

TOTAL YEARLY COST—$11,516

Minnesota Reciprocity

Tuition—16 credit semester $2,064

General Activity Fee—$22 per credit / 16 credit semester $352

University Support Fee—$67 per credit / 16 credit semester $1,072

Books—Estimate, per semester $350

Residence Hall Rent (double occupancy)—$1,120

Average Meal Plan per semester—$1,000

TOTAL SEMESTER COST—$5,998

TOTAL YEARLY COST—$11,996

FINANCIAL AID

The Jackrabbit Guarantee, a revolutionary student financial aid award, has raised the academic bar of our entering freshmen. Offered to all first-time students who score a 24 or higher on the ACT, the scholarship program guarantees $4,000 in aid over four years ($1,000 per year). SDSU was the first university in our region to present this opportunity to incoming students.

Approximately 85% of the SDSU students attending full-time receive some type of financial assistance to help pay their educational costs. Financial assistance includes both need-based financial aid (grants, loans, work) as determined by the Free Application for Federal Student Aid, and other financial aid (scholarship, agency assistance, etc.) not based on need. Financial need is defined as the portion of educational costs not covered by family contributions. Average educational costs are determined by the Financial Aid Office and family contribution is calculated from information on the Free Application for Federal Student Aid (FAFSA).

To apply for federal financial aid the student (and if applicable the student's parents) need to complete a FAFSA; please go to FAFSA on the Web SDSU School Code is 003471. Financial Aid packages consist of federal loans, federal grants, federal work-study, and scholarships, in combination with the student's family contribution.

STUDENT ORGANIZATIONS AND ACTIVITIES

South Dakota State University has over 200 recognized Student Organizations, including: Cultural Organizations Departmental Associations, Honorary Organizations Religious Organizations, Special Interest Sports Clubs, Student Government and Program Boards, Men's Fraternities & Women's Fraternities

Intercollegiate Athletics

South Dakota State University is a Division I, National Collegiate Athletic Association member and offers competition in eleven sports for women and ten sports for men. The National Collegiate Athletic Association (NCAA) governs competition for both women and men.

Women compete in cross country, equestrian, indoor and outdoor track and field, volleyball, basketball, swimming, golf, tennis, softball and soccer. Men compete in cross country, indoor and outdoor track and field, football, basketball, swimming, golf, tennis, wrestling and baseball.

Intramurals and Recreational Sports and Sports Clubs

The purpose of the Intramural Program is to provide the opportunity for all activity-fee-paying women and men students, both undergraduate and graduate, to participate in organized and informal sports as regularly as their time and interests permit. From informal settings such as open swim and gyms, to league play in traditional sports such as football, basketball, softball, and volleyball, it is hoped that the individual will develop a good and lasting attitude toward physical activity and the worthy use of leisure time.

For further information, contact the Intramural Office at 605-688-4724 or website: http://www3.sdstate.edu/Athletics/Intramurals

ADMISSIONS PROCESS

Application Procedures

The SDSU Admissions Office processes applications on a rolling basis. Students are encouraged to apply well in advance (six to ten months) of the semester they wish to attend in order to arrange housing, apply for financial assistance, and to attend new student orientation/early

registration programs.

All applicants must submit the following to be considered for admission:

• Admission Application

• $20 Application Fee

If you have previously attended SDSU or another South Dakota public university as a degree-seeking student, you are not required to pay the application fee to SDSU.

• Official High School Transcript

• Official Report of ACT Scores

In addition, all transfer applicants must provide:

• Official College Transcript(s)

Questions regarding admission can be sent to:

South Dakota State University

Admissions Office

Box 2201

Brookings, SD 57007

605-688-4121—1-800-952-3541 (Toll Free)

e-mail: sdsu.admissions@sdstate.edu

www3.sdstate.edu

STATE UNIVERSITY OF NEW YORK— COLLEGE OF ENVIRONMENTAL SCIENCE AND FORESTRY

AT A GLANCE

ESF is the premier college in the United States for Academic Programs focused on the science, design, engineering, and management of our environment and natural resources. In fact, before there was "Earth Day" there was ESF, which was founded in 1911 as the New York State College of Forestry at Syracuse University. Over the past 97 years the College's mission has expanded to provide a fuller understanding of the range of environmental issues facing our global society. The College was re-chartered in 1972 as the State University of New York College of Environmental Science and Forestry, and is part of the state's 64 campus system for higher education. ESF currently offers 22 undergraduate and 28 graduate degree programs, including 8 Ph.D. programs, and is nationally-recognized for outstanding value, small class size, and student engagement in learning.

Our students share a common concern for the environment. They are hardworking, active learners who want to use their knowledge and experience to confront society's tough questions and make the world a better place to live. They arrive at the College as freshmen and transfers from throughout the United States to pursue professional education leading to a vast array of career pathways and advanced study.

The College's Academic Programs serve some of the largest and most productive sectors of the national economy. Students are broadly educated, prepared to take on responsibilities as citizens, and trained to be problem-solvers, managers and leaders. The hallmarks of the undergraduate educational experience at ESF include career-oriented programs with an unmatched range of course offerings, experiential learning provided through field experiences, internships and research activities, and highly developed analytical and problem solving skills. The Faculty is responsible for delivering all undergraduate instruction in addition to their research, graduate level teaching and public service responsibilities. More than 90% of the Faculty have completed a Ph.D. or terminal degree, and more than 75% are employed full-time.

ESF graduates experience excellent employment opportunities and are admitted to the nation's best graduate schools. More than 95% are employed or enrolled in advanced study within six months of graduation.

The academic, cultural, and social lives of ESF students are enhanced through the College's long-standing partnership with neighboring Syracuse University. ESF students live in SU residence halls and access all of the University's resources while paying affordable State University of new York tuition rates. The College also owns more than 25,000 acres of forest property located throughout NY State, and operates several regional campuses and field stations that provide special research and experiential learning opportunities. The ESF Ranger School campus at Wanakena, in the heart of the 6 million acre Adirondack State Park, offers degree programs in surveying and forest technology.

LOCATION AND ENVIRONMENT

Syracuse, a metropolitan area of nearly 465,000 people located in the heart of upstate NY, is a leader in the manufacture of china, air conditioning, drugs, and automotive parts, medical and lighting equipment. It offers many cultural and recreational opportunities, including a symphony orchestra, museums, live theater, and historic places. The driving time to Syracuse from New York City, Philadelphia, Boston, Toronto, and Montreal is about five hours; from Buffalo and Albany, about three hours. The city is served by a modern international airport and major bus and rail lines. Syracuse has recently become recognized as one of America's "greenest" cities for its environmental efforts.

MAJORS AND DEGREES OFFERED

The College of Environmental Science and Forestry offers three undergraduate degrees: the Bachelor of Science (BS), the Bachelor of Landscape Architecture (BLA), and the Associate's degree in Applied Science (AAS). BS degree programs include aquatic and fisheries science, bioprocess engineering, biotechnology, chemistry, conservation biology, construction management, environmental biology, environmental science, environmental studies, environmental resources and forest engineering, forest ecosystem science, forest health, forest resources management, natural history and interpretation, natural resources management, paper engineering, paper science, wildlife science, and wood products engineering. The BLA degree, which requires five years of study, is awarded in landscape architecture. AAS degrees are awarded in forest technology or land surveying technology at ESF's Ranger School campus.

ACADEMIC PROGRAMS

ESF offers an undergraduate Honors Program and more than 60 service-learning courses. Specialized study options within the biology program include plant physiology, entomology, environmental microbiology, pest management, plant physiology, plant science, zoology, and additional areas. A five week period of summer field study, usually taken at ESF's Cranberry Lake Biological Station, is a required part of the biology program. Options for specialization within the chemistry program include biochemistry and polymer chemistry. The College also offers four engineering programs focused on environmental and chemical engineering specializations. The natural resources management curriculum offers concentrations in environmental, water, and recreation resources and requires a four week period of summer field study. The environmental studies program offers options in environmental communication, environmental policy, and biological science applications. The nationally-ranked landscape architecture curriculum requires participation in an off-campus independent study project in the fifth year. Students majoring in biology or chemistry may complete teacher certification through a joint program with Syracuse University. Many undergraduates complete some of their liberal arts requirements through courses offered at SU while paying State University of new York tuition. Transfer agreements also exist with State University of new York Upstate Medical University in Syracuse to offer several health-related programs, including a 3+3 degree in physical therapy. ESF's new bioprocess engineering program is focused on the production of biofuels, and is the first program of its kind in the Northeast.

CAMPUS FACILITIES AND EQUIPMENT

Specialized facilities and equipment include electron microscopes, plant growth chambers, air conditioned greenhouses, an animal environmental simulation chamber, a bioacoustical laboratory, a radioisotope laboratory, nuclear magnetic resonance spectrometers, gas chromatography apparatus, a mass spectrometer, ultracentrifuges, and X ray and infrared spectrophotometers. The photogrammetric and geodetic facilities of the environmental and forest engineering department are among the most extensive available in the United States. The paper science and engineering laboratory has a semicommercial paper mill with accessory equipment. The construction management and wood products engineering faculty has a complete strength of materials laboratory, a pilot scale plywood laboratory, and a machining laboratory. The landscape architecture faculty has a one of a kind environmental simulation laboratory with a visual simulator. Eight greenhouses and a forest insectary are used to produce plant and insect materials for the classroom and laboratory. Extensive collections are available, including wood samples from all over the world, botanical materials, insects, birds, mammals, and fishes. A new six-story chemistry facility with 36 laboratories opened in 1997. Laboratories for forest engineering, wood products engineering and construction management, as well as student computing labs, were totally renovated in 2007.

The F. Franklin Moon Library contains more than 135,000 cataloged items, more than 800 print journals, and hundreds more electronically. Library facilities and services are supplemented by the collections available to ESF students through Syracuse University and the STATE UNIVERSITY OF NEW YORK Upstate Medical University at Syracuse, both of which are within easy walking distance.

ESF's regional campuses in Tully, Warrensburg, Cranberry Lake, Newcomb, and Wanakena NY offer a great diversity of forest sites used as outdoor teaching laboratories and for intensive research. ESF operates several field stations to support its instruction, research, and public service programs, including one in Costa Rica.

FINANCIAL AID

Many Financial Aid programs are available for ESF students, and more than 85 percent receive support. Types of Financial Aid include academic (merit) and need-based scholarships, low interest student loans, and student employment. Students are encouraged to apply for aid by completing the Free Application for Federal Student Aid (FAFSA).

STUDENT ORGANIZATIONS AND ACTIVITIES

The College has a representative Undergraduate Student Association, and representatives also participate in student government at Syracuse University. ESF's student government organizes and presents social activities, and its representatives attend College administrative meetings, communicate concerns and ideas to the administration, and serve as a conduit of information back to the student body. ESF students participate in more than 300 clubs and organizations at Syracuse University, in addition to 40 offered on the ESF campus. Student community service efforts have led to the College being listed among a select group of institutions on the President's Higher Education Community Service Honor Roll.

ADMISSIONS PROCESS

Students interested in the Academic Programs offered at ESF have four enrollment options: Early Action, Regular Freshman Admission, Guaranteed Transfer Admission, and Regular Transfer Admission.

The Early Action option is for freshman candidates who wish to complete the Admission Process early in their senior year of high school. Early Action candidates must have their application completed by November 15 and are notified of the decision by January 1.

Students not admitted under the Early Action option are considered for Regular (Rolling) Freshman Admission. The Regular Admission plan has a suggested application deadline of January 15, and students are notified on a rolling basis until the entering class is filled. All freshman candidates should demonstrate strong academic performance in a college preparatory program with emphasis on mathematics and science. Freshman candidates may apply for admission to a specific program of study or enter the College's "undeclared" program option.

Guaranteed Transfer Admission (GTA) candidates apply to ESF as high school seniors but are offered delayed admission to their sophomore or junior year of college. Students who plan to attend another college prior to transferring to ESF select this option to ensure a place at ESF for their chosen entry date. This option may be offered to students who do not meet the freshman admissions criteria. Those who are accepted for admission receive a letter of acceptance for their sophomore or junior year of college, contingent upon the successful completion of specific prerequisite courses required for the curriculum they have selected. The prerequisite courses are outlined and described in an enclosure with the student's acceptance letter.

Students applying as transfer students from other institutions are admitted to ESF on the basis of their previous college coursework and overall academic aptitude. Consideration is given to both the quality and the appropriateness of each student's prior academic experience. Students normally spend one or two years at any college of their choice. ESF, working in cooperation with other four year and two year colleges in New York, Connecticut, Maryland, Massachusetts, New Jersey, Pennsylvania, and Rhode Island, has developed several Cooperative Transfer Programs. In addition, since many ESF students have been previously enrolled at Syracuse University, the two institutions have an articulated program through which students can move from Syracuse University to ESF after the sophomore year with no loss of credits. All admission acceptances are conditional upon satisfactory completion of coursework in progress.

Students may apply for fall or spring admission. Admission decisions are made on a rolling basis until the class is filled. Decisions for the fall semester are made beginning on or about December 15, and decisions for the spring semester are made beginning on or about October 15. Application forms are available at New York State high schools and at all State University of new York campuses. Out-of-state students should request an application form directly from the Office of Undergraduate Admissions at ESF. Application Forms are also available for submission online at www.State University of New York.edu or at www.esf.edu.

Requests for more information should be directed to:

Office of Undergraduate Admissions

State University of New York College of Environmental Science and Forestry

1 Forestry Drive

Syracuse, NY 13210 2779

Telephone: 315-470-6600

800-777-7373 (toll free)

Fax: 315-470-6933

Email: esfinfo@esf.edu

World Wide Web: www.esf.edu

STATE UNIVERSITY OF NEW YORK— PURCHASE COLLEGE

AT A GLANCE

Combining the energy and excitement of professional training in the performing and the visual arts with the intellectual traditions and spirit of discovery of the liberal arts and sciences, Purchase College encourages our students to "think wide open."

Purchase College emphasizes creativity, individual accomplishment, and diversity. Your Purchase education culminates in a Senior Project you and your professor choose that is an excellent springboard to a career or to graduate or professional school. The conservatories of the School of the Arts offer many apprenticeships and other professional opportunities in near-by New York City.

Maybe that's why actors Edie Falco, Parker Posey and Stanley Tucci; filmmaker Chris Wedge ("Ice Age," "Robots"); a Pulitzer Prize winning playwright; a MacArthur Genius Award winning author and environmentalist; an internationally known cancer researcher; several top business executives; the Chief Political Correspondent for The New York Times; Broadway stage designers and lighting technicians; award-winning choreographers and dancers; singer/songwriter Regina Spektor, and hip-hop artist Amanda Diva are all alumni of Purchase College.

LOCATION AND ENVIRONMENT

On a wooded 500-acre suburban campus only 35 minutes by train from Grand Central Station in New York City, Purchase College features a learning environment that's typical of a small, private college. At Purchase, you might share a class with someone from NYC, take in a concert with someone else from the Midwest or the West Coast, and hang out with another student from overseas. About 65 percent of students are enrolled in the humanities, natural and social sciences; the other 35 percent study in one of the professional performing and visual arts programs.

The campus is home to a Performing Arts Center that hosts more than 600 performances a year and to the Neuberger Museum of Art, one of the nation's ten largest university-based art museums. Both will enrich your studies and provide ample opportunity for entertainment. The College believes that artists and scholars inspire and stimulate one another and that both forms of knowledge and discovery are essential to success in the 21st century.

OFF-CAMPUS OPPORTUNITIES

Purchase College students can master the culture, language, and perspectives of another nation by studying in Spain, Italy or France. Purchase students may also study virtually anywhere else in the world, through any of the other State University of New York overseas exchange programs.

Closer to home, dozens of major companies and organizations offer internships for Purchase students. Carefully integrated with your academic studies, internships add a real-life dimension to your Purchase College degree. The College also assists with service-learning opportunities for students who wish to volunteer during semester breaks for such experiences as helping rebuild New Orleans, working in an AIDS clinic in Philadelphia, or participating in the clean-up of Florida's Everglades.

MAJORS AND DEGREES OFFERED

The College features rewarding undergraduate majors, including anthropology, art history, biochemistry, biology, chemistry, math and computer science, economics, English literature, foreign languages and cultures, history, math, philosophy, political science, psychology and sociology, as well as majors in relatively new, interdisciplinary fields such as Afro-American & African studies; arts management, Asian studies; cinema studies, drama studies, Latin American studies; women's studies; creative and dramatic writing; journalism; environmental studies; new media, and media, society and the arts. Innovative new areas of study that integrate the College's strengths in the arts, liberal arts and the sciences are being added each year.

Purchase also provides nationally recognized training in acting; dance; dramatic writing; film; music composition and performance; jazz studies; studio production; theatre design/technology; drawing; painting; sculpture; 3-D media and graphic design; book and/or printmaking; and photography.

Purchase College awards the B.A., B.S., B.F.A., Mus.B., Music Performer's Certificate and Music Artists Diploma, as well as the M.A. and M.F.A.

ACADEMIC PROGRAMS

The humanities, natural sciences or social sciences at Purchase emphasize interdisciplinary learning and thinking, and study in these subjects can open the door to virtually any career. Over 95 percent of the liberal arts and sciences faculty at the college have earned a Ph.D. or equivalent degree, and your professors will include widely published authors, scientists and scholars.

Purchase College conservatory and art/design school courses are taught in the master-apprentice tradition by true professionals, just one reason Purchase College alumni are so successful and so highly regarded throughout the nation.

As a liberal arts and sciences freshman, you may take part in a Freshman Learning Community. There, you share with others in your dorm courses taught by a resident faculty member, who is also available for consultation and friendly conversation.

The Senior Project, the capstone of a Purchase College education, is often the springboard to a career, medical or law school, graduate school, or the arts. And, the recent merger of Student Affairs and Academic Affairs means that your education and your extra-curricular life on campus are more integrated. Community outreach, service-learning programs, career-related internships and volunteer opportunities all help you develop leadership and a greater civic engagement with the world beyond campus.

CAMPUS FACILITIES AND EQUIPMENT

Purchase College offers its nearly 4,200 students wonderful amenities, small classes and laboratories in all disciplines, a Dance Building that is the first in America designed specifically for dancers-in-training, 80 Steinway pianos, 75 music practice rooms and professional recording studios, 160,000 square feet of studio and exhibition space in the visual arts, and fully equipped science laboratories designated for undergraduate use.

The College features three recently renovated dining halls, each with unique menus (including vegetarian and vegan meals). In fact, the Terra Ve café at Purchase College was recently named the fifth best "vegetarian-friendly" dining option at a U.S. college or university.

Some 2,500 students live on campus. Upper-class students can choose among three apartment/townhouse-style residences, with kitchens, dining/living rooms and separate bedrooms. All residences are wired with T-1 lines for Internet access and students receive their own free e-mail accounts.

In addition, one of the largest collections of contemporary art on a college campus is resides in the famous Neuberger Museum of Art, while the popular Purchase College Performing Arts Center presents more than 600 world-class performances each year that are open to the public.

TUITION, ROOM, BOARD AND FEES

Purchase College is an exceptional educational bargain. Full-time students in 2008-09 will pay State University of New York tuition: $4,350 per year for state residents and $10,610 for out-of-state residents (Fall 2007). Room (a double) and full board are estimated to amount to $10,000 and student service fees come to $1,647. (There is also an applied fee for selected music students.)

FINANCIAL AID

Purchase is committed to seeing that every qualified student who wants to can attend the College, regardless of his or her financial situation.

In 2007-08, for example, the average need-based Financial Aid package for full-time students entering Purchase College as freshmen was more than $7,900 per student, with need-based scholarships or grants for beginning students amounting to nearly $5,350 per student. Eight-five percent of incoming freshmen received one or more types of financial assistance that year.

For information and help from a Financial Aid advisor, please contact:

Office of Student Financial Services

Tele.: (914) 251-6598

E-mail: www.purchase.edu/Departments/Admissions/FinancialAid

STUDENT ORGANIZATIONS AND ACTIVITIES

Students make a difference in everything that happens on campus. The Purchase College Student Government is a strong advocate for students' views, and there are more than 20 active clubs and organizations, including the Jazz Club, the Literary Society, the Pre-Med Club, the Organization of African Peoples in America, Hillel, the Gay, Lesbian and Transgendered Union, the Anime Club and the X-Gen/Christian Fellowship.

The student radio station and a student-run newspaper are always looking for talent. The Purchase College Panthers field a dozen varsity men's and women's NCAA Division III teams; and there are plenty of intramural sports and activities for every interest and experience level.

Even with NYC so near, Purchase students enjoy local bands, poetry slams, art shows, special events, dance concerts, plays and music recitals right on campus. The College boasts its own dance troupe, symphony orchestra, opera company, repertory theatre, jazz orchestra, and contemporary music ensemble. And, the Terra Ve café on campus was recently named the fifth best "vegetarian-friendly" dining option at a U.S. college or university.

You can hear more directly from some of your future classmates at the "Experience Purchase" page of the College's Web site: www.purchase.edu

ADMISSIONS PROCESS

Admission to Purchase College is competitive and involves a thorough evaluation of high school coursework, standardized test scores (SAT or ACT), an essay, and other supporting documents.

Overall, the Admissions Committee looks for indicators that a student will be academically successful in a college curriculum and graduate within four years. We recommend that freshman applicants complete a minimum of 16 college preparatory courses (which in New York State includes Regents coursework) during high school, including a minimum of 4 units of English, 3 units of math, 2 units of lab science, 2 units of social science, 2 units of foreign language, and 3 units of electives. The SAT or the ACT are required.

All freshman applicants to Purchase College must complete a State University of New York application and should expect to provide SAT, ACT or GED scores. Liberal Arts and Sciences applicants are asked to complete a one-page Supplemental Admission Form, while applicants to the Performing and Visual Arts programs, including Dramatic Writing, provide either a résumé or repertoire list, writing sample or essay, and take part in a audition, portfolio review or screening interview, depending upon the program. The college also requires freshman entering the Creative Writing program to provide a creative writing portfolio.

Transfer students need official transcripts from all the colleges they have attended.

Many adult and non-traditional learners take classes at Purchase College through The School of Liberal Studies and Continuing Education, either for their degrees or as non-matriculated students. The School of LS&CE also offers classes that provide professional development for teachers, graduate test preparation, and certification for arts managers, fundraisers, engineers and early childhood educators.

For more details and assistance, please contact:

Office of Admissions

Purchase College, State University of New York

Tele.: (914) 251-6300

E-mail: admissions@purchase.edu

STEVENS INSTITUTE OF TECHNOLOGY

AT A GLANCE

Founded in 1870 as the first American college to devote itself exclusively to engineering education based on scientific principles, Stevens Institute of Technology is a prestigious independent university for study and research. In 2004, Stevens was ranked by the Princeton Review as one of the nation's Most Entrepreneurial Campuses, for having tailored their undergraduate business and technology curricula to encourage young entrepreneurs, providing them with the training and guidance they need to start their own businesses. In 2006, Stevens was ranked among the nation's Top 20 "Most Wired Campuses" by PC Magazine and the Princeton Review. In 2007, a Princeton Review survey placed Stevens' Office of Career Development among the nation's top 20.

At the undergraduate level, Stevens' broad-based education leads to prestigious degrees in business, the sciences, computer science, engineering, or the humanities. Research activities are vital to the university's educational mission; thus, Stevens attracts world-renowned faculty to complement its exceptional on-campus facilities. In addition, Stevens maintains an Honor System that has been in existence since 1908. Stevens' 2,040 undergraduates come from more than 42 states and 28 countries, creating a diverse, dynamic environment.

LOCATION AND ENVIRONMENT

Stevens is in one of the most exciting small towns in America. Hoboken, New Jersey, is a quaint one-mile-square town with old Victorian brownstones and tree-lined streets dotted with great restaurants and trendy shops. Located on a high bank of the majestic Hudson River, the 55-acre campus, with stretches of deep green lawns, old-growth elms and maples, and historic classroom buildings, offers the best view of the New York City skyline. Stevens students take advantage of being just minutes away from Manhattan by car, bus, train, and cab, and the Office of Student Life also plans various trips to Broadway plays, museums, and cultural and sporting events throughout the year.

Approximately 90 percent of first-year undergraduate students live on campus; housing is guaranteed for undergraduates for all four years. Ten national fraternities and five sororities have chapters on campus and most maintain houses where members may live. Over 30 percent of undergraduates join a Greek organization.

OFF-CAMPUS OPPORTUNITIES

In addition to the popular internship, undergraduate research, and cooperative education opportunities, Stevens offers other off-campus programs. Juniors may spend the year abroad at the University of Dundee in Scotland, University of Sydney, Australia, or choose from a variety of institutions through the International Exchange Program.

Hoboken, New York City, and the surrounding area also offer numerous artistic, cultural, athletic, and recreational opportunities.

MAJORS AND DEGREES OFFERED

Stevens Institute of Technology consists of three schools that award the Bachelor of Engineering (BE), Bachelor of Science (BS), and Bachelor of Art (BA) degrees.

BE degree: Biomedical Engineering, Chemical Engineering, Civil Engineering, Computer Engineering, Electrical Engineering, Engineering Management, Environmental Engineering, Information Systems Engineering, Mechanical Engineering, and Naval Engineering.

BS degree: Bioanalytical Chemistry, Bioinformatics, Chemical Biology, Chemistry, Computational Science, Computer Science, Cybersecurity, Engineering Physics, Information Systems, Mathematical Sciences, Physics, Science and Law, and Service Oriented Computing. Students can also earn a BS in Business, which provides a comprehensive background in principles of management and entrepreneurship.

BA degree: Art and Technology, English and American Literature, History, Music and Technology, Philosophy, and Science and Technology Studies. Stevens students may pursue a dual degree or a pre-professional program in dentistry, medicine, or law.

ACADEMIC PROGRAMS

Stevens offers a number of unique educational programs.

Research opportunities and summer internships are available for all major fields of study. The Cooperative Education program alternates semesters of on-campus study with semesters of paid, professional work experience. Currently, 40 percent of the undergraduate body elects to co-op and many earn more than $52,000 by the end of the five-year period.

Technogenesis is the educational frontier, pioneered by Stevens, where faculty, students and industry jointly nurture research concepts to commercialization and back to the classroom. This unique initiative is the cornerstone of a curriculum that emphasizes a strong and versatile background in business, engineering, the sciences, computer science, management, and the humanities. The concept is reinforced through classes, coursework, projects, guest speakers and a summer research program.

The Stevens Scholars Program allows exceptional students to participate in summer research or accelerate their course work and graduate with a bachelor's and master's degree in four years at no additional cost. Stevens Technical Enrichment Program (STEP) helps broaden the access of minority and economically disadvantaged students to careers in engineering, science, and technology through pre-college and in-college programs and support services.

All Stevens students take eight humanities courses and four or six physical education courses to balance with the technical, scientific, and management subjects at Stevens.

CAMPUS FACILITIES AND EQUIPMENT

Stevens operates within a computer-intensive environment to meet the needs of a highly computer-fluent campus, including a variety of centralized, departmental, and individual desktop computing resources. Various departmental computing facilities are also available, including "smart" classrooms, computer-aided design and manufacturing labs, graphics labs, robotic sites, a computer-aided education lab, and an instructional business lab. In addition, Stevens offers its community an extensive wireless networking system with access from anywhere on campus, indoors and out. This environment led PC Magazine and the Princeton Review to name Stevens among the Top 20 "Most Wired Campuses" in 2006.

Unique to Stevens is its educational environment, called Technogenesis, where students, faculty, and industry jointly nurture new technologies from concept to marketplace realization.

There are many specialized laboratory facilities on campus used for academic and research functions, applied research, technology transfer, and educational programs in telecommunications systems integration, which meet and support the needs of government and industry. Their areas of focus include: Wireless Network Security, Maritime Systems, Environmental Systems, Microchemical Systems, and Computer Vision.

The Samuel C. Williams Library has access to 30 million volumes and participates in a 12-million-volume New Jersey network, with next-day book delivery. It is open seven days a week.

TUITION, ROOM, BOARD AND FEES

Stevens estimated tuition for 2007-2008 is $33,300. Room and board total $10,500 (typical on-campus, double occupancy/typical meal plan; other plans vary). Required fees amount to $1,800. This fee consists of a student activity/SGA fee, health insurance, technology fee, and freshman orientation fee.

FINANCIAL AID

Stevens is committed to assisting, investing in, and ensuring the highest quality of service to its prospective and current students. The university offers a wide range of institutional need- and merit-based scholarships and grants, and state and federal grant, loan, and work opportunity programs. Stevens encourages students to file the Free Application for Federal Student Aid (FAFSA) by February 15 (Early Decision I applicants submit the Stevens Early Decision Financial Aid Form by December 15.). To apply for merit-based scholarships, no other application is needed except for the Stevens Application for Admission.

STUDENT ORGANIZATIONS AND ACTIVITIES

There are more than 150 student organizations, clubs, and teams on campus, including Student Government; The Stute, the weekly campus newspaper; Link, the yearbook; WCPR radio; Glee Club; Drama Society; brass and jazz ensembles; ethnic and religious groups; and national, honor, and professional societies. Offices are located in Jacobus Hall, the Stevens student center, and all organizations utilize areas on campus to host events, sponsor guest speakers, and organize social activities or volunteer work.

The Schaefer Athletic and Recreation Center features a NCAA competition-size pool with Jacuzzi, four-court basketball gymnasium, racquetball courts, and a fitness center. Newly renovated DeBaun Field has been surfaced in NexTurf, a state-of the-art, durable, year-round playing surface for varsity and intramural competition. Walker Gym has an elevated indoor track plus a new weightlifting facility and dance studios. There are also six outdoor tennis courts and a sand volleyball court.

Stevens competes in NCAA Division III in the following sports: for men: baseball, basketball, cross-country, fencing, golf, indoor/outdoor track and field, lacrosse, soccer, swimming, tennis, volleyball and wrestling; and for women: basketball, cross-country, equestrian, fencing, field hockey, indoor/outdoor track and field, lacrosse, soccer, swimming, tennis, and volleyball. Students may also join a club team or play intramural sports.

ADMISSIONS PROCESS

Stevens is highly competitive. Undergraduate applicants must submit an Application for Admission; an official high school transcript including four years of English, four years of mathematics, and a minimum of three years of science; official SAT I or ACT scores; and meet with an admissions representative for a personal interview. SAT II scores are required for those applying to an accelerated program. Two recommendations (one by a guidance counselor and one by a faculty member) are required and a personal statement or essay is required. Stevens typically accepts less than 50 percent of its applicants and enrolls over 570 students each fall; SAT scores (from the twenty-fifth to seventy-fifth percentile) range from 1170-1360; average high school GPA is 3.8. The application deadline for the fall semester is February 1 (early decision November 15 and January 15).

STONEHILL COLLEGE

AT A GLANCE

Stonehill College's focus is truly on the students, as it has created an environment that caters to them exclusively. Life at Stonehill equates to what many imagine to be the ideal collegiate setting: a 2,350 full-time student body with a comparatively large faculty and expansive campus setting in a charming New England town just outside of Boston. In addition, the curriculum is not only academically challenging but mind expanding, aiming to foster effective skills such as communication, critical thinking, and problem solving. Stonehill provides a powerful learning environment where students are known, safe, and valued.

Founded in 1948 as a college of arts, sciences and pre-professional studies, Stonehill continues to adhere to its mission of providing a rigorous education centered on Catholic values. The College offers 31 academic majors, international and U.S. internships, study abroad programs, undergraduate research opportunities as well as practicum and field work experiences.

LOCATION AND ENVIRONMENT

Life in suburbia is the best. Especially when that suburban town is on the outskirts of Boston. You get it all, the charm and accessibility of small-town life and the excitement and opportunities of the big city.

Easton, in the heart of southeastern Massachusetts, has a population of 23,242. This is truly a best-of-both-worlds situation, a 375-acre campus is all yours to be shared with only 2,350 other students. This is a vast expanse of space that includes a pond, rolling fields, and stretches of woods. Boston is a mere 22 miles away, and offers countless cultural, social, internship, and academic opportunities. Museums, theater, professional athletic teams, a vibrant music scene, and thousands of other college students are all found in Boston. Second only to Boston as popular student retreats are the beaches and activities of Cape Cod and Newport and Providence, Rhode Island, all within 45 minutes from Easton.

The College does provide a free shuttle service to Boston's subway system. The student government association also has vans that students can reserve for trips to sporting events, concerts, skiing, and other activities.

OFF-CAMPUS OPPORTUNITIES

When it comes to Off-Campus Opportunities, the Stonehill administration actively recruits students and solicits programs in all of the big three: study abroad, consortium programs, and internships.

Study Abroad: Stonehill sponsors study abroad programs at over 130 institutions in more than 40 countries throughout the world. The most popular destinations are Italy, Ireland, England, and Australia.

Local Consortium: Stonehill belongs to a consortium that allows its students to take classes at eight area colleges. Stonehill is also a member of the Marine Studies Consortium in Boston.

Internships: Over eighty-one percent of Stonehill students by graduation participate in either a domestic or international internship experience. Stonehill's internship program affords each student the opportunity to gain valuable work experience for academic credit while networking with professionals from a wide variety of corporate and nonprofit agencies. Students intern at organizations such as Grant Thornton UK, Serono Pharmaceutical, Reebok International, UBS, Marvel Comics, Children's Hospital Boston, NCIS, PriceWaterhouseCoopers, Fidelity Investments, the Boston Globe, and more.

Full-time internships are available in New York City, Washington D.C., Dublin, London, Paris, and Geneva, Switzerland.

MAJORS AND DEGREES OFFERED

Stonehill College offers the Bachelor of Arts degree in American Studies, Chemistry, Communication, Criminology, Economics, Education Studies (early childhood, elementary, middle and secondary certification), English, Environmental Studies, Fine Arts, Foreign Languages, Gender Studies, Health Care Administration, History, International Studies, Mathematics, Multidisciplinary Studies, Philosophy, Political Science, Psychology, Public Administration, Religious Studies, and Sociology. Bachelor of Science degrees are offered in Biochemistry, Biology, Chemistry, Computer Science, Computer Science/Computer Engineering, and Neuroscience. The Bachelor of Science degree in Business is offered in Accounting, Finance, International Business, Management, and Marketing.

Pre-professional programs are offered in dentistry, education, law, and medicine. Students interested in the field of education can receive early childhood, elementary, middle and secondary school teacher certification. Students may also design their own major by combining various departmental courses into a comprehensive multidisciplinary program.

ACADEMIC PROGRAMS

Stonehill College's academic program doesn't follow the traditional model that so many schools employ. Rather then focusing the academic program on requirements, Stonehill focuses its program on exploration. The primary mission of the school is to encourage students to challenge themselves by experiencing academic offerings to begin a lifelong quest for intellectual excellence and a dedication to service. All students receive a foundation in liberal arts courses and expert training in one or more major field. The goal of this liberal arts foundation is to help students understand their culture, find and analyze information, develop critical-thinking skills, become effective communicators, and master proficient writing skills. The exploration can continue through the middle of junior year, when students must declare their major. At Stonehill, faculty and student interaction is an essential element to the academic process. Advisers help students choose a major and discuss course selections, study abroad opportunities, internships, as well as graduate school and full-time employment prospects.

Students take five courses each semester, and need 40 courses to graduate with a Bachelor's degree.

CAMPUS FACILITIES AND EQUIPMENT

Kaplan's Insiders Guide of the 320 Most Interesting Colleges listed Stonehill as one of the colleges with the "Best Freshman Housing". Upper-class housing is equally nice and that's perhaps why almost everyone lives on campus all four years! Housing is guaranteed and 89% of all students live on-campus.

A new 89,000 square foot state-of-the-art science center will be opened in the

Fall 2009. This exciting science facility will include research labs with advanced technology and instrumentation for the biology, chemistry, physics, and psychology departments along with the neuroscience, biochemistry, and environmental studies programs.

The MacPhaidin Library and Networked Information Center provides students with features such as wireless access, multimedia computers, and electronic resources such as E-Journals, WorldCat for locating books worldwide as well as technology workshops focused on library research skills.

Stanger Hall is a 100% wireless building providing 4 multimedia classrooms, over 100 computers in 4 computer classrooms and labs for student use. In addition to software for Computer Science, Robotics and other specialized courses, the labs also include laser printers and scanners, as well as the Bloomberg Stock Trading Computer System. The Information Technology Help Desk, a central point of assistance for students, is located in Stanger Hall and is open over 90 hours per week.

The Joseph W. Martin Institute for Law and Society serves as a regional center for education, research, and public service. The Martin Insititute features an archival research center, the Center for Regional and Policy Analysis, the Stonehill Education Project, and the papers of Joseph W. Martin, the former Speaker of the U.S. House of Representatives, as well as the papers of Stonehill graduate Michael Novak. Michael Novak was awarded the very prestigious internationally recognized Templeton Award.

TUITION, ROOM, BOARD AND FEES

Full-time tuition (including fees) for the 2007-2008 academic year is $28,440 and room and board is $11,430.

FINANCIAL AID

The College is committed to helping each qualified student find the resources to meet the cost of a Stonehill education. In fact, Stonehill distributes more than $37 million a year in scholarships and Financial Aid to a full-time student body of only 2,350 students. Last year, the average Financial Aid package awarded to first-year applicants who demonstrated a need was $20,397. Stonehill also awards a competitive number of merit-based scholarships to outstanding students who do not demonstrate a financial need. Stonehill's merit fund program awards scholarships ranging from $7,500 to $20,000 per year.

To file for Stonehill scholarship and/or Financial Aid consideration, simply complete the online CSS PROFILE form at http://profileonline.collegeboard.com. Stonehill's CSS PROFILE code number is 3770. In addition, file the Free Application for Federal Student Aid Assistance (FAFSA) online at www.fafsa.ed.gov in order to be considered for government funds to Stonehill. The College's federal code number is 002217 for the FAFSA form.

For more information, contact the Stonehill College Student Aid and Finance Office at 508-565-1088.

STUDENT ORGANIZATIONS AND ACTIVITIES

Stonehill College competes on the NCAA Division II level and offers a multitude of recreational, intramural, and intercollegiate club sports.

The Student Government Association (SGA) is an influential group of student leaders who represent the voice of Stonehill students to the President, the Board of Trustees, the Alumni Council, and the Faculty Senate.

Over 70 organized student groups representing academic societies, multicultural interests, music as well as performance, community service and shared interests in areas such as Amnesty International, the environment and the EMS Club enable our student population of 2,350 to actually become involved.

Just 22 miles south of Boston and connected to the "T" via a free campus shuttle service, many Stonehill students venture into the city to attend major sporting events and concerts, to shop or dine, or simply stated, just to have fun!

ADMISSIONS PROCESS

Most successful candidates have prepared for the rigors of Stonehill by taking a demanding college preparatory program in high school. Stonehill's Admissions Committee considers a student's academic performance, strength of curriculum, SAT or ACT scores, recommendations, essay, co-curricular activities, and work experience. Beginning the Fall 2008, standardized testing scores for admission are optional.

Stonehill awards credit for high scores on Advancement Placement, CLEP, and upper level International Baccalaureate exams.

All high school candidates are encouraged to participate in a Group Information Session (GIS) conducted by a professional admissions staff member with the assistance of Stonehill students. Following each GIS, a student-led campus tour completes the visit. Contact 508-565-1373 to arrange your campus visit.

To apply to Stonehill, simply submit the Common Application (CA). Stonehill College is a member of the Common Application Program. The Stonehill/Common Application is available online at https://app.commonapp.org. Your application information will be securely transmitted to Stonehill along with your completed Stonehill Supplemental Information Form and filing fee payment. The CA is also available in paper form at your high school guidance office or online for downloading at www.stonehill.edu.

SUSQUEHANNA UNIVERSITY

AT A GLANCE

Susquehanna is a national liberal arts college enrolling approximately 2,000 undergraduates in its three schools: the School of Arts, Humanities and Communications; the Sigmund Weis School of Business; and the School of Natural and Social Sciences. The University offers the best qualities of a residential college and a challenging university. Distinctive liberal arts programs such as biology and writing are enhanced by equally strong professional programs in areas like music and business. A Susquehanna education builds the broad base of knowledge needed to help students become educated citizens of the world while offering the in-depth preparation needed to succeed in graduate or professional school or in a job after graduation. Susquehanna is affiliated with the Evangelical Lutheran Church in America, and since its founding in 1858, the University has worked to design the programs and educational opportunities common to a challenging university while maintaining the tightly knit community typical of a residential college.

LOCATION AND ENVIRONMENT

Selinsgrove is a town of about 6,000 inhabitants. It is approximately 90 minutes west of the Pocono Mountain resort areas; about an hour from State College and Harrisburg, PA; about a 3-hour drive from Philadelphia, New York City, and Washington, D.C.; and about a 4-hour drive from Pittsburgh. Cultural, dining, recreational and shopping opportunities abound. Susquehanna has close ties with the community, where a number of students participate in internships and many take part in the university's extensive, award-winning volunteer program. Susquehanna is one of three universities in the area.

Susquehanna University boasts a 220-acre residential campus with upwards of 50 buildings that span a period of more than 140 years. Approximately 80 percent of the students live on campus in seven residence halls, six apartment-style units, several academic or volunteer student project suites and houses, a scholar's house, and eight fraternity and sorority houses.

OFF-CAMPUS OPPORTUNITIES

Susquehanna students participate in a variety of off-campus programs, including the Washington Center in the nation's capital, the Washington Semester of American University, the United Nations Semester of Drew University, and the Philadelphia Center Program. Each semester, the University approves numerous off-campus departmental internships, some of which are in other countries. Students are encouraged to study abroad, and Susquehanna is a participating member of the Institute of European Studies. The University is a coordinating institution with Senshu University in Japan, exchanges students with University of Macau, and offers a semester in London for juniors majoring in business. Susquehanna-designed Focus programs complement special groups of courses with travel to the country being studied. Recent trips have included southern Africa, Australia, and Martinique. All of these programs carry academic credit.

MAJORS AND DEGREES OFFERED

Susquehanna University offers the Bachelor of Science degree with majors in Biochemistry, Biology, Chemistry, Computer Science, Earth and Environmental Science, Ecology, Physics, and Psychology, and the Bachelor of Arts degree with majors in Art History, Chemistry, Communications (with emphases in: Broadcasting, Communications Studies, Corporate Communications, Journalism, Mass Communications, Public Relations, and Speech Communication), Computer Science, Earth and Environmental Science, Economics, English, French, German, Graphic Design, History, Information Systems, International Studies, Liberal Studies (Education), Mathematics, Music, Philosophy, Physics, Political Science, Psychology, Religion, Sociology, Spanish, Studio Art, Theatre, and Writing. The Bachelor of Music is offered in Music Education and Performance. The Bachelor of Science in Business is offered in Accounting, Business Administration (with emphases in Entrepreneurship, Finance, Global or Human Resource Management, Information Systems and Marketing), and Economics. There are also a number of program options with interdisciplinary and self-designed majors. Nearly fifty academic minors, including programs in diversity studies, film, health care studies, Jewish studies, and legal studies are available.

Pre-professional studies may be pursued in the fields of law, medicine and allied health, and the ministry. Teaching certification is offered at the early childhood, elementary (K-6) and secondary (7-12) levels. Certification for grades K-12 is available for music education and foreign language.

Two dual-degree programs are available: a joint degree program with Temple University's School of Dentistry and a 3-2 program in forestry or environmental management with Duke University. BS/MS programs in allied health are offered with Thomas Jefferson University. Army ROTC is available under a cross-enrollment program with Bucknell University.

ACADEMIC PROGRAMS

Susquehanna's central curriculum provides the breadth of knowledge needed for graduate school or a career through exposure to the humanities and natural sciences. Other core courses help students develop intellectual skills and understand relationships among individuals, organizations, and the natural world. Susquehanna's central curriculum also encourages participation in cross-cultural experiences. The Center for Career Services, which developed the nation's first required course on career planning, provides resources assisting students throughout their academic lives.

Susquehanna offers a competitive four-year interdisciplinary Honors Program affiliated with the National Collegiate Honors Council.

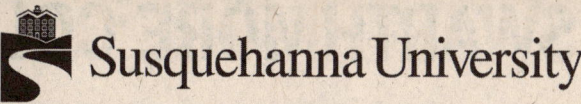
CAMPUS FACILITIES AND EQUIPMENT

Susquehanna is an undergraduate university. All facilities and equipment are for the exclusive use of undergraduate students. The Blough-Weis Library houses Susquehanna's language lab, music and sound media, the Film Institute and 350 individual study spaces. The general collection includes 265,000 volumes as well as periodicals, language and music tapes and videos. Fisher Science Hall provides facilities for all the sciences, including experimental psychology. The Center for Music and Art, completed in 2002, includes 32 practice rooms, two Music Technology lab rooms, two recording studios, Stretansky Hall (a 320-seat concert venue designed specifically for the singing voice), art studio and exposition space, a dark room, and a graphic design computer lab. Apfelbaum Hall provides the business and communications programs with multimedia computer labs, two "smart" classrooms which are equipped with the latest presentation hardware and software, a TV studio, and two audio-visual editing rooms. The Charles B. Degenstein Campus Center houses the Lore Degenstein Gallery and a state-of-the-art 450-seat teaching theatre. The James W. Garrett Sports Complex, completed in 2001, includes a fitness center, racquetball courts and a 51,000-square-foot field house equipped for indoor track meets, volleyball, tennis, and basketball. Nicholas Lopardo Stadium is equipped for day and night use by a multiplicity of sports teams, and the Sassafras Fields provide lighted, synthetic playing areas for rugby, lacrosse and softball. Seibert Hall and Selinsgrove Hall appear on the National Registry of Historic Places. Trax, a new social space featuring a dance floor, game area, performance stage, and outdoor patio, opened in spring 2006.

TUITION, ROOM, BOARD AND FEES

Tuition and fees for 2007-2008 are $29,330. Room and board costs are $8,000. A student's personal expenses, including books, travel and other costs are estimated at $1,800 to $2,700 per year.

FINANCIAL AID

Susquehanna University offers renewable academic and music scholarships, which are awarded on a competitive basis without regard to financial need. In addition, need-based Financial Aid is awarded to permit attendance by full-time students whose personal and family resources are not sufficient to meet the costs. The amount of Financial Aid is based on need, not on family income alone. The level of need is determined annually by information provided on the PROFILE and the Free Application for Federal Student Aid (FAFSA). More than half of all students receive financial assistance that ranges from $1,000 to full need. Aid is provided in packages that may include grants, scholarships, loans, and jobs.

STUDENT ORGANIZATIONS AND ACTIVITIES

As a residential university, Susquehanna believes that extracurricular activities should be an integral part of each student's experience. There are 23 varsity sports teams as well as an extensive intramural program, numerous academic clubs for projects and initiatives tied to students' majors, abundant opportunities to explore Pennsylvania's natural geography through skiing, camping, kayaking, and hiking; and the third most powerful student-run radio station in the state, 88.9 WQSU - The Pulse. With over 100 student organizations to choose from, Susquehanna students have a hard time exhausting extracurricular options. A host of musical activities include a chorale, bands, an orchestra, a cappella groups, a hand-bell choir and a Gospel choir. The Student Government Association (SGA) provides a representative student organization to assure students a voice in university governance. The Student Senate provides a forum for student opinion, deals with issues of concern to the entire student body, and is responsible for the allocation of funds to the student-run organizations. The nationally recognized Project House system allows students in community service projects to live together in special housing. There are groups that promote diversity, among them the Hispanic Organization for Latino Awareness (HOLA), the Black Student Union, the Gender and Sexuality Alliance (GSA) and WomenSpeak; groups that promote environmental and political activism: Green SU, Student Liberals, Activists and Progressives (SLAP), SU Republicans; groups that seek to increase awareness of social issues: Students Promoting AIDS Awareness (SPAA), America Reads, SU Health; and groups that support religious life on campus: Chapel Council, Bible study groups, Hillel, Chancel Drama, Lutheran Student Movement (LSM). A large number of activities are focused upon service to various populations within the local community of which the following is a small sampling: Habitat for Humanity, Big Brothers/Big Sisters, Senior Friends, Study Buddy. Additionally, there are opportunities to be involved in a variety of communications efforts: WQSU, the weekly newspaper, the student yearbook, literary magazines and publications, and the student-run public relations firm Sterling Communications.

ADMISSIONS PROCESS

Susquehanna admits students without regard for race, color, religion, national or ethnic origin, age, sex, sexual orientation, or handicap. Students who gain admission are those whom the Admissions Committee deems able to profit from and contribute to the Susquehanna experience. Graduation from an accredited secondary school or a high school equivalency certificate is required. Experience has shown that the best preparation includes at least four years of English, four years of mathematics, three years of laboratory science, three years of social studies, two years of one foreign language, and three or more units of electives. In evaluating a candidate, the committee considers academic performance, major interests, test scores, recommendations, extracurricular activities and demonstrated interest in the University. In addition to the application and secondary school records, the candidate must submit scores from either the SAT or the ACT, unless he or she chooses the Write Option and submits two graded writing samples instead of standardized test scores. Students for whom English is not their native language must submit official score reports of the TOEFL. Applications for early decision are encouraged when Susquehanna is clearly a student's first choice, and deferred admission is available. Interviews and campus tours are strongly suggested for all students interested in Susquehanna. Applicants to the Bachelor of Music or the Bachelor of Arts in music must audition, and applicants to the Bachelor of Arts majors in writing and graphic design must submit portfolios. Transfer candidates can be considered for either semester, and the University recognizes the Advanced Placement and CLEP programs of the College Board and the International Baccalaureate program.

Application materials and introductory and departmental information may be obtained by contacting the Office of Admissions. All interview appointments should be made two weeks in advance to allow time for faculty contact and the scheduling of student-conducted tours. The priority application deadline is March 1 (for Early Decision I—November 15; for Early Decision II—January 1). The University adheres to the Candidate's Reply Date of May 1 and is a Common Application and Universal Application participant.

SWARTHMORE COLLEGE

AT A GLANCE

Swarthmore, one of the nation's finest institutions of higher learning, is a college like no other. Private, yet open to all regardless of financial need. American, yet decidedly global in outlook and diversity, drawing students from around the world and all 50 states. Small, yet with the financial strength to offer students and faculty generous resources to push their own and the world's understanding of disciplines from Arabic to plasma physics, from microbiology to dance, from engineering to art history.

Swarthmoreans are CEO patent-holders who bring technology to underserved markets, investment bankers looking for alternative forms of energy, lawyers who become college presidents, doctors who serve in Congress, winners of the Nobel Prize. A Swarthmorean founded the first liberal arts college in Ghana. Another led the team that developed the Hubble Space Telescope. Swarthmoreans invented hypertext and helped women win the right to vote.

So much of what Swarthmore stands for, from its commitment to curricular breadth and rigor to its demonstrated interest in facilitating discovery and fostering ethical intelligence among exceptional young people, lies in the quality and passion of its faculty. Professors at Swarthmore are leading scholars and researchers in their fields, yet remain deeply committed to serving their students as outstanding teachers and mentors. A student/faculty ratio of 8:1 ensures that students have close, meaningful engagement with their professors, preparing them to translate the skills and understanding gained at Swarthmore into the mark they want to make on the world.

LOCATION AND ENVIRONMENT

Located 11 miles southwest of Philadelphia, Swarthmore's idyllic, 357-acre campus is a designated arboretum, complete with rolling lawns, creek, wooded hills, and hiking trails. From its state-of-the-art science complex to its new, environmentally friendly residence hall, Swarthmore's buildings and architecture stand as national models of curricular and co-curricular undergraduate facilities.

OFF-CAMPUS OPPORTUNITIES

Swarthmore College is a member of the Tri-College consortium, linking our campus to Bryn Mawr and Haverford Colleges, academically and socially. Students are also able to take courses at the University of Pennsylvania. The College offers shuttles to the other tri-co schools, local community service sites, movie theaters and shopping complexes, as well as to the city of Philadelphia. Public transportation is readily available with a train station located on campus; the ride to Philadelphia takes approximately 20 minutes.

MAJORS AND DEGREES OFFERED

Swarthmore College awards two degrees, the Bachelor of Arts and the Bachelor of Science. The following courses of study are offered at the College:

Art and Art History

Asian Studies

Astronomy

Biology

Black Studies

Chemistry and Biochemistry

Classics

Cognitive Science

Comparative Literature

Computer Science

Dance

Economics

Educational Studies

Engineering

English Literature

Environmental Studies

Film and Media Studies

German Studies

History

Interpretation Theory

Latin American Studies

Linguistics

Mathematics and Statistics

Medieval Studies

Modern Languages and Literatures (including Arabic, Chinese, French, German, Japanese, Russian, and Spanish)

Music

Peace and Conflict Studies

Philosophy

Physics

Political Science

Psychology

Public Policy

Religion

Sociology and Anthropology

Theater

Women's Studies

ACADEMIC PROGRAMS

The College offers more than 600 courses a year; an exceptional honors program; individual special majors; a program in education that leads to Pennsylvania secondary school certification; and undergraduate research opportunities in the sciences, social sciences, humanities, and engineering.

The Honors Program features faculty working with small groups of dedicated and accomplished students; an emphasis on independent learning; students entering into a dialogue with peers, teachers, and examiners; a demanding program of study in major and minor fields; and an examination at the end of two years' study by outside scholars.

CAMPUS FACILITIES AND EQUIPMENT

The Campus is a 357-acre, nationally registered arboretum. The Lang Performing Arts Center's resources include an art gallery, dance studios, cinema, and theater performance space. Highlights of Swarthmore's library facilities include the Friends Historical Library and the Peace Collection. The athletics facilities include a lighted stadium complex, a 400-meter dual durometer track, and synthetic grass playing field, state-of-the-art fitness center and three indoor tennis courts with Rebound Ace surface. The Science Center has been recognized by the U.S. Green Building Council for "leadership in energy and environmental design."

TUITION, ROOM, BOARD, AND FEES

For 2008–2009, the College charges including tuition, room, board, and student activity fee total to $47,804. The activity fee covers not only the usual student services—health, library, laboratory fees, for example—but admission to all social, cultural, and athletic events on campus.

FINANCIAL AID

Admission and financial aid decisions for U.S. citizens and permanent residents are made independently at Swarthmore. financial aid awards meet demonstrated need for all admitted students. Beginning with the 2008–09 academic year all Swarthmore aid awards will be loan free.

STUDENT ORGANIZATIONS AND ACTIVITIES

With more than 100 student clubs and organizations on campus, dozens of community service groups, 22 varsity athletic teams, free lectures and performances occurring daily on campus, and full academic schedules, Swarthmore students are rarely idle. The student culture encourages involvement and a strong sense of community.

ADMISSIONS PROCESS

In an effort to seek a variety of students leading to a well-rounded class, the admissions staff carefully considers a number of criteria without a rigid emphasis on any one factor in particular. Applicants are evaluated based upon the following:

- High school record (as well as strength of curriculum)
- Rank in class (if high school ranks)
- Standardized tests
- Extracurricular commitments
- Essays (included in application)
- Recommendations (two from academic teachers, one from counselor)
- Interview (highly recommended but not required)

SWEET BRIAR COLLEGE

AT A GLANCE

Since its founding in 1901, Sweet Briar College has been deeply committed to the education of women. It is consistently ranked as one of the top, national liberal arts and sciences colleges in the country. The excellent academic reputation, beautiful campus, and attention to the individual, attract smart, confident women who want to excel.

At Sweet Briar, faculty and staff members are committed to helping each individual young woman reach her full potential both inside and outside the classroom. As a result, the College has crafted put together a series of guarantees (titled "The Sweet Briar Promise") to ensure that every student has a college experience that will land her exactly where she wants to be after college.

The College has a wide geographic, ethnic, and socioeconomic representation. About 650–700 women from more than forty states and fifteen countries are enrolled at Sweet Briar's Virginia campus; another 150 students are enrolled in Sweet Briar's coed Junior Year in France and Junior Year in Spain programs.

A Sweet Briar education sets in motion the conviction that any goal is achievable, and prepares young women for a lifetime of success. Classes average twelve students, and a student to faculty ratio of 8:1 ensures academic interaction and personal attention.

LOCATION AND ENVIRONMENT

Sweet Briar is located in central Virginia in the foothills of the Blue Ridge Mountains. The spacious campus of 3,250 acres contains hiking trails, nature preserves, and spectacular views. The core buildings, designed by Ralph Adams Cram, form the Sweet Briar College National Historic District.

Recent additions to campus include a student commons that opened in 2002 and a fine arts facility that opened in 2006. The College will break ground on a new Fitness and Athletic Center in May 2008, scheduled to be open and ready for use for the 2009-2010 academic year. This facility will include multiple volleyball/tennis courts, a climbing wall, a movie theater, racquetball courts, and student common space with large-screen TV and pool table. Sweet Briar is the only college in the country with a residential artists' colony on its campus, the Virginia Center for the Creative Arts. The on-campus equestrian center, one of the largest and best-designed college facilities in the country, attracts both competitive and recreational riders.

The community atmosphere of the College is enhanced by the large proportion of faculty and administrators who also live on campus.

The College is 12 miles north of Lynchburg, Virginia; less than an hour south of Charlottesville, VA; and about 3 hours southwest of Washington, D.C.

OFF-CAMPUS OPPORTUNITIES

By the time they graduate, more than a third of each Sweet Briar class will have studied abroad.

Sweet Briar owns and operates two study abroad programs (in France and in Spain); maintains formal exchange agreements with universities in Germany, Italy, Japan, and Scotland; and allows students to explore any study abroad program offered through another college or university giving students almost unlimited opportunity for an international study experience. Scholarship assistance is available for students who wish to study abroad.

The Sweet Briar Junior Year in France Program (JYF) is the oldest coeducational intercollegiate American program in Paris. The Sweet Briar Junior Year in Spain Program (JYS) offers students the opportunity to study at the University of Seville, one of Spain's most prestigious universities. In 2006, both the JYF and JYS programs began offering a 5-week session in May/June so that students are able to have an international study experience and not miss an academic semester on campus. In addition, Sweet Briar works with students to select appropriate programs and destinations throughout the world for study during the academic year or for a summer session.

Sweet Briar participates in the Tri-College Consortium along with Randolph College and Lynchburg College. In addition to taking courses at the other colleges, students can also participate in social and cultural activities on those college campuses.

MAJORS AND DEGREES OFFERED

Sweet Briar awards the Bachelor of Arts, Bachelor of Science, or Bachelor of Fine Arts degree in the following majors: Anthropology, Archaeology, Art History, Biochemistry and Molecular Biology, Biology, Business Management, Chemistry, Classics, Computer Science, Dance, Economics, Engineering Science, English, English and Creative Writing, Environmental Science, Environmental Studies, French, German, German Studies, Government, History, International Affairs, Italian Studies, Liberal Studies (Education), Mathematics, Mathematics-Physics, Modern Languages and Literatures, Music, Philosophy, Physics, Psychology, Religion, Sociology, Spanish, Studio Art, and Theatre.

Additional area studies, minors, and certificate programs include: Archaeology, Arts Management, Communications, Equine Studies, Film Studies, Italian, Latin American Studies, Law & Society, Leadership, Musical Theatre, Pre-Law, Pre-Med, Pre-Vet, and Women and Gender Studies.

Students may design interdisciplinary majors focusing on a topic of special interest or may construct a personalized major.

In May 2004, Sweet Briar began offering the Master of Education and the Master of Arts in Teaching degrees. The MAT is a full-time program, which can be completed in 11 months (including teacher licensure requirements); the M.Ed. can be completed full-time or part-time to allow working professionals the opportunity to join the program. Both graduate programs are coed.

ACADEMIC PROGRAMS

Sweet Briar College supports students in realizing their full potential through the "Sweet Briar Promise" - a series of six guarantees that provides each student the opportunity to have a resume-building internship, study abroad, develop and apply her leadership skills, personalize her academic program, conduct primary research with a faculty mentor, and build an advising team of faculty, staff, and alumnae professionals so that she is best prepared for success after college.

The general education program has 4 components: English 104 (composition), Skills Requirements, Experiences Requirements, and Knowledge Area Requirements. Our general education approach is based on the belief that students will benefit more from their college experience and be better prepared for life after college if they understand the value of a liberal arts curriculum and actively cultivate, in and out of the classroom, their intellectual, social, cultural, creative, and recreational potential to prepare for a life of continual growth, responsibility, and fulfillment. The curriculum emphasizes comprehensive understanding, analysis, reflection, creation, and communication across disciplines. Independent studies, available at all levels, and seminars are included in most majors, with a culminating senior course or exercise required in most majors.

Sweet Briar has ten honorary societies including a chapter of Phi Beta Kappa.

The four-year Honors Program is nationally recognized for its innovative partnering of interdisciplinary academic and co-curricular programs. Honors students take special tutorials, known as honors variants and honors seminars. Seniors may choose to complete a yearlong research project culminating in an honors thesis on an original topic in the major department.

Sweet Briar provides free of charge to all students academic support services that include assistance with papers and study strategies, a personalized time management system, stress management advice, tutoring information, and one-on-one peer mentoring. The Academic Resource Center (ARC) also provides support and learning strategies for students with a diagnosed learning difference.

Sweet Briar operates on a traditional, two-semester calendar.

CAMPUS FACILITIES AND EQUIPMENT

Sweet Briar has the largest private undergraduate library collection in the state of Virginia with resources including more than 240,000 volumes, 1,000 journal subscriptions, 430,000 microforms, 6,800 audiovisual materials, and special libraries in art, music, and the sciences.

A recently upgraded fiber-optic backbone allows high-speed Internet access from all academic and administrative buildings, as well as residence hall rooms. Many of the buildings and areas on campus are equipped for wireless connection to the College network.

Students enrolled in science courses use modern equipment that enhances faculty-student collaborative research. A sample of equipment used by students on a regular basis includes a scanning electron microscope with digital imaging system, DNA sequencing equipment, two nuclear magnetic resonance spectrometers (NMR; 400 MHz and 60 MHz), an atomic absorption spectrometer (AAS), a modular LASER laboratory, a gas chromatograph/mass spectrograph (GC/MS), a scanning tunneling microscope, a 10-inch diameter reflecting telescope, a 20,000 Pound Capacity Universal Testing Machine, a Rockwell Hardness Tester, and many additional pieces of equipment provided from grant funds provided by the National Science Foundation.

TUITION, ROOM, BOARD AND FEES

For the 20067-20078 academic year, tuition was $24,7403,540, and room and board totaled $10,0409,480. Books, supplies, and fees average about $1500. Personal expenses average $1000.

FINANCIAL AID

Sweet Briar offers merit scholarships to qualified applicants that range up to $15,000 per year. Scholarships are awarded based on the applicant's high school gpa and best standardized test score. There is no separate application required.

Need-based Financial Aid is offered based on a family's demonstrated need as determined by the Free Application for Federal Student Aid (FAFSA). More than 90% of students receive some type of institutional financial support.

Scholarships for non-U.S. citizens are also available on a competitive basis.

STUDENT ORGANIZATIONS AND ACTIVITIES

Students who benefit the most from the Sweet Briar experience are those who get involved in the co-curricular activities on campus. Sweet Briar students recognize that one of the advantages of a women's college is the opportunity for women to be involved and to hold leadership roles in organizations and activities.

More than fifty campus organizations are available, including honor societies, community service groups, a multicultural club, a student newspaper, drama and dance clubs, a radio station, and singing groups. Students plan and participate in an extensive array of concerts, films, and dance and theatre productions as well as workshops and master classes by visiting scholars and performers. Recent visitors have included writer, Salman Rushdie; environmental attorney, Robert F. Kennedy, Jr.; and columnist, Christine Brennan.

Varsity athletes compete in NCAA Division III field hockey, lacrosse, soccer, softball, swimming, tennis, and volleyball. Sweet Briar's riding program, both competitive and instructional, has consistently garnered national recognition.

Students participate actively in the governance of the College through offices and committee positions of the Student Government Association. The Association and its committees are largely responsible for the self-governance of the student body.

ADMISSIONS PROCESS

Sweet Briar seeks talented women who are adventurous, enthusiastic about learning, and want to take an active part in their education. In addition to academic achievement, the Admissions Committee looks for qualities such as academic promise, independent thinking, upholding of ethical principles, creativity, and an appreciation of diversity. Sweet Briar welcomes students of all economic, ethnic, geographic, religious, and social backgrounds.

Requirements include a minimum of 4 units in English, 3 in mathematics, 3 in social studies, 2 sequential years in a foreign language, and 3 units in science, as well as additional units in these subjects to total 16. Most candidates have 20 such academic units. Special attention is given to the difficulty of the applicant's curriculum, her class rank, and the school attended; scores on the SAT I or ACT (including optional writing section) are required. An interview at the College is recommended but not required.

Early decision applications are due by December 1 of the senior year; regular decision applications are due by February 1. Transfer applications for the fall semester are due by May 1. A completed application includes a transcript of the candidate's academic work, scores on the required tests, recommendations from the guidance counselor and a teacher, and an essay written by the candidate. There is a $40 application fee, but it may be waived if it is deemed to be a financial burden. Sweet Briar also accepts the Common Application. All materials should be sent to the address below; information may be requested from the same office.

Dean of Admissions

Box B

Sweet Briar College

Sweet Briar, Virginia 24595

Telephone: 434-381-6142

800-381-6142 (toll-free)

Fax: 434-381-6152

E-mail: admissions@sbc.edu

World Wide Web: http://www.sbc.edu

TEMPLE UNIVERSITY

AT A GLANCE

Temple University attracts the nation's brightest and most motivated minds from all 50 states and 130 foreign countries. Offering the perfect combination of large-school resources and a small-school feel, Temple has something for every kind of student. At home in Philadelphia, Pennsylvania, Temple is nationally recognized for innovative achievements in teaching and research. Students have the opportunity to choose between suburban and city campuses. Temple University strives to instill a sense of global perspective in our students and offers the ability to study at our campuses in Rome, Italy and Tokyo, Japan. On all of our campuses, the Temple faculty includes instructors who are distinguished and active members in their fields. Professors bring the critical perspective of scholars and the practical knowledge of their discipline to their classrooms. With an average class-size of just 27, students have the access they need to thrive within the classroom. Temple is renowned in areas such as Business, Communications, Education, Art, Music, Science, and the Health Professions, and Temple graduates have the know-how and confidence to achieve success and make lasting contributions. Driven by the knowledge that the greatest students are students that are having fun, Temple goes to great lengths to make sure students are never at a loss for things to do. With a campus that is home to 19,000 students, activities are as diverse as the student body. In addition to cultural, athletic, and social events on campus, students always have the nation's 5th largest city at their fingertips.

LOCATION AND ENVIRONMENT

The city of Philadelphia is the cornerstone of life at Temple. One of the largest cities on the East Coast, Philadelphia is home to a variety of forward-looking businesses, progressive work in technology and science, and thriving artistic output. While the city is the product of a rich history, it is also a center for 21st century innovation and culture. With plays, concerts, museums, major league sporting events, shopping, clubs, and restaurants, Philadelphia provides students with tremendous opportunities for resources and fun. As an alternative to the urban setting, students can attend Temple University Ambler, set on 187 acres 30 minutes outside of the city. Ambler is a great choice for students who want all the resources of a world-renowned research university in a small and quiet setting. Temple also offers four additional campuses/sites in the Philadelphia region. Free shuttles connect all of our campuses giving Temple students ample opportunities to experience the many sides of Temple University.

OFF-CAMPUS OPPORTUNITIES

For Temple, "off-campus" is synonymous with opportunity. Whether it's hopping the subway to an internship with a Fortune 500 Company, hailing a cab to see priceless works of art at Philadelphia's museums, or flying to one of the dozens of study-abroad programs we have to offer, the world off-campus serves us as a classroom without walls.

Temple students are encouraged to incorporate travel and study into their academic experience. In addition to the tremendous opportunities of Philadelphia, the world abroad presents students with an exciting and affordable way to gain invaluable global perspective. Boasting a list of locales from Scotland to France and from Ghana to Beijing, a Temple education becomes more than just books and papers - it's about experience.

MAJORS AND DEGREES OFFERED

Temple University offers 123 undergraduate majors through 12 schools and colleges. Temple has become nationally recognized in areas such as business, communications, education, engineering, health professions, liberal arts, science and technology, tourism and hospitality, horticulture, music and the arts.

ACADEMIC PROGRAMS

Temple University offers an extensive breadth of Academic Programs that provide graduates with an esteemed education. Temple's mission is to provide students with the resources they need to become leaders in their fields. Whether it's cutting-edge technology, a diverse educational experience, or small classes, Temple succeeds in producing graduates that are critical thinkers in addition to working professionals. By integrating the foundations of a student's field in major coursework with a scholarly approach to conceptual ideas through our general education curriculum, Temple prepares students for the rigors of the workplace and the complexity of the world around them. Temple recognizes that education should be personalized to meet the diverse needs of a diverse student body. First-year students can participate in courses and programs that are designed to meet their unique needs. Additionally, the University Honors Program provides tremendous opportunities for students seeking a more rigorous intellectual challenge. Wholly, Temple University's Academic Programs are founded on a comprehensive and personalized approach to education that enables students to thrive.

CAMPUS FACILITIES AND EQUIPMENT

Temple University's facilities are on the cutting-edge of technology and expose today's students to tomorrow's innovation. Home to the TECH Center, the largest student computer lab in the country, Temple students have access to nearly 2,000 computers in over a dozen computer labs across campus. With a campus that is nearly 90% wireless, students have limitless access to information and 24-hour access to their courses through the Temple Blackboard® system. Temple also strives to bring technology into the classroom by outfitting them with "smart" technology as can be seen in Temple's Tuttleman Learning Center, which offers 20 high-tech classrooms. On the social scene, Temple's new Student Center offers students lounges, a food court, a non-alcoholic nightclub, and a movie theater. Temple's Liacouras Walk is home to restaurants and shops that make campus a city within a city. To stave off that weight from the world-famous Philly cheese steaks, students have access to the Independence Blue Cross Student Recreation Center where they can workout with state-of-the art equipment, take fitness classes, or run the top-floor indoor track. Also, Temple is the proud home of the 11,000 seat Liacouras Center that serves campus as the state-of-the-art home for men's and women's basketball and a variety of top-ticket concerts throughout the year. Temple has been called a "boomtown" as it continues to make improvements and additions to an already vibrant and modern campus.

TUITION, ROOM, BOARD AND FEES

In 2007-2008, full-time undergraduates that are Pennsylvania residents pay $10,252 per year. Students that are residents of other states pay $18,770 per year. Room and board and annual fees cost an additional $8,000 per year on average. Specific schools and colleges within the university, including the Boyer College of Music and Dance, the Tyler School of Art, the College of Health Professions and the Fox School of Business, may charge slightly different tuitions.

FINANCIAL AID

Two-thirds of Temple attendees are awarded Financial Aid in the form of a combination of grants, loans, and work-study programs. Those seeking Financial Aid are asked to submit the Free Application for Federal Student Aid (FAFSA). The deadline for the FAFSA is March 1st. Students transferring to Temple need to submit a Financial Aid transcript whether they received aid at their previous institution or not. Merit-based scholarships are awarded to top students annually and vary in value. These scholarships may be renewed for each of a student's four years.

STUDENT ORGANIZATIONS AND ACTIVITIES

Temple's campuses are always pulsating with activity. Whether it's a movie night in the residence halls or grabbing a slice of pizza at the campus food court, the Temple experience centers upon living on campus. With 10,000 students that live on or around campus, Temple students never run out of things to do. More than 200 clubs and organizations provide opportunities for socializing, political debate and community service. Temple is also home to 23 NCAA Division I athletics and offers students free tickets to games. For the student who wants to do more than watch, students can get involved with a large variety of intramural sports teams. For students who wish to indulge their cultural side, Temple's prestigious art, music, dance, and theater departments offer over 75 performances and exhibitions annually. Temple University also offers plenty of opportunities for students to take a break from the books with events like "Free Food and Fun Fridays" and an array of low-priced trips to ski resorts, amusements parks, and local attractions. But with downtown Philadelphia only a 10-minute ride from campus, Temple students take advantage of the city they call home. With attractions like the Philadelphia Museum of Art, Olde City, South Street, the Italian Market, Main Street Manayunk and the Avenue of the Arts, students find a world of fun to be experienced in their backyard.

ADMISSIONS PROCESS

Temple University takes a holistic approach to the Admissions Process by taking into consideration every piece of information that a student chooses to provide. Applications are reviewed by the admissions committee in an individualized context. But to standardize the process for all of our applicants, the admissions committee will look at three things specifically. The first and most important piece of information is the student's high school record. Generally, students should have a strong and consistent 3.30 GPA (B+) in academic coursework. Students are required to submit scores from college entrance exams (SAT or ACT). For the SAT, the admissions committee would like to see that a student has a score that is close to Temple's combined-score average, which ranges from 1050-1150 on the Math and Critical Reading sections of the SAT. The Writing secion of the SAT will be considered as part of the admissions review process for the class of 2009. Temple's average for the ACT is a 23 composite score, and the Writing section of this test is required. Given our holistic approach, Temple also gives consideration to the student's essay, extracurricular activities, recommendation letters and special awards and honors. All applicants are automatically assessed for merit scholarships and the University Honors Program.

The best way to apply to Temple is online at www.temple.edu/undergrad .Temple's application deadline is March 1st. For questions, Temple encourages students to visit our website at www.temple.edu/undergrad or email us at tuadm@temple.edu

THOMAS MORE COLLEGE

AT A GLANCE

With just the right balance of suburban calm and big-city excitement, modern facilities and old-fashioned attention, Thomas More College is the perfect place to earn your college degree. Our small campus and small class sizes ensure you never get lost in the crowd. Our wide range of programs and activities helps you pursue any dream or interest. The College's affiliation with the Roman Catholic Church emphasizes your spiritual and personal growth along with academic achievement. As a result, you thoroughly enjoy your time here, and you leave with critical thinking and ethical leadership skills so important in life. There's more to learn and more to like at Thomas More College.

LOCATION AND ENVIRONMENT

Thomas More College is ideally located in beautiful Crestview Hills, Northern Kentucky, just 10 minutes from downtown Cincinnati, and 10 minutes from the Greater Cincinnati International Airport. This region of the country is accessible via automobile to much of the Midwest and southern U.S.

MAJORS AND DEGREES OFFERED

Accountancy°

Art

Biology

Business Administration°

Chemistry°

Computer Information Systems°

Communication

Criminal Justice

Drama°

Economics°

Education

English°

Exercise Science°°

Foreign Languages

Forensic Science

Gerontology°°

History°

International Studies

Mathematics

Medical Technology

Nursing

Philosophy°

Physics°

Political Science°

Pre-Engineering

Pre-Legal Studies°°

Psychology°

Recall Program

Sociology and Criminal Justice°

Spanish°

Speech Communication°

Theology°

°Also offered as a two-year degree program.

°°Only offered as a two-year degree program

CAMPUS FACILITIES AND EQUIPMENT

With more than 40% of our students living on campus in four residence halls, residence life at Thomas More College is an important part of the total Thomas More experience.

Our residence halls create a comfortable and safe living-learning environment, which encourages personal growth and development through a variety of activities and social interaction. Each resident is a 'citizen' in this special community, contributing to an atmosphere of harmony and maturity.

Even for those who choose not to live on campus, residence life permeates the core values of our college. Forming the nucleus of the campus community, resident students experience first hand the important interaction and life skills that will help shape their lives.

The Thomas More experience transcends the classroom. For a small, private, liberal arts school, Thomas More is packed with big ideas, featured facilities and powerful programs that are sure to make a big impact on your life stretching your mind, feeding your soul, and lifting your spirit.

The River Station biology field research center, the fully-equipped Observatory, the state-of-the-art Library Center and the Holbrook Student Center are just some of the featured cornerstones of excellence and opportunity for Thomas More students.

TUITION, ROOM, BOARD AND FEES

For the school year of 2008-2009 the cost per semester is:

Tuition

Full-Time student 12-18 credit hours	$10,750
Part-Time student 1-11 credit hours	$515 per credit hour
Nursing Differential	$30 per credit hour

Fees

Technology Fee for full-time student	$300
Technology Fee for part-time student	$30/ credit hour, max $300
Student Activity Fee	$60
Reservation Deposit	$100
Housing Security Deposit	$100

Room

Single Occupancy	$1,750
Double Occupancy	$1,450
Two Bedroom Suites	$1,750

Board

19 meal plan with $50 flex dollars	$1,675
14 meal plan with $100 flex dollars	$1,425
10 meal plan with $100 flex dollars	$1,205

FINANCIAL AID

The Office of Financial Aid works to keep tuition affordable for students and their families, while maintaining high standards of quality throughout the College's academic and extracurricular programs. Our track record of helping students experience a high-quality private education at the most affordable price underscores our mission of expanding access to educational opportunities.

Located in the Administrative Building at Thomas More College, the Office of Financial Aid is staffed with professionals eager to assist you and your family with the application process or answer any questions about Financial Aid. We are here to inform you of the many sources of financial support and help you navigate your way through the process.

Given the high percentage of Thomas More students receiving awards, chances are you may be eligible for a combination of grants, loans, scholarships and part-time work as part of a Financial Aid package. Students are encouraged to get their applications in by March 1st for full consideration of our scholarships and awards. But don't leave it to chance, contact the Office of Financial Aid to learn more and earn more for your education.

ADMISSIONS PROCESS

3 Ways to Apply

Save $25 by applying online at www.thomasmore.edu.

Complete a paper application and submit by mail with your $25 application fee.

Download a paper application from www.thomasmore.edu and submit by mail with your $25 application fee.

Do You Qualify?

Freshman must rank in the top half of their high school class, have a high school average of C or better, and a minimum of 20 on the ACT or 980 on the SAT. Transfer students with less than 24 hours of transferable credit must meet the freshman admission criteria, while those with more than 24 hours must have a GPA of 2.0 or higher. We also look at your extracurricular activities, as well as life or work experience, as important indicators of your ability to succeed at Thomas More.

TRANSYLVANIA UNIVERSITY

AT A GLANCE

Transylvania, a small, private liberal arts college of about 1,120 men and women, is consistently ranked among the best of its kind in the nation. The name_from the Latin that means across the woods refers to the heavily forested Transylvania settlement in which the University was founded in 1780. Transylvania was the first college west of the Allegheny Mountains and the sixteenth in the nation. The University established the first schools of medicine and law in what was then the West and educated the doctors, lawyers, ministers, political leaders, and others who helped shape the young nation. Transylvania also founded the first college literary magazine in the West, The Transylvanian, still published by students today.

Transylvania continues as a pioneer in higher education, preparing future leaders in business, government, education, the sciences, and the arts. Students work closely with professors in small classes, many with fewer than 10 students. Due in large part to these close collaborations with faculty, a high percentage of graduates attend selective medical, law, and other graduate and professional programs.

Transylvania offers more than fifty cocurricular organizations, covering a range of student interests, and most students participate in several of these. The Lampas Circle of the national leadership honorary society Omicron Delta Kappa, which recently moved its national headquarters to Transylvania, recognizes students for academic excellence and campus leadership. The athletics program includes seven varsity sports for men, nine for women, and more than a dozen intramural sports. Transylvania also has four national sororities and four national fraternities.

LOCATION AND ENVIRONMENT

Transylvania is located in Lexington, Kentucky, a city of 270,000 and a growing center of commerce, culture, research, and education. Known as the horse capital of the world, Lexington is surrounded by the rolling green pastures of the famous Bluegrass region of central Kentucky. The area is also home to over 30,000 college students. Transylvania's park-like campus is just a 5-minute walk from downtown, with easy access to restaurants, shops, and entertainment. The proximity to downtown is also an advantage for students who want convenient part-time jobs and internship opportunities in law offices, accounting firms, hospitals, and other organizations.

OFF-CAMPUS OPPORTUNITIES

Experiencing diverse cultures through international study is a vital part of a Transylvania education. It is common for Transylvania students to study abroad for a summer, a term, or a year. A program at Regent's College, London, allows students to study there for the same cost and course credit as a semester at Transylvania. Scholarships are available for both semester-long and summer study abroad. Summer study programs, including those in Austria, Brazil, China, Costa Rica, Ecuador, France, Germany, Italy, Japan, Mexico, and Spain, are available through Transylvania's affiliation with the Kentucky Institute for International Studies. Transylvania also cooperates with the English-Speaking Union to offer advanced students scholarships for summer study at Cambridge and Oxford Universities. Students may participate in seminars or internships in Washington, D.C., through the Washington Center and in the Canadian Parliamentary Internship Program in Ottawa. Internships with congressional offices, Kentucky state government, city government, and local firms are easily arranged.

MAJORS AND DEGREES OFFERED

The Bachelor of Arts degree is awarded in the following majors: accounting, anthropology, art history, art studio, biology, business administration (concentrations in finance; hospitality management, management; and marketing), chemistry, classics, computer science, drama, economics, education, English, exercise science, French, history, mathematics, music, music technology, philosophy, physical education, physics, political science, psychology, religion, sociology, and Spanish. Individually designed majors also may be arranged. Minors are available in most majors and in; classical studies; communication; environmental studies, German; hospitality management; international affairs; multicultural studies; and women's studies. Advising and undergraduate preparation are provided for pre-professional programs in dentistry, engineering, law, medicine, ministry, pharmacy, physical therapy, and veterinary medicine. A cooperative program in engineering allows students to earn a B.A. in physics or liberal studies from Transylvania in three years and a B.S. in engineering from the University of Kentucky or Vanderbilt University in two years. A cooperative program in accounting allows students to earn a B.A. in accounting from Transylvania in four years and an M.S. in accounting from the University of Kentucky in one year; graduates qualify to take the CPA exam.

ACADEMIC PROGRAMS

The academic year is based on a 4-4-1 academic calendar, with two 14-week terms (fall and winter) and a one-month May term. During the May term, students may participate in a variety of programs on or off campus. Students normally take four courses in each of the fall and winter terms and one course in the May term. Thirty-six courses are required to graduate. Freshmen participate in a two-term program called Foundations of the Liberal Arts, which features small-group discussions with a faculty leader; lectures, films, concerts, and other presentations; and a tutorial program in basic communication, critical thinking, and study skills. Students must complete requirements designed to ensure broad familiarity with the major areas of learning and human endeavor in the humanities and fine arts, social sciences, natural sciences and mathematics, logic, and languages.

CAMPUS FACILITIES AND EQUIPMENT

Two new Georgian-style buildings combine elegance with high-tech facilities to offer the latest advances in teaching and learning. The Cowgill Center for Business, Economics, and Education includes a multimedia classroom where professors from any discipline can use a large display screen to show the entire class information from one of the twenty-five networked student computers or from a TV, video, CD-ROM, or satellite. A specialized area for education majors includes a laboratory classroom for teacher training. The new Lucille C. Little Theater, used for faculty- and student-directed productions and drama classes, is a technically innovative facility that includes computerized lighting and sound, flexible staging options, and movable seating. The Frances Carrick Thomas/J. Douglas Gay, Jr. Library offers sophisticated computerized databases, which are invaluable for research and can be accessed from any computer connected to Transylvania's server, including PCs in dorm rooms. The Mitchell Fine Arts Center provides music program facilities, including practice rooms, a recital hall, and an auditorium. It also houses the Career Development Center, which provides free interest testing and helps students research careers, improve job search skills, arrange internships and part-time jobs, and apply to graduate schools. The recently acquired Shearer Art Building is dedicated to instructional space, student and faculty studios, and a student gallery. Other modern facilities include the newly renovated L. A. Brown Science Center, the Haupt Humanities Building, and the Clive M. Beck Athletic and Recreation Center, which opened in January 2002. About 80 percent of students live on campus in six residence halls_two for men, one for women, and three for men and women. These include traditional-style accommodations, apartment-style living for upperclass students, and suite-style rooms. All rooms are air-conditioned and completely furnished, offer private telephone service with voice mail, and access to Transylvania's cable television and computer networks. Each residence hall has ample lounge and study space and easy access to computer labs and recreational facilities. Dining options include a cafeteria, two grills, and a coffee shop. The William T. Young Campus Center offers a competition-size indoor pool, a gymnasium, a fitness center, and other facilities.

TUITION, ROOM, BOARD AND FEES

Transylvania charges an annual tuition that covers fall, winter, and May terms for a normal full-time schedule of courses. Special instruction fees are charged in addition for certain designated courses, such as applied music and May Term travel courses. For 2007-08, tuition and fees were $22,300 and room and board (double occupancy) were $7,130

FINANCIAL AID

Transylvania is committed to providing Financial Aid to students and their families. Four types of financial assistance are available: scholarships, which are based on academic performance, leadership, and citizenship; and grants, loans, and work-study, which are based on financial need. About 90 percent of Transylvania students receive some form of financial assistance and many receive more than one type of aid. Outstanding entering freshmen may qualify for one of twenty William T. Young Scholarships, each worth more than $85,000 over four years, which cover tuition and fees. Submission of Transylvania's Application for Admission and Scholarships by the appropriate deadline is all that is necessary to be considered for all scholarships at Transylvania. Students who are interested in need-based aid must file the Free Application for Federal Student Aid (FAFSA).

STUDENT ORGANIZATIONS AND ACTIVITIES

Transylvania offers more than fifty cocurricular organizations, covering a range of student interests, and most students participate in several of these. The Lampas Circle of the national leadership honorary society Omicron Delta Kappa, which recently moved its national headquarters to Transylvania, recognizes students for academic excellence and campus leadership. The athletics program, in NCAA Division III, includes seven varsity sports for men, nine for women, and more than a dozen intramural sports. Transylvania also has four national sororities and four national fraternities.

ADMISSIONS PROCESS

Each applicant is considered individually on the basis of academic records, SAT scores and/or ACT scores, activities, interests, essays, and recommendations. Admission is also offered to transfer students, international students and nontraditional students. High school students who graduate at the end of their junior year may also be considered for admission.

Transylvania enrolled 349 new students for the 2007-08 academic year. The middle 50 percent composite ACT score for the freshman class was 23 to 29; the middle 50 percent combined SAT score was 1060 to 1260. Fifty percent were in the top 10 percent of their high school class.

Submission of a Transylvania Application for Admission and Scholarships or submission of the Common Application is all that is necessary to be considered for admission and most merit scholarships at Transylvania. Application deadlines vary with particular scholarships and types of Financial Aid.

The early action deadline is December 1 for applicants who wish to learn of their admission by January 15 and who want to be considered for all Transylvania scholarships. February 1 is the regular admission and scholarships deadline for applicants who wish to be considered for all Transylvania scholarships except the William T. Young Scholarship. Applicants who apply after February 1 are considered on a space-available basis. The deadline for applications for the winter term, which begins in January, is December 1. The same deadlines apply to electronic applications, which may be submitted on the Internet at the Web address listed below.

Students considering Transylvania are urged to visit the campus, and high school seniors are encouraged to stay overnight in a dorm with a student admissions assistant. Weekday visits may include a customized campus tour, the opportunity to attend classes; talk with professors, coaches, students, and admissions and Financial Aid counselors; and enjoy meals on campus. Visits should be arranged with the Office of Admissions, preferably one to two weeks in advance. Open houses are held in the fall and winter, and a college planning workshop for high school juniors and sophomores is held in the spring.

To request application materials and additional information, contact:

Office of Admissions

Transylvania University

300 North Broadway

Lexington, KY 40508-1797

Telephone: (859) 233-8242 or (800) 872-6798

E-mail: admissions@transy.edu

Web site: www.transy.edu

TRINITY COLLEGE

AT A GLANCE

Trinity College is an independent, nonsectarian liberal arts college located in the historic capital city of Hartford, Connecticut. Founded in 1823, Trinity is one of the oldest colleges in the country, and is consistently ranked among the best. It brings the great tradition of the liberal arts into the 21st century with a dynamic living and learning community where education doesn't stop at the classroom door.

Our 2,200 students work closely with faculty and extend their education through campus activities and organizations. They engage with the city of Hartford through internships, community learning and service, and explore the wider world through study abroad and international initiatives on campus. With an 11 to 1 student-faculty ratio, each and every student is challenged and encouraged by Trinity's outstanding faculty. Students are offered a rigorous curriculum that is firmly grounded in the traditional liberal arts, but that also incorporates newer fields, an interdisciplinary approach, and urban engagement.

With 38 majors and more than 970 courses to choose from, students are immersed in a community of learning that is facilitated by a stimulating academic environment, small classes, and exceptional facilities, including fully networked classrooms and dorms. Opportunities to explore the arts abound on campus and students can nurture and hone artistic skills. More than 40 percent of our students play varsity and club sports, and many more participate in intramurals and fitness activities.

As a student at Trinity College, you will explore new worlds, thoughts, and ideas, and become prepared for the challenge and change of a successful, fulfilling life.

LOCATION AND ENVIRONMENT

Trinity is situated on a beautiful, 100-acre campus in Connecticut's capital city of Hartford, midway between Boston and New York. Hartford is a city with a rich history that offers many opportunities for urban engagement. Mark Twain lived here, as did Harriet Beecher Stowe. Dentist Horace Wells discovered anesthesia here. It is the home of the oldest continuously published newspaper in America as well as the oldest public art museum, the Wadsworth Atheneum. Trinity effectively uses the city as a classroom with access to assets and resources that is matched by few liberal arts colleges of our size.

Anyone who visits the College sees the beauty of the campus, with its hilltop location, mix of historic and contemporary buildings, and abundant trees and lawns. Trinity is one of the earliest examples of "Collegiate Gothic"; many of the original buildings are modeled after the architecture of Oxford and Cambridge and symbolize Trinity's roots in the classical liberal arts. A major campus and community revitalization initiative has created several new state-of-the-art facilities, including the Raether Library and Information Technology Center on campus and the neighboring innovative Learning Corridor of magnet schools and academic resources. Also, in 2006, the award-winning Koeppel Community Sports Center opened its doors as a multi-use athletic facility on the southern edge of campus.

Off campus, the 256-acre Field Station at Church Farm in Ashford, Connecticut, is dedicated to research in the natural sciences and a wide range of environmental educational endeavors. Plans are being developed for use of Church Farm buildings to support programs in the arts.

As a Trinity student, you have numerous opportunities to engage in volunteer work, internships, research and community learning projects. Many courses—from art history to political science and from economics to neuroscience—incorporate aspects of city life. There are hundreds of internships that allow you to continue your education while exploring career opportunities. And whatever your tastes, there are cultural and entertainment events throughout the city and a shuttle service provided by the College.

OFF-CAMPUS OPPORTUNITIES

Trinity students have a wide variety of opportunities to take advantage of the College's special relationship to the City of Hartford. The Community Learning Initiative comprises nearly 30 courses each year that weave direct contact with local people and institutions directly into the learning process. Such urban engagement builds on Trinity's liberal arts foundation, and for some students, has led to independent studies or collaborative research papers published in scholarly journals.

Trinity offers over 200 internship opportunities that represent excellent preparation for life after college. Students can explore career interests in a wide variety of fields, including law, banking, journalism, communications, health, engineering, computer science, government, and non-profit organizations. Trinity challenges its students to make a difference in the real world—starting with their Hartford community. Students can choose from a wide range of community service activities, from child-mentoring programs to senior citizen buddy programs, from the Boys and Girls Club at Trinity to Habitat for Humanity.

Trinity's study abroad programs provide unforgettable learning experiences that broaden perspectives and deepen understanding. Among the rich menu of study abroad choices are Trinity's own campus in Rome, our Shanghai semester, and our network of global learning sites, as well as intercollegiate exchange and study abroad programs. Equally valuable are many study-away programs in the U.S., including Trinity/La Mama Performing Arts in New York City, research and internships in Washington D.C., maritime studies at Mystic Seaport, and theater courses at the National Theater Institute. Students can also take advantage of the Twelve College Exchange Program.

Trinity also created the new Center for Urban and Global Studies to integrate the College's well-established tradition of urban engagement with its strong global programs. The center, which is the first of its kind at a liberal arts college in the United States, takes advantage of Trinity's location and will strengthen the long-standing mutually beneficial relationship between the College and Hartford. Playing off Trinity's global reach, it will improve existing and develop new learning and research opportunities in world cities.

MAJORS AND DEGREES OFFERED

Undergraduates completing the necessary requirements receive the Bachelor of Arts or the Bachelor of Science degrees from Trinity College. There is also a five-year Trinity/Rensselaer at Hartford program in engineering and computer science, which leads to both a bachelor's degree and a master's degree.

Trinity offers more than 970 courses in 38 majors. Options include cross-disciplinary majors, such as American studies, and self-designed majors, such as environmental studies, as well as interdisciplinary minors, such as human rights. At Trinity, your education is student-centered, and our array of curricular options will provide you with the tools to help you to meet your goals.

Trinity offers majors in: American Studies, Anthropology, Art History, Biochemistry, Biology, Chemistry, Classical Civilization, Classics, Computer Coordinate, Computer Science, Economics, Educational Studies, Engineering, English, Environmental Science, French, German, History, International Studies, Italian, Jewish Studies, Mathematics, Modern Languages (including Chinese and Japanese), Music, Neuroscience, Philosophy, Physics, Political Science, Psychology, Public Policy, Religion, Russian, Sociology, Spanish, Studio Arts, Theater and Dance, and Women, Gender and Sexuality.

As you can see, Trinity's curriculum is both broad and flexible, encouraging you to challenge yourself as you follow your interests and select a major.

ACADEMIC PROGRAMS

At Trinity, the curriculum features the First-Year Seminar Program, where a small group of students and a faculty member explore a topic through critical reading and discussion, analysis and writing. It's a shared introduction to intellectual life at Trinity and an important way to meet other students and make friends because students in the same seminar live in the same residence hall together with a student mentor.

There are many special curricular options, including the Guided Studies, Interdisciplinary Science, InterArts and Cities Programs, as well as the Trinity/La MaMa Performing Arts Program in New York. Trinity is also home to the first undergraduate Human Rights Program in the United States, as well as the unique Center for Urban and Global Studies.

The key words here are variety and flexibility—if you don't see exactly what you want, that doesn't mean we don't have it. Independent study? Study abroad? Open semester? Engineering? Neuroscience? Law courses? How about an academic leave of absence to work on a political campaign or hike the Appalachian Trail? Many Trinity students pursue these and other existing opportunities. And it is very easy to work with faculty to create your own opportunities. Your motivation and imagination are your only limits.

CAMPUS FACILITIES AND EQUIPMENT

The campus is fully wired, with every student room connected to the campus network and the Internet. The newly expanded Raether Library and Information Technology Center combines the resources of one of the leading small-college library facilities in the nation with an array of electronic resources, including digital media labs and video-conferencing capabilities. The library houses more than 900,000 volumes and more than 12,000 periodicals, as well as the Watkinson Library rare-book collections.

The science labs offer our undergraduates an opportunity to work hands-on with sophisticated equipment, including a research nuclear magnetic resonance spectrometer, a scanning electron microscope, incubators and climatically controlled growth chambers.

Focal points for the visual arts are the Widener Gallery in the Austin Arts Center and the Broad Street Gallery. In addition to a proscenium theater and a more intimate black box performance space, each art medium has its own studio.

The Ferris Athletic Center houses a fully-equipped fitness center, an Olympic-size pool, premier international-size squash courts, crew tanks, an indoor track, a field house, basketball and tennis courts. Outdoor features include an all-weather track, soccer fields, softball and baseball diamonds, tennis courts, an artificial turf field hockey field, and a new field turf playing surface for football and lacrosse. In addition, the new Koeppel Community Sports Center serves as home-ice for Trinity men's and women's ice hockey teams, as well as a place for community academic and athletic mentoring programs..

TUITION, ROOM, BOARD AND FEES

Estimated college fees for 2007-2008 are as follows:

Tuition: $35,110

Room & Board: $9,420

General Fee: $1,760

FINANCIAL AID

Through the generosity of alumni and friends, the College has an endowment sufficient to give our students an education that's worth considerably more than the actual tuition charged. If you decide that Trinity is the right college for you, we are determined not to let money stand in your way. We are committed to making a Trinity education accessible to promising students who are unable to meet the full educational costs. Approximately 40 percent of our students receive need-based Financial Aid in the form of grants, low-interest loans, and campus employment. If you have any questions about Financial Aid at Trinity during any point in your college search, you should not hesitate to contact the Office of Student Financial Services at 860-297-2046 or e-mail financial_aid@trincoll.edu.

STUDENT ORGANIZATIONS AND ACTIVITIES

While the number in our student body is relatively small, their interests are incredibly diverse. With over a hundred student organizations on campus, the opportunities for active involvement are wide open – whether continuing something in which you've already been involved or something that is completely new to you. Student organizations include community service organizations, cultural organizations, media groups, such as the College newspaper and radio station, academic clubs, fraternities, and club sports. And if you have an interest that isn't covered by an existing organization, then start one! It will probably be impossible for you not to find at least one activity that appeals to you, whether on campus or in the city. Academics are the most important part of your education, but they aren't the only part. We encourage you to get involved beyond the classroom. The opportunities are right at hand.

ADMISSIONS PROCESS

Selecting candidates for admission to Trinity is a complex but personalized process. The components of your evaluation include your academic credentials. Your grades are very important, but so is the strength of the Academic Programs in which you participated. We require one form of standardized test; either the SAT I, ACT, or any two SAT II subject tests. Non-native speakers of English are encouraged to submit the TOEFL.

In addition, two teachers' recommendations are required. Teachers give us insight into your scholarship, work habits, and classroom contributions. Personal qualities are considered, too. What talents, skills, or qualities can you bring to the life of the campus? What contributions have you made to your school and community? We aren't as concerned with the number of your activities as we are with the quality and depth of them.

If we may be of assistance, please don't hesitate to call upon us in the Office of Admissions at 860-297-2180 or e-mail admissions.office@trincoll.edu.

TRI-STATE UNIVERSITY

AT A GLANCE

Tri-State University is a private, independent, coeducational institution offering associate, baccalaureate and masters degrees. Our 1,250 students receive a private, career-oriented education and personal attention, within a hands-on learning environment. Our teaching-focused faculty are experts in the fields of engineering, technology, business, education, criminal justice, sport management, golf management, mathematics, science, and computer science. TSU has a full-time faculty of 70 members. Most hold doctoral degrees and/or are registered professional engineers. The student/faculty ratio is 15:1.

LOCATION AND ENVIRONMENT

TSU's 400-acre main campus is located in Angola, the heart of northeast Indiana's scenic lake resort region. With more than 100 lakes, the area offers fishing, camping, skiing, boating, and fine dining. Pokagon State Park is five miles from campus. TSU is situated near the crossroads of two major interstate highways (Interstate 80/90 and Interstate 69), less than a three-hour drive from Toledo, Detroit, Chicago, Cincinnati and Indianapolis.

MAJORS AND DEGREES OFFERED

The Allen School of Engineering and Technology awards bachelor of science degrees in chemical, civil, computer, electrical, and mechanical engineering; and computer-aided drafting and design technology. It awards a master of engineering (civil and mechanical majors) . The Ketner School of Business awards bachelor of science in business administration degrees in accounting, entrepreneurship, finance, hospitality and tourism management, sports management, health promotion and recreational programming, management, management information systems, marketing, and golf management. The Jannen School of Arts and Sciences awards Bachelor of Arts degrees in communication and psychology. It awards Bachelor of Science degrees in biology, chemistry, computer science, criminal justice, forensic science, mathematics, and premed. The Franks School of Education awards Bachelor of Science degrees in elementary education, physical education, and secondary education. Secondary education majors include health, mathematics, science, and social studies.

ACADEMIC PROGRAMS

TSU's goal is to provide graduates with skills and perspectives to enhance life-long learning opportunities and to improve communication with persons in other professions. Our Academic Programs are designed to ensure breadth of knowledge and to promote intellectual inquiry. All students are required to gain competencies in computer literacy, humanities, mathematics, science, social science, oral communication, and written communication. The Allen School of Engineering and Technology concentrates on providing a fundamental, application-oriented engineering education. In addition to specialized fields, students are required to successfully complete courses in communication skills, socio-humanistic studies, and analysis and design. The Ketner School of Business includes a broad range of hands-on, practical experiences that acquaint students with the practices, procedures, and problems of contemporary business. Guest lecturers are frequent visitors to campus, and internships and field trips are considered vital to the total educational experience.

CAMPUS FACILITIES AND EQUIPMENT

TSUs Upper Campus is completely wireless and includes the Aerospace Engineering Building (which contains 4-by-4-by-6-foot subsonic and 4-inch supersonic wind tunnels, aircraft structures, a machine shop, and student project laboratory), Best Hall (which houses the Jannen School of Arts and Sciences), C.W. Sponsel Administrative Center (home to the presidents office, advancement, and academic affairs), Fawick Hall (state-of-the-art technology facility home to Allen School of Engineering and Technology), Forman Hall (which contains Centennial Station, TSUs coffeehouse, the Trine Welcome Center), Shambaugh Hall (home to Ketner School of Business, Taylor Hall (Humanities Institute, Wells Theatre), Ford Hall (which includes the Franks School of Education), and the Student Villas (upperclassmen townhouse style residences). Lower Campus is home to Hershey Hall (which contains the Ketner Sports Complex, Gettig Fitness Center, two racquetball courts, three basketball courts, and weight room), University Center and Center for Online Technology is home to commons, bookstore, mailroom, Fabiani Theatre, radio station, rock climbing wall, IPOD filling station, and Center for Learning and Technology. Zollner Golf Course, an 18-hole championship course, sits on the southwest corner. TSUs seven residence halls offer various living options including apartment-style, townhouse and traditional options: Alwood Hall, Cameron Hall, Conrad Hall, Honors Residence, Kinney Apartments, Platt Hall, and University Apartments. Every residence is wireless and each room is wired to the university network and the Internet. Four new residence halls, a new stadium (housing football, lacrosse and soccer), and a new field house (to include a 200 meter track) are currently under construction (completion January 2009).

TUITION, ROOM, BOARD AND FEES

Tuition for the 2008-2009 academic year is $23,350; standard room and board is $6,700.

STUDENT ORGANIZATIONS AND ACTIVITIES

TSU supports and encourages student participation in extracurricular activities. More than half of our students participate in MIAA Conference intercollegiate athletics. Thunder athletics offers 21 varsity sports: baseball (M), basketball (M/W), cross- country (M/W), football (M), golf (M/W), indoor track and field (M/W), lacrosse (M/W), soccer (M/W), softball (W), tennis (M/W), track and field (M/W), volleyball (W), and wrestling (M). Of the more than 60 clubs and student organizations, two have had recent success in national competitions: the American Criminal Justice Association and the Bass Anglers Club. Other groups include Cheer Squad, Christian Campus House, Dance Team, Drama Club, Habitat for Humanity, Pep Band, Ski Club, Student Senate, student newspaper (The Triangle), student yearbook (The Modulus), and student radio station (The Revolution, WEAX 88.3FM). Also active on campus are professional and honorary societies.

ADMISSIONS PROCESS

TSU admits applicants on the basis of scholastic achievement and academic potential; selection is made without regard to race, religion, color, gender, sexual orientation, or age. Interested students are encouraged to visit campus—especially for a Campus Visit Day—and talk with faculty and students. TSU has a rolling Admission Process with no deadlines. Applicants are notified of their status within two weeks after the application is complete. Applications are considered complete once the Office of Admission has received the following: application (online, no application fee), official high school transcript, and official ACT or SAT score. Standard admission requirements include English (4 years), mathematics (3 years), science (3 years), and social studies (2 years). In addition to the standard admission requirements, the Allen School of Engineering and Technology requires 1 semester of trigonometry, 1 year chemistry, and 1 year physics.

TRUMAN STATE UNIVERSITY

AT A GLANCE

Truman State University is Missouri's premier liberal arts and sciences university and the only highly selective public institution in the state. As one of the very few publicly funded liberal arts schools in the nation, Truman successfully combines affordability with the type of education and personal attention typically only offered at a private institution.

Truman has established an impeccable reputation in the Midwest and throughout the nation for the high-quality undergraduate programs offered. In fact, for the eleventh consecutive year, *U.S. News & World Report* has ranked Truman State University as the number one master's level public institution in the Midwest. A commitment to student achievement and learning is the focus of the University.

OFF-CAMPUS OPPORTUNITIES

More than 500 students participate in Truman's enriching and life-changing study abroad experiences each year. Truman is ranked eighth in the nation among master's level institutions for number of students studying abroad, according to the latest "Open Doors" survey conducted by the Institute of International Education.

In cooperation with the Washington Center, Truman offers a wide variety of experiential internships in Washington, D.C. Included are work-experience opportunities in such areas as foreign affairs/diplomacy, government affairs, criminal justice, international relations, health and human services and communications as well as other areas.

Truman requires internships in education, health science, and exercise science and annually offers internship opportunities with the Missouri State Legislature. In recent years, students have completed internships with United States sena-

tors, the governor of Missouri, business and industry managers, advertising agencies, physical therapists, artists, and the United States Supreme Court.

In addition, Truman is affiliated with the Gulf Coast Research Laboratory at Ocean Springs, Mississippi. Marine biology courses may be taken at the laboratory during the summer with credit awarded at Truman. In-depth study of the Ozark habitats is also available through Truman's affiliation with Reis Biological Station located near Steelville, Missouri. Students interested in medical technology may complete clinical classes at one of several medical technology schools in Missouri, Illinois and Iowa.

MAJORS AND DEGREES OFFERED

Undergraduate degrees offered by Truman include the Bachelor of Arts (B.A.), Bachelor of Science (B.S.), Bachelor of Music: Performance (B.M.), Bachelor of Fine Arts (B.F.A.), and Bachelor of Science in Nursing (B.S.N.). Truman offers more than forty areas of study in the following disciplines: accounting, agricultural science, art, art history, athletic training, biology, business administration, chemistry, classics, communication, communication disorders, computer science, economics, English, exercise science, French, German, health science, history, interdisciplinary studies, justice systems, linguistics, mathematics, music, music: performance, nursing, philosophy and religion, physics, political science, psychology, romance language, Russian, sociology/anthropology, Spanish and theater.

Professional paths include but are not limited to dentistry, engineering, law, medicine, optometry, pharmacy, physical therapy, physician's assistant, occupational therapy and veterinary medicine.

The teaching degree at Truman is the Master of Arts in Education. Students wishing to pursue a teaching career first complete a bachelor's degree in an academic discipline and then apply for admission into professional study at the master's level. Master's programs in special education, early childhood education, elementary education, middle school education, and secondary education are available.

Truman also offers Master's level degrees in Accountancy (MAc), Music (MA), Communication Disorders (MA), English (MA) and Biology (MS).

ACADEMIC PROGRAMS

The Liberal Studies program is the heart of Truman's curriculum and is intended to serve as a foundation for all major programs of study.

The philosophy behind the Liberal Studies Program is based upon a commitment that Truman has made to provide students with essential skills needed for lifelong learning, breadth across the traditional liberal arts and sciences through exposure to various discipline-based modes of inquiry, and interconnecting perspectives that stress interdisciplinary thinking and integration as well as linkage to other cultures and experiences.

All students at Truman complete a "capstone," or culminating experience their senior year. This experience prompts seniors to reflect on the knowledge they have gained throughout their learning experience and to integrate the knowledge, skills, and attitudes of liberal learning with an in-depth understanding of the major.

Truman also offers an especially challenging General Honors Program. Students have the opportunity to select the most rigorous honors courses to satisfy the liberal arts component of their respective programs. Those who successfully complete this program benefit from an even richer academic experience at Truman and receive special recognition at graduation. Departmental honors are also available in several disciplines.

CAMPUS FACILITIES AND EQUIPMENT

The Truman campus is beautifully situated on 140 acres near downtown Kirksville.

Improvements to campus facilities have included the $20-Million renovation and expansion of Truman's Science facility, Magruder Hall, was completed for the Spring 2006 semester and includes new research labs, a greenhouse, classrooms, meeting areas, and a cyber café. The brand new West Campus Suites opened to students in the fall of 2006. The suites are equipped with a living room, two bedrooms housing two students each, closet space, a large bathroom, and central air conditioning. Missouri Hall, which serves as home to over 500 students, re-opened for the 2007 Fall Semester after a $16-Million renovation and expansion to this facility. Renovations are underway on Blanton-Nason-Brewer Hall.

Additional facilities include a student media center with a TV studio and a radio station, a biofeedback laboratory, a speech and hearing clinic for communication disorder students, an organic chemistry lab, an independent learning center for nursing students, an observatory, a 5,000-seat football stadium, a 3,000-seat arena with three basketball courts and an Olympic-size swimming pool, a multicultural affairs center, student health center, and a career center.

TUITION, ROOM, BOARD AND FEES

Tuition for Missouri residents for the 2007-08 academic year is $ 6,210; out-of-state tuition is $10,820 . Room and board totals for both Missouri residents and non-residents start at $5,815. Additional fees include a $250 Truman Week fee, an annual $72 Activities Fee, a $50 Student Health Center fee, a $50 Parking Fee for those with a vehicle, a $100 Athletic Fee and costs of books and personal expenses.

FINANCIAL AID

Truman offers automatic scholarships ranging from $1,000 to $2,000. Competitive scholarship awards vary from $500 up to full tuition, room and board, plus a $4,000 study-abroad stipend. The application for admission also serves as the application for the automatic and competitive scholarship programs.

Several scholarships are awarded to students for excellence in music, theater, or art. These scholarships are available for instrumental, strings, or vocal music; acting or dramatic production; and studio art or art history. Of special interest to piano students is the Truman Piano Fellowship Competition.

The National Collegiate Athletic Association and the University authorize a limited number of grants to outstanding athletes. The value of this aid may vary with each individual recipient.

Truman accepts the Free Application for Federal Student Aid (FASFA) and participates in all Federal Title IV Financial Aid programs. Financial Aid estimates are available upon request.

STUDENT ORGANIZATIONS AND ACTIVITIES

Truman was recently ranked by the Princeton Review as number eight in the social category based upon the number of social opportunities available on campus. With over 250 university organizations to choose from, encompassing service, Greek, honorary, professional, religious, social, political and recreational influences, Truman students have tremendous opportunities to become involved on campus and in the Kirksville community.

The Kohlenberg Lyceum Series also provides a variety of cultural programs that interest students throughout the year. Past programs have included a lively performance by the Peking Acrobats, an elite group of hand-selected gymnasts and tumblers from the Peoples Republic of China, the Vienna Boys Choir and the Polish Philharmonic. All Kohlenberg Lyceum events are free for students.

ADMISSIONS PROCESS

Each applicant is evaluated for admission based upon academic and co-curricular record, ACT or SAT results and the admission essay. Truman requires the following high school core; 4 units of English, 3 units of mathematics (4 recommended), 3 units of social studies/history, 3 units of natural science, 1 unit of fine arts and 2 units of the same foreign language.

To ensure consideration for all Truman scholarships and Financial Aid programs Students are encouraged to apply by the priority application date of December 15. There is no application fee. Students may apply online at the website listed below. For further information or to schedule a campus visit, students should contact:

Office of Admission

Truman State University

205 McClain Hall

100 East Normal

Kirksville, Missouri 63501

Telephone: 660.785.4114

        800.892.7792 (Missouri only)

Fax: 660785.7456

Email: admissions@truman.edu

http://admissions.truman.edu

TULANE UNIVERSITY

AT A GLANCE

Founded in 1834 in New Orleans, Tulane is one of the most respected universities in the country, known worldwide for its teaching and research. It is consistently ranked among the top 50 universities in the nation and is one of only four private research institutions in the South that is a member of the prestigious Association of American Universities, an organization of the top research institutions in the United States and Canada. Tulane was named by Kaplan/Newsweek's college guide as one of the nine "Hot Schools" in the nation in 2002 and its Latin American Studies program is ranked second in the country by the Gourman Report of Undergraduate and Professional Programs.

With research and educational partnerships that span the globe and top-ranked programs in both undergraduate and professional schools, Tulane has the intimacy of a small liberal arts college and the resources of a major research institution located in one of the world's greatest cities.

LOCATION AND ENVIRONMENT

Tulane's 110-acre campus is located in the heart of New Orleans' beautiful and historic Uptown neighborhood on oak-lined St. Charles Avenue, home to the country's oldest streetcar line. Tulane's campus combines old and new styles of architecture interspersed among live oaks, azaleas, magnolias and the occasional banana tree or bamboo grove. Tulane's semi-tropical location makes outdoor classes and activities possible almost year-round.

OFF-CAMPUS OPPORTUNITIES

Across the street from Tulane is the world-famous Audubon Park and Zoo. Restaurants and shopping are only a few blocks away. The historic St. Charles Avenue streetcar, which stops directly in front of campus, takes students the four miles to downtown New Orleans where many pursue internships and cultural activities in the Central Business District and French Quarter. New Orleans, with a half a million residents, is the second-largest port in the United States and is internationally known for its music, food and rich confluence of cultures and traditions. Many of Tulane's programs are based in the living laboratory that is New Orleans.

MAJORS AND DEGREES OFFERED

Tulane offers more than 70 undergraduate majors and minors including accounting, African and African Diaspora studies, American studies, anthropology, architecture, art history, art studio, Asian studies, biological chemistry, biomedical engineering, business, cell and molecular biology, chemical engineering, chemistry, classical studies, cognitive studies, communication, consumer behavior, dance, entrepreneurship, engineering physics, earth and environmental sciences, ecology and evolutionary biology, economics, English, film studies, finance, French, geology, German cultural studies, German Languages and literatures, global and community health, Greek, health informatics, history, international development, Italian, Italian studies, jazz studies, Jewish studies, Latin, Latin American studies, legal studies in business, linguistics, literature, management, marketing, mathematical economics, mathematics, medieval and early modern studies, music, neuroscience, philosophy, physics, political economy, political science, Portuguese, psychology, religious studies, Russian cultural studies, Russian Languages and literatures, social policy and practice, sociology, Spanish, theatre and women's studies. Minors include architecture studies, cultural studies, film studies and urban sociology.

Because Tulane provides many educational options advisors are available to new students from their first days on campus. This support network of faculty advisors, resident advisors, deans and professional academic counselors guides students through questions of course selection and major and ensures that they are on track to meet their degree and graduation goals.

ACADEMIC PROGRAMS

The 9 schools and colleges of Tulane University offer undergraduate, graduate and professional degrees in architecture, business, engineering, law, liberal arts and sciences, medicine, public health and tropical medicine and social work. Tulane's Academic Programs are considered among the best in the country. At Tulane, traditional classroom instruction is enhanced by experiential, hands-on

learning. Examples of this include a myriad of service learning programs that give students real-life experience in their chosen field, internships for students during the summer or school year, and cutting-edge research opportunities with professors. For example of service learning, a psychology student might be assigned service learning hours at a local mental health facility or an English major assigned as a tutor at an adult literacy program. Other hands-on opportunities include the archaeological excavations sponsored through Tulane's Latin American program and the award-winning Burkenroad Reports through which business majors produce stock analyses used by investors across the country.

CAMPUS FACILITIES AND EQUIPMENT

Tulane's facilities are designed to optimize its students' intellectual and social experiences. Tulane's libraries hold 2.5 million volumes, 10,000 periodicals and 800,000 government documents. The main Howard-Tilton Memorial Library houses the Latin American Library and the Maxwell Music Library. The Rudolph Matas Medical Library is located in the School of Medicine.

The university's Special Collections Division includes the Hogan Jazz Archive, Southeastern Architectural Archive, university archives, rare books and manuscripts and the Louisiana collection. Other libraries include architecture, botany, business, law, mathematics, natural history, primate research, race relations and ethnic history, and women's studies.

In 2003, the Goldring/Woldenberg Hall II, a $25 million addition to Tulane's A.B. Freeman School of Business, opened. With more than 60,000 square feet of classroom and lab space, the building includes a 130-seat lecture theater, four 65-seat MBA classrooms configured for case-method-style study and a $1.5 million electronic trading room.

Several new Tulane student residences have recently been completed. These include the award-winning $15 million 300-bed Willow Residences, which Architecture magazine called an "endearing little jewel," and Wall Residential College, which features 267 beds in 80,500 square feet of space at a cost of approximately $11.9 million. With 55 single rooms and 106 doubles, Wall Residential College offers students a modern residential community with the convenience of campus living. A second, 270-bed residence hall is currently in the design stage.

Two of Tulane's main sports arenas have been the focus for change. Greer Field at Turchin Stadium, home of the Green Wave baseball team, recently received a $7.5 million renovation that was completed in time for the team to open the 2008 season there. Fogelman, home to the men's and women's basketball teams, and volleyball team, will soon undergo a $25 million renovation, as well.

The Lavin-Bernick Center for University Life, the heart of Tulane student life, recently completed a $37 million renovation that serves as home to dozens of student organizations, the campus bookstore, a food court, student-related administrative offices and more than 6,000 annual meetings.

TUITION, ROOM, BOARD AND FEES

$36,610, undergraduate schools, A.B. Freeman School of Business, and Law School

$47,234, School of Medicine (tuition only, first year)

$832/credit hour (tuition only), School of Public Health and Tropical Medicine

$263/credit hour (tuition only), School of Continuing Studies

$8,690 Room and Board

FINANCIAL AID

Students should not hesitate to apply for financial assistance to attend Tulane. Between Tulane-funded grants, scholarships and other sources, more than $111 million is available to subsidize undergraduate education at Tulane each year. The average need-based Financial Aid package given to 2006-2007 entering freshman was $29,417. Financial Aid packages are typically composed of grants and need-based scholarships, loans and part-time student employment. Merit, ROTC and athletic scholarships are also available. High-performing Louisiana students may also qualify for special awards. Approximately 75% of incoming freshmen for the fall of 2007 received some form of need or merit based aid.

STUDENT ORGANIZATIONS AND ACTIVITIES

Much of the learning that takes place in college happens when students pursue interests outside of class. Such learning plays an important role in the Tulane experience. With more than 200 student organizations on campus, including student government; pre-professional and multicultural organizations; media groups; performance; service and education organizations; honor societies; fraternities and sororities; club and intramural sports and military; and religious and political organizations, every student has opportunities to join, lead, expand horizons, make friends and have fun. Campus programming brings concerts, lectures, and special events year-round to Tulane. Students also enjoy supporting Tulane's athletics teams, known as the GreenWave, who play at the highest level (Division I-A) of the NCAA.

First-year students also have the opportunity to take part in the Tulane Interdisciplinary Experiences or TIDES program, a unique opportunity to get to know some of the university's most distinguished faculty and their fellow students both as scholars and friends. Students select a TIDE program from a list that includes themes such as politics, religion, the arts, women's studies, popular culture and more.

ADMISSIONS PROCESS

Tulane enrolls 6,488 undergraduates (48 percent males and 52 percent females) from all 50 states and many foreign countries. A higher percentage of Tulane students travel farther to school than students of any other college or university in the nation. More than 75 percent of entering Tulane freshmen come from more than 500 miles away, making the student body geographically, socially and academically diverse.

An additional 4,073 students are enrolled in the university's graduate programs and professional schools. Admission to Tulane is highly competitive with evaluators looking for high levels of achievement in all areas of student life, including leadership and community involvement. The average SAT score for the 2006-2007 entering freshmen class was 1300, which is 274 points above the national average

Each year approximately 63 percent of enrolling freshmen rank in the top 10 percent of their high school class; more than 75 percent rank in the top 25 percent and 95 percent rank in the top half of their class.

Candidates for admission are expected to present strong high school programs of study consisting of 18 or more academic courses taken over the four-year period. The following minimum preparation is recommended for each subject area.

English: Four years with extensive work in reading and writing

Mathematics: Three years (students entering scientific fields should have four years including advanced algebra, trigonometry, geometry, and calculus)

Foreign Language: At least two years, preferably three, of a classical or modern language

Science: At least two years of a laboratory science (biology, chemistry, or physics); students entering scientific fields should have at least four years

Social Studies: At least two years with an emphasis on history

Application Deadlines for Admission to Tulane are:

Early Action (Nonbinding)

By September: Take TOEFL, SAT I, or ACT no later than September if applying for Early Action.

October 1: Submit CSS PROFILE Registration to College Scholarship Service.

November 1: Application deadline. Submit CSS PROFILE application packet to College Scholarship Service.

December 15: Last day for notification of admission. All Deans' Honor Scholarship projects must be submitted.

January 15: Community Service Scholarship applications due.

February 1: Submit FAFSA to federal processor.

February 20: Deans' Honor Scholarship winners announced.

April 15: Last day for notification of Financial Aid decision.

May 1: Enrollment commitment deposit due for Early Action candidates. Deadline for accepting Financial Aid offers.

Regular Decision

Take SAT or ACT no later than December if applying for Regular Decision.

By December 15: Applicants for Deans' Honors Scholarships must submit application materials and projects.

January 1: Submit CSS PROFILE Registration to College Scholarship Service.

January 15: Regular Decision application deadline (if not applying for Deans' Honor Scholarship). Community Service Scholarship application due.

By February 1: Submit CSS PROFILE Application packet to College Scholarship Service. Submit FAFSA to Federal Processor.

February 20: Deans' Honor Scholarship winners announced.

April 1: Last day for notification of admission decision.

April 15: Last day for notification of Financial Aid decision.

May 1: Enrollment commitment deposit due for Regular Decision candidates. Deadline for accepting Financial Aid offers.

UNION COLLEGE (NY)

AT A GLANCE

Union College, founded in 1795 as the first college chartered by the New York State Board of Regents, offers programs in the liberal arts and engineering to students of high academic promise and strong personal motivation. With its long history of blending disciplines, Union is a leader in educating students to be engaged, innovative, and ethical contributors to an increasingly diverse, global and technologically complex society. Union's curriculum emphasizes collaboration with students and faculty through small classes and undergraduate research, an international experience in all disciplines and learning through service to the campus and community. Students are also afforded opportunities through the College's unique Minerva residential program for meaningful interaction outside the classroom. Each year, the Admissions Committee selects a diverse class of 560 from approximately 4,600 candidates. The student population of 2,100 full-time undergraduates, with nearly equal numbers of men and women, comes from 37 different U.S. states and 26 foreign countries. Roughly one out of three graduates goes straight on to graduate or professional school.

LOCATION AND ENVIRONMENT

Union is located in the small upstate city of Schenectady, which is within 15 miles of Albany, the capital of New York. The Capital District area has a population of approximately 900,000, including 55,000 college and university students. The Union campus is three hours from New York City or Boston, and approximately four hours from Montreal. Nearby natural attractions include the Catskills, Adirondacks, Green Mountains and the Massachusetts Berkshires. Students enjoy the gardens, natural woodland and grassy areas that are elements of the 120-acre campus.

OFF-CAMPUS OPPORTUNITIES

Union offers study-abroad programs in more than two dozen countries and more than 60 percent of Union students participate. Closer to home, students may cross-register for classes offered at any of the member schools in the Hudson-Mohawk Association of Colleges and Universities, all located in the Capital District. The Association also enables Union students to enroll in the Reserve Officers' Training Corps (ROTC) programs of the Army, Navy, and Air Force.

ACADEMICS

The College has implemented a new set of General Education requirements called the Core Components curriculum. The first-year seminar and sophomore research seminar promote skills in reading, writing, research and analyzing texts. Distribution requirements in the humanities, literature, social sciences, linguistic and cultural competency, quantitative mathematical reasoning and the sciences promote breadth of knowledge about the social and natural world, and key skills in analysis, literacy, and numeracy. Approved interdisciplinary "clusters" centered on particular intellectual themes are designed to prompt awareness of interdisciplinary connections and understanding of issues from multiple perspectives. The Union Scholars program was created to provide an enriched educational experience for entering students with unusual academic capabilities and talents through a more extensive and enhanced first-year seminar, the opportunity to begin working individually with faculty on independent study projects during the sophomore year, increased opportunities for study abroad, and participation in scholars colloquia and departmental honors programs during the junior and senior years. Union vigorously encourages student research in all disciplines and annually sends one of the largest contingents to the National Conference on Undergraduate Research. At Union's own Steinmetz Symposium each year, more than 400 students present the results of their scholarly activities. Converging Technologies (CT) is a new interdisciplinary approach that brings together students from engineering and the liberal arts so that they graduate with a broad background that goes beyond that provided by the traditional major. This element in Union's academic program is designed to address a major challenge facing our society—the discovery and application of scientific and technological advances that will shape the next century. Many programs offer internship opportunities. Students can spend a 10-week term in Washington, D.C., or participate in a legislative internship in Albany, New York. In order to graduate, students must successfully complete a minimum of 36 courses (up to 40 for engineering degrees) and all departmental and general education requirements must be satisfied. The academic calendar is based on three 10-week terms, starting in early September and running through early June. Students normally take three classes per term.

MAJORS AND DEGREES OFFERED

Union grants the Bachelor of Arts degree in anthropology, art, astronomy, classics, economics, English, history, modern languages, philosophy, political science, and sociology. The Bachelor of Science is awarded in biology, chemistry, computer science, computer engineering, electrical engineering, geology, mathematics, mechanical engineering, physics, and psychology. Students may undertake one of the formal interdepartmental programs available in Africana studies; American studies; Biochemistry; East Asian studies; environmental studies; Latin American and Caribbean studies; managerial economics; neuroscience; Russian and Eastern European studies; science, medicine & technology in culture; and women's and gender studies. Union offers dual and student-designed majors, as well as the Leadership in Medicine program (eight year B.S., M.S. or M.B.A., M.D. joint program with Albany Medical College and Union Graduate College) and the Law and Public Policy program (six-year B.A./J.D. with Albany Law School); and five year bachelor's/M.B.A. or bachelor's M.A.T. programs with Union Graduate College.

ADMISSIONS

Assessment of the application begins with a careful analysis of the applicant's academic credentials, particularly secondary school academic performance and the quality of courses selected, including honors and advanced courses. Recommendations from the secondary school—teachers or counselors—are also important. Successful applicants present a strong and varied curriculum including English, a foreign language, mathematics, social studies, and science. Additional courses are encouraged, and honors, advanced and AP courses strengthen an application. The College also considers extracurricular activities, talents and personal attributes. Testing is optional except for combined programs. Applicants for the Leadership in Medicine or Law and Public Policy programs are required to submit the SAT I and two SAT II tests and must complete the necessary tests no later than December of the senior year. Students may arrange an on-campus interview from May through January. Students desiring an alumni interview should request one by December 15. The deadline for regular applications is January 15. Applications to combined programs must be received by January 1, with the exception of the Leadership in Medicine program which has a deadline of December 15. Applicants will receive notification in early April. Two early-decision options are available. Applications received by November 15 will have a response by December 15. Those who have their materials in by January 15 will hear by February 1. All accepted students must reply to Union by May 1.

CAMPUS LIFE

Union College encourages students to complement their classroom learning with extracurricular experiences. More than 100 student-run clubs and organizations provide venues for any interest. Many students attend on-campus cultural events, such as concerts, lectures, and movies. Union also offers athletic opportunities ranging from intercollegiate competition to intramural leagues, club sports, and casual recreational games. Seven social and academic spaces in the center of campus make up the student-run Minerva House System. Each student belongs to one of the houses and all faculty members have house affiliations. This initiative was designed to encourage all students and faculty members to contribute in a variety of ways to Union's social, residential, and intellectual life.

CAMPUS FACILITIES AND EQUIPMENT

Schaffer Library houses more than 600,000 volumes and approximately 1,600 periodical subscriptions, a periodicals reading room, faculty studies, and more than 500 individual study spaces. The F.W. Olin Center is a high-technology classroom and laboratory building. The Science and Engineering Center contains a number of specialized research tools available for student use. The College's arts program is greatly enhanced by the Morton and Helen Yulman Theater and the recently renovated and expanded Taylor Music Building. Union's central computer facility consists of several multi-user servers on a campus wide fiber-optic-based network that includes UNIX, Windows Server and Apple Macintosh Xserves. Connected to the network are more than 1,500 College-owned personal computers and workstations. More than 40 electronic classrooms are used to enhance the integration of technology and academic studies. At least 85% of the faculty use the Blackboard LMS (Learning Management System) as a component of their teaching. Facilities with Windows and Macintosh computers as well as UNIX workstations are available for student use. Each residence hall room is wired, providing access to the College's computing resources and the Internet. In addition, the College's wireless network extends to all public/study areas on campus (including the public areas in the residence halls), all classrooms, the library, all academic buildings and most other buildings. The Reamer Campus Center provides space for social and community activities and services for the entire campus. The Center houses dining facilities, an auditorium, a two-level bookstore, a radio station, and multiple student activities spaces. The 16-sided Nott Memorial has been renovated to become a display and discussion center and has been designated a National Historic Landmark. Among the athletic facilities are the Alumni Gymnasium with an eight-lane swimming/diving pool, multi-use rooms for dance, aerobics and yoga programs, a new fitness center, and squash and racquetball courts, the 3,000-seat Messa ice rink, an Astroturf field, an all-weather track, and the state-of-the-art Viniar Athletic Center for basketball and volleyball. Residential options for students include apartment-style housing, theme houses, residence halls, and the newest facility (2004), College Park Hall, which houses upper class students.

STUDENT ORGANIZATIONS AND ACTIVITIES

Union College encourages students to complement their classroom learning with extracurricular experiences. More than 100 student-run clubs and organizations provide venues for any interest. Many students attend on-campus cultural events, such as concerts, lectures, and movies. Union also offers athletic opportunities ranging from intercollegiate competition to intramural leagues, club sports, and casual recreational games.

Seven social and academic spaces in the center of campus make up the student-run Minerva House System. Each student belongs to one of the houses and all faculty members have house affiliations. This initiative was designed to encourage all students and faculty members to contribute in a variety of ways to Union's social, residential, and intellectual life.

TUITION AND FEES

The comprehensive fee for 2007–08 is $46,245. This includes tuition, mandatory fees, and room and board.

FINANCIAL AID

For the 2007–08 academic year, the amount of Union-funded grants, loans and work-study totals approximately $28 million. Scholarship awards are based on academic performance and financial need. All financial aid applicants must submit both the Free Application for Federal Student Aid (FAFSA) and the College Scholarship Service's PROFILE form. These should be submitted directly to the appropriate agencies by February 1.

UNION UNIVERSITY

AT A GLANCE

Union University is an institution of higher learning grounded in a Christian world and life view. In the words of Union President David S. Dockery, "You will find an education characterized by rigorous academic pursuit and authentic Christian commitment—an education involving head, heart and hands."

Union alumni enjoy a high acceptance rate to top graduate schools. Nearly 100 percent of our faculty-recommended health science students have been accepted to medical school or professional graduate study. Within three months of receiving their degrees, more than 80 percent of all graduates are accepted by graduate schools or employed, many with Fortune 500 companies. Among Union seniors, 60 percent plan to complete postgraduate work.

Union has consistently received national recognition for academic excellence and value. *U.S.News & World Report* has ranked Union in the top tier of either "Baccalaureate Colleges" or more recently "Best Universities–Master's" each year since 1997. Independent research by *America's 100 Best College Buys* ranks Union among the nation's best for combining academic quality and affordable price.

More than 3,300 undergraduate and graduate students attend classes in Jackson and Germantown (suburban Memphis), Tennessee. Forty states and thirty-five countries are represented in the student body.

On its Jackson campus, the university provides each resident a private bedroom with an Internet connection. The suites are located within apartment-style complexes with gathering areas, laundry facilities, and other services. All units have kitchens.

LOCATION AND ENVIRONMENT

The 290-acre campus is located in suburban Jackson, Tennessee, a growing community with a population of about 100,000. Jackson is located 80 miles east of Memphis and 120 miles west of Nashville along the I-40 corridor.

Students find convenient access to entertainment, shopping, and many other services. Jackson hosts many cultural, recreational and sporting events. Daily commercial flights are available at airports in Memphis and Nashville.

OFF-CAMPUS OPPORTUNITIES

Union offers study abroad programs throughout the world and short-term international projects. The university affiliates with several organizations in offering numerous cross-discipline selections.

Yanbian University of Science and Technology, which ranks among China's top 100 universities, partners with Union in an exchange of students and visiting professors.

Global Outreach (GO) trips occur during school breaks. Students work in teams on mission service projects regionally, nationally and internationally. Recently, for example, Union engineering students conducted a feasibility study on solar energy in rural North Africa.

Although students may work and study all over the world, they also invest time and helpfulness in our local community. Each fall, the entire campus shuts down for a day so students, faculty and staff can complete service projects throughout West Tennessee. These efforts receive national recognition: Union is listed on the President's Higher Education Community Service Honor Roll.

MAJORS AND DEGREES OFFERED

Art: Ceramics; Digital Media Studies; Drawing; Graphic Design; Painting; Photography; Sculpture

Biology: General Biology; Cell and Molecular Biology; Zoology; Conservation

Business Administration: Accounting; Economics and Finance; International Business; Management; Marketing; Organizational Leadership

Chemistry: Chemical Physics; Chemistry; Medical Technology

Christian Studies: Biblical Studies; Biblical Studies –Languages; Christian Ethics; Church History; Philosophy—Christian Studies; Philosophy – General Studies; Sport Ministry; Youth Ministry

Communication Arts: Broadcasting; Digital Media Studies; Film Studies

Journalism: Photojournalism; Public Relations/Advertising; Theatre and Speech°

Computer Science: Computer Information Systems; Computer Science; Digital Media Studies

Education: Liberal Studies, Grades 4-8; Learning Foundations, PreK-3 or K-6; Special Education K-12; Teacher Licensure, Secondary Areas

Engineering: Mechanical; Electrical

English: Literature; Writing

History

Honors: Interdisciplinary Honors; Interdisciplinary Studies; Intercultural Studies

Global: Regional

Language: French; Spanish; Teaching English as a Second Language

Mathematics: Actuarial Science; Mathematics

Music: Church Music; Christian Studies; Communication Arts; Music Management; Music Marketing; Music Education; Band; Choral; Music Theory; Performance (Organ, Piano, Voice)

Nursing

Physical Education, Wellness and Sport: Athletic Training; Physical Education & Health; Sport Communication; Sport Management; Sport Marketing; Sports Medicine - Exercise Science; Sport Ministry

Physics: Engineering Physics; Physical Science; Physics

Political Science: Pre-professional Programs; Chiropractry; Cytotechnology; Dental Hygiene; Dentistry; Health Information Management; Medicine; Occupational Therapy; Optometry; Pharmacy; Physical Therapy; Physician Assistant; Podiatry; Veterinary Medicine

Psychology

Social Work

Sociology and Family Studies: Criminal Justice; Family Studies; Sociology

Degrees: Bachelor of Arts; Bachelor of Science; Bachelor of Music; Bachelor of Business Administration; Bachelor of Science in Nursing; Bachelor of Science in Medical Technology; Master of Business Administration; Master of Education; Master of Arts in Education; Master of Christian Studies; Master of Science in Nursing; Master of Social Work; Master of Arts in Intercultural Studies; Educational Specialist; Doctor of Education

ACADEMIC PROGRAMS

Union University requires those seeking a bachelor's degree to complete 46 hours of general core curriculum, 18 to 21 hours of specific core curriculum, a minimum of 30 hours in the major academic program, and 18 hours in the minor academic program. The completion of the required 128 hours usually takes four years with 32 hours per year.

For each undergraduate degree granted, at least 25 percent of the required semester hours must be earned through instruction at Union University. The last 56 semester hours of credit for a bachelor's degree must be earned at an accredited senior college.

The academic calendar is divided into fall semester (August to December), a January winter term, spring semester (February to May), and three summer terms. Evening accelerated courses are available each term.

Faculty

The faculty members at Union put a priority on classroom teaching but also join students in the pursuit of significant research, especially at the undergraduate level. Among full-time faculty members, more than 83 percent hold doctorates or the highest degree offered in their field of study. Classes at Union are small, with a student-faculty ratio of 11:1.

Faculty members also serve as student advisers. Advisers are assigned within the department of the student's major. Faculty advisers assist students in planning schedules and defining educational and career goals. The student and adviser meet at least once each semester.

CAMPUS FACILITIES AND EQUIPMENT

During the past decade, Union has invested more than $62 million in campus improvements. Additions include a 64,000 square foot science building, an athletic field house, and two other major classroom buildings. New on-campus housing and a banquet facility are under construction.

Union provides more than 300 computers for student use, with full access to e-mail and the Internet. In addition, each residential student has a port for the campus network and Internet access in their private bedroom. Wireless access is available in many areas on campus.

The Emma Waters Summar Library has immediate access to a collection of over 150,000 books, 19,000 e-journals and 40,000 e-books. Through its membership in cooperatives there is easy access to the combined collections of over 41,000 libraries worldwide. The library provides knowledgeable reference service, in-depth research assistance, personalized training, and group instructional sessions to facilitate the effective use of these resources. It also maintains a safe comfortable environment for both individual and group study.

Other academic amenities include top-quality lecture facilities, fine and performing arts practice rooms, theaters, broadcast studios, digital media labs, and science laboratories. Union is among a small group of nursing schools in the region training students with human patient simulators.

TUITION, ROOM, BOARD AND FEES

Tuition (up to 16 hours per semester): $18,980

Fees: $630 per year

Room: $4,900

Board: (150/semester) $2,360

Total Annual Cost: $26,870

FINANCIAL AID

Nearly 90 percent of Union students receive some Financial Aid based on need or merit. Union commits very competitive scholarships and grants to qualified students. The university helps connect students with other financial resources such as loans, student work programs, privately funded scholarships, and a host of state and federal assistance programs.

STUDENT ORGANIZATIONS AND ACTIVITIES

Campus organizations offer opportunities for social and academic pursuits and hosts seven Greek fraternal organizations.

Union's Student Government Association (SGA), composed of all students enrolled in Union University, functions through its executive, legislative, and judicial branches. Its elected officers and representatives serve as the official voice of the students in institutional affairs. The SGA seeks to foster university unity, promote student welfare and provide students with programs, activities and services designed to meet their needs and interests.

Intramural sports—including soccer, volleyball, basketball, flag football and softball—involve many Union students. Union competes in the National Association of Intercollegiate Athletics (NAIA-Division I). Varsity sports include basketball, baseball, golf, soccer, softball, volleyball, tennis and cross-country.

ADMISSIONS PROCESS

Applicants must graduate from an accredited high school with at least 20 units in the areas of English, foreign language, mathematics, social and natural sciences, and approved electives.

In addition, students who qualify for unconditional admission must meet or exceed two of the following three admissions criteria: a 2.5 core GPA, a composite score of 22 on the ACT or 1020 (math and critical reading combined) on the SAT, and a ranking in the top 50 percent of their high school class. Union also actively admits home-schooled students. A state high school equivalency diploma is accepted in lieu of a high school diploma.

Transfer students who have completed at least 24 semester hours of transferable credit at an accredited college may also apply. Transfer students with less than 24 semester hours must meet freshman and transfer admission requirements. Transfer student must have a 2.3 cumulative GPA to qualify for unconditional admission.

Applicants must complete and return the Union University application for undergraduate admission along with the $35 application fee. All official transcripts must be requested and mailed directly to the Office of Undergraduate Admissions. Results of either the ACT or SAT must also be sent.

For more information or to request an application, students should contact:

Office of Undergraduate Admissions

Union University

1050 Union University Drive

Jackson, Tennessee 38305-3697

United States

Phone: 800-33-UNION (toll-free) or 731.661.5100

E-mail: info@uu.edu

Web site: http://www.uu.edu

UNITED STATES AIR FORCE ACADEMY

AT A GLANCE

The Air Force Academy was established in 1954 to train and motivate Air Force cadets pursuing careers in the military. The academy emphasizes character building, military discipline, physical fitness, and academic excellence. An academy education builds valuable leadership skills in all areas.

Approximately 4,000 students attend the academy, of whom about 1,300 are entering students (fourth-class). The makeup of the student body reflects that of the corps of Air Force officers: approximately 20 percent women and 24 percent minority. Cadets arrive from all 50 states and a number of other countries. They share a common bond: the aspiration to become military officers. All cadets must live on campus and wear uniforms.

The Academy is accredited by the North Central Association of Colleges and Schools. Engineering programs are approved by the Engineering Accreditation Commission of the Accreditation Board for Engineering and Technology. Computer courses are approved by the Computing Sciences Accreditation Board. The Commission on Professional Training of the American Chemical Society establishes the requirements made of biochemistry and chemistry majors.

Cadets are required to engage in club, intramural, and intercollegiate athletics each semester. Options for intramural activity include basketball, boxing (men), cross-country, flag football, flickerball, mountain biking, racquetball, rugby (men's & women's), soccer, softball, team handball, tennis, ultimate Frisbee, volleyball, and wallyball.

The Academy fields intercollegiate teams in Division I of the NCAA; its teams compete both regionally and nationally. The men compete in baseball, basketball, boxing (men), cheerleading, cross-country, diving, fencing, football, golf, gymnastics, ice hockey, lacrosse, rifle, soccer, swimming, tennis, track, water polo, and wrestling teams. Women compete in basketball, cheerleading, cross-country, diving, fencing, gymnastics, rifle, soccer, swimming, tennis, track, and volleyball. Over 80 extracurricular activities are available to cadets; including competitive and recreational clubs, hobby clubs, mission support, professional organizations, and sports groups.

Qualified graduates of the academy may commence flight training after graduating. About three-quarters of all cadets undertake graduate study within 10 years of graduation. Every year, many graduates of the academy are given graduate fellowships and scholarships; including the Guggenheim, Marshall, National Collegiate Athletic Association, National Science Foundation, and Rhodes awards.

LOCATION AND ENVIRONMENT

Located in the foothills of the Rocky Mountains' Rampart Range, the Academy is truly surrounded by natural beauty. The campus sits upon a 7,000-foot mesa; the campus and its immediate area are among the state's most popular tourist attractions. Contemporary architecture is featured on campus; the space age Cadet Chapel, with its seventeen 150-foot aluminum spires, set the tone for the entire cadet area. This modern setting aptly reflects the campus' mission: to train tomorrow's Air Force leaders and officers. The campus is located just north of Colorado Springs, a city of nearly 360,000; which sits at the foot of Pikes Peak (14,100 feet). The state capital, Denver, is just 55 miles to the north; this metropolis of over 2.5 million offers a plethora of cultural, educational, and recreational opportunities. Cadets also enjoy horseback riding, hunting, skiing, whitewater rafting, and many other outdoor activities in the nearby mountains and its resorts.

OFF-CAMPUS OPPORTUNITIES

Cadets chosen to participate in exchange programs may visit the Military Academy, Naval Academy, Coast Guard Academy, or any of 15 foreign air force academies around the world. International programs are usually one to two weeks in duration; exchange programs with other U.S. service academies generally run for a single semester, as do exchange programs with air force academies in Germany and France.

MAJORS AND DEGREES OFFERED

Graduates receive a Bachelor of Science degree and a commission as second lieutenants in the Air Force. Students may pursue a BS in any of 32 majors: aeronautical engineering; astronautical engineering; basic sciences; behavioral sciences; biology; chemistry; civil engineering; computer engineering; computer science; economics; electrical engineering; engineering mechanics; English; environmental engineering; foreign area studies; general engineering; geospatial science; history; humanities; legal studies; management; mathematical sciences; mechanical engineering; meteorology; military strategic studies; operations research; physics; political science; social sciences; space operations; system engineering; and system engineering management. Cadets may minor in foreign languages and philosophy.

ACADEMIC PROGRAMS

The school year for entering students begins in late June or early July; incoming cadets commence their tenure at the academy with a rigorous 38-day summer training program designed to test their physical and mental abilities. This training is conducted by upper-class cadets; commissioned officers serve as advisers. Cadets who successfully complete this program are admitted as fourth-class cadets in the Cadet Wing. Academic courses begin in early August and run through May. Cadets in their first two years focus on core curriculum courses in engineering, humanities, science, and the social sciences. Cadets pursue a specialized academic major during their final two years.

Core courses are designed to prepare cadets for a wide range of duties as Air Force officers. They include courses in academic subjects; military training and leadership; and athletics and physical education. All cadets must also complete the requirements of an academic major. Other graduation requirements include: demonstration of ability to serve and to lead; demonstration of character befitting a member of a professional military; along with maintenance of a minimum Military Performance Average (MPA) and Grade Point Average (GPA) of 2.0. Cadets have numerous options in selecting elective courses.

All cadets must enter as freshmen. Cadets who have previously completed comparable core course work at other institutions may earn transfer or validation credit for their work. Those who receive transfer credit may take other courses at the academy in place of their core courses. Advanced study classes are open to cadets who meet academic prerequisites, including a minimum grade point average. Cadets learn all operational procedures of the Air Force through the academy's aviation program. Optional courses are available in basic flying, navigation, parachuting, and soaring. Students who complete these courses may earn pilot or glider certificates issued by the Federal Aviation Administration. Once they have graduated from the academy, select cadets may enter Air Education and Training Command flight programs to train as pilots or navigators. Cadets may pursue summer studies in aviation and military training; these programs prepare them for the responsibilities of an Air Force officer. A number of optional assignments are available, both at the Air Force Academy and at other military installations.

CAMPUS FACILITIES AND EQUIPMENT

The Air Force Academy has excellent facilities to sustain the academic, athletic, and military goals of its programs. Classrooms are designed to accommodate small sessions of 12 to 20 students. A few larger classes meet in lecture halls, as do assemblies. The academy provides its science students with fully equipped laboratories, as well as an Aeronautics Laboratory that houses rocket engines, shock tubes, and wind tunnels. A LAN links every classroom, dorm room, laboratory, and faculty and staff office on campus; all entering cadets are required to purchase microcomputers, which they may use for both academic and personal purposes. The library houses over 1.5 million volumes; its collection includes many historical materials pertaining to aeronautics.

TUITION, ROOM, BOARD AND FEES

The government of the United States bears the entire cost of an Air Force Academy education. There are no charges for tuition, room, board, medical, or dental care. Academy cadets earn a monthly salary, with which they are expected to purchase clothing, supplies, and personal items. Cadets who manage their money carefully will meet all obligations and have a small sum left over for personal expenses.

FINANCIAL AID

All cadets attend the Air Force Academy on full scholarship, as described above.

STUDENT ORGANIZATIONS AND ACTIVITIES

Cadets learn important leadership skills through their duties in the Cadet Wing, an organization though which upper-class cadets take responsibility for enforcing the honor system and honor education, leading under-class cadets in military drills, and enforcing the human relations, ethics, and character development programs of the academy. First-class cadets (fourth-year students) supervise the operations of the Cadet Wing; they hold the rank of cadet officer and command its groups, squadrons, flights, and elements.

ADMISSIONS PROCESS

Every year, young U.S. citizens both men and women receive appointment to the academy. They arrive from all of the nation's states and territories. A limited number of foreign nationals are also admitted. Applicants must be between the ages of 17 and 23 as of July 1 of their projected year of admission, must be unmarried and without dependents. They must be principled individuals; and must be physically fit. An official nomination is a required part of any application to the academy. Most nominations come from Members of Congress and are submitted for students living in their districts and states. Representatives and Senators nominate high school juniors who have demonstrated academic excellence, who possess leadership qualities (as demonstrated by academic and extracurricular records), who are physically fit, who have the respect of their peers and associates, and who desire a career in the military. It is not necessary for applicants to know their congressional representatives personally to receive their nomination. Other categories than congressional exist; interested applicants should consult their guidance counselor or local Air Force Admissions Liaison Officer to learn more about other available nomination categories. Students wishing to enter the academy upon completion of high school should submit applications as soon after January 31 of their junior year as possible. Applicants who receive a nomination must pass a physical fitness exam and a medical exam; they must also submit standardized test scores (SAT I or ACT). Applicants should carefully read the instructions that accompany the application package. These instructions clearly detail the proper procedure for submitting an application. The application package includes, among other materials, sample letters to members of Congress, senators, and the President requesting nomination to the academy. Applicants seeking help with application requirements should contact an Air Force Admissions Liaison Officer; there is at least one in every state.

Applications are available to high school juniors; to request an application, write to:

HQ USAFA/RRS

2304 Cadet Drive, Suite 2300

USAF Academy, CO 80840-5025

Telephone: 719-333-2520

Website: www.academyadmissions.com

UNITED STATES MILITARY ACADEMY

AT A GLANCE

As the nation's oldest service academy, the United States Military Academy at West Point, offers young men and women a first-rate and highly respected college education. Through progressive development in four complementary programs—academic, military, physical, and moral-ethical—everything cadets experience during their 47 months at West Point is focused on developing them as educated leaders of character who, upon graduation, will serve at least five years on active duty in a variety of exciting career opportunities while serving as commissioned officers in the U.S. Army.

LOCATION AND ENVIRONMENT

West Point is located approximately 50 miles north of New York City in the picturesque Hudson Valley region. Flanked by the Hudson River and the Storm King Mountain, the U.S. Military Academy maintains some of the finest educational and military-training facilities in the nation on its 16,000 acres.

MAJORS AND DEGREES OFFERED

Every West Point graduate earns a Bachelor of Science degree and a commission as a second lieutenant in the U.S. Army. The curriculum complements the core program by providing the opportunity for in-depth study through the elective program. There are more than 40 majors available. The majors cover virtually all the liberal arts, sciences and engineering disciplines one would expect to find in a high-quality, selective college or university of comparable size. At West Point, cadets may enter most majors without restriction. No special grade-point averages are established for entry, but there may be a limitation as to the number of cadets in a particular major. Cadets choose to major in specialized areas, including philosophy and literature, basic science, chemical engineering, chemistry, civil engineering, computer science, economics, electrical engineering, electronic and information technology systems, engineering management, engineering psychology, environmental engineering, environmental geography, environmental science, environmental studies, foreign area studies (Latin America, Europe, Middle East, Eurasia, East Asia), foreign languages (Arabic, Chinese, French, German, Portuguese, Russian, Spanish), geospatial information science, history, human geography, information systems engineering, law and legal studies, kinesiology, leadership, life science, management, mathematical sciences, mathematical studies, mechanical engineering, mechanical engineering studies, military art and science, nuclear engineering, nuclear engineering science, operations research, physics, political science, psychology, sociology, systems engineering, and systems management.

ACADEMIC PROGRAMS

In addition to offering a top-notch college education, the West Point curriculum develops character, competence, and intellectual abilities – the essential broad base of knowledge necessary for success as a commissioned officer in the U.S. Army. A broad background in the arts and sciences is the focal point of the academic program, which also prepares cadets for future graduate study. The core curriculum ranges in size from 26 to 30 courses depending on the major.

West Point classes are small, averaging 12 to 18 cadets. Consequently, cadets receive individual attention and may request tutorial sessions, if needed. Cadets with exceptional ability may take advanced and honors courses.

West Point's Centers of Excellence serve to enhance the quality of the academic program. They coordinate professional expertise and concentrate technical resources in order to enrich cadet education, enhance cadet academic performance, improve faculty teaching, promote faculty and cadet research, and provide outreach and support to the Army.

Cadets study military science and participate in class instruction on the principles of small-unit tactics and leadership during a two-week intercession period between the first and second semesters. Field training is concentrated on during the summer as each cadet gains opportunities to learn and practice the military skills and principles that are learned in the classroom.

CAMPUS FACILITIES AND EQUIPMENT

West Point has carefully crafted an electronic environment in which virtually every course offered has integrated computer use. Cadets and faculty at West Point enjoy the benefits of a first-class information technology environment. Every cadet has a notebook computer and a PDA, and everyone is connected to a large array of powerful academic computing services at West Point and has unlimited access to the internet.

Computer-aided math, design, and simulation, dynamic news sources, world-wide electronic mail, spreadsheets, statistical analysis, database access, library bibliographic research, and electronic bulletin boards, document preparation, and printing all contribute to an academic environment rich with information resources and electronic media tools. Cadets also register for classes, get grades and counseling reports, and receive and send homework assignments using the USMA network.

Graduates of the United States Military Academy are well versed in the use of information technology and services, and are ready for the challenges awaiting them in the high technology Army of the present and future.

TUITION, ROOM, BOARD AND FEES

The cost of a four-year education at West Point, including tuition, room, board, and medical and dental expenses, is paid by the U.S. government. As members of the Army, cadets also receive an annual salary of more than $10,000. This helps to pay for uniforms, books, a notebook computer, supplies, and incidental living expenses. An initial deposit of about $3,000 is required to cover uniform costs and initial expenses during the first year.

FINANCIAL AID

There are no Financial Aid programs at West Point because most expenses are paid by the U.S. Government. Scholarship awards may offset the cost of the required initial deposit.

STUDENT ORGANIZATIONS AND ACTIVITIES

Cadets, like college students everywhere, find time for social activities. Frequent dances bring students from neighboring campuses. Cadets hold social functions in the ski lodge, the golf club, a remodeled railroad depot, two lake cabins, and even on West Point's excursion boats.

Throughout the year special weekends are held for each class, which include a formal banquet and dance, and other activities. Events surrounding the traditional Army-Navy game culminate the first semester of activities. Movies, plays, concerts, other live entertainment, and dances are held in Eisenhower Hall, the cadet activities center, on many weekends.

There are more than 100 extracurricular clubs to enhance athletic, recreational, hobby, academic and religious interests of the individual cadet.

In addition to an intercollegiate athletic program that features 25 varsity teams, there are more than 25 competitive club sports teams and an extensive intramural program. There are sailing and crew teams, cycling, marathon and triathlon teams, sport parachuting, orienteering, mountaineering, and skeet and trap teams as well as a ski team.

There are flying, fishing and inline hockey clubs, as well as a ballroom dance club, a chess club, close-combat team, mountain bike club and whitewater canoe club. The Cadet Glee Club is one of the most well-known collegiate singing groups in the world. Their nationwide concert schedule often includes appearances throughout the United States and on national television. There are a radio station, pipes and drums, a hop band, and a Gospel choir. There are many academic clubs, a scoutmaster's council and numerous religious clubs.

ADMISSIONS PROCESS

Each year the United States Military Academy admits approximately 1,200 young men and woman. These new members of the cadet corps come from all corners of the United States and represent every race, religion, and culture in the country.

To become a cadet you must meet the requirements specified by public law, and you must be qualified academically, physically, and medically. Each candidate must also obtain a nomination from a member of Congress (Each candidate can apply to two United States Senators, local representative in Congress, and the vice president of the United States.) or from the Department of the Army in one of the service-connected categories.

Candidates are evaluated for admission on the basis of academic performance (high school academic record and SAT and/or ACT scores), demonstrated leadership potential, fitness assessment, and medical qualification.

A candidate must be at least 17 but not older than 23 on July 1st of the year of admission; be a U.S. citizen at the time of enrollment; be unmarried; not be pregnant or have a legal obligation to support a child or children. A candidate must have an above-average high school or college academic record and turn in a strong performance on the timed ACT and/or the SAT tests.

West Point encourages a strong college-preparatory academic background as a prerequisite for admission. The Admissions Committee looks for four years of English with a strong emphasis on composition, grammar, literature, and speech; four years of math, including algebra, plane geometry, intermediate algebra and trigonometry; two years of a foreign language; two years of a laboratory science, such as chemistry and physics; and one year of U.S. history. Additional courses in geography, government, and economic are helpful. Courses in pre-calculus and calculus, and a basic computer course are extremely helpful.

Candidates for admission should begin the Admissions Process in the winter of their junior year of high school and should begin the nomination process at the same time.

THE UNIVERSITY OF ALABAMA AT BIRMINGHAM

AT A GLANCE

The University of Alabama at Birmingham (UAB) is a fully accredited research university and academic health center with an annual enrollment of more than 16,000 students. In a short time, UAB has established outstanding programs through six liberal arts and professional schools, six health professional schools, and graduate programs serving all major units. As the University has grown, so have its contributions to the state, the nation, and the world. UAB is committed to education, research, and service programs of excellent quality and far-reaching scope. In terms of federal research and development funding, UAB ranks twenty-sixth nationally and first in the state of Alabama, receiving more funding than all Alabama universities combined. In such an environment, undergraduate students can pursue a wide array of research opportunities and gain valuable experience that pays off later in graduate studies or career development.

LOCATION AND ENVIRONMENT

Birmingham earned the name "The Magic City" during its first boom days. The expression still rings true as the metropolitan area continues to mirror UAB's phenomenal growth and reflects the many cultural opportunities available within the city. Birmingham is easily reached from major national routes (Interstates 20, 59, and 65) and UAB is only minutes away from the Birmingham International Airport.

MAJORS AND DEGREES OFFERED

School of Arts and Humanities: African-American Studies, Art (concentrations in art education, art history, ceramic sculpture, drawing, graphic design, painting, photography, printmaking, sculpture), Communication Studies [concentrations in Communication Management, Mass Communications (journalism, broadcasting, public relations), English (concentration in creative writing, linguistics, professional writing and public discourse), Foreign Language (concentrations in French, Spanish), Music (concentrations in music education, music technology), Philosophy, Theatre (concentrations in design/technology, performance)

School of Business: Accounting (concentrations in forensic accounting and information technology/auditing), Economics (concentrations in economic analysis and policy, philosophy and political economy, quantitative methods), Finance (concentrations in investments and institutions, financial management), Industrial Distribution (concentrations in medical equipment and supplies marketing, industrial products), Information Systems, Management, Marketing

School of Education: Early Childhood Education, Elementary Education, Health Education, High School Education, Physical Education, Special Education

School of Engineering: Biomedical Engineering, Civil Engineering, Electrical Engineering, Materials Engineering, Mechanical Engineering

School of Health Professions: Cytotechnology, Health Information Management, Health Sciences, Medical Technology, Nuclear Medicine Technology, Radiologic Sciences (concentrations in advanced imaging, radiation therapy), Respiratory Therapy

School of Natural Sciences and Mathematics: Biology (concentrations in marine science, molecular biology), Chemistry (concentrations in biochemistry, forensic chemistry, polymer/materials science, chemistry education), Computer and Information Sciences (concentration in computer networking), Mathematics (concentrations in applied math, scientific computation), Natural Science, Physics (concentrations in biophysics, physics education)

School of Nursing: Nursing

School of Social and Behavioral Sciences: Anthropology, Criminal Justice, Economics, History, International Studies, Political Science, Psychology, Social Work, Sociology (concentration in social psychology).

General Studies: Undeclared Majors

Pre-Professional Programs: pre-dentistry, pre-medicine, pre-optometry, pre-nurse anesthesia, pre-law, pre-occupational therapy, pre-physical therapy, pre-surgical physician assistant.

ACADEMIC PROGRAMS

The UAB Honors Academy offers several special programs that present rare and valuable opportunities to explore knowledge from new angles, enriching the overall educational experience for future success. Students can take advantage of smaller class sizes, individual attention from faculty, and a community of like-minded, motivated students.

The University Honors Program concentrates the vast resources of a major research university in a small, liberal arts setting. Students participate in challenging interdisciplinary courses, honors seminars, independent research projects, extracurricular activities and community service.

The Science and Technology Honors Program offers students interested in a science or technology career the opportunity to work closely with world-renowned researchers. Students combine research experience with specialized courses in a scientifically focused learning community and can earn up to 12 hours of graduate credit toward a doctorate as an undergraduate.

The Global and Community Leadership Honors Program is designed to provide unique learning opportunities for students throughout their academic experience. Students will be able to participate in special honors courses relating to global and community issues, and in international and community learning experiences, with the objective of becoming prepared for leadership roles on a global, national, or local level.

Qualified students interested in a career in medicine, optometry, or dentistry may be accepted to professional school at UAB before they even begin college through the Early Admission to Medical Professional Schools Program. Students enjoy specialty seminars, classes, and research opportunities.

CAMPUS FACILITIES AND EQUIPMENT

The UAB campus occupies more than 100 major buildings, more than 11 million gross square feet, and almost 90 square blocks near downtown Birmingham. The undergraduate area of campus is concentrated within an eight-square-block area, however, giving students the convenience and togetherness that is so important to the college experience.

The new "Campus Green" includes a state-of-the-art Campus Recreation Center offering free weights, court sports, swimming pools/lazy river, fitness classes, nutrition education, fitness areas, a climbing wall, a juice bar and much more. A brand new freshman residence hall as well as a new dining facility, "Commons on the Green", which also includes a diner and "C-Store", opened Fall 2006. The new 95,000-square-foot Heritage Hall is one of the anchor buildings for the Campus Green and houses the School of Social & Behavioral Sciences programs, labs for mathematics, and communication studies.

The Mervyn H. Sterne Library houses a collection of more than 1.5 million items selected to support teaching and research at UAB. In addition to books and subscriptions to more than 1,600 periodicals, the collection consists of microforms and other print and nonprint materials. In addition to Sterne Library, the Lister Hill Library of the Health Sciences provides a comprehensive collection of materials for medical study and research.

UAB is home to the Alys Robinson Stephens Performing Arts Center, with state-of-the-art concert halls and practice facilities. This beautiful facility draws national and international performers, enhancing the strong cultural opportunities in Birmingham.

TUITION, ROOM, BOARD AND FEES

Enjoy the benefits of a world-class university at a fraction of the cost.

Tuition and fees shown are based on fall 2007 rates and a course load of 12 credit hours each semester (fall and spring). Because tuition and fees are billed per semester hour, the actual costs may vary.

Fall 2008 First-Year Freshman (estimated)

First-Year Freshman	In-State	Out-of-State
Tuition and Fees	$4,208	$9,296
Books and Supplies	$900	$900
Meal Plan	$3,380–$3,650	$3,380–$3,650
Residence Hall	$4,100	$4,100
Grand Total	$12,588–$12,858	$17,676–$17,946

FINANCIAL AID

UAB's Financial Aid package consists of loans, employment, and grants and scholarships, enabling students from all economic backgrounds to attend UAB. UAB offers a growing number of scholarships to provide support for eligible students who attend UAB. Newly admitted students are considered for all academic scholarships for which they are qualified. Awards are distributed on a first-come, first-served basis; students are encouraged to apply as early as possible. Financial Aid applications are available in early January for the following academic year, with a priority packaging deadline of April 1.

STUDENT ORGANIZATIONS AND ACTIVITIES

Part of the UAB experience is student life, consisting of a rich mix of academic organizations, honor clubs, social fraternities and sororities, volunteer groups, and activities ranging from intramural sports and SGA to supporting Blazer sports as a member of the "Gang Green" spirit group. With more than 150 campus organizations to keep students involved, UAB offers the chance to make lifelong friendships while assisting in the development of skills essential to leadership and teamwork.

The South is the place for sports year-round, and UAB is no exception. The athletic program is a Division I member of the NCAA and a founding member of Conference USA. UAB athletes participate in seventeen intercollegiate teams including men's and women's basketball, golf, rifle, soccer, and tennis; men's baseball and football; and women's cross-country, track, softball, synchronized swimming, and volleyball.

A new Campus Recreation Center offers free weights, court sports, swimming pools/lazy river, fitness classes, nutrition education, fitness areas, a climbing wall, a juice bar and much more. A brand new freshman residence hall as well as a new state-of-the-art dining facility, "Commons on the Green", which also includes a diner and "C-Store", opened Fall 2006.

ADMISSIONS PROCESS

UAB is an equal educational opportunity institution. The requirements for regular admission for entering freshmen include minimum high school GPA of 2.25 on a 4.0 scale in core subjects; a minimum ACT score of 20 or SAT I score of 950; and completion of no fewer than 17 core courses including four years of English, three years of social studies, three years of math (including algebra 1 and 2, geometry, and either algebra 3, pre-cal, trigonometry, AP calculus, or other senior college-preparatory math), three years of science (including two with lab components),one year of foreign language and three additional courses of the student's choice.

For tentative action, a transcript may be sent during the student's senior year in high school. A final transcript must be sent upon graduation.

An application may be submitted as early as one year prior to admission. A completed application, a nonrefundable $35 application fee ($30 for online U.S. applications), and all supporting documentation must be received by the Office of Undergraduate Admission by the priority deadline for the term for which admission is requested. The application priority deadline for fall term is March 1. For an application and further information, students should contact:

UAB Undergraduate Admission

Hill University Center, Room 260

1530 3rd Avenue, South

Birmingham, Alabama 35294-1150

United States

Phone: 205-934-8221

800-421-8473 (toll-free)

E-mail: undergradadmit@uab.edu

Web site: www.uab.edu

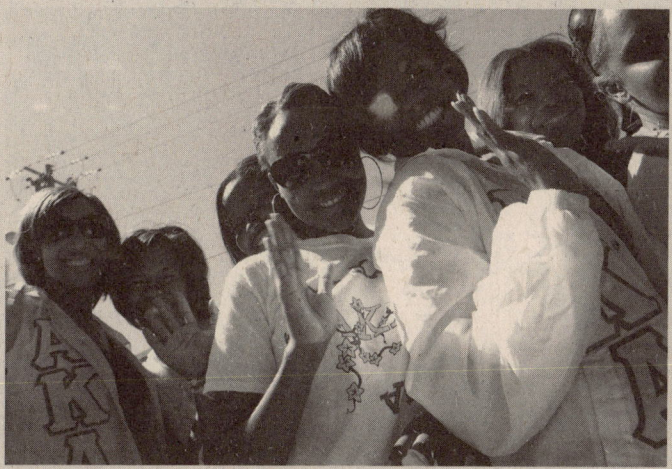

UNIVERSITY OF ARKANSAS—FAYETTEVILLE

AT A GLANCE

Located in Fayetteville, the University of Arkansas, founded in 1871, is both the major land-grant university for Arkansas and the state's flagship university. It has a proud legacy of internationally significant scientific and intellectual achievements in many academic fields. It also enjoys a reputation of being a great educational institution, producing over its 137-year history more than 125,000 graduates who have provided leadership in all walks of life. On July 1, 2005, the University of Arkansas completed the Campaign for the Twenty-First Century, raising more than a billion dollars. The success of this campaign places the University among only 13 public institutions in America to reach the billion dollar mark during similar campaigns and significantly augments the institution's endowment funds and ability to serve students. The university offers more than 200 areas of study in a comprehensive range of fields and is moderate in size among major research institutions with more than 18,600 students, of which over 14,000 are undergraduates. Its diverse student population includes almost 900 international students from 100 countries.

ACADEMIC PROGRAMS

The school operates on a traditional two-semester academic year schedule, with two regular summer sessions and some special concurrent summer sessions. The majority of undergraduate degree offerings follow a four-year plan requiring from 124 to 136 course hours for graduation; however, there are some exceptions to this requirement, such as the five-year, design-oriented architecture program, which requires 163 hours. A course in English as a second language is offered in five 9-week sessions throughout the year. Classes focus on all language skills grammar, reading, writing, and conversational skills. The endowed Honors College enables students to pursue honors programs in any college or department and provides undergraduate research and study abroad opportunities. Requirements vary among programs and schools. More information is available by visiting http://honorscollege.uark.edu.

CAMPUS FACILITIES AND EQUIPMENT

The University of Arkansas Libraries consist of the David W. Mullins Library (the main facility), the Fine Arts Library, Chemistry Library, Physics Library, and the Robert A. and Vivian Young Law Library. These libraries contain more than 1.7 million volumes, 4.5 million microforms, 25,300 audio-visual items, and 22,400 periodical subscriptions. The University Libraries also offer electronic access to more than 16,700 online journals in a wide variety of subject areas. The University is a member of Internet2, providing a high speed connection to other national and international research networks. In addition, a wide variety of computing resources are available including e-mail, free internet connections, and Web page development to all students, faculty, and staff.

ADMISSIONS PROCESS

Students interested in applying to the University of Arkansas for the fall semester are urged to apply through the early Admission Process. By applying prior to November 15th, students take advantage of scholarship, housing, and orientation privileges; however, regular fall applications will be accepted until August 15. Entering freshmen are advised to prepare for admission in high school by taking 4 units of English, 4 units of math, 3 units of social studies, and 3 units of natural sciences, as well as 2 units of academic electives. A minimum of a 3.0 high school GPA and an ACT superscore of 20 (930 SAT, combined critical reading/verbal and math scores) are required for general admission, but other students may be admitted after an individual review. The ACT code is 0144, and the SAT code is 6866. Transfer students need a cumulative GPA of at least 2.0 on all college courses taken and must be in good academic standing when applying for admission. Students completing fewer than 24 transferable hours will need to meet all requirements for freshman admission in addition to those for transfer students. International students must have above-average secondary school records, and those who are not native speakers of English must submit a minimum TOEFL score of 550 (paper) or 213 (computer) or 80 (internet) or an IELTS score of 6.5. The university offers qualified applicants conditional admission to the Spring International Language Center, with academic admission granted upon reaching a satisfactory English language level. To apply, submit a completed Application for Undergraduate Admission and an application fee of $40. An admission form can be found online at http://apply.uark.edu. The application deadline for the fall semester is August 15; the spring deadline is January 1. The student must also request that official transcripts be mailed to the Office of Admissions. A preliminary admission is provided for those high school seniors who have a transcript of six or seven semesters, but a final transcript is needed to certify high school graduation. Official ACT or SAT scores no more than 5 years old must be submitted by all entering freshmen and transfer students with fewer than 24 transferable hours. Students wishing to apply for scholarships must complete and return a separate scholarship application to the Office of Academic Scholarships with all appropriate materials no later than February 1. All students are encouraged to apply by the November 15 priority date for maximum scholarship consideration. Scholarship applications can be downloaded via the Internet (http://honorscollege.uark.edu). International students must submit an application for admission with a $50 application fee. A financial statement, a TOEFL score, and official secondary and postsecondary academic record are also required. The application deadline for fall is April 1 for a graduate student and May 31 for an undergraduate student. The deadline for the summer term is March 1, and the deadline for the spring term is October 1. International students should visit the international programs web site at http://international.uark.edu.

For further information, students should contact the following:

Office of Admissions

232 Silas H. Hunt Hall

1 University of Arkansas

Fayetteville, AR 72701

Telephone: 1-800-377-UOFA (toll free) or (+1) 479-575-6246 (international)

Fax: 479-575-7515

Email: uofa@uark.edu or iao@uark.edu (international)

Website: www.uark.edu

UNIVERSITY OF BALTIMORE

AT A GLANCE

The University of Baltimore welcomes undergraduate, graduate and professional students, associate degree recipients and transfer and re-entering students to an urban learning environment where they can benefit from small-college contact with professors and advisers. Our pre-professional and undergraduate programs in business and applied liberal arts focus on Knowledge That Works, offering you practical, hands-on experience that will prepare you to enter or move up in the career to which you aspire.

As UB is a member of the University System of Maryland, you can take advantage of varied, system-wide resources and programs while studying in a city full of inspiration and excitement. Flexible day, evening and weekend scheduling, built around the needs of both full-time students and working adults, provides career-focused education options for those juggling busy professional and personal lives.

Fully accredited, exclusively online programs in both business and liberal arts also contribute to Knowledge That Works. You can participate in programs offering the same rigorous educational quality as do our onsite courses, but with the convenience of being able to access classes from home, work or anywhere with an Internet connection.

Visit UB online at www.ubalt.edu.

Contact the Office of Undergraduate Admissions at admissions@ubalt.edu or 410.837.4777 or 1.877.ApplyUB for an undergraduate viewbook, admission application and financial aid/scholarship information.

Contact the Office of Graduate Admissions at gradadmissions@ubalt.edu, 410.837.6565 or 1.877.ApplyUB for a graduate viewbook and more information.

Call law admissions at 410.837.4459 to request the School of Law prospectus and application.

UNIVERSITY OF CALIFORNIA—LOS ANGELES

AT A GLANCE

As one of the world's premier research universities, UCLA offers unimagined diversity, unmatched depth of scholarship, and limitless possibility. At UCLA, everything is extra large: 3,800 faculty, 5,000 courses, 130 undergraduate majors, more than 880 student organizations, and the cultural and social opportunities equal to a large city.

LOCATION AND ENVIRONMENT

UCLA is located on 419 acres in the community of Westwood, a wooded suburban neighborhood of West Los Angeles that is bordered by Beverly Hills, Bel-Air, and Brentwood. The campus has an average year-round temperature of 73 degrees, low humidity, and 330 days of sunshine.

OFF-CAMPUS OPPORTUNITIES

The UCLA campus is 15 minutes from the beach, two hours to the mountains, and near to Santa Monica, Hollywood, the ocean, mountain and national park recreation areas, and the vibrant social, cultural, artistic, and sports scenes of greater Los Angeles.

UCLA itself is a major part of the Los Angeles cultural scene, offering more art, music, culture, and sports than most cities. On campus are seven major performance halls and theaters, special exhibitions, two world-class museums, and art galleries. UCLA hosts performances by world-renowned musicians and theater companies, first-run film sneak previews (often featuring stars and directors in attendance and in conversation), unique art and cultural events, and programs from the world's largest university-based film and television archive.

MAJORS AND DEGREES OFFERED

UCLA offers 190 fields of study, 180 majors, and some 3,000 undergraduate courses taught by 3,800 faculty. Bachelors, Masters, and Ph.D.s are offered in all of the liberal arts and science fields, as well as in 11 professional school programs. At UCLA, 31 Academic Programs are ranked among the top 20 in their fields, representing all the most popular undergraduate majors.

ACADEMIC PROGRAMS

At UCLA students have immediate, first-year access to a virtually limitless selection of studies that only a world-class university can offer.

Incoming freshmen can begin their UCLA experience with a *Freshman Cluster* (www.ugeducation.ucla.edu/clusters), an innovative program that involves stimulating, multidisciplinary exploration of challenging, timely topics. Clusters become year-long learning communities.

Or, students can choose among 200 small group seminars in the *Fiat Lux* program (www.ugeducation.ucla.edu/fiatlux). *Fiat Lux* offers more than 200 classes each year to bring the talents and expertise of a premier research university into a small classroom setting where students and faculty engage in critical thinking together.

Undergraduate students can perform important, publishable research in close collaboration with senior faculty—often as early as their freshman year (www.ugeducation.ucla.edu/ugresearch). Each year, thousands of UCLA students participate in seminars, research tutorials, and departmental honors programs. Two undergraduate research centers—Humanities and Social Sciences; Life Sciences and Physical Sciences—help undergraduates identify faculty mentors from every discipline.

The *Honors Program* (www.ugeducation.ucla.edu/ugresearch) provide an enriched educational experience through interdisciplinary seminars, engaging classroom presentations, individualized mentoring, and special honors courses designed to encourage and reward critical thinking. The *Honors Program* also offers the *Honors Collegium*, which is open to all UCLA students. The Collegium creates a community atmosphere in small, interdisciplinary courses with extensive interaction between students and faculty from throughout the campus, including the graduate professional schools. More than 75 Collegium courses are offered each year.

At UCLA, community service is a cornerstone of undergraduate education. The Center for Community Learning (www.ugeducation.ucla.edu/communitylearning) sends students into the diverse communities of Los Angeles in programs that merge a volunteer experience with academic coursework. Programs include tutoring, research and credit-earning internships, AmeriCorps service—even academic minors in Civic Engagement and Disability Studies.

Want to study abroad? UCLA's Education Abroad Program (www.international.ucla.edu/eap) offers opportunities in 33 countries taught at 140 universities. You can go abroad for a year, a summer, or an academic quarter, or work on international internships, independent research, and field studies.

CAMPUS FACILITIES AND EQUIPMENT

UCLA houses many of the most advanced educational facilities for undergraduate study and research, including the top-ranked UCLA library system that includes two major general collections—the Charles E. Young Research Library and the College Library for undergraduates—and special-subject libraries in the arts, medicine, languages, law, management, music, science, and engineering. Laboratories for undergraduate study are often closely linked with faculty research. The recent new additions to the campus residential community include advanced computing labs, academic counseling, classroom, a working TV station and a theater for stage productions—right where most students live.

UCLA is home to the nation's most successful collegiate athletic program, with teams winning 100 national championships. On campus is Pauley Pavilion, home to the legendary teams in basketball, volleyball, and women's gymnastics.

For recreation, campus facilities include the huge new workout facilities at the John Wooden Center, more than 45 intramural sports, and the UCLA Aquatic Center on Santa Monica Bay.

At UCLA, diversity is a core value, and the campus is one of the most ethnically and culturally diverse universities in the nation. UCLA is home to the Academic Advancement Program, the nation's largest and most successful university student diversity program.

TUITION, ROOM, BOARD AND FEES

To attend UCLA, California residents pay $7,038 for annual university fees, plus $13,935 for room, board, books, and supplies.

For non-California residents, annual fees are $8,265 and $13,935 for room, board, books, and supplies; plus $19,620 for non-resident tuition.

See (www.registrar.ucla.edu/fees) for updates.

FINANCIAL AID

UCLA's Financial Aid Office (www.fao.ucla.edu) evaluates eligibility for aid and ensures delivery of funds to undergraduate and graduate students. Need and non-need based aid is available. Assessment of financial need and eligibility for aid (university scholarships, grants, work-study and loans) is based on the evaluation of the Free Application for Federal Student Aid (FAFSA).

STUDENT ORGANIZATIONS AND ACTIVITIES

At UCLA, the opportunities for involvement are endless: some 880 student organizations—more than any other university—spanning social, political, personal, ethnic, and cultural interests, as well as a daily student newspaper, seven specialized student magazines, a campus radio station, a yearbook, three undergraduate research journals, and a literary magazine. Fraternities and sororities are both available, along with many local community service and religious organizations near campus.

ADMISSIONS PROCESS

UCLA selects students using the carefully designed Holistic Review Process, which takes into account an applicant's achievements, both academic and non-academic, in the context of the opportunities available to the student. Among other factors, the Holistic Review process specifically considers academic grade-point average; performance on standardized tests; the quality, quantity, and level of coursework taken; sustained participation in activities that develop academic and intellectual abilities; leadership and initiative; employment and personal responsibilities; and, overcoming life challenges relating to personal and family situations.

UNIVERSITY OF CENTRAL FLORIDA

AT A GLANCE

The University of Central Florida is a comprehensive research university with approximately 48,000 students. As one of the nation's fastest growing universities and the 6th largest in the nation, UCF enrolls a diverse student body representing 50 states and over 120 countries. The University offers educational and research programs that complement the economy, with strong components in aerospace engineering, business, education, film, health, nursing, social sciences, and hospitality management. UCF's programs in communication and the fine arts help to meet the cultural and recreational needs of a growing metropolitan area. The University also offers many graduate programs leading to masters and doctoral degrees.

UCF has established extensive partnerships with businesses and industry in the central Florida area that provide students with exceptional research and learning experiences. These partnerships bring practical learning environments to UCF students through co-op and internship programs. Joint curriculum development strategies include BE2020, which is a widely modeled business curriculum incorporating classes taught by local business and industry executives.

The on-campus and campus-affiliated housing facilities include traditional residence halls, apartment-style options, and Greek housing that accommodates approximately 10,000 students. Several thousand students live in apartments located within walking distance of the campus. Approximately 400 students live in on-campus Greek housing.

Students participate in more than 300 organizations, including special interest clubs, multicultural associations, fraternities and sororities, honor societies, and academic and preprofessional organizations. The Offices of Student Life and Student Activities schedule a wide array of extracurricular programs, including concerts, movies, and guest speakers.

LOCATION AND ENVIRONMENT

The University of Central Florida: Competitive Advantages

A Focus on Undergraduate Education: We're committed to teaching and providing advising and academic support services for all students. Our undergraduates have access to state-of-the-art wireless buildings, high-tech classrooms and research labs, Web-based classes and an undergraduate Research and Mentoring program.

A Talented Student Body: As one of the fastest growing universities in the southeast, total enrollment has reached 48,000; 38,000 are undergraduates. Our emphasis on excellence in undergraduate education has produced many rewarding results: a Goldwater Scholarship awardee, a Rhodes Scholarship finalist, a Clarion awardee in Radio/Television, a Zonta International Amelia Earhart fellowship awardee, and a nationally ranked Computer Science programming team.

Career Opportunities: Our Career Services professionals help students gain practical experiences at NASA, schools, hospitals, high-tech companies, local municipalities, and the entertainment industry. UCF faculty sit on boards and planning committees, and our graduates make their mark in engineering, business, computer science, education, health care, science, tourism, film and public service.

An International Presence: With an international focus to our curricula and research programs, we currently enroll international students from 122 nations. Our study abroad programs and other study and research opportunities include agreements with 98 institutions and 36 countries, including Australia, France, Germany, Holland, Italy, Russia, South Africa, Spain and Wales.

A Spacious, Modern Campus, plus Orlando: UCF's 1,415-acre campus provides a safe and serene setting for learning, with natural lakes and woodlands. The university provides housing for 10,000 students on campus and through affiliated housing. The bustle of Orlando lies a short distance away: the Orlando Magic, the Orlando Predators, the Kennedy Space Center, major film studios, Walt Disney World, Universal Orlando, Sea World, and sandy beaches are all nearby.

OFF-CAMPUS OPPORTUNITIES

Career Services and Experiential Learning offers programs in which student's alternate semesters of classroom study with equal periods of paid employment in government, industry, or business. The Department of Foreign Languages offers summer study programs in Canada, Eastern Europe, France, Germany, Italy, Japan, Poland, Spain, Sweden, and Russia. Courses are available in the subject areas of language (all levels), art, and civilization. UCF is also a participant in the National Student Exchange Consortium.

Students participate in more than 300 organizations, including special interest clubs, multicultural associations, fraternities and sororities, honor societies, and academic and preprofessional organizations. The Offices of Student Life and Student Activities schedule a wide array of extracurricular programs, including concerts, movies, and guest speakers.

MAJORS AND DEGREES OFFERED

The University offers the degrees of Bachelor of Arts, Bachelor of Engineering Technology, Bachelor of Fine Arts, Bachelor of Science, Bachelor of Science in Business Administration, Bachelor of Science in Education, Bachelor of Science in Engineering, Bachelor of Science in Nursing, and Bachelor of Science in Social Sciences.

These degrees are available in the colleges listed below, with majors or areas of specialization as indicated.

The College of Arts and Humanities offers degrees in art, cinema studies, digital media, English, film, modern language combination, French, history, humanities, music, music education, philosophy, Spanish and theater.

The College of Business Administration offers degrees in accounting, economics, finance, general business administration, management, management information systems, and marketing. The College also offers a minor in international business.

The College of Education offers degrees in art education, early childhood education, elementary education, English language arts education, exceptional education, foreign language education, mathematics education, science education, sports and fitness, social science education, and technical education and industry training.

The College of Engineering and Computer Science offers degrees in aerospace engineering, civil engineering, computer engineering, computer science, electrical engineering, environmental engineering, industrial engineering, and mechanical engineering. The Bachelor of Science in Engineering Technology (B.S.E.T.) is awarded in computer, design, electronics, information systems, operations engineering technology, and space science technology.

The College of Health and Public Affairs offers degrees in athletic training, cardiopulmonary sciences, communicative disorders, criminal justice, health information management, health services administration, health sciences, legal studies, medical laboratory sciences, physical therapy (master's program), public administration, radiological sciences, and social work.

The College of Nursing offers degrees in nursing.

The College of Sciences offers degrees in actuarial science, advertising/public relations, anthropology, biology, chemistry, forensic science, interpersonal and organizational communications, journalism, mathematics, physics, political science, psychology, radio/television, sociology, and statistics.

The Rosen College of Hospitality Management offers degrees in Hospitality Management and in restaurant and foodservice management.

The Burnett School of Biomedical Sciences and Biotechnology offers degrees in biomedical sciences and molecular biology and microbiology. Pre-professional programs are offered in chiropractic, medicine, optometry, osteopathy, pharmacy, physical therapy, physical assistant, podiatry, dentistry and veterinary medicine.

Degrees in liberal studies are available through the Office of Undergraduate Studies.

CAMPUS FACILITIES AND EQUIPMENT

In addition to the Academic Programs offered on the Orlando campus, students can work toward a degree at campuses located in Cocoa, Daytona Beach and South Lake. These regional campuses work cooperatively with local community colleges to provide all four years of course work in many academic areas. The library houses nearly 1.4 million volumes and subscribes to more than 10,000 periodicals and journals. In addition, students have access to an online computer catalog that provides information on the collections of the State University System libraries. An extensive online network of more than 500 computer terminals and a network of nearly 1,000 IBM PC's cover the campus. The Institute for Simulation and Training gives students the opportunity to pursue undergraduate research. The School of Optics allows faculty members and students to work directly with industrial personnel in conducting basic and applied research at the regional and national level. The Central Florida Research Park, located next to the UCF campus, houses more than ninety important high-technology firms and agencies. This proximity fosters relationships between industry and the University, which strengthens the Academic Programs at UCF.

TUITION, ROOM, BOARD AND FEES

Approximate Tuition, Health Fee, Room and Board Annual Rates 2007-2008

	Florida Resident	Non-Florida Resident
Tuition and Fees	$3,677	$17,878
Room	$4,900	$4,900
Board	$3,200	$3,200
Books (estimate)	$800	$800
Approximate Total	$12,600	$26,800

Based on 15 credit hours per semester, double room and meal plan.

FINANCIAL AID

Financial Aid is awarded according to each student's demonstrated need in relation to college costs and may include grants, loans, scholarships and part-time employment. Programs based on need include the Federal Perkins Loan, Federal Pell Grant, Florida Student Assistance Grant, Federal Work-Study, Florida College Career Work-Study Program, and Federal Stafford Student Loan. To qualify for these programs, students must complete the Free Application for Federal Student Aid. The priority application deadline is March 1. Approximately 70 percent of UCF students receive some form of Financial Aid.

STUDENT ORGANIZATIONS AND ACTIVITIES

Students participate in more than 300 organizations, including special interest clubs, multicultural associations, fraternities and sororities, honor societies, and academic and preprofessional organizations. The Offices of Student Life and Student Activities schedule a wide array of extracurricular programs, including concerts, movies, and guest speakers.

The University of Central Florida is a member of the NCAA and Conference USA. All teams compete on the NCAA Division 1 Level. UCF's men's teams compete in intercollegiate baseball, basketball, cross-country, football, golf, soccer, and tennis. Women's teams compete in basketball, cross-country, golf, rowing, soccer, softball, tennis, track, and volleyball. Intercollegiate coed club activities include championship cheerleading, crew, and waterskiing teams. The university intramural sports program offers disc golf, flag football, floor hockey, racquetball, soccer, softball, tennis, and volleyball.

ADMISSIONS PROCESS

A freshman applicant is a student with fewer than 12 hours of college coursework after high school graduation. The most important criteria in the admission decision for these applicants is the high school academic record, quality and level of difficulty of courses, grade point average, grade trends, and SAT I or ACT test scores. UCF operates on a rolling admission basis. Students are generally notified of their admission decision within two to three weeks after receipt of the application and all supporting documents. If the number of qualified applicants exceeds the number that the university is permitted to enroll, a waiting list will be established.

All applicants must have earned a minimum of 18 high school academic units (yearlong courses that are not remedial in nature). These include 4 units of English (3 must include substantial writing), 3 units of mathematics at or above algebra I, 3 units of natural science (2 must include a laboratory), 3 units of social science, 2 units of one foreign language, and 3 units of academic electives. Grades in honors courses, International Baccalaureate, Advanced Placement and dual enrollment courses are given additional weight in the GPA computation. Students must meet the Department of Education minimum eligibility to be considered for admission. Applicants should understand that the satisfaction of minimum requirements does not automatically guarantee admission to UCF.

Transfer applicants with fewer than 60 semester hours of college course work must submit official high school transcripts, SAT I or ACT test scores, and all official college transcripts. Transfer students with more than 60 semester hours or who have earned an Associate in Arts degree or a state-wide articulated Associate in Science degree from a Florida public community college need only to submit all official college transcripts. A transfer credit summary evaluation is provided to students once they are offered admission to UCF.

Students are encouraged to apply several months in advance and can apply online at www.admissions.ucf.edu. It is recommended that freshman students apply early during the fall semester of their senior year. Applications are accepted up to one year prior to the start of the term for which entry is desired. Priority application deadlines are May 1 for the fall term (July 1 for transfers), November 1 for the spring term, and March 1 for the summer term.

UNIVERSITY OF CHICAGO

AT A GLANCE

A private university chartered in 1890, the University of Chicago has a longstanding reputation for academic excellence, and for good reason. The birthplace of both sociology and political science, Chicago does not just teach scholarly disciplines, it creates them. Across the entire range of its strong liberal arts and sciences curriculum, the University's distinguished faculty reflects this commitment to fundamentals and to breaking new intellectual ground. Chicago's 4,500 undergraduates are deeply involved in those enterprises. Small classes and spirited give-and-take characterize the undergraduate experience at Chicago. Drawn to theoretical inquiry and open discussion, Chicago students thrive on a free exchange of ideas. With abundant opportunities for involvement in research, some undergraduates even coauthor journal articles before graduation. Many others undertake independent projects, guided and challenged by dedicated faculty and their own high standards. The University of Chicago encourages a close-knit learning environment on campus, and promotes this by guaranteeing each student on-campus housing for four years. Chicago's ten residence halls, including modern dorm complexes and neo-Gothic buildings, as well as converted former luxury hotels and apartment buildings, are distinct communities made up of undergraduate students as well as Resident Heads, who are advanced graduate students or faculty members. These communities are a focal point for campus life.

LOCATION AND ENVIRONMENT

The campus is 7 miles south of the main business district of Chicago, the Midwest's largest and the nation's third-largest city. The city's size and importance make it a valuable resource to students, an internationally acclaimed symphony, world-renowned museums, and numerous cultural opportunities are all accessible by public transportation. The University's neighborhood, Hyde Park, is a residential community of 41,000 situated on the shores of Lake Michigan. Home to more than 60 percent of the faculty, the neighborhood is often cited as a model of urbane and multi-ethnic city living. The University's 211-acre campus is distinguished by its English Gothic style architecture and its designation as a botanic garden. Campus buildings designed by Eero Saarinen, Ludwig Mies van der Rohe, Walter Netsch, and Frank Lloyd Wright, as well as newer buildings designed by Cesar Pelli and Ricardo Legorreta, contribute further eloquence to the learning environment.

ACADEMIC PROGRAMS

Bachelor of Arts or Bachelor of Science degrees are awarded in the following 53 major programs: Environmental Studies, African/Afro-American Studies, Latin American and Caribbean Studies, Russian Civilization, South Asian Studies, Gender Studies, Computer Science, Education, Linguistics, Comparative Literature, East Asian Languages and Civilizations, Slavic Languages and Literatures, Germanic Studies, South Asian Languages and Literatures, Romance Languages and Literatures, Early Christian Literature, Near Eastern Languages and Civilizations, Classical Languages and Literatures, Classical Studies, Ancient Studies, English Language and Literature, Fundamentals:Issues and Texts, Tutorial Studies, Interdisciplinary Studies in the Humanities, Religion and Humanities, Biological Sciences, Biological Chemistry, Mathematics, Statistics, Medieval Studies, Philosophy, Jewish Studies, Religious Studies, Chemistry, Biological Chemistry, Geophysical Sciences, Physics, Psychology, Human Development, Public Policy Studies, General Studies in the Social Sciences, Anthropology, Economics, Geographical Studies, International Studies, Political Science, Sociology, Law Letters and Society, Cinema and Media Studies, Art History, Music, Visual Arts, History, Hist. Phil. and Social Sci. of Med.

CAMPUS FACILITIES AND EQUIPMENT

Campus facilities offer a broad array of academic, cultural, and other resources, including the Oriental Institute Museum; the David and Alfred Smart Museum of Art; Court Theatre; the University of Chicago Hospitals; and the Department of Ecology and Evolution's rooftop greenhouse. The Biological Sciences Learning Center is the most up-to-date biology teaching and medical facility of its kind in the nation. Each student has a college advisor, and other support is offered by staff in the residence halls, counselors in the career and planning office, tutors, and the campus ministries. All dorm rooms are hard-wired for Ethernet connection use, allowing access to electronic mail, networked information and printers, and the Internet.

TUITION, ROOM, BOARD AND FEES

For freshmen living on campus, the cost of attending the University of Chicago for the 2007-2008 academic year is $50,800. Of that, tuition amounts to $35,169, room and board totals $11,139, fees come to $1,523, and average personal expenses and books are estimated at $2,969.

STUDENT ORGANIZATIONS AND ACTIVITIES

Chicago students are involved in more than 500 student organizations. Community service, academic interest, and cultural awareness groups provide a wide range of opportunities, perspectives, and support. In addition to three student newspapers, a campus radio station, and music, art, theater, and film organizations, the award-winning Model United Nations Team, Debate Society, and College Bowl Team offer forums for competition. An annual scavenger hunt and the winter festival Kuviasungnerk (from an Eskimo word roughly translated as "pursuit of happiness") are among the traditional and very "Chicago" events on campus. With one of the most extensive intramural and club sports programs in the country, Chicago students take athletics seriously, more than 70 percent participate in intramurals. Varsity athletics attract 14 percent of the undergraduate student population, where competition at the NCAA Division III level has resulted in numerous Academic All-American awards plus team league championships in women's cross-country, soccer, and softball, and men's basketball, wrestling, and cross country.

ADMISSIONS PROCESS

No formula exists for the successful Chicago applicant; all have displayed the capacity to inquire, to contribute to their schools and communities, and to succeed at the tasks before them. Among 1301 students in the Class of 2011(High School graduation year 2007), approximately 83 percent graduated in the top 10 percent of their high school classes. The middle 50 percent of admitted students had a combined score of between 1330 and 1530 on the SAT or between 28 and 33 on the ACT.

To apply for admission or to obtain more information about the University of Chicago, please write to the Office of College Admissions, The University of Chicago, 1101 East 58th Street, Suite 105, Chicago, Illinois 60637, or call 773-702-8650.

Information can also be obtained on the web from the University of Chicago College Admissions home page at collegeadmissions.uchicago.edu

UNIVERSITY OF DALLAS

AT A GLANCE

The University of Dallas, known as "the Catholic university for independent thinkers," is a private, Catholic,. co-educational liberal arts university dedicated to the pursuit of wisdom, of truth, and of virtue as the proper and primary goals of education. Founded in 19571956, the University of Dallas received its Phi Beta Kappa charter when the school was just 32 years, the youngest college or university in the 20th century to be so honored.

In 1996, UD was the first liberal arts college to be accredited by the American Academy of Liberal Education (AALE). It is also consistently recognized by the Templeton Foundation for scholarly excellence and character building, and is ranked as one of the top national liberal arts schools in the country by The National Review. Most recently, UD was selected for inclusion in the Intercollegiate Studies Institute guide, Choosing the Right College, described by Thomas Sowell as "the best college guide in America."

On our main campus in Irving, Texas (a suburb of Dallas), 1,200 bright, motivated students drawn from 4449 states and 1118 countries thrive on a rigorous academic program distinguished by our Core Curriculum and our Rome Program. UD is one of the few schools in the country that adhere to a classical Core Curriculum, encompassing the greatest thoughts, deeds, and creations of the Western theological intellectual tradition. Core studies are enhanced through our unique Rome Program. Approximately 80% of our students choose to spend a semester at Due Santi, our residential campus in Rome, Italy.

After completing the Core at the end of the sophomore year, UD's students are, in essence, better educated than most college graduates. They are well-prepared to excel in any of our 29 majors and nine pre-professional programs, and they do. Approximately 80% eventually enroll in graduate school. More impressive, over 8580% of pre-med and over 90% of pre-law graduates are accepted by their first-choice professional school.

LOCATION AND ENVIRONMENT

UD students derive special benefits from each of the University's two campuses.

UD Texas: Our 750-acre landscaped Texas campus is located in Irving, Texas, a city of 191,600 in the middle of the Dallas/Fort Worth Metroplex, with its population of nearly 3 million. It is just 10 miles from the Dallas-Fort Worth International Airport and 15 minutes from downtown Dallas.

The campus is a self-contained community, with academic facilities, a church, residence halls, a dining hall, performance spaces, and athletic facilities that support participation in our NCAA Division III intercollegiate teams, club sports, intramurals, and individual recreation. Stand-out facilities include the Braniff Memorial Tower, the beautiful 500-seat Church of the Incarnation which also includes the St. Thomas Aquinas Eucharistic Chapel, the five-building Haggerty Art Village complex, Haggerty Science Center, and the intimate Jonsson Theatre.

In nearby Dallas-Fort Worth, our students have access to over 7,000 restaurants, dozens of music clubs, seven major professional sports teams, and over 150 museums and galleries, as well as professional theatre, ballet, and opera companies and classical orchestras. Internship opportunities abound with the city's many financial, legal, and medical institutions, as well as with local businesses, non-profit agencies, and others.

UD Italy: Our 12-acre Due Santi campus 18 kilometers outside of Rome, Italy sits among the olive groves and vineyards at the foot of the hill crowned by the Papal summer residence of Castel Gandalfo. It features suite-style student housing, classrooms, a library, swimming pool, and tennis courts.

The city of Rome, with its ancient monuments and ruins, museums and art galleries, churches and castles, is an extended classroom for UD students. Vatican City is of special significance to our students, who visit it frequently both to worship and to enjoy its vast art collections. Students in Rome also spend 10 days in Greece and have ample opportunities to travel in Europe at large, expanding their international experience.

MAJORS AND DEGREES OFFERED

UD's undergraduate college offers 24 majors leading to a Bachelor of Arts or a Bachelor of Science degree. Majors include: art history, biochemistry, biology, business leadership, chemistry, classical philology (Greek and Latin), classics (Greek and Latin), comparative literary traditions, drama, economics, economics and finance, education, English, French, German, history, mathematics, philosophy, physics, politics, psychology, Spanish, studio art (ceramics, painting, printmaking, sculpture), and theology. Students also have the option of combining any two programs to create their own distinctive double major.

Undergraduate students may double major or create their own major subject to faculty approval.

UD Faculty

UD's full-time faculty numbers 121, 90% of whom hold a doctorate or equivalent highest academic degree in their discipline. Top scholars in their fields, they value the academic freedom UD offers them to freely explore intellectual inquiries, both within their disciplines and outside them. Teachers first and foremost, they, as much as our students, benefit from UD's 1213:1 student to faculty ratio and small classes in which they can give each student the individual attention he or she deserves.

Braniff Graduate School's Liberal Arts Division also offers a doctoral program in the Institute of Philosophic Studies, and a Master of Fine Arts, and Master of Art programs The College of Business's Graduate School of Management offers a Master of Business Administration and Master of Management.

ACADEMIC PROGRAMS

Our undergraduate academic program is based on the supposition that truth and virtue exist and are the proper objects of search in an education. To that end, we developed our Core Curriculum, a two-year course of study through which every UD student directly encounters Western civilization's greatest authors, leaders, and artists by reading the classic original works that comprise our Core reading list. Within this heritage, the Christian intellectual tradition is an essential element, and the American experience merits special consideration.

The Core Curriculum is comprehensive, encompassing English, philosophy, mathematics, fine arts, science, classics, modern language, American civilization, Western civilization, politics, economics, and theology. The Core foundation enables all UD students to embark on their major studies at an advanced level, well-prepared for the intellectual challenges they encounter.

The Rome Program. All UD's students are encouraged to spend one semester on UD's Rome campus and approximately 80% do so. The Rome curriculum is a coherent and integral part of UD's undergraduate education, regardless of major. The courses are selected from the Core Curriculum, which concern the development of Western civilization and are most appropriate to the Rome semester experience.

Majors. Any two of UD's 24 majors can be combined in double majors that exactly match student's interests and goals. The academic program can be customized even more by adding one or more of our 23 minors.

Pre-professional programs. UD is justly renowned for its pre-professional programs in pre-architecture, pre-dentistry, pre-engineering, pre-law, pre-medicine, pre-physical therapy, pre-ministry, teaching certification. Students who complete these programs consistently are accepted by some of the top national and international graduate programs.

The Princeton Review's Complete Book of Colleges

TUITION, ROOM, BOARD AND FEES

The 2007–2008 comprehensive fee for undergraduate students at the University of Dallas is $30,83732,655 (tuition: $21,81923,250; room and board: $7,6157,885; and fees: $1,4031,520).

FINANCIAL AID

The University of Dallas administers comprehensive programs of merit-based scholarships and need-based Financial Aid. Approximately 94% of our current students receive Financial Aid in the form of scholarships and/or need-based award packages.

Merit-based scholarships awarded on the basis of academic achievement as demonstrated by high school class rank and standardized test scores (SAT and/or ACT) range from $1,000 to full tuition per year. Scholarships awarded on the basis of co-curricular achievement range from $1,000 to $12,000 per year. Other scholarships based on leadership accomplishments or on special talents range from $1,000 to $3,000 per year. We also offer half-tuition scholarships to members of Phi Theta Kappa honor society. The UD Application for Admission serves also as the application for most merit-based scholarship programs.

We award need-based Financial Aid funded by federal and state government agencies in compliance with government regulations for determining eligibility. Applicants for need-based aid must complete the Free Application for Federal Student Aid (FAFSA) to be considered for any need-based awards. UD's FAFSA school code is 003651.

First-time freshmen applicants submit an application for admission on or before January 15 of senior year of high school receive priority scholarship consideration. Applicants that apply for admission between January 16 and March 1 receive regular scholarship consideration. Applicants that apply after March 1 receive admission evaluation based on available space and receive scholarship consideration based on available funding. Complete information about all aid programs, requirements, and deadlines is available from the Office of Admission and Financial Aid 972-721-5266 or 800-628-6999 or www.udallas.edu.

STUDENT ORGANIZATIONS AND ACTIVITIES

UD students grow spiritually, intellectually, socially, and creatively on our campus. We have over 40 student clubs and organizations, representing interests from chess to rugby and from the Jane Austen Society to Investment Club. There are also numerous opportunities to engage in meaningful service activities through groups such as Best Buddies and Hearts and Hammers. The yearly calendar is filled with theatrical performances, concerts, and displays of art that showcase student talents. Annually, we also bring many distinguished guests to campus; they have included recently Maya Lin, architect of the Vietnam Veterans Memorial in Washington, DC; Mikhail Gorbachev, last premier of the Soviet Union, and Francis Cardinal Arinze, Prefect of the Congregation for Divine

Worship. Favorite campus traditions include the annual Groundhog celebration, Mallapolooza, and regular "Thank God It's Thursday" (TGIT) evenings in the Rathskellar.

ADMISSIONS PROCESS

The University is open to applicants without regard to ethnic or national origin, creed, or sex. Applicants for admission must furnish evidence of good character and of sufficient academic preparation and ability to succeed academically within the University of Dallas curriculum.

Interested students must submit a completed application, required application essay, academic letter of recommendation completed by an instructor or counselor, and $40 application fee.

Freshman candidates (high school seniors and students with fewer than 24 transferable hours) also must submit an official high school transcript, high school class rank, and official results of SAT or ACT.

Transfer applicants also must submit official transcripts from all colleges attended, whether or not credit was earned, an official high school transcript showing final class rank, and SAT or ACT.

International candidates must also submit official transcript (with certified English translations) showing all secondary and post-secondary courses and grades, "O" and "A" levels (or other national examination results), if applicable, official results of the TOEFL, the University of Dallas Educational History Form, the Confirmation of Financial Resources, certified by a bank official, and a copy of your passport, if applicable.

Important Deadlines: November 1, Early Action I (non-binding); December 1, Early Action II (non-binding); January 15, Freshmen Priority Scholarship Deadline; February 15, Regular Admission Deadline for International Students; March 1, Regular Admission Deadline for domestic students; March 1- August 1, rolling admission; July 1, Transfer Student Deadline for Fall entry; December 1, Transfer Student Deadline for Spring entry.

The University of Dallas

OFFICE OF ADMISSION AND FINANCIAL AID

1845 East Northgate Drive

Irving, TX 75062

Phone: 972-721-5266 or toll-free 800-628-6999

www.udallas.edu

UNIVERSITY OF DELAWARE

AT A GLANCE

Founded in 1743, the University of Delaware is one of very few institutions who are both public and private (state-assisted with private charter). Students from every state and 100 foreign countries choose Delaware due to its medium size (15,000 undergraduate and 3,000 graduate students) and private offerings, including a $1 billion+ endowment, 125+ majors and 75 minors, smaller classes with 95% taught by full-time faculty, and a vibrant arts community. Located on a beautiful campus at the center of the East Coast, Delaware is home to a winning Division I athletic program (Go Blue Hens!), the first Study Abroad Program in the U.S. (now on all 7 continents), one of the country's oldest honors programs, and a nationally-recognized Undergraduate Research Program.

LOCATION AND ENVIRONMENT

One of the most beautiful campuses on the East Coast, the University of Delaware in Newark, Delaware, is located at the center of the "megacity" that stretches from New York City to Washington, D.C. The town of Newark is a charming place, with its very own Main Street full of shops, restaurants, and nightspots catering to the college community. Delaware's location, in a state known as the "Corporate Capital of America," benefits students through access to intellectual resources, professional relationships, and countless opportunities for internships, jobs, and entry into top graduate schools. Delaware's 1,000-acre campus is minutes from I-95 and is easily accessible by car, train, and air, with two airports less than an hour away (Philadelphia & BWI), and both New York City and Washington, D.C. accessible in about two hours by train or car.

Students at the University and visitors to UD believe that Delaware's central campus looks as a college campus should, with lush green lawns, winding brick paths, and grand Georgian architecture. A glimpse beyond the classical setting reveals miles of cables and wires running beneath the ground and into the walls of the library, residence halls, classrooms, labs, and every building on campus. Students are encouraged to bring laptops so that they can plug in for class, for research, and for staying in touch with friends, faculty, and the world.

OFF-CAMPUS OPPORTUNITIES

University of Delaware graduates are in demand due to the opportunities they take advantage of during their undergraduate years. About 20 percent of Delaware grads continue directly on to graduate school. The Univerity's Bank of America Career Services Center reports that over 90 percent of Delaware grads who don't go on to graduate schools find full-time jobs within six months of leaving the University. Fifteen major career fairs are hosted on campus each year with over 600 employers in attendance. In addition, more than 300 corporations and nonprofits participate in the Campus Interview Program and contribute to the 20,000 employment possibilities listed at the Career Services Center.

MAJORS AND DEGREES OFFERED

From Accounting to Wildlife, students at the University of Delaware can choose from over 125 majors and 75 minors. In fact, over one-third of Delaware students choose to do more, pursuing double majors and multiple minors. Academic Programs of study are found in our seven colleges: Arts & Sciences; Agriculture & Natural Resources; Lerner College of Business & Economics; Engineering; Health Sciences; Human Services, Education, & Public Policy (CHEP); and Marine & Earth Studies. Students can explore the many options with our major finder at http://admissions.udel.edu/udcms/

125+ Majors (and 75 Minors): Accounting; Agriculture & Natural Resources; Agricultural Education; Animal Science; Anthropology; Anthropology Education; Apparel Design; Applied Nutrition; Art Interests (includes Fine Arts, BFA or BA, and Visual Communications, BFA); Art Conservation; Art History; Athletic Training; Biochemistry; Biological Sciences; Business - Undeclared; Chemical Engineering; Chemistry (BA or BS); Chemistry Education; Civil Engineering; Communication; Comparative Literature; Computer Engineering; Computer Science (BA or BS); Computer Science - Information Systems; Continental European Studies; Criminal Justice (includes Law & Society); Dietetics; Early Childhood Education; Earth Science Education; East Asian Studies; Economics (BA or BS); Economics Education; Electrical Engineering; Elementary Teacher Education (with certification options in: Elementary Education, Middle School English, Middle School Mathematics & Middle School Science, Middle School Social Studies, and Special Education); English; English Education; Engineering - Undeclared; Engineering Technology; Entomology; Environmental Engineering; Environmental Science; Exercise Science; Fashion Merchandising; Finance; Food & Agribusiness Management; Food Science & Technology; Foreign Languages & Literatures; Geography; Geography Education; Geology (BA or BS); Health Behavior Science; History; History Education; History - Foreign Languages; International Business Studies; International Relations; Hotel, Restaurant & Institutional Management; Human Services; Landscape Horticulture; Latin American Studies; Leadership; Management; Management Information Systems; Marketing; Mathematical Sciences (BA or BS); Mathematics & Economics; Mathematics Education; Mechanical Engineering; Medical Technology; Music; Music, Applied - Instrumental; Music, Applied - Piano; Music, Applied - Voice; Music Education - General/Choral; Music Education - Instrumental; Music Theory/Composition; Natural Resource Management; Nursing; Nutritional Sciences; Operations Management; Philosophy; Physics (BA or BS); Physics Education; Plant Science; Political Science; Political Science Education; Psychology (BA or BS); Psychology Education; Resource Economics; Sociology; Sport Management; Statistics; Theatre Production; University Studies - Undeclared; Wildlife Conservation; Women's Studies

ACADEMIC PROGRAMS

Delaware students benefit from a series of signature Academic Programs, including the First Year Experience, University Honors Program, Service-Learning, Study Abroad, and Undergraduate Research.

First Year Experience

All freshmen at UD have a First Year Experience (FYE) that allows them to meet other students in their major, learn about resources at Delaware, and feel more at home on campus. FYE is designed to help students succeed in any major, including University Studies.

University Honors Program

At the intellectual heart of the University is the University Honors Program (UHP). Entrance into the Program is highly selective, with about 400 new freshmen enrolled each year. Advantages of the Honors Program include smaller classes, private music instruction, academic scholarships, superb teaching, special housing options, personal attention, interdisciplinary colloquia, "great books" tutorials, lectures, and student-run activities and field trips.

Service-Learning

Service-Learning at UD allows students to participate in an organized service experience that heightens their academic experience. As part of their course work, students will provide a service to a community—From Newark to Wilmington to Costa Rica to Vietnam—and then reflect on these real-world experiences in light of the academic theories and information being taught in the course.

Study Abroad

Over 40% of our student body choose to study abroad at least once with 12% (and rising each year) studying abroad more than once. The reasons are compelling: UD credits applicable toward any major; UD faculty; UD's reasonable tuition rate; special study abroad scholarships; & exotic destinations on any of the seven continents including—that's right—Antarctica.

Undergraduate Research

The University of Delaware is recognized as a national leader in fostering undergraduate research by offering research apprenticeships with faculty mentors in a variety of disciplines. About 700 undergraduates (including freshmen) take advantage of the opportunity each year.

CAMPUS FACILITIES AND EQUIPMENT

The University continues to enhance its appearance and accessibility to the UD community, with almost $400 million spent on campus improvements in the past 10 years. Since 1990, 22 new buildings were erected at the University, including MBNA America Hall, the $48 million Roselle Center for the Arts, the $17.5 million Gore Hall, the $3 million Rullo Field Hockey Stadium, Bayard Sharpe Hall, and – a technologically enhanced gothic cathedral, and a $23.5 million renovation of DuPont Hall is under way. A five-year program to refurbish all of the residence halls on the mall has been completed. According to President David P. Roselle, by the year 2004, "everything built before 1950 will have had a major overhaul."

Extensive facilities and resources exist to meet the needs of UD students. Over 7,000 students live on campus in one of 65 residence halls and dine in any of more than 18 eateries. Morris Library, a six-acre structure, houses millions of books, journals, and items on microtext, with additional access to over 75 networked databases. Students can plug in their own computers or log on at one of 28 microcomputing sites on campus. Socializing, performing, and engaging in a variety of entertainment options takes place at Perkins Student Center, Trabant University Center, Hartshorn Hall (home of the top-rated Graduate Professional Theatre Training Program), on the MallGreen, in the residence halls, or at one of the smaller theatres on campus. Athletic facilities abound at the University, including the 23,000-seat Delaware Stadium; 5,000-seat Bob Carpenter Sports/Convocation Center; Rust & Gold Ice Skating Arenas (home of the Ice Skating Development Center and training ground for 20 Olympic skaters, including Oksana Baiul); outdoor hockey rink; track, softball, and practice fields; indoor and outdoor swimming pools; Outdoor Recreation Resource Center; and indoor climbing wall, fitness centers, and weight rooms. The Student Services Center, a "one-stop shopping" model for colleges across the country, puts course registration, Financial Aid, housing, dining, student accounts, ID cards, telephone service, and parking all under one roof.

TUITION, ROOM, BOARD AND FEES

Delaware Residents

Tuition $6,9807,340

Room°° $4,336 4,748

Board°° $3,0303,200

Health Service Fee $410 440

Comprehensive Student Fee $144 156

Student Center Fee $206 214

TOTAL $15,10616,098

Cost Per Credit Hour $291 306

Non-Residents

Tuition $17,69018,590

Room°° $4,3364,748

Board°° $3,0303,200

Health Service Fee $410 440

Comprehensive Student Fee $144 156

Student Center Fee $206 214

TOTAL $25,81627,348

Cost Per Credit Hour $737 775

° Optional Winter and Summer Sessions are charged separately.

FINANCIAL AID

The University of Delaware awards more than $100 million annually in aid. Our commitment to making a University of Delaware education affordable is seen in our reasonable tuition for in-state and out-of-state students and in our variety of scholarships, Financial Aid programs, and financing plans. These include Merit Scholarships, Athletic Scholarships, Music Scholarships, Art Scholarships, Additional Scholarships, Need-based Aid, and Outside Resources.

Additional information can be found online at http://admissions.udel.edu/finance/tuitionfees.shtml

STUDENT ORGANIZATIONS AND ACTIVITIES

The Fightin' Blue Hens are a spirited community with the mix of academics, campus activities, and athletics that fit the profile of a national university. UD supports 23 varsity sports, 11 men's and 12 women's, all NCAA Division I members of the Colonial Athletic Association, except for the football team, which is a Division I-AA member of the Atlantic 10 Conference. More than half of the undergraduate body participates in intramurals, varsity, club, band, cheerleading, or other sports.

In addition to athletics, the University is home to more than 200 275 campus organizations covering a spectrum of interests and communities. Visit the Web at www.udel.edu/RSO/ for a complete list. The UD undergraduate experience begins with DelaWorld 101, the summer and fall orientation program for new students. Annual events on the green Greengrass of the Mall, at the Bob Carpenter Center, in theatres across campus, and in the Trabant University or Perkins Student Centers keep students entertained and active. Delaware students fill their free time with movie nights; Mallstock; and concerts and performances such as Chris Rock, Tori Amos, LIVE, the Goo Goo Dolls, the Harlem Globetrotters, and Alanis Morissette, Elton John, Jon Stewart, Kanye West, and Black Eyed Peas. In addition, there are 38 Greek letter organizations, including 17 NIC fraternities, 11 NPC sororities, and 5 National PanHellenic Council chapters (traditionally African-American membership).

ADMISSIONS PROCESS

The complete Admissions Process and requirements can be found on the UD website at www.udel.edu/apply.

THE UNIVERSITY OF FINDLAY

AT A GLANCE

Recognized as one of America's Best Private Colleges, The University of Findlay has much to offer! Affiliated with the Church of God since our beginnings, we are a comprehensive university founded in 1882 with a strong liberal arts tradition. UF offers more than 65 exciting majors, 23 varsity D-II NCAA sports, 75 clubs and organizations, theatre, art, music and so much more, there is something for every type of student! Our most popular majors include pre-veterinary medicine, business, health professions, equestrian studies and education.

Our Fall 2007 enrollment of more than 4,600 students includes full-time and part-time students pursuing associate's, bachelor's or master's degrees. The diverse student body encompasses 1,200 students living on campus. In addition, 465 international students from 41 countries attend Findlay.

Faculty and staff are focused on students, with personal attention, individual academic advising and a caring environment cited by students and alumni as hallmarks of their education at Findlay. Classes are taught by professors, not graduate assistants. Most faculty have worked in their chosen professions, bringing a wealth of experience to the classroom, where their true love is teaching.

The University of Findlay is situated in Findlay, Ohio, a small mid-western city that has been named one of "100 Best Community for Young People" and a "dream-town" by Demographics Daily. The city has many internship and job opportunities, as well as shopping and entertainment.

Discover who you will be at The University of Findlay!

LOCATION AND ENVIRONMENT

The University of Findlay is located in a small city that is pleasant and progressive. The city of Findlay has been designated as a "dreamtown" by Demographics Daily, an online newsletter that rated the quality of life in 632 small cities nationwide.

Findlay also has been named one of the top 100 small towns in the United States by Site Selection magazine, and one of the "100 Best Communities for Young People."

The campus has a great location and is within 45 minutes of Toledo, Ohio; 2 hours from Cleveland and Columbus, Ohio; and 5 hours from Chicago.

The region offers a wide range of internship and full-time job opportunities, and shopping and entertainment venues.

OFF-CAMPUS OPPORTUNITIES

The University of Findlay is known for providing career-based education for its students. The University offers career planning and placement services that assist students in determining career goals, developing job search skills, and finding paid employment in their field, and in selecting and applying to graduate programs.

The Professional Experience Program (PEP) and the Office of Career Services on campus assists students in finding internship, cooperative education, and degree-related work experience prior to graduation.

MAJORS AND DEGREES OFFERED

College of Business

The College of Business is home to some of the most popular majors at The University of Findlay. Building on a strong foundation that promotes problem solving, sound decision-making and the integration of the latest technological applications, UF's business programs allow you the opportunity to declare majors in one or two disciplines.

College of Education

UF's teacher education program is constantly evolving to meet the changing requirements of the state and national education systems. Accredited by the National Council for Accreditation of Teacher Education and the Higher Learning Commission, our program emphasizes practical experience, the integration of technology in classrooms and the benefits of service learning.

College of Liberal Arts

The College of Liberal Arts offers 28 successful programs that will equip you with the indispensable tools you will need for that first job and for a lifetime of achievements. Our programs range from social work and political science to English and history.

College of Science

From environmental management to Internet security, UF's College of Sciences can train you for many of the fastest-growing careers in today's marketplace.

At UF, you can observe an equine surgery, study gene replication, develop new computer software, analyze exposure risks to hazardous chemicals and more. Our rigorous Academic Programs, experience faculty and focus on hands-on training will prepare you for a successful career in the sciences.

TUITION, ROOM, BOARD AND FEES

Tuition: $22,906

Room & Board: $8,026

Student Fees: $984

FINANCIAL AID

For students new to the University, Financial Aid is awarded on the basis of merit and need. The award will use grade point average and standardized test scores (ACT or SAT) in determining the award amounts.

The Office of Financial Aid prepares aid awards on a rolling basis once the office has received the FAFSA and the student has been accepted for enrollment. Each year more than 90 percent of students attending The University of Findlay receive some form of financial assistance.

We participate in all federal loan programs including Perkins, Stafford, Parent Plus. Students received $21.1 million in institutional Financial Aid in 2004-2005, and 90 percent of UF students receive Financial Aid, either in scholarships, work study grants, or government loans.

Scholarships:

If eligible, scholarships range from $7,500 to $13,000 per year. These scholarships are deducted from your tuition each year subject to the student staying in good academic standing. UF also awards (if eligible) the following: Federal Pell Grant ($400-$4050), Ohio Institutional Grant ($444-$5466), Ohio Student Choice Grant (approx. $1000), Federal Supplemental Educational Opportunity Grant (SEOG), Pennsylvania Higher Education Grant, Professional Advancement for Teachers.

STUDENT ORGANIZATIONS AND ACTIVITIES

Extracurricular Activities

Students may participate in any of more than 75 organizations, including special interest clubs, student media, student government, music and theatre groups, service clubs, and academic honorary organizations.

The fine arts flourish on campus with a variety of theatre productions, art exhibits and vocal and instrumental music concerts that offer creative outlets and training for students and serve as a source of cultural enrichment for the community.

Some additional activities include:

Music & theater groups

Greek system

Student Government Association

WLFC-FM radio station

UF-TV student television station

Spiritual life groups

Academic honorary organizations

Student-run newspaper, The Pulse

As a Division II member of the National Collegiate Athletic Association (NCAA), Findlay participates in 23 intercollegiate sports. The University of Findlay is a member of the Great Lakes Intercollegiate Athletic Conference (GLIAC), Midwest Intercollegiate Volleyball Association (MIVA) and International Horse Show Association.

The NCAA Division II sports that The University of Findlay participates in are:

BASEBALL (M)

BASKETBALL (M)

BASKETBALL (W)

CROSS COUNTRY (M)

CROSS COUNTRY (W)

FOOTBALL

GOLF (M)

GOLF (W)

SOCCER (M)

SOCCER (W)

SOFTBALL (W)

SWIMMING (M)

SWIMMING (W)

INDOOR TRACK (M)

INDOOR TRACK (W)

OUTDOOR TRACK (M)

OUTDOOR TRACK (W)

TENNIS (M)

TENNIS (W)

VOLLEYBALL (W)

WRESTLING (M)

ENGLISH EQUESTRIAN

WESTERN EQUESTRIAN

ADMISSIONS PROCESS

Admission as a first-time, full-time undergraduate student to The University of Findlay requires an earned diploma from an accredited high school in a college preparatory course of study or a GED certificate. Candidates for admission should successfully complete the following requirements: 4 units of English, 2 units of social science, 3 units of mathematics, and 2 units of foreign language.

In addition all candidates must submit results from the ACT or SAT. A letter of recommendation from a guidance counselor or teacher is required. Other indicators of academic and personal success may also be considered. All applicants must submit the secondary school report and an essay in their application packet. In addition to the criteria listed above, Canadian residents must submit an Affidavit of Financial Support and obtain an I-20. Students for whom English is not the primary language spoken in the home may be required to submit results of the TOEFL. Home-schooled candidates should contact the Office of Admissions for specific criteria.

Admission decisions are made on a rolling basis. We encourage all candidates for admission to submit their application packet as soon as possible as the entering class fills quickly.

Students who intend to major in equestrian studies, equine business management or pre-veterinary medicine are encouraged to complete the application as early as possible, due to limited space available in these programs.

The profile for the Fall 2007 class was: SAT Average of 1561, ACT Average of 23, and a GPA average of 3.41.

Application Instructions

Students should complete the Application for Undergraduate Admission after they've finished their junior year course work. The University can provide students who apply early with information on scholarships, services, and special programs. Students can also apply online at www.findlay.edu. No application fee is required.

Applicants should send an official high school transcript that includes class rank, attendance information, a calculated GPA, and proficiency tests results. Post-secondary option participants should submit transcripts of all college-level work.

The results of the ACT or SAT should be submitted to the University. Applicants may send the results of these tests directly to Findlay by listing the following codes during test registration: ACT-3272, SAT-1223.

In order to enroll, all candidates must submit their final transcript after graduation.

UNIVERSITY OF HARTFORD

AT A GLANCE

The University of Hartford, a fully accredited, independent, nonsectarian institution, is composed of the College of Arts and Sciences; the College of Engineering, Technology and Architecture; the College of Education, Nursing, and Health Professions; Hillyer College; the Barney School of Business; the Hartford Art School; and The Hartt School.

Our students come from nearly all 50 states and 61 countries make up the full-time undergraduate enrollment of approximately 4,800 men and women. Students participate in about 100 organized student groups, including clubs devoted to special interests or political, professional, religious, or civic activities. Athletics include intercollegiate (NCAA Division I) and intramural sports. These activities, as well as the recreational and fitness needs of the university, are served by a modern 130,000-square-foot Sports Center. Students are also involved in school publications and AM and FM radio stations, and the Hartt School, the Hartford Art School, and the University Players present a variety of concerts, exhibitions, and theatrical productions each year.

The university's Career Development and Placement Center provides career counseling and information on occupations, employers, testing, and graduate schools; serves as a reference and credential source; and provides graduating students with an on-campus recruiting program. Courses, programs, and educational counseling are provided by the Office of Graduate and Adult Academic Services for part-time adult students.

LOCATION AND ENVIRONMENT

The university is located in the peaceful residential suburb of West Hartford. The West Hartford area offers hundreds of shops and restaurants along with many opportunities for students to discover new cultural and intellectual experiences. With museums, theaters, libraries, the XL Center, other colleges, a symphony orchestra, shopping, great restaurants, an international airport, and local and intercity transportation systems, the opportunities are only limited by the individual's imagination.

OFF-CAMPUS OPPORTUNITIES

Through the Hartford Consortium for Higher Education, Hartford students have the opportunity to register for select courses at the Connecticut School of Dance, Saint Joseph College, and Trinity College. Opportunities are available to teaching and human services majors in the College of Education, Nursing, and Health Professions for field and/or clinical experiences where applicable. The cooperative education office is available to custom-tailor work experiences within many of the University's programs.

MAJORS AND DEGREES OFFERED

The Bachelor of Arts is offered in art history, biology, chemistry, cinema, communication, computer science, criminal justice, drama, economics, English, foreign languages and literatures, history, multimedia and web design & development, international studies, Judaic studies, mathematics, music, philosophy, physics, political economy, politics and government, rhetoric and professional writing, psychology, and sociology.

The Bachelor of Science in secondary education is offered in the College of Education, Nursing, and Health Professions with a major in English and mathematics.

Students can earn the Bachelor of Fine Arts in ceramics, dance, drawing, illustration, music theater, painting, photography, printmaking, actor training, sculpture, video, and visual communication design.

The Bachelor of Music is offered at the Hartt School with majors in performance (guitar, orchestral instrument, organ, piano, and voice), composition, jazz studies, music education, music history, music management, music production and technology, opera, performing arts management, piano accompanying and ensemble, and theory.

The Bachelor of Science is awarded in biology, clinical lab science-lab tech, chemistry, chemistry-biology, computer science, early childhood education, elementary education, health sciences (upper division only), human services, mathematics, mathematics-management science, nursing (for registered nurses only), physics, radiological technology, respiratory therapy, and special education (offering dual certification and covering emotional disabilities, learning disabilities, and mental retardation).

The Bachelor of Science in Business Administration (BSBA) is offered in accounting, economics and finance, entrepreneurial studies, finance and insurance, management, and marketing.

Additional BS programs are offered in the College of Engineering, Technology and Architecture and include ABET-accredited BSEE, BSME, BSCE, BSCompE, and interdisciplinary BSE options. The most popular BSE options are acoustics/music, biomedical engineering, and environmental engineering

Bachelor of Science degrees are also offered in architectural engineering technology, computer engineering technology, electronic engineering technology, and mechanical engineering technology.

Additional special programs include the five-year music education program; five-year double-major programs; Bachelor of Music with an emphasis in management, offered by the Hartt School in conjunction with the Barney School of Business; and the Bachelor of Science in Engineering with a music-acoustics major, offered by the College of Engineering.

ACADEMIC PROGRAMS

The University of Hartford is known nationally for the breadth and depth of its program. Hartford's seven schools and colleges offer more than 80 undergraduate majors. The university encourages students to sample a variety of academic areas and enroll in courses in any of the colleges in campus. Students interested in interdisciplinary majors can combine courses from the different schools within the university. Students are assigned academic advisors who help guide them in curriculum choices, career exploration, and the transition to university life. The All-University curriculum was developed in order to help students learn more about how different academic disciplines approach related problems. Courses in different fields of expertise are team taught, and topics are examined from the perspective of several academic disciplines. Students who are undecided on their majors are assisted by a special program at the university. Individual students will also find help in the areas of writing proficiency, reading comprehension, and research and test-taking skills at the reading and writing center, which is available to the entire student body. The Math Tutoring Lab, which is staffed by full-time faculty members and math majors, offers further help for students in math. Selected students are encouraged to participate in the Honors Program. Honors students have the opportunity to graduate with an Honors degree.

CAMPUS FACILITIES AND EQUIPMENT

The West Hartford campus houses the buildings and facilities of our seven colleges and schools.

The newest additions to the campus are the Integrated Science, Engineering and Technology Complex with 37,000 square feet of new state-of-the-art classrooms and laboratories as well as a complete renovation of the existing science and engineering facilities. The Renee Samuels Center provides state-of-the art digital equipment and studios specifically designed for Media Arts and Photography.

The Harry Jack Gray Center is the home of the Mildred P. Allen Memorial Library; the William H. Mortensen Library; the Museum of American Political Life; the Harry J. Gray Conference Center; the Joseloff Gallery; the University Bookstore; the School of Communication; and studios for art, radio, and television. The library has approximately 572,000 items, including books, musical scores, recordings, periodicals, journals, and microfilm units. The Hartford Consortium for Higher Education, the Hartford Library, and the Interlibrary-Loan systems also offer extensive resources.

The University of Hartford has a Computer Center that houses the central computer systems and operates a high-performance campus wide network that connects student residential housing, all academic buildings on campus, and the university's remote locations. A high-speed T1 line connects the university's network to the Internet. Each student resident has his or her own Ethernet connection to the campus network. The library is connected to the campus network and provides network access in study carrels and study rooms. The library's online systems include the online catalog for book, audio, and video collection; CD-ROM databases; and Internet resources, including 1,000 electronic journals. Easy-to-use Web access for many of the library's online resources and electronic reserves are part of the ongoing improvements to the library's systems. Access is available to all of the university network resources—on campus at university facilities and off campus by using computers with modems. Computing labs, used by all students of the university, are provided at three locations around the campus. The labs are equipped with PCs and Macs, computer workstations, and are connected to the campus network and the Internet. Word processing, spreadsheet, database management, and graphics programs are some of the types of software made available to students. On-duty lab assistants are available to help students with any questions or problems. There are also specialized computer facilities for instruction and learning, including the Gilman Center for Communication Technology for English and journalism instruction; Information Technology Center for business students; the Computer Assisted Learning Center; the Center for Computer and Electronic Music; the Computer Aided Design/Computer Aided Manufacturing Laboratory; and the Dana Computer Lab with workstations for computer science. Additional facilities consist of the Hoffman Computer Lab for health professions, the Graphic Design Lab for art instruction, the Educational Computing Lab, and the GIS Computer Lab for engineering instruction.

Tuition, Room, Board, and Fees:

Costs for 2007-2008

Tuition $25,806

Double Room (Complexes) $6,424

Freshman Meal Plan $3,996

Fees $1,1900

Total $37,416

Over 90 percent of University of Hartford students receive a scholarship or grant from the university. For most students, the cost of a University of Hartford education is significantly reduced by financial assistance.

The average "out of pocket" expense for new students this year was $18,100.

FINANCIAL AID

The university's Financial Aid program, which administers over $90 million annually including student loans, consists of scholarships, grants, loans, and work-study opportunities provided through the federal government, private agencies, interested individuals, and the University. Factors contributing to disbursal of university funds are the college or school in which the student is enrolled, availability of funds, applicant pool, and competition for funds. About 92 percent of all full-time undergraduate students receive assistance; the average amount is $18,407 per year. Students who have demonstrated outstanding academic achievement are eligible for full and partial-tuition scholarships.

STUDENT ORGANIZATIONS AND ACTIVITIES

The Student Government Association (SGA) represents all full-time students at the University. Through SGA, students and faculty work together to develop and coordinate the co-curriculars of the university. In addition, students are represented on all major administrative committees, including the Board of Regents.

ADMISSIONS PROCESS

The admissions decision is based on a combination of the following: quality of the secondary school curriculum, course selection, academic performance in secondary school, recommendations of the secondary school principal or guidance counselor, ACT or SAT scores, evidence of a desire to succeed, and leadership qualities shown by academic and extracurricular activities. Music and art applicants are required to audition, show portfolios, and take other tests depending upon the program to which they are applying.

The University has a rolling admission policy.

For more information, students should contact:

Richard A. Zeiser

Dean of Admission

University of Hartford

West Hartford, CT 06117-0395

Phone: 860-768-4296

Toll free: 800-947-4303

Fax: 860-768-4961

E-mail: admission@hartford.edu

Website: http://admission.hartford.edu

UNIVERSITY OF HOUSTON—CLEAR LAKE

AT A GLANCE

University of Houston-Clear Lake specializes in upper-level undergraduate and graduate programs, and maintains partnerships with NASA's Johnson Space Center, Texas Medical Center, more than 20 independent school districts, and the petrochemical and high-technology industries. These community partners afford UH-Clear Lake students many opportunities for internships, research and employment.

UHCL enrolls approximately 7,500 students and employs 203 full-time and 407 adjunct faculty, creating an average student-to-instructor ratio of 16 to one.

Founded in 1974, UHCL consists of four schools: Business, Education, Human Sciences and Humanities, and Science and Computer Engineering. The university offers bachelor's degrees in more than 30 fields of study and master's degrees in over 40 fields of study as well as a doctoral degree in educational leadership.

UHCL continuously expands and enhances its Web-based and distance learning programs. These programs give UHCL students greater flexibility as they pursue their degrees, offering viable alternatives to working adults and professionals with busy schedules. The university also offers off-campus courses, degrees and certificate programs at locations throughout the Houston Metro area. Most recently, the Texas Higher Education Coordinating Board approved a UHCL branch campus to be built in Pearland, Texas.

UHCL is accredited by the Commission on Colleges of the Southern Association of Colleges and Schools. Additionally, each school is accredited by the appropriate professional agencies.

LOCATION AND ENVIRONMENT

University of Houston Clear Lake is located in the suburbs of Houston, adjacent to Clear Lake, Galveston Bay and the Gulf of Mexico. The UH Clear Lake campus borders NASA's Johnson Space Center and Armand Bayou Nature Center. Since the former opened more than 40 years ago, the aerospace industry has been the largest employer in the region, providing work for approximately 15,000 people. In addition, more than 9,000 people work for software development and computer services companies, and more than 8,000 for specialty chemical firms.

Ellington Field, located in the Clear Lake area, is home to the Wings Over Houston Airshow which features aerial performances of classic and contemporary aircraft. The Johnson Space Center hosts the RE/MAX Ballunar Liftoff Festival, the highlight of which is a multiple hot air balloon ascension. Clear Lake has seven marinas and offers opportunities for windsurfing, parasailing and jet skiing.

Five main buildings—Arbor, Bayou, Central Services, Delta, and Students Services and Classroom are situated on the university's 524-acre campus. The Alfred R. Neumann Library houses 416,000 print volumes, which includes more than 2,000 periodical subscriptions and 1.6 million microforms. The UH Clear Lake library catalog is electronically connected to the library catalogs of the University of Houston and University of Houston Downtown. UH Clear Lake's telecommunications system affords its students many opportunities to interact with peers in partner universities throughout Europe, Asia and Latin America.

MAJORS AND DEGREES OFFERED

School of Business: Accounting, Environmental Management, Finance, General Business, Healthcare Administration, Legal Studies (BS), Management (BBA), Management Information Systems Marketing (BBA), Political Science (BS), Professional Accounting

School of Education: Geography , Interdisciplinary Studies

School of Human Sciences and Humanities: Applied Design and Visual Arts, Behavioral Sciences, Behavioral Sciences, Anthropology, Psychology , Sociology, Communication (BA), Criminology (BS, MA), Cross-Cultural Studies, Fitness and Human Performance, History Humanities, Literature Social Work (BSW), Women's Studies (BA)

School of Science and Computer Engineering: Biological Sciences, Chemistry, Computer Science, Computer Information Systems, Computer Systems Engineering, Environmental Science, Mathematical Sciences, Physical Sciences, Campus Facilities and Equipment, Study Facilities

Areas where computers are available: library, computer labs, some classrooms, laptops to check-out

Total number of computers available to students: 702

Internet access provided to all students: yes

Email services/accounts provided to all students: yes

Library on Campus: yes

TUITION, ROOM, BOARD AND FEES

Expenses at a Glance (in $US)

°Annual tuition noted includes fees.

°°Residence prices do not include meals.

Annual Tuition

In-State: $4080°

Out-of-State: $12,840°

International: $12,840°

Other Expenses

Books and Materials: $1431

Miscellaneous Expenses: $2,968

Accommodation

Private: $4,714 (homestay)°°

Residence: $7,361°°

Required to live on Campus: no

FINANCIAL AID AND ASSISTANTSHIPS

Graduate students at UHCL are qualified to receive financial aid from a variety of sources. State grants, except TPEG, are usually unavailable to graduate students. Graduate and professional students may qualify for the Federal Perkins and Stafford Loans. Part-time employment is open to graduate students. International students may qualify for some state grants, university scholarships and private student loans.

STUDENT ORGANIZATIONS AND ACTIVITIES

Total enrollment: 7,522

Graduate Enrollment: 3,240

Male/Female ratio: 34%/66%

% Students from Out-of-State: 11%

Off campus employment opportunities for graduate students are: Careerlink, co-ops, job fairs, alumni career network, career library

Student Affairs

Numerous student services are available through the offices of the Student Services and the Dean of Students: Career and Counseling Services, Health and Disability Services, Intercultural and International Student Services, Student Assistance Center and Student Life. These services are designed to encourage students to participate in various cultural, recreational and social programs.

Social Activities: Accounting Association/Institute of Management Accountants Student Chapter; American College of Healthcare Executives; American Marketing Association; Financial Management Association; Healthcare Financial Management Association; Healthcare Student Association; The Management Association; Management Information Systems Organization; Medical Group Management Association; Society for Human Resource Management; Education; Association for Childhood Education International; Bilingual Education Student Organization; Student Council for Exceptional Children; Student Reading Council; Texas State Teachers Association Student Program; Honor Societies that are registered UHCL organizations; Alpha Chi; Alpha Phi Sigma; Beta Alpha Psi; Chi Sigma Iota; I/O Psi; Omicron Delta Kappa; Phi Alpha Delta; Phi Alpha Theta; Phi Kappa; Phi Theta Kappa Alumni Association; Pi Alpha Alpha; Psi Chi; Sigma Tau Delta; Upsilon Phi Delta

Human Science: Clinical Psychology Student Association; Family Therapy Student Association; The Bridge; Psychology Club; Social Work Student Association; Sociology Student Association; Student Futurists Association

Humanities: Art Association; Film and History Club; History Club; Literature Club; Women's Studies Student Association

International: Indian Students Association; Sri Lanka Student Pride; Taiwanese Student Organization; Vietnamese Students Association

Natural and Applied Science: Biology Club; Institute of Electrical and Electronics Engineers (IEEE) Student Branch; Society of Environmental Toxicology and Chemistry

Religious: Baptist Student Ministry; Campus Crusade for Christ; Jewish Students Association; Muslim Student Association; Women's Christian Fellowship

Special Interest: Asian/Pacific Islander Student Organization; Black Students Association; Child Care Advocates of UHCL; College Republicans; Gamers' Guild; Helping Other People thru Endeavors; Hispanic Leaders in Business; Hispanics Advancing Culture and Education; Rugby Club; Student Alumni Association; Student Government Association; Studies of the World Student Association; Unity Club

ADMISSIONS PROCESS

Graduate students must have a bachelor's degree from a regionally accredited institution and be eligible to return to the last institution attended. Applications are term specific, but may be updated by submitting an Application Update Request Form. Admission to the university is a separate process from admission to degree candidacy.

To be considered for graduate admission, applicants must submit: 1) an application for admissions, 2) $35 nonrefundable application fee for domestic applications, $75 for international applications or $95 for doctoral applications, 3) official transcripts and 4) standardized test score reports, such as the GMAT, GRE or MAT. The application form can be submitted in person, by mail or fax, or online. All supporting documentation should be submitted to the Office of Admissions by the deadline, where applicable.

Students are not obligated to submit graduate test score requirements if they have: 1) a doctorate from a U.S. institution, 2) M.D. degree and license to practice in the U.S., 3) J.D. degree from an accredited US law school, or 4) graduate degree from a business school accredited by the AACSB International The Association to Advance Collegiate Schools of Business (for applicants to the School of Business). Students applying to a doctoral program must submit a GRE score.

Applicants seeking admission to the School of Business should apply by August 1 for fall admission, December 1 for spring admission or May 1 for summer admission. Those seeking admission to the School of Human Sciences and Humanities' Professional Psychology Programs must apply between December 10 and January 25 for the next fall semester. Applicants seeking admission to the School of Education's Counseling Program should apply by June 1 for fall admission, October 1 for spring admission or February 1 for summer admission. Those seeking admission to the School of Education's Superintendent's Certificate Program should apply by July 15 for fall admission, November 15 for spring admission or April 15 for summer admission. Students applying to a doctoral program must apply by March 1 for the following fall term and August 1 for the following spring term.

Transfer Students Accepted: yes

International Students Accepted: yes

Deadlines (Early): March 1 (summer and fall), October 1 (spring)

Deadlines (Regular): August 18 (fall), January 12 (spring)

Deadlines (International): March 1 (summer and fall), October 1(spring)

Entrance Semester: Fall, Spring, Summer

Preferred Tests: GRE, GMAT, MAT, IELTS, TOEFL

Minimum Test Scores: TOEFL 79-80 (ibt), IELTS 6, others vary

Notification of Admission for Fall Term: varies

Acceptance of Admission: 1251

Acceptance Rate: 80%

School Says . . .

UNIVERSITY OF MAINE—FORT KENT

AT A GLANCE

The University of Maine at Fort Kent is a small liberal arts university, part of the seven-campus University of Maine system. We are located in northern Maine nestled in the heart of the St. John Valley in Aroostook County among gentle, rolling rivers; clear, fish-filled lakes; snow-draped mountains in the winter; and lush, green carpets of farmland and forest in the summer. Autumn welcomes in clean, crisp air on brisk fall nights, and days burst with a kaleidoscope of color from leaves preparing for the first flakes of winter.

We started out as the Madawaska Training School for teachers back in 1878. Today, we offer baccalaureate and associate degrees to just under a thousand students of diverse backgrounds.

LOCATION AND ENVIRONMENT

The St. John Valley offers some of the best canoeing, kayaking, fishing, ice fishing, hiking, and biking opportunities anywhere in the country. We have hundreds of miles of the highest rated snowmobile trails in New England. The Maine Winter Sports Center, located in our community, is a world-class training facility for biathlon athletes and cross-country skiers, some of them Olympians. In March, Fort Kent's population swells as the town hosts the Can-Am Crown Sled Dog Race, the largest race in the eastern U.S. that serves as a qualifier for the Ididarod. Summer enthusiasts can tee off on challenging golf courses or just enjoy the peacefulness of a walk along the water's edge surrounded by wildflowers and wildlife.

MAJORS AND DEGREES OFFERED

The University of Maine at Fort Kent's programs are accredited by The New England Association of Schools and Colleges, the National League of Nursing, the Society of American Foresters, and the Maine State Department of Education. We operate on a two-semester calendar and offer two six-week summer sessions plus courses of special interest.

Undergraduate bachelor programs include behavioral science; biology; business management; computer applications; electronic commerce; education (elementary and secondary); English; environmental studies with concentration in aquatic ecology, environmental assessment & measurement, field naturalist, forestry, game warden, geographic information systems, plant ecology, social policy & activism, and wildlife ecology; French; nursing; public safety administration; social science field; teacher certification (elementary and secondary); and university studies (self-designed).

Associate programs include bicultural studies, business, computer science, criminal justice, forest technology, general studies, and human services.

We also offer minors in art, behavioral science, biology, education, English, environmental science, forestry, French, history, mathematics, music, oral communication, social science, and theater.

CAMPUS FACILITIES AND EQUIPMENT

Nursing students can take advantage of a brand new building, Nadeau Hall, which houses the Northern Maine Center for Rural Health Services, home to UMFK's nursing division. Nadeau Hall also houses 35 new student computer workstations equipped with Pentium IV computers and 17" flat screens in the new Northern Aroostook Center for Technology. For outdoor enthusiasts, our environmental studies program provides hands-on learning in the field. You'll have the opportunity to study in the very rustic setting of the University's Violette Wilderness Camp, located on the outskirts of the Allagash Wilderness Waterway. We also provide distance education through interactive television, known as our ITV system. All seven University campuses are connected to the network. Classes are electronically transmitted to a broadcast classroom where students at other locations participate through an audio talkback system. For those students interested in living on campus, UMFK has two co-educational residence halls, Crocker Hall and a new suite-style residence hall, The Lodge. The Lodge offers students the option to live in suites, which include a kitchenette, bedrooms, a living room and a bathroom.

TUITION, ROOM, BOARD AND FEES

Expenses for the 2007-2008 academic year, based on 30 credit hours, are $5,100 tuition for in-state students, $7,710 tuition for out-of-state-students, and $6,620 for room and board. Books, supplies, and fees are estimated at $1,992.

FINANCIAL AID

Each year, more than 75 percent of students at University of Maine at Fort Kent receive some form of financial assistance. Financial Aid is awarded based on need and academic achievement or special talent and is renewable yearly. A variety of grants are available, including the Federal Pell Grant, which is based on need and doesn't have to be repaid. We also offer a list of student loans, including the Stafford Student of Parent Loan, plus alternative financial packages through various lenders. To apply for Financial Aid, students must complete the FAFSA as soon as possible. You can also contact the Financial Aid office at 888-TRY-UMFK.

STUDENT ORGANIZATIONS AND ACTIVITIES

There are more than 25 student clubs and organizations on campus and among them are honor societies, student government, a writer's group, and a theatre group to name just a few. Athletically, we compete in six sports and are part of Division II of the National Association of Intercollegiate Athletics as a member of the Sunrise Conference. We also offer intramural and club sports and our Sports Center houses a Gold's Standard Gym.

ADMISSIONS PROCESS

The University of Maine at Fort Kent's admission is offered on a rolling basis and we welcome applications from qualified students. The office of admissions requires a completed application form with essay, $40 application fee, and official transcript from the applicant's secondary school with recommendation from the guidance counselor.

SAT and ACT scores, letters of recommendation, and a campus interview/visit are not required but are strongly recommended.

College Portrait available at: http://www.umfk.maine.edu/ie/profile/default.cfm

University of Massachusetts DartmouthAt A GlanceIn 1895, the Massachusetts legislature chartered the New Bedford Textile School and the Bradford Durfee Textile School, laying the foundation for the modern University of Massachusetts Dartmouth. Since then, the base of local economy has slowly changed from textiles to manufacturing and service, and the university's programs have grown along with the economy, continually expanding to meet modern needs. In 1988, the Swain School of Design was incorporated into the University of Massachusetts Dartmouth's College of Visual and Performing Arts.In 1962, the Southeastern Massachusetts Technological Institute was founded, later to become the more comprehensive Southeastern Massachusetts University in 1969. In 1991, the University of Massachusetts Amherst, Boston, and Dartmouth campuses joined with the University of Lowell, Southeastern Massachusetts University, and the Medical Center in Worcester to create a new University of Massachusetts educational system.Today, UMass Dartmouth is a comprehensive teaching and research university, offering a variety of educational programs, research opportunities, and extension and continuing education programs in the liberal arts, creative arts, sciences, andprofessional fields. Undergraduate enrollment is roughly 8,500 and graduateenrollment is about 1,000. Currently, about 90 percent of students are from Massachusetts; however, every year, the university attracts a growing number of students from other U.S. states and foreign countries.Location and EnvironmentThe University of Massachusetts Dartmouth is located on 710 acres in southeastern Massachusetts, near the historic cities of Fall River and New Bedford. The renowned architect Paul Rudolph, former dean of the Yale University School of Art and Architecture, designed the university's extraordinary, modern campus. In addition to the main campus, the university's arts programs are located in a renovated retail store in downtown New Bedford. There are a variety of shops and restaurants within walking distance of the university and ample public transportation servicing areas outside the immediate vicinity. Massachusetts state beaches, hiking trails, and neighboring cities offer a variety of social, cultural, and recreational activities in the surrounding region. Beyond local resources, the world-class cities of Boston and Providence are an hour from campus, offering a large number of museums, libraries, performances, concerts, and sporting events. In addition, New York City, New Hampshire, and Vermont's famous mountain ranges are only four hours away. Boston and Providence both offer extensive, national air, bus, and rail lines.Off-Campus OpportunitiesBecause UMass Dartmouth is a member of SACHEM (Southeastern Association for Cooperation in Higher Education in Massachusetts), students can cross register for courses at neighboring public and private colleges for full course credit.In addition, the university operates exchange programs with the University of Grenoble (France), the Lycee du Gresivaudanat Meylan and the Lycee Aristide Berges; Nottingham Trent University (England); the Baden-Wurttemburg universities (Germany); Centro de Arte e Communicacao (Portugal); Nova Scotia College of Art and Design; Ben Gurion University of the Negev (Israel); and the Ecole Nationale Superieure des Industries Textiles, Universite de Haute Alsace (France). In addition to the formal exchange programs, students often earn course credit through individually arranged overseas programs.Majors and Degrees OfferedThe university is divided into five colleges: The colleges of Arts and Sciences, which offers 20 major fields, the Charlton College of Business, which offers 7 major fields, The College of Engineering, which offers 7 major fields, the College of Visual and Performing Arts, which offers 7 major fields, and the College of Nursing. Students may also study at the Graduate School of Marine Sciences and Technology.Students at UMass Dartmouth may pursue a bachelor of arts, bachelor of fine arts, or bachelor of science degree. Many of the programs offer opportunities for internships, and there is an engineering co-op education program. The university also operates an undergraduate honors program, supports interdisciplinary studies, offers pre-law, pre-med, and numerous minor programs, and emphasizes undergraduate academic advising. Students may also earn course credit through independent study, directed study courses, and contract learning programs.Academic ProgramsThe academic year consists of two semesters, beginning in September and ending in mid-May. Between the conclusion of the fall semester in December and the start of the spring semester in late January, the university offers a three-week January term. From the end of May through the end of August, the university offers summer sessions through the Division of Professional and Continuing Education. To earn an undergraduate degree, students must complete at least 120 credits of course work. Students generally earn three credits for each semester course and take four or five courses per semester. In some major fields, students must complete 133 credits to graduate.In addition to coursework required by their major field, students must complete General Education Requirements in the areas of: ethics and social responsibility; mathematics, natural science, and technology; global awareness and diversity; written and oral communications; cultural and artistic literacy; and information and computer literacy.Campus Facilities and EquipmentAn understanding of, and access to, the latest trends in computers and technology is fundamental to the university's educational program. Every academic building and residence hall is connected to the campus computer network and there are computer clusters in the library and most academic buildings, which jointly hold about 400 Mac and IBM microcomputers or terminals. Students who live off campus have access to the campus network via modem.The university library is a complete research center, containing over 460,000 titles and online access to 22,000-plus electronic journals and newspapers. The library subscribes to numerous electronic and Web-based educational databases, and operates a modern, electronic catalog and search system. In addition, the university participates in an extensive interlibrary loan and delivery program, which gives students the ability to search and borrow from millions of volumes at other libraries.All five academic colleges have their own academic facilities, including classrooms, modern laboratories, study areas, art galleries and performance spaces, faculty and administrative offices, and student lounges.Tuition, Room, Board and FeesTuition and fees for in-state residents total $8,592 annually. Tuition for out-of-state students is about $18,174 annually. Room and board costs vary according to the dorm and meal plan selected; a double room and 19 meals per week averages $8,844. Students should expect to spend $1,200 to $2,000 on books and supplies, though this cost varies by major.Financial AidMost students at UMass receive some form of financial assistance from a federal, state, or institutional source. The university defines financial need as the difference between a family's expected contribution and the costs of attending college.The Financial Aid Services Office evaluates a student's financial need in the context of the total costs of attending college, considering the price of tuition and fees, as well as the cost of books, room and board, transportation, and living expenses.To be considered for any form of Financial Aid, students must complete the Free Application for Federal Student Aid (FAFSA). The university recommends that all Financial Aid applicants submit the FAFSA no later than February 15.In addition to need-based awards, the university offers a number of merit-based scholarships, based on a student's grade point average, standardized test scores, and class rank.Student Organizations and ActivitiesAt UMass Dartmouth, there are a wide variety of extracurricular clubs, organizations, and events on campus, giving students of every background and interest the opportunity to participate in campus life. There are over 70 student-run organizations, including the Outing Club, Theater Company, Society of Women Engineers, and the university FM radio station WUMD 89.3 The university also competes in 25 intercollegiate athletic teams. The Student Senate, the Campus Center Board of Governors, Residence Hall Congress, and Student Judiciary are elected students organizations that help determine campus policies. In addition to clubs and activities, the university brings a multitude of events to campus, such as well-known entertainers and musicians, noted lecturers, movie screenings, and art exhibits.Admissions ProcessAdmission to the university is selective and every prospective student is evaluated by the general university standards, as well as by the standards of the academic departments in which they intend to study. In some departments, there are a limited number of spaces available each year. Candidates are evaluated on the strength of their secondary school academic program, weighted GPA, class rank, SAT I or ACT scores, and their personal essay. Transfer students must also submit transcripts from all previous college or university work.Prospective students are encouraged to visit the campus for a tour and meet with an admissions counselor. Students are admitted to the university on a rolling basis until each program is filled.The university is committed to providing equal admissions opportunity to all qualified students through standard and alternative admission programs. The university offers an alternative admissions program, College Now, specially designed for students from a low-income family, or who have limited English speaking ability.To apply for freshman admission, candidates must submit a completed application along with an application fee. The application fee is $40 for in-state applicants and $60 for out-of-state applicants. In addition to these materials, the university requires a secondary school transcript, official scores from the SAT I or ACT, and any other supporting documents the Admissions Committee should consider.Transfer students make up about one third of all incoming students annually. To apply for transfer status, students must submit the preceding materials as well as official records of all work at the college or university they attended previously.Transfer candidates are evaluated by the same standards as freshman applicants, with a stronger emphasis on their college or university achievement. Students may apply for admission to the January or September semester. The application procedures are the same for either term. The university recommends that all international students submit their credentials no later than June 1 for September entrance and no later than November 1 for January entrance.In addition to its own standards, the university evaluates students by the Massachusetts State Board of Higher Education admission standards. Massachusetts State Board of Higher Education evaluates applicants based on the strength of their secondary school curriculum, the level of course work, and standardized test results. Undergraduate students may be admitted as freshman, transfer, or College Now students

UNIVERSITY OF MARYLAND— BALTIMORE COUNTY

AT A GLANCE

University of Maryland, Baltimore County (UMBC) attracts motivated students and rewards them with the resources and attention they need to succeed. A selective, medium-sized public research university, UMBC provides students with opportunities for hands-on research experience working with professors at the top of their fields. The University was recognized by Kaplan/Newsweek's "How to Get Into College" guide as one of the twelve hottest schools in the country. For three consecutive years, Cosmogirl! has selected UMBC as one of the 50 best colleges for women. The Carnegie Foundation ranks UMBC in the category of Research Universities with high research activity. UMBC is a two-time winner of the U.S. Presidential Award for Excellence in Science, Mathematics and Engineering Mentoring. The University's academic reputation and industry partnerships help place students in promising careers and leading graduate programs. One third of UMBC students immediately go on to leading graduate or professional schools such as Harvard, Johns Hopkins, Stanford, and Yale. At UMBC, students find out quickly that learning at an honors university can take place in many ways. Undergraduates have access to the latest technology in areas from geography to art history to chemistry. The International Media Center offers students multilingual word processing, worldwide databases, and satellite feeds from the International Channel, Deutsche Welle, and international stations. The Goddard Earth Science and Technology Center brings NASA scientists, UMBC professors, and students together to study the earth.. Students in UMBC's Imaging Research Center (IRC) gain professional experience with companies such as the Discovery Channel, CNN, and PBS; students use the IRC's high-end equipment for applications such as molecular imaging and three-dimensional cartography. UMBC also has a Howard Hughes Medical Institute laboratory, a privately sponsored research facility dedicated to the study of the structural building blocks of the AIDS virus. The UMBC climate is friendly and energetic; 9,400 undergraduates have enough ideas and interests to support more than 200 groups, including Greek organizations, recreational sports clubs, community outreach efforts, and campus events.. Students enthusiastically follow UMBC NCAA Division I athletic teams and attend games in the UMBC Stadium and Retriever Activities Center. UMBC students are from 41 states and 90 countries. Approximately 72% of freshman students live on campus, with 14% from out of state. The undergraduate student population is 50% female, 54% Caucasian, 2% Asian American, 15% African American, 4% Hispanic American, and .04% Native American. UMBC houses nearly 3,900 students, 1,600 live in UMBC's three new residence suites and apartment communities. Residential communities feature nine living-learning programs including the Center for Women and Information Technology; Intercultural Living Exchange; Shriver Living Learning Center; Visual and Performing Arts.

An Honors University with the teaching and student support traditions of a small liberal arts college, UMBC is also among the most rapidly developing and diverse research universities in the nation.

LOCATION AND ENVIRONMENT

Located a few miles south of Baltimore, UMBC is 15 minutes from downtown Baltimore and 45 minutes from Washington, D.C. The Baltimore-Washington area is known for its music, sports, museums, restaurants, and historical traditions. UMBC's 530-acre campus includes more than 40 buildings accessed by a two-mile elliptical drive, with housing and dining facilities on one side and core facilities (classroom/lab buildings, a library, galleries, a student union, a bookstore, a gymnasium, an Olympic-size pool, and tennis courts) surrounding a central walkway. BWTech@UMBC Research and Technology Park, adjacent to the campus, attracts firms in the high-technology fields, including engineering, information technology, and the life sciences. Close to the campus, techcenter@UMBC is a magnet for high-technology start-up and emerging companies and offers students internship opportunities with cutting-edge firms.

ACADEMICS

UMBC's academic calendar consists of fall and spring semesters, a four-week mini session in January, and summer sessions from six to eight weeks. To receive a UMBC degree, students complete 120 to 128 credits plus two physical education courses. In addition to the requirements for the chosen major, the general education program (GEP), provides a solid basis for a lifetime of learning. GEP courses encompass humanities and fine arts, mathematics and natural sciences, social sciences, and languages and culture. The Honors College at UMBC is a special option for students seeking a community of like-minded people for whom the quest for knowledge is its own reward. All Honors College students must take at least one honors course per semester. Students choose from honors versions of core courses, special honors seminars, and plenty of other honors courses.

CAMPUS FACILITIES AND EQUIPMENT

UMBC's landmark building, the Albin O. Kuhn Library and Gallery, contains one million books and bound volumes of journals, an extensive reference collection, 4,200 journal and database subscriptions, more than 200 computers, wireless and wired connections for laptops, and more than 3 million other items, including slides, photographs, maps, musical scores, recordings, and microforms. The Commons, UMBC's state-of-the-art student center, the hub of campus life includes a food court, general lounges, the University bookstore, meeting spaces, a student recreation center, a full-service bank, student organization offices, administrative offices, retail-type spaces, wireless computer connectivity and Web-accessible kiosks. UMBC students have access to research opportunities and equipment such as conducting AIDS research on one of the world's largest nuclear magnetic resonance spectrometers in the only Howard Hughes Medical Institute lab at a public university in Maryland. New facilities include a Public Policy Building and a state-of-the-art Information Technology/Engineering Building. In the next few years, UMBC will open a new Performing Arts and Humanities Facility, housing seven departments and new performance space that will showcase the University's strong arts and humanities programs and create a regional and national appreciation of UMBC as a cultural attraction.

CAMPUS LIFE

The campus climate is friendly and energetic. UMBC's more than 9,400 undergraduates have enough ideas and interests to support more than 200 student groups, including Greek organizations and recreational sports clubs, such as fencing and sailing; community outreach efforts, such as Habitat for Humanity; and campus events, including lectures, films, concerts, and plays. Students enthusiastically follow UMBC NCAA Division I athletic teams, such as basketball, lacrosse, and soccer and attend games in the UMBC Stadium and Retriever Activities Center, which includes a multipurpose gym, auxiliary gym, weight room, and classrooms. Elections are held each year for officers in UMBC's Student Government Association (SGA). The SGA represents the student body on a number of administrative committees, including the Undergraduate Council, the Library Committee and the Student Health Advisory Committee.

FINANCIAL AID

Scholarships, grants, loans, student employment, and other financial aid programs are available to qualified undergraduates. Interested students must have their FAFSA received and accepted by the FAFSA processor by February 15 in order to receive consideration for maximum need-based financial assistance; this is the University's priority financial aid deadline. Students who are talented academically or creatively are eligible for several merit scholarships that the University proudly offers. Each year, around $4 million is awarded through these scholarships. Students who wish to be considered for these scholarships must submit an admission application by December 1. Sixty-nine percent of full-time students who applied for financial aid last year received it, and they were awarded an average of $7,445.

STUDENT ORGANIZATIONS AND ACTIVITIES

All undergraduates are members of Maryland's self-governing student body. The Student Government Association is a major component of the shared governance of the University, and it regularly speaks to the president of the University, the campus senate, and the state legislature. There are over 450 student clubs and organizations sponsored by the University, and the University hosts countless social, athletic, academic, and recreational activities every week. Approximately 10 percent of students participate in 26 fraternities and 20 sororities. Students enjoy a wide spectrum of intramural and club sports as well as a new campus recreation center, which boasts indoor and outdoor swimming pools, free weights, fitness machines, courts, climbing wall, and a running track. An 18-hole golf course, a soccer/track complex and playing fields are part of the University's outdoor sports facilities. Finally, men's and women's teams in 27 NCAA sports are hosted at Maryland—Go Terps!—and they compete in the Atlantic Coast Conference.

ADMISSIONS PROCESS

As prescribed by the Board of Regents, the university expects all freshman applicants, at a minimum, to have completed by graduation the following coursework: 4 years of English, 3 years of mathematics, including algebra I or applied math I and II, formal logic or geometry, 3 years of history or social science, 3 years of science that involves at least 2 lab experiences and 2 years of a foreign language. Most of our students have a strong A-/B+ averages in their high school course work and have taken the most challenging classes available to them, including honors, Advancement Placement (AP) and International Baccalaureate (IB) courses. About 86 percent of our students finished in the top quarter of their high school class, with about two-thirds in the top tenth. Successful transfer applicants have earned 30 semester hours or 45 quarter hours (one full year of college), above-average grades from all schools previously attended, good academic and judicial standing at all previous schools, completion of an English composition class that transfers as ENGL 101 and a college-level math course such as college algebra, probability, statistics or pre-calculus. Transfer applicants are also encouraged to submit an essay and statement of activities for consideration. Maryland's priority freshman application deadline for the fall semester is December 1, and students are urged to meet this deadline to receive the best consideration for admission, merit-based scholarships, and invitations to special programs. The regular freshman application deadline is January 20. The deadline for freshman applications for the spring semester is December 1. Applications for fall transfer admission should be received by the priority deadline of March 1 or the regular deadline of June 1. The deadline for transfers for the spring semester is November 15. International students and students with any non-U.S. academic records must meet the December 1 deadline for fall freshman admission and March 1 for fall transfer admission. Both freshman and transfer international students and students with non-U.S. academic records must meet a deadline of August 1 for Spring admission.

UNIVERSITY OF MASSACHUSETTS—BOSTON

AT A GLANCE

Notable for its solid academic reputation, active faculty, modest class size and flexible schedules, the University of Massachusetts Boston is Boston's only public university. Its proximity to the city's cultural and social riches and urban sophistication, moderate cost structure, and dedicated, highly diverse student body make the campus a desirable academic destination. The picturesque harborside campus is accessible by both public and private transportation, and help is available to locate appropriate housing options. A rich mix of student organizations provides social options connecting to both the campus and the surrounding metropolitan environs. With more than 100 undergraduate programs, 38 masters and 13 doctoral degree programs, UMass Boston surely has something for you.

ACADEMIC PROGRAMS

Five undergraduate colleges award bachelor's degrees: the College of Liberal Arts and the College of Science and Mathematics (32 majors, and 17 programs of study between them,) the College of Management, the College of Nursing and Health Sciences (both a regular and an accelerated BSN and an online RN-to-BSN program, as well as a program in Exercise & Health Sciences,) and the College of Public and Community Service (five majors and three career concentrations.) Pre-med, pre-law, and teacher licensure programs are also offered, along with programs for honors study, credit by examination, and advanced placement.

These colleges offer graduate level programs, as well, including master's and doctoral degree programs and graduate certificate programs. In addition, two graduate colleges — the Graduate College of Education and the McCormack Graduate School of Policy Studies — offer graduate degree programs, graduate certificate and CAGS programs. Altogether, UMass Boston offers 38 master's degree programs, 13 doctoral degrees and more than 20 graduate certificate programs.

The academic calendar runs from early September through the end of May, with a one-month optional winter session in January and summer school sessions in June, July and August.

COLLEGE OF LIBERAL ARTS AND COLLEGE OF SCIENCE AND MATHEMATICS

Distribution, core curriculum, and writing comprise the 3 required elements of our general education curriculum. Requirements of the major must also be fulfilled. The Colleges both offer an individual major option.

COLLEGE OF MANAGEMENT

Fulfilling the general education, management, and elective course requirements, earns graduates a BS degree with a strong liberal arts foundation and the theoretical, technical, and functional training needed to succeed in business.

COLLEGE OF NURSING AND HEALTH SCIENCES

A BS program in nursing offers a liberal arts foundation and intensive study in the principles and practices of nursing. The program in Exercise & Health Sciences prepares graduates for the technical aspects of a professional discipline with a foundation in liberal arts.

COLLEGE OF PUBLIC AND COMMUNITY SERVICE

Nationally acclaimed as a model for competency-based education, the college offers an innovative curriculum with strong emphasis on social justice. Students draw upon a variety of learning options including classroom study, self-directed study, project-based learning, and the demonstration of competence gained through relevant prior experience.

Honors programs are open to high achievers in all colleges.

CAMPUS FACILITIES AND EQUIPMENT

The University s Healey Library holds a collection of more than 600,000 volumes, 25,000 electronic and print journals and newspapers, 30,000 electronic books, 85 databases, and over 2,500 videos, DVDs, and films representing all fields of study on the campus. The library s electronic resources are available on and off campus, 24/7. UMass Boston is a member of three library consortia, and participates in the state-wide virtual catalog providing yet wider accessibility to scholarly and study resources. The Information Technology Division (ITD) provides seven-day-a-week access to general purpose computer labs with some 220 Dell Pentium Four and 60 Apple Macintosh G5/G4s, as well as other specialized, course-related facilities including Adaptive Computer, Graduate and Faculty, and Media and Language Labs, and a media viewing center. ITD houses equipment from Dell, Sun and Apple, and operating systems include Windows XP, Unix, Linux and Apple OS. With more than 70 Smart Classrooms, network connections throughout the campus, and wireless access in the Library and Campus Center, a wide variety of IT and data communications resources is available to students. The campus uses a WebCT/Blackboard learning management system, a fiber optic infrastructure with Gigabit backbone and 10 MB switched connectivity. The Kennedy Presidential Library is linked to UMass Boston by a variety of educational programs, enabling students to utilize the more than 28 million pages of documents, 6.5 million feet of film, and 100,000+ still photographs in the library s archives. Next door, the Archives of the Commonwealth of Massachusetts are also a rich depository covering more than 550 years of Massachusetts history. A state-of-the-art Campus Center provides easy access to student services, dining services and spectacular meeting spaces, along with computer terminals and wireless Internet access.

STUDENT ORGANIZATIONS AND ACTIVITIES

No matter your interest, UMass Boston has an activity to engage you socially and intellectually. Be it student government, literary endeavors, championship chess, working with inner city youth, academically affiliated clubs, affinity groups, athletics opportunities, or a course-credit-based leadership development program, you can find the right activity to complement your classroom experience. UMass Boston is a community of scholars with pride in academic excellence, diversity, research, and service, tightly woven into the public and community service needs of Greater Boston. Our students come from an extraordinary range of backgrounds, talents and interests and represent all levels of the economic, political, spiritual and ethnic spectra. Many come straight from high school, others transfer from two- and four-year colleges; most are from Massachusetts, but many arrive from other states and countries.

ADMISSIONS PROCESS

Freshman candidates must have at least 16 academic units in high school including four years of English, three of mathematics, three of science including two with laboratory requirements, two years of social science including one of US history, two years of a single foreign language, and two of electives in the arts or computer science (excluding vocational training.) Candidates must present satisfactory scores on either the SAT I or ACT. Students must have a strong academic background (as determined by a re-calculated GPA.) Academic program choices, motivation, achievement and annual progress are closely scrutinized. Reading and writing skills are measured using English grades, the application essay and standardized test scores. A separate international application is required of international students. The Test of English as a Foreign Language (TOEFL) is required of all students educated in a non-English educational system. We consider transfer students by reviewing all college academic credentials. In general, a minimum 2.5 GPA is required, though specific programs require higher. A campus visit with a group information session is strongly encouraged. Contact 617-287-6000 or www.umb.edu for more information.

UNIVERSITY OF MASSACHUSETTS—DARTMOUTH

AT A GLANCE

In 1895, the Massachusetts legislature chartered the New Bedford Textile School and the Bradford Durfee Textile School, laying the foundation for the modern University of Massachusetts Dartmouth. Since then, the base of local economy has slowly changed from textiles to manufacturing and service, and the university's programs have grown along with the economy, continually expanding to meet modern needs. In 1988, the Swain School of Design was incorporated into the University of Massachusetts Dartmouth's College of Visual and Performing Arts.

In 1962, the Southeastern Massachusetts Technological Institute was founded, later to become the more comprehensive Southeastern Massachusetts University in 1969. In 1991, the University of Massachusetts Amherst, Boston, and Dartmouth campuses joined with the University of Lowell, Southeastern Massachusetts University, and the Medical Center in Worcester to create a new University of Massachusetts educational system.

Today, UMass Dartmouth is a comprehensive teaching and research university, offering a variety of educational programs, research opportunities, and extension and continuing education programs in the liberal arts, creative arts, sciences, and professional fields.

Undergraduate enrollment is roughly 8,500 and graduate enrollment is about 1,000. Currently, about 90 percent of students are from Massachusetts; however, every year, the university attracts a growing number of students from other U.S. states and foreign countries.

LOCATION AND ENVIRONMENT

The University of Massachusetts Dartmouth is located on 710 acres in southeastern Massachusetts, near the historic cities of Fall River and New Bedford. The renowned architect Paul Rudolph, former dean of the Yale University School of Art and Architecture, designed the university's extraordinary, modern campus. In addition to the main campus, the university's arts programs are located in a renovated retail store in downtown New Bedford. There are a variety of shops and restaurants within walking distance of the university and ample public transportation servicing areas outside the immediate vicinity. Massachusetts state beaches, hiking trails, and neighboring cities offer a variety of social, cultural, and recreational activities in the surrounding region.

Beyond local resources, the world-class cities of Boston and Providence are an hour from campus, offering a large number of museums, libraries, performances, concerts, and sporting events. In addition, New York City, New Hampshire, and Vermont's famous mountain ranges are only four hours away. Boston and Providence both offer extensive, national air, bus, and rail lines.

OFF-CAMPUS OPPORTUNITIES

Because UMass Dartmouth is a member of SACHEM (Southeastern Association for Cooperation in Higher Education in Massachusetts), students can cross register for courses at neighboring public and private colleges for full course credit.

In addition, the university operates exchange programs with the University of Grenoble (France), the Lycee du Gresivaudanat Meylan and the Lycee Aristide Berges; Nottingham Trent University (England); the Baden-Wurttemburg universities (Germany); Centro de Arte e Communicacao (Portugal); Nova Scotia College of Art and Design; Ben Gurion University of the Negev (Israel); and the Ecole Nationale Superieure des Industries Textiles, Universite de Haute Alsace (France). In addition to the formal exchange programs, students often earn course credit through individually arranged overseas programs.

MAJORS AND DEGREES OFFERED

The university is divided into five colleges: The colleges of Arts and Sciences, which offers 20 major fields, the Charlton College of Business, which offers 7 major fields, The College of Engineering, which offers 7 major fields, the College of Visual and Performing Arts, which offers 7 major fields, and the College of Nursing. Students may also study at the Graduate School of Marine Sciences and Technology.

Students at UMass Dartmouth may pursue a bachelor of arts, bachelor of fine arts, or bachelor of science degree. Many of the programs offer opportunities for internships, and there is an engineering co-op education program. The university also operates an undergraduate honors program, supports interdisciplinary studies, offers pre-law, pre-med, and numerous minor programs, and emphasizes undergraduate academic advising. Students may also earn course credit through independent study, directed study courses, and contract learning programs.

ACADEMIC PROGRAMS

The academic year consists of two semesters, beginning in September and ending in mid-May. Between the conclusion of the fall semester in December and the start of the spring semester in late January, the university offers a three-week January term. From the end of May through the end of August, the university offers summer sessions through the Division of Professional and Continuing Education. To earn an undergraduate degree, students must complete at least 120 credits of course work. Students generally earn three credits for each semester course and take four or five courses per semester. In some major fields, students must complete 133 credits to graduate.

In addition to coursework required by their major field, students must complete General Education Requirements in the areas of: ethics and social responsibility; mathematics, natural science, and technology; global awareness and diversity; written and oral communications; cultural and artistic literacy; and information and computer literacy.

CAMPUS FACILITIES AND EQUIPMENT

An understanding of, and access to, the latest trends in computers and technology is fundamental to the university's educational program. Every academic building and residence hall is connected to the campus computer network and there are computer clusters in the library and most academic buildings, which jointly hold about 400 Mac and IBM microcomputers or terminals. Students who live off campus have access to the campus network via modem.

The university library is a complete research center, containing over 460,000 titles and online access to 22,000-plus electronic journals and newspapers. The library subscribes to numerous electronic and Web-based educational databases, and operates a modern, electronic catalog and search system. In addition, the university participates in an extensive interlibrary loan and delivery program, which gives students the ability to search and borrow from millions of volumes at other libraries.

All five academic colleges have their own academic facilities, including classrooms, modern laboratories, study areas, art galleries and performance spaces, faculty and administrative offices, and student lounges.

TUITION, ROOM, BOARD AND FEES

Tuition and fees for in-state residents total $8,592 annually. Tuition for out-of-state students is about $18,174 annually. Room and board costs vary according to the dorm and meal plan selected; a double room and 19 meals per week averages $8,844. Students should expect to spend $1,200 to $2,000 on books and supplies, though this cost varies by major.

FINANCIAL AID

Most students at UMass receive some form of financial assistance from a federal, state, or institutional source. The university defines financial need as the difference between a family's expected contribution and the costs of attending college.

The Financial Aid Services Office evaluates a student's financial need in the context of the total costs of attending college, considering the price of tuition and fees, as well as the cost of books, room and board, transportation, and living expenses.

To be considered for any form of financial aid, students must complete the Free Application for Federal Student Aid (FAFSA). The university recommends that all financial aid applicants submit the FAFSA no later than February 15.

In addition to need-based awards, the university offers a number of merit-based scholarships, based on a student's grade point average, standardized test scores, and class rank.

STUDENT ORGANIZATIONS AND ACTIVITIES

At UMass Dartmouth, there are a wide variety of extracurricular clubs, organizations, and events on campus, giving students of every background and interest the opportunity to participate in campus life. There are over 70 student-run organizations, including the Outing Club, Theater Company, Society of Women Engineers, and the university FM radio station WUMD 89.3 The university also competes in 25 intercollegiate athletic teams. The Student Senate, the Campus Center Board of Governors, Residence Hall Congress, and Student Judiciary are elected students organizations that help determine campus policies. In addition to clubs and activities, the university brings a multitude of events to campus, such as well-known entertainers and musicians, noted lecturers, movie screenings, and art exhibits.

ADMISSIONS PROCESS

Admission to the university is selective and every prospective student is evaluated by the general university standards, as well as by the standards of the academic departments in which they intend to study. In some departments, there are a limited number of spaces available each year. Candidates are evaluated on the strength of their secondary school academic program, weighted GPA, class rank, SAT I or ACT scores, and their personal essay. Transfer students must also submit transcripts from all previous college or university work.

Prospective students are encouraged to visit the campus for a tour and meet with an admissions counselor. Students are admitted to the university on a rolling basis until each program is filled.

The university is committed to providing equal admissions opportunity to all qualified students through standard and alternative admission programs. The university offers an alternative admissions program, College Now, specially designed for students from a low-income family, or who have limited English speaking ability.

To apply for freshman admission, candidates must submit a completed application along with an application fee. The application fee is $40 for in-state applicants and $60 for out-of-state applicants. In addition to these materials, the university requires a secondary school transcript, official scores from the SAT I or ACT, and any other supporting documents the Admissions Committee should consider.

Transfer students make up about one third of all incoming students annually. To apply for transfer status, students must submit the preceding materials as well as official records of all work at the college or university they attended previously.

Transfer candidates are evaluated by the same standards as freshman applicants, with a stronger emphasis on their college or university achievement. Students may apply for admission to the January or September semester. The application procedures are the same for either term. The university recommends that all international students submit their credentials no later than June 1 for September entrance and no later than November 1 for January entrance.

In addition to its own standards, the university evaluates students by the Massachusetts State Board of Higher Education admission standards. Massachusetts State Board of Higher Education evaluates applicants based on the strength of their secondary school curriculum, the level of course work, and standardized test results. Undergraduate students may be admitted as freshman, transfer, or College Now students.

UNIVERSITY OF MASSACHUSETTS—LOWELL

AT A GLANCE

The academic experience at UML offers students comprehensive, broad-based programs characterized by a continuing effort to break down traditional barriers between disciplines, and between the classroom and the "real world." Most programs include an internship that provides an opportunity for students to put into practice what they've learned in the classroom. Resources including an Honors program, multimedia computer labs, and an active peer tutoring program ensure that all students have access to the opportunities and services that support their success.

UMass Lowell offers 15 doctoral, 31 master's and 38 bachelor's degree programs that incorporate 74 concentrations in science, engineering, health, humanities, social sciences, fine arts, education and management. Signature programs include sound recording technology, plastics engineering and meteorology. Internationally recognized for excellence in science and engineering, the campus is a leader in nanotechnology, nanomanufacturing, biomanufacturing, bioinformatics and advanced materials research.

LOCATION AND ENVIRONMENT

UMass Lowell is surrounded by a region rich with heritage and culture. The campus is located 25 miles from Boston and within an hour of ocean beaches and New Hampshire mountains.

The City of Lowell, a thriving city of 110,000, offers everything from the Merrimack Repertory Theater to white water rafting, the Kerouac Festival to great baseball with the Red Sox-affiliated minor league Lowell Spinners. Ethnic restaurants, cobblestone streets, a lively arts community—it's a renaissance city.

ACADEMIC PROGRAMS

Supporting Success

Part of the culture of UMass Lowell is the commitment we make to help every student reach his or her potential. That's why students are encouraged to ask harder questions and dig deeper for the answers. That's why tutoring, advising and learning skills workshops are available to make sure each student masters the content of their courses.

We believe that you deserve the opportunity to excel—that's the UMass Lowell formula for success.

First Year Program: www.uml.edu/firstyear

We want you to start off on the right foot. So the First Year program provides learning communities, a commuter mentor program, a freshman leadership program and an ongoing schedule of educational and recreational activities. There's even a parents' network, so we can help them help you succeed.

Centers for Learning: www.class.uml.edu

Everyone needs a little help sometime & and it's available at the Centers for Learning and Academic Support Services. CLASS offers individual and group tutoring (peer tutors cover more than 70 subject areas) and help choosing your courses, editing a paper or boosting your study skills.

Honors Program: www.uml.edu/honors

The Honors Program is for people who want to take their academics to another level. The University-wide program offers students in-depth study in small classes, individualized advising, relationships with faculty mentors, research opportunities, professional development grants for workshops and conferences and scholarships. Honors students may choose to live on honors floors in campus residence halls and may be eligible to earn a degree with the designation "Commonwealth Honors Program Scholar."

Career Services: career.uml.edu

In addition to helping you find a job when you graduate, the Career Services office is a resource for internships, co-ops and part-time and summer jobs. The staff will help you identify a career path and how to get there, connect you to alumni so you can get feedback on a career, facilitate on-campus and virtual employer interviews, hold daily drop-in hours and conduct multiple skill-building workshops throughout the year. Career Services maintains a resource library and searchable databases with thousands of positions.

CAMPUS FACILITIES AND EQUIPMENT

The UMass Lowell campus stretches over 100 acres along both sides of the Merrimack River. Academic buildings are clustered on UMass Lowell North and South, while UMass Lowell East is home to residence halls and research labs.

UMl East also houses a 12,000-square-foot, state-of-the- art Campus Recreation Center that attracts hundreds of students daily to its basketball, racquetball and squash courts, its one-eighth-mile seamless rubber compound running track and its dual-level fitness area that houses dozens of pieces of cardiovascular and strength training equipment.

The first of two multi-story parking garages was opened in 2007. There are plans on the drawing board for a nanotechnology research center and new residence halls.

We are determined to provide you with the right tools in classrooms, laboratories and residence halls. The multimedia labs on campus are regularly upgraded. Every student has a free email account, and the campus is completely wireless. Our electronic library, which ranks among the best, can be accessed anywhere on-and-off campus, including in residence halls.

TUITION, ROOM, BOARD AND FEES

Annual Undergraduate Costs 2007-2008

Total Tuition and Fees

In-State Residents: $8,906

Out-of-State Residents : $20,559 ,714

New England Regional Program: $9,633

Residence Hall Room $4,331

Meals (Full Plan) $2,492

Total Room and Board $6,823

FINANCIAL AID

Maintaining Access

UMass Lowell is committed to making quality higher education accessible to all qualified students. In 2007, the campus met 93 percent of need for its students. In the same year, the campus awarded more than $48 million in need and non-need based aid.

Scholarships for Freshmen

More than 150 UMass Lowell scholarships are available to eligible students each year. Scholarships are awarded by the academic college or department

STUDENT ORGANIZATIONS AND ACTIVITIES

UMass Lowell's 6,000 undergraduate students are ethnically, culturally, and economically diverse. Students are active in a wide variety of community service activities and volunteer work throughout the community.

There are dozens of clubs and organizations that offer activities as diverse as publishing a weekly newspaper, producing multicultural festivals and learning to crochet. Academic clubs avoid the all-work-and-no-play principle by going skiing, canoeing and spelunking.

In addition to a nationally-ranked Division I hockey team and 15 other varsity sports, the University sponsors an active recreational sports program.

Whatever you do, you'll be surrounded by one of UMass Lowell's great assets: the people. Among your classmates, professors and administrators, you'll encounter a wide range of ideas, traditions and languages—people who share your aspirations and commitment, people who offer you support and encouragement. You'll be welcomed into the community and form friendships that last a lifetime.

Eight residence halls offer a choice of living environments. All residence halls are secured 24/7 with electronic access and overnight professional security. Building exteriors and parking lots are lit, scanned by security cameras and regularly patrolled. Between 7 P.M. and 1 A.M., our Student Escort Vans are available to shuttle students around campus.

ADMISSIONS PROCESS

UMass Lowell has a rolling admissions policy, meaning that applications are reviewed and decisions made as soon as a student's application package is complete. However, there is a preferred deadline of February 15 for fall semester applications. We encourage high school seniors to apply as soon as their first quarter grades are in. We will continue to accept applications until June 1st.

Check on the website (www.uml.edu/admissions) to see everything required and to download an Application Checklist.

UNIVERSITY OF NEW ENGLAND

AT A GLANCE

The University of New England (UNE) is an independent, coeducational, comprehensive university committed to academic excellence and the enhancement of the quality of life for the people, organizations, and communities it serves. The university fosters critical inquiry through a student-centered, academic environment rich in research, scholarship, creative activity, and service while providing opportunities for acquiring and applying knowledge in selected clinical, professional, and community settings.

UNE's 3,553 students are enrolled in a wide variety of Academic Programs at the undergraduate, graduate, and first-professional levels in four colleges: the College of Arts and Sciences, the College of Health Professions, the College of Pharmacy, and the College of Osteopathic Medicine (housing Maine's only medical school). At the undergraduate level, we have approximately 1,986 students enrolled from 35 different states and several foreign countries in over 40 undergraduate degree programs.

UNE traces its history to 1831 with the founding of Westbrook College, one of Maine's oldest institutions of learning. Today's university represents the joining of three unique higher education institutions through the combining of St. Francis College and the New England College of Osteopathic Medicine in 1978, and Westbrook College in 1996.

LOCATION AND ENVIRONMENT

The University of New England has two campuses located in the picturesque southern coastal beach communities of Maine. The 540-acre University Campus in Biddeford, home to the College of Arts and Sciences and the College of Osteopathic Medicine, is situated on a beautiful coastal site where the Saco River flows into the Atlantic Ocean and includes more than 4,000 feet of water frontage. Located 20 miles to the north is the Westbrook College Campus, home to the College of Health Professions, set on 41 acres in a quiet residential setting in Portland. Students at both campuses can joy the vibrant social life offered in nearby metropolitan Boston (located 90 miles to the south of Biddeford) or Portland and the dynamic outdoor recreational activities that have made Maine a prime tourist destination. Southern Maine is conveniently serviced by a number of airlines at the Portland International Jetport and by bus and train service with stations in Biddeford/Saco and Portland, making our campuses very accessible to all areas of the Northeastern United States and beyond.

OFF-CAMPUS OPPORTUNITIES

The university is committed to supplementing the traditional learning process with practical applications. All students are encouraged to participate in cooperative education programs, field placements, and practicums. These experiences provide valuable learning situations and increase a student's exposure to job-related opportunities, and are required for graduation by most majors. Students also have the opportunity to arrange a study abroad experience. The Office for Study Abroad and International Programs promotes the goals of international cooperation and understanding through rigorous Academic Programs, overseas study opportunities, student-faculty research projects and a host of special programs designed to address current issues in international relations and cultural studies.

MAJORS AND DEGREES OFFERED

UNE offers highly competitive undergraduate and graduate programs in a variety of areas. The university confers the Associates of Science, Bachelor of Arts, Bachelor of Science, Master of Public Health, Master of Science, Master of Science in Education, Master of Social Work, Doctor of Physical Therapy, Doctor of Pharmacy, and Doctor of Osteopathic Medicine degrees along with several postgraduate and graduate certificate programs.

Associate degrees are offered in dental hygiene and nursing. Bachelor degrees are offered in: applied exercise science, aquaculture and aquarium science, art education, athletic training, biochemistry, biological sciences, business, chemistry, communications, dental hygiene, elementary education, English, environmental science, environmental studies, health sciences (for occupational therapy five-year entry-level master's degree), health services management (bachelor degree completion program), history, liberal studies (including pre-law), marine biology, mathematics, medical biology (health and medical sciences tracks for pre-dental, pre-medicine, and pre-veterinary), nursing, political science, psychobiology, psychology, psychology and social relations, sociology, and sport management.

Individualized majors, various minors, pre-physical therapy designation, accelerated pre-physician assistant programs, pre-pharmacy with an early assurance path to the Pharm. D. program, and secondary education certification (Teacher Certification Program) is also available at the undergraduate level.

Masters degree programs are offered in applied biosciences, education, medical education leadership, nurse anesthesia, marine sciences, occupational therapy, physician assistant, public health, and social work. Doctor degree programs are offered in osteopathic medicine, pharmacy, and physical therapy. Graduate certificate programs are offered in addictions counseling, gerontology, and public health.

ACADEMIC PROGRAMS

All undergraduate programs at UNE have a core curriculum as a common thread. Designed to provide a foundation in the liberal arts, the core reflects the values of the college and is designed to prepare students for living informed, thoughtful, and active lives in a complex and changing society. It provides an innovative common learning experience for all UNE undergraduates. It invites students to explore four college-wide themes - (1) Environmental Awareness, (2) Social and Global Awareness, (3) Critical Thinking: Human Responses to Problems and Challenges, and (4) Citizenship. Skills of communications, mathematics, and critical thinking are taught throughout the core.

Student Support Services provides a wide-range of services to assist students with psychological and emotional health, academic support, educational and career planning, and equal opportunities during their academic experience. The Office of Career Services provides academic and career exploration assistance, assistance in applying to graduate schools, self-assessment and personal interest exploration, resume help, job listings, and job fairs. Learning Assistance Services, another department within Student Support Services, offers a comprehensive array of academic support including placement testing, courses, workshops, tutoring, and individual consultations.

CAMPUS FACILITIES AND EQUIPMENT

Both the University and Westbrook College Campuses feature 38 buildings with a variety of uses to support the needs of the university community. The $8 million Marine Science Education and Research Center on the university Campus is the only facility of its kind on any university campus. It features flow-through seawater laboratories and a marine mammal rehabilitation center. The Harold Alfond Center for Health Sciences on the university Campus is a state-of-the-art science education facility and a major medical, health and natural sciences resource for the region. The collections of the Jack S. Ketchum Library (University Campus) and Josephine S. Abplanalp Library (Westbrook College Campus) provide access to over 150,000 volumes and print journals, more than 22,000 print and electronic full-text journal titles, and 6,000 electronic books.

Several computer laboratories are conveniently located throughout each campus and in each library (also providing access via the Internet to many computer databases) along with campus-wide wireless technology service. Other academic facilities include Decary Hall, Gregory Hall, Marcil Hall, and Stella Maris Hall on the University Campus and Alexander Hall, Alumni Hall, Blewett Science Center, Coleman Dental Hygiene Building, Hersey Hall, Parker Pavillion, and Proctor Hall on the Westbrook College Campus.

Both campuses also provide a variety of facilities in support of community life. The 55,000 square-foot Campus Center on the university Campus houses both a sports complex and student union. The sports complex includes a gymnasium with indoor track, collegiate swimming pool, fully equipped fitness center, racquetball courts and athletic training room. The student union provides multipurpose rooms, snack bar, University bookstore, and offices. The Finley Recreation Center on the Westbrook College Campus provides a variety of fitness, health, wellness, and recreational programs and includes a gymnasium, fitness center, and multi-purpose room. Both campuses provide residence halls and dining halls for residential students. The University Campus has nine residence halls, including the recently completed South Hall. The Westbrook College Campus has three residence halls.

TUITION, ROOM, BOARD AND FEES

For 2007-2008, full-time (12 to 18 credits) undergraduate comprehensive annual costs are $35,190. This includes:

Full-time tuition $24,440

Room and Board $9,860 (traditional double occupancy)

General Services Fee $890

FINANCIAL AID

In 2007-2008, approximately 90 percent of all full-time freshmen received some form of financial assistance. The Financial Aid Office uses the Free Application for Federal Student Aid (FAFSA) as its primary application for institutional, federal, and state aid programs. The average financial award was approximately $22,000 and includes scholarships, grants, loans, and employment. The University of New England has a generous scholarship program based on academic performance, scholarships range from $2,000 to over $17,000 per year.

STUDENT ORGANIZATIONS AND ACTIVITIES

Both campuses offer a variety of cultural and social events.

The Student Senate plays a vital role in the student life at both campuses and supports various events and programs through funding derived from the General Services Fee.

The university encourages students to become involved in activities, clubs, and sports. Popular interests include scuba diving, skiing, hiking, biking, swimming, photography, and community service. There are over forty student clubs and organizations between the two campuses as well as an extensive student leadership development program.

UNE's Athletic Department operates an NCAA Division III varsity athletics program. Varsity sports for men are basketball, cross-country, golf, lacrosse, soccer, and a pre-varsity program in ice hockey that will move to a varsity program in 2010; varsity sports for women are basketball, cross-country, field hockey, lacrosse, soccer, softball, swimming and volleyball. Intramural teams in basketball, floor hockey, softball, skiing, and volleyball are popular.

ADMISSIONS PROCESS

The university welcomes applications from students who are seriously pursuing an education of high quality. UNE has a February 15 freshman application deadline, and a December 1st priority application deadline with a December 31st notification date. . Transfer and international students have a Dec 1st application deadline for January admission, and a March 15th application deadline for September admission. Applications received after deadline dates are reviewed on a space available basis.

Students applying for admission are expected to submit a completed application, a $40 nonrefundable application fee, transcripts of all academic work (high school and college), and scores on either the ACT or SAT (TOEFL is required of students whose primary language is not English). International students must also complete an International Student Supplemental Application. Students applying for admission should have completed a curriculum that includes English, mathematics, science, and social sciences. Those considering majors in the life or health sciences should show strength and preparation in mathematics and science. All prospective students are strongly encouraged to visit the campuses of the University of New England for an interview and tour. Interviews are held weekdays from 9:00 A.M. to 4:00 P.M., and tours are also available on select Saturdays. Appointments may be requested by letter, online at our website, or telephone.

UNIVERSITY OF NORTH CAROLINA—ASHEVILLE

AT A GLANCE

The University of North Carolina at Asheville is the designated undergraduate liberal arts university in the sixteen-campus University of North Carolina system. The university enrolls 3,500 students in programs in the arts and humanities, natural and social sciences, and selected pre-professional areas. Emphasizing the liberal arts since its beginning in 1927 as a small junior college, UNCA joined the University of North Carolina system in 1969 with the distinct mission to provide an undergraduate liberal arts education of superior quality for serious and able students.

Consistently rated a "best buy," UNC Asheville earns praise for its strong academics, close faculty-student interactions, small classes, and beautiful mountain setting. The university also has received national recognition for its Undergraduate Research, Integrative Liberal Studies core curriculum, and Humanities programs. Additional special academic opportunities include the honors, study abroad, UNC in Washington semester, and N.C. Teaching Fellows Scholarship programs.

With an average class size of nineteen, UNC Asheville focuses on providing a personalized undergraduate education. Twenty-eight graduates in as many years have received the prestigious Fulbright Scholarships to study abroad. UNC Asheville offers unique opportunities for community service, co-curricular learning, and outdoor recreation in the surrounding Blue Ridge Mountains. In athletics, UNC Asheville competes at the Division I level of the NCAA in fourteen men's and women's sports, including basketball, cross country, track, soccer, tennis, baseball, and volleyball. Student athletes' graduation rates are among the highest in the NCAA.

LOCATION AND ENVIRONMENT

Situated one mile north of downtown Asheville, the 265-acre UNC Asheville campus overlooks the city, Mount Pisgah, and the surrounding Blue Ridge Mountains. It's close to Asheville's shops and nightlife, yet minutes from outdoor adventure amid a million acres of public lands. The campus comprises thirty buildings, situated on two landscaped quadrangles, housing classroom, administration, recreation, and residence facilities.

An All American City, Asheville has been described as one of the country's most livable cities. The nearby Great Smoky Mountains National Park, Blue Ridge Parkway, and Pisgah and Nantahala national forest offer plenty of space for hiking, backpacking, rock climbing, mountain biking, canoeing, kayaking, and more. Asheville's revitalized downtown blends modern life and mountain culture. A varied nightlife, shopping, restaurants, and entertainment appeal to many tastes. Theatre UNCA, the Cultural and Special Events, and the Music and Art departments' activities contribute to the year-round line-up of regional concerts, theatre productions, music and dance festivals, crafts fairs, and other cultural events that are held each year in Asheville.

With a growing population of 75,000, Asheville is the business, cultural, and population center of the Western North Carolina region. There is easy highway access via Interstates 40 and 26, and major commercial carriers serve the Asheville Regional Airport. Asheville is 240 miles west of Raleigh, 175 miles north of Atlanta, and 120 miles east of Knoxville.

OFF-CAMPUS OPPORTUNITIES

The university conducts summer programs in Cambridge, France, Honduras, Ecuador, and Greece, and Spain. UNC Asheville has exchange programs with University College, Chester, England and nine German universities. Many other study abroad locations are available through the N.C. Consortium for Study Abroad.

The UNCA Classics Department offers a special archaeological summer program that takes place on site at Lithares, Boeotia, Greece. For students who truly want an interdisciplinary experience, UNCA offers special summer study programs, such as the Desert Ecology Study Tour of the American Southwest.

MAJORS AND DEGREES OFFERED

Students select from thirty majors leading to the Bachelor of Arts, Bachelor of Fine Arts, and Bachelor of Science degrees, with teacher licensure available. The most popular majors according to enrollment figures are management, biology, environmental studies, and psychology. The university offers these majors and minors: art, classics, drama, French, German, history, literature and language, music, philosophy, Spanish, atmospheric sciences, biology, chemistry, computer science, environmental studies, health & wellness promotion, mathematics, physics, economics, management, mass communication, multimedia arts, political science, psychology, sociology, accounting, industrial engineering, mechatronics engineering, and a 2+2 joint engineering degree with NC State University.

In addition to the above areas, minors are available in all majors plus: Africana studies, anthropology, art history, creative writing, dance, humanities, legal studies, religious studies and sports medicine. Special advising programs are available for pre-health and pre-law. A master of liberal arts program also is offered.

CAMPUS FACILITIES AND EQUIPMENT

The university's comprehensive high-speed fiber-optic network connects all campus computers to each other and the rest of the world via Internet. Allowing such innovations as student class registration on the Internet, the network ensures a capability-rich information technology environment that enhances teaching, learning, and the quality of campus life. Our completely wired campus provides extensive computing and networking resources to students, who are encouraged but not required to buy computers.

Notable campus facilities include two teleconference centers for distance learning, a renovated and expanded library, versatile 200-seat theatre, music recital halls, new state-of-the-art health and fitness center, new computer labs for the mass communication and multimedia programs, and the University botanical gardens. The Asheville Graduate Center, North Carolina Center for Creative Retirement and Key Center for Service-Learning benefit UNCA undergraduates and the people of the region.

Several of UNC Asheville's Academic Programs, including environmental studies and atmospheric sciences, enjoy cooperative relationships with agencies such as the National Climatic Data Center and U.S. Forest Service, whose offices are in Asheville. Students use the natural "laboratories" of nearby national parks and forests.

TUITION, ROOM, BOARD AND FEES

Tuition and fees for the 2007–08 academic year are about $4,165 for in-state students and $15,160 for out-of-state students. Estimated annual room and board costs total about $6,230 for both in-state and out-of-state residents. Single- or double-occupancy rooms in one of UNC Asheville's seven residence halls have an estimated annual average cost of about $3,450. The meal plans are $2,780, with Dining Hall service provided by Chartwell's.

FINANCIAL AID

Many UNC Asheville students receive need or merit-based scholarships, grants, loans and work-study positions. Full and partial merit awards are available, ranging from $500 to full scholarships at in-state tuition and fees costs. Awards are unified under the University Laurels Scholarships, given to high school seniors with high academic or artistic promise. Some merit scholarships are based on demonstrated financial need. UNCA participated in federal and state financial aid programs. Eligibility is determined from the Free Application for Federal Student Aid (FAFSA). Other scholarships include the North Carolina Teaching Fellowships and UNC Asheville's Leadership Scholarships. To learn more about scholarships, please call the Office of Admissions at 828-251-6481 or 1-800-531-9842.

STUDENT ORGANIZATIONS AND ACTIVITIES

Students may join about eighty clubs and interest groups, including a campus newspaper, theatre and musical performance groups, student activities board, departmental clubs and honor societies, Greek-letter sororities and fraternities, and an active Student Government Association. Of special note are the Outdoor and Recreation programs that take advantage of UNC Asheville's ideal Blue Ridge Mountain location. Outdoor trips for mountain biking, hiking, camping, rock climbing, and other activities are geared for both novices and experts. The new Health and Fitness Center is a hub of camps activity, offering state-of-the-art weight training equipment and indoor track and multipurpose courts. Intramurals, club sports and Division I NCAA athletic events are popular with students. Concerts, movies, comedy shows, lectures, art exhibitions, and entertainment of all types are part of the lineup throughout the year. The Cultural and special Events Committee brings nationally known performers to UNCA and the community.

Service learning is an important part of the UNC Asheville experience. Students are introduced to community service early in their careers. During orientation they participate in a community-wide service day, Bulldog Day: A Time of Service, when students work with area organizations such as Manna Food Bank, Habitat for Humanity, Big Brothers/Big Sisters, and others. Often the activities students begin on Bulldog Day continue throughout their years at UNCA. The Key Center for Service-Learning helps faculty and students integrate community service into the curriculum.

ADMISSIONS PROCESS

UNC Asheville is looking for students with diverse backgrounds who thrive on active learning. We believe this happens best on a campus where classes are small, faculty want the best from and for their students, and where there is opportunity for personal growth.

Please refer to the www.unca.edu/admissions for the current schedule of application deadlines and notification dates.

Admissions professionals review your application individually and evaluate how well your goals and strengths match our educational mission. Additionally, we look for students with a strong, academic high school curriculum with demonstrated achievement and ability to succeed; extra-curricular activities in school and the community, including athletics participation; honors, awards and special talents and skills; and travel and other experiences that support academic achievement.

In order to be considered for admission, all applicants must fulfill North Carolina's Minimum Course Requirements: high school diploma from a regionally accredited secondary school; four units of college preparatory English; four units of mathematics including Algebra I, Algebra II and Geometry, and an additional mathematics course beyond Algebra II; three units of science including one unit of biological science, one unit of physical science and one laboratory course; two units of social studies, including one unit of United States history; two units of a foreign language (recommended one unit taken in the 12th grade).

Transfer students should follow the regular application procedures and must have a 2.5 cumulative grade-point average from all colleges or universities previously attended. Additional information may be requested including an official high school transcript and standardized test scores.

Estimated cost for a full-time international student attending UNC Asheville for nine months is approximately $30,000. This includes tuition, fees, room, food, books, health insurance, at least one trip home and miscellaneous expenses. There are no UNC Asheville scholarships available to international students.

In order to study in the United States, UNC Asheville assists international students in obtaining a U.S. visa. The I-20 form required to obtain a student visa will be mailed to you with your acceptance letter. UNC Asheville cannot release this form to you until you have been accepted and the university has received a notarized Affidavit of Support and bank statement.

UNIVERSITY OF OREGON

AT A GLANCE

At the University of Oregon (UO), you'll live the university motto, which translates loosely as Minds Move Mountains. Whether you want to change a community, a law, or one person's mind, the UO will provide you with all the inspiration and resources you'll need to succeed.

You'll discover that many of the UO's 273 Academic Programs are internationally recognized for academic excellence. Chemistry, economics, English, psychology, molecular biology, biochemistry, physics, neuroscience, and sports marketing departments all rank among the top ten in the U. S. Programs in comparative literature, finance, historic preservation, and mathematics rank in the top twenty in the U.S.

Set in a 295-acre arboretum, the University of Oregon is quite literally green. Both academic and outdoor programs will bring you into contact with forests, mountains, rivers, and lakes. The world's first green chemistry teaching methods were developed by UO students and faculty. The Lillis Business Complex is the only green facility of a top-ranked business school world-wide. Nationally-recognized programs in sustainable business, architecture, and technology demonstrate the UO's ongoing commitment to the environment.

With a student-teacher ratio of 18:1 and an average class size of 22 students, you'll discover that it's easy to connect with faculty members and your peers. You'll also have all the resources of a major research university, with 273 comprehensive Academic Programs and more than 250 student organizations.

The UO was recognized by the American Council on Education as one of the nation's leaders in internationalization. You'll attend UO classes alongside students from all fifty states, four U.S. territories and eighty-four other countries and learn from people with religious, cultural, and ethnic heritages different from your own. You'll thrive as you learn to see the world differently.

LOCATION AND ENVIRONMENT

The UO is located in the center of Eugene (metropolitan area population 256,380), a classic college town that's small enough to bike across, but large enough to offer diverse art, music, and social venues. The Hult Center for the Performing Arts and the Grammy-winning Oregon Bach Festival lure a variety of nationally acclaimed musical acts each year. *Rolling Stone* named Eugene to its list of top ten college town music scenes.

Eugene is a great place for those who love the outdoors, and offers more than 100 city parks, 250 miles of bicycle trails, rock climbing areas, and beautiful public gardens, all within the city limits. Getting here is easy. Eugene is served by several major airlines and is on the main north-south Amtrak line that runs between Seattle and San Diego.

With 11 NCAA Division 1 teams, as well as 44 club sports, you'll have your choice of sports to play or teams to cheer. The excitement begins in the fall, when you'll root for Ducks' football team at Autzen Stadium. In the winter, the men's and women's basketball teams thrill the crowds at McArthur Court. In the spring, UO track stars compete at Hayward Field, often the site for NCAA championships and U.S. Olympic Track and Field Trials.

Four museums on campus are valuable resources in the sciences and visual arts. The Jordan Schnitzer Museum of Art offers exhibitions of classical and contemporary art. Three theaters offer students an opportunity to produce and perform. Films, lectures, and cultural events are an everyday part of campus life.

OFF-CAMPUS OPPORTUNITIES

The Career Center offers off-campus internships in fields related to your academic major or extracurricular interests. Both paid and volunteer internships are widely available to all majors. Global Graduates is an international program that provides academic credit while you gain career-related work experience through overseas internships.

The UO offers 190 overseas study programs in 84 countries. You'll experience the history, arts, social institutions, customs, and beliefs of a new culture, all while earning credit toward your UO degree.

Pine Mountain Observatory, near Bend, Oregon, offers study options in physics and astronomy. You can participate in an annual Archaeology Field School in central Oregon's Northern Great Basin. The Oregon Institute of Marine Biology on the Pacific coast gives you access to deep sea, coastal watershed, and estuary habitat.

Cooperatively run by students, the top-ranked Outdoor Program takes you beyond the campus to Oregon's great outdoors. You can choose from activities like snowboarding, skiing, rock climbing, hiking, surfing, white water rafting, and kayaking.

MAJORS AND DEGREES OFFERED

The 273 undergraduate academic majors, minors, certificates, and preparatory programs offered are:

School of Architecture and Allied Arts

Architecture, art, art history, ceramics, community arts, digital arts, fibers, historic preservation, interior architecture, landscape architecture, metalsmithing and jewelry, material and product studies, multimedia, nonprofit administration, painting, photography, planning, public policy, and management, printmaking, product design, sculpture, and visual design.

College of Arts and Sciences

African studies, anthropology, Asian studies, biochemistry, biology chemistry, Chinese, classical civilization, classics, clinical laboratory science-medical technology°, comparative literature, computer and information science, computer information technology, dentistry,° East Asian studies, economics, engineering,° English, environmental science, environmental studies, ethnic studies, European studies, film studies, folklore, forensic science,° French, general science, geography, geological sciences, German, German studies, Greek, health sciences,° history, humanities, human physiology, independent study, international studies, Italian, Japanese, Judaic studies, Latin, Latin American studies, law,° linguistics, marine biology, mathematics, mathematics and computer science, medicine,° medieval studies, nursing,° occupational therapy,° optometry,° peace studies, pharmacy,° philosophy, physical therapy,° physician assistant,° physics, podiatry,° political science, psychology, religious studies, Romance languages, Russian and East European studies, Scandinavian, second-language acquisition and teaching, social work,° sociology, Southeast Asian studies, Spanish, theater arts, veterinary medicine,° women's and gender studies.

Charles H. Lundquist College of Business

Accounting, business administration with concentrations in entrepreneurship, finance, information systems and operations, management, marketing, and sports business, global management.

College of Education

Communication disorders and sciences, educational studies, family and human services, special education, teacher education.°

School of Journalism and Communication

Communication studies, journalism, journalism: advertising, journalism: communication studies, journalism: electronic media, journalism: magazine, journalism: news-editorial, and journalism: public relations.

School of Music

Dance, music, music composition, music education, music education: elementary education, music: jazz studies, and music performance.

An ° denotes preparatory programs.

ACADEMIC PROGRAMS

You'll spend about one third of your UO education on each of three areas of course work: the general education requirements, requirements for your major, and elective credit. The university is on a quarter system.

First-year Interest Groups (FIGs) bring together a small group of freshmen interested in the same academic area in three related courses. Freshman Seminars are small-group discussion courses taught by some of the University's most outstanding faculty members.

Architecture

The UO architecture department is ranked 11th in the nation by *Design Intelligence* magazine.

Arts and Sciences

The faculty of the College of Arts and Sciences ranks fifteenth nationally, according to the Graham-Diamond Report.

Business

The Lundquist College of Business is ranked 1st in Oregon, 2nd in the NW , and 17th nationally (U.S. News and World Reports).

Education

The UO's College of Education is ranked 3rd in the U.S. for special education and 6th among public colleges overall (U.S. News and World Reports. It is the only top-tier college of education in the Pacific Northwest.

Journalism and Communication

The UO's School of Journalism and Communication is ranked among the top 25 in the nation.

Music and Dance

The UO School of Music and Dance is the only comprehensive school of music in Oregon.

CAMPUS FACILITIES AND EQUIPMENT

The University of Oregon Library System is the second largest in the Pacific Northwest. You'll find more than two million volumes and more than 17,000 journals.

Wireless internet connection is available in the majority of UO buildings and computer labs are open in the library, residence halls, and in academic facilities across campus.

Science facilities at the UO are among the best in the nation. Research and laboratory courses offer students firsthand experience with electron microscopes and microprobes, advanced optical microscopy, seismic array, and atomic absorption and emissions.

TUITION, ROOM, BOARD AND FEES

Resident: Undergraduate tuition and fees for the 2007-08 academic year were $6,174. On-campus residence halls, including room and board, $7,848 per academic year for double occupancy. Books and supplies, $900. Personal expenses, $2,376. Total, $17,298.

Nonresident: Undergraduate tuition and fees for the 2007-08 academic year were, $19,388. On-campus residence halls, including room and board, $7,848 per academic year for double occupancy. Books and supplies, $900. Personal expenses, $2,376. Total, $30,512.

FINANCIAL AID

The UO makes a concerted effort to enable you to attend the UO regardless of your family's income. Financial Aid in the form of grants, loans, and employment is available to qualifying students. More than 65% of our students receive scholarships that are awarded through the university, academic departments, and private sources.

Eligibility information

To apply for Financial Aid, you must file the Free Application for Federal Student Aid (FAFSA) in early February. The UO's federal school code is 003223.

Scholarship application deadline: January 15, 2009 (postmark) for the following fall term.

• All required materials must be postmarked by January 15, 2009

• Submit admission materials, transcripts, SAT or ACT scores, and application fee to the Office of Admissions

• Submit scholarship application and essays to the Office of Student Financial Aid and Scholarships

Competition for scholarships is very strong. Unless exceptional circumstances exist, applicants must have minimum GPAs of 3.50. For scholarship applications and eligibility requirements, visit financialaid.uoregon.edu.

Dean's Scholarships

These scholarships are awarded each year to academically successful entering freshmen and range from $1,000 to $6,000 per year.

General University, Laurel, and Presidential Scholarships

For the 2007-08 school year, more than 1,000 students were offered these scholarships, which ranged from $1000 to $6,500.

Diversity-Building Scholarships (DBS)

DBS awards are tuition-remission scholarships with awards ranging from partial to full tuition and fee waivers.

Staton Scholarships

These $5,000 scholarships, renewable for up to four years, are awarded each year to incoming Oregon students with extraordinary financial need.

Western Undergraduate Exchange (WUE)

WUE offers selected freshmen from certain western states the opportunity to study at the University of Oregon for 150 percent of UO resident tuition.

STUDENT ORGANIZATIONS AND ACTIVITIES

The Associated Student of University of Oregon offers more than 250 student organizations, including cultural organizations, fraternities and sororities, student government, campus ministries, political groups, performing arts groups, international student clubs, and honor societies. Learn more at asuo.uoregon.edu.

The UO Student Vote Coalition led the nation in registering student voters in each of the past three presidential elections. The UO also ranks 11th in the nation for current Peace Corps volunteers.

ADMISSIONS PROCESS

The early notification deadline for fall 2009 is November 1, 2008. The standard admission deadline for fall 2009 is January 15, 2009. To be eligible for freshman admission, you must have a high school GPA of at least 3.00, be a graduate of a standard or accredited high school, and submit SAT or ACT scores. A cumulative GPA of 3.25 or better on a 4.00 scale and completion of at least sixteen units of academic course work qualifies you for guaranteed admission.

We require the following college-preparatory courses: Four years of English in preparatory composition and literature; three years of mathematics including first-year algebra and two additional years of college-preparatory mathematics; two years of science in such areas as biology, chemistry or physics; and three years of Social science which could include one year of U.S. history, one year of global studies such as world history or geography, and one elective. Two years of the same second-language in high school or two college terms of the same second language are also required.

Other factors considered for admission include the strength of high school coursework, grade trend, class rank, and senior-year course load. Academic potential and special talents are also considered.

To apply, submit a completed application for admission, transcripts, SAT or ACT scores and nonrefundable $50 application fee to the Office of Admissions.

For information and an application, contact:

Office of Admissions

1217 University of Oregon

Eugene, OR 97403-1217]

United States

Phone: 541-346-3201

Toll-free: 800-BE-A-DUCK

Website: http://admissions.uoregon.edu

School Says . . .

UNIVERSITY OF ROCHESTER

AT A GLANCE

Founded in 1850, the University of Rochester is one of 63 member schools of the eminent Association of American Universities. It is also one of the eight members of the University Athletic Association, a consortium of national research institutions that share a unique approach to academics and athletics.

Rochester's moderate size and the range of its academic and research programs allow for both individual attention and uncommon flexibility in designing undergraduate studies.

LOCATION AND ENVIRONMENT

The University is located in Rochester, NY, the third largest urban area in the state. The region is home to over one million people. The 85-acre River Campus is situated just two miles south of downtown Rochester, along the Genesee River. The Medical Center, the South Campus, and the Mt. Hope Campus are located nearby. The University's renowned Eastman School of Music and the Memorial Art Gallery are a free 10-minute bus ride away in downtown Rochester.

Roughly 4,600 undergraduates and 2,900 graduate students attend the University of Rochester.

Eighty-six percent of undergraduates in the College of Arts, Sciences, and Engineering live and take classes on the River Campus.

OFF-CAMPUS OPPORTUNITIES

With Lake Ontario on its northern border, and the scenic Finger Lakes to the south, Rochester has been rated among the most livable cities in the United States. *Places Rated Almanac 2007* named Rochester the 6th best out of 343 metropolitan areas in the U.S. and Canada. Rochester offers a wide range of cultural and recreational opportunities through its museums, parks, orchestras, theater companies, and professional sports teams.

MAJORS AND DEGREES OFFERED

The University of Rochester offers Bachelor of Arts and/or Bachelor of Science programs through the College: available majors include African and African-American Studies, American Sign Language, anthropology, art history, biological sciences (biochemistry, cell and developmental biology, ecology and evolutionary biology, microbiology, molecular genetics, or neuroscience), biology, brain and cognitive sciences, chemistry, classics, comparative literature, computer science, economics, English, environmental science, environmental studies, film and media studies, financial economics, economics and business strategies, French, geological sciences, geomechanics, German, health and society, history, interdepartmental studies, international relations, Japanese, linguistics, mathematics, mathematics-applied, mathematics-statistics, music, philosophy, physics, physics and astronomy, political science, psychology, public health, religion and classics, Russian, Russian studies, Spanish, statistics, studio arts, visual and cultural studies, and women's studies.

The School of Engineering and Applied Sciences offers study in biomedical engineering, chemical engineering, electrical and computer engineering, mechanical engineering, geomechanics, optics, engineering and applied sciences, and engineering science.
Rochester not only offers a Bachelor of Arts in music through the College, but also a Bachelor of Music degree through the Eastman School of Music; available majors include applied music, jazz studies and contemporary media, music composition, music education, and music theory. Private instruction through the Eastman School is available to students in the College.

The College offers certificate programs in actuarial studies, Asian studies, biotechnology, international relations, literary translation studies, management studies, and Polish and Central European studies. These programs complement traditional majors.

ACADEMIC PROGRAMS

The Rochester Curriculum is driven by students. There are no required subjects. Undergraduates take responsibility and build their education out of their own interests, goals, and aspirations. At Rochester, students are invited to learn what they love. The unique curriculum allows undergraduates to choose their major from among the three branches of learning – natural sciences, social sciences, and humanities – and take a cluster of three related courses in each of the other two.

Rochester's distinctive Quest courses offer freshmen the benefits of small classes, mentorship and collaboration, and the opportunity to conduct original research. Students learn the value and skills of independent study through Quest courses, a lesson that serves them both during their undergraduate careers and after.

Through the "Take Five" Scholars Program, selected students may undertake a tuition-free fifth year so that they may pursue their diverse interests.

Exceptional undergraduates interested in studying medicine, business, or education may pursue one of the following combined degree programs, upon successful completion of undergraduate studies:

• Rochester Early Medical Scholars (REMS) program, an eight-year BA/BS–MD program. Admitted students enter the University with a guarantee of admission to the School of Medicine and Dentistry.

• Rochester Early Business Scholars (REBS) program, a six-year BA/BS–MBA program. Admitted students enter the University with a guarantee of admission to the William E. Simon School of Business Administration.

• Guaranteed Rochester Accelerated Degree in Education (GRADE), a five-year BA/BA–MS program. Admitted students enter the University with a guarantee of admission to the Margaret Warner Graduate School of Education.

Rochester students may take advantage of full-year and semester-long opportunities for study abroad; summer and winter trips are also available. In all, Rochester offers more than 60 study abroad programs. Destinations include Australia, Austria, Belgium, China, Egypt, France, Germany, Ireland, Italy, Japan, Mexico, Poland, Russia, Spain, Sweden, and Taiwan. Internships are available in Brussels, London, Paris, Berlin, Bonn, and Madrid.

For those interested in an exciting and enlightening domestic field experience, the Department of Political Science directs the Washington Semester Program; this program allows selected undergraduates to participate actively in the national legislative process.

CAMPUS FACILITIES AND EQUIPMENT

The University's Laboratory for Laser Energetics houses the 60-beam OMEGA laser, the world's most powerful fusion laser. The Medical Center includes Strong Memorial Hospital, the James P. Wilmot Cancer Center, and the Golisano Children's Hospital. Resources in downtown Rochester include the Memorial Art Gallery, Eastman Theatre, and the Sibley Music Library – the largest academic music library in North America. The River Campus is home to the Frederick Douglass Institute for African and African-American Studies, the Susan B. Anthony Institute for Gender and Women's Studies, and the M.K. Gandhi Institute for Nonviolence. Additional campus facilities include a virtual reality lab, optics institute, observatory, and an 11,000 square-foot athletic center.

TUITION, ROOM, BOARD, AND FEES

In 2007–08, tuition and fees cost $35,190; room and board averaged $10,640; and books, transportation, and other expenses averaged $2,320.

FINANCIAL AID

Academic merit scholarships, loans, grants, tuition payment plans, and part-time jobs all contribute to the University of Rochester's strong financial assistance program. Those applying for financial aid should submit both the Free Application for Federal Student Aid (FAFSA) and the College Scholarship Service (CSS) PROFILE application.

Merit scholarships are awarded to eligible incoming undergraduate students. Candidates are considered based upon their application for admissions, reviewing academic performance, involvement, and leadership. Although separate applications are not required, students should be aware of earlier deadlines that may apply. Merit scholarships are awarded regardless of financial need. Information on specific scholarship programs is available at www.enrollment.rochester.edu/admissions.

STUDENT ORGANIZATIONS AND ACTIVITIES

With more than 220 student organizations, ranging from cultural and political to religious and athletic, students at Rochester can easily find communities of friends who share their interests and passions. When it's time for recreation, Rochester students flock to the Goergen Athletic Center. The Center includes an 11,000 square-foot fitness facility; an indoor track and activity field; a swimming pool and diving well; numerous courts for basketball, indoor tennis, racquetball, squash, and volleyball; a state-of-the-art athletic training facility; and the Palestra, home for 22 Division III varsity teams and host to various campus events.

ADMISSIONS PROCESS

The University of Rochester seeks to admit students who will take advantage of its resources, be strongly motivated to do their best, and contribute to the life of the University community. An applicant's character, extracurricular activities, job experience, academic accomplishments, and career goals are considered. More than three quarters of last year's enrolled students ranked in the top tenth of their secondary school classes. The University accepts the Common Application. An electronic online application is available from the University's Web site. Applicants for freshman admission are required to submit scores from either the SAT or the ACT. An interview is recommended. SAT Subject Test results are reviewed, but not required.

The recommended application filing date for freshman applicants is January 1 for fall admission and October 1 for spring. An early decision plan is available. The deadline for Early Decision applications is November 1; applicants are notified in December.

The University welcomes applications from transfer students for either semester. The application deadline is June 1 for the fall semester, and November 1 for spring enrollment.

UNIVERSITY OF SAN FRANCISCO

AT A GLANCE

When the Jesuits founded the University of San Francisco in 1855, it was a one-room schoolhouse. Now, it is one of the West Coast's largest Catholic universities. Some things haven't changed: class size is still small, and student/faculty ratio is still low. USF has been dedicated to helping students learn the skills they need to improve their world for over 150 years. USF's Jesuit education is committed to providing all students with individual attention. Both love of learning and the willingness to face the challenge of serving society are fostered in programs in the arts, the sciences, business, education, nursing, and law.

San Francisco itself is a laboratory for students. The city and its university have interconnected histories, and today, this vibrant partnership gives students the wonderful opportunity to bring classroom theory into real, twenty-first-century life. There are 4,793 undergraduates on the 54-acre residential campus, and these students come from all 50 states and 76 countries. All students under the age of 21 and within two years of graduation must live on campus unless they have permanent residence within thirty miles of the university. Students have access to facilities including libraries, a health and recreation center with an Olympic-size swimming pool, a coffeehouse, and several dining areas. Right outside is the city of San Francisco and it has "facilities" of its own: the ballet, opera, museum exhibits, concerts, theater, and sports events. In addition, students have the opportunity to live with their peers in a cozy, laid-back environment within the residence halls. There are traditional residence halls and also University apartment-style facilities on campus. Both Hayes-Healy and Gillson Hall are for freshmen students. Sophomores are assigned to live in Phelan Hall while most of the upperclassmen live in Lone Mountain Hall and Loyola Village. Double rooms are standard, but there are a few single rooms for upperclassmen. There are laundry facilities, study/computer rooms, and television lounges in every residence hall. Most floors in each dormitory also contain a community kitchen.

There are several dining facilities on campus that are convenient to the residence halls and classrooms. The Market has a dining environment similar to a food court with options for vegetarians and those who only consume organic foods. Other selections include a student-run coffeehouse, Jamba Juice, and a convenient store/cafe.

There are over 80 student-run associations for undergraduates at USF, including culturally focused clubs, leadership and community service organizations, honor and professional societies and club sports and intramural programs. These associations include the oldest continuously performing theater group west of the Mississippi River: The College Players, an award-winning FM radio station, a weekly newspaper, and a literary magazine. The Career Services Center is one of the most active offices, aiding students in choosing a career path and learning about employment and internship opportunities. The exciting Koret Health and Recreation Center offers facilities for exercise, racquetball, swimming, court games, and socializing.

There are graduate programs in the arts and sciences, business, education, law, and nursing.

LOCATION AND ENVIRONMENT

The beautiful University of San Francisco campus is 54 acres, and is located in a residential neighborhood. Downtown San Francisco and the Pacific Ocean are just minutes away, and the 1,000-acre Golden Gate Park is only a few blocks away. There are many benefits of an urban campus, and San Francisco's diversity and compact geography allow students to discover research facilities, community involvement options, and work opportunities found in few other cities.

OFF-CAMPUS OPPORTUNITIES

USF students have many opportunities for university-sponsored study abroad programs, such as ones to Sophia University (Tokyo), Oxford (England), and Innsbruck (Austria), through USF's St. Ignatius Institute, a program at Universidad Iberoamericana in Mexico City, and a joint program with Hungary's Péter Pázmány Catholic University in Budapest. USF is connected to Gonzaga University's study abroad program in Florence (Italy) and to Loyola University of Chicago's program in Rome. The Institute of European and Asian Studies, of which USF is an associate member, offers programs in Durham and London, England; Paris, Dijon, and Nantes, France; Berlin and Freiburg, Germany; Vienna, Austria; Madrid and Salamanca, Spain; Milan, Italy; Tokyo and Nagoya, Japan; Moscow, Russia; Adelaide and Canberra, Australia; Beijing, China; and Singapore. There are many other study abroad opportunities as well. Students receive assistance from USF in all aspects of the program: choosing a location, completing applications, arranging financial matters, registering for academic credit, obtaining a passport and visa, and organizing travel plans.

MAJORS AND DEGREES OFFERED

BA and BS degrees are available through USF. The College of Arts and Sciences offers majors in Architecture and Community Design, Arts History/Arts Management, Asia Pacific Studies, Asian Studies, Biology, Chemistry, Communication studies, Comparative Literature and Culture, Computer Science, Economics, Engineering 3/2, English, Environmental Science, Environmental Studies, Exercise and Sports Science, Fine Arts, French, Graphic Design, History, Latin American studies, Mathematics, Media Studies, Performing Arts and Social Justice, Philosophy, Physics, Politics, Pre-Professional Health Studies, Psychology, Sociology, Spanish, Theology and Religious Studies, undeclared arts/science, and Visual Arts. The McLaren College of Business offers degrees in Accounting, Business Administration, Entrepreneurship, Finance, Hospitality Industry Management, International Business, Management, and Marketing. Qualified high school graduates and second-baccalaureate candidates can pursue a four-year baccalaureate program through the School of Nursing. Students can receive teacher certification at the elementary or secondary level by completing a fifth year of study.

The Pre-Professional Health Committee at USF advises and recommends students to medical and dental professional health schools, as well as to schools for pharmacy, optometry, veterinary medicine, and podiatry. The pre-medical or other pre-health science requirements can be taken as part of, or in addition to, the requirements of an academic major. The Pre-Professional Health Committee helps students with the application process, creates a professional file for each student, gathers and sends recommendations to professional schools, gives interviews in preparation for application, and endorses approved candidates through a committee letter of recommendation that is sent to all professional schools the student selects.

ACADEMIC PROGRAMS

It is hoped that students leave USF with a well-rounded education with a focus and awareness of social justice. A curriculum of 128 units is required for the degree. General education from six particular categories of knowledge make up 51 units of the curriculum, including a nine-unit block of basic skills courses and 80 to 83 units divided between major requirements and electives. Superior students may be selected for an honors program that provides a high academic challenge.

USF urges qualified high school students to study subjects traditionally reserved for colleges as early as possible. To this end, advanced placement courses, as certified by the College Board's Advanced Placement Program tests, are honored. USF also cooperates with the College-Level Examination Program (CLEP). Students interested in obtaining this credit are required to take the CLEP tests before registering for their freshman courses.

A special program is available through the St. Ignatius Institute. The institute has a core curriculum that is based on the Western civilization's great books, with an emphasis on the great works of Christianity. General education course requirements can be met through courses at the institute, no matter what the student's major. Army ROTC is also available at USF, and qualified applicants and continuing students have access to ROTC scholarships.

Two semesters make up the academic year, and there are also summer sessions and a January intersession.

CAMPUS FACILITIES AND EQUIPMENT

USF students enjoy access to the more than 700,000 volumes at Gleeson Library and to the Computer Center, the Applied Math Laboratory, the Institute of Chemical Biology, and the Physics Research Laboratories, all in the Harney Science Center. The Instructional Media Center is located in Cowell Hall, along with the home base of nursing classes and the Nursing Skills Laboratory. KDNZ and KUSF, the University's AM and FM radio stations, make their home in Phelan Hall. The Headquarters for the McLaren College of Business is Malloy Hall, which also holds an additional computer laboratory and special seminar rooms.

TUITION, ROOM, BOARD AND FEES

Tuition for the 2007-2008 school year is $30,840. Room and board are $10,730 for the academic year. An additional $4,210 per year is generally required for books, fees, travel, and other expenses.

FINANCIAL AID

Many scholarships, grants, loans, and work-study programs are available for USF students, and all students must submit the Free Application for Federal Student Aid (FAFSA). Over two-thirds of all University students receive some form of financial assistance. Students have access to many jobs both on and off campus.

New freshman applicants with a minimum cumulative grade point average of 3.8 and a combined SAT I score of 1320 (Critical Reading + Math sections only) or an ACT composite score of 30 can participate in the University Scholars Program. University Scholars receive a non-need-based scholarship that covers a large portion of tuition costs for four years of undergraduate work. Scholars must maintain a GPA of 3.25 to remain eligible. Students eligible for University Scholars are identified during the Admission Process, and interested students must apply for admission by the November 15 early action deadline.

STUDENT ORGANIZATIONS AND ACTIVITIES

Every undergraduate student is a member of the Associated Students of the University of San Francisco (ASUSF). There are three purposes to the ASUSF: to represent the official student viewpoint, to recommend policies, and to fund activities and services. There are three branches: the executive branch, the Student Senate, and the Student Court. The main representative body of the undergraduate day students is the Senate, and it monitors the expenditures of the $200,000-plus student budget.

USF offers over 80 different clubs and organizations. They give students opportunities to be involved in leadership and professional organizations, honor societies, culturally focused clubs, fraternities and sororities, club sports and intramurals.

ADMISSIONS PROCESS

Students with a desire to obtain a well-rounded education are sought after by USF. Admission is selective, and each application receives an individual review. USF desires a high-quality and diverse student body, and so encourages applications from men and women of all races, nationalities, and religious beliefs. Prospective students are evaluated on many criteria, including high school grade point average, the application essay, a personal recommendation, and satisfactory test scores. All applicants must take the SAT I or the ACT, and international applicants must take the TOEFL. A completed application file is made up of the application form, an essay, all academic transcripts, SAT I or ACT scores, and one letter of recommendation. For the fall semester, November 15 is the deadline for early action and January 15 is the deadline for regular action.

For additional information, please contact:

Office of Admission

University of San Francisco

2130 Fulton Street

San Francisco, CA 94117-1046

Telephone: 415-422-6563

800-CALL-USF (toll free outside California)

Fax: 415-422-2217

E-mail: admission@usfca.edu

World Wide Web: www.usfca.edu

THE UNIVERSITY OF SCRANTON

AT A GLANCE

A Jesuit university in Pennsylvania's Pocono northeast region, The University of Scranton is known for many things, especially its outstanding academics, state-of-the art campus and technology, and exceptional sense of community. Founded in 1888, the University offers more than 80 undergraduate and graduate Academic Programs of study through four colleges and schools.

For 14 consecutive years, *U.S. News & World Report* has ranked Scranton among the 10 finest master's universities in the North—10th in the 2008 edition. For the past four years, Scranton has been listed among the *U.S. News* selections of Universities-Masters in the North in the category "Great Schools at a Great Price," a ranking that relates academic quality to the cost of attendance. For the past six years, The Princeton Review has included Scranton among its "366 Best Colleges."

For the third consecutive year, Scranton's Kania School of Management has been included among the elite colleges listed in the Princeton Review's "Best 290 Business Schools." Scranton is also the only college in Northeastern Pennsylvania to be listed in Kaplan/*Newsweek's* publication *How to Get into College*, which included Scranton as one of the nation's "372 Most Interesting Schools." Scranton was listed among the 247 colleges in the nation included in the ninth edition of Barron's "Best Buys in College Education." Only 19 schools in Pennsylvania were listed.

Of the 319 senior applicants to medical schools over the last eight years, an average of 81% were accepted. In addition to senior applicants, 102 alumni, graduate students and post-baccalaureate students applied to health-professions schools between 2000 and 2007; 79 of these individuals (77%) gained acceptance to health professions doctoral programs. Well over half of successful applicants in the past eight years have received more than one acceptance. From 2003 - 2006, over 200 Scranton graduates have received acceptance into law schools from over 65 schools, including some of the nation's most prestigious. These include the University of California at Berkeley, Boston College, Cornell University, Duke University, Fordham University, Georgetown University, New York University, the University of Notre Dame and the University of Pennsylvania.

Since 1972, students have received 117 Fulbrights and other prestigious fellowships. In the past five years alone, students earned four Truman Scholarships and six Goldwater Scholarships. Five students were also named to USA Today's All-USA Academic Team. In 2006, Scranton was the only college in Pennsylvania and the only Jesuit university in the United States to have a student among the 20 in the nation listed on the first academic team.

Scranton has always had high rates of both graduation and retention. The University's average fall-to-fall freshman retention rate is 90.4%. The average rate, nationally, for selective Bachelor's/Master's institutions is 80%. Its five-year graduation rate averages 79%. The average rate, nationally, for selective Bachelor's/Master's Institutions is 64%.

Its average five-year graduation rate is 79%. The national average for selective Bachelor's/Master's Institutions is 64%.

LOCATION AND ENVIRONMENT

Easily reached by major highways, The University of Scranton is about two hours from New York City, Philadelphia, Syracuse, and Danbury (Connecticut) and only about four hours from Baltimore and Washington. An urban campus, The University of Scranton offers all of the opportunities of a city location. Students can also take advantage of the University's Conference and Retreat Center at Chapman Lake, just 25 minutes from campus. One visit to our 56-acre campus is enough to experience the friendliness and enthusiasm that is the cornerstone of the Scranton community.

Located in the City of Scranton (population 70,000), The University of Scranton is within walking distance of internships, cultural opportunities, a downtown mall, movie theater, and the Steamtown National Historic Site. Students can intern at one of three hospitals within a mile of campus, law offices, businesses, local television stations and newspapers, service agencies and other organizations.

Just a 10-minute drive away is Snow Mountain with its winter ski area and snow tubing park, as well as the Toyota Pavilion at Montage Mountain concert amphitheater. The nearby 12,000-seat Lackawanna County Stadium is home to the Scranton/Wilkes-Barre Yankees, the AAA franchise of the New York Yankees. The Wachovia Arena, just 15 minutes away from Montage, offers national concert tours, arena football and professional ice hockey featuring a minor-league affiliate of the Pittsburgh Penguins. Other attractions include the Pocono Motor Speedway, Elk Mountain ski resort, several state parks, and two museums.

MAJORS AND DEGREES OFFERED

Accounting; Accounting Information Systems; Biochemistry ; Biochemistry, Cell and Molecular Biology; Biology; Biomathematics; Biophysics; Business Administration; Chemistry; Chemistry/Business; Chemistry/Computers; Classical Languages; Communication; Community Health Education; Computer Engineering; Computer Information Systems; Computer Science; Counseling and Human Services ; Criminal Justice; Early Childhood/Special Education; Economics (Business); Economics (Social Science); Electrical Engineering; Electronic Commerce; Electronics/Business; Elementary/Early Childhood Education; Elementary/Special Education; English; Environmental Science; Exercise Science; Finance; Forensic Chemistry; French ; German; Gerontology; Health Administration; History; Human Resources Studies; International Business; International Language/Business; International Studies; Management; Marketing; Mathematics; Media and Information Technology; Medical Technology; Military Science; Modern Languages; Neuroscience; Nursing; Occupational Therapy; Operations Management; Philosophy; Physical Therapy (D.P.T.); Physics; Political Science; Pre-Engineering ; Pre-Law; Pre-Medical; Psychology; Secondary Education; Sociology; Spanish; Special Education; Theatre; Theology/Religious Studies

Applicants are allowed to enroll as undecided and choose a major in their sophomore year.

ACADEMIC PROGRAMS

We offer a full range of undergraduate programs of study to match your interests and prepare you to meet the future with confidence.

The newest additions to the University's 60 undergraduate majors include forensic chemistry, community health education, business administration, and biochemistry, cell and molecular biology. Scranton also offers 44 minors, 31 concentrations and tracks, 22 master's degree programs and a doctor of physical therapy program.

You can choose our highly successful pre-law and pre-medical programs. You can even enhance study in a particular field through double majors, bachelor's/master's degree combinations, ROTC, foreign study, internships, clinicals, research, and three programs of advanced study.

Each year we select between 50 and 60 of the most qualified freshmen to join the Special Jesuit Liberal Arts Program (SJLA), a program that allows them to fulfill their general education credits in a community atmosphere encouraging excellence and service to others.

Open to all majors, the Honors Program each year accepts between 40 and 50 of our most able sophomores, giving them the opportunity to take seminars together and to work one-on-one with professors both in tutorials and on projects.

Open to students from all majors, our Business Leadership Program helps students develop the talents and skills necessary to succeed in a variety of leadership settings, especially in the world of business. This highly selective program accepts 15 sophomores each spring to explore basic theories and concepts of leadership through special seminars and courses in management, ethics, strategy, and analysis.

The Office of Fellowship Programs builds on Scranton's remarkable success in securing Fulbrights by supporting students who wish to compete for the nation's other top fellowships and scholarships.

CAMPUS FACILITIES AND EQUIPMENT

The university is in the midst of more than $60 million in campus improvements. Scranton has built 25 new buildings and renovated 38 others since 1984. The new Patrick & Margaret DeNaples Center, a $35 million, 118,000 square-foot campus center, opened in January 2008. The four-story DeNaples Center provides dining and meeting space for students, as well as rooms for community events. Key features of the building are a grand lobby, Starbucks, Chick-fil-A and Quiznos, and a main dining area featuring the innovative "Fresh Food Company," where food is prepared right in front of you. The building also offers a fireplace lounge, student forum for clubs and activities, a theater and a ballroom that accommodates more than 400 for dinner and 200 for lectures.

Construction is also underway on Christopher & Margaret Condron Hall, a 386-bed suite-style residence hall scheduled to open for the fall 2008 semester.

TUITION, ROOM, BOARD AND FEES

Annual tuition for the 2007-2008 academic year is $28,458, with mandatory fees of $300. Room Charges range from $6,256 to $7,276. Meal plans range from $3,068 to $4,354.

FINANCIAL AID

Financial Aid assists about 91 percent of freshman, and includes scholarships, grants, loans and work-study. There are full- and partial-tuition academic scholarships available, which are awarded on a merit basis, taking into consideration high academic achievement and extracurricular activities. The University also offers a special Arrupe Scholarship for academically qualified minority students and a Claver Award for those who have demonstrated financial need.

STUDENT ORGANIZATIONS AND ACTIVITIES

Because learning does not stop at the classroom door, we provide opportunities to participate in an array of social, educational, wellness, and retreat activities.

You will be able to participate in more than 75 clubs and organizations. If your interests are journalism or writing you can become involved in *The Aquinas* (student newspaper), *Esprit* (literary journal), *Windhover* (yearbook), or Royal Network News (campus electronic news). You can become active in the arts through the University Players, University Bands and University Singers. You can develop as a leader through student government or explore politics with the Campus Democrats and College Republicans. You can even choose clubs that link to academic majors or that celebrate ethnic and cultural roots. And you can experience the satisfaction of helping others through Students for Social Justice, Habitat for Humanity, and the Community Outreach Office.

Scranton fields NCAA Division III varsity teams in 10 sports for men and nine sports for women. The University is affiliated with the National Collegiate Athletic Association, the Middle Atlantic States Collegiate Athletic Conferences, Freedom Conference and Eastern Collegiate Athletic Conference. In addition, more than 3,000 students each year participate in leagues, weekend special events and tournaments through the Intra-mural and Recreation Program.

ADMISSIONS PROCESS

Scranton welcomes men and women of all races, national origins, and religious beliefs. We look for high-achieving students who have shown that they are prepared for a challenging college program through their high school course selection and level, grades, class rank, and SAT/ACT scores. Also important are involvement in activities, athletics, and service, and work experience. Physical therapy and occupational therapy students must submit documentation of experience in their field. A campus visit with an informational interview or small group presentation is encouraged.

The University of Scranton offers an Early Action program with a November 15 deadline. Students who apply early will receive notification of admission on December 15. The application deadline for students interested in applying for the physical therapy program is January 15. For students who choose not to apply for Early Action, we operate on a rolling admissions basis, with an application deadline of March 1 and a confirmation deadline of May 1.

UNIVERSITY OF SOUTH FLORIDA

AT A GLANCE

The University of South Florida is a place where the unforgettable is part of the everyday — where intellectual, social and professional growth is the norm. With more than 45,000 students, USF is among America's largest and most dynamic national research universities. Located in the beautiful Tampa Bay region of Florida's Gulf Coast, USF offers nearly 200 degree programs at the bachelor's, masters, specialist and doctoral level, including the doctor of medicine. Undergraduate programs are offered in the Colleges of Arts and Sciences, Business, Education, Engineering, Visual and Performing Arts and Nursing.

USF creates a dynamic learning environment where students actively participate in the discovery of new knowledge. The university's faculty are world-class scholars and dedicated teachers who often provide research opportunities to undergraduates, including freshmen. With a 19:1 student to faculty ratio and a freshman class average of 37 students, USF students work side-by-side with professors in a dynamic learning environment as active participate in the discovery of new knowledge.

USF is nationally recognized for its diverse student body and is ranked in the top 20 on the Diverse Student Population List for the last three years by The Princeton Review's The Best 361 Colleges. USF students come from every state in the U.S. and more than 125 countries around the world, and more than a third of USF undergraduate students are African American, Black, Asian American, Hispanic or Native American.

While USF's main research campus is located in Tampa, more than 11,000 students study at our three regional campuses located in Lakeland, St. Petersburg, and Sarasota-Manatee. Our regional campuses offer the atmosphere of a small college coupled with the resources and prestige of one of the country's fastest-growing research universities.

USF is accredited by the Commission on Colleges of the Southern Association of Colleges and Schools. In addition, a number of scientific, professional, and academic bodies confer accreditation in specific disciplines and groups of disciplines.

LOCATION AND ENVIRONMENT

In addition to the cultural and recreational opportunities afforded by the university's residential campus, USF students benefit from myriad internship and employment options available in Tampa. The thriving metropolitan area is nationally recognized as a hub for cutting-edge technology and economic growth, as Tampa houses 60 percent of Florida's high-technology corridor and has been ranked by Forbes Magazine as "15th Best in the Nation for Business and Careers."

While the Tampa area has hot professional contacts, its proximity to theme parks and the nation's top beaches is a popular choice for many USF students. The Tampa Bay region also offers a wealth of arts and leisure activities, a professional orchestra, Broadway theatrical series, world-class concert halls, art museums, big-city nightlife, and professional sports teams. The Gulf beaches are less than an hour from campus, with Atlantic Ocean beaches only two hours away.

OFF-CAMPUS OPPORTUNITIES

USF offers many options to add an international dimension to a degree program: study abroad and exchange programs, international internships, service learning, and dual degree programs are available in many different countries on at least six continents.

Off campus opportunities, such as internships and part-time jobs, can be explored through the Career Center, which helps students plan, identify, refine and implement their career goals and job search campaign; provides current information on employment opportunities and labor market trends; creates venues that allow students to network and interview with hiring employers; and fosters and maintains active partnerships with academic departments to ensure seamless referrals between the Career Center, the academic community and employers.

MAJORS AND DEGREES OFFERED

As one of America's top metropolitan research universities, USF offers world-class Academic Programs. USF has more than 200 majors and programs in its 13 colleges and schools, ranging from engineering to education, criminal justice, anthropology, biochemistry and geology, business and music, to name but a few. USF offers students a well-rounded education through a core curriculum of general education and liberal arts requirements.

The Honors College, University Experience and TAPS (Tracking the Academic Progress of Students) are programs that help students broaden their horizons, expand their critical thinking skills and receive proactive academic advising partnered with career focus.

The University also features the Joint Military Science Center which represents a unique, national leadership development model that supplements and strengthens the intellectual and pedagogical expertise of a major, public research university and a strong Air Force, Army and Naval Reserve Officer Training Corps (ROTC) tradition. For students interested in pursuing medical careers and advanced education, numerous internship and volunteer opportunities abound at the four hospitals located on campus.

ACADEMIC PROGRAMS

The Honors College at USF is an extraordinary environment that nurtures exceptional students' talents and pushes them to live up to their tremendous potential.

The Honors College at USF offers the only undergraduate research major in the country, a unique course of study that is based on the Ph.D. model. Students in the Honors Research Major spend an intensive year-and-a-half working with senior faculty members on individualized research projects.

For students who plan to pursue an advanced degree immediately following their undergraduate years, USF offers several accelerated degree programs, including a seven-year medical degree, six-year doctorate in physical therapy, and five-year programs for master's degrees in public health and engineering.

Honors College students enjoy classes that are never bigger than 25 students and intense debate and discussion is the norm. In addition to tangible research opportunities, accelerated degree programs and academic rigor, the Honors College is a close-knit community where students share ideas and form friendships with like-minded individuals — friendships that last much longer than their four years at the Honors College.

CAMPUS FACILITIES AND EQUIPMENT

USF students enjoy access to a world of educational and entertainment opportunities all in walking, biking, rollerblading or driving distance. Among the on-campus facilities are science, engineering and medical laboratories, broadcasting studios, performing arts theaters and practice rooms and an award-winning student newspaper.

USF is home to the world renowned Graphic Studio, Contemporary Art Museum and the Florida Institute of Oceanography. USF offers its students a 2 million volume library with 20,500 periodical subscriptions and access to hundreds of databases through its Library User Information System (LUIS).

All residence halls are wired for email and Internet access. The university offers a number of open-use computer labs and wireless hubs across campus.

State-of-the-art athletic and recreational facilities, a 10,000 seat arena, the student health center and multiple dining options give all students ample opportunity to stay healthy and have fun.

College wouldn't be complete without sports, and USF is home to 18 unbelieva-BULL teams competing in the Big East Conference. Cheer on the Bulls at Raymond James Stadium, home of the Tampa Bay Buccaneers or in the USF Sun Dome, which houses men's and women's basketball.

TUITION, ROOM, BOARD AND FEES

At Florida's public colleges and universities, tuition is still among the lowest in the nation. For 2007-08, annual tuition costs were as follows: $3,340 for Florida residents and $16,040 for non-Florida resident undergraduate students attending full-time. Per credit hour tuition and fees vary according to class time, course load, and location.

Room and board costs are $7,590, which is based on a double occupancy room and mid-priced dining plan. Room and board charges vary according to board plan, housing facility, and location. Costs are subject to change each academic year.

FINANCIAL AID

The University of South Florida awards an average of $7,600 of Financial Aid to 32,000 students in 2006-07. Financial Aid is awarded according to each student's need, academic standing, and/or talents in relation to college costs and may include grants, loans, scholarships, and/or part-time employment.

The priority application deadline is December 31 for academic scholarships and March 1 for federal and institutional aid.

Programs based on need include Federal programs such as Pell Grant, Work-Study, and Stafford and Perkins Loans. State aid includes programs such as the Florida Student Assistance Grant, Florida College Career Work-Study Program, and the Florida Bright Futures Scholarship program. To qualify for federal and state aid, students should submit the Free Application for Federal Student Aid (FAFSA), which is available in both English and Spanish.

STUDENT ORGANIZATIONS AND ACTIVITIES

USF has more than 350 student organizations including national fraternities and sororities, multicultural organizations and honor societies. Students can also participate in intramural and club sports, community service and volunteer organizations or one of many special interest groups.

USF's 18 varsity sports teams compete at the NCAA Division I level and are members of the Big East Conference. USF students are provided with free tickets to all home athletic events.

Theaters and concert stages provide venues for student performances, top-name entertainment, concerts, and a university lecture series. Recreational facilities include a multi-million dollar fitness center, 18 tennis courts, an indoor and several outdoor pools, a private riverfront park, an 18-hole championship golf course and an extensive outdoor recreation program featuring hiking, camping, kayaking and river rafting.

ADMISSIONS PROCESS

When considering your application for admission as a first-time-in-college freshman, the admissions office calculates a student's GPA in core academic courses — English, mathematics, science, social science and foreign language. The rigor of high school curriculum as measured by Advanced Placement, International Baccalaureate, honors and dual enrollment course selection plays a major factor in the admission decision, followed by scores on the SAT or ACT (essay required). Ultimately, all applications are considered on an individual basis, taking into account grade trends, a student's personal profile, involvement in extracurricular activities or work experience.

Transfer applications are reviewed according to the number of transferable credit hours earned, with priority given to transfers who have earned an Associate in Arts degree from a public community college in Florida. Additionally, an official high school transcript and SAT or ACT score is required of all freshman and sophomore-level transfer applicants with less than 60 transferable credit hours.

Both freshman and transfer admission decisions are made on a rolling basis. That means that decisions are made as application files are completed. In some cases, a decision might be deferred for additional information, especially seventh semester senior grades for freshman applicants.

In order to be guaranteed priority consideration for merit scholarships administered by the Office of Undergraduate Admissions, freshman applicants must apply by January 2; freshman scholarships are awarded to Summer/Fall applicants only and first take effect for the Fall semester. Otherwise, the priority deadline for freshman admission is March 1. Transfer scholarships are awarded to Summer/Fall and Spring applicants; transfer applicants who wish to be considered must apply by April 1 or November 1, respectively. Any applicant who applies to USF after the published deadlines above will be considered for admission and scholarship on a space- or fund-available basis.

UNIVERSITY OF TAMPA

AT A GLANCE

The University of Tampa is a private, medium-sized, comprehensive university in the heart of Tampa. The university offers exciting learning experiences in over 100 fields of study. All programs offer students a combination of challenging coursework and real world experience. Situated on a beautiful 100 acre campus, the university is adjacent to the Hillsborough River and downtown Tampa. Students enjoy a traditional self-contained campus, only steps away from the excitement and opportunities of the bustling city. At the center of campus lies Plant Hall, once a luxurious hotel for the rich and famous. This historical landmark is complemented by modern surroundings and excellent facilities including a student union, art studios and gallery, theatres, computer resource center, complete athletic facilities, science labs, and new residence halls. Over 5,600 students (4,500 full-time undergraduates) are enrolled at the university. UT students represent 50 states and over 100 countries. Students choose from more than 120 different clubs and organizations including honors societies, social clubs, Greek Life, community service and others. The University of Tampa has one of the top NCAA Division II sports programs in the nation, winning twelve national championships including recent championships in Baseball (2006 & 2007), Women's Volleyball (2006), and Women's Soccer (2007).

LOCATION AND ENVIRONMENT

Located on the west central coast of Florida, Tampa has far more to offer than just beautiful beaches and a pleasant climate. Tampa Bay is one of the fastest growing areas in the United States. The city is a leading center for the arts, international business, law, education, media, and health and scientific research. Forbes magazine and Newsweek magazine consistently pick Tampa Bay as one of the best places to live in the United States.

OFF-CAMPUS OPPORTUNITIES

Across the river in downtown Tampa is the Museum of Art, Tampa Bay Center for the Performing Arts, the Florida Aquarium, the St. Petersburg Times Forum, and an outstanding public library. Busch Gardens is only several miles from campus and Walt Disney World and Universal Studios are only 90 minutes away. Tampa International Airport is five miles from campus.

MAJORS AND DEGREES OFFERED

The University of Tampa offers Bachelor's degrees in accounting, advertising & public relations, art, athletic training & sports medicine, biochemistry, biology, chemistry, communication, criminology, digital arts, economics, education (elementary and secondary certification), electronic media arts & technology, English, entrepreneurship, environmental science, exercise science & sport studies, film & media arts, finance, financial services operations & systems, forensic science, government and world affairs, graphic design, history, international business, international & cultural studies, liberal studies, management, management information systems, marine science (biology and chemistry), marketing, mathematical programming, mathematics, music, music education, nursing, perform-

ing arts, philosophy, physical education, psychology, public health, social sciences, sociology, Spanish, sport management, theatre, and writing. Minors and concentrations are offered in adult fitness, advertising, aerospace studies, American Government, art history, arts administration & management, biology/business, biology/molecular, biology/organismal & evolutionary, business administration, dance/theatre, French, humanities, international studies, law & government, law & justice, military science, recreation, speech/theatre, urban studies, women's studies, and world affairs. Pre-professional programs offered include pre-dentistry, pre-law, pre-medicine, pre-veterinary science, allied health, art therapy, and chemistry. Certificate programs include early childhood education, European studies, French, German, gerontology, international studies, Italian, Latin American studies, Spanish and TESOL. An undergraduate Evening College (School of Continuing Studies) offers fifteen degree programs designed for adults who want to study part-time. Three summer sessions also offer excellent learning and professional advancement opportunities. At the graduate level, the business school offers the Master of Business Administration degree and Master of Science degrees in accounting, finance, innovation management, and marketing. A Master of Science in Nursing, Master of Arts in Teaching, and Master of Education degrees are also offered to students.

ACADEMIC PROGRAMS

The University of Tampa's undergraduate curriculum is designed to give students a broad academic and cultural background as well as a concentrated study in a major. Students complete a comprehensive core curriculum known as the Baccalaureate Experience, which is highlighted by the unique and innovative first year program known as Gateways. Gateways is an extensive orientation program which encourages student development via exploration of global issues, career possibilities, and development of critical thinking and communication skills. International experience has always been a major focus at the University of Tampa. Students are essentially educated and prepared to live and work internationally. Academic opportunities in this area are available to students immediately and in 2008 there are 20 faculty led study abroad opportunities available to students. For qualifying students, the university has a rigorous and rewarding Honors Program of expanded instruction and student research.

CAMPUS FACILITIES AND EQUIPMENT

$201 million has been invested in new academic facilities, technology, and residence halls since 1998, making this national historic landmark the model of a modern university. 82% of all residence halls are new within the last decade and most of the others have been renovated. The Vaughn Student Center and residence hall complex serves as the hub of student life. Here students find food courts, a two-story cyber cafe, recreational areas, the Reeves Theatre, student office space, Barnes & Noble campus store and a 9th floor conference center with magical views of downtown Tampa. The new Stadium Center residence hall opened in Fall 2007 with state-of-the-art amenities and eight separate dining venues. Other outstanding facilities and resources include The John H. Sykes College of Business, a waterfront Marine Science Field Station and research vessels, the library's online computer catalog system, the Ferman Music Center, Reeves Theatre, 1,000-seat Falk Theatre, the R.K. Bailey Art Studio, and excellent sports facilities.

TUITION, ROOM, BOARD AND FEES

The cost for the 2007-2008 academic year is $20,682 for tuition & fees and $7,616 for room & board. The average Financial Aid award for students at the University of Tampa in 2007 was $17,500 with 87% of students receiving financial assistance.

FINANCIAL AID

A high-quality, private education at the University of Tampa presents students with exceptional value and is not as difficult to finance as some students may think. Each family's situation is evaluated individually for need-based assistance. Academic achievements, leadership potential, athletic skills, and other special talents are also recognized, regardless of need. Academic scholarships are awarded to all entering first year students with a 3.2 unweighted grade point average or above. Transfer, leadership, departmental, Phi Theta Kappa, International Baccalaureate and ROTC scholarships are also available.

STUDENT ORGANIZATIONS AND ACTIVITIES

Students choose from more than 120 student clubs and organizations including honors societies, social clubs, and community service groups amongst many others. Visit The University of Tampa website at www.ut.edu to learn more about Student Organizations and Activities.

ADMISSIONS PROCESS

The University of Tampa is an academically competitive institution with a 49% acceptance rate. Check The University of Tampa website at www.ut.edu for specific admission details.

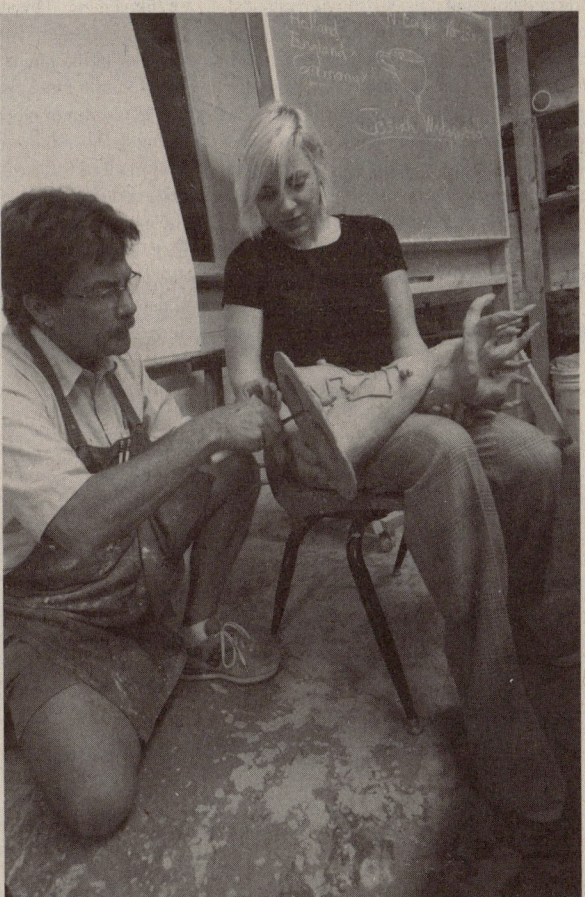

UNIVERSITY OF THE ARTS

AT A GLANCE

The only university in the nation devoted exclusively to education and training in art and design, the performing arts, and media and communication, The University of the Arts (UArts) is located in the heart of Philadelphia's professional arts community. More than 2,300 students from forty states and thirty countries are enrolled in the undergraduate and graduate programs.

Composed of the College of Art and Design, the College of Performing Arts, and the College of Media and Communication, the University offers intensive concentration within a major field as well as creative challenges in multidisciplinary exploration. Our accomplished faculty members are working artists, designers, performers, and authors, as well as educators—people who do as well as teach—and win awards while pursuing their artistic passion.

The graduate programs offer an impressive combination of strengths: exceptionally accomplished faculty, a remarkably individualized and interactive learning environment, access to outstanding facilities and resources, specialized studios, and programs of study that are both highly focused and highly flexible.

LOCATION AND ENVIRONMENT

UArts' location on the exciting Avenue of the Arts in Philadelphia provides students with a vital urban experience at the crossroads of culture and business. The Avenue of the Arts is a neighborhood of theaters, hotels, restaurants, clubs, museums, galleries, and shops that draws thousands of visitors to the heart of the city. Students find that inspiration, energy, style, and opportunity are around every corner.

MAJORS AND DEGREES OFFERED

Undergraduate Programs

College of Art and Design

B.F.A. — Animation, crafts, film/animation, film/digital video, graphic design, illustration, multi-disciplinary fine arts, painting/drawing, photography, printmaking/book arts, and sculpture

B.S. — Industrial design

Postbaccalaureate Certificate — Crafts

College of Performing Arts

School of Dance

B.F.A.—Ballet, Dance Education, Jazz/Theater, Modern,

School of Music

B.M. — Composition, instrumental performance (with a jazz/contemporary focus), and vocal performance

School of Theater Arts

B.F.A. — Acting, musical theater, theater design and technology, and theater management and production

Two-year certificate — Dance and music

Four-year diploma—music

College of Media and Communication

B.F.A.—Multimedia and writing for film and television

B.S. — Communication

Graduate Programs

Master's degree programs — Art education, book arts/printmaking, ceramics, painting, sculpture, industrial design, jazz studies, museum communication, museum education, museum exhibition planning & design, music education, and teaching visual arts

Minors

Students can choose from more than a dozen minors in various degree programs at The University of the Arts.

ACADEMIC PROGRAMS

Students are attracted to UArts because of its dynamic, creative atmosphere. Whether majoring in dance, sculpture, graphic design, or multimedia, they enjoy interacting with their talented peers in other disciplines. The Freshman Project, the culmination of the required first-year writing course in liberal arts, provides the first opportunity for freshmen to work with students in other majors on a cross-disciplinary creative project. All students take a total of 42 credits in liberal arts, which gives them substantial exposure to the humanities, social science, and science and provides them with the historical and theoretical framework of their major field. Students are further encouraged, to the extent that their busy schedules allow, to take elective courses outside their chosen major.

The freshman year in the College of Art and Design is devoted to the Foundation Program; its focus is exploratory, allowing students to investigate various disciplines before deciding on a specific major. Students are assigned to small sections, each with a team of 3 instructors. In the fall, students take two-dimensional design, three-dimensional design, and drawing; in the spring, they may substitute a Time and Motion course for one of these.

General program requirements vary from department to department. At the end of the freshman year, students select a major in animation, crafts, film/TV, fine arts, graphic design, illustration, or photography, and they may add a concentration in art education or art therapy. A wide variety of internship experiences is available to qualified students. A minimum of 123 credits is required for graduation, including 18 credits in the Foundation Program, 42 credits in the major, 42 credits in liberal arts, 15 credits in electives (9 credits of which must be taken in a department other than the major), and 6 credits in other areas outside the major. Students may request credit by examination in liberal arts subjects and by portfolio examination in studio art subjects.

In the College of Performing Arts, the School of Music program stresses individualized training, with a performance emphasis. Students undergo intensive training in theory and musicianship. Private lessons are supplemented by master classes and ensemble work. In the School of Dance, two years of ballet, modern, and jazz dance are required before students choose a major in the junior year. Electives include improvisation, repertory, partnering, Spanish dance, ethnic dance, character, and mime. The School of Theater Arts concentrates on developing the student's skill as an actor. In addition to the acting studio, requirements include courses in movement, stage combat, mime, and modern dance. In the College of Performing Arts, a minimum of 126 to 130 credits is required for graduation, 42 of which must be in liberal arts. Participation in the 17-credit MATPREP Program enables students to complete bachelor's and master's degrees in teaching music in five years. The University has close working relationships, including internships, with professional theater, dance, and music groups in Philadelphia and elsewhere. Students are also encouraged to seek professional roles.

The College of Media and Communication recognizes new artistic opportunities that have arisen from the latest advances in digital technology. In the B.F.A. program in Writing for Film and Television, students learn to create original narrative prose and to adapt stories to different media through intensive creative writing experiences as well as through the study of mainstream and experimental literature, emphasizing the art of storytelling. In addition, students take courses in film history, history of television, video production, and acting and directing for writers. The B.F.A. program in multimedia is designed to prepare students to work in fields in which close interaction among arts disciplines, digital fluency, collaboration, and effective communication is important. Students learn to combine text, image, video, animation, and sound to educate, entertain, and communicate. The B.S. program in communication enables students to develop, in the first two years, the conceptual understanding, creative problem-solving and technical skills, and storytelling ability required for effective communication in all media. After selecting a concentration in digital journalism, documentary media production, or advertising and social marketing, students work in the studio and on location, both collaboratively and individually, on creative projects using primarily digital media. Internships in professional settings provide students with real-life experience in the field. Freshmen who want to learn more about the world of media and communication before choosing a major can enroll in The UArts Discovery Year. This 30-credit program provides an overview of media and communication while students take courses in the college's three majors - communication, multimedia, and writing for film and television - before students decide on a major. Students also take foundation courses in liberal arts to satisfy their general education requirements.

Internships

Internships in professional settings provide students with real-life experience in the field. A wide variety of internship opportunities are available to qualified students.

Study Abroad

UARts offers International Study Abroad programs. The Study Abroad Office can assist students in finding suitable overseas programs, apply, and, to some degree, arrange for Financial Aid.

CAMPUS FACILITIES AND EQUIPMENT

The University facilities are composed of numerous buildings, with studios, classrooms, galleries, theaters, lounges, cafes, dormitories, and administrative offices. The Terra Building provides seventeen floors of studios, computer labs, classrooms, performing spaces, and TV and video production and recording studios. All design departments provide individual workstations for seniors and exhibition spaces that feature student and faculty work throughout the year. The University also maintains several public galleries, where students may exhibit their work along with curator-managed exhibitions of the work of distinguished guest artists. Student performances are held in the University's formal theaters, such as the 200-seat Dance Theater, the historic 1,800-seat Merriam Theater, the black box theater, the music recital hall, the Arts Bank, and a 239-seat state-of-the-art theater and rehearsal hall, and in the many informal spaces on campus.

As part of a multimillion-dollar telecommunications project, the campus provides free Internet access in all classroom, labs, and dormitories. Academic computing resources include more than twenty labs on Macintosh and PC platforms that are used for animation, digital imaging, 3-D modeling, multimedia, music, CAD, Web page design, and for word processing. Several "smart" classrooms enable faculty members to use computer applications and Internet access in their presentations; smart studios allow students to function as they would in the professional world.

Students work in a large number and variety of specialized facilities throughout the campus that support the learning of their craft. Among these are the Typography Lab, the Borowsky Center for Publication Arts, digital video editing suites, photo/film/animation labs and darkrooms, a scanner lab, an SGI lab, a bronze foundry and plaster workshop, and crafts studios and workshops for ceramics, metals, wood, glassblowing, papermaking, and fibers. The performing arts facilities include a recording studio; music technology (MIDI) studios; editing suites; chamber music studios and practice rooms; computer labs; dance and movement studios, with barres, mirrors, and resilient floors; and acting studios.

TUITION, ROOM, BOARD AND FEES

Tuition for the 2007-08 academic is $29,500 plus a general student fee of $950. Accommodations in 3- or 4-person apartment-style dormitory units average $6,600.

FINANCIAL AID

Last year, UArts provided more than $7 million in scholarships and grants to new students alone. Roughly one-third of these awards went to students demonstrating financial need; the rest were awarded in the form of talent- or merit-based scholarships. Overall, UArts students receive $30 million in scholarships, grants, loans, and part-time employment each year.

Typically, 80 percent of our students enrolled on a full-time basis are eligible for some type of need-based aid. All students should apply. UArts financial counselors will assist in meeting costs within our available resources.

STUDENT ORGANIZATIONS AND ACTIVITIES

The student activities office sponsors a variety of activities to complement Academic Programs, including an annual Halloween event, "open mike" nights, fall carnival, concerts, movie nights, ski trips, ice skating parties, and trips to nearby New York and Washington, D.C.

Besides serving as the voice of the students, Student Council supports a variety of arts-oriented student organizations, including a dance/step troupe, a Web radio station, and a student-run gallery, among many others.

ADMISSIONS PROCESS

In addition to submitting a portfolio or auditioning, applicants should submit their high school transcript, SAT or ACT scores, one letter of recommendation, and a personal statement of purpose.

The placement of transfer students is made after an evaluation of their portfolio or audition and a determination of their approved credits. Transfer students may be given advanced standing.

International applicants are required to submit scores on the Test of English as a Foreign Language (TOEFL); a minimum score of 550 on the paper-based TOEFL or 213 on the computer-based TOEFL is required. Early entrance and deferred entrance are possible.

Application Information

The University of the Arts follows a system of rolling admission. All students are notified within two weeks of the receipt of all required materials. Students are encouraged to submit applications by March 15 for fall admission and December 1 for spring admission.

For additional information, students should contact:

Office of Admission

University of the Arts

320 South Broad Street

Philadelphia, Pennsylvania 19102

United States

Telephone: 215-717-6030

800-616-ARTS (toll-free)

Fax: 215-717-6045

World Wide Web: http://www.uarts.edu

UNIVERSITY OF THE CUMBERLANDS

AT A GLANCE

Founded in 1889, Cumberland College officially became the University of the Cumberlands on July 1, 2005. In keeping with its commitment to providing a superior education in an exceptional Christian atmosphere, the University emphasizes the growth of the individual student and strives to instill in students the desire to be agents of change in the world and to use knowledge for the benefit of others, as well as themselves.

University of the Cumberlands is a four-year, coed liberal arts college offering a broad curriculum with more than 46 programs of study from which to choose. A graduate program leading to the Master of Arts in Education is also offered.

The student body consists of 1,843 students representing 40 states and 27 countries. Most students live on campus in the University's eleven residence halls. A director assisted by student staff members supervises each hall.

Students benefit from such special services as the Career Services Center, Center for Leadership Studies, Student Health Center, Academic Resource Center, and free tutorial assistance.

University of the Cumberlands is accredited by the Commission on Colleges of the Southern Association of Colleges and Schools (1866 Southern Lane, Decatur, GA 30033-4097; telephone: 404-679-4501) to award the Bachelor of Arts, Bachelor of General Studies, Bachelor of Music, Bachelor of Science, and Master of Arts in Education degrees.

LOCATION AND ENVIRONMENT

University of the Cumberlands is located in Williamsburg, Kentucky, which is in the southern part of the mountains of Eastern Kentucky. Williamsburg is about two hundred miles south of Cincinnati, about an equal distance from Louisville, about eighty miles north of Knoxville, and about 100 miles south of Lexington. The business section of the city lies in a small valley of the Cumberland River; the University and chief residence section are situated on the surrounding hills. It is a place of natural beauty and healthful surroundings.

Williamsburg is one of the older cities of the state. It has long been known for its larger number of beautiful residences, for its churches and schools, and for the hospitality of its people.

UC offers a picturesque campus with stately buildings and rolling green lawns nestled in the foothills of the Appalachian mountain range with the main campus situated on three hills which divide it into three distinct parts and afford a magnificent view of the surrounding area. The University's buildings, which are situated on these hills and a viaduct, spanning the south and middle hills, provide an easy and pleasant passageway to each part of the campus.

Within a few miles of campus are Laurel Lake, Cumberland Falls State Park, Cumberland Gap National Park, and the Daniel Boone National Forest.

OFF-CAMPUS OPPORTUNITIES

Study Abroad

Ministry Opportunities

Internships

MAJORS AND DEGREES OFFERED

University of the Cumberlands confers the Bachelor of Arts, Bachelor of Science, Bachelor of General Studies, and Bachelor of Music. Major fields of study include accounting, art°, biological science°, biology, business administration, chemistry, church music, communication arts, communication and theatre arts°, early elementary education°, English°, exercise and sport science°, fitness and sport management, health, health education°, history, history and political science, human services, management information systems, mathematics°, middle school education°, music°, philosophy and religion, physical science°, physics, political science, psychology, public health, religion, social studies°, Spanish°, special education°, and theatre arts. Minor fields of study include biblical languages, French°, geography, and journalism. Pre-professional and special curricula are offered in medical technology, military science, pre-dentistry, pre-engineering, pre-law, pre-medicine, pre-optometry, pre-pharmacy, pre-physical therapy, pre-veterinary medicine, and religious vocations.

°Denotes teacher certification available

ACADEMIC PROGRAMS

University of the Cumberlands seeks to provide academic specialization within the broad framework of a liberal arts education. To supplement the in-depth knowledge acquired within each major, 47 semester hours of general studies from the areas of Christian faith and values, cultural and aesthetic values, the English language, humanities, leadership and community service, natural and mathematical sciences, physical education, and social sciences are required. Students must earn 128 semester hours to graduate with a bachelor's degree.

The academic year begins in late August, with the first semester ending in mid-December. The second semester runs from early January to early May. Two five-week undergraduate summer sessions and two four-week graduate summer sessions are also offered. Orientation, pre-registration, and academic advising by faculty members begin in the summer preceding entrance.

Students may receive credit for passing the College Board, the College-Level Examination Programs (CLEP), and special departmental tests. Highly qualified students have the opportunity to undertake advanced independent study.

CAMPUS FACILITIES AND EQUIPMENT

UC's campus contains 34 buildings in the architectural style of the early 1900s. Recent additions to campus include the state-of-the-art Hutton School of Business, a 27,000 square foot addition to the science building, featuring well-equipped labs providing graduate-level research opportunities, a new women's residence hall and a baseball complex. The McGaw Music Building contains individual rehearsal and studio areas as well as a recital hall. The Norma Perkins Hagan Memorial Library houses more than 190,312 book titles, 518 current serial subscriptions, and 770,875 microform titles. Sophisticated computer equipment provides access to an additional 20 million or more items from many of the nation's outstanding libraries. The instructional media center includes a children's library, a computerized language lab, and a listening library.

Other special academic features include a computer center, an art gallery, a word processing center for English composition, a theatre, the Career Services Center, a 600-seat chapel, three large lecture halls, and the Distance Learning laboratory.

TUITION, ROOM, BOARD AND FEES

For 2008-2009, the basic academic year expenses are $14,658 for tuition and fees and $6,626 for room and board. The average cost for books and supplies is approximately $800 per academic year.

FINANCIAL AID

University of the Cumberlands sponsors a large Financial Aid program that coordinates money from federal, state, private, and University sources. Last year, 95 percent of UC students shared more than $20 million in aid. Academic, athletic, church-related and community service scholarships are available.

STUDENT ORGANIZATIONS AND ACTIVITIES

Don't let the small size of our campus fool you. There are enough activities going on every day at UC to fill a dozen college careers. Whether your interest lies in athletics, creative expression, student government, academic enrichment, community service, spiritual development, or in any combination of these areas, you'll find an outlet here for your energy.

Many academic departments sponsor clubs and academic honor societies for students with a particular interest in the discipline, so be sure to visit the departments that interest you or contact a faculty member in that department for more information.

Each year, University of the Cumberlands hosts numerous guest performers and speakers and celebrates the talents of its students and faculty through a variety of lectures, concerts, art exhibitions, and theatrical productions. Many of these events are free of charge, and most are open to the public.

In addition, UC offers ten varsity sports for both men and women. Competing in the Mid-South Conference, UC is a member of the NAIA and is Division I.

The Student Government Association is dedicated to giving students a voice through elected representatives. In addition to promoting student concerns and working as a liaison between students and college administrators, the SGA provides a number of important services, and sponsors a number of student-centered events throughout the year.

ADMISSIONS PROCESS

The purpose of the Admission Process is to identify applicants who are likely to succeed academically at University of the Cumberlands and at the same time contribute positively to the campus community. The process considers such factors as high school records (including courses taken, grade trends, and rank in class), scores on the American College Test (ACT), or on the Scholastic Aptitude Test (SAT), application essay (not required of all applicants), extracurricular activities and honors, and personal contact.

School Says . . .

UNIVERSITY OF WYOMING

AT A GLANCE

The University of Wyoming (UW), a public land-grant institution founded in 1886, is a reflection of the global community it serves. The extensive range of Academic Programs offered at UW inspires the development of new thinking and promotes fulfilling careers in our rapidly evolving world. As a major research institution, UW's research goals, which benefit Wyoming and the world, are continually being pushed to the boundaries and beyond by its professors and students. It is this academic ambition that has allowed UW to provide high-quality undergraduate and graduate education, research, and service since 1886. UW continues to remain true to its goal of serving the educational needs of students today while preparing them for the complex world of tomorrow. UW's number of Rhodes, Goldwater, and Truman Scholars in the past decade demonstrates this commitment. Wyoming, unique among the 50 state, has only one university. UW enjoys tremendous support from within its state as well as from an alumni network that spans the globe. More than 13,203 students from all parts of the U.S. and 77 other countries attend UW classes in Laramie and at outreach sites around the state. The variety of students at UW enriches the educational experience for all by fostering a multicultural environment that encourages sharing and learning about those with different heritages and cultural backgrounds. It is this dialogue that continues to promote respect and appreciation for diversity. Undergraduate education is a high priority at UW with almost 90 percent of undergraduate courses taught by faculty and not graduate assistants. With an average class size of 30 students, UW students receive more individual attention in the classroom making their educational experience rewarding and valuable. Opportunities for excitement and involvement are abundant at UW! There are more than 200 recognized campus clubs and organizations, including 15 national fraternities and sororities, honor and professional societies, political and religious organizations and special interest groups. Students also have the opportunity to participate in over 60 different intramural and club sports. UW competes in the Division I NCAA Mountain West Conference athletics in 17 men and women's sports. UW houses 2,400 students in six residence halls and freshmen are required to live on campus their first year. While primarily coed, the residence halls offer a number of unique living environments, including quiet/study floors, special interest floors, honors floors, single sex floors and other academic living environments.

ACADEMIC PROGRAMS

The UW academic calendar consists of two semesters and a complete summer session. Depending on their degree program, students will be required to complete 120 to 164 credit hours for graduation. Undergraduate programs for most majors can be completed in four years. Student may choose to double major within the same college or they may pursue majors in two separate colleges for a cross college major. Minors are also available in many areas. UW offers a unique breadth of Academic Programs of study because it is the only four-year public university in Wyoming. Students entering undecided or who want to tailor their education have many options. UW hosts colleges in Agriculture, Arts & Sciences, Business, Education, Engineering, and Health Sciences. At a professional level, UW also has a Law School and Pharmacy School.

UW prepares students to choose rewarding careers and to lead successful lives that make positive contributions in a complex multicultural society. This foundation is centered in the University Studies Program, which provides students a core curriculum that assists in developing oral and written communication, mathematics, science, diversity, global awareness, government and cultures. The University Honors Program provides academically and ambitious undergraduates innovative and intellectual learning opportunities. Award-winning faculty, unique and challenging course work and senior research projects are the hallmarks of this program. UW is also committed to providing its students an international experience through actively recruiting international students and providing resources for students to study abroad.

CAMPUS FACILITIES AND EQUIPMENT

UW's students, faculty and staff are what make the university truly exceptional. The modern facilities of the campus reinforce UW's commitment as an extensive research university to both students and faculty. In the last five years UW has spent more than $120 million on major renovation and building projects and another $200 million in construction projects are underway. Students have the opportunity to take classes in state of the art classrooms while benefiting from the individual attention UW offers.

URSINUS COLLEGE

STUDENT ORGANIZATIONS AND ACTIVITIES

Students at the University of Wyoming have lots of opportunities to be involved; with UW having over 200 recognized student organizations. There is an organization to fit everyone's interests, from honoraries to Greek life to religious groups to sports activities. Check out all the current groups available by going to www.uwyo.edu/rso. Because Laramie is a small town, campus activities are abundant to keep students engaged and having fun.

UW's Outdoor Adventure Program provides organized activities from white water rafting, climbing, hiking, fishing and camping in the nearby Snowy Range (25 minutes from Laramie), Vedauwoo rock formation (15 minutes from campus) and many other breathtaking locations in the nearby Rocky Mountains.

UW's proximity to the Denver and the Colorado Front Range allows students to take advantage of activities associated with a larger metro area while living and studying in a smaller community.

ADMISSIONS PROCESS

High school graduates with less than 30 transferable college credit hours should have successfully completed thirteen high school courses that include 4 years of English, 3 years of mathematics, 3 years of science (including a physical science), and 3 years of cultural context courses (behavioral or social sciences, visual or performing arts, humanities or foreign languages) A minimum cumulative grade point average (GPA) of 2.75 and an ACT score of 20 or combined math and verbal SAT score of 960 is required. Admissions with conditions is available to students who do not meet these standards but have a minimum 2.25 GPA and an ACT score of 20 or an combined math and verbal SAT score of 960. Transfer students with 30 or more transferable semester credit hours must have a minimum cumulative GPA of 2.0. To be considered for admission, students must submit a completed UW Application for Admission, submit official high school/college transcripts, submit ACT or SAT scores, and pay a $40, non-refundable application fee. Students may apply and pay the application fee online via the internet at the address listed below. UW strongly encourages all prospective students and their parents to visit the campus.

For more information or to schedule a campus visit, students should contact:

Admissions Office Department 3435

1000 East University Avenue

Laramie, Wyoming 82070

Telephone: 307.766.5160 800.

DIAL.WYO (342.5996) (toll free)

Email: why-wyo@uwyo.edu

World Wide Web: www.uwyo.edu

URSINUS COLLEGE

AT A GLANCE

Ursinus College is a highly selective, national liberal arts college located in suburban Philadelphia. Founded in 1869, the mission of the college is to enable students to become independent, responsible, and thoughtful individuals through a program of liberal education. Ursinus prepares students for an interdependent world, and teaches them how to put their ideas to work. At Ursinus, the emphasis is on student achievement, undergraduate research, and multiple opportunities to participate in broadening and enriching Academic Programs. In recent years, the programs and facilities have undergone dramatic improvement, leading a recent team of evaluators to call the Ursinus experience "nothing short of astonishing."

LOCATION AND ENVIRONMENT

Known for the beauty of its campus setting, Ursinus is part of the richly varied higher educational community of the greater Philadelphia region. Our wooded 170-acre campus is just 28 miles from downtown Philadelphia. The village ambiance of Collegeville contrasts with busy Philadelphia and the huge corporate and retail complexes within a 10-miles radius in Upper Providence, Valley Forge and King of Prussia, and with the biotechnology research concentration just outside the town.

OFF-CAMPUS OPPORTUNITIES

Ursinus students prepare for the world by experiencing it first hand—through academic and cultural programs at locations from Japan to Mexico to Africa. An Ursinus student learns Wolof from native speakers in Senegal. A student with a dual major in biology and Spanish gains premedical experience in a hospital in Bogotá, Colombia. A business major learns the ropes of cross-border trade in Barcelona. Each year, dozens of Ursinus students spend from a month to a year abroad earning academic credit and gaining invaluable life experience. Ursinus believes that students in every field can be transformed by contact with another culture. We have created programs, as well as research, volunteer and internship opportunities, that turn our small college into a global gateway.

MAJORS AND DEGREES OFFERED

Ursinus offers two degrees, the Bachelor of Arts and the Bachelor of Science. It has 27 majors, 50 minors and an International Studies Certificate. Biology, Business & Economics, English and Psychology are four of the majors with the largest numbers of students.

Majors are offered in American Studies, Anthropology and Sociology, Art, Biochemistry and Molecular Biology, Biology, Business and Economics, Chemistry, Classics, Computer Science, Dance, East Asian Studies, English, Environmental Studies, Exercise and Sport Science, French, German, History, International Relations, Mathematics, Media and Communication Studies, Neuroscience, Philosophy, Physics, Politics, Psychology, Spanish, and Theater. Students are also permitted, with approval of the Dean, to initiate their own major combining two or more fields of study.

The faculty of Ursinus is primarily dedicated to teaching excellence. The student-faculty ratio is a low 12:1, which means students have the opportunity to benefit from an independent project, completed and presented to their peers under the close supervision of a faculty member. There is no better way to develop critical thinking, discipline and intellectual independence.

ACADEMIC PROGRAMS

Ursinus is committed to undergraduate liberal education and requires students to select from among a wide range of choices to complete both the core curriculum requirements and a concentration in a major. A minimum of 128 credits is required for the bachelor's degree.

The best-known of the Ursinus core requirements is the Common Intellectual Experience or CIE, a two-semester seminar required of every first-year student. In this course, students gather in small groups to read, discuss, write and reflect on the great questions of human existence. Students read the works of the most profound thinkers throughout the ages, and consider creative works of art, music, theater and dance. The class syllabus is designed and taught by professors from every discipline.

All students are required to complete an Independent Learning Experience (ILE) which may take the form of an internship, an independent research project, a study-abroad program, or a student teaching experience. The College offers funded summer research opportunities with its aggressive undergraduate research scholars program of 75 students.

CAMPUS FACILITIES AND EQUIPMENT

Ursinus facilities include 25 academic and administrative buildings and 41 residence halls. Among these is The Kaleidoscope, a new $25 million, 55,000-square-foot performing arts center, which provides dance studios, two theaters, as well as technical spaces for lighting and sound equipment, recording, scenery building, costume and prop storage and more. The Kaleidoscope serves both majors in theater and dance, and students interested in taking performing arts courses outside their fields of study. The Floy Lewis Bakes Center features a regulation indoor track, indoor tennis courts, and a fully equipped recreation and weight room, a swimming pool, basketball courts, a wrestling room and ample locker rooms. Wismer Student Center houses a cafeteria; a food court; the Ursinus Bookstore; a television lounge; dance and movie facilities. The Residential Village, comprising 25 renovated Victorian homes used as dormitories, complements the campus culture. The campus also is home to the Berman Museum of Art and the recently renovated Myrin Library. During the academic year, the library is open 110 hours per week. A café just inside the library entrance offers a comfortable and relaxing space where students and faculty may meet to read, talk or study, while enjoying coffee, tea and other light refreshments.

Every Ursinus student is issued a laptop computer during new-student orientation. The computer is exchanged for a newer version before the junior year.

TUITION, ROOM, BOARD AND FEES

Basic student charges at Ursinus College include tuition and room and board for resident students. Fees and a laptop computer are included in the basic charges.

For 2008-2009, the following rates apply for first-year, full-time students:

Tuition: $36,750

Room and Board: $8,800

Fees: $160

FINANCIAL AID

To help meet these charges, the Student Financial Services Office administers a comprehensive program of aid from Ursinus, federal, state and other private sources. Approximately 85 percent of all students receive some form of assistance. Both merit and need-based aid is available.

STUDENT ORGANIZATIONS AND ACTIVITIES

Ursinus students are known for their involvement. Here you will discover nearly 100 Ursinus clubs and organizations providing political voice, religious community, creative outlets, networking opportunities and fun. From clubs and organizations to Greek life, New Student Orientation to Campus Activities, Student Activities has an activity to fit just about any interest, from fencing to community service to computer gaming.

Ursinus students compete in the NCAA Division III's Centennial Conference, among the country's most prestigious collections of colleges with Swarthmore, Haverford, Dickinson, Gettysburg, and Franklin and Marshall Colleges as members.

ADMISSIONS PROCESS

Ursinus students are intelligent, motivated and academically curious. All admitted freshmen have successfully completed advanced college prep high school programs and are active outside of the classroom. Fifty percent achieve top 10th ranking in their high school classes, and the middle 50 percent range on the SATs are Math 560-660 and Verbal 550-660. Reporting of the SAT score or other standardized test results to the Ursinus Admissions Office is optional if: A) your high school reports class rank and you are in the top 10 percent, or B) your high school does not report class rank and you have a 3.5 GPA or better on a 4.0 scale. All other candidates for admission to the freshman class are required to take the SAT or ACT. Interviews are strongly encouraged.

VANDERBILT UNIVERSITY

AT A GLANCE

In 1873, Commodore Cornelius Vanderbilt endowed Vanderbilt University in the hope that it would "strengthen the ties which should exist between all sections of our common country." Today, Vanderbilt is a highly selective, medium-sized university with a total enrollment of just over 11,000. In line with the Commodore's dream, students join the campus from all over the country and around the world.

There are 6,532 undergraduates at Vanderbilt, all of whom live on campus in residence halls that are shared by students in all four undergraduate schools. The university has a strong sense of community, and the housing staff works with the Vanderbilt Student Government to organize social, cultural, and educational events on campus. Housing options include traditional single and double rooms, apartments, townhouses, and suites. About 42 percent of undergraduates participate in Greek life, and though fraternities and sororities do not have residential houses, Greek organizations play an active role in undergraduate life.

The fall of 2008 will see the arrival of the Commons, Vanderbilt's new living-learning area for first-year students. The Commons will include five recently renovated and five newly constructed residence halls, which will allow the university to house all freshmen in the same area of campus. Each residence hall (or "house") will also have a faculty member in residence, who will serve as a mentor to students and oversee programming for the house. The Sarratt Student Center is the hub of student life, boasting recreational facilities such as a movie theater, a pub, and a game room, as well as meeting rooms, an art gallery, craft and darkroom facilities, and a student-produced FM radio station. Other student facilities include a state-of-the-art recreation center.

LOCATION AND ENVIRONMENT

Vanderbilt is located in the city of Nashville, home to a diverse population of 1.25 million and marked by a special touch of Southern charm. As the capital of Tennessee, Nashville is an important cultural and commercial hub in the mid-South, and is often called the music industry's "third coast." Located equidistant from the northern and southern U.S. borders, Nashville sits at the intersection of three major interstate highways, and 18 airlines serve the city. Beyond the city limits, the surrounding area contains 81 parks and recreation areas, and over 30,000 acres of lakes, offering ample opportunity for sports year round.

OFF-CAMPUS OPPORTUNITIES

During their undergraduate career, students are encouraged to study overseas in Vanderbilt's 60 programs in 19 countries, giving them the opportunity to develop language skills and a deeper cultural awareness. Students receive course credit for overseas study and do not pay extra tuition to participate in programs abroad; financial aid packages also apply to all Vanderbilt study abroad programs. Most programs allow students to participate without extending their graduation date. Students may also participate in programs sponsored by other universities.

MAJORS AND DEGREES OFFERED

Degrees are offered in African American and Diaspora studies; American studies; Ancient Mediterranean studies; art; biological sciences; biomedical engineering; chemical engineering; chemistry; child development; child studies; civil engineering; classical languages; classics; cognitive studies; communication of science and technology; communication studies; comparative literature; computer engineering; computer science; earth and environmental sciences; East Asian studies; ecology, evolution, and organismal biology; economics; economics and history; education (early childhood, elementary, secondary, and special education); electrical engineering; engineering science; English; English and history; European studies; French; French and European studies; film studies; German; German studies; history; history of art; human and organizational development; Jewish studies; Latin American and Iberian studies; mathematics; mechanical engineering; medicine, health, and society; molecular and cellular biology; musical arts; musical arts and teacher education; music composition and theory; music performance; neuroscience; philosophy; physics and astronomy; political science; psychology; public policy studies; religious studies; Russian; Russian studies; Russian and European studies; sociology; Spanish, Spanish and European studies; Spanish and Portuguese; Spanish, Portuguese, and European studies; theatre; women's and gender studies; and individually designed majors.

ACADEMIC PROGRAMS

Students apply to one of the four undergraduate schools: the College of Arts and Science, the School of Engineering, Peabody College of Education and Human Development, and the Blair School of Music. The College of Arts and Science provides all Vanderbilt students the opportunity to experience a wide range of academic disciplines and subjects. While there is no "core curriculum," the distribution requirements of AXLE (Achieving excellence in Liberal Education) allow students to refine their skills in writing, mathematics, foreign languages, the humanities, natural sciences, and the social sciences. The School of Engineering educates engineers for practice in industry, government, consulting, teaching, and research careers. In addition to technical courses, each student's program includes a rich complement of course work in the humanities and social sciences, resulting in a balanced foundation for future achievement and for the assumption of leadership roles in his or her chosen field. Peabody College offers degree programs leading to teacher certification and to careers in other areas of education and human development. The degree reflects a strong liberal arts foundation, combined with a solid program of pre-professional courses and a multitude of internship and practicum requirements. Peabody undergraduates must complete requirements in communication, the humanities, mathematics, the natural sciences, and the social sciences. The Blair School offers majors in composition and theory, musical arts, musical arts and teacher education, and performance. Instruction is available in all orchestral instruments, as well as piano, organ, euphonium, multiple woodwinds, saxophone, classical guitar, and voice. The curriculum combines intensive musical training with liberal arts studies.

CAMPUS FACILITIES AND EQUIPMENT

Vanderbilt University sits 1.5 miles southwest of downtown Nashville on a 330-acre, park-like campus that was designated a national arboretum in 1988. The university comprises 229 buildings, including a world-class medical center, 30 residence halls, and 9 libraries. Recently completed buildings include Buttrick Hall, which houses several interdisciplinary centers; the Ingram Studio Arts Center; an 18,000 square foot Student Life Center; and Sutherland House and Crawford House, which house first-year students.

TUITION, ROOM, BOARD AND FEES

The costs for 2007-2008 include: tuition, $34,414; room and board, $11,446; books and supplies, $1,140; and the student activities and recreation fee, $864. First-year engineering students have an equipment fee of $2850. All costs are subject to change.

FINANCIAL AID

About 60 percent of the university's undergraduates receive some type of financial aid. Vanderbilt's undergraduate admissions process is need-blind for domestic students, and the university will meet 100% of demonstrated need for all admitted students. Need-based aid is awarded based on the CSS/Financial Aid PROFILE and the FAFSA. Each year, Vanderbilt awards approximately 300 merit-based scholarships to applicants who demonstrate exceptional accomplishment and intellectual promise. Three signature scholarship programs comprise the majority of these honor scholarships. Recipients are guaranteed full-tuition awards, plus summer stipends for study abroad, research, or service projects. All three programs require a separate application in addition to the application for admission. The signature programs are the Cornelius Vanderbilt Scholarships (for students who combine outstanding academic achievements with strong leadership and contributions outside the classroom), the Ingram Scholarships (for students who have demonstrated an exceptional commitment to community service), and the Chancellor's Scholarships (for students who have worked to build strong high school communities by bridging gaps among economically, socially, and racially diverse groups). Vanderbilt also offers scholarships to National Merit Finalists.

STUDENT ORGANIZATIONS AND ACTIVITIES

Vanderbilt Student Government is responsible for maintaining a lively educational atmosphere on campus. Elected representatives of VSG work in conjunction with the nearly 400 student-run organizations to bring noted speakers and events to campus. Students can join a variety of pre-professional, cultural, religious, political, and social organizations. Vanderbilt operates under an Honor Code, a backbone of the undergraduate academic experience. Every year, one senior has the honor of serving a four-year term as the Young Alumni Trustee of the university's Board of Trust. Vanderbilt has a thriving college athletics program. Recent accomplishments include a Sweet Sixteen berth for the men's basketball team, Southeastern Conference regular season and tournament championships for the baseball team, and a national championship for the women's bowling team. A founding member of the SEC, Vanderbilt sponsors 16 Division I (FBS) teams.

ADMISSIONS PROCESS

Vanderbilt seeks accomplished students who are prepared to benefit from a demanding undergraduate program. The Admissions Committee evaluates every aspect of a candidate's application and achievements, both academic and extracurricular. The typical applicant will have completed 20 or more units in a challenging high school curriculum, including two years of foreign language study. School of Engineering applicants must complete at least 4 units of mathematics; calculus is strongly recommended. Admissions decisions are based on strength of high school transcript, extracurricular activities, official recommendations, personal essays, and standardized test results (either the SAT Reasoning Test or ACT With Writing). SAT Subject Tests are not required. In addition to standard application materials, candidates for the Blair School of Music must audition on their primary instrument. Campus visits are recommended, although a student's demonstrated interest in Vanderbilt is not a consideration in admissions decisions. Students can contact the Office of Undergraduate Admissions directly for information on group information sessions, campus tours, and opportunities to attend classes and to "shadow" a current Vanderbilt student. Vanderbilt does not conduct on-campus interviews. Vanderbilt offers Early Decision for students who have selected Vanderbilt as their first choice. Early Decision I applications are due November 1; admissions decisions are mailed by December 15. Early Decision II applications are due January 3, with a response date of February 15. Regular Decision applications are due January 3, and a decision will be mailed by April 1. Vanderbilt exclusively accepts the Common Application for freshman and transfer admission. Applicants must submit "Part 1: The Vanderbilt Common Application Supplement," the Common Application, and a $50 application fee. Part 1 and the application fee may be submitted before or with the Common Application itself. All parts of the application should be submitted electronically or postmarked by the appropriate deadline.

VAUGHN COLLEGE OF AERONAUTICS AND TECHNOLOGY

AT A GLANCE

Located in New York City, Vaughn College of Aeronautics and Technology has offered a quality, small campus experience to students since 1932. We have an enrollment of more than 1,100 students, and offer master's, bachelor's and associate degree programs in engineering, technology, management, and aviation. What sets Vaughn College apart is its small size, unique faculty and student interaction, and ideal location in the heart of the New York metropolitan area. Additionally, Vaughn College is committed to making education affordable for students. Vaughn's reasonable tuition can be an important consideration in your decision-making process. In recent years, the opportunities generated by technology have crossed all segments of American industry. There is a high demand for jobs in electronics, engineering firms, computer software companies, fiber optics communication corporations, local, state and federal government, defense and airport authorities, as well as major transportation companies. Accordingly, our distinguished alumni enjoy positions in many varied fields, from airport management and engineering to manufacturing and electronics. They have built successful careers in organizations such as the Federal Aviation Administration (FAA), IBM and Xerox, Kodak, the Metropolitan Transit Authority (MTA), The Port Authority of New York and New Jersey (PANYNJ), United Technologies, Cessna Citation, and Sikorsky. The analytical, technical, and communications skills developed by more than 5,000 Vaughn alumni make them integral parts of any corporate team, as well as lifelong students of the high-tech world in which we all live.

LOCATION AND ENVIRONMENT

Vaughn College of Aeronautics and Technology is located at 86-01 23rd Avenue, Flushing, NY 11369. Located in the New York City borough of Queens, Vaughn offers many opportunities for a vast array of technology and aviation companies. Vaughn has a six-acre campus and is convenient to major transportation routes. As part of the institution's strategic plan, a 200-bed residential building just opened, a new master's degree in airport management and a bachelor of science in engineering have also been added.

OFF-CAMPUS OPPORTUNITIES

Vaughn is located in New York City and students can take advantage of every opportunity this amazing city has to offer.

MAJORS AND DEGREES OFFERED

Vaughn offers master's, bachelor's and associate degree programs in engineering, electronic engineering technology, mechanical engineering technology, mechatronic engineering, flight, general management, airline management, airport management, aviation maintenance management, aviation maintenance, animation and digital technologies, aeronautical engineering technology, and air traffic control (a non-degree program). Most Popular Majors: general management, airline management, airport management, animation and digital technologies, electronic engineering technology, aircraft operations, and aviation maintenance technology. Most Interesting Majors: aircraft operations (flight), airline management, airport management electronic technology, general management, aeronautical, and engineering technology.

ACADEMIC PROGRAMS

All students in associate and baccalaureate degree programs complete a core curriculum as part of their degree requirements. The core curriculum is derived from the mission of the College and reflects what the institution believes is important and elemental to students' education and development. In general, the core instills in students critical-thinking skills, values appropriate to an educated person, the ability to communicate, and the curriculum provides context for advanced learning. The baccalaureate core consists of three components - academic skills (13 credits, including a year of English composition, a course in oral communication, and pre-calculus), the liberal arts (12 credits, including a year of world and American literature), and math and science (15 credits).

CAMPUS FACILITIES AND EQUIPMENT

Each laboratory provides the work/study environment suited to the requirements of each program. Students experience the technology that they will ultimately use once employed. This practical, hands-on experience helps qualify students for immediate employment upon graduation. From the new photonics laboratory to the CATIA/NASTRAN computer center, the College's faculty members are committed to providing students with the knowledge and tools they are likely to find in today's businesses. The FRASCA 142 flight simulator is a major component of the flight students on campus. Over the last several years, the College has invested significant resources in both hardware and software technology. The College maintains a stable and robust infrastructure which supports processing at 10/100/1000 Megabits. The system supports other operating systems, including Windows NT, Windows 2000, Windows 2003, Windows XP, Macintosh OSX, and UNIX as well as all the previous server versions of windows operating systems. Our network can be accessed both internally and externally via the Internet, using VPN connections. At present we have upgraded our wireless capability to 108 mbps. Eight Cisco access points have been installed in various areas of the building. More information can be found on the College's Web site, www.vaughn.edu. Plans are underway for the construction of a new library. The new library will incorporate the new technologies that are currently being used in the existing library in addition to providing more complete references to meet more of the needs of a traditional student body and new graduate-level academic programs.

TUITION, ROOM, BOARD AND FEES

In 2007-08, full-time tuition (12 to 18 credits per semester) is $7,350. Students taking fewer than 11 credits pay $500 per credit. The semester fee, which covers the cost of orientation courses, Internet and computer usage, and student-support services, activities, and leadership programs, is $200.

Estimated fees for room and board are approximately $10,000, depending on room size and meal plan selected.

FINANCIAL AID

Vaughn College of Aeronautics and Technology provides financial aid packages, which may include scholarships, grants, loans and work study to students with strong academic records and/or demonstrated need. Counseling and assistance is available at the financial aid office at the College. All financial information is confidential to the extent possible.

Applicants for financial aid must complete the Free Application for Federal Student Aid (FAFSA) and a New York State Tuition Assistance Program (TAP) application if appropriate.

Financial aid is determined by a variety of factors, such as income, assets, family size and other family information. Every applicant has unique circumstances and the financial aid office is committed to helping students and their parents through the process. It is strongly recommended that students file for financial assistance as early in the year prior to enrollment as possible.

Financial aid eligibility requires that the student maintain satisfactory academic progress and program pursuit after enrolling.

STUDENT ORGANIZATIONS AND ACTIVITIES

Vaughn College supports a variety of student organizations. Activities are moderated by members of the faculty and staff. Distinguished professional societies have chartered student chapters. Students interested in joining should contact the office of student activities and development.

ADMISSIONS PROCESS

Vaughn College offers equal educational opportunity to all students without regard to age, citizenship status, color, disability, marital status, national origin, race, religion, creed, veteran status, gender or sexual orientation. Applications are accepted throughout the year. Applicants for admission must provide: Vaughn College of Aeronautics and Technology admissions application an official copy of their high school transcript official college transcript(s) - if applicable a copy of their high school diploma or GED with scores immunization records SAT I for all Bachelor of Science applicants. The admissions counseling staff is available to advise applicants and their parents and to provide up-to-date advisement material to high school guidance offices. Each applicant is evaluated individually and is kept informed about his or her status by admission status notices, which are issued as changes in status occur. For more information, contact the office of admissions at: 1.866.6VAUGHN, ext. 118.

WEBBER INTERNATIONAL UNIVERSITY

AT A GLANCE

Webber International University was established in 1927 by world-renowned economist Roger Babson. This four-year nonaffiliated coeducational institution is situated on a stunning 110-acre campus perched along the Lake Caloosa shoreline. Webber International University's location offers students convenient access to popular attractions such as Disney World and Cypress Gardens, among others. Webber receives its accreditation from the Southern Association of Colleges and Schools. The University prides itself on its strong tradition of high moral standards and exemplary academic achievement. Webber has cultivated an atmosphere that promotes success through hard work and scholastic merit. Roughly 160 women and 310 men are enrolled in Webber's undergraduate program. About 80 percent of those students are Florida residents; the remaining 20 percent come from 21 states across the nation and nearly 36 countries around the world. The University's off-campus placement programs provide students with practical, on-the-job business experience. Webber also offers field trips designed to enhance undergraduates' business education pursuits.

The University fields intercollegiate sports teams in baseball, basketball, cross-country, football, golf, soccer, tennis, and track and field for men and in basketball, cheerleading, cross-country, golf, soccer, softball, tennis, track and field, and volleyball for women. Students may also participate in Webber's intramural athletics program. The University's sports complex includes a beach volleyball court, a fitness room, two gymnasiums, racquetball courts, a soccer field, a junior Olympic-size swimming pool, and tennis courts. Undergraduates may also participate in lakeside and water sports such as beach volleyball, canoeing, fishing, and kayaking.

Webber International University offers a large assortment of social clubs and organizations including athletic boosters, Eta Sigma Delta and the Society of Hosteurs, FCA, an international club, a marketing club, Phi Beta Lambda, a sport management club, a student government association, a tourism society, and Webber ambassadors. These organizations, among others, help to fund the numerous social events at Webber.

LOCATION AND ENVIRONMENT

Webber International University is located in the small rural community of Babson Park, which lies at the center of Florida's citrus groves near a variety of freshwater lakes. The area has a welcoming and tranquil atmosphere. Babson Park is convenient to the many popular recreational amenities and tourist attractions of Florida's central region.

OFF-CAMPUS OPPORTUNITIES

Webber International University offers study abroad opportunities to undergraduates pursuing a bachelor's degree. Students may complete either one or two semesters in Paris, Nice, and Lille, France, or Barcelona, Spain.

The hospitality tourism and marketing departments offer internship programs with major restaurants and hotels in the Orlando region. In-state and out-of-state internships with prominent retail outlets are also available.

The finance department offers internship opportunities in a variety of financial organizations and in the financial divisions of regional corporations.

Additional Off-Campus Opportunities include elective programs in which undergraduates survey and evaluate business procedures and operations of area companies, then report their conclusions in a presentation. In this way, students gain valuable experience in the field of business consultancy.

A special departmental program is available that allows undergraduates in all 8 majors to spend the summer semester abroad and to observe business methods in an international setting.

ACADEMIC PROGRAMS

Webber International University students may pursue bachelor's and associate degrees in business administration. The school offers eight majors: accounting, computer information systems mangement, finance, hospitality and tourism management, management, marketing, pre-law, and sport management.

Webber International University follows a semester calendar with 15-week semesters, and two 6-week summer terms. Webber requires its students to complete 60 credit hours for the Associate of Science degree and 120 credit hours for the Bachelor of Science degree with a 2.0 minimum GPA. Students typically carry a 15 hour course load per semester. Undergraduates pursuing the Bachelor of Science degree must complete roughly 30 hours in the major, 36 hours in the business core, 36 hours in the general education core, and 18 hours of tailored electives. Undergraduates pursuing the Associate of Science degree must complete 27 hours in the business core, 18 hours in the general education core, and 15 hours in the major and tailored elective. Students pursuing the Bachelor of Science degree in general business studies must complete 45 hours in the general business studies core, 39 hours in the general education core, and 36 hours of tailored electives. All undergraduates are required to complete 30 of the last 33 hours at Webber International University to earn a degree. Students who earn exemplary scores on Advanced Placement (AP) and College-Level Examination Program (CLEP) general tests are awarded credit.

CAMPUS FACILITIES AND EQUIPMENT

Situated at the center of the campus is the Roger Babson Learning Center, a state-of-the-art business library. The facility presently holds approximately 15,000 volumes and a wide variety of audiovisual resources. The library has computers available for undergraduate use. Numerous research databases are on hand for students to use as well.

Webber's computer resources centers are data processing hubs and teaching facilities whose equipment offers the most up-to-date technology, encouraging outstanding student performance in business, communication, and creativity.

TUITION, ROOM, BOARD AND FEES

For the 2007-2008 academic year, the annual fee (including room and board, the student activities fee, and tuition) is $24,070. The annual fee for commuting students totaled $16,760. These costs are adjusted periodically. Webber International University projects that $1,200 is sufficient for books and supplies. Laboratory fees are not included in this amount.

FINANCIAL AID

The Student Financial Aid Department is available to guide and assist students in meeting educational costs. Financial Aid is distributed on the basis of academic performance, applicant need, and potential. Roughly 90 percent of undergraduates at the University are awarded financial assistance. Students applying for need-based assistance must file the Free Application for Federal Student Aid (FAFSA). Numerous forms of aid, such as Federal Work-Study awards, grants, loans, and scholarships are employed to meet undergraduate needs. A small number of non-need-based scholarships are also offered; these are awarded based on academic achievement, on college and community service, or on athletic performance in basketball, cheerleading, cross-country, football, golf, soccer, softball, tennis, track and field, or volleyball. Students seeking aid must resubmit applications annually. Webber International University participates in the Federal Perkins Loan, Federal Supplemental Educational Opportunity Grant, and Federal Work-Study programs. Prospective applicants must apply for any government-funded grant for which they are qualified, such as the Federal Pell Grant; Florida residents are required to apply for a Florida Student Assistance Grant and the Florida Tuition Voucher Program. Federal Stafford Student Loans are offered as well. Students seeking Financial Aid should submit their applications prior to April 1 in order to qualify for specific Financial Aid opportunities.

STUDENT ORGANIZATIONS AND ACTIVITIES

At Webber International University, not all learning takes place in the classroom. Active involvement in social programs, recreational activities and personal-growth experiences create special moments and long-lasting university memories. The Student Government Association, Webber's primary governing organization, is comprised of elected undergraduate representatives and a staff advisor. The SGA addresses nonacademic aspects of campus life. It oversees the activities of student organizations and involves undergraduates in campus procedures and policies. Representatives from many different undergraduate organizations participate in the Student Government Association, as do elected representatives from the University's student body.

ADMISSIONS PROCESS

Prospective students must be high school graduates. It is recommended that applicants have completed at least 4 years of English and 2 to 3 years of mathematics as well as preparation in seven other academic subjects. The majority of prospective students rank in the top half of their graduating class. Applicants must present their SAT I or ACT scores before being considered for admission. International applicants are required to present scores on the Test of English as a Foreign Language (TOEFL).

Early admission is an option for exceptional juniors with test scores near the top 15th percentile in the state or country, a grade point average of at least 3.0 (on a 4.0 scale), a favorable letter of reference from a counselor or principal, and a letter of permission from their parents or legal guardian. Applicants are required to interview with the dean of student development.

Transfer student applications are welcome, as well as applications from students resuming their education as nontraditional adult students. Transfer students must have satisfactory records at their previous institution.

Applicants who fall short of regular entrance requirements may be considered individually as candidates for the Fresh Start program by the Fresh Start admissions committee. All Fresh Start applicants must appear for a personal interview.

The Admissions Committee formally considers an application once it has received the $35 domestic student application fee or the $75 international student application fee, all necessary test scores and recommendations, and transcripts from all learning institutions attended. The University operates on a rolling admissions basis. It is strongly suggested that application forms be submitted at the earliest possible date, as on-campus housing is in high demand. (Freshmen must reside in the dormitory unless they share a residence with a parent, guardian, or spouse.)

To receive application forms, catalogs, and other information, applicants should contact:

Webber International University

1201 North Scenic Highway

PO Box 96

Babson Park, FL 33827-9990

Telephone: 863-638-2910

E-mail: admissions@webber.edu

World Wide Web: www.webber.edu

WELLS COLLEGE

AT A GLANCE

Wells College is a coeducational, private, liberal arts college enrolling 550 students from across the United States and throughout the world. Today, true to its heritage, Wells maintains a national reputation for academic excellence. The College prides itself on offering one of the most collaborative learning environments in higher education today. The top five reasons to consider Wells: (1) Wells offers students education of the highest quality at an affordable price. This impressive combination makes us a best value among national liberal arts colleges (2) 94% of Wells faculty members have doctoral degrees and all classes are taught by professors - not teaching assistants (3) Wells students prepare for careers and entrance into top graduate and professional schools through experiential learning: internships, research with faculty members, and community service (4) Wells offers an extensive study abroad program with affiliated programs in 14 different countries (5) All students at Wells benefit from an academic experience similar to honors programs available only to a small number of students at other institutions. Throughout their four years, they work toward a senior thesis that is comparable to graduate-level study. Wells prides itself on offering one of the most collaborative learning environments in higher education.

LOCATION AND ENVIRONMENT

The beautiful 365-acre lakeside campus is situated in the heart of the Finger Lakes Resort Region of New York State in the historical village of Aurora. The campus is 30 minutes from Ithaca, one hour from Syracuse and Rochester, and approximately five hours from New York City.

MAJORS AND DEGREES OFFERED

Wells College offers the Bachelor of Arts degree with majors in the following areas (concentrations within the majors appear in parentheses): American Studies (African-American Studies, American Cultures); Biological and Chemical Sciences (Biochemistry, Molecular Biology, Biology, Chemistry); Economics and Management (Economics, Management); English (Creative Writing, Literature); Environmental Studies (Environmental Policies and Values, Environmental Sciences); Foreign Languages, Literatures, and Cultures (French, German, Spanish); History; International Studies; Mathematical and Physical Sciences (Computer Science, Mathematics, Physics); Performing Arts (Music, Theatre and Dance); Psychology; Public Affairs: Ethics, Politics, and Social Policy (Ethics and Philosophy, Government and Politics); Religion (Historical and Comparative Studies, Religion and Culture); Sociology and Anthropology (Sociology, Anthropology/Cross-cultural Sociology), Visual Arts (Art History, Studio Art); Women's Studies. In consultation with the dean and faculty, students may also design their own concentrations and majors. In addition, Wells offers programs that lead to provisional certification in elementary and secondary education.

ACADEMIC PROGRAMS

This is not your ordinary education. The Wells experience is deeply personal and intensely focused on superior academic achievement. Wells offers 16 majors and over 35 minors. With one professor for every nine students, professors really get to know everyone. The average class size has twelve students and is taught seminar-style, with discussions taking precedence over lectures. Fundamental to the Wells curriculum is an interdisciplinary approach to the liberal arts with the opportunity to experience intimate classes and innovative teaching methods. Through Wells' experiential learning program, students have opportunities to participate in quality internships, off campus study programs, and academic research projects. Experiential learning in the curriculum enables students to test theories learned in the classroom with real-life situations and intertwine it with a rigorous academic program.

TUITION, ROOM, BOARD AND FEES

For the 2007-08 year: Tuition: $16,510 Room and board: $8,100 Fees: $1,300.

STUDENT ORGANIZATIONS AND ACTIVITIES

Wells students enjoy all of the advantages of living in a closely-knit community. A well-respected Honor Code shapes the educational and social atmosphere of the campus. Wells supports more than 40 clubs and organizations including a literary magazine and newspaper, music and drama groups, and political organizations, in addition to student-sponsored events, lectures, and performances. Wells is also a Division III member of the NCAA. Wells women compete in six intercollegiate sports: soccer, lacrosse, softball, field hockey, tennis, and swimming. Wells also offers a co-ed cross-country team. Wells men compete in four intercollegiate sports: soccer, lacrosse, basketball and swimming. Women's basketball will begin at the club level next year and be elevated to intercollegiate status in 2009-10.

ADMISSIONS PROCESS

Wells students are intellectually curious, open-minded, and creative. They are comfortable expressing themselves, listening to others and sharing ideas. They are caring citizens of the world, eager to travel beyond the campus and outside their comfort zones. Wells students love to learn. If you love learning, you'll love the Wells experience.

Candidates for admission are expected to complete a solid college preparatory program throughout their four years in secondary school. The college recommends a program which provides the best background for study at Wells, including four years of English grammar, composition, and literature; three years of History; three years of mathematics; two years of history; two years of laboratory science; and coursework in a foreign language. Student's records are enhanced by the addition of courses such as computer science, art, and music, when appropriate curricular choices are offered. To apply for admission to Wells College candidates must submit completed application forms to the Admissions Office by March 1 of the year of entrance.

In addition, the following credentials are required: a transcript of all secondary school work, including the recommendation of the high school principal or school counselor; scores from either the College Entrance Examination Board Scholastic Aptitude Test (SAT I) or the American College Testing Program (ACT); two letters of recommendation from teachers in academic subject areas. A personal interview is recommended.

Admissions Deadline Options:

Early Decision. December 15: Students whose first choice is Wells College are encouraged to apply under the early decision option. This is a binding admissions option; if admitted; early decision applicants agree to accept Wells offer of admission and agree to withdraw their applications from all other colleges.

Early Action. December 15: Students who would like to receive an early review of their application files are encouraged to apply under the early action option. This is a non-binding admissions option.

Regular Admission. March 1: All other applications to the college should be received by the regular admission deadline. Applications are reviewed after this date and decisions are mailed by April 1.

School Says . . .

WESTERN MICHIGAN UNIVERSITY

AT A GLANCE

Students who choose Western Michigan University get an edge in work and life by taking full advantage of a school that combines the resources of a national research university with the personal attention and atmosphere often found at a smaller institution. WMU focuses on providing the tools students need to become successful alumni, and its top-notch programs, faculty and facilities have attracted national as well as international attention.

• The Carnegie Foundation classifies WMU as one of the nation's 139 public research universities.

• *U.S. News & World Report* names WMU among the top-100 public institutions in the nation and the top 30 in the Midwest.

• WMU is just one of 97 public universities nationwide authorized to have its own chapter of Phi Beta Kappa.

WMU was founded in 1903 and enrolls more than 24,000 students from across the United States and 84 other countries. Twenty percent of the student body is composed of graduate students, while minorities make up 11 percent and international students 4 percent.

The University places equal emphasis on offering high-quality Academic Programs at both the undergraduate and graduate levels through its seven degree-granting colleges: Arts and Sciences, Aviation, Education, Engineering and Applied Sciences, Fine Arts, Haworth College of Business, and Health and Human Services.

Students may choose from 237 programs, including 140 bachelor's programs, 29 doctoral programs and 67 master's programs. A wide variety of these offerings have earned a national or international reputation, such as those in aviation, blindness and low vision studies, creative writing, engineering management, evaluation, jazz studies, and medieval studies.

But despite its size and complexity, the University offers the personal attention and support crucial to helping students succeed. At WMU, students don't have to look far to find first-year mentoring programs, extensive career and employment services, or experienced advisors and tutors.

LOCATION AND ENVIRONMENT

Kalamazoo is a vibrant college town in southwest Michigan's Kalamazoo County, which has a population of more than 238,000 people. The campus is located midway between Detroit and Chicago, about two and one-half hours from each city. The region offers a wide array of entertainment: sports, such as professional baseball, hockey and soccer; music of every variety; intimate coffee houses and comedy clubs; and dining, from fast food to international cuisine. In addition, the area is dotted with lakes, parks, golf courses, and hiking, biking and cross country ski trails. It also is situated just 45 minutes from Lake Michigan's sandy beaches and 30 minutes from excellent local skiing.

OFF-CAMPUS OPPORTUNITIES

WMU's business-industry partnerships and exchange agreements with institutions around the world provide countless opportunities for students to gain field experience, conduct research and study abroad. The University's West Michigan location provides plenty of opportunities for employment, from service and seasonal jobs to positions at Fortune 500 companies like Haworth Inc., the Whirlpool Corp. and the Kellogg Co. Many of the larger employers offer internships to WMU students.

MAJORS AND DEGREES OFFERED

WMU offers bachelor's degree programs in these fields:

Accountancy; Advertising and Promotion; Aeronautical Engineering; Africana Studies; Anthropology; Art; Art Education; Art History; Athletic Training Program; Aviation Flight Science; Aviation Maintenance Technology; Aviation Science and Administration; Biochemistry; Biology; Biomedical Sciences; Business (General); Business-Oriented Chemistry; Chemical Engineering; Chemistry; Civil Engineering; Communication Studies; Computer Engineering; Computer Information Systems; Computer Science (General); Computer Science (Theory and Analysis); Construction Engineering; Criminal Justice; Dance; Dietetics; Early Childhood Professional Education; Earth Science; Economics; Electrical Engineering; Electronic Business Design; Elementary Professional Education; Engineering Graphics and Design Technology; Engineering Management Technology; English; Environmental Studies; Exercise Science; Family and Consumer Science Teacher Education; Family Studies; Film Video and Media Studies; Finance; Food and Consumer Packaging Goods Marketing; Food Service Administration; French; Geochemistry; Geography; Geology; Geophysics; German; Global and International Studies; Graphic Design; Health Education (Community); Health Education (School); Health Services (Interdisciplinary); Health Services (Interdisciplinary Occupational Therapy); History; Human Resource Management; Hydrogeology; Imaging; Industrial Engineering; Industrial Technology; Integrated Supply Matrix Management; Interior Design; Interpersonal Communication; Journalism; Latin; Management; Manufacturing Engineering Technology; Manufacturing Engineering; Marketing; Mathematics; Mechanical Engineering; Music; Music Composition; Music Education; Music (Elementary Education); Music (Jazz Studies); Music Performance; Music Theatre Performance; Music Therapy; Nursing (B.A.); Nursing (R.N.); Occupational Education Studies; Organizational Communication; Paper Engineering; Paper Science; Personal Financial Planning; Philosophy; Physical Education (Teacher/Coach); Physics; Political Science; Psychology; Public History; Public Relations; Recreation; Religion (Comparative); Sales and Business Marketing; Secondary Education in Business; Secondary Education in Marketing; Social Work; Sociology; Spanish; Special Education (Cognitive Impairments); Special Education (Emotional Impairments); Speech Pathology and Audiology; Statistics; Student Integrated Curriculum; Student Planned Curriculum; Student Planned Major; Technology and Design; Telecommunications and Information Management; Textile and Apparel Studies; Theatre; Tourism and Travel; and Women's Studies.

ACADEMIC PROGRAMS

Instructional programs are designed so graduating students are ready to immediately add value to their work places and prepared to achieve success in whatever endeavors they pursue. The rich blend of majors and minors is supplemented by programs such as the Lee Honors College, which is one of the oldest honors programs in the nation and offers the intimacy of a small college with the resources of a major university; BroncoJobs Plus, which conveniently puts many of WMU's career and job-search resources online; and University Curriculum, which helps undecided students select a major.

Faculty

WMU attracts faculty members who have been trained at the world's leading universities and who have well-established research and teaching careers. The University's commitment to academic excellence means that many of its 860 full-time and 441 part-time faculty members conduct research. In addition to having a passion for teaching, these scholars welcome students into their research labs and creative studios as well as bring a global perspective to the classroom because of their overseas academic and research experiences.

CAMPUS FACILITIES AND EQUIPMENT

The campus learning environment is bolstered by some of the best instructional, cultural and recreational facilities in the Midwest. New construction and equipment has continuously transformed the campus, giving students access to acclaimed performance spaces; a large, well-equipped student recreation center; a state-of-the-art science pavilion; a world-class aviation college; a sophisticated health and human services college; and a cutting-edge engineering campus adjacent to a thriving Business Technology and Research Park.

The University Libraries, with the fourth-largest holdings in Michigan, and the University Computing Center together provide campuswide access to worldwide information resources. Computer labs are available across the campus, many in residence halls, and wireless computing is commonplace. In fact, Intel ranks WMU second on its list of America's 100 "Most Unwired College Campuses."

TUITION, ROOM, BOARD AND FEES

WMU's tuition and fees are among the most affordable in Michigan. For 2007-08, tuition and fees for full-time freshmen and sophomores cost $7,260, while the cost of room and board is $7,042. Books and supplies as well as personal and travel expenses vary based on individual factors.

A student/WMU compact called the *Western Edge* is making the University even more affordable. Started in fall 2007, the compact helps students find the right career path and earn their degrees quickly—bucking what has become the national trend of taking about six years to graduate. Less time in school automatically saves money, and it allows students to head for graduate school or enter the job market sooner.

FINANCIAL AID

In 2006-07, some 18,000 students received financial assistance totaling nearly $200 million. Merit-based programs include the Medallion Scholarships, which are valued at $40,000 over four years and are WMU's most prestigious award for entering freshmen. Need-based loans, grants, college work-study and other aid options are provided for students who demonstrate particular financial need. To be considered, students should complete the Free Application for Federal Student Aid (FAFSA).

STUDENT ORGANIZATIONS AND ACTIVITIES

There are nearly 300 registered student organizations, including a wide range of Greek, academic honorary and professional organizations. In addition, the University has nationally recognized arts programs, a lively cultural calendar, and NCAA Division I-A teams in the Mid-American Conference and Central Collegiate Hockey Association. Six men's and 10 women's varsity sports, intramural teams, and club sports add vitality to campus life.

ADMISSIONS PROCESS

Admission to WMU is based on a combination of factors, including grade point average, ACT scores, number and kinds of college-prep courses, and trend of grades. Admission of high school students to the University is based on a combination of quantitative and qualitative factors. Quantitative factors include grade point average and ACT or SAT scores. Qualitative factors include, but are not limited to, the number and type of academic classes taken, personal recommendations and trend of grades. The Office of Admissions reviews each application for these criteria. To be considered for the Medallion Scholarship, students must apply by Dec. 1.

Transfer students with a minimum of 26 transferable hours (39 quarter hours) at the time of application and a GPA of at least 2.0 (C average) are considered for admission. The trend of the most recent grades is also taken into account. Applicants with fewer than 26 transferable hours (39 quarter hours) at the time of application also must submit a high school transcript. In such cases, admission is based on both college and high school records.

For an application or additional information, students should contact:

Office of Admissions

Western Michigan University

1903 W. Michigan Avenue

Kalamazoo, Michigan 49008-5211

United States

Telephone: 269-387-2000

World Wide Web: www.wmich.edu/admi/undergradapp

WESTERN NEW ENGLAND COLLEGE

AT A GLANCE

Western New England College prepares you for your future from the first moment you step on campus. Beginning with our First Year Program and continuing straight through Commencement and beyond, Western New England College prepares you for professional careers or graduate studies within its five schools: Arts and Sciences, Business, Engineering, Law, and Pharmacy.

Founded in 1919, Western New England College is ranked among the North Region's "Best Universities-Master's Category," those which provide a full range of bachelor's and master's programs, in the annual "America's Best Colleges" ranking, by *U.S. News & World Report*.

By The Numbers

9	Residence facilities
15:1	Student-faculty ratio
19	NCAA Division III sponsored sports
20	Average class size
28	States represented by the student body
29	NCAA Tournament appearances since 2000
39	Undergraduate Academic Programs
60%	Out-of-state student body
60	Student clubs and organizations
79%	Students living on campus
90%	Freshmen receiving Financial Aid
92%	Faculty holding doctoral degrees
92%	Freshmen living on campus
215	Total acreage of the campus
2,500	Full-time undergraduate enrollment
3,700	Total College enrollment
38,000	Total College alumni

Excellence in Athletics

You'll have plenty of opportunities to cheer for the Golden Bears during your time at Western New England College. The College's 19 NCAA Division III teams enjoy a growing reputation having earned 29 NCAA tournament berths and captured numerous conference titles since 2000. The College is a member of The Commonwealth Coast Conference (TCCC).

Men's Sports: Baseball; Basketball; Cross Country; Football; Golf; Ice Hockey; Lacrosse; Soccer; Tennis; Wrestling

Women's Sports: Basketball; Cross Country; Field Hockey; Lacrosse; Soccer; Softball; Swimming; Tennis; Volleyball; Non-NCAA Sports; Bowling; Martial Arts

A Beautiful Campus is Just the Beginning

Western New England College students enjoy a beautiful 215-acre suburban campus at the "Crossroads of New England." Western New England College is located a mere 30 minutes from Hartford and Bradley International Airport, 90 minutes from Boston, and less than three hours from New York City. The Connecticut River Valley along Interstate 91 is called New England's "Knowledge Corridor" because of its abundance of institutions of higher education. In fact, the region boasts 35 colleges and universities, which enroll 149,200 students.

Success in Your First Year

The College's First Year Program is a structured support system to help you make a smooth transition from high school to college. Part of the support program includes the First Year Seminar taught by faculty who also serve as your advisor. This seminar will help you improve information literacy skills, explore careers, learn to think critically, and give oral presentations.

Major in success: Today's most popular programs

Do you want to pursue a career with a professional basketball franchise? Our business-oriented sport management major would be a great fit. Maybe medical school is in your future. Then biomedical engineering, a preferred major of medical school acceptance committees, would be best suited for you. Perhaps you want to anchor a national news broadcast? Our state-of-the-art television studio, the jewel of the communication department, will give you the hands-on experience you need. From creative writing to forensic chemistry, Western New England College offers these and other exciting majors that lead to jobs in some of the fastest growing fields in the world.

Western New England College also offers an accelerated 3+3 Law Program, Six-year Biomedical Engineering/Law program, and the Five-year Bachelor/MBA and MSA programs which allow you to complete your undergraduate and graduate studies in less time than it would take to do separately.

Experience a World of Opportunity

Western New England College emphasizes the importance of gaining real-world experience with a global perspective during your education. Internships, guest speakers, alumni mentoring programs, study abroad, and industry symposiums are just a few of the opportunities offered by the College to increase your exposure to the world outside of campus. Western New England College students have completed internships for:

Baystate Health; General Dynamics; Invesco Field at Mile High; MassMutual Financial Group; Naismith Memorial Basketball Hall of Fame; New England Center for Children; Pratt and Whitney; Walt Disney World; Willie Ross School for the Deaf

OFF-CAMPUS OPPORTUNITIES

Springfield is the third largest city in Massachusetts. Home to 152,000 people, it sits on the banks of the Connecticut River at the intersection of Interstate 91 and the Massachusetts Turnpike (I-90).

The Springfield area has numerous attractions including:

- Naismith Memorial Basketball Hall of Fame
- Six Flags New England
- The Big E—Eastern States Exposition
- MassMutual Center—home of the Springfield Falcons of the American Hockey League
- CityStage and Symphony Hall
- Forest Park—home to the annual Bright Nights at Forest Park celebration
- Dr. Seuss National Memorial Sculpture Garden
- Numerous libraries and museums

Boston; New York City; popular ski resorts in Vermont, Massachusetts, and New Hampshire; and the beaches of Cape Cod, Connecticut, Maine, New Hampshire, and Rhode Island are all within driving distance of campus.

School of Business—One of the Best in the World

The Association to Advance Collegiate Schools of Business (AACSB) International is considered the gold standard for schools of business. Less than 10 percent of the business schools in the world hold this accreditation. Western New England College School of Business is proud to have its name included on this illustrious list. AACSB International accreditation is prized among the corporate world and graduate school admissions councils.

Coming 2009: Western New England College Pharmacy

Coming in the fall of 2009, Western New England College will admit the first class in the Pre-pharmacy program. Students who graduate from this six-year professional program will earn a Doctor of Pharmacy (Pharm.D.) degree. The jewel of the program will be a new state-of-the-art academic building slated for completion in 2010.

MAJORS AND DEGREES OFFERED

Accounting; Biology (General and Molecular concentrations); Biomedical Engineering; Business Information Systems; Chemistry; Communication (Interpersonal Communication and Mass Media concentrations); Computer Science; Creative Writing; Criminal Justice; Economics; Education (Elementary and Secondary); Electrical Engineering (Computer and Electrical concentration); English; Finance; Forensic Biology; Forensic Chemistry; General Business; History; Industrial Engineering; Information Technology; International Studies (Developing Societies, Economics and Commerce, and European Area concentrations); Law and Society; Management; Marketing; Marketing Communication/Advertising; Mathematical Sciences; Mechanical Engineering (Manufacturing and Mechanical concentrations); Philosophy; Political Science; Pre-pharmacy; Psychology; Social Work; Sociology; Sport Management; Five-year Bachelor/MBA; Five-year Bachelor/MSA; 3+3 Law Program (bachelor's degree and a law degree in six years of study); Six-year BME/Law (bachelor's degree in Biomedical Engineering and a law degree in six years of study)

Pre-professional Studies: Law; Medicine

Accelerated Programs

3+3 Law Program

The 3+3 Law Program offers eligible students the opportunity to earn their bachelor's degree from the College and Juris Doctor degrees from Western New England College School of Law, located on campus, in six years instead of seven.

Five-year Bachelor/MBA or MSA

Gain a competitive advantage for your future with the Five-year Bachelor/MBA or MSA program. The MBA program is open to students in most majors.

Six-year Biomedical Engineering/Law

This unique program fills a dire need for professionals with training in both engineering and the law. Pursue careers as attorneys working for the government, private industry, or in private practice.

Accreditation

The College is accredited by the New England Association of Schools and Colleges, the School of Business is fully accredited by AACSB International—The Association to Advance Collegiate Schools of Business, and all majors in the School of Engineering are accredited by ABET—The Accreditation Board for Engineering and Technology. Various programs have additional accreditation.

Faculty

All classes are taught by faculty members; there are no graduate student teaching assistants. The average class size consists of about 20 students, and classes are not taught in large lecture halls. The typical classroom holds a maximum of 35 students. The student/faculty ratio is 15 to 1.

CAMPUS FACILITIES AND EQUIPMENT

Classes are held in five centrally located classroom-laboratory buildings, which contain more than 65 classrooms. Many classrooms feature multimedia-teaching stations with projection units. The campus features a network of hundreds of PCs and a large number of microcomputers and specialized equipment are available to engineering students. Each semester, approximately 150 faculty members and hundreds of students communicate and study online using the *Manhattan* Virtual Classroom, a software package developed at the College and used by schools and universities around the world.

Tuition, Room, Board, and Fees

Note: These figures are for the 2008-09 Academic Year.

$1,718   Fees

$9,998   Room and board

$24,224   Schools of Arts and Science and Business tuition

$25,316   School of Engineering tuition

FINANCIAL AID

Western New England College offers comprehensive programs of financial assistance to students who demonstrate financial need. The programs include merit and need-based scholarships, grants, loans, and on-campus employment. Students seeking Financial Aid must submit the Free Application for Federal Student Aid (FAFSA) and a copy of the federal income tax return and W2. Approximately 90 percent of Western New England College students annually receive assistance.

ADMISSIONS PROCESS

Admission is offered to students on a rolling basis for all programs. Decisions begin in late fall after the first quarter marking period grades are released. Students must submit the Western New England College application, SAT I or ACT scores, an official secondary school transcript, and a recommendation from a guidance counselor or teacher. International students can substitute the Test of English as a Foreign Language (TOEFL) for the SAT or ACT test. American students for whom English is not their first language are encouraged to submit TOEFL scores. Transfer students must also submit official transcripts for any collegiate work. An essay is not required, but essays and personal statements are welcome.

Applicants must have graduated from an approved secondary school or have obtained a General Equivalency Diploma (GED). The minimum units of high school preparation should include four units of English, two units of mathematics, one unit of laboratory science, and one unit of U.S. history. Students seeking admission to the School of Business and various majors within the School of Arts and Sciences are required to have three units of mathematics while engineering applicants are required to have four units of mathematics. The School of Engineering and various Arts and Sciences majors require more than one unit of laboratory science. The Office of Admissions should be contacted for specific admissions requirements.

Visit our website at www.wnec.edu and we'll create a customized digital viewbook all about you—your major, your sport, your interests emailed directly to you. You can also take a virtual tour of campus and create an account to apply for admission online.

Telephone 413-782-1321 or

800-325-1122, ext. 1321

FAX 413-782-1777

Email: ugradmis@wnec.edu

www.wnec.edu

WESTMINSTER COLLEGE

AT A GLANCE

Westminster College offers students an unique learning environment, a vibrant community, and a track record of success. Enrolling approximately 2500 students, Westminster College is the only private, comprehensive liberal arts college in Utah. Students are encouraged to take advantage of a dynamic urban setting with unparalleled access to an ecological wonderland and the college uses that larger setting as an extension of its classrooms through internships, field work, undergraduate research and an impressive outdoor recreation program. The learning environment is led by faculty members who are here because they love to teach. Deeply committed to each student's success, Westminster College is a challenging and supportive community of learners.

LOCATION AND ENVIRONMENT

Located where Salt Lake City meets the Rocky Mountains, Westminster is tucked into the quaint and eclectic Sugarhouse neighborhood of Salt Lake City and provides a welcome academic haven for learners. Distinguished by old-growth trees, a small creek, and a graceful blend of old and new architecture, the urban College campus still provides plenty of green space to enjoy in the midst of the city. The Colleges on-campus housing, which accommodates 500 students, includes new apartment-style suites featuring entertainment systems and cooking facilities. Off-campus rental housing is readily available in the neighborhood.

In 2007, Outside magazine gave Salt Lake plenty of kudos for its progressive thinking, and describes it as "a near-perfect location for avid outdoor adventures" and in 2008 Forbes magazine ranked SLC #1 for job growth. Salt Lake City, a metropolitan area of approximately 1.3 million people, has also been rated as one of the ten most fun places to live, was home of the 2002 Winter Olympics, and offers easy access to the Sundance Film Festival.

OFF-CAMPUS OPPORTUNITIES

Downtown Salt Lake is 10 minutes away from campus by bus, car, or bicycle. Attractions include professional sports events, ballet, theater, concerts, and shopping to suit all tastes. A new Campus Concierge program facilitates student access to cultural events, recreational and entertainment options, student discounts, and volunteer opportunities.

Salt Lake and the surrounding areas have four distinct seasons, with limited amounts of rain and snow in the valley and moderate temperatures. However, the Wasatch Mountains, a section of the Rockies that borders the Salt Lake Valley on the east, are famous for the "greatest snow on earth." With approximately 500 inches of annual snowfall, these mountains are ideal for winter sports enthusiasts as well as for those who enjoy summer hiking, biking, and camping. Ten world-class ski and snowboard resorts lie within an hours drive of campus, and sixteen national parks and recreational areas are within a days drive or less. Golf, backpacking, mountain biking, kayaking, wakeboarding, mountain climbing, canyoneering, spelunking, and rafting are all within easy reach of campus.

Westminster students may participate in travel/study trips (for credit) during May term and the summer session. Students can also make individual arrangements for international study by advisement from the college's International Studies Chair and the Career Resource Center and through a cooperative agreement with the Foreign Study Office at a nearby University. Westminster is also a member of the Utah Asian Studies Consortium, which promotes connections between faculty members and students in Utah and businesses and schools in Asia, offering May-term trips, internships, semester study-abroad programs, and other opportunities in several Asian countries.

MAJORS AND DEGREES OFFERED

Westminster College offers over seventy Academic Programs. Bachelor of Arts and Bachelor of Science degrees are awarded in the following areas: Accounting, Art, Aviation, Biology, Business (Accounting, Finance, General Business, Human Resource Management, Information Resource Management, Management, and Marketing,) Chemistry, Communication, Computer Science, Economics, Education (Early Childhood, Elementary, Secondary, and Special Education), English, Financial Services, History, International Business, Justice Studies, Mathematics, Neuroscience, Nursing, Philosophy, Physics, Political Studies, Pre-Professional Programs (Dentistry, Law, Medicine, Veterinary Medicine, and 3-2 Engineering), Psychology, Social Science, And Sociology. In addition to the above-listed majors, the college offers minors in many of those program areas plus minors only in the following areas: Anthropology, Environmental Studies, French, Gender Studies, Music, Political Science, Religion, Spanish, and Theater Arts.

ACADEMIC PROGRAMS

Westminster encourages students to think for themselves, draw conclusions … and change their minds. Through engaging college-wide learning goals, students experiment with ideas, raise questions, and critically examine alternatives. That philosophy is just one reason that Westminster offers a unique environment for learning. Others include our commitment to students and their learning; our emphasis on an active and engaged style of learning; a campus that is warm, welcoming and active; and graduates who have mastered the skills that employers want and society needs. By integrating a liberal arts foundation with professional education, Westminster exhibits features of both a liberal arts college and a comprehensive university.

Courses are designed to involve students in active, experiential, cross-disciplinary and collaborative learning. Each student must complete at least 124 semester hours to receive a bachelor's degree and while approximately 40 hours consist of liberal arts students are also exposed to practical, career-oriented experiences. Credit is awarded for successful scores on Advanced Placement and CLEP examinations. The College has a 4-4-1 calendar, consisting of two 15-week semesters followed by a one-month May term, as well as a summer session. May Term is Westminster's intensive semester: a month of offbeat and inspiring classes, laid-back trips around Utah and adventures outside of the U.S. After a year of hitting the books, May Term is a truly unique experience taking you outside of the classroom and leading you to discoveries about yourself and the world. And the best part is it's free. Students who attend full-time during fall and spring semesters earn free May-term tuition.

Students may also enroll in Reserve Officer Training Corps programs through cooperative agreements with a nearby University.

TUITION, ROOM, BOARD AND FEES

Tuition and fees for 2007-08 were $22,374 for the academic year for a full-time student (12 to 16 semester credit hours). This figure includes costs for the fall semester, spring semester, and May term. Room and board costs were $6354 for the same period. Books and supplies were estimated at $1000 per year.

FINANCIAL AID

Ninety-six percent of freshmen at Westminster receive some form of Financial Aid, averaging approximately $17,713 each year per student. Aid programs include need-based institutional grants and need-based federal aid programs, such as grants, loans, and employment (Federal Work-Study Program). The Free Application for Federal Student Aid (FAFSA) is the only form required for new students seeking Financial Aid. Students wishing to apply for federal aid programs should plan to submit applications by early April. Merit-based scholarships are available to incoming freshmen and transfer students as well as to continuing students through a generous endowment and institutional aid programs. Every full-time student is automatically considered for merit-based scholarships awarded by the College. The scholarships are based on their GPA from previous academic course work. Scholarships are also offered for music, theatre, athletics and extra curricular achievements.

ADMISSIONS PROCESS

We seek students who will thrive in our classrooms and bring vibrancy to our campus. We review each application individually and take into consideration quality of academic preparation, which includes both difficulty of course work and grades, extracurricular activities, individual talents and character, recommendations, and ACT or SAT scores. Westminster admits students whose academic records indicate that they possess the skills and maturity necessary for success in college work. Students are admitted without discrimination as to race, color, nationality, creed, sex, physical handicaps, or veteran status. Although the college does not require a specific pattern of school subjects, it does strongly recommend a solid college preparatory high school academic program.

Transfer students must have a minimum 2.5 academic GPA to be considered for admission. In addition to all other admissions criteria, international students must have at least a 3.0 GPA in non U.S. high school or college work and a Test of English as a Foreign Language (TOEFL) score of at least 550 (or equivalent).

Application and Information

To apply for admission, a student must submit an application for admission, personal essay, a recommendation, an application fee, and official transcripts of previous high school and/or college class work. Freshman applicants must submit ACT or SAT scores. Applicants are notified of their admission status within two weeks of receipt of all required materials. Westminster operates rolling admissions, so it's best to send your application in as soon as possible. To preserve the faculty-student ratio, classes are limited. Westminster College reserves the right to close the class earlier than dates specified if enrollment goals are met before those dates. New applicants are accepted for the start of all sessions. For application forms and additional information, students should contact:

Office of Admissions

Westminster College

1840 South 1300 East

Salt Lake City, Utah 84105

United States

Phone: 801-832-2200 800-748-4753 (toll-free)

Web site: http://www.westminstercollege.edu

WHEATON COLLEGE

AT A GLANCE

Wheaton College offers Academic Programs rooted in the classic liberal arts tradition, taught from an evangelical Christian perspective. It's a top-ranked college that challenges students to grow their intellect in the context of developing a whole life—a school that combines serious study and academic rigor with Christian distinctiveness.

Ranked by U.S. News and World Report as one of the top national liberal arts colleges, Wheaton attracts exceptional high school students from all 50 states and more than 40 countries. Established in 1860 as a co-ed, interdenominational Christian liberal arts college, Wheaton takes the pursuit of faith and learning seriously. Seeking to create a diverse, service-oriented community, Wheaton offers a rich curriculum that emphasizes global awareness and engagement. Students participate in a vibrant, growing multicultural community of talented, capable learners who are distinct in their desire to grow intellectually, to grow in relationship with one another, and to grow in Christ.

Wheaton's concern for values is a long-standing tradition, not a trend. Wheaton has consistently appeared on the Honor Roll of Character Building Colleges established by The John Templeton Foundation. Such recognition reflects Wheaton's commitment to character building programs such as its Center for Applied Christian Ethics, Urban Studies Program, Human Needs and Global Resources Program (HNGR), Honduras Project, HoneyRock's Wheaton Passage Wilderness Program, and the many services and ministries of the Office of Christian Outreach.

A profile of the Class of 2007 demonstrates the caliber of students that choose Wheaton. Of the 577 students who entered in the fall of 2003, 45 were National Merit Finalists. The group's average high school GPA was 3.7 and 61% graduated in the top 10% of their class. The middle 50% scored between 1250 and 1400 on the Critical Reasoning and Math sections of the SAT and between 27 and 31 on the ACT.

15% of Wheaton's students are multicultural, and approximately 80% will graduate on time. Wheaton, with its emphasis on faith, learning, and service, is a place where students like this can thrive.

LOCATION AND ENVIRONMENT

Wheaton, Illinois, population 54,000, is a family-oriented community known for its good schools, pleasant neighborhoods, and many churches. Major airports, OHare and Midway, are easily accessible for domestic and international travel. A 45-minute train ride links suburban Wheaton to downtown Chicago and all the excitement a world-class city offers, including a magnificent lakeshore. Chicago provides Wheaton students with a focus for their interests in art, music, science, sports, and ministry.

ACADEMIC PROGRAMS

Academically, Wheaton compares with the finest schools in the nation. It boasts a rigorous curriculum, a top-tier science department, a nationally regarded conservatory of music, and outstanding summer research programs. Distinguished graduate schools such as those at Yale, Princeton, Harvard, and the University of Chicago regularly enroll Wheaton graduates in various fields.

With top quality faculty, sophisticated instrumentation, and abundant resources, Wheaton is ranked 21st among baccalaureate schools that produce the best science graduates. Here, careers in medicine, energy, natural resources, biological science, environmental science, engineering, law, and higher education get a strong start; one-third of our science graduates go on to complete doctorates.

Those with a flair for the visual arts, a gift for music, or a special way with words will find courses they are looking for within the Division of Arts, Media and Communication. This academic division sustains a creative environment that includes the plays of Arena Theatre, fine art from the studios of Adams hall, original audio and video productions, and outstanding musical performances. Wheaton's Conservatory of Music is one of the finest music schools in the nation. The reasons why? A talented faculty, an 80-member orchestra, several outstanding music ensembles, interesting workshops, opportunities for travel abroad, and a long list of renowned alumni.

CAMPUS FACILITIES AND EQUIPMENT

Recent additions to campus facilities include the Sports and Recreation Complex (2000); the Wade Center (2001), which houses the books and papers of seven British authors, including C. S. Lewis and J. R. R. Tolkien; the Beamer Student Center (2004); and a jumbo-tron at McCully stadium (2007). In 2008, Wheaton's Memorial Student Center will re-open after an extensive renovation to house the J. Dennis Hastert Center for Economics, Government, and Public Policy, with classroom, research, and public discussion space geared towards the study of economics, politics, and values in business, government, and ministry.

Wheaton's current capital campaign aims to, among other things, strengthen the sciences, stimulate the arts, and enliven the library. For the sciences, a new $80 million science facility with expanded teaching labs and research equipment will soon be built. For the arts, an $11 million renovation of Adams Hall will add art gallery and studio space, and a $9 million renovation of Edman Chapel will further enhance this venue that is often home to concerts from world-class musicians. In addition, the library will be renovated to adequately house its expansive collections.

Approximately 90% of undergraduate students live on-campus in residence halls or in college-owned apartments and houses. All residence halls have been renovated within the last ten years.

TUITION, ROOM, BOARD AND FEES

For 2007-2008 the costs are:

Tuition $23,730

Room $4,288

Board $2,964

The cost of a Wheaton College education is remarkably low compared to private institutions of similar quality. The 2007 Kiplinger's Personal Finance Report ranks Wheaton #16 in its list of the "100 Best Values in Private Colleges."

FINANCIAL AID

Wheaton offers a comprehensive Financial Aid program. In 2006-2007 the average need-based Financial Aid package for freshmen was $16,297. Several merit-based scholarships are also available. See www.wheaton.edu/finaid for more details on all types of aid.

STUDENT ORGANIZATIONS AND ACTIVITIES

Chicago may beckon, but students don't have to catch the train when they're looking for things to do. Right on campus there are College Union Concerts, college-sponsored dances, the talent show, Homecoming, coffee house performances, late night skates, plays, class films, brother/sister floor activities in the dorms, and a versatile place to play and work out called the Sports and Recreation Complex.

Wheaton offers men and women intercollegiate participation in 22 different sports as a member of the NCAA Division III. Through the years Wheaton has won 157 conference championships, including a league-best 54 in women's sports. Wheaton has won six NCAA Championships in team sports and accumulated individual championships in several other sports. More than 100 students have earned All-American recognition and more than 35 have earned Academic All-American honors. Dozens of club and intramural sports are also offered.

ADMISSIONS PROCESS

Wheaton selects candidates for admission from those who evidence a vital Christian experience, high academic ability, moral character, personal integrity, and social concern. The College seeks to enroll, from its over 2200 applicants, a well rounded freshman class; a class composed of about 586 dynamic individuals with a wide variety of attributes, accomplishments, backgrounds, and interests.

Wheaton offers both regular admission and early action application options. The deadline for early action is November 1 and for regular action January 10. The application includes biographical data and essays. The recommended high school curriculum includes 4 years of English, 3-4 years each of mathematics, science, social studies and 2-3 years of foreign language. Students are encouraged to include honors, advanced and AP/IB courses in their curricula. Applicants must submit their official high school transcript as well as official results from the SAT or ACT, including the writing section. Students are encouraged to use the online applications available through Wheaton's website—www.wheaton.edu/admissions.

WHEELOCK COLLEGE

AT A GLANCE

Founded in Boston in 1888, Wheelock College® is a four-year, private, coeducational college with the mission of improving the lives of children and families. We offer comprehensive programs in the Arts and Sciences and the professional areas of Child Life, Education, Juvenile Justice and Youth Advocacy, and Social Work.

The Wheelock experience will thoroughly prepare you for success — both professionally and personally. From your first moments on campus, you will be a welcomed, valued member of a learning community that shares your passion for making the world a better place. We are known nationally and internationally for our programs in Education, the Arts and Sciences, and some of the fastest-growing and most meaningful professions anywhere.

A staple of a Wheelock education is innovative professional internships and field work opportunities. Right from your start at Wheelock, you will gain real-world experience that combines your professional discipline and classroom learning. Boston and environs provide a wealth of fieldwork and professional choices. So you can graduate with a valuable degree and a strong resumé – key elements in landing the jobs you want in a wide range of careers. The College's extensive connections in the Greater Boston community ensure a wide range of high-quality placements for students in all of our programs. Our students have worked with varied organizations, such as:

• Afterschool programs • Museums• Non-profit organizations • Public schools• Child care centers • Hospitals• Head start programs • Youth advocacy agencies

LOCATION AND ENVIRONMENT

In the heart of Boston, Wheelock is within walking distance of several Boston landmarks like Fenway Park, Newbury Street, the Freedom Trail, the Prudential Center, and the Charles River Esplanade. Close to campus there is easy access to the MBTA green line which connects to all of Boston and the surrounding suburbs.

OFF-CAMPUS OPPORTUNITIES

Wheelock is just a short walk from some incredible

Museums such as the Museum of Fine Arts and the

Isabella Stewart Gardner Museum

The city also serves as an exciting crossroads for meeting

people and making new friends. Boston provides access

to unlimited opportunities to enjoy your time outside of

the classroom, too, whether your interests are in good

music, cinema, food, or just hanging out. There are also

plenty of opportunities to help the community in

which you live through many volunteer opportunities

during the school year. Wheelock students spend time

volunteering in homeless shelters, cleaning the parks

around campus, and fundraising and working with

different non-profit t organizations.

MAJORS AND DEGREES OFFERED

Our Programs:

Early Childhood Education

Elementary Education

Special Education

Child Life

Social Work

Juvenile Justice and Youth Advocacy

Math/Science

Human Development

Psychology • Sociology

Arts

Music • Theater • Visual Arts

American Studies

Popular Culture • Race & Ethnic Studies • Women's Studies

Humanities

History • Literature • PhilosophyAcademic Programs

First Year Seminar and First Year Experience program

Honors Program

Summer Bridge

Study Abroad

Service Learning Trips

Academic Advising

Tuition, Room, Board, and Fees

2008-2009

Undergraduate Costs

Tuition: $26,225

R&B: $10,825

Fees: $875 (general)

Fees: $105 (student activity)

Total: $38,030

FINANCIAL AID

Wheelock has an extensive Financial Aid program that includes scholarships, loans, grants, and work-study. Eighty-five percent of Wheelock students receive some form of Financial Aid.

Wheelock College offers merit scholarships to incoming first-year students who start in the fall semester. To be eligible you must apply for admission to Wheelock by March 1. If you are accepted, have a high school GPA of at least 3.0 and an SAT score of 1050 (Critical Reading and Math) or higher, you will automatically receive a merit scholarship between $4,000 and $12,000.Student Organizations and Activities

Clubs and Organizations

Student Government Association

- Asian-American, Latino, African-American and Native-American Society (ALANA)
- Best Buddies
- Bible Study
- Boston Association for the Education of Young Children (BAEYC)
- Campus Activities Board
- Campus Association of Social Workers (CASW)
- Child Life Organization
- Dance Team
- Divine Harmony
- Math Mania
- Pi Gamma Mu
- Queer Co-Op
- Sign Choir
- Students Against Destructive Decisions (SADD)

Women's Varsity Sports

- Field Hockey
- Soccer
- Basketball
- Swimming & Diving
- Softball
- Cross-Country

Men's Varsity Sports

- Basketball
- Tennis
- Cross-Country

ADMISSIONS PROCESS

Undergraduate First Year Application

We are very happy that you are interested in applying to Wheelock College. Please see below for details about the different ways to complete and submit your application, as well as application deadlines. If you have any questions, please contact us.

How to Apply

1. Fill out and submit a completed application. You can submit the Wheelock paper application (download below), the paper Common Application or the Online Common Application. Wheelock College gives equal consideration to the Wheelock application and Common Application.

- Apply online using the Common Application.

- Download our Traditional Paper Application: 2008-2009 Undergraduate Application. If you would prefer to have a paper application mailed to you, please call (800) 734-5212.

2. Please also submit:

3. A writing sample. Please submit a copy of a graded paper you have written within the past year. It should be a minimum of 250 words and can be on any subject. Some examples are an English composition, a history thesis, a psychology report or a literary critique. Wheelock College will accept the Common Application essay in place of a graded writing sample.

4. Secondary school report — to be filled out by your guidance counselor

5. Academic recommendation — to be filled out by an English, Math, History, Science, or Foreign Language instructor

6. Transcripts — first-year applicants must submit their high school transcript. All transcripts must be official copies.

7. Test scores — first-year applicants are required to submit official SAT I Scores or ACT Scores. Students for whom English is not their native language are also required to submit TOEFL scores.

8. Application fee — $35 for the paper application or $15 for the online application. Please send a check made out to Wheelock College.

9. Financial Aid — if you wish to apply for Financial Aid, you must submit the FAFSA (Free Application for Federal Student Assistance) by February 15, 2008. Instructions can be found at the Financial Aid website.

Priority Deadlines

January 2008 Start: December 1, 2007

Early Action: December 1, 2007

Regular Decision: March 1, 2008

Early Action

Students who are interested in learning about their admission decision early in the application cycle may apply under the Early Action Plan. Students must submit their application and credentials by the December 1 deadline and are notified of the admission decision by January 1. The tuition deposit must be submitted by May 1.

Regular Decision

The deadline for regular decision applications is March 1. Wheelock uses rolling decision and students will be notified of a decision within 4 weeks of completing their application. The tuition deposit must be submitted by May 1.

WHITMAN COLLEGE

AT A GLANCE

Whitman College's programs in the arts, humanities, social sciences, and natural sciences have earned the college a national reputation. Whitman's students acquire the knowledge and talents to succeed in whatever career and life paths they choose. Whitman fosters a closely-knit community of dedicated teachers and students working together to achieve lives of intellectual vitality, personal confidence, social responsibility, and the flexibility to adapt to a rapidly changing world. With 1,450 students and a student-faculty ratio of ten-to-one, a rigorous, personalized education is ensured. College rating guides recognize Whitman as one of the nation's top liberal arts institutions. Believing that every moment should be a "learning moment," we offer extensive, extracurricular and residential programs. Our student body is extremely active, with more than 100 interest groups and clubs that are student-run. The Outdoor Program sponsors numerous wilderness activities. Three-quarters of Whitman students live on campus in a wide variety of living arrangements, including coeducational and apartment-style residence halls; 11 special interest houses, dedicated to foreign language study, environmental awareness, the arts, and multi-cultural living; four fraternity houses; and an all-women's residence hall that provides living space and chapter rooms for three national sororities. About 45% of Whitman students study abroad.

ACADEMIC PROGRAMS

Whitman strives to equip all students with the intellectual tools they need to become life-long learners. All students undertake the general studies program, which hones skills in reasoning, critical thinking, leadership, and expository writing. First-years take Antiquity and Modernity, an interdisciplinary seminar focused on reading, writing, and in-class discussion about many of the great books of Western intellectual thought. Whitman's distribution requirements include fine arts, social sciences, humanities, sciences, and alternate voices. Students must complete a class in quantitative analysis. The capstone to each academic major is a comprehensive oral examination. Whitman was the first college in the nation to require such exams. In addition, most departments also require a written exam or thesis. Top students receive honors distinctions in their respective majors. Whitman follows the semester system.

CAMPUS FACILITIES AND EQUIPMENT

Students at Whitman have access to the facilities and technology they need to conduct their own research and independent academic work. The Penrose Memorial Library contains more than 350,000 volumes and 85 online databases. Penrose is open 24/7 during the academic year. Students can request any of the 25 million titles available through the ORCA library consortium. The Hunter Conservatory houses the Center for Communication Arts and Technology including facilities for video conferencing, video editing, and multimedia production. Whitman's debate team (ranked #1 in the nation in 2006-2007) works from Hunter, as does the campus writing center. Internet Life Magazine acknowledged Whitman's advanced technological status by naming it one of America's Most Wired Colleges. Whitman's renovated science building opened in 2002 as did the $13 million Reid Campus Center. In 2006 the Welty Health and Wellness Center, also open 24/7 during the academic year, and the Baker Ferguson Fitness Center and Harvey Pool opened. A new visual arts complex is under construction and will be completed in the fall of 2008.

TUITION, ROOM, BOARD AND FEES

In the 2007-2008 school year, tuition totaled $32,980°. Room and board cost $8,310. Students spend approximately $1,400 more on books, supplies, and personal expenses.

°Includes student government fee.

STUDENT ORGANIZATIONS AND ACTIVITIES

Students complement their classroom learning with extracurricular activities. Most people can find a group that shares their interests within one of the college's 100 student organizations. Students are welcome to found new clubs and groups. Those interested in communications may participate in KWCW, the student radio station, The Blue Moon, an award-winning literary magazine, or The Pioneer, Whitman's newspaper. Physically active students enjoy Whitman's Outdoor Program, ten clubs sports, and twelve intramural sports. The men's and women's road cycling team won the National College Cycling Association's Overall Team National Championship in 2004-2005 and 2005-2006 in addition to numerous individual titles. Varsity athletes compete in the NCAA's Division III. Exceptions to this are the men's and women's Division I alpine and Nordic skiing teams. The men field teams in alpine skiing, baseball, basketball, cross-country, golf, Nordic skiing, soccer, swimming, and tennis. The women compete in alpine skiing, basketball, cross-country, golf, Nordic skiing, soccer, swimming, tennis, and volleyball. Students undertake volunteer work arranged by the Whitman College Center for Community Service. The college's forensics team excels on the national level. The theatre program stages up to ten major productions a year as well as numerous smaller performances. Students interested in music have 16 groups to choose from, and an opera or musical is staged annually. Students do not need to major in music or theatre to participate.

ADMISSIONS PROCESS

Whitman's admission committee seeks applicants who demonstrate academic excellence, motivation, a dedication to learning, and the potential to contribute to the college community. Each admitted class includes students from diverse backgrounds. Gaining admission to Whitman is a competitive process. More than 60 percent of enrolled students graduated in the top ten percent of their high school class. The middle fifty percent of enrolled students score between 620-730 on the Critical Reasoning section of the SAT, 620-700 on the Math section, and 610-700 on the Writing section. The middle fifty percent of enrolled students taking the ACT scored between 27-32. Whitman offers two rounds of Early Decision. The deadline for Early Decision I is November 15, and for Early Decision II, January 1. The Regular Decision deadline is January 15. Those seeking spring admission must meet a November 15 deadline. Students may apply to Whitman online at www.whitman.edu/admission/apply.html.

Students may also complete the Common Application, www.commonapp.org, along with the Whitman Supplement form. Official scores from the SAT or the ACT are mandatory.

Candidates must submit the application fee of $50 with their materials. In addition, international students are required to send TOEFL scores and the College Board's International Student Financial Aid Application and Certification form.

WILKES UNIVERSITY

AT A GLANCE

The difference between doing something ordinary or extraordinary can come down to a simple cup of coffee. And those people who think enough of you to take that extra time to connect with you and to mentor you. At more than 2,300 undergraduates, Wilkes University's small size provides a personal, intimate experience. Experience access to professors unlike that found elsewhere. Get plenty of face time with instructors. Professors can get to know you well enough to learn your strengths and tune into your interests and goals. And you'll have the chance to put your education to work quickly, whether it's starting a business under the wing of a professor who's built million-dollar businesses or researching a genome with a biologist.

Founded in 1933, Wilkes University is a private, co-ed, nondenominational institution in historic Wilkes-Barre, Pa. The academic calendar includes two 15-week semesters, with optional sessions held during the summer and winter breaks. Students hail from 20 states and eight foreign countries. Some other numbers to know: 87% of our faculty have earned their Ph.D. or highest degree in their field; 15:1 student:faculty ratio; our undergraduate classes average 22 students for freshmen, 17 students for upper-level classes, and 15 students for graduate classes.

LOCATION AND ENVIRONMENT

Spend some time at the Wilkes campus, and you'll feel right at home. Each residence hall is as unique as you are, from the contemporary dorms to Tudor mansions. One even boasts a rope swing in the backyard.

Outside the classroom and your dorm, you'll find the Wilkes campus has a lot going on. Stop by the Farley Library for Thursday night study group and pick up a DVD for later. Hit the fitness center. Drop by the Rifkin Café or Starbucks (located right in the Barnes & Noble Wilkes Bookstore) for a cup of coffee. Join your dorm mates for an all-you-care-to-eat dinner in the Henry Student Center food court—or for a late-night breakfast all through finals.

OFF-CAMPUS OPPORTUNITIES

Wilkes-Barre is located in northeastern Pennsylvania, on the western edge of the Pocono Mountains region, right on the Susquehanna River. You'll find a lot to explore, from the campus rock wall or ropes course, to the 14-screen movie theater just a block from campus. Then there are the arts exhibits, plays, concerts, poetry slams, comedians and other goings-on to keep your life fun and exciting. Hike, fish or raft in one of our nearby state parks. Ride two of the top 20 roller coasters in the country at Knoebels Amusement Resort. Take in a hockey game. And enjoy the beauty and hit the slopes of the rambling Pocono Mountains.

MAJORS AND DEGREES OFFERED

Each student must complete a major in a discipline or area of concentration in order to graduate. The major must be declared prior to the first semester of the student's junior year.

Bachelor of Arts Degree — Majors

Biochemistry

Biology

Chemistry

Communication Studies

Computer Science

Criminology

Earth and Environmental Sciences

Elementary Education

English

French

History

Individualized Studies

Integrative Media

International Studies

Mathematics

Musical Theatre

Philosophy

Political Science

Psychology

Sociology

Spanish

Theatre Arts

Bachelor of Science Degrees — Majors

Accounting

Applied and Engineering Sciences

Biochemistry

Biology

Chemistry

Clinical Lab Sciences (Medical Technology)

Computer Information Systems

Computer Science

Earth and Environmental Sciences

Engineering, Electrical

Engineering, Environmental

Engineering Management

Engineering, Mechanical

Health Sciences

Individualized Studies

Mathematics

Nursing

Pharmaceutical Sciences

Pharmacy (Guaranteed Seat Doctor of Pharmacy)

Bachelor of Business Administration Degree — Majors

Business Administration

Entrepreneurship

Minors

Air and Space Studies (Air Force ROTC)

Art History

Computer Engineering

Dance

Economics

Education:

Early Childhood

Reading

Secondary

Special

Geology

Marketing

Music

Neuroscience

Physics

Policy Studies

Statistics

Studio Art

Women's Studies

Programs

Pre-dentistry

Pre-doctoral

Pre-law

Pre-medical

Pre-occupational therapy

Pre-optometry

Pre-osteopathic medicine

Pre-physical therapy

Pre-podiatry

Pre-veterinary

ROTC (Army)

Study Abroad

FINANCIAL AID

Wilkes University maintains a comprehensive program of Financial Aid sources that includes scholarships, grants, loans, and part-time employment. The University also participates in the federal campus-based programs and is approved by the Federal Pell Grant Program, the Federal Family Education Loan Programs, the Pennsylvania Higher Education Assistance Agency and individual aid programs as described in the sections that follow.

-More than 80% of students receive Financial Aid.

-More than 95% of freshmen receive aid. Merit and need-based aid is available.

-Honor scholarships are available. They include University, Presidential, Achievement and Transfer.

Costs for the 2006-2007 academic year were as follows:

Tuition and fees: $24,080

Room and board: $10,100

STUDENT ORGANIZATIONS AND ACTIVITIES

Think high school had a lot of activities? Check out Club Day, where you can explore all 67 student clubs. Maybe build a house with Habitat for Humanity or devise a radio broadcast. Try student government, or design, build and race an off-road vehicle with the Baja team. From community service to career development to just plain fun, find a club to suit your interests.

About a third of Wilkes freshmen participate in athletics. The Colonels battle in the fiercely competitive Mid-Atlantic Division in 14 NCAA Division III sports. Varsity programs for women include basketball, field hockey, lacrosse, soccer, softball, tennis and volleyball; men compete at the varsity level in baseball, basketball, football, golf, soccer, tennis and wrestling. The University recently reinstated cross country teams for both men and women.

Intramurals bring students, faculty and staff together in individual, dual and team competitions in traditional sports. Or you can try plyometrics, free-throw competition and aerobics.

ADMISSIONS PROCESS

Individual admissions decisions are based upon secondary-school or preparatory-school record, class rank, and results of the SAT/ACT examination. Interviews are not required but are highly recommended.

RECOMMENDED HIGH SCHOOL PREPARATION

Preparation for your Wilkes experience should include a college preparatory curriculum. Such a curriculum generally includes four years of progressive courses in English, mathematics, science (including at least one laboratory component) and social science. While four years of each are not required, they are recommended for college preparation and admission. Choose elective courses in academic subject areas pertaining to individual interest. That may be computer science, foreign language, and communications and may include the fine arts and technical courses as they relate to desired college majors. Depending on the academic discipline desired, different emphases might be placed on the high school curriculum completed by the applicant. Students whose preparation does not follow the pattern described above may still qualify for admission. But you'll have to provide other strong evidence that you prepared for the academic rigors of college.

APPLICATION FOR ADMISSION

Applications for admission and instructions regarding secondary school transcripts and records, letters of recommendation, standardized test reports and entrance examinations may be obtained by contacting the Admissions Office. Send completed applications directly to the Admissions Office. The Scholastic Aptitude Test (SAT) of the College Entrance Examination Board or the Achievement College Test (ACT) is generally required of all applicants entering Wilkes University directly from high school. Take this examination before the second semester of your senior year in high school.

WILLIAM JEWELL COLLEGE

AT A GLANCE

Among the oldest colleges west of the Mississippi, William Jewell College is one of a select group of 218 national liberal arts colleges named by the Carnegie Foundation for the Advancement of Teaching. Distinctive programs include the internationally renowned Oxbridge Honors and Pryor Leadership programs. The Harriman-Jewell Series is considered one of the great performing artist series in the country. More than 700 world-class performances and 17 American recital debuts, including that of Luciano Pavarotti in 1973, have come to Kansas City by way of this program. Acknowledging completion of the college's 38-hour liberal arts core—plus three "applied learning experiences." Jewell offers a recognized major in Applied Critical Thought and Inquiry. This means that virtually all students can graduate with double majors and some with triple majors in just four years.

LOCATION AND ENVIRONMENT

Just 20 minutes from downtown Kansas City, Jewell offers 1,100 students all the amenities of a beautiful liberal arts campus setting. The 200-acre campus is perched above the town of Liberty and its historic town square, among the beautiful rolling hills of western Missouri. With more than 900 students living on campus and 60 clubs and organizations, life at Jewell is vibrant. Students have the opportunity to learn and apply practical life and business skills while making friends and participating in the life of the College.

ACADEMIC PROGRAMS

Pursuing a liberal arts education at William Jewell guarantees that students have the opportunity to graduate with the academic credentials to face the challenges of the twenty-first century with a demonstrated ability to apply learning to complex ethical, scientific and cultural problems. One distinctive way William Jewell proves this is by acknowledging completion of the college's 38-hour liberal arts core plus three "applied learning experiences" as a recognized major in Applied Critical Thought and Inquiry. This means that virtually all students can graduate with double majors and some with triple majors. A number of distinctive programs are available to Jewell students. The internationally recognized Oxbridge Honors Program, supported by the Hall Family Foundation, combines British tutorial methods of instruction with opportunities for a year of study in Oxford or Cambridge. It is the only one of its kind in the nation. Jewell's new Non-Profit Leadership major is one of only 13 nationwide. It allows students to fulfill all of the nonprofit competencies established by American Humanics and meets the guidelines for graduate study in philanthropy, the nonprofit sector and nonprofit leadership established by the Nonprofit Academic Centers Council (NACC). The Pryor Leadership Studies Program includes course work, community service projects and internships that help students enhance their leadership skills in a variety of settings.

CAMPUS FACILITIES AND EQUIPMENT

In 2006, the College dedicated a new academic building to support our leadership development programs, the Fred and Shirley Pryor Center for Leadership Development. Also housed in the building is the Tucker Leadership Lab, which facilitates team-building exercises on our high and low ropes course, also located on campus. In May, the College will break ground on a $13 million sorority complex, which will complement the four multi-million dollar fraternity houses. A number of residence halls have also been renovated in recent years. Students also have access to a newly-constructed campus wellness center and a renovated and expanded student union. Students in the sciences have access to state-of-the-art research equipment as undergraduates. Examples of equipment include a flow cytometer, atomic absorption spectrometer, nuclear magnetic resonance spectrometer, and a scanning UV-Visible spectrophotometer. The Pillsbury Observatory is equipped with at 14-inch Celestron telescope on a Byers Class 2 mount in a 5-meter dome and is also available for student research. Jewell's renowned music department is housed in the Pillsbury Music Center, which includes large and small rehearsal space, practice facilities, keyboard/computer lab and the Forbis recital hall. The Liberty Symphony Orchestra offers our string and wind students the opportunity to gain invaluable orchestral experience at a high level, often playing alongside their teachers and other area professionals. William Jewell is the home of the Quimby Pipe Organ Company's Op. 55, a magnificent instrument that is housed in Gano Chapel and is used for Jewell and area wide events. Organ students regularly practice and perform on this outstanding instrument.

TUITION, ROOM, BOARD AND FEES

For the 2008-2009 academic year, tuition for all students is $23,000, and room and board is $6,130. William Jewell participates in Tuition Exchange, Midwest Student Exchange, the Council of Independent Colleges and Baptist Student Exchange.

ADMISSIONS PROCESS

Students interested in admission to William Jewell must complete a secondary school curriculum that includes at least 15 credits in college-preparatory courses; four additional academic electives are recommended as well. Required credits include 4 years of English, 3 years of math, 3 years of social science, 3 years of science, and 2 years of foreign language. Applicants must complete either the William Jewell College application or the Common Application and provide an official secondary school transcript, standardized test scores (SAT I or ACT, writing sections recommended), a writing sample, and a secondary school report form. Students interested in Oxbridge Honors must also submit two academic letters of recommendation. Homeschooled students must submit one letter of recommendation and complete the homeschool supplement. Applicants to the direct-entry nursing program must submit the nursing essay and supplement form. The $25 application fee is waived for online applications. Applications are reviewed on a rolling basis. Priority consideration for merit scholarships is given to applications postmarked by Dec. 1. Additional application materials are required for consideration for the Jewell Scholarship.

WILLIAM PATERSON UNIVERSITY

AT A GLANCE

William Paterson University, a public school founded in 1855, has grown to become a comprehensive, liberal arts institution committed to academic excellence and student success. Accredited by the Middle States Association of Schools and Colleges, it offers 35 undergraduate and 19 graduate degrees and professional development programs through its five colleges: Arts and Communication; Christos M. Cotsakos College of Business; Education; Humanities and Social Sciences; and Science and Health.

William Paterson is located in suburban Wayne, New Jersey. The approximately 11,000 full- and part-time students, who enjoy the resources of a large university as well as the individual attention available at a smaller school, relax and study on the 370-acre campus amid the University's woods and waterfalls. It offers a wide variety of student activities, modern on-campus housing, and the most up-to-date educational facilities. Financial Aid is also available to qualified students.

LOCATION AND ENVIRONMENT

Each course of study at William Paterson is enhanced by world-class academic facilities and resources; curricula that address classic and contemporary issues in higher education; and a distinguished faculty comprised of award-winning teacher-scholars—eighty-nine percent of fulltime faculty hold the highest degree in their field.

Many social, cultural, and recreational opportunities complement Academic Programs. Two new residence halls, High Mountain East and West, bring the University's residential capacity to nearly 2,700 students in ten residence halls... A 4,000-seat recreation center is a short walk from the residence halls, and Wightman Gym houses a competition-sized pool. The "Pioneer spirit" is evident in the University's 12 intercollegiate sports with numerous NCAA Division III post-season tournament appearances.

The University also presents many enlightening and entertaining cultural events, among them the Distinguished Lecturer Series, concerts, art exhibitions, and theatrical productions. In addition, it offers a wide variety of continuing education programs designed for both professionals and the general public.

OFF-CAMPUS OPPORTUNITIES

Students participate in internships in many leading area companies and businesses that both help them clarify career goals and forge relationships that can result in post-graduation jobs. Study abroad programs are also available to sophomores and juniors. Students may also elect to study in the University's distance learning programs.

MAJORS AND DEGREES OFFERED

Students can pursue B.A., B.S., B.F.A., and B.M. degrees in any of the University's five colleges. Bachelor of arts degrees are granted in African, African American, and Caribbean studies, anthropology, art, Asian studies, communication, English, French and Francophone studies, geography, history, Latin American studies, liberal studies, mathematics, music, philosophy, political science, psychology, sociology, Spanish, and women's studies.

Bachelor of science program degrees include accounting, applied chemistry, athletic training, biology, biotechnology, business administration, community health/school health education, computer science, environmental science, exercise science, nursing, professional sales, and physical education.

The bachelor of fine arts program degree is awarded in fine arts. And, in the bachelor of music program, students can choose between performance, jazz, and music management.

Students may also pursue certification in early childhood, elementary, secondary, and special education.

ACADEMIC PROGRAMS

In order to graduate, the baccalaureate degree requires 128 credits. Sixty of those credits are earned in general education classes. Another 30 to 60 come from work in the student's major, and 20 to 40 can be earned in electives. The general education specifications and major requirements vary for degrees, including the B.F.A. and the B.M. Counseling and advising are available to students who are undecided as to their major. And, students seeking guidance on their career choices can take advantage of the University's Career Development Center.

Programs in the University Honors College offer students further challenges and include biopsychology, cognitive science, humanities, life science and environmental ethics, music, performing and literary arts, and social sciences. There are also pre-professional programs in dentistry, engineering, law, medicine (which includes dentistry, optometry, podiatry, and veterinary science), pharmacy, physical therapy, and speech-language pathology. Military experience may also be evaluated for credit.

CAMPUS FACILITIES AND EQUIPMENT

Facilities are easily accessible to undergraduate students in various academic, cultural, and recreational programs. A recent renovation increased the David and Lorraine Cheng Library's bound collection area by 33 percent and its seating capacity by 100 percent. Cultural activities are supported by Shea Center for Performing Arts, which contains a 922-seat theater, as well as band, choral, and orchestral practice rooms and classrooms. The Ben Shahn Center for Visual Arts features an extensive art gallery, as well as art studios and classrooms, while the Power Art Center houses faculty offices and studios for three-dimensional design, photography, sculpture, ceramics, printmaking, woodworking, and painting.

Athletic facilities include an indoor pool, outdoor tennis courts, and a lighted athletics field complex. Also, the recreation center includes a 4,000-seat facility with various athletic courts and exercise rooms. Hobart Hall, a state-of-the-art communication facility, houses television studios, a multipurpose computer lab, film studio, a radio station, and an uplink and four downlink satellite dishes. The Atrium, an academic building, contains a writing center, multimedia language lab, tutorial center, and computing support facilities. Among other academic resources are a nursing instructional facility, speech and hearing clinic, a child-care center, and comprehensive science research facilities.

The site of the Allan and Michele Gorab Alumni House contains a pond, wetlands, woods, as well as a living laboratory for courses in biology and the environmental sciences. The 1600 Valley Road facility houses the Christos M. Cotsakos College of Business and its state-of-the-art Financial Learning Center, the Russ Berrie Institute, the Russ Berrie Professional Sales Lab, the College of Education, the Center for Continuing and Professional Education, and classrooms. A full-service cafeteria is located in Wayne Hall.

The brand new University Commons complex, including the redesigned John Victor Machuga Student Center, is the heart of the campus, where the entire University community gathers and interacts. This state-of-the-art campus center provides students with an exquisite setting for a vast array of social and extracurricular activities, dining venues, and student support services, all under one roof..

TUITION, ROOM, BOARD AND FEES

Full-time students from New Jersey pay $9,996 for tuition and fees in 2007-2008. Tuition for out-of-state students is $16,242. Room and board runs roughly $9,442 annually. For those in-state residents who want to live on-campus, the total is approximately $19,436, and for out-of-state residents, approximately $25,682. These totals may vary subject to decisions by the University's Board of Trustees.

FINANCIAL AID

William Paterson provides a first-rate education at a highly reasonable cost. In accordance with the University's commitment to value in education, federal and state need-based Financial Aid programs are offered in the forms of grants, loans, scholarships, and work-study programs. In order to apply for Financial Aid, students should submit Free Application for Federal Student Aid (FAFSA) with the United States Department of Education by April 1.

Recently, scholarship/grant awards totaling approximately $20,000,000 were distributed at the University. First-year students and upperclassmen compete for academic scholarships. And, both the William Paterson Foundation and the Alumni Association award more than 200 scholarships for academic achievement, exceptional character qualities, leadership excellence, and financial need.

STUDENT ORGANIZATIONS AND ACTIVITIES

There are more than 50 student clubs covering interests from anthropology to the student-run television station. The University also offers various opportunities for students to become involved in leadership roles. They may pursue leadership opportunities in student government or in one of the many academic, social, programmatic, and media groups on campus.

William Paterson's athletic teams participate in the NCAA's Division III, as well as in club and intramural sports. Both men and women have teams in basketball, soccer, and swimming. In addition, the men field baseball and football teams (the baseball team won national championships in 1992 and 1996). Women also participate in field hockey, softball, tennis, and volleyball.

ADMISSIONS PROCESS

Application Deadlines

Application, fee, and supporting official transcripts for freshman, transfer, second-degree and re-admit students must be received by the deadline dates shown below:

Fall   June 1

Spring   December 1

All forms, transcripts, and the $50 application fee must be received from first-year applicants or transfer students by those dates. Candidates should bear in mind that the cut-off dates may be earlier if the combination of continuing students and new applications begin to exceed availability.

Proof of High School Graduation

In order to comply with state and federal regulations regarding Financial Aid, all applicants (freshman, transfer, second baccalaureate, and re-admit students) MUST submit proof of high school graduation or equivalency (copy of high school diploma or high school transcripts with date of graduation posted) prior to enrollment. A high school equivalency diploma recognized by New Jersey may be presented in place of the above requirements.

Freshman Application Process

Admission criteria include having passed a minimum of sixteen (16) Carnegie Units and having demonstrated good academic ability. To strengthen academic success, it is strongly recommended that you take more than the minimum courses.

SAT/ACT Requirements

Entering freshman students must have taken the SAT I or the American College Test (ACT) and have their scores sent to the Office of Admissions, William Paterson University. To submit your scores, indicate code 2518 for the SAT and code 2584 for the ACT.

Transfer Applicants

William Paterson accepts students for the fall and spring semesters (June 1 and January 9) for full- or part-time study. When applying, students must present at least 12 college-level credits with a minimum 2.0 grade point average (GPA); computer science and nursing majors must have a GPA of at least 2.5, and teacher certification program applicants must have a GPA of at least 2.75. There are some limitations on the number of credits accepted, e.g., a maximum of 70 credits from a two-year institution or 90 credits from a four-year college or university. More details on transferring credits may be obtained from our Admissions staff.

William Paterson University welcomes all visitors and requests for information. Campus tours are conducted weekdays by appointment. The Office of Admissions will gladly schedule a tour for you or answer any questions. To make arrangements to visit the University or for more information about our programs, contact:

Office of Admissions

William Paterson University of New Jersey

Wayne, NJ 07470

Telephone: 973-720-2125

Toll-free: 877-WPU-EXCEL

Fax: 973-720-2910

E-mail: admissions@wpunj.edu

World Wide Web: www.wpunj.edu

WILSON COLLEGE

AT A GLANCE

Develop Your Potential at Wilson College - Wilson fosters the development of your leadership abilities in a collaborative, rather than a competitive, environment. We give you opportunities to try new things. We offer a rigorous liberal arts and sciences education that encourages you to question, debate and develop your ability to reason. We expose you to global perspectives, prepare you for a career and provide the support you need to become your best self.

LOCATION AND ENVIRONMENT

Wilson College sits on a 300-acre campus of gracious lawns, rolling hills, waterways and handsome Victorian architecture. The College was founded in 1869 and the campus is designated as a National Historic District in Chambersburg, PA.

OFF-CAMPUS OPPORTUNITIES

Downtown Chambersburg is within walking distance of campus. Students display their artwork in town, take music lessons from the Cumberland Valley School of Music on campus and volunteer in community organizations. Wilson's cultural events and enrichment programs are resources to the local and regional communities. Students can take advantage of nearby parks and recreation areas, such as Caledonia State Park, part of the Appalachian Trail. Wilson is within an easy travel distance to Baltimore, Washington, DC, Philadelphia, New York City and historic Gettysburg.

MAJORS AND DEGREES OFFERED

Accounting
  Managerial
  Financial
Biology
Business and Economics
  Management Information Systems
  Economics
  International Business
  Management
Chemistry
Elementary Education
English
  Literary Studies
  Writing
Environmental Science
  Ecological Perspectives
  Natural and Sustainable Systems
  Social Systems
Equestrian Studies
  Equestrian Management
  Equine Management
Equine Facilitated Therapeutics
Exercise Sport Science
Fine Arts
  Art History
  Studio Art
Foreign Language
  French
  Spanish

History and Political Science
  History
  International Relations
  Political Science
International Studies
Mass Communications
  Media Studies
  Professional Writing
Mathematics/Computer Science
Philosophy
Psychobiology
Psychology
Religion
Sociology
Veterinary Medical Technology
  Veterinary Biology
  Veterinary Business Management
Secondary Education Certification
  Biology
  Chemistry
  Citizenship Education (formerly Social Studies)
  English
  Environmental Studies
  Mathematics
  Spanish
Pre-Professional Programs:
  Pre-Health Sciences
  Pre-Law
  Pre-Medicine
  Pre-Veterinary Medicine

ACADEMIC PROGRAMS

Study Abroad
Internships
The Washington Center
Summer Sessions
Off-Campus Study
College Level Examination Program (CLEP)

CAMPUS FACILITIES AND EQUIPMENT

There are 30 buildings and seven residence halls, along with various on-campus facilities including: Penn Hall Equestrian Center, Helen M. Beach '24 Veterinary Medical Center, the 100-acre Fulton Center for Sustainable Living, Lenfest Student Commons, Hankey Center (which houses the C. Elizabeth Boyd '33 Archives and Barron Blewett Hunnicutt Classics Gallery), Bogigian Art Gallery, Natural History Museum, a child care center and dance and art studios.

Tuition, Room, Board, and Fees

Tuition & Fees: 23,770

Room & Board: 8,236

FINANCIAL AID

Wilson College is committed to helping students receive a high-quality education. More than 90% of our students receive some form of Financial Aid. Because we know the value of a Wilson College education, we consider every student for all available Financial Aid in the form of scholarships, grants and need-based Financial Aid.

Aid offered includes:

Merit Scholarships

Presidential $10,000

Dean's 7,500

Faculty 5,000

Competitive Scholarships

Curran—based on community service

TASC—leadership potential, character and academic excellence

SEMLAR—Scholarship to Enhance Mathematics, Learning and Research (funded by the National Science Foundation)

Transfer Student Merit Scholarship

Phi Theta Kappa

Affiliation Scholarships

Alumna Daughter

Presbyterian Student

Pony Club

Girl Scout Gold Award

Franklin County, PA

Transfer Student Articulation

Specialty Scholarships

National Presbyterian College

Twin & Triplets Scholarship

STUDENT ORGANIZATIONS AND ACTIVITIES

There are more than 26 student organizations and clubs on campus that are sponsored by the Wilson College Student Government Association (WCGA). Each student may also start her own organization if she meets specific requirements and gathers a minimum of seven members.

Current clubs/organizations:

Allies

Archery Club

Athletic Association

Behavioral Sciences Club

Billboard (Student Newspaper)

Black Student Union

Bottom Shelf Review

Campus Activities Board (CAB)

Choir

Conococheague (yearbook)

Education Club

Environmental Club

Joko

Kittochtinny Players (drama club)

Muhibbah International Club

Orchesis (Modern Dance)

Students in Free Enterprise (SIFE)

Veterinary Medical Technology Club

WCGA (Student Government)

Women with Children Club

Equestrian Teams:

Dressage

Hunt Seat

Western

Eventing

Musical Drill

ADMISSIONS PROCESS

First-Year Applicants are required to submit the following:

Completed Application Form

Official high school transcripts

Teacher Recommendation Form

Graded English paper

SAT or ACT results

Transfer Applicants are required to submit:

Completed Application Form

Official transcripts from every college attended along with college catalogs or course descriptions

Teacher Recommendation Form

Graded paper written for a college class

Final high school transcript

WORCESTER POLYTECHNIC INSTITUTE

AT A GLANCE

You want to be on the first Mars mission, find alternative energy sources, or work on cancer research. WPI believes in the power of our students to make an impact. Students do much more than study science and technology in the classroom and lab. They delve into the arts and humanities. They complete projects on campus and around the globe where they connect what they've learned in the classroom with pressing real-life challenges, from human health and the environment to business and engineering. Students grow—personally, professionally, and intellectually—as they discover how to apply their talents and turn ideas into tangible solutions.

WPI's aim is to educate students broadly, so they achieve greatly. Though WPI has an over 140 year history, the curriculum, like its students, is both innovative and practical. Small classes, a flexible curriculum, and one-on-one interaction with professors at the top of their fields make learning at WPI an experience unlike any other.

WPI has been widely recognized for its academic program. WPI was the only technological university out of sixteen national Leadership Institutions selected by the Association of American Colleges and Universities to serve as models of outstanding practices in liberal education. WPI consistently ranks among the top national universities by *U.S. News & World Report*. In the National Survey of Student Engagement, WPI ranked number one for student-faculty interactions, a measure of the quality and quantity of time faculty members spend with undergraduates.

LOCATION AND ENVIRONMENT

With its beautiful architecture, grassy quad and ivy-covered walls, WPI has a traditional New England campus. Students stop and chat with their friends and professors on tree-lined paths. Play pool between classes at the Campus Center or get a coffee with friends at Dunkin' Donuts. Study in the sun by the fountain in Reunion Plaza. Get a group together for bowling at Gompeii's Gutters funky Galactic Bowling Nights. Stop and smell the roses in the formal English garden behind Higgins House. See a student play at the new Little Theatre.

Home to twelve other colleges and universities and over 35,000 college students, Worcester is a great college town. WPI is a member of the Colleges of Worcester Consortium, through which WPI students may register for courses at other colleges and may take advantage of a wide range of cultural programming offered by consortium members. A shuttle provides free transportation between campuses.

Late-night diners, clubs, museums, concert venues and theaters are right down the hill from WPI in Worcester's vibrant downtown. Boston is less than an hour away by commuter rail if you want to catch Red Sox fever. There's great skiing and boarding at nearby Wachusett Mountain. If you want to go a bit farther, Worcester is centrally located with easy access to Providence, New York City, the Berkshires and White Mountains and Cape Cod.

OFF-CAMPUS OPPORTUNITIES

In Worcester you'll find:

35,000+ college students at 13 colleges and universities

14,800 seats at the DCU Center for arena concerts and sporting events

5,000 objects of arms and armor at the Higgins Armory Museum

53 parks including the largest urban nature sanctuary in New England

and the Olmstead-designed Elm Park

36 galleries and 5,000 years of art at the Worcester Art Museum

20 ski trails at nearby Wachusett Mountain

2 minor league sports teams (Tornadoes, baseball; Sharks, hockey)

2 polar bears, one residing at the Ecotarium, and the other on the roof of Polar Beverages

1 Gompei the goat (WPI mascot)

MAJORS AND DEGREES OFFERED

WPI offers over 35 areas of study in engineering, science, management and the liberal arts leading to the Bachelor of Science (B.S.) or Bachelor of Arts (B.A.) degree. Exciting, new interdisciplinary programs are driven by real-world demand, like interactive media and game development, environmental engineering and the first undergraduate program in robotics engineering in the nation.

We offer pre-professional programs (law, medicine, dentistry and veterinary) and a five year BS/MS program. You can even create your own major or minor program. Not surprisingly, over forty percent of students change their major at least once. A comprehensive academic advising program and a wide array of academic support services help students make the right choices and reach their goals.

WPI students have received some of the nation's highest academic honors; two students have received the prestigious Marshall Scholarship, twelve have been awarded Goldwater scholarships, four have received the Rotary Ambassadorial Scholarship over the last six years.

ACADEMIC PROGRAMS

Students take the equivalent of three courses (as either courses or project work) during each of four 7-week terms (two in the fall and two in the spring). At WPI, learning is about more than just theories and ideas. Students learn how to put ideas into practice through its project-enriched curriculum. WPI undergraduates complete two projects: one directly related to your major and one working with a team of students to solve a problem at the intersection of society and technology—helping to bring electricity to remote villages in Thailand, or studying the bioethics of cloning, for example. Students gain valuable professional skills, a talent for team work, the confidence to dive right in, no matter what the challenge.

WPI's academic program encourages collaboration—not competition. Students work closely together in project-oriented classes. Learning how to work in teams will prepare students to achieve results and become a leader in life after college —no matter what path they take.

WPI's award-winning Global Perspective Program is one of the most comprehensive and highly regarded global studies programs in the nation. About half of WPI students complete projects outside the United States and the majority complete projects off-campus. With WPI's Global Perspective Program, you'll not only experience the challenge of solving real-life problems with your fellow students, you'll immerse yourself in another culture. Complete your projects on campus or at any of our more than 20 project centers located on five continents around the globe including in Thailand, Australia, Costa Rica, South Africa or within the U.S. Recent project sponsors include NASA Johnson Space Center, Johnson & Johnson, Morgan Stanley, Environmental Protection Agency and UNESCO.

Top-tier employers seek out WPI graduates for their real-world experience and ability to work collaboratively. With a placement rate of over 90 percent, students are recruited by leading organizations such as Pfizer, General Electric, Fidelity Investments, IBM and Google. Not surprisingly, WPI graduates' starting salaries are higher than those of many other college graduates, according to the National Association of Colleges and Employers. Each year, WPI graduates are accepted at many prestigious graduate schools, including MIT, Yale University, Princeton University, Johns Hopkins University and Tufts University Medical School.

CAMPUS FACILITIES AND EQUIPMENT

With all of the amazing things WPI students and faculty do, our outstanding research facilities should come as no surprise. Our campus is equipped with hundreds of computers in 24/7 computer labs and offer high-speed wireless access. WPI is one of only 208 universities with Internet2—the next generation Internet.

Gateway Park, a new life-sciences-based campus, will provide top-tier bioscience facilities for WPI and bioscience companies, providing tremendous opportunities for collaboration. Our two atomic force microscopes let you see individual atoms on a material's surface. A new $11 million Undergraduate Life Sciences Laboratory Center at WPI will open in February 2009. The center will become WPI's main facility for undergraduate teaching and research in biology and biotechnology, biomedical engineering, chemistry and biochemistry, and chemical engineering.

The Fire Science Laboratory enables students and faculty to evaluate fire safety measures in actual fire simulations. A newly constructed chemistry laboratory facilitates team-based laboratory work. Laser holography labs, computer music labs, medical imaging labs, a bioprocess lab—they're all here. And lots more.

TUITION, ROOM, BOARD AND FEES

2007-2008 Tuition and Fees

Tuition: $34,300.00

Social Fee: $250.00

Health Fee: $280.00

Total: $34,830.00

Typical Room: $6,104.00

Typical Board Plan: $4,306.00

Books and Supplies: $1,000.00

Personal Expenses: $1,000.00

New Student Orientation: $200.00

Total: $47,440.00

FINANCIAL AID

It's no secret. A great education costs a lot of money, but think about the return on your investment. College graduates in general earn over the course of their careers at least $1 million more than those without a degree. For WPI graduates, starting salaries frequently exceed the national averages and graduates are able to move quickly up the ranks to positions of influence as a result of their excellent preparation.

APPLYING FOR FINANCIAL AID

Students should file the FAFSA and CSS Profile on or near their admissions application deadline. WPI should receive all Financial Aid materials by February 1. Applications after this date will be reviewed subject to funds available.

Most applicants (including early applicants) will receive a Financial Aid package within two weeks of their acceptance. We'll inform you of the Financial Aid Committee's decision no later than April 15 for regular decision admissions, and you'll have until the Candidates Common Reply Date (May 1) to either accept or decline the offer.

Academic Scholarships

WPI offers academic scholarships to freshman applicants based upon academic performance, standardized test scores, leadership, extracurricular involvement and community service. All admitted applicants are considered and there is no separate application required.

Scholarships vary in amounts, but typically range between $10,000 and $25,000, and are renewable for four years. Valedictorians and Salutatorians are guaranteed a minimum scholarship of $12,500. National Merit, National Achievement, and National Hispanic Recognition Finalists are guaranteed a minimum of $17,000.

STUDENT ORGANIZATIONS AND ACTIVITIES

WPI has twenty varsity (NCAA Division III) athletics teams and thirty-four club and intramural athletics. WPI won the "Worcester Cup" for the third time in four years, recognizing it as the top collegiate program in Worcester County. WPI has eleven fraternities and three sororities, fifteen music and theater ensembles, dozens of academic clubs, international organizations, religious groups and other organizations. There are more than 200 student clubs and activities.

ADMISSIONS PROCESS

WPI Admissions offers a variety of application options. Students can apply using the WPI application (paper or on-line). We also accept the Common Application. A $60 application fee is required for all applicants. (WPI endorses the fee waiver policy of the College Board, as well as accepts fee waivers from high school guidance or college counselors.)

Academic Requirements

four years of math (including pre-calculus)

four years of English

two years of lab science

Other requirements include:

High school transcript

Science or math teacher's recommendation

Guidance counselor's recommendation

Personal essay

SAT I or ACT scores or alternate materials through WPI's "Flex Path"

TOEFL or IELTS Exam scores for international students whose first language is not English

Interviews

While interviews are optional, this is your chance to meet one-on-one with an Admissions staff member or a trained Admissions intern. We'll have the chance to learn more about you, and can answer specific questions you may have.

Deadlines

Early Action (Round 1)—Nov. 15

Early Action (Round 2)—Jan. 1

Regular Decision—Feb. 1

January Admission—Freshmen and Transfer Students—Nov. 15 (Rolling notification)

Fall Admission—Transfer Students—Apr. 15 (Rolling notification)

INDEXES

ALPHABETICAL INDEX

X

Y

INDEX BY LOCATION

UNITED STATES

INDEX BY SIZE
(in descending order)

10,000 TO 4,000 STUDENTS

Index by Size

UP TO 4,000 STUDENTS

INDEX BY COST
(in ascending order)

MORE THAN $15,000

INDEX BY SELECTIVITY

72

American International College	37, 1054
Averett University	66
Benedictine College	84
Bennett College for Women	85
Boise State University	103
Bowling Green State University	107
Central Methodist University	154
Central State University	156
Chaminade University of Honolulu	159, 1112
Daniel Webster College	236
East Tennessee State University	260, 1027
Emporia State University	279, 1028
Evergreen State College, The	283
Faulkner University	286
Franciscan University, The	302
Frostburg State University	307, 1178
Goldey-Beacom College	322
Holy Family University	355
Humboldt State University	360
Judson College (AL)	390
Keene State College	395
Kent State University—Kent Campus	398
Kentucky Christian College	398
Laboratory Institute of Merchandising	407, 1228
Louisiana Tech University	439
MacMurray College	448
Marian College	456
Midway College	488
Morrisville State College	515
Mount Marty College	518
Newberry College	543
Northwestern State University	562, 1033
Notre Dame de Namur University	566
Ohio Dominican University	572
Robert Morris University	643, 1340
Saginaw Valley State University	660
South Dakota State University	709, 1386
Southern Wesleyan University	723
Spalding University	727
State University of New York—	
The College at Old Westbury	745
Suffolk University	767
Taylor University—Fort Wayne Campus	774, 1036
University of Akron, The	811
University of Central Missouri	827
University of Michigan—Flint	869, 1040
University of Northern Iowa	893
University of Pittsburgh—Greensburg	899
University of Saint Francis (IN), The	906
University of Sioux Falls	911
University of Southern Maine	918
University of Wisconsin—Milwaukee	940
Utah State University	949, 1044
Utica College	949, 1044
Viterbo University	960, 1044
West Virginia University Institute	
of Technology	984
Western Carolina University	985
Western Kentucky University	987

71

Adrian College	22
Alvernia College	34, 1052
Ball State University	71, 1023
Bloomfield College	99, 1088
Brewton-Parker College	111
Caldwell College	122, 1100
Cazenovia College	149
Chicago State University	163
Clarion University of Pennsylvania	178, 1025
Concordia University at Austin	217
D'Youville College	257, 1146
Eastern Illinois University	261
Elms College	272
Fairleigh Dickinson University—	
College at Florham	284
Grand View College	328
Hartwick College	342
Illinois State University	366
Indiana State University	369
Kean University	395, 1216
LaGrange College	408
Lakeland College	411, 1029
Lander University	414, 1030
Lock Haven University of Pennsylvania	433
Long Island University—C.W. Post	435
Mesa State College	481
Mitchell College	503
Mount Saint Mary College	520
Northern Illinois University	555
Northwood University	563, 1033, 1296
Pennsylvania State University—Abington	598
Pennsylvania State University—Altoona	599
Pennsylvania State University—	
Fayette, The Eberly Campus	602
Pennsylvania State University—	
Lehigh Valley	604
Presentation College	622
Quincy University	627
Radford University	629, 1326
Saint Charles Borromeo Seminary	663
Silver Lake College	701
Southern University and A&M College	721
State University of New York—Plattsburgh	756
Stephen F. Austin State University	762
Thiel College	785
University of Central Oklahoma	828
University of Maine—Farmington	857
University of Maine at Machias	859
University of Minnesota—Crookston	870, 1040
University of Pittsburgh—Bradford	898
University of Pittsburgh—Johnstown	899
University of Wisconsin—Stout	944, 1043
University of Wisconsin—Superior	944
Virginia Wesleyan College	960
Webber International University	975, 1486
Weber State University	976
West Texas A&M University	983
Western Michigan University	988, 1490
Western Oregon University	989
Youngstown State University	1019

70

Alaska Pacific University	25, 1022
Cabrini College	122, 1098
Castleton State College	147, 1106
Central Connecticut State University	154, 1110
Concordia College—New York	217
Delaware State University	241
East Texas Baptist University	260
Edinboro University of Pennsylvania	268
Ferrum College	289
Fort Hays State University	299, 1028
Greensboro College	330
Indiana University—Northwest	371
Indiana University—Southeast	373
Kansas Wesleyan University	394
Keuka College	402
La Roche College	406
Lake Superior State University	411
Life Pacific College	427, 1030
Lourdes College	439
Mansfield University of Pennsylvania	455, 1031
Marian College of Fond Du Lac	456
Mount Mary College	518
New Jersey City University	537
New York Institute of Technology	541
Pace University—Pleasantville/Briarcliff	591
Pennsylvania State University—Berks	600
Pennsylvania State University—	
Delaware County	600
Pennsylvania State University—	
Greater Allegheny	602
Pennsylvania State University—Mont Alto	604
Pennsylvania State University—	
New Kensington	605
Pennsylvania State University—Wilkes-Barre	607
Pennsylvania State University—York	608
Plymouth State University	615
Saint Augustine's College	662
Saint Thomas Aquinas College	677
Salem International University	679
Sam Houston State University	682
Southern Connecticut State University	715
Southern Illinois University—Carbondale	716
Tarleton State University	773
Thomas College	786
Troy University—Dothan	800
Unity College	810
University of Bridgeport	819, 1038
University of Mary	860
University of Massachusetts—	
Lowell	866, 1040, 1456
University of Nebraska—Omaha	880
University of North Carolina at Pembroke, The	888
University of Southern Indiana	917
Valley City State University	950
Washburn University	968
Western State College of Colorado	990
William Paterson University	1004, 1506

69

Cleveland State University	185
Dickinson State University	247, 1027
Eastern Connecticut State University	261
Husson College	363, 1202
Indiana University—Kokomo	370
Lynn University	446, 1250
Metropolitan State College of Denver	483
Missouri Baptist College	499
Montana State University—Billings	506
Pennsylvania State University—Hazleton	603
Shaw University	695
Southern Vermont College	722
Virginia State University	959
Wayne State College	973
Winona State University	1010

68

Dakota State University	233
Indiana University—East	370
Lees-McRae College	420
Minnesota State University—Moorhead	495
New England College	535, 1032
Norfolk State University	545
North Carolina Agriculture and Technical State University	546
Northeastern Illinois University	552
Pennsylvania State University—Beaver	599
Saint Martin's University	670
Texas A&M University—Corpus Christi	778
University of Maine—Presque Isle	859
University of Minnesota—Duluth	870
University of Texas at El Paso, The	925
University of Texas of the Permian Basin, The	927

67

Black Hills State University	97
Centenary College	151
Central Baptist College	152
Columbia College—Chicago (IL)	211, 1128
Indiana University—South Bend	373
Lyndon State College	446
Northwestern Oklahoma State University	562
Pennsylvania State University—DuBois	601
Pennsylvania State University—Schuylkill	605
Pennsylvania State University—Worthington Scranton	607
Regis College	633
Rivier College	641
Southeastern Louisiana University	712, 1035
West Liberty State College	982
Western Illinois University	987, 1044

66

Becker College	79, 1080
Bethune-Cookman College	94
Dowling College	251
Elizabeth City State University	269
Felician College	288, 1170
Indiana University of Pennsylvania	374
Jacksonville State University	380
Nichols College	545, 1290
North Central University	549
Peru State College	609
Texas A&M University at Galveston	779
University of Wisconsin—Platteville	942
University of Wisconsin—Whitewater	945
Urbana University	947
William Penn University	1005

65

Angelo State University	43
Bethel College (TN)	93
Bluefield State College	101
College of Saint Elizabeth	198
College of St. Joseph in Vermont	203
Fayetteville State University	287
Humphreys College	361
Indiana University— Purdue University Fort Wayne	371
Norwich University	565
Oklahoma Panhandle State University	580
Pennsylvania State University—Shenango	606
Pine Manor College	613
Purdue University—North Central	625
State University of New York—Cobleskill	744
Sterling College (VT)	764

64

Baptist College of Florida	72, 1023
Georgian Court University	318
Hilbert College	350
Johnson State College	389
Milwaukee Institute of Art and Design	493
Mount Senario College	522
North Carolina Central University	546
Roanoke Bible College	642
Saint Cloud State University	663
Saint Paul's College	675
St. Thomas University	739
University of Maine—Fort Kent	858, 1446
University of Montana—Western, The	877
Upper Iowa University	946, 1043

63

Anna Maria College	43, 1058
Colorado State University—Pueblo	209
Curry College	232, 1144
Fairmont State College	285
Kendall College of Art and Design of Ferris State University	397, 1218
Lincoln University (MO)	429
Massachusetts Maritime Academy	469
Minnesota State University—Mankato	496
Missouri Southern State University—Joplin	500
Ohio State University at Lima, The	573
Philander Smith College	611
Purdue University—Calumet	625
Saint Mary's College of Ave Maria University (MI)	672
University of New Hampshire—Manchester	883
University of Texas—San Antonio	927

62

Cameron University	137
City University of New York—Medgar Evers College	174
Huston-Tillotson University	363
Indiana Institute of Technology	368
Iowa Wesleyan College	379
Missouri Western State College	503
Ohio State University—Mansfield, The	575
Ohio State University at Marion, The	574
Ohio State University—Newark, The	575
Robert Morris College (IL)	643, 1338
Shawnee State University	695
State University of New York— Broome Community College	743
Sul Ross State University	768
University of Wisconsin—Parkside	941

61

Arkansas Baptist College	49
Arlington Baptist College	51
Art Institute of California—San Francisco, The	54
California Maritime Academy of California State University	126
Cincinnati Bible College and Seminary	167
Gratz College	329
Jarvis Christian College	383
Madonna University	449
Metropolitan College of New York	483
Miles Community College	490
Morris College	514
National-Louis University	531
North Carolina Wesleyan College	548
Ohio University—Zanesville	577
State University of New York— Niagara County Community College	754
Villa Maria College of Buffalo	955
Winston-Salem State University	1010

60*

NOTES

NOTES

NOTES

NOTES

NOTES

NOTES

NOTES

NOTES